THE SCHOTTENSTEIN EDITION

The ArtScroll Series®

THE DAVIDOWITZ FAMILY
RENOV STAHLER ROSENWALD PERLYSKY EDITION OF SEDER NEZIKIN

מסכת בבא בתרא
TRACTATE BAVA BASRA

A PROJECT OF THE

Mesorah Heritage Foundation

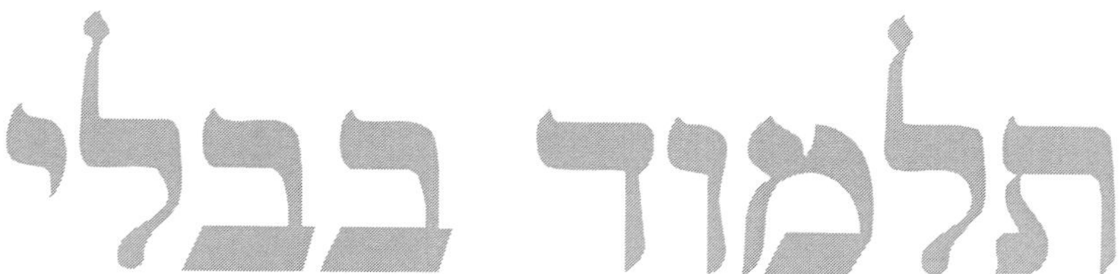

THE DAVIDOWITZ FAMILY
RENOV STAHLER ROSENWALD PERLYSKY EDITION OF SEDER NEZIKIN

מסכת בבא בתרא
TRACTATE BAVA BASRA
VOLUME I

Elucidated by
Rabbi Yosaif Asher Weiss

and edited by a team scholars
under the General Editorship of
R' Hersh Goldwurm

The Schottenstein Edition

THE GEMARA: THE CLASSIC VILNA EDITION,
WITH AN ANNOTATED, INTERPRETIVE ELUCIDATION,
AS AN AID TO TALMUD STUDY

The Hebrew folios are reproduced from the newly typeset and enhanced Oz Vehadar Edition of the Classic Vilna Talmud

Published by
Mesorah Publications, ltd

We gratefully acknowledge the outstanding
Torah scholars who contributed to this volume:

Rabbi Yosaif Asher Weiss and
Rabbis Yehezkel Danziger, Hillel Danziger,
Yosef Davis, Eliezer Herzka, Nesanel Kasnett,
Henoch Morris and **Feivel Wahl**
together with
Rabbis Avraham Berman, Dovid Katz, Abba Zvi Naiman,
Avrohom Yoseif Rosenberg, Eliyahu Shulman,
Michoel Weiner and **Chaim Weinfeld**

Rabbi Hersh Goldwurm,
Rabbi Yisroel Simcha Schorr and **Rabbi Chaim Malinowitz**
reviewed and commented on the entire manuscript.

Rabbi Yehezkel Danziger
is the Editorial Director of this project.

FIRST EDITION
Three Impressions ... December 1992 — August 1998

SECOND EDITION
Seventeen Impressions ... November 2001 — December 2022
Eighteenth Impression ... June 2023

Published and Distributed by
MESORAH PUBLICATIONS, Ltd.
313 Regina Avenue / Rahway, N.J. 07065

Distributed in Europe by
LEHMANNS
Unit E, Viking Business Park
Rolling Mill Road
Jarrow, Tyne & Wear NE32 3DP
England

Distributed in Israel by
SIFRIATI / A. GITLER — BOOKS
POB 2351
Bnei Brak 51122

Distributed in Australia & New Zealand by
GOLDS WORLD OF JUDAICA
3-13 William Street
Balaclava, Melbourne 3183
Victoria Australia

Distributed in South Africa by
KOLLEL BOOKSHOP
Northfield Centre, 17 Northfield Avenue
Glenhazel 2192, Johannesburg, South Africa

THE ARTSCROLL® SERIES / SCHOTTENSTEIN EDITION
TALMUD BAVLI / TRACTATE BAVA BASRA VOL. I

ITEM CODE: TBB1
ISBN 10: 0-89906-738-7
ISBN 13: 978-0-89906-738-4

Typography by CompuScribe at ArtScroll Studios, Ltd.
Custom bound by **Sefercraft, Inc.,** Rahway, NJ

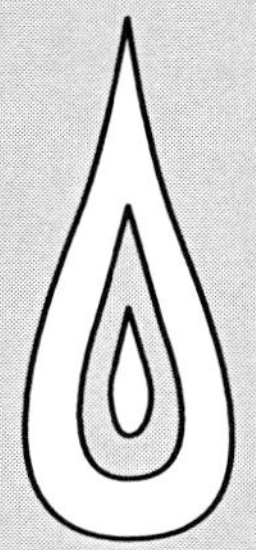

לעילוי נשמת

ר׳ מנחם מענדל

בן אלימלך יהושע העשל ע״ה

פאר אישים וכשרון מעללים

להיטיב חשב לילות וימים

זכרו לא יסוף לדור דורים

כ״ג אדר תש״נ

והאשה חיה בת יהושע הכהן ע״ה

אשת חיל חשובה ויקרה

פיה פתחה בחכמה

חמדה לבה לגדל בניה בדרך הישר

יראת השם ושומרת מצותיו

כ״ח תשרי תשמ״ז

תנצב״ה

is reverently dedicated to the memory of
the patron of this Talmud
and of countless other noble causes in Jewish life

יעקב מאיר חיים בן אפרים אליעזר הכהן ע״ה

נפטר ה׳ אדר ב׳ תשנ״ב

Jerome Schottenstein ע״ה

and to the memory of his parents

אפרים אליעזר בן יהושע הכהן ע״ה — נפטר ב׳ אייר תשט״ז

חנה בת צבי הירש ע״ה — נפטרה ט״ו מנחם אב תשט״ו

Ephraim and Anna Schottenstein ע״ה

by

Geraldine Schottenstein

Saul and Sonia Schottenstein

and

Jay and Jeanie Schottenstein

and their children

Joseph Aaron and Lindsay Brooke,
Jacob Meir, Jonah Philip, Emma Blake

Jonathan Richard and Nicole Lauren,
Winnie Simone, Teddi Isabella,
Allegra Giselle, Elodie Yael

Jeffrey Adam and Ariella
Jerome Meir

Ann and Ari Deshe

and their children

Elie Michael, David Scott, Dara Lauren, Daniel Matthew

Susan and Jon Diamond

and their children

Jillian Leigh, Joshua Louis, Jacob Meyer

and

Lori Schottenstein

PATRONS OF THE SEDARIM

Recognizing the need for the holy legacy of the Talmud
to be available to its heirs in their own language,
these generous and visionary patrons have each dedicated
one of the six Sedarim/Orders of the Talmud.

THE FORMAN EDITION OF SEDER ZERAIM

is lovingly dedicated by

Mr. and Mrs. Sam Forman, Brett and Wendy

in memory of their beloved parents and grandparents

Mr. and Mrs. George Forman ע״ה **Dr. and Mrs. Morey Chapman ע״ה**

THE HORN EDITION OF SEDER MOED

is lovingly dedicated to the memory of

ר׳ משה מניס ב״ר יעקב יצחק ע״ה — Moishe Horn ע״ה

נפטר ב׳ מנחם אב תשנ״ד

by his wife **Malkie**

his parents **Jacob ע״ה and Genia Horn ע״ה**

and his children

Shimmie and Alissa
Ari Shana Michal Tali

Devorah and Dov Elias
Moishe Ariella Eli Chaviva Tehilla Tova

Shandi and Sruli Glaser
Ruthi Jack Miri Rachelli

THE ELLIS A. SAFDEYE EDITION OF SEDER NASHIM

is reverently dedicated to the memory of

המנוח יהודה אצלאן ומרת צלחה ויקטוריא ע״ה

Aslan and Victoria Safdeye ע״ה

and

המנוח יהודה ומרת מרגלית ע״ה

Judah and Margie Sultan ע״ה

by their children

Ellis A. and Altoon Safdeye

and grandchildren

Alan Judah and Rachel Safdeye
Ezra and Victoria Esses
Joseph and Rochelle Safdeye
Michael and Bobbi Safdeye

PATRONS OF THE SEDARIM

THE DAVIDOWITZ FAMILY
RENOV STAHLER ROSENWALD PERLYSKY EDITION OF SEDER NEZIKIN

is lovingly dedicated to

Rozi and Morty Davis-Davidowitz

builders of this dynasty

by their children and grandchildren

Esti and Ushi Stahler
Jamie, Danny, Duvi, Lisi, Avi, Eli, Malka and Loni

Rivki and Lindsay Rosenwald
Doni, Joshy, Demi, Davey and Tamar Rina

Ruki and Kal Renov
Tova, Tani, Eli, Ari, Yoni, Yael, Emi and Benji

Laya and Dov Perlysky
Ayala Malka, Tova Batsheva, Naftali Yonatan, Atara Yael, Eitan Moshe, Shira Avital, Akiva Yair, Avigail and Gavriel Yehuda

and is lovingly dedicated to the memory of our grandparents

Emily and Nathan Selengut ע״ה

נפתלי ב״ר יעקב ע״ה ומלכה בת ר׳ אלתר חיים ע״ה

THE SCHWARTZ EDITION OF SEDER KODASHIM

is lovingly dedicated by

Avrohom Yeshaya and Sally Schwartz

and their children

Ari and Daniella, Moshe, Dani, and Dovi

in memory of their beloved parents and grandparents

Isaac and Rebecca Jarnicki ז״ל — ר׳ יצחק ב״ר אשר ז״ל וחיה רבקה בת הרב בצלאל הירש ז״ל

נפ׳ יג׳ תמוז תשנ״ז   נפ׳ ג׳ אדר תשס״ד

and their beloved grandmother

Mrs. Pearl Septytor ע״ה — פערל בת ר׳ מרדכי ע״ה

and in honor of their parents and grandparents יבלח״ט

Rabbi and Mrs. Gedalia Dov Schwartz שליט״א

and in memory of our grandparents

Rabbi Eliezer and Pesha Chaya Poupko ז״ל   **Abraham Schwartz ז״ל**

Betzalel Hersh and Hendel Berliner ז״ל   **Asher and Gittel Jarnicki ז״ל**

PATRONS OF THE TALMUD

With generosity, vision, and devotion to the perpetuation of Torah study,
the following patrons have dedicated individual volumes of the Talmud

INTRODUCTION TO THE TALMUD: **Robin and Warren Shimoff**
In honor of **Kollel Yisroel V'Shimshon** of the West Side
In memory of our parents
Lynn and Irving Shimoff
ישראל דוב בן אהרן יעקב ז״ל חיה רבקה לאה בת אליעזר יהודה ע״ה

BERACHOS I: In memory of
Jerome Schottenstein ע״ה
יעקב מאיר חיים בן אפרים אליעזר הכהן ע״ה

BERACHOS II: **Zvi and Betty Ryzman**
Mickey and Shelly Fenig — Aliza, Yissachar David, Batsheva, Aharon Yakov and Elazar
Elie and Adina Ryzman — Leora, Yonatan, Ari and Shai
Avi and Zahava Ryzman — Sarah Chloe and Eliana Shayna
Rafi and Elimor Ryzman — Ora and Nava
In memory of
Rabbi Yehoshua Heschel Ryzman ז״ל — הרב יהושע השיל ב״ר חיים ז״ל נפ׳ י׳ טבת, תשס״ט
Halina Shaindel Ryzman ע״ה — מרת הלינה שיינדל בת ר׳ צבי ע״ה נפ׳ ה׳ מנחם אב, תשנ״ז
and in honor of Mrs. Mila Kornwasser שתחי׳
and in memory of
Rabbi Aharon Yaakov Kornwasser ז״ל — הרב אהרן יעקב ב״ר אליעזר ז״ל נפ׳ ז׳ תמוז, תשס״ב

Malcolm and Joy Lyons
in honour of their parents שיחי׳
Eve Lyons
Cecil and Mona Jacobs
and in memory of his father
Leopold Lyons ע״ה — יהודה בן גרשון ע״ה נפ׳ כ״ב שבט תשס״ג

SHABBOS I: **Nachshon and Bruria Minucha [Nuchi] Draiman and Family**
in memory of
הר״ר יהודה ליב מנדלקורן זצ״ל בן הר״ר צבי הי״ו
Rabbi Yehuda Leib Mandelcorn זצ״ל — נפטר כ׳ תמוז, תשנ״ג

A Hebrew edition of the Talmud Bavli is now in progress.
The Hebrew edition is dedicated by

Jay and Jeanie Schottenstein

and their children

Joseph Aaron and Lindsay Brooke, Jonathan Richard, and Jeffrey Adam

— in honor of their cherished loved ones who have left indelible marks on their own lives and the lives of countless others, as models of inspiration, generosity, integrity, and devotion to the noblest causes in Jewish life:
his parents **JEROME ז״ל AND GERALDINE SCHOTTENSTEIN**,
her parents **LEONARD AND HEDDY RABE**
and **SAUL AND SONIA SCHOTTENSTEIN**

JAY AND JEANIE SCHOTTENSTEIN
have a perspective that transcends time and community.
Through their dedication of these editions of the Talmud, they spread Torah study around the globe and across generations.
Multitudes yet unborn will be indebted to them for their vision and generosity.

PATRONS OF THE TALMUD

SHABBOS II: **David and Bonnie Anfang** **Chaim and Ruthie Anfang**
Rachel, Julie and Elliot **Ariella Hope** **Michael Brett**
In loving memory of
ר׳ אריה ליב ב״ר דוד אביגדור ע״ה — Leib Anfang ע״ה
בשה לאה בת ר׳ אלימלך דוב ע״ה — Barbara Anfang ע״ה

Mimi Rosenbaum **Joseph and Sharon Prawer** **Alan and Louisa Prawer**
Stacey and Danny **Dovid and Natalie White,** **Ruben Pinchas**
Shlomo Haim, Sarah Meira, Yishai Shalom
Dena and Adam Ballew, Shlomo Gavriel, Ariella Shira, Daniella Elise
Alana and Meir Popowitz **Naomi White**
In loving memory of
ר׳ פנחס ב״ר יוסף ברוך הלוי ע״ה גילה בת אשר יונה ע״ה — Pinkus and Genia Prawer ע״ה, and
שרה בת שמעון ליב ע״ה — Sarah Cukierman ע״ה

Rabbi Eliyahu and Yehudit Fishman
Rivka and Zvi Silberstein and Leah **Akiva Yitzchak Fishman**
Rabbi Yechiel Meir and Chagit Fishman **Rabbi Yosef and Aliza Fishman**
Talia Chanah, Ariel Yishai and Daniel
In loving memory of
ר׳ יוסף ב״ר טוביה ע״ה רודע רבקה בת ר׳ הירש מאיר ע״ה — Yosef and Rude Rivka Fishman ע״ה
and their children Yechiel Meir, Leah and Chanah הי״ד who perished in the Holocaust

SHABBOS III: **Stanley and Ellen Wasserman**
and their children
Alan and Svetlana Wasserman **Mark and Anne Wasserman**
Neil and Yael Wasserman **Stuart and Rivka Berger**
and families
In loving memory of
יוסף בן דוב בער ע״ה בילא בת יעקב ע״ה — Joseph and Bess Wasserman ע״ה, and
שמריהו בן משה ע״ה רבקה בת הרב יוסף הכהן ע״ה — Sascha and Regina (Czaczkes) Charles ע״ה

SHABBOS IV: לעילוי נשמות
הורינו היקרים **ר׳ לוי ב״ר יהודה הלוי ע״ה וצירל בת ר׳ מרדכי ע״ה לוינגר**
זקנינו היקרים **ר׳ יהודה ב״ר אליעזר צבי הלוי ע״ה וטלצא בת פרומט ע״ה לווינגר**
ר׳ מרדכי ב״ר שמואל ע״ה ומלכה בת ר׳ נתן ע״ה אדלר
אחינו **שמואל הלוי ע״ה יהודה הלוי ע״ה יהונתן הלוי הי״ד**
אחותנו **לאה בת ר׳ לוי סג״ל ע״ה ובעלה ר׳ טוביה ע״ה**
גיסינו **ר׳ מיכאל ב״ר ברוך שמואל ע״ה שוויצר ר׳ שמואל ב״ר יעקב ע״ה מיכל**
ולעילוי נשמות דודינו ודודותינו ויוצאי חלוציהם שנפטרו ושנהרגו על קידוש השם הי״ד
Dedicated by **Louis and Morris Lowinger**
Teri Schweitzer **Kato Michel** **Margit Baldinger** **Eva Lowinger**

ERUVIN: [two volumes] **Jerome and Geraldine Schottenstein** **Saul and Sonia Schottenstein**
Jay and Jeanie Schottenstein **Ann and Ari Deshe**
Susan and Jon Diamond **Lori Schottenstein**
in memory of
אפרים אליעזר בן יהושע הכהן ע״ה — Ephraim Schottenstein ע״ה
חנה בת צבי הירש ע״ה — Anna Schottenstein ע״ה

The Edmond J. Safra Edition of the Talmud Bavli in French,
adapted from the Schottenstein Edition, is now in progress.

The Edmond J. Safra Edition
was dedicated by
Lily Safra לאה בת דוב הכהן וחנה ע״ה
in memory of her beloved husband
Edmond J. Safra רפאל אדמון עזרא בן אסתר ע״ה

His desire is in the Torah of HASHEM, and in His Torah he meditates day and night.
He shall be like a tree deeply rooted alongside brooks of water;
that yields its fruit in due season, and whose leaf never withers,
and everything that he does will succeed (Psalms 1:2-3).

PATRONS OF THE TALMUD

PESACHIM I: **Vera and Soli Spira and Family**
in memory of
ברוך בן חיים ע״ה — Baruch Spira ע״ה
בילה בת נתן שלום ע״ה — Bella Spira ע״ה
שמואל בן אברהם ע״ה — Shmuel Lebovits ע״ה
and their respective families הי״ד who perished in the Holocaust
and in honor of
שפרה בת משה — Caroline Lebovits תחי׳

PESACHIM II: **Vera and Soli Spira and Family**
in memory of an uncle who was like a father
and a cousin who was like a brother
ישראל בן נתן שלום ע״ה — Israel Stern ע״ה
נתן שלום בן ישראל ע״ה — Noussi Stern ע״ה

PESACHIM III: **Lorraine and Mordy Sohn** **Ann and Pinky Sohn**
in memory of
ר׳ צבי ב״ר אלעזר ע״ה — Dr. Harry Sohn ע״ה
מרת הענדיל דבורה ב״ר אברהם שלמה ע״ה — Dora F. Sohn ע״ה
ר׳ יחזקאל ב״ר אליקים חנוך הלוי ע״ה — Harold Levine ע״ה
רבקה הענא בת שמעון הלוי ע״ה — Ruth Levine ע״ה
רייזל ב״ר שמשון ע״ה — Rosalie Sohn ע״ה

SHEKALIM: In loving memory of
Mr. Maurice Lowinger ז״ל
ר׳ מאיר משה ב״ר בן ציון הלוי ז״ל
נפ׳ כ״ז אדר תשס״א

YOMA I: **A. Joseph and Rochelle Stern**
Moshe Dov, Zev, Shani, Esty, and Shaye
in honor of their parents and grandparents
Eli and Frieda Stern שיחיו
Frida Weiss שתחי׳
and in memory of
ר׳ ישעי׳ בן ר׳ ישראל שמואל ווייס ז״ל

YOMA II: **A. Leibish and Edith Elbogen**
and Family
לזכר נשמות
מוה״ר אהרן בן מוה״ר יעקב קאפל עלבוגן ז״ל
וזו׳ אלטע חנה חיה מלכה בת מוה״ר חיים יצחק מאיר ע״ה
אחותי פערל עם בעלה ושבע בנים ובנות
ושלשה אחי: חיים יצחק מאיר, משה יוסף, יעקב קאפל הי״ד
בני אהרן עלבוגן שנהרגו עקד״ה
מוה״ר נתן פייטל בן מוה״ר אברהם וואלד ז״ל
וזו׳ ברכה בת מוה״ר דוד יהודה הי״ד שנאספה עקד״ה באוישוויץ

SUCCAH I: **Howard and Roslyn Zuckerman** **Steven and Shellie Zuckerman**
Leo and Rochelle Goldberg
in memory of their parents
ר׳ פסח יהודה ב״ר יצחק אייזיק ע״ה וחוה בת ר׳ יהודה לייב ע״ה — Philip and Evelyn Zuckerman ע״ה

in honor of their children
Yisroel and Shoshana Pesi Zuckerman שיחי׳
Pesach Yehudah and Asher Anshel שיחי׳
Michael (Ezra) and Lauren Zuckerman שיחי׳
Adrianne & Shawn Meller, Elliot, & Joshua Goldberg שיחי׳

in honor of their children
Glenn and Heidi, Jamie Elle, Benjamin,
Brett and Robin, Brandon Noah, Ross and T.J. שיחי׳
and in honor of their parents
Marilyn and Aaron Feinerman שיחי׳

in memory of
ר׳ ישראל צבי ב״ר ברוך ע״ה ושיינדל בת ר׳ ישראל ע״ה — Israel and Shaindel Ray ע״ה
and in memory of Mrs. Rose Ray (Glass) ע״ה

PATRONS OF THE TALMUD

SUCCAH I: [continued] **Arthur and Randi Luxenberg**
in honor of their parents
Irwin and Joan Luxenberg שיחי' Bernard and Evelyn Beeber שיחי'
their children Elizabeth Jewel and Jacqueline Paige שיחי'
in memory of his grandparents
ר' אברהם בן אהרן מרדכי ז"ל ורחל בת ר' משה ע"ה — Abraham and Rose Luxenberg ע"ה
ישעיהו צבי בן הרב טוביה ז"ל ושרה צירל בת ר' יעקב ע"ה — Jesse and Celia Aronson ע"ה

SUCCAH II: **Thomas and Lea Schottenstein** **William and Amy Schottenstein**
in memory of
אריה ליב בן אפרים אליעזר הכהן ע"ה — Leon Schottenstein ע"ה
מאיר אבנר בן דוד הלוי ע"ה — Meir Avner Levy ע"ה
and in honor of
Mrs. Jean S. Schottenstein שתחי' Bertram and Corinne Natelson שיחי'
Mrs. Flory Levy שתחי'

BEITZAH: **Paul and Suzanne Peyser** **Irwin and Bea Peyser**
in memory of
דוד בן פינחס ע"ה פריידע רייזעל בת יהושע ע"ה — David and Rose Peyser ע"ה

ROSH HASHANAH: **Steve and Genie Savitsky** **David and Roslyn Savitsky**
In memory of
יואל בן אברהם ע"ה — Jerry J. Savitsky ע"ה
ישראל בן מנחם מאנעס ע"ה — Irving Tennenbaum ע"ה
שמואל בן יצחק ע"ה — George Hillelsohn ע"ה
רחל בת דוד הלוי ע"ה — Ruth Hillelsohn ע"ה
אהרן בן יהודה אריה ע"ה — Aaron Seif ע"ה

TAANIS: **David and Jean Bernstein**
Matthew Bernstein, Owen and Kei
Scott and Andrea Bernstein, Samara, Jonah, and Jesse
Albert and Gail Nassi, Jessica and Garrett
in memory of
Annna and Harry Bernstein ע"ה Sarah and Joseph Furman ע"ה
Mr. Samuel Nassi ע"ה

MEGILLAH: Special Commemorative Edition published in conjunction with the Sh'loshim of the patron of this edition of the Talmud
Jerome Schottenstein ע"ה
יעקב מאיר חיים בן אפרים אליעזר הכהן ע"ה

MOED KATAN: **Solomon T. and Leah Scharf**
and their children
David and Tzipi Diamond **Alexander and Naomi Scharf**
Joseph and Lisa Scharf **Dovid and Chani Scharf**
לזכרון עולם
ר' אליהו בן משה יעקב ע"ה — R' Eliyahu Scharf ע"ה
שרה בת אלכסנדר זיסקינד ע"ה — Sara Scharf ע"ה
ר' יוסף בן צבי הירש ע"ה — R' Joseph Felder ע"ה
עטיל בת מוה"ר שמעון ע"ה — Mrs. Ettel Felder-Hollander ע"ה

CHAGIGAH: **The Alvin E. Schottenstein Family**
In memory of
חיים אברהם יונה בן אפרים אליעזר הכהן ז"ל — Alvin E. Schottenstein ז"ל
יצחק אייזיק בן עקיבא הכהן ז"ל — Irving Altman ז"ל
הדס בת אברהם אביש ע"ה — Helen Altman ע"ה
שרגא פייוול בן יצחק אייזיק הכהן ז"ל — Frank Altman ז"ל

YEVAMOS I: **Phillip and Ruth Wojdyslawski and Family**
In memory of his beloved parents
Abraham Michel and Ora Wojdyslawski ע"ה
ר' אברהם מיכאל ב"ר פינחס ע"ה
אורה בת ר' צבי הירש ע"ה

PATRONS OF THE TALMUD

YEVAMOS II: **Phillip and Ruth Wojdyslawski and Family**
In memory of her beloved mother
Chaya (Cytryn) Valt ע״ה
חיה צירל בת ר׳ שלמה זלמן ע״ה

YEVAMOS III: **Phillip and Ruth Wojdyslawski and Family**
In honor of
Benjamin C. Fishoff לאוי״ט
To the public he is a leader with vision and dedication.
To us he has always been a role model, a father,
and a constant inspiration.

KESUBOS I: **The Fishoff Families**
in memory of their beloved mother
מינדל בת ר׳ ישראל ע״ה — Mrs. Marilyn Fishoff ע״ה
נפ׳ כד תשרי תשמ״ט
and in memory of their dear grandparents
Fishoff — ר׳ דוב ב״ר מנחם אשר ע״ה מרת מירל בת ר׳ מנחם מענדל ע״ה
Neider — ר׳ ישראל ב״ר אברהם ע״ה מרת חיה זיסא בת ר׳ שרגא פייוועל ע״ה

KESUBOS II **Arthur A. and Carla Rand**
in memory of their parents
ר׳ ישראל ב״ר צבי Rand ומרת ליבא מלכה ב״ר יהודה Marcus ע״ה
ר׳ שלמה ב״ר מרדכי יהודה Ratzersdorfer ומרת חוה ב״ר חיים Finkelstein ע״ה
and in honor of their children
ר׳ אריה יהושע ב״ר אליהו דוב ומרת ליבא מלכה שיחי׳ — Lydia M. and Lionel S. Zuckier
ר׳ יואל אשר ב״ר חיים שלמה ומרת גנענדל חנה שיחי׳ — Gigi A. and Joel A. Baum
ר׳ ישראל יהודה ומרת צפורה געלא ב״ר יצחק חיים שיחי׳ — Jay J. and Cyndi G. Finkel-Rand
and grandchildren
דניאל יעקב, נפתלי צבי, חוה, בנימין, צפורה מרים, רחל, בתשבע Baum שיחי׳
שלמה יצחק, שירה חיה, צבי, שפרה לאה, בן ציון Zuckier שיחי׳
אליהו אריה לייב, יעקב שלמה, צבי, חסיה ליבא, מתתיהו דוד Rand שיחי׳

KESUBOS III **ישימך אלהים כשרה רבקה רחל ולאה**
May God make you like Sarah, Rebecca, Rachel and Leah

NEDARIM I: **Mrs. Goldy Golombeck**
Hyman P. and Elaine Golombeck **Blanche B. Lerer**
Moishe Zvi and Sara Leifer **Avrohom Chaim and Renee Fruchthandler**
In memory of
ר׳ משה יוסף ב״ר חיים פנחס ע״ה — Morris J. Golombeck ע״ה
and by Moishe Zvi and Sara Leifer in memory of
הרב ברוך יוסף ב״ר משה צבי ע״ה – האשה הצנועה מרים יוטא בת ר׳ לוי יצחק ע״ה
Mr. and Mrs. Baruch Leifer ע״ה

NEDARIM II: **The Rothstein Family**
In loving memory of
וועלוועל ב״ר יוסף ע״ה — Warren Rothstein ע״ה
David and Esther Rothstein ע״ה Max and Gussie Gottlieb ע״ה
and in honor of
Howard and Beatrice Rothstein

NAZIR I: **Albert and Gail Nassi**
Garrett A. Nassi
Jessica Lea Nassi
in memory of
Samuel Nassi ע״ה
Albert and Leona Nassi ע״ה
Benjamin and Adell Eisenberg ע״ה
Arthur and Sarah Dector ע״ה

Daniel and Susan Kane
Jessica, Adam and Stacey
in memory of
Abraham and Rose Kanofsky ע״ה
Benjamin and Sophie Gornstein ע״ה
Elie and Irma Darsa ע״ה
Mack and Naomi Mann ע״ה

PATRONS OF THE TALMUD

NAZIR II: **Alan and Myrna Cohen, Alison and Matthew**
in memory of
Harry and Kate Cohen ע״ה Harry and Pauline Katkin ע״ה

SOTAH: **Motty and Malka Klein**
for the merit of their children שיחי׳
Esther and Chaim Baruch Fogel Dovid and Chavie Binyomin Zvi ז״ל
Elana Leah and Natan Goldstein Moshe Yosef and Rikki Yaakov Eliyahu and Tammy
In honor of his mother שתחי׳
Mrs. Suri Klein לאוי״ט
In memory of his father
ר׳ יהודה ב״ר דוד הלוי ז״ל נפ׳ כ״ז אדר ב׳ תשס״ג – Yidel Klein
In memory of her parents
ר׳ אשר אנשיל ב״ר משה יוסף ז״ל נפ׳ ג׳ שבט תשנ״ט – Anchel Gross
שרה בת ר׳ חיים אליהו ע״ה נפ׳ כ״ד סיון תשס״א – Suri Gross
And in memory of their grandparents who perished על קידוש השם in the Holocaust
ר׳ דוד ב״ר יעקב הלוי ע״ה ופערל בת ר׳ צבי ע״ה הי״ד – Klein
ר׳ מרדכי ב״ר דוד הלוי ע״ה ולאה בת ר׳ יעקב הלוי ע״ה הי״ד – Klein
ר׳ משה יוסף ב״ר בנימין צבי ע״ה ומלכה בת ר׳ יחיאל מיכל ע״ה הי״ד – Gross
ר׳ חיים אליהו ב״ר מרדכי ע״ה ויוטא בת ר׳ שלמה אליעזר ע״ה הי״ד – Gartenberg

GITTIN I: **Mrs. Kate Tannenbaum**
Elliot and Debra Tannenbaum Edward and Linda Zizmor
and Families
commemorating the first yahrzeit of beloved husband, father and grandfather
ר׳ נפתלי ב״ר יהודה אריה ע״ה — Fred Tannenbaum ע״ה
נפטר ח׳ ניסן תשנ״ב

GITTIN II: **Richard and Bonnie Golding**
in honor of Julian and Frances Golding Lawrence Cohen and Helen Lee Cohen
and in memory of Vivian Cohen ע״ה
Irving and Ethel Tromberg Clarence and Jean Permut
in memory of
Benjamin and Sara Tromberg ע״ה Harry and Lena Brown ע״ה
Molly and Julius Permut ע״ה Lizzie and Meyer Moscovitz ע״ה

KIDDUSHIN I: **Ellis A. and Altoon Safdeye**
in memory of their beloved parents
המנוח יהודה אצלאן ומרת צלחה ויקטוריא ע״ה — Aslan and Victoria Safdeye ע״ה
המנוח יהודה ומרת מרגלית ע״ה — Judah and Margie Sultan ע״ה
and in memory of his brother יוסף ע״ה — Joseph Safdeye ע״ה

KIDDUSHIN II: **Mr. and Mrs. Ben Heller**
in memory of his father
יואל נתן ב״ר חיים הלוי ע״ה — Joseph Heller ע״ה
and in honor of his mother
צפורה שתחי׳ לאוי״ט בת ר׳ בנימין ע״ה — Fanya Gottesfeld-Heller שתחי׳

BAVA KAMMA I: **Yitzchok and Shoshana Ganger**
and Children
in memory of
ר׳ יצחק ישעיהו ב״ר שלמה זלמן ע״ה–רויזא גיטל בת ר׳ משה ע״ה — Ganger
מיכאל ב״ר אברהם מרדכי ע״ה–מרים יוכבד בת ר׳ בנימין ע״ה — Ferber
ר׳ משה דוד ב״ר יצחק זעליג מקוצק ע״ה–פיגא בת ר׳ אברהם מרדכי ע״ה — Morgenstern
ר׳ מתתיהו ב״ר שמואל דוב ע״ה–אסתר מלכה בת ר׳ אריה ליב ע״ה — Newman

PATRONS OF THE TALMUD

BAVA KAMMA II: **William and Esther Bein, and**
Joseph Hillel, Abraham Chaim Zev, and Bella Leah
In memory of parents and grandparents
מנחם מענדל ב"ר שמואל יצחק הכהן ע"ה — Edward (Mendus) Bein ע"ה
לאה בת חיים זאב הכהן ע"ה — Ilus Hartstein Bein ע"ה
מרדכי בן יוסף ע"ה — Mordochej Szer ע"ה
בילה בת אברהם ע"ה — Baila Silber Szer ע"ה
שמואל יצחק הכהן ושרה ביין ע"ה — חיים זאב הכהן ושרה הרטשטיין ע"ה
יוסף ויענטה שער ע"ה — אברהם ואסתר זילבר ע"ה

BAVA KAMMA III: **Dedicated to Klal Yisrael,**
and particularly to the Six Million.
הקב"ה שוכן בתוך בני ישראל והוא חד עם כנסת ישראל
"The Holy One Blessed is He dwells among the children of Israel;
He and the congregation of Israel are one." — *Tzidkas Hatzaddik* 179

BAVA METZIA I: **Drs. Robert and Susan Schulman**
Howard and Tzila Schulman **Fred and Cindy Schulman**
and Families
in memory of
מיכאל בן צבי הירש ע"ה ומלכה בת ר' יוסף ע"ה — Milton and Molly Schulman ע"ה

BAVA METZIA II: **Donald E. and Eydie R. Garlikov, and Jennifer**
in memory of beloved son and brother
צבי שלמה בן דן ע"ה — Kenneth Scott Garlikov ע"ה
and in memory of parents and grandparents
עזריאל וועלוויל ב"ר אנשיל ע"ה טשארנא בת ר' אריה לייב ע"ה
Irve W. and Cecelia (Kiki) Garlikov ע"ה
and in honor of parents and grandparents, brother and uncle
מרדכי ואסתר פריידל ריטטער — Marcus and Elfrieda Ritter
נפתלי חיים ריטטער — Dr. Nathaniel Ritter

BAVA METZIA III: **The David H. Gluck Foundation**
in memory of
The Gluck Family
זאב בן דוד צבי ע"ה ואסתר בת אשר זעליג ע"ה — Zev and Esther Gluck ע"ה
ליבא, אשר זעליג, דוד צבי, שמואל, מנשה, יחזקאל שרגא ע"ה —
Lee, George, David H., Samuel C., Emanuel M., Henry ע"ה, and
יעקב יצחק בן זאב ע"ה ומיימי בת זאב ע"ה — Dr. Jack I. and Mrs. Mae Saks ע"ה
and in memory of
זאב בן חיים דוד וחיה ביילע בת יצחק יעקב ע"ה — Wolf and Chaye Beilah Saks ע"ה
יחיאל בן משה ע"ה — Elie Neustadter ע"ה

BAVA BASRA I: In memory of
מנחם מענדל בן אלימלך יהושע העשל ע"ה
חיה בת יהושע הכהן ע"ה

BAVA BASRA II: **Paul and Beth Guez and Family**
in memory of
Felix (Mazal) Guez ע"ה

BAVA BASRA III: **Irving and Frances Schottenstein**
in honor of their beloved parents
מאיר בן יהושע הכהן ע"ה ליבא בת הרב יצחק משה ע"ה — Meyer and Libbie Schottenstein
טוביה ע"ה ויבדל"ח שיינדל תחי' — Tobias ע"ה and Jennie Polster תחי'
Melvin ע"ה and Lenore תחי' Schottenstein
in honor of their beloved parents
אברהם יוסף בן יהושע הכהן ע"ה ויבדל"ח בליה זילפה בת יצחק תחי'
Abe J. ע"ה and Bessie (Stone) תחי' Schottenstein
יצחק ע"ה ויבדל"ח שרה תחי' — Isadore J. ע"ה and Sophie תחי' Green

PATRONS OF THE TALMUD

SANHEDRIN I: **Mortimer and Barbara Klaus** **Lester and Esther Klaus**
Arthur and Vivian Klaus
in memory of their beloved parents
ר׳ שמשון ב״ר יעקב ע״ה באשא בת ר׳ מרדכי נתן ע״ה
Samuel and Bessie Klaus ע״ה
and in memory of their sister
Rosalie Klaus Sohn — רייזל בת ר׳ שמשון ע״ה

SANHEDRIN II: Dedicated by a fellowship of people who revere the Talmud, its sanctity and wisdom, who foster its study, and who join in helping bring its treasures to future generations, the world over.

SANHEDRIN III: **Joseph and Adina Russak**
Dr. Leonard and Bobbee Feiner
Larry and Rochelle Russak
in memory of
Mr. and Mrs. Harry Russak ע״ה — צבי הירש ורחל רוסק ע״ה
Mr. and Mrs. Eliezer Deutsch ע״ה — אליעזר ובריינדל דייטש ע״ה
Mr. and Mrs. Jacob Feiner ע״ה — יעקב ורבקה לאה פיינר ע״ה

MAKKOS: **Mr. and Mrs. Marcos Katz**
in honor of הרב אפרים לייבוש בן הרב מרדכי דוד הכהן כ״ץ שליט״א
Rabbi Ephraim Leibush Katz שליט״א

SHEVUOS: Dedicated by
Michael and Danielle Gross
(London)

AVODAH ZARAH I: **The Kuhl Family**
in memory of
Dr. Julius Kuhl ע״ה — יחיאל ב״ר יצחק אייזיק ע״ה
Mrs. Yvonne Kuhl ע״ה — פרומט בת ר׳ שמואל הלוי ע״ה
Sydney Kuhl ע״ה — שמואל ב״ר יחיאל ע״ה

AVODAH ZARAH II: In memory of
Jerome Schottenstein ע״ה
יעקב מאיר חיים בן אפרים אליעזר הכהן ע״ה

HORAYOS-EDUYOS: **Woli and Chaja Stern** (Sao Paulo, Brazil)
in memory of his parents
Stern – ר׳ צבי בן ר׳ חיים הלוי ומרת מרים ז״ל
Tager – מרת דאכא בת ר׳ פרץ ומרת ברכה ע״ה
and in memory of her parents
Brenner – ר׳ דוד אריה בן ר׳ יעקב ומרת שיינדל ז״ל
Stern – מרת איטלה בת ר׳ חיים ומרת מדל ע״ה
and in memory of their mechutanim
Landau – ר׳ ישראל מרדכי ב״ר צבי יוסף סג״ל ז״ל
Weitman – ר׳ יששכר טוביה ב״ר יוסף ז״ל
Kierszenbaum – ר׳ שמואל עקיבא ב״ר שלמה צבי ז״ל
and in memory of their brother and sister-in-law
Stern – ר׳ אריה בן ר׳ צבי הלוי ומרת דאכא ע״ה
Stern – מרת זלטה פסל בת ר׳ אברהם יעקב ומרת חנה גיטל ע״ה
and in honor of their children
Jacques and Ariane Stern   Jaime and Ariela Landau   Michaël and Annete Kierszenbaum

ZEVACHIM I: **Mr. and Mrs. Samson Bitensky**

ZEVACHIM II: **Victor Posner**

PATRONS OF THE TALMUD

ZEVACHIM III: **Friends of Value City Department Stores**
In memory of
Jerome Schottenstein ע״ה — יעקב מאיר חיים בן אפרים אליעזר הכהן ע״ה

MENACHOS I: **Terumah Foundation**

MENACHOS II: **Terumah Foundation**

MENACHOS III: **Terumah Foundation**

CHULLIN I: **The Kassin Family**
in memory of
Rabbi Dr. Jacob Saul Kassin זצ״ל — הרב יעקב שאול קצין זצ״ל
The late Chief Rabbi of the Syrian-Sephardic Community
and in honor of
Rabbi Saul Jacob Kassin שליט״א — הרב שאול יעקב קצין שליט״א
Chief Rabbi of the Syrian-Sephardic Community

CHULLIN II: **Marty Silverman**
in memory of
Joseph and Fannie Silverman ע״ה and Dorothy Silverman ע״ה

CHULLIN III: **Harold and Ann Platt**
in memory of their beloved parents
Eliezer and Sarah Feiga (Olshak) Platkowski ע״ה of Malkinia, Poland — אליעזר ושרה פיגא ע״ה
Baruch and Laura Bienstock ע״ה of Lwow, Poland — ברוך ולאה ע״ה
and in memory of their entire families who perished in the Holocaust

CHULLIN IV: **Terumah Foundation**

BECHOROS I: **Howard Tzvi and Chaya Friedman**
Gabrielle and Noam Charnowitz Aryeh Yerachmiel Alexander and Daniella
in memory of their father and grandfather
Yerachmiel Friedman ז״ל — הרב ירחמיאל ברוך בן הרה״ח ר׳ אלעזר ז״ל

BECHOROS II: **Howard and Chaya Balter**
Nachum and Perri Augenbaum Gavriel Shmuel, Rachel
Naftali and Perele Balter Aryeh Leib Akiva
in memory of our parents and grandparents
David Balter ז״ל — דוד זאב בן ר׳ שלמה ז״ל, נפ׳ ז׳ תמוז תשס״ח
Ruth L. Balter ע״ה — רחל בת ר׳ חיים ע״ה, נפ׳ ז׳ שבט תשנ״ט
and in honor of their parents and grandparents שיחי׳
Noah and Shirley Schall
and in beloved memory of their grandparents and great grandparents
Balter — ר׳ שלמה ב״ר דוד ז״ל אדעל בת ר׳ זאב ע״ה
Lelling — ר׳ חיים ב״ר לייב ז״ל פערל בת ר׳ בייניש הערש ע״ה
Zabrowsky — ר׳ דוב בער ב״ר אליעזר ז״ל ליבה בת ר׳ ישראל ע״ה
Schall — ר׳ נפתלי ב״ר יעקב שלמה ז״ל שרה בת ר׳ רפאל ע״ה

ARACHIN: **Chanoch and Hadassah Weisz and Family**
in memory of his father:
Weisz — לעי״נ אביו ר׳ צבי ב״ר שמחה הלוי ע״ה, נפ׳ כ״ז מנחם אב תשמ״ה
his maternal grandfather:
Grunwald — לעי״נ ר׳ שלמה ב״ר יצחק ע״ה, נפ׳ ה׳ סיון תש״א
his maternal grandmother and their children who perished in the Holocaust:
Grunwald — לעי״נ מרת גנדל בת ר׳ חנוך העניך ע״ה, שנהרגה עקה״ש כ״ז סיון תש״ד הי״ד
ולעי״נ בניהם משה ב״ר שלמה, יעקב ב״ר שלמה, יצחק ב״ר שלמה, בנימין ב״ר שלמה,
שנהרגו עקה״ש כ״ז סיון תש״ד הי״ד

and in memory of her grandparents:
Aryeh — לעי״נ ר׳ חייא בן חכם ר׳ רפאל ע״ה, נפ׳ כ״ד מנחם אב תשל״ה
וזוגתו מרת מלכה בת ר׳ אליהו ע״ה, נפ׳ י״ח טבת תשל״ד

PATRONS OF THE TALMUD

TEMURAH: **Dr. and Mrs. Walter Silver**
Shlomo, Chani, and Avi Cohen
Sheri, Terri, Jennifer and Michelle Kraut
Evan and Alison Silver
in memory of our parents, and great grandparents
צבי יצחק ב״ר שמואל ע״ה — Harry Silver ע״ה
שרה פיגא בת מענדל ע״ה — Sarah Silver ע״ה
אברהם משה בן הרב שלמה זאלי ע״ה — Morris Bienenfeld ע״ה
גוטקה טובה בת אברהם דוד ע״ה — Gertrude Bienenfeld ע״ה

KEREISOS: **Mouky and Charlotte Landau** (Antwerp)
in honor of their children
Natalie and Chemi Friedman **Yanky and Miriam Landau**
Steve and Nechama Landau
and in beloved memory of their parents
חיים יעקב ב״ר יהושע ז״ל — Chaim Yaakov Landau ז״ל
אסתר בת ר׳ יעקב קאפל הכהן ע״ה — Esther Landau ע״ה
בן ציון ב״ר יצחק צבי ז״ל — Benzion Gottlob ז״ל
צילה בת ר׳ שמואל יהודה לייב ע״ה — Cila Herskovic ע״ה
and in beloved memory of our partner
מורנו הרב ר׳ יוסף יצחק בן מורנו ורבנו הרה״ג ר׳ מרדכי רוטנברג זצ״ל אבדק״ק אנטווערפן

ME'ILAH, TAMID, MIDDOS, KINNIM: **Steven and Renée Adelsberg**
Sarita and Rubin Gober **Israel Joseph and Menachem Yechezkel**
David and Joclyn **Sammy** **Avi**
in loving memory of
שמואל שמעלקא ב״ר גדליה ז״ל — Samuel Adelsberg ז״ל
and in honor of
Helen Adelsberg Weinberg שתחי׳
and
Chaim and Rose Fraiman שיחי׳

NIDDAH I: In memory of
Joseph and Eva Hurwitz ע״ה
יוסף ב״ר מרדכי הלוי וחוה פיגא ב״ר אליעזר הלוי ע״ה
and
Lorraine Hurwitz Greenblott — לאה בילא חיה בת ר׳ יוסף ע״ה
by
Marc and Rachel Hurwitz,
Elisheva Ruchama, Michal, and Nechama Leah;
Martin and Geraldine Schottenstein Hoffman,
Jay and Jeanie Schottenstein, Ann and Ari Deshe,
Susan and Jon Diamond, and Lori Schottenstein;
and Pam and Neil Lazaroff, Frank Millman, and Dawn Petel

NIDDAH II: In memory of
Jerome Schottenstein ע״ה
יעקב מאיר חיים בן אפרים אליעזר הכהן ע״ה

*Guardians of the Talmud**

A society of visionary people who recognize the primacy of the Jewish people's commitment to intellect, ethics, integrity, law, and religion — and pursue it by presenting the treasures of the eternal Talmud in the language of today . . . for the generations of tomorrow.

David and Jean Bernstein
Matthew Bernstein
Scott and Andrea Bernstein

in memory of
Mr. and Mrs. Harry Bernstein ע״ה
Mr. and Mrs. Joseph Furman ע״ה

The publishers pay tribute to the memory of a couple that embodied Torah knowledge and service to our people

Rabbi Yitzchok Filler ז״ל — הרב יצחק בן ר׳ שמואל ז״ל
נפטר ל״ג בעומר תש״ל

Mrs. Dorothy Filler ע״ה — הרבנית דבורה בת ר׳ אברהם בצלאל ע״ה
נפטרה כ״א מרחשון תשס״ג

and the memory of a man of integrity and sensitivity

George May ז״ל — ר׳ יוסף בן הרב יהודה אריה ז״ל
נפטר כ״ז שבט תש״ס

תנצב״ה

We also honor a matriarch and role model

Mrs. Sylvia May תחי׳

Stephen L. and Terri Geifman and children
Leonard and Linda Comess and children
Alan and Cherie Weiss and children

in loving memory of
Morris M. Geifman — משה מרדכי בן יחיאל מיכאל ז״ל
and in honor of
Geraldine G. Geifman

Elliot and Debbie Gibber
Daniel and Amy Gibber and family, Jacob and Jennifer Gibber and family,
Marc, Michael, Mindy, and David

in memory of our parents and grandparents
Charles Goldner ז״ל — אלימלך חיים בן ירמיה הלוי ז״ל
נפ׳ כ׳ חשון תשס״ב
who completed Shas many times
Kate Ettlinger Goldner ע״ה — מינדל בת משולם ע״ה
נפ׳ כ״א תמוז תשכ״ח

*In formation

The Written Word is Forever

Guardians of the Talmud*

A society of visionary people who recognize the primacy of the Jewish people's commitment to intellect, ethics, integrity, law, and religion — and pursue it by presenting the treasures of the eternal Talmud in the language of today . . . for the generations of tomorrow.

❦ ❦ ❦

Milton and Rita Kramer

in honor of their 50th wedding anniversary and Milton's 80th birthday (April 1999),
in honor of the marriage of Ellen to George Gross (September 18, 2000),
and in honor of their children and grandchildren

Daniel and Gina Kramer and Children **Jonathan and Marian Kramer and Children**

Ellen K. and George Gross and their Children

and in everlasting memory of their beloved parents and grandparents
חיים שניאור זלמן הלוי (חזק) ופייגע דינה ע״ה — Hyman S. and Fannie D. Kramer ע״ה
חיים אלטער ושרה חנה ע״ה — Adolph H. and Sadie A. Gross ע״ה
משה אליעזר הלוי ורחל עלקא ע״ה — Morris L. and Rachel E. Kramer ע״ה
דוב בער הכהן ודבורה ע״ה — Barney and Dvorah Cohen ע״ה
משולם צבי ולאה ע״ה — Herman M. and Leah Gross ע״ה
פסח אלכסנדר וחנה ע״ה — Peisach and Hannah Neustadter ע״ה

❦ ❦ ❦

Helene and Moshe Talansky **Ida Bobrowsky** **Irene and Kalman Talansky** **Shoshana Silbert**

in honor of

Rebecca Talansky's 100th birthday עמו״ש

and in memory of
הרב דוד בן הרב אברהם חיים ז״ל — Rabbi David Talansky ז״ל
בלומא בת ר׳ שלמה הלוי ע״ה — Blanche Moshel ע״ה
ר׳ אברהם חיים בן הרב דוד ז״ל — Abraham R. Talansky ז״ל
הרב יעקב בן ר׳ אברהם ז״ל — Rabbi Jacob Bobrowsky ז״ל
תמר בת הרב יעקב ע״ה — Tema Bobrowsky ע״ה
ר׳ משה בן ר׳ לייב ז״ל — ברײנה בת ר׳ זלמן ע״ה — Rebecca and Morris Weisinger ז״ל
הרב אברהם בן ר׳ נחמיה ז״ל — Rabbi Avraham Silbert ז״ל
ר׳ מרדכי בן ר׳ שאול ז״ל — שפרה רייזל בת ר׳ צבי ע״ה — Ruth and Marek Stromer ז״ל
ר׳ אהרון בן ר׳ שלמה אריה ז״ל — רחל בת ר׳ יהושע אהרון ע״ה — Rose and Aaron Lerer ז״ל

❦ ❦ ❦

Thomas R. and Janet F. Ketteler

in memory of his mentor

Jerome Schottenstein ע״ה

❦ ❦ ❦

Alan and Myrna Cohen

in honor of

their children

Alison and Matthew

*In formation

The Written Word is Forever

Guardians of the Talmud*

A society of visionary people who recognize the primacy of the Jewish people's commitment to intellect, ethics, integrity, law, and religion — and pursue it by presenting the treasures of the eternal Talmud in the language of today . . . for the generations of tomorrow.

Rona and Edward Jutkowitz

In honor of our family's continuing commitment to Torah learning and Klal Yisrael.
We dedicate this volume to our daughters, **Rebecca and Mollie,**
who are the light of our lives and our blessings, and always fill our hearts with nachas;
and to their zeide, **Mr. Herman Jutkowitz**, who is a constant source of guidance and inspiration;

and in memory of our beloved parents
Martin W. and Ruth Trencher ז״ל — משה בן מאניס ז״ל ורחל בת אברהם הכהן ע״ה
Bernice Jutkowitz ע״ה — ברכה בת שניאור זלמן ע״ה

May our daughters have the honor to teach the value of Torah to their own children,
and may Torah be the guiding light for all of Klal Yisrael.

לעילוי נשמת

Franky Ehrenberg — הבחור מרדכי גדליהו ז״ל בן משה ואסתר שיחי׳

June 22, 2003 / נפ׳ כ״ג סיון תשס״ג

With a life of Torah study and service to Klal Yisrael ahead of him,
our beloved son, brother, and uncle was plucked from this life at only twenty-three.

כי מרדכי . . . דרש טוב לעמו ודבר שלום לכל זרעו

Dr. Martin and Esther Ehrenberg

Elisheva and Dr. Scott Leon Ehrenberg

Dr. Judy and Hillel Olshin
Yonatan Eliezer Sara Elisheva Shmuel Abba

Richard Bookstaber and Janice Horowitz

In memory of his son

May his memory be a blessing
to all those whose lives he touched.

Michael and Patricia Schiff
Sophia, Juliette and Stefan

in memory and appreciation of
Jerome Schottenstein ז״ל

and in honor of beloved parents and grandparents
Shirlie and Milton Levitin Solange and Joseph Fretas Judy and Robert Schiff

and Torah scholars
Rabbi Mordechai Schiff ז״ל and **Rabbi Ephraim Schiff ז״ל**

May we all bring honor to Hashem

*In formation

Community Guardians of the Talmud

A community is more than a collection of individuals. It is a new entity that is a living expression of support of Torah and dedication to the heritage of Klal Yisrael.

In honor of

Rabbi Reuven Fink and the *maggidei shiur* of **Young Israel of New Rochelle**

Dr. Joey and Lisa Bernstein
in memory of
שרה אלטע בת אברהם ע״ה
Mrs. Sondra Goldman ע״ה

Meyer and Ellen Koplow
in honor of their children
Tovah and Michael Koplow, Jonathan, and Aliza

Stanley and Sheri Raskas
in memory of his parents
ראובן ב״ר חיים שבתי לייב ע״ה וחנה בת הרב טוביה ע״ה
Ralph and Annette Raskas ז״ל

Stanley and Ellen Wasserman
in memory of
חיה פיגא בת שמריהו — Viola Charles ע״ה
רות גולדה בת שמריהו — Ruth Schreiber ע״ה
לאה בת יוסף — Lee Salzberg ע״ה

Stanley and Vivian Bernstein and children
in honor of their parents and grandparents
Jules and Adele Bernstein
Andrew and Renee Weiss

Dr. Ronald and Susan Moskovich
in honor of their children
Adam Moshe, Leah Rivka, and David
"עשה תורתך קבע"

Drs. Arthur and Rochelle Turetsky
in honor of their children and grandson
Avi and Melissa, Jonathan and Nili, Yehuda
Shmuel Chaim

Gerald and Judith Ziering
in memory of
יחיאל מיכל בן אפרים פישל ז״ל וזלטא בת נחמן ע״ה
Jesse and Laurette Ziering ז״ל

Aaron and Carol Greenwald
in honor of their children and grandchildren
Ira and Jamie Gurvitch and children
Shlomo and Tobi Greenwald and children

Karen and Michael Raskas and Family

Mark and Anne Wasserman
in honor of their children
Joseph, Bailey, Erin, Rebeccah and Jordyn

Daf Yomi shiur
in honor of their wives

Lakewood Links
in honor of
Rabbi Abish Zelishovsky

The Community of Great Neck, New York

YOUNG ISRAEL OF GREAT NECK
Rabbi Yaacov Lerner
Rabbi Eric Goldstein
Dr. Leeber Cohen
Professor Lawrence Schiffman

GREAT NECK SYNAGOGUE
Rabbi Ephraim R. Wolf ז״ל
Rabbi Dale Polakoff
Rabbi Shalom Axelrod
Rabbi Yoel Aryeh
Rabbi Yossi Singer

In Memoriam
Rabbi Ephraim R. Wolf ז״ל,
a pioneer of *harbotzas Torah,* a *kiruv* visionary, and a gifted spiritual leader. His legacy is the flourishing Torah community of Great Neck, New York.

The Community of Columbus, Ohio

In memory of **Jerome Schottenstein** Of Blessed Memory
and in honor of **Geraldine Schottenstein and Family**

Jay And Jeanie Schottenstein
Joseph, Jonathan, Jeffrey
Ann And Ari Deshe
Elie, David, Dara, Daniel
Susie And Jon Diamond
Jillian, Joshua, Jacob
Lori Schottenstein
Saul And Sonia Schottenstein

Sarah and Edward Arndt & Family
Irwin and Beverly Bain
Daniela & Yoram Benary
Liron & Alexandra, Oron, Doreen
Deborah & Michael Broidy
Michelle & Daniel
Families of Columbus Kollel
Naomi & Reuven Dessler
Sylvia & Murray Ebner & Family

Tod and Cherie Friedman
Rachel, Ross & Kara
Jim & Angie Gesler
Gerald & Karon Greenfield
Ben & Tracy Kraner & Family
Mike, Heidi, Brian, Deena & Leah Levey
Helene & Michael Lehv
Gary Narin
Ira & Laura Nutis & Family

Lea & Thomas Schottenstein & Family
Jeff & Amy Swanson
Jon
Marcy, Mark, Sam, & Adam Ungar
Drs. Philip & Julia Weinerman
Michael & Channa Weisz & Family
Dr. Daniel & Chaya Wuensch & Family
Main Street Synagogue
Howard Zack, Rabbi

The Talmud Associates*

A fellowship of benefactors dedicated to the dissemination of the Talmud

Audrey and Sargent Aborn and Family

Dr. Mark and Dr. Barbara Bell,
Bentzion Yosef and Mordechai Yehudah

The Belz Family

Richard Bookstaber and Janice Horowitz
In memory of his son

Michael and Bettina Bradfield
Gabrielle and Matthew
(London)

Nachi and Zippi Brown,
Jessica, Daniella, Shachar and Mindy
in honor of their parents and grandparents

Columbus Jewish Foundation

Milton Cooper and Family

Dr. and Mrs. David Diamond

Nahum and Feige Hinde Dicker and Family

Sophia, Alberto and Rose Djmal

Dr. Richard Dubin

Kenneth and Cochava Dubin

Dr. Martin and Esther Ehrenberg

David and Simone Eshaghian

Rabbi Judah and Ruth Feinerman

In honor of
Mr. and Mrs. Yehoshua Chaim Fischman
by their children

Mayer and Ruthy Friedman
Ari, Yitzy, Suri, Dovi

Dr. Michael and Susan Friedman
לזכות בניהם, כלתם, ונכדם; בנותיהם, וחתניהם שיחי׳

Yeshaya and Perel Friedman

Julius Frishman

David and Sally Frenkel
לזכות בניהם וכלתם היקרים שיחיו:
דניאל שמואל ומאשה שושנה, אורי גבריאל, רונית פרימיט

Daniel and Ruth Furmanovich

Shimmy and Devorah Gardyn

Gorfine Schiller Gardyn

Sander and Tracy Gerber
לזכות בניהם היקרים יעקב עקיבא, אסתר פערל, טליה גולדה,
חנה טובה, רותי רבקה, שרה אורה, ושושנה חוה שיחי׳
שיתעלו בתורה ויראת שמים

Leon and Agi Goldenberg
in honor of the marriage of their children
Mendy and Estie Blau

Robert and Rita Gluck
לרפו״ש טויבא רחל בת פריידא שתחי׳

Shari and Jay Gold and Family

Dr. Martin and Shera Goldman and Family

Esther Henzel

Hirtz, Adler and Zupnick Families

Hashi and Miriam Herzka

Norman and Sandy Nissel Horowitz

Mrs. Farokh Imanuel, Kamram Imanuel
Dr. Mehran and Sepideh Imanuel
Eli and Fariba Maghen

David and Trudy Justin and Family
in honor of their parents
Zoltan and Kitty Justin

Nosson Shmuel and Ann Kahn and Family
ולזכות בניהם היקרים שיחיו:
חיים דוד, צבי מנחם, אברהם יצחק, ומשפחתם

David J. and Dora Kleinbart

In honor of
Mr. and Mrs. Label Kutoff
by their children

The Landowne Family

Ezriel and Miriam Langer

Mr. and Mrs. Chaim Leibel

Yehuda and Rasie Levi

Donald Light

Rudolph and Esther Lowy

Raphael and Blimie Manela
לזכות בניהם היקרים שיחיו:
מתתיהו, ישראל, ישעיהו, חיים משה, ושמעון

*In formation

The Talmud Associates*

A fellowship of benefactors dedicated to the dissemination of the Talmud

Howard and Debra Margolin and Family
Mendy and Phyllis Mendlowitz
Robby and Judy Neuman and Family
לזכות בניהם היקרים שיחיו:
אברהם לייב ושרה מאטיל, מרדכי שרגא וזיסל,
שמואל שמעלקא ונחמה, רחל ברכה וישראל זכריהו,
מנשה ברוך וחיה רחל
RoAnna and Moshe Pascher
לזכות בניהם היקרים שיחיו:
נח צבי, דוד ישראל, אילנה שירה בתיה
Naftali Binyomin and Zypora Perlman
Kenneth Ephraim and Julie Pinczower
לרפו״ש ישראל חיים בן פייגלא שיחי׳
Dr. Douglas and Vivian Rabin
Michael G. Reiff
Ingeborg and Ira Leon Rennert
Alan Jay and Hindy Rosenberg
Aviva and Oscar Rosenberg
John and Sue Rossler Family
Mr. and Mrs. David Rubin and Family
Dinah Rubinoff and Family
Ms. Ruth Russ
Mr. and Mrs. Alexander Scharf
Mark and Chani Scheiner
Avi and Michou Schnur
Rubin and Marta Schron
Rivie and Leba Schwebel and Family
Shlomo Segev (Smouha)
Bernard and Chaya Shafran
לזכות בניהם היקרים שיחיו:
דבורה, יעקב חיים, דוד זאב, אסתר מנוחה

Jeffrey and Catherine Shachat
in honor of Rabbeim Howard Zack and Judah Dardik
Steven J. Shaer
Joel and Malka Shafran
לזכות בניהם היקרים שיחיו:
אשר נחמן, טובה חיה, תמר פעסיל, שרה חוה
Robin and Warren Shimoff
Nathan B. and Malka Silberman
The Soclof Family
Dr. Edward L. and Judith Steinberg
Avrohom Chaim and Elisa Taub
Hadassah, Yaakov Yehuda Aryeh, Shifra, Faige, Devorah Raizel, and Golda Leah
Max Taub
and his son Yitzchak
Jay and Sari Tepper
Walter and Adele Wasser
Melvin, Armond and Larry Waxman
William and Noémie Wealcatch
The Wegbreit Family
Robert and Rachel Weinstein and Family
Dr. Zelig and Evelyn (Gutwein) Weinstein
Yaakov, Daniella, Aliza and Zev
Erwin and Myra Weiss
Morry and Judy Weiss
Shlomo and Esther Werdiger
Leslie M. and Shira Westreich
Willie and Blimie Wiesner
The Yad Velvel Foundation
Moshe and Venezia Zakheim
Dr. Harry and Holly Zinn
Mrs. Edith Zukor and Family

*In formation

In Memoriam — לזכרון עולם

Dedicated by the Talmud Associates to those who forged eternal links

Friedman — ר׳ אברהם ב״ר אלטר יצחק אייזיק ע״ה
Frishman — מרים בת ר׳ יוסף מרדכי ע״ה
Frishman — יצחק אריה ב״ר יהודה ע״ה ומרים לאה בת ר׳ יצחק ע״ה
Furmanovich — לע״נ שרה הניה בת פסח הלוי ע״ה
Furmanovich — לע״נ גדליה דב בן אברהם יואל ז״ל
Gardyn — הרב משה בן הרב צבי זצ״ל
Gardyn — חיה פריידל בת שמעון פנחס ע״ה
Goldman — אביו, צבי יעקב בן חיים ז״ל
Goldman — אמו, שפרה בת ר׳ קלונימוס קלמן ע״ה
Goldberger — אברהם צבי בן מתתיהו ע״ה
Gugenheim — החבר אפרים בן רפאל ע״ה
Gugenheim — בריינדל בת החבר נתן הכהן ע״ה
Hanz — חיים בן מרדכי הי״ד
Henzel — אברהם בן ר׳ מנחם זאב ע״ה
Hirtz — אליעזר בן ישעיה ז״ל ולאה בת יוסף הלוי ע״ה
Honig — ר׳ פנחס בן ר׳ יצחק חיים ז״ל
Honig — בלומה לאה בת ר׳ מרדכי ע״ה
Horowitz — שלמה יהודה ב״ר זלמן יוסף הלוי ז״ל ומרים בת אברהם הכהן ע״ה
Imanuel — מרדכי בן רחמים ז״ל
Kahn — ר׳ ישראל אריה ב״ר שמואל הכהן ז״ל
Kahn — גיטל בת נתן ע״ה
Katzef — פרומה באדענה בת אלחנן ע״ה
Kleinbart — משה ב״ר אריה לייב ע״ה
Kleinbart — בתיה בת ר׳ משה אברהם ע״ה
Kriegel — רויזא מינצא בת הרב ישראל יהודה ע״ה
Kulefsky — הילד יהודה לייב ע״ה בן נתן נטע לאי״ט
Langer — משה בן יצחק הי״ד
Landowne — שלמה בן יוסף ע״ה
Lasry — שאול ב״ר אברהם ע״ה וזהרה אסתר בת משה ע״ה
Lazar — אליעזר שאול בן זאב מאיר ע״ה
Lefkovich — ר׳ זאב וועלוול ב״ר יצחק אייזיק ע״ה
Lemberger — יצחק בן אריה ע״ה
Leibel — יחזקאל שרגא ב״ר חיים ע״ה
Leibel — רויזא בת ר׳ אברהם משה ע״ה
Levi — הרב חיים מאיר בן ר׳ מנחם ע״ה
Levi — שושנה טייבא רייזל בת ר׳ יחזקאל גרשון ע״ה
Light — משה גבריאל בן אברהם אליהו ז״ל וחנה בת נתן ע״ה
Lowy — מרדכי אריה ב״ר רפאל הלוי ז״ל ומינדל בת ר׳ שלמה זלמן ע״ה
May — ר׳ יוסף בן הרב יהודה אריה ע״ה
Meizner — מרדכי חיים ב״ר זבולן יצחק חייא ז״ל
Miller — אלטער משה יוסף ב״ר צבי אריה ז״ל
Moskowitz — אליעזר ב״ר אברהם ברוך ז״ל וזהבה בת ר׳ משה ע״ה
Neuman — ר׳ יצחק אייזיק צבי בן מאיר אהרן ז״ל
Dr. Moshe Neuman — ר׳ משה ב״ר יצחק אייזיק ז״ל

Abraham — שמחה בן ר׳ יהודה לייב הכהן ע״ה
דוד חי ב״ר שלום הכהן ע״ה וחנה בת ר׳ עזרא ע״ה
אהרן בן חיים זאב ע״ה גאלדע בת ר׳ דוד ע״ה
Ashkenazy — ר׳ שלמה ב״ר יצחק זצ״ל ורעיתו עלי׳ מינדעל בת ר׳ יעקב ע״ה
Sarah T. Belz — שרה בת אהרן צבי הלוי ע״ה
Ben-Ari — אליעזר בן מרדכי ע״ה ושרה בת ר׳ אברהם ע״ה
Ben-Ari — מרדכי בן אליעזר ע״ה
Berber — משה ורחל
Menashe Bernath — ר׳ מנשה בן שמואל שמעלקא ז״ל
Hency Bernath — הענצה רייזעל בת אברהם ארי׳ ע״ה
Biegeleisen — שמעון דוד ז״ל ב״ר יעקב שלמה שיחי׳ לאוי״ט
Blitz — דוב מאיר ב״ר דוד הכהן ע״ה
Freddy Bradfield — יעקב בן צבי ע״ה
אהרן ב״ר דוד הכהן ז״ל
Elihu Brodsky — אליהו ב״ר חיים ע״ה
Vera (Greif) Brodsky — יונה בת ר׳ פינחס ע״ה
Cooperberg — שימה רייזל בת ר׳ אהרן שלמה ע״ה
Cooperberg — אברהם אשר בן ר׳ מאיר ע״ה
Cumsky — דוב בער בן אברהם יששכר ע״ה ופעשא מאטלא בת יוסף ע״ה
צבי טעביל בן ישראל ע״ה וליבע בת דוד ע״ה
Diamant — אשר ב״ר יהושע מרדכי הכהן ע״ה
Diamant — שרה בת ר׳ אריה ע״ה
Diamant — ר׳ דוב ב״ר משה ע״ה ורייזל בת ר׳ אברהם ע״ה
Diamond — דר. ר׳ יצחק ב״ר ברוך בענדיט ע״ה
Dicker — מרדכי צבי ב״ר יעקב ע״ה
Dicker — קיילא בת ר׳ משה ע״ה
Djmal — טופיק טוביה בן משה ושושנה ע״ה
Paul and Jeannette Dubin ע״ה
Mollie Dubinsky ע״ה
Abram B. Efroymson ע״ה
Sylvia Spira Efroymson ע״ה
Ehrenberg — אברהם בן עמנואל ע״ה ויוכבד בת ר׳ אלימלך ע״ה
Einhorn — משה בן ברוך ז״ל ורבקה נעכא בת חיים צבי ע״ה
Eshaghian — אברהם בן דוד ע״ה
Esrig — דוד בן שלמה ע״ה וחיה אייגא בת שלום ע״ה
Feiden — ישראל בן אהרן ע״ה
Feinerman — אליעזר בן יוסף ע״ה ולאה בת ישראל יצחק ע״ה
יוסף בן צבי יחזקאל ע״ה ושרה בת ר׳ משה ע״ה
Feinstein — הרה״ג ר׳ דוד בן הרה״ג ר׳ משה זצ״ל
Freier — ישעיה צבי ב״ר חיים אלכסנדר יוסף ע״ה
Freier — שיינדל בת ר׳ משה הלוי ע״ה
Freilich — הרב יצחק דוב ב״ר אברהם יעקב ז״ל
Frenkel — גרשון בן יחיאל דוד ע״ה Rottenstreich — דוד בן עקיבא ע״ה
Friedman — ר׳ אהרן ב״ר יעקב מאיר ע״ה

In Memoriam — לזכרון עולם

Dedicated by the Talmud Associates to those who forged eternal links

Bobi Neuman — פייגא יכט בת שרגא פייבל ע״ה
Rochel Neuman — רחל בת משה הכהן ע״ה
Nissel — שלמה מאיר בן הרב חיים לייב עזריאל ז״ל
Paneth — אלטע חיה שרה ע״ה בת ר׳ פנחס שיחי׳ לאוי״ט
Parnes — אריה לייבש בן יוסף יצחק ועטיא בת אשר ראובן ע״ה
Parnes — הרב אברהם זאב ב״ר ישכר ע״ה
Parsons — משה זלמן בן אהרן דוב ע״ה
Perlman — יוסף ב״ר נפתלי בנימין ז״ל ורעכל לאה בת ר׳ שלמה ע״ה
Perlowitz — הרב משה ב״ר אליעזר הלל ע״ה
Pinczower — אפרים ב״ר ישראל חיים ופייגלא בת ר׳ יעקב ע״ה
Rabin — ישראל בן נחום ע״ה
Reiff — לוי יצחק ב״ר עזריאל ז״ל ויהודית בת ר׳ יצחק אייזיק ע״ה
Rennert — שרה בת יצחק יעקב ע״ה
Rennert — יונה מנחם בן אהרן ע״ה
Rosenberg — חיים נחמן ב״ר דוד ולאה בת יוסף ע״ה
Sam and Leah Rosenbloom ע״ה
Roth — ר׳ צבי יהודה ז״ל ב״ר אברהם יצחק שיחי׳ לאוי״ט
Roth — משה ב״ר יעקב הכהן ע״ה   Weisner — יצחק ב״ר זאב ע״ה
In memory of the Sanz-Klausenburger Rebbe זצוק״ל
כ״ק אדמו״ר אבדק״ק צאנז-קלויזענבורג זי״ע
מרן הרהגה״צ ר׳ יקותיאל יהודה בהרהגה״צ ר׳ צבי זצוק״ל
נלב״ע ש״ק פ׳ חקת, ט׳ תמוז תשנ״ד
William Shachat ע״ה and Israel Ira Shachat ע״ה
Scharf — אליהו ב״ר משה יעקב ושרה בת אלכסנדר זיסקינד ע״ה
Scherman — ר׳ אברהם דוב ב״ר שמואל נטע ע״ה
Scherman — ליבא בת ר׳ זאב וואלף ע״ה
Schneerson — כ״ק אדמו״ר יוסף יצחק בן כ״ק אדמו״ר שלום דובער זצ״ל
Schneerson — חי׳ מושקא בת כ״ק אדמו״ר יוסף יצחק ע״ה
Schneerson — כ״ק אדמו״ר מנחם מענדל בן הרב לוי יצחק זצ״ל
Schnur — אברהם יצחק בן אהרן הי״ד   וחנה בת חיים יעקב ע״ה
Schonbrun — שרגא פייבל ב״ר יעקב הכהן ז״ל
Schonbrun — מאטל אסתר בת מרדכי הלוי ע״ה
Schron — אליעזר דוב בן חיים משה ע״ה
Schron — חוה בת שמעון ע״ה
Schulman — חיים חייקל בן ר׳ שמואל ע״ה
Schulman — חיה בת הרב ישראל יהודה ע״ה
Schwebel — אברהם זכריה מנחם בן יוסף ז״ל
Schwebel — מחלה בת ישראל מרדכי ע״ה
Scherman — חיים שמואל ב״ר אברהם דוב ע״ה
Scherman — הילד אברהם דוב ע״ה ב״ר זאב יוסף שיחי׳
Sol Scheiner — שלמה טוביה בן יהושע מנחם הלוי ע״ה
Rose Schwartz — רייזל בת הרה״ג ר׳ אברהם יצחק ע״ה
Shafran — ר׳ יהושע ב״ר אברהם ע״ה

Shayovich — משה יעקב ב״ר נחום ועטיא פייגא בת מרדכי ע״ה
Shimoff — ר׳ ישראל דוב ב״ר אהרן יעקב ז״ל
Shimoff — חיה רבקה לאה בת ר׳ אליעזר יהודה ע״ה
Shubow — יוסף שלום בן משה ע״ה
Silberman — ר׳ צבי ב״ר זאב הלוי ע״ה
Silberman — דבורה אסתר בת ישראל ע״ה
Silbermintz — יהושע ב״ר יוסף שמריהו ע״ה
Singer — צבי בן ר׳ חיים ע״ה
Singer — הינדי בת ר׳ שלמה ע״ה
Soclof — אברהם אבא ב״ר שמריהו ע״ה
Soclof — חיה ברכה בת צבי הירש הלוי ע״ה
Smouha — הרב אליהו בן מאיר הלוי ע״ה
Steir — משה בן מיכאל ע״ה
Steinberg – יצחק גדליה בן יהודה לייב ע״ה
Steinberg – מלכה בת מאיר לוי ע״ה
Stern — ר׳ חיים מאיר ב״ר שמחה ז״ל ובינה בת ר׳ יוסף מרדכי ע״ה
Tabak — שיינא רחל בת יוסף מרדכי ע״ה
Taub — ר׳ יעקב ב״ר יהודה אריה ע״ה נפ׳ ד׳ מנחם אב תשל״ט
Taub — אליעזר יוסף בן מענדל ע״ה
Taub — מענדל בן אליעזר יוסף   חיה בת הירש ע״ה
Taub — רויזא בת ר׳ משה ע״ה
Wealcatch — חיים דוב ב״ר זאב ואסתר בת ר׳ יוסף אייזיק ע״ה
Weiss — צבי בן יואל ע״ה
Weiss — גיטל בת ישראל ע״ה
Werdiger — ר׳ שלמה אלימלך ב״ר ישראל יצחק ע״ה
Westreich — הרב יהושע בן הרב יוסף יאסקא ז״ל
Leo Werter ע״ה
Wiesner — הרב שמעיה בן הרב זאב ע״ה
Wiesner — שרה לאה בת ר׳ צבי אריה ע״ה
Zakheim-Brecher — בתיה רחל ע״ה בת ר׳ משה יוסף שיחי׳ לאוי״ט
Zalstain — שמעון בן מרדכי יוסף הלוי ע״ה
Zimmer — ר׳ אברהם יעקב בן אהרן אליעזר ע״ה
הרב אהרן ב״ר מאיר יעקב ע״ה
הרבנית פרומא בת ר׳ חיים צבי ע״ה
Zinn — צבי יהודה בן שמעון ע״ה
Zinn — דבורה בת יחיאל מרדכי ע״ה
Leslie Zukor — ר׳ יצחק חיים ב״ר יוסף ע״ה
Zlatow — ר׳ שמואל דוד ב״ר מאיר יעקב ז״ל
הרב אהרן ב״ר מאיר יעקב זצ״ל
הרבנית פרומא בת ר׳ חיים צבי ע״ה
צבי יהודה ז״ל בן אברהם יצחק לאוי״ט
חיים מאיר בן שמחה ז״ל ובינה בת יוסף מרדכי הכהן ע״ה
אליעזר ב״ר אברהם ברוך ז״ל וגולדה זהבה בת משה הלוי ע״ה

תנצב״ה

We express our appreciation to the distinguished patrons
who have dedicated volumes in the

HEBREW ELUCIDATION OF THE SCHOTTENSTEIN EDITION OF THE TALMUD

Dedicated by

JAY AND JEANIE SCHOTTENSTEIN

and their children

Joseph Aaron and Lindsay Brooke, Jonathan Richard and Nicole Lauren, Jeffrey Adam and Ariella

Jacob Meir Jonah Philip Emma Blake Winnie Simone Teddi Isabella Allegra Giselle Elodie Yael Jerome Meir

SEDER ZERA'IM: **Mrs. Margot Guez and Family**
Paul Vivianne Michelle Hubert Monique Gerard Aline Yves

SEDER MOED: **Jacob M. M. and Pnina (Rand) Graff** (Los Angeles)
Malka Ita and Aaron Rubenstein Chaya Rivka Graff
Meira and Dr. Elie Portnoy Joy and Adam Kushnir
Meir and Itta Graff Ahuva and Yehuda Levin and Families

SEDER NASHIM: **Geoffrey and Mimi Rochwarger** (Bet Shemesh)
Tehila Rivka Naftali Zvi Atara Kaila Aryeh Shalom Dalia Eliana

SEDER NEZIKIN: **Yisrael and Gittie Ury and Family** (Los Angeles)

SEDER KODASHIM: **Yaakov and Beatrice Herzog and Family** (Toronto)

INTRODUCTION TO THE TALMUD: **Robin and Warren Shimoff**

BERACHOS I: **Jay and Jeanie Schottenstein** (Columbus, Ohio)
BERACHOS II: **Zvi and Betty Ryzman** (Los Angeles)
SHABBOS I: **Moshe and Hessie Neiman** (New York)
SHABBOS II: **David and Elky Retter and Family** (New York)
SHABBOS III: **Mendy and Itta Klein** (Cleveland)
SHABBOS IV: **Mayer and Shavy Gross** (New York)
ERUVIN I: **The Schottenstein Family** (Columbus, Ohio)
ERUVIN II: **The Schottenstein Family** (Columbus, Ohio)
PESACHIM I: **Serge and Nina Muller** (Antwerp)
PESACHIM II: **The Cohen Family**
PESACHIM III: **Morris and Devora Smith** (New York / Jerusalem)
SHEKALIM: **The Rieder, Wiesen and Karasick Families**
YOMA I: **Peretz and Frieda Friedberg** (Toronto)
YOMA II: **Mr. and Mrs. Avrohom Noach Klein** (New York)
SUCCAH I: **The Pruwer Family** (Jerusalem)
SUCCAH II: **The Pruwer Family** (Jerusalem)
BEITZAH: **Chaim and Chava Fink** (Tel Aviv)
ROSH HASHANAH: **Avi and Meira Schnur** (Savyon)
TAANIS: **Mendy and Itta Klein** (Cleveland)
MEGILLAH: **In memory of Jerome Schottenstein ז״ל**
MOED KATTAN: **Yisroel and Shoshana Lefkowitz** (New York)
CHAGIGAH: **Steven and Hadassah Weisz** (New York)
YEVAMOS I: **Phillip and Ruth Wojdyslawski** (Sao Paulo, Brazil)
YEVAMOS II: **Phillip and Ruth Wojdyslawski** (Sao Paulo, Brazil)

פטרוני התלמוד

YEVAMOS III: **Phillip and Ruth Wojdyslawski** (Sao Paulo, Brazil)
KESUBOS I: **Ben Fishoff and Family** (New York)
KESUBOS II: **Jacob and Esther Gold** (New York)
KESUBOS III: **David and Roslyn Lowy** (Forest Hills)
NEDARIM I: **Soli and Vera Spira** (New York / Jerusalem)
NEDARIM II: **Mr. and Mrs. Yehudah Klein** **Mr. and Mrs. Moshe Klein**
NAZIR: **Shlomo and Esther Ben Arosh** (Jerusalem)
SOTAH: **Motty and Malka Klein** (New York)
GITTIN I: **Mrs. Kate Tannenbaum;**
Elliot and Debra Tannenbaum; Edward and Linda Zizmor
GITTIN II: **Mordchai Aron and Dvorah Gombo** (New York)
KIDDUSHIN I: **Dr. Allan and Dr. Chaikie Novetsky** (Jerusalem)
KIDDUSHIN II: **Jacqui and Patty Oltuski** (Savyon)
BAVA KAMMA I: **Lloyd and Hadassah Keilson** (New York)
BAVA KAMMA II: **Faivel and Roiza Weinreich** (New York)
BAVA KAMMA III: **David and Fanny Malek**
BAVA METZIA I: **Joseph and Rachel Leah Neumann** (Monsey)
BAVA METZIA II: **Shlomo and Tirzah Eisenberg** (Bnei Brak)
BAVA METZIA III: **A. George and Stephanie Saks** (New York)
BAVA BASRA I: **Ezra and Debbie Beyman** (New York)
BAVA BASRA II: **Ezra and Debbie Beyman** (New York)
BAVA BASRA III: **Ezra and Debbie Beyman** (New York)
SANHEDRIN I: **Martin and Rivka Rapaport** (Jerusalem)
SANHEDRIN II: **Aryeh and Faige Lebovic** **Avrom and Susie Lebovic** (Toronto)
SANHEDRIN III: In honor of **Joseph and Anita Wolf** (Tel Aviv)
MAKKOS: **Hirsch and Raquel Wolf** (New York)
SHEVUOS: **Jacques and Miriam Monderer** (Antwerp)
AVODAH ZARAH I: **Mr. and Mrs. Eli Kaufman** (Petach Tikva)
AVODAH ZARAH II: **Mr. and Mrs. Chaim Schweid** (New York)
HORAYOS-EDUYOS: **Woli and Chaja Stern, Jacques and Ariane Stern** (Sao Paulo, Brazil)
ZEVACHIM I: **Mr. and Mrs. Eli Kaufman** (Petach Tikva)
ZEVACHIM II: **Mr. and Mrs. Eli Kaufman** (Petach Tikva)
ZEVACHIM III: **Mr. and Mrs. Eli Kaufman** (Petach Tikva)
MENACHOS I: **Yaakov and Beatrice Herzog and family** (Toronto)
MENACHOS II: **Yaakov and Beatrice Herzog and family** (Toronto)
MENACHOS III: **Yaakov and Beatrice Herzog and family** (Toronto)
CHULLIN I: **The Pluczenik Families** (Antwerp)
CHULLIN II: **Avrohom David and Chaya Baila Klein** (Monsey)
CHULLIN III: **Avrohom David and Chaya Baila Klein** (Monsey)
CHULLIN IV: **The Frankel Family** (New York)
BECHOROS I: **Mordchai Aron and Dvorah Gombo** (New York)
BECHOROS II: **Howard and Chaya Balter** (New York)
ARACHIN: **Mr. and Mrs. Eli Kaufman** (Petach Tikva)
TEMURAH: **Abraham and Bayla Fluk** (Tel Aviv)
KEREISOS: **Mr. and Mrs. Eli Kaufman** (Petach Tikva)
ME'ILAH, TAMID, MIDDOS KINNIM: In memory of **ר׳ אליהו אלעזר ב״ר יוסף ברוך ז״ל**
NIDDAH I: **Daniel and Margaret, Allan and Brocha, and David and Elky Retter and Families**
NIDDAH II: **Jay and Jeanie Schottenstein** (Columbus, Ohio)

PATRONS OF THE TALMUD ❖ DAF YOMI EDITION

We express our appreciation to the distinguished patrons
who have dedicated volumes in

Dedicated by

JAY AND JEANIE SCHOTTENSTEIN

and their children

Joseph Aaron and Lindsay Brooke, Jonathan Richard and Nicole Lauren, Jeffrey Adam and Ariella

Jacob Meir Jonah Philip Emma Blake Winnie Simone Teddi Isabella Allegra Giselle Elodie Yael Jerome Meir

INTRODUCTION TO THE TALMUD:	**Robin and Warren Shimoff**
BERACHOS I:	**Jay and Jeanie Schottenstein** (Columbus, Ohio)
BERACHOS II:	**Zvi and Betty Ryzman** (Los Angeles)
SHABBOS I:	**Dr. Paul and Esther Rosenstock Jake and Dr. Helaine Harman Mrs. Faigy Harman**
SHABBOS II:	**Stanley and Ellen Wasserman**
SHABBOS III:	**Stanley and Ellen Wasserman**
SHABBOS IV:	**Malkie and Nachum Silberman, Leonard and Cassia Friedlander, Elkie Friedlander**
ERUVIN I:	**Jerome and Geraldine Schottenstein**
ERUVIN II:	**Jerome and Geraldine Schottenstein**
PESACHIM I:	**Tommy and Judy Rosenthal**
PESACHIM II:	**Yisroel and Rochi Zlotowitz**
PESACHIM III:	**Lorraine and Mordy Sohn Ann and Pinky Sohn**
SHEKALIM:	**Laibish and Tanya Kamenetsky**
BEITZAH:	**Eric and Joyce Austein**
ROSH HASHANAH:	**Steve and Genie Savitsky**
YOMA I:	**Mrs. Ann Makovsky and Family** (Cleveland)
YOMA II:	**Mr. and Mrs. David Justin**
SUCCAH II:	**The Lowy and Fasman Families** (Los Angeles)
TAANIS:	**David and Jean Bernstein**
MEGILLAH:	**Jay and Jeanie Schottenstein** (Columbus, Ohio)
MOED KATAN:	**Leon and Olga Klein Allen and Sylvia Klein Daniel and Esther Ollech**
CHAGIGAH:	**Benzi and Esther Dunner**
YEVAMOS I:	**Phillip and Ruth Wojdyslawski and Family**
YEVAMOS II:	**Phillip and Ruth Wojdyslawski and Family**
YEVAMOS III:	**Phillip and Ruth Wojdyslawski and Family**
KESUBOS I:	**The Fishoff Families**
KESUBOS II:	**Moise & Angie Hendeles Hayim & Miriam Hendeles Jerry & Cecille Cohen**
KESUBOS III:	**Brenda and Isaac Gozdzik** (Los Angeles)
NEDARIM I:	**Fradie Rapp and Children**
NEDARIM II:	**In memory of Laurence A. Tisch**
NAZIR I:	**Andrew and Nancy Neff**
NAZIR II:	**Andrew and Nancy Neff**
SOTAH I:	**Motty and Malka Klein and Family**
SOTAH II:	**Motty and Malka Klein and Family**
GITTIN I:	**Mrs. Kate Tannenbaum; Elliot and Debra Tannenbaum Edward and Linda Zizmor**
GITTIN II:	**Mrs. Kate Tannenbaum; Elliot and Debra Tannenbaum Edward and Linda Zizmor**

PATRONS OF THE TALMUD ✦ DAF YOMI EDITION

KIDDUSHIN I:	**Leslie and Shira Westreich** **Adam and Dayna, Rayna and Dina**
KIDDUSHIN II:	**In honor of Berish and Hannah Fuchs**
BAVA KAMMA I:	**Yitzchok and Shoshana Ganger and Family**
BAVA KAMMA II:	**The Maggid Families** (Sao Paulo, Brazil)
BAVA KAMMA III:	**Robert and Malka Friedlander** (Sao Paulo, Brazil)
BAVA METZIA I:	**Fred and Cindy Schulman**
BAVA METZIA II:	**Suzy and Yussie Ostreicher**
BAVA METZIA III:	**Stephanie and George Saks**
BAVA BASRA I:	**Nachum and Malkie Silberman**
BAVA BASRA II:	**Roger and Caroline Markfield**
BAVA BASRA III:	**Jaime and Marilyn Sohacheski**
SANHEDRIN I:	**Martin and Rivka Rapaport**
SANHEDRIN II:	**Martin and Rivka Rapaport**
SANHEDRIN III:	**Marvin and Roz Samuels**
SHEVUOS:	**Michael and Danielle Gross** (Herzlia and London)
MAKKOS:	**David and Joan Tepper and Family**
AVODAH ZARAH I:	**The Kuhl Family**
AVODAH ZARAH II:	**In memory of Mr. Jerome Schottenstein ז״ל**
HORAYOS-EDUYOS:	**Woli and Chaja Stern, Jacques and Ariane Stern** (Sao Paulo, Brazil)
ZEVACHIM I:	**Robin and Warren Shimoff**
ZEVACHIM II:	**Abbie Spetner** **Ari and Chaya** **Sara and Dovi Nussbaum** **Chanoch** **Moshe**
ZEVACHIM III:	**Yaakov and Yona Spinner**
MENACHOS I:	**Terumah Foundation**
MENACHOS II:	**Terumah Foundation**
MENACHOS III:	**Terumah Foundation**
CHULLIN I:	**Rabbi Heshie and Rookie Billet**
CHULLIN II:	**The Kleinman Family**
CHULLIN IV:	**Terumah Foundation**
BECHOROS I:	**Jeff and Leslie Gould**
BECHOROS II:	**Hilda and Yitz Applbaum**
ARACHIN:	**The Brown Family**
TEMURAH:	**Dr. Thomas and Anne Kohn** **Dr. Allan and Susan Seidenfeld**
KEREISOS:	**In memory of Rabbi Meir Shapiro זצ״ל, the Lubliner Rav**
ME'ILAH, TAMID, MIDDOS KINNIM:	**Steven and Renée Adelsberg**
NIDDAH I:	**Martin and Geraldine Schottenstein Hoffman** **Marc and Rachel Hurwitz**
NIDDAH II:	**In memory of Mr. Jerome Schottenstein ז״ל**

We express our appreciation to the distinguished patrons
who have dedicated volumes in the

COMPACT SIZE HEBREW ELUCIDATION OF THE SCHOTTENSTEIN EDITION OF THE TALMUD

Dedicated by

JAY AND JEANIE SCHOTTENSTEIN

and their children

Joseph Aaron and Lindsay Brooke, Jonathan Richard and Nicole Lauren, Jeffrey Adam and Ariella

Jacob Meir   Jonah Philip   Emma Blake   Winnie Simone   Teddi Isabella   Allegra Giselle   Elodie Yael   Jerome Meir

INTRODUCTION TO THE TALMUD: **Robin and Warren Shimoff**

BERACHOS I: **Jay and Jeanie Schottenstein** (Columbus, Ohio)
BERACHOS II: **Zvi and Betty Ryzman** (Los Angeles)
SHABBOS I: **Yussie and Suzy Ostreicher**
SHABBOS II: in memory of **R' Shimon ben R' Shlomo Zalman ע"ה**
SHABBOS III: **Mendy and Itta Klein** (Cleveland)
SHABBOS IV: **Mayer and Shavy Gross** (New York)
ERUVIN I: **The Schottenstein Family** (Columbus, Ohio)
ERUVIN II: **The Schottenstein Family** (Columbus, Ohio)
PESACHIM I: **Serge and Nina Muller** (Antwerp)
PESACHIM II: **The Cohen Family**
PESACHIM III: **Morris and Devora Smith** (New York / Jerusalem)
SHEKALIM: **Avrohom David and Chaya Baila Klein** (Monsey)
ROSH HASHANAH: **Joseph and Nina**
YOMA I: **Hirsch and Raquel Wolf**
YOMA II: **Mr. and Mrs. Avrohom Noach Klein**
SUCCAH I: **Lloyd and Harriet Keilson**
SUCCAH II: **Joel and Joyce Yarmak**
BEITZAH: **Benjy and Adina Goldstein**
TAANIS: **Mendy and Itta Klein** (Cleveland)
MEGILLAH: **Leibel and Myrna Zisman**
MOED KATTAN: **Binyamin and Dvorah Chanah;** and **Moshe Rubinstein**
CHAGIGAH: **Steven and Hadassah Weisz**
YEVAMOS I: **Phillip and Ruth Wojdyslawski** (Sao Paulo)
YEVAMOS II: **Phillip and Ruth Wojdyslawski** (Sao Paulo)
YEVAMOS III: **Phillip and Ruth Wojdyslawski** (Sao Paulo)
KESUBOS I: **Ben Fishoff and Family**
KESUBOS II: **Judah and Bayla Septimus**
KESUBOS III: **Yitzchak Fund and Zalli Jaffe**
NEDARIM I: **Soli and Vera Spira and Family**
NEDARIM II: **Judah and Yuta Klein   Moshe and Shaindel Klein**
NAZIR I: **Shlomo and Esther Ben Arosh** (Jerusalem)
NAZIR II: **Shlomo and Esther Ben Arosh** (Jerusalem)
GITTIN I: **Mrs. Kate Tannenbaum;**
Elliot and Debra Tannenbaum; Edward and Linda Zizmor

פטרוני התלמוד • מהדורת ״בכל דרכיך״

GITTIN II: **Mordchai Aron and Dvorah Gombo**
KIDDUSHIN I: **David and Fanny Malek**
KIDDUSHIN II: **Peter and Debbie Rabenwurzel**
SOTAH: **Motty and Malka Klein**
BAVA KAMMA I: **Yussie and Estie Fettman** (Miami)
BAVA KAMMA II: **Faivel and Roiza Weinreich**
BAVA KAMMA III: **David and Fanny Malek**
BAVA METZIA I: **Hyman P. Golombeck** **Avrohom Chaim and Renee Fruchthandler**
BAVA METZIA II: **Shlomo and Tirzah Eisenberg** (Bnei Brak)
BAVA METZIA III: **A. George and Stephanie Saks**
BAVA BASRA I: **Ezra and Debbie Beyman**
BAVA BASRA II: **Ezra and Debbie Beyman**
BAVA BASRA III: **Ezra and Debbie Beyman**
SANHEDRIN I: **Martin and Rivka Rapaport** (Jerusalem)
SANHEDRIN II: **Aryeh and Faige Lebovic** **Avrom and Susie Lebovic** (Toronto)
SANHEDRIN III: In honor of **Joseph and Anita Wolf** (Tel Aviv)
MAKKOS: **Hirsch and Raquel Wolf**
SHEVUOS: **Jacques and Miriam Monderer** (Antwerp)
AVODAH ZARAH I: **Mr. and Mrs. Eli Kaufman** (Petach Tikva)
AVODAH ZARAH II: **Mr. and Mrs. Chaim Schweid** (New York)
HORAYOS-EDUYOS: **Woli and Chaja Stern** (Sao Paulo, Brazil)
ZEVACHIM I: **Mr. and Mrs. Eli Kaufman** (Petach Tikva)
ZEVACHIM II: **Mr. and Mrs. Eli Kaufman** (Petach Tikva)
ZEVACHIM III: **Mr. and Mrs. Eli Kaufman** (Petach Tikva)
MENACHOS I: **Yaakov and Beatrice Herzog and family** (Toronto)
MENACHOS II: **Yaakov and Beatrice Herzog and family** (Toronto)
MENACHOS III: **Yaakov and Beatrice Herzog and family** (Toronto)
CHULLIN I: **The Pluczenik Families** (Antwerp)
CHULLIN II: **Avrohom David and Chaya Baila Klein** (Monsey)
CHULLIN III: **Avrohom David and Chaya Baila Klein** (Monsey)
CHULLIN IV: **Levin Family**
BECHOROS I: **Mordchai Aron and Dvorah Gombo** (New York)
BECHOROS II: **Howard and Chaya Balter** (New York)
ARACHIN: **Mr. and Mrs. Eli Kaufman** (Petach Tikva)
TEMURAH: **Abraham and Bayla Fluk** (Tel Aviv)
KEREISOS: **Mr. and Mrs. Eli Kaufman** (Petach Tikva)
ME'ILAH, TAMID, MIDDOS KINNIM: In memory of **ר׳ אליהו אלעזר ב״ר יוסף ברוך ז״ל**
NIDDAH I: **Mrs. Shoshanah Lefkowitz and Family**
NIDDAH II: **Jay and Jeanie Schottenstein** (Columbus, Ohio)

The Schottenstein Edition of the Talmud

They never surrendered the principles of Judaism or the love of Torah that they had absorbed in Lithuania.

This pioneering elucidation of the entire Talmud was named **THE SCHOTTENSTEIN EDITION** in memory of **EPHRAIM AND ANNA SCHOTTENSTEIN** ז״ל, of Columbus, Ohio. Mr. and Mrs. Schottenstein came to the United States as children, but they never surrendered the principles of Judaism or the love of Torah that they had absorbed in their native Lithuania. Tenacious was their devotion to the Sabbath, kashruth, and halachah; their support of needy Jews in a private, sensitive manner; their generosity to Torah institutions; and their refusal to speak ill of others.

This noble and historic gesture of dedication was made by their sons and daughters-in-law **JEROME** ז״ל **AND GERALDINE SCHOTTENSTEIN** and **SAUL AND SONIA SCHOTTENSTEIN.**

Jerome left numerous memorials of accomplishment and generosity, but surely the Schottenstein Edition of the Talmud – spanning centuries – will be the most enduring.

With the untimely passing of JEROME SCHOTTENSTEIN ז״ל, it became our sad privilege to rededicate THE SCHOTTENSTEIN EDITION to his memory, in addition to that of his parents.

Jerome Schottenstein ז״ל was a dear friend and inspirational patron. He saw the world through the lens of eternity, and devoted his mind, heart and resources to the task of assuring that the Torah would never be forgotten by its people. He left numerous memorials of accomplishment and generosity, but surely the **SCHOTTENSTEIN EDITION OF THE TALMUD** – spanning centuries – will be the most enduring.

The Schottensteins are worthy heirs to the traditions and principles of Jerome and his parents. Gracious and generous, kind and caring, they have opened their hearts to countless causes and people.

The Schottensteins are worthy heirs to the traditions and principles of Jerome and his parents. Gracious and generous, kind and caring, they have opened their hearts to countless causes and people. Quietly and considerately, they elevate the dignity and self-respect of those they help; they make their beneficiaries feel like benefactors; they imbue institutions with a new sense of mission to be worthy of the trust placed in them.

THE MESORAH HERITAGE FOUNDATION is proud and grateful to be joined with the Schottenstein family as partners in this monumental endeavor.

We pray that this great undertaking will be a source of merit for the continued health and success of the entire Schottenstein family, including the children and grandchildren:

JAY and JEANIE SCHOTTENSTEIN and their children, Joseph Aaron and Lindsay Brooke, Jonathan Richard, and Jeffrey Adam; **ANN and ARI DESHE** and their children, Elie Michael, David Scott, Dara Lauren, and Daniel Matthew; **SUSAN and JON DIAMOND** and their children, Jillian Leigh, Joshua Louis, and Jacob Meyer; and **LORI SCHOTTENSTEIN.**

The Schottensteins will be remembered with gratitude for as long as English-speaking Jews are nourished by the eternity of the Talmud's wisdom, for, thanks to them, millions of Jews over the generations will become closer to their heritage.

A Jew can accomplish nothing more meaningful or lasting in his sojourn on earth.

ACKNOWLEDGMENTS

The *Roshei HaYeshivah* and *Gedolei Torah* of the previous generation and this one have been unstintingly generous with their time and wisdom. Their guidance has shaped the ArtScroll Series from its inception, and the same holds true for this edition of the Talmud.

MARAN HARAV MORDECHAI GIFTER שליט"א has been more than an inspiration and counselor; he has been a father and mentor of ArtScroll from its very beginning. He encouraged us to embark on the elucidation of the Talmud and guided us in arriving at its final format.

HARAV DAVID FEINSTEIN שליט"א graciously maintained steady communication, and offered wise and erudite suggestions.

HARAV DAVID COHEN שליט"א has unstintingly placed the treasury of his knowledge at our disposal whenever it was needed.

HARAV HILLEL DAVID שליט"א has been a valued friend, counselor, and source of comment.

As overall editor, we are fortunate to have a *talmid chacham* of exceptional proportions, whose humility cannot mask his greatness. The participation of RABBI HERSH GOLDWURM, who also wrote portions of this volume and reviewed and commented on much of the rest, enhances the stature of any project in which he has a role. RABBI YISROEL SIMCHA SCHORR, Rosh Yeshivah of Ohr Sameach-Monsey and RABBI CHAIM MALINOWITZ, Rosh HaKollel of Kollel Beis Medrash Eeyun HaTalmud of Monsey. have joined Rabbi Goldwurm in reviewing and commenting on this work. Its quality is a testament to their outstanding scholarship.

As this project has developed, the efforts of more and more people have become critical to its success, particularly in the writing and editing. We are proud to acknowledge them and express our pride in being associated with so distinguished a group of scholars. The writers of this volume are:

RABBI YOSAIF ASHER WEISS, a highly regarded member of the Kollel of Yeshiva of Staten Island and a member of the faculty of Yeshiva Tiferes Torah, wrote the great majority of the manuscript; portions were also contributed by RABBIS AVROHOM BERMAN, DOVID KATZ, AVROHOM YOSEIF ROSENBERG, ELIYAHU SHULMAN, MICHOEL WEINER, and CHAIM WEINFELD.

The editors of this volume are: RABBIS YEHEZKEL DANZIGER, HILLEL DANZIGER, YOSEF DAVIS, NESANEL KASNETT, HENOCH MORRIS, ABBA ZVI NAIMAN and FEIVEL WAHL.

The participation of all these scholars lends distinction to this volume and the entire Schottenstein Talmud. We are grateful for their selfless efforts and valuable contributions.

The author expresses his profound gratitude to his father-in-law, HARAV REUVEN FEINSTEIN שליט"א, Rosh Yeshiva of Staten Island, who made his time and vast knowledge available to help clarify numerous points of difficulty.

May the author's efforts in the creation of this work be a *z'chus* to the *neshamah* of his father, ר' אהרן צבי ב"ר מאיר ע"ה.

We express our gratitude to RABBI AVROHOM YOSEIF ROSENBERG for performing the difficult task of vowelizing the Aramaic text of the Talmud. We also thank RABBI MOSHE LIEBER for his contributions to the glossary.

The trustees of the Mesorah Heritage Foundation join the Schottenstein family in acknowledging RABBI DR. NORMAN LAMM for his warm encouragement and invaluable assistance; despite his many responsibilities, he has been gracious and understanding whenever called upon.

Among those whose guidance was invaluable in this Talmud project are such leaders of organizational and rabbinic life as LORD RABBI IMMANUEL JAKOBOVITS, RABBI MOSHE SHERER, RABBI PINCHAS STOLPER, RABBI JOSHUA FISHMAN, RABBI MOSHE GLUSTEIN, RABBI DAVID STAVSKY, MR. DAVID H. SCHWARTZ, RABBI MICHAEL LEVI, RABBI YISRAEL H. EIDELMAN, RABBI BURTON JAFFA, RABBI YAAKOV REISMAN, RABBI YAAKOV BENDER, RABBI ZALMAN GIFTER, RABBI YAAKOV M. KATZ, and RABBI TZVI MORGENSTERN.

We are grateful to RABBI ALAN CINER of Columbus, Ohio, a spiritual leader whose goal is to turn Jews into *better* Jews.

Warm acknowledgment is expressed to RABBI RAPHAEL BUTLER, National Director, Orthodox Union/NCSY, whose creative insight, constant good cheer, and inspired leadership have brought multitudes to Torah Judaism.

The manuscript was read by RABBI YOSEF GESSER, as well as by MRS. JUDI DICK and MRS. FAIGIE WEINBAUM. Their meticulous attention to detail was vital to the final product. They are more than proofreaders; many of their insightful suggestions were incorporated into this volume. We also thank MRS. DICK for producing the glossary and Scriptural index.

The typesetting of these volumes is an especially difficult and demanding task; it requires conscientious devotion to the goal of Torah dissemination, as well as a high level of technical skill. To all the members of our typesetting staff who worked long and hard on this volume, sometimes late into the night, we wish to express our deepest appreciation. They are: MISS NICHIE FENDRICH, MR. YEHUDA GORDON, MR. YITZCHOK SAFTLAS, MRS. BASSIE GUTMAN, MRS. CHAVIE FRIEDMAN, MISS MINDY KOHN, MRS. ESTHER FEIERSTEIN, MRS. ZISSI LANDAU, MISS CHAYA GITTY ZAIDMAN and MRS. MIRYAM STAVSKY.

Much cooperative spirit and effort on the part of the administrative and support staffs of the Mesorah Heritage Foundation and ArtScroll/Mesorah Publications are required to enable such a work to be published. We express our gratitude, therefore, to them all. Of the Foundation: RABBI AVIE GOLD, SHMUEL BLITZ, MANNY HENZEL, MS. JUDITH CALDER, MRS. ESTIE DICKER, MRS. ETHEL GOTTLIEB, MRS. LIBBY GLUSTEIN, ELI KROEN and AVROHOM SCHORR.

Of ArtScroll/mesorah Publications: EFRAIM PERLOWITZ, AVROHOM BIDERMAN, YOSEF TIMINSKY, AVRAHAM KAY, SAID KOHAN FOLAD, YURI GUTKIN, SHEILA TENNENBAUM, LEA FREIER, MRS. ESTIE SCHREIBER, MRS. DVORAH MORGENSTERN, RAIZY BRANDER and JOSHUA J. GROSSMAN of Mesorah Mafitzim/Jerusalem.

Finally, enough cannot be said in praise of our dear friend and colleague RABBI SHEAH BRANDER, whose graphics genius continues to set new standards of excellence in Torah publishing. That this Gemara is a thing of beauty and a *Kiddush Hashem* is a tribute to him. Along with the Torah world, we are deeply and eternally grateful.

A huge investment of time and resources is required to make this edition of the Talmud a reality. Only through the generous support of many people is it possible not only to undertake and sustain such a huge and ambitious undertaking, but to keep the price of the published volumes within the reach of the average family and student. We are grateful to the many people who have made such work possible over the years.

This work was made possible by the support of the MESORAH HERITAGE FOUNDATION, whose Trustees saw the need to support the scholarship and production of outstanding works of Torah scholarship.

We are especially grateful to:

MR. ALBERT REICHMANN, whose quiet magnanimity for Torah causes is legend; MR. LAURENCE A. TISCH and his sons, JAMES S. and THOMAS J., who have been more than gracious on numerous occasions; MR. HIRSCH WOLF, who has taken the initiative in offering to assist and in recruiting others; MR. JOEL L. FLEISHMAN, whose sage advice and active intervention was a turning point in our work; MR. ABRAHAM FRUCHTHANDLER, who has placed support for Torah institutions on a new plateau; MR. AND MRS. LOUIS GLICK, whose sponsorship of the ArtScroll Mishnah series with the YAD AVRAHAM commentary is a jewel in the crown of Torah scholarship and dissemination; MR. IRVING STONE, whose name has justly become a legend as a supporter of Torah and other Jewish causes; MR. MORRY WEISS, who is a shining example of responsible and dynamic lay leadership; MR. JOSEPH STERN whose warmth and concern for people and causes are justly legendary; MR. SHLOMO SEGEV of Bank Leumi, who has been a responsible and effective friend; MR. DAN SUKENIK and MR. MOSHE SUKENIK, who are synonymous with kindness and generosity; MR. ELLIS A. SAFDEYE, a legendary supporter of worthy causes and a treasured friend; MR. JUDAH SEPTIMUS and MR. NATHAN B. SILBERMAN, who have made their skills and resources available in too many ways to mention; and to the many other good friends who have stepped forward when their help was needed most, among them: DR. and MRS. YISROEL BLUMENFRUCHT, RABBI YECHEZKEL KAMINSKY, MR. MORDECHAI LIPSCHITZ, RABBI CHAIM LEIBEL, RABBI YEHUDAH LEVI, and MR. WILLY WEISNER.

We conclude with gratitude to *Hashem Yisbarach* for His infinite blessings and for the opportunity to have been the quill that records His word. It has been said that when a Jew prays, he speaks to God; when he learns, God speaks to him. May this volume help the Jew listen, and may God continue to guide our work for the benefit of His people.

Rabbi Nosson Scherman / Rabbi Meir Zlotowitz

Kislev, 5752 / December, 1992

With sadness and a deep sense of personal loss, we note the passing of

Rabbi Simcha Wasserman זצ״ל

הרה״ג ר׳ אליעזר שמחה בן הרה״ג ר׳ אלחנן זצ״ל

and the Rebbetzin

מרת פייגא ע״ה

For sixty years, Reb Simcha founded and led Torah institutions on three continents. More than that, he was the personification of Torah wisdom and life. He tried mightily to conceal his vast knowledge of *Shas* and the rest of Torah, but it was impossible for him to hide the inspiration and guidance, the light and warmth that he and the Rebbetzin provided to countless individuals who revered them and depended on them.

One of the very few precious links to the generation of the Chofetz Chaim, Reb Chaim Ozer, and Reb Elchonon has been severed, and a ray of sunshine removed from the world.

Their memory will continue to illuminate dark paths and refresh heavy hearts.

תנצב״ה

מסכת בבא בתרא
TRACTATE BAVA BASRA

מסכת בבא בתרא / Bava Basra

General Introduction

Bava Basra, literally, the last gate, is the third tractate in the fourth order of the Mishnah, the order known as *Nezikin*, literally, torts or damages. It is also the third and final part of a sub-group of tractates within this order, comprised of *Bava Kamma, Bava Metzia* and *Bava Basra*. According to the Amora Rav Yosef, these three tractates are not separate tractates but merely three subdivisions, each consisting of ten chapters, of a larger tractate known as *Nezikin* (*Avodah Zarah* 7a with *Rashi*; see *Ramban* to *Shevuos* 2a). Together, these tractates define the bulk of the Torah's civil law — damages, litigations, personal liabilities and responsibilities, and property rights and transactions. *Bava Basra* deals primarily with the last of these categories — property rights and transactions.

ש מוּחְזָק, Muchzak One of the most basic principles of civil litigation is the concept of *muchzak*, possession. The general rule is that in cases of doubt, הַמּוֹצִיא מֵחֲבֵרוֹ עָלָיו הָרְאָיָה, *the burden of proof is upon the one who seeks to exact property from another.* That is, if one person is in possession of property and another claims it as his own, the court will not act to remove it from the person who is in possession of it unless the claimant can prove that it does not belong to the current holder. The Gemara (*Bava Kamma* 46b) holds this principle to be so logically self-evident that no Scriptural basis for it is necessary. This principle does not, however, establish a presumption of ownership on the part of the person in possession of the object; it merely predicates that whenever the evidence is insufficient to establish the facts, the object is granted to the person who is in prior possession of it (see *Kuntres HaSefeikos* 1:5). According to some, there is also a presumption (in most cases) that whatever is in one's possession is his (see *Tosafos* to *Bava Metzia* 2a ד״ה ויחלקו).

ש חֲזָקָה, Three-year Chazakah Physical possession — holding the object in question on one's person or in one's property — establishes a position of *muchzak* only in the case of movable property [מִטַּלְטְלִין]. The law concerning real property is different. Doubts regarding ownership are, in the absence of evidence, resolved in favor of the last person known to have owned the property (מָרָא קַמָּא), and it is up to the person trying to establish his claim to the property to prove that it no longer belongs to the original owner. For someone to supersede the last-known owner and achieve the presumptive right to the property [thereby removing the necessity for him to prove that the land is his], he must occupy the property for three consecutive years without any protest from the original owner. This rule is the subject of Chapter Three.

ש קִנְיָן, Kinyan Another basic principle of civil law is that the transfer of ownership must be accomplished through a formal act of acquisition (save in the case of inheritance). A *kinyan* is a legally defined act whose performance accomplishes the change of ownership, thereby finalizing the transaction. Once the *kinyan* has been performed, the transfer is complete and neither side may retract. The method of *kinyan* necessary to accomplish the transfer varies according to the article being transferred and the domain in which the transfer takes place. This will be discussed in Chapter Five of this tractate.

In the absence of an act of *kinyan*, property does not change hands, an agreement does not become binding, and either party can retract. This applies whether the transfer is a sale or a gift. Similarly, property and monetary agreements of any kind (e.g. easements, waivers) are finalized with an appropriate *kinyan*. The *kinyan* is performed either by the two principals together (e.g. one giving and the other receiving money or a document of transfer), or by the person acquiring the property alone at the behest of the one giving it up (e.g. lifting the object being acquired).

Chapter One

Introduction

The beginning of the first chapter deals primarily with the right of privacy; i.e. the right of an owner to use his property for private activities free from observation.

הֶיזֵּק רְאִיָּה, visual trespass Observing another's activities inside his private property is considered a form of trespass on his domain. In certain circumstances , the Rabbis considered this trepass to be a form of a damage, and required that proper steps be taken to prevent the trepass. There are different types of properties, each with its own laws regarding visual trespass.

In a property where private activities are constantly performed, such as a house, all agree that the neighbors are required to prevent any visual trespass. In a property where no private activities are performed, such as a grain field, there is no requirement to prevent visual trepass. The first Mishnah discusses another type of property, a חָצֵר, i.e. a courtyard in front of the house where, in Talmudic times, one would perform many of his everyday activities (see below). In a case of two neighboring courtyards, the Gemara cites two views as to whether the Rabbis require each neighbor to participate in the building of a wall between them to prevent visual trespass. Other types of properties, such as vegetable gardens and roofs, will also be discussed in this chapter.

חָצֵר, chatzeir Literally: a yard. In the Mishnah, *chatzeir* refers to the courtyard in front of the home, where such activities as cooking, unloading animals and transacting business were commonly performed. If a courtyard is jointly owned, it falls into one of two categories: (1) יֵשׁ בָּהּ דִּין חֲלוּקָה, *[a courtyard] subject to the law of division* — This is a parcel large enough to be useful to both partners even after being divided between them. Either partner can compel the other to dissolve the partnership in a courtyard of this type. (2) אֵין בָּהּ דִּין חֲלוּקָה, *[a courtyard] not subject to the law of division* — This is a parcel that, after division, would not be useful to either partner, due to its small size. Such a courtyard may be divided only if both partners agree to do so.

Beginning with a discussion of the basic laws of privacy, the chapter moves on to a number of related topics. The following is a brief outline of the subjects considered in this chapter: which types of property are protected by privacy laws; duties owed by neighbors to construct barriers to protect one another's privacy; the physical details (i.e. materials and dimensions) of these barriers; the various obligations incurred by the residents of a city, and the powers of appointed city administrators.

Pursuant to this chapter's treatment of privacy laws, the Gemara discusses situations in which partnerships may be dissolved, as well as methods of equitable dissolution.

Tangentially introduced topics discussed in the chapter include: an extensive discussion of the merits and rewards of charity, a listing of the authors of all the books of the Holy Scriptures and a comprehensive homiletic discourse on the Book of *Job.*

Chapter One

Mishnah הַשּׁוּתָּפִין שֶׁרָצוּ לַעֲשׂוֹת מְחִיצָה בֶּחָצֵר — **Partners who agreed to make a partition**[1] **in a courtyard**[2] that they own jointly בּוֹנִין אֶת הַכּוֹתֶל בָּאֶמְצַע — **must build the wall in their portions** of the courtyard,[3] each partner providing half of the land upon which to build.[4]

The Mishnah now discusses the physical requirements of the wall:

מְקוֹם שֶׁנָּהֲגוּ לִבְנוֹת — If they live in **a place where** people **are accustomed to building** courtyard partitions with, for example, גְּוִיל — **rough-edged stones,** גָּזִית — smooth, **planed stones,** כְּפִיסִין — **half-size bricks,**[5] לְבֵינִין — or whole **bricks,** בּוֹנִין — **they must build** with that material.[6]

The Mishnah states the general rule:

הַכֹּל כְּמִנְהַג הַמְּדִינָה — **All** construction **should conform to local custom.**[7]

The Mishnah now cites width requirements for the various types of partitions:

גְּוִיל — If the wall is constructed **with**[8] **rough-edged stones,** זֶה נוֹתֵן שְׁלֹשָׁה טְפָחִים — **this** partner **must provide three** ***tefachim***[9] of land for the foundation, וְזֶה נוֹתֵן שְׁלֹשָׁה טְפָחִים — **and that** other partner **must provide three** ***tefachim*** of land for the foundation.[10] בְּגָזִית — If the wall is built with smooth, **planed stones,** זֶה נוֹתֵן טְפָחַיִים וּמֶחֱצָה וְזֶה נוֹתֵן טְפָחַיִים וּמֶחֱצָה — **this** partner **must provide two and one-half** ***tefachim*** **and that** other partner **must provide two and one-half** ***tefachim.***[11] בִּכְפִיסִין — If the wall is built **with half-size bricks,** זֶה נוֹתֵן טְפָחַיִים וְזֶה נוֹתֵן טְפָחַיִים — **this** partner **must provide two** ***tefachim*** **and that** other partner **must provide two** ***tefachim***, for a total of four *tefachim.* בִּלְבֵינִין — If the wall is built **with** whole **bricks,** זֶה נוֹתֵן טֶפַח וּמֶחֱצָה וְזֶה נוֹתֵן טֶפַח וּמֶחֱצָה — **this** partner **must provide one and one-half** ***tefachim*** **and that** other partner **must provide one and one-half** ***tefachim.***[12] לְפִיכָךְ — **Therefore,** since one partner can legally compel the other to provide half of the land and material to build the wall, אִם נָפַל הַכּוֹתֶל — **if** after many years **the wall collapsed,** הַמָּקוֹם וְהָאֲבָנִים שֶׁל שְׁנֵיהֶם — the law presumes that the wall was built by both, and so **the place and the stones** of the fallen wall **belong** equally **to both** of them.[13]

The Mishnah establishes which other types of land are subject to this ruling:

וְכֵן בְּגִינָּה — **And, similarly, regarding a** jointly owned vegetable **garden,** whose owners have agreed to make a partition, מְקוֹם שֶׁנָּהֲגוּ לִגְדּוֹר — in **a place where** neighbors **are accustomed to erecting partitions** between the gardens,[14] מְחַיְּיבִין אוֹתוֹ — the authorities **obligate [each partner]** to contribute toward the building of the partition.[15] אֲבָל בְּבִקְעָה — **However, concerning a valley** containing fields of grain, מְקוֹם שֶׁנָּהֲגוּ שֶׁלֹּא לִגְדּוֹר — **in a place where they are accustomed not to erect partitions** between the fields,[14] אֵין מְחַיְּיבִין אוֹתוֹ — the authorities **do not obligate [each partner]** to contribute toward the building of the partition when they divide the field.[16] אֶלָּא אִם רָצָה — **But if** one of the partners **should desire** to build the wall without the assistance of his neighbor, כּוֹנֵס לְתוֹךְ שֶׁלּוֹ וּבוֹנֶה — **he must enter into his own field**[17] **and build** the wall, וְעוֹשֶׂה חֲזִית מִבַּחוּץ — **and he makes a sign**[18] **on the outside** of the wall to indicate his ownership. לְפִיכָךְ — **Therefore,** since he had

NOTES

1. The Gemara will discuss the definition of the word partition in this context (see also introduction).

2. The courtyard generally discussed in the Mishnah consisted of a central area surrounded by houses which opened into it. It was there that most household chores were performed (*Rashi; see also Maharam*) [Although generally, a courtyard was surrounded by many houses which opened into it, the discussion here concerns a courtyard shared by two people.]

3. I.e. either partner can legally compel the other one to provide half of the land and material to build the wall, which will ensure privacy for each of the partners.

4. *Rashi.* See *Shitah Mekubetzes* who infers from *Rashi* that they share equally in building the wall even if their portions in the courtyard are not equal (See also *Yad Ramah*; cf. *Rashash*).

5. Using this material, two walls were built with a space in between that was filled with mortar (below, 3a).

6. I.e. with the material customarily used for erecting courtyard partitions, and not with material customarily used for constructing buildings (*Rambam, Hil. Shecheinim* 2:18; see also *Maggid Mishneh* there).

7. Hence, if in a particular locale partitions were customarily built with rough-edged stone, one partner cannot say to the other, "I wish to build only with smooth, planed stones" (*Rashi*). The *thickness* of the wall, however, is not dictated by custom; the specifications presently cited by the Mishnah were established by the Sages to ensure that the walls would endure (*Rosh, Nemukei Yosef*). See *Tosafos* ד״ה בגויל for a dissenting opinion.

8. In *Tosafos'* version בְּגְוִיל is written, since the Mishnah refers to a type of wall mentioned previously (see also *Bach*). Our translation follows their emendation.

9. Literally: handbreadths. A common measurement of those times, the *tefach* measures between 3.5 and 4 inches.

10. For a total thickness of six *tefachim* (*Rashi*).

11. For a total thickness of five *tefachim* (*Rashi*). *G'vil* required an extra *tefach* for the protruding rough edges (below, 3a).

12. For a total thickness of three *tefachim* (*Rashi*). *K'fisin* required an extra *tefach* for the mortar between the two walls (below, 3a).

13. Hence, any one partner is prevented from claiming that he alone provided the land and the stones for the wall, even when his presumption of ownership is greater [such as when the wall fell into his portion, and he physically possesses the stones] (*Rashi*). See *Tosafos* ד״ה לפיכך and the Gemara below (4a) for a major discussion of this topic.

14. The Gemara below (4a) discusses the law in a locale without an established custom.

15. That is to say, if either one of them desires to build a wall between them, he can legally compel the other one to share in its building. Although private acts are not usually performed in a garden, a fence protects the garden's produce from an evil eye (*ayin hara*), as explained in the Gemara below (2b). [See however, *Yad Ramah* and *Shitah Mekubetzes* who explain that at times a garden may also require a wall for privacy.

16. Private acts are not performed in a grain field (see also below, 2b note 22 regarding the problem of *ayin hara*).

17. Since the neighbor is not required to contribute any land, the *entire* wall must be situated within the builder's property.

18. The Gemara below (4a-4b) will discuss the exact nature and placement of the sign.

השותפין

א שרצו לעשות מחיצה בחצר בונין את הכותל באמצע מקום שנהגו לבנות גויל גזית כפיסין לבינין בונין ב הכל כמנהג המדינה (א) בגויל ג זה נותן ג' טפחים וזה נותן ג' טפחים בגזית זה נותן טפחיים ומחצה וזה נותן טפחיים ומחצה בכפיסין זה נותן טפחיים וזה נותן טפחיים בלבינין זה נותן טפח ומחצה וזה נותן טפח ומחצה ד לפיכך אם נפל הכותל המקום והאבנים של שניהם ה וכן בגינה מקום שנהגו לגדור מחייבין אותו ו אבל בבקעה ז מקום שנהגו שלא לגדור אין מחייבין אותו אלא אם רצה כונס לתוך שלו ובונה ועושה חזית מבחוץ ח לפיכך אם נפל הכותל המקום והאבנים שלו אם עשו מדעת שניהם בונין את הכותל באמצע ועושין חזית מכאן ומכאן לפיכך אם נפל הכותל המקום והאבנים של שניהם: **גמ'** סברוה מאי מחיצה גודא א) כדתניא ט מחיצת הכרם שנפרצה אומר לו גדור חזרה ונפרצה אומר לו גדור נתיאש

קידש

השותפין. שיש להן חצר בשותפות ובתי שניהן פתוחין לתוכו וכל חצירות שנו חכמים לפני הבתים הן ורוב תשמישן בחצר: **באמצע.** זה נותן מחלקו חצי מקום עובי הכותל וכן זה: **גויל גזית כפיסין.** הכל מפרש בגמרא: **הכל כמנהג המדינה.** אם מנהג לבנות בגויל אין חבירו יכול לומר איני חפץ אלא גזית: **זה נותן ג' טפחים כו'.** שעובי כותל גויל ו' טפחים ושל גזית חמשה ושל כפיסים ד' ושל לבינים ג': **לפיכך.** הואיל ובתחלת הבנין חייבום חכמים לבנות בין שניהם אם נפל הכותל לאחר שנים רבים אין האחד יכול לומר כל הכותל נבנה בחלקי ומשלי היו האבנים אע"פ שהוחזק יותר מחבירו וכגון שנפל הכותל בחלקו כדמפרש בגמ': **וכן בגינה.** מחייבין את שניהן לבנות במקום שנהגו לגדור באמצע: **אבל בבקעה.** שדה הלבן: **מקום שנהגו כו'.** בגמ' מפרש מאי קאמר: **ועושה חזית מבחוץ.** מפרש בגמ': **ועושין חזית מכאן ומכאן.** להודיע ששניהם עשאוהו: **גמ' גודא.** כותל: ג) (כדתנן). דקרי תנא לגודא מחיצה: **מחיצת הכרם.** שסמוך לשדה הלבן של חבירו: **אומר לו.** לבעל הכרם גדור אתה שלא יאסרו גפניך את תבואת השדה משום כלאים לפי שסמך בעל השדה את זרעיו סמוך לגדר כדתנן בפרק שני (דף כו.) היה גדר בינתים זה סומך לגדר מכאן את אילנותיו וזה סומך לגדר את זרעיו מכאן וכשאין שם גדר תנן בפ' שני לא יטע אדם אילן סמוך לשדה חבירו אא"כ הרחיק ממנו ד' אמות כדי עבודת הכרם דבהכי הוי כלאים: **חזרה ונפרצה אומר לו.** לגדור:

השותפין. כולה נזיקין חדא מסכתא היא כדאמרינן בהגוזל קמא (ב"ק דף קב.) ובפ"ק דע"ז (דף ז.) ואפי' לא הוי חדא מסכתא צריך לפרש למה נשנית מסכתא זו אחר ב"מ דהאשכחן דדייק גמ' בריש מס' שבועות (דף ג:) מכדי תנא ממכות סליק מ"ש דקתני שבועות וכן בכמה מקומות והא דאמר (ב"ק קב.) בתרי מסכתות אין סדר למשנה היינו לענין מחלוקת ואח"כ סתם משום דרבי לא שנה לתלמידיו כסדר המסכתות ופעמים שנה האחרונה קודם הראשונה ואור"י דהיינו טעמא משום דקאי אהך פירקא דלעיל (ב"מ דף קטז:) הבית והעלייה של ב' שנפלו חולקים בעצים וכו' וקרי להו התם בגמ' שותפין וקתני נמי (שם דף קיז:) ב' גנות זו ע"ג זו וירק בינתים דהוי ענין שותפות: **כפיסין.** מפרש בגמ' ארחי וקשה לר"י והכתיב (חבקוק ב) וכפיס מעץ יעננה משמע שהוא של עץ ואור"י דשמא היו מניחין עצים מלמעלה ומלמטה: **בגויל זה נותן ג' טפחים כו'.** והא דלא קאמר בגויל ו' טפחים משום דלא נטעי למימר ו' לכל אחד ואחד וא"ת ואמאי אצטריך למיתני מדת גויל וגזית כיון דתנן הכל כמנהג המדינה כמו שנהגו כן יעשו וי"ל דאם נהגו יותר מו' בגויל לא יעשה וכן כולם אלא כשיעור המפורש ומיהו אם נהגו לעשות פחות מו' יעשה דאפילו אם נהגו בהוצא ודפנא יעשה כדמפרש בגמרא וא"ת ומאי בעי בגמ' הכל כמנהג המדינה לאתויי מאי ומשני לאתויי אתרא דנהיגי בהוצא ודפנא לימא לאתויי כמנהג כל המקומות כמו שנהגו ונראה לר"ת דדוקא בהוצא ודפנא אבל פחות מכאן אפילו נהגו הדיוט הוא ומוכיח מכאן דיש מנהגים שאין לסמוך עליהם אפילו היכא דתנן הכל כמנהג המדינה: **לפיכך** אם נפל הכותל וכו'. פי' לפי שבונים הכותל בעל כרחם או משום דהקנו זה לזה לעשות גודא ללישנא קמא וכגון דידוע לנו עדיין וחוכרים שהקנו זה לזה וללישנא בתרא משום היזק ראיה וא"ת ומאי איריא משום דבונין הכותל בעל כרחם בלאו הכי נמי הוי של שניהם אפי' נפל לרשותא דחד מינייהו כיון דאין חזית לא לזה ולא לזה כדפריך בגמרא גבי בקעה לא יעשה חזית לא לזה ולא לזה ואי הוה ההיא דנפל לרשותו מאי פריך הא צריך לעשות חזית שלא יפול לרשות אחר ויאמר שלו הן והא דאמרינן בהשואל (ב"מ דף ק.) גבי מחליף פרה בחמור וכן בריש הבית והעלייה (שם דף קטז:) וליחזי ברשות דמאן קיימא וליהוי אידך המוציא מחבירו עליו הראיה היינו משום דהתם מתחילה מבורר היה הדבר וברשות אחד מהן נולד הספק אבל הכא מעיקרא נולד הספק ואם היו באין לחלוק בעוד שהכותל קיים היו חולקין בשוה מספק אפילו לרבנן דסומכוס דלית להו ממון המוטל בספק חולקין הכא מודו כיון דליכא הכא חזקה לזה יותר מלזה הילכך אפילו נפל לרשותא דחד מינייהו לא יפסיד האחר כחו והא דלא אמר הכא כל דאלים גבר כמו בזה אומר של אבותי (לקמן דף לד:) התם הוא דליכא דררא דממונא אבל הכא איכא דררא דממונא ומתרץ ר"י דהיינו הך דפריך בגמרא פשיטא כדפירש בקונטרס דאפילו לא פסיק לן דינא דמתניתין שמתחילה בין שניהם עשאוה בעל כרחם היו חולקין בשוה ואפילו דנפל לרשותא דחד מינייהו כדמוכח גבי בקעה ומשני לא צריכא דנפל לרשותא דחד מינייהו פירוש ושהו ברשותו הרבה מהו דתימא כיון דשהו ברשותו הרבה ניהמניה שעשאוה כולה ◦ מיגו דאיבעי אמר ממך לקחתיה והיה נאמן משום דשהו הרבה ואף על גב דאמר בריש הבית והעלייה דשותפין לא קפדי אהדדי הכא מיירי דשהו יותר מכדי רגילות דאטו משום דשותפין נינהו לא יקפידו עד עולם ולא דמי לגודרות דאין להם חזקה (לקמן דף לו.) לפי שאין ידוע ביד מי הם אבל הכא לא היה לו להשהותו כל כך ברשותו קמ"ל כיון דמעיקרא על שניהם היה לעשות לא מהימן לומר שהוא עשה הכל דמיגו במקום עדים הוא דאנן סהדי שלא עשאה לבדו כיון שהיה יכול לדחוק את חבירו בדין שהיה עושה עמו אבל בבקעה אם שהו הרבה היה נאמן לומר שעשאה במיגו דאי בעי אמר לקחתיה והאי שינויא אינו אלא מאבנים אבל מקום הכותל לעולם פשיטא שחולקין אותו ואיידי דנקט אבנים נקט המקום:

סברוה מאי מחיצה גודא. אע"ג דלבסוף קאי קאמר סברוה לפי שזה הלשון אינו עיקר מחמת פירכא דלקמן ודיחוי בעלמא הוא האי דמשני וכלשון שני הלכה וכן פוסק ר"ת ואגב דנקט בהאי לישנא סברוה נקט נמי בלישנא אחריתי ועוד אור"י דבפרק קמא דנדרים (דף יח.) איכא סברוה אע"ג דלבסוף קאי ומסיק הכי: **כדתניא** מחיצת הכרם שנפרצה. יש ספרים דגרסי דתנן ואומר ר"ת שאינה משנה בשום מקום ג) (וא"כ) היכי פשיט מינה בהגוזל קמא (ב"ק דף ק. ושם) דר"מ דאין דינא דגרמי ואם היתה משנה הוה אתי שפיר דסתם משנה ר"מ היא ואומר ר"ת דמשמע ליה דאתיא כר"מ מכח מתניתין דכלאים דמייתי התם המסכך [את] גפנו על גבי תבואתו של חבירו [ה"ז] קידש וחייב באחריותו וההיא סתם משנה היא הילכך ההיא נמי דקתני קידש רבי מאיר היא ואין להאריך כאן יותר: **אומר** לו גדור. פירוש לבעל הכרם (ב) והוא המזיק דארבע אמות שאמרו להרחיק הוא בשביל עבודת הכרם כדאמרי' בפ' שני לקמן (דף כו.) ואפילו ר' יוסי דקאמר לקמן (דף יח: כה:) על הניזק להרחיק את עצמו האמר רב אשי לקמן (דף כה:) מודי ר' יוסי בגירי דיליה ואומר ר"י דלהכי קתני אומר לו גדור ולא קתני חייב לגדור לפי שצריך להתרות בו ואם לא התרו בו לגדור אינו חייב באחריותו ולהכי נקט נמי תרי זימני נפרצה אומר לו גדור אף פעם שניה כשנפרצה צריך להתרותו שאינו סבור להיות חייב לגדור כל שעה ונפרצה פעם שלישית מספקא לר"י אם צריך להתרותו כל שעה או שמא סגי בתרי זימני ואין צריך להתרות בו יותר ור"ת מפרש דלהכי נקט תרי זימני לאשמועינן שאם יש תוספת מאתים בין מה שהוסיף בנפרצה ראשונה ובין מה שהוסיף בנפרצה שניה דאין מצטרפין לאסור ומראשונה ראשונה בטלי והארכתי בהגוזל קמא (ב"ק דף ק: ושם) ובפרק במה אשה (שבת דף סה:):

עין משפט נר מצוה

א א מיי' פ"ב מהל' שכנים הל' יז סמג עשין פב טוש"ע ח"מ סי' קנז סעיף א:
ב ב מיי' שם הלכה טו טוש"ע שם סעיף ד:
ג ג מיי' שם הלכה יח טור שם:
ד ד מיי' שם טוש"ע שם סעיף ה:
ה ה ו ז מיי' שם הלכה טז וסמג שם טוש"ע ח"מ סי' קנח סעיף א:
ו ח מיי' שם טוש"ע שם סעיף ז:
ז ט מיי' פ"ז מהל' כלאים הל' יז סמג לאוין רפ טוש"ע י"ד סי' רצו סעיף מז:

מסורת הש"ס

א) [לקמן ג.] ב"ק ק. [תוספתא כלאים פרק ג], ב) [צ"ל כדתנא], ג) נ"א ולא"כ.

הגהות הב"ח

(א) במשנה בגויל זה נותן: (ב) תוס' ד"ה אומר וכו' והוא המזיק:

גליון הש"ס

תוס' ד"ה לפיכך וכו' מיגו דאי בעי אמר ממך לקחתיה. קשה לי למ"ל מדין מגו ולא דשמעינן כי היכי דנאמן לקחתיה מכח דשהה הרבה מוכח שהוא שלו ה"נ יהא נאמן מהאי טעמא ומאי אולמי טענת לקוח מטענת אני בניתי:

ליקוטי רש"י

גויל. אבנים דלא משפיין דמורשי דידהו מעפי בה טפח [ב"מ קיז.]. גזית. לשון גוזה שמפולין כבן. נפסלים ומקורותות [מלכים א, ה, לא]. כפיסין. כפים חתיכת עץ כמו כפיסין בבבא בתרא (ב.) [חגיגה טז.]. ארחי. חצאי לבינים ודקים ומלמטה ונותן ארים מכאן וארים מכאן ועושה אבנים דקות וסיד בינייהם וזה עובי החומה ארבעה טפחים. לבינים. שלימות ואין עוביו של כותל אלא כמדת רוחבן והן שלשה טפחים [ב"מ שם]. חזית. לשון קלה ונכנס כן פותחו ומכירו (תהלים קז) על מחה תפלה ולא חזית מה שלבשון משנה כך הוא כנדר מערכת התמיד (תמיד כט.) [מלכים א, ז, ה]. סברוה. האי סברוה במסכתא נמי קאי [ר"ן נדרים יא.]. מחיצת הכרם שנפרצה. קיימא לן היה גדר בנתיים זה סומך ועושים לגדר מכאן וזה סומך גפנים לגדר מכאן שלא יתפור לו (ב"ק כו.) [ב"ק ק.]. גדור. שלא יוסיף התבואה אחד ממאתים בעוד התבואה פרוצה ותאסר [שם]. [מכאן שייך לע"ב] נתיאש היינו ולא גדרה. ונתוך קך הולא הורע אחד מן המאתים ובנס בה כהנה. ה"ז קידש. ואין בעל אלא באחד ומאתים וכאן יש קנ"ע מן הסותר ומן לאיסור [ב"ק ק.]. ותהי מחצת העדה. כך וכך [במדבר לא, מג]. במספים. מחילה מגולה של חתיכות עצים [עירובין עב. וכעי"ז ע"ש]. אסור לאדם כו'. שלא יסתכלו בענין הרע [ב"מ קז.]. כותל חצר וכו' מחייבין אותו לבנות עד ד' אמות. דהכי סגי להיזק ראיה [לקמן ה.].

פירוש רבינו גרשום מאור הגולה

השותפין דאית להו חצר בשותפות ונתרצו לחלוק ולעשות מחיצה: **בונין את הכותל לאמצע: גמ' גודא.** כותל: **כדתנן** א) **מחיצת הכרם שנפרצה** לזה היה לו שדה תבואה ולזה היה לו כרם והיתה כותל מחיצה מפסקת בין השדה לכרם. ועכשיו נפרצה מחיצת כרמו דיש לחוש שלא יתערבו הזרעים בכרם. **אומרים לו** בית דין לבעל הכרם **גדור.** [מכאן שייך לע"ב] **נתייאש** מן הזמן שקבעו לו ב"ד **ולא גדרה** ונתערבו הזרעים בכרם **הרי זה קידש** וטעונין שריפה ככלאי הכרם כדכתיב פן תקדש המלאה ודרשי' לה (חולין קטו) פן תוקד אש. ואותו בעל מחיצה **חייב באחריות** זרעוני של זה שהופסדו וחייב לשלם דמיהן. השתא כיון דאשכחן דהאי מחיצה דמתני' כותל הוא דילפי' לה ממחיצת הכרם דייקא מתני' **טעמא דרצו** שניהן לעשות מחיצה משום הכי בונין אותו באמצע שניהן ביחד **הא לא רצו** שניהם לבנות ביחד אלא אחד רוצה ואחד אינו רוצה **אין מחייבין אותו** שאינו רוצה לבנות חלקו בעל כרחו. והואיל דאין כופין אותו לבנות **ש"מ** שזה שהמעכב רואה בחצר חבירו אותו **היזק ראיה לא שמיה היזק:** ומקשה מאן לימא לן דהאי מחיצה דמתני' גודא דאיכא למידק כדקאמרת דהיזק ראיה לאו שמיה היזק. **אימא מאי מחיצה דמתני' פלוגתא.** חלוקה שנתרצו לעשות חלוקה. והכי פריש למתני' השותפין שרצו לחלוק חצירן בונין את הכותל באמצע. ואידוק הכי **כיון דנתרצו** לחלוק אם זה מעכב שאינו רוצה לעשות עמו את הכותל הואיל דמקפידין זה על זה שלא ישתמש הא' בחלק של חבירו (היו) כופין אותו **ובונין את הכותל** באמצע **בעל כרחו** משום **דהיזק ראיה** [דיליה] שמסתכל בחצר חבירו **הוי היזק.** ומהדר ליה **אי הכי** דפלוגתא הוי אמאי קתני **שרצו לעשות מחיצה** שרצו לחצות מיבעי ליה: **אלא מאי גודא.** אמאי קתני תו **בונין את הכותל.** והא כל לשון משנה לשון קצרה הוא. וכיון דההיא שרצו לעשות מחיצה היינו כותל **בונין אותו מיבעי ליה** ולא איצטריך למיתני כותל. ואכתי היזק ראיה שמיה היזק: ומתרץ ליה לעולם מחיצה גודא. ודקשיא לך בונין אותו מיבעי ליה משום הכי איצטריך למתני כותל **דאי תנא** בונין **אותו הוה אמינא במסיפס בעלמא** סגי. מחיצת הקנים עראי שקורין בל"ע פלפי"ט. **קמ"ל כותל.** דצריכי למיעבד כותל של קיימא ולעולם כדאמינא דמחיצה גודא היא וכדדייקי דהיזק ראיה לאו שמיה היזק: **בונין את הכותל באמצע פשיטא.** אכתי מקשה למאן דאמר גודא כי האי גוונא ב) בשלמא אי אמרי' מאי מחיצה פלוגתא מש"ה איצטריך למיתני בונין את הכותל דלא סגי בלאו הכי דאיצטריך לאדכר כותל. והאי דקתני באמצע ודאי לא איצטריך למיתנייה הואיל דקאמר פלוגתא. אלא אגב דאיצטריך למתני כותל קתני באמצע ולא משום דוקא אלא אי אמרת דהאי מחיצה גודא היא בשלמא כותל לא מיותר הוא משום דאתי למעוטי מסיפס ולא לגופיה איצטריך. אלא ודאי באמצע מיותר הוא דכיון דשותפין נינהו בהאי חצר ורצו לעשות גודא פשיטא דבאמצע בונין אותו והשתא לא מצית למימר אגב דאיצטריך למתני כותל קתני באמצע משום דכותל גופיה לא אתא אלא לאפוקי מסיפס בודאי לא איצטריך באמצע אלא לעולם כדאמר' מחיצה פלוגתא והיזק ראיה שמיה היזק. לעולם אימא לך מחיצה גודא ודקא קשיא לך באמצע למה לי (לא) צריכי דודאי לא מייתר הוא דהכא במאי עסקינן **דאקדים חד** מינייהו **וארציה לחבריה** שלא רצו שניהן מתחלה אלא אחד פייסו לחבירו עד שנתרצה לו שיעשה כותל. עכשיו אי לא תני דבונין באמצע בחלק שניהן **הוה אמינא** דיכול למימר ליה **כי נתרציתי** לעשות מחיצה בכך נתרציתי שלא אשתמש **באוירא** דידך אבל למעוטי **בתשמיש** שלי ליתן מקום חצי הכותל **לא נתרציתי: קמ"ל.** דכיון דנתרצה בונין את הכותל באמצע חצי בחלק זה וחצי בחלק זה. ולהכי איצטריך למתני באמצע ולעולם מחיצה גודא הוא ואכתי היזק ראיה לאו שמיה היזק: **ת"ש וכן בגינה** מקום שנהגו לגדור. בגינה העומדת בעיר קא מיירי דאיכא היזק ראיה שרואה מה שבחצר חבירו. קתני וכן בגינה דמחייבין אותו לגדור. אלמא היזק ראיה שמיה היזק: לא לעולם אימא לך לאו שמיה היזק **ושאני גינה** לאו משום דטעמא דהיזק ראיה. אלא משום דמסתכלין בגינתו ומכניסין בו עין הרע **[כדר'] אבא:** א"כ כדקאמרת דמשום טעמא דעין הרעה מחייבין לגדור בגינה ולאו משום היזק ראיה **מאי וכן** בגינה כלומר דמשמע דאותו דין [דין] עצמו שנוהג בחצר אותו דין עצמו שנוהג בגינה ולטעמיך אינו דין א'. בשלמא לדידי דאמינא אידי ואידי משום היזק ראיה להכי אתי שפיר וכן בגינה אלא לדידך מאי וכן: ומשני האי וכן לא מהדר כלל ארישא אבונין את הכותל דתידוק מינה כשם שמחייבין לבנות כותל בחצר משום היזק ראיה כן בגינה אלא האי דקתני וכן בגינה **אגויל וגזית** מה בחצר מקום שנהגו לבנות בגויל ובגזית בונין כן בגינה ולעולם לא קשיא לי:

חשק שלמה על רבינו גרשום א) עי' בתוס' כאן ד"ה כדתניא: ב) פשיטא היא:

constructed the wall with his own resources, אִם נָפַל הַכּוֹתֶל – **if** eventually **the wall collapsed,** הַמָּקוֹם וְהָאֲבָנִים שֶׁלּוֹ – **the land** beneath the wall **and the stones are his.**[19] אִם עָשׂוּ מִדַּעַת שְׁנֵיהֶם – **If,** however, **they acted** to erect the wall **by mutual consent,** בּוֹנִין אֶת הַכּוֹתֶל בָּאֶמְצַע – **they must build the wall in between** their fields, each providing half of the necessary land and materials, וְעוֹשִׂין חָזִית מִכָּאן וּמִכָּאן – **and they make a sign on *both* sides of the wall**[20] to indicate joint ownership.[21] לְפִיכָךְ – **Therefore,** since this wall was a joint undertaking, אִם נָפַל הַכּוֹתֶל – **if** over time **the wall collapsed,** הַמָּקוֹם וְהָאֲבָנִים שֶׁל שְׁנֵיהֶם – **the land** under the foundation **and the stones belong to them both** equally.

Gemara By precisely defining the word *mechitzah,* the Gemara elucidates a deeper implication of the Mishnah's opening statement:[22]

סַבְרוּהָ – The Rabbis **maintained:** מַאי מְחִיצָה – **What is** the meaning of the word ***mechitzah*** as it appears in our Mishnah? גּוּדָא – **A wall!**

The Gemara digresses to offer support for this translation:

כִּדְתַנְיָא – **As it was taught in a Baraisa:** מְחִיצַת הַכֶּרֶם שֶׁנִּפְרְצָה – Concerning A VINEYARD WALL[23] THAT WAS BREACHED,[24] אוֹמֵר לוֹ גְּדוֹר – [THE OWNER OF THE FIELD][25] MAY SAY TO [THE VINEYARD OWNER]: REBUILD THE WALL.[26] חָזְרָה וְנִפְרְצָה – If after repair IT WAS BREACHED AGAIN, אוֹמֵר לוֹ גְּדוֹר – the owner of the field MAY SAY TO [THE VINEYARD OWNER] a second time:[27] REBUILD THE WALL.

NOTES

19. I.e. if a neighbor claims that the wall was constructed jointly, he is not believed.

20. Literally: from here and from here.

21. Since most walls in valleys are of private construction (see *Rosh* §6 and *Nemukei Yosef*), the double sign is necessary. One might wonder why jointly owned walls were not distinguished simply by the absence of any sign – in contrast to the private walls, which all had signs. This question is discussed in the Gemara below (4b).

22. The Mishnah stated: *Partners who agreed to make a mechitzah in a courtyard.* By clarifying the meaning of *mechitzah,* the Gemara will determine whether neighbors enjoy an enforceable right of privacy.

23. The wall had separated the vineyard from an adjoining field of grain, and thereby satisfied the requirement of the law of כִּלְאֵי הַכֶּרֶם, *mixtures of the vineyard*, for the Torah (*Deut.* 22:9) forbids the planting of grains and grapevines together. This prohibition applies when both species were planted at the same time, or when grains were planted in an existing vineyard and grew there. Such growth is called *kilayim* (mixture), and must be destroyed. The Mishnah (*Kilayim* 4:1, 4:5) further requires that the vineyard and the grain planting be separated by at least four *amos.* Since the oxen plowing around the vines require this amount of "working space," the four *amos* are considered part of the vineyard proper (see *Rashi* to *Eruvin* 93a). Thus, planting grain within four *amos* of a vineyard is tantamount to planting in the vineyard itself, and the growth is prohibited (*Rambam, Hil. Kilayim* 5:7). [This prohibition is Rabbinic in nature, for most authorities maintain that the Biblical prohibition applies only to vines and grain planted at one time (see *Kessef Mishneh* for a discussion).] However, if a wall is built between the vines and the grain, no other separation is required (below, 26a). The Baraisa deals with this latter instance, and discusses what steps must be taken if the wall is breached.

24. *Rashi* (here and to *Shabbos* 84b ד״ה ואחת באמצע) explains that while the wall was standing, both grain and vines were permissibly planted next to the wall itself, since the latter clearly distinguished the two growths. However, since with the breaching of the wall the vines and grain would appear intermingled, a timely repair of the wall was required to maintain the appearance of separation.

25. The version of the Baraisa cited by *Rabbeinu Gershom* states that the warning issues from *beis din,* not from the owner of the field. See *Meiri* and *Chasam Sofer* for a discussion of whether *beis din's* warning is required.

26. So that the vines will not render the mixture prohibited as *kilayim.* The Baraisa places the onus of repairing the wall on the vineyard owner, even though both types of growth are necessary to create *kilayim,* because, as explained in note 23, it is considered as if the vineyard itself extends four *amos* into the field of grain, so that the vineyard is causing the *kilayim* (*Rashi* as explained by the Chidushei R' Nachum and Shiurei R' Shmuel). *Tosafos* offer a different explanation why the obligation is placed on the vineyard owner; namely, because he is obligated to make the repair in any case. That is, the Mishnah below (26a) requires anyone planting any type of tree or vine next to a grain field to withdraw four *amos* from his boundary, so that his plowing and digging around the trees do not damage the grain. This law applies only to the vineyard owner; hence, he is obligated to repair the wall regardless, and if he neglects the repair, he is solely responsible for all resultant liabilities, including those arising from the prohibition of *kilayim* (*Tosafos* ד״ה אומר, as explained by *Maharam*). Nevertheless, *Tosafos* (ibid.) add that the Baraisa implies that if the owner of the field fails to warn the owner of the vineyard, the latter is not liable for damages (see following note).

27. *Tosafos* (ibid.) are uncertain whether a *third* warning is necessary if the partition was breached for a third time, since it is possible that the second warning alerted the vineyard owner to his obligation to keep the wall in constant repair.

השותפין. שיש להן חצר בשותפות ובתי שניהן פתוחין לתוכו וכל חצירות ששנו חכמים לפני הבתים הן ורוב תשמישן בחצר: **באמצע.** זה נותן מחלקו חצי מקום עובי הכותל וכן זה: **גויל גזית כפיסין.** הכל מפרש בגמרא: **הכל כמנהג המדינה.** אם מנהג לבנות בגויל אין חבירו יכול לומר איני חפץ אלא גזית: **זה נותן ג' טפחים כו'.** שעובי כותל גויל ו' טפחים ושל גזית חמשה ושל כפיסים ד' ושל לבינים ג': **לפיכך.** הואיל ובתחלת הבנין חייבום חכמים לבנות בין שניהם אם נפל הכותל לאחר שנים רבים אין האחד יכול לומר כל הכותל נבנה בחלקי ומשלי היו האבנים אע"פ שהמוחזק יותר מחבירו וכגון שנפל הכותל בחלקו כדמפרש בגמ': **וכן בגינה.** מחייבין את שניהן לבנות במקום שנהגו לגדור באמצע: **אבל בבקעה.** שדה הלבן: **מקום שנהגו כו'.** בגמ' מפרש מאי קאמר: **ועושה חזית מבחוץ.** מפרש בגמ': **ועושין חזית מכאן ומכאן.** להודיע ששניהם עשאוהו: **גמ' גודא.** כותל: (ב) **כדתנן.** דקרי תנא לגודא מחיצה: **מחיצת הכרם.** שסמוך לשדה הלבן של חבירו: **אומר לו.** לבעל הכרם גדור אתה שלא יאסרו גפניך את תבואת השדה משום כלאים לפי שסמוך בעל השדה את זרעיו סמוך לגדר כדתנן בפרק שני (דף כו.) היה גדר בינתים זה סומך לגדר מכאן את אילנותיו וזה סומך לגדר את זרעיו מכאן וכשאין שם גדר תנן בפ' שני לא יטע אדם אילן סמוך לשדה חבירו אא"כ הרחיק ממנו ד' אמות כדי עבודת הכרם דבהכי הוי כלאים: **חזרה ונפרצה אומר לו.** לגדור:

קידש

השותפין. כולה מזיקין חדא מסכתא היא כדאמרינן בהגוזל קמא (ב"ק דף קב.) ובפ"ק דע"ז (דף ז.) ואפי' הכי הוי חדא מסכתא צריך לפרש למה נשנית מסכתא זו אחר ב"מ דהא דייק גמ' בריש מס' שבועות (דף ג:) מכדי תנא ממכות סליק מ"ש דקתני שבועות וכן בכמה מקומות והא דאמר (ב"ק קב.) בתרי מסכתות אין סדר למשנה היינו לענין מחלוקת ואח"כ סתם משום דרבי לא שנה לתלמידיו כסדר המסכתות ופעמים שנה האחרונה קודם הראשונה ואור"י דהיינו טעמא משום דקאי אהך פירקא דלעיל (ב"מ דף קטז:) הבית והעלייה של ב' שנפלו חולקים בעצים וכו' וקרי להו התם בגמ' שותפין וקתני נמי (שם דף קיז:) ב' גנות זו ע"ג זו וירק בינתים דהוי ענין שותפות: **כפיסין.** מפרש בגמ' ארחי וקשה לר"י והכתיב (חבקוק ב) וכפיס מעץ יעננה משמע שהוא של עץ ואור"י דשמא היו מניחין עצים מלמעלה ולמטה: **בגויל זה נותן ג' טפחים כו'.** והא דלא קאמר בגויל ו' טפחים משום דלא נטעי למימר ו' לכל אחד ואם תאמר ואמאי אצטריך למיתני מדת גויל וגזית כיון דתנן הכל כמנהג המדינה כמו שנהגו יעשו וי"ל דאם נהגו יותר מו' בגויל לא יעשה וכן כולם אלא כשיעור המפורש ומיהו אם נהגו לעשות פחות מו' יעשה דאפילו אם נהגו בהוצא ודפנא יעשה כדמפרש בגמרא וא"ת ומאי בעי בגמ' הכל כמנהג המדינה לאתויי מאי ומשני לאתויי אתרא דנהיגי בהוצא ודפנא לימא לאתויי כמנהג כל המקומות כמו שנהגו ונראה לר"ת דדוקא בהוצא ודפנא אבל פחות מכאן אפילו נהגו מנהג הדיוט הוא ומוכיח מכאן דיש מנהגים שאין לסמוך עליהם אפילו היכא דתנן הכל כמנהג המדינה:

השותפין

א שרצו לעשות מחיצה בחצר בונין את הכותל באמצע מקום שנהגו לבנות גויל גזית כפיסין לבינין בונין ב הכל כמנהג המדינה (א) בגויל זה נותן ג' טפחים וזה נותן ג' טפחים בגזית זה נותן טפחיים ומחצה וזה נותן טפחיים ומחצה בכפיסין זה נותן טפחיים וזה נותן טפחיים בלבינין זה נותן טפח ומחצה וזה נותן טפח ומחצה ד לפיכך אם נפל הכותל המקום והאבנים של שניהם ה וכן בגינה מקום שנהגו לגדור מחייבין אותו ו אבל בבקעה ז מקום שנהגו שלא לגדור אין מחייבין אותו אלא אם רצה כונס לתוך שלו ובונה ועושה חזית מבחוץ ח לפיכך אם נפל הכותל המקום והאבנים שלו אם עשו מדעת שניהם בונין את הכותל באמצע ועושין חזית מכאן ומכאן לפיכך אם נפל הכותל המקום והאבנים של שניהם: **גמ'** סברוה מאי מחיצה גודא (א) כדתניא ט מחיצת הכרם שנפרצה אומר לו גדור חזרה ונפרצה אומר לו גדור

נתיאש

לפיכך אם נפל הכותל וכו'. פי' לפי שבונים הכותל בעל כרחם או משום דהקנו זה לזה לעשות גודא ללישנא קמא וכגון דידוע לנו עדיין חוכרים שהקנו זה לזה וללישנא בתרא משום היזק ראיה וא"ת ומאי איריא משום דבונין הכותל בעל כרחם בלאו הכי נמי הוי של שניהם אפי' נפל לרשותא דחד מינייהו כיון דלאין חזית לא לזה ולא לזה כדפריך בגמרא גבי בקעה לא יעשה חזית לא לזה ולא לזה ואי הוה דהאיך דנפל לרשותו מאי פריך הא צריך לעשות חזית שלא יפול לרשות אחר ויאמר שלו הן והא דאמרינן בהשואל (ב"מ דף ק.) גבי מחליף פרה בחמור וכן בריש הבית והעלייה (שם דף קטז:) וליחזי ברשות דמאן קיימא וליהוי אידך המוציא מחבירו עליו הראיה היינו משום דהתם מתחילה מבורר היה הדבר וברשות אחד מהן נולד הספק אבל הכא מעיקרא נולד הספק ואם היו באין לחלוק בעוד שהכותל קיים היו חולקין בשוה מספק אפילו לרבנן דסומכוס דלית להו ממון המוטל בספק חולקין הכא מודו כיון דליכא הכא חזקה לזה יותר מלזה הילכך אפילו נפל לרשותא דחד מינייהו לא יפסיד האחר כחו והא דלא אמר הכא כל דאלים גבר כמו בזה אומר של אבותי (לקמן דף לד:) התם הוא דליכא דררא דממונא אבל הכא איכא דררא דממונא ומתרץ ר"י דהיינו הך דפריך בגמרא פשיטא כדפירש בקונטרס דאפילו לא פסיק לן דינא דמתניתין שמתחילה בין שניהם עשאוה בעל כרחם היו חולקין בשוה ואפילו דנפל לרשותא דחד מינייהו כדמוכח גבי בקעה ומשני לא צריכא דנפל לרשותא דחד מינייהו פירוש ושהו ברשותו הרבה מהו דתימא כיון דשהו ברשותו הרבה ניהמניה שעשאוה כולה * מיגו דאיבעי אמר ממך לקחתיה והיה נאמן משום דשהו הרבה ואף על גב דאמר בריש הבית והעלייה דשותפין לא קפדי אהדדי הכא מיירי דשהו יותר מכדי רגילות דאטו משום דשותפין נינהו לא יקפידו עד עולם ולא דמי לגודרות דאין להם חזקה (לקמן דף לו.) לפי שאין ידוע ביד מי הם אבל הכא לא היה לו להשהותו כל כך ברשותו קמ"ל כיון דמעיקרא על שניהם היה לעשות לא מהימן לומר שהוא עשה הכל דמיגו במקום עדים הוא דאין סהדי שלא עשאה לבדו כיון שהיה יכול לדחוק את חבירו בדין שהיה עושה עמו אבל בבקעה אם שהו הרבה היה נאמן לומר שעשאה במיגו דאי בעי אמר לקחתיה והאי שינויא אינו אלא מאבנים אבל מקום הכותל לעולם פשיטא שחולקין אותו ואיידי דנקט אבנים נקט המקום:

סברוה מאי מחיצה גודא. אע"ג דלבסוף קאי קאמר סברוה לפי שזה הלשון אינו עיקר מחמת פירכא דלקמן ודיחוי בעלמא הוא האי דמשני וכלשון שני הלכה וכן פוסק ר"ת ואגב דנקט בהאי לישנא סברוה נקט נמי בלישנא אחריתי ועוד אור"י דבפרק קמא דנדרים (דף יא.) איכא סברוה אע"ג דלבסוף קאי ומסיק הכי: **כדתניא** מחיצת הכרם שנפרצה. יש ספרים דגרסי דתנן ואומר ר"ת שאינה משנה בשום מקום ג) (וא"כ) היכי פשיט מינה בהגוזל קמא (ב"ק דף ק. ושם) דר"מ דאין דינא דגרמי ואם היתה משנה הוה אתי שפיר דסתם משנה ר"מ היא ואומר ר"ת דמשמע ליה דאתיא כר"מ מכח מתניתין דכלאים דמייתי התם המסכך [את] גפנו על גבי תבואתו של חבירו [ה"ז] קידש וחייב באחריותו והיא סתם משנה היא הילכך ההיא נמי דקתני קידש רבי מאיר היא ואין להאריך כאן יותר: **אומר** לו גדור. פירוש לבעל הכרם (ג) והוא המזיק דארבע אמות שאמרו להרחיק הוא בשביל עבודת הכרם כדאמרי' בפ' שני לקמן (דף כו.) ואפילו ר' יוסי דקאמר לקמן (דף יח: כה:) על הניזק להרחיק את עצמו האמר רב אשי לקמן (דף כה:) מודי ר' יוסי בגירי דיליה ואומר ר"י דלהכי קתני אומר לו גדור ולא קתני חייב לגדור לפי שצריך להתרות בו ואם לא התרו בו לגדור אינו חייב באחריותו ולהכי נקט נמי תרי זימני נפרצה אומר לו גדור אף פעם שניה כשנפרצה צריך להתרותו שאינו סבור להיות חייב לגדור כל שעה ונפרצה פעם שלישית מספקא לר"י אם צריך להתרותו כל שעה או שמא סגי בתרי זימני ואין צריך להתרות בו יותר ור"ת מפרש דלהכי נקט תרי זימני לאשמועינן שאם יש תוספת מאתים בין מה שהוסיף בנפרצה ראשונה ובין מה שהוסיף בנפרצה שניה דאין מצטרפין לאסור ומראשונה ראשונה בטלי והארכתי בהגוזל קמא (ב"ק דף ק: ושם) ובפרק במה אשה (שבת דף סה:):

פירוש רבינו גרשום מאור הגולה

השותפין דאית להו חצר בשותפות ונתרצו לחלוק ולעשות מחיצה: **בונין את הכותל לאמצע:** **גמ' גודא.** כותל: **כדתנן** א) **מחיצת הכרם שנפרצה** לזה היה לו שדה תבואה ולזה היה לו כרם והיתה כותל מחיצה מפסקת בין השדה לכרם ועכשיו נפרצה מחיצת כרמו כמו דיש לחוש שלא יתערבו הזרעים בכרם: **אומרים לו** בית דין לבעל הכרם **גדור.** [מכאן שייך לע"ב] **נתייאש** מן הזמן שקבעו לו ב"ד **ולא גדרה** ונתערבו הזרעים בכרם **הרי זה קידש** וטעונין שריפה ככלאי הכרם כדכתיב פן תקדש המלאה ודרשי' לה (חולין קטו.) פן תוקד אש. ואותו בעל מחיצה **חייב באחריות** זרעוני של זה שהופסדו וחייב לשלם דמיהן. השתא כיון דאשכחן דהאי מחיצה דמתני' כותל הוא דילפי' לה ממחיצת הכרם דמיקרי מתני' **טעמא דרצו** שניהן לעשות מחיצה משום הכי בונין הכותל באמצע שניהן ביחד **הא לא רצו** שניהם לבנות ביחד אלא אחד רוצה ואחד אינו רוצה **אין מחייבין אותו** שאינו רוצה לבנות חלקו בעל כרחו. והואיל דאין כופין אותו לבנות ש"מ שזה שהמעכב רואה בחצר חבירו אותו **היזק ראיה לא שמיה היזק:** ומקשה מאן לימא לן דהאי מחיצה דמתני' גודא דאיכא למידק כדקאמרת דהיזק ראיה לאו שמיה היזק. **אימא מאי מחיצה דמתני' פלוגתא.** חלוקה. שנתרצו לעשות חלוקה. והכי פריש למתני' השותפין שרצו לחלוק חצירן בונין את הכותל באמצע. ואידוק הכי כיון **דנתרצו** לחלוק אם זה מעכב שאינו רוצה לעשות עמו הכותל הואיל דמקפידין זה על זה שלא ישתמש הא' בחלק חבירו (היו) כופין אותו **ובונין את הכותל באמצע בעל כרחו** משום דהיזק **ראיה** [דיליה] שמסתכל בחצר חבירו **הוי היזק.** ומהדר ליה **אי הכי** דפלוגתא הוי אמאי קתני **שרצו לעשות מחיצה שרצו לחצות מיבעי ליה: אלא מאי גודא.**

אמאי קתני תו **בונין את הכותל.** והא כל לשון משנה לשון קצרה הוא. וכיון דההיא שרצו לעשות מחיצה היינו כותל **בונין אותו מיבעי ליה** ולא איצטריך למיתני כותל. ואכתי היזק ראיה שמיה היזק: ומתרץ ליה לעולם מחיצה גודא. ודקשיא לך בונין אותו מיבעי ליה משום הכי איצטריך למתני כותל **דאי תנא** בונין **אותו הוה אמינא במסיפס בעלמא** סגי. מחיצת הקנים עראי שקורין בל"ע פלפי"ט. **קמ"ל כותל.** דצריכי למיעבד כותל של קיימא ולעולם כדאמינא דמחיצה גודא היא וכדדייקי דהיזק ראיה לאו שמיה היזק: **בונין את הכותל באמצע פשיטא.** אכתי מקשה למאן דאמר גודא כי האי גוונא ב) בשלמא אי אמרי' מאי מחיצה פלוגתא מש"ה איצטריך למיתני בונין את הכותל דלא סגי בלאו הכי דאיצטריך לאדכר כותל. והאי דקתני באמצע ודאי לא איצטריך למיתנייה הואיל דקאמר פלוגתא. אלא אגב דאיצטריך למתני כותל קתני באמצע ולא משום דוקא אלא אי אמרת דהאי מחיצה גודא היא בשלמא כותל לא מיותר הוא משום דאתי לאפוקי מסיפס ולא לגופיה איצטריך. אלא ודאי באמצע מיותר הוא דכיון דשותפין נינהו בהאי חצר ורצו לעשות גודא פשיטא דבאמצע בונין אותו והשתא לא מצית למימר אגב דאיצטריך למתני כותל קתני באמצע משום דכותל גופיה לא אתא אלא לאפוקי מסיפס בודאי לא איצטריך באמצע אלא לעולם כדאמר' מחיצה פלוגתא והיזק ראיה שמיה היזק. לעולם אימא לך מחיצה גודא ודקא קשיא לך באמצע למה לי (לא) צריכי דודאי לא מייתר הוא דהכא במאי עסקינן **דאקדים חד** מינייהו **וארציה לחבריה** שלא רצו שניהן מתחלה אלא אחד פייס לחבירו עד שנתרצה לו שיעשה כותל. עכשיו אי לא תני דבונין באמצע בחלק שניהן **הוה אמינא** דיכול למימר ליה **כי נתרציתי** לעשות מחיצה בכך נתרציתי שלא אשתמש **באוירא** דידך אבל למעוטי **בתשמיש** שלי ליתן מקום חצי הכותל **לא נתרציתי: קמ"ל.** דכיון דנתרצה בונין את הכותל באמצע חצי בחלק זה וחצי בחלק זה. ולהכי איצטריך למתני באמצע ולעולם מחיצה גודא הוא ואכתי היזק ראיה לאו שמיה היזק: **ת"ש וכן בגינה** מקום שנהגו לגדור. בגינה העומדת בעיר קא מיירי דאיכא היזק ראיה שרואה מה שבחצר חבירו. קתני וכן בגינה דמחייבין אותו לגדור. אלמא היזק ראיה שמיה היזק: לא לעולם אימא לך לאו שמיה היזק **ושאני גינה** לאו משום דטעמא דהיזק ראיה. אלא משום דמסתכלין בגינתו ומכניסין בו עין הרע **[כדר'] אבא:** א"כ כדקאמרת דמשום טעמא דעין הרעה מחייבין לגדור בגינה ולאו משום היזק ראיה **מאי וכן** בגינה כלומר דמשמע דאותו דין עצמו נוהג בגינה ולטעמיך אינו דין א'. בשלמא לדידי דאמינא אידי ואידי משום היזק ראיה להכי אתי שפיר וכן בגינה אלא לדידך מאי וכן: ומשני האי וכן לא מהדר אכולה אבונין את הכותל דתידוק מינה כשם שמחייבין לבנות כותל בחצר משום היזק ראיה כן בגינה אלא האי דקתני וכן בגינה **אגויל וגזית** מה בחצר מקום שנהגו לבנות בגויל ובגזית בונין כן בגינה ולעולם לא קשיא לי:

חשק שלמה על רבינו גרשום א) עי' בתוס' כאן ד"ה כדתניא: ב) פשיטא היא:

עין משפט נר מצוה

א א מיי' פ"ב מהל' שכנים הל' יד סמג עשין פב טוש"ע ח"מ סי' קנז סעיף א:
ב ב מיי' שם הלכה טו טוש"ע שם סעיף ד:
ג ג מיי' שם הלכה יח טור שם:
ד ד מיי' שם טוש"ע שם סעיף ה:
ה ה ו ז מיי' שם הלכה טז וסמג שם טוש"ע ח"מ סי' קנח סעיף א:
ו ח מיי' שם טוש"ע שם סעיף ד:
ז ט מיי' פ"ו מהל' כלאים הל' ו סמג לאוין רפ טוש"ע י"ד סי' רצו סעיף מז:

מסורת הש"ס

א) [לקמן ג.], ב"ק ק. [תוספתא כלאים פרק ג], ב) [נ"ל כדתנן], ג) נ"ל ול"ש.

הגהות הב"ח

(א) במשנה בגויל זה נותן: (ב) תוס' ד"ה אומר וכו' דהוא המזיק:

גליון הש"ס

תוס' ד"ה לפיכך וכו' מיגו דאי בעי אמר ממך לקחתיה. קשה לי למ"ל מדין מגו ולא בפשיטות כי היכי דנאמן לקחתיה מכח שהו הרבה...

ליקוטי רש"י

גויל. אבנים דלא מספיין למורשי דידהו מטפי בה ספק [ב"מ קיז:]. גזית. לשון גזיזה שמספין ומכתתן בברזל [שמות כ, כב]. נסכלות ומסותתות [מלכים א, ה, לא]. כפיסין. כפיס חתיכת עץ כמו כפיסין בבבא בתרא (ג.) [חגיגה טז.]. ... אומר לאדם כו'. ... כותל חצר וכו' מחייבין אותו לבנות עד ד' אמות דבהכי סגי להיזק ראיה [לקמן ה.].

עין משפט
נר מצוה

ח א מיי' פ"ג מהל' שכנים הלכה ו ועיין בהשגות סמג עשין פב טוש"ע ח"מ סי' קנז סעיף ג וסי' קס סעיף א:

רבינו גרשום

[תחילת הפירוש ששייך לכאן נדפס בעמוד הקודם] כותל חצר שבין שני חצירות שנפל אם א' מהן מעכב מלבנותו מחייבין אותו לבנותו בעל כרחו עד שיהא גבוה ד"א דלא מצי איניש לאסתכולי דרך היכתו עד שיהא גבוה ד' אמות אלמא משום היזק ראיה הוא. ומשני דהיכא דנפל שאני האויל דהוי מעיקרא הכותל בדין הוא דמחייבין אותו עד ד' אמות דפחות מכאן לא מצי למיבניה דהכי שמה מחיצה אבל גבי מתני' שלא היה מעולם מחיצה אין מחייבין המעכב: ודקארי לה מאי קארי לה כלו' המקשה שהיה מקשה קושי' זו מאי מקשה לה. וכי לא היה יודע דהיכא דנפל שאני ומה ראה להקשותה. ומשני לעולם משום קושיא מייתינן לה משום דהוא בסיפא איצטריך ליה למיתני' דקתני סיפא מד' אמות ולמעלה אין מחייבין אותו לבנות גבוה כדמעיקרא אלמא ש"מ משום היזק ראייה הוא ומשה"ה אין מחייבין אותו אלא כשיעור שאינו יכול לראות. והמתרץ מתרץ [לעולם] כדמעיקרא נפל שאני. והאי דאמר עד ד' אמות דבהכי הוא דין מחיצה ולאו משום היזק ראייה: ת"ש בתים הפתוחים לחצר וחצר פתוח לרה"ר ונפל בית שער החצר. וכל בני החצר נתרצו לבנות. כופין לא' מבני החצר המעכב לבנות בית שער ודלת עמהן משום היזק ראייה דבני רה"ר. אלמא היזק ראייה שמיה היזק: היזק דרבים שאני. אבל היכא דאיכא היזק ראייה דיחיד כגון האי חצר השותפין לאו שמיה היזק: ת"ש קתני מתני' אין חולקין את החצר. האחין שבאו לחלוק בנכסי אביהן אין חולקין את החצר עד שיהא בה ד"א לזה וד"א לזה דהכי חזי לדירה. וכשהן חולקין מאי לאו כותל מצליא בעו למיעבד בינייהו משום היזק ראייה: לא במסיפס בעלמא. חולקין דאע"ג דזה יכול לראות בזה: ת"ש חלונות שיש להם חזקה כדאמר לקמן מלמעלן מלמטן ומכנגדן ד' אמות כלומר אם רוצה זה לבנות כותל בחצר שהחלון פתוח בחצירו לבנות כותל בצד חלון. מלמעלה שאם רצה להגביה כותל (מן) החלון צריך להגביהו ד' אמות על החלון. אי נמי למטה (מן) החלון ד' נמוך (מן) הכותל מן (הצד) שצריך להנמיכו ד' אמות ואם בא אצל החלון צריך להרחיק ד' אמות או כותלו כן עד שיהא יש לו חזקת חלון בחצירו של זה צריך להרחיק ד' אמות כדי שלא יאפיל חלונותי': ותני עלה מלמעלה להם צריך שיהא גבוה ד' אמות על החלון כדי שלא יציץ ויראה

ב.

נתיאש הימנה ולא גדרה ה"ז קידש וחייב באחריות׳: (א) טעמא דרצו הא לא רצו אין מחייבין אותו אלמא א) היזק ראיה לאו שמיה היזק ואימא (ב) מחיצה פלוגתא כדכתיב א) ותהי מחצת העדה וכיון דרצו בונין את הכותל בעל כרחו אלמא ג) היזק ראיה שמיה היזק אי הכי האי שרצו לעשות מחיצה שרצו לחצות מבעי ליה אלא מאי גודא בונין את הכותל בונין אותו מבעי ליה אי תנא אותו הוה אמינא במסיפס בעלמא קמ"ל כותל: בונין את הכותל באמצע וכו': פשיטא לא צריכא דקדים חד ורצייה לחבריה מהו דתימא מצי א"ל כי איתרצאי לך באוירא בתשמישתא לא איתרצאי לך קמ"ל והיזק ראיה לאו שמיה היזק (סימן גינה כותל כופין וחולקין חלונות דרב נחמן) ת"ש וכן בגינה שאני גינה דר' אבא ג) דאמר ר' אבא אמר רב הונא אמר רב אסור לאדם לעמוד בשדה חבירו בשעה שהיא עומדת בקמותיה והא וכן קתני אגויל וגזית ת"ש ד) כותל חצר שנפל מחייבין אותו לבנות עד ד' אמות נפל שאני ה) ודקארי לה מאי קארי לה סיפא איצטריכא ליה מד' אמות ולמעלה אין מחייבין אותו ת"ש ו) כופין אותו לבנות בית שער ודלת לחצר ש"מ היזק ראיה שמיה היזק הזיקא דרבים שאני ודיחיד לא ת"ש ז) אין חולקין את החצר עד שיהא בה ד' אמות לזה וד' אמות לזה הא יש בה כדי לזה וכדי לזה חולקין מאי לאו בכותל לא במסיפס בעלמא תא שמע ז) החלונות בין מלמעלה בין מלמטה ובין מכנגדן ד' אמות ותני עלה ח) מלמעלן כדי שלא יציץ ויראה מלמטן כדי שלא יעמוד ויראה מכנגדן כדי שלא יאפיל הזיקא דבית שאני תא שמע ט) דאמר רב נחמן אמר שמואל גג אהסמוך לחצר חבירו עושין לו מעקה גבוה ד' אמות שאני התם דאמר ליה בעל החצר לבעל הגג לדידי קביעה לי (ג) תשמישי לדידך לא קביעה לך תשמישתך ולא ידענא בהי עידנא סליקא ואתית

תוספות

נתיאש הימנה ולא גדרה. דוקא נתיאש אבל לא נתיאש ועוסק כל שעה לגדור אע"פ שהוסיף מאתים מותר כדתנן במסכת כלאים (פ"ה מ"ו) הרואה ירק בכרם ואמר כשאגיע לשם אלקטנו הוסיף מאתים מותר לכשאחזור אלקטנו הוסיף מאתים אסור אלמא כשהוא מחזר אחר לקיטתו אפילו הוסיף מאתים מותר והטעם יש לפרש משום דכתיב (דברים כב) לא תזרע כרמך כלאים דומיא דזריעה דניחא ליה: וחייב באחריותו. אע"ג דהיזק שאינו ניכר לא שמיה היזק (גיטין נג.) נראה לר"י דהאי חשיב היזק ניכר שהרי ניכר הוא שהוא כלאים כשרואה הגפנים בשדה וטומאה אע"פ שרואין השרץ על הטהרות לא חשיב היזק ניכר דמי יודע אם הוכשרו אבל אין לומר דה"ט הוי היזק שאינו ניכר וקנסוהו כמו במטמא (שם) שלא יהא כל אחד הולך ומטמא טהרותיו של חבירו דהכא ליכא למיחש להכי שבעל הכרם נמי מפסיד ועוד אי קנס הוא במזיד דוקא היה לו להתחייב: ואימא מאי מחיצה פלוגתא. מפרש ר"י משום דעל לשון גודא יש כמה קושיות כדפריך בסמוך לפיכך דוחק לפרש מחיצה פלוגתא אע"ג דבכל מקום הוי מחיצה גודא: וכיון דרצו בונין את הכותל בעל כרחו. לקמן מוקי לה כשאין בה דין חלוקה ותימה לר"י דלמאי נקט מתני' כשאין בה דין חלוקה וקתני רצו לא ליתני רצו ולאיירי בשיש בה דין חלוקה ומי' קמ"ל דס"ד בשאין בה דין חלוקה דמצי למימר כי (ה) איתרצאי לך לחלוק ע"מ שלא לעשות גודא אבל על מנת לעשות גודא לא איתרצאי לך. ויש ספרים דמקשין ומתרץ כן להדיא בשילהי שמעתין: הוה אמינא במסיפס בעלמא. פי' ורצו דקתני אמסיפס ואע"ג דבלאו רצו נמי עושין מסיפס בעל כרחם כדמוכח בסמוך דקאמר מאי לאו בכותל לא במסיפס היינו מסיפס גרוע אבל כי רצו עושין מסיפס מגויל וגזית כמנהג המדינה ומקרי מסיפס לפי שהוא מלא חלונות כדפי' בערוך ואינו מגין מהיזק ראיה א"נ לפי שאינו גבוה י' כדמוכח לקמן גבי גג הסמוך י) לחצר דאמר ר"נ עושה לו מעקה גבוה י' ופריך למאי אי להיזק ראיה ד"א בעינן ואי לנתפס כגנב במסיפס סגי ובקונטרס פי' דרצו דקתני אחלוקה קאי ותימה דהא אסיק דמחיצה היינו גודא דאי פלוגתא לחצות מיבעי ליה ועוד היכי מצי למימר דה"א במסיפס בעלמא הא שמעינן ליה מסיפא דקתני אבל בזמן ששניהם רוצים אפילו פחות מכאן יחלוקו והיינו לכל הפחות במסיפס ועוד היכא המ"ל במסיפס בעלמא הא בהדיא קתני במתני' גזית וגויל: בונין את הכותל באמצע פשיטא. למ"ד גודא פריך כמו כל הנך פירכי דלקמן דכשהקנו לעשות גודא כך הקנה זה כמו זה ופשיטא דבאמצע אבל למ"ד פלוגתא איצטריך למימר סד"א דמשום היזק ראיה יש לו לסייע בבנין הכותל אבל אין לו לבנות בחלקו בשביל כך: תא שמע וכן בגינה. לקמן מסקינן דה"ק וכן בגינה סתם כמקום שנהגו לגדור דמי הלכך דייק שפיר דהיזק ראיה שמיה היזק: גינה שאני כדרבי אבא וכו'. וא"ת ומהאי טעמא יתחייב נמי לגדור בבקעה ויש לומר דשאני גינה שמגדלין בה ירק לאכילה וכל שעה היא עומדת בקמותיה אבל בקעה אינה עומדת בקמותיה אלא חדש אחד בשנה ולא מחייב לגדור אבל אסור לעמוד בשעה שעומדת בקמותיה וא"ת ולמ"ד פלוגתא כיון דאשמועינן דאפילו בחצר שמיה היזק כל שכן בגינה ואמאי איצטריך תו למיתני וכן בגינה וי"ל דאיצטריך וכן בגינה למיתני משום גויל וגזית: נפל שאני. שהורגלו לעשות דבר הצנע בחצר ולא למדו ליזהר זה מזה: ודקארי לה מאי קארי לה. כלומר פשיטא דנפל שאני ואדרבה היה לו להוכיח מדקתני נפל מכלל דבעלמא לא שמיה היזק: הזיקא דרבים שאני. ואע"ג דלקמן משמע דאיירי בחצר שאינה סמוכה לרה"ר מ"מ איכא היזקא דרבים דזימנין דדחקי רבים ועיילי להתם כדאמרי' לקמן ורשב"ג אע"ג דלית ליה האי טעמא דזימנין דדחקי רבים מ"מ מרחוק יכולין לראות לפנים ולכך לא פליג אלא אבית שער אבל בדלת מודה דכופין אותו לבנות: מאי לאו בכותל. תימה ויהא בכותל דילמא הכי פי' אין חולקין את החצר אפי' האחד רוצה לבנות את הכותל בתוך שלו עד שיהא בה ד' אמות לכל אחד הא אם יש בה ד' אמות לכל אחד חולקין אם רצה לכנוס ולבנות בתוך שלו וי"ל דחולקין משמע באמצע דאי אשמועינן כדפי' הוה ליה למיתני אין עושין כותל בחצר עד שיהא בה כו': שאני התם דאמר ליה בעל החצר לבעל הגג כו'. תימה אמאי לא מייתי מדתנן לקמן (דף ו:) שתי חצירות זו למעלה מזו לא יאמר העליון הריני בונה כנגדי ועולה אלא מסייע מלמטה ועולה אלמא שמיה היזק:

רש"י

קידש. התבואה אם הוסיף מאתים לשנא דקרא נקט פן תוקדש (דברים כב): וטעמא דרצו. לבנות כותל (ד) דמדעת שניהן הוא דחייביה חכמים שיבנו בין שניהן ולקמן פריך כשרצו מאי הוי ליהדר בהו אבל לא רצו שניהן שהיה אחד אומר דייה לחלוקה במסיפס של יתדות עלים תקועים בארץ נמוכים לא כייפינן ליה ואע"ג דיכול לומר לו איני חפץ שתראה עסקי: פלוגתא. חלוקת חצר שהושוו לדעתם לחולקה וכגון שלא היה בה ד' אמות כדי לזה וכדי לזה שאין האחד יכול לכוף את חבירו לחולקה ולהכי תני רצו שכיון שרצו לחולקה בונין כותל אבנים על כרחם ואם בא האחד לומר לא איפשי בכך אלא מסיפס בעלמא אין שומעין לו: הוה אמינא במסיפס בעלמא. מיירי מתני' דאיהו נמי מחילה איקרו והוה דקתני אחלוקה קאי וכשאין בה דין חלוקה קמ"ל כותל והוא דקתני משום כותל דאי לא רצו פלגי לה במסיפס: דרצייה חד מינייהו לחבריה. ביקש ממנו לחולקה במחילה: מהו דתימא א"ל כשנתרציתי לך. במחילה מחילה דקה נתרציתי ולמעוטי באוירא כגון של נסרים שהיא דקה והזיק ראיה אין בה לא תמשכן עובי הכותל בחלקך חוץ מדבר מועט אבל לבנות כותל אבנים עב ולמעוטי נמי תשמישתי לא נתרציתי: אסור לאדם שיעמוד כו'. שלא יזיקנו בעין רעה: והא וכן קתני. דמשמע מרוייהו חד טעמא הוא גינה וחצר: מחייבין אותו. והכא לא קתני רצו אלא על כרחו: נפל שאני. שכבר נתרצו הראשונים בכותל: ודקארי לה מאי קארי לה. וכי לא ידע דנפל שאני: סיפא איצטריך ליה. כלומר הוא הדין נמי מעיקרא והאי דקתני נפל משום סיפא לאשמועינן דיותר מד' אמות אין מחייבין ואע"פ שהראשון היה גבוה יותר לא מחייבין ליה: כופין אותו. כל אחד מבני החצר לתת חלקו בבנין: בית השער. שבונים כותל נגד השער עגול סביב ועושין באותו היקף פתח קטן מן הכלל משום היזק ראיית בני רה"ר שלא יראו תוך החצר: הזיקא דרבים. שכל בני רה"ר מסתכלין שם: אין חולקין. אין האחד כופה את חבירו לחלוק: החלונות. אחד מבני השותפין הבונה כותל בחצר כנגד חלונותיו של חבירו בין מלמעלה וכו' אם הכותל גבוה יותר מן החלונות צריך להגביה למעלה מהן ד"א כדמפרש ואזיל כדי שלא יסמוך על כותלו וישחה ויראה בחלונותיו של חבירו: בין מלמטה. אם הכותל נמוך מן החלונות צריך להשפילו מהן ד"א כדי שלא יעמוד על עובי כותלו ויראה: ומכנגדן. צריך להרחיק את הכותל מן החלונות ד' אמות כדי שלא יאפיל: הזיקא דבית שאני. שאדם עושה בביתו דברי הצנע: מעקה גבוה ארבע אמות. כדי שלא יראה בחצר חבירו כשהוא משתמש בגגו: ולא ידענא בהי עידנא דקא אתית. להשתמש בגגך:

דאיצטנע

מסורת הש"ס

א) [לקמן נט:], ב) [שם], ג) ב"מ קז. ע"ש, ד) לקמן ה, ה) לקמן ז:, ו) לקמן יא., ז) לקמן דף כב., ח) [שם:], ט) לקמן ו:, י) נ"ל לגג:

הגהות הב"ח

(א) גמ' וטעמא דרצו: (ב) שם ואימא מאי מחיצה פלוגתא: (ג) שם קביעא לי תשמישתי: (ד) רש"י ד"ה וטעמא וכו' מדעת שניהן הוא דחייבום חכמים: (ה) תוס' ד"ה וכיון וכו' כי איתרצאי לך וכו' לא איתרצאי לך ויש ספרים דמקשה ומתרץ:

גליון הש"ס

גמ' ודקארי לה. עי' בחדושי הרמב"ן לקמן דף ז ע"ב ד"ה גירסת רש"י: שם ודקארי לה. כתובות טו ע"ב וש"נ:

תורה אור השלם

א) וַתְּהִי מֶחֱצַת הָעֵדָה מִן הַצֹּאן שְׁלֹשׁ מֵאוֹת אֶלֶף וּשְׁלֹשִׁים אֶלֶף שִׁבְעַת אֲלָפִים וַחֲמֵשׁ מֵאוֹת: [במדבר לא, מג]

ליקוטי רש"י

[תחילת ליקוטי רש"י ששייך לכאן נדפס בעמוד הקודם] כופין אותו לבנות בית שער. את בן החצר שאינו רוצה לסייע את בני החצר לבנות להן בית שער להיות שומר הפתח יושב שם בצל ומרחיק את בני רשות הרבים מלהכיר בחצר [לקמן ז:]. בית שער. בית קטן לפני שער [יומא יא.]. בית כניסה שער החצר ולהשתפף שם שומר החצר [סוטה מג.]. בית קטן שעושין בצל שערי חצירות ויושב שם שומר הפתח [מנחות לג:]. ודלת. לשער החצר לנעלו [לקמן ז:]. החלונות. מי שיש לו חלונות פתוחים לחצר חבירו והוחזק בדבר זה שלש שנים ובא בעל החצר לבנות שם כותל צריך לשער ד' אמות. בין מלמעלה. אם בא להגביה יגביה כותלו ד' אמות מן החלונות. בין מלמטה. אם בא לבנותו נמוך צריך להשפילו מן החלונות ד' אמות וטעמא מפרש בגמ'. בין מכנגדן. צריך להרחיקו מהן ד' אמות [לקמן כב.]. מלמעלן. צריך להגביה שיעור שלא יוכל להשענו על כותלו ויסתכל דרך חלונות ויראה בבית חבירו. שלא יעמוד. על ראש עובי כותלו ויראה. מכנגדן. צריך להרחיק כדי שלא יאפיל. שלא יאפיל. חלונות [שם]. מעקה גבוה ד' אמות. משום היזק ראיה [לקמן ו:]. [מכאן שייך לדף ג.] אפילו פחות מכאן חולקין. משום דבעי למיתני וכתבי הקדש אע"פ ששניהם רוצים לא יחלוקו תני רישא. כתבי הקדש. כ"ד ספרים והיו רגילים לכותבן בגליון כ"ט שלו ולפיכך גוללי הדבר למתכן כל כתבי הקדש. כגון תורה נביאים וכתובים

[קטו.] כל אלה אבנים יקרות. כל האבנים הללו עשויות כמדות. כמדות גזית. כמדת אבני גזית מדה אחת היתה להם לאבני גזית במדינה [מלכים א ז, ט]. למורשא דקרנתא. המורשא דידהו מטפי טפח. לבני אורבי. בין שורות אבני הבנין. והא אמה טרקסין וכו'. כך נקראת כותל מחיצה שמפסקת במקדש בין ההיכל לבין קדש הקדשים [יומא נא:]. טרקסין. לשון פנים ולשון חוץ [ברכות לה:] למדנו שטרקסין לשון כניסה פנים הוא [יומא נב.].

ויציץ ויראה בחלון ומלמטן צריך לנמוך ד' אמות שלא יעמוד זקוף על גבי הכותל ויראה בבית אלמא היזק ראיה שמיה היזק: הזיקא דבית שני. דאינש צניע דשמיש בבית טפי מבחצר: גג הסמוך לחצר חבירו. דחצר גבוה קרקעיתה ושוותה לגג בעל הגג צריך לעשות מעקה גבוה ד' אמות שלא יסתכל בתוך חצר חבירו אלמא היזק ראיה שמיה היזק: לא לעולם אימא בחצר של שנים לאו שמיה היזק ושאני התם דאמר ליה בעל החצר לבעל הגג לדידי קביעא תשמישתאי בכל שעה בחצר אבל לגג ולהכי בעי למיעבד מעקה:

חשק שלמה על רבינו גרשום א) [נראה דל"ל ואם לא לבנות כותל מנגד כותל החצר והוא יש לו חזקת וכו']: ב) [נראה דל"ל לא לכך יכול להגביה וכו' להנמיכו ד' אמות וכו']: ג) [אולי צ"ל דאינש צניע בתשמישיה טפי מבחצר]:

נִתְיָאֵשׁ הֵימֶנָּה וְלֹא גְּדָרָהּ — If, however, **HE ABANDONED [THE PROJECT]**[1] **AND DID NOT REBUILD [THE WALL]**, and the grain grew[2] without a wall separating them, הֲרֵי זֶה קִידֵּשׁ — the vineyard **RENDERS [THE GRAIN] UNFIT,**[3] וְחַיָּיב בְּאַחֲרָיוּתָהּ — **AND** the vineyard's owner **IS RESPONSIBLE FOR ANY LOSS** incurred by the owner of the grain. This concludes the Baraisa, in which we find that the word *mechitzah* connotes a "wall."

The Gemara now explains the implication of employing this translation of *mechitzah* in our Mishnah:

טַעְמָא דְּרָצוּ — And[4] **the reason** that *beis din* can compel the two partners to jointly build a solid wall **is because** originally **they had agreed** to erect just such a structure.[5] הָא לֹא רָצוּ — **But had they not** specifically **agreed** to do so,[6] אֵין מְחַיְּיבִין אוֹתוֹ — *beis din* **would not obligate [the reluctant partner]** to contribute toward the building of a wall as a result of his agreement to divide. אַלְמָא הֶיזֵּק רְאִיָּה לָאו שְׁמֵיהּ הֶיזֵּק — **We see** therefore that **visual trespass is not considered damaging.**[7]

The Gemara suggests an alternative definition of *mechitzah*, one which reverses the Mishnah's implied position on the right to privacy in a courtyard:

וְאֵימָא מַאי מְחִיצָה — **But say, what is**[8] meant by the word ***mechitzah?*** פְּלוּגְתָּא — **A division!** כִּדְכְתִיב: ,,וַתְּהִי מֶחֱצַת הָעֵדָה" — **As it is written:**[9] ***And the division***[10] ***of the congregation was...*** This translation changes the meaning of the Mishnah, for the Mishnah now reads: *Partners who agreed to divide*[11] *must build a wall.* That is, וְכֵיוָן דְּרָצוּ — **since they agreed** to the division of the courtyard (with an irrevocable agreement), בּוֹנִין אֶת הַכּוֹתֶל בְּעַל כָּרְחוֹ — **they must build a** stone **wall notwithstanding** the objection of either party.[12] The Mishnah thus implies that in agreeing to divide the courtyard they became obligated to contribute to the erection of a solid wall as well. אַלְמָא הֶיזֵּק רְאִיָּה שְׁמֵיהּ הֶיזֵּק — **We** therefore **see** that **visual trespass** is considered damaging, for only if a right to privacy existed would each partner be obligated to build a wall.

The Gemara explains its objection to incorporating the second translation into the Mishnah:

אִי הָכִי— **If it is so,** that *mechitzah* means "division," הַאי שֶׁרָצוּ לַעֲשׂוֹת מְחִיצָה — **this** segment, **WHO AGREED TO MAKE A DIVISION,** is poorly worded. שֶׁרָצוּ לַחֲצוֹת מִבָּעֵי לֵיהּ — The Mishnah **should have said, WHO AGREED TO DIVIDE** — for the expression לַחֲצוֹת can mean only "to divide" (i.e. the courtyard), and in no way implies the building of a wall. The expression לַעֲשׂוֹת מְחִיצָה, however, implies making something in the courtyard.[13] **— ? —**

The Gemara counters by pointing out a difficulty with the first translation:

אֶלָּא מַאי גּוּדָא — **Rather, what** is the alternative definition of *mechitzah* **— a wall?** If this is the appropriate translation, בּוֹנִין אֶת הַכּוֹתֶל — why does the Mishnah state, **THEY MUST BUILD THE WALL?** בּוֹנִין אוֹתוֹ מִבָּעֵי לֵיהּ — **It should have said, THEY MUST BUILD IT,** since the word *wall* has already been mentioned.[14]

The Gemara resolves this difficulty:[15]

אִי תָּנָא אוֹתוֹ — **If the Mishnah had taught, [THEY MUST BUILD] IT,** הֲוָה אֲמִינָא בִּמְסִיפָּס בְּעָלְמָא — **I would have thought** that the Mishnah requires only **an ordinary boundary marker.**[16] קָא מַשְׁמַע לָן כּוֹתֶל — Therefore, **[the Mishnah] informs us** explicitly that they must erect **a** solid stone **wall.**

NOTES

1. The vineyard owner must actually abandon any intent to repair the wall for the produce to become prohibited as *kilayim*. However, so long as he is actively engaged in the process of repair, the mixture will not become prohibited — even if much time elapses and the mixture grows in the interim (see following note) [*Tosafos* ד״ה נתיאש, based on a Scriptural inference].

2. The amount of growth necessary to prohibit is an increase of 1/200th of the produce (*Rashi*). *Rambam* (*Hilchos Kilayim* 5:22) explains that this is measured in time: If the grain were cut and would wither in 100 hours, and the crops grew unseparated for 1/200th of that time (½ hour), the grain is prohibited.

3. Not only is *kilayim* of the vineyard unfit (i.e. prohibited) for consumption, it must also be burnt. For the Torah states (*Deut.* 22:9): פֶּן־תִּקְדַּשׁ, which we read as תּוּקַד אֵשׁ, *it shall be burnt in fire.* Thus, the term קִידֵּשׁ is used here, as is found in the Torah *(Rashi).*

Although the word מְקַדֵּשׁ is commonly translated as *sanctify, Targum* (ibid.) renders תִּקְדַּשׁ as תִּסְתָּאַב, *it will become unfit. Rashi* there explains that a common idea links the two definitions: Wherever an object is unfit for man — whether because it is holy or it is proscribed — a derivative of the root קדש may be used to convey the sense of its inaccessibility.

[The vineyard, of course, is also rendered unfit. However, since the Baraisa is discussing his responsibility to pay, it only mentions the grain becoming unfit.]

[It should be noted that he is liable for the loss even though he did not directly damage the field but only caused the damage by not repairing the wall. See *Bava Kamma* 100a-100b, where the liability is explained to be for *garmi - directly causing* damage (see Schottenstein edition of *Bava Kamma*, 98b note 15 for further explanation of this law.)]

4. In *Rashi's* version the conjunction וְ, *and,* precedes the word טַעְמָא, *reason,* thus connecting the inference to the definition. In our version the connection is assumed.

5. As the Mishnah explicitly states: "Partners who agreed to build a *[solid] wall."* Hence, neither party may later renege on the agreement. [The Gemara below (3a) will explain why such an agreement is binding.]

6. Rather, one of the parties thought it sufficient to mark the division of the courtyard with a line of short wooden pegs driven into the ground (*Rashi*).

7. If loss of privacy in a courtyard were considered actual damage, one partner could compel the other to assist in building the wall even without a prior agreement to do so. For once they decided to divide the courtyard, the partners could rightfully declare to one another: "I do not want you to observe my private activities!" (*Rashi*). Thus, in stating that the partners must *agree* to build a wall, the Mishnah teaches that no right of privacy exists in a courtyard setting.

[For an explanation as to what damage is being done by visual trespass that would require building a wall, see *Chidushei R' Reuven* and *Chidushei R' Nachum.*]

8. *Bach* adds מאי, *what,* to conform with the prior manner of expression.

9. *Numbers* 31:43. The Torah speaks of the division of spoils following Israel's successful military campaign against the Midianites.

10. Although the sense of מֶחֱצַת as it appears in this particular verse is *half-share,* the Gemara translates it as *result of dividing* (i.e. a division), just as "half" implies "result of halving."

11. Ordinarily, one party may unilaterally dissolve a partnership. However, here mutual consent is required, since the Mishnah speaks of a legally indivisible courtyard (i.e. one whose division would not yield four *amos* by four *amos* to each former partner) [*Rashi;* see Mishnah 11a and note 21 there; see Gemara below, 3a for a detailed discussion of this interpretation of the Mishnah].

12. Neither may decline to bear the expense of a stone wall in favor of using wooden pegs to demarcate the two new courtyards (*Rashi*).

13. *Yad Ramah.* In addition, the expression לַחֲצוֹת is more concise, and the Tannaim always strove for brevity (see *Bava Kamma* 6b).

14. As the Mishnah states initially: *Partners who agreed to make a wall.*

15. The other difficulty is resolved below (3a).

16. For a boundary marker, too, is called a *mechitzah*. According to this translation of the word, the agreement between the partners would concern the division of the courtyard and not the erection of a wall. The Mishnah would thus be teaching that partners may agree to divide an extremely small (normally indivisible) courtyard, a matter discussed by the Gemara below (3a). Hence, the Mishnah would not be addressing the subject of visual trespass at all. It is therefore necessary to use the word כּוֹתֶל, *wall,* in the Mishnah to underscore that the agreement concerned building a wall, and that — had no such agreement been made — the partners could be required to erect only a boundary marker, thus establishing that visual trespass is not considered injurious (*Rashi;* see *Tosafos* who raise questions on *Rashi's* explanation, see *Maharam* and *Ramban* to resolve the difficulties).

נתיאש הימנה ולא גדרה ה"ז קידש וחייב באחריות' (א) טעמא דרצו הא לא רצו אין מחייבין אותו אלמא א) היזק ראיה לאו שמיה היזק ואימא (ב) מחיצה פלוגתא כדכתיב א) ותהי מחצת העדה וכיון דרצו בונין את הכותל בעל כרחו אלמא ב) היזק ראיה שמיה היזק אי הכי האי שרצו לעשות מחיצה שרצו לחצות מבעי ליה אלא מאי גודא בונין את הכותל בונין אותו מבעי ליה אי תנא אותו הוה אמינא במסיפס בעלמא קמ"ל כותל: בונין את הכותל באמצע וכו': פשיטא לא צריכא דקדים חד ורצייה לחבריה מהו דתימא מצי א"ל כי איתרצאי לך באוירא בתשמישתא לא איתרצאי לך קמ"ל והיזק ראיה לאו שמיה היזק (סימן גינה כותל כופין וחולקין חלונות דרב נחמן) ת"ש וכן בגינה גינה שאני כדר' אבא ג) דאמר ר' אבא אמר רב הונא אמר רב אסור לאדם לעמוד בשדה חבירו בשעה שהיא עומדת בקמותיה והא וכן קתני אגויל וגזית ת"ש ד) כותל חצר שנפל מחייבין אותו לבנות עד ד' אמות נפל שאני ה) ודקארי לה מאי קארי לה סיפא איצטריכא ליה מד' אמות ולמעלה אין מחייבין אותו ת"ש ו) כופין אותו לבנות בית שער ודלת לחצר ש"מ היזק ראיה שמיה היזק הזיקא דרבים שאני ודיחיד לא ת"ש ז) אין חולקין את החצר עד שיהא בה ד' אמות לזה וד' אמות לזה הא יש בה כדי לזה וכדי לזה חולקין מאי לאו בכותל לא במסיפס בעלמא תא שמע ח) החלונות בין מלמעלה ובין מלמטה ובין מכנגדן ד' אמות ותני עלה ט) מלמעלן כדי שלא יציץ ויראה מלמטן כדי שלא יעמוד ויראה מכנגדן כדי שלא יאפיל הזיקא דבית שאני תא שמע י) דאמר רב נחמן אמר שמואל גג א) הסמוך לחצר חבירו עושין לו מעקה גבוה ד' אמות שאני התם דאמר ליה בעל החצר לבעל הגג לדידי קביעה לי (ג) תשמישי לדידך לא קביעה לך תשמישתך ולא ידענא בהי עידנא סליקא ואתית

רש"י

קידש. התבואה אם הוסיף מאתים לישנא דקרא נקט פן תוקדש (דברים כב): **וטעמא דרצו.** לבנות כותל (ד) דמדעת שניהן הוא דחייביה חכמים שידעו בין שניהן ולקמן פריך כשרצו מאי הוי ליהדרי בהו אבל לא רצו שניהן שהיה אחד אומר דייה לחלקה במסיפס של יתדות עלים תקועים בארץ נמוכים לא כייפינן ליה ואין זה יכול לומר לו איני חפץ שתראה עסקי: **פלוגתא.** חלוקת חצר שהושוו דעתם לחולקה וכגון שלא היה בה ח' אמות כדי לזה וכדי לזה שאין האחד יכול לכוף את חבירו לחולקה והכי תני שרצו שכיון שרצו לחולקה בונין כותל אבנים על כרחם ואם בא האחד לומר אי איפשי ביגיעה זו אלא מסיפס בעלמא אין שומעין לו משום היזק הראיה: **הוה אמינא במסיפס בעלמא.** מיירי מתני' דאיהו נמי מחילה איקרו ורצו דקתני אחלוקה קאי וכשאין בה דין חלוקה קמ"ל כותל ורצו דקתני משום כותל דאי לא רצו פלגי לה במסיפס: **דרצייה חד מינייהו לחבריה.** ביקש ממנו לחולקה במחילה: **מהו דתימא א"ל כשנתרציתי לך.** במחילה מחילה דקה נתרציתי ולמעוטי באוירא כגון של נסרים שהיא דקה והיזק ראיה אין בה או תמשוך עובי הכותל בחלקך חוץ מדבר מועט אבל לבנות כותל אבנים עב למעוטי נמי תשמישתי לא נתרציתי: **אסור לאדם שיעמוד כו'.** שלא יזיקנו בעין רעה: **והא וכן קתני.** דמשמע תרוייהו חד טעמא הוא גינה וחצר: **מחייבין אותו.** והכא לא קתני רצו אלא על כרחו: **נפל שאני.** שכבר נתרצו הראשונים בכותל: **ודקארי לה מאי קארי לה.** וכי לא ידע דנפל שאני: **סיפא איצטריך ליה.** כלומר הוא הדין נמי מעיקרא והאי דקתני נפל משום סיפא לאשמועינן דיותר מד' אמות אין מחייבין ואע"פ שהראשון היה גבוה יותר לא מחייבין ליה: **כופין אותו.** כל אחד מבני החצר לתת חלקו בבנין: **בית השער.** שבונים כותל נגד השער עגול סביב ועושין באותו היקף פתח קטן מן הצד משום היזק ראיות בני רה"ר שלא יראו תוך החצר: **הזיקא דרבים.** שכל בני רה"ר מסתכלין שם: **אין חולקין.** אין האחד כופה את חבירו לחלוק: **החלונות.** אחד מבני השותפין הבונה כותל בחצר כנגד חלונותיו של חבירו בין מלמעלה וכו' אם הכותל גבוה יותר מן החלונות צריך להגביה למעלה מהן ד"א כדמפרש ואזיל כדי שלא יסמוך על כותלו וישחה ויראה בחלונותיו של חבירו: **בין מלמטה.** אם הכותל נמוך מן החלונות צריך להשפילו מהן ד"א כדי שלא יעמוד על עובי כותלו ויראה: **ומכנגדן.** צריך להרחיק את הכותל מן החלונות ד' אמות כדי שלא יאפיל: **הזיקא דבית שאני.** שאדם עושה בביתו דברי הצנע: **מעקה גבוה ארבע אמות.** כדי שלא יראה בחצר חבירו כשהוא משתמש בגגו: **ולא ידענא בהי עידנא דקא אתית.** להשתמש בגגך: דאיצטנע

תוספות

נתיאש הימנה ולא גדרה. דוקא נתיאש אבל לא נתיאש ועוסק כל שעה לגדור אע"פ שהוסיף מאתים מותר כדתנן במסכת כלאים (פ"ה מ"ו) הרואה ירק בכרם ואמר כשאגיע לשם אלקטנו הוסיף מאתים מותר לכשאחזור אלקטנו הוסיף מאתים אסור אלמא כשהוא מחזר אחר לקיטתו אפילו הוסיף מאתים מותר והטעם יש לפרש משום דכתיב (דברים כב) לא תזרע כרמך כלאים דומיא דזריעה דניחא ליה:

וחייב באחריותו. אע"ג דהיזק שאינו ניכר לא שמיה היזק (גיטין נג.) נראה לר"י דהאי חשיב היזק ניכר שהרי ניכר הוא שהוא כלאים כשרואה הגפנים בשדה ומטמא אע"פ שרואין הסרך על הטהרות לא חשיב היזק ניכר דמי יודע אם הוכשרו אבל אין לומר דה"נ הוי היזק שאינו ניכר וקנסוהו כמו במטמא (שם) שלא יהא כל אחד הולך ומטמא טהרותיו של חבירו דהכא ליכא למיחש להכי שבעל הכרם נמי מפסיד ועוד אי קנס הוא במזיד דוקא היה לו להתחייב: **ואימא** מאי מחיצה פלוגתא. מפרש ר"י משום דעל לשון גודא יש כמה קושיות כדפריך בסמוך לפיכך דוחק לפרש מחילה פלוגתא אע"ג דבכל מקום הוי מחילה גודא: **וכיון** דרצו בונין את הכותל בעל כרחו. לקמן מוקי לה כשאין בה דין חלוקה ותימה לר"י דאמאי נקט תנא דמתני' באין בה דין חלוקה וקתני רצו לא ליתני רצו ולאיירי בשיש בה דין חלוקה ותי' דקמ"ל דס"ד בשאין בה דין חלוקה דמצי למימר כי (ה) איתרצאי לך לחלוק ע"מ שלא לעשות גודא אבל על מנת לעשות גודא לא איתרצי לך. ויש ספרים דמקשין ומתרץ כן להדיא בשילהי שמעתין: **הוה** אמינא במסיפס בעלמא. פי' ורצו דקתני אמסיפס ואע"ג דבלאו רצו נמי עושין מסיפס בעל כרחם כדמוכח בסמוך דקאמר מאי לאו בכותל לא במסיפס היינו מסיפס גרוע אבל כי רצו עושין מסיפס מגויל וגזית כמנהג המדינה ומקרי מסיפס לפי שהוא מלא חלונות כדפי' בערוך ואינו מגין מהיזק ראיה א"נ לפי שאינו גבוה י' כדמוכח לקמן גבי גג הסמוך י) לחצר דאמר ר"נ עושה לו מעקה גבוה י' ופריך למאי אי להיזק ראיה ד"א בעינן ואי לנתפס כגנב במסיפס סגי ובקונטרס פי' דרצו דקתני אחלוקה קאי ותימה דהא אסיק דמחילה היינו גודא דאי פלוגתא לחצות מיבעי ליה ועוד היכי מצי למימר דה"א במסיפס בעלמא הא שמעינן ליה מסיפא דקתני אבל בזמן ששניהם רוצים אפילו פחות מכאן יחלוקו והיינו לכל הפחות במסיפס ועוד היכא הוה ס"ל במסיפס בעלמא הא בהדיא קתני במתני' גזית וגויל: **בונין** את הכותל באמצע פשיטא. למ"ד גודא פריך כמו כל הנך פירכי דלקמן דכשהקנו לעשות גודא כך הקנה זה כמו זה ופשיטא דבאמצע אבל למ"ד פלוגתא איצטריך למימר סד"א דמשום היזק ראיה יש לו לסייע בבנין הכותל אבל אין לו לבנות בחלקו בשביל כך: **תא** שמע וכן בגינה. לקמן מסקינן דה"ק וכן בגינה סתם כמקום שנהגו לגדור דמי הלכך דייק שפיר דהיזק ראיה שמיה היזק: **גינה** שאני כדרבי אבא וכו'. וא"ת ומהאי טעמא יתחייב נמי לגדור בבקעה ויש לומר דשאני גינה שמגדלין בה ירק לאכילה וכל שעה היא עומדת בקמותיה אבל בקעה אינה עומדת בקמותיה אלא חדש אחד בשנה ולא מחייב לגדור אבל אסור לעמוד בשעה שעומדת בקמותיה וא"ת ולמ"ד פלוגתא כיון דאשמועינן דאפילו בחצר שמיה היזק כל שכן בגינה ואמאי איצטריך תו למיתני וכן בגינה וי"ל דאיצטריך וכן בגינה למיתני משום גויל וגזית: **נפל** שאני. שהורגלו לעשות דבר הצנע בחצר ולא למדו ליזהר זה מזה: **ודקארי** לה מאי קארי לה. כלומר פשיטא דנפל שאני ואדרבה היה לו להוכיח מדקתני ונפל מכלל דבעלמא לא שמיה היזק: **הזיקא** דרבים שאני. ואע"ג דלקמן משמע דאיירי בחצר שאינה סמוכה לרה"ר מ"מ איכא היזקא דרבים דזימנין דדחקי רבים ועיילי להתם כדאמרי' לקמן ורשב"ג אע"ג דלית ליה האי טעמא דזימנין דדחקי רבים מ"מ מרחוק יכולין לראות לפנים ולכך לא פליג אלא אבית שער אבל בדלת מודה דכופין אותו לבנות: **מאי** לאו בכותל. תימה ויהא בכותל דילמא הכי פי' אין חולקין את החצר אפי' האחד רוצה לבנות את הכותל בתוך שלו עד שיהא בה ד' אמות לכל אחד הא אם יש בה ד' אמות לכל אחד חולקין אם רצה לכנוס ולבנות בתוך שלו וי"ל דחולקין משמע באמצע דאי אשמועינן כדפי' הוה ליה למיתני אין עושין כותל בחצר עד שיהא כו': **שאני** התם דאמר ליה בעל החצר לבעל הגג כו'. תימה אמאי לא מייתי מדתניא לקמן (דף ו:) שתי חצירות זו למעלה מזו לא יאמר העליון הריני בונה מכנגדי ועולה אלא מסייע מלמטה ובונה אלמא שמיה היזק:

עין משפט נר מצוה

ח א מיי' פ"ג מהל' שכנים הלכה ו ועיין בהשגות סמג עשין פב טוש"ע ח"מ סי' קנט סעיף ג וסי' קס סעיף א:

רבינו גרשום

[תחילת הפירוש ששייך לכאן נדפס בעמוד הקודם] **כותל חצר** שבין שני חצירות **שנפל** אם א' מהן מעכב מלבנותו **מחייבין אותו לבנותו** בעל כרחו **עד** שיהא גבוה **ד"א** דלא מצי איניש לאסתכולי דרך הליכתו עד שיהא גבוה ד' אמות אלמא משום היזק ראיה הוא. ומשני דהיכא **דנפל שאני** הואיל דהוי מעיקרא הכותל בדין הוא דמחייבין אותו עד ד' אמות דפחות מכן לא מצי למיבניה דהכי שמה מחיצה אבל גבי מתני' שלא היה מעולם מחיצה אין מחייבין המעכב: **ודקארי לה אמאי קארי לה** כלו' המקשה שהיה מקשה קושי' זו אמאי מקשה לה. וכי לא היה יודע דהיכא דנפל שאני ומה ראה להקשותה. ומשני לעולם משום קושיא מייתינן לה משום דחזא **בסיפא איצטריך ליה** למיתניי' בלשון קושיא דקתני סיפא **מד' אמות ולמעלה אין מחייבין אותו** לבנות גבוה כדמעיקרא אלמא ש"מ משום היזק ראייה הוא ומש"ה אין מחייבין אותו אלא כשיעור שאינו יכול לראות. והמתרץ מתרץ [לעולם] כדמעיקרא נפל שאני. והאי דאמר עד ד' אמות דבהכי הוא דין מחיצה ולא משום היזק ראייה: ת"ש בתים הפתוחים לחצר וחצר פתוח לרה"ר ונפל בית שער החצר. וכל בני החצר נתרצו לבנות. [**כופין** לא' מבני החצר המעכב **לבנות] בית שער ודלת** עמהן משום היזק ראייה דבני רה"ר. אלמא היזק ראייה שמיה היזק: **היזק דרבים שאני.** אבל היכא דאיכא היזק ראייה **דיחיד** כגון האי חצר השותפין **לאו** שמיה היזק: **ת"ש** קתני מתני' **אין חולקין את החצר.** האחין שבאו לחלוק בנכסי אביהן אין חולקין את החצר **עד שיהא בה ד' אמות לזה וד' אמות לזה** דהכי חזי לדירה. וכשהן חולקין **מאי לאו כותל** מעליא בעו למיעבד בינתייהו משום היזק ראייה: **לא במסיפס בעלמא.** חולקין דאע"ג דזה יכול לראות בזה: **ת"ש חלונות** שיש להם חזקה כדאמר לקמן **מלמעלן ומלמטן ומכנגדן ד' אמות** כלומר אם רוצה זה בעל החצר שהחלון פתוח בחצירו לבנות כותל בצד חלון. **מלמעלה** שאם רצה להגביה כותל (מן) החצר יותר מן החלון צריך להגביהו ד' אמות על החלון. אי נמי **למטה** אם רוצה א) נמוך (מן) הכותל מן (הצד) שצריך להנמיכו ד' אמות ואם בא לבנות כותלו ב) עד הכותל ולזה יש לו חזקת חלון בחצירו של זה צריך להרחיק ד' אמות ויבנה כדי שלא יאפיל חלונותי': **ותני עלה מלמעלה** להם צריך שיהא גבוה ד' אמות על החלון **כדי שלא** יעמוד ע"ג הכותל ויגחין **ויציץ ויראה** בחלון **ומלמטן** צריך לנמוך ד' אמות **שלא יעמוד** זקוף על גבי הכותל **ויראה** בבית אלמא היזק ראיה שמיה היזק: **הזיקא דבית שני** טפי מחצר. דאינש ג) צניע דשמיש בבית טפי מבחצר: **גג הסמוך לחצר חבירו.** דחצר גבוה קרקעיתה ושוותה לגג חבירו צריך בעל הגג **לעשות** (מעשה) **מעקה גבוה ד' אמות** שלא יסתכל בתוך חצר חבירו אלמא היזק ראיה שמיה היזק: לא לעולם אימא בחצר של שנים לא אמרי' היזק ראיה שמיה היזק **ושאני התם** לגבי חצר וגג **דאמר בעל החצר לבעל הגג לדידי קביעא תשמישתאי** בכל שעה בחצרי **לדידך לא קביעא תשמישתך** בכל שעה לגג ולהכי בעי למיעבד מעקה:

חשק שלמה על רבינו גרשום א) [נראה דצ"ל אם רוצה להנמיך הכותל מן החלון צריך להנמיכו ד' אמות וכו']: ב) [נראה דצ"ל ואם בא לבנות כותל החצר ולזה יש לו חזקת וכו']: ג) [אולי צ"ל דאיניש צניע בתשמישו דבית טפי מבחצר]:

מסורת הש"ס

א) [לקמן נט:], ב) [שם], ג) ב"מ קז. ע"ש, ד) [לקמן ה., ה) לקמן ז:, ו) לקמן יא., ז) לקמן דף כב., ח) [שם:], ט) לקמן ו:, י) צ"ל גגג:

הגהות הב"ח

(א) גמ' וטעמא דרצו: (ב) שם ואימא מאי מחיצה פלוגתא: (ג) שם קביעא לי תשמישתי: (ד) רש"י ד"ה וטעמא וכו' מדעת שניהן הוא דחייבום חכמים: (ה) תוס' ד"ה וכיון וכו' כי איתרצאי לך וכו' לא איתרצאי לך ויש ספרים דמקשה ומתרץ:

גליון הש"ס

גמ' ודקארי לה. עי' בחדושי הרמב"ן לקמן דף יז ע"ב ד"ה גירסת רש"י: שם ודקארי לה. כתובות עז ע"א וש"נ:

תורה אור השלם

א) וַתְּהִי מֶחֱצַת הָעֵדָה מִן הַצֹּאן שְׁלֹשׁ מֵאוֹת אֶלֶף וּשְׁלֹשִׁים אֶלֶף שִׁבְעַת אֲלָפִים וַחֲמֵשׁ מֵאוֹת: [במדבר לא, מג]

ליקוטי רש"י

[תחילת ליקוטי רש"י ששייך לכאן נדפס בעמוד הקודם] **כופין אותו לבנות בית שער.** את בן החצר שאינו רוצה לסייע את בני החצר לבנות להן בית שער להיות שומר הפתח יושב שם בצל ומרחיק את בני רשות הרבים מלהציץ בחצר [לקמן ז:]. **בית שער.** בית קטן לפני בית שער [יומא יא.]. בית כניסת שער החצר להסתופף בו שומר הפתח [סוטה מג.]. בית קטן שעושין בצד שערי חצירות ויושב שם שומר הפתח [מנחות לג.]. **ודלת.** לשער החצר לנעלו [לקמן ז:]. **החלונות.** מי שהיו לו חלונות פתוחים לחצר חבירו והוחזק בדבר זה שלא מיחו בו ובא זה לבנות שם כותל צריך לשער ד' אמות. **בין מלמעלה.** אם בא להגביה כותלו ד' אמות מן החלונות. **בין מלמטה.** אם בא לבנותו נמוך צריך להשפילו מן החלונות ד' אמות וטעמא מפרש בגמ'. **בין מכנגדן.** צריך להרחיקו מהן ד' אמות [לקמן כב.]. **מלמעלן.** צריך להגביה שיעור שלא יציץ בהשענו על כותלו ויטפיל ראשו ויראה דרך חלונות ויראה בבית חבירו. **שלא יעמוד.** על ראש עובי כותלו ויראה. **מכנגדן.** צריך להרחיק כדי שלא יאפיל. **שלא יאפיל.** בשיש חלונות [שם:]. **מעקה גבוה ד' אמות.** משום היזק ראיה [לקמן ו:]. [מכאן שייך לדף ג.] **אפילו פחות מכאן חולקין.** משום דבעי למיתני וכתבי הקדש אע"פ ששניהם רוצים לא יחלוקו תני רישא. **כתבי הקדש.** כ"ד ספרים והיו רגילים לכותבן בגליון כס"ת שלנו לפיכך גנאי הדבר לחתכן [לקמן יא.]. **כתבי הקדש.** כגון תורה נביאים וכתובים [שבת קטו.]. **כל אלה אבנים יקרות.** כל האבנים האלה עשויות כבדות. **כמדות גזית.** כמדת אבני גזית מדה אחת היתה לאבני גזית במדינה [מלכים א, ז, ט]. **למורשא דקרנתא.** למורשי דידהו מטפי בה טפח [ב"מ קיז:]. **לביני אורבי.** בין שורות הבנין בכותל [ב"מ מב.]. **והא אמה טרקסין וכו'.** כך נקראת כותל מחיצה שהפסיק במקדש ראשון אבל במקדש שני שהיה גבוה (מאה) [גי' תוי"ט מ'] אמה לא עשאוהו לפי שלא היו עוביה אלא אמה ואינה יכולה לעמוד בגובה (מאה) [גי' תוי"ט מ'] אמה ולהוסיף על עוביה אי אפשר דכתיב הכל בכתב מיד ה' עלי השכיל (דברי הימים א כח) [יומא נא:]. שעשה שלמה בבנין ראשון אף ואנשי הגולה עשו את ההיכל גבוה מאד ולא יכול בנין בעובי אמה להתקיים בגובה כזה והרחיבו לא יכלו לפי שמקריבים את ההיכל או את קדשי הקדשים ועשו שתי פרכות וביניהם אמה כדאמרינן במסכת יומא (נא:) [כתובות קו.]. **טרקסין.** לשון פנים וחוץ הוא כך ראיתי בתלמוד ירושלמי וראיה לדבר חסידים הראשונים היו מכניסין פירותיהן דרך טרקסמון כדי לחייבן במעשר (ברכות לה:) למדנו שטרק לשון כניסת פנים הוא [יומא נב.].

The Mishnah stated:

בּוֹנִין אֶת הַכּוֹתֶל בְּאֶמְצַע וכו׳ — **THEY MUST BUILD THE WALL IN THE CENTER** of the courtyard **etc.**[17]

The Gemara asks:

פְּשִׁיטָא — This is **obvious!** If they are building jointly, surely the wall must be in the middle!

The Gemara replies:

לֹא צְרִיכָא — **No, it is necessary** to teach this law in a case דְּקְדִים חַד וְרַצְיֵיהּ לְחַבְרֵיהּ — **where one** of them **went ahead and appealed to his friend** to commit himself to divide the courtyard with a partition. מַהוּ דְּתֵימָא מָצֵי אָמַר לֵיהּ — In such a case, **you might have said** that the accommodating partner **can say to [the other]:** כִּי אִיתְרַצַּאי לָךְ בְּאֲוִירָא — **When I acceded to you,** it was only **with respect to the view;**[18] בְּתַשְׁמִישְׁתָּא לֹא אִיתְרַצַּאי לָךְ — however, **with respect to** my **use** of the courtyard **I never acceded to you.**[19] קָא מַשְׁמַע לָן — **[The Mishnah] thus informs us** that he may not so claim, but, having agreed to build a wall, he must provide half the land necessary for a stone wall.

The Gemara now attempts to prove that visual trespass is considered injurious:

וְהֶיזֵּק רְאִיָּה לָאו שְׁמֵיהּ הֶיזֵּק — **Is** there an opinion that **visual trespass is not considered injurious?**

The Gemara prefaces its presentation of six proofs with a mnemonic aid:

(סִימָן: גִּינָּה כּוֹתֶל כּוֹפִין וְחוֹלְקִין חַלּוֹנוֹת דְּרַב נַחְמָן) — **(A sign: garden, wall, compel, and divide, windows, of Rav Nachman.)**[20]

The Gemara's first proof comes from our Mishnah:

תָּא שְׁמַע — **Come, learn** a proof. Our Mishnah stated: וְכֵן בְּגִינָּה — **AND, SIMILARLY, IN A** vegetable **GARDEN** a wall must be built![21] By stating that one gardener can force his neighbor to assist in erecting a wall without agreeing to do so, we may infer that visual trespass is considered damaging.

The Gemara responds:

גִּינָּה שָׁאנֵי כִּדְרַבִּי אַבָּא — The case of **a** vegetable **garden differs** from that of a courtyard, **in line with** the statement **of R' Abba,** דְּאָמַר רַבִּי אַבָּא אָמַר רַב הוּנָא אָמַר רַב — **for R' Abba said in the name of Rav Huna, who said in the name of Rav:** אָסוּר לְאָדָם לַעֲמוֹד בִּשְׂדֵה חֲבֵירוֹ — **It is forbidden for a person to stand in his friend's field** בְּשָׁעָה שֶׁהִיא עוֹמֶדֶת בְּקָמוֹתֶיהָ — **during the time it displays a standing crop,** lest he become jealous and cast an evil eye (*ayin hara*) on the field. Thus, the Sages required construction of a wall in a garden,[22] where the gaze of a neighbor can cause actual monetary damage through *ayin hara.* However, since in a courtyard the absence of a wall can cause only inconvenience and loss of privacy, the Gemara cannot prove from the case of the garden that visual trespass is likewise considered injurious in a courtyard.

The Gemara objects to this explanation:

וְהָא וְכֵן קָתָנֵי — **But the Mishnah stated AND SIMILARLY,** implying that *one* reason compels construction of a wall in both a garden and a courtyard — namely, to prevent visual trespass. — **?** —

The Gemara answers:

אַגְּוִיל וְגָזִית — The phrase "and similarly" refers only **to** the building materials, **rough-edged stones or** smooth, **planed stones,** that are used for constructing walls in both courtyards and gardens, according to local custom. The phrase does *not* suggest a commonality of function in the two cases.

The Gemara offers a second proof that visual trespass is considered damaging:

תָּא שְׁמַע — **Come, learn** a proof from the following Mishnah:[23] כּוֹתֶל חָצֵר שֶׁנָּפַל — Concerning **A COURTYARD WALL**[24] **THAT COLLAPSED,** מְחַיְּיבִין אוֹתוֹ לִבְנוֹת עַד אַרְבַּע אַמּוֹת — the authorities **OBLIGATE [EACH NEIGHBOR] TO REBUILD [THE WALL] TO** a height of **FOUR AMOS.**[25] Since the obligation to rebuild the wall is imposed, and not voluntarily assumed by the two parties, we may infer that visual trespass is an unlawful violation of a property right.

The Gemara refutes the proof:

נָפַל שָׁאנֵי — The case of a pre-existing wall that **collapsed is different,** since the original courtyard owners had previously agreed to build the wall.[26]

Since this distinction is so obvious, the Gemara asks:

וּדְקָארֵי לָהּ מַאי קָארֵי לָהּ — **And the one who involved this** Mishnah in the discussion [i.e. who advanced this proof], **why did**

NOTES

17. The Gemara does not cite this statement of the Mishnah to discuss it per se (see *Rashash*). Rather, the Gemara uses it to pose a difficulty on those who would define *mechitzah* as a "wall." That is, if the partners specifically agreed to make a wall, then obviously they must contribute equally toward every aspect of the project. Thus, the Mishnah need not tell us that each must provide land for the wall. If, however, *mechitzah* is defined as a "division," then although one partner may be compelled to build a wall to prevent visual trespass, still it is not obvious that he must also surrender land for that purpose, since he may claim that he is not obligated to lose a part of his courtyard in order to provide privacy to his neighbor courtyard. According to this opinion, then, the Mishnah is justified in expressly teaching that he incurs this obligation as well (*Tosafos* ד״ה בונין, see *Chidushei R' Nachum*).

18. I.e. I agreed to obstruct my view of your half of the courtyard, thereby affording you privacy there, with the erection of a thin partition composed of boards, which are suitable for that purpose. Or, if you insist on a thick wall, all but a narrow slice thereof must be withdrawn into your property (*Rashi*).

19. I.e. I never agreed to build a thick stone wall between our two properties and thereby diminish the area available for my use (*Rashi*).

20. This mnemonic device is composed of a word taken from the beginning of each of the six proffered proofs. Since the Gemara was transmitted orally, such methods of memory-enhancement were frequently employed (see *Rashi, Shabbos* 104a ד״ה סימנים).

21. Although the Mishnah seems to say that a wall must be built only if local custom so dictates, which would indicate that no absolute requirement exists and hence that visual trespass is not considered damaging, the Gemara's proof is based on the definitive interpretation of the Mishnah (rendered below, 4a) — that gardens in general are regarded as places where people customarily do erect walls. Hence, the Mishnah implies that visual trespass violates a property right (*Tosafos, Ran*).

22. The Sages do not, however, require construction of a wall between grain fields to deter *ayin hara*, as they do in the case of adjoining gardens, because a grain field is subject to *ayin hara* damage for only a brief period each year — when the grain is fully grown and before it is harvested. In a garden, however, various species of vegetables sprout throughout the year, continually attracting attention and possibly an *ayin hara* (*Tosafos*). [See *Rashba* and *Ran* who explain that we can not obligate him to construct a wall in the case of a grain field, since he can claim that for that short period of time, he will be able to control himself and not gaze at the other field, so that there will not be any *ayin hara* damage. But in a garden this claim is not accepted, for one can not control himself indefinitely.)

23. Below, 5a.

24. I.e. the wall had divided two contiguous courtyards.

25. Approximately seven to seven and one-half feet. This measurement is sufficient to protect against visual trespass, since it exceeds the height of most individuals even if they stretch themselves upward to look (*Tosafos, Shabbos* 92a ד״ה אישתכח; see also *Tosafos* to 100b, ד״ה והכוכין).

26. *Rashi.* [Hence, each succeeding owner was bound by the terms of their agreement, which essentially redefined each property as a private yard.] Alternatively, *Tosafos* (ד״ה נפל) explain that the owners of the yards had become accustomed to the privacy afforded by the wall, commonly performing private activities in their courtyards. Since it would be difficult for them to adjust their behavior to the changed circumstances, in a case such as this visual trespass would be deemed injurious.

עין משפט נר מצוה

ח א מיי' פ"ג מהל' שכנים הלכה ו ועיין בהשגות סמג עשין פב טוש"ע ח"מ סי' קנז סעיף ג וסי' קס סעיף א:

מסורת הש"ס

א) [לקמן נט:], ב) [עס], ג) ב"מ קז. ע"ש, ד) לקמן ה., ה) לקמן ז., ו) לקמן יא., ז) לקמן דף כב., ח) [עס], ט) לקמן ו:, י) צ"ל לגג:

נתיאש הימנה ולא גדרה ה"ז קידש וחייב באחריות' (א) טעמא דרצו הא לא רצו אין מחייבין אותו אלמא [א] היזק ראיה לאו שמיה היזק ואימא (ב) מחיצה פלוגתא כדכתיב [א] ותהי מחצת העדה וכיון דרצו בונין את הכותל בעל כרחו אלמא [ב] היזק ראיה שמיה היזק אי הכי האי שרצו לעשות מחיצה שרצו לחצות מבעי ליה אלא מאי גודא בונין את הכותל בונין אותו מבעי ליה אי תנא אותו הוה אמינא במסיפס בעלמא קמ"ל כותל: בונין את הכותל באמצע וכו': פשיטא לא צריכא דקדים חד ורצייה לחבריה מהו דתימא מצי א"ל כי איתרצאי לך באוירא בתשמישתא לא איתרצאי לך קמ"ל והיזק ראיה לאו שמיה היזק (סימן גינה כותל כופין וחולקין חלונות דרב נחמן) ת"ש וכן בגינה גינה שאני כדר' אבא [ג] דאמר ר' אבא אמר רב הונא אמר רב אסור לאדם לעמוד בשדה חבירו בשעה שהיא עומדת בקמותיה והא וכן קתני אגויל וגזית ת"ש [ד] כותל חצר שנפל מחייבין אותו לבנות עד ד' אמות נפל שאני [ה] ודקארי לה מאי קארי לה סיפא איצטריכא ליה מד' אמות ולמעלה אין מחייבין אותו ת"ש [ו] כופין אותו לבנות בית שער ודלת לחצר ש"מ היזק ראיה שמיה היזק הזיקא דרבים שאני ודיחיד לא ת"ש [ז] אין חולקין את החצר עד שיהא בה כדי ד' אמות לזה וד' אמות לזה הא יש בה כדי לזה וכדי לזה חולקין מאי לאו בכותל לא במסיפס בעלמא תא שמע [ח] החלונות בין מלמעלה בין מלמטה ובין מכנגדן ד' אמות ותני עלה [ט] מלמעלן כדי שלא יציץ ויראה מלמטן כדי שלא יעמוד ויראה מכנגדן כדי שלא יאפיל הזיקא דבית שאני תא שמע [י] דאמר רב נחמן אמר שמואל גג [כ] הסמוך לחצר חבירו עושין לו מעקה גבוה ד' אמות שאני התם דאמר ליה בעל החצר לבעל הגג לדידי קביעה לי (ג) תשמישי לדידך לא קביעה לך תשמישתך ולא ידענא בהי עידנא סליקא ואתית

רש"י

קידש. התבואה אם הוסיף מאתים לישנא דקרא נקט פן תוקדש (דברים כב): וטעמא דרצו. לבנות כותל (ד) דמדעת שניהן הוא דחייביה חכמים שיבנו בין שניהן ולקמן פריך כשרצו מאי הוי ליהדרי בהו אבל לא רצו שניהן שהיה אחד אומר דייה לחלקה במסיפס של יתדות עצים תקועים בארץ נמוכים לא כייפינן ליה ואין זה יכול לומר לו איני חפץ שתראה עסקי: פלוגתא. חלוקת חצר שהושוו דעתם לחלוקה וכגון שלא היה בה ח' אמות כדי לזה וכדי לזה שאין האחד יכול לכוף את חבירו לחלוקה ולהכי תני שרצו שכיון שרצו לחלוקה בונין כותל אבנים על כרחם ואם בא האחד לומר אי איפשי ביגיאה זו אלא מסיפס בעלמא אין שומעין לו משום היזק הראיה: הוה אמינא במסיפס בעלמא. מיירי מתני' דאיהו נמי מחיצה איקרו ורצו דקתני אחלוקה קאי וכשאין בה דין חלוקה קמ"ל כותל ורצו דקתני משום כותל דאי לא רצו פלגי לה במסיפס: דרצייה חד מינייהו לחבריה. ביקש ממנו לחלוקה במחילה: מהו דתימא א"ל כשנתרציתי לך. במחילה מחילה דקה נתרציתי ולמעוטי באוירא כגון של נסרים שהיא דקה והיזק ראיה אין בה או תמשוך עובי הכותל בחלקך חוץ מדבר מועט אבל לבנות כותל אבנים עב למעוטי נמי תשמישתי לא נתרציתי: אסור לאדם שיעמוד כו'. שלא יזיקנו בעין רעה: והא וכן קתני. דמשמע תרוייהו חד טעמא הוא גינה וחצר: מחייבין אותו. והכא לא קתני רצו אלא על כרחו: נפל שאני. שכבר נתרצו הראשונים בכותל: ודקארי לה מאי קארי לה. וכי לא ידע דנפל שאני: סיפא איצטריך ליה. כלומר הוא הדין נמי מעיקרא והאי דקתני נפל משום סיפא לאשמועינן דיותר מד' אמות אין מחייבין ואע"פ שהראשון היה גבוה יותר לא מחייבין ליה: כופין אותו. כל אחד מבני החצר לתת חלקו בבנין: בית השער. שבונים כותל נגד השער עגול סביב ועושין באותו היקף פתח קטן מן הצד משום היזק ראיית בני רה"ר שלא יראו תוך החצר: הזיקא דרבים. שכל בני רה"ר מסתכלין שם: אין חולקין. אין האחד כופה את חבירו לחלוק: החלונות. אחד מבני החצר כנגד חלונותיו של חבירו בין מלמעלה וכו' אם הכותל גבוה יותר מן החלונות צריך להגביה למעלה מהן ד"א כדמפרש ואזיל כדי שלא יסמוך על כותלו וישחה ויראה בחלונותיו של חבירו: בין מלמטה. אם הכותל נמוך מן החלונות צריך להשפילו מהן ד"א כדי שלא יעמוד על עובי כותלו ויראה: ומכנגדן. צריך להרחיק את הכותל מן החלונות ד' אמות כדי שלא יאפיל: הזיקא דבית שאני. שאדם עושה בביתו דברי הצנע: מעקה גבוה ארבע אמות. כדי שלא יראה בחצר חבירו כשהוא משתמש בגגו: ולא ידענא בהי עידנא דקא אתית. להשתמש בגגך: דאיצטנע

תוספות

נתיאש הימנה ולא גדרה. דוקא נתיאש אבל לא נתיאש ועוסק כל שעה לגדור אע"פ שהוסיף מאתים מותר כדתנן במסכת כלאים (פ"ה מ"ו) הרואה ירק בכרם ואמר כשאגיע לשם אלקטנו הוסיף מאתים מותר לכשאחזור אלקטנו הוסיף מאתים אסור אלמא כשהוא מחזר אחר לקיטתו אפילו הוסיף מאתים מותר והטעם יש לפרש משום דכתיב (דברים כב) לא תזרע כרמך כלאים דומיא דזריעה דניחא ליה: וחייב באחריותו. אע"ג דהיזק שאינו ניכר לא שמיה היזק (גיטין נג.) נראה לר"י דהאי חשיב היזק ניכר שהרי ניכר הוא שהוא כלאים כשרואה הגפנים בשדה ומטמא אע"פ שרואין הסרך על הטהרות לא חשיב היזק ניכר דמי יודע אם הוכשרו אבל אין לומר דה"נ הוי היזק שאינו ניכר וקנסוהו כמו במטמא (שם) שלא יהא כל אחד הולך ומטמא טהרותיו של חבירו דהכא ליכא למיחש להכי שבעל הכרם נמי מפסיד ועוד אי קנס הוא במזיד דוקא היה לו להתחייב: ואימא מאי מחיצה פלוגתא. מפרש ר"י משום דעל לשון גודא יש כמה קושיות כדפריך בסמוך לפיכך דוחק לפרש מחיצה פלוגתא אע"ג דבכל מקום הוי מחיצה גודא: וכיון דרצו בונין את הכותל בעל כרחו. לקמן מוקי לה כשאין בה דין חלוקה ותימה לר"י דלמאי נקט תנא דמתני' באין בה דין חלוקה וקתני רצו לא ליתני רצו ולאיירי בשיש בה דין חלוקה ותי' דקמ"ל דס"ד בשאין בה דין חלוקה דמצי למימר כי (ה) איתרצאי לך לחלוק ע"מ שלא לעשות גודא אבל על מנת לעשות גודא לא איתרצי לך. ויש ספרים דמקשין ומתרץ כן להדיא בשילהי שמעתין: הוה אמינא במסיפס בעלמא. פי' ורצו דקתני אמסיפס ואע"ג דבלאו רצו נמי עושין מסיפס בעל כרחם כדמוכח בסמוך דקאמר מאי לאו בכותל לא במסיפס היינו מסיפס גרוע אבל כי רצו עושין מסיפס מגויל וגזית כמנהג המדינה ומקרי מסיפס לפי שהוא מלא חלונות כדפי' בערוך ואינו מגין מהיזק ראיה א"נ לפי שאינו גבוה י' כדמוכח לקמן גבי גג הסמוך [ג] לחצר דאמר ר"נ עושה לו מעקה גבוה י' ופריך למאי אי להיזק ראיה ד"א בעינן ואי לנתפס כגנב במסיפס סגי ובקונטרס פי' דרצו דקתני אחלוקה קאי ותימה דהא אסיק דמחיצה היינו גודא דאי פלוגתא לחלות מיבעי ליה ועוד היכי מצי למימר דה"א במסיפס בעלמא הא שמעינן ליה מסיפא דקתני אבל בזמן ששניהם רוצים אפילו פחות מכאן יחלוקו והיינו לכל הפחות במסיפס ועוד היכא המ"ל במסיפס בעלמא הא בהדיא קתני במתני' גזית וגויל: בונין את הכותל באמצע פשיטא. למ"ד גודא פריך כמו כל הנך פירכי דלקמן דכשהקנו לעשות גודא כך הקנה זה כמו זה ופשיטא דבאמצע אבל למ"ד פלוגתא איצטריך למימר סד"א דמשום היזק ראיה יש לו לסייע בבנין הכותל אבל אין לו לבנות בחלקו בשביל כך: תא שמע וכן בגינה. לקמן מסקינן דה"ק וכן בגינה סתם כמקום שנהגו לגדור דמי הלכך דייק שפיר דהיזק ראיה שמיה היזק: גינה שאני כדרבי אבא וכו'. וא"ת ומהאי טעמא יתחייב נמי לגדור בבקעה ויש לומר דשאני גינה שמגדלין בה ירק לאכילה וכל שעה היא עומדת בקמותיה אבל בקעה אינה עומדת בקמותיה אלא חדש אחד בשנה ולא מיחייב לגדור אבל אסור לעמוד בשעה שעומדת בקמותיה וא"ת ולמ"ד פלוגתא כיון דאשמועינן דאפילו בחצר שמיה היזק כל שכן בגינה ואמאי איצטריך תו למיתני וכן בגינה וי"ל דאיצטריך וכן בגינה למיתני משום גויל וגזית: נפל שאני. שהורגלו לעשות דבר הצנע בחצר ולא למדו ליזהר זה מזה: ודקארי לה מאי קארי לה. כלומר פשיטא דנפל שאני ואדרבה היה לו להוכיח מדקתני ונפל מכלל דבעלמא לא שמיה היזק: הזיקא דרבים שאני. ואע"ג דלקמן משמע דאיירי בחצר שאינה סמוכה לרה"ר מ"מ איכא היזקא דרבים דזימנין דדחקי רבים ועיילי להתם כדאמרי' לקמן ורשב"ג אע"ג דלית ליה האי טעמא דזימנין דדחקי רבים מ"מ מרחוק יכולין לראות לפנים ולכך לא פליג אלא אבית שער אבל בדלת מודה דכופין אותו לבנות: מאי לאו בכותל. תימה ויהא בכותל דילמא הכי פי' אין חולקין את החצר אפי' האחד רוצה לבנות את הכותל בתוך שלו עד שיהא בה ד' אמות לכל אחד הא אם יש בה ד' אמות לכל אחד חולקין אם רצה לכנוס ולבנות בתוך שלו וי"ל דחולקין משמע באמצע דאי אשמועינן כדפי' הוה ליה למיתני אין עושין כותל בחצר עד שיהא כו': שאני התם דאמר ליה בעל החצר לבעל הגג כו'. תימה אמאי לא מייתי מדתניא לקמן (דף ו:) שתי חצירות זו למעלה מזו לא יאמר העליון הריני בונה מכנגדי ועולה אלא מסייע מלמטה ובונה אלמא שמיה היזק:

רבינו גרשום

[תחילת הפירוש ששייך לכאן נדפס בעמוד הקודם] כותל חצר שבין שני חצירות שנפל אם א' מהן מעכב מלבנותו מחייבין אותו לבנותו בעל כרחו עד שיהא גבוה ד"א דלא מצי איניש לאסתכולי דרך הליכתו עד שיהא גבוה ד' אמות אלמא משום היזק ראיה הוא. ומשני דהיכא דנפל שאני הואיל דהוי מעיקרא הכותל בדין הוא דמחייבין אותו עד ד' אמות דפחות מכאן לא מצי למיבניה דהכי שמה מחיצה אבל גבי מתני' שלא היה מעולם מחיצה המעכב: ודקארי לה מאי קארי לה. כלו' המקשה שהיה מקשה קושי' זו מאי מקשה לה. וכי לא היה יודע דהיכא דנפל שאני ומה ראה להקשותה. ומשני לעולם משום קושיא מייתינן לה משום דחזא איצטריך ליה למיתני' בלשון קושיא דקתני סיפא מד' אמות ולמעלה אין מחייבין אותו לבנות גבוה כדמעיקרא אלמא ש"מ משום היזק ראייה הוא ומש"ה אין מחייבין אותו אלא כשיעור שאינו יכול לראות. והמתרץ מתרץ [לעולם] והאי דאמר עד ד' אמות דבהכי הוא דין מחיצה ולא משום היזק ראייה: ת"ש בתים הפתוחים לחצר וחצר פתוח לרה"ר ונפל בית שער החצר. וכל בני החצר נתרצו לבנות. [כופין] אותו לבנות בית שער ודלת עמהן משום היזק ראייה דבני רה"ר. אלמא היזק ראייה שמיה היזק: היזק דרבים שאני. אבל דיחיד כגון האי חצר השותפין לאו שמיה היזק: ת"ש קתני מתני' אין חולקין את החצר. האחין שבאו לחלוק בנכסי אביהן אין חולקין את החצר עד שיהא בה ד' אמות לזה וד' אמות לזה דהכי חזי לדירה. וכשהן חולקין מאי לאו כותל מעליא בעו לבנות ביניהו משום היזק ראייה: לא במסיפס בעלמא. דאע"ג דזה יכול לראות בזה: ת"ש חלונות שיש להם חזקה כדאמר לקמן מלמעלן ומלמטן ומכנגדן ד' אמות כלומר אם רצה זה בעל החצר שהחלון פתוח בחצירו לבנות כותל בצד חלון. שאם רצה להגביה כותל (מן) החצר יותר מן החלון צריך להגביהו ד' אמות על החלון. אי נמי למטה (מן) הכותל מן (הצד) שצריך להנמיכו ד' אמות ואם בא לבנות (ב) עד הכותל ולזה יש לו חזקת חלון בחצירו של זה צריך להרחיק ד' אמות ויבנה כדי שלא יאפיל חלונותי': ותני עלה מלמעלה להם על החלון כדי שלא יעמוד ע"ג הכותל ויציץ ויראה בחלון ומלמטן צריך לנמוך ד' אמות שלא יעמוד זקוף על גבי הכותל ויראה בבית אלמא היזק ראיה שמיה היזק: הזיקא דבית שאני טפי מחצר. דאיניש (ג) צניע דשמיש בבית טפי מבחצר: גג הסמוך לחצר חבירו. דחצר גבוה קרקעיתה ושוותה לגג חבירו צריך בעל הגג לעשות (מעשה) מעקה גבוה ד' אמות שלא יסתכל בתוך חצר חבירו אלמא היזק ראיה שמיה היזק: ומשני לעולם אימא בחצר של שנים לא אמרי' היזק ראיה שמיה היזק ושאני התם לגבי חצר וגג דאמר בעל החצר לבעל הגג לדידי קביעא תשמישתאי בכל שעה בחצרי לדידך לא קביעא תשמישתך בכל שעה לגג ולהכי בעי למיעבד מעקה:

חשק שלמה על רבינו גרשום א) [נראה דצ"ל אם הוא להנמיך הכותל צריך להנמיכו ד' אמות וכו'] ב) [נראה דצ"ל ואם בא לבנות כותל מנגד כותל החלון צריך להרחיק ד' אמות וכו'] ג) [אולי צ"ל דאיניש צנע מתשמש דבית טפי מבחצר].

הגהות הב"ח

(א) גמ' וטעמא דרצו: (ב) שם ואימא מאי מחיצה פלוגתא: (ג) שם קביעא לי תשמישאי: (ד) רש"י ד"ה וטעמא וכו' מדעת שניהן הוא דחייבום חכמים: (ה) תוס' ד"ה וכיון וכו' כי איתרצאי לך וכו' לא איתרצאי לך וכו' וה"פ ספרים דמקשה ומתרץ:

גליון הש"ס

גמ' ודקארי לה. ע' בחדושי הרמב"ן לקמן דף יט ע"ב ד"ה גירסת רש"י: שם ודקארי לה. כתובות טז ע"א וש"נ:

תורה אור השלם

א) וַתְּהִי מֶחֱצַת הָעֵדָה מִן הַצֹּאן שְׁלֹשׁ מֵאוֹת אֶלֶף וּשְׁלֹשִׁים אֶלֶף שִׁבְעַת אֲלָפִים וַחֲמֵשׁ מֵאוֹת: [במדבר לא, מג]

ליקוטי רש"י

[תחילת ליקוטי רש"י ששייך לכאן נדפס בעמוד הקודם] כופין אותו לבנות בית שער. את בן החצר שאינו רוצה לסייע את בני החצר לבנות להן בית שער להיות שומר הפתח יושב שם בצל ומרחיק את בני רשות הרבים מלהלך בחצר [לקמן ז:]. בית שער. בית קטן לפני שער [יומא יא.]. בית כניסת שער החצר להסתופף שם שומר [סוטה מג.]. בית קטן עושים בצד שערי חצירות ויושב שם שומר הפתח [מנחות לג:]. ודלת. לשער החצר לנעלו [לקמן ז:]. החלונות. מי שהיו לו חלונות פתוחים לחצר חבירו והוחזק בכך זה שלש שנים ובא בעל החצר לבנות שם כותל צריך לשער ד' אמות. בין מלמעלה. אם בא להגביה יגביה כותלו ד' אמות מן החלונות. בין מלמטה. אם בא לבנותו נמוך צריך להשפילו מן החלונות ד' אמות כמפרש בגמ'. בין מכנגדן. צריך להרחיקו מהן ד' אמות [לקמן כב.]. מלמעלן. צריך להגביה שיעור שלא יוכל להשענו על כותלו ויציץ ויראה. שלא יעמוד. על ראש עובי כותלו ויראה. מכנגדן. צריך להרחיק כדי שלא יאפיל. שלא יאפיל. את חלונות [שם]. מעקה גבוה ד' אמות. משום היזק ראיה [לקמן ו:]. [מכאן שייך לדף ג.] אפילו פחות מכאן חולקין. משום דבעי למיתני וכתבי הקדש אע"פ ששניהם רוצים לא יחלוקו תני רישא. כתבי הקדש. כ"ד ספרים וכיון רגילים לכתבן בגליון כס"ת שלנו לפיכך נגנאי הדבר לחתכן [לקמן יא.]. כתבי הקדש. כגון תורה נביאים וכתובים [שבת קטו.]. כל אלה אבנים יקרות. כל האבנים האלה עשויות כבדות. כמדות גזית. כמדת אבני גזית במדינה [מלכים א, ז, ט]. למורשא דקרנתא. למורשי דידהו מטפי בה טפח [ב"מ קיז:]. לביני אורבי. בין שורות הבנין בכותל [ב"מ מב.]. והא אמה טרקסין וכו'. כך נקראת כותל מחיצה שהפסיק במקדש ראשון בין הקדש לקדשי הקדשים (מאה) [גי' תוי"ט מ'] אמה לא עשאוהו לפי שלא היו עוביה אלא אמה ואינה יכולה לעמוד בגובה (מאה) והוסיף על עוביה אי אפשר דכתיב הכל בכתב מיד ה' עלי השכיל (דברי הימים א כח) [יומא נא:]. (ברכות לה:) למדנו שטרקסין לשון כניסת פנים הוא (יומא נב.)

he involve it? Did he not know that the case of a collapsed wall might be different?[27]

The Gemara answers:

סֵיפָא אִיצְטְרִיכָא לֵיהּ — The questioner held that the Baraisa's choice of a collapsed wall **was required for** formulating **a later ruling** in that Mishnah, which states: מד׳ אַמּוֹת וּלְמַעְלָה אֵין מְחַיְּיבִין אוֹתוֹ — WE DO NOT OBLIGATE [EITHER NEIGHBOR] to rebuild the wall HIGHER THAN FOUR AMOS, even though the original wall exceeded that height, since no additional protection is provided thereby.[28]

The Gemara offers a third proof:

תָּא שְׁמַע — **Come, learn** a proof. The Mishnah states:[29] כּוֹפִין אוֹתוֹ לִבְנוֹת בֵּית שַׁעַר וְדֶלֶת לֶחָצֵר — WE COMPEL [EACH RESIDENT] of a common courtyard[30] TO contribute toward the BUILDING OF A GATEHOUSE AND A DOOR[31] FOR THE COURTYARD. The purpose of the gatehouse was to prevent people from looking through the gate, and the Mishnah states that all residents were required to assist in its construction! שְׁמַע מִינָּה הֶיזֵּק רְאִיָּה שְׁמֵיהּ הֶיזֵּק — Hence, **infer from [this Mishnah]** that **visual trespass is damaging.**

The Gemara replies:

הֶזֵּיקָא דְּרַבִּים שָׁאנֵי — **Damage** caused by the viewing **of the public is different.**[32]

The Gemara objects to this distinction:

וּדְיָחִיד לֹא — **And** the visual trespass of **an individual is not** damaging?

The Gemara therefore presents a proof that involves visual trespass by an individual:

תָּא שְׁמַע — **Come, learn** a proof. The Mishnah states:[33] אֵין חוֹלְקִין אֶת הֶחָצֵר — Partners MAY NOT be compelled to DIVIDE A COURTYARD עַד שֶׁיְּהֵא בָּהּ אַרְבַּע אַמּוֹת לָזֶה וְאַרְבַּע אַמּוֹת לָזֶה — UNLESS THERE ARE a minimum of FOUR AMOS FOR THIS partner AND FOUR AMOS FOR THAT partner[34] after division is made.

From this the Gemara infers:

הָא יֵשׁ בָּהּ כְּדֵי לָזֶה וּכְדֵי לָזֶה — **But** if the courtyard **contains enough for this** partner **and enough for that** other partner, חוֹלְקִין — **they may divide** even against the will of one partner. מַאי לָאו בְּכוֹתֶל — **Does this not mean** that one partner can force the other to divide **with a** stone **wall,**[35] proving that visual trespass, even by a single person, is considered an injury?

The Gemara rejects this inference:

לֹא — The Mishnah does **not** imply that one may force his partner to divide a larger courtyard with a stone wall.[36] בִּמְסִיפָס בְּעָלְמָא — Rather, **an ordinary boundary marker** is all that is necessary. Hence, the Mishnah does not prove that visual trespass is damaging.

The Gemara adduces as proof a fifth Mishnah:

תָּא שְׁמַע — **Come, learn** a proof. The Mishnah states:[37] הַחַלּוֹנוֹת — One who erects a wall in his courtyard opposite THE WINDOWS of his neighbor's house,[38] בֵּין מִלְמַעְלָה בֵּין מִלְמַטָּה — must ensure that EITHER ABOVE OR BELOW the windows, וּבֵין מִכְּנֶגְדָּן — AND OPPOSITE THEM, אַרְבַּע אַמּוֹת — there is a space of FOUR AMOS between the windows and the wall.[39] וְתָנֵי עֲלָהּ — **And a Baraisa was taught on [the Mishnah]** to explain the rationale of these rulings: מִלְמַעְלָן — When the wall reaches ABOVE [THE WINDOWS], it must be built four *amos* higher, כְּדֵי שֶׁלֹּא יָצִיץ וְיִרְאֶה — SO THAT [THE OWNER] CANNOT LOWER HIMSELF from atop his wall AND GAZE into his neighbor's windows; מִלְמַטָּן — when the top of the wall is BELOW [THE WINDOWS], it must be four *amos* lower, כְּדֵי שֶׁלֹּא יַעֲמוֹד וְיִרְאֶה — SO THAT HE CANNOT STAND atop the wall AND GAZE into the windows; מִכְּנֶגְדָּן — and if the wall stands OPPOSITE THEM, a distance of four *amos* must be maintained, כְּדֵי שֶׁלֹּא יַאֲפִיל — SO AS NOT TO DARKEN the neighbor's home.[40] The first two rulings clearly evidence the Rabbis'

NOTES

27. *Rashi,* who does not explain why the Gemara considered this distinction to be obvious. *Tosafos* suggest that the very fact that the Tanna of the Baraisa chose to discuss the case of a collapsed wall, and not a wall being initially constructed, should have alerted the questioner to the distinction between a collapsed wall and initial construction. [See *Shitah Mekubetzes* who points out that from the answer of the Gemara we may clearly infer that this was the question, and indeed this is how *Rashi* understood it.]

28. The questioner reasoned that once we accept the principle that visual trespass is considered damage in the case of a collapsed wall, logic dictates that the same principle would apply even pertaining to initial construction. This is not contradicted by the Baraisa's choice of a collapsed wall to illustrate this principle, since that might have been required for the purpose of formulating the later ruling of the Baraisa, which indeed is relevant only to the case of a collapsed wall (see *Rashi*).

29. Below, 7b.

30. Unlike the courtyards mentioned previously, this courtyard was shared by many houses. It was surrounded by a wall and its gate opened to a main thoroughfare.

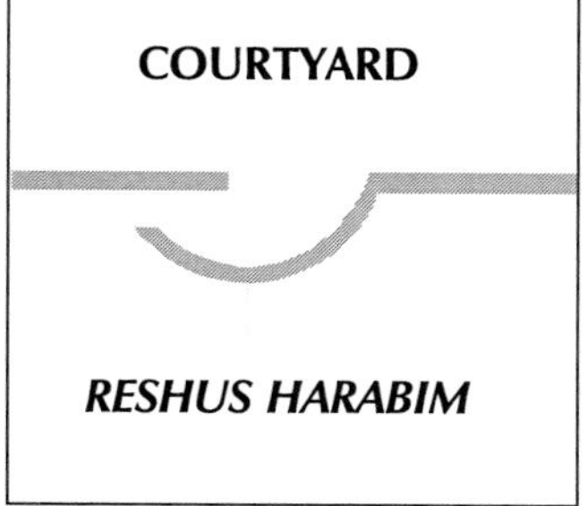

31. The gatehouse was a semicircular wall built in front of the gate (see diagram) with an opening in its side (*Rashi*). The public was thus prevented from gazing into the courtyard. The "door" referred to by the Mishnah is in the gate itself, which was locked at night for protection but was often kept open during the day. Hence, the Gemara's proof derives from the residents' obligation to construct the gatehouse (see *Ramban, Rashba* and *Chidushei HaRan;* cf. *Tosafos* with *Pnei Shlomo*).

32. Since all passersby would gaze into the courtyard, a constant visual trespass would result. This would cause a total loss of privacy to perform even less private acts, that one would perhaps perform in a neighbor's presence. Such a loss of privacy is definitely injurious. The dispute in the Gemara, however, concerns viewing by a single neighbor, which restricts him to a much lesser degree.

33. Below, 11a.

34. Four *amos* by four *amos* is the minimum area required for those activities commonly performed in a courtyard.

35. *Ramban* questions why the Gemara understands the Mishnah to imply a stone wall more than it does an ordinary boundary marker. He answers that at this point the Gemara does not interpret the Mishnah's ruling literally — that one is *completely* precluded from compelling the division of an excessively small courtyard. Rather, since even a tiny area can be used for unloading packages, the Mishnah indeed sanctions a forced division. However, since no private activity can be performed there, protection from visual trespass is unnecessary. Hence, the Mishnah is actually teaching that a forced division of such a small courtyard need not be accomplished *with a wall,* for no right of privacy exists. Rather, an ordinary boundary marker would suffice. The Mishnah thus implies that when a larger courtyard is divided, the division must be effected with a stone wall, in order to shield the private activities of the former partners (see also *Chidushei HaRan*).

36. According to *Ramban,* the Gemara now interprets the Mishnah literally — that one may not compel any division of an exceedingly small courtyard, because each half by itself is unsuitable for any use.

37. Below, 22a.

38. I.e. the neighbor's windows opened onto the friend's courtyard (*Rashi* to 22a).

39. I.e. if the wall was built higher than the windows, it must be at least four *amos* taller; if lower, it must be at least four *amos* shorter. In the first case, it must be built no closer than four *amos* from the neighboring house.

40. A homeowner's right to have unobstructed windows for sources of

ח א מיי' פ"ג מהל' שכנים הלכה ו ועיין בהשגות סמג עשין פב טוש"ע ח"מ סי' קנז סעיף ג וסי' קס סעיף א:

נתיאש הימנה ולא גדרה ה"ז קידש וחייב באחריות' (א) טעמא דרצו הא לא רצו אין מחייבין אותו אלמא [א] היזק ראיה לאו שמיה היזק ואימא (ב) מחיצה פלוגתא כדכתיב [א] ותהי מחצת העדה וכיון דרצו בונין את הכותל בעל כרחו אלמא [ג] היזק ראיה שמיה היזק אי הכי האי שרצו לעשות מחיצה שרצו לחצות מבעי ליה אלא מאי גודא בונין את הכותל בונין אותו מבעי ליה אי תנא אותו הוה אמינא במסיפס בעלמא קמ"ל כותל: בונין את הכותל באמצע וכו': פשיטא לא צריכא דקדים חד ורצייה לחבריה מהו דתימא מצי א"ל כי איתרצאי לך באוירא בתשמישתא לא איתרצאי לך קמ"ל והיזק ראיה לאו שמיה היזק (סימן גינה כותל כופין וחולקין חלונות דרב נחמן) ת"ש וכן בגינה גינה שאני כדר' אבא [ג] דאמר ר' אבא אמר רב הונא אמר רב אסור לאדם לעמוד בשדה חבירו בשעה שהיא עומדת בקמותיה והא וכן קתני אגויל וגזית ת"ש [ד] כותל חצר שנפל מחייבין אותו לבנות עד ד' אמות נפל שאני [ה] ודקארי לה מאי קארי לה סיפא איצטריכא ליה מד' אמות ולמעלה אין מחייבין אותו ת"ש [ו] כופין אותו לבנות בית שער ודלת לחצר ש"מ היזק ראיה שמיה היזק היזקא דרבים שאני ודיחיד לא ת"ש [ז] אין חולקין את החצר עד שיהא בה ד' אמות לזה וד' אמות לזה הא יש בה כדי לזה וכדי לזה חולקין מאי לאו בכותל לא במסיפס בעלמא תא שמע [ח] החלונות בין מלמעלה בין מלמטה ובין מכנגדן ד' אמות ותני עלה [ט] מלמעלן כדי שלא יציץ ויראה מלמטן כדי שלא יעמוד ויראה מכנגדן כדי שלא יאפיל היזקא דבית שאני תא שמע [י] דאמר רב נחמן אמר שמואל גג (ג) הסמוך לחצר חבירו עושין לו מעקה גבוה ד' אמות שאני התם דאמר ליה בעל החצר לבעל הגג לדידי קביעה לי (ג) תשמישי לדידך לא קביעה לך תשמישתך ולא ידענא בהי עידנא סליקא ואתית

רש"י

קידש. התבואה אם הוסיף מאתים ליסנא דקרא נקט פן תוקדש (דברים כב): וטעמא דרצו. לבנות כותל (ד) דמדעת שניהן הוא דחייביה חכמים שידנו בין שניהן ולקמן פריך כשרצו מאי הוי ליהדרי בהו אבל לא רצו שניהן שהיה אחד אומר דייה לחלקה במסיפס של יתדות עלים תקועים בארץ נמוכים לא כייפינן ליה ואין זה יכול לומר לו איני חפץ שתראה עסקי: פלוגתא. חלוקת חצר שהושוו דעתם לחולקה וכגון שלא היה בה ח' אמות כדי לזה וכדי לזה שאין האחד יכול לכוף את חבירו לחולקה ולהכי תני שרצו שכיון שרצו לחולקה בונין כותל אבנים על כרחם ואם בא האחד לומר אי איפשי ביגיאה זו אלא מסיפס בעלמא אין שומעין לו משום היזק הראיה: הוה אמינא במסיפס בעלמא. מיירי מתני' דאיהו נמי מחיצה איקרו ורצו דקתני אחלוקה קאי וכשאין בה דין חלוקה קמ"ל כותל ורצו דקתני משום כותל דאי לא רצו פלגי לה במסיפס: דרצייה חד מינייהו לחבריה. ביקש ממנו לחולקה במחיצה: מהו דתימא א"ל כשנתרציתי לך. במחיצה מחיצה דקה נתרציתי ולמעוטי באוירא כגון של נסרים שהיא דקה והיזק ראיה אין בה או תמסוך עובי הכותל בחלקך חוץ מדבר מועט אבל לבנות כותל אבנים עב למעוטי נמי תשמישתי לא נתרציתי: אסור לאדם שיעמוד כו'. שלא יזיקנו בעין רעה: והא וכן קתני. דמשמע תרוייהו חד טעמא הוא גינה וחצר: מחייבין אותו. והכא לא קתני רצו אלא על כרחו: נפל שאני. שכבר נתרצו הראשונים בכותל: ודקארי לה מאי קארי לה. וכי לא ידע דנפל שאני: סיפא איצטריך ליה. כלומר הוא הדין נמי מעיקרא והאי דקתני נפל משום סיפא לאשמועינן דיותר מד' אמות אין מחייבין ואע"פ שהראשון היה גבוה יותר לא מחייבין ליה: כופין אותו. כל אחד מבני החצר לתת חלקו בבנין: בית השער. שבונים כותל נגד השער עגול סביב ועושין באותו היקף פתח קטן מן הצד משום היזק ראיות בני רה"ר שלא יראו תוך החצר: היזקא דרבים. שכל בני רה"ר מסתכלין שם: אין חולקין. אין האחד כופה את חבירו לחלוק: החלונות. אחד מבני השותפין הבונה כותל בחצר כנגד חלונותיו של חבירו בין מלמעלה וכו' אם הכותל גבוה יותר מן החלונות צריך להגביה למעלה מהן ד"א כדמפרש ואזיל כדי שלא יסמוך על כותלו וישחה ויראה בחלונותיו של חבירו: בין מלמטה. אם הכותל נמוך מן החלונות צריך להשפילו מהן ד"א כדי שלא יעמוד על עובי כותלו ויראה: ומכנגדן. צריך להרחיק את הכותל מן החלונות ד' אמות כדי שלא יאפיל: היזקא דבית שאני. שאדם עושה בביתו דברי הצנע: מעקה גבוה ארבע אמות. כדי שלא יראהו בעל החצר חבירו כשהוא משתמש בגגו: ולא ידענא בהי עידנא דקא אתית. להשתמש בגגך:

תוספות

נתיאש הימנה ולא גדרה. דוקא נתיאש אבל לא נתיאש ועוסק כל שעה לגדור אע"פ שהוסיף מאתים מותר כדתנן במסכת כלאים (פ"ה מ"ו) הרואה ירק בכרם ואמר כשאגיע לשם אלקטנו הוסיף מאתים מותר לכשאחזור אלקטנו הוסיף מאתים אסור אלמא כשהוא מחזר אחר לקיטתו אפילו הוסיף מאתים מותר והטעם יש לפרש משום דכתיב (דברים כב) לא תזרע כרמך כלאים דומיא דזריעה דניחא ליה: וחייב באחריותו. אע"ג דהיזק שאינו ניכר לא שמיה היזק (גיטין נג.) נראה לר"י דהאי חשיב היזק ניכר שהרי ניכר הוא שהוא כלאים כשרואה הגפנים בשדה ומטמא אע"פ שרואין השרץ על הטהרות לא חשיב היזק ניכר דמי יודע אם הוכשרו אבל אין לומר דה"נ הוי היזק שאינו ניכר וקנסוהו כמו במטמא (שם) שלא יהא כל אחד הולך ומטמא טהרותיו של חבירו דהכא ליכא למיחש להכי שבעל הכרם נמי מפסיד ועוד אי קנס הוא במזיד דוקא היה לו להתחייב: ואימא מאי מחיצה פלוגתא. מפרש ר"י משום דעל לשון גודא יש כמה קושיות כדפריך בסמוך לפיכך דוחק לפרש מחיצה פלוגתא אע"ג דבכל מקום הוי מחיצה גודא: וכיון דרצו בונין את הכותל בעל כרחו. לקמן מוקי לה כשאין בה דין חלוקה ותימה לר"י דאמאי נקט תנא דמתני' באין בה דין חלוקה וקתני רצו לא ליתני רצו ולאיירי בשיש בה דין חלוקה ותי' דקמ"ל דס"ד בשאין בה דין חלוקה דמצי למימר כי (ה) איתרצאי לך לחלוק ע"מ שלא לעשות גודא אבל על מנת לעשות גודא לא איתרצי לך. ויש ספרים דמקשין ומתרץ כן להדיא בשילהי שמעתין: הוה אמינא במסיפס בעלמא. פי' ורצו דקתני אמסיפס ואע"ג דבלאו רצו נמי עושין מסיפס בעל כרחם כדמוכח בסמוך דקאמר מאי לאו בכותל לא במסיפס היינו מסיפס גרוע אבל כי רצו עושין מסיפס מגויל וגזית כמנהג המדינה ומקרי מסיפס לפי שהוא מלא חלונות כדפי' בערוך ואינו מגין מהיזק ראיה א"נ לפי שאינו גבוה י' כדמוכח לקמן גבי גג הסמוך [י] לחצר דאמר ר"נ עושה לו מעקה גבוה י' ופריך למאי אי להיזק ראיה ד"א בעינן ולא סגי ובקונטרס פי' דרצו דקתני אחלוקה קאי ותימה דהא לקמן בסמוך מפרש מחיצה היינו גודא דאי פלוגתא לחצות מבעי ליה ועוד היכי מצי למימר דס"ד במסיפס בעלמא הא שמעינן ליה מסיפא דקתני אבל בזמן שאינם רוצים אפילו פחות מכאן יחלוקו והיינו בכל דפחות במסיפס ועוד היכי הס"ל במסיפס בעלמא הא בהדיא קתני במתני' גזית וגויל: בונין את הכותל באמצע פשיטא. למ"ד גודא פריך כמו כל הנך פירכי דלקמן דכשהקנו לעשות גודא כך הקנה זה כמו זה ופשיטא דבאמצע אבל למ"ד פלוגתא איצטריך למימר סד"א משום היזק הוא דבעי גודא אבל אין לו לסייע בבנין הכותל אלא לבנות בחלקו בשביל כך: תא שמע וכן בגינה. לקמן מסקינן דה"ק וכן בגינה סתם במקום שנהגו לגדור דמי הלכך דייק שפיר דהיזק ראיה שמיה היזק: גינה שאני כדרבי אבא כו'. וא"ת ומהאי טעמא יתחייב נמי לגדור בבקעה ויש לומר דשאני גינה שמגדלין בה ירק לאכילה וכל שעה היא עומדת בקמותיה אבל בקעה אינה עומדת בקמותיה אלא חדש אחד בשנה ולא מחייב לגדור אבל אסור לעמוד בשעה שעומדת בקמותיה וא"ת ולמ"ד פלוגתא כיון דאשמועינן דאפילו בחצר שמיה היזק כל שכן בגינה ולמאי איצטריך תו למיתני וכן בגינה וי"ל דאיצטריך וכן בגינה למיתני משום גויל וגזית: נפל שאני. שהסוגלו לעשות דבר הצנע בחצר ולא למדו ליזהר זה מזה: ודקארי לה מאי קארי לה. כלומר פשיטא דנפל שאני ולדרכו היה לו להוכיח מדקתני נפל מכלל דבעלמא לא שמיה היזק: היזקא דרבים שאני. ואע"ג דלקמן משמע דאיירי בחצר שאינה סמוכה לרה"ר מ"מ איכא היזקא דרבים דזימנין דדחקי רבים ועיילי להתם כדאמרי' לקמן ורשב"א אע"ג דליכא ליה האי טעמא דזימנין דדחקי רבים מ"מ מרחוק יכולין לראות לפנים ולכך לא פליג אלא אבית שער אבל בדלת מודה דכופין אותו לבנות: מאי לאו בכותל. תימה ויהא בכותל דילמא הכי פי' אין חולקין את החצר אפי' האחד רוצה לבנות את הכותל בתוך שלו עד שיהא בה ד' אמות לכל אחד הא אם יש בה ד' אמות לכל אחד חולקין אם רצה לכנוס ולבנות בתוך שלו וי"ל דחולקין משמע באמצע דאי לאשמועינן כדפי' הוה ליה למיתני אין עושין כותל בחצר עד שיהא כו': שאני התם דאמר ליה בעל החצר לבעל הגג כו'. תימה אמאי לא מייתי מדתניא לקמן (דף ו:) שתי חצירות זו למעלה מזו לא יאמר העליון הריני בונה מכנגדי ועולה אלא מסייע מלמטה ובונה אלמא שמיה היזק:

רבינו גרשום

[תחלת הפירוש ששייך לכאן נדפס בעמוד הקודם] כותל חצר שבין שני חצירות שנפל אם א' מהן מעכב מלבנותו מחייבין אותו לבנותו בעל כרחו עד שיהא גבוה ד"א דלא מצי איניש לאסתכולי דרך הליכתו עד שיהא גבוה ד' אמות אלמא משום היזק ראיה הוא. ומשני דהיכא דנפל שאני הואיל דהוי מעיקרא הכותל בדין הוא דמחייבין אותו עד ד' אמות דפחות מכן לא מצי למיבניה דהכי שמה מחיצה אבל גבי מתני' שלא היה מעולם מחיצה אין מחייבין המעכב: ודקארי לה מאי קארי לה כלו' המקשה שהיה מקשה קושי' זו אמאי מקשה לה. וכי לא היה יודע דהיכא דנפל שאני ומה ראה להקשותה. ומשני לעולם משום קושיא מייתינן לה משום דהוא בסיפא איצטריך ליה למיתני' בלשון קושיא דקתני סיפא מד' אמות ולמעלה אין מחייבין אותו לבנות גבוה כדמעיקרא אלמא ש"מ משום היזק ראייה הוא ומשה"ה אין מחייבין אותו אלא כשיעור שאינו יכול לראות. והמתרץ מתרץ [לעולם] כדמעיקרא נפל שאני. והאי דאמר עד ד' אמות דבהכי הוא דין מחיצה ולא משום היזק ראייה: ת"ש בתים הפתוחים לחצר וחצר פתוח לרה"ר ונפל בית שער החצר. וכל בני החצר נתרצו לבנות. [כופין לא' מבני החצר המעכב לבנות] בית שער ודלת עמהן משום היזק ראייה דבני רה"ר. אלמא היזק ראייה שמיה היזק: היזקא דרבים שאני. אבל דיחיד כגון האי חצר השותפין לאו שמיה היזק: ת"ש קתני מתני' אין חולקין את החצר. האחין שבאו לחלוק בנכסי אביהן אין חולקין את החצר עד שיהא בה ד' אמות לזה וד' אמות לזה דהכי חזי לדירה. וכשהן חולקין מאי לאו כותל מעליא בעו למיעבד בינייהו משום היזק ראייה: לא במסיפס בעלמא. חולקין אע"ג דזה יכול לראות בזה: ת"ש חלונות שיש להם חזקה כדאמר לקמן מלמעלן ומלמטן ומכנגדן ד' אמות כלומר אם רוצה זה לבנות כותל בצד החצר שהחלון פתוח בחצירו לבנות כותל בצד חלון. מלמעלה שאם רצה להגביה כותל (מן) החצר עד (מן) החלון צריך להגביהו ד' אמות על החלון. אי נמי למטה אם רוצה לא נמוך (מן) הכותל מן (הצד) שצריך להנמיכו ד' אמות ואם בא לבנות כנגד החלון עד הכותל ולזה יש לו חזקת חלון בחצירו של זה צריך להרחיק ד' אמות כדי שלא יאפיל חלונותיו: ותני עלה מלמעלה להם צריך שיהא גבוה ד' אמות על החלון כדי שלא יעמוד ע"ג הכותל ויציץ ויראה בחלון ומלמטן כדי שלא יעמוד זקוף על גבי הכותל ויראה בבית אלמא היזק ראיה שמיה היזק: היזקא דבית שאני טפי מחצר: גג הסמוך לחצר חבירו. עושין לו מעקה גבוה ד' אמות שלא יסתכל בתוך חצר חבירו אלמא היזק ראיה שמיה היזק: שאני התם דאמר ליה בעל החצר לבעל הגג לדידי קביעא תשמישתאי בכל שעה בחצר לדידך לא קביעא תשמישתך:

מסורת הש"ס

א) [לקמן נט:], ב) [שם], ג) ב"מ קז. ע"ש, ד) לקמן ה., ה) לקמן ז:, ו) לקמן יא., ז) לקמן דף כב., ח) [שם], ט) לקמן ו:, י) ל"ל לגג.

הגהות הב"ח

(א) גמ' וטעמא דרצו: (ב) שם ואימא מאי מחיצה פלוגתא: (ג) שם קביעה לי תשמישי: (ד) רש"י ד"ה וטעמא וכו' מדעת שניהן הוא דחייבוהו חכמים: (ה) תוס' ד"ה וכיון וכו' כי איתרצאי לך וכו' לא איתרצאי לך ויש ספרים דמקשה ומתרץ:

גליון הש"ס

גמ' ודקארי לה. ע' בחדושי הרמב"ן לקמן דף יז ע"ב ד"ה גירסת רש"י: שם ודקארי לה. כתובות טז ע"א וש"נ:

תורה אור השלם

א) וַתְּהִי מֶחֱצַת הָעֵדָה מִן הַצֹּאן שְׁלֹשׁ מֵאוֹת אֶלֶף וּשְׁלֹשִׁים אֶלֶף שִׁבְעַת אֲלָפִים וַחֲמֵשׁ מֵאוֹת: [במדבר לא, מג]

ליקוטי רש"י

[תחילת ליקוטי רש"י ששייך לכאן נדפס בעמוד הקודם] כופין אותו לבנות בית שער. אם בן החצר שאינו רוצה לסייע את בני החצר לבנות להן בית שער להיות שומר הפתח יושב שם בצל ומרחיק את בני רשות הרבים מלהכנס לחצר [לקמן ז:]. בית שער. בית קטן לפני שער [יומא יא.]. בית כניסת שער החצר להסתופף שם שומר [סוטה מג.]. בית קטן שעושין בצד שערי חצירות ויושב שם שומר הפתח [מנחות לג:]. ודלת. לשער החצר לנעלו [לקמן ז:]. החלונות. מי שיש לו חלונות פתוחים לחצר חבירו והוסמך בדבר זה שלא שנים וכא חבירו לבנות שם כותל צריך לשער ד' אמות. בין מלמעלה. אם בא להגביה יגביה כותלו ד' אמות מן החלונות. בין מלמטה. אם בא לבנותו נמוך צריך להשפילו מן החלונות ד' אמות וטעמא מפרש בגמ'. בין מכנגדן. צריך להרחיקו מהן ד' אמות [לקמן כב.]. מלמעלן. צריך להגביה שיעור שלא יציץ השכנו על כותלו ויסתכל ראשו בחלון ויראה דרך חלונות ויראה בבית חבירו. שלא יעמוד. על ראש עובי כותלו ויראה. מכנגדן. צריך להרחיק כדי שלא יאפיל ולא יהיה מגה דבריש' שיעורא. שלא יאפיל. בשם חלונות [שם]. מעקה גבוה ד' אמות. משום היזק ראיה [לקמן ו:]. [מכאן שייך לדף ג.] אפילו פחות מכאן חולקין. משום דבעי למיתני ובכתבי הקדש אע"פ שניהם רוצים לא יחלוקו תני רישא. כתבי הקדש. כ"ד ספרים והיו רגילים לכותבן בגליון כא' שלא לפרק יפה כבר הוו לכתבן. כתבי הקדש. כגון תורה נביאים וכתובים.

חשק שלמה על רבינו גרשום א) [נראה דל"ל אם רוצה להנמיך הכותל מן החלון צריך להנמיכו ד' אמות וכו']: ב) [נראה דל"ל שלא]. ג) [אולי צ"ל דאינם לאו בתשמישים דעות של תכלתן]:

concern for safeguarding an individual's privacy. Obviously, then, visual trespass is considered injurious.

The Gemara answers:

הֶזֵּיקָא דְּבַיִת שָׁאנֵי — **Damage** caused by visual trespass into a **home is different,** since intimate activities are routinely performed there. Our discussion, however, concerns whether a right to privacy pertains also in a courtyard.

The Gemara attempts a sixth and final proof:

תָּא שְׁמַע — **Come, learn** a proof from a ruling דְּאָמַר רַב נַחְמָן אָמַר שְׁמוּאֵל — **that Rav Nachman said in Shmuel's name:** גַּג הַסָּמוּךְ לַחֲצַר חֲבֵירוֹ — If one's **roof adjoins the courtyard of his neighbor,** עוֹשִׂין לוֹ מַעֲקֶה גָּבוֹהַּ אַרְבַּע אַמּוֹת — **he must make for [the roof] a fence four *amos* high.**[41] Since the purpose of such a tall fence is to prevent him, while he is working on his roof, from viewing the neighbor's actions below, Rav Nachman's ruling thus implies that visual trespass is damaging.

The Gemara rebuts the proof:

שָׁאנֵי הָתָם — The situation **there is different,** and all would agree that a tall fence is required, דְּאָמַר לֵיהּ בַּעַל הֶחָצֵר לְבַעַל הַגַּג — **for the courtyard owner can say to the owner of the roof:** לְדִידִי קְבִיעָא לִי תַּשְׁמִישִׁי — **As for me, my use** of the courtyard **is a regular** occurrence; לְדִידָךְ לֹא קְבִיעָא לָךְ תַּשְׁמִישְׁתָּךְ — but **as for you, your use** of the roof **is irregular.** וְלֹא יָדַעְנָא בְּהֵי עִידָּנָא סְלִיקָא וְאָתֵית — Hence, **I do not know at which times you may be coming up**

NOTES

light is not absolute. The Gemara below (59a) will discuss under which conditions it exists. However, in this Mishnah's case it is assumed that the neighbor possesses such a right.

41. Although the Torah requires for reasons of safety the erecting of fences around roofs (*Deut.* 22:8), their minimum height is set at only ten *tefachim (Rambam, Hil. Rotzeach* 11:3, from *Sifri*). The increment demanded by Rav Nachman was therefore for the purpose of protecting against visual trespass.

דְּאִיצְטְנַע מִינָּךְ – **so that I can conceal from you** my private activities. Thus, a wall is required to protect the courtyard owner in this atypical case.[1]

The Gemara now presents a different version of its earlier discussion (on 2a-b) of the meaning of the word *mechitzah.* Although much of the material is familiar, a question left unresolved before is now answered: לִישָּׁנָא אַחֲרִינָא אָמְרֵי לַהּ – **Another version** of the previous discussion **was quoted,** as follows: סַבְרוּהָ – The Rabbis **maintained:** מַאי מְחִיצָה – **What is** the meaning of the word ***mechitzah,*** as it appears in our Mishnah? פְּלוּגְתָּא – **A division.** דִּכְתִיב ,,וַתְּהִי מֶחֱצַת הָעֵדָה״ – **As it is written:**[2] ***And the division***[3] ***of the congregation was . . .***[4]

The Gemara explains the implication of this translation with regard to the Mishnah's position on visual trespass:

וְכֵיוָן דְּרָצוּ – **And since they agreed** to divide the yard, even though they did not stipulate to build a wall, בּוֹנִין אֶת הַכּוֹתֶל בְּעַל כּוֹרְחָן – **they must build a** stone **wall, notwithstanding** the objection of either party. The Mishnah thus implies that agreeing to divide the courtyard results in an obligation to contribute to the erection of a solid wall as well. אַלְמָא הֶיזֵּק רְאִיָּה שְׁמֵיהּ הֶיזֵּק – **We** therefore **see that visual trespass is considered damaging,** for only if a right to privacy existed would each partner be required to build a wall.

The Gemara suggests an alternative definition of *mechitzah,* one which reverses the Mishnah's implicit position on the right to privacy in a courtyard:

אֵימָא מַאי מְחִיצָה – **But say, what is** meant by the word ***mechitzah?*** גּוּדָא – **A wall.** (דתנן) דְּתַנְיָא – **For it was taught in a Baraisa:** מְחִיצַת הַכֶּרֶם שֶׁנִּפְרְצָה – Concerning A VINEYARD WALL[5] THAT WAS BREACHED,[6] אוֹמֵר לוֹ גְּדוֹר – the owner of the field MAY SAY TO [THE VINEYARD OWNER]: "REBUILD THE WALL."[7] נִפְרְצָה – If after repair IT WAS BREACHED again, אוֹמֵר לוֹ גְּדוֹר – the owner of the field MAY SAY TO [THE VINEYARD OWNER] a second time:[8] "REBUILD THE WALL." נִתְיָאֵשׁ הֵימֶנָּה וְלֹא גְדָרָהּ – If, however, HE ABANDONED [THE PROJECT][9] AND DID NOT REBUILD [THE WALL,] and the grain and the vines grew[10] without a wall separating them, הֲרֵי זֶה קִידֵּשׁ – THE vineyard RENDERS [THE GRAIN] UNFIT,[11] וְחַיָּיב בְּאַחֲרָיוּתָהּ – AND the vineyard owner IS RESPONSIBLE FOR ANY LOSS incurred by the owner of the grain. This concludes the Baraisa, in which we find that the word *mechitzah* connotes a "wall."

The Gemara now explains the implication of employing this translation of *mechitzah* in our Mishnah:

וְטַעְמָא דְּרָצוּ – **And the reason** that *beis din* can compel both partners to assist in building a wall **is because** originally **they had agreed** to erect just such a structure.[12] הָא לֹא רָצוּ – **But had they not** specifically **agreed** to do so,[13] אֵין מְחַיְּיבִין אוֹתוֹ – *beis din* **would not obligate [the reluctant partner]** to contribute toward the building of a wall as a result of his agreement to divide. אַלְמָא הֶיזֵּק רְאִיָּה לָאו שְׁמֵיהּ הֶיזֵּק – **We** therefore **see** that **visual trespass is not considered damaging,** for if it were, once they decided to divide the courtyard either party could rightfully demand his privacy and compel the other to join in building a wall.

The Gemara explains its objection to incorporating this second translation into the Mishnah:

אִי הָכִי – **If it is so** that *mechitzah* means "wall," בּוֹנִין אֶת הַכּוֹתֶל – why does the Mishnah state, THEY MUST BUILD A WALL? בּוֹנִין אוֹתוֹ מִבָּעֵי לֵיהּ – **[The Mishnah] should have said,** [THEY MUST BUILD] IT, since the word *wall* has already been mentioned.[14]

The Gemara counters by pointing out a difficulty with the other translation of *mechitzah:*

אֶלָּא מַאי פְּלוּגְתָּא – **Rather, what** is the alternative definition of *mechitzah* – **a division?** אִי הָכִי – **If it is so,** שֶׁרָצוּ לַעֲשׂוֹת מְחִיצָה – why does the Mishnah state, WHO AGREED TO MAKE A DIVISION? שֶׁרָצוּ לַחֲצוֹת מִבָּעֵי לֵיהּ – **[The Mishnah] should have said,** WHO AGREED TO DIVIDE – for the expression לַחֲצוֹת can mean only "to divide" (i.e. the courtyard), and in no way implies the building of a wall. The expression לַעֲשׂוֹת מְחִיצָה, however, implies making something in the courtyard. – ? –

For this difficulty, however, the Gemara has a solution:

כִּדְאָמְרֵי אִינָשֵׁי תָּא נַעֲבִיד פְּלוּגְתָּא – The Tanna wrote in the vernacular, **for people** commonly **say: "Come, let us make a division."** Thus, he sacrificed some clarity to use a popular expression.

The Gemara questions the interpretation that has *mechitzah* meaning "division" and the Mishnah implying, as a corollary, that visual trespass is considered damaging.

וְאִי הֶיזֵּק רְאִיָּה שְׁמֵיהּ הֶיזֵּק – **But if visual trespass is considered damaging,** מַאי אִירְיָא רָצוּ – **why does** the Mishnah **mention** the case of partners who **agreed** to divide the courtyard? אֲפִילוּ לֹא רָצוּ נַמִּי – **Even if they never agreed** to divide the courtyard, either partner should in any event be able to force the other to divide and build a wall – for each partner has a right to demand a division and the subsequent building of a wall to protect against the damage of visual trespass. – ? –

The Gemara answers:

אָמַר רַב אַסִּי אָמַר רַבִּי יוֹחָנָן – **Rav Assi said in the name of R' Yochanan:** מִשְׁנָתֵנוּ כְּשֶׁאֵין בָּהּ דִּין חֲלוּקָה – **Our Mishnah** speaks of a courtyard that **is not subject to legal division,**[15] וְהוּא דְּרָצוּ – **and** thus **[the ruling]** that one partner can compel the other to build a wall applies only because **they agreed** to divide the courtyard, for only then is each partner entitled to demand privacy in his portion.

The Gemara questions the logic of this answer:

מַאי קָא מַשְׁמַע לָן – **What** additional ruling **does** the Mishnah **teach us** with the case of an "indivisible" courtyard that is divided by

NOTES

1. However, since in a shared courtyard each partner frequently and routinely makes use of his half, neither would perform private activities there in the first place (*Rashi*). Hence, no proof can be adduced from Rav Nachman's ruling to require erecting a wall in a shared courtyard on account of visual trespass.

2. *Numbers* 31:43.

3. See above, 2b note 10.

4. According to this translation of *mechitzah,* the Mishnah reads: "Partners who agreed to *divide* must build a wall."

5. See above, 2a note 23.

6. See above, 2a note 24.

7. See above, 2a note 26.

8. See above, 2a note 27.

9. See above, 2b note 1.

10. See above, 2b note 2.

11. See above, 2b note 3.

12. See above, 2b note 5.

13. See above, 2b note 6.

14. If *mechitzah* means "division," however, this problem obviously does not arise.

15. A courtyard that measures less than 8 x 4 *amos* is too small to afford each partner a usable portion if divided (see below, 11a and chapter introduction), and thus one partner cannot compel the other to divide – even if visual trespass is regarded as injurious.

ט א ב ג מיי' פ"ב מהל' שכנים הל' יד סמג עשין פב טוש"ע ח"מ סי' קנז סעיף א:
י ד ה ו מיי' שם הל' י טוש"ע שם סעיף ג:

א) [נ"ל דתניא], ב) [לעיל ב. וש"נ], ג) [לקמן יא.], ד) [שם], ה) ב"מ לא מיעו, ו) [ב"מ טו. וש"נ], ז) [ב"מ לד], ח) [נ"ל מגררות במגרה וכן הגיה בערוך ערך שף א'], ט) [לקמן ה.], י) [עי' תוי"ט ריש פ"ה דיומא ד"ה לבין שתי דגרס מ' אמות], כ) ס"א ומירך מהרש"ל ולפי גירסתו צ"ל כשרצו והגי' שלפנינו הוא גי' מהרש"א, ל) [וע"ע תוס' כתובות נד: ד"ה אע"פ]:

דאיצטנע מינך לישנא אחרינא אמרי לה סברוה מאי מחיצה פלוגתא (א) דכתיב א) ותהי מחצת העדה א וכיון דרצו בונין את הכותל בעל כורחן אלמא ב היזק ראיה שמיה היזק (ב) אימא מאי מחיצה גודא א) (דתנן) ג) מחיצת הכרם שנפרצה אומר לו גדור נפרצה אומר לו גדור נתיאש הימנה ולא גדרה הרי זה קידש וחייב באחריותה וטעמא דרצו הא לא רצו אין מחייבין אותו אלמא היזק ראיה לאו שמיה היזק אי הכי בונין את הכותל בונין אותו מבעי ליה אלא מאי פלוגתא אי הכי שרצו לעשות מחיצה שרצו לחצות מבעי ליה כדאמרי אינשי תא נעביד פלוגתא ואי היזק ראיה שמיה היזק מאי איריא רצו אפי' לא רצו נמי א"ר אסי א"ר יוחנן משנתנו ג כשאין בה דין חלוקה והוא דרצו מאי קמ"ל (ג) דכי לית ביה דין חלוקה כי רצו פליגי תנינא ג אימתי בזמן שאין שניהם רוצים אבל בזמן ששניהם רוצים אפילו פחות מכאן חולקין אי מהתם הוה אמינא אפילו פחות מכאן במסיפס בעלמא קמ"ל הכא כותל וליתני הא ולא ליתני הך סיפא איצטריכא ליה ה וכתבי הקדש אע"פ ששניהם רוצים לא יחלוקו (ד) ו) (ל"א וכי רצו מאי הוי ליהדר ביה אמר רב אסי א"ר יוחנן בשקנו מידו כו' אדאשמעינן בשאין בה דין חלוקה והוא דרצו לישמעינן ביש בה דין חלוקה ואע"ג דלא רצו אי אשמעינן ביש בה דין חלוקה ואע"ג דלא רצו הוה אמינא שאין בה דין חלוקה אפילו רצו נמי לא קמ"ל ומי מצית אמרת הכי והא קתני סיפא אימתי בזמן שאין שניהם רוצים אבל בזמן ששניהם רוצים יחלוקו מאי לאו אכותל לא אמסיפס בעלמא וליתני האי ולא ליתני האי סיפא אצטריכא ליה ובכתבי הקדש אע"פ ששניהם רוצים לא יחלוקו): במאי אוקימתא למתני' בשאין בה דין חלוקה אי בשאין בה דין חלוקה כי רצו מאי הוי נהדרו בהו א"ר אסי א"ר יוחנן ו שקנו מידן אז וכי קנו מידן מאי הוי קנין דברים בעלמא הוא ה בשקנו מידן ברוחות רב אשי אמר ט כגון שהלך זה בתוך שלו והחזיק וזה בתוך שלו והחזיק: מקום שנהגו לבנות כו': ז גויל אבני דלא משפיא גזית אבני דמשפיא דכתיב ב כל אלה אבנים יקרות כמדות גזית ח (וגו') כפיסין ארחי לבנין ליבני אמר ליה רבה בריה דרבא לרב אשי ממאי דגויל אבני דלא משפיא נינהו והאי טפח יתירא למורשא דקרנתא דילמא פלגא דגזית הוא והאי טפח יתירא לביני אורבי ולטעמיך כפיסין ארחי מנלן אלא גמרא גמירי לה גויל נמי אבני דלא משפיא גמרא גמירי לה איכא דאמרי אמר ליה רב אחא בריה דרב אויא לרב אשי ממאי דהאי כפיסין ארחי נינהו והאי טפח יתירא לביני אורבי דילמא מאי כפיסין אבני דלא משפיין והאי טפח יתירא למורשא דקרנתא כדקאמרינן גויל אבני דלא משפיין גזית אבני דמשפיין והאי טפח יתירא למורשא דקרנתא אמר ליה ולטעמיך גויל אבני דלא משפיין מנלן אלא גמרא גמירי לה הכא נמי גמרא גמירי לה אמר אביי שמע מינה כל ביני אורבי טפח הני מילי בטינא אבל בריכסא בעי טפי ואיכא דאמרי הני מילי בריכסא אבל בטינא לא בעי כולי האי למימרא דבגזית (ה) דכל ד' אמות גובה אי הוי פותיא חמשא קאי אי לא לא קאי והא אמה טרקסין דהואי גבוה תלתין אמהתא ולא הוה פותיא אלא שית פושכי וקם כיון דאיכא טפח יתירא קאי ובמקדש שני מ"ט לא עבוד אמה טרקסין כי קאי בתלתין קאי טפי לא קאי ומנלן דהוה גבוה טפי דכתיב ג גדול יהיה כבוד הבית הזה האחרון מן הראשון רב ושמואל ואמרי לה ר' יוחנן ור"א חד אמר בבנין וחד אמר

רש"י

דאיצטנע מינך. דברי הלנע אבל אחר החלוקה לתרוייהו קביעא תשמישתי' לכל אחד בחלקו כל שעה ולא עבדי בה מילי דלנעא: כיון דרצו. לחלוק ולקמן פריך מאי איריא רצו אפילו לא רצו הרי הן יכולין לכוף זה את זה: בונין כותל. של אבנים: גודא. כותל אבנים ובחצר שיש בה דין חלוקה ועל כרחן חולקים: וטעמא דרצו. שהתנו לחולקה בכותל אבנים הא לא רצו אין מחייבין אותו אלא מסיפס בעלמא: כדאמרי אינשי כו'. תירוצא הוא: שאין בה דין חלוקה. ח' אמות לא יחלוקו: ובכתבי הקדש. ספר תורה שהוא בכרך אחד וכן נביאים וכתובים הכתובים בגליון כס"ת: קנין דברים הוא. ואין חליפין קונין אלא דבר הנקנה או (ו) מכר או מתנה או שעבוד קרקעות שהקנין חל עליו או מטלטלין: ברוחות. זה בורר לו חלק מזרחי וזה בורר לו חלק מערבי וקנו מידם ומעתה נקנה חלק מזרחי לזה ואין לזה חלק בו וכן השני לחבירו: והחזיק. בחלקו רפק ביה פורתא וקרקע נקנה בחזקה אחרי אשר רצו בשעת חלוקה: אריח. חצי לבינה והלבינה ג' טפחים והאריח טפח ומחצה ועובי הכותל אריח מכאן ואריח מכאן וטפח באמצע שנותן שם טיט לחברו: לבינים ליבני. שלימות לבינה לעובי הכותל: למורשא דקרנת'. ראשי האבנים בולטות לחוץ שאינן חלקות ולהכי בעי רוחב טפח יתירא: לביני אורבי. בין דימוס שמכאן ובין דימוס שמכאן ונותן טיט באמצע: ה"ג אימא לביני דלא משפיין: ש"מ כו'. ונפקא מינה למקבל עליו לבנות כותל לחבירו: בריכסא. אבנים דקות וטיט בין שני הדימוסות: למימרא דבגזית כו' כל ד' אמות גובה אי הוה פותיא ה' טפחים קאי ואי לא לא קאי. כדתנן במתני' בגזית זה נותן טפחיים ומחצה וזה נותן טפחיים ומחצה וקתני סיפא ט) מחייבין אותן לבנותו עד ד' אמות ולפי חשבון זה לגובה שמנה צריך י' טפחים רוחב: והא אמה טרקסין. דבנין שלמה דגזית הוה דכתיב אבני גזית (מלכים א ה) והוי שלשים אמה קומתה ואין עוביו אלא אמה להבדיל בין ההיכל לקדשי הקדשים: דאיכא טפח יתירא. ומשום האי טפח פותיא מצי לאגבוה טובא ואין צריך לתת לכל ארבע אמות ה' טפחים רוחב: בבנין. שהיה גובהו (ז) י) מאה אמות כדתנן במסכת מדות (פרק ד מ"ו):

תוספות

מאי קא משמע לן בשאין בה דין חלוקה. אע"ג דקא משמע לן דשמיה היזק ה"פ מאי קמ"ל במאי דאיירי באין בה דין חלוקה לישמעינן בשיש בה דין חלוקה [אע"ג דלא רצו] (כשרצו) פלגי כ) תימה הא קמ"ל דאפילו באין בה דין חלוקה דאיכא למימר על מנת לעשות גודא לא איתרצאי כדפירש לעיל: כי רצו מאי הוי ניהדרו בהו. למ"ד מחיצה גודא לא פריך דאיכא למימר דקנו ושיעבדו נכסיהן לבנין הכותל אלא למ"ד פלוגתא לא מהני קנין דקנין דברים בעלמא הוא דלא מסיק אדעתיה שקנו ברוחות: קנין דברים בעלמא הוא. בפרק השוכר את הפועלים (ב"מ דף צד.) דתנן מתנה ש"ח להיות כשואל ומוקי לה בקנו מידו התם לאו קנין דברים הוא אלא קנין גמור הוא שמשעבד את עצמו שאם יאנס שישלם ל): רב אשי אמר כגון שהלך כו'. תימה לר"י מה בא רב אשי להוסיף וכי איצטריך לאשמועינן דחזקה מועלת כמו קנין ונראה לר"י דהא קמ"ל דאע"ג דקאמר לקמן בחזקת הבתים (דף נג.) שלא בפניו צריך למימר לו לך חזק וקני הכא כיון שאמרו אתה תקח רוח צפונית ואני רוח דרומית והלך והחזיק לו כל אחד בשלו זה שלא בפני זה נעשה כמי שקנו מידם ברוחות אע"פ שלא אמרו זה לזה לך חזק וקני: ארבע אמות גובה אפותיא דה' קאי טפי לא קאי. וקשיא לר"ת הא לבינין דגריעי קאי בשלשה טפחים ועוד הא קא חזינן דקאי בגזית טפי אפורתא ותירץ דהכי קאמר טפי לא קאי כמשפט גזית שרוצים בני אדם לבנותו שיעמוד ימים רבים כשבונים בגזית: טרקסין. אומר ר"ת דטרק הוי כמו טרוקי גלי (ברכות דף כח.) וסין הוי סיני כלומר שהיה מפסיק וסוגר את הלוחות שנתנו בסיני שהיו מונחות בארון שהיה בבית קדשי הקדשים וי"מ טרקסין פנים וחוץ שאותה אמה היתה ספק אם מקודשת פנים או חוץ ולכך היו שם שתי פרוכת כדאמרינן ביומא (דף נא:): שאני התם דאיכא טפח יתירא. ה"מ לשנויי דאגב תקרה ומעזיבה קאי טפי כדאמרי' בסמוך: אמר

רבינו גרשום

ל"א [מפיך] כולה הלכה דכיון שרצו לחלוק אם מעכב א' מלעשות כותל בונין אותו בעל כרחו: א) וטעמא דרצו לעשות [כותל] מש"ה בונין הא לא רצו בין שניהן אלא א' רוצה וא' מעכב אין מחייבין אותו אלמא היזק ראיה לאו שמיה היזק: שרצו לחצות מיבעי ליה. כלומר אם איתא דמחיצה דמתני' פלוגתא אמאי תני לעשות ליתני לחצות בשלמא אי אמרת גודא אמטא להכי תני לעשות דלא מיתני בלא לעשות. ומשני לעולם מחיצה פלוגתא ודקא קשיא לך שרצו לחצות מיבעי ליה לא קשיא דמתני' משתעי בלשון בני אדם דאמרי תא ונעביד פלוגתא ולעולם היזק ראיה שמיה היזק: מאי אריא דתני מתני' רצו לחלוק מש"ה בונין את הכותל באמצע בעל כרחו משום היזק ראיה דהואיל דנתרצו לחלוק בונין אפי' לא רצו שניהן לחלוק הואיל דנתרצה א' מהן לחלוק בדין הוא דבונין את הכותל לאמצע אע"ג דלא נתרצה אידך משום היזק ראיה: משנתנו בשאין בה דין חלוקה שאין בה ד' אמות לזה וד' אמות לזה מש"ה אם נתרצו שניהן לחלוק בונין את הכותל בעל כרחו הואיל דנתרצו לחלוק משום היזק ראיה ואם לא נתרצו א' מהן לחלוק אע"ג דמעכב אידך אין בונין הואיל דאין בה דין חלוקה: תנינא. בסיפא דמתני' אימתי אמרי' דאין חלוקה הואיל דלית בה דין חלוקה בזמן שאין שניהן רוצין: במסיפס בעלמא. חולקין הואיל ונתרצו קמ"ל רישא דמתני' דקתני כותל דלא סגי בלא כותל משום היזק ראיה: וליתני הא רישא דמתני' ולא בעי סיפא למיתני. ומשני סיפא איצטריכא לה למיתני דקתני וכתבי הקדש לא יחלוקו. משום דקא נהוג בהו מנהג בזיון ואגב סיפא תני רישא אימתי בזמן כו': בשקנו מידן. דלא מצי למיהדר בהו: קנין דברים בעלמא הוא כלומר (אין זה) [איזהו] קנין הוא עיקר כגון מתנה או מכירה או שום דבר שמראה לו החפץ שנותן למקבל וקונין מידו על כך אבל הכא שאדם אומר לחבירו ניטול קנין שנחלוק כגון זה קנין דברים בעלמא הוא דלא נגמר על מה נוטל קנין ואכתי ליהדרו בהו: שקנו מידן ברוחות. דזה הקנה לזה אותו חלק שבצד רוח מזרח וזה לזה חלק שבצד רוח מערב דהיינו קנין גמור הואיל וידוע על מה קנו: רב אשי אומר מש"ה לא מצי למיהדר בהו הואיל דקני אע"ג דלית בה דין חלוקה כגון שהלך זה לאחר קנין להחזיק בחלקו דנעל גדר ופרץ כל שהוא ודאי בתר הכי לא מצי למיהדר: פיסקא גויל. אבנים שנחצבו מן ההר דעדיין לא משופין והם ו' טפחים: גזית. אבנים משופין והם ה' טפחים. כפיסין, ארחי חצי לבינה שלימה לבינה היא ג' טפחים. מקום שנהגו לבנות בגויל דמן ו' טפחים [illegible]

[illegible]

הגהות הב"ח

(א) גמ' כדכתיב ותהי מחצת: (ב) שם ואימא מאי מחיצה גודא כדתנן מחיצת הכרם שנפרצה אומר לו גדור מחיצה ונפרצה: (ג) שם מאי קמ"ל דכי לית ביה דין חלוקה) תא"מ ונ"ב ג"י תוס' שאין בה דין חלוקה: (ד) שם לא יחלוקו וכי רצו מאי הוי ניהדרו בהו כו' ובקנו מידן כו' לישנא אחרינא דלאשמעינן בשאין בה: (ה) שם למימרא דבגזית כל ב"ל ואות ד' נמחק: (ו) רש"י ד"ה קנין וכו' או מכר או מתנה: (ז) ד"ה בבנין שהיה גובהו ק' [illegible]

גליון הש"ס

גמרא כגון שהלך זה. עי' בתשובת רשב"א סי' אלף רכ"ו ול"ע:

הגהות מהר"ב רנשבורג

א] גמרא וכי קנו מידן מאי הוי. נ"ב עי' רש"י ד"ה קנין דברים כו' והתוס' ד"ה קנין כו' [illegible]

ליקוטי רש"י

[נדפס בעמוד הקודם]

תורה אור השלם

א) וַתְּהִי מֶחֱצַת הָעֵדָה מִן הַצֹּאן שְׁלֹשׁ מֵאוֹת אֶלֶף וּשְׁלֹשִׁים אֶלֶף שִׁבְעַת אֲלָפִים וַחֲמֵשׁ מֵאוֹת: [במדבר לא, מג]

ב) כָּל אֵלֶּה אֲבָנִים יְקָרֹת כְּמִדֹּת גָּזִית מְגֹרָרוֹת בַּמְּגֵרָה מִבַּיִת וּמִחוּץ וּמִמַּסָּד עַד הַטְּפָחוֹת וּמִחוּץ עַד הֶחָצֵר הַגְּדוֹלָה: [מלכים א ז, ט]

ג) גָּדוֹל יִהְיֶה כְּבוֹד הַבַּיִת הַזֶּה הָאַחֲרוֹן מִן הָרִאשׁוֹן אָמַר יְיָ צְבָאוֹת וּבַמָּקוֹם הַזֶּה אֶתֵּן שָׁלוֹם נְאֻם יְיָ צְבָאוֹת: [חגי ב, ט]

[illegible]

חשק שלמה על רבינו גרשום א) [נראה דל"ל בונין אותו בעל כרחו ...] ג) [נ"ל לריך לבנות בלמלע וכו']:

agreement?[16] דְּכִי לֵית בֵּיהּ דִּין חֲלוּקָה כִּי רָצוּ פְּלִיגִי – **That** partners must **divide** a courtyard **that is not subject to division once they have agreed** to do so?[17] תְּנֵינָא – This cannot be, for **we have learned** this ruling **from** another **Mishnah,**[18] which states: אֵימָתַי – WHEN must indivisible property remain whole? בִּזְמַן שֶׁאֵין שְׁנֵיהֶם רוֹצִים – WHEN BOTH partners DO NOT CONSENT to divide it. אֲבָל בִּזְמַן שֶׁשְּׁנֵיהֶם רוֹצִים – BUT WHEN THEY BOTH CONSENT to divide it, אֲפִילוּ פָּחוֹת מִכָּאן חוֹלְקִין – **even if** the property is **smaller than [the measure of divisibility], they** must proceed to **divide it** (unless both consent to abrogate the agreement). Thus, we cannot say that our Mishnah chose the case of an "indivisible" courtyard in order to teach this additional ruling. Why, then, did it not teach the the law of visual trespass with the case of the larger, divisible courtyard?

The Gemara answers:

אִי מֵהָתָם – **If** the "additional ruling" were derived **from there** (the Mishnah on 11a), הֲוָה אֲמִינָא אֲפִילוּ פָּחוֹת מִכָּאן – **I might have thought** that although an agreement to divide property **even smaller than [the measure of divisibility]** is binding, בְּמְסִיפַס בְּעָלְמָא – the division may be created **with an ordinary marker.**[19] קָא מַשְׁמַע לָן הָכָא כּוֹתֶל – The Mishnah **here** therefore **informs us** that once an agreement is reached to divide an "indivisible" courtyard, one partner can compel the other to build **a wall,** and neither partner can retract.

Still, the Gemara asks:

וְלִיתְנֵי הָא וְלָא לִיתְנֵי הַךְ – **But teach** only **this** Mishnah (on 2a),[20] **and do not teach that** other Mishnah (on 11a), which is at best superfluous and even unclear! – ? –

The Gemara answers:

סֵיפָא אִיצְטְרִיכָא לֵיהּ – The second Mishnah was taught because **the latter case** in that Mishnah **was needed,** for it states: וְכִתְבֵי הַקֹּדֶשׁ אַף עַל פִּי שֶׁשְּׁנֵיהֶם רוֹצִים לֹא יַחֲלוֹקוּ – BUT scrolls of THE HOLY SCRIPTURES MAY NOT BE DIVIDED, EVEN IF THEY BOTH CONSENT.[21] Hence, restating the law that an agreement to divide "indivisible" property is binding, while unnecessary in itself, does serve to introduce the case of Holy Scriptures as the exception to the rule.

The Gemara now records a variant text[22] of the previous discussion. This version commences at the point in the Gemara above where Rav Assi explained that the Mishnah is speaking of a courtyard that is not subject to legal division.[23]

(לִישָּׁנָא אַחֲרִינָא – In **another version** of the previous discussion, a question was raised regarding [R' Assi's] explanation: וכי) רצו מאי הוי ליהדר ביה אמר רב אסי אמר רבי יוחנן בשקנו מידו כו') אַדְּאַשְׁמְעִינָן בְּשֶׁאֵין בָּהּ דִּין חֲלוּקָה – **Instead of teaching** the law of visual trespass **in** the case of **[a courtyard] that is not subject to legal division,** וְהוּא דְּרָצוּ – and therefore dealing **only** with a case **where [the partners] agreed** to divide the courtyard,[24] לִישְׁמְעִינַן בְּיֵשׁ בָּהּ דִּין חֲלוּקָה – **let [the Mishnah] teach** the law of visual trespass as it applies **to [a courtyard] that *is* subject to legal division,** וְאַף עַל גַּב דְּלָא רָצוּ – **and** then the ruling would apply **even when [the partners] did not agree** to divide, since either partner has the right to force division of a large courtyard. – ? –

The Gemara answers:

אִי אַשְׁמְעִינַן בְּיֵשׁ בָּהּ דִּין חֲלוּקָה – **If [the Mishnah] would teach** the law of visual trespass as it applies **to [a courtyard] that is subject to legal division,** וְאַף עַל גַּב דְּלָא רָצוּ – **and** the ruling that visual trespass mandates the building of a wall would apply **even though [the partners] did not agree** to divide, הֲוָה אֲמִינָא – **I would have** mistakenly **said** שֶׁאֵין בָּהּ דִּין חֲלוּקָה – that **regarding [a courtyard] that is not subject to legal division,** אֲפִילוּ רָצוּ נַמִּי לֹא – even if they agreed to divide the courtyard, one partner still **cannot** force the other to build a wall.[25] קָא מַשְׁמַע לָן – **[The Mishnah]** therefore speaks of a courtyard that is not subject to legal division to **inform us** that once an agreement to divide is made, a wall must be built.

The Gemara questions whether such a conclusion is defensible even if the Mishnah had not chosen the case of "indivisible" courtyard to prove it incorrect:

וּמִי מָצֵית אָמְרַתְּ הָכִי – **But are you able to say this** [i.e. that without the Mishnah's specific ruling to the contrary, the law could be that agreement to divide an "indivisible" courtyard would not bind the partner to construct a wall]? וְהָא קָתָנֵי סֵיפָא – **But it is taught in the latter case:**[26] אֵימָתַי – WHEN must indivisible property remain whole? בִּזְמַן שֶׁאֵין שְׁנֵיהֶם רוֹצִים – WHEN BOTH partners DO NOT CONSENT to divide it. אֲבָל בִּזְמַן שֶׁשְּׁנֵיהֶם רוֹצִים – BUT WHEN THEY BOTH CONSENT to divide it, יַחֲלוֹקוּ – even if the property is smaller than the measure of divisibility,[27] THEY must proceed to DIVIDE IT (unless both consent to abrogate the agreement). מַאי לָאו אַכּוֹתֶל – **Is this** ruling ("they must divide") **not** referring **to** the type of division mentioned in the

NOTES

16. I.e. if the Mishnah wishes to teach only that visual trespass is injurious, it should have done so with the case of a larger, divisible courtyard, instructing that even though one partner is *unwilling* to divide, the other may compel him to do so, and to then erect a wall between their properties. Since the Mishnah eschewed this more novel elucidation of the law of visual trespass, it must have intended an additional teaching that only the case of an "indivisible" courtyard could convey. The Gemara seeks to demonstrate, however, that no such additional teaching exists (*Tosafos, Ramban, Rashba* et al.).

17. I.e. that once they have committed themselves to divide the courtyard, neither may abrogate the agreement by claiming that his consent was based on the mistaken belief that he could tolerate the cramped quarters of the divided courtyard (*Rashba, Chidushei HaRan*).

18. This other Mishnah, which appears below (on 11a), establishes the measure of divisibility for various types of real property. The section quoted by the Gemara modifies the general rule stated there: *Anything that is divided and retains its name, we divide; but if not, we do not divide it.*

19. Because either partner could claim that his consent to divide was based on the assumption that he would not be required to build a wall (*Tosafos* above, 2b ד״ה וכיון, and *Maharam* here).

20. Which teaches both that an agreement to divide an "indivisible" courtyard is binding and that neither partner can retract, and that they are required agreement binds them to build a wall.

21. For to cut up and divide a scroll of the Prophets or Writings constitutes an indignity (*Rashi* to 11a and 13b). However, separate scrolls may be divided among partners by mutual consent.

22. Our Gemara (i.e. the *Vilna Shas*; see also *Mesoras HaShas*) presents this entire section in parentheses, thus indicating that it should be omitted. *Maharam*, however, writes that only a small segment is invalid, but that the rest of the section (which our texts leave in parentheses) is part of the valid text (see also *Dikdukei Sofrim*). We have therefore punctuated and translated only that segment which *Maharam* deems valid, and left the segment which even he considers incorrect without punctuation or translation.

23. This variant text of the Gemara's discussion does not differ from the preceding version in any essential matter, and comes to the same conclusions as the first version. The difference between the versions lies only in their presentation of the various difficulties that arise.

24. For one partner cannot force the other to divide an "indivisible" courtyard.

25. See note 19.

26. I.e. to the first section of the second Mishnah (on 11a).

27. The Gemara paraphrases the Mishnah here, omitting the words אֲפִילוּ פָּחוֹת מִכָּאן.

ט א ב ג ד מיי' פ"ב מהל' שכנים הל' יד סמג עשין פב טוש"ע ח"מ סי' קנז סעיף א: י ד ה ו מיי' שם הל' י טוש"ע שם סעיף ב:

דאיצטנע מינך לישנא אחרינא אמרי לה סברוה מאי מחיצה פלוגתא (א) דכתיב א) ותהי מחצת העדה *וכיון דרצו בונין את הכותל בעל כורחן אלמא היזק ראיה שמיה היזק (ג) אימא מאי מחיצה גודא (דתנן) מחיצת הכרם שנפרצה אומר לו גדור נפרצה אומר לו גדור נתיאש הימנה ולא גדרה הרי זה קידש וחייב באחריותה וטעמא דרצו הא לא רצו אין מחייבין אותו אלמא היזק ראיה לאו שמיה היזק אי הכי בונין את הכותל בונין אותו מבעי ליה אלא מאי פלוגתא אי הכי שרצו לעשות מחיצה שרצו לחצות מבעי ליה כדאמרי אינשי תא נעביד פלוגתא ואי היזק ראיה שמיה היזק מאי איריא רצו אפי' לא רצו נמי א"ר אסי א"ר יוחנן משנתנו בשאין בה דין חלוקה והוא דרצו מאי קמ"ל (ג) דכי לית ביה דין חלוקה כי רצו פליגי תנינא אימתי בזמן שאין שניהם רוצים אבל בזמן ששניהם רוצים אפילו פחות מכאן חולקין אי מהתם הוה אמינא אפילו פחות מכאן במסיפס בעלמא קמ"ל הכא כותל וליתני הא ולא ליתני הך סיפא איצטריכא ליה וכתבי הקדש אע"פ ששניהם רוצים לא יחלוקו (ד) (ל"א וכי רצו מאי הוי ליהדר ביה אמר רב אסי א"ר יוחנן בשקנו מידו כו' אדאשמעינן בשאין בה דין חלוקה והוא דרצו לישמעינן ביש בה דין חלוקה ואע"ג דלא רצו אי אשמעינן ביש בה דין חלוקה ואע"ג דלא רצו הוה אמינא שאין בה דין חלוקה אפילו רצו נמי לא קמ"ל ומי מצית אמרת הכי והא קתני סיפא אימתי בזמן שאין שניהם רוצים אבל בזמן ששניהם רוצים יחלוקו מאי לאו אכותל לא אמסיפס בעלמא וליתני האי ולא ליתני האי סיפא אצטריכא ליה ובכתבי הקדש אע"פ ששניהם רוצים לא יחלוקו): במאי אוקימתא למתני' בשאין בה דין חלוקה אי בשאין בה דין חלוקה כי רצו מאי הוי נהדרו בהו א"ר אסי א"ר יוחנן שקנו מידן וכי קנו מידן מאי הוי קנין דברים בעלמא הוא בשקנו מידן ברוחות רב אשי אמר כגון שהלך זה בתוך שלו והחזיק וזה בתוך שלו והחזיק: מקום שנהגו לבנות כו': גויל אבני דלא משפיא גזית אבני דמשפיא דכתיב ב) כל אלה אבנים יקרות כמדות גזית (וגו') כפיסין ארחי לבנין ליבני אמר ליה רבה בריה דרבא לרב אשי ממאי דגויל אבני דלא משפיא נינהו והאי טפח יתירא למורשא דקרנתא דילמא פלגא דגזית הוא והאי טפח יתירא לביני אורבי הוא כדקאמרינן כפיסין ארחי לבנין ליבני והאי טפח יתירא לביני אורבי אמר ליה וליטעמיך כפיסין ארחי מנלן אלא גמרא גמירי לה גויל נמי אבני דלא משפיא גמרא גמירי לה איכא דאמרי אמר ליה רב אחא בריה דרב אויא לרב אשי ממאי דהאי כפיסין ארחי נינהו והאי טפח יתירא לביני אורבי דילמא מאי כפיסין אבני דלא משפיין והאי טפח יתירא למורשא דקרנתא כדקאמרינן גויל אבני דלא משפיין גזית אבני דמשפיין והאי טפח יתירא למורשא דקרנתא אמר ליה וליטעמיך גויל אבני דלא משפיין מנלן אלא גמרא גמירי לה הכא נמי גמרא גמירי לה אמר אביי שמע מינה כל ביני אורבי טפח הני מילי בטינא אבל בריכסא בעי טפי ואיכא דאמרי הני מילי בריכסא אבל בטינא לא בעי כולי האי למימרא דבגזית (ה) דכל ד' אמות גובה אי הוי פותיא חמשא קאי אי לא לא קאי והא אמה טרקסין דהואי גבוה תלתין אמתא ולא הוה פותיא אלא שית פושכי וקם וכיון דאיכא טפח יתירא קאי ובמקדש שני מ"ט לא עבוד אמה טרקסין כי קאי בתלתין קאי טפי לא קאי ומנלן דהוה גבוה טפי דכתיב ג) גדול יהיה כבוד הבית הזה האחרון מן הראשון רב ושמואל ואמרי לה ר' יוחנן ור"א חד אמר בבנין וחד אמר

רש"י

דאיצטנע מינך. דברי הלנע אבל אחר החלוקה לתרוייהו קביעא תשמישתי' לכל אחד בחלקו כל שעה ולא עבדי בה מילי דלנעא: כיון דרצו. לחלוק ולקמן פריך מאי איריא רצו אפילו לא רצו הרי הן יכולין לכוף זה את זה: בונין כותל. של אבנים: גודא. כותל אבנים ובמאי שיש בה דין חלוקה ועל כרחן חולקים: וטעמא דרצו. שהתנו לחלוקה בכותל אבנים הא לא רצו אין מחייבין אותו אלא מסיפס בעלמא: כדאמרי אינשי כו'. מירולא הוא: שאין בה דין חלוקה. ד' אמות לא יחלוקו: ובכתבי הקדש. ספר תורה שהוא בכרך אחד וכן נביאים וכתובים הכתובים בגליון כס"ת: קנין דברים הוא. ואין חליפין קונין אלא דבר הנקנה או (ו) מכר או מתנה או שעבוד קרקעות שסקנין על עליו או מטלטלין: ברוחות. זה בורר לו חלק מזרחי וזה בורר לו חלק מערבי וקנו מידם ומעתה נקנה חלק מזרחי לזה ואין לזה חלק בו וכן השני לחבירו: והחזיק. בחלקו רפק ביה פורתא וקרקע נקנה בחזקה אחרי אשר רצו בשעת חלוקה: אריח. חצי לבינה והלבינה ג' טפחים והאריח טפח ומחצה ועובי הכותל אריח מכאן ואריח מכאן וטפח באמצע שנותן שם טיט לחברו: לבינים ליבני. שלימות לבינה לעובי הכותל: למורשא דקרנתא. ראשי האבנים בולטות לחוץ שאינן חלוקות ולהכי בעי רוחב טפח יתירה: לביני אורבי. בין דימוס מכאן ובין דימוס מכאן ונותן טיט באמצע: ה"ג אימא לביני דלא משפיין: ש"מ כו'. ונפקא מינה למקבל עליו לבנות כותל לחבירו: בריכסא. אבנים דקות וטיט בין שני הדימוסות: למימרא דבגזית כו' כל ד' אמות גובה אי הוה פותיא ה' טפחים קאי ואי לא לא קאי. כדתנן במתני' בגזית זה נותן טפחיים ומחצה וזה נותן טפחיים ומחצה וקתני סיפא מחייבין אותו לבנותו עד ד' אמות ולפי חשבון זה לגובה שמנה צריך י' טפחים רוחב: והא אמה טרקסין. דבנין שלמה בגזית הוה דכתיב אבני גזית (מלכים א ה) והוי שלשים אמה קומתה ואין עוביו אלא אמה להבדיל בין ההיכל לקדשי הקדשים: דאיכא טפח יתירא. ומשום האי טפח פותיא מצי לאגבוה טובא ואין צריך לתת לכל ארבע אמות ה' טפחים רוחב: בבנין. שהיה גובהו (ז) מאה אמה כדתנן במסכת מדות (פרק ד מ"ו):

תוספות

מאי קא משמע לן בשאין בה דין חלוקה. אע"ג דקא משמע לן דשמיה היזק ה"ס מאי קמ"ל במאי דאיירי באין בה דין חלוקה לישמעינן בשיש בה דין חלוקה [אע"ג דלא רצו] (כשרצו) פליגי תימה הא קמ"ל דאפילו באין בה דין חלוקה כו' למימר על מנת לעשות גודא לא מיתרצו לכפייהו לעיל: כי רצו מאי הוי ניהדרו בהו. למ"ד מחיצה גודא לא פריך דאיכא למימר דקנו ושיעבדו נכסיהן לבנין הכותל אלא למ"ד פלוגתא לא מהני קנין דקנין דברים בעלמא הוא דלא מסיק אדעתיה שקנו ברוחות: קנין דברים בעלמא הוא. בפרק השוכר את הפועלים (ב"מ דף עו:) דתנן מתנה ש"מ להיות כשואל ומוקי לה בקנו מידו התם לאו קנין דברים הוא אלא קנין גמור הוא שמשעבד את עצמו שאם יאנס ישלם: רב אשי אמר כגון שהלך כו'. תימה לר"י מה בא רב אשי להוסיף ומי איצטריך לאשמועינן דחזקה מועלת כמו קנין ונראה לר"י דהא קמ"ל דאע"ג דקאמר לקמן בחזקת הבתים (דף נג.) שלא בפניו צריך למימר לו לך חזק וקני הכא כיון שאמרו אתה תקח רוח צפונית ואני רוח דרומית והלך והחזיק לו כל אחד בשלו זה שלא בפני זה נעשה כמי שקנו מידם ברוחות אע"פ שלא אמרו זה לזה לך חזק וקני: ארבע אמות גובה אפותיא דה' קאי טפי לא קאי. וקשיא לר"ת הא לבנין דגריעי קאי בשלשה טפחים ועוד דהא קא חזינן דקאי בגזית טפי אפורתא ותירץ ר"ת דקאמר טפי לא קאי כמשפט גזית שרוצים בני אדם לבנותו שיעמוד ימים רבים כשבונים בגזית: טרקסין. אומר ר"ת דטרק הוי כמו טרוקי גלי (ברכות דף כח.) וסין הוי סיני כלומר שהיה מפסיק וסוגר את הלוחות שנתנו בסיני שהיו מונחות בארון שהיה בבית קדשי הקדשים וי"מ טרקסין פנים וחוץ שאותה אמה היתה ספק אם מקודשת פנים או חוץ ולכך היו שם שתי פרוכות כדאמרינן ביומא (דף נא:) שאני התם דאיכא טפח יתירא. ה"מ אתא לאגבוה תקרה ומעזיבה קאי טפי כדאמרי' בסמוך:

רבינו גרשום

ל"א [מפיך] כולה הלכה דכיון שרצו לחלוק אם מעכב א' מלעשות כותל בונין אותו בעל כרחו: א) וטעמא דרצו לעשות [כותל] מש"ה בונין הא לא רצו בין שניהן אלא א' רוצה וא' מעכב אין מחייבין אותו אלמא היזק ראיה לאו שמיה היזק: שרצו לחצות מיבעי ליה. כלומר אם איתא דמחיצה דמתני' פלוגתא אמאי תני לעשות ליתני לחצות בשלמא אי אמרת גודא אמטא להכי תני לעשות דלא מיתני בלא לעשות. ומשני לעולם מחיצה פלוגתא ודקא קשיא לך שרצו לחצות מיבעי ליה לא קשיא דמתני' משתעי בלשון בני אדם דאמרי תא ונעביד פלוגתא ולעולם היזק ראיה שמיה היזק: מאי אריא דתני מתני' רצו לחלוק מש"ה בונין את הכותל באמצע בעל כרחו משום היזק ראיה דהואיל דנתרצו לחלוק בונין אפי' לא רצו שניהן לחלוק הואיל דנתרצה א' מהן לחלוק בדין הוא דבונין את הכותל לאמצע אע"ג דלא נתרצה אידך משום היזק ראיה: משנתנו בשאין בה דין חלוקה שאין בה ד' אמות לזה וד' אמות לזה מש"ה אם נתרצו שניהן לחלוק בונין את הכותל בעל כורחו הואיל דנתרצו לחלוק משום היזק ראיה ואם לא נתרצה א' מהן לחלוק אע"ג דמעכב אידך אין בונין הואיל דאין בה דין חלוקה: תנינא. בסיפא דמתני' אימתי אמרי' דאין חלוקה הואיל דלית בה דין חלוקה בזמן שאין שניהן רוצין: במסיפס בעלמא. חולקין הואיל ונתרצו קמ"ל רישא דמתני' דקתני כותל דלא סגי בלא כותל משום היזק ראיה: וליתני הא רישא דמתני' ולא בעי סיפא למיתני. ומשני סיפא איצטריכא לה למיתני דקתני וכתבי הקדש לא יחלוקו. משום דקא נהוג בהו מנהג בזיון ואגב סיפא דלא סגי דלא ליתני קתני רישא אימתי בזמן כו': בשקנו מידן. דלא מצי למיהדר בהו: קנין דברים בעלמא הוא כלומר (אין זה) [איזה] קנין הוא עיקר כגון מתנה או מכירה או שום דבר שמראה לו החפץ שנותן למקבל וקונין מידו על כך אבל הכא שאדם אומר לחבירו ניטול קנין שנחלוק כגון זה קנין דברים בעלמא הוא דלא נברר על מה נוטל קנין ואכתי ליהדרו בהו: שקנו מידן ברוחות. דזה הקנה לזה אותו חלק שבצד רוח מזרח וזה לזה חלק שבצד רוח מערב דהיינו קנין גמור הואיל והוברר על מה קנו: רב אשי אומר מש"ה לא מצי למיהדר בהו הואיל דקני אע"ג דלית בה דין חלוקה כגון שהלך זה לאחר קנין החזיק בחלקו לנעל גדר ופרץ כל שהוא ודאי בתר הכי לא מצי למיהדר: פיסקא גויל. אבנים שנחצבו מן ההר דעדיין אין משופין והם ו' טפחים: גזית. אבנים משופין והן של ה' טפחים. כפיסין, ארחי חצי לבינה

תורה אור השלם

א) וַתְּהִי מֶחֱצַת הָעֵדָה מִן הַצֹּאן שְׁלֹשׁ מֵאוֹת אֶלֶף וּשְׁלֹשִׁים אֶלֶף שִׁבְעַת אֲלָפִים וַחֲמֵשׁ מֵאוֹת: [במדבר לא, מג]

ב) כָּל אֵלֶּה אֲבָנִים יְקָרֹת כְּמִדֹּת גָּזִית מְגֹרָרוֹת בַּמְּגֵרָה מִבַּיִת וּמִחוּץ וּמִמַּסָּד עַד הַטְּפָחוֹת וּמִחוּץ עַד הֶחָצֵר הַגְּדוֹלָה: [מלכים א ז, ט]

ג) גָּדוֹל יִהְיֶה כְּבוֹד הַבַּיִת הַזֶּה הָאַחֲרוֹן מִן הָרִאשׁוֹן אָמַר יְיָ צְבָאוֹת וּבַמָּקוֹם הַזֶּה אֶתֵּן שָׁלוֹם נְאֻם יְיָ צְבָאוֹת: [חגי ב, ט]

previous Mishnah — namely, division by construction of **a wall?**[28] It would be impossible, then, to conclude mistakenly that an agreement to divide does not bind them to build a wall in an "indivisible courtyard." Why, then, can the Mishnah not speak of a larger courtyard?

The Gemara replies:

לא — I would **not** conclude from the latter case (i.e. the Mishnah on 11a) that the partners are bound to build a wall; **אַמְסִיפָס בְּעָלְמָא** — rather, I would assume that they are bound to divide the courtyard by means **of an ordinary marker.** It would still be possible, however, to assume that in an "indivisible" courtyard an agreement to divide does not bind them to build a wall; thus, our Mishnah chose to teach the case of such a courtyard to illustrate that even in "indivisible" courtyards an agreement to divide binds them to build a wall.[29]

Still, the Gemara asks:

לִיתְנֵי הַאי וְלֹא לִיתְנֵי הַאי — **But teach** only **this Mishnah** (on 2a), **and do not teach that Mishnah** (on 11a)? Once our Mishnah teaches us that even the agreement to divide binds them to build a wall, it is superfluous to teach us that the agreement to divide cannot be abrogated. — ? —

The Gemara answers:

סֵיפָא אִיצְטְרִיכָא לֵיהּ — The second Mishnah was taught because **the latter case** in that Mishnah **was needed,** for it states: **וּבְכִתְבֵי הַקֹּדֶשׁ אַף עַל פִּי שֶׁשְּׁנֵיהֶם רוֹצִים לֹא יַחֲלוֹקוּ** — BUT scrolls of THE HOLY SCRIPTURES MAY NOT BE DIVIDED EVEN IF THEY BOTH CONSENT.[30] Hence, restating the law that an agreement to divide "indivisible" property is binding, while unnecessary in itself, does serve to introduce the case of Holy Scriptures as the exception to the rule.)

The Gemara continues to challenge Rav Assi's explanation of the Mishnah's case:

בְּמַאי אוֹקִימְתָּא לְמַתְנִיתִין — **What** case **have you established the Mishnah** to be discussing? **בְּשֶׁאֵין בָּהּ דִּין חֲלוּקָה** — The case of a courtyard **that is not subject to legal division.** **אִי בְּשֶׁאֵין בָּהּ דִּין חֲלוּקָה** — **If** it is discussing a courtyard **that is not subject to legal division,** **כִּי רָצוּ מַאי הָוֵי** — **what does it matter if they agreed** to divide? **נֶהְדְּרוּ בְּהוּ** — **They can** always **recant!**[31]

Rav Assi offers an answer:

אָמַר רַב אַסִּי אָמַר רַבִּי יוֹחָנָן — **Rav Assi said in the name of R' Yochanan:** **שֶׁקָּנוּ מִיָּדָן** — The Mishnah speaks of a case **where** the partners **"acquired" from one another**[32] to formalize their agreement. With this act the agreement becomes irrevocable, for each partner "acquires" the commitment of the other to divide, and so neither can retract his word.

The Gemara questions this explanation:

וְכִי קָנוּ מִיָּדָן מַאי הָוֵי — **But what does it matter if they "acquired" from one another?** **קִנְיַן דְּבָרִים בְּעָלְמָא הוּא** — **It is an acquisition of mere words** — and *chalifin* can work to transfer only tangible items, which are acquired by sale, gift or lien. Hence, even if their promises to divide were conveyed by *chalifin,* no binding agreement was created.

The Gemara answers:

בְּשֶׁקָּנוּ מִיָּדָן בְּרוּחוֹת — In the Mishnah's case **they "acquired" from one another** their respective **sides** in the courtyard.[33] These acquisitions accomplish the division, thus rendering retraction an impossibility.

Rav Ashi offers an alternative approach:

רַב אַשִׁי אָמַר — **Rav Ashi says:** **כְּגוֹן שֶׁהָלַךְ זֶה בְּתוֹךְ שֶׁלּוֹ וְהֶחֱזִיק** — The Mishnah refers to a case **where this** partner went **into his** half of the courtyard and **performed an** act of ***chazakah,***[34] thereby acquiring his half irrevocably, **וְזֶה בְּתוֹךְ שֶׁלּוֹ וְהֶחֱזִיק** — **and this** other partner **went into his** half of the courtyard **and performed an** act of ***chazakah.***[35] These acts of acquisition, too, accomplish the division of the courtyard and eliminate the possibility of retraction.[36]

NOTES

28. *Maharam* explains the question as follows: Once the first Mishnah would have taught regarding a divisible courtyard that visual trespass is considered injurious and that a wall must be built to protect against it, we would have understood the ruling of the second Mishnah in the same light. Thus, the second Mishnah's ruling would be that an "indivisible" courtyard is the same as a "divisible" courtyard once an agreement to divide is in place, and that there would be a requirement to build a wall.

29. And neither partner can claim that he agreed to divide only with an ordinary marker (see note 19).

30. See note 21.

31. The Gemara is asking its question according to the explanation that the Mishnah is asking of where they agreed to divide the "indivisible" courtyard. However the same question may be asked according to the explanation that the Mishnah is speaking where they agreed to build a wall; why are they not able to recant? (*Rashi* above 2b ד״ה וטעימא דרצו, and *Rashba* there; cf. *Tosafos* ד״ה כי).

[However, the next question of the Gemara would not be posed according to that explanation. For since each one is obligating himself to build the wall through an act of acquisition (*chalifin*), he is, in effect, creating a lien on his property to build it. Thus, each one is aquiring the rights to the other's property, for the building of the wall, which constitutes a proper legal acquisition. This would not be considered an "acquisition of words," as it is in the case where they agreed to divide the courtyard. (*Rashba* ibid. in explanation of *Rashi* there; see also *Tosafos* ibid.)]

32. The Gemara refers to an act of acquisition called *chalifin*, "exchange," whereby the buyer typically hands the seller a small item, such as a glove or handkerchief, and in exchange acquires title to the object being sold. Hence, the seller may not subsequently repudiate the sale and withhold the object. See *Ruth* 4:7-8, where Boaz used *chalifin* to transfer the inheritance of Elimelech. Similarly, in our Mishnah, *chalifin* is used to transfer the "word" of each partner (i.e. his agreement to divide) to the other, so that neither can retract it.

33. I.e. each partner selects one particular side of the courtyard and acquires the other's property rights in that half through an act of *chalifin* (*Rashi*).

This, in fact, was the meaning of R' Assi's answer all along. The Gemara, however, did not initially comprehend his reply.

34. One of the methods of acquiring real estate involves performing an act of *improving* the property, such as enclosing it with a fence or plowing it in preparation for planting. This act of acquisition is called *chazakah* (*Rashi,* and see *Kiddushin* 26a).

35. Although the Gemara says that each partner performs a *chazakah*, it does not mean that both are required to do so. Rather, once one of them performs an act of acquisition in his half, his interest in the other half automatically reverts to his former partner (*Rosh, Nimukei Yosef*).

However, some commentators accept the Gemara's case at face value, because they rule that the type of *chazakah* made here need not be the full *chazakah* normally required for acquisition. Since the partners already own the land and are now only dividing it, it is sufficient for each of them to walk along the borders of his share. Since this *chazakah* is inferior to the standard *chazakah*, however, they must both perform the act in order for it to be effective [and it is for this reason that the Gemara speaks of both having made a *chazakah*] (*Beis Yosef* to *Choshen Mishpat* 157, from *Hagahos Maimonios*).

36. Seemingly, Rav Ashi provides no new insight here, for obviously *chazakah* will just as effectively precipitate the courtyard's division as will *chalifin. Tosafos* (ד״ה רב) therefore explain that, ordinarily, the seller must expressly direct the purchaser to perform the act of *chazakah* if he will not actually witness it. Here, however, neither partner was present when the other performed *chazakah* in his half of the courtyard. Rav Ashi therefore informs us that their verbal agreement to divide the courtyard by each performing *chazakah* in his side effectively substitutes for the requisite verbal directive from the seller (see also *Rosh*).

דאיצטנע מינך לישנא אחרינא אמרי לה סברוה מאי מחיצה פלוגתא (א) דכתיב א) ותהי מחצת העדה א וכיון דרצו בונין את הכותל בעל כורחן אלמא ב היזק ראיה שמיה היזק (ג) אימא מאי מחיצה גודא א) (דתנן) ג) מחיצת הכרם שנפרצה אומר לו גדור נפרצה אומר לו גדור נתיאש הימנה ולא גדרה הרי זה קידש וחייב באחריותה וטעמא דרצו הא לא רצו אין מחייבין אותו אלמא היזק ראיה לאו שמיה היזק אי הכי בונין את הכותל בונין אותו מבעי ליה אלא מאי פלוגתא אי הכי שרצו לעשות מחיצה שרצו לחצות מבעי ליה כדאמרי אינשי תא נעביד פלוגתא ואי היזק ראיה שמיה היזק מאי איריא רצו אפי' לא רצו נמי א"ר אסי א"ר יוחנן משנתנו ג כשאין בה דין חלוקה והוא דרצו מאי קמ"ל (ג) דכי לית ביה דין חלוקה כי רצו פליגי תנינא ג) אימתי בזמן שאין שניהם רוצים אבל בזמן ששניהם רוצים אפילו פחות מכאן חולקין אי מהתם הוה אמינא אפילו פחות מכאן במסיפס בעלמא קמ"ל הכא כותל וליתני הא ולא ליתני הך סיפא איצטריכא ליה ד) וכתבי הקדש אע"פ ששניהם רוצים לא יחלוקו ה) (ד) (ל"א וכי רצו מאי הוי ליהדר ביה אמר רב אסי א"ר יוחנן בשקנו מידו כו' אדאשמעינן בשאין בה דין חלוקה והוא דרצו לישמעינן ביש בה דין חלוקה ואע"ג דלא רצו אי אשמעינן ביש בה דין חלוקה ואע"ג דלא רצו הוה אמינא שאין בה דין חלוקה אפילו רצו נמי לא קמ"ל ומי מצית אמרת הכי והא קתני סיפא אימתי בזמן שאין שניהם רוצים אבל בזמן ששניהם רוצים יחלוקו מאי לאו אכותל לא אמסיפס בעלמא ליתני האי ולא ליתני האי סיפא אצטריכא ליה ובכתבי הקדש אע"פ ששניהם רוצים לא יחלוקו): במאי אוקימתא למתני' בשאין בה דין חלוקה אי בשאין בה דין חלוקה כי רצו מאי הוי נהדרו בהו א"ר אסי א"ר יוחנן ו) שקנו מידן אז ד וכי קנו מידן מאי הוי קנין דברים בעלמא הוא ה בשקנו מידן ברוחות רב אשי אמר ו כגון שהלך זה בתוך שלו והחזיק וזה בתוך שלו והחזיק: מקום שנהגו לבנות כו': ז) גויל אבני דלא משפיא גזית אבני דמשפיא דכתיב ב) כל אלה אבנים יקרות כמדות גזית ח) (וגו') כפיסין ארחי לבינין ליבני אמר ליה רבה בריה דרבא לרב אשי ממאי דגויל אבני דלא משפיא נינהו והאי טפח יתירא למורשא דקרנתא דילמא פלגא דגזית הוא והאי טפח יתירא לביני אורבי הוא דכדאמרינן כפיסין ארחי לבינין ליבני והאי טפח יתירא לביני אורבי אמר ליה וליטעמיך כפיסין ארחי מנלן אלא גמרא גמירי לה הכא נמי גמרא גמירי לה איכא דאמרי אמר ליה רב אחא בריה דרב אויא לרב אשי ממאי דהאי כפיסין ארחי נינהו והאי טפח יתירא לביני אורבי דילמא מאי כפיסין אבני דלא משפיין והאי טפח יתירא למורשא דקרנתא כדקאמרינן גויל אבני דלא משפיין גזית אבני דמשפיין והאי טפח יתירא למורשא דקרנתא אמר ליה וליטעמיך גויל אבני דלא משפיין מנלן אלא גמרא גמירי לה הכא נמי גמרא גמירי לה אמר אביי שמע מינה כל ביני אורבי טפח הני מילי בטינא אבל בריכסא בעי טפי ואיכא דאמרי הני מילי בריכסא אבל בטינא לא בעי כולי האי למימרא דבגזית (ה) דכל ד' אמות גובה אי הוי פותיא חמשא קאי אי לא לא קאי והא אמה טרקסין דהואי גבוה תלתין אמהתא ולא הוה פותיא אלא שית פושכי וקם כיון דאיכא טפח יתירא קאי ובמקדש שני מ"ט לא עבוד אמה טרקסין כי קאי בתלתין קאי טפי לא קאי ומנלן דהוה גבוה טפי דכתיב ג) גדול יהיה כבוד הבית הזה האחרון מן הראשון רב ושמואל ואמרי לה ר' יוחנן ור"א חד אמר בבנין וחד אמר

רש"י

דאיצטנע מינך. דברי הלעג אבל אחר החלוקה לתרוייהו קביעא תשמישתי' לכל אחד בחלקו כל שעה ולא עבדי מילי דלגנאי: **כיון דרצו.** לחלוק ולקמן פריך מאי איריא רצו אפילו לא רצו הרי הן יכולין לכוף זה את זה: **בונין כותל.** של אבנים: **גודא.** כותל אבנים ובתר שיש בה דין חלוקה ועל כרחן חולקים: **וטעמא דרצו.** שהסכימו לחלוקה בכותל אבנים הא לא רצו אין מחייבין אותו אלא מסיפס בעלמא: **כדאמרי אינשי כו'.** מילתא היא: **שאין בה דין חלוקה.** שאין בו ד' אמות לזה ולזה: **וכתבי הקדש.** ספר תורה שהוא בכרך אחד וכן נביאים וכתובים הכתובים בגליון אחד: **קנין דברים הוא.** ואין קונין אלא דבר הנקנה או (ו) מכר או מתנה או שעבוד קרקעות שהקנין חל עליו או מטלטלין: **ברוחות.** זה בורר לו חלק מזרחי וזה בורר לו חלק מערבי וקנו מידם ומעתה נקנה חלק מזרחי לזה ואין לזה חלק בו וכן השני לחבירו: **והחזיק.** בחלקו דפק ביה פורתא וקרקע נקנה בחזקה ואחרי אשר רצו לא בשעת חלוקה: **אריח.** חצי לבינה והלבינה ג' טפחים והאריח טפח ומחצה ועובי הכותל אריח מכאן ואריח מכאן וטפח באמצע שנותן שם טיט לחברו: **לבינים ליבני.** שלימות לבינה לעובי הכותל: **למורשא דקרנתא.** ראשי האבנים בולטות לחוץ שאינן חלקות ולכך בעי רוחב טפח יתירה: **לביני אורבי.** בין דימוס שמכאן ובין דימוס שמכאן ונותן טיט באמצע: ה"ג אימא לביני דלא משפיין: **ש"מ כו'.** ונפקא מינה למקבל עליו לבנות כותל לחבירו: **בריכסא.** אבנים דקות וטיט בין שני הדימוסות: **למימרא דבגזית כו'** כל ד' אמות גובה אי הוה פותיא ה' טפחים קאי ואי לא לא קאי. כדתנן במתני' בגזית זה נותן ב' טפחים ומחצה וזה נותן טפחים ומחצה וקתני סיפא מחייבין אותן לבנותו עד ד' אמות ולפי חשבון זה לגובה שמנה צריך י' טפחים רוחב: **והא אמה טרקסין.** דבנין שלמה דגזית הוה דכתיב אבני גזית (מלכים א ה) והוי שלשים אמה קומתה ואין עוביו אלא אמה להבדיל בין ההיכל לקדשי הקדשים: **דאיכא טפח יתירא.** ומשום האי טפח פותיא מלי לאגבוה טובא ואין צריך לתת לכל ארבע אמות ה' טפחים רוחב: **בבנין.** שהיה גובהו (ז) מאה אמות כדתנן במסכת מדות (פרק ד מ"ו):

תוספות

מאי קא משמע לן בשאין בה דין חלוקה. אע"ג דקא משמע לן דשמיה היזק ה"פ מאי קמ"ל במאי דאיירי באין בה דין חלוקה לישמעינן בשיש בה דין חלוקה [אע"ג דלא רצו] (כשרצו) פלגי ט) תימה הא קמ"ל דאפילו באין בה דין חלוקה דאיכא למימר על מנת לעשות גודא לא איתרצאי כדפירש לעיל: **כי** רצו מאי הוי ניהדרו בהו. למ"ד מחיצה גודא לא פריך דאיכא למימר דקנו ושיעבדו נכסיהן לבנין הכותל אלא למ"ד פלוגתא לא מהני קנין דקנין דברים בעלמא הוא דלא מסיק אדעתיה שקנו ברוחות: **קנין** דברים בעלמא הוא. בפרק השוכר את הפועלים (ב"מ דף צד.) דתנן מתנה ש"ח להיות כשואל ומוקי לה בקנו מידו התם לאו קנין דברים הוא אלא קנין גמור הוא שמשעבד את עצמו שאם יאנס שישלם ל): **רב** אשי אמר כגון שהלך כו'. תימה לר"י מה בא רב אשי להוסיף וכי איצטריך לאשמועינן דחזקה מועלת כמו קנין ונראה לר"י דהא קמ"ל דאע"ג דקאמר לקמן בחזקת הבתים (דף נג.) שלא בפניו צריך למימר לו לך חזק וקני הכא כיון שאמרו אתה תקח רוח צפונית ואני רוח דרומית והלך והחזיק לו כל אחד בשלו זה שלא בפני זה נעשה כמי שקנו מידם ברוחות אע"פ שלא אמרו זה לזה לך חזק וקני: **ארבע** אמות גובה אפותיא דה' קאי טפי לא קאי. וקשיא לר"ת הא לבנין דגריעי קאי בשלשה טפחים ועוד הא קא חזינן דקאי בגזית טפי אפורתא ותירץ דהכי קאמר טפי לא קאי כמשפט גזית שרוצים בני אדם לבנותו שיעמוד ימים רבים כשבונים בגזית: **טרקסין.** אומר ר"ת דטרק הוי כמו טרוקי גלי (ברכות דף כח.) וסין הוי סיני כלומר שהיה מפסיק וסוגר את הלוחות שנתנו בסיני שהיו מונחות בארון שהיה בבית קדשי הקדשים וי"מ טרקסין פנים וחוץ שאותה אמה היתה ספק אם מקודשת פנים או חוץ ולכך היו שם שתי פרוכת כדאמרינן ביומא (דף נא:): **שאני** התם דאיכא טפח יתירא. ה"מ לשנויי דאגב תקרה ומעזיבה קאי טפי כדאמרי' בסמוך: אמר

עין משפט נר מצוה

ט א ב ג מיי' פ"ב מהל' שכנים הל' יד סמג עשין פב טוש"ע ח"מ סי' קנז סעיף א:
י ד ה ו מיי' שם הל' י טוש"ע שם סעיף ג:

רבינו גרשום

ל"א [מפיך] כולה הלכה **דכיון שרצו** לחלוק אם מעכב א' מלעשות כותל בונין אותו **בעל כרחו:** א) **וטעמא דרצו** לעשות [כותל] מש"ה בונין **הא לא רצו** בין שניהן אלא א' רוצה וא' מעכב **אין מחייבין אותו אלמא היזק ראיה לאו שמיה היזק: שרצו לחצות מיבעי ליה.** כלומר אם איתא דמחיצה דמתני' פלוגתא אמאי תני לעשות ליתני לחצות בשלמא אי אמרת גודא אמטא להכי תני לעשות דלא מיתני בלא לעשות. ומשני לעולם מחיצה פלוגתא ודקא קשיא לך שרצו לחצות מיבעי ליה לא קשיא דמתני' משתעי בלשון בני אדם דאמרי **תא ונעביד פלוגתא** ולעולם היזק ראיה שמיה היזק: **מאי אריא** דתני מתני' **רצו** לחלוק מש"ה בונין את הכותל באמצע בעל כרחו משום היזק ראיה דהואיל דנתרצו לחלוק בונין **אפי' לא רצו** שניהן לחלוק הואיל דנתרצה א' מהן לחלוק בדין הוא דבונין את הכותל לאמצע אע"ג דלא נתרצה אידך משום היזק ראיה: **משנתנו בשאין בה דין חלוקה** שאין בה ד' אמות לזה וד' אמות לזה מש"ה **אם נתרצו** שניהן לחלוק בונין את הכותל בעל כורחו הואיל דנתרצו לחלוק משום היזק ראיה ואם לא נתרצה א' מהן לחלוק אע"ג דמעכב אידך אין בונין הואיל דאין בה דין חלוקה: **תנינא.** בסיפא דמתני' אימתי אמרי' דאין חלוקה הואיל דלית בה דין חלוקה **בזמן שאין שניהן רוצין: במסיפס בעלמא.** חולקין הואיל ונתרצו קמ"ל רישא דמתני' דקתני **כותל** דלא סגי בלא כותל משום היזק ראיה: **וליתני הא** רישא דמתני' **ולא** בעי סיפא **למיתני.** ומשני **סיפא איצטריכא לה** למיתני דקתני **וכתבי הקדש לא יחלוקו.** משום דקא נהוג בהו מנהג בזיון ואגב סיפא דלא סגי דלא ליתני קתני רישא אימתי בזמן כו': **בשקנו מידן.** דלא מצי למיהדר בהו: **קנין דברים בעלמא הוא** כלומר (אין זה) [איזה] קנין הוא עיקר כגון מתנה או מכירה או שום דבר שמראה לו החפץ שנותן למקבל וקונין מידו על כך אבל הכא שאדם אומר לחבירו ניטול קנין שנחלוק כגון זה קנין דברים בעלמא הוא דלא נברר על מה נוטל קנין ואכתי ליהדרו בהו: **שקנו מידן ברוחות.** דזה הקנה לזה אותו חלק שבצד רוח מזרח וזה לזה חלק שבצד רוח מערב דהיינו קנין גמור הואיל והוברר על מה קנו: **רב אשי אומר** מש"ה לא מצי למיהדר בהו הואיל דקני אע"ג דלית בה דין חלוקה **כגון שהלך זה** לאחר קנין להחזיק בחלקו דנעל גדר ופרץ כל שהוא ודאי בתר הכי לא מצי למיהדר: **פיסקא גויל.** אבנים שנחצבו מן ההר דעדיין אין משופין והם ו' טפחים: **גזית.** אבנים משופין והן של ה' טפחים. **כפיסין, ארחי** חצי לבינה לבינה שלימה היא ג' טפחים. **מקום שנהגו לבנות בגויל** דמן ו' טפחים זה נותן ג' טפח מחלקו בקרקע וזה ג' טפח. **בגזית** של חמש טפחים זה נותן טפחיים ומחצה בקרקע וזה נותן טפחיים ומחצה. **כפיסין** שהן טפח ומחצה זה נותן טפחיים וזה נותן טפחיים לפי שכשיתן זה כפיס אחד מטפח ומחצה וזה כפיס אחד מטפח ומחצה דהיינו ג' טפחים עדיין צריך טינא **ביני אורבי** לפי שכשמניחין כפיס מכאן וכפיס מכאן ג) ובאמצע כשיעור טפח של סיד כדי שיהיו מדובקות בטינא יפה והיינו ב' טפחים מן הקרקע לכל אחד: **לבינים.** כותל של לבינים לא הוי אלא ג' טפחים שאין מניחין לבינה כנגד לבינה אלא זו על גב זו: **דלא משפיין.** שאין משופות ומסותתות: **ארחי.** חצי לבינה: **לבינים ליבני.** הכי קרו להו בלשון [המון]. (האי) **ממאי דהאי טפח יתירא** דמייתרי מתני' בגויל טפי משום דצריך הוא טפח **למורש' דקרנתא** מן הכותל טפי מכותל של גזית משום דגזית משפייא וגויל לא משפייא **דילמא** האי גויל לאו מו' טפחים הוי כי אם **פלגא דגזית** דהיינו ב' טפחים ומחצה ומש"ה צריך ליתן לכל חד וחד ג' טפחים מן הקרקע משום דהאי יהיב גויל מב' טפחים ומחצה [וכן] אידך הכי (טפי) וטפח דמייתר מתני' [בגויל] על אבני גזית משום טינא שמניחין **ביני ארבי כדאמרי' כפיסין ארחי** כול' **וממאי** דהני **כפיסין** דקתני מתני' **ארחי נינהו** דהיינו חצי לבינה **והאי טפח יתירא** דמייתר בכפיסין טפי מליבנא משום (דביה) [דביני] ארבי **דלמא** האי כפיסין דקתני מתני' **אבנים דלא משפיין** נינהו ולא מתוקנות כשאר ליבני. **והאי טפח יתירא דמייתר למורשא דקרנתא** שבולט מן הכותל הוא מי לא קאמרת נמי הכי כול': **אמר אביי ש"מ** ממתני' דקתני בכפיסים זה נותן טפחיים וזה נותן טפחיים איכא למשמע מינה **כל ביני ארבי טפח** ליתן בלי סיד. **והני מילי** דסגי בטפח **בטינא** שמגובל במים ועפר הואיל ואינו מדובק יפה **בעי** ודאי **טפי** מטפח: **למימרא** דכל כותל (בוני) [שבונין] **מגזית גבוה ד'** כגון זה שהיא להיזק ראיה שאין צריך להגביהו אלא ד' אמות כדתנן כותל חצר שנפל וכו' והוא מאבני גזית שהם ה' טפחים ההוא כותל דגבוה ד' אמות מצי **קאי** טפחים וקמ"ל מתני' **דאי פותיא ה'** טפחים רוחב: **לא קאי** בה' **והא אמה טרקסין.** הכותל שהיה מפסיק בין ההיכל לקודש הקדשים קרי ליה אמה טרקסין דעובי הכותל הוי אמה בת ו' טפחים ואי קשיא אמאי מקשה מגזית טפי מגויל וכפיסין וליבני תריץ משום דבעי לאקשויי ליה מאמה טרקסין (דביני) [דבנו] מאבני גזית ומקדש ראשון היה גבוה ל' וההיא אמה טרקסין **לא הוה פותייה אלא י' פושכי** ואפ"ה קם ההוא כותל **והיכי אמרת עד ד' אמות בגובה קאי כותל דעבה ה'** טפחים **ותו לא שאני התם הואיל ואיכא טפח יתירא** על ה' טפחים מצי קאי עד גובה ל': **ובמקדש שני מאי טעמא לא עביד אמה טרקסין.** אלא פרוכת כדתנן בפ' הוציאו לו (יומא נא.) שתי פרוכות היו שם וביניהם אמה וכו': **אתלתין קאי.** כלומר מקדש ראשון שהיה גבוה ל' אמה כעובי אמה מצי קאי **טפי לא קאי: וחד אמר בבנין.** שהיה גבוה יותר מן הראשון:

חשק שלמה על רבינו גרשום א) [נראה דצ"ל בונין אותו בעל כרחו משום דהיזק ראיה שמיה היזק ולימא מאי מחיצה גודא וכו' וטעמא דרצו וכו']: ב) [צ"ל צריך להניח באמצע וכו']:

מסורת הש"ס

א) [צ"ל דתניא], ב) [לעיל ב. וש"נ], ג) [לקמן יא.], ד) [שם], ה) ב"מ לא:, ו) [ב"מ טו.], ז) [ב"מ לד], ח) [צ"ל מגררות במגרה וכן הגי' בערוך ערך קס א'], ט) [לקמן ה.], י) [עי' תוס' ריש פ"ה דיומא ד"ה לבין שתי דגרס מ' אמות וכתב דנתקן מ' למאה ע"ש], כ) ומיהו מהרש"ם ולפי גירסתו צ"ל כשלא והגי' שלפנינו הוא גי' מהרש"א], ל) [וע"ע תוס' כתובות נד: ד"ה אע"פ]:

הגהות הב"ח

(א) גמ' כדכתיב ותהי מחצת: (ב) שם ואימא מאי מחיצה גודא כדתנן מחיצת הכרם שנפרצה אומר לו גדור חזרה ונפרצה: (ג) שם מאי קמ"ל דכי לית ביה דין חלוקה) תא"מ ונ"ב גי' תוס' כשאין בה דין חלוקה: (ד) שם לא יחלוקו וכו' מאי הוי ליהדר ביה וכו' מידן כו' ל"א אלישנא אחרינא דאשמעינן בשאין בה: (ה) שם למימרא דבגזית כל כ"ל ואות ד' נמחק: (ו) רש"י ד"ה קנין וכו' או מכר או מתנה: (ז) ד"ה בבנין שהיה גובהו ק' נ"ב נראה דזה הוא בית שני דבית ראשון היה גבוה ל' אמה ובית שני הוסיף עליו ק' אמה ועי' ר"ל ל' מעלה ע"ש תוספות ולפי זה ק' הוא רק מאה אמה וע"ל דף ג' ע"ב:

גליון הש"ס

גמרא כגון שהלך זה. עי' בתשובת רשב"א סי' אלף רכ"ו וצ"ע:

הגהות מהר"ב רנשבורג

אז גמרא וכי קנו מידן מאי הוי. כ"ה עי' רש"י ד"ה קנין דברים כו' והש"ך בח"מ סימן קג ס"ק ח' נראה שלא זכר זה ועיין ערכין דף כ"ט ע"א תוס' ד"ה וא"ת ודו"ק:

ליקוטי רש"י

[נדפס בעמוד הקודם]

תורה אור השלם

א) וַתְּהִי מֶחֱצַת הָעֵדָה מִן הַצֹּאן שְׁלֹשׁ מֵאוֹת אֶלֶף וּשְׁלֹשִׁים אֶלֶף שִׁבְעַת אֲלָפִים וַחֲמֵשׁ מֵאוֹת: [במדבר לא, מג]

ב) כָּל אֵלֶּה אֲבָנִים יְקָרֹת כְּמִדֹּת גָּזִית מְגֹרָרוֹת בַּמְּגֵרָה מִבַּיִת וּמִחוּץ וּמִמַּסָּד עַד הַטְּפָחוֹת וּמִחוּץ עַד הֶחָצֵר הַגְּדוֹלָה: [מלכים א' ז, ט]

ג) גָּדוֹל יִהְיֶה כְּבוֹד הַבַּיִת הַזֶּה הָאַחֲרוֹן מִן הָרִאשׁוֹן אָמַר יְיָ צְבָאוֹת וּבַמָּקוֹם הַזֶּה אֶתֵּן שָׁלוֹם נְאֻם יְיָ צְבָאוֹת: [חגי ב, ט]

The Mishnah stated:
מָקוֹם שֶׁנָּהֲגוּ לִבְנוֹת כו׳ – In **A PLACE WHERE PEOPLE ARE ACCUSTOMED TO BUILDING** etc.

The Gemara identifies the various building materials mentioned in the Mishnah:
גָּזִית אַבְנֵי .גְּוִיל אַבְנֵי דְּלָא מְשַׁפְיָא – ***G'vil*** denotes **unplaned stones.** דְּמְשַׁפְיָא – ***Gazis*** refers to **stones that have been planed,** דִּכְתִיב – **as it is written:**[37] "כָּל־אֵלֶּה אֲבָנִים יְקָרֹת כְּמִדּוֹת גָּזִית (וגו׳)" – ***All these were of precious stones, according to the measures of planed (gazis) stones***[38] (*trimmed with a plane*).[39] כְּפִיסִין אַרְחֵי – ***K'fisin*** are **half-size bricks,**[40] לְבֵינִין לִיבְנֵי – and ***l'veinin*** are **full-size bricks.**[41]

The Gemara challenges these identifications:
אָמַר לֵיהּ רַבָּה בְּרֵיהּ דְּרָבָא לְרַב אַשִׁי – **Rabbah the son of Rava said to Rav Ashi:** מִמַּאי דִּגְוִיל אַבְנֵי דְּלָא מְשַׁפְיָא נִינְהוּ – **How** do we know **that *g'vil* means unplaned stones** וְהַאי טֶפַח יְתֵירָא לְמוֹרְשָׁא דְּקַרְנָתָא – **and that extra *tefach*** of thickness[42] **is for** their **protruding edges?** דִּילְמָא פַּלְגָא דְּגָזִית הוּא – **Perhaps [*g'vil*] is half of a smooth *gazis*** stone וְהַאי טֶפַח יְתֵירָא לְבֵינֵי אוּרְבֵי הוּא – **and that extra *tefach* is for** an intervening space **between the** two **sides** of the wall into which mortar is poured. – ? –

כִּדְקָאָמְרִינַן כְּפִיסִין אַרְחֵי לְבֵינִין לִיבְנֵי – **For similarly we explained** that ***k'fisin* are half-size bricks** and ***l'veinin* are full-size bricks,** וְהַאי טֶפַח יְתֵירָא לְבֵינֵי אוּרְבֵי – **and that extra *tefach*** mentioned in the Mishnah[43] **is for** an intervening space **between the** two **sides** of the wall into which mortar is poured.[40]

The Gemara parries the challenge:
אָמַר לֵיהּ – **[Rav Ashi] said to [Rabbah]:** וְלִיטַעֲמִיךְ – **And according to your reasoning,** כְּפִיסִין אַרְחֵי מְנָלַן – **from where do we know that *k'fisin*** are **half-size bricks?** This accepted interpretation also has no apparent source! אֶלָּא גְּמָרָא גְּמִירֵי לָהּ – **Rather,** you must admit that **they taught it as a tradition.**[44] גְּוִיל נַמִּי אַבְנֵי דְּלָא מְשַׁפְיָא גְּמָרָא גְּמִירֵי לָהּ – That ***g'vil* are unplaned stones** – and not half-size planed *gazis* stones – **is also taught as a tradition.**

The Gemara records a different version of this discussion:
אִיכָּא דְּאָמְרֵי – **There are those who say** that the dialogue actually proceeded as follows: אָמַר לֵיהּ רַב אַחָא בְּרֵיהּ דְּרַב אַוְיָא לְרַב אַשִׁי – **Rav Acha the son of Rav Avya said to Rav Ashi:** מִמַּאי דְּהַאי כְּפִיסִין אַרְחֵי נִינְהוּ – **How do we know that these *k'fisin*** mentioned in the Mishnah **are half-size bricks,** וְהַאי טֶפַח יְתֵירָא לְבֵינֵי אוּרְבֵי – **and that extra *tefach***[43] **is for** an intervening space **between the** two **sides** of the wall into which mortar is poured? דִּילְמָא מַאי כְּפִיסִין – **Perhaps, what are *k'fisin*?** אַבְנֵי דְּלָא מְשַׁפְיָין – **Unplaned bricks!**[45] וְהַאי טֶפַח יְתֵירָא לְמוֹרְשָׁא דְּקַרְנָתָא – **And that extra *tefach*** of thickness **is for** their **protruding edges.** – ? –

כִּדְקָאָמְרִינַן גְּוִיל אַבְנֵי דְּלָא מְשַׁפְיָין – **For similarly we explained** that ***g'vil* means unplaned stones** גָּזִית אַבְנֵי דִּמְשַׁפְיָין – **and *gazis* means planed stones,** וְהַאי טֶפַח יְתֵירָא לְמוֹרְשָׁא דְּקַרְנָתָא – **and that extra *tefach*** of thickness in a wall of *g'vil*[42] **is for the protruding edges** of the *g'vil* stone.

The Gemara rejects this suggestion:
אָמַר לֵיהּ – **[Rav Ashi said to [Rav Acha]:** וְלִיטַעֲמִיךְ – **And according to your reasoning,** גְּוִיל אַבְנֵי דְּלָא מְשַׁפְיָין מְנָלַן – **from where do we know that *g'vil* are unplaned stones?** This accepted interpretation also has no apparent source! אֶלָּא גְּמָרָא גְּמִירֵי לָהּ – **Rather,** you must admit that **they taught it as a tradition.**[44] הָכָא נַמִּי – **Here, also,** we know that *k'fisin* are half-size bricks – and not unplaned bricks – גְּמָרָא גְּמִירֵי לָהּ – because **it is taught as a tradition.**

Abaye derives a practical application of a rule in the Mishnah:
אָמַר אַבַּיֵי – **Abaye said:** שְׁמַע מִינָּהּ – **Infer from [the Mishnah],** which states that a wall of half-size bricks must be one *tefach* thicker than a wall of full-size bricks, כָּל בֵּינֵי אוּרְבֵי טֶפַח – that the intervening space **between the** two **sides** of a wall of half bricks, into which mortar is poured, **is always a *tefach*.**[46]

Abaye now qualifies his ruling:
הָנֵי מִילֵּי בְּטִינָא – **These words** apply only when the mortar is made **of** pure **mud,** which adheres well; אֲבָל בְּרִיכְּסָא בָּעֵי טְפֵי – **however,** if the mortar is composed **of pebbles and mud, more** than a *tefach* **is needed,** since this type of mortar does not adhere as well. Hence, in our Mishnah's case the first type of mortar was used.

The Gemara now presents another version of Abaye's qualification:
וְאִיכָּא דְּאָמְרֵי – **And there are those that say** that Abaye said as follows: הָנֵי מִילֵּי בְּרִיכְּסָא – **These words** that establish the width of the void at a *tefach* apply only when the mortar is composed **of pebbles and mud;** אֲבָל בְּטִינָא לֹא בָּעֵי כּוּלֵּי הַאי – **however, if** the mortar consists **of pure mud, not so much** intervening space **is necessary,** for the superior adhesion of this type of mortar allows for the use of a smaller amount. According to this version, in the Mishnah's case the inferior grade of mortar was used.

The Gemara now discusses whether the width measurements specified in the Mishnah are relative to the wall's height, or are absolute:
לְמֵימְרָא דִּבְגָזִית – **Does** the Mishnah mean **to say that, regarding** a wall built of **planed stones,** דְּכָל אַרְבַּע אַמּוֹת גּוֹבַהּ – **for every four *amos* of height,** אִי הָוֵי פּוּתְיָא חַמְשָׁא – **if there exists five *tefachim* of width** קָאֵי – the wall **will stand,** אִי לֹא לֹא קָאֵי – **and if not,** the wall **will not stand?**[47] וְהָא אַמָּה טְרַקְסִין – But

NOTES

37. *I Kings* 7:9. The verse speaks of the stones used for building the *Beis HaMikdash*.

38. All planed stones were cut to a uniform size (*Rashi* ibid.).

39. *Mesoras HaShas* inserts this clause (מְגֹרָרוֹת בַּמְּגֵרָה) into the text in place of (וגו׳), since the Gemara's proof essentially derives therefrom.

40. Each half-size brick measured 1.5 *tefachim* in width, and they were laid to form two parallel sides one *tefach* apart. The empty space was filled with mortar to hold the two sides of the wall together (*Rashi*). Hence, a wall constructed of half-size bricks measured four *tefachim* wide, as is indicated in the Mishnah: "This (partner) must provide two *tefachim* etc."

41. Full-size bricks were each three *tefachim* wide, and were laid in a single piling to form the wall (*Rashi*). Hence, a wall constructed of full-size bricks was three *tefachim* in width, as is indicated in the Mishnah: "This (partner) must provide one and one-half *tefachim* etc."

42. The Mishnah specified that walls of *g'vil* must be six *tefachim* thick, whereas walls of *gazis* were only five *tefachim* thick.

43. The Mishnah specified that walls constructed of half-size bricks must measure four *tefachim* in width, while those of full-size bricks were only three *tefachim* wide.

44. I.e. as an oral teaching that was transmitted by the sages from generation to generation.

45. Our translation follows *Rashi*, who emends אַבְנֵי דְּלָא מְשַׁפְיָין (*unplaned stones*) to לְבֵינֵי דְּלָא מְשַׁפְיָין (*unplaned bricks*), for if *k'fisin* meant unplaned *stones*, it would have the same meaning as *g'vil*. Unplaned *bricks*, however, are man-made.

46. The legal implication of Abaye's statement is that one who contracts to build such a wall for another must leave a void one *tefach* wide in the interior of the wall and fill it with mortar (*Rashi*).

47. The Mishnah specified that a wall built of planed stones must be five *tefachim* wide. Further, the Mishnah below (5a) specified that any courtyard wall must be at least four *amos* high. Hence, if the Mishnah has indeed established a height-width ratio, then a *gazis* wall eight *amos* tall, for instance, would have to measure ten *tefachim* wide (*Rashi*).

דאיצטנע מינך לישנא אחרינא אמרי לה סברוה מאי מחיצה פלוגתא (א) דכתיב א) ותהי מחצת העדה א וכיון דרצו בונין את הכותל בעל כורחן אלמא ב היזק ראיה שמיה היזק (ג) אימא מאי מחיצה גודא א) (דתנן) ג) מחיצת הכרם שנפרצה אומר לו גדור נפרצה אומר לו גדור נתיאש הימנה ולא גדרה הרי זה קידש וחייב באחריותה וטעמא דרצו הא לא רצו אין מחייבין אותו אלמא היזק ראיה לאו שמיה היזק אי הכי בונין את הכותל בונין אותו מבעי ליה אלא מאי פלוגתא אי הכי שרצו לעשות מחיצה שרצו לחצות מבעי ליה כדאמרי אינשי תא נעביד פלוגתא ואי היזק ראיה שמיה היזק מאי איריא רצו אפי' לא רצו נמי א"ר אסי א"ר יוחנן משנתנו ג בשאין בה דין חלוקה והוא דרצו מאי קמ"ל (ג) דכי לית ביה דין חלוקה כי רצו פליגי תנינא ג) אימתי בזמן שאין שניהם רוצים אבל בזמן ששניהם רוצים אפילו פחות מכאן חולקין אי מהתם הוה אמינא אפילו פחות מכאן במסיפס בעלמא קמ"ל הכא כותל וליתני הא ולא ליתני הך סיפא איצטריכא ליה ד) וכתבי הקדש אע"פ ששניהם רוצים לא יחלוקו (ד) ה) (ל"א וכי רצו מאי הוי ליהדר ביה אמר רב אסי א"ר יוחנן בשקנו מידו כו' אדאשמעינן בשאין בה דין חלוקה והוא דרצו לישמעינן ביש בה דין חלוקה ואע"ג דלא רצו אי אשמעינן ביש בה דין חלוקה ואע"ג דלא רצו הוה אמינא שאין בה דין חלוקה אפילו רצו נמי לא קמ"ל ומי מצית אמרת הכי והא קתני סיפא אימתי בזמן שאין שניהם רוצים אבל בזמן ששניהם רוצים יחלוקו מאי לאו אכותל לא אמסיפס בעלמא ליתני האי ולא ליתני האי סיפא אצטריכא ליה ובכתבי הקדש אע"פ ששניהם רוצים לא יחלוקו): במאי אוקימתא למתני' בשאין בה דין חלוקה אי בשאין בה דין חלוקה כי רצו מאי הוי נהדרו בהו א"ר אסי א"ר יוחנן ו) שקנו מידן א"ו וכי קנו מידן מאי הוי קנין דברים בעלמא הוא ה בשקנו מידן ברוחות רב אשי אמר ט) ו כגון שהלך זה בתוך שלו והחזיק וזה בתוך שלו והחזיק: מקום שנהגו לבנות כו': ז) גויל אבני דלא משפיא גזית אבני דמשפיא דכתיב ב) כל אלה אבנים יקרות כמדות גזית ח) (וגו') כפיסין ארחי לבינין ליבני אמר ליה רבה בריה דרבא לרב אשי ממאי דגויל אבני דלא משפיא נינהו והאי טפח יתירא למורשא דקרנתא דילמא פלגא דגזית הוא והאי טפח יתירא לביני אורבי הוא בדקאמרינן כפיסין ארחי לבינין ליבני והאי טפח יתירא לביני אורבי אמר ליה וליטעמיך כפיסין ארחי מנלן אלא גמרא גמירי לה גויל נמי אבני דלא משפיא גמרא גמירי לה איכא דאמרי אמר ליה רב אחא בריה דרב אויא לרב אשי ממאי דהאי כפיסין ארחי נינהו והאי טפח יתירא לביני אורבי דילמא מאי כפיסין אבני דלא משפיין והאי טפח יתירא למורשא דקרנתא בדקאמרינן גויל אבני דלא משפיין גזית אבני דמשפיין והאי טפח יתירא למורשא דקרנתא אמר ליה וליטעמיך גויל אבני דלא משפיין מנלן אלא גמרא גמירי לה הכא נמי גמרא גמירי לה אמר אביי שמע מינה כל ביני אורבי טפח הני מילי בטינא אבל בריכסא בעי טפי ואיכא דאמרי הני מילי בריכסא אבל בטינא לא בעי כולי האי למימרא דבגזית (ה) דכל ד' אמות גובה אי הוי פותיא חמשא קאי אי לא לא קאי והא אמה טרקסין דהואי גבוה תלתין אמהתא ולא הוה פותיא אלא שית פושכי וקם כיון דאיכא טפח יתירא קאי ובמקדש שני מ"ט לא עבוד אמה טרקסין כי קאי בתלתין קאי טפי לא קאי ומנלן דהוה גבוה טפי דכתיב ג) גדול יהיה כבוד הבית הזה האחרון מן הראשון רב ושמואל ואמרי לה ר' יוחנן ור"א חד אמר בבנין וחד אמר

רש"י

דאיצטנע מינך. דברי הצנע אבל חצר החלוקה לתרוייהו קביעא תשמישתי' לכל אחד בחלקו כל שעה ולא עבדי בה מילי דצנעא: כיון דרצו. לחלוק ולקמן פריך מאי איריא רצו אפילו לא רצו הרי הן יכולין לכוף זה את זה: בונין כותל. של אבנים: גודא. כותל אבנים ובחצר שיש בה דין חלוקה ועל כרחן חולקים: וטעמא דרצו. שהתנו לחלוקה בכותל אבנים הא לא רצו אין מחייבין אותו אלא מסיפס בעלמא: כדאמרי אינשי כו'. תירוצא הוא: שאין בה דין חלוקה. ד' אמות לא יחלוקו: ובכתבי הקדש. ספר תורה שהוא בכרך אחד וכן נביאים וכתובים הכתובים בגליון כס"ת: קנין דברים הוא. ואין חליפין קונין אלא דבר הנקנה או (ו) מכר או מתנה או שעבוד קרקעות שהקנין חל עליו או מטלטלין: ברוחות. זה בורר לו חלק מזרחי וזה בורר לו חלק מערבי וקנו מידם ומעתה נקנה חלק מזרחי לזה ואין לזה חלק בו וכן השני לחבירו: והחזיק. בחלקו דפסק ביה פורתא וקרקע נקנית בחזקה אחרי אשר רצו בשעת חלוקה: ארחי. חצי לבינה ולבינה ג' טפחים והאריח טפח ומחצה ועובי הכותל אריח מכאן ואריח מכאן וטפח באמצע שנותן שם טיט לחבירו: לבינים ליבני. שלימות לבינה לעובי הכותל: למורשא דקרנתא. ראשי האבנים בולטות לחוץ שאינן חלקות ולהכי בעי רוחב טפח יתירה: לביני אורבי. בין דימוס שמכאן ובין דימוס שמכאן ונותן טיט באמצע: הנ"מ. לביני דלא משפיא: ש"מ כו'. ונפקא מינה למקבל עליו לבנות כותל לחבירו: בריכסא. אבנים דקות וטיט בין שני הדימוסות: למימרא דבגזית כו' כל ד' אמות גובה אי הוה פותיא ה' טפחים קאי ואי לא לא קאי. כדתנן במתני' בגזית זה נותן טפחיים ומחצה וזה נותן טפחיים ומחצה וקתני סיפא ט) מחייבין אותן לבנותו עד ד' אמות ולפי חשבון זה לגובה שמנה צריך י' טפחים רוחב: והא אמה טרקסין. דבנין שלמה הוה דכתיב אבני גזית (מלכים א ה) והוי שלשים אמה קומתה ואין עוביו אלא אמה להבדיל בין ההיכל לקדשי הקדשים: דאיכא טפח יתירא. ומשום הכי טפח מוסיף מלי לאגבוה טובא ואין צריך לתת לכל ארבע אמות ה' טפחים רוחב: בבנין. שהיה גובהו (ז) י) מאה אמות כדתנן במסכת מדות (פרק ד מ"ו):

תוספות

מאי קא משמע לן בשאין בה דין חלוקה. אע"ג דקא משמע לן דשמיה היזק ה"פ מאי קמ"ל במאי דאיירי באין בה דין חלוקה לישמעינן בשיש בה דין חלוקה [אע"ג דלא רצו] (כשרצו) פלגי ט) תימה הא קמ"ל דאפילו באין בה דין חלוקה דאיכא למימר על מנת לעשות גודא לא איתרצאי כדפירש לעיל: כי רצו מאי הוי ניהדרו בהו. למ"ד מחיצה גודא לא פריך דאיכא למימר דקנו ושיעבדו נכסיהן לבנין הכותל אלא למ"ד פלוגתא לא מהני קנין דקנין דברים בעלמא הוא דלא מסיק אדעתיה שקנו ברוחות: קנין דברים בעלמא הוא. בפרק השוכר את הפועלים (ב"מ דף עד.) דתנן מתנה ש"ח להיות כשואל ומוקי לה בקנו מידו התם לאו קנין דברים הוא אלא קנין גמור הוא שמשעבד את עצמו שאם יאנס שישלם ל): רב אשי אמר כגון שהלך כו'. תימה לר"י מה בא רב אשי להוסיף וכי איצטריך לאשמועינן דחזקה מועלת כמו קנין ונראה לר"י דהא קמ"ל דאע"ג דקאמר לקמן בחזקת הבתים (דף נג.) שלא בפניו צריך למימר לו לך חזק וקני הכא כיון שאמרו אתה תקח רוח צפונית ואני רוח דרומית והלך והחזיק לו כל אחד בשלו זה שלא בפני זה נעשה כמי שקנו מידם ברוחות אע"פ שלא אמרו זה לזה לך חזק וקני: ארבע אמות גובה אפותיא דה' קאי טפי לא קאי. וקשיא לר"ת הא לבינין דגריעי קאי בשלשה טפחים ועוד הא קא חזינן דקאי בגזית טפי אפורתא ותירץ דהכי קאמר טפי לא קאי כמשפט גזית שרוצים בני אדם לבנותו שיעמוד ימים רבים כשבונים בגזית: טרקסין. אומר ר"ת דטרק הוי כמו טרוקי גלי (ברכות דף כח.) וסין הוי סיני כלומר שהיה מפסיק וסוגר את הלוחות שנתנו בסיני שהיו מונחות בארון שהיה בבית קדשי הקדשים וי"מ טרקסין פנים וחוץ שאותה אמה היתה ספק אם מקודשת פנים או חוץ ולכך היו שם שתי פרוכת כדאמרינן ביומא (דף נא:): שאני התם דאיכא טפח יתירא. ה"מ לשנוי דאגב תקרה ומעזיבה קאי טפי כדאמרי' בסמוך: אמר

רבינו גרשום

ל"א [מפין] כולה הלכה דכיון שרצו לחלוק אם מעכב א' מלעשות כותל בונין אותו בעל כרחו: א) וטעמא דרצו לעשות [כותל] מש"ה בונין הא לא רצו בין שניהן אלא א' רוצה וא' מעכב אין מחייבין אותו אלמא היזק ראיה לאו שמיה היזק: שרצו לחצות מיבעי ליה. כלומר אם איתא דמחיצה דמתני' פלוגתא אמאי תני לעשות ליתני לחצות בשלמא אי אמרת גודא אמטא להכי תני לעשות דלא מיתני בלא לעשות. ומשני לעולם מחיצה פלוגתא ודקא קשיא לך שרצו לחצות מיבעי ליה לא קשיא דמתני' משתעי בלשון בני אדם דאמרי תא ונעביד פלוגתא ולעולם היזק ראיה שמיה היזק: מאי אריא דתני מתני' רצו לחלוק מש"ה בונין את הכותל באמצע בעל כרחו משום היזק ראיה דהואיל דנתרצו לחלוק בונין אפי' לא רצו שניהן לחלוק הואיל דנתרצה א' מהן לחלוק בדין הוא דבונין את הכותל לאמצע אע"ג דלא נתרצה אידך משום היזק ראיה: משנתנו בשאין בה דין חלוקה שאין בה ד' אמות לזה וד' אמות לזה מש"ה אם נתרצו שניהן לחלוק בונין את הכותל בעל כורחו הואיל דנתרצו לחלוק משום היזק ראיה ואם לא נתרצה א' מהן לחלוק אע"ג דמעכב אידך אין בונין הואיל דאין בה דין חלוקה: תנינא. בסיפא דמתני' אימתי אמרי' דאין חלוקה הואיל דלית בה דין חלוקה בזמן שאין שניהן רוצין: במסיפס בעלמא. חולקין הואיל ונתרצו קמ"ל רישא דמתני' דקתני כותל דלא סגי בלא כותל משום היזק ראיה: וליתני הא רישא דמתני' ולא בעי סיפא למיתני: ומשני סיפא איצטריכא לה למיתני דקתני וכתבי הקדש לא יחלוקו. משום דקא נהוג בהו מנהג בזיון והאי סיפא דלא סגי דלא ליתני קתני רישא אימתי בזמן כו': בשקנו מידן. דלא מצי למיהדר בהו: קנין דברים בעלמא הוא כלומר (אין זה) [איזה] קנין הוא ואי עיקר כגון מתנה או מכירה או שום דבר שמראה לו החפץ שנותן למקבל וקונין מידו על כך אבל הכא שאדם אומר לחבירו נטול קנין שנחלוק כגון זה קנין דברים בעלמא הוא דלא נברר על מה נוטל קנין ואכתי ליהדרו בהו: שקנו מידן ברוחות. דזה הקנה לזה אותו חלק שבצד מזרח ולזה חלק שבצד רוח מערב דהיינו קנין גמור הואיל והודיעו על מה קנו: רב אשי אומר מש"ה לא מצי למיהדר בהו הואיל דקני אע"ג דלית בה דין חלוקה כגון שהלך זה לאחר קנין להחזיק בחלקו דנעל גדר ופרץ כל שהוא ודאי בתר הכי לא מצי למיהדר: פיסקא גויל. אבנים שנחצבו מן ההר דעדיין אין משופין והם ו' טפחים: גזית. אבנים משופין והן של ה' טפחים. כפיסין, ארחי חצי לבינה לבינה שלימה היא ג' טפחים. מקום שנהגו לבנות בגויל דמן ו' טפחים מחלקו בקרקע וזה ג' טפח. בגזית של חמש טפחים זה נותן טפחיים ומחצה בקרקע וזה נותן טפחיים ומחצה. כפיסין שהן טפח ומחצה זה נותן טפחיים וזה נותן טפחיים לפי שכשיתן זה כפיס אחד מטפח ומחצה וזה כפיס אחד מטפח ומחצה עדיין צריך טינא ביני אורבי לפי שכשמניחין כפיס מכאן וכפיס מכאן ב) ובאמצע כשיעור טפח של סיד כדי שיהיו מדובקות בטינא יפה והיינו ב' טפחים מן הקרקע לכל אחד: לבינים. כותל של לבינים לא הוי אלא ג' טפחים שאין מניחין לבינה כנגד לבינה אלא זו על גב זו: דלא משפיין. שאין משופות ומסותתות: ארחי. חצי לבינה: לבינים ליבני. הכי קרו להו בלשון [המון]. (האי) ממאי דהאי טפח יתירא דמייתרי מתני' בגויל טפי משום דצריך ההוא טפח למורש' דקרנתא מן הכותל טפי משום דגזית משפייא וגויל לא משפייא דילמא האי גויל לאו מר' טפחים הוי כי אם פלגא דגזית דהיינו ב' טפחים ומחצה ומש"ה צריך ליתן לכל חד וחד ג' טפחים מן הקרקע משום דהאי יהיב גויל מב' טפחים ומחצה [וכן] אידך הכי (טפי) [בגויל] על אבני גזית משום טינא שמניחין ביני ארבי כדאמרי' כפיסין ארחי כול' וממאי דהני כפיסין דקתני מתני' ארחי נינהו דהיינו חצי לבינה והאי טפח יתירא דמייתר בכפיסין טפי מלבינא משום (דביה) [דביני] ארבי דלמא האי אבנים דלא משפיין נינהו ולא מתוקנות כשאר ליבני. והאי טפח יתירא דמייתר למורשא דקרנתא שבולט מן הכותל הוא מי לא קאמרת נמי הכי כול': אמר אביי ש"מ ממתני' דקתני בכפיסים זה נותן טפחיים וזה נותן טפחיים איכא למשמע מינה כל ביני ארבי טפח ליתן בלי סיד. והני מילי דסגי בטפח בטינא שמגובל במים ועפר הואיל ואינו מדובק יפה בעי ודאי טפי מטפח: למימרא דכל כותל (בוני) [שבונין] מגזית גבוה ד' כגון זה שאין צריך להגביהו אלא ד' אמות כדתנן כותל חצר שנפל וכו' והוא מאבני גזית שהם ה' טפחים וקמ"ל מתני' דאי פותיא ה' טפחים ההוא כותל דגבוה ד' אמות מצי קאי הכותל אבל אי גבוה טפי מד' לא קאי בה' טפחים רוחב: והא אמה טרקסין. הכותל שהיה מפסיק בין ההיכל לקודש הקדשים קרי ליה אמה טרקסין דעובי הכותל הוי אמה בת ו' טפחים ואי קשיא אמאי מקשה מגזית טפי מגויל וכפיסין וליבני תריץ משום דבעי לאקשויי ליה מאמה טרקסין (דביני) [דבנו] מאבני גזית ומקדש ראשון היה גבוה ל' וההיא אמה טרקסין לא הוה פותיה אלא ו' פושכי ואפ"ה קם ההוא כותל והיכי אמרת עד ד' אמות בגובה קאי כותל דעבה ה' טפחים ותו לא שאני התם הואיל ואיכא טפח יתירא על ה' טפחים מצי קאי עד גובה ל': ובמקדש שני מאי טעמא לא עביד אמה טרקסין. אלא פרוכת כדתנן בפ' הוציאו לו (יומא נא.) שתי פרוכות היו שם וביניהם אמה וכו': אתלתין קאי. כלומר מקדש ראשון שהיה גבוה ל' אמה כעובי אמה מצי קאי טפי לא קאי: וחד אמר בבנין. שהיה גבוה

חשק שלמה על רבינו גרשום א) [נראה דל"ל בונין אותו בעל כרחו משום דהיזק דראיה שמיה היזק ולימא מאי מחיצה גודא וכו' וטעמא דרצו וכו']: ב) [נ"ל לריך להניח באמצע וכו']:

עין משפט נר מצוה

ט א ב ג מיי' פ"ב מהל' שכנים הל' יד סמג עשין פב טוש"ע ח"מ סי' קנז סעיף א:
י ד ה ו מיי' שם הל' י טוש"ע שם סעיף ג:

מסורת הש"ס

א) [ל"ל דתניא], ב) [לעיל ב. וש"נ], ג) [לקמן יא.], ד) [שם], ה) ב"מ כ"ו לוט., ו) [כ"ל טו. וש"נ], ז) [ל"ל לד], ח) [ע' מגרורות במגרה וכן הגי' בערוך ערך שף א'], ט) [לקמן ה.], י) [ע' תוי"ט רים פ"ה דיומא ד"ה לבין שתי דגרס מ' אמות וכתב דנתחלף לו למאה ע"ש], כ) ש"ל ותירך מהרש"א ולפי גירסתו ל"ל כשרלו והגי' שלפנינו הוא גי' מהרש"א, ל) [וע"ע תוס' כתובות נד: ד"ה אע"ש].

הגהות הב"ח

(א) גמ' כדכתיבא ותהי מחצת: (ב) שם ולמאי מאי מחילה גודא כדתנן מחילת הכרם שנפרלה אומר לו גדור נפרלה: (ג) שם מאי קמ"ל (דכי לית ביה דין חלוקה) תא"מ וכ"ב גי' תוס' בשאין בה דין חלוקה: (ד) שם לא יחלוקו וכי רלו מאי הוי ליהדר ביה וכו' ובעקנו מידן כו' לישנא אחרינא דלאשמעינן בשאין בה: (ה) שם למימרא דבגזית כל כל"ל ואות ד' נמחק: (ו) רש"י ד"ה קנין וכו' או מכר או מתנה: (ז) ד"ה בבנין שהיה גובהו כ"ל נראה דזה ט"ם דהכי הוא תירוצו דכבר ירלה ראשון היה גבוה ק' אמה והיה גבוה ק"ל אמה כמו דכתיב ג' מעליה ראשונה ועתה ג'... א"כ מקדש ראשון היה גבוה יותר וע"כ ל"ל מ' ומשיב הא לא תמה ר"ח רק שלשים ושני מ' הוא רק ל' ע"ש ועי"ל דף נ"ח ע"ב:

גליון הש"ס

גמרא כגון שהלך זה. ע' בתשובת רשב"א סי' אלף רכ"ו וצ"ע:

הגהות מהר"ב רנשבורג

א] גמרא וכי קנו מידן מאי הוי. נ"ב ע' רש"י ד"ה קנין דברים כו' ק"ק נמ"ש סימן רג ס"ק ב' ונראה שלא זכר זה ועיין ערכין דף ל' ע"א תוס' ד"ה ולא דעינה כו' ודו"ק:

ליקוטי רש"י

[נדפס בעמוד הקודם]

תורה אור השלם

א) וַתְּהִי מֶחֱצַת הָעֵדָה מִן הַצֹּאן שְׁלֹשׁ מֵאוֹת אֶלֶף וּשְׁלֹשִׁים אֶלֶף שִׁבְעַת אֲלָפִים וַחֲמֵשׁ מֵאוֹת: [במדבר לא, מג]

ב) כָּל אֵלֶּה אֲבָנִים יְקָרֹת כְּמִדֹּת גָּזִית מְגֹרָרוֹת בַּמְּגֵרָה מִבַּיִת וּמִחוּץ וּמִמַּסָּד עַד הַטְּפָחוֹת וּמִחוּץ עַד הֶחָצֵר הַגְּדוֹלָה: [מלכים א' ז, ט]

ג) גָּדוֹל יִהְיֶה כְּבוֹד הַבַּיִת הַזֶּה הָאַחֲרוֹן מִן הָרִאשׁוֹן אָמַר יְיָ צְבָאוֹת וּבַמָּקוֹם הַזֶּה אֶתֵּן שָׁלוֹם נְאֻם יְיָ צְבָאוֹת: [חגי ב, ט]

there is the ***amah traksin***,[48] i.e. the wall separating the Holy of Holies from the rest of the *Heichal* in the First Temple, **דַּהֲוַאי גְּבוֹהָהּ תְּלָתִין אַמְּהָתָא — which was thirty *amos* high, וְלֹא הֲוָה פּוּתְיָא אֶלָּא שִׁית פּוּשְׁכֵי — but was only six *tefachim* wide, וְקָם — and** yet **it stood!**[49] — ? —

The Gemara answers that, in fact, no such ratio exists:

כֵּיוָן דְּאִיכָּא טֶפַח יְתֵירָא — Since there was an extra (sixth) ***tefach*** of thickness, **קָאֵי** — the *amah traksin* **stood** securely, for the extra *tefach* strengthened the wall enabling it to stand much higher than four *amos.*

The Gemara thereupon asks:

וּבְמִקְדָּשׁ שֵׁנִי מַאי טַעְמָא לֹא עָבוּד אַמָּה טְרַקְסִין — And why was an *amah traksin* not made in the Second Temple?[50]

The Gemara answers:

כִּי קָאֵי בִּתְלָתִין קָאֵי — Although the *amah traksin* **stood** at a width of six *tefachim,* **it stood** only at a height of **thirty** *amos.* **טְפֵי לֹא קָאֵי** — A wall of **greater** height **would not stand** at that width. Thus, since the *Heichal* was forty *amos* high in the Second Temple,[51] and since it was impossible to construct a wider *amah traksin*, as the measurements of the *Heichel* may not be altered, a curtain was hung instead.

The Gemara asks:

וּמְנָלַן דַּהֲוָה גָּבוֹהַּ טְפֵי — And from where do we know that the *Heichal* in the Second Temple **was taller** than its predecessor?

The Gemara cites the source:

דִּכְתִיב — For it is written:[52] **„גָּדוֹל יִהְיֶה כְּבוֹד הַבַּיִת הַזֶּה הָאַחֲרוֹן מִן־הָרִאשׁוֹן" — *The honor of this later*[53] *House will be greater than that of the first.*** **רַב וּשְׁמוּאֵל וְאָמְרֵי לָהּ רַבִּי יוֹחָנָן וְרַבִּי אֶלְעָזָר — Rav and Shmuel — and some say, R' Yochanan and R' Eliezer** — argue as to which preeminence Scripture intends: **חַד אָמַר בְּבִנְיָן — One said** that the superiority of the Second Temple lay **in the edifice** itself,[54] **וְחַד אָמַר — while the other said**

NOTES

48. The term *"amah traksin"* is a composite of three words: *"amah"*, for the wall was an *amah* (six *tefachim*) thick; *"trak,"* which means "to close," as in טְרוֹקוּ גַּלֵּי, *close the gates* (*Berachos* 28a); and *"sin,"* "Sinai." Hence, the entire expression denotes the ***amah***-wide wall that **closed in** the Tablets of the Law (which reposed in the Holy Ark in the Holy of Holies), which were given at Mt. **Sinai** (*Tosafos*).

49. Although the *amah traksin* was constructed with planed stones (see *I Kings* 5), its height-width ratio fell far short of the four *amos:* five *tefachim*-standard seemingly implied by our two Mishnahs.

50. In that edifice a curtain was hung between the two sections of the *Heichal* to replace the *amah traksin.*

The Gemara's question here is related to its previous reply — that once a wall of planed stones is six *tefachim* thick, it will stand even if built to great heights. The Gemara asks why there was no *amah traksin* in the Second Temple, for a wall six *tefachim* thick should have been able to stand even if built to the Second Temple's height.

51. *Midos* 4:6. [Although *Rashi's* commentary (ד״ה בבנין) states that the *Heichal* stood 100 *amos* tall, *Tos. Yom Tov* in *Yoma* (5:1) explains that most probably the printer mistook the letter מ, *Rashi's* abbreviation for 40, to mean מֵאָה, 100. (See, however, *Yad Ramah*, who also states that its height was 100.)]

52. *Haggai* 2:9.

53. אַחֲרוֹן does not always mean *last* (since, God willing, another Temple will soon be built). It can also imply something that is *later* in a series (see *Tos. Yom Tov* to *Demai* 7:3 and *Hagahos Maharam Strashun* here).

54. I.e. in the fact that its *Heichal* exceeded the height of the *Heichal* in the First Temple by ten *amos,* as discussed above.

דאיצטנע מינך. דברי הצנע אבל חצר השותפין לתרוייהו קביעה תשמישתי' לכל אחד בחלקו כל שעה ולא עבדי בה מילי דצנעה: **כיון דרצו.** לחלוק ולקמן פריך מאי איריא רצו אפילו לא רצו הרי הן יכולין לכוף זה את זה: **בונין כותל.** של אבנים: **גודא.** כותל אבנים ובחצר שיש בה דין חלוקה ועל כרחן חולקים: **וטעמא דרצו.** שהתנו לחולקה בכותל אבנים הא לא רצו אין מחייבין אותו אלא מסיפס בעלמא: **כדאמרי אינשי כו'.** תירוצא הוא: **שאין בה דין חלוקה.** ח' אמות לא יחלוקו: **ובכתבי הקדש.** ספר תורה שהוא בכרך אחד וכן נביאים וכתובים הכתובים בגליון כס"ת: **קנין דברים הוא.** ואין חליפין קונין אלא דבר הנקנה או (ו) מכר או מתנה או שעבוד קרקעות שהקנין חל עליו או מטלטלין: **ברוחות.** זה בורר לו חלק מזרחי וזה בורר לו חלק מערבי וקנו מידם ומעתה נקנה חלק מזרחי לזה ואין לזה חלק בו וכן השני לחבירו: **והחזיק.** בחלקו רפק ביה פורתא וקרקע נקנה בחזקה אחרי אשר רצו בשעת חלוקה: **אריח.** חצי לבינה והלבינה ג' טפחים והאריח טפח ומחצה ועובי הכותל אריח מכאן ואריח מכאן וטפח באמצע שנותן שם טיט לחברו: **לבינים ליבני.** שלימות לבינה לעובי הכותל: **למורשא דקרנת'.** ראשי האבנים בולטות לחוץ שאינן חלקות ולהכי בעי רוחב טפח יתירא: **לביני אורבי.** בין דימוס שמכאן ובין דימוס שמכאן ונותן טיט באמצע: ה"ג אימא לביני דלא משפיין: **ש"מ כו'.** ונפקא מינה למקבל עליו לבנות כותל לחבירו: **בריכסא.** אבנים דקות וטיט בין שני הדימוסות: **למימרא דבגזית כו'** כל ד' אמות גובה אי הוה פותיא ה' טפחים קאי ואי לא לא קאי. כדתנן במתני' בגזית זה נותן טפחיים ומחצה וזה נותן טפחיים ומחצה וקתני סיפא ט) מחייבין אותן לבנותו עד ד' אמות ולפי חשבון זה לגובה שמנה צריך י' טפחים רוחב: **והא אמה טרקסין.** דבנין שלמה דגזית הוה דכתיב אבני גזית (מלכים א ה) והוי שלשים אמה קומתה ואין עוביו אלא אמה להבדיל בין ההיכל לקדשי הקדשים: **דאיכא טפח יתירא.** ומשום האי טפח פותיא מלי לאגבוה טובא ואין צריך לתת לכל ארבע אמות ה' טפחים רוחב: **בבנין.** שהיה גובהו (ז) י) מאה אמות כדתנן במסכת מדות (פרק ד מ"ו):

דאיצטנע מינך לישנא אחרינא אמרי לה סברוה מאי מחיצה פלוגתא (א) דכתיב א) ותהי מחצת העדה א) וכיון דרצו בונין את הכותל בעל כורחן אלמא ב) היזק ראיה שמיה היזק (ב) אימא מאי מחיצה גודא א) (דתנן) ג) מחיצת הכרם שנפרצה אומר לו גדור נפרצה אומר לו גדור נתיאש הימנה ולא גדרה הרי זה קידש וחייב באחריותה וטעמא דרצו הא לא רצו אין מחייבין אותו אלמא היזק ראיה לאו שמיה היזק אי הכי בונין את הכותל בונין אותו מבעי ליה אלא מאי פלוגתא אי הכי שרצו לעשות מחיצה שרצו לחצות מבעי ליה כדאמרי אינשי תא נעביד פלוגתא ואי היזק ראיה שמיה היזק מאי איריא רצו אפי' לא רצו נמי א"ר אסי א"ר יוחנן משנתנו ג) בשאין בה דין חלוקה והוא דרצו מאי קמ"ל (ג) דכי לית ביה דין חלוקה כי רצו פליגי תנינא ד) אימתי בזמן שאין שניהם רוצים אבל בזמן ששניהם רוצים אפילו פחות מכאן חולקין אי מהתם הוה אמינא אפילו פחות מכאן במסיפס בעלמא קמ"ל הכא כותל וליתני הא ולא ליתני הך סיפא איצטריכא ליה ה) וכתבי הקדש אע"פ ששניהם רוצים לא יחלוקו (ד) (ל"א וכי רצו מאי הוי ליהדר ביה אמר רב אסי א"ר יוחנן בשקנו מידו כו' אדאשמעינן בשאין בה דין חלוקה והוא דרצו לישמעינן ביש בה דין חלוקה ואע"ג דלא רצו אי אשמעינן ביש בה דין חלוקה ואע"ג דלא רצו הוה אמינא שאין בה דין חלוקה אפילו רצו נמי לא קמ"ל ומי מצית אמרת הכי והא קתני סיפא אימתי בזמן שאין שניהם רוצים אבל בזמן ששניהם רוצים יחלוקו מאי לאו אכותל לא אמסיפס בעלמא וליתני האי ולא ליתני האי סיפא אצטריכא ליה ובכתבי הקדש אע"פ ששניהם רוצים לא יחלוקו): במאי אוקימתא למתני' בשאין בה דין חלוקה אי בשאין בה דין חלוקה כי רצו מאי הוי נהדרו בהו א"ר אסי א"ר יוחנן ו) שקנו מידן א] וכי קנו מידן מאי הוי קנין דברים בעלמא הוא ה) בשקנו מידן ברוחות רב אשי אמר ו) כגון שהלך זה בתוך שלו והחזיק וזה בתוך שלו והחזיק: מקום שנהגו לבנות כו': ז) גויל אבני דלא משפיא גזית אבני דמשפיא דכתיב ב) כל אלה אבנים יקרות כמדות גזית ח) (וגו') כפיסין ארחי לבינין ליבני אמר ליה רבה בריה דרבא לרב אשי ממאי דגויל אבני דלא משפיא ניניהו והאי טפח יתירא למורשא דקרנתא דילמא פלגא דגזית הוא והאי טפח יתירא לביני אורבי הוא כדקאמרינן כפיסין ארחי לבינין ליבני והאי טפח יתירא לביני אורבי אמר ליה וליטעמיך כפיסין ארחי מנלן אלא גמרא גמירי לה גויל נמי אבני דלא משפיא גמרא גמירי לה איכא דאמרי אמר ליה רב אחא בריה דרב אויא לרב אשי ממאי דהאי כפיסין ארחי ניניהו והאי טפח יתירא לביני אורבי דילמא מאי כפיסין אבני דלא משפיין והאי טפח יתירא למורשא דקרנתא כדקאמרינן גויל אבני דלא משפיין גזית אבני דמשפיין והאי טפח יתירא למורשא דקרנתא אמר ליה וליטעמיך גויל אבני דלא משפיין מנלן אלא גמרא גמירי לה הכא נמי גמרא גמירי לה אמר אביי שמע מינה כל ביני אורבי טפח הני מילי בטינא אבל בריכסא בעי טפי ואיכא דאמרי הני מילי בריכסא אבל בטינא לא בעי כולי האי למימרא דבגזית (ה) דכל ד' אמות גובה אי הוי פותיא חמשא קאי אי לא לא קאי והא אמה טרקסין דהואי גבוה תלתין אמהתא ולא הוה פותיא אלא שית פושכי וקם כיון דאיכא טפח יתירא קאי ובמקדש שני מ"ט לא עבוד אמה טרקסין כי קאי בתלתין קאי טפי לא קאי ומנלן דהוה גבוה טפי דכתיב ג) גדול יהיה כבוד הבית הזה האחרון מן הראשון רב ושמואל ואמרי לה ר' יוחנן ור"א חד אמר בבנין וחד אמר

מאי קא משמע לן בשאין בה דין חלוקה. אע"ג דקא משמע לן דשמיה היזק ה"פ מאי קמ"ל במאי דאיירי באין בה דין חלוקה לישמעינן בשיש בה דין חלוקה [אע"ג דלא רצו] (כשרצו) פלגי כ) תימה הא קמ"ל דאפילו באין בה דין חלוקה דאיכא למימר על מנת לעשות גודא לא איתרצאי כדפירש לעיל: **כי** רצו מאי הוי נידהדרו בהו. למ"ד מחילה גודא לא פריך דאיכא למימר דקנו ושיעבדו נכסיהן לבנין הכותל אלא למ"ד פלוגתא לא מהני קנין דקנין דברים בעלמא הוא דלא מסיק אדעתיה שקנו ברוחות: **קנין** דברים בעלמא הוא. בפרק השוכר את הפועלים (ב"מ דף צד.) דתנן מתנה ש"ח להיות כשואל ומוקי לה בקנו מידו התם לאו קנין דברים הוא אלא קנין גמור הוא שמשעבד את עצמו שאם יאנס שישלם ל): **רב** אשי אמר כגון שהלך כו'. תימה לר"י מה בא רב אשי להוסיף וכי איצטריך לאשמועינן דחזקה מועלת כמו קנין ונראה לר"י דהא קמ"ל דאע"ג דקאמר לקמן בחזקת הבתים (דף נג.) שלא בפניו צריך למימר לו לך חזק וקני הכא כיון שאמרו אתה תקח רוח צפונית ואני רוח דרומית והלך והחזיק לו כל אחד בשלו זה שלא בפני זה נעשה כמי שקנו מידם ברוחות אע"פ שלא אמרו זה לזה לך חזק וקני: **ארבע** אמות גובה אפותיא דה' קאי טפי לא קאי. וקשיא לר"ת הא לבינין דגריעי קאי בשלשה טפחים ועוד הא קא חזינן דקאי בגזית טפי אפורתא ותירץ דהכי קאמר טפי לא קאי כמשפט גזית שרולים בני אדם לבנותו שיעמוד ימים רבים כשבונים בגזית: **טרקסין.** אומר ר"ת דטרק הוי כמו טרוקי גלי (ברכות דף כח.) וסין הוי סיני כלומר שהיה מפסיק וסוגר את הלוחות שנתנו בסיני שהיו מונחות בארון שהיה בבית קדשי הקדשים וי"מ טרקסין פנים וחוץ שאותה אמה היתה ספק אם מקודשת פנים או חוץ ולכך היו שם שתי פרוכת כדאמרינן ביומא (דף נא:): **שאני** התם דאיכא טפח יתירא. ה"מ לשני דאגב תקרה ומעזיבה קאי טפי כדאמרי' בסמוך: אמר

רבינו גרשום

ל"א [מפיק] כולה הלכה דכיון שרצו לחלוק אם מעכב א' מלעשות כותל בונין אותו **בעל כרחו:** א) **וטעמא דרצו** לעשות [כותל] מש"ה בונין הא **לא רצו** בין שניהן אלא א' רוצה וא' מעכב **אין מחייבין אותו אלמא היזק ראיה לאו שמיה היזק: שרצו לחצות מיבעי ליה.** כלומר אם איתא דמחיצה דמתני' פלוגתא אמאי תני לעשות ליתני לחצות בשלמא אי אמרת גודא אמטא להכי תני לעשות דלא מיתני בלא לעשות. ומשני לעולם מחיצה פלוגתא ודקא קשיא לך שרצו לחצות מיבעי ליה לאו קשיא דמתני' משתעי בלשון בני אדם דאמרי **תא ונעביד פלוגתא** ולעולם היזק ראיה שמיה היזק: **מאי איריא** דתני מתני' **רצו** לחלוק מש"ה בונין את הכותל באמצע בעל כרחו משום היזק ראיה דהואיל דנתרצו לחלוק בונין **אפי' לא** רצו שניהן לחלוק הואיל דנתרצה א' מהן לחלוק בדין הוא דבונין את הכותל לאמצע אע"ג דלא נתרצה אידך משום היזק ראיה: **משנתנו בשאין בה דין חלוקה** שאין בה ד' אמות לזה וד' אמות לזה מש"ה **אם נתרצו** שניהן לחלוק בונין את הכותל בעל כורחו הואיל דנתרצו לחלוק משום היזק ראיה ואם לא נתרצה א' מהן לחלוק אע"ג דמעכב אידך אין בונין הואיל דאין בה דין חלוקה: **תנינא.** בסיפא דמתני' אימתי אמרי' דאין חלוקה הואיל דלית בה דין חלוקה **בזמן שאין שניהן רוצין: במסיפס בעלמא.** חולקין הואיל ונתרצו קמ"ל רישא דמתני' דקתני **כותל** הלכה לא סגי בלא כותל משום היזק ראיה: **וליתני הא רישא** דמתני' **ולא** בעי סיפא **למיתני.** ומשני **סיפא איצטריכא לה** למיתני דקתני **וכתבי הקדש לא יחלוקו.** משום דקא נהוג בהו מנהג בזיון ואגב סיפא דלא סגי דלא ליתני קתני רישא אימתי בזמן כו': **בשקנו מידן.** דלא מצי למיהדר בהו: **קנין דברים בעלמא הוא** כלומר (אין זה) [איזה] קנין הוא עיקר כגון מתנה או מכירה או שום דבר שמראה לו החפץ שנותן למקבל וקונין מידו על כך אבל הכא שאדם אומר לחבירו ניטול קנין שנחלוק כגון זה קנין דברים בעלמא הוא דלא נברר על מה נוטל קנין ואכתי ליהדרו בהו: **שקנו מידן ברוחות.** דזה הקנה לזה אותו חלק שבצד רוח מזרח וזה לזה חלק שבצד רוח מערב דהיינו קנין גמור הואיל והוברר על מה קנו: **רב אשי אומר** מש"ה לא מצי למיהדר בהו הואיל דקני אע"ג דלית בה דין חלוקה **כגון שהלך זה** לאחר קנין להחזיק בחלקו דנעל גדר ופרץ כל שהוא ודאי בתר הכי לא מצי למיהדר: **פיסקא גויל.** אבנים שנחצבו מן ההר דעדיין אין משופין והם ו' טפחים: **גזית.** אבנים משופין והן של ה' טפחים. **כפיסין, ארחי** חצי לבינה לבינה שלימה היא ג' טפחים. **מקום שנהגו לבנות בגויל** דמן ו' טפחים זה נותן ג' טפח מחלוקו בקרקע וזה ג' טפח. **בגזית** של חמש טפחים זה נותן טפחיים ומחצה וזה נותן טפחיים ומחצה. **כפיסין** שהן טפח ומחצה זה נותן טפחיים וזה נותן טפחיים לפי שכשיתן זה כפיס אחד מטפח ומחצה וזה כפיס אחד מטפח ומחצה דהיינו ג' טפחים עדיין צריך לתת **ביני אורבי** לפי שכשמניחין כפיס מכאן וכפיס מכאן ב) ובאמצע כשיעור טפח של סיד כדי שיהיו מדובקות בטינא יפה והיינו ב' טפחים מן הקרקע לכל אחד: **לבינים.** כותל של לבינים לא הוי אלא ג' טפחים שאין מניחין לבינה כנגד לבינה אלא ג' על גב זה: **דלא משפיין.** שאין משופות ומסותתות: **ארחי.** חצי לבינה: **לבינים ליבני.** הכי קרו להו בלשון [המון]. (האי) **ממאי דהאי טפח יתירא** דמייתרי מתני' בגויל טפי משום דצריך ההוא טפח **למורש' דקרנתא** מן הכותל טפי מכותל של גזית משום דגזית משפיא וגויל לא משפייא **דילמא** האי גויל לאו מר' טפחים הוי כי אם **פלגא דגזית** דהיינו ב' טפחים ומחצה ומש"ה צריך ליתן לכל חד וחד ג' טפחים מן הקרקע משום דהאי יהיב גויל מב' טפחים ומחצה [וכן] אידך הכי (טפי) וטפח דמייתר מתני' [בגויל] על אבני גזית משום טינא שמניחין **ביני ארבי כדאמרי' כפיסין ארחי** כול' **וממאי** דהני **כפיסין** דקתני מתני' **ארחי ניניהו** דהיינו חצי לבינה **והאי טפח יתירא** דמייתר בכפיסין טפי מליבנא משום (דביה) [דביני] ארבי **דלמא** האי כפיסין דקתני מתני' אבנים דלא משפיין ניניהו ולא מתוקנות כשאר ליבני. הכי קאמרת נמי הכי כול': **אמר אביי ש"מ** ממתני' דקתני בכפיסים זה נותן טפחיים וזה נותן טפחיים איכא למשמע מינה **כל ביני** ארבי טפח ליתן לגבי סיד. **והני מילי** דסגי בטפח **בטינא** שמגובל מחול וסיד **אבל בריכסא** היינו טיט חוצות שמגובל במים ועפר הואיל ואינו מדובק יפה **בעי** ודאי **טפי** מטפח: **למימרא** דכל כותל (בוני) [שבונין] **מגזית גבוה ד'** כגון זה שהיא להזק ראיה שהיה צריך להגביהו אלא ד' אמות כדתנן כותל חצר שנפל וכו' והוא מאבני גזית שהם ה' טפחים וקמ"ל מתני' **דאי פותיא ה'** טפחים ההוא כותל דגבוה ד' אמות מצי **קאי** הכותל אבל אי גבוה טפי מד' **לא קאי** בה' טפחים רוחב: **והא אמה טרקסין.** הכותל שהיה מפסיק בין ההיכל לקודש הקדשים קרי ליה אמה טרקסין דעובי הכותל הוי אמה בת ו' טפחים ואי קשיא אמאי מקשה מגזית טפי מגויל וכפיסין וליבני תריץ משום דבעי לאקשויי ליה מאמה טרקסין (דביני) [דבנו] מאבני גזית ומקדש ראשון היה גבוה ל' והיא אמה טרקסין **לא הוה פותייה אלא י' פושכי** ואפ"ה **קם** ההוא כותל **והיכי אמרת עד ד' אמות בגובה קאי כותל דעבה ה' טפחים ותו לא שאני התם הואיל ואיכא טפח יתירא** על ה' טפחים מצי **קאי** עד גובה ל': **ובמקדש שני מאי טעמא לא עביד אמה טרקסין.** אלא פרוכת כדתנן בפ' הוציאו לו (יומא נא.) שתי פרוכות היו שם וביניהם אמה וכו': **אתלתין קאי.** כלומר מקדש ראשון שהיה גבוה ל' אמה כעובי אמה מצי קאי **טפי לא קאי: וחד אמר בבנין.** שהיה גבוה יותר מן הראשון:

חשק שלמה על רבינו גרשום א) [נראה דל"ל בונין אותו בעל כרחו משום דהזיק ראיה שמיה היזק ולימא מאי מחילה גודא וכו' וטעמא דרצו וכו']: ב) [נ"ל לריך להניח באמלע וכו']:

ט א ב ג מיי' פ"ב מהל' שכנים הל' יד סמג עשין פב טוש"ע ח"מ סי' קנז סעיף ה:
י ד ה ו מיי' שם הל' י טוש"ע שם סעיף ג:

א) [ל"ל דתניא], ב) [לעיל ב. וש"נ], ג) [לקמן יא.], ד) [שם], ה) [ב"מ לד. אינו], ו) [ב"מ טו. וש"נ], ז) [ב"מ לד], ח) [נ"ל מגררות במגרה וכן הגי' בערוך ערך שף א'], ט) [לקמן ה.], י) [עי' תוי"ט ריש פ"ה דיומא ד"ה לבין שתי דגרס מ' אמות וכתב דנתחלף בין מ' למאה ע"ש], כ) ס"א ותירץ מהר"ם ולפי גירסתו צ"ל כשרצו והגי' שלפנינו הוא גי' מהרש"א, ל) [וע"ע תוס' כתובות נד: ד"ה אע"פ].

הגהות הב"ח

(א) גמ' כדכתיב ותהי מחצת. נ"ב ולימא מאי מחילה גודא כדתנן מחילת הכרם שנפרצה אומר לו גדור חזרה ונפרצה: (ב) שם מאי קמ"ל דכי לית ביה דין חלוקה תא"מ ונ"ב ג"ר תוס' שבאין בה דין חלוקה: (ג) שם לא יחלוקו וכו' מאי הוי ליהדר ביה וכו' בשקנו מידן כו' לישנא אחרינא דלאשמעינן באין בה: (ה) שם למימרא דבגזית כל כ"ל ואות ד' נמחק: (ו) רש"י ד"ה קנין וכו' או מכר או מתנה: (ז) ד"ה בבנין שהיה גובהו כ"ג נ"ב נראה דזה היה טעות הסופר דהא בית ראשון היה גבוה ק"כ אמה דהיינו ל' מעליה ראשונה והבית גופיה ל"א משקדש ראשון גבוה יותר וע"כ צ"ל ותשיב עד העלייה דראשון לא הוה רק שלשים ושני מ' וע"ל דף ג"מ ע"ב:

גליון הש"ס

גמרא כגון שהלך זה. עי' בתשובת רשב"א סי' אלף רכ"ו וק"ע:

הגהות מהר"ב רנשבורג

א] גמרא וכי קנו מידן מאי הוי. נ"ב ע' רש"י ד"ה קנין דברים כו' הש"ך בח"מ סי' קנו ס"ק ד' כ"ב נראה שלא זכר רבינו ועיין ערכין דף כ' ע"א תוס' ד"ה ולא יחנה גו' ודו"ק:

ליקוטי רש"י

[נדפס בעמוד הקודם]

תורה אור השלם

א) וַתְּהִי מֶחֱצַת הָעֵדָה מִן הַצֹּאן שְׁלֹשׁ מֵאוֹת אֶלֶף וּשְׁלֹשִׁים אֶלֶף שִׁבְעַת אֲלָפִים וַחֲמֵשׁ מֵאוֹת: [במדבר לא, מג]

ב) כָּל אֵלֶּה אֲבָנִים יְקָרֹת כְּמִדֹּת גָּזִית מְגֹרָרוֹת בַּמְּגֵרָה מִבַּיִת וּמִחוּץ וּמִמַּסָּד עַד הַטְּפָחוֹת וּמִחוּץ עַד הֶחָצֵר הַגְּדוֹלָה: [מלכים א ז, ט]

ג) גָּדוֹל יִהְיֶה כְּבוֹד הַבַּיִת הַזֶּה הָאַחֲרוֹן מִן הָרִאשׁוֹן אָמַר יְיָ צְבָאוֹת וּבַמָּקוֹם הַזֶּה אֶתֵּן שָׁלוֹם נְאֻם יְיָ צְבָאוֹת: [חגי ב, ט]

עין משפט נר מצוה

יא א מיי' פ"ב מהלכות שכנים הלכה יח סמג עשין פב טוש"מ סי' קנז:
יב ב מיי' פי"א מהל' שבת הל' יג סמג עשין מד טוש"ע א"ח סי' שסג סעיף ח:
יג ג ד מיי' פי"א מהל' תפלה הל' יב סמג עשין יט טוש"ע א"ח סי' קנב [וברב אלפס פרק בני העיר דף רסד]:
יד ה ו מיי' פ"ח מהל' מתנות עניים הל' יא סמג עשין קסב טוש"ע י"ד סי' רנב סעיף ד:
טו ז מיי' פי"א מהל' תפלה הלכה יב סמג עשין יט טוש"ע א"ח סי' קנב [וברב אלפס פרק בני העיר דף רסד]:

מסורת הש"ס

א) עירובין יג:, ב) מגלה כו:, ג) נ"א דוכתא לצלויי, רש"א, ד) נ"א מלתא דמצוה ויהבי, רש"ל, ה) [ערכין ו.], ו) [שם], ז) קדושין ע"ב,

בשנים ואיתא להא ואיתא להא וניעבדו תלתין אמין בבנין ואידך ניעביד פרוכת כי קאי תלתין אמהתא נמי אגב תקרה ומעזיבה (א) הוה קאי בלא תקרה ומעזיבה לא הוה קאי וליעביד מה דאפשר בבנין וליעביד אידך פרוכת אמר אביי גמירי אי כולהו בבנין אי כולהו בפרוכת אי כולהו בבנין ממקדש אי כולהו בפרוכת ממשכן איבעיא להו הן וסידן או דילמא הן בלא סידן אמר ר"נ בר יצחק [א] מסתברא הן וסידן דאי ס"ד הן בלא סידן ליתנייה לשיעוריה אלא לאו ש"מ הן וסידן לא לעולם אימא לך הן בלא סידן וכיון דלא הוי טפח לא תני והא קתני (ב) בלבינין זה נותן טפח ומחצה וזה נותן טפח ומחצה התם חזי לאיצטרופי ת"ש [ב] הקורה שאמרו רחבה כדי לקבל אריח והאריח חצי לבינה של ג' טפחים התם ברברבתא דיקא נמי דקתני של שלשה טפחים מכלל דאיכא זוטרא ש"מ: אמר רב חסדא [ג] לא ליסתור איניש בי כנישתא עד דבני בי כנישתא אחריתי איכא דאמרי [ד] משום פשיעותא ואיכא דאמרי משום צלויי מאי בינייהו איכא בינייהו דאיכא [ג] (בי כנישתא אחריתי) מרימר ומר זוטרא סתרי ובנו בי קייטא בסיתווא (ג) ובנו בי סיתווא בקייטא א"ל רבינא לרב אשי גבו זוזי ומחתי מאי אמר ליה [ה] דילמא מיתרמי להו [ו] פדיון שבויים ויהבי להו שריגי ליבני והדרי הודרי ומחתי כשורי מאי א"ל [ז] זמנין דמתרמי להו פדיון שבויים מזבני ויהבי להו א"ה אפי' בנו נמי אמר ליה דירתיה דאינשי לא מזבני ולא אמרן [ז] אלא דלא חזי בה תיוהא אבל חזי בה תיוהא סתרי ובני כי הא דרב אשי חזא בה תיוהא בכנישתא דמתא מחסיא סתריה ועייל לפוריי' להתם ולא אפקיה עד דמתקין ליה שפיכי ובבא בן בוטא היכי אסביה ליה עצה להורדוס למיסתריה לבית המקדש והאמר רב חסדא לא ליסתור איניש בי כנישתא עד דבני בי כנישתא אחריתא אי בעית אימא תיוהא חזא ביה איבעית אימא [ח] מלכותא שאני דלא הדרא ביה דאמר [ט] שמואל אי אמר מלכותא עקרנא טורי עקר טורי ולא הדר ביה הורדוס עבדא דבית חשמונאי הוה נתן עיניו באותה תינוקת יומא חד (ד) שמע ההוא גברא בת קלא דאמר כל עבדא דמריד השתא מצלח קם קטלינהו לכולהו מרותיה ושיירה לההיא ינוקתא כי חזת ההיא ינוקתא דקא בעי למינסבה סליקא לאיגרא (ה) ורמא קלא אמרה [י] כל מאן דאתי ואמר מבית חשמונאי קאתינא עבדא הוא דלא אישתיירא מינייהו אלא ההיא ינוקתא וההיא ינוקתא נפלה מאיגרא לארעא טמנה שבע שנין בדובשא איכא דאמרי בא עליה איכא דאמרי לא בא עליה דאמרי לה בא עליה הא דטמנה ליתובי ליצריה ודאמרי לה לא בא עליה האי דטמנה כי היכי דנאמרו בת מלך נסב אמר מאן דריש [א] מקרב אחיך תשים עליך מלך רבנן קם קטלינהו לכולהו רבנן שבקיה לבבא בן בוטא למשקל עצה מניה

רש"י

בשנים. בית ראשון עמד ד' מאות ועשר ובית שני ד' מאות ועשרים: אגב תקרה ומעזיבה. שהעלייה היתה נתונה עליו ומעזיבה של טיט טרכש על גגה וכובד המשא מעמיד הכותל שלא יטה לצדדין הלכך במקדש שני שלא היה כותל ל' מגיע לעלייה לא יוכל לעמוד: הן וסידן או הן בלא סידן. הני שיעורי דמתני' עם עובי הטיח קא חשיב להן או דילמא מקום האבנים הוי בפותיא לבד טיח הסיד: והא קתני טפחיים ומחצה. אלמא חצי טפח נמי חשיב: חזי לאיצטרופי. של זה ושל זה מצטרפין לטפח: הקורה שאמרו. לענין הכשר מבוי: ג' טפחים. אלמא ג' טפחים דקתני לגבי מתני' גבי לבינין כדקתני זה נותן טפח ומחצה וזה נותן טפח ומחצה הן בלא סידן קאמר דהא לבינה לחודה שלשה טפחים: התם ברברבתא. ומתני' בזוטרתא דעם סידן לא הוו אלא ג' טפחים: משום פשיעותא. דילמא מתרמי אונס ופשעי ולא בנו אחריתי: משום צלויי. כל זמן הבנין: בי קייטא בסיתווא. בית הכנסת היא להם לימות החורף נמוך בכתלים רחבים וחלונות מועטין מפני הצינה ובימות החמה בית הכנסת אחר שאויר שולט בו: זוזי. לצורך בית הכנסת החדש ומונחים ביד הגבאי מי איכא למיחש לפשיעות או לא: שריגי ליבני. מסודרים הלבינים זה על גב זה ומזומנים לנתן בבנין: הדרי הודרי. משופין ומתוקנין רהיטי הגג קיברונ"ש: כי בנו נמי. בי כנישתא חדתא לא נסתרוה לעתיקא דדילמא מתרמי פדיון שבויין ומזבני ליה: ולא אמרן. דלא ליסתרוה לעתיקא: אלא דלא חזו ביה תיוהא. ביקוע שיהא מזומן ליפול: עייליה לפורייה התם. כדי שלא יתייאש בבנינו שהחמה והגשמים מלערין אותו: שפכי. מרזבין: היכי אסביה עצה להורדוס. כדאמרי' לקמן בשמעתין וכתובה היא ביוסיפון בן גוריון: אהדר

תוספות

אמר אביי גמירי. השתא לא צריך לשנויא קמא: מכלל דאיכא זוטרתי. וא"ת ודילמא מכלל דאיכא רברבתא ומה דיקא הוא זה ותירץ ר"י דאם אין פחות משלשה אבל גדולות יש א"כ בכדי נקט חצי לבינה של ג' טפחים דלא הוה צריך למתני אלא והאריח חצי לבינה ותו לא וממילא הייתי משער בקטנה הואיל ולא מפרש שיעורא: הג"ה בי קייטא ובי סיתווא הוי כמו איכא תיוהא ושרי ואם שתי בתי כנסיות היו בב' מקומות של קייטא ושל סיתווא איירי כגון דחזו בה תיוהא ועוד נראה כיון דיש שם בהכ"נ אחר אין לחוש אם לא יבנו זאת והא דקאמר דאיכא דוכתא לצלויי היינו שאין בהכ"נ ועוד מחמת קור וחום אין לחוש שמא יפשעו או בזמן גדול כל כך אין לחוש. ע"כ הגה"ה: אי הכי כי בנייה נמי. פירוש עד שיתפללו בה: ועייליה לפורייה להתם. ותימה והא אמרת בתי כנסיות אין ישנים בהם לא שינת קבע ולא שינת עראי ואין לתרץ משום דבבבל הוי ואמר רב אסי בפ' בתרא דמגילה (דף כח: ושם ד"ה בתי) בתי כנסיות של בבל על תנאי הן עשויות ופ"ה התם נפקא מינה לענין הא דקתני לעיל אין אוכלין בהן ואין שותים בהן ואין נכנסין בהן בחמה מפני החמה ובגשמים מפני הגשמים ושל בבל מותר דהא קאמר התם בתר הכי רבינא ורב אדא הוו קיימי ושיילי שמעתא מרבא אתא זילחא דמטרא עלייהו ועיילי לבי כנישתא ולא משום מטרא אלא משום דשמעתא בעי' צילותא והשתא והלא בהכ"נ של בבל היה והיו יכולין ליכנס בה מפני המטר וי"ל דלאו ממש לבהכ"נ עיילה לפוריי' אלא בסמוך לבהכ"נ במקום שהאורחין רגילין לישן שם ולאכול כדאמרינן בע"פ (פסחים דף קא. ושם ד"ה דאכלי) ושמואל למה לי' לקדושי בבי כנישתא לאפוקי אורחים ידי חובתן דאכלו ושתו וגנו בבי כנישתא והא דאמר דעל תנאי הן עשויין מפרש ר"י לענין שאם יחרבו יעשו מהן מה שירצו לבד מקלות ראש כדאמרי' התם: כל דאמר מבית חשמונאי אתינא עבדא הוא. וכן הוא דהכי נמי אמר שמואל בפרק עשרה יוחסין (קדושין דף ע:) ומכאן קשה על פ"ה באלו נאמרים (סוטה דף מא.) דאמר אמרו לו לאגריפס אחינו אתה ופ"ה התם שאמרו לו אחינו לפי שהיתה אמו מישראל דא"כ כיון דבני הורדוס היה שמואל גופיה אית ליה עובד כוכבים ועבד הבא על בת ישראל הולד כשר בפסולו (יבמות דף מה.) וי"ל שלא נשאו ישראליות וקראוהו אחינו אתה לפי שעבד אחינו [הוא] במצות:

מאן דריש מקרב אחיך רבנן. דפשטי' דקרא לא משמע למעוטי עבד שהוא אחיך במצות אלא עובד כוכבים ורבנן דרשו (ב"ק פח.) ממובחר שבאחיך [וע"ע תוס' יבמות מה: ד"ה כיון דאמו]: קטלינהו לכולהו רבנן. לאו דוקא לכולהו דהא הוו בני בתירה שהיו נשיאים כשעלה הלל מבבל כדאמרינן בפסחים בפרק אלו דברים (דף סו.) והלל היה בפני הבית מאה שנה כדאמרינן בפרק קמא דשבת (דף טו.) ומלכות הורדוס היה בפני הבית ק"ג שנה כדאמרינן בפרק קמא דע"ז (דף ט.):

רבינו גרשום

איתא להא ואית' להא. דהא בין בבנין בין בשנים היה גדול: כי קאי נמי תלתין אמה בעובי אמה בבית הראשון משום דהתקרה והמעזיב' מונחת עליו וסומכתו שלא יפול אם לא הוי הכי לא קאי אפי' בתלתין: ונעבד כמה דאפשר. לעמוד בגובה בבנין כותל ומכאן ולמעלה עד התקרה ליעבד פרוכת: אי כוליה בפרוכת. ממשכן [דכתיב] והבדילה הפרוכת וגו': הן וסידן. כלומר הא דתנינן בגויל זה נותן ג' טפחים וזה נותן ג' טפחים תני שמסידו מבחוץ צריך ג' טפחים (דאי לא הכי) [דליכא הכא] ו' טפחים שלימות בדבר שיעור מקום הסיד: או הן בלא סידן כלומר דלמקום גויל גרידא בעי למיתן זה ג' טפחים וזה ג' טפחים חוץ ממקום הסיד: דאי ס"ד הן בלא סידן. ו' טפחים (ולמקום) [ולעולם] בעי למיתב תרוייהו א"כ ניתנייה לשיעורא דסיד ולימא הכי זה נותן ג' טפחים ומשהו למקום הסיד וזה נותן ג' טפחים ומשהו למקום הסיד השני כמו כן בכולהו אלא מדלא תני הכי ש"מ מקום הגויל ומקום הסיד לא הוי אלא ו' טפחים (אלא) [לא] לעולם אימא לך הן בלא סידן ואי אמרת אמאי לא תני שיעורא דסיד כיון דלא הוי טפח לא חשיב למתנייה: התם חזי לאצטרופי. ב' חצאי טפח לטפח אבל מקום הסיד לא חזי לאצטרופי לשום חשבון: קורה שאמרו. לגבי מבוי מדתני לבינה של ג' טפחים מכלל דג' טפחים שלימות הוי כל לבינה וש"מ דלמקום לבינה בענין ג' טפחים שלימות לבד ממקום הסיד הוה"ה לגויל וכפים וגזית: (מיהו) [דהתם דמהא] לא תידוק דמקום לבינה ג' טפחים שלימות דאותן טפחים גדולים [א] מדי גבי לבינות אבל מתני' בטפחים בינונים הן ומשה"ה הן וסידן ו' טפחים: משום פשיעותא. דדלמא מטריד בשאר מילי ולא בני ליה: משום לצלויי. דלא הוה להו דוכתא לצלויי עד שיעסוק בבנין: סתרו ובנו בי קייטא בסיתוא. שמעתי [דשתי] בתי כנסיות היו להם באחד היו מתפללין בימות הגשמים ובאחד בימות החמה אותו של ימות החמה היו מחזקין אותו בימות הגשמים ושל ימות הגשמים בימות החמה כדי שיהא להם מקום תפלה בכל שעה: גבו זוזי. מציבורא לצורך בית הכנסת: ומחתי. ומונחין הן במקום אחד [מי] אמרינן הואיל והמעות גבויין לא פשעי ומצי למיסתריה או דלמא ניחוש דלמא יהבינהו למצוה אחריתי. אם תמצא לומר דהמעות יתנו לפדיון שבוים. הדרי הודרי. מתוקנים הזיזין. שריגי ליבני שמתוקנין וערוכין הלבינים. ומחתי כשורי ומונחין הקורות והכל [שקנו] להתחיל הבנין מאי יכול לסתור הישן קודם שיתחילו החדש או לאו: אי הכי דאכתי איכא למיחש אפי' כי מיבני האי לא ליסתור אחרינא דאיכא למיחש דמתרמי להו פדיון שבוים ומזבני ליה ואיכא פשיעותא ומשני דירתא דאינשא לא מזדבן כ"ש בית הכנסת הואיל ומתוקן הוא וליכא למיחש: ולא אמרן דלא לסתור עד דבני אחרינא אלא דלא חזו ביה תיוהא. רעוע או סדק אבל חזו ביה תיוהא סתר לאלתר: ועיילה לפורייה להתם. כדי שיהיו הגשמים יורדין ומנטפין עליו והוא ימהר במלאכת בהכ"נ יותר: שפיכי. מרזבין: אי הכי דלא ליסתור עד דבני אחרינא. בבא בן בוטא היכי אסביה עצה כו'. מלכא שאני דכיון דאמר למיבנייה לא הדר ביה וליכא למיחש לפשיעות': באותה תינוקת. דבית חשמונאי:

חשק שלמה על רבינו גרשום א) [ונראה דל"ל דאותן לבינות דתני גבי מבוי לבינות גדולות של ג"ט אבל מתני' בלבינות בינונים הן וכו']:

הגהות הב"ח

(א) גמ' ומעזיבה קאי בלא תקרה ומעזיבה לא קאי כצ"ל ותיבת הוה נמחק ב' פעמים: (ב) שם לא תני והא קתני בגזית זה נותן טפחים ומחצה וזה נותן טפחים ומחצה התם חזי לאצטרופי: (ג) שם בי קייטא בסיתווא וסתרי ובנו בי סיתווא: (ד) שם יומא חד שמעיה לבת קלא דאמר כצ"ל ותיבת ההוא גברא נמחק: (ה) שם ורמת קלא:

תורה אור השלם

א) שׂוֹם תָּשִׂים עָלֶיךָ מֶלֶךְ אֲשֶׁר יִבְחַר יְיָ אֱלֹהֶיךָ בּוֹ מִקֶּרֶב אַחֶיךָ תָּשִׂים עָלֶיךָ מֶלֶךְ לֹא תוּכַל לָתֵת עָלֶיךָ אִישׁ נָכְרִי אֲשֶׁר לֹא אָחִיךָ הוּא: [דברים יז, טו]

לעזי רש"י

קיברונ"ש. פירוש רהיטי הגג, קורות הגג, זחין (רבינו גרשום דף ג ע"ב ודף ו ע"א ועיין רש"י שם ד"ה אחזיק לכשורי)

ליקוטי רש"י

רחבה כדי לקבל אריח. שתהא דומה לקביעות לבנות עליה בנין. והאריח חצי לבנה של שלשה טפחים. נמצא אריח טפח ומחצה רוחב [עירובין יג:]. משום פשיעותא. שמא יפשעו (אלא) ויתייאשו ולא יבנה אחר [מגילה כו:]. תיוהא. קלקול [ב"ק כ.]. טורי. הרים [ברכות נד.]. כל מאן דאתי ואמר מבית חשמונאי קאתינא עבדא הוא. כגון זרעו של הורדוס שהיה עבד לבית חשמונאי ונכרת ידו ומלך [כתובות יד:]. שכל זרעו של הורדוס ועבד היה ומלך והחזיק וקרא בניו על שם בית חשמונאי ומשפחתו לאו בנות ישראל נשא והוו כולם עבדים [קידושין ע:]. איגרא. גגין [פסחים פה:]. עליה [תענית כג. וקידושין מה:]. [מכאן שייך לדף ד.]. גם במדעך מלך. אפי' במחשבתך בלבך דכור. גם אפילו, מלך על כן קרא לה רבינא למלכו של עולם. ד"ה כמשמעו מלך בשר ודם. עוף השמים וגו'. ולפי משמעו השומעים והסבי' יש לך לדאג מכל בריה שמא יש שומעין ויגיד לאחרים [קהלת י, כ]. ובויקרא רבה. בן המלוכי כי עוף השמים יוליך את הקול [קהלת י]

זה עורב וחכמת טואלרי [דה"י ב, ט, ד]. אברך. כתרגומו דין אבא למלכא רך בלשון ארמי מלך בהשותפין [...] [בראשית מא מג וכעי"ז רש"י שבת נג.]. שישא. שיש לבוע לא לבן ולא שחור אלא כעין ירוק בלע"ז בי"ש. ומרמרא. שיש לבן. כוחלא. שישא לבוע ככחול. אפיק שפה. שורה של אבנים נכנסה ושורה יוצאה. דמיחזי כי אידוותא דימא. שהאבנים משונים במראיהן זו מזו והעינים המסתכלות בהן שוטטות ונראות כאילו גלי הים הם נדים ונעים [סוכה נא:]. להן מלכא. באמת אתה מלך שמע לעצתי. מלכי. עצתי כמו איעצך אמלכינך. ישפר עלך. עצתי מיטב בעיניך לשמוע מילי [דניאל ד, כד]. דניאל אמר לנבוכדנצר כשפתר לו החלום שיהא נטרד מן האנשים ולהיות עם בהמה ושיה להן מלכא [...] ישפר עליך עצתי מיטב בעיניך להאמין לעצתי [סוטה כ:]. וחטאיך בצדקה פרוק. וחטאתך בצדקה פרוק [...] [דניאל שם]. חטאך ע"י צדקה פדה [סוטה שם]. ועויתך במחן עניין. ועונותיך פרוק בחנינת עניים [דניאל שם] [...] העניים [סוטה שם]. הן תהוה ארכא לשלותך. אולי תהא שהות לשלומך שלא תמהר הרעה לבא [...] טובה לנבוכדנצר ראה ישראל עניים שפלי גולה מחזירין על הפתחים והשיאו עצה לחנגס אמר לו עניים [...] פרנסם וכן עשה פתח אוצרותיו והיה מפרנסם כל י"ב חדש [דניאל שם]. ואז תהא אור זמן לשלומך שלא [...] עשה נבוכדנצר היה מקבץ בכל יום עניי ישראל שהביא בגולה והיו צריכין מזונות ומפרנסם ואף דניאל [...] נתכוין שראה את ישראל בגולה מחזרין על הפתחים [סוטה כא.]. וכתיב כולא מטא. כל הפתרון [...] שם, כה]. כל הפורענות הגיע על נבוכדנצר. ולקצת ירחין. תלה לו הזכות י"ב חדש [...]

בְּשָׁנִים — that it lay **in the years** of its existence.[1]

The Gemara notes that there is no dispute between these two opinions:

וְאִיתָא לְהָא וְאִיתָא לְהָא — **And this is true and that is true** — i.e. the Second Temple exceeded the first in both height and longevity.

The Gemara suggests that the *amah traksin* could have been preserved in the Second Temple:

וְנֶיעֶבְדוּ תְּלָתִין אַמִּין בְּבִנְיָן — **But let us make thirty *amos*** of [**the partition] as a** stone **structure,** similar to the one that stood securely in the First Temple, וְאִידָךְ נֶיעֱבִיד פָּרוֹכֶת — **and the other** (i.e. uppermost) ten *amos* **let us make** with **a curtain.** Why discontinue the *amah traksin* entirely?

The Gemara answers that under those circumstances the wall would not be structurally sound:

כִּי קָאֵי תְּלָתִין אַמְּהָתָא נַמִּי — **Even when** an *amah traksin* **stood thirty *amos*** high at a width of six *tefachim,* אַגַּב תִּקְרָה וּמַעֲזִיבָה הֲוָה קָאֵי — **it stood** only **on account of the ceiling and plaster** weighing upon it.[2] בְּלֹא תִּקְרָה וּמַעֲזִיבָה לֹא הֲוָה קָאֵי — However, **without** the support of **the ceiling and plaster,** an *amah traksin* **would not stand** securely. Thus, since in the Second Temple a thirty-*amah* wall would be a freestanding structure, the Gemara's alternative is rejected as unfeasible.

The Gemara suggests another means of retaining some form of *amah traksin* in the Second Temple:

וְלֶיעֱבִיד מַה דְּאֶפְשָׁר בְּבִנְיָן — **But make as much** of the partition **as possible as a** freestanding **structure,**[3] וְלֶיעֱבִיד אִידָךְ פָּרוֹכֶת — **and make the rest** with **a curtain.** Why was it necessary to abandon altogether the concept of an *amah traksin?*

Abaye rejects this suggestion:

אָמַר אַבַּיֵי — **Abaye said:** גְּמִירִי — **They taught** a tradition[4] that the partition between the Holy and the Holy of Holies must be created אִי כּוּלְּהוּ בְּבִנְיָן אִי כּוּלְּהוּ בְּפָרוֹכֶת — **either entirely with a structure or entirely with a curtain,** but not with a combination of the two. Thus, since constructing a freestanding stone wall forty *amos* tall was not feasible, there was no choice but to forego erecting an *amah traksin* as the partition in the Second Temple and to hang a curtain instead.[5]

The Gemara provides the source for this rule:

אִי כּוּלְּהוּ בְּבִנְיָן מִמִּקְדָּשׁ — That the partition was created **either entirely with a structure** is learned **from the** First **Temple,** where a wall divided the Holy from the Holy of Holies, אִי כּוּלְּהוּ בְּפָרוֹכֶת מִמִּשְׁכָּן — **or** that, in the alternative, it was created **entirely with a curtain** is learned **from the Tabernacle** constructed by Moses, where a curtain effected the division.[6]

It was customary in the time of the Mishnah to strengthen walls by plastering them with a layer of lime. The Gemara now discusses whether the thickness of this application is reflected in the width measurements dictated by the Mishnah:

אִיבַּעְיָא לְהוּ — **[A group of sages] asked:** הֵן וְסִידָן — Do the width measurements of the various types of stone wall include **[the walls] and their plastering** as well,[7] אוֹ דִילְמָא הֵן בְּלֹא סִידָן — **or, perhaps,** do they indicate **[the walls] without their plastering?**[8]

Rav Nachman attempts to answer the question:

אָמַר רַב נַחְמָן בַּר יִצְחָק — **Rav Nachman bar Yitzchak said:** מִסְתַּבְּרָא הֵן וְסִידָן — **It is logical** to assume that the width measurements specified by the Mishnah include **[the walls] and their plastering,** דְּאִי סַלְקָא דַּעְתָּךְ הֵן בְּלֹא סִידָן — **for if it enters your mind that** they indicate **[the walls] without their plastering,** לִיתְנְיֵיהּ לְשִׁיעוּרֵיהּ — **let** the Mishnah **teach the** required **measure [of plaster]** as well,[9] so as to project the actual amount of land that must be donated for the wall. אֶלָּא לָאו שְׁמַע מִינַּהּ הֵן וְסִידָן — **Rather,** since the Mishnah states only one measure for each type of wall, **can we not infer from it** (from the fact that the width of the plastering is not mentioned in the Mishnah) that the measurements include **[the walls] and their plastering?!**

The Gemara rejects this argument:

לֹא — This is **not** a conclusive proof, לְעוֹלָם אֵימָא לָךְ הֵן בְּלֹא סִידָן — for **actually I can say to you that** the Mishnah's measurements indicate **[the walls] without their plastering,** וְכֵיוָן דְּלָא הָוֵי טֶפַח — **and** to justify that exclusion, thereby depriving Rav Nachman of his proof, we can explain that **since [the plastering] is not** even **a *tefach*** wide, לֹא תָּנֵי — the Mishnah **did not** bother to **teach** its rather insignificant measurement, and that this omission does not render the Mishnah's schedule of allotments incorrect.

The Gemara objects to this reply, noting that the Mishnah does mention measurements of less than a *tefach:*

וְהָא קָתָנֵי — **But has it not been taught** in the Mishnah: בִּלְבֵינִין זֶה נוֹתֵן טֶפַח וּמֶחֱצָה וְזֶה נוֹתֵן טֶפַח וּמֶחֱצָה — If the wall is built WITH WHOLE BRICKS, THIS partner MUST PROVIDE ONE AND ONE-HALF *TEFACHIM* of land for the wall's base AND THAT partner MUST PROVIDE ONE AND ONE-HALF *TEFACHIM* for the wall's base?[10] Thus, since fractional measurements are worthy of mention, had the thickness of the plaster not been included in the width measurement of the wall, it would have been stated. — ? —

The Gemara answers this objection:

הָתָם חָזֵי לְאִיצְטָרוּפֵי — The two half-*tefachim* mentioned **there combine** to form a full *tefach*, which is significant. The plastering,

NOTES

1. The Second Temple stood for 420 years, while its predecessor endured for only 410 (*Rashi*).

2. A ceiling of beams rested upon the *amah traksin*, and a layer of plaster was spread across the beams. Hence, the weight of the ceiling stabilized the partition and prevented it from toppling. This support was unavailable in the Second Temple, where the ceiling rose forty *amos* above the floor of the Heichal, clearly beyond the reach of an *amah traksin (Rashi)*.

3. Although a freestanding stone wall thirty *amos* tall lacks stability, one of lesser height would not.

4. The word גְּמִירִי normally indicates an oral transmission from Sinai. However, here the reference is to specific Biblical sources, which are mentioned in the Gemara below.

5. Abaye's refutation [which cites a legal impediment to constructing a composite partition] supersedes the first refutation [which cited impracticality] (*Tosafos*).

6. The particulars of the curtain, or *paroches,* are discussed in *Exodus* 26:31-33.

7. So that, for instance, in the case of a wall constructed of unplaned *g'vil* stones, the stones themselves would provide slightly less than the required width of six *tefachim*, with the layer of plaster comprising the remainder (*Rabbeinu Gershom*).

8. So that each type of wall would occupy slightly more space than the specification in the Mishnah called for (*Rabbeinu Gershom*).

9. By stating: "Each partner must provide three *tefachim* of land *plus* a small amount for plaster [i.e. for a wall of unplaned stones]" (*Rabbeinu Gershom*).

10. In *Rashi's* text of the Gemara, a different case from the Mishnah — the first to state a fractional measurement — is quoted: בְּגָזִית זֶה נוֹתֵן טְפָחַיִים וּמֶחֱצָה וְזֶה נוֹתֵן טְפָחַיִים וּמֶחֱצָה, *(If the wall is built) with planed stones, this (partner) must provide two and one-half tefachim and that (partner) must provide two and one-half tefachim* (see also *Bach,* who emends our Gemara to conform with *Rashi's* text).

בשנים ואיתא להא ואיתא להא וניעבדו תלתין אמין בבנין ואידך ניעביד פרוכת כי קאי תלתין אמהתא נמי אגב תקרה ומעזיבה (א) הוה קאי בלא תקרה ומעזיבה לא הוה קאי וליעביד מה דאפשר בבנין וליעביד אידך פרוכת אמר אביי גמירי אי כולהו בבנין ממקדש אי כולהו בפרוכת ממשכן איבעיא להו הן וסידן או דילמא הן בלא סידן אמר ר"נ בר יצחק [א] מסתברא הן וסידן דאי ס"ד הן בלא סידן ליתנייה לשיעוריה אלא לאו ש"מ הן וסידן לא לעולם אימא לך הן בלא סידן וכיון דלא הוי טפח לא תני והא קתני (ב) בלבינין זה נותן טפח ומחצה וזה נותן טפח ומחצה התם חזי לאיצטרופי ת"ש [ב] הקורה שאמרו רחבה כדי לקבל אריח והאריח חצי לבינה של ג' טפחים התם ברברבתא דיקא נמי דקתני של שלשה טפחים מכלל דאיכא זוטרא ש"מ: אמר רב חסדא [ג] לא ליסתור איניש בי כנישתא עד דבני בי כנישתא אחריתי איכא דאמרי [ד] משום פשיעותא ואיכא דאמרי משום צלויי מאי בינייהו איכא בינייהו דאיכא (בי כנישתא אחריתי) מרימר ומר זוטרא סתרי ובנו בי קייטא בסיתווא (ג) ובנו בי סיתווא בקייטא א"ל רבינא לרב אשי גבו זוזי ומחתי מאי אמר ליה [ה] דילמא מיתרמי להו [ו] פדיון שבויים ויהבי להו שריגי ליבני והדרי הודרי ומחתי כשורי מאי א"ל זימנין דמתרמי להו פדיון שבויים מזבני ויהבי להו א"ה אפי' בנו נמי אמר ליה דירתיה דאינשי לא מזבני ולא אמרן [ז] אלא דלא חזי בה תיוהא אבל חזי בה תיוהא סתרי ובני כי הא דרב אשי חזא בה תיוהא בכנישתא דמתא מחסיא סתריה ועייל לפורייה להתם ולא אפקיה עד דמתקין ליה שפיכי ובבא בן בוטא היכי אסביה ליה עצה להורדוס למיסתריה לבית המקדש והאמר רב חסדא לא ליסתור איניש בי כנישתא עד דבני בי כנישתא אחריתא אי בעית אימא תיוהא חזא ביה אי בעית אימא מלכותא שאני דלא הדרא ביה דאמר שמואל אי אמר מלכותא עקרנא טורי עקר טורי ולא הדר ביה הורדוס עבדא דבית חשמונאי הוה נתן עיניו באותה תינוקת יומא חד (ד) שמע ההוא גברא בת קלא דאמר כל עבדא דמריד השתא מצלח קם קטלינהו לכולהו מרותיה ושיירה לההיא ינוקתא כי חזת ההיא ינוקתא דקא בעי למינסבה סליקא לאיגרא (ה) ורמא קלא אמרה כל מאן דאתי ואמר מבית חשמונאי קאתינא עבדא הוא דלא אישתיירא מינייהו אלא ההיא ינוקתא וההיא ינוקתא נפלה מאיגרא לארעא טמנה שבע שנין בדובשא איכא דאמרי בא עליה איכא דאמרי לא בא עליה ודאמרי לה בא עליה הא דטמנה ליתובה ליצריה ודאמרי לה לא בא עליה האי דטמנה כי היכי דנאמרו בת מלך נסב מאן דריש [א] מקרב אחיך תשים עליך מלך רבנן קם קטלינהו לכולהו רבנן שבקיה לבבא בן בוטא למשקל עצה מניה

בשנים. בית ראשון עמד ד' מאות ועשר ובית שני ד' מאות ועשרים: **אגב תקרה ומעזיבה.** שהעלייה היתה נתונה עליו ומעזיבה של טיט טרכסין על גבה וכובד המשא מעמיד הכותל שלא יטה לצדדין הלכך במקדש שני שלא היה כותל ג' מגיע לעלייה לא יוכל לעמוד: **הן וסידן או הן בלא סידן.** הני שיעורי דמתני' עם עובי הטיח קא חשיב להן או דילמא מקום האבנים הוי בפותיא לבד טיח הסיד: **והא קתני טפחיים ומחצה.** אלמא חצי טפח נמי חשיב: **חזי לאיצטרופי.** של זה ושל זה מצטרפין לטפח: **הקורה שאמרו.** לענין הכשר מבוי: **ג' טפחים.** אלמא ג' טפחים דקתני לגבי מתני' גבי לבינין דקתני זה נותן טפח ומחצה וזה נותן טפח ומחצה הן בלא סידן קאמר דהא לבינה לחודה שלשה טפחים: **התם ברברבתא.** ומתני' בזוטרתא דעם סידן לא הוו אלא ג' טפחים: **משום פשיעותא.** דילמא מתרמי אונס ופשעי ולא בנו אחריתי: **משום צלויי.** כל זמן הבנין: **בי קייטא בסיתווא.** בית הכנסת היה לימות החורף נמוך בכתלים רחבים וחלונות מועטין מפני הצינה ולימות החמה בית הכנסת אחר שאויר שולט בו: **זוזי.** לצורך בית הכנסת החדש ומונחים ביד הגבאי מי איכא למיחש לפשיעות או לא: **שריגי ליבני.** מסודרים הלבינים זה על גב זה ומזומנין לתתן בבנין: **הדרי הודרי.** משופין ומתוקנין רהיטי הגג קיברונ"ש: **כי בנו נמי.** בי כנישתא חדתא לא נסתרה לעתיקא דדילמא מתרמי פדיון שבויין ומזבני ליה: **ולא אמרן.** דלא ליסתרוה לעתיקא: **אלא דלא חזו ביה תיוהא.** ביקוע שיהא מזומן ליפול: **ועיילה לפורייה התם.** כדי שלא יתעצלו בבנינו שהחמה והגשמים מצערין אותו: **שפיכי.** מרזבין: **היכי אסביה עצה להורדוס.** כדאמרי' לקמן בשמעתין וכתובה היא ביוסיפון בן גוריון: אהדר

אמר אביי גמירי. השתא לא צריך לשנויא קמא דאיכא זוטרתי. וא"ת ודילמא מכלל דאיכא רברבתא ומה דיקא הוא זה ותירץ ר"י דאם אין פחות משלשה אבל גדולות יש א"כ בכדי נקט חצי לבינה של ג' טפחים דלא הוה צריך למתני אלא והאריח חצי לבינה ותו לא וממילא הייתי משער בקטנה הואיל ולא מפרש שיעורא: **הג"ה** בי קייטא ובי סיתווא הוי כמו היכא תיוהא ושרי ואם שתי בתי כנסיות היו בב' מקומות של קייטא ושל סיתווא איירי כגון לחזו בה תיוהא ועוד נראה כיון דיש שם בהכ"נ אחר אין לחוש אם לא יבנו זאת והא דקאמר דליכא דוכתא לצלויי היינו שאין בהכ"נ ועוד מחמת קור וחום אין לחוש שמא יפשעו או בזמן גדול כל כך אין לחוש. ע"כ הגה"ה: **אי הכי כי בנייה נמי.** פירוש עד שיתפללו בה: **ועייליה לפורייה להתם.** ותימה והא אמרת בתי כנסיות אין ישנים בהם לא שינת קבע ולא שינת עראי ואין לתרץ משום דבבבל הוי ואמר רב אסי בפ' בתרא דמגילה (דף כח. ושם ד"ה בתי) בתי כנסיות של בבל על תנאי הן עשויות ופ"ה התם נפקא מינה לענין הא דקתני לעיל אין אוכלין בהן ואין שותים בהן ואין נכנסין בהן בחמה מפני החמה ובגשמים מפני הגשמים ובשל בבל מותר והא דקאמר התם בתר הכי רבינא ורב אדא הוו קיימי ושיילי שמעתא מרבא אתא זילחא דמיטרא עלייהו ועיילי לבי כנישתא ולא משום מיטרא אלא משום דשמעתא בעי' צילותא והשתא הלא בהכ"נ של בבל היה והיו יכולין ליכנס בה מפני המטר וי"ל דלאו ממש לבהכ"נ עיילה לפורי' אלא בסמוך לבהכ"נ במקום שהאורחין רגילין לישן שם ולאכול כדאמרינן בע"פ (פסחים דף קא. ושם ד"ה דאכלו) ושמואל למה לי' לקדושי בבי כנישתא לאפוקי אורחים ידי חובתן דאכלו ושתו וגנו בבי כנישתא והא דאמר דעל תנאי הן עשויין מפרש ר"י לענין שאם יחרבו יעשו מהן מה שירצו לבד מקלות ראש כדאמרי' התם: **כל דאמר מבית חשמונאי אתינא עבדא הוא.** וכן הוא דהכי נמי אמר שמואל בפרק עשרה יוחסין (קדושין דף ע:) ומכאן קשה על פ"ה באלו נאמרים (סוטה דף מא.) דאמר אמרו לו לאגריפס אחינו אתה ופ"ה התם שאמרו לו אחינו לפי שהיתה אמו מישראל דא"כ כיון דבני הורדוס נשאו ישראליות אמאי עבדא הוה הא שמואל גופיה אית ליה עובד כוכבים ועבד הבא על בת ישראל הולד כשר בהחולץ (יבמות דף מה.) וי"ל שלא נשאו ישראליות וקראוהו אחינו אתה לפי שעבד אחינו [הוא] במצות: [וע"ע תוס' יבמות מה: ד"ה כיון דלאו]: **מאן דריש מקרב אחיך רבנן.** דפשטי' דקרא לא משמע למעוטי עבד שהוא אחיך במצות אלא עובד כוכבים ורבנן דרשו (ב"ק פח.) ממובחר שבאחיך: **קטלינהו לכולהו רבנן.** לאו דוקא לכולהו דהא הוו בני בתירא שהיו נשיאים כשעלה הלל מבבל כדאמרינן בפסחים בפרק אלו דברים (דף סו.) והלל היה בפני הבית מאה שנה כדאמרינן בפרק קמא דשבת (דף טו.) ומלכות הורדוס היה בפני הבית ק"ג שנה כדאמרינן בפרק קמא דע"ז (דף ט.):

עין משפט נר מצוה

יא א מיי' פ"ב מהלכות שכנים הלכה יח סמג עשין פב טוש"מ סי' קנז:
יב ב מיי' פי"ז מהל' שבת הל' יג סמג עשין מד סא טוש"ע א"ח סי' שסג סעיף יז:
יג ג ד מיי' פי"א מהל' תפלה הל' יב סמג עשין יט טוש"ע א"ח סי' קנב [וברב אלפס פרק בני העיר דף רסד]:
יד ה ו מיי' פ"ח מהל' מתנות עניים הל' יא סמג עשין קסב טוש"ע י"ד סי' רנב סעיף א:
טו ז מיי' פי"א מהל' תפלה הלכה יב סמג עשין יט טוש"ע א"ח סי' קנב [וברב אלפס פרק בני העיר דף רסד]:

מסורת הש"ס

א) עירובין יג:, ב) מגילה כו:, ג) נ"א דוכתא לצלויי. רש"א, ד) נ"א מלתא דמצוה ויהבי. רש"ל, ה) [ערכין ו.], ו) [שם], ז) קדושין ע ע"ב:

הגהות הב"ח

(א) גמ' ומעזיבה קאי בלא תקרה ומעזיבה לא קאי כצ"ל ותיבת הוה נמחק ב' פעמים: (ב) שם לא תני והא קתני בגזית זה נותן טפחים ומחצה וזה נותן טפחים ומחצה התם חזי לאצטרופי: (ג) שם בי קייטא בסיתווא וסתרי ובנו בי סיתווא: (ד) שם יומא חד שמעיה לבת קלא דאמר כצ"ל ותיבת ההוא גברא נמחק: (ה) שם ורמת קלא:

תורה אור השלם

א) שׂוֹם תָּשִׂים עָלֶיךָ מֶלֶךְ אֲשֶׁר יִבְחַר יְיָ אֱלֹהֶיךָ בּוֹ מִקֶּרֶב אַחֶיךָ תָּשִׂים עָלֶיךָ מֶלֶךְ לֹא תוּכַל לָתֵת עָלֶיךָ אִישׁ נָכְרִי אֲשֶׁר לֹא אָחִיךָ הוּא: [דברים יז, טו]

לעזי רש"י

קיברונ"ש. פירוש רהיטי הגג, קורות הגג, זיזין (רבינו גרשום דף ג ע"ב ודף ו ע"א ועיין רש"י שם ד"ה אמזיק להורדי):

רבינו גרשום

איתא להא ואית' להא. דהא בין בבנין בין בשנים היה גדול: **כי קאי נמי תלתין אמה** בעובי אמה בבית ראשון משום **דהתקרה והמעזיב'** מונחת עליו וסומכתו שלא יפול הא לאו הכי **לא קאי** אפי' בתלתין: **ונעבד כמה דאפשר.** לעמוד בגובה בבנין כותל ומכאן ולמעלה עד התקרה **ליעבד פרוכת: אי כוליה בפרוכת.** ממשכן [כדכתיב] והבדילה הפרוכת וגו': **הן וסידן.** כלומר הא דתנינן בגויל זה נותן ג' טפחים וזה נותן ג' טפחים תני מקום אבנים בהדי סיד שמסיידו מבחוץ צריך ג' טפחים (דאי לא הכי) [דליכא הכא] ו' טפחים שלימות דבצר שיעור מקום הסיד. **או הן בלא סידן** כלומר דלמקום גויל גרידא בעי למיתן זה ג' טפחים וזה ג' טפחים חוץ ממקום הסיד: **דאי ס"ד הן בלא סידן.** ו' טפחים (ולמקום) [ולעולם] בעי למיתב תרוייהו א"כ **ניתנייהו לשיעורא** דסיד ולימא הכי זה נותן ג' טפחים ומשהו למקום הסיד והשני כמו כן וכן בכולהו **אלא** מדלא תני הכי **ש"מ** מקום הגויל ומקום הסיד לא הוי אלא ו' טפחים (אלא) **[לא] לעולם אימא לך הן ולא סידן** ואי אמרת אמאי לא תני שיעורא דסיד **כיון דלא הוי טפח** לא חשיב למתנייה: **התם חזי לאצטרופי.** ב' חצאי טפח לטפח אבל מקום הסיד לא חזי לאצטרופי לשום חשבון: **קורה שאמרו.** לגבי מבוי מדתני **לבינה של ג' טפחים** מכלל דג' טפחים שלימות הוי כל לבינה וש"מ דלמקום לבינה בעינן ג' טפחים שלימות לבד ממקום הסיד וה"ה לגויל וכפיס וגזית: (מיהו) [ודחיה דמהא] לא תידוק דמקום לבינה ג' טפחים שלימות דאותן טפחים א) דתני גבי לבינות מבוי גדולים טפח בגודל אבל מתני' בטפחים בינונים הן ומש"ה הן וסידן ג' טפחים: **משום פשיעותא.** דדלמא מטריד בשאר מילי ולא בני ליה: **משום לצלויי.** דלא הוה להו דוכתא לצלויי עד שיעסוק בבנין: **סתרו ובנו בי קייטא בסיתוא.** שמעתי [דשתי] בתי כנסיות היו להם באחד היו מתפללין בימות הגשמים ובאחד בימות החמה היו מחזקין אותו בימות הגשמים ושל ימות הגשמים בימות החמה כדי שיהא להם מקום תפלה בכל שעה: **גבו זוזי.** מציבורא לצורך בית הכנסת: **ומחתי.** ומונחין הן במקום אחד [מי] אמרינן הואיל והמעות גבויין לא פשעי ומצי למיסתריה או **דלמא** ניחוש דלמא יהבינהו למצוה אחריתי. אם תמצא לומר דהמעות יתנו **לפדיון שבוים. הדרי הודרי.** מתוקנים הזיזין. **שריגי ליבני** שמתוקנין וערוכין הלבינים. **ומחתי כשורי** ומונחין הקורות והכל [שקנו] להתחיל הבנין **מאי** יכול לסתור הישן קודם שיתחילו החדש או לאו: **אי הכי** דאכתי איכא למיחש אפי' כי מיבני האי לא ליסתור אחרינא דאיכא למיחש דמתרמי להו פדיון שבוים ומזבני ליה ואיכא פשיעותא ומשני **דירתא דאינשא לא מזדבן** כ"ש בית הכנסת הואיל ומתוקן הוא וליכא למיחש: **ולא אמרן** דלא לסתור עד דבני אחרינא **אלא דלא חזו ביה תיוהא.** רעוע או סדק **אבל חזו ביה תיוהא סתר** לאלתר: **ועיילה לפורייה להתם.** כדי שיהיו הגשמים יורדין ומנטפין עליו והוא ימהר במלאכת בהכ"נ יותר: **שפיכי.** מרזבין: **אי הכי** דלא ליסתור עד דבני אחרינא. בבא בן בוטא היכי אסביה עצה כו'. מלכא שאני דכיון דאמר למיבנייה **לא הדר ביה** וליכא למיחש לפשיעות': **באותה תינוקת.** דבית חשמונאי:

חשק שלמה על רבינו גרשום א) [ונראה דצ"ל דאומן לבינות דתני גבי מבוי לבינות גדולות של ג"ט אבל מתני' בלבינות בינונים הן וכו']:

ליקוטי רש"י

רחבה כדי לקבל אריח. שתהא דומה לקביעות לבנות עליה בנין. **והאריח חצי לבנה של שלשה טפחים.** נמצא אריח טפח ומחצה רוחב [עירובין יג:]. **משום פשיעותא.** שמא יפשע (אלא) ויתייאש ולא יבנה אחר [מגילה כו:]. **תיוהא.** קלקול [ב"מ עג.]. **טורי.** הרים [ברכות נד:]. **כל מאן דאתי ואמר מבית חשמונאי קאתינא עבדא הוא.** כגון זרעו של הורדוס שהי' עבד לבית חשמונאי וגברה ידו ומלך [כתובות יד.]. שכל זרעו הרגם הורדוס ועבד היה ומלך מתחילה וקרא בניו על שם בית חשמונאי ומסתמא לאו בנות ישראל נסיב דמוזהרים הם להשיא בנותם לעבדים והוו להו כולם עבדים [קידושין ע:]. **איגרא.** גגין [פסחים פה:]. עלייה [תענית כג: וקידושין מה:]. [מכאן שייך לדף ד.] **גם במדעך מלך.** אפי' במחשבותיך אלא דבור, גם אפילו, מלך אל תקלל לא תרגיז למלכו של עולם. ד"א כמשמעו מלך בשר ודם. **עוף השמים וגו'.** ולפי משמעו העופות והשדי' יש לך לדאג מכל בריה שמא יש שומעין ויגיד לאחרים [קהלת י, כ]. ובויקרא רבה בפ' בן המצרי כי עוף השמים יוליך את הקול (קהלת י) זה עורב וחכמת טוילארי [דה"י ב, ט, ד]. **אברך.** כתרגומו דין אבא למלכא רך בלשון ארמי מלך בהשותפין לא ריכא ולא בר ריכא. [בראשית מא מג וכעי"ז רש"י שבת נג.]. **שישא.** שיש צבוע לא לבן ולא שחור אלא כעין ירוק בלע"ז בי"ש. **ומרמרא.** שיש לבן. **כוחלא.** שישא צבוע ככחול. **אפיק שפה.** שורה של אבנים נכנסה ושורה יוצאה. **דמיחזי כי אידוותא דימא.** כגלי הים שהאבנים משונים במראיהן זו מזו והעינים המסתכלות בהן שוטטות ונראות כאילו גלי הים הם נדים ונעים [סוכה נא:]. **להן מלכא.** באמת אתה מלך שמע לעצתי. **מלכי.** עצתי כמו איעצך אמלכינך. **ישפר עלך.** עצתי תיטב בעיניך לשמוע מילי [דניאל ד, כד]. דניאל אמר לנבוכדנצר כשפתר לו החלום שיהא נטרד מן האנשים ולהיות עם בהמה ושיה להן מלכא אמנם המלך מלכי ישפר עליך עצתי תיטב בעיניך להאמין לעצתי [סוטה כ:]. **וחטאיך בצדקה פרוק.** וחטאתך בצדקה פרוק מעל צוארך [דניאל שם]. חטאך ע"י צדקה פדה [סוטה שם]. **ועויתך במחן עניין.** ועונותיך פרוק בחנינת עניים [דניאל שם]. ועונותיך בחנינת העניים [סוטה שם]. **הן תהוה ארכא לשלותך.** אולי תהא שהות לשלומך שלא תמהר הרעה לבא ומה ראה דניאל להשיא עצה טובה לנבוכדנצר ראה ישראל עניים שפלי גולה מחזירין על הפתחים והשיאו עצה לחננם אמר לו עניים אלו שהגליתם רעבים הם פרנסם וכן עשה פתח אוצרותיו והיה מפרנסם כל י"ב חדש [דניאל שם]. ולא תהא אור זמן לשלומך שלא יבאו עליך הפורענות וכן עשה נבוכדנצר היה מקבץ בכל יום עניי ישראל שהביא בגולה והיו צריכין מזונות ומפרנסם ואף דניאל כשהשיאו עצה זו לכך נתכוין שראה את ישראל בגולה מחזירין על הפתחים [סוטה כא.]. **וכתיב כולא מטא.** כל הפתרון הגיע על נבוכדנצר [דניאל שם, כה]. כל הפורענות הגיע על נבוכדנצר. **ולקצת ירחין.** תלה לו הזכות י"ב חדש [סוטה שם].

however, measures only a fraction of a *tefach*, which is an insignificant amount undeserving of mention.

The Gemara again attempts to determine the scope of the Mishnah's width measurements:

תָּא שְׁמַע — Come, learn a Mishnah[11] that answers our question: **הַקּוֹרָה שֶׁאָמְרוּ — THE BEAM OF WHICH THEY SPOKE** in the previous Mishnah[12] **רְחָבָה כְּדֵי לְקַבֵּל אָרִיחַ** — must be **WIDE ENOUGH TO ACCOMMODATE A HALF-SIZE BRICK.**[13] **וְהָאָרִיחַ חֲצִי לְבֵינָה שֶׁל שְׁלֹשָׁה טְפָחִים — AND A HALF-SIZE BRICK IS HALF** as wide as **A FULL-SIZE BRICK OF THREE *TEFACHIM.*** Hence, the width measurements in our Mishnah do not include the plastering.[14]

The Gemara rejoins that, on the contrary, the *Eruvin* Mishnah proves that the layer of plastering *is* included:

הָתָם בִּרְבְרְבָתָא — There, in *Eruvin,* the Mishnah makes reference **to large** bricks, which are three *tefachim* wide without the plastering. **דַּיְקָא נַמִּי — And one can infer this as well from** a **precise** reading of the Mishnah, **דְּקָתָנֵי שֶׁל שְׁלֹשָׁה טְפָחִים — for the Mishnah taught:** A full-size brick **OF THREE *TEFACHIM,*** **מִכְּלַל דְּאִיכָּא זוּטְרָא — implying that there exists a smaller** version of the full-size brick[15] that the Mishnah sought to exclude. Our Mishnah, which does not specify "full-size bricks *of three tefachim,*" must then refer to the smaller version. Hence, their width measurement of three *tefachim* must include the layer of plaster.

The Gemara accepts this reasoning and concludes:

שְׁמַע מִינָּהּ — Learn from [the *Eruvin* Mishnah] that the plastering is included in our Mishnah's measurements.

The following passage of Gemara is not germane to our analysis of the Mishnah. However, it is recorded here because it eventually discusses the remodeling of the Temple, whose architecture was discussed above (3a):

אָמַר רַב חִסְדָּא — Rav Chisda said: **לֹא לִיסְתּוֹר אִינִישׁ בֵּי כְּנִישְׁתָּא — A person may not demolish a synagogue** **עַד דְּבָנֵי בֵּי כְּנִישְׁתָּא אַחֲרִיתִי — until he has built another synagogue** in its place.

The Gemara offers two reasons for Rav Chisda's ruling:

אִיכָּא דְּאָמְרֵי מִשּׁוּם פְּשִׁיעוּתָא — There are those that say that the restriction is **because of negligence.**[16] **וְאִיכָּא דְּאָמְרֵי מִשּׁוּם צַלּוּיֵי — And there are those that say** that it is **out of concern** that during the period of rebuilding there would be no place to congregate **for praying.** For that reason Rav Chisda required that the new synagogue be constructed before the other was razed.

The Gemara asks:

מַאי בֵּינַיְיהוּ — What is the practical difference **between [the two reasons]?**

And the Gemara replies:

אִיכָּא בֵּינַיְיהוּ דְּאִיכָּא (בי כנישתא אחריתי) [**דּוּכְתָּא לְצַלּוּיֵי**] **— There is** a difference **between them when there exists** another **place to pray**[17] during the period of construction. According to the first reason, the prohibition will still apply, since the possibility remains that they will neglect to complete the new structure. According to the second reason, demolition may occur immediately, since temporary accommodations are available.

The Gemara illustrates Rav Chisda's ruling with the following incident:

מְרֵימָר וּמָר זוּטְרָא סָתְרֵי וּבָנוּ בֵּי קַיְיטָא בְּסִיתְוָוא — Mereimar and Mar Zutra demolished and built anew **a summer synagogue**[18] **during the winter,** [**וְסָתְרֵי**] **וּבָנוּ בֵּי סִיתְוָוא בְּקַיְיטָא — and they demolished**[19] **and built** anew **a winter synagogue**[20] **during the summer.** Since another, temporary place to pray[21] was available, Mereimar and Mar Zutra allowed immediate demolition of the out-of-season synagogue, in keeping with the second explanation of Rav Chisda's ruling.[22]

Addressing now the first explanation of Rav Chisda's ruling, the Gemara considers various methods of insuring against negligence in order to allow immediate demolition of the old synagogue:[23]

אָמַר לֵיהּ רָבִינָא לְרַב אָשֵׁי — Ravina said to Rav Ashi: **גָּבוּ זוּזֵי וּמַחְתֵּי — If they collected money** for the new construction **and it is deposited** with the synagogue officials, **מַאי — what is** the law? Since the necessary funds are already in hand, may demolition

NOTES

11. *Eruvin* 13b.

12. That earlier Mishnah (*Eruvin* 11b) discussed methods for adjusting a *mavoi* (alley) entrance to permit carrying inside the *mavoi* on the Sabbath. One such method involves placing a *korah,* or crossbeam, atop the entrance of the *mavoi.* The Mishnah on 13b, which our Gemara is citing, discusses various attributes that the beam must possess. Among them is a minimum width.

13. A brick is not actually placed there. Nevertheless, the beam must be wide enough to hold a half-size brick in order to project the semblance of permanence (see Gemara there, where it is established that the beam itself need be only one *tefach* wide, since this width is sufficient to hold the half-brick in place).

14. The full-size brick cited for purposes of illustration by the *Eruvin* Mishnah obviously lacks the protective plastering that the full-size bricks in our Mishnah receive. Nevertheless, its measure is three *tefachim.* Thus, when our Mishnah states that a wall composed of full-size bricks must be three *tefachim* wide, clearly it does not include the layer of plaster in that measurement (*Rashi*).

15. To infer the opposite — that there exists a version of the full-size brick *larger* than three *tefachim* and that the three-*tefachim* version is the smallest — is impossible, for if so the Mishnah need not have specified: "a full-size brick *of three tefachim.*" Rather, by simply stating "a full-size brick" it would have implied the smallest version, since if a larger size were appropriate, specification would be necessary to prevent misunderstanding and assure compliance with the laws of *korah* (*Tosafos,* as explained by *Maharam; see also Tos HaRosh*).

16. Rav Chisda was concerned that following the razing of the old synagogue, unforeseen circumstances would cause the townspeople to neglect the construction of a replacement [thereby leaving the community without a permanent place of worship] (*Rashi*).

[It should be noted, that these reasons are needed in a situation where the old synagogue is being replaced with a new one. To destroy a synagogue without replacing it, is itself a forbidden act, comparable to destroying a part of the *Beis Hamikdash* (see *Mishnah Berura* 152:11 and *Beur Halachah* there ד״ה אא״כ).

17. *Mesoras HaShas* and most Rishonim (*Ran, Rosh* and *Rif*) change בֵּי כְּנִישְׁתָּא אַחֲרִיתִי, *another synagogue,* to דּוּכְתָּא לְצַלּוּיֵי, *a place to pray.* The emendation, which our translation has adopted, implies that if there is another synagogue in town, (large enough to accommodate everyone) all would agree that the old synagogue may be demolished immediately, for even if construction of the new building is neglected, a formal place of worship still exists (see *Taz* to *Orach Chaim* 152:1 for a major discussion of this subject).

18. The "summer synagogue" was an airy building suitable for use in the warm months (*Rashi*).

19. Emendation and translation follow *Bach,* who adds וְסָתְרֵי, *and they demolished,* to the text.

20. The "winter synagogue" was built low to the ground, with thick walls and few windows, to keep out the cold (*Rashi*).

21. I.e. the synagogue currently "in season."

22. This is *Rosh's* interpretation. Cf. *Tosafos,* who explain Mar Zutra and Mereimar in various ways also according to the first explanation of Rav Chisda's ruling; and see *Maharsha.*

23. The need for immediate demolition would arise, for instance, when a community wanted to erect the new synagogue on the site of the old, or when they wished to expand the old synagogue (see *Rosh* and *Rama* to *Orach Chaim* 152).

בשנים ואיתא להא ואיתא להא ונעבדו תלתין אמין בבנין ואידך ניעביד פרוכת כי קאי תלתין אמהתא נמי אגב תקרה ומעזיבה (א) הוה קאי בלא תקרה ומעזיבה לא הוה קאי וליעביד מה דאפשר בבנין וליעביד אידך פרוכת אמר אביי גמירי אי כולהו בבנין אי כולהו בפרוכת אי כולהו בבנין ממקדש אי כולהו בפרוכת ממשכן איבעיא להו הן וסידן או דילמא הן בלא סידן אמר ר"נ בר יצחק [א]מסתברא הן וסידן דאי ס"ד הן בלא סידן ליתנייה לשיעוריה אלא לאו ש"מ הן וסידן לא לעולם אימא לך הן בלא סידן וכיון דלא הוי טפח לא תני והא קתני (ג) בלבינין זה נותן טפח ומחצה וזה נותן טפח ומחצה התם חזי לאיצטרופי ת"ש [ב] הקורה שאמרו רחבה כדי לקבל אריח והאריח חצי לבינה של ג' טפחים התם ברברבתא דיקא נמי דקתני של שלשה טפחים מכלל דאיכא זוטרא ש"מ: [ג] אמר רב חסדא [ג]לא ליסתור איניש בי כנישתא עד דבני בי כנישתא אחריתי איכא דאמרי [ד]משום פשיעותא ואיכא דאמרי משום צלויי מאי בינייהו איכא בינייהו דאיכא (ג) (בי כנישתא אחריתי) מרימר ומר זוטרא סתרי ובנו בי קייטא בסיתווא (ג) ובנו בי סיתווא בקייטא א"ל רבינא לרב אשי גבו זוזי ומחתי מאי אמר ליה [ה]דילמא מיתרמי להו [ד] פדיון שבויים ויהבי להו שריגי ליבני והדרי הודרי ומחתי כשורי מאי א"ל [ו]זמנין דמתרמי להו פדיון שבויים מזבני ויהבי להו א"ה אפי' בנו נמי אמר ליה דירתיה דאינשי לא מזבני ולא אמרן [ז]אלא דלא חזי בה תיוהא אבל חזי בה תיוהא סתרי ובני כי הא דרב אשי חזא בה תיוהא בבנישתא דמתא מחסיא סתריה ועייל לפוריי' להתם ולא אפקיה עד דמתקין ליה שפיכי ובבא בן בוטא היכי אסביה ליה עצה להורדוס למיסתריה לבית המקדש והאמר רב חסדא לא ליסתור איניש בי כנישתא עד דבני בי כנישתא אחריתי איבעית אימא תיוהא חזא ביה איבעית אימא [ח] מלכותא שאני דלא הדרא ביה דאמר [ט] שמואל אי אמר מלכותא עקרנא טורי עקר טורי ולא הדר ביה הורדוס עבדא דבית חשמונאי הוה נתן עיניו באותה תינוקת יומא חד (ד) שמע ההוא גברא בת קלא דאמר כל עבדא דמריד השתא מצלח קם קטלינהו לכולהו מרותיה ושיירה לההיא ינוקתא כי חזת ההיא ינוקתא דקא בעי למינסבה סליקא לאיגרא (ה) ורמא קלא אמרה [י] כל מאן דאתי ואמר מבית חשמונאי קאתינא עבדא הוא דלא אישתיירא מינייהו אלא ההיא ינוקתא וההיא ינוקתא נפלה מאיגרא לארעא טמנה שבע שנין בדובשא איכא דאמרי בא עליה איכא דאמרי לא בא עליה הא דטמנה ליתוביה ליצריה ודאמרי לה לא בא עליה האי דטמנה כי היכי דנאמרו בת מלך נסב אמר מאן דריש א) מקרב אחיך תשים עליך מלך רבנן קם קטלינהו לכולהו רבנן שבקיה לבבא בן בוטא למשקל עצה מניה

רש"י

בשנים. בית ראשון עמד ד' מאות ועשר ובית שני ד' מאות ועשרים: **אגב תקרה ומעזיבה.** שהעלייה היתה נתונה עליו ומעזיבה של טיט טרכסין על גבה וכובד המשא מעמיד הכותל שלא יטה לצדדין הלכך במקדש שני שלא היה כותל ל' מגיע לעלייה לא יוכל לעמוד: **הן וסידן או הן בלא סידן.** הני שיעורי דמתני' עם עובי הטיח קא חשיב להן או דילמא מקום האבנים הוי בפותיא לבד טיח הסיד: **והא קתני טפחיים ומחצה.** אלמא חצי טפח נמי חשיב: **חזי לאיצטרופי.** של זה ושל זה מצטרפין לטפח: **הקורה שאמרו.** לענין הכשר מבוי: **ג' טפחים.** אלמא ג' טפחים דקתני לגבי מתני' גבי לבינין דקתני זה נותן טפח ומחצה וזה נותן טפח ומחצה הן בלא סידן קאמר דהא לבינה לחודה שלשה טפחים: **התם ברברבתא.** ומתני' בזוטרתא דעם סידן לא הוו אלא ג' טפחים: **משום פשיעותא.** דילמא מתרמי אונס ופשעי ולא בנו אחריתי: **משום צלויי.** כל זמן הבנין: **בי קייטא בסיתווא.** בית הכנסת היה להם לימות החורף נמוך בכתלים רחבים וחלונות מועטין מפני הצינה ולימות החמה בית הכנסת אחר שאויר שולט בו: **זוזי.** לצורך בית הכנסת החדש ומונחים ביד הגבאי מי איכא למיחש לפשיעות או לא: **שריגי ליבני.** מסודרים הלבינים זה על גב זה ומזומנין לתתן בבנין: **הדרי הודרי.** משופין ומתוקנין רהיטי הגג קיברונ"ש: **כי בנו נמי.** בי כנישתא חדתא לא נסתרוה לעתיקא דדילמא מתרמי פדיון שבויין ומזבני ליה: **ולא אמרן.** דלא ליסתרוה לעתיקא: **אלא דלא חזו ביה תיוהא.** ביקוע שיהא מזומן ליפול: **עיילה לפורייה התם.** כדי שלא יתייאש בבנינו שהחמה והגשמים מלערין אותו: **שפכי.** מרזבין: **היכי אסביה עצה להורדוס.** כדאמרי' לקמן בשמעתין וכתובה היא ביוסיפון בן גוריון: אהדר

תוספות

אמר אביי גמירי. השתא לא צריך לשנויא קמא: **מכלל** דאיכא זוטרתי. וא"ת ודילמא מכלל דאיכא רברבתא ומה דיקא הוא זה ותירץ ר"י דאם אין פחות משלשה אבל גדולות יש א"כ בכדי נקט חצי לבינה של ג' טפחים דלא הוה צריך למתני אלא והאריח חצי לבינה ותו לא וממילא הייתי משער בקטנה הואיל ולא מפרש שיעורה: **הג"ה** בי קייטא ובי סיתווא הוי כמו איכא תיוהא ושרי ואם שתי בתי כנסיות היו בב' מקומות של קייטא ושל סיתווא איירי כגון דחזו בה תיוהא ועוד נראה כיון דיש שם בהכ"נ אחר אין לחוש אם לא יבנו זאת והא דקאמר דאיכא דוכתא לצלויי היינו שאין בהכ"נ ועוד מחמת קור וחום אין לחוש שמא יפשעו או בזמן גדול כל כך אין לחוש. ע"כ הגה"ה: **אי** הכי בי בנייה נמי. פירוש עד שיתפללו בה: **ועייליה** לפורייה להתם. ותימה והא אמרת בתי כנסיות אין ישנים בהם לא שינת קבע ולא שינת עראי ואין לתרץ משום דבבבל הוי ואמר רב אסי בפ' בתרא דמגילה (דף כח: ושם ד"ה בתי) בתי כנסיות של בבל על תנאי הן עשויות ופ"ה התם נפקא מינה לענין הא דקתני לעיל אין אוכלין בהן ואין שותים בהן ואין נכנסין בהן בחמה מפני החמה ובגשמים מפני הגשמים ושבבל מותר דהא קאמר התם בתר הכי רבינא ורב אדא הוו קיימי ושיילי שמעתא מרבא אתא זילפא דמטרא עלייהו ועיילי לבי כנישתא ולא משום מטרא אלא משום דשמעתא בעי' צילותא והשתא והלא בהכ"נ של בבל היה והיו יכולין ליכנס בה מפני המטר וי"ל דלאו ממש בהכ"נ עיילה לפוריי' אלא בסמוך לבהכ"נ במקום שהאורחין רגילין לישן שם ולאכול כדאמרינן בע"פ (פסחים דף קא. ושם ד"ה דאכלי) ושמואל למה לי' לקדושי בבי כנישתא לאפוקי אורחים ידי חובתן דאכלו ושתו וגנו בבי כנישתא והא דאמר דעל תנאי הן עשויין מפרש ר"י לענין שאם יחרבו יעשו מהן מה שירצו לבד מקלות ראש כדאמרי' התם: **כל** דאמר מבית חשמונאי אתינא עבדא הוא. וכן הוא דהכי נמי אמר שמואל בפרק עשרה יוחסין (קדושין דף ע:) ומכאן קשה על פ"ה באלו נאמרים (סוטה דף מא.) דאמר אמרו לו לאגריפס אחינו אתה ופ"ה התם שאמרו לו אחינו לפי שהיתה אמו מישראל דא"כ כיון דבני הורדוס נשאו ישראלית אמאי עבדא הוה הא שמואל גופיה אית ליה עובד כוכבים ועבד הבא על בת ישראל הולד כשר בהחולץ (יבמות דף מה.) וי"ל שלא נשאו ישראלית וקראוהו אחינו אתה לפי שעבד אחינו [הוא] במצות: [וע"ע תוס' יבמות מה: ד"ה כיון דאמו]: **מאן** דריש מקרב אחיך רבנן. דפשטי' דקרא לא משמע למעוטי עבד שהוא אחיך במצות אלא עובד כוכבים ורבנן דרשו (ב"ק פח.) ממובחר שבאחיך: **קטלינהו** לכולהו רבנן. לאו דוקא לכולהו דהא הוו בני בתירא שהיו נשיאים כשעלה הלל מבבל כדאמרינן בפסחים בפרק אלו דברים (דף סו.) והלל היה בפני הבית מאה שנה כדאמרינן בפרק קמא דשבת (דף טו.) ומלכות הורדוס היה בפני הבית ק"ג שנה כדאמרינן בפרק קמא דע"ז (דף ט.):

עין משפט נר מצוה

יא א מיי' פ"ב מהלכות שכנים הלכה יב סמג עשין פב טוש"ע ח"מ סי' קנז:

יב ב מיי' פ"ו מהל' שבת הל' יג סמג לאוין סה טוש"ע א"ח סי' שטז סעיף יז:

יג ג ד מיי' פי"א מהל' תפלה הל' יב סמג עשין יט טוש"ע א"ח סי' קנב [וברב אלפס פרק בני העיר דף רסד]:

יד ה ו מיי' פ"ח מהל' מתנות עניים הל' יא סמג עשין קסב טוש"ע י"ד סי' רנב סעיף א:

טו ז מיי' פי"א מהל' תפלה הלכה יג סמג עשין יט טוש"ע א"ח סי' קנב [וברב אלפס פרק בני העיר דף רסד]:

רבינו גרשום

איתא להא ואית' להא. דהא בין בבנין בין בשנים היה גדול: **כי נמי תלתין אמה** בעובי אמה בבית ראשון משום התקרה והמעזיב' מונחת עליו וסומכתו שלא יפול הא לאו הכי לא קאי אפי' בתלתין: **ונעביד כמה דאפשר.** לעמוד בגובה בבנין כותל ומכאן ולמעלה עד התקרה **ליעבד פרוכת:** **אי כוליה בפרוכת.** ממשכן [כדכתיב] והבדילה הפרוכת וגו': **הן וסידן.** כלומר הא דתנינן בגויל זה נותן ג' טפחים וזה נותן ג' טפחים תני מקום אבנים בהדי סיד שמסידו מבחוץ צריך ג' טפחים (דאי לא תני) [דליכא הכא] ו' טפחים שלימות דבצר שיעור מקום הסיד: **או הן בלא סידן** כלומר דלמקום גויל גרידא בעי למיתן זה ג' טפחים וזה ג' טפחים חוץ ממקום הסיד: **דאי ס"ד הן בלא סידן** ו' טפחים (ולעולם) [ולמקום] למיתב תרוייהו א"כ **ניתנייהו לשיעורא** דסיד ולימא הכי זה נותן ג' טפחים ומשהו למקום הסיד והשני כמו כן וכן הכי ש"מ מקום הגויל ומקום הסיד לא הוי אלא ו' טפחים (אלא) [לא] **לעולם אימא לך הן ולא סידן** ואי אמרת אמאי לא תני שיעורא דסיד **כיון דלא הוי טפח** לא חשיב למתנייה: **התם חזי לאצטרופי.** ב' חצאי טפח לטפח אבל מקום הסיד לא חזי לאצטרופי לשום חשבון: **קורה שאמרו.** לגבי מבוי מדתני **לבינה של ג' טפחים** מכלל דג' טפחים שלימות הוי כל לבינה וש"מ דלמקום לבינה בעינן ג' טפחים שלימות לבד ממקום הסיד וה"ה לגויל וכפיס וגזית: (מיהו) [ודחיה דמהא] לא תידוק דמקום לבינה ג' טפחים שלימות דאותן טפחים א) דתני גבי לבינות מבוי גדולים טפח בגודל אבל מתני' בטפחים בינונים הן ומש"ה הן וסידן ג' טפחים: **משום פשיעותא.** דדלמא מטריד בשאר מילי ולא בני ליה: **משום לצלויי.** דלא הוה להו דוכתא לצלויי עד שיעסוק בבנין: **סתרו ובנו בי קייטא בסיתוא.** שמעתי [דשתי] בתי כנסיות היו להם באחד היו מתפללין בימות הגשמים ובאחד בימות החמה אותו של ימות החמה היו מחזקין אותו בימות הגשמים ושל ימות הגשמים בימות החמה כדי שיהא להם מקום תפלה בכל שעה: **גבו זוזי.** מציבורא לצורך בית הכנסת: **ומחתי.** ומונחין הן במקום אחד [מי] אמרינן הואיל והמעות גביין לא פשעי ומצי למיסתריה או **דלמא** ניחוש דלמא יהבינהו למצוה אחריתי. אם תמצא לומר דהמעות יתנו **לפדיון שבוים. הדרי הודרי.** מתוקנים הזיזין. **שריגי ליבני** שמתוקנין וערוכין הלבינים. **ומחתי כשורי** ומונחין הקורות והכל [שקנו] להתחיל הבנין **מאי** יכול לסתור הישן קודם שיתחילו החדש או לאו: **אי הכי** דאכתי איכא למיחש אפי' כי מיבני האי לא ליסתור אחרינא דאיכא למיחש דמתרמי להו פדיון שבוים ומזבני ליה ואיכא פשיעותא ומשני **דירתא דאינשא לא מזבנן** כ"ש בית הכנסת הואיל ומתוקן הוא וליכא למיחש: **ולא אמרן** דלא לסתור עד דבני אחרינא **אלא דלא חזו ביה תיוהא.** רעוע או סדק **אבל חזו ביה תיוהא סתר** לאלתר: **ועיילה לפורייה להתם.** כדי שיהיו הגשמים יורדין ומנטפין עליו והוא ימהר במלאכת בהכ"נ יותר: **שפיכי.** מרזבין: **אי הכי** דלא ליסתור עד דבני אחרינא. בבא בן בוטא היכי אסביה עצה כו'. מלכא שאני דכיון דאמר למיבנייה **לא הדר ביה** וליכא למיחש לפשיעות': **באותה תינוקת.** דבית חשמונאי:

חשק שלמה על רבינו גרשום א) [ונראה דל"ל דאותן לבינות דתני גבי מבוי לבינות גדולות של ג"ט אבל מתני' בלבינות בינונים הן וכו']:

מסורת הש"ס

א) עירובין יג:, ב) מגילה כו:, ג) נ"א דוכתא לצלויי. רש"א, ד) נ"א מלתא דמצוה ויהבי. רש"ל, ה) [ערכין ו.], ו) [שם], ז) קדושין ע ע"ב:

הגהות הב"ח

(א) גמ' ומעזיבה קאי בלא תקרה ומעזיבה לא קאי כצ"ל ותיבת הוה נמחק ב' פעמים: (ב) שם לא תני והא קתני בגזית זה נותן טפחים ומחצה וזה נותן טפחים ומחצה התם חזי לאצטרופי: (ג) שם בי קייטא בסיתווא וסתרי ובנו בי סיתווא: (ד) שם יומא חד שמעיה לבת קלא דאמר כצ"ל ותיבת ההוא גברא נמחק: (ה) שם ורמת קלא:

תורה אור השלם

א) שׂוֹם תָּשִׂים עָלֶיךָ מֶלֶךְ אֲשֶׁר יִבְחַר יְיָ אֱלֹהֶיךָ בּוֹ מִקֶּרֶב אַחֶיךָ תָּשִׂים עָלֶיךָ מֶלֶךְ לֹא תוּכַל לָתֵת עָלֶיךָ אִישׁ נָכְרִי אֲשֶׁר לֹא אָחִיךָ הוּא: [דברים יז, טו]

לעזי רש"י

קיברונ"ש. פירוש רהיטי הגג, קורות הגג, זיזין (רבינו גרשום דף ג ע"ב ודף ו ע"א ועיין רש"י שם ד"ה אחזיק להורדי):

ליקוטי רש"י

רחבה כדי לקבל אריח. שתהא דומה לקביעות לבנות עליה בנין. **והאריח חצי לבנה של שלשה טפחים.** נמצא אריח טפח ומחצה רוחב [עירובין יג:]. **משום פשיעותא.** שמא יפשעו (אלא) ויתייאשו ולא יבנו אחר [מגילה כו:]. **תיוהא.** קלקול [ב"מ עג.]. **טורי.** הרים [ברכות נד:]. **כל מאן דאתי ואמר מבית חשמונאי קאתינא עבדא הוא.** כגון זרעו של הורדוס שהי' עבד לבית חשמונאי וגברה ידו ומלך [כתובות יד:]. שכל זרעו של הרגם הורדוס ועבד היה ומלך תחתיהן וקרא בניו על שם בית חשמונאי ומתחמא לאו בנות ישראל נסיב דמוזהרים הם להשיא בנותם לעבדים והוו להו כולם עבדים [קידושין ע:]. **איגרא.** גגין [פסחים פה:]. עלייה [תענית כג: וקידושין מה:].

[מכאן שייך לדף ד.]

גם במדעך מלך. אפי' במחשבותיך בלא דבור, גם אפילו, מלך אל תקלל לא תרגיז למלכו של עולם. ד"א כמשמעו מלך בשר ודם. **עוף השמים וגו'.** ולפי משמעו העוברים והשבי' יש לך לדאג מכל בריה שמא יש שומעין ויגיד לאחרים [קהלת י, כ]. ובויקרא רבה בפ' בן המלרי כי עוף השמים יוליך את הקול (קהלת י)

זה עורב וחכמת טוולארי [דה"י ב, ט, ד]. **אברך.** כתרגומו דין אבא למלכא רך בלשון ארמי מלך בהשותפין לא ריכא ולא בר ריכא. [בראשית מא מג וכעי"ז רש"י שבת נג.]. **שישא.** שיש לבוע לא לבן ולא שחור אלא כעין ירוק בלע"ז בי"ש. **ומרמרא.** שיש לבן. **כוחלא.** שישא לבוע ככחול. **אפיק שפה.** שורה של אבנים נכנסה ושורה יוצאה. **דמיחזי כי אידוותא דימא.** כגלי הים שהאבנים משוים במראיהן זו מזו והעינים המסתכלות בהן שוטטות ונראות כאלו גלי הים הם נדים ונעים [סוכה נא:]. **להן מלכא.** באמת אתה מלך שמע לעצתי. **מלכי.** עצתי כמו איעצך אמלכינך. **ישפר עלך.** עצתי תיטב בעיניך לשמוע מילי [דניאל ד, כד]. דניאל אמר לנבוכדנצר כשפתר לו החלום שיהא נטרד מן האנשים ולהיות עם בהמה וחיה להן מלכא אמנם המלך מלכי ישפר עליך עצתי תיטב בעיניך להאמין לעצתי [סוטה כ:]. **וחטאיך בצדקה פרוק.** וחטאתך בלדקה פרוק מעל לוארך [דניאל שם]. חטאך ע"י לדקה פדה [סוטה שם]. **ועויתך במחן עניין.** ועוונותיך פרוק בחנינת עניים [דניאל שם]. ועוונותיך בחנינת העניים [סוטה שם]. **הן תהוה ארכא לשלותך.** אולי תהא שהות לשלומך שלא תמהר הרעה לבא ומה ראה דניאל להשיא עלה טובה לנבוכדנצר ראה ישראל עניים שפלי גולה מחזירין על הפתחים והשיאו עלה לחנם אמר לו עניים אלו שהגליתם רעבים הם פרנסם וכן עשה פתח אולרותיו והיה מפרנסם כל י"ב חדש [דניאל שם]. ולא תהא אור זמן לשלומך שלא יבאו עליך הפורעניות וכן עשה נבוכדנצר היה מקבץ בכל יום עניי ישראל שהביא בגולה והיו לריכין מזונות ומפרנסם ואף דניאל כשהשיאו עלה זו לכך נתכוין שראה את ישראל בגולה מחזירין על הפתחים [סוטה כא.]. **וכתיב כולא מטא.** כל הפתרון הגיע על נבוכדנצר [דניאל שם, כה]. כל הפורענות הגיע על נבוכדנצר. **ולקצת ירחין.** תלה לו הזכות י"ב חדש [סוטה שם].

proceed forthwith? Or should they still be concerned that unforeseen circumstances will cause them to neglect the project?

Rav Ashi replies:

אָמַר לֵיהּ – Rav Ashi **said to [Ravina]:** The availability of funds earmarked for construction does not affect the ruling, since דִּילְמָא מִיתְרַמֵּי לְהוּ פִּדְיוֹן שְׁבוּיִים – **perhaps** an opportunity for **redeeming captives will arise**[24] וְיָהֲבֵי לְהוּ – **and** the synagogue officials **will give [the money]** to the captors. Thus, even when the funds are in hand, construction must precede demolition.

Ravina proposes another method of insuring construction:

שְׁרִיגֵי לִיבְנֵי וְהַדְרֵי הוּדְרֵי וּמְחַתֵּי כְּשׁוּרֵי – If **bricks** for the new synagogue **are stacked and rafters are planed and beams are deposited,** מַאי – **what is** the law?[25]

Rav Ashi is unreceptive:

אָמַר לֵיהּ – Rav Ashi **said [to Ravina]:** זִמְנִין דְּמִתְרַמֵּי לְהוּ פִּדְיוֹן שְׁבוּיִים – **Sometimes** an opportunity for **redeeming captives will arise,** מְזַבְּנֵי וְיָהֲבֵי לְהוּ – and the synagogue officials **will sell** the materials **and give [the money]** to the captors. Thus, even when the materials are purchased, immediate demolition of the old synagogue is forbidden.

Ravina counters:

אִי הָכִי – **If so,** if the imperative of redeeming captives is so great that assets are liquidated to obtain the necessary funds, אֲפִילּוּ בָּנוּ נַמִּי – **even after they have built** the new synagogue they should not raze the old one, for if the need arises they might sell the new synagogue[26] to raise money for redeeming captives.[27] – ? –

Rav Ashi refutes this argument:

אָמַר לֵיהּ – **[R' Ashi] said [to Ravina]:** דִּירְתֵיהּ דְּאִינִשׁ לָא מְזַבְּנֵי – **People do not sell their dwellings,** even to redeem captives. Thus, a synagogue, which serves the entire town, would certainly not be sold. Communal funds and materials, on the other hand, would be requisitioned for the performance of this great mitzvah.

The Gemara notes an important exception to Rav Chisda's rule:

וְלָא אֲמָרַן אֶלָּא – **And they stated [this prohibition]** against prematurely razing the old synagogue **only** דְּלָא חֲזֵי בָּהּ תִּיוּהָא – **when cracks are not seen in [the old synagogue's structure];** אֲבָל חֲזֵי בָּהּ תִּיוּהָא – **however, if cracks are seen in it** and the building is in danger of collapse,[28] סָתְרֵי וּבָנֵי – the townspeople **may demolish** it **and** then **build** a new synagogue. Since the old synagogue is unsafe to use, nothing is gained[29] by requiring it to stand until the new one is built.

The Gemara relates an incidence of early demolition based on this exception:

כִּי הָא דְּרַב אַשִׁי – **Like that** case **of Rav Ashi,** חֲזָא בָּהּ תִּיוּהָא בִּכְנִישְׁתָּא דְּמָתָא מְחַסְיָא – who **saw cracks in the synagogue of Masa Machasya.** סָתְרֵיהּ – **He** immediately **demolished it,** וְעַיֵּיל לְפוּרְיֵיהּ לְהָתָם – **and** then, in order to ensure that the townspeople would expeditiously erect a new one,[30] **he brought his bed there** (to the construction site), וְלָא אַפְקֵיהּ עַד דְּמִתַקְּנִין לֵיהּ שְׁפִיכֵי – **and he did not remove it until they attached leaders** to the roof gutters.[31] Only when every last detail of construction had been accomplished did he return to sleep in his home.

The Gemara applies Rav Chisda's ruling to the case of the Holy Temple itself:

וּבָבָא בֶּן בּוּטָא – **And** concerning **Bava ben Buta,** הֵיכִי אַסְבְּיהּ לֵיהּ עֵצָה לְהוּרְדוֹס לְמִיסְתְּרֵיהּ לְבֵית הַמִּקְדָּשׁ – **how could he advise Herod to raze the Holy Temple** and then rebuild it?[32] וְהָאָמַר רַב חִסְדָּא – **But did Rav Chisda not say:** לָא לִיסְתּוֹר אִינִישׁ בֵּי כְּנִישְׁתָּא עַד דְּבָנֵי בֵּי כְּנִישְׁתָּא אַחֲרִיתָא – **"A person may not demolish a synagogue until he has built another synagogue** in its place?"[33] Surely, a great sage such as Bava ben Buta would not have encouraged Herod to contravene Rav Chisda's ruling. – ? –

The Gemara offers two explanations:

אִי בָּעֵית אֵימָא – **If you prefer, say:** תִּיוּהָא חֲזָא בֵּיהּ – Bava ben Buta **saw cracks in [the Temple],** and under such circumstances immediate demolition was allowed.[34] אִיבָּעֵית אֵימָא – **Or, if you prefer, say:** מַלְכוּתָא שָׁאנֵי – **A king is different,** דְּלָא הָדְרָא בֵּיהּ – **for he will not renege on [his pledge],**[35] דְּאָמַר שְׁמוּאֵל – **as Shmuel said:** אִי אָמַר מַלְכוּתָא עָקַרְנָא טוּרֵי – **If a king says, "I will uproot mountains,"** עָקַר טוּרֵי וְלָא הָדַר בֵּיהּ – **he will uproot mountains and will not renege on [his pledge].** Thus, since Herod would not be deterred from rebuilding the Temple, Bava ben Buta's counsel was not inconsistent with Rav Chisda's ruling.

The Gemara now relates the story of Herod – his ascent to the monarchy and his rebuilding the Beis Hamikdash:

NOTES

24. Redeeming captives is considered "a great mitzvah" (Gemara below, 8a-b). Therefore, the possibility always exists that communal money will be diverted for this purpose if the need arises. [For discussion about whether it would be permitted to use the funds for other mitzvos, see *Yad Ramah*, *Nimukei Yosef*, *Taz* to *Yoreh Deah* 252:1.]

25. In this case the construction materials have already been purchased, thus eliminating the possibility that funds earmarked for the new synagogue will be used for other purposes. Hence, Ravina inquires whether immediate demolition is permitted, or whether a cause for concern still exists.

26. The new synagogue may be sold only until they actually begin to pray there (*Tosafos*).

27. And since this procedure is not followed, even though the possibility exists that the new synagogue would have to be sold in order to redeem captives, it is clear that we need not anticipate that exigency. Hence, demolition of the old synagogue should be permitted once materials for constructing its replacement have been procured.

28. *Rashi.*

29. I.e. whether the reason for Rav Chisda's ruling is possible negligence, or the lack of an interim place to pray.

30. He knew that they would not want to prolong his suffering from exposure to the sun and the rain (*Rashi*).

31. Rav Ashi did not actually sleep in the new synagogue, since that is prohibited (see *Megillah* 28b). Rather, he slept in quarters located near the synagogue that were provided for visitors (*Tosafos*; see however, *Rashi* to *Megillah* there, cited in *Tosafos*; see also *Ran*).

32. The Gemara will relate the incident below.

33. Certainly, the Gemara's question accords with the first explanation of Rav Chisda's ruling, for in the case of the Temple as well the possibility exists that unforeseen circumstances will cause them to neglect to rebuild. However, the commentators dispute whether the second explanation is also relevant here. *Yad Ramah* asserts that since during the period of reconstruction the Temple service was perforce suspended, the situation at that time was analogous to lacking an interim place of worship in the case of the razed synagogue. Hence, the Gemara's question accords also with the second explanation. *Rashash*, however, contends that if curtains were hung around the Temple court, the sacrificial service could proceed during the period of reconstruction. Thus, according to *Rashash*, the Gemara's question accords only with the first explanation.

34. Even though the sacrificial service was interrupted during the period of reconstruction (*Yad Ramah*).

35. Although others may fail to honor their commitments due to a shortage of funds, a king can wield any of his enormous powers to raise what is needed.

This answer accords only with the first interpretation of Rav Chisda's ruling (which the halachah follows (*Yad Ramah*); see above, note 33).

אמר אביי גמירי. השתא לא צריך לשנויא קמא: **מכלל** דאיכא זוטרתי. וא"ת ודילמא מכלל דאיכא רברבתא ומה דיקא הוא זה ותירץ ר"י דאם אין פחות משלשה אבל גדולות יש א"כ בכדי נקט חצי לבינה של ג' טפחים דלא הוה צריך למתני אלא והאריח חצי לבינה ותו לא וממילא הייתי משער בקטנה הואיל ולא מפרש שיעורא: **הג"ה** כי קייטא וכי סיתווא הוי כמו איכא תיוהא ושרי ואם שתי בתי כנסיות היו בב' מקומות של קייטא ושל סיתווא איירי כגון דחזו בה תיוהא ועוד נראה כיון דיש שם בהכ"נ אחר אין לחוש אם לא יבנו זאת והא דקאמר דאיכא דוכתא לצלויי היינו שאין בהכ"נ ועוד מחמת קור וחום אין לחוש שמא יפשעו או בזמן גדול כל כך אין לחוש. ע"כ הגה"ה: **אי** הכי כי בנייה נמי. פירוש עד שיתפללו בה: **ועייליה** לפורייה להתם. ותימה והא אמרת בתי כנסיות אין ישנים בהם לא שינת קבע ולא שינת עראי ואין לתרץ משום דבבבל הוי ואמר רב אסי בפ' בתרא דמגילה (דף כח: ושם ד"ה בתי) בתי כנסיות של בבל על תנאי הן עשויות ופ"ה התם נפקא מינה לענין הא דקתני לעיל אין אוכלין בהן ואין שותים בהן ואין נכנסין בהן בחמה מפני החמה ובגשמים מפני הגשמים ושל בבל מותר דהא קאמר התם בתר הכי רבינא ורב אדא הוו קיימי ושיילי שמעתא מרבא אתא זילחא דמטרא עלייהו ועיילי לבי כנישתא ולא משום מטרא אלא משום דשמעתא בעי' צילותא והשתא והלא בהכ"נ של בבל היה והיו יכולין ליכנס בה מפני המטר וי"ל דלאו ממש לבהכ"נ עיילה לפוריי' אלא בסמוך לבהכ"נ במקום שהאורחין רגילין לישן שם ולאכול כדאמרינן בע"פ (פסחים דף קא. ושם ד"ה דאכלי) ושמואל למה לי' לקדושי בבי כנישתא לאפוקי אורחים ידי חובתן דאכלו ושתו וגנו בבי כנישתא והא דאמר דעל תנאי הן עשויין מפרש ר"י לענין שאם יחרבו יעשו מהן מה שירצו לבד מקלות ראש כדאמרי' התם: **כל** דאמר מבית חשמונאי אתינא עבדא הוא. וכן הוא דהכי נמי אמר שמואל בפרק עשרה יוחסין (קדושין דף ע:) ומכאן קשה על פ"ה באלו נאמרים (סוטה דף מא.) דאמר אמרו לו לאגריפס אחינו אתה ופ"ה התם שאמרו לו אחינו לפי שהיתה אמו מישראל דא"כ כיון דבני הורדוס נשאו ישראלית אמאי עבדא הוה הא שמואל גופיה אית ליה עובד כוכבים ועבד הבא על בת ישראל הולד כשר בהחולץ (יבמות דף מה.) וי"ל שלא נשאו ישראלית וקראוהו אחינו אתה לפי שעבד אחינו [הוא] במצות: [וע"ע תוס' יבמות מה: ד"ה כיון דאמו]

בשנים ואיתא להא ואיתא להא וניעבדו תלתין אמין בבנין ואידך ניעביד פרוכת כי קאי תלתין אמהתא נמי אגב תקרה ומעזיבה (א) הוה קאי בלא תקרה ומעזיבה לא הוה קאי וליעביד מה דאפשר בבנין וליעביד אידך פרוכת אמר אביי גמירי אי כולהו בבנין אי כולהו בפרוכת אי כולהו בבנין ממקדש אי כולהו בפרוכת ממשכן איבעיא להו הן וסידן או דילמא הן בלא סידן אמר ר"נ בר יצחק [א]מסתברא הן וסידן דאי ס"ד הן בלא סידן ליתנייה לשיעוריה אלא לאו ש"מ הן וסידן לא לעולם אימא לך הן בלא סידן וכיון דלא הוי טפח לא תני והא קתני (ב) בלבינין זה נותן טפח ומחצה וזה נותן טפח ומחצה התם חזי לאיצטרופי ת"ש (א) [ב]הקורה שאמרו רחבה כדי לקבל אריח והאריח חצי לבינה של ג' טפחים התם ברברבתא דיקא נמי דקתני של שלשה טפחים מכלל דאיכא זוטרא ש"מ: (ב) אמר רב חסדא [ג]לא ליסתור איניש בי כנישתא עד דבני בי כנישתא אחריתי איכא דאמרי [ד]משום פשיעותא ואיכא דאמרי משום צלויי מאי בינייהו איכא בינייהו דאיכא (ג) (בי כנישתא אחריתי) מרימר ומר זוטרא סתרי ובנו בי קייטא בסיתווא (ג) ובנו בי סיתווא בקייטא א"ל רבינא לרב אשי גבו זוזי ומחתי מאי אמר ליה [ה]דילמא מיתרמי להו (ד) פדיון שבויים ויהבי להו שריגי ליבני והדרי הודרי ומחתי כשורי מאי א"ל [ו]זמנין דמתרמי להו פדיון שבויים מזבני ויהבי להו א"ה אפי' בנו נמי אמר ליה דירתיה דאינשי לא מזבני ולא אמרן [ז]אלא דלא חזי בה תיוהא אבל חזי בה תיוהא סתרי ובני כי הא דרב אשי חזא בה תיוהא בכנישתא דמתא מחסיא סתריה ועייל לפורייה להתם ולא אפקיה עד דמתקין ליה שפיכי ובבא בן בוטא היכי אסביה ליה עצה להורדוס למיסתריה לבית המקדש והאמר רב חסדא לא ליסתור איניש בי כנישתא עד דבני בי כנישתא אחריתי איבעית אימא תיוהא חזא ביה איבעית אימא (ח) מלכותא שאני דלא הדרא ביה דאמר (ו) שמואל אי אמר מלכותא עקרנא טורי עקר טורי ולא הדר ביה הורדוס עבדא דבית חשמונאי הוה נתן עיניו באותה תינוקת יומא חד (ד) שמע ההוא גברא בת קלא דאמר כל עבדא דמריד השתא מצלח קם קטלינהו לכולהו מרותיה ושייריה לההיא ינוקתא כי חזת ההיא ינוקתא דקא בעי למינסבה סליקא לאיגרא (ה) ורמא קלא אמרה (ז) כל מאן דאתי ואמר מבית חשמונאי קאתינא עבדא הוא דלא אישתיירא מינייהו אלא ההיא ינוקתא וההיא ינוקתא נפלה מאיגרא לארעא טמנה שבע שנין בדובשא איכא דאמרי בא עליה איכא דאמרי לא בא עליה דאמרי לה בא עליה הא דטמנה ליתובי יצריה ודאמרי לה לא בא עליה האי דטמנה כי היכי דנאמרו בת מלך נסב מאן דריש (א) מקרב אחיך תשים עליך מלך רבנן קם קטלינהו לכולהו רבנן שבקיה לבבא בן בוטא למשקל עצה מניה

בשנים. בית ראשון עמד ד' מאות ועשר ובית שני ד' מאות ועשרים: **אגב תקרה ומעזיבה.** שהעלייה היתה נתונה עליו ומעזיבה של טיט טורכס על גבה וכובד המשא מעמיד הכותל שלא יטה לצדדין הלכך במקדש שני שלא היה כותל ל' מגיע לעלייה לא יוכל לעמוד: **הן וסידן או הן בלא סידן.** הני שיעורי דמתני' עם עובי הטיח קא חשיב להן או דילמא מקום האבנים הוי בפותיא לבד טיח הסיד: **והא קתני טפחיים ומחצה.** אלמא חצי טפח נמי חשיב: **חזי לאיצטרופי.** של זה ושל זה מצטרפין לטפח: **הקורה שאמרו.** לענין הכשר מבוי: **ג' טפחים.** אלמא ג' טפחים דקתני לגבי מתני' גבי לבינין כדקתני זה נותן טפח ומחצה וזה נותן טפח ומחצה הן בלא סידן קאמר דהא לבינה לחודה שלשה טפחים: **התם ברברבתא.** ומתני' בזוטרתא דעם סידן לא הוו אלא ג' טפחים: **משום פשיעותא.** דילמא מתרמי אונס ופשעי ולא בנו אחריתי: **משום צלויי.** כל זמן הבנין: **בי קייטא בסיתווא.** בית הכנסת היה להם לימות החורף נמוך בכתלים רחבים וחלונות מועטין מפני הצינה ובימות החמה בית הכנסת אחר שאויר שולט בו: **זוזי.** לצורך בית הכנסת החדש ומונחים ביד הגבאי מי איכא למיחש לפשיעות או לא: **שריגי ליבני.** מסודרים הלבינים זה על גב זה ומזומנין לתתן בבנין: **הדרי הודרי.** משופין ומתוקנין רהיטי הגג קיברונ"ש: **כי בנו נמי.** בי כנישתא חדתא לא נסתרוה לעתיקא דדילמא מתרמי פדיון שבויין ומזבני ליה: **ולא אמרן.** דלא ליסתרוה לעתיקא: **אלא דלא חזו ביה תיוהא.** ביקוע שיהא מזומן ליפול: **עייליה לפורייה התם.** כדי שלא יתייאש בבניינו שהחמה והגשמים מצערין אותו: **שפכי.** מרזבין: **היכי אסביה עצה להורדוס.** כדאמרי' לקמן בשמעתין וכתובה היא ביוסיפון בן גוריון: אהדר

מאן דריש מקרב אחיך רבנן. דפשטי' דקרא לא משמע למעוטי עבד שהוא אחיך במצות אלא עובד כוכבים ורבנן דרשו (ב"ק פח.) ממובחר שבאחיך: **קטלינהו** לכולהו רבנן. לאו דוקא לכולהו דהא הוו בני בתירא שהיו נשיאים כשעלה הלל מבבל כדאמרינן בפסחים בפרק אלו דברים (דף סו.) והלל היה בפני הבית מאה שנה כדאמרינן בפרק קמא דשבת (דף טו.) ומלכות הורדוס היה בפני הבית ק"ג שנה כדאמרינן בפרק קמא דע"ז (דף ט.)

עין משפט נר מצוה

יא א מיי' פ"ב מהלכות שכנים הלכה יח סמג עשין פב טוש"ע ח"מ סי' קנז:
יב ב מיי' פי"ז מהלכ' שבת הל' יב סמג עשין מד טוש"ע א"ח סי' שסג סעיף יז:
יג ג ד מיי' פי"א מהל' תפלה הל' יב סמג עשין יט טוש"ע א"ח סי' קנב [וברב אלפס פרק בני העיר דף רסד]:
יד ה ו מיי' פ"ח מהל' מתנות עניים הל' יא סמג עשין קסב טוש"ע י"ד סי' רנב סעיף א:
טו ז מיי' פי"א מהל' תפלה הלכה יג סמג עשין יט טוש"ע א"ח סי' קנב [וברב אלפס פרק בני העיר דף רסד]:

רבינו גרשום

איתא להא ואית' להא. דהא בין בבנין בין בשנים היה גדול: כי קאי נמי תלתין אמה בעובי אמה בבית ראשון משום דהתקרה והמעזיבה מונחת עליו וסומכתו שלא יפול הא לאו הכי לא קאי אפי' בתלתין: ונעבד כמה דאפשר. לעמוד בגובה בבנין כותל ומכאן ולמעלה עד התקרה ליעבד פרוכת: אי כוליה בפרוכת. ממשכן [כדכתיב] והבדילה הפרוכת וגו': הן וסידן. כלומר הא דתנינן בגויל זה נותן ג' טפחים וזה נותן ג' טפחים תני מקום אבנים בהדי סיד שמסידו מבחוץ צריך ג' טפחים (דאי לא הכי) [דליכא הכא] ד' טפחים שלימות דבצר שיעור מקום הסיד. או הן בלא סידן כלומר דלמקום גויל גרידא בעי למיתן זה ג' טפחים וזה ג' טפחים חוץ ממקום הסיד: דאי ס"ד הן בלא סידן. ג' טפחים (למקום) (ולעולם) בעי למיתב תרווייהו א"כ ליתנייה לשיעורא דסיד ולימא הכי זה נותן ג' טפחים ומשהו למקום הסיד והשני כמו כן וכן בכולהו אלא מדלא תני הכי ש"מ מקום הגוויל ומקום הסיד לא הוי אלא ו' טפחים (אלא) [לא] לעולם אימא לך הן ולא סידן ואי אמרת אמאי לא תני שיעורא דסיד כיון דלא הוי טפח לא חשיב למתנייה: התם חזי לאצטרופי. ב' חצאי טפח מקום אבנים של מקום הסיד לא חזי לאצטרופי לשום חשבון: קורה שאמרו. לגבי מבוי מדתני לבינה של ג' טפחים מכלל דג' טפחים שלימות הוו כל לבינה וש"מ דלמקום לבינה בעינן ג' טפחים שלימות לבד למקום הסיד וה"ה לגויל וכפים וגזית: (מיהו) [ודידיה דמהא] לא תידוק דמקום לבינה ג' טפחים שלימות דאותן טפחים (א) דתני גבי לבינות מבוי גדולים הוו לבינה טפח בגדול אבל משנה דגבינים בינונים הן ומש"ה הן וסידן הוו ג' טפחים: משום פשיעותא. דדלמא מטריד בשאר מילי ולא

מסורת הש"ס

א) ערכין יג, ב) מגילה כו. ג) נ"א דוכתא לצלויי. רש"ל, ד) נ"א מלתא דמצוה ויהבי. רש"ל, ה) [ערכין ו.], ו) [שם], ז) קדושין ע ע"ב:

הגהות הב"ח

(א) גמ' ומעזיבה קאי בלא תקרה ומעזיבה לא קאי כצ"ל ותיבת הוה נמחק ב' פעמים: (ב) שם לא תני והא קתני בגויל זה נותן טפחים וזה נותן טפחים ומחצה התם חזי לאצטרופי: (ג) שם בי קייטא בסיתווא וסתרי ובנו בי סיתווא וכו' בי סיתווא: (ד) שם יומא חד שמעיה לבת קלא דאמר כצ"ל ותיבת ההוא גברא נמחק: (ה) שם ורמת קלא:

תורה אור השלם

א) שׂוֹם תָּשִׂים עָלֶיךָ מֶלֶךְ אֲשֶׁר יִבְחַר יְיָ אֱלֹהֶיךָ בּוֹ מִקֶּרֶב אַחֶיךָ תָּשִׂים עָלֶיךָ מֶלֶךְ לֹא תוּכַל לָתֵת עָלֶיךָ אִישׁ נָכְרִי אֲשֶׁר לֹא אָחִיךָ הוּא: [דברים יז, טו]

לעזי רש"י

קיברונ"ש. פירוש רהיטי הגג, קורות הגג, זיזין (רבינו גרשום דף ג ע"ב ודף ו ע"א ועיין רש"י שם ד"ה אמוק להודרי).

ליקוטי רש"י

רחבה כדי לקבל אריח. שתהא דומה לקביעות לבנות עליה בנין. והאריח חצי לבנה של שלשה טפחים. נמלא אריח טפח ומחצה רוחב [עירובין יג:]. משום פשיעותא. שמא יפשעו (אלא) ויתייאשו ולא יבנה אחר [מגילה כו:]. תיוהא. קלקול [ב"מ עג.]. טורי. הרים [ברכות נד:]. כל מאן דאתי ואמר מבית חשמונאי קאתינא עבדא הוא. כגון הורדוס וזרעו שהי' עבד לבית חשמונאי וגברה ידו ומלך [כתובות יא:]. שכל זרעו הכהנים הגדולים ועבד היה ומלך מתמיהין וקורא בניו על שם בית חשמונאי ומתמהלך אחר בנות ישראל בנושה לעבדים הם להשיא עבדים וכולהו להו כולם עבדים [קידושין ע:]. איגרא. גגין [פסחים פה:]. עליה [תענית כג. וקידושין מה:].

[מכאן שייך לדף ד.]

גם במדעך מלך. אפי' במחשבותיך בלא דבור, גם פילו, מלך אל תקלל לא תרגין ולמלכו של עולם. ד"ה כמשמעו מלך בשר ודם. עוף השמים וגו'. ולפי משמעו העוברים והשבי' יש לך לדאג שלא בריא שמא יש שומען וילך לאמרים [קהלת י, כ]. ונוקרא רבה בפ' בן המלך כי עוף השמים יוליך את הקול (קהלת י)

בני ליה: משום צלויי. דלא הוה להו דוכתא לצלויי עד שיעסוק בבנין: סתרו ובנו בי קייטא בסיתוא. שמעתי [דשתי] בתי כנסיות היו להם באחד היו מתפללין בימות הגשמים ובאחד בימות החמה היו מתפללין אותו בית של ימות החמה היה פתוח לרוחות והיה עשוי לימות הגשמים ושל ימות הגשמים בימות החמה כדי שיהא להם מקום תפלה בכל שעה: גבו זוזי. מציבורא לצורך בית הכנסת: ומחתי. ומונחין הן במקום אחד [מי] אמרינן הואיל והמעות מזומנין לבנין לא פשעי ומצי למיסתריה או דלמא ניחוש דלמא יהבינהו לבנים: ומחתי כשורי מאי. ואם תמצא לומר דהמעות יתנו לפדיון שבוים מהו בקורות דאינן מזומנין אלא לבנין: שריגי ליבני. שמוקפין ומסודרין הלבינים: הדרי הודרי. מתוקנים הזיזין. שריגי ליבני שמתוקנין ומוכנים להתחלת הבנין קודם שיתחילו החדש הישן והבנין למיסתר: מאי. מי יכול לסתור הישן קודם שיתחיל החדש או לאו: אי הכי דאבתי איכא למיחש אפי' כי מיבני האי לא ליסתור אחרינא דאיכא למיחש דמתרמי להו פדיון שבוים ומזבני להו לאחרינא: אמר ליה דדירתא דאינשי לא מזבני ולא אמרן דלא לסתור עד דבני אחרינא אלא דלא חזו ביה תיוהא. רעוע עד סדק אבל חזו ביה תיוהא סתר לאלתר: ועיילה לפורייה להתם. כדי שיהיו הגשמים יורדין ומנטפין עליו והוא ימהר במלאכת בהכ"נ יותר: שפיכי. מרזבין: אי הכי דלא ליסתור עד דבני אחרינא. בבא בן בוטא היכי אסביה עצה כו'. מלכא שאני דכיון דאמר למיבנייה לא הדר ביה וליכא למיחש לפשיעה: באותה תינוקת. דבית חשמונאי:

זה עורב וחכמת טוולדי [דה"י ב, ט, ד]. אברך. כתרגומו דין אבא למלכא רך בלשון ארמי מלך [illegible] ... יפה נוף ויפה קיבוץ ... סישא ... בוזלא ... אפיק שפה ... שיחה ... [illegible] ... מלכא ... [illegible] ... ולקצת ירחין. אלא לו הזמות י"ב חדש [סוטה שם].

חשק שלמה על רבינו גרשום א) [ונראה דל"ל דאותן לבינות דתני גבי מבוי גדולות של ג"ט אבל מתני' בלבינות בינונים הן וכו']:

הוּרְדוֹס עַבְדָּא דְּבֵית חַשְׁמוֹנָאִי הֲוָה – **Herod was** originally **a slave in the house of the Hasmoneans.**[36] נָתַן עֵינָיו בְּאוֹתָהּ תִּינוֹקֶת – **He had set his eyes on a certain young girl** from that illustrious family.[37] יוֹמָא חַד שָׁמַע (ההוא גברא) בַּת קָלָא דְּאָמַר – **One day he**[38] **heard a Heavenly voice that said:** כָּל עַבְדָּא דְּמָרִיד הַשְׁתָּא מַצְלַח – **Any slave that revolts now will succeed** in his rebellion. קָם קַטְלִינְהוּ לְכוּלְּהוּ מַרְוָתֵיהּ – Herod thereupon **rose and killed all of his masters,** exterminating the house of the Hasmoneans,[39] וְשַׁיְּירָהּ לְהַהִיא יְנוּקְתָּא – **but he spared** the life of **that maiden** in order to marry her.[40]

The girl, however, thwarted his plan:

כִּי חָזַת הַהִיא יְנוּקְתָּא דְּקָא בָּעֵי לְמִינְסְבָהּ – **When that maiden saw that** Herod **wanted to marry her,** סְלִיקָא לְאִיגָּרָא – **she ascended to the roof** וְרָמָא קָלָא אָמְרָה – **and raised her voice, saying:** כָּל מַאן דְּאָתֵי וְאָמַר – **"Whoever comes** in future years **and says:** מִבֵּית חַשְׁמוֹנָאִי קָאָתֵינָא – **'I am descended from the house of the Hasmoneans,'** עַבְדָּא הוּא – **is** in truth **a slave,**[41] דְּלָא אִישְׁתַּיַּירָא מִינַּיְיהוּ אֶלָּא הַהִיא יְנוּקְתָּא – **for no one remains from [the Hasmonean family] save this maiden** (a reference to herself), וְהַהִיא יְנוּקְתָּא נָפְלָה מֵאִיגָּרָא לְאַרְעָא – **and this maiden is hurling**[42] **herself from the roof to the ground."** After completing her declaration, she leaped from the roof to her death.[43]

The Gemara records the aftermath of this tragic episode:

טְמָנָהּ שְׁבַע שְׁנִין בְּדוּבְשָׁא – Herod **preserved [her body] in honey for seven years.** אִיכָּא דְּאָמְרֵי בָּא עָלֶיהָ – **There are those that say** that **he copulated with [her corpse],** אִיכָּא דְּאָמְרֵי לֹא בָּא עָלֶיהָ – **and there are those that say** that **he did not copulate with [her corpse].** דְּאָמְרֵי לָהּ בָּא עָלֶיהָ – According to those **that relate** that **he did copulate with [her corpse],** הָא דִּטְמָנָהּ לִיתוּבֵיהּ לְיִצְרֵיהּ – **that which he preserved her was to satisfy his desires.** וּדְאָמְרֵי לָהּ לֹא בָּא עָלֶיהָ – **But** according to those **that relate** that **he did not copulate with [her corpse],** הַאי דִּטְמָנָהּ כִּי הֵיכִי דְּנֵאמְרוּ – **that which he preserved her was so that it should be said** בַּת מֶלֶךְ נָסַב – that **he married a king's daughter,** and thus ascended to the throne by right.

Having usurped the throne, Herod sought to consolidate his position by eliminating any opposition:

אָמַר – Herod **said** to himself: מַאן דָּרִישׁ – **Who** are the ones that **expound** the verse,[44] ,,מִקֶּרֶב אַחֶיךָ תָּשִׂים עָלֶיךָ מֶלֶךְ״ – ***From the midst of your brothers shall you place a king over you,*** in such a way that it excludes slaves?[45] רַבָּנָן – **The Rabbis!** Perceiving the Rabbis as potential detractors, קָם קַטְלִינְהוּ לְכוּלְּהוּ רַבָּנָן – **he rose** and **slew all**[46] **of the Rabbis.** שַׁבְקֵיהּ לְבָבָא בֶּן בּוּטָא לְמִשְׁקַל עֵצָה מִנֵּיהּ – **He spared Bava ben Buta,** however, **to take counsel from him.**

NOTES

36. The Hasmonean revolt against the Syrian-Greek oppressors of the Jewish nation was led by the sons of Matisyahu, the *Kohen Gadol*. In the year 3597 (165 B.C.E.) the Holy Temple was recaptured and the miracle of Chanukah occurred. More than twenty years passed, however, until the final military victory was achieved. In the year 3621 (140 B.C.E.) the Sanhedrin and the people proclaimed the Hasmonean Shimon, the last surviving son of Matisyahu, "Prince of the Jews." The Hasmonean dynasty ruled from that year until 3725 (36 B.C.E.), when it was overthrown by Herod in a manner described presently by the Gemara. The Herodian dynasty and various Roman governors ruled Eretz Yisrael from 3725 (36 B.C.E.) until 3828 (68 C.E.), at which time the Second Temple was destroyed by the Romans.

37. Herod's motivation will be explained by the Gemara below.

38. Emendation follows *Bach,* who removes הַהוּא גַּבְרָא, *that man,* from the text.

39. *Ramban* (to *Genesis* 49:10) explains that the Hasmoneans were punished because they usurped the throne, which was promised by Jacob to the tribe of Judah.

40. *Maharsha* explains that not only did Herod desire the maiden, but he intended specifically to marry her for personal reasons. At that time he was a slave, the property of the Hasmonean family, whose only surviving member was now his master. The Gemara (*Gittin* 39b-40a) states that when a master marries his/her slave, the slave automatically gains his/her freedom. Thus, Herod's only hope of shedding the ignominious status of a slave was to marry the young Hasmonean girl, his master.

41. Whether the Gemara means that any descendant of Herod is actually a slave, or merely *descends from slaves* (and so lacks royal blood), is a question debated by Rishonim. See *Tosafos* here and to *Yevamos* (45b ד״ה כיון), and *Ritva* to *Kiddushin* 70b; and see *Sefer HaMiknah* to *Kiddushin* 7b.

42. Although our text states נָפְלָה, *she hurled herself, Pnei Shlomo* cites *Ein Yaakov's* version, which states תִּיפּוֹל, *she is hurling herself.*

43. As to whether the maiden was actually permitted to commit suicide to avoid marrying Herod, see *Dibros Moshe, Bava Basra I,* 12:11.

44. *Deuteronomy* 17:15.

45. The simple reading of the verse indicates that the Torah disqualifies only gentiles from assuming the office of king, for slaves are to some extent considered "brothers," since they are obligated to observe the mitzvos that are incumbent upon women. The Rabbis (in *Bava Kamma* 88a), however, interpreted *from the midst of your brothers* as *from the select of your brothers* — thereby excluding slaves like Herod (*Tosafos* ד״ה מאן).

46. *Tosafos* (ד״ה קטלינהו) note that not *all* of the Sages were killed, for the sons of Beseira survived the purge. Rather, Herod had a majority of the Sages murdered.

אַהֲדַר לֵיהּ כְּלִילָא דְיָלֵי — Nevertheless, Herod **placed around** [Bava ben Buta's] head **a crown of porcupine** hide נַקְרִינְהוּ לְעֵינֵיהּ — and **put out his eyes.**[1]

Despite this precaution Herod still feared that Bava ben Buta would agitate against him; hence, the king resolved to test his loyalty:

יוֹמָא חַד אֲתָא וְיָתִיב קַמֵּיהּ — **One day** Herod **came and sat before** [Bava ben Buta], pretending to be a commoner. אֲמַר חֲזִי מַר הַאי עַבְדָּא בִּישָׁא מַאי קָא עָבֵיד — **[He] said** to Bava ben Buta: **See, master, what this wicked slave is doing!** Herod was insinuating that Bava ben Buta should act against the king.

Bava ben Buta replied:

אֲמַר לֵיהּ מַאי אֶעֱבֵיד לֵיהּ — **[Bava] said to [Herod]: What shall I do to him?**[2]

Herod offered a plan:

אֲמַר לֵיהּ נִלַטְיֵיהּ מַר — **[Herod] said to [Bava]: Let master curse him!**

Bava refused:

אֲמַר לֵיהּ [כְּתִיב] — **[Bava] said to [Herod]: [It is written:]**[3] ,,גַּם בְּמַדָּעֲךָ מֶלֶךְ אַל־תְּקַלֵּל" — ***Even in your thoughts do not curse a king.*** Hence, I may not curse him.

Herod rejoined:

אֲמַר לֵיהּ הַאי לָאו מֶלֶךְ הוּא — **[Herod] said to [Bava]:** But **this** man **is not a** true **king;** he is a slave who seized the throne by force! Thus, there is no reason to refrain from cursing him.

Bava still refused:

אֲמַר לֵיהּ וְלֶיהֱוֵי עָשִׁיר בְּעָלְמָא — **[Bava] said to [Herod]: But were he simply a wealthy man** I could not curse him, וּכְתִיב: ,,וּבְחַדְרֵי מִשְׁכָּבְךָ אַל־תְּקַלֵּל עָשִׁיר" — **for it is written** further in that verse: ***. . . and even in your bedroom do not curse the rich.*** וְלָא יְהֵא אֶלָּא נָשִׂיא — **And were he only a leader**[4] I could not curse him, וּכְתִיב: ,,וְנָשִׂיא בְעַמְּךָ לֹא תָאֹר" — **for it is** also **written:**[5] ***And a leader among your people you shall not curse.*** Although Herod lacks royal blood, he is nevertheless a ruler.

Herod persisted:

אֲמַר לֵיהּ בְּעוֹשֶׂה מַעֲשֵׂה עַמְּךָ — **[Herod] said to [Bava]:** The prohibition against cursing *a leader among your people* applies only **to one that "acts in the manner of your people,"**[6] וְהַאי לָאו עוֹשֶׂה מַעֲשֵׂה עַמְּךָ — **and this** king **is not one that "acts in the manner of your people,"** for he is wicked! Why, then, do you refuse to curse him?

Realizing that Scriptural sources would not satisfy his companion,[7] Bava tried a simpler approach:

אֲמַר לֵיהּ מִסְתְּפִינָא מִינֵּיהּ — **[Bava] said to [Herod]: I am afraid of [the king].**[8]

Herod assured him that the king would never know:

אֲמַר לֵיהּ לֵיכָּא אִינִישׁ דְּאָזִיל דְּלֵימָא לֵיהּ — **[Herod] said to [Bava]: There is no one that will go and tell [the king]** that you have cursed him, דַּאֲנָא וְאַתְּ יָתִיבְנָא — **for you and I are sitting** here alone, and no one hears us!

Bava still refused:

אֲמַר לֵיהּ כְּתִיב — **[Bava] said to [Herod]: It is written:**[9] ,,כִּי עוֹף הַשָּׁמַיִם יוֹלִיךְ אֶת־הַקּוֹל וּבַעַל כְּנָפַיִם יַגֵּיד דָּבָר" — ***For a bird of the sky will carry the sound, and a winged creature will betray the matter.*** One can never be assured that a private conversation will remain secret.

Astounded by Bava's self-control, Herod revealed his identity:

אֲמַר לֵיהּ אֲנָא הוּא — **[Herod] said to [Bava]: I am he,** the king himself! אִי הֲוַאי יָדַעְנָא דִּזְהִירֵי רַבָּנַן כּוּלֵּי הַאי — **If I had known that the Rabbis were so circumspect,** לֹא הֲוָה קְטִילְנָא לְהוּ — **I would not have killed them.** Herod realized that Bava exemplified the entire group of Rabbis, and that none of them would have acted to depose him.

Stricken with remorse, Herod asked Bava to prescribe a course of repentance:

הַשְׁתָּא מַאי תַּקַּנְתֵּיהּ דְּהַהוּא גַּבְרָא — **Now, what is the remedy for this particular person?** What can I do to gain God's forgiveness?

Bava replied allegorically:

אֲמַר לֵיהּ — **[Bava] said to [Herod],** addressing the king in the third person: הוּא כִּבָּה אוֹרוֹ שֶׁל עוֹלָם — **He extinguished the light of the world** by annihilating the Rabbis, whose Torah knowledge is compared to light, דִּכְתִיב: ,,כִּי נֵר מִצְוָה וְתוֹרָה אוֹר" — **as it is written:**[10] ***For the commandments are a candle, and the Torah is light.*** יֵלֵךְ וְיַעֲסוֹק בְּאוֹרוֹ שֶׁל עוֹלָם — Therefore, in order to gain forgiveness, **he should go and occupy himself with** restoring **the light of the world** by rebuilding the Holy Temple,[11] which is also associated with "light," דִּכְתִיב: ,,וְנָהֲרוּ אֵלָיו כָּל־הַגּוֹיִם" — **for it is written** regarding the Third Temple: ***And all the nations will be drawn to it.***[12]

The Gemara records another version of Bava's response:

אִיכָּא דְּאָמְרֵי הָכִי אֲמַר לֵיהּ — **There are those that say** that **[Bava] replied to [Herod] thus:** הוּא סִימֵּא עֵינוֹ שֶׁל עוֹלָם — **He** (Herod) **blinded the eye of the world** by annihilating the Sages, who are the "eyes" of the nation, דִּכְתִיב: ,,וְהָיָה אִם מֵעֵינֵי הָעֵדָה" — **as it is written:**[13] ***And if through the "eyes" of the congregation.*** יֵלֵךְ וְיִתְעַסֵּק בְּעֵינוֹ שֶׁל עוֹלָם — Therefore, in order to achieve atonement, **he should go and occupy himself with** restoring **the "eye" of the world** by rebuilding the Holy Temple, which is also associated with "eyes," דִּכְתִיב: ,,הִנְנִי מְחַלֵּל אֶת־מִקְדָּשִׁי גְּאוֹן עֻזְּכֶם מַחְמַד עֵינֵיכֶם" — **as it is written:**[14] ***Behold, I will destroy My Temple, the pride of your strength, and the desire of your "eyes."*** In

NOTES

1. Wishing to incapacitate Bava so he would not foment rebellion, Herod fashioned a headband from porcupine hide (with quills attached) and bound it around Bava's head, so that the quills blinded him.

2. This reply did not condemn Bava in Herod's eyes, for Herod had blinded him and murdered most of his colleagues. Hence, Bava could scarcely be expected to profess love for the king. Rather, Herod was testing to see whether Bava would take any action against him.

3. *Ecclesiastes* 10:20.

4. Bava cited the prohibition against cursing a wealthy man first because it is derived from the verse (already mentioned) that prohibits cursing a king.

5. *Exodus* 22:27.

6. I.e. he observes the laws of the Torah (see *Yevamos* 22b).

7. Since Herod ignored Bava's second rationale (the prohibition against cursing a rich man), Bava realized that his companion would not be swayed by quotes from Scripture. Hence, he simply professed to be afraid.

8. *Bach* adds: "I am afraid that someone will overhear me and go inform the king."

9. *Ecclesiastes* 10:20.

10. *Proverbs* 6:23.

11. Although the Second Temple was still standing in Herod's time, it was badly in need of repair, as mentioned in the Gemara above (3b). Bava therefore advised Herod to raze the old structure and build anew.

12. *Isaiah* 2:2. Bava translated וְנָהֲרוּ as a derivative of נְהוֹרָא, *light* (cf. commentaries there). In the Messianic era the gentile nations will be drawn to the Holy Temple as if to light.

13. *Numbers* 15:24, wherein a sacrifice is prescribed if a majority of the nation unwittingly sins pursuant to a decision permitting some form of idol worship, which was erroneously rendered by the "eyes" of the nation — the *beis din.*

14. *Ezekiel* 24:21.

אהדר ליה כלילא דיילי נקרינהו לעיניה יומא חד אתא ויתיב קמיה אמר חזי מר האי עבדא בישא מאי קא עביד אמר ליה מאי אעביד ליה א"ל נלטייה מר אמר ליה [כתיב] א) גם במדעך מלך אל תקלל אמר ליה האי לאו מלך הוא א"ל ולהוי עשיר בעלמא וכתיב א) ובחדרי משכבך אל תקלל עשיר ולא יהא אלא נשיא וכתיב ב) ונשיא בעמך לא תאור א"ל בעושה מעשה עמך והאי לאו עושה מעשה עמך א"ל מסתפינא (א) מיניה א"ל ליכא איניש דאזיל דלימא ליה דאנא ואת יתיבנא א"ל כתיב א) כי עוף השמים יוליך את הקול ובעל כנפים יגיד דבר א"ל אנא הוא אי הואי ידענא דזהירי רבנן כולי האי לא הוה קטילנא להו השתא מאי תקנתיה דההוא גברא א"ל הוא כבה אורו של עולם דכתיב ג) כי נר מצוה ותורה אור ילך ויעסוק באורו של עולם דכתיב ד) ונהרו אליו כל הגוים איכא דאמרי הכי א"ל הוא סימא עינו של עולם דכתיב ה) והיה אם מעיני העדה ילך ויתעסק בעינו של עולם דכתיב ו) הנני מחלל את מקדשי גאון עוזכם מחמד עיניכם א"ל מסתפינא ממלכותא א"ל שדר שליחא וליזיל שתא וליעכב שתא ולהדר שתא אדהכי והכי סתרית [ליה] ובניית [ליה] עבד הכי שלחו ליה אם לא סתרתה אל תסתור ואם סתרתה אל תבני ואם סתרתה ובנית עבדי בישא בתר דעבדין מתמלכין אם זיינך עלך ספרך כאן לא רכא ולא בר רכא הורדוס [עבדא] קלניא מתעביד מאי רכא מלכותא דכתיב ז) אנכי היום רך ומשוח מלך ואי בעית אימא מהכא ח) ויקראו לפניו אברך אמרי מי שלא ראה בנין הורדוס לא ראה בנין נאה [מימיו] במאי בנייה אמר רבה באבני שישא ומרמרא איכא דאמרי באבני כוחלא שישא ומרמרא אפיק שפה ועייל שפה כי היכי דנקביל סידא סבר (ב) למשעייה בדהבא אמרו ליה רבנן שבקיה דהכי שפיר טפי דמיחזי כי אידוותא דימא ובבא בר בוטא היכי עבד הכי והאמר רב יהודה אמר רב ואיתימא ר' יהושע בן לוי מפני מה נענש דניאל מפני שהשיא עצה לנבוכד נצר שנאמר ט) להן מלכא מלכי ישפר עלך וחטאיך בצדקה פרוק ועויתך במיחן עניין הן תהוי ארכא לשלותך וגו' וכתיב י) כולא מטא על נבוכד נצר מלכא וכתיב כ) ולקצת ירחין תרי עשר וגו' איבעית אימא שאני עבדא דאיחייב במצות ואיבעית אימא שאני בית המקדש דאי לא מלכות לא מתבני ודניאל מנלן דאיענש אילימא משום דכתיב ל) ותקרא אסתר להתך ואמר רב התך זה דניאל הניחא למ"ד שחתכוהו מגדולתו אלא למ"ד שכל דברי מלכות נחתכין על פיו מאי איכא למימר דשדיוהו לגובא דארייוותא: הכל כמנהג המדינה: הכל לאתויי מאי לאתויי אתרא דנהיגי בהוצא ודפנא: לפיכך אם נפל הכותל המקום והאבנים של שניהם: פשיטא לא צריכא דנפל לרשותא דחד מינייהו אי נמי דפנינהו חד לרשותא דידיה מהו דתימא ניהוי אידך המוציא מחבירו עליו הראיה קמ"ל: וכן בגינה מקום שנהגו לגדור מחייבין אותו: הא גופא קשיא אמרת וכן בגינה מקום שנהגו לגדור מחייבין אותו הא סתמא אין מחייבין אותו אימא סיפא אבל בקעה מקום שנהגו שלא לגדור אין מחייבין אותו הא סתמא מחייבין אותו השתא סתם גינה אמרת לא סתם בקעה מיבעיא אמר אביי ה"ק וכן סתם גינה ובמקום שנהגו לגדור בבקעה מחייבין אותו אמר ליה רבא אם כן מאי אבל אלא אמר רבא הכי קתני וכן סתם גינה כמקום שנהגו לגדור דמי ומחייבין אותו אבל סתם בקעה כמקום שלא נהגו דמי ואין מחייבין אותו: אלא אם רצה כונס לתוך שלו ובונה ועושה חזית: מאי חזית אמר רב הונא אכפיה ליה לקרנא לבר ונעביד מלגיו עביד חבריה נמי מלבר ואמר דידי ודידיה הוא אי הכי השתא נמי גייז ליה חבריה ואמר דידי ודידיה הוא גיזוזא מידע ידיע איכא דאמרי אמר רב הונא מיכפא לקרנא מלגיו ונעבד מלבר גייז ליה חבריה ואמר דידי ודידיה הוא אי הכי השתא נמי לייף ליה חבריה ואמר דידי ודידיה הוא ליפופא מידע ידיע והא מבחוץ קתני קשיא רבי יוחנן אמר נשעייה

רש"י

אהדר ליה כלילא דיילי. הלנקה מתרגמינן ילא (ויקרא יא) והוא שרץ שקורין הרצו"ן ושערו קשה כמחטין ועשה לו עטרה מעורו סביבות עיניו: השתא מיהא [דאנא ואת]. אנא ואת שנינו כאן ואין שומע: הנני מחלל את מקדשי. סיפיה דקרא מחמד עיניכם: מסתפינא ממלכותא. כפופים היו למלכות רומיים: מתמלכין. נוטלין רשות: אי זיינך עלך ספרך כאן. אם נתגאית בכלי מלחמתך שהרגת בית אדונך ספר יוחסין שלך בידינו הוא [ידענו] שאתה עבד: לא רכא כו'. לא מלך ולא בן מלך: קלניא מתעביד. נעשה בן חורין מאליו: שישא. שיש ירוק שקורין ביי"ש: ומרמרא. שיש לבן: כוחלא. שיש צבוע כעין כחול: אידוותא דימא. גלי הים [שהם נעים ונדים והעין] מתעששת בראייתן: נענש דניאל. לקמיה מפרש עונשו: מלכי ישפר עלך. עצתי תיטב בעיניך: במיחן עניין. בחנינת עניים: בכן תהא ארכא לשלותך. [יהא ארוכה] לשלומך: כולא מטא. כל השלום של פורענות בא עליו: לקצת ירחין תרי עשר. בשביל עצמו של דניאל תלה לו שנים עשר חדש: בהוצא. לולבי דקלים: ודפנא. ענפי עץ ערמונים שקורין לו"ר ופרי שלו קורין ביי"ש: פשיטא. דהאבנים של שניהם דלפי' לא פסק לן דינא דמתני' המלמדנו שמתחלה בין שניהם עשאוה על כרחם היו חולקין בשוה האבנים שהרי ברשות שניהם מונחים ויד מי מהם תגבר: (הג"ה בפי' ר"ח קמ"ל דלא בעינן ראיה אלא שותף מפיק מיניה בלא ראיה ואיהו דטעין דדיליה נינהו עליו הראיה וכל כה"ג הכי דיינינן ליה וזה הדין מפורש עוד כמו כן בפרק הבית והעלייה בתחלתו איבעית אימא בשותפין כי האי גוונא אמרי אבנים ברשות חבירו לא קפדי וחזקת רשות לאו כלום הוא שמעינן מינה דלכהאי גוונא דמילתא דידיעא בשותפתא לתרוייהו אע"ג דמנחי ברשותא דחד מינייהו לא יכול למיטען דידי נינהו דברשותי מנחי דקי"ל שותפין לא קפדי אהדדי ע"כ): השתא סתם גינה אמרת לא. אע"פ שהיזק ראיה קשה: אמר אביי כו'. הכי מקום שנהגו לגדור דקתני מתני' אבקעה קאי: א"כ מאי אבל בבקעה. הא מינה סליק והכי איבעי (ג) למיתני אבל מקום שנהגו שלא לגדור אין מחייבין אותו: מכפייה לקרנא לבר. ראשי הכותל יכוף לצד חבירו. וכל חזית לשון קצה הוא וכן שנינו בתמיד (פ"ג מ"ד) גבי מערכה וחזיתה מזרחה ראשי הגזירין וכן מחזה מול מחזה דמלכים (א ז) ראשי הגסרים מוסבין זה מול זה ועבי' מאבראי כופה לצדי ראשי הכותל שמחבר בראשו אבנים וטיט ומעבהו: דידי ודידיה הוא. כדקתני מתניתין כשעושין אותו בין שניהם עושין חזית מכאן ומכאן: השתא נמי גייז לה. להסיר כפופה שהיא לצדו ואימא דידי ודידיה הוא ולא עשינו חזית: מלגיו. לצד שלו ולקמיה פריך הא מבחוץ קתני: לייף ליה. מחבר חזית אחרת לצדו:

תוספות

שכל דברי מלכות נחתכין על פיו. לפי תרגום [של] אחשורוש (ט) נענש הרבה שנהרג דכתיב ויגידו למרדכי את דברי אסתר ולא כתב התם התך לפי שהרגו המן על שהיה משיב דברים בין אסתר למרדכי ומיהו גמ' שלנו אין תופס כן דדרשינן במגילה (דף טו.) והתך להיכן הלך ומפרש לפי שאין משיבין על הקלקלה:

הכי קתני וכן בגינה סתם כו'. וסיפא נמי יש לפרש כן אבל סתם בקעה ומקום שלא נהגו לגדור בגינה אין מחייבין אותו:

והא מבחוץ קתני קשיא. ותיובתא היא דמלינן למימר היינו שבולט חוץ לחומה מ"מ קשיא היא דה"ל מחוץ הוה ליה למיתני:

גייז ליה חבריה ושדי ליה. אע"ג דלעיל אמר גזוזא מידע ידיע בהולא לא ידיע: לאפוקי

מסורת הש"ס

א) [יבמות כב: ב"ק לד: ב"מ מח: סב. סנהדרין מז. פה. מכות ח:], ב) סוכה נא: ע"ש, ג) [שם איתא רבא], ד) נ"א דלא סגיא ליה בלא מלכא, ה) מגילה טו., ו) משתעשעת, ז) ס"א ועציו, ח) [וכן בפירקי דר"א פ"ג], ט) שייך לע"ב:

הגהות הב"ח

(א) גמ' א"ל מסתפינא איכא איניש דשמע מלתא ואזיל ומודע ליה א"ל השתא מיהא ליכא איניש גבן דלזיל ולימא ליה: (ב) שם סבר למתפייה בדהבא: (ג) רש"י ד"ה א"כ מאי וכו' איבעי ליה למיתנא:

ליקוטי רש"י

[תחילת ליקוטי רש"י ששייך לכאן נדפס בעמוד הקודם] שחתכוהו מגדולתו. בימי אחשורוש שהרי בלשצר הגדילו במלכותו וכן דריוש המדי שנאמר ועלא מנהון סרכין תלתא די דניאל חד מנהון (דניאל ו) וכן כורש שנאמר ודניאל הצלח במלכות דריוש ובמלכות כורש פרסאה (שם) ובמלכות אחשורוש חתכוהו מגדולתו (מגילה טו.). ... חזית. (תהלים קד ו) כל מחזה פנים... (מלכים א, ז, ד).

עין משפט נר מצוה

טו א ב ג מיי' פכ"ו מהל' סנהדרין הל' א סמג לאוין רטו:

יז ד ה מיי' פי"ב מהל' רוצח הלכה טו:

יח ו מיי' פ"ב מהל' שכנים הל' טו סמג עשין פב טוש"ע ח"מ סי' קנז סעיף ד:

יט ז ח מיי' שם הלכה יח טוש"ע שם סעיף ה:

כ ט מיי' שם הל' ח סמג שם טוש"ע ח"מ סי' קנח סעיף א:

לעזי רש"י

הרצו"ן. פירוש הלנקה (רש"י ויקרא יא, ל), קופר (רש"י שבת דף נד ע"ב), הקופד (רא"ש כלאים פ"ח מ"ה), קפוד (רש"י ישעיה יד, כג). ביי"ש. פירוש כעין ירוק (רש"י סוכה דף נא ע"ב ד"ה שישא), להוב (עיין רש"י ויקרא יג, מט ותוספות סוכה דף לא ע"ב ד"ה הירוק). לו"ר. פירוש עץ הער (רש"י גיטין דף סט ע"ב ד"ה אטרפא ועיין אסף הרופא כ"י מינכן דף סט ע"ב), לורברבייס. ביי"ש. פירוש עץ הער (רש"י כנ"ל).

רבינו גרשום

כלילא דיילי. כתר של מיני האנקה שהן עלוקות נתן סביב ראשו ונעקרו עיניו: כי נר מצוה ותורה אור. אלו תלמידי חכמים שעוסקין בתורה אלו סנהדרין: ממלכותא. זו מלכות רומי שהיה משועבד להם: שלחו ליה. ממלכות רומיים אם זיינך עלך ספרך כאן. כלומר אם מלחמתך עליך שאתה מתגבר לשם ייחוסך כאן שיודעין אנו מאיזה משפחה אתה לפי שהורדוס אביו של הורדוס פעם אחת הלך על הרומים להלחם ונצח וראה בשביה שפחה אחת יפת תואר וחמדה ועשה לה כדין תורה ובא עליה והוליד ממנה אותו הורדוס ולפיכך היו מחרפין אותו מיחוסו: קלניא. בן חורין נעשה: שישא. שיש לבן: ומרמרא. מנומרין: כוחלא. שחורין: כאדוותא דימא. כגלי הים שזו יורדת וזו עולה: שאני עבד משום דהוי שייך במצות עשה (שהזמן) [שאין הזמן] גרמא והורדוס עבד היה: בהוצא ודפנא. שנוהגין לעשות גדר מכפות תמרים: ודפנא עץ של (עור) [ערמון] שקורין לו"ר וכיון דנתרצו לעשות כותל על זה ועל זה לעכב שלא יעשו אלא כמנהג המדינה: קמ"ל. כיון דזה נותן מחצה וזה נותן מחצה אין צריך להביא ראיה: פיסקא וכן בגינה מקום שנהגו לגדור בגויל או בגזית וחבירו מעכב היו כופין אותו משום דאיכא היזק ראיה כדאוקימנא [לעיל ב:] בגינה הסמוכה לעיר אבל בבקעה של שדות כו': הא סתמא. דיש שגודרין ויש שאין גודרין: השתא סתם גינה. דאיכא היזק ראיה אמרת לא דאין מחייבין סתם בקעה דליכא היזק ראיה מחייב: אמר אביי ה"ק. כלומר כגון חסורא מיחסרא וכן גינה סתם משום דאיכא היזק ראיה ובמקום שנהגו לגדור בבקעה מחייבין אותו: א"ל רבא. לאביי אי הכי כדקא תרצת א"כ מאי אבל דקתני במתני' אבל בבקעה אי אמרת בשלמא דרישא לא איירי בדינא דבקעה כלל היינו דקתני בסיפא אבל בבקעה דעד השתא לא איירי בדינא דבקעה אלא לדעתך דתרצת דרישא איירי בבקעה מאי אבל בבקעה תו דתני בסיפא: אלא אמר רבא. אנא מתריצנא דלא תקשי אבל ולא תקשי סתמא דרישא לסתמא דסיפא וה"ק וכן בגינה סתם דינא דגינה סתם כדינא דמקום שנהגו לגדור בבקעה דמחייבין לגדור ועדיין לא שמעי' דינא דסתם בקעה ואמטו להכי צריך למתני בסיפא אבל בבקעה לאשמעינן דינא דסתם בקעה דכמקום שנהגו שלא לגדור דמי דאין מחייבין לגדור דהשתא מיתרצא כולה מתני': ועושה לכותל חזית. סימן היכרא שידעו בני אדם שזה בנאו כולו בקרקע שלו משלו לפיכך כיון דעשה חזית אם נפל הכותל כו': דכייף ליה קרנא מלבר. דלשקע בראש הכותל בסופו קנים בטיט ויכוף ראשם של קנים מבחוץ לצד הכותל לצד אויר חבירו: אזיל אידך חבירו וכייף ליה נמי מלבר לצד שלו ואמר הרי אית לי נמי חזית ודידי ודידך הוא הכותל ומקומו הלכך לא כייף אלא מלבר: אכתי אתי האי וגייז לההיא חזית שהוא (פצע) [לצד] שלו ואמר דידי ודידך הוא: השתא נמי לייף ליה. כלומר יחברם לכותל בטיט בלא שקיעה: מידע ידיע. יכולין להבין ולהבחין בין דבוקה לשקיעה: והא מבחוץ קתני. ועושה לו חזית מבחוץ קשיא להך לישנא דאיכא דאמרי: ור' יוחנן אמר. היינו חזית:

תורה אור השלם

א) גַּם בְּמַדָּעֲךָ מֶלֶךְ אַל תְּקַלֵּל וּבְחַדְרֵי מִשְׁכָּבְךָ אַל תְּקַלֵּל עָשִׁיר כִּי עוֹף הַשָּׁמַיִם יוֹלִיךְ אֶת הַקּוֹל וּבַעַל כְּנָפַיִם יַגִּיד דָּבָר: [קהלת י, כ]

ב) אֱלֹהִים לֹא תְקַלֵּל וְנָשִׂיא בְעַמְּךָ לֹא תָאֹר: [שמות כב, כז]

ג) כִּי נֵר מִצְוָה וְתוֹרָה אוֹר וְדֶרֶךְ חַיִּים תּוֹכְחוֹת מוּסָר: [משלי ו, כג]

ד) וְהָיָה בְּאַחֲרִית הַיָּמִים נָכוֹן יִהְיֶה הַר בֵּית יְיָ בְּרֹאשׁ הֶהָרִים וְנִשָּׂא מִגְּבָעוֹת וְנָהֲרוּ אֵלָיו כָּל הַגּוֹיִם: [ישעיה ב, ב]

ה) וְהָיָה אִם מֵעֵינֵי הָעֵדָה נֶעֶשְׂתָה לִשְׁגָגָה וְעָשׂוּ כָל הָעֵדָה פַּר בֶּן בָּקָר אֶחָד לְעֹלָה לְרֵיחַ נִיחֹחַ לַייָ וּמִנְחָתוֹ וְנִסְכּוֹ כַּמִּשְׁפָּט וּשְׂעִיר עִזִּים אֶחָד לְחַטָּת: [במדבר טו, כד]

ו) אֱמֹר לְבֵית יִשְׂרָאֵל כֹּה אָמַר אֲדֹנָי יְיָ הִנְנִי מְחַלֵּל אֶת מִקְדָּשִׁי גְּאוֹן עֻזְּכֶם מַחְמַד עֵינֵיכֶם וּמַחְמַל נַפְשְׁכֶם וּבְנֵיכֶם וּבְנוֹתֵיכֶם אֲשֶׁר עֲזַבְתֶּם בַּחֶרֶב יִפֹּלוּ: [יחזקאל כד, כא]

ז) וְאָנֹכִי הַיּוֹם רַךְ וּמָשׁוּחַ מֶלֶךְ וְהָאֲנָשִׁים הָאֵלֶּה בְּנֵי צְרוּיָה קָשִׁים מִמֶּנִּי יְשַׁלֵּם יְיָ לְעֹשֵׂה הָרָעָה כְּרָעָתוֹ: [שמואל ב' ג, לט]

ח) וַיַּרְכֵּב אֹתוֹ בְּמִרְכֶּבֶת הַמִּשְׁנֶה אֲשֶׁר לוֹ וַיִּקְרְאוּ לְפָנָיו אַבְרֵךְ וְנָתוֹן אֹתוֹ עַל כָּל אֶרֶץ מִצְרָיִם: [בראשית מא, מג]

ט) לָהֵן מַלְכָּא מִלְכִּי יִשְׁפַּר עֲלָךְ וַחֲטָאָךְ בְּצִדְקָה פְרֻק וַעֲוָיָתָךְ בְּמִחַן עֲנָיִן הֵן תֶּהֱוֵה אַרְכָה לִשְׁלֵוְתָךְ: [דניאל ד, כד]

י) כֹּלָּא מְטָא עַל נְבוּכַדְנֶצַּר מַלְכָּא: [דניאל ד, כה]

כ) לִקְצָת יַרְחִין תְּרֵי עֲשַׂר עַל הֵיכַל מַלְכוּתָא דִּי בָבֶל מְהַלֵּךְ הֲוָה: [דניאל ד, כו]

ל) וַתִּקְרָא אֶסְתֵּר לַהֲתָךְ מִסָּרִיסֵי הַמֶּלֶךְ אֲשֶׁר הֶעֱמִיד לְפָנֶיהָ וַתְּצַוֵּהוּ עַל מָרְדֳּכַי לָדַעַת מַה זֶּה וְעַל מַה זֶּה: [אסתר ד, ה]

both versions Bava prescribed reconstructing the Second Temple as a penance for Herod.

To this advice Herod replied:

אָמַר לֵיהּ מִסְתְּפִינָא מִמַּלְכוּתָא — Herod said to [Bava]: I am afraid of the Roman **government,** to which Herod himself was subject.[15] Herod feared that the imperial Roman authorities would disapprove of his strengthening the focal point of Jewish life, the Holy Temple, and so would oppose his efforts.

Bava provided a solution:

אָמַר לֵיהּ שְׁדַר שְׁלִיחָא — Bava said to [Herod]: Send an emissary to Rome to request permission for the reconstruction. **וְלֵיזִיל שַׁתָּא —** However, the agent **should travel** for **a year** before reaching Rome, **וְלִיעַכֵּב שַׁתָּא — and remain** in Rome for **a year,** prolonging the negotiations, **וְלֶהְדַר שַׁתָּא — and** then spend **a year returning** home, thus gaining for you three uninterrupted years. **אַדְּהָכִי וְהָכִי סָתְרִית [לֵיהּ] וּבָנֵית [לֵיהּ] — In the meantime, you can demolish [the existing structure] and build [the Temple]** anew and Rome cannot retaliate, for you requested permission! **עֲבַד הָכִי — [Herod]** agreed to this plan and **did so,** dispatching the emissary and building a new Temple during the three years that the agent was away.

When the emissary finally returned, he bore a message that indicated that Rome had seen through Herod's stratagem:

שְׁלַחוּ לֵיהּ — [The Roman government] sent a reply **to [Herod]: אִם לֹא סָתַרְתָּה אַל תִּסְתּוֹר — If you have not** yet **demolished [the existing structure], do not demolish** it; **וְאִם סָתַרְתָּה אַל תִּבְנֵי — and if you have** already **demolished it, do not build;**[16] **וְאִם סָתַרְתָּה וּבָנִיתָ — and if you have** already **demolished it and have built** anew, we have this to say to you: **עַבְדֵי בִּישָׁא בָּתַר דְּעָבְדִין מִתְמַלְּכִין — Wicked slaves seek permission** only **after they do** as they wish. **אִם זַיְינָךְ עֲלָךְ סִפְרָךְ כָּאן — If you are proud of your weaponry, your book** of lineage **is here** before us.[17] **לֹא רֵכָא וְלֹא בַּר רֵכָא —** You are **not a *reicha* or the son of a *reicha;*** **הוֹרְדוֹס [עַבְדָּא] קַלְנָיָא מִתְעַבֵּיד —** you are merely **"Herod the slave, who made himself free."**

The Gemara defines the unfamiliar word *reicha:*

מַאי רֵכָא — What is the meaning of ***reicha*? מַלְכוּתָא — King! דִּכְתִיב: ,,אָנֹכִי הַיּוֹם רַךְ וּמָשׁוּחַ מֶלֶךְ" — As it is written: *I am today a tender and anointed king.***[18] **וְאִי בָּעֵית אֵימָא מֵהָכָא — And if you prefer, I shall cite** a proof **from here: ,,וַיִּקְרְאוּ לְפָנָיו אַבְרֵךְ" — *And they called before him*** (Joseph) ***"avreich."***[19]

The Gemara now discusses some of the physical details of the Temple built by Herod:

אָמְרֵי מִי שֶׁלֹּא רָאָה בִּנְיַן הוֹרְדוֹס לֹא רָאָה בִּנְיָן נָאֶה [מִיָּמָיו] — It was said: Whoever did not see the Temple **building** erected by **Herod — has not seen a** truly **beautiful building in his lifetime. בְּמַאי בַּנְיֵיהּ — With what** materials **was it built? אָמַר רַבָּה בְּאַבְנֵי שִׁישָׁא וּמַרְמְרָא — Rabbah said: With stones of green and white marble. אִיכָּא דְּאָמְרֵי בְּאַבְנֵי כוּחְלָא שִׁישָׁא וּמַרְמְרָא — There are those that say: With stones of blue, green and white marble. אַפִּיק שָׁפָה וְעַיֵּיל שָׁפָה — One row of stones protruded and the other row was recessed**[20] **כִּי הֵיכִי דְּנִקַבֵּיל סִידָא — in order to** provide a space to **hold the cement.**[21] **סָבַר לְמִשְׁעֲיֵיהּ בְּדַהֲבָא —** Herod **thought to cover**[22] **[the entire Temple] with** a **gold** plating, **אָמְרוּ לֵיהּ רַבָּנַן שַׁבְקֵיהּ — but the Rabbis**[23] **said to him: Leave it** as it is, **דְּהָכִי שַׁפִּיר טְפֵי — for this way is more attractive, דְּמֶחֱזֵי כִּי אִידְווֹתָא דְּיַמָּא — since** the swirling coloration of the marble facade **appears like the waves of the sea.**[24]

The Gemara questions Bava's actions:

וּבָבָא בַּר בּוּטָא הֵיכִי עָבַד הָכִי — And Bava ben Buta — how could he do this? Why did he divulge the appropriate act of penance to Herod, thereby enabling the wicked king to alter his Divine punishment? **וְהָאָמַר רַב יְהוּדָה אָמַר רַב — But did Rav Yehudah not say in Rav's name, וְאִיתֵּימָא רַבִּי יְהוֹשֻׁעַ בֶּן לֵוִי — and some say** it was **R' Yehoshua ben Levi: מִפְּנֵי מָה נֶעֱנַשׁ דָּנִיֵּאל— For what** reason **was Daniel punished? מִפְּנֵי שֶׁהִשִּׁיא עֵצָה לִנְבוּכַדְנֶצַּר — Because** he **proffered advice to Nebuchadnezzar** on how to escape God's wrath,[25] **שֶׁנֶּאֱמַר: ,,לָהֵן מַלְכָּא מִלְכִּי יִשְׁפַּר עֲלָךְ וַחֲטָאָךְ בִּצְדְקָה פְרֻק וַעֲוָיָתָךְ בְּמִחַן עֲנָיִן הֵן תֶּהֱוֵה אַרְכָה לִשְׁלֵוְתָךְ וגו׳" — as it says:**[26] ***Nevertheless, O king, let my advice be agreeable to you; redeem your sins with charity and your iniquities with graciousness to the poor; in this way there will be an extension of your tranquility etc.*** **וּכְתִיב: ,,כֹּלָּא מְטָא עַל־נְבוּכַדְנֶצַּר מַלְכָּא" — And** afterward **it is written:**[27] ***All*** (the punishments foretold in the dream) ***befell King Nebuchadnezzar.*** **וּכְתִיב: ,,לִקְצָת יַרְחִין תְּרֵי־עֲשַׂר וגו׳" — And it is** further **written:**[28] ***At the end of twelve months etc.*** (the decree indeed befell him). Thus, because he heeded Daniel's advice, Nebuchadnezzar escaped retribution for an entire year. Since Daniel's actions were judged improper,

NOTES

15. *Rashi.*

16. Although Rome was obviously reluctant to antagonize the God of Israel, as evidenced by their separate, first order (not to destroy the Temple), they nonetheless opposed the reconstruction of the Temple (see also *Maharsha*).

17. I.e. if you have become haughty on account of your prowess in battle, having exterminated the house of your master, we have your genealogy here in Rome; we know that you are a slave (*Rashi*).

18. *II Samuel* 3:39. Although the commentators translate רַךְ as *tender* (see *Radak* and *Metzudos Tzion*), the Gemara understands it to connote *royalty,* so as to say: *I am today royalty and an anointed king.*

19. *Genesis* 41:43. אַבְרֵךְ is a composite of אָב, *father,* and רַךְ, *king.* That is, Joseph was the *father* (i.e. adviser) to the *king* (Pharaoh) [see *Targum* there].

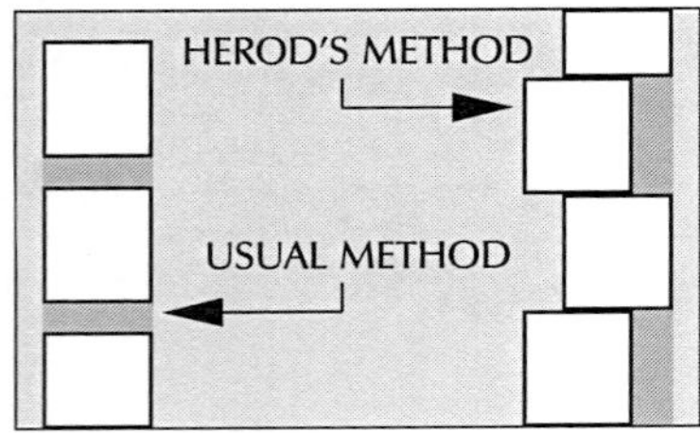

20. Literally: it sent out an edge and drew in an edge.

21. Builders customarily place cement between each brick in order to hold them together. Herod eschewed this procedure, however, since it would mar the beauty of the marble face of the Temple. Instead, he had the rows of stones overlap — i.e. every other row recessed slightly toward the inside — so that cement could be placed in the pockets created in the back side of the wall by the recessing (see diagram) [*Yad Yosef* to *Ein Yaakov*].

22. *Bach* changes לְמִשְׁעֲיֵיהּ to לְמִחַפְיֵיהּ.

23. These were the survivors of Herod's purge (see above, 3b note 46). Although Herod had retained Bava ben Buta as an adviser, Bava was unable to help in this matter — for he was blind.

24. And the eye delights in the undulations of the sea (*Rashi*).

25. Daniel had interpreted Nebuchadnezzar's "dream of the tree" (*Daniel* 4:7-15) as a presaging of the dire punishment that awaited the wicked emperor for his erecting a golden image, an act that demonstrated his arrogance and defiance of God's will (see ArtScroll *Daniel,* introduction to chapter 3 and Appendix). Then, without solicitation, Daniel advised Nebuchadnezzar that the retribution would possibly be averted if the king undertook to dispense gifts of charity among the poor. Daniel's punishment for so aiding the idolater will be discussed by the Gemara below.

26. *Daniel* 4:24.

27. Ibid. v. 25.

28. Ibid. v. 26.

אהדר ליה כלילא דיילי נקרינהו לעיניה יומא חד אתא ויתיב קמיה אמר חזי מר האי עבדא בישא מאי קא עביד אמר ליה מאי אעביד ליה א"ל נלטייה מר אמר ליה [כתיב] א) גם במדעך מלך אל תקלל אמר ליה האי לאו מלך הוא א"ל וליהוי עשיר בעלמא וכתיב א) ובחדרי משכבך אל תקלל עשיר ולא יהא אלא נשיא וכתיב ב) ונשיא בעמך לא תאור א"ל בעושה מעשה עמך והאי לאו עושה מעשה עמך א"ל מסתפינא (א) מיניה א"ל ליכא איניש דאזיל דלימא ליה דאנא ואת יתיבנא א"ל כתיב א) כי עוף השמים יוליך את הקול ובעל כנפים יגיד דבר א"ל אנא הוא אי הואי ידענא דזהירי רבנן כולי האי לא הוה קטילנא להו השתא מאי תקנתיה דההוא גברא א"ל הוא כבה אורו של עולם דכתיב ג) כי נר מצוה ותורה אור ילך ויעסוק באורו של עולם דכתיב ד) ונהרו אליו כל הגוים איכא דאמרי הכי א"ל הוא סימא עינו של עולם דכתיב ה) והיה אם מעיני העדה ילך ויתעסק בעינו של עולם דכתיב ו) הנני מחלל את מקדשי גאון עוזכם מחמד עיניכם א"ל מסתפינא ממלכותא א"ל שדר שליחא וליזיל שתא וליעכב שתא ולהדר שתא אדהכי והכי סתרית [ליה] ובניית [ליה] עבד הכי שלחו ליה אם לא סתרתה אל תסתור ואם סתרתה אל תבני ואם סתרתה ובנית עבדי בישא בתר דעבדין מתמלכין אם זיינך עלך ספרך כאן לא רכא ולא בר רכא הורדוס [עבדא] קלניא מתעביד מאי רכא מלכותא דכתיב ז) אנכי היום רך ומשוח מלך ואי בעית אימא מהכא ח) ויקראו לפניו אברך אמרי מי שלא ראה בנין הורדוס לא ראה בנין נאה [מימיו] במאי בנייה אמר רבה באבני שישא ומרמרא איכא דאמרי באבני כוחלא שישא ומרמרא אפיק שפה ועייל שפה כי היכי דנקביל סידא סבר (ב) למשעייה בדהבא אמרו ליה רבנן שבקיה דהכי שפיר טפי דמיחזי כי אידוותא דימא ובבא בר בוטא היכי עבד הכי והאמר רב יהודה אמר רב ואיתימא ר' יהושע בן לוי מפני מה נענש דניאל מפני שהשיא עצה לנבוכד נצר שנאמר ט) להן מלכא מלכי ישפר עלך וחטאך בצדקה פרוק ועויתך במיחן עניין הן תהוי ארכא לשלותך וגו' וכתיב י) כולא מטא על נבוכד נצר מלכא וכתיב כ) ולקצת ירחין תרי עשר וגו' איבעית אימא שאני עבדא דאיחייב במצות ואיבעית אימא שאני בית המקדש דאי לא מלכות לא מתבני ודניאל מנלן דאיענש אילימא משום דכתיב ל) ותקרא אסתר להתך ואמר רב התך זה דניאל הניחא למ"ד שחתכוהו מגדולתו אלא למ"ד שכל דברי מלכות נחתכין על פיו מאי איכא למימר דשדיוהו לגובא דאריוותא: הכל כמנהג המדינה: הכל לאתויי מאי לאתויי אתרא דנהיגי בהוצא ודפנא: לפיכך אם נפל הכותל המקום והאבנים של שניהם: פשיטא לא צריכא דנפל לרשותא דחד מינייהו אי נמי דפנינהו חד לרשותא דידיה מהו דתימא ניהוי איהך המוציא מחבירו עליו הראיה קמ"ל: וכן בגינה מקום שנהגו לגדור מחייבין אותו: הא גופא קשיא אמרת וכן בגינה מקום שנהגו לגדור מחייבין אותו הא סתמא אין מחייבין אותו אימא סיפא אבל בבקעה מקום שנהגו שלא לגדור אין מחייבין אותו הא סתמא מחייבין אותו השתא סתם גינה אמרת לא סתם בקעה מיבעיא אמר אביי ה"ק וכן סתם גינה ובמקום שנהגו לגדור בבקעה מחייבין אותו אמר ליה רבא אם כן מאי אבל אלא אמר רבא הכי קתני וכן סתם גינה כמקום שנהגו לגדור דמי ומחייבין אותו אבל סתם בקעה כמקום שלא נהגו דמי ואין מחייבין אותו: אלא אם רצה כונס לתוך שלו ובונה ועושה חזית: מאי חזית אמר רב הונא אכפיה ליה לקרנא לבר ונעביד מלגיו עביד חבריה נמי מלבר ואמר דידי ודידיה הוא אי הכי השתא נמי גייז ליה חבריה ואמר דידי ודידיה הוא גיזוזא מידע ידיע איכא דאמרי אמר רב הונא מיכפא לקרנא מלגיו ונעבד מלבר גייז ליה חבריה ואמר דידי ודידיה הוא אי הכי השתא נמי לייף ליה חבריה ואמר דידי ודידיה הוא ליפופא מידע ידיע והא מבחוץ קתני קשיא רבי יוחנן אמר נשעייה

רש"י

אהדר ליה כלילא דיילי. האנקה מתרגמינן ילא (ויקרא יא) והוא שרץ שקורין הרצו"ן ושערו קשה כמחטין ועשה לו עטרה מעורו סביבות עיניו: השתא מיהא [דאנא ואת]. אנא ואת שנינו כאן ואין שומע: הנני מחלל את מקדשי. סיפיה דקרא מחמד עיניכם: מסתפינא ממלכותא. כפופים היו למלכות רומיים: מתמלכין. נוטלין רשות: אי זיינך עלך ספרך כאן. אם נתגאית בכלי מלחמתך שהרגת בית אדוניך ספר יוחסין שלך בידינו הוא [ידענו] שאתה עבד: לא רכא כו'. לא מלך ולא בן מלך: קלניא מתעביד. נעשה בן חורין מאליו: שישא. שיש ירוק שקורין ביי"ש: ומרמרא. שיש לבן: כוחלא. שיש צבוע כעין כחול: אידוותא דימא. גלי הים [שהם נעים ונדים והעין ^י) מתעששת בראייתן]: נענש דניאל. לקמיה מפרש עונשו: מלכי ישפר עלך. עצתי תיטב בעיניך: במיחן עניין. בחנינת עניים: בכן תהא ארכא לשלותך. [יהא אורך] לשלומך: כולא מטא. כל החלום של פורענות בא עליו: לקצת ירחין תרי עשר. בשביל עצתו של דניאל תלה לו שנים עשר חדש: בהוצא. לולבי דקלים: ודפנא. ענפי עץ ערמונים שקורין לו"ר ופרי שלו קורין ביי"ש: פשיטא. דהאבנים של שניהם דאפי' לא פסק לן דינא דמתני' המלמדנו שמתחלה בין שניהם עשאוה על כרחם היו חולקין בשוה האבנים שהרי ברשות שניהם מונחים ויד מי מהם תגבר: (הג"ה בפי' ר"ח קמ"ל דלא בעינן ראיה אלא שותף מפיק מיניה בלא ראיה ואיהו דטעין דדיליה ניהו עליו הראיה וכל כה"ג הכי דיינינן ליה וזה הדין מפורש עוד כמו כן בפרק הבית והעלייה בתחילתו איבעית אימא בשותפין כי האי גוונא אנוחי אבנים ברשות חבירו לא קפדי וחזקת רשות לאו כלום הוא שמעינן מינה דכל כהאי גוונא דמילתא דידיעא בשותפתא לתרוייהו אע"ג דמנחי ברשותא דחד מינייהו לא יכול למיטען דידי ניהו דברשותי מנחי דקי"ל שותפין לא קפדי אהדדי ע"כ): השתא סתם גינה אמרת לא. אע"פ שהיזק ראיה קשה: אמר אביי כו'. האי מקום שנהגו לגדור דקתני מתני' אבקעה קאי: א"כ מאי אבל בבקעה. הא מינה סליק והכי איבעי (ג) למיתני אבל מקום שנהגו שלא לגדור אין מחייבין אותו: מכפייה לקרנא לבר. ראשי הכותל יכוף לצד חבירו. וכל חזית לשון קצה הוא וכן שנינו בתמיד (פ"ג מ"ד) גבי מערכה וחזיתה מזרחה ראשי הגזירין וכן מחזה מול מחזה דמלכים (א ז) ראשי הנסרים מוסבין זה מול זה ^ז) ועבי' מאבראי כופה לצדי ראשי הכותל שמחבר בראשו אבנים וטיט ומעבהו: דידי ודידיה הוא. כדקתני מתניתין כשעושין אותו בין שניהם עושין חזית מכאן ומכאן: השתא נמי גייז לה. להזיא כפופה שהיא לצדו ואימא דידי ודידיה הוא ולא עשינו חזית: מלגיו. לצד שלו ולקמיה פריך הא מבחוץ קתני: לייף ליה. מחבר חזית אחרת לצדו: נשעייה

תוספות

שכל דברי מלכות נחתכין על פיו. לפי תרגום [שלו] אחשורוש ^ט) נענש הרבה שנהרג דכתיב ויגידו למרדכי את דברי אסתר ולא כתב התם התך לפי שהרגו המן על שהיה משיב דברים בין אסתר למרדכי ומיהו גמ' שלנו אין תוספת כן דדרשינן במגילה (דף טו.) והתך להיכן הלך ומפרש לפי שאין משיבין על הקלקלה:

הכי קתני וכן בגינה סתם כו'. וסיפא נמי יש לפרש כן אבל סתם בקעה ומקום שלא נהגו לגדור בגינה אין מחייבין אותו:

והא מבחוץ קתני קשיא. ותימה איכא דמלגיו למימר היינו שבולט חוץ לחומה מ"מ קשיא היא דא"כ מחוץ הוה ליה למיתני:

גייז ליה חבריה ושדי ליה. אע"ג דלעיל אמר גזוזא מידע ידיע בהולא לא ידיע: לאפוקי

רבינו גרשום

כלילא דיילי. כתר של מיני האנקה שהן עלוקות נתן סביב ראשו ונקרו עיניו: כי נר מצוה ותורה אור. אלו תלמידי חכמים שעוסקין בתורה אלו סנהדרין: ממלכותא. זו מלכות רומאי שהיה משועבד להם: שלחו ליה. מלכות רומיים אם זיינך עלך ספרך כאן. כלומר אם מלחמתך עליך שאתה מתגבר לשם ייחוסך שידעינן אנו מאיזה משפחה אתה לפי שהורקנוס אביו של הורדוס פעם אחת הלך על הרומים להלחם ונצח וראה בשביה שפחה אחת יפת תואר וחמדה ועשה לה כדין תורה ובא עליה והוליד ממנה אותו הורדוס ולפיכך היו מחרפין אותו מיחוסו: קלניא. בן חורין נעשה. שישא. שיש לבן: ומרמרא. מגומרין: כוחלא. שחורין: כאדוותא דימא. כגלי הים שזו יורדת וזו עולה: שאני עבד משום דהוי שייך במצות עשה (שהזמן) [שאין הזמן] גרמא והורדוס עבד היה: בהוצא ודפנא. שנוהגין לעשות גדר מכפות תמרים ודפנא עץ של (עור) [ערמון] שקורין לו"ר וכיון דנתרצו לעשות כותל על זה ועל זה לעכב שלא יעשו אלא כמנהג המדינה: קמ"ל. כיון דזה נותן מחצה וזה נותן מחצה אין צריך להביא ראיה: פיסקא וכן בגינה מקום שנהגו לגדור בגויל או בגזית וחבירו מעכב היו כופין אותו משום דאיכא היזק ראיה כדאוקימנא [לעיל ב:] בגינה הסמוכה לעיר אבל בבקעה של שדות כו': הא סתמא. דיש שגודרין ויש שאין גודרין: השתא סתם גינה. דאיכא היזק ראיה אמרת לא דאין מחייבין סתם בקעה דליכא היזק ראיה מחייב: אמר אביי ה"ק. כלומר כגון חסורא מיחסרא וכן גינה סתם משום דאיכא היזק ראיה ובמקום שנהגו לגדור בבקעה מחייבין אותו: א"ל רבא. לאביי אי הכי כדקא תרצת א"כ מאי אבל דקתני במתני' אבל בבקעה אי אמרת בשלמא דרישא לא איירי בדינא דבקעה כלל היינו דקתני בסיפא אבל בבקעה דעד השתא לא איירי בדינא דבקעה אלא לדעתך דתרצת דרישא איירי בבקעה מאי אבל בבקעה תו דתני בסיפא: אלא אמר רבא. אנא מתריצנא דלא תקשי אבל ולא תקשי סתמא דרישא לסתמא דסיפא וה"ק וכן בגינה סתם דינא דגינה סתם כדינא דמקום שנהגו לגדור בבקעה דמחייבין לגדור ועדיין לא שמעי' דינא דסתם בקעה ואמטו להכי צריך למתני בסיפא אבל בבקעה לאשמעינן דינא דסתם בקעה דכמקום שנהגו שלא לגדור דמי דאין מחייבין לגדור דהשתא מיתרצא כולה מתני': ועושה לכותל חזית. סימן היכרא שידעו בני אדם שזה בנאו כולו בקרקע שלו משלו לפיכך כיון דעשה חזית אם נפל הכותל כו': דכייף ליה קרנא מלבר. דלשקע בראש הכותל בסופו קנים בטיט ויכוף ראשם של קנים מבחוץ לצד הכותל לצד אויר חבירו: אזיל אידך חבירו וכייף ליה נמי מלבר לצד שלו ואמר הרי אית לי נמי חזית ודידי ודידך הוא הכותל ומקומו הלכך לא כייף אלא מלבר: אכתי אתי האי וגייז להיא חזית שהוא (פצע) [לצד] שלו ואמר דידי ודידך הוא: השתא נמי לייף ליה. כלומר יחברם לכותל בטיט בלא שקיעה: מידע ידיע. יכולין להבין ולהבחין בין דבוקה לשקיעה: והא מבחוץ קתני. ועושה לו חזית מבחוץ קשיא להך לישנא דאיכא דאמרי: ור' יוחנן אמר. היינו חזית:

עין משפט נר מצוה

טז א ב ג מיי' פכ"ו מהל' סנהדרין הל' א סמג לאוין רט:
יז ד ה מיי' פי"ב מהל' רוצח הלכה טו:
יח ו מיי' פ"ב מהל' שכנים הל' טו סמג עשין פב טוש"ע ח"מ סי' קנז סעיף ד:
יט ז ח מיי' שם הלכה יח טוש"ע שם סעיף ט:
כ ט מיי' שם הל' יז סמג שם טוש"ע ח"מ סי' קנח סעיף א:

לעזי רש"י

הרצו"ן. פירוש האנקה (רש"י ויקרא יא, ל), קופר (רש"י שבת דף נד ע"ב), קפוד (רש"י כלאים פ"ח מ"ה), קפוד (רש"י ישעיה יד, כג). ביי"ש. פירוש כעין ירוק (רש"י סוכה דף לא ע"ב ד"ה שישלת), לגוץ (עיין רש"י ויקרא יג, לו ותוספות סוכה דף לא ע"ב ד"ה סירוק). לור"ר. פירוש עץ הער (רש"י גיטין דף סט ע"ב ד"ה אטרפא ועיין אסף הרופא כת"י מינכן דף סט ע"ב), לורבריט. ביי"ש. פירוש עץ הער (רש"י כנ"ל).

מסורת הש"ס

א) [יבמות כב: ב"ק צד: ב"מ מח: סנהדרין פה. מכות ח:], ב) סוכה לא. ע"ש, ג) [שם איתא רבא], ד) ב"ה דלא סגיא ליה בלא מלכא, ה) מגילה טו., ו) משעשעת, ז) ר"א ועביו, ח) [וכן בפירקין דר"א פ"ג], ט) שייך לע"ב.

הגהות הב"ח

(א) גמ' א"ל מסתפינא איכא מינייהו דשמע אנא וזיל ומודע ליה א"ל השתא מיהא ליכא איניש בהדן וליתא אנא ואת גבן דאזיל ולימא ליה: (ב) שם סבר למשעייה בדהבא: (ג) רש"י ד"ה א"כ מאי וכו' איבעי ליה למיתני:

ליקוטי רש"י

[תחילת ליקוטי רש"י ששייך לכאן נדפס בעמוד הקודם] שחתכוהו מגדולתו. בימי אחשורוש שהרי בלשצר השליטו שלישי במלכותו וכן מנוהו המדי שנאמר ועלא מנהון סרכין תלתא די דניאל חד מנהון (דניאל ו) וכן כורש שנאמר ודניאל הצלח במלכות דריוש ובמלכות כורש פרסאה (שם) וכשמלך אחשורוש חתכו מגדולתו [מגילה טו.]. ויהי דניאל. בגדולתו בבבל עד שנת אחת לכורש המלך לדברי האומר התך זה דניאל ולמה נקרא שמו התך שחתכוהו מגדולתו צריכין אנו לומר שזהו כורש הראשון שלפני אחשורוש ולדברי האומר שכל דברי מלכות נחתכין על פיו נאמר כורש זה הוא דריוש השני אחר אחשורוש שהוא בן אסתר המדי שהשליכו לגוב אריות (דניאל ו) ודניאל דנה הצלח במלכות דריוש ובמלכות כורש פרסאה והיא בגדולה כורש הראשון היה בגדולה [דניאל א, כא]. בהוצא ודפנא. הוצא לולבי דקל. דפנא ענפי עץ שקורין לור"ר וגדל בו פרי שקורין ביי"ש [סוכה כב.]. עליו הראיה. [ב"ב מב.] עליו להביא עדים לברר את הספק ולהוציא היא בבבא קמא (מו:) מי בעל דברים יגש אליהם (שמות כד) יגיש ראיה אליהם [גיטין מח:]. חזית. לשון קצה והמנסים כן פי' מחזה ופנים וכבר (תהלים קד) ופני חבם מלאכי החזון אבל חזית בכל חזית מערכת התמיד מזרחה קצה הוא [מלכים א, ז, ה].

תורה אור השלם

א) גַּם בְּמַדָּעֲךָ מֶלֶךְ אַל תְּקַלֵּל וּבְחַדְרֵי מִשְׁכָּבְךָ אַל תְּקַלֵּל עָשִׁיר כִּי עוֹף הַשָּׁמַיִם יוֹלִיךְ אֶת הַקּוֹל וּבַעַל כְּנָפַיִם יַגֵּיד דָּבָר: [קהלת י, כ]

ב) אֱלֹהִים לֹא תְקַלֵּל וְנָשִׂיא בְעַמְּךָ לֹא תָאֹר: [שמות כב, כז]

ג) כִּי נֵר מִצְוָה וְתוֹרָה אוֹר וְדֶרֶךְ חַיִּים תּוֹכְחוֹת מוּסָר: [משלי ו, כג]

ד) וְהָיָה בְּאַחֲרִית הַיָּמִים נָכוֹן יִהְיֶה הַר בֵּית יְיָ בְּרֹאשׁ הֶהָרִים וְנִשָּׂא מִגְּבָעוֹת וְנָהֲרוּ אֵלָיו כָּל הַגּוֹיִם: [ישעיה ב, ב]

ה) וְהָיָה אִם מֵעֵינֵי הָעֵדָה נֶעֶשְׂתָה לִשְׁגָגָה וְעָשׂוּ כָל הָעֵדָה פַּר בֶּן בָּקָר אֶחָד לְעֹלָה לְרֵיחַ נִיחֹחַ לַייָ וּמִנְחָתוֹ וְנִסְכּוֹ כַּמִּשְׁפָּט וּשְׂעִיר עִזִּים אֶחָד לְחַטָּת: [במדבר טו, כד]

ו) אֱמֹר לְבֵית יִשְׂרָאֵל כֹּה אָמַר אֲדֹנָי יְיָ הִנְנִי מְחַלֵּל אֶת מִקְדָּשִׁי גְּאוֹן עֻזְּכֶם מַחְמַד עֵינֵיכֶם וּמַחְמַל נַפְשְׁכֶם וּבְנֵיכֶם וּבְנוֹתֵיכֶם אֲשֶׁר עֲזַבְתֶּם בַּחֶרֶב יִפֹּלוּ: [יחזקאל כד, כא]

ז) וְאָנֹכִי הַיּוֹם רַךְ וּמָשׁוּחַ מֶלֶךְ וְהָאֲנָשִׁים הָאֵלֶּה בְּנֵי צְרוּיָה קָשִׁים מִמֶּנִּי יְשַׁלֵּם יְיָ לְעֹשֵׂה הָרָעָה כְּרָעָתוֹ: [שמואל ב' ג, לט]

ח) וַיַּרְכֵּב אֹתוֹ בְּמִרְכֶּבֶת הַמִּשְׁנֶה אֲשֶׁר לוֹ וַיִּקְרְאוּ לְפָנָיו אַבְרֵךְ וְנָתוֹן אֹתוֹ עַל כָּל אֶרֶץ מִצְרָיִם: [בראשית מא, מג]

ט) לָהֵן מַלְכָּא מִלְכִּי יִשְׁפַּר עֲלָךְ וַחֲטָאָךְ בְּצִדְקָה פְרֻק וַעֲוָיָתָךְ בְּמִחַן עֲנָיִן הֵן תֶּהֱוֵא אַרְכָה לִשְׁלֵוְתָךְ: [דניאל ד, כד]

י) כֹּלָּא מְטָא עַל נְבוּכַדְנֶצַּר מַלְכָּא: [דניאל ד, כה]

כ) לִקְצָת יַרְחִין תְּרֵי עֲשַׂר עַל הֵיכַל מַלְכוּתָא דִּי בָבֶל מְהַלֵּךְ הֲוָה: [דניאל ד, כו]

ל) וַתִּקְרָא אֶסְתֵּר לַהֲתָךְ מִסָּרִיסֵי הַמֶּלֶךְ אֲשֶׁר הֶעֱמִיד לְפָנֶיהָ וַתְּצַוֵּהוּ עַל מָרְדֳּכַי לָדַעַת מַה זֶּה וְעַל מַה זֶּה: [אסתר ד, ה]

and he himself was punished therefor, why did Bava ben Buta offer advice to Herod?

The Gemara offers two explanations:

אִיבָּעִית אֵימָא שָׁאנֵי עַבְדָּא — If you prefer, say that the case of **a slave** (such as Herod) is **different, דְּאִיחַיַּיב בְּמִצְוֹת — for** a slave **is obligated** to observe **the commandments.**[29] Hence, Bava acted properly in assisting Herod to achieve atonement. However, Nebuchadnezzar was a gentile, and so Daniel's counsel was improper. **וְאִיבָּעִית אֵימָא שָׁאנֵי בֵּית הַמִּקְדָּשׁ— And if you prefer, say** that the case of **the Holy Temple is different, דְּאִי לָא מַלְכוּת לָא מִתְבְּנֵי — for without** the involvement of **the monarchy it could not be built,** so enormous was the undertaking. Thus, in this particular instance Bava ben Buta was justified in suggesting a penance for Herod, even though the wicked king would benefit therefrom.

The Gemara finds evidence of Daniel's punishment in the Scriptures:

וְדָנִיֵּאל מְנָלַן דְּאִיעֲנַשׁ — And Daniel? How do we know that he was punished for advising Nebuchadnezzar? **אילֵימָא מִשּׁוּם דִּכְתִיב: "וַתִּקְרָא אֶסְתֵּר לַהֲתָךְ" — If you say because it is written,**[30] ***And Esther called to Hasach,*** **וְאָמַר רַב הֲתָךְ זֶה דָּנִיֵּאל — and** interpreting the verse **Rav said:** ***Hasach*** **— this is Daniel. הָנִיחָא לְמַאן דְּאָמַר שֶׁחֲתָכוּהוּ מִגְּדוּלָּתוֹ — This** approach **is acceptable according to the one that says that** Daniel was so named because **they "cut him down" from his greatness.**[31] Daniel's fall from high office was indeed a punishment! **אֶלָּא לְמַאן דְּאָמַר שֶׁכָּל דִּבְרֵי מַלְכוּת נֶחְתָּכִין עַל פִּיו — But according to the one that says that** he was so named because **all affairs of state were decided by him,**[32] **מַאי אִיכָּא לְמֵימַר — what is there to say** in explanation of Daniel's punishment?

The Gemara answers:

דְּשַׁדְיוּהוּ לְגוּבָּא דְּאַרְיְוָותָא — He was punished in **that they threw him into a den of lions.**[33]

The Mishnah had stated:

הַכֹּל כְּמִנְהַג הַמְּדִינָה — ALL SHOULD CONFORM TO LOCAL CUSTOM.

The Gemara inquires about the function of this clause:

הַכֹּל לְאַתּוּיֵי מַאי — "All" is written in the Mishnah **to include what** other local building custom?[34]

The Gemara answers:

לְאַתּוּיֵי אַתְרָא דִּנְהִיגֵי בְּהוּצָא וְדַפְנָא — The extra clause is written **to include a place where they are accustomed** to building partitions **with palm fronds and laurel** branches.[35] Although this type of partition is qualitatively inferior to those mentioned in the Mishnah, the Sages considered it strong enough to endure. The Mishnah thus informs us that local custom should be followed in such a case, so that neither one may be forced by the other to build a stronger wall.[36]

The Gemara quotes another section of the Mishnah:

לְפִיכָךְ אִם נָפַל הַכּוֹתֶל הַמָּקוֹם וְהָאֲבָנִים שֶׁל שְׁנֵיהֶם — THEREFORE, IF THE WALL eventually **COLLAPSED, THE LAND** underneath **AND THE STONES BELONG TO THEM BOTH.**

The Gemara challenges the notion of a causal connection implied by the word לְפִיכָךְ, *therefore,* in the above statement:

פְּשִׁיטָא — This law is **obvious!** Even if the Mishnah had not just taught us that partners must contribute equally toward the building of the wall, this ruling — that the scattered stones are to be divided equally — is self-evident.[37]

The Gemara answers:

לָא צְרִיכָא — No, it is necessary to predicate this law on the first ruling **דְּנָפַל לִרְשׁוּתָא דְּחַד מִינַּיְיהוּ — where** the wall **collapsed into the property of one of them.** Had the Mishnah not previously ruled that they must contribute equally toward building the wall, the partner in possession of the stones could claim them as his own,[38] and the other partner would have to bring proof that half of the stones were his. **אִי נַמִּי דְּפַנִּינְהוּ חַד לִרְשׁוּתָא דִּידֵיהּ — Alternatively,** it is necessary to predicate the second ruling on the first **when** after the wall collapsed **one** partner **cleared [the stones] into his property,** thereby establishing exclusive possession of them.[39] **מַהוּ דְּתֵימָא— In** either of these cases **what would you have said? נֶיהֱוֵי אִידָךְ הַמּוֹצִיא מֵחֲבֵירוֹ עָלָיו הָרְאָיָה — To the other** partner, the claimant, **should apply** the dictum, **"the** burden of **proof is on the one who** seeks to **exact** property from the possession **of his fellow,"**[40] for the other has sole possession of all the stones. **קָא מַשְׁמַע לָן — [The Mishnah] therefore informs us** that since the law allows either partner to demand that the other pay for the

NOTES

29. The slave of a Jew (called an עֶבֶד כְּנַעֲנִי, *Canaanite slave*) must observe all the commandments that a Jewish woman is obligated to keep. Thus, assisting him to achieve atonement is a meritorious act.

30. *Esther* 4:5.

31. This opinion maintains that Achashveirosh demoted Daniel from the high position he held in the courts of the previous kings — Belshazzar, Darius and Cyrus.

The letters ה and ח are, for homiletic purposes, interchangeable. Thus, הֲתָךְ, *Hasach,* is equivalent to חֲתָךְ, *cut.*

32. This opinion maintains that Daniel retained his high office during Achashveirosh's reign, for נֶחְתָּכִין, *decided,* also derives from the root חתך (see previous note). Hence, according to this view, the name "Hasach" does not intimate that Daniel suffered retribution for advising Nebuchadnezzar.

33. As related in *Daniel* 6. Although Daniel was not harmed by the lions, the exposure to danger was itself a punishment.

34. Since the Mishnah already enumerated several types of brick and stone that are used in various localities, this clause appears superfluous. Hence, the Gemara understands that it comes to add a type of material whose acceptability is not apparent.

35. The laurel branches were fixed into the ground at intervals and palm fronds were woven between them to form the fence.

36. However, where partitions are built of less sturdy material, local custom is not followed, for such a wall will not stand (*Tosafos* 2a ד״ה בגויל).

37. The Gemara here assumes that the stones are more or less evenly scattered over both courtyards. Hence, neither partner has a superior claim to them. Why, then, would we assume that one of them prevails? (*Rashi,* see *Tosafos* above (2a ד״ה לפיכך) for an alternate interpretation of our Gemara.

38. If the only reason for dividing them equally would be due to the fact that neither one has a superior claim, then in this situation, where the stones are in the possession of one of them, he would keep them with the claim that they are his alone. [As the Gemara will explain, this follows the rule of הַמּוֹצִיא מֵחֲבֵירוֹ עָלָיו הָרְאָיָה, which teaches that if a person is in possession of an object, another may not claim ownership without proper proof.]

39. *Rashba* explains that clearing the stones into one's property establishes exclusive possession only when there were no witnesses to the act. Otherwise, the stones are in the possession of the one into whose property they initially fell (which is when the question of ownership first arose).

Rabbeinu Yonah adds that this second explanation does not conflict with the first, but simply provides another instance (i.e. when the stones fell into both yards) when the causal connection between the Mishnah's two rulings is relevant.

40. The Gemara (*Bava Kamma* 46b) considers this rule to be logically self-evident. As the Gemara states: דְּכָאִיב לֵיהּ כְּאֵיבָא אָזִיל לְבֵי אַסְיָא, *the one who is in pain, he is the one who goes to the physician*; i.e. the one with the complaint is the one who has the burden of establishing the grounds for redress.

אהדר ליה כלילא דיילי נקרינהו לעיניה יומא חד אתא ויתיב קמיה אמר חזי מר האי עבדא בישא מאי קא עביד אמר ליה מאי אעביד ליה א"ל נלטייה מר א"ל [כתיב] גם במדעך מלך אל תקלל אמר ליה האי לאו מלך הוא א"ל וליהוי עשיר בעלמא וכתיב ובחדרי משכבך אל תקלל עשיר ולא יהא אלא נשיא וכתיב ונשיא בעמך לא תאור א"ל בעושה מעשה עמך והאי לאו עושה מעשה עמך א"ל מסתפינא מיניה א"ל ליכא איניש דאזיל דלימא ליה דאנא ואת יתיבנא א"ל כתיב כי עוף השמים יוליך את הקול ובעל כנפים יגיד דבר א"ל אנא הוא אי הואי ידענא דזהירי רבנן כולי האי לא הוה קטילנא להו השתא מאי תקנתיה דההוא גברא א"ל הוא כבה אורו של עולם דכתיב כי נר מצוה ותורה אור ילך ויעסוק באורו של עולם דכתיב ונהרו אליו כל הגוים איכא דאמרי הכי א"ל הוא סימא עינו של עולם דכתיב והיה אם מעיני העדה ילך ויתעסק בעינו של עולם דכתיב הנני מחלל את מקדשי גאון עוזכם מחמד עיניכם א"ל מסתפינא ממלכותא א"ל שדר שליחא וליזיל שתא וליעכב שתא ולהדר שתא אדהכי והכי סתרית [ליה] ובניית [ליה] עבד הכי שלחו ליה אם לא סתרתה אל תסתור ואם סתרתה אל תבני ואם סתרתה ובנית עבדי בישא בתר דעבדין מתמלכין אם זיינך עלך ספרך כאן לא רכא ולא בר רכא הורדוס [עבדא] קלניא מתעביד מאי רכא מלכותא דכתיב אנכי היום רך ומשוח מלך ואי בעית אימא מהכא ויקראו לפניו אברך אמרי מי שלא ראה בנין הורדוס לא ראה בנין נאה [מימיו] במאי בנייה אמר רבה באבני שישא ומרמרא איכא דאמרי באבני כוחלא שישא ומרמרא אפיק שפה ועייל שפה כי היכי דנקביל סידא סבר למשעייה בדהבא אמרו ליה רבנן שבקיה דהכי שפיר טפי דמיחזי כי אידוותא דימא ובבא בר בוטא היכי עבד הכי והאמר רב יהודה אמר רב ואיתימא ר' יהושע בן לוי מפני מה נענש דניאל מפני שהשיא עצה לנבוכד נצר שנאמר להן מלכא מלכי ישפר עלך וחטאך בצדקה פרוק ועויתך במיחן עניין הן תהוי ארכא לשלותך וגו' וכתיב כולא מטא על נבוכד נצר מלכא וכתיב ולקצת ירחין תרי עשר וגו' איבעית אימא שאני עבדא דאיחייב במצות ואיבעית אימא שאני בית המקדש דאי לא מלכות לא מתבני ודניאל מנלן דאיענש אילימא משום דכתיב ותקרא אסתר להתך ואמר רב התך זה דניאל הניחא למ"ד שחתכוהו מגדולתו אלא למ"ד שכל דברי מלכות נחתכין על פיו מאי איכא למימר דשדיוהו לגובא דאריוותא: **הכל כמנהג המדינה:** הכל לאתויי מאי לאתויי אתרא דנהיגי בהוצא ודפנא: **לפיכך אם נפל הכותל המקום והאבנים של שניהם:** פשיטא לא צריכא דנפל לרשותא דחד מינייהו אי נמי דפנינהו חד לרשותא דידיה מהו דתימא ניהוי אידך המוציא מחבירו עליו הראיה קמ"ל: **וכן בגינה מקום שנהגו לגדור מחייבין אותו:** הא גופא קשיא אמרת וכן בגינה מקום שנהגו לגדור מחייבין אותו הא סתמא אין מחייבין אותו אימא סיפא אבל בבקעה מקום שנהגו שלא לגדור אין מחייבין אותו הא סתמא מחייבין אותו השתא סתם גינה אמרת לא סתם בקעה מיבעיא אמר אביי ה"ק וכן סתם גינה ובמקום שנהגו לגדור בבקעה מחייבין אותו אמר ליה רבא אם כן מאי אבל אלא אמר רבא הכי קתני וכן סתם גינה כמקום שנהגו לגדור דמי ומחייבין אותו אבל סתם בקעה כמקום שלא נהגו דמי ואין מחייבין אותו: **אלא אם רצה כונס לתוך שלו ובונה ועושה חזית:** מאי חזית אמר רב הונא אכפיה ליה לקרנא לבר ונעביד מלגיו עביד חבריה נמי מלבר ואמר דידי ודידיה הוא אי הכי השתא נמי גייז ליה חבריה ואמר דידי ודידיה הוא גיזוזא מידע ידיע איכא דאמרי אמר רב הונא מיכפא לקרנא מלגיו ונעבד מלבר גייז ליה חבריה ואמר דידי ודידיה הוא אי הכי השתא נמי לייף ליה חבריה ואמר דידי ודידיה הוא ליפופא מידע ידיע והא מבחוץ קתני קשיא רבי יוחנן אמר נשעייה

אהדר ליה כלילא דיילי. האנקה מתרגמינן ילא (ויקרא יא) והוא שרץ שקורין הרצו"ן ושערו קשה כמחטין ועשה לו עטרה מעורו סביבות עיניו: **השתא מיהא [דאנא ואת].** אנא ואת שנינו כאן ואין שומע: **הנני מחלל את מקדשי.** סיפיה דקרא מחמד עיניכם: **מסתפינא ממלכותא.** כפופים היו למלכות רומיים: **מתמלכין.** נוטלין רשות: **אי זיינך עלך ספרך כאן.** אם נתגאית בכלי מלחמתך שהרגת בית אדוניך ספר יוחסין שלך בידינו הוא [ידענו] שאתה עבד: **לא רכא כו'.** לא מלך ולא בן מלך: **קלניא מתעביד.** נעשה בן חורין מאליו: **שישא.** שיש ירוק שקורין ביי"ש: **ומרמרא.** שיש לבן: **כוחלא.** שיש צבוע כעין כחול: **אידוותא דימא.** גלי הים [שהים נעים ונדים והעין מתעשטשת בראייתן]: **נענש דניאל.** לקמיה מפרש עונשו: **מלכי ישפר עלך.** עצתי תיטב בעיניך: **במיחן עניין.** בחנינת עניים: **בכן תהא ארכא לשלותך.** [יהא אורך] לשלומך: **כולא מטא.** כל השלום של פורענות בא עליו: **לקצת ירחין תרי עשר.** בשביל עצתו של דניאל תלה לו שנים עשר חדש: **בהוצא.** לולבי דקלים: **ודפנא.** ענפי עץ ערמונים שקורין לו"ר ופרי שלו קורין ביי"ש: **פשיטא.** דהאבנים של שניהם דהא לא פסק לן דינא דמתני' המלמדנו שמתחלה בין שניהם עשאוה על כרחם היו חולקין בשוה האבנים שהרי ברשות שניהם מונחים ויד מי מהם תגבר: (הג"ה בפי' ר"ח קמ"ל דלא בעינן ראיה אלא שותף מפיק מיניה בלא ראיה ואיהו דטעין דדיליה נינהו עליו הראיה וכל כה"ג הכי דיינין ליה וזה הדין מפורש עוד כמו כן בפרק הבית והעלייה בתחלתו איבעית אימא בשותפין כי הלי גוונא אנוחי אבנים ברשות חבירו לא קפדי וחזקת רשות לאו כלום הוא שמעינן מינה דכל כהאי גוונא דמילתא דידיעא בשותפתא לתרוייהו אע"ג דמנחי ברשותא דחד מינייהו לא יכול למיטען דידי נינהו דברשותי מנחי דקי"ל שותפין לא קפדי אהדדי ע"כ): **השתא סתם גינה אמרת לא.** אע"פ שהיזק ראיה קשה: **אמר אביי כו'.** הא מקום שנהגו לגדור דקתני מתני' אבקעה קאי: **א"כ מאי אבל בבקעה.** הא מינה סליק והכי איבעי (ג) למיתני אבל מקום שנהגו שלא לגדור אין מחייבין אותו: **מכפיה לקרנא לבר.** ראשי הכותל יכוף לצד חבירו. וכל חזית לשון קצה הוא וכן שנינו בתמיד (פ"ב מ"ד) גבי מערכה וחזיתה מזרחה ראשי הגזירין וכן מחזה מול מחזה דמלכים (א ז) ראשי הנסרים מוסכין זה מול זה ועבי' מאברא' כופה לצדי ראשי הכותל שמחבר בראשו אבנים וטיט ומעבהו: **דידי ודידיה הוא.** כדקתני מתניתין כשעושין אותו בין שניהם עושין חזית מכאן ומכאן: **השתא נמי גייז לה.** להאי כפופה שהיא לצדו ואימא דידי ודידיה הוא ולא עשינו חזית: **מלגיו.** לצד שלו ולקמיה פריך הא מבחוץ קתני: **לייף ליה.** מחבר חזית אחרת לצדו:

שכל דברי מלכות נחתכין על פיו. לפי תרגום [של] אחשורוש נענש הרבה שנהרג דכתיב ויגידו למרדכי את דברי אסתר ולא כתב התם התך לפי שהרגו המן על שהיה משיב דברים בין אסתר למרדכי ומיהו גמ' שלנו אין תופס כן דדרשינן במגילה (דף טו.) והתך להיכן הלך ומפרש לפי שאין משיבין על הקלקלה:

הכי קתני וכן בגינה סתם כו'. וסיפא נמי יש לפרש כן אבל סתם בקעה ומקום שלא נהגו לגדור בגינה אין מחייבין אותו:

והא מבחוץ קתני קשיא. ומיוכחא הכא דמלינן למימר היינו שבולט חוץ לחומה מ"מ קשיא היא דא"כ מחוץ הוה ליה למיתני:

גייז ליה חבריה ושדי ליה. אע"ג דלעיל אמר גיזוזא מידע ידיע בהולא לא ידיע:

לאפוקי

עין משפט נר מצוה

טז א ב ג מיי' פכ"ו מהל' סנהדרין הל' א סמג לאוין רע:
יז ד ה מיי' פי"ב מהל' רוצח הלכה טו:
יח ו מיי' פ"ב מהל' שכנים הל' טו סמג עשין פב טוש"ע ח"מ סי' קנז סעיף ד:
יט ז ח מיי' שם הלכה יח טוש"ע שם סעיף ה:
כ ט מיי' שם הל' יז סמג שם טוש"ע ח"מ סי' קנח סעיף א:

לעזי רש"י

הרצו"ן. פירוש האנקה (רש"י ויקרא יא, ל), קופד (רש"י שבת דף נד ע"ב), הקופד (רא"ש כלאים פ"ח מ"ה), קפוד (רש"י ישעיה יד, כג). ביי"ש. פירוש כעין ירוק (רש"י סוכה דף לא ע"ב ד"ה שיישא), להוב (עיין רש"י ויקרא יג, לז ותוספות סוכה דף לא ע"ב ד"ה הירוק). לו"ר. פירוש עץ הער (רש"י גיטין דף סט ע"ב ד"ה אטרפא ועיין אסף הרופא כת"י מינכן דף סט ע"ב), לורברבוי"ס. ביי"ש. פירוש עץ הער (רש"י כנ"ל):

רבינו גרשום

כלילא דיילי. כתר של מיני האנקה שהן עלוקות נתן סביב ראשו **וניקרו עיניו: כי נר מצוה ותורה אור.** אלו תלמידי חכמים שעוסקין בתורה אלו סנהדרין: **ממלכותא.** זו מלכות רומאי שהיה משועבד להם: **שלחו ליה.** ממלכות רומיים **אם זיינך עלך ספרך כאן.** כלומר אם מלחמתך עליך שאתה מתגבר לשם ייחוסך כאן שיודעין אנו מאיזה משפחה אתה לפי שהורקנוס אביו של הורדוס פעם אחת הלך על הרומים להלחם ונצח וראה בשביה שפחה אחת יפת תואר וחמדה ועשה לה כדין תורה ובא עליה והוליד ממנה אותו הורדוס ולפיכך היו מחרפין אותו מיחוסו: **קלניא.** בן חורין נעשה: **שישא.** שיש לבן: **ומרמרא.** מגומרין: **כוחלא.** שחורין: **כאדוותא דימא.** כגלי הים שזו יורדת וזו עולה: שאני עבד משום דהוי שייך במצות עשה (שהזמן) [שאין הזמן] גרמא והורדוס עבד היה: **בהוצא ודפנא.** שנוהגין לעשות גדר מכפות תמרים **ודפנא** עץ של (עור) [ערמון] שקורין לו"ר וכיון דנתרצו לעשות כותל על זה ועל זה לעכב שלא יעשו אלא כמנהג המדינה: **קמ"ל.** כיון דזה נותן מחצה וזה נותן מחצה אין צריך להביא ראיה: **פיסקא וכן בגינה מקום שנהגו לגדור** בגזית וחבירו מעכב היו כופין אותו משום דאיכא היזק ראיה כדאוקימנא [לעיל ב:] בגינה הסמוכה לעיר **אבל בבקעה** של שדות כו': **הא סתמא.** דיש שגודרין ויש שאין גודרין: **השתא סתם גינה.** דאיכא היזק ראיה **אמרת לא** דאין מחייבין **סתם בקעה** דליכא היזק ראיה מחייב: **אמר אביי ה"ק.** כלומר כגון חסורא מיחסרא **וכן גינה סתם** משום דאיכא היזק ראיה **ובמקום שנהגו לגדור בבקעה מחייבין אותו: א"ל רבא.** לאביי אי הכי כדקא תרצת **א"כ מאי אבל** דקתני במתני' אבל בבקעה אי אמרת בשלמא דרישא לא איירי בבקעה כלל היינו דקתני בסיפא אבל בבקעה דעד השתא לא איירי בדינא דבקעה אלא לדעתך דתרצת דרישא איירי בבקעה מאי אבל בבקעה תו דתני בסיפא: **אלא אמר רבא.** אנא מתריצנא דלא תקשי אבל ולא תקשי סתמא דסיפא והכי קתני ה"ק **וכן בגינה סתם** דינא דגינה סתם כדינא **דמקום שנהגו** לגדור בבקעה דמחייבין לגדור ועדיין לא שמעינן דינא דסתם בקעה ואמטו להכי צריך למתני בסיפא **אבל בבקעה** לאשמעינן דינא **דסתם בקעה דכמקום שנהגו** שלא לגדור דמי **דאין מחייבין** לגדור דהשתא מיתרצא כולה מתני': **ועושה לכותל חזית.** סימן היכרא שידעו בני אדם שזה בנאו כולו בקרקע שלו משלו לפיכך כיון דעשה חזית אם נפל הכותל כו': **דכייף ליה קרנא מלבר.** דלשקע קנים בטיט ויכוף ראשם של קנים מבחוץ לצד הכותל לצד אויר חבירו: **אזיל** אידך חבירו וכייף ליה **ואמר** הרי אית לי נמי חזית **ודידי ודידך הוא** הכותל ומקומו הלכך לא כייף אלא מלבר: **אכתי אתי האי וגייז** להאי חזית שהוא (פצע) [לצד] שלו **ואמר דידי ודידך הוא: השתא נמי לייף ליה.** כלומר יחברם לכותל בסופו **מידע ידיע.** יכולין להבין ולהבחין בין דבוקה לשקיעה: **והא מבחוץ קתני.** ועושה לו חזית מבחוץ קשיא להך לישנא דאיכא דאמרי: **ור' יוחנן אמר.** היינו חזית:

מסורת הש"ס

א) [יבמות כב: ב"ק לד: ב"מ מח: סב. סנהדרין מז. פה. מכות ח:], ב) סוכה לא: ע"ש, ג) [שם איתא רבא], ד) נ"א דלא סגיא ליה בלא מלכא, ה) מגילה טו., ו) משתעשעת, ז) ס"א ועביו, ח) [וכן בפירקי דר"א פ"ג], ט) שייך לע"ב:

הגהות הב"ח

(א) גמ' א"ל מסתפינא איכא איניש דשמע מלתא ואזיל ומודע ליה א"ל השתא מיהא ליכא איניש גבן דאזיל ולימא ליה: (ב) שם סבר למחפייה בדהבא: (ג) רש"י ד"ה א"כ מאי וכו' איבעי ליה למיתנא:

ליקוטי רש"י

[תחילת ליקוטי רש"י ששייך לכאן נדפס בעמוד הקודם] **שחתכוהו מגדולתו.** בימי אחשורוש שהרי בלשצר השליטו תלתא במלכותו וכן דריוש המדי שנאמר ועלא מנהון סרכיא תלתא די דניאל חד מנהון (דניאל ו) וכן כורש שנאמר ודניאל הצלח במלכות דריוש ובמלכות כורש פרסאה (שם) וכשמלך אחשורוש חתכו מגדולתו [מגילה טו.]. ויהי דניאל. בגדולה בבבל עד שנת אחת לכורש המלך לדברי האומר התך זה דניאל ולמה נקרא שמו התך שחתכוהו מגדולתו צריכין אנו לומר שזהו כורש הראשון שלפני אחשורוש ולדברי האומר שכל דברי מלכות נחתכין על פיו נאמר כורש זה הוא דריוש השני אחר אחשורוש ובימי דריוש המדי שהשליכו לגוב אריות לא ירד מגדולתו שנאמר (דניאל ו) ודניאל דנה הצלח במלכות דריוש ובמלכות כורש פרסאה [דניאל א, כא]. **בהוצא ודפנא.** הוצא ענפי עץ שקורין דפנא ענפי עץ שקורין לורי"ר ולגד גו פרי שקורין באיי"ש [סוכה כב:]. **עליו הראיה.** עליו להביא עדים לברר את הספק והראיה היא בבבא קמא (מו:) [...] **חזית.** לשון קצה ומנוסים כן פותרו [...] מערכת התמיד [מלכים א, ז, ד].

תורה אור השלם

א) גַּם בְּמַדָּעֲךָ מֶלֶךְ אַל תְּקַלֵּל וּבְחַדְרֵי מִשְׁכָּבְךָ אַל תְּקַלֵּל עָשִׁיר כִּי עוֹף הַשָּׁמַיִם יוֹלִיךְ אֶת הַקּוֹל וּבַעַל כְּנָפַיִם יַגֵּיד דָּבָר: [קהלת י, כ]

ב) אֱלֹהִים לֹא תְקַלֵּל וְנָשִׂיא בְעַמְּךָ לֹא תָאֹר: [שמות כב, כז]

ג) כִּי נֵר מִצְוָה וְתוֹרָה אוֹר וְדֶרֶךְ חַיִּים תּוֹכְחוֹת מוּסָר: [משלי ו, כג]

ד) וְהָיָה בְּאַחֲרִית הַיָּמִים נָכוֹן יִהְיֶה הַר בֵּית יְיָ בְּרֹאשׁ הֶהָרִים וְנִשָּׂא מִגְּבָעוֹת וְנָהֲרוּ אֵלָיו כָּל הַגּוֹיִם: [ישעיה ב, ב]

ה) וְהָיָה אִם מֵעֵינֵי הָעֵדָה נֶעֶשְׂתָה לִשְׁגָגָה וְעָשׂוּ כָל הָעֵדָה פַּר בֶּן בָּקָר אֶחָד לְעֹלָה לְרֵיחַ נִיחֹחַ לַייָ וּמִנְחָתוֹ וְנִסְכּוֹ כַּמִּשְׁפָּט וּשְׂעִיר עִזִּים אֶחָד לְחַטָּת: [במדבר טו, כד]

ו) אֱמֹר לְבֵית יִשְׂרָאֵל כֹּה אָמַר אֲדֹנָי יְיָ הִנְנִי מְחַלֵּל אֶת מִקְדָּשִׁי גְּאוֹן עֻזְּכֶם מַחְמַד עֵינֵיכֶם וּמַחְמַל נַפְשְׁכֶם וּבְנֵיכֶם וּבְנוֹתֵיכֶם אֲשֶׁר עֲזַבְתֶּם בַּחֶרֶב יִפֹּלוּ: [יחזקאל כד, כא]

ז) וְאָנֹכִי הַיּוֹם רַךְ וּמָשׁוּחַ מֶלֶךְ וְהָאֲנָשִׁים הָאֵלֶּה בְּנֵי צְרוּיָה קָשִׁים מִמֶּנִּי יְשַׁלֵּם יְיָ לְעֹשֵׂה הָרָעָה כְּרָעָתוֹ: [שמואל ב' ג, לט]

ח) וַיַּרְכֵּב אֹתוֹ בְּמִרְכֶּבֶת הַמִּשְׁנֶה אֲשֶׁר לוֹ וַיִּקְרְאוּ לְפָנָיו אַבְרֵךְ וְנָתוֹן אֹתוֹ עַל כָּל אֶרֶץ מִצְרָיִם: [בראשית מא, מג]

ט) לָהֵן מַלְכָּא מִלְכִּי יִשְׁפַּר עֲלָךְ וַחֲטָאָךְ בְּצִדְקָה פְרֻק וַעֲוָיָתָךְ בְּמִחַן עֲנָיִן הֵן תֶּהֱוֵא אַרְכָה לִשְׁלֵוְתָךְ: [דניאל ד, כד]

י) כֹּלָּא מְטָא עַל נְבוּכַדְנֶצַּר מַלְכָּא: [דניאל ד, כה]

כ) לִקְצָת יַרְחִין תְּרֵי עֲשַׂר עַל הֵיכַל מַלְכוּתָא דִּי בָבֶל מְהַלֵּךְ הֲוָה: [דניאל ד, כו]

ל) וַתִּקְרָא אֶסְתֵּר לַהֲתָךְ מִסָּרִיסֵי הַמֶּלֶךְ אֲשֶׁר הֶעֱמִיד לְפָנֶיהָ וַתְּצַוֵּהוּ עַל מָרְדֳּכָי לָדַעַת מַה זֶּה וְעַל מַה זֶּה: [אסתר ד, ה]

building of the wall, the halachah presumes that the wall was built by both. Hence, the stones and land are equally divided, regardless of who actually possesses them.

The Gemara cites two additional rulings from the Mishnah, noting that they give rise to irreconcilable implications. The first ruling:

וְכֵן בְּגִינָּה מָקוֹם שֶׁנָּהֲגוּ לִגְדּוֹר מְחַיְּיבִין אוֹתוֹ – AND, SIMILARLY, REGARDING A GARDEN, in A PLACE WHERE THEY ARE ACCUSTOMED TO ERECTING PARTITIONS, WE OBLIGATE [EACH NEIGHBOR] to assist in building the partition.

The Gemara asks:

הָא גּוּפָא קַשְׁיָא – This statement is intrinsically difficult! אָמְרַתְּ וְכֵן בְּגִינָּה מָקוֹם שֶׁנָּהֲגוּ לִגְדּוֹר מְחַיְּיבִין אוֹתוֹ – You (i.e. the Mishnah) have said: AND, SIMILARLY, REGARDING A GARDEN, in A PLACE WHERE THEY ARE ACCUSTOMED TO ERECTING PARTITIONS, WE OBLIGATE [EACH NEIGHBOR] to assist. This ruling implies: הָא סְתָמָא אֵין מְחַיְּיבִין אוֹתוֹ – But ordinarily, in the absence of a specific custom, we would not obligate him to assist.

The Gemara cites the second ruling:

אֵימָא סֵיפָא – But state the latter case of the Mishnah, which says:

אֲבָל בְּבִקְעָה מָקוֹם שֶׁנָּהֲגוּ שֶׁלֹּא לִגְדּוֹר אֵין מְחַיְּיבִין אוֹתוֹ – HOWEVER, CONCERNING A VALLEY containing fields of grain, IN A PLACE WHERE THEY ARE ACCUSTOMED NOT TO ERECT PARTITIONS between the fields, WE DO NOT OBLIGATE [EACH NEIGHBOR] to do so. This second ruling implies: הָא סְתָמָא מְחַיְּיבִין אוֹתוֹ – But ordinarily, in the absence of a specific custom against erecting partitions, we would obligate [each neighbor] to assist in building one.

The Gemara finds this second implication indefensible:

הַשְׁתָּא סְתָם גִּינָּה – Now that in the case of an ordinary garden, i.e. one not encumbered by local custom, אָמְרַתְּ לֹא – you have said that there is no inherent right for either neighbor to demand a wall,[41] סְתָם בִּקְעָה מִיבַּעְיָא – is there any need to mention that an ordinary valley, i.e. one similarly unencumbered by local custom, follows the same ruling?[42] Yet, inexplicably, the Mishnah implies that there, the right to demand a wall exists!

Abaye attempts to resolve this difficulty with a novel reading of the Mishnah:

אָמַר אַבַּיֵי הָכִי קָאָמַר – Abaye said: This is what the Mishnah is saying: וְכֵן סְתָם גִּינָּה – AND, SIMILARLY, REGARDING AN ORDINARY GARDEN, וּבְמָקוֹם שֶׁנָּהֲגוּ לִגְדּוֹר בְּבִקְעָה – OR IN A PLACE WHERE THEY ARE ACCUSTOMED TO ERECTING PARTITIONS IN A VALLEY, מְחַיְּיבִין אוֹתוֹ – WE OBLIGATE [EACH NEIGHBOR] to assist in building the partition.[43]

Rava objects to Abaye's interpretation of the Mishnah:

אָמַר לֵיהּ רָבָא אִם כֵּן – Rava said to [Abaye]: If it is so that this section of the Mishnah refers to two separate cases,[44] מַאי אֲבָל – what is the meaning of the Mishnah's next statement, "But in a valley," which implies that no case of a valley had previously been taught?[45]

Rava, therefore, offers his own interpretation:

אֶלָּא אָמַר רָבָא הָכִי קָתָנֵי – Rather, Rava said: The Mishnah taught thus: וְכֵן סְתָם גִּינָּה כְּמָקוֹם שֶׁנָּהֲגוּ לִגְדּוֹר דָּמֵי – AND, SIMILARLY, AN ORDINARY GARDEN IS LIKE A PLACE WHERE THEY ARE ACCUSTOMED TO ERECTING PARTITIONS, וּמְחַיְּיבִין אוֹתוֹ – AND so WE OBLIGATE [EACH NEIGHBOR] to assist. אֲבָל סְתָם בִּקְעָה כְּמָקוֹם שֶׁלֹּא נָהֲגוּ דָּמֵי – BUT AN ORDINARY VALLEY IS LIKE A PLACE WHERE THEY ARE NOT ACCUSTOMED to erecting partitions, וְאֵין מְחַיְּיבִין אוֹתוֹ – AND so WE DO NOT OBLIGATE [EITHER NEIGHBOR] to assist.[46]

The next section of the Mishnah said:

אֶלָּא אִם רָצָה כּוֹנֵס לְתוֹךְ שֶׁלּוֹ וּבוֹנֶה וְעוֹשֶׂה חָזִית – BUT IF [ONE NEIGHBOR] in a valley SHOULD DESIRE to build the fence himself, HE MUST ENTER INTO HIS OWN field AND BUILD, AND HE MAKES A SIGN, to indicate his sole ownership of the fence.

The Gemara discusses the nature of this sign:

מַאי חָזִית – What exactly is the sign mentioned in the Mishnah?

Rav Huna provides one explanation:

אָמַר רַב הוּנָא אַכְפִּיָּה לֵיהּ לְקַרְנָא לְבַר – Rav Huna said: He must bend the top[47] of the wall toward the outside, i.e. to his neighbor's side.

The Gemara asks:

וְנַעֲבִיד מִלְּגָיו – But let him make the sign on the inside of the wall! Why have it face his neighbor's property?

The Gemara answers:

עָבִיד חַבְרֵיהּ נַמִּי מִלְּבַר – If the owner placed the sign on his side of the wall, his neighbor may also make a sign on the outside (which faces his property) וְאָמַר דִּידִי וְדִידֵיהּ הוּא – and say, "[The wall] is mine and yours," pointing to the two signs as proof.[48] Thus, the owner of the wall should position his sign on the outer face of the wall, thereby preempting that side, while obviously denying the neighbor access to the inside face of the wall.[49]

The Gemara persists:

NOTES

41. Even though the potential for visual trespass in a garden (i.e. damage to the produce caused by *ayin hara,* the evil eye) is very great (*Rashi;* see above, 2a note 15).

42. Where the potential for damage caused by *ayin hara* is much less (see above, 2b note 22).

43. Originally, the Gemara understood וְכֵן בְּגִינָּה מָקוֹם שֶׁנָּהֲגוּ *(and, similarly, regarding a garden in a place where they are accustomed to erecting partitions)* as one case, and thus inferred that absent such custom no inherent right to a wall exists in a garden. The Gemara therefore questioned how the law of an ordinary valley, where the danger posed by visual trespass is minimal, could be more stringent than the law of an ordinary garden, where such danger is serious indeed. Abaye now suggests that וְכֵן בְּגִינָּה refers to one case (an ordinary garden), while מָקוֹם שֶׁנָּהֲגוּ refers to a second case — that of a valley where they customarily erect partitions. In the case of the *ordinary garden* the Mishnah expressly posits an inherent right to demand a partition. Additionally, Abaye will interpret the Mishnah below as teaching that in an *ordinary valley* no such right exists (*Tosafos*). Hence, according to Abaye's reading of the Mishnah the law of the ordinary garden is more stringent than that of the ordinary valley — not less so.

44. And, specifically, that the second case concerns a valley encumbered by local custom.

45. According to Abaye, the Mishnah should have simply stated: "But in a place where they are accustomed not to erect partitions, we do not obligate [either neighbor]" (*Rashi*; see also *Tosafos* with *Maharsha*).

46. This interpretation of the Mishnah is consistent with the Gemara's long-held presumption that the law of an ordinary garden, where the danger posed by visual trespass is great, must not be *less* stringent than the law of an ordinary valley, where such danger is minimal. According to Rava's interpretation, the law of the ordinary garden is, indeed, *more* stringent.

47. According to this interpretation, חָזִית means קָצֶה, *extremity.* The sign is formed by widening the outer face of the wall's upper extremity with stones and cement (*Rashi*).

48. For the Mishnah below states that if neighbors undertake to build a wall jointly, they must create signs on both sides of the wall to signal their mutual ownership (*Rashi*).

49. The owner, however, must be careful to recess the wall so that his sign on the outer face will not project over his neighbor's property (*Yad Ramah*).

אהדר ליה כלילא דיילי נקרינהו לעיניה יומא חד אתא ויתיב קמיה אמר חזי מר האי עבדא בישא מאי קא עביד אמר ליה מאי אעביד ליה א"ל נלטייה מר אאמר ליה [כתיב] א) גם במדעך מלך אל תקלל אמר ליה האי לאו מלך הוא א"ל בולהוי עשיר בעלמא וכתיב א) ובחדרי משכבך אל תקלל עשיר גולא יהא אלא נשיא וכתיב ב) ונשיא בעמך לא תאור א"ל (א) בעושה מעשה עמך והאי לאו עושה מעשה עמך א"ל מסתפינא (א) מיניה א"ל ליכא איניש דאזיל דלימא ליה דאנא ואת יתיבנא א"ל כתיב א) כי עוף השמים יוליך את הקול ובעל כנפים יגיד דבר א"ל אנא הוא אי הואי ידענא דזהירי רבנן כולי האי לא הוה קטילנא להו השתא מאי תקנתיה דההוא גברא א"ל הוא כבה אורו של עולם דכתיב ג) כי נר מצוה ותורה אור ילך ויעסוק באורו של עולם דכתיב ד) ונהרו אליו כל הגוים איכא דאמרי הכי א"ל הוא סימא עינו של עולם דכתיב ה) והיה אם מעיני העדה ילך ויתעסק בעינו של עולם דכתיב ו) הנני מחלל את מקדשי גאון עוזכם מחמד עיניכם א"ל מסתפינא ממלכותא א"ל שדר שליחא וליזיל שתא וליעכב שתא ולהדר שתא אדהכי והכי סתרית [ליה] ובניית [ליה] עבד הכי שלחו ליה אם לא סתרתה אל תסתור ואם סתרתה אל תבני ואם סתרתה ובנית עבדי בישא בתר דעבדין מתמלכין אם זיינך עלך ספרך כאן לא רכא ולא בר רכא הורדוס [עבדא] קלניא מתעביד מאי רכא מלכותא דכתיב ז) אנכי היום רך ומשוח מלך ואי בעית אימא מהכא ח) ויקראו לפניו אברך ג) אמרי מי שלא ראה בנין הורדוס לא ראה בנין נאה [מימיו] במאי בנייה אמר ג) רבה באבני שישא ומרמרא איכא דאמרי באבני כוחלא שישא ומרמרא אפיק שפה ועייל שפה כי היכי דנקביל סידא סבר (ב) למשעייה בדהבא אמרו ליה רבנן שבקיה דהכי שפיר טפי דמיחזי כי אידוותא דימא ובבא בר בוטא ד)היכי עבד הכי והאמר רב יהודה אמר רב ואיתימא ר' יהושע בן לוי ה)מפני מה נענש דניאל מפני שהשיא עצה לנבוכד נצר שנאמר ט) להן מלכא מלכי ישפר עלך וחטאיך בצדקה פרוק ועויתך במיחן עניין הן תהוי ארכא לשלותך וגו' וכתיב י) כולא מטא על נבוכד נצר מלכא וכתיב כ) ולקצת ירחין תרי עשר וגו' איבעית אימא שאני עבדא דאיחייב במצות ואיבעית אימא שאני בית המקדש ו) דאי לא מלכות לא מתבני ודניאל מנלן דאיענש אילימא משום דכתיב ל) ותקרא אסתר להתך ו) ואמר רב התך זה דניאל הניחא למ"ד שחתכוהו מגדולתו אלא למ"ד שכל דברי מלכות נחתכין על פיו מאי איכא למימר דשדיוהו לגובא דאריוותא: הכל כמנהג המדינה: הכל לאתויי מאי ילאתויי אתרא דנהיגי בהוצא ודפנא: לפיכך אם נפל הכותל המקום והאבנים של שניהם: פשיטא לא צריכא ז)דנפל לרשותא דחד מינייהו אי נמי ח)דפנינהו חד לרשותא דידיה מהו דתימא ניהוי אידך המוציא מחבירו עליו הראיה קמ"ל: וכן בגינה מקום שנהגו לגדור מחייבין אותו: הא גופא קשיא אמרת וכן בגינה מקום שנהגו לגדור מחייבין אותו הא סתמא אין מחייבין אותו אימא סיפא אבל בקעה מקום שנהגו שלא לגדור אין מחייבין אותו הא סתמא מחייבין אותו השתא סתם גינה אמרת לא סתם בקעה מיבעיא אמר אביי ה"ק וכן סתם גינה ובמקום שנהגו לגדור בבקעה מחייבין אותו אמר ליה רבא אם כן מאי אבל אלא אמר רבא ט)הכי קתני וכן סתם גינה כמקום שנהגו לגדור דמי ומחייבין אותו אבל סתם בקעה כמקום שלא נהגו דמי ואין מחייבין אותו: אלא אם רצה כונס לתוך שלו ובונה ועושה חזית: מאי חזית אמר רב הונא אכפיה ליה לקרנא לבר ונעביד מלגיו עביד חבריה נמי מלבר ואמר דידי ודידיה הוא אי הכי השתא נמי גייז ליה חבריה ואמר דידי ודידיה הוא גיזוזא מידע ידיע איכא דאמרי אמר רב הונא מיכפא לקרנא מלגיו ונעבד מלבר גייז ליה חבריה ואמר דידי ודידיה הוא אי הכי השתא נמי לייף ליה חבריה ואמר דידי ודידיה הוא ליפופא מידע ידיע והא מבחוץ קתני קשיא רבי יוחנן אמר נשעייה

רש"י

אהדר ליה כלילא דיילי. האנקה מתרגמינן ילא (ויקרא יא) והוא שרץ שקורין הרצו"ן ושערו קשה כמחטין ועשה לו עטרה מעורו סביבות עיניו: השתא מיהא [דאנא ואת]. אנא ואת שנינו כאן ואין שומע: הנני מחלל את מקדשי. סיפיה דקרא מחמד עיניכם: מסתפינא ממלכותא. כפופים היו למלכות רומיים: מתמלכין. נוטלין רשות: אי זיינך עלך ספרך כאן. אם נתגאית בכלי מלחמתך שהרגת בית אדוניך ספר יוחסין שלך בידינו הוא [ידענו] שאתה עבד: לא רכא כו'. לא מלך ולא בן מלך: קלניא מתעביד. נעשה בן חורין מאליו: שישא. שיש ירוק שקורין ביי"ש: ומרמרא. שיש לבן: כוחלא. שיש צבוע כעין כחול: אידוותא דימא. גלי הים [שהם נעים ונדים והעין ו) מתעטשת בראייתן]: נענש דניאל. לקמיה מפרש עונשו: מלכי ישפר עלך. עצתי תיטב בעיניך: במיחן עניין. בחנינת עניים: בכן תהא ארכא לשלותך. [יהא אורך] לשלומך: כולא מטא. כל החלום של פורענות בא עליו: לקצת ירחין תרי עשר. בשביל עצתו של דניאל תלה לו שנים עשר חדש: בהוצא. לולבי דקלים: ודפנא. ענפי עץ ערמונים שקורין לו"ר ופרי שלו קורין ביי"ש: פשיטא. דהאבנים של שניהם דאפי' לא פסק לן דינא דמתני' המלמדנו שמתחלה בין שניהם עשאוהו על כרחם היו חולקין בשוה האבנים שהרי ברשות שניהם מונחים ויד מי מהם תגבר: (הג"ה בפי' ר"ח קמ"ל דלא בעינן ראיה אלא שותף מפיק מיניה בלא ראיה ואיהו דטעין דדליה ניהו עליו הראיה וכל כה"ג הכי דיינינן ליה וזה הדין מפורש עוד כמו כן בפרק הבית והעלייה בתחילתו איבעית אימא בשותפין כי האי גוונא אנוחי אבנים ברשות חבירו לא קפדי וחזקת רשות לאו כלום הוא שמעינן מינה דכל כהאי גוונא דמילתא דידיעא בשותפתא לתרוייהו אע"ג דמנחי ברשותא דחד מינייהו לא יכול למיטען דידי ניניה דברשותי מנחי דקי"ל שותפין לא קפדי אהדדי ע"כ): השתא סתם גינה אמרת לא. אע"פ שהיזק ראיה קשה: אמר אביי כו'. הא מקום שנהגו לגדור דקתני מתני' אבקעה קאי: א"כ מאי אבל בבקעה. הא מינה סליק והכי איבעי (ג) למיתני אבל מקום שנהגו שלא לגדור אין מחייבין אותו: מכפיה לקרנא לבר. ראשי הכותל יכוף לצד חבירו. וכל חזית לשון קצה הוא וכן שנינו בתמיד (פ"ב מ"ד) גבי מערכה וחזיתה מזרחה ראשי הגזירין וכן מחזה מול מחזה דמלכים (א ז) ראשי הנסרים מוסבין זה מול זה ז) ועבי' מאבראי כופה לצד ראשי הכותל שמחבר בראשו אבנים וטיט ומעבהו: דידי ודידיה הוא. דקתני מתמיהין כשעושין אותו בין שניהם עושין חזית מכאן ומכאן: השתא נמי גייז לה. להסיר כפופה שהיא לצדו ולימא דידי ודידיה הוא ולא עשינו חזית: מלגיו. לצד שלו ולקמיה פריך הא מבחוץ קתני: לייף ליה. מחבר חזית אחרת לצדו: נשעייה

תוספות

שכל דברי מלכות נחתכין על פיו. לפי תרגום [של] אחשורוש ט) נענש הרבה שנהרג דכתיב ויגדו למרדכי את דברי אסתר ולא כתב התם התך לפי שהרגו המן על שהיה משיב דברים בין אסתר למרדכי ומיהו גמ' שלנו אין תופס כן דדרשינן במגילה (דף טו.) והתך להיכן הלך ומפרש לפי שאין משיבין על הקלקלה:

הכי קתני וכן בגינה סתם כו'. וסיפא נמי יש לפרש כן אבל סתם בקעה ומקום שלא נהגו לגדור בגינה אין מחייבין אותו:

והא מבחוץ קתני קשיא. ותיובתא היא דמצינן למימר היינו שבולט חוץ לחומה מ"מ קשיא היא דא"כ מחוץ הוה ליה למיתני:

ט) גיין ליה חבריה ושדי ליה. אע"ג דלעיל אמר גוזא מידע ידיע בהולא לא ידיע: לאפוקי

מסורת הש"ס

א) [יבמות כב: ב"ק צד: ב"מ מח: סנ. סנהדרין פה. מכות ט:], ב) סוכה נא: ע"ש, ג) [שם איתא רבא], ד) נ"א דלא סניא ליה בלא מלכא, ה) מגילה טו. ו) מתמעטעת, ז) ס"א ועביו, ח) [וכן בפירקין דף ה' ע"ג], ט) שייך לע"ב:

הגהות הב"ח

(א) גמ' א"ל מסתפינא איכא איניש דשמע ואזיל ומודע ליה א"ל השתא מיהא ליכא איניש א"ל גבן דאזיל ולימא ליה: (ב) שם סבר למשעייה בדהבא: (ג) רש"י ד"ה א"כ מאי וכו' איבעי ליה למיתנא:

ליקוטי רש"י

[תחילת ליקוטי רש"י שייך לכאן נדפס בעמוד הקודם] שהתכוהו מגדולתו. בימי אחשורוש שכבר נבלשו מלכות מלכותן וכן דריוש המדי שנאמר ועלה הרגישו תלתא די דניאל חד מנהון (דניאל ו) וכן כורש שנאמר ודניאל הצלח במלכות דריוש ובמלכות כורש פרסאה (שם) ובימי אחשורוש התכוהו מגדולתו [מגילה טו.]. ויהי דניאל. בגדולה בבבל עד שנת אחת לכורש המלך לדברי האומר התך זה דניאל ולמה נקרא שמו התך שהתכוהו מגדולתו צריכין אנו לומר שזהו כורש הראשון שלפני אחשורוש ולדברי האומר שכל דברי מלכות נחתכין על פיו נאמר כורש זה הוא כורש השני אחר אחשורוש ובימיו היה דריוש המדי שהכשילו גבוה מלכות לא ירד מגדולתו שנאמר (דניאל ו) ודניאל דנה הצלח במלכות דריוש ובמלכות כורש פרסאה וכורש הראשון היה בגדולה [דניאל א, כא]. בהוצא ודפנא. הוצא לולבי דקל. דפנא ענפי עץ שקורין לור"ו וגדל בו פרי שקורין באי"ש [סוכה לב:]. עליו הראיה. עליו להביא עדים [ב"ק מו:]. עליו להביא עדים לברר את הספק והמוציא היא בבבא קמא (מו:) מי בעל דברים יגש אליהם (שמות כד) יש ראיה עליהם [גיטין מח:]. חזית. לשון קצה ובמנסים כן פותרו ותדברו (תהלים קיט) על מחוז חפצם ולכל חזות שבלשון משנה כן הוא כבסדר מערכת התמיד (תמיד כח.) [מלכים א, ז, ה].

תורה אור השלם

א) גַּם בְּמַדָּעֲךָ מֶלֶךְ אַל תְּקַלֵּל וּבְחַדְרֵי מִשְׁכָּבְךָ אַל תְּקַלֵּל עָשִׁיר כִּי עוֹף הַשָּׁמַיִם יוֹלִיךְ אֶת הַקּוֹל וּבַעַל כְּנָפַיִם יַגֵּיד דָּבָר: [קהלת י, כ]

ב) אֱלֹהִים לֹא תְקַלֵּל וְנָשִׂיא בְעַמְּךָ לֹא תָאֹר: [שמות כב, כז]

ג) כִּי נֵר מִצְוָה וְתוֹרָה אוֹר וְדֶרֶךְ חַיִּים תּוֹכְחוֹת מוּסָר: [משלי ו, כג]

ד) וְהָיָה בְּאַחֲרִית הַיָּמִים נָכוֹן יִהְיֶה הַר בֵּית יְיָ בְּרֹאשׁ הֶהָרִים וְנִשָּׂא מִגְּבָעוֹת וְנָהֲרוּ אֵלָיו כָּל הַגּוֹיִם: [ישעיה ב, ב]

ה) וְהָיָה אִם מֵעֵינֵי הָעֵדָה נֶעֶשְׂתָה לִשְׁגָגָה וְעָשׂוּ כָל הָעֵדָה פַּר בֶּן בָּקָר אֶחָד לְעֹלָה לְרֵיחַ נִיחֹחַ לַייָ וּמִנְחָתוֹ וְנִסְכּוֹ כַּמִּשְׁפָּט וּשְׂעִיר עִזִּים אֶחָד לְחַטָּת: [במדבר טו, כד]

ו) אֱמֹר לְבֵית יִשְׂרָאֵל כֹּה אָמַר אֲדֹנָי יְיָ הִנְנִי מְחַלֵּל אֶת מִקְדָּשִׁי גְּאוֹן עֻזְּכֶם מַחְמַד עֵינֵיכֶם וּמַחְמַל נַפְשְׁכֶם וּבְנֵיכֶם וּבְנוֹתֵיכֶם אֲשֶׁר עֲזַבְתֶּם בַּחֶרֶב יִפֹּלוּ: [יחזקאל כד, כא]

ז) וְאָנֹכִי הַיּוֹם רַךְ וּמָשׁוּחַ מֶלֶךְ וְהָאֲנָשִׁים הָאֵלֶּה בְּנֵי צְרוּיָה קָשִׁים מִמֶּנִּי יְשַׁלֵּם יְיָ לְעֹשֵׂה הָרָעָה כְּרָעָתוֹ: [שמואל ב ג, לט]

ח) וַיַּרְכֵּב אֹתוֹ בְּמִרְכֶּבֶת הַמִּשְׁנֶה אֲשֶׁר לוֹ וַיִּקְרְאוּ לְפָנָיו אַבְרֵךְ וְנָתוֹן אֹתוֹ עַל כָּל אֶרֶץ מִצְרָיִם: [בראשית מא, מג]

ט) לָהֵן מַלְכָּא מִלְכִּי יִשְׁפַּר עֲלָךְ וַחֲטָאָךְ בְּצִדְקָה פְרֻק וַעֲוָיָתָךְ בְּמִחַן עֲנָיִן הֵן תֶּהֱוֵא אַרְכָה לִשְׁלֵוְתָךְ: [דניאל ד, כד]

י) כֹּלָּא מְּטָא עַל נְבוּכַדְנֶצַּר מַלְכָּא: [דניאל ד, כה]

כ) לִקְצָת יַרְחִין תְּרֵי עֲשַׂר עַל הֵיכַל מַלְכוּתָא דִּי בָבֶל מְהַלֵּךְ הֲוָה: [דניאל ד, כו]

ל) וַתִּקְרָא אֶסְתֵּר לַהֲתָךְ מִסָּרִיסֵי הַמֶּלֶךְ אֲשֶׁר הֶעֱמִיד לְפָנֶיהָ וַתְּצַוֵּהוּ עַל מָרְדֳּכָי לָדַעַת מַה זֶּה וְעַל מַה זֶּה: [אסתר ד, ה]

עין משפט נר מצוה

טז א ב ג מיי' פכ"ו מהל' סנהדרין הל' א סמג לאוין רט:

יז ד ה מיי' פ"ב מהל' רוצח הלכה טו:

יח ו מיי' פ"ב מהל' שכנים הל' טו סמג עשין פב טוש"ע ח"מ סי' קנז סעיף ד:

יט ז ח מיי' שם הלכה יח טוש"ע שם סעיף ה:

כ ט מיי' שם הל' יח סמג שם טוש"ע ח"מ סי' קנח סעיף א:

לעזי רש"י

הרצו"ן. פירוש האנקה (רש"י ויקרא יא, ל), קופר (רש"י שבת דף נד ע"ב), הקופד (רש"ש כלאים פ"ח מ"ה), קפוד (רש"י ישעיה יד, כג). ביי"ש. פירוש כעין ירוק (רש"י סוכה דף נא ע"ב ד"ה שישא), להוב (עיין רש"י ויקרא יג, לז ותוספות סוכה דף נא ע"ב ד"ה הירוק). לו"ר. פירוש עץ הער (רש"י גיטין דף סט ע"ב ד"ה אטרפא ועיין אסף הרופא כת"י מינכן דף סט ע"ב), לורברבו"ס. ביי"ש. פירוש פרי עץ הער (רש"י כנ"ל).

רבינו גרשום

כלילא דיילי. כתר של מיני האנקה שהן עלוקות נתן סביב ראשו וניקרו עיניו: כי נר מצוה ותורה אור. אלו תלמידי חכמים שעוסקין בתורה אלו סנהדרין: ממלכותא. זו מלכות רומאי שהיה משועבד להם: שלחו ליה. ממלכות רומיים אם זיינך עלך ספרך כאן. כלומר אם מלחמתך עליך שאתה מתגבר לשם ייחוסך כאן שיודעין אנו מאיזה משפחה אתה לפי שהורקנוס אביו של הורדוס פעם אחת הלך על הרומים להלחם ונצח וראה בשביה שפחה אחת יפת תואר וחמדה ועשה לה כדין תורה ובא עליה והוליד ממנה אותו הורדוס ולפיכך היו מחרפין אותו מיחוסו: קלניא. בן חורין נעשה: שישא. שיש לבן. ומרמרא. מנומרין: כוחלא. שחורין: כאדוותא דימא. כגלי הים שזו יורדת וזו עולה: שאני עבד משום דהוי שייך במצות עשה (שהזמן) [שאין הזמן] גרמא והורדוס עבד היה: בהוצא ודפנא. שנהגין לעשות גדר מכפות תמרים ודפנא עץ של (עור) [ערמון] שקורין לו"ר וכיון דנתרצו לעשות כותל על זה ועל זה לעכב שלא יעשו אלא כמנהג המדינה: קמ"ל. כיון דזה נותן מחצה וזה נותן מחצה אין צריך להביא ראיה: פיסקא וכן בגינה מקום שנהגו לגדור בגויל או בגזית וחבירו מעכב היו כופין אותו משום דאיכא היזק ראיה כדאוקימנא [לעיל ב:] בגינה הסמוכה לעיר אבל בבקעה של שדות כו': הא סתמא. דיש שגודרין ויש שאין גודרין השתא סתם גינה. דאיכא היזק ראיה אמרת לא דאין מחייבין סתם בקעה דליכא היזק ראיה מחייב: אמר אביי ה"ק. כלומר כגון חסורא מיחסרא וכן גינה סתם משום דאיכא היזק ראיה ובמקום שנהגו לגדור בבקעה מחייבין אותו: א"ל רבא. לאביי אי הכי כדקא תרצת א"כ מאי אבל דקתני במתני' אבל בבקעה אי אמרת בשלמא דרישא לא איירי בדינא דבקעה כלל היינו דקתני בסיפא אבל בבקעה דעד השתא לא איירי בדינא דבקעה אלא לדעתך דתרצת דרישא איירי בבקעה מאי אבל בבקעה תו דתני בסיפא: אלא אמר רבא. אנא מתריצנא דלא תקשי אבל ולא תקשי סתמא דסיפא ה"ק וכן בגינה סתם דהא גינה סתם כדינה במקום שנהגו לגדור דמי ומחייבין לגדור ועדיין לא שמעי' דינא דסתם בקעה ואמטו להכי צריך למתני בסיפא אבל בבקעה לאשמעינן דינא דסתם בקעה כמקום שנהגו שלא לגדור דמי דאין מחייבין לגדור דהשתא מיתרצא כולה מתני': ועושה לכותל חזית. סימן היכרא שיהו בני אדם יודעין שהכותל כולו בקרקע שלו משלו ולפיכך כיון דעשה חזית מצדו הוי כולו שלו: דכיף ליה קרנא מלבר. דלשקע בראש הכותל בסופו קנים בטיט ויכוף ראשם מבחוץ לצד הכותל לצד אויר חבירו: אזיל איניש אידך בחצר חבירו ויכוף אף הוא לצד שלו ויאמר הרי יש לי נמי חזית ודידי ודידך הוא הכותל ומקומו: נמי מלבר: אכתי אתי האי וגייז ליה להאי חזית שהוא (פצע) [לצד] שלו ואמר דידי ודידך הוא: נמי לייף ליה. כלומר יעשה החזית בכותל בטיט בלא שקיעה: מידע ידיע. יכולין להבין ולהבחין בין דבוקה לשקיעה: והא מבחוץ קתני. ועושה לו חזית מבחוץ קשיא להך לישנא דאיכא דאמרי: ור' יוחנן אמר. היינו חזית:

אִי הָכִי – **If** it is **so** that the neighbor's integrity is a factor, **הַשְׁתָּא נַמִּי גָּיֵיז לֵיהּ חַבְרֵיהּ** – **even now** that the sign faces outward **his neighbor can shear it** **וְאָמַר דִּידִי וְדִידֵיהּ הוּא** – **and say, "[The wall] is mine and yours,"**[50] and there will be no sign to disprove him! What, then, is the advantage of projecting the sign from the wall's outer face?

The Gemara answers:

גִּיזוּזָא מֵידַע יְדִיעַ – The **shearing** of a projection **is discernible;** hence, the neighbor will be unable to claim half the wall by surreptitiously removing the sign. Therefore, it is clearly advantageous for the sign to project outward.

The Gemara presents another version of this dialectic:

אִיכָּא דְּאָמְרֵי – **There are those that say** that the dialogue proceeded as follows: **אָמַר רַב הוּנָא מִיכְפָּא לְקַרְנָא מִלְּגָיו** – **Rav Huna said: He** must **bend the top of the wall toward the inside,**[51] i.e. toward his own property.

The Gemara asks:

וְנַעֲבֵד מִלְּבַר – **But let him make** the sign **on the outside** of the wall (to prevent his neighbor from doing so)!

The Gemara answers:

גָּיֵיז לֵיהּ חַבְרֵיהּ – If the sign projects outward **his neighbor can shear it** **וְאָמַר דִּידִי וְדִידֵיהּ הוּא** – **and say, "[The wall] is mine and yours!"**[52] Thus, we position the sign on the inside face of the wall, where the neighbor cannot reach it.

The Gemara persists:

אִי הָכִי – **If** it is **so** that the neighbor's integrity is a factor, **הַשְׁתָּא נַמִּי לָיֵיף לֵיהּ חַבְרֵיהּ** – **even now** that the sign projects inward, **his neighbor can attach [another sign]** on his side of the wall **וְאָמַר דִּידִי וְדִידֵיהּ הוּא** – **and say, "[The wall] is mine and yours!"** What, then, is the advantage of projecting the sign from the wall's inner face?

The Gemara answers:

לִיפוּפָא מֵידַע יְדִיעַ – **An attachment is discernible;** hence, the neighbor will be unable to claim half the wall by surreptitiously adding a sign of his own. Therefore, it is clearly advantageous for the sign to project inward.

The Gemara raises an objection to this version of Rav Huna's statement:

וְהָא מִבַּחוּץ קָתָנֵי – **But the Mishnah teaches:** He makes a sign ON THE OUTSIDE! How, then, can Rav Huna say that the sign must project inward?

The Gemara answers:

קַשְׁיָא – This is indeed **a difficulty.**[53]

R' Yochanan prescribed a different method for making a sign:

רַבִּי יוֹחָנָן אָמַר – **R' Yochanan said:**

NOTES

50. I.e. although we built the wall in concert, we failed to add the obligatory signs (*Rashi*).

51. This statement does not dovetail with the language of the Mishnah: "He makes a sign *on the outside.*" The Gemara will raise this difficulty below (*Rashi*).

52. According to this version, one would be unable to detect a shearing of his sign.

53. *Tosafos* explain that since the Gemara did not say תְּיוּבְתָּא, *a refutation,* it does not completely refute this version of Rav Huna's statement, for it is possible to translate מִבַּחוּץ as *outward* since the sign protruded from the wall into the property. Nevertheless, this interpretation remains problematic, for it would be conveyed more clearly had the Mishnah stated מִחוּץ, which means *"outward,"* rather than מִבַּחוּץ, which connotes *"on* the outside."

אהדר ליה כלילא דיילי נקרינהו לעיניה יומא חד אתא ויתיב קמיה אמר חזי מר האי עבדא בישא מאי קא עביד אמר ליה מאי אעביד ליה א"ל נלטייה מר אמר ליה [כתיב] גם במדעך מלך אל תקלל אמר ליה האי לאו מלך הוא א"ל וליהוי עשיר בעלמא וכתיב ובחדרי משכבך אל תקלל עשיר ולא יהא אלא נשיא וכתיב ונשיא בעמך לא תאור א"ל בעושה מעשה עמך והאי לאו עושה מעשה עמך א"ל מסתפינא (א) מיניה א"ל ליכא איניש דאזיל דלימא ליה דאנא ואת יתיבנא א"ל כתיב כי עוף השמים יוליך את הקול ובעל כנפים יגיד דבר א"ל אנא הוא אי הואי ידענא דזהירי רבנן כולי האי לא הוה קטילנא להו השתא מאי תקנתיה דההוא גברא א"ל הוא כבה אורו של עולם דכתיב כי נר מצוה ותורה אור ילך ויעסוק באורו של עולם דכתיב ונהרו אליו כל הגוים איכא דאמרי הכי א"ל הוא סימא עינו של עולם דכתיב והיה אם מעיני העדה ילך ויתעסק בעינו של עולם דכתיב הנני מחלל את מקדשי גאון עוזכם מחמד עיניכם א"ל מסתפינא ממלכותא א"ל שדר שליחא וליזיל שתא וליעכב שתא ולהדר שתא אדהכי והכי סתרית [ליה] ובניית [ליה] עבד הכי שלחו ליה אם לא סתרתה אל תסתור ואם סתרתה אל תבני ואם סתרתה ובנית עבדי בישא בתר דעבדין מתמלכין אם זיינך עלך ספרך כאן לא רכא ולא בר רכא הורדוס [עבדא] קלניא מתעביד מאי רכא מלכותא דכתיב אנכי היום רך ומשוח מלך ואי בעית אימא מהכא ויקראו לפניו אברך אמרי מי שלא ראה בנין הורדוס לא ראה בנין נאה [מימיו] במאי בנייה אמר רבה באבני שישא ומרמרא איכא דאמרי באבני כוחלא שישא ומרמרא אפיק שפה ועייל שפה כי היכי דנקביל סידא סבר (ב) למשעייה בדהבא אמרו ליה רבנן שבקיה דהכי שפיר טפי דמיחזי כי אידוותא דימא ובבא בר בוטא היכי עבד הכי והאמר רב יהודה אמר רב ואיתימא ר' יהושע בן לוי מפני מה נענש דניאל מפני שהשיא עצה לנבוכד נצר שנאמר להן מלכא מלכי ישפר עלך וחטאך בצדקה פרוק ועויתך במיחן עניין הן תהוי ארכא לשלותך וגו' וכתיב כולא מטא על נבוכד נצר מלכא וכתיב ולקצת ירחין תרי עשר וגו' איבעית אימא שאני עבדא דאיחייב במצות ואיבעית אימא שאני בית המקדש דאי לא מלכות לא מתבני ודניאל מנלן דאיענש אילימא משום דכתיב ותקרא אסתר להתך ואמר רב התך זה דניאל הניחא למ"ד שחתכוהו מגדולתו אלא למ"ד שכל דברי מלכות נחתכין על פיו מאי איכא למימר דשדיוהו לגובא דארייוותא: הכל כמנהג המדינה: הכל לאתויי מאי לאתויי אתרא דנהיגי בהוצא ודפנא: לפיכך אם נפל הכותל המקום והאבנים של שניהם: פשיטא לא צריכא דנפל לרשותא דחד מינייהו אי נמי דפנינהו חד לרשותיה דידיה מהו דתימא ניהוי המוציא מחבירו עליו הראיה קמ"ל: וכן בגינה מקום שנהגו לגדור מחייבין אותו: הא גופא קשיא אמרת וכן בגינה מקום שנהגו לגדור מחייבין אותו הא סתמא אין מחייבין אותו אימא סיפא אבל בבקעה מקום שנהגו שלא לגדור אין מחייבין אותו הא סתמא מחייבין אותו השתא סתם גינה אמרת לא סתם בקעה מיבעיא אמר אביי ה"ק וכן סתם גינה ובמקום שנהגו לגדור בבקעה מחייבין אותו אמר ליה רבא אם כן מאי אבל אלא אמר רבא הכי קתני וכן סתם גינה כמקום שנהגו לגדור דמי ומחייבין אותו אבל סתם בקעה כמקום שלא נהגו דמי ואין מחייבין אותו: אלא אם רצה כונס לתוך שלו ובונה ועושה חזית: מאי חזית אמר רב הונא אכפיה ליה לקרנא לבר ונעביד מלגיו עביד חבריה נמי מלבר ואמר דידי ודידיה הוא אי הכי השתא נמי גייז ליה חבריה ואמר דידי ודידיה הוא גיזוא מידע ידיע איכא דאמרי אמר רב הונא מיכפא לקרנא מלגיו ונעבד מלבר גייז ליה חבריה ואמר דידי ודידיה הוא אי הכי השתא נמי לייף ליה חבריה ואמר דידי ודידיה הוא ליפופא מידע ידיע והא מבחוץ קתני קשיא רבי יוחנן אמר נשעייה

רש"י

אהדר ליה כלילא דיילי. האנקה מתרגמינן יילא (ויקרא יא) והוא שרץ שקורין הרצו"ן ושערו קשה כמחטין ועשה לו עטרה מעורו סביבות עיניו: **השתא מיהא [דאנא ואת].** אנא ואת שנינו כאן ואין שומע: **הנני מחלל את מקדשי.** סיפיה דקרא מחמד עיניכם: **מסתפינא ממלכותא.** כפופים היו למלכות רומיים: **מתמלכין.** נוטלין רשות: **אי זיינך עלך ספרך כאן.** אם נתגאית בכלי מלחמתך שהרגת בית חשמונאי ספר יוחסין שלך בידינו הוא [ידענו] שאתה עבד: **לא רכא כו'.** לא מלך ולא בן מלך: **קלניא מתעביד.** נעשה בן חורין מאליו: **שישא.** שיש ירוק שקורין ביי"ש: **ומרמרא.** שיש לבן: **כוחלא.** שיש צבוע כעין כחול: **אידוותא דימא.** גלי הים [שהם נעים ונדים] והעין מתעשתת בראייתן: **נענש דניאל.** לקמיה מפרש עונשו: **מלכי ישפר עלך.** עצתי תיטב בעיניך: **במיחן עניין.** בחנינת עניים: **בכן תהא ארכא לשלותך.** [יהא אורך] לשלומך: **כולא מטא.** כל החלום של פורענות בא עליו: **לקצת ירחין תרי עשר.** בשביל עצתו של דניאל תלה לו שנים עשר חדש: **בהוצא.** לולבי דקלים: **ודפנא.** ענפי עץ ערמונים שקורין לו"ר ופרי שלו קורין ביי"ש: **פשיטא.** דהכונס של שניהם דהפי' לא פסק לן דינא דמתני' המלמדנו שמתחלה בין שניהם עשאוה על כרחם היו חולקין בשוה הכונס שכרי ברשות שניהם מונחים ויד מי מהם תגבר: (הג"ה בפי' ר"ח קמ"ל דלא בעינן ראיה אלא שותף מפיק מיניה בלא ראיה ואיהו דטעין דדליה ניהו עליו הראיה וכל כה"ג הכי דיינינן ליה וזה הדין מפורש עוד כמו כן בפרק הבית והעלייה בתחלתו איבעית אימא בשותפין כי האי גוונא אוזי אבנים ברשות חבירו לא קפדי וחזקת רשות לאו כלום הוא שמעינן מינה דכל כהאי גוונא למילתא דידיעה בשותפות לתרווייהו אע"ג דמנחי ברשותא דחד מינייהו לא יכול למיטען דידי ניהו דברשותי מנחי דקי"ל שותפין לא קפדי אהדדי ע"כ): **השתא סתם גינה אמרת לא.** אע"פ שהיזק ראיה קשה: **אמר אביי כו'.** האי מקום שנהגו לגדור דקתני מתני' אבקעה קאי: **א"כ מאי אבל בבקעה.** הא מינה סליק והכי איבעי (ג) למיתני אבל מקום שנהגו שלא לגדור אין מחייבין אותו: **מכפייה לקרנא לבר.** ראשי הכותל יכוף לצד חבירו. וכל חזית לשון קצה הוא וכן שנינו בתמיד (פ"ב מ"ד) גבי מערכה וחזיתה מזרחה ראשי הגזירין וכן מחזה מול מחזה דמלכים (א ז) ראשי הנסרים מוסבין זה מול זה ועבי' מאבראי כופה לצד ראשי הכותל שמחבר בראשו אבנים וטיט ומעגהו: **דידי ודידיה הוא.** דקתני מתחילין כשעושין אותו בין שניהם עושין חזית מכאן ומכאן: **השתא נמי גייז לה.** להסיר כפופה שהיא לצדו ולימא דידי ודידיה הוא ולא עשינו חזית: **מלגיו.** לצד שלו ולקמיה פריך הא מבחוץ קתני: **לייף ליה.** מחבר חזית אחרת לצדו: נשעייה

תוספות

שכל דברי מלכות נחתכין על פיו. לפי תרגום [של] אחשורוש נענש הרבה שנהרג דכתיב ויגידו למרדכי את דברי אסתר ולא כתב התם התך לפי שהרגו המן על שהיה משיב דברים בין אסתר למרדכי ומיהו גמ' שלנו אין תופס כן דדרשינן במגילה (דף טו.) והתך להיכן הלך ומפרש לפי שאין משיבין על הקלקלה: **הכי** קתני וכן בגינה סתם כו'. וסיפא נמי יש לפרש כן אבל סתם בקעה ומקום שלא נהגו לגדור בגינה אין מחייבין אותו: **והא** מבחוץ קתני קשיא. ותיובתא אינה דמלינן למימר היינו שבולט חוץ לחומה מ"מ קשיא היא דא"כ מחוץ הוה ליה למיתני: **גייז** ליה חבריה ושדי ליה. אע"ג דלעיל אמר גזוזא מידע ידיע בהולא לא ידיע: לאפוקי

עין משפט נר מצוה

טז א ב ג מיי' פכ"ו מהל' סנהדרין הל' א סמג לאוין רעו:
יז ד ה מיי' פי"ב מהל' רוצח הלכה טו:
יח ו מיי' פ"ב מהל' שכנים הל' טו סמג עשין פב טוש"ע ח"מ סי' קנז סעיף ד:
יט ז ח מיי' שם הלכה יח טוש"ע שם סעיף ה:
כ ט מיי' שם הל' יז סמג שם טוש"ע ח"מ סי' קנח סעיף א:

לעזי רש"י

הרצו"ן. פירוש האנקה (רש"י ויקרא יא, ל), קופר (רש"י שבת דף נד ע"ב), הקופד (רא"ש כלאים פ"ח מ"ה), קפוד (רש"י ישעיה יד, כג). ביי"ש. פירוש כעין ירוק (רש"י סוכה דף נא ע"ב ד"ה שישא), לאוב (עיין רש"י ויקרא יג, לז ותוספות סוכה דף לא ע"ב ד"ה הירוק). לו"ר. פירוש עץ הער (רש"י גיטין דף סט ע"ב ד"ה אטרפא ועיין אסף הרופא כת"י מינכן דף סט ע"ב), לורברבוי"ס. ביי"ש. פירוש עץ הער (רש"י כנ"ל):

רבינו גרשום

כלילא דיילי. כתר של מיני האנקה שהן עלוקות נתן סביב ראשו **וניקרו עיניו: כי נר מצוה ותורה אור.** אלו תלמידי חכמים שעוסקין בתורה אלו סנהדרין: **ממלכותא.** זו מלכות רומאי שהיה משועבד להם: **שלחו ליה.** ממלכות רומיים **אם זיינך עלך ספרך כאן.** כלומר אם מלחמתך עליך שאתה מתגבר לשם ייחוסך כאן שיודעין אנו מאיזה משפחה אתה לפי שהורקנוס אביו של הורדוס פעם אחת הלך על הרומים להלחם ונצח וראה בשביה שפחה אחת יפת תואר וחמדה ועשה לה כדין תורה ובא עליה והוליד ממנה אותו הורדוס ולפיכך היו מחרפין אותו מיחוסו: **קלניא.** בן חורין נעשה: **שישא.** שיש לבן: **ומרמרא.** מנומרין: **כוחלא.** שחורין: **כאדוותא דימא.** כגלי הים שזו יורדת וזו עולה: **שאני עבד** משום דהוי שייך במצות עשה (שהזמן) [שאין הזמן] גרמא והורדוס עבד היה: **בהוצא ודפנא.** שנוהגין לעשות גדר מכפות תמרים **ודפנא** עץ של (עור) [ערמון] שקורין לו"ר וכיון דנתרצו לעשות כותל על זה ועל זה לעכב שלא יעשו אלא כמנהג המדינה: **קמ"ל.** כיון דזה נותן מחצה וזה נותן מחצה אין צריך להביא ראיה: **פיסקא וכן בגינה מקום שנהגו לגדור** בגויל או בגזית וחבירו מעכב היו **כופין אותו** משום דאיכא היזק ראיה כדאוקימנא [לעיל ב:] בגינה הסמוכה לעיר **אבל בבקעה** של שדות כו': **הא סתמא.** דיש שגודרין ויש שאין גודרין: **השתא סתם** גינה. דאיכא היזק ראיה **אמרת לא** דאין מחייבין **סתם בקעה** דליכא היזק ראיה מחייב: **אמר אביי ה"ק.** כלומר כגון חסורא מיחסרא **וכן גינה סתם** משום דאיכא היזק ראיה **ובמקום שנהגו לגדור בבקעה מחייבין אותו: א"ל רבא.** לאביי אי הכי כדקא תרצת א"כ **מאי אבל** דקתני במתני' אבל בבקעה אלא לדעתך דרישא לא איירי בדינא דבקעה כלל היינו דקתני בסיפא אבל בבקעה דעד השתא לא איירי בדינא דבקעה אלא לדעתך דתרצת דרישא איירי בבקעה מאי אבל בבקעה תו דתני בסיפא: **אלא אמר רבא.** אנא מתרצינא דלא תקשי אבל ולא תקשי סתמא דרישא לסתמא דסיפא ה"ק **וכן בגינה סתם** דינא דגינה סתם כדינא **דמקום שנהגו** לגדור בבקעה דמחייבין לגדור ועדיין לא שמעי' דינא דסתם בקעה ומשום הכי צריך למתני בסיפא **אבל בבקעה** לאשמעינן דינא **דסתם בקעה דכמקום שנהגו** שלא לגדור **דמי** דאין מחייבין לגדור דהשתא מיתרצא כולה מתני': **ועושה לכותל חזית.** סימן היכרא שידעו בני אדם שזה בנאו כולו בקרקע שלו משלו לפיכך כיון דעשה חזית אם נפל הכותל כו': **דכייף ליה קרנא מלבר.** דלשקע בראש הכותל בסופו קנים בטיט ויכוף ראשם של קנים מבחוץ לצד הכותל לצד אויר חבירו: **אזיל** אידך חבירו וכייף ליה **נמי מלבר** לצד שלו **ואמר** הרי אית לי נמי חזית **ודידי ודידך הוא** הכותל ומקומו הלכך לא כייף אלא מלבר: **אכתי אתי האי וגייז** לההיא חזית שהוא (פצע) [לצד] שלו **ואמר דידי ודידך הוא: השתא נמי לייף ליה.** כלומר יחברם לכותל בטיט בלא שקיעה: **מידע ידיע.** יכולין להבין ולהבחין בין דבוקה לשקיעה: **והא מבחוץ קתני.** ועושה לו חזית מבחוץ **קשיא** להך לישנא דאיכא דאמרי: **ור' יוחנן אמר.** היינו חזית:

מסורת הש"ס

א) [יבמות כב: ב"ק לד: ב"מ מח: סנהדרין מז. פה. מכות ח:], ב) סוכה נא: ע"ש, ג) [ע"ש איתא רבא], ד) כ"ה דלא כבא ליה בלא מלכא, ה) מגילה טו., ו) מתעשעת, ז) ר"ח ועיניו, ח) [וכן בפירקין דר"א פ"נ], ט) שייך לע"ב:

הגהות הב"ח

(א) גמ' א"ל מסתפינא מיכא אינש דשמע מלתא ואזיל ומודע ליה א"ל השתא מיהא ליכא איניש גבן דאזיל ולימא ליה: (ב) שם סבר למשעייה בדהבא: (ג) רש"י ד"ה א"כ מאי וכו' איבעי ליה למיתנא:

ליקוטי רש"י

[תחילת ליקוטי רש"י ששייך לכאן נדפס בעמוד הקודם] **שחתכוהו מגדולתו.** בימי אחשורוש שכבר בלשצר הפליטו מלכותו למלכותו וכן דריוש המדי שנאמר ועלה מנהון סרכין תלתא די דניאל חד מנהון (דניאל ו) וכן כורש שנאמר ודניאל הצלח במלכות דריוש ובמלכות כורש פרסאה (שם) וכשעמד אחשורוש חתכו מגדולתו (מגילה טו.). **הוצא.** ענפי עץ שקורין לו"ר וגלל בו פרי שקורין בא"ש (סוכה כב.). **עליו הראיה.** כעדים. עליו להביא עדים לברר את הספק (שמות כב). **חזית.** לשון קצה (גיטין מח:):

תורה אור השלם

א) גַּם בְּמַדָּעֲךָ מֶלֶךְ אַל תְּקַלֵּל וּבְחַדְרֵי מִשְׁכָּבְךָ אַל תְּקַלֵּל עָשִׁיר כִּי עוֹף הַשָּׁמַיִם יוֹלִיךְ אֶת הַקּוֹל וּבַעַל כְּנָפַיִם יַגֵּיד דָּבָר: [קהלת י, כ]
ב) אֱלֹהִים לֹא תְקַלֵּל וְנָשִׂיא בְעַמְּךָ לֹא תָאֹר: [שמות כב, כז]
ג) כִּי נֵר מִצְוָה וְתוֹרָה אוֹר וְדֶרֶךְ חַיִּים תּוֹכְחוֹת מוּסָר: [משלי ו, כג]
ד) וְהָיָה בְּאַחֲרִית הַיָּמִים נָכוֹן יִהְיֶה הַר בֵּית יְיָ בְּרֹאשׁ הֶהָרִים וְנִשָּׂא מִגְּבָעוֹת וְנָהֲרוּ אֵלָיו כָּל הַגּוֹיִם: [ישעיה ב, ב]
ה) וְהָיָה אִם מֵעֵינֵי הָעֵדָה נֶעֶשְׂתָה לִשְׁגָגָה וְעָשׂוּ כָל הָעֵדָה פַּר בֶּן בָּקָר אֶחָד לְעֹלָה לְרֵיחַ נִיחֹחַ לַייָ וּמִנְחָתוֹ וְנִסְכּוֹ כַּמִּשְׁפָּט וּשְׂעִיר עִזִּים אֶחָד לְחַטָּת: [במדבר טו, כד]
ו) אֱמֹר לְבֵית יִשְׂרָאֵל כֹּה אָמַר אֲדֹנָי אֱלֹהִים הִנְנִי מְחַלֵּל אֶת מִקְדָּשִׁי גְּאוֹן עֻזְּכֶם מַחְמַד עֵינֵיכֶם וּמַחְמַל נַפְשְׁכֶם וּבְנֵיכֶם וּבְנוֹתֵיכֶם אֲשֶׁר עֲזַבְתֶּם בַּחֶרֶב יִפֹּלוּ: [יחזקאל כד, כא]
ז) וְאָנֹכִי הַיּוֹם רַךְ וּמָשׁוּחַ מֶלֶךְ וְהָאֲנָשִׁים הָאֵלֶּה בְּנֵי צְרוּיָה קָשִׁים מִמֶּנִּי יְשַׁלֵּם יְיָ לְעֹשֵׂה הָרָעָה כְּרָעָתוֹ: [שמואל ב ג, לט]
ח) וַיַּרְכֵּב אֹתוֹ בְּמִרְכֶּבֶת הַמִּשְׁנֶה אֲשֶׁר לוֹ וַיִּקְרְאוּ לְפָנָיו אַבְרֵךְ וְנָתוֹן אֹתוֹ עַל כָּל אֶרֶץ מִצְרָיִם: [בראשית מא, מג]
ט) לָהֵן מַלְכָּא מִלְכִּי יִשְׁפַּר עֲלָךְ וַחֲטָאָךְ בְּצִדְקָה פְרֻק וַעֲוָיָתָךְ בְּמִחַן עֲנָיִן הֵן תֶּהֱוֵא אַרְכָא לִשְׁלֵוְתָךְ: [דניאל ד, כד]
י) כֹּלָּא מְטָא עַל נְבוּכַדְנֶצַּר מַלְכָּא: [דניאל ד, כה]
כ) לִקְצָת יַרְחִין תְּרֵי עֲשַׂר עַל הֵיכַל מַלְכוּתָא דִּי בָבֶל מְהַלֵּךְ הֲוָה: [דניאל ד, כו]
ל) וַתִּקְרָא אֶסְתֵּר לַהֲתָךְ מִסָּרִיסֵי הַמֶּלֶךְ אֲשֶׁר הֶעֱמִיד לְפָנֶיהָ וַתְּצַוֵּהוּ עַל מָרְדֳּכָי לָדַעַת מַה זֶּה וְעַל מַה זֶּה: [אסתר ד, ה]

[כ א מיי' פ"ג מהל' שכנים הלכה טו טוש"ע ח"מ סי' קנח סעיף ז]: כא ב ג ד ה מיי' פ"ג מהל' שכנים הל' ג סמג עשין פב טוש"ע ח"מ סי' קנח סעיף ו:

[א] נשעייה באמתא מלבר וניעבד מלגיו ועביד חבריה מלבר ואמר דידי ודידיה הוא אי הכי השתא נמי דקפיל ליה חבריה ואמר דידי ודידיה הוא ° א) קילופא מידע ידיע הוצא אמר רב נחמן סינופי ב) יריכי מלבר וניעבד מלגיו עביד נמי חבריה מלבר ואמר דידי ודידיה הוא אי הכי השתא נמי גייז ושדי ליה ואמר דידי ודידיה הוא משריק ליה טינא השתא נמי אתי חבריה וקליף ליה קילופא מידע ידיע אביי אמר הוצא לית ליה תקנתא אלא בשטרא: אבל אם עשו מדעת שניהם: אמר ליה רבא מפרזיקא לרב אשי לא יעשו לא זה ולא זה א"ל לא צריכא דקדים חד מנייהו ועבד דידיה ואי לא עביד חבריה אמר דידיה הוא (א) ותנא תקנתא לרמאי קמ"ל א"ל ורישא לאו תקנתא לרמאי הוא א"ל בשלמא רישא תנא דינא ומשום דינא תנא תקנתא אלא סיפא דינא קתני דקתני תקנתא אמר רבינא הכא בהוצי עסקינן לאפוקי מדאביי דאמר הוצא לית ליה תקנתא אלא בשטרא קמ"ל דבחזית סגיא:

מתני' ג) א המקיף את חבירו משלש רוחותיו וגדר את הראשונה ואת השניה ואת השלישית אין מחייבין אותו רבי יוסי אומר ב אם עמד וגדר את הרביעית מגלגלין עליו את הכל:

גמ' אמר רב יהודה אמר שמואל הלכה כר' יוסי דאמר אם עמד וגדר את הרביעית מגלגלין עליו את הכל ג ל"ש עמד ניקף ל"ש עמד מקיף איתמר רב הונא אמר ד הכל לפי מה שגדר חייא בר רב אמר הכל לפי דמי קנים בזול תנן המקיף את חבירו משלש רוחותיו וגדר את הראשונה ואת השניה ואת השלישית אין מחייבין אותו הא רביעית מחייבין אותו אימא סיפא רבי יוסי אומר אם עמד וגדר את הרביעית מגלגלין עליו את הכל בשלמא לרב הונא דאמר הכל לפי מה שגדר היינו דאיכא בין ת"ק (ב) ורבי יוסי ת"ק סבר דמי קנים בזול אין ומה שגדר לא ורבי יוסי סבר הכל לפי מה שגדר אלא לחייא בר רב דאמר הכל לפי דמי קנים בזול מאי איכא בין ת"ק לר' יוסי אי דמי קנים בזול לא קיהיב ליה לת"ק מאי קיהיב ליה אי בעית אימא אגר נטירא איכא בינייהו תנא קמא סבר אגר נטירא אין דמי קנים בזול לא ורבי יוסי סבר דמי קנים בזול ואי בעית אימא ראשונה שניה ושלישית איכא בינייהו ת"ק סבר רביעית הוא דיהיב ליה אבל ראשונה שניה ושלישית לא יהיב ליה ור' יוסי סבר ראשונה שניה ושלישית נמי יהיב ליה איבעית אימא מקיף וניקף איכא בינייהו דת"ק סובר טעמא דעמד ניקף (ג) דמגלגלין עליו את הכל אבל עמד מקיף אינו נותן לו אלא דמי רביעית ורבי יוסי סבר ל"ש ניקף ול"ש מקיף אם עמד וגדר מגלגלין עליו את הכל לישנא אחרינא מקיף וניקף איכא בינייהו ת"ק סבר אם גדר מקיף את הרביעית נמי יהיב ליה ורבי יוסי סבר אם עמד ניקף וגדר את הרביעית הוא דיהיב ליה דגלי דעתיה דניחא ליה אבל אם גדר מקיף לא יהיב ליה מידי

רוניא

נשעייה באמתא מלבר. יהא טח בטיט אמה בראש הכותל מבחוץ ומקפל ליה. (ד) מקפלו: **הוצא.** אם עשו מחילת נגרים כיצד יעשו חזית: **סינופי** ה) **יריכי לבר.** ראשי ההוצים יעבר לצד שדה חבירו וכשיהיה סוף ההוצים כשיכלה האחד ויתן את חבירו יכפפנו מבחוץ: הג"ה יריכי דאמרי' לעיל טפח יתירה לבניו (ה) אורכי תמ"ש. ור"ח פי' מולא ראשי הקנים ודפנא (ו) שהוא הקנים העומדים לחזוק המחילה לחוץ מתוך פירושו משמע שהקנים שמעמידין מן הצד לסמוך הכותל והוא לשון סניפין ע"כ: **אלא בשטרא.** אם עשה האחד יביא עדים ויחתמו לו ואם (ז) עשוהו שניהם יעידו עדים ויחתמו דס"ל קופלא דטינא מעליוה הוא לא ידיע: **ולא יעשו.** חזית לא לזה ולא לזה והרי סימן שלא עשאה האחד בשלו שאילו עשאה היה עושה חזית מבחוץ: **ועביד דידיה.** עשה חזית מבחוץ: **ותקנתא לרמאי.** בתמיה וכי מפני לאגת רמאין איכפל תנא למיתני הא מתני': **ורישא.** דקתני ועושה חזית מבחוץ לאו תקנתא משום רמאי הוא דלא לימא חבריה של שניהם הוא: **תנא דינא.** הואיל ובקעה אין מנהג לגדור אין יכול לכופו אלא כונס לתוך שלו ובונה ואידי דתנא דינא תנא תקנתא ועושה חזית משום רמאי אלא סיפא דינא לא תנא דהא פשיטא דאם עשו מדעת שניהם תעשה משל שניהם וכולה משום תקנתא הוא דתנייה: **מתני' המקיף את חבירו משלש רוחותיו.** שקנה ג' שדות סביב שדה חבירו לשלשה צדדיו וגדר את שלשתן ונמצא שדהו של אמצעי זה מוקף משלש רוחותיו: **אין מחייבין אותו.** לתת כלום כדאמרי' דסתם בקעה מקום שנהגו שלא לגדור הוא: הג"ה תמ"ש ול"נ טעמא משום דאכתי לא מהני ליה מידי שהכל יכולים ליכנס מרוח רביעית אבל אם גדר רביעית מחייבין אותו כדאמרינן בגמ' ולע"ג דאמרינן לעיל דסתם בקעה מקום שנהגו שלא לגדור הוא ה"מ בין בקעה לבקעה וכותל גבוה ד' אמות לשם הוא דלא בעינן (ח) מ"מ דליכא היזק ראיה אבל בשביל היזק בהמות שלא יכנסו לשדה צריך לגדור גדר שלו עשרה טפחים המונע מליכנס הבהמות: ה"ג **ר' יוסי אומר אם עמד וגדר את הרביעית.** ו) ולא גרסי' ניקף: הג"ה וכן בפירוש ר"ח ומיהו אניקף מפרשינן לה לקמן. תוס' והכי מוכח בפ"ב דב"ק והלשון מוכיח דקתני אם עמד ולא קתני אם גדר מכלל דלאו בההוא דגדר השלש מיירי. ת' מו' שמ' ע"כ: **מגלגלין עליו את הכל.** לתת חלקו בשלשת הראשונות דכיון דגדר את הצד הפתוח גלי דעתיה דניחא ליה במאי דגדר חבריה: **גמ' לפי מה שגדר.** בכל יציאות שהוציא בהן הראשון יחזיר לו מחצה: **דמי קנים.** דאמר ליה לדידי סגי לי בגדר קנים ואי אפשי בהוצאה של גדר אבנים: ה"ג **תנן המקיף את חבירו מג' רוחותיו אין מחייבין אותו הא רביעית מחייבין אותו אימא סיפא ר' יוסי אומר כו' וגדר את הראשונה כו' אין מחייבין אותו.** דהא לא אהני ליה מידי שהרי גלוי הוא מצד רביעית הא אם גדר עוד מקיף את הרביעית מחייבין אותו דאהני ליה: **אימא סיפא רבי יוסי אומר.** בשלמא לרב הונא דאמר הכל דר' יוסי במה שגדר הוא היינו דאיכא בין ת"ק לר' יוסי דת"ק דלא נקט לישנא דהכל סבר דמי קנים בזול הוא דמחייבין אותו ור' יוסי סבר כו' דהא ליכא למימר דת"ק דוקא אם גדר מקיף את הרביעית הוא דמחייבין אותו אבל אם גדר ניקף לא דכ"ש הוא השתא היכא דלא גלי דעתיה דניחא ליה בהיקיפא קא מחייב ליה כ"ש היכא דגלי ולר' יוסי נמי קס"ד השתא דתנא ניקף וה"ה למקיף אלא בגלגול דהכל הוא דפליגי: **אלא לת"ק דמי קנים נמי לא יהיב ליה אלא מאי יהיב ליה.** מאי מחייבין אותו דדייקינן ממילתיה: **יהב ליה אגר נטירא.** דבר מועט שהיה צריך ליתן לשומר בכל שנה כשהיא בקמותיה: **דתנא קמא סבר.** דמי רביעית יהיב ליה אם גדרה מקיף אבל דמי הראשונות לא יהיב ליה שסבר יצא מהם זכאי בבית דין שהיו שם ימים רבים ולא הועילו לו ואם גדרה ניקף לרביעית לא יהיב ליה מידי כדפיר' שסבר יצא ידי בית דין מהם ולר' יוסי לא שנא גדרה ניקף ולא שנא מקיף מגלגלין עליו (ט) את הכל בכולן דמי קנים: **ואיבעית אימא מקיף וניקף איכא בינייהו.** דתנא קמא אית ליה דרבי יוסי היכא דגדרה ניקף אבל רבי יוסי לית ליה דתנא קמא תנא קמא בגדר מקיף תנא קמא סבר לא שנא ניקף ולא שנא מקיף כי גדר לרביעית מחייבין אותו דהא תנא קמא במקיף איירי ודייקינן ממילתיה הא רביעית מחייבין אותו וכל שכן כשגדרה ניקף דגלי דעתיה:

ורבי

לאפוקי מדאביי. ואביי סבר דשפיר אית ליה למיתני תקנתא לרמאי: **אם** עמד וגדר את הרביעית. ל"ג אם עמד ניקף דהא לכולהו ליתני דגמרא קאי אמקיף בר מלישנא בתרא דקאמר מקיף וניקף איכא בינייהו והא דדייק בפרק כילד הרגל (ב"ק דף כ: ושם) טעמא דניקף הא מקיף פטור היינו להנהו לישנא: **דמי** קנים בזול. וא"ת מאי שנא משדה שאינה עשויה ליטע דאם נטעה חבירו שלא ברשות אמר רב ושמואל בהשואל (ב"מ דף קא.) שמין לו וידו על התחתונה ואור"י דשאני הכא דמצי א"ל לדידי סגי לי בנטירא בר זוזא ומ"מ דמי קנים בזול יהיב ליה דאכן סהדי דאם היה מוצאם כ"כ בזול היה גודר בהם: **שניה** ושלישית לא. אומר ר"י דהיינו טעמא דאין לך אדם שלא היה מסייע לרביעית ע"מ שיהא גדור מד' רוחותיו ובקונטרס פירש לפי שסבר יצא מן השלשה מב"ד זכאי: הג"ה וקצת קשה דא"כ גם ברביעית יצא זכאי עד טפח אחרון ע"כ: **ורבי** יוסי סבר אם עמד ניקף וגדר את הרביעית. אע"ג דעד השתא היה מתמיר כדמשמע לישנא דמגלגלין עליו את הכל להכי לישנא לא הוי הכי דלשון אם עמד משמע ניקף:

רבינו גרשום

נשעייה עליה אמה מלבר. שאמה העליונה מייסד אותה בסיד על פני כולה לאורך הכותל מבחוץ לצד חבירו: **קפיל ליה.** שיבא חבירו בסתר ומקליף אותו הסיד: **מידע ידיע.** מקום הקילוף ולא יועיל לו: כל הני דאמרן היינו בכותל של אבנים אבל [אם] אותו כותל מקני **הוצא** הוא מאי חזית מצי למקבע ביה **דסניף** ליה **ריבי מלבר** דלכי גדיל להו להוצא ליכוון דליהוי רישיהו דהוצא כייפי לבר לאותו צד של חבירו (שדין) **[ושריק] ליה טינא** דלא מצי חבירו לגזוז להו (ולא למישדינהו) [ולמישדינהו] דאיכא היכרא ומקשינן אפ"ה **אתי חבריה (ומקבל) [ומקפל]** להההוא טינא ושדי ליה **ואמר דידי ודידך הוא** (וישנו) [ומשני] **קילופא מידע ידיע: אביי אמר.** בשום ענין לכותל **הוצין אין לו תקנה** לעשות שום היכר שיהא כולו שלו שחבירו לא יכול לרמותו **אלא בשטרא** אא"כ יכתבו לו שטר שכולו שלו ואין לחבירו בו כלום: **ואם עשו מדעת שניהם.** כותל בבקעה בונין אותו שניהן בשותפות ועושין חזית מכאן ומכאן להיכרא שהכותל של שניהם הוא: **ולא יעשה חזית לא זה ולא זה.** וממילא ידעינן דשל שניהם הוא דכיון דלאחד אין לו חזקה בו יותר מחבירו לא יוכל לטוענו דכולו שלו הוא: **לא צריכא. דאקדים חד ועביד** חזית מצד שלו להכי צריך למעבד אידך: **אמר לו וכי תנא** דמתני' לא אתי לאשמועינן בהא סיפא אלא **תקנתא דרמאי. בשלמא רישא תנא דינא ותנא תקנתא.** תנא אם רוצה כונס בתוך שלו דאף על גב דחבירו אינו רוצה שימעט לו באויר אינו יכול לעכב עליו היינו דינא ואגב דאיצטריך למיתני דינא תנא נמי תקנתא אבל סיפא לא אית ביה דינא כלל דהא דקתני מתני' אבל אם עשו מדעת שניהם בונין את הכותל באמצע לאו דינא הוא דמדעתייהו עבדי: **רבינא אמר בהוצא עסקינן כו'.** כלומר אפי' סיפא לא אתי לאורויי תקנתא כלל לרמאי אלא לאורויי אכותל דהוצא לאפוקי מדאביי דאמר לית ליה תקנתא אלא בשטרא קמ"ל דבחזית סגי בלא שטרא: **מתני' המקיף את חבירו מג' רוחותיו.** כגון שהיו לו למקיף ד' שדות מכאן וא' מכאן ואדם אחר שהיה באמצעיתן של אותן שדות ורצה בעל שדותיו לגדור **את הא'** ואת הב' ואת הג' ומאותן גדרים של אותן שדות לא היתה משתמרת שדהו של זה הואיל שלא גדר שדה רביעית **אין מחייבין** הניקף ליתן חלקו המגיעו באותן ג' גדרים הואיל ועדיין אינו משומר שדהו שעדיין פתוח מרוח א': **ר' יוסי אומר אם עמד מקיף וגדר שדה רביעית מגלגלין לו את הכל** לניקף ליתן בכל אותן ג' גדרים לפי חלקו המגיעו דעכשיו שדהו משתמרת בכל צד: **גמ' הכל כמה שגדר.** כלומר אם זה המקיף גדר שדותיו בכותל יפה של אבנים חייב ליתן לו זה הניקף לפי חלקו במה שהוציא זה על אותן גדרים ואין יכול לטעון לדידי סגי לי בכותל רעוע של מחיצת קנים: **חייא בר רב אמר.** מצי ליטען ליה ולא יהיב ליה אלא **דמי קנים בזול** כמו שאם היו גדרים של קנים: **בשלמא לרב הונא דאמר במה שגדר היינו דאיכא בין ת"ק ור' יוסי.** דדייקי הכי הא רביעית **לת"ק** מחייבין אותו **דמי קנים בזול** ואתי **ר' יוסי** למימר לחלוק על ת"ק ואמר את אמרת דמי קנים בזול ואנא אמינא **במה שגדר** כעין שהוציא: **אלא לחייא בר רב דאמר.** לטעמא דר' יוסי דמחייב לניקף ליתן **דמי קנים בזול מאי איכא בין ת"ק לר' יוסי.** כלומר מאי יהיב לת"ק בציר מדמי קנים בזול (ולטעמיה) אי האי פורתא דלא יהיב דמי קנים בזול מאי יהיב ליה. לעולם כדאמר חייא בר רב דלר' יוסי לא יהיב ליה אלא דמי קנים בזול והאי דמקשית מאי איכא בין ת"ק לר' יוסי **איכא בינייהו ראשונה שניה ושלישית דת"ק סבר** אם עמד מקיף וגדר את הרביעית מחייבין ליה לניקף דמי קנים בזול מאותה **רביעית** אבל מאינך אחרינא **לא יהיב ליה** כלל **ור' יוסי סבר דראשונה ושניה ושלישית נמי יהיב ליה דמי קנים בזול: ואיבעית אימא מקיף וניקף איכא בינייהו. דת"ק סבר אם עמד מקיף** נמי וגדר את הרביעית מחייבי ליה לניקף ליתן דמי קנים בזול מאותה רביעית ולא יותר דמצי ליטען ניקף אנא הוינא יתיב ומנטר לשדה שלי. **ור' יוסי אומר אם עמד** ניקף **וגדר את הרביעית** ה' גדרים דמי קנים בזול דהואיל והוא עצמו גדר את הרביעית גלי אדעתיה דניחא ליה באינך גדרים. **אבל אם** עמד מקיף **וגדר** את הרביעית **לא יהיב** ליה כלל דמצי למימר אנא הויתי מנטר שדה שלי: **אגר נטירא איכא בינייהו.** האי דקשיא ליה לעיל לת"ק מאי קיהיב ליה אגר נטירא מאי דהאי ניקף הוי יהיב לשומר שדהו דעכשיו לא צריך דהיינו בציר מדמי קנים בזול. **ור' יוסי סבר מגלגלין עליו את הכל** דיהיב ניקף דמי קנים בזול מכלהו גדרים:

א) [גי' הערוך ערך קפל ג' קיפולא], ב) נ"א ריבי. רש"ל, ג) ב"ק כ:, ד) נ"א יריי. רש"ל, ה) נ"א יכפ, ו) הן ול"ג ניקף אינו מפירש"י רק שייך בהג"ה. רש"ל.

הגהות הב"ח

(א) גמ' דידיה הוא א"ל ותנא תקנתא לרמאי וכו' א"ל הכי קאי בשלמא רישא: (ב) שם היינו דאיכא בין ת"ק לר' יוסי ת"ק סבר דמי קנים כו' ומיבת הכל לפי נמחק: (ג) שם דעמד ניקף הוא דמגלגלין: (ד) רש"י ד"ה ומקפל ליה מקפלו הס"ד: (ה) ד"ה הג"ה יריכי וכו' יתירה לבניו יריכי תמ"ש. נ"ב כך היה גורס בעל הג"ה וכך הוא גי' רמינו יוסף: (ו) בא"ד ודפנא שהן הקנים: (ז) ד"ה אלא כו' אם עשאוהו שניהם: (ח) ד"ה הג"ה תמ"ש וכו' דלא בעינן דליכא כל"ל ותיבת מ"מ נמחק: (ט) ד"ה דת"ק סבר וכו' מגלגלין עליו בכולן כל"ל ותיבת את הכל נמחק:

גליון הש"ס

גמרא קילופא מידע ידיע. בתשב"ץ ח"ג סי' ק"ג היה לו הגירסא כאן קיפולא וכ' שהוא היפוך הלשון מלשון קילוף וכעין מ"ש רש"י תולין על ע"ג ד"ה לאקפל.

ליקוטי רש"י

משלש רוחותיו. שהיו לו לראובן שלש שדות אצל שדה שמעון משלש רוחותיו. **וגדר.** ראובן את הראשונה סמוך לשדה שמעון לבד מאותן מחיצות שהיו לו בינו לשאר הבקעות. **אין מחייבין אותו.** אין מחייבין את שמעון כלום דאמר ליה הרי שדה פתוחה מצד רביעית. **אם עמד וגדר את הרביעית.** גלי דעתיה דניחא ליה בהקיפו של ראובן ומגלגלים עליו את הכל לתת את חלקו בג' מחיצות פנימיות של ראובן. **הא רביעית.** הא אם היה לו לראובן ד' שדות מארבע רוחות של שמעון וגדרן מחייבין את שמעון לתת את חלקו במחיצות פנימיות שבינו לראובן. **גדר מקיף לא יהיב ליה מידי.** אם קנה מקיף עוד שדה רביעית אצל שמעון וגדרה פטור שמעון [ב"ק כ:].

נִשַׁעְיֵיהּ בְּאַמְּתָא מִלְּבַר – Let him simply **smear [the wall]** with lime **on the outside** at the top **to the extent of an *amah*.** According to R' Yochanan, the owner need not create a protrusion of stones and cement.

The Gemara asks:

וְנֶיעֱבַד מִלְּגָיו – **But let him make** the sign **on the inside?** Why have it face his neighbor's property?

The Gemara answers:

עָבִיד חַבְרֵיהּ מִלְּבַר וְאָמַר – If the owner makes the sign on his side, **his neighbor may make** another **on the outside and say,** **דִּידִי וְדִידֵיהּ הוּא** – **["The wall] is mine and yours,"** pointing to both signs as proof. Thus, the builder should position his sign on the outer face of the wall, thereby preempting that side, while obviously denying the neighbor access to the inside face of the wall.

The Gemara persists:

אִי הָכִי – **If** it is **so** that the neighbor's integrity is a factor, **הַשְׁתָּא נַמִּי** – **even** now that the sign faces outward **דְּקָפִיל לֵיהּ חַבְרֵיהּ וְאָמַר** – be concerned **that his neighbor will peel off [the coating of lime] and say,** **דִּידִי וְדִידֵיהּ הוּא** – **"[The wall] is mine and yours.** We simply failed to add the obligatory signs after building it together." What, then, is the advantage of placing the sign on the outside of the wall, if the neighbor can destroy it?

The Gemara answers:

קִילוּפָא מֵידַע יְדִיעַ – **A peeling** of the lime coating **is discernible;** hence, the neighbor will be unable to claim half the wall by surreptitiously removing the sign. Therefore, it is clearly advantageous to apply the sign to the outer face of the wall.

The Gemara continues its discussion of "signs":

הוּצָא – If the wall is made of **palm fronds,**[1] how is a sign made?[2]

אָמַר רַב נַחְמָן סִינוּפֵי יְרִיכֵי מִלְּבַר – **Rav Nachman said: The tips of the palm fronds should be attached on the outside.**[3]

The Gemara asks:

וְנֶיעֱבַד מִלְּגָיו – **But let him make** the fence so that the tips are joined **on the inside?** Why should they face his neighbor's property?

The Gemara answers:

עָבִיד נַמִּי חַבְרֵיהּ מִלְּבַר וְאָמַר – If the tips are joined on the inside, **his neighbor may also** add some branches and **arrange** the tips **on the outside** (which is his side) **and say,** **דִּידִי וְדִידֵיהּ הוּא** – **"[The wall] is mine and yours,"** pointing to the signs as proof. Thus, the owner places the tips on the outside, thereby preventing the neighbor from adding his own signs and claiming partnership.

The Gemara persists:

אִי הָכִי – **If** it is **so** that the neighbor's integrity is a factor, **הַשְׁתָּא נַמִּי** – **even now** that the tips face outward **גָּיֵיז וְשָׁדֵי לֵיהּ** – the neighbor **can lop off [the tips] and discard them** **וְאָמַר דִּידִי וְדִידֵיהּ הוּא** – **and say, "[The wall] is mine and yours,** but we simply failed to create signs to prove it."

The Gemara suggests a deterrent:

מַשְׁרִיק לֵיהּ טִינָא – The builder should **coat [the fence] with mud** so that the tips cannot be removed, thus preserving the sign.

The Gemara faults this method:

הַשְׁתָּא נַמִּי אָתֵי חַבְרֵיהּ וְקָלֵיף לֵיהּ – **Even now** the owner is not protected, for **his neighbor will come and scrape [the mud]** from the tips and then lop them off, claiming that the fence was jointly constructed!

The Gemara answers this objection:

קִילוּפָא מֵידַע יְדִיעַ – The **scraping** of mud from the palm leaves **is discernible** at the place just below the cut. Hence, any attempt to tamper with the sign will be noticed.

Abaye takes issue with this assertion:

אַבַּיֵי אָמַר הוּצָא לֵית לֵיהּ תַּקַּנְתָּא – **Abaye said:** (One who builds) **a fence of palm leaves has no remedy** against false claims of ownership[4] **אֶלָּא בִּשְׁטָרָא** – **except with a document.**[5]

The Mishnah further stated:

אֲבָל אִם עָשׂוּ מִדַּעַת שְׁנֵיהֶם – BUT IF THEY ACTED to erect the wall BY MUTUAL CONSENT etc.

The Mishnah states that when a wall is built by mutual consent between two fields, two signs must be erected to indicate joint ownership. The Gemara raises an obvious question:

אָמַר לֵיהּ רָבָא מִפַּרְזִיקָא לְרַב אַשִׁי – **Rava from** the town of **Prazika said to Rav Ashi:** **לֹא יַעֲשׂוּ לֹא זֶה וְלֹא זֶה** – **Let neither this** neighbor **nor that** neighbor **make** a sign, and still we would know that the wall is jointly owned![6] Why bother to fashion two signs?

Rav Ashi answers:

אָמַר לֵיהּ לֹא צְרִיכָא – Rav Ashi **said to [Rava]: No, it is necessary** to make two signs in a case **דְּקָדִים חַד מִנַּיְיהוּ וְעָבֵד דִּידֵיהּ** – **where one [of the neighbors] went ahead and made his** sign while the wall was being built,[7] **וְאִי לֹא עָבִיד חַבְרֵיהּ** – **and if his neighbor does not make** another sign immediately, **אָמַר דִּידֵיהּ הוּא** – **he will say** that **[the wall] is his.**[8] Thus, the absence of signs indeed indicates joint ownership. However, in a case of fraud such as this the Mishnah advises the other partner to make a second sign.[9]

Rava from Prazika questions this explanation:[10]

[אָמַר לֵיהּ – **[Rava] said to [Rav Ashi]:]** **וְתַנָּא תַּקַּנְתָּא לְרַמָּאֵי קָא מַשְׁמַע לַן** – **But does the Tanna teach us a remedy against deceivers?!**[11]

NOTES

1. This is the type of wall mentioned in the Gemara above (4a). It consists of laurel branches fixed at intervals and palm leaves woven between them to form the fence.

2. Neither method mentioned above is feasible with such a fence.

3. I.e. when weaving the palm branches around the laurel branches, the tips of the palm branches should be joined on the neighbor's side of the fence (*Rashi*).

4. Abaye maintains that it is possible to scrape mud from a palm branch without leaving a trace (*Rashi*). [Hence, a dishonest neighbor could effectively remove the sign and claim partial ownership.]

5. Hence, if the fence is built unilaterally, the owner should have witnesses attest to that fact in writing. If the neighbors built it jointly, the witnesses who observed the partnership agreement should attest to the joint construction in writing (*Rashi*; see *Rashash*, *Shiurei R' Shmuel*).

6. The absence of signs is itself a sign that the wall was built in partnership, for if one had acted alone he would have placed a sign on the outer face of the wall (*Rashi*; see also *Tosafos* above 2a ד״ה לפיכך, *Ramban*, *Rashba*).

7. Although his sign must be placed on his neighbor's side of the wall (which is normally off limits to him), here he acted while engaged in constructing the wall, when it was possible for him to place the sign there (*R' Yonah, Rashba, Nimukei Yosef*).

8. If the second sign is made at a later date, the unscrupulous neighbor will claim that the other was attempting to defraud him.

9. This interpretation follows our text, which states: דְּקָדִים, *where he went ahead*, implying that the Mishnah's rule applies only to this specific case, i.e. where one neighbor had already attempted a deception. *Rashash,* however, cites the emendation of *Nimukei Yosef*: דִּילְמָא קָדִים, *perhaps he will go ahead,* which implies that in *all* cases of joint construction two signs are required as a precautionary measure.

10. The following emendation follows *Bach,* who adds אָמַר לֵיהּ, *[Rava] said to [Rav Ashi],* at this point in the text.

11. Does the Tanna bother to author a ruling in the Mishnah simply out of concern for unscrupulous individuals? (*Rashi;* see *Chason Ish* 1:11, *Nachalas Moshe*).

עין משפט נר מצוה

[כ א מיי' פ"ב מהל' שכנים הלכה ט סמג עשין פב טוש"ע ח"מ סי' קנח סעיף ד]: כא ב ג ד מיי' פ"ג מהל' שכנים הל' ג סמג עשין פב טוש"ע ח"מ סי' קנח סעיף ו:

[א] נשעייה באמתא מלבר וניעבד מלגיו עביד חבריה מלבר ודידיה הוא אי הכי השתא נמי דקפיל ליה חבריה ואמר דידי ודידיה הוא * קילופא מידע ידיע הוצא אמר רב נחמן סינופי יריכי מלבר וניעבד מלגיו עביד נמי חבריה מלבר ואמר דידי ודידיה הוא אי הכי השתא נמי גייז ושדי ליה ואמר דידי ודידיה הוא משריק ליה טינא השתא נמי אתי חבריה וקליף ליה קילופא מידע ידיע אביי אמר הוצא לית ליה תקנתא אלא בשטרא: אבל אם עשו מדעת שניהם: אמר ליה רבא מפרזיקא לרב אשי לא יעשו לא זה ולא זה א"ל לא צריכא דקדים חד מנייהו ועבד דידיה ואי לא עביד חבריה אמר דידיה הוא (א) ותנא תקנתא לרמאי קמ"ל א"ל ורישא לאו תקנתא לרמאי הוא א"ל בשלמא רישא תנא דינא ומשום דינא תנא תקנתא אלא סיפא דינא קתני דקתני תקנתא אמר רבינא הכא בהוצי עסקינן לאפוקי מדאביי דאמר הוצא לית ליה תקנתא אלא בשטרא קמ"ל דבחזית סגיא:

מתני' המקיף את חבירו משלש רוחותיו וגדר את הראשונה ואת השניה ואת השלישית אין מחייבין אותו רבי יוסי אומר אם עמד וגדר את הרביעית מגלגלין עליו את הכל:

גמ' אמר רב יהודה אמר שמואל הלכה כר' יוסי דאמר אם עמד וגדר את הרביעית מגלגלין עליו את הכל ל"ש עמד ניקף ל"ש עמד מקיף איתמר רב הונא אמר הכל לפי מה שגדר חייא בר רב אמר הכל לפי דמי קנים בזול תנן המקיף את חבירו משלש רוחותיו וגדר את הראשונה ואת השניה ואת השלישית אין מחייבין אותו הא רביעית מחייבין אותו אימא סיפא רבי יוסי אומר אם עמד וגדר את הרביעית מגלגלין עליו את הכל בשלמא לרב הונא דאמר הכל לפי מה שגדר היינו דאיכא בין ת"ק (ג) ורבי יוסי ת"ק סבר הכל לפי דמי קנים בזול ורבי יוסי סבר הכל לפי מה שגדר אלא לחייא בר רב דאמר הכל לפי דמי קנים בזול מאי איכא בין ת"ק לר' יוסי אי דמי קנים בזול לא קיהיב ליה מאי קיהיב ליה אי בעית אימא אגר נטירא איכא בינייהו תנא קמא סבר אגר נטירא אין דמי קנים בזול לא ורבי יוסי סבר דמי קנים בזול ואי בעית אימא ראשונה שניה ושלישית איכא בינייהו ת"ק סבר רביעית הוא דיהיב ליה אבל ראשונה שניה ושלישית לא יהיב ליה ור' יוסי סבר ראשונה שניה ושלישית נמי יהיב ליה איבעית אימא מקיף וניקף איכא בינייהו דת"ק סובר טעמא דעמד ניקף (ג) דמגלגלין עליו את הכל אבל עמד מקיף אינו נותן לו אלא דמי רביעית ורבי יוסי סבר ל"ש ניקף ול"ש מקיף אם עמד וגדר מגלגלין עליו את הכל לישנא אחרינא מקיף וניקף איכא בינייהו ת"ק סבר אם גדר מקיף את הרביעית נמי יהיב ליה ורבי יוסי סבר אם עמד ניקף וגדר את הרביעית הוא דיהיב ליה דגלי דעתיה דניחא ליה אבל אם גדר מקיף לא יהיב ליה מידי

רוניא

נשעייה באמתא מלבר. יטח בטיט אמה בראש הכותל מבחוץ: ומקפל ליה. (ד) מקפלו: הוצא. אם עשו מחיצת הוצים כיצד יעשו חזית: סינופי (ה) יריכי לבר. ראשי ההוצים יהיו לצד שדה חבירו וכשיהיה סוף ההוצים כשיכלה האחד ויתחיל את חבירו יכפפו מבחוץ:

הג"ה יריכי כדאמרי' לעיל טפח יתירה לבינ (ה) אורכי תמ"ש. ור"ח פי' מולים ראשי הקנים ודפנא (ו) שהוא הקנים העומדים לחיזוק המחיצה לחוץ מתוך פירושו משמע שהקנים שמעמידין מן הצד לסמוך הכותל וזהו לשון סניפין ע"כ: אלא בשטרא. אם עשה האחד יביא עדים ויחתמו לו ואם (ז) עשהו שנים יעידו עדים ויחתמו דס"ל קופלא דטינא מעלויה הוא לא ידיע: ולא יעשו. חזית לא לזה ולא לזה והרי סימן שלא עשאה האחד בשלו שאילו עשאה היה עושה חזית מבחוץ: ועביד דידיה. עשה חזית מבחוץ: ותקנתא לרמאי. בתמיה וכי מפני דאגת רמאין איכפל תנא לאשמעינן הא מתני': ורישא. דקתני ועושה חזית מבחוץ לאו תקנתא משום רמאי הוא דלא לימא חבריה של שניהם הוא: תנא דינא. הואיל ובקעה אין מנהג לגדור אין יכול לכופו אלא כונס לתוך שלו ובונה ואיידי דתנא דינא תנא תקנתא ועושה חזית משום רמאי אלא סיפא דינא לא תנא דהא פשיטא דאם עשו מדעת שניהם תעשה משל שניהם וכולה משום תקנתא הוא דתנייה: מתני' המקיף את חבירו משלש רוחותיו. שקנה ג' שדות סביב שדה חבירו לשלשה מצריה וגדר את שלשתן ונמצא שדהו של אמצעי זה מוקף משלש רוחותיו: אין מחייבין אותו. לתת כלום כדאמרי' דסתם בקעה מקום שנהגו שלא לגדור הוא: הג"ה תמ"ש ול"נ טעמא משום דאכתי לא מהני ליה מידי שהכל יכולים ליכנס מרוח רביעית אבל אם גדר רביעית מחייבין אותו כדאמרינן בגמ' ולעיל נמי לגדור הוא ה"מ בין בקעה לבקעה וכותל גבוה ד' אמות לשם הוא דלא בעינן (ח) מ"ט דליכא היזק ראיה אבל בשביל היזק בהמות שלא יכנסו לשדה צריך לגדור גדר שלו עשרה טפחים המונע מליכנס הבהמות: ה"ג ר' יוסי אומר אם עמד וגדר את הרביעית. ולא גרסי' ניקף: הג"ה וכן בפירוש ר"ח ומיהו אניקף מפרשינן לה לקמן. תוס' והכי מוכח בפ"ב דב"ק והלשון מוכיח דקתני אם עמד ולא קתני אם גדר מכלל דלאו בההוא דגדר השלש איירי. ת' מו' שמ' ע"כ: מגלגלין עליו את הכל. לתת חלקו בשלשת הראשונות דכיון דגדר את הצד הפתוח גלי דעתיה דניחא ליה במאי דגדר חבריה: **גמ'** לפי מה שגדר. בכל יציאות שהוציא בהן הראשון יחזיר לו מחצה: דמי קנים. דאמר ליה לדידי סגי לי בגדר קנים ולא אפשי בהוצאה של גדר אבנים: ה"ג תנן המקיף את חבירו מג' רוחותיו וגדר את הראשונה כו' אין מחייבין אותו הא רביעית מחייבין אותו אימא סיפא ר' יוסי אומר כו' וגדר את הראשונה כו' אין מחייבין אותו. דהא לא אהני ליה מידי שהרי גלוי הוא מצד רביעית הא אם גדר עוד מקיף את הרביעית מחייבין אותו דאהני ליה: אימא סיפא רבי יוסי אומר. בשלמא לרב הונא דאמר הכל דר' יוסי במה שגדר הוא היינו דאיכא בין ת"ק לר' יוסי דת"ק דלא נקט לישנא דהכל סבר דמי קנים בזול הוא דמחייבין אותו ור' יוסי סבר כו' דהא ליכא למימר דת"ק דוקא אם גדר מקיף את הרביעית הוא דמחייבין אותו אבל אם גדר ניקף לא דכ"ש הוא השתא היכא דלא גלי דעתיה דניחא ליה בהיקיפא קא מחייב ליה כ"ש היכא דגלי ולר' יוסי נמי קס"ד השתא דתנא ניקף וה"ה למקיף אלא בגלגול דהכל הוא דפליגי: אלא לת"ק דמי קנים נמי לא יהיב ליה אלא מאי יהיב ליה. מאי מחייבין אותו דדייקינן ממילתיה: יהב ליה אגר נטירא. דבר מועט שהיה צריך ליתן לשומר בכל שנה כשהיא בקמותיה: דתנא קמא סבר. דמי רביעית יהיב ליה אם גדרה מקיף אבל דמי הראשונות לא יהיב ליה שכבר יצא מהם וזכאי בבית דין שהיו שם ימים רבים ולא הועילו לו ואם גדרה ניקף לרביעית לא יהיב ליה מידי כדפיר' שכבר יצא ידי בית דין מהם ולר' יוסי לא שנא גדרה ניקף ולא שנא מקיף מגלגלין עליו (ט) את הכל בכולן דמי קנים: ואיבעית אימא מקיף וניקף איכא בינייהו. דתנא קמא אית ליה דרבי יוסי היכא דגדרה ניקף אבל רבי יוסי לית ליה דתנא קמא בגדר מקיף תנא קמא סבר לא שנא ניקף ולא שנא מקיף כי גדר לרביעית מחייבין אותו דהא תנא קמא במקיף איירי ודייקינן ממילתיה הא רביעית מחייבין אותו וכל שכן כשגדרה ניקף דגלי דעתיה:

ורבי

לאפוקי מדאביי. ואביי סבר דשפיר אית ליה למיתני תקנתא לרמאי: אם עמד וגדר את הרביעית. ל"ג אם עמד ניקף דהא לכולהו לישני דגמרא קאי אמקיף בר מלישנא בתרא דקאמר מקיף וניקף איכא בינייהו והא דדייק בפרק כיצד הרגל (ב"ק דף כ: ושם) טעמא דניקף הא מקיף פטור היינו להההוא לישנא: דמי קנים בזול. וא"ת מאי שנא משדה שאינה עשויה ליטע דאם נטעה חבירו שלא ברשות אמר רב ושמואל בהשואל (ב"מ דף קא.) שמין לו וידו על התחתונה ואור"י דשאני הכא דמצי א"ל לדידי סגי לי בנטירה בר זוזא ומ"מ דמי קנים בזול יהיב ליה דלאו שהדי דאם היה מוצאם כ"כ בזול היה גודר בהם: שניה ושלישית לא. אומר ר"י דהיינו טעמא דאין לך אדם שלא היה מסייע לרביעית ע"מ שיהיה גודר מג' רוחותיו וקונטרס פירש לפי שכבר יצא מן השלשה מב"ד זכאי: הג"ה וקצת קשה דא"כ גם ברביעית יצא זכאי עד טפח אחרון ע"כ: ורבי יוסי סבר אם עמד ניקף וגדר את הרביעית. אע"ג דעד השתא היה מחמיר כדמשמע לישנא דמגלגלין עליו את הכל להך לישנא לא הוי הכי לשון אם עמד משמע ניקף:

רבינו גרשום

נשעייה עליה אמה מלבר. שאמה העליונה מייסד אותה בסיד על פני כולה לאורך הכותל מבחוץ לצד חבירו: קפיל ליה. שיבא חבירו בסתר ומקליף אותו הסיד: מידע ידיע. מקום הקילוף ולא יועיל לו: כל הני דאמרן היינו בכותל של אבנים אבל [אם] אותו כותל מקני הוצא הוא מאי חזית מצי למקבע ביה דסניף ליה: רבי נחמן: ירכי מלבר דלכי גדיל להו להוצא ליכון דליהוי רישייהו דהוצא כייפי לבר לאותו צד של חבירו (שדין) [ושריק] ליה טינא דלא מצי חבירו לגזוז להו (ולא למישדינהו) [ולמישדינהו] ואיכא היכירא ומקשינן אפ"ה אתי חבריה (ומקבל) [ומקפל] להוהא טינא ושדי ליה ואמר דידי ודידך הוא (ורשנו) [ומשנו] קילופא מידע ידיע: אביי אמר. בשום ענין לכותל הוצין אין לו תקנה לעשות שום היכר שיהא כולו שלו שחבירו לא יכול לרמותו אלא בשטרא אא"כ יכתבו לו שטר שכותל שלו ואין לחבירו בו כלום: ואם עשו מדעת שניהם. כותל בבקעה בבנין אותו שניהן בשותפות ועושין חזית מכאן ומכאן להיכרא שהכותל של שניהם הוא: ולא יעשה חזית לא זה ולא זה. וממילא ידעינן דשל שניהם הוא כיון דלאחד אין לו חזקה בו יותר מחבירו לא יוכל לטוענו דכולו שלו הוא: לא צריכא. דאקדים חד ועביד חזית מצד שלו להכי צריך למעבד אידך: אמר לו ותני תנא דמתני' לא אתי לאשמועינן בהא סיפא אלא תקנתא לרמאי. בשלמא רישא תנא דינא ותנא תקנתא. תנא אם רוצה כונס בתוך שלו דאף על גב דחבירו אינו רוצה שימעט לו באויר אינו יכול לעכב עליו היינו דינא ואגב דאיצטריך למיתני דינא תנא נמי תקנתא אבל סיפא לא אית ביה דינא כלל דהא דקתני מתני' אבל אם עשו מדעת שניהם בונין את הכותל באמצע לאו דינא הוא דמדעתייהו עבדי: רבינא בהוצא עסקינן כו'. כלומר אפי' סיפא לא אתי לאורויי כלל לרמאי אלא לאורויי אכותל דהוצא לאפוקי מדאביי דאמר לית ליה תקנתא אלא בשטרא קמ"ל דבחזית סגי בלא שטרא: מתני' המקיף את חבירו מג' רוחותיו. כגון שהיו לו למקיף ד' שדות א' מכאן וא' מכאן לשדה של אדם אחר שהיה באמצעיתן של אותן שדות ורצה בעל אותן ד' שדות לגדור שדותיו וגדר את הא' ואת הב' ואת הג' ומאותן גדרים של אותן שדות לא היתה משתמרת שדהו של זה הואיל שלא גדר שדה רביעית **אין מחייבין** הניקף ליתן חלקו המגיעו באותן ג' גדרים הואיל ועדיין אינו משומר שדהו שעדיין פתוח מרוח א': **ר' יוסי אומר אם עמד מקיף וגדר שדה רביעית מגלגלין לו את הכל** לניקף ליתן בכל אותן ג' גדרים לפי חלקו המגיעו דעכשיו שדהו משתמרת בכל צד: **גמ' הכל כמה שגדר.** כלומר אם זה המקיף גדר שדותיו בכותל יפה של אבנים חייב ליתן לו זה הניקף לפי חלקו במה שהוציא זה על אותן גדרים ואין יכול לטעון לדידי סגי לי בכותל רעוע של מחיצת קנים: **חייא בר רב אמר.** מצי ליטען ליה ולא יהיב ליה אלא **דמי קנים בזול** כמו שאם היו גדרים של קנים: **בשלמא לרב הונא דאמר במה שגדר היינו דאיכא בין ת"ק ור' יוסי.** דדייקי הכי הא רביעית **לת"ק** מחייבין אותו **דמי קנים בזול** ואתי **ר' יוסי** למימר לחלוק על ת"ק ואמר את אמרת דמי קנים בזול ואנא אמינא דמחייבין אותו **במה שגדר** כעין שהוציא: **אלא לחייא בר רב דאמר.** לטעמא דר' יוסי דמחייב לניקף ליתן **דמי קנים בזול מאי איכא בין ת"ק לר' יוסי.** כלומר מאי יהיב לת"ק בציר מדמי קנים בזול (ולטעמיה) אי האי פורתא דלא יהיב ליה דמי קנים בזול מאי יהיב ליה. לעולם כדאמר חייא בר רב דלר' יוסי לא יהיב ליה אלא דמי קנים בזול והאי דמקשית מאי איכא בין ת"ק לר' יוסי **איכא בינייהו ראשונה שניה ושלישית דת"ק סבר** אם עמד מקיף וגדר את הרביעית מחייבין ליה לניקף דמי קנים בזול מאותה **רביעית** אבל מאינך אחרינא **לא יהיב ליה** כלל **ור' יוסי סבר דראשונה ושניה ושלישית נמי יהיב ליה דמי קנים בזול: ואיבעית אימא מקיף וניקף איכא בינייהו. דת"ק סבר אם עמד מקיף** וגדר את הרביעית מחייבי ליה לניקף ליתן דמי קנים בזול מאותה רביעית ולא יותר דמצי ליטען ניקף אנא הוינא יתיב ומנטר לשדה שלי. **ור' יוסי אומר אם עמד ניקף וגדר את הרביעית** יהיב ליה מכוליה גדרים דמי קנים בזול דהואיל והוא עצמו גדר את הרביעית גלי אדעתיה דניחא ליה באינך גדרים. **אבל אם** עמד **מקיף וגדר** את הרביעית **לא יהיב** ליה כלל דמצי למימר אנא הויתי מנטר שדה שלי: **אגר נטירא איכא בינייהו.** דהאי דקשיא ליה לעיל לת"ק מאי קיהיב ליה אגר נטירא מאי דהאי ניקף הוי יהיב לשומר שדהו דעכשיו לא צריך דהיינו בציר מדמי קנים בזול. **ור' יוסי סבר מגלגלין עליו את הכל** דיהיב ניקף דמי קנים בזול מכולהו גדרים:

מסורת הש"ס

א) [גי' הערוך ערך קפל ג' קיפולא], ב) נ"א ריבי, רש"ל, ג) ב"ק כ, ד) נ"א ריבי, רש"ל, ה) נ"ל יסב, רש"ל, ו) כן ול"ג ניקף אינו מפירש"י רק שייך בהג"ה. רש"א.

הגהות הב"ח

(א) גמ' דידיה הוא ותנא תקנתא לרמאי וכו' א"ל הא מאי בשלמא רישא: (ב) שם (ג) שם היינו דאיכא בין ת"ק לר' יוסי ת"ק סבר דמי קנים כל"ל ותיבת הכל לפני נמחק: (ג) שם דעמד ניקף הוא דמגלגלין: (ד) רש"י ד"ה ומקפל ליה מקלפו הס"ד: (ה) ד"ה הג"ה יריכי וכו' יתירה לבינ יריכי תמ"ש. נ"ב כך היה גורס בעל הג"ה וכך הוא גי' נימוקי יוסף: (ו) בא"ד ודפנא שהן הקנים: (ז) ד"ה אלא כו' ואם עשאוהו שנים: (ח) ד"ה הג"ה תמ"ש וכו' דלא בעינן דליכא כל"ל ותיבת מ"ט נמחק: (ט) ד"ה דת"ק סבר וכו' מגלגלין עליו בכולן כל"ל ותיבת את הכל נמחק:

גליון הש"ס

גמרא קילופא מידע ידיע. בתשב"ץ ח"ג סי' ג"ג היה לו הגירסא כאן קיפולא וכ' שהוא הכיפוף הלשון מלשון קילוף וכעין מ"ש רש"י חולין דף מד ע"א ד"ה לאקפל:

ליקוטי רש"י

משלש רוחותיו. שהיה לו לראובן שלש שדות אצל שדה שמעון משלש רוחותיו. וגדר. ראובן את הראשונה סמוך לשדה שמעון לצד שלש מחיצות שהיו לו בינו לשאר הבקעות. אין מחייבין אותו. את שמעון לתת כלום דמאי אהני ליה הרי שדהו פתוחה מצד רביעית. אם עמד וגדר את הרביעית. גלי אדעתיה דניחא ליה בהקיפו של ראובן ומגלגלים עליו את הכל ומחייבין לתת את חלקו בג' מחיצות פנימיות של ראובן. הא רביעית. הא אם היה לו לראובן ד' שדות מארבע רוחות של שמעון וגדרן מחייבין את שמעון לתת את חלקו במחיצות פנימיות שבינו לראובן. גדר מקיף לא יהיב ליה מידי. אם קנה מקיף את שדה רביעית אצל שמעון וגדרה פטור שמעון [ב"ק כ:].

Rav Ashi retorts:

אָמַר לֵיהּ – Rav Ashi **said to [Rava]:** וְרֵישָׁא לָאו תַּקַּנְתָּא לְרַמָּאֵי הוּא – And is not the prior ruling[12] also only **a remedy against deceivers,** designed to prevent the neighbor from fraudulently claiming joint ownership? Hence, the Tanna does consider it worthwhile simply to teach us how to protect our property.

Rava distinguishes between the two cases:

אָמַר לֵיהּ בִּשְׁלָמָא רֵישָׁא – Rava **said to [Rav Ashi]:** The inclusion of the remedy in **the prior ruling is understandable,** תְּנָא דִּינָא – for **[the Tanna] taught a** substantive **law,**[13] וּמִשּׁוּם דִּינָא תְּנָא תַּקַּנְתָּא – **and along with the law he taught a remedy** against one who would take advantage of the situation created by that law. אֶלָּא סֵיפָא – **But in the latter case,** where they agreed to build jointly, דִּינָא קָתָנֵי דְּקָתָנֵי תַּקַּנְתָּא – **did [the Tanna] teach us a** substantive **law that he** was able to **teach** incidentally **a remedy?**[14]

The Gemara answers that, in truth, in the latter case the Tanna does not concern himself with providing a remedy against deceivers; rather, he decides a substantive issue:[15]

אָמַר רָבִינָא הָכָא בְּהוּצֵי עָסְקִינַן – **Ravina said: Here** in this latter case **we are dealing with** a wall made of **palm fronds.**[16] לְאַפּוּקֵי מִדְּאַבַּיֵי – And the case specifically entails the use of signs **in order to refute [the view] of Abaye,** דְּאָמַר הוּצָא לֵית לֵיהּ תַּקַּנְתָּא אֶלָּא בִּשְׁטָרָא – **who said** that (one who builds) a fence of **palm leaves has no remedy** against false claims of ownership **except with a document.** קָא מַשְׁמַע לָן דִּבְחָזִית סַגְיָא – The Mishnah therefore **informs us that a sign is sufficient** to prove ownership of such a wall.[17]

Mishnah The first Mishnah stated that farmers do not ordinarily erect fences between fields in a valley, and therefore one cannot obligate his neighbor to participate in the building of such a fence. This Mishnah presents a case where one farmer unilaterally did so. The Gemara discusses under what conditions his neighbor will be liable to help defray the cost of the fences, and to what extent.

הַמַּקִּיף אֶת חֲבֵירוֹ מִשָּׁלֹשׁ רוּחוֹתָיו – If **one surrounds his neighbor's [field] on three** of its four **sides,** וְגָדַר אֶת הָרִאשׁוֹנָה וְאֶת הַשְּׁנִיָּה וְאֶת הַשְּׁלִישִׁית – **and [the outer neighbor] fenced the first, second and third** sides, so that the inner field is now enclosed on three sides,[18] אֵין מְחַיְּיבִין אוֹתוֹ – **we do not obligate [the owner of the inner field]** to help defray the cost of the fences.[19] רַבִּי יוֹסֵי אוֹמֵר – **R' Yose says:** אִם עָמַד וְגָדַר אֶת הָרְבִיעִית – **If he rose and fenced the fourth** side, מְגַלְגְּלִין עָלָיו אֶת הַכֹּל – **we devolve upon him** the obligation to share in the expense of **all** the partitions.[20]

Gemara The Gemara rules in accordance with R' Yose, and further clarifies his opinion:

אָמַר רַב יְהוּדָה אָמַר שְׁמוּאֵל – **Rav Yehudah said in the name of Shmuel:** הֲלָכָה כְּרַבִּי יוֹסֵי דְּאָמַר – **The halachah accords with** the view of **R' Yose, who said:** אִם עָמַד וְגָדַר אֶת הָרְבִיעִית מְגַלְגְּלִין עָלָיו אֶת הַכֹּל – IF HE ROSE AND FENCED THE FOURTH side, WE DEVOLVE UPON HIM the obligation to share in the expense of ALL the partitions.[21] לֹא שְׁנָא עָמַד נִיקָּף לֹא שְׁנָא עָמַד מַקִּיף – And **it makes no difference whether the "surrounded one"** (i.e. the owner of the inner field) **rose** to fence the fourth side **or whether the "surrounding one"** (i.e. the owner of the outer fields) **rose** to fence it. Either way, R' Yose maintains that the owner of the inner field must pay his share of the cost of all the walls once he derives benefit from them.

The Gemara discusses the measure of the inner neighbor's contribution, according to R' Yose. The discussion centers on the connotation of the word הַכֹּל, *all,* that appears in R' Yose's statement (מְגַלְגְּלִין עָלָיו אֶת הַכֹּל):

אִיתְּמַר – **It was stated:** רַב הוּנָא אָמַר הַכֹּל לְפִי מַה שֶּׁגָּדַר – **Rav Huna says:** He must pay his share for **all** (הַכֹּל) the expenses **according to what** his neighbor actually spent to **erect the fences.** Thus, even if the neighbor used expensive materials, the owner of the inner field must pay half the actual expenses.[22]

NOTES

12. Which stated that one who unilaterally erects a wall in a valley should make a sign on the outer face of the wall (*Rashi*).

13. The Mishnah established that since ordinarily farmers in a valley do not erect fences between their fields, one who desires a fence has no legal right to compel his neighbor's assistance in building one. Rather, he must erect the fence on his own property and at his own expense (*Rashi*).

14. There was no need for the Tanna to teach us that partners in the construction of a wall must share the expenses. Hence, he authored the latter ruling only for the sake of teaching the remedy (*Rashi*). Rava's question therefore remains unanswered: Why did the Tanna bother to teach ways of protecting one's property from devious individuals?

15. *Rabbeinu Yonah.*

16. Although this particular type of wall is not mentioned in the Mishnah, Ravina reasoned that the seemingly superfluous latter case was teaching something about signs, and thus concluded that a fence made of palm leaves was the subject of that teaching.

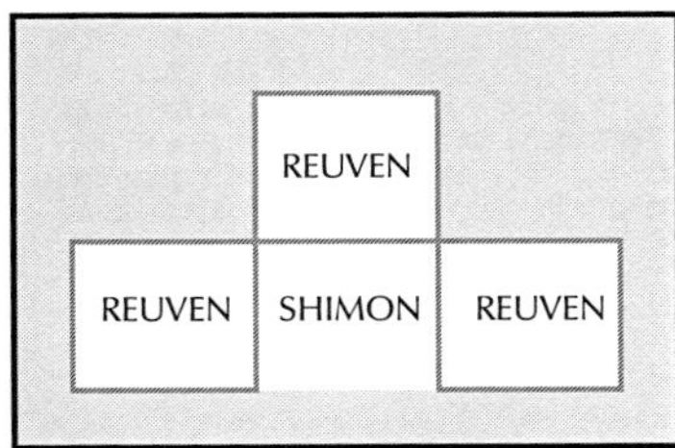

17. According to Abaye, on the other hand, it is acceptable for the Tanna to concern himself solely with providing a remedy against deceitful practices (*Tosafos*).

18. One farmer purchased three fields that bounded his neighbor's field on three sides. He then erected fences around these three fields, thereby enclosing his neighbor's field on three sides (*Rashi*). See diagram.

19. Since in an ordinary valley farmers customarily refrain from erecting fences to protect against visual trespass, the fence builder has no legal right to demand compensation from his neighbor [*Rashi;* cf. *Tosafos* (to *Bava Kamma* 20b ד״ה את), who explain that the Mishnah refers to where the outer neighbor erected fences only along the outer perimeter of his fields, and did not erect walls between his property and the inner neighbor's property at all. This interpretation necessitates an entirely different approach to the Gemara. The gloss to *Rashi* may also follow this interpretation (*Nachalas David*)].

20. The Gemara explains that this clause refers to the erection of the fourth fence by the *inner neighbor.* By enclosing the open fourth side, the owner of the inner field indicates that he approves of the construction of the other three fences [and we construe that approval as an ex post facto agreement between the two neighbors to build the three fences in partnership]. Hence, the owner of the inner field is now obligated to pay his share of the cost (*Rashi;* see *Maharsha,* who maintains that *Rashi's* text of this clause of the Mishnah stated explicitly that the inner neighbor erected the fence).

Whether this law applies if the outer neighbor erected the fourth fence is discussed in the Gemara.

The Gemara will also explain the nature of the dispute between the Tanna Kamma and R' Yose.

21. The Gemara will discuss below the extent of this obligation.

22. *Rashi.*

עין משפט
נר מצוה

[כ א מיי' פ"ג מהל' שכנים הלכה כו טוש"ע ח"מ סי' קנח סעיף ד]:
כא א ב ג ד מיי' פ"ג מהל' שכנים הל' ג סמג עשין פב טוש"ע ח"מ סי' קנח סעיף ו:

מסורת הש"ס

א) [גי' הערוך ערך קפל ג' קיפולא], ב) נ"א ריבי. רש"ל, ג) ב"ק כב, ד) נ"א ריבי. רש"ל, ה) נ"ל יושב. רש"ל, ו) הך ול"ג ניקף אינו מפירש רק שייך בהג"ה רש"ל:

[א] נשעייה באמתא מלבר וניעבד מלגיו עביד חבריה מלבר ואמר דידי ודידיה הוא אי הכי השתא נמי דקפיל ליה חבריה ואמר דידי ודידיה הוא • א) קילופא מידע ידיע הוצא אמר רב נחמן סינופי ב) יריכי מלבר וניעבד מלגיו עביד נמי חבריה מלבר ואמר דידי ודידיה הוא אי הכי השתא נמי גייז ושדי ליה ואמר דידי ודידיה הוא משריק ליה טינא השתא נמי אתי חבריה וקליף ליה קילופא מידע ידיע אביי אמר הוצא לית ליה תקנתא אלא בשטרא: אבל אם עשו מדעת שניהם: אמר ליה רבא מפרזיקא לרב אשי לא יעשו לא זה ולא זה א"ל לא צריכא דקדים חד מנייהו ועבד דידיה ואי לא עביד חבריה אמר דידיה הוא (א) ותנא תקנתא לרמאי קמ"ל א"ל ורישא לאו תקנתא לרמאי הוא א"ל בשלמא רישא תנא דינא ומשום דינא תנא תקנתא אלא סיפא דינא קתני דקתני תקנתא אמר רבינא הכא בהוצי עסקינן לאפוקי מדאביי דאמר הוצא לית ליה תקנתא אלא בשטרא קמ"ל דבחזית סגיא:

מתני' ג) א המקיף את חבירו משלש רוחותיו וגדר את הראשונה ואת השניה ואת השלישית אין מחייבין אותו רבי יוסי אומר ב אם עמד וגדר את הרביעית מגלגלין עליו את הכל:

גמ' אמר רב יהודה אמר שמואל הלכה כר' יוסי דאמר אם עמד וגדר את הרביעית מגלגלין עליו את הכל ג) ל"ש עמד ניקף ול"ש עמד מקיף איתמר רב הונא אמר ד הכל לפי מה שגדר חייא בר רב אמר הכל לפי דמי קנים בזול תנן המקיף את חבירו משלש רוחותיו וגדר את הראשונה ואת השניה ואת השלישית אין מחייבין אותו הא רביעית מחייבין אותו אימא סיפא רבי יוסי אומר אם עמד וגדר את הרביעית מגלגלין עליו את הכל בשלמא לרב הונא דאמר הכל לפי מה שגדר היינו דאיכא בין ת"ק (ב) ורבי יוסי ת"ק סבר הכל לפי דמי קנים בזול אין ומה שגדר לא ורבי יוסי סבר הכל לפי מה שגדר אלא לחייא בר רב דאמר הכל לפי דמי קנים בזול מאי איכא בין ת"ק לר' יוסי אי דמי קנים בזול לא קיהיב ליה מאי קיהיב ליה אי בעית אימא אגר נטירא איכא בינייהו תנא קמא סבר אגר נטירא אין דמי קנים בזול לא ורבי יוסי סבר דמי קנים בזול ואי בעית אימא ראשונה שניה ושלישית איכא בינייהו ת"ק סבר רביעית הוא דיהיב ליה אבל ראשונה שניה ושלישית לא יהיב ליה ור' יוסי סבר ראשונה שנייה ושלישית נמי יהיב ליה איבעית אימא מקיף וניקף איכא בינייהו דת"ק סובר טעמא דעמד ניקף (ג) דמגלגלין עליו את הכל אבל עמד מקיף אינו נותן לו אלא דמי רביעית ורבי יוסי סבר ל"ש ניקף ול"ש מקיף אם עמד וגדר מגלגלין עליו את הכל לישנא אחרינא מקיף וניקף איכא בינייהו ת"ק סבר אם גדר מקיף את הרביעית נמי יהיב ליה ורבי יוסי סבר אם עמד ניקף וגדר את הרביעית הוא דיהיב ליה דגלי דעתיה דניחא ליה אבל אם גדר מקיף לא יהיב ליה מידי

רוניא

רש"י

נשעייה באמתא מלבר. יהא טח בטיט אמה בראש הכותל מבחוץ: ומקפל ליה. (ד) מקלפו: הוצא. אם עשו מחילת נצרים כילד יעשו חזית: סינופי ה) יריכי לבר. ראשי ההוצים ו) ישב לצד שדה חבירו וכשיהיה סוף ההוצים כשיכלה האחד ויתן את חבירו יסנפנו מבחוץ: הג"ה יריכי כדאמרי' לעיל טפח יתירא לביני (ה) אורבי תמ"ש. ור"ח פי' מוליא ראשי הקנים ודפנא (ו) שהוא הקנים העומדים לחיזוק המחילה לחוץ מתוך פירושו משמע שהקנים שמעמידין מן הצד לסמוך הכותל וזהו לשון סניפין ע"כ: אלא בשטרא. אם עשה האחד יביא עדים ויחתמו לו ואם (ז) עשהו שנים יעידו עדים ויחתמו דס"ל קופלא דטינא מעילויה הוצא לא ידיע: ולא יעשו. חזית לא לזה ולא לזה והרי סימן שלא עשאה האחד בשלו שאילו עשאה היה עושה חזית מבחוץ: ועביד דידיה. עשה חזית מבחוץ: ותקנתא לרמאי. בתמיה וכי מפני דאגת רמאין איכפל תנא למיתני הא מתני': ורישא. דקתני ועושה חזית מבחוץ לאו תקנתא משום רמאי הוא דלא לימא חבריה של שניהם הוא: תנא דינא. הואיל ובקעה אין מנהג לגדור אין יכול לכופו אלא כונס לתוך שלו ובונה ואיידי דתנא דינא תנא תקנתא ועושה חזית משום רמאי אלא סיפא דינא לא תנא דהא פשיטא דאם עשו מדעת שניהם תעשה משל שניהם וכולה משום תקנתא הוא דתנייה: מתני' המקיף את חבירו משלש רוחותיו. שקנה ג' שדות סביב שדה חבירו לשלשת מצריה וגדר את שלשתן ונמצא שדהו של אמצעי זה מוקף משלש רוחותיו: אין מחייבין אותו. לתת כלום כדאמרי' דסתם בקעה מקום שנהגו שלא לגדור הוא: הג"ה תמ"ש ול"נ טעמא משום דאכתי לא מהני ליה מידי שהכל יכולים ליכנס מרוח רביעית אבל אם גדר רביעית מחייבין אותו כדאמרינן בגמ' ואע"ג דאמרינן לעיל דסתם בקעה מקום שנהגו שלא לגדור הוא ה"מ בין בקעה לבקעה וכותל גבוה ד' אמות לשם הוא דלא בעינן (ח) מ"ט דליכא היזק ראיה אבל בשביל היזק בהמות שלא יכנסו לשדה צריך לגדור גדר שלו עשרה טפחים המונע מליכנס הבהמות: ה"ג ר' יוסי אומר אם עמד וגדר את הרביעית. ו) ולא גרסי' ניקף: הג"ה וכן בפירוש ר"ח ומיהו אניקף מפרשינן לה לקמן. תוס' והכי מוכח בפ"ב דב"ק והלשון מוכיח דקתני אם עמד ולא קתני אם גדר מכלל דלאו בההוא דגדר השלש מיירי. ת' מו' שמ' ע"כ: מגלגלין עליו את הכל. לתת חלקו בשלשת הראשונות דכיון דגדר את הצד הפתוח גלי דעתיה דניחא ליה במאי דגדר חבריה: גמ' לפי מה שגדר. בכל יציאות שהוציא בהן הראשון יחזיר לו מחצה: דמי קנים. דאמר ליה לדידי סגי לי בגדר קנים ואי אפשי בהוצאה של גדר אבנים: ה"ג תנן המקיף את חבירו מג' רוחותיו כו' וגדר את הראשונה כו' אין מחייבין אותו. הא רביעית מחייבין אותו אימא סיפא ר' יוסי אומר כו' דהא לא אהני ליה מידי שסכרי גלוי הוא מצד רביעית הא אם גדר עוד מקיף את הרביעית מחייבין אותו דאהני ליה: אימא סיפא רבי יוסי אומר. בשלמא לרב הונא דאמר הכל לפי מה שגדר הוא היינו דאיכא בין ת"ק לר' יוסי דת"ק לא נקט לישנא דהכל סבר דמי קנים בזול הוא דמחייבין אותו ור' יוסי סבר כו' דהא ליכא למימר דת"ק דוקא אם גדר מקיף את הרביעית הוא דמחייבין אותו אבל אם גדר ניקף לא דכ"ש הוא השתא היכא דלא גלי דעתיה דניחא ליה בהקיפה קא מחייב ליה כ"ש היכא דגלי ולר' יוסי נמי קס"ד השתא דתנא ניקף והוא הדין למקיף אלא בגלגול דהכל הוא דפליגי: אלא לת"ק דמי קנים נמי לא יהיב ליה אלא מאי יהיב ליה. מאי מחייבין אותו דדייקינן ממתני': יהב ליה אגר נטירא. דבר מועט שהיה צריך ליתן לשומר בכל שנה כשהיה בקמותיה: דתנא קמא סבר. דמי רביעית יהיב הא אם גדרה מקיף אבל דמי הראשונות לא יהיב ליה שכבר יצא מהם וזכה בהן דבית דין שהיו ימים רבים ולא הועילו לו ואם גדרה ניקף לרביעית לא יהיב ליה מידי דלפיכך שכבר יצא מהם ולר' יוסי לא שנא גדרה ניקף ולא שנא מקיף מגלגלין עליו (ט) את הכל בכולן דמי קנים: ואיבעית אימא מקיף וניקף איכא בינייהו. דתנא קמא אית ליה דרבי יוסי היכא דגדרה ניקף אבל רבי יוסי לית ליה דתנא קמא בגדר מקיף תנא קמא סבר לא שנא ניקף ולא שנא מקיף כי גדר לרביעית מחייבין אותו דהא תנא קמא במקיף איירי ודייקינן ממילתיה הא רביעית מחייבין אותו וכל שכן כשגדרה ניקף דגלי דעתיה:

ורבי

תוספות

לאפוקי מדאביי. ואביי סבר דשפיר אית ליה למיתני תקנתא לרמאי: אם עמד וגדר את הרביעית. לר"ג אם עמד ניקף דהא לכולהו לישני דגמרא קאי אמקיף בר מלישנא בתרא דקאמר מקיף וניקף איכא בינייהו והא דדייק בפרק כיצד הרגל (ב"ק דף כ: ושם) טעמא דניקף הא מקיף פטור היינו להההוא לישנא: דמי קנים בזול. וא"ת מאי שנא משדה שאינה עשויה ליטע דאם נטעה חבירו שלא ברשות אמר רב ושמואל בהשואל (ב"מ דף קא.) שמין לו וידו על התחתונה ואור"י דשאני הכא דמצי א"ל לדידי סגי לי בנטירא בר זוזא ומ"מ דמי קנים בזול יהיב ליה דאנן סהדי דאם היה מוצאם כ"כ בזול היה גודר בהם: שניה ושלישית לא. אומר ר"י דהיינו טעמא דאין לך אדם שלא היה מסייע לרביעית ע"מ שיהא גדור מד' רוחותיו ובקונטרס פירש לפי שכבר יצא מן השלשה מב"ד זכאי: הג"ה וקצת קשה דא"כ גם ברביעית יצא זכאי עד טפח אחרון ע"כ: ורבי יוסי סבר אם עמד ניקף וגדר את הרביעית. אע"ג דעד השתא היה מחמיר כדמשמע לישנא דמגלגלין עליו את הכל להך לישנא לא הוי הכי דלשון אם עמד משמע ניקף:

רבינו גרשום

נשעייה עליה אמה מלבר. שאמה העליונה מיסד אותה בסיד על פני כולה לאורך הכותל מבחוץ לצד חבירו: קפיל ליה. שיבא חבירו בסתר ומקליף אותו הסיד: מידע ידיע. מקום הקילוף ולא יועיל לו: כל הני דאמרן היינו בכותל של אבנים אבל [אם] אותו כותל מקני הוצא הוא מאי חזית מצי למקבע ביה דסניף ליה ריבי מלבר דכל גדיל להו להוצא ליכוון דליהוי רישיהו דהוצא כייפי לבר לאותו צד של חבירו (שדין) [ושריק] ליה טינא דלא מצי חבירו לגזוז להו (ולא למשדינהו) [ולמשדינהו] דאיכא היכרא ומקשינן אפ"ה אתי חבריה (ומקבל) [ומקפל] להההוא טינא ושדי ליה ואמר דידי ודידך הוא (וישנו) [ומשנן] קילופא מידע ידיע: אביי אמר. בשום ענין לכותל הוצין אין לו תקנה לעשות שום היכר שיהא כולו שלו שחבירו לא יכול לרמותו אלא בשטרא אא"כ יכתבו לו שטר שכולו שלו ואין לחבירו בו כלום: ואם עשו מדעת שניהם. כותל בבקעה בבנין או שניהן בשותפות ועושין חזית מכאן ומכאן להיכרא שהכותל של שניהם הוא: ולא יעשה חזית לא זה ולא זה. וממילא ידעינן דשל שניהם הוא דכיון דלאחד אין לו חזקה בו יותר מחבירו לא יכול לטוענו דכולו שלו הוא: לא צריכא. דאקדים חד ועביד חזית מצד שלו להכי צריך למעבד איך: אמר לו וכי תנא מתני' לא אתי לאשמעינן בהא סיפא אלא תקנתא דרמאי. בשלמא רישא תנא דינא ותנא תקנתא. תנא אם רוצה כונס בתוך שלו דאף על גב דחבירו אינו רוצה שימעט לו באויר אינו יכול לעכב עליו היינו דינא ואגב דאיצטריך למיתני דינא תנא נמי תקנתא אבל סיפא לא אית ביה דינא כלל דהא דקתני מתני' אבל אם עשו מדעת שניהם בונין את הכותל באמצע לאו דינא הוא דמדעתיהו עבדי: רבינא אמר בהוצא עסקינן כו'. כלומר אפי' סיפא לא אתי לאורויי תקנתא כלל לרמאי אלא לאורויי אכותל הוצין לאפוקי מדאביי דאמר לית ליה תקנתא אלא בשטרא קמ"ל דבחזית סגי בלא שטרא: מתני' המקיף את חבירו מג' רוחותיו. כגון שהיו לו למקיף ד' שדות א' מכאן וא' מכאן לשדה של אדם אחר שהיה באמצעיתן של אותן שדות ורצה בעל אותן ד' שדות לגדור שדותיו וגדר את הא' ואת הב' ואת הג' ומאותן גדרים של אותן שדות לא היתה משתמרת שדהו של זה הואיל שלא גדר שדה רביעית אין מחייבין הניקף ליתן חלקו המגיעו באותן ג' גדרים הואיל ועדיין אינו משומר שדהו שעדיין פתוח מרוח א': ר' יוסי אומר אם עמד מקיף וגדר שדה רביעית מגלגלין לו את הכל לניקף ליתן בכל אותן ג' גדרים לפי חלקו המגיעו דעכשיו שדהו משתמרת בכל צד: גמ' הכל כמה שגדר. כלומר אם זה המקיף גדר שדותיו בכותל יפה של אבנים חייב ליתן לו זה הניקף לפי חלקו במה שהוציא זה על אותן גדרים ואין יכול לטעון לדידי סגי לי בכותל רעוע של מחיצת קנים: חייא בר רב אמר. מצי ליטען ליה ולא יהיב ליה אלא דמי קנים בזול כמו שאם היו גדרים של קנים: בשלמא לרב הונא דאמר במה שגדר היינו דאיכא בין ת"ק ור' יוסי. דדייקי הכי הא רביעית לת"ק מחייבין אותו דמי קנים בזול ואתי ר' יוסי למימר לחלוק על ת"ק ואמר את אמרת דמי קנים בזול ואנא אמינא דמחייבין אותו במה שגדר כעין שהוציא: אלא לחייא בר רב דאמר. לטעמא דר' יוסי דמחייב לניקף ליתן דמי קנים בזול מאי איכא בין ת"ק לר' יוסי. כלומר מאי יהיב לת"ק בציר מדמי קנים בזול (ולטעמיה) אי האי פורתא דלא יהיב ליה דמי קנים בזול מאי יהיב ליה. לעולם כדאמר חייא בר רב דלר' יוסי לא יהיב ליה אלא דמי קנים בזול והאי דמקשית מאי איכא בין ת"ק לר' יוסי איכא בינייהו ראשונה שניה ושלישית דת"ק סבר אם עמד מקיף וגדר את הרביעית מחייבין ליה לניקף דמי קנים בזול מאותה רביעית אבל מאינך אחרינא לא יהיב ליה כלל ור' יוסי סבר דראשונה ושניה ושלישית נמי יהיב ליה דמי קנים בזול: ואיבעית אימא מקיף וניקף איכא בינייהו. דת"ק סבר אם עמד מקיף נמי וגדר את הרביעית מחייבי ליה לניקף ליתן דמי קנים בזול מאותה רביעית ולא יותר דמצי ליטען ניקף אנא הוינא יתיב ומנטר לשדה שלי. ור' יוסי אומר אם עמד ניקף וגדר את הרביעית יהיב ליה מכוליה גדרים דמי קנים בזול דהואיל והוא עצמו גדר את הרביעית גלי אדעתיה דניחא ליה באינך גדרים. אבל אם עמד מקיף וגדר את הרביעית לא יהיב ליה כלל דמצי למימר אנא הויתי מנטר שדה שלי: אגר נטירא איכא בינייהו. דהאי דקשיא ליה לעיל לת"ק מאי קיהיב ליה אגר נטירא מאי דהאי ניקף הוי יהיב לשומר שדהו דעכשיו לא צריך דהיינו בציר מדמי קנים בזול. ור' יוסי סבר מגלגלין עליו את הכל דיהיב ניקף דמי קנים בזול מכולהו גדרים:

הגהות הב"ח

(א) גמ' דידיה הוא א"ל ותנא תקנתא לרמאי וכו' א"ל הא לאו מאי בשלמא רישא: (ב) שם בינו דאיכא בין ת"ק לר' יוסי ת"ק סבר דמי קנים כצ"ל ותיבת הכל נמחק: (ג) שם דעמד ניקף הוא דמגלגלין: (ד) רש"י ד"ה ומקפל ליה מקלפו הס"ד: (ה) ד"ה הג"ה ירכי וכו' יתירא לביני ירכי תמ"ש. נ"ב כך היה גורס בעל הג"ה וכך הוא גי' נימוקי יוסף: (ו) בא"ד ודפנא שהן הקנים: (ז) ד"ה אלא כו' ואם עשאוה שנים: (ח) ד"ה הג"ה תמ"ש וכו' דלא בעינן דליכא כל"ל ותיבת מ"ט נמחק: (ט) ד"ה דת"ק סבר וכו' מגלגלין עליו בכולן כל"ל ותיבת את הכל נמחק:

גליון הש"ס

גמרא קילופא מידע ידיע. בתשב"ץ ח"א סי' כ"ג היה לו הגירסא כאן קיפולא וכו' שהוא היפוך הלשון מלשון קילוף ועיין מ"ש רש"י חולין דף מד ע"א ד"ה דקפל:

ליקוטי רש"י

משלש רוחותיו. שהיה לו לראובן שלש שדות אצל שדה שמעון משלש רוחותיו. וגדר. ראובן את הראשונה סמוך לשדה שמעון לצד מחילות מילוטה ולא כונו לשאר הנקעות. אין מחייבין אותו. אין מחייבין את שמעון כלום דמאי אהני ליה הרי שדהו פתוחה מצד רביעית. עמד וגדר את הרביעית. גלי אדעתיה דניחא ליה בהקיפו של ראובן ומגלגלים עליו את הכל לתת את חלקו בג' מחיצות פנימיים של ראובן. הא רביעית. אם היה לו לראובן ד' שדות מארבע רוחות של שמעון וגדרן מחייבין את שמעון לתת את חלקו במחיצות הפנימיים שבינו לראובן. גדר מקיף לא יהיב ליה מידי. אם קנה מקיף עוד שדה רביעית אצלו שמעון וגדרה פטור שמעון [ב"ק כ:].

חִיָּיא בַּר רַב אָמַר הַכֹּל לְפִי דְּמֵי קָנִים בְּזוֹל — **Chiya bar Rav said:** He must pay his share for **all** (הַכֹּל) the fences **commensurate with the cost of reeds** bought **cheaply.**[23]

The Gemara questions Chiya's interpretation of R' Yose's opinion:

תְּנַן הַמַּקִּיף אֶת חֲבֵירוֹ מִשָּׁלֹשׁ רוּחוֹתָיו וְגָדַר אֶת הָרִאשׁוֹנָה וְאֶת הַשְּׁנִיָּה וְאֶת הַשְּׁלִישִׁית אֵין מְחַיְּיבִין אוֹתוֹ — **We learned in** our **Mishnah:** IF ONE SURROUNDS HIS NEIGHBOR ON THREE SIDES, AND [THE OUTER NEIGHBOR] FENCED THE FIRST, SECOND AND THIRD sides, WE DO NOT OBLIGATE [THE OWNER OF THE INNER FIELD] to share the expense of the fences.[24]

The Gemara infers:

הָא רְבִיעִית — **But** if the outer neighbor fenced **the fourth** side as well, מְחַיְּיבִין אוֹתוֹ — **we would obligate [the inner neighbor]** to contribute his share.[25]

The Gemara continues to develop the question:

אֵימָא סֵיפָא — Now **state the latter part** of the Mishnah, which says: רַבִּי יוֹסֵי אוֹמֵר אִם עָמַד וְגָדַר אֶת הָרְבִיעִית מְגַלְגְּלִין עָלָיו אֶת הַכֹּל — R' YOSE SAYS: IF HE ROSE AND FENCED THE FOURTH side, WE DEVOLVE UPON HIM the obligation to share in the expense of ALL the partitions. Apparently, the Tanna Kamma and R' Yose both maintain that when the inner field is completely enclosed, its owner becomes obligated to pay his share in all four fences. On what issue, then, do they disagree? בִּשְׁלָמָא לְרַב הוּנָא — **There is no difficulty according to Rav Huna,** דְּאָמַר הַכֹּל לְפִי מַה שֶּׁגָּדַר בָּהּ — **who said** that according to R' Yose the owner of the inner field must pay his share for **all** the expenses **according to what** his neighbor actually spent to **enclose [the inner field],** הַיְינוּ דְּאִיכָּא בֵּין תַּנָּא קַמָּא וְרַבִּי יוֹסֵי — as **this** very point **is** at issue **between the Tanna Kamma and R' Yose.** תַּנָּא קַמָּא סָבַר הַכֹּל לְפִי דְּמֵי קָנִים בְּזוֹל אִין — That is, **the Tanna Kamma held** that the inner field's owner **is indeed** liable commensurate with **the cost of** building a fence with **reeds** bought **cheaply,**[26] וּמַה שֶּׁגָּדַר לֹא — **but not** for half the cost of **what** the outer field's owner actually **erected,** וְרַבִּי יוֹסֵי סָבַר הַכֹּל לְפִי מַה שֶּׁגָּדַר — **while R' Yose held** that he is liable for his share of **all** the expenses **according to what** his neighbor actually spent to **erect the fences.**[27] אֶלָּא לְחִיָּיא בַּר רַב — **However, according to Chiya bar Rav,** דְּאָמַר הַכֹּל לְפִי דְּמֵי קָנִים בְּזוֹל — **who said that** according to R' Yose he must pay his share for **all** the fences **commensurate with the cost of reeds** bought **cheaply,** מַאי אִיכָּא בֵּין תַּנָּא קַמָּא לְרַבִּי יוֹסֵי — **what is** at issue **between the Tanna Kamma and R' Yose?** אִי דְּמֵי קָנִים בְּזוֹל לֹא קָיָהִיב לֵיהּ — **If** according to the Tanna Kamma the inner field's owner **does not give [his neighbor]** half **the cost of** a fence of **reeds** bought **cheaply,** מַאי קָיָהִיב לֵיהּ — **what,** then, **does he give him?**[28] It would seem, then, that according to Chiya's interpretation of R' Yose it is impossible to understand the dispute in the Mishnah. — **?** —

The Gemara advances the first of four alternate ways of understanding the dispute between R' Yose and the Tanna Kamma, according to Chiya:

אִי בָּעֵית אֵימָא אֲגַר נְטִירָא אִיכָּא בֵּינַיְיהוּ — **If you prefer say** that **the hire of a watchman is** at issue **between them.** תַּנָּא קַמָּא סָבַר אֲגַר נְטִירָא אִין — **The Tanna Kamma held** that the owner of the inner field **is indeed** liable for an amount equal to **the hire of a watchman,**[29] דְּמֵי קָנִים בְּזוֹל לֹא — but **not** for half **the** greater **cost of** a fence of **reeds** bought **cheaply,** since he can claim that he would have employed a watchman rather than build a fence. וְרַבִּי יוֹסֵי סָבַר דְּמֵי קָנִים בְּזוֹל — **And R' Yose held** that he must pay half the **cost of** a fence of **reeds** bought **cheaply.** Hence, R' Yose would impose the greater liability.

The Gemara offers a second explanation:

וְאִי בָּעֵית אֵימָא רִאשׁוֹנָה שְׁנִיָּה וּשְׁלִישִׁית אִיכָּא בֵּינַיְיהוּ — **Or, if you prefer say** that the expense of the **first, second and third** fences **is** the point of contention **between them.** However, all agree that payment is based on the cost of a fence constructed with reeds bought cheaply.[30] תַּנָּא קַמָּא סָבַר רְבִיעִית הוּא דְּיָהֵיב לֵיהּ — **The Tanna Kamma held** that **it is** his share of **the fourth** fence **that** the inner field's owner **must give [his neighbor],**[31] אֲבָל רִאשׁוֹנָה שְׁנִיָּה וּשְׁלִישִׁית לֹא יָהֵיב לֵיהּ — **but he does not give him** half the cost of the **first, second and third** fences, for until the

NOTES

23. [Since the owner of the inner field must pay only for benefit he receives] he can claim that he would have been satisfied with an inexpensive fence of reeds bought cheaply and did not need a costly stone wall. Hence, his share is based on the cost of a fence of reeds (*Rashi*). The dispute between Rav Huna and Chiya bar Rav thus concerns whether the word הַכֹּל connotes *all of the expenses* incurred by the outer neighbor, or connotes nothing more than its plain meaning — *all of the fences.*

The term קָנִים בְּזוֹל, *reeds bought cheaply,* includes two leniencies: (1) The inner neighbor need pay only for reeds and not for more costly material; and (2) he need pay only for what reeds would cost *when bought cheaply* (i.e. two-thirds of the retail price — see *Rashbam* below, 146b ד״ה ושמין), since he can claim that he would not have built the fence until he found reeds being sold at the cheaper price (*Ramban*; cf. *Ritva*).

24. See above, note 19.

25. By completely enclosing the inner field, the outer neighbor has conferred a benefit upon its owner (as his field is now completely protected). Halachah thus regards him as "one who improves his neighbor's field without permission," הַיּוֹרֵד לְתוֹךְ שְׂדֵה חֲבֵירוֹ שֶׁלֹּא בִּרְשׁוּת. Such a "benefactor" is entitled to receive reimbursement for his expenses if it is a type of improvement that people usually make (שָׂדֶה הָעֲשׂוּיָה לִיטַּע — see Bava Metzia 101a) In the Mishnah's case, as long as the owner of the inner field did not protest when his neighbor erected the fourth fence, he became obligated to pay the cost of the benefit he received (*Maharsha* on *Rashi* ד״ה המקיף את חבירו; see also *Ran*).

[*Rashi* notes that there is no such obligation when the outer neighbor erected only three walls, since there is no benefit to the owner of the inner field when one side is open.]

[See also *Ramban* and *Rashba,* who elaborate on this theme, explaining that the dispute between Rav Huna and Chiya bar Rav as to the extent of the inner neighbor's liability revolved around the exact category of "benefactor" to which the outer neighbor belongs.]

26. *Bach* deletes הַכֹּל לְפִי from the text.

27. We may infer that this is their point of disagreement from the word הַכֹּל added by R' Yose. According to Rav Huna, this word denotes that he must pay for all the expenses, not just the cost of reeds bought cheaply (*Rashi*).

Rashi notes that at this point the Gemara assumes that the rulings of the Tanna Kamma and R' Yose apply irrespective of which neighbor erected the fourth wall.

28. Previously, the Gemara inferred that the Tanna Kamma also requires the inner neighbor to contribute if a fourth partition is built. Further, since R' Yose stated, "...we devolve upon him *all* (הַכֹּל)," instead of merely noting liability, the Gemara assumes that he prescribes a larger contribution than that imposed by the Tanna Kamma (see *Rashi* ד״ה אימא סיפא). The Gemara thus questions: If, according to Chiya, R' Yose prescribes the smaller of the two measures, what measure of payment remains for the Tanna Kamma to impose?

29. This is a small amount of money paid annually to a watchman to guard the crop for the short period between full growth and harvesting (*Rashi; see Meiri*). The watchman's salary is less than half the cost of a reed fence.

30. The Gemara's alternative explanations are also all introduced to explain the dispute between the Tanna Kamma and R' Yose according to Chiya bar Rav; thus, all payments discussed refer to payments based on the cost of reeds bought cheaply (*Rashba*).

31. I.e. if the outer neighbor erected the fourth fence (*Rashi*).

עין משפט נר מצוה

[כ א מיי׳ פ״ב מהל׳ שכנים הלכה טז טוש״ע ח״מ סי׳ קנח סעיף ד]: **כא ב ג ד** מיי׳ פ״ג מהל׳ שכנים הל׳ ג סמג עשין פב טוש״ע ח״מ סי׳ קנח סעיף ו:

[א] נשעייה באמתא מלבר וניעבד מלגיו עביד חבריה מלבר ואמר דידי ודידיה הוא אי הכי השתא נמי דקפיל ליה חבריה ואמר דידי ודידיה הוא • [א] קילופא מידע ידיע הוא אמר רב נחמן סינופי [ג] ירוכי מלבר וניעבד מלגיו עביד נמי חבריה מלבר ואמר דידי ודידיה הוא אי הכי השתא נמי גייז ושדי ליה ואמר דידי ודידיה הוא משריק ליה טינא השתא נמי אתי חבריה וקליף ליה קילופא מידע ידיע אביי אמר הוצא לית ליה תקנתא אלא בשטרא: אבל אם עשו מדעת שניהם: אמר ליה רבא מפרזיקא לרב אשי לא יעשו לא זה ולא זה א״ל לא צריכא דקדים חד מנייהו ועבד דידיה ואי לא עביד חבריה אמר דידיה הוא (א) ותנא תקנתא לרמאי קמ״ל א״ל ורישא לאו תקנתא לרמאי הוא א״ל בשלמא רישא תנא דינא ומשום דינא תנא תקנתא אלא סיפא דינא קתני דקתני תקנתא אמר רבינא הכא בהוצי עסקינן לאפוקי מדאביי דאמר הוצא לית ליה תקנתא אלא בשטרא קמ״ל דבחזית סגיא:

מתני׳ [ג] [א] המקיף את חבירו משלש רוחותיו וגדר את הראשונה ואת השניה ואת השלישית אין מחייבין אותו רבי יוסי אומר [ב] אם עמד וגדר את הרביעית מגלגלין עליו את הכל: **גמ׳** אמר רב יהודה אמר שמואל הלכה כר׳ יוסי דאמר אם עמד וגדר את הרביעית מגלגלין עליו את הכל [ג] ל״ש עמד ניקף ל״ש עמד מקיף איתמר רב הונא אמר [ד] הכל לפי מה שגדר חייא בר רב אמר הכל לפי דמי קנים בזול תנן המקיף את חבירו משלש רוחותיו וגדר את הראשונה ואת השניה ואת השלישית אין מחייבין אותו הא רביעית מחייבין אותו אימא סיפא רבי יוסי אומר אם עמד וגדר את הרביעית מגלגלין עליו את הכל בשלמא לרב הונא דאמר הכל לפי מה שגדר היינו דאיכא בין ת״ק (ב) ורבי יוסי ת״ק סבר הכל לפי דמי קנים בזול ומה שגדר לא ורבי יוסי סבר הכל לפי מה שגדר אלא לחייא בר רב דאמר הכל לפי דמי קנים בזול מאי איכא בין ת״ק לר׳ יוסי אי דמי קנים בזול לא קיהיב ליה מאי קיהיב ליה אי בעית אימא אגר נטירא איכא בינייהו תנא קמא סבר אגר נטירא אין דמי קנים בזול לא ורבי יוסי סבר דמי קנים בזול ואי בעית אימא ראשונה שניה ושלישית איכא בינייהו ת״ק סבר רביעית הוא דיהיב ליה אבל ראשונה שניה ושלישית לא יהיב ליה ור׳ יוסי סבר ראשונה שנייה ושלישית נמי יהיב ליה איבעית אימא מקיף וניקף איכא בינייהו דת״ק סובר טעמא דעמד ניקף (ג) דמגלגלין עליו את הכל אבל עמד מקיף אינו נותן לו אלא דמי רביעית ורבי יוסי סבר ל״ש ניקף ול״ש מקיף אם עמד וגדר מגלגלין עליו את הכל לישנא אחרינא מקיף וניקף איכא בינייהו ת״ק סבר אם גדר מקיף את הרביעית נמי יהיב ליה ורבי יוסי סבר אם עמד ניקף וגדר את הרביעית הוא דיהיב ליה דגלי דעתיה דניחא ליה אבל אם גדר מקיף לא יהיב ליה מידי

רוניא

נשעייה באמתא מלבר. יהא טח בטיט אמה בראש הכותל מבחוץ: ומקפל ליה. (ד) מקפלו: הוצא. אם עשו מחיצת הוצים כיצד יעשו חזית: סינופי (ה) ירוכי לבר. ראשי ההוצים ישב לצד שדה חבירו וכשיהיה סונף ההוצים כשיכלה האחד ויתן את חבירו יסקפנו מבחוץ: הג״ה ירוכי כדאמרי׳ לעיל טפח יתירה לגיני (ה) אורכי תמ״ש. ור״ח פי׳ מוציא ראשי הקנים ודפנא לבר (ו) שהוא הקנים העומדים לחיזוק המחיצה לחוץ מתוך פירושו משמע שהקנים שמעמידין מן הצד לסמוך הכותל וזהו לשון סניפין ע״כ: אלא בשטרא. אם עשה האחד יביא עדים ויחתמו לו ואם (ז) עשאו שנים יעידו עדים ויחתמו דס״ל קופלא דטינא מעליותא הוא לא ידיע: ולא יעשו. חזית לא לזה ולא לזה והרי סימן שלא עשאה האחד בשלו שאילו עשאה היה עושה חזית מבחוץ: ועביד דידיה. עשה חזית מבחוץ: ותקנתא לרמאי. בתמיה וכי מפני דאגת רמאין איכפל תנא למיתני הא מתני׳: ורישא. דקתני ועושה חזית מבחוץ לאו תקנתא משום רמאי הוא דלא לימא חבריה של שניהן הוא: תנא דינא. הואיל ובקעה אין מנהג לגדור אין יכול לכופו אלא כונס לתוך שלו ובונה ואיידי דתנא דינא תנא תקנתא ועושה חזית משום רמאי אלא סיפא דינא לא תנא דהא פשיטא דאם עשו מדעת שניהם תעשה משל שניהם וכולה משום תקנתא הוא דתנייה: מתני׳ המקיף את חבירו משלש רוחותיו. שקנה ג׳ שדות סביב שדה חבירו לשלשה צדדיה וגדר את שלשתן ונמצא שדהו של אמצעי זה מוקף משלש רוחותיו: אין מחייבין אותו. לתת כלום כדאמרי׳ דסתם בבקעה מקום שנהגו שלא לגדור הוא: הג״ה תמ״ש ול״נ טעמא משום דלאכתי לא מהני ליה מידי שהכל יכולים ליכנס מרוח רביעית אבל אם גדר רביעית מחייבין אותו כדאמרינן בגמ׳ ואע״ג דאמרינן לעיל דסתם בבקעה מקום שנהגו שלא לגדור הוא ה״מ בין בקעה לבקעה וכותל גבוה ד׳ אמות לאסור הוא דלא בעינן (ח) מ״מ לצילה היזק ראיה אבל בשביל היזק בהמות שלא יכנסו לשדה צריך לגדור גדר שלו עשרה טפחים המונע מליכנס הבהמות: הג״ה ר׳ יוסי אומר אם עמד וגדר את הרביעית. (ט) ולא גרסי׳ ניקף: הג״ה וכן בפירוש ר״ח ומיהו הניקף מפרשינן לה לקמן. תוס׳ והכי מוכח בפ״ב דב״ק והלשון מוכיח דקתני אם עמד ולא קתני אם גדר מכלל דלאו בההוא דגדר השלש מיירי. ת׳ מו׳ שמ׳ ע״כ: מגלגלין עליו את הכל. לתת חלקו בשלשת הראשונות דכיון דגדר את הצד הפתוח גלי דעתיה דניחא ליה במאי דגדר חבריה: גמ׳ לפי מה שגדר. בכל יציאות שהוציא בהן הראשון יחזיר לו מחצה: דמי קנים. דאמר ליה לדידי סגי לי בגדר קנים ואי אפשי בהוצאה של גדר אבנים: ה״ג תנן המקיף את חבירו מג׳ רוחותיו וגדר את הראשונה כו׳ אין מחייבין אותו הא רביעית מחייבין אותו אימא סיפא ר׳ יוסי אומר כו׳ וגדר את הראשונה כו׳ אין מחייבין אותו. דהא לא אהני ליה מידי שהרי גלוי הוא מצד רביעית הא אם גדר עוד מקיף את הרביעית מחייבין אותו דאהני ליה: אימא סיפא רבי יוסי אומר. בשלמא לרב הונא דאמר הכל דר׳ יוסי במה שגדר הוא היינו דאיכא בין ת״ק לר׳ יוסי דת״ק דלא נקט לישנא דהכל סבר דמי קנים בזול הוא דמחייבין אותו ור׳ יוסי סבר כו׳ דהא ליכא למימר דת״ק דוקא אם גדר מקיף את הרביעית הוא דמחייבין אותו אבל אם גדר ניקף לא דכ״ש הוא השתא היכא דלא גלי דעתיה דניחא ליה בהקיפא קא מחייב ליה כ״ש היכא דגלי ולר׳ יוסי נמי קס״ד השתא דתנא ניקף וה״ה למקיף אלא בגלגול דהכל הוא דפליגי: אלא לת״ק דמי קנים נמי לא יהיב ליה אלא מאי יהיב ליה. מאי מחייבין אותו דדייקינן ממילתיה: יהב ליה אגר נטירא. דבר מועט שהיה צריך ליתן לשומר בכל שנה כשהיא בקמותיה: דתנא קמא סבר. דמי רביעית יהיב ליה אם גדרה מקיף אבל דמי הראשונות לא יהיב ליה שכבר יצא מהם וזכאי בבית דין שהיו שם ימים רבים ולא הועילו לו ואם גדרה ניקף לרביעית לא יהיב ליה מידי כדפיר׳ שכבר יצא ידי בית דין מהם ולר׳ יוסי לא שנא גדרה ניקף ולא שנא מקיף מגלגלין עליו (ט) את הכל בכולן דמי קנים: ואיבעית אימא מקיף וניקף איכא בינייהו. דתנא קמא אית ליה דרבי יוסי היכא דגדרה ניקף אבל רבי יוסי לית ליה דתנא קמא בגדר מקיף תנא קמא סבר לא שנא ניקף ולא שנא מקיף כי גדר לרביעית מחייבין אותו דהא תנא קמא במקיף איירי ודייקינן ממילתיה הא רביעית מחייבין אותו וכל שכן כשגדרה ניקף דגלי דעתיה:

ורבי

לאפוקי מדאביי. ואביי סבר דשפיר אית ליה למיתני תקנתא לרמאי: **אם** עמד וגדר את הרביעית. ל״ג אם עמד ניקף דהא לכולהו לישני דגמרא קאי אמקיף בר מלישנא בתרא דקאמר מקיף וניקף איכא בינייהו והא דדייק בפרק כילד הרגל (ב״ק דף כ: ושם) טעמא דניקף הא מקיף פטור היינו להאי לישנא: **דמי** קנים בזול. וא״ת מאי שנא משדה שאינה עשויה ליטע דאם נטעה חבירו שלא ברשות אמר רב ושמואל בהשואל (ב״מ דף קא.) שמין לו וידו על התחתונה ואור״י דשאני הכא דמצי א״ל לדידי סגי לי בנטירא בר זוזא ומ״מ דמי קנים בזול יהיב ליה דאנן סהדי דאם היה מוצאם כ״כ בזול היה גודר בהם: **שניה** ושלישית לא. אומר ר״י דהיינו טעמא דאין לך אדם שלא היה מסייע לרביעית ע״מ שיהא גדור מד׳ רוחותיו ובקונטרס פירש לפי שכבר יצא מן השלשה מב״ד זכאי: הג״ה וקצת קשה דא״כ גם ברביעית יצא זכאי עד טפח אחרון ע״כ: **ורבי** יוסי סבר אם עמד ניקף וגדר את הרביעית. אע״ג דעד השתא היה מחמיר כדמשמע לישנא דמגלגלין עליו את הכל להך לישנא לא הוי הכי דלשון אם עמד משמע ניקף:

רבינו גרשום

נשעייה עליה אמה מלבר. שאמה העליונה מייסד אותה בסיד על פני כולה לאורך הכותל מבחוץ לצד חבירו: **קפיל ליה.** שיבא חבירו בסתר ומקליף אותו הסיד: **מידע ידיע.** מקום הקילוף ולא יועיל לו: כל הני דאמרן היינו בכותל של אבנים אבל [אם] אותו כותל מקני **הוצא** הוא מאי חזית מצי למקבע ביה **דסניף** ליה **ריבי מלבר** דלכי גדיל להו להוצא ליכוון דליהוי רישייהו דהוצא כייפי לבר לאותו צד של חבירו (שדין) **[ושריק] ליה טינא** דלא מצי חבירו לגזוז להו (ולא למישדינהו) [ולמישדינהו] דאיכא היכרא ומקשינן אפ״ה **אתי חבריה** (ומקבל) **[ומקפל]** להאי טינא ושדי ליה **ואמר דידי ודידך הוא** (וישנו) [ומשני] **קילופא מידע ידיע: אביי אמר.** בשום ענין לכותל **הוצין אין לו תקנה** לעשות שום היכר שיהא כולו שלו שחבירו לא יכול לרמותו **אלא בשטרא** אא״כ יכתבו לו שטר שכולו שלו ואין לחבירו בו כלום: **ואם עשו מדעת שניהם.** כותל בבקעה בונין אותו שניהן בשותפות ועושין חזית מכאן ומכאן להיכרא שהכותל של שניהם הוא: **ולא יעשה חזית לא זה ולא זה.** וממילא ידעינן דשל שניהם הוא דכיון דלאחד אין לו חזקה בו יותר מחבירו לא יוכל לטוענו דכולו שלו הוא: **לא צריכא. דאקדים חד ועביד** חזית מצד שלו להכי צריך למעבד אידך: **אמר לו וכי תנא דמתני׳** לא אתי לאשמועינן בהא סיפא אלא **תקנתא דרמאי. בשלמא רישא תנא דינא ותנא תקנתא.** תנא אם רוצה כונס בתוך שלו דאף על גב דחבירו אינו רוצה שימעט לו באויר אינו יכול לעכב עליו היינו דינא ואגב דאיצטריך למיתני דינא תנא נמי תקנתא אבל סיפא לא אית ביה דינא כלל דהא דקתני מתני׳ אבל אם עשו מדעת שניהם בונין את הכותל באמצע לאו דינא הוא דמדעתייהו עבדי: **רבינא אמר בהוצא עסקינן כו׳.** כלומר אפי׳ סיפא לא אתי לאורויי תקנתא כלל לרמאי אלא לאורויי אכותל דהוצא לאפוקי מדאביי דאמר לית ליה תקנתא אלא בשטרא קמ״ל דבחזית סגי בלא שטרא: **מתני׳ המקיף את חבירו מג׳ רוחותיו.** כגון שהיו לו למקיף ד׳ שדות א׳ מכאן וא׳ מכאן לשדה של אדם אחר שהיה באמצעיתן של אותן שדות ורצה בעל אותן ד׳ שדות לגדור שדותיו **וגדר את הא׳** **ואת הב׳ ואת הג׳** ומאותן גדרים של אותן שדות לא היתה משתמרת שדהו של זה הואיל שלא גדר שדה רביעית **אין מחייבין** הניקף ליתן חלקו המגיעו באותן ג׳ גדרים הואיל ועדיין אינו משומר שדהו שעדיין פתוח מרוח א׳: **ר׳ יוסי אומר אם עמד מקיף וגדר שדה רביעית מגלגלין לו את הכל** לניקף ליתן בכל אותן ג׳ גדרים לפי חלקו המגיעו דעכשיו שדהו משתמרת בכל צד: **גמ׳ הכל כמה שגדר.** כלומר אם זה המקיף גדר שדותיו בכותל יפה של אבנים חייב ליתן לו זה הניקף לפי חלקו במה שהוציא זה על אותן גדרים ואין יכול לטעון לדידי סגי לי בכותל רעוע של מחיצת קנים: **חייא בר רב אמר.** מצי ליטען ליה ולא יהיב ליה אלא **דמי קנים בזול** כמו שאם היו גדרים של קנים: **בשלמא לרב הונא דאמר במה שגדר היינו דאיכא בין ת״ק ור׳ יוסי.** דדייקי הכי הא רביעית **לת״ק** מחייבין אותו **דמי קנים בזול** ואתי **ר׳ יוסי** למימר לחלוק על ת״ק ואמר את אמרת דמי קנים בזול ואנא אמינא דמחייבין אותו **במה שגדר** כעין שהוציא: **אלא לחייא בר רב דאמר.** לטעמא דר׳ יוסי דמחייב לניקף ליתן **דמי קנים בזול מאי איכא בין ת״ק לר׳ יוסי.** כלומר מאי יהיב לת״ק בציר מדמי קנים בזול (ולטעמיה) אי האי פורתא דלא יהיב ליה דמי קנים בזול מאי יהיב ליה. לעולם כדאמר חייא בר רב דלר׳ יוסי לא יהיב ליה אלא דמי קנים בזול והאי דמקשית מאי איכא בין ת״ק לר׳ יוסי **איכא בינייהו ראשונה שניה ושלישית דת״ק סבר** אם עמד מקיף וגדר את הרביעית מחייבין ליה לניקף דמי קנים בזול מאותה **רביעית** אבל מאינך אחרינא **לא יהיב ליה** כלל **ור׳ יוסי סבר דראשונה ושניה ושלישית נמי יהיב ליה דמי קנים בזול: ואיבעית אימא מקיף וניקף איכא** בינייהו. דת״ק **סבר אם עמד מקיף** נמי וגדר את הרביעית מחייבי ליה לניקף ליתן דמי קנים בזול מאותה רביעית ולא יותר דמצי ליטען ניקף אנא הוינא יתיב ומנטר לשדה שלי. **ור׳ יוסי אומר אם עמד** ניקף **וגדר את הרביעית** יהיב ליה מכולהו גדרים דמי קנים בזול דהואיל והוא עצמו גדר את הרביעית גלי אדעתיה דניחא ליה באינך גדרים. **אבל אם** עמד **מקיף וגדר** את הרביעית **לא יהיב** ליה כלל דמצי למימר אנא הויתי מנטר שדה שלי: **אגר נטירא** איכא בינייהו. והאי דקשיא ליה לעיל לת״ק מאי קיהיב ליה אגר נטירא מאי דהאי ניקף הרי יהיב לשומר שדהו דעכשיו לא צריך דהיינו בציר מדמי קנים בזול. **ור׳ יוסי סבר מגלגלין עליו את הכל** דיהיב ניקף דמי קנים בזול מכולהו גדרים:

מסורת הש״ס

א) [גי׳ הערוך ערך קפל ג׳ קיפולא], ב) נ״א ריבי. רש״ל, ג) ב״ק כ:, ד) נ״א ריזי. רש״ל, ה) נ״ל יסב, ו) כך ול״ג ניקף אינו מפירש״י רק שייך בהג״ה. רש״א:

הגהות הב״ח

(א) גמ׳ דידיה הוא א״ל ותנא תקנתא לרמאי וכו׳ א״ל הא מאי בשלמא רישא: (ב) שם היינו דאיכא בין ת״ק לר׳ יוסי ת״ק סבר דמי קנים כצ״ל ותיבת הכל לפי נמחק: (ג) שם דעמד ניקף הוא דמגלגלין: (ד) רש״י ד״ה ומקפל ליה מקלפו הס״ד: (ה) ד״ה הג״ה ירוכי וכו׳ יתירא לביני ירכי תמ״ש. נ״ב כך היה גורס בעל הג״ה וכך הוא גי׳ נימוקי יוסף: (ו) בא״ד ודפנא שהן הקנים: (ז) ד״ה אלא כו׳ ואם עשאוה שנים: (ח) ד״ה הג״ה תמ״ש וכו׳ דלא בעינן דליכא כצ״ל ותיבת מ״ט נמחק: (ט) ד״ה דת״ק סבר וכו׳ מגלגלין עליו בכולן כצ״ל ותיבת את הכל נמחק:

גליון הש״ס

גמרא קילופא מידע ידיע. בתשב״ץ ח״א סי׳ נ״ג היה לו הגירסא כאן קיפולא וכו׳ שהוא היפוך הלשון מלשון קילוף וכעין מ״ש רש״י חולין דף מד ע״א ד״ה דאקפל:

ליקוטי רש״י

משלש רוחותיו. שהיה לו לראובן שלש שדות אצל שדה שמעון משלש רוחותיו. וגדר. ראובן את הראשונה סמוך לשדה שמעון לצד מחיצות מחיצות שהיו לו בינו לשאר הבקעות. אין מחייבין אותו. אין מחייבין את שמעון כלום דמאי אהני ליה הרי שדהו פתוחה מצד רביעית. אם עמד וגדר את הרביעית. גלי אדעתיה דניחא ליה בהקיפו של ראובן ומגלגלים עליו את הכל לתת את חלקו בג׳ מחיצות פנימיות של ראובן. הא רביעית. הא אם היה לו לראובן ד׳ שדות מארבע רוחות של שמעון וגדרן מחייבין את שמעון לתת את חלקו במחיצות הפנימיות שבינו לראובן. גדר מקיף לא יהיב ליה מידי. אם קנה מקיף עוד שדה רביעית אצל שמעון וגדרה פטור שמעון [ב״ק כ:].

fourth fence was built they afforded him no benefit, and he has already been exempted by the court from paying for them.[32] Therefore, his liability is limited to his share of the fourth fence. וְרַבִּי יוֹסֵי סָבַר רִאשׁוֹנָה שְׁנִיָּה וּשְׁלִישִׁית נַמִּי יָהִיב לֵיהּ – **And R' Yose held** that **he must give [his neighbor]** half the cost of **the first, second and third** fences **as well,**[33] based on the cost of a fence of reeds bought cheaply, since he benefits from them now.[34]

The Gemara advances a third interpretation:

אִיבָּעֵית אֵימָא מַקִּיף וְנִיקָּף אִיכָּא בֵּינַיְיהוּ – **If you prefer say** that the dispute **between them is** whether it matters if **"the surrounding one"** (i.e. the owner of the outer fields) **or "the surrounded one"** (i.e. the owner of the inner field) built the fourth partition. דְּתַנָּא קַמָּא סוֹבֵר טַעְמָא דְּעָמַד נִיקָּף – **For the Tanna Kamma holds** that **it is because the surrounded** neighbor **rose** and built the fourth fence himself דִּמְגַלְגְּלִין עָלָיו אֶת הַכֹּל – **that we devolve upon him** the obligation to pay his share for **all** the fences.[35] For by fencing the fourth side he signals his approval of the construction of the first three, and must therefore share in their cost. אֲבָל עָמַד מַקִּיף – **But if the surrounding** neighbor **rose** and built the fourth fence as well,[36] אֵינוֹ נוֹתֵן לוֹ אֶלָּא דְּמֵי רְבִיעִית – the "surrounded" neighbor **gives him only** half **the cost of a fourth** fence, since in fact he benefits from its construction. However, he is exempt from contributing toward the other three fences, since he never evinced his approval of their construction. וְרַבִּי יוֹסֵי סָבַר לֹא שְׁנָא נִיקָּף וְלֹא שְׁנָא מַקִּיף – **And R' Yose held** that **it makes no difference whether** the builder **is the surrounded** neighbor **or the surrounding** neighbor. אִם עָמַד וְגָדַר – **If** either one **rose and fenced** the fourth side, מְגַלְגְּלִין עָלָיו אֶת הַכֹּל – **we devolve upon [the surrounded neighbor]** the obligation to share the expense of **all** the fences.[37] Hence, R' Yose rules more stringently than does the Tanna Kamma in that he imposes liability on the owner of the inner field for all the fences regardless of who erects the fourth fence.

The Gemara presents a fourth explanation of the dispute. In this variation of the previous explanation R' Yose adopts the more lenient position:

לִישָּׁנָא אַחֲרִינָא – **Another version** of the previous interpretation: מַקִּיף וְנִיקָּף אִיכָּא בֵּינַיְיהוּ – The dispute **between them is** whether it matters if **the surrounding one or the surrounded one** built the fourth fence. תַּנָּא קַמָּא סָבַר אִם גָּדַר מַקִּיף אֶת הָרְבִיעִית – **The Tanna Kamma held that if the surrounding** neighbor **fenced the fourth** side, נַמִּי יָהִיב לֵיהּ – the surrounded neighbor **also gives him** money for all the fences, since in fact he benefits from them.[38] וְרַבִּי יוֹסֵי סָבַר אִם עָמַד נִיקָּף וְגָדַר אֶת הָרְבִיעִית – **And R' Yose held** that **if the surrounded** neighbor **rose and fenced the fourth** side, הוּא דְיָהִיב לֵיהּ – only **then must he give [the surrounding neighbor]** payment for the other fences, דְּגַלֵּי דַּעְתֵּיהּ דְּנִיחָא לֵיהּ – **for** in building the fourth fence **he evinced his satisfaction** with their construction. אֲבָל אִם גָּדַר מַקִּיף – **But if the surrounding** neighbor **fenced** the fourth side, לֹא יָהִיב לֵיהּ מִידֵי – the surrounded neighbor **need not give him anything,** since he has not indicated his approval of their construction.[39]

NOTES

32. *Rashi,* who adds that for this very reason the owner of the inner field is exempt from liability for the first three fences even if he himself completes the enclosure by erecting the fourth fence.

The Rishonim explain that this ruling is based on the law of קַם דִּינָא – once a person has been exempted by law for any liability, he can no longer be held liable for it (*Baal Hamor*, *Rabbeinu Yonah*, *Rashba*, based on *Yevamos* 37b).

Tosafos question *Rashi's* explanation, arguing that according to his reasoning the owner of the inner field should be exempt from all but the cost of the final *tefach* of the fourth fence, since until that point he receives no benefit from the fences. *Tosafos* therefore explain that since being completely enclosed is an undeniable benefit, one that any farmer would want, we assume that the inner neighbor, even if he would not have willingly shared in the cost of all four walls, would have willingly consented to the cost of the erection of a fourth and final partition – the one that effects the enclosure. [See *Rashash* for a defense of *Rashi*.]

33. Irrespective of who erected the fourth fence (*Rashi*).

34. According to this explanation of the dispute, הַכֹּל, *all,* is interpreted literally: R' Yose rules more stringently than does the Tanna Kamma in that he imposes liability for *all* four fences, whereas the Tanna Kamma restricts liability to the fourth fence.

35. The Tanna Kamma expressly stated that if three fences are built by the outer neighbor and the inner neighbor does not react, he incurs no liability at all. Implied by this statement is that if the inner neighbor does react by erecting the fourth fence, he will incur liability for the first three (based on the cost of a reed fence; see note 30 above).

An apparent difficulty with this interpretation: The Tanna Kamma requires the surrounded neighbor to pay for the first three fences only if *he* erected the fourth fence, and exempts him if the surrounding neighbor did so. If the reason for the exemption is due to the fact that the court has exempted him from the first three fences (see above note 32), it should apply regardless of who erected the fence (as *Rashi* himself said in the previous interpretation, which makes no such distinction). For this reason and others, *Chidushei Chasam Sofer* maintains that *Rashi* deletes this interpretation from the Gemara – and, indeed, *Rashi* does not mention it at all (see also *Rashba*, *Ran*).

[It should be noted, however, that *Baal Hamaor* also explains the exemption from the first three walls as *Rashi* does, and yet he does quote this third interpretation. See *Chidushei R' Nachum* §80 for a resolution of this difficulty.]

36. The Tanna Kamma does not expressly rule on this contingency. However, the Gemara is making a reasoned interpretation of what his position would be, drawing also from its assumption that the Tanna Kamma treats the inner neighbor more leniently than does R' Yose (see above, note 28).

37. According to R' Yose, the inner field's owner need not indicate his approval of the first three fences; since he now in fact benefits from them, he must help defray their cost. [As noted above, his liability applies only to the cost of a reed fence.]

38. Certainly, if the inner field's owner erected the fourth fence (thereby showing his desire for the fences), he would be liable to help pay for the other three fences.

39. In this interpretation the Gemara abandons the assumption that הַכֹּל indicates a greater liability for the owner of the inner field. Instead, the Gemara assumes that the term "rose" refers only to the inner field's owner, since he has remained passive until now. Thus, R' Yose's ruling applies only when that neighbor erects the fourth fence. Since the Gemara previously inferred that the Tanna Kamma's ruling applies even when the outer neighbor builds the fourth fence, we see that in this explanation the Tanna Kamma stakes out the more stringent position.

[This interpretation disagrees with that which Rav Yehudah said in Shmuel's name (above, at the beginning of the Gemara's discussion), that R' Yose required payment regardless of who erected the fourth wall.]

The Gemara in *Bava Kamma* (20b) interprets our Mishnah in accord with this last interpretation, that R' Yose exempts the inner neighbor if the outer neighbor erected all four fences. The Gemara there gives two possible reasons for this ruling. According to the opinion that זֶה נֶהֱנֶה וְזֶה לֹא חָסַר פָּטוּר – one is exempt from paying for receiving a benefit if the benefactor has suffered no loss, here too he has suffered no loss on account of his neighbor's benefit. The second reason the Gemara gives for the exemption is because he can claim there is no benefit at all for him to have the fences, for it would be sufficient to him to have protection costing only one *zuz*. See *Tosafos* there (ד"ה טעמא) for further discussion.

The Gemara relates an incident similar to the case of the Mishnah:

רוּנְיָא אַקְפֵיהּ רָבִינָא מֵאַרְבַּע רוּחוֹתָיו — Ravina surrounded Runia's field **on** all **four of its sides.**[1] **אָמַר לֵיהּ הַב לִי כַּמָּה דְּגַדְרִי —** Attempting to recoup half of the cost of the fences, Ravina **said to [Runia]: "Give me** reimbursement **commensurate with the fences I erected."**[2]

Runia refused to pay:

לָא יְהֵיב לֵיהּ — Runia **did not give [Ravina]** what he demanded, maintaining that since he had done nothing to indicate his satisfaction with the fences, he was not liable to pay.[3]

Ravina then offered to settle for a lesser amount:

הַב לִי לְפִי קָנִים בְּזוֹל — Ravina said: "At least **give me** reimbursement **according to** the cost of a fence of **reeds** bought **cheaply.** Surely the fence is worth at least that much to you."

Runia refused:

לָא יְהֵיב לֵיהּ — Runia **did not give [Ravina]** even this amount.

Ravina attempted to recoup an even smaller amount:

הַב לִי אֲגַר נְטִירוּתָא — Ravina said: **"Give me** at least **the hire of a watchman.**[4] Surely you wish to protect your crop!"

Runia refused even this offer:

לָא יְהֵיב לֵיהּ — Runia **did not give [Ravina]** even this minimal amount, and so the two remained deadlocked.

When subsequently an opportunity to win his case arose, Ravina seized it:

יוֹמָא חַד הֲוָה קָא גָדַר דִּיקְלֵי — One day Runia **was harvesting dates from his palm trees,** which were located in the field that Ravina had surrounded with fences. **אָמַר לֵיהּ לַאֲרִיסֵיהּ — [Ravina] said to his sharecropper: זִיל שְׁקוֹל מִנֵּיהּ קִיבּוּרָא דַּאֲהִינֵי — "Go** into Runia's field and **take a cluster of dates from him,** in his presence." **אָזַל לְאַתּוּיֵי —** The sharecropper **went to bring [the dates]. רָמָא בֵּיהּ קָלָא —** Upon witnessing the brazen act of thievery, Runia **shouted at [the sharecropper]** to stop.

Ravina thereupon confronted Runia:

אָמַר לֵיהּ — [Ravina] said to [Runia]: גַּלֵּית דַּעְתָּךְ דְּמֵינַח נִיחָא לָךְ — "In rebuking my agent **you have indicated** that the palm trees are dear to you and **that you are** therefore **agreeable** to their being protected.[5] **לָא יְהָא אֶלָּא עִיזָא בְּעָלְמָא —** Even **if [the threat] were merely a** foraging **goat, מִי לָא בָּעֵי נְטִירוּתָא — would** your trees **not need protection?**[6] Thus, you must share in the expense of the fences!"

Runia replied:

אָמַר לֵיהּ — [Runia] said to [Ravina]: עִיזָא בְּעָלְמָא (לאו) לְאַכְלוּיֵי בָּעְיָא — "A mere goat requires[7] only **to be shouted at** to be kept away. Hence, I do not need a fence for protection!"

Ravina countered:

אָמַר לֵיהּ — [Ravina] said to [Runia]: וְלָא גַּבְרָא בָּעֵית דְּמִיכְלֵי לָהּ — "But do you not need a person who will stay in the field and **shout at it** when it approaches? Pay me at least for a watchman!"

אָתוּ לְקַמֵּיהּ דְּרָבָא — They came before Rava for a judgment, since they could not settle their dispute.

Rava instead offered counsel:

אָמַר לֵיהּ — [Rava] said to [Runia]: זִיל פַּיְיסֵיהּ בְּמַאי דְּאִיפַּיֵּיס — "Go and appease Ravina with [the amount] with which he has agreed to **be appeased**. Since he will accept the equivalent of a watchman's pay, you can fulfill your obligation by giving him that. **וְאִי לָא — But if** you do **not** pay him at all, **דָּאֵינָא לָךְ דִּינָא כְּרַב הוּנָא אַלִּיבָּא דְּרַבִּי יוֹסֵי — I will judge you in accordance with Rav Huna's interpretation of R' Yose's** ruling,[8] and you will be forced to pay half of the actual cost of the fences that Ravina erected."

The Gemara relates another incident involving Runia and Ravina:

רוּנְיָא זְבַן אַרְעָא אַמֵּיצְרָא דְּרָבִינָא — Runia bought a parcel of land on the boundary of (i.e. adjacent to) **Ravina's field.**[9] **סְבַר רָבִינָא לְסַלּוּקֵי — Ravina thought to oust [Runia]** from the field and purchase it himself **מִשּׁוּם דִּינָא דְּבַר מִצְרָא — in accordance with the law** pertaining to **the owner of the adjacent property** ("one who shares a boundary"), which provides that a Jew who wishes to sell a tract of land must give his neighbor the right of first refusal.[10] Thus, Ravina sought to acquire the field for himself, since it bordered his property.

Rav Safra dissuaded Ravina from depriving Runia, who was a poor man, of the field:

אָמַר לֵיהּ רַב סַפְרָא בְּרֵיהּ דְּרַב יֵיבָא לְרָבִינָא — Rav Safra the son of Rav Yaiva said to Ravina: אָמְרֵי אִינְשֵׁי אַרְבְּעָה לְצַלָּא אַרְבְּעָה לְצַלְּלָא — "People say, 'Four for the hide, and four for the tanner.'"[11]

NOTES

1. Ravina owned four fields that completely bounded Runia's field, and he erected a fence along each common border (*Rashi*).

2. Ravina's demand follows the view of R' Yose as interpreted by Rav Huna (above, 4b), which states that upon the fencing of the fourth side the owner of the inner field is liable for half of the actual cost of all the fences. The Gemara below indicates that this view constitutes accepted halachah (*Rashi*).

3. As will become evident, Runia subscribed to R' Yose's opinion as presented in the fourth interpretation of the Mishnah above (4b).

4. Which is less than half the cost of a reed fence, as explained in the Gemara above (4b).

5. *Rashi.* As mentioned above (note 3), Runia subscribed to the view that since he had not built the fourth fence, he was not liable at all to share in the cost of the fences. However, his action (shouting at Ravina's sharecropper) undermined his case — for even R' Yose, who exempts the surrounded neighbor where he did not erect the final fence, does so only where there is no indication from *any* source that the surrounded neighbor is agreeable to the protection which the fences afford. If, however, any such indication exists, R' Yose too requires the surrounded neighbor to help pay for the fences (*Meiri* to 4b; see also *Be'ur HaGra* to *Choshen Mishpat* 158:7).

[Ravina did not intend to equate this case with that of R' Yose, for in that case, if the inner neighbor puts up the fourth fence, it is an indication of his willingness to pay for the protection of fences, and he would therefore be liable to share the entire cost of erecting the fences. Here, however, there was no such indication, for even a person who does not feel a need to have fences will definitely not allow someone to steal his possessions! Rather, (as *Rashi* explains), it is just an indication that he values his fruit, and therefore would obviously be willing to pay for some sort of protection. Ravina therefore ruled that Runia could not refuse to give at least minimal payment for the fence's protection (*Yad Ramah*).]

[See *Ritva* for possible reasons why it would be permissible to take Runia's dates without his consent in this situation.]

6. I.e. even if you do not fear thieves, you must still protect your trees from foraging animals (*Rashi*).

7. Emendation and translation follow *Bach,* who deletes לָאו from the text.

8. The Gemara here implies that this view is the established halachah (gloss to *Rashi;* see above, note 2; see *Rashba* here; see also *Tosafos* ד״ה ואי).

9. *Rashi* presents several interpretations of this incident (see below, note 11). According to the interpretation we have followed, this episode is unrelated to the previous one; hence, different fields are involved.

10. Literally: the law of the person of the boundary. This law is elucidated in tractate *Bava Metzia* (108a-108b). Its source is *Deuteronomy* 6:18, which states: *And you shall do what is right and good.* Since having contiguous fields reduces the cost of labor and security, among other advantages, it is only proper to allow an adjoining neighbor to purchase the property at a fair market price.

11. Runia was a shoemaker, who would purchase hides and then pay

ג) ור' יוסי סבר. דוקא גדרה ניקף דגלי דעתיה אבל גדרה מקיף לא: רוניא אקפיה רבינא. ד' שדות היו לרבינא סביבות ארבעה מצריו של רוניא וגדרן: הב לי כמה דגדרי. כרב הונא אליבא דר' יוסי דאמר הכל לפי מה שגדר דהכי קי"ל כדמוכח לקמן: יומא חד הוה גדר. רוניא היה גודר תמרים מדקל שבשדהו: קיבורא דאהיני. אשכול של תמרים משל רוניא ובפניו: רמא ביה קלא. גער בו רוניא באריסיה דרבינא: א"ל. רבינא גלית אדעתיך שחביבין הדקלין עליך וניחא לך בשמירתן: לא יהא אלא עיזי בעלמא מי לא בעית כו'. כלומר אפי' אינך ירא מן הגנבים צריך אתה לשמרן מן העזים: ולאו גברא בעית לאכלויי. להזעיק ולגעור בהן ד) וירעם מתרגמי' אכלי (תהלים יח) וכן כל לשון הכרזה בתרגום יהונתן: פייסיה במה דאיפיים. טוב לך (ג) להתפייס באגר נטירא הואיל ונתרצה לכך: הגה"ה ואי לא דאיננא לך כר' יוסי כו' מכלל דהכי הלכתא. וכן פסק ר"ח. תמ"ש: ארבעה לצלא וד' לצללא. אני שמעתי צלא רצען עני וצללא רצען עשיר וכך אמר לו ארבע ככרות צריכין לרצען עני למאכלות ביתו ליום כמו שצריכין לעשיר וזה עני הוא וצריך לו השדה לפרנסה וכשם שאתה אומר לו הסתלק מעלי בדינא דבר מצרא משום ועשית הישר והטוב כך אני אומר לך עשה ישר וטוב לעני זה ואל תסלקהו ויש לגמגם דהעור קרוי צלא ולא הרצען כדאמרי' בעלמא (נדרים דף נו:) מאי דרגש ערסא דצלא ואומר אני רוניא רצען היה (ד) ונותן עורות לעבדנין לעשות מהן מנעלין למוכרן בשוק וכך אמר לו רב ספרא לרבינא העני זה שכרו מועט שהוא צריך ליתן שכר הרבה לעבדנין דאמרי אינשי ארבעה זוזי לצורך מקח העור וארבעה זוזי לשכר העבדנין והיינו צללא לפיכך עשה ישר וטוב ותהי לו שדה זו לפרנסת ביתו ה) ול"נ ד' לצלא ד' ככרות צריך לעבדן עני וד' לצללא כמו כן ד' לצורך עבדן עשיר ומשל הוא כנגד רוניא שהיה לו שדה אחת בתוך שדות של רבינא כדאמר לעיל דרבינא אקפיה מארבע רוחותיו ועכשיו קנה לו שדה אצל מצר רבינא ומפסיק שדה רבינא בין שדותיו וא"ל רב ספרא לרבינא שיעשה הישר והטוב להניח לרוניא אותה (ה) דעכשיו יהיה לו שנים שכמו שצריך שמירה לשני שדות [צריך] ג"כ לאחד ומכמה דברים יציאת האחד מרובה כיציאת שנים ונמצא רוניא משתכר: מתני' מחייבין אותו לבנותו עד ד' אמות. דהכי סגי להיזק ראיה: בחזקת שנתן. אם אמר האחד לאחר שבנאו אני עשיתיו משלי שלא רצה זה לסייעני ותובעו חצי היציאה וזה אומר נתתי חלקי נאמן: עד שיביא התובע. עדים שתבעו ולא נתן לו דכיון דחובה עליו לסייעו ומשפט זה לכל גלוי לא היה בונה משלו אלא היה צועק עליו בב"ד: סמך לו כותל אחר. לאחר שבנאו האחד למעלה מד' אמות הרבה ולא רצה האחר לסייעו בהגבהתו סמך השני כותל אחר כנגד כותל זה כדי לסכך ולתת עליו תקרה מכותל לכותל אע"פ שלא נתן עליו עדיין התקרה: מגלגלין עליו את הכל. דגלי דעתיה דניחא ליה בהגבהה דהילך: בחזקת שלא נתן. אם בא הראשון ותבעו לדין לאחר שסמך את כותלו לכותל ראשון ואומר לו תן לי חלקך במה שהגבהתי וזה אומר נתתי חלקי אינו נאמן אלא בעדים שאין משפט זה גלוי לכל ועד שיחייבוהו בית דין אינו עשוי ליתן: גמ' הקובע זמן לחבירו. במלוה שהלוהו אלימא אבל בסתם הלוואה לא חשיב ליה תוך שלשים תוך זמנו: ובא בזמנו ואמר פרעתיך תוך זמני אינו נאמן. ונראה לי שיש עדים שחייב לו וקבע לו זמן דאי לאו הכי מהימניה שפרעו תוך זמן במיגו דאי בעי אמר לא הלוית לי כלום או לא קבעת לי שום זמן ולקמן מיבעי ליה אי

רוניא אקפיה רבינא מארבע רוחותיו א"ל הב לי כמה דגדרי לא יהיב ליה הב לי לפי (א) קנים בזול לא יהיב ליה הב לי אגר נטירותא לא יהיב ליה יומא חד הוה קא גדר דיקלי אמר ליה לאריסיה זיל שקול מניה קיבורא דאהיני אזל לאתויי רמא ביה קלא א"ל גלית דעתך דמינח ניחא לך לא יהא אלא עיזא בעלמא מי לא בעי נטירותא א"ל עיזא בעלמא (ב) לאו לאכלויי בעיא א"ל ולא גברא בעית דמיכלי לה אתא לקמיה דרבא א"ל זיל פייסיה במאי דאיפיים ואי לא דאיננא לך דינא כר"ה אליבא דרבי יוסי רוניא זבן ארעא אמיצרא דרבינא סבר רבינא לסלוקי משום דינא דבר מצרא א"ל רב ספרא בריה דרב ייבא לרבינא אמרי אינשי ארבעה לצלא ארבעה לצללא:

מתני' (א) אכותל חצר שנפל מחייבין אותו לבנותו בעד ארבע אמות בחזקת שנתן עד שיביא ראיה שלא נתן גמד' אמות ולמעלן אין מחייבין אותו דסמך לו כותל אחר אע"פ שלא נתן עליו את התקרה מגלגלין עליו את הכל הבחזקת שלא נתן עד שיביא ראיה שנתן:

גמ' אמר ריש לקיש הקובע זמן לחבירו ג) ואמר לו פרעתיך בתוך זמני אינו נאמן ולואי שיפרע בזמנו אביי ורבא דאמרי תרוייהו עביד איניש דפרע בגו זימניה זימנין דמתרמו ליה זוזי אמר איזיל איפרעיה

י) הגה"ה כתב בספרים אבל מקיף לא יהיב ליה אלא דמי רביעית. וקשה דמנלן דיהיב ליה אפי' דמי רביעית דילמא לא יהיב ליה כלל וכן משמע בפ' כיצד הרגל (ב"ק דף כ: ושם ד"ה טעמא) דקאמר טעמא (ו) דניקף הא מקיף פטור ש"מ זה נהנה וזה לא חסר פטור ודחי שאני התם דא"ל לדידי סגי לי בנטירא בר זוזא מיהו יש לדחות דה"ק לדידי סגי לי בנטירא בר זוזא הלכך פטור מלסייע לד' רוחות אבל רביעית יסייע דאין לך אדם שלא יסייע לרביעית שיהיה גדור מארבע רוחותיו: ואי לא דאיננא לך כרב הונא אליבא דר' יוסי. קצת היה נראה שלא להפחידו היה אומר כן מדלא קאמר ואי לא מגבינא לאפדנא מינך או מחינא לך בסילוואה דלא מבע דמא ואע"ג דבלולב הגזול (סוכה דף לד: ושם ד"ה ולדרוש) אמר שמואל להנהו דמזבני אסא אשוו זבינייכו ואי לא דרשינן לכו כר' טרפון ובעי למימר התם דלהפחידם היה אומר כן הכא נראה דהכי ס"ל כדפירש רש"י ועוד מדקאמר ליה זיל פייסיה במאי דאיפיים משמע דמן הדין היה לו יותר אם לא בשביל שכבר נתפייס: ארבעה לצלא כו'. לפירוש הקונטרס מקשה ר"ת [הא] אין מרחמים בדין ז) ועוד דקאמר סבר רבינא לסלוקי משמע שטעה רבינא ועוד מה שייך כאן האי מעשה אי משום דאיירי ברבינא ורוניא לייתי נמי מעשה דהמקבל (ב"מ דף קט.) רוניא שתלא דרבינא הוה והנך תרי עובדי דשמעתין לייתי נמי התם ועוד דצלא הוא עור כדאמרי' (מו"ק דף כז.) מאי דרגש ערסא דצלא ואומר ר"ת דזבן ארעא אמיצרא דרבינא היינו אמיצר אותם שדות דאקפיה רבינא מארבע רוחות והיה רבינא מצרן מג' רוחות ורוניא מרוח אחת ואף על גב דאמר בהמקבל (ב"מ דף קח:) הני ארבע בני מצרא דקדים חד מינייהו וזבן מאי דזבן זבן מ"מ סבר רבינא לסלוקי משום שהיה מצרן מג' לדדין ורוניא רק מרוח אחת א"ל רב ספרא אמרי אינשי ארבעה לצלא פירוש לעור גדול צריך ליתן לעבדן ד' זוזי וד' לצללא עור קטן כלומר צריך ליתן מן הקטן כמו מן הגדול שיש טורח בקטן כמו בגדול ה"נ מאי טעמא דינא דבר מצרא משום שיהיו כל שדותיו סמוכין שיוכל לחורשן בבת אחת ולכך הוא מצרן מרוח אחת כמו אתה מג' רוחות וה"ר אברהם פירש דהך ארעא דזבן רוניא אמיצרא דרבינא היינו אמצרא דאותן שדות שהיה רוניא אריס בהן כדאמרי' רוניא שתלא דרבינא הוה וה"ק ליה רב ספרא לרבינא אע"פ שאין לרוניא בגוף הקרקע כלום מכל מקום הואיל שהוא עובדן הרי הוא מצרן (ז) כמו דאמרי אינשי ארבעה לצלא נותנין ד' זוז על העור וכמו כן צריך ליתן לצללא לאומן המעבד את העור: מארבע אמות ולמעלה אין מחייבין אותו כו' בחזקת שלא נתן. איירי כגון דידעינן דקדם חד ואצליה לחבריה והיה מסרהב כדמשמע לישנא אין מחייבין אותו ולכך הוי בחזקת שלא נתן וא"ל להעמיד בשעשה חזית: אע"פ שלא נתן (ח) תקרה מגלגלין עליו את הכל. אע"ג דזה נהנה וזה לא חסר פטור מ"מ כיון דגלי דעתיה דניחא ליה בהגבהה חייב וכן משמע נמי בכיצד הרגל (ב"ק דף כ: ושם) דקאמר טעמא דניקף הא מקיף פטור ש"מ זה נהנה וזה לא חסר פטור ואפ"ה כשעמד ניקף חייב כן נראה לי אי נמי הכא זה חסר הוא שגורם לו שהגביה הכותל למעלה מד' אמות כדי שלא יהיה לו היזק ראיה בשום ענין ממנו: הקובע זמן לחבירו. אור"י דוקא קובע זמן

מסורת הש"ס
א) [לעיל ג:], ב) ג"א ובא בזמנו. רש"ל, ג) שייך לעמוד הקודם, ד) [אלכווי לשון הרמת קול ירעם מתרגמינן וכו' כצ"ל וכן הוא בש"ב כב וכן הוא בס"ח], ה) ס"א ל"ג ול"נ רק הוא הגה"ה עד הס"ד. רש"ל, ו) שייך לעמוד הקודם, ז) [כדאיתא בכתובות פד.]

הגהות הב"ח
(א) גמ' הב לי לפי דמי קנים: (ב) שם בעלמא לאכלויי בעיא כצ"ל ותיבת לאו נמחק: (ג) רש"י ד"ה פייסיה וכו' טוב לך שנילות להתפייס: (ד) ד"ה ארבעה לצלא וכו' רצען היה ולוקח עורות ונותן עורות לעבדנין: (ה) בא"ד אותה שדה דעכשיו: (ו) תוס' ד"ה הגה"ה וכו' דקאמר טעמא דגדר ניקף: (ז) ד"ה ארבעה וכו' והרי הוא מצרן כמוך דאמרי אינשי: (ח) ד"ה אע"פ שלא נתן עליו את התקרה מגלגלין וכו' טעמא דגדר ניקף:

ליקוטי רש"י
קיבורא דאהיני. אשכול תמרים [שבת קנו:]. כמין אשכול יש תמרים הרבה בענף אחד [סנהדרין כו:]. לימויי"ש [חולין צה:]. דצלא. עור [מו"ק כז.].

עין משפט נר מצוה
כב א מיי' פ"ג מהל' שכנים הל' א סמג עשין פב טוש"ע ח"מ סי' קנז סעיף ד:
כג ב מיי' שם הל' ג טוש"ע שם סעיף ח:
כד ג ד מיי' שם הל' א טוש"ע שם סעיף י:
כה ה מיי' שם הל' ג טוש"ע שם סעיף יא:

רבינו גרשום
הב לי כמה דגדרי. הואיל והוקפת שדך מד' רוחותיה ומשתמרת תן לי לפי חלקך המגיעך מהוצאותי: הב לי דמי קנים בזול. כלומר אם לא תרצה ליתן שיעור גדר טוב תן לי מיהו שיעור דמי קנים בזול: הוה קא גדר דיקלא. היה (ולקט) [לוקט] דיקלא: א"ל רבינא לאריסיה זיל אייתי לי קיבורא. כגון אשכול של ג' או ד' תמרים תלוים בקנה א' מאותו דקל: רמא קלא. גער בו באותו אריס שלא יגע בתמרים: דניחא לך. בהני גדרים דגדרי: אלא עיזא בעלמא. כלומר מי לא בעית למעביד נטירותא מחמת עיזי דלא ליפסדו בשדך והשתא לא צריכת: פסיקנא לך כרב הונא אליבא דר' יוסי. דאמר הכל כמה שגדר: ארבעה לצלא ארבעה לצללא. כלומר דהיכי דצריכי לאושכף עשיר שהוא (דלא) [צלא] ד' ככרות למזונותיו ואנשי ביתו כך צריכין לעבדן עני משל אמר לו כלומר מעשה זה דבר מיצרא אינו אלא משום ועשית הישר והטוב וכיון דזה רוניא עני הוא (אעפ"כ) אינו יכול לחיות בלא שדה (שאם) [ואם] לא יקח עכשיו יפסיד מעותיו ואין לו במה להתפרנס משום הכי לא תוכל לסלוקיה דאין לך ועשית הישר והטוב גדול מזה דתשבקיה ליה למיזבן: פיסקא כותל חצר שבין ב' חצירות שנפל מחייבין אותו למעכב שיסייע לבנות עד ד' אמות משום היזק ראיה והואיל דמחייבין ליה לסיועיה אם טוען הלה לא נתן לי כלום אלא אני לבדי בניתי לי משלי וזה אומר נתתי הרי הוא בחזקת שנתן עד שיביא ראיה עדים שלא נתן: מד' אמות ולמעלה אין מחייבין אותו. לסייעו לבנותו דהשתא ליכא היזק ראיה: סמך לו זה. שלא נתן מד' אמות ולמעלה ובנה זה בחלקו כותל אחר גבוה כמו זה שהגביה חבירו משלו שנתכוין לבנות שניהן ביחד ושיהיה כותל זה שהגביה חבירו אחד מכותל הבית: אע"פ שלא נתן עליו את התקרה. על כותל זה שהגביה חבירו ולא כיון קונדסין ונתן עליהם את התקרה מצד אחד על כותליו אפע"כ מגלגלין עליו את הכל מה שהרציא זה על אותו גובה יותר על ד' שאע"פ שלא נתן התקרה עליו נהנה הוא מן הכותל א) וההנאה היא בביתו מחמת אותו כותל: והואיל דמארבע אמות ולמעלה אין מחייבין אותו לבנות אם טוען הלה ואמר אני נתתי והגבהתי עמו והלה אומר לא נתת הרי הוא בחזקת שלא נתן עד שיביא ראיה שנתן: הקובע זמן לחבירו. לפרוע לו את חובו:

חשק שלמה על רבינו גרשום א) נראה דצ"ל וההנאה היא מחמת שהוא דר בביתו ע"י אותו כותל.

Mishnah As explained in the first Mishnah, owners of adjoining courtyards may compel each other to share in the expense of building an intervening partition to protect their privacy, and they are therefore assumed to be partners in any wall that separates them. The following Mishnah discusses obligations created when that original wall collapses, and presumptions that arise thereafter:

כּוֹתֶל חָצֵר שֶׁנָּפַל — If **a courtyard wall**[12] **collapsed,** **מְחַיְּיבִין אוֹתוֹ לִבְנוֹתוֹ עַד אַרְבַּע אַמּוֹת** — **we obligate [each neighbor] to rebuild it to** a height of **four *amos*.**[13] **בְּחֶזְקַת שֶׁנָּתַן** — After the wall is rebuilt each neighbor is **presumed to have contributed** to the cost of construction[14] **עַד שֶׁיָּבִיא רְאָיָה שֶׁלֹּא נָתַן** — **until** the other neighbor **brings proof that he did not contribute.**[15] **מֵאַרְבַּע אַמּוֹת וּלְמַעְלָן אֵין מְחַיְּיבִין אוֹתוֹ** — However, **we do not obligate him** to rebuild the wall **from four *amos* and upward.**[16] Nevertheless, if one neighbor extended the height of the new wall beyond four *amos* at his own expense, and then **סָמַךְ לוֹ כּוֹתֶל אַחֵר** — the other neighbor **juxtaposed another wall** parallel to **[the first one],** with the intent of placing a roof across the two walls, **אַף עַל פִּי שֶׁלֹּא נָתַן עָלָיו אֶת הַתִּקְרָה** — **even though he did not** yet **place the roof on [the walls]** **מְגַלְגְּלִין עָלָיו אֶת הַכֹּל** — **we devolve upon him** the obligation to pay his share of **the entire** wall, even the section above four *amos,* for he has indicated that he is agreeable to the extension.[17] **בְּחֶזְקַת שֶׁלֹּא נָתַן**— Further, the builder of the parallel wall **is presumed not to have contributed** toward the cost of the extension[18] **עַד שֶׁיָּבִיא רְאָיָה שֶׁנָּתַן** — **until he brings proof that he did contribute.**[19]

Gemara The Gemara attempts to resolve a dispute regarding the early repayment of loans with proof from our Mishnah:

אָמַר רֵישׁ לָקִישׁ — **Reish Lakish said:** **הַקּוֹבֵעַ זְמַן לַחֲבֵירוֹ** — **If one establishes a time for** repayment of a loan that he made to **his friend,** **וְאָמַר לוֹ** — **and** when approached upon the arrival of that date the borrower **said to him,** **פְּרַעְתִּיךָ בְּתוֹךְ זְמַנִּי** — **"I repaid you within my** allotted **time** period (i.e. before the loan came due)," **אֵינוֹ נֶאֱמָן** — the borrower **is not believed,** for there is a presumption that people do not repay loans early[20] — **וּלְוַאי שֶׁיִּפְרַע בִּזְמַנּוֹ** — **and would that** a borrower **repay on time!**[21]

Abaye and Rava differ with Reish Lakish:

אַבַּיֵּי וְרָבָא דְּאָמְרֵי תַּרְוַיְיהוּ — **Abaye and Rava both said:** The borrower is believed, for **עֲבִיד אִינִישׁ דְּפָרַע בְּגוֹ זִימְנֵיהּ** — **it happens that a person repays** a loan **within his** allotted **time.** **זִימְנִין דְּמִתְרַמּוּ לֵיהּ זוּזֵי** — **For sometimes money** unexpectedly **becomes available to him,** **אָמַר אֵיזִיל אִיפְרְעֵיהּ** — and **he says** to himself, **"I will go and pay him** ahead of time

---

NOTES

tanners to prepare the leather that he would fashion into shoes for sale in the market. Rav Safra therefore explained to Ravina: "Runia is a poor man who makes little profit, for he must pay the tanner handsomely, as per the adage: 'Four *zuzim* to purchase the hides, and four *zuzim* for the tanner's wages.' The purchase of this field will therefore better enable him to support his family. Thus, you should not preempt him, for the source for the law of '*bar metzra*' is: *And you shall do what is right and good*. Usually, it is 'right and good' to give preference to a neighbor over a stranger when selling a field. However, in this case the 'right and good' thing is to leave the field in the indigent Runia's hands" (*Rashi;* see there for two other interpretations, and see *Tosafos,* who challenge all three interpretations and advance two others).

12. I.e. the wall separating two courtyards.

13. A height of four *amos* is sufficient to protect against visual trespass (*Rashi*). The Gemara (2b; see note 26 there) explained that in the case of a collapsed wall all opinions concur that the resulting visual trespass is considered damaging, and that the wall must be rebuilt.

14. Thus, if one neighbor claims that since the other refused to assist in the reconstruction he bore all the expenses himself, and so demands reimbursement for half of his outlay, the other neighbor is believed to say that he already paid his share. The reason we presume that he has already paid his share is because the obligation of each neighbor to contribute is so well known; hence, the halachah presumes that the claimant would have sued in court for his neighbor's assistance rather than undertaken the reconstruction unilaterally (*Rashi*).

[*Rashi* interprets the words בְּחֶזְקַת שֶׁנָּתַן to mean that we presume he had paid his share, because the other neighbor would not have built the wall without his assistance. Obviously, therefore, he is claiming that he paid before the wall was built, and we presume this to be true.

Other Rishonim (*Yad Ramah, Rashba, Ritva*), however, explain that the Mishnah is speaking of a case where we know that one of them built the wall by himself. [See there for how this is known.] The other neighbor is not disputing this. He is, however, claiming that after his neighbor built the wall, he paid the money owed to the neighbor for the wall. The Mishnah is teaching us that he is believed. (This may be compared to a loan, where the borrower would be believed to say that he repaid the loan). The Gemara below seems to support this interpretation (see 5b note 1).]

15. To be successful, the claimant (see previous note) must prove through the testimony of witnesses that he solicited his neighbor's contribution and that the latter refused. (*Rashi;* see *Rosh*).

16. I.e. even if the neighbors built the original wall higher, they are not obligated to restore it beyond the height that ensures privacy — four *amos* (*Rashi* to 2b ד״ה סיפא איצטריך ליה, *Meiri*).

17. *Rashi. Tosafos* understand that the neighbor is obligated to pay because he was benefited by the wall (similar to the previous Mishnah). *Rashba* and *Nimukei Yosef,* however, question what benefit he has received prior to his building any adjoining structure. They explain that since the neighbor has shown his desire to eventually use this wall as part of his structure, he automatically acquires the part of the wall that is in his portion, and therefore must pay for it. [See *Kehilos Yaakov* for a defense of *Tosafos.*]

18. Thus, if the builder of the extension sues his neighbor after the latter erected the parallel wall, the neighbor is not believed to claim that he already paid his share, but must bring witnesses to testify that he did so (*Rashi*).

19. The burden of proof devolves upon this neighbor because his obligation to contribute toward the extension is not obvious. Hence, the halachah presumes that he would not readily pay until he was directed by *beis din* to do so (*Rashi*).

This presumption applies even to one who is cognizant of his obligation, for if not, anyone could claim that knowledge and assert that he already paid (*Yad Ramah*).

20. This presumption (*chazakah*) has the status of fact; hence, one who claims that he has repaid early is not believed, for the *chazakah* informs otherwise.

21. *Tosafos* note that concerning a loan whose due date is unspecified, which halachah regards as a thirty-day loan, the concept of early repayment does not apply. Hence, in such a case there is no *chazakah* weighing against his claim of repayment within thirty days. (See *Rabbeinu Yonah, Nachalas David, Shiurei R' Shmuel,* and *Chidushei R' Nachum*). In the Gemara's case, however, a due date was specified.

רוניא אקפיה רבינא מארבע רוחותיו א"ל הב לי כמה דגדרי לא יהיב ליה הב לי לפי (א) קנים בזול לא יהיב ליה הב לי אגר נטירותא לא יהיב ליה יומא חד הוה קא גדר דיקלי אמר ליה לאריסיה זיל שקול מניה קיבורא דאהיני אזל לאתויי רמא ביה קלא א"ל גלית דעתך דמינח ניחא לך לא יהא אלא עיזא בעלמא מי לא בעי נטורותא א"ל עיזא בעלמא (ב) לאו לאכלויי בעיא א"ל ולא גברא בעית דמיכלי לה אתא לקמיה דרבא א"ל זיל פייסיה במאי דאיפיים ואי לא דאיננא לך דינא כר"ה אליבא דרבי יוסי רוניא זבן ארעא אמיצרא דרבינא סבר רבינא לסלוקי משום דינא דבר מצרא א"ל רב ספרא בריה דרב ייבא לרבינא אמרי אינשי ארבעה לצלא ארבעה לצללא:

מתני' [א] כותל חצר שנפל מחייבין אותו לבנותו [ב] עד ארבע אמות בחזקת שנתן עד שיביא ראיה שלא נתן [ג] מד' אמות ולמעלן אין מחייבין אותו [ד] סמך לו כותל אחר אע"פ שלא נתן עליו את התקרה מגלגלין עליו את הכל [ה] בחזקת שלא נתן עד שיביא ראיה שנתן:

גמ' אמר ריש לקיש הקובע זמן לחבירו ואמר לו פרעתיך בתוך זמני אינו נאמן ולואי שיפרע בזמנו אביי ורבא דאמרי תרוייהו עביד איניש דפרע בגו זימניה זימנין דמתרמו ליה זוזי אמר איזיל איפרעיה

רש"י

ג) **ור' יוסי סבר.** דוקא גדלה ניקף דגלי דעתיה אבל גדלה מקיף לא: **רוניא אקפיה רבינא.** ד' שדות היו לרבינא סביבות ארבעה מצריו של רוניא וגדרן: **הב לי כמה דגדרי.** כרב הונא אליבא דר' יוסי דאמר הכל לפי מה שגדר דהכי קי"ל כדמוכח לקמן: **יומא חד הוה גדר.** רוניא היה גודר תמרים מדקל שבשדהו: **קיבורא דאהיני.** אשכול של תמרים משל רוניא ובפניו: **רמא ביה קלא.** גער בו רוניא באריסיה דרבינא: **א"ל.** רבינא גלית אדעתיך שחביבין הדקלין עליך וניחא לך בשמירתן: **לא יהא אלא עיזי בעלמא מי לא בעית כו'.** כלומר אפי' אינך ירא מן הגנבים צריך אתה לשמרן מן העזים: **ולאו גברא בעית לאכלויי.** להזעיק ולגעור בהן ד) וירעם מתרגמי' אכלי (תהלים יח) וכן כל לשון הכרזה בתרגום יהונתן: **פייסיה במה דאיפיים.** טוב לך (ג) להתפייס באגר נטירא הואיל ונתרצה לכך: הגה"ה ואי לא דאיננא לך כר' יוסי כו' מכלל דהכי הלכתא. וכן פסק ר"ח. תמ"ס: **ארבעה לצלא וד' לצללא.** אני שמעתי ללא רצען עני ולצללא רצען עשיר וכך אמר לו ארבע ככרות צריכין לרצען לעשיר לאמלכות ביתו ליום כמו שצריכין לעני וזה עני הוא וצריך לו השדה לפרנסה וכשם שאתה אומר לו הסתלק מעלי בדינא דבר מצרא משום ועשית הישר והטוב כך אני אומר לך עשה ישר וטוב לעני זה ואל תסלקהו ויש לגמגם דהעור קרוי צלא ולא הרצען כדאמרי' בעלמא (נדרים דף טו:) מאי דרגש ערסא דצלא ואומר אני רוניא רצען היה (ד) וקונה עורות לעבדנין לעשות מהן מנעלין למוכרן בשוק וכך אמר לו רב ספרא לרבינא העני זה שכרו מועט שהוא צריך ליתן שכר הרבה לעבדנין דאמרי אינשי ארבעה זוזי לצורך מקח העור וארבעה זוזי לשכר העבדנין והיינו לצללא לפיכך עשה ישר וטוב ותהי לו שדה זו לפרנסת ביתו ה) ול"נ ד' לצלא ד' ככרות צריך לעבדן עני וד' לצללא כמו כן ד' לצורך עבדן עשיר ומשל הוא כנגד רוניא שהיה לו שדה אחת בתוך שדות של רבינא כדאמר לעיל דרבינא אקפיה מארבע רוחותיו ועכשיו קנה לו שדה אצל מצר רבינא ומפסיק שדה רבינא בין שדותיו וא"ל רב ספרא לרבינא שיעשה הישר והטוב להניח לרוניא אותה (ה) דעכשיו יהיו לו שנים כמו שצריך שמירה לשני שדות [צריך] ג"כ לאחד ומכמה דברים יצילה האחד מרובה כיצילת שנים ונמצא רוניא משתכר:

מתני' מחייבין אותו לבנותו עד ד' אמות. דבהכי סגי להיזק ראיה: **בחזקת שנתן.** אם אמר האחד לאחר שבנאו אני עשיתי משלי שלא רצה זה לסייעני ותובעו אני הייתי וזה אומר נתתי חלקי נאמן: **עד שיביא ראיה התובע.** עדים שתבעו ולא נתן לו דכיון דחובה עליו לסייעו ומשפט זה לכל גלוי לא היה בונה משלו אלא היה צועק עליו בב"ד: **סמך לו כותל אחר.** לאחר שבנאו האחד למעלה מד' אמות הרבה ולא רצה האחר לסייעו בהגבהתו סמך השני כותל אחר כנגד כותל זה כדי לסכך ולתת עליו תקרה מכותל לכותל אע"פ שלא נתן עליו עדיין התקרה: **מגלגלין עליו את הכל.** דגלי דעתיה דניחא ליה בהגבהה דהיזקו: **בחזקת שלא נתן.** אם בא הראשון ותבעו לדין לאחר שסמך את כותלו לכותל ראשון ואומר לו תן לי חלקך במה שהגבהתי וזה אומר נתתי חלקי אינו נאמן אלא בעדים שאין משפט זה גלוי לכל ועד שיחייבוהו בית דין אינו עשוי ליתן: **גמ' הקובע זמן לחבירו.** במלוה שהלוהו: אלימא **ובא** בזמנו ואמר פרעתיך תוך זמני אינו נאמן. ונראה לי שיש עדים שחייב לו וקבע לו זמן דאי לאו הכי ניהמניה שפרעו תוך זמן במיגו דאי בעי אמר לא הלוית לי כלום או לא קבעת לי שום זמן ולקמן מיבעי ליה אי

תוספות

י) **הגה"ה** כתב בספרים אבל מקיף לא יהיב ליה אלא דמי רביעית. וקשה דמנלן דיהיב ליה אפי' דמי רביעית דילמא לא יהיב ליה כלל וכן משמע בפ' כילד הרגל (ב"ק דף כ: ושם ד"ה טעמא) דקאמר טעמא (ו) דניקף הא מקיף פטור ש"מ זה נהנה וזה לא חסר פטור ודחי שאני התם דא"ל לדידי סגי לי בנטירא בר זוזא מיהו יש לדחות דה"ק לדידי סגי לי בנטירא בר זוזא הלכך פטור מלסייע לד' רוחות אבל רביעית יסייע דאין לך אדם שלא יסייע לרביעית שיהיה גדור מארבע רוחותיו: **ואי לא דאיננא לך כרב הונא אליבא דר' יוסי.** קצת היה נראה שלא להפחידו היה אומר כן מדלא קאמר ואי לא מגבינא לאפדנא מינך או מחינא לך בסילואה דלא מבע דמא ואע"ג דבלולב הגזול (סוכה דף לד: ושם ד"ה ולדרוש) אמר שמואל להנהו דמזבני אסא אשוו זבינייכו ואי לא דרשינן לכו כר' טרפון ובעי למימר התם דלהפחידם היה אומר כן הכא נראה דהכי ס"ל כדפירש רש"י ועוד מדקאמר ליה זיל פייסיה במאי דאיפיים משמע דמן הדין היה לו יותר אם לא בשביל שכבר נתפיים: **ארבעה לצלא כו'.** לפירוש הקונטרס מקשה ר"ת [הא] אין מרחמים בדין ז) ועוד דקאמר סבר רבינא לסלוקי משמע שטעה רבינא ועוד מה שייך כאן האי מעשה אי משום דאיירי ברבינא ורוניא לייתי נמי מעשה דהמקבל (ב"מ דף קט.) רוניא שתלא דרבינא הוה והנך תרי עובדי דשמעתין לייתי נמי התם ועוד דצלא הוא עור כדאמרי' (מו"ק דף כז.) מאי דרגש ערסא דצלא ואומר ר"ת דזבן ארעא אמיצרא דרבינא היינו אמיצר אותם שדות דאקפיה רבינא מארבע רוחות והיה רבינא מצרן מג' רוחות ורוניא מרוח אחת ואף על גב דאמר בהמקבל (ב"מ דף קח:) הני ארבע בני מצרא דקדים חד מינייהו וזבן מאי דזבן זבן מ"מ סבר רבינא לסלוקי משום שהיה מצרן מג' לדדין ורוניא רק מרוח אחת א"ל רב ספרא אמרי אינשי ארבעה לצלא פירוש לעור גדול צריך ליתן לעבדן ד' זוזי וד' לצללא עור קטן כלומר צריך ליתן מן הקטן כמו מן הגדול שיש טורח בקטן כמו בגדול ה"נ מאי טעמא דינא דבר מצרא משום שיהיו כל שדותיו סמוכין שיוכל לחורשן בבת אחת ולכך הוא מצרן מרוח אחת כמו אתה מג' רוחות וה"ר אברהם פירש דהך ארעא דזבן רוניא אמיצרא דרבינא היינו אמצרא דאותן שדות שהיה רוניא אריס בהן כדאמרי' רוניא שתלא דרבינא הוה וה"ק ליה רב ספרא לרבינא אע"פ שאין לרוניא בגוף הקרקע כלום מכל מקום הואיל שהוא עובדן הרי הוא מצרן (ז) כמו דאמרי אינשי ארבעה לצלא נותנין ד' זוז על העור וכמו כן צריך ליתן לצללא לאומן המעבד את העור: **מארבע** אמות ולמעלה אין מחייבין אותו כו' בחזקת שלא נתן. איירי כגון דידעינן דקדם חד ואגביה לחבריה והיה מסרהב כדמשמע לישנא אין מחייבין אותו ולכך הוי בחזקת שלא נתן וא"ל להעמיד בשעשה חזית: **אע"פ** שלא נתן (ח) תקרה מגלגלין עליו את הכל. אע"ג דזה נהנה וזה לא חסר פטור מ"מ כיון דגלי דעתיה דניחא ליה בהגבהה חייב וכן משמע נמי בכילד הרגל (ב"ק דף כ: ושם) דקאמר טעמא דניקף הא מקיף פטור ש"מ זה נהנה וזה לא חסר פטור ואפ"ה כשעמד ניקף חייב כן נראה לי אי נמי הכא זה חסר הוא שגורם לו שהגביה הכותל למעלה מד' אמות כדי שלא יהיה לו היזק ראיה בשום ענין ממנו: **הקובע** זמן לחבירו. אור"י דוקא קובע זמן אבל בסתם הלואה לא חשיב ליה תוך שלשים תוך זמנו:

מסורת הש"ס

א) [לעיל ג:], ב) נ"א ובא בזמנו. רש"ל, ג) שייך לעמוד הקודם, ד) [אלכויי לשון הרמת קול וירעם מתרגמינן וכו' כצ"ל רש"ל] והוא בש"ב כב וכן הוא בס"ע, ה) ס"א ול"נ רק הוא הגה"ה עד הס"ד רש"ל, ו) שייך לעמוד הקודם, ז) [כתובות פד.]

הגהות הב"ח

(א) גמ' הב לי לפי דמי קנים: (ב) שם בעלמא לאכלויי בעיא כצ"ל ותיבת לאו נמחק: (ג) רש"י ד"ה פייסיה וכו' טוב לך שיאות להתפייס: (ד) ד"ה ארבעה לצלא וכו' רצען היה וקונה עורות ונותן עורות לעבדנין: (ה) בא"ד אותה שדה דעכשיו: (ו) תוס' ד"ה הגה"ה וכו' דקאמר טעמא דגדר ניקף: (ז) ד"ה ארבעה וכו' הרי הוא מצרן כמו דאמרי אינשי: (ח) ד"ה אע"פ שלא נתן עליו את התקרה מגלגלין וכו' טעמא דגדר ניקף:

ליקוטי רש"י

קיבורא דאהיני. אשכול תמרים [שבת קנו.]. כמין אשכול יש תמרים הרבה בענף אחד [סנהדרין כו.]. לימוסי"ל [חולין צה.]. דצלא. עור [מו"ק כז.].

עין משפט נר מצוה

כב א מיי' פ"ג מהל' שכנים הל' א סמג עשין פב טוש"ע ח"מ סי' קנז סעיף י:
כג ב מיי' שם הל' ב טוש"ע שם סעיף ח:
כד ג ד מיי' שם הל' א טוש"ע שם סעיף י:
כה ה מיי' שם הל' ג טוש"ע שם סעיף יא:

רבינו גרשום

הב לי כמה דגדרי. הואיל והוקפת שדך מד' רוחותיה ומשתמרת תן לי לפי חלקך המגיעך מהוצאותי: **הב לי דמי קנים בזול.** כלומר אם לא תרצה ליתן שיעור גדר טוב תן לי מיהו שיעור דמי קנים בזול: **הוה קא גדר דיקלא.** היה (ולקט) [לוקט] דיקלא: **א"ל** רבינא **לאריסיה זיל אייתי לי קיבורא.** כגון אשכול של ג' או ד' תמרים תלוים בקנה א' מאותו דקל: **רמא קלא.** גער בו באותו אריס שלא יגע בתמרים: **דניחא לך.** בהני גדרים דגדרי: **אלא עיזא בעלמא.** כלומר מי לא **בעית** למעביד **נטירותא** מחמת עיזי דלא ליפסדו בשדך והשתא לא צריכת: **פסיקנא לך כרב הונא אליבא דר' יוסי.** דאמר הכל כמה שגדר: **ארבעה לצלא ארבעה לצללא.** כלומר דהיכי דצריכי לאושכף עשיר שהוא (דלא) [צלא] ד' ככרות למזונותיו ואנשי ביתו כך צריכין לעבדן עני משל אמר לו כלומר מעשה זה דבר מיצרא אינו אלא משום ועשית הישר והטוב וכיון דזה רוניא עני הוא (אעפ"כ) אינו יכול לחיות בלא שדה (שאם) [ואם] לא יקח עכשיו יפסיד מעותיו ואין לו במה להתפרנס משום הכי לא תוכל לסלוקיה דאין לך ועשית הישר והטוב גדול מזה דתשבקיה ליה למיזבן: **פיסקא כותל חצר** שבין ב' חצירות **שנפל מחייבין אותו** למעכב שיסייע **לבנות עד ד'** אמות משום היזק ראיה והואיל דמחייבין ליה לסיועיה אם טוען הלה לא נתן לי כלום אלא אני לבדי בניתי לי משלי וזה אומר נתתי הרי הוא **בחזקת שנתן עד שיביא ראיה** עדים שלא נתן: **מד' אמות ולמעלה אין מחייבין אותו.** לסייעו לבנות דהשתא ליכא היזק ראיה: **סמך לו זה.** שלא נתן מד' אמות ולמעלה ובנה זה בחלקו **כותל אחר** גבוה כמו זה שהגביה חבירו משלו שנתכוין לבנות שניהן ביחד ושיהיה כותל זה שהגביה חבירו אחד מכותלי הבית: **אע"פ שלא נתן עליו את התקרה.** על כותל זה שהגביה חבירו אלא כעין קונדסין ונתן עליהם את התקרה מצד אחד על כותליו אעפ"כ מגלגלין עליו **את הכל** מה שהוציא זה על אותו גובה יותר על ד' שאע"פ שלא נתן התקרה עליו נהנה הוא מן הכותל א) ההנאה היא בביתו מחמת אותו כותל: והואיל דמארבע אמות ולמעלה אין מחייבין אותו לבנות אם טוען הלה ואמר אני נתתי והלה אומר לא נתת הרי הוא **בחזקת שלא נתן עד שיביא ראיה שנתן: הקובע זמן לחבירו.** לפרוע לו את חובו:

חשק שלמה על רבינו גרשום א) נראה דצ"ל והכותל היא מחמת שהוא על בניינו של אותו כותל.

עין משפט נר מצוה

כו א ב מיי' פי"ד מהל' מלוה הל' א סמג עשין צד טוש"ע ח"מ סי' עח סעיף א:

כז ג מיי' שם סמג עשין צג טוש"ע ח"מ סי' קח סעיף יז:

כח ד ה מיי' שם סמג שם טוש"ע ח"מ סי' עח סעיף א:

גמרא

כי היכי דלא ליטרדן תנן בחזקת שנתן עד שיביא ראיה שלא נתן היכי דמי אילימא דאמר ליה פרעתיך בזמני פשיטא בחזקת שנתן אלא לאו דאמר ליה פרעתיך בתוך זמני אלמא עביד איניש דפרעיה בתוך זמניה שאני הכא דכל א) שפא ושפא זימניה הוא ת"ש בחזקת שלא נתן עד שיביא ראיה שנתן היכי דמי אילימא דאמר ליה פרעתיך בזמני אמאי לא אלא לאו דאמר ליה פרעתיך בתוך זמני אלמא לא עביד איניש דפרע בגו זימניה שאני הכא דאמר מי יימר דמחייבו לי רבנן רב פפא ורב הונא בריה דרב יהושע עבדי כאביי ורבא מר בר רב אשי עבד כר"ל א והלכתא כר"ל ב ואפילו מיתמי ואע"ג ג) דאמר מר ג הבא ליפרע מנכסי יתומים לא יפרע אלא בשבועה ד חזקה לא עביד איניש דפרע בגו זימניה ה איבעיא להו תבעו לאחר זמן ואמר לו פרעתיך בתוך זמני מהו ו מי אמרינן ° במקום חזקה (א) אמרינן ז) מה לי לשקר או

רש"י

אילימא דא"ל פרעתיך בזמני. כשהשלמת את גובה ארבע אמות: פשיטא. דנאמן שהרי זו טענת מנה לי בידך והלה אומר אין לך בידי כלום: אלא לאו דאמר ליה פרעתיך בתוך זמני. קודם שהשלמת לארבע אמות: ת"ש. מסיפא בחזקת שלא נתן כו': אילימא דא"ל פרעתיך בזמני. כשגמרתי את כותלי וידעתי כמה נתחייבתי לסייע בהגבהתך: מי יימר דמחייבו לי רבנן. הילכך אפילו אמר פרעתיך בזמני לא מהימן: ואפילו מיתמי. אם מת הלוה בתוך זמנו וגובה חובו מן היתומים בלא שבועה ולא חיישינן דילמא פרעיה: מה לי לשקר. אי בעי אמר ליה פרעתיך בזמני הילכך כי א"ל נמי פרעתיך בתוך זמני נאמן בשבועה: או

תוספות

אי אמרינן מיגו במקום חזקה ומ"מ אין להוכיח מכאן דקסבר ר"ל לקיש המלוה את חבירו בעדים אין צריך לפורעו בעדים דאפשר דמיירי הכא שהלוהו שלא בעדים אלא הודה לו בפני עדים דאפילו למ"ד צריך לפורעו בעדים ה"מ היכא דהלוהו בפני עדים מעיקרא דלא הימניה אלא בפני עדים ואם תאמר מכל מקום ניפשוט מהכא דלא אמרינן מיגו דאי בעי אמר פרעתיך עתה ואומר ר"י דהא לא חשיב מיגו כיון דמיירי דקיימי ביום אחרון של זמן ואע"ג דמסקינן בשילהי דהשואל (ב"מ דף קב: ושם) דעביד איניש דפרע ביומא דמישלם זימניה מ"מ אין זה מיגו דלא חליף איניש למימר פרעתיך היום אבל רגיל הוא לומר פרעתיך אתמול ושכחת:

כי היכי דלא ליטרדן. אע"ג דבפ' יש בכור (בכורות דף מט. ושם) תנן בכור בתוך שלשים יום בחזקת שלא נפדה ואומר ר"י דהתם לא שייך האי טעמא דלא ליטרדן דהוי ממון שאין לו תובעין מיהו קשיא לרבי מפרק השואל (ב"מ דף קב: ושם) דאמר בעו מיניה מרבי ינאי שוכר אומר נתתי ומשכיר אומר לא נטלתי על מי להביא ראיה אימת אי בתוך זמנו תנינא מת (ב) בתוך שלשים יום בחזקת שלא נפדה והשתא היכי מדמי לה לבכור דהתם לא שייך למימר לא ליטרדן ולכך צריך לומר דבכור נמי איכא טירדא דמלוה שצריך מיד ליתן דזריזין מקדימין ומפרש ר"י טעם אחר דהכא כיון דחייב לו ואיתרמי ליה זוזי פורע לו תוך הזמן דלא ליטרדן אבל גבי בכור דאכתי לא איחייב כלל עד לאחר ל' יום ושמא ימות בתוך ל' ויפטר וכן שוכר שמא יפול ביתו של משכיר ויצטרך שוכר לצאת דלא עדיף מיניה ומיהו קשיא הא דפריך לר"ל מכותל חצר שנפל ודייק מיניה דעביד איניש דפרע בגו זימניה ורבא נמי תיקשי דמודו התם דלא עביד דפרע דשמא לא יבנה זה את הכותל ומיהו בכמה מקומות יכול לומר וליטעמיך ולא קאמר:

אילימא דא"ל פרעתיך בזמני פשיטא. וא"ת ואמאי פשיטא הא כיון דאין אדם פורע תוך זמנו ואנן סהדי שזה עשה כותל איצטריך לאשמועינן דאין צריך לפורעו בעדים וי"ל דאפילו מ"ד גבי מלוה חבירו בעדים צריך לפורעו בעדים התם משום דלא הימניה מעיקרא אבל הכא ליכא שום הוכחה דלא הימניה הילכך פשיטא דאין צריך לפורעו בעדים:

ואפילו מיתמי. ואע"ג דאמור רבנן הבא ליפרע כו'. נראה דביתומים גדולים מיירי אבל בקטנים לא גבי אפי' תוך זמנו (ג) לרב פפא דמפרש טעמא דאין נזקקין משום פריעת בעל חוב מלוה ויתמי לאו בני מיעבד מלוה נינהו ואפילו לרב הונא בריה דרב יהושע דמפרש טעמא משום נררי לא גבי מיתמי קטנים אפילו תוך זמנו דאין מקבלים עדים שלא בפני בעל דין דקטנים חשוב שלא בפניו כדמוכח בריש פרק הגוזל בתרא (ב"ק דף קיב.) ואפילו נתקבלה עדות בחיי האב (ד) מצית למימר דחיישינן לנררי אפילו תוך הזמן בקטנים כדאשכחן גבי אלמנה בפרק השולח (גיטין דף לד: ושם) דתנן אין האלמנה נפרעת מנכסי יתומים אלא בשבועה וטעמא משום שמא התפיסה הבעל נררי אע"פ שהוא תוך הזמן ומיהו מאלמנה אין ראיה דהתם חיישינן לנררי אפילו בגדולים משום דאית לה בתנאי בית דין כדאמרינן בהנושא (כתובות דף קב: ושם) דחיישינן טפי לנררי בבנותיו מבבת אשתו משום כיון דאיתנהו בתנאי בית דין אימור נררי אתפסינהו ואין להביא ראיה מדלא קאמר הכא אע"ג דאמור רבנן אין נזקקין לנכסי יתומים קטנים אא"כ רבית אוכלת בהן כו' דלא מיירי בקטנים אלא דוקא בגדולים דשמא משום רב פפא נקט ההוא דהבא ליפרע לאשמועינן דגבי אפילו בלא שבועה ואין להביא ראיה משלהי דמכילתין (דף קעד:) דקאמר מאי בינייהו דרב פפא ורב הונא בריה דרב יהושע ולא קאמר איכא בינייהו כגון דמית לוה תוך הזמן דלרב הונא גבי דהא רב הונא ורב פפא אמר בשמעתין דלית להו חזקה דריש לקיש ועוד דבכמה מקומות יכול למצוא איכא בינייהו טובא ואינו חושש לומר אלא דבר אחד או שנים כדאמרינן בהמניח (ב"ק דף לג. ושם ד"ה הקדישו) גבי פלוגתא דיוסף השור מיהו יש להביא ראיה דאפילו רב הונא דמפרש טעמא משום נררי לא גבי מיתומים קטנים אפילו תוך הזמן דפריך עליה דרב אסי בפ' שום היתומים (ערכין דף כב. ושם) ודחיק עלה לשנויי בבעל חוב שקיבל עליו לזו ולא לזו ולא משני הכא במאי עסקינן בשלא הגיע הזמן בחיי האב ואין לומר דההיא סוגיא סברה כטעמא דרב פפא דהא במסקנא משני כשחייב מודה והאי שינויא ליתא אליבא דטעמא דרב פפא וכן יש להוכיח מגופיה דמילתיה דרב אסי דקאמר אלא אם כן רבית אוכלת בהן ור' יוחנן אינו מוסיף כי אם כתובת אשה משום מזוני משמע בעל חוב לא משתכח בשום ענין דנפרעין ומסתמא רב אסי ורבי יוחנן אית להו חזקה דריש לקיש דהכי הלכתא כדפסיק בשמעתין ועוד אי לית להו חזקה דריש לקיש א"כ קי"ל כריש לקיש בארבעה דברים וברים החולץ (יבמות דף לו. ושם) לא פסיק רבא כוותיה אלא בתלת אע"ג דרבא ודאי פליג אריש לקיש בשמעתין מ"מ גם לדידן מוכח דלא קי"ל כריש לקיש אלא בתלת ובפרק ד' וה' (ב"ק דף לט. ושם) דפריך לרבי יוחנן דאמר מעליית יתומים והאמר רבי יוחנן אין נזקקין לנכסי יתומים אלא לכתובת אשה אע"ג דקיימא לן דטעמא הוי משום נררי והתם בשור שנגח לא שייך נררי מ"מ פריך שפיר דרבי יוחנן אית ליה אין נזקקין בכל ענין אפילו במלוה הבאה מחמת עצמו דלא שייך נררי מטעם דאין מקבלין עדות שלא בפני בעל דין:

אע"ג דאמור רבנן הבא ליפרע מנכסי יתומים כו'. ותניא נמי בפ' הכותב (כתובות דף פז. ושם) אבל מה אעשה שהרי אמרו חכמים הבא ליפרע כו' משמע שהיא משנה בשום מקום ותימה היכא אמרו חכמים דמאלמנה ליכא למילף דשאני אלמנה דאית לה בתנאי ב"ד וחיישינן לנררי טפי ואומר ר"י מדתנן בפרק הכותב (שם דף פד.) גבי מי שמת והניח אשה ובעל חוב והיה לו מלוה ופקדון ביד אחרים כו' יתנו ליורשים שכולם צריכים שבועה ואין היורשין צריכין שבועה ועוד תנן בשבועות (דף מה.) וכן היתומים מן היתומים לא יפרעו אלא בשבועה וכו' שלא מצינו בין שטרותיו של אבא ששטר זה פרוע אלמא גם האב היה נשבע שאינו פרוע מכאן משמע שאם הוציא שטר חוב על חבירו וא"ל אישתבע לי דלא פרעתיך בגו זימניה אין צריך לעשות שבועה:

מי אמרי' במקום חזקה מה לי לשקר או לא. הקשה הר"י בר מרדכי והא הך חזקה עדיפא משטר דבשטר איהו גובה אלא בשבועה ובהך חזקה גובה בלא שבועה וא"כ מאי קא מיבעיא ליה הא פשיטא דמיגו במקום עדים לא אמרינן כ"ש במקום חזקה דעדיפא טפי ואור"י דלא קשה כלל דודאי עדים עדיפי מחזקה דאי אמרי שפרעו אפי' בתוך הזמן פטור ואי אמרי אפילו אחר זמן ידענו שלא פרעו היה גובה מן היתומים בלא שבועה ומה שצריך שבועה ביש לו שטר זהו לפי שאינו מוכיח מתוך השטר אם פרע ואם לאו דזימנין דזייר ליה אפסיטי דספרא כדאמרינן בפ"ק דב"מ (דף טז:) אך קשה דמ"מ תפשוט דלא אמרי' מיגו במקום חזקה מדרמי בר חמא דאמר בפרק כל הנשבעין (שבועות דף מה: ושם) המפקיד אצל חבירו בשטר צריך להחזיר לו ה) (בשטר) ולא מהימן לומר החזרתי לך במיגו דאי בעי אמר דנאנסו משום דמלי א"ל שטרך בידי מאי בעי וכ"ש דלא אמר מיגו במקום חזקה דחזקה עדיפא דאין צריך שבועה וטעמא דשטרך בידי מאי בעי לא מהני לפוטרו משבועה ושמא סוגיא דהכא לא סברה כרמי בר חמא ולא דמי כלל לההוא ו) דפרק האומר (דף סד: ושם) דאמר היכא דמוחזק לן דאית ליה אחים ואמר יש לי בנים דנאמן במיגו דאי בעי פטר לה בגיטא וכן ההיא דהאשה שלום (יבמות דף קטו. ושם) דבעי החזיקה היא מלחמה בעולם מי אמר מיגו דאי בעי אמרה שלום בעולם או דלמא כיון דהחזיקה היא ואמרה בדדמי לא אתי מה לי לשקר ומרע לחזקה ומייתי התם מעין ההיא בעיא לא דמי כלל להך דהכא ומיהו קשה מדתנן ביבמות בפרק בית שמאי (דף קיא:) יבמה שאמרה תוך שלשים יום לא נבעלתי כופין אותו אחר שלשים מבקשים הימנו ומפרש התם דעד שלשים יום מוקי איניש אנפשיה טפי לא מוקי ולכך לאחר שלשים יום אין כופין דלא מהימנא אף על גב דאית לה מיגו ° דאי בעיא אמרה אינו יכול לבא עלי דנאמנת כדמוכח בסוף נדרים (דף צא.):

ואמר

רבינו גרשום

כי היכי דלא ליטרדן. שלא יתבעו בזמנו: אילימא בזמנו. בשעת השלמת ד' אמות פשיטא דנאמן דמי איכא למאן דאמר דבזמנו לא הוי נאמן: אלא בתוך זמנו. קודם השלמת ד' אמות קתני דנאמן דבחזקת שנתן הוא אלמא עביד איניש דפרע בגו זמניה ותיובתא דריש לקיש. אמר לך ריש לקיש בעלמא אימא לך דלא עביד איניש דפרע בגו זימניה ושאני הכא גבי כותל אמאי נאמן דליכא תוך זמנו דכל שעה ושעה כל דימוס ודימוס שבנה זמנו הוא לסייע ומש"ה נאמן: ת"ש מסיפא. הא סיפא קשיא לאביי ורבא אמרי לך אביי ורבא בעלמא אימא לך דעביד איניש דפרע בגו זימניה ושאני הכא גבי סמוך לו כותל דמש"ה אינו נאמן כי טוען דפרע חלקו קודם שסמך לו א) דאמרי' ליה אימר אמר סבר בדעתו הואיל ואינו חייב עכשיו לסייע בהגבהה למה ליה למיתן ליה מי יימר דמחייבי (ליה) [לי] רבנן למיתן כשאסמוך הכותל ומשום האי סברא לא יהיב ליה מידי ואי טעין דיהיב אינו נאמן: ואפי' מיתמי. שאם טען אחד לחבירו פרעתיך תוך זמנו ומת והניח יתומים חייבין היתומין לשלם דלא יכלי למטען שמענו מאבינו שאמר שפרע לו בתוך זמנו ואע"ג דאמרי' הבא ליפרע מנכסי יתומים אע"פ שיש לו שטר לא יפרע אלא בשבועה דאמרי' אלו הוה אבוהון קיים הוה מפיק שובר ומרע ליה לשטרא אפ"ה דמהמרינן כל כך בנכסי יתמי אפ"ה אי אמר אבוהון לבעל חובו פרעתיך בתוך זמנו ומת מגבי מיתמי: מה לי לשקר במקום חזקה. כלומר הואיל ויכול הוא לטעון לפטור עצמו ולומר שפרע בזמנו ב) בחזקה דאדם פורע בזמנו והואיל ויכול לפטור עצמו בזמנו ואמר תוך זמנו אמרי' מה לי לשקר:

חשק שלמה על רבינו גרשום

א) [נראה דצ"ל דאמרי' ליה דהואיל אמר וכו' סבר בדעתו הואיל וכו']. ב) [אולי צ"ל שפרע בזמנו דאמרינן מה לי לשקר ולמאן דנטען שפרע תוך זמנו ואף שהוא נגד החזקה דאדם פורע בזמנו והואיל ויכול לפטור עצמו ולומר שפרע בזמנו].

מסורת הש"ס

א) [גי' הערוך בערך סף ד' ספא וספא פי' כל נדבך ונדבך זמניה הוא], ב) [לקמן נג. גיטין לד:] כתובות פז., ג) [וער' תוס' כתובות יט. ד"ה חזקה וכו' מה שהניחו בצ"ע], ד) [קדושין סד: וש"נ], ה) [נ"ל בעדים], ו) [נ"ל דקדושין פרק]:

הגהות הב"ח

(א) גמ' במקום חזקה מה לי כצ"ל ותיבת אמרי' נמחק: (ב) תוס' ד"ה כי היכי וכו' זמנו תנינא מת האב בתוך: (ג) ד"ה ואפי' וכו' תוך זמנו (לרב פפא למפרש וכו' ואפילו לרב הונא בריה דרב יהושע) תא"מ ונ"ב ס"א וכ"ה באשר"י ולא מיבעיא לרב פפא וכו' אלא אפי' לרב הונא בריה דרב יהושע וכו': (ד) בא"ד עדות בחיי האב נמי מלית למימר:

גליון הש"ס

גמ' במקום חזקה אמרי' מה לי לשקר. עי' ב"ק דף קו ע"א: תוס' ד"ה מי כו' דאי בעיא אמרה א"י בבא עלי. לא זכיתי להבין הא שם בנדרים מבואר הטעם דנאמנת בהכי משום דאין אשה מעיזה פניה בפני בעלה והכא לא"ש כן הכא בדבריו דבא עליה אינו בעלה עוד ותו לא"ל ליכא חזקה זו דהא ממ"נ אינו בעלה ולהרבה כפי דבריה עדיין זקוקה לו וצ"ע:

ליקוטי רש"י

הבא ליפרע מנכסי יתומים לא יפרע אלא בשבועה. וכל זמן שלא נשבע אין לנו רשות בהם [כתובות פז.]. ואפילו הוציא שטר דאי הוה אבוהון דיתמי קיים דלמא הוה טוען ואמר לאשתבע לי דלא פרעתיך ומשבעינן ליה כדאמרינן בשבועות (מא.) [גיטין נ.]. צריך שבועה שלא נתקבל חוב [שבועות מב.].

כִּי הֵיכִי דְּלָא לִיטְרְדָן – **so that he will not bother me** for the money when the loan comes due."

The Gemara attempts to refute Reish Lakish's opinion by citing our Mishnah:

תְּנַן – **It was taught in the Mishnah** regarding the rebuilding of the first four *amos* of a collapsed wall: בְּחֶזְקַת שֶׁנָּתַן עַד שֶׁיָּבִיא רְאָיָה שֶׁלֹּא נָתַן – Each neighbor IS PRESUMED TO HAVE CONTRIBUTED to the cost of the wall UNTIL the other neighbor BRINGS PROOF THAT HE DID NOT CONTRIBUTE. הֵיכִי דָּמֵי – **What is this case like?**[1] אִילֵימָא דְּאָמַר לֵיהּ פְּרַעְתִּיךְ בִּזְמַנִּי – **If we will say that** the neighbor **told [the builder]: "I paid you at my** allotted **time,"**[2] פְּשִׁיטָא בְּחֶזְקַת שֶׁנָּתַן – **it is obvious** that **he is presumed to have contributed,** and so is believed![3] אֶלָּא לָאו דְּאָמַר לֵיהּ – **Rather, is this not** a case **where** the neighbor **said to [the builder],** פְּרַעְתִּיךְ בְּתוֹךְ זְמַנִּי – **"I paid you within my** allotted **time,"** i.e. before the wall was built to a height of four *amos;* and yet the Mishnah states that the neighbor is presumed to have paid! אַלְמָא עָבִיד אִינִישׁ דְּפָרְעֵיהּ בְּתוֹךְ זִמְנֵיהּ – **We** therefore **see** that **it happens that a person pays [his creditor] within his** allotted **time,** in accordance with the view of Abaye and Rava and in direct contradiction to the view of Reish Lakish.

The Gemara rejects this proof:

שָׁאנֵי הָכָא – The case **here** in the Mishnah **is different,** דְּכָל שָׁפָא וְשָׁפָא זִמְנֵיהּ הוּא – **for as each and every row** of stones is set in place, **it is his time** to pay. Hence, this case of the Mishnah does not refute Reish Lakish, since the neighbor did not claim to have paid before the loan came due.[4]

The Gemara now attempts to discredit the view of Abaye and Rava:

תָּא שְׁמַע – **Come, learn** a refutation of Abaye and Rava from the second case of the Mishnah, which stated:

בְּחֶזְקַת שֶׁלֹּא נָתַן עַד שֶׁיָּבִיא רְאָיָה שֶׁנָּתַן – HE IS PRESUMED NOT TO HAVE CONTRIBUTED UNTIL HE BRINGS PROOF THAT HE DID CONTRIBUTE.[5]

Developing its challenge, the Gemara analyzes the case:

הֵיכִי דָּמֵי – **What is** this case **like?** אִילֵימָא דְּאָמַר לֵיהּ – **If we say that he** (the one who built the parallel wall) **said to [the builder of the extension]:** פְּרַעְתִּיךְ בִּזְמַנִּי – **"I paid you** my share **at my** allotted **time,"**[6] אַמַּאי לֹא – **why** is he **not** believed? He is merely claiming that he paid his debt when it came due! אֶלָּא לָאו דְּאָמַר לֵיהּ – **Rather,** is this **not** a case **where he said to him:** פְּרַעְתִּיךְ בְּתוֹךְ זְמַנִּי – **"I paid you** my share **within my** allotted **time"**;[7] and yet the Mishnah states that in this case he is not believed?! אַלְמָא לֹא עָבִיד אִינִישׁ דְּפָרַע בְּגוֹ זִמְנֵיהּ – **We** therefore **see** that **it does not happen that a person pays** his creditor **within his** allotted **time** – a refutation of the view of Abaye and Rava!

The Gemara dismisses this proof:

שָׁאנֵי הָכָא – The case **here differs** from that of a regular debt, דְּאָמַר – **for** the builder of the parallel wall **said** to himself, מִי יֵימַר דִּמְחַיְּיבוּ לִי רַבָּנַן – **"Who says that the Rabbis will obligate me** to contribute toward the extension?" Since this liability is not obvious, the halachah presumes that he will not pay until ordered by the court to do so.[8]

NOTES

1. The Gemara understands from the Mishnah that altough both neighbors are required to rebuild the wall, only one of them built it without any assistance from the second one, expecting to be repaid after its completion. Upon being asked for payment, the second one replied that he had already repaid him for the rebuilding of the wall. In developing its challenge to Reish Lakish, the Gemara clarifies the neighbor's response.

This entire section of the Gemara would seem to be inconsistent with *Rashi's* statement in the Mishnah (see above, 5a note 14) that the reason we assume the second neighbor has paid is because the first neighbor would not construct a wall unilaterally, but would sue in court for his neighbor's assistance. The Gemara here is based on an opposite premise – namely, that the Mishnah deals with an instance where the first neighbor claims that he built the wall unilaterally. The second neighbor agrees, but claims to have paid his share after the wall was completed (or during its construction). Several commentators offer intricate solutions to this difficulty (see *Urim V'Tumim* 78:4 and *Nachalas David*; see also *Chidushei R' Nachum* and *Nachalas Moshe*).

2. I.e. when you erected the wall to a height of four *amos* (*Rashi*). A request to be paid in full was made by the builder only after the wall was completed (see previous note). Thus, in essence, the Mishnah is stating that if the builder requests payment, the neighbor can reply that he paid at the proper time.

Rabbeinu Yonah raises an obvious question: The Gemara is stating that the time of payment is after the wall is built, for before it is finished payment is not yet due. Based on this, the question on Reish Lakish is posed. This would seem to be problematic, for Reish Lakish stated that a person would not repay a loan before the payment is due, since he is not yet obligated to do so. That is not the case here, as even before the wall is finished, the neighbor is already obligated to pay; for as soon as the old wall fell down, he was obligated to contribute towards a replacement! Seemingly, then, even according to Reish Lakish, he may rightfully claim to have paid before the wall was finished, since he already was obligated to do so!

Rabbeinu Yonah answers that the Gemara assumes that although indeed they are both obligated to rebuild the wall, when one of them begins to do so unilaterally, he is in effect undertaking to rebuilt it for both of them, expecting to be reimbursed after the wall is finished. Therefore, the other neighbor has no obligation to pay until the wall is completed.

3. This situation is analogous to the case of one who purports to have lent money to another and sues for repayment, and the other says he no longer owes anything to the claimant (*Rashi*). [The burden of proof naturally falls on the claimant, since there is no basis to presume that the other owes him money. Here, too, there is no basis to presume that the neighbor still owes his share of the wall, since the time for repayment has passed.]

4. Thus, the Mishnah does not speak of a case where the neighbor claims to have paid for the entire wall; he merely claims to have paid for the row of bricks just constructed (*Rabbeinu Yonah*; cf. *Tur Choshen Mishpat* 157:24). Although the fact that the neighbor is believed to claim that he paid is in itself obvious (for he is merely claiming that he paid on time), the novelty of the ruling lies in the very fact that payment for each row is due as it is completed, and a claim that the payment has been made is therefore accepted (*Rabbeinu Yonah* and *Ri MiGash*; cf. *Ritva* and *Shach* to *Choshen Mishpat* 78:12).

5. The Mishnah had stated that neither neighbor is permitted to compel the other to rebuild the collapsed wall higher than four *amos*. However, if one of them extended the wall (at his own expense) and the other subsequently juxtaposed a parallel wall near or equal in height to the extended first wall, the latter becomes liable to pay his share of the extension. The section of the Mishnah quoted by the Gemara charges the owner of the parallel wall with the burden of proving that he met his obligation.

6. I.e. upon completion of my parallel wall, when it can be ascertained how much I am obligated to contribute toward your extension (*Rashi*). [The neighbor's liability corresponds to the amount of the extension that he actually intends to use, and not necessarily to the entire extension.]

7. I.e. before completing my parallel wall, as I already estimated how high I would build, and could thus calculate my share of the extension. [It is still considered to be within the allotted time, however, since the other neighbor cannot obligate him to pay his share of the entire extension until he builds his parallel wall to the same height.]

8. *Rashi* 5a ד״ה בחזקת. Thus, he is not believed even if he claims that he paid *after* incurring liability – i.e. after completing the parallel wall (*Rashi* here). [See, however, *Ritva*, who explains why he would be believed if he claims to have maden payment after completion of the

כי היכי דלא ליטרדן תנן בחזקת שנתן עד שיביא ראיה שלא נתן היכי דמי אילימא דאמר ליה פרעתיך בזמני פשיטא בחזקת שנתן אלא לאו דאמר ליה פרעתיך בתוך זמני אלמא עביד איניש דפרעיה בתוך זמניה שאני הכא דכל א) שפא ושפא זימניה הוא ת"ש בחזקת שלא נתן עד שיביא ראיה שנתן היכי דמי אילימא דאמר ליה פרעתיך בזמני אמאי לא אלא לאו דאמר ליה פרעתיך בתוך זמני אלמא לא עביד איניש דפרע בגו זמניה שאני הכא דאמר מי יימר דמחייבו לי רבנן רב פפא ורב הונא בריה דרב יהושע עבדי כאביי ורבא מר בר רב אשי עבד כר"ל והלכתא כר"ל ואפילו מיתמי ואע"ג דאמר מר הבא ליפרע מנכסי יתומים לא יפרע אלא בשבועה חזקה לא עביד איניש דפרע בגו זמניה איבעיא להו תבעו לאחר זמן ואמר לו פרעתיך בתוך זמני מהו מי אמרינן במקום חזקה (א) אמרינן מה לי לשקר או

אילימא דא"ל פרעתיך בזמני. כשהשלמת את גובה ארבע אמות: **פשיטא.** דנאמן שהרי זו טענת מנה לי בידך והלה אומר אין לך בידי כלום: **אלא לאו דאמר ליה פרעתיך בתוך זמני.** קודם שהשלמת לארבע אמות: **ת"ש.** מסיפא בחזקת שלא נתן כו': **אילימא דא"ל פרעתיך בזמני.** כשגמרתי את כותלי וידעתי כמה נתחייבתי לסייע בהגבהתו: **מי יימר דמחייבו לי רבנן.** הילכך אפילו אמר פרעתיך בזמני לא מהימן: **ואפילו מיתמי.** אם מת הלוה בתוך זמנו גובה חובו מן היתומים בלא שבועה ולא חיישינן דילמא פרעיה: **מה לי לשקר.** אי בעי אמר ליה פרעתיך בזמני הילכך כי א"ל נמי פרעתיך בתוך זמני נאמן בשבועה: או

אי אמרינן מיגו במקום חזקה ומ"מ אין להוכיח מכאן דקסבר ר"ל המלוה את חבירו בעדים אין צריך לפורעו בעדים דאפשר דמיירי הכא שהלוהו שלא בעדים אלא הודה לו בפני עדים דאפילו למ"ד צריך לפורעו בעדים ה"מ היכא דהלוהו בפני עדים מעיקרא דלא הימניה אלא בפני עדים ואם תאמר מכל מקום ניפשוט מהכא דלא אמרינן מיגו דאי בעי אמר פרעתיך עתה ואומר ר"י דהא לא חשיב מיגו כיון דמיירי דקיימי ביום אחרון של זמן ואע"ג דמסקינן בשילהי השואל (ב"מ דף קב: ושם) דעביד איניש דפרע ביומא דמישלם זימניה מ"מ אין זה מיגו דלא חציף איניש למימר פרעתיך היום אבל רגיל הוא לומר פרעתיך אתמול ושכחת: **כי היכי דלא ליטרדן.** אע"ג דבפ' יש בכור (בכורות דף מט. ושם) תנן בכור בתוך שלשים יום בחזקת שלא נפדה ואומר ר"י דהתם לא שייך האי טעמא דלא ליטרדן דהוי ממון שאין לו תובעין מיהו קשיא לרבי מפרק השואל (ב"מ דף קב: ושם) דאמר בעו מיניה מרבי ינאי שוכר אומר נתתי ומשכיר אומר לא נטלתי על מי להביא ראיה אי בתוך זמנו תניא מת (ב) בתוך שלשים יום בחזקת שלא נפדה והשתא היכי מדמי לה לבכור דהתם לא שייך למימר לא ליטרדן ולכך צריך לומר דבכור נמי איכא טירדא למלוה שצריך מיד ליתן דזריזין מקדימין ומפרש ר"י טעם אחר דהכא כיון דחייב לו ואיתרמי ליה זוזי פורע לו תוך הזמן דלא ליטרדן אבל גבי בכור דאכתי לא איחייב כלל עד לאחר ל' יום ושמא ימות בתוך ל' ויפטר וכן שוכר שמא יפול ביתו של משכיר וליטרף שוכר לאלתר דלא עדיף מיניה ומיהו קשיא הא דפריך הא דר"ל מכותל חצר שנפל ודייק מיניה דעביד איניש דפרע בגו זימניה ורבא נמי מיקשי דמודו התם דלא עביד דפרע דשמא לא יבנה זה את הכותל ומיהו בכמה מקומות יכול לומר וליטעמיך ולא קאמר: **אילימא דא"ל פרעתיך בזמני פשיטא.** וא"ת ואמאי פשיטא הא כיון דאין אדם פורע תוך זמנו ואין סהדי שזה עשה כותל איצטריך לאשמועינן דאין צריך לפורעו בעדים וי"ל דאפילו למ"ד גבי מלוה חבירו בעדים צריך לפורעו בעדים התם משום דלא הימניה מעיקרא אבל הכא ליכא שום הוכחה דלא הימניה הילכך פשיטא דאין צריך לפורעו בעדים: **ואפילו מיתמי.** ואע"ג דאמור רבנן הבא ליפרע כו'. נראה דביתומים גדולים מיירי אבל בקטנים לא גבי אפי' תוך זמנו (ג) לרב פפא דמפרש טעמא דאין מזקקין משום פריעת בעל חוב מצוה ויתמי לאו בני מיעבד מצוה נינהו ואפילו לרב הונא בריה דרב יהושע דמפרש טעמא משום דררי לא גבי מיתמי קטנים אפילו תוך זמנו דאין מקבלים עדים שלא בפני בעל דין וקטנים חשוב שלא בפניו כדמוכח בריש פרק הגוזל בתרא (ב"ק דף קיב:) ואפילו נתקבלה עדות בחיי האב (ד) מלית למימר דחיישינן לדררי אפילו תוך הזמן בקטנים כדאשכחן גבי אלמנה בפרק השולח (גיטין דף לד: ושם) דתנן אין האלמנה נפרעת מנכסי יתומים אלא בשבועה וטעמא משום שמא התפיסה הבעל לכרי אע"פ שהוא תוך הזמן ומיהו מאלמנה אין ראיה דהתם חיישינן לכרי אפילו בגדולים משום דלית לה בתנאי בית דין כדאמרינן בהנושא (כתובות דף קג: ושם) דחיישינן טפי לכרי בבנותיו מבבת אשתו משום כיון דאיתנהו בתנאי בית דין אימור כרכי אתפסינהו ואין להביא ראיה מדלא קאמר הכא אע"ג דאמור רבנן אין נזקקין לנכסי יתומים קטנים אא"כ רבית אוכלת בהן כו' דלא מיירי בקטנים אלא דוקא בגדולים דשמא משום רב פפא נקט מילתיה בגדולים אי נמי ניקט הבא ליפרע דנוהגין דגבי אפילו בלא שבועה ואין להביא ראיה משילהי דמכילתין (דף קעד:) דקאמר מאי בינייהו דרב פפא ורב הונא בריה דרב יהושע ולא קאמר איכא בינייהו כגון דמית לוה תוך הזמן דלרב הונא גבי דהא רב הונא ורב פפא אמר בשמעתין דלית להו חזקה דריש לקיש ועוד דבכמה מקומות יכול למצוא איכא בינייהו טובא ואינו חושש לומר אלא דבר אחד או שנים כדאמרינן בהמניח (ב"ק דף לג. ושם ד"ה הקדישו) גבי פלוגתא דיוסי הגלילי [?] רב הונא דמפרש טעמא משום דררי לא גבי מיתמי קטנים אפילו תוך הזמן דפריך עליה דרב אסי בפ' שום היתומים (ערכין דף כב. ושם) ודחיק עלה לשנויי בבעל חוב שקיבל עליו לוז ולא לוז ולא משני הכא במאי עסקינן בשלא הגיע הזמן בחיי האב ואין לומר דההיא סוגיא סברה כטעמא דרב פפא דהא במסקנא משני כשחייב מודה והאי שינויא ליתא אליבא דטעמא דרב פפא וכן יש להוכיח מגופיה דמילתיה דרב אסי דקאמר אלא אם כן רבית אוכלת בהן ור' יוחנן אינו מוסיף כי אם כתובת אשה משום מזוני משמע בעל חוב לא משתכח בשום ענין דנפרעין ומסתמא רב אסי ורבי יוחנן אית להו חזקה דריש לקיש דהכי הלכתא כדפסיק בשמעתין ועוד אי לית להו חזקה דריש לקיש א"כ קי"ל כריש לקיש בארבעה דברים וכריש החולץ (יבמות דף לו. ושם) לא פסיק רבא כוותיה אלא בתלת אע"ג דרבא ודאי פליג אריש לקיש בשמעתין מ"מ גם לדידן מוכח דלא קי"ל כריש לקיש אלא בתלת ובפרק ד' וה' (ב"ק דף נג. ושם) דפריך לרבי יוחנן דאמר מעלין יתומים והאמר רבי יוחנן אין נזקקין לנכסי יתומים אלא לכתובת אשה אע"ג דקיימא לן דטעמא הוי משום דררי והתם בשור שנגח לא שייך לררי מ"מ פריך שפיר דרבי יוחנן אית ליה דאין נזקקין בכל ענין אפילו בא מלוה הבא מחמת עצמו דלא שייך לררי מטעם שלא בפני בעל דין: **אע"ג דאמור רבנן הבא ליפרע מנכסי יתומים כו'.** ותנית נמי בפ' הכותב (כתובות דף פז. ושם) אבל מה עשה שהרי אמרו חכמים הבא ליפרע כו' משמע שהיא משנה בשום מקום ותימה היכא אמרו חכמים דמאלמנה ליכא למילף דשאני אלמנה דלית לה בתנאי ב"ד וחיישינן לכרי טפי ואומר ר"י מדתנן בפרק הכותב (שם דף פד.) גבי מי שמת והניח אשה ובעל חוב והיה לו מלוה ופקדון ביד אחרים כו' יתנו ליורשים שכולם צריכים שבועה ואין היורשין צריכין שבועה ועוד תנן בשבועות (דף מה.) וכן היתומים מן היתומים לא יפרעו אלא בשבועה וכו' שלא מצינו בין שטרותיו של אבא ששטר זה פרוע אלמא גם האב היה נשבע שאינו פרוע מכאן משמע שאם הוציא שטר חוב על חבירו וא"ל אישתבע לי דלא פרעתיך בגו זימניה אין צריך לעשות שבועה: **מי אמרי' במקום חזקה מה לי לשקר או לא.** הקשה הר"י בר מרדכי והא הך חזקה עדיפא משטר דבשטר אינו גובה אלא בשבועה ובהך חזקה גובה בלא שבועה וא"כ מאי קא מיבעיא ליה הא פשיטא דמיגו במקום עדים לא אמרינן כ"ש במקום חזקה דעדיפא טפי ואור"י דלא קשה כלל דודאי עדים עדיפי מחזקה דאי אמרי אפי' בתוך הזמן פטור ואי אמרי אפילו אחר זמן ידענו שלא פרעו היה גובה מן היתומים בלא שבועה ומה שצריך שבועה בי"ש לו שטר זהו לפי שאינו מוכיח מתוך השטר אם פרע ואם לאו דזימנין דזייר ליה אפסיטי דספרא כדאמרינן בפ"ק דב"מ (דף טז:) אך קשה דמ"מ תפשוט דלא אמרי' מיגו במקום חזקה מדרמי בר חמא דאמר בפרק כל הנשבעין (שבועות דף מה: ושם) המפקיד אצל חבירו בשטר צריך להחזיר לו [ה] (בשטר) ולא מהימן לומר החזרתי לך במיגו דאי בעי אמר דנאנסו משום דמאי א"ל שטרך בידי מאי בעי וכ"ש דלא אמר מיגו במקום חזקה עדיפא דאין צריך שבועה וטעמא דשטרך בידי מאי בעי לא מהני לפוטרו משבועה ושמא סוגיא דהכא לא סברה כרמי בר חמא ולא דמי כלל להווא [ו] דפרק האומר (דף סד: ושם) דאמר היכא דמוחזק לן דאית ליה אחים ואמר יש לי בנים דנאמן במיגו דאי בעי פטר לה בגיטא וכן ההיא דהאשה שלום (יבמות דף קטו. ושם) דבעי החזיקה היא מלחמה בעולם מי אמר מיגו דאי בעי אמרה שלום בעולם או דלמא כיון דהחזיקה היא ואמרה בדדמי לא אתי מה לי לשקר ומרע לחזקה ומייתי התם מעין ההיא בעיא לא דמי כלל להך דהכא ומיהו קשה מדתנן ביבמות בפרק בית שמאי (דף קיא:) יבמה שאמרה תוך שלשים יום לא נבעלתי כופין אותו אחר שלשים מבקשים הימנו ומפרש התם דעד שלשים יום מוקי איניש אנפשיה טפי לא מוקי ולכך לאחר שלשים יום אין כופין דלא מהימנא אף על גב דאית לה מיגו [ט] דאי בעיא אמרה אינו יכול לבא עלי דנאמנת כדמוכח בסוף נדרים (דף צא.):

ואמר

כו א ב מיי' פי"ד מהל' מלוה הל' א סמג עשין פד טוש"ע ח"מ סי' עח סעיף א:
כז ג מיי' שם סמג עשין לד טוש"ע ח"מ סי' קח סעיף יז:
כח ד ה מיי' שם סמג שם טוש"ע ח"מ סי' עח סעיף א:

רבינו גרשום

כי היכי דלא ליטרדן. שלא יתבעו בזמנו: **אילימא בזמנו.** בשעת השלמת ד' אמות **פשיטא** דנאמן דמי איכא למאן דאמר דבזמנו לא הוי נאמן: **אלא בתוך זמנו.** קודם השלמת ד' אמות ואפ"ה קתני דנאמן דבחזקת שנתן הוא **אלמא עביד איניש דפרע בגו זימניה** ותיובתא דריש לקיש. אמר לך ריש לקיש בעלמא אימא לך דלא עביד איניש דפרע בגו זימניה **ושאני הכא** גבי כותל אמאי נאמן דליכא תוך זמנו דכל שעה ושעה כל דימוס ודימוס שבנה **זמנו הוא** לסייע ומש"ה נאמן: **ת"ש** מסיפא. הא סיפא קשיא לאביי ורבא אמרי לך אביי ורבא בעלמא אימא לך דעביד איניש דפרע בגו זימניה **ושאני הכא** גבי סמך לו כותל דמש"ה אינו נאמן כי טעין דפרע חלקו קודם שסמך א) דאמרי' ליה אימר **אמר** סבר בדעתו הואיל ואינו חייב עכשיו לסייע בהגבהה למה ליה למיתן ליה **מי יימר דמחייבי** (ליה) [לי] **רבנן** למיתן כשאסמוך הכותל ומשום האי סברא לא יהיב ליה מידי ואי טעין דיהיב אינו נאמן: **ואפי' מיתמי.** שאם טעין אחד לחבירו פרעתיך תוך זמנו ומת והניח יתומים חייבין היתומין לשלם דלא יכלי למטען שמענו מאבינו שאמר שפרע לו בתוך זמנו **ואע"ג דאמרי' הבא ליפרע מנכסי יתומין** אע"פ שיש לו שטר **לא יפרע אלא בשבועה** דאמרי' אלו הוה אבוהן קיים הוה מפיק שובר ומרע ליה לשטרא אפ"ה דמחמרינן כל כך בנכסי יתמי אפ"ה אי אמר אבוהן לבעל חובו פרעתיך בתוך זמנו ומת מגבי מיתמי: **מה לי לשקר במקום חזקה.** כלומר הואיל ויכול הוא לטעון לפטור עצמו ולומר שפרע בזמנו ב) בחזקה דאדם פורע בזמנו והואיל ויכול לפטור עצמו בזמנו ואמר תוך זמנו אמרי' מה לי לשקר:

חשק שלמה על רבינו גרשום

א) [נראה דל"ל דאמרי' ליה דודאי אמר וסבר בדעתו הואיל וכו']. ב) [אולי צ"ל שפרע בזמנו אמרינן מה לו לשקר ונאמן לטעון שפרע תוך זמנו ואף שהוא נגד החזקה דאדם פורע בזמנו והואיל ויכול לפטור עצמו ולומר שפרע בזמנו].

מסורת הש"ס

א) [גי' הערוך בערך סף ד' ספא וספא פי' כל נדבך ונדבך זימניה הוא], ב) [לקמן לג. גיטין לד:] כתובות פז., ג) [ועי' תוס' כתובות יט. ד"ה חזקה וכו' מה שהניחו בצ"ע], ד) [קדושין סד: וש"נ], ה) [ל"ל בעדים], ו) [ל"ל קדושין פרק].

הגהות הב"ח

(א) גמ' במקום חזקה מה לי כל"ל ותיבת אמרי' נמחק: (ב) תוס' ד"ה כי היכי וכו' זמנו תניא מת האב בתוך: (ג) ד"ה ואפי' וכו' תוך זמנו (לרב פפא דמפרש וכו' ואפילו לרב הונא בריה דרב יהושע תא"מ ונ"ב ס"א וכ"ה באשר"י ולא מיבעיא לרב פפא וכו' אלא אפי' לרב הונא בריה דרב יהושע וכו': (ד) בא"ד עדות בחיי האב נמי מלית למימר:

גליון הש"ס

גמ' במקום חזקה אמרי' מה לי לשקר. עי' ב"ק קדושין דף לה ע"א: תוס' ד"ה מי כו' דאי בעיא אמרה א"י לבא עלי. לא זכיתי להבין הא שם בנדרים מבואר הטעם דנאמנת בהכי משום דאין אשה מעיזה פניה בפני בעלה והכא ל"ש כן הכא בידה וכפי דבריו דבא עליה אינו נאמן עוד ואי ליכא חזקה זו דהא מ"מ אינו נאמנת והדרנא כפי דבריי עדיין זקוקה לו וצע"ג:

ליקוטי רש"י

הבא ליפרע מנכסי יתומים לא יפרע אלא בשבועה. וכל זמן שלא נשבע אין להם רשות בהם [כתובות פז.]. ואפילו הוציא שטר דאי הוה אבוהון דיתמי קיים דלמא הוה טוען לדידיה אמר לי דלא פרעתיך ומשבעינן ליה כדאמרינן בשבועות (מא.) [גיטין ג.]. צריך שבועה שלא נתקבל חוב. [שבועות מב:].

Having failed to discredit the opinions of either Reish Lakish or Abaye and Rava, the Gemara cites positions taken by various authorities and then renders a final, definitive ruling on the question of early repayment:

רַב פָּפָּא וְרַב הוּנָא בְּרֵיהּ דְּרַב יְהוֹשֻׁעַ עָבְדֵי כְּאַבַּיֵי וְרָבָא – **Rav Pappa and Rav Huna the son of Rav Yehoshua acted in accordance with** the view of **Abaye and Rava,** who held that one is believed to claim that he paid his debt prematurely. מַר בַּר רַב אַשִׁי עָבֵד כְּרֵישׁ לָקִישׁ – **Mar the son of Rav Ashi acted in accordance with** the view of **Reish Lakish,** who held one is not believed to claim that he paid his debt prematurely. וְהִלְכְתָא כְּרֵישׁ לָקִישׁ – **And the law accords with** the view **of Reish Lakish.** Thus, halachah presumes that a debtor would not satisfy his obligation before the due date, and so one who claims to have done so bears the burden of proving it.

The Gemara notes how strong this presumption is:

וַאֲפִילוּ מִיַּתְמֵי – **And** we may rely on this presumption **even** to collect **from orphans** without an oath.[9] וְאַף עַל גַּב דְּאָמַר מַר – **And even though the master said:**[10] הַבָּא לִיפָּרַע מִנִּכְסֵי יְתוֹמִים – **One who comes to collect** a debt **from the** inherited **property of orphans** לֹא יִפָּרַע אֶלָּא בִשְׁבוּעָה – **may not collect without** first **swearing** that he has not been paid, חֲזָקָה לֹא עָבִיד אִינִישׁ דְּפָרַע בְּגוֹ זִימְנֵיהּ – nevertheless, there is **a legal presumption** that **a person does not pay** a debt **before his** allotted **time.** Thus, if a borrower died before his loan came due, the presumption establishes that the loan has not been paid, and so releases the creditor from having to swear to that effect.

The Gemara raises a related question:

אִיבַּעְיָא לְהוּ – **They asked:** תְּבָעוֹ לְאַחַר זְמַן – If a lender **sued [a borrower]** for repayment **after the time** period of the loan had lapsed, וְאָמַר לוֹ פְּרַעְתִּיךְ בְּתוֹךְ זְמַנִּי – **and** the borrower **told [the lender], "I paid you within my** allotted **time,"** מַהוּ – **what is [the law]?** מִי אַמְרִינַן בִּמְקוֹם חֲזָקָה אַמְרִינַן[11] מַה לִּי לְשַׁקֵּר – **Do we apply** the logic of **"why should I lie,"**[12] and believe the borrower even **in the face of a legal presumption** that one does not repay his debts prematurely?[13]

NOTES

parallel wall; See also *Rashba.*]

9. That is, if a borrower died before his loan came due, the creditor may collect from the orphaned heirs without having to take the customary oath (discussed by the Gemara below), for we are not concerned that the deceased paid his debt prematurely (*Rashi*).

Tosafos (ד״ה ואפילו) note that this ruling applies only to adult orphans; however, a creditor may not collect from minors, even if their father died before the debt fell due. *Tosafos* mention two reasons for this: 1) Repayment of a debt is a mitzvah, and minors are not obligated to perform mitzvos. 2) The creditor must establish the existence of a debt through the testimony of witnesses, who may testify only in the presence of the opposing litigant. However, a minor is not considered "present" at a legal proceeding. See *Tosafos* for a lengthy discussion of this matter.

10. *Tosafos'* version of the Gemara (which reads: "even though the Rabbis said") and also a Baraisa they cite from *Kesubos* (87a) both indicate that the requirement to swear is of Rabbinic origin, designed to protect orphans, who are often unfamiliar with their father's affairs, from unscrupulous individuals.

11. *Bach* deletes the second אַמְרִינַן, since it is superfluous.

12. I.e. if the borrower wanted to lie, he would have stated that he paid when the loan came due, and his claim would have been accepted as true. Hence, we believe him when he swears that he paid prematurely (*Rashi*; see *Kovetz Shiurim* §34). This legal rule of procedure is referred to in the Talmud as a *"migo"*; literally: since.

13. In the case disputed by Reish Lakish and Abaye and Rava, however, the lender sued for repayment on the day that the loan came due, and the logic of "why should I lie" cannot be applied to that case. (*Tosafos* above, 5a ד״ה ובא בזמנו; see there for an explanation why this logic would not apply to that case, despite the fact that the borrower would be believed to say that he paid on that day).

אוֹ דִילְמָא בִּמְקוֹם חֲזָקָה לָא אַמְרִינַן מָה לִי לְשַׁקֵּר – **Or, perhaps, in the face of a** conflicting **presumption we do not apply "why should I lie."**[1]

The Gemara attempts to resolve this question with proof from our Mishnah, as before:

תָּא שְׁמַע – **Come, learn** a proof from the Mishnah, which stated: בְּחֶזְקַת שֶׁנָּתַן עַד שֶׁיָּבִיא רְאָיָה שֶׁלֹּא נָתַן – Each neighbor **IS PRESUMED TO HAVE CONTRIBUTED** his share of the cost of the first four *amos* **UNTIL** the other neighbor **BRINGS PROOF THAT HE DID NOT CONTRIBUTE.** הֵיכִי דָּמֵי – **What is** this case **like?**[2] אִילֵימָא שֶׁתְּבָעוֹ לְאַחַר זְמַן – **If we say that** the builder **sued [his neighbor]** for reimbursement **after the time** it was due,[3] וְאָמַר לוֹ פְּרַעְתִּיךָ בִּזְמַנִּי – **and** the neighbor **told him, "I paid you at my** allotted **time,"** פְּשִׁיטָא – **it is obvious** that the neighbor is presumed to have contributed and is therefore believed, for he claimed that he repaid the loan at the expected time.[4] Hence, the Mishnah need not teach us this ruling. אֶלָּא לָאו דְּאָמַר לֵיהּ – **Rather,** is this **not** a case **where** the money was demanded after it was due and the neighbor **said to [the builder],** פְּרַעְתִּיךָ בְּתוֹךְ זְמַנִּי – **"I paid you within my** allotted **time,"** i.e. before the wall was built to a height of four *amos;* and yet the Mishnah states that the neighbor is presumed to have paid even though there is a countervailing legal presumption that one does not pay his debt prematurely?! אַלְמָא אֲפִילּוּ בִּמְקוֹם חֲזָקָה – **We** therefore **see** that **even in the face of** a conflicting **presumption** אַמְרִינַן מָה לִי לְשַׁקֵּר – **we apply** the logic of **"why should I lie"** and believe him when he swears that he paid prematurely, because he could have responded with the inherently credible claim that he paid when the loan came due.

The Gemara rejects this proof, as before:

שָׁאנֵי הָכָא – The case **here** in the Mishnah **is different,** דְּכָל שָׁפָא וְשָׁפָא זִמְנֵיהּ הוּא – **for** as **each and every row** of stones is set in place, **it is his time**[5] to pay. Hence, the neighbor is believed not because the logic of "why should I lie" overcomes the presumption that debtors do not pay prematurely. Rather, since in essence he claimed that he paid after the debt came due, there is no conflicting presumption.

The Gemara attempts a different resolution of the question with proof from the latter case of the Mishnah:

תָּא שְׁמַע – **Come, learn** a proof from the Mishnah, which stated: מֵאַרְבַּע אַמּוֹת וּלְמַעְלָה אֵין מְחַיְּיבִין אוֹתוֹ – To rebuild the wall **FROM FOUR *AMOS* AND UPWARD WE DO NOT OBLIGATE [EITHER NEIGHBOR].** Nevertheless, if one neighbor extended the height of the new wall beyond four *amos* at his own expense, and then סָמַךְ לוֹ כּוֹתֶל אַחֵר כו׳ – the other neighbor **JUXTAPOSED ANOTHER WALL** parallel **TO [THE FIRST ONE] etc.,** the latter must contribute even toward the cost of the extension. Further, the builder of the parallel wall is presumed not to have contributed toward the extension עַד שֶׁיָּבִיא רְאָיָה שֶׁנָּתַן – **UNTIL HE BRINGS PROOF THAT HE DID CONTRIBUTE.**

Developing its proof the Gemara analyzes the case:

הֵיכִי דָּמֵי – **What is** this case **like?** אִילֵימָא שֶׁתְּבָעוֹ לְאַחַר זְמַנּוֹ – **If we say that** the builder of the extension **sued [his neighbor]** for reimbursement **after [the latter's]** allotted **time,** וְאָמַר לוֹ פְּרַעְתִּיךָ בִּזְמַנִּי – **and** the neighbor **said to him, "I paid you** for the extension **at my** allotted **time,"**[6] אַמַּאי לָא – **why** is the neighbor **not** believed? He is simply claiming that he repaid his obligation on time! אֶלָּא לָאו דְּאָמַר – **Rather,** is this **not** a case **where he replied,** פְּרַעְתִּיךָ בְּתוֹךְ זְמַנִּי – **"I paid you** my share **within my** allotted **time,"**[7] and the Mishnah states that the neighbor is presumed not to have paid even though the logic of "why should I lie"[8] should persuade us that his claim of premature payment is true? אַלְמָא בִּמְקוֹם חֲזָקָה – **We** therefore **see** that **in the face of a** conflicting **presumption** לָא אַמְרִינַן מָה לִי לְשַׁקֵּר – **we do not apply** the logic of **"why should I lie";** indeed, here the presumption that debtors do not repay prematurely weakens his actual claim to have done so.

The Gemara dismisses this proof, as before:

שָׁאנֵי הָכָא – The case **here differs** from that of a regular debt, דְּאָמַר – **for** the builder of the parallel wall **said** to himself, מִי יֵימַר דִּמְחַיְּיבִי לִי רַבָּנָן – **"Who says that the Rabbis will obligate me** to contribute toward the extension?" Since that liability is not obvious, the halachah presumes that he will not pay unless ordered by the court to do so.[9] Hence, neither case of the Mishnah assists in resolving the question of whether "why should I lie" applies despite the existence of a conflicting presumption.[10]

Rav Acha attempts to resolve the Gemara's question with proof from another Mishnah:

אָמַר לֵיהּ רַב אַחָא בְּרֵיהּ דְּרָבָא לְרַב אַשִׁי – **Rav Acha the son of Rava said to Rav Ashi:** תָּא שְׁמַע – **Come, learn** a proof that we do not apply this logic in the face of a conflicting presumption, for the Mishnah states:[11] מָנֶה לִי בְיָדְךָ – If a man said to his fellow, **"YOU OWE ME[12] A *MANEH*,"[13]** אָמַר לוֹ הֵין – and the fellow **TOLD HIM** in agreement, **"YES";**[14] לְמָחָר אָמַר לוֹ תְּנֵהוּ לִי – and **THE NEXT DAY**[15] the lender **SAID TO [THE BORROWER], "GIVE IT** (i.e. the

NOTES

1. I.e. we do not believe the borrower because he could have made the more credible claim (that he paid on time), since his actual claim (that he paid within his allotted time) is weakened by the legal presumption that one does not repay his debt prematurely (*Rashi*; see *Chidushei R' Nachum*).

2. The Gemara understands that the Mishnah's case is where one party unilaterally rebuilt the collapsed wall to a height of four *amos*. He then seeks reimbursement for half of his expenses from his neighbor. In developing its proof, the Gemara clarifies the neighbor's response.

3. I.e. after the four *amos* were built.

4. See above, 5b note 3.

5. Since the two neighbors are mutually required to build the wall to a height of four *amos*, they are jointly obligated to bear the expense of every step of construction. Hence, it is impossible to claim that one satisfied his obligation prematurely. (*Urim V'Tumim* 78:4 following the opinion of *Rashi*; see above, 5b note 4 for a different explanation by *Rabbeinu Yonah*).

6. I.e. after he completed the parallel wall. See above, 5b note 6.

7. See above, 5b note 7.

8. I.e. since payment was not demanded until after it came due, he could have successfully claimed that he paid on time; hence, believe his claim of premature payment.

9. Thus, he is not believed even if he claims that he paid *after* incurring liability – i.e. after completing the parallel wall.

10. *Tosafos* write that the Gemara could have retorted that in the Mishnah's case payment was demanded as soon as it became due, or before, and the neighbor replied: "I paid you early." Thus, since the timing of the demand precludes a theoretical claim of post-due-date payment, there is no "why should I lie" *migo* (see above, 5b note 13). However, the Gemara did not wish to refute implicitly the view of Abaye and Rava, who maintain that debtors sometimes do pay prematurely. Thus, it attributes the presumption of non-payment to the special nature of the liability imposed in this case.

11. *Shevuos* 38b.

12. Literally: I have a *maneh* in your hand.

13. A *maneh* equals 100 *zuzim.*

14. This admission was made in front of witnesses (*Rashi*), as is evident from the Gemara below.

15. Not necessarily the next day, but at a future time – for the Mishnah states that the borrower is believed to claim that he paid between the admission and the demand.

או דילמא. כיון דמוחזק לן דאין אדם פורע בתוך זמנו לא אמרינן במקום דאיכא חזקה דמרעיה לדבוריה מה לי לשקר וליהמנוהו: **אמר לו הין.** ובפני עדים: **אין לך בידי.** מפרש ואזיל מאי היא: **לא היו דברים מעולם.** הלכך חייב לשלם שהרי יש עדים שהודה לו בפניהם וכיון דאמר לא לויתי מודה הוא שלא פרע שכל מי שאינו לוה אינו פורע הלכך כאומר לא פרעתי דמי דאילו אמר פרעתי נאמן אפילו לוה בפני עדים דקי"ל בשבועות (דף מא:) המלוה את חבירו בעדים אין צריך לפורעו בעדים: **סמך לפלגא.** שלא היה כותל חדש ארוך ככותל הראשון אלא בחציו או בגובהו לא הגיע לגובהו של ראשון: **סמך לכולה.** חייב ליתן לו חלקו בכותל הראשון כאילו סמך כותל שני כנגד כל הראשון דכיון דהתחיל סופו לגמור ויתן תקרה ותנן אע"פ שלא נתן עליו את התקרה נותן מיד: תוס'. ויעשה עליות ע"ג תקרה ויצטרך לו כותל שהגביה חבירו. ע"כ: **ומודה רב הונא בקרנא ולופתא.** בחיבור שבקרן זוית. לופתא חיבור הרי שהיה סוף ביתו של ראובן דבוק לכותל זה שבין שתי חצרות ולאחר זמן נמלך ראובן זה וחיבר בנין מועט בקרן זוית של סוף ביתו ובליטת הבנין משוכה כנגד מקצת אורך הכותל המבדיל בין החצרות מודה רב הונא דלמאי דלא סמך לא סמך שאין בנין כזה עשוי לימשך (ה): **ומודה רב נחמן באפריזא ובאקבועי כשורי.** לענין גובה דקאמר רב נחמן דלמאי דלא סמך לא סמך מודה הוא שאם עשה בכותל שסמך מקום הנחת ראשי קורות עלייה על פני כולה סופו להגביהו עוד כשיעור גובה עלייה וניחא ליה בגובה דכותל ראשון ונותן חלק בכל גובהו: **אפריזא.** עץ ארוך ועב שנותן על פני כל אורך הכותל להניח עליו ראשי קורות ומגין עליהם שלא ירקבו מחמת ליחלוח הכותל ובלשון משנה קרוי מלטוטין ומי שאין לו (ו) עץ עב עושה הכותל ונותן נסרים קטנים למעלה ולמטה ולצדדין ומניח בתוכו ראשי קורות והיינו אקבעתא דכשורי: **בי כוי לא הוי חזקה.** שמעון שהגביה כותל החולק בחצר למעלה מד' אמות ועשה בו חלונות לצד ראובן להנחת ראשי קורות כמו שפירשתי לא הויא חזקה לגבי ראובן לומר אני סייעתיך להגביהו שאלולי שסייעתיך לא הייתי עושה לי הנחת קורות שאם אבא לסמוך לו כותל אחר לאחר זמן שאתן עליה תקרה ואף על גב דמתנת ביה הימלטי הם נסרים עבים שנותנים בגדי החורים להגין על ראשי הקורות ולא מצי למימר ראובן אי לאו דסייעי בהדך לא עבדית כל האי טירחא: **דא"ל שמעון (ז) דכי מפייסת לי לא תתרע אשיתאי.** אמרתי בלבי שמא תמלך לסמוך לי כותל אחר ולתת תקרה ותפייסני בממון במה שהגבהתי לא אצטרך לקלקל כותלי לנקוב בו חורים להנחת ראשי קורותיך: תוס'. **אחזיק להודרי.** כל חזקות הללו דשמעתין אינן חזקות שלא שנים דלא שייך שלש שנים אלא גבי חזקת קרקע שמחזיק בשדה חבירו ואומר לקחתיו ממך אבל הכא בחזקת תשמישין בעלמא מיירי משתמש בשל חבירו ובעטה אחת משתמש בפניו ושותק הויא חזקה כדמוכח לקמן דאמרי' ולי חבריה בטילא לאלתר הויא חזקה וטעמא משום דאמרינן לא שביק איניש לאישתמושי בתוך שלו תשמיש של קביעות בלא רשותו וכיון דמשתמש זה לפניו ושותק ש"מ דנטל רשות ממנו או נתן לו ממון ומכר לו תשמיש זה והני מילי דהויא חזקה ° כגון שטוען הוא מכר לי או נתן לי במתנה אבל אם טוען שנשתמשתי בפניו ושתק איצה חזקה דתנן לקמן בחזקת הבתים (דף מא.) כל חזקה שאין עמה טענה אינה חזקה כיצד אמר לו מה אתה עושה בתוך שלי והוא א"ל שלא אמר לי אדם דבר מעולם אינה חזקה כו' וכל חזקות מיירי דלא בעינן ג' שנים חזקת יום אחד כי הני. ע"כ: **אחזיק להודרי.** להניח ראשי רהיטים דקים על כותל חבירו: **לא אחזיק לכשורי.** להניח עלי קורות כבדות תחת אלו: הכי גרסינן **אחזיק לנטפי אחזיק לשפכי אחזיק לשפכי לא אחזיק לנטפי.** היתה לו מזחילה ומחקה בחצר חבירו שיטפטף גגו מן גשמים לתוכו על פני כל אורך גגו בלא מרזב: **אחזיק לשפכי.** אם רצה עושה מרזב ויקלח כל מי הגג במקום אחד דהא עדיפא ליה לבעל החצר: **א"ד אמר רב נחמן כו'. אבל לצריפא דאורבני לא.** גג של צריף שרדי"ל בלע"ז שמכסין אותו בענפי ערבה והיינו אורבני ומתוך שהטיפין סמוכין מאד אין בעל החצר יכול להשתמש תחתיהם:

או דילמא במקום חזקה לא אמרינן מה לי לשקר ת"ש בחזקת שנתן עד שיביא ראיה שלא נתן היכי דמי אילימא שתבעו לאחר זמן ואמר לו פרעתיך בזמני פשיטא אלא לאו דאמר ליה פרעתיך בתוך זמני אלמא אפילו במקום חזקה אמרי' מה לי לשקר הכא דכל שפא ושפא זמניה הוא ת"ש מד' אמות ולמעלה אין מחייבין אותו סמך לו כותל אחר כו' עד שיביא ראיה שנתן ה"ד אילימא שתבעו לאחר זמנו ואמר לו פרעתיך בזמני אמאי לא אלא לאו דאמר (א) פרעתיך בתוך זמני אלמא במקום חזקה לא אמרינן מה לי לשקר שאני הכא דאמר מי יימר דמחייבי לי רבנן א"ל רב אחא בריה דרבא לרב אשי ת"ש (א) [א] מנה לי בידך אמר לו הין למחר אמר לו תנהו לי אם אמר נתתיו לך פטור אין לך בידי חייב מאי לאו נתתיו לך דא"ל פרעתיך בזמני אין לך בידי דא"ל פרעתיך בתוך זמני וקתני חייב אלמא במקום חזקה לא אמרינן מה לי לשקר לא מאי אין לך בידי לא היו דברים מעולם (ב) דאמר מר [ב] כל האומר לא לויתי כאומר לא פרעתי דמי: סמך לו כותל אחר מגלגלין עליו את הכל כו': א"ר הונא סמך לפלגא סמך לכולה ורב נחמן אמר [ג] למאי דסמך סמך למאי דלא סמך לא סמך (ג) ומודה רב הונא בקרנא ולופתא [ד] ומודה ר"נ באפריזא (ג) ובקבעתא דכשורי אמר רב הונא [ה] בי כוי לא הוי חזקה ואע"ג (ו) דעבד ליה הימלטי דא"ל אמינא לכי פייסת לי לא ליתרע אשיתאי (ג) אמר ר"נ אחזיק להודרי לא אחזיק לכשורי לכשורי אחזיק להודרי רב יוסף אמר אחזיק להודרי אחזיק לכשורי א"ד אמר רב נחמן [ו] אחזיק להודרי אחזיק לכשורי לכשורי אחזיק להודרי אמר רב נחמן אחזיק לנטפי אחזיק לשפכי אחזיק לשפכי לא אחזיק לנטפי ורב יוסף אמר אפילו אחזיק לשפכי אחזיק לנטפי א"ד אמר רב נחמן [ז] אחזיק לשפכי אחזיק לנטפי אחזיק לנטפי אחזיק לשפכי אבל לצריפא דאורבני לא רב יוסף אמר [ח] אפי' צריפא דאורבני עבד רב יוסף עובדא בצריפא דאורבני אמר רבה בר רב נחמן אמר רבה בר אבוה המשכיר בית לחבירו

ואמר לו פרעתיך בזמני אמאי לא כו'. הוה מצי לשנויי הא דקתני בחזקת שלא נתן היינו בתוך זמנו או בזמנו ואמר פרעתיך בתוך הזמן דליכא מיגו כדפרי' לעיל אבל לאחר זמנו הוי בחזקת שנתן דבמקום חזקה אמרינן מה לי לשקר אך ניחא ליה לשנויי התם מימר אמר מי יימר דמחייבי לי רבנן דלא תיקשי נמי לאביי ולרבא: **כל** האומר לא לויתי כאומר כו'. הקשה ה"ר יצחק מה צריך כאן לטעם כל האומר כו' הא ודאי כיון שכבר הודה תו לא מהימן לומר שלא לוה דבשלמא בשבועות (דף מא:) ושם ד"ה כל) צריך להאי טעמא שאומר לו מנה לי בידך והלה אומר להד"מ ואתו עדים ואמרי ראינו שלוה ופרע השתא הא דקאמרי סהדי שלוה מהימני והא דקאמרי (ח) פרע לא מהימני דהא איהו קמכחיש להו דאמר לא לויתי והאומר לא לויתי כאומר לא פרעתי דמי אבל הכא לא צריך כלל ואומר ר"י דאיצטריך לאשמועינן דלא מצי למימר האומר לא לויתי לא שלא לוה כלל אלא כאילו לא לויתי לפי שפרעתי קמ"ל דכאילו אומר לא פרעתי בהדיא: **סמך** לפלגא סמך לכולה. האי לפלגא מיירי בין לאורך בין לגובה: (ז) **ומודה** רב הונא בקרנא ולופתא. מפרש ר"ח קרנא היכר שלא יאריך החומה יותר שבסוף אותו כותל שסמך (ט) כייפיה לקרנא כלפי כותלו של חבירו ולופתא נמי היכר שלא יגביה הכותל יותר כגון שעשה היכר בראש החומה לפי שרגילין לעשות החומה רחב למעלה שיפלו הגשמים מחוץ לחומה ולא ישהו שם ומודה רב נחמן באפריזא היא היכר שיאריך עדיין הכותל שבסוף אורך החומה אינו שוה אלא אבן אחת בולטת ואחת שוקעת דודאי עדיין יאריכו ואקבעתא דכשורי היינו שעשה מקום הנחת ראשי קורות דמוכח שסופו להגביה עד שיעור גובה עלייה: הסי

רבינו גרשום

והלה אומר לפני עדים הן. אין לך בידי מעולם חייב הואיל והודה לו מעיקרא: **פרעתיך בזמני.** באותו [היום] שתבעו. **אלמא דבמקום חזקה לא אמרי' מה לי לשקר.** לא לעולם בעלמא אמרי' מה לי לשקר והכא כי אמר ליה אידך אין לך בידי משום מאי חייב לאו זמן ותוך זמן איכא הכא. אלא מש"ה חייב אתמול אמר לו הן בפני עדים ועכשיו אמר ליה אין לך בידי כמאן דכפר ליה בתר הודאתו דמי א) הכא אמר לויתי ויש עדים שלא יכול לומר לא פרעתי דמי וחייב לפרוע ולעולם דליכא למשמע מינה: **פיסקא סמך לו כותל אחר.** כדפרישית לעיל: **סמך לפלגא סמך לכולה.** שאם סמך זה כותל כנגד אותו כותל שהגביהו חבירו משלו ולא האריכו כשיעור אותו כותל כולו אלא כנגד חציו (משום דאמר' סמך לכולה) אעפ"כ אמר רב הונא מגלגלין עליו את הכל ויתן חלקו המגיע בכל הכותל אע"פ שלא סמך אלא כנגד חציו משום דאמרי' היום או למחר ימלך בעצמו ויאריכנו כנגד כולו: **מה דסמך סמך.** שכנגד אותו שיעור שסמך יתן חלקו ותו לא דלא מחייבי' עכשיו משום היום ומחר: **בקרנא ולופתא. קרנא.** שאם התחיל אותו כותל שסמך מרחוק שלא כנגד אותו כותל שהגביה חבירו אלא סופו של אותו כותל שסמך אותו כנגד זוית של אותו כותל שהגביה חבירו בהא מודה רב הונא שאין מגלגלין עליו ליתן אלא כנגד חלקו באותו קרן שאם היה דעתו לסומכו היום ומחר כולו כנגד אותו כותל לא היה בונה משך בנינו לצד אחר. **לופתא,** אנפנדי"ף בלע"ז כלומר שלא סמך האי כותל כנגד גובה של כותל חבירו אלא הגביהו כנגד מחצית כותלו של חבירו ולא משום בית אלא לקרות עליו מעט בהא מודה רב הונא שלא יתן אלא כנגד אותו לופתא לפי שאין בדעתו להגביהו יותר: **ומודה רב נחמן באפריזא.** היינו

א) שבועות לח:, ב) שם מא:, כתובות פח., ג) [בערוך ערך לפתא הארוך בפי' סוגיא זו], ד) לפי' מהרש"א הד"א.

הגהות הב"ח

(א) גמ' דאמר ליה פרעתיך בתוך: (ב) שם ומודה רב נחמן באפריזא ובאקבעתא דכשורי אמר רב הונא בי כוי לא הוי חזקה ואע"ג דמתנת ביה הימלטי דאמר ליה אמינא לכי מפייסת: (ג) שם ואמר רב נחמן אחזיק להודרי לא אחזיק לכשורי לכשורי אחזיק להודרי רב יוסף אמר אחזיק לכשורי אחזיק להודרי איכא דאמרי אמר ר"נ אפי' לכשורי לא אחזיק להודרי איכא דאמרי אמר רב נחמן אחזיק להודרי כצ"ל וג"כ ה"ג בלבספ ועי' פי' בנמוקי יוסף: (ד) רש"י ד"ה סמך לכולה וכו' אף התקרה עדיין נותן מיד: (ה) ד"ה ומודה רב הונא וכו' לימשך יותר הס"ד: (ו) ד"ה אפריזא וכו' ומי שאין לו אותו עץ עב: (ז) ד"ה דא"ל מעטן לכי מפייסת וכו' ומעיטתה ותפייסני כו' ולא אצטרך: (ח) תוס' ד"ה כל וכו' שפרע לא מהימני וכו' דלא מצי למימר לא כאומר דאמרי לא לויתי כלל: (ט) ד"ה ומודה וכו' שסמך כייפיה לקרנא וכו' ראש החומה כמו שרגילים:

גליון הש"ס

גמרא דעבד ליה הימלטי. מלשון הכתוב ותמתכתם בתמלט (ירמיה מג ט'). רש"י ד"ה אחזיק להודרי כו' כגון שטוען הוא מכר לי. עי' לקמן דף כג ע"א תוס' ד"ה והא:

לעזי רש"י

שרדי"ל. פירוש לריף, כוך (רש"י שבת דף ע"ב וסוכה דף יג ע"ב ודף יט ע"ב ועיין רש"י שמות דף כב ע"ב ד"ה בסוכה לדידי), בית קטן עגול כמין כובע (רש"י ב"מ דף מב ע"ב).

ליקוטי רש"י

מנה לי בידך אמר לו הין. ואמר עדים ולא לאחר עדי. נתתיו לך פטור. מגלגל ומתבונן לפורעו. אין לך בידי. לא היו דברים מעולם. חייב. שלאו ולא נאמן לומר פרעתי שהרי הוחזק כפרן [שבועות מב.]. כאומר לא פרעתי דמי. כיון דאמר לא לוה הוא לא מודה הוא שלא פרע [כתובות פח.]. דכיון דלא לוה לא פרע אלא שלא לוה פרע [שבועות מא.]. כשורי. קורות [שבת פו]. אשיתאי. חומה [ב"מ סו.]. בי כוי.

עין משפט נר מצוה

כט א מיי' פ"ו מהל' טוען הל' ו ופי"ו הלכה ה סמג עשין לה טוש"ע ח"מ סי' עט סעיף ו:
ל ב מיי' שם פ"א הל' ג סמג שם טוש"ע ח"מ סי' קנז סעיף ח וסמ"ג:
לא ג ד מיי' פי"ג מהל' שכנים הל' א סמג עשין פב טוש"ע ח"מ סי' קנז סעיף י:
לב ה מיי' פ"ח מהל' שכנים הל' ט סמג עשין פב טוש"ע ח"מ סי' קנג סעיף יא:
לג ו מיי' שם הל' ז טוש"ע שם סעיף טז:
לד ז ח מיי' שם הל' ו טוש"ע שם סעיף יז:

מורפט"א בל"ע אע"ג דאמר רב נחמן למאי דסמך סמך דלא יתן אלא כנגד שיעורא דסמך מודה שאם סמך כותלו כנגד חציו גבוה כמו אותו שהגביה חבירו וחציו נמוך ועשה בו כעין מורפט"א שבולט בכותל לסימן שדעתו להגביהו כולו. ואית דאמרי אפריזא (נתר) [נסר] ארוך שמשקיעין באורך הכותל ובונין עליו כדי שתקשר הכותל יפה וכן **בקבעתא דכשורי** שאם עשה באותו מחיצה הנמוך מקום שקובע בו קורות אפריזא בשוה לאחר ומגביה לאחר והאי מודה רב נחמן מגלגלין עליו את הכל. ואית דאמרי אפריזא [נסר] עליה ויגביהו: **בי כוי לא הוי חזקה.** כגון כותל שהגביהו בו לצד חבירו ועשה בו חלונות אחורי החלונות לצד חצר חבירו אין יכול חבירו להחזיק בזה הכותל מחמת אלו החורין לרשותו **ואע"ג דעבד ביה** החומר ואע"פ שטוען בעל חצר אני עשיתי כל זה הנה לטעון שיש לו חלק בכותל מחמת אותן המלטות משום

החלונות מקום כניסת הקורות בתוך החומה [רשב"ם לקמן נה:]. **אמר ר"נ אחזיק וכו'.** כל חזקה שאין עמה טענה אינה חזקה על כל לטעון דאין מכר ולא ידע ממני שהוא לך ואם יש לו בית מדרש נגד ג' שנים דקרקעות ובתים ואילנות בין בחזקת יום אחד כגון דהם דאמרינן ... לטעון מתנה ... אמרינן שמכר לו והכא רב נחמן ... לכן מחזיק לאו לטעון ... שפכי. מרזב (לעיל נ.). **צריפא דאורבני.** בית קטן של ערבה (ב"מ מב.). כמין כובע עגול וכו'. שעושין עגול מלמעלה וקלוע ואינו מחזיק בו ... עשוי מענפי ערבה עבות ... בחזקת אינו עשוי אלא לצרכים ...

דמצי **אמר** בעל הכותל האי דעבדי הכי מצד שלך להכי עבדי **דכי מפייסת לי** ותקנה ממני שיהא לך רשות להשתמש בכותלי ולקבוע בו קורות שיהיו מזומנין החורין ולא תצטרך לחתור בכותל **דלא מיתרע אשיתאי: אחזיק להודרי.** שאם היה לאחר שתחזיק בזה הכותל לשום בו קורות דיכול לשום בו עד היכי שהוא רוצה להשתמש ולהניח לזיזין שהם דקין ואין משאן כבד לפיכך אפי' אם החזיק בו להשתמש בכשורי אחזיק נמי להודרי: **איכא דאמרי אחזיק להודרי אחזיק לכשורי.** הואיל והחזיק בו בכותל קובע מה שירצה: **אחזיק לשפכי.** שאם יש לא' חזקה שמרזבו מקלח לחצר חבירו מקום א' מתקרו ורוצה לסלק את מרזיבו ולהניח לכותלו שלו שיטפו המים מכל גגו בניטוף ג) תקרתו בנוטפין יכול חבירו לעכב עליו ולומר לו כבר מיחל (ופ') לך מקום א' יותר מכמה מקומות: **איכא דאמרי.** אחזיק נמי לנטפי דיכול לומר לו בנטפי. **אבל לצריפא דאורבני.** כלומר הני מילי דאמרינן דמי שיש לו חזקה לנטפי מחזיק לשפכי וה"ה כן אגודות אורבני כגון בית המים שמקלחת המים שבה הן סוכת גג שבעו כן מסוכה הצריף והיא עשויה ... מגוסף ... שבולים מן הגג וכולה שאין בה אלא ...

חשק שלמה על רבינו גרשום א) [אולי צ"ל כמו דאמר לא לויתי ויש עדים שלוה דלאו יכול לומר לא פרעתי דמי וחייב לפרוע וכו']: ב) [אולי צ"ל לאפוקי אם מיחלו לו מתחלה ואם שהיה המים מכל תקרתו ממנה וכו']: ג) [נ"ל דליכא למימר פירוש על בצריפא דאורבני]:

money you admitted owing) TO ME." אִם אָמַר נְתַתִּיו לָךְ פָּטוּר – IF the borrower SAID, "I GAVE IT TO YOU between the time of admission and now," he is believed and IS NOT LIABLE to pay. אֵין לָךְ בְּיָדִי חַיָּיב – If, however, he says, "I HOLD NOTHING OF YOURS,"[16] HE IS LIABLE to pay.

Developing his proof, Rav Acha interprets these two disparate replies:

מַאי לָאו – **Is not** the difference between the two replies as follows: נְתַתִּיו לָךְ דְּאָמַר לֵיהּ פְּרַעְתִּיךָ בִּזְמַנִּי – **"I gave it to you"** means **that** the borrower **said to [the lender], "I paid you at my** allotted **time,"** i.e. when the loan came due; hence, he is believed. אֵין לָךְ בְּיָדִי – And **"I hold nothing of yours"** means דְּאָמַר לֵיהּ פְּרַעְתִּיךָ בְּתוֹךְ זְמַנִּי – **that** the borrower **said to [the lender], "I paid you within my** allotted **time,"** i.e. before the loan came due, וְקָתָנֵי חַיָּיב – **and the Mishnah teaches** that in this latter case **he is liable** to pay, even though he could have said, "I paid you on time!" אַלְמָא בִּמְקוֹם חֲזָקָה – We therefore **see** that **in the face of** a conflicting **legal presumption**[17] לֹא אָמְרִינַן מַה לִי לְשַׁקֵּר – **we do not apply** the logic of **"why should I lie"** and believe his claim of premature payment.

The Gemara rejects this proof:

לֹא – This is **not** the correct explanation of the borrower's second reply. Rather, מַאי אֵין לָךְ בְּיָדִי – **what is** the meaning of **"I hold nothing of yours"?** לֹא הָיוּ דְּבָרִים מֵעוֹלָם – It is: **"These things never occurred,"** which constitutes a complete denial of the loan. However, since the borrower had previously acknowledged his debt before witnesses, his denial is ignored. Further, in denying the loan he in effect admits that he has not paid, דְּאָמַר מַר כָּל הָאוֹמֵר לֹא לָוִיתִי – **for the master said:**[18] **Anyone who says, "I have not borrowed,"** כְּאוֹמֵר לֹא פָּרַעְתִּי דָּמֵי – **is like one who says, "I have not paid,"** for one who did not borrow certainly has made no repayment.[19] Thus, since the second reply does not concern premature payment, the Gemara's question remains unresolved.

The Mishnah had also stated:

סָמַךְ לוֹ כּוֹתֶל אַחֵר מְגַלְגְּלִין עָלָיו אֶת הַכֹּל כו׳ – If the second neighbor JUXTAPOSED ANOTHER WALL parallel TO [THE FIRST ONE], which divides the courtyards,[20] WE DEVOLVE UPON HIM the obligation to pay his share of the ENTIRE wall etc.

Amoraim differ in the application of this statement:

אָמַר רַב הוּנָא סָמַךְ לְפַלְגָּא – **Rav Huna said:** If **he juxtaposed** the parallel wall **to half** of the dividing wall,[21] סָמַךְ לְכוּלָּהּ – he is liable for the entirety of the extension as though **he had juxtaposed** his parallel wall **to the entire** dividing wall.[22] וְרַב נַחְמָן אָמַר לְמַאי דְּסָמַךְ סָמַךְ – **And Rav Nachman said: To that which he juxtaposed, he juxtaposed** – and is liable accordingly. לְמַאי דְּלֹא סָמַךְ לֹא סָמַךְ – **To that which he did not juxtapose, he did not juxtapose** – and we do not obligate him now for the entire extension, since he has done nothing to indicate that he will complete the parallel wall to the size of the extended dividing wall.[23]

The Gemara qualifies these two statements:

וּמוֹדֶה רַב הוּנָא בְּקַרְנָא וְלוּפְתָּא – **But Rav Huna will concede** that **in** the case of **an attachment to the corner** of his house the second neighbor pays only for that part of the extension that he is actually about to use.[24] וּמוֹדֶה רַב נַחְמָן בְּאַפְרִיזָא וּבְקְבַעְתָּא דִּכְשׁוּרֵי – **And Rav Nachman will concede** that **in** the cases of **a king-beam**[25] **and a setting for crossbeams**[26] the second neighbor must pay his share of the entire height of the dividing wall, for these preparations indicate that he plans to lay beams from his wall to the dividing wall for the floor of an upper story, and will thus extend his wall upward to serve as a wall for the upper story, using the extended portion of the dividing wall for the same purpose.[27]

The Gemara presents a related ruling:

אָמַר רַב הוּנָא בֵּי כַּוֵּי – **Rav Huna said: Windows** constructed in the outer face of a dividing wall[28] לֹא הָוֵי חֲזָקָה – **do not create a presumption** that the neighbor has assisted in building the extension.[29] וְאַף עַל גַּב דְּעָבַד לֵיהּ הִימַלְטֵי – **And even though** the builder **made casings for [the beams],**[30] there is still no proof

NOTES

16. Literally: you have nothing in my hand.

17. In our case, that debtors do not repay prematurely.

18. *Shevuos* 41b.

19. However, if the borrower expressly claims that he repaid the loan he is believed, since the Gemara (*Shevuos* 41b) states that a loan made before witnesses [e.g. our case, where he admitted liability in the presence of witnesses] need not be repaid before witnesses (*Rashi*).

Tosafos question the necessity of applying this ruling here – that is, since the borrower previously admitted liability before witnesses, he is no longer believed to claim that he never borrowed; hence, there is no need to construe his denial as an admission that he never paid. *Tosafos* therefore explain that the master is teaching that the borrower's denial, "I did not borrow," cannot be interpreted as, "it is as if I did not borrow, since I have paid." Rather, his denial must be construed as an outright admission that he has not paid his debt.

20. In the Mishnah's case, after a collapsed wall had been restored to the required height of four *amos,* one neighbor (at his own expense) extended it even higher. The other neighbor is not liable to contribute toward the extension until he erects a parallel wall and thereby signals his desire to use the extension. The Mishnah stated that his liability commences even before he places a roof across the two walls. Our Gemara discusses the extent of his liability when his parallel wall is not initially built equal to the first wall.

21. I.e. if either the length or the height of the parallel wall failed to equal the corresponding dimension of the dividing wall (*Rashi*).

22. Since he commenced the parallel wall, we assume that he will eventually complete it and place a roof across the two equal walls. Hence, he becomes liable for the entire extension even at this point, as the Mishnah states: *Even though he did not* (yet) *place the roof on the walls, we* (still) *devolve upon him* (the obligation to pay his share of) *the entire* (wall immediately) [*Rashi*].

23. See *Rashi* ד״ה ומודה רב נחמן; cf. *Rabbeinu Gershom.* [Hence, he is liable only for that part of the extension he actually has readied for his use, even before he attaches a roof to the face of the extended dividing wall.]

24. In this case one end of a neighbor's house abutted the restored and extended wall dividing two courtyards. At the corner of his house and the wall, the neighbor subsequently created a small structure by building a wall that projected from his house parallel to part of the dividing wall. In such a case, Rav Huna will concede that the neighbor pays only for that part of the dividing wall's extension that his small attachment actually parallels, inasmuch as this type of structure is not usually enlarged (*Rashi*; cf. *Tosafos*). [Hence, it is certain that he will not eventually utilize the entire extension for purposes of this attachment.]

25. This is a long, thick beam attached along the entire length of the top of the parallel wall, upon which the ends of crossbeams for an upper floor would rest. This arrangement protected the crossbeams from the dampness of the stone wall, for if attached directly to the wall the crossbeams would rot (*Rashi*).

26. One who did not possess a king-beam would build holes into the wall and line them with small, thick wooden boards in order to protect the crossbeams from the wall's dampness. He would then insert the ends of the beams into these sockets (*Rashi*).

27. *Rashi.*

28. In this case Shimon extended the height of the wall dividing his courtyard from that of his neighbor Reuven, intentionally constructing sockets for holding beams in Reuven's side of the wall (*Rashi*).

29. I.e. Reuven is not believed to claim that he helped defray the cost of the extension with the argument that Shimon would not have provided sockets for Reuven's beams had Reuven not assisted in the construction (*Rashi*).

30. He fixed thick boards to the walls of the sockets for the protection of the beams (*Rashi*).

או דילמא במקום חזקה לא אמרינן מה לי לשקר ת"ש בחזקת שנתן עד שיביא ראיה שלא נתן היכי דמי אילימא שתבעו לאחר זמן ואמר לו פרעתיך בזמני פשיטא אלא לאו דאמר ליה פרעתיך בתוך זמני אלמא אפילו במקום חזקה אמרי' מה לי לשקר שאני הכא דכל שפא ושפא זמניה הוא ת"ש מד' אמות ולמעלה אין מחייבין אותו סמך לו כותל אחר כו' עד שיביא ראיה שנתן ה"ד אילימא שתבעו לאחר זמנו ואמר לו פרעתיך בזמני אמאי לא אלא לאו דאמר (א) פרעתיך בתוך זמני אלמא במקום חזקה לא אמרינן מה לי לשקר שאני הכא דאמר מי יימר דמחייבי לי רבנן א"ל רב אחא בריה דרבא לרב אשי ת"ש א מנה לי בידך אמר לו הין למחר אמר לו תנהו לי אם אמר נתתיו לך פטור אין לך בידי חייב מאי לאו נתתיו לך דא"ל פרעתיך בזמני אין לך בידי דא"ל פרעתיך בתוך זמני וקתני חייב אלמא במקום חזקה לא אמרינן מה לי לשקר לא מאי אין לך בידי לא היו דברים מעולם ב דאמר מר כל האומר לא לויתי כאומר לא פרעתי דמי: סמך לו כותל אחר מגלגלין עליו את הכל כו': א"ר הונא סמך לפלגא סמך לכולה ורב נחמן אמר ג למאי דסמך סמך למאי דלא סמך לא סמך ומודה רב הונא בקרנא ולופתא ד ומודה ר"נ באפריזא (ב) ובקבעתא דכשורי אמר רב הונא ה בי כוי לא הוי חזקה ואע"ג דעבד ליה הימלטי דא"ל אמינא לכי פייסת לי לא ליתרע אשיתאי (ג) אמר ר"נ אחזיק להורדי לא אחזיק לכשורי לכשורי אחזיק להורדי רב יוסף אמר אחזיק להורדי אחזיק לכשורי א"ד אמר רב נחמן ו אחזיק להורדי אחזיק לכשורי לכשורי אחזיק להורדי אמר רב נחמן אחזיק לנטפי אחזיק לשפכי לשפכי לא אחזיק לנטפי ורב יוסף אמר אפילו אחזיק לשפכי אחזיק לנטפי א"ד אמר רב נחמן ז אחזיק לנטפי אחזיק לשפכי אבל לצריפא דאורבני לא רב יוסף אמר ח אפי' צריפא דאורבני עבד רב יוסף עובדא בצריפא דאורבני אמר רב נחמן אמר רבה בר אבוה המשכיר בית לחבירו

רש"י

או דילמא. כיון דמוחזק לן דאין אדם פורע בתוך זמנו לא אמרינן במקום דאיכא חזקה דמרעיה לדבוריה מה לי לשקר וליהמנוהו: **אמר לו הין.** ובפני עדים: **אין לך בידי.** מפרש ואזיל מאי היא: **לא היו דברים מעולם.** הלכך חייב דשלא שהרי יש עדים שהודה לו בפניהם וכיון דאמר לא לויתי מודה הוא שלא פרע שכל מי שאינו לוה אינו פורע הלכך כאומר לא פרעתי דמי דאילו אמר פרעתי נאמן אפילו לוה בפני עדים דקי"ל בשבועות (דף מא:) המלוה את חבירו בעדים אין צריך לפורעו בעדים: **סמך לפלגא.** שלא היה כותל חדש ארוך ככותל הראשון אלא בחציו או בגובהו לא הגיע לגובהו של ראשון: **סמך לכולה.** חייב ליתן לו חלקו בכותל הראשון כאילו סמך כותל שני כנגד כל הראשון דכיון דהתחיל סופו לגמור ויתן תקרה ותנן אע"פ שלא נתן עליו את התקרה (ד) נותן מיד: תוס'. ויעשה עליות ע"ג תקרה ויצטרך לו כותל שהגביה חבירו. ע"כ: **ומודה רב הונא בקרנא ולופתא.** בחיבור שבקרן זוית. לופתא חיבור הרי שהיה סוף ביתו של ראובן דבוק לכותל זה שבין שתי חצרות ולאחר זמן נמלך ראובן זה וחיבר בנין מועט בקרן זוית של סוף ביתו ובליטת הבנין משוכה כנגד מקצת אורך הכותל המבדיל בין החצרות מודה רב הונא דלמאי דלא סמך לא סמך שאין בנין כזה עשוי לימשך (ה): **ומודה רב נחמן באפריזא ובאקבועי כשורי.** לענין גובה דקאמר רב נחמן למאי דלא סמך לא סמך מודה הוא שאם עשה בכותל שסמך מקום הנחת ראשי קורות עלייה על פני כולה סופו להגביהו עוד כשיעור גובה עלייה ונימא ליה בגובה דכותל ראשון ונותן חלק בכל גובהו: **אפריזא.** עץ ארוך ועב שנותן על פני כל אורך הכותל להניח עליו ראשי קורות ומגין עליהם שלא ירקבו מחמת ליחלוח הכותל ובלשון משנה קרוי מלטיסין ומי שאין לו (ו) עץ עב עושה חורים בכותל ונותן נסרים קטנים למעלה ולמטה ולצדדין ומניח בתוכו ראשי קורות והיינו אקבעתא דכשורי: **בי כוי לא הוי חזקה.** שמעון שהגביה כותל החולק בחצר למעלה מד' אמות ועשה בו חלונות לצד ראובן להנחת ראשי קורות כמו שפירשתי לא הויא חזקה לגבי ראובן לאמר אני סייעתיך להגביהו שאלולי שסייעתיך לא היית עושה לי הנחת קורות שאם אבא לסמוך לו כותל אחר לאחר זמן שאתן עליה תקרה ואף על גב דמתנח ביה הימלטי הם נסרים עבים שנותנים בלדי החורים להגין על ראשי הקורות ולא מצי למימר ראובן אי לאו דסייעי בהדך לא טרחית כל האי טירחא: **דא"ל שמעון** (ז) **דכי מפייסת לי לא תתרע אשיתאי.** אמרתי בלבי שמא תמלך לסמוך לי כותל אחר ולתת תקרה ותפייסני בממון במה שהגבהתי לא אצטרך לקלקל כותלי לנקוב בו חורים להנחת ראשי קורותיך: תוס'. **אחזיק להורדי.** כל חזקות הללו דשמעתין אינן חזקות שלש שנים דלא שייך שלש שנים אלא גבי חזקת קרקע שמחזיק בשדה חבירו ואומר לקחתיו ממך אבל הכא בחזקת תשמישין בעלמא מיירי שמשתמש בשל חבירו ובשעה אחת משתמש בפניו ושותק הויא חזקה כדמוכח לקמן דאמרי' ואי חבריה בטינא לאלתר הויא חזקה וטעמא משום דאמרינן לא שביק איניש לאישתמושי בתוך שלו תשמיש של קביעות בלא רשותו וכיון דמשתמש זה לפניו ושותק י"ל דנטל רשות ממנו או נתן לו ממון ומכר לו תשמיש זה והני מילי דהויא חזקה ° כגון שטוען הוא מכר לי או נתן לי במתנה אבל אם טוען נשתמשתי בפניו ושתק אינה חזקה כדתנן לקמן בחזקת הבתים (דף מא.) כל חזקה שאין עמה טענה אינה חזקה כיצד אמר לו מה אתה עושה בתוך שלי והוא א"ל שלא אמר לי אדם דבר מעולם אינה חזקה כו' ובכל חזקות מיירי לא שנא חזקת שלש שנים ל"ש חזקת יום אחד כי הני. ע"כ: **אחזיק להורדי.** להניח ראשי רהיטים דקים על כותל חבירו: **לא אחזיק לכשורי.** להניח עלי קורות כבדות תחת אלו: הכי גרסינן **אחזיק לנטפי אחזיק לשפכי לא אחזיק לנטפי.** היתה לו חזקה בחצר חבירו שיטפטף גגו מי גשמים לתוכו על פני כל אורך גגו בלא מרזב: **אחזיק לשפכי.** אם רצה עושה מרזב ומקלח כל מי הגג במקום אחד דהא עדיפא ליה לבעל החצר: **א"ד אמר רב נחמן כו'. אבל לצריפא דאורבני לא.** גג של צריף שרד"ל בלע"ז שמכסין אותו בענפי ערבה והיינו אורבני ומתוך שהטיפין סמוכין מאד אין בעל החצר יכול להשתמש תחתיהם: בירה

תוספות

ואמר לו פרעתיך בזמני אמאי לא כו'. הוה מצי לשנויי הא דקתני בחזקת שלא נתן היינו בתוך זמנו או בזמנו ואמר פרעתיך בתוך הזמן דליכא מיגו כדפרי' לעיל אבל לאחר זמנו הוי בחזקת שנתן דבמקום חזקה אמרינן מה לי לשקר אך ניחא ליה לשנויי התם מימר אמר מי יימר דמחייבי לי רבנן דלא תיקשי נמי לאביי ולרבא:

כל האומר לא לויתי כאומר כו'. הקשה ה"ר יצחק מה צריך כאן לטעם כל האומר כו' הא ודאי כיון שכבר הודה תו לא מהימן לומר שלא לוה דבשלמא בשבועות (דף מא: ושם ד"ה כל) צריך להאי טעמא שאומר לו מנה לי בידך והלה אומר להד"מ ואתו עדים ואמרי דאינו שלוה ופרע השתא הא דקאמרי סהדי שלוה מהימני והא דקאמרי (ח) פרע לא מהימני דהא איהו קמכחיש להו דאמר לא לויתי והאומר לא לויתי כאומר לא פרעתי דמי אבל הכא לא צריך כלל ואומר ר"י דאיצטריך לאשמועינן דלא מצי למימר האומר לא לויתי לא שלא לוה כלל אלא כאילו לא לויתי לפי שפרעתי קמ"ל דכאילו אומר לא פרעתי בהדיא: **סמך** לפלגא סמך לכולה. האי לפלגא איירי בין לאורך בין לגובה: ד **ומודה** רב הונא בקרנא ולופתא. מפרש ר"ת קרנא להיכר שלא יאריך החומה יותר שבסוף אותו כותל שסמך (ט) כייפיה לקרנא כלפי כותלו של חבירו ולופתא הוי היכר שלא יגביה הכותל יותר כגון שעשה היכר בראש החומה לפי שרגילין לעשות החומה צרה למעלה שיפלו הגשמים מחוץ לחומה ולא ישהו שם ומודה רב נחמן באפריזא היא היכר שיאריך עדיין הכותל שבסוף אורך החומה אינו שוה אלא אבן אחת בולטת ואחת שוקעת דודאי עדיין יאריכנו ואקבעתא דכשורי היינו שעשה מקום הנחת ראשי קורות דמוכח שסופו להגביה עד שיעור גובה עלייה:

האי

כט א מיי' פ"ו מהל' טוען ונטען הל' ו ופי"ו מהל' מלוה ולוה הל' ה סמג עשין צד טוש"ע ח"מ סי' עט סעיף י:

ל ב מיי' שם פ"ו הל' ג סמג שם טוש"ע ח"מ שם סעיף ח ובהג"ה:

לא ג ד מיי' פ"ג מהל' שכנים הל' א סמג עשין פב טוש"ע ח"מ סי' קנז סעיף י:

לב ה מיי' פ"ח מהל' שכנים הל' ט סמג עשין פה טוש"ע ח"מ סי' קנג סעיף יט:

לג ו מיי' שם הל' ו טוש"ע שם סעיף כח:

לד ז ח מיי' שם הל' ו טוש"ע שם סעיף יז:

רבינו גרשום

והלה אומר לפני עדים הן. אין לך בידי מעולם חייב הואיל והודה לו מעיקרא: פרעתיך בזמנו. באותו [היום] שתבעו. אלמא דבמקום חזקה לא אמרי' מה לי לשקר. לא לעולם בעלמא אמרי' מה לי לשקר והכא כי אמר ליה אידך אין לך בידי משום מאי חייב לאו זמן ותוך זמן איכא הכא. אלא מש"ה חייב אתמול אמר לו הן בפני עדים ועכשיו אמר ליה אין לך בידי כמאן דכפר ליה בתר הודאתו דמי (א) הכא אמר לויתי ויש עדים שלא יכול לומר לא פרעתי דמי וחייב לפרוע ולעולם מיהא ליכא למישמע מינה: פיסקא סמך לו כותל אחר. כדפרישית לעיל: סמך לפלגא סמך לכולה. שאם סמך זה כותלו כנגד אותו כותל שהגביהו חבירו משלו ולא האריכו כשיעור אותו כותל כולו אלא כנגד חציו (משום דאמר סמך לכולה) אעפ"כ אמר רב הונא מגלגלין עליו את הכל ויתן חלקו המגיע בכל הכותל אע"פ שלא סמך אלא כנגד חציו משום דאמרי' היום או למחר ימלך בעצמו ויאריכנו כנגד כולו: מה דסמך סמך. שכנגד אותו שיעור שסמך יתן חלקו ותו לא הוו מחייבי ליה עכשיו משום היום ומחר: בקרנא ולופתא. קרנא שאם התחיל אותו כותל שסמך מרחוק שלא כנגד אותו כותל שהגביה חבירו אלא סופו של אותו כותל שסמך אותו כנגד זוית של אותו כותל שהגביה חבירו בהא מודה רב הונא שאין מגלגלין עליו ליתן אלא כנגד חלקו באותו קרן שאם היה דעתו לסומכו היום ומחר כולו כנגד אותו כותל לא היה בונה משך בינו לצד אחר. לופתא, אפנדר"ף בלע"ז כלומר שלא סמך האי כותל כנגד גובה של כותל חבירו אלא הגביהו כנגד מחצית כותלו של חבירו ולא משום בית אלא לקרות עליו מעט בהא מודה רב הונא שלא יתן אלא כנגד אותו גובה של אותו לופתא לפי שאין בדעתו להגביהו יותר: ומודה רב נחמן באפריזא. היינו

א) שבועות מא:, ב) שם מא. כתובות פח., ג) [בערוך ערך לפתא האריך בפי' קרנא ולופתא], ד) לפי' מהרש"א הד"א:

הגהות הב"ח

(א) גמ' דאמר ליה פרעתיך בתוך: (ב) שם ומודה רב נחמן באפריזא ובקבעתא דכשורי אמר רב נחמן בי כוי לא הוי חזקה ואע"ג דמתנח ביה הימלטי דאמר ליה אמינא לכי מפייסת: (ג) שם אמר רב נחמן אחזיק להורדי לא אחזיק לכשורי לכשורי אחזיק להורדי רב יוסף אמר אחזיק להורדי אחזיק לכשורי איכא דאמרי אמר רב נחמן אחזיק להורדי אחזיק לכשורי: (ד) רש"י ד"ה סמך לכולה וכו' את התקרה נותן מיד: (ה) ד"ה ומודה רב הונא וכו' לימשך יותר הס"ד: (ו) ד"ה אפריזא וכו' ומי שאין לו עץ עב: (ז) ד"ה דא"ל שמעון לכי מפייסת וכו' לא אצטרך: (ח) תוס' ד"ה כל וכו' שפרע לא מהימני וכו' דהא לא מצי למימר הא דאמר לא לויתי או לא לויתי כלל: (ט) ד"ה ומודה וכו' שסמך כייפיה לקרנא וכו' בראש החומה כמו שרגילים:

גליון הש"ס

גמרא דעבד ליה הימלטי. מלשון הכתוב ותמלטהו בלבנים (ירמיה מג ט'). רש"י ד"ה אחזיק להורדי כו' כגון שטוען הוא מכר לי. עי' לקמן דף כג ע"א תוס' ד"ה והא:

לעזי רש"י

שרד"ל. פירוש צריף, כוך (רש"י שבת דף ט ע"ב וסוכה דף יג ע"ב ודף יט ע"ב ועיין רש"י לקמן דף כג ע"א ד"ה כבולא לדידי), בית קטן עגול כמין כובע (רש"י ב"מ דף מב ע"א):

ליקוטי רש"י

מנה לי בידך אמר לו הין. ובפני עדים ואמר לו אתם עדי. נתתיו לך פטור. מלשלם ומשבועה דאורייתא. אין לך בידי. לא היו דברים מעולם. חייב. לשלם ואינו נאמן לומר פרעתי שהרי הוחזק כפרן [שבועות מב.]. כאומר לא פרעתי דמי. דכיון דאמר לא לויתי מודה הוא שלא פרע דלא נמצא לוה לא פרע [כתובות פח.]. כיון דלוה לא היו דברים לא פרע [שבועות מא.]. כשורי. קורות [שבת סו.]. אשיתא. חומה [ב"מ סו.]. בי כוי.

החלונות מקום כניסת הקורות בתוך החומה (רשב"ם לקמן נח:). אמר ר"נ אחזיק וכו'. כל חזקה שאין עמה טענה אינה חזקה [illegible]

מורפט"א בל"ע אע"ג דאמר רב נחמן למאי דסמך סמך דלא יתן אלא כנגד שיעורא דסמך מודה שאם סמך כותלו כנגד חציו גבוה של כותל שהגביה חבירו וחציו האחר עשה נמוך והניח על הנמוך אפריזא ודאי גלי דעתיה דהיום ומחר יניח על אותו אפריזא קורות ויגביהנו בשוה לאותו הגבוה. ובהאי מודה ר"נ דמגלגלין עליו את הכל. ואית דאמרי אפריזא (נתר) [נסר] ארוך שמשקיעין באורך הכותל ובונין עליו כדי שלא יסתור. ובקבעתא דכשורי שאם עשה באותה מחיצה המקום שקובעין בה הקורות ע"ג דהשתא לא קבע בהן כשורי מגלגלין עליו את הכל דגילה דעתו דלאחר זמן יעשה שם עליה ויגביהנו: בי כוי לא הוי חזקה. [illegible]

דמצי אמר בעל הכותל האי דעבדיה הכי [illegible] אחזיק להורדי. [illegible] איכא דאמרי אחזיק להורדי אחזיק לכשורי [illegible]

חשק שלמה על רבינו גרשום א) [אולי צ"ל כמו הודאתו דמי וכשיכול לומר לא לויתי ויש עדים שלא יכול לומר לא פרעתי דמי וחייב לפרוע וכו'] ב) [illegible] ג) [illegible]

that the neighbor contributed,[31] דְּאָמַר לֵיהּ – **for** the builder **can say to [his neighbor]:** אֲמִינָא – **I said** to myself before building the extension, לִכִי פַּיְיסַתְּ לִי – **if** at some future date **you** erect a parallel wall and **reconcile me** (with a payment of money) to allowing you to attach beams to my extension upon which to construct a roof, לֹא לִיתְרַע אֲשִׁיתָאִי – **my wall need not be damaged** by boring holes therein in order to accommodate your beams. Rather, as I construct the extension I shall provide windows in your side of the wall for that possibility.[32] Hence, the existence of windows with casings does not prove that the neighbor assisted in building the extension.

Starting with the case of placing beams on a neighbor's wall, the Gemara discusses various situations where a person has established a right[33] to use his neighbor's property, delineating the extent of each right:

אָמַר רַב נַחְמָן אַחֲזִיק לְהוּרְדֵי – **Rav Nachman said:** If **one has established the right to** rest narrow **rafters** on his neighbor's wall, לֹא אַחֲזִיק לְכְשׁוּרֵי – **he has not** automatically **established the right to** rest thick **beams** on the wall, for the neighbor can claim that he specifically did not grant (or sell) the right to rest the heavier beams as well, since they could damage his wall.[34] לְכְשׁוּרֵי – However, if he has established the right **to** rest thick **beams** on his neighbor's wall, אַחֲזִיק לְהוּרְדֵי – **he has** automatically **established the right to** rest narrow **rafters** on the wall, for since they are less likely to cause damage, the right is subsumed into the expressly established right to rest beams.

Rav Yosef takes issue with this ruling:

רַב יוֹסֵף אָמַר אַחֲזִיק לְהוּרְדֵי – **Rav Yosef said:** If **he established the right to** rest narrow **rafters** on the wall, אַחֲזִיק לְכְשׁוּרֵי – **he has also established the right to** rest thick **beams** on the wall, for once he has established his right to use the wall for the purpose of setting objects on it, he may set there any type of beam he desires.[35]

In another version of the ruling Rav Nachman espouses Rav Yosef's view:

אִיכָּא דְּאָמְרֵי – **There are those that say:** אָמַר רַב נַחְמָן אַחֲזִיק לְהוּרְדֵי – **Rav Nachman said:** If **he established the right to** rest narrow **rafters** on his neighbor's wall, אַחֲזִיק לְכְשׁוּרֵי – **he has** thereby **established the right to** rest heavy **beams** on the wall; לְכְשׁוּרֵי – and if he established the right **to** rest heavy **beams,** אַחֲזִיק לְהוּרְדֵי – **he has** certainly **established the right to** rest narrow **rafters** as well.

Rav Nachman and Rav Yosef rule similarly in a related case:

אָמַר רַב נַחְמָן אַחֲזִיק לְנַטְפֵי – **Rav Nachman said:** If **one has established the right to** let rainwater **drip** onto his neighbor's courtyard from along the entire length of his roof, אַחֲזִיק לְשַׁפְכֵי – **he has** automatically **established the right to** let the water **pour** onto the courtyard in one spot.[36] אַחֲזִיק לְשַׁפְכֵי – If, however, **he established a right to** let rainwater **pour** from a drainspout onto one area of his neighbor's courtyard, לֹא אַחֲזִיק לְנַטְפֵי – **he has not established the right to** let the water **drip** from along the entire length of his roof.[37] וְרַב יוֹסֵף אָמַר אֲפִילּוּ אַחֲזִיק לְשַׁפְכֵי – **And Rav Yosef said: Even** if **he established** only **the right to** let rainwater **pour** from his drainspout, אַחֲזִיק לְנַטְפֵי – **he has** automatically **established the right to** let the water **drip** from his entire roof, for once the neighbor is legally bound to receive the runoff, it is irrelevant how the runoff occurs.[38]

The Gemara presents a second version of these rulings:

אִיכָּא דְּאָמְרֵי – **There are those that say:** אָמַר רַב נַחְמָן אַחֲזִיק לְשַׁפְכֵי – **Rav Nachman said:** If **one established the right to** let rainwater **pour** from his drainspout onto one area of his neighbor's courtyard, אַחֲזִיק לְנַטְפֵי – **he has** also established **the right to** let the water **drip** from his roof onto the entire courtyard.[39] לְנַטְפֵי – And if he established the right **to** let the water **drip** from his roof onto the entire courtyard, אַחֲזִיק לְשַׁפְכֵי – **he has** certainly **established the right to** let the water **pour** from a drainspout onto one area; אֲבָל לִצְרִיפָא דְּאוּרְבָנֵי לֹא – **but to** let rainwater drip from **a shack** whose roof is composed **of willow branches,** he has established **no** right, for the dripping from such a roof is concentrated and thus prevents the courtyard owner from using the affected area.[40] רַב יוֹסֵף אָמַר אֲפִילּוּ צְרִיפָא דְּאוּרְבָנֵי – **Rav Yosef said:** In such a case he has **even** established the right **to** let rainwater drip from **a shack** whose roof is composed **of willow branches,** since the courtyard owner is legally bound to receive any type of runoff. עָבַד רַב יוֹסֵף עוּבְדָא בִּצְרִיפָא דְּאוּרְבָנֵי – And, indeed, **Rav Yosef** actually **decided a case involving** the runoff from **a shack** whose roof was composed **of willow branches,** ruling in favor of the shack's owner.

The Gemara discusses another teaching of Rav Nachman that concerns automatically acquired rights:

אָמַר רַב נַחְמָן אָמַר רַבָּה בַּר אֲבוּהּ – **Rav Nachman said in the name of Rabbah bar Avuha:** הַמַּשְׂכִּיר בַּיִת לַחֲבֵירוֹ – If **one rents an apartment to his fellow**

NOTES

31. I.e. it is futile for Reuven even to argue that Shimon would not have troubled himself so much (to build the casings) had Reuven not assisted in the construction (*Rashi*).

32. *Rashi.*

33. The "established rights" (or *chazakos*) mentioned here do not involve holding property undisturbed for three years and claiming acquisition of title from the prior owner, for that type of possessing (also called *chazakah*) is necessary only for establishing ownership of real property. Rather, our Gemara discusses "established rights" of ordinary usage, which are created when one makes use of another's property in the latter's presence and the latter fails to object. The user is later believed to claim that the owner had gratuitously extended permission for the use or that the owner had sold him a right of use, for under no other circumstances would a property owner silently countenance another's making a permanent use of his property. However, if a user merely claims that he performed an uncontested act of usage, but fails to claim how he acquired a *right* of usage, his claim is dismissed, in accordance with the Mishnah below (41a), which states: כָּל חֲזָקָה שֶׁאֵין עִמָּהּ טַעֲנָה אֵינָהּ חֲזָקָה, *Any act of possession* (חֲזָקָה) *unaccompanied by a claim* (as to how ownership was acquired) *does not establish ownership.* This ruling applies to *chazakos* involving real property as well as to those involving usage (gloss to *Rashi*). [This view, however, is not universally accepted — see *Rashi* to 7a ד״ה בדנפשאי, *Rashbam* to 41a ד״ה כל, and *Rashbam* to 57a ד״ה אלו, with *Nachalas David* here; see *Tosafos* below, 23a ד״ה והא, *Shiurei R' Shmuel* and *Chidushei R' Nachum*; see also *Tur* and *Shulchan Aruch Choshen Mishpat* 153:6 and 154:12.]

34. *Rabbeinu Gershom.*

35. *Rabbeinu Gershom.* See *Rosh*, who explains that when one acquires rights of usage, we assume that he has aquired full rights for that usage, rather than just partial rights (cf. *Ramban*). [He would, however, be liable for any actual damage caused by his beams, since obviously the wall's owner did not convey a right to inflict damage.]

36. I.e. he may attach a gutter and leader to his roof to allow the rainwater to drain off onto one area of his neighbor's courtyard. This right is assumed, since the neighbor would surely prefer to have the runoff confined to one section of his yard (*Rashi*).

37. Hence, he may not remove his gutter and leader over his neighbor's objection and allow the rainwater to run off along the entire length of his roof, for the neighbor may claim that it is better for him if the runoff is confined to one area (*Rabbeinu Gershom*).

38. *Rabbeinu Gershom* ד״ה איכא דאמרי. [See *Rosh* cited above, note 35.]

39. The reason of Rav Nachman according to this version is that there is no significant difference between the two [as opposed to a runoff from a shack of willow branches, where the potential damage is significantly greater] (*Ramban, Rashba, Ran*).

40. *Rashi;* cf. *Rabbeinu Gershom.*

או דילמא במקום חזקה לא אמרינן מה לי לשקר ת"ש בחזקת שנתן עד שיביא ראיה שלא נתן היכי דמי אילימא שתבעו לאחר זמן ואמר לו פרעתיך בזמני אלמא לאו דאמר ליה פרעתיך בתוך זמני אלמא אפילו במקום חזקה אמרי' מה לי לשקר שאני הכא דכל שפא ושפא זמניה הוא ת"ש מד' אמות ולמעלה אין מחייבין אותו סמך לו כותל אחר כו' עד שיביא ראיה שנתן ה"ד אילימא שתבעו לאחר זמנו ואמר לו פרעתיך בזמני אמאי לא אלא לאו דאמר (א) פרעתיך בתוך זמני אלמא במקום חזקה לא אמרינן מה לי לשקר שאני הכא דאמר מי יימר דמחייבי לי רבנן א"ל רב אחא בריה דרבא לרב אשי ת"ש [א] מנה לי בידך אמר לו הין למחר אמר לו תנהו לי אם אמר נתתיו לך פטור אין לך בידי חייב מאי לאו נתתיו לך דא"ל פרעתיך בתוך זמני אין לך בידי דא"ל פרעתיך בתוך זמני וקתני חייב אלמא במקום חזקה לא אמרינן מה לי לשקר לא מאי אין לך בידי לא היו דברים מעולם [ב] דאמר מר [ב] כל האומר לא לויתי כאומר לא פרעתי דמי: סמך לו כותל אחר מגלגלין עליו את הכל כו': א"ר הונא סמך לפלגא סמך לכולה ורב נחמן אמר [ג] למאי דסמך סמך למאי דלא סמך לא סמך [ג] ומודה רב הונא בקרנא ולופתא [ד] ומודה ר"נ באפריזא (ב) ובקבעתא דכשורי אמר רב הונא [ה] בי כוי לא הוי חזקה ואע"ג [ו] דעבד ליה הימלטי דא"ל אמינא לכי פייסת לי לא ליתרע אשיתאי (ג) אמר ר"נ אחזיק להורדי לא אחזיק לכשורי לכשורי אחזיק להורדי רב יוסף אמר אחזיק להורדי אחזיק לכשורי א"ד אמר רב נחמן [ו] אחזיק להורדי אחזיק לכשורי לכשורי אחזיק להורדי אמר רב נחמן אחזיק לנטפי אחזיק לשפכי אחזיק לשפכי לא אחזיק לנטפי ורב יוסף אמר אפילו אחזיק לשפכי אחזיק לנטפי א"ד אמר רב נחמן [ז] אחזיק לנטפי אחזיק לשפכי אבל לצריפא דאורבני לא רב יוסף אמר [ח] אפי' צריפא דאורבני עבד רב יוסף עובדא בצריפא דאורבני אמר רבה בר רב נחמן אמר רבה בר אבוה המשכיר בית לחבירו

רש"י

או דילמא. כיון דמוחזק לן דאין אדם פורע בתוך זמנו לא אמרינן במקום דאיכא חזקה דמרעיה לדבוריה מה לי לשקר וליהמניה: אמר לו הין. ובפני עדים: אין לך בידי. מפרש ואזיל מאי היא: לא היו דברים מעולם. הלכך חייב לשלם שהרי יש עדים שהודה לו בפניהם וכיון דאמר לא לויתי מודה הוא שלא פרע שכל מי שאינו לוה אינו פורע הלכך כאומר לא פרעתי דמי דאילו אמר פרעתי נאמן אפילו לוה בפני עדים דקי"ל בשבועות (דף מא.) המלוה את חבירו בעדים אין צריך לפורעו בעדים: סמך לפלגא. שלא היה כותל חדש ארוך ככותל הראשון אלא בחציו או בגובהו לא הגיע לגובהו של ראשון: סמך לכולה. חייב ליתן לו חלקו בכותל הראשון כאילו סמך כותל שני כנגד כל הראשון דכיון דהתחיל סופו לגמור ויתן תקרה ותנן אע"פ שלא נתן עליו את התקרה (ד) נותן מיד: תוס'. ויעשה עליות ע"ג תקרה ויצטרך לו כותל שהגביה חבירו. ע"כ: ומודה רב הונא בקרנא ולופתא. בחיבור שבקרן זוית. לופתא חיבור הרי שהיה סוף ביתו של ראובן דבוק לכותל זה שבין שתי חצרות ולאחר זמן נמלך ראובן זה וחיבר בנין מועט בקרן זוית של סוף ביתו ובליטת הבנין משוכה כנגד מקצת אורך הכותל המבדיל בין החצרות מודה רב הונא דלמאי דלא סמך לא סמך שאין בנין כזה עשוי לימשך (ה): ומודה רב נחמן באפריזא ובאקבועי כשורי. לענין גובה דקאמר רב נחמן דלמאי דלא סמך לא סמך מודה הוא שאם עשה בכותל שסמך מקום הנחת ראשי קורות עלייה על פני כולה סופו להגביהו עוד כשיעור גובה עלייה וניחא ליה בגובה דכותל ראשון ונותן חלק בכל גובהו: אפריזא. עץ ארוך ועב שנותן על פני כל אורך הכותל להניח עליו ראשי קורות ומגין עליהם שלא ירקבו מחמת ליחלוח הכותל ובלשון משנה קרוי מלטיסין ומי שאין לו (ו) עץ עב עושה חורים בכותל ונותן נסרים קטנים למעלה ולמטה ולצדדין ומניח בתוכו ראשי קורות והיינו אקבעתא דכשורי: בי כוי לא הוי חזקה. שמעון שהגביה כותל החולק בחצר למעלה מד' אמות ועשה בו חלונות לצד ראובן להנחת ראשי קורות כמו שפירשתי לא הויא חזקה לגבי ראובן לאמר אני סייעתיך להגביהו שאלולי שסייעתיך לא היית עושה לי הנחת קורות שאם אבא לסמוך לו כותל אחר ולאחר זמן שאתן עליה תקרה ואף על גב דמתנח ביה הימלטי הם נסרים עבים שנותנים בצדי החורים להגין על ראשי הקורות ולא מצי למימר ראובן אי לאו דסייעי בהדך לא טרחית כל האי טירחא: דא"ל שמעון (ז) דכי מפייסת לי לא תתרע אשיתאי. אמרתי בלבי שמא תמלך לסמוך לי כותל אחר ולתת תקרה ותפייסני בממון במה שהגבהתי לא אצטרך לקלקל כותלי לנקוב בו חורים להנחת ראשי קורותיך: תוס'. אחזיק להורדי. כל חזקות הללו דשמעתין אינן חזקות שלש שנים דלא שייך שלש שנים אלא גבי חזקת קרקע שמחזיק בשדה חבירו ואומר לקחתיו ממך אבל הכא בחזקת תשמישין בעלמא איירי שמשתמש בשל חבירו ובשעה אחת משתמש בפניו ושותק הויא חזקה כדמוכח לקמן דאמרי' ואי חבריה בטינא לאלתר הויא חזקה וטעמא משום דאמרינן לא שביק איניש לאשתמושי בתוך שלו תשמיש של קביעות בלא רשותו וכיון דמשתמש זה לפניו ושותק י"ל דנטל רשות ממנו או נתן לו ממון ומכר לו תשמיש זה והני מילי דהויא חזקה [ט] כגון שטוען הוא מכר לי או נתן לי במתנה אבל אם טוען נשתמשתי בפניו ושתק אינה חזקה כדתנן לקמן בחזקת הבתים (דף מא.) כל חזקה שאין עמה טענה אינה חזקה כיצד אמר לו מה אתה עושה בתוך שלי והוא א"ל שלא אמר לי אדם דבר מעולם אינה חזקה כו' ובכל חזקות מיירי לא שנא חזקת שלש שנים ל"ש חזקת יום אחד כי הני. ע"כ: אחזיק להורדי. להניח ראשי רהיטים דקים על כותל חבירו: לא אחזיק לכשורי. להניח עלי קורות כבדות תחת אלו: הכי גרסינן אחזיק לנטפי אחזיק לשפכי לא אחזיק לנטפי. היתה לו זוקה בחצר חבירו שיטפטף גגו מי גשמים לתוכו על פני כל אורך גגו בלא מרזב: אחזיק לשפכי. אם רצה עושה מרזב ויקלח כל מי הגג במקום אחד דהא עדיפא ליה לבעל החצר: א"ד אמר רב נחמן כו'. אבל לצריפא דאורבני לא. גג של צריף שרד"ל בלע"ז שמכסין אותו בענפי ערבה והיינו אורבני ומתוך שהטיפין סמוכין מאד אין בעל החצר יכול להשתמש תחתיהם:

דירה

תוספות

ואמר לו פרעתיך בזמני אמאי לא כו'. הוה מצי לשנויי הא דקתני בחזקת שלא נתן היינו בתוך זמנו או בזמנו ואמר פרעתיך בתוך הזמן דליכא מיגו כדפרי' לעיל אבל לאחר זמנו הוי בחזקת שנתן דבמקום חזקה אמרינן מה לי לשקר אך ניחא ליה לשנויי התם מימר אמר מי יימר דמחייבי לי רבנן דלא תיקשי נמי לאביי ולרבא: כל האומר לא לויתי כאומר כו'. הקשה ה"ר יצחק מה צריך כאן לטעם כל האומר כו' הא ודאי כיון שכבר הודה תו לא מהימן לומר שלא לוה דבשלמא בשבועות (דף מא: ושם ד"ה כל) צריך להאי טעמא שאומר לו מנה לי בידך והלה אומר להד"מ ואתו עדים ואמרי ראינו שלוה ופרע השתא הא דקאמרי סהדי שלוה מהימני והא דקאמרי (ח) פרע לא מהימני דהא איהו קמכחיש להו דאמר לא לויתי והאומר לא לויתי כאומר לא פרעתי דמי אבל הכא לא צריך כלל ואומר ר"י דאיצטריך לאשמועינן דלא מצי למימר האומר לא לויתי לא שלא לוה כלל אלא כאילו לא לויתי לפי שפרעתי קמ"ל דכאילו אומר לא פרעתי בהדיא: סמך לפלגא סמך לכולה. האי לפלגא איירי בין לאורך בין לגובה: [ד] ומודה רב הונא בקרנא ולופתא. מפרש ר"ת קרנא להיכר שלא יאריך החומה יותר שבסוף אותו כותל שסמך (ט) כייפיה לקרנא כלפי כותלו של חבירו ולופתא הוי היכר שלא יגביה הכותל יותר כגון שעשה היכר בראש החומה לפי שרגילין לעשות החומה צרה למעלה שיפלו הגשמים מחוץ לחומה ולא ישהו שם ומודה רב נחמן באפריזא היא היכר שיאריך עדיין הכותל שבסוף אורך החומה אינו שוה אלא אבן אחת בולטת ואחת שוקעת דודאי עדיין יאריכנו ואקבעתא דכשורי היינו שעשה מקום הנחת ראשי קורות דמוכח שסופו להגביה עד שיעור גובה עלייה:

האי

מסורת הש"ס

א) שבועות לח:, ב) שם מא: כתובות פח., ג) [עערך עכך לפתח האחר בפי' סוגיא זו], ד) לפי' מהרש"א הד"א.

הגהות הב"ח

(א) גמ' דאמר ליה פרעתיך בתוך: (ב) שם ומודה רב נחמן באפריזא ובאקבעתא דכשורי אמר רב נחמן בי כוי לא הוי חזקה ואע"ג דמתנח ביה הימלטי דאמר ליה אמינא לכי מפייסת: (ג) שם אמר רב נחמן אחזיק להורדי לא אחזיק לכשורי לכשורי אחזיק להורדי רב יוסף אמר אחזיק להורדי אחזיק לכשורי איכא דאמרי אמר ר"נ אפי' אחזיק לכשורי לא אחזיק להורדי אמר רב נחמן אחזיק להורדי כצ"ל ונ"ב ה"ג בהלכות ופי' בנמוקי יוסף: (ד) רש"י ד"ה סמך לכולה וכו' את התקרה עדיין נותן מיד: (ה) ד"ה ומודה רב הונא וכו' לימשך יותר הס"ד: (ו) ד"ה אפריזא וכו' ומי שאין לו אותו עץ: (ז) ד"ה דא"ל שמעון לכי מפייסת וכו' תקרה ותפייסני כו' לא אצטרך: (ח) תוס' ד"ה כל וכו' שפרע לא מהימני דהא לאמרי לא לויתי לא שלא לוה כלל: (ט) ד"ה וכו' כרי שסמך עושה כיפיה לקרנא וכו' בראש החומה כמו שרגילים:

גליון הש"ס

גמרא דעבד ליה הימלטי. מלשון הכתוב ותמלטם במלט (ירמיה מג ע"ש): רש"י ד"ה אחזיק להורדי כו' כגון שטוען הוא מכר לי. עי' לקמן דף כט ע"א תוס' ד"ה והא:

לעזי רש"י

שרד"ל. פירוש צריף, כוך (רש"י שבת דף נ ע"ב וסוכה דף יג ע"ב ודף כא ע"א וע"ע רש"י תענית דף כב ע"א ד"ה כוכלה לדייג), בית קטן עגול כמין כובע (רש"י ב"מ דף מב ע"א).

ליקוטי רש"י

מנה לי בידך אמר לו הין. ובפני עדים ולמחר אמר להם אתם עדי. נתתיו לך פטור. דנאמן כדאמרינן מלוה בעדים אין צריך לפורעו בעדים. אין לך בידי. לא היו דברים מעולם. חייב. שאינו נאמן בשבועה שהרי הודה בפניהם [שבועות מא:]. כאומר לא פרעתי דמי. דכיון דאמר לא לוה מודה הוא שלא פרע [כתובות פח.]. שלא פרע [שבועות מא:]. כשורי. קורות [שבת פז.]. אשיתא. חומה. בי כוי [ב"מ פו.].

עין משפט נר מצוה

כט א מיי' פ"ו מהל' טוען ונטען הל' ו ופ"ו הלכה ה סמג עשין צה טוש"ע ח"מ סי' עט סעיף י:
ל ב מיי' שם פ"ו הל' ג סמג שם טוש"ע ח"מ שם סעיף א והגה"ה:
לא ג ד מיי' פ"ג מהל' שכנים הל' א סמג עשין פב טוש"ע ח"מ סי' קמ סעיף י:
לב ה מיי' פ"ח מהל' שכנים הל' ט סמג עשין פה טוש"ע ח"מ סי' קנג סעיף יט:
לג ו מיי' שם הל' ו טוש"ע שם סעיף טו:
לד ז ח מיי' שם הל' ו טוש"ע שם סעיף י:

רבינו גרשום

והלה אומר לפני עדים הן. אין לך בידי מעולם חייב הואיל והודה לו מעיקרא: פרעתיך בזמנו. באותו [היום] שתבעו. אלמא דבמקום חזקה לא אמרי' מה לי לשקר. לא לעולם בעלמא אמרי' מה לי לשקר והכא כי אמר ליה אידך אין לך בידי משום מאי חייב לאו זמן ותוך זמן איכא הכא. אלא מש"ה חייב אתמול אמר לו הן בפני עדים ועכשיו אמר ליה אין לך בידי כמאן דכפר ליה בתר הודאתו דמי א) הכא אמר לויתי ויש עדים שלא יכול לומר לא פרעתי דמי וחייב לפרוע ולעולם מיהא ליכא למשמע מינה: פיסקא סמך לו כותל אחר. כדפרישית לעיל: סמך לפלגא סמך לכולה. שאם סמך זה כותל כנגד אותו כותל שהגביה חבירו משלו ולא הארכו כשיעור אותו כותל כולו אלא כנגד חציו (משום דאמר' סמך לכולה) אעפ"כ אמר רב הונא מגלגלין עליו את הכל ויתן חלקו המגיע בכל הכותל אע"פ שלא סמך אלא כנגד חציו משום דאמרי' היום או למחר ימלך בעצמו ויאריכנו כנגד כולו: מה דסמך סמך. שכנגד אותו שיעור שסמך יתן חלקו ותו לא דלא מחייבי ליה עכשיו משום היום ומחר: בקרנא ולופתא. קרנא. שאם התחיל אותו כותל שסמך מרחוק שלא כנגד אותו כותל שהגביה חבירו אלא אם סופו של אותו כותל שסמך אותו כנגד זוית של אותו כותל שהגביה חבירו בהא מודה רב הונא שאין מגלגלין עליו ליתן אלא כנגד חלקו באותו קרן שאם היה דעתו לסומכו היום ומחר כולו כנגד אותו כותל לא היה בונה משך בנינו לצד אחר. לופתא. אנפנדי"ר בלע"ז כלומר שלא סמך כנגד האי כותל כנגד גובה של כותל חבירו אלא הגביהו כנגד מחצית כותלו של חבירו ולא משום בית אלא לקרות עליו מעט בהא מודה רב הונא שלא יתן אלא כנגד אותו ולופתא לפי שאין בדעתו להגביהו יותר: ומודה רב נחמן באפריזא. היינו

אמר ר"נ אחזיק וכו'. כל חזקה שאין עמה טענה אינה [illegible]

מורפט"א בל"ע אע"ג דאמר רב נחמן למאי דסמך סמך דלא יתן אלא כנגד שיעורא דסמך מודה שאם [illegible] גבוה כמו אותו כותל שהגביה חבירו וחציו האחר עשה נמוך והניח על הנמוך אפריזא ודאי גלי דעתיה [illegible] אותו אפריזא קורות ויגביהו בשוה לאחר זמן ובהאי מודה רב נחמן דמגלגלין עליו את הכל. ואית דאמרי [illegible] ארוך שמשקעין באורך הכותל ובונין עליו כדי שתקשר הכותל יפה וכן בקבעתא דכשורי שאם עשה [illegible] מקום חוריץ כדי לקבוע בהן לאחר זמן קורות אע"ג דהשתא לא קבע בהן מגלגלין עליו את הכל דגילה [illegible]

חשק שלמה על רבינו גרשום [illegible]

עין משפט
נר מצוה

לה א ב ג מיי' פ"ו מהל' שכירות הל' א סמג עשין סט טוש"ע ח"מ סי' שיג סעיף א:
לו ד ה ו מיי' פ"ח מהל' שכנים הל' ז סמג עשין פב טוש"ע ח"מ סי' קנג סעיף יז:
לז ז ח מיי' שם פ"ג הלכה ה סמג שם טוש"ע ח"מ סי' קנט סעיף א:
לח ט מיי' שם הל' ו ועי' בהשגות סמג שם טוש"ע שם סעיף ב וסי' קס סעיף א:
לט י כ מיי' וסמג שם טוש"ע ח"מ סי' קנט סעיף ב:
מ ל מיי' שם הלכה ז ועי' בהשגות ובמ"מ ובכ"מ סמג שם טוש"ע ח"מ סי' קס סעיף ג:
מא מ מיי' שם טוש"ע שם סעיף א וסעיף ב:

אבירה גדולה משתמש (א) בזיזיה ובכתליה עד ד' אמות ובעובי הכותל במקום שנהגו אבל בתרבץ אפדני לא ורב נחמן דידיה אמר באפילו בתרבץ אפדני אבל רחבה שאחורי הבתים לא ורבא אמר גאפילו רחבה שאחורי הבתים אמר רבינא דהאי כשורא דמטללתא עד תלתין יומין לא הוי חזקה בתר תלתין יומין הוי חזקה הואי סוכה דמצוה היא עד שבעה יומין לא הוי חזקה בתר שבעה יומין הוי חזקה ואי חבריה בטינא לאלתר הוי חזקה אמר אביי זשני בתים בשני צדי רשות הרבים זה עושה מעקה לחצי גגו וזה עושה מעקה לחצי גגו זה שלא כנגד זה ומעדיף מאי איריא ברשות הרבים חאפילו רשות היחיד נמי רשות הרבים איצטריכא ליה מהו דתימא נימא ליה סוף סוף הא בעית לאצטנועי מבני רשות הרבים קמ"ל דא"ל רבים ביממא חזו לי בליליא (ב) לא חזו לי את בין ביממא בין בליליא חזית לי א"נ רבים כי קאימנא חזו לי כי יתיבנא לא חזו לי את חזית לי בין כי קאימנא בין כי יתיבנא רבים כי מעיינו חזו לי כי לא מעיינו לא חזו לי את ממילא נמי חזית לי אמר מר זה עושה מעקה לחצי גגו וזה עושה מעקה לחצי גגו זה שלא כנגד זה ומעדיף פשיטא לא צריכא דקדים חד מנייהו ועבד (ג) מהו דתימא נימא ליה אידך שקול אוזינקא ועבדיה את כוליה קמ"ל דא"ל את מ"ט לא עבדת משום דמיתרע אשיתך אנא נמי מיתרע ליה אשיתאי אמר ר"נ אמר שמואל טגג הסמוך לחצר חבירו עושה לו מעקה גבוה ד' אמות אבל בין גג לגג לא ור"נ דידיה אמר יאינו זקוק לד"א אבל זקוק למחיצת עשרה למאי אי להזיק ראיה ארבע אמות בעינן אי לנתפס עליו כגנב במסיפס בעלמא סגי אי לגדיים וטלאים בכדי שלא יזדקר בבת ראש סגי כלעולם לנתפס עליו כגנב במסיפס מצי משתמיט ליה ג) [אמר ממצורי קממצירנא] במחיצת עשרה לא מצי משתמיט ליה מיתיבי אם היה חצרו למעלה מגגו של חבירו אין נזקקין לו מאי לאו אין נזקקין לו כלל לא לד' אמות אבל נזקקין לו למחיצת עשרה איתמר שתי חצרות זו למעלה מזו אמר רב הונא תחתון בונה מכנגדו ועולה ועליון בונה מכנגדו ועולה ורב חסדא אמר עליון מסייע מלמטה ובונה תניא כוותיה דרב חסדא לשתי חצרות זו למעלה מזו לא יאמר העליון הריני בונה מכנגדי ועולה אלא מסייע מלמטה ובונה מואם היתה חצרו למעלה מגגו של חבירו אינו זקוק לו הנהו בי תרי דהוו דיירי חד הוה דייר עילאי וחד הוה דייר תתאי (ד) איתבר תתאי א"ל תתאי לעילאי תא ונבנייה א"ל אנא שפיר קא דאירנא אמר

רש"י

בירה גדולה. בית ארוך מאד וחלוק מתוכו להרבה חדרים (ה) קטנות והשכיר לזה אחד מהן הרי זה משתמש בכתליה בחורי הכתלים על פני ארכה מבחוץ עד ד' אמות אף שלא כנגד ביתו ובזיזים היוצאים מכתלים: ובעובי הכותל. ברחבו כגון אם השכיר לו בה עלייה: אבל בתרבץ אפדני לא. דרך בוני בירה חשובה להניח לה כנגד פתח הטרקלין החשוב שבה כעין גינה קטנה לאויר ועולין בה דשאים ויפה המראה לעיניים ושם אין רשות לזה לתלות בכתלים כלום שאינו עשוי ליכנס לתוכו: אבל רחבה שאחורי הבתים. כל היקף שאחורי הבתים קרוי רחבה ושלפני הבתים קרוי חצר (ו) אין הרחבה מושכרת לו להשתמש: לא הויא חזקה. אם סמכה על כותל חבירו ולא מיחה בתוך שלשים [יום] לא הויא חזקה לטעון ולומר פייסתיך במעות עד עולם דכל תלתין יומין לא קפיד איניש ולא מחי סבור חברי זה צריך לצל ולימים מועטים יטלנו משם: ואי סוכה דמצוה היא לבתר ז' הויא חזקה. דכיון דשבקוה עלה יותר מן הצורך הוה ליה למחויי: תוס'. ומדלא מיחה איכא למימר דזה פייסו במעות עד עולם שכן היה דרכם לקבוע סוכתן לצורך כל השנים והלכך מיד לאחר ז' הויא חזקה דלא דמי לסוכה דמטללתא דלא הוי חזקה עד תלתין יומין דהפיא לצל בעלמא הוא דעבדה אבל סוכה זו לצורך כל ימות החג שבכל שנה עשאה. ע"כ: זה שלא כנגד זה. זה סותם גגו לצד צפון וזה לצד דרום: ומעדיף. מושך המעקה יותר מחצי הגג כדי שיהיה במקצת כנגד סתימתו של זה ומתוך כך לא יראה בהדיא לגגו של חבירו: פשיטא. דהאי פלגא והאי פלגא: לא צריכא דקדים חד ועביד דידיה. מעקה לחצי גגו קודם שבא לב"ד ואח"כ תבע את חבירו לעשות בשלו מהו דתימא הואיל והתחיל לעשות יגמור המעקה בגגו וזה יתן לו חצי הוצאה: אוזינקא. יציאה: תוס'. (ז) דלאי לא קדים אלא בא לב"ד על עסק המעקה ולא זה רוצה לעשות בגגו פשיטא דב"ד עושה פשרה ביניהם לעשות כל אחד חצי מעקה או האחד יעשה כולו וחבירו יחזיר לו שכר הוצאה אשיותא אבל השתא דקדים יכול לטעון אידך אילו לא קדמת אותי הייתי עושה כולו בגגי אבל לאלאין לא עבידנא דטריחא לי לחזור אחר פועלין בשביל דבר מועט. ע"כ: לא תתרע אשיתאי. מכובד הבנין שמכבידין על חומה טיט ממהרת לקלקל למעלה: גבוה ארבע אמות. משום היזק ראיה: אבל בין גג לגג. לא צריך כדאמרינן בשמעתין קמייתא חצר קביעא תשמישיה וגג לא קביעא תשמישיה ולא ידענא בהי עדנא (ח) דסלקת דאיטנע ממך: אין זקוק לו. בין גג לגג לארבע אמות גובה: אם נתפס כגנב. שאם יכנס לפניס מן המחילה לשם גניבה נכנס: מצי משתמיט ליה. ולומר חפץ נפל מידי על גגך ונכנסתי אלך ליטול: היתה חצירו למעלה מגגו של חבירו. שהיה קרקע החצר גבוה מקרקע הבית: אין זקוק לו. בעל החצר לעשות לו מחילה בין חצר לגג דכיון דגג לא קביע תשמישיה נוח ליזהר משכיניו שלא יראוהו: זו למעלה מזו. קרקעית האחד גבוה מחבירתה: זה בונה מכנגדו ועולה. התחתון בונה משלו מלמטה עד שמגיע לגובה קרקעיתו של חבירו ואחר כך מתחיל זה לסייעו ונותן חלקו מכנגדו ומעלה ולא יהא עליון נפסד בשפלות קרקעיתו של תחתון: דהוו דיירי חד עילאי וחד תתאי. כשחלקו האחין נטל זה בית וזה עלייה: (ט) איתבר תתאי. נטבעו הכתלים התחתונים בארץ עד ששפלה תקרת העלייה ואין התחתון יכול ליכנס בתוכו אלא אם כן שוחה: תא ונבנייה. בוא ונסתור את כל הבית ונבננו: איבנייה אנא. משלי: אמר ליה. עליון לית לי דוכתא דדיירנא ביה: לא קא מתדר לי. איני יכול לדור בביתי מפני עלייתך:

סוף

תוספות

האי כשורא דמטללתא. אומר ר"ת דלמתני' קאי דעד שלשים יום לא הוי חזקה והוי בחזקת שלא נתן מכאן ואילך הוי בחזקת שנתן ואתי שפיר דנקטיה הכא ולא בחזקת הבתים: עד שבעה יומי. לאו דוקא שבעה דבשמיני עלרת לא יוכל לסתור: ואי חבריה בטינא לאלתר הוי חזקה. ואומר רבינו שמואל דחזקות דלעיל לאו דשלש שנים אלא לאלתר כדאמרינן הכא: בשני צדי רשות הרבים. אומר ר"י דוקא בשני צדי רשות הרבים שאין האחד מרגיש בחבירו כשעולה בגגו שיזהר ממנו מדאמרינן בסמוך אבל בין גג לגג לא: מהו דתימא מצי א"ל שקול אוזינקא כו'. וא"ת והיכי הוי ס"ד דמצי למימר ליה הכי דאטו משום דקדם זה ועשה הורע כחו ויכול לדוחקו זה לעשות כל הכותל ויש לומר דס"ד כיון דאם לא קדם זה ועשה (י) זה הוה מצי למימר שקול אוזינקא וזיל ועשה כל הכותל או הב לי אוזינקא ואעשה אני הכל ונרויח בין שנינו שלא נצטרך להעדיף השתא נמי מצי למימר ליה הכי קמ"ל דלא מצי אמר ליה כיון שכבר עשה זה ולא אמר לו קודם: שתי חצרות זו למעלה מזו. וא"ת ותחתון למה יסייע לעליון דמכי מטי לארבע אמות ולא יוכל התחתון לראות בחצר העליון יבנה העליון ואומר ר"ת כגון שחצר התחתון אינו נמוך אלא אצל חצרו של עליון (אלא מצד א') ומצד א' הוא גבוה כחצר העליון שיוכל לראות שם ור"י מפרש דהתחתון מזיק לעליון כי קאי עליון (כ) כדאמרי' לעיל כי קאימנא חזו לי ולכך צריך לסייע עד ד' אמות בחצר העליון:

מסורת הש"ס

א) לעיל ב:, ב) [ערוך ערך מצר], ג) בדפוס ישן איתא ולא זה רוצה לעשות בגגו, ד) [שייך לדף ז.], ה) ס"א ל"ג:

הגהות הב"ח

(א) גמ' משתמש בכתליה ובזיזיה עד ארבע אמות: (ב) שם לא חזו לי. נ"ב ע"ל דף ס': (ג) שם ועבד דידיה מהו דתימא: (ד) שם איתבר תתאי: (ה) רש"י ד"ה בירה וכו' חדרים קטנים והשכיר: (ו) ד"ה אבל רחבה [וכו'] חצר הס"ד ואח"כ מה"ד לא אין הרחבה: (ז) ד"ה תוס' פשיטא לא"ל דקדים דאי לא קדים: (ח) ד"ה אבל וכו' בהי עדנא סלקת כצ"ל ואות ד' נמחק: (ט) ד"ה איתבר תתאי: (י) תוס' ד"ה מהו כו' ועשה הוה מצי כצ"ל ותיבת זה נמחק: (כ) ד"ה שתי וכו' כי קאי עליון בשפת חצירו כדאמרי' לעיל:

ליקוטי רש"י

מעקה גבוה ארבע אמות. די שלא יראה בחצר חבירו כשהוא משתמש בגגו [לעיל ב:]. במסיפס. מחילה נמוכה של מחיצות עצים [עירובין עו.] וכעי"ז ע"ז ע:]. של יתדות עצים תקועים בארץ נמוכים [לעיל ב:].

רבינו גרשום

מנטף אלא משני עברי הבית אבל בנוי כעין צריף הוט"א בל"ע שהוא עגול ומנטף בכל סביבותיו לא [אחזיק] ויכול לעכב עליו: בבירה גדולה. כעין מגדל גדול ובונין בתוכה בתים הרבה סביבותיה ויש סביבותיה חצר וגנות ופרדסין הרי זה השוכר משתמש חוץ לביתו בכתליה דבירה הסמוכות א) לכותל אם יש בה חורין או זיזין שתולין בה חפציהן עד ד' אמות סמוך לבית דשייך בתר בית: ובעובי הכותל במקום שנהגו. לישתמש על גב ב) הבית משתמש חוץ לגג בעובי החומה ד' אמות: אבל בתרבץ אפדני. גינת ביתן שסמוך לפלטין אינו משתמש לבתים אלא לפלטין: אבל רחבה גדולה שאחורי הבתים. היא ודאי עשויה לצורך הפלטין עצמה: האי כשורא דמטללתא. אם נעץ אחד קורתו בכותל חבירו מדעתו של בעל הכותל לסכך עליה מפני החמה אם נעוצה בו הקורה יותר מל' יום ולא מיחה בעל הכותל הוי חזקה לזה שנעצה לקובעה שם לעולם שסתם שאלה משאיל כותלו לחבירו לנעוץ בו [מידי] ל' יום ותו לא: ואי סוכה דמצוה היא. כלומר אם הרשהו לנעוץ קורה לצורך סוכת החג דמצוה ודאי אם הניחה שם יותר על ז' ימים בפני בעל הכותל שלא מיחה יכול להחזיק בה לעולם: ואי חבריה לקורה בטינא. כלומר שקבעה לקורה בכותל בחומר ובלבנים בקביעות בפני בעל הכותל ולא מיחה הוה חזקה לאלתר דאיכא למימר דמחל לו: ב' בתים משני צדי רה"ר. אם מקום הוא שמשתמשין על הגגות זה עושה לחצי גגו מעקה גבוה ד' אמות משום היזק ראיה וכן השני זה שלא כנגד זה ומעדיף מעט זה כנגד זה כדי שלא יוכל א' להציץ בתוך גג חבירו ג) אלא ברה"ר מצי למימר חבריה דמעכב מאי [נפקא] לך מינה אי לא עבידנא מעקה כוותך סוף סוף אי לא הואי אנא הכא אפ"ה קבעית לאצטנועי מבני רה"ר קמ"ל דמצי אמר ליה אידך ד) אי לא מבני רה"ר יכילנא לאצטנועי דכי יתיבנא לא חזו לי קמ"ל ה) דאפ"ה יכול לכופו שיעשה חצי מעקה לגגו: דקדים חד מינייהו ועביד. מעקה לחצי גגו: אזינקא. חצי הוצאתך שתוציא בכולו: משום דאיתרע אשיתך. שלא יכביד על הכותל ויפול הכותל אנא נמי מסתפינא הכי: גג הסמוך לחצר חבירו. דמקום החצר גבוה ושוה לגגו עושה מעקה ד' אמות לגג שלא יציץ לחצר חבירו. ואי קשיא למה אין מחייבין בעל חצר לעשות מחיצה לחצירו שלא יסתכל לגג חבירו. הא לא תיקשי דהיזקא דחצר עדיף מהיזקא דגג דחצר קביעא תשמישתא וגג לא קביעא תשמישתיה: אבל בין גג לגג דלא קביעא תשמישתייהו לא להאי ולא להאי לא: אי לנתפס עליו כגנב. כלומר אי לכך צריך מחיצה דלא יכנס חבירו לשם בלא רשות ויתפס כגנב דיכול לומר לו לגנוב באת: במסיפס בעלמא סגי. אפי' במחיצה כל שהוא אם יעבור עליו בלא רשות יתפס כגנב: במסיפס יכול לאישתמוטי. דטעין דכיון דלא הוי האי מחיצה גבוה י' טפחים לא הוה ידענא אי משום מחיצה הוי משום הכי עברנא ולא משום גניבה: למעלה מגגו של חבירו. שקרקעית החצר גבוה יותר על הגג: מאי לאו אין נזקקין לו כלל לעשות מחיצה וקשיא לעיל דתרצת ו) זקוק למחיצה: שתי חצירות זו למעלה מזו. שהאחת גבוה יותר מן האחרת תחתון יחקוק מחיצה בקרקע עליון ובונה עד שיהיה הכותל שוה לחצר העליון ושוב יגביהו העליון עד ד' אמות: ורב חסדא אמר עליון מסייע מלמטה עם התחתון. לפי שהעליון יכול לראות התחתון ולא תחתון העליון לפיכך צריך העליון לעשות רוב הבנין כפי שלא יזיק לתחתון מראייתו: ואם היתה חצירו למעלה מגג של חבירו אין זקוק לו. משום דגג לא קביעא תשמישתיה: איתבר ביתא דתתאי. שנפלו קצת מכותלי התחתון וירד בית העליון ונח על אותו קצת כותל התחתון שנשתיירו: אמר ליה תתאי לעילאי תא נבניה. כלומר סייע לי לבנות הבית כבראשונה: שפיר דאירנא. כלומר איני צריך שאני יפה דר שלא נפלה עלייתי:

חשק שלמה על רבינו גרשום א) [אולי צ"ל בכותליה דבירה הסמוכות לכותל ביתו אם יש בה חורין וכו']: ב) [נראה דצ"ל על גג הבית וכו']: ג) [נראה דצ"ל רה"ר איצטריכא ליה דמהו דתימא דמצי למימר ליה חבריה וכו']: ד) [נראה דצ"ל דמצי למימר ליה אידך אי לא את מבני רה"ר וכו']: ה) [אולי צ"ל דכי יתיבנא לא חזו לי ומש"ה יכול לכופו שיעשה חצי מעקה לגגו]: ו) [אולי צ"ל דקאמרת דזקוק למחילה י']:

מִשְׁתַּמֵּשׁ בְּזִיזֵיהָ וּבִכְתָלֶיהָ[1] בְּבִירָה גְּדוֹלָה – **in a large residence** the tenant **may use [the building's]** projecting **beams and** the crevices in its **walls**[2] עַד אַרְבַּע אַמּוֹת – **up to four** ***amos*****,**[3] for use of the walls and beams is included in the apartment's rental. וּבְעוֹבִי הַכּוֹתֶל – **And** he may also use **the thickness of the** top of the **wall** to store objects[4] בְּמָקוֹם שֶׁנָּהֲגוּ – **in a place where [homeowners] are accustomed** to storing objects there.[5] אֲבָל בְּתַרְבַּץ אַפַּדְנֵי לֹא – **But** he may **not** use the section of wall that faces the garden of **the reception hall of the residence.**[6]

Having presented the opinion of Rabbah bar Avuha, Rav Nachman offers his own view of the matter:

וְרַב נַחְמָן דִּידֵיהּ אָמַר – **But Rav Nachman himself said:** אֲפִילּוּ בְּתַרְבַּץ אַפַּדְנֵי – He may use **even** the section of wall that faces the garden of **the reception hall of the residence,** since it is possible for him to enter there. אֲבָל רְחָבָה שֶׁאֲחוֹרֵי הַבָּתִּים לֹא – **But** he may **not** use **the expanse**[7] of land **behind the apartments,** since use of this area is not included in the rental.

Rava has a third view:

וְרָבָא אָמַר אֲפִילּוּ רְחָבָה שֶׁאֲחוֹרֵי הַבָּתִּים – **And Rava said:** He may use **even the expanse** of land **behind the apartments,** for that, too, is included in the rental.

The Gemara now discusses instances of uncontested usage that do not immediately establish a right to use a neighbor's property:

אָמַר רָבִינָא – **Ravina said:** הַאי כְּשׁוּרָא דִּמְטַלַּלְתָּא – Regarding **this beam** of a hut built **for shade** that rests on a neighbor's wall for support[8] – עַד תְּלָתִין יוֹמִין – if it remains there for **up to thirty days** and the owner of the wall does not object, לָא הָוֵי חֲזָקָה – that **does not create a presumption** that the hut's owner purchased the right to rest his beam there permanently;[9] בָּתַר תְּלָתִין יוֹמִין – if, however, the beam remains in place **longer than**[10] **thirty days** and the wall's owner does not object, הָוֵי חֲזָקָה – that **does create a presumption** that the hut's owner purchased the right to rest his beam there permanently.[11]

Ravina distinguishes this case from the case of a hut built for the Yom Tov of Succos:

וְאִי סוּכָּה דְּמִצְוָה הִיא – **But if [the hut] is a succah**[12] built for observance **of the commandment** to dwell in a succah[13] (and the succah's beam rested on the neighbor's wall), then the following rule applies: עַד שִׁבְעָה יוֹמִין – If the succah stood only **until** the **seven days** of Succos[14] had passed and the wall's owner remained silent, לָא הָוֵי חֲזָקָה – that **does not create a presumption** that the succah's owner purchased the right to rest his beam permanently on this neighbor's wall;[15] בָּתַר שִׁבְעָה יוֹמִין – if, however, the succah remains standing **longer than seven days** and the wall's owner does not protest, הָוֵי חֲזָקָה – that **does create a presumption** that the succah's owner purchased the right to rest his beam permanently on his neighbor's wall.[16]

Ravina issues an important qualification to the previous rulings:

וְאִי חַבְרֵיהּ בְּטִינָא – **And if he affixed [the beam]** to the neighbor's wall **with cement,** and the neighbor saw this and did not protest, לְאַלְתַּר הָוֵי חֲזָקָה – that act **immediately creates a presumption** that the owner of the hut (or succah) purchased the right to rest his beam permanently on his neighbor's wall.[17]

The Gemara returns to the subject of visual trespass, and discusses specifically the rooftop area of a private residence:

אָמַר אַבָּיֵי – **Abaye said:** שְׁנֵי בָתִּים בִּשְׁנֵי צִדֵּי רְשׁוּת הָרַבִּים – Regarding **two houses** standing **on two** opposite **sides of a public domain,**[18] זֶה עוֹשֶׂה מַעֲקֶה לַחֲצִי גַּגּוֹ – **this** homeowner **must make a fence** four *amos*[19] high **along half of his roof,**

NOTES

1. This is a very long building divided internally into many small apartments that were rented separately (*Rashi*).

2. In Mishnaic times beams projected from the outside of the walls of buildings, and objects were commonly hung on them. Further, crevices in the outside of the walls were used for storage. Rav Nachman thus rules that a tenant is entitled to use these features of the building according to their common usage.

3. He may use any of the beams or crevices that are within four *amos* of the section of wall opposite his room (*Rashi*).

4. If he rented a room on the top floor of the building (*Rashi*).

5. Since the owners themselves are not concerned that the weight of the storage on top will damage the wall, halachah presumes that when they rent out their buildings they allow their tenants this right of storage (*Ran, Nimukei Yosef*; cf. *Rabbeinu Yonah* and *Ri Migash*).

6. It was customary to plant a small ornamental garden to beautify the entrance to the main reception hall of a large, imposing residence. Since tenants were not wont to enter this area, use of the wall facing the garden was not included in the rental agreement (*Rashi*).

7. רְחָבָה, *expanse,* refers to the area behind an apartment building, while חָצֵר, *courtyard,* denotes the area in front (*Rashi*).

8. The Gemara refers to a beam [or beams] upon which a roof for shade is placed (*Rabbeinu Gershom*).

9. I.e. the hut's owner is not believed to claim that he purchased this right of usage, pointing to the silence of the wall's owner as proof, for until thirty days have elapsed the wall's owner can explain that he failed to object because he thought that the neighbor would remove the hut after a short while, since it was erected only for shade (*Rashi*).

10. Literally: after thirty days.

11. I.e. the hut's owner is believed to claim that he purchased this right, for the wall's owner would not otherwise have countenanced an unauthorized use of such duration without voicing a protest. [As before, the hut's owner must claim that he actually acquired the right; he cannot claim it solely on the basis of his uncontested usage (see above, 6a note 33).]

12. A temporary dwelling whose size and roofing must conform to specifications promulgated in tractate *Succah.*

13. The Torah commands: *You shall dwell in succos for seven days (Leviticus* 23:42). This mitzvah is performed annually during the festival of Succos, which commences on the 15th day of Tishrei.

14. *Tosafos* point out that a succah will actually remain standing for eight days, since the eighth day is a Yom Tov, Shemini Atzeres, when the labor of dismantling (סְתִירָה) is forbidden.

15. I.e. the succah's owner is not believed to claim that he purchased this right of usage, pointing to the silence of the wall's owner as proof, since the wall's owner can explain that he refrained from protesting because he did not wish to disturb his neighbor's holiday by demanding the dismantling of the succah.

16. [I.e. the succah's owner is believed to claim that he purchased this right] for since he allowed the succah to stand longer than necessary, the wall's owner should have objected (*Rashi*).

During the Talmudic era people customarily erected succos that stood from year to year; hence, if the wall's owner did not protest immediately upon the completion of the Succos holiday, the succah's owner is believed to claim that he purchased the right to use his neighbor's wall to support a permanent succah. This case differs from the previous case, since there the hut was inherently a temporary structure, serving only to provide shade for a short period of time. Hence, until the passage of thirty days the wall's owner can attribute his silence to his willingness to tolerate what he perceived as only a brief arrogation of the wall (gloss to *Rashi*; cf. *Yad Ramah*).

17. I.e. he is believed to claim that he purchased this right, for otherwise the wall's owner would not have allowed him to make a permanent attachment.

18. Although the Gemara below states that adjacent roofs do not require protection from visual trespass, the situation is different when the roofs are separated by a public thoroughfare, since the distance prevents one homeowner from noticing that his neighbor has ascended to the other roof. Hence, the possibility of the first one being caught off-guard while engaged in a private activity on his own roof is substantial (*Tosafos*).

19. Although the Torah requires for reasons of safety the erecting of

עין משפט
נר מצוה

לה א ב ג מיי' פ"ו מהל' שכירות הל' א סמג עשין קט טוש"ע ח"מ סי' שיג סעיף א:

לו ד ה ו מיי' פ"ז מהל' שכנים הל' ז סמג עשין פב טוש"ע ח"מ סי' קנג סעיף יז:

לז ז ח מיי' שם פ"ג הלכה ה סמג שם טוש"ע ח"מ סי' קנט סעיף א:

לח ט מיי' שם הל' ו וע"ש בהשגות סמג שם טוש"ע שם סעיף ב וסי' קס סעיף א:

לט י כ מיי' שם טוש"ע ח"מ סי' קנט סעיף ג:

מ ל מיי' שם הלכה ז וע"ש בהשגות ובמ"מ ובכ"מ סמג שם טוש"ע ח"מ סי' קס סעיף ג:

מא מ מיי' שם טוש"ע שם סעיף א וסעיף ב:

[א] בבירה גדולה משתמש (א) בזויזה ובכתליה עד ד' אמות ובעובי הכותל במקום שנהגו אבל בתרבץ אפדני לא ורב נחמן דידיה אמר [ב] אפילו בתרבץ אפדני אבל רחבה שאחורי הבתים לא ורבא אמר [ג] אפילו רחבה שאחורי הבתים אמר רבינא [ד] האי כשורא דמטללתא עד תלתין יומין לא הוי חזקה בתר תלתין יומין הוי חזקה [ה] ואי סוכה דמצוה היא עד שבעה יומין לא הוי חזקה בתר שבעה יומין הוי חזקה [ו] ואי חבריה בטינא לאלתר הוי חזקה אמר אביי [ז] שני בתים בשני צדי רשות הרבים זה עושה מעקה לחצי גגו וזה עושה מעקה לחצי גגו זה שלא כנגד זה ומעדיף מאי איריא ברשות הרבים [ח] אפילו רשות היחיד נמי רשות הרבים איצטריכא ליה מהו דתימא נימא ליה סוף סוף הא בעית לאצטנועי מבני רשות הרבים קמ"ל דא"ל רבים בימָמא חזו לי בליליא (ב) לא חזו לי את בין בימָמא בין בליליא חזית לי א"נ רבים כי קאימנא חזו לי כי יתיבנא לא חזו לי את חזית לי בין כי קאימנא בין כי יתיבנא רבים כי מעיינו חזו לי כי לא מעיינו לא חזו לי את ממילא נמי חזית לי אמר מר זה עושה מעקה לחצי גגו וזה עושה מעקה לחצי גגו זה שלא כנגד זה ומעדיף פשיטא לא צריכא דקדים חד מנייהו ועבד (ג) מהו דתימא נימא ליה איהך שקול אוזינקא ועבדיה את כוליה קמ"ל דא"ל את מ"ט לא עבדת משום דמיתרע אשיתך אנא נמי מיתרע ליה אשיתאי א) אמר ר"נ אמר שמואל [ט] גג הסמוך לחצר חבירו עושה לו מעקה גבוה ד' אמות אבל בין גג לגג לא ור"נ דידיה אמר [י] אינו זקוק לד"א אבל זקוק למחיצת עשרה למאי אי להיזק ראיה ארבע אמות בעינן אי לנתפס עליו כגנב במסיפס בעלמא סגיא אי לגדיים וטלאים בבדי שלא יזדקר בבת ראש סגי [כ] לעולם לנתפס עליו כגנב במסיפס מצי משתמיט ליה ב) [אמר ממצורי קממצירנא] במחיצת עשרה לא מצי משתמיט ליה מיתיבי אם היה חצרו למעלה מגגו של חבירו אין נזקקין לו מאי לאו אין נזקקין לו כלל לא לד' אמות אבל נזקקין למחיצת עשרה איתמר שתי חצרות זו למעלה מזו אמר רב הונא תחתון בונה מכנגדו ועולה ועליון בונה מכנגדו ועולה ורב חסדא אמר עליון מסייע מלמטה ובונה תניא כוותיה דרב חסדא [ל] שתי חצרות זו למעלה מזו לא יאמר העליון הריני בונה מכנגדי ועולה אלא מסייע מלמטה ובונה [מ] ואם היתה חצרו למעלה מגגו של חבירו אינו זקוק לו הנהו בי תרי דהוו דיירי חד הוה דייר עילאי וחד הוה דייר תתאי (ד) איתבר תתאי א"ל תתאי לעילאי תא ונבנייה א"ל אנא שפיר קא דאירנא

אמר

בירה גדולה. בית ארוך מאד וחלוק מתוכו להרבה חדרים (ה) קטנות והשכיר לזה אחד מהן הרי זה משתמש בכתליה בחורי הכתלים על פני ארכה מבחוץ עד ד' אמות אף שלא כנגד ביתו ובזיזים היוצאים מכתלים: **ובעובי הכותל.** בראשו כגון אם השכיר לו בה עלייה: **אבל בתרבץ אפדני לא.** דרך בוני בירה חשובה להניח לה כנגד פתח הטרקלין החשוב שבה כעין גינה קטנה לאויר ועולין בה דשאים ויפה המראה לעיניים ושם אין רשות לזה לתלות בכתלים כלום שאינו עשוי ליכנס לתוכו: **אבל רחבה שאחורי הבתים.** כל היקף שאחורי הבתים קרוי חצר (ו) ואין הרחבה מושכרת לו להשתמש: **לא הויא חזקה.** אם סמכה על כותל חבירו ולא מיחה בתוך שלשים [יום] לא הויא חזקה לטעון ולומר פייסתיך במעות עד עולם דכל תלתין יומין לא קפיד איניש ולא מחי סבור חברי זה צריך לכך ולימים מועטים יטלנו משם: **ואי סוכה דמצוה היא לבתר ז' הויא חזקה.** דכיון דשבקוה עלה יותר מן הצורך הוה ליה למחויי: תוס'. ומדלא מיחה איכא למימר דזה פייסו במעות עד עולם שכן היה דרכם לקבוע סוכתן לצורך כל השנים והלכך מיד לאחר ז' הויא חזקה דלא דמי לסוכה דמטללתא דלא הוי חזקה עד תלתין יומין דהתם איכא למימר הוא דעבדה אבל סוכה זו לצורך כל ימות החג שבכל שנה ושנה עשאה. ע"כ: **זה שלא כנגד זה.** זה סותם גגו לצד צפון וזה לצד דרום: **ומעדיף.** מוסף המעקה יותר מחצי הגג כדי שיהיה במקצת כנגד סתימתו של זה ומתוך כך לא יראה בהדיא לגגו של חבירו: **פשיטא.** דהאי פלגא והאי פלגא: **לא צריכא דקדים חד ועביד דידיה.** מעקה לחצי גגו קודם שבא לב"ד ואח"כ תבע את חבירו לעשות בשלו מהו דתימא הואיל והתחיל לעשות יגמור המעקה בגגו וזה יתן לו חצי הוצאה: **אוזינקא.** יציאה: תוס'. (ז) דאי לא קדים אלא בא לב"ד על עסק המעקה ולא זה רוצה לעשות בגגו ג) פשיטא דב"ד עושה פשרה ביניהם לעשות כל אחד חצי מעקה או האחד יעשה כולו וחבירו יחזיר לו שכר הורעת אשיותא אבל השתא דקדים יכול לטעון אידך אילו לא קדמת אותי הייתי עושה כולו בגגי אבל לאנאין לא עבידנא דטריחא לי לחזור אחר פועלין בשביל דבר מועט. ע"כ: **לא תתרע אשיתאי.** מכובד הבנין שמכבידין על חומה טיט מתהרס לקלקל למעלה: **גבוה ארבע אמות.** משום היזק ראיה: **אבל בין גג לגג.** לא צריך כדאמרינן בשמעתין קמייתא חצר קביעא תשמישיה וגג לא קביעא תשמישיה ולא ידענא בהי עדנא (ח) דסלקת דלאיטמרנא מינך: **אין זקוק לו.** בין גג לגג לארבע אמות גובה: **אם נתפס כגנב.** שאם יכנס לפנים מן המחיצה לגגו נכנס: **מצי משתמיט ליה.** ולומר חפץ נפל מידי על גגך ונכנסתי אצלך ליטול: **היתה חצירו למעלה מגגו של חבירו.** שהיה קרקע החצר גבוה מקרקע הבית: **אין זקוק לו.** בעל החצר לעשות לו מחיצה בין חצר לגג דכיון דגג לא קביע תשמישיה נוח ליזהר משכיניו שלא יראוהו: **זו למעלה מזו.** קרקעית האחד גבוה מחבירתה: **זה בונה מכנגדו ועולה.** התחתון בונה משלו מלמטה עד שמגיע לגובה קרקעיתו של חבירו ואחר כך מתחיל זה לסייעו ונותן חלקו מכנגדו ומעלה ולא יהא עליון נפסד בשפלות קרקעיתו של תחתון: **דהוו דיירי חד עילאי וחד תתאי.** כשחלקו האחין נטל זה בית וזה עלייה: (ט) **איתבר תתאי.** נטבעו הכתלים התחתונים בארץ עד ששפלה תקרת העלייה ואין התחתון יכול ליכנס בתוכו אלא אם כן שוחה: **תא ונבנייה.** בוא ונסתור את כל הבית ונבננו: ז) **איבנייה אנא.** משלי: **אמר ליה.** עליון לית לי דוכתא דדיירנא ביה: **לא קא מתדר לי.** איני יכול לדור בביתי מפני עלייתך:

סוף

האי כשורא דמטללתא. אומר ר"ת דלמתני' קאי דעד שלשים יום לא הוי חזקה והוי בחזקת שלא נתן מכאן ואילך הוי בחזקת שנתן ולתני שפיר דנקטיה הכא ולא בחזקת הבתים: **עד שבעה יומי.** לאו דוקא שבעה דבשמיני עצרת לא יוכל לסתור: **ואי חבריה בטינא לאלתר הוי חזקה.** ואומר רבינו שמואל דחזקות דלעיל לאו דשלש שנים אלא לאלתר כדאמרינן הכא:

בשני צדי רשות הרבים. אומר ר"י דוקא בשני צדי רשות הרבים שאין האחד מרגיש בחבירו כשעולה בגגו שיזהר ממנו מדאמרינן בסמוך אבל בין גג לגג לא:

מהו דתימא מצי א"ל שקול אוזינקא כו'. וא"ת והיכי הוי ס"ד דמצי למימר ליה הכי דלמא משום דקדם זה ועשה הורע כחו ויכול לדוחקו זה לעשות כל הכותל ויש לומר דס"ד כיון דאם לא קדם זה ועשה (י) זה הוה מצי למימר שקול אוזינקא וזיל ועשה כל הכותל או הב לי אוזינקא ואעשה אני הכל ונרויח בין שנינו שלא נצטרך להעדיף השתא נמי מצי למימר ליה הכי קמ"ל דלא מצי אמר ליה כיון שכבר עשה זה ולא אמר לו קודם:

שתי חצרות זו למעלה מזו. וא"ת ותחתון למה יסייע לעליון דמכי מטי לארבע אמות ולא יוכל התחתון לראות בחצר העליון יבנה העליון ואומר ר"ת כגון שחצר התחתון אינו נמוך אלא אמה אבל חצרו של עליון (ה) [אלא מלא א'] ומלא א' הוא גבוה מחצר העליון שיוכל לראות שם ור"י מפרש דהתחתון מזיק לעליון כי קאי עליון (כ) כדאמרי' לעיל כי קאימנא חזו לי ולכך צריך לסייע עד ד' אמות בחצר העליון:

מסורת הש"ס

א) לעיל ב:, ב) [ערוך ערך מצר], ג) בדפוס ישן איתא ולא זה רוצה לעשות בגגו, ד) [שייך לדף ז.], ה) ס"א ל"ג:

רבינו גרשום

מנטף אלא משני עברי הבית אבל בנוי כעין צריף הוט"א בל"ע שהוא עגול ומנטף בכל סביבותיו לא [אחזיק] ויכול לעכב עליו: **בבירה גדולה.** כעין מגדל גדול ובונין בתוכה בתים הרבה סביבותיה ויש סביבותיה חצר וגנות ופרדסין הרי זה השוכר **משתמש** חוץ לביתו **בכתליה** דבירה הסמוכות א) לכותל אם יש בה חורין או זיזין שתולין בה חפציהן **עד ד' אמות** סמוך לבית דשייך בתר בית: **ובעובי הכותל במקום שנהגו.** לישתמש על גב ב) הבית משתמש חוץ לגג בעובי החומה ד' אמות: **אבל בתרבץ אפדני.** גינת ביתן שסמוך לפלטין אינו משתמש לבתים אלא לפלטין: **אבל רחבה גדולה שאחורי הבתים.** היא ודאי עשויה לצורך הפלטין עצמה: **האי כשורא דמטללתא.** אם נעץ אחד קורתו בכותל חבירו מדעתו של בעל הכותל לסכך עליה מפני החמה אם נעוצה בו הקורה יותר מל' יום ולא מיחה בעל הכותל **הוי חזקה** לזה שנעצה לקובעה שם לעולם שסתם שאלה משאיל כותלו לחבירו לנעוץ בו [מידי] ל' יום ותו לא: **ואי סוכה דמצוה היא.** כלומר אם הרשהו לנעוץ קורה לצורך סוכת החג דמצוה ודאי אם הניחה שם יותר על ז' ימים בפני בעל הכותל שלא מיחה יכול להחזיק בה לעולם: **ואי חבריה לקורה בטינא.** כלומר שקבעה לקורה בכותל בחומר ובלבנים בקביעות בפני בעל הכותל ולא מיחה **הוה חזקה לאלתר** דאיכא למימר דמחל לו: **ב' בתים משני צדי רה"ר.** אם מקום הוא שמשתמשין על הגגות **זה עושה לחצי גגו מעקה** גבוה ד' אמות משום היזק ראיה וכן השני **זה שלא כנגד זה ומעדיף** מעט זה כנגד זה כדי שלא יוכל א' להציץ בתוך גג חבירו ג) אלא ברה"ר מצי למימר חבריה מעכב מאי [נפקא] לך מינה אי לא עבידנא מעקה כוותך סוף סוף אי לא הויה אנא הכא אפ"ה קבעית לאצטנועי מבני רה"ר קמ"ל דמצי אמר ליה אידך ד) אי לא מבני רה"ר יכילנא לאצטנועי דכי יתיבנא לא חזו לי קמ"ל דאפ"ה יכול לכופו שיעשה חצי מעקה לגגו: **דקדים חד מיניהו ועביד.** מעקה לחצי גגו: **אזינקא.** חצי הוצאתך שתוציא בכולו: **משום דאיתרע אשיתך.** שלא יכביד על הכותל ויפול הכותל **אנא נמי** מסתפינא הכי: **גג הסמוך לחצר חבירו.** דמקום החצר גבוה ושוה לגגו **עושה מעקה ד' אמות** לגג שלא יציץ לחצר חבירו. ואי קשיא למה אין מחייבין בעל חצר לעשות מחיצה לחצירו שלא יסתכל לגג חבירו. הא לא תיקשי דהיזקא דחצר עדיף מהיזקא דגג דחצר קביעא תשמישתא וגג לא קביעא תשמישתיה: **אבל בין גג לגג** דלא קביעא תשמישתייהו לא להאי ולא להאי **לא: אי לנתפס עליו כגנב.** כלומר אי לכך צריך מחיצה דלא יכנס חבירו לשם בלא רשות ויתפס כגנב דיכול לומר לו לגנוב באת. אפי' במחיצה כל שהוא אם יעבור עליו בלא רשות יתפס כגנב: **במסיפס בעלמא סגי. במסיפס יכול לאישתמוטי.** דטעין דכיון דלא הוי האי מחיצה גבוה י' טפחים לא הוה ידענא אי משום מחיצה הוי משום הכי עברנא ולא משום גניבה: **למעלה מגגו של חבירו.** שקרקעית החצר גבוה יותר על הגג: **מאי לאו אין נזקקין לו כלל** לעשות מחיצה וקשיא לעיל דתרצת ו) זקוק למחיצה: **שתי חצירות זו למעלה מזו.** שהאחת גבוה יותר מן האחרת **תחתון** יחקוק מחיצה בקרקע עליון **ובונה** עד שיהיה הכותל שוה לחצר העליון ושוב יגביהו העליון עד ד' אמות: **ורב חסדא אמר עליון מסייע מלמטה** עם התחתון. לפי שהעליון יכול לראות התחתון ולא תחתון העליון לפיכך צריך העליון לעשות רוב הבנין כפי שלא יזיק לתחתון מראייתו: **ואם היתה חצירו למעלה** גבוה מגג **של חבירו אין זקוק לו.** משום דגג לא קביעא תשמישתיה: **איתבר ביתא דתתאי.** שנפלו קצת מכותלי התחתון וירד בית העליון ונח על אותו קצת כותל התחתון שנשתיירו: **אמר ליה תתאי לעילאי תא נבניה.** כלומר סייע לי לבנות הבית כבראשונה: **שפיר דאירנא.** כלומר איני צריך שאני יפה דר שלא נפלה עלייתי:

חשק שלמה על רבינו גרשום א) [אולי צ"ל בכותליה דבירה הסמוכות לכותל ביתו אם יש בה חורין וכו']: ב) [נראה דצ"ל על גג הבית וכו']: ג) [נראה דצ"ל רה"ר איצטריכא ליה דמהו דתימא דמצי למימר ליה חבריה וכו']: ד) [נראה דצ"ל דמצי למימר ליה אידך אי לא את מבני רה"ר וכו']: ה) [אולי צ"ל דכי יתיבנא לא חזו לי ומש"ה יכול לכופו שיעשה חצי מעקה לגגו]: ו) [אולי צ"ל דתרצת דזקוק למחיצה י']:

הגהות הב"ח

(א) גמ' משתמש בכתליה ובזויזה עד ארבע אמות: (ב) שם לא חזו לי. נ"ב ע"ל דף ח': (ג) שם ועבד דידיה מהו דתימא: (ד) שם איתבר תתאי: (ה) רש"י ד"ה בירה וכו' חדרים קטנים והשכיר: (ו) ד"ה אבל רחבה [וכו'] חצר הס"ד ואח"כ מה"ד לא הויא חזקה: (ז) ד"ה תוס' פשיטא נ"ל דקדים דאי לא קדים: (ח) ד"ה אבל וכו' בהי עדנא סלקת כל"ל ואות ד' נמחק: (ט) ד"ה איתבר תתאי: (י) תוס' ד"ה מהו כו' ועשה זה הוה מצי: (כ) ד"ה שתי וכו' כי קאי עליון בשפת חצירו כדאמרי' לעיל:

ליקוטי רש"י

מעקה גבוה ארבע אמות. די שלא יראה בחצר חבירו כשהוא משתמש בגגו [לעיל ב:]. **במסיפס.** מחיצה נמוכה של חתיכות עצים [עירובין עב. וכעי"ז ע"ז] של יתדות עצים תקועים בארץ נמוכים [לעיל ב:].

וְזֶה עוֹשֶׂה מַעֲקֶה לַחֲצִי גַגּוֹ – **and this** other homeowner **must make a fence** four *amos* high **along half of his roof;** זֶה שֶׁלֹּא כְּנֶגֶד זֶה – and **this** fence must be built **not directly opposite this** other fence,[20] וּמַעֲדִיף – **and** each homeowner must **extend** his fence beyond the halfway mark, so that the two fences slightly overlap.[21]

The Gemara questions Abaye's formulation of the law:

מַאי אִירְיָא בִּרְשׁוּת הָרַבִּים – **Why is it mentioned** that the two houses are separated by **a public domain?** אֲפִילוּ רְשׁוּת הַיָּחִיד נַמִּי – **Even** if they faced each other across **a private domain,**[22] is it not **also** necessary to erect fences to ensure rooftop privacy?[23]

The Gemara answers:

רְשׁוּת הָרַבִּים אִיצְטְרִיכָא לֵיהּ – Although Abaye's ruling applies to both cases, **it was necessary** to formulate it in the case of **a public domain.** מַהוּ דְּתֵימָא נֵימָא לֵיהּ – For otherwise **you might have said** that one homeowner[24] **can say to [the other],** סוֹף סוֹף הָא בָּעֵית לְאִצְטְנוּעֵי מִבְּנֵי רְשׁוּת הָרַבִּים – "What does it matter to you if I do not erect my fence? **In any case you will have to conceal yourself from [passersby] in the public domain** if you wish to perform private acts on your roof." קָא מַשְׁמַע לָן – Abaye therefore **informs us** that this claim is not valid, דְּאָמַר לֵיהּ – **for** the willing owner **can** successfully **respond to [the unwilling owner],** "I can protect myself from visual trespass by the public without a fence, for רַבִּים בִּימָמָא חָזוּ לִי – **the public sees me during the day,** when they frequent the street, בְּלֵילְיָא לָא חָזוּ לִי – but **at night,** when they are not usually in the street, **they do not see me!**[25] אַתְּ בֵּין בִּימָמָא בֵּין בְּלֵילְיָא חָזֵית לִי – **You,** however, **can see me both during the day and at night!** Thus, I require a fence specifically to protect myself from you."

The Gemara suggests two other replies:

אִי נַמִּי – **Alternatively,** he can reply, רַבִּים כִּי קָאֵימְנָא חָזוּ לִי – **"The public can see me** only **when I am standing,**[26] כִּי יָתִיבְנָא לָא חָזוּ לִי – but **when I am sitting they cannot see me.** Hence, at the very least I can perform my private activities without the protection of a fence while sitting. אַתְּ חָזֵית לִי בֵּין כִּי קָאֵימְנָא בֵּין כִּי יָתִיבְנָא – **You,** however, **can see me whether I am standing or sitting;** hence, it is necessary for you to assist in building a fence. Additionally, רַבִּים כִּי מְעַיְּינוּ חָזוּ לִי – **the public can see me** only **when they make a conscious effort** to do so,[27] and that does not happen often;[28] כִּי לָא מְעַיְּינוּ לָא חָזוּ לִי – but **when they do not make a conscious effort they do not see me.** אַתְּ מִמֵּילָא נַמִּי חָזֵית לִי – **You,** however, **also see me involuntarily,** since my roof is level to yours. Thus, while I might tolerate the rare instance of visual trespass from the street, I am precluded by you from performing private activities on my roof. Hence, you must also build a fence."

The Gemara analyzes Abaye's statement further:

אָמַר מַר – **The master** (Abaye) had **said:** זֶה עוֹשֶׂה מַעֲקֶה לַחֲצִי גַגּוֹ וְזֶה עוֹשֶׂה מַעֲקֶה לַחֲצִי גַגּוֹ – **This** owner **must make a fence along half** of **his roof, and this** other owner **must make a fence along half** of **his roof;** זֶה שֶׁלֹּא כְּנֶגֶד זֶה וּמַעֲדִיף – **this** first fence must be built **not directly opposite this** other fence, **and** each owner must **extend** his fence beyond the halfway point, so that the two fences slightly overlap.

The Gemara asks:

פְּשִׁיטָא – Inasmuch as the two neighbors bear equal responsibility for preventing visual trespass, that each must build half of the fence is **obvious!** Why, then, does Abaye belabor this point?[29]

The Gemara answers:

לָא צְרִיכָא – **No,** Abaye's accentuating the obligation of each **is necessary** for a case דְּקָדִים חַד מִנַּיְיהוּ וְעָבֵד – **where one of [the owners] went ahead and made his** half of the fence before going to *beis din.*[30] מַהוּ דְּתֵימָא נֵימָא לֵיהּ אִידָךְ – **You might have said** that **the other** owner **could say to him,** שְׁקוֹל אוּזִינְקָא וְעַבְדֵיהּ אַתְּ כּוּלֵּיהּ – **"Take the expense** of building the rest of the fence from me, **and you build the entire** fence on your side."[31] קָא מַשְׁמַע לָן – Abaye therefore **informs us** that we do not compel the first owner to build the rest of the fence on his roof, דְּאָמַר לֵיהּ – **for he can say to [the other owner],** אַתְּ מַאי טַעְמָא לָא עָבְדַתְּ –

NOTES

fences around all roofs that are in use (*Deuteronomy* 22:8), their minimum height is set at only ten *tefachim* (*Rambam, Hil. Rotzeach* 11:3, from *Sifri*). The increment required by Abaye is for the purpose of protecting against visual trespass.

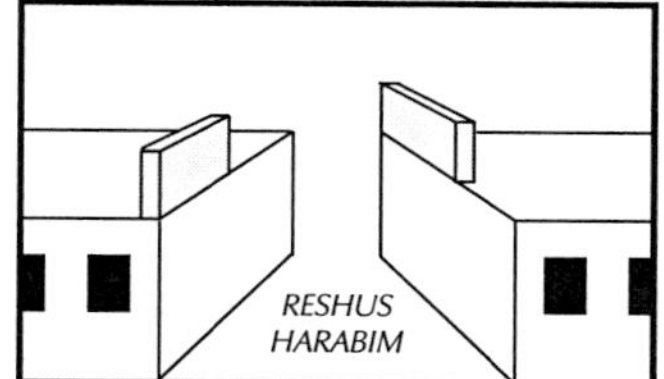

20. For example, if the sides of their roofs bordering the public domain extended from north to south, one neighbor would fence the northern half of his side, while the other neighbor would begin construction from the southern end of his side (Rashi). See diagram.

21. The slight overlap prevents one neighbor from gazing *directly* into the other's rooftop area (*Rashi*); and even though one could stand at the edge of his roof and look diagonally across onto part of his neighbor's roof, still the Rabbis had no suitable alternative to this measure. For to require both owners to erect a complete fence is wasteful, while to require one to do so is impractical, since each would insist that the other accept the responsibility and thus suffer any damage that the weight of the fence caused to his wall (*Ran;* see also *Rabbeinu Yonah*). However, precisely because a slight overlap is only partially effective, other Rishonim (*HaRav Av Beis Din,* cited in *Shitah Mekubetzes; Ramban* below, 59a; second opinion in *Meiri*) understand the Gemara to require an overlap sufficient to obstruct completely the view from one roof to the other. Obviously, the distance between and the lengths of the roofs will determine the measure of overlap in each particular case.

22. The intervening "private domain" is not a third-party courtyard, for if so each homeowner would have to fence completely his bordering side, so as not to violate the privacy of the courtyard. Rather, the Gemara refers to an unused parcel of land, where visual trespass is not a factor.

23. I.e. since a private domain is usually narrower than a public domain, and so causes less of a separation between the roofs, one might think that in the case of an intervening private domain the homeowners would notice each other's ascension to the roof and could protect themselves from visual trespass — thus obviating the need for fences. Hence, Abaye should have promulgated the "fence" requirement in the case of an intervening private domain in order to clarify this point (*Rabbeinu Yonah, Ritva*).

24. Who does not wish to build a fence.

25. Hence, to avoid the scrutiny of the public I can use my roof at night.

26. Due to the angle of vision from street level to roof, it is impossible to see a person on a roof unless he is standing.

27. Since the roof is overhead, a passerby must intentionally raise his head to observe me.

28. For generally people do not consciously and obviously gaze into another's property (see *Rashbam* below, 59a ד״ה ר׳ אילעא).

29. *Rashi.* According to *Rabbeinu Yonah*, however, the Gemara questions why Abaye bothered to state that the two fences should not be directly opposite one another.

30. Afterward he brought suit against his neighbor, demanding that the latter fulfill his obligation (*Rashi*).

31. I.e. since you have begun remedying the situation, complete the fence on your roof (*Rashi*). *Rashi's* explanation — indeed, the Gemara — is difficult to understand, for why should the first builder (Reuven) disadvantage himself by having summarily discharged his obligation (see *Tosafos* ד״ה מהו and *Rashba*)? The gloss to *Rashi* therefore explains that the other owner (Shimon) can claim that Reuven's precipitate action precluded Shimon from offering to construct the fence entirely on *his* roof (with Reuven paying half the costs plus compensation for any resulting weakening of the wall). That would

עין משפט נר מצוה

לה א ב ג מיי' פ"ו מהל' שכירות הל' א סמג עשין קט טוש"ע ח"מ סי' שיג סעיף א:

לו ד ה ו מיי' פ"ח מהל' שכנים הל' ז סמג עשין פב טוש"ע ח"מ סי' קנג סעיף יז:

לז ז ח מיי' פ"ג הלכה ה סמג שם טוש"ע ח"מ סי' קסד סעיף א:

לח ט מיי' שם הל' ו ועי' בהשגות סמג שם טוש"ע ח"מ סי' קנח סעיף א:

לט י כ מיי' וסמג שם טוש"ע ח"מ סי' קסב סעיף ג:

מ ל מיי' שם הלכה ז ועי' בהשגות ובמ"מ ובכ"מ סמג שם טוש"ע ח"מ סי' קס סעיף ג:

מא מ מיי' שם טוש"ע שם סעיף א וסעיף ב:

הגהות הב"ח

(א) גמ' משתמש בכתליה ובזיזיה עד ארבע אמות: (ב) שם לא חזו לי. נ"ב ע"ל דף ס': (ג) שם ועבד דידיה מהו דתימא: (ד) שם איתבר תתאי: (ה) רש"י ד"ה בירה וכו' חדרים קטנים והשכיר: (ו) ד"ה אבל רחבה וכו' חצר הס"ד ואח"כ מה"ד לא אין הרחבה: (ז) ד"ה תוס' פשיטא נ"ל לקדים דלאו לא קדים: (ח) ד"ה אבל וכו' בהי עדנא סלקת כצ"ל ואות ד' נמחק: (ט) ד"ה איתבר תתאי: (י) תוס' ד"ה מהו כו' ועשה זה הוה מצי כצ"ל ותיבת זה נמחק: (כ) ד"ה דמי וכו' כי קאי עליון בשפת חצירו כדאמרי' לעיל:

ליקוטי רש"י

מעקה גבוה ארבע אמות. די שלא יראה בחצר חבירו כשהוא בגגו [לעיל ב:]. במסיפס. מחילה נמוכה של מחיצות עלים [עירובין עט. ובכ"י ע"ז ע.]. של יחדות עלים תקועים בארץ נמוכים [לעיל ב:].

מסורת הש"ס

א) לעיל ב:, ב) [ערכין לג.], ג) כדפוס ישן איתא ולא זה רוצה לעשות בגגו, ד) [שייך לדף ז.], ה) ס"א ל"ג:

גמרא

א בבירה גדולה משתמש (א) בזיזיה ובכתליה עד ד' אמות ובעובי הכותל במקום שנהגו אבל בתרבץ אפדני לא ורב נחמן דידיה אמר ב אפילו בתרבץ אפדני אבל רחבה שאחורי הבתים לא ורבא אמר ג אפילו רחבה שאחורי הבתים אמר רבינא ד האי כשורא דמטללתא עד תלתין יומין לא הוי חזקה בתר תלתין יומין הוי חזקה ה ואי סוכה דמצוה היא עד שבעה יומין לא הוי חזקה בתר שבעה יומין הוי חזקה ו ואי חבריה בטינא לאלתר הוי חזקה אמר אביי ז שני בתים בשני צדי רשות הרבים זה עושה מעקה לחצי גגו וזה עושה מעקה לחצי גגו זה שלא כנגד זה ומעדיף מאי איריא ברשות הרבים ח אפילו רשות היחיד נמי רשות הרבים איצטריכא ליה מהו דתימא נימא ליה סוף סוף הא בעית לאצטנועי מבני רשות הרבים קמ"ל דא"ל רבים ביממא חזו לי בליליא (ב) לא חזו לי את בין ביממא בין בליליא חזית לי א"נ רבים כי קאימנא חזו לי כי יתיבנא לא חזו לי את חזית לי בין כי קאימנא בין כי יתיבנא רבים כי מעיינו חזו לי כי לא מעיינו לא חזו לי את ממילא נמי חזית לי אמר מר זה עושה מעקה לחצי גגו וזה עושה מעקה לחצי גגו זה שלא כנגד זה ומעדיף פשיטא לא צריכא דקדים חד מנייהו ועבד (ג) מהו דתימא נימא ליה אידך שקול אוזינקא ועבדיה את כוליה קמ"ל דא"ל את מ"ט לא עבדת משום דמיתרע אשיתך אנא נמי מיתרע ליה אשיתאי אמר ר"נ אמר שמואל ט גג הסמוך לחצר חבירו עושה לו מעקה גבוה ד' אמות אבל בין גג לגג לא ור"נ דידיה אמר י אינו זקוק לד"א אבל זקוק למחיצת עשרה למאי אי להיזק ראיה ארבע אמות בעינן אי לנתפס עליו כגנב במסיפס בעלמא סגיא אי לגדיים וטלאים בכדי שלא יזדקר בבת ראש סגי כ לעולם לנתפס עליו כגנב במסיפס מצי [אמר ממצורי קממצירנא] במחיצת עשרה לא מצי משתמיט ליה מיתיבי אם היה חצרו למעלה מגגו של חבירו אין נזקקין לו מאי לאו אין נזקקין לו כלל לא אין נזקקין לד' אמות אבל נזקקין למחיצת עשרה איתמר שתי חצרות זו למעלה מזו אמר רב הונא תחתון בונה מכנגדו ועולה ועליון בונה מכנגדו ועולה ורב חסדא אמר עליון מסייע מלמטה ובונה תניא כוותיה דרב חסדא ל שתי חצרות זו למעלה מזו לא יאמר העליון הריני בונה מכנגדי ועולה אלא מסייע מלמטה ובונה מ ואם היתה חצרו למעלה מגגו של חבירו אינו זקוק לו הנהו בי תרי דהוו דיירי חד הוה דייר עילאי וחד הוה דייר תתאי (ד) איתבר תתאי א"ל תתאי לעילאי תא ונבנייה א"ל אנא שפיר קא דאירנא אמר

תוספות

האי כשורא דמטללתא. אומר ר"ת דלמתני' קאי דעד שלשים יום לא הוי חזקה והוי בחזקת שלא נתן מכאן ואילך הוי בחזקת שנתן ואתי שפיר דנקטיה הכא ולא בחזקת הבתים: עד שבעה יומי. לאו דוקא שבעה דבשמיני עצרת לא יוכל לסתור: ואי חבריה בטינא לאלתר הוי חזקה. ואומר רבינו שמואל דחזקות דלעיל לאו דשלש שנים אלא לאלתר כדאמרינן הכא: בשני צדי רשות הרבים. אומר ר"י דוקא בשני צדי רשות הרבים שאין האחד מרגיש בחבירו כשעולה בגגו שיזהר ממנו מדאמרינן בסמוך אבל בין גג לגג לא: מהו דתימא מצי א"ל שקול אוזינקא כו'. וא"ת והיכי הוי ס"ד דמצי למימר ליה הכי דלאטו משום דקדם זה ועשה הורע כחו ויכול לדוחקו זה לעשות כל הכותל ויש לומר דס"ד כיון דלאם לא קדם זה ועשה (י) זה הוה מצי למימר שקול אוזינקא וזיל ועשה כל הכותל או הב לי אוזינקא ואעשה אני הכל ונרויח בין שנינו שלא נצטרך להעדיף השתא נמי מצי למימר ליה הכי קמ"ל דלא מצי אמר ליה כיון שכבר עשה זה ולא אמר לו קודם: שתי חצרות זו למעלה מזו. וא"ת ותחתון למה יסייע לעליון דמכי מטי לארבע אמות ולא יוכל התחתון לראות בחצר העליון יבנה העליון ואומר ר"ת כגון שחצר התחתון אינו נמוך אלא אלא מכותל של עליון (ה) (אלא מלא א') ומלא א' הוא גבוה מחצר העליון שיוכל לראות שם ור"י מפרש דהתחתון מזיק לעליון כי קאי עליון (כ) כדאמרי' לעיל כי קאימנא חזו לי ולכך צריך לסייע עד ד' אמות בחצר העליון:

רש"י

בירה גדולה. בית ארוך מאד וחלוק מתוכו להרבה חדרים (ה) קטנות והשכיר לזה אחד מהן הרי זה משתמש בכתליה בחורי הכתלים על פני ארכה מבחוץ עד ד' אמות אף שלא כנגד ביתו ובזיזים היוצאים מכתלים: ובעובי הכותל. בראשו כגון אם השכיר לו בה עלייה: אבל בתרבץ אפדני לא. דרך בוני בירה חשובה להניח לה כנגד פתח הטרקלין החשוב שבה כעין גינה קטנה לאויר ועולין בה דשאים ויפה המראה לעיניים ושם אין רשות לזה לתלות בכתלים כלום שאינו עשוי ליכנס לתוכו: אבל רחבה שאחורי הבתים. כל היקף שאחורי הבתים קרוי רחבה ושלפני הבתים קרוי חצר (ו) אין הרחבה מושכרת לו להשתמש: לא הויא חזקה. אם סמכה על כותל חבירו ולא מיחה בתוך שלשים [יום] לא הויא חזקה לטעון ולומר פייסתיך במעות עד עולם דכל תלתין יומין לא קפיד איניש ולא ממי סבור חברי זה לצריך לגג ולימים מועטים יטלנו משם: ואי סוכה דמצוה היא לבתר ז' הויא חזקה. דכיון דשבקוה עלה יותר מן הצורך הוה ליה למחויי: תוס'. ומדלא מיחה איכא למימר דזה פייסו במעות עד עולם שכן היה דרכם לקבוע סוכתן לצורך כל השנים והלכך מיד לאחר ז' הויא חזקה דלא דמי לסוכה דמטללתא דלא הוי חזקה עד תלתין יומין דהסיא לצל בעלמא הוא דעבדה אבל סוכה זו לצורך כל ימות החג שבכל שנה עשאה. ע"כ: זה שלא כנגד זה. זה סותם גגו לצד צפון וזה לצד דרום: ומעדיף. מושך המעקה יותר מחצי הגג כדי שיהיה במקצת כנגד סתימתו של זה ומתוך כך לא יראה בהדיא לגגו של חבירו: פשיטא. דהאי פלגא והאי פלגא: לא צריכא דקדים חד ועביד דידיה. מעקה לחצי גגו קודם שבא לב"ד ואח"כ תבע את חבירו לעשות בשלו מהו דתימא הואיל והתחיל לעשות יגמור המעקה בגגו וזה יתן לו חצי הוצאה: אוזינקא. יציאה: תוס'. (ז) דלאו לא קדים אלא בא לב"ד על עסק המעקה ולא זה רוצה לעשות בגגו ג) פשיטא דב"ד עושה פשרה ביניהם לעשות כל אחד חצי מעקה או האחד יעשה כולו וחבירו יחזיר לו שכר הורעת אשיותא אבל השתא דקדים יכול לטעון אידך אילו לא קדמת אותי הייתי עושה כולו בגגי אבל לתלאין לא עבידנא דטריחא לי לחזור אחר פועלין בשביל דבר מועט. ע"כ: לא תתרע אשיתאי. מכובד הבנין שמכבידין על חומה טיט ממהרת לקלקל למעלה: גבוה ארבע אמות. משום היזק ראיה: אבל בין גג לגג. לא צריך כדאמרינן בשמעתין קמייתא חצר קביעא תשמישיה וגג לא קביעא תשמישיה ולא ידענא בהי עדנא (ח) דסלקת דאיצטנע ממך: אין זקוק לו. בין גג לגג לארבע אמות גובה: אם נתפס כגנב. שאם יכנס לפנים מן המחיצה לשם גניבה נכנס: מצי משתמיט ליה. ולומר חפץ נפל מידי על גגך ונכנסתי אלך ליטול: היתה חצירו למעלה מגגו של חבירו. שהיה קרקע החצר גבוה מקרקע הבית: אין זקוק לו. בעל החצר לעשות לו מחיצה בין חצר לגג דכיון דגג לא קביע תשמישיה נוח ליזהר משכיניו שלא יראוהו: זו למעלה מזו. קרקעית האחד גבוה מחבירתה: זה בונה מכנגדו ועולה. התחתון בונה משלו מלמטה עד שמגיע לגובה קרקעיתו של חבירו ואחר כך מתחיל זה לסייעו ונותן חלקו מכנגדו ומעלה ולא יהא עליון נפסד בשפלות קרקעיתו של תחתון: דהוו דיירי חד עילאי וחד תתאי. כשחלקו האחין נטל זה בית וזה עלייה: (ט) איתבר תתאי. נטבעו הכתלים התחתונים בארץ עד ששפלה תקרת העלייה ואין התחתון יכול ליכנס בתוכו אלא אם כן שוחה: תא ונבנייה. בוא ונסתור את כל הבית ונבננו: ד) איבנייה אנא. מסלי: אמר ליה. עליון לית לי דוכתא דדיירנא ביה: לא קא מתדר לי. איני יכול לדור בביתי מפני עלייתך: סוף

רבינו גרשום

מנטף אלא משני עברי הבית אבל בנוי כעין צריף הוט"א בל"ע שהוא עגול ומנטף בכל סביבותיו לא [אחזיק] ויכול לעכב עליו: בבירה גדולה. כעין מגדל גדול ובונין בתוכה בתים הרבה סביבותיה ויש סביבותיה חצר וגנות ופרדסין הרי זה השוכר משתמש חוץ לביתו בכתליה דבירה הסמוכות א) לכותל אם יש בה חורין או זיזין שתולין בה חפציהן עד ד' אמות סמוך לבית דשייך בתר בית: ובעובי הכותל במקום שנהגו. לישתמש על גב ב) הבית משתמש חוץ לגג בעובי החומה ד' אמות: אבל בתרבץ אפדני. גינת ביתן שסמוך לפלטין אינו משתמש לבתים אלא לפלטין: אבל רחבה גדולה שאחורי הבתים. היא ודאי עשויה לצורך הפלטין עצמה: האי כשורא דמטללתא. אם נעץ אחד קורתו בכותל חבירו מדעתו של בעל הכותל לסכך עליה מפני החמה אם נעוצה בו הקורה יותר מל' יום ולא מיחה בעל הכותל הוי חזקה לזה שנעצה לקובעה שם לעולם שסתם שאלה משאיל כותלו לחבירו לנעוץ בו [מידי] ל' יום ותו לא: ואי סוכה דמצוה היא. כלומר אם הרשהו לנעוץ קורה לצורך סוכת החג דמצוה ודאי אם הניחה שם יותר על ז' ימים בפני בעל הכותל שלא מיחה יכול להחזיק בה לעולם: ואי חבריה לקורה בטינא. כלומר שקבעה לקורה בכותל בחומר ובלבנים בקביעות בפני בעל הכותל ולא מיחה הוה חזקה לאלתר דאיכא למימר דמחל לו: ב' בתים משני צדי רה"ר. אם מקום הוא שמשתמשין על הגגות זה עושה לחצי גגו מעקה גבוה ד' אמות משום היזק ראיה וכן השני זה שלא כנגד זה ומעדיף מעט זה כנגד זה כדי שלא יוכל א' להציץ בתוך גג חבירו ג) אלא ברה"ר מצי למימר חבריה למעכב מאי [נפקא] לך מינה אי לא עבידנא מעקה כוותך סוף סוף אי לא הוא אנא הוה אפ"ה קבעת לאצטנועי מבני רה"ר קמ"ל דמצי אמר ליה אידך ד) אי לא מבני רה"ר יכילנא לאצטנועי דכי יתיבנא לא חזו לי קמ"ל ה) דאפ"ה יכול לכופו שיעשה חצי מעקה לגגו: דקדים חד מינייהו ועביד. מעקה לחצי גגו: אוזינקא. חצי הוצאתך שתוציא בכולו: משום דאיתרע אשיתך. שלא יכביד על הכותל ויפול הכותל אנא נמי מסתפינא הכי: גג הסמוך לחצר חבירו. דמקום החצר גבוה ושוה לגגו עושה מעקה ד' אמות לגג שלא יציץ לחצר חבירו. ואי קשיא למה אין מחייבין בעל חצר לעשות מחיצה לחצירו שלא יסתכל לגג חבירו. הא לא תיקשי דהיזקא דחצר עדיף מהיזקא דגג דחצר קביעא תשמישתא וגג לא קביעא תשמישתיה: אבל בין גג לגג דלא קביעא תשמישתייהו לא להאי ולא להאי לא: אי לנתפס עליו כגנב. כלומר אי לכך צריך מחיצה דלא יכנס חבירו לשם בלא רשות ויתפס כגנב דיכול לומר לו לגנוב באת: במסיפס בעלמא סגי. אפי' במחיצה כל שהוא אם יעבור עליו בלא רשות יתפס כגנב: במסיפס יכול לאישתמוטי דטעין דכיון דלא הוי האי מחיצה גבוה י' טפחים לא הוה ידענא אי משום מחיצה הוי משום הכי עברנא ולא משום גניבה: למעלה מגגו של חבירו. שקרקעית החצר גבוה יותר על הגג: מאי לאו אין נזקקין לו כלל לעשות מחיצה וקשיא לעיל דתרצת ו) זקוק למחיצה: שתי חצירות זו למעלה מזו. שהאחת גבוה יותר מן האחרת תחתון יחקוק מחיצה בקרקע עליון ובונה עד שיהיה הכותל שוה לחצר העליון ושוב יגביהו העליון עד ד' אמות: ורב חסדא אמר עליון מסייע מלמטה עם התחתון. לפי שהעליון יכול לראות התחתון ולא תחתון העליון לפיכך צריך העליון לעשות רוב הבנין כפי שלא יזיק לתחתון מראייתו: ואם היתה חצירו למעלה גבוה מגג של חבירו אין זקוק לו. משום דגג לא קביעא תשמישתיה: איתבר ביתא דתתאי. שנפלו קצת מכותלי התחתון וירד בית העליון ונח על אותו קצת כותל התחתון שנשתיירו: אמר ליה תתאי לעילאי תא נבניה. כלומר סייע לי לבנות הבית כבראשונה: שפיר דאירנא. כלומר איני צריך שאני יפה דר שלא נפלה עלייתי:

חשק שלמה על רבינו גרשום א) [אולי צ"ל בכותליה דבירה הסמוכות לכותל ביתו אם יש בה חורין וכו']: ב) [נראה דצ"ל על גג הבית וכו']: ג) [נראה דצ"ל רה"ר איצטריכא ליה דמהו דתימא דמצי למימר ליה חבריה וכו']: ד) [נראה דצ"ל דמצי למימר ליה אידך אי לא את מבני רה"ר וכו']: ה) [אולי צ"ל דכי יתיבנא לא חזו לי ומש"ה יכול לכופו שיעשה חצי מעקה לגגו]: ו) [אולי צ"ל דתרצת דזקוק למחיצה י']:

"What is the reason that **you did not,** in fact, **make** the entire fence on your roof?[32] מִשּׁוּם דְּמִיתְּרַע אֲשִׁיתָךְ – Is it not **because your** house's **wall will be damaged** by the weight of a fence?[33] אֲנָא נַמִּי מִיתְּרַע לֵיהּ אֲשִׁיתָאִי – **I also** decline to build the entire fence on my roof, since **my** house's **wall will be damaged!"** Abaye teaches us that this claim is valid.[34]

The Gemara discusses other cases of visual trespass involving rooftops:

אָמַר רַב נַחְמָן אָמַר שְׁמוּאֵל – **Rav Nachman said in the name of Shmuel:** גַּג הַסָּמוּךְ לַחֲצַר חֲבֵירוֹ – One owning **a roof that adjoins** (and overlooks) **his neighbor's courtyard** עוֹשֶׂה לוֹ מַעֲקֶה גָּבוֹהַּ אַרְבַּע אַמּוֹת – **must make for [the roof] a fence four** ***amos*** **high** to obstruct his view of the courtyard. אֲבָל בֵּין גַּג לְגַג לֹא – **But between** two adjacent **rooftops** there is **no** need for a fence.[35] וְרַב נַחְמָן דִּידֵיהּ אָמַר – **And Rav Nachman himself** amplified this ruling and **said:** אֵינוֹ זָקוּק לְאַרְבַּע אַמּוֹת – The border of adjacent rooftops **does not require** a fence **four** ***amos*** high, since visual trespass can be avoided. אֲבָל זָקוּק לִמְחִיצַת עֲשָׂרָה – **But it does require a partition of ten** *tefachim* in height.

The Gemara explores the reason for building a partition of that height:

לְמַאי – **For what** purpose is a partition ten *tefachim* tall required? אִי לְהֶיזֵּק רְאִיָּה – **If for** the purpose of preventing **visual trespass,** אַרְבַּע אַמּוֹת בְּעֵינַן – a height of **four** ***amos*** **is required,** as in the first case taught by Shmuel. אִי לְנִתְפַּס עָלָיו כְּגַנָּב – **If for** the neighbor **to be apprehended as a thief on account of [the trespass],**[36] בְּמְסִיפַּס בְּעָלְמָא סַגְיָא – **an ordinary boundary marker**[37] of less than ten *tefachim* **would suffice!** אִי לִגְדָיִים וּטְלָאִים – **If for** preventing **kids and lambs** from wandering onto the neighbor's roof, בִּכְדֵי שֶׁלֹּא יִזְדַּקֵּר בְּבַת רֹאשׁ סַגִּי – a height **so that** animals **cannot run headlong over** the partition **would suffice.**[38]

The Gemara clarifies the function of the partition:

לְעוֹלָם לְנִתְפַּס עָלָיו כְּגַנָּב – **Actually,** the purpose of the ten-*tefachim*-high partition is for a trespassing neighbor **to be apprehended as a thief on account of it,** and yet an ordinary boundary marker will not perform this function. בִּמְסִיפַּס מָצֵי מִשְׁתַּמֵּיט לֵיהּ – For **in** the case of **a boundary marker** the trespassing neighbor **can put off [the owner]** by claiming that he stepped over the marker to retrieve a fallen object.[39] [אמר ממצורי קממצירנא] בִּמְחִיצַת עֲשָׂרָה לֹא מָצֵי מִשְׁתַּמֵּיט לֵיהּ – However, **in** the case of **a partition of ten** ***tefachim*** **he cannot put off [the owner],** for a partition of such height signifies that the owner forbids unauthorized entry, so that a traversing of the partition would indicate felonious intent.

The Gemara challenges Rav Nachman's ruling:

מֵיתִיבֵי – **They responded** to Rav Nachman from the evidence of a Baraisa, which states: אִם הָיָה חֲצֵרוֹ לְמַעְלָה מִגַּגּוֹ שֶׁל חֲבֵירוֹ – IF ONE'S COURTYARD WAS HIGHER THAN THE ROOF OF HIS NEIGHBOR,[40] אֵין נִזְקָקִין לוֹ – the courtyard owner IS NOT BOUND[41] TO [THE ROOF'S OWNER].[42] מַאי לָאו אֵין נִזְקָקִין לוֹ כְּלָל – **Does this not** mean that **he is not bound to him at all,** even to help him build a partition ten *tefachim* high to discourage physical trespass?[43] The Baraisa thus refutes Rav Nachman's ruling. **– ? –**

The Gemara answers:

לֹא – **No,** this is not the meaning of the Baraisa. Rather, the Baraisa teaches that אֵין נִזְקָקִין לְאַרְבַּע אַמּוֹת – the courtyard owner **is not bound** to build a fence of **four** ***amos,*** for visual trespass can be avoided.[44] אֲבָל נִזְקָקִין לִמְחִיצַת עֲשָׂרָה – **But he is bound to** contribute toward **a partition of ten** ***tefachim,***[45] in accordance with Rav Nachman's ruling.

NOTES

have been preferable to his building a second half-fence, for such an undertaking would involve expending much effort to locate workers willing to take on such a small project. For other explanations of the Gemara, see *Tosafos* (ibid.), *Rashba* and *Rabbeinu Yonah.*

32. I.e. your claim is spurious, for had you really been willing to erect a complete fence on your roof you would have stopped me immediately and made your offer. Why, then, did you allow me to complete my partial fence? (*Maharam;* see also *Rosh*).

33. The top of a mud wall is quickly ruined by such weight (*Rashi*).

34. Had they initially taken their dispute to *beis din,* the court could have arranged a settlement, whereby one neighbor would build a complete fence on his roof and the other would pay his share of the fence and, in addition, compensation for the expected damage to his neighbor's wall (gloss to *Rashi*). However, one neighbor cannot compel his fellow to complete a partial fence, for the other can refuse to incur even compensated damage.

35. *Rashi* points out that the Gemara above (2b-3a) explained that in the case of an adjoining courtyard and rooftop a fence of four *amos* is required because of the disparity between these two areas. That is, since a courtyard is used regularly while a rooftop is used only occasionally, the owner of the courtyard can never predict when his neighbor will ascend to the roof, and thus cannot effectively conceal his private activities. Hence, the rooftop owner must erect a fence to ensure that he does not violate his neighbor's right to privacy. [However, no fence is required in the case of two adjoining rooftops, since one would notice the ascension of his neighbor and could thus limit his occasional private activities to other times. Where, however, two roofs are separated by a public or even private domain, timely detection is impossible; hence, the construction of two partial fences is required, as Abaye ruled above.]

36. For if he traversed the partition and entered onto the other's roof, he must have entered with intent to steal (*Rashi*).

37. A line of short wooden pegs (see *Rashi* above, 2b ד״ה וטעמא) would mark the boundary between the roofs and so expose any trespasser as a thief.

38. I.e. the partition need not exceed three *tefachim* in height (see *Rashi* to *Succah* 16a ד״ה שלשה).

39. *Rashi.* The following bracketed text in our Gemara reads: *He can say, "I was walking along the boundary* (and accidentally stepped over)." *Rabbeinu Gershom* may have had this version, but *Rashi* apparently did not. Cf. *Nimukei Yosef* here, and *Rashi* to *Avodah Zarah* 70b ד״ה אמצרי.

40. The surface of the rooftop was lower than the level of the courtyard (*Rashi*).

41. I.e. he is not obligated to help defray the cost of a fence, even though he can gaze onto his neighbor's rooftop. [This translation follows *Rashi,* whose text reads "אֵין זָקוּק לוֹ" in the singular form. The plural form found in our text can be translated to refer to the court; i.e. *[the court] will not obligate* itself to assist the owner of the rooftop (by compelling the courtyard owner to help pay for the fence).]

42. The reason for this law is as follows: Since a person does not use his roof with regularity, he can schedule the occasional usage for those times that his neighbor does not occupy the courtyard (*Rashi*). Hence, since the rooftop owner can avoid being victimized by visual trespass, the courtyard owner need not contribute toward the cost of a fence four *amos* tall.

The owner of the rooftop, however, must unilaterally erect a fence four *amos* high to prevent visual trespass, for although his roof is lower than the neighboring courtyard, he can nevertheless see his neighbor when he is standing at the edge of his courtyard (*Rosh* §17; see, however, *Yad Ramah* and *Ritva*).

43. The Baraisa does not specify the height differential between the courtyard and the roof. This implies that the courtyard owner is exempt from helping to defray the wall's cost even if the difference in height is less than ten *tefachim* (i.e. where Rav Nachman's ruling requiring a partition ten *tefachim* high to discourage trespass should apply).

44. See above, note 42.

45. Thus, both the rooftop owner and the courtyard owner are required to construct a ten-*tefach*-high wall. This liability, however, is diminished by the height differential between the roof and the courtyard — e.g. if

[א] בבירה גדולה משתמש (א) בזיזיה ובכתליה עד ד' אמות ובעובי הכותל במקום שנהגו אבל בתרבץ אפדני לא ורב נחמן דידיה אמר [ב] אפילו בתרבץ אפדני אבל רחבה שאחורי הבתים לא ורבא אמר [ג] אפילו רחבה שאחורי הבתים אמר רבינא [ד] האי כשורא דמטללתא עד תלתין יומין לא הוי חזקה בתר תלתין יומין הוי חזקה [ה] ואי סוכה דמצוה היא עד שבעה יומין לא הוי חזקה בתר שבעה יומין הוי חזקה [ו] ואי חבריה בטינא לאלתר הוי חזקה אמר אביי [ז] שני בתים בשני צדי רשות הרבים זה עושה מעקה לחצי גגו וזה עושה מעקה לחצי גגו זה שלא כנגד זה ומעדיף מאי איריא ברשות הרבים [ח] אפילו רשות היחיד נמי רשות הרבים איצטריכא ליה מהו דתימא נימא ליה סוף סוף הא בעית לאצטנועי מבני רשות הרבים קמ"ל דא"ל רבים ביממא חזו לי בליליא (ב) לא חזו לי את בין ביממא בין בליליא חזית לי א"נ רבים כי קאימנא חזו לי כי יתיבנא לא חזו לי את חזית לי בין כי קאימנא בין כי יתיבנא רבים כי מעיינו חזו לי כי לא מעיינו לא חזו לי את ממילא נמי חזית לי אמר מר זה עושה מעקה לחצי גגו וזה עושה מעקה לחצי גגו זה שלא כנגד זה ומעדיף פשיטא לא צריכא דקדים חד מנייהו ועבד (ג) מהו דתימא נימא ליה אידך שקול אוזינקא ועבדיה את כוליה קמ"ל דא"ל את מ"ט לא עבדת משום דמיתרע אשיתך אנא נמי מיתרע ליה אשיתאי [א] אמר ר"נ אמר שמואל [ט] גג הסמוך לחצר חבירו עושה לו מעקה גבוה ד' אמות אבל בין גג לגג לא ור"נ דידיה אמר [י] אינו זקוק לד"א אבל זקוק למחיצת עשרה למאי אי להיזק ראיה ארבע אמות בעינן אי לנתפס עליו כגנב במסיפס בעלמא סגיא אי לגדיים וטלאים בכדי שלא יזדקר בבת ראש סגי [כ] לעולם לנתפס עליו כגנב במסיפס מצי משתמיט ליה [ב] [אמר ממצורי קממצירנא] במחיצת עשרה לא מצי משתמיט ליה מיתיבי אם היה חצרו למעלה מגגו של חבירו אין נזקקין לו מאי לאו אין נזקקין לו כלל לא אין נזקקין לד' אמות אבל נזקקין למחיצת עשרה איתמר שתי חצרות זו למעלה מזו אמר רב הונא תחתון בונה מכנגדו ועולה ורב חסדא אמר עליון מסייע מלמטה ובונה תניא כוותיה דרב חסדא [ל] שתי חצרות זו למעלה מזו לא יאמר העליון הריני בונה מכנגדי ועולה אלא מסייע מלמטה ובונה [מ] ואם היתה חצרו למעלה מגגו של חבירו אינו זקוק לו הנהו בי תרי דהוו דיירי חד הוה דייר עילאי וחד הוה דייר תתאי (ד) איתבר תתאי א"ל תתאי לעילאי תא ונבנייה א"ל אנא שפיר קא דאירנא

אמר

בירה גדולה. בית ארוך מאד וחלוק מתוכו להרבה חדרים (ה) קטנות והשכיר לזה אחד מהן הרי זה משתמש בכתליה בחורי הכתלים על פני ארכה מבחוץ עד ד' אמות אף שלא כנגד ביתו ובזיזים היוצאים מכתלים: ובעובי הכותל. ברחבו כגון אם השכיר לו בה עלייה: אבל בתרבץ אפדני לא. דרך בוני בירה חשובה להניח לה כנגד פתח הטרקלין החשוב שבה כעין גינה קטנה לאויר ועולין בה דשאים ויפה המראה לעינים ושם אין רשות לזה לתלות בכתלים כלום שאינו עשוי ליכנס לתוכו: אבל רחבה שאחורי הבתים. כל היקף שאחורי הבתים קרוי רחבה ושלפני הבתים קרוי חצר (ו) אין הרחבה מושכרת לו להשתמש: לא הויא חזקה. אם סמכה על כותל חבירו ולא מיחה בתוך שלשים [יום] לא הויא חזקה לטעון ולומר פייסתיך במעות עד עולם דכל תלתין יומין לא קפיד איניש ולא מחי סבור חברי זה צריך לגל ולימים מועטים יטלנו משם: ואי סוכה דמצוה היא לבתר ז' הויא חזקה. דכיון דשבקוה עלה יותר מן הצורך הוה ליה למחויי: תום'. ומדלא מיחה איכא למימר דזה פייסו במעות עד עולם שכן היה דרכם לקבוע סוכתן לצורך כל השנים והלכך מיד לאחר ז' הויא חזקה דלא דמי לסוכה דמטללתא דלא הוי חזקה עד תלתין יומין דההיא לגל בעלמא הוא דעבדה אבל סוכה זו לצורך כל ימות החג שבכל שנה עשאה. ע"כ: זה שלא כנגד זה. זה סותם גגו לצד צפון וזה לצד דרום: ומעדיף. מושך המעקה יותר מחצי הגג כדי שיהיה במקצת כנגד סתימתו של זה ומתוך כך לא יראה בהדיא לגגו של חבירו: פשיטא. דהאי פלגא והאי פלגא: לא צריכא דקדים חד ועביד דידיה. מעקה לחצי גגו קודם שבא לב"ד ואח"כ תבע את חבירו לעשות בשלו מהו דתימא הואיל והתחיל לעשות יגמור המעקה בגגו וזה יתן לו חצי הוצאה: אוזינקא. יציאה: תום'. (ז) דאי לא קדים אלא בא לב"ד על עסק המעקה ולא זה רוצה לעשות בגגו [ג] פשיטא דב"ד עושה פשרה ביניהם לעשות כל אחד חצי מעקה או האחד יעשה כולו וחבירו יחזיר לו שכר הורעת אשיותא אבל השתא דקדים יכול לטעון אידך אילו לא קדמת אותי הייתי עושה כולו בגגי אבל לאלאין לא עבידנא דטריחא לי לחזור אחר פועלין בשביל דבר מועט. ע"כ: לא תתרע אשיתאי. מכובד הבנין שמכבידין על חומה טיט ממהרת לקלקל למעלה: גבוה ארבע אמות. משום היזק ראיה: אבל בין גג לגג. לא צריך כדאמרינן בשמעתין קמייתא חצר קביעא תשמישיה וגג לא קביעא תשמישיה ולא ידענא בהי עדנא (ח) דסלקת דאיטנע ממך: אין זקוק לו. בין גג לגג לארבע אמות גובה: אם נתפס כגנב. שאם יכנס לפנים מן המחילה לשם גניבה נכנס: מצי משתמיט ליה. ולומר חפץ נפל מידי על גגך ונכנסתי אלך ליטול: היתה חצירו למעלה מגגו של חבירו. שהיה קרקע החצר גבוה מקרקע הבית: אין זקוק לו. בעל החצר לעשות לו מחילה בין חצר לגג דכיון דגג לא קביע תשמישיה נוח ליזהר משכיניו שלא יראוהו: זו למעלה מזו. קרקעית האחד גבוה מחבירתה: זה בונה מכנגדו ועולה. התחתון בונה משלו מלמטה עד שמגיע לגובה קרקעיתו של חבירו ואחר כך מתחיל זה לסייעו ונותן חלקו מכנגדו ומעלה ולא יהא עליון נפסד בשפלות קרקעיתו של תחתון: דהוו דיירי חד עילאי וחד תתאי. כשחלקו האחין נטל זה בית וזה עלייה: (ט) איתבר תתאי. נטבעו הכתלים התחתונים בארץ עד ששפלה תקרת העלייה ואין התחתון יכול ליכנס בתוכו אלא אם כן שוחה: תא ונבנייה. בוא ונסתור את כל הבית ונבננו: [ד] איבנייה אנא. משלי: אמר ליה. עליון לית לי דוכתא דדיירנא ביה: לא קא מתדר לי. איני יכול לדור בביתי מפני עלייתך:

סוף

האי כשורא דמטללתא. אומר ר"ת דלהכי קאי דעד שלשים יום לא הוי חזקה והוי בחזקת שלא נתן מכאן ואילך הוי בחזקת שנתן ואתי שפיר דנקטיה הכא ולא בחזקת הבתים: עד שבעה יומי. לאו דוקא שבעה דבשמיני עצרת לא יוכל לסתור: ואי חבריה בטינא לאלתר הוי חזקה. ואומר רבינו שמואל דחזקות דלעיל לאו דשלש שנים אלא לאלתר כדאמרינן הכא:

בשני צדי רשות הרבים. אומר ר"י דוקא בשני צדי רשות הרבים שאין האחד מרגיש בחבירו כשעולה בגגו שיזהר ממנו מדאמרינן בסמוך אבל בין גג לגג לא:

מהו דתימא מצי א"ל שקול אוזינקא כו'. וא"ת והיכי הוי ס"ד דמצי למימר ליה הכי דאטו משום דקדם זה ועשה הורע כחו ויכול לדוחקו זה לעשות כל הכותל ויש לומר דס"ד כיון דאם לא קדם זה ועשה (י) זה הוה מצי למימר שקול אוזינקא וזיל ועשה כל הכותל או הב לי אוזינקא ואעשה אני הכל ונראה בין שניהו שלא נצטרך להעדיף השתא נמי מצי למימר ליה הכי קמ"ל דלא מצי אמר ליה כיון שכבר עשה זה ולא אמר לו קודם:

שתי חצרות זו למעלה מזו. וא"ת ותחתון למה יסייע לעליון דמכי מטי לארבע אמות ולא יוכל התחתון לראות בחצר העליון יבנה העליון ואומר ר"ת כגון שחצר התחתון אינו נמוך אלא אצל חצרו של עליון [ה] (אלא מצד א') ומצד א' הוא גבוה כחצר העליון שיוכל לראות שם ור"י מפרש דהתחתון מזיק לעליון כי קאי עליון (כ) כדאמרי' לעיל כי קאימנא חזו לי ולכך צריך לסייע עד ד' אמות בחצר העליון:

עין משפט
נר מצוה

לה א ב ג מיי' פ"ו מהל' שכירות הל' א סמג עשין סט טוש"ע ח"מ סי' שיג סעיף א:
לו ד ה ו מיי' פ"ח מהל' שכנים הל' ז סמג עשין פב טוש"ע ח"מ סי' קנג סעיף יח:
לז ז ח מיי' שם פ"ג הלכה ה סמג שם טוש"ע ח"מ סי' קנט סעיף א:
לח ט מיי' שם הל' ו ועי' בהשגות סמג שם טוש"ע שם סעיף ב וסי' קס סעיף א:
לט י כ מיי' וסמג שם טוש"ע ח"מ סי' קנט סעיף ב:
מ ל מיי' שם הלכה ז ועי' בהשגות ובמ"מ ובכ"מ סמג שם טוש"ע ח"מ סי' קס סעיף ג:
מא מ מיי' שם טוש"ע שם סעיף א וסעיף ב:

מסורת הש"ס

א) לעיל ב:, ב) [ערוך ערך מצר], ג) בדפוס ישן איתא ולא זה רוצה לעשות בגגו, ד) [שייך לדף ז.], ה) ס"א ל"ג:

הגהות הב"ח

(א) גמ' משתמש בכתליה ובזיזיה עד ארבע אמות: (ב) שם לא חזו לי. נ"ב ע"ל דף ס': (ג) שם ועבד דידיה מהו דתימא: (ד) שם איתבר תתאי: (ה) רש"י ד"ה בירה וכו' חדרים קטנים והשכיר: (ו) ד"ה אבל רחבה [וכו'] חצר הס"ד ואח"כ מה"ד לא אין הרחבה: (ז) ד"ה תום' פשיטא נ"ב דקדים דאי לא קדים: (ח) ד"ה אבל וכו' בהי עדנא סלקת כצ"ל ואות ד' נמחק: (ט) ד"ה איתבר תתאי: (י) תום' ד"ה מהו כו' ועשה הוה מצי כצ"ל ותיבת זה נמחק: (כ) ד"ה שתי וכו' כי קאי עליון בשפת חצירו כדאמרי' לעיל:

ליקוטי רש"י

מעקה גבוה ארבע אמות. די שלא יראה בחצר חבירו כשהוא משתמש בגגו [לעיל ב:]. במסיפס. מחילה נמוכה של חתיכות עצים [עירובין עב. וכעי"ז ע"ז ע:]. של יתדות עצים תקועים בארץ נמוכים [לעיל ב:].

רבינו גרשום

מנטף אלא משני עברי הבית אבל בנוי כעין צריף הוט"א בל"ע שהוא עגול ומנטף בכל סביבותיו לא [אחזיק] ויכול לעכב עליו: בבירה גדולה. כעין מגדל גדול ובונין בתוכה בתים הרבה סביבותיה ויש סביבותיה חצר וגנות ופרדסין הרי זה השוכר משתמש חוץ לביתו בכתליה דבירה הסמוכות א) לכותל אם יש בה חורין או זיזין שתולין בה חפציהן עד ד' אמות סמוך לבית דשייך בתר בית: ובעובי הכותל במקום שנהגו. לישתמש על גב ב) הבית משתמש חוץ לגג בעובי החומה ד' אמות: אבל בתרבץ אפדני. גינת ביתן שסמוך לפלטין אינו משתמש לבתים אלא לפלטין: אבל רחבה גדולה שאחורי הבתים. היא ודאי עשויה לצורך הפלטין עצמה: האי כשורא דמטללתא. אם נעץ אחד קורתו בכותל חבירו מדעתו של בעל הכותל לסכך עליה מפני החמה אם נעוצה בו הקורה יותר מל' יום ולא מיחה בעל הכותל הוי חזקה לזה שנעצה לקובעה שם לעולם שסתם שאלה משאיל כותלו לחבירו לנעוץ בו [מידי] ל' יום ותו לא: ואי סוכה דמצוה היא. כלומר אם הרשהו לנעוץ קורה לצורך סוכת החג דמצוה ודאי אם הניחה שם יותר על ד' ימים בפני בעל הכותל שלא מיחה יכול להחזיק בה לעולם: ואי חבריה לקורה בטינא. כלומר שקבעה לקורה בכותל בחומר ובלבנים בקביעות בפני בעל הכותל ולא מיחה הוה חזקה לאלתר דאיכא למימר דמחל לו: ב' בתים משני צדי רה"ר. אם מקום הוא שמשתמשין על הגגות זה עושה לחצי גגו מעקה גבוה ד' אמות משום היזק ראיה וכן השני זה שלא כנגד זה ומעדיף מעט זה כנגד זה כדי שלא יוכל א' להציץ בתוך גג חבירו ג) אלא ברה"ר מצי למימר חבריה דמעכב מאי [נפקא] לך מינה אי לא עבידנא מעקה כוותך סוף סוף אי לא הואי אנא הכא אפ"ה קבעית לאצטנועי מבני רה"ר קמ"ל דמצי אמר ליה אידך ד) אי לא מבני רה"ר יכילנא לאצטנועי דכי יתיבנא לא חזו לי קמ"ל ה) דאפ"ה יכול לכופו שיעשה חצי מעקה לגגו: דקדים חד מינייהו ועביד. מעקה לחצי גגו: אזינקא. חצי הוצאתך שתוציא בכולו: משום דאיתרע אשיתך. שלא יכביד על הכותל ויפול הכותל אנא נמי מסתפינא הכי: גג הסמוך לחצר חבירו. דמקום החצר גבוה ושוה לגגו עושה מעקה ד' אמות לגג שלא יציץ לחצר חבירו. ואי קשיא למה אין מחייבין בעל חצר לעשות מחיצה לחצירו שלא יסתכל לגג חבירו. הא לא תיקשי דהיזקא דחצר עדיף מהיזקא דגג דחצר קביעא תשמישתא וגג לא קביעא תשמישתיה: אבל בין גג לגג דלא קביעא תשמישתייהו לא להאי ולא להאי לא: אי לנתפס עליו כגנב. כלומר אי לכך צריך מחיצה דלא יכנס חבירו לשם בלא רשות ויתפס כגנב דיכול לומר לו לגנוב באת: במסיפס בעלמא סגי. אפי' במחיצה כל שהוא אם יעבור עליו בלא רשות יתפס כגנב: במסיפס יכול לאישתמוטי. דטעין דכיון דלא הוי האי מחיצה גבוה י' טפחים לא הוה ידענא אי משום מחיצה הוי משום הכי עברנא ולא משום גניבה: למעלה מגגו של חבירו. שקרקעית החצר גבוה יותר על הגג: מאי לאו אין נזקקין לו כלל לעשות מחיצה וקשיא לעיל דתרצת ו) זקוק למחיצה: שתי חצירות זו למעלה מזו. שהאחת גבוה יותר מן האחרת תחתון יחקוק מחיצה בקרקע עליון ובונה עד שיהיה הכותל שוה לחצר העליון ושוב יגביהו העליון עד ד' אמות: ורב חסדא אמר עליון מסייע מלמטה עם התחתון. לפי שהעליון יכול לראות התחתון ולא תחתון העליון לפיכך צריך העליון לעשות רוב הבנין כפי שלא יזיק לתחתון מראייתו: ואם היתה חצירו למעלה גבוה מגג של חבירו אין זקוק לו. משום דגג לא קביעא תשמישתיה: איתבר ביתא דתתאי. שנפלו קצת מכותלי התחתון וירד בית העליון ונח על אותו קצת כותל התחתון שנשתיירו: אמר ליה תתאי לעילאי תא נבניה. כלומר סייע לי לבנות הבית כבראשונה: שפיר דאירנא. כלומר איני צריך שאני יפה דר שלא נפלה עלייתי:

חשק שלמה על רבינו גרשום א) [אולי צ"ל בכותליה דבירה הסמוכות לכותל ביתו אם יש בה חורין וכו']: ב) [נראה דצ"ל על גג הבית וכו']: ג) [נראה דצ"ל רה"ר איצטריכא ליה דמהו דתימא דמצי למימר ליה חבריה וכו']: ד) [נראה דצ"ל דמצי למימר ליה אידך אי לא את מבני רה"ר וכו']: ה) [אולי צ"ל דכי יתיבנא לא חזו לי ומש"ה יכול לכופו שיעשה חצי מעקה לגגו]: ו) [אולי צ"ל דתרצת דזקוק למחיצה י']:

The Gemara discusses another case of adjoining properties on different levels:

אִיתְּמַר – It was said: שְׁתֵּי חֲצֵרוֹת זוֹ לְמַעְלָה מִזּוֹ – Concerning **two** adjoining **courtyards, this** one **higher than this** other one,[46] אָמַר רַב הוּנָא – **Rav Huna said:** תַּחְתּוֹן בּוֹנֶה מִכְּנֶגְדּוֹ וְעוֹלֶה – The owner of **the lower** courtyard **must build** a wall **upward from his level** to the level of his neighbor's courtyard at his own expense, and from there extend the wall in partnership with his neighbor.[47] וְעֶלְיוֹן בּוֹנֶה מִכְּנֶגְדּוֹ וְעוֹלֶה – **And** the owner of **the upper** courtyard **must build** only **from his level and upward;** he does not have to participate in the building of that part of the wall below his level.[48] וְרַב חִסְדָּא אָמַר – **And Rav Chisda said:** עֶלְיוֹן מְסַיֵּיעַ מִלְּמַטָּה וּבוֹנֶה – The owner of **the upper** courtyard **must assist in constructing the lower portion** as well.[49]

The Gemara cites a Baraisa that corroborates Rav Chisda's opinion:

תַּנְיָא כְּוָותֵיהּ דְּרַב חִסְדָּא – **A Baraisa was taught in accordance with Rav Chisda**'s view: שְׁתֵּי חֲצֵרוֹת זוֹ לְמַעְלָה מִזּוֹ – Concerning **TWO** adjoining **COURTYARDS, THIS** one **HIGHER THAN THIS** other one, לֹא יֹאמַר הָעֶלְיוֹן – the owner of **THE UPPER** courtyard **MAY NOT SAY,** הֲרֵינִי בּוֹנֶה מִכְּנֶגְדִּי וְעוֹלֶה – **"I SHALL BUILD** the wall **FROM MY LEVEL AND UPWARD."** אֶלָּא מְסַיֵּיעַ מִלְּמַטָּה וּבוֹנֶה – **RATHER, HE MUST ASSIST IN BUILDING THE LOWER PORTION** of the wall as well. וְאִם הָיְתָה חֲצֵרוֹ לְמַעְלָה מִגַּגּוֹ שֶׁל חֲבֵירוֹ – **BUT IF HIS COURTYARD WAS ABOVE HIS NEIGHBOR'S ROOF,** אֵינוֹ זָקוּק לוֹ – **HE IS NOT BOUND [TO THE ROOF'S OWNER].**[50] The first ruling in this Baraisa expressly confirms Rav Chisda's view.

Having discussed cases involving neighboring properties of disparate heights, the Gemara considers "upper" and "lower" neighbors of a different sort:

הָנְהוּ בֵּי תְּרֵי דַּהֲווּ דָּיְירֵי – There were once **these two** brothers **that lived** together in a house they inherited.[51] חַד הֲוָה דָּיֵיר עִילָּאֵי – **One** of the brothers **lived** in **the upper** apartment of the house, וְחַד הֲוָה דָּיֵיר תַּתָּאֵי – **and one lived** in **the lower** apartment. אִיתְּבַר תַּתָּאֵי – After a time the walls of **the lower** apartment **began sinking**[52] into the ground, causing the floor of the upper apartment to descend until the downstairs resident could not enter his house without stooping. אָמַר לֵיהּ תַּתָּאֵי לְעִילָּאֵי – Thereupon, the brother owning **the lower** apartment **said to** the one that dwelt in **the upper** apartment, תָּא וְנִבְנְיֵיהּ – **"Come, and let us** demolish the old house and **rebuild it**, so that I can dwell comfortably in my apartment."

The brother declined:

אָמַר לֵיהּ – The brother living upstairs **said to [the one living downstairs],** אֲנָא שַׁפִּיר קָא דָּאִירְנָא – **"I am living comfortably** in my apartment. Hence, I do not wish to destroy the building."

NOTES

the courtyard was six *tefachim* higher than the roof, only four *tefachim* of wall are necessary to fulfill the requirement of a ten-*tefach*-high wall. Thus, the courtyard owner must pay for two of the four *tefachim* (*Rosh* §17; cf. *Rabbeinu Yonah;* see also *Ketzos HaChoshen* 160:4 and *Nesivos HaMishpat* 160:2).

46. The ground level of one courtyard was higher than that of the other (*Rashi*). *Rabbeinu Yonah* explains that even if the height differential exceeded four *amos,* it would still be possible to observe activity in the upper courtyard from the lower (cf. *Tosafos*). Hence, the owner of the lower courtyard must join with the owner of the upper courtyard to prevent the commission of visual trespass from one area to the other.

47. *Rashi.* Rav Huna does not specify how high above the ground of the upper courtyard the owner of the lower courtyard must build. *Rosh* (§17) rules that the owner of the lower courtyard must help defray the cost of the entire wall – since until a wall four *amos* high is in place at the edge of the courtyard, he can still observe what transpires at the edge of the courtyard (see also Rambam; cf. *Rabbeinu Yonah*).

48. He must, however, contribute half the land needed for the base of the wall by allowing his neighbor to excavate a portion of the ground beneath his courtyard (*Rabbeinu Yonah, Ritva*).

49. Since the upper courtyard owner wants half of the width of the wall to rest on his neighbor's property, the lower portion perforce serves as the foundation of the (upper) portion with which he discharges his obligation to prevent visual trespass. Hence, he must help defray the cost of the lower portion as well. This is the reasoning of Rav Chisda. However, Rav Huna exempts the upper courtyard owner from contributing toward the lower portion, even though it functions as the foundation of his wall, because the lower courtyard owner is able to use the lower portion – while he cannot (*Rabbeinu Yonah*; see there for a second explanation of Rav Huna's position).

50. I.e. he is not obligated to help defray the cost of a fence four *amos* high, for although he can gaze onto his neighbor's rooftop, the neighbor can avoid being victimized by visual trespass (see note 42 above). [This is the Baraisa that the Gemara adduced above in its challenge to Rav Nachman.]

51. *Rashi.*

52. *Rashi. Bach* emends אִיתְּבַר to אִיתְּבַס.

The distressed brother then offered to pay for the construction:

אָמַר לֵיהּ אִיסְתְּרֵיהּ אֲנָא וְאֶבְנְיֵיהּ – The brother living downstairs **said to [the upstairs resident], "I shall raze**[1] **[the house] and rebuild it** with my own funds, if you do not wish to contribute."

This offer was rejected:

אָמַר לֵית לִי דוּכְתָּא לְמֵידַר בָּהּ – His brother **replied, "I do not have a place to live in** during the reconstruction; therefore, I do not allow you to demolish the house."

The distressed brother offered to solve this problem:

אָמַר לֵיהּ אֲנָא אוֹגַר לָךְ דוּכְתָּא – The downstairs resident **said to [the upstairs resident], "I shall rent a place for you** to serve as a temporary dwelling."

This offer was rejected as well:

אָמַר לֵיהּ לָא טַרְחְנָא – His brother **told him, "I do not** want to **bother** moving my belongings to another house. Since legally you cannot force me to do so, I reject your offer."

The brother living downstairs protested:

לָא קָא מִתְדַּר לִי – "But **I am not able to live** in my house!" For the house was sinking into the ground, and passage through the doorway had become difficult.[2]

The upstairs resident merely said:

שׁוּף אַכְּרֵיסָךְ וְעוּל וְשׁוּף אַכְּרֵיסָךְ וּפוּק – **"Bend over to your stomach and enter, and bend over to your stomach and leave;**[3] your discomfort is not my concern."

The dispute was brought before Rav Chama, who rendered a decision:

אָמַר רַב חָמָא בְּדִינָא קָא מְעַכֵּב – **Rav Chama stated: By law** the upstairs resident **can prevent** the downstairs resident from demolishing the house. Since the downstairs dwelling is still considered habitable, its occupant has no right to inconvenience his sibling by forcing him to move temporarily, even if the distressed brother is willing to bear all the expenses.

Rav Chama then qualified his ruling in two respects. The Gemara recounts the first:

וְהָנֵי מִילֵּי דְּלָא מָטוּ כְּשׁוּרֵי לְמַטָּה מֵעֲשָׂרָה – **And this statement** of the law **applies** only **if the** sunken floor **beams** of the upper story **did not reach below ten** *tefachim* from the ground. Since it is possible to live in a house whose ceiling is ten *tefachim* high,[4] the downstairs apartment is still considered habitable, and rebuilding is not required by law. **אֲבָל מָטוּ כְּשׁוּרֵי לְמַטָּה מֵעֲשָׂרָה** – **But if the** floor **beams** of the upper story **did reach below ten** *tefachim* from the ground, thus rendering the lower dwelling uninhabitable, **מָצֵי אָמַר לֵיהּ** – the downstairs resident **can say to [his upstairs neighbor], לְמַטָּה מֵעֲשָׂרָה רְשׁוּתָא דִּידִי הוּא** – "The airspace **below ten** *tefachim* **is my property, וְלָא מִשְׁעַבַּד לָךְ** – **and is not subject to your** use. Therefore, since your floor has invaded my space and rendered my apartment useless, you must share the expense of demolishing and reconstructing the building."[5]

The Gemara recounts the second qualification of Rav Chama's ruling:

וְהָנֵי מִילֵּי דְּלָא אַתְנוּ גַּבֵּי הֲדָדֵי – **And this statement applies** only **if** the brothers **did not stipulate between themselves** when they divided the house that if the upper story ever sank, they would jointly demolish and rebuild the house. **אֲבָל אַתְנוּ גַּבֵּי הֲדָדֵי** – **But if** initially **they** so **stipulated between themselves, סָתְרֵי וּבָנוּ** – **they must raze** the house **and rebuild** it together.

The Gemara questions how much settling must occur before this condition is invoked:[6]

וְכִי אַתְנוּ בַּהֲדֵי הֲדָדֵי – **And if they stipulated** thus **between themselves, עַד כַּמָּה** – **how much** must the building settle before the downstairs resident may compel his upstairs neighbor to help demolish and rebuild the house?

The Gemara answers:

אָמְרוּ רַבָּנָן קַמֵּיהּ דְּרַבָּה מִשְּׁמֵיהּ דְּמָר זוּטְרָא בְּרֵיהּ דְּרַב נַחְמָן – **The Rabbis said before Rabbah**[7] **in the name of Mar Zutra the son of Rav Nachman דְּאָמַר מִשְּׁמֵיהּ דְּרַב נַחְמָן** – **who said in the name of Rav Nachman: כְּאוֹתָהּ שֶׁשָּׁנִינוּ** – The minimum height of a dwelling **is like that which we learned in a Mishnah:**[8] **רוּמוֹ כַּחֲצִי אָרְכּוֹ וְכַחֲצִי רָחְבּוֹ** – **[A DWELLING'S] HEIGHT MUST EQUAL TO HALF OF ITS LENGTH PLUS HALF OF ITS WIDTH.** Thus, in our case, when the height of the lower apartment falls below this measure, the stipulation that allows for total reconstruction may be invoked.

Rabbah disputes this version of Rav Nachman's statement, and offers another:

אָמַר לְהוּ רַבָּה – **Rabbah said to [the rabbis], לָאו אֲמִינָא לְכוּ לָא תִּיתְלוּ בֵּיהּ בּוּקֵי סְרִיקֵי בְּרַב נַחְמָן** – **"Have I not** previously **told you, 'Do not hang empty pitchers**[9] **on Rav Nachman'?"**[10] He did

NOTES

1. *Bach* deletes אִיסְתְּרֵיהּ, *I shall raze it,* from the text.

2. The height of the interior of the house was also reduced, as is evident from the Gemara below. However, the problem of entry was more severe, since the doorway did not extend to the ceiling. That the complaint specifically concerned passage through the doorway is indicated by the brother's reply.

3. *Rashi* translates שׁוּף as "bend," i.e. bend your body to stomach level. *Tosafos,* however, understand שׁוּף to mean "rub," as in שִׁפְשׁוּף. Hence, the brother told him to crawl into his house, which necessarily involves *rubbing* the stomach against the ground.

4. Approximately 35.5 inches.

5. Actually, the entire original height of the lower apartment is still his property, and therefore, even if the building sank only a little, the upper neighbor would still be intruding into the lower one's airspace. However, this would not give the lower one the right to evict him. For they are partners in this building, and among the rights of partership is the right of the upper neighbor to use the lower apartment whenever necessary. Therefore, as long as the lower neighbor still has a functional place to live, the upper one has the right to use the airspace of the lower one for his apartment. Once, however, the lower apartment is no longer considered a dwelling, this no longer applies, for the rights of the upper one do not include ruining the lower dwelling. It is at this point that the lower one can say: "You have no right to enter my airspace, and you must share the expense of demolishing and reconstructing the building" (See *Rabbeinu Yonah, Nimukei Yosef, Shiurei R' Shmuel, Chidushei R' Nachum*). [See *Rashba*, who explains that the lower neighbor rebuilds his apartment, and the upper neighbor rebuilds his (cf. *Ramban*).]

6. The Gemara assumes that a minuscule settling would not warrant forcing the upstairs dweller to share in the large expense of demolishing the house and rebuilding it. At the same time, the condition was obviously meant to provide relief for the downstairs dweller *before* his apartment became useless. Therefore, the Gemara seeks to ascertain the point at which the condition becomes operative.

7. Others read "Rava."

8. The Mishnah below (98b) establishes separate minimum length and width measurements, to which building contractors must adhere, for various types of structures. A single formula for determining minimum height, however, applies to all types of structures. The Mishnah there states that the height of a given structure is determined by adding half the measure of its length to half the measure of its width. This formula is derived from the dimensions of the *Heichal,* which measured 40 *amos* long, 20 *amos* wide and 30 *amos* high (*I Kings* 6:2) [*Rashi*]. Thus, if in the Gemara's case the lower apartment measured 10x12 *amos* and the ceiling was originally 15 *amos* high, the condition would become operative once the ceiling sank below eleven *amos* from the ground.

9. The translation follows *Rashi* (to *Avodah Zarah* 37b; cf. *Aruch*). [*Tosafos* here cite a *Targum* to show that סְרִיקֵי means *empty.*]

10. I.e. do not attribute unreasonable statements to him (*Rashi, Avodah Zarah* 37b ד"ה בוקי סריקי). Rabbah deemed this an unrealistic measurement, for although this might be the optimal height for building

שוף אכריסך. שחה קומתך עד כריסך: כשורי. קורות העלייה: אבל אתנו אהדדי. כשחלקו אם תשפל עלייה (ו) יסתרוהו הבית ויבנוהו: עד כמה. תשפיל העלייה ויגביה את העליון לסתור ולבנות: כאותה ששנינו. בהמוכר פירות המקבל עליו מחבירו לבנות לו בית עושה רומו כחצי ארכו וחצי רחבו כבנין ההיכל שהיה ארכו ארבעים ורחבו עשרים וגבהו שלשים: איסוריתא. חבילות קנים ארוכין: והדר. מחזיר עצמו לכל לדדין: סכרנא לך הכא. אסתום לך חלונותיך באבנים וטיט ואפתח לך למעלה מכותלי בגובה כנגדך חלונות אחרים שיאירו (ז) בביתך: קמרעת לאשיתאי. כשתפתח בה חלונות תנוע החומה מחמת המכה: סתרנא לך. הכותל מראש גובהו עד שיגיע למקום החלונות שאעשה לך: לא קיימא. שאין טיט החדש נדבק יפה בטיט הישן שיבש כבר: דאע"ג דקא משתמש בה ציבי ותיבני. ואין הוא עצמו דר בתוכו מלי א"ל לא מצינא לאטרוח להוציא העצים והתבן: אספלידא. טרקלין יפה: תרביצא. גינה שבצד הטרקלין שהיתה מאירה לתוכו: בדנפשאי אנא בנינא. בשלי אני בונה ואתה אין לך עלי חזקת אורה של שלש שנים להשתא הוא דפלגינהו: ד' אמות לעבודת הכרם. שהיו חורשין אותה בשוורים: דעלו אהדדי. שנתן בעל הכרם לבעל השדה לבן דמים של עילוי הכרם הילכך כרם בעי למשקל עם עבודתו: בשופטני עסקינן. וכי שוטה היה שנטל גינה חלקה כנגד בית בנוי ולא נטל עילוי דמים: והשתא (ח) אידרונא. חדר אפל ואני על מנת אספלידא נתתי עילוי דמים: שמא בעלמא. (ט) אם אספלידא שמא ואע"פ שאינו כשאר אספלידא לא בטיל שמו: בית כור. לפי חשבון (י) סאתים כחצר המשכן:

נהרדעי

א"ל (א) איסתריה אנא ואבנייה אמר ליה לית לי דוכתא למידר בה א"ל אנא אוגר לך דוכתא א"ל לא [א] טרחנא (ב) לא קא מתהדר לי שוף אכריסך ועול ושוף אכריסך ופוק אמר רב חמא [א] בדינא קא מעכב והני מילי דלא מטו כשורי למטה מעשרה [ב] אבל מטו כשורי למטה מעשרה מצי א"ל למטה מי' רשותא דידי הוא ולא משעבד לך וה"מ דלא אתנו גבי הדדי [ג] אבל אתנו גבי הדדי סתרי ובנו וכי אתנו בהדי הדדי עד כמה אמרו רבנן קמיה [ד] דרבה משמיה דמר זוטרא בריה דרב נחמן דאמר משמיה דר"נ כאותה ששנינו [ג] רומו כחצי ארכו וכחצי רחבו אמר להו [ד] רבה [ה] לאו אמינא לכו לא תיתלו ביה בוקי סריקי ברב נחמן הכי אמר ר"נ (ג) כי דדיירי אינשי וכמה אמר רב הונא בריה דרב יהושע [ו] כי היכי דעיילי איסוריתא דמחוזא והדר [ה] ההוא גברא דהוה בני אשיתא אחורי כווי דחבריה אמר ליה קא מאפלת עלי א"ל סכרנא לך הכא ועבידנא לך כווי לעיל מאשיתאי א"ל קא מרעת ליה לאשיתאי א"ל סתרנא לך לאשיתך עד דוכתא דכווי ובנינא לה ועבידנא לך כווי בבנינא לעיל מאשיתאי א"ל אשיתא מתתאה עתיקא ומלעיל חדתא לא קיימא אמר ליה סתרנא לה עד לארעא ובנינא לה ועבידנא לך כווי בגוה א"ל חדא אשיתא חדתא בכוליה ביתא עתיקא לא קיימא א"ל סתרנא לה לכוליה ביתא ובנינא לך כווי בבנינא א"ל לית לי דוכתא למידר בה א"ל אגירנא לך דוכתא א"ל לא [ט] טרחנא אמר רב חמא [י] בדין קא מעכב [ס] היינו הך והא תו למה לי הא קמ"ל דאע"ג דלא משתמש [ז] אלא תיבנא (ד) ובי ציבי בעלמא [ח] הנהו בי תרי אחי דפלגי בהדי הדדי חד מטייה אספלידא וחד מטייה תרביצא אזל ההוא דמטייה תרביצא וקא בני אשיתא אפומא דאספלידא א"ל קא מאפלת עלי א"ל בדידי קא בנינא אמר רב חמא [ט] בדין קאמר ליה א"ל רבינא לרב אשי מאי שנא מהא דתניא [י] שני אחין שחלקו אחד מהן נטל שדה כרם ואחד מהן נטל שדה לבן יש לו לבעל הכרם ד' אמות בשדה לבן שעל מנת כן חלקו א"ל התם דעלו להדדי אבל הכא מאי דלא עלו להדדי [י] וכי בשופטני עסקינן דהאי שקיל אספלידא והאי שקיל תרביצא ולא עלו להדדי א"ל [כ] נהי דעלו להדדי דמי לבני כשורי והודרי דמי אוירא לא עלו להדדי ולימא ליה מעיקרא אספלידא פלגת לי השתא משוית לי (ה) אידרונא אמר רב שימי בר אשי שמא בעלמא פלג ליה מי לא תניא [ל] האומר בית כור עפר אני מוכר לך אע"פ שאינו אלא לתך הגיעו שלא מכר לו אלא שמא והוא דמיתקרי בית כור [מ] פרדס אני מוכר לך אע"פ שאין בו רמונים הגיעו שלא מכר לו אלא שמא והוא דמיתקרי פרדס [נ] כרם אני מוכר לך אע"פ שאין בו גפנים הגיעו שלא מכר לו אלא שמא והוא דמיתקרי כרמא מי דמי התם מצי אמר ליה מוכר ללוקח שמא זביני לך הכא מצי א"ל אדעתא דהכי פלגי דדאירנא ביה כי היכי דדרו אבהתן אמרו ליה

שוף אכריסך. פ"ה שחה קומתך ולר"י נראה שוף לשון שפשוף שמתחכך בארץ: **בוקי** סריקי. אנשים רקים מתרגמינן גוברין סריקין (שופטים יא): **היינו** הך. וא"ת והא אשמעינן בהאי עובדא לחדתא אעתיקא לא קאי דלא שמעינן מההיא דלעיל ולעיל איצטריך כדאמרינן וה"מ דלא מטו כשורי למטה מי' וכו' וי"ל דמילתא דפשיטא היא דחדא אחדתא וכולה עתיקא לא קאי ומשום הא לא הוה צריך לאתויי האי עובדא: **אספלידא.** פרש"י טרקלין יפה ובערוך פירש מערה כדמתרגם (תהלים נז) מפני שאול במערה באספלידא ואור"י דאספלידא דהכא א"א להיות מערה מדקאמר [ט] נמי דעלו להדדי בכשורי והודרי ובמערה ליכא כשורי והודרי ועוד מדקאמר מעיקרא אספלידא והשתא [י] אידרונא ובמערה ליכא אורה כלל ומפרש ר"י דאספלידא דהכא הוי אכסדרה שיש בה אורה גדולה שפרוצה ברוח אחד כדאמרינן בלא יחפור (לקמן דף כה.) עולם דומה לאכסדרה וכו' וכן מוכח בהקומץ רבה (מנחות דף לג: ושם ד"ה אספלידא) דאמר אביי חזינא להו לאספלידי דבי מר דאית להו פלימי ולית להו מזוזה ופריך מיתיבי בית שער ואכסדרה ומרפסת חייבין במזוזה: **א"ל** בדידי קבנינא. פ"ה אתה אין לך עלי חזקת אורה של שלש שנים ותימה שהיה יכול להאפילו עליו שלא יהא לו בטרקלין אורה כלל ועוד דמאי קאמר באוירא לא עלו אהדדי פשיטא דעלו נמי באוירא דבית בלא אורה אינו שוה כלום ומפרש ר"ת שמאספלידא היה יכול לראות לשדותיו דרך התרביצא ודקאמר מאפלת עילווי היינו שהיה מעכבו שלא היה יכול לראות שדותיו וקרי לה נמי אידרונא שלא היה יכול להביט למרחוק וכן מפרש ההוא דלקמן אין להם חלונות זה על זה ומיהו קשיא לר"י דמאי קפריך מאי שנא מהא דתניא כו' התם ודאי יש לו ד' אמות לפי שהם צורך לעבודת הכרם אבל הכא זה לא היה צורך האספלידא מש"ה בדין קאמר ליה ונראה לר"י דודאי היה מאפיל עליו האורה שלא היה בו אורה גדולה כאשר צריך לאכסדרה אבל עדיין היה בו אור גדול והא דאמר ומכנגדן מרחיק ד' אמות שלא יאפיל היינו שלא יאפיל לגמרי עד שלא יהא ראוי להשתמש בו יפה ומש"ה קרי ליה אידרונא משום דלגבי אכסדרה אידרונא היא והשתא נמי אתי שפיר דלא עלו להדדי באוירא שהוא צורך האכסדרה: **והוא** דקרו ליה בית כור. וכגון שהלוקח יודע שיש לו קרקע שקרוי בית כור דאל"כ הרי הטעהו ואפי' אם רואה בשעת מכירה שאין שם בית כור יכול לומר סבור הייתי שהיית משלים לי בית כור ואם תאמר ונימא דדמים מודיעים ואם נתן לו דמי בית כור אפילו קרו ליה בית כור ישלים לו בית כור שלם ויש לומר דמיירי כגון דאחיל גביה ואינו נותן לו אפילו דמי לתך ואי קרו ליה בית כור אפילו אין בו אלא לתך הגיעו ואי לא קרו ליה בית כור חייב לתת לו בית כור שלם אי נמי דלא אחיל גביה וכגון דנתן לו דמי לתך והשתא אי לא קרו ליה בית כור היה יכול לומר לוקח אם תרצה לתת לי בית כור עמוד ואם לאו תחזור לי מעותי אבל אי קרו ליה בית כור הגיעו אע"פ שאין בו אלא לתך:

מר

עין משפט נר מצוה

מב א ב ג ד מיי' פ"ד מהל' שכנים הל' ו ז סמג עשין פב טוש"ע ח"מ סימן קסד סעיף ג ועיין בהג"ה:

מג ה ו מיי' שם פ"ז הלכה ח סמג עשין פב טוש"ע ח"מ סי' קנד סעיף יג:

מד ז טוש"ע שם וסימן קסד סעיף ב:

מה ח ט מיי' שם הל' י סמג שם טוש"ע ח"מ סי' קנד סעיף ט:

מו י מיי' פכ"ח מהל' מכירה הל' י סמג שם טוש"ע ח"מ סי' קעו סעיף ד:

מז כ מיי' פ"ז מהלכות שכנים הל' י סמג עשין פב טוש"ע ח"מ סי' קנד סעיף טו:

מח ל מיי' פכ"ח מהל' מכירה הל' יד סמג עשין פב טוש"ע ח"מ סי' ריח סעיף ח:

מט מ נ מיי' שם הל' יד טוש"ע שם סעיף יח:

רבינו גרשום

לא מצינא דאטרח (לבנות) [לפנות] ביתי: שוף אכריסך עול. כלומר הואיל וגרם מולך א) חפור בארץ וכפוף בטנך וצא והכנס. דינא קאמר ליה דבתוך שלו יבנה: לא אמרן דדינא קאמר ליה אלא דלא מטו כשורי. שלא ירדה העליה למטה מי' אז יכול לטעון לו דור בדוחק בתוך עשרה: [דלא] אתנו בהדי הדדי. שלא התנו זה לזה לבנות אחר נפילה: עד כמה. גבוה יכול לכופו שיסייע לו: כאותה ששנינו. בפ' המוכר: רומו כחצי ארכו וכחצי רחבו. שאם היה הבית כ' אמה באורך והרוחב י' אמה עושה גבוה חצי כ' וחצי י' שהם ט"ו אמה וראויה לדבר מהיכל: לא תיתלו בוקי סריקי. כלומר לא תאמינו בדברים רקים הללו מעולם לא אמר ר' נחמן שיבנהו גבוה כזה: שיעור איסוריתא דמחוזא כדי שיהא יכול לישא משאוי על גבו כמשאוי של אנשי מחוזא ויכול לחזור בריוח בהכי מצי לכופו טפי לא: אשיתא ג) אגב כוי דחבריה. שהיה בונה כותלו כנגד חלון חבירו שהיה לו חזקה לחלון ולא הרחיק ד' אמות: מרעת אשיתאי. שתחתור בו חלונות אחרות: סתרנא לך. עד חלונות אלו ובינא לך מחדש: דינא אמר ליה. דלא מצי למיטרח לפנות ביתו: היינו הך. דקאמר רב חמא בהנהו בי תרי וכו': והא תו למה לי: הא איצטריך למיתני. שאפי' אלו חלונות שיש לו בהן חזקה: בי תבני וציבי. שאין צריך בהן לאורה כל כך אפ"ה לא מצי לכופו לפנות: אספלידא. חדר שלועזין קמערא: תרביצא. גינה שסמוך לה: אפומא דאספלידא. לפני הפתח: אחד של שדה לבן. שדה תבואה: יש לו לבעל הכרם ד' אמות בשדה לבן. כמלא

מסורת הש"ס

א) נ"א מצינן דאיטרח, ב) פ"א דרבא, ג) פ"א רבא, ד) [לקמן קנא: עי' לז: חולין נג.], ה) נ"א מצינן דאיטרח, ו) [ע' מ"ש בב"ק פה. על הגליון], ח) ב"מ קד., ט) נ"ל נמי ועי' רש"ש, י) [אידרונא וכן בסמוך].

הגהות הב"ח

(א) גמ' א"ל איבנייה אנא א"ל לית לי דוכתא כל"ל ותיבת איסתריה נמחק: (ב) שם לא טרחנא א"ל לא קא מתהדר לי א"ל שוף אכריסך ועול: (ג) שם אמר ר"נ כי דדיירי כל"ל ותיבת כי נמחק: (ד) שם אלא תיבנא וציבי בעלמא כל"ל ותיבת ובי נמחק: (ה) שם משוית לי אידרונא: (ו) רש"י ד"ה אבל וכו' יסתרו הבית: (ז) ד"ה סכרנא וכו' שיאירו לך בביתך: (ח) ד"ה אידרונא: (ט) ד"ה שמא בעלמא אספלידא שמא כל"ל ותיבת אם נמחק: (י) ד"ה בית כור לפי חשבון. נ"ב עיין לקמן בפ' רשב"ם ריש פ' בית כור:

גליון הש"ס

גמ' היינו הך. עי' ריטב"א שבועות דף לו ע"א ד"ה תרתי למ"ל:

ליקוטי רש"י

רומו כחצי ארכו כו'. אכולהו קאי והיינו בית מתנות שהוא ארכו ד' על ו' רומו כ' דהיינו חצי ארכו וחצי רחבו בבית קטן שבע ושתא בבית גדול ועשר ותריסר בטרקלין [רשב"ם לקמן צח:]. בוקי סריקי. כדים ריקים כלומר דברים שאין טעם [ע"ז לד:]. כדים רקים כלומר דברים [חולין ג.]. אשיתא. חומה [ב"מ פו.]. כווי. חלונות [שם]. ציבי. עצים [שם פב:]. בשופטני. שוטים [בב"ב מ.]. לתך. ... אידרונא. [מנחות לג:]. בעלמא. ...

צמד בקר ובליו כדי לחרוש גפניו העומדין על המיצר ששם היו ג) עומדים גפנותיהם בחרישה: שעל מנת כן חלקו השדות. ... אספלידא דהדיא ... אמר רב שימי בר אשי שמא בעלמא פלג ליה ... מי לא תניא כו' ... דדיירנא ביה כי דדרו ... ביה אבהתן:

חשק שלמה על רבינו גרשום א) [אולי צ"ל שוף בארץ ועי' בתוס' ד"ה שוף]. ב) [לפניגו הגי' אחורי כוי דחבריה]. ג) [הלשון צריך תיקון ואולי דצ"ל דלא סוי מעמידין גפנותיהם ע"ש תרישה]:

not grant a right to rebuild in such cases, for the height would still be adequate, particularly if the apartment was large. הָכִי אָמַר רַב נַחְמָן – Rather, **Rav Nachman stated thus:** כִּי דְדַיְירֵי אִינְשֵׁי – The upstairs neighbor cannot be forced to rebuild as long as the lower tenant can dwell **as**[11] **people** normally **dwell.**

The Gemara clarifies this ambiguous statement:

וְכַמָּה – **And how much** space is required for "normal dwelling"? אָמַר רַב הוּנָא בְּרֵיהּ דְּרַב יְהוֹשֻׁעַ – **Rav Huna the son of Rav Yehoshua said:** כִּי הֵיכִי דְעַיְילֵי אִיסוּרְיָתָא דִמְחוּזָא וְהָדַר – Enough space **so that he can bring into** the house **bundles** of long reeds **from Mechuza and turn around** with them in all directions.[12] If the house has settled to the point where this is no longer possible, the condition is triggered and the upper neighbor can be compelled to rebuild.

The Gemara recounts a related incident, also decided by Rav Chama:

הַהוּא גַּבְרָא דַּהֲוָה בָּנֵי אֲשִׁיתָא אֲחוֹרֵי כַּוֵּי דְּחַבְרֵיהּ – **A certain person was building a wall behind the windows of his neighbor's** house. The wall blocked the sunlight from entering the house.

The neighbor thereupon protested:

אָמַר לֵיהּ קָא מַאְפַּלְתְּ עָלַי – **He said to [the builder], "You are darkening my** house!" He then demanded the demolition of the offending wall.[13]

The builder offered a solution:

אָמַר לֵיהּ סָכַרְנָא לָךְ הָכָא – **He replied to [his neighbor], "I shall close up** your windows **here** with stones and mortar, וַעֲבִידְנָא לָךְ כַּוֵּי לְעֵיל מֵאֲשִׁיתָאי – **and I shall make** new **windows for you** that will be **higher than my wall."**[14]

The neighbor objected to this solution:

אָמַר לֵיהּ קָא מְרַעַתְּ לֵיהּ לַאֲשִׁיתָאי – **[The neighbor] said to him, "You will damage my** house's **wall** if you construct new windows!"[15]

The builder offered to solve this problem as well:

אָמַר לֵיהּ סָתַרְנָא לָךְ לַאֲשִׁיתָךְ – **He said to [the neighbor], "I shall dismantle your wall,** עַד דּוּכְתָּא דְכַוֵּי – starting from the top **until the place of the** new **windows,** וּבָנֵינָא לָהּ – **and I shall rebuild it;** וַעֲבִידְנָא לָךְ כַּוֵּי בְּבִנְיָנָא – **and I shall make for you** new **windows in the structure** לְעֵיל מֵאֲשִׁיתָאי – that will be **higher than my wall.** With this method no pounding is necessary, and your wall will not be damaged."

The neighbor found a flaw in this plan also:

אָמַר לֵיהּ אֲשִׁיתָא מִתַּתָּאָה עַתִּיקָא וּמִלְּעֵיל חַדְתָּא – **[The neighbor] told [the builder], "A wall that is old at the bottom and new at the top** לָא קַיְימָא – **will not endure,** for new cement does not adhere well to old cement, since the latter has already dried.[16] Hence, your plan will ruin the wall of my house."

The builder suggested another remedy:

אָמַר לֵיהּ סָתַרְנָא לָהּ עַד לְאַרְעָא – **He said to [the neighbor], "I shall tear [the wall]** of your house **down to the ground** וּבָנֵינָא לָהּ – and then **rebuild it;** וַעֲבִידְנָא לָךְ כַּוֵּי בְּגַוָּהּ – **and I shall make** new, unobstructed **windows in it for you."**

The neighbor still refused:

אָמַר לֵיהּ חֲדָא אֲשִׁיתָא חַדְתָּא בְּכוּלֵּיהּ בֵּיתָא עַתִּיקָא – **[The neighbor] said to him, "One new wall** attached **to an entire house that is old** לָא קַיְימָא – **will not endure,** for it will not adhere to the rest of the house."

The builder offered to solve this problem, too:

אָמַר לֵיהּ סָתַרְנָא לָהּ לְכוּלֵּיהּ בֵּיתָא – **[The builder] said to [the neighbor], "I shall raze the entire house** וּבָנֵינָא לָךְ כַּוֵּי בְּבִנְיָנָא – **and shall build** unobstructed **windows for you in an** entirely reconstructed **edifice."**

The neighbor still refused:

אָמַר לֵיהּ לֵית לִי דוּכְתָּא לְמֵידַר בָּהּ – **[The neighbor] said to him, "I do not have a place in which to live** during the reconstruction."

The builder countered:

אָמַר לֵיהּ אָגִירְנָא לָךְ דּוּכְתָּא – **He said to [the neighbor], "I will rent** another dwelling **place for you** for that period of time."

The neighbor replied:

אָמַר לֵיהּ לָא טָרַחְנָא – **He said to [the builder], "I do not** wish to **bother** moving to another house."

The dispute came before Rav Chama for judgment:

אָמַר רַב חָמָא בְּדִין קָא מְעַכֵּב – **Rav Chama stated: By law** the neighbor **can prevent** the builder from blocking his light; hence, the wall must be demolished.

The Gemara asks:

הַיְינוּ הָךְ – **This** ruling **is** identical to **this** first ruling of Rav Chama! וְהָא תּוּ לָמָּה לִי – **Why do I need** to hear it **again?**[17]

The Gemara answers:

הָא קָא מַשְׁמַע לָן – **This** second ruling **informs us** דְּאַף עַל גַּב דְּלָא מִשְׁתַּמֵּשׁ אֶלָּא תִּיבְנָא וּבֵי צִיבֵי בְּעָלְמָא – **that even though** the neighbor **uses** his building **only** to store **ordinary straw and twigs,**[18] still he may refuse to vacate the building on the grounds that removing his straw and wood would be too bothersome.[19]

The Gemara recounts another related incident, also decided by Rav Chama:

הָנְהוּ בֵּי תְּרֵי אַחֵי דִּפְלַגֵי בַּהֲדֵי הֲדָדֵי – Regarding **these two brothers that divided** an inheritance **between them** – חַד מְטְיֵיהּ אִסְפְּלִידָא – **one received a mansion** as his portion, וְחַד מְטְיֵיהּ

NOTES

a dwelling, we could not require rebuilding if an upper apartment sinks below this height, since the lower apartment would still function as a normal dwelling.

11. *Bach* emends כִּי דְדַיְירֵי to כִּדְדַיְירֵי. We have followed his emendation in the translation.

12. *Rashi.* [Presumably, one of the directions is "up" – i.e. he must be able to hold the bundles in a vertical position without impediment.] *Rambam* (*Hil. Shecheinim* 4:7), however, understands that he must be able to enter the doorway with a medium-size bundle on his head without bending.

[See *Rivta* (below ד״ה אמר רב חמא), who explains that this is just an example of the height that was needed in that time and place. This rule would be followed in other places and times – the ceiling must be high enough to allow one to easily maneuver his possesions.]

13. Once a homeowner has an established right (*chazakah*) to enjoy sunlight through his window, a neighbor may not erect any structure that blocks the light, even if the structure stands completely on the builder's property (Mishnah below, 22a; see also Mishnah below, 58b). This *chazakah* is acquired only after the window has stood unobstructed for three years (*Rashi* ד״ה בדנפשאי). In the Gemara's case, the neighbor had an established right to sunlight, and thus could legally object to the wall's construction.

14. I.e. I shall open new windows in the wall of your house *above* my wall, so that the sun's light will continue to illuminate your home (*Rashi*).

15. The blows of your hammer will cause the wall to sway (*Rashi*).

16. *Rashi.*

[There is an apparent difficulty here: We learned above (4a) that an ordinary garden is subject to visual trespass

17. Although the two cases concern fundamentally different rights – the one, dwelling space and the other, light – no new law can be derived from the second case that was not stated either in the Mishnah below (22a) or in the first case. Thus, the second case appears redundant, and the Gemara questions why it was taught.

18. I.e. he does not reside in the structure (*Rashi*).

19. *Rashi.*

מסורת הש"ס

א) נ"א מצינן דאיטרח, ב) פ"א דרבא, ג) לקמן לה., ד) פ"א רבא, ה) [לקמן קנג: ע"ש] חולין נ:, ו) נ"א מצינן דאיטרחא, ז) [עי' מ"ש בב"ק פט. על הגליון], ח) ב"מ קד, ט) ל"ל נהי ועי' רש"ש, י) [אידרונא וכן בסמוך]

עין משפט נר מצוה

מב א ב ג ד מיי' פ"ד מהל' שכנים הל' ו ז סמג עשין פב טוש"ע ח"מ סימן קסד סעיף ב ועיין בהג"ה:

מג ה ו מיי' שם פ"ז הלכה ח סמג עשין פב טוש"ע ח"מ סי' קנד סעיף יג:

מד ז טוש"ע שם וסימן קסד סעיף ג:

מה ח ט מיי' שם הל' י סמג שם טוש"ע שם סי' קנד סעיף ט:

מו י מיי' פכ"ח מהל' מכירה הל' ו סמג שם טוש"ע ח"מ סי' קטג סעיף ד:

מז כ מיי' פ"ז מהלכות שכנים הל' י סמג עשין פב טוש"ע ח"מ סי' קנד סעיף ט:

מח ל מיי' פכ"ח מהל' מכירה הל' יד סמג עשין פב טוש"ע ח"מ סי' רים סעיף יח:

מט מ נ מיי' שם הל' יד טוש"ע שם סעיף יח:

א"ל (א) א) איסתריה אנא ואבנייה אמר ליה לית לי דוכתא למידר בה א"ל אנא אוגר לך דוכתא א"ל לא ב) טרחנא (ג) לא קא מתדר לי שוף אכריסך ועול ושוף אכריסך ופוק אמר רב חמא א בדינא קא מעכב והני מילי דלא מטו כשורי למטה מעשרה ב אבל מטו כשורי למטה מעשרה מצי א"ל למטה מי' רשותא דידי הוא ולא משעבד לך וה"מ דלא אתנו גבי הדדי ג אבל אתנו גבי הדדי סתרי ובנו וכי אתנו בהדי הדדי עד כמה אמרו רבנן קמיה ג) דרבה משמיה דמר זוטרא בריה דרב נחמן דאמר משמיה דר"נ כאותה ששנינו ג רומו כחצי ארכו וכחצי רחבו אמר להו ד) רבה ה) לאו אמינא לכו לא תיתלו ביה בוקי סריקי ברב נחמן הכי אמר ר"נ (ג) כי דדיירי אינשי וכמה אמר רב הונא בריה דרב יהושע ד כי היכי דעיילי איסוריתא דמחוזא והדר ה ההוא גברא דהוה בני אשיתא אחורי כווי דחבריה אמר ליה קא מאפלת עלי א"ל סכרנא לך הכא ועבידנא לך כווי לעיל מאשיתאי א"ל קא מרעת ליה לאשיתאי א"ל סתרנא לך לאשיתך עד דוכתא דכווי ובנינא לה ועבידנא לך כווי בבנינא לעיל מאשיתאי א"ל אשיתא מתתאה עתיקא ומלעיל חדתא לא קיימא אמר ליה סתרנא לה עד לארעא ובנינא לה ועבידנא לך כווי בגוה א"ל חדא אשיתא חדתא בכוליה ביתא עתיקא לא קיימא א"ל סתרנא לה לכוליה ביתא ובנינא לך כווי בבנינא א"ל לית לי דוכתא למידר בה א"ל אגירנא לך דוכתא א"ל לא י) טרחנא אמר רב חמא ו בדין קא מעכב • היינו הך והא תו למה לי הא קמ"ל דאע"ג דלא משתמש ז אלא תיבנא (ד) וכי ציבי בעלמא ח הנהו בי תרי אחי דפלגי בהדי הדדי חד מטייה אספלידא וחד מטייה תרביצא אזל ההוא דמטייה תרביצא וקא בני אשיתא אפומא דאספלידא א"ל קא מאפלת עלי א"ל בדידי קא בנינא אמר רב חמא ט בדין קאמר ליה א"ל רבינא לרב אשי מאי שנא מהא דתניא י שני אחין שחלקו אחד מהן נטל שדה כרם ואחד מהן נטל שדה לבן יש לו לבעל הכרם ד' אמות בשדה לבן שעל מנת כן חלקו א"ל התם דעלו להדדי אבל הכא מאי דלא עלו להדדי ו) וכי בשופטני עסקינן דהאי שקיל אספלידא והאי שקיל תרביצא ולא עלו להדדי א"ל ט) נהי דעלו להדדי דמי ליבני כשורי והודרי דמי אוירא לא עלו להדדי ולימא ליה מעיקרא אספלידא פלגת לי השתא משוית לי (ה) אידרונא אמר רב שימי בר אשי שמא בעלמא פלג ליה מי לא תניא ה) ל האומר בית כור עפר אני מוכר לך אע"פ שאינו אלא לתך הגיעו שלא מכר לו אלא שמא והוא דמיתקרי בית כור מ פרדס אני מוכר לך אע"פ שאין בו רמונים הגיעו שלא מכר לו אלא שמא והוא דמיתקרי פרדס נ כרם אני מוכר לך אע"פ שאין בו גפנים הגיעו שלא מכר לו אלא שמא והוא דמיתקרי כרמא מי דמי התם מצי אמר ליה מוכר ללוקח שמא זבינו לך הכא מצי א"ל אדעתא דהכי פלגי דדאירנא ביה כי היכי דדרו אבהתן אמרו ליה

רש"י

שוף אכריסך. שחה קומתך עד כריסך: כשורי. קורות העלייה: אבל אתנו אהדדי. כשחלקו אם תשפל עלייה (ו) יסתרוהו הבית ויבנוהו: עד כמה. תשפיל העלייה ויכוף את העליון לסתור ולבנות: כאותה ששנינו. בהמוכר פירות המקבל עליו מחבירו לבנות לו בית עושה רומו כחצי ארכו וחצי רחבו כבנין ההיכל שהיה ארכו ארבעים ורחבו עשרים וגבהו שלשים: איסוריתא. חבילות קנים ארוכין: והדר. מחזיר עצמו לכל לדדין: סכרנא לך הכא. אסתום לך חלונותיך באבנים וטיט ואפתח לך למעלה מכותלי בגובה כתלך חלונות אחרים שיאירו (ז) בביתך: קמרעת לאשיתאי. כשתפתח בה חלונות תנוע החומה מחמת המכה: סתרנא לך. הכותל מראשו וגובהו עד שיגיע למקום החלונות שאעשה לך: לא קיימא. שאין טיט חדש נדבק יפה בטיט הישן שיבש כבר: דאע"ג דקא משתמש בה בציבי ותיבני. ואין הוא עצמו דר בתוכו אלא א"ל לא מצינא לאטרוח להוציא העצים והתבן: אספלידא. טרקלין יפה: תרביצא. גינה שבצד הטרקלין שהיתה מאירה לתוכו: בדנפשאי אנא בנינא. בשלי אני בונה ואתה אין לך עלי חזקת אורה של שלש שנים דהשתא הוא דפלגינהו: ד' אמות לעבודת הכרם. שהיו חורשין אותה בשוורים: דעלו אהדדי. שנתן בעל הכרם לבעל השדה לבן דמים של עילוי הכרם הילכך כרם בעי למשקל עם עבודתו: בשופטני עסקינן. וכי שוטה היה שנטל גינה חלקה כנגד בית בנוי ולא נטל עילוי דמים: והשתא (ח) אידרונא. חדר אפל ואני על מנת אספלידא נתתי עילוי דמים: שמא בעלמא. (ט) אם אספלידא שמא ואע"פ שאינו כשאר אספלידא לא בטיל שמו: בית כור. לפי חשבון (י) סאתים כחצר המשכן:

נהרדעי

תוספות

שוף אכריסך. פ"ה שחה קומתך ולר"י נראה שוף לשון שפשוף שמתחכך בכרסך: בוקי סריקי. פ"ה כלים ריקים. אנשים רקים מתרגמינן גוברין סריקין (שופטים יא): היינו הך. וא"ת והא אשמעינן בהאי עובדא דלחדתא מעתיקא לא קאי דלא שמעינן מההיא דלעיל ולעיל איצטריך כדאמרינן וה"מ דלא מטו כשורי למטה מי' וכו' וי"ל דמילתא דפשיטא היא דלחדא חדתא וכולה עתיקא לא קאי ומשום הא לא הוה צריך לאתויי האי עובדא: אספלידא. פרש"י טרקלין יפה ובערוך פירש מערה כדמתרגם (תהלים מ) מפני שאול במערה באספלידא ואור"י דאספלידא דהכא א"א להיות מערה מדקאמר נמי דעלו להדדי בכשורי והודרי ובמערה ליכא כשורי והודרי ועוד מדקאמר מעיקרא אספלידא והשתא אידרונא ובמערה ליכא אורה כלל ומפרש ר"י דאספלידא דהכא הוי אכסדרא שיש בה אורה גדולה שפרוצה ברוח אחד כדאמרינן בלא יחפור (לקמן דף כה.) עולם דומה לאכסדרא וכו' וכן מוכח בהקומץ רבה (מנחות דף לג: ושם ד"ה אספלידא) דקאמר אביי חזינא להו לאספלידי דבי מר דאית להו פלימי ולית להו מזוזה ופריך מיתיבי בית שער ואכסדרא ומרפסת חייבין במזוזה: א"ל בדידי קבנינא. פ"ה אתה אין לך עלי חזקת אורה של שלש שנים ותימה שהיה יכול להאפילו עליו שלא יהא לו בטרקלין אורה כלל ועוד דמאי קאמר באורה לא עלו אהדדי פשיטא דעלו נמי באורה דבית בלא אורה אינו שוה כלום ומפרש ר"ת שמאספלידא היה יכול לראות לשדותיו דלכך התרביצא ודקאמר מאפלת עילוי היינו שהיה מעכבו שלא היה יכול לראות שדותיו וקרי לה נמי אידרונא שלא היה יכול להביט למרחוק וכן מפרש ההוא דלקמן אין להם חלונות זה על זה ומיהו קשיא לר"י דמאי קפריך מאי שנא מהא דתניא כו' התם ודאי יש לו ד' אמות לפי שהם צורך לעבודת הכרם אבל הכא זה לא היה צורך האספלידא מש"ה בדין קאמר ליה ונראה לר"י דודאי היה מאפיל עליו האורה שלא היה בו אורה גדולה כשאר אכסדרא אבל עדיין היה בו אור גדול והא דאמר ומכנגדן מרחיק ד' אמות שלא יאפיל היינו שלא יאפיל לגמרי עד שלא יהא ראוי להשתמש בו יפה ומש"ה קרי ליה אידרונא משום דלגבי אכסדרא אידרונא היא והשתא נמי אתי שפיר דלא עלו להדדי באורה שהוא צורך האכסדרא: והוא דקרו ליה בית כור. וכגון שהלוקח יודע שיש לו קרקע שקרוי בית כור דאל"כ הרי הטעהו ואפי' אם רואה בשעת מכירה שאין שם בית כור יכול לומר סבור הייתי שהיית משלים לי בית כור ואם תאמר וניזיל דדמים מודיעים ואם נתן לו דמי בית כור אפילו קרו ליה בית כור ישלים לו בית כור שלם ויש לומר דמיירי כגון דאזיל גביה ואינו נותן לו אפילו דמי לתך ואי קרו ליה בית כור אפילו אין בו אלא לתך הגיעו ואי לא קרו ליה בית כור חייב לתת לו בית כור שלם אי נמי דלא אזיל גביה וכגון דנתן לו דמי לתך והשתא אי לא קרו ליה בית כור היה יכול לומר לוקח אם תרצה לתת לי בית כור שלם ולעמוד במקחך עמוד ואם לאו תחזור לי מעותי אבל אי קרו ליה בית כור הגיעו אע"פ שאין בו אלא לתך:

מר

רבינו גרשום

לא מצינא דאטרח (לבנות) [לפנות] ביתי: שוף אכריסך עול. כלומר הואיל וגרם מזלך (א) חפור בארץ וכפוף בטנך וצא והכנס. דינא קאמר ליה דבתוך שלו יבנה: לא אמרן דדינא קאמר ליה אלא דלא מטו כשורי. שלא ירדה העליה למטה מי' אז יכול לטעון לו דור בדוחק בתוך עשרה: [דלא] אתנו בהדי הדדי. שלא התנו זה לזה לבנות אחר נפילה: עד כמה. גבוה יכול לכופו שיסייע לו: כאותה ששנינו. בפ' המוכר: רומו כחצי ארכו וכחצי רחבו. שאם היה הבית כ' אמה אורך ורוחב י' אמה עושה גבהו חצי כ' וחצי י' שהם ט"ו אמה וראיה לדבר מהיכל: לא תיתלו בוקי סריקי. כלומר לא תאמינו בדברים רקים הללו מעולם לא אמרן ר' נחמן שיבנהו גבוה כזה: שיעור איסוריתא דמחוזא כדי שיהא יכול לישא משאוי על גבו כמשאוי של אנשי מחוזא ויכול לחזור ברוחה בהכי מצי לכופו טפי לא: אשיתא (ב) אגב כוי דחבריה. שהיה בונה כותלו כנגד חלון חבירו שהיה לו חזקה לחלון ולא הרחיק ד' אמות: מרעת אשיתאי. שתחתור בו חלונות אחרות: סתרנא לך. עד חלונות אלו ובנינא לך מחדש: דינא אמר ליה. דלא מצי למיטרח לפנות ביתו: היינו הך. דקאמר רב חמא בהני בי תרי והא תו למה לי: הא איצטריך למיתני. שאפי' אלו חלונות שיש לו בהן חזקה: בי תבני וציבי. שאין צריך בהן לאורה כלל כך אפ"ה לא מצי לכופו לפנות: אספלידא. חדר שלועזין קמערה: תרביצא. גינה שסמוך לה: אפומא דאספלידא. לפני הפתח: אחד של שדה לבן. שדה תבואה: יש לו לבעל הכרם ד' אמות בשדה לבן:

תַּרְבִּיצָא – **and one received a garden.**[20] אָזַל הַהוּא דְּמַטְיֵיה תַּרְבִּיצָא וְקָא בָּנֵי אֲשִׁיתָא אַפּוּמָא דְּאַסְפְּלִידָא – **The one that received the garden went and built a wall at the entrance of the mansion**, thereby obstructing the sunlight that illuminated the mansion.

The owner of the mansion protested:

אָמַר לֵיהּ קָא מַאֲפַלְתְּ עֲלַי – **He said to [his brother], "You are darkening my** residence!"

The owner of the garden replied:

אָמַר לֵיהּ בְּדִידִי קָא בָּנֵינָא – **[The offender] said to [his brother], "I am building on my own** property! You do not have an established right (*chazakah*) to the light, which is attained only after three years of undisturbed enjoyment, since we have just divided our father's estate.[21] Hence, you cannot prevent me from building this wall."

The dispute was brought before Rav Chama for judgment:

אָמַר רַב חָמָא בְּדִין קָאָמַר לֵיהּ – **Rav Chama stated:** The owner of the garden **has replied in accordance with the law.** That is, since the owner of the mansion has no established right to benefit from the sunlight, he is powerless to prevent the construction of the wall.

Ravina questions Rav Chama's decision:

אָמַר לֵיהּ רָבִינָא לְרַב אַשִׁי – **Ravina said to Rav Ashi:** מַאי שְׁנָא מֵהָא דְּתַנְיָא – **How is** this ruling **different from [the ruling] that was taught in a Baraisa:** שְׁנֵי אַחִין שֶׁחָלְקוּ – Regarding **TWO BROTHERS THAT DIVIDED** an estate, אֶחָד מֵהֶן נָטַל שְׂדֵה כֶּרֶם – **ONE OF THEM TOOK A VINEYARD** as his portion וְאֶחָד מֵהֶן נָטַל שְׂדֵה לָבָן – **AND ONE OF THEM TOOK AN** adjoining **FIELD OF GRAIN**[22] as his portion. יֵשׁ לוֹ לְבַעַל הַכֶּרֶם אַרְבַּע אַמּוֹת בִּשְׂדֵה לָבָן – In this case **THE OWNER OF THE VINEYARD HAS** the right to a strip of land **FOUR *AMOS*** wide **IN THE GRAIN FIELD,**[23] שֶׁעַל מְנַת כֵּן חָלְקוּ – **FOR** we assume that **IT WAS ON THIS CONDITION** that **THEY DIVIDED** the estate. The Baraisa thus teaches that when brothers divide an estate, each receives any additional right that promotes the full and proper utilization of his portion. Why, then, did Rav Chama rule against the brother that inherited the mansion? Surely the mansion cannot be fully utilized without the illumination provided by sunlight. It follows, then, that the obstructing wall violates his right to benefit from the sunlight. – ?–

Rav Ashi replied:

אָמַר לֵיהּ הָתָם דְּעַלּוּ לַהֲדָדֵי – Rav Ashi **said to [Ravina]: There**, in the case of the Baraisa, **they assessed** their portions **one against the other** in order to achieve parity.[24]

Ravina rejects this distinction:

אֲבָל הָכָא מַאי – **But here,** in the case of the mansion and the garden, **what** transpired? דְּלָא עַלּוּ לַהֲדָדֵי – **That they did not assess** their portions **one against the other?** וְכִי בְּשׁוּפְטָנֵי עַסְקִינַן – **Are we, then, dealing with fools,** דְּהַאי שָׁקֵיל אַסְפְּלִידָא – **that this** brother **took a** finished **mansion** for his portion וְהַאי שָׁקֵיל תַּרְבִּיצָא – **and this** other one **took** only **an** empty **garden,** וְלָא עַלּוּ לַהֲדָדֵי – **and they did not assess** them **one against the other?!** Obviously, the inheritor of the mansion must have paid his brother the difference in value between the two portions. Therefore, we should assume that he paid for a functional residence – one that would receive illumination from sunlight – in line with the ruling of the Baraisa. – ? –

Rav Ashi replied:

אָמַר לֵיהּ נְהִי דְּעַלּוּ לַהֲדָדֵי – Rav Ashi **said to [Ravina]: It is true that they assessed one against the other** דְּמֵי לִיבְנֵי כְּשׁוּרֵי וְהוּדְרֵי – **the value of the bricks, support beams and ornamental beams,** since these materials constitute the essential difference between a finished building and a garden; דְּמֵי אֲוִירָא לָא עַלּוּ לַהֲדָדֵי – however, **they did not assess one against the other the value of the open space** surrounding the mansion, since that is not an integral component of a house. Thus, the owner of the mansion does not receive a right to unobstructed sunlight for his payment.[25]

Ravina suggests other grounds for opposing Rav Chama's decision:

וְלֵימָא לֵיהּ – **Let** the mansion owner **say to [the garden owner]:** מֵעִיקָּרָא אַסְפְּלִידָא פְּלַגְתְּ לִי – **Originally, you allotted me a mansion;** הַשְׁתָּא מְשַׁוֵּית לִי אִידְרוֹנָא – **now,** by building the wall, **you have created a dark room for me!** Hence, you have violated the terms of our agreement, inasmuch as I compensated you for having received a mansion.[26] –?–

The Gemara objects to this reasoning:

אָמַר רַב שִׁימִי בַּר אַשִׁי – **Rav Shimi bar Ashi said:** שְׁמָא בְּעָלְמָא פְּלַג לֵיהּ – The garden owner agreed merely to **allot [his brother]** a mansion **in name only,** and this building is nonetheless called a "mansion."[27] Thus, the division is valid, even though the light is

NOTES

20. The garden was located next to the mansion, and the light from the garden area entered and illuminated the mansion (*Rashi*).

[There is an apparent difficulty here: We learned above (4a) that an ordinary garden is subject to visual trespass, so the owner of the mansion should actually be obligated to build a wall to block his view of the garden! For discussion of this question, see *Ritva, Yad Ramah*.]

21. *Rashi*.

22. Literally, "field of white." A grain field is called שְׂדֵה לָבָן because grain turns white when it ripens, or because the field is exposed to the white light of the sun (*Rash* to *Pe'ah* 3:1, and see *Tos. Yom Tov* there).

23. He does not own the strip of land itself, which runs along the border of the two fields; rather, he owns the right to use it while plowing his vineyard (*Ritva*). That is, the strip of land is subject to his עֲבוֹדַת הַכֶּרֶם (*cultivation of the vineyard*), which means that he is allowed to turn his oxen around on the strip when plowing his vineyard in order to avoid damaging the vines. Normally, for this purpose, it is the vineyard owner that must leave over four *amos* at the edge of his vineyard, so as not to encroach with his plow upon the neighboring field (see Mishnah below, 26a). In the Baraisa's case, however, the vineyard and the grain field belonged to one person (the father), so that there was no clear demarcation between the two fields at the time the estate was divided. Hence, whether or not the inheritor of the vineyard has to relinquish four *amos* of previously cultivated land is an issue unique to this case, and one decided by the Baraisa.

24. A vineyard is more valuable than a grain field, and so the inheritor of the vineyard compensated his brother with a cash payment. Therefore, we assume that he paid for a functional vineyard – one that necessarily included four additional *amos* for turning the oxen. In Rav Chama's case, however, no compensation was paid (*Rashi*).

25. Since in the other case, however, a vineyard is worthless if it cannot be plowed, with his payment the inheritor of the vineyard necessarily acquired the right to use his neighbor's land for the purpose of turning his oxen.

[This is the interpretation of Rosh as cited by Tur 154:37. Other Rishonim, however, explain that the right of an unobstructed view is indeed an integral componet of a house. The discussion here is of a case where the assessment specified that the difference between them consisted of the value of the bricks, support beams and ornamental beams, but did not include the value of the open space around the house (see *Rashba, Rivta, Ran*; see also *Nachalas David*).]

26. *Rashi*.

According to the Rishonim cited in the previous note, who explain that the assessment specified the difference as consisting only of the materials of the building, his claim is neverthless valid for the agreement stated that the brother was to receive a mansion, and without light, the building is not considered a mansion.]

27. Even though it is not like other mansions, for the wall darkens its interior, the building nevertheless retains its designation of "mansion" (*Rashi*).

א"ל (א) איסתריה אנא ואבנייה אמר לית לי דוכתא למידר בה א"ל אנא אוגר לך דוכתא א"ל לא [א] טרחנא (ב) לא קא מתדר לי שוף אכריסך ועול ושוף אכריסך ופוק אמר רב חמא [א] בדינא קא מעכב והני מילי דלא מטו כשורי למטה מעשרה [ב] אבל מטו כשורי למטה מעשרה מצי א"ל למטה מי' רשותא דידי הוא ולא משעבד לך והני מילי דלא אתנו גבי הדדי [ג] אבל אתנו גבי הדדי סתרי ובנו וכי אתנו בהדי הדדי עד כמה אמרו רבנן קמיה [ג] דרבה משמיה דמר זוטרא בריה דרב נחמן דאמר משמיה דר"נ כאותה ששנינו [ד] רומו כחצי ארכו וכחצי רחבו אמר להו [ד] רבה [ה] לאו אמינא לכו לא תיתלו ביה בוקי סריקי ברב נחמן הכי אמר ר"נ (ג) כי דדיירי אינשי וכמה אמר רב הונא בריה דרב יהושע [ו] כי היכי דעיילי איסוריתא דמחוזא והדר [ה] ההוא גברא דהוה בני אשיתא אחורי כווי דחבריה אמר ליה קא מאפלת עלי א"ל סכרנא לך הכא ועבידנא לך כווי לעיל מאשיתאי א"ל קא מרעת ליה לאשיתאי א"ל סתרנא לך לאשיתך עד דוכתא דכווי ובנינא לה ועבידנא לך כווי בבנינא לעיל מאשיתאי א"ל אשיתא מתתאה עתיקא ומלעיל חדתא לא קיימא אמר ליה סתרנא לה עד לארעא ובנינא לה ועבידנא לך כווי בגוה א"ל חדא אשיתא חדתא בכוליה ביתא עתיקא לא קיימא א"ל סתרנא לה לכוליה ביתא ובנינא לך כווי בבנינא א"ל לית לי דוכתא למידר בה א"ל אגירנא לך דוכתא א"ל לא [ז] טרחנא אמר רב חמא [ח] בדין קא מעכב [ט] היינו הך והא תו למה

לי הא קמ"ל דאע"ג דלא משתמש [י] אלא תיבנא (ד) ובי ציבי בעלמא [ח] ההנהו בי תרי אחי דפלגי בהדי הדדי חד מטייה אספלידא וחד מטייה תרביצא אזל ההוא דמטייה תרביצא וקא בני אשיתא אפומא דאספלידא א"ל קא מאפלת עלי א"ל בדידי קא בנינא אמר רב חמא [ט] בדין קאמר ליה א"ל רבינא לרב אשי מאי שנא מהא דתניא [י] שני אחין שחלקו אחד מהן נטל שדה כרם ואחד מהן נטל שדה לבן יש לו לבעל הכרם ד' אמות בשדה לבן שעל מנת כן חלקו א"ל התם דעלו להדדי אבל הכא מאי דלא עלו להדדי [י] וכי בשופטני עסקינן דהאי שקיל אספלידא והאי שקיל תרביצא ולא עלו להדדי א"ל [כ] נהי דעלו להדדי דמי ליבני כשורי והודרי דמי אוירא לא עלו להדדי ולימא ליה מעיקרא אספלידא פלגת לי השתא משוית לי (ה) אידרונא אמר רב שימי בר אשי שמא בעלמא פלג ליה מי לא תניא [ל] [ל] האומר בית כור עפר אני מוכר לך אע"פ שאינו אלא לתך הגיעו שלא מכר לו אלא שמא והוא דמיתקרי בית כור [מ] פרדס אני מוכר לך אע"פ שאין בו רמונים הגיעו שלא מכר לו אלא שמא והוא דמיתקרי פרדס [נ] כרם אני מוכר לך אע"פ שאין בו גפנים הגיעו שלא מכר לו אלא שמא והוא דמיתקרי כרמא מי דמי התם מצי אמר ליה מוכר ללוקח שמא זביני לך הכא מצי א"ל אדעתא דהכי פלגי דדאירנא ביה כי היכי דדרו אבהתן אמרו ליה

רש"י

שוף אכריסך. שחה קומתך עד כריסך: כשורי. קורות העלייה: אבל אתנו אהדדי. כשחלקו אם תשפל עלייה (ו) יסתרוהו הבית ויבנוהו: עד כמה. תשפיל העלייה ויכוף את העליון לסתור ולבנות: כאותה ששנינו. בהמוכר פירות המקבל עליו מחבירו לבנות לו בית עושה רומו כחצי ארכו וחצי רחבו כבנין ההיכל שהיה ארכו ארבעים ורחבו עשרים וגבהו שלשים: איסוריתא. חבילות קנים ארוכין: והדר. מחזיר עצמו לכל לצדדין: סכרנא לך הכא. אסתום לך חלונותיך באבנים וטיט ואפתח לך למעלה מכותלי בגובה כתליך חלונות אחרים שיאירו (ז) בביתך: קמרעת לאשיתאי. כשתפתח בה חלונות תנוע החומה מחמת המכה: סתרנא לך. הכותל מראשו וגובהו עד שיגיע למקום החלונות שאעשה לך: לא קיימא. שאין טיט החדש נדבק יפה בטיט הישן שיבש כבר: דאע"ג דקא משתמש בה בציבי ותיבני. ואין הוא עצמו דר בתוכו אפי' א"ל לא מצינא לאטרח להוציא העצים והתבן: אספלידא. טרקלין יפה: תרביצא. גינה שבצד הטרקלין שהיתה מאירה לתוכו: בדנפשאי אנא בנינא. בשלי אני בונה ואתה אין לך עלי חזקת אורה של שלש שנים להשתא הוא דפלגינוהו: ד' אמות לעבודת הכרם. שהיו חורשין אותה בשוורים: דעלו אהדדי. שנתן בעל הכרם לבעל השדה לבן דמים של עילוי הכרם הילכך כרם בעי למשקל עם עבודתו: בשופטני עסקינן. וכי שוטה היה שנטל גינה חלוקה כנגד בית בנוי ולא נטל עילוי דמים: והשתא (ח) אידרונא. חדר אפל ואני על מנת אספלידא נתתי עילוי דמים: שמא בעלמא. (ט) אם אספלידא שמה ואע"פ שאינו כשאר אספלידא לא בטיל שמו: בית כור. לפי חשבון (י) סאתים כחצר המשכן נהרדעי

תוספות

שוף אכריסך. פ"ה שחה קומתך ולר"י נראה שוף לשון שפשוף שמתחכך בארץ: בוקי סריקי. אנשים רקים מתרגמינן גוברין סריקין (שופטים יא) בהאי עובדא דהדתא אעתיקא לא קאי דלא שמעינן מההיא **היינו** הך. וא"ת והא אשמעינן דלעיל ולעיל איצטריך כדאמרינן וה"מ דלא מטו כשורי למטה מי' וכו' וי"ל דמילתא דפשיטא היא דחדא חדתא וכולה עתיקא לא קאי ומשום הא לא הוה צריך לאתויי האי עובדא: **אספלידא**. פרש"י טרקלין יפה ובערוך פירש מערה כדמתרגם (תהלים נז) מפני שאול במערה באספלידא ואור"י דאספלידא דהכא א"א להיות מערה מדקאמר [ט] נמי דעלו להדדי בכשורי והודרי ובמערה ליכא כשורי והודרי ועוד מדקאמר מעיקרא אספלידא והשתא [י] אידרונא ובמערה ליכא אורה כלל ומפרש ר"י דאספלידא דהכא הוי אכסדרה שיש בה אורה גדולה שפרוצה ברוח אחד כדאמרינן בלא יחפור (לקמן דף כה.) עולם דומה לאכסדרה וכו' וכן מוכח בהקומץ רבה (מנחות דף לג: ושם ד"ה אספלידא) דאמר אביי חזינא להו לאספלידי דבי מר דאית להו פלימי ולית להו מזוזה ופריך מיתיבי בית שער ואכסדרה ומרפסת חייבין במזוזה: **א"ל** בדידי קבנינא. פ"ה אתה אין לך עלי חזקת אורה של שלש שנים ותימה שהיה יכול להאפילו עליו שלא יהא לו בטרקלין אורה כלל ועוד דמאי קאמר באוירא לא עלו אהדדי פשיטא דעלו נמי באוירא דבית בלא אורה אינו שוה כלום ומפרש ר"ת שמאספלידא היה יכול לראות לשדותיו דרך התרביצא ודקאמר מאפלת עילווי היינו שהיה מעכבו שלא היה יכול לראות שדותיו וקרי לה נמי אידרונא שלא היה יכול להביט למרחוק וכן מפרש ההוא דלקמן אין להם חלונות זה על זה ומיהו קשיא לר"י דמאי קפריך מאי שנא מהא דתניא כו' התם ודאי יש לו ד' אמות לפי שהם צורך לעבודת הכרם אבל הכא זה לא היה צורך האספלידא מש"ה בדין קאמר ליה ונראה לר"י דודאי היה מאפיל עליו האורה שלא היה בו אורה גדולה כאשר צריך לאכסדרה אבל עדיין היה בו אור גדול והא דאמר ומכנגדן מרחיק ד' אמות שלא יאפיל היינו שלא יאפיל לגמרי עד שלא יהא ראוי להשתמש בו יפה ומש"ה קרי ליה אידרונא משום דלגבי אכסדרה אידרונא היא והשתא נמי אתי שפיר דלא עלו להדדי באוירא שהוא צורך האכסדרה: **והוא** דקרו ליה בית כור. וכגון שהלוקח יודע שיש לו קרקע שקרוי בית כור דאל"כ הרי הטעהו ואפי' אם רואה בשעת מכירה שאין שם בית כור יכול לומר סבור הייתי שהיית משלים לי בית כור ואם תאמר ונימא דדמים מודיעים ואם נתן לו דמי בית כור אפילו קרו ליה בית כור ישלים לו בית כור שלם ויש לומר דמיירי כגון דאוזיל גביה ואינו נותן לו אפילו דמי לתך ואי קרו ליה בית כור אפילו אין בו אלא לתך הגיעו ואי לא קרו ליה בית כור חייב לתת לו בית כור שלם אי נמי דלא אוזיל גביה וכגון דנתן לו דמי לתך והשתא אי לא קרו ליה בית כור היה יכול לומר לוקח אם תרצה לתת לי בית כור שלם ולעמוד במקחך עמוד ואם לאו תחזור לי מעותי אבל אי קרו ליה בית כור הגיעו אע"פ שאין בו אלא לתך:

מר

עין משפט נר מצוה

מב א ב ג ד מיי' פ"ד מהל' שכנים הל' ו ז סמג עשין פב טוש"ע ח"מ סימן קסד סעיף ג ועיין בהגה"ה:

מג ה ו מיי' שם פ"ז הלכה ח סמג שם טוש"ע ח"מ סי' קנד סעיף יג:

מד ז טוש"ע שם וסימן קסד סעיף ג:

מה ח ט מיי' שם הל' ח סמג שם טוש"ע ח"מ סי' קנד סעיף ד:

מו י מיי' פכ"ד מהל' מכירה הל' י סמג שם טוש"ע ח"מ סי' קעג סעיף ד:

מז כ מיי' פ"ז מהלכות שכנים הל' י סמג עשין פב טוש"ע ח"מ סי' קנד סעיף ט:

מח ל מיי' פכ"ח מהל' מכירה הל' יד סמג עשין פב טוש"ע ח"מ סי' ריח סעיף יח:

מט מ נ מיי' שם הל' יד טוש"ע שם סעיף יח:

רבינו גרשום

לא מצינא דאטרח (לבנות) [לפנות] ביתי: שוף אכריסך עול. כלומר הואיל וגרם מולך א) חפור בארץ וכפוף בטנך וצא והכנס. דינא קאמר ליה דבתוך שלו יבנה: לא אמרן דדינא קאמר ליה אלא דלא מטו כשורי. שלא ירדה העליה למטה מי' אז יכול לטעון לו דור בדוחק בתוך עשרה: [דלא] אתנו בהדי הדדי. שלא התנו זה לזה לבנות אחר נפילה: עד כמה. גבהו יכול לכופו שיסייע לו: כאותה ששנינו. בפ' המוכר: רומו כחצי ארכו וכחצי רחבו. שאם היה הבית כ' אמה באורך ורוחב י' אמה עושה גבהה חצי כ' וחצי י' שהם ט"ו אמה וראיה לדבר מההיכל: לא תיתלו בוקי סריקי. כלומר לא תאמינו בדברים רקים הללו מעולם לא אמר ר' נחמן שיבנהו גבוה כזה. שיעור איסוריתא דמחוזא כדי שיהא יכול לישא משאוי על גבו כמשאוי של אנשי מחוזא ויכול לחזור בריוח בהדי מצי לכופו טפי לא: אשיתא ג) אגב כווי דחברי'. שהיה בונה כותלו כנגד חלון חבירו שהיה לו חזקה לחלון ולא הרחיק ד' אמות: מרעית אשיתאי. שתחתור את חלונות אחרות: סתרנא לך. עד חלונות אלו ובנינא לך מחדש: דינא אמר ליה. דלא מצי למיטרח לפנות ביתו: היינו הך. דקאמר רב חמא בהנהו בי תרי וכו' והא תו למה לי: הא איצטריך למיתני. שאפי' אלו חלונות שיש לו בהן חזקה: בי תבני וציבי. שאין צריך בהן לאורה כל כך אפ"ה לא מצי לכופו לפנות. אספלידא. חדר שלועזין קמערא: תרביצא. גינה שסמוך לה: אפומא דאספלידא. לפני הפתח: אחד של שדה לבן. שדה תבואה: יש לו לבעל הכרם ד' אמות בשדה לבן. כמלא

צמד בקר וכליו כדי לחרוש גפניו העומדים על המיצר ששם היו ג) עומדים גפנותיהם בחרישה: שעל מנת כן חלקו השדות. והכי קאמר ליה רבינא: ה"נ מאחר שנטל אחד האספלידא שלו כדי שיהא לו אורה וקאמר לו לא תאפיל עלי: א"ל התם. משו"ה יש לו לבעל הכרם ד' אמות בשדה לבן משום דעלו להדדי שמעלה זה לבעל הכרם לבעל שדה לבן יותר מחלק שדה כרם כדי שיהא לו ד' אמות לעבודת הכרם אבל הכא מאי עלו אהדדי. דלא מעלו אספלידא לא העלהו יותר מתרביצא ולא נתן לו קרקע יותר ובדין קאמר בדידי קא בנינא: א"ל וכי בשופטני עסקינן. כלומר וכי באנשים שוטים עסקינן דבלא עלוי קרקע נטל זה תרביצא תחת האספלידא והלא זה בנוי [אינן] בנוי ואיך אלו אהדדי ברמים: כשורי והודרי. ולא עלו אווירא ולא נתן לו קרקע יותר ובדין קאמר בדידי קא בנינא: ולימא ליה. בעל האספלידא מעיקרא אספלידא פלגת לי בתחילה אין לך אורה וזה לא האספלידא דאינו דאידרונא אי השתא אי בית אשיתא קא מאפלת עלי והוה לה אדרונא חשוכה: אמר רב שימי בר אשי שמא בעלמא פליג ליה. דהשתא נמי שם אספלידא קרי ליה אע"פ שאין בו שתים ואחת וכו'. מי לא תניא כו'. דדירינא ביה כדדרו ביה אבהתי. כלומר להכי איכוונא למיתב חלק אספלידא שאהי' דר כשדרו בו אבותי שהיה לה מאור גדול:

מסורת הש"ס

א) נ"א מצינן דאיטרחא, ב) פ"א דרבא, ג) לקמן לח:, ד) פ"א רבא, ה) [לקמן קנא: ע"ז לג: חולין נ.], ו) נ"א מצינן דאיטרחא, ז) [ער' מ"ש בב"ק פה. על הגליון, ח) ב"מ קד., ט) נ"ל נדי וער' רש"י, י) [אידרונא וכן בסמוך]

הגהות הב"ח

(א) גמ' א"ל אבנייה אנא ולא אמרת לית לי דוכתא כצ"ל ותיבת איסתריה נמחק: (ב) שם לא טרחנא לא קא מתדר לי א"ל שוף אכריסך ועול: (ג) שם אמר ר"ן כדדיירי כצ"ל ותיבת כי נמחק: (ד) שם לא תיבנא וציבי בעלמא כצ"ל ותיבת ובי נמחק: (ה) שם משוית לי אידרונא: (ו) רש"י ד"ה אבל וכו' יסתרוהו ויבנוהו: (ז) ד"ה סכרנא וכו' שיאירו לך בביתך: (ח) ד"ה והשתא אידרונא: (ט) ד"ה שמא בעלמא אספלידא שמה כצ"ל ותיבת אם נמחק: (י) ד"ה בית כור לפי חשבון. נ"ב עיין לקמן בפי' רשב"ם ריש פ' בית כור:

גליון הש"ס

גמ' היינו הך. ע' ריטב"א שבועות דף לו ע"א ד"ה תרתי למ"ל:

ליקוטי רש"י

רומו כחצי ארכו כו'. אכולהו קאי והיינו בית מתנות שהוא ארכו ד' על ו' [גי' ב"מ של רוחב ד'] רומו ה' דהיינו חצי ארכו וחצי רחבו בבית קטן שבע ושמנה בבית גדול ועשר בטרקלין [רשב"ם לקמן צח:]. בוקי סריקי. כדים ריקים כלומר דברים שאין טעם [ע"ז לז:] כדים רקים כלומר דברים ריקים [חולין נ.]. אשיתא. חומה [ב"מ פו.]. כווי. חלונות [עירובין ס.]. ציבי. עצים [שם סב:]. בשופטני. שוטים [ב"מ פב:]. לתך. חצי כור הוא שמונה עשר סאין [שבת קכז.]. חצי כור לפי חשבון סאתים כחצר המשכן שהוא כ"ט אמה ושליש על כ"ט אמה ושליש הוי בית סאה [ב"מ קד.]. אידרונא. קתבנ"א [מנחות לג:]. שמא בעלמא. כך היא נקראת [ב"מ קד.] [שייך לע"ב] מר ינוקא ומר קשישא. שני בניו היו לרב חסדא ושם שניהם שוין אלא שהגדול קורין לו מר קשישא ולצעיר קורין לו מר ינוקא [כתובות פה:]. האחין שחלקו. שניהם מוכרין זה לזה. אין להן לא דרך זה על זה. אם חלקו שני בתים אחד נטל חיצון ואחד נטל פנימי אין לפנימי יכול ליכנס לשדהו אלא דרך חיצון שהיה אביו נכנס בו לפנימי דרך על חיצון שהוא מוכר לו שיהא לו דרך לעצמו וכיון שמכר לו לאחיו חלקו שבחיצון בעין יפה מכר לו כל השדה והדרך ולא שייר לעצמו במכירה זו כלום והיינו שמואל לטעמיה דפסק לקמן בפרק המוכר את הבית (דף סד:) דמוכר בעין יפה מוכר דבר שלא בעין יפה מוכר דבר שאם אמר ליה למוכר דלאו לבר מן הדרך מכר לו כל הדרך אבל אין לו ליכנס בחיצון שום דבר וגם לכל אלה נלקח ובלבד שלא יהא לו גם על מה שהוא מוכר בשדה זה החיצון לא שייר לעצמו דרך שהרי היה לו להשאיר לעצמו ומה שהאחין שחלקו לא נתן לבנות חלון כנגד חלון של חבירו ויש מבחוץ קנין מילתא דסבר הלכה כן. (ורבא) [ורב] אמר יש להן. למוכר בעין רעה מוכר ומשייר לעצמו כמו כן דרך ודרך אם עשה לו לפנים וגם לפנים כלל. ולא חלונות. ולא חלונות. זה לא עשה כנגדם והלכה כשמואל. ויתר לו חזקה על הבית וכולי. [רשב"ם לקמן סה.] תברא. סוכר [ב"מ קג.]. בית שער. בית קטן לפני שער החצר [יומא יא.]. בית כניסה שער הבית והשוער שם שומר ספתח [סוטה מג.] שערי חצרות ויושב שם שומר ספתח [מנחות לג.]. ויהא כאנשי העיר. ליתן לצורכי העיר [סנהדרין קיב.]. פותחת. מפתח [ביצה לא.]. לספר. ער שמבדלת בין ארץ ישראל לגבול האומות [עירובין מה.]. לא צריכי נטירותא. מורה משמירתם כדכתיב (משלי ו) בשכבך תשמר עליך [ב"מ קח.]

חשק שלמה על רבינו גרשום

א) אולי צ"ל שוף בארץ וער' בתום' ד"ה שוף: ב) לפנינו הגי' אחורי כוי דאחבריה: ג) הלשון צריך תיקון ואולי צ"ל דלא היו מעמידין גפנותיהם ע"י חרישה:

blocked, for the compensation he paid does not entitle the mansion's owner to demand elimination of the wall.[28]

Rav Shimi cites a Baraisa to support his reasoning: מִי לֹא תַנְיָא – **Was it not taught in a Baraisa:** הָאוֹמֵר בֵּית כּוֹר עָפָר אֲנִי מוֹכֵר לְךָ – Regarding ONE WHO SAYS to another, "I AM SELLING TO YOU A *BEIS KOR*[29] OF LAND,"[30] אַף עַל פִּי שֶׁאֵינוֹ אֶלָּא לֶתֶךְ – EVEN THOUGH [THE TRACT] of land IS ONLY A *LESSECH*[31] in size, הִגִּיעוֹ – the buyer OBTAINS IT, i.e. the sale is valid, שֶׁלֹּא מָכַר לוֹ אֶלָּא שְׁמָא – FOR [THE SELLER] ONLY purported to SELL HIM a parcel of land whose NAME is a *"beis kor,"* even though it actually measures substantially less. וְהוּא דְּמִיתְקְרֵי בֵּית כּוֹר – AND [THE SALE] IS valid only IF [THE PARCEL OF LAND] IS, in fact, CALLED A *"BEIS KOR"* by the public?[32] – Thus, the Baraisa demonstrates that so long as an item is at least called publicly by the name by which it is sold, the sale is valid. Similarly, so long as a darkened mansion is known as a "mansion," the division of the estate is valid.

The Baraisa continues, applying its rationale to other cases: פַּרְדֵּס אֲנִי מוֹכֵר לְךָ – If one says, "I AM SELLING TO YOU this POMEGRANATE FIELD," אַף עַל פִּי שֶׁאֵין בּוֹ רִמּוֹנִים – EVEN THOUGH IT CONTAINS NO POMEGRANATE trees, הִגִּיעוֹ – the buyer OBTAINS IT, i.e. the sale is valid, שֶׁלֹּא מָכַר לוֹ אֶלָּא שְׁמָא – FOR HE ONLY purported to SELL HIM a parcel of land whose NAME is a "pomegranate field." וְהוּא דְּמִיתְקְרֵי פַּרְדֵּס – AND [THIS SALE] IS valid only IF [THE FIELD] IS CALLED A "POMEGRANATE FIELD" by the public. Similarly, with respect to a vineyard, כֶּרֶם אֲנִי מוֹכֵר לְךָ – if one says, "I AM SELLING TO YOU this VINEYARD," אַף עַל פִּי שֶׁאֵין בּוֹ גְּפָנִים – EVEN THOUGH [THE FIELD] CONTAINS NO GRAPEVINES, הִגִּיעוֹ – the buyer OBTAINS IT, שֶׁלֹּא מָכַר לוֹ אֶלָּא שְׁמָא – FOR HE ONLY purported to SELL HIM a field whose NAME is "vineyard." וְהוּא דְּמִיתְקְרֵי כַּרְמָא – AND [THIS SALE] IS valid only IF [THE FIELD] IS CALLED A "VINEYARD" by the public. This concludes the Baraisa, which teaches that items are legitimately sold "in name only." Thus, in Rav Chama's case, the owner of the garden may claim that his brother in fact received a "mansion," albeit in name only![33]

The Gemara distinguishes between the case of the inheritance and the cases of the Baraisa: מִי דָּמֵי – **Are** these cases **similar?** הָתָם מָצֵי אָמַר לֵיהּ מוֹכֵר לְלוֹקֵחַ – **There,** in the cases of the Baraisa, **the seller can say to the buyer,** שְׁמָא זַבֵּינִי לָךְ – **"I sold you** only **a name."** The buyer cannot affect what the seller intended to include in the sale. הָכָא מָצֵי אָמַר לֵיהּ – But **here,** in Rav Chama's case, the one who took the mansion **can say to [his brother],** אַדַּעְתָּא דְּהָכִי פְּלַגִי – "It was **with this intention** that I agreed to **divide** the estate as we did – namely, דְּדָאֵירְנָא בֵּיהּ כִּי הֵיכִי דְּדָרוּ אֲבָהָתָן – **that I would reside in [the mansion] in the manner that our forefathers resided** there." Here, the inheritor of the garden, who in effect is the "seller" of the mansion, cannot exclusively define the sale item, since the division of the estate was mutually conceived. Hence, the mansion's owner may claim that he is entitled to receive a mansion as usable as it was in his father's lifetime. This claim would entitle him to unobstructed light and empower him to have the wall dismantled, contrary to Rav Chama's ruling.

The Gemara concludes that Rav Chama does not honor the claim, "I wish to live in my portion as did my father": אָמְרוּ לֵיהּ –

NOTES

28. The garden owner can claim that compensation entitled his brother only to a "mansion," which the latter indeed received. A vineyard without working space, however, does not retain the name of a "vineyard," for it is unusable. Although a Baraisa cited below states that the sale of a "vineyard" without vines is valid, this is because allowance for adequate working space can be made when replanting the empty field.

29. Literally: house of a *kor*. A *beis kor* is the amount of land needed for planting a *kor* (approximately 120 or, according to other opinions, 67.5 gallons) of barley seeds (*Rashi* to *Kiddushin* 60b; see there, note 27, for the sources of the measurements of a *beis kor*). It measures 75,000 square *amos* and is thus thirty times the size of a *beis se'ah*, which is 2,500 square *amos*. The *beis kor* measurement is constant; it is not affected by the quality of the land (*Maharsha* to Gemara 102b).

30. Literally, earth. The significance of this word choice is discussed in the Gemara below (102b; see *Rashbam* and *Tosafos* ד״ה בית כור עפר).

31. A *lessech* is one-half of a *kor*.

32. *Rambam* (*Hil. Mechirah* 28:14) writes that the seller must bring witnesses to attest that the field was called *"beis kor"* by the public. *Rambam* thus implies that if witnesses so testify, the sale is valid even if the buyer is unaware of the common designation. *Tosafos* (ד״ה והוא), however, rule that unless the buyer actually knew that the seller possessed a field called a *"beis kor,"* the buyer may claim that he was misled, and the sale is void. This ruling applies even if the buyer saw at the time of the sale that the land did not measure a *beis kor*, since he can claim that he thought that other tracts would be conveyed to complete the stipulated amount.

33. One might think that – on the contrary – the Baraisa actually refutes Rav Chama's position, for it validates only the sale of a *previously empty* field. However, if after the sale the seller were to uproot existing vines and then claim that he sold a vineyard "in name only," presumably his actions would invalidate the sale. How, then, is the garden owner permitted to obstruct the mansion's light *after* the division of the estate? *Rashba* answers that the garden owner did not actively *remove* light from the mansion (which would constitute a direct act to the item of sale, analogous to uprooting vines). Rather, he merely *prevented* light from reaching the mansion through the airspace of his garden, so that any damage is only an incidental consequence of the separate act of building the wall. Hence, Rav Chama's ruling is consistent with the Baraisa (see also *Ritva*).

א"ל (א) איסתריה אנא ואבנייה אמר ליה לית לי דוכתא למידר בה א"ל אנא אוגר לך דוכתא א"ל לא ו) טרחנא (ב) לא קא מתדר לי שוף אכריסך ועול ושוף אכריסך ופוק אמר רב חמא א בדינא קא מעכב והני מילי דלא מטו כשורי למטה מעשרה ב אבל מטו כשורי למטה מעשרה מצי א"ל למטה מי' רשותא דידי הוא ולא משעבד לך וה"מ דלא אתנו גבי הדדי ג אבל אתנו גבי הדדי סתרי ובנו וכי אתנו בהדי הדדי עד כמה אמרו רבנן קמיה ד דרבה משמיה דמר זוטרא בריה דרב נחמן דאמר משמיה דר"נ כאותה ששנינו ז) רומו כחצי ארכו וכחצי רחבו אמר להו ח) רבה ט) לאו אמינא לכו לא תיתלו ביה בוקי סריקי ברב נחמן הכי אמר ר"נ (ג) כי דדיירי אינשי וכמה אמר רב הונא בריה דרב יהושע ד כי היכי דעיילי איסוריתא דמחוזא והדר ה ההוא גברא דהוה בני אשיתא אחורי כווי דחבריה אמר ליה קא מאפלת עלי א"ל סכרנא לך הכא ועבידנא לך כווי לעיל מאשיתאי א"ל קא מרעת ליה לאשיתאי א"ל סתרנא לך לאשיתך עד דוכתא דכווי ובנינא לה ועבידנא לך כווי בבנינא לעיל מאשיתאי א"ל אשיתא מתתאה עתיקא ומלעיל חדתא לא קיימא אמר ליה סתרנא לה עד לארעא ובנינא לה ועבידנא לך כווי בגוה א"ל חדא אשיתא חדתא בבוליה ביתא עתיקא לא קיימא א"ל סתרנא לה לכוליה ביתא ובנינא לך כווי בבנינא א"ל לית לי דוכתא למידר בה א"ל אגירנא לך דוכתא א"ל לא י) טרחנא אמר רב חמא ו בדין קא מעכב ס) היינו הך והא תו למה לי הא קמ"ל דאע"ג דלא משתמש י) אלא תיבנא (ד) וכי ציבי בעלמא ח ההנהו בי תרי אחי דפלגי בהדי הדדי חד מטייה אספלידא וחד מטייה תרביצא אזל ההוא דמטייה תרביצא וקא בני אשיתא אפומא דאספלידא א"ל קא מאפלת עלי א"ל בדידי קא בנינא אמר רב חמא ט בדין קאמר ליה א"ל רבינא לרב אשי מאי שנא מהא דתניא י שני אחין שחלקו אחד מהן נטל שדה כרם ואחד מהן נטל שדה לבן יש לו לבעל הכרם ד' אמות בשדה לבן שעל מנת כן חלקו א"ל התם דעלו להדדי אבל הכא מאי דלא עלו להדדי י) וכי בשופטני עסקינן דהאי שקיל אספלידא והאי שקיל תרביצא ולא עלו להדדי א"ל כ נהי דעלו להדדי דמי ליבני כשורי והודרי דמי אוירא לא עלו להדדי ולימא ליה מעיקרא אספלידא פלגת לי השתא משוית לי (ה) אידרונא אמר רב שימי בר אשי שמא בעלמא פלג ליה מי לא תניא מ) ל האומר בית כור עפר אני מוכר לך אע"פ שאינו אלא לתך הגיעו שלא מכר לו אלא שמא והוא דמיתקרי בית כור מ פרדס אני מוכר לך אע"פ שאין בו רמונים הגיעו שלא מכר לו אלא שמא והוא דמיתקרי פרדס נ כרם אני מוכר לך אע"פ שאין בו גפנים הגיעו שלא מכר לו אלא שמא והוא דמיתקרי כרמא מי דמי התם מצי אמר ליה מוכר ללוקח שמא זביני לך הכא מצי א"ל אדעתא דהכי פלגי דדאירנא ביה כי היכי דדרו אבהתן אמרו ליה

רש"י

שוף אכריסך. שחה קומתך עד כריסך: כשורי. קורות העלייה: אבל אתנו אהדדי. כשחלקו אם תשפל עלייה (ו) יסתרוהו הבית ויבנוהו: עד כמה. תשפיל העלייה ויכוף את העליון לסתור ולבנות: כאותה ששנינו. בהמוכר פירות המקבל עליו מחבירו לבנות לו בית עושה רומו כחצי ארכו וחצי רחבו כבנין ההיכל שהיה ארכו ארבעים ורחבו עשרים וגבהו שלשים: איסוריתא. חבילות קנים ארוכין: והדר. מחזיר עלמו לכל לצדדין: סכרנא לך הכא. אסתום לך חלונותיך באבנים וטיט ואפתח לך למעלה מכותלי בגובה כתליך חלונות אחרים שיאירו (ז) בביתך: קמרעת לאשיתאי. כשתפתח בה חלונות תנוע החומה מחמת המכה: סתרנא לך. הכותל מראש גובהו עד שיגיע למקום החלונות שאעשה לך: לא קיימא. שאין טיט החדש נדבק יפה בטיט הישן שיבש כבר: דאע"ג דקא משתמש בה צביבי ותיבני. ואין הוא עלמו דר בתוכו מלי א"ל לא מלינא לאטרחה להוליך העצים והתבן: אספלידא. טרקלין יפה: תרביצא. גינה שבלד הטרקלין שהיתה מאירה לתוכו: בדנפשאי אנא בנינא. בשלי אני בונה ואתה אין לך עלי חזקת אורה של שלש שנים להשתא הוא דפלגינהו: ד' אמות לעבודת הכרם. שהיו חורשין אותה בשוורים: דעלו אהדדי. שנתן בעל הכרם לבעל השדה לבן דמים של עילוי הכרם הילכך כרם בעי למשקל עם עבודתו: בשופטני עסקינן. וכי שוטה היה שנטל גינה חלקה כנגד בית בנוי ולא נטל עילוי דמים: והשתא (ח) אידרונא. חדר אפל ואני על מנת אספלידא נתתי עילוי דמים: שמא בעלמא. (ט) אם אספלידא שמא ואע"פ שאינו כשאר אספלידא לא בטיל שמו: בית כור. לפי חשבון (י) סאתים כחצר המשכן:

תוספות

שוף אכריסך. פ"ה שחה קומתך ולר"י נראה שוף לשון שפשוף שמתחכך בגופך: בוקי סריקי. אנשים רקים מתרגמינן גוברין סריקין (שופטים יא): היינו הך. וא"ת והא אשמעינן בהאי עובדא דחדתא אעתיקא לא קאי דלא שמעינן מההיא דלעיל ולעיל איצטריך כדאמרינן וה"מ דלא מטו כשורי למטה מי' וכו' וי"ל דמילתא דפשיטא היא דחדא חדתא וכולה עתיקא לא קאי ומשום הא לא הוה צריך לאתויי האי עובדא: אספלידא. פרש"י טרקלין יפה ובערוך פירש מערה כדמתרגם (תהלים נז) מפני שאול במערה באספלידא ואור"י דאספלידא דהכא א"א להיות מערה מדקאמר ט) נמי דעלו להדדי בכשורי והודרי ובמערה ליכא כשורי והודרי ועוד מדקאמר מעיקרא אספלידא והשתא י) אידרונא ובמערה ליכא אורה כלל ומפרש ר"י דאספלידא דהכא הוי אכסדרה שיש בה אורה גדולה שפרוצה ברוח אחד כדאמרינן בלא יחפור (לקמן דף כה.) עולם דומה לאכסדרה וכו' וכן מוכח בהקומץ רבה (מנחות דף לג: ושם ד"ה אספלידא) דאמר אביי חזינא להו לאספלידי דבי מר דאית להו פלימי ולית להו מזוזה ופריך מיתיבי בית שער ואכסדרה ומרפסת חייבין במזוזה: א"ל בדידי קבנינא. פ"ה אתה אין לך עלי חזקת אורה של שלש שנים ותימה שהיה יכול להאפילו עליו שלא יהא לו בטרקלין אורה כלל ועוד דמאי קאמר באוירא לא עלו אהדדי פשיטא דעלו נמי באוירא דבית בלא אורה אינו שוה כלום ומפרש ר"ת שמאספלידא היה יכול לראות לשדותיו דרך התרביצא ודקאמר מאפלת עילוי היינו שהיה מעכבו שלא היה יכול לראות שדותיו וקרי לה נמי אידרונא שלא היה יכול להביט למרחוק וכן מפרש ההוא דלקמן אין להם חלונות זה על זה ומיהו קשיא לר"י דמאי קפריך מאי שנא מהא דתניא כו' התם ודאי יש לו ד' אמות לפי שהם צורך לעבודת הכרם אבל הכא זה לא היה צורך האספלידא מש"ה בדין קאמר ליה ונראה לר"י דודאי היה מאפיל עליו האורה שלא היה בו אורה גדולה כאשר צריך לאכסדרה אבל עדיין היה בו אור גדול והא דאמר ומכנגדן מרחיק ד' אמות שלא יאפיל היינו שלא יאפיל לגמרי עד שלא יהא ראוי להשתמש בו יפה ומש"ה קרי ליה אידרונא משום דלגבי אכסדרה אידרונא היא והשתא נמי אתי שפיר דלא עלו להדדי באוירא שהוא צורך האכסדרה: והוא דקרו ליה בית כור. וכגון שהלוקח יודע שיש לו קרקע שקרוי בית כור דאל"כ הרי הטעהו ואפי' אם רואה בשעת מכירה שאין שם בית כור יכול לומר סבור הייתי שהיית משלים לי בית כור ואם תאמר וניחא דדמים מודיעים ואם נתן לו דמי בית כור אפילו קרו ליה בית כור ישלים לו בית כור שלם ויש לומר דמיירי כגון דאזיל גביה ואינו נותן לו אפילו דמי לתך ואי קרו ליה בית כור אפילו אין בו אלא לתך הגיעו ואי לא קרו ליה בית כור חייב לתת לו בית כור שלם אי נמי דלא אזיל גביה וכגון דנתן לו דמי לתך והשתא אי לא קרו ליה בית כור היה יכול לומר לוקח אם תרצה לתת לי בית כור שלם ולעמוד במקחך עמוד ואם לאו תחזור לי מעותי אבל אי קרו ליה בית כור הגיעו אע"פ שאין בו אלא לתך:

מר

רבינו גרשום

לא מצינא דאטרח (לבנות) [לפנות] ביתי: שוף אכריסך עול. כלומר הואיל וגרום מולך א) חפור בארץ וכפוף בטנך וצא והכנס. דינא קאמר ליה דבתוך שלו יבנה: לא אמרן דדינא קאמר ליה אלא דלא מטו כשורי. שלא ירדה העליה למטה מי' אז יכול לטעון לו דור בדוחק בתוך עשרה: [דלא] אתנו בהדי הדדי. שלא התנו זה לזה לבנות אחר נפילה: עד כמה. גבוה יכול לכופו שיסייע לו: כאותה ששנינו. בפ' המוכר: רומו כחצי ארכו וכחצי רחבו. שאם היה הבית כ' אמה באורך ורוחב י' אמה עושה גבוה חצי כ' וחצי י' שהם ט"ו אמה וראיה לדבר מהיכל: לא תיתלו בוקי סריקי. כלומר לא תאמינו בדברים רקים הללו מעולם לא אמרן ר' נחמן שיבנהו גבוה כזה: שיעור אסוריתא דמחוזא כדי שיהא יכול לישא משאוי על גבו כמשאוי של אנשי מחוזא ויכול לחזור בריוח בהכי מצי לכופו טפי לא: אשיתא ב) אגב כוי דחבריה. שהיה בונה כותלו כנגד חלון חבירו שהיה לו חזקה לחלון והרחיק ד' אמות: מרעת אשיתאי. שתחתור בו חלונות אחרות: סתרנא לך. עד חלונות אלו ובנינא לך מחדש: דינא אמר ליה. דלא מצי למיטרח לפנות ביתו: היינו הך. דקאמר רב חמא בהני בי תרי וכו' והא תו למה לי: הא איצטריך למיתני. שאפי' אלו חלונות שיש לו בהן חזקה: בי תבני וציבי. שאין צריך בהן לאורה כל כך אפ"ה לא מצי לכופו לפנות: אספלידא. חדר שלועדין קמארא: תרביצא. גינה שסמוך לה: אפומא דאספלידא. לפני הפתח: אחד של שדה לבן. שדה תבואה: יש לו לבעל הכרם ד' אמות בשדה לבן. כמלא צמד בקר וכליו כדי לחרוש גפניו העומדין על המיצר ששם היו ג) עומדים גפנותיהם בחרישה: שעל מנת כן חלקו השדות. והכי נמי לא יבנה כותלו לאספלידא שלו כדי שלא לאפיל עליו: א"ל התם. מש"ה יש לו לבעל הכרם ד' אמות בשדה לבן משום דעלו להדדי שמעלה זה בעל הכרם לבעל שדה משדה לבן יותר מחלק שדה כרם כדי שיהא לו ד' אמות אבל הכא בני אספלידא לא העלהו יותר בתרביצא ומש"ה מצי למימר ליה בדידי קבנינא: א"ל וכי בשופטני עסקינן. דהאי כלומר וכי באנשים שוטים עסקינן דבלא עלוי קרקע נטל זה תרביצא תחת האספלידא והלא זה בנוי וזה [אינו בנוי] עלו אהדדי בדמים: כשורי והודרי. ולא עלו באוירא ולא נתן לו בקרקע יותר ובדין קאמר בדידי קא בנינא: ולימא ליה. בעל האספלידא עד האידנא הויא לה אספלידא דהויא לה נהורא מעליא אבל השתא אי בנית אשיתא קא מאפלת עלי והוה לי אדרונא דחשיכה טפי ובהא טענה מצי מעכב עלויה: אמר רב שימי בר אשי שמא בעלמא פליג ליה. דהשתא נמי שם אספלידא קרי ליה אע"ג דמאפלא: מי לא תניא כו'. אע"פ שאין שם גפנים שתים כנגד שתים ואחת יוצא זנב (אילנות): דדיירנא ביה אבהתי. כלומר להכי איכוונא למיתב חלק אספלידא שאהי' דר כשדרו בה אבותי שהיה לה מאור גדול:

חשק שלמה על רבינו גרשום א) [אולי צ"ל שוף באוך ועי' בתוס' ד"ה שוף]: ב) [לפנינו הגי' אחורי כוי דחבריה]: ג) [הלשון צריך תיקון ואולי דצ"ל דאז היו מעמידין גפנותיהם ע"י חרישה]:

מסורת הש"ס

א) נ"א מצינא דאיטרח, ב) מ"א דרבא, ג) לקמן ג:, ד) מ"א רבא, ה) [לקמן קנא. עי' תוס' לו: חולין נ.], ו) נ"א מצינא דאיטרח, ז) [עי' מ"ש בב"ק פה. על הגליון], ח) ב"מ קז., ט) נ"א נהי ועי' רש"ש, י) [אידרונא וכן בסמוך].

הגהות הב"ח

(א) גמ' א"ל אבנייה אנא אמר ליה לית לי דוכתא כל"ל ותיבת איסתריה נמחק: (ב) שם לא טרחנא לא קא מתדר לי א"ל שוף אכריסך ועול: (ג) שם אמר ר"נ כדדיירי כל"ל ותיבת כי נמחק: (ד) שם אלא תיבנא וציבי בעלמא כל"ל ותיבת וכי נמחק: (ה) שם משוית לי אידרונא: (ו) רש"י ד"ה אבל וכו' יסתרו הבית: (ז) ד"ה סכרנא וכו' שיאירו לך בביתך: (ח) ד"ה והשתא אידרונא: (ט) ד"ה שמא בעלמא אספלידא שמא כל"ל ותיבת אם נמחק: (י) ד"ה בית כור לפי חשבון. נ"ב עיין לקמן בפי' רשב"ם ריש פ' בית כור:

גליון הש"ס

גמ' היינו הך. עי' ריטב"א שבועות דף לו ע"א ד"ה תרתי למ"ל:

ליקוטי רש"י

רומו כחצי ארכו כו'. אכולהו קאי והיינו בית מתנות שהוא ארכו ד' על ו' [גב' ב"ב שש על רוחב ד'] רומו ה' דהיינו חצי ארכו וחצי רחבו בבית קטן שבע ושמנה בבית גדול ועשר בטרקלין [רשב"ם לקמן צח:]. בוקי סריקי. כדים ריקים כלומר דברים שאין טעם [ע"ז לו:]. כדים רקים כלומר דברים שאין [חולין ג.]. אשיתא. חומה [ב"מ פו.]. כווי. חלונות [עירובין ס.]. ציבי. עצים [שם פב]. בשופטני. שוטים [בב"מ מ.]. לתך. חצי כור ט"ו סאה [שבת קכז.]. חצי כור לפי חשבון סאתים כחצר המשכן חמשים על חמשים הוי בית סאה [ב"מ קד.]. אידרונא. קמנב"א [מנחות לג:]. שמא בעלמא. כך הוא נקראת [ב"מ קד.]. [שייך לע"ב] מר ינוקא ומר קשישא. שני בניו היו לרב חסדא ושם שניהם שוין אלא שהגדול קורין לו מר קשישא ולצעיר קורין לו מר ינוקא [כתובות פה:]. האחין שחלקו. שניהם מוכרין זה לזה. אין להן לא דרך זה על זה. אם חלקו שני שדות אחד נטל חילון ואחד נטל פנימי ואין הפנימי יכול ליכנס לשדהו אלא דרך חילון דכיון דכך שהיה אביו נכנס אף הוא יכנס לפנימי דרך על חילון משום דמוכר עין יפה מוכר ולא שייר לעצמו וכיון שמכר לו לאחיו חלקו שבחילון בעין יפה מכר לו כל השדה והדרך ולא שייר לעצמו במכירה זו כלום והיינו שמואל לטעמיה דפסק כר' עקיבא דמוכר בעין יפה מוכר דלגבי פנימי שייך למימר עין יפה דאע"פ שצריך לפרוע באויר לא שייר לעצמו כלל אבל גבי חילון לא שייך עין רעה במה שאינו נותן לו את הדרך שהרי אינו מוכר בשדה זו החילון אלא לוקח ובלוקח לא שייך עין יפה אבל בשדה הפנימי הוי הוא מוכר שמכר לאחיו חלקו וההוא שמכר לא שייר לעצמו גביה כלל. ולא חלונות כו'. ואם רצה לבנות בחצירו כנגד חלון אחיו בונה. קבועות. כלומר שהלכה כן. (ורבא) [ורב] אמר יש להן. דמוכר בעין רעה מוכר ומשייר לעצמו במה שמכר לאחיו דבר הצריך לו כגון דרך ואורה [רשב"ם לקמן סה.]. תברא. שובר [ב"מ קג.]. בית שער. בית קטן לפני שער החצר [יומא יא:]. בית כניסת השער ששם שומר הפתח [סוטה מג.]. שערי חצירות ויושב שם שומר הפתח [מנחות לג:]. ויהא כאנשי העיר. ליתן בצורכי העיר [סנהדרין קיב.]. פותחת. מפתח [ביצה לא.]. לספר. עיר שמבדלת בין גבול ישראל לגבול האומות [עירובין מה:]. לא צריכי נטירותא. תורתו משמרתו כדכתיב (משלי ו) בשכבך תשמור עליך [ב"מ קח.].

עין משפט נר מצוה

מב א ב ג ד ה מיי' פ"ד מהל' שכנים הל' ו ז סמג עשין פב טוש"ע ח"מ סי' קנד סעיף ב ועיין בהג"ה:
מג ה ו מיי' שם פ"ז הלכה ח סמג עשין פב טוש"ע ח"מ סי' קנד סעיף יג:
מד ז טוש"ע שם וסימן קסד סעיף ג:
מה ח ט מיי' שם הל' י סמג שם טוש"ע שם סי' קנד סעיף ד:
מו י מיי' פ"ל מהל' מכירה הל' י סמג שם טוש"ע ח"מ סי' קיט סעיף ד:
מז כ מיי' פ"ו מהלכות שכנים הל' י סמג עשין פב טוש"ע ח"מ סי' קנד סעיף ט:
מח ל מיי' פכ"ח מהל' מכירה הל' יד סמג עשין פב טוש"ע ח"מ סי' ריח סעיף ח:
מט מ נ מיי' שם הל' יד טוש"ע שם סעיף יח:

מר ינוקא ומר קשישא בריה דרב חסדא לרב אשי נהרדעי לטעמייהו (א) דאמר ר"נ אמר שמואל א האחין שחלקו אין להן לא דרך זה על זה ולא חלונות זה על זה ולא סולמות זה על זה ולא אמת המים זה על זה והזהרו בהן שהלכות קבועות הן (א) ורבא אמר יש להן: ההוא שטרא דיתמי דנפיק עליה תברא אמר רב חמא ב אגבויי לא מגבינן ליה ומיקרע לא קרעינן ליה אגבויי לא מגבינן ליה דנפק תברא עליה מיקרע לא קרעינן ליה דכי גדלי יתמי דילמא מייתו ראיה ומרעי ליה אמר ליה רב אחא בריה דרבא לרבינא הלכתא מאי א"ל בכולהו הלכתא כרב חמא לבר מתברא דסהדי בשקרי לא מחזקינן מר זוטרא בריה דרב מרי אמר ג בהא נמי הלכתא כרב חמא דאם איתא דתברא מעליא הוא איבעי ליה לאפוקי בחיי אבוהון ומדלא אפקיה שמע מינה זויפי זייפיה: מתני' ד כופין אותו לבנות בית שער ודלת לחצר רבן שמעון בן גמליאל אומר לא כל החצרות ראויות לבית שער ה כופין אותו לבנות לעיר חומה ודלתים ובריח רשב"ג אומר לא כל העיירות ראויות לחומה ו כמה יהא בעיר ויהא כאנשי העיר י"ב חדש ז קנה בה בית דירה הרי הוא כאנשי העיר מיד: גמ' למימרא דבית שער מעליותא היא והא ההוא חסידא דהוה רגיל אליהו דהוה משתעי בהדיה עבד בית שער ותו לא משתעי בהדיה לא קשיא הא מגואי הא (ב) מבראי ואי בעית אימא הא והא מבראי ולא קשיא הא דאית ליה דלת הא דלית ליה דלת ואבע"א הא והא דאית ליה דלת ולא קשיא הא דאית ליה פותחת הא דלית ליה פותחת אי בעית אימא הא והא דאית ליה פותחת ולא קשיא הא דפותחת דידיה מגואי הא דפותחת דידיה (ג) מבראי: כופין אותו לבנות בית שער ודלת לחצר: תניא רבן שמעון בן גמליאל אומר לא כל חצרות ראויות לבית שער אלא חצר הסמוכה לרשות הרבים ראויה לבית שער ושאינה סמוכה לרשות הרבים אינה ראויה לבית שער ורבנן זימנין דדחקי בני רשות הרבים ועיילו ואתו: כופין אותו לבנות לעיר כו': (ת"ר כופין אותו לעשות לעיר דלתים ובריח) ורבן שמעון בן גמליאל אומר לא כל העיירות ראויות לחומה אלא עיר הסמוכה לספר ראויה לחומה ושאינה סמוכה לספר אינה ראויה לחומה ורבנן זימנין דמקרו ואתי גייסא בעא מיניה רבי אלעזר מרבי יוחנן כשהן גובין לפי נפשות גובין או דילמא לפי שבח ממון גובין אמר ליה לפי ממון גובין ואלעזר בני קבע בה מסמרות איכא דאמרי בעא מיניה רבי אלעזר מרבי יוחנן כשהן גובין לפי קירוב בתים הן גובין או דילמא לפי ט ממון גובין אמר ליה ח לפי קירוב בתים הן גובין ואלעזר בני קבע בה מסמרות רבי יהודה נשיאה רמא דשורא אדרבנן אמר (ד) ריש לקיש ט רבנן לא צריכי נטירותא דכתיב א אספרם מחול ירבון לצדיקים למאן אילימא לצדיקים דנפישי מחלא השתא כולהו ישראל כתיב בהו ב כחול אשר על שפת הים צדיקים עצמם מחול ירבון אלא הכי קאמר אספרם למעשיהם של צדיקים מחול ירבון וק"ו ומה חול שמועט מגין על הים מעשיהם של צדיקים שהם מרובים לא כל שכן שמגינים עליהם כי אתא לקמיה דרבי יוחנן אמר ליה מאי טעמא לא תימא ליה מהא ג אני חומה ושדי כמגדלות

רש"י

נהרדעי לטעמייהו. רב חמא דמן נהרדעא הוא דלא ס"ל הא דאמור בה כללו אבהתי ולהכי לא חילקו אזיל לטעמייהו דנהרדעי דאמר שמואל דהוא מנהרדעא: האחין שחלקו. ונטל זה שדה לצפון וזה לדרום והיה אביו רגיל להיות לו ליכנס דרך זו לתוך זו אין יכול לומר דרך לי עליך: ולא חלונות. לערער על סתימת אורו: ולא סולמות. אם נטל זה בית ואחר זה נטל עלייה אין לו לקבוע סולם בחלקו של זה לעלות לעלייתו: ולא אמת המים. להביאה מן הנהר דרך שדהו של זה לתוך שלו: תברא. שובר שהוא פרוע לאביהם: ומרעי ליה. לשובר שהן עדי שקר: מתני' כופין אותו. את בן החצר שאינו רוצה לסייע את בני החצר לבנות להן בית שער להיות שומר הפתח יושב שם בצלו ומרחיק את בני רשות הרבים מלהסתכל בחצר: ודלת. לשער החצר לנועלו: לא כל החצרות ראויות לבית שער. בגמ' מפרש אזו היא הראויה: ויהא כאנשי העיר. לשאת עמהם בעול: גמ' ולא אישתעי בהדיה. לפי שמפסיק בעניים הצועקין ואין קולם נשמע: מגואי. לחצר גריעותא הוא לפי שדלת החצר נעול והעני צועק ובית שער שבפנים מפסיק הקול: מבראי. אינו מפסיק בפניו שהרי נכנס לתוכו וכשאין לו דלת עסקינן: פותחת דידיה מאבראי. העני פותחו ונכנס. פותחת שירודי"ר בלע"ז והוא של עץ ותמיד המפתח בתוכו: שאינה סמוכה. שמסובה להלן מרשות הרבים: כשהם גובים. לחומת העיר: קבע בה מסמרות. הזהר לדון כן ולא תזוז ממנה: קירוב בתים. בית הקרוב לחומה צריך לחומת העיר יותר מן הרחוק: רמא דשורא אדרבנן. הטיל יציאת חומת העיר על החכמים כמו על שאר בני אדם: חול. שהוא מועט ממעשיהם של צדיקים: מגין על הים. והוא לו לחומה כדכתיב אשר שמתי חול גבול לים (ירמיה ה): אלו

תוספות

מר ינוקא. הוא הגדול ועל שם שנולד בינקותו של רב חסדא קרי ליה מר ינוקא ומר קשישא הוא הצעיר ונולד בקשישותו של רב חסדא (ועיין רש"י כתובות סט: ד"ה מר): נהרדעי לטעמייהו. רב חמא נהרדעי הוא כדאמרינן בפרק קמא דסנהדרין (דף יז:) [אמוראי] דנהרדעי רב חמא ושמואל נמי נהרדעי הוא כדאמר שמואל (ברכות דף נח:) נהירין לי שבילי דרקיע כשבילי דנהרדעי: אין להם דרך זה על זה. טעמא משום דספיק שמואל בפרק המוכר את הבית (לקמן דף סה.) כר"ע דאמר מוכר בעין יפה מוכר ולפיכך אין להם דרך זה על זה שלא שייר לעצמו כלום כל אחד (ה) חלק בחלק חבירו אלא לו כמוכר ואף על גב דאמרינן המוכר בית ושייר אחר מכר לו עם הדרך למ"ד מוכר בעין יפה מוכר לא דמי דהכא כולם מוכרין וכל אחד מכר ולא שייר לעצמו כלום בחלק חבירו וה"ל כמוכר אחר ושייר בית דצריך ליקח לו דרך מבעל השדה: ולא סולמות זה על זה. פי' בקונט' אם נטל זה בית ואחר זה נטל עלייה אין לו לקבוע סולם בחלקו של זה לעלות לעלייתו וקשה לר"י דהיינו דרך ונראה לר"י כגון שלקח זה בית וזה עלייה וחלק אין לו לסמוך הסולם בכותל של זה ולעלות בעלייתו: ואי בעית אימא הא והא מבראי. ולא גרסינן הא והא מגואי דמגואי אין שייך לחלק בין אית ליה דלת ללית ליה ובין אית ליה פותחת ללית ליה דבכל ענין הוא רע כיון שאין יכול לבא אלא עד פתח החצר ואין לפרש הא דאית ליה דלת כו' אחצר קאי דהא במתני' בהדיא קתני כופין אותו לבנות דלת לחצר ולמאי דגרסי' מבראי קצת קשה דלא הוי כשאר שינויי דנקט לב דלא מעלי הא והא דאית ליה דלת והא והא דאית ליה פותחת והכא נקיט ההוא דמעלי: לפי שבח ממון הן גובין. כיון דאין (ו) סכנת נפשות לא אזלינן אלא בתר ממון והכי נמי אמר בהגוזל בתרא (ב"ק דף קטז:) שיירא ההולכת במדבר ועמד עליה גייס מחשבין לפי ממון דליכא סכנת נפשות כיון דאין הגייס בא רק בשביל ממון ואף על גב דאמר בפ' בן סורר (סנהדרין דף עב.) דהבא במחתרת נידון על שם סופו ומפרש רבא טעמא בגמ' משום חזקה דאין אדם מעמיד עצמו על ממונו כו' ואפי' הכי אין מחשבין אלא לפי ממון כיון דהגייס ברצונו אינו בא על הנפשות דאם לא יעמדו נגדם לא יזיק לגופם הילכך לא חשיב סכנת נפשות לפיכך אם יעמדו עליהם לסטים ונתפשרו עמהם גובין לפי ממון אבל היכי (ז) דטעו במדבר אמר התם דמחשבין אף לפי הנפשות משום כיון דטעו איכא סכנת נפשות: לפי קירוב בתים הן גובין. פירש ר"ת ונותנין עניים קרובים יותר מרחוקים וכן עשירים קרובים יותר מעשירים רחוקים אבל עשירים רחוקים נותנין יותר מעניים קרובים דלפי שבח ממון נמי הן גובין: אילימא לצדיקים כו'. דבהכי מיירי קרא דלעיל מיניה כתיב ולי מה יקרו רעיך אל מה עצמו ראשיהם וכתיב בתריה אספרם מחול ירבון:

עין משפט נר מצוה

נ א מיי' פ"ג מהלכות שכנים הל' יב סמג עשין פב טוש"ע ח"מ סי' קעג סעיף ג:

נא ב ג מיי' פי"ז מהל' מלוה הל' ח סמג עשין צד טוש"ע ח"מ סי' קח סעיף טז:

נב ד מיי' פ"ה מהל' שכנים הל' א סמג עשין פב טוש"ע ח"מ סי' קסא סעיף א:

נג ה מיי' שם פ"ו הל' א סמג שם טוש"ע ח"מ סי' קסג סעיף א:

נד ו ז מיי' שם הל' ה טוש"ע שם סעיף ב:

נה ח מיי' שם הל' ד טוש"ע שם סעיף ג:

נו ט מיי' שם הלכה ו טוש"ע שם סעיף ד וטוש"ע י"ד סי' רמג סעיף ב:

רבינו גרשום

נהרדעי לטעמייהו. דרב נחמן ושמואל ורב חמא מנהרדעי: האחין שחלקו אין להם דרך זה על זה. כגון בתחלה היו כל השדות בחיזוק א' של אביהם ולא הוה בכולהו אלא דרך אחד לילך מזה לזה והשתא כשחלקו אין להם דרך אם לא יקנו זה מזה וחלונות. שאם הגיע חצר לזה ולזה בית והיו חלונות הבית פתוחים לחצר יכול זה לבנות כנגדן ולסותמן וכן לאמת המים צריך ליקח דרך זה מזה. כה"נ יכול בעל תרביצא לבנות אשיתא נגד אספלידא: שהלכות קבועות הן. לדון הכי: דנפיק עליה תברא. דפריע השטר של יתומין: דגדלי יתמי. (למייתי) [דלמא מייתו] ראיה דהאי תברא מזויף הוא שהוחזק בפני עדים לאחר מיתת אביהן שעדיין היה חייב לו: לבר מהא. דודאי קרעי' לשטר. דסהדי דחתימי על שובר בשקרי לא מחזקינן: א) לעולם לא קרעי' לשטרא כדרב חמא. דאם כן הוה מפיק ליה האי שובר בחיי האב מדלית עדים דאפקה בחיי האב משום הכי לא קרעי' לשטרא: בית שער. ג) מקום שהשומר ישן שמשומר החצר כופין לא' מבני חצר המעכב: מעליותא הוא. בית שער: ולא אשתעי אליהו בהדיה. משום דכי אתי עני צועק על פתח שער מפסיק אותו בית שער קולו ואינו נשמע לבעל הבית: הא מגואי. גריעותא הוא. כלומר אם נעשה בנין בית שער מבפנים לחצר מפסיק הקול שאין העני יכול ליכנס לתוכו אבל אם בנו מאבראי ברה"ר והיו כופין אותו לבנות הואיל והחצר פתוח לרה"ר יכול העני ליכנס בתוך מחיצות בית שער עד השער וצועק ושומעין דאין מפסיק אלא שער לחודיה: אית ליה דלת. לבית שער גריעותא. שהשער והדלת מעכבין קולו. אית ליה פותחת. מנעול לאו מעליותא היא שאין העני יכול לפותחו מפני המנעול. הא דמשנתנו דכופין לבנות בית שער דלית ליה פותחת לבית שער. ואי קשיא הא דתנא כופין לבנות בית שער ודלת הא תני דלת [לחצר] במתני' ולחצר תנן לא לבית השער: חצר הסמוכה לרה"ר. צריכה בית שער. כלומר [illegible]

מסורת הש"ס

א) [לקמן סה.], ב) [לעיל ז:], ג) [סנהדרין קיב.], ד) רש"ל מ"ז וצ"ל תניא רשב"ג כו', ה) [שבח ממון וכן הוא ברא"ש], ו) [לקמן ח. ב"מ קח.], ז) [פסחים פז.]:

הגהות הב"ח

(א) גמ' ורבא אמר יש להן: (ב) שם הא מאבראי וכו' הא והא מאבראי: (ג) שם דפותחת דידיה מאבראי רשב"ג אומר וכו' תניא רשב"ג אומר לא כל כצ"ל ופיסקא כופין אותו לבנות בית שער ודלת לחצר נמחק: (ד) שם אמר ליה ר"ל רבנן: (ה) תוס' ד"ה אין להם וכו' כל אחד בחלק חבירו כצ"ל ותיבת חלק נמחק: (ו) ד"ה לפי כו' דאין בה סכנת: (ז) באו"ד אבל היכא דטעו במדבר וכו' כיון דטעו איכא:

תורה אור השלם

א) אֶסְפְּרֵם מֵחוֹל יִרְבּוּן הֱקִיצֹתִי וְעוֹדִי עִמָּךְ: [תהלים קלט, יח]

ב) כִּי בָרֵךְ אֲבָרֶכְךָ וְהַרְבָּה אַרְבֶּה אֶת זַרְעֲךָ כְּכוֹכְבֵי הַשָּׁמַיִם וְכַחוֹל אֲשֶׁר עַל שְׂפַת הַיָּם וְיִרַשׁ זַרְעֲךָ אֵת שַׁעַר אֹיְבָיו: [בראשית כב, יז]

ג) אֲנִי חוֹמָה וְשָׁדַי כַּמִּגְדָּלוֹת אָז הָיִיתִי בְעֵינָיו כְּמוֹצְאֵת שָׁלוֹם: [שיר השירים ח, י]

לעזי רש"י

שירודו"ר. פירוש פותחת, מנעול (רש"י עירובין דף קא ע"ב ד"ה למקומו):

ליקוטי רש"י

[מה ששייך לכאן נדפס בע"א. מכאן שייך לדף ח.] אלו ת"ח. המגינין אחרים כחומות הללו. כמגדלות. שמגינים על הדור [פסחים פז.]. אני חומה. חזקה באהבת דודי. ושדי כמגדלות. אלו בתי כנסיות ובתי מדרשות המניקים את ישראל בדברי תורה [שיר השירים ח, י]. כרגא. כסף גולגלתא שהיו כל היהודים כל אחד נותן כסף גולגלתו למלך [ב"מ עג:]. אפילו בשעה שאתה מחבב עמים וכו'. אף בשעת חבתן של אומות העולם שהראית להם פנים שוחקות ומסרת את ישראל בידם. כל קדושיו יהיו בידך. כל צדיקים וטוביהם דבקו בך ולא משו מאחריך ואתה שומרם. והם תכו לרגלך. והם מתמצעים ומתכנסים לתחת צלך. ישא מדברותיך. מקבלין גזירותיך ודתותיך בשמחה [דברים לג, ג]. מנדה בלו והלך. מיני מסים הם וכסף גולגלות [עזרא ד, יג]. מנת המלך. ארנונא שהיו נותנין מתבואותיהן ומבהמותיהן [ע"ז עא.]. והלך זו ארנונא. סעודת המלך כשהולך ממקום למקום ארנונא. בלשון יון סעודה. לשון אחר שותפות שיש לו למלך בבהמות לארנונא לשון שותפות מלכותא (במדבר כא) כי ארנון גבול מואב בין מואב ובין האמורי [ר"ן נדרים סב:]. [illegible]

מַר יְנוּקָא וּמַר קְשִׁישָׁא בְּרֵיהּ דְּרַב חִסְדָּא לְרַב אַשִׁי – **Mar Yenuka and Mar Keshisha,**[1] **the sons of Rav Chisda, said to Rav Ashi:** נְהַרְדָּעֵי לְטַעְמַיְיהוּ – The two **natives of Nehardea** (Rav Chama and Shmuel,[2] who is quoted below) **follow their** common **reasoning** in such matters,[3] דְּאָמַר רַב נַחְמָן אָמַר שְׁמוּאֵל – **for Rav Nachman said in the name of Shmuel:** הָאַחִין שֶׁחָלְקוּ – Concerning **brothers that divided** an inherited estate – אֵין לָהֶן לֹא דֶּרֶךְ זֶה עַל זֶה – **they do not have a right-of-way against each other,**[4] וְלֹא חַלּוֹנוֹת זֶה עַל זֶה – **nor** do they have the right to unobstructed **windows against each other,**[5] וְלֹא סוּלָּמוֹת זֶה עַל זֶה – **nor** do they have a right of **ladders against each other,**[6] וְלֹא אַמַּת הַמַּיִם זֶה עַל זֶה – **nor** do they have the right to **a water channel against each other.**[7] וְהִזָּהֲרוּ בָהֶן שֶׁהֲלָכוֹת קְבוּעוֹת הֵן – **And be zealous in [these matters], for they are established laws.**[8] וְרָבָא אָמַר יֵשׁ לָהֶן – **And Rav**[9] **said: [The brothers] do have** these rights in each other's portion. Hence, we see that the Nehardean Shmuel denies inheritors the right to enjoy their inheritance in the manner to which their father was entitled. Rav Chama, also from Nehardea, took this position in the case of the mansion.

The Gemara relates a fourth case that was brought to Rav Chama for judgment:

הַהוּא שְׁטָרָא דְּיַתְמֵי דִּנְפִיק עֲלֵיהּ תַּבְרָא – There was **a certain promissory note** belonging to young orphans,[10] **against which a receipt was produced.**[11] Since the orphans claimed that the receipt was forged, the case was brought before Rav Chama.

Rav Chama rendered a decision:

אָמַר רַב חָמָא – **Rav Chama stated:** אַגְבּוּיֵי לֹא מַגְבִּינַן לֵיהּ – **We surely shall not collect on [the note]** on behalf of the orphans, וּמִיקְרַע לֹא קָרְעִינַן לֵיהּ – **nor shall we tear it up.** Although *beis din* routinely destroys a promissory note when a receipt is produced,[12] Rav Chama was suspicious of the fact that the receipt had not been introduced until after the father's death.[13]

Rav Chama then explained his ruling:

אַגְבּוּיֵי לֹא מַגְבִּינַן לֵיהּ – **Surely we shall not collect on [the note],** דִּנְפַק תַּבְרָא עֲלֵיהּ – **for a receipt has been produced against it,** and the receipt may be genuine. מִיקְרַע לֹא קָרְעִינַן לֵיהּ – Nevertheless, **we shall certainly not tear up [the note],** דְּכִי גָּדְלֵי יַתְמֵי דִּילְמָא מַיְיתוּ רְאָיָה וּמָרְעֵי לֵיהּ – **for when the orphans mature perhaps they will adduce proof**[14] **and** thereby **invalidate [the receipt].** Hence, the note will be required to prove the existence of a debt. The best course, then, is to maintain the status quo, and do nothing.

Rav Acha inquired whether Rav Chama's four rulings should be accepted as practical halachah:

אָמַר לֵיהּ רַב אַחָא בְּרֵיהּ דְּרָבָא לְרָבִינָא – **Rav Acha the son of Rava said to Ravina:** הִלְכְתָא מַאי – **What is the law** in these four cases?

Ravina replied:

אָמַר לֵיהּ בְּכוּלְּהוּ הִלְכְתָא כְּרַב חָמָא – Ravina **said to him: In all** of these cases **the halachah accords with** the ruling of **Rav Chama,** לְבַר מִתַּבְרָא – **except for** the case of **the receipt.** דְּסַהֲדֵי בְּשִׁקְרֵי לֹא מַחְזְקִינַן – **For we do not presume that witnesses are liars.** By refusing to accept the receipt as genuine, Rav Chama in effect challenged the credibility of the witnesses, who attested to the debt's repayment with their signatures. In doing so, he acted contrary to the established rule that *beis din* must accept the testimony of two unimpeached witnesses.

Mar Zutra disagrees with Ravina's assessment:

מַר זוּטְרָא בְּרֵיהּ דְּרַב מָרִי אָמַר – **Mar Zutra the son of Rav Mari said:** בְּהָא נַמִּי הִלְכְתָא כְּרַב חָמָא – **In this** case (of the receipt) **as well the halachah accords with Rav Chama's** ruling, דְּאִם אִיתָא דְּתַבְרָא מְעַלְּיָא הוּא – **for if, in fact, it was a genuine receipt,** אִיבְּעֵי לֵיהּ לְאַפּוּקֵי בְּחַיֵּי אֲבוּהוֹן – the borrower **should have produced it during the father's lifetime.**[15] וּמִדְּלָא אַפְּקֵיהּ – **And since he did not produce [the receipt]** until after the father's death, שְׁמַע מִינָּהּ זִיּוּפֵי זַיְּיפֵיהּ – **we can infer** that

NOTES

1. *Rashi* (*Kesubos* 89b ד״ה מר) writes that the real names of these two sons of Rav Chisda were identical. Hence, the younger was called Mar Yenuka (literally: child) and the elder was called Mar Keshisha (literally: old man) in order to distinguish them. *Tosafos* here, however, write that Mar Yenuka was actually the older son, but was so called because he was born in Rav Chisda's youth, while Mar Keshisha, the younger son, was born during Rav Chisda's later years.

2. That both Rav Chama and Shmuel hailed from Nehardea is stated in *Sanhedrin* (17b) and *Berachos* (58b), respectively (*Tosafos*).

3. I.e. Rav Chama's decision in the case of the mansion followed the opinion, expressed by Shmuel below, of the sages of his native Nehardea, that an inheritor's claim of "I wish to live as my father did" is invalid (*Rashi*).

4. If, for instance, the brothers inherited separate fields, and their father had regularly traversed one to reach the other, still neither brother may claim that he also inherited this right-of-way (*Rashi*).

Tosafos explain that since each brother is considered a "seller" vis-a-vis his sibling [i.e. he "sells" him his rights to one field in return for possession of the other field], and since Shmuel follows the ruling of R' Akiva, that a seller relinquishes *all* his rights to the property being sold (מוֹכֵר בְּעַיִן יָפָה מוֹכֵר; see below, 64a), thus, when each brother conveys his share in the other field, he does not retain a right-of-way in that field for himself.

5. I.e. neither may protest if the other blocks his light (*Rashi*), since he has not established a right (*chazakah*) to unobstructed sunlight (see above, 7a note 13).

6. For example, if one brother inherited the courtyard and lower apartment of a residence and the other brother inherited the upper apartment, the second brother may not anchor a ladder in his sibling's courtyard for ascending to his apartment (*Rashi;* cf. *Tosafos*).

7. Neither brother may dig a canal through the other's property in order to channel water from a river into his own field (*Rashi*). [See Ramban, who points out that Rashi seems to imply that if a canal was already running through the poperty, or a ladder was already anchored there, he may not remove them.]

8. *Rashbam* (below, 65a) understands this expression to mean "for thus is the halachah."

9. *Bach* emends our text to read רַב, consistent with the Gemara below (65a). [See Rashbam there, ד״ה ורב אמר, who explains that Rav holds the view that a seller retains the rights that are necessary to him (מוֹכֵר בְּעַיִן רָעָה מוֹכֵר, see above, note 4), such as the right for airspace and the right of passage (cf. *Ritva*).]

10. The orphans were minors, as is evident from the Gemara below.

11. These orphans inherited a promissory note from their father and sought to collect from the debtor. The latter claimed that he had repaid their father before his death, and produced a receipt from their father to corroborate his claim. However, witnesses testified that the father himself had (unsuccessfully) attempted to collect the loan (after the date marked on the receipt), and that the borrower had not produced a receipt on that occasion (*Rashba, Nimukei Yosef;* cf. *Rosh* and *Ri Migash*).

12. *Ritva,* from *Shevuos* 48b.

13. See note 11, above.

14. [When they are old enough to investigate the matter themselves] perhaps they will discover proof that the witnesses on the receipt attested falsely (*Rashi*).

15. See note 11, above.

עין משפט נר מצוה

נ א מיי' פ"ב מהלכות שכנים הל' יב סמג עשין פב טוש"ע ח"מ סי' קעג סעיף ג:
נא ב ג מיי' פי"ג מהל' מלוה הל' ח סמג עשין לד טוש"ע ח"מ סי' קח סעיף טז:
נב ד מיי' פ"ה מהל' שכנים הל' א סמג עשין פב טוש"ע ח"מ סי' קסא סעיף א:
נג ה מיי' שם הל' א סמג שם טוש"ע ח"מ סי' קסג סעיף א:
נד ו ז מיי' שם הל' ה טוש"ע שם סעיף ב:
נה ח מיי' שם הל' ד טוש"ע שם סעיף ג:
נו ט מיי' שם הלכה ו טוש"ע שם סעיף ד וטוש"ע י"ד סי' רמג סעיף ב:

מר ינוקא ומר קשישא בריה דרב חסדא לרב אשי נהרדעי לטעמייהו דאמר ר"נ אמר שמואל האחין שחלקו אין להן לא דרך זה על זה ולא חלונות זה על זה ולא סולמות זה על זה ולא אמת המים זה על זה והזהרו בהן שהלכות קבועות הן (א) ורבא אמר יש להן: ההוא שטרא דיתמי דנפיק עליה תברא אמר רב חמא אגבויי לא מגבינן ליה ומיקרע לא קרעינן ליה אגבויי לא מגבינן ליה דנפק תברא עליה מיקרע לא קרעינן ליה דכי גדלי יתמי דילמא מייתו ראיה ומרעי ליה אמר ליה רב אחא בריה דרבא לרבינא הלכתא מאי א"ל בכולהו הלכתא כרב חמא לבר מתברא דסהדי בשקרי לא מחזקינן מר זוטרא בריה דרב מרי אמר בהא נמי הלכתא כרב חמא דאם איתא דתברא מעליא הוא איבעי ליה לאפוקי בחיי אבוהון ומדלא אפקיה שמע מינה זיופי זייפיה: **מתני'** כופין אותו לבנות בית שער ודלת לחצר רבן שמעון בן גמליאל אומר לא כל החצרות ראויות לבית שער כופין אותו לבנות לעיר חומה ודלתים ובריח רשב"ג אומר לא כל העיירות ראויות לחומה כמה יהא בעיר ויהא כאנשי העיר י"ב חדש קנה בה בית דירה הרי הוא כאנשי העיר מיד: **גמ'** למימרא דבית שער מעליותא היא והא ההוא חסידא דהוה רגיל אליהו דהוה משתעי בהדיה עבד בית שער ותו לא משתעי בהדיה לא קשיא הא מגואי הא (ב) מבראי ואי בעית אימא הא והא מבראי ולא קשיא הא דאית ליה דלת הא דלית ליה דלת ולא קשיא הא דאית ליה דלת אבע"א הא והא דאית ליה דלת ולא קשיא הא דאית ליה פותחת הא דלית ליה פותחת אי בעית אימא הא והא דאית ליה פותחת ולא קשיא הא דפותחת דידיה מגואי הא דפותחת דידיה (ג) מבראי: כופין אותו לבנות בית שער ודלת לחצר: תניא רבן שמעון בן גמליאל אומר לא כל חצרות ראויות לבית שער אלא חצר הסמוכה לרשות הרבים ראויה לבית שער ושאינה סמוכה לרשות הרבים אינה ראויה לבית שער ורבנן זימנין דדחקי בני רשות הרבים ועיילו ואתו: כופין אותו לבנות לעיר כו': (ת"ר כופין אותו לעשות לעיר דלתים ובריח) ורבן שמעון בן גמליאל אומר לא כל העיירות ראויות לחומה אלא עיר הסמוכה לספר ראויה לחומה ושאינה סמוכה לספר אינה ראויה לחומה ורבנן זימנין דמקרו ואתי גייסא בעא מיניה רבי אלעזר מרבי יוחנן כשהן גובין לפי נפשות גובין או דילמא לפי שבח ממון גובין אמר ליה לפי ממון גובין ואלעזר בני קבע בה מסמרות איכא דאמרי בעא מיניה רבי אלעזר מרבי יוחנן כשהן גובין לפי קירוב בתים הן גובין או דילמא לפי ממון גובין אמר ליה לפי קירוב בתים הן גובין ואלעזר בני קבע בה מסמרות רבי יהודה נשיאה רמא דשורא אדרבנן אמר (ד) ריש לקיש רבנן לא צריכי נטירותא דכתיב א) אספרם מחול ירבון למאן אילימא לצדיקים דנפישי מחלא השתא כולהו ישראל כתיב בהו ב) כחול אשר על שפת הים צדיקים עצמם מחול ירבון אלא הכי קאמר אספרם למעשיהם של צדיקים מחול ירבון וק"ו ומה חול שמועט מגין על הים מעשיהם של צדיקים שהם מרובים לא כל שכן שמגינים עליהם כי אתא לקמיה דרבי יוחנן אמר ליה מאי טעמא לא תימא ליה מהא ג) אני חומה ושדי כמגדלות אני חומה זו תורה ושדי כמגדלות

רש"י

נהרדעי לטעמייהו. רב חמא דמן נהרדעא הוא דלא ס"ל הא דאידור בה כדדרו אבהתי ואם כך חלקנו אזיל לטעמייהו דנהרדעי דאמר שמואל דהוה מנהרדעא: האחין שחלקו. ונטל זה שדה לצפון וזה לדרום והיה אביו רגיל להיות לו ליכנס דרך זו לתוך זו אין יכול לומר דרך לי עליך: ולא חלונות. לערער על סתימת אורו: ולא סולמות. אם נטל זה בית וחצר וזה נטל עלייה אין לו לקבוע סולם בחצירו של זה לעלות לעלייתו: ולא אמת המים. להביאה מן הנהר דרך שדהו של זה לתוך שלו: תברא. שובר שהוא פרוע לאביהם: ומרעי ליה. לשובר שהן עדי שקר: מתני' כופין אותו. את בן החצר שאינו רוצה לסייע את בני החצר לבנות להן בית שער להיות שומר הפתח יושב שם בצל ומרחיק את בני רשות הרבים מלהלך בחצר: ודלת. לשער החצר לנועלו: לא כל החצרות ראויות לבית שער. בגמ' מפרש איזו היא הראויה: ויהא כאנשי העיר. לשאת עמהם בעול: גמ' ולא אישתעי בהדיה. לפי שמפסיק בעניים הצועקין ואין קולם נשמע: מגואי. לחצר גריעותא הוא לפי שדלת החצר נעול והעני צועק ובית שער שבפנים מפסיק הקול: מבראי. אינו מפסיק בפניו שהרי נכנס לתוכו וכשאין לו דלת עסקינן: פותחת דידיה מאבראי. העני פותחה ונכנס. פותחת שירוד"ר בלע"ז והוא של עץ ותמיד המפתח לתוכו: שאינה סמוכה. שמשוכה להלן מרשות הרבים: כשהם גובים. לחומת העיר: קבע בה מסמרות. הזהר לדון כן ולא תזוח ממנה: קירוב בתים. בית הקרוב לחומה צריך לחומת העיר יותר מן הרחוק: רמא דשורא אדרבנן. הטיל יציאת חומת העיר על החכמים כמו על שאר בני אדם: חול. שהוא מועט ממעשיהם של צדיקים: מגין על הים. והוא לו לחומה כדכתיב אשר שמתי חול גבול לים (ירמיה ה): אלו

תוספות

מר ינוקא. הוא הגדול ועל שם שנולד בינקותו של רב חסדא קרי ליה מר ינוקא ומר קשישא הוא הצעיר ונולד בקשישותו של רב חסדא (ועיין רש"י כתובות פט: ד"ה מר): נהרדעי לטעמייהו. רב חמא נהרדעי הוא כדאמרינן בפרק קמא דסנהדרין (דף יז:) [אמוראי] דנהרדעי רב חמא ושמואל נמי נהרדעי הוא כדאמר שמואל (ברכות דף נח:) נהירין לי שבילי דרקיע כשבילי דנהרדעי: אין להם דרך זה על זה. טעמא משום דפסיק שמואל בפרק המוכר את הבית (לקמן דף סה.) כר"ע דאמר מוכר בעין יפה מוכר ולפיכך אין להם דרך זה על זה שלא שייר לעצמו כלום כל אחד (ה) חלק בחלק חבירו והוה לו כמוכר ואף על גב דאמרינן המוכר בית ושייר חצר מכר לו עם הדרך למ"ד מוכר בעין יפה מוכר לא דמי דהכא כולם מוכרין וכל אחד מכר ולא שייר לעצמו כלום בחלק חבירו וה"ל כמוכר חצר ושייר בית דצריך ליקח לו דרך מבעל החצר: ולא סולמות זה על זה. פי' בקונט' אם נטל זה בית וחצר וזה נטל עלייה אין לקבוע סולם בחצירו של זה לעלות לעלייתו וקשה לר"י דהיינו ולא דרך זה על זה ונראה לר"י כגון שלקח זה בית וזה עלייה וחצר אין לו לסמוך הסולם בכותל של זה ולעלות בעלייתו: ואי בעית אימא הא והא מבראי. ולא גרסינן הא והא מגוואי דמגוואי אין שייך לחלק בין אית ליה דלת ללית ליה ובין אית ליה פותחת ללית ליה דבכל ענין הוא רע כיון שאין יכול לבא אלא עד פתח החצר ואין לפרש הא דאית ליה דלת כו' אחצר קאי דהא במתני' בהדיא קתני כופין אותו לבנות דלת לחצר ולמאי דגרסי' מבראי קצת קשה דלא הוי כשאר שינויי דנקט בד דלא מעלי הא והא דאית ליה דלת והא והא דאית ליה פותחת והכא נקיט ההוא דמעלי: לפי שבח ממון הן גובין. כיון דאין (ו) סכנת נפשות לא אזלינן אלא בתר ממון והכי נמי אמר בהגוזל בתרא (ב"ק דף קטז:) שיירא ההולכת במדבר ועמד עליה גיים מחשבין לפי ממון דליכא סכנת נפשות כיון דאין הגיים בא רק בשביל ממון ואף על גב דאמר בפ' בן סורר (סנהדרין דף עב.) דהבא במחתרת נידון על שם סופו ומפרש רבא טעמא בגמ' משום חזקה דאין אדם מעמיד עצמו על ממונו כו' ואפי' הכי אין מחשבין אלא לפי ממון כיון דהגיים ברצונו אינו בא על הנפשות דאם לא יעמדו נגדם לא יזיק לגופם הילכך לא חשיב סכנת נפשות לפיכך אם יעמדו עליהם לסטים ונתפשרו עמהם גובין לפי ממון אבל היכי (ז) דטעו במדבר אמר התם דמחשבינן אף לפי הנפשות משום כיון דטעו איכא סכנת נפשות: לפי קירוב בתים הן גובין. פירש ר"ת ונותנין עניים קרובים יותר מרחוקים וכן עשירים קרובים יותר מעשירים רחוקים אבל עשירים רחוקים נותנין יותר מעניים קרובים דלפי שבח ממון נמי הן גובין: אילימא לצדיקים כו'. דבהאי מיירי קרא דלעיל מיניה כתיב ולי מה יקרו רעיך אל מה עצמו ראשיהם וכתיב בתריה אספרם מחול ירבון:

רבינו גרשום

נהרדעי לטעמייהו. דרב נחמן ושמואל ורב חמא מנהרדעי: האחין שחלקו אין להם דרך זה על זה. כגון בתחלה היו כל השדות בחיזוק א' של אביהם ולא הוה בכולהו אלא דרך אחד לילך מזה לזה והשתא כשחלקו אין להם דרך אם לא יקנו זה מזה וחלונות. שאם הגיע חצר לזה ולזה בית והיו חלונות הבית פתוחים לחצר יכול זה לבנות כנגדן ולסותמן וכן לאמת המים צריך ליקח דרך זה מזה. כה"נ יכול בעל תרביצא לבנות אשיתא נגד אספלידא: שהלכות קבועות הן. לדון הכי: דנפיק עליה תברא. דפריע השטר של יתומין: דגדלי יתמי. (למייתי) [דלמא מייתו] ראיה דהאי תברא מזויף הוא שהוחזק בפני עדים לאחר מיתת אביהן שעדיין היה חייב לו: לבר מהא. דודאי קרעי' לשטר. דסהדי דחתימי על שובר בשקרי לא מחזקינן: א) לעולם לא קרעי' לשטרא כדרב חמא. דאם כן הוה מפיק ליה האי שובר בחיי האב מדלית עדים דאפקה בחיי האב משום הכי לא קרעי' לשטרא: בית שער. ב) מקום שהשומר ישן ששומר החצר כופין לא' מבני חצר המעכב: מעליותא הוא. בית שער: ולא אשתעי אליהו בהדיה. משום דכי אתי עני וצועק על פתח שער מפסיק אותו בית שער קולו ואינו נשמע לבעל הבית: הא מגואי. גריעותא הוא. כלומר אם נעשה בנין בית שער מבפנים לחצר מפסיק הקול שאין העני יכול ליכנס לתוכו אבל אם בנו מאבראי ברה"ר ודאי מעליותא היא והיו כופין אותו לבנות הואיל והחצר פתוח לרה"ר יכול העני ליכנס בתוך מחיצות בית שער עד השער וצועק ויכול לשומעו דאין מפסיק ולא שער לחודיה: אית ליה דלת. לבית שער גריעותא. שהשער והדלת מעכבין קולו. אית ליה פותחת. מנעול לדלת לאו מעליותא היא שאין העני יכול לפותחו מפני המנעול. הא דמשנתנו דכופין לבנות בית שער דלית ליה דלת לבית שער. ואי קשיא הא תנא כופין לבנות בית שער [illegible]

מסורת הש"ס

א) [לקמן סה.], ב) [לעיל ב:], ג) [סנהדרין קיז.], ד) רש"ל מ"ז וכ"ל תניא רשב"ג כו', ה) [שבת ממון וכן הוא ברש"ש], ו) [לקמן ת. ב"מ קח.], ז) [פסחים פז.]

הגהות הב"ח

(א) גמ' ורבא אמר יש להן: (ב) שם הא מאבראי וכו' הא והא מאבראי: (ג) שם דפותחת דידיה מאבראי רשב"ג אומר וכו' תניא רשב"ג אומר לא כל כצ"ל ותיבת כופין אותו לבנות בית שער ודלת לחצר נמחק: (ד) שם אמר ליה ר"ל רבנן: (ה) תוס' ד"ה אין להם וכו' כל אחד בחלק חבירו כצ"ל ותיבת חלק נמחק: (ו) ד"ה לפי כו' דאין בה סכנת: (ז) בא"ד אבל היכא דטעו במדבר וכו' כיון דטעו איכא:

תורה אור השלם

א) אֶסְפְּרֵם מֵחוֹל יִרְבּוּן הֱקִיצֹתִי וְעוֹדִי עִמָּךְ: [תהלים קלט, יח]
ב) כִּי בָרֵךְ אֲבָרֶכְךָ וְהַרְבָּה אַרְבֶּה אֶת זַרְעֲךָ כְּכוֹכְבֵי הַשָּׁמַיִם וְכַחוֹל אֲשֶׁר עַל שְׂפַת הַיָּם וְיִרַשׁ זַרְעֲךָ אֵת שַׁעַר אֹיְבָיו: [בראשית כב, יז]
ג) אֲנִי חוֹמָה וְשָׁדַי כַּמִּגְדָּלוֹת אָז הָיִיתִי בְעֵינָיו כְּמוֹצְאֵת שָׁלוֹם: [שיר השירים ח, י]

לעזי רש"י

שירוד"ר. פירוש פותחת, מנעול (רש"י עירובין דף קא ע"ב ד"ה [מקומו]).

ליקוטי רש"י

[מה ששייך לכאן נדפס בע"א. מכאן שייך לדף ח.] אלו ת"ח. המניקין אחרים כשדיים הללו. כמגדלות. שמגינין על הדור [פסחים פז.]. אני חומה. חזקה באהבת דודי. ושדי כמגדלות. אלו בתי כנסיות ובתי מדרשות המניקים את ישראל בדברי תורה [שיר השירים ח, י]. [illegible]

חשק שלמה על רבינו גרשום א) נ"ל דהא נמי הלכתא כרב חמא ולעולם לא קרעינן וכו'. ב) נ"ל מקום ששומר החצר [illegible]

[illegible]

possibly the borrower **forged [the receipt].**[16] Because of this possibility, Rav Chama allowed the orphans to retain the promissory note, thus inviting them to investigate for any incidence of fraud when they matured.

Mishnah The Mishnah now rules on the responsibility of those whose homes adjoin a common courtyard to contribute toward maintaining the privacy and security of the courtyard. It also rules on the responsibility of citizens of a city to share in the expenses of protecting the city:

כּוֹפִין אוֹתוֹ לִבְנוֹת בֵּית שַׁעַר וְדֶלֶת לֶחָצֵר – **We compel [an unwilling resident]** of a courtyard **to** help **build a gatehouse and a door for the courtyard.**[17] **רַבָּן שִׁמְעוֹן בֶּן גַּמְלִיאֵל אוֹמֵר** – **Rabban Shimon ben Gamliel says: לֹא כָּל הַחֲצֵירוֹת רְאוּיוֹת לְבֵית שַׁעַר** – **Not all courtyards require a gatehouse.**[18]

A similar dispute exists with regard to the security of a city:

כּוֹפִין אוֹתוֹ לִבְנוֹת לָעִיר חוֹמָה וּדְלָתַיִם וּבְרִיחַ – **We compel [an unwilling citizen]** of a city **to** help **build for a city a** surrounding **wall, and double-doors and a crossbar** for locking the city's gates. **רַבָּן שִׁמְעוֹן בֶּן גַּמְלִיאֵל אוֹמֵר** – **Rabban Shimon ben Gamliel says: לֹא כָּל הֶעֲיָירוֹת רְאוּיוֹת לְחוֹמָה** – **Not all cities require a** surrounding **wall.**[19]

The Mishnah turns to the question of who qualifies as a citizen:

כַּמָּה יְהֵא בָעִיר וִיהֵא כְּאַנְשֵׁי הָעִיר – **How long must one be in the city to be** treated **like one of the citizens of the city,** and so be obligated to help bear these municipal expenses? **שְׁנֵים עָשָׂר חֹדֶשׁ** – He must reside there for **twelve months.**[20] **קָנָה בָהּ בֵּית דִּירָה** – If, however, **he bought a house** in the city, **הֲרֵי הוּא כְּאַנְשֵׁי הָעִיר מִיָּד** – **he is immediately** treated **like** one of **the citizens of the city,** for he obviously plans to reside there permanently.

Gemara In ruling that *beis din* may compel courtyard residents to build a gatehouse, the Mishnah implies that such a structure is desirable. The Gemara, however, relates an incident that seems to indicate just the opposite:

לְמֵימְרָא דְּבֵית שַׁעַר מְעַלְּיוּתָא הִיא – Is this **to say that a gatehouse is a good thing? וְהָא הַהוּא חֲסִידָא דַּהֲוָה רָגִיל אֵלִיָּהוּ דַּהֲוָה מִשְׁתַּעֵי בַּהֲדֵיהּ** – **But** there was **a certain pious man with whom Elijah** the prophet **would regularly** visit and **converse. עֲבַד בֵּית שַׁעַר וְתוּ לֹא מִשְׁתַּעֵי בַּהֲדֵיהּ** – **[The pious man]** once **constructed a gatehouse, and Elijah conversed with him no more!**[21] Obviously, then, a gatehouse is an undesirable structure. – ? –

The Gemara answers:

לֹא קַשְׁיָא – **This is not a difficulty. הָא** – **This** gatehouse built by the pious man **מִגַּוַּאי** – was located **inside** the door of the courtyard.[22] Hence, the cries of the paupers could not be heard by the courtyard residents. **הָא** – However, **that** gatehouse discussed in the Mishnah **מִבַּרַאי** – was constructed **outside** the door of the courtyard, and so did not constitute an additional barrier.[23]

The Gemara offers an alternative explanation:

וְאִי בָּעֵית אֵימָא הָא וְהָא מִבַּרַאי – **And if you want, say** that both **this** desirable **and that** undesirable gatehouse were built **outside** the courtyard door, **וְלֹא קַשְׁיָא** – **and** yet there is **no difficulty,** since the buildings were constructed differently: **הָא דְּאִית לֵיהּ דֶּלֶת** – **This** gatehouse in the incident **had a door,** which the poor were afraid to open; hence, they remained behind a double barrier. **הָא דְּלֵית לֵיהּ דֶּלֶת** – However, **that** gatehouse in the Mishnah **has no door;** hence, the poor are able to enter the gatehouse freely and call to the residents through the closed courtyard door.

The Gemara presents a third difference:

אִי בָּעֵית אֵימָא הָא וְהָא דְּאִית לֵיהּ דֶּלֶת – **If you want, say** that **this** desirable **and that** undesirable gatehouse each **has a door, וְלֹא קַשְׁיָא** – **and** yet there is **no difficulty. הָא דְּאִית לֵיהּ פּוֹתַחַת** – **This** gatehouse in the incident **has a lock,**[24] and so paupers are not able to open the door and enter. **הָא דְּלֵית לֵיהּ פּוֹתַחַת** – **That** gatehouse in the Mishnah **had no lock,** and so the poor could enter the gatehouse.

The Gemara presents a fourth alternative:

אִי בָּעֵית אֵימָא הָא וְהָא דְּאִית לֵיהּ פּוֹתַחַת – **If you want, say** that **this** desirable **and that** undesirable gatehouse each **has a lock, וְלֹא קַשְׁיָא** – **and** yet there is **no difficulty. הָא דְּפוֹתַחַת דִּידֵיהּ מִגַּוַּאי** – **The lock of this** gatehouse in the incident was **on the inside** of the gatehouse door; hence, paupers were unable to open it and enter. **הָא דְּפוֹתַחַת דִּידֵיהּ מִבַּרַאי** – However, **the lock of that** gatehouse in the Mishnah **is on the outside** of the door, and so the poor are able to enter the gatehouse and call out.

The Mishnah stated:

כּוֹפִין אוֹתוֹ לִבְנוֹת בֵּית שַׁעַר וְדֶלֶת לֶחָצֵר – WE COMPEL [AN UNWILLING

NOTES

16. Thus, Rav Chama did not impugn the credibility of the witnesses on the receipt. Rather, he allowed for the possibility that *no witnesses ever signed the receipt*, but that the borrower had forged the signatures so well that even the "witnesses" thought they had signed, so that even if the witnesses themselves affirm that the signatures are theirs, we still suspect forgery (*Rashba*, *Ritva*).

17. That is, any resident may be compelled to contribute toward the construction of a gatehouse and the erection of a door. A gatekeeper would sit in the shade of the gatehouse and prevent passersby on the public road from gazing into the courtyard. The door was used to keep outsiders from actually entering the courtyard (*Rashi*, see above, 2b note 31).

18. The Gemara will explain which courtyards require a gatehouse and which do not. It should be noted that Rabban Shimon agrees that a door is always required (*Tosafos* above, 2b ד״ה הזיקא).

19. Here, Rabban Shimon means that double-doors and a crossbar are also not required. The Gemara will explain which cities do not require a wall.

20. One who has lived in a place for less than a year, and has not yet bought a house, may yet decide to leave, and is thus considered a transient. [However, if it is known that he has decided to make this his permanent residence, he would be obligated immediately. Conversely, if one bought a home, but intends to stay there only temporarily, he would not be obligated. Furthermore, if he has not purchased the home, but rather inherited it or received it as a gift, there would be no indication of any intention to reside permanently, and he would not be obligated (*Rama, Choshen Mishpat* 163:2)

21. Because a gatehouse intervenes between paupers in the street and courtyard residents, and muffles the sound of the paupers' cries for help (*Rashi*).

22. In that case the closed courtyard door and the gatehouse formed a double barrier to impede the sound of the paupers' cries coming from the street. Hence, construction of the gatehouse inside the courtyard was a reprehensible act [that earned Elijah's disapproval] (*Rashi*).

23. For paupers are able to enter the gatehouse and call out for help, and the single barrier created by the courtyard door does not muffle their cries. The Gemara here assumes that the gatehouse has an opening on one side, but no door (*Rashi*).

24. Literally: opener. This was a wooden locking mechanism, in which the key remained permanently in place (*Rashi* below ד״ה פותחת; cf. *Yad Ramah, Chasam Sofer* to *Tosafos* ד״ה ואי).

מר ינוקא ומר קשישא בריה דרב חסדא לרב אשי נהרדעי לטעמייהו א) דאמר ר"נ אמר שמואל א האחין שחלקו אין להן לא דרך זה על זה ולא חלונות זה על זה ולא סולמות זה על זה ולא אמת המים זה על זה והזהרו בהן שהלכות קבועות הן (א) ורבא אמר יש להן: ההוא שטרא דיתמי דנפיק עליה תברא אמר רב חמא ב אגבויי לא מגבינן ליה ומיקרע לא קרעינן ליה אגבויי לא מגבינן ליה דנפק תברא עליה מיקרע לא קרעינן ליה דכי גדלי יתמי דילמא מייתו ראיה ומרעי ליה אמר ליה רב אחא בריה דרבא לרבינא הלכתא מאי א"ל בכולהו הלכתא כרב חמא לבר מתברא דסהדי בשקרי לא מחזקינן מר זוטרא בריה דרב מרי אמר ג בהא נמי הלכתא כרב חמא דאם איתא דתברא מעליא הוא איבעי ליה לאפוקי בחיי אבוהון ומדלא אפקיה שמע מינה זיופי זייפיה:

מתני' ד כופין אותו לבנות בית שער ודלת לחצר רבן שמעון בן גמליאל אומר לא כל החצרות ראויות לבית שער ה כופין אותו לבנות לעיר חומה ודלתים ובריח רשב"ג אומר לא כל העיירות ראויות לחומה ו כמה יהא בעיר ויהא כאנשי העיר י"ב חדש ז קנה בה בית דירה הרי הוא כאנשי העיר מיד:

גמ' למימרא דבית שער מעליותא היא והא ההוא חסידא דהוה רגיל אליהו דהוה משתעי בהדיה עבד בית שער ותו לא משתעי בהדיה לא קשיא הא מגואי הא (ב) מבראי ואי בעית אימא הא והא מבראי ולא קשיא הא דאית ליה דלת הא דלית ליה דלת ואבע"א הא והא דאית ליה דלת ולא קשיא הא דאית ליה פותחת הא דלית ליה פותחת אי בעית אימא הא והא דאית ליה פותחת ולא קשיא הא דפותחת דידיה מגואי הא דפותחת דידיה (ג) מבראי: ודלת לחצר: תניא רבן שמעון בן גמליאל אומר לא כל חצרות ראויות לבית שער אלא חצר הסמוכה לרשות הרבים ראויה לבית שער ושאינה סמוכה לרשות הרבים אינה ראויה לבית שער ורבנן זימנין דדחקי בני רשות הרבים ועיילו ואתו: כופין אותו לבנות לעיר כו': (ת"ר כופין אותו לעשות לעיר דלתים ובריח) ורבן שמעון בן גמליאל אומר לא כל העיירות ראויות לחומה אלא עיר הסמוכה לספר ראויה לחומה ושאינה סמוכה לספר אינה ראויה לחומה ורבנן זימנין דמקרו ואתי גייסא בעא מיניה רבי אלעזר מרבי יוחנן כשהן גובין לפי נפשות גובין או דילמא לפי שבח ממון גובין אמר ליה לפי ממון גובין ואלעזר בני קבע בה מסמרות איכא דאמרי בעא מיניה רבי אלעזר מרבי יוחנן כשהן גובין הן גובין או דילמא לפי ממון גובין אמר ליה ח לפי קירוב בתים הן גובין ואלעזר בני קבע בה מסמרות רבי יהודה נשיאה רמא דשורא אדרבנן אמר (ד) ריש לקיש ט רבנן לא צריכי נטירותא דכתיב א) אספרם מחול ירבון למאן אילימא לצדיקים דנפישי מחלא השתא כולהו ישראל כתיב בהו ב) כחול אשר על שפת הים צדיקים עצמם מחול ירבון אלא הכי קאמר אספרם למעשיהם של צדיקים מחול ירבון וק"ו ומה חול שמועט מגין על הים מעשיהם של צדיקים שהם מרובים לא כל שכן שמגינים עליהם כי אתא לקמיה דרבי יוחנן אמר ליה מאי טעמא לא תימא ליה מהא ג) אני חומה ושדי כמגדלות אני חומה זו תורה ושדי כמגדלות אלו

נהרדעי לטעמייהו. רב חמא דמן נהרדעא הוא דלא ס"ל הא דאידור בה כדדרו אבהתי ולשם כך חילקנו אזיל לטעמייהו דנהרדעי דאמר שמואל דהוא מנהרדעא: האחין שחלקו. ונטל זה שדה לצפון וזה לדרום והיה אביו רגיל להיות לו ליכנס דרך זו לתוך זו אין יכול לומר דרך לי עליך: ולא חלונות. לערער על סתימת אורו: ולא סולמות. אם נטל זה בית ואחר וזה נטל עלייה אין לו לקבוע סולם בחצירו של זה לעלות לעלייתו: ולא אמת המים. להביאה מן הנהר דרך שדהו של זה לתוך שלו: תברא. שובר שהוא פרוע לאביהם: ומרעי ליה. לשובר שהן עדי שקר: מתני' כופין אותו. את בן החצר שאינו רוצה לסייע את בני החצר לבנות להן בית שער להיות שומר הפתח יושב שם בצלו ומרחיק את בני רשות הרבים מלהליץ בחצר: ודלת. לשער החצר לנעלו: לא כל החצרות ראויות לבית שער. בגמ' מפרש איזו היא הראויה: ויהא כאנשי העיר. לשאת עמהם בעול: גמ' ולא אישתעי בהדיה. לפי שמפסיק בעניים הצועקין ואין קולם נשמע: מגואי. לחצר גריעותא הוא לפי שדלת החצר נעול והעני צועק ובית שער שבפנים מפסיק הקול: מבראי. אינו מפסיק בפניו שהרי נכנס לתוכו וכשאין לו דלת עסקינן: פותחת דידיה מבראי. העני פותחה ונכנס. פותחת שירו"ר בלע"ז והוא של עץ ותמיד המפתח תחובה בה: שאינה סמוכה. לתוכה להכן מדרסת הרבים: כשהם גובים. לחומת העיר: קבע בה מסמרות. הזהר לדון כן ולא תזוח ממנו: קירוב בתים. בית הקרוב לחומה צריך לחומת העיר יותר מן הרחוק: רמא דשורא אדרבנן. הטיל יציאת חומת העיר על החכמים כמו על שאר בני אדם: חול. שהוא מועט מעשיהם של צדיקים: מגין על הים. והוא לו לחומה כדכתיב אשר שמתי חול גבול לים (ירמיה ה): אלו

מר ינוקא ומר קשישא בריה דרב חסדא. הוא הגדול ועל שם שנולד בינקותו של רב חסדא קרי ליה מר ינוקא ומר קשישא הוא הצעיר ונולד בקשישותו של רב חסדא (ועיין רש"י כתובות פט: ד"ה מר): **נהרדעי** לטעמייהו. רב חמא נהרדעי הוא כדאמרינן בפרק קמא דסנהדרין (דף יז:) [אמוראי] דנהרדעי רב חמא ושמואל נמי נהרדעי הוא כדאמר שמואל (ברכות דף נח:) נהירין לי שבילי דרקיע כשבילי דנהרדעי: **אין** להם דרך זה על זה. טעמא משום דשמואל בפרק המוכר את הבית (לקמן דף סה.) כר"ע דאמר מוכר בעין יפה מוכר ולפיכך אין להם דרך זה על זה שלא שייר לעצמו כלום כל אחד (ה) חלק בחלק חבירו והוה לו כמוכר ואף על גב דאמרינן המוכר בית ושייר חצר מכר לו עם הדרך למ"ד מוכר בעין יפה מוכר לא דמי דהכא כולם מוכרין וכל אחד מכר ולא שייר לעצמו כלום בחלק חבירו וה"ל כמוכר חצר ושייר בית דצריך ליקח לו דרך מבעל החצר: **ולא** סולמות זה על זה. פי' בקונט' אם נטל זה בית ואחר וזה נטל עלייה אין לו לקבוע סולם בחצירו של זה לעלות לעלייתו וקשה לר"י דהיינו ולא דרך זה על זה ונראה לר"י כגון שלקח זה בית וזה עלייה ואחר אין לו לסמוך הסולם בכותל של זה ולעלות בעלייתו: **ואי** בעית אימא הא והא מבראי. ולא גרסינן הא והא מגואי דמגואי אין שייך לחלק בין אית ליה דלת ללית ליה ובין אית ליה פותחת ללית ליה דבכל ענין הוא רע כיון שאין יכול לבא אלא עד פתח החצר ואין לפרש הא דאית ליה דלת כו' אחצר קאי דהא במתני' בהדיא קתני כופין אותו לבנות דלת לחצר ולמאי דגרסי' מבראי קאמר קשה דלא הוי כשאר שינוי דנקט לד דמעלי הא והא דאית ליה דלת והא דאית ליה פותחת והכא נקיט ההוא דמעלי: **לפי** שבח ממון הן גובין. כיון דאין (ו) סכנת נפשות לא אזלינן אלא בתר ממון והכי נמי אמר בהגוזל בתרא (ב"ק דף קטז:) שיירא ההולכת במדבר ועמד עליה גייס מחשבין לפי ממון דליכא סכנת נפשות כיון דאין הגייס בא רק בשביל ממון ואף על גב דאמר בפ' בן סורר (סנהדרין דף עב.) דהבא במחתרת נידון על שם סופו ומפרש רבא טעמא בגמ' משום חזקה דאין אדם מעמיד עצמו על ממונו כו' ואפי' הכי אין מחשבין אלא לפי ממון כיון דהגייס ברצונו אינו בא על הנפשות דאם לא יעמדו נגדם לא יזיק לגופם הילכך לא חשיב סכנת נפשות לפיכך אם יעמדו עליהם לסטים ונתפשרו עמהם גובין לפי ממון אבל היכי (ז) דטעו במדבר אמר התם דמחשבינן אף לפי הנפשות משום כיון דטעו איכא סכנת נפשות: **לפי** קירוב בתים הן גובין. פירש ר"ת ונותנין עניים קרובים יותר מרחוקים וכן עשירים קרובים יותר מעשירים רחוקים אבל עשירים רחוקים נותנין יותר מעניים קרובים דלפי שבח ממון נמי הן גובין: **אילימא** לצדיקים כו'. דבכי מיירי קרא דלעיל מיניה כתיב ולי מה יקרו רעיך אל מה עצמו ראשיהם וכתיב בתריה אספרם מחול ירבון:

עין משפט נר מצוה

נ א מיי' פי"ג מהלכות שכנים הל' ה סמג עשין פב טוש"ע ח"מ סי' קנג סעיף ב:

נא ב ג מיי' פ"ג מהל' מלוה הל' ח סמג עשין לד טוש"ע ח"מ סי' קח סעיף טז:

נב ד מיי' פ"ו מהל' שכנים הל' א סמג עשין פב טוש"ע ח"מ סי' קסא סעיף א:

נג ה מיי' שם פ"ו הל' ג סמג שם טוש"ע שם סי' קסג סעיף א:

נד ו ז מיי' שם הל' ב טוש"ע שם סעיף ג:

נה ח מיי' שם הל' ד טוש"ע שם סעיף ג:

נו ט מיי' שם הלכה ו טוש"ע שם סעיף ד וטוש"ע י"ד סי' רמג סעיף ב:

רבינו גרשום

נהרדעי לטעמייהו. דרב נחמן ושמואל ורב חמא מנהרדעי: האחין שחלקו אין להם דרך זה על זה. כגון בתחלה היו כל השדות בחיזוק א' של אביהם ולא הוה בכולהו אלא דרך אחד לילך מזה לזה והשתא כשחלקו אין להם דרך אם לא יקנו זה מזה וחלונות. שאם הגיע חצר לזה ולזה בית והיו חלונות הבית פתוחים לחצר יכול זה לבנות כנגדן ולסותמן וכן לאמת המים צריך ליקח דרך זה מזה. כה"נ יכול בעל תרביצא לבנות אשיתא נגד אספלידא: שהלכות קבועות הן. לדון הכי: דנפיק עליה תברא. דפריע השטר של יתומין: דגדלי יתמי. (למייתי) [דלמא מייתו] ראיה דהאי תברא מזויף הוא שהוחזק בפני עדים לאחר מיתת אביהן שעדיין היה חייב לו: לבר מהא. דודאי קרעי' לשטר. דסהדי דחתימי על שובר בשקרי לא מחזקינן: א) לעולם לא קרעי' לשטרא כדרב חמא. דאם כן הוה מפיק ליה האי שובר בחיי האב מדלית עדים דאפקה בחיי האב משום הכי לא קרעי' לשטרא: בית שער. ב) מקום שהשומר ישן ששומר החצר כופין לא' מבני חצר המעכב: מעליותא הוא. בית שער: ולא אשתעי אליהו בהדיה. משום דכי אתי עני צועק על פתח שער מפסיק אותו בית שער קולו ואינו נשמע לבעל הבית: הא מגואי, גריעותא הוא. כלומר אם נעשה בנין בית שער מבפנים לחצר מפסיק הקול שאין העני יכול ליכנס לתוכו אבל אם בנו מאבראי ברה"ר ודאי מעליותא היא והיו כופין אותו לבנות הואיל והחצר פתוח לרה"ר יכול העני ליכנס בתוך מחיצות בית שער עד השער וצועק ויכול לשומעו דאין מפסיק אלא שער לחודיה: אית ליה דלת. לבית שער גריעותא. שהשער והדלת מעכבין קולו. אית ליה פותחת, מנעול לדלת לאו מעליותא היא שאין העני יכול לפותחו מפני המנעול. הא דמשנתנו דכופין לבנות בית שער דלית ליה דלת לבית שער. ואי קשיא דהא תנא כופין לבנות בית שער ודלת הא לא תקשי דהא תני דלת [לחצר] במתני' ולחצר תנן לא לבית השער: חצר הסמוכה לרה"ר, צריכה בית שער. כלומר אם מבוי שאינו מפולש ויש בו חצירות אותן שבפנים אין צריכות בית שער ולא היו כופין אבל אותה הסמוכה לרה"ר היו כופין: ורבנן דמתני' דלא פליגי בין סמוכה לשאינה סמוכה דזימנין דדחקי רבים ועיילו ואתו [illegible] ואיכא היזק ראיה מבני רה"ר: הסמוכה לספר. משום גייסות: כשהן גובין. לצורך חומה ודלתים: לפי שבח ממון. מי שיש לו ממון הרבה נותן יותר: קבע בה מסמרות. קבע בה הלכה: לפי קירוב בתים. כלומר אותן בתים חיצונות שצריכין לחומה יותר לפי שהן קרובים לחומה יותר מן הפנימיות ויתנו יותר: רמא דשורא אדרבנן. שפסק עליהם ליתן חלקן לבנות החומה: רבנן לא צריכי נטירותא. שתורה שעוסקין מגינה להן: השתא כל ישראל. [illegible]: וק"ו. ומה חול שמועט מגין על הים [illegible] מעשיהם של צדיקים על אחת כמה וכמה: אני חומה. זו תורה: ושדי כמגדלות [illegible]

חשק שלמה על רבינו גרשום א) [נ"ל הכא נמי הלכתא כרב חמא ולעולם לא קרעינן וכו']: ב) [נ"ל מקום ששומר החצר ישן שם וכו']:

מסורת הש"ס

א) [לקמן סה.], ב) [לעיל ג:], ג) [סנהדרין קיג.], ד) רש"ל מ"ז וע"ל תניא רשב"ג כו', ה) [שבת מטון וכן הוא בכל"ש], ו) [לקמן ח. ב"מ קח.], ז) [פסחים פז.]

הגהות הב"ח

(א) גמ' ורבא אמר יש להן: (ב) שם הא מאבראי וכו' הא מאבראי: (ג) שם דפותחת דידיה מאבראי רשב"ג אומר וכו' [illegible]: (ד) שם אמר ריש לקיש רבנן: (ה) תוס' ד"ה אין להם וכו' כל אחד בחלק חבירו: (ו) ד"ה לפי כו' דאין בה סכנת: (ז) בא"ד אבל היכא דטעו [illegible]

תורה אור השלם

א) אֶסְפְּרֵם מֵחוֹל יִרְבּוּן הֱקִיצֹתִי וְעוֹדִי עִמָּךְ: [תהלים קלט, יח]

ב) כִּי בָרֵךְ אֲבָרֶכְךָ וְהַרְבָּה אַרְבֶּה אֶת זַרְעֲךָ כְּכוֹכְבֵי הַשָּׁמַיִם וְכַחוֹל אֲשֶׁר עַל שְׂפַת הַיָּם וְיִרַשׁ זַרְעֲךָ אֵת שַׁעַר אֹיְבָיו: [בראשית כב, יז]

ג) אֲנִי חוֹמָה וְשָׁדַי כַּמִּגְדָּלוֹת אָז הָיִיתִי בְעֵינָיו כְּמוֹצְאֵת שָׁלוֹם: [שיר השירים ח, י]

לעזי רש"י

שירו"ר. פירוש פותחת, מנעול (רש"י עירובין דף קא ע"ב ד"ה למקומו).

ליקוטי רש"י

[illegible]

RESIDENT] TO help BUILD A GATEHOUSE AND A DOOR FOR THE COURTYARD.

A Baraisa explains Rabban Shimon ben Gamliel's dissenting opinion:

תַּנְיָא – It was taught in a Baraisa: רַבָּן שִׁמְעוֹן בֶּן גַּמְלִיאֵל אוֹמֵר – **Rabban Shimon ben Gamliel says:** לֹא כָּל חֲצֵרוֹת רְאוּיוֹת לְבֵית שַׁעַר – **Not all courtyards require a gatehouse.** אֶלָּא חָצֵר הַסְּמוּכָה לִרְשׁוּת הָרַבִּים – RATHER, A COURTYARD ADJOINING A PUBLIC THOROUGHFARE[25] רְאוּיָה לְבֵית שַׁעַר – REQUIRES A GATEHOUSE, since many people pass by the courtyard entrance; hence, a gatehouse is needed to protect the privacy of the courtyard's inhabitants. וְשֶׁאֵינָהּ סְמוּכָה לִרְשׁוּת הָרַבִּים – AND [A COURTYARD] THAT DOES NOT ADJOIN A PUBLIC THOROUGHFARE[26] אֵינָהּ רְאוּיָה לְבֵית שַׁעַר – DOES NOT REQUIRE A GATEHOUSE, for travelers rarely pass by.

The Gemara asks:

וְרַבָּנָן – **And** what is the rationale of **the Rabbis?** Why do they rule that even a courtyard far from the public thoroughfare requires a gatehouse?

The Gemara answers:

זִימְנִין דְּדָחֲקֵי בְּנֵי רְשׁוּת הָרַבִּים – **Sometimes travelers on the public thoroughfare are crowded,** וְעָיְילוּ וְאָתוּ – **and** some **will go up** the *mavoi* **and come** by a courtyard far from the entrance in order to escape the traffic. Thus, any courtyard requires the construction of a gatehouse.

The Mishnah further stated:

כּוֹפִין אוֹתוֹ לִבְנוֹת לָעִיר כו׳ – WE COMPEL [AN UNWILLING RESIDENT] TO help BUILD FOR THE CITY ETC. (a surrounding wall).

The Gemara again quotes a Baraisa that explains the dissenting opinion of Rabban Shimon ben Gamliel:

(תָּנוּ רַבָּנָן כּוֹפִין אוֹתוֹ לַעֲשׂוֹת לָעִיר דְּלָתַיִם וּבְרִיחַ) – (**The Rabbis taught in a Baraisa:** WE COMPEL HIM TO MAKE FOR THE CITY DOORS AND A CROSSBAR.)[27] וְרַבָּן שִׁמְעוֹן בֶּן גַּמְלִיאֵל אוֹמֵר – AND RABBAN SHIMON BEN GAMLIEL SAYS: לֹא כָּל הָעֲיָירוֹת רְאוּיוֹת לְחוֹמָה – NOT ALL CITIES REQUIRE A WALL. אֶלָּא עִיר הַסְּמוּכָה לַסְּפָר רְאוּיָה לְחוֹמָה – RATHER, A CITY NEAR THE BORDER of the country REQUIRES A WALL to defend itself from an invading legion, וְשֶׁאֵינָהּ סְמוּכָה לַסְּפָר אֵינָהּ רְאוּיָה לְחוֹמָה – AND A CITY THAT IS NOT NEAR THE BORDER, but lies in the interior of the country, REQUIRES NO WALL for defense.

The Gemara asks:

וְרַבָּנָן – **And** what is the rationale of **the Rabbis?** Why do they require a wall even for those far from the border?

The Gemara responds:

זִימְנִין דְּמִקְרוּ וְאָתֵי גַּיְיסָא – **It sometimes happens that invaders will** penetrate far beyond the border and **come** to attack a city in the interior. Thus, all cities need the protection of a wall.

The Gemara discusses how to apportion the cost of a wall among a city's residents:

בְּעָא מִינֵּיהּ רַבִּי אֶלְעָזָר מֵרַבִּי יוֹחָנָן – **R' Elazar inquired of R' Yochanan:** כְּשֶׁהֵן גּוֹבִין – **When [the city administrators] collect** funds from the citizenry to build a wall around the city, לְפִי נְפָשׁוֹת גּוֹבִין – **do they collect according to** the number of **persons** in each household? אוֹ דִילְמָא לְפִי שֶׁבַח מָמוֹן גּוֹבִין – **Or, perhaps, they collect according to** the relative **wealth** of each household.[28] – ? –

R' Yochanan replied:

אָמַר לֵיהּ – **[R' Yochanan] said to [R' Elazar]:** לְפִי מָמוֹן גּוֹבִין – **[The administrators] collect** from each household **according to** its relative **wealth,** since invading pillagers pose no danger to life.[29]

R' Yochanan added:

וְאֶלְעָזָר בְּנִי קְבַע בֵּיהּ מַסְמְרוֹת – **And Elazar, my son, fix nails in [this ruling].** I.e. be careful to judge in accord with my ruling, and do not deviate from it.[30]

The Gemara records another version of the previous exchange. In this version R' Elazar was aware that the size of individual contributions was based on wealth; his question to R' Yochanan involved whether to consider a *second* factor:

אִיכָּא דְאָמְרֵי – **There are those who say** that the dialogue went as follows: בְּעָא מִינֵּיהּ רַבִּי אֶלְעָזָר מֵרַבִּי יוֹחָנָן – **R' Elazar inquired of R' Yochanan:** כְּשֶׁהֵן גּוֹבִין – **When [administrators] collect** funds for a wall, לְפִי קֵירוּב בָּתִּים הֵן גּוֹבִין – **do they collect** also **according to the proximity of houses** to the edge of the city?[31] אוֹ דִילְמָא לְפִי מָמוֹן גּוֹבִין – **Or, perhaps, they collect** solely **according to the** relative **wealth** of each household. – ? –

R' Yochanan replied:

אָמַר לֵיהּ – **[R' Yochanan] said to [R' Elazar]:** לְפִי קֵירוּב בָּתִּים הֵן גּוֹבִין – **[The administrators] collect** from each household **according to the proximity of houses** to the city's edge, as well as according to relative wealth; וְאֶלְעָזָר בְּנִי קְבַע בָּהּ מַסְמְרוֹת – **and Elazar, my son, fix nails in [this ruling].** I.e. be careful to judge in accord with my ruling, and do not deviate from it.

NOTES

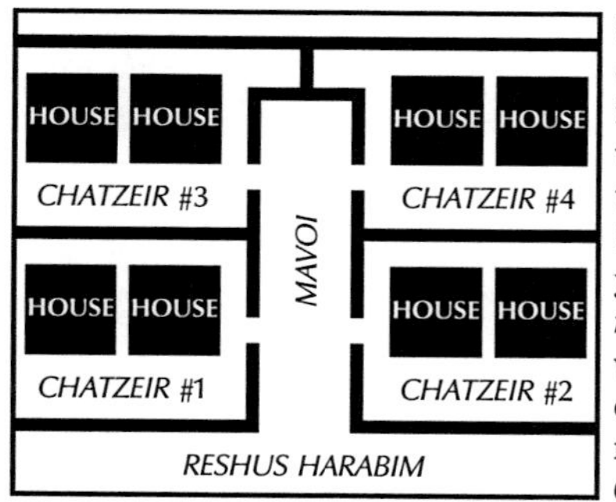

25. In Mishnaic times several courtyards commonly opened into one alleyway (*mavoi*), which in turn led to a public thoroughfare (*reshus harabim*) [see diagram]. Those courtyards near the entrance to the *mavoi* (#1 or #2 in diagram) would require a gatehouse, even according to Rabban Shimon ben Gamliel (*Rabbeinu Gershom*).

26. Such as #3-4 in the diagram accompanying note 25 above.

27. This section is deleted by *Maharshal*. It should read תַּנְיָא רַבָּן שִׁמְעוֹן בֶּן גַּמְלִיאֵל אוֹמֵר.

28. R' Elazar queried as follows: Do we say that since most invaders are interested only in plundering the wealth of a city, each household must contribute toward the cost of the protective wall according to the degree it stands to benefit therefrom (i.e. the rich will pay more and the poor less)? Or, perhaps, since occasionally invaders will come with a murderous intent, the number of persons in each household is also taken into account (*Ritva;* cf. *Nimukei Yosef*).

According to the first possibility, when reckoning the relative wealth of each household only movable property is taken into account, since invaders do not usually damage buildings and despoil fields and vineyards. However, if it is known that the invaders intend to capture the city or burn it to the ground, even a household's real property is taken into account, since each family stands to lose everything (ibid.).

29. If plunderers are not physically resisted, they will not harm their victims. Thus, since there is no danger to life, the only factor in determining the contribution of each household is its relative wealth (see *Tosafos*).

30. *Rashi*. [Perhaps R' Yochanan was concerned that wealthy, influential citizens adversely affected by his ruling would protest it; he therefore admonished R' Elazar to stand firm.]

31. A house on the outskirts of a city is more likely to be attacked; hence, it has a greater need for protection.

Thus, if this other factor were also considered, a rich person living in the center of town would contribute less than a rich man living on the edge of town. Both, however, would be required to donate more than a poor person, even one that lived on the outskirts of town (*Tosafos;* cf *Yad Ramah*).

עין משפט
נר מצוה

נ א מיי' פ"ב מהלכות שכנים הל' יב סמג עשין פב טוש"ע ח"מ סי' קעג סעיף ג:
נא ב ג מיי' פי"ז מהל' מלוה הל' ח סמג עשין לד טוש"ע ח"מ סי' קח סעיף טו:
נב ד מיי' פ"ה מהל' שכנים הל' א סמג עשין פב טוש"ע ח"מ סי' קסא סעיף א:
נג ה מיי' שם פ"ו הל' א סמג שם טוש"ע ח"מ סי' קסג סעיף א:
נד ו ז מיי' שם הל' ה טוש"ע שם סעיף ב:
נה ח מיי' שם הל' ד טוש"ע שם סעיף ג:
נו ט מיי' שם הלכה ו טוש"ע שם סעיף ד וטוש"ע י"ד סי' רמג סעיף ב:

רבינו גרשום

נהרדעי לטעמייהו. דרב נחמן ושמואל ורב חמא מנהרדעי: **האחין שחלקו אין להם דרך זה על זה.** כגון בתחלה היו כל השדות בחיזוק א' של אביהם ולא הוה בכולהו אלא דרך אחד לילך מזה לזה והשתא כשחלקו אין להם דרך אם לא יקנו זה מזה **וחלונות.** שאם הגיע חצר לזה ולזה בית והיו חלונות הבית פתוחים לחצר יכול זה לבנות כנגדן ולסותמן וכן **לאמת המים** צריך ליקח דרך זה מזה. כה"נ יכול בעל תרביצא לבנות אשיתא נגד אספלידא: **שהלכות קבועות הן.** לדון הכי: **דנפיק עליה תברא.** דפריע השטר של יתומין: **דגדלי יתמי.** (למייתי) **[דלמא מייתו] ראיה** דהאי תברא מזויף הוא שהוחזק בפני עדים לאחר מיתת אביהן שעדיין היה חייב לו: **לבר מהא.** דודאי קרעי' לשטר. **דסהדי** דחתימי על שובר **בשקרי לא מחזקינן:** א) לעולם לא קרעי' לשטרא כדרב חמא. דאם כן הוה מפיק ליה האי שובר בחיי האב מדלית עדים דאפקה בחיי האב משום הכי לא קרעי' לשטרא: **בית שער.** ב) מקום שהשומר ישן ששומר החצר כופין לא' מבני חצר המעכב: **מעליותא הוא.** בית שער: **ולא אשתעי אליהו בהדיה.** משום דכי אתי עני צועק על פתח שער מפסיק אותו בית שער קולו ואינו נשמע לבעל הבית: **הא מגואי,** גריעותא הוא. כלומר אם נעשה בנין בית שער מבפנים לחצר מפסיק הקול שאין העני יכול ליכנס לתוכו אבל אם בנו **מאבראי** ברה"ר ודאי מעליותא היא והיו כופין אותו לבנות הואיל והחצר פתוח לרה"ר יכול העני ליכנס בתוך מחיצות בית שער עד השער וצועק ויכול לשומעו דאין מפסיק אלא שער לחודיה: **אית ליה דלת.** לבית שער גריעותא. שהשער והדלת מעכבין קולו. **אית ליה פותחת,** מנעול לדלת לאו מעליותא היא שאין העני יכול לפותחו מפני המנעול. **הא** דמשנתנו דכופין לבנות בית שער **דלית ליה דלת** לבית שער. ואי קשיא דהא תנא כופין לבנות בית שער ודלת הא לא תקשי דהא תני דלת [לחצר] במתני' ולחצר תנן לא לבית השער: **חצר הסמוכה לרה"ר,** צריכה בית שער. כלומר אם מבוי שאינו מפולש ויש בו חצירות אותן שבפנים אין צריכות שער ולא היו כופין אבל אותה הסמוכה לרה"ר צריך והיו כופין: **ורבנן** דמתני' דלא פליגי בין סמוכה לשאינה סמוכה **דזימנין דדחקי רבים** במבוי **ועיילי ואתי** וקא חזו להההוא ואיכא היזק ראיה מבני רה"ר: **הסמוכה לספר.** משום גייסות: **כשהן גובין** מבני העיר. לצורך חומה ודלתים: **לפי שבח ממון.** מי שהוא עשיר נותן יותר **או לפי נפשות** שבעיר שכולן יתנו בשוה: **קבע בה מסמרות.** קבע הלכה (שם) [יתחד] הוא שלא תמוט: **לפי קירוב בתים.** כלומר אותן בתים חיצוניות שצריכין להם יותר לחיזוק החומה יותר מן הפנימית ויתנו יותר אי לא: **דשורא אדרבנן.** שפסק עליהם ליתן חלקם לבנות החומה: **רבנן לא צריכי נטירותא.** שתורה ומעשים טובים שלהם משמרים אותן: **השתא כל ישראל** עם הצדיקים **כחול וצדיקים לבדם יותר מחול** בתמיה. ומה חול שמועט ממעשיהם של צדיקים מגין על הים שאין עוברין אותו גלי ים. על אחת כמה וכמה שמגינין עליהם מעשיהם ולא צריכי נטירותא: **כי אתא.** ריש לקיש **לקמיה דר' יוחנן: אני חומה. זו תורה** שמגינה על לומדיה כחומה שמגינה על אנשי העיר: **ושדי כמגדלות**

חשק שלמה על רבינו גרשום א) נ"ל בהא נמי הלכתא כרב חמא ולעולם לא קרעינן וכו'] ב) נ"ל מקום ששומר החצר ישן כופין וכו']:

מר ינוקא ומר קשישא בריה דרב חסדא לרב אשי נהרדעי לטעמייהו [א] דאמר ר"נ אמר שמואל [א] האחין שחלקו אין להן לא דרך זה על זה ולא חלונות זה על זה ולא סולמות זה על זה ולא אמת המים זה על זה והזהרו בהן שהלכות קבועות הן (א) ורבא אמר יש להן: ההוא שטרא דיתמי דנפיק עליה תברא אמר רב חמא [ב] אגבויי לא מגבינן ליה ומיקרע לא קרעינן ליה אגבויי לא מגבינן ליה דנפק תברא עליה מיקרע לא קרעינן ליה דכי גדלי יתמי דילמא מייתו ראיה ומרעי ליה אמר ליה רב אחא בריה דרבא לרבינא הלכתא מאי א"ל בכולהו הלכתא כרב חמא לבר מתברא דסהדי בשקרי לא מחזקינן מר זוטרא בריה דרב מרי אמר [ג] בהא נמי הלכתא כרב חמא דאם איתא דתברא מעליא הוא איבעי ליה לאפוקי בחיי אבוהון ומדלא אפקיה שמע מינה זיופי זייפיה: **מתני'** [ד] כופין אותו לבנות בית שער ודלת לחצר רבן שמעון בן גמליאל אומר לא כל החצרות ראויות לבית שער [ה] כופין אותו לבנות לעיר חומה ודלתים ובריח רשב"ג אומר לא כל העיירות ראויות לחומה [ו] כמה יהא בעיר ויהא כאנשי העיר י"ב חדש [ז] קנה בה בית דירה הרי הוא כאנשי העיר מיד: **גמ'** למימרא דבית שער מעלייתא היא והא ההוא חסידא דהוה רגיל אליהו דהוה משתעי בהדיה עבד בית שער ותו לא משתעי בהדיה לא קשיא הא מגואי הא (ג) מבראי ואי בעית אימא הא והא מבראי ולא קשיא הא דאית ליה דלת הא דלית ליה דלת ואב"א הא והא דאית ליה דלת ולא קשיא הא דאית ליה פותחת הא דלית ליה פותחת אי בעית אימא הא והא דאית ליה פותחת ולא קשיא הא דפותחת דידיה מגואי הא דפותחת דידיה (ג) מבראי: כופין אותו לבנות בית שער ודלת לחצר: תניא רבן שמעון בן גמליאל אומר לא כל חצרות ראויות לבית שער אלא חצר הסמוכה לרשות הרבים ראויה לבית שער ושאינה סמוכה לרשות הרבים אינה ראויה לבית שער ורבנן זימנין דדחקי בני רשות הרבים ועיילו ואתו: כופין אותו לבנות לעיר כו': (ת"ר כופין אותו לעשות לעיר דלתים ובריח) ורבן שמעון בן גמליאל אומר לא כל העיירות ראויות לחומה אלא עיר הסמוכה לספר ראויה לחומה ושאינה סמוכה לספר אינה ראויה לחומה ורבנן זימנין דמקרו ואתי גייסא בעא מיניה רבי אלעזר מרבי יוחנן כשהן גובין לפי נפשות גובין או דילמא לפי שבח ממון גובין אמר ליה לפי ממון גובין ואלעזר בני קבע בה מסמרות איכא דאמרי בעא מיניה רבי אלעזר מרבי יוחנן כשהן גובין לפי קירוב בתים הן גובין או דילמא לפי [ח] ממון גובין אמר ליה [ט] לפי קירוב בתים הן גובין ואלעזר בני קבע בה מסמרות רבי יהודה נשיאה רמא דשורא אדרבנן אמר (ד) ריש לקיש [י] רבנן לא צריכי נטירותא דכתיב [א] אספרם מחול ירבון למאן אילימא לצדיקים דנפישי מחלא השתא כולהו ישראל כתיב בהו [ב] כחול אשר על שפת הים צדיקים עצמם מחול ירבון אלא הכי קאמר אספרם למעשיהם של צדיקים מחול ירבון וק"ו ומה חול שמועט מגין על הים מעשיהם של צדיקים שהם מרובים לא כל שכן שמגינים עליהם כי אתא לקמיה דרבי יוחנן אמר ליה מאי טעמא לא תימא ליה מהא [ג] אני חומה ושדי כמגדלות אני חומה זו תורה ושדי כמגדלות אלו

רש"י

נהרדעי לטעמייהו. רב חמא דמן נהרדעא הוא דלא ס"ל הא דאידור בה כדדרו אבהתי ולשם כך חילקנו אזיל לטעמייהו דנהרדעי דאמר שמואל דהוא מנהרדעא: **האחין שחלקו.** ונטל זה שדה לצפון וזה לדרום והיה אביו רגיל להיות לו ליכנס דרך זו לתוך זו אין יכול לומר דרך לי עליך: **ולא חלונות.** לערער על סתימת אורו: **ולא סולמות.** אם נטל זה בית ואחר זה נטל עלייה אין לו לקבוע סולם בחדרו של זה לעלות לעלייתו: **ולא אמת המים.** להביאה מן הנהר דרך שדהו של זה לתוך שלו: **תברא.** שובר שהוא פרוע לאביהם: **ומרעי ליה.** לשובר שהן עדי שקר: **מתני' כופין אותו.** את בן החצר שאינו רוצה לסייע את בני החצר לבנות להן בית שער להיות שומר הפתח יושב שם בצל ומרחיק את בני רשות הרבים מלהציץ בחצר: **ודלת.** לשער החצר לנעלו: **לא כל החצרות ראויות לבית שער.** כדמפרש אזיל היא כולה: **ויהא כאנשי העיר.** לשאת עמהם בעול: **גמ' ולא אישתעי בהדיה.** לפי שמפסיק בעניים הצועקין ואין קולם נשמע: **מגואי.** לחצר גריעותא הוא לפי שדלת החצר נעול והעני צועק ובית שער שבפנים מפסיק הקול: **מבראי.** אינו מפסיק בפניו שהרי נכנס לתוכו וכשאין לו דלת עסקינן: **פותחת דידיה מבראי.** העני פותחה ונכנס. פותחת שירוד"ר בלע"ז של עץ ותמיד המפתח לתוכו: **שאינה סמוכה.** שמסוכה להכין מרעות הרבים: **כשהם גובים.** לחומת העיר: **קבע בה מסמרות.** הזהר לדון כן ולא תזוח ממנה: **קירוב בתים.** בית הקרוב לחומה צריך לחומת העיר יותר מן הרחוק: **רמא דשורא אדרבנן.** הטיל יציאת חומת העיר על החכמים כמו על שאר בני אדם: **חול.** שהוא מועט ממעשיהם של צדיקים: **מגין על הים.** והוא לו לחומה כדכתיב אשר שמתי חול גבול לים (ירמיה ה): אלו

תוספות

מר ינוקא. הוא הגדול ועל שם שנולד בינקותו של רב חסדא קרי ליה מר ינוקא ומר קשישא הוא הצעיר ונולד בקשישותו של רב חסדא (ועיין רש"י כתובות פט: ד"ה מר): **נהרדעי לטעמייהו.** רב חמא נהרדעי הוא כדאמרינן בפרק קמא דסנהדרין (דף יז:) [אמוראי] דנהרדעי רב חמא ושמואל נמי נהרדעי הוא כדאמר שמואל (ברכות דף נח:) נהירין לי שבילי דרקיע כשבילי דנהרדעי: **אין להם דרך זה על זה.** טעמא משום דפסיק שמואל בפרק המוכר את הבית (לקמן דף סה.) כר"ע דאמר מוכר בעין יפה מוכר ולפיכך אין להם דרך זה על זה שלא שייר לעצמו כלום כל אחד (ה) חלק בחלק חבירו והוה לו כמוכר ואף על גב דאמרינן המוכר בית ושייר אחר מכר לו עם הדרך לת"ד מוכר בעין יפה מוכר לא דמי דהכא כולם מוכרין וכל אחד מכר ולא שייר לעצמו כלום בחלק חבירו וה"ל כמוכר אחר ושייר בית דצריך ליקח לו דרך מבעל החצר:

ולא סולמות זה על זה. פי' בקונט' אם נטל זה בית ואחר זה נטל עלייה אין לקבוע סולם בחדרו של זה לעלות לעלייתו וקשה לר"י דהיינו ולא דרך זה על זה ונראה לר"י כגון שלקח זה בית וזה עלייה ואחר אין לו לסמוך הסולם בכותל של זה ולעלות בעלייתו:

ואי בעית אימא הא והא מבראי. ולא גרסינן הא והא מגואי דמגואי אין שייך לחלק בין אית ליה דלת ללית ליה ובין אית ליה פותחת ללית ליה דבכל ענין הוא רע כיון שאין יכול לבא אלא עד פתח החצר ואין לפרש הא דלית ליה דלת כו' אחצר קאי דהא במתני' בהדיה קתני כופין אותו לבנות דלת לחצר ולמאי דגרסי' מבראי קצת קשה דלא הוי כשאר שינויי דנקט לך הא מעלי הא והא דאית ליה פותחת והכא נקיט הוה למעלי:

לפי שבח ממון הן גובין. כיון דאין (ו) סכנת נפשות לא אזלינן אלא בתר ממון והכי נמי אמר בהגוזל בתרא (ב"ק דף קטז:) שיירא ההולכת במדבר ועמד עליה גייס מחשבין לפי ממון ולא לפי נפשות כיון דאין הגייס בא רק בשביל ממון ואף על גב דאמר בפ' בן סורר (סנהדרין דף עב.) דהבא במחתרת נידון על שם סופו ומפרש רבא טעמא בגמ' משום חזקה דאין אדם מעמיד עצמו על ממונו כו' ואפ"ה הכי אין מחשבין אלא לפי ממון כיון דהגייס ברצונו אינו בא על הנפשות דאם לא יעמדו נגדם לא יזיק לגופם הילכך לא חשיב סכנת נפשות לפיכך אם יעמדו עליהם לסטים ונתפשרו עמהם גובין לפי ממון אבל היכי (ז) דטעו במדבר אמר התם דמחשבין אף לפי הנפשות משום כיון דטעו איכא סכנת נפשות:

לפי קירוב בתים הן גובין. פירש ר"ת ונותנין עניים קרובים יותר מרחוקים וכן עשירים קרובים יותר מעשירים רחוקים אבל עשירים רחוקים נותנין יותר מעניים קרובים דלפי שבח ממון נמי הן גובין: **אילימא** לצדיקים כו'. דבהכי מיירי קרא דלעיל מיניה כתיב ולי מה יקרו רעיך אל מה עצמו ראשיהם וכתיב בתריה אספרם מחול ירבון:

מסורת הש"ס

א) [לקמן סה.], ב) [לעיל ג:], ג) [סנהדרין קיב.], ד) רש"ל מ"ז וכ"ל תניא רשב"ג כו', ה) [שבח ממון וכן הוא ברא"ש], ו) [לקמן ח. ב"מ קח.], ז) [פסחים פז.]

הגהות הב"ח

(א) גמ' ורבא אמר יש להן: (ב) שם הא מאבראי וכו' הא והא מאבראי: (ג) שם דפותחת דידיה מאבראי רשב"ג אומר וכו' תניא רשב"ג אומר לא כל כל"ל ופיסקא כופין אותו לבנות בית שער ודלת לחצר נמחק: (ד) שם אמר ליה ר"ל רבנן: (ה) תוס' ד"ה אין להם וכו' כל אחד בחלק חבירו כל"ל ותיבת חלק נמחק: (ו) ד"ה לפי כו' דאין בה סכנת: (ז) בא"ד אבל היכא דטעו במדבר וכו' כיון דטעו איכא:

תורה אור השלם

א) אֶסְפְּרֵם מֵחוֹל יִרְבּוּן הֱקִיצֹתִי וְעוֹדִי עִמָּךְ: [תהלים קלט, יח]

ב) כִּי בָרֵךְ אֲבָרֶכְךָ וְהַרְבָּה אַרְבֶּה אֶת זַרְעֲךָ כְּכוֹכְבֵי הַשָּׁמַיִם וְכַחוֹל אֲשֶׁר עַל שְׂפַת הַיָּם וְיִרַשׁ זַרְעֲךָ אֵת שַׁעַר אֹיְבָיו: [בראשית כב, יז]

ג) אֲנִי חוֹמָה וְשָׁדַי כַּמִּגְדָּלוֹת אָז הָיִיתִי בְעֵינָיו כְּמוֹצְאֵת שָׁלוֹם: [שיר השירים ח, י]

לעזי רש"י

שירוד"ר. פירוש פותחת, מנעול (רש"י עירובין דף קא ע"ב ד"ה למקומו).

ליקוטי רש"י

[מה ששייך לכאן נדפס בע"א. מכאן שייך לדף ח.] **אלו ת"ח.** המגינין אחרים כשדיים הללו. כמגדלות. שמגינין על הדור [פסחים פז.]. **אני חומה.** מוקף באהבת דודי. **ושדי כמגדלות.** אלו בתי כנסיות ובתי מדרשות המניקים את ישראל בדברי תורה [שיר השירים ח, י]. **כרגא.** כסף גולגלתא שהיו כל היהודים כל אחד נותן כסף גולגלתו למלך [ב"מ עג:]. **אפילו** בשעה שאתה מחבב עמים וכו'. אף בשעת חבתן של אומות העולם שהראית להם פנים שוחקות ומסרת את ישראל בידם. **כל קדושיו יהיו בידך.** כל צדיקיהם וטוביהם דבקו בך ולא משו מאחריך ואתה שומרם. **והם תכו לרגלך.** והם מתמצעים ומתכנסים לתחת צלך. **ישא מדברותיך.** מקבלין גזירותיך ודתותיך בשמחה [דברים לג, ג]. **מנדה בלו והלך.** מיני מסים הם וכסף גולגלת [עזרא ד, יג]. **מנת המלך.** ארנונא שהיו נותנין מתבואותיהן ומבהמותיהן [ע"ז עא.]. **והלך זו ארנונא.** סעודת המלך כשהולך ממקום למקום ארנונא. בלשון יון סעודה. לשון אחר שותפות שיש לו למלך בבהמות לארנונא לשון שותפות מדכתיב (במדבר כא) כי ארנון גבול מואב בין מואב ובין האמורי [ר"ן נדרים סב:]. מס שגובה המלך מן התבואות כך וכך כורין מן השדה לשנה [סנהדרין כו.]. **לאגלי גפא.** הכל מסייעין לגדור חומת העיר ולהעמיד שעריה שלא יכנס לבא שודאים לעיר. **אגלי.** שערים כמו ברכות (כח.) טרוקו גלי. **גפא.** סתימת העיר כדתנן (ב"מ כה:) מגא אחר הגפה גוולות. **לא צריכי נטירותא.** תורתו משמרתו כדכתיב (משלי ו) בשכבך תשמור עליך. **לכריא פתיא.** לכרות מעין או בורות למים לשתות. **אפי' מרבנן.** שהרי גם הם צריכים לשתות ועל שם כלי שנותין בו מקקין שקורין פתיא בלשון ארמי קרי ליה כריא דפתיא. **דלא נפקי באכלוזא.** שאין יוצאין בעלי בתים עצמן באכלוזא ובאוכלוסא לחפור אלא גובין מעות ושוכרין פועלים. **לאו בני מיפק וכו'.** גגלי הוא לכן [ב"מ קח.]. **כעורב.** עורב אכזרי על בניו כדכתיב (תהלים קמז) לבני עורב אשר יקראו והקדוש ברוך הוא מזמן להן יתושים ונכנסין לתוך פיהן [עירובין כב.]. **כלילא.** קרונ"א בלע"ז כמו נזר [יחזקאל טז, יד]. כתר מלכות. **דשדו.** הטילו על אלו לעשותה [רשב"ם לקמן קמג.]. **הא לבני מתא הא ליתובי מתא.** שיהא נקרא כבני העיר אין נקרא בפחות משנים עשר חדש אבל להקרות מיושבי העיר כיון ששהה שלשים יום נקרא מאנשי העיר וקרינן בהו את יושבי העיר הסוה. **המודר הנאה.** שאומר הרי עלי קונם אם אהנה [סנהדרין קיב.]. המודר הנאה מאנשי העיר ובא אדם אחד ונשתהא עמהם כל ששהא שם שנים עשר חדש אסור ליהנות ממנו [ר"ן נדרים פד.]. **תמחוי.** קערה גדולה היא וגובין בה גבאים מאכל מבעלי בתים ומחלקין לעניים ב' סעודות ליום מיום ליום [שבת קיח.]. מאכל לחם ומיני מאכל שגובין לחלק [פסחים יג. וכעי"ז ב"מ לח.]. **קופה.** מעות הן לפרנס עניים בני טובים דזיל להו מילתא דתמחוי ומחלקין מע"ש לע"ש [שבת שם]. **לטרזינא.** נכרי היה ממונה על כלי זיין העשוין לשמירת העיר להלחם על הגרים ודר בעיר [עירובין פ.]. **איפרא הורמיז.** כך שמה איפרא מן יופי שדים היה לה [תענית כד: ועי' תוס' גיטין יא. ד"ה הורמן]. נכרית היתה וכן שמה ולעפ"כ היתה משמרת עצמה מנדות וקרובה להתגייר ואף קרבנות היתה שולחת ולשון יוני איפרא חן כמו אפריון נמטייה לרבי שמעון (ב"מ יט.).

The Gemara records a related incident:

רַבִּי יְהוּדָה נְשִׂיאָה רָמָא דְּשׁוּרָא אַדְּרַבָּנָן – **R' Yehudah Nesiyah**[32] once **placed** the burden of bearing the expense **of a** protective **wall upon the Rabbis** along with the other city residents.

R' Yehudah's action was opposed:

אָמַר רֵישׁ לָקִישׁ – **Reish Lakish said [to him]:**[33] רַבָּנָן לֹא צְרִיכֵי נְטִירוּתָא – **The Rabbis do not require** our **protection** – God protects them! Hence, they should be exempt from the obligation to contribute toward the wall.

Reish Lakish supported his objection with an interpretation of Scripture:

דִּכְתִיב: ,,אֶסְפְּרֵם מֵחוֹל יִרְבּוּן" – **For it is written:**[34] ***Were I [Hashem] to count them, they would outnumber the grains of sand*** (on the seashore). ,,אֶסְפְּרֵם" לְמַאן – Now, **to whom** does ***Were I to count them*** refer? אִילֵימָא לְצַדִּיקִים – **If we say** that it refers **to the righteous men,**[35] דִּנְפִישֵׁי מֵחָלָא – can we say **that they are more numerous than the grains of sand?!** הַשְׁתָּא כּוּלְּהוּ יִשְׂרָאֵל כְּתִיב בְּהוּ – **Now, it is written with respect to the entire** nation of **Israel:**[36] ,,כַּחוֹל אֲשֶׁר עַל־שְׂפַת הַיָּם" – *I shall greatly increase your offspring. . .* ***like the sand on the seashore.*** צַדִּיקִים עַצְמָם ,,מֵחוֹל" יִרְבּוּן – Can we then say of **the righteous themselves,** who comprise only a small segment of the Jewish nation: ***they would outnumber the grains of sand?*** Obviously not! אֶלָּא הָכִי קָאָמַר – **Rather, this is** what Scripture actually **said:** ,,אֶסְפְּרֵם" לְמַעֲשֵׂיהֶם שֶׁל צַדִּיקִים ,,מֵחוֹל יִרְבּוּן" – ***Were I to count*** **the good deeds of the righteous,** ***they would outnumber the grains of sand.*** וְקַל וָחוֹמֶר – **And** from the fact that the deeds of the righteous outnumber the grains of sand, we can deduce that the righteous need no human protection by employing the following ***kal vachomer*** argument:[37] וּמַה חוֹל שֶׁמּוּעָט – **If the grains of sand, which are fewer** than the deeds of the righteous, מֵגֵין עַל הַיָּם – **protect** the shore **from the sea,**[38] מַעֲשֵׂיהֶם שֶׁל צַדִּיקִים שֶׁהֵם מְרוּבִּים – **the good deeds of the righteous, which are numerous,** לֹא כָּל שֶׁכֵּן שֶׁמְּגִינִים עֲלֵיהֶם – **certainly protect them** from harm! Reish Lakish thus demonstrated that the Rabbis of the town, who were all righteous men, should have been exempted from contributing toward the protective wall.

R' Yochanan suggests a different source for the exemption:

כִּי אָתָא לְקַמֵּיהּ דְּרַבִּי יוֹחָנָן – **When [Reish Lakish] came before R' Yochanan,** אָמַר לֵיהּ – **[R' Yochanan] said to him:** מַאי טַעְמָא לֹא תֵּימָא לֵיהּ מֵהָא – **Why did you not tell him** that we derive that the Rabbis need no human protection **from this** verse:[39] ,,אֲנִי חוֹמָה וְשָׁדַי כַּמִּגְדָּלוֹת" – ***I am a wall, and my breasts are like towers?*** ,,אֲנִי חוֹמָה" זוֹ תּוֹרָה – ***I am a wall*** – **this is** a reference to the **Torah,** which protects those who study it as a wall protects the residents of a city;[40] ,,וְשָׁדַי כַּמִּגְדָּלוֹת" – ***and my breasts are like towers*** –

NOTES

32. R' Yehudah Nesiyah was a son and disciple of Rabban Gamliel of Tiberias and a contemporary of R' Yochanan and Reish Lakish. He should not be confused with his granfather, R' Yehudah HaNasi, codifier of the Mishnah.

33. *Bach* adds לֵיהּ, *to him,* to the text.

34. *Psalms* 139:18.

35. The Gemara entertains this suggestion because the preceding verse speaks of righteous men (*Tosafos*).

36. *Genesis* 22:17.

37. I.e. the a fortiori argument, one of the thirteen methods of Biblical exegesis (preface to *Sifra*).

38. By Divine decree the sands act as a protective wall to prevent the sea from inundating the land, as the prophet wrote (*Jeremiah* 5:22): *I have placed the sand [as] a border for the sea* [*Rashi;* see Gemara below, 73a, with *Rashbam*; cf. *Maharal Chidushei Aggados*].

39. *Song of Songs* 8:10.

40. *Rabbeinu Gershom.* This part of the verse indicates that Torah scholars need not depend on human devices for their protection (cf. *Maharsha, Maharal Chidushei Aggados*).

אֵלּוּ תַּלְמִידֵי חֲכָמִים – **these** are a reference to **the scholars,** who learn Torah from one another as eagerly as a child suckles from his mother's breast.[1] Why, then, did Reish Lakish not buttress his opposition to R' Yehudah Nesiyah with the more explicit teaching of this verse?

The Gemara explains:

וְרֵישׁ לָקִישׁ סָבַר לָהּ כִּדְדָרֵשׁ רָבָא – **But Reish Lakish thought** to expound this verse **as Rava expounded** it: ,,אֲנִי חוֹמָה" זוֹ כְּנֶסֶת יִשְׂרָאֵל – ***I am a wall*** – **this is** a reference to **the Assembly of Israel;** ,,וְשָׁדַי כַּמִּגְדָּלוֹת" אֵלּוּ בָּתֵּי כְנֵסִיּוֹת וּבָתֵּי מִדְרָשׁוֹת – ***and my breasts are like towers*** – **these are** a reference to **houses of prayer and houses of study.**[2] Since he did not understand *I am a wall* as alluding to the protective nature of Torah vis-a-vis its students, Reish Lakish was compelled to adduce another, albeit less explicit, source for the exemption of Torah scholars.

The Gemara relates another incident in which the Rabbis were unjustifiably taxed:

רַב נַחְמָן בַּר רַב חִסְדָּא רָמָא כַּרְגָּא אַרַבָּנָן – **Rav Nachman bar Rav Chisda** once **imposed a head tax on the Rabbis** as a part of a general levy.[3]

This action encountered opposition:

אָמַר לֵיהּ רַב נַחְמָן בַּר יִצְחָק – **Rav Nachman bar Yitzchak said to him:** עֲבַרְתְּ אַדְּאוֹרַיְיתָא וְאַדִּנְבִיאֵי וְאַדִּכְתוּבֵי – **You have violated** a precept **of the Torah, of the** Book of **Prophets and of the Writings,**[4] that Torah scholars are generally exempt from taxation.

Rav Nachman now elucidates the three teachings, citing the verse from the Torah first:

אַדְּאוֹרַיְיתָא דִּכְתִיב – You have transgressed a precept **of the Torah, for it is written:**[5] ,,אַף חֹבֵב עַמִּים כָּל־קְדֹשָׁיו בְּיָדֶךָ" – ***Even as He loves the peoples, all His holy ones – they are in Your hand.*** This verse is explained as follows: אָמַר מֹשֶׁה לִפְנֵי הַקָּדוֹשׁ בָּרוּךְ הוּא – **Moses said before the Holy One, Blessed is He:** רִבּוֹנוֹ שֶׁל עוֹלָם – **Master of the Universe,** אֲפִילּוּ בְּשָׁעָה שֶׁאַתָּה מְחַבֵּב עַמִּים – **even at a time when You cherish the peoples,** כָּל קְדוֹשָׁיו יִהְיוּ בְּיָדֶךָ – **all the holy men** of Israel **will be in Your hand.**[6]

The Gemara interprets the second half of the verse to explain why the Sages are deserving of God's special protection:

,,וְהֵם תֻּכּוּ לְרַגְלֶךָ" – The verse continues: ***and they sit at Your feet.*** תָּנֵי רַב יוֹסֵף – **Rav Yosef taught** the meaning of these words: אֵלּוּ תַּלְמִידֵי חֲכָמִים – **These are the scholars,** שֶׁמְּכַתְּתִים רַגְלֵיהֶם מֵעִיר לְעִיר וּמִמְּדִינָה לִמְדִינָה לִלְמוֹד תּוֹרָה – **who trudge**[7] **from city to city and from country to country to study Torah** under many different teachers, as the verse concludes: ,,יִשָּׂא מִדַּבְּרֹתֶיךָ" – ***receiving of Your words*** – that is, לִישָּׂא וְלִיתֵּן בְּדִבּוּרוֹתָיו שֶׁל מָקוֹם – **to debate**[8] **the words of the Omnipresent.**[9]

Rav Nachman now elucidates the second verse:

אַדִּנְבִיאֵי דִּכְתִיב – You have also transgressed a precept **of the** Book of **Prophets, for it is written:**[10] ,,גַּם כִּי־יִתְנוּ בַגּוֹיִם עַתָּה אֲקַבְּצֵם וַיָּחֵלּוּ מְּעָט מִמַּשָּׂא מֶלֶךְ (ו)שָׂרִים" – ***Even when they ingratiate themselves with the nations, I will gather them now;***[11] ***and they will be somewhat humbled by the burdens of kings (and) officers.***[12]

Ulla interprets the verse homiletically:

אָמַר עוּלָּא פָּסוּק זֶה בִּלְשׁוֹן אֲרָמִית נֶאֱמַר – **Ulla said:** Part of **this verse is stated in the Aramaic language.**[13] Thus, the meaning of the verse is as follows: אִי תָּנוּ כּוּלְּהוּ – **If all**[14] the Jews **study** the Torah in exile, עַתָּה אֲקַבְּצֵם – **I will gather** and return **them** to

NOTES

1. *Rabbeinu Gershom.* (cf. *Rashi* to *Pesachim* 87a ד״ה ושדי)

[See also *Rashi* there ד״ה כמגדלות, who interprets the comparison of scholars to towers, for they protect the people from harm. *Rashi* here says that we see from this verse that no wall is needed when scholars are present. It would seem, therefore, that *Rashi* understands that Torah Scholars should not be obligated to contribute towards a protective wall, for they serve as a greater protection than any wall (See *Rif* to *Ein Yaakov*).]

2. With respect to the aspect suggested by the metaphor of "a wall," Scripture regards the children of Israel as equals in the sense that all the Jewish people insulate themselves from the contaminating influence of the idolaters by surrounding themselves with a protective wall (*Rashi*) [and constant attendance in the houses of prayer and Torah study creates that wall].

3. The head tax was so named because it was imposed upon each "head," or person, equally – without regard to his financial state. The revenue generated by the tax was deposited in a discretionary, general purpose fund; the government did not necessarily apply it to defense. Thus, opposition to the tax was not based on the principle that "Rabbis do not need protection," but on the principle that Rabbis are exempt from *all* taxation (except for levies for specific projects from which they will derive benefit, as the Gemara explains below).

4. The Pentateuch, the Books of Prophets and the Writings (Hagiographa) comprise the three parts of the Bible.

5. *Deuteronomy* 33:3.

6. I.e. even when You shine Your countenance upon the nations to allow them to subjugate Your children, the holy ones (Torah scholars) will remain under your protection (*Rashi*). As the Gemara states below (see note 41), any decree by the nations against Israel comes only because of the unlearned people. Torah scholars, however, are protected from such decrees. Therefore it is only proper that when any tax is levied against the Jews, the Rabbis should be exempted (*Bach, Yoreh Deah* 243:2).

[The verse refers to Torah Scholars as "holy ones." *Yad Ramah* and *Ritva* say that we may infer from this that it is speaking only of Torah Scholars who also posses exemplary fear of Heaven. Scholars of Torah who are lacking in their fear of Heaven are no better than the unlearned in meriting protecting from Heaven.]

7. שֶׁמְּכַתְּתִים רַגְלֵיהֶם – literally: who pound their feet [i.e. on the road; colloquially: pound the pavement]. Rav Yosef's explication derives from inverting תֻּכּוּ, *they sit,* to yield כתּ(ת)וּ, *they pound.*

8. לִישָּׂא וְלִיתֵּן – literally: to receive and give – connotes the "give and take" of Talmudic debate. This idea is intimated by the conclusion of the verse: יִשָּׂא מִדַּבְּרֹתֶיךָ, *receiving of Your words.*

9. *Maharsha* understands that the conclusion of the verse implies that scholars who wander from place to place to study Torah are, in fact, *legally* entitled to an exemption from all taxes. For the Mishnah stated that one may not be taxed as a citizen of a city unless he has resided there twelve months. Since these migrant Torah scholars never remain in one place for that length of time, they never qualify as legal residents.

10. *Hosea* 8:10.

11. Even though certain of the exiled Jews will form close friendships with gentiles of ill repute, God promises not to postpone their redemption when the appointed time arrives (*Rashi* there).

12. They will be somewhat humbled by the fear of having to bear the yoke of their subjugating rulers (ibid.).

[וַיָּחֵלּוּ is normally translated as *humbled.* In the following homiletical interpretation of Ulla, it is translated as *nullifield* (as in לֹא יַחֵל דְּבָרוֹ – *Numbers* 30:3), meaning that the burden of taxes on Torah scholars will be nullifield (*Rashi*).]

13. יִתְנוּ (translated here as *they ingratiate*) is the Aramaic equivalent of the Hebrew יִשְׁנוּ, *they study* or *teach* – as in *Deuteronomy* 6:7: וְשִׁנַּנְתָּם, which *Onkelos* translates as וּתְתַנֵּינוּן (*Rashi*). Ulla thus proposes to explain the verse according to the Aramaic translation of the word יִתְנוּ.

14. *Rashi* adds that this promise of redemption applies even if only a *majority* of the exiles engages in Torah study.

Although this part of the verse speaks neither of a majority nor of a minority, *Rashi* based his interpretation on the second half of the verse: וַיָּחֵלּוּ מְּעָט, *the few* (i.e. minority) that study Torah *will be released* from all obligations to the authorities, which implies that if the *majority* studies Torah, total redemption will shortly follow (*Maharsha*).

אלו ת"ח ור"ל סבר לה כדדרש רבא אני חומה זו כנסת ישראל ושדי כמגדלות אלו בתי כנסיות ובתי מדרשות רב נחמן בר רב חסדא רמא כרגא ארבנן א"ל רב נחמן בר יצחק עברת אדאורייתא ואדנביאי ואדכתובי אדאורייתא דכתיב אף חובב עמים כל קדושיו בידך אמר משה לפני הקב"ה רבונו של עולם אפילו בשעה שאתה מחבב עמים כל קדושיו יהיו בידך והם תכו לרגלך תני רב יוסף אלו תלמידי חכמים שמכתתים רגליהם מעיר לעיר וממדינה למדינה ללמוד תורה ישא מדברותיך לישא וליתן בדברותיו של מקום אדנביאי דכתיב גם כי יתנו בגוים עתה אקבצם ויחלו מעט ממשא מלך ושרים אמר עולא פסוק זה בלשון ארמית נאמר אי תנו כולהו עתה אקבצם ואם מעט מהם יחלו ממשא מלך ושרים אדכתובי דכתיב מנדה בלו והלך לא שליט למרמא עליהם ואמר רב יהודה מנדה זו מנת המלך בלו זו כסף גולגלתא והלך זו ארנונא רב פפא רמא כריא חדתא איתמי א"ל רב שישא בריה דרב אידי לרב פפא ודילמא לא מידויל א"ל מישקל שקילנא מנייהו אי מידויל מידויל ואי לא מהדרנא להו ניהליהו אמר רב יהודה הכל לאגלי גפא אפילו מיתמי אבל רבנן לא צריכי נטורותא הכל לכריא פתיא אפי' מרבנן ולא אמרן אלא דלא נפקי באכלוזא אבל נפקי באכלוזא רבנן לאו בני מיפק באכלוזא נינהו: רבי פתח אוצרות בשני בצורת אמר יכנסו בעלי מקרא בעלי משנה בעלי גמרא בעלי הלכה בעלי הגדה אבל עמי הארץ אל יכנסו דחק רבי יונתן בן עמרם ונכנס אמר לו רבי פרנסני אמר לו בני קרית אמר לו לאו שנית א"ל לאו אם כן במה אפרנסך [א"ל] פרנסני ככלב וכעורב פרנסיה בתר דנפק יתיב רבי וקא מצטער ואמר אוי לי שנתתי פתי לעם הארץ אמר לפניו ר' שמעון בר רבי שמא יונתן בן עמרם תלמידך הוא שאינו רוצה ליהנות מכבוד תורה מימיו בדקו ואשכח אמר רבי יכנסו הכל רבי לטעמיה דאמר רבי אין פורענות בא לעולם אלא בשביל עמי הארץ כההוא דמי כלילא דשדו אטבריא אתו לקמיה דרבי ואמרו ליה ליתבו רבנן בהדן אמר להו לא אמרו ליה ערוקינן [א"ל] ערוקו ערקו פלגיהון דליוה פלגא אתו הנהו פלגא קמי דרבי א"ל ליתבו רבנן בהדן אמר להו לא ערוקינן ערקו כולהו פש ההוא כובס שדיוה אכובס ערק כובס פקע כלילא א"ר ראיתם שאין פורענות בא לעולם אלא בשביל עמי הארץ: וכמה יהא בעיר ויהא כאנשי העיר וכו': ורמינהי החמרת והגמלת העוברת ממקום למקום ולנה בתוכה והודחה עמהן הן בסקילה וממונן פלט ואם נשתהו שם שלשים יום הן בסייף וממונן אבד אמר רבא לא קשיא הא לבני מתא הא ליתובי מתא כדתניא המודר הנאה מאנשי העיר כל שנשתהא שם שנים עשר חדש אסור ליהנות ממנו פחות מכאן מותר מיושבי העיר כל שנשתהא שם שלשים יום אסור ליהנות ממנו פחות מכאן מותר ליהנות ממנו ולכל מילי מי בעינן י"ב חדש והתניא שלשים יום לתמחוי שלשה חדשים לקופה ששה לכסות תשעה לקבורה שנים עשר לפסי העיר אמר ר' אסי אמר ר' יוחנן כי תנן נמי מתניתין שנים עשר חדש לפסי העיר תנן: וא"ר אסי אמר ר' יוחנן הכל לפסי העיר ואפי' מיתמי אבל רבנן לא דרבנן לא צריכי נטירותא אמר רב פפא לשורא ולפרשאה ולטרזינא אפילו מיתמי אבל רבנן לא צריכי נטירותא כללא דמילתא כל מילתא דאית להו הנאה מיניה אפילו מיתמי רבה רמא צדקה איתמי דבי בר מריון א"ל אביי והתני רב שמואל בר יהודה אין פוסקין צדקה על היתומים אפילו לפדיון שבוים א"ל אנא לאחשובינהו קא עבידנא איפרא הורמיז אימיה דשבור מלכא שדרה ארנקא דדינרי לקמיה דרב יוסף אמרה ליהוי למצוה רבה יתיב רב יוסף וקא מעיין בה מאי מצוה רבה א"ל אביי מדתני רב שמואל בר יהודה אין פוסקין צדקה על היתומים אפילו לפדיון שבוים שמע מינה פדיון

רש"י

אלו תלמידי חכמים. אלמא אין צריכין חומה: [זו] כנסת ישראל. כולם שוין לענין חומה וגודרים עצמן מלטמע בעובדי כוכבים: מחבב עמים. שאתה מגביה להם פניך להשליטן על בניך: כל קדושיו. של ישראל בידך [הם] לשומרן: בלשון ארמי נאמר. יתנו תרגום של ישנו כמו ושננתם ותנינון (דברים ו): אם תנו כולם. וכן רובן יהיו שונין ועוסקים בתורה כשיגלו בעמים: עתה אקבצם. בקרוב אקבצם: ויחלו מעט וגו'. ואף [אם] מועטין הן השונין בעמים יחלו ממשא מלך ושרים יהיו בטלים מלשאת משא מלך ושרים. יחלו כמו לא יחל דברו (במדבר ל): מנדה בלו והלך. דריוש צוה את פחת עבר הנהר על אנשי כנסת הגדולה: מנת המלך. מגבת מסים שהן מטילין תמיד על בני המדינה: ארנונא. עישורי תבואות ובהמות מדי שנה בשנה: כריא חדתא. יציאת כריית באר מים חיים לשתות: לא מידויל. לא ימצאו בו מים והפסדתם חנם ויתמי לאו בני מחילה נינהו דליחלו: לאגלי גפא. לשערי חומות העיר להציב בהן דלתות. אגלי דלתות כמו טרוקו גלי (ברכות דף כח.). גפא סתימה כמו מלא אחר הגפה באלו מציאות (ב"מ דף כה:): לכריא פתיא. חפירת בור לשתות מים ועל שם הכלי המונח שם בבור תמיד לשתות בו עוברי דרכים קורהו פתיא: אפילו מרבנן. שהכל צריכין למים: דלא נפקי באכלוזא. שאין הן עצמם יוצאין בהכרזה לחפור אלא שוכרים פועלים: ככלב וכעורב. שחס הקב"ה עליהם (שבת קנה:) שנאמר יודע צדיק דין דלים (משלי כט) לפי שהכלב מזונותיו מועטין לפיכך שוהה אכילתו במעיו שלשת ימים וגבי עורב כתיב לבני עורב אשר יקראו (תהלים קמז) לפי שהעורב אכזרי על בניו והקב"ה מזמין להן יתושין מתוך צואתם ואוכלין: דמי כלילא. עטרה למלך קיסר: אתו. עמי הארץ לקמיה דרבי: דליוה לפלגא. מחל המלך דמי החצי וסילקה מעליהן: שדיוה אכובס. הטילוה פחתי המלך על הכובס: החמרת והגמלת. שיירא של חמרים ושל גמלים: הרי אלו בסקילה. כדין שאר יחידים: יתובי מתא. בשלשים יום וגבי עיר הנדחת כתיב יושבי העיר (דברים יג): ולכל מילי. ומקמי הכי לא יהיב מידי עם בני העיר: שלשים יום לתמחוי. כיון ששהה שם שלשים יום גובין הימנו [גבאי] תמחוי מאכל לעניים: לקופה. לצדקה: לכסות. עניי העיר: לקבורה. לקבור עניי העיר שהיא יציאה יתירא: לשורא. לתיקון החומה: לפרשא. פרש (ב) שהולך סביבות העיר לשומר' ולידע מה היא צריכה: לטרזינא. שומר כלי זיין של בני העיר ויושב בבית אצל השער:

תוספות

לא שליט למרמא עליהם. לפי שהיו עסוקים במלאכת שמים בבנין בית המקדש ה"נ אין להטיל מס על לומדי תורה:

והלך זו ארנונא. פי' בקונטרס עישור בהמות ותבואה כו' ור"ח פי' ארוחה דורון לשלטון העובר ממקום למקום שנותן לו כל עיר ועיר ארוחה ופירושו מלשון ויבא הלך לאיש העשיר (שמואל ב יב):

כריא פתיא. פירש ר"ח להסיר גבשושית מרחוב העיר:

איפרא הורמיז. פר"ח למשמעות הלשון חן מאת המקום איפרא כמו אפריון נמטייה לר"ש (ב"מ דף קיט.) הורמיז שם שכינה כי ההיא דס"פ אחד דיני ממונות (סנהדרין דף לט. ושם ד"ה דהורמיז) מפלגא דידך ולעיל דהורמיז בזיי"ן מפלגא ולתחת דהורמין בנו"ן כמו הורמין בר לילתא (לקמן דף עג.): (לעיל)

ככלב וכעורב. כמו שפי' הקונטרס והיינו דכתיב נותן לבהמה לחמה לבני עורב וגו' בהמה בגימטריא כלב:

יתיב רב יוסף וקא מעיין בה. וא"ת וכי לית ליה ביבש קצירה תשברנה וגו' (ישעיה כז) כדאמרי' בפירקין (דף י:) וי"ל דקבל' משום שלום מלכות כדעבד רבא לקמן (שם) וכי היכי דפלגינהו רבא לעניי עובדי כוכבים ה"נ פדה בהו רב יוסף שבויי עובדי כוכבים ומיהו לא צריכי להכי אלא כדפירש הקונט' (ג) דרבא דקבלה משום שלום מלכות וכיון שאמר לו ליתן למצוה רבה לא היה אפשר לחלקם לעניי עובדי כוכבים דאסור לגנוב דעת הבריות ואפי' דעתו של עובד כוכבים (חולין צד.) אבל מעות המתחלקים לעניים אין כאן גניבת דעת דאינהו נמי ידעי שישראל רגילין לפרנס כדאמר בהמזקין (גיטין דף סא.) מפרנסים עניי עכו"ם עם עניי ישראל מפני דרכי שלום והא דקבל מההוא טייעא דנדב שרגא לבי כנישתא בפ"ק דערכין (דף ו: ושם ד"ה עד) אע"ג דהתם לא היה שלום מלכות התם טעמא משום דהוו כמו קרבן ואמרינן (נזיר סב.) איש איש לרבות נכרים שנודרים נדרים ונדבות כישראל:

רבינו גרשום

אלו ת"ח. שלומדין זה מזה כתינוק יונק משדי אמו: ודריש לקיש דמפיק מאספים מחול יובין דריש האי אני חומה בכל ישראל ולא בצדיקים בלבד: כרגא. כסף גולגלתא: אע"פ שאתה מחבב אומות העולם. שאתה נותן להם על ישראל ממשלה בזמן שישראל בגלות אעפ"כ קדושיו של ישראל העוסקים בתורה יהיו מסורין בידך: לרגלך. משמע בשבילך ומשמע רגל ממש: יתנו בגוים. בלשון ארמי כמו ושננתם ותתנינון כלומר גם יתנון שעוסקים בתורה כולהו עתה אקבצם מגלותם ואם מעט מהם יעסקו ויחלו אותו מעט ויחלו כמו לא יחל דברו: מנת המלך. שנותנין מתנות למלך מסים: ארנונא. מס של קרקע: כריא חדתא. חפירה גדולה שחופרין ליכנס שם מים הרבה להשקות ממנה שדות ע"י דלייה ודרך נגרים ופסק א) ליתן ליתומין חלק בחפירה זו שהן נהנין ממנה כאחרים: לא מידויל. שלא יגבעו המים ונמצאת מוציא מעות יתומים בכדי: לאגלי גפא. זהו שעושין מחיצה או גדר סמוך לחומת העיר מבחוץ כדי להגן על החומה ועל שם כך קרי אגלי גפא לשון הגפת דלתות כלומר לנעול שערים שעושין לפני פנות העיר משום מצור העיר: לכריא פתיא. שחופרין למלאות ממנו מים לשתות ועל שם כך קרי ליה כריא פתיא שדולין בכלי חרס כמו (ברכות נ ש"מ) פתיא אוכמא: אפי' מרבנן. שהן שותין ממנו כאחרים: ואי קא נפקי באכלוזא. כלומר שיוצאין חבורות בני העיר הן עצמן (ואינן) [ואינהו] חופרין ואינן שוכרין רבנן לא עבדי הכי מפני כבוד תורה: פתח אוצר בשני בצורת. [illegible] עניים: בעל הלכות. זה ששונה ברייתות. אף על גב דבדוכתא אחרינא אמרי' בעלי הלכות אלו בעלי משנה הכא הואיל ותני בעלי משנה צריכין למימר דהלכות אלו ברייתות הן: ככלב וכעורב. דכתיב ורחמיו [illegible] לטעמיה. שלא היה רוצה לפרנס עם הארץ: דההוא דמי כלילא. שהשליך המלך מס על יושבי טבריא כדי שיקנו לו כתר: אמר להו. לא תסייען [לכון] רבנן: ערקינן. דלא מצינן למיתן כולי דמי כלילא אמר [illegible] לדמי כלילא. על ההוא פלגא דאשתייר: פקע כלילא. בטל גזירת הכתר: הראיתם שאין פורעניות בא לעולם אלא בשביל עמי הארץ. דכיון דלא נשארו שם אלא רבנן לא גזרו עליהן ליתן דמי כתר ש[illegible] הארץ היה שם גזרו ושוב לא גזרו: פיסקא ויהא כאנשי העיר. ליתן בכל מילי שנותנין בני העיר שנים עשר חדש: החמרת והגמלת. שיירא של חמרין וגמלין העוברים ממקום למקום ולנה בתוך עיר הנ[illegible] כדכתיב וידיחו את יושבי עירם הן בסייף וממונן אבד כאנשי עיר הנדחת כדכתיב הכה תכה את יושבי העיר וגו': הן נדונין בסקילה וממונן פלט. הואיל ולא נשתהו שם כלל אלא כדי לינה אלמא דל' יום הוי [illegible] למתני' דבעי י"ב חדש ב) למיקרייא מיתבא מתא לא בעינן אלא ל' יום ונידון כמותם משום דהכתוב מיירי בלשון יושבי כדכתיב הכה תכה את יושבי העיר וגו' אבל למיקרייא מבני מתא להיותן כאנשי העיר ל[illegible] לא הוי עד י"ב חודש כדתניא המודר וכו': ולכל מילי. כלומר דמשמע במתני' שלא יתן כלום בדבר עד י"ב חודש והא תניא נמי הבא לעיר ונשתהה שם ל' יום חייב ליתן לתמחוי היינו כלי שבו נותנין מ[illegible] מבני העיר ליתן מנות ממאכלים בתמחוי להאכיל לעניי העולם העוברים עליהם ואם נשתהה שם ג' חדשים יתן חלקו לקופה של צדקה שגובין מע"ש לערב שבת לפרנס עניי אותה העיר ואם נשתהה ו' חדשים [illegible] העיר שקורין שפיצ"א ותירות שעושין חוץ לחומה לחזוק העיר אלמא לכל מילי לא בעינן י"ב חדש: הכל לפסי. מן הכל גובין לצורך תקון פסי העיר: לשורא. לחזוק החומה: לפרשא. שקונים סוסים לפרשים [illegible] חוץ לעיר לעיין אם [באו] גייסות: לטורזינא. לצורך [כלי] זיין שנושאין אותן שומרי חומות העיר: בר מריון. איש א' היה עשיר גדול: אנא לאחשובינהו בעינא. שיהיו חשובין בכל דבר מצוה [illegible]

חשק שלמה על רבינו גרשום א) נראה דל"ל ופסק שיתנו היתומים חלק וכו'. ב) נ"ל הא למיקרייא מיתבא מתא וכו'. ג) נ"ל חייב ליתן חלקו בכסות: לפסי העיר שקורין שפילא וכו':

מסורת הש"ס

א) [פסחים פז.], ב) ס"א רב הונא, ג) ס"א רבא, ד) נדרים סב:, ה) ב"מ קח., ו) [שם ולעיל ז:], ז) [שבת קמג.], ח) [שם קלג. ע"ש יבמות סג. ע"ש], ט) [פי' עגגא גר המלך אמר המלך הואיל ופשטו היהודים בשמירת העיר ישלמו דמי המס. ערוך ערך כלל א'], י) סנהדרין קיב. ע"ש, כ) [סנהדרין שם תוספתא נדרים פ"ב], ל) [תוספתא דפאה פ"ד], מ) [פי' קרשי עץ לחזק שערי העיר. ערוך ערך סף], נ) [עי' פירש"י נדה כ: ובמעונות כד:], ס) נ"ל דרב יוסף. רש"א.

הגהות הב"ח

(א) גמ' רב נחמן בר רב חסדא רמא כרגא וכו' עבר מר אדאורייתא: (ב) רש"י ד"ה לפרשא פרש הרוכב סביבות: (ג) תוס' ד"ה יתיב וכו' כדפי' הקונטרס דרב יוסף קבלה הכא משום שלום. נ"ב לקמן דף י' ד"ה רבא קיימוה:

גליון הש"ס

גמרא המודר הנאה מאנשי העיר. עיין בר"ן נדרים דף סג ע"ב ד"ה ר"י אמר: שם דרבנן לא צריכי נטירותא. עי' רבינו יונה פ"ק דברכות דף ד ע"ב ד"ה שנאמר:

תורה אור השלם

א) אֲנִי חוֹמָה וְשָׁדַי כַּמִּגְדָּלוֹת אָז הָיִיתִי בְעֵינָיו כְּמוֹצְאֵת שָׁלוֹם: [שיר השירים ח, י]

ב) אַף חֹבֵב עַמִּים כָּל קְדֹשָׁיו בְּיָדֶךָ וְהֵם תֻּכּוּ לְרַגְלֶךָ יִשָּׂא מִדַּבְּרֹתֶיךָ: [דברים לג, ג]

ג) גַּם כִּי יִתְנוּ בַגּוֹיִם עַתָּה אֲקַבְּצֵם וַיָּחֵלּוּ מְּעָט מִמַּשָּׂא מֶלֶךְ שָׂרִים: [הושע ח, י]

ד) וּלְכֹם מְהוֹדְעִין דִּי כָל כָּהֲנַיָּא וְלֵוָיֵא זַמָּרַיָּא תָרָעַיָּא נְתִינַיָּא וּפָלְחֵי בֵּית אֱלָהָא דְנָה מִנְדָּה בְלוֹ וַהֲלָךְ לָא שַׁלִּיט לְמִרְמֵא עֲלֵיהֹם: [עזרא ז, כד]

ליקוטי רש"י

[תחילת ליקוטי רש"י ששייך לכאן נדפס בעמוד הקודם] הורמיז. לקמן עג. הורמין בר לילית כלומר יופי שדים היה לה [נדה כ:].

עין משפט נר מצוה

נז א מיי' פ"ו מהלכות ת"ת הלכה י סמג עשין יב טוש"ע י"ד סי' רמג סעיף ב וטוש"ע י"ד סי' רמג סעיף ג:

נח ב ג ד מיי' פ"ו מהל' שכנים הל' ו ז סמג עשין פב טוש"ע ח"מ סי' קסג סעיף ז:

נט ה ו ז מיי' פ"ו מהל' ת"ת הל' י סמג עשין יב טוש"ע י"ד סי' רמג סעיף ב וטוש"ע י"ד סי' רנג סעיף א ב:

ס ח טוש"ע י"ד סי' רנג סעיף יא:

סא ט מיי' פ"ד מהל' ע"ז הל' ט:

סב י מיי' פ"ט מהל' נדרים הל' יח סמג לאוין רמג טוש"ע י"ד סי' ריז סעיף לב:

סג כ מיי' פ"ט מהל' מתנות עניים הל' יב סמג עשין קסב טוש"ע י"ד סי' רנו סעיף ה:

סד ל מיי' פ"ו מהל' שכנים הל' ה סמג עשין פב טוש"ע ח"מ סי' קסג סעיף ג:

סה מ מיי' שם הל' ו סמג שם טוש"ע שם סעיף ז:

סו נ ס ע מיי' שם ופ"ו מהל' ת"ת הלכה י סמג שם טוש"ע שם וטוש"ע י"ד סי' רמג סעיף ב:

סז פ צ מיי' פ"ח מהל' מתנות עניים הלכה יב סמג עשין קסב טוש"ע י"ד סי' רמח סעיף ג:

סח ק מיי' שם הל' ט סמג עשין קסב טוש"ע י"ד סי' רנב סעיף ג:

סט ר מיי' שם הל' י סמג שם טוש"ע י"ד סי' רנב סעיף א:

Eretz Yisrael **now.**[15] וְאִם מְעַט מֵהֶם – **And if** only **a few of them** study in exile, יָחֵלּוּ מִמַּשָּׂא מֶלֶךְ וְשָׂרִים – [those scholars] **will be released from the burdens of kings and officers.** From here we see that God exempts Torah scholars from the "burden" of taxes, among other obligations owed to the government.

Rav Nachman elucidates the third verse:

אַדִּכְתוּבֵי דִּכְתִיב – You have transgressed a precept **of the Writings, for it is written:**[16] "מִנְדָּה בְלוֹ וַהֲלָךְ לָא שַׁלִּיט לְמִרְמֵא עֲלֵיהֹם" – *It shall be unlawful to impose upon them levies, taxes and tithes.*[17] **וְאָמַר רַב יְהוּדָה** – **And Rav Yehudah said:** "מִנְדָּה" זוֹ מְנַת הַמֶּלֶךְ – *Levies* – **this is the king's portion;**[18] "בְּלוֹ" זוֹ כֶּסֶף גּוּלְגַּלְתָּא – *taxes* – **this is the head tax;** "וַהֲלָךְ" זוֹ אַרְנוֹנָא – *and tithes* – **this is the** annual **tithe** of produce and livestock, which was given to the government. Thus, it is obvious from all three sources that Rav Nachman bar Rav Chisda wrongfully imposed a head tax on the Rabbis of his town, since Rabbis are generally exempt from taxation.

The Gemara discusses other taxes, and who must pay them:

רַב פָּפָּא רָמָא כְּרְיָא חַדְתָּא – **Rav Pappa imposed** a tax for the purpose of **digging a new** well to provide drinking water for the town, **אַיְתָמֵי** – and he levied the tax even **upon orphans.**[19]

An objection is raised:

אָמַר לֵיהּ רַב שִׁישָׁא בְּרֵיהּ דְּרַב אִידִי לְרַב פָּפָּא – **Rav Shisha the son of Rav Idi said to Rav Pappa:** וְדִילְמָא לָא מִידְּוִיל – **But perhaps [water] will never be drawn** from the well, for the digging may prove unsuccessful![20] – ? –

Rav Pappa dismisses this concern:

אָמַר לֵיהּ מִישְׁקַל שָׁקִילְנָא מִנַּיְיהוּ – **[Rav Pappa] told [Rav Shisha]: I shall collect** the tax **from [the orphans],** אִי מִידְּוִיל – and **if [water] will** ultimately **be drawn** from the well, מִידְּוִיל – **it will be drawn** (i.e. there will be no problem)! וְאִי לָא – **And if** the digging is **not** successful, מַהְדַּרְנָא לְהוּ נִיהֲלַיְיהוּ – **I shall** simply **return [the money] to them.** On this basis it was permitted to include minor orphans in the tax.

Rav Yehudah issues two rulings:

אָמַר רַב יְהוּדָה הַכֹּל לְאַגְלֵי גַּפָּא – **Rav Yehudah said:** We collect from **everyone for** installing **doors to enclose**[21] the city's gates – אֲפִילוּ מִיַּתְמֵי – **even from orphans,** for they also need protection. אֲבָל רַבָּנָן לָא צְרִיכֵי נְטִירוּתָא – **But the Rabbis do not need** human **protection,** and so they are exempt from this tax. הַכֹּל לִכְרְיָא פַּתְיָא – Further, we collect from **everyone for the digging of a well**[22] אֲפִילּוּ מֵרַבָּנָן – **even from the Rabbis,** for they also require drinking water.

Rav Yehudah qualifies his second ruling:

וְלָא אֲמָרָן אֶלָּא – **And we have said** that the Rabbis must contribute toward the well **only** דְּלָא נָפְקֵי בְּאַכְלוֹזָא – **when [the townspeople] do not go out** in turns **when called**[23] to dig the well themselves, but hire workers to do so. In such a case, the Rabbis must help bear the cost of the project. אֲבָל נָפְקֵי בְּאַכְלוֹזָא – **But if [the townspeople] go out** in turns **when called** to dig the well themselves, the Rabbis are excused from performing this duty, רַבָּנָן לָאו בְּנֵי מִיפַּק בְּאַכְלוֹזָא נִינְהוּ – for **Rabbis are not people who go out** and perform manual labor **when called.** To do so would bring dishonor on the Torah, which they represent.[24]

The Gemara relates an incident:

רַבִּי פָּתַח אוֹצָרוֹת בִּשְׁנֵי בַצּוֹרֶת – **Rebbi**[25] **opened storehouses** of food to feed the poor **during the years of famine.** אָמַר יִכָּנְסוּ בַּעֲלֵי מִקְרָא בַּעֲלֵי מִשְׁנָה בַּעֲלֵי גְּמָרָא בַּעֲלֵי הֲלָכָה בַּעֲלֵי הַגָּדָה – However, **[Rebbi] said:** Only those who are **students**[26] **of Scripture,** or **students of Mishnah,** or **students of Gemara,**[27] or **students of halachah,**[28] or **students of the homiletic literature may enter** and take food from the storehouses. אֲבָל עַמֵּי הָאָרֶץ אַל יִכָּנְסוּ – **But unlearned folk may not enter.**[29] דָּחַק רַבִּי יוֹנָתָן בֶּן עַמְרָם וְנִכְנַס – **R' Yonasan ben Amram,** a disciple of Rebbi's, disguised himself[30] and **pushed his way into** the storehouse. אָמַר לוֹ רַבִּי

NOTES

15. *Rashi* writes: "I will gather them *soon*."

16. *Ezra* 7:24.

17. *Rashi* explains that in this verse King Darius II, son of Esther and Achashveirosh, commanded the pasha whose dominion included Eretz Yisrael to exempt the Men of the Great Assembly from these taxes and levies. *Rashash* points out, however, that the first part of the verse explicitly mentions only the Temple personnel as deserving of this exemption (see *Hagahos R' Matisyahu Strashun*). [Perhaps *Rashi* reckons the Men of the Great Assembly among the Temple personnel because they convened for judgment in the Temple.] *Tosafos* explain that devotion to Torah study is equivalent to involvement in the Temple service. Thus, the Gemara's proof is as follows: Just as the Temple personnel were exempt from taxes because of their participation in the sacred Temple services, so, too, Torah scholars are exempt because of their sacred Torah study.

18. I.e. revenue from various taxes imposed routinely upon the citizenry (*Rashi*).

19. I.e. who were minors and thus entitled to special treatment. Although minor orphans must also contribute to communal projects from which they benefit, digging a new well poses a special problem, as the Gemara now explains.

20. Rav Shisha argued that if water is not found, Rav Pappa will have caused a needless loss of the orphans' money, and that since they are minors the orphans are not legally competent to forgive the administrators' inadvertant misuse of their funds (*Rashi*).

Rav Shisha's objection does not imply that every failed public works project signifies a misuse of funds collected from the general populace, so that the public's forgiveness would be required to absolve the city administrators of wrongdoing, for administrators are authorized to use communal funds as they see fit (see Gemara below, 8b). Rather, it is only the money of minor orphans that may not be expended needlessly, for they have no real obligation to contribute to communal projects. We may only take funds from them when they actually benefit from their use (see *Yad Ramah, Rabbeinu Gershom*).

21. אַגְלֵי means *doors* (see *Berachos* 28a), and גַּפָּא means *closure* (see *Bava Metzia* 25b) [*Rashi*].

22. פַּתְיָא actually means *drinking vessel*, not "well." Rav Yehudah called the well "a drinking vessel" because such vessels were permanently placed at wells for the use of wayfarers that required a drink (*Rashi*).

23. *Rashi*, who understands that אַכְלוֹזָא is derived from הַכְרָזָה, *public announcement. Rabbeinu Gershom* and others translate אַכְלוֹזָא as "in rotations." According to these commentators אַכְלוֹזָא derives from אוּכְלוּסָא, which means *a large group of people.*

24. *Rabbeinu Gershom. Nimukei Yosef* cites a ruling from *Tosafos* (which is not found in our text), that in this case the Rabbis are totally exempt, and do not have to hire others to go in their stead.

25. Rabbi Yehudah HaNasi, codifier of the Mishnah.

26. Literally, masters of Scripture etc.

27. This refers to the oral elucidation of the Mishnah, for the Gemara (*Talmud Bavli*) was not redacted until later.

28. Although normally בַּעֲלֵי הֲלָכָה refers to students of the Mishnah, here it means students of the Baraisa, since the former category is already explicitly mentioned (*Rabbeinu Gershom*). *Rashash*, however, understands the expression to refer to students of the various codes of halachah that existed at that time.

29. Rebbi was concerned that his food supplies were insufficient to feed everyone, and that the unlearned people would therefore sustain themselves at the expense of the Torah scholars (*Ritva*, cited in *Beis Yosef* to *Tur Yoreh Deah* 251; see also *Maharsha*).

30. As a common, unlearned person. The Gemara below will explain his reason for doing so.

אלו ת"ח ור"ל סבר לה כדדרש רבא אני חומה זו כנסת ישראל ושדי כמגדלות אלו בתי כנסיות ובתי מדרשות רב נחמן בר רב חסדא רמא כרגא ארבנן א"ל רב נחמן בר יצחק עברת אדאורייתא ואדנביאי ואדכתובי אדאורייתא דכתיב אף חובב עמים כל קדושיו בידך אמר משה לפני הקב"ה רבונו של עולם אפילו בשעה שאתה מחבב עמים כל קדושיו יהיו בידך והם תכו לרגלך תני רב יוסף אלו תלמידי חכמים שמכתתים רגליהם מעיר לעיר וממדינה למדינה ללמוד תורה ישא מדברותיך לישא וליתן בדברותיו של מקום אדנביאי דכתיב גם כי יתנו בגוים עתה אקבצם ויחלו מעט ממשא מלך ושרים אמר עולא פסוק זה בלשון ארמית נאמר אי תנו כולהו עתה אקבצם ואם מעט מהם יחלו ממשא מלך ושרים אדכתובי דכתיב מנדה בלו והלך לא שליט למרמא עליהם ואמר רב יהודה מנדה זו מנת המלך בלו זו כסף גולגלתא והלך זו ארנונא רב פפא רמא כריא חדתא איתמי א"ל רב שישא בריה דרב אידי לרב פפא ודילמא לא מידויל מידויל ואי לא מהדרנא לה ניהליהו אמר רב יהודה הכל לאגלי גפא אפילו מיתמי אבל רבנן לא צריכי נטירותא הכל לכריא פתיא אפי' מרבנן ולא אמרן אלא דלא נפקי באכלוזא אבל נפקי באכלוזא רבנן לאו בני מיפק באכלוזא נינהו: רבי פתח אוצרות בשני בצורת אמר יכנסו בעלי מקרא בעלי משנה בעלי גמרא בעלי הלכה בעלי הגדה אבל עמי הארץ אל יכנסו דחק רבי יונתן בן עמרם ונכנס אמר לו רבי פרנסני אמר לו בני קרית אמר לו לאו שנית א"ל לאו אם כן במה אפרנסך [א"ל] פרנסני ככלב וכעורב פרנסיה בתר דנפק יתיב רבי וקא מצטער ואמר אוי לי שנתתי פתי לעם הארץ אמר לפניו ר' שמעון בר רבי שמא יונתן בן עמרם תלמידך הוא שאינו רוצה ליהנות מכבוד תורה מימיו בדקו ואשכח אמר רבי יכנסו הכל רבי לטעמיה דאמר רבי אין פורענות בא לעולם אלא בשביל עמי הארץ כי ההוא דמי כלילא דשדו אטבריא אתו לקמיה דרבי ואמרו ליה ליתבו רבנן בהדן אמר להו לא אמרו ליה ערוקינן [א"ל] ערוקו פלגיהון דליוה פלגא אתו הנהו פלגא קמי דרבי א"ל ליתבו רבנן בהדן אמר להו לא ערוקינן ערוקו כולהו פש ההוא כובס שדיוה אכובס ערק כובס פקע כלילא א"ר ראיתם שאין פורענות בא לעולם אלא בשביל עמי הארץ: וכמה יהא בעיר ויהא כאנשי העיר וכו': ורמינהי החמרת והגמלת העוברת ממקום למקום ולנה בתוכה והודחה עמהן הן בסקילה וממונן פלט ואם נשתהו שם שלשים יום הן בסייף וממונן אבד אמר רבא לא קשיא הא לבני מתא הא ליתובי מתא כדתניא המודר הנאה מאנשי העיר כל שנשתהא שם שנים עשר חדש אסור ליהנות ממנו פחות מכאן מותר מיושבי העיר כל שנשתהא שם שלשים יום אסור ליהנות ממנו פחות מכאן מותר ליהנות ממנו ולכל מילי מי בעינן י"ב חדש והתניא שלשים יום לתמחוי שלשה חדשים לקופה ששה לכסות תשעה לקבורה שנים עשר לפסי העיר אמר ר' אסי אמר ר' יוחנן כי תנן נמי מתניתין שנים עשר חדש לפסי העיר תנן: וא"ר אסי אמר ר' יוחנן הכל לפסי העיר ואפי' מיתמי אבל רבנן לא דרבנן לא צריכי נטירותא אמר רב פפא לשורא ולפרשאה ולטרזינא אפילו מיתמי אבל רבנן לא צריכי נטירותא כללא דמילתא כל מילתא דאית להו הנאה מיניה אפילו מיתמי רבה רמא צדקה איתמי דבי בר מריון א"ל אביי והתני רב שמואל בר יהודה אין פוסקין צדקה על היתומים אפילו לפדיון שבוים א"ל אנא לאחשובינהו קא עבידנא איפרא הורמיז אימיה דשבור מלכא שדרה ארנקא דדינרי לקמיה דרב יוסף אמרה ליהוי למצוה רבה יתיב רב יוסף וקא מעיין בה מאי מצוה רבה א"ל אביי מדתני רב שמואל בר יהודה אין פוסקין צדקה על היתומים אפילו לפדיון שבוים שמע מינה פדיון

רש"י

אלו תלמידי חכמים. הלכך אין צריכין חומה: [זו] כנסת ישראל. כולם שוין לענין חומה וגודרים עצמן מלהטמע בעובדי כוכבים: שאתה מחבב עמים. שאתה מגביה להם פניך להשליטן על בניך: כל קדושיו. של ישראל בידך [הם] לשומרן: בלשון ארמי נאמר. יתנו תרגום של ישנו כמו ושננתם ותניתנון (דברים ו): אם תנו כולם. וכן רובן יהיו שונין ועוסקים בתורה כשגלו בעמים: עתה אקבצם. בקרוב אקבצם: ויחלו מעט וגו'. ואף [אם] מועטין הן השונין בעמים יחלו ממשא מלך ושרים יהיו בטלים מלשאת משא מלך ושרים. יחלו כמו לא יחל דברו (במדבר ל): מנדה בלו והלך. דריוש צוה את פחת עבר הנהר על אנשי כנסת הגדולה: מנת המלך. מגבת מסים שהן מטילין תמיד על בני המדינה: ארנונא. עישורי תבואות ובהמות מדי שנה בשנה: כריא חדתא. יציאת כריית באר מים חיים לשתות: לא מידויל. לא ימצאו בו מים והפסדתם חנם ויתמי לאו בני מחילה נינהו ליחלו: לאגלי גפא. לשערי חומות העיר להגיף בהן דלתות. אגלי דלתות כמו ערוקו גלי (ברכות דף מג.) גפא סתימה כמו מצא אחר הגפה בהלו מציאות (ב"מ דף כה:): לכריא פתיא. חפירת בור לשתות מים ועל שם הכלי המונח שם בבור תמיד לשתות בו עוברי דרכים קורהו פתיא: אפילו מרבנן. שהכל צריכין למים: דלא נפקי באכלוזא. שאין הן עצמם יוצאין בהכרזה לחפור אלא שוכרים פועלים: ככלב וכעורב. שחס הקב"ה עליהם (שבת קנה:) שנאמר יודע צדיק דין דלים (משלי כט) לפי שהכלב מזונותיו מועטין לפיכך שוהה אכילתו במעיו שלשת ימים וגבי עורב כתיב לבני עורב אשר יקראו (תהלים קמז) לפי שהעורב אכזרי על בניו והקב"ה מזמין להן יתושין מתוך צואתם ואוכלין: דמי כלילא. עטרה למלך קיסר: אתו. עמי הארץ לקמיה דרבי: דליוה לפלגא. מחל המלך דמי החצי וסילקה מעליהן: שדיוה אכובס. הטילוה פחתי המלך על הכובס: החמרת והגמלת. שיירא של חמרים ושל גמלים: הרי אלו בסקילה. כדין שאר יחידים: ליתובי מתא. בשלשים יום וגבי עיר הנדחת כתיב יושבי העיר (דברים יג): ולכל מילי. ומקמי הכי לא יהיב מידי עם בני העיר: שלשים יום לתמחוי. כיון ששהה שם שלשים יום גובין הימנו [גבאי] תמחוי מאכל לעניים: לקופה. לצדקה. לכסות. עניי העיר: לקבורה. לקבור עניי העיר שהיא יצאה יחידה: לשורא. לתיקון החומה: לפרשא. פרש (ג) שהולך סביבות העיר לשומרה ולידע מה היא צריכה: לטרזינא. שומר כלי זיין של בני העיר ויושב בבית אצל השער:

תוספות

לא שליט למרמא עליהם. לפי שהיו עסוקים במלאכת שמים בבנין בית המקדש ה"נ אין להטיל מס על לומדי תורה: והלך זו ארנונא. פי' בקונטרס עישור בהמות ותבואה כו' ור"ח פי' ארוחה דורון לשלטון העובר ממקום למקום שנותן לו כל עיר ועיר ארוחה ופירושו מלשון ויבא הלך לאיש העשיר (שמואל ב יב): כריא פתיא. פירש ר"ח להסיר גבשושית מרחוב העיר: איפרא הורמיז. פר"ח משמעות הלשון חן מאת המקום איפרא כמו אפריון נמטייה לר"ש (ב"מ דף קיט.) הורמיז שם שכינה כי הוא דס"פ אחד דיני ממונות (סנהדרין דף לט.) (ושם ד"ה הורמיז) מפלגא דידך ולעיל להורמיז בזי"ן מפלגא ולמטה דהורמין בנו"ן כמו הורמין בר לילתא (לקמן דף עג.): (לעיל) ככלב וכעורב. כמו שפי' הקונטרס והיינו דכתיב נותן לבהמה לחמה לבני עורב וגו' בהמה בגימטריא כלב: יתיב רב יוסף וקא מעיין בה. וא"ת ולית ליה דינא בקצור קצירה תשברנה וגו' (ישעיה כז) כדאמרי' בפירקין (דף י:) וי"ל דקבלי' משום שלום מלכות לדעבד רבא לקמן (שם) וכי היכי דפלגינהו רבא לעניי עובדי כוכבים ה"נ בעי למיעבד בהו רב יוסף שבויי עובדי כוכבים ומיהו לא צריכי להכי אלא לכדפירש הקונט' (ג) דרבא דקבלה משום שלום מלכות וכיון שאמר לו ליתן למצוה רבה לא היה אפשר לחלקם לעניי עובדי כוכבים דאסור לגנוב דעת הבריות ואפי' דעתו של עובד כוכבים (חולין צד.) אבל מעות המתחלקים לעניים אין כאן גניבת דעת דאינהו נמי ידעי דישראל רגילין לפרנסם כדאמר בהנזקין (גיטין דף סא.) מפרנסים עניי עכו"ם עם עניי ישראל מפני דרכי שלום והא דקבל מההוא טייעא דנדר שרגא לבי כנישתא בפ"ק דערכין (דף ו: ושם ד"ה עד) אע"ג דהתם לא היה שלום מלכות התם טעמא משום דהוו כמו קרבן ואמרינן (נזיר סב.) איש איש לרבות נכרים שנודרים נדרים ונדבות כישראל:

רבינו גרשום

אלו ת"ח. שלומדין זה מזה כתינוק יונק משדי אמו: ווריש לקיש דמפיק מאספרם מחול ירבון דריש האי אני חומה בכל ישראל ולא בצדיקים בלבד: כרגא. כסף גולגלתא: אע"פ שאתה מחבב אומות העולם. שאתה נותן להם על ישראל ממשלה בזמן שישראל בגלות אעפ"כ קדושיו של ישראל העוסקים בתורה יהיו מסורין בידך: לרגלך. משמע בשבילך ומשמע רגל ממש: יתנו בגוים. בלשון ארמי כמו ושננתם ותתנינון כלומר גם יתנון שעוסקים בתורה כולהו עתה אקבצם מגלותם ואם מעט מהם יעסקו ויחלו אותו מעט ויחלו כמו לא יחל דברו: מנת המלך. שנותנין מתנות למלך מסים: ארנונא. מס של קרקע: כריא חדתא. חפירה גדולה שחופרין ליכנס שם מים הרבה להשקות ממנה שדות ע"י דלייה ודרך נגרים ופסק א) ליתן ליתומין חלק בחפירה זו שהן נהנין ממנה כאחרים: לא מידויל. שלא ינבעו המים ונמצאת מוציא מעות יתומים בכדי: לאגלי גפא. זהו שעושין מחיצה או גדר סמוך לחומת העיר מבחוץ כדי להגן על החומה ועל שם כך קרי אגלי גפא לשון הגפת דלתות כלומר לנעול שערים שעושין לפני פינת העיר משום מצור העיר: לכריא פתיא. שחופרין למלאות ממנו מים לשתות ועל שם כך קרי ליה כריא פתיא שדולין בכלי חרס כמו (ברכות נ וש"מ) פתיא אוכמא: אפי' מרבנן. שהן שותין ממנו כאחרים: ואי קא נפקי באכלוזא. כלומר שיוצאין חבורות בני העיר הן עצמן (ואינן) [ואינהו] חופרין ואינן שוכרין רבנן לא עבדי הכי מפני כבוד תורה: פתח אוצר בשני בצורת. לפרנס עניים: בעל הלכות. זה ששונה ברייתות. אף על גב דבדוכתא אחרינא אמרי' בעלי הלכות אלו בעלי משנה הכא הואיל ותני בעלי משנה צריכין למימר דהלכות אלו ברייתות הן: ככלב וכעורב. דכתיב ורחמיו על כל מעשיו: רבי לטעמיה. שלא היה רוצה לפרנס עם הארץ: דההוא דמי כלילא. שהשליך המלך מס על יושבי טבריא כדי שיקנו לו כתר: אמר להו. לא תסייעו [לכון] רבנן: ערקינן. דלא מצינן למיתן כולי דמי כלילא אמר להו ערוקו: דלייה לדמי כלילא. על ההוא פלגא דאשתייר: פקע כלילא. בטל גזירת הכתר: הראיתם שאין פורענות בא לעולם אלא בשביל עמי הארץ. דכיון דלא נשארו שם אלא רבנן לא גזרו עליהן ליתן דמי כתר שכל זמן שאחד מעמי הארץ היה שם גזרו ושוב לא גזרו: פיסקא ויהא כאנשי העיר. ליתן בכל מילי שנותנין בני העיר שנים עשר חדש: החמרת והגמלת. שיירא של חמרין וגמלין העוברים ממקום למקום ולנה בתוך עיר הנדחת והודחה עמה כדכתיב וידיחו את יושבי עירם הן בסייף וממונן אבד כאנשי עיר הנדחת כדכתיב הכה תכה את יושבי העיר וגו': הן נדונין בסקילה וממונן פלט. הואיל ולא נשתהו שם כלל אלא כדי לינה אלמא דל' יום הוי כיושבי העיר וקשיא למתני' דבעי י"ב חדש ב) למיקרייה מיתבא מתא לא בעינן אלא ל' יום ונידון כמותם משום דהכתוב מיירי בלשון יושבי כדכתיב הכה תכה את יושבי העיר וגו' אבל למיקרייה מבני מתא להיותן כאנשי העיר ליתן עמהם לכל דבר לא הוי עד י"ב חודש כדתניא המודר וכו': ולכל מילי. כלומר דמשמע במתני' שלא יתן כלום בדבר עד י"ב חודש והא תניא נמי הבא לעיר ונשתהה שם ל' יום חייב ליתן לתמחוי היינו כלי שבו נותנין מאכל ומקבצין וגובין מבני העיר ליתן מנות ממאכלים בתמחוי להאכיל לעניי העולם העוברים עליהם ואם נשתהה שם ג' חדשים יתן חלקו לקופה של צדקה שגובין מע"ש לערב שבת לפרנס עניי אותה העיר ואם נשתהה ו' חדשים חייב ליתן ג) חלקו לכסות: הכל לפסי. מן הכל גובין לצורך תקון פסי העיר: לשורא. לחזוק החומה: לפרשא. שקונים סוסים לפרשים (כפי) [כדין] שיצאו חוץ לעיר לעיין אם [באו] גייסות: לטורזינא. לצורך [כלי] זיין שנושאין אותן שומרי חומות העיר: בר מריון. איש א' היה עשיר גדול: אנא לאחשובינהו בעינא. שיהיו חשובין בכל דבר מצוה כמו אביהן:

חשק שלמה על רבינו גרשום א) נראה דל"ל ופסק שיתנו היתומים חלק וכו'. ב) נ"ל הא למיקרייה מיתבא מתא וכו'. ג) נ"ל חייב ליתן חלקו בכסות: לפסי העיר שקורין שפילא וכו':

מסורת הש"ס

א) [פסחים פז.], ב) ס"א רב הונא, ג) ס"א רבא, ד) נדרים סב., ה) [שם ע"ש], ו) [עי' תוס' קמ.], ז) [שבת קנה:], ח) [פי' כגנב נזר המלך אמר המלך הואיל ופשעו היהודים בשמירת העיר ישלמו דמי הנזר. ערוך ערך כלל א'], ט) סנהדרין קיב. ע"ש, י) [סנהדרין שם תוספתא נדרים פ"ב], כ) [תוספתא דפאה פ"ד], ל) פי' קרשי עץ לחזק שערי העיר. ערוך ערך פס א'], מ) [לעיל ז:], נ) [עי' פירש"י ובתענית כד:] ס) צ"ל דרב יוסף. רש"א.

הגהות הב"ח

(א) גמ' רב נחמן בר רב חסדא רמא כרגא וכו' עבר מר אדאורייתא: (ב) רש"י ד"ה לפרנסא פרש הרוכב סביבות: (ג) תוס' ד"ה יתיב וכו' כדפי' הקונטרס דרב יוסף קבלם הכא משום שלום. נ"ב לקמן דף י' ע"ב ד"ה דלא פיימוה:

גליון הש"ס

גמרא המודר הנאה מאנשי העיר. עיין בר"ן נדרים דף סג ע"ב ד"ה ר"נ אמר: שם דרבנן לא"צ נטירותא. עי' רבינו יונה פ"א דברכות דף ד ע"ב ד"ה שנאמר:

תורה אור השלם

א) אֲנִי חוֹמָה וְשָׁדַי כַּמִּגְדָּלוֹת אָז הָיִיתִי בְעֵינָיו כְּמוֹצְאֵת שָׁלוֹם: [שיר השירים ח, י]

ב) אַף חֹבֵב עַמִּים כָּל קְדֹשָׁיו בְּיָדֶךָ וְהֵם תֻּכּוּ לְרַגְלֶךָ יִשָּׂא מִדַּבְּרֹתֶיךָ: [דברים לג, ג]

ג) גַּם כִּי יִתְנוּ בַגּוֹיִם עַתָּה אֲקַבְּצֵם וַיָּחֵלּוּ מְּעָט מִמַּשָּׂא מֶלֶךְ שָׂרִים: [הושע ח, י]

ד) וּלְכֹם מְהוֹדְעִין דִּי כָל כָּהֲנַיָּא וְלֵוָיֵא זַמָּרַיָּא תָרָעַיָּא נְתִינַיָּא וּפָלְחֵי בֵּית אֱלָהָא דְנָה מִנְדָּה בְלוֹ וַהֲלָךְ לָא שַׁלִּיט לְמִרְמֵא עֲלֵיהֹם: [עזרא ז, כד]

ליקוטי רש"י

[תחילת ליקוטי רש"י ששייך לכאן נדפס בעמוד הקודם] הורמיז. כמו (לקמן עג.) הורמין בר לילתא כלומר שדים היה לה [נדה כ:].

עין משפט נר מצוה

נז א מיי' פ"ו מהלכות ת"ת הלכה י סמג עשין יב טוש"ע י"ד סי' רמג סעיף ב:
נח ב ג ד מיי' פ"ו מהל' שכנים הל' א וז סמג עשין פב טוש"ע ח"מ סי' קסג סעיף ד:
נט ה ו ז מיי' שם ופ"ו מהל' ת"ת הל' י סמג שם וסי' יב טוש"ע שם וטוש"ע י"ד סי' רמג סעיף ג:
ס ח טוש"ע י"ד סי' רנו סעיף יא:
סא ט מיי' פ"ד מהל' ע"ז הל' ט:
סב י מיי' פ"ט מהל' נדרים הל' יח סמג לאוין רמב טוש"ע י"ד סי' ריז סעיף לג:
סג כ ל מיי' פ"ט מהל' מתנות עניים הל' יב סמג עשין קסב טוש"ע י"ד סי' רנו סעיף ה:
סד ל מיי' פ"ו מהל' שכנים הל' ה סמג עשין פב טוש"ע ח"מ סי' קסג סעיף ג:
סה מ מיי' שם הל' ו סמג שם טוש"ע שם סעיף ב:
סו נ ס ע מיי' שם וסי' מהל' ת"ת הלכה י סמג שם וטוש"ע שם וטוש"ע י"ד סי' רמג סעיף ב:
סז פ צ מיי' פ"ז מהל' מתנות עניים הלכה יב סמג עשין קסב טוש"ע י"ד סי' רמח סעיף ג:
סח ק מיי' פ"ח מהל' ע הל' ט סמג עשין קסב טוש"ע י"ד סי' רנד סעיף א:
סט ר מיי' שם הל' י סמג עשין קסב טוש"ע י"ד סי' רנב סעיף א:

פַּרְנְסֵנִי – Once inside **he said to [Rebbi]: "Master,**[31] please **sustain me."**

Not recognizing his disciple, Rebbi set about to determine the supplicant's eligibility:

אָמַר לוֹ בְּנִי קָרִיתָ – **[Rebbi] said to him: "My son, do you read"** (i.e. do you study Scripture)? **אָמַר לוֹ לָאו** – **[R' Yonasan] said to him: "No."** Rebbi inquired further: **שָׁנִיתָ** – **"Have you studied** other sections of the Torah?"[32] **אָמַר לֵיהּ לָאו** – **[R' Yonasan] said to him: "No."** Remaining resolute, Rebbi then said: **אִם כֵּן בַּמֶּה אֲפַרְנֶסְךָ** – **"If it is so** that you are totally unlearned, **on what** merit **shall I sustain you?** I do not give precious food to unlearned people!"

R' Yonasan declined to reveal himself, but instead pleaded with Rebbi for food:

אָמַר לֵיהּ פַּרְנְסֵנִי כְּכֶלֶב וּכְעוֹרֵב – **[R' Yonasan] said to [Rebbi]: "Sustain me as** you would **a dog or a raven.** Even though I am unlearned, surely I deserve as much compassion as is shown an animal!"[33] **פַּרְנְסֵיהּ** – **[Rebbi]** relented and gave him food, and thereby **sustained him.**

Rebbi immediately regretted his decision:

בָּתַר דִּנְפַק – **After [R' Yonasan] departed, יָתִיב רַבִּי וְקָא מִצְטָעֵר** – **Rebbi was sitting and became distressed** by what he had done, **וְאָמַר אוֹי לִי שֶׁנָּתַתִּי פִּתִּי לְעַם הָאָרֶץ** – and he said: **"Woe is me, for I have given** of **my bread to an unlearned person."**[34]

Rebbi's son, who suspected the truth, sought to comfort his father:

אָמַר לְפָנָיו רַבִּי שִׁמְעוֹן בַּר רַבִּי – **R' Shimon bar Rebbi said before [Rebbi]: שֶׁמָּא יוֹנָתָן בֶּן עַמְרָם תַּלְמִידְךָ הוּא** – **"Perhaps [that unlearned man]** was actually **Yonasan ben Amram, your disciple,**[35] **שֶׁאֵינוֹ רוֹצֶה לֵיהָנוֹת מִכְּבוֹד תּוֹרָה מִימָיו** – **who does not wish to benefit ever from the honor** due **the Torah** and Torah scholars. Thus, he disguised himself as an unlearned person and begged for food." **בָּדְקוּ וְאַשְׁכַּח** – Subsequently, **they investigated** the matter **and found** that the supplicant was indeed R' Yonasan.

Realizing that other humble scholars might follow R' Yonasan's example, or might refuse to seek help altogether, Rebbi rescinded the restriction:

אָמַר רַבִּי יִכָּנְסוּ הַכֹּל – **Rebbi said: Let everyone enter** the storehouses to receive food.

The Gemara explains that Rebbi's original decree was consistent with his own position:

רַבִּי לְטַעְמֵיהּ – **Rebbi** was going **according to his own opinion** on the matter when he excluded unlearned people, **דְּאָמַר רַבִּי** – **for Rebbi said: אֵין פּוּרְעָנוּת בָּא לָעוֹלָם אֶלָּא בִּשְׁבִיל עַמֵּי הָאָרֶץ** – **Misortune comes to the world only because of unlearned people.**[36]

The Gemara illustrates this truth:

כְּהַהוּא דְּמֵי כְּלִילָא דְּשָׁדוּ אַטְבֶרְיָא – It is **like [the case]** of the tax to raise **money for a crown that was imposed on** the inhabitants of **Tiberias.**[37] Rebbi exempted the Rabbis of the town from the tax. **אָתוּ לְקַמֵּיהּ דְּרַבִּי** – **[The unlearned townsfolk] came before Rebbi וְאָמְרוּ לֵיהּ לִיתְּבוּ רַבָּנָן בַּהֲדָן** – **and said to him: "Let the Rabbis contribute** along **with us!" אָמַר לְהוּ לָא** – **[Rebbi] said to them: "No!** They will not help you pay the tax." Whereupon the townspeople threatened:

אָמְרוּ לֵיהּ עָרוֹקִינַן – **"We shall flee** the city, for we cannot bear the tax burden ourselves."[38]

Rebbi did not oppose this idea:

[אָמַר לְהוּ] עֲרוֹקוּ – **[Rebbi] said to them: "Flee!"**[39] **עָרְקוּ פַּלְגֵּיהוֹן** – Subsequently, **half of them fled. דַּלְיוּהָ פַּלְגָּא** – When the king heard of this, **he waived half** of the expected tax revenue, but still demanded that the remaining inhabitants pay their share.

The townspeople again protested to Rebbi:

אָתוּ הָנְהוּ פַּלְגָּא קַמֵּי דְּרַבִּי – **That** remaining **half** of the populace **came before Rebbi. אָמְרוּ לֵיהּ לִיתְּבוּ רַבָּנָן בַּהֲדָן** – **They said to him: "Let the Rabbis contribute** along **with us!"**

Rebbi again rejected their demand:

אָמַר לְהוּ לָא – **[Rebbe] said to them: "No."** Whereupon the townspeople threatened: **עָרוֹקִינַן** – **"We will** also **flee!"**

Rebbi replied:

עֲרוֹקוּ – **"Flee!" עָרְקוּ כּוּלְּהוּ** – **All** the townspeople **fled;**[40] **פָּשׁ הַהוּא כּוֹבֵס** – however, **a certain launderer remained** in town. **שַׁדְיוּהָ אַכּוֹבֵס** – Thereupon **[the imperial governors] imposed [the entire remaining tax] on the launderer. עָרַק כּוֹבֵס** – **The launderer** himself then **fled, פָּקַע כְּלִילָא** – and the tax for **the crown was canceled,** even though the Rabbis were still residing in Tiberias.

Rebbi drew the following conclusion from this episode:

אָמַר רַבִּי רְאִיתֶם שֶׁאֵין פּוּרְעָנוּת בָּא לָעוֹלָם אֶלָּא בִּשְׁבִיל עַמֵּי הָאָרֶץ – **Rebbi said:** From here **you see that misfortune comes to the world only because of unlearned people.**[41]

The Mishnah stated:

וְכַמָּה יְהֵא בָעִיר וִיהֵא כְּאַנְשֵׁי הָעִיר וכו׳ – AND HOW LONG MUST ONE BE

NOTES

31. The word רַבִּי in this address is not Rebbi's name, but the title "Master."

32. Here the word שָׁנִיתָ does not refer specifically to the study of מִשְׁנָה, *Mishnah*, but to general study — i.e. of Gemara, Baraisa or halachah (see *Rashash;* cf. *Iyun Yaakov* to *Ein Yaakov*).

33. R' Yonasan chose the example of a dog and a raven because God shows extra kindness to these creatures: Since a dog's meals are few and far between, it retains food in its system for three days; and since a mother raven does not feed its young, God provides the chicks with food from within their own excrement (*Rashi*, from *Shabbos* 155b, and see *Tosafos;* cf. *Maharsha, Iyun Yaakov*).

34. If R' Yonasan correctly demonstrated from the examples of the dog and raven that he was certainly deserving of Rebbi's compassion, why did Rebbi regret his action? *Iyun Yaakov* explains that it would have sufficed for Rebbi to provide the "unlearned" supplicant with food of inferior quality (for God sustains the dog and raven with food that is unsuitable for human consumption). Thus, Rebbe was troubled by the fact that he gave R' Yonasan פִּתִּי, "*my* bread" — that is, bread of superior quality. See *Ben Yehoyada* for a different explanation.

35. R' Shimon knew R' Yonasan to be a humble man, and therefore suspected that he would attempt such a deception.

36. Only material entities can be diminished, which is the effect of misfortune. Unlearned, boorish folk are pure material entities, since they lack active intellects. Hence, misfortune comes to the world because of them, since they are susceptible to diminution and loss (*Maharal, Chidushei Aggados*).

37. The tax revenue would be used to purchase a crown for the Roman emperor (*Rashi*). [*Aruch*, cited by *Masores Hashas*, relates that the royal crown had been placed in Tiberias for safekeeping, but was stolen. The emperor placed the blame on the Jews of the city, and imposed on them a tax to replace it.]

38. *Rabbeinu Gershom.*

39. Rebbi did not compel the unlearned townsfolk to pay the tax; in fact, he approved of their plan to flee Tiberias. For their departure would trigger the cancellation of the tax [inasmuch as the town was originally visited with that misfortune only because of them] (*Ramban*).

40. The Rabbis, however, did not join them.

41. The governors could have shifted the tax burden to the Rabbis, as they had previously done to the launderer, but they did not do so. Rebbi demonstrated from this episode that the unlearned townsfolk were the root cause of the onerous tax. Once they left town, the tax was rescinded.

אלו ת"ח ור"ל סבר לה כדדרש רבא אני חומה זו כנסת ישראל ושדי כמגדלות אלו בתי כנסיות ובתי מדרשות רב נחמן בר רב חסדא רמא כרגא ארבנן א"ל רב נחמן בר יצחק עברת אדאורייתא ואדנביאי ואדכתובי אדאורייתא דכתיב אף חובב עמים כל קדושיו בידך אמר משה לפני הקב"ה רבונו של עולם אפילו בשעה שאתה מחבב עמים כל קדושיו יהיו בידך והם תכו לרגלך תני רב יוסף אלו תלמידי חכמים שמכתתים רגליהם מעיר לעיר וממדינה למדינה ללמוד תורה ישא מדברותיך לישא וליתן בדבורותיו של מקום אדנביאי דכתיב גם כי יתנו בגוים עתה אקבצם ויחלו מעט ממשא מלך ושרים אמר עולא פסוק זה בלשון ארמית נאמר אי תנו כולהו עתה אקבצם ואם מעט מהם יחלו ממשא מלך ושרים אדכתובי דכתיב מנדה בלו והלך לא שליט למרמא עליהם ואמר רב יהודה מנדה זו מנת המלך בלו זו כסף גולגלתא והלך זו ארנונא רב פפא רמא כריא חדתא איתמי א"ל רב שישא בריה דרב אידי לרב פפא ודילמא לא מידויל א"ל משקל שקילנא מנייהו אי מידויל מידויל ואי לא מהדרנא לה ניהליהו אמר רב יהודה הכל לאגלי גפא אפילו מיתמי אבל רבנן לא צריכי נטירותא הכל לכריא פתיא אפי' מרבנן ולא אמרן אלא דלא נפקי באכלוזא אבל נפקי באכלוזא רבנן לאו בני מיפק באכלוזא נינהו: רבי פתח אוצרות בשני בצורת אמר יכנסו בעלי מקרא בעלי משנה בעלי גמרא בעלי הלכה בעלי הגדה אבל עמי הארץ אל יכנסו דחק רבי יונתן בן עמרם ונכנס אמר לו רבי פרנסני אמר לו בני קרית אמר לו לאו שנית א"ל לאו אם כן במה אפרנסך [א"ל] פרנסני ככלב וכעורב פרנסיה בתר דנפק יתיב רבי וקא מצטער ואמר אוי לי שנתתי פתי לעם הארץ אמר לפניו ר' שמעון בר רבי שמא יונתן בן עמרם תלמידך הוא שאינו רוצה ליהנות מכבוד תורה מימיו בדקו ואשכח אמר רבי יכנסו הכל רבי לטעמיה דאמר רבי אין פורענות בא לעולם אלא בשביל עמי הארץ כההוא דמי כלילא דשדו אטבריא אתו לקמיה דרבי ואמרו ליה ליתבו רבנן בהדן אמר להו לא אמרו ליה ערוקינן [א"ל] ערוקו פלגיהון דליוה פלגא אתו הנהו פלגא קמי דרבי א"ל ליתבו רבנן בהדן אמר להו לא ערוקינן ערקו כולהו פש ההוא כובס שדיוה אכובס ערק כובס פקע כלילא א"ר ראיתם שאין פורענות בא לעולם אלא בשביל עמי הארץ: וכמה יהא בעיר ויהא כאנשי העיר וכו': ורמינהי החמרת והגמלת העוברת ממקום למקום ולנה בתוכה והודחה עמהן הן בסקילה וממונן פלט ואם נשתהו שם שלשים יום הן בסייף וממונן אבד אמר רבא לא קשיא הא לבני מתא הא ליתובי מתא כדתניא המודר הנאה מאנשי העיר כל שנשתהא שם שנים עשר חדש אסור ליהנות ממנו פחות מכאן מותר מיושבי העיר כל שנשתהא שם שלשים יום אסור ליהנות ממנו פחות מכאן מותר ליהנות ממנו ולכל מילי מי בעינן י"ב חדש והתניא שלשים יום לתמחוי שלשה חדשים לקופה ששה לכסות תשעה לקבורה שנים עשר לפסי העיר אמר ר' אסי אמר ר' יוחנן כי תנן נמי מתניתין שנים עשר חדש לפסי העיר תנן: וא"ר אסי אמר ר' יוחנן הכל לפסי העיר ואפי' מיתמי אבל רבנן לא דרבנן לא צריכי נטירותא אמר רב פפא לשורא ולפרשאה ולטרזינא אפילו מיתמי אבל רבנן לא צריכי נטירותא כללא דמילתא כל מילתא דאית להו הנאה מיניה אפילו מיתמי רבה רמא צדקה איתמי דבי בר מריון א"ל אביי והתני רב שמואל בר יהודה אין פוסקין צדקה על היתומים אפילו לפדיון שבוים א"ל אנא לאחשובינהו קא עבידנא איפרא הורמיז אימיה דשבור מלכא שדרה ארנקא דדינרי לקמיה דרב יוסף אמרה ליהוי למצוה רבה יתיב רב יוסף וקא מעיין בה מאי מצוה רבה א"ל אביי מדתני רב שמואל בר יהודה אין פוסקין צדקה על היתומים אפילו לפדיון שבוים שמע מינה פדיון

IN THE CITY TO BE treated **LIKE ONE OF THE CITIZENS OF THE CITY ETC.** [i.e. and so become subject to taxation]?

The Mishnah answered that after twelve months a new resident is considered a citizen, and must help bear all the municipal expenses. The Gemara challenges this ruling by citing a Baraisa:

וּרְמִינְהִי – But pit [this Mishnah and a Baraisa] against one another, and see a contradiction! For a Baraisa states: הַחַמֶּרֶת וְהַגַּמֶּלֶת הָעוֹבֶרֶת מִמָּקוֹם לְמָקוֹם – **IF A CARAVAN TRAVELING ON DONKEYS OR CAMELS THAT PASSES FROM PLACE TO PLACE** וְלָנָה בְּתוֹכָהּ – **TOOK LODGING IN [A PARTICULAR CITY],** וְהוּדְּחָה עִמָּהֶן – **AND [THE PEOPLE IN THE CARAVAN] WERE SEDUCED** into committing idolatry along **WITH [THE INHABITANTS OF THE CITY],**[42] הֵן בִּסְקִילָה – **[THE TRAVELERS]** are punished with death **BY STONING,**[43] וּמָמוֹנָן פָּלֵט – **AND THEIR PROPERTY ESCAPES** destruction.[44] Since the travelers are only transients, they are not punished as citizens of the *ir hanidachas,* but as individuals.

The Baraisa continues:

וְאִם נִשְׁתַּהוּ שָׁם שְׁלֹשִׁים יוֹם – BUT IF [THE TRAVELERS] HAD STAYED THERE in the city for **THIRTY DAYS** before the populace was seduced into idol worship, הֵן בְּסַיִיף וּמָמוֹנָן אָבֵד – **[THE TRAVELERS]** are executed **BY THE SWORD AND THEIR POSSESSIONS ARE LOST** (i.e. burned) along with those of the inhabitants. From the fact that the travelers receive the same punishments that the longtime residents do, we see that a newcomer attains citizen status after only a thirty-day residency. The Baraisa thus contradicts the Mishnah, which states that citizenship is accorded after a twelve-month period. – ? –

Rava resolves the contradiction:

אָמַר רָבָא לֹא קַשְׁיָא – Rava said: There is no difficulty. הָא לִבְנֵי מָתָא – **This** ruling of the Mishnah refers **to the citizens**[45] **of the city.** One does not acquire full citizenship, and with it tax liability, until he has dwelt in a city for twelve months. הָא לִיתוּבֵי מָתָא – However, **that** ruling of the Baraisa refers **to the residents of the city.** To be subject to the law of the *ir hanidachas,* one need reside in the city only thirty days.[46]

Rava proves this distinction between a "resident of a city" and a "citizen" from the evidence of a Baraisa: **כִּדְתַנְיָא – This is similar to what was taught in a Baraisa:** הַמּוּדָּר הֲנָאָה מֵאַנְשֵׁי הָעִיר – Regarding **ONE WHO IS FORBIDDEN THROUGH A VOW TO DERIVE BENEFIT FROM THE "CITIZENS" OF A CITY** – כָּל שֶׁנִּשְׁתַּהָא שָׁם שְׁנֵים עָשָׂר חֹדֶשׁ – **ANYONE THAT HAS REMAINED THERE** in the city for **TWELVE MONTHS** prior to the vow אָסוּר לֵיהָנוֹת מִמֶּנּוּ – **[THE VOWER] IS FORBIDDEN TO DERIVE ANY BENEFIT FROM HIM,** for such inhabitants are considered citizens of the city. פָּחוֹת מִכָּאן מוּתָּר – But the vower **IS PERMITTED** to derive benefit from anyone who has lived in the city for **LESS THAN [TWELVE MONTHS],** for such inhabitants are not considered citizens. מִיּוֹשְׁבֵי הָעִיר – If, however, he vowed not to benefit from **THE "RESIDENTS" OF THE CITY,** כָּל שֶׁנִּשְׁתַּהָא שָׁם שְׁלֹשִׁים יוֹם – then **ANYONE WHO HAS REMAINED THERE** in the city for even **THIRTY DAYS** אָסוּר לֵיהָנוֹת מִמֶּנּוּ – **[THE VOWER] IS FORBIDDEN TO DERIVE BENEFIT FROM HIM,** for such inhabitants are considered residents of the city. פָּחוֹת מִכָּאן – And anyone who has lived in the city for **LESS THAN [THIRTY DAYS]** prior to the vow מוּתָּר לֵיהָנוֹת מִמֶּנּוּ – **[THE VOWER] IS PERMITTED TO DERIVE BENEFIT FROM HIM,** for such people are not considered residents. Thus, the Baraisa clearly states that to achieve "citizen" status one must reside in a city for twelve months, while thirty days of dwelling renders one a "resident."

The Mishnah stated that until one has resided in a city for twelve months he is not required to contribute toward the cost of communal projects. The Gemara questions this ruling:

וּלְכֹל מִילֵּי מִי בְּעִינַן שְׁנֵים עָשָׂר חֹדֶשׁ – And for all things (i.e. all types of communal expenses) **do we need** to wait **twelve months** before collecting from a new resident? Is he not required to make any contributions before that time? **וְהָתַנְיָא – But it was taught in a Baraisa:** שְׁלֹשִׁים יוֹם לְתַמְחוּי – After a new resident has lived in a city for **THIRTY DAYS,** the charity collectors can require him to contribute **TO THE** communal **"PLATTER";**[47] שְׁלֹשָׁה חֳדָשִׁים לְקוּפָּה – after he has resided there for **THREE MONTHS,** they can require him to contribute **TO THE** communal "charity **BOX";**[48] שִׁשָּׁה לִכְסוּת – after **SIX** months of residence, he must contribute **FOR CLOTHING** for the poor of the city; תִּשְׁעָה לִקְבוּרָה – after **NINE** months of residence, he must contribute **TOWARD THE BURIAL** of the city's poor;[49] שְׁנֵים עָשָׂר לְפַסֵּי הָעִיר – and after **TWELVE** months he must contribute **TOWARD** the cost of **BOARDS** to fortify the gates **OF THE CITY.** We see, therefore, that a new resident must help bear various communal expenses even before his first twelve months have elapsed. – ? –

The Gemara answers:

אָמַר רַבִּי אַסִּי אָמַר רַבִּי יוֹחָנָן – R' Assi said in the name of R' Yochanan: כִּי תְּנַן נַמִּי מַתְנִיתִין שְׁנֵים עָשָׂר חֹדֶשׁ – **When our Mishnah also taught** that a newcomer is not required to contribute until after **twelve months** of residency, לְפַסֵּי הָעִיר תְּנַן – **it taught** that ruling with regard to contributing **toward** the cost of **boards** to fortify the gates **of the city,** or other safeguards protecting the city, in agreement with the Baraisa on that point. The Mishnah does not, however, discuss other communal expenses, and would therefore concur with the schedule outlined in the Baraisa.

The Gemara cites a related ruling by R' Assi in R' Yochanan's name:

וְאָמַר רַבִּי אַסִּי אָמַר רַבִּי יוֹחָנָן – And R' Assi also **said in the name of R' Yochanan:** הַכֹּל לְפַסֵּי הָעִיר – **All** must contribute **toward** the cost of **boards** to fortify the gates **of the city,** וַאֲפִילוּ מִיַּתְמֵי – **and** the officials may collect **even from orphans,** for they also require protection. **אֲבָל רַבָּנָן לֹא – However, the Rabbis** are **not** required to contribute, **דְּרַבָּנָן לֹא צְרִיכֵי נְטִירוּתָא – for the Rabbis do not need** human **protection.**

NOTES

42. This Baraisa discusses the law of the *ir hanidachas, the city led astray* to idol worship (see *Deuteronomy* 13:13-19). If at least a majority of the inhabitants of a city is seduced by proselytizers into committing idolatry, then those who committed idolatry are executed by *beis din* through the method of *sword*, and the city and all the property within it are burned. For a full discussion of this subject, see Mishnah *Sanhedrin* 10:4-6.

43. This is the method of capital punishment for *individuals* that commit idolatry (*Rashi*).

44. Their property escapes the fate of the citizens' possessions, which are publicly burned (see *Deuteronomy* 13:17).

45. Literally: sons of the city.

46. Regarding the punishment meted out to the inhabitants of an *ir hanidachas,* Scripture states (*Deuteronomy* 13:16): הַכֵּה תַכֶּה אֶת־יֹשְׁבֵי הָעִיר הַהִוא לְפִי־חָרֶב, *You shall surely smite the residents of that city with the edge of the sword*. The condemned are called יֹשְׁבֵי הָעִיר, *residents of the city,* as opposed to אַנְשֵׁי or בְּנֵי הָעִיר, literally *men* or *sons* of the city – both terms that connote the status of citizens (see *Rashi*).

47. The communal soup kitchen. People donated cooked food, which was distributed daily to the very poor (see below, 8b).

48. The general charity fund, from which weekly allotments of money were distributed to the needy (ibid.).

49. This was a larger expense [and so the more recent arrivals were not required to contribute] (*Rashi*).

אלו ת"ח ור"ל סבר לה (א) כדדרש רבא א) אני חומה זו כנסת ישראל ושדי כמגדלות אלו בתי כנסיות ובתי מדרשות ג) רב (א) נחמן בר רב חסדא רמא כרגא ארבנן א"ל רב נחמן בר יצחק עברת אדאורייתא ואדנביאי ואדכתובי אדאורייתא דכתיב ב) אף חובב עמים כל קדושיו בידך אמר משה לפני הקב"ה רבונו של עולם אפילו בשעה שאתה מחבב עמים כל קדושיו יהיו בידך והם תכו לרגלך תני רב יוסף אלו תלמידי חכמים שמכתתים רגליהם מעיר לעיר וממדינה למדינה ללמוד תורה ישא מדברותיך לישא וליתן בדברותיו של מקום אדנביאי דכתיב ג) גם כי יתנו בגוים עתה אקבצם ויחלו מעט ממשא מלך ושרים אמר ג) עולא פסוק זה בלשון ארמית נאמר אי תנו כולהו עתה אקבצם ואם מעט מהם יחלו ממשא מלך ושרים אדכתובי דכתיב ד) מנדה בלו והלך לא שליט למרמא עליהם ד) ואמר רב יהודה מנדה זו מנת המלך בלו זו כסף גולגלתא והלך זו ארנונא רב פפא ב) רמא כריא חדתא איתמי א"ל רב שישא בריה דרב אידי לרב פפא ודילמא לא מדויל א"ל משקיל שקילנא מנייהו אי מדויל מדויל ואי לא ג) מהדרנא להו ניהליהו ה) אמר רב יהודה ד) הכל לאגלי גפא אפילו מיתמי ו) ה) אבל רבנן לא צריכי נטירותא ו) הכל לכריא פתיא אפי' מרבנן ז) ולא אמרן אלא דלא נפקי באכלוזא אבל נפקי באכלוזא רבנן לאו בני מיפק באכלוזא נינהו: רבי פתח אוצרות בשני בצורת אמר יכנסו בעלי מקרא בעלי משנה בעלי גמרא בעלי הלכה בעלי הגדה אבל עמי הארץ אל יכנסו דחק רבי יונתן בן עמרם ונכנס אמר לו רבי פרנסני אמר לו בני קרית אמר לו לאו שנית א"ל לאו אם כן במה אפרנסך [א"ל] פרנסני ככלב וכעורב פרנסיה בתר דנפק ח) יתיב רבי וקא מצטער ואמר אוי לי שנתתי פתי לעם הארץ אמר לפניו ר' שמעון בר רבי שמא יונתן בן עמרם תלמידך הוא שאינו רוצה ליהנות מכבוד תורה מימיו בדקו ואשכח אמר רבי יכנסו הכל רבי לטעמיה דאמר רבי ז) אין פורענות בא לעולם אלא בשביל עמי הארץ כההוא דמי ח) כלילא דשדו אטבריא אתו לקמיה דרבי ואמרו ליה ליתבו רבנן בהדן אמר להו לא אמרו ליה ערוקינן [א"ל] ערוקו פלגיהון ערקו דליוה פלגא אתו הנהו פלגא קמי דרבי א"ל ליתבו רבנן בהדן אמר להו לא ערוקינן ערוקו כולהו פש ההוא כובס שדיוה אכובס ערק כובס פקע כלילא א"ר ראיתם שאין פורענות בא לעולם אלא בשביל עמי הארץ: וכמה יהא בעיר ויהא כאנשי העיר וכו': ורמינהי ט) ט) החמרת והגמלת העוברת ממקום למקום ולנה בתוכה והודחה עמהן הן בסקילה וממונן פלט ואם נשתהו שם שלשים יום הן בסייף וממונן אבד אמר רבא לא קשיא הא לבני מתא הא ליתובי מתא כדתניא י) י) המודר הנאה מאנשי העיר כל שנשתהא שם שנים עשר חדש אסור ליהנות ממנו פחות מכאן מותר מיושבי העיר כל שנשתהא שם שלשים יום אסור ליהנות ממנו פחות מכאן מותר ולכל מילי מי בעינן י"ב חדש והתניא כ) כ) שלשים יום לתמחוי שלשה חדשים לקופה ששה לכסות תשעה לקבורה שנים עשר ל) לפסי העיר אמר ר' אסי אמר ר' יוחנן ל) כי תנן נמי מתניתין שנים עשר חדש לפסי העיר תנן: וא"ר אסי אמר ר' יוחנן מ) הכל לפסי העיר ואפי' מיתמי נ) אבל רבנן לא מ) דרבנן לא צריכי נטירותא אמר רב פפא ס) לשורא ולפרשאה ולטרזינא אפילו מיתמי ע) אבל רבנן לא צריכי נטירותא כללא דמילתא כל מילתא דאית להו הנאה מיניה אפילו מיתמי רבה רמא צדקה איתמי דבי בר מריון א"ל אביי והתני רב שמואל בר יהודה פ) אין פוסקין צדקה על היתומים אפילו לפדיון שבוים א"ל אנא צ) לאחשובינהו קא עבידנא נ) ק) איפרא הורמיז אימיה דשבור מלכא שדרה ארנקא דדינרי לקמיה דרב יוסף אמרה ליהוי למצוה רבה יתיב רב יוסף וקא מעיין בה מאי מצוה רבה א"ל אביי מדתני רב שמואל בר יהודה אין פוסקין צדקה על היתומים אפילו לפדיון שבוים ר) שמע מינה פדיון

רש"י

אלו תלמידי חכמים. אלמא אין צריכין חומה: כולם שוין לענין חומה וגודרים עצמן מלטמע בעובדי כוכבים: שאתה מחבב עמים. שאתה מגביה להם פניך להשליטן על בניך: כל קדושיו של ישראל בידך [הם] לשומרן: בלשון ארמי נאמר. יתנו תרגום של ישנו כמו ושננתם ותנינן (דברים ו): אם תנו כולם. וכן רוצן יהיו שונין ועוסקים בתורה כשיגלו בעמים: עתה אקבצם. בקרוב אקבצם: ויחלו מעט וגו'. ואף [אם] מועטין הן השונין בעמים יחלו ממשא מלך ושרים יהיו בטלים מלשאת משא מלך ושרים. יחלו כמו לא יחל דברו (במדבר ל): מנדה בלו והלך. דריוש לוה את פחת עבר הנהר על אנשי כנסת הגדולה: מנת המלך. מגבת מסים שהן מטילין תמיד על בני המדינה: ארנונא. עישורי תבואות ובהמות מדי שנה בשנה: כריא חדתא. יציאת כריית באר מים חיים לשתות: לא מידויל. לא ימצאו בו מים והפסדתם הנס ויתמי לאו בני מחילה נינהו דליחלו: לאגלי גפא. לשערי חומות העיר להציב בהן דלתות. אגלי דלתות כמו טרוקו גלי (ברכות דף כח.). גפא סתימה כמו מלא אחר הגפה באלו מציאות (ב"מ דף כה:): לכריא פתיא. חפירת בור לשתות מים ועל שם הכלי המונח שם בבור תמיד לשתות בו עוברי דרכים קורהו פתיא: אפילו מרבנן. שהכל צריכין למים: דלא נפקי באכלוזא. שאין הן עצמם יוצאין בהכרזה לחפור אלא שוכרים פועלים: ככלב וכעורב. שחס הקב"ה עליהם (שבת קנה:) שנאמר יודע צדיק דין דלים (משלי כט) לפי שהכלב מזונותיו מועטין לפיכך שוהה אכילתו במעיו שלשת ימים וגבי עורב כתיב לבני עורב אשר יקראו (תהלים קמז) לפי שהעורב אכזרי על בניו והקב"ה מזמין להן יתושין מתוך צואתם ואוכלין: דמי כלילא. עטרה למלך קיסר: אתו. עמי הארץ לקמיה דרבי: דליוה לפלגא. מחל המלך דמי החצי וסילקה מעליהן: שדיוה אכובס. הטילוה פחתי המלך על הכובס: החמרת והגמלת. שיירא של חמרים ושל גמלים: הרי אלו בסקילה. כדין שאר יחידים: יתובי מתא. בשלשים יום וגבי עיר הנדחת כתיב יושבי העיר (דברים יג): ולכל מילי. ומקמי הכי לא יהיב מידי עם בני העיר: שלשים יום לתמחוי. כיון ששהה שם שלשים יום גובין הימנו [גבאי] תמחוי מאכל לעניים: לקופה. לצדקה: לכסות. עניי העיר: לקבורה. לקבור עניי העיר שהיא יציאה יתירה: לשורא. לתיקון החומה: לפרשא. פרש (ב) שהולך סביבות העיר לשומר' ולידע מה היא צריכה: לטרזינא. שומר כלי זיין של בני העיר ויושב בבית אצל השער:

תוספות

לא שליט למרמא עליהם. לפי שהיו עסוקים במלאכת שמים בבנין בית המקדש ה"נ אין להטיל מס על לומדי תורה:

והלך זו ארנונא. פי' בקונטרס עישור בהמות ותבואה כו' ור"ח פי' ארוחת דורון לשלטון העובר ממקום למקום שנותן לו כל עיר ועיר ארוחה ופירושו מלשון ויבא הלך לאיש העשיר (שמואל ב יב):

כריא פתיא. פירש ר"ח להסיר גבשושית מרחוב העיר:

איפרא הורמיז. פר"ח דמשמעות הלשון חן מאת המקום איפרא כמו אפריון נמטייה לר"ש (ב"מ דף קיט.) הורמיז שם שכינה כי ההיא דס"פ אחד דיני ממונות (סנהדרין דף לט. ושם ד"ה דהורמיז) מפלגא דידך ולעיל דהורמיז בזיי"ן מפלגא ולתחת דהורמין בנו"ן כמו הורמין בר לילתא (לקמן דף עג.): (לעיל)

ככלב וכעורב. כמו שפי' הקונטרס והיינו דכתיב נותן לבהמה לחמה לבני עורב וגו' בהמה בגימטריא כלב:

יתיב רב יוסף וקא מעיין בה. וא"ת וכי לית ליה ביבש קצירה תשברנה וגו' (ישעיה כז) כדאמרי' בפירקין (דף י:) וי"ל דקבל' משום שלום מלכות כדעבד רבא לקמן (שם) וכי היכי דפלגינהו רבא לעניי עובדי כוכבים ה"נ פדה בהו רב יוסף שבויי עובדי כוכבים ומיהו לא צריכי להכי אלא כדפירש הקונט' (ג) ס) דרבא דקבלה משום שלום מלכות וכיון שאמר לו ליתן למצוה רבה לא היה אפשר לחלקם לעניי עובדי כוכבים דאסור לגנוב דעת הבריות ואפי' דעתו של עובד כוכבים (חולין צד.) אבל מעות המתחלקים לעניים אין כאן גניבת דעת דאינהו נמי ידעי שישראל רגילין לפרנסם כדאמר בהנזקין (גיטין דף סא.) מפרנסים עניי עכו"ס עם עניי ישראל מפני דרכי שלום והא דקבל מההוא טייעא דנדב שרגא לבי כנישתא בפ"ק דערכין (דף ו: ושם ד"ה עד) אע"ג דהתם לא היה שלום מלכות התם טעמא משום דהוו כמו קרבן ואמרינן (נזיר סב.) איש איש לרבות נכרים שנודרים נדרים ונדבות כישראל:

מסורת הש"ס

א) [פסחים סו.], ב) ס"א רב הונא, ג) ס"א רבא, ד) נדרים סב., ה) ב"מ קח., ו) [שם ולעיל ז:], ז) [שבת קנה.] ע"ש יבמות סג. ע"ש, ח) ע"ש מלך המלך אמר המלך הואיל ופשעו היהודים בשמירת העיר ישלמו דמי השמר. ערוך ערך כלל א', ט) סנהדרין קיב. ע"ש, י) [סנהדרין שם תוספתא נדרים פ"ב], כ) [תוספתא פ"ג], ל) פי' קרשי עץ לחזק שערי העיר. ערוך ערך פס א', מ) [לעיל ז:], נ) [עי' פירש"י נדה כ:], ס) נ"ל דרב יוסף. רש"ל.

הגהות הב"ח

(א) גמ' רב נחמן בר רב חסדא רמא כרגא וכו' עבר מר אדאורייתא: (ב) רש"י ד"ה לפרשא פרש ההולך סביבות: (ג) תוס' ד"ה יתיב וכו' כדפי' הקונטרס דרב יוסף קבלה משום שלום. נ"ב לקמן דף י"א ד"ה דלא קיימוה:

גליון הש"ס

גמרא המודר הנאה מאנשי העיר. עיין נדרים דף מט ע"ב ד"ה ר"ג אמר: שם דרבנן ל"צ נטירותא. עי' רבינו יונה פ"ח דברכות דף ד ע"ב ד"ה שנאמר:

תורה אור השלם

א) אֲנִי חוֹמָה וְשָׁדַי כַּמִּגְדָּלוֹת אָז הָיִיתִי בְעֵינָיו כְּמוֹצְאֵת שָׁלוֹם: [שיר השירים ח, י]

ב) אַף חֹבֵב עַמִּים כָּל קְדֹשָׁיו בְּיָדֶךָ וְהֵם תֻּכּוּ לְרַגְלֶךָ יִשָּׂא מִדַּבְּרֹתֶיךָ: [דברים לג, ג]

ג) גַּם כִּי יִתְנוּ בַגּוֹיִם עַתָּה אֲקַבְּצֵם וַיָּחֵלּוּ מְּעָט מִמַּשָּׂא מֶלֶךְ שָׂרִים: [הושע ח, י]

ד) וּלְכֹם מְהוֹדְעִין דִּי כָל כָּהֲנַיָּא וְלֵוָיֵא זַמָּרַיָּא תָרָעַיָּא נְתִינַיָּא וּפָלְחֵי בֵּית אֱלָהָא דְנָה מִנְדָּה בְלוֹ וַהֲלָךְ לָא שַׁלִּיט לְמִרְמֵא עֲלֵיהֹם: [עזרא ז, כד]

ליקוטי רש"י

[תחילת ליקוטי רש"י ששייך לכאן נדפס בעמוד הקודם] הורמיז. כמו (לקמן עג.) הורמין בר ליליתא כלומר יופי שדים היה לה [נדה כ:].

עין משפט נר מצוה

נז א מיי' פ"ו מהלכות ת"ת הלכה י סמג עשין יב טוש"ע ח"מ סי' קסג סעיף ה וטוש"ע י"ד סי' רמג סעיף ב:

נח ב ג ד מיי' פ"ו מהל' שכנים הל' ו ז סמג עשין פב טוש"ע ח"מ סי' קסג סעיף ד:

נט ה ו ז מיי' שם ופ"ו מהל' ת"ת הל' י סמג שם וסי' יב טוש"ע ח"מ שם וטוש"ע י"ד סי' רמג סעיף ב:

ס ח טוש"ע י"ד סי' רנא סעיף יא:

סא ט מיי' פ"ג מהל' ע"ז הל' ו:

סב י מיי' פ"ו מהל' נדרים הל' ח סמג לאוין רמב טוש"ע י"ד סי' ריז סעיף לב:

סג כ מיי' פ"ט מהל' מתנות עניים הל' יב סמג עשין קסב טוש"ע י"ד סי' רנו סעיף ה:

סד ל מיי' פ"ו מהל' שכנים הל' ה סמג עשין פב טוש"ע ח"מ סי' קסג סעיף ב:

סה מ מיי' שם הל' ו טוש"ע שם סעיף ד:

סו נ ס ע מיי' שם ופ"ו מהל' ת"ת הלכה י סמג שם וטוש"ע ח"מ שם וטוש"ע י"ד סי' רמג סעיף ב:

סז פ צ מיי' פ"ז מהל' מתנות עניים הלכה יב סמג עשין קסב טוש"ע י"ד סי' רמח סעיף ג:

סח ק מיי' שם פ"ח הל' ט סמג עשין קסב טוש"ע י"ד סי' רנד סעיף ב:

סט ר מיי' שם הל' י סמג שם טוש"ע י"ד סי' רנב סעיף א:

רבינו גרשום

אלו ת"ח. שלומדין זה מזה כתינוק יונק משדי אמו: ודריש לקיש דמפיק מאספסו מחול ירבון דריש האי אני חומה בכל ישראל ולא בצדיקים בלבד: כרגא. כסף גולגלתא: אע"פ שאתה מחבב אומות העולם. שאתה נותן להם על ישראל ממשלה בזמן שישראל בגלות אעפ"כ קדושיו של ישראל העוסקים בתורה יהיו מסורין בידך: לרגלך. משמע בשבילך ומשמע רגל ממש: יתנו בגוים. בלשון ארמי כמו ושננתם ותתנינן כלומר גם יתנון שעוסקים בתורה כולהו עתה אקבצם מגלותם ואם מעט מהם יעסקו ויחלו אותו מעט ויחלו כמו לא יחל דברו: מנת המלך. שנותנין מתנות למלך מסים: ארנונא. מס של קרקע: כריא חדתא. חפירה גדולה שחופרין ליכנס שם מים הרבה להשקות מהמה שדות ע"י דלייה ודרך נגרים ופסק א) ליתן ליתומים חלק בחפירה זו שהן נהנין ממנה כאחרים: לא מידויל. שלא יובעו המים ונמצאת מוציא מעות יתומים בכדי: לאגלי גפא. זהו שעושין מחיצה או גדר סמוך לחומת העיר מבחוץ כדי להגן על החומה ועל שם כך קרי אגלי גפא לשון הגפת דלתות כלומר לנעול שערים שעושין לפני פינת העיר משום מצור העיר: לכריא פתיא. שחופרין למלאות ממנו מים לשתות ועל שם כך קרי כריא פתיא שדולין בכלי חרס כמו (ברכות נ ושם) פתיא אוכמא: **אפי' מרבנן.** שהן שותין ממנו כאחרים: **ואי קא נפקי באכלוזא.** כלומר שיוצאין חבורות בני העיר הן עצמן (ואינן) [ואינהו] חופרין ואינן שוכרין רבנן לא עבדי הכי מפני כבוד תורה: **פתח אוצר בשני בצורת.** לפרנס עניים: **בעל הלכות.** זה ששונה ברייתות. אף על גב דבדוכתא אחרינא אמרי' בעלי הלכות אלו בעלי משנה הכא הואיל ותני בעלי משנה צריכין למימר דהלכות אלו ברייתות הן: **ככלב וכעורב.** דכתיב ורחמיו על כל מעשיו: **רבי לטעמיה.** שלא היה רוצה לפרנס עם הארץ: **דההוא דמי כלילא.** שהשליך המלך מס על יושבי טבריא כדי שיקנו לו כתר: **אמר להו.** לא תסייען [לכו] רבנן: **ערקינן.** דלא מצינן למיתן כולי דמי כלילא **אמר להו ערוקו: דליוה** לדמי כלילא. על ההוא פלגא דאשתייר: **פקע כלילא.** בטל גזירת הכתר: **הראיתם שאין פורעניות בא לעולם אלא בשביל עמי הארץ.** דכיון דלא נשארו שם אלא רבנן לא גזרו עליהן ליתן דמי כתר שכל זמן שאחד מעמי הארץ היה שם גזרו ושוב לא גזרו: **פיסקא ויהא כאנשי העיר.** ליתן בכל מילי שנותנין בני העיר שנים עשר חדש: **החמרת והגמלת.** שיירא של חמרין וגמלין **העוברים ממקום למקום ולנה** בתוך עיר הנדחת **עמהן הן** כדכתיב וידיחו את יושבי עירם **הן בסייף וממונן אבד** כאנשי עיר הנדחת כדכתיב הכה תכה את יושבי העיר וגו': **הן** נדונין **בסקילה וממונן פלט.** הואיל ולא נשתהו שם כלל אלא כדי לינה אלמא דל' יום הוי כיושבי העיר וקשיא למתני' דבעי י"ב חדש ב) למיקרייא **מיתבא מתא** לא בעינן אלא ל' יום ונידון כמותם משום דהכתוב מיירי בלשון יושבי כדכתיב הכה תכה את יושבי העיר וגו' אבל למיקרייא **מבני מתא** להיותן כאנשי העיר ליתן עמהם לכל דבר לא הוי עד י"ב חודש **כדתניא המודר וכו': ולכל מילי.** כלומר דמשמע במתני' שלא יתן כלום בדבר עד י"ב חודש **והא תניא** נמי הבא לעיר ונשתהה שם **ל' יום** חייב ליתן **לתמחוי** היינו כלי שבו נותנין מאכל לעניים מבני העיר ליתן מנות ממאכלים בתמחוי להאכיל לעניי העולם העוברים עליהם ואם נשתהה שם ג' **חדשים** יתן חלקו **לקופה** של צדקה שגובין מע"ש לערב שבת לפרנס עניי אותה העיר ואם נשתהה **ו' חדשים** חייב ליתן ג) חלקו העיר שקורין שפיצ"א ותירות שעושין חרן לחומה לחזוק העיר אלמא לכל מילי לא בעינן י"ב חדש: **הכל לפסי.** מן הכל גובין לצורך תקון פסי העיר: **לשורא.** לחזוק החומה: **לפרשא.** שקונים סוסים לפרשים (כפי) [כדי] שיצאו חרן לעיר לעיין אם [באון] גייסות: **לטורזינא.** לצורך [כלי] זיין שנושאין אותן שומרי חומות העיר: **בר מריון.** איש א' היה עשיר גדול: **אנא לאחשובינהו בעינא.** שיהיו חשובין בכל דבר מצוה כמו אביהן:

חשק שלמה על רבינו גרשום א) נראה דל"ל ופסק שיתנו היתומים חלק וכו'. ב) נ"ל הא למיקרייא מיתבא מתא וכו'. ג) נ"ל חייב ליתן חלקו בכסות: לפסי העיר שקורין שפילא וכו'.

The Gemara discusses other communal expenses:

אָמַר רַב פָּפָּא לְשׁוּרָא וּלְפָרְשָׁאָה וּלְטַרְזִינָא – Rav Pappa said: Funds **for** repairing **the** city **wall, and for** hiring **a horseman**[50] **and a weapons guard,**[51] **אֲפִילוּ מִיַּתְמֵי** – may be collected **even from orphans,** for they also require protection. **אֲבָל רַבָּנָן לֹא צְרִיכֵי נְטִירוּתָא – However, the Rabbis do not require** such **protection,** and so they are exempt from these taxes.

Rav Pappa offers a guideline:

כְּלָלָא דְּמִילְּתָא – The general rule of the matter[52] is: **כָּל מִילְּתָא דְּאִית לְהוּ הֲנָאָה מִינֵּיהּ** – For **any [project] from which [people] derive benefit** a tax may be collected, **אֲפִילוּ מִיַּתְמֵי – even from orphans,** so long as they are beneficiaries.

The Gemara reports a related incident:

רַבָּה רָמָא צְדָקָה אַיַּתְמֵי דְּבֵי בַּר מֶרְיוֹן – Rabbah levied a tax for **charity on the orphans of the house of Bar Meryon.**[53]

Abaye questioned this action:

אָמַר לֵיהּ אַבַּיֵי – Abaye said to [Rabbah]: וְהָתָנֵי רַב שְׁמוּאֵל בַּר יְהוּדָה – But Rav Shmuel bar Yehudah taught אֵין פּוֹסְקִין צְדָקָה עַל הַיְתוֹמִים – that **we do not impose charity** payments **on orphans, אֲפִילוּ לְפִדְיוֹן שְׁבוּיִם – even for** the purpose of **redeeming captives**[54] with the funds! Why, then, did you levy a charity tax on these orphans?

Rabbah replied:

אָמַר לֵיהּ – [Rabbah] said to [Abaye]: אֲנָא לְאַחְשׁוּבִינְהוּ קָא עֲבִידְנָא – I did this to make them prominent in every charitable cause, as their father had been.[55] Thus, since the tax actually benefited the orphans from the house of Bar Meryon, it complied with the guideline established by Rav Pappa above.

The Gemara relates an incident involving Rav Shmuel bar Yehudah's teaching:

אִיפְרָא הוּרְמִיז אִימֵּיהּ דְּשָׁבוּר מַלְכָּא – Ifra Hurmiz,[56] **the mother of King Shapur,**[57] **שְׁדְרָה אַרְנְקָא דְּדִינָרֵי** – once **sent a pouch of gold** ***dinar*** **coins**[58] **לְקַמֵּיהּ דְּרַב יוֹסֵף – before Rav Yosef. אָמְרָה – She said** to him, **לֶיהֱוֵי לְמִצְוָה רַבָּה – "Let [the money] be** used **for a great mitzvah,"** but she did not specify which mitzvah she had in mind.

Rav Yosef was perplexed:

יָתִיב רַב יוֹסֵף וְקָא מְעַיֵּין בָּהּ – Rav Yosef was sitting and analyzing [the question of] מַאי מִצְוָה רַבָּה – which act of charity is considered a **great mitzvah.**[59]

Abaye suggested an answer:

אָמַר לֵיהּ אַבַּיֵי – Abaye said to [Rav Yosef]: מִדְּתָנֵי רַב שְׁמוּאֵל בַּר יְהוּדָה – Inasmuch as Rav Shmuel bar Yehudah taught אֵין פּוֹסְקִין צְדָקָה עַל הַיְתוֹמִים –that **we do not impose charity** payments **on orphans, אֲפִילוּ לְפִדְיוֹן שְׁבוּיִם** – even for the purpose of **redeeming captives** with the funds, **שְׁמַע מִינָּהּ – derive from [this teaching]**

NOTES

50. He rode constantly around the city, to watch over it and to see what needed attention and repair (*Rashi*).

51. The word טַרְזִינָא derives from טור, *watch*, and זַיִן, *weapon*. The guard lived in a house near the city gate [near where the inhabitants' weapons were kept] (*Rashi*).

52. I.e. the rule for determining when we would collect from orphans for communal needs.

[The Rishonim explain that this ruling excludes other communal needs from which orphans derive no benefit; e.g. building of synagogues or purchasing of Torah scrolls etc., which are not considered to be beneficial to minor orphans, since they are not obligated to fulfill *Mitzvos* (*Ramban, Ran, Nimukei Yosef*).]

53. Their father had been a very rich man (*Rabbeinu Gershom*; see also below, 12b).

54. Which is a very great mitzvah, as the Gemara explains below (8b).

55. *Rabbeinu Gershom.*

56. Ifra (אִיפְרָא) derives from אַפִּרְיוֹן, and means *grace.* Hurmiz suggests the Divine Presence. Hence, this name means "Grace from God" (*Tosafos*). But *Rashi* to *Taanis* 24b and *Niddah* 20b understands Hurmiz as the name of a demon (see Gemara below, 73a). Hence, the name connotes that she had the bewitching beauty of a demon.

57. He was an emperor of the Sassanid dynasty, which ruled in Persia and Mesopotamia.

58. One gold *dinar* equaled 25 silver *dinars*.

59. Obviously, any act of charity is a great mitzvah, but Ifra Hurmiz indicated that she wished the funds to be used to perform the greatest act of charity possible.

אלו ת"ח ור"ל סבר לה א) כדדרש רבא א) אני חומה זו כנסת ישראל ושדי כמגדלות אלו בתי כנסיות ובתי מדרשות ג) רב א) נחמן בר רב חסדא רמא כרגא ארבנן א"ל רב נחמן בר יצחק עברת אדאורייתא ואדנביאי ואדכתובי אדאורייתא דכתיב ב) אף חובב עמים כל קדושיו בידך אמר משה לפני הקב"ה רבונו של עולם אפילו בשעה שאתה מחבב עמים כל קדושיו יהיו בידך והם תכו לרגלך תני רב יוסף אלו תלמידי חכמים שמכתתים רגליהם מעיר לעיר וממדינה למדינה ללמוד תורה ישא מדברותיך לישא וליתן בדברותיו של מקום אדנביאי דכתיב ג) גם כי יתנו בגוים עתה אקבצם ויחלו מעט ממשא מלך ושרים אמר ג) עולא פסוק זה בלשון ארמית נאמר אי תנו כולהו עתה אקבצם ואם מעט מהם יחלו ממשא מלך ושרים אדכתובי דכתיב ד) מנדה בלו והלך לא שליט למרמא עליהם ד) ואמר רב יהודה מנדה זו מנת המלך בלו זו כסף גולגלתא והלך זו ארנונא רב פפא ב) רמא כריא חדתא איתמי א"ל רב שישא בריה דרב אידי לרב פפא ודילמא לא מידויל א"ל מישקל שקילנא מנייהו אי מידויל מידויל ואי לא ג) מהדרנא להו ניהלייהו ה) אמר רב יהודה ד) הכל לאגלי גפא אפילו מיתמי ו) ה) אבל רבנן לא צריכי נטירותא ו) הכל לכריא פתיא אפי' מרבנן ז) ולא אמרן אלא דלא נפקי באכלוזא אבל נפקי באכלוזא רבנן לאו בני מיפק באכלוזא נינהו: רבי פתח אוצרות בשני בצורת אמר יכנסו בעלי מקרא בעלי משנה בעלי גמרא בעלי הלכה בעלי הגדה אבל עמי הארץ אל יכנסו דחק רבי יונתן בן עמרם ונכנס אמר לו רבי פרנסני אמר לו בני קרית אמר לו לאו שנית א"ל לאו אם כן במה אפרנסך [א"ל] פרנסני ככלב וכעורב פרנסיה בתר דנפק ח) יתיב רבי וקא מצטער ואמר אוי לי שנתתי פתי לעם הארץ אמר לפניו ר' שמעון בר רבי שמא יונתן בן עמרם תלמידך הוא שאינו רוצה ליהנות מכבוד תורה מימיו בדקו ואשכח אמר רבי יכנסו הכל רבי לטעמיה דאמר רבי י) אין פורענות בא לעולם אלא בשביל עמי הארץ כ) כההוא דמי כלילא דשדו אטבריא אתו לקמיה דרבי ואמרו ליה ליתבו רבנן בהדן אמר להו לא אמרו ליה ערוקינן [א"ל] ערוקו ערקו פלגיהון דליהוי פלגא אתו הנהו פלגא קמי דרבי א"ל ליתבו רבנן בהדן אמר להו לא ערוקינן ערוקו ערקו כולהו פש ההוא כובס שדיוה אכובס ערק כובס פקע כלילא א"ר ראיתם שאין פורענות בא לעולם אלא בשביל עמי הארץ: וכמה יהא בעיר ויהא כאנשי העיר וכו': ורמינהי ט) החמרת והגמלת העוברת ממקום למקום ולנה בתוכה והודחה עמהן הן בסקילה וממונן פלט ואם נשתהו שם שלשים יום הן בסייף וממונן אבד אמר רבא לא קשיא הא לבני מתא הא ליתובי מתא כדתניא י) המודר הנאה מאנשי העיר כל שנשתהא שם שנים עשר חדש אסור ליהנות ממנו פחות מכאן מותר מיושבי העיר כל שנשתהא שם שלשים יום אסור ליהנות ממנו פחות מכאן מותר ליהנות ממנו ולכל מילי מי בעינן י"ב חדש והתניא כ) שלשים יום לתמחוי שלשה חדשים לקופה ששה לכסות תשעה לקבורה שנים עשר ל) לפסי העיר אמר ר' אסי אמר ר' יוחנן כי תנן נמי מתניתין שנים עשר חדש לפסי העיר תנן: וא"ר אסי אמר ר' יוחנן מ) הכל לפסי העיר ואפי' מיתמי נ) אבל רבנן לא מ) דרבנן לא צריכי נטירותא אמר רב פפא ס) לשורא ולפרשאה ולטרזינא אפילו מיתמי ע) אבל רבנן לא צריכי נטירותא כללא דמילתא כל מילתא דאית להו הנאה מיניה אפילו מיתמי רבה רמא צדקה איתמי דבי בר מריון א"ל אביי והתני רב שמואל בר יהודה פ) אין פוסקין צדקה על היתומים אפילו לפדיון שבוים א"ל אנא צ) לאחשובינהו קא עבידנא ק) איפרא הורמיז אימיה דשבור מלכא שדרה ארנקא דדינרי לקמיה דרב יוסף אמרה ליהוי למצוה רבה יתיב רב יוסף וקא מעיין בה מאי מצוה רבה א"ל אביי מדתני רב שמואל בר יהודה אין פוסקין צדקה על היתומים אפילו לפדיון שבוים ר) שמע מינה פדיון

רש"י

אלו תלמידי חכמים. אלמא אין צריכין חומה: [זו] כנסת ישראל. כולם שוין לענין חומה וגודרים עצמן מלטמע בעובדי כוכבים: שאתה מחבב עמים. שאתה מלהיב להם פניך להשליטן על בניך: כל קדושיו. של ישראל בידך [הם] לשומרן: בלשון ארמי נאמר. יתנו תרגום של ישנו כמו ושננתם ותניתם (דברים ו): אם תנו כולם. וכן רובן יהיו שונין ועוסקים בתורה כשיגלו בעמים: עתה אקבצם. בקרוב אקבצם: ויחלו מעט וגו'. ואף [אם] מועטין הן השונין בעמים יחלו ממשא מלך ושרים יהיו בטלים מלשאת משא מלך ושרים. יחלו כמו לא יחל דברו (במדבר ל): מנדה בלו והלך. דריוש צוה את פחת עבר הנהר על אנשי כנסת הגדולה: מנת המלך. מגבת מסים שהן מטילין תמיד על בני המדינה: ארנונא. עישורי תבואות ובהמות מדי שנה בשנה: כריא חדתא. יציאת כריית באר מים חיים לשתות: לא מידויל. לא ימלאו בו מים והפסדתם תנס ויתמי לאו בני מחילה נינהו דליחלו: לאגלי גפא. לשערי חומות העיר להגיה בהן דלתות. אגלי דלתות כמו טרוקו גלי (ברכות דף כח.). גפא סתימה כמו מלא אחר הגפה באלו מציאות (ב"מ דף כה:): לכריא פתיא. חפירת בור לשתות מים ועל שם הכלי המונח שם בבור תמיד לשתות בו עוברי דרכים קורהו פתיא: אפילו מרבנן. שהכל צריכין למים: דלא נפקי באכלוזא. שאין הן עצמם יוצאין בהכרזה לחפור אלא שוכרים פועלים: ככלב וכעורב. שחס הקב"ה עליהם (שבת קנה:) שנאמר יודע צדיק דין דלים (משלי כט) לפי שהכלב מזונותיו מועטין לפיכך שוהה אכילתו במעיו שלשה ימים וגבי עורב כתיב לבני עורב אשר יקראו (תהלים קמז) לפי שהעורב אכזרי ואינו חס על בניו והקב"ה מזמין להן יתושין מתוך צואתם ואוכלין: דמי כלילא. עטרה למלך קיסר: אתו. עמי הארץ לקמיה דרבי: דליהוי לפלגא. מחצה המלך דמי החצי וסילקה מעליהן: שדיוה אכובס. הטילוה פחתי המלך על הכובס: החמרת והגמלת. שיירא של חמרים ושל גמלים: הרי אלו בסקילה. כדין שאר יחידים: יתובי מתא. בשלשים יום וגבי עיר הנדחת כתיב יושבי העיר (דברים יג): ולכל מילי. ומקמי הכי לא יהיב מידי עם בני העיר: שלשים יום לתמחוי. כיון ששהה שם שלשים יום גובין הימנו [גבאי] תמחוי מאכל לעניים: לקופה. לצדקה: לכסות. עניי העיר: לקבורה. לקבור עניי העיר שהיא יוצאה יתירה: לשורא. לתיקון החומה: לפרשא. פרש (ג) שהולך סביבות העיר לשומר' ולידע מה היא צריכה: לטרזינא. שומר כלי זיין של בני העיר ויושב בבית אצל השער:

תוספות

לא שליט למרמא עליהם. לפי שהיו עסוקים במלאכת שמים בבנין בית המקדש ה"נ אין להטיל מס על לומדי תורה:

והלך זו ארנונא. פי' בקונטרס עישור בהמות ותבואה כו' ור"ת פי' ארוחת דורון לשלטון העובר ממקום למקום שנותן לו כל עיר ועיר ארוחה ופירושו מלשון ויבא הלך לאיש העשיר (שמואל ב יב):

כריא פתיא. פירש ר"ח להסיר גבשושית מרחוב העיר:

איפרא הורמיז. פר"ח דמשמעות הלשון חן מאת המקום איפרא כמו אפריון נמטייה לר"ש (ב"מ דף קיט.) הורמיז שם שכינה כי ההיא דס"פ אחד דיני ממונות (סנהדרין דף לט. ושם ד"ה דהורמיז) מפלגא דידך ולעיל דהורמיז בזיי"ן מפלגא ולתחת דהורמין בנו"ן כמו הורמין בר לילתא (לקמן דף עג.): (לעיל)

ככלב וכעורב. כמו שפי' הקונטרס והיינו דכתיב נותן לבהמה לחמה לבני עורב וגו' בהמה בגימטריא כלב:

יתיב רב יוסף וקא מעיין בה. וא"ת וכי לית ליה ביבש קצירה תשברנה וגו' (ישעיה מ) כדאמרי' בפירקין (דף י:) וי"ל דקבל' משום שלום מלכות כדעבד רבא לקמן (שם) וכי היכי דפלגינהו רבא לעניי עובדי כוכבים ה"נ פדה בהו רב יוסף שבויי עובדי כוכבים ומיהו לא צריכי להכי אלא כדפירש הקונט' (ג) דרבא דקבלה משום שלום מלכות וכיון שאמר לו ליתן למצוה רבה לא היה אפשר לחלקם לעניי עובדי כוכבים דאסור לגנוב דעת הבריות ואפי' דעתו של עובד כוכבים (חולין צד.) אבל מעות המתחלקים לעניים אין כאן גניבת דעת דאינהו נמי ידעי שישראל רגילין לפרנסם כדאמר בהמקין (גיטין דף סא.) מפרנסים עניי עכו"ם עם עניי ישראל מפני דרכי שלום והא דקבל מההוא טייעא דנדב שרגא לבי כנישתא בפ"ק דערכין (דף ו: ושם ד"ה עד) אע"ג דהתם לא היה שלום מלכות התם טעמא משום דהוו כמו קרבן ואמרינן (נזיר סב.) איש איש לרבות נכרים שנודרים נדרים ונדבות כישראל:

הגהות הב"ח

(א) גמ' רב נחמן בר רב חסדא רמא כרגא וכו'. (ב) רש"י ד"ה לפרשא פרש הרוכב סביבות: (ג) תוס' ד"ה יתיב וכו' כדפי' הקונטרס לדרב יוסף קבלם הכא משום שלום.

גליון הש"ס

גמרא המודר הנאה מאנשי העיר. עיין ר"ן נדרים דף מט ע"ב ד"ה ר"נ אמר: שם דרבנן לא צריכי נטירותא. עי' רבינו יונה פ"א דברכות דף ד ע"ב ד"ה שנאמר:

תורה אור השלם

א) אֲנִי חוֹמָה וְשָׁדַי כַּמִּגְדָּלוֹת אָז הָיִיתִי בְעֵינָיו כְּמוֹצְאֵת שָׁלוֹם: [שיר השירים ח, י]

ב) אַף חֹבֵב עַמִּים כָּל קְדֹשָׁיו בְּיָדֶךָ וְהֵם תֻּכּוּ לְרַגְלֶךָ יִשָּׂא מִדַּבְּרֹתֶיךָ: [דברים לג, ג]

ג) גַּם כִּי יִתְנוּ בַגּוֹיִם עַתָּה אֲקַבְּצֵם וַיָּחֵלּוּ מְּעָט מִמַּשָּׂא מֶלֶךְ שָׂרִים: [הושע ח, י]

ד) וּלְכֹם מְהוֹדְעִין דִּי כָל כָּהֲנַיָּא וְלֵוָיֵא זַמָּרַיָּא תָרָעַיָּא נְתִינַיָּא וּפָלְחֵי בֵּית אֱלָהָא דְנָה מִנְדָּה בְלוֹ וַהֲלָךְ לָא שַׁלִּיט לְמִרְמֵא עֲלֵיהֹם: [עזרא ז, כד]

ליקוטי רש"י

[תחלת ליקוטי רש"י ששייך לכאן נדפס בעמוד הקודם] הורמיז. כמו (לקמן עג.) הורמין בר ליליתא כלומר יופי שדים היה לה [נדה כ:].

רבינו גרשום

אלו ת"ח. שלומדין זה מזה כתינוק יונק משדי אמו: ודריש לקיש דמפיק מאספרים מחול ירבון דריש האי אני חומה בכל ישראל ולא בצדיקים בלבד: כרגא. כסף גולגלתא: אע"פ שאתה מחבב אומות העולם. שאתה נותן להם על ישראל ממשלה בזמן שישראל בגלות אעפ"כ קדושיו של ישראל העוסקים בתורה כולהו יהיו מסורין בידך: לרגלך. משמע בשבילך ומשמע רגל ממש: יתנו בגוים. בלשון ארמי כמו ושננתם ותניתם כלומר גם יתנו שעוסקים בתורה כולהו עתה אקבצם מגלותם ואם מעט מהם יעסקו ויחלו אותו מעט ויחלו כמו לא יחל דברו: מנת המלך. שנותנין מתנות למלך מסים: ארנונא. מס של קרקע: כריא חדתא. חפירה גדולה שחופרין ליכנס שם מים הרבה להשקות ממנה שדות ע"י דלייה ודרך נגרים ופסק א) ליתן ליתומין חלק בחפירה זו שהן נהנין ממנה כאחרים: לא מידויל. שלא יתנבעו המים ונמצאת מוציא מעות יתומים בכדי: לאגלי גפא. זהו שעושין מחיצה או גדר סמוך לחומת העיר מבחוץ כדי להגן על החומה ועל שם כך קרי אגלי גפא לשון הגפת דלתות כלומר לנעול שערים שעושים לפני פינת העיר משום מצור העיר: לכריא פתיא. שחופרין למלאות ממנו מים לשתות ועל שם כך קרי ליה כריא פתיא שדולין בכלי חרס כמו (ברכות ג וש"מ) פתיא

רש"י

אוכמא: אפי' מרבנן. שהן שותין ממנו כאחרים: ואי קא נפקי באכלוזא. כלומר שיוצאין חבורות בני העיר הן עצמן (ואינן) [ואינהו] חופרין ואינן שוכרין רבנן לא עבדי הכי מפני כבוד תורה: פתח אוצר בשני בצורת. לפרנס עניים: בעל הלכות. זה ששונה ברייתות. אף על גב דבדוכתא אחרינא אמרי' בעלי הלכות אלו בעלי משנה הכא הואיל ותני בעלי משנה צריכין למימר דהלכות אלו ברייתות הן: ככלב וכעורב. דכתיב לטעמיה. שלא היה רוצה לפרנס עם הארץ: דההוא דמי כלילא. שהשליך המלך מס על יושבי טבריא כדי שיקנו לו כתר: אמר להו. לא תסייען [לכון] רבנן: ערקינן. דלא מצינן למיתן כולי דמי כלילא לדמי כלילא. על ההוא פלגא דאשתייר: פקע כלילא. בטל גזירת הכתר: הראיתם שאין פורענות בא לעולם אלא בשביל עמי הארץ. דכיון דלא נשארו שם אלא רבנן לא גזרו עליהן ליתן דמי הארץ היה שם גזרו ושוב לא גזרו: פיסקא ויהא כאנשי העיר. ליתן בכל מילי שנותנין בני העיר שנים עשר חדש: החמרת והגמלת. שיירא של חמרין וגמלין העוברים ממקום למקום ולנה בתוכה והודחה עמה כדכתיב וידיחו את יושבי עירם הן בסייף וממונן אבד כאנשי עיר הנדחת כדכתיב הכה תכה את יושבי העיר וגו': הן נדונין בסקילה וממונן פלט. הואיל ולא נשתהו שם כלל אלא כדי לינה אלמא דלי

עין משפט
נר מצוה

ע א ב ג מיי׳ פ״ט מהל׳ מתנות עניים הל׳ ה סמג עשין קסב טוש״ע י״ד סי׳ רנו סעיף ג:
עא ד ה ו מיי׳ שם הל׳ ו ז טוש״ע שם סעיף ד:
עב ז מיי׳ פי״ד מהל׳ מכירה הל׳ ט סמג לאוין קע טוש״ע ח״מ סי׳ רלא סעיף כו כח:
עג ח ט מיי׳ פ״ט מהל׳ מתנות עניים הל׳ ה סמג עשין קסב טוש״ע י״ד סי׳ רנו סעיף ג:
עד י מיי׳ שם פ״ז הל׳ י סמג שם טוש״ע י״ד סי׳ רמח סעיף ב:
עה כ מיי׳ שם הל׳ י והל׳ יא טוש״ע שם סעיף א וסעיף ז:
עו ל מ נ מיי׳ שם פ״ט הל׳ ח ט סמג שם טוש״ע י״ד סי׳ רנז סעיף א:
עז ס ע מיי׳ שם הל׳ יא טוש״ע שם סעיף ב:
עח פ מיי׳ שם הל׳ י טוש״ע שם סעיף א:

רבינו גרשום

נהרג בחרב מינויל. דמתלכלך בדמו: נגבית בשנים. משום דמתחלקת לעניי העיר ודבר קצוב הוא שיודעין כמה כל אחד ואחד צריך ליתן בקצוב ונותנין בשוה וליכא א) אלא סידורי בעלמא דגובין אותו גבאי צדקה מהם: ומתחלקת בג׳. מפני שהיא כדיני ממונות מה דיני ממונות נוטלין מזה ונותנין לזה אף מחלקי צדקה מרבין לא׳ וממעטין לא׳ לפי שיראו צרכי עניים: גיבויו וחילוקיו שוה. שגובין מכל א׳ לפי מה שידו משגת וכעין דין שמעיינין בדין על מי להרבות ועל מי למעט משא״כ בקופה שאין גובין מכל אחד אלא לפי מה שרוצה ליתן ג) וקרוב נותנין כולן בשוה: לעשות קופה תמחוי. שאם ניתותר בקופה יותר על צורך עניי העיר ונתמעט בתמחוי לעניי כל אדם שבאו עניים הרבה וכן תמחוי לקופה כמו כן: להתנות על המדות. להגדילן או למעטן מכמות שהיו: ועל השער. שאם היה השער ביוקר רשאין להתנות שילך בזול: ועל שכר הפועלין. שאם נשכרין פועלים בג׳ פשי׳ ביום רשאין להתנות שלא ישכרום אלא בב׳: ולהסיע על קיצתן. לקנוס על מי שעובר על תנאי שקצבו אנשי העיר: והם יקחו. ואין הם פחות משנים: שררות הוא דלא עבדי פחות משנים. כלומר דמשמע טעמו דשררות הוא דבעינן ב׳ ולא לשום דין ולא לשום עדות הלכך (הא) המוני מהמני אפי׳ ב׳ קרובים למנות על הקופה והיינו ג) מאי שררות איכא בגבאי צדקה הואיל דדבר קצוב הוא ונותנין ברצון: ממשכנין. אם מעכב ליתן צדקה בקופה. ואפי׳ בע״ש דטרידי אינשי בתיקון מאכלם: הא דאמיד. אם אומדין אותו שהוא עשיר וממאן ליתן ממשכנין אותו בעל כרחו: והא דלא אמיד שאין לו מה ליתן אם (לוה) [ליה] ממשכנין עליו נאמר ופקדתי על כל לוחציו: שקל מיניה [ד׳ מאה] זוזי לצדקה. דהוה אמיד שהיה עשיר גדול: זה דיין. שמשכיל לדין הדין לאמתו.
ומצדיקי הרבים אלו גבאי צדקה שמעשין בני אדם ליתן צדקה ומצדיקין אותן: שבקת לאומנותך. שהיה מלמד תינוקות כלומר אם היית מלמד עדיין לא היית מבטל לעמוד בגינה: דעתי עלייהו. על התינוקות שלא הסחתי דעתי מהם שלא לזוזם ממקום זה שאני עומד: ורבנן מאי. כלומר כיון דלדיין נתת זוהר הרקיע לעתיד לבא [ולגבאין] צדקה נתת אור הכוכבים רבנן עצמן מאי לאיזה אור יזכו הן: כצאת השמש בגבורתו. דעדיף מכולהו: לפרוש זה מזה. בשוק משום חשדא שלא יחשדו זה לזה שא׳ מהם יתן לתוך כיסו ולא לכיס של צדקה אבל רשאי לפרוש זה לשער לשאול הצדקה וזה לחנות משום דקרובין זה לזה: פורטין לאחרים. שאם יש בכיס של צדקה פרוטות ורוצה לחלפן בסלע כסף פורטין לאחרים חלפי לאחרים ולא לעצמן שלא יחשדום שמרויחים בצדקה: אין מונין אותן שתים שתים כשפורטין לאחרים אלא מונה אחת אחת שלא יטעה: לא יתיב מר. רבה: אציפי. אמחצלאות שפורסין על כותלי בית הכנסת והיו קניות מצדקה: מחצלאות. ששוכבין עליהן עניים: עביד חד

חשק שלמה על רבינו גרשום א) נראה דל״ל וליכא רק שררותא בעלמא: ב) נראה דל״ל וע״פ הרוב נותנין כולן בשוה או דל״ל וקרוב שנותנין כולן בשוה כל״ל: ג) נראה דל״ל והיינו כר׳ חנינא וכו׳:

פדיון שבוים מצוה רבה. והא דאמר בפרק בני העיר (מגילה דף כז.) אין מוכרין ס״ת אלא ללמוד תורה ולישא אשה ולא קתני פדיון שבוים שמא מילתא דפשיטא היא ולא איצטריך למיתני: **ומתחלקת** בג׳ מפני שהוא כדיני ממונות. וא״ת מהאי טעמא נמי תהא נגבית בג׳ ופר״ת לפי שהיה ידוע סכום של כל אחד ואחד כמה יתן: **ולשנותה** לכל מה שירצו. נראה לר״ת דיכולים לשנותו אף לדבר הרשות אע״ג דאמרינן בערכין בפ״ק (דף ו: ושם) האי מאן דנדר שרגא לבי כנשתא אסור לשנותה לדבר הרשות ואמר נמי התם האומר פרוטה זו לצדקה עד שלא באה ליד הגבאי מותר לשנותה משבאה ליד הגבאי אסור לשנותה (ד) לדבר הרשות הכא שבני העיר משנים אותה שאני דמיקר מותר לשנותה אפילו לדבר הרשות ואפילו באה ליד הגבאי וכן היה ר״ת נוהג לתת מעות הקופה לשומרי העיר לפי שעל דעת בני העיר נותנים אותם: **כי הא דרבא אכפיה.** אמר היה עמו דאין עושין שררה על הצבור פחות מב׳ ולא חשיב ליה י) מפני כבודו של רבא: **אכפיה** לרב נתן. וא״ת והא בפרק כל הבשר (חולין דף קי: ושם ד״ה כל) אמר כל מ״ע שמתן שכרה ז) [כתובה] בצדה אין ב״ד של מטה מוזהרים עליה וגבי צדקה כתיב כי בפתוח תפתח את ידך לו וכתיב כי בגלל הדבר הזה יברכך (דברים טו) ואר״ת דהאי כפיה בדברים כמו כפייה (ה) ועל בפרק נערה שנתפתתה (כתובות דף נג.) ועוד תירץ דהכא קבלו עליהם שיכופו אותן הגבאי ולר״י נראה דבצדקה כופין משום דאית בה לאו דכתיב בה לא תאמץ את לבבך ולא תקפוץ וגו׳ ולריצב״א נראה דהא דאין ב״ד מוזהרין על מצות עשה שמתן (ו) שכרן בצדה היינו דאין נענשין וכן משמע בירושלמי דהמוכר את הספינה והיא דכל הבשר (שם) דלא הוה מוקיר אבוה וכפתוהו ואמר להו שבקוהו ה״פ איכנס מוזהרין להכריחו עד שיעשה כשאר מצות עשה דאם א״ל עשה סוכה ולולב ואינו עושה מכין אותו עד שתצא נפשו כדאמר בהכותב (כתובות דף פו. ושם) [וע״ע תוס׳ כתובות מט: ד״ה אכפייה ותוס׳ חולין קי: ד״ה כל]: **דין** אמת לאמתו. אמת לאפוקי דין מרומה אע״ג שהעדים מעידין אותו ח) [אין מחתכים אותו] כיון שיודעים שמשקרים כדדרשינן (בסנהדרין דף ז.) [צ״ל בשבועות ל:] לאמתו שלא יטו את הדין [וע״ע תוס׳ מגילה טו: ד״ה זה]: **ומצדיקי** הרבים וגו׳ אלו מלמדי תינוקות. אומר ר״י דלריך לומר דרקיע מזהיר טפי מכוכבים דהא בס״פ אלו עוברין (פסחים מט: ושם ד״ה לא) משמע דגבאי צדקה עדיפי ממלמדי תינוקות דאמר לא מצא בת תלמיד חכם ישא בת גבאי צדקה לא מצא בת גבאי צדקה ישא בת מלמדי תינוקות ואריב״א כי מצא בפרקי דרבי אליעזר דרקיע דהאי קרא דהמשכילים יזהירו כזוהר הרקיע היינו רקיע שעל ראשי החיות שמזהירין מכוכבים שאורו כאור החמה והאי דקאמר ורבנן מאי אמר רבינא ואוהביו כצאת השמש היינו שמש של עתיד לבא דהוא שבעתים כאור שבעת הימים ואור שבעת ימי בראשית היה שבעתים מאור חמה של עכשיו כדמפרש תרגום של רני ושמחי (זכריה ב):

פדיון שבוים מצוה רבה היא אמר ליה רבא לרבה בר מרי מנא הא מילתא דאמור רבנן דפדיון שבוים מצוה רבה היא א״ל דכתיב א) והיה כי יאמרו אליך אנה נצא ואמרת אליהם כה אמר ה׳ אשר למות למות ואשר לחרב לחרב ואשר לרעב לרעב ואשר לשבי לשבי ואמר רבי יוחנן כל המאוחר בפסוק זה קשה מחבירו חרב קשה ממות אי בעית אימא קרא ואי בעית אימא סברא סברא האי קא מינוול והאי לא קא מינוול ואבע״א קרא ב) יקר בעיני ה׳ המותה לחסידיו רעב קשה מחרב איבעית אימא (א) סברא האי קא מצטער והאי לא קא מצטער איבעית אימא קרא ג) טובים היו חללי חרב מחללי רעב שבי [קשה מכולם] דכולהו איתנהו ביה: תנו רבנן קופה של צדקה נגבית בשנים ומתחלקת בשלשה נגבית בשנים שאין עושים שררות על הצבור פחות משנים ומתחלקת בשלשה כדיני ממונות תמחוי נגבית בשלשה ומתחלקת בשלשה שגבויה וחלוקה שוים תמחוי בכל יום קופה מערב שבת לערב שבת תמחוי לעניי עולם קופה לעניי העיר ורשאים בני העיר לעשות קופה תמחוי ותמחוי קופה ולשנותה לכל מה שירצו ורשאין בני העיר להתנות על המדות ועל השערים ועל שכר פועלים ולהסיע על קיצתן אמר מר אין עושין שררות על הצבור פחות משנים מנא הני מילי אמר רב נחמן אמר קרא ד) והם יקחו את הזהב וגו׳ שררות הוא דלא עבדי הא הימוני מהימן מסייע ליה לרבי חנינא דאמר רבי חנינא מעשה ומינה רבי שני אחין על הקופה מאי שררותא דאמר רב נחמן אמר רבה בר אבוה לפי שממשכנין על הצדקה ואפילו בע״ש איני והא כתיב ה) ופקדתי על כל לוחציו ואמר ר׳ יצחק בר שמואל בר מרתא משמיה דרב ואפי׳ על גבאי צדקה לא קשיא הא דאמיד הא דלא אמיד כי הא דרבא אכפיה לרב נתן בר אמי ושקיל מיניה ארבע מאה זוזי לצדקה ו) והמשכילים יזהירו כזוהר הרקיע וגו׳ (המשכילים יזהירו כזוהר הרקיע) זה דיין שדן דין אמת לאמתו ומצדיקי הרבים ככוכבים לעולם ועד אלו גבאי צדקה במתניתא תנא והמשכילים יזהירו כזוהר הרקיע זה דיין שדן דין אמת לאמתו וגבאי צדקה ומצדיקי הרבים ככוכבים לעולם ועד אלו מלמדי תינוקות כגון מאן אמר רב כגון רב שמואל בר שילת דרב אשכחיה לרב שמואל בר שילת דהוה קאי בגינתא א״ל שבקתיה להימנותך אמר ליה (ג) הא תליסר שנין דלא חזיא לי והשתא נמי דעתאי עלויהו ורבנן מאי אמר רבינא ז) ואוהביו כצאת השמש בגבורתו ת״ר גבאי צדקה אינן רשאין לפרוש זה מזה אבל פורש זה לשער וזה לחנות מצא מעות בשוק לא יתנם בתוך כיסו אלא נותנן לתוך ארנקי של צדקה ולכשיבא לביתו יטלם כיוצא בו היה נושה בחבירו מנה ופרעו בשוק לא יתננו לתוך כיסו אלא נותנן לתוך ארנקי של צדקה ולכשיבא לביתו יטלם תנו רבנן גבאי צדקה שאין להם עניים לחלק פורטין לאחרים ואין פורטין לעצמן גבאי תמחוי שאין להם עניים לחלק מוכרין לאחרים ואין מוכרין לעצמן מעות של צדקה אין מונין אותן שתים (ג) אלא אחת אחת אמר אביי מריש לא הוה יתיב מר אציפי דבי כנישתא כיון דשמעה להא דתניא ולשנותה לכל מה שירצו הוה יתיב אמר אביי מריש הוה עביד מר תרי כיסי חד לעניי דעלמא וחד לעניי דמתא כיון דשמעה להא דאמר ליה שמואל לרב תחליפא בר אבדימי עביד חד כיסא

שבי כולהו איתנהו ביה. שהוא ביד העכו״ם לעשות בו כל חפצו אם למות [אם לחרב] אם לרעב: מפני שהוא כדיני ממונות. לעיין ולתת לכל אחד כפי טפלים התלויין בו: שגבויה וחלוקה שוה. בכל יום מדי יום ביום כדקתני לקמיה לפיכך אין גבוין בשנים שלא יצטרכו לטרוח ולבקש את השלישי לחלק: לעשות קופה תמחוי. לחלק לעניי עולם אם ירבו עליהן: להתנות על המדות. להגדיל קלת העיר או להקטין: ועל השערים. שער חטין והיין שלא ימכרנה שנה זו יותר מכך וכך דמים: להסיע על קיצתם. לקנוס את העובר על קלת כדבריהם להסיעם מדת דין תורה: הא הימוני מהימן. יחיד להיות גזבר: שני אחים. נגבי המנותות כמד דמו: מאי שררותיה. דקופה דקאמרת עלה לפי שאין עושין שררה על הצבור כו׳: אפילו בע״ש. שיש פתחון פה בע״ש לומר טרוד אני: ופקדתי וגו׳. אלמא אסור למשכן: אמיד. עשיר ט): גבאי צדקה. המשכילים אל דל מהו לריך: מלמדי תינוקות. מלדיקי רבים כן שמלמדין ומחנכין אותן בדרך טובה: שבקתיה להמנותיך. שהיית רגיל ללמדם באמונה וללמד ולישב על גבם תמיד: דעתאי להתם. לתינוקות: ורבנן מאי. תלמידי חכמים העוסקים בתורה תמיד מאי כתיב בהו: לפרוש זה מזה. מפני החשד שלא יאמרו זה הגונב יחידי דעתו לגנוב: אבל זה פורש לחנות וזה לשער. זה לגבות מיושבי השער וזה לגבות מיושבי החנות ולבלד שיראו זה את זה: לא יתנם לתוך כיסו. שלא יאמרו מעות של לדקה הוא גונב: פורטין. פרוטות שגבו לוקחין דינרי כסף לפי שהפרוטות של נחושת מחלידות: ואין פורטין לעצמם. פן יחשדום שפורטין בזול: אין מונין אותם שנים שנים. פן יאמרו שנים הוא נוטל ואינו מונה אלא אחד: אציפי דבי כנישתא. מחללות של בית הכנסת משום דמזבני להו ממעות הקופה: ואתני

אשר למות וגו׳. כל המאוחר בפ׳ קשה מחבירו חרב קשה ממות מיתת חרב מנוולת ומיתה על מטתו אינה מנוולת וכן הוא אומר (תהלים קטז) יקר בעיני ה׳ המותה לחסידיו רעב קשה מחרב שזה מצטער וזה אינו מצטער וכן הוא אומר טובים היו חללי חרב מחללי רעב שבי כולהו איתנהו בגוה [ירמיה טו, ב]. יקר בעיני ה׳. הראני הקב״ה שדבר קשה וכבד הוא בעיניו להמית את חסידיו. המותה. המות כמ׳ הביתה המולה (בראשי׳ לט) [תהלים קטז, טו]. טובים היו חללי חרב. טובים היו אילו חללי חרב היו מעכשיו שהם חללי רעב [ישעיה כב, ב]. נגבית בשנים ומתחלקת בשלשה. והמחלקים אותה עליהם לבדוק לפי הלריך לכל אחד ואחד ופעמים שקרובין לעתם לרחם על זה ולחלוק יותר מן הלורך שאומדין אותו בהרווחה ואומדין את חסרו כגלמום [שבת קיח:]. שממשכנין על הצדקה. נוטלי׳ משכונות על לדקה שיפסקו עליו ואינו נותנה. ואפילו בערב שבת. שהאדם טרוד [קידושין עו:]. גבאי. גוזה [סנהדרין צח:]. ממונה [בכורות לא.]. דרבא אכפיה. על הלדקה [כתובות מט:]. והמשכילים. שעסקו בתורה ובמלות יזהירו כזוהר הרקיע [דניאל יב, ג]. ואוהביו כצאת השמש בגבורתו. לעתיד לבא [שופטים ה, לא]. פורטין. פרוטות של נחשת שגבו ללדקה וכשמשהין אותם מחלידות לריך לפורטן בכסף [פסחים יג.]. מחליפין פרוטות נחושת בסלעי כסף מפני שהפרוטות מתעפשות ונפסלות [ב״מ לח.]. תמחוי. מאכל לחם ומיני מאכל שגובין לחלק [פסחים שם וכעי״ז ב״מ שם]. קערה גדולה היא וגובין בה גבאים מאכל מבעלי בתים ומחלקין לעניים שתי סעודות ליום מיום ליום [שבת קיח.]. ואין מוכרין לעצמן. שמא יחשדום שלקחום בזול [פסחים שם].

מסורת הש״ס

א) [ברכות ד: וש״נ], ב) [פאה פ״ח מ״ז סנהדרין יז:], ג) שקלים פ״ה מ״ב, ד) [קדושין עו:], ה) כתובות מט:, ו) [בילקוט ליתא וכן בע״י ליתא], ז) נ״א להתם, ח) [בשאלתות פרשת תשא איתא ורבנן אמרו מאי דכתיב ואוהביו כצאת השמש בגבורתו אלו גבאי צדקה ופרנסי העיר], ט) [תוספתא פאה פ״ד], י) פסחים יג. ב״מ לח., כ) [מבואר היטב בפירש״י גיטין נב: ד״ה ולא אמיד], ל) יעב״ן, מ) [כ״ה בדפו״י]:

הגהות הב״ח

(א) גמ׳ רעב קשה מחרב איבעית אימא קרא ואיבעית אימא סברא אב״א סברא האי קא מצטער: (ב) שם א״ל לאו הא תליסר שנין דלא חזיא לי: (ג) שם אין מונין אותן שתים שתים אלא: (ד) תוס׳ ד״ה ולשנות׳ וכו׳ משבאה ליד הגבאי אסור לשנות׳ הכא כצ״ל ותיבות לדבר הרשות נמחק: (ה) ד״ה אכפיה וכו׳ כמו כפייה רב פפא לרב יהודה בפ׳ נערה: (ו) בא״ד שמתן שכרה כתובה בצדה:

גליון הש״ס

תוס׳ ד״ה כי כו׳ מפני כבודו של רבא. ועיין דאיתא בר״ה דף כב ע״ב גיטין דף ג ע״ב סנהדרין דף יא ע״ב:

תורה אור השלם

א) וְהָיָה כִּי יֹאמְרוּ אֵלֶיךָ אָנָה נֵצֵא וְאָמַרְתָּ אֲלֵיהֶם כֹּה אָמַר יְיָ אֲשֶׁר לַמָּוֶת לַמָּוֶת וַאֲשֶׁר לַחֶרֶב לַחֶרֶב וַאֲשֶׁר לָרָעָב לָרָעָב וַאֲשֶׁר לַשְּׁבִי לַשֶּׁבִי: [ירמיה טו, ב]
ב) יָקָר בְּעֵינֵי יְיָ הַמָּוְתָה לַחֲסִידָיו: [תהלים קטז, טו]
ג) טוֹבִים הָיוּ חַלְלֵי חֶרֶב מֵחַלְלֵי רָעָב שֶׁהֵם יָזוּבוּ מְדֻקָּרִים מִתְּנוּבֹת שָׂדָי: [איכה ד, ט]
ד) וְהֵם יִקְחוּ אֶת הַזָּהָב וְאֶת הַתְּכֵלֶת וְאֶת הָאַרְגָּמָן וְאֶת תּוֹלַעַת הַשָּׁנִי וְאֶת הַשֵּׁשׁ: [שמות כח, ה]
ה) וְהָיוּ בָנָיו כְּקֶדֶם וַעֲדָתוֹ לְפָנַי תִּכּוֹן וּפָקַדְתִּי עַל כָּל לֹחֲצָיו: [ירמיה ל, כ]
ו) וְהַמַּשְׂכִּלִים יַזְהִרוּ כְּזֹהַר הָרָקִיעַ וּמַצְדִּיקֵי הָרַבִּים כַּכּוֹכָבִים לְעוֹלָם וָעֶד: [דניאל יב, ג]
ז) כֵּן יֹאבְדוּ כָל אוֹיְבֶיךָ יְיָ וְאֹהֲבָיו כְּצֵאת הַשֶּׁמֶשׁ בִּגְבֻרָתוֹ וַתִּשְׁקֹט הָאָרֶץ אַרְבָּעִים שָׁנָה: [שופטים ה, לא]

ליקוטי רש״י

ואע״פ

פִּדְיוֹן שְׁבוּיִם מִצְוָה רַבָּה הִיא – that **redeeming captives is a great mitzvah.**[1] Since Rav Shmuel stressed that orphans' funds are exempt even from the mitzvah of redeeming captives, we see that this mitzvah surpasses all other acts of charity. Abaye therefore advised Rav Yosef to use Ifra Hurmiz's donation to redeem captives.[2]

The Gemara explains how we know that redeeming captives is such a great mitzvah:

אֲמַר לֵיהּ רָבָא לְרַבָּה בַּר מָרִי – **Rava said to Rabbah bar Mari:** מְנָא הָא מִילְּתָא דְּאָמוּר רַבָּנַן – **From where do** we derive **this point that the Rabbis have said,** namely, דְּפִדְיוֹן שְׁבוּיִם מִצְוָה רַבָּה הִיא – **that redeeming captives is a great mitzvah?**

Rabbah bar Mari provides a source:

אֲמַר לֵיהּ דִּכְתִיב – **[Rabbah] said to [Rava]: For it is written:**[3] ,,וְהָיָה כִּי־יֹאמְרוּ אֵלֶיךָ אָנָה נֵצֵא – ***And it will be when they say to you, "To where shall we depart?"*** וְאָמַרְתָּ אֲלֵיהֶם כֹּה אָמַר ה' – ***And you shall say to them: "Thus said Hashem,*** אֲשֶׁר לַמָּוֶת לַמָּוֶת – ***'Those*** destined ***for death***[4] depart ***to death,*** וַאֲשֶׁר לַחֶרֶב – ***and those*** destined ***for*** death by ***the sword*** לַחֶרֶב – *depart* ***to*** *death by* ***the sword,*** וַאֲשֶׁר לָרָעָב – ***and those*** *destined* ***for*** *death from* ***hunger*** לָרָעָב – *depart* ***to*** *death from* ***hunger,*** וַאֲשֶׁר לַשְּׁבִי לַשֶּׁבִי" – ***and those*** *destined* ***for captivity*** *depart* ***to captivity.'"*** Rabbah bar Mari uses R' Yochanan's insight to explain the proof of the verse:

וְאָמַר רַבִּי יוֹחָנָן – **And R' Yochanan said** regarding this verse: כָּל הַמְּאוּחָר בְּפָסוּק זֶה קָשֶׁה מֵחֲבֵירוֹ – **Each subsequent [calamity] in this verse is harsher than the one** preceding it.

R' Yochanan establishes the truth of his insight:

חֶרֶב קָשֶׁה מִמָּוֶת – Death by the **sword** (the calamity mentioned second) **is harsher than death** from natural causes (the calamity first mentioned). אִי בָּעֵית אֵימָא קְרָא – **If you wish, say** that this point is established by a Biblical **verse,** וְאִי בָּעֵית אֵימָא סְבָרָא – **or if you wish, say** that it can be deduced through **rational argument.** אִי בָּעֵית אֵימָא סְבָרָא – **If you wish, say** that it can be deduced through **rational argument,** as follows:[5] הַאי קָא מִינַּוֵּול – **This one** put to death by sword **is disfigured,**[6] וְהַאי לָא קָא מִינַּוֵּול – **and that one,** who died naturally, **is not disfigured.** וְאִי בָּעֵית אֵימָא קְרָא – **And if you wish, say** that the point is established by the following **verse:**[7] ,,יָקָר בְּעֵינֵי ה' הַמָּוְתָה לַחֲסִידָיו" – ***Honorable in the eyes of God is the*** (natural) ***death of His pious ones.***[8]

R' Yochanan now proves that death by sword is preferable to starvation:

רָעָב קָשֶׁה מֵחֶרֶב – Death from **hunger** (mentioned third in the verse) **is harsher than** death by the **sword** (which is mentioned second). אִיבָּעֵית אֵימָא סְבָרָא – **If you wish, say** that this fact can be deduced by **rational argument,** as follows: הַאי קָא מִצְטַעֵר – **This** person who starves to death **suffers** in the process, וְהַאי לָא קָא מִצְטַעֵר – **and that one** killed by the sword **does not suffer,** for he dies quickly. אִיבָּעֵית אֵימָא קְרָא – And **if you wish, say** that the point is clearly established by the following Biblical **verse:** ,,טוֹבִים הָיוּ חַלְלֵי־חֶרֶב מֵחַלְלֵי רָעָב" – ***More fortunate were the victims of the sword than the victims of the famine.***[9]

R' Yochanan now establishes that captivity is the harshest fate of all:

שְׁבִי [קָשֶׁה מִכּוּלָּם] – **Captivity** (which is mentioned last in the verse) **is harsher than all** the previously enumerated calamities, דְּכוּלְּהוּ אִיתְנְהוּ בֵּיהּ – **for all of them are** included **in it.**[10] Thus, since the captive faces such a high risk of dying, it is truly a great mitzvah to effect his release.

The Gemara now discusses the rules for administering two charities mentioned previously (8a) in passing:

תָּנוּ רַבָּנַן – **The Rabbis taught in a Baraisa:**[11] קוּפָּה שֶׁל צְדָקָה נִגְבֵּית בִּשְׁנַיִם – Contributions to THE "CHARITY BOX"[12] ARE COLLECTED BY TWO [PEOPLE] וּמִתְחַלֶּקֶת בִּשְׁלֹשָׁה – AND the funds ARE DISTRIBUTED to the poor BY THREE [PEOPLE].

The Baraisa elucidates its ruling:

נִגְבֵּית בִּשְׁנַיִם – Contributions are COLLECTED BY a delegation of at least TWO [PEOPLE], שֶׁאֵין עוֹשִׂים שְׂרָרוּת עַל הַצִּבּוּר פָּחוֹת מִשְּׁנַיִם – FOR with respect monetary matters WE DO NOT ESTABLISH AN AUTHORITY[13] OVER THE PUBLIC consisting of LESS THAN TWO [PEOPLE].[14] וּמִתְחַלֶּקֶת בִּשְׁלֹשָׁה – AND the funds ARE DISTRIBUTED BY a panel of THREE, כְּדִינֵי מָמוֹנוֹת – for the distribution of charity funds is treated LIKE a case of MONETARY LAW.[15]

NOTES

1. *Rambam (Hil. Matanos Aniyim* 8:10) writes that there is no greater mitzvah than redeeming captives — that this duty takes priority over even feeding or clothing the poor. For a captive is regarded as one who is suffering from both hunger and thirst, and who is naked and in mortal danger. Thus, if one disregards this mitzvah, he violates several prohibitions and several positive commandments of the Torah.

2. Ordinarily, one should not afford an idolater the opportunity to achieve merit by allowing him to contribute to Jewish charitable causes (see Gemara below, 10b). Here, Rav Yosef was allowed to accept Ifra's donation, since rejecting it would antagonize King Shapur. Further, he was constrained to use the funds to redeem only Jewish captives because she expected him to do so, and Rav Yosef was not permitted to deceive her [and use the donation to redeem gentile captives, thereby limiting Ifra's merit] (*Tosafos* above, 8a ד״ה יתיב, as explained by *Maharam*; cf, *Bais Yosef* to *Yoreh Deah* 254:2, *Kovetz Shiurim* 55-56).

3. *Jeremiah* 15:2. God tells the prophet Jeremiah how to respond when asked by the people what the future exile holds in store for them.

4. The term "death" here refers to death from natural causes.

5. The Gemara first explains the option last quoted, since it is freshest in the student's mind (see *Nedarim* 3a).

6. In that his corpse becomes soiled with his blood (*Rabbeinu Gershom*). Hence, death by the sword is a harsher form of punishment than natural death, since the latter does not mar the outward appearance of the body.

7. *Psalms* 116:15.

8. [In the simple meaning of the verse, יָקָר is translated as "difficult" — i.e. the death of His pious ones is difficult for God to bear. R' Yochanan's interpretation, however, renders יָקָר as "honorable."] God regards dying naturally in one's bed — as opposed to dying by violence or from starvation — as an honorable demise for the pious (*Maharsha*).

9. *Lamentations* 4:9. The conclusion of the verse states explicitly that victims of famine suffer an agonizing death: *for they pine away, stricken, lacking the fruits of the field.*

10. The captive is totally at the mercy of his captor, who may slay the captive or starve him to death if he chooses. Although the captor cannot precipitate the captive's natural death, this first-mentioned calamity may nonetheless result from the circumstances of captivity itself, for some people cannot acclimate to foreign surroundings, and thus will die there of natural causes (*Rashi*, as explained by *Maharsha*).

11. The Baraisa elaborates on the Mishnah in *Pe'ah* 8:7.

12. The general charity fund, from which money was distributed weekly to the poor of the city.

13. [See Mishnah *Shekalim* 5:2; Rif, Rosh, Rambam (Hil. Matanos Aniyim 9:5).] The Gemara below will explain why this is considered a form of "authority."

14. The Gemara below will discuss the source of this rule.

15. Since the amount each beneficiary receives is determined by the number and circumstances of the dependents in his household, the administrators must exercise discernment and judgment in making these disbursements. Hence, they function in the manner of a *beis din* judiciously deciding a monetary dispute. Just as such a *beis din* must be comprised of three judges, so distribution of the charity's funds must be accomplished by a panel of three officials (see *Rashi* and *Ritva*; cf. *Rabbeinu Gershom*). *Collecting* the charity funds, however, need

עין משפט נר מצוה

ע א ב ג מיי' פ"ט מהל' מתנות עניים הל' ה סמג עשין קסב טוש"ע יו"ד סי' רנו סעיף ג:
עא ד ה ו מיי' שם הל' ו ז טוש"ע שם סעיף ד:
עב ז מיי' פ"ד מהל' מכירה הל' ו סמג לאוין קע טוש"ע ח"מ סי' רלא סעיף כז כח:
עג ח ט מיי' פ"ט מהל' מתנות עניים הל' ה סמג עשין קסב טוש"ע יו"ד סי' רנו סעיף ג:
עד י מיי' שם הל' ו סמג שם טוש"ע יו"ד סי' רמח סעיף ב:
עה כ מיי' שם הל' ז ופ"ט הל' יא טוש"ע שם סעיף ז וסעיף ח:
עו ל מ נ מיי' שם פ"ט הל' יא טוש"ע שם סעיף ב:
עז ס ע מיי' שם הל' יא טוש"ע שם סעיף ג:
עח פ מיי' שם הל' יא טוש"ע שם סעיף ה:

פדיון שבוים מצוה רבה היא אמר ליה רבא לרבה בר מרי מנא הא מילתא דאמור רבנן דפדיון שבוים מצוה רבה היא א"ל דכתיב והיה כי יאמרו אליך אנה נצא ואמרת אליהם כה אמר ה' אשר למות למות ואשר לחרב לחרב ואשר לרעב לרעב ואשר לשבי לשבי ואמר רבי יוחנן כל המאוחר בפסוק זה קשה מחבירו חרב קשה ממות אי בעית אימא קרא ואי בעית אימא סברא סברא האי קא מינוול והאי לא קא מינוול ואבע"א קרא יקר בעיני ה' המותה לחסידיו רעב קשה מחרב איבעית אימא (א) סברא האי קא מצטער והאי לא קא מצטער איבעית אימא קרא טובים היו חללי חרב מחללי רעב שבי [קשה מכולם] דכולהו איתנהו ביה:

תנו רבנן קופה של צדקה נגבית בשנים ומתחלקת בשלשה נגבית בשנים שאין עושים שררות על הצבור פחות משנים ומתחלקת בשלשה כדיני ממונות תמחוי נגבית בשלשה ומתחלקת בשלשה שגבויה וחלוקה שוים תמחוי בכל יום קופה מערב שבת לערב שבת תמחוי לעניי עולם קופה לעניי העיר ורשאים בני העיר לעשות קופה תמחוי ותמחוי קופה ולשנותה לכל מה שירצו ורשאין בני העיר להתנות על המדות ועל השערים ועל שכר פועלים ולהסיע על קיצתן אמר מר אין עושין שררות על הצבור פחות משנים מנא הני מילי אמר רב נחמן אמר קרא והם יקחו את הזהב וגו' שררות הוא דלא עבדי הא הימוני מהימן מסייע ליה לרבי חנינא דאמר רבי חנינא מעשה ומינה רבי שני אחין על הקופה מאי שררותא דאמר רב נחמן אמר רבה בר אבוה לפי שממשכנין על הצדקה ואפילו בע"ש איני והא כתיב ופקדתי על כל לוחציו ואמר ר' יצחק בר שמואל בר מרתא משמיה דרב ואפי' על גבאי צדקה לא קשיא הא דאמיד הא דלא אמיד כי הא דרבא אכפיה לרב נתן בר אמי ושקיל מיניה ארבע מאה זוזי לצדקה והמשכילים יזהירו כזוהר הרקיע וגו' (המשכילים יזהירו כזוהר הרקיע) זה דיין שדן דין אמת לאמתו ומצדיקי הרבים ככוכבים לעולם ועד אלו גבאי צדקה במתניתא תנא והמשכילים יזהירו כזוהר הרקיע זה דיין שדן דין אמת לאמתו וגבאי צדקה ומצדיקי הרבים ככוכבים לעולם ועד אלו מלמדי תינוקות כגון מאן אמר רב כגון רב שמואל בר שילת דרב אשכחיה לרב שמואל בר שילת דהוה קאי בגינתא א"ל שבקתיה להימנותך אמר ליה (ב) הא תליסר שנין דלא חזיא לי והשתא נמי דעתאי עלויהו ורבנן מאי אמר רבינא ואוהביו כצאת השמש בגבורתו ת"ר גבאי צדקה אינן רשאין לפרוש זה מזה אבל פורש זה לשער וזה לחנות מצא מעות בשוק לא יתנם בתוך כיסו אלא נותנן לתוך ארנקי של צדקה ולכשיבא לביתו יטלם כיוצא בו היה נושה בחבירו מנה ופרעו בשוק לא יתננו לתוך כיסו אלא נותנן לתוך ארנקי של צדקה ולכשיבא לביתו יטלם תנו רבנן גבאי צדקה שאין להם עניים לחלק פורטין לאחרים ואין פורטין לעצמן גבאי תמחוי שאין להם עניים לחלק מוכרין לאחרים ואין מוכרין לעצמן מעות של צדקה אין מונין אותן שתים (ג) אלא אחת אחת אמר אביי מריש לא הוה יתיב מר אציפי דבי כנישתא כיון דשמעה להא דתניא ולשנותה לכל מה שירצו הוה יתיב אמר אביי מריש הוה עביד מר תרי כיסי חד לעניי דעלמא וחד לעניי דמתא כיון דשמעה להא דאמר ליה שמואל לרב תחליפא בר אבדימי עביד חד כיסא

רש"י

שבי כולהו איתנהו ביה. שהוא ביד העכו"ם לעשות בו כל חפצו אם למות [אם לחרב] אם לרעב: מפני שהוא כדיני ממונות. לעיין ולתת לכל אחד כפי טפלים התלויין בו: שגבויה וחלוקה שוה. בכל יום מדי יום ביום דקתני לקמיה לפיכך אין גבויו בשנים שלא יטרכו לטרוח ולבקש את השלישי לחלק: לעשות קופה תמחוי. לחלק לעניי עולם אם ירבו עליהן: להתנות על המדות. להגדיל סאת העיר או להקטין: ועל השערים. שער חטין והיין שלא ימכרנה שנה זו יותר מכך וכך דמים: להסיע על קיצתם. לקנוס את העובר על קיצת דבריהם להסיעם מדת דין תורה: הא הימוני מהימן. יחיד להיות גזבר: שני אחים. המשועבדים כחד דמו: מאי שררותיה. דקופה דקאמרת עלה לפי שאין עושין שררה על הצבור כו': אפילו בע"ש. שיש פתחון פה לבעה"ב לומר טרוד אני: ופקדתי וגו'. אלמא אסור למשכן: אמיד. עשיר: גבאי צדקה. המשכילים אל דל מהו לריך: מלמדי תינוקות. מלדיקים רבים הן שמלמדין ומחנכין אותן בדרך טובה: שבקתיה להימנותך. שהיית רגיל ללמדם באמונה וללמד ולישב על גבם תמיד: דעתאי להתם. לתינוקות: ורבנן מאי. תלמידי חכמים העוסקים בתורה תמיד מאי כתיב בהו: לפרוש זה מזה. מפני החשד שלא יאמרו זה הגזבר יחידי בעתו לגנוב: אבל זה פורש לחנות וזה לשער. זה לגבות מיושבי השער וזה לגבות מיושבי החנות ובלבד שיראו שניהם כאחד: לא יתנם לתוך כיסו. שלא יאמרו מעות של צדקה הוא גונב: פורטין. פרוטות שגבו לוקחין דינרי כסף לפי שהפרוטות של נחושת מחלידות: ואין פורטין לעצמם. פן יחשדום שפורטין בזול: אין מונין אותם שנים שנים. פן יאמרו שנים הוא נוטל ואינו מונה אלא אחד: אציפי דבי כנישתא. מחצלות של בית הכנסת משום דמזבני להו ממעות הקופה: ואתני

תוספות

פדיון שבוים מצוה רבה. והא דאמר בפרק בני העיר (מגילה דף כז.) אין מוכרין ס"ת אלא ללמוד תורה ולישא אשה ולא קתני פדיון שבוים שמא מילתא דפשיטא היא ולא איצטריך למיתני:

ומתחלקת בג' מפני שהוא כדיני ממונות. וא"ת מאי טעמא נמי תהא נגבית בג' ופר"ת לפי שהיה ידוע סכום של כל אחד ואחד כמה יתן:

ולשנות' לכל מה שירצו. נראה לר"ת דיכולים לשנותו אף לדבר הרשות וע"ג דאמרינן בערכין בפ"ק (דף ו: ושם) האי מאן דנדר שרגא לבי כנישתא אסור לשנותה לדבר הרשות ואמר נמי התם האומר פרוטה זו לצדקה עד שלא באה ליד הגבאי מותר לשנותה משבאה ליד הגבאי אסור לשנותה (ד) לדבר הרשות הכא שבני העיר משנים אותה שאני לפיכך מותר לשנותה אפילו לדבר הרשות ואפילו באה ליד הגבאי וכן היה ר"ת נוהג לתת מעות הקופה לשומרי העיר לפי שעל דעת בני העיר נותנים אותם:

כי הא דרבא אכפיה. אחר היה עמו דאין עושין שררה על הצבור פחות מב' ולא חשיב ליה מפני כבודו של רבא:

אכפיה לרב נתן. וא"ת והא בפרק כל הבשר (חולין דף קי: ושם ד"ה כל) אמר כל מ"ע שמתן שכרה [כתובה] בצדה אין ב"ד של מטה מוזהרים עליה וגבי צדקה כתיב כי פתוח תפתח את ידך לו וכתיב כי בגלל הדבר הזה יברכך (דברים טו) ואר"ת דהאי כפיה בדברים כמו כפייה (ה) דעל בפרק נערה שנתפתתה (כתובות דף נג.) ועוד תירץ דהכא קבלו עליהם שיכופו אותן הגבאי ולר"י נראה דבצדקה כופין משום דאית בה לאו דכתיב בה לא תאמץ את לבבך ולא תקפוץ וגו' ולריצב"א נראה דהא דאין ב"ד מוזהרין על מצות עשה שמתן (ו) שכרן בצדה היינו דאין נענשין וכן משמע בירושלמי דהמוכר את הספינה והיא דכל הבשר (שם) דלא הוה מוקיר אבוה וכפתוהו ואמר להו שבקוהו ה"פ אינכם מוזהרין להכריחו עד שיעשה כשאר מצות עשה דאם א"ל עשה סוכה ולולב ואינו עושה מכין אותו עד שתצא נפשו כדאמר בהכותב (כתובות דף פו. ושם) [וע"ע תוס' כתובות מט: ד"ה אכפייה ותוס' חולין קי: ד"ה כל]:

דין אמת לאמתו. אמת לאפוקי דין מרומה אע"ג שהעדים מעידין אותו [אין מחתכים אותו] כיון שיודעים שמשקרים כדדרשינן (בסנהדרין דף ז.) [צ"ל בשבועות ל:] לאמתו שלא יטו את הדין [וע"ע תוס' מגילה טו: ד"ה זה]:

ומצדיקי הרבים וגו' אלו מלמדי תינוקות. אומר ר"י דצריך לומר דרקיע מזהיר טפי מכוכבים דהא בס"פ אלו עוברין (פסחים מט: ושם ד"ה לא) משמע דגבאי צדקה עדיפי ממלמדי תינוקות דקאמר לא מצא בת תלמיד חכם ישא בת גבאי צדקה לא מצא בת גבאי צדקה ישא בת מלמדי תינוקות ואריב"א כי מצא בפרקי דרבי אליעזר דרקיע דהאי קרא דהמשכילים יזהירו כזוהר הרקיע היינו רקיע שעל ראשי החיות שמזהירין מכוכבים שאורו כאור החמה והאי דקאמר ורבנן מאי אמר רבינא ואוהביו כצאת השמש בגבורתו היינו שמש של עתיד לבא דהוא שבעתים כאור שבעת הימים ואור שבעת ימי בראשית היה שבעתים מאור חמה כדמפרש תרגום של רני ושמחי (זכריה ב):

מסורת הש"ס

א) [ברכות ד: וש"נ], ב) [פאה פ"ח מ"ז סנהדרין יז:], ג) שקלים פ"ה מ"ב, ד) [קדושין עו:], ה) כתובות מט:, ו) [ילקוט ליתא וכן בע"י ליתא], ז) נ"א להתם, ח) [בתוספתא פרשה קשא ליתא ורבנן אמרו מאי דכתיב ואוהביו כצאת השמש בגבורתו אלו גבאי צדקה ופרנסי העיר], ט) [תוספתא פ"ד], י) פסחים יג., כ) ב"מ לח., ל) [מהרש"א], מ) [עי' ד"ה ולא אמיד], נ) יעב"ץ, ס) [כ"ה בדפו"י]

הגהות הב"ח

(א) גמ' רעב קשה מחרב איבעית אימא קרא ואיבעית אימא סברא אב"א קבלה הכי קא מצטער: (ב) שם א"ל לאו הא תליסר שנין דלא חזיא לי: (ג) שם אין מונין אותם שתים שתים אלא: (ד) תוס' ד"ה ולשנות' וכו' משבאה ליד הגבאי אסור לשנות' הכא בצ"ל ותיבות לדבר הרשות נמחק: (ה) ד"ה אכפיה וכו' כמו כפייה רב פפא לרב יהודה בפ' נערה: (ו) בא"ד שמתן שכרה כתובה בצדה:

גליון הש"ס

תוס' ד"ה כי כו' מפני כבודו של רבא. וכעין לאותה כה"ג דף כב ע"ג גיטין דף ג ע"ב סנהדרין דף יא ע"ב:

תורה אור השלם

א) וְהָיָה כִּי יֹאמְרוּ אֵלֶיךָ אָנָה נֵצֵא וְאָמַרְתָּ אֲלֵיהֶם כֹּה אָמַר יְיָ אֲשֶׁר לַמָּוֶת לַמָּוֶת וַאֲשֶׁר לַחֶרֶב לַחֶרֶב וַאֲשֶׁר לָרָעָב לָרָעָב וַאֲשֶׁר לַשְּׁבִי לַשֶּׁבִי: [ירמיה טו, ב]
ב) יָקָר בְּעֵינֵי יְיָ הַמָּוְתָה לַחֲסִידָיו: [תהלים קטז, טו]
ג) טוֹבִים הָיוּ חַלְלֵי חֶרֶב מֵחַלְלֵי רָעָב שֶׁהֵם יָזוּבוּ מְדֻקָּרִים מִתְּנוּבֹת שָׂדָי: [איכה ד, ט]
ד) וְהֵם יִקְחוּ אֶת הַזָּהָב וְאֶת הַתְּכֵלֶת וְאֶת הָאַרְגָּמָן וְאֶת תּוֹלַעַת הַשָּׁנִי וְאֶת הַשֵּׁשׁ: [שמות כח, ה]
ה) וְהָיוּ בָנָיו כְּקֶדֶם וַעֲדָתוֹ לְפָנַי תִּכּוֹן וּפָקַדְתִּי עַל כָּל לֹחֲצָיו: [ירמיה ל, כ]
ו) וְהַמַּשְׂכִּלִים יַזְהִרוּ כְּזֹהַר הָרָקִיעַ וּמַצְדִּיקֵי הָרַבִּים כַּכּוֹכָבִים לְעוֹלָם וָעֶד: [דניאל יב, ג]
ז) כֵּן יֹאבְדוּ כָל אוֹיְבֶיךָ יְיָ וְאֹהֲבָיו כְּצֵאת הַשֶּׁמֶשׁ בִּגְבֻרָתוֹ וַתִּשְׁקֹט הָאָרֶץ אַרְבָּעִים שָׁנָה: [שופטים ה, לא]

רבינו גרשום

נהרג בחרב מינוול. דמתלכלך בדמו: נגבית בשנים. משום דמתחלקת לעניי העיר ודבר קצוב הוא שיודעין כמה כל אחד ואחד צריך ליתן בקצוב ונותנין בשוה וליכא (א) אלא סידורי בעלמא דגובין אותו גבאי צדקה מהם: ומתחלקת בג'. מפני שהיא כדיני ממונות מה דיני ממונות נוטלין מזה ונותנין לזה אף מחלקי צדקה מרבין לא' וממעטין לא' לפי שיראו צרכי עניים: גבויה וחילוקה שוה. שגובין מכל א' לפי מה שידו משגת וכמין דין שמעיינין בדין על מי להרבות ועל מי למעט משא"כ בקופה שאין גובין מכל אחד אלא לפי מה שרוצה ליתן ב) וקרוב נותנין כולן בשוה: לעשות קופה תמחוי. שאם ניתותר בקופה יותר על צורך עניי העיר תמעט בתמחוי לעניי כל אדם שבאו עניים הרבה וכן תמחוי לקופה כמו כן: להתנות על המדות. אם להגדיל אם למעטן ממכמות שהיו: ועל השער. שאם היה השער ביוקר רשאין להתנות שילך בזול: ועל שכר הפועלין. שאם נשכרין פועלים בב' פשיטי ביום רשאין להתנות שלא ישכרום אלא בב': ולהסיע על קיצתן. לקנוס על מי שעובר על מה שקצבו אנשי העיר: והם יקחו. ואין הם פחות משנים. שררות הוא דלא עבדי פחות משנים. כלומר דמשמע טעמו דשררות הוא דבעינן ב' ולא לשום דין ולא לשום עדות הלכך (הא) המוני מהימן אפי' ב' קרובים למנות על הקופה והיינו ג) מאי שררות איכא בגבאי צדקה הואיל ודבר קצוב הוא ונותנין ברצון: ממשכנין. אם מעכב ליתן צדקה בקופה. ואפי' בע"ש דטרידי בהכנת שבת לאכלם: הא דאמיד. אם אומדין אותו שהוא עשיר וממאן ליתן ממשכנין אותו בעל כרחו: והא דלא אמיד שאין לו מה ליתן אם (לוה) [ליה] ממשכנין עליו נאמר ופקדתי על כל לוחציו: שקל מיניה [ד' מאה] זוזי לצדקה. דהוה אמיד שהיה עשיר גדול: זה דיין. שמשכיל לדין הדין לאמתו. ומצדיקי הרבים אלו גבאי צדקה שמעשין בני אדם ליתן צדקה ומצדקין אותן: שבקת לאומנותך. שהיה מלמד תינוקות כלומר אם היית מלמד עדיין לא היית מבטל לעמוד בגינה: דעתי עלייהו. על התינוקות שלא הסחתי דעתי מהם שלא לזוזם ממקום זה שאני עומד: ורבנן מאי. כלומר כיון דלדיין נתת זוהר הרקיע לעתיד לבא [ולגבאי] צדקה נתת אור הכוכבים רבנן עצמן מאי לאיזה אור יזכו הן: כצאת השמש בגבורתו. דעדיף מכולהו: לפרוש זה מזה. בשוק משום חשדא שלא יחשדו זה לזה שא' מהם יתן לתוך כיסו ולא לכיס של צדקה אבל רשאי לפרוש זה לשער לשאול הצדקה וזה לחנות משום דקרובין זה לזה: פורטין לאחרים. שאם יש בכיס של צדקה פרוטות ורוצה לחלפן בסלע כסף פורטין לאחרים חלפי לאחרים ולא לעצמן שלא יחשדום שמרויחים בצדקה: אין מונין אותן שתים שתים כשפורטין לאחרים אלא מונה אחת אחת שלא יטעה: לא יתיב מר. רבה: אציפי. אמחצלאות שפורסין על כותלי בית הכנסת והיו קנויות מצדקה: מחצלאות. ששוכבין עליהן עניים: עביד חד

חשק שלמה על רבינו גרשום א) נראה דצ"ל וליכא רק שררותא בעלמא: ב) נראה דצ"ל וע"פ הרוב נותנין כולן בשוה או דצ"ל וקרוב שנותנין כולן בשוה כצ"ל: ג) נראה דצ"ל והיינו כו' מגילה וכו':

ליקוטי רש"י

אשר למות וגו'. כל המאוחר בפ' קשה מחבירו חרב קשה ממות מיתת חרב מנוולת ומיתה על מטתו אינה מנוולת וכן הוא אומר (תהלים קטז) יקר בעיני ה' המותה לחסידיו רעב קשה מחרב שזה מצטער וזה אינו מצטער וכן הוא אומר טובים היו חללי חרב מחללי רעב שבי כולהו איתנהו בגוה [ירמיה טו, ב]. יקר בעיני ה'. הראני הקב"ה שדבר קשה וכבד הוא בעיניו להמית את חסידיו. המותה. המות כמו הביתה החוצה (בראשית לט) [תהלים קטז, טו]. טובים היו חללי חרב. טובים היו אלו חללי חרב היו מעכשיו שהם חללי רעב [ישעיה כב, ב]. נגבית בשנים ומתחלקת בשלשה. והמחלקים אותה עליהם לבדוק לפי הצריך לכל אחד ואחד ופעמים שקרובין דעתם לרחם על זה ולחלוק יותר מן הצורך שאומדין אותו בהרווחה ואומדין את חברו בצמצום [שבת קיח:]. שממשכנין על הצדקה. נוטלי' משכונות על צדקה שיפסקו עליו ואינו נותנה. ואפילו בערב שבת. שהאדם טרוד [קידושין עו:]. גבאי. גובה [סנהדרין צח:]. ממונה [בכורות לא.]. דרבא אכפיה. על הצדקה [כתובות מט:]. והמשכילים. שעסקו בתורה ובמצות יזהירו כזוהר הרקיע [דניאל יב, ג]. ואוהביו כצאת השמש בגבורתו. לעתיד לבא [שופטים ה, לא]. פורטין. פרוטות של נחשת שגבו לצדקה וכשמשהין אותם מחלידות צריך לפורטן בכסף [פסחים יג.]. מחליפין פרוטות נחושת בסלעי כסף מפני שהפרוטות מתעפשות ונפסלות [ב"מ לח.]. תמחוי. מאכל לאם ומיני מאכל שגובין לחלק. קערה גדולה היא וגובין בה גבאים מאכל מבעלי בתים ומחלקין לעניים שתי סעודות ליום מיום ליום [שבת קיח.]. ואין מוכרין לעצמן. שמא יחשדום שלקחום בזול [פסחים שם].

The Baraisa continues:

תַּמְחוּי נִגְבֵּית בִּשְׁלֹשָׁה וּמִתְחַלֶּקֶת בִּשְׁלֹשָׁה – Food for THE communal "PLATTER"[16] IS COLLECTED BY THREE [PEOPLE], AND IS DISTRIBUTED BY THREE [PEOPLE]. שֶׁגְּבוּיָיהּ וְחִלּוּקָהּ שָׁוִים – FOR ITS COLLECTION AND ITS DISBURSEMENT ARE ON THE SAME DAY.[17]

The Baraisa now presents distinctive laws of the "charity box" and of the "platter":[18]

תַּמְחוּי בְּכָל יוֹם – Food from the communal "PLATTER" was distributed once EACH DAY to paupers who lacked provisions for the next day. קוּפָּה מֵעֶרֶב שַׁבָּת לְעֶרֶב שַׁבָּת – Money from the "CHARITY BOX" was distributed once a week, FROM FRIDAY TO FRIDAY. Paupers who had food for several days, but needed additional money to feed their families for the rest of the week, would receive supplemental funds from the "charity box." תַּמְחוּי לַעֲנִיֵּי עוֹלָם – The communal "PLATTER" provides food TO ANY POOR PERSON,[19] קוּפָּה לַעֲנִיֵּי הָעִיר – while THE "CHARITY BOX," which provides larger sums for support, is accessible only TO THE POOR OF THE CITY. Paupers who were residents of the city, received weekly cash stipends to provide for their family for the entire week.

The Baraisa teaches that transferring money between the funds was permissible:

וְרַשָּׁאִים בְּנֵי הָעִיר לַעֲשׂוֹת קוּפָּה תַּמְחוּי – AND THE OFFICIALS OF THE CITY ARE AUTHORIZED TO RENDER THE "CHARITY BOX" A "PLATTER" וְתַמְחוּי קוּפָּה – AND A "PLATTER" A "CHARITY BOX" if necessary.[20]

The Baraisa adds a general rule:

וּלְשַׁנּוֹתָהּ לְכָל מַה שֶּׁיִּרְצוּ – AND they are authorized TO DIVERT [EXCESS CHARITY FUNDS] TO ANY [PURPOSE] THAT THEY DESIRE.[21]

The Baraisa concludes by enumerating other powers of the communal leaders:

וְרַשָּׁאִין בְּנֵי הָעִיר לְהַתְנוֹת עַל הַמִּדּוֹת – AND THE CITY OFFICIALS ARE AUTHORIZED TO STIPULATE REGARDING THE MEASURES,[22] וְעַל הַשְּׁעָרִים – AND REGARDING THE PRICES[23] וְעַל שְׂכַר פּוֹעֲלִים – AND REGARDING LABORERS' WAGES;[24] וּלְהַסִּיעַ עַל קִיצָתָן – AND the officials are further authorized TO FINE THOSE WHO TRANSGRESS THEIR STIPULATIONS.[25]

The Gemara teaches the source of an earlier ruling:

אָמַר מַר – The master stated previously: אֵין עוֹשִׂין שְׂרָרוּת עַל הַצִּבּוּר פָּחוֹת מִשְּׁנַיִם – We do not establish an authority over the public consisting of less that two [people]. מְנָא הָנֵי מִילֵּי – From where do we derive [this principle]? אָמַר רַב נַחְמָן אָמַר קְרָא – Rav Nachman said: The verse stated:[26] "וְהֵם יִקְחוּ אֶת־הַזָּהָב וגו׳" – *And they shall take the gold etc.* Scripture refers to the officials that collected donations from the public for the construction of the Tabernacle, and it stated "they," in the plural.[27] This teaches that with respect to money matters, we may not establish an authority over the public consisting of one individual.[28]

The Gemara infers from this ruling:

שְׂרָרוּת הוּא דְּלָא עָבְדִי – It is an authority that we do not make of one individual; הָא הֵימוּנֵי מְהֵימַן – but with regard to trusting an individual, he would be trusted to serve as the administrator of a charity fund. מְסַיֵּיעַ לֵיהּ לְרַבִּי חֲנִינָא – [This inference] supports R' Chanina, דְּאָמַר רַבִּי חֲנִינָא – for R' Chanina said: מַעֲשֶׂה וּמִינָּה רַבִּי שְׁנֵי אַחִין עַל הַקּוּפָּה – It once happened that Rebbi appointed two brothers to serve as administrators for the charity fund. Concerning matters of trust, two brothers are regarded as one individual, for one may not testify against the other; hence, it was as if Rebbi appointed one person to administer the charity fund.

The Gemara stated above that collecting for the "charity box" must be performed by at least two people because one individual may not be appointed an authority over the public. The Gemara now inquires:

מַאי שְׂרָרוּתָא – What element of authority does collecting donations for the charity fund entail?[29]

The Gemara replies:

דְּאָמַר רַב נַחְמָן אָמַר רַבָּה בַּר אֲבוּהָ – There is, nevertheless, an

NOTES

not be accomplished by a group of three, since the amount that each contributor gives is known in advance. Thus, the collectors do not need to exercise their judgment to determine the size of each individual's contribution (*Tosafos*; see *Rabbeinu Gershom*).

16. The communal soup kitchen. People donated cooked food, which was distributed daily to the very poor.

17. Distribution of food to the poor was necessarily performed by a panel of three, since they functioned in the manner of a *beis din* deciding a case of monetary law, judiciously determining the size of each allotment (as in the case of the "charity box" – see above, note 14). Although no such determinations were required for the collections (cf. *Rabbeinu Gershom, Rif, Rosh* and *Ritva*), still three people were appointed for that function as well. For since the food in the communal "platter" was distributed on a daily basis, the Sages wanted to eliminate the bother of always having to obtain a third official to participate in the disbursement. Hence, they required three people to participate in the collection so that three would be available later for a timely disbursement (*Rashi*; see *Nachalas Moshe*).

18. *Maharam* says that according to Rashi's explanation (see previous note), the Baraisa now gives the reason why collection for the "platter" requires three, and for the "charity box" only two.

19. Literally: the poor of the world.

20. I.e. if a particular city receives an influx of paupers from the outside, thus overburdening the resources of its "platter," it may provide for these poor with *excess* funds from the "charity box," even though this money is normally reserved for the local poor. Similarly, the city may sell *excess* food in the "platter" to meet an extraordinary demand for donations from the "charity box" (*Rashi, Rabbeinu Gershom*).

21. *Ri Migash, Ramah* and other commentators understand the Gemara to authorize the diversion of these charity assets only to projects that benefit paupers in other ways. Thus, for example, although money was donated to the "charity box" in order to provide the impoverished with food, those funds may be used to provide them with clothing or shelter as well. However, to divert that money to a general community project would constitute גֶּזֶל עֲנִיִּים, *stealing from the poor. Rashi, Tosafos* and *Ramban* disagree with this interpretation, and contend that the diverted funds may be used to meet any public need, since the donors initially intended to rely on the discretion of the charity administrators (*Ritva*). See *Rabbeinu Yonah, Rashba* and *Ritva* for important qualifications of this second opinion.

22. I.e. to decree that a specific volume measure be made larger or smaller (*Rashi, Rabbeinu Gershom*).

23. I.e. to set a certain ceiling price for commodities such as wheat and wine in any given year (*Rashi*).

24. I.e. to decree that laborers be paid less than the prevailing rate (*Rabbeinu Gershom*).

25. Literally: to transport regarding their regulations.

Rashi explains that the unusual use of לְהַסִּיעַ, *to transport,* suggests that the city officials' stipulations transport the townspeople from normative Torah law through the imposition of fines for violations of those stipulations.

26. *Exodus* 28:5.

27. "They" implies a minimum of two people (*Rabbeinu Gershom*).

28. The Gemara below will explain in what sense the collection of taxes and other levies constitutes an authority.

29. Since every city resident was required to donate to the fund (see Gemara above, 8a), in what way did the collectors exercise authority?

פדיון שבוים מצוה רבה היא אמר ליה רבא לרבה בר מרי מנא הא מילתא דאמור רבנן דפדיון שבוים מצוה רבה היא א"ל דכתיב א) והיה כי יאמרו אליך אנה נצא ואמרת אליהם כה אמר ה' אשר למות למות ואשר לחרב לחרב ואשר לרעב לרעב ואשר לשבי לשבי ואמר רבי יוחנן כל המאוחר בפסוק זה קשה מחבירו חרב קשה ממות א) אי בעית אימא קרא ואי בעית אימא סברא סברא האי קא מינוול והאי לא קא מינוול ואבע"א קרא ב) יקר בעיני ה' המותה לחסידיו רעב קשה מחרב איבעית אימא (א) סברא האי קא מצטער והאי לא קא מצטער איבעית אימא קרא ג) טובים היו חללי חרב מחללי רעב שבי [קשה מכולם] דכולהו איתנהו ביה:

תנו רבנן ב) א קופה של צדקה נגבית בשנים ומתחלקת בשלשה נגבית בשנים ג) ב שאין עושים שררות על הצבור פחות משנים ומתחלקת בשלשה כדיני ממונות ג תמחוי נגבית בשלשה ומתחלקת בשלשה שגבויה וחלוקה שוים ד תמחוי בכל יום קופה מערב שבת לערב שבת ה תמחוי לעניי עולם קופה לעניי העיר ו ורשאים בני העיר לעשות קופה תמחוי ותמחוי קופה ולשנותה לכל מה שירצו ז ורשאין בני העיר להתנות על המדות ועל השערים ועל שכר פועלים ולהסיע על קיצתן אמר מר אין עושין שררות על הצבור פחות משנים מנא הני מילי אמר רב נחמן אמר קרא ד) והם יקחו את הזהב וגו' שררות הוא דלא עבדי ח הא הימוני מהימן מסייע ליה לרבי חנינא דאמר רבי חנינא מעשה ט ומינה רבי שני אחין על הקופה מאי שררותא דאמר רב נחמן אמר רבה בר אבוה לפי ד) י שממשכנין על הצדקה ואפילו בע"ש איני והא כתיב ה) ופקדתי על כל לוחציו ואמר ר' יצחק בר שמואל בר מרתא משמיה דרב ואפי' על גבאי צדקה לא קשיא כ הא דאמיד הא דלא אמיד ה) כי הא דרבא אכפיה לרב נתן בר אמי ושקיל מיניה ארבע מאה זוזי לצדקה ו) והמשכילים יזהירו כזוהר הרקיע וגו' ו) (המשכילים יזהירו כזוהר הרקיע) זה דיין שדן דין אמת לאמתו ומצדיקי הרבים ככוכבים לעולם ועד אלו גבאי צדקה במתניתא תנא והמשכילים יזהירו כזוהר הרקיע זה דיין שדן דין אמת לאמתו וגבאי צדקה ומצדיקי הרבים ככוכבים לעולם ועד אלו מלמדי תינוקות כגון מאן אמר רב כגון רב שמואל בר שילת דרב אשכחיה לרב שמואל בר שילת דהוה קאי בגינתא א"ל שבקתיה להימנותך אמר ליה (ב) הא תליסר שנין דלא חזיא לי והשתא נמי דעתאי עלוייהו ורבנן מאי אמר רבינא ז) ואוהביו כצאת השמש בגבורתו ת"ר ל גבאי צדקה אינן רשאין לפרוש זה מזה אבל פורש זה לשער וזה לחנות מ מצא מעות בשוק לא יתנם בתוך כיסו אלא נותנן לתוך ארנקי של צדקה ולכשיבא לביתו יטלם כיוצא בו נ היה נושה בחבירו מנה ופרעו בשוק לא יתננו לתוך כיסו אלא נותנן לתוך ארנקי של צדקה ולכשיבא לביתו יטלם תנו רבנן ס גבאי צדקה שאין להם עניים לחלק פורטין לאחרים ואין פורטין לעצמן ע גבאי תמחוי שאין להם עניים לחלק מוכרין לאחרים ואין מוכרין לעצמן פ מעות של צדקה אין מונין אותן שתים (ג) אלא אחת אחת אמר אביי מריש לא הוה יתיב מר אציפי דבי כנישתא כיון דשמעה להא דתניא ולשנותה לכל מה שירצו הוה יתיב אמר אביי מריש הוה עביד מר תרי כיסי חד לעניי דעלמא וחד לעניי דמתא כיון דשמעה להא דאמר ליה שמואל לרב תחליפא בר אבדימי עביד חד כיסא

רש"י

שבי כולהו איתנהו ביה. שהוא ביד העכו"ם לעשות בו כל חפצו אם למות [אם לחרב] אם לרעב: מפני שהוא כדיני ממונות. לעיין ולתת לכל אחד כפי טפלים התלויין בו: שגבויה וחלוקה שוה. בכל יום מדי יום ביום כדקתני לקמיה לפיכך אין גבויו בשנים שלא יצטרכו לטרוח ולבקש את השלישי לחלק: לעשות קופה תמחוי. לחלק לעניי עולם אם ירבו עליהן: להתנות על המדות. להגדיל סאת העיר או להקטין: ועל השערים. שער חטין והיין שלא ימכרנה שנה זו יותר מכך וכך דמים: להסיע על קיצתם. לקנוס את העובר על קיצת דבריהם להסיעם מדת דין תורה: הא הימוני מהימן. יחיד להיות גזבר: שני אחים. לגבי המנותא כחד דמו: מאי שררותיה. דקופה דקאמרת עלה לפי שאין עושין שררה על הצבור כו': אפילו בע"ש. שיש פתחון פה לבעה"ב לומר טרוד אני: ופקדתי וגו'. אלמא אסור למשכן: אמיד. עשיר ל): גבאי צדקה. המשכילים אל דל מהו צריך: מלמדי תינוקות. מצדיקי רבים הן שמלמדין ומחנכין אותן בדרך טובה: שבקתיה להמנותיך. שהיית רגיל ללמדם באמונה וללמד ולישב על גבם תמיד: דעתאי להתם. לתינוקות: ורבנן מאי. תלמידי חכמים העוסקים בתורה תמיד מאי כתיב בהו: לפרוש זה מזה. מפני החשד שלא יאמרו זה הגובה יחידי דעתו לגנוב: אבל זה פורש לחנות וזה לשער. זה לגבות מיושבי השער וזה לגבות מיושבי החנות ובלבד שיראו שניהן כאחד: לא יתנם לתוך כיסו. שלא יאמרו מעות של צדקה הוא גונב: פורטין. פרוטות שגבו לוקחין דינרי כסף לפי שהפרוטות של נחושת מחלידות: ואין פורטין לעצמם. פן יחשדום שפורטין בזול: אין מונין אותם שנים שנים. פן יאמרו שנים הוא נוטל ואינו מונה אלא אחד: אציפי דבי כנישתא. מחצלות של בית הכנסת משום דמזבני להו ממעות הקופה: ואתני

תוספות

פדיון שבוים מצוה רבה. והא דאמר בפרק בני העיר (מגילה דף כז.) אין מוכרין ס"ת אלא ללמוד תורה ולישא אשה ולא קתני פדיון שבוים שמא מילתא דפשיטא היא ולא איצטריך למיתני: ומתחלקת בג' מפני שהוא כדיני ממונות. וא"ת מהאי טעמא נמי תהא נגבית בג' ופר"ת לפי שהיה ידוע סכום של כל אחד ואחד כמה יתן: ולשנות' לכל מה שירצו. נראה לר"ת דיכולים לשנותו אף לדבר הרשות אע"ג דאמרינן בערכין בפ"ק (דף ו: ושם) האי מאן דנדב שרגא לבי כנישתא אסור לשנותה לדבר הרשות ואמר נמי התם האומר פרוטה זו לצדקה עד שלא באה ליד הגבאי מותר לשנותה משבאה ליד הגבאי אסור לשנותה (ד) לדבר הרשות הכא שבני העיר משנים אותה שאני לפיכך מותר לשנותה אפילו לדבר הרשות ואפילו באה ליד הגבאי וכן היה ר"ת נוהג לתת מעות הקופה לשומרי העיר לפי שעל דעת בני העיר נותנים אותם: כי הא דרבא אכפיה. אחר היה עמו דאין עושין שררה על הצבור פחות מב' ולא חשיב ליה ס) מפני כבודו של רבא: אכפיה לרב נתן. וא"ת והא בפרק כל הבשר (חולין דף קי: ושם ד"ה כל) אמר כל מ"ע שמתן שכרה ל) [כתובה] בצדה אין ב"ד של מטה מוזהרים עליה וגבי צדקה כתיב כי פתוח תפתח את ידך לו וכתיב כי בגלל הדבר הזה יברכך (דברים טו) ואר"ת דהאי כפיה בדברים כמו כפייה (ה) ועל בפרק נערה שנתפתתה (כתובות דף נג.) ועוד תירץ דהכא קבלו עליהם שיכופו אותן הגבאי ולר"י נראה דבצדקה כופין משום דאית בה לאו דכתיב בה לא תאמץ את לבבך ולא תקפוץ וגו' ולריצב"א נראה דהא דאין ב"ד מוזהרין על מצות עשה שמתן (ו) שכרן בצדה היינו דאין נענשין וכן משמע בירושלמי דהמוכר את הספינה והיא דכל הבשר (שם) דלא הוה מוקיר אבוה וכפתוהו ואמר להו שבקוהו ה"פ איכנס מוזהרין להכריחו עד שיעשה כשאר מצות עשה דאם א"ל עשה סוכה ולולב ואינו עושה מכין אותו עד שתצא נפשו כדאמר בהכותב (כתובות דף פו. ושם) [וע"ע תוס' כתובות מט: ד"ה אכפייה ותוס' חולין קי: ד"ה כל]: דין אמת לאמתו. אמת לאפוקי דין מרומה אע"ג שהעדים מעידין אותו מ) [אין מחתכים אותו] כיון שיודעים שמשקרים כדדרשינן (בסנהדרין דף ז.) [צ"ל בשבועות ל:] לאמתו שלא יטו את הדין [וע"ע תוס' מגילה טו: ד"ה זה]: ומצדיקי הרבים וגו' אלו מלמדי תינוקות. אומר ר"י דצריך לומר דרקיע מזהיר טפי מכוכבים דהא בס"פ אלו עוברין (פסחים מט: ושם ד"ה לא) משמע דגבאי צדקה עדיפי ממלמדי תינוקות דאמר לא מצא בת תלמיד חכם ישא בת גבאי צדקה לא מצא בת גבאי צדקה ישא בת מלמדי תינוקות ואריב"א כי מצא בפרקי דרבי אליעזר דרקיע דהאי קרא דהמשכילים יזהירו כזוהר הרקיע היינו רקיע שעל ראשי החיות שמזהירין מכוכבים שאורו כאור החמה והאי דקאמר ורבנן מאי אמר רבינא ואוהביו כצאת השמש היינו שמש של עתיד לבא דהוא שבעתים כאור שבעת הימים ואור שבעת ימי בראשית היה שבעתים מאור חמה של עכשיו כדמפרש תרגום של רני ושמחי (זכריה ב):

ואע"פ

עין משפט נר מצוה

ע א ב ג מיי' פ"ט מהל' מתנות עניים הל' ה סמג עשין קסב טוש"ע י"ד סי' רנו סעיף ג:

עא ד ה ו מיי' שם הל' ו ז טוש"ע שם סעיף ד:

עב ז מיי' פ"ט מהל' מכירה הל' ט סמג לאוין קע טוש"ע ח"מ סי' רלא סעיף כח:

עג ח ט מיי' פ"ט מהל' מתנות עניים הל' ה סמג עשין קסב טוש"ע י"ד סי' רנו סעיף ג:

עד י מיי' שם פ"ז הל' י סמג שם טוש"ע י"ד סי' רמח סעיף ג:

עה כ מיי' שם הל' י והל' יא טוש"ע שם סעיף ה וסעיף ז:

עו ל מ נ מיי' שם פ"ט הל' ח ט סמג שם טוש"ע י"ד סי' רנז סעיף א:

עז ס ע מיי' שם הל' יא טוש"ע שם סעיף ב:

עח פ מיי' שם הל' י טוש"ע שם סעיף ג:

רבינו גרשום

נהרג בחרב מינויל. דמתלכלך בדמו: נגבית בשנים. משום דמתחלקת לעניי העיר והכל קצוב הוא שיודעין כמה כל אחד ואחד צריך ליתן בקצוב ונותנין בשוה וליכא א) אלא סידורי בעלמא דגובין אותו גבאי צדקה מהם: ומתחלקת בג'. מפני שהוא כדיני ממונות מה דיני ממונות נוטלין מזה ונותנין לזה אף מחלקי צדקה מרבין לא' וממעטין לא' לפי שיראו צרכי עניים: גיבויו וחילוקו שוה. שגובין מכל א' לפי מה שידו משגת וכעין דין שמעיינין בדין על מי להרבות ועל מי למעט משא"כ בקופה שאין גובין מכל אחד אלא לפי מה שרוצה ליתן ב) וקרוב נותנין כולן בשוה: לעשות קופה תמחוי. שאם ניתותר בקופה יותר על צורך עניי העיר ותתמעט בתמחוי לעניי כל אדם שבאו עניים הרבה וכן תמחוי לקופה כמו כן: להתנות על המדות. להגדיל או למעטן מכמות שהיו: ועל השער. שאם היה השער ביוקר רשאין להתנות שילך בזול: ועל שכר הפועלים. שאם נשכרין פועלים בב' פשי' ביום רשאין להתנות שלא ישכרום אלא בב': ולהסיע על קיצתן. לקנוס על העובר על מה שקבעו אנשי העיר: והם יקחו. ואין הם פחות משנים: שררות הוא דלא עבדי פחות משנים. כלומר דמשמע טעמו דשררות הוא דבעינן ב' ולא משום דין ולא לשום עדות הלכך (הא) המוני מהמני אפי' ב' קרובים למנות על הקופה והיינו ג) מאי שררות איכא בגבאי צדקה הואיל דדבר קצוב הוא ונותנין משמשכנין. אם מעכב ליתן צדקה בקופה. ואפי' בע"ש דטרידי עצמו מאי איכא למיעבד ביה: הא דאמיד. אותו שהוא עשיר וממאן ליתן ממשכנין אותו ואפי' בעל כרחו: הא דלא אמיד שאין לו מה ליתן אם (לוה) [ליה] ממשכנין עליו נאמר ופקדתי על כל לוחציו: ושקל מיניה [ד' מאה] זוזי לצדקה. דהוה אמיד שהיה עשיר: זה דיין. שמשכיל לדין הדין לאמתו.

ומצדיקי הרבים אלו גבאי צדקה שמעשין בני אדם ליתן צדקה ומצדיקין אותן: שבקת לאומנותך. שהיה מלמד תינוקות כלומר אותו התלמוד עדיין לא היית מבטל לעמוד בגינה: דעתי עלייהו. על התינוקות שלא הסחתי דעתי מהם שלא לזרום ממקומם זה שאני עומד: ורבנן מאי. כלומר כיון דלדיין נתת זוהר הרקיע לעתיד לבא [ולגבאי] צדקה נתת אור הכוכבים רבנן עצמן מאי יזכו הן: כצאת השמש בגבורתו. דעדיף מכולהו: לפרוש זה מזה. בשוק משום חשדא שלא יחשדו זה לזה שא' מהם יתן לתוך כיסו ולא לכיס של צדקה אבל רשאי לפרוש זה לשער לשאול הצדקה וזה לחנות משום דקרובין זה לזה: פורטין לאחרים. שאם יש בכיס של צדקה פרוטות ורוצה לחלפן בסלע כסף פורטין לאחרים חלפי לאחרים ולא לעצמן שמא יאמרו שמרויחים בצדקה: אין מונין אותן שתים שתים כשפורטין לאחרים אלא מונה אחת אחת שלא יטעה: לא יתיב מר. רבה: אציפי. אמחצלאות שפורסין על כותלי בית הכנסת והיו קנויות מצדקה: מחצלאות. ששוכבין עליהן עניים: עביד חד

חשק שלמה על רבינו גרשום א) נראה דצ"ל וליכא רק שררותא בעלמא: ב) נראה דצ"ל וע"פ הרוב טומנין כולן בשוה או דצ"ל וקרוב שטומנין כולן בשוה כצ"ל: ג) נראה דצ"ל והיינו כר' חנינא וכו':

מסורת הש"ס

א) [ברכות ד: וש"נ], ב) [פאה פ"ח מ"ז סנהדרין יז:], ג) שקלים פ"ה מ"ב, ד) [קדושין עו:], ה) כתובות מט:, ו) [ילקוט איתא וכן בע"י איתא], ז) ר"ל להתם, ח) [בשאלתות פרשת תשא איתא ורבנן אמרו מאי דכתיב ואוהביו כצאת השמש בגבורתו אלו גבאי צדקה ופרנסי העיר], ט) [תוספתא פאה פ"ד], י) פסחים יג., כ) ב"מ לח., ל) יעב"ץ, מ) [כ"ה בדפו"י].

הגהות הב"ח

(א) גמ' רעב קשה מחרב איבעית אימא סברא ואיבעית אימא קרא. סברא א"ל סברא האי קא מצטער: (ב) שם א"ל לאו הא אידנא תליסר שנין דלא חזיא לי: (ג) שם אין מונין אותן שתים שתים אלא: (ד) תוס' ד"ה ולשנות' וכו' משבאה ליד הגבאי אסור לשנות' הכא ל"ל ותיבות לדבר הרשות נמחק: (ה) ד"ה אכפיה וכו' כמו כפיה רב פפא לרב יהודה בפ' נערה: (ו) בא"ד שמתן שכרה בצדה.

גליון הש"ס

תוס' ד"ה כי כו' מפני כבודו של רבא. ועיין לעיל בר"ה דף כב ע"ב גיטין דף ג ע"ב סנהדרין דף יא ע"ב:

תורה אור השלם

א) וְהָיָה כִּי יֹאמְרוּ אֵלֶיךָ אָנָה נֵצֵא וְאָמַרְתָּ אֲלֵיהֶם כֹּה אָמַר יְיָ אֲשֶׁר לַמָּוֶת לַמָּוֶת וַאֲשֶׁר לַחֶרֶב לַחֶרֶב וַאֲשֶׁר לָרָעָב לָרָעָב וַאֲשֶׁר לַשְּׁבִי לַשֶּׁבִי: [ירמיה טו, ב]

ב) יָקָר בְּעֵינֵי יְיָ הַמָּוְתָה לַחֲסִידָיו: [תהלים קטז, טו]

ג) טוֹבִים הָיוּ חַלְלֵי חֶרֶב מֵחַלְלֵי רָעָב שֶׁהֵם יָזוּבוּ מְדֻקָּרִים מִתְּנוּבֹת שָׂדָי: [איכה ד, ט]

ד) וְהֵם יִקְחוּ אֶת הַזָּהָב וְאֶת הַתְּכֵלֶת וְאֶת הָאַרְגָּמָן וְאֶת תּוֹלַעַת הַשָּׁנִי וְאֶת הַשֵּׁשׁ: [שמות כח, ה]

ה) וְהָיוּ בָנָיו כְּקֶדֶם וַעֲדָתוֹ לְפָנַי תִּכּוֹן וּפָקַדְתִּי עַל כָּל לֹחֲצָיו: [ירמיה ל, כ]

ו) וְהַמַּשְׂכִּלִים יַזְהִרוּ כְּזֹהַר הָרָקִיעַ וּמַצְדִּיקֵי הָרַבִּים כַּכּוֹכָבִים לְעוֹלָם וָעֶד: [דניאל יב, ג]

ז) כֵּן יֹאבְדוּ כָל אוֹיְבֶיךָ יְיָ וְאֹהֲבָיו כְּצֵאת הַשֶּׁמֶשׁ בִּגְבֻרָתוֹ וַתִּשְׁקֹט הָאָרֶץ אַרְבָּעִים שָׁנָה: [שופטים ה, לא]

ליקוטי רש"י

אשר למות וגו'. כל המאוחר בפ' קשה מחבירו חרב קשה ממות מיתת חרב מנוולת ומיתה על מטתו אינה מנוולת וכן הוא אומר (תהלים קטז) יקר בעיני ה' המותה לחסידיו רעב קשה מחרב שזה מצטער וזה אינו מצטער וכן הוא אומר טובים היו חללי חרב מחללי רעב שבי כולהו איתנהו ביה [ירמיה טו, ב]. יקר בעיני ה'. הראהו הקב"ה שדבר קשה וכבד הוא בעיניו להמית את חסידיו. המותה. המות (כראשי' לט) [תהלים קטז, טו]. טובים היו חללי חרב. טובים היו אילו חללי חרב היו מעכשיו שהם חללי רעב. נגבית בשנים ומתחלקת בשלשה. והמחלקים אותה עליהם לבדוק לפי הצריך לכל אחד ואחד ופעמים שקרובין דעתם לרחם על זה ולחלוק יותר מן הצורך שאומדין אותו בהרווחה ואומדין את חברו בצמצום [שבת קיח:]. שממשכנין על הצדקה. נוטלי' משכונות על צדקה שיפסקו עליו ואינו נותנה. ואפילו בערב שבת. שהאדם טרוד [קידושין עו:]. גבאי. גובה [סנהדרין צח:]. ממונה [בכורות לא.]. דרבא אכפיה. על הצדקה [כתובות מט:]. והמשכילים. יזהירו כזוהר הרקיע [דניאל יב, ג]. ואוהביו כצאת השמש בגבורתו. לעתיד לבא [שופטים ה, לא]. נחשת שגבו לצדקה וכשמשהין אותם מחלידות צריך לפורטן בכסף [פסחים יג.]. מחליפין פרוטות נחושת שהפרוטות מתעפשות ונפסלות [ב"מ לח.]. תמחוי. מאכל לחם ומיני מאכל שגובין לחלק גדולה היא וגובין בה גבאים מאכל מבעלי בתים ומחלקין לעניים שתי סעודות ליום מיום ליום [שבת קיח.]. ואין מוכרין לעצמן. שמא יחשדום שלקחום בזול [פסחים שם].

element of authority, **for Rav Nachman said in the name of Rabbah bar Avuha:** לְפִי שֶׁמְּמַשְׁכְּנִין עַל הַצְּדָקָה – **Because [collectors]** are authorized to **seize a pledge for an** unpaid **charity** obligation – וַאֲפִילוּ בְּעֶרֶב שַׁבָּת – **and even on the Sabbath eve**[30] – their function entails an exercise of authority, and so two collectors must be assigned to the task.

The Gemara objects to Rav Nachman's statement:

אֵינִי – **Is it so** that collectors may seize pledges? וְהָא כְּתִיב: "וּפָקַדְתִּי עַל כָּל־לֹחֲצָיו" – **But is it not written:** ***And I will visit evil upon all of their oppressors?***[31] וְאָמַר רַבִּי יִצְחָק בַּר שְׁמוּאֵל בַּר מַרְתָּא מִשְּׁמֵיהּ דְּרַב – **And R' Yitzchak the son of Shmuel bar Marsa said in Rav's name:** וַאֲפִילוּ עַל גַּבָּאֵי צְדָקָה – **And** God will visit evil **even upon charity collectors!** Since collecting that which the people are willing to give is not oppressive – indeed, it is a great service to the community – R' Yitzchak must mean that the collectors occasionally oppress the people by over-zealously seizing their property for collateral, and for that they will be punished. We see, then, that collectors are forbidden to seize pledges for unpaid charity obligations. – ? –

The Gemara replies:

לֹא קַשְׁיָא – This is **not a difficulty.** הָא דַּאֲמִיד – **This** law of Rav Nachman applies **when** the contributor is **wealthy,**[32] and he has not contributed what he is capable of giving. הָא דְּלָא אֲמִיד – **That** law of R' Yitzchak applies **when** the contributor **is not wealthy.** To seize from him more than he is capable of giving, is an oppressive act.

The Gemara relates an incident to illustrate that wealthy people are treated differently:

כִּי הָא דְּרָבָא – We see that the rich may even be compelled to contribute, **as in that** case **of Rava,** אַכְפְּיֵהּ לְרַב נָתָן בַּר אַמֵּי – who while collecting for charity[33] **coerced**[34] Rav **Nassan bar Ami,** a wealthy man, וְשָׁקִיל מִינֵּיהּ אַרְבַּע מְאָה זוּזֵי לִצְדָקָה – **and took from [Rav Nassan] four hundred** ***zuzim*** **for charity.** Similarly, collectors are permitted to seize collateral from wealthy contributors.

The Gemara extols the virtues of charity collectors:

"וְהַמַּשְׂכִּלִים יַזְהִרוּ כְּזֹהַר הָרָקִיעַ וגו׳" – Scripture states:[35] – ***And the wise will shine like the radiance of the firmament etc.***[36] (הַמַּשְׂכִּלִים יַזְהִרוּ כְּזֹהַר הָרָקִיעַ) זֶה דַּיָּין שֶׁדָּן דִּין אֱמֶת לַאֲמִתּוֹ – **This** refers to **a judge who renders an absolutely truthful judgment.**[37] His virtues will cause him to shine.

The Gemara expounds upon the end of the verse:

"וּמַצְדִּיקֵי הָרַבִּים כַּכּוֹכָבִים לְעוֹלָם וָעֶד" – ***And those who make the many righteous*** (will shine) ***like the stars forever and ever.*** אֵלּוּ גַּבָּאֵי צְדָקָה – **This** refers to **charity collectors,** who in the merit of causing the many to be charitable will shine like the stars.[38]

The Gemara presents a different version of the above:

בְּמַתְנִיתָא תָּנָא – **It was taught in a Baraisa:** "וְהַמַּשְׂכִּלִים יַזְהִרוּ כְּזֹהַר הָרָקִיעַ" – ***And the wise will shine like the radiance of the firmament*** – זֶה דַּיָּין שֶׁדָּן דִּין אֱמֶת לַאֲמִתּוֹ וְגַבָּאֵי צְדָקָה – **this** refers to **a judge who renders an absolutely truthful judgment and** to **charity collectors;**[39] "וּמַצְדִּיקֵי הָרַבִּים כַּכּוֹכָבִים לְעוֹלָם וָעֶד" – ***and those who make the many righteous*** (will shine) ***like the stars forever and ever*** – אֵלּוּ מְלַמְּדֵי תִּינוֹקוֹת – **these are teachers of children.**[40]

The Gemara asks:

כְּגוֹן מַאן – **Who, for example,** fits this description of a teacher? אָמַר רַב – **Rav said:** כְּגוֹן רַב שְׁמוּאֵל בַּר שִׁילַת – A teacher **such as Rav Shmuel bar Shilas,** who was extremely dedicated to his students.

The Gemara relates an incident that illustrates Rav Shmuel's extraordinary dedication:

דְּרַב אַשְׁכְּחֵיהּ לְרַב שְׁמוּאֵל בַּר שִׁילַת דַּהֲוָה קָאֵי בְּגִינְתָא – **For Rav** once **found Rav Shmuel bar Shilas standing in a garden.**[41] אָמַר לֵיהּ שְׁבַקְתֵּיהּ לְהֵימְנוּתָךְ – **[Rav] said to him: "Have you abandoned your trust?"**[42] אָמַר לֵיהּ – **[Rav Shmuel] said to [Rav]:** הָא תְּלֵיסַר שְׁנִין דְּלָא חֲזְיָא לִי – **"It has been thirteen years that I have not seen** this garden, וְהַשְׁתָּא נַמִּי דַּעְתַּאי עִלָּוַיְהוּ – **and even now my mind is on [the children]."** A teacher who always thinks of his students is truly making the "many" (the future generation) righteous, and like the stars will shine forever.[43]

NOTES

30. When every Jew has the excuse that he is busy preparing for the Sabbath [and therefore cannot tender his contribution] (*Rashi*).

[*Kovetz Shiurim* asks: the source of the requirment for two collectors is the collection of donations for the Tabernacle, where it was totally voluntary and no one was forced to donate. How then can the Gemara state the reason for requiring two people is to allow collectors to seize donations? See there for his answer.]

31. *Jeremiah* 30:20. The prophet refers to the time of the final redemption, when God will punish all the nations that oppressed the Jewish people.

32. Literally: estimated. *Rashi* in *Gittin* (52b ד״ה ולא אמיד) explains that "estimated" connotes "wealthy" because people constantly estimate a rich man's worth; nobody, however, bothers to estimate the worth of a pauper.

33. *Tosafos* note that Rava was certainly accompanied by another collector, for authority to collect is not given to an individual. In deference to Rava, however, the companion's name is not mentioned.

34. There are various opinions as to the nature of the coercion mentioned here, since *beis din* is not authorized to use physical coercion to enforce a positive commandment (such as giving charity) whose reward for compliance is recorded in the Torah (see *Chullin* 110b). *Rabbeinu Tam* (cited in *Tosafos* ד״ה אכפיה) therefore explains that Rava employed verbal persuasion. *Ri* (ibid.) suggests that since the act of charity involves a negative precept as well (*You shall not harden your heart, and you shall not shut your hand, from your needy brother – Deuteronomy* 15:7), physical coercion may be used. See *Tosafos* for other explanations.

35. *Daniel* 12:3. The verse speaks of the luminosity that God will bestow upon the deserving after the final redemption.

36. רָקִיעַ, *firmament,* denotes the section of the heavens above the heads of the holy *chayos*, and it is exceedingly brilliant (*Tosafos* ד״ה ומצדיקי, citing *Pirkei D' Rabbi Eliezer* 4).

37. He will reject unimpeached testimony if he suspects the witnesses are lying (*Tosafos*). Such a judge, because of his wisdom and integrity, perceives the truth through the camouflage of the witnesses' dissembling, and does not fall back on the principle אֵין לְדַיָּין אֶלָּא מַה שֶּׁעֵינָיו רוֹאוֹת, *a judge decides only on the basis of the testimony and evidence before him.* He therefore merits to shine like the *true* radiance of the firmament, which, although distorted into many hues by the earth's atmosphere, is indeed the color of sapphire – the very color of God's Holy Throne (*Maharsha*).

38. Just as the stars exert their influence both day and night but illuminate only at night, so the charity collectors are solicitous of the needs of the poor both day and night but shine forth only at night – i.e. they distribute charity discreetly, so as not to embarrass the recipient (*Maharsha*).

39. The word מַשְׂכִּלִים can be translated "those who know"; charity collectors discern the needs of the poor (*Rashi*).

40. They are among "those who make others righteous" because they teach the children and train them in the proper path (*Rashi*).

41. *Rif's* text reads "in *his* garden." According to this version, Rav Shmuel did not take time even to tend his own garden!

42. Rav Shmuel was so dedicated that he taught and supervised his students constantly. Rav was therefore amazed to see Rav Shmuel alone (*Rashi*). According to *Rabbeinu Gershom*, Rav questioned whether Rav Shmuel had quit his job.

43. Just as the stars exert their influence even when they are not visible, so the conscientious and dedicated teacher will not relinquish

עין משפט נר מצוה

ע א ב ג מיי' פ"ט מהל' מתנות עניים הל' ה סמג עשין קסב טוש"ע י"ד סי' רנו סעיף ג:
עא ד ה ו מיי' שם הל' ו ז טוש"ע שם סעיף ד:
עב ז מיי' פי"ד מהל' מכירה הל' ט סמג לאוין קע טוש"ע ח"מ סי' רלא סעיף כז כח:
עג ח ט מיי' פ"ט מהל' מתנות עניים הל' ה סמג עשין קסב טוש"ע י"ד סי' רנו סעיף ג:
עד י מיי' שם פ"ז הל' י סמג שם טוש"ע י"ד סי' רמח סעיף ג:
עה כ מיי' שם הל' י והל' יא טוש"ע שם סעיף א וסעיף ז:
עו ל מ נ מיי' שם פ"ט הל' ח ט סמג שם טוש"ע י"ד סי' רנז סעיף א:
עז ס ע מיי' שם הל' יא טוש"ע שם סעיף ג:
עח פ מיי' שם הל' י טוש"ע שם סעיף א:

פדיון שבוים מצוה רבה היא אמר ליה רבא לרבה בר מרי מנא הא מילתא דאמור רבנן דפדיון שבוים מצוה רבה היא א"ל דכתיב א) והיה כי יאמרו אליך אנה נצא ואמרת אליהם כה אמר ה' אשר למות למות ואשר לחרב לחרב ואשר לרעב לרעב ואשר לשבי לשבי ואמר רבי יוחנן כל המאוחר בפסוק זה קשה מחבירו חרב קשה ממות א) אי בעית אימא קרא ואי בעית אימא סברא אי בעית אימא סברא האי קא מינוול והאי לא קא מינוול ואבע"א קרא ב) יקר בעיני ה' המותה לחסידיו רעב קשה מחרב איבעית אימא (א) סברא האי קא מצטער והאי לא קא מצטער איבעית אימא קרא ג) טובים היו חללי חרב מחללי רעב שבי [קשה מכולם] דכולהו איתנהו ביה:

תנו רבנן א קופה של צדקה נגבית בשנים ומתחלקת בשלשה ב) נגבית בשנים ב שאין עושים שררות על הצבור פחות משנים ומתחלקת בשלשה כדיני ממונות ג תמחוי נגבית בשלשה ומתחלקת בשלשה שגבויה וחלוקה שוים ד תמחוי בכל יום קופה מערב שבת לערב שבת ה תמחוי לעניי עולם קופה לעניי העיר ו ורשאים בני העיר לעשות קופה תמחוי ותמחוי קופה ולשנותה לכל מה שירצו ז ורשאין בני העיר להתנות על המדות ועל השערים ועל שכר פועלים ולהסיע על קיצתן אמר מר אין עושין שררות על הצבור פחות משנים מנא הני מילי אמר רב נחמן אמר קרא ד) והם יקחו את הזהב וגו' שררות הוא דלא עבדי ח הא הימוני מהימן מסייע ליה לרבי חנינא דאמר רבי חנינא מעשה ט ומינה רבי שני אחין על הקופה מאי שררותא דאמר רב נחמן אמר רבה בר אבוה לפי י) שממשכנין על הצדקה ואפילו בע"ש איני והא כתיב ה) ופקדתי על כל לוחציו ואמר ר' יצחק בר שמואל בר מרתא משמיה דרב ואפי' על גבאי צדקה לא קשיא כ הא דאמיד הא דלא אמיד ל) כי הא דרבא אכפיה לרב נתן בר אמי ושקיל מיניה ארבע מאה זוזי לצדקה ו) והמשכילים יזהירו כזוהר הרקיע וגו' מ) (המשכילים יזהירו כזוהר הרקיע) זה דיין שדן דין אמת לאמתו ו) ומצדיקי הרבים ככוכבים לעולם ועד אלו גבאי צדקה במתניתא תנא והמשכילים יזהירו כזוהר הרקיע זה דיין שדן דין אמת לאמתו וגבאי צדקה ומצדיקי הרבים ככוכבים לעולם ועד אלו מלמדי תינוקות כגון מאן אמר רב כגון רב שמואל בר שילת דרב אשכחיה לרב שמואל בר שילת דהוה קאי בגינתא א"ל שבקתיה להימנותך א"ל (ג) הא תליסר שנין דלא חזיא לי והשתא נמי דעתאי עלויהו ורבנן מאי אמר רבינא ז) ואוהביו כצאת השמש בגבורתו ת"ר ס גבאי צדקה אינן רשאין לפרוש זה מזה אבל פורש זה לשער וזה לחנות ע מצא מעות בשוק לא יתנם בתוך כיסו אלא נותנן לתוך ארנקי של צדקה ולכשיבא לביתו יטלם כיוצא בו היה נושה בחבירו מנה ופרעו בשוק לא יתננו לתוך כיסו אלא נותנו לתוך ארנקי של צדקה ולכשיבא לביתו יטלם תנו רבנן פ גבאי צדקה שאין להם עניים לחלק פורטין לאחרים ואין פורטין לעצמן גבאי תמחוי שאין להם עניים לחלק מוכרין לאחרים ואין מוכרין לעצמן מעות של צדקה אין מונין אותן שתים (ג) אלא אחת אחת אמר אביי מריש לא הוה יתיב מר אציפי דבי כנישתא כיון דשמעה להא דתניא ולשנותה לכל מה שירצו הוה יתיב אמר אביי מריש הוה עביד מר תרי כיסי חד לעניי דעלמא וחד לעניי דמתא כיון דשמעה להא דאמר ליה שמואל לרב תחליפא בר אבדימי עביד חד כיסא

רש"י

שבי כולהו איתנהו ביה. שהוא ביד העכו"ם לעשות בו כל חפצו אם למות [אם לחרב] אם לרעב: מפני שהוא כדיני ממונות. לעיין ולתת לכל אחד כפי טפלים התלויין בו: שגבויה וחלוקה שוה. בכל יום מדי יום ביום כדקתני לקמיה לפיכך אין גבויו בשנים שלא יטרטרו לטרוח ולבקש את השלישי לחלק: לעשות קופה תמחוי. לחלק לעניי עולם אם ירבו עליהן: להתנות על המדות. להגדיל סאת העיר או להקטין: ועל השערים. שער חטין והיין שלא ימכרנה סאה זו יותר מכך וכך דמים: להסיע על קיצתם. לקנוס את העובר על קיצת דבריהם להסיעם מדת דין תורה: הא הימוני מהימן. יחיד להיות גזבר: שני אחים. לגבי המנותא כחד דמו: מאי שררותיה. דקופה דקאמרת עלה לפי שאין עושין שררה על הצבור כו': אפילו בע"ש. שיש פתחון פה לבעה"ב לומר טרוד אני: ופקדתי וגו'. אלמא אסור למשכן: אמיד. עשיר ה): גבאי צדקה. המשכילים אל דל מהו צריך: מלמדי תינוקות. מצדיקי רבים הן שמלמדין ומחנכין אותן בדרך טובה: שבקתיה להמנותיך. שהיית רגיל ללמדם באמונה וללמד ולישב על גבם תמיד: דעתאי להתם. לתינוקות: ורבנן מאי. תלמידי חכמים העוסקים בתורה תמיד מאי כתיב בהו: לפרוש זה מזה. מפני החשד שלא יאמרו זה הגובה יחידי דעתו לגנוב: אבל זה פורש לחנות וזה לשער. זה לגבות מיושבי השער וזה לגבות מיושבי החנות ובלבד שיראו שניהן כאחד: לא יתנם לתוך כיסו. שלא יאמרו מעות של צדקה הוא גונב: פורטין. פרוטות שגבו לוקחין דינרי כסף לפי שהפרוטות של נחושת מחלידות: ואין פורטין לעצמם. פן יחשדום שפורטין בזול: אין מונין אותם שנים שנים. פן יאמרו שנים הוא נוטל ואינו מונה אלא אחד: אציפי דבי כנישתא. מחצלות של בית הכנסת משום דמזבני להו ממעות הקופה: ואתני

תוספות

פדיון שבוים מצוה רבה. והא דאמר בפרק בני העיר (מגילה דף כז.) אין מוכרין ס"ת אלא ללמוד תורה ולישא אשה ולא קתני פדיון שבוים שמא מילתא דפשיטא היא ולא איצטריך למיתני: ומתחלקת בג' מפני שהיא כדיני ממונות. וא"ת מהאי טעמא נמי תהא נגבית בג' ופר"ת לפי שהיה ידוע סכום של כל אחד ואחד כמה יתן: ולשנות' לכל מה שירצו. נראה לר"ת דיכולים לשנותו אף לדבר הרשות אע"ג דאמרינן בערכין בפ"ק (דף ו: ושם) האי מאן דנדב שרגא לבי כנשתא אסור לשנותה לדבר הרשות ואמר נמי התם האומר פרוטה זו לצדקה עד שלא באה ליד הגבאי מותר לשנותה משבאה ליד הגבאי אסור לשנותה (ד) לדבר הרשות הכא שבני העיר משנים אותה שאני לפיכך מותר לשנותה אפילו לדבר הרשות ואפילו באה ליד הגבאי וכן היה ר"ת נוהג לתת מעות הקופה לשומרי העיר לפי שעל דעת בני העיר נותנים אותם: כי הא דרבא אכפיה. אחר היה עמו דאין עושין שררה על הצבור פחות מב' ולא חשיב ליה ° מפני כבודו של רבא: אכפיה לרב נתן. וא"ת והא בפרק כל הבשר (חולין דף קי: ושם ד"ה כל) אמר כל מ"ע שמתן שכרה ל) [כתובה] בצדה אין ב"ד של מטה מוזהרים עליה וגבי צדקה כתיב כי פתוח תפתח את ידך לו וכתיב כי בגלל הדבר הזה יברכך (דברים טו) ואר"ת דהאי כפיה בדברים כמו כפייה (ה) ועל בפרק נערה שנתפתתה (כתובות דף נג.) ועוד תירץ דהכא קבלו עליהם שיכופו אותן הגבאי ולר"י נראה דבצדקה כופין משום דאית בה לאו דכתיב בה לא תאמץ את לבבך ולא תקפוץ וגו' ולריב"א נראה דהא דאין ב"ד מוזהרין על מצות עשה שמתן (ו) שכרן בצדה היינו דאין נענשין וכן משמע בירושלמי דהמוכר את הספינה והיא דכל הבשר (שם) דלא הוה מוקיר אבוה וכפתוהו ואמר להו שבקוהו ה"פ אינכס מוזהרין להכריחו עד שיעשה כשאר מצות עשה דאם א"ל עשה סוכה ולולב ואינו עושה מכין אותו עד שתצא נפשו כדאמר בהכותב (כתובות דף פו. ושם) [וע"ע תוס' כתובות מט: ד"ה אכפייה ותוס' חולין קי: ד"ה כל]: דין אמת לאמתו. אמת לאפוקי דין מרומה אע"ג שהעדים מעידין אותו מ) [אין מחתכים אותו] כיון שיודעים שמשקרים כדדרשינן (בסנהדרין דף ז.) [נ"ל בשבועות ל:] לאמתו שלא יטו את הדין [וע"ע תוס' מגילה טו: ד"ה זה]: ומצדיקי הרבים וגו' אלו מלמדי תינוקות. אומר ר"י דצריך לומר דרקיע מזהיר טפי מכוכבים דהא בס"פ אלו עוברין (פסחים מט: ושם ד"ה לא) משמע דגבאי צדקה עדיפי ממלמדי תינוקות דאמר לא מצא בת תלמיד חכם ישא בת גבאי צדקה לא מצא בת גבאי צדקה ישא בת מלמדי תינוקות ואריב"א כי מצא בפרקי דרבי אליעזר דרקיע דהאי קרא דהמשכילים יזהירו כזוהר הרקיע היינו רקיע שעל ראשי החיות שמזהירין מכוכבים שאורו כאור החמה והאי דקאמר ורבנן מאי אמר רבינא ואוהביו כצאת השמש היינו שמש של עתיד לבא דהוא שבעתים כאור שבעת הימים ואור שבעת ימי בראשית היה שבעתים מאור חמה של עכשיו כדמפרש תרגום של רני ושמחי (זכריה ב):

ואע"פ

רבינו גרשום

נהרג בחרב מינויל. דמתלכלך בדמו: נגבית בשנים. משום דמתחלקת לעניי העיר ודבר קצוב הוא שיודעין כמה כל אחד ואחד צריך ליתן בקצוב ונותנין בשוה וליכא א) אלא סידורי בעלמא דגובין אותו גבאי צדקה מהם: ומתחלקת בג'. מפני שהיא כדיני ממונות מה דיני ממונות נוטלין מזה ונותנין לזה אף מחלקי צדקה מרבין לא' וממעטין לא' לפי שיראו צרכי עניים: גיבויו וחילוקיו שוה. שגובין מכל א' לפי מה שידו משגת וכעין דין שמעיינין בדין על מי להרבות ועל מי למעט משא"כ בקופה שאין גובין מכל אחד אלא לפי מה שרוצה ליתן ב) וקרוב נותנין כולן בשוה: לעשות קופה תמחוי. שאם ניתותר בקופה יותר על צורך עניי העיר ונתמעט בתמחוי לעניי כל אדם שבאו עניים הרבה וכן תמחוי לקופה כמו כן: להתנות על המדות. להגדילן או למעטן מכמות שהיו: ועל השער. שאם היה השער ביוקר רשאין להתנות שילך בזול: ועל שכר הפועלין. שאם נשכרין פועלים בג' פשי' ביום רשאין להתנות שלא ישכרום אלא בב': ולהסיע על קיצתן. לקנוס על מי שעובר על תנאי שקצבו אנשי העיר: והם יקחו. ואין הם פחות משנים: שררות הוא דלא עבדי פחות משנים. כלומר דמשמע טעמו דשררות הוא דבעינן ב' ולא לשום דין ולא לשום עדות הלכך (הא המוני מהמני) אפי' ב' קרובים למנות על הקופה והיינו ג) מאי שררות איכא בגבאי צדקה הואיל דדבר קצוב הוא ונותנין ברצון: ממשכנין. אם מעכב ליתן צדקה בקופה. ואפי' בע"ש דטרידי אינשי בתיקון מאכלם: הא דאמיד. אם אומדין אותו שהוא עשיר וממאן ליתן ממשכנין אותו בעל כרחו: והא דלא אמיד שאין לו מה ליתן אם (לוה) [ליה] ממשכנין עליו נאמר ופקדתי על כל לוחציו: שקל מיניה [ד' מאה] זוזי לצדקה. דההוא אמיד שהיה עשיר גדול: זה דיין. שמשכיל לדין הדין לאמתו. ומצדיקי הרבים אלו גבאי צדקה שממשכנין בני אדם ליתן צדקה ומצדיקין אותן: שבקת להימנותך. שהיה מלמד תינוקות והיה עומד בגינה: דעתי עלייהו. על התינוקות שלא הסחתי דעתי מהם: ורבנן מאי. כלומר כיון דדיינין נתת זוהר הרקיע ולגבאי צדקה נתת אור הכוכבים רבנן עצמן מאי: כצאת השמש בגבורתו: לפרוש זה מזה. בשוק משום חשדא: אבל פורש זה לשער וזה לחנות: פורטין לאחרים. אין מונין אותן שתים שתים: לא יתיב מר. רבה: אציפי. אמחצלאות שפורשין על כותלי בית הכנסת שקנויות מצדקה: עביד חד

מסורת הש"ס

א) [ברכות ד: וש"נ], ב) [פאה פ"ח מ"ז סנהדרין יז:], ג) שקלים פ"ה מ"ב, ד) [קדושין עו:], ה) כתובות מט., ו) [ילקוט ליתא וכן בע"י ליתא], ז) כ"א להתם, ח) [בשאלתות פרשת תשא איתא ורבנן אמרו מאי דכתיב ואוהביו כצאת השמש בגבורתו אלו גבאי צדקה ופרנסי העיר], ט) [תוספתא פאה פ"ד], י) פסחים יג. ב"מ לח., כ) [מבואר היטב בפירש"י גיטין נג: ד"ה ולא אמיד], ל) יעב"ץ, מ) [כ"ה בדפו"י]:

הגהות הב"ח

(א) גמ' רעב קשה מחרב איבעית אימא קרא ואיבעית אימא סברא אב"א סברא האי קא מצטער: (ב) שם א"ל לאו הא אידנא תליסר שנין דלא חזיא לי: (ג) שם אין מונין אותן שתים שתים אלא: (ד) תוס' ד"ה ולשנות' וכו' משבא' ליד הגבאי אסור לשנות' הכא כצ"ל ותיבות לדבר הרשות נמחק: (ה) ד"ה אכפיה וכו' כמו כפייה רב פפא לרב יהודה בפ' נערה: (ו) בא"ד שמתן שכרה כתובה בצדה:

גליון הש"ס

תוס' ד"ה כי כו' מפני כבודו של רבא. ועיין דאיתא בר"ה דף כב ע"ב גיטין דף ג ע"ב סנהדרין דף יא ע"ב:

תורה אור השלם

א) וְהָיָה כִּי יֹאמְרוּ אֵלֶיךָ אָנָה נֵצֵא וְאָמַרְתָּ אֲלֵיהֶם כֹּה אָמַר יְיָ אֲשֶׁר לַמָּוֶת לַמָּוֶת וַאֲשֶׁר לַחֶרֶב לַחֶרֶב וַאֲשֶׁר לָרָעָב לָרָעָב וַאֲשֶׁר לַשְּׁבִי לַשֶּׁבִי: [ירמיה טו, ב]

ב) יָקָר בְּעֵינֵי יְיָ הַמָּוְתָה לַחֲסִידָיו: [תהלים קטז, טו]

ג) טוֹבִים הָיוּ חַלְלֵי חֶרֶב מֵחַלְלֵי רָעָב שֶׁהֵם יָזוּבוּ מְדֻקָּרִים מִתְּנוּבֹת שָׂדָי: [איכה ד, ט]

ד) וְהֵם יִקְחוּ אֶת הַזָּהָב וְאֶת הַתְּכֵלֶת וְאֶת הָאַרְגָּמָן וְאֶת תּוֹלַעַת הַשָּׁנִי וְאֶת הַשֵּׁשׁ: [שמות כח, ה]

ה) וְהָיוּ בָנָיו כְּקֶדֶם וַעֲדָתוֹ לְפָנַי תִּכּוֹן וּפָקַדְתִּי עַל כָּל לֹחֲצָיו: [ירמיה ל, כ]

ו) וְהַמַּשְׂכִּלִים יַזְהִרוּ כְּזֹהַר הָרָקִיעַ וּמַצְדִּיקֵי הָרַבִּים כַּכּוֹכָבִים לְעוֹלָם וָעֶד: [דניאל יב, ג]

ז) כֵּן יֹאבְדוּ כָל אוֹיְבֶיךָ יְיָ וְאֹהֲבָיו כְּצֵאת הַשֶּׁמֶשׁ בִּגְבֻרָתוֹ וַתִּשְׁקֹט הָאָרֶץ אַרְבָּעִים שָׁנָה: [שופטים ה, לא]

ליקוטי רש"י

אשר למות וגו'. כל המאוחר בפ' קשה מחבירו חרב קשה ממות מיתת חרב מנוולת ומיתה על מטתו אינה מנוולת וכן הוא אומר (תהלים קטז) יקר בעיני ה' המותה לחסידיו רעב קשה מחרב שזה מצטער וזה אינו מצטער וכן הוא אומר טובים היו חללי חרב מחללי רעב שבי קשה מכולם שכולהו איתנהו ביה [ירמיה טו, ב]. יקר בעיני ה'. המותה. טובים היו חללי חרב. נגבית בשנים ומתחלקת בשלשה. ואפילו בערב שבת. גבאי. גובה [סנהדרין כו:]. ממונה [כתובות לא.]. דרבא אכפיה. על הצדקה [כתובות מט:]. והמשכילים. ומצדיקי הרבים. [דניאל יב, ג]. ואוהביו כצאת השמש בגבורתו. [שופטים ה, לא]. פורטין. תמחוי. ואין מוכרין לעצמן.

חשק שלמה על רבינו גרשום א) נראה דצ"ל וליכא אלא וכו'. ב) נראה דצ"ל וקרוב. ג) נראה דצ"ל והיינו מאי וכו'.

After revealing the tremendous honors these worthy people will receive, the Gemara asks:

וְרַבָּנָן מַאי – **And what** is written about **the Rabbis,** who study Torah constantly?[44]

The Gemara answers:

אָמַר רָבִינָא – **Ravina said** that the honor to be accorded the Rabbis is described in the following verse:[45] ,,וְאֹהֲבָיו כְּצֵאת הַשֶּׁמֶשׁ בִּגְבֻרָתוֹ" – ***But they who love Him shall be as the sun going forth in its might.***[46] The light that Torah scholars merit is the most brilliant light by far.

The Gemara discusses various laws designed to protect the reputations of charity collectors:

תָּנוּ רַבָּנָן – **The Rabbis taught in a Baraisa:** גַּבָּאֵי צְדָקָה אֵינָן רַשָּׁאִין לִפְרוֹשׁ זֶה מִזֶּה – CHARITY COLLECTORS ARE NOT PERMITTED TO SEPARATE FROM ONE ANOTHER while collecting, for one person collecting alone might be suspected of stealing. אֲבָל פּוֹרֵשׁ זֶה לַשַּׁעַר וְזֶה לֶחָנוּת – HOWEVER, THIS one MAY SPLIT OFF TO THE GATE AND THIS other one may split off TO THE STORE.[47] So long as both are seen together, they will arouse no suspicions.[48]

A second ruling:

מָצָא מָעוֹת בַּשּׁוּק – IF [A CHARITY COLLECTOR] FOUND COINS IN THE MARKETPLACE while collecting, לֹא יִתְּנֵם בְּתוֹךְ כִּיסוֹ – HE MUST NOT PUT THEM INTO HIS POCKET, lest observers suspect that he is stealing money that belongs to charity. אֶלָּא נוֹתְנָן לְתוֹךְ אַרְנְקֵי שֶׁל צְדָקָה – RATHER, HE SHOULD PUT [THE COINS] INTO THE CHARITY [FUND'S] PURSE, וְלִכְשֶׁיָּבֹא לְבֵיתוֹ יִטְּלֵם – AND WHEN HE REACHES HIS HOUSE HE MAY TAKE THEM. כַּיּוֹצֵא בּוֹ – SIMILARLY, הָיָה נוֹשֶׁה בַּחֲבֵירוֹ מָנֶה וּפְרָעוֹ בַּשּׁוּק – IF [A CHARITY COLLECTOR] WAS OWED A *MANEH*[49] BY HIS FELLOW AND [THE DEBTOR] REPAID HIM IN THE MARKETPLACE, לֹא יִתְּנֶנּוּ לְתוֹךְ כִּיסוֹ – HE MUST NOT PUT [THE MONEY] INTO HIS OWN POCKET. אֶלָּא נוֹתְנָן לְתוֹךְ אַרְנְקֵי שֶׁל צְדָקָה – RATHER, HE SHOULD PUT [THE MONEY] INTO THE CHARITY [FUND'S] PURSE, וְלִכְשֶׁיָּבֹא לְבֵיתוֹ יִטְּלֵם – AND WHEN HE REACHES HIS HOUSE HE MAY TAKE [THE PAYMENT].

The Gemara quotes another Baraisa that further instructs how to protect the reputation of charity collectors:

תָּנוּ רַבָּנָן – **The Rabbis taught in a Baraisa:** גַּבָּאֵי צְדָקָה שֶׁאֵין לָהֶם עֲנִיִּים לְחַלֵּק – ADMINISTRATORS OF A CHARITY [FUND] THAT HAVE NO POOR PEOPLE to whom TO DISTRIBUTE money, and thus are left holding a surplus of coins in the fund, פּוֹרְטִין לַאֲחֵרִים – SHOULD EXCHANGE the copper coins FOR OTHER PEOPLE,[50] וְאֵין פּוֹרְטִין לְעַצְמָן – BUT MAY NOT EXCHANGE them FOR THEMSELVES, lest people suspect that the collectors are allowing themselves a favorable exchange rate and are thereby stealing from the charity fund. גַּבָּאֵי תַמְחוּי שֶׁאֵין לָהֶם עֲנִיִּים לְחַלֵּק – Similarly, ADMINISTRATORS OF A communal "PLATTER" THAT HAVE NO POOR PEOPLE to whom TO DISTRIBUTE the food that was collected[51] מוֹכְרִין לַאֲחֵרִים – SHOULD SELL the surplus food TO OTHERS, and hold the proceeds for purchasing other food as needed, וְאֵין מוֹכְרִין לְעַצְמָן – BUT MAY NOT SELL it TO THEMSELVES, for they may be suspected of paying a deflated price.

The Baraisa teaches a third law:

מָעוֹת שֶׁל צְדָקָה אֵין מוֹנִין אוֹתָן שְׁתַּיִם [שְׁתַּיִם][52] – CHARITY FUNDS SHOULD NOT BE COUNTED TWO coins AT A TIME;[53] אֶלָּא אַחַת אַחַת – RATHER, they should be counted ONE BY ONE to avoid giving the appearance of a dishonest accounting.

Abaye relates certain practices of his teacher, Rabbah, that concerned communal charity matters:

אָמַר אַבַּיֵי מֵרֵישׁ לֹא הֲוָה יָתִיב מָר אַצִּיפֵּי דְּבֵי כְּנִישְׁתָּא – **Abaye said: Originally, the master** (Rabbah) **would not sit upon the mats belonging to the** city's **synagogue.** The mats had been purchased with money from the charity fund, and Rabbah did not wish to benefit from what he felt was a misuse of public monies. כֵּיוָן דִּשְׁמָעָהּ לְהָא דְּתַנְיָא – However, **once [Rabbah] heard that which was taught in the Baraisa** mentioned above, וּלְשַׁנּוֹתָהּ לְכָל מַה שֶּׁיִּרְצוּ – AND the city officials are authorized TO DIVERT [EXCESS CHARITY FUNDS] TO ANY [COMMUNAL PURPOSE] THAT THEY DESIRE,[54] הֲוָה יָתִיב – **he would sit** upon the mats, for he realized that the allocation was valid.

Abaye relates a second practice of Rabbah's:

אָמַר אַבַּיֵי מֵרֵישׁ הֲוָה עָבֵיד מָר תְּרֵי כִּיסֵי – **Abaye said: Originally, the master** (Rabbah) **would make two purses** for donations he collected – חַד לַעֲנִיֵּי דְעָלְמָא – one purse to hold money to be distributed **to all paupers,** וְחַד לַעֲנִיֵּי דְמָתָא – **and one** purse to hold money to be distributed **to the poor of the city.** Rabbah originally kept separate accounts, since some contributions were designated specifically for the local poor. כֵּיוָן דִּשְׁמָעָהּ לְהָא דְּאָמַר לֵיהּ שְׁמוּאֵל לְרַב תַּחֲלִיפָא בַּר אַבְדִּימִי – However, **once he heard that which Shmuel said to Rav Tachalifa bar Avdimi**[55] – עָבֵיד חַד כִּיסָא – **"Make one purse,**

NOTES

supervision of his students even when he is not with them (*Maharsha*).

44. Inasmuch as the truthful judges will receive the radiance of the firmament and the charity collectors will be rewarded with the light of the stars, what light remains for the Rabbis themselves to merit? (*Rabbeinu Gershom*).

45. *Judges* 5:31.

46. This is the sunlight that will be unsheathed in the messianic future. It will be seven times more brilliant than the light of the seven days of creation, which itself was 49 times brighter than today's sun (*Tosafos* ד״ה מצדיקי and *Rashi* to *Judges* [ibid.]).

47. One to collect from the residents who live near the gate, and the other to collect from those living near the store (*Rashi*).

48. *Rabbeinu Gershom* interprets the Gemara differently. He writes that two charity collectors are forbidden to separate lest one suspect the other of stealing the donations.

49. A *maneh* equals one hundred *zuzim*.

50. Small copper coins (*perutos*) cannot be held for any great length of time, for they tend to become moldy. Hence, the administrators are authorized to exchange them for silver *dinar* coins belonging to others (*Rashi*).

51. I.e. there was not a demand for all the food in the "platter," and what remains will eventually spoil.

52. Emendation follows Bach.

53. Lest observers suspect the collector of taking a donation of two coins but recording only one [and pocketing the other for himself] (*Rashi*). *Rabbeinu Gershom*, however, understands this ruling as a corollary of a previous one: When exchanging copper coins for silver *dinars*, the administrator must count the coins individually, so as to avoid mistakes.

54. [This Gemara would seem to support the view of the Rishonim that charity funds may be diverted to other communal needs (see above, note 21). However, see *Rif* communal needs (see above, note 21). However, see *Rif* for a different version of the *Gemara* (see also *Ramban*, *Rashba*, *Ritva*).]

55. Like Rabbah, Rav Tachalifa kept two purses – one for donations to the local poor and the other for the benefit of any pauper. Shmuel advised him that such duplication was unnecessary.

וְאַתְנֵי עֲלָהּ — **and stipulate** with the community **regarding it"**[1] — אִיהוּ נַמִּי עֲבַד חַד כִּיסָא וְאַתְנֵי עֲלָהּ — **[Rabbah] also made one purse and stipulated regarding it.**

Rav Ashi was able to simplify the procedure:

רַב אַשִׁי אָמַר אֲנָא אַתְנוּיֵי נַמִּי לָא צְרִיכְנָא — **Rav Ashi said: I need not even stipulate,** דְּכָל דְּקָא אָתֵי — **for anyone that comes** to donate money to the city's charity fund (which Rav Ashi administered) אַדַּעְתָּא דִּידִי אָתֵי — **comes** to donate with the understanding that I shall distribute the funds **at my discretion;**[2] וּלְמָאן דְּבָעֵינָא יָהֵיבְנָא לֵיהּ — **and** so **I may give to whomever I wish** without stipulating beforehand.

The Gemara relates an incident involving the law, quoted previously (8b), that authorizes penalizing those who violate communal edicts.

הָנְהוּ בֵּי תְּרֵי טַבָּחֵי — There were **those two butchers** דְּעָבְדֵי עֲנְיָינָא בַּהֲדֵי הֲדָדֵי — **who stipulated between themselves:**[3] דְּכָל מַאן דְּעָבִיד בְּיוֹמָא דְּחַבְרֵיהּ — **If anyone slaughters** an animal[4] **on a day reserved for his colleague,**[5] נִקְרְעוּהּ לְמַשְׁכֵיהּ — **we** [the other butchers] **will** penalize him and **rend [the animal's] hide** to prevent him from profiting from his wrongdoing.

One of the butchers acted wrongfully:

אֲזַל חַד מִינַּיְיהוּ עֲבַד בְּיוֹמָא דְּחַבְרֵיהּ — **One of [the butchers] went** and **slaughtered** an animal **on a day reserved for his colleague.** קָרְעוּ לְמַשְׁכֵיהּ — **[The other butchers,]** as per the stipulation, **rent [the animal's] hide.**

The offending butcher sought damages for the ruined hide, maintaining that the agreement was not binding.

אָתוּ לְקַמֵּיהּ דְּרָבָא — **[The litigants] came before Rava** for a judgment. חַיְּיבִינְהוּ רָבָא לְשַׁלּוּמֵי — **Rava obligated [the other butchers] to pay** for the hide, for he concurred that the butchers had no authority to make such an agreement.

Rav Yeimar challenged Rava's ruling from the Baraisa quoted above (8b):

אֵיתִיבֵיהּ רַב יֵימַר בַּר שֶׁלֶמְיָא לְרָבָא — **Rav Yeimar bar Shlamya retorted to Rava:** וּלְהַסִּיעַ עַל קִיצָתָם — But the Baraisa stated: AND the officials are further authorized TO FINE THOSE WHO TRANSGRESS THEIR STIPULATIONS! We see that the community is empowered to enforce its edicts. Why, then, were the city's butchers not entitled to damage the offending butcher's hides, as per their stipulation?[6]

לָא אַהְדַּר לֵיהּ רָבָא — **Rava did not reply to [Rav Yeimar],** but let his own ruling stand.

The Gemara explains the reason for Rava's silence:

אָמַר רַב פָּפָּא שַׁפִּיר עֲבַד דְּלָא אַהְדַּר לֵיהּ מִידֵּי — **Rav Pappa said: [Rava] did well not to offer [Rav Yeimar] any reply,** הָנֵי מִילֵּי הֵיכָא דְּלֵיכָּא אָדָם חָשׁוּב — **for these words** of the Baraisa apply **where there is no distinguished person**[7] in the city. אֲבָל הֵיכָא דְּאִיכָּא אָדָם חָשׁוּב — **However, where there is a distinguished person** in the city, לָאו כָּל כְּמִינַּיְיהוּ דְּמַתְנוּ — **[the community officials] are not empowered to stipulate** without his participation.[8] Certainly, Rava qualified as a "distinguished person." Thus, since the butchers of his city acted without consulting him, their stipulation was invalid, and for that reason Rava declared them liable for the damaged hides. It was due to his humility that Rava withheld this reasoning from Rav Yeimar.

The Gemara discusses another law pertaining to charity collectors:

תָּנוּ רַבָּנַן — **The Rabbis taught in a Baraisa:** אֵין מְחַשְּׁבִין בִּצְדָקָה עִם גַּבָּאֵי צְדָקָה — WE DO NOT RECKON the disbursements OF CHARITY FUNDS WITH THE CHARITY COLLECTORS, וְלֹא בְּהֶקְדֵּשׁ עִם הַגִּזְבָּרִין — AND, similarly, we do NOT reckon the expenditures OF TEMPLE FUNDS WITH THE Temple TREASURERS. וְאַף עַל פִּי שֶׁאֵין רְאָיָה לַדָּבָר — AND EVEN THOUGH THERE IS NO PROOF FOR THE PRACTICE,[9] זֵכֶר לַדָּבָר שֶׁנֶּאֱמַר — there is AN ALLUSION TO THE PRACTICE in the verse that exempts Temple treasurers from giving an accounting of their expenditures, FOR IT IS STATED:[10] "וְלֹא יְחַשְּׁבוּ אֶת־הָאֲנָשִׁים — *AND THEY WOULD NOT RECKON WITH THE MEN* (the treasurers) אֲשֶׁר יִתְּנוּ אֶת־הַכֶּסֶף עַל־יָדָם לָתֵת לְעֹשֵׂי הַמְּלָאכָה — *INTO WHOSE HAND THEY DELIVERED THE MONEY TO GIVE TO THOSE WHO PERFORMED THE WORK* (of repairing the Temple)," כִּי בֶאֱמֻנָה הֵם עֹשִׂים — *FOR THEY* (the treasurers) *DEALT FAITHFULLY.*[11]

NOTES

1. I.e. have them approve beforehand of your distributing money from the unified charity fund to any needy applicant (*Rashi*).

2. Since Rav Ashi was a great man and knew what he was doing, the people contributed with the understanding that Rav Ashi would disburse the funds to whomever he wished. Hence, Rav Ashi did not need to stipulate with the community beforehand (*Rabbeinu Gershom*).

[See *Yad Ramah*, *Ritva*, who explain why *Rabbah* was unable to use this procedure.]

3. Whether individual members of a profession or guild may stipulate amongst themselves, or whether these business agreements are not binding unless all the members make themselves parties thereto, is an issue debated by *Rishonim* (see *Ramban* and *Rashba*). The text of our Gemara implies that two individual artisans may enter into a binding agreement. *Bach*, however, deletes בֵּי תְּרֵי, *two*, either because the narrative below clearly indicates that at least three butchers were involved in the incident, or because he holds that all members of the guild must ratify any such agreement. [*Rif* and other *Rishonim*, also delete these words]

4. Literally: performed.

5. In Amoraic times it was unprofitable for butchers to operate competing businesses, since meat unsold by day's end would quickly spoil. To alleviate this problem, each butcher was assigned his own day to slaughter animals and sell all the meat. The agreement mentioned in the Gemara was designed to strengthen compliance with this practice by penalizing violations.

6. Although the Baraisa grants the power of enforcement only to בְּנֵי הָעִיר, *the city officials*, Rav Yeimar regarded each guild as an independent community, which would thus be empowered to regulate and punish its own members (*Ramban* and *Ritva*).

[We may infer from this that the stipulation would only be valid if agreed upon all members of that group (see above, note 3), for only then would it have the status of בְּנֵי הָעִיר (*Rambam, Ran, Nimukei Yosef*).]

7. I.e. a Torah scholar who is also a community leader (*Ri Migash*, cited by *Ritva, Ran* and *Meiri*; see also *Rashba* and *Tur Choshen Mishpat* 231:30).

8. For two reasons: (a) It would be disrespectful to exclude him; and (b) he would protect city residents from injudicious expenditures of public funds and (in the case of the guilds) consumers from "price-fixing" and other unfair business practices (*Ramban, Ritva* and *Ran*). [According to the second reason, if the stipulation could not possibly result in any loss to the public, there would be no need to consult him (*Ramban, Ran*).]

9. I.e. of exempting charity collectors from giving an accounting of their disbursements, for the verse soon to be quoted concerns only the Temple treasurers (*Rashi*; cf. *Tosafos* with *Maharsha* and *Maharam*).

10. *II Kings* 12:16.

11. A great many artisans and laborers were employed to perform a multitude of tasks necessary to repair the Holy Temple. Hence, it was impossible to keep an accurate accounting of monies expended for payroll and supplies, for the treasurers were kept continually busy and could not remember every expenditure (*Rashi* and *Nimukei Yosef*). [Thus, reliance was placed instead on the honesty and integrity of the treasurers.]

Although charity collectors are not distracted to the extent that the Temple treasurers were — and so proof of their exemption from giving an accounting cannot be drawn from this verse — still the Baraisa finds in the verse a slight intimation that they, too, should be exempted (*Nimukei Yosef*).

ואתני עלה איהו נמי עבד חד כיסא ואתני עלה רב אשי אמר אנא אתנויי נמי לא צריכנא דכל דקא אתי אדעתא דידי אתי ולמאן דבעינא יהיבנא ליה הנהו (א) בי תרי טבחי דעבדי עניינא בהדי הדדי דכל מאן דעביד ביומא דחבריה נקרעוה למשכיה אזל חד מנייהו עבד ביומא דחבריה קרעו למשכיה אתו לקמיה דרבא חייבינהו רבא לשלומי איתיביה רב יימר בר שלמיא לרבא ולהסיע על קיצתם לא אהדר ליה רבא אמר רב פפא שפיר עבד דלא אהדר ליה מידי [א] ה"מ היכא דליכא אדם חשוב אבל היכא דאיכא אדם חשוב לאו כל כמינייהו דמתנו ת"ר [ב] אין מחשבין בצדקה עם גבאי צדקה ולא בהקדש עם הגזברין ואע"פ שאין ראיה לדבר זכר לדבר שנאמר א) ולא יחשבו את האנשים אשר יתנו את הכסף על ידם לתת לעושי המלאכה כי באמונה הם עושים א"ר אלעזר אע"פ שיש לו לאדם גזבר נאמן בתוך ביתו יצור וימנה שנאמר ב) ויצורו וימנו אמר רב הונא בודקין למזונות ואין בודקין לכסות (א) אי בעית אימא קרא ואי בעית אימא סברא אב"א סברא האי קא מבזי והאי לא קא מבזי אי בעית אימא קרא [ג] הלא ג) פרוש לרעב לחמך בשי"ן כתיב פרוש והדר הב ליה והתם כתיב ג) כי תראה ערום וכסיתו כי תראה לאלתר ורב יהודה אמר [ג] בודקין לכסות ואין בודקין למזונות אי בעית אימא סברא ואי בעית אימא קרא אי בעית אימא סברא האי קמצערא ליה והאי לא קמצערא ליה אי בעית אימא קרא הכא כתיב הלא פרום לרעב לחמך פרום לאלתר וכדקרינן והתם כתיב כי תראה ערום וכסיתו כשיראה לך תניא כוותיה דרב יהודה אמר כסוני בודקין אחריו פרנסוני אין בודקין [ג] תנן התם [ד] אין פוחתין לעני העובר ממקום למקום מככר בפונדיון מארבע סאין בסלע לן נותנין לו פרנסת לינה מאי פרנסת לינה אמר רב פפא [ה] פוריא ובי סדיא שבת נותנין לו מזון שלש סעודות תנא [ו] אם היה מחזיר על הפתחים אין נזקקין לו ההוא עניא דהוה מחזיר על הפתחים דאתא לקמיה דרב פפא לא מזדקיק ליה א"ל רב סמא בריה דרב ייבא לרב פפא אי מר לא מזדקיק ליה אינש אחרינא לא מזדקיק ליה לימות (ב) ליה והא תניא אם היה עני המחזיר על הפתחים אין נזקקין לו א"ל [ז] אין נזקקין לו למתנה מרובה אבל נזקקין לו למתנה מועטת אמר רב אסי [ח] לעולם אל ימנע אדם עצמו [מלתת] שלישית השקל בשנה שנא' ד) והעמדנו עלינו מצות לתת עלינו שלישית השקל בשנה לעבודת בית אלהינו ואמר רב אסי שקולה צדקה כנגד כל המצות שנאמר והעמדנו עלינו מצות וגו' מצוה אין כתיב כאן אלא מצות (סימן גדול מקדש משה) א"ר אלעזר [ח] גדול המעשה יותר מן העושה שנאמר ה) והיה מעשה הצדקה שלום ועבודת הצדקה השקט ובטח עד עולם זכה הלא פרוש לרעב לחמך לא זכה ועניים מרודים תביא בית אמר להו רבא לבני מחוזא במטותא מנייכו עושו בהדי הדדי כי היכי דליהוי לכו שלמא במלכותא וא"ר אלעזר בזמן שבהמ"ק קיים אדם שוקל שקלו ומתכפר לו עכשיו שאין בהמ"ק קיים אם עושין צדקה מוטב ואם לאו באין עובדי כוכבים ונוטלין בזרוע [ט] ואעפ"כ נחשב להן לצדקה שנא' ו) ונוגשיך צדקה אמר רבא האי מילתא אישתעי לי עולא

רש"י

ואתני. מתנה עם הלבור לחלקס לכל הבא: דכל דאתי. לתת מעות לקופה: עניינא. תנאי: למשכיה. עור הבהמה: לאו כל כמינייהו דמתנו. אלא בפניו: אין מחשבין. לומר היכן נתתם מעות שגביתם: שאין ראיה לדבר. דלא בגבאי לדקה כתיב אלא בגיזברי הקדש הנותנים (ג) לבס לעושי המלאכה שהפועלים מרוצין למלאכות הרבה לגודרין ולחוצבי האבן לכתפים ולחמרים ולקנות עלים ואבני מחלב וא"א לעמוד על החשבון כדאמרינן בעלמא (שבועות דף מה.) בעל הבית טרוד בפועליו הוא ואינשי: יצור וימנה. הכסף שהוא מוסר בידו ואע"פ שאינו בא עמו לחשבון לאחר מכאן יצור וימנה שנאמר ויצורו וימנו וגו' והדר ונתנו את הכסף המתוכן המנוי על ידי עושי המלאכה וגו': בודקין למזונות. אם בא עני ואמר פרנסוני בודקין שלא יהיה רמאי: ואין בודקין לכסות. בא ערום ואמר כסוני לוקחין כסות מיד: פרוש. דרוש וחקור תחלה: לכשיראה לך. שאינו רמאי: מככר בפונדיון. ככר הלקוח בפונדיון כשלוקחין ארבע סאין חטין בסלע ומגיע לפונדיון חצי קב שהסלע מ"ח פונדיונין וארבע סאין מ"ח חצאי קבין והחנוני שהוא טוחן ואופה ומוכר בשוק משתכר מחצה הרי שנותן ככר של רובע הקב בפונדיון: לן. בלילה: פרנסת לינה. צרכי לינה: בי סדיא. כר לתת מראשותיו: אין נזקקין לו. לתת מעות מן הקופה אחרי שלמד לחזר על הפתחים דיו בכך: ולא אזדקיק ליה. אפי' (י) לפרנסה: מעשה הצדקה. טורח המעשים את חבריהם מדלא כתיב והיתה הצדקה שלום: זכה. למזל טוב: עניים מרודים. זו ממשלת רומי שצועקת תמיד הבו הבו שאנו צריכין: מרודים. קונפליינ"ט בלע"ז כמו אריד בשיחי (תהלים נה): עולא משגש ארחתיה דאימיה. לרב ששת קרו ליה הכי עולל המשגש דרכי אמו שגרס (ד) להטותה מדרך אחר שאר נשים כדלקמן:

תוספות

ואע"פ שאין ראיה לדבר זכר לדבר. ראיה גמורה אינה דשאני התם שהיו צדיקים גמורים: אין פוחתין לעני העובר ממקום למקום מככר בפונדיון כו'. הככר עולה ששה ביצים דלא מהן מחצה לחנווני והוא מזון שתי סעודות כדתניא בפרק כילד משתתפין (עירובין דף פב:) וקשה לר"י דבפרק כל כתבי (שבת דף קיח. ושם) משמע שהוא רגילות דאיכא סעודה בהדיה דקאמר התם דכי אזיל מלווינא ליה סעודה בהדיה דכי אזיל לאו בריקן אזיל וא"כ למה נותנין לו שתי סעודות די לו בסעודה אחת ההיא סעודה דאיכא בהדיה יאכל מיד וסעודה שנותנין לו עכשיו יוליכנו עמו ונראה לר"י דאין מחלקין תמחוי בלילה לפי שאין יכולין להבחין למי נתנו ולמי לא נתנו וכן משמע מדקאמר לן נותנים לו פרנסת לינה ומפרש דהיינו פוריא ובי סדיא אבל ככר אין נותנין לו ולכך נותנין לו ב' סעודות שיאכל אחת בלילה ואחת למחר (ה) דכי אזיל לאו בריקן אזיל וטעמא דבעינן שלא ילך ריקם דאינו דומה מי שיש לו פת בסלו למי שאין לו ולא יהא רעב כל כך אבל אין לפרש דהטעם שמא לא יגיע בין היהודים ויהא לו מה לאכול דאי חיישינן להכי היה ליתן לו שלש סעודות כי גם בלילה לא יתנו אף כשיגיע בין היהודים שאין מחלקין תמחוי בלילה ואין לומר דלעולם מחלקין ולכך נותנין שתים דחיישינן שמא לא יגיע בין היהודים שתי פעמים אי נמי לא חיישינן אלא לפעם אחת והשניה נותנין לו כדי שיהא לו פת בסלו דאם כן היכי קאמר התם דמלווין ליה סעודה אחת בהדיה ואם יש לחוש שמא לא יגיע בין היהודים היה לו ליתן שתים לכך נראה כדפרישית: שבת נותנין לו מזון שלש סעודות. פירוש בשבת בצהרים (ו) אותן שתי סעודות שנתן לו אתמול בערב שבת אכל ליל שבת ושבת שחרית ושלש סעודות שנותנים לו בשבת יאכל אחת בשבת בסעודה שלישית ואחת למוצאי שבת ושלישית ישאר לו למחר בדרך שלא ילך ריקם ואין להאריך וקשה לרשב"א הא דתנן במסכת פאה (פ"ח מ"ז) ומייתי לה בפרק כל כתבי (שבת דף קיח. ושם) מי שיש לו מזון שתי סעודות בביתו לא יטול מן התמחוי ואמאי הא אחד יאכל מיד ואחד בלילה וא"כ כי אזיל ריקם אזיל וצריך לפרש דמזון שתי סעודות דקאמר היינו בלא אותה שיש לו לאכול מיד וא"ת שבת אמאי נותנין לו שלש סעודות והא הך מתני' ר"ע היא דקתני רישא כל מי שיש לו מזון י"ד סעודות לא יטול מן הקופה ופריך בפרק כל כתבי הקדש (שם) מני אי רבנן תמיסר הויין אי רבי חדקא שיתסר הויין ומשני הא מני ר"ע היא דאמר עשה שבתך חול ונראה לרשב"א דבשביל סעודת שבת אין לו להתחיל וליטול אבל בשכבר צריך ליטול נוטל גם כדי לסעודת שבת: לא אזדקיק ליה. רב פפא גבאי היה ולא נתן לו מן הקופה כדתניא אין נותנין לו מן הקופה כיון שמחזר על הפתחים וא"ל רב סמא אי מר לא אזדקיק ליה לתת לו מן הקופה (ז) היינו כדי סעודה כ"ש שגם אחרים לא יתנו לו ומסיק הא דתניא אין נזקקין לו מן הקופה היינו כדי סעודה אבל דבר מועט יתנו לו: שנאמר והעמדנו עלינו מצות. ולע"ג דהאי קרא גבי בית אלהינו כתיב דהיינו בדק הבית כ"ש לצדקה:

מסורת הש"ס

א) [כרמות ד: וש"נ], ב) [כל הספרים מדויקים כתיב פרוש ולכאורה היא פליאה ולריכין לומר ע"פ מ"ש תוס' שבת נה: ד"ה מעבירים כתיב ועיין במהרש"א בח"א שעמד על פליאה זו ונכנס לשנות דבזוקק בשיטה הגירסא קצת שלא כמקומו ד"ה הלא פרוס בשי"ן כתיב], ג) פאה פ"ח שבת קיח., ד) [תוספ' פאה פ"ד], ה) נ"א אמר מר עוקבא כו', ו) ס"א לפרוסה.

הגהות הב"ח

(א) גמ' הנהו טבחי כל"ל ותיבת בי תרי נמחק: (ב) שם לימות אמר ליה והא תניא אם היה: (ג) רש"י ד"ה שאין ראיה וכו' הנותנים לעושי המלאכה כל"ל ותיבת לבס נמחק: (ד) ד"ה עולא וכו' שגרס לה להטות וכו' נשים כהתכוות כדלקמן: (ה) תוס' ד"ה אין פוחתין וכו' ואחת למחר כשילך דכי אזיל לאו: (ו) ד"ה שבת וכו' בלהריס כי אותן: (ז) ד"ה לא וכו' לתת לו מן הקופה כ"ש שגם אחרים כל"ל ותיבות היינו כדי סעודה נמחק:

תורה אור השלם

א) וְלֹא יְחַשְּׁבוּ אֶת הָאֲנָשִׁים אֲשֶׁר יִתְּנוּ אֶת הַכֶּסֶף עַל יָדָם לָתֵת לְעֹשֵׂי הַמְּלָאכָה כִּי בֶאֱמֻנָה הֵם עֹשִׂים: [מלכים ב יב, טז]

ב) וַיְהִי כִּרְאוֹתָם כִּי רַב הַכֶּסֶף בָּאָרוֹן וַיַּעַל סֹפֵר הַמֶּלֶךְ וְהַכֹּהֵן הַגָּדוֹל וַיָּצֻרוּ וַיִּמְנוּ אֶת הַכֶּסֶף הַנִּמְצָא בֵית יְיָ: [מלכים ב יב, יא]

ג) הֲלוֹא פָרֹס לָרָעֵב לַחְמֶךָ וַעֲנִיִּים מְרוּדִים תָּבִיא בָיִת כִּי תִרְאֶה עָרֹם וְכִסִּיתוֹ וּמִבְּשָׂרְךָ לֹא תִתְעַלָּם: [ישעיה נח, ז]

ד) וְהֶעֱמַדְנוּ עָלֵינוּ מִצְוֹת לָתֵת עָלֵינוּ שְׁלִשִׁית הַשֶּׁקֶל בַּשָּׁנָה לַעֲבֹדַת בֵּית אֱלֹהֵינוּ: [נחמיה י, לג]

ה) וְהָיָה מַעֲשֵׂה הַצְּדָקָה שָׁלוֹם וַעֲבֹדַת הַצְּדָקָה הַשְׁקֵט וָבֶטַח עַד עוֹלָם: [ישעיה לב, יז]

ו) תַּחַת הַנְּחֹשֶׁת אָבִיא זָהָב וְתַחַת הַבַּרְזֶל אָבִיא כֶסֶף וְתַחַת הָעֵצִים נְחֹשֶׁת וְתַחַת הָאֲבָנִים בַּרְזֶל וְשַׂמְתִּי פְקֻדָּתֵךְ שָׁלוֹם וְנֹגְשַׂיִךְ צְדָקָה: [ישעיה ס, יז]

לעזי רש"י

קונפליינ"ט. פירוש נלחצים ונאנקים (רש"י ישעיה נח, ז) (על לרחס).

ליקוטי רש"י

ולא יחשבו את האנשים וגו'. לא היו מחשבים עם הממונים אשר יתנו את הכסף ביד המלאכה לפי שלא היו חשודים לעשות שקר. שאין לפי שלא היו חשודים כי באמונה הם עושים [מלכים ב, יב, טז].

עין משפט נר מצוה

עט א מיי' פ"ד מהל' מכירה הלכה יא סמג לאוין קע טוש"ע ח"מ סי' רלא סעיף כח וטוש"ע י"ד סי' רנו סעיף ז:

פ ב מיי' פ"ט מהלכות מתנות עניים הל' יא סמג עשין קסב טוש"ע י"ד סי' רנא סעיף י:

פא ג מיי' שם פ"ז הל' ו סמג שם טוש"ע י"ד סי' רנא סעיף י:

פב ד ה מיי' שם הל' ח סמג שם טוש"ע י"ד סי' רנ סעיף ד:

פג ו מיי' שם הל' ז טוש"ע שם סעיף ג:

פד ז מיי' שם הל' ה סמג שם טוש"ע י"ד סי' רמט סעיף ג:

פה ח מיי' שם פ"י הל' ו סמג עשין קסב טוש"ע שם סעיף ה:

רבינו גרשום

ואתני. אם יצטרכו לעניי העיר שיהיו לעניי העיר ואם לאו שיותירו על עניי העיר שיהיו לעניי כל אדם: דכל דאתי אדעתא דידי אתיא. כל מי שנותן לי על דעת כן נותן לי שאני אתנן לכל עני שארצה משום דרב אשי היה אדם גדול והיה יודע מה הוא עושה: [הנהו בי תרי טבחי]. התנו ביניהן שכל א' מהן ישחוט ביומו: קרעוה למשכיה. דחיותא: וחייביה רבא לשלם. דמי העור שקרע: ולהסיע על קיצתן. והלא רשאין לקנוס כל מי שעבר על תנאן: הני מילי. דיכולין להתנות ולהסיע על קיצתן: היכא דליכא אדם חשוב. להתנות לפניו: אבל אי איכא אדם חשוב. ולא אתנו קמיה לאו תנאיהו תנאה ואיכא דאמר היכא דליכא אדם חשוב עביד אינש דינא לנפשיה אבל אי איכא אדם חשוב נקיט ליה בדינא קמיה: אין מחשבין בצדקה עם הגבאין. מה גבו ומה נתנו דאין צריך לחשוד: אע"פ שאין ראיה לדבר זכר לדבר. גבי גבאי צדקה זכר לדבר ממקדש שנא' (מ"ב יב) אך לא יחשב וגו' אבל גבי גזברין של הקדש הוי ראיה גמורה: יצור. בעה"ב בקשר ובחותם וימנה דכתיב ויצורו וימנו כלומר אע"ג דהגזברין היו נאמנין אף על פי כן הגזברין עצמן היו צרין ומונין: בודקין למזונות. שאם אמר עני תנו לי מזונות בודקין אחריו קודם שיתנו לו אם רמאי הוא שאין צריך אם לאו: ואין בודקין לכסות. שאם בא עני ערום ואמר כסוני אין בודקין אחריו אלא נותנין מיד: פרוש כתיב. כלומר צריך אתה לידע בפירוש אם צריך ואם לאו: (פרוש) [פרוס] לאלתר (פרוש) [פרוס] הלחם ותן לו: לכשיראה לך. שהוא צריך כשתבדוק אחריו: העובר ממקום למקום. שאין לן אלא דרך עברה עובר: ככר בפונדיון. ככר שקונין בפונדיון כשנותנין ד' סאין בסלע דהוי ככר של ה' סאים כיצד בסלע יש מ"ח פונדיונות דסלע ד' דינר ודינר שש מעות ומעה ב' פונדיונות נמצא מ"ח פונדיונות בסלע וכיצד הוי חצי קב בפונדיון [ד' סאין] אחד ממ"ח בד' [סאין]

הערות

דסאה ו' קבים נמצא כ"ד קבין שהם מ"ח חצאי קבין בסלע שהוא מ"ח פונדיונות ושיערו חכמים דבהדם איך ליה ב' סעודות א' לכאן ואי' קודם שיגיע לישוב: פוריא ובי סדיא. כר וכסת: אין נזקקין לתת לו. מכיס של צדקה. הדואיל (ומחזר) [ומחסר] על הפתח הכל נותנין לו וא"צ ליטול מכיס של צדקה: משליש שקל. בצדקה: לעבודת אלהינו. דהיינו צדקה: מצות. הרבה משמע: מ) [עבודת (הצדקה)]. מעשה הוא: עכשיו באין וכו'. ודאי יתן לו לעובדי כוכבים ולא לצדקה: מאי לרעב שיתנהו לעניים אם לא זכה ליתנהו לעניים אעפ"כ יתן לעובדי כוכבים בשביל שהיה חייב לעניים: ואם זכה הלא פרוש מרודים כלומר עובדי כוכבים הרודים לביתו ונטלוהו בזרוע: ונוגשיך צדקה. מה שתתן לנוגשיך: עולא. עלם אחד כמו עול [ימים] (א"ה היינו שמו עולא אלא אחד בלי) [אחרבוני]:

חשק שלמה על רבינו גרשום א) [רבינו מפרש דגדול המעשה זה המעשה לגדול המעשה מה מפיקה דקרא דכתיב ועבודת הלדקה וגו' ודלא כפירש"י]:

ליקוטי רש"י: כי באמונה הם עושים [מלכים ב, יב, טז]. אין פותחין לעני העובר ממקום למקום. שאין לו בלילה ללכת. מככר. הלקוח בפונדיון כשהשער ארבע סאין בסלע והפונדיון אחד מארבעים ושמונה בסלע ואם בסלע ד' סאין נמצא לפונדיון חצי קב והחנוני נוטל מחצה בשכרו הוי ככר רובע. לן נותנין לו פרנסת לינה. לקמן מפרש מאי פרנסת לינה ובי סדיא. מזון שתי סעודות לעירובין (פב:) [שבת קיח.]. שבת. שבת בצהרים לנו בבית נותנין לו שלש סעודות [שם]. פוריא ובי סדיא. מטה וכר [שם]. עניים מרודים. נלחצים ונאנקים על לרחס (מיכה ג) אריד בשיחי (תהלים נה) [ישעיה נח, ז].

R' Elazar recommends a procedure used in the Temple: אָמַר רַבִּי אֶלְעָזָר אַף עַל פִּי שֶׁיֵּשׁ לוֹ לְאָדָם גִּזְבָּר נֶאֱמָן בְּתוֹךְ בֵּיתוֹ – **R' Elazar said: Even though a person has a trusted treasurer in his household,** יָצוּר וְיִמְנֶה – **he should bind and count** his money before giving it to the treasurer,[12] שֶׁנֶּאֱמַר: ,,וַיָּצֻרוּ וַיִּמְנוּ" – **for it is stated:** ***And they bound up and counted*** *the money.*[13]

The Gemara now discusses which applicants for assistance must be investigated:

אָמַר רַב הוּנָא בּוֹדְקִין לִמְזוֹנוֹת – **Rav Huna said: We investigate** the eligibility of a pauper that asks **for food,** וְאֵין בּוֹדְקִין לִכְסוּת – **but we do not investigate** the eligibility of an inadequately dressed pauper that asks **for clothing.** Rather, we fulfill his request immediately.

Rav Huna offers two sources for his ruling:

אִי בָּעֵית אֵימָא קְרָא – **If you wish, say** that my ruling is established by a Biblical **verse,** וְאִי בָּעֵית אֵימָא סְבָרָא – **or if you wish, say** that it can be deduced by **rational argument.** אִי בָּעֵית אֵימָא סְבָרָא – **If you wish, say** that it can be deduced by **rational argument,** as follows: הַאי קָא מִבַּזֵּי – **This** inadequately clothed applicant **debases himself** by appearing before the charity administrators in his woeful attire. If he were not truly in need, he would not do so. Thus, there is no reason to investigate whether he owns proper clothing. וְהַאי לָא קָא מִבַּזֵּי – **And this** other applicant **does not debase himself** by merely *claiming* that he is hungry. Thus, the administrators must investigate whether he is telling the truth.

Rav Huna now advances his Scriptural source:

אִי בָּעֵית אֵימָא קְרָא – **If you wish, say** that the ruling is established by the following **verse:**[14] ,,הֲלוֹא פָּרוֹשׂ לָרָעֵב לַחְמֶךָ" – ***Will you not break your bread for the hungry?*** בְּשִׂי"ן כְּתִיב – The word *break,* פָּרוֹשׂ, **is written with** the letter ***sin*** (שׂ) and not *samech* (ס),[15] so that it can be read as פָּרוֹשׁ, *clarify.*[16] Thus, the verse instructs us פָּרוֹשׁ – first to investigate and **clarify** whether the supplicant is truly hungry, וַהֲדַר הַב לֵיהּ – **and then give him** food if he is deserving. וְהָתָם כְּתִיב – **But there,** with regard to those who lack adequate clothing, **it is written:**[17] ,,כִּי־תִרְאֶה עָרֹם וְכִסִּיתוֹ" – ***When you see the naked, you shall cover him.*** כִּי תִרְאֶה לְאַלְתַּר – The verse implies that clothing should be provided **"when you see"** him – that is, **immediately** upon being apprised of his need, without first investigating whether it is authentic.

Interpreting the two verses differently, Rav Yehudah reverses Rav Huna's ruling:

וְרַב יְהוּדָה אָמַר בּוֹדְקִין לִכְסוּת – **And Rav Yehudah said: We investigate** the eligibility of an inadequately dressed pauper that asks **for clothing,** וְאֵין בּוֹדְקִין לִמְזוֹנוֹת – **but we do not investigate** the eligibility of a pauper that asks **for food.**

Rav Yehudah also offers two sources for his ruling:

אִי בָּעֵית אֵימָא סְבָרָא – **If you wish, say** that my ruling can be deduced by **rational argument,** וְאִי בָּעֵית אֵימָא קְרָא – **and if you wish, say** that it is established by a Biblical **verse.** אִי בָּעֵית אֵימָא סְבָרָא – **If you wish, say** that it can be deduced by **rational argument,** as follows: הַאי קָמִצְטַעֲרָא לֵיהּ – **This** one who asks for food is possibly **suffering** the pangs of hunger, and we should not prolong his suffering while we verify his claim. וְהַאי לָא קָמִצְטַעֲרָא לֵיהּ – **But this** one who requests clothing **does not suffer** physically.[18] Hence, he must wait while we authenticate his claim.

Rav Yehudah now advances his Scriptural source:

אִי בָּעֵית אֵימָא קְרָא – **If you wish, say** that the ruling is established by a Biblical **verse:** הָכָא כְּתִיב – **Here,** regarding one who requests food, **it is written:** ,,הֲלוֹא פָּרוֹס לָרָעֵב לַחְמֶךָ" – ***Will you not break***[19] ***your bread for the hungry?*** The verse implies that one must פָּרוֹס לְאַלְתַּר – **break** the bread for him **immediately;** וּכְדִקְרֵינַן – **just as we read** the word פָּרוֹשׂ.[20] The administrators may not delay feeding the supplicant in order to investigate him. וְהָתָם כְּתִיב – **But there,** regarding those who lack adequate clothing, **it is written:** ,,כִּי־תִרְאֶה עָרֹם וְכִסִּיתוֹ" – ***When you see the naked, you shall cover him,*** which implies that only כְּשֶׁיֵּרָאֶה לְךָ – **when it is apparent to you**[21] that the supplicant is not deceiving (i.e. after you have investigated the matter) may you provide him with the garments he requests.

The Gemara offers corroborations of Rav Yehudah's position:

תַּנְיָא כְּוָותֵיהּ דְּרַב יְהוּדָה – **It was taught in a Baraisa like the** opinion of **Rav Yehudah:** אָמַר כַּסּוּנִי – IF [A PAUPER] SAID, "CLOTHE ME," בּוֹדְקִין אַחֲרָיו – WE INVESTIGATE HIM to determine if he is truly needy. פַּרְנְסוּנִי – If, however, he said, "PROVIDE ME WITH SUSTENANCE," אֵין בּוֹדְקִין – WE DO NOT INVESTIGATE.

NOTES

12. Even though he has no intention of demanding an accounting afterward (*Rashi*).

13. *II Kings* 12:11. When the Temple treasury chest was filled, the king's scribe and the Kohen Gadol would count the money and bind it into packages. Verse 12 reports that they then gave the counted money to the treasurers, who were in charge of the workers. Verse 16, cited by the Gemara above, states that the treasurers were not required to provide an accounting of how they disbursed the funds. Nevertheless, the king's scribe and the Kohen Gadol deemed it prudent to count and package the entrusted money beforehand [so as to preclude any unwarranted suspicions (*Meiri*; see *Maharsha* for a novel explanation of this practice)]. R' Elazar bethought this a wise practice for everyone (see *Rashi*).

14. *Isaiah* 58:7.

15. *Mesoras HaShas* notes that in all exact texts of the Book of *Isaiah* the word *break* indeed appears as פָּרֹס – with a *samech* (ס). Citing *Tosafos* (*Shabbos* 55b ד"ה מעבירם) for support, *Mesoras HaShas* suggests that our Gemara, in fact, disputes the version contained in those texts. Cf. *Maharsha,* who emends our Gemara to resolve this problem. See also *Yad Ramah* and *Ritva*.

16. The Hebrew word for "breaking bread" is normally written with a *samech,* as פָּרֹס. The replacement of the *samech* with the homophonous *sin* (שׂ) indicates that a halachic interpretation of the word is in order. Rav Huna therefore explicates the word as פָּרוֹשׁ (with a *shin*), since for exegetic purposes the *sin* (שׂ) and *shin* (שׁ) are interchangeable.

17. *Isaiah* 58:7. This is the conclusion of the verse mentioned above.

18. The Gemara speaks of a case where the supplicant appears in clothing that is sufficient to protect him from the cold, for if not, he, too, qualifies as one who suffers from his poverty and the administrators would be required to provide him with warm clothing immediately. Rather, this supplicant is merely embarrassed and debased by the inappropriateness of his attire (*Ritva*).

19. Here, the Gemara records פָּרוֹס in its quotation of the verse, whereas before it established that the word is written with the letter *sin* (שׂ) – פָּרוֹשׂ (see above, note 15). Perhaps the Gemara means to underscore that Rav Yehudah rejects the interpretation of Rav Huna, who explains פרוש as if it were written with a *shin* – פָּרוֹשׁ, *clarify*. Rather, because Rav Yehudah interprets the word the way it is read (פָּרוֹשׂ, with a *sin*), as being synonymous with the homophonous פרוס (*break bread*), the Gemara records the word as פָּרוֹס.

In *Rosh's* text, however, the Gemara indeed records פָּרוֹשׂ – with a *sin* and not a *samech* – in its quotation of the verse.

20. I.e. with the letter *sin* (שׂ) at the end of the word. Hence, פרוש is synonymous with פרוס – *break bread.*

21. Rav Yehudah interprets תראה as if it were written in the passive form – תֵּרָאֶה, *when it is seen* (i.e. apparent) *to you.*

ואתני עלה איהו נמי עבד חד כיסא ואתני עלה רב אשי אמר אנא אתנויי נמי לא צריכנא דכל דקא אתי אדעתא דידי אתי ולמאן דבעינא יהיבנא ליה הנהו (א) בי תרי טבחי דעבדי עניינא בהדי הדדי דכל מאן דעביד ביומא דחבריה נקרעוה למשכיה אזל חד מנייהו עבד ביומא דחבריה קרעו למשכיה אתו לקמיה דרבא חייבינהו רבא לשלומי איתיביה רב יימר בר שלמיא לרבא ולהסיע על קיצתם לא אהדר ליה רבא אמר רב פפא שפיר עבד דלא אהדר ליה מידי ה"מ היכא דליכא אדם חשוב אבל היכא דאיכא אדם חשוב לאו כל כמינייהו דמתנו ת"ר אין מחשבין בצדקה עם גבאי צדקה ולא בהקדש עם הגזברין ואע"פ שאין ראיה לדבר זכר לדבר שנאמר [א] ולא יחשבו את האנשים אשר יתנו את הכסף על ידם לתת לעושי המלאכה כי באמונה הם עושים א"ר אלעזר אע"פ שיש לו לאדם גזבר נאמן בתוך ביתו יצור וימנה שנאמר [ב] ויצורו וימנו אמר רב הונא בודקין למזונות ואין בודקין לכסות אי בעית אימא קרא ואי בעית אימא סברא אב"א סברא האי קא מבזי והאי לא קא מבזי אי בעית אימא קרא [ג] הלא פרוש לרעב לחמך בשי"ן כתיב פרוש והדר הב ליה והתם כתיב כי תראה ערום וכסיתו כי תראה לאלתר ורב יהודה אמר בודקין לכסות ואין בודקין למזונות אי בעית אימא סברא ואי בעית אימא קרא אי בעית אימא סברא האי קמצערא ליה והאי לא קמצערא ליה אי בעית אימא קרא הכא כתיב הלא פרוס לרעב לחמך פרוס לאלתר וכדקרינן והתם כתיב כי תראה ערום וכסיתו כשיראה לך תניא כוותיה דרב יהודה אמר כסוני בודקין אחריו פרנסוני אין בודקין תנן התם אין פוחתין לעני העובר ממקום למקום מככר בפונדיון מארבע סאין בסלע לן נותנין לו פרנסת לינה מאי פרנסת לינה אמר רב פפא פוריא ובי סדיא שבת נותנין לו מזון שלש סעודות תנא אם היה מחזיר על הפתחים אין נזקקין לו ההוא עניא דהוה מחזיר על הפתחים דאתא לקמיה דרב פפא לא מזדקיק ליה א"ל רב סמא בריה דרב ייבא לרב פפא אי מר לא מזדקיק ליה אינש אחרינא לא מזדקיק ליה לימות (ב) ליה והא תניא אם היה עני המחזיר על הפתחים אין נזקקין לו א"ל אין נזקקין לו למתנה מרובה אבל נזקקין לו למתנה מועטת אמר רב אסי לעולם אל ימנע אדם עצמו [מלתת] שלישית השקל בשנה שנא' [ד] והעמדנו עלינו מצות לתת עלינו שלישית השקל בשנה לעבודת בית אלהינו ואמר רב אסי שקולה צדקה כנגד כל המצות שנאמר והעמדנו עלינו מצות וגו' מצוה אין כתיב כאן אלא מצות (סימן גדול מקדש משה) א"ר אלעזר גדול המעשה יותר מן העושה שנאמר [ה] והיה מעשה הצדקה שלום ועבודת הצדקה השקט ובטח עד עולם זכה הלא פרוש לרעב לחמך לא זכה ועניים מרודים תביא בית אמר להו רבא לבני מחוזא במטותא מניכו עושו בהדי הדדי כי היכי דליהוי לכו שלמא במלכותא וא"ר אלעזר בזמן שבהמ"ק קיים אדם שוקל שקלו ומתכפר לו עכשיו שאין בהמ"ק קיים אם עושין צדקה מוטב ואם לאו באין עובדי כוכבים ונוטלין בזרוע ואעפ"כ נחשב להן לצדקה שנא' [ו] ונוגשיך צדקה אמר רבא האי מילתא אישתעי לי עולא

רש"י

ואתני. מתנה עם הצבור לחלקם לכל הבא: דכל דאתי. לתת מעות לקופה: עניינא. תנאי: למשכיה. עור הבהמה: לאו כל כמינייהו דמתנו. אלא בפניו: אין מחשבין. לומר היכן נתתם מעות שגביתם: שאין ראיה לדבר. דלא בגבאי צדקה כתיב אלא בגיזברי הקדש הנותנים (ג) לבס לעושי המלאכה שהפועלים מרובין למלאכות הרבה לגודרין ולחוצבי האבן לכתפים ולחמרים ולקנות עצים ואבני מחצב וא"א לעמוד על החשבון כדאמרינן בעלמא (שבועות דף מה.) בעל הבית טרוד בפועליו הוא ואינשי: יצור וימנה. הכסף שהוא מוסר בידו ואע"פ שאינו בא עמו לחשבון לאחר מכאן יצור וימנה שנאמר ויצורו וימנו וגו' והדר ונתנו את הכסף המתוכן המנוי על ידי עושי המלאכה וגו': בודקין למזונות. אם בא עני ואמר פרנסוני בודקין שלא יהיה רמאי: ואין בודקין לכסות. בא ערום ואמר כסוני לוקחין כסות מיד: פרוש. דרוש וחקור תחלה: לכשיראה לך. שאינו רמאי: מככר בפונדיון. ככר הלקוח בפונדיון כשלוקחין ארבע סאין חטין בסלע ומגיע לפונדיון חצי קב שהסלע מ"ח פונדיונין וארבע סאין מ"ח חצאי קבין והחנוני שהוא טוחן ואופה ומוכר בשוק משתכר מחצה הרי שנותן ככר של רובע הקב בפונדיון: לן. בלילה: פרנסת לינה. צרכי לינה: בי סדיא. כר לתת מראשותיו: אין נזקקין לו. לתת מעות מן הקופה אחרי שלמד לחזר על הפתחים דיו בכך: ולא אזדקיק ליה. אפי' (י) לפרנסה: מעשה הצדקה. טורח המעשים את חבריהם מדלא כתיב והיתה הצדקה שלום: זכה. למזל טוב: עניים מרודים. זו ממשלת רומי שצועקת תמיד הבו הבו שאנו צריכין: מרודים. קונפליינ"ט בלע"ז כמו אריד בשיחי (תהלים נה): עולא משגש ארחתיה דאימיה. לרב ששת קרו ליה הכי עולל המשגש דרכי אמו שגרס (ד) להטותה מדרך שאר נשים כדלקמן:

תוספות

ואע"פ שאין ראיה לדבר זכר לדבר. ראיה גמורה אינה דשאני התם שהיו צדיקים גמורים: **אין** פוחתין לעני העובר ממקום למקום מככר בפונדיון כו'. הככר עולה ששה ביצים דלא מהן מחצה לחנווני והוא מזון שתי סעודות כדתניא בפרק כילד משתתפין (עירובין דף פב:) וקשה לר"י דבפרק כל כתבי (שבת דף קיח. ושם) משמע שהוא רגילות דאיכא סעודה בהדיה דקאמר התם דכי אזיל מלוינא ליה סעודה בהדיה דכי אזיל לאו בריקן אזיל וא"כ למה נותנין לו שתי סעודות די לו בסעודה אחת ההיא סעודה דאיכא בהדיה יאכל מיד וסעודה שנותנין לו עכשיו יוליכנו עמו ונראה לר"י דאין מחלקין תמחוי בלילה לפי שאין יכולין להבחין למי נתנו ולמי לא נתנו וכן משמע מדקאמר לן נותנים לו פרנסת לינה ומפרש דהיינו פוריא ובי סדיא אבל ככר אין נותנין לו ולכך נותנין לו ב' סעודות שיאכל אחת בלילה ואחת למחר (ה) דכי אזיל לאו בריקן אזיל וטעמא דבעינן שלא ילך ריקם דאינו דומה מי שיש לו פת בסלו למי שאין לו ולא יהא רעב כל כך אבל אין לפרש דהטעם שמא לא יגיע בין היהודים ויהא לו מה לאכול דאי חיישינן להכי היה ליתן לו שלש סעודות כי גם בלילה לא יתנו אף כשיגיע בין היהודים שאין מחלקין תמחוי בלילה ואין לומר דלעולם מחלקין ולכך נותנין שתים דחיישינן שמא לא יגיע בין היהודים שתי פעמים אי נמי לא חיישינן אלא לפעם אחת והשניה נותנין לו כדי שיהא לו פת בסלו דאם כן היכי קאמר התם דמלוינן ליה סעודה אחת בהדיה ואם יש לחוש שמא לא יגיע בין היהודים היה לו ליתן שתים לכך נראה כדפרישית: **שבת** נותנין לו מזון שלש סעודות. פירוש בשבת בצהרים (ו) אותן שתי סעודות שנתן לו אתמול בערב שבת אכל ליל שבת ושבת שחרית ושלש סעודות שנותנים לו בשבת יאכל אחת בשבת בסעודה שלישית ואחת למוצאי שבת ושלישית ישאר לו למחר בדרך שלא ילך ריקם ואין להאריך וקשה לרשב"א הא דתנן במסכת פאה (פ"ח מ"ז) ומייתי לה בפרק כל כתבי (שבת דף קיח. ושם) מי שיש לו מזון שתי סעודות בביתו לא יטול מן התמחוי ואמאי הא אחד יאכל מיד ואחד בלילה וא"כ כי אזיל ריקם אזיל וצריך לפרש דמזון שתי סעודות דקאמר היינו בלא אותה שיש לו לאכול מיד וא"ת שבת אמאי נותנין לו שלש סעודות והא הך מתני' ר"ע היא דקתני רישא כל מי שיש לו מזון י"ד סעודות לא יטול מן הקופה ופריך בפרק כל כתבי הקדש (שם) מני אי רבנן חמיסר הויין אי רבי חדקא שיתסר הויין ומשני הא מני ר"ע היא דאמר עשה שבתך חול ונראה לרשב"א דבשביל סעודת שבת אין לו להתחיל וליטול אבל בשכבר צריך ליטול נוטל גם כדי לסעודת שבת: **לא** אזדקיק ליה. רב פפא גבאי היה ולא נתן לו מן הקופה כדתניא אין נותנין לו מן הקופה כיון שמחזר על הפתחים וא"ל רב סמא אי מר לא אזדקיק ליה לתת לו מן הקופה (ז) היינו כדי סעודה כ"ש שגם אחרים לא יתנו לו ומסיק הא דתניא אין נזקקין לו מן הקופה היינו כדי סעודה אבל דבר מועט יתנו לו: **שנאמר** והעמדנו עלינו מצות. ואע"ג דהאי קרא גבי בית אלהינו כתיב דהיינו בדק הבית כ"ש צדקה:

מנין

עין משפט נר מצוה

עט א מיי' פי"ד מהל' מכירה הלכה יא סמג לאוין קע טוש"ע ח"מ סי' רלא סעיף כח וטוש"ע י"ד סי' רנו סעיף ד:
פ ב מיי' פ"ט מהלכות מתנות עניים הל' יא סמג עשין קסב טוש"ע י"ד סי' רנז סעיף ג:
פא ג מיי' שם הל' ו סמג שם טוש"ע י"ד סי' רנא סעיף י:
פב ד ה מיי' שם הל' ח סמג שם טוש"ע שם סי' רנ סעיף ד:
פג ו מיי' שם הל' ו טוש"ע שם סעיף ג:
פד ז מיי' שם הל' ה סמג שם טוש"ע י"ד סי' רמט סעיף ג:
פה ח מיי' שם פ"י הל' ו סמג עשין קסב טוש"ע שם סעיף ה:

רבינו גרשום

ואתני. אם יצטרכו לעניי העיר שיהיו לעניי העיר ואם לאו שיוזירו על עניי העיר שיהיו לעניי כל אדם: דכל דאתי אדעתא דידי אתיא. כל מי שנותן לי על דעת כן נותן לי שאני אתנן לכל עני שארצה משום דרב אשי היה אדם גדול והיה יודע מה הוא עושה: [הנהו בי תרי טבחין]. התנו ביניהן שכל א' מהן ישחוט ביומו: קרעוה למשכיה. דחיותא: וחייביה רבא לשלם. דמי העור שקרע: ולהסיע על קיצתן. והלא רשאין לקנוס כל מי שעבר על תנאן: הני מילי. דיכולין להתנות ולהסיע על קיצתן: היכא דליכא אדם חשוב. להתנות לפניו: אבל אי איכא אדם חשוב. ולא אתנו קמיה לאו תנאיהו תנאה ואיכא דאמר היכא דליכא אדם חשוב עביד אינש דינא לנפשיה אבל אי איכא אדם חשוב נקיט ליה בדינא קמיה: אין מחשבין בצדקה עם הגבאין. מה גבו ומה נתנו דאין צריך לחשדן: אע"פ שאין ראיה לדבר זכר לדבר. גבי גבאי צדקה זכר לדבר ממקדש שנא' (מ"ב כב) אך לא יחשב וגו' אבל גבי גזברין של הקדש הוי ראיה גמורה: יצור. בעה"ב בקשר ובחותם וימנה דכתיב ויצורו וימנו כלומר אע"ג דהגזברין היו נאמנין אף על פי כן הגזברין עצמן היו צרין ומונין: בודקין למזונות. שאם אמר עני תנו לי מזונות בודקין אחריו קודם שיתנו לו אם רמאי הוא שאין צריך אם לאו: ואין בודקין לכסות. שאם בא עני ערום ואמר כסוני אין בודקין אחריו אלא נותנין מיד: פרוש כתיב. כלומר צריך אתה לידע בפירוש אם צריך ואם לאו: (פרוש) [פרוס] לאלתר (פרוש) [פרוס] הלחם ותן לו: לכשיראה לך. שהוא צריך כשתבדוק אחריו: העובר ממקום למקום. שאין לן אלא דרך עברה עובר: ככר בפונדיון. ככר שקונין בפונדיון כשנותנין ד' סאין בסלע דהוי ככר של חצי קב כיצד בסלע הם מ"ח פונדיונות דסלע ד' דינר ודינר שש מעות ומעה ב' פונדיונות נמצא מ"ח פונדיונות בסלע וכיצד הוי חצי קב בפונדיון דחצי קב אחד ממ"ח בד' [סאין] דסאה ו' קבים נמצא כ"ד קבין בסלע שהם מ"ח חצאי קבין בסלע שהוא מ"ח פונדיונות ושיערו חכמים דבהם אית ליה ב' סעודות א' לכאן וא' קודם שיגיע לישוב: פוריא ובי סדיא. כר וכסת: אין נזקקין לתת לו. מכיס של צדקה. דהואיל (ומחסר) [ומחזר] על הפתח הכל נותנין לו וא"צ ליטול מכיס של צדקה: משליש שקל. בצדקה: לעבודת אלהינו. דהיינו צדקה: מצות. הרבה משמע: א) ועבודת [הצדקה]. מעשה הוא: עכשיו באין וכו'. ודאי יתן או לעובדי כוכבים או לצדקה. אם זכה הלא פרוש לרעב שיתנהו לעניים אם לא זכה יתנהו לעובדי כוכבים אעפ"כ יתן לעובדי כוכבים בשביל שהיה חייב ליתן לעניים. באים [עניים] מרודים כלומר עובדי כוכבים הרודים לביתו ונוטלוהו בזרוע: ונוגשיך צדקה. מה שתתן לנוגשיך: עולא. עלם אחד כמו עול [ימים] לא יהיה שמו עולא אלא אחד בלין [אחדבוי]:

חשק שלמה על רבינו גרשום א) [דעתו מפרש דגדול המעשה נלמד מסיפא דקרא דכתיב ועבודת הצדקה וגו' ודלא כפירש"י]:

מסורת הש"ס

א) [ברכות ד: וש"נ], ב) [בכל הספרים מדוקים כתיב פרוש ולכאורה היא פליאה וצריכין ליישב ע"פ מ"ש תוס' שבת נה: ד"ה מעבירים כתיב ועיין במהרש"א בח"א שעמד על פליאה זו ונכנס בדוחק בשינוי הגירסא קצת שלא במקומו ד"ה הלא פרוש בשי"ן כתיב], ג) פאה פ"ח מ"ז, ד) [תוספ' פאה פ"ד], ה) כ"א אמר מר עוקבא כו', ו) ל"א לפרוסה. רש"ל.

הגהות הב"ח

(א) גמ' הנהו עבדי כל"ל ותיבת בי תרי נמחק: (ב) שם לימות אמר ליה והא תניא אם היה: (ג) רש"י ד"ה שאין ראיה וכו' הנותנים לעושי המלאכה כל"ל ותיבת לבס נמחק: (ד) ד"ה עולא וכו' שגרס לה להטות וכו' נשים כדלקמן: (ה) תוס' ד"ה אין פוחתין וכו' ואחת למחר כשילך דכי אזיל לאו: (ו) ד"ה שבת וכו' בצהרים כי אותן: (ז) ד"ה לא וכו' לתת לו מן הקופה כ"ש שגם אחרים כל"ל ותיבות היינו כדי סעודה נמחק:

תורה אור השלם

א) ולא יחשבו את האנשים אשר יתנו את הכסף על ידם לתת לעשי המלאכה כי באמנה הם עשים: [מלכים ב יב, טז]
ב) ויהי כראותם כי רב הכסף בארון ויעל ספר המלך והכהן הגדול ויצרו וימנו את הכסף הנמצא בית יי: [מלכים ב יב, יא]
ג) הלוא פרס לרעב לחמך ועניים מרודים תביא בית כי תראה ערם וכסיתו ומבשרך לא תתעלם: [ישעיה נח, ז]
ד) והעמדנו עלינו מצות לתת עלינו שלשית השקל בשנה לעבדת בית אלהינו: [נחמיה י, לג]
ה) והיה מעשה הצדקה שלום ועבדת הצדקה השקט ובטח עד עולם: [ישעיה לב, יז]
ו) תחת הנחשת אביא זהב ותחת הברזל אביא כסף ותחת העצים נחשת ותחת האבנים ברזל ושמתי פקדתך שלום ונגשיך צדקה: [ישעיה ס, יז]

לעזי רש"י

קונפליינ"ט. פירוש נאנחים ונאנקים (על צרתם) (רש"י ישעיה נח, ז):

ליקוטי רש"י

ולא יחשבו את האנשים וגו'. לא היו המארכלין באין לחשבון עם האנשים הגזברין אשר יתנו המארכלין את הכסף תמיד על ידם לתתו לעושי המלאכה לפי שלא היו חשודים בעיניהם כי באמונה הם עושים [מלכים ב, יב, טז]. אין פוחתין לעני העובר ממקום למקום. שאינו לן בלילה אלא עובר. מככר. הלקוח בפונדיון כשהשער ארבע סאין בסלע והפונדיון אחד משנים עשר בדינר דהוא אחד מארבעים ושמונה בסלע ושיערו לו חכמים ככר זו לשתי סעודות היום והלילה. לן נותנין לו פרנסת לינה. לקמן מפרש מאי היא שהרי סעודה של לילה בכלל ככר היא וככר זו משערין בעירובין (פב:) למזון שתי סעודות לעירובי תחומין. מאי פרנסת לינה. בי סדיא. לבדין שקורין פלטר"ש ועושין לקפלן תחתיו ולהניח תחת מראשותיו [שבת קיח.]. שבת. אכלה בשבת [שם קיח.]. ועניים מרודים. נאנחים ונאנקים על צרתם כגון עני ומרודי (איכה ג) אריד בשיחי (תהלים נה) [ישעיה נח, ז].

A Mishnah establishes the criteria for determining eligibility for different forms of public assistance:

תְּנַן הָתָם — **We learned there in a Mishnah:**[22] אֵין פּוֹחֲתִין לְעָנִי הָעוֹבֵר מִמָּקוֹם לְמָקוֹם — WE DO NOT GIVE A POOR MAN WHO TRAVELS FROM PLACE TO PLACE[23] LESS מִכִּכָּר בְּפוּנְדְּיוֹן מֵאַרְבַּע סְאִין בְּסֶלַע — THAN A LOAF of bread THAT COSTS A *PUNDYON* WHEN FOUR *SE'AHS* of flour COST A *SELA*.[24] לָן — IF HE STAYS OVERNIGHT, נוֹתְנִין לוֹ פַּרְנָסַת לִינָה — WE GIVE HIM PROVISIONS FOR NIGHT-LODGING.

The Gemara asks:

מַאי פַּרְנָסַת לִינָה — **What are provisions for night-lodging?**

The Gemara answers:

אָמַר רַב פָּפָּא — **Rav Pappa said:** פּוּרְיָא וּבֵי סַדְיָא — **A bed, and a pillow** for his head.

The Gemara again quotes the Mishnah:

שַׁבָּת — If the poor person spends THE SABBATH in the city, נוֹתְנִין לוֹ מְזוֹן שָׁלֹשׁ סְעוּדוֹת — WE GIVE HIM FOOD FOR THREE MEALS, for on the Sabbath one must eat a third meal.[25]

The Gemara qualifies the above rulings:

תָּנָא — **It was taught in a Baraisa:** אִם הָיָה מַחֲזִיר עַל הַפְּתָחִים — IF [THE POOR PERSON] HAD BEEN COLLECTING DOOR-TO-DOOR, אֵין נִזְקָקִין לוֹ — WE ARE NOT BOUND TO assist HIM with a donation of money from the public charity fund. Once he has learned to collect on his own, he will be able to support himself.[26]

The Gemara relates an incident in which this Baraisa is invoked and reinterpreted:

הַהוּא עַנְיָא דַּהֲוָה מַחֲזִיר עַל הַפְּתָחִים — There was **a certain pauper, who had been collecting door-to-door,** דְּאָתָא לְקַמֵּיה דְּרַב פָּפָּא — **who came before Rav Pappa** to request assistance from the public charity fund.[27] לָא מִזְדַּקֵּיק לֵיהּ — **[Rav Pappa] did not bother with him,** even to give him money from the charity fund for a slice of bread,[28] in accordance with the Baraisa.

Rav Pappa was subsequently challenged:

אָמַר לֵיהּ רַב סַמָּא בְּרֵיהּ דְּרַב יֵיבָא לְרַב פָּפָּא — **Rav Samma the son of Rav Yeiva said to Rav Pappa:** אִי מָר לָא מִזְדַּקֵּיק לֵיהּ — **If the master** (Rav Pappa) **will not bother with [this pauper],** to assist him, אִינִישׁ אַחֲרִינָא לָא מִזְדַּקֵּיק לֵיהּ — **no other person will bother with him,** for they will assume that he is dishonest! לֵימוּת — **Should he** therefore **die** from hunger?[29]

Rav Pappa attempted to justify his decision:

[אָמַר] לֵיהּ וְהָא תַּנְיָא — **[Rav Pappa said] to [Rav Samma]:**[30] **But it was taught in a Baraisa:** אִם הָיָה עָנִי הַמַּחֲזִיר עַל הַפְּתָחִים — IF HE WAS A POOR PERSON WHO COLLECTS DOOR-TO-DOOR, אֵין נִזְקָקִין לוֹ — WE ARE NOT BOUND TO assist HIM with a donation from the charity fund. Hence, your concern that others will be deterred from contributing their private funds to such a pauper is unfounded.

Rav Samma challenged Rav Pappa's interpretation of the Baraisa:

אָמַר לֵיהּ — **[Rav Samma] said to [Rav Pappa]:** אֵין נִזְקָקִין לוֹ לְמַתָּנָה מְרוּבָּה — When the Baraisa says that **we are not bound to** assist **him,** it means **with a large donation.**[31] This is not necessary, since the pauper can support himself by collecting door-to-door. אֲבָל נִזְקָקִין לוֹ לְמַתָּנָה מוּעֶטֶת — **However, we are bound to** assist **him with a small donation,** in order to signal to the residents of the city that he is truly a needy person.

The Gemara establishes the minimum annual charity contribution:

אָמַר רַב אַסִּי — **Rav Assi said:** לְעוֹלָם אַל יִמְנַע אָדָם עַצְמוֹ [מִלִּתֵּת] שְׁלִישִׁית הַשֶּׁקֶל בַּשָּׁנָה — **A person should never restrain himself from donating** to charity at least **one-third of a** ***shekel*** **each year,**[32] שֶׁנֶּאֱמַר: ,,וְהֶעֱמַדְנוּ עָלֵינוּ מִצְוֹת לָתֵת עָלֵינוּ שְׁלִישִׁית הַשֶּׁקֶל בַּשָּׁנָה לַעֲבֹדַת בֵּית אֱלֹהֵינוּ" — **for it is stated:**[33] ***And we took upon ourselves commandments***[34] ***to give ourselves one-third of a shekel each year for the work of the House of our God.*** Rav Assi draws an analogy between donations to charity and donations for the upkeep of the Temple, which is the subject of this verse.[35]

NOTES

22. *Pe'ah* 8:7.

23. I.e. a pauper who will leave the city before nightfall.

24. If a poor person who is traveling from place to place passes through a community, that community's official charity organization must see to it that he has enough food for the day — i.e. two meals' worth (the norm in those days). Thus, he must receive at the very minimum the amount of bread that a *pundyon* will buy when a *sela* buys four *se'ahs* of wheat. When wheat is at this price, a *pundyon* will buy a loaf of bread containing a quarter-*kav* [or the volume of six eggs] of flour, and it is a loaf of bread this size that a poor person must be provided with daily (*Rav, Rash* and *Rosh* to Mishnah; see also *Rashi* here). A loaf this size is sufficient for two meals (*Rashi* to *Shabbos* 118a).

That a loaf costing a *pundyon* contains a quarter-*kav* of flour is ascertained in the following way: A *se'ah* is a unit of volume equal to six *kavs*, so that four *se'ahs* are equal to 24 *kavs*. A *sela* is a coin equal in value to 24 silver *ma'os*; a *ma'ah* (singular of *ma'os*) is equal to two *pundyons,* so that there are 48 *pundyons* in a *sela*. Thus, when four *se'ahs* [24 *kavs*] of wheat sell for a *sela* [48 *pundyons*], two *pundyons* will buy a *kav* of wheat, and one *pundyon* will buy a half-*kav*. A finished loaf of bread, however, costs twice as much as the wheat content, since the loaf's price reflects the additional cost of the baker's labor. Therefore, when a *pundyon* buys a half-*kav* of wheat, it will buy a loaf of bread containing a quarter-*kav* of flour (*Rav, Rash* and *Rosh* to Mishnah; see also *Rashi* here).

See, however, *Rabbeinu Gershom,* who writes that the loaf that can be acquired for a *pundyon* contains a half-*kav* of flour [he does not subtract the baker's charge], and it is a loaf this size that is sufficient for two meals. *Yad Ramah* indeed sets the size of the loaf at a quarter-*kav*, but considers this enough for only one meal.

25. *Shabbos* 118a. Hence, of the two meals' worth of food he was given on Friday, the pauper eats half for his Sabbath (Friday) night meal and the other half for his Sabbath morning meal. [His Friday morning (or afternoon) meal consisted of food he brought with him from the place of the previous night's lodging.] Of the three meals' worth of food he is given on the Sabbath, the pauper eats one-third for his third (afternoon) Sabbath meal and one-third on Saturday night. He takes the final third with him when he resumes his journey on Sunday morning, so that he does not travel empty-handed (*Tosafos*).

26. The public charity fund was intended mainly for the assistance of those who were unable to collect door-to-door, either because of physical limitations or pride. See *Ritva*, who writes that we still provide him with sleeping provisions.

27. Rav Pappa was the administrator of the charity fund (*Tosafos* ד״ה לא).

28. See *Rashi* and *Tosafos*.

29. Rav Samma argued that other people will not realize that Rav Pappa refrained only from giving from the charity fund, but will think that Rav Pappa declined to donate his own money because the supplicant was unworthy. Consequently, the public will withhold their own funds, and the pauper's welfare would then be seriously jeopardized. Rav Samma therefore suggested that Rav Pappa give the pauper a small contribution from the charity fund, so that others will be encouraged to donate privately (*Maharsha*, explaining *Tosafos*).

30. The word אמר, *said*, is missing from the text; it is inserted by *Bach*.

31. I.e. the equivalent of a full meal (*Tosafos*).

32. *Rambam* (*Hil. Matanos Aniyim* 7:5) writes that although the norm is to donate one-tenth of one's income to charity, the absolute annual minimum is the amount mentioned here. Donating less than one-third of a *shekel* does not constitute a fulfillment of the mitzvah.

33. *Nehemiah* 10:33.

34. The reason for using the plural "commandments" [when only the one commandment of charity is involved] is discussed by the Gemara below.

35. Although there is a Biblical commandment to contribute a *half-shekel* annually toward the purchase of animals for the sacrificial

ואתני עלה איהו נמי עבד חד כיסא ואתני עלה רב אשי אמר אנא אתנויי נמי לא צריכנא דכל דקא אתי אדעתא דידי אתי ולמאן דבעינא יהיבנא ליה הנהו (א) בי תרי טבחי דעבדי עניינא בהדי הדדי דכל מאן דעביד ביומא דחבריה נקרעוה למשכיה אזל חד מנייהו עבד ביומא דחבריה קרעו למשכיה אתו לקמיה דרבא חייבינהו רבא לשלומי איתיביה רב יימר בר שלמיא לרבא ולהסיע על קיצתם לא אהדר ליה רבא אמר רב פפא שפיר עבד דלא אהדר ליה מידי א ה"מ היכא דליכא אדם חשוב אבל היכא דאיכא אדם חשוב לאו כל כמינייהו דמתנו ת"ר ב אין מחשבין בצדקה עם גבאי צדקה ולא בהקדש עם הגזברין ואע"פ שאין ראיה לדבר זכר לדבר שנאמר א) ולא יחשבו את האנשים אשר יתנו את הכסף על ידם לתת לעושי המלאכה כי באמונה הם עושים א"ר אלעזר אע"פ שיש לו לאדם גזבר נאמן בתוך ביתו יצור וימנה שנאמר ב) ויצורו וימנו אמר רב הונא בודקין למזונות ואין בודקין לכסות (ב) אי בעית אימא קרא ואי בעית אימא סברא אב"א סברא האי קא מבזי והאי לא קא מבזי אי בעית אימא קרא ג הלא ג) פרוש לרעב לחמך בשי"ן כתיב פרוש והדר הב ליה והתם כתיב ג) כי תראה ערום וכסיתו כי תראה לאלתר ורב יהודה אמר ג בודקין לכסות ואין בודקין למזונות אי בעית אימא סברא ואי בעית אימא קרא אי בעית אימא סברא האי קמצערא ליה והאי לא קמצערא ליה אי בעית אימא קרא הכא כתיב הלא פרוס לרעב לחמך פרוס לאלתר וכדקרינן והתם כתיב כי תראה ערום וכסיתו כשיראה לך תניא כוותיה דרב יהודה אמר כסוני בודקין אחריו פרנסוני אין בודקין ג) תנן התם ד אין פוחתין לעני העובר ממקום למקום מככר בפונדיון מארבע סאין בסלע לן נותנין לו פרנסת לינה מאי פרנסת לינה אמר רב פפא ה פוריא ובי סדיא שבת נותנין לו מזון שלש סעודות תנא ו אם היה מחזיר על הפתחים אין נזקקין לו ההוא עניא דהוה מחזיר על הפתחים דאתא לקמיה דרב פפא לא מזדקיק ליה א"ל רב סמא בריה דרב ייבא לרב פפא אי מר לא מזדקיק ליה איניש אחרינא לא מזדקיק ליה לימות (ג) ליה והא תניא אם היה עני המחזיר על הפתחים אין נזקקין לו א"ל ז אין נזקקין לו למתנה מרובה אבל נזקקין לו למתנה מועטת אמר רב אסי ח לעולם אל ימנע אדם עצמו [מלתת] שלישית השקל בשנה שנא' ד) והעמדנו עלינו מצות לתת עלינו שלישית השקל בשנה לעבודת בית אלהינו ואמר רב אסי שקולה צדקה כנגד כל המצות שנאמר והעמדנו עלינו מצות וגו' מצוה אין כתיב כאן אלא מצות (סימן גדול מקדש משה) א"ר אלעזר ט גדול המעשה יותר מן העושה שנאמר ה) והיה מעשה הצדקה שלום ועבודת הצדקה השקט ובטח עד עולם זכה הלא פרוש לרעב לחמך לא זכה ועניים מרודים תביא בית אמר להו רבא לבני מחוזא במטותא מנייכו עושו בהדי הדדי כי היכי דליהוי לכו שלמא במלכותא וא"ר אלעזר בזמן שבהמ"ק קיים אדם שוקל שקלו ומתכפר לו עכשיו שאין בהמ"ק קיים אם עושין צדקה מוטב ואם לאו באין עובדי כוכבים ונוטלין בזרוע ואעפ"כ נחשב להן לצדקה שנא' ו) ונוגשיך צדקה אמר רבא האי מילתא אישתעי לי עולא

רש"י

ואתני. מתנה עם הצבור לחלקם לכל הבא: דכל דאתי. לתת מעות לקופה: עניינא. תנאי: למשכיה. עור הבהמה: לאו כל כמינייהו דמתנו. אלא בפניו: אין מחשבין. לומר היכן נתתם מעות שגביתם: שאין ראיה לדבר. דלא בגבאי צדקה כתיב אלא בגיזברי הקדש הנותנים (ג) לבם לעושי המלאכה שהפועלים מרובין למלאכות הרבה לגודרין ולחוצבי האבן לכתפים ולתמרים ולקונות עלים ואבני מאלב וא"א לעמוד על החשבון כדאמרינן בעלמא (שבועות דף מה.) בעל הבית ערוד בפועליו הוא ואינשי: יצור וימנה. הכסף שהוא מוסר בידו ואע"פ שאינו בא עמו לחשבון לאחר מכאן יצור וימנה שנאמר ויצורו וימנו וגו' והדר ונתנו את הכסף המתוכן המנוי על ידי עושי המלאכה וגו': בודקין למזונות. אם בא עני ואמר פרנסוני בודקין שלא יהיה רמאי: ואין בודקין לכסות. אם בא ערום ואמר כסוני לוקחין כסות מיד: פרוש. דרוש וחקור תחלה: לכשיראה לך. שאינו רמאי: מככר בפונדיון. ככר הלקוח בפונדיון כשלוקחין ארבע סאין חטין בסלע ומגיע לפונדיון חצי קב שהסלע מ"ח פונדיונין וארבע סאין מ"ח חצאי קבין והחנוני שהוא טוחן ואופה ומוכר בשוק משתכר מחצה הרי שנותן ככר של רובע הקב בפונדיון: לן. בלילה: פרנסת לינה. צרכי לינה: בי סדיא. כר לתת מראשותיו: אין נזקקין לו. לתת מעות מן הקופה אחרי שלמד לחזר על הפתחים דיו בכך: ולא אזדקיק ליה. אפי' (ו) לפרנסה: מעשה הצדקה. טורח המעשים את אחרים מלאה כתיב והיתה הצדקה שלום: זכה. למזל טוב: עניים מרודים. זו ממשלת רומי שצועקת תמיד הבו הבו שאנו צריכין: מרודים. קונפליינ"ט בלע"ז כמו אריד בשיחי (תהלים נה): עולא משגש ארחתיה דאימיה. לרב ששת קרו ליה הכי עולא המשגש דרכי אמו שגרס (ד) להטותה מדרך שאר נשים כדלקמן:

תוספות

ואע"פ שאין ראיה לדבר זכר לדבר. ראיה גמורה אינה דשאני התם שהיו צדיקים גמורים: אין פוחתין לעני העובר ממקום למקום מככר בפונדיון כו'. הככר עולה ששה ביצים דלא מהן מחצה לחנווני והוא מזון שתי סעודות כדתניא בפרק כילד משתתפין (עירובין דף פב:) וקשה לר"י דבפרק כל כתבי (שבת דף קיח. ושם) משמע שהוא רגילות דאיכא סעודה בהדיה דקאמר התם דכי אזיל מלווינא ליה סעודה בהדיה דכי אזיל לאו בריקן אזיל וא"כ למה נותנין לו שתי סעודות די לו בסעודה אחת ההיא סעודה דאיכא בהדיה יאכל מיד וסעודה שנותנין לו עכשיו יוליכנו עמו ונראה לר"י דאין מחלקין תמחוי בלילה לפי שאין יכולין להבחין למי נתנו ולמי לא נתנו וכן משמע מדקאמר לן נותנים לו פרנסת לינה ומפרש דהיינו פוריא ובי סדיא אבל ככר אין נותנין לו ולכך נותנין לו ב' סעודות שיאכל אחת בלילה ואחת למחר (ה) דכי אזיל לאו בריקן אזיל וטעמא דבעינן שלא ילך ריקם דאינו דומה מי שיש לו פת בסלו למי שאין לו ולא יהא רעב כל כך אבל אין לפרש דהטעם שמא לא יגיע בין היהודים ויהא לו מה לאכול דאי חיישינן להכי היה ליתן לו שלש סעודות כי גם בלילה לא יתנו אף כשיגיע בין היהודים שאין מחלקין תמחוי בלילה ואין לומר דלעולם מחלקין ולכך נותנין שתים דחיישינן שמא לא יגיע בין היהודים שתי פעמים אי נמי לא חיישינן אלא לפעם אחת והשניה נותנין לו כדי שיהא לו פת בסלו דאם כן היכי קאמר התם דמלוינן ליה סעודה אחת בהדיה ואם יש לחוש שמא לא יגיע בין היהודים היה לו ליתן שתים לכך נראה כדפרישית: שבת נותנין לו מזון שלש סעודות. פירוש בשבת בצהרים (ו) אותן שתי סעודות שנתן לו אתמול בערב שבת אכל ליל שבת ושבת שחרית ושלש סעודות שנותנים לו בשבת יאכל אחת בשבת בסעודה שלישית ואחת למוצאי שבת ושלישית ישאר לו למחר בדרך שלא ילך ריקם ואין להאריך וקשה לרשב"א הא דתנן במסכת פאה (פ"ח מ"ז) ומייתי לה בפרק כל כתבי (שבת דף קיח. ושם) מי שיש לו מזון שתי סעודות בביתו לא יטול מן התמחוי ואמאי הא לאחד יאכל מיד ואחד בלילה וא"כ כי אזיל ריקם אזיל וצריך לפרש דמזון שתי סעודות דקאמר היינו בלא אותה שיש לו לאכול מיד וא"ת שבת מאי נותנין לו שלש סעודות והא הך מתני' ר"ע היא דקתני רישא כל מי שיש לו מזון י"ד סעודות לא יטול מן הקופה ופריך בפרק כל כתבי הקדש (שם) מני אי רבנן תמני סרי הוין ואי רבי חדקא שיתסר הוין ומשני הוין מני ר"ע היא דאמר עשה שבתך חול ונראה לרשב"א דבשביל סעודת שבת אין לו להתחיל וליטול אבל בשביל שצריך ליטול נוטל גם כדי לסעודת שבת: לא אזדקיק ליה. רב פפא גבאי היה ולא נתן לו מן הקופה דתניא אין נותנין לו מן הקופה כיון שמחזר על הפתחים וא"ל רב סמא אי מר לא אזדקיק ליה לתת לו מן הקופה (ז) היינו כדי סעודה כ"ש שגם אחרים לא יתנו לו ומסיק הא דתניא דאין נזקקין לו מן הקופה היינו כדי סעודה אבל דבר מועט יתנו לו: שנאמר והעמדנו עלינו מצות. ואע"ג דהאי קרא גבי בית אלהינו כתיב דהיינו בדק הבית כ"ש לצדקה:

מנין

מסורת הש"ס

א) [ברכות ד: וש"נ], ב) [בכל הספרים מדויקים כתיב פרוס ולכאורה היא פליאה וצריכין ליישב ע"פ מ"ש תוס' שבת נה: ד"ה מעבירים כתיב ועיין במהרש"א בח"א שעמד על פליאה זו ונכנס לשטות דבוק בשיורי הגירסא קלת שלא במקומו ד"ה הלא פרוש בשי"ן כתיב], ג) פאה פ"ח מ"ז שבת קיח., ד) [תוספ' פאה פ"ד], ה) כ"ל אמר מר עוקבא כו', ו) ת"א לפרוסה. רש"ל:

הגהות הב"ח

(א) גמ' הנהו טבחי כל"ל ותיבת בי תרי נמחק: (ב) שם לימות ואמר ליה והא תניא אם היה: (ג) רש"י ד"ה שאין ראיה וכו' הנותנים לעושי המלאכה כל"ל ותיבת לבם נמחק: (ד) ד"ה עולא וכו' שגרס לה להטות דרכם וכו' נשים להטותה כדלקמן: (ה) תוס' ד"ה אין פוחתין וכו' ואחת למחר שילך לא אזיל לאו: (ו) ד"ה שבת וכו' בצהרים כי אותן: (ז) ד"ה לא וכו' לתת לו מן הקופה כ"ש שגם אחרים כל"ל ותיבות היינו כדי סעודה נמחק:

תורה אור השלם

א) וְלֹא יְחַשְּׁבוּ אֶת הָאֲנָשִׁים אֲשֶׁר יִתְּנוּ אֶת הַכֶּסֶף עַל יָדָם לָתֵת לְעֹשֵׂי הַמְּלָאכָה כִּי בֶאֱמֻנָה הֵם עֹשִׂים: [מלכים ב יב, טז]

ב) וַיְהִי כִּרְאוֹתָם כִּי רַב הַכֶּסֶף בָּאָרוֹן וַיַּעַל סֹפֵר הַמֶּלֶךְ וְהַכֹּהֵן הַגָּדוֹל וַיָּצֻרוּ וַיִּמְנוּ אֶת הַכֶּסֶף הַנִּמְצָא בֵית יְיָ: [מלכים ב יב, יא]

ג) הֲלוֹא פָרֹס לָרָעֵב לַחְמֶךָ וַעֲנִיִּים מְרוּדִים תָּבִיא בָיִת כִּי תִרְאֶה עָרֹם וְכִסִּיתוֹ וּמִבְּשָׂרְךָ לֹא תִתְעַלָּם: [ישעיה נח, ז]

ד) וְהֶעֱמַדְנוּ עָלֵינוּ מִצְוֹת לָתֵת עָלֵינוּ שְׁלִשִׁית הַשֶּׁקֶל בַּשָּׁנָה לַעֲבֹדַת בֵּית אֱלֹהֵינוּ: [נחמיה י, לג]

ה) וְהָיָה מַעֲשֵׂה הַצְּדָקָה שָׁלוֹם וַעֲבֹדַת הַצְּדָקָה הַשְׁקֵט וָבֶטַח עַד עוֹלָם: [ישעיה לב, יז]

ו) תַּחַת הַנְּחֹשֶׁת אָבִיא זָהָב וְתַחַת הַבַּרְזֶל אָבִיא כֶסֶף וְתַחַת הָעֵצִים נְחֹשֶׁת וְתַחַת הָאֲבָנִים בַּרְזֶל וְשַׂמְתִּי פְקֻדָּתֵךְ שָׁלוֹם וְנֹגְשַׂיִךְ צְדָקָה: [ישעיה ס, יז]

לעזי רש"י

קונפלייני"ש. פירוש נאנקים (על צרתם) (רש"י ישעיה נח, ז).

ליקוטי רש"י

ולא יחשבו את האנשים. לא היו המלכרכין באין לחשבון עם האנשים אשר יתנו את הכסף על ידם לתת לעושי המלאכה לפי שלא היו חשודים בעיניהם כי באמונה הם עושים [מלכים ב, יב, טז]. אין פוחתין לעני העובר ממקום למקום. מככר. הלקוח בפונדיון כשהחטין נמכרות ארבע סאין בסלע והפונדיון אחד מארבעים ושמונה בסלע ונמצא מגיע חצי קב לפונדיון ומחצה לחנוני [שבת קיח.]. לן נותנין לו פרנסת לינה. לקמן מפרש פרנסת לינה. בי סדיא. כר [שם]. שבת. שלש סעודות [שם]. ועניים מרודים. נאנקים על צרתם כגון עני ומרודי (איכה ג) אריד בשיחי (תהלים נה) [ישעיה נח, ז].

עין משפט נר מצוה

עט א מיי' פ"ד מהל' מכירה הלכה יא סמג לאוין קע טוש"ע ח"מ סי' רלא סעיף כח וטוש"ע י"ד סי' רנו סעיף ד:

פ ב מיי' פ"ט מהלכות מתנות עניים הל' יא סמג עשין קסב טוש"ע י"ד סי' רנז סעיף ג:

פא ג מיי' שם פ"ז הל' ו סמג שם טוש"ע י"ד סי' רנא סעיף י:

פב ד ה מיי' שם פ"ז הל' ח סמג שם טוש"ע י"ד סי' רנ סעיף ג:

פג ו מיי' שם הל' ז טוש"ע שם סעיף ג:

פד ז מיי' שם הל' ח סמג שם טוש"ע י"ד סי' רמט סעיף ג:

פה ח מיי' שם פ"י הל' ו סמג עשין קסב טוש"ע שם סעיף ה:

רבינו גרשום

ואתני. אם יצטרכו לעניי העיר שיהיו לעניי העיר ואם לאו שיחזרו על עניי העיר שיהיו לעניי כל אדם: דכל דאתי למיתן צדקה אדעתא דידי אתיא. כל מי שנותן לי על דעת כן נותן לי שאני אתנן לכל עני שארצה משום דרב אשי היה אדם גדול והיה יודע מה הוא עושה: [הנהו בי תרי טבחי]. התנו ביניהן שכל א' מהן ישחוט ביומו: קרעוה למשכיה. דחיותא: וחייביה רבא לשלם. דמי העור שקרעו: ולהסיע על קיצתן. והלא רשאין לקנוס כל מי שעבר על תנאן: הני מילי. דיכולין להתנות ולהסיע על קיצתן: היכא דליכא אדם חשוב. להתנות לפניו: אבל אי איכא אדם חשוב. ולא אתנו קמיה לאו תנאיהו תנאה ואיכא דאמר היכא דליכא אדם חשוב עביד איניש דינא לנפשיה אבל אי איכא אדם חשוב בעי למיקם ליה בדינא קמיה: אין מחשבין בצדקה עם הגבאין. מה גבו ומה נתנו דאין צריך לחשדן: אע"פ שאין ראיה לדבר זכר לדבר. גבי גבאי צדקה זכר לדבר ממקדש שנא' (מ"ב כב) אך לא יחשב וגו' אבל גבי גזברין של הקדש הוי ראיה גמורה: יצור. בעה"ב בקשר ובחותם וימנה דכתיב ויצורו וימנו כלומר אע"ג דהגזברין היו נאמנין אף על פי כן הגזברין עצמן היו צרין ומונין: בודקין למזונות. שאם אמר עני תנו לי מזונות בודקין אחריו קודם שיתנו לו אם רמאי הוא אם לאו: ואין בודקין לכסות. שאם בא עני ערום ואמר כסוני אין בודקין אחריו אלא נותנין לו מיד: פרוש כתיב. כלומר צריך אתה לידע בפירוש אם צריך ואם לאו: [פרוס] לאלתר. (פרוש) [פרוס] הלחם ותן לו: לכשיראה לך. שהוא צריך כשתבדוק אחריו: העובר ממקום למקום. שאין לו אלא דרך עברה עובר: מככר בפונדיון. ככר שקונין בפונדיון כשנותנין ד' סאין בסלע כיצד בסלע הם מ"ח פונדיונות דסלע ד' דינר דינר שש מעות מעה ב' פונדיונות נמצא מ"ח פונדיונות בסלע וכיצד הוי חצי קב בפונדיון כיון אחד מ"ח בד' [סאין] דסאה ו' קבים נמצא כ"ד קבין שהם מ"ח חצאי קבין בסלע שהוא מ"ח פונדיונות ושיערו חכמים דבהם איכא ליה ב' סעודות א' לכאן וא' קודם שיגיע לישוב: פוריא ובי סדיא. כר וכסת: אין נזקקין לתת לו. מכיס של צדקה: דהואיל ומחזר [ומחזר] הפתח הכל נותנין לו וא"צ ליטול מכיס של צדקה: משליש שקל. בצדקה: לעבודת אלהינו. דהיינו צדקה: מצות. הרבה משמע: א) ועבודת [הצדקה]. מעשה הוא: עכשיו באין וכו'. ודאי אין לו לעובדי כוכבים או לצדקה: אם זכה הלא פרוש לרעב שיתנו לעניים אם לא זכה ליתנו לעניים לעובדי כוכבים בשביל שהוא חייב לתת לעניים: באים [עניים] מרודים כלומר עובדי כוכבים ההורדים לביתו ונוטלות בזרוע: ונוגשיך צדקה. מה שתתן לנוגשיך: עולא. עלם אחד כמו עול [ימים] לא היה שמו עולא אלא (אחד בלי) [אחדברי]:

חשק שלמה על רבינו גרשום

א) [רבינו מפרש דקרא] במעשה הצדקה ועבודת הצדקה וגו' וצ"ל כפירש"י:

Rav Assi now interprets the verse homiletically:
וְאָמַר רַב אַסִּי — And Rav Assi also **said:** **שְׁקוּלָה צְדָקָה כְּנֶגֶד כָּל הַמִּצְוֹת — The** commandment of giving **charity is equivalent to all** the other **commandments combined,** **שֶׁנֶּאֱמַר— for it is stated** in the previously mentioned verse: ,,וְהֶעֱמַדְנוּ עָלֵינוּ מִצְוֹת וגו׳ " — ***And we took upon ourselves commandments etc.*** מִצְוָה אֵין כְּתִיב כָּאן — **"Commandment"** in the singular form **is not written here;** אֶלָּא מִצְוֹת — **rather,** the plural **"commandments"** is written, to teach that the mitzvah of charity[36] is equivalent to all the other mitzvos.[37]

The Gemara prefaces three homiletic statements by R' Elazar with a mnemonic device:
(סִימָן גָּדוֹל מִקְדָּשׁ מֹשֶׁה) — **(A mnemonic — Greater, Sanctuary, Moses)** Each of the above is a key word in one of the three statements.

The first of R' Elazar's statements:
אָמַר רַבִּי אֶלְעָזָר גָּדוֹל הַמְעַשֶּׂה יוֹתֵר מִן הָעוֹשֶׂה — R' Elazar said: The one who causes the performance of charitable deeds **is greater than the one who** actually **performs** the deed, since often much effort must be expended to convince others to assist in charitable works.

R' Elazar adduces support for his statement:
שֶׁנֶּאֱמַר: ,,וְהָיָה מַעֲשֵׂה הַצְּדָקָה שָׁלוֹם וַעֲבֹדַת הַצְּדָקָה הַשְׁקֵט וָבֶטַח עַד־עוֹלָם" — **For it is stated:**[38] ***And it will be that the act of charity*** (will bring) ***peace; and the work of charity*** (will cause) ***everlasting tranquility and security.***[39]

R' Elazar adds a warning to those who do not give charity:
זָכָה — If [a person] merits good fortune, he will give money that Heaven decrees he must lose to needy people, as Scripture says:[40] ,,הֲלוֹא פָרֹשׂ לָרָעֵב לַחְמֶךָ" — ***You will break your bread for the hungry.*** **לֹא זָכָה — If he does not merit** good fortune, ,,וַעֲנִיִּים מְרוּדִים תָּבִיא בָיִת" — then ***wailing poor will come to his house.***[41] The Roman government, which constantly cries out that it is in need of funds, will come and confiscate that money, which could have been given as charity, so that its owner will derive no benefit from it.

Rava, who was the Rabbi of Mechuza, urged his community to be mindful of this warning:
אָמַר לְהוּ רָבָא לִבְנֵי מְחוֹזָא — Rava said to the inhabitants of Mechuza:[42] **בְּמָטוּתָא מִינַּייכוּ — I beg of you,** **עוּשׂוּ בַּהֲדֵי הֲדָדֵי — do** charitable acts **amongst yourselves,** **כִּי הֵיכִי דְּלֶיהֱוֵי לְכוּ שְׁלָמָא בְּמַלְכוּתָא — so that you will have peaceful relations with the** gentile **government,** i.e. so that the authorities will not confiscate your money.

The Gemara presents R' Elazar's second statement regarding charity:
וְאָמַר רַבִּי אֶלְעָזָר — And R' Elazar also **said:** **בִּזְמַן שֶׁבֵּית הַמִּקְדָּשׁ קַיָּים — At the time the Holy Temple stood,** **אָדָם שׁוֹקֵל שִׁקְלוֹ וּמִתְכַּפֵּר לוֹ — a person would donate his *shekel***[43] for the daily sacrifices, which were offered on behalf of the entire Jewish nation, **and would gain atonement.** **עַכְשָׁיו שֶׁאֵין בֵּית הַמִּקְדָּשׁ קַיָּים** — However, **now that the Holy Temple is no** longer **standing,** **אִם עוֹשִׂין צְדָקָה מוּטָב — if [people] perform** acts of **charity all will be well,** for these selfless deeds will atone for their sins.[44] **וְאִם לָאו — But if** they do **not** perform charitable deeds, **בָּאִין עוֹבְדֵי כּוֹכָבִים וְנוֹטְלִין בִּזְרוֹעַ — the idolaters will come and take by force** funds that should have been donated to charity; **וְאַף עַל פִּי כֵן נֶחְשָׁב לָהֶן לִצְדָקָה — and even so, [these confiscated assets] will be regarded for their [sakes] as** contributions to **charity,**[45] שֶׁנֶּאֱמַר: ,,וְנֹגְשַׂיִךְ צְדָקָה" — **as it says:**[46] ***And I shall make*** ***your taskmasters charity.*** God promises that after the Final Redemption He will regard all Jewish property confiscated by their gentile taskmasters as donations to charity.

Rava relates another homily on the subject of charity:
אָמַר רָבָא הַאי מִילְּתָא אִישְׁתָּעֵי לִי עוּלָּא — Rava said: This matter was mentioned to me by the child[47]

NOTES

services, Rav Assi regarded donations to charity as being more analogous to the *one-third shekel* contribution to *bedek habayis*, the Temple maintenance fund — inasmuch as the sanctity of *bedek habayis*, which could be removed by an act of פִּדְיוֹן, *redemption*, was less than the sanctity of the animal sacrifices, which were intrinsically and irrevocably holy. Hence, Rav Assi set the minimum yearly charity requirement at one-third, rather than one-half, of a *shekel* (*Maharsha*).

However, see *Ritva,* who writes that the verse indeed refers to the Biblical half-*shekel,* which in the time of Nehemiah was valued at one-third of a *shekel.*

36. *Tosafos* note that this verse does not concern donations for the poor, but for the upkeep of the Temple, as the end of the verse explicitly states. Nevertheless, since supporting the needy is more commendable than donating to the Temple [which itself is equated to all the mitzvos], then certainly giving charity is equivalent to performing all the mitzvos.

37. The commentators offer various explanations of this teaching. *Ben Yehoyada* writes that with a gift of charity one can revive a starving or critically ill pauper, and thereby share in the merit of all the many and tremendous mitzvos of the Torah that the pauper will perform during the remaining years of his life, which the donor made possible. See *Maharsha* and *Maharal* for other interpretations.

38. *Isaiah* 32:17.

39. The word מַעֲשֵׂה *(act of)* is superfluous, since Scripture could have stated simply: "... *and charity* (הַצְּדָקָה) *will bring peace.*" R' Elazar therefore expounds homiletically that the verse refers to מְעַשֵּׂה הַצְּדָקָה — *those who effectuate the performance of charity* (*Rashi*). Thus, since genuine peace is a greater blessing than tranquility or security (*Ritva, Maharsha*), R' Elazar derives from here that one who motivates another to perform an act of charity is the greater of the two. Cf. *Rabbeinu Gershom, Malbim.*

40. *Isaiah* 58:7.

41. This is a continuation of the verse just mentioned. The simple translation of עֲנִיִּים מְרוּדִים is *suffering poor* (as in זְכָר־עָנְיִי וּמְרוּדִי, *Eichah* 3:19). However, R' Elazar translates מְרוּדִים as *wailing*, and understands that the verse refers to the Roman government (see *Rashi*).

42. Mechuza was a wealthy city (see *Bava Kamma* 119a). Hence, Rava worried that its residents would be lax in performing the mitzvah of charity, and not give as much as they should.

43. Although under Biblical law the required annual donation to the Temple was only a half-*shekel,* in the currency used for sacred (Temple) purposes the coins were doubled in size (see below, 90b). Thus, a half-*shekel* in Temple currency equaled one *shekel* in common currency. Alternatively, the term *shekel* was used when referring to the coin that was contributed, even when it was actually only a half-*shekel* (see *Ramban, Exodus* 30:13)

44. Just as the consumption of animal sacrifices on the Altar effected atonement for the people during the Temple era, so afterward the consumption of food by the poor (i.e. their deriving benefit from charity) will effect atonement for the donors (*Maharsha*).

45. Since the idolaters collect taxes from the rich and then do not bother to collect from the poor (*Maharsha*). This, also, is a form of charity (cf. *Meiri*).

46. *Isaiah* 60:17.

47. עוּלָּא derives from עוֹלֵל, *child* (*Rashi*).

ואתני עלה איהו נמי עבד חד כיסא ואתני עלה רב אשי אמר אנא אתנויי נמי לא צריכנא דכל דקא אתי אדעתא דידי אתי ולמאן דבעינא יהיבנא ליה הנהו (א) בי תרי טבחי דעבדי עניינא בהדי הדדי דכל מאן דעביד ביומא דחבריה נקרעוה למשכיה אזל חד מנייהו עבד ביומא דחבריה קרעו למשכיה אתו לקמיה דרבא חייבינהו רבא לשלומי איתיביה רב יימר בר שלמיא לרבא ולהסיע על קיצתם לא אהדר ליה רבא אמר רב פפא שפיר עבד דלא אהדר ליה מידי א ה"מ היכא דליכא אדם חשוב אבל היכא דאיכא אדם חשוב לאו כל כמיניהו דמתנו ת"ר ב אין מחשבין בצדקה עם גבאי צדקה ולא בהקדש עם הגזברין ואע"פ שאין ראיה לדבר זכר לדבר שנאמר א ולא יחשבו את האנשים אשר יתנו את הכסף על ידם לתת לעושי המלאכה כי באמונה הם עושים א"ר אלעזר אע"פ שיש לו לאדם גזבר נאמן בתוך ביתו יצור וימנה שנאמר ב ויצורו וימנו אמר רב הונא בודקין למזונות ואין בודקין לכסות ו אי בעית אימא קרא ואי בעית אימא סברא אב"א סברא האי קא מבזי והאי לא קא מבזי אי בעית אימא קרא ג הלא ג פרוש לרעב לחמך בשי"ן כתיב פרוש והדר הב ליה והתם כתיב ג כי תראה ערום וכסיתו כי תראה לאלתר ורב יהודה אמר ג בודקין לכסות ואין בודקין למזונות אי בעית אימא סברא ואי בעית אימא קרא אי בעית אימא סברא האי קמצערא ליה והאי לא קמצערא ליה אי בעית אימא קרא הכא כתיב הלא פרוס לרעב לחמך פרוס לאלתר וכדקרינן והתם כתיב כי תראה ערום וכסיתו כשיראה לך תניא כוותיה דרב יהודה אמר כסוני בודקין אחריו פרנסוני אין בודקין ג תנן התם ד אין פוחתין לעני העובר ממקום למקום מככר בפונדיון מארבע סאין בסלע לן נותנין לו פרנסת לינה מאי פרנסת לינה אמר רב פפא ה פוריא ובי סדיא שבת נותנין לו מזון שלש סעודות תנא ו אם היה מחזיר על הפתחים אין נזקקין לו ההוא עניא דהוה מחזיר על הפתחים דאתא לקמיה דרב פפא לא מזדקיק ליה א"ל רב סמא בריה דרב ייבא לרב פפא אי מר לא מזדקיק ליה אינש אחרינא לא מזדקיק ליה לימות (ג) ליה והא תניא אם היה עני המחזיר על הפתחים אין נזקקין לו א"ל ז אין נזקקין לו למתנה מרובה אבל נזקקין לו למתנה מועטת אמר רב אסי ח לעולם אל ימנע אדם עצמו [מלתת] שלישית השקל בשנה שנא' ד והעמדנו עלינו מצות לתת עלינו שלישית השקל בשנה לעבודת בית אלהינו ואמר רב אסי שקולה צדקה כנגד כל המצות שנאמר והעמדנו עלינו מצות וגו' מצוה אין כתיב כאן אלא מצות (סימן גדול מקדש משה) א"ר אלעזר ח גדול המעשה יותר מן העושה שנאמר ה והיה מעשה הצדקה שלום ועבודת הצדקה השקט ובטח עד עולם זכה הלא פרוש לרעב לחמך לא זכה ועניים מרודים תביא בית אמר להו רבא לבני מחוזא במטותא מנייכו עושו בהדי הדדי כי היכי דליהוי לכו שלמא במלכותא וא"ר אלעזר בזמן שבהמ"ק קיים אדם שוקל שקלו ומתכפר לו עכשיו שאין בהמ"ק קיים אם עושין צדקה מוטב ואם לאו באין עובדי כוכבים ונוטלין בזרוע ט ואעפ"כ נחשב להן לצדקה שנא' ו ונוגשיך צדקה אמר רבא האי מילתא אישתעי לי עולא

רש"י

ואתני. מתנה עם הצבור לחלקם לכל הבא: דכל דאתי. לתת מעות לקופה: עניינא. תנאי: למשכיה. עור הבהמה: לאו כל כמיניהו דמתנו. אלא בפניו. לומר היכן נתתם מעות שגביתם: שאין ראיה לדבר. דלא בגבאי צדקה כתיב אלא בגזברי הקדש הטוענים (ג) לבא לעושי המלאכה שהפועלים מרובין למלאכות הרבה לגודרין ולחוצבי האבן לכתפים ולחמרים ולקנות עצים ואבני מזבח וא"א לעמוד על החשבון כדאמרינן בעלמא (שבועות דף מה.) בעל הבית טרוד בפועליו הוא ואינשי: יצור וימנה. הכסף שהוא מוסר בידו ואע"פ שאינו בא עמו לחשבון לאחר מכאן יצור וימנה שנאמר ויצורו וימנו וגו' ויהבו ונתנו את הכסף המתוכן המנוי על ידי עושי המלאכה וגו': בודקין למזונות. אם בא עני ואמר פרנסוני בודקין שלא יהיה רמאי: ואין בודקין לכסות. בא ערום ואמר כסוני לוקחין כסות מיד: פרוש. דרוש וחקור תחלה: לכשיראה לך. שאינו רמאי: מככר בפונדיון. ככר הלקוח בפונדיון כשלוקחין ארבע סאין חטין בסלע ומגיע לפונדיון חצי קב שהסלע מ"ח פונדיונין וארבע סאין מ"ח חצאי קבין והחנוני שהוא טוחן ואופה ומוכר בשוק משתכר מחצה הרי שנותן ככר של רובע הקב בפונדיון: לן. בלילה: פרנסת לינה. צרכי לינה: בי סדיא. כר לתת מראשותיו: אין נזקקין לו. לתת מעות מן הקופה אחרי שלמד לחזר על הפתחים דיו בכך: ולא אזדקיק ליה. אפי' לפרנסה: מעשה הצדקה. טורח המעשים את אחרים מעלה כתיב והיתה הצדקה שלום: זכה. למזל טוב: ועניים מרודים. זו ממשלת רומי שצועקת תמיד הבו הבו שאנו צריכין: מרודים. קונפליינ"ט בלע"ז: שלא משגש ארחתיה (תהלים) דאימיה. לרב ששת קרו ליה הכי עולא המשגש דרכי אמו שגרס (ד) להטומאה מלדך אשר נשים כדלקמן:

תוספות

ואע"פ שאין ראיה לדבר זכר לדבר. ראיה גמורה אינה דשאני התם שהיו צדיקים גמורים: אין פוחתין לעני העובר ממקום למקום מככר בפונדיון כו'. הככר עולה ששה ביצים דלא מהן מתלה לחנוני והוא מזון שתי סעודות כדתניא בפרק כיצד משתתפין (עירובין דף פב:) וקשה לר"י דבפרק כל כתבי (שבת דף קיח. ושם) משמע שהוא לרגילות דאיכא סעודה בהדיה דקאמר התם דכי אזיל מלווינא ליה סעודה בהדיה דכי אזיל לאו בריקן אזיל וא"כ למה נותנין לו שתי סעודות די לו בסעודה אחת ההיא סעודה דאיכא בהדיה יאכל מיד וסעודה שנותנין לו עכשיו יוליכנו עמו ונראה לר"י דאין מחלקין תמחוי בלילה לפי שאין יכולין להבחין למי נתנו ולמי לא נתנו וכן משמע מדקאמר לן נותנים לו פרנסת לינה ומפרש דהיינו פוריא ובי סדיא אבל ככר אין נותנין לו ולכך נותנין לו ב' סעודות שיאכל אחת בלילה ואחת למחר (ה) דכי אזיל לאו בריקן אזיל וטעמא דבעינן שלא ילך ריקם דאינו דומה מי שיש לו פת בסלו למי שאין לו ולא יהא רעב כל כך אבל אין לפרש דהטעם שמא לא יגיע בין היהודים ויהא לו מה לאכול דאי חיישינן להכי היה ליתן לו שלש סעודות כי גם בלילה לא יתנו לו אף כשיגיע בין היהודים שאין מחלקין תמחוי בלילה ואין לומר דלעולם מחלקין ולכך נותנין שתים דחיישינן שמא לא יגיע בין היהודים שתי פעמים אי נמי לא חיישינן אלא לפעם אחת והשניה נותנין לו כדי שיהא לו פת בסלו דאם כן היכי קאמר התם דמלוינן ליה סעודה אחת בהדיה ואם יש לחוש שמא לא יגיע בין היהודים היה לו ליתן שתים לכך נראה כדפרישית: שבת נותנין לו מזון שלש סעודות. פירוש בשבת בצהרים (ו) אותן שתי סעודות שנתן לו אתמול בערב שבת אכל ליל שבת ושבת שחרית ושלש סעודות שנותנים לו בשבת יאכל אחת בשבת בסעודה שלישית ואחת למוצאי שבת ושלישית ישאר לו למחר בדרך שלא ילך ריקם ואין להאריך וקשה לרשב"א הא דתנן במסכת פאה (פ"ח מ"ז) ומייתי לה בפרק כל כתבי (שבת דף קיח. ושם) מי שיש לו מזון שתי סעודות בביתו לא יטול מן התמחוי ואמאי הא אחד יאכל מיד ואחד בלילה וא"כ כי אזיל ריקם אזיל וצריך לפרש דמזון שתי סעודות דקאמר היינו בלא אותה שיש לו לאכול מיד וא"ת שבת אמאי נותנין לו שלש סעודות והא הך מתני' ר"ע היא דקתני רישא כל מי שיש לו מזון י"ד סעודות לא יטול מן הקופה ופריך בפרק כל כתבי הקדש (שם) מני אי רבנן חמיסר הוין אי רבי חדקא שיתסר הוין ומשני הא מני ר"ע היא דאמר עשה שבתך חול ונראה לרשב"א דבשביל סעודת שבת אין לו להתחיל וליטול אבל בשכבר צריך ליטול נוטל גם כדי לסעודת שבת: לא אזדקיק ליה. רב פפא גבאי היה ולא נתן לו מן הקופה כדתניא אין נותנין לו מן הקופה כיון שמחזר על הפתחים וא"ל רב סמא אי מר לא אזדקיק ליה לתת לו מן הקופה (ז) היינו כדי סעודה כ"ש שגם אחרים לא יתנו לו ומסיק הא דתניא אין נזקקין לו מן הקופה היינו כדי סעודה אבל דבר מועט יתנו לו: שנאמר והעמדנו עלינו מצות. ואע"ג דהאי קרא גבי בית אלהינו כתיב דהיינו בדק הבית כ"ש לצדקה:

מנין

מסורת הש"ס

א) [ברכות ד: וש"נ], ב) [בכל הספרים מדויקים כתיב פרוס ולכאורה היא פליאה וצריכין ליישב ע"פ מ"ש תוס' שבת נה: ד"ה מעבירים כתיב ועיין במהרש"א בח"א שעמד על פליאה זו ונכנס לשנות בדוחק בשינוי הגירסא קצת שלא במקומו ד"ה הלא פרוש בשי"ן כתיב], ג) פאה פ"ח מ"ז שבת קיח., ד) [תוספ' פאה פ"ד], ה) נ"א אמר מר עוקבא כו', ו) ס"א לפרוסה. רש"ל:

הגהות הב"ח

(א) גמ' הנהו טבחי כצ"ל ותיבת בי תרי נמחק: (ב) שם לימות אמר ליה והא תניא אם היה: (ג) רש"י ד"ה שאין ראיה וכו' הנותנים לעושי המלאכה כצ"ל ותיבת לבס נמחק: (ד) ד"ה עולא וכו' שגרס לה להטות וכו' נשים להתבזות כדלקמן: (ה) תוס' ד"ה אין פוחתין וכו' ואחת למחר כשילך דכי אזיל לאו: (ו) ד"ה שבת וכו' בצהרים כי אותן: (ז) ד"ה לא וכו' לתת לו מן הקופה כ"ש שגם אחרים כצ"ל ותיבות היינו כדי סעודה נמחק:

תורה אור השלם

א) וְלֹא יְחַשְּׁבוּ אֶת הָאֲנָשִׁים אֲשֶׁר יִתְּנוּ אֶת הַכֶּסֶף עַל יָדָם לָתֵת לְעֹשֵׂי הַמְּלָאכָה כִּי בֶאֱמֻנָה הֵם עֹשִׂים: [מלכים ב יב, טז]

ב) וַיְהִי כִּרְאוֹתָם כִּי רַב הַכֶּסֶף בָּאָרוֹן וַיַּעַל סֹפֵר הַמֶּלֶךְ וְהַכֹּהֵן הַגָּדוֹל וַיָּצֻרוּ וַיִּמְנוּ אֶת הַכֶּסֶף הַנִּמְצָא בֵית יְיָ: [מלכים ב יב, יא]

ג) הֲלוֹא פָרֹס לָרָעֵב לַחְמֶךָ וַעֲנִיִּים מְרוּדִים תָּבִיא בָיִת כִּי תִרְאֶה עָרֹם וְכִסִּיתוֹ וּמִבְּשָׂרְךָ לֹא תִתְעַלָּם: [ישעיה נח, ז]

ד) וְהֶעֱמַדְנוּ עָלֵינוּ מִצְוֹת לָתֵת עָלֵינוּ שְׁלִשִׁית הַשֶּׁקֶל בַּשָּׁנָה לַעֲבֹדַת בֵּית אֱלֹהֵינוּ: [נחמיה י, לג]

ה) וְהָיָה מַעֲשֵׂה הַצְּדָקָה שָׁלוֹם וַעֲבֹדַת הַצְּדָקָה הַשְׁקֵט וָבֶטַח עַד עוֹלָם: [ישעיה לב, יז]

ו) תַּחַת הַנְּחֹשֶׁת אָבִיא זָהָב וְתַחַת הַבַּרְזֶל אָבִיא כֶסֶף וְתַחַת הָעֵצִים נְחֹשֶׁת וְתַחַת הָאֲבָנִים בַּרְזֶל וְשַׂמְתִּי פְקֻדָּתֵךְ שָׁלוֹם וְנֹגְשַׂיִךְ צְדָקָה: [ישעיה ס, יז]

לעזי רש"י

קונפליינ"ט. פירוש נאנקים ונאנחים (על צרתם) (רש"י ישעיה נח, ז):

ליקוטי רש"י

ולא יחשבו את האנשים וגו'. לא היו המרכלין באין לחשבון עם האנשים הגזברין אשר יתנו המרכלין את הכסף תמיד על ידם לתתו לעושי המלאכה לפי שלא היו חשודים בעיניהם כי באמונה הם עושים [מלכים ב, יב, טז]. אין פוחתין לעני העובר ממקום למקום. שאינו לן בלילה אצלם. מככר. הלקוח בפונדיון כשהשער ארבע סאין בסלע והפונדיון אחד משנים עשר בדינר דהוא אחד מארבעים ושמונה בסלע ושיערו לו חכמים ככר זו לשתי סעודות היום והלילה. לן נותנין לו פרנסת לינה. לקמן מפרש מאי היא שהרי סעודה של לילה בכלל כיכר היא וככר זו משערינן בעירובין (פב:) למזון שתי סעודות לעירובי תחומין. מאי פרנסת לינה. הא קבל ליה סעודת הלילה. בי סדיא. לבדין פולטר"א להניח תחת מראשותיו [שבת קיח.]. לבדין שקורין פלטר"ש ועשויין לקפלן תחתיו במקום הכר או הכסת [שם קמו:]. שבת. אלגס בשבת [שם קיח.]. ועניים מרודים. נאנחים ונאנקים על צרתם כגון עניי ומרודי (איכה ג) אריד בשיחי (תהלים נה) [ישעיה נח, ז].

עין משפט נר מצוה

עט א מיי' פי"ד מהל' מכירה הלכה יא סמג לאוין קע טוש"ע ח"מ סי' רלא סעיף כח וטוש"ע י"ד סי' רנו סעיף ד:
פ ב מיי' פ"ט מהלכות מתנות עניים הל' יא סמג עשין קסב טוש"ע י"ד סי' רנז סעיף ב:
פא ג מיי' שם פ"ז הל' ו סמג שם טוש"ע י"ד סי' רנא סעיף י:
פב ד ה מיי' שם הל' ח סמג שם טוש"ע י"ד סי' רנ סעיף ד:
פג ו מיי' שם הל' ז טוש"ע שם סעיף ג:
פד ז מיי' שם הל' ה סמג שם טוש"ע י"ד סי' רמט סעיף ב:
פה ח מיי' שם פ"י הל' ו סמג עשין קסב טוש"ע שם סעיף ה:

רבינו גרשום

ואתני. אם יצטרכו לעניי העיר שיהיו לעניי העיר ואם לאו שיותירו על עניי העיר שיהיו לעניי כל אדם: דכל דאתי למיתן צדקה אדעתא דידי אתיא. כל מי שנותן לי על דעת כן נותן לי שאני אתנן לכל עני שארצה משום דרב אשי היה אדם גדול והיה יודע מה הוא עושה: [הנהו בי תרי טבחי]. התנו ביניהן שכל א' מהן ישחוט ביומו: קרעוה למשכיה. דחיותא: וחייביה רבא לשלם. דמי העור שקרע: ולהסיע על קיצתן. והלא רשאין לקנוס כל מי שעבר על תנאן: הני מילי. דיכולין להתנות ולהסיע על קיצתן: היכא דליכא אדם חשוב. להתנות לפניו: אבל אי איכא אדם חשוב. ולא אתנו קמיה לאו תנאיהו תנאה ואיכא דאמר היכא דליכא אדם חשוב עביד אינש דינא לנפשיה אבל אי איכא אדם חשוב נקיט ליה בדינא קמיה: אין מחשבין בצדקה עם הגבאין. מה גבו ומה נתנו דאין צריך לחשדן: אע"פ שאין ראיה לדבר זכר לדבר. גבי גבאי צדקה זכר לדבר ממקדש שנא' (מ"ב כב) אך לא יחשב וגו' אבל גבי גזברין של הקדש הוי ראיה גמורה: יצור. בעה"ב בקשר ובחותם וימנה דכתיב ויצורו וימנו כלומר אע"ג דהגזברין היו נאמנין אף על פי כן הגזברין עצמן היו צרין ומונין: בודקין למזונות. שאם אמר עני תנו לי מזונות בודקין אחריו קודם שיתנו לו אם רמאי הוא שאין צריך אם לאו: ואין בודקין לכסות. שאם בא עני ערום ואמר כסוני אין בודקין אחריו אלא נותנין מיד: פרוש כתיב. כלומר צריך אתה לידע בפירוש אם צריך ואם לאו: (פרוש) [פרוס] לאלתר (פרוש) [פרוס] הלחם ותן לו: לכשיראה לך. שהוא צריך כשתבדוק אחריו: העובר ממקום למקום. שאין לן אלא דרך עברה עובר: ככר בפונדיון. ככר שקונין בפונדיון כשנותנין ד' סאין בסלע דהוי ככר של חצי קב כיצד בסלע הם מ"ח פונדיונות דסלע ד' דינר ודינר שש מעות ומעה ב' פונדיונות נמצא מ"ח פונדיונות בסלע וכיצד הוי חצי קב בפונדיון דחצי קב אחד ממ"ח בד' [סאין] דסאה ו' קבים נמצא כ"ד קבין שהם מ"ח חצאי קבין בסלע שהוא מ"ח פונדיונות ושיערו חכמים דבהם אית ליה ב' סעודות א' לכאן וא' קודם שיגיע לישוב: פוריא ובי סדיא. כר וכסת: אין נזקקין לתת לו. מכיס של צדקה. דהואיל (ומחסר) [ומחזר] על הפתח הכל נותנין לו וא"צ ליטול מכיס של צדקה: משליש שקל. בצדקה: לעבודת אלהינו. דהיינו צדקה: מצות. הרבה משמע: א) ועבודת [הצדקה]. מעשה הוא: עכשיו באין וכו'. ודאי יתן או לעובדי כוכבים או לצדקה. אם זכה הלא פרוש לרעב שיתנהו לעניים אם לא זכה ליתנהו לעניים אעפ"כ יתן לעובדי כוכבים בשביל שהיה חייב לעניים. באים [עניים] מרודים כלומר עובדי כוכבים הרודים לביתו ונטלוהו בזרוע: ונוגשיך צדקה. מה שתתן לנוגשיך: עולא. עלם אחד כמו עול [ימים] לא היה שמו עולא אלא (אחד בלי) [אחדבוי]:

חשק שלמה על רבינו גרשום א) [רבינו מפרש דגדול המעשה נלמד מסיפא דקרא דכתיב ועבודת הצדקה וגו' ודלא כפירש"י]:

משגש ארחתיה דאימיה משמיה דר' אלעזר מאי דכתיב א) וילבש צדקה כשריון לומר לך מה שריון זה כל קליפה וקליפה מצטרפת לשריון גדול אף צדקה כל פרוטה ופרוטה מצטרפת לחשבון גדול רבי חנינא אמר מהכא ב) וכבגד עדים כל צדקותינו מה בגד זה כל נימא ונימא מצטרפת לבגד גדול אף צדקה כל פרוטה ופרוטה מצטרפת לחשבון גדול אמאי קרו ליה עולא משגש ארחתיה דאימיה דבעא מיניה רב אחדבוי בר אמי מרב ששת מנין למצורע בימי ספורו שמטמא אדם אמר לו הואיל ומטמא בגדים מטמא אדם א"ל דילמא טומאה בחבורים שאני דהא הסיט נבילה דמטמא בגדים ואינו מטמא אדם אמר ליה ואלא שרץ דמטמא אדם מנלן לאו משום דמטמא בגדים א"ל שרץ בהדיא כתיב ביה ג) או איש אשר יגע בכל שרץ אלא שכבת זרע דמטמא אדם מנלן לאו משום דהואיל ומטמא בגדים מטמא אדם א"ל שכבת זרע נמי בהדיא כתיב ביה ד) או איש לרבות את הנוגע אהדר ליה בבדיחותא חלש דעתיה דרב ששת אישתיק רב אחדבוי בר אמי ואתיקר תלמודיה אתיא אימיה וקא בכיא קמיה צווחה צווחה ולא אשגח בה אמרה ליה חזי להני חדיי דמצית מינייהו בעא רחמי עליה ואיתסי ודאתאן עלה מנא לן דכדתניא ר"ש בן יוחי אומר נאמר כבוס בגדים בימי ספורו ונאמר כבוס בגדים בימי חלוטו מה להלן מטמא אדם אף כאן מטמא אדם אמר רבי אלעזר גדול העושה צדקה בסתר יותר ממשה רבינו דאילו במשה רבינו כתיב ה) כי יגורתי מפני האף והחמה ואילו בעושה צדקה כתיב ו) מתן בסתר יכפה אף [ושחד בחיק חמה עזה] ופליגא דרבי יצחק דאמר ר' יצחק אף כופה חמה אינו כופה שנא' ושחד בחיק חמה עזה אע"פ ששוחד בחיק חמה עזה איכא דאמרי א"ר יצחק כל דיין שנוטל שחד מביא חמה עזה לעולם [שנאמר ושחד בחיק וגו'] ואמר רבי יצחק כל הנותן פרוטה לעני מתברך בשש ברכות והמפייסו בדברים מתברך בי"א ברכות הנותן פרוטה לעני מתברך בשש ברכות דכתיב ז) הלא פרוש וגו' ועניים מרודים תביא בית וגו' כי תראה ערום וגו' (א) והמפייסו בדברים מתברך באחת עשרה ברכות שנאמר ח) ותפק לרעב נפשך ונפש נענה תשביע וזרח בחשך אורך ואפלתך כצהרים ונחך ה' תמיד והשביע בצחצחות נפשך (ב) וגו' ובנו ממך חרבות עולם מוסדי דור ודור תקומם וגו' ואמר רבי יצחק מאי דכתיב ט) רודף צדקה וחסד ימצא חיים צדקה וכבוד משום דרודף צדקה ימצא צדקה אלא לומר לך כל הרודף אחר צדקה הקדוש ברוך הוא ממציא לו מעות ועושה בהן צדקה רב נחמן בר יצחק אמר הקדוש ברוך הוא ממציא לו בני אדם המהוגנים לעשות להן צדקה כדי לקבל עליהם (ג) שכרו לאפוקי מאי לאפוקי מדדרש רבה דדרש רבה מאי דכתיב י) ויהיו מוכשלים לפניך בעת אפך עשה בהם אמר ירמיה לפני הקדוש ברוך הוא רבונו של עולם [אפילו] בשעה שכופין את יצרן ומבקשין לעשות צדקה לפניך הכשילם בבני אדם שאינן מהוגנין כדי שלא יקבלו עליהן שכר רבי יהושע בן לוי אמר כל הרגיל לעשות צדקה (ד) זוכה הויין לו בנים בעלי חכמה בעלי עושר בעלי אגדה דכתיב

ימצא

רש"י

משגש. לשון מהומה ושגעון: קליפה. מייל"א בלע"ז: וכבגד עדים כל צדקותינו. כלומר אף כל צדקותינו נמאסו מחמת רשעינו כבגד מאוס שהאדם מסירו מעליו: עדים. כדמתרגמינן ויסר ואעדי וכן מעדה בגד ביום קרה (משלי כה) מ"מ מקיש צדקה לבגד צדקת הצדיקים לבגד הגון: בימי ספורו. בשבעת ימים שבין טהרת הצפרים להבאת קרבנותיו בשלמא בימי חלוטו איתקש למת לטמא אף באהל: הואיל ומטמא בגדים. דהא ביום השביעי כתיב וכבס בגדיו: טומאה בחבורין. כגון בגדי לבושו הרי הן כמוהו אבל שאר בגדים הנוגע בהן וכן אם יגע באדם לא מטמא תדע שהרי המסיט נבילה כתיב ביה והנושא את נבלתה יכבס בגדיו (ויקרא יא) ולא אשכחן דלהוי אב הטומאה לטמא אדם ושאר בגדים: שכבת זרע מטמא בגדים. וכל בגד וכל עור אשר יהיה עליו שכבת זרע וגו': בהדיא כתיב ביה כו'. ה"ה נמי דהוה מצי למיפרך דהא טומאת בגדים לא דמיא לבגדים דימי ספורו דהא בגדים דהכא לאו בגדי לבוש שרץ הן וטומאת מגע הוא אלא דעדיפא מיניה קא מותיב ליה: או לרבות הנוגע. דהכי תניא במסכת נדה (דף מג:) מנין לרבות הנוגע בשכבת זרע ת"ל או איש: הוה קמהדר ליה. רב אחדבוי לרב ששת בבדיחותא לפי שהיה רב ששת נכשל בתשובותיו: אשתתק רב אחדבוי. נעשה אלם: אתיא אימיה. דרב ששת: צווחה קמיה. שיתפלל עליו: להני חדיי. הדדים הללו. חדיי תרגום של חזה: דמצית מינייהו. שינקת מהן: ודאתאן עלה. ואחרי שבא לידינו שאלה זו לקובעה בגמ' מנלן דמטמא אדם: נאמר כיבוס בגדים בימי ספורו. והיה ביום השביעי יגלח את כל שערו וגו' ונאמר כיבוס בגדים למעלה ביום טהרת הצפרים כשיוצא מטומאת החלט וכבס המטהר את בגדיו: אף וחימה. שני לגיונות קשים הם ליפרע מן החוטאים: אע"פ ששוחד בחיק. שהוא עושה צדקה בסתר: חימה עזה. עדיין היא בתוקפה ורבי אלעזר סבר דהאי שוחד בחיק ארישא קאי ושוחד בחיק יכפה חימה עזה: ותפק לרעב נפשך. הוא פיוס דברי נחומים: רודף צדקה. משמע יצא לידי עניות וימצא בני אדם שיעשו לו צדקה: ויהיו מוכשלים לפניך. את אנשי ענתות היה מקלל שהיו מבקשין נפשו:

תוספות

מנין למצורע בימי ספורו שמטמא אדם. פשיטא לן דמטמא כדתנן בריש מס' כלים (פ"א מ"א) אבות הטומאות השרץ ושכבת זרע (ה) ונבלה וטמא מת ומצורע בימי ספורו כו' הרי אלו מטמאין אדם וכלים במגע וכלי חרס באויר ולכך בעי מנלן דמטמא דהא כתיב ורחץ במים וטהר משמע דבאותה טבילה נטהר: דהא הסיט נבלה מטמא בגדים ואינו מטמא אדם. (ו) לאו משום דטומאה בחבורין שאני. פ"ה דאינו מטמא אלא בגדים שהוא לבוש וקשה לריב"ס דבתורת כהנים פ' ויהי ביום השמיני (ז) מרבה שמטמא אפילו כלים (בחבורים) אע"ג דלא שייך בהו לבישה ואינו ממעט מבגדיו אלא אדם וכלי חרס שנוגע בהן אלא ודאי מטמא בגדים בשעה שמסיט אפילו אין לבוש בהן וכן משמע מדקאמר אלא מעתה שרץ דמטמא אדם מנלן לאו משום דמטמא בגדים מטמא אדם נמי כו' ואי קרי חבורים בגדים שהוא לבוש מאי פריך משרץ דלא שייך ביה לבישה התם ודאי ילפינן אדם מבגדים ונראה לריב"ס דלא גרס (ח) בחבורים אלא הכי גרס ודילמא טומאת בגדים שאני תדע דהא מסיט נבלה דמטמא בגדים ואינו מטמא אדם ולא גרסינן מ"ט לאו משום דטומאה בחבורים שאני דלא מהדר אלא שיש חילוק בין טומאת בגדים לטומאת אדם וכן משמע דאיהו גופיה לא קא מיבעיא ליה אם מטמא בגדים וכלים במגע אלא אאדם בעי:

אתיא אימיה וקא בכיא קמיה. פר"ח דהיינו אימיה דרב אחדבוי ולדידיה קרי עולא משגש אורחא דאימיה שגרם לאמו להתבזות לפני רב ששת והיא היתה מניקתו של רב ששת לכך אמר חזי הני חדיי דמלית מינייהו:

מה כיבוס בגדים האמור בימי חלוטו כו'. בכמה דברים חמור ימי חלוטו מימי ספורו ולא גמר מהיקשא והיינו טעמא משום דלגמרי לא מצי למגמר דהא כתב וטהר דמשמע דנטהר מכמו שהיה מתחלה אלא דוקא להך מילתא גמרי לפי שהן שוין דאין אדם וכלים מקבלין טומאה אלא מאב הטומאה:

גדול העושה צדקה בסתר יותר ממשה רבינו. פירוש יותר משכך חמה ממשה רבינו בתפלתו ואע"ג דמשה נמי עשה צדקה בסתר שמא אותה שעה לכך פסק אותו זכות:

חמה אינו כופה. תימה דבפרק ארבעה נדרים (דף לב.) אמרינן דחמה משה הרגו (ט):

והמפייסו בדברים מתברך בי"א. יש מגיהין והנותן פרוטה לעני והמפייסו משום דמשמע להו דקרא איירי בנותן צדקה דכתיב ותפק לרעב נפשך ונפש נענה תשביע ולאו מילתא היא דנפש נענע תשביע היינו תשביע בדברים שתפייסנו בדברים וע"כ לא גרסי' ליה דלהאי גיר' הוה ליה למימר מתברך בי"ז הנך שש דלעיל והני אחת עשרה:

ולאו

עין משפט נר מצוה

פו א מיי' פ"א מהל' טומאת צרעת הל' ג:

פז ב מיי' פ"ד מהל' אבות הטומאה הל' ג:

פח ג מיי' שם פ"ה הלכה ו:

פט ד מיי' פ"י מהל' מתנות עניים הלכה ד ה סמג עשין קסב טוש"ע י"ד סי' רמט סעיף ג וסעיף ז:

רבינו גרשום

משגש. מבזה ארחתיה דאימיה שהצריכה להתבזות במה שדרכה להצניע שגלתה דדיה בשבילו כדאמר לקמן: וכבגד עדים. אלו אותן בגדים בלוים ונסחבים שמשימין שם התינוק כשהוא נולד ולפיכך נקראו עדים א) כמו ועדיאתו: בימי ספורו. היינו אותן ימים דכתיב וישב מחוץ לאהלו שבעת ימים דבכך עבר לימי חלוטו והאתו: אמר ליה הואיל ומטמא בגדים. בימי ספורו דכתיב והיה ביום השביעי יגלח שערו וגו' וכבס בגדיו והואיל דמטמא בגדים דטעונין כבוס הכי נמי מטמא אדם: אמר ליה דלמא טומאה בחבורין שני דהני בגדים מחוברין עליו שלובש בהן הלכך לעולם אימא לך אם יגע בבגדים אחרים אינו מטמאן וכי היכי דלא מטמא בגדים מעלמא אימא נמי דלא מטמא אדם תדע דהנה אשכחן דמטמא בגדים בחבורין ולא מטמא אדם: היסט נבלה. אדם שהסיט נבלה ומטמא בגדים דכתיב והנושא את נבלתה יכבס בגדיו וטמא עד הערב ומטמא בגדים טמאים הן ואינו [מטמא אדם] דכתיב וטמא עד הערב הוא טמא ואין מטמא אדם: היסט בכלל נושא. כדתניא וקרינן נשא (חולין קכד:): אמר ליה רב ששת. ולטעמיך דקא אמרת דטומאה בחבורין שאני מש"ה אין מטמא אדם אלא שרץ דמטמא אדם מנא לן לאו משום הואיל דמטמא בגדים דכתיב וכל אשר יפול עליו מהם במותם יטמא מכל כלי עץ או בגד או עור או שק והני לאו בחבורין נינהו: אמר ליה רב אחדבוי. שרץ דמטמא אדם בהדיא כתיב או איש אשר יגע בכל שרץ אלא פריך הכי ולטעמיך דאמרת דטומאה בחבורין שני שכבת זרע דמטמא אדם מנא לן משום דהואיל ומטמא בגדים דכתיב ואיש (אשר) [כי] תצא ממנו שכבת זרע וכתיב וכל בגד וכל עור אשר יהיה עליו שכבת זרע וכבס במים וטמא עד הערב ה"נ אם מטמא אדם ה"נ גבי מצורע: אמר ליה רב אחדבוי. שכבת זרע בהדיא כתיב ביה דמטמא כל אדם הנוגע בו דכתיב או דמייתר דמצי למכתב איש אשר תצא ממנו וגו' או ל"ל לרבות את הנוגע ואכתי מנין למצורע שמטמא בימי ספורו: הוה קא מהדר ליה בבדיחותא. כלומר שמח היה רב אחדבוי שנצחו לרב ששת שלא היה לו להשיב: אישתתק. נאלם: אתיא אימא. ג) דרב אחדבוי בכיא קמיה דרב ששת שהיתה מינקת שלו בשביל בנה דלימחל ליה דרב אחדבוי ובעי רחמי עליה דרב אחדבוי ולא אשגח בה עד דמפקי דדיה לפניו כלומר עשה בשביל אלו דדין שינקת מהן ולהכי שהצריכה לכך קרי ליה עולא משגש ארחתיה דאימיה: ודאתאן עלה מיהא. הואיל ובאת לידינו שאילה זו דרב אחדבוי נעסוק בה: מנלן. דמצורע מטמא אדם בימי ספורו: כבוס בגדים בימי חלוטו. דכתיב וכבס המטהר את בגדיו דנטמאו בימי חלוטו: מה להלן בימי חלוטו מטמא אדם. דכתיב כל ימי אשר הנגע בו יטמא וגו': מתן בסתר [יכפה] אף ושוחד בחיק. כלומר מי שנותן בחיק של עני בצנעה כופה נמי חימה עזה: אע"פ ששוחד בחיק. של עני אעפ"כ חימה עזה שאינה נכפית בשביל השוחד בחיק: והמפייסו בדברים. שמנחמו ומדבר על לבו דברי נחומין: דכתיב ותפק לרעב נפשך וגו'. כלומר משתוציא מנפשך דברים טובים לנחם הרעב ונפש נענה תשביע בדברים טובים אז תזכה לדברים הללו: משום דרודף צדקה. שעושה צדקה משלו בא לידי צדקה שיצטרך לבריות בתמיה:

חשק שלמה על רבינו גרשום א) [לכאורה משמע דכוון לתרגום אונקלוס על ותהר ועדיאת אבל צ"ע דמשם זה לא שייך לקרותם עדים וצ"ע]. ג) [עי' בתוס' כאן ד"ה אתיא מה שכתב בשם ר"ח]:

מסורת הש"ס

א) רש"ל, ב) [נ"ל פרוש], ג) ב"ק נח: [ושם איתא רבא], ד) רש"ל מ"ז, ה) אולי נ"ל אמרה:

הגהות הב"ח

(א) גמ' כי תראה ערום וגו' וכתיב לא יבוש בשער ותפק וכו' וזרח בחשך אורך ואפלתך כצהרים מהרה תצמח והלך לפניך צדקך כבוד ה' יאספך וכתיב אז תקרא וה' יענה תשוע ויאמר הנני והמפייסו בדברים: (ב) שם ושם בצחצחות נפשך ובנו כצ"ל ותיבת וגו' נמחק: (ג) שם עליהם שכר כצ"ל ואות ו' נמחק: (ד) שם כל הרגיל לעשות [צדקה] הווין כצ"ל ותיבת זוכה נמחק: (ה) תוס' ד"ה מנין וכו' אבות הטומאות השרץ ושכבת זרע וטמא מת כצ"ל ותיבת ונבלה נמחק: (ו) ד"ה דהא הסיט כו' ואינו מטמא אדם מ"ט לאו משום: (ז) בא"ד פרשת ויהי ביום השמיני מוכח שמטמא אפי' כלים אע"ג דלא כצ"ל ותיבת בחיבורים נמחק: (ח) בא"ד ונראה לריב"ס דלא גרס ודילמא טומאה בחיבורים שאני אלא הכי: (ט) ד"ה חמה וכו' משה הרגו. נ"ב ועי' בע"ז ריש דף ד' בתוס':

גליון הש"ס

תוס' ד"ה חמה כו' דחמה משה הרגו. ע"ל שבת דף נה ע"ב תד"ה קנף:

לעזי רש"י

מייל"א. פירוש קליפה, קשקשת (תרגום ויקרא יא, ט ועיין רש"י ש"א יז, ה וערוך ערך קלף א').

ליקוטי רש"י

כשריון. שריון קשקשים. כמין קשקשות דגים שעשוין מברזל נוטפים על גב השריון [ש"א יז, ה]. מתן בסתר. צדקה. ושוחד בחיק. אף חמה עזה [משלי כא, יד]. ותפק לרעב נפשך. בתנחומי דברים טובים [ישעיה נח, י].

תורה אור השלם

א) וַיִּלְבַּשׁ צְדָקָה כַּשִּׁרְיָן וְכוֹבַע יְשׁוּעָה בְּרֹאשׁוֹ וַיִּלְבַּשׁ בִּגְדֵי נָקָם תִּלְבֹּשֶׁת וַיַּעַט כַּמְעִיל קִנְאָה: [ישעיה נט, יז]

ב) וַנְּהִי כַטָּמֵא כֻּלָּנוּ וּכְבֶגֶד עִדִּים כָּל צִדְקֹתֵינוּ וַנָּבֶל כֶּעָלֶה כֻּלָּנוּ וַעֲוֹנֵנוּ כָּרוּחַ יִשָּׂאֻנוּ: [ישעיה סד, ה]

ג) אוֹ אִישׁ אֲשֶׁר יִגַּע בְּכָל שֶׁרֶץ אֲשֶׁר יִטְמָא לוֹ אוֹ בְאָדָם אֲשֶׁר יִטְמָא לוֹ לְכֹל טֻמְאָתוֹ: [ויקרא כב, ה]

ד) אִישׁ אִישׁ מִזֶּרַע אַהֲרֹן וְהוּא צָרוּעַ אוֹ זָב בַּקֳּדָשִׁים לֹא יֹאכַל עַד אֲשֶׁר יִטְהָר וְהַנֹּגֵעַ בְּכָל טְמֵא נֶפֶשׁ אוֹ אִישׁ אֲשֶׁר תֵּצֵא מִמֶּנּוּ שִׁכְבַת זָרַע: [ויקרא כב, ד]

ה) כִּי יָגֹרְתִּי מִפְּנֵי הָאַף וְהַחֵמָה אֲשֶׁר קָצַף יְיָ עֲלֵיכֶם לְהַשְׁמִיד אֶתְכֶם וַיִּשְׁמַע יְיָ אֵלַי גַּם בַּפַּעַם הַהִוא: [דברים ט, יט]

ו) מַתָּן בַּסֵּתֶר יִכְפֶּה אָף וְשֹׁחַד בַּחֵק חֵמָה עַזָּה: [משלי כא, יד]

ז) הֲלוֹא פָרֹס לָרָעֵב לַחְמֶךָ וַעֲנִיִּים מְרוּדִים תָּבִיא בָיִת כִּי תִרְאֶה עָרֹם וְכִסִּיתוֹ וּמִבְּשָׂרְךָ לֹא תִתְעַלָּם: [ישעיה נח, ז]

ח) וְתָפֵק לָרָעֵב נַפְשֶׁךָ וְנֶפֶשׁ נַעֲנָה תַּשְׂבִּיעַ וְזָרַח בַּחֹשֶׁךְ אוֹרֶךָ וַאֲפֵלָתְךָ כַּצָּהֳרָיִם: וְנָחֲךָ יְיָ תָּמִיד וְהִשְׂבִּיעַ בְּצַחְצָחוֹת נַפְשֶׁךָ וְעַצְמֹתֶיךָ יַחֲלִיץ וְהָיִיתָ כְּגַן רָוֶה וּכְמוֹצָא מַיִם אֲשֶׁר לֹא יְכַזְּבוּ מֵימָיו: וּבָנוּ מִמְּךָ חָרְבוֹת עוֹלָם מוֹסְדֵי דוֹר וָדוֹר תְּקוֹמֵם וְקֹרָא לְךָ גֹּדֵר פֶּרֶץ מְשֹׁבֵב נְתִיבוֹת לָשָׁבֶת: [ישעיה נח, י-יב]

ט) רֹדֵף צְדָקָה וָחָסֶד יִמְצָא חַיִּים צְדָקָה וְכָבוֹד: [משלי כא, כא]

י) וְאַתָּה יְיָ יָדַעְתָּ אֶת כָּל עֲצָתָם עָלַי לַמָּוֶת אַל תְּכַפֵּר עַל עֲוֹנָם וְחַטָּאתָם מִלְּפָנֶיךָ אַל תֶּמְחִי וְיִהְיוּ מֻכְשָׁלִים לְפָנֶיךָ בְּעֵת אַפְּךָ עֲשֵׂה בָהֶם: [ירמיה יח, כג]

מְשַׂגֵּשׂ אָרְחָתֵיהּ דְּאִימֵּיהּ מִשְּׁמֵיהּ דְּרַבִּי אֶלְעָזָר – **that debased the ways of his mother,**[1] **in R' Elazar's name:** מַאי דִּכְתִיב: ,,וַיִּלְבַּשׁ צְדָקָה כַּשִּׁרְיָן" – **What** is the meaning of that **which is written:**[2] ***And He donned charity like a coat of mail?*** Why is charity compared to a coat of mail? לוֹמַר לָךְ – **To tell you:** מַה שִּׁרְיוֹן זֶה כָּל קְלִיפָּה וּקְלִיפָּה מִצְטָרֶפֶת לְשִׁרְיוֹן גָּדוֹל – **Just as** in the manufacture of **this mail each and every scale combines** with all the others **to** form **a large coat of mail,**[3] אַף צְדָקָה כָּל פְּרוּטָה וּפְרוּטָה מִצְטָרֶפֶת לְחֶשְׁבּוֹן גָּדוֹל – **so** with respect to giving **charity each and every *perutah***[4] one donates **combines** with all the others **to** comprise **a large sum.**[5]

R' Chanina adduces a different source:

רַבִּי חֲנִינָא אָמַר מֵהָכָא – **R' Chanina says:** This principle can be derived **from here:**[6] ,,וּכְבֶגֶד עִדִּים כָּל־צִדְקֹתֵינוּ" – ***And all our** acts of **charity are like a repulsive garment.***[7] מַה בֶּגֶד זֶה כָּל נִימָא וְנִימָא מִצְטָרֶפֶת לְבֶגֶד גָּדוֹל – **Just as** in the weaving of **this garment each and every thread combines** with all the others **to** form **a large garment,**[8] אַף צְדָקָה כָּל פְּרוּטָה וּפְרוּטָה מִצְטָרֶפֶת לְחֶשְׁבּוֹן גָּדוֹל – **so** with respect to giving **charity each and every *perutah*** one donates **combines** with all the others **to** comprise **a large sum.**[9]

The Gemara inquires about Rav Sheishess' unusual title:

אַמַּאי קָרוּ לֵיהּ עוּלָּא מְשַׂגֵּשׂ אָרְחָתֵיהּ דְּאִימֵּיהּ – **Why did [Rava] call [Rav Sheishess] "the child that debased the ways of his mother"?**

The Gemara relates the incident that gave rise to this designation:

דִּבְעָא מִינֵּיהּ רַב אַחֲדְבוֹי בַּר אַמֵּי מֵרַב שֵׁשֶׁת – **Because** it once happened that **Rav Achadvoi bar Ami inquired of Rav Sheishess:** מִנַּיִן לִמְצוֹרָע בִּימֵי סְפוּרוֹ שֶׁמְּטַמֵּא אָדָם – **From where** do we derive the law **that a *metzora***[10] **during the days of his counting**[11] **renders a person** whom he touches ***tamei*?**[12]

Rav Sheishess replied:

אָמַר לוֹ – **[Rav Sheishess] said to [Rav Achadvoi]:** הוֹאִיל וּמְטַמֵּא בְּגָדִים – **Since [a *metzora*] ritually defiles the clothes** he wears during the seven days of counting,[13] מְטַמֵּא אָדָם – it follows that **he** also **ritually defiles** another **person.**[14]

Rav Achadvoi challenged this explanation:

אָמַר לֵיהּ – **[Rav Achadvoi] said to [Rav Sheishess]:** דִּילְמָא טוּמְאָה בְּחִבּוּרִים שָׁאנֵי – **Perhaps the *tumah* of [objects]** directly **connected** to the *metzora* **is different.** Clothing *worn* by the *metzora* becomes *tamei* because it is accorded his status; however, clothing – or people – that the *metzora* merely touches do not become *tamei*.

Rav Achadvoi offers support for this distinction:

דְּהָא הֶסֵּיט נְבֵילָה דִּמְטַמֵּא בְּגָדִים – **For one who** becomes *tamei* from having **moved the carcass** of an animal **ritually defiles the clothes** he wears,[15] וְאֵינוֹ מְטַמֵּא אָדָם – **but does not defile a person** or clothing he touches! Hence, one who defiles the clothing he wears is not necessarily an *av hatumah,* with the capability of rendering other people *tamei* through touching. – ? –

Rav Sheishess advances another source:

אָמַר לֵיהּ – **[Rav Sheishess] said to [Rav Achadvoi]:** וְאֶלָּא שֶׁרֶץ דִּמְטַמֵּא אָדָם מְנָלַן – **But from where do we [derive]** that the carcass of a **crawling animal**[16] **ritually defiles a person** who touches it? לָאו מִשּׁוּם דִּמְטַמֵּא בְּגָדִים – **Is it not because it defiles clothing,**[17] from which we derive that it defiles people as well? Similarly, let us infer that a *metzora* defiles people he touches from the fact that he defiles his clothing.

NOTES

1. He caused her to deviate from the normal behavior of women (*Rashi* to 9a above ד״ה עולא) and thereby debase herself (see *Bach* there). The incident is described by the Gemara below. *Rashi* (ibid.) identifies this "child" as Rav Sheishess; but see below, note 26, for *Tosafos'* view.

2. *Isaiah* 59:17.

3. Mail is flexible armor made either of interlinked rings or of small protective scales or plates.

4. A small copper coin worth 1/192 of a *zuz.*

5. Giving charity is unlike performing other mitzvos. When, for example, one removes *challah* from several batches of dough, he performs a commensurate number of mitzvos, since each batch of dough requires its own *challah* separation. However, each *perutah* given for charity is indistinguishable; hence, every donation combines with all the others to form one large gift of charity, which reflects more favorably upon the donor than do many small gifts (*Maharal*).

6. *Isaiah* 64:5. The prophet is decrying the spiritual state of the Jewish nation.

7. I.e. all of Israel's righteous and charitable deeds have been polluted by their evil natures; their deeds are like a repulsive garment that one must remove (the word עִדִּים actually means *removed*) [*Rashi*].

8. Even though the verse speaks of the charitable deeds of the wicked and creates the metaphor of a repulsive garment, the Gemara nonetheless derives from there an analogy between the charitable deeds of the righteous and a worthy garment (*Rashi*).

9. Regarding the additional insight R' Chanina's analogy offers, see *Maharsha* and *Ben Yehoyada.*

10. A *metzora* is a person who has contracted *tzaraas,* an affliction mentioned in *Leviticus* (ch. 13,14). *Tzaraas* manifests itself (on people) as white or light-colored spots on the body. A Kohen (priest) must examine any such spots to determine if they are indeed *tzaraas;* if he declares them as such, the *metzora* is called *muchlat* – confirmed – and is rendered *tamei*, or ritually impure.

The purification of a *metzora* whose spots have receded (certain guidelines exist – see *Leviticus* 13) consists of several steps. First, the Kohen performs an act of purification with two birds (*Leviticus* 14:1-8). This ritual is known as *taharas hatzipporim*, and is followed by a seven-day waiting period, during which the *metzora* is still encumbered by certain restrictions. This is the period called "days of counting" to which the Gemara refers. After these days pass, a second act of purification, involving various rituals and sacrifices (see *Leviticus* 14:10-32), is performed, following which the status of *metzora* is completely removed.

11. The Gemara asks only about a *metzora* during the days of his counting, for there is a Biblical source equating a "confirmed" *metzora* with a corpse, teaching us that a "confirmed" *metzora* defiles objects that are under the same אֹהֶל, *roof,* as he (under certain conditions), as a corpse does (*Rashi;* see Mishnah *Keilim* 1:4 and *Negaim* 13:7).

12. *Tamei* means contaminated by *tumah,* a state of ritual impurity that carries certain laws and restrictions.

13. For it says in the Torah: *On the seventh day. . .he shall wash his clothing* (*Leviticus* 14:9) [i.e., they must undergo ritual purification in a *mikveh* which implies that during the seven days of his counting he defiled them] (*Rashi*).

14. Rav Sheishess derived from the fact that a *metzora* defiles clothing that he has the status of an *av hatumah,* a primary source of *tumah,* which can render persons or utensils *tamei* (see glossary).

15. As Leviticus 11:40 states: *And one who carries its carcass must wash his clothing* (*Rashi*). [*Rashi* makes a distinction between clothing that the person wears and clothing that he touches. *Tosafos* and other Rishonim, however, quote sources that one who carries the carcass of an animal would indeed ritually defile clothing that he touches. See there for an alternate explanation, making a distinction between touching clothing and touching another person.]

16. Leviticus (11:29-30) enumerates eight types of crawling creatures (שְׁרָצִים, *sheratzim*) whose carcasses transmit *tumah.*

17. As is stated in *Leviticus* 11:32: *And when they* (i.e. crawling animals) *are dead, anything upon which part of them falls becomes defiled, whether it is a wooden utensil, a garment. . .* (*Rabbeinu Gershom*).

פו א מיי' פ"ד מהל' טומאת צרעת הל' ב:
פז ב מיי' פ"ד מהל' אבות הטומאה הל' ב:
פח ג מיי' שם פ"ה הלכה ו:
פט ד מיי' פ"י מהל' מתנות עניים הלכה ז ה סמג עשין קסב טוש"ע י"ד סי' רמט סעיף ג וסעיף ד:

משגש ארחתיה דאימיה משמיה דר' אלעזר מאי דכתיב (א) וילבש צדקה כשריון לומר לך מה שריון זה כל קליפה וקליפה מצטרפת לשריון גדול אף צדקה כל פרוטה ופרוטה מצטרפת לחשבון גדול רבי חנינא אמר מהכא (ב) וכבגד עדים כל צדקותינו מה בגד זה כל נימא ונימא מצטרפת לבגד גדול אף צדקה כל פרוטה ופרוטה מצטרפת לחשבון גדול אמאי קרו ליה עולא משגש ארחתיה דאימיה דבעא מיניה רב אחדבוי בר אמי מרב ששת *מנין למצורע בימי ספורו שמטמא אדם אמר לו הואיל ומטמא בגדים מטמא אדם א"ל דילמא טומאה בחבורים שאני דהא הסיט נבילה דמטמא בגדים ואינו מטמא אדם אמר ליה ואלא שרץ *דמטמא אדם מנלן לאו משום דמטמא בגדים א"ל שרץ בהדיא כתיב ביה (ג) או איש אשר יגע בכל שרץ אלא *שכבת זרע דמטמא אדם מנלן לאו משום דהואיל ומטמא בגדים מטמא אדם א"ל שכבת זרע נמי בהדיא כתיב ביה (ד) או איש לרבות את הנוגע אהדר ליה בבדיחותא חלש דעתיה דרב ששת אישתיק רב אחדבוי בר אמי ואתיקר תלמודיה אתיא אימיה וקא בכיא קמיה צווחה ולא אשגח בה אמרה ליה חזי להני חדיי דמצית מינייהו בעא רחמי עליה ואיתסי ודאתאן עלה מנא לן כדתניא ר"ש בן יוחי אומר נאמר כבוס בגדים בימי ספורו ונאמר כבוס בגדים בימי חלוטו מה להלן מטמא אדם אף כאן מטמא אדם אמר רבי אלעזר גדול העושה צדקה בסתר יותר ממשה רבינו דאילו במשה רבינו כתיב (ה) כי יגורתי מפני האף והחמה ואילו בעושה צדקה כתיב (ו) מתן בסתר יכפה אף (א) [ושחד בחיק חמה עזה] ופליגא דרבי יצחק דאמר ר' יצחק אף כופה חמה אינו כופה שנא' ושחד בחיק חמה עזה אע"פ ששוחד בחיק חמה עזה איכא דאמרי א"ר יצחק כל דיין שנוטל שחד מביא חמה עזה לעולם [שנאמר ושחד בחיק וגו'] ואמר רבי יצחק כל הנותן פרוטה לעני מתברך בשש ברכות והמפייסו בדברים מתברך בי"א ברכות הנותן פרוטה לעני מתברך בשש ברכות דכתיב (ז) הלא פרוש וגו' ועניים מרודים תביא בית וגו' כי תראה ערום וגו' (א) והמפייסו בדברים מתברך באחת עשרה ברכות שנאמר (ח) ותפק לרעב נפשך ונפש נענה תשביע וזרח בחשך אורך ואפלתך כצהרים ונחך ה' תמיד והשביע בצחצחות נפשך (ב) וגו' ובנו ממך חרבות עולם מוסדי דור ודור תקומם וגו' ואמר רבי יצחק מאי דכתיב (ט) רודף צדקה וחסד ימצא חיים צדקה וכבוד משום דרודף צדקה ימצא צדקה אלא לומר לך כל הרודף אחר צדקה הקדוש ברוך הוא ממציא לו מעות ועושה בהן צדקה רב נחמן בר יצחק אמר הקדוש ברוך הוא ממציא לו בני אדם המהוגנים לעשות להן צדקה כדי לקבל שכרו עליהם (ג) לאפוקי מדדרש רבה דדרש רבה מאי דכתיב (י) ויהיו מוכשלים לפניך בעת אפך עשה בהם אמר ירמיה לפני הקדוש ברוך הוא רבונו של עולם [אפילו] בשעה שכופין את יצרן ומבקשין לעשות צדקה לפניך הכשילם בבני אדם שאינן מהוגנין כדי שלא יקבלו עליהן שכר רבי יהושע בן לוי אמר כל הרגיל לעשות צדקה (ד) זוכה הויין לו בנים בעלי חכמה בעלי עושר בעלי אגדה דכתיב ימצא

רשב"ם

משגש. לשון מהומה וקגנון: קליפה. מייל"א בלע"ז: וכבגד עדים כל צדקותינו. כלומר אף כל צדקותינו נמאסו מחמת רשעינו כבגד מאוס שהאדם מסירו מעליו: עדים. כדמתרגמינן ויסר ואעדי וכן מעדה בגד ביום קרה (משלי כה) מ"מ מקיש צדקה לבגד צדקת הצדיקים לבגד הגון: בימי ספורו. בשבעת ימים שבין טהרת הצפרים להבאת קרבנותיו בשלמא בימי חלוטו איתקש למת לטמא אף באהל: הואיל ומטמא בגדים. דהא ביום השביעי כתיב וכבס בגדיו: טומאה בחבורין. כגון בגדי לבושו הרי הן כמוהו אבל שאר בגדים הנוגע בהן וכן אם יגע באדם לא מטמא תדע שהרי המסיט נבילה כתיב ביה והנושא את נבלתה יכבס בגדיו (ויקרא יא) ולא אשכחן דלהוי אב הטומאה לטמא אדם ושאר בגדים: שכבת זרע מטמא בגדים. וכל בגד וכל עור אשר יהיה עליו שכבת זרע וגו': בהדיא כתיב ביה כו'. ה"ה נמי דהוה מצי למיפרך דהא טומאת בגדים לא דמיא לבגדים דימי ספורו דהא בגדים דהכא לאו בגדי לבוש שרץ הן וטומאת מגע הוא אלא דעדיפא מיניה קא מותיב ליה: או לרבות הנוגע. דהכי תניא במסכת נדה (דף מג:) מנין לרבות הנוגע בשכבת זרע ת"ל או איש: הוה קמהדר ליה. רב אחדבוי לרב ששת בבדיחותא לפי שהיה רב ששת נכשל בתשובותיו: אשתתק רב אחדבוי. נעשה אלם: אתיא אימיה. דרב ששת: צווחה קמיה. שיתפלל עליו: להני חדיי. הדדים הללו. חדיי תרגום של חזה: דמצית מינייהו. שינקת מהן: ודאתאן עלה. ואחרי שבא לידינו שאלה זו לקובעה בגמ' מנלן דמטמא אדם: נאמר כיבוס בגדים בימי ספורו. והיה ביום השביעי יגלח את כל שערו וגו' ונאמר כיבוס בגדים למעלה ביום טהרת הצפרים כשיוצא מטומאת החלט וכבס המטהר את בגדיו: אף וחימה. שני לגיונות קשים הם ליפרע מן החוטאים: אע"פ ששוחד בחיק. שהוא עושה צדקה בסתר: חימה עזה. עדיין היא בתוקפה ורבי אלעזר סבר דהאי שוחד בחיק ארישא קאי ושוחד בחיק יכפה חימה עזה: ותפק לרעב נפשך. הוא פיוס דברי נחומים: ימצא צדקה. משמע יבא לידי עניות וימלא בני אדם שיעשו לו צדקה: ויהיו מוכשלים לפניך. את אנשי ענתות היה מקלל שהיו מבקשין נפשו:

תוספות

מנין למצורע בימי ספורו שמטמא אדם. פשיטא לן דמטמא דתנן בריש מס' כלים (פ"א מ"א) אבות הטומאות השרץ ושכבת זרע (ה) ונבלה וטמא מת ומצורע בימי ספורו כו' הרי אלו מטמאין אדם וכלים במגע וכלי חרס באויר ולכך בעי מנלן דמטמא דהא כתיב ורחץ במים וטהר משמע דבלאו טבילה טהור: דהא הסיט נבלה מטמא בגדים ואינו מטמא אדם. (ו) לאו משום דטומאה בחבורין שאני. פי' דאינו מטמא אלא בגדים שהוא לבוש וקשה לרי"ם דבתורת כהנים פ' ויהי ביום השמיני (ז) מרבה שמטמא אפילו כלים (בחבורים) אע"ג דלא שייך בהו לבישה ואינו ממעט מבגדיו אלא אדם וכלי חרס שנוגע בהן אלא ודאי מטמא בגדים בשעה שמסיט אפילו אין לבוש בהן וכן משמע מדקאמר אלא מעתה שרץ דמטמא אדם מנלן לאו משום דמטמא בגדים ואי קרי חבורים בגדים שהוא לבוש מאי פריך משרץ דלא שייך ביה לבישה התם ודאי ילפינן אדם מבגדים ונראה לרי"ם דלא גרס (ח) בחבורים אלא הכי גרס ודילמא טומאת בגדים שאני תדע דהא מסיט נבלה מטמא בגדים ואינו מטמא אדם ולא גרסינן מ"ט לאו משום דטומאה בחבורים שאני דלא מהדר אלא שיש חילוק בין טומאת בגדים לטומאת אדם וכן משמע דאיהו גופיה לא קא מיבעיא ליה אם מטמא בגדים וכלים במגע אלא אאדם בעי:

אתיא אימיה וקא בכיא קמיה. פר"ח דהיינו אימיה דרב אחדבוי ולדידיה קרי עולא משגש אורחא דאימיה שגרם לאמו להתבזות לפני רב ששת והיא היתה מניקתו של רב ששת לכך (י) אמר חזי הני חדיי דמצית מינייהו: מה כיבוס בגדים האמור בימי חלוטו כו'. בכמה דברים חמור ימי חלוטו מימי ספורו ולא גמר מהיקשא והיינו טעמא משום דלגמרי לא מצי למגמר דהא כתב וטהר דמשמע דנטהר מכמו שהיה מתחלה אלא דוקא להך מילתא גמרי לפי שהן שוין דאין אדם וכלים מקבלין טומאה אלא מאב הטומאה:

גדול העושה צדקה בסתר יותר ממשה רבינו. פירוש יותר משכך חמה ממשה רבינו בתפלתו ואע"ג דמשה נמי עשה צדקה בסתר שמא אותה שעה כבר פסק אותו זכות:

חמה אינו כופה. תימה דבפרק ארבעה נדרים (דף לב.) אמרינן ° דחמה משה הרגו (ט):

והמפייסו בדברים מתברך בי"א. יש מגיהין והנותן פרוטה לעני והמפייסו משום דמשמע להו דקראי איירי בנותן צדקה דכתיב ותפק לרעב נפשך ונפש נענה תשביע ולאו מילתא היא דנפש נענה תשביע היינו תשביע בדברים שתפייסנו בדברים וע"כ לא גרסי' ליה דלהאי גיר' הוה ליה למימר מתברך בי"ז הנך שש דלעיל והני אחת עשרה:

ואיזו

רבינו גרשום

משגש. מבזה ארחתיה דאימיה שהצריכה להתבזות במה שדרכה להצניע שגלתה דדיה בשבילו כדאמר לקמן: וכבגד עדים. אלו אותן בגדים בלוים ונסחבים שמשימין עם התינוק כשהוא נולד ולפיכך נקראו עדים (א) כמו ועדיאתו: בימי ספורו. היינו אותן ימים דכתיב וישב מחוץ לאהלו שבעת ימים דבתר עבורו לימי חלוטו והזאתו: אמר ליה הואיל ומטמא בגדים. בימי ספורו דכתיב והיה ביום השביעי יגלח שערו וגו' וכבס בגדיו והואיל דמטמא בגדים דטעונין כבוס הכי נמי מטמא אדם: אמר ליה דלמא טומאה בחבורין שני דהני בגדים מחוברין עליו שלובש בהן אבל לעולם אימא לך אם יגע בבגדים אחרים אינו מטמאן וכי היכי דלא מטמא בגדים מעלמא אימא נמי דלא מטמא אדם תדע דהנה אשכחן דמטמא בגדים בחבורין ולא מטמא אדם: הסיט נבלה. אדם שהסיט נבלה ומטמא בגדים בחבורין דכתיב והנושא את נבלתה יכבס בגדיו וטמא עד הערב אלמא הבגדים טמאים הן ואינו [מטמא אדם] כדכתיב וטמא עד הערב הוא טמא ואינו מטמא אדם: הסיט בכלל נשוא. כדכתיב נישא וקרינן נושא (חולין קכד:): אמר ליה רב ששת. ולטעמיך דקא אמרת דטומאה בחבורין שאני משה"א אין מטמא אדם אלא שרץ דמטמא אדם מנא לן לאו משום הואיל דמטמא בגדים דכתיב וכל אשר יפול עליו מהם במותם יטמא מכל כלי עץ או בגד או עור או שק והני לאו בחבורין נינהו: אמר ליה רב אחדבוי. שרץ דמטמא אדם בהדיא כתיב או איש אשר יגע בכל שרץ אלא פריך הכי ולטעמיך דאמרת דטומאה בחבורין שני שכבת זרע דמטמא אדם מנלן משום דהואיל ומטמא בגדים דכתיב ואיש (אשר) [כי] תצא ממנו שכבת זרע וכתיב וכל בגד וכל עור אשר יהיה עליו שכבת זרע וכבס במים וטמא עד הערב הה"נ גבי מצורע: אמר ליה רב אחדבוי. שכבת זרע בהדיא כתיב ביה דמטמא כל אדם הנוגע בו דכתיב או איש דמייתר דמצי למכתב איש אשר תצא ממנו וגו' או ל"ל לרבות את הנוגע ואכתי מנין למצורע שמטמא בימי ספורו: הוה קא מהדר ליה בבדיחותא. כלומר שמח היה רב אחדבוי שנצחו לרב ששת שלא היה לו להשיב: אישתתק. נאלם: אתיא אימיה. ד) דרב אחדבוי בכיא קמיה דרב ששת שהיתה מינקת שלו בשביל בנה דלימחול ליה ובעי רחמי עליה דרב אחדבוי ולא אשגח בה עד דמפקי דדיה לפניו כלומר עשה בשביל אלו דדין שינקת מהן ולהכי שהצריכה לכך קרי ליה עולא משגש ארחתיה דאימיה: ודאתאן עלה מהכא. הואיל ובאת לידינו שאילה זו דרב אחדבוי נעסוק בה: מנלן. דמצורע מטמא אדם בימי ספורו: כבוס בגדים בימי חלוטו. דכתיב וכבס המטהר את בגדיו: מה להלן בימי חלוטו מטמא אדם. דכתיב כל ימי אשר הנגע בו יטמא: מתן בסתר [יכפה] אף ושוחד בחיק. כלומר מי שנותן שוחד בחיק של עני אפ"ה חימה עזה: אע"פ ששוחד בחיק. של עני אע"פ חימה עזה: המפייסו בדברים. שמנחמו ומדבר על לבו דברי נחומין: דכתיב ותפק לרעב נפשך. כלומר שמפייסו בדברים טובים לנחם העני ונפש נענה תשביע: משום דרודף צדקה. שעושה צדקה משלו בא לידי עניות שיצטרך לבריות בתמיה:

מסורת הש"ס

א) רש"ל, ב) [נ"ל פרוס], ג) ב"ק נח: [וכס איתא רבא], ד) רש"ל מ"ז, ה) אולי נ"ל אמרה:

הגהות הב"ח

(א) גמ' כי תראה ערום וגו' וכתיב אז יבקע כשחר אורך וארוכתך מהרה תצמח והלך לפניך צדקך כבוד ה' יאספך וכתיב אז תקרא וה' יענה תשוע ויאמר הנני והמפייסו בדברים: (ב) שם והשביע בצחצחות נפשך ובנו כצ"ל ותיבת וגו' נמחק: (ג) שם עליהם שכר כצ"ל ואות ו' נמחק: (ד) שם כל הרגיל לעשות [צדקה] הוויין כצ"ל ותיבת זוכה נמחק: (ה) תוס' ד"ה מנין וכו' אבות הטומאות השרץ ושכבת זרע וטמא מת כצ"ל ותיבת ונבלה נמחק: (ו) ד"ה דהא הסיט כו' ואינו מטמא אדם מ"ט לאו משום: (ז) בא"ד פרשת ויהי ביום השמיני מוכח שמטמאה אפי' כלים אע"ג דלא כצ"ל ותיבת בחיבורים נמחק: (ח) בא"ד ונראה לרי"ם דלא גרס ודלמא טומאה בחיבורים שאני אלא הכי: (ט) ד"ה חמה וכו' משה הרגו. נ"ב ועי' בע"ז ריש דף ד' בתוס':

גליון הש"ס

תוס' ד"ה חמה כו' דחמה משה הרגו. עי' שבת דף נה ע"ב תד"ה קלף:

לעזי רש"י

מייל"א. פירוש קליפה, קשקשת (תרגום ויקרא יא, ט ועיין רש"י שם יא, ה וערוך ערך קלף א'):

ליקוטי רש"י

כשריון. שריון קשקשים. כמין קשקשות דגים עשוין מנבלע טפולים על גב השריון [רש"י נקוי השריון] קשקשת לכל נקב (שמואל א, יז, ה). מתן בסתר. לצדקה. ושוחד בחיק. אף חמה עזה וגו' אם לו לדקה יכפה אף חמה עזה (משלי כא, יד). ותפק לרעב נפשך. בתנחומי דברים טובים [ישעיה נח, י].

תורה אור השלם

א) וַיִּלְבַּשׁ צְדָקָה כַּשִּׁרְיָן וְכוֹבַע יְשׁוּעָה בְּרֹאשׁוֹ וַיִּלְבַּשׁ בִּגְדֵי נָקָם תִּלְבֹּשֶׁת וַיַּעַט כַּמְעִיל קִנְאָה: [ישעיה נט, יז]

ב) וַנְּהִי כַטָּמֵא כֻּלָּנוּ וּכְבֶגֶד עִדִּים כָּל צִדְקֹתֵינוּ וַנָּבֶל כֶּעָלֶה כֻּלָּנוּ וַעֲוֹנֵנוּ כָּרוּחַ יִשָּׂאֻנוּ: [ישעיה סד, ה]

ג) אוֹ אִישׁ אֲשֶׁר יִגַּע בְּכָל שֶׁרֶץ אֲשֶׁר יִטְמָא לוֹ אוֹ בְאָדָם אֲשֶׁר יִטְמָא לוֹ לְכֹל טֻמְאָתוֹ: [ויקרא כב, ה]

ד) אִישׁ אִישׁ מִזֶּרַע אַהֲרֹן וְהוּא צָרוּעַ אוֹ זָב בַּקֳּדָשִׁים לֹא יֹאכַל עַד אֲשֶׁר יִטְהָר וְהַנֹּגֵעַ בְּכָל טְמֵא נֶפֶשׁ אוֹ אִישׁ אֲשֶׁר תֵּצֵא מִמֶּנּוּ שִׁכְבַת זָרַע: [ויקרא כב, ד]

ה) כִּי יָגֹרְתִּי מִפְּנֵי הָאַף וְהַחֵמָה אֲשֶׁר קָצַף יְיָ עֲלֵיכֶם לְהַשְׁמִיד אֶתְכֶם וַיִּשְׁמַע יְיָ אֵלַי גַּם בַּפַּעַם הַהִוא: [דברים ט, יט]

ו) מַתָּן בַּסֵּתֶר יִכְפֶּה אָף וְשֹׁחַד בַּחֵק חֵמָה עַזָּה: [משלי כא, יד]

ז) הֲלוֹא פָרֹס לָרָעֵב לַחְמֶךָ וַעֲנִיִּים מְרוּדִים תָּבִיא בָיִת כִּי תִרְאֶה עָרֹם וְכִסִּיתוֹ וּמִבְּשָׂרְךָ לֹא תִתְעַלָּם: [ישעיה נח, ז]

ח) וְתָפֵק לָרָעֵב נַפְשֶׁךָ וְנֶפֶשׁ נַעֲנָה תַּשְׂבִּיעַ וְזָרַח בַּחֹשֶׁךְ אוֹרֶךָ וַאֲפֵלָתְךָ כַּצָּהֳרָיִם: וְנָחֲךָ יְיָ תָּמִיד וְהִשְׂבִּיעַ בְּצַחְצָחוֹת נַפְשֶׁךָ וְעַצְמֹתֶיךָ יַחֲלִיץ וְהָיִיתָ כְּגַן רָוֶה וּכְמוֹצָא מַיִם אֲשֶׁר לֹא יְכַזְּבוּ מֵימָיו: וּבָנוּ מִמְּךָ חָרְבוֹת עוֹלָם מוֹסְדֵי דוֹר וָדוֹר תְּקוֹמֵם וְקֹרָא לְךָ גֹּדֵר פֶּרֶץ מְשֹׁבֵב נְתִיבוֹת לָשָׁבֶת: [ישעיה נח, י-יב]

ט) רֹדֵף צְדָקָה וָחָסֶד יִמְצָא חַיִּים צְדָקָה וְכָבוֹד: [משלי כא, כא]

י) וְאַתָּה יְיָ יָדַעְתָּ אֶת כָּל עֲצָתָם עָלַי לַמָּוֶת אַל תְּכַפֵּר עַל עֲוֹנָם וְחַטָּאתָם מִלְּפָנֶיךָ אַל תֶּמְחִי וְיִהְיוּ מֻכְשָׁלִים לְפָנֶיךָ בְּעֵת אַפְּךָ עֲשֵׂה בָהֶם: [ירמיה יח, כג]

חשק שלמה על רבינו גרשום א) [לכאורה משמע דגרס [illegible]] ב) [עי' בתוס' כאן ד"ה אתיא מה שכתב בשם ר"ח]

Rav Achadvoi rejects this source also:

אָמַר לֵיהּ – [Rav Achadvoi] said to [Rav Sheishess]: שֶׁרֶץ בְּהֶדְיָא כְּתִיב בֵּיהּ – **Regarding a crawling creature, it is explicitly written:**[18] "אוֹ־אִישׁ אֲשֶׁר יִגַּע בְּכָל־שֶׁרֶץ" – ***Or a man who touches any creeping thing*** (will become *tamei*). Since we do not deduce that a *sheretz* defiles people from the fact that it defiles clothing (for Scripture expressly teaches that law!), there is no precedent for similarly deducing that a *metzora* defiles people because he defiles his clothing.[19] – ? –

Rav Sheishess proposes a third source:

אֶלָּא שִׁכְבַת זֶרַע דִּמְטַמֵּא אָדָם מְנָלַן – **But from where do we [derive]** that **semen ritually defiles a person** who touches it? לָאו מִשּׁוּם דְּהוֹאִיל וּמְטַמֵּא בְּגָדִים – **Is it not because** of the following deduction: **Since [semen] defiles clothing** it touches,[20] מְטַמֵּא אָדָם – **it** has the status of an *av hatumah* and therefore **defiles a person** as well? Similarly, let us infer that a *metzora* defiles people he touches from the fact that he defiles his clothing.

Rav Achadvoi rejects this source as well:

אָמַר לֵיהּ – [Rav Achadvoi] said to [Rav Sheishess]: שִׁכְבַת זֶרַע נַמִּי בְּהֶדְיָא כְּתִיב בֵּיהּ – **Regarding semen, it is also explicitly written:** "אוֹ־אִישׁ" – ***Or a man,*** לְרַבּוֹת אֶת הַנּוֹגֵעַ – which comes **to include one who touches** semen among the *tamei*.[21] Since we do not deduce this law from the law that semen defiles clothing (for Scripture expressly[22] teaches it!), there is no precedent for similarly deducing that a *metzora* defiles people because he defiles his clothing. – ? –

With each of Rav Sheishess' failures to provide a source, Rav Achadvoi made a fateful mistake:

אַהְדַר לֵיהּ בִּבְדִיחוּתָא – **[Rav Achadvoi] responded to [Rav Sheishess]** each time in a humorous manner, חֲלַשׁ דַּעְתֵּיהּ דְּרַב שֵׁשֶׁת – and as a result **Rav Sheishess became distressed.** אִישְׁתִּיק רַב אַחַדְבוֹי בַּר אַמֵּי – Thereupon, **Rav Achadvoi bar Ami was struck dumb** וְאִתְיַקַּר תַּלְמוּדֵיהּ – **and forgot his learning**[23] in Heavenly retribution for vexing Rav Sheishess.

Rav Sheishess' mother[24] entreated her son to pray for Rav Achadvoi's recovery:

אֲתְיָא אִימֵּיהּ וְקָא בָּכְיָא קַמֵּיהּ – **[Rav Sheishess'] mother came and cried before [Rav Sheishess],** pleading with him to intercede on Rav Achadvoi's behalf.[25] צְווֹחָה צְווֹחָה וְלֹא אַשְׁגַּח בָּהּ – **She cried out and cried out, but he paid no attention to her.**

Rav Sheishess' mother then took more drastic action:

אָמְרָה לֵיהּ – **She said to [Rav Sheishess],** חֲזִי לְהָנֵי חַדְיֵי דְּמָצִית מִינַּיְיהוּ – **"See these breasts of mine that you suckled from** as a child![26] Repay that kindness by acceding to my request." בְּעָא רַחֲמֵי עֲלֵיהּ – Moved by his mother's desperate plea, **[Rav Sheishess] prayed** that God have **mercy on [Rav Achadvoi],** וְאִיתַּסֵּי – **and he was healed.** Thus, because his initial reluctance to pray for Rav Achadvoi caused his mother to expose herself before him, Rav Sheishess became known as "the child that debased the ways of his mother."

The Gemara now answers the question posed by Rav Achadvoi:

וְדַאֲתָאן עֲלָהּ – **And now that we have come upon [this question]** in the course of our discussing the origin of Rav Sheishess' unusual designation, מְנָא לָן – **from where,** indeed, **do we [derive]** that a *metzora* defiles people he touches during the "days of his counting"?

The Gemara answers:

כִּדְתַנְיָא – The source **is as was taught in a Baraisa:** רַבִּי שִׁמְעוֹן בֶּן יוֹחַי אוֹמֵר – **R' SHIMON BEN YOCHAI SAYS:** נֶאֱמַר כִּבּוּס בְּגָדִים בִּימֵי סְפוּרוֹ – A requirement of IMMERSING CLOTHING[27] IS STATED WITH RESPECT TO garments the *metzora* wore during THE DAYS OF HIS COUNTING, וְנֶאֱמַר כִּבּוּס בְּגָדִים בִּימֵי חִלּוּטוֹ – AND a similar requirement of IMMERSING CLOTHING[28] IS STATED WITH RESPECT TO garments he wore during THE DAYS OF HIS CONFIRMATION as a *metzora*. Since the two stages of the *tzaraas* affliction are exegetically connected[29] by the common requirement of immersion, the law of defilement may be extrapolated from one stage to the other, as follows:

מָה לְהַלָּן מְטַמֵּא אָדָם – JUST AS THERE [A CONFIRMED *METZORA*] RITUALLY DEFILES PEOPLE by touching them,[30] אַף כָּאן מְטַמֵּא

NOTES

18. *Leviticus* 22:5.

19. Rav Achadvoi could have refuted Rav Sheishess with the distinction he drew previously, arguing: Since a *sheretz* defiles a garment merely by touching it, it is an *av hatumah,* a primary source of *tumah* that defiles even people. A *metzora*, on the other hand, defiles only those garments that he actually wears; hence, we could not conclude that he defiles people through touching. Rav Achadvoi chose, however, an even more convincing rebuttal (see *Rashi* ד״ה בהדיא כתיב ביה).

Other Rishonim offer an alterate interpretation, based on their explanation above (see note 15).]

20. As is stated in *Leviticus* 15:17: *Any garment or leather article upon which there shall be semen shall be washed in water (Rashi).*

21. In *Leviticus* 22:4 it is written: **Or a man** *from whom a seminal discharge issues.* The following verse records: **Or a man** *who touches any creeping thing* (*sheretz*). The Gemara (*Niddah* 43b) interprets: Just as a *sheretz* defiles a person through mere contact, so semen defiles a person through mere contact (*Rashi*).

22. Scripture does not actually state the law, as it did in the case of *sheretz* (ibid. v. 5). The law is, however, derived from Scripture exegetically; it is not merely deduced from another law.

23. Literally: his learning became heavy. These were Heavenly signs to Rav Achadvoi that he had misused his *mouth* and his *scholarship* to distress Rav Sheishess. [Clearly, Rav Achadvoi never intended to degrade Rav Sheishess, and was just expressing satisfaction with his convincing Torah arguments. Rav Sheishess, however, misunderstood his reaction, and Rav Achadvoi was punished for not preventing this misunderstanding (see *Rabbeinu Gershom*).

24. This follows *Rashi;* but see note 26 below.

25. Her motive for doing this is unclear. Perhaps she wished to prevent her son (Rav Sheishess) from falling into the category of "one whose fellow was punished on account of him," for such people do not reach lofty levels of spirituality in the World to Come (see *Shabbos* 149b; also *Tosafos* below, 22a ד״ה אנא).

[See *Chasam Sofer*, who explains that Rav Sheishness paid no need to his mother's pleas because he felt that if was a matter of defending the honor of Torah.]

26. The woman's statement is the basis for *Rashi's* interpreting that the "child" Rava quoted was Rav Sheishess, for who else but her child would the woman nurse? *Rabbeinu Chananel* (cited by *Tosafos*) and *Rabbeinu Gershom* explain, however, that the "child" was actually Rav Achadvoi who, by his vexing remark, ultimately caused his mother to debase herself before Rav Sheishess. These Rishonim further explain that Rav Achadvoi's mother had been Rav Sheishess' wet nurse; hence, she was able to say to Rav Sheishess, "See these breasts from which you suckled."

27. On the seventh day of his days of counting (see note 10 above) the *metzora* must shave off all his hair, and immerse the clothing he wore during the "days of counting" and immerse himself in a *mikveh*; see *Leviticus* 14:9 (*Rashi*). This is the final stage of the purification process.

28. During the ritual of *taharas hatzipporim,* which is performed when the *metzora* leaves the state of being a *confirmed metzora* (see note 10 above), the *metzora* must shave off all his hair, and immerse the garments he wore while he was a "confirmed" *metzora* and immerse himself in a *mikveh*; see *Leviticus* 14:8 (*Rashi*).

29. See *Tosafos* ד״ה מה.

30. *Rashi* above (ד״ה בימי ספורו) equated a "confirmed" *metzora* to a corpse. Hence, just as a corpse defiles people through physical contact,

עין משפט נר מצוה

פו א מיי' מהל' טומאת צרעת הל' ב:
פז ב מיי' פ"ד מהל' אבות הטומאה הל' ב:
פח ג מיי' שם פ"ה הלכה ו:
פט ד מיי' פ"י מהל' מתנות עניים הלכה ד ה סמג עשין קסב טוש"ע י"ד סי' רמט סעיף ג וסעיף ד:

משגש ארחתיה דאימיה משמיה דר' אלעזר מאי דכתיב א וילבש צדקה כשריון לומר לך מה שריון זה כל קליפה וקליפה מצטרפת לשריון גדול אף צדקה כל פרוטה ופרוטה מצטרפת לחשבון גדול רבי חנינא אמר מהכא ב וכבגד עדים כל צדקותינו מה בגד זה כל נימא ונימא מצטרפת לבגד גדול אף צדקה כל פרוטה ופרוטה מצטרפת לחשבון גדול אמאי קרו ליה עולא משגש ארחתיה דאימיה דבעא מיניה רב אחדבוי בר אמי מרב ששת מנין למצורע בימי ספורו שמטמא אדם אמר לו הואיל ומטמא בגדים מטמא אדם א"ל דילמא טומאה בחבורים שאני דהא הסיט נבילה דמטמא בגדים ואינו מטמא אדם אמר ליה ואלא שרץ דמטמא אדם מנלן לאו משום דמטמא בגדים א"ל שרץ בהדיא כתיב ביה ג או איש אשר יגע בכל שרץ אלא שכבת זרע דמטמא אדם מנלן לאו משום דהואיל ומטמא בגדים מטמא אדם א"ל שכבת זרע נמי בהדיא כתיב ביה ד או איש לרבות את הנוגע אהדר ליה בבדיחותא חלש דעתיה דרב ששת אישתיק רב אחדבוי בר אמי ואתיקר תלמודיה אתיא אימיה וקא בכיא קמיה צווחה ולא אשגח בה אמרה ליה חזי להני חדיי דמצית מינייהו בעא רחמי עליה ואיתסי ודאתאן עלה מנא לן דכדתניא ר"ש בן יוחי אומר נאמר כבוס בגדים בימי ספורו ונאמר כבוס בגדים בימי חלוטו מה להלן מטמא אדם אף כאן מטמא אדם אמר רבי אלעזר גדול העושה צדקה בסתר יותר ממשה רבינו דאילו במשה רבינו כתיב ה כי יגורתי מפני האף והחמה ואילו בעושה צדקה כתיב ו מתן בסתר יכפה אף (א) [ושחד בחיק חמה עזה] ופליגא דרבי יצחק דאמר ר' יצחק אף כופה חמה אינו כופה שנא' ושחד בחיק חמה עזה אע"פ ששוחד בחיק חמה עזה איכא דאמרי א"ר יצחק כל דיין שנוטל שחד מביא חמה עזה לעולם [שנאמר ושחד בחיק חמה עזה וגו'] ואמר רבי יצחק כל הנותן פרוטה לעני מתברך בשש ברכות והמפייסו בדברים מתברך בי"א ברכות הנותן פרוטה לעני מתברך בשש ברכות דכתיב ז הלא פרוש לרעב לחמך ועניים מרודים תביא בית וגו' כי תראה ערום וגו' (א) והמפייסו בדברים מתברך באחת עשרה ברכות שנאמר ח ותפק לרעב נפשך ונפש נענה תשביע וזרח בחשך אורך ואפלתך כצהרים ונחך ה' תמיד והשביע בצחצחות נפשך (ב) וגו' ובנו ממך חרבות עולם מוסדי דור ודור תקומם וגו' ואמר רבי יצחק מאי דכתיב ט רודף צדקה וחסד ימצא חיים צדקה וכבוד משום דרודף צדקה ימצא צדקה אלא לומר לך כל הרודף אחר צדקה הקדוש ברוך הוא ממציא לו מעות ועושה בהן צדקה רב נחמן בר יצחק אמר הקדוש ברוך הוא ממציא לו בני אדם המהוגנים לעשות להן צדקה כדי לקבל עליהם (ג) שכרו לאפוקי מאי לאפוקי מדדרש רבה דדרש רבה מאי דכתיב י ויהיו מוכשלים לפניך בעת אפך עשה בהם אמר ירמיה לפני הקדוש ברוך הוא רבונו של עולם [אפילו] בשעה שכופין את יצרן ומבקשין לעשות צדקה לפניך הכשילם בבני אדם שאינן מהוגנין כדי שלא יקבלו עליהן שכר רבי יהושע בן לוי אמר כל הרגיל לעשות צדקה (ד) זוכה הויין לו בנים בעלי חכמה בעלי עושר בעלי אגדה דכתיב

ימצא

רש"י

משגש. לשון מהומה ושגעון: קליפה. מייל"א בלע"ז: וכבגד עדים כל צדקותינו. כלומר אף כל צדקותינו נמאסו מחמת רשעינו כבגד מאוס שהאדם מסירו מעליו: עדים. כדמתרגמינן ויסר ואעדי וכן מעדה בגד ביום קרה (משלי כה) מ"מ מקיש צדקה לבגד צדקת הצדיקים לבגד הגון: בימי ספורו. בשבעת ימים שבין טהרת הצפרים להבאת קרבנותיו בשלמא בימי חלוטו איתקש למת לטמא אף באהל: הואיל ומטמא בגדים. דהא ביום השביעי כתיב וכבס בגדיו: טומאה בחבורין. כגון בגדי לבושו הרי הן כמוהו אבל שאר בגדים הנוגע בהן וכן אם יגע באדם לא מטמא תדע שהרי המסיט נבילה כתיב ביה והנושא את נבלתה יכבס בגדיו (ויקרא יא) ולא אשכחן דלהוי אב הטומאה לטמא אדם ושאר בגדים: שכבת זרע מטמא בגדים. וכל בגד וכל עור אשר יהיה עליו שכבת זרע וגו': בהדיא כתיב ביה כו'. ה"ה נמי דהוה מצי למיפרך דהא טומאת בגדים לא דמיא לבגדים דבימי ספורו דהא בגדים דהכא לאו בגדי לבוש שרץ הן וטומאת מגע הוא אלא דעדיפא מיניה קא מותיב ליה: או לרבות הנוגע. דהכי תניא במסכת נדה (דף מג:) מנין לרבות הנוגע בשכבת זרע ת"ל או איש: הוה קמהדר ליה. רב אחדבוי לרב ששת בבדיחותא לפי שהיה רב ששת נכשל בתשובותיו: אשתתק רב אחדבוי. נעשה אלם: אתיא אימיה. דרב ששת: צווחה קמיה. שיתפלל עליו: להני חדיי. הדדים הללו. חדיי תרגום של חזה: דמצית מינייהו. שינקת מהן: ודאתאן עלה. ואחרי שבא לידינו שאלה זו לקובעה בגמ' מנלן דמטמא אדם: נאמר כיבוס בגדים בימי ספורו. והיה ביום השביעי יגלח את כל שערו וגו' ונאמר כיבוס בגדים למעלה ביום טהרת הצפרים כשיוצא מטומאת החלט וכבס המטהר את בגדיו: אף וחימה. שני לגיונות קשים הם ליפרע מן החוטאים: אע"פ ששוחד בחיק. שהוא עושה צדקה בסתר: חימה עזה. עדיין היא בתוקפה ורבי אלעזר סבר דהאי שוחד בחיק ארישא קאי ושוחד בחיק יכפה חימה עזה: ותפק לרעב נפשך. הוא פיוס דברי נחומים: ימצא צדקה. משמע יבא לידי עניות וימצא בני אדם שיעשו לו צדקה: ויהיו מוכשלים לפניך. אם אנשי ענתות היה מקלל שהיו מבקשין נפשו:

תוספות

מנין למצורע בימי ספורו שמטמא אדם. פשיטא לן למטמא כדתנן בריש מס' כלים (פ"א מ"א) אבות הטומאות השרץ ושכבת זרע (ה) ונבלה וטמא מת ומצורע בימי ספורו כו' הרי אלו מטמאין אדם וכלים במגע וכלי חרס באויר ולכך בעי מנלן דמטמא דהא כתיב ורחץ במים וטהר משמע דבאותה טבילה נטהר:

דהא הסיט נבלה מטמא בגדים ואינו מטמא אדם. (ו) לאו משום דטומאה בחבורין שאני. פ"ה דאינו מטמא אלא בגדים שהוא לבוש וקשה לריב"ס דבתורת כהנים פ' ויהי ביום השמיני (ז) מרבה שמטמא אפילו כלים (בחבורים) אע"ג דלא שייך בהו לבישה ואינו ממעט מבגדיו אלא אדם וכלי חרס שנוגע בהן אלא ודאי מטמא בגדים בשעה שמסיט אפילו אין לבוש בהן וכן משמע מדקאמר אלא מעתה שרץ דמטמא אדם מנלן לאו משום דמטמא בגדים מטמא אדם נמי כו' ואי קרי חבורים בגדים שהוא לבוש מאי פריך משרץ דלא שייך ביה לבישה התם ודאי ילפינן אדם מבגדים ונראה לריב"ס דלא גרס (ח) בחבורים אלא הכי גרס ודילמא טומאת בגדים שאני תדע דהא מסיט נבלה דמטמא בגדים ואינו מטמא אדם ולא גרסינן מ"ט לאו משום דטומאה בחבורים שאני דלא מהדר אלא שיש חילוק בין טומאת בגדים לטומאת אדם וכן משמע דאיהו גופיה לא קא מיבעיא ליה אם מטמא בגדים וכלים במגע אלא אאדם בעי:

אתיא אימיה וקא בכיא קמיה. פר"ח דהיינו אימיה דרב אחדבוי ולדידיה קרי עולא משגש אורחא דאימיה שגרם לאמו להתבזות לפני רב ששת והיא היתה מניקתו של רב ששת לכך אמר חזי הני חדיי דמלית מינייהו:

מה כיבוס בגדים האמור בימי חלוטו כו'. בכמה דברים חמור ימי חלוטו מימי ספורו ולא גמר מהיקשא והיינו טעמא משום דלגמרי לא מצי למגמר דהא כתב וטהר דמשמע דנטהר מכמו שהיה מתחלה אלא דוקא להך מילתא גמרי לפי שהן שוין דאין אדם וכלים מקבלין טומאה אלא מאב הטומאה:

גדול העושה צדקה בסתר יותר ממשה רבינו. פירוש יותר משכר חמה ממשה רבינו בתפלתו ואע"ג דמשה נמי עשה צדקה בסתר שמא אותה שעה כבר פסק אותו זכות:

חמה אינו כופה. תימה דבפרק ארבעה נדרים (דף לב.) אמרינן דחמה משה הרגו (ט):

והמפייסו בדברים מתברך בי"א. יש מגיהין והנותן פרוטה לעני והמפייסו משום דמשמע להו דקראי איירי בנותן צדקה דכתיב ותפק לרעב נפשך ונפש נענה תשביע ולאו מילתא היא דנפש נענה תשביע היינו תשביע בדברים שתפייסנו בדברים וע"כ לא גרסי' ליה דלהאי גיר' הוה ליה למימר מתברך בי"ז הנך שש דלעיל והני אחת עשרה:

רבינו גרשום

משגש. מבזה ארחתיה דאימיה שהצריכה להתבזות במה שדרכה להצניע שגלתה דדיה בשבילו כדאמר לקמן: וכבגד עדים. אלו אותן בגדים בלוים ונסחבים שמשימין שם התינוק כשהוא נולד ולפיכך נקראו עדים א) כמו ועדיאתו: בימי ספורו. היינו אותן ימים דכתיב וישב מחוץ לאהלו שבעת ימים דכבר עברו לימי חלוטו והזאתו: אמר ליה הואיל ומטמא בגדים. בימי ספורו דכתיב והיה ביום השביעי יגלח שערו וגו' וכבס בגדיו והואיל דמטמא בגדים דטעונין כבוס הכי נמי מטמא אדם: אמר ליה דלמא טומאה בחבורין שני דהני בגדים מחוברין עליו שלובש בהן אבל לעולם אימא לך אם יגע בבגדים אחרים אינו מטמאן וכי היכי דלא מטמא בגדים מעלמא אימא נמי דלא מטמא אדם תדע דהנה אשכחן דמטמא בגדים בחבורין ולא מטמא אדם: היסט נבלה. אדם שהסיט נבלה ומטמא בגדים דכתיב והנושא את נבלתה יכבס בגדיו וטמא עד הערב אלמא דבגדים טמאים הן ואינו [מטמא אדם] כדכתיב וטמא עד הערב הוא טמא ואינו מטמא אדם: היסט בכלל נושא. כדכתיב נישא וקרינן נושא (חולין קכד:): אמר ליה רב ששת. ולטעמיך דקא אמרת דטומאה בחבורין שאני מש"ה אין מטמא אדם אלא שרץ דמטמא אדם מנא לן לאו משום הואיל דמטמא בגדים דכתיב וכל אשר יפול עליו מהם במותם יטמא מכל כלי עץ או בגד או עור או שק והני לאו בחבורין נינהו: אמר ליה רב אחדבוי. שרץ דמטמא אדם בהדיא כתיב או איש אשר יגע בכל שרץ אלא פריך הכי ולטעמיך דאמרת טומאה בחבורין שני שכבת זרע דמטמא אדם מנלן משום דהואיל ומטמא בגדים דכתיב ואיש (אשר) [כי] תצא ממנו שכבת זרע וכתיב וכל בגד וכל עור אשר יהיה עליו שכבת זרע וכבס במים וטמא עד הערב ה"נ מטמא אדם ה"נ גבי מצורע: אמר ליה רב אחדבוי. שכבת זרע בהדיא כתיב ביה דמטמא כל אדם הנוגע בו דכתיב או דמייתר דמצי למכתב איש אשר תצא ממנו וגו' או ל"ל לרבות את הנוגע ואכתי מנין למצורע שמטמא בימי ספורו: הוה קא מהדר ליה בבדיחותא. כלומר שמח היה רב אחדבוי שנצחו לרב ששת שלא היה לו להשיב: אישתתק. נאלם: אתיא אימא. ג) דרב אחדבוי בכיא קמיה דרב ששת שהיתה מינקת שלו בשביל בנה דלימחל ליה ובעי רחמי עליה דרב אחדבוי ולא אשגח בה עד דמפקי דדיה לפניו כלומר עשה בשביל אלו דדין שינקת מהן ולהכי שהצריכה לכך קרו ליה עולא משגש ארחתיה דאימיה: ודאתאן עלה מיהא. הואיל ובאת לידינו שאילה זו דרב אחדבוי נעסוק בה: מנלן. דמצורע מטמא אדם בימי ספורו: כבוס בגדים בימי חלוטו. דכתיב וכבס המטהר את בגדיו ודנימטמו בימי חלוטו: מה להלן. בימי חלוטו מטמא אדם. דכתיב כל ימי אשר הנגע בו יטמא: מתן בסתר [יכפה] אף ושחד בחיק. כלומר מי שנותן צדקה בחיק של עני בצנעה כופה נמי חימה עזה: אע"פ ששוחד בחיק. של עני אעפ"כ חימה עזה שאינה נכפית בשביל השוחד בחיק: והמפייסו בדברים. שמנחמו ומדבר על לבו בדברי נחומין: דכתיב ותפק לרעב נפשך וגו'. כלומר משתדל מנפשך בדברים טובים לנחם הרעב ונפש נענה תשביע בדברים טובים או תוכה לדברים הללו: משום דרודף צדקה. שעושה צדקה משלו בא לו כבוד ברבים שיצטרך לבריות בתמיה:

מסורת הש"ס

א) רש"ע, ב) [ע"ל פרוש], ג) ב"ק נח: [ושם איתא רבא], ד) רש"א מ"ז, ה) אולי צ"ל אמרה:

הגהות הב"ח

(א) גמ' כי תראה ערום וגו' וכתיב אז יבקע כשחר אורך וארוכתך מהרה תצמח והלך לפניך צדקך כבוד ה' יאספך וכתיב אז תקרא וה' יענה תשוע ויאמר הנני והמפייסו בדברים: (ב) שם ונפש נענה תשביע בצחצחות נפשך ועצמותיך וכו' כצ"ל ותיבת וגו' נמחק: (ג) שם עליהם שכר כצ"ל ואות ו' נמחק: (ד) שם כל הרגיל לעשות צדקה הויין כצ"ל ותיבת זוכה נמחק: (ה) תוס' ד"ה מנין וכו' אבות הטומאות השרץ ושכבת זרע וטמא מת כצ"ל ותיבת ונבלה נמחק: (ו) ד"ה דהא הסיט כו' ואינו מטמא אדם מ"ט לאו כו': (ז) בא"ד פרשת ויהי ביום השמיני מוכח שמטמא אפי' כלים אע"ג דלא כצ"ל ותיבת בחיבורים נמחק: (ח) בא"ד ונראה לריב"ס דלא גרס ודלמא טומאה בחיבורים שאני אלא הכי: (ט) ד"ה חמה וכו' משה הרגו. נ"ב וע' בע"ז ריש דף ד' בתוס':

גליון הש"ס

תוס' ד"ה חמה כו' דחמה משה הרגו. עי' שבת דף נה ע"א תד"ה קלף:

לעזי רש"י

מייל"א. פירוש קליפה, קשקשת (תרגום ויקרא יא, ט ועיין רש"י ש"א יז, ה וערוך ערך קלף א'):

ליקוטי רש"י

כשריון. שריון קשקשים. כמין קשקשים דגים עשוין מברזל ומוסלים על גב השריון [ש"א יז, ה] קשקשת לכל נקב [ישעיה נט, יז]. מתן בסתר. צדקה. ושוחד בחיק. אף זו צדקה יכפה חמה עזה [משלי כא, יד]. ותפק לרעב נפשך. בתנחומי דברים [ישעיה נח, י].

תורה אור השלם

א) וַיִּלְבַּשׁ צְדָקָה כַּשִּׁרְיָן וְכוֹבַע יְשׁוּעָה בְּרֹאשׁוֹ וַיִּלְבַּשׁ בִּגְדֵי נָקָם תִּלְבֹּשֶׁת וַיַּעַט כַּמְעִיל קִנְאָה: [ישעיה נט, יז]
ב) וַנְּהִי כַטָּמֵא כֻּלָּנוּ וּכְבֶגֶד עִדִּים כָּל צִדְקֹתֵינוּ וַנָּבֶל כֶּעָלֶה כֻּלָּנוּ וַעֲוֹנֵנוּ כָּרוּחַ יִשָּׂאֻנוּ: [ישעיה סד, ה]
ג) אוֹ אִישׁ אֲשֶׁר יִגַּע בְּכָל שֶׁרֶץ אֲשֶׁר יִטְמָא לוֹ אוֹ בְאָדָם אֲשֶׁר יִטְמָא לוֹ לְכֹל טֻמְאָתוֹ: [ויקרא כב, ה]
ד) אִישׁ אִישׁ מִזֶּרַע אַהֲרֹן וְהוּא צָרוּעַ אוֹ זָב בַּקֳּדָשִׁים לֹא יֹאכַל עַד אֲשֶׁר יִטְהָר וְהַנֹּגֵעַ בְּכָל טְמֵא נֶפֶשׁ אוֹ אִישׁ אֲשֶׁר תֵּצֵא מִמֶּנּוּ שִׁכְבַת זָרַע: [ויקרא כב, ד]
ה) כִּי יָגֹרְתִּי מִפְּנֵי הָאַף וְהַחֵמָה אֲשֶׁר קָצַף יְיָ עֲלֵיכֶם לְהַשְׁמִיד אֶתְכֶם וַיִּשְׁמַע יְיָ אֵלַי גַּם בַּפַּעַם הַהִוא: [דברים ט, יט]
ו) מַתָּן בַּסֵּתֶר יִכְפֶּה אָף וְשֹׁחַד בַּחֵק חֵמָה עַזָּה: [משלי כא, יד]
ז) הֲלוֹא פָרֹס לָרָעֵב לַחְמֶךָ וַעֲנִיִּים מְרוּדִים תָּבִיא בָיִת כִּי תִרְאֶה עָרֹם וְכִסִּיתוֹ וּמִבְּשָׂרְךָ לֹא תִתְעַלָּם: [ישעיה נח, ז]
ח) וְתָפֵק לָרָעֵב נַפְשֶׁךָ וְנֶפֶשׁ נַעֲנָה תַּשְׂבִּיעַ וְזָרַח בַּחֹשֶׁךְ אוֹרֶךָ וַאֲפֵלָתְךָ כַּצָּהֳרָיִם: וְנָחֲךָ יְיָ תָּמִיד וְהִשְׂבִּיעַ בְּצַחְצָחוֹת נַפְשֶׁךָ וְעַצְמֹתֶיךָ יַחֲלִיץ וְהָיִיתָ כְּגַן רָוֶה וּכְמוֹצָא מַיִם אֲשֶׁר לֹא יְכַזְּבוּ מֵימָיו: וּבָנוּ מִמְּךָ חָרְבוֹת עוֹלָם מוֹסְדֵי דוֹר וָדוֹר תְּקוֹמֵם וְקֹרָא לְךָ גֹּדֵר פֶּרֶץ מְשֹׁבֵב נְתִיבוֹת לָשָׁבֶת: [ישעיה נח, י-יב]
ט) רֹדֵף צְדָקָה וָחָסֶד יִמְצָא חַיִּים צְדָקָה וְכָבוֹד: [משלי כא, כא]
י) וְאַתָּה יְיָ יָדַעְתָּ אֶת כָּל עֲצָתָם עָלַי לַמָּוֶת אַל תְּכַפֵּר עַל עֲוֹנָם וְחַטָּאתָם מִלְּפָנֶיךָ אַל תֶּמְחִי וְיִהְיוּ מֻכְשָׁלִים לְפָנֶיךָ בְּעֵת אַפְּךָ עֲשֵׂה בָהֶם: [ירמיה יח, כג]

חשק שלמה על רבינו גרשום א) [לכאורה משמע דכוון אתכלכים ועתר ועדילמא אבל לע"ע משמם זה לא שייך לקרותם עדים וצ"ע]: ג) [עי' בתוס' כאן ד"ה אתיא מה שכתב בשם ר"ח]:

אָדָם – HERE, TOO, [A *METZORA* DURING THE DAYS OF HIS COUNTING] DEFILES PEOPLE by touching them.

The Gemara now resumes discussing the merits of giving charity, and quotes the third statement made by R' Elazar:

אָמַר רַבִּי אֶלְעָזָר – R' Elazar said: גָּדוֹל הָעוֹשֶׂה צְדָקָה בְּסֵתֶר יוֹתֵר מִמֹּשֶׁה רַבֵּינוּ – **One who performs charitable acts in secret is greater than Moses, our teacher,**[31] דְּאִילּוּ בְּמֹשֶׁה רַבֵּינוּ כְּתִיב – **for while regarding Moses, our teacher, it is written:**[32] ,,כִּי יָגֹרְתִּי מִפְּנֵי הָאַף וְהַחֵמָה" – ***For I was in dread of the anger and the wrath;***[33] וְאִילּוּ בְּעוֹשֶׂה צְדָקָה כְּתִיב – **and regarding one who performs charitable acts** in secret **it is written:**[34] ,,מַתָּן בַּסֵּתֶר יִכְפֶּה־אָף וְשֹׁחַד בַּחֵק חֵמָה עַזָּה" – ***A gift in secret pacifies***[35] ***anger, and a present***[36] ***in the bosom*** (pacifies) ***strong wrath.*** Thus, one who performs charitable deeds in secret can triumph over the very anger and wrath that Moses himself feared, and in this sense he is greater than Moses.

R' Yitzchak interprets the latter part of the verse differently:

וּפְלִיגָא דְּרַבִּי יִצְחָק – **And** this interpretation by R' Elazar **differs with that of R' Yitzchak.** דְּאָמַר רַבִּי יִצְחָק אַף כּוֹפֶה – **For R' Yitzchak said: [Charity performed secretly] will pacify anger,** חֵמָה אֵינוֹ כּוֹפֶה – but **will not pacify wrath,** שֶׁנֶּאֱמַר: ,,וְשֹׁחַד בַּחֵק חֵמָה עַזָּה" – **for it is stated** in the verse: ***And a present in the bosom, strong wrath.*** אַף עַל פִּי שֶׁשּׁוֹחַד בַּחֵיק – This implies that **although a present is in the bosom** (i.e. even though charity was given in secret), חֵמָה עַזָּה – the Divine **wrath** remains **strong.** Thus, according to R' Yitzchak, an anonymous act of charity has the power to turn aside only the Divine anger,[37] while according to R' Elazar it can vanquish the Divine wrath as well.[38]

Another version of R' Yitzchak's statement:

אִיכָּא דְּאָמְרִי אָמַר רַבִּי יִצְחָק – **There are those who say** that **R' Yitzchak said** a different interpretation of the verse: כָּל דַּיָּין שֶׁנּוֹטֵל שֹׁחַד מֵבִיא חֵמָה עַזָּה לָעוֹלָם – **Any judge that takes a bribe brings strong wrath to the world,** [שֶׁנֶּאֱמַר: ,,וְשֹׁחַד בַּחֵק וגו׳ "] – **as it is stated:** ***And a bribe***[39] ***in the bosom etc.*** According to this version, the latter part of the verse does not concern the effects of charity, but the terrible consequences of accepting bribes.

Having mentioned R' Yitzchak, the Gemara records other statements by him on the subject of charity:

וְאָמַר רַבִּי יִצְחָק כָּל הַנּוֹתֵן פְּרוּטָה לְעָנִי – **And R' Yitzchak** also **said: Anyone who gives** even **a *perutah*** [a small copper coin] **to a pauper** מִתְבָּרֵךְ בְּשֵׁשׁ בְּרָכוֹת – **is blessed with six** Heavenly **blessings.** וְהַמְפַיְּיסוֹ בִּדְבָרִים – **And one who comforts [a pauper] with words** מִתְבָּרֵךְ בְּאַחַת עֶשְׂרֵה בְּרָכוֹת – **is blessed with eleven** Heavenly **blessings.**[40]

The Gemara enumerates the blessings that a donor receives:

הַנּוֹתֵן פְּרוּטָה לְעָנִי מִתְבָּרֵךְ בְּשֵׁשׁ בְּרָכוֹת דִּכְתִיב – **One who gives a *perutah* to a pauper is blessed with six** Heavenly **blessings, as it is written:** ,,הֲלוֹא פָרֹשׂ וגו׳ וַעֲנִיִּים מְרוּדִים תָּבִיא בָיִת וגו׳ כִּי־תִרְאֶה עָרֹם וגו׳" – ***Will you not break etc.*** *[your bread for the hungry]* ***and the wailing poor bring to your house etc.; when you see the naked*** *[you shall cover him].*[41]

The Gemara now enumerates the blessings that a comforter receives:

וְהַמְפַיְּיסוֹ בִּדְבָרִים מִתְבָּרֵךְ בְּאַחַת עֶשְׂרֵה בְּרָכוֹת – **And one who comforts [a pauper] with words is blessed with eleven** Heavenly **blessings.** שֶׁנֶּאֱמַר: ,,וְתָפֵק לָרָעֵב נַפְשֶׁךָ וְנֶפֶשׁ נַעֲנָה תַּשְׂבִּיעַ וְזָרַח בַּחֹשֶׁךְ אוֹרֶךָ וַאֲפֵלָתְךָ כַּצָּהֳרָיִם" – **For it is stated:**[42] ***And if you draw out*** (from) ***your soul to the hungry and satisfy the afflicted spirit,***[43] – then ***your light will shine through the darkness, and your gloom will be like the noonday.***

The next verse continues to shower blessings on the comforter:

,,וְנָחֲךָ ה׳ תָּמִיד וְהִשְׂבִּיעַ בְּצַחְצָחוֹת נַפְשֶׁךָ וגו׳ " – ***And God will guide you continually, and satisfy your soul*** (even) ***in*** (times of) ***drought etc.***

The next verse offers more blessings:

,,וּבָנוּ מִמְּךָ חָרְבוֹת עוֹלָם מוֹסְדֵי דוֹר־וָדוֹר תְּקוֹמֵם וגו׳ " – ***And through you*** (i.e. your good deeds) ***the ancient ruins will be rebuilt; you will raise up the foundations of many generations etc.*** All these blessings[44] will come to one who comforts the poor with words of kindness and compassion.

NOTES

so does a confirmed *metzora.* See *Rambam Comm.* to Mishnah *Keilim* 1:1, and *Mishnah Acharonah* there, and *Rabbeinu Gershom* here.

31. I.e. in the sense that his anonymous deeds more effectively appease the Divine wrath than did Moses' prayer (*Tosafos*). Anonymous charity is praiseworthy for two reasons: (1) the poor person is not embarrassed; (2) the giver receives no honor for his act, and it is thus performed purely for the sake of heaven (*Rabbeinu Yonah* to *Mishlei* 21:14).

32. *Deuteronomy* 9:19. Moses was describing his efforts to persuade God to spare the Jews after the sin of the Golden Calf.

33. Despite having interceded with God on behalf of the Jews, Moses still feared an awful retribution by the "anger" and the "wrath," those "two harsh legions (of angels) that punish sinners" (in the words of *Rashi*).

34. *Proverbs* 21:14.

35. Literally: inverts.

36. Literally: bribe. A gift to the poor resembles a bribe that one gives to God to obtain His favor. "In the bosom" connotes "in secret," since the bosom is a concealed part of the body (*Maharsha*).

37. It would be possible to interpret the Gemara to mean that R' Yitzchak, while disagreeing with R' Elazar on whether one who gives secret charity conquers "wrath," concurs that such a benefactor is greater than Moses. For Moses feared both "anger" *and* "wrath," while according to R' Yitzchak secret charity does conquer "anger." *Maharsha,* however, understands the Gemara to mean that R' Yitzchak disputes R' Elazar's very statement (that one who performs charity in secret is greater than Moses). He explains that R' Yitzchak's rebuttal is actually predicated on the fact that Moses indeed *slew* "wrath" (see *Nedarim* 32a), something which R' Yitzchak here establishes that secret charity is unable to do. Thus, it is impossible to declare the practitioner of secret charity superior to Moses, for even though the former is superior to Moses vis-a-vis "anger," Moses is superior vis-a-vis "wrath." Hence, they are equal (see also *Tosafos* ד״ה חמה and *Maharsha*).

38. R' Elazar understands *a present in the bosom* as belonging at the beginning of the verse, as the subject (along with *a gift in secret*) of the verb *pacify* [so that the second part of the verse means: "A present in the bosom pacifies strong anger"] (*Rashi*).

39. In this version R' Yitzchak interprets the word שֹׁחַד literally: *bribe.*

40. R' Yitzchak speaks of one who has no money to give, for otherwise one cannot fulfill his obligation to assist the poor merely with comforting words. Nevertheless, the comforter is more richly blessed than the donor, for the comforter gives of himself (a greater act of charity), while the donor merely parts with his money (*Maharsha*).

However, one who succors the poor both financially *and* emotionally will receive all seventeen blessings (*Tosafos*).

41. *Isaiah* 58:7. The six blessings, enumerated and inserted by *Bach,* are found in the following two verses (ibid. v. 8 and 9). They are: (1) יִבָּקַע כַּשַּׁחַר אוֹרֶךָ, *your light shall break forth like the morning.* (2) וַאֲרֻכָתְךָ מְהֵרָה תִצְמָח, *and your healing shall spring forth speedily.* (3) וְהָלַךְ לְפָנֶיךָ צִדְקֶךָ, *and your righteousness shall go before you.* (4) כְּבוֹד ה׳ יַאַסְפֶךָ, *the glory of God shall be your reward.* (5) אָז תִּקְרָא וַה׳ יַעֲנֶה, *Then you shall call, and God will answer.* (6) תְּשַׁוַּע וְיֹאמַר הִנֵּנִי, *you shall cry, and He will say, "Here I am."* [See *Rashi* and *Metzudas David* there.]

42. *Isaiah* 58:10.

43. I.e. if you offer to the poor heartfelt words of comfort and kindness, you will merit the blessings that the prophet now pronounces (*Rabbeinu Gershom*; cf. *Radak* and *Metzudos David* there).

44. Actually, the Gemara has only partially recounted the eleven blessings. The full list, which appears in verses 10-12 of *Isaiah* 58, is as follows: (1) וְזָרַח בַּחֹשֶׁךְ אוֹרֶךָ, *your light will shine through the darkness.* (2)

עין משפט נר מצוה

פו א מיי' פ"א מהל' טומאת צרעת הל' ב:
פז ב מיי' פ"ד מהל' אבות הטומאות הל' ב:
פח ג מיי' שם פ"ה הלכה א:
פט ד מיי' פ"י מהל' מתנות עניים הלכה ד ה סמג עשין קסב טוש"ע י"ד סי' רמט סעיף ו וסעיף ז:

משגש ארחתיה דאימיה משמיה דר' אלעזר מאי דכתיב א) וילבש צדקה כשריון לומר לך מה שריון זה כל קליפה וקליפה מצטרפת לשריון גדול אף צדקה כל פרוטה ופרוטה מצטרפת לחשבון גדול רבי חנינא אמר מהכא ב) וכבגד עדים כל צדקותינו מה בגד זה כל נימא ונימא מצטרפת לבגד גדול אף צדקה כל פרוטה ופרוטה מצטרפת לחשבון גדול אמאי קרו ליה עולא משגש ארחתיה דאימיה דבעא מיניה רב אחדבוי בר אמי מרב ששת א מנין למצורע בימי ספורו שמטמא אדם אמר לו הואיל ומטמא בגדים מטמא אדם א"ל דילמא טומאה בחבורים שאני דהא הסיט נבילה דמטמא בגדים ואינו מטמא אדם אמר ליה ואלא שרץ ב דמטמא אדם מנלן לאו משום דמטמא בגדים א"ל שרץ בהדיא כתיב ביה ג) או איש אשר יגע בכל שרץ אלא ג שכבת זרע דמטמא אדם מנלן לאו משום דהואיל ומטמא בגדים מטמא אדם א"ל שכבת זרע נמי בהדיא כתיב ביה ד) או איש לרבות את הנוגע אהדר ליה בבדיחותא חלש דעתיה דרב ששת אישתיק רב אחדבוי בר אמי ואתיקר תלמודיה אתיא אימיה וקא בכיא קמיה צווחה צווחה ולא אשגח בה אמרה ליה חזי להני חדיי דמצית מינייהו בעא רחמי עליה ואיתסי ודאתאן עלה מנא לן כדתניא ר"ש בן יוחי אומר נאמר כבוס בגדים בימי ספורו ונאמר כבוס בגדים בימי חלוטו מה להלן מטמא אדם אף כאן מטמא אדם אמר רבי אלעזר גדול העושה צדקה בסתר יותר ממשה רבינו דאילו במשה רבינו כתיב ה) כי יגורתי מפני האף והחמה ואילו בעושה צדקה כתיב ו) מתן בסתר יכפה אף ה) [ושחד בחיק חמה עזה] ופליגא דרבי יצחק דאמר ר' יצחק אף כופה חמה אינו כופה שנא' ושחד בחיק חמה עזה אע"פ ששוחד בחיק חמה עזה איכא דאמרי א"ר יצחק כל דיין שנוטל שחד מביא חמה עזה לעולם [שנאמר ושחד בחיק וגו'] ואמר רבי יצחק כל הנותן פרוטה לעני מתברך בשש ברכות והמפייסו בדברים מתברך בי"א ברכות הנותן פרוטה לעני מתברך בשש ברכות דכתיב ז) הלא ו פרוש לרעב לחמך ועניים מרודים תביא בית וגו' כי תראה ערום וגו' (א) ד והמפייסו בדברים מתברך באחת עשרה ברכות שנאמר ח) ותפק לרעב נפשך ונפש נענה תשביע וזרח בחשך אורך ואפלתך כצהרים ונחך ה' תמיד והשביע בצחצחות נפשך (ב) וגו' ובנו ממך חרבות עולם מוסדי דור ודור תקומם וגו' ואמר רבי יצחק מאי דכתיב ט) רודף צדקה וחסד ימצא חיים צדקה וכבוד משום דרודף צדקה ימצא צדקה אלא לומר לך כל הרודף אחר צדקה הקדוש ברוך הוא ממציא לו מעות ועושה בהן צדקה רב נחמן בר יצחק אמר הקדוש ברוך הוא ממציא לו בני אדם המהוגנים לעשות להן צדקה כדי לקבל עליהם (ג) שכרו לאפוקי מאי לאפוקי מדרבה ז דדרש רבה מאי דכתיב י) ויהיו מוכשלים לפניך בעת אפך עשה בהם אמר ירמיה לפני הקדוש ברוך הוא רבונו של עולם [אפילו] בשעה שכופין את יצרן ומבקשין לעשות צדקה לפניך הכשילם בבני אדם שאינן מהוגנין כדי שלא יקבלו עליהן שכר רבי יהושע בן לוי אמר כל הרגיל לעשות צדקה (ד) זוכה הווין לו בנים בעלי חכמה בעלי עושר בעלי אגדה דכתיב ימצא

רש"י

משגש. לשון מהומה ושגעון: קליפה. מייל"א בלע"ז: וכבגד עדים כל צדקותינו. כלומר אף כל צדקותינו נמאסו מחמת רשעינו כבגד מאוס שהאדם מסירו מעליו: עדים. כדמתרגמינן ויסר ואעדי וכן מעדה בגד ביום קרה (משלי כה) מ"מ מקיש צדקה לבגד צדקת הצדיקים לבגד הגון: בימי ספורו. בשבעת ימים שבין טהרת הצפרים להבאת קרבנותיו בשלמא בימי חלוטו איתקש למת לטמא אף באהל: הואיל ומטמא בגדים. דהא ביום השביעי כתיב וכבס בגדיו: טומאה בחבורין. כגון בגדי לבושו הרי הן כמוהו אבל שאר בגדים הנוגע בהן וכן אם יגע באדם לא מטמא מדע שהרי המסיט נבילה כתיב ביה והנושא את נבלתה יכבס בגדיו (ויקרא יא) ולא אשכחן להאי אב הטומאה לטמא אדם ושאר בגדים: שכבת זרע מטמא בגדים. וכל בגד וכל עור אשר יהיה עליו שכבת זרע וגו': בהדיא כתיב ביה כו'. ה"נ דהוה מצי למיפרך דהא טומאת בגדים לא דמיא לבגדים דימי ספורו דהא בגדים דהכא לאו בגדי לבוש שרץ הן וטומאת מגע הוא אלא דעדיפא מיניה קא מותיב ליה: או לרבות הנוגע. דהכי תניא במסכת נדה (דף מג.) מנין לרבות הנוגע בשכבת זרע ת"ל או איש: הוה קמהדר ליה. רב אחדבוי לרב ששת בבדיחותא לפי שהיה רב ששת נכשל בתשובותיו: אשתתק רב אחדבוי. נעשה אלם: אתיא אימיה. דרב ששת: צווחה קמיה. שיתפלל עליו: להני חדיי. הדדים הללו. חדיי שדים בלע"ז: דמצית מינייהו. שינקת מהן: ודאתאן עלה. ואחרי שבא לידינו שאלה זו לקובעה בגמ' מנלן למטמא אדם: נאמר כיבוס בגדים בימי ספורו. והיה ביום השביעי יגלח את כל שערו וגו' ונאמר כיבוס בגדים למעלה ביום טהרת הצפרים כשיוצא מטומאת החלט וכבס המטהר את בגדיו: אף וחימה. שני מלאכים קשים הם ליפרע מן החוטאים: אע"פ ששוחד בחיק. שהוא עושה צדקה בסתר: חימה עזה. עדיין היא בתוקפה ורבי אלעזר סבר דהאי שוחד בחיק אריישא קאי ושוחד בחיק יכפה חימה עזה: ותפק לרעב נפשך. הוא פיוס דברי נחומים: ימצא צדקה. משמע יבא לידי עניות שיהיו בני אדם צריכין לו: ויהיו מוכשלים לפניך. את אנשי ענתות היה מקלל שהיו מבקשין נפשו:

תוספות

מנין למצורע בימי ספורו שמטמא אדם. פשיטא לן דמטמא כדתנן בריש מס' כלים (פ"א מ"א) אבות הטומאות השרץ ושכבת זרע (ה) ונבלה וטמא מת ומצורע בימי ספורו כו' הרי אלו מטמאין אדם וכלים במגע וכלי חרס באויר ולכך בעי מנלן דמטמא דהא כתיב ורחץ במים וטהר משמע דבאותה טבילה נטהר: דהא הסיט נבלה מטמא בגדים ואינו מטמא אדם. (ו) לאו משום דטומאה בחבורין שאני. פ"ה דאינו מטמא אלא בגדים שהוא לבוש וקשה לריב"ס דבתורת כהנים פ' ויהי ביום השמיני (ז) מרבה שמטמא אפילו כלים ד) (בחבורים) אע"ג דלא שייך בהו לבישה ואינו ממעט מבגדיו אלא אדם וכלי חרס שנוגע בהן אלא ודאי מטמא בגדים בשעה שמסיט אפילו אין לבוש בהן וכן משמע מדקאמר אלא מעתה שרץ דמטמא אדם מנלן לאו משום דמטמא בגדים מטמא אדם נמי כו' ואי קרי חבורים בגדים שהוא לבוש מאי פריך משרץ דלא שייך ביה לבישה התם ודאי ילפינן אדם מבגדים ונראה לריב"ס דלא גרס (ח) בחבורים אלא הכי גרס ודילמא טומאת בגדים שאני תדע דהא מסיט נבלה דמטמא בגדים ואינו מטמא אדם ולא גרסינן מ"ט לאו משום דטומאה בחבורים שאני דלא מהדר אלא שיש חילוק בין טומאת בגדים לטומאת אדם וכן משמע דאיהו גופיה לא קא מיבעיא ליה אם מטמא בגדים וכלים במגע אלא אאדם בעי:

אתיא אימיה וקא בכיא קמיה. פר"ח דהיינו אימיה דרב אחדבוי ולדידיה קרי עולא משגש אורחא דאימיה שגרם לאמו להתבזות לפני רב ששת והיא היתה מניקתו של רב ששת לכך ה) אמר חזי הני חדיי דמצית מינייהו: מה כיבוס בגדים האמור בימי חלוטו כו'. בכמה דברים חמור ימי חלוטו מימי ספורו ולא גמר מהיקשא והיינו טעמא משום דלגמרי לא מצי למגמר דהא כתב וטהר דמשמע דנטהר מכמו שהיה מתחלה אלא דוקא להך מילתא גמרי לפי שהן שוין דאין אדם וכלים מקבלין טומאה אלא מאב הטומאה: גדול העושה צדקה בסתר יותר ממשה רבינו. פירוש יותר משכך חמה ממשה רבינו בתפלתו ואע"ג דמשה נמי עשה צדקה בסתר שמא אותה שעה כבר פסק אותו זכות: חמה אינו כופה. תימה דבפרק ארבעה נדרים (דף לב.) אמרינן ט) דחמה משה הרגו (ט): והמפייסו בדברים מתברך בי"א. יש מגיהין והנותן פרוטה לעני והמפייסו משום דמשמע להו דקרא איירי בנותן צדקה דכתיב ותפק לרעב נפשך ונפש נענה תשביע ולאו מילתא היא דנפש נענע תשביע היינו תשביע בדברים שתפייסנו בדברים וע"כ לא גרסי' ליה דלההיא גיר' הוה ליה למימר מתברך בי"ז הנך שש דלעיל והני אחת עשרה: ואיזו

מסורת הש"ס

א) רש"ל, ב) [ל"ל פרוס], ג) ב"ק נח: [ושם איתא רבא], ד) רש"א מ"ז, ה) אולי צ"ל אמרה:

הגהות הב"ח

(א) גמ' כי תראה ערום וגו' וכתיב אז יבקע כשחר אורך וארוכתך מהרה תצמח והלך לפניך צדקך כבוד ה' יאספך וכתיב אז תקרא וה' יענה תשוע ויאמר הנני והמפייסו בדברים: (ב) שם והשביע בצחצחות נפשך ובנו כצ"ל ותיבת וגו' נמחק: (ג) שם עליהם שכר כצ"ל ואות ו' נמחק: (ד) שם כל הרגיל לעשות [צדקה] הוין כצ"ל ותיבת זוכה נמחק: (ה) תוס' ד"ה מנין וכו' אבות הטומאות השרץ ושכבת זרע וטמא מת כצ"ל ותיבת ונבלה נמחק: (ו) ד"ה דהא הסיט כו' ואינו מטמא אדם מ"ט לאו משום: (ז) בא"ד פרשת ויהי ביום השמיני מוכח שמטמא אפי' כלים אע"ג דלא כצ"ל ותיבת בחיבורים נמחק: (ח) בא"ד ונראה לריב"ס דלא גרס טומאה בחיבורים שאני אלא הכי: (ט) ד"ה חמה וכו' משה הרגו. נ"ב ועי' בע"ז ריש דף ד' כתוס':

גליון הש"ס

תוס' ד"ה חמה כו' דחמה משה הרגו. עי' שבת דף נה ע"א תד"ה קלף:

לעזי רש"י

מייל"א. פירוש קליפה, קשקשת (תרגום ויקרא יא, ט ועיין רש"י ש"ח ה וערוך ערך קלף א').

ליקוטי רש"י

כשריון. שריון קשקשים. כמין קשקשות דגים עשוין מברזל תופלים על גב השריון [פ"א נקבי השריון] קשקשים לכל נקב [שמואל א, יז, ה]. מתן בסתר. צדקה. ושוחד בחיק. אף זו צדקה יכפה אף חמה עזה [משלי כא, יד]. ותפק לרעב נפשך. בתנחומי דברים טובים [ישעיה נח, י].

תורה אור השלם

א) וילבש צדקה כשרין וכובע ישועה בראשו וילבש בגדי נקם תלבשת ויעט כמעיל קנאה: [ישעיה נט, יז]
ב) ונהי כטמא כלנו וכבגד עדים כל צדקתינו ונבל כעלה כלנו ועוננו כרוח ישאנו: [ישעיה סד, ה]
ג) או איש אשר יגע בכל שרץ אשר יטמא לו או באדם אשר יטמא לו לכל טמאתו: [ויקרא כב, ה]
ד) איש איש מזרע אהרן והוא צרוע או זב בקדשים לא יאכל עד אשר יטהר והנגע בכל טמא נפש או איש אשר תצא ממנו שכבת זרע: [ויקרא כב, ד]
ה) כי יגרתי מפני האף והחמה אשר קצף יי עליכם להשמיד אתכם וישמע יי אלי גם בפעם ההוא: [דברים ט, יט]
ו) מתן בסתר יכפה אף ושחד בחק חמה עזה: [משלי כא, יד]
ז) הלוא פרס לרעב לחמך ועניים מרודים תביא בית כי תראה ערם וכסיתו ומבשרך לא תתעלם: [ישעיה נח, ז]
ח) ותפק לרעב נפשך ונפש נענה תשביע וזרח בחשך אורך ואפלתך כצהרים: ונחך יי תמיד והשביע בצחצחות נפשך ועצמתיך יחליץ והיית כגן רוה וכמוצא מים אשר לא יכזבו מימיו: ובנו ממך חרבות עולם מוסדי דור ודור תקומם וקרא לך גדר פרץ משבב נתיבות לשבת: [ישעיה נח, י-יב]
ט) רדף צדקה וחסד ימצא חיים צדקה וכבוד: [משלי כא, כא]
י) ואתה יי ידעת את כל עצתם עלי למות אל תכפר על עונם וחטאתם מלפניך אל תמחי ויהיו מכשלים לפניך בעת אפך עשה בהם: [ירמיה יח, כג]

רבינו גרשום

משגש. מבזה ארחתיה דאימיה שהצריכה להתבזות במה שדרכה להצניע שגלתה דדיה בשבילו כדאמר לקמן: וכבגד עדים. אלו אותן בגדים בלוים ונסחבים שמשימין את התינוק כשהוא נולד ולפיכך נקראו עדים לשון א) כמו ועדיאתו: בימי ספורו. היינו אותן ימים דכתיב וישב מחוץ לאהלו שבעת ימים דכבר עברו ימי חלוטו והזאתו: אמר ליה הואיל ומטמא בגדים. בימי ספורו דכתיב והיה ביום השביעי יגלח שערו וגו' וכבס בגדיו והואיל דמטמא בגדים דטעונין כבוס הכי נמי מטמא אדם: אמר ליה דלמא טומאה בחבורין שני דהני בגדים מחוברין עליו שלובש בהן אבל לעולם אימא לך אם יגע בבגדים אחרים אינו מטמאן וכי היכי דלא מטמא בגדים מעלמא אימא נמי דלא מטמא אדם תדע דהנה אשכחן דמטמא בגדים בחבורין ולא מטמא אדם: הסיט נבלה. אדם שהסיט נבלה ומטמא בגדים דכתיב והנושא את נבלתה יכבס בגדיו וטמא עד הערב אלמא דבגדים טמאים הן ואינו [מטמא אדם] דכתיב וטמא עד הערב הוא ואינו מטמא אדם: הסיט בכלל נשא. כדכתיב נישא וקרינן נושא (חולין קכד:): אמר ליה רב ששת. ולטעמיך דקא אמרת דטומאה בחבורין שאני משו"ה אין מטמא אדם אלא שרץ דמטמא אדם מנ לן לאו משום הואיל דמטמא בגדים דכתיב וכל אשר יפול עליו מהם במותם יטמא מכל כלי עץ או בגד או עור או שק והני לאו בחבורין נינהו: אמר ליה רב אחדבוי. שרץ דמטמא אדם בהדיא כתיב ביה או איש אשר יגע בכל שרץ אלא פריך הכי ולטעמיך דאמרת טומאה בחבורין שני שכבת זרע דמטמא אדם מנלן לאו משום הואיל ומטמא בגדים דכתיב ואיש (אשר) [כי] תצא ממנו שכבת זרע וכתיב וכל בגד וכל עור אשר יהיה עליו שכבת זרע וכבס במים וטמא עד הערב ה"נ גבי מצורע: אמר ליה רב אחדבוי. שכבת זרע בהדיא כתיב ביה דמטמאה כל אדם הנוגע בו דכתיב או דמייתר מדאי דמכתב איש אשר תצא ממנו וגו' ה"ל או לרבות את הנוגע ואכתי מנין למצורע שמטמא בימי ספורו: הוה קא מהדר ליה בבדיחותא. כלומר שמחה הוה אחדבוי שנצחו לרב ששת שלא היה לו להשיב: אישתתק. נאלם: אתיא אימא. ג) דרב אחדבוי בכיא קמיה דרב ששת שהיתה מניקת שלו בשביל בנה דלימחל ליה ובעי רחמי עליה ובכי רחמי עליה ולא אשגח בה עד דמפקי דדיה לפני רב ששת כלומר בשביל אלו דדין שינקת מהן ולהכי שהצריכה לכך קרי ליה עולא משגש ארחתיה דאימיה: ודאתאן עלה מיהא. הואיל ובאת לידינו שאלה זו דרב אחדבוי נעסוק בה: מנלן. למצורע דמטמא אדם בימי ספורו: מה להלן בימי חלוטו מטמא אדם. אף כאן מטמא אדם: כבוס בגדים. וכבס המטהר את בגדיו: מתן בסתר [יכפה] אף ושוחד בחיק. כלומר מי שנותן בחיק של עני בצנעה כופה נמי חימה עזה: אע"פ ששוחד בחיק. של עני אע"פ כן חימה עזה שאינה נכפית בשביל השוחד בחיק: והמפייסו בדברים. שמנחמו ומדבר על לבו דבר נחומין: דכתיב ותפק לרעב נפשך וגו'. כלומר אם תפייסנו בדברים טובים אז תזכה לדברים הללו: משום דרודף צדקה. שעושה צדקה משלו בא לידי עושר שיצטרך לבריות בתמיה:

חשק שלמה על רבינו גרשום א) [בלשון] משמע דסון לתרגום אונקלוס ...

The Gemara records another statement by R' Yitzchak on the topic of charity:

וְאָמַר רַבִּי יִצְחָק – **And R' Yitzchak** also **said:** מַאי דִּכְתִיב – **What** is the meaning of that **which is written:**[45] ,,רֹדֵף צְדָקָה וָחֶסֶד יִמְצָא חַיִּים צְדָקָה וְכָבוֹד״ – ***He who pursues*** (opportunities to perform acts of) ***charity and kindness will find life, charity and honor*** (from God)? מִשּׁוּם דְּרוֹדֵף צְדָקָה יִמְצָא צְדָקָה – **Because one pursues charity he will find charity?!** Scripture implies that he will become poor and find people to give *him* charity, which is hardly a just reward! אֶלָּא לוֹמַר לְךָ – **Rather,** the verse comes **to tell you** that כָּל הָרוֹדֵף אַחַר צְדָקָה – concerning **anyone who pursues** opportunities to perform acts of **charity,** הַקָּדוֹשׁ בָּרוּךְ הוּא מַמְצִיא לוֹ מָעוֹת – **the Holy One, Blessed is He, provides him with funds** וְעוֹשֶׂה בָּהֶן צְדָקָה – and he uses them for charity. Thus, the reward for pursuing charity is prosperity.[46]

The Gemara presents another interpretation of the verse:

רַב נַחְמָן בַּר יִצְחָק אָמַר – **Rav Nachman bar Yitzchak said:** הַקָּדוֹשׁ בָּרוּךְ הוּא מַמְצִיא לוֹ בְּנֵי אָדָם הַמְהוּגָּנִים – Concerning one who pursues opportunities to do charity, **the Holy One, Blessed is He, provides him with worthy people** לַעֲשׂוֹת לָהֶן צְדָקָה – **for whom to perform** acts of **charity,** כְּדֵי לְקַבֵּל עֲלֵיהֶם שְׂכָרוֹ – **in order for [the donor] to receive a**[47] **reward for [his deeds].**

The Gemara wonders when charity is *not* rewarded:

לְאַפּוּקֵי מַאי – **What** situation does Rav Nachman's interpretation come **to exclude?**

The Gemara answers:

לְאַפּוּקֵי מִדְּדָרַשׁ רַבָּה – It comes **to exclude** the situation **that Rabbah expounded** upon, דְּדָרַשׁ רַבָּה – **for Rabbah expounded:** מַאי דִּכְתִיב – **What** is the meaning of that **which is written:**[48] ,,וְיִהְיוּ מֻכְשָׁלִים לְפָנֶיךָ בְּעֵת אַפְּךָ עֲשֵׂה בָהֶם״ – ***And let them be made to stumble before You; deal with them at the time of Your anger.***[49] אָמַר יִרְמְיָה לִפְנֵי הַקָּדוֹשׁ בָּרוּךְ הוּא – **Jeremiah said before the Holy One, Blessed is He:** רִבּוֹנוֹ שֶׁל עוֹלָם [אֲפִילוּ] בְּשָׁעָה שֶׁכּוֹפִין אֶת יִצְרָן – **Master of the Universe! [Even] at a time when [the inhabitants of Anasos] subdue their** evil **inclinations** וּמְבַקְּשִׁין לַעֲשׂוֹת צְדָקָה לְפָנֶיךָ – **and seek to perform** acts of **charity before You,**[50] הַכְשִׁילֵם בִּבְנֵי אָדָם שֶׁאֵינָן מְהוּגָּנִין – **make them stumble** by providing them **with people that are not worthy** of receiving charity, כְּדֵי שֶׁלֹּא יְקַבְּלוּ עֲלֵיהֶן שָׂכָר – **so that they will not receive a reward for [their deeds].**[51] Jeremiah's prayer thus clarifies Rav Nachman's interpretation: One who pursues opportunities to perform charity ensures that God will provide him with deserving recipients, so that – unlike the inhabitants of Anasos – he will be fully rewarded for his deeds.

The Gemara mentions another reward for giving charity:

רַבִּי יְהוֹשֻׁעַ בֶּן לֵוִי אָמַר – **R' Yehoshua ben Levi said:** כָּל הָרָגִיל לַעֲשׂוֹת צְדָקָה – **Anyone who habitually performs** acts of **charity** (זוכה) הָוְיָין לוֹ בָּנִים בַּעֲלֵי חָכְמָה בַּעֲלֵי עוֹשֶׁר בַּעֲלֵי אַגָּדָה – **will have**[52] **sons who possess wisdom, wealth and** knowledge of the **Aggadah.**[53]

R' Yehoshua provides Scriptural support for his dictum:

בַּעֲלֵי חָכְמָה דִּכְתִיב – They will **possess wisdom, as it is written:**

NOTES

וַאֲפֵלָתְךָ כַּצָּהֳרָיִם, *and your gloom will be like the noonday.* (3) וְנָחֲךָ ה׳ תָּמִיד, *and God will guide you continually.* (4) וְהִשְׂבִּיעַ בְּצַחְצָחוֹת נַפְשֶׁךָ, *and satisfy your soul in drought.* (5) וְעַצְמֹתֶיךָ יַחֲלִיץ, *and make strong your bones.* (6) וְהָיִיתָ כְּגַן רָוֶה, *and you shall be like a watered garden.* (7) וּכְמוֹצָא מַיִם אֲשֶׁר לֹא־יְכַזְּבוּ מֵימָיו, *and like a spring of water, whose waters fail not.* (8) וּבָנוּ מִמְּךָ חָרְבוֹת עוֹלָם, *And through you the ancient ruins will be rebuilt.* (9) מוֹסְדֵי דוֹר־וָדוֹר תְּקוֹמֵם, *you will raise up the foundations of many generations.* (10) וְקֹרָא לְךָ גֹּדֵר פֶּרֶץ, *and you shall be called "the repairer of the breach."* (11) מְשׁוֹבֵב נְתִיבוֹת לָשָׁבֶת, *"the restorer of paths to dwell in."* [See *Rashi*, *Radak*, and *Metzudas David* there.]

45. *Proverbs* 21:21.

46. I.e. he will always have money to donate to charity. *Maharsha* explains differently: One who cannot afford to give charity, but *pursues others* to persuade them to give, will become prosperous and thus able to contribute himself.

47. Our translation follows *Bach,* who deletes the letter ו (*vav*) from שְׂכָרוֹ.

48. *Jeremiah* 18:23, wherein the prophet curses the men of Anasos, who wished to kill him (*Rashi*).

49. So that the punishment meted out be especially severe (*Metzudos David*).

50. [See *Tosafos*, *Shitah Mekubetzes* and *Maharsha* to *Bava Kamma* 16b, who explain how we may infer that this verse is speaking of acts of charity.]

51. [It should be noted that only wicked people receive no reward at all. However, if a righteous person gives charity to an unworthy person inadvertantly , he receives some measure of reward for his act, since it was done for the sake of Heaven (see *Nimukei Yosef* to *Bava Kamma* 16b, see also *Pnei Shlomo*).]

52. Emendation and translation follows *Bach,* who deletes זוֹכֶה, *merit.*

53. He will be rewarded measure for measure (מִדָּה כְּנֶגֶד מִדָּה), as follows: Because with his gift of charity he revived the poor, his sons will achieve wisdom, for it is written: *Wisdom will revive its possessors (Ecclesiastes* 7:12). Because he depleted his financial resources to give charity, he will have wealthy sons. And because his donations allowed the poor to live respectably in the eyes of society, his sons [will become masters of homiletic discourse and] will be honored by all the people (*Ben Yehoyada*; see *Rashi* below, 10a ד״ה בעלי אגדה).

יִמְצָא חַיִּים – ***He*** (who pursues charity) ***will find life,***[1] which refers to wisdom;[2] בַּעֲלֵי עוֹשֶׁר דִּכְתִיב: ,,צְדָקָה" – further, his sons will **possess wealth, for it is written** that the pursuer of charity will also find ***charity;***[3] בַּעֲלֵי אַגָּדָה דִּכְתִיב: ,,וְכָבוֹד" – and, finally, his sons will **possess** knowledge of **Aggadah, for it is** also **written** there: ***and honor.***[4]

The Gemara proves that the honor mentioned here is accorded specifically for Torah knowledge:

כְּתִיב הָכָא: ,,וְכָבוֹד" – **It is written here** in the verse just quoted: ***and honor;*** וּכְתִיב הָתָם: ,,כָּבוֹד חֲכָמִים יִנְחָלוּ" – **and it says there:**[5] ***The wise men shall inherit honor.*** The second verse teaches that the honor promised to the sons of one who pursues charity will be accorded for their knowledge of Torah.

The Gemara continues to discuss the merits of giving charity:

תַּנְיָא הָיָה רַבִּי מֵאִיר אוֹמֵר – **It was taught in a Baraisa:** R' MEIR WAS WONT TO SAY: יֵשׁ לוֹ לְבַעַל הַדִּין לְהָשִׁיבְךָ וְלוֹמַר לְךָ – THE LITIGANT[6] HAS an argument TO ANSWER YOU AND TELL YOU, and it is the following: אִם אֱלֹהֵיכֶם אוֹהֵב עֲנִיִּים הוּא – IF YOUR GOD IS truly A LOVER OF THE POOR, מִפְּנֵי מָה אֵינוֹ מְפַרְנְסָן – FOR WHAT REASON[7] DOES HE NOT SUSTAIN THEM? Since God does not provide for them, they must have fallen into His disfavor; hence, you Jews certainly should not assist them with gifts of charity!

R' Meir provides us with the correct reply to this argument:

אֱמוֹר לוֹ – However, you should SAY TO HIM: כְּדֵי שֶׁנִּיצּוֹל אָנוּ בָּהֶן מִדִּינָהּ שֶׁל גֵּיהִנֹּם – God does not cause the poor to suffer because they are wicked; rather, He impoverishes people SO THAT WE MAY BE SAVED, THROUGH giving THEM charity, FROM THE JUDGMENT OF GEHINNOM.[8] Thus, the poor may even be righteous individuals; they suffer poverty for our benefit!

The Gemara relates that this argument was, in fact, once advanced by a Roman general:

וְזוֹ שְׁאֵלָה שָׁאַל טוּרְנוּסְרוּפוּס הָרָשָׁע אֶת רַבִּי עֲקִיבָא – **And this** very **question the wicked Turanus Rufus**[9] **asked of R' Akiva:** אִם אֱלֹהֵיכֶם אוֹהֵב עֲנִיִּים הוּא – **If your God is a lover of the poor,** מִפְּנֵי מָה אֵינוֹ מְפַרְנְסָם – **for what reason does He not sustain them?**

R' Akiva offered the reply previously mentioned:

אָמַר לוֹ כְּדֵי שֶׁנִּיצּוֹל אָנוּ בָּהֶן מִדִּינָהּ שֶׁל גֵּיהִנֹּם – **[R' Akiva] said to [Turanus Rufus]:** God makes people needy **in order that, through** our giving **them** charity, **we may be saved from the judgment of Gehinnom.**

Turanus Rufus took issue with this response:

אָמַר לוֹ אַדְּרַבָּה – **[Turanus Rufus] said to [R' Akiva]: On the contrary!** זוֹ שֶׁמְּחַיַּיבְתָּן לַגֵּיהִנֹּם – **This** giving of charity **is what** actually **condemns you to** be punished in **Gehinnom!**

Turanus Rufus explained himself allegorically:

אֶמְשׁוֹל לְךָ מָשָׁל – **I shall illustrate** this concept **for you with a parable.** לְמָה הַדָּבָר דּוֹמֶה – **To what is this matter similar?** לְמֶלֶךְ בָּשָׂר וָדָם שֶׁכָּעַס עַל עַבְדּוֹ – It is analogous **to** the case of **a human**[10] **king who was angry at his servant** וַחֲבָשׁוֹ בְּבֵית הָאֲסוּרִין – **and confined [the servant] in prison** וְצִוָּה עָלָיו שֶׁלֹּא לְהַאֲכִילוֹ וְשֶׁלֹּא לְהַשְׁקוֹתוֹ – **and ordered that** no one **feed him or give him drink.** וְהָלַךְ אָדָם אֶחָד וְהֶאֱכִילוֹ וְהִשְׁקָהוּ – **And one man** subsequently **went and fed [the servant] and gave him drink** in defiance of the king's order. כְּשֶׁשָּׁמַע הַמֶּלֶךְ לֹא כּוֹעֵס עָלָיו – **When the king hears** about this man's actions, **is he not angry at [the man]?** וְאַתֶּם קְרוּיִן עֲבָדִים – **And you** Jews **are called servants** of God, שֶׁנֶּאֱמַר: ,,כִּי-לִי בְנֵי-יִשְׂרָאֵל עֲבָדִים" – **as it says:**[11] ***For unto Me the children of Israel are servants!***[12] Hence, by giving charity you actually violate the edict of God, your King, and so *incur* the judgment of Gehinnom.

R' Akiva countered with a parable of his own:

אָמַר לוֹ רַבִּי עֲקִיבָא אֶמְשׁוֹל לְךָ מָשָׁל – **R' Akiva said to [Turanus Rufus]: I shall illustrate** the situation **for you with a** different **parable.** לְמָה הַדָּבָר דּוֹמֶה – **To what is this matter** of giving charity **similar?** לְמֶלֶךְ בָּשָׂר וָדָם שֶׁכָּעַס עַל בְּנוֹ וַחֲבָשׁוֹ בְּבֵית הָאֲסוּרִין – It is analogous **to** the case of **a human king who was angry at his son and confined [the son] in prison** וְצִוָּה עָלָיו שֶׁלֹּא לְהַאֲכִילוֹ וְשֶׁלֹּא לְהַשְׁקוֹתוֹ – **and ordered that** no one **feed him or give him drink.** וְהָלַךְ אָדָם אֶחָד וְהֶאֱכִילוֹ וְהִשְׁקָהוּ – **And one man** subsequently **went and fed [the son] and gave him drink,** thereby saving his life. כְּשֶׁשָּׁמַע הַמֶּלֶךְ לֹא דּוֹרוֹן מְשַׁגֵּר לוֹ – **When the king hears** about this man's actions, **does he not send [the man] a gift?**[13] וַאֲנַן קְרוּיִן בָּנִים – **And we** Jews **are called sons** of God, דִּכְתִיב: ,,בָּנִים אַתֶּם לַה' אֱלֹהֵיכֶם" – **as it is written:**[14] ***Sons you are to Hashem, your God.*** Thus, although imprisoned in exile, the Jewish people are still God's children,[15] and one who sustains the poor among them with gifts of charity earns God's gratitude and is thus absolved from the judgment of Gehinnom.

Turanus Rufus objected to this explanation:

אָמַר לוֹ אַתֶּם קְרוּיִם בָּנִים וּקְרוּיִן עֲבָדִים – **[Turanus Rufus] said to**

NOTES

1. R' Yehoshua's source for all three rewards is the verse cited previously (9b): *He who pursues charity and kindness will find life, charity and honor (Proverbs* 21:21).

2. For Scripture states (*Proverbs* 8:35): כִּי מֹצְאִי מָצָא חַיִּים, *For one who finds me* [Wisdom narrates this verse] *has found life (Rashi;* cf. *Maharsha).*

3. I.e. they will be blessed by God with prosperity and thus have the wherewithal to give charity, as R' Yitzchak explained above (9b).

4. I.e. they will be honored by all because, as masters of the Aggadah, they will inspire the public with their homiletic discourses (*Rashi*).

5. *Proverbs* 3:35.

6. I.e. a wicked Jew or an idolater [who is attempting to dissuade Jews from giving charity] (*Rashi*; cf. *Rabbeinu Gershom*). He is called a "litigant" because he has a vested interest in preventing charitable gifts, for charity properly given saves the Jewish people from being subjugated by gentile regimes (*Ben Yehoyada*).

7. The expression מִפְּנֵי מָה, *for what reason,* implies that the questioner understood that two (or more) reasons are possible, and he therefore asks which one is applicable. Here, too, the idolater understood that God does not sustain the poor for one of two reasons: 1) He wishes to afford the Jews an opportunity to be saved from the judgment of Gehinnom; or (2) to be saved from subjugation under gentile regimes. R' Meir cunningly replied that the first reason is correct, for he feared that had he indicated the second reason the Roman idolaters would legally ban the giving of charity in order to retain their stranglehold over the subjugated Jewish people (*Ben Yehoyada*; see previous note).

8. A metaphysical realm where souls are punished.

9. He plowed under the ruins of the *Heichal* after the destruction of the Second Temple — see *Taanis* 29a.

10. Literally: flesh and blood.

11. *Leviticus* 25:55.

12. It would appear that the wicked Turanus Rufus conceded that when the Jews occupy their own land, they are obligated to give charity and are thereby saved from the judgment of Gehinnom. However, when the Jews are cast into exile, they are like the imprisoned servant in the parable, to whom the king forbade offering any food or drink. Similarly, argued Turanus Rufus, God has cast His servant nation into the prison of exile and subjugation, and has forbidden everyone to alleviate their suffering with gifts of charity (*Maharsha*).

13. Although the king imprisoned his son, we know that he did not want the son to die, for no father ever desires to kill his child (see *Sanhedrin* 72a,b). Thus, although the king may have been compelled to imprison his son, he would undoubtedly reward anyone who sustained the child.

14. *Deuteronomy* 14:1.

15. See *Maharsha*.

מסורת הש"ס

א) [תוספ' פאה פ"ד] כתובות סח., ב) [תוס' פאה פ"ד], ג) [בילקוט ובע"י ליתא] והגי' אמר ר"ח ב"א אר"י:

הגהות הב"ח

(א) גמרא פש גבייהו כצ"ל ואות ו' נמחק: (ב) שם בעי למיפל חלש דעתיה אמר השתא: (ג) שם ברזל קשה אש מפעפעו אש קשה מים: (ד) שם ומיתה קשה (מכולם) תז"מ ונ"ב ס"א משינה: (ה) שם והדר מצלי אמר כתיב כצ"ל ואות ד' נמחק: (ו) רש"י ד"ה חזא להו בחלמא במוצאי ראש השנה הס"ד:

גליון הש"ס

גמרא כי הא דבני אחתיה. וכעין זה איתא במדרש רבה ויקרא פרשה לד בבני אחתיה דרשב"י:

תורה אור השלם

א) כָּבוֹד חֲכָמִים יִנְחָלוּ וּכְסִילִים מֵרִים קָלוֹן: [משלי ג, לה]

ב) כִּי לִי בְנֵי יִשְׂרָאֵל עֲבָדִים עֲבָדַי הֵם אֲשֶׁר הוֹצֵאתִי אוֹתָם מֵאֶרֶץ מִצְרָיִם אֲנִי יְיָ אֱלֹהֵיכֶם: [ויקרא כה, נה]

ג) בָּנִים אַתֶּם לַייָ אֱלֹהֵיכֶם לֹא תִתְגֹּדְדוּ וְלֹא תָשִׂימוּ קָרְחָה בֵּין עֵינֵיכֶם לָמֵת: [דברים יד, א]

ד) הֲלוֹא פָרֹס לָרָעֵב לַחְמֶךָ וַעֲנִיִּים מְרוּדִים תָּבִיא בָיִת כִּי תִרְאֶה עָרֹם וְכִסִּיתוֹ וּמִבְּשָׂרְךָ לֹא תִתְעַלָּם: [ישעיה נח, ז]

ה) הִשָּׁמֶר לְךָ פֶּן יִהְיֶה דָבָר עִם לְבָבְךָ בְלִיַּעַל לֵאמֹר קָרְבָה שְׁנַת הַשֶּׁבַע שְׁנַת הַשְּׁמִטָּה וְרָעָה עֵינְךָ בְּאָחִיךָ הָאֶבְיוֹן וְלֹא תִתֵּן לוֹ וְקָרָא עָלֶיךָ אֶל יְיָ וְהָיָה בְךָ חֵטְא: [דברים טו, ט]

ו) יָצְאוּ אֲנָשִׁים בְּנֵי בְלִיַּעַל מִקִּרְבֶּךָ וַיַּדִּיחוּ אֶת יֹשְׁבֵי עִירָם לֵאמֹר נֵלְכָה וְנַעַבְדָה אֱלֹהִים אֲחֵרִים אֲשֶׁר לֹא יְדַעְתֶּם: [דברים יג, יד]

ז) כִּי כֹה אָמַר יְיָ אַל תָּבוֹא בֵּית מַרְזֵחַ וְאַל תֵּלֵךְ לִסְפּוֹד וְאַל תָּנֹד לָהֶם כִּי אָסַפְתִּי אֶת שְׁלוֹמִי מֵאֵת הָעָם הַזֶּה נְאֻם יְיָ אֶת הַחֶסֶד וְאֶת הָרַחֲמִים: [ירמיה טז, ה]

ח) כֹּה אָמַר יְיָ שִׁמְרוּ מִשְׁפָּט וַעֲשׂוּ צְדָקָה כִּי קְרוֹבָה יְשׁוּעָתִי לָבוֹא וְצִדְקָתִי לְהִגָּלוֹת: [ישעיה נו, א]

ט) לֹא יוֹעִילוּ אוֹצְרוֹת רֶשַׁע וּצְדָקָה תַּצִּיל מִמָּוֶת: [משלי י, ב] י) אֲנִי בְּצֶדֶק אֶחֱזֶה פָנֶיךָ אֶשְׂבְּעָה בְהָקִיץ תְּמוּנָתֶךָ: [תהלים יז, טו] כ) מַלְוֵה יְיָ חוֹנֵן דָּל וּגְמֻלוֹ יְשַׁלֶּם לוֹ: [משלי יט, יז] ל) עָשִׁיר בְּרָשִׁים יִמְשׁוֹל וְעֶבֶד לֹוֶה לְאִישׁ מַלְוֶה: [משלי כב, ז] מ) לֹא יוֹעִיל הוֹן בְּיוֹם עֶבְרָה וּצְדָקָה תַּצִּיל מִמָּוֶת: [משלי יא, ד] נ) יוֹם עֶבְרָה הַיּוֹם הַהוּא יוֹם צָרָה וּמְצוּקָה יוֹם שֹׁאָה וּמְשׁוֹאָה יוֹם חֹשֶׁךְ וַאֲפֵלָה יוֹם עָנָן וַעֲרָפֶל: [צפניה א, טו]

ימצא חיים בעלי עושר דכתיב צדקה בעלי אגדה דכתיב וכבוד כתיב הכא וכבוד וכתיב התם א) כבוד חכמים ינחלו תניא היה רבי מאיר אומר יש לו לבעל הדין להשיבך ולומר לך אם אלהיכם אוהב עניים הוא מפני מה אינו מפרנסן אמור לו כדי שניצול אנו בהן מדינה של גיהנם וזו שאלה שאל טורנוסרופוס הרשע את ר"ע אם אלהיכם אוהב עניים הוא מפני מה אינו מפרנסם א"ל כדי שניצול אנו בהן מדינה של גיהנם א"ל [אדרבה] זו שמחייבתן לגיהנם אמשול לך משל למה הדבר דומה למלך בשר ודם שכעס על עבדו וחבשו בבית האסורין וצוה עליו שלא להאכילו ושלא להשקותו והלך אדם אחד והאכילו והשקהו כששמע המלך לא כועס עליו ואתם קרוין עבדים שנאמר ב) כי לי בני ישראל עבדים אמר לו ר"ע אמשול לך משל למה הדבר דומה למלך בשר ודם שכעס על בנו וחבשו בבית האסורין וצוה עליו שלא להאכילו ושלא להשקותו והלך אדם אחד והאכילו והשקהו כששמע המלך לא דורון משגר לו ואנן קרוין בנים דכתיב ג) בנים אתם לה' אלהיכם אמר לו אתם קרוים בנים וקרוין עבדים בזמן שאתם עושין רצונו של מקום אתם קרוין בנים ובזמן שאין אתם עושין רצונו של מקום אתם קרוין עבדים ועכשיו אין אתם עושין רצונו של מקום אמר לו הרי הוא אומר ד) הלא פרוס לרעב לחמך ועניים מרודים תביא בית אימתי עניים מרודים תביא בית האידנא וקאמר הלא פרוס לרעב לחמך: דרש ר"י ברבי שלום כשם שמזונותיו של אדם קצובין לו מראש השנה כך חסרונותיו של אדם קצובין לו מראש השנה זכה הלא פרוס לרעב לחמך לא זכה ועניים מרודים תביא בית * כי הא דבני אחתיה דרבן יוחנן בן זכאי חזא להו בחילמא דבעו למיחסר שבע מאה דינרי עשינהו שקל מינייהו לצדקה (א) פוש גבייהו שיבסר דינרי כי מטא מעלי יומא דכיפורי שדור דבי קיסר נקטינהו אמר להו רבן יוחנן בן זכאי לא תדחלון שיבסר דינרי גבייכו שקלינהו מינייכו אמרי ליה מנא ידעת אמר להו חלמא חזאי לכו א"ל ואמאי לא אמרת לן [דניתבינהו] אמר להו אמינא כי היכי דתעבדו מצוה לשמה רב פפא הוה סליק בדרגא אישתמיט כרעיה בעי למיפל (ב) אמר השתא כן איחייב מאן דסני לן כמחללי שבתות וכעובדי עבודת כוכבים א"ל חייא בר רב מדפתי לרב פפא שמא עני בא לידך ולא פרנסתו א) דתניא רבי יהושע בן קרחה אומר כל המעלים עיניו מן הצדקה כאילו עובד עבודת כוכבים כתיב הכא ה) השמר לך פן יהיה דבר עם לבבך בליעל וכתיב התם ו) יצאו אנשים בני בליעל מה להלן עבודת כוכבים אף כאן עבודת כוכבים תניא ב) א"ר אלעזר בר' יוסי כל צדקה וחסד שישראל עושין בעולם הזה שלום גדול ופרקליטין גדולין בין ישראל לאביהן שבשמים שנאמר ז) כה אמר ה' אל תבא בית מרזח ואל תלך לספוד ואל תנוד להם כי אספתי את שלומי מאת העם הזה [וגו' את] החסד ואת הרחמים חסד זו גמילות חסדים רחמים זו צדקה תניא ר"י אומר גדולה צדקה שמקרבת את הגאולה שנאמר ח) כה אמר ה' שמרו משפט ועשו צדקה כי קרובה ישועתי לבא וצדקתי להגלות הוא היה אומר עשרה דברים קשים נבראו בעולם הר קשה ברזל מחתכו ברזל קשה (ג) אור מפעפעו אור קשה מים מכבין אותו מים קשים עבים סובלים אותן עבים קשים רוח מפזרתן רוח קשה גוף סובלו גוף קשה פחד שוברו פחד קשה יין מפיגו יין קשה שינה מפכחתו ומיתה קשה (ד) מכולם [וצדקה מצלת מן המיתה] דכתיב ט) וצדקה תציל ממות דרש רבי דוסתאי ברבי ינאי בוא וראה שלא כמדת הקב"ה מדת בשר ודם מדת בשר ודם אדם מביא דורון גדול למלך ספק מקבלין אותו הימנו ספק אין מקבלין אותו הימנו [ואם תמצא לומר מקבלים אותו ממנו] ספק רואה פני המלך ספק אינו רואה פני המלך והקדוש ברוך הוא אינו כן אדם נותן פרוטה לעני זוכה ומקבל פני שכינה שנאמר י) אני בצדק אחזה פניך אשבעה בהקיץ תמונתך רבי אלעזר ג) יהיב פרוטה לעני והדר מצלי אמר (ה) דכתיב אני בצדק אחזה פניך מאי אשבעה בהקיץ תמונתך אמר רב נחמן בר יצחק אלו תלמידי חכמים שמנדדין שינה מעיניהם בעולם הזה והקב"ה משביען מזיו השכינה לעולם הבא א"ר יוחנן מאי דכתיב כ) מלוה ה' חונן דל מקרא כתוב אי אפשר לאומרו כביכול ל) עבד לוה לאיש מלוה א"ר חייא בר אבא א"ר יוחנן ג) (רמי) כתיב מ) לא יועילו אוצרות רשע וצדקה תציל ממות וכתיב נ) לא יועיל הון ביום עברה וצדקה תציל ממות שתי צדקות הללו למה אחת שמצילתו ממיתה משונה ואחת שמצילתו מדינה של גיהנם ואי זו היא שמצילתו מדינה של גיהנם ההוא דכתיב ביה עברה דכתיב ס) יום עברה היום ההוא ואי זו היא שמצילתו ממיתה משונה

רש"י

ימצא חיים. וכתיב גבי חכמה כי מוצאי מצאי חיים: בעלי אגדה. מתוך שהן דרשנין ומושכין את הלב הכל מכבדין אותם: לבעל הדין. רשע או עובד כוכבים: להנצל אנו בהן כו'. שהצדקה מצלת מגיהנם כדאמרי' לקמן בשמעתין: שמזונותיו של אדם. שכר שיתפרנס ממנו: חסרונותיו. הפסד שעתיד להפסיד: זכה. למזל טוב יתן אותו חסרון לעניים: חזא [להו] בחלמא. במוצאי (ו) יה"כ: דבעו מחסר שבע מאה דינרין. באותה שנה: שקיל צדקה מינייהו. כל השנה היה כופן בדברים וגובה מהן לצדקה: פש גבייהו. ערב ראש השנה שיבסר דינרי שלא נתנו לצדקה משבע מאה דינרי: לא תדחלו. למיפסד יותר: אמאי לא אמרת לן. מתחלה שכך חלמת והיינו נותנין כולן: השתא כן. אם נפלתי: איחייב מאן דסני לן. כאדם שתולה קללתו בחבירו: מחללי שבת ועובדי עבודת כוכבים. בסקילה ואמר מר (כתובות דף ל:) מי שנתחייב סקילה או נופל מן הגג או חיה דורסתו דדמי לסקילה דתנן (סנהדרין דף מה.) בית הסקילה היה גבוה שתי קומות וכו': פרקליטין. מליצי יושר [של מלאכי השרת]: כי אספתי את שלומי מאת העם הזה. ומהו השלום את החסד ואת הרחמים שהיו רגילין לעשות: מפעפעו. מרככו: הגוף סובלו. [כל הגוף] מלא רוח: ואני בצדק. בתחלה ואח"כ אחזה פניך בתפלה: אשבעה בהקיץ תמונתך. בשכר הקילה אשבע תמונתך: מלוה ה' חונן דל. הנותן לדלים נעשה מלוה להקב"ה וכתיב ועבד לוה לאיש מלוה (משלי כב): ואיזו היא צדקה המצלת מדינה של גיהנם. כלומר איזה מן המקראות הללו מדבר מדין של גיהנם אותו שכתוב לא יועיל הון ביום עברה: נותנה

תוספות

ואיזו שמצלת ממיתה משונה נותנה ואינו יודע למי נותנה. וא"ת אדרבה זאת שהיא מצוה רבה היה לה להציל מדינה של גיהנם שהוא רע ביותר ואומר ר"י דרוב דברים אין עומדין לאדם בעולם הזה אלא לאחר מיתה ובעולם הזה אין עומדין לאדם אלא מצות גדולות כדתנן (קדושין דף לט:) אלו דברים שאדם אוכל מפירותיהן בעולם הזה והקרן קיימת לעולם הבא לכך קאמר דאפילו ממיתה משונה דהוי בעולם הזה מצלת:

עין משפט נר מצוה

צ א מיימוני פ"י מהל' מתנות עניים הל' ג סמג עשין קסב טוש"ע י"ד סי' רמז סעיף א:

צא ב מיי' שם הל' טו [טוש"ע א"ח סי' לג סעי' ין] וטוש"ע י"ד סי' רמט סעי' יד:

רבינו גרשום

צדקה. זו עושר שיהיו לו נכסים ועושר שיעשה מהם צדקה: כבוד. זו אגדה בשביל שיודע לדרוש באגדות מכבדין אותו: יש לו לבעל הדין. יצר הרע להשיבך ולהטעותך ולומר לך: ועכשיו אי אתם עושין רצונו של מקום. לפי שאתם בגלות ואי אתם יכולים לקיים כל התורה: עניים מרודים. שנרדים מבני אדם שללום: איכי השתא נפלי. הייתי נידון בסקילה כדאמר בית הסקילה היה גבוה ב' קומות (סנהדרין מה.) וכעובדי עבודת כוכבים דכתיב (דברי' יז) וסקלתם באבני' ומתו: ופרקליטין. מלמדי סניגוריאה: כי אספתי את שלומי. בשביל שאינם עושים לא חסד ולא רחמים. הא עושין יהיה להם שלום גדול: מפעפעו. עושהו רך: אני בצדק. שאעשה צדקה מתחילה והדר אחזה פניך בתפלה:

ליקוטי רש"י

ועניים מרודים. זו ממשלת רומי שצועקת תמיד הבו הבו שאנו צריכין. מרודים. קונפליינ"ט בלע"ז כמו אריד בשיחי (תהלים נה) [לעיל ט.]. נאנחים ונאנקים על צרתם כגון עניי ומרודי (איכה ג) אריד בשיחי (תהלים נה) [ישעיה נח, ז]. דרגא. סולם [שבת קנה.]. סולם של עלייה [ע"פ גיטין נט.]. פרקליט. מליץ טוב [זבחים ז:]. בית מרזח. משתה בספרי בפרשת בית פעור ראיתי חזרו לעשות להם מרזיחין אבל רבותינו פירשו מרזח אבל. תנוד. תקונן. כי אספתי את שלומי וגו'. כשהיה אברהם אביהם עושה צדקה ומשפט נתתי לזרעו חסד ורחמים ושמר ה' אלהיך לך וגו' (דברים ז) ונתן לך רחמים (שם יג) הם הפכו ללענה משפט וצדקה לארץ הניחו (עמוס ה) אף אני חזרתי ואספתי אלי את חסדי ואת רחמי. אספתי. אטולי"ש בלעז כמו אסף אלהים את חרפתי (בראשית ל) [ירמיה טז, ה]. מלוה ה' חונן דל. קרי ביה מלוה את המקום מי שחונן את הדל [ברכות יח.]. יום עברה היום ההוא. ביום הדין משתעי בנבואת צפניה [לקמן בעמ' ב']. ביום הדין משתעי קרא שנידונין עובדי כוכבים לגיהנם [ע"ז יח.]

[R' Akiva]: You Jews **are called** God's **"children"** in one verse **and are called** His **"servants"** in another verse. The explanation for this seeming discrepancy is that בִּזְמַן שֶׁאַתֶּם עוֹשִׂין רְצוֹנוֹ שֶׁל מָקוֹם **– at the time you do the Omnipresent's will** [i.e. you observe His commandments] אַתֶּם קְרוּיִן בָּנִים **– you are called** His **"children,"** and it is appropriate to give charity to the poor among you. וּבִזְמַן שֶׁאֵין אַתֶּם עוֹשִׂין רְצוֹנוֹ שֶׁל מָקוֹם **– But at the time you do not do the Omnipresent's will,** אַתֶּם קְרוּיִן עֲבָדִים **– you are called** His **"servants,"** and do not merit charity. וְעַכְשָׁיו **– And now,** at the present time, אֵין אַתֶּם עוֹשִׂין רְצוֹנוֹ שֶׁל מָקוֹם **– you are *not* doing the Omnipresent's will,** for He has subjugated you to the Romans! It is therefore improper to give charity to the poor at this time.

R' Akiva proved conclusively that charity must be given at all times, thereby defeating Turanus Rufus' argument:

אָמַר לוֹ הֲרֵי הוּא אוֹמֵר **– [R' Akiva] said to [Turanus Rufus]: Behold, [Scripture] states:**[16] "הֲלוֹא פָרֹס לָרָעֵב לַחְמֶךָ וַעֲנִיִּים מְרוּדִים תָּבִיא בָיִת" **– *You will break your bread for the hungry, and wailing poor*[17] *you will bring to the house.*** אֵימָתַי "עֲנִיִּים מְרוּדִים תָּבִיא בָיִת" **– When** does the verse, ***wailing poor you will bring to the house,*** apply? הָאִידָנָא **– Now,** when we must pay tribute to the subjugating Roman authorities! וְקָאָמַר: "הֲלוֹא פָרֹס לָרָעֵב לַחְמֶךָ" **– And [the verse] stated** that even in such times ***you will break your bread for the hungry!*** Scripture thus teaches that God desires us to give charity even when we have earned His condemnation because of our transgressions.[18]

The Gemara offers another interpretation of the aforementioned verse:

דָּרַשׁ רַבִּי יְהוּדָה בְּרַבִּי שָׁלוֹם **– R' Yehudah the son of R' Shalom expounded:** כְּשֵׁם שֶׁמְּזוֹנוֹתָיו שֶׁל אָדָם קְצוּבִין לוֹ מֵרֹאשׁ הַשָּׁנָה **– Just as a person's sustenance**[19] for the coming year **is apportioned for him from Rosh Hashanah,**[20] כָּךְ חֶסְרוֹנוֹתָיו שֶׁל אָדָם קְצוּבִין לוֹ מֵרֹאשׁ הַשָּׁנָה **– so a person's losses** for the coming year **are apportioned for him from Rosh Hashanah.** זָכָה "הֲלוֹא פָרֹס לָרָעֵב לַחְמֶךָ" **– If one merited** good fortune, he will give the amount he must lose to the poor, in compliance with the verse, ***You will break your bread for the hungry.*** לֹא זָכָה **– But if he did not merit** good fortune, "וַעֲנִיִּים מְרוּדִים תָּבִיא בָיִת" **–** the government will confiscate that amount, in fulfillment of the verse, ***and wailing poor you will bring to the house.***

The following incident illustrates this principle:

כִּי הָא דִּבְנֵי אַחְתֵיהּ דְּרַבָּן יוֹחָנָן בֶּן זַכַּאי **– An application of the above is like that case of the nephews**[21] **of Rabban Yochanan ben Zakkai.** חֲזָא לְהוּ בְּחֶילְמָא דְּבָעוּ לְמֵיחְסַר שְׁבַע מְאָה דִּינְרֵי **– For once [Rabban Yochanan] saw in a dream**[22] **that [the nephews] were required to lose seven hundred *dinars*** during the coming year. עַשְׂינְהוּ **– Thus,** over the course of the year **[Rabban Yochanan] would convince them** to donate money, שְׁקַל מִינַּיְיהוּ לִצְדָקָה **– and he took from them** most of the seven hundred *dinars* **for charity.** פּוּשׁ גַּבַּיְיהוּ שִׁיבְסַר דִּינְרֵי **– However, seventeen *dinars*** from the seven hundred **remained in their possession.**[23] כִּי מְטָא מַעֲלֵי יוֹמָא דְּכִיפּוּרֵי **– When the eve of Yom Kippur**[24] **arrived,** שְׁדוּר דְּבֵי קֵיסָר נַקְטִינְהוּ **– the Roman government dispatched** emissaries, who **confiscated [the seventeen *dinars*]** from Rabban Yochanan's nephews.

The nephews were frightened that the officers would return. Rabban Yochanan therefore reassured them:

אָמַר לְהוּ רַבָּן יוֹחָנָן בֶּן זַכַּאי **– Rabban Yochanan ben Zakkai told [his nephews]:** לֹא תִּדְחֲלוּן **– Do not be afraid** of losing more money. שִׁיבְסַר דִּינְרֵי גַּבַּיְיכוּ שַׁקְלִינְהוּ מִינַּיְיכוּ **– They took from you** the **seventeen *dinars*** that remained **in your possession** from the seven hundred you were destined to lose; hence, no more will be taken. אָמְרֵי לֵיהּ מְנָא יָדְעַתְּ **– Puzzled, [the nephews] said to [Rabban Yochanan]: From where do you know** that no more than seventeen *dinars* will be taken? אָמַר לְהוּ חֶלְמָא חֲזַאי לְכוּ **– [Rabban Yochanan] said to [his nephews]: I saw a dream concerning you,** that you were required to lose a certain amount of money during this past year, and I calculated how much remained to be lost.[25] אָמְרוּ לֵיהּ וְאַמַּאי לֹא אָמַרְתְּ לָן **– Realizing** now why Rabban Yochanan had been urging them to give charity throughout the year, **[the nephews] said to [Rabban Yochanan]: And why did you not tell us** that we were required to lose seven hundred *dinars* this year, [דְּנֵיתְבִינְהוּ] **– so that we would have given** all **[the money] to charity?** What a pity to have part of it confiscated!

Rabban Yochanan replied:

אָמַר לְהוּ **– [Rabban Yochanan] said to [his nephews]:** אֲמִינָא **– I said** to myself: It is better not to inform you, כִּי הֵיכִי דְּתַעַבְדוּ מִצְוָה לִשְׁמָהּ **– so that you will perform a mitzvah** (i.e. of giving charity) **for its own sake.** If you had known that you were destined to lose a particular sum of money, your intent in giving would be simply to avoid its confiscation, and not to benefit the poor.[26]

The Gemara relates an incident that illustrates the importance of responding readily to a request for charity:

NOTES

16. *Isaiah* 58:7.

17. Above (9a), R' Elazar interpreted עֲנִיִּים מְרוּדִים as *wailing poor* — a reference to the Roman government, which constantly bemoaned its lack of funds and taxed its subject nations accordingly. R' Akiva here utilizes R' Elazar's interpretation in refutation of Turanus Rufus (*Maharsha*).

18. In fact, even when Jews violate the Torah's laws they are called God's "children," as it says: *Behold, a sinful people. . .destructive children; they abandoned God (Isaiah* 1:4; see *Kiddushin* 36a) [*Maharsha*]. [Hence, when Scripture refers to Jews as "servants," it means that every Jew is obligated to follow God's commands like a *servant* — i.e. fully and without complaint or question.]

19. I.e. the income from which he will support himself and his family (*Rashi*).

20. On Rosh Hashanah, the day of Divine judgment, God decrees each person's fortunes for the coming year (see *Rosh Hashanah* 16a). For average people the period of decision actually extends until Yom Kippur, which falls ten days later. Only the decrees of wholly righteous (or wholly wicked) people are sealed on Rosh Hashanah itself.

21. Literally: the sons of his sister.

22. Rabban Yochanan's dream occurred on the night following Yom Kippur, for presumably his nephews were among the average people, whose judgments are concluded on Yom Kippur (*Rashi* with *Maharsha*; see note 20 above; cf. *Bach*).

23. I.e. on the eve of the following Rosh Hashanah (*Rashi*). But see *Maharsha*, who emends *Rashi* to read: "on the eve of [the following] Yom Kippur." This reading conforms with the next line of the Gemara (which reports that Roman agents seized the remaining seventeen *dinars* on Yom Kippur eve of the following year), and also conforms with the fact that the decree of average people is not concluded until Yom Kippur. Hence, the final day of the previous annual decree (which required the nephews to lose 700 *dinars)* was Yom Kippur eve of the following year.

24. This refers to the *following* Yom Kippur eve — the conclusion of the twelve-month period during which the nephews were to lose 700 *dinars.*

25. Rabban Yochanan explained to them that he had subtracted the amount of charity he had convinced them to give from the figure he had seen in the dream.

26. This incident teaches an important lesson. Although the *amount* of charity given by the nephews was less than what they were destined to lose, Rabban Yochanan felt that it was better for them to give a smaller amount with the proper intent than to give the larger sum with an ulterior motive.

ימצא חיים בעלי עושר דכתיב צדקה בעלי אגדה דכתיב וכבוד כתיב הכא וכבוד וכתיב התם א) כבוד חכמים ינחלו תניא היה רבי מאיר אומר יש לו לבעל הדין להשיבך ולומר לך אם אלהיכם אוהב עניים הוא מפני מה אינו מפרנסן אמור לו כדי שניצול אנו בהן מדינה של גיהנם וזו שאלה שאל טורנוסרופוס הרשע את ר"ע אם אלהיכם אוהב עניים הוא מפני מה אינו מפרנסם א"ל כדי שניצול אנו בהן מדינה של גיהנם א"ל [אדרבה] זו שמחייבתן לגיהנם אמשול לך משל למה הדבר דומה למלך בשר ודם שכעס על עבדו וחבשו בבית האסורין וצוה עליו שלא להאכילו ושלא להשקותו והלך אדם אחד והאכילו והשקהו כששמע המלך לא כועס עליו ואתם קרוין עבדים שנאמר ב) כי לי בני ישראל עבדים אמר לו ר"ע אמשול לך משל למה הדבר דומה למלך בשר ודם שכעס על בנו וחבשו בבית האסורין וצוה עליו שלא להאכילו ושלא להשקותו והלך אדם אחד והאכילו והשקהו כששמע המלך לא דורון משגר לו ואנן קרוין בנים דכתיב ג) בנים אתם לה' אלהיכם אמר לו אתם קרוים בנים וקרוים עבדים בזמן שאתם עושין רצונו של מקום אתם קרוין בנים ובזמן שאין אתם עושין רצונו של מקום אתם קרוין עבדים ועכשיו אין אתם עושין רצונו של מקום אמר לו הרי הוא אומר ד) הלא פרוס לרעב לחמך ועניים מרודים תביא בית אימתי עניים מרודים תביא בית האידנא וקאמר הלא פרוס לרעב לחמך: דרש ר' ברבי שלום כשם שמזונותיו של אדם קצובין לו מראש השנה כך חסרונותיו של אדם קצובין לו מראש השנה זכה הלא פרוס לרעב לחמך לא זכה ועניים מרודים תביא בית * כי הא דבני אחתיה דרבן יוחנן בן זכאי חזא להו בחילמא דבעו למיחסר שבע מאה דינרי עשינהו שקל מינייהו לצדקה (א) פוש גבייהו שיבסר דינרי כי מטא מעלי יומא דכיפורי שדור דבי קיסר נקטינהו אמר להו רבן יוחנן בן זכאי לא תדחלון שיבסר דינרי גבייכו שקלינהו מינייכו אמרי ליה מנא ידעת אמר להו חלמא חזאי לכו א"ל ואמאי לא אמרת לן [דניתבינהו] אמר להו אמינא כי היכי דתעבדו מצוה לשמה רב פפא הוה סליק בדרגא אישתמיט כרעיה בעי למיפל (ב) אמר השתא כן איחייב מאן דסני לן כמחללי שבתות וכעובדי עבודת כוכבים א"ל חייא בר רב מדפתי לרב פפא שמא עני בא לידך ולא פרנסתו דתניא רבי יהושע בן קרחה אומר כל המעלים עיניו מן הצדקה כאילו עובד עבודת כוכבים כתיב הכא ה) השמר לך פן יהיה דבר עם לבבך בליעל וכתיב התם ו) יצאו אנשים בני בליעל מה להלן עבודת כוכבים אף כאן עבודת כוכבים תניא א"ר אלעזר בר' יוסי כל צדקה וחסד שישראל עושין בעולם הזה שלום גדול ופרקליטין גדולין בין ישראל לאביהן שבשמים שנאמר ז) כה אמר ה' אל תבא בית מרזח ואל תלך לספוד ואל תנוד להם כי אספתי את שלומי מאת העם הזה [וגו' את] החסד ואת הרחמים חסד זו גמילות חסדים רחמים זו צדקה תניא ר"י אומר גדולה צדקה שמקרבת את הגאולה שנאמר ח) כה אמר ה' שמרו משפט ועשו צדקה כי קרובה ישועתי לבא וצדקתי להגלות הוא היה אומר עשרה דברים קשים נבראו בעולם הר קשה ברזל מחתכו ברזל קשה (ג) אור מפעפעו אור קשה מים מכבין אותו מים קשים עבים סובלים אותן עבים קשים רוח מפזרתן רוח קשה גוף סובלו גוף קשה פחד שוברו פחד קשה יין מפיגו יין קשה שינה מפכחתו ומיתה קשה (ד) מכולם [וצדקה מצלת מן המיתה] דכתיב ט) וצדקה תציל ממות דרש רבי דוסתאי ברבי ינאי בוא וראה שלא כמדת הקב"ה מדת בשר ודם מדת בשר ודם אדם מביא דורון גדול למלך ספק מקבלין אותו ממנו ספק אין מקבלין אותו הימנו [ואם תמצא לומר מקבלים אותו ממנו] ספק רואה פני המלך ספק אינו רואה פני המלך והקדוש ברוך הוא אינו כן אדם נותן פרוטה לעני זוכה ומקבל פני שכינה שנאמר י) אני בצדק אחזה פניך אשבעה בהקיץ תמונתך רבי אלעזר יהיב פרוטה לעני והדר מצלי אמר (ה) דכתיב אני בצדק אחזה פניך מאי אשבעה בהקיץ תמונתך אמר רב נחמן בר יצחק אלו תלמידי חכמים שמנדדין שינה מעיניהם בעולם הזה והקב"ה משביען מזיו השכינה לעולם הבא א"ר יוחנן מאי דכתיב כ) מלוה ה' חונן דל אלמלא מקרא כתוב אי אפשר לאומרו כביכול ל) עבד לוה לאיש מלוה א"ר חייא בר אבא א"ר יוחנן (רמי) כתיב ט) לא יועילו אוצרות רשע וצדקה תציל ממות וכתיב מ) לא יועיל הון ביום עברה וצדקה תציל ממות שתי צדקות הללו למה אחת שמצילתו ממיתה משונה ואחת שמצילתו מדינה של גיהנם ואי זו היא שמצילתו מדינה של גיהנם הוא דכתיב ביה עברה דכתיב נ) יום עברה היום ההוא ואי זו היא שמצילתו ממיתה משונה

רש"י

ימצא חיים. וכתיב גבי חכמה כי מוצאי מצא חיים: בעלי אגדה. מתוך שהן דרשנין ומושכין את הלב הכל מכבדין אותם: לבעל הדין. רשע או עובד כוכבים: להנצל אנו בהן כו'. שהצדקה מצלת מגיהנם כדאמרי' לקמן בשמעתין: שמזונותיו של אדם. שכר שיתפרנס ממנו: חסרונותיו. הפסק שעתיד להפסיד: זכה. למזל טוב יתן אותו חסרון לעניים: חזא [להון] בחלמא. במוצאי (ו) יה"כ: דבעו מחסר שבע מאה דינרין. באותה שנה: שקיל צדקה מינייהו. כל השנה היה כופן בדברים וגובה מהן לצדקה: פש גבייהו. ערב ראש השנה שיבסר דינרי שלא נתנו לצדקה משבע מאה דינרי: לא תדחלו. למיספד יותר: אמאי לא אמרת לן. מתחלה שהיינו נותנין כולן: השתא כן. אם נפלתי: איחייב מאן דסני לן. כאדם שתולה קללתו בחבירו: מחללי שבת ועובדי עבודת כוכבים. בסקילה ואמר מר (כתובות דף ל:) מי שנתחייב סקילה או נופל מן הגג או חיה דורסתו דדמי לסקילה דתנן (סנהדרין דף מה.) בית הסקילה היה גבוה שתי קומות וכו': פרקליטין. מליצי יושר [של מלאכי השרת]: כי אספתי את שלומי מאת העם הזה. ומהו השלום את החסד ואת הרחמים שהיו רגילין לעשות: מפעפעו. מרככו: הגוף סובלו. [כל הגוף] מלא רוח: ואני בצדק. בתחלה ואח"כ אחזה פניך בתפלה: אשבעה בהקיץ תמונתך. בשכר הקיצה אשבע תמונתך: מלוה ה' חונן דל. החונן דלים נעשה מלוה להקב"ה וכתיב ועבד לוה לאיש מלוה (משלי כב): ואיזו היא צדקה המצלת מדינה של גיהנם. כלומר איזה מן המקראות הללו מדבר מדין של גיהנם אותו שכתוב לא יועיל הון ביום עברה: נותנה

תוספות

ואיזו שמצלת ממיתה משונה נותנה ואינו יודע למי נותנה. וא"ת אדרבה זאת שהיא מלוה רבה היא לו להציל מדינה של גיהנם שהוא רע ביותר ואומר ר"י דרוב דברים אין עומדין לאדם בעולם הזה אלא לאחר מיתה ובעולם הזה אין עומדין לאדם אלא מלות גדולות כדתנן (קדושין דף לט:) אלו דברים שאדם אוכל מפירותיהן בעולם הזה והקרן קיימת לעולם הבא לכך קאמר דאפילו ממיתה משונה דהוי בעולם הזה מצלת:

אלא

מסורת הש"ס

א) [תוספ' פאה פ"ד] כתובות סח., ב) [תוס' פאה פ"ד], ג) [בילקוט ובע"י ליתא] והגי' אמר ר"ח ב"א אר"י:

הגהות הב"ח

(א) גמרא פש גבייהו כצ"ל ואות ו' נמחק: (ב) שם בעי למיפל חלש דעתיה אמר השתא: (ג) שם ברזל קשה אש מפעפעו אש קשה מים: (ד) שם ומיתה קשה (מכולם) תז"מ ונ"ב ס"א משינה: (ה) שם והדר מצלי אמר כתיב כצ"ל ואות ד' נמחק: (ו) רש"י ד"ה חזא להו בחלמא במוצאי ראש השנה הס"ד:

גליון הש"ס

גמרא כי הא דבני אחתיה. וכעין זה איתא במדרש רבה ויקרא פרשה לד בבני אחתיה דרשב"י:

תורה אור השלם

א) כָּבוֹד חֲכָמִים יִנְחָלוּ וּכְסִילִים מֵרִים קָלוֹן: [משלי ג, לה]

ב) כִּי לִי בְנֵי יִשְׂרָאֵל עֲבָדִים עֲבָדַי הֵם אֲשֶׁר הוֹצֵאתִי אוֹתָם מֵאֶרֶץ מִצְרָיִם אֲנִי יְיָ אֱלֹהֵיכֶם: [ויקרא כה, נה]

ג) בָּנִים אַתֶּם לַייָ אֱלֹהֵיכֶם לֹא תִתְגֹּדְדוּ וְלֹא תָשִׂימוּ קָרְחָה בֵּין עֵינֵיכֶם לָמֵת: [דברים יד, א]

ד) הֲלוֹא פָרֹס לָרָעֵב לַחְמֶךָ וַעֲנִיִּים מְרוּדִים תָּבִיא בָיִת כִּי תִרְאֶה עָרֹם וְכִסִּיתוֹ וּמִבְּשָׂרְךָ לֹא תִתְעַלָּם: [ישעיה נח, ז]

ה) הִשָּׁמֶר לְךָ פֶּן יִהְיֶה דָבָר עִם לְבָבְךָ בְלִיַּעַל לֵאמֹר קָרְבָה שְׁנַת הַשֶּׁבַע שְׁנַת הַשְּׁמִטָּה וְרָעָה עֵינְךָ בְּאָחִיךָ הָאֶבְיוֹן וְלֹא תִתֵּן לוֹ וְקָרָא עָלֶיךָ אֶל יְיָ וְהָיָה בְךָ חֵטְא: [דברים טו, ט]

ו) יָצְאוּ אֲנָשִׁים בְּנֵי בְלִיַּעַל מִקִּרְבֶּךָ וַיַּדִּיחוּ אֶת יֹשְׁבֵי עִירָם לֵאמֹר נֵלְכָה וְנַעַבְדָה אֱלֹהִים אֲחֵרִים אֲשֶׁר לֹא יְדַעְתֶּם: [דברים יג, יד]

ז) כִּי כֹה אָמַר יְיָ אַל תָּבוֹא בֵּית מַרְזֵחַ וְאַל תֵּלֵךְ לִסְפּוֹד וְאַל תָּנֹד לָהֶם כִּי אָסַפְתִּי אֶת שְׁלוֹמִי מֵאֵת הָעָם הַזֶּה נְאֻם יְיָ אֶת הַחֶסֶד וְאֶת הָרַחֲמִים: [ירמיה טז, ה]

ח) כֹּה אָמַר יְיָ שִׁמְרוּ מִשְׁפָּט וַעֲשׂוּ צְדָקָה כִּי קְרוֹבָה יְשׁוּעָתִי לָבוֹא וְצִדְקָתִי לְהִגָּלוֹת: [ישעיה נו, א]

ט) לֹא יוֹעִילוּ אוֹצְרוֹת רֶשַׁע וּצְדָקָה תַּצִּיל מִמָּוֶת: [משלי י, ב]

י) אֲנִי בְּצֶדֶק אֶחֱזֶה פָנֶיךָ אֶשְׂבְּעָה בְהָקִיץ תְּמוּנָתֶךָ: [תהלים יז, טו] כ) מַלְוֵה יְיָ חוֹנֵן דָּל וּגְמֻלוֹ יְשַׁלֶּם לוֹ: [משלי יט, יז] ל) עָשִׁיר בְּרָשִׁים יִמְשׁוֹל וְעֶבֶד לֹוֶה לְאִישׁ מַלְוֶה: [משלי כב, ז] מ) לֹא יוֹעִיל הוֹן בְּיוֹם עֶבְרָה וּצְדָקָה תַּצִּיל מִמָּוֶת: [משלי יא, ד] נ) יוֹם עֶבְרָה הַיּוֹם הַהוּא יוֹם צָרָה וּמְצוּקָה יוֹם שֹׁאָה וּמְשׁוֹאָה יוֹם חֹשֶׁךְ וַאֲפֵלָה יוֹם עָנָן וַעֲרָפֶל: [צפניה א, טו]

עין משפט נר מצוה

צ א מיימוני פ"י מהל' מתנות עניים הל' ג סמג עשין קסב טוש"ע י"ד סי' רמז סעיף א:

צא ב מיי' שם הל' טו [טוש"ע א"ח סי' לב סעי' ז] וטוש"ע י"ד סי' רמט סעי' יד:

רבינו גרשום

צדקה. זו עושר שיהיו לו נכסים ועושר שיעשה מהם צדקה: כבוד. זו אגדה בשביל שיודע לדרוש באגדות מכבדין אותו: יש לו לבעל הדין. יצר הרע להשיבך ולהטעותך ולומר לך: ועכשיו אי אתם עושין רצונו של מקום. לפי שאתם בגלות ואי אתם יכולים לקיים כל התורה: עניים מרודים. שנרדים מבני אדם ששללום: איכי השתא נפלי. הייתי נידון בסקילה כדאמר בית הסקילה היה גבוה ב' קומות (סנהדרין מה.) וכעובדי עבודת כוכבים דכתיב (דברי' יז) וסקלתם באבני' ומתו: ופרקליטין. מלמדי סניגוריאה: כי אספתי את שלומי. בשביל שאינם עושים לא חסד ולא רחמים. הא עושין יהיה להם שלום גדול: מפעפעו. עושהו רך: אני בצדק. שאעשה צדקה מתחילה והדר אחזה פניך בתפלה:

ליקוטי רש"י

ועניים מרודים. זו ממשלת רומי שגועקת תמיד הבו הבו שאנו צריכין. מרודים. קונפליינ"ט בלע"ז כמו אריד בשיחי (תהלים נה) [לעיל ט.]. נאנחים ונאנקים על צרתם כגון עניי ומרודי (איכה ג) אריד בשיחי (תהלים נה) [ישעיה נח, ז]. דרגא. סולם [שבת קנה.]. סולם של עלייה [ע"פ גיטין נט.]. פרקליט. מליץ טוב [זבחים ז:]. בית מרזח. משתה בספרי בפרשת בית פעור ראיתי חזרו לעשות להם מרזיחין אבל רבותינו פירשו מרזח אבל. תנוד. תקונן. כי אספתי את שלומי וגו'. כשהיה אברהם אביהם עושה צדקה ומשפט נתתי לזרעו חסד ורחמים ושמר ה' אלהיך לך וגו' (דברים ז) ונתן לך רחמים (שם יג) הם הפכו לענה משפט וצדקה לארץ הניחו (עמוס ה) אף אני חזרתי ואספתי אלי את חסדי ואת רחמי. אספתי. אטולי"ש בלעז כמו אסף אלהים את חרפתי (בראשית ל) [ירמיה טז, ה]. מלוה ה' חונן דל. קרי ביה מלוה את המקום מי שחונן את הדל [ברכות יח.]. יום עברה היום ההוא. ביום הדין משתעי בנבואת צפניה [לקמן בעמ' ב']. ביום הדין משתעי קרא שנידונין עובדי כוכבים לגיהנם [ע"ז יח:].

רַב פָּפָּא הֲוָה סָלִיק בְּדַרְגָּא – **Rav Pappa was climbing a ladder.** אִישְׁתַּמֵּיט כַּרְעֵיהּ – **His foot slipped** on one of the rungs, בָּעֵי לְמִיפַּל – and **he nearly fell** off the ladder. אָמַר הַשְׁתָּא כֵּן – In retrospect **[Rav Pappa] said: Now,** if an accident had **indeed** occurred, and I had fallen to my death, אִיחַיַּיב מָאן דְּסָנֵי לָן – **the one whom we hate**[27] **would have been liable** and thus punished כִּמְחַלְּלֵי שַׁבָּתוֹת וּכְעוֹבְדֵי עֲבוֹדַת כּוֹכָבִים – **like those who desecrate the Sabbath and like idol worshipers.**[28] Rav Pappa did not understand why he deserved this particular brush with death.[29]

An explanation was proposed:

אָמַר לֵיהּ חִיָּיא בַּר רַב מִדִּפְתִּי לְרַב פָּפָּא – **Chiya bar Rav, from** the city of **Difti, said to Rav Pappa:** שֶׁמָּא עָנִי בָּא לְיָדְךָ וְלֹא פַּרְנַסְתּוֹ – **Perhaps a pauper came to you and you did not sustain him** with a gift of charity.[30] For such indifference one could incur a punishment as severe as that meted out to idolaters.

Chiya bar Rav offered support for this explanation:

דְּתַנְיָא – **For it was taught in a Baraisa:** רַבִּי יְהוֹשֻׁעַ בֶּן קָרְחָה אוֹמֵר – R' YEHOSHUA BEN KARCHAH SAYS: כָּל הַמַּעֲלִים עֵינָיו מִן הַצְּדָקָה – If ANYONE AVERTS HIS EYES FROM giving CHARITY, כְּאִילּוּ עוֹבֵד עֲבוֹדַת כּוֹכָבִים – IT IS AS IF HE WORSHIPS IDOLS. כְּתִיב הָכָא: ,,הִשָּׁמֶר לְךָ פֶּן־יִהְיֶה דָבָר עִם־לְבָבְךָ בְלִיַּעַל" – For IT IS WRITTEN HERE:[31] *BEWARE LEST THERE BE AN IRRESPONSIBLE* (בְלִיַּעַל)[32] *THOUGHT IN YOUR HEART.* וּכְתִיב הָתָם: ,,יָצְאוּ אֲנָשִׁים בְּנֵי־בְלִיַּעַל" – AND IT IS WRITTEN THERE:[33] *IRRESPONSIBLE* (בְלִיַּעַל) *MEN WENT OUT* [to seduce the inhabitants of a city into committing idolatry]. מָה לְהַלָּן עֲבוֹדַת כּוֹכָבִים – JUST AS THERE in the passage of *ir hanidachas* the Torah refers to IDOLATRY, אַף כָּאן עֲבוֹדַת כּוֹכָבִים – SO HERE the Torah teaches that refusing to assist the poor is akin to committing IDOLATRY.[34] Thus, one who spurns the opportunity to give charity may incur a punishment analogous to stoning, which is the punishment for idolatry.

The Gemara continues to discuss the merits of giving charity:

תַּנְיָא אָמַר רַבִּי אֶלְעָזָר בְּרַבִּי יוֹסֵי – **It was taught in a Baraisa:** R' ELAZAR THE SON OF R' YOSE SAID: כָּל צְדָקָה וָחֶסֶד שֶׁיִּשְׂרָאֵל עוֹשִׂין בָּעוֹלָם הַזֶּה – ALL acts of CHARITY AND KINDNESS THAT the nation of ISRAEL PERFORMS IN THIS WORLD שָׁלוֹם גָּדוֹל וּפְרַקְלִיטִין גְּדוֹלִין בֵּין יִשְׂרָאֵל לַאֲבִיהֶן שֶׁבַּשָּׁמַיִם – create GREAT PEACE AND DEFENDING ANGELS BETWEEN the nation of ISRAEL AND THEIR FATHER IN HEAVEN, שֶׁנֶּאֱמַר – FOR IT IS STATED:[35] ,,כֹּה אָמַר ה׳ אַל־תָּבוֹא בֵּית מַרְזֵחַ וְאַל־תֵּלֵךְ לִסְפּוֹד וְאַל־תָּנֹד לָהֶם כִּי־אָסַפְתִּי אֶת־שְׁלוֹמִי מֵאֵת הָעָם הַזֶּה [וגו׳ אֶת־] הַחֶסֶד וְאֶת־הָרַחֲמִים" – *SO SAID GOD: "DO NOT ENTER THE HOUSE OF MOURNING, NOR GO TO LAMENT, AND DO NOT BEMOAN THEM, FOR I HAVE GATHERED UP MY PEACE FROM THIS NATION. . .THE KINDNESS AND MERCY."*

R' Elazar explicates the verse:

,,חֶסֶד" זוֹ גְּמִילוּת חֲסָדִים – **"Kindness" – this** relates to the **acts of kindness** performed by the Jewish people; ,,רַחֲמִים" זוֹ צְדָקָה – and **"mercy" – this** relates to the acts of **charity** performed by the Jewish people. When Jews perform acts of kindness and charity, God shows them kindness and mercy – His "peace."

The Gemara extols another virtue of giving charity:

תַּנְיָא רַבִּי יְהוּדָה אוֹמֵר – **It was taught in a Baraisa:** R' YEHUDAH SAYS: גְּדוֹלָה צְדָקָה שֶׁמְּקָרֶבֶת אֶת הַגְּאוּלָּה – CHARITY IS GREAT, BECAUSE IT BRINGS THE REDEMPTION CLOSER, שֶׁנֶּאֱמַר – AS IT IS STATED:[36] ,,כֹּה אָמַר ה׳ שִׁמְרוּ מִשְׁפָּט וַעֲשׂוּ צְדָקָה כִּי־קְרוֹבָה יְשׁוּעָתִי לָבוֹא וְצִדְקָתִי לְהִגָּלוֹת" – *SO SAID GOD: "KEEP JUSTICE AND DO CHARITY, FOR MY SALVATION IS NEAR TO COME, AND MY CHARITY TO BE REVEALED."*[37]

The Gemara quotes another statement by R' Yehudah on the power of charity:

הוּא הָיָה אוֹמֵר – **[R' Yehudah] was wont to say:** עֲשָׂרָה דְבָרִים קָשִׁים נִבְרְאוּ בָּעוֹלָם – **Ten strong**[38] **things were created in the world.** הַר קָשֶׁה – A **mountain is strong,** בַּרְזֶל מְחַתְּכוֹ – but **iron cleaves it.** בַּרְזֶל קָשֶׁה אוּר מְפַעְפְּעוֹ – **Iron is strong,** but **fire softens it.** אוּר קָשֶׁה מַיִם מְכַבִּין אוֹתוֹ – **Fire is strong,** but **water extinguishes it.** מַיִם קָשִׁים עָבִים סוֹבְלִים אוֹתָן – **Water is strong,** but **clouds bear it.** עָבִים קָשִׁים רוּחַ מְפַזַּרְתָּן – **Clouds are strong,** but **wind scatters them.** רוּחַ קָשֶׁה גּוּף סוֹבְלוֹ – **Wind is strong,** but **a body bears it.**[39] גּוּף קָשֶׁה פַּחַד שׁוֹבְרוֹ – **A body is strong,** but **fear breaks it.** פַּחַד קָשֶׁה יַיִן מְפִיגוֹ – **Fear is strong,** but **wine dispels it.** יַיִן קָשֶׁה שֵׁינָה מְפַכַּחְתּוֹ – **Wine is strong,** but **sleep lessens its effect.** וּמִיתָה קָשָׁה מִכּוּלָּם – **And death is stronger than all of these!**[40] [וּצְדָקָה מַצֶּלֶת מִן הַמִּיתָה] – **Yet** the merit of **charity saves** a person **from death,** דִּכְתִיב: ,,וּצְדָקָה תַּצִּיל מִמָּוֶת" – **as it is written:**[41] ***And charity will save from death!*** Charity has the power to rescue a person from the most powerful force in creation.[42]

NOTES

27. Rav Pappa did not wish to relate the potentially fatal mishap to himself; hence, he spoke of it as if it happened to another party (see *Rashi*).

28. The punishment for both of these transgressions is death by stoning (*Sanhedrin* 53a). This method of execution was initiated when the condemned was thrown from a height of two stories (*Sanhedrin* 45a). Although capital punishment ceased well before Rav Pappa's time, the Gemara states (*Kesubos* 30b) that God causes those deserving execution to die unnaturally. Hence, those deserving to be stoned would be killed in a similar fashion – either by falling from a roof or by being torn apart by wild animals (*Rashi*).

29. I.e. he did not recall a sin he had committed that was akin to Sabbath desecration or idolatry.

30. Perhaps Chiya was alluding to the incident reported above (9a), where Rav Pappa ignored the supplication of a pauper that collected door-to-door (*Maharsha*; cf. *Maharshal* to *Shabbos* 118b).

31. *Deuteronomy* 15:9. The Torah cautions against refusing to lend money to the poor out of concern that the approaching *Shemittah* year will eradicate the debt.

32. "בְּלִיַּעַל" is a compound word, from בְּלִי עֹל, *without yoke* or responsibility (*Rashi* to *Deuteronomy* 13:14).

33. *Deuteronomy* 13:14, which speaks of the *ir hanidachas,* the city that was proselytized by idolaters. For further explanation, see above, 8a note 42.

34. Although the word בְּלִיַּעַל appears frequently in the Scriptures, it is found in the Pentateuch only in these two places. Hence, the connection between the two passages wrought by the common word is compelling (*Maharsha*; see there for an explanation why it is compared to idolatry; see also *Toras Chaim*).

35. *Jeremiah* 16:5.

36. *Isaiah* 56:1.

37. The acts of charity performed by the Jewish people will bring the Final Redemption, and at that time there will be a revelation of God's acts of charity, which now are concealed (*Maharsha*).

Ben Yehoyada questions why the verse mentions "justice," inasmuch as R' Yehudah said only that "charity" brings the redemption closer. He explains that charity has this effect only when the money donated was *justly* obtained by the giver. Money acquired by dishonest means is not acceptable to God when offered as charity. Hence, "charity" alone *does* have the power to bring closer the redemption; Scripture mentions "justice" as well in order to define which type of charity is meant.

38. Literally: hard.

39. The entire body is filled with air (*Rashi*).

40. For sleep is stronger than all the other enumerated forces, and sleep is but 1/60 of death (*Berachos* 57b). Hence, death is the most powerful force in the physical creation (*Maharsha*).

41. *Proverbs* 10:2.

42. Giving charity is essentially a supranatural and Godly act [for it goes against human nature to make a gratuitous offering of oneself or of one's

ימצא חיים. וכתיב גבי חכמה כי מוצאי מצא חיים: בעלי אגדה. מתוך שהן דרשנין ומושכין את הלב הכל מכבדין אותם: לבעל הדין. רשע או עובד כוכבים: להנצל אנו בהן כו'. שהצדקה מצלת מגיהנם כדאמרי' לקמן בשמעתין: שמזונותיו של אדם. שכר שיתפרנס ממנו: חסרונותיו. הפסד שעתיד להפסיד: זכה. למזל טוב יתן אותו חסרון לעניים: חזא [להו] בחלמא. במוצאי (ו) יה"כ: דבעו מחסר שבע מאה דינרין. באותה שנה: שקיל צדקה מינייהו. כל השנה היה כופן בדברים וגובה מהן לצדקה: פש גבייהו. ערב ראש השנה שיבסר דינרי שלא נתנו לצדקה משבע מאה דינרי: לא תדחלו. למיפסד יותר: אמאי לא אמרת לן. מתחלה שכך חלמת והיינו נותנין לון: השתא כן. אם נפלתי: איחייב מאן דסני לן. כלומר שתולה קללתו בחבירו: מחללי שבת ועובדי עבודת כוכבים. בסקילה ואמר מר (כתובות דף ל:) מי שנתחייב סקילה או נופל מן הגג או חיה דורסתו דדמי לסקילה דתנן (סנהדרין דף מה.) בית הסקילה היה גבוה שתי קומות וכו': פרקליטין. מליצי יושר [של מלאכי השרת]: כי אספתי את שלומי מאת העם הזה. ומהו השלום את החסד ואת הרחמים שהיו רגילין לעשות: מפעפעו. מרככו: הגוף סובלו. [כל הגוף] מלא רוח: ואני בצדק. בתחלה ואח"כ אחזה פניך בתפלה: אשבעה בהקיץ תמונתך. בשכר הקיצה אשבע תמונתך: מלוה ה' חונן דל. החונן דלים נעשה מלוה להקב"ה וכתיב ועבד לוה לאיש מלוה (משלי כב): ואיזו היא צדקה המצלת מדינה של גיהנם. כלומר איזה מן המקראות הללו מדבר מדין של גיהנם אותו שכתוב לא יועיל הון ביום עברה: נותנה

ימצא חיים בעלי עושר דכתיב צדקה בעלי אגדה דכתיב וכבוד כתיב הכא וכבוד וכתיב התם א) כבוד חכמים ינחלו תניא היה רבי מאיר אומר יש לו לבעל הדין להשיבך ולומר לך אם אלהיכם אוהב עניים הוא מפני מה אינו מפרנסן אמור לו כדי שניצול אנו בהן מדינה של גיהנם וזו שאלה שאל טורנוסרופוס הרשע את ר"ע אם אלהיכם אוהב עניים הוא מפני מה אינו מפרנסם א"ל כדי שניצול אנו בהן מדינה של גיהנם א"ל [אדרבה] זו שמחייבתן לגיהנם אמשול לך משל למה הדבר דומה למלך בשר ודם שכעס על עבדו וחבשו בבית האסורין וצוה עליו שלא להאכילו ושלא להשקותו והלך אדם אחד והאכילו והשקהו כששמע המלך לא כועס עליו ואתם קרוין עבדים שנאמר ב) כי לי בני ישראל עבדים אמר לו ר"ע אמשול לך משל למה הדבר דומה למלך בשר ודם שכעס על בנו וחבשו בבית האסורין וצוה עליו שלא להאכילו ושלא להשקותו והלך אדם אחד והאכילו והשקהו כששמע המלך לא דורון משגר לו ואנן קרוין בנים דכתיב ג) בנים אתם לה' אלהיכם אמר לו אתם קרוים בנים וקרוים עבדים בזמן שאתם עושין רצונו של מקום אתם קרוין בנים ובזמן שאין אתם עושין רצונו של מקום אתם קרוין עבדים ועכשיו אין אתם עושין רצונו של מקום אמר לו הרי הוא אומר ד) הלא פרוס לרעב לחמך ועניים מרודים תביא בית אימתי עניים מרודים תביא בית האידנא וקאמר הלא פרוס לרעב לחמך: דרש ר' ברבי שלום כשם שמזונותיו של אדם קצובין לו מראש השנה כך חסרונותיו של אדם קצובין לו מראש השנה זכה הלא פרוס לרעב לחמך לא זכה ועניים מרודים תביא בית * כי הא דבני אחתיה דרבן יוחנן בן זכאי חזא להו בחילמא דבעו למיחסר שבע מאה דינרי עשינהו שקל מינייהו לצדקה (א) פוש גבייהו שיבסר דינרי כי מטא מעלי יומא דכיפורי שדור דבי קיסר נקטינהו אמר להו רבן יוחנן בן זכאי לא תדחלון שיבסר דינרי גבייכו שקלינהו מינייכו אמרי ליה מנא ידעת אמר להו חלמא חזאי לכו א"ל ואמאי לא אמרת לן [דניתבינהו] אמר להו אמינא כי היכי דתעבדו מצוה לשמה רב פפא הוה סליק בדרגא אישתמיט כרעיה בעי למיפל (ב) אמר השתא בן איחייב מאן דסני לן כמחללי שבתות וכעובדי עבודת כוכבים א"ל חייא בר רב מדפתי לרב פפא שמא עני בא לידך ולא פרנסתו א) דתניא רבי יהושע בן קרחה אומר א כל המעלים עיניו מן הצדקה כאילו עובד עבודת כוכבים כתיב הכא ה) השמר לך פן יהיה דבר עם לבבך בליעל וכתיב התם ו) יצאו אנשים בני בליעל מה להלן עבודת כוכבים אף כאן עבודת כוכבים תניא ב) א"ר אלעזר בר' יוסי כל צדקה וחסד שישראל עושין בעולם הזה שלום גדול ופרקליטין גדולין בין ישראל לאביהן שבשמים שנאמר ז) כה אמר ה' אל תבא בית מרזח ואל תלך לספוד ואל תנוד להם כי אספתי את שלומי מאת העם הזה [וגו' את] החסד ואת הרחמים חסד זו גמילות חסדים רחמים זו צדקה תניא ר' יהודה אומר גדולה צדקה שמקרבת את הגאולה שנאמר ח) כה אמר ה' שמרו משפט ועשו צדקה כי קרובה ישועתי לבא וצדקתי להגלות הוא היה אומר עשרה דברים קשים נבראו בעולם הר קשה ברזל מחתכו ברזל קשה (ג) אור מפעפעו אור קשה מים מכבין אותו מים קשים עבים סובלים אותן עבים קשים רוח מפזרתן רוח קשה גוף סובלו גוף קשה פחד שוברו פחד קשה יין מפיגו יין קשה שינה מפכחתו ומיתה קשה (ד) מכולם [וצדקה מצלת מן המיתה] דכתיב ט) וצדקה תציל ממות דרש רבי דוסתאי ברבי ינאי בוא וראה שלא כמדת הקב"ה מדת בשר ודם מדת בשר ודם אדם מביא דורון גדול למלך ספק מקבלין אותו הימנו ספק אין מקבלין אותו הימנו [ואם תמצא לומר מקבלים אותו ממנו] ספק רואה פני המלך ספק אינו רואה פני המלך והקדוש ברוך הוא אינו כן אדם נותן פרוטה לעני זוכה ומקבל פני שכינה שנאמר י) אני בצדק אחזה פניך אשבעה בהקיץ תמונתך רבי אלעזר ג) יהיב פרוטה לעני והדר מצלי אמר (ה) דכתיב אני בצדק אחזה פניך מאי אשבעה בהקיץ תמונתך אמר רב נחמן בר יצחק אלו תלמידי חכמים שמנדדין שינה מעיניהם בעולם הזה והקב"ה משביען מזיו השכינה לעולם הבא א"ר יוחנן מאי דכתיב כ) מלוה ה' חונן דל אלמלא מקרא כתוב אי אפשר לאומרו כביכול ל) עבד לוה לאיש מלוה א"ר חייא בר אבא א"ר יוחנן ג) (רמי) כתיב ט) לא יועילו אוצרות רשע וצדקה תציל ממות וכתיב מ) לא יועיל הון ביום עברה וצדקה תציל ממות שתי צדקות הללו למה אחת שמצילתו ממיתה משונה ואחת שמצילתו מדינה של גיהנם ואי זו היא שמצילתו מדינה של גיהנם ההוא דכתיב ביה עברה דכתיב נ) יום עברה היום ההוא ואי זו היא שמצילתו ממיתה משונה

ואיזו שמצלת ממיתה משונה נותנה ואינו יודע למי נותנה. וא"ת אדרבה זאת שהיא מצלה מדינה רבה היה לה להציל מדינה של גיהנם שהוא רע ביותר ואומר ר"י דרוב דברים אין עומדין לאדם בעולם הזה אלא לאחר מיתה ובעולם הזה אין עומדין לאדם אלא מצות גדולות כדתנן (קדושין דף לט:) אלו דברים שאדם אוכל מפירותיו בעולם הזה והקרן קיימת לעולם הבא לכך קאמר דאפילו ממיתה משונה דהוי בעולם הזה מצלת: אלא

עין משפט נר מצוה

צ א מיימוני פ"י מהל' מתנות עניים הל' ג סמג עשין קסב טוש"ע י"ד סי' רמז סעיף א:

צא ב מיי' שם הל' טו [טוש"ע א"ח סי' לב סעי' ין] וטוש"ע י"ד סי' רמט סעי' יד:

רבינו גרשום

צדקה. זו עושר שיהיו לו נכסים ועושר שיעשה מהם צדקה: כבוד. זו אגדה בשביל שיודע לדרוש באגדות מכבדין אותו: יש לו לבעל הדין. יצר הרע להשיבך ולהטעותך ולומר לך: ועכשיו אי אתם עושין רצונו של מקום. לפי שאתם בגלות ואי אתם יכולים לקיים כל התורה: עניים מרודים. שנרדים מבני אדם ששללום: איכי השתא נפלי. הייתי נידון בסקילה כדאמר בית הסקילה היה גבוה ב' קומות (סנהדרין מה.) וכעובדי עבודת כוכבים דכתיב (דברי' יז) וסקלתם באבני' ומתו: ופרקליטין. מלמדי סניגוריאה: כי אספתי את שלומי. בשביל שאינם עושים לא חסד ולא רחמים. הא עושין יהיה להם שלום גדול: מפעפעו. עושהו רך: אני בצדק. שאעשה צדקה מתחילה והדר אחזה פניך בתפלה:

ליקוטי רש"י

ועניים מרודים. זו ממשלת רומי שלועקת תמיד הבו הבו שאנו לריכין. מרודים. קונפליינ"ט בלע"ז כמו אריד בשיחי (תהלים נה) [לעיל ט.]. נאנחים ונאנקים על לרתם כגון עניי ומרודי (איכה ג) אריד בשיחי (תהלים נה) [ישעיה נח, ז]. דרגא. סולם [שבת קנה.]. סולם של עלייה [ע"פ גיטין נט.]. פרקליט. מליץ טוב [זבחים ז:]. בית מרזח. משתה בספרי בפרשת בית פעור ראיתי חזרו לעשות להם מרזיחין אבל רבותינו פירשו מרזח אבל. תנוד. תקונן. כי אספתי את שלומי וגו'. כשהיה אברהם אביהם עושה לדקה ומשפט נתתי לזרעו חסד ורחמים ושמר ה' אלהיך לך וגו' (דברים ז) ונתן לך רחמים (שם יג) הם הפכו ללענה משפט ולדקה לארץ הניחו (עמוס ה) אף אני חזרתי ואספתי אלי את חסדי ואת רחמי. אספתי. אטולי"ש בלעז כמו אסף אלהים את חרפתי (בראשית ל) [ירמיה טז, ה]. מלוה ה' חונן דל. קרי ביה מלוה את המקום מי שחונן את הדל [ברכות יח.]. יום עברה היום ההוא. ביום הדין משתעי בנבואת לפניה [לקמן בעמ' ב']. ביום הדין משתעי קרא שנידונין עובדי כוכבים לגיהנם [ע"ז יח:].

מסורת הש"ס

א) [תוספ' פאה פ"ד] כתובות סח., ב) [תוס' פאה פ"ד], ג) [בילקוט ובע"י ליתא] והגי' אמר ר"ח ב"א אר"י:

הגהות הב"ח

(א) גמרא פש גבייהו כצ"ל ואות ו' נמחק: (ב) שם בעי למיפל חלש דעתיה אמר השתא: (ג) שם ברזל קשה אש מפעפעו אש קשה מים: (ד) שם ומיתה קשה (מכולם) תז"מ ונ"ב ס"א משינה: (ה) שם והדר מצלי אמר כתיב כצ"ל ואות ד' נמחק: (ו) רש"י ד"ה חזא להו בחלמא במוצאי ראש השנה הס"ד:

גליון הש"ס

גמרא כי הא דבני אחתיה. וכעין זה איתא במדרש רבה ויקרא פרשה לד בבני אחתיה דרשב"י:

תורה אור השלם

א) כבוד חכמים ינחלו וכסילים מרים קלון: [משלי ג, לה]

ב) כי לי בני ישראל עבדים עבדי הם אשר הוצאתי אותם מארץ מצרים אני יי אלהיכם: [ויקרא כה, נה]

ג) בנים אתם ליי אלהיכם לא תתגדדו ולא תשימו קרחה בין עיניכם למת: [דברים יד, א]

ד) הלוא פרס לרעב לחמך ועניים מרודים תביא בית כי תראה ערם וכסיתו ומבשרך לא תתעלם: [ישעיה נח, ז]

ה) השמר לך פן יהיה דבר עם לבבך בליעל לאמר קרבה שנת השבע שנת השמטה ורעה עינך באחיך האביון ולא תתן לו וקרא עליך אל יי והיה בך חטא: [דברים טו, ט]

ו) יצאו אנשים בני בליעל מקרבך וידיחו את ישבי עירם לאמר נלכה ונעבדה אלהים אחרים אשר לא ידעתם: [דברים יג, יד]

ז) כי כה אמר יי אל תבוא בית מרזח ואל תלך לספוד ואל תנד להם כי אספתי את שלומי מאת העם הזה נאם יי את החסד ואת הרחמים: [ירמיה טז, ה]

ח) כה אמר יי שמרו משפט ועשו צדקה כי קרובה ישועתי לבוא וצדקתי להגלות: [ישעיה נו, א]

ט) לא יועילו אוצרות רשע וצדקה תציל ממות: [משלי י, ב]

י) אני בצדק אחזה פניך אשבעה בהקיץ תמונתך: [תהלים יז, טו] כ) מלוה יי חונן דל וגמלו ישלם לו: [משלי יט, יז] ל) עשיר ברשים ימשול ועבד לוה לאיש מלוה: [משלי כב, ז] מ) לא יועיל הון ביום עברה וצדקה תציל ממות: [משלי יא, ד] נ) יום עברה היום ההוא יום צרה ומצוקה יום שאה ומשואה יום חשך ואפלה יום ענן וערפל: [צפניה א, טו]

More on the power of charity:

דָּרַשׁ רַבִּי דּוֹסְתָּאי בְּרַבִּי יַנַּאי – **R' Dusta'i the son of R' Yanai expounded:** בּוֹא וּרְאֵה שֶׁלֹּא כְּמִדַּת הַקָּדוֹשׁ בָּרוּךְ הוּא מִדַּת בָּשָׂר וָדָם – **Come and see that the ways of man**[43] **are not like the ways of the Holy One, Blessed is He.** מִדַּת בָּשָׂר וָדָם – **The way of man** is: אָדָם מֵבִיא דּוֹרוֹן גָּדוֹל לְמֶלֶךְ – When **a man brings a large gift to a king,** סָפֵק מְקַבְּלִין אוֹתוֹ הֵימֶנּוּ – **it is a question whether [the king's servants] will accept [the gift] from him** סָפֵק אֵין מְקַבְּלִין אוֹתוֹ הֵימֶנּוּ – **or whether they will not accept it from him.** [וְאִם תִּמְצָא לוֹמַר מְקַבְּלִים אוֹתוֹ מִמֶּנּוּ] – **And if you conclude and say** that **they accept it from him,** סָפֵק רוֹאֶה פְּנֵי הַמֶּלֶךְ – **it is** still **a question whether he will see the face of the king** [i.e. be granted a personal audience] סָפֵק אֵינוֹ רוֹאֶה פְּנֵי הַמֶּלֶךְ – **or whether he will not see the face of the king.** וְהַקָּדוֹשׁ בָּרוּךְ הוּא אֵינוֹ כֵן – **But the Holy One, Blessed is He, is not so.** אָדָם נוֹתֵן פְּרוּטָה לֶעָנִי – When **a person gives a** ***perutah*** [a small coin] **to a pauper,** זוֹכֶה וּמְקַבֵּל פְּנֵי שְׁכִינָה – **he is deserving**[44] **and receives the Divine Presence** directly, שֶׁנֶּאֱמַר – **for it is stated:**[45] "אֲנִי בְּצֶדֶק אֶחֱזֶה פָנֶיךָ אֶשְׂבְּעָה בְהָקִיץ תְּמוּנָתֶךָ" – ***I shall behold Your face through charity; through awakening I shall be sated by Your image.***[46]

R' Elazar relied on this interpretation in practice:

רַבִּי אֶלְעָזָר יָהִיב פְּרוּטָה לֶעָנִי – **R' Elazar would give a** ***perutah*** **to a pauper** וַהֲדַר מְצַלֵּי – **and then** proceed **to pray.** אָמַר דִּכְתִיב – **[R' Elazar] said** in explanation: **For it is written:** "אֲנִי בְּצֶדֶק אֶחֱזֶה פָנֶיךָ" – ***I shall behold Your face*** **through** (giving) ***charity.*** Thus, one should proffer a gift of charity before engaging in prayer.[47]

The Gemara now expounds upon the end of the verse:

מַאי: "אֶשְׂבְּעָה בְהָקִיץ תְּמוּנָתֶךָ" – **What** is the meaning of ***through awakening I shall be sated by Your image?***

The Gemara explains:

אָמַר רַב נַחְמָן בַּר יִצְחָק – **Rav Nachman bar Yitzchak said:** אֵלּוּ תַּלְמִידֵי חֲכָמִים שֶׁמְּנַדְּדִין שֵׁינָה מֵעֵינֵיהֶם בָּעוֹלָם הַזֶּה – **These are the scholars who banish sleep from their eyes** to study Torah continuously **in this world,**[48] וְהַקָּדוֹשׁ בָּרוּךְ הוּא מַשְׂבִּיעָן מִזִּיו הַשְּׁכִינָה לָעוֹלָם הַבָּא – **and the Holy One, Blessed is He, satiates them from the radiance of** His **Presence in the World to Come.**[49]

R' Yochanan discusses the power of charity:

אָמַר רַבִּי יוֹחָנָן מַאי דִּכְתִיב – **R' Yochanan said: What** is meant by that **which is written:**[50] "מַלְוֵה ה׳ חוֹנֵן דָּל" – ***He who is gracious to the poor has lent to God?*** אִלְמָלֵא מִקְרָא כָּתוּב – **If the verse were not** explicitly **written,** אִי אֶפְשָׁר לְאוֹמְרוֹ – **it would be impossible to utter [its implication].** כִּבְיָכוֹל – **As if it were possible** to speak in this manner,[51] we interpret the verse with another verse:[52] "עֶבֶד לֹוֶה לְאִישׁ מַלְוֶה" – ***A borrower is a servant to the lender.*** As it were, God is beholden to one who gives charity.[53]

More on the protective power of charity:

אָמַר רַבִּי חִיָּיא בַּר אַבָּא רַבִּי יוֹחָנָן (רמי) – **R' Chiya bar Abba said in R' Yochanan's name:**[54] כְּתִיב: "לֹא יוֹעִיל הוֹן בְּיוֹם עֶבְרָה וּצְדָקָה תַּצִּיל מִמָּוֶת" – In one verse **it is written:**[55] ***Wealth will not help on the day of anger, and charity saves from death;*** וּכְתִיב: "לֹא־יוֹעִילוּ אוֹצְרוֹת רֶשַׁע וּצְדָקָה תַּצִּיל מִמָּוֶת" – **and** in a second verse **it is written:**[56] ***Treasures of wickedness will not help, and charity saves from death.*** שְׁתֵּי צְדָקוֹת הַלָּלוּ לָמָּה – **Why are these two [statements about] charity** delivering from death both necessary?

The Gemara explains:

אַחַת שֶׁמַּצִּילַתּוֹ מִמִּיתָה מְשׁוּנָּה – **One** verse is necessary to teach **that [charity] rescues [the donor] from an unnatural death;** וְאַחַת שֶׁמַּצִּילַתּוֹ מִדִּינָהּ שֶׁל גֵּיהִנֹּם – **and one** verse teaches **that [charity] rescues [the donor] from the judgment of Gehinnom.**

The Gemara now matches each of the verses to the protection it affords:

וְאֵי זוֹ הִיא שֶׁמַּצִּילַתּוֹ מִדִּינָהּ שֶׁל גֵּיהִנֹּם – **And which** of the verses **is the one that** speaks of **saving [the donor] from the judgment of Gehinnom?** הַהוּא דִּכְתִיב בֵּיהּ: "עֶבְרָה" – **The one in which** the word ***anger*** **is written** – for "anger" refers to the time of judgment, דִּכְתִיב: "יוֹם עֶבְרָה הַיּוֹם הַהוּא" – **as it is written** elsewhere[57] regarding the day of judgment: ***A day of anger is that day.***

The Gemara inquires:

וְאֵי זוֹ הִיא שֶׁמַּצִּילַתּוֹ מִמִּיתָה מְשׁוּנָּה – **And which** type of charity **is it that rescues [the donor] from an unnatural death?**[58]

NOTES

property to another]. Death, on the other hand, is a function of the impermanence of material things, and so belongs to this material world. Thus, since charity has a transcendent quality, it overwhelms and eliminates death (*Maharal*).

43. Literally: flesh and blood.

44. *Ben Yehoyada* notes that the word "deserving" appears to be extraneous. See there for a beautiful interpretation of this passage.

45. *Psalms* 17:15.

46. On the simple level, the verse refers to the future resurrection of the dead (*techias hameisim*). However, the Gemara interprets the first part of the verse to mean that giving charity entitles one to an audience with God. The Gemara will expound upon the end of the verse below.

47. The gift of charity parallels the gift to the king mentioned in the Gemara's parable. It should precede one's audience with the King of all earthly kings – i.e. it should precede the act of prayer, when one petitions God for all his personal needs (*Maharsha*).

R' Elazar understood that *I shall behold Your face* refers to prayer because during prayer one must create the mental image that he is actually standing before God (*Ben Yehoyada*).

48. This is the meaning of *through awakening* – i.e. in the merit of their constantly awakening themselves to study Torah (see *Rashi*).

49. When a person sleeps he is a completely physical entity, for his intellectual soul is inactive. Conversely, when one banishes sleep in order to study Torah, he overcomes and banishes his physicality. It is thus fitting that these scholars be sated from the radiance of the Divine Presence in the World to Come, where they will completely transcend physicality (*Maharal;* cf. *Maharsha*).

50. *Proverbs* 19:17.

51. כִּבְיָכוֹל – *as if it were possible.* This term introduces an anthropomorphic statement. In post-Talmudic Hebrew, it is sometimes used as a designation for God.

52. *Proverbs* 22:7.

53. *Maharal* explains the concept: God is obligated, as it were, to complete the world He created, and thus must provide sustenance for those individuals He created to be poor. Hence, *he who is gracious to the poor* with gifts of charity *has lent to God,* in that he has paid God's obligation. For that reason God is *beholden* (מְשֻׁעְבָּד, from עֶבֶד, *servant*) to the donor, in the sense that He must reimburse him. Hence, *a borrower* (God) *is a servant* (i.e. is beholden) *to the lender* (the donor).

54. The word רמי, *noted a contradiction,* is not appropriate, for R' Yochanan presents no contradiction. Our translation follows the emendation of *Mesoras HaShas* (cf. *Maharsha*).

55. *Proverbs* 11:4.

56. Ibid. 10:2.

57. *Zephaniah* 1:15.

58. Having identified the verse that refers to the judgment of Gehinnom, the Gemara necessarily understands that the other verse refers to unnatural death. Hence, the Gemara now poses a different question than it did before [even though the two questions are expressed identically].

ימצא חיים. וכתיב גבי חכמה כי מוצאי מצא חיים: בעלי אגדה. מתוך שהן דרשנין ומושכין את הלב הכל מכבדין אותם: לבעל הדין. רשע או עובד כוכבים: להנצל אנו בהן כו'. שהצדקה מצלת מגיהנם כדאמרי' לקמן בשמעתין: שמזונותיו של אדם. שכר שיתפרנס ממנו: חסרונותיו. הפסד שעתיד להפסיד: זכה. למזל טוב יתן אותו חסרון לעניים: חזא [להו] בחלמא. במוצאי (ו) יה"כ: דבעו מחסר שבע מאה דינרין. באותה שנה: שקיל צדקה מינייהו. כל השנה היה כופן בדברים וגובה מהן לצדקה: פש גבייהו. ערב ראש השנה שיבסר דינרי שלא נתנו לצדקה משבע מאה דינרי: לא תדחלו. למיפסד יותר: אמאי לא אמרת לן. מתחלה שכך חלמת והיינו נותנין כולן: השתא כן. אם נפלתי: איחייב מאן דסני לן. כלפי שתולה קללתו בחבירו: מחללי שבת ועובדי עבודת כוכבים. בסקילה ואמר מר (כתובות דף ל:) מי שנתחייב סקילה או נופל מן הגג או חיה דורסתו דדמי לסקילה דתנן (סנהדרין דף מה.) בית הסקילה היה גבוה שתי קומות וכו': פרקליטין. מלאכי יושר [של מלאכי השרת]: כי אספתי את שלומי מאת העם הזה. ומהו השלום את החסד ואת הרחמים שהיו רגילין לעשות: מפעפעו. מרככו: הגוף סובלו. [כל הגוף] מלא רוח: ואני בצדק. בתחלה ואח"כ אחזה פניך בתפלה: אשבעה בהקיץ תמונתך. בשכר הקיצה אשבע תמונתך: מלוה ה' חונן דל. החונן לדל נעשה מלוה להקב"ה וכתיב ועבד לוה לאיש מלוה (משלי כב): ואיזו היא צדקה המצלת מדינה של גיהנם. כלומר איזה מן המקראות הללו מדבר מדין של גיהנם אותו שכתוב לא יועיל הון ביום עברה:

עוברה

ימצא חיים בעלי עושר דכתיב צדקה בעלי אגדה דכתיב וכבוד כתיב הכא וכבוד וכתיב התם א) כבוד חכמים ינחלו תניא היה רבי מאיר אומר יש לו לבעל הדין להשיבך ולומר לך אם אלהיכם אוהב עניים הוא מפני מה אינו מפרנסן אמור לו כדי שניצול אנו בהן מדינה של גיהנם וזו שאלה שאל טורנוסרופוס הרשע את ר"ע אם אלהיכם אוהב עניים הוא מפני מה אינו מפרנסם א"ל כדי שניצול אנו בהן מדינה של גיהנם א"ל [אדרבה] זו שמחייבתן לגיהנם אמשול לך משל למה הדבר דומה למלך בשר ודם שכעס על עבדו וחבשו בבית האסורין וצוה עליו שלא להאכילו ושלא להשקותו והלך אדם אחד והאכילו והשקהו כששמע המלך לא כועס עליו ואתם קרוין עבדים שנאמר ב) כי לי בני ישראל עבדים אמר לו ר"ע אמשול לך משל למה הדבר דומה למלך בשר ודם שכעס על בנו וחבשו בבית האסורין וצוה עליו שלא להאכילו ושלא להשקותו והלך אדם אחד והאכילו והשקהו כששמע המלך לא דורון משגר לו ואנן קרוין בנים דכתיב ג) בנים אתם לה' אלהיכם אמר לו אתם קרוים בנים וקרוין עבדים בזמן שאתם עושין רצונו של מקום אתם קרוין בנים ובזמן שאין אתם עושין רצונו של מקום אתם קרוין עבדים ועכשיו אין אתם עושין רצונו של מקום אמר לו הרי הוא אומר ד) הלא פרוס לרעב לחמך ועניים מרודים תביא בית אימתי עניים מרודים תביא בית האידנא וקאמר הלא פרוס לרעב לחמך: דרש ר' יהודה ברבי שלום כשם שמזונותיו של אדם קצובין לו מראש השנה כך חסרונותיו של אדם קצובין לו מראש השנה זכה הלא פרוס לרעב לחמך לא זכה ועניים מרודים תביא בית * כי הא דבני אחתיה דרבן יוחנן בן זכאי חזא להו בחילמא דבעו למיחסר שבע מאה דינרי עשינהו שקל מינייהו לצדקה (א) פוש גבייהו שיבסר דינרי כי מטא מעלי יומא דכיפורי שדור דבי קיסר נקטינהו אמר להו רבן יוחנן בן זכאי לא תדחלון שיבסר דינרי גבייכו שקלינהו מינייכו אמרי ליה מנא ידעת אמר להו חלמא חזאי לכו א"ל ואמאי לא אמרת לן [דניתבינהו] אמר להו אמינא כי היכי דתעבדו מצוה לשמה רב פפא הוה סליק בדרגא אישתמיט כרעיה בעי למיפל (ב) אמר השתא כן איחייב מאן דסני לן כמחללי שבתות וכעובדי עבודת כוכבים א"ל חייא בר רב מדפתי לרב פפא שמא עני בא לידך ולא פרנסתו דתניא רבי יהושע בן קרחה אומר * כל המעלים עיניו מן הצדקה כאילו עובד עבודת כוכבים כתיב הכא ה) השמר לך פן יהיה דבר עם לבבך בליעל וכתיב התם ו) יצאו אנשים בני בליעל מה להלן עבודת כוכבים אף כאן עבודת כוכבים תניא א"ר אלעזר בר' יוסי כל צדקה וחסד שישראל עושין בעולם הזה שלום גדול ופרקליטין גדולין בין ישראל לאביהן שבשמים שנאמר ז) כה אמר ה' אל תבא בית מרזח ואל תלך לספוד ואל תנוד להם כי אספתי את שלומי מאת העם הזה [וגו' את] החסד ואת הרחמים חסד זו גמילות חסדים רחמים זו צדקה תניא ר"י אומר גדולה צדקה שמקרבת את הגאולה שנאמר ח) כה אמר ה' שמרו משפט ועשו צדקה כי קרובה ישועתי לבא וצדקתי להגלות הוא היה אומר עשרה דברים קשים נבראו בעולם הר קשה ברזל מחתכו ברזל קשה (ג) אור מפעפעו אור קשה מים מכבין אותו מים קשים עבים סובלים אותן עבים קשים רוח מפזרתן רוח קשה גוף סובלו גוף קשה פחד שוברו פחד קשה יין מפיגו יין קשה שינה מפכחתו ומיתה קשה (ד) מכולם [וצדקה מצלת מן המיתה] דכתיב ט) וצדקה תציל ממות דרש רבי דוסתאי ברבי ינאי בוא וראה שלא כמדת הקב"ה מדת בשר ודם מדת בשר ודם אדם מביא דורון גדול למלך ספק מקבלין אותו הימנו ספק אין מקבלין אותו הימנו [ואם תמצא לומר מקבלים אותו ממנו] ספק רואה פני המלך ספק אינו רואה פני המלך והקדוש ברוך הוא אינו כן אדם נותן פרוטה לעני זוכה ומקבל פני שכינה שנאמר י) אני בצדק אחזה פניך אשבעה בהקיץ תמונתך רבי אלעזר יהיב פרוטה לעני והדר מצלי אמר (ה) דכתיב אני בצדק אחזה פניך מאי אשבעה בהקיץ תמונתך אמר רב נחמן בר יצחק אלו תלמידי חכמים שמנדדין שינה מעיניהם בעולם הזה והקב"ה משביען מזיו השכינה לעולם הבא א"ר יוחנן מאי דכתיב כ) מלוה ה' חונן דל אלמלא מקרא כתוב אי אפשר לאומרו כביכול ל) עבד לוה לאיש מלוה א"ר חייא בר אבא א"ר יוחנן ג) (רמי) כתיב מ) לא יועיל הון ביום עברה וצדקה תציל ממות וכתיב ט) לא יועילו אוצרות רשע וצדקה תציל ממות שתי צדקות הללו למה אחת שמצילתו ממיתה משונה ואחת שמצילתו מדינה של גיהנם ואי זו היא שמצילתו מדינה של גיהנם ההוא דכתיב ביה עברה דכתיב נ) יום עברה היום ההוא ואי זו היא שמצילתו ממיתה משונה

ואיזו שמצלת ממיתה משונה נותנה ואינו יודע למי נותנה. וא"ת אדרבה זאת שהיא מעלה רבה היה לה להציל מדינה של גיהנם שהוא רע ביותר ואומר ר"י דרוב דברים אין עומדין לאדם בעולם הזה אלא לאחר מיתה ובעולם הזה אין עומדין לאדם אלא מצות גדולות כדתנן (קדושין דף לט:) אלו דברים שאדם אוכל מפירותיו בעולם הזה והקרן קיימת לעולם הבא לכך קאמר דאפילו ממיתה משונה דהוי בעולם הזה מצלת:

אלא

מסורת הש"ס

א) [תוספ' פאה פ"ד] כתובות סח., ב) [תוס' פאה פ"ד], ג) [בילקוט ובע"י ליתא] והגי' אמר ר"ח ב"א אר"י:

הגהות הב"ח

(א) גמרא פש גבייהו כצ"ל ואות ו' נמחק: (ב) שם בעי למיפל חלש דעתיה אמר השתא: (ג) שם ברזל קשה אש מפעפעו אש קשה מים: (ד) שם ומיתה קשה (מכולם) תז"מ ונ"ב ס"א מסיני: (ה) שם והדר מצלי אמר כתיב כצ"ל ואות ד' נמחק: (ו) רש"י ד"ה חזא להו בחלמא במוצאי ראש השנה הס"ד:

גליון הש"ס

גמרא כי הא דבני אחתיה. ועיין זה איתא במדרש רבה ויקרא פרשה לד בבני אחתיה דרשב"י:

תורה אור השלם

א) כבוד חכמים ינחלו וכסילים מרים קלון: [משלי ג, לה]

ב) כי לי בני ישראל עבדים עבדי הם אשר הוצאתי אותם מארץ מצרים אני יי אלהיכם: [ויקרא כה, נה]

ג) בנים אתם ליי אלהיכם לא תתגדדו ולא תשימו קרחה בין עיניכם למת: [דברים יד, א]

ד) הלוא פרס לרעב לחמך ועניים מרודים תביא בית כי תראה ערם וכסיתו ומבשרך לא תתעלם: [ישעיה נח, ז]

ה) השמר לך פן יהיה דבר עם לבבך בליעל לאמר קרבה שנת השבע שנת השמטה ורעה עינך באחיך האביון ולא תתן לו וקרא עליך אל יי והיה בך חטא: [דברים טו, ט]

ו) יצאו אנשים בני בליעל מקרבך וידיחו את ישבי עירם לאמר נלכה ונעבדה אלהים אחרים אשר לא ידעתם: [דברים יג, יד]

ז) כי כה אמר יי אל תבוא בית מרזח ואל תלך לספוד ואל תנד להם כי אספתי את שלומי מאת העם הזה נאם יי את החסד ואת הרחמים: [ירמיה טז, ה]

ח) כה אמר יי שמרו משפט ועשו צדקה כי קרובה ישועתי לבוא וצדקתי להגלות: [ישעיה נו, א]

ט) לא יועילו אוצרות רשע וצדקה תציל ממות: [משלי י, ב]

י) אני בצדק אחזה פניך אשבעה בהקיץ תמונתך: [תהלים יז, טו] כ) מלוה יי חונן דל וגמלו ישלם לו: [משלי יט, יז] ל) עשיר ברשים ימשול ועבד לוה לאיש מלוה: [משלי כב, ז] מ) לא יועיל הון ביום עברה וצדקה תציל ממות: [משלי יא, ד] נ) יום עברה היום ההוא יום צרה ומצוקה יום שאה ומשואה יום חשך ואפלה יום ענן וערפל: [צפניה א, טו]

עין משפט נר מצוה

צ א מיימוני פ"י מהל' מתנות עניים הל' ג סמג עשין קסב טוש"ע י"ד סי' רמז סעיף א:

צא ב מיי' שם הל' טו [טוש"ע א"ח סי' לב סעי' ז] וטוש"ע י"ד סי' רמט סעי' יד:

רבינו גרשום

צדקה. זו עושר שיהיו לו נכסים ועושר שיעשה מהם צדקה: כבוד. זו אגדה בשביל שיודע לדרוש באגדות מכבדין אותו: יש לו לבעל הדין. יצר הרע להשיבך ולהטעותך ולומר לך: ועכשיו אי אתם עושין רצונו של מקום. לפי שאתם בגלות ואי אתם יכולים לקיים כל התורה: עניים מרודים. שנרדים מבני אדם ששללום: איכי השתא נפלי. הייתי נידון בסקילה כדאמר בית הסקילה היה גבוה ב' קומות (סנהדרין מה.) וכעובדי עבודת כוכבים דכתיב (דברי' יז) וסקלתם באבני' ומתו: ופרקליטין. מלמדי סניגוריאה: כי אספתי את שלומי. בשביל שאינם עושים לא חסד ולא רחמים. הא עושין יהיה להם שלום גדול: מפעפעו. עושהו רך: אני בצדק. שאעשה צדקה מתחילה והדר אחזה פניך בתפלה:

ליקוטי רש"י

ועניים מרודים. זו ממשלת רומי שצועקת תמיד הבו הבו שאנו צריכין. מרודים. קונפליינ"ט בלע"ז כמו אריד בשיחי (תהלים נה) [לעיל ט.]. נאנחים ונאנקים על צרתם כגון עניי ומרודי (איכה ג) אריד בשיחי (תהלים נה) [ישעיה נח, ז]. דרגא. סולם [שבת קנה.]. סולם של עלייה [ע"פ גיטין נט.]. פרקליט. מליץ טוב [זבחים ז:]. בית מרזח. משתה בספרי בפרשת בית פעור ראיתי חזרו לעשות להם מרזיחין אבל רבותינו פירשו מרזח אבל. תנוד. תקונן. כי אספתי את שלומי וגו'. כשהיה אברהם אביהם עושה צדקה ומשפט נתתי לזרעו חסד ורחמים ושמר ה' אלהיך לך וגו' (דברים ז) ונתן לך רחמים (שם יג) הם הפכו ללענה משפט וצדקה לארץ הניחו (עמוס ה) אף אני חזרתי ואספתי אלי את חסדי ואת רחמי. אספתי. אטולי"ש בלעז כמו אסף אלהים את חרפתי (בראשית ל) [ירמיה טז, ה]. מלוה ה' חונן דל. קרי ביה מלוה את המקום מי שחונן את הדל [ברכות יח.]. יום עברה היום ההוא. ביום הדין משתעי בנבואת לפניה [לקמן בעמ' ב']. ביום הדין משתעי קרא שנידונין עובדי כוכבים לגיהנם [ע"ז יח:].

נותנה ואינו יודע למי נותנה נוטלה ואינו יודע ממי נוטלה נותנה ואינו יודע למי נותנה לאפוקי מדמר עוקבא נוטלה ואינו יודע ממי נוטלה לאפוקי מדרבי אבא ואלא היכי ליעביד ליתיב לארנקי של צדקה מיתיבי מה יעשה אדם ויהיו לו בנים זכרים ר"א אומר יפזר מעותיו לעניים ר' יהושע אומר ישמח אשתו לדבר מצוה ר' אליעזר בן יעקב אומר לא יתן אדם פרוטה לארנקי של צדקה אלא א"כ ממונה עליה כר' חנניא בן תרדיון כי קא אמרינן דממני עלה כר' חנניא בן תרדיון א"ר אבהו אמר משה לפני הקב"ה רבש"ע במה תרום קרן ישראל אמר לו בכי תשא וא"ר אבהו שאלו את שלמה בן דוד עד היכן כחה של צדקה אמר להן צאו וראו מה פירש דוד אבא פזר נתן לאביונים צדקתו עומדת לעד קרנו תרום בכבוד רבי אבא אמר מהכא הוא מרומים ישכון מצדות סלעים משגבו לחמו נתן מימיו נאמנים מה טעם מרומים ישכון מצדות סלעים משגבו משום דלחמו נתן ומימיו נאמנים וא"ר אבהו שאלו את שלמה איזהו בן העולם הבא אמר להם כל שכנגד זקניו כבוד כי הא (א) דיוסף בריה דר' יהושע חלש אינגיד א"ל אבוה מאי חזית א"ל עולם הפוך ראיתי עליונים למטה ותחתונים למעלה א"ל עולם ברור ראית ואנן היכי חזיתינן [א"ל] כי היכי דחשבינן הכא חשבינן התם ושמעתי שהיו אומרים אשרי מי שבא לכאן ותלמודו בידו ושמעתי שהיו אומרים הרוגי מלכות אין כל בריה יכולה לעמוד במחיצתן מאן נינהו אילימא ר"ע וחבריו משום הרוגי מלכות ותו לא פשיטא בלאו הכי נמי אלא הרוגי לוד תניא אמר להן רבן יוחנן בן זכאי לתלמידיו בני מהו שאמר הכתוב צדקה תרומם גוי וחסד לאומים חטאת נענה רבי אליעזר ואמר צדקה תרומם גוי אלו ישראל דכתיב ומי כעמך ישראל גוי אחד בארץ וחסד לאומים חטאת כל צדקה וחסד שאומות עובדי כוכבים עושין חטא הוא להן שאינם עושין אלא להתגדל בו כמו שנאמר די להוון מהקרבין ניחוחין לאלהה שמיא ומצליין לחיי מלכא ובנוהי ודעביד הכי לאו צדקה גמורה היא והתניא האומר סלע (ב) זה לצדקה בשביל שיחיו בני ובשביל שאזכה לעולם הבא הרי זה צדיק גמור לא קשיא כאן בישראל כאן בעובד כוכבים נענה רבי יהושע ואמר צדקה תרומם גוי אלו ישראל דכתיב ומי כעמך ישראל גוי אחד וחסד לאומים חטאת כל צדקה וחסד שאומות עובדי כוכבים עושין חטא הוא להן שאין עושין אלא כדי שתמשך מלכותן שנאמר להן מלכא מלכי ישפר עליך וחטיך בצדקה פרוק ועויתך במיחן עניין הן תהוי ארכא לשלותיך וגו' נענה רבן גמליאל ואמר צדקה תרומם גוי אלו ישראל דכתיב ומי כעמך ישראל [וגו'] וחסד לאומים חטאת כל צדקה וחסד שעכו"ם עושין חטא הוא להן שאין עושין אלא להתיהר בו וכל המתיהר נופל בגיהנם שנאמר זד יהיר לץ שמו עושה בעברת זדון ואין עברה אלא גיהנם שנאמר יום עברה היום ההוא אמר רבן גמליאל עדיין אנו צריכין למודעי רבי אליעזר המודעי אומר צדקה תרומם גוי אלו ישראל דכתיב ומי כעמך ישראל גוי אחד וחסד לאומים חטאת כל צדקה וחסד שעכו"ם עושין חטא הוא להן שאין עושין אלא לחרף אותנו בו שנאמר ויבא ויעש ה' כאשר דבר כי חטאתם לה' ולא שמעתם בקולו והיה לכם הדבר הזה נענה רבי נחוניא בן הקנה ואמר צדקה תרומם גוי וחסד לישראל ולאומים חטאת אמר להם רבן יוחנן בן זכאי לתלמידיו נראין דברי רבי נחוניא בן הקנה מדברי ומדבריכם לפי שהוא נותן צדקה וחסד לישראל ולעכו"ם חטאת מכלל דהוא נמי אמר מאי היא דתניא אמר להם רבן יוחנן בן זכאי כשם שהחטאת מכפרת על ישראל כך צדקה מכפרת על אומות העולם: איפרא הורמיז אימיה דשבור מלכא שדרה ארבע מאה דינרי לקמיה דרבי אמי ולא קבלינהו (ג) שדרינהו קמיה דרבא וקבלינהו משום שלום מלכות שמע רבי אמי איקפד אמר לית ליה ביבש קצירה תשברנה נשים באות מאירות אותה ורבא משום שלום מלכות ורבי אמי נמי משום שלום מלכות דאיבעי ליה למפלגינהו לעניי עובדי כוכבים ורבא נמי לעניי עובדי כוכבים יהבינהו ור' אמי דאיקפד הוא דלא

נותנה ואינו יודע למי נותנה. כדמסיים בסיפיה יתננה בכיס של גבאי צדקה: דרב עוקבא ור' אבא במס' כתובות (דף סז:) מר עוקבא הוה שדי לענייא דשבבותיה כל יומא ארבעה זוזי בצינורא דדשא הרי שהעני אינו יודע ממי נוטלה והוא יודע למי נותנה ור' אבא הוה צייר בסודריה ושדי לאחוריה וממציא נפשיה לביני עניי והעני נוטלה ויודע ממי נוטלה ואינו יודע למי נותנה: לדבר מצוה. לפני תשמיש: אמר לו בכי תשא. אם באת לשאת ראשם בהגבהה קח מהם כופר לצדקה: כנגד זקניו כבוד. אותם שחולקין להם כבוד בעולם הזה מחמת חכמת זקנתם: עליונים למטה. אותם שהם עליונים כאן מחמת עושרן ראיתי שם שהם למטה: ותחתונים למעלה. ראיתי עניים שהם בינינו שפלים שם ראיתים חשובים: ואנן. בעלי תורה היאך אתינן היאך יש חשיבותינו: כי היכי. דאיתינן הכא חשובים ונכבדים הכי איתינן התם: הרוגי מלכות ותו לא. כלומר הך מלתא לחודא הוא דהוי בהו שנהרגו על קידוש השם ותו לא הוה בהו: הרוגי לוד. לולייוס ופפוס אחים שהרגם (ט) טורנוסרופוס הרשע בלודקיא כדאמרינן במסכת תענית (דף יח:) על ידי גזירה שנגזרה על ישראל להשמיד על שנמצאת בת מלך הרוגה וחשדו את ישראל עליה ועמדו האחים הללו ואמרו מה לכם על ישראל אנו הרגנוה: ה"ז צדיק גמור. ולא אמרינן שלא לשמה הוא: כאן בישראל. וכאן בעובד כוכבים. ישראל לבם לשמים בין יחיה בין לא יחיה אינו מהרהר אחר מדת הדין אבל עכו"ם אינו נותן אלא ע"מ כן ואם לאו מתחרט: יום עברה היום ההוא. ביום הדין משתעי בנבואת צפניה: המודעי. מהר המודעי היה: ויבא ויעש ה' כאשר דבר כי חטאתם לה' וגו'. נבוזראדן קאמר ליה לירמיה כשהיה מגלה את ישראל לבבל: ביבש קצירה תשברנה. כשתכלה זכות שבידן וייבש לחלוחית מעשה צדקה שלהן אז ישברו: דלא

אלא א"כ ממונה עליה כרבי חנניא בן תרדיון. פי' נאמן כמותו אבל צדיק כמותו לא דהא גבאים דבימי אמוראים לא היו צדיקים כמותו והכי נקט ר' חנניא בן תרדיון משום מעשה שבא לידו דאמר פ"ק דמסכת ע"ז (דף יז:) מעות פורים נתחלפו לי במעות של צדקה וחלקתים לעניים וכן בפרק במה טומנין (שבת דף מט. ושם) דאמר תפילין צריכין גוף נקי כאלישע לא צדיק כאלישע קאמר אלא גוף נקי שידע ליזהר שלא ישן בהם ושלא יפיח בהם קאמר ולא נקט אלישע אלא משום דאיתרחיש ביה ניסא:

עליונים למטה ותחתונים למעלה. פי' ר"ח דאמרו הגאונים שקבלה בידם רב מפי רב דעולם הפוך היינו שראה שמואל דהוה יתיב קמיה דרב יהודה תלמידיה משום דמיחה בשמואל בפר' במה בהמה (שם דף נה.) גבי ההיא איתתא דאתיא וצוחא קמיה דשמואל ולא אשגח בה א"ל רב יהודה לית ליה למר אוטם אזנו מזעקת דל וגו':

ויבא ויעש ה' כאשר דבר כי חטאתם וגו'. ואותה שעה עשה צדקה שהיה (ד) מקנא להקב"ה א"נ שהיה מתיר את ירמיה מן הזיקים כדכתיב התם:

ולא

עין משפט נר מצוה

צב א ב מיי' פ"י מהל' מתנות עניים הלכה ח סמג עשין קסב טוש"ע י"ד סי' רמט סעיף ז:
צג ג מיי' שם הלכה ט סמג שם טוש"ע י"ד סימן רנד סעיף ב:

הגהות הב"ח

(א) גמרא כי הא דרב יוסף בריה דר' יהושע: (ב) שם סלע זו לצדקה: (ג) שם שדרינהו קמיה דרבא: (ד) תוס' ד"ה ויבא וכו' עשה צדקה שהיה נראה כמקנא להקב"ה:

רבינו גרשום

ואינו יודע למי נותנה. לאפוקי ממר עוקבא דמנח לצדקה אצינורא דדשא של ביתו והעני לא היה יודע מי נותנה שם ומר עוקבא יודע איזה עני נוטלה. נוטלה העני ואינו יודע ממי נוטלה. לאפוקי דר' אבא דצייר בסודריה ומפשילו לאחוריו ואתי עני ושרי ושקיל. עני היה יודע ממי נוטל ור' אבא אינו יודע איזה עני נוטלה: יתן לארנקי של צדקה ולא ידע העני מי נתן והנותן לא ידע מי נוטל: ישמח אשתו בדבר מצוה. שיפרנסה שלא בזמן עונה: אלא א"כ ממונה עליה כר' חנינא בן תרדיון. שהיה אדם גדול והיה יודע לבדוק למי יתן אלמא (דלא) [דאי לא] מצינן למשכח ממונה כגון זה. הוא מפזר ונותן. כי אמרינן נמי דיתן לארנקי בשיש ממונה עליה כר' חנינא בן תרדיון. אי לא יפזרן הוא עצמו: אמר לו בכי תשא. משום דכתי' שם ונתנו איש כופר נפשו: אמר להן כל שכנגד זקניו כבוד. זה שקנה חכמה כלומר כל שחולקין לו כבוד בשביל חכמתו ולא משום עושרו: עליונים למטה. כלומר אותן שהן עליונים בעולם הזה בשביל עושרם ולא בגין חכמתם ושם בעולם הבא שרוין למטה: ותחתונים. בעולם הזה שהם חכמים ומסכינין ובני מעשים טובים לא חשיבי הכא. לעולם הבא שרוין למעלה: ואנן מאי כלומר איך תלמידי חכמים (האיך) חושבין אותו שם: כי היכי דחשבינן הכא חשיבין התם והיינו נגד זקניו כבוד: ותלמודו בידו. בגירסא: ר' עקיבא ועשרה חביריו. פשיטא כלומר בלא זכותא דהריגה דהוו צדיקין גמורים: הרוגי לוד. שפעם אחת נמצאת בת מלך הרוגה ומושלכת ברחוב ולא נודע מי הרגה וחשדו לכל היהודים ורצה המלך לשלוח יד בכולן עד שבאו שנים ומסרו עצמן ואמרו שהן הרגוה והצילו את כולם על ידן: כאן בישראל. ודאי מעליותא היא דאעפ"כ לבו לשמים

מסורת הש"ס

א) ע"ז דף יז, ב) [בע"י איתא רבא], ג) פסחים נ. [וש"נ איתא כי הא דיוסף בריה דר' יהושע בן לוי חלש ואיתנגיד כי הדר א"ל כו'], ד) [מ"ק כח. כתובות עז:], ה) ס"א דהא איכא מעשים טובים בלאו הכי אלא כו', ו) ס"א לפי שאין עושין כו' וכן בכולן, ז) פסחים ח. ר"ה ד., ח) [לקמן עה: ע"ש] ע"ז יח., ט) צ"ל טוריינוס.

תורה אור השלם

א) פִּזַּר נָתַן לָאֶבְיוֹנִים צִדְקָתוֹ עֹמֶדֶת לָעַד קַרְנוֹ תָּרוּם בְּכָבוֹד: [תהלים קיב, ט]

ב) הוּא מְרוֹמִים יִשְׁכֹּן מְצָדוֹת סְלָעִים מִשְׂגַּבּוֹ לַחְמוֹ נִתָּן מֵימָיו נֶאֱמָנִים: [ישעיה לג, טז]

ג) וְחָפְרָה הַלְּבָנָה וּבוֹשָׁה הַחַמָּה כִּי מָלַךְ יְיָ צְבָאוֹת בְּהַר צִיּוֹן וּבִירוּשָׁלַיִם וְנֶגֶד זְקֵנָיו כָּבוֹד: [ישעיה כד, כג]

ד) צְדָקָה תְרוֹמֵם גּוֹי וְחֶסֶד לְאֻמִּים חַטָּאת: [משלי יד, לד]

ה) וּמִי כְעַמְּךָ כְּיִשְׂרָאֵל גּוֹי אֶחָד בָּאָרֶץ אֲשֶׁר הָלְכוּ אֱלֹהִים לִפְדּוֹת לוֹ לְעָם וְלָשׂוּם לוֹ שֵׁם וְלַעֲשׂוֹת לָכֶם הַגְּדוּלָּה וְנֹרָאוֹת לְאַרְצֶךָ מִפְּנֵי עַמְּךָ אֲשֶׁר פָּדִיתָ לְּךָ מִמִּצְרַיִם גּוֹיִם וֵאלֹהָיו: [שמואל ב ז, כג]

ו) דִּי לֶהֱוֹן מְהַקְרְבִין נִיחוֹחִין לֶאֱלָהּ שְׁמַיָּא וּמְצַלַּיִן לְחַיֵּי מַלְכָּא וּבְנוֹהִי: [עזרא ו, י]

ז) לָהֵן מַלְכָּא מִלְכִּי יִשְׁפַּר עֲלָךְ וַחֲטָאָךְ בְּצִדְקָה פְרֻק וַעֲוָיָתָךְ בְּמִחַן עֲנָיִן הֵן תֶּהֱוֵא אַרְכָה לִשְׁלֵוְתָךְ: [דניאל ד, כד]

ח) זֵד יָהִיר לֵץ שְׁמוֹ עוֹשֶׂה בְּעֶבְרַת זָדוֹן: [משלי כא, כד]

ט) יוֹם עֶבְרָה הַיּוֹם הַהוּא יוֹם צָרָה וּמְצוּקָה יוֹם שֹׁאָה וּמְשׁוֹאָה יוֹם חֹשֶׁךְ וַאֲפֵלָה יוֹם עָנָן וַעֲרָפֶל: [צפניה א, טו]

י) וַיָּבֵא וַיַּעַשׂ יְיָ כַּאֲשֶׁר דִּבֵּר כִּי חֲטָאתֶם לַייָ וְלֹא שְׁמַעְתֶּם בְּקוֹלוֹ וְהָיָה לָכֶם הַדָּבָר הַזֶּה: [ירמיה מ, ג]

כ) בִּיבֹשׁ קְצִירָהּ תִּשָּׁבַרְנָה נָשִׁים בָּאוֹת מְאִירוֹת אוֹתָהּ כִּי לֹא עַם בִּינוֹת הוּא עַל כֵּן לֹא יְרַחֲמֶנּוּ עֹשֵׂהוּ וְיֹצְרוֹ לֹא יְחֻנֶּנּוּ: [ישעיה כז, יא]

ליקוטי רש"י

אינגד. איגניד, גוע ופרחה רוחו. עליונים למטה. אותן שהיו כאן חשובים ראיתי קלים. ואנן. תלמידי חכמים היאך אנו חשובים שם. הרוגי

נוֹתְנָהּ וְאֵינוֹ יוֹדֵעַ לְמִי נוֹתְנָהּ – He must give [charity] without knowing to whom he is giving it, נוֹטְלָהּ וְאֵינוֹ יוֹדֵעַ מִמִּי נוֹטְלָהּ – while **[the pauper] takes it without knowing from whom he has taken it.**[1] This is the highest level of charity – for a pauper does not feel beholden to an anonymous donor, and a donor cannot develop a patronizing attitude toward an anonymous recipient.[2]

The Gemara contrasts this superior method of giving charity with two lesser models:

נוֹתְנָהּ וְאֵינוֹ יוֹדֵעַ לְמִי נוֹתְנָהּ – To attain the highest level of charity, **one must give it without knowing to whom he is giving it; לְאַפּוּקֵי מִדְּמָר עוּקְבָא** – this standard **excludes Mar Ukva's** method.[3] נוֹטְלָהּ וְאֵינוֹ יוֹדֵעַ מִמִּי נוֹטְלָהּ – Additionally, in the highest form of charity **[the pauper] must take [the charity] without knowing from whom he has taken it; לְאַפּוּקֵי מִדְּרַבִּי אַבָּא** –this standard **excludes R' Abba's** method.[4]

The Gemara queries:

וְאֶלָּא הֵיכִי לֶיעֱבִיד – But how, then, should one optimally **perform** the act of giving charity? What method will preserve both the dignity of the recipient and the good character of the donor?

The Gemara answers:

לֵיתִיב לְאַרְנְקִי שֶׁל צְדָקָה – One should donate to the communal **charity purse.** With this method the donor and the recipient remain unaware of each other's identity, for the charity is distributed by the administrators of the charity fund.

The Gemara objects to this method:

מֵיתִיבֵי – They retorted from the evidence of a Baraisa, which states: מַה יַּעֲשֶׂה אָדָם וְיִהְיוּ לוֹ בָּנִים זְכָרִים – WHAT SHOULD A MAN DO IN ORDER TO merit HAVING MALE CHILDREN?[5] רַבִּי אֱלִיעֶזֶר אוֹמֵר יְפַזֵּר מְעוֹתָיו לַעֲנִיִּים – R' ELIEZER SAYS: HE SHOULD LIBERALLY DISTRIBUTE HIS MONEY TO THE POOR.[6] רַבִּי יְהוֹשֻׁעַ אוֹמֵר יְשַׂמַּח אִשְׁתּוֹ לִדְבַר מִצְוָה – R' YEHOSHUA SAYS: HE SHOULD MAKE HIS WIFE HAPPY in preparation FOR THE MITZVAH of marital relations.[7] רַבִּי אֱלִיעֶזֶר בֶּן יַעֲקֹב אוֹמֵר לֹא יִתֵּן אָדָם פְּרוּטָה לְאַרְנְקִי שֶׁל צְדָקָה – R' ELIEZER BEN YAAKOV SAYS: A PERSON SHOULD NOT GIVE even A *PERUTAH* TO THE communal CHARITY PURSE אֶלָּא אִם כֵּן מְמוּנֶּה עָלֶיהָ כְּרַבִּי חֲנַנְיָא בֶּן תְּרַדְיוֹן – UNLESS the person APPOINTED OVER IT is as honest[8] AS R' CHANANYA BEN TERADYON.[9] The Baraisa implies that not all charity fund administrators are trustworthy. Why, then, does the Gemara recommend donating to the communal charity fund as the most desirable method of giving charity?

The Gemara answers:

כִּי קָא אָמְרִינַן – When [the Gemara] said that donating to the communal charity fund is the highest form of charity, דִּמְמַנֵּי עֲלַהּ כְּרַבִּי חֲנַנְיָא בֶּן תְּרַדְיוֹן – it was referring to a fund **over which** an administrator as honest **as R' Chananya ben Teradyon was appointed.** In other instances, however, the Gemara would recommend that the donor personally distribute his charity money.

The Gemara discusses the benefits that accrue to the Jewish people from their giving charity:

אָמַר רַבִּי אַבָּהוּ – R' Abahu said: אָמַר מֹשֶׁה לִפְנֵי הַקָּדוֹשׁ בָּרוּךְ הוּא – Moses said before the Holy One, Blessed is He: רִבּוֹנוֹ שֶׁל עוֹלָם בַּמֶּה תָּרוּם קֶרֶן יִשְׂרָאֵל – Master of the Universe, with what is the strength[10] **of Israel exalted?** Which deeds will cause them to ascend to a higher level as a nation? **אָמַר לוֹ בְּכִי תִשָּׂא – [God] said to [Moses]:** ***When you raise*** (them) ***up.***[11] When you collect charity from the Jewish people, they become elevated above the nations.

Another statement by R' Abahu on the subject of charity:

וְאָמַר רַבִּי אַבָּהוּ – And R' Abahu also **said: שָׁאֲלוּ אֶת שְׁלֹמֹה בֶּן דָּוִד – They asked** King **Solomon, the son of** King **David: עַד הֵיכָן כֹּחָהּ שֶׁל צְדָקָה – How far** does **the power of charity** extend? I.e. how great is the reward that accrues to the donor? **אָמַר לְהֶן – [Solomon] said to them: צְאוּ וּרְאוּ מַה פֵּירַשׁ דָּוִד אַבָּא – Go out and see what** my **father David explained** regarding the reward for charity; indeed, he wrote:[12] ״פִּזַּר נָתַן לָאֶבְיוֹנִים צִדְקָתוֹ עֹמֶדֶת לָעַד קַרְנוֹ תָּרוּם בְּכָבוֹד״ – ***He distributed widely to the poor; his charity endures forever; his strength will be exalted with honor.*** Thus, the charitable man will be blessed with eternal honor.

NOTES

1. The Gemara below will instruct how to accomplish this.

2. *Tosafos* (above, 10a ד״ה ואיזו) question: Such an elevated fulfillment of the mitzvah of charity should protect the donor even from the judgment of Gehinnom, which is a far worse punishment than unnatural death. Why is the scope of its protective power so limited? They answer by explaining that the reward for most mitzvos is reserved for the World to Come. Only from the very greatest of his mitzvos does a person benefit in this world. Scripture therefore teaches that charity given in this perfect manner is so great a mitzvah that it protects even against unnatural death, a terrible occurrence of *this world.*

3. Each day Mar Ukva would place four *zuzim* in the hole of a poor neighbor's door hinge. Although the pauper did not know the identity of his benefactor, Mar Ukva knew the recipient (*Rashi,* citing *Kesubos* 67b).

4. R' Abba would walk among the poor with a kerchief filled with money slung over his shoulder. The poor would then come and take what they needed. Even though R' Abba never knew the identity of the recipients, they nevertheless recognized their benefactor (ibid.). Hence, his method also fell short of the highest level of charity.

5. "[Although] the world cannot exist without [both] males and females, fortunate is he whose children are males" (below, 16b; see *Maharal*).

6. In Rabbinic literature the male is termed a מַשְׁפִּיעַ, an influencing force. The female is termed the מֻשְׁפָּע, the one who receives and nurtures the male's influences. The human reproductive process is the model for this relationship. One who generously gives charity is a מַשְׁפִּיעַ, for he showers beneficial, life-giving influences upon others. The Gemara tells us that he will be rewarded measure for measure with the blessing of many male children, who are themselves intrinsically מַשְׁפִּיעִים, influential forces (*Ben Yehoyada;* cf. *Maharsha*).

7. The Gemara (*Niddah* 31a) states that if the woman is the first to issue a climactic discharge during intercourse, the resulting offspring will be male. Hence, a husband should engage his wife in pleasant and jovial conversation to put her in a happy state of mind prior to having relations. This will increase her desire, causing her to discharge first, so that the resulting offspring will be male (*Ben Yehoyada*).

8. Charity administrators need not, however, be as *righteous* as R' Chananya ben Teradyon, since in the time of the Gemara they no longer attained that level of righteousness.

R' Eliezer chose R' Chananya as his standard for honesty because of a particular incident reported in *Avodah Zarah* (17b): Once communal charity funds were inadvertently misspent, and R' Chananya voluntarily replaced them with his own money (*Tosafos* cf. *Rabbeinu Gershom*).

9. R' Eliezer also comes to answer the question posed at the beginning of the Baraisa: "What should a man do in order to [merit] having male children?" He therefore states that one who is careful to give his charity donations to a trustworthy administrator will be rewarded measure for measure with sons, because only an honest and conscientious administrator is a true influencing force (מַשְׁפִּיעַ; see note 6 above) [*Ben Yehoyada*].

10. The word קֶרֶן can mean *strength*, as in קַרְנוֹ תָּרוּם בְּכָבוֹד, *his strength will be exalted in honor* (*Psalms* 112:9).

11. *Exodus* 30:12, which [speaks of each individual Jew giving a half-*shekel* donation and] is addressed in the singular as an answer to Moses rather than in the plural as a commandment (as in *Numbers* 1:2) [*Maharsha*].

12. *Psalms* 112:9. [See gloss to *Yad Ramah* 128 for a lenghty discussion

עין משפט נר מצוה

צב א ב מיי' פ"י מהל' מתנות עניים הלכה ח סמג עשין קסב טוש"ע י"ד סי' רמט סעיף ז:
צג ג ד מיי' שם פ"א הלכה ט סמג שם טוש"ע י"ד סימן רנד סעיף ב:

הגהות הב"ח

(א) גמרא כי הא דרב יוסף בריה דר' יהושע: (ב) שם סלע זו לצדקה: (ג) שם שדרינהו קמיה דרבא: (ד) תוס' ד"ה ויבא וכו' עשה צדקה שהיה נראה כמקנא להקב"ה:

רבינו גרשום

ואינו יודע למי נותנה. לאפוקי ממר עוקבא דמנח לצדקה אצינורא דדשא של עני העני לא היה יודע מי נתנה שם ומר עוקבא יודע איזה עני נטלה. נוטלה העני ואינו יודע ממי נטלה. לאפוקי דר' אבא דצייר בסודריה ומפשילו לאחוריה ואתי עני ושרי ושקל. עני היה יודע ממי נוטל ור' אבא אינו יודע איזה עני נוטלה: יתן לארנקי של צדקה ולא ידע העני מי נתן והנותן לא ידע מי נטל: ישמח אשתו בדבר מצוה. שיפקדנה שלא בזמן עונה: אלא א"כ ממונה עליה כר' חנינא בן תרדיון. שהיה אדם גדול והיה יודע לבדוק למי יתן אלמא (דלא) [דאי לא] מצינן למשכח ממונה כגון זה. הוא עצמו מפזרן ונותן. כי אמרינן נמי דיתן לארנקי בשיש ממונה עליה כר' חנינא בן תרדיון. אי לא יפזרן הוא עצמו: אמר לו בכי תשא. משום דכתי' שם ונתנו איש כופר נפשו: אמר להן כל שכנגד זקניו כבוד. זה שקנה חכמה כלומר כל שחולקין לו כבוד בשביל חכמתו ולא משום עושרו: עליונים למטה. כלומר אותן שהן עליונים בעולם הזה בשביל עושרם ולא בגין חכמתם ושם בעולם הבא שרוין למטה: ותחתונים בעולם הזה שהם חכמים ומסכינין ובני מעשים טובים לא חשיבי הכא. לעולם הבא שרוין למעלה: ואנן מאי כלומר איך תלמידי חכמים (האיך) חושבין אותם שם: כי היכי דחשיבין הכא חשיבין התם והיינו נגד זקניו כבוד: ותלמודו בידו. בגירסא: ר' עקיבא ועשרה חביריו. פשיטא כלומר בלא זכותא דהריגה דהוו צדיקין גמורים: הרוגי לוד. שפעם אחת נמצאת בת מלך הרוגה ומושלכת ברחוב ולא נודע מי הרגה וחשדו לכל היהודים ורצה המלך לשלוח יד בכולן עד שבאו שנים ומסרו עצמן ואמרו שהן הרגוה והצילו את כולם על ידן: כאן בישראל. ודאי מעליותא היא דאעפ"כ לבו לשמים לשם מצוה אבל הרבה אומות אין עושין אלא לצורך עצמן ולא לשם שמים ומשום הכי דלא עבדיתו צדקה כו': ויבא ויעש וגו' כי האי גונא מחרפין אותן. ור' נחוניא דריש הכי צדקה תרומם ישראל וחסד דמשים צדקה וחסד לישראל. וכל מה שאמרו הרבה אומות עושין חטאת הוא להן מכלל דהא ריב"ז דריש האי קרא כשם שחטאת קרבן חטאת מכפר על ישראל: לקמיה דר' אמי דהוי גבאי ליתנם לצדקה: איקפד על רבא דקבלינהו: אמר לית ליה לרבא ביבש קצירה תשברנה. כלומר כעין שהקציר מבושל יפה משברין אותו כך כשימלא ספקם ומגרש אותם מחטאתם תשבר זרועם נשים באות מאירות כגון אריתי מורי כלומר שאפי' הנשים (אין) יכולין למשול בם והיכי עביד רבא דקביל צדקה מהן להימשך מלכותן בזכות הצדקה: ור' אמי דאקפד

תוספות

אלא א"כ ממונה עליה כרבי חנניא בן תרדיון. פי' נאמן כמותו אבל לצדיק כמותו לא דהא גבאים דבימי אמוראים לא היו לצדיקים כמותו ולהכי נקט ר' חנניא בן תרדיון משום מעשה שבא לידו דאמר פ"ק דמסכת ע"ז (דף יז:) מעות פורים נתחלפו לי במעות של צדקה וחלקתים לעניים וכן בפרק במה טומנין (שבת דף מט. ושם) דאמר תפילין צריכין גוף נקי כאלישע בעל כנפים לאו לצדיק כאלישע קאמר אלא גוף נקי שידע ליזהר שלא ישן בהם ושלא יפיח בהם קאמר ולא נקט אלישע אלא משום דאיתרחיש ביה ניסא:

עליונים למטה ותחתונים למעלה. פי' ר"ח דאמרו הגאונים שקבלה בידם רב מפי רב דעולם הפוך היינו שראה שמואל דהוה יתיב קמיה דרב יהודה תלמידיה משום דמיחה בשמואל בפר' במה בהמה (שם דף נה.) גבי ההיא איתתא דאתיא וצווחה קמיה דשמואל ולא אשגח בה א"ל רב יהודה לית ליה למר אוטם אזנו מזעקת דל וגו':

ויבא ויעש ה' כאשר דבר כי חטאתם וגו'. ואותה שעה עשה צדקה שהיה (ד) מקנא להקב"ה א"כ שהיה מתיר ירמיה מן הזיקים כדכתיב התם:

ולא

רש"י

נותנה ואינו יודע למי נותנה. כדמסיים בסיפיה יתננה בכיס של גבאי צדקה: דרב עוקבא ור' אבא במס' כתובות (דף סז:) מר עוקבא הוה שדי לענייא דשבבותיה כל יומא ארבעה זוזי בצינורא דדשא הרי שהעני אינו יודע ממי נוטלה והוא יודע למי נותנה ור' אבא הוה צייר בסודריה ושדי לאחוריה וממציא נפשיה לביני עניי והעני נוטלה ויודע ממי נוטלה ואינו יודע למי נותנה: לדבר מצוה. לפני תשמיש: אמר לו בכי תשא. אם באת לשאת ראשם בהגבהה קח מהם כופר לצדקה: כנגד זקניו כבוד. אותם שחולקין להם כבוד בעולם הזה מחמת חכמת זקנתם: עליונים למטה. אותם שהם עליונים כאן מחמת עושרן ראיתי שם שהם למטה: ותחתונים למעלה. ראיתי עניים שהם בינינו שפלים שם ראיתים חשובים: ואנן. בעלי תורה היאך אתינן היאך יש חשיבותינו: כי היכי. דאיתינן הכא חשובים ונכבדים הכי איתינן התם: הרוגי מלכות ותו לא. כלומר הך מעלה לחודה הוא דהוי בהו שנהרגו על קידוש השם ותו לא הוה בהו: הרוגי לוד. לולייגוס ופפוס אחים שהרגם (טורנוסרופוס) [טוריינוס] הרשע בלודקיא כדאמרינן במסכת תענית (דף יח:) על ידי גזירה שנגזרה על ישראל להשמיד על שנמצאת בת מלך הרוגה וחשדו את ישראל עליה ועמדו האחים הללו ואמרו מה לכם על ישראל אנו הרגנוה: הרי זה צדיק גמור. על דבר זה ומחשבה זו: כאן בישראל וכאן בעובד כוכבים. ישראל דעתן לשמים בין יחיה בין לא יחיה אינו מהרהר אחר מדת הדין אבל עכו"ם אינו נותן אלא ע"מ כן ואם לאו מתחרט: יום עברה היום ההוא. ביום הדין משתעי בנבואה לפניה: המודעי. מהר המודעי היה: ויבא ויעש ה' כאשר דבר כי חטאתם לה' וגו'. נבוזראדן קאמר ליה לירמיה כשהיה מגלה את ישראל לבבל: ביבש קצירה תשברנה. כשתכלה זכות שבידן וייבש לחלוחית מעשה צדקה שלהן אז ישברו:

דלא

גמרא

נותנה ואינו יודע למי נותנה נוטלה ואינו יודע ממי נוטלה נותנה ואינו יודע למי נותנה לאפוקי מדמר עוקבא נוטלה ואינו יודע ממי נוטלה לאפוקי מדרבי אבא ואלא היכי ליעביד ליתיב לארנקי של צדקה מיתיבי מה יעשה אדם ויהיו לו בנים זכרים ר"א אומר יפזר מעותיו לעניים ר' יהושע אומר ישמח אשתו לדבר מצוה ר' אליעזר בן יעקב אומר לא יתן אדם פרוטה לארנקי של צדקה אלא א"כ ממונה עליה כר' חנניא בן תרדיון כי קא אמרינן דממני עלה כר' חנניא בן תרדיון א"ר אבהו אמר משה לפני הקב"ה רבש"ע במה תרום קרן ישראל אמר לו בכי תשא וא"ר אבהו שאלו את שלמה בן דוד עד היכן כחה של צדקה אמר להן צאו וראו מה פירש דוד אבא פזר נתן לאביונים צדקתו עומדת לעד קרנו תרום בכבוד רבי אבא אמר מהכא הוא מרומים ישכון מצדות סלעים משגבו לחמו נתן מימיו נאמנים מה טעם מרומים ישכון מצדות סלעים משגבו משום דלחמו נתן ומימיו נאמנים וא"ר אבהו שאלו את שלמה איזהו בן העולם הבא אמר להם כל שכנגד זקניו כבוד כי הא (א) דיוסף בריה דר' יהושע חלש אינגיד א"ל אבוה מאי חזית א"ל עולם הפוך ראיתי עליונים למטה ותחתונים למעלה א"ל עולם ברור ראית ואנן היכי חזיתינן [א"ל] כי היכי דחשבינן הכא חשבינן התם ושמעתי שהיו אומרים אשרי מי שבא לכאן ותלמודו בידו ושמעתי שהיו אומרים הרוגי מלכות אין כל בריה יכולה לעמוד במחיצתן מאן נינהו אילימא ר"ע וחבריו משום הרוגי מלכות ותו לא פשיטא בלאו הכי נמי אלא הרוגי לוד תניא אמר להן רבן יוחנן בן זכאי לתלמידיו בני מהו שאמר הכתוב צדקה תרומם גוי וחסד לאומים חטאת נענה רבי אליעזר ואמר צדקה תרומם גוי אלו ישראל דכתיב ומי כעמך ישראל גוי אחד בארץ וחסד לאומים חטאת כל צדקה וחסד שאומות עובדי כוכבים עושין חטא הוא להן שאינם עושין אלא להתגדל בו כמו שנאמר די להוון מהקרבין ניחוחין לאלהה שמיא ומצליין לחיי מלכא ובנוהי ודעביד הכי לאו צדקה גמורה היא והתניא האומר סלע (ב) זה לצדקה בשביל שיחיו בני ובשביל שאזכה לעולם הבא הרי זה צדיק גמור לא קשיא כאן בישראל כאן בעובד כוכבים נענה רבי יהושע ואמר צדקה תרומם גוי אלו ישראל דכתיב ומי כעמך ישראל גוי אחד וחסד לאומים חטאת כל צדקה וחסד שאומות עובדי כוכבים עושין חטא הוא להן שאין עושין אלא כדי שתמשך מלכותן שנאמר להן מלכא מלכי ישפר עליך וחטיך בצדקה פרוק ועויתך במיחן עניין הן תהוי ארכא לשלותיך וגו' נענה רבן גמליאל ואמר צדקה תרומם גוי אלו ישראל דכתיב ומי כעמך ישראל [וגו'] וחסד לאומים חטאת כל צדקה וחסד שעכו"ם עושין חטא הוא להן שאין עושין אלא להתיהר בו וכל המתיהר נופל בגיהנם שנאמר זד יהיר לץ שמו עושה בעברת זדון ואין עברה אלא גיהנם שנאמר יום עברה היום ההוא אמר רבן גמליאל עדיין אנו צריכין למודעי רבי אליעזר המודעי אומר צדקה תרומם גוי אלו ישראל דכתיב ומי כעמך ישראל גוי אחד וחסד לאומים חטאת כל צדקה וחסד שעכו"ם עושין חטא הוא להן שאין עושין אלא לחרף אותנו בו שנאמר ויבא ויעש ה' כאשר דבר כי חטאתם לה' ולא שמעתם בקולו והיה לכם הדבר הזה נענה רבי נחוניא בן הקנה ואמר צדקה תרומם גוי וחסד לישראל ולאומים חטאת אמר להם רבן יוחנן בן זכאי לתלמידיו נראין דברי רבי נחוניא בן הקנה מדברי ומדבריכם לפי שהוא נותן צדקה וחסד לישראל ולעכו"ם חטאת מכלל דהוא נמי אמר מאי היא דתניא אמר להם רבן יוחנן בן זכאי כשם שהחטאת מכפרת על ישראל כך צדקה מכפרת על אומות העולם: איפרא הורמיז אימיה דשבור מלכא שדרה ארבע מאה דינרי לקמיה דרבי אמי ולא קבלינהו (ג) שדרינהו קמיה דרבא וקבלינהו משום שלום מלכות שמע רבי אמי איקפד אמר לית ליה ביבש קצירה תשברנה נשים באות מאירות אותה ורבא משום שלום מלכות ורבי אמי נמי משום שלום מלכות דאיבעי ליה למפלגינהו לעניי עובדי כוכבים ורבא נמי לעניי עובדי כוכבים יהבינהו ור' אמי דאיקפד הוא

דלא

מסורת הש"ס

א) ע"ז דף יז:, ב) [בע"י איתא רבא], ג) פסחים נ. [ושם איתא כי הא דיוסף בריה דר' יהושע בן לוי חלש ואיתנגיד כי הדר א"ל כו'], ד) [מ"ק כח. כתובות עז:], ה) ס"א דהא איכא מעשים טובים בלאו ה"נ אלא כו', ו) ס"א לפי שאין עושין כו' וכן בכולן, ז) פסחים ח. ר"ה ד., ח) [לקמן עח: ע"ש] ע"ז יח:, ט) נ"ל טוריינוס:

תורה אור השלם

א) פִּזַּר נָתַן לָאֶבְיוֹנִים צִדְקָתוֹ עֹמֶדֶת לָעַד קַרְנוֹ תָּרוּם בְּכָבוֹד: [תהלים קיב, ט]

ב) הוּא מְרוֹמִים יִשְׁכֹּן מְצָדוֹת סְלָעִים מִשְׂגַּבּוֹ לַחְמוֹ נִתָּן מֵימָיו נֶאֱמָנִים: [ישעיה לג, טז]

ג) וְחָפְרָה הַלְּבָנָה וּבוֹשָׁה הַחַמָּה כִּי מָלַךְ יְיָ צְבָאוֹת בְּהַר צִיּוֹן וּבִירוּשָׁלַ͏ִם וְנֶגֶד זְקֵנָיו כָּבוֹד: [ישעיה כד, כג]

ד) צְדָקָה תְרוֹמֵם גּוֹי וְחֶסֶד לְאֻמִּים חַטָּאת: [משלי יד, לד]

ה) וּמִי כְעַמְּךָ כְּיִשְׂרָאֵל גּוֹי אֶחָד בָּאָרֶץ אֲשֶׁר הָלְכוּ אֱלֹהִים לִפְדּוֹת לוֹ לְעָם וְלָשׂוּם לוֹ שֵׁם וְלַעֲשׂוֹת לָכֶם הַגְּדוּלָּה וְנֹרָאוֹת לְאַרְצֶךָ מִפְּנֵי עַמְּךָ אֲשֶׁר פָּדִיתָ לְּךָ מִמִּצְרַיִם גּוֹיִם וֵאלֹהָיו: [שמואל ב ז, כג]

ו) דִּי לֶהֱוֺן מְהַקְרְבִין נִיחוֹחִין לֶאֱלָהּ שְׁמַיָּא וּמְצַלַּיִן לְחַיֵּי מַלְכָּא וּבְנוֹהִי: [עזרא ו, י]

ז) לָהֵן מַלְכָּא מִלְכִּי יִשְׁפַּר עֲלָךְ וַחֲטָאָךְ בְּצִדְקָה פְרֻק וַעֲוָיָתָךְ בְּמִחַן עֲנָיִן הֵן תֶּהֱוֵא אַרְכָה לִשְׁלֵוְתָךְ: [דניאל ד, כד]

ח) זֵד יָהִיר לֵץ שְׁמוֹ עוֹשֶׂה בְּעֶבְרַת זָדוֹן: [משלי כא, כד]

ט) יוֹם עֶבְרָה הַיּוֹם הַהוּא יוֹם צָרָה וּמְצוּקָה יוֹם שֹׁאָה וּמְשׁוֹאָה יוֹם חֹשֶׁךְ וַאֲפֵלָה יוֹם עָנָן וַעֲרָפֶל: [צפניה א, טו]

י) וַיָּבֵא וַיַּעַשׂ יְיָ כַּאֲשֶׁר דִּבֵּר כִּי חֲטָאתֶם לַייָ וְלֹא שְׁמַעְתֶּם בְּקוֹלוֹ וְהָיָה לָכֶם הַדָּבָר הַזֶּה: [ירמיה מ, ג]

כ) בִּיבֹשׁ קְצִירָהּ תִּשָּׁבַרְנָה נָשִׁים בָּאוֹת מְאִירוֹת אוֹתָהּ כִּי לֹא עַם בִּינוֹת הוּא עַל כֵּן לֹא יְרַחֲמֶנּוּ עֹשֵׂהוּ וְיֹצְרוֹ לֹא יְחֻנֶּנּוּ: [ישעיה כז, יא]

ליקוטי רש"י

אינגד. איתנגיד, גוע ופרחה רוחו. עליונים למטה. אותן שהיו כאן חשובים ראיתי קלים. ואנן. תלמידי חכמים היכי איתינן התם. הרוגי מלכות ותו לא. לא היתה בהן מעלה אחרת שיחשבו עליה אלא זו בלבד. הרוגי לוד. שני אחים היו שמסרו עצמן על ישראל שהודו על עצמן הריגת בת מלך שהיו מטילין אותה על כל ישראל [פסחים נ.]. לוליינוס ופפוס אחים צדיקים גמורים היו. בלודקיא היא לוד ויש אומרין שנהרגו על בתו של מלך שנמצאת הרוגה ואמרו היהודים הרגוה וגזרו גזרה על שונאיהן של ישראל ועמדו אלו ופדו את ישראל ואמרו אנו הרגנוה והרג המלך לאלו בלבד [תענית יח:]. הרי זה צדיק גמור. בדבר זה ולא אמרינן שלא לשמה עושה אלא קיים מצות בוראו שצוהו לעשות צדקה ומתכוין אף להנאת עצמו שיזכה בה לעולם הבא או שיחיו בניו [פסחים ח.]. אם רגיל בכך [ר"ה ד.]. וחסד לאומים חטאת. שהיו נוטלי' מזה ונותנים לזה [משלי יד, לד]. ומי כעמך ישראל גוי אחד. ממה הם מיוחדים מכל העמים מזה אשר הלך אלהים בעצמו לפדותם לו לעם כמו שכתוב אני יוצא בתוך מצרים (שמות יב) מזה אנו מיוחדים שלא עשה זה לשום אומה בעולם [דברי הימים א, יז, כא]. להן מלכא. באמת אתה מלך שמע לעצתי. מלכי. עצתי כמו איעצך אמלכיך. ישפר עליך. עצתי תיטב בעיניך לשמוע מילי [דניאל ד, כד]. דניאל אמר לנבוכדנצר כשפתר לו החלום שיהא נטרד מן האנשים ולהיות עם בהמה וחיה להן מלכא אמנם המלך מלכי ישפר עליך עצתי תיטב בעיניך להאמין לעצתי [סוטה כ:]. וחטיך בצדקה פרוק. וחטאתך בצדקה פרוק מעל צוארך [דניאל שם]. חטאך ע"י צדקה פדה [סוטה שם]. ועויתך במיחן עניין. ועוונותיך פרוק בחנינת עניים [דניאל שם]. ועוונותיך בחנינת העניים [סוטה שם]. הן תהוי ארכא לשלותיך. אולי תהא שהות לשלומך שלא תמהר הרעה לבא ומה ראה דניאל להשיא עצה טובה לנבוכדנצר ראה ישראל עניים שפלי גולה מחזירין על הפתחים והשיאו עצה לחננם אמר לו עניים אלו שהגליתם לעבדים הם פרנסם וכן עשה פתח אוצרותיו והיה מפרנסם כל י"ב חדש [דניאל שם]. איפרא הורמיז. כך שמה איפרא מן יופי שדים היה לה [תענית כד: ועי' תוס' גיטין יא. ד"ה הורמין]. נכרית היתה וכן שמה ואעפ"כ היתה משמרת עצמה מנדות וקרובה להתגייר ואף קרבנות היתה שולחת ולשון יוני איפרא חן כמו אפריון נמטייה לרבי שמעון (ב"מ קיט.). הורמיז. כמו (לקמן עג.) הורמיז בר ליליתא כלומר יופי שדים היה לה [נדה כ:]. ביבש קצירה. קצירי שרשיה כמו תשלח קציריה (תהלים פ) ועשה קציר (איוב יד) כלומר כשתכלה זכות מעט שבידה אז תשברנה סעיפיה. וכן רבותינו שאסרו לקבל מהן צדקה מפני הטעם הזה [ישעיה כז, יא]. [מכאן שייך לדף יא.] אמת מארץ תצמח וגו'. כשהיו ישראל דוברים אמת וישקפו מן השמים לצדקה שהם עושים בארץ [תהלים פה, יב]. פרי צדיק עץ חיים. גמול פירות מעשה הצדיקים עץ חיים הם לעולם. ולוקח נפשות חכם. מי שהוא חכם קונה לו נפשות שמלמד דרך טוב והרי הם לו כאילו קנאם כענין שנאמר ואת הנפש אשר עשו בחרן (בראשית יב) [משלי יא, ל]. אין חולקין. אין האחד כופה את חבירו לחלוק [לעיל ב:]. חצי קב. שזה שיעור גנה. ר' עקיבא אומר בית רובע. הוא שיעור גנה [כתובות צח.]. בית הבד. בית לעצור זיתים [ב"מ קיז:]. בית השלחין. ארץ יבשה קרויה בית השלחין וצריך להשקותה תמיד ושדה בית הבעל יפה הימנו [שיר השירים ד יג]. קרקע יבישה דלא דייה במי הגשמים וממעיין שבה משקה אותה [ב"מ קג.]. שדה שהיא עומדת בחר וצריך להשקותה תמיד [מו"ק ב.]. ושמו עליו. כל דבר שיש בו שיעור שאם תחלקו עדיין יהא עליו שמו הראשון [לקמן יג:].

R' Abba cites a different verse:
רַבִּי אַבָּא אָמַר מֵהָכָא — **R' Abba said:** We derive how great is the reward for giving charity **from here:**[13] ,,הוּא מְרוֹמִים יִשְׁכֹּן מְצָדוֹת סְלָעִים מִשְׂגַּבּוֹ לַחְמוֹ נִתָּן מֵימָיו נֶאֱמָנִים" — ***He shall dwell on high; fortresses of rock shall be his stronghold;***[14] ***his bread shall be given, his waters shall be sure.*** R' Abba interprets the second part of the verse as the cause of the first, as follows: מַה טַּעַם ,,מְרוֹמִים יִשְׁכֹּן מְצָדוֹת סְלָעִים מִשְׂגַּבּוֹ" — **What is the reason** that this person deserves to ***dwell on high*** and that ***fortresses of rock shall be his stronghold?*** מִשּׁוּם דְּ,,לַחְמוֹ נִתָּן וּמֵימָיו נֶאֱמָנִים" — Because ***his bread was given*** to the poor ***and his waters were sure*** to assist the needy. His great rewards are the result of the charity he gave.

The Gemara records a third statement by R' Abahu:
וְאָמַר רַבִּי אַבָּהוּ שָׁאֲלוּ אֶת שְׁלֹמֹה — **And R' Abahu** also **said: They asked** King **Solomon:** אֵיזֶהוּ בֶּן הָעוֹלָם הַבָּא — **Who is destined for** eternal reward in **the World to Come?** אָמַר לָהֶם כָּל שֶׁכְּנֶגֶד זְקֵנָיו כָּבוֹד — **[Solomon] said to them: Anyone who is honored** in this world **for** the wisdom of **his old age.**[15] However, someone honored in this world for his wealth would not necessarily merit a place in the World to Come.

The Gemara relates an incident that illustrates this point:
כִּי הָא דְּיוֹסֵף בְּרֵיהּ דְּרַבִּי יְהוֹשֻׁעַ — It is **like that** case **of [Rav]**[16] **Yosef the son of R' Yehoshua,** חֲלַשׁ אִיתְנְגִיד — **who took ill and slipped into a comatose state.**[17] אָמַר לֵיהּ אֲבוּהּ — When he regained consciousness **his father asked him:** מַאי חָזִית — **"What did you see** in the next world?" אָמַר לֵיהּ — **[Rav Yosef] said to [his father]:** עוֹלָם הָפוּךְ רָאִיתִי — **"I saw an inverted world.** עֶלְיוֹנִים לְמַטָּה — **The uppermost** in this world[18] **are below** in the World to Come, וְתַחְתּוֹנִים לְמַעְלָה — **and the lowly** in this world **are above** in the World to Come."[19] אָמַר לֵיהּ עוֹלָם בָּרוּר רָאִיתָ — **[R' Yehoshua] said to [his son]: "You have seen a well-ordered world,** for in the World to Come material possessions and accomplishments have no significance."

R' Yehoshua inquired further:
וַאֲנַן הֵיכִי חֲזִיתִינַן — **"And we** Torah scholars? **How do we appear** in the next world?" אָמַר לֵיהּ כִּי הֵיכִי דַּחֲשִׁבִינַן הָכָא — **[Rav Yosef] said to [his father]: "Just as we are considered important** and are honored **here** in this world,[20] חֲשִׁבִינַן הָתָם — so **we are important** and honored **there,** for the value of Torah wisdom is eternal." This incident corroborates R' Abahu's teaching, that one honored in this world for his wisdom is destined for eternal life in the World to Come.

Rav Yosef continued to relate what he had experienced:
וְשָׁמַעְתִּי שֶׁהָיוּ אוֹמְרִים — **"And** in the next world **I heard them saying:** אַשְׁרֵי מִי שֶׁבָּא לְכָאן וְתַלְמוּדוֹ בְּיָדוֹ — **'Fortunate is he who comes here and his learning is in his hand,** i.e. he remembers what he has learned.'[21] וְשָׁמַעְתִּי שֶׁהָיוּ אוֹמְרִים — **And I** also **heard them saying:** הֲרוּגֵי מַלְכוּת אֵין כָּל בְּרִיָּה יְכוֹלָה לַעֲמוֹד בִּמְחִיצָתָן — **'Those executed by the** Roman **government** have reached such an exalted level in the World to Come that **no** other **creature can** bear to **stand in their enclosure.** The level of holiness they have attained is beyond the reach of other beings.' "

The Gemara inquires:
מַאן נִינְהוּ — **Who are these** holy martyrs of whom Rav Yosef speaks? אִילֵימָא רַבִּי עֲקִיבָא וַחֲבֵרָיו — **If we say** that he refers to **R' Akiva and his colleagues,**[22] מִשּׁוּם הֲרוּגֵי מַלְכוּת — is it merely **because they were executed by the** Roman **government**[23] that they attained this lofty level, וְתוּ לֹא — **and for no other** reason? פְּשִׁיטָא בְּלָאו הָכִי נַמִּי — **It is obvious** that even **without this** distinction they would merit a unique station in the World to Come — by virtue of their unparalleled righteousness and wisdom!

The Gemara answers:
אֶלָּא הֲרוּגֵי לוֹד — **Rather,** the martyrs of whom Rav Yosef spoke were those **executed** in the city of **Lod.**[24] Their enormous sacrifice entitled them to such a rarified place in the World to Come.

The Gemara discusses the difference between the charity of Jews and the charity of idolaters:
תַּנְיָא אָמַר לָהֶן רַבָּן יוֹחָנָן בֶּן זַכַּאי לְתַלְמִידָיו — **It was taught in a Baraisa:** RABBAN YOCHANAN BEN ZAKKAI SAID TO HIS STUDENTS: בָּנַי מַהוּ שֶׁאָמַר הַכָּתוּב — MY CHILDREN! WHAT IS the explanation of that WHICH SCRIPTURE SAID:[25] ,,צְדָקָה תְּרוֹמֵם־גּוֹי וְחֶסֶד לְאֻמִּים חַטָּאת" — ***CHARITY EXALTS A NATION, AND THE KINDNESS OF NATIONS IS A SIN?*** Rabban Yochanan found two difficulties in this verse: 1) Why is kindness considered a sin? 2) What is the difference between " a nation" and "nations"?

Rabban Yochanan's disciples answered the question in turns:
נַעֲנָה רַבִּי אֱלִיעֶזֶר וְאָמַר — R' ELIEZER SPOKE UP AND SAID: ,,צְדָקָה

NOTES

why it was permitted for King Solomon to refer to his father by his first name (see *Yoreh Deah* 240:2).]

13. *Isaiah* 33:16, which on the simple level announces the rewards awaiting those who follow the virtuous practices described by the prophet in the preceding verses (*Ibn Ezra*). Our Gemara understands that these rewards accrue to the charitable man as well.

14. He will be protected from his enemies (by God) as if he lived on impregnable heights in fortresses of rock (*Metzudas David*).

15. [The Gemara is paraphrasing *Isaiah* 24:23, which states, וְנֶגֶד זְקֵנָיו כָּבוֹד, *and before His elders shall be honor,* and refers to the glory that will cloak the faithful when the Final Redemption occurs.] However, here the Gemara intends the honor bestowed for wisdom achieved over the course of a lifetime (*Rashi;* cf. *Rabbeinu Gershom* and *Maharsha*).

16. *Bach* adds the title Rav.

17. During this period his soul temporarily left his body and ascended to Heaven (see *Rashi* to *Pesachim* 50a ד"ה איתנגיד).

18. I.e. those esteemed because of their wealth (*Rashi*).

19. The poor, whom we perceive as lowly, are considered important in the next world (*Rashi*). *Maharal* explains that since the poor are divorced from the materiality of this world, they are worthy of entering a world that transcends all materiality.

20. I.e. the intellect is esteemed even in this world, for without his intellect man is considered nothing (*Maharal*).

21. *Maharsha* interprets "in his hand" as a reference to the original insights and explanations that a Torah scholar commits to writing. Thus, fortunate indeed is the scholar who records his Torah thoughts, for his primary learning — and that which makes the greatest impression on him — occurs when he composes those works. For that reason Torah scholars are called סוֹפְרִים, *scribes.*

22. These are the Ten Martyrs whose story is recounted in the cantor's repetition of the Yom Kippur *Mussaf* service. They were ten sages of the Mishnaic period who were brutally put to death to satisfy the anti-Semitic caprice of a Roman ruler. As a pretext for these executions, the Roman claimed that the sages were being punished in place of the ten sons of Jacob that participated in the sale of their brother, Joseph. Halachah specifies the death penalty for one who kidnaps a fellow Jew, forces him to work and then sells him (*Exodus* 21:16).

23. And so died in sanctification of God's Name — a supreme sacrifice and source of merit (*Rashi*).

24. Once, during the time of the Roman occupation of Eretz Yisrael, the emperor's daughter was found murdered and the Jews were accused of the crime. The Jews were threatened with annihilation unless they produced the murderers. To save their people, two righteous brothers, Lilianus and Pappus, stepped forward and falsely confessed to the crime. They were executed by the wicked Turyanus (*Rashi* here and to *Taanis* 18b).

25. *Proverbs* 14:34.

צב א ב מיי' פ"י מהל' מתנות עניים הלכה ח סמג עשין קסב טוש"ע י"ד סי' רמט סעיף ז:
צג ג ד מיי' שם הלכה יג טו סמג שם טוש"ע י"ד סימן רנד סעיף ב:

הגהות הב"ח

(א) גמרא כי הא דרב יוסף בריה דר' יהושע: (ב) שם סלע זו לצדקה: (ג) שם שדרתינהו קמיה דרבא: (ד) תוס' ד"ה ויבא וכו' עשה צדקה שהיה נראה כמקנא להקב"ה:

אלא א"כ ממונה עליה כרבי חנניא בן תרדיון. פי' נאמן כמותו אבל צדיק כמותו לא דהא גבאים דימי אמוראים לא היו צדיקים כמותו ולהכי נקט ר' חנניא בן תרדיון משום מעשה שבא לידו דאמר פ"ק דמסכת ע"ז (דף יח:) מעות פורים נתחלפו לי במעות של צדקה וחלקתים לעניים וכן בפרק במה טומנין (שבת דף מט. ושם) דאמר תפילין צריכין גוף נקי כאלישע לא צדיק כאלישע קאמר אלא גוף נקי שידע ליזהר שלא יישן בהם ושלא יפיח בהם קאמר ולא נקט אלישע אלא משום דאיתרחיש ביה ניסא:

עליונים למטה ותחתונים למעלה. פי' ר"ח דאמרו הגאונים שקבלה בידם רב מפי רב דעולם הפוך היינו שראה שמואל דהוה יתיב קמיה דרב יהודה תלמידיה משום דמיתה בשמואל בפר' במה בהמה (שם דף נה.) גבי ההיא איתתא דאתיא וצווחא קמיה דשמואל ולא אשגח בה א"ל רב יהודה לית ליה למר אוטם אזנו מזעקת דל וגו':

ויבא ויעש ה' כאשר דבר כי חטאתם וגו'. ואותה שעה עשה צדקה שהיה (ד) מקנא להקב"ה א"נ שהיה מתיר את ירמיה מן הזיקים כדכתיב התם: ולא

[א] נותנה ואינו יודע למי נותנה נוטלה ואינו יודע ממי נוטלה נותנה ואינו יודע למי נותנה לאפוקי מדמר עוקבא נוטלה ואינו יודע ממי נוטלה לאפוקי מדרבי אבא ואלא היכי ליעביד ליתיב לארנקי של צדקה מיתיבי מה יעשה אדם ויהיו לו בנים זכרים ר"א אומר יפזר מעותיו לעניים ר' יהושע אומר ישמח אשתו לדבר מצוה [א] ר' אליעזר בן יעקב אומר [ב] לא יתן אדם פרוטה לארנקי של צדקה אלא א"כ ממונה עליה כר' חנניא בן תרדיון כי קא אמרינן דממני עלה כר' חנניא בן תרדיון א"ר אבהו אמר משה לפני הקב"ה רבש"ע במה תרום קרן ישראל אמר לו בכי תשא וא"ר אבהו שאלו את שלמה בן דוד עד היכן כחה של צדקה אמר להן צאו וראו מה פירש דוד אבא [א] פזר נתן לאביונים צדקתו עומדת לעד קרנו תרום בכבוד [ג] רבי אבא אמר מהכא [ב] הוא מרומים ישכון מצדות סלעים משגבו לחמו נתן מימיו נאמנים מה טעם מרומים ישכון מצדות סלעים משגבו משום דלחמו נתן ומימיו נאמנים וא"ר אבהו שאלו את שלמה איזהו בן העולם הבא אמר להם כל [ג] שכנגד זקניו כבוד [ג] כי הא (א) דיוסף בריה דר' יהושע חלש אינגיד א"ל אבוה מאי חזית א"ל עולם הפוך ראיתי עליונים למטה ותחתונים למעלה א"ל עולם ברור ראית ואנן היכי חזיתינן [א"ל] כי היכי דחשבינן הכא חשבינן התם ושמעתי שהיו אומרים [ד] אשרי מי שבא לכאן ותלמודו בידו ושמעתי שהיו אומרים הרוגי מלכות אין כל בריה יכולה לעמוד במחיצתן מאן נינהו אילימא ר"ע וחבריו משום הרוגי מלכות ותו לא פשיטא [ה] בלאו הכי נמי אלא הרוגי לוד תניא אמר להן רבן יוחנן בן זכאי לתלמידיו בני מהו שאמר הכתוב [ד] צדקה תרומם גוי וחסד לאומים חטאת נענה רבי אליעזר ואמר צדקה תרומם גוי אלו ישראל דכתיב [ה] ומי כעמך ישראל גוי אחד בארץ וחסד לאומים חטאת כל צדקה וחסד שאומות עובדי כוכבים עושין חטא הוא להן [ו] שאינם עושין אלא להתגדל בו כמו שנאמר [ו] די להוון מהקרבין ניחוחין לאלהה שמיא ומצליין לחיי מלכא ובנוהי ודעביד הכי לאו צדקה גמורה היא [ז] והתניא האומר סלע (ב) זו לצדקה בשביל שיחיו בני ובשביל שאזכה לעולם הבא הרי זה צדיק גמור לא קשיא כאן בישראל כאן בעובד כוכבים נענה רבי יהושע ואמר צדקה תרומם גוי אלו ישראל דכתיב ומי כעמך ישראל גוי אחד וחסד לאומים חטאת כל צדקה וחסד שאומות עובדי כוכבים עושין חטא הוא להן שאין עושין אלא כדי שתמשך מלכותן שנאמר [ז] להן מלכא מלכי ישפר עליך וחטיך בצדקה פרוק ועויתך במיחן עניין הן תהוי ארכא לשלותך וגו' נענה רבן גמליאל ואמר צדקה תרומם גוי אלו ישראל דכתיב ומי כעמך ישראל [וגו'] וחסד לאומים חטאת כל צדקה וחסד שעכו"ם עושין חטא הוא להן שאין עושין אלא להתיהר בו [ח] וכל המתיהר נופל בגיהנם שנאמר [ח] זד יהיר לץ שמו עושה בעברת זדון ואין עברה אלא גיהנם שנאמר [ט] יום עברה היום ההוא אמר רבן גמליאל עדיין אנו צריכין למודעי רבי אליעזר המודעי אומר צדקה תרומם גוי אלו ישראל דכתיב ומי כעמך ישראל גוי אחד וחסד לאומים חטאת כל צדקה וחסד שעכו"ם עושין חטא הוא להן שאין עושין אלא לחרף אותנו בו שנאמר [י] ויבא ויעש ה' כאשר דבר כי חטאתם לה' ולא שמעתם בקולו והיה לכם הדבר הזה נענה רבי נחוניא בן הקנה ואמר צדקה תרומם גוי וחסד לישראל ולאומים חטאת אמר להם רבן יוחנן בן זכאי לתלמידיו נראין דברי רבי נחוניא בן הקנה מדברי ומדבריכם לפי שהוא נותן צדקה וחסד לישראל ולעכו"ם חטאת מכלל דהוא נמי אמר מאי היא דתניא אמר להם רבן יוחנן בן זכאי כשם שהחטאת מכפרת על ישראל כך צדקה מכפרת על אומות העולם: איפרא הורמיז אימיה דשבור מלכא שדרה ארבע מאה דינרי לקמיה דרבי אמי ולא קבלינהו (ג) שדרינהו קמיה דרבא [ג] וקבלינהו משום שלום מלכות שמע רבי אמי איקפד אמר לית ליה [כ] ביבש קצירה תשברנה נשים באות מאירות אותה ורבא משום שלום מלכות ורבי אמי נמי משום שלום מלכות [ד] דאיבעי ליה למפלגינהו לעניי עובדי כוכבים ורבא נמי לעניי עובדי כוכבים יהבינהו ור' אמי דאיקפד הוא דלא

נותנה ואינו יודע למי נותנה. כדמסיים בסיפיה יתננה בכיס של גבאי צדקה: דרב עוקבא ור' אבא במס' כתובות (דף סז:) מר עוקבא הוה שדי לעניא דשבבותיה כל יומא ארבעה זוזי בצינורא דדשא הרי שהעני אינו יודע ממי נוטלה והוא יודע למי נותנה ור' אבא הוה צייר בסודריה ושדי לאחוריה וממציא נפשיה לביני עניי והעני נוטלה ויודע ממי נוטלה ואינו יודע למי נותנה: לדבר מצוה. לפני תשמיש: אמר לו בכי תשא. אם באת לשאת ראשם בהגבהה קח מהם כופר לצדקה: כנגד זקניו כבוד. אותם שחולקין להם כבוד בעולם הזה מחמת חכמת זקנתם: עליונים למטה. אותם שהם עליונים כאן מחמת עושרן ראיתי שם שהם למטה: ותחתונים למעלה. ראיתי עניים שהם בינינו שפלים שם ראיתים חשובים: ואנן. בעלי תורה היאך אתינן היאך יש חשיבותינו: כי היכי. דאיתינן הכא חשובים ונכבדים הכי איתינן התם: הרוגי מלכות ותו לא. כלומר הך מלתא לחודא הוא דהוי בהו שנהרגו על קידוש השם ותו לא הוה בהו: הרוגי לוד. לולייינוס ופפוס אחים שהרגם (ט) טורנוסרופוס הרשע בלודקיא כדאמרינן במסכת תענית (דף יח:) על ידי גזירה שנגזרה על ישראל להשמיד על שנמצאת בת מלך הרוגה וחשדו את ישראל עליה ועמדו האחי' הללו ואמרו מה לכם על ישראל אנו הרגנוה: ה"ז צדיק גמור. על דבר זה ומחשבה זו: כאן בישראל וכאן בעובד כוכבים. ישראל דעתן לשמים בין יחיה בין לא יחיה אינו מהרהר אחר מדת הדין אבל עכו"ם אינו נותן אלא ע"מ כן ואם לאו מתחרט: יום עברה היום ההוא. ביום הדין משתעי בנבואת צפניה: המודעי. מהר המודעי היה: ויבא ויעש ה' כאשר דבר כי חטאתם לה' וגו'. נבוזראדן קאמר ליה לירמיה כשהיה מגלה את ישראל לבבל: ביבש קצירה תשברנה. כשתכלה זכות שבידן וייבש לחלוחית מעשה צדקה שלהן אז ישברו: דלא

רבינו גרשום

ואינו יודע למי נותנה. לאפוקי ממר עוקבא דמנח לצדקה אצינורא דדשא על שני העני דלא היה יודע מי נתנה שם ומר עוקבא יודע איזה עני נטלה. נוטלה העני ואינו יודע ממי נטלה. לאפוקי דר' אבא דצייר בסודריה ומפשילו לאחוריו ואתי עני ושרי ושקל. עני היה יודע ממי נוטל ור' אבא אינו יודע איזה עני נוטלה: יתן לארנקי של צדקה ולא ידע העני מי נתן והנותן לא ידע מי נוטל: ישמח אשתו בדבר מצוה. שיפקדנה שלא בזמן עונה: אלא א"כ ממונה עליה כר' חנינא בן תרדיון. שהיה אדם גדול והיה יודע לבדוק למי יתן אלמא (דלא) [דאי לא] מצינן למשכח ממונה כגון זה. הוא עצמו מפזרן ונותן. כי אמרינן נמי דיתן לארנקי בשיש ממונה עליה כר' חנינא בן תרדיון. אי לא יפזרן הוא עצמו: אמר לו בכי תשא. משום דכתי' שם ונתנו איש כופר נפשו: אמר להן כל שכנגד זקניו כבוד. זה שקנה חכמה כלומר כל שחולקין לו כבוד בשביל חכמתו ולא משום עושרו: עליונים למטה. כלומר אותן שהן עליונים בעולם הזה בשביל עושרם ולא בגין חכמתם ושם בעולם הבא שרוין למטה: ותחתונים בעולם הזה שהם חכמים ומסכינן ובני מעשים טובים לא חשיבי הכא. לעולם הבא שרוין למעלה: ואנן מאי. כלומר איך תלמידי חכמים (האיך) חושבין אותם שם: כי היכי דחשיבינן הכא חשיבין התם והיינו נגד זקניו כבוד: ותלמודו בידו. בגירסא: ר' עקיבא ועשרה חביריו. פשיטא כלומר בלא זכותא דהרוגא דהוו צדיקין גמורים: הרוגי לוד. שפעם אחת נמצאת בת מלך הרוגה ומושלכת ברחוב ולא נודע מי הרגה וחשדו לכל היהודים ורצה המלך לשלוח יד בכולן עד שבאו שנים ומסרו עצמן ואמרו שהן הרגוה והצילו את כולם על ידן: כאן בישראל. ודאי מעליותא היא דאעפ"כ לבו לשמים לשם מצוה

[...]גות אין עושין אלא לצורך עצמן ולא לשם שמים ומשום הכי דלא עבדיתו צדקה כו': ויבא ויעש וגו' כי האי [...]ותן. ור' נחוניא דריש הכי צדקה תרומם ישראל וחסד דמשים צדקה וחסד לישראל. וכל מה שאמרו הרבה [...]טאת הוא להן מכלל דהא ריב"ז דריש האי קרא כשם שחטאת קרבן חטאת מכפר על ישראל: לקמיה דר' אמי [...]נם לצדקה: איקפד על רבא דקבלינהו: אמר לית ליה לרבא ביבש קצירה תשברנה. כלומר כעין שהקציר [...]שברין אותו כך כשימלא ספקם ומגרש אותם מחטאתם תשבר זרועם נשים באות מאירות כגון אריתי מורי כלומר (אין) יכולין למשול בם והיכי עביד רבא דקביל צדקה מהן להימשך מלכותן בזכות הצדקה: ור' אמי דאקפד

מסורת הש"ס

א) ע"ז דף יח, ב) [בע"י איתא רבא], ג) פסחים נ. [ושם איתא כי הא דיוסף בריה דר' יהושע בן לוי חלש ואיתנגיד כי הדר א"ל כו'], ד) [מ"ק כח. כתובות עז:], ה) ס"א דהא איכא מעשים טובים בלאו ה"נ אלא כו', ו) ס"א לפי שאין עושין כו' וכן בכולן, ז) פסחים ח. ר"ה ד., ח) [לקמן עח: ע"ש] ע"ז יח:, ט) ע"ל טורייינוס.

תורה אור השלם

א) פִּזַּר נָתַן לָאֶבְיוֹנִים צִדְקָתוֹ עֹמֶדֶת לָעַד קַרְנוֹ תָּרוּם בְּכָבוֹד: [תהלים קיב, ט]

ב) הוּא מְרוֹמִים יִשְׁכֹּן מְצָדוֹת סְלָעִים מִשְׂגַּבּוֹ לַחְמוֹ נִתָּן מֵימָיו נֶאֱמָנִים: [ישעיה לג, טז]

ג) וְחָפְרָה הַלְּבָנָה וּבוֹשָׁה הַחַמָּה כִּי מָלַךְ יְיָ צְבָאוֹת בְּהַר צִיּוֹן וּבִירוּשָׁלַיִם וְנֶגֶד זְקֵנָיו כָּבוֹד: [ישעיה כד, כג]

ד) צְדָקָה תְרוֹמֵם גּוֹי וְחֶסֶד לְאֻמִּים חַטָּאת: [משלי יד, לד]

ה) וּמִי כְעַמְּךָ כְּיִשְׂרָאֵל גּוֹי אֶחָד בָּאָרֶץ אֲשֶׁר הָלְכוּ אֱלֹהִים לִפְדּוֹת לוֹ לְעָם וְלָשׂוּם לוֹ שֵׁם וְלַעֲשׂוֹת לָכֶם הַגְּדוּלָּה וְנֹרָאוֹת לְאַרְצֶךָ מִפְּנֵי עַמְּךָ אֲשֶׁר פָּדִיתָ לְּךָ מִמִּצְרַיִם גּוֹיִם וֵאלֹהָיו: [שמואל ב ז, כג]

ו) דִּי לֶהֱוֺן מְהַקְרְבִין נִיחוֹחִין לֶאֱלָהּ שְׁמַיָּא וּמְצַלַּיִן לְחַיֵּי מַלְכָּא וּבְנוֹהִי: [עזרא ו, י]

ז) לָהֵן מַלְכָּא מִלְכִּי יִשְׁפַּר עֲלָךְ וַחֲטָאָךְ בְּצִדְקָה פְרֻק וַעֲוָיָתָךְ בְּמִחַן עֲנָיִן הֵן תֶּהֱוֵא אַרְכָה לִשְׁלֵוְתָךְ: [דניאל ד, כד]

ח) זֵד יָהִיר לֵץ שְׁמוֹ עוֹשֶׂה בְּעֶבְרַת זָדוֹן: [משלי כא, כד]

ט) יוֹם עֶבְרָה הַיּוֹם הַהוּא יוֹם צָרָה וּמְצוּקָה יוֹם שֹׁאָה וּמְשׁוֹאָה יוֹם חֹשֶׁךְ וַאֲפֵלָה יוֹם עָנָן וַעֲרָפֶל: [צפניה א, טו]

י) וַיָּבֵא וַיַּעַשׂ יְיָ כַּאֲשֶׁר דִּבֵּר כִּי חֲטָאתֶם לַייָ וְלֹא שְׁמַעְתֶּם בְּקוֹלוֹ וְהָיָה לָכֶם הַדָּבָר הַזֶּה: [ירמיה מ, ג]

כ) בִּיבֹשׁ קְצִירָהּ תִּשָּׁבַרְנָה נָשִׁים בָּאוֹת מְאִירוֹת אוֹתָהּ כִּי לֹא עַם בִּינוֹת הוּא עַל כֵּן לֹא יְרַחֲמֶנּוּ עֹשֵׂהוּ וְיֹצְרוֹ לֹא יְחֻנֶּנּוּ: [ישעיה כז, יא]

ליקוטי רש"י

אינגד. איתנגיד, גוע ופרכס רוחו. עליונים למטה. אותן שהיו כאן חשובים ראיתי קלים. ואנן. תלמידי חכמים היכי איתינן התם. הרוגי מלכות ותו לא. לא היתה בהן מעלה אחרת שיחשבו עליה אלא זו בלבד. הרוגי לוד. שני אחים היו [...] שהודו על עצמן הריגת בת מלך שהיו מטילין אותה על כל ישראל [פסחים נ.]. לולייינוס ופפוס אחים צדיקים [...] היא לוד ויש אומרין שנהרגו על בתו של מלך שנמצאת הרוגה ואמרו היהודים הרגוה וגזרו גזרה על [...] אלו ופדו את ישראל ואמרו אנו הרגנוה והרג המלך לאלו בלבד [תענית יח:]. הרי זה צדיק גמור. בד[...] לשמה עושה אלא קיים מצות בוראו שצוהו לעשות צדקה ומתכוין אף להנאת עצמו שיזכה בה לעולם הב[א ...] ח:]. אם רגיל בכך [ר"ה ד.]. וחסד לאומים חטאת. שהיו נוטלי' מזה ונותנים לזה [משלי יד, לד]. ומ[י כעמך ... גוי] אחד. ממה הם מיוחדים מכל העמים מזה אשר הלך אלהים בעצמו לפדותם לו לעם כמו שכתוב אני יו[...] [...]וחדים שלא עשה זה לשום אומה בעולם [דברי הימים א, יז, כא]. להן מלכא. באמת אתה מלך שמע לעצתי. מלכי. עצתי כמו איעצך אמלכיך. ישפר עליך. עצתי תיטב בעיניך לשמוע מילי [דניאל ד, כד]. דניאל אמר לנבוכ[דנצר ...] האנשים ולהיות עם בהמה ומיה להן מלכא אמנם המלך מלכי ישפר עליך עצתי תיטב בעיניך להאמין לעצתי [סוטה כ:]. וחטיך בצדקה פרוק. וחטאתך בצדקה פרוק מעל צוארך [דניאל שם]. חטאך ע"י צדקה פדה [סוטה שם]. [ועויתך במיחן עניין. ועונותי]ך פרוק בחנינת עניים. ועונותיך בחנינת העניים [סוטה שם]. הן תהוי ארכא לשלותיך. אולי תהא שהות לשלומך שלא תמהר הרעה לבא ומה ראה דניאל להשיא עצה טובה לנבוכדנצר ראה ישראל עניים [...]לו עלה לחננם אמר לו עניים אלו שהגליתם רעבים הם פרנסם וכן עשה פתח אוצרותיו והיה מפרנסם כל י"ב חדש [דניאל שם]. איפרא הורמיז. כך שמה איפרא מן יופי שדים היה לה [תענית כד: ועי' תוס' גיטין יא. ד"ה ה[...]] [...]היתה משמרת עצמה מנדות וקרובה להתגייר ואף קרבנות היתה שולחת ולשון יוני איפרא חן כמו אפריון נמטייה לרבי שמעון (ב"מ קיט.). הורמיז. כמו (לקמן עג.) הורמיז בר ליליתא כלומר יופי שדים היה לה [נדה כ:]. [...]שלא קצירה (תהלים פ) ועשה קציר (איוב יד) כלומר כשתכלה זכות מעט שבידם את אביו אז תשברנה סעיפיה. וכן רבותינו שאסרו לקבל מהן צדקה מפני הטעם הזה [ישעיה כז, יא]. [מכאן שייך לדף יא.] אמת מארץ תצמ[ח ...] ישקפו מן השמים צדקה שהם עושים בארץ [תהלים פה, יב]. פרי צדיק עץ חיים. גמול פירות מעשה הצדיקים עץ חיים הם לעולם. ולוקח נפשות חכם. מי שהוא חכם קונה לו נפשות שמלמד דרך טוב והרי הם לו כ[...]ר עשו בחרן (בראשית יב) [משלי יא, ל]. אין חולקין. אין האחד כופה את חבירו לחלוק [לעיל ב:]. חצי קב. שזה שיעור גנה. הוא שיעור גנה [כתובות צח.]. ר' עקיבא אומר בית רובע. בית הבד. בית לעצור [...]ן יבשה קרויה בית השלחין וצריך להשקותה תמיד ושדה בית הבעל יפה הימנו [שיר השירים ד יג]. קרקע יבישה דלא דייה במי הגשמים וממעיין שבה משקה אותה [ב"מ קג:]. שדה שהיא עומדת בהר וצריך להשקותה תמיד [מו[...]] דבר שיש בו שיעור שאם תחלקנו עדיין יהא עליו שמו הראשון [לקמן יג:].

תְּרוֹמֵם-גּוֹי" אֵלּוּ יִשְׂרָאֵל — *CHARITY EXALTS A NATION* — THESE ARE the Children of ISRAEL, who constitute a unique nation and are therefore mentioned in the singular, דִּכְתִיב: ,,וּמִי כְעַמְּךָ כְּיִשְׂרָאֵל גּוֹי אֶחָד בָּאָרֶץ" — AS IT IS WRITTEN:[26] *AND WHO IS LIKE YOUR PEOPLE, ISRAEL, A UNIQUE NATION IN THE LAND.*[27] The Jewish nation is exalted by the charity it gives. ,,וְחֶסֶד לְאֻמִּים חַטָּאת" — *AND THE KINDNESS OF NATIONS IS A SIN* — this refers to the heathen nations. כָּל צְדָקָה וָחֶסֶד שֶׁאוּמּוֹת עוֹבְדֵי כּוֹכָבִים עוֹשִׂין — ANY act of CHARITY OR KINDNESS THAT THE IDOLATROUS NATIONS PERFORM חֵטְא הוּא לָהֶן — IS CONSIDERED A SIN FOR THEM, שֶׁאֵינָם עוֹשִׂין אֶלָּא לְהִתְגַּדֵּל בּוֹ — FOR THEY PERFORM a good deed ONLY TO LIVE LONGER[28] IN ITS merit, כְּמוֹ שֶׁנֶּאֱמַר: ,,דִּי-לֶהֱוֹן מְהַקְרְבִין נִיחוֹחִין לֶאֱלָהּ שְׁמַיָּא וּמְצַלַּיִן לְחַיֵּי מַלְכָּא וּבְנוֹהִי" — AS IT IS STATED:[29] *SO THAT THEY MAY OFFER PLEASING SACRIFICES TO THE GOD OF HEAVEN AND PRAY FOR THE LIVES OF THE KING AND HIS SONS.* Thus, because the charity of a gentile is performed for the ulterior motive of attaining longevity, it is considered sinful.[30]

The Gemara questions R' Eliezer's basic explanation:

וּדְעָבִיד הָכִי — **And if one performs** charitable acts **in this manner** (i.e. for an ulterior motive), לָאו צְדָקָה גְּמוּרָה הִיא — **is it not charity in the fullest sense?** וְהָתַנְיָא הָאוֹמֵר סֶלַע זֶה לִצְדָקָה בִּשְׁבִיל שֶׁיִּחְיוּ בָנַי — **Was it not taught in a Baraisa:** Concerning ONE WHO SAYS, "THIS *SELA*[31] is donated TO CHARITY SO THAT MY SONS SHALL LIVE in the merit of the mitzvah," וּבִשְׁבִיל שֶׁאֶזְכֶּה לָעוֹלָם הַבָּא — OR if he says, "SO THAT I SHALL MERIT a portion in THE WORLD TO COME" — הֲרֵי זֶה צַדִּיק גָּמוּר — THIS [DONOR] IS A COMPLETELY RIGHTEOUS PERSON,[32] even though his contribution was given for a self-serving purpose. The Baraisa thus teaches that to give charity for an ulterior motive is *not* a sin. — ? —

The Gemara answers:

לָא קַשְׁיָא — This is **not a difficulty.** כָּאן בְּיִשְׂרָאֵל — **Here** the Baraisa speaks **of a Jew,** who donates wholeheartedly to fulfill God's will. Since he would not regret his donation if his son did not recover, his gift is an unblemished act of charity. כָּאן בְּעוֹבֵד כּוֹכָבִים — **There,** however, R' Eliezer speaks **of an idolater,** who donates to charity only for selfish reasons. If his purpose is not achieved, he regrets his donation. This is not charity, but a sin, for the idolater may ultimately regret his good deed.

A second disciple advanced a slightly different explanation of the twofold enigmatic verse:

נַעֲנָה רַבִּי יְהוֹשֻׁעַ וְאָמַר — R' YEHOSHUA then SPOKE UP AND SAID: ,,צְדָקָה תְּרוֹמֵם-גּוֹי" אֵלּוּ יִשְׂרָאֵל — *CHARITY EXALTS A NATION* — *THESE ARE* the Children of *ISRAEL,* דִּכְתִיב: ,,וּמִי כְעַמְּךָ כְּיִשְׂרָאֵל גּוֹי אֶחָד" — AS IT IS WRITTEN: *AND WHO IS LIKE YOUR PEOPLE, ISRAEL, A UNIQUE NATION.* ,,וְחֶסֶד לְאֻמִּים חַטָּאת" — *AND THE KINDNESS OF NATIONS IS A SIN* — this refers to the heathen nations. כָּל צְדָקָה וָחֶסֶד שֶׁאוּמּוֹת עוֹבְדֵי כּוֹכָבִים עוֹשִׂין — ANY act of CHARITY OR KINDNESS THAT THE IDOLATROUS NATIONS PERFORM חֵטְא הוּא לָהֶן — IS A SIN FOR THEM, שֶׁאֵין עוֹשִׂין אֶלָּא כְּדֵי שֶׁתִּמָּשֵׁךְ מַלְכוּתָן — FOR THEY PERFORM a good deed ONLY TO PERPETUATE THEIR REIGN in its merit,[33] שֶׁנֶּאֱמַר: ,,לָהֵן מַלְכָּא מִלְכִּי יִשְׁפַּר עֲלָךְ וַחֲטָאָךְ בְּצִדְקָה פְרֻק וַעֲוָיָתָךְ בְּמִחַן עֲנָיִן הֵן תֶּהֱוֵא אַרְכָה לִשְׁלֵוְתָךְ וגו'" — AS IT IS STATED:[34] *NEVERTHELESS, O KING, LET MY ADVICE BE AGREEABLE TO YOU; REDEEM YOUR SINS WITH CHARITY, AND YOUR INIQUITIES WITH KINDNESS TO THE POOR — THERE WILL BE AN EXTENSION TO YOUR TRANQUILITY ETC.* Thus, Nebuchadnezzar performed charitable deeds only to prolong his rule.

Another disciple offered a third explanation:

נַעֲנָה רַבָּן גַּמְלִיאֵל וְאָמַר — RABBAN GAMLIEL SPOKE UP AND SAID: ,,צְדָקָה תְּרוֹמֵם-גּוֹי" אֵלּוּ יִשְׂרָאֵל — *CHARITY EXALTS A NATION* — THESE ARE the Children of ISRAEL, דִּכְתִיב: ,,וּמִי כְעַמְּךָ כְּיִשְׂרָאֵל" [וגו'] — AS IT IS WRITTEN: *AND WHO IS LIKE YOUR PEOPLE, ISRAEL [ETC.]* ,,וְחֶסֶד לְאֻמִּים חַטָּאת" — *AND THE KINDNESS OF NATIONS IS A SIN* — this refers to the heathens. כָּל צְדָקָה וָחֶסֶד שֶׁעוֹבְדֵי כּוֹכָבִים עוֹשִׂין — ANY act of CHARITY OR KINDNESS THAT IDOLATERS PERFORM חֵטְא הוּא לָהֶן — IS A SIN FOR THEM, שֶׁאֵין עוֹשִׂין אֶלָּא לְהִתְיַהֵר בּוֹ — FOR THEY PERFORM a good deed ONLY TO GLORIFY THEMSELVES THROUGH IT; וְכָל הַמִּתְיַהֵר נוֹפֵל בְּגֵיהִנֹּם — AND ANYONE THAT GLORIFIES HIMSELF FALLS INTO GEHINNOM for punishment. שֶׁנֶּאֱמַר: ,,זֵד יָהִיר לֵץ שְׁמוֹ עוֹשֶׂה בְּעֶבְרַת זָדוֹן" — FOR IT IS STATED:[35] *A PROUD AND HAUGHTY MAN, SCOFFER IS HIS NAME; HE PERFORMS IN ANGRY* (בְּעֶבְרַת) *PRIDE.* The verse mentions עֶבְרָה in connection with haughtiness and pride, born of self-glorification. וְאֵין עֶבְרָה אֶלָּא גֵיהִנֹּם — AND the word ANGER (עֶבְרָה) REFERS ONLY TO GEHINNOM, שֶׁנֶּאֱמַר: ,,יוֹם עֶבְרָה הַיּוֹם הַהוּא" — AS IT IS STATED:[36] *THAT DAY* [the day of judgment] *IS A DAY OF ANGER,* for then the wicked will be punished in Gehinnom. Thus, because the nations perform good deeds for purposes of self-glorification only, their acts of kindness and charity are considered sinful, and they will suffer the punishment of Gehinnom for them.

Rabban Gamliel appended the explanation of another Tanna to his own:

אָמַר רַבָּן גַּמְלִיאֵל עֲדַיִין אָנוּ צְרִיכִין לַמּוֹדָעִי — RABBAN GAMLIEL SAID: WE STILL NEED the explanation of THE scholar from Mt. MODA'I, for it substantiates and amplifies my own interpretation.[37] רַבִּי אֱלִיעֶזֶר הַמּוֹדָעִי אוֹמֵר — For R' ELIEZER OF Mt. MODA'I SAYS: ,,צְדָקָה תְּרוֹמֵם-גּוֹי" אֵלּוּ יִשְׂרָאֵל — *CHARITY EXALTS A NATION* — THESE ARE the Children of ISRAEL, דִּכְתִיב: ,,וּמִי כְעַמְּךָ כְּיִשְׂרָאֵל גּוֹי אֶחָד" — AS IT IS WRITTEN: *AND WHO IS LIKE YOUR PEOPLE, ISRAEL, A UNIQUE NATION.* ,,וְחֶסֶד לְאֻמִּים חַטָּאת" — *AND THE KINDNESS OF NATIONS IS A SIN* — this refers to the heathens. כָּל צְדָקָה וָחֶסֶד שֶׁעוֹבְדֵי כּוֹכָבִים עוֹשִׂין חֵטְא הוּא לָהֶן — ANY act of CHARITY

NOTES

26. *II Samuel* 7:23.

27. Their uniqueness lies in their being especially designated for the service of God (*Ralbag* there).

28. See *Maharsha.*

29. *Ezra* 6:10. King Darius II ordered his satraps to participate actively in the reconstruction of the Holy Temple for selfish reasons (i.e. so that he and his sons would attain longevity), as the following verse attests.

30. R' Eliezer's proof presumes that Darius was a gentile, and yet this is difficult, for tradition maintains that he was Queen Esther's son, and was therefore Jewish (see *Tosafos* to *Rosh Hashanah* 3b ד״ה שנת and *Chidushei Beis Meir* there; for a possible explanation, see *Dibros Moshe* to *Yevamos* §13).

31. One *sela* equals four *dinars.*

32. I.e. he is completely righteous with respect to this particular donation and intent (*Rashi*). See *Rabbeinu Chananel* to *Rosh Hashanah* 4a, where he cites a variant text: "This [gift] is a complete [act of] charity." See also *Ahavas Chessed* 23:2 and gloss there.

33. This is a sin, for if the gift of charity or good deed does not achieve its purpose, the idolater will regret having done it, as explained above.

34. *Daniel* 4:24, in which Daniel advises Nebuchadnezzar, an idolater and blasphemer, how to escape Divine retribution and retain his monarchy (see Gemara above, 4a).

35. *Proverbs* 21:24.

36. *Zephaniah* 1:15.

37. Rabban Gamliel did not originally support his interpretation by citing Scripture, as did the first two Tannaim. Rather, he built on their explanations to suggest that idolaters seek longevity and extended dominion in order to glorify themselves in these things. Thus, he now attaches R' Eliezer's explanation as a supplement to his own, in order to provide for it the Scriptural basis and amplification that the Gemara now sets forth (*Maharsha*; see also *Ben Yehoda*).

עין משפט נר מצוה

צב א ב מיי' פ"י מהל' מתנות עניים הלכה ח סמג עשין קסב טוש"ע י"ד סי' רמט סעיף ז:

צג ג ד מיי' שם פ"ח הלכה ט סמג שם טוש"ע י"ד סימן רנד סעיף ב:

הגהות הב"ח

(א) גמרא כי הא דר' יוסף בריה דר' יהושע: (ב) שם סלע זו לצדקה: (ג) שם שדרתינהו קמיה דרבא: (ד) תוס' ד"ה ויבא וכו' עשה צדקה שהיה נראה כמקנא להקב"ה:

גמרא

נותנה ואינו יודע למי נותנה נוטלה ואינו יודע ממי נוטלה נותנה ואינו יודע למי נותנה לאפוקי מדמר עוקבא נוטלה ואינו יודע ממי נוטלה לאפוקי מדרבי אבא ואלא היכי ליעביד ליתיב לארנקי של צדקה מותיבי מה יעשה אדם ויהיו לו בנים זכרים ר"א אומר יפזר מעותיו לעניים ר' יהושע אומר ישמח אשתו לדבר מצוה ר' אליעזר בן יעקב אומר לא יתן אדם פרוטה לארנקי של צדקה אלא א"כ ממונה עליה כר' חנניא בן תרדיון כי קא אמרינן דממני עלה כר' חנניא בן תרדיון א"ר אבהו אמר משה לפני הקב"ה רבש"ע במה תרום קרן ישראל אמר לו בכי תשא וא"ר אבהו שאלו את שלמה בן דוד עד היכן כחה של צדקה אמר להן צאו וראו מה פירש דוד אבא פזר נתן לאביונים צדקתו עומדת לעד קרנו תרום בכבוד רבי אבא אמר מהכא הוא מרומים ישכון מצדות סלעים משגבו לחמו נתן מימיו נאמנים מה טעם מרומים ישכון מצדות סלעים משגבו משום דלחמו נתן ומימיו נאמנים וא"ר אבהו שאלו את שלמה איזהו בן העולם הבא אמר להם כל שכנגד זקניו כבוד כי הא (א) דיוסף בריה דר' יהושע חלש אינגיד א"ל אבוה מאי חזית א"ל עולם הפוך ראיתי עליונים למטה ותחתונים למעלה א"ל עולם ברור ראית ואנן היכי חזיתינן [א"ל] כי היכי דחשבינן הכא חשבינן התם ושמעתי שהיו אומרים אשרי מי שבא לכאן ותלמודו בידו ושמעתי שהיו אומרים הרוגי מלכות אין כל בריה יכולה לעמוד במחיצתן מאן נינהו אילימא ר"ע וחבריו משום הרוגי מלכות ותו לא פשיטא בלאו הכי נמי אלא הרוגי לוד תניא אמר להן רבן יוחנן בן זכאי לתלמידיו בני מהו שאמר הכתוב צדקה תרומם גוי וחסד לאומים חטאת נענה רבי אליעזר ואמר צדקה תרומם גוי אלו ישראל דכתיב ומי כעמך ישראל גוי אחד בארץ וחסד לאומים חטאת כל צדקה וחסד שאומות עובדי כוכבים עושין חטא הוא להן שאינם עושין אלא להתגדל בו כמו שנאמר די להוון מהקרבין ניחוחין לאלהה שמיא ומצליין לחיי מלכא ובנוהי ודעביד הכי לאו צדקה גמורה היא והתניא האומר סלע (ב) זה לצדקה בשביל שיחיו בני ובשביל שאזכה לעולם הבא הרי זה צדיק גמור לא קשיא כאן בישראל כאן בעובד כוכבים נענה רבי יהושע ואמר צדקה תרומם גוי אלו ישראל דכתיב ומי כעמך ישראל גוי אחד וחסד לאומים חטאת כל צדקה וחסד שאומות עובדי כוכבים עושין חטא הוא להן שאין עושין אלא כדי שתמשך מלכותן שנאמר להן מלכא מלכי ישפר עליך וחטיך בצדקה פרוק ועויתך במיחן עניין הן תהוי ארכא לשלותיך וגו' נענה רבן גמליאל ואמר צדקה תרומם גוי אלו ישראל דכתיב ומי כעמך ישראל [וגו'] וחסד לאומים חטאת כל צדקה וחסד שעכו"ם עושין חטא הוא להן שאין עושין אלא להתיהר בו וכל המתיהר נופל בגיהנם שנאמר זד יהיר לץ שמו עושה בעברת זדון ואין עברה אלא גיהנם שנאמר יום עברה היום ההוא אמר רבן גמליאל עדיין אנו צריכין למודעי רבי אליעזר המודעי אומר צדקה תרומם גוי אלו ישראל דכתיב ומי כעמך ישראל גוי אחד וחסד לאומים חטאת כל צדקה וחסד שעכו"ם עושין חטא הוא להן שאין עושין אלא לחרף אותנו בו שנאמר ויבא ויעש ה' כאשר דבר כי חטאתם לה' ולא שמעתם בקולו והיה לכם הדבר הזה נענה רבי נחוניא בן הקנה ואמר צדקה תרומם גוי וחסד לישראל ולאומים חטאת אמר להם רבן יוחנן בן זכאי לתלמידיו נראין דברי רבי נחוניא בן הקנה מדברי ומדבריכם לפי שהוא נותן צדקה וחסד לישראל ולעכו"ם חטאת מכלל דהוא נמי אמר מאי היא דתניא אמר להם רבן יוחנן בן זכאי כשם שהחטאת מכפרת על ישראל כך צדקה מכפרת על אומות העולם: איפרא הורמיז אימיה דשבור מלכא שדרה ארבע מאה דינרי לקמיה דרבי אמי ולא קבלינהו (ג) שדרינהו קמיה דרבא וקבלינהו משום שלום מלכות שמע רבי אמי איקפד אמר לית ליה ביבש קצירה תשברנה נשים באות מאירות אותה ורבא משום שלום מלכות ורבי אמי נמי משום שלום מלכות דאיבעי ליה למפלגינהו לעניי עובדי כוכבים ורבא נמי לעניי עובדי כוכבים יהבינהו ור' אמי דאיקפד הוא

דלא

תוספות

אלא א"כ ממונה עליה כרבי חנניא בן תרדיון. פי' נאמן כמותו אבל לדיק כמותו לא דהא גבאים דמי אמורלאים לא היו לדיקים כמותו והכי נקט ר' חנניא בן תרדיון משום מעשה שבא לידו דאמר פ"ק דמסכת ע"ז (דף יז:) מעות פורים נתחלפו לי במעות של לדקה וחלקתים לעניים וכן בפרק במה טומנין (שבת דף מט. ושם) דאמר תפילין לריכין גוף נקי כאלישע בעל כנפים לא לדיק כאלישע קאמר אלא גוף נקי שידע ליזהר שלא ישן בהם ושלא יפיח בהם קאמר ולא נקט אלישע אלא משום דאיתרחיש ביה ניסא:

עליונים למטה ותחתונים למעלה. פי' ר"ח דאמרו הגאונים שקבלה בידם רב מפי רב דעולם הפוך היינו שראה שמואל דהוה יתיב קמיה דרב יהודה תלמידיה משום דמיתה בשמואל בפר' במה בהמה (שם דף נה.) גבי הסיא איתתא דאתיא ונפקא קמיה דשמואל ולא אשגח בה א"ל רב יהודה לית ליה למר אוטם אזנו מזעקת דל וגו':

ויבא ויעש ה' כאשר דבר כי חטאתם וגו'. ואותה שעה עשה לדקה שהיה (ד) מקנא להקב"ה א"כ שהיה מתיר את ירמיה מן הזיקים כדכתיב התם: ולא

רשב"ם

נותנה ואינו יודע למי נותנה. כדמפרש בספיה יתננה בכיס של גבאי לדקה: דרב עוקבא ור' אבא במס' כתובות (דף סז:) מר עוקבא הוה שדי לעניא דשבבותיה כל יומא ארבעה זוזי בציגורא דדשא הרי שהעני אינו יודע ממי נוטלה והוא יודע למי נותנה ור' אבא הוה לייר בסודריה ושדי לאחוריה ומשוי נפשיה לבני עניי והעני נוטלה ויודע ממי נוטלה ואינו יודע למי נותנה: לדבר מצוה. לפני תשמיש: אמר לו בכי תשא. אם באת לשאת ראשם בהגבהה קח מהם כופר לדקה: כנגד זקניו כבוד. אותם שחולקין להם כבוד בעולם הזה מחמת חכמת זקנתם: עליונים למטה. אותם שהם עליונים כאן מחמת עושרן ראיתי שם שהם למטה: ותחתונים למעלה. ראיתי עניים שהם ביזוין שפלים כאן ראיתים חשובים: ואנן. בעלי תורה היאך אתינן היאך יש חשיבותינו: כי היכי. דאתינן הכא חשובים ונכבדים הכי איתינן התם: הרוגי מלכות ותו לא. כלומר הך מעלה אמאי לאחרים לא דהוי בהו שנהרגו על קידוש השם ותו לא הוה בהו: הרוגי לוד. לולינוס ופפוס אחים שהרגם (ט) טורנוסרופוס הרשע בלודקיא כדאמרינן במסכת תענית (דף יח:) על ידי גזירה שנגזרה על ישראל להשמיד על שנמצאת בת מלך הרוגה וחשדו את ישראל עליה ועמדו האחי' הללו ואמרו מה לכם על ישראל אנו הרגנוה: ה"ז צדיק גמור. על דבר זה ומחשבה זו: כאן בישראל וכאן בעובד כוכבים. ישראל דעתן לשמים בין יחיה בין לא יחיה אינו מהרהר אחר מדת הדין אבל עכו"ם אינו נותן אלא ע"מ כן ואם לאו מתחרט: יום עברה היום ההוא. ביום הדין משתעי בנבואת לפניה: המודעי. מהר המודעי היה: ויבא ויעש ה' כאשר דבר לה' וגו'. נבוזראדן קאמר ליה לירמיה כשהיה מגלה את ישראל לבבל: ביבש קצירה תשברנה. כשתכלה זכות שבידן וייבש לחלוחית מעשה לדקה שלהן אז ישברו: דלא

רבינו גרשום

ואינו יודע למי נותנה. לאפוקי ממר עוקבא דמנח לצדקה אצינורא דדשא של עני והעני לא היה יודע מי נתנה שם ומר עוקבא היה יודע איזה עני נוטלה. ואינו יודע ממי נוטלה. לאפוקי דר' אבא דצייר בסודריה ומפשילו לאחוריה ואתי עני ושרי ושקיל. עני היה יודע ממי נוטל ור' אבא אינו יודע איזה עני נוטלה: יתן לארנקי של צדקה ולא ידע העני מי נתן והנותן לא ידע מי נטל: ישמח אשתו בדבר מצוה. שיפקדנה שלא בזמן עונה: אלא א"כ ממונה עליה כר' חנינא בן תרדיון. שהיה אדם גדול והיה יודע לבדוק למי יתן אלמא (דלא) [דאי לאו] מצינן למשכח ממונה כגון זה. הוא עצמו מפזרן ונותן. כי אמרינן נמי דיתן לארנקי בשיש ממונה עליה כר' חנינא בן תרדיון. אי לא יפזרן הוא עצמו: אמר לו בכי תשא. משום דכתי' שם ונתנו איש כופר נפשו: אמר להן כל שכנגד זקניו כבוד. זה שקנה חכמה כלומר כל שחולקין לו כבוד בשביל חכמתו ולא משום עושרו: עליונים למטה. כלומר אותן שהן עליונים בעולם הזה בשביל עושרן ולא בגין חכמתם ושם בעולם הבא שרוין למטה: ותחתונים. בעולם הזה שהם חכמים ומסכינין ובני מעשים טובים לא חשיבי הכא. לעולם הבא שרוין למעלה: ואנן מאי. כלומר תלמידי חכמים איך (האיך) חשובין אותם שם: כי היכי דחשיבין הכא חשיבין התם והיינו נגד זקניו כבוד: ותלמודו בידו. בגירסא: ר' עקיבא ועשרה חביריו: פשיטא. כלומר בלא זכותא דהרוגיה הוו צדיקין גמורים: הרוגי לוד. שפעם אחת נמצאת בת מלך הרוגה ומושלכת ברחוב ולא נודע מי הרגה וחשדו לכל היהודים ורצה המלך לשלוח יד בכולן עד שבאו שנים ומסרו עצמן ואמרו שהן הרגוה והצילו את כולם על ידן: כאן בישראל. ודאי מעליותא היא דאעפ"כ לבו לשמים לשם מצוה אבל הרבה אומות אין עושין אלא לצורך עצמן ולא לשם שמים ומשום הכי דלא עבדיתו צדקה כו': ויבא ויעש וגו' כי האי גונא מחרפין אותן. ור' נחוניא דריש הכי צדקה תרומם ישראל וחסד דמשים צדקה וחסד לישראל. וכל מה שאמרו הרבה אומות עושין חטאת הוא להן מכלל דהא ריב"ז דריש האי קרא כשם שחטאת קרבן חטאת מכפר על ישראל: לקמיה דר' אמי דהוי גבאי ליתנם לצדקה: איקפד על רבא דקבלינהו: אמר לית ליה לרבא ביבש קצירה תשברנה. כלומר כעין שהקציר מבושל יפה משברין אותו כך כשימלא ספקם ומגרש אותם מחטאתם תשבר זרועם נשים באות מאירות כגון אריתי מורי כלומר שאפי' הנשים (אין) יכולין למשול בם והיכי עביד רבא דקביל צדקה מהן להימשך מלכותן בזכות הצדקה: ור' אמי דאקפד

מסורת הש"ס

א) ע"ז דף יח. ב) [בע"י איתא רבא], ג) פסחים נ. [וגם איתא כי הא דיוסף בריה דר' יהושע בן לוי חלש ואיתנגיד כי הדר א"ל כו'], ד) [מ"ק כח. כתובות עז:], ה) מ"ח דהא איכא מעשים טובים בלאו ה"נ אלא כו', ו) ס"א לפי שאין עושין כו' וכן בכולן, ז) פסחים ח. ר"ה ד., ח) [לקמן עמ' ע"ש] ע"ז יח., ט) ל"ל טורנוסרופוס.

תורה אור השלם

א) פִּזַּר נָתַן לָאֶבְיוֹנִים צִדְקָתוֹ עֹמֶדֶת לָעַד קַרְנוֹ תָּרוּם בְּכָבוֹד: [תהלים קיב, ט]

ב) הוּא מְרוֹמִים יִשְׁכֹּן מְצָדוֹת סְלָעִים מִשְׂגַּבּוֹ לַחְמוֹ נִתָּן מֵימָיו נֶאֱמָנִים: [ישעיה לג, טז]

ג) וְחָפְרָה הַלְּבָנָה וּבוֹשָׁה הַחַמָּה כִּי מָלַךְ יְיָ צְבָאוֹת בְּהַר צִיּוֹן וּבִירוּשָׁלַיִם וְנֶגֶד זְקֵנָיו כָּבוֹד: [ישעיה כד, כג]

ד) צְדָקָה תְרוֹמֵם גּוֹי וְחֶסֶד לְאֻמִּים חַטָּאת: [משלי יד, לד]

ה) וּמִי כְעַמְּךָ כְּיִשְׂרָאֵל גּוֹי אֶחָד בָּאָרֶץ אֲשֶׁר הָלְכוּ אֱלֹהִים לִפְדּוֹת לוֹ לְעָם וְלָשׂוּם לוֹ שֵׁם וְלַעֲשׂוֹת לָכֶם הַגְּדוּלָּה וְנֹרָאוֹת לְאַרְצֶךָ מִפְּנֵי עַמְּךָ אֲשֶׁר פָּדִיתָ לְּךָ מִמִּצְרַיִם גּוֹיִם וֵאלֹהָיו: [שמואל ב ז, כג]

ו) דִּי לֶהֱוֺן מְהַקְרְבִין נִיחוֹחִין לֶאֱלָהּ שְׁמַיָּא וּמְצַלַּיִן לְחַיֵּי מַלְכָּא וּבְנוֹהִי: [עזרא ו, י]

ז) לָהֵן מַלְכָּא מִלְכִּי יִשְׁפַּר עֲלָךְ וַחֲטָאָךְ בְּצִדְקָה פְרֻק וַעֲוָיָתָךְ בְּמִחַן עֲנָיִן הֵן תֶּהֱוֵא אַרְכָא לִשְׁלֵוְתָךְ: [דניאל ד, כד]

ח) זֵד יָהִיר לֵץ שְׁמוֹ עוֹשֶׂה בְּעֶבְרַת זָדוֹן: [משלי כא, כד]

ט) יוֹם עֶבְרָה הַיּוֹם הַהוּא יוֹם צָרָה וּמְצוּקָה יוֹם שֹׁאָה וּמְשׁוֹאָה יוֹם חֹשֶׁךְ וַאֲפֵלָה יוֹם עָנָן וַעֲרָפֶל: [צפניה א, טו]

י) וַיָּבֵא וַיַּעַשׂ יְיָ כַּאֲשֶׁר דִּבֵּר כִּי חֲטָאתֶם לַייָ וְלֹא שְׁמַעְתֶּם בְּקוֹלוֹ וְהָיָה לָכֶם הַדָּבָר הַזֶּה: [ירמיה מ, ג]

כ) בִּיבֹשׁ קְצִירָהּ תִּשָּׁבַרְנָה נָשִׁים בָּאוֹת מְאִירוֹת אוֹתָהּ כִּי לֹא עַם בִּינוֹת הוּא עַל כֵּן לֹא יְרַחֲמֶנּוּ עֹשֵׂהוּ וְיֹצְרוֹ לֹא יְחֻנֶּנּוּ: [ישעיה כז, יא]

ליקוטי רש"י

אינגד. איתנגיד, גוע ופרכס רוחו. עליונים למטה. אותן שהיו כאן חשובים ראיתים קלים. ואנן. תלמידי חכמים היכי איתינן התם. הרוגי מלכות ותו לא. לא היתה בהן מעלה אחרת שיחשבו עליה אלא זו בלבד. הרוגי לוד. שני אחים היו שמסרו עצמן על ישראל שהודו על עצמן הריגת בת מלך שהיו מטילין אותה על כל ישראל [פסחים נ.]. לולייאנוס ופפוס אחים צדיקים גמורים היו. בלודקיא היא לוד ויש אומרין שנהרגו על בתו של מלך שנמצאת הרוגה ואמרו היהודים הרגוה וגזרו גזרה על שונאיהן של ישראל ועמדו אלו ופדו את ישראל ואמרו אנו הרגנוה והרג המלך לאלו בלבד [תענית יח:]. הרי זה צדיק גמור. בדבר זה ולא אמרינן שלא לשמה עושה אלא קיים מצות בוראו שצוהו לעשות צדקה ומתכוין אף להנאת עצמו שיזכה בה לעולם הבא או שיחיו בניו [פסחים ח:]. אם רגיל בכך [ר"ה ד.]. וחסד לאומים חטאת. שהיו נוטלי' מזה ונותנים לזה [משלי יד, לד]. ומי כעמך ישראל גוי אחד. ממה הם מיוחדים מכל העמים מזה אשר הלך אלהים בעצמו לפדותם לו לעם כמו שכתוב אני יוצא בתוך מצרים (שמות יב) מזה אנו מיוחדים שלא עשה זה לשום אומה בעולם [דברי הימים א, יז, כא]. להן מלכא. באמת אתה מלך שמע לעצתי. מלכי. עצתי כמו איעצך אמלכינך. ישפר עליך. עצתי תיטב בעיניך לשמוע מילי [דניאל ד, כד]. דניאל אמר לנבוכדנצר כשפתר לו החלום שיהא נטרד מן האנשים ולהיות עם בהמה וחיה להן מלכא אתנם המלך מלכי ישפר עליך עצתי תיטב בעיניך להאמין לעצתי [סוטה כ:]. וחטיך בצדקה פרוק. וחטאתך בצדקה פרוק מעל צוארך [דניאל שם]. חטאך ע"י צדקה פדה [סוטה שם]. ועויתך במיחן עניין. ועונותיך פרוק בחנינת עניים [דניאל שם]. ועונותיך בחנינת העניים [סוטה שם]. הן תהוי ארכא לשלותיך. אולי תהא שהות לשלומך שלא תמהר הרעה לבא ומה ראה דניאל להשיא עצה טובה לנבוכדנצר ראה ישראל עניים שפלי גולה מחזירין על הפתחים והשיאו עצה לחננם אמר לו עניים אלו שהגליתם רעבים הם פרנסם וכן עשה פתח אוצרותיו והיה מפרנסם כל י"ב חדש [דניאל שם]. איפרא הורמיז. כך שמה איפרא חן יופי שדים היה לה [תענית כד: ועי' תוס' גיטין יא. ד"ה הורמין]. נכרית היתה וכן שמה ואעפ"כ היתה משמרת עצמה מנדות וקרובה להתגייר ואף קרבנות היתה שולחת ולשון יוני איפרא חן כמו אפריון נמטייה לרבי שמעון (ב"מ קיט.). הורמיז. כמו (לקמן עג.) הורמיז בר ליליתא כלומר יופי שדים היה לה [נדה כ:]. ביבש קצירה. קצירי שרשיה כמו תשלח קצירה (תהלים פ) ועשה קציר (איוב יד) כלומר כשתכלה זכות מעט שבידם אז תשברנה סעיפיה. וכן רבותינו שאסרו לקבל מהן צדקה מפני הטעם הזה [ישעיה כז, יא]. [מכאן שייך לדף יא.] אמת מארץ תצמח וגו'. כשהיו ישראל דוברים אמת וישקפו מן השמים צדקה שהם עושים בארץ [תהלים פה, יב]. פרי צדיק עץ חיים. גמול פירות מעשה הצדיקים עץ חיים הם לעולם. ולוקח נפשות חכם. מי שהוא חכם קונה לו נפשות שמלמד דרך טוב והרי הם לו כאילו קנאם כענין שנאמר ואת הנפש אשר עשו בחרן (בראשית יב) [משלי יא, ל]. אין חולקין. אין האחד כופה את חבירו לחלוק [לעיל ב:]. חצי קב. שזה שיעור גנה. ר' עקיבא אומר בית רובע. הוא שיעור גנה [כתובות צח.]. בית הבד. בית לעצור זיתים [ב"מ קיז:]. בית השלחין. ארץ יבשה קרויה בית השלחין וצריך להשקותה תמיד ושדה בית הבעל יפה הימנו [שיר השירים ד יג]. קרקע יבישה דלא דייה במי הגשמים וממעיין שבה משקה אותה [ב"מ קג:]. שדה שהיא עומדת בהר וצריך להשקותה תמיד [מו"ק ב.]. ושמו עליו. כל דבר שיש בו שיעור שאם תחלקנו עדיין יהא עליו שמו הראשון [לקמן יג:].

OR KINDNESS THAT IDOLATERS PERFORM IS A SIN FOR THEM, שֶׁאֵין עוֹשִׂין אֶלָּא לְחָרֵף אוֹתָנוּ בּוֹ – FOR THEY PERFORM a good deed ONLY to chide and REVILE US WITH IT,[38] שֶׁנֶּאֱמַר: ,,וַיָּבֵא וַיַּעַשׂ ה׳ כַּאֲשֶׁר דִּבֵּר כִּי־חֲטָאתֶם לַה׳ וְלֹא־שְׁמַעְתֶּם בְּקוֹלוֹ וְהָיָה לָכֶם הַדָּבָר הַזֶּה״ – AS IT IS STATED:[39] *AND GOD HAS BROUGHT* it *AND HAS DONE AS HE HAD SPOKEN; BECAUSE YOU HAVE SINNED AGAINST GOD AND HAVE NOT HEARKENED TO HIS VOICE, THIS THING HAS BEFALLEN YOU.* According to this opinion, the idolaters perform charitable deeds for the most heinous of ulterior motives – to revile through them the Jewish people. This is a most grievous sin.

The next disciple pursued a novel approach:

נַעֲנָה רַבִּי נְחוּנְיָא בֶּן הַקָּנָה וְאָמַר – R' NECHUNYA BEN HAKANEH SPOKE UP AND SAID: ,,צְדָקָה תְּרוֹמֵם־גּוֹי וְחֶסֶד״ – *CHARITY EXALTS A NATION, AND KINDNESS* – לְיִשְׂרָאֵל – both types of good works[40] apply TO the Children of ISRAEL. וּלְאֻמִּים חַטָּאת – *AND TO THE NATIONS – SIN!* "Kindness" belongs with the first part of the verse, and – along with "charity" – pertains to the "nation" mentioned there – Israel. Thus, for the idolatrous "nations" there is nothing but "sin."

Rabban Yochanan declared this the superior interpretation:

אָמַר לָהֶם רַבָּן יוֹחָנָן בֶּן זַכַּאי לְתַלְמִידָיו – RABBAN YOCHANAN BEN ZAKKAI SAID TO HIS STUDENTS: נִרְאִין דִּבְרֵי רַבִּי נְחוּנְיָא בֶּן הַקָּנָה מִדְּבָרַי וּמִדִּבְרֵיכֶם – THE WORDS OF R' NECHUNYA BEN HAKANEH ARE MORE ACCEPTABLE THAN MY WORDS[41] OR YOUR WORDS, לְפִי שֶׁהוּא נוֹתֵן צְדָקָה וְחֶסֶד לְיִשְׂרָאֵל – BECAUSE HE ATTRIBUTES CHARITY AND KINDNESS TO THE JEWS, וּלְעוֹבְדֵי כּוֹכָבִים חַטָּאת – AND TO THE IDOLATERS he attributes only SIN!

The Gemara draws an inference:

מִכְּלָל דְּהוּא נַמִּי אָמַר – From the fact that Rabban Yochanan said, "My words," it follows **by implication that he also said** an explanation of this verse! מַאי הִיא – **What,** then, **is it?**

Rabban Yochanan's interpretation is found in a Baraisa:

דְּתַנְיָא אָמַר לָהֶם רַבָּן יוֹחָנָן בֶּן זַכַּאי – **For it was taught in a Baraisa:** RABBAN YOCHANAN BEN ZAKKAI SAID TO [HIS DISCIPLES]: כְּשֵׁם שֶׁהַחַטָּאת מְכַפֶּרֶת עַל יִשְׂרָאֵל – JUST AS A *CHATAS* OFFERING ATONES FOR THE JEWS, כָּךְ צְדָקָה מְכַפֶּרֶת עַל אוּמּוֹת הָעוֹלָם – SO CHARITY ATONES FOR THE NATIONS OF THE WORLD. In our verse חַטָּאת does not mean "sin," but a "sin offering" (the *chatas* sacrifice). Thus, the nations' acts of kindness and charity[42] function as a *chatas* to effect atonement for them.

The Gemara relates an incident involving a gentile who donated charity:

אִיפְרָא הוּרְמִיז אִימֵּיהּ דִּשְׁבוּר מַלְכָּא – **Ifra Hurmiz, mother of King Shapur,**[43] שַׁדְּרָה אַרְבַּע מְאָה דִּינְרֵי לְקַמֵּיהּ דְּרַבִּי אַמִּי – **sent four hundred golden** ***dinars***[44] **before R' Ami** for distribution to the needy, וְלָא קַבְּלִינְהוּ – **and he did not accept them,** since he did not want the gentile to receive the reward due to one who gives charity. שַׁדְּרִינְהוּ קַמֵּיהּ דְּרָבָא – **She** then **sent [the money] before Rava,** וְקַבְּלִינְהוּ מִשּׁוּם שְׁלוֹם מַלְכוּת – **and he accepted it for the sake of peaceful relations with the monarchy.** Had Rava slighted the king's mother by rejecting her gift of charity, the king would have been insulted and angered. שָׁמַע רַבִּי אַמִּי אִיקְפַּד – **R' Ami heard** about Rava's actions, and **he took exception.** אָמַר לֵית לֵיהּ: ,,בִּיבֹשׁ קְצִירָהּ תִּשָּׁבַרְנָה נָשִׁים בָּאוֹת מְאִירוֹת אוֹתָהּ״ – **[Rav Ami] said: Does [Rava] not accept** the teaching of the verse:[45] ***When her boughs are withered, they shall be broken; women will come and set them on fire?***[46] Certainly, then, we should not accept charity from the nations and thereby afford them the opportunity to generate additional merit.

The Gemara explains Rava's position:

וְרָבָא מִשּׁוּם שְׁלוֹם מַלְכוּת – **And Rava** did not disagree with R' Ami; rather, he was forced to accept Ifra's gift **for the sake of peaceful relations with the monarchy.**[47]

The Gemara asks:

וְרַבִּי אַמִּי נַמִּי מִשּׁוּם שְׁלוֹם מַלְכוּת – **And R' Ami** should have **also** acknowledged the necessity of accepting the gift **for the sake of peaceful relations with the monarchy.** – ? –

The Gemara answers:

דְּאִיבְּעֵי לֵיהּ לְמִפְלְגִינְהוּ לַעֲנִיֵּי עוֹבְדֵי כּוֹכָבִים – R' Ami did not object to Rava's *accepting* the gift. Rather, he felt **that [Rava] should have distributed the money to poor idolaters,** so as to deny the gentile donor the merit of sustaining Jews!

The Gemara explains that, unbeknownst to R' Ami, Rava did exactly that:

וְרָבָא נַמִּי לַעֲנִיֵּי עוֹבְדֵי כּוֹכָבִים יַהֲבִינְהוּ – **And,** in fact, **Rava** ***did*** **give [the money] to poor idolaters;** וְר׳ אַמִּי דְּאִיקְפַּד הוּא – **and R' Ami, who took exception** to Rava's actions, did so

NOTES

38. I.e. they perform good deeds only to glorify themselves at the Jews' expense, by humiliating and harshly rebuking them: "Had you acted kindly and charitably as we did, you would not suffer such a terrible fate" (see *Maharsha* and previous note).

39. *Jeremiah* 40:3. Nebuzaradan, captain of the guard, here rebukes Jeremiah as the captive Israelites are exiled to Babylonia (*Rashi*).

40. "Charity" and "kindness" are closely related. However, charity is performed only with one's wealth, whereas kindness is performed with one's very person as well. Hence, kindness is the greater of the two. The previous Tannaim therefore taught that Israel was exalted even by the lesser act of charity, while even the greater act of kindness failed to elevate the idolaters. R' Nechunya now comes to teach that the attribute of kindness is entirely *foreign* to idolaters (*Maharsha*).

41. The Gemara below infers from this statement that Rabban Yochanan had devised his own interpretation of the verse.

42. Rabban Yochanan understands that the first part of the verse, *Charity exalts a nation,* also applies to the gentile nations (*Maharsha*).

43. See above, 8a notes 56 and 57.

44. "דִּינְרֵי" – without a "ן" at the end – refers to *golden dinars* (see below, 166a), each worth twenty-five regular *dinars.* Thus, the gift was 10,000 *dinars.*

45. *Isaiah* 27:11.

46. The prophet analogizes the merit generated by acts of charity to the moisture that vivifies a tree. Should the moisture be depleted, the wood of the tree becomes brittle and easily broken. Similarly, once the merit of the nations' charitable deeds has dissipated, they become weak and easily broken – even by nations as weak as women (*women will come and set them on fire*) [*Rashi*].

[It should be noted, that although the Gemara above established that acts of charity performed by the nations are considered "sin" because of their intentions, neverthless, the merit of the charity will protect them.]

47. Rava lived in Babylonia which was under the Persian rule of King Shapur. R' Ami, however, lives in Eretz Yisrael which was under Roman rule; thus, there was no necessity for R' Ami to appease the Persian rulers (*Hagahos Yaavetz*; cf. *Maharsha*).]

דְּלָא סַיְּימוּהָ קַמֵּיהּ – **because they did not complete [the account]** of the incident **before him.** R' Ami was not informed that Rava had distributed the funds to non-Jewish poor, and so he voiced his objections. Rava, however, acted properly, since he was compelled to accept the donation in order to avoid offending the king.[1]

The Gemara relates how charity gives life to the donor:

תַּנְיָא – **It was taught in a Baraisa:** אָמְרוּ עָלָיו עַל בִּנְיָמִין הַצַּדִּיק – THEY RELATED the following story ABOUT BENJAMIN THE RIGHTEOUS, שֶׁהָיָה מְמוּנֶּה עַל קוּפָּה שֶׁל צְדָקָה – WHO WAS APPOINTED administrator OVER THE communal CHARITY FUND. פַּעַם אַחַת בָּאתָה אִשָּׁה לְפָנָיו בִּשְׁנֵי בַצּוֹרֶת – ONCE, DURING YEARS OF FAMINE, A WOMAN CAME BEFORE [BENJAMIN] and requested assistance. אָמְרָה לוֹ רַבִּי פַּרְנְסֵנִי – SHE SAID TO HIM: MY MASTER, SUSTAIN ME!

Benjamin the Righteous replied:

אָמַר לָהּ הָעֲבוֹדָה – [BENJAMIN] SAID TO [THE WOMAN]: I swear by THE Holy Temple SERVICE[2] שֶׁאֵין בְּקוּפָּה שֶׁל צְדָקָה כְּלוּם – THAT THERE IS NOTHING IN THE CHARITY FUND for me to distribute to you.

The woman recounted her desperate plight:

אָמְרָה לוֹ רַבִּי אִם אֵין אַתָּה מְפַרְנְסֵנִי – [THE WOMAN] SAID TO [BENJAMIN]: MY MASTER, IF YOU DO NOT SUSTAIN ME, הֲרֵי אִשָּׁה וְשִׁבְעָה בָנֶיהָ מֵתִים – A WOMAN AND HER SEVEN SONS WILL PERISH! עָמַד וּפִרְנְסָהּ מִשֶּׁלּוֹ – Moved by the woman's plea, [BENJAMIN] ROSE AND PROVIDED HER WITH SUSTENANCE FROM HIS own funds.[3]

Benjamin's selfless act of charity rebounded to sustain him as well:

לְיָמִים חָלָה וְנָטָה לָמוּת – AFTER A TIME [BENJAMIN] TOOK ILL AND WAS CLOSE TO DYING. אָמְרוּ מַלְאֲכֵי הַשָּׁרֵת לִפְנֵי הַקָּדוֹשׁ בָּרוּךְ הוּא – THE MINISTERING ANGELS thereupon SAID TO THE HOLY ONE, BLESSED IS HE: רִבּוֹנוֹ שֶׁל עוֹלָם – MASTER OF THE UNIVERSE! אַתָּה אָמַרְתָּ כָּל הַמְקַיֵּים נֶפֶשׁ אַחַת מִיִּשְׂרָאֵל – YOU HAVE SAID[4] that ONE WHO PRESERVES ONE JEWISH SOUL כְּאִילּוּ קִיֵּים עוֹלָם מָלֵא – IS regarded AS IF HE PRESERVED AN ENTIRE WORLD,[5] וּבִנְיָמִין הַצַּדִּיק שֶׁהֶחֱיָה אִשָּׁה וְשִׁבְעָה בָנֶיהָ – AND BENJAMIN THE RIGHTEOUS, WHO PRESERVED A WOMAN AND HER SEVEN SONS during a famine, יָמוּת בְּשָׁנִים מוּעָטוֹת הַלָּלוּ – SHOULD DIE AFTER THESE FEW YEARS on earth?!

The angels were persuasive:

מִיָּד קָרְעוּ לוֹ גְּזַר דִּינוֹ – IMMEDIATELY upon hearing this argument [THE HEAVENLY COURT] TORE UP [BENJAMIN'S] DECREE, and in the merit of his charity he was spared.

A second Baraisa relates the extent of Benjamin's reward:

תָּנָא הוֹסִיפוּ לוֹ עֶשְׂרִים וּשְׁתַּיִם שָׁנָה עַל שְׁנוֹתָיו – **It was taught in a Baraisa:** [THE HEAVENLY COURT] ADDED TWENTY-TWO YEARS TO HIS LIFETIME in the merit of this single act of charity.

The Gemara relates the transcendent qualities of charity:

תָּנוּ רַבָּנַן – **The Rabbis taught in a Baraisa:** מַעֲשֶׂה בְּמוּנְבַּז הַמֶּלֶךְ – There was once AN EPISODE INVOLVING KING MUNBAZ,[6] שֶׁבִּזְבֵּז אוֹצְרוֹתָיו וְאוֹצְרוֹת אֲבוֹתָיו – IN WHICH HE DEPLETED HIS TREASURIES AND THE TREASURIES OF HIS FOREBEARS בִּשְׁנֵי בַצּוֹרֶת – to feed the poor DURING YEARS OF FAMINE. וְחָבְרוּ עָלָיו אֶחָיו וּבֵית אָבִיו – AND HIS BROTHERS AND HIS FATHER'S FAMILY BANDED TOGETHER AGAINST HIM וְאָמְרוּ לוֹ – AND SAID TO HIM in protest: אֲבוֹתֶיךָ גָּנְזוּ וְהוֹסִיפוּ עַל שֶׁל אֲבוֹתָם – YOUR FATHERS HOARDED their wealth, AND ADDED TO the fortune OF THEIR FOREFATHERS, וְאַתָּה מְבַזְבְּזָם – AND YOU, instead of increasing the family riches, ARE LIBERALLY EXPENDING THEM! Why are you destroying the work of generations?

Munbaz replied by enumerating various advantages of giving charity over hoarding wealth:

אָמַר לָהֶם אֲבוֹתַי גָּנְזוּ לְמַטָּה – [MUNBAZ] SAID TO [HIS FAMILY]: MY FATHERS HOARDED wealth BELOW on the earth, וַאֲנִי גָּנַזְתִּי לְמַעְלָה – BUT by giving charity I HAVE HOARDED merit ABOVE in Heaven, שֶׁנֶּאֱמַר: ,,אֱמֶת מֵאֶרֶץ תִּצְמָח וְצֶדֶק מִשָּׁמַיִם נִשְׁקָף" – AS IT IS STATED:[7] *[WHEN] TRUTH WILL SPROUT FROM THE EARTH, CHARITY WILL GAZE DOWN FROM HEAVEN.*[8]

Munbaz replied further:

אֲבוֹתַי גָּנְזוּ בְּמָקוֹם שֶׁהַיָּד שׁוֹלֶטֶת בּוֹ – MY FATHERS HOARDED their wealth IN AN INSECURE PLACE,[9] וַאֲנִי גָּנַזְתִּי בְּמָקוֹם שֶׁאֵין הַיָּד שׁוֹלֶטֶת בּוֹ – BUT I HAVE HOARDED my "wealth" IN A SECURE PLACE, שֶׁנֶּאֱמַר: ,,צֶדֶק וּמִשְׁפָּט מְכוֹן כִּסְאֶךָ" – AS IT IS STATED:[10] *CHARITY AND JUSTICE ARE YOUR THRONE'S FOUNDATION.*[11]

Munbaz said further:

אֲבוֹתַי גָּנְזוּ דָּבָר שֶׁאֵין עוֹשֶׂה פֵּירוֹת – MY FATHERS HOARDED SOMETHING THAT DOES NOT PRODUCE FRUITS,[12] וַאֲנִי גָּנַזְתִּי דָּבָר שֶׁעוֹשֶׂה פֵּירוֹת – BUT I HAVE HOARDED SOMETHING THAT DOES PRODUCE FRUITS, שֶׁנֶּאֱמַר: ,,אִמְרוּ צַדִּיק כִּי־טוֹב כִּי־פְרִי מַעַלְלֵיהֶם יֹאכֵלוּ" – AS IT IS STATED:[13] *SAY OF THE RIGHTEOUS MAN THAT IT*

NOTES

1. Above (8a), when Ifra Hurmiz contributed money for the redemption of captives, Rav Yosef was compelled to use the money to redeem only Jewish captives (and thereby enhance her merit), for she expected him to do so and he was not allowed to deceive her (see above, 8b note 2). Here, however, Rava was permitted to disburse Ifra's charity donation to non-Jewish paupers. For since Jews customarily distributed charity to gentiles for purposes of maintaining peaceful relations (see *Gittin* 61a), Ifra fully expected Rava to follow suit, and so he did not deceive her in any way (*Rashi*).

2. It was a common practice in those times that when swearing, one mentioned the Holy Temple or something connected to it, instead of mentioning the name of God (see also *Kiddushin* 71a; *Tos. Yom Tov* to *Kesubos* 2:9).

3. Benjamin did not realize initially that the woman's situation was critical, and therefore held back his limited resources for himself, in accordance with halachah. Had he appreciated the extent of her difficulty, he would have channeled his donation through the communal charity fund, so as not to cause her embarrassment (see 10b above) [*Maharsha*].

4. I.e. from Your Torah we have learned (*Rashi*).

5. The Mishnah (*Sanhedrin* 37a) states that God initially created a solitary human being (Adam) to teach that preserving a single Jew's life is tantamount to preserving an entire world. For God told Cain after he killed his brother Abel (*Genesis* 4:10): *The voice of your brother's bloods cry out to me;* and the Mishnah (ibid.) interprets the plural *bloods* to mean Abel's blood and the blood of his unborn descendants. Thus, if a murderer is condemned for destroying future generations, then certainly one who preserves a life is regarded as preserving all of that person's unborn progeny — for God rewards good more abundantly than He punishes evil (*Rashi*).

6. One of the Hasmonean kings, he was a son of Queen Helene (*Rashi*). *Maharsha,* however, cites a Midrash that identifies Munbaz as a gentile king who converted to Judaism.

7. *Psalms* 85:12.

8. When the Jews are observing the mitzvos, then the merit of their charitable deeds — which abides in Heaven — will gaze down to bestow reward (*Rashi*).

9. Literally: a place that the hand (of others) controls. I.e. no one's fortune is perfectly safe from loss or destruction in this world.

10. *Psalms* 89:15.

11. I.e. the merit of my charitable deeds is concealed under the foundation of God's throne — a most secure repository (*Rashi*).

12. I.e. the wealth they hoarded did not produce any fruits from which they could benefit (see *Rashi*).

13. *Isaiah* 3:10. Here and in the next quoted verse Munbaz interprets the word "צַדִּיק," *righteous man,* as צְדָקָה, *charity.*

דלא סיימוה קמיה. דר' אמי לעניי עובדי כוכבים חלקן רבא והנך דאמרן לעיל (דף ח.) דשדרה נמי איפרא הורמיז למלוה רבה משום שלום מלכות נמי קבלינהו ולא אפשר ליה לחלקן לעניי עובדי כוכבים דאסור לגנוב דעת הבריות ואפילו דעתו של עובד כוכבים אבל במעות המתחלקות לעניים אין גניבת דעת דאינהו נמי ידעי שישראל רגילים לפרנס עניי עובדי כוכבים כדאמרי' במס' גיטין (דף סא.) מפרנסין עניי עובדי כוכבים עם עניי ישראל מפני דרכי שלום: אתה אמרת כו'. מתורתך למדנו לפיכך נברא אדם יחידי לומר לך כל המקיים נפש אחת [מישראל] כאילו קיים העולם מלא וכתיב (בראשית ד) קול דמי אחיך דמו ודם זרעיותיו אף כשאתה מקיים דמי אחיך עמך מעלה עליך חייו וחיי זרעיותיו שמדה טובה מרובה ממדת פורענות: מונבז המלך. בנה של הילני המלכה מזרע החשמונאים: כשאמת מארץ תצמח. אף משמים נשקף הצדק לשלם גמול: נשקף. מביט כמו נשקפה ותייבב (שופטים ה) כלומר זכות הצדקה מביט ומסתכל למטה: מכון כסאך. גנוזתן תחת מכון הכסא: (במקום) [דבר] שעושה פירות. והקרן קיים לעוה"ב והפירות אוכל בחייו שנאמר כי פרי מעלליהם יאכלו: אוצרות נפשות. שנאמר ולוקח נפשות חכם בהאי קרא: מתני' טרקלין ומורן. מיני פלטין: בית השלחין. מתוך שיש לו מעיין ובידו להשקותו תדיר אם אין בו ט' קבין זורעין בו שאר זרעים לפיכך אפילו בפחות מכאן יש בו דין חלוקה: אפילו בפחות מכאן יחלוקו. משום דבעי למיתני וכתבי הקדש אע"פ ששניהם רוצים לא יחלוקו תני רישא (א): כתבי הקדש. כ"ד ספרים והיו רגילים לכותבן בגליון כס"ת שלנו לפיכך גנאי הדבר לחתכן: גמ' חוץ משל פתחים. אלא של שותפים שני בתים פתוחין לתוכה ולפני הפתח ארבע אמות לאורך הבית הן לפרק משאו מעל חמורו וחוץ מאותן ד' אמות צריך שיהא ארבע אמות לשאר תשמישין: חצר מתחלקת לפתחי'. היתה לו חצר ובה שני בתים ואחד מהן פתוחין לו שני פתחים לחצר ולבית השני אין פתוח לחצר אלא פתח אחד וחולק נכסיו על פיו ונותן האחד לראובן בנו והשני לשמעון וחצר לא חילק אם באו לחלוק את החצר זה שיש לו שני פתחים נוטל שני חלקים בחצר ואחיו נוטל חלק אחד: נותן לכל פתח (ב) ד' אמות. כנגד הרוחב להלן מן הפתח כנגד הרוחב כפי רוחב הפתח: נוטל שמונה אמות. דהיינו כנגד רוחב הפתח ולארבע אמות ברוחב החצר להלן מן הפתח: האי פירא דסופלי. מי שיש לו חפירה בחצר שנותנין בה גרעיני תמרים למאכל בהמה יש לו ארבע אמות בחצר לכל סביבותיה: דלא מייחד ליה פיתחא. שלא היה לו פתח אצל חפירה אלא דרך פתח ביתו שהוא יוצא ונכנס בו היה לו דרך לצאת לחצר ולילך אחר החפירה שלפני סוף ביתו ומשתמש: אבל

דלא סיימוה קמיה תניא אמרו עליו על בנימין הצדיק שהיה ממונה על קופה של צדקה פעם אחת באתה אשה לפניו בשני בצורת אמרה לו רבי פרנסני אמר לה העבודה שאין בקופה של צדקה כלום אמרה לו רבי אם אין אתה מפרנסני הרי אשה ושבעה בניה מתים עמד ופרנסה משלו לימים חלה ונטה למות אמרו מלאכי השרת לפני הקב"ה רבש"ע אתה אמרת כל המקיים נפש אחת מישראל כאילו קיים עולם מלא ובנימין הצדיק שהחיה אשה ושבעה בניה ימות בשנים מועטות הללו מיד קרעו לו גזר דינו תנא הוסיפו לו עשרים ושתים שנה על שנותיו ת"ר מעשה במונבז המלך שבזבז אוצרותיו ואוצרות אבותיו בשני בצורת וחברו עליו אחיו ובית אביו ואמרו לו אבותיך גנזו והוסיפו על של אבותם ואתה מבזבזם אמר להם אבותי גנזו למטה ואני גנזתי למעלה שנאמר א) אמת מארץ תצמח וצדק משמים נשקף אבותי גנזו במקום שהיד שולטת בו ואני גנזתי במקום שאין היד שולטת בו שנאמר ב) צדק ומשפט מכון כסאך אבותי גנזו דבר שאין עושה פירות ואני גנזתי דבר שעושה פירות שנאמר ג) אמרו צדיק כי טוב כי פרי מעלליהם יאכלו אבותי גנזו אוצרות [אוצרות] ממון ואני גנזתי אוצרות נפשות שנאמר ד) פרי צדיק עץ חיים ולוקח נפשות חכם אבותי גנזו לאחרים ואני גנזתי לעצמי שנאמר ה) ולך תהיה צדקה אבותי גנזו לעולם הזה ואני גנזתי לעולם הבא שנאמר ו) והלך לפניך צדקך כבוד ה' יאספך: ואם קנה בה בית דירה הרי הוא כאנשי העיר: מתניתין דלא כרשב"ג דתניא רבן שמעון בן גמליאל אומר אם קנה בה קרקע כל שהוא הרי הוא כאנשי העיר והא תניא רבן שמעון בן גמליאל אומר אם קנה שם קרקע הראויה לבית דירה הרי הוא כאנשי העיר תרי תנאי ואליבא דרבן שמעון בן גמליאל: מתני' אין חולקין את החצר עד שיהא ארבע אמות לזה וארבע אמות לזה ולא את השדה עד שיהא בה תשעה קבין לזה ותשעה קבין לזה ר' יהודה אומר עד שיהא בה תשעת חצי קבין לזה ותשעת חצי קבין לזה ולא את הגינה עד שיהא בה חצי קב לזה וחצי קב לזה ר' עקיבא אומר בית רובע ולא את הטרקלין ולא את המורן ולא את השובך ולא את הטלית ולא את המרחץ ולא את בית הבד ולא את בית השלחין עד שיהא בהן כדי לזה וכדי לזה זה הכלל כל שיחלק ושמו עליו חולקין ואם לאו אין חולקין אימתי בזמן שאין שניהם רוצים אבל בזמן ששניהם רוצים אפי' פחות מכאן יחלוקו וכתבי הקדש אע"פ ששניהם רוצים לא יחלוקו: גמ' א"ר אסי א"ר יוחנן ארבע אמות שאמרו חוץ משל פתחים תניא נמי הכי אין חולקים את החצר עד שיהא בה שמונה אמות לזה ושמונה אמות לזה והא אנן תנן ארבע אמות לזה וארבע אמות לזה אלא ש"מ כדרבי אסי שמע מינה ואיכא דרמי להו מירמא תנן אין חולקין את החצר עד שיהא בה ארבע אמות לזה וארבע אמות לזה והתניא שמונה אמות לזה ושמונה אמות לזה א"ר אסי אמר ר' יוחנן ארבע אמות שאמרו חוץ משל פתחים אמר רב הונא חצר מתחלקת לפי פתחיה ורב חסדא אמר נותנין ארבע אמות לכל פתח ופתח והשאר חולקין בשוה תניא כוותיה דרב חסדא פתחים שבחצר יש להן ארבע אמות היה לזה פתח אחד ולזה שני פתחים זה שיש לו פתח אחד נוטל ארבע אמות וזה שיש לו שני פתחים נוטל שמונה אמות והשאר חולקין בשוה היה לזה פתח רחב שמונה אמות נוטל שמונה אמות כנגד הפתח וארבע אמות בחצר ארבע אמות בחצר מאי עבידתייהו אמר אביי הכי קאמר נוטל שמונה אמות באורך החצר וארבע אמות ברוחב החצר אמר אמימר האי פירא דסופלי יש לו ארבע אמות לכל רוח ורוח ולא אמרן אלא דלא מייחד ליה פתחא אבל

ולא את השדה עד שיהיה בה ט' קבין וכו'. אף על גב דבכל דהו מקרי שדה כדאמרינן בפרק האומר בקידושין (דף סא.) אין לי (ג) אלא בית כור זרע חומר שעורים מנין לרבות סאה ותלי סאה תרקב ותלי תרקב ת"ל שדה מ"מ אינו חשוב לטרוח לחרוש ולזרוע בפחות מט' קבין והא דאמר בסוף כתובות (דף קיב.) אמר ההוא מינא לר' חנינא יאות משבחיתו (ד) בארעייכו בית סאה הניח לי אבא ממנה משח [ממנה חמר] ממנה עיבור ממנה קטנית כו' התם היה במקום שמתברך ביותר:

מסורת הש"ס

א) [סנהדרין דף לז.], ב) [תוס' פאה פ"ד], ג) [לעיל ג:] סוכה ג., ד) [לקמן קג: כתובות לא.], ה) [לעיל ג.], ו) [לקמן יג: לעיל ג.], ז) [סוכה ג:]:

הגהות הב"ח

(א) רש"י ד"ה אפי' וכו' תני רישא יחלוקו הס"ד: (ב) ד"ה נותן לכל פתח ד' אמות להלן מן הפתח כנגדו והרוחב כפי רוחב הפתח כצ"ל ותיבת ברוחב החצר נמחק ואח"כ מ"ה הכי קאמר נוטל ח' אמות באורך החצר דהיינו וכו' מן הפתח כנגדו הס"ד: (ג) תוס' ד"ה ולא וכו' אין לי אלא זרע חומר שעורים בחמשים מנין לרבות לתך סאה תרקב כצ"ל ותיבת בית כור ותיבת ותלי סאה ותלי סאה נמחק: (ד) בא"ד משבחיתו לארעייכו:

תורה אור השלם

א) אֱמֶת מֵאֶרֶץ תִּצְמָח וְצֶדֶק מִשָּׁמַיִם נִשְׁקָף: [תהלים פה, יב]

ב) צֶדֶק וּמִשְׁפָּט מְכוֹן כִּסְאֶךָ חֶסֶד וֶאֱמֶת יְקַדְּמוּ פָנֶיךָ: [תהלים פט, טו]

ג) אִמְרוּ צַדִּיק כִּי טוֹב כִּי פְרִי מַעַלְלֵיהֶם יֹאכֵלוּ: [ישעיה ג, י]

ד) פְּרִי צַדִּיק עֵץ חַיִּים וְלֹקֵחַ נְפָשׁוֹת חָכָם: [משלי יא, ל]

ה) הָשֵׁב תָּשִׁיב לוֹ אֶת הָעֲבוֹט כְּבוֹא הַשֶּׁמֶשׁ וְשָׁכַב בְּשַׂלְמָתוֹ וּבֵרְכֶךָּ וּלְךָ תִּהְיֶה צְדָקָה לִפְנֵי יְיָ אֱלֹהֶיךָ: [דברים כד, יג]

ו) אָז יִבָּקַע כַּשַּׁחַר אוֹרֶךָ וַאֲרֻכָתְךָ מְהֵרָה תִצְמָח וְהָלַךְ לְפָנֶיךָ צִדְקֶךָ כְּבוֹד יְיָ יַאַסְפֶךָ: [ישעיה נח, ח]

ליקוטי רש"י

[תחילת לקוטי רש"י ששייך לכאן נדפס בדף י:] וכתבי הקדש. כגון תורה נביאים וכתובים [שבת קטו.]. ספר תורה שהוא בכרך אחד וכן נביאים וכתובים הכתובים בגליון כס"ת [לעיל ג.]. חצר מתחלקת לפי פתחיה. חצר שהיו בתים פתוחין לה ומלוקו שני אחין ביניהם זה נטל שלשה בתים קטנים וזה נטל כנגדן בית גדול אם באו לחלק אוירה של חצר זה שנטל שלשה בתים הקטנים נוטל שלשה חלקים כמנין שלשה פתחים וזה נוטל רביע לפי שהחצר עשוי ליציאה וביאה שדרך החצר נכנסין ויוצאין מן הבתים לרשות הרבים ומכניסין משאותיהן ופורקין לפני פתחיהם לפיכך חצר מתחלקת לפי הפתחים. ורב חסדא אמר. אין צריך ליתן לכל פתח אלא ד"א כנגדן מן הפתח והלאה ורחבן ברוחב הפתח ואפילו הוא רחב י' אמות נוטל ד' אמות במשך וכנגד כל רחבו לפרק משאו [סוכה ג:]. פירא דסופלי. חפירה העשויה להטיל שם גרעיני תמרים למאכל בהמות [קידושין עג:]. שוחה עמוקה ושם היו מניחין גרעיני התמרים לאכול השוורים. פירא. שוחה כמו פירא דכוורי במס' תענית (כז.) [עירובין כו.].

עין משפט נר מצוה

צד א מיי' פ"א מהל' רוצח ושמירת נפש הלכה טז:

צה ב ג ד מיי' פ"א מהל' שכנים הל' ד ופ"ב הלכה א סמג עשין פב טוש"ע ח"מ סי' קעא סעיף ג:

צו ה מיי' שם פ"א הל' ה סמג שם:

צז ו מיי' שם הל' ד סמג שם טוש"ע שם סעיף ג:

צח ז ח מיי' שם פ"ב הלכה ט סמג שם טוש"ע ח"מ סי' קעב סעיף א:

צט ט מיי' שם הל' א וסמג שם טוש"ע ח"מ סי' קעא סעיף ג:

ק י כ ל מיי' שם וסמג שם טוש"ע ח"מ סי' קעב סעיף א:

קא מ נ מיי' שם הל' ג טוש"ע שם ס"ג:

רבינו גרשום

לא סיימוה קמיה. דחילקו לעניי עובדי כוכבים דאין להם זכות בכך: מונבז ממלכי חשמונים היה: במקום שאין עושין פירות. שהממון המונח באוצר אינו מייתר כלום: אם קנה בה קרקע הראוי לבית דירה אע"פ שלא עשה בה דירה: פיס': ארבע אמות לזה וד' אמות לזה שאמרו בחצר חוץ משל פתחים דלכל פתח יש לו בחצר ד' אמות לפרק משאו. ועכשיו אם יהיה חצר ט"ז אמה דמטי לפתחים ח' ולחלוק ח' (חלקים) והיינו ח' אמות לכל אחד עם הפתח שלו: אמר רב הונא חצר מתחלקת לפי פתחיה. שאם הניח להם אביהן לזה בית אחד של ב' פתחים ולזה בית אחד של פתח אחד ולפני בתים הללו היתה חצר, מתחלקת אותה חצר לפי פתחיה וזה שיש לו ב' פתחים נוטל ב' ידות מן החצר וזה שאין לו אלא פתח אחד נוטל שליש דלפי שיש חזקה לזה טפי: ורב חסדא אמר ד' אמות לכל פתח ופתח. ולא כל שתי ידות החצר דאי מייתר מד' ד' לכל פתח חולקין בשוה: נוטל ח' אמות באורך החצר כנגד ח' אמות של רוחב הפתח וד' אמות ברוחב החצר כנגד הפתח כלומר דלא שקיל אלא (על) ח' ברוחב ד': פירא דסופלי אם הגיעם חצר אחרת גדולה ובתוך אותה חצר היתה פירא דסופלי חפירה שמשימין גרעיני תמרים לצורך מאכל בהמה והגיע ליורש אחד אותה פירא דסופלי. יש לו ד' אמות בחצר זה הואיל דעדיין לא נעשה פתח ודרך לאותה חפירה אמרינן דיש לו ד' אמות לכל רוח ליכנס באיזה רוח שירצה ולהשתמש ד' אמות לכל רוח: אלא שלא ייחד אביהן פתח. לאותה חפירא דסופלי: אבל וכו'. ל"א אם יש לאחד מן השותפים פירות דסופלי חריץ שמשימין בו תבן ומספוא לשוורים בהאי חצר נוטל ד' אמות לכל רוח של חריץ זו כלומר כשיעור תשמיש ועבודת טלטול החריץ לבד החלוקה שחולקין בשוה דיש לו ליטול לפי חזקה דאית ליה בתוך החצר. למורי הרב: [מכאן שייך לע"ב:] אכסדרה גג מקורה הקבוע על ד' קונדסין ופתוחה מכל צדדיה ואינה עשויה אלא לצל בעלמא כשחולקין את החצר למי שיגיע לו האכסדרה אין נוטל ד' אמות חוץ לאכסדרה כמו לפתח דטעמא מאי אמרו דנוטל ד' אמות כנגד פתחו בחצר כדי עבודת הפתח לפרק משאו מעל גבי בהמתו בהני ד' אמות דאינו רוצה לפרק ולטנף ביתו מזבל בהמתו אבל הכא באכסדרה זו הואיל שאין לה דפנות סביב אפשר לו דעייל באכסדרה זו (דבי בי רב שלומדין שם תלמידים שיש לה ג' דפנות) ומפרק דבלאו הכי נמי מטונפות מן הזבלים ומן הגשמים ולהכי אין צריכין ד' אמות: באכסדרה דבי רב שלומדין בה תלמידין שיש לה ג' דפנות עד הסכך (ופ') ודופן רביעית אינה מגעת לסכך משום שיהא אורה ופתח אותה אכסדרה יש לו ד' אמות ומקשינן אכסדרה דבי רב אידרונא חדר מעליא הוא ולא צריך למימר דיש לה ד' אמות: באכסדרה רומיתא דיש לה ג' מחיצות מגיעות לסכך ומחיצה רביעית נמוכה ובונין עליה על פני כולה חלונות גדולות על גבי פצימין כעין אותם שקורין קלוסטי"ר ופתח באמצעיות אותה מחיצה נמוכה ולאותו פתח יש לו ד' אמות אף על גב דיש הרבה סביב חלונות גדולות אבל לא לאכסדר' העומדת על קונדסין. (כלומר) בית שער יש לו ד' אמות במבוי מרפסת היינו עלייה שיש לה ד' פתחים או יותר בשורה אחת ועושין לפניהם נסר ארוך שרופסין עליו ולסוף אותו נסר סולם שיורדין בו לארץ ולפני אותו סולם יש פתח שנועל בעד המרפסת כל אותן ד' פתחים של עלייה אין להם בחצר אלא ד' אמות שלפני פתח הסולם שכולם יוצאין באותו פתח: לול של תרנגולים. ארובה של עלייה שמשימין דרך אותה ארובה תרנגולין לעלייה כלומר אם אין לאותן היורשין שום פתח לשם אלא לול של תרנגולין משום חזקת אותו לול אינו נוטל ד' אמות בחצר כמו לפתח דליכא התם משום פריקת משוי שהתרנגול מטפס ועולה (ניסרין). יש לו לאחד מן היורשין בית שחציו מקורה וחציו אינו מקורה. מי אמרי' כיון דחציו אינו מקורה יכול לפרק משאו באותו צד שאינו מקורה ואין לו ד' אמות בחצר או דילמא כיון דיש לו ד' מחיצות ופתח כשאר בית אע"פ שחציו אינו מקורה יש לו ד' אמות: לא מיבעיא. היכא דהוה אותו חצי (קורה) [קירוי] כלפי פנים הבית כלומר לאחורי הבית והא דאינו מקורה סמוך לחצר דאע"ג דאיכא פתח בית הפתוח לחצר דאינו נוטל ד' אמות בחצר מתוך דהכא מצי לפרק משאו בהאי חצי דאינו מקורה שסמוך לחצר אלא אע"פ אי הוה אותו חצי קירוי לצד חרץ סמוך לחצר ושאינו מקורה לצד אחורי הבית אפי' הכי אינו נוטל ד' אמות בחצר כנגד פתח הבית משום דיכול להכניס באותו חצי שאחורי הכותל שאינו מקורה ומפרק שם לחצר: פתחו למבוי אחר. שאם היה פתחו פתוח למבוי זה ואחרי פתחו איכא מבוי אחר ורוצה לסתום פתחו מיכן ולפותחו למבוי שאחורי ביתו: בני מבוי. שעכשיו רוצה לפתוח פתחו לשם יכולין לעכבו לצאת ולבוא דרך מבואן הואיל ועד עתה לא החזק באותו מבוי או לא. ותו בעא מיניה אכסניא. אכסנאין של מלך שעוברין בעיר ומחלקין אותן בבתי העיר ליתן להם לינה ופרנסה השתא בעי לפי בני מבוי שיש להם בתים לכל בית מחלקים או לפי פתחיה מחלקים שאם יש בבית ב' פתחים שיתנו לו ב' חלקים מן האכסנאין שיעור שני בתים: זבל שבחצר לפי פתחים מתחלק. שאם היו בבית ב' פתחים ולבית אחר פתח א' שמוציאין זבל ובאו לחלקן זה של שני פתחים נוטל פי שנים וחלק שלישי [נוטל האחר] לפי שיעור הפתחים היו מוציאים הזבל: לסתום כנגד פתחו. שכשם שיש לו לפתח ד' אמות בחצר כך יש לו לכל פתח חצר ד' אמות במבוי וזה בקש לסתום אותן ד' אמות שלו ולהקיפן בגדר בני מבוי שכניו מעכבין עליו שמרבה עליהן את הדרך להקיף אותו סתום (מבוי): ה' חצרות זו בצד זו הפתוחות למבוי אותה הסמוכה לרשות הרבים קרויה חיצונה ואותה שבסוף המבוי מצד אחר קרויה פנימית כולן הד' משתמשות עם חיצונית. כלומר דיש לכולן רשות לעבור לפני פתח החיצונה והחיצונה משתמשת לעצמה. שרשאה לסתום כנגד פתחה הד' אמות ולהשתמש בתוכן. והם. הני השאר משתמשות עם השניה שעוברין לפני פתחיה ושניה משתמשת לעצמה. שרשאה לסתום ד' אמות נגד פתחה ומשתמשת עם החיצונה שמקפת ד' אמות ויוצאת לחוץ. נמצאת הפנימית שבמבוי שהיא משתמש' עם כולן שעוברת עליהן ומשתמשת לעצמה קשיא לרב הונא:

SHALL BE GOOD, FOR THEY SHALL EAT THE FRUIT OF THEIR (good) ***DEEDS.***[14]

Munbaz continued:

אֲבוֹתַי גָּנְזוּ אוֹצָרוֹת מָמוֹן – **MY FATHERS HOARDED STORES OF MONEY,** וַאֲנִי גָּנַזְתִּי אוֹצָרוֹת נְפָשׁוֹת – **AND I HAVE HOARDED STORES OF SOULS** (i.e. those people whom I have preserved through my gifts of charity), שֶׁנֶּאֱמַר: ,,פְּרִי־צַדִּיק עֵץ חַיִּים וְלֹקֵחַ נְפָשׁוֹת חָכָם" – **AS IT IS STATED:**[15] ***THE FRUIT OF THE RIGHTEOUS IS A TREE OF LIFE; AND ONE WHO ACQUIRES SOULS IS WISE.***

Another advantage of charity:

אֲבוֹתַי גָּנְזוּ לַאֲחֵרִים – **MY FATHERS HOARDED** their wealth **FOR OTHERS** to use, וַאֲנִי גָּנַזְתִּי לְעַצְמִי – **BUT I HAVE HOARDED** the reward for my charitable deeds **FOR MYSELF,** שֶׁנֶּאֱמַר: ,,וּלְךָ תִּהְיֶה צְדָקָה" – **AS IT IS STATED:**[16] ***AND FOR YOU IT SHALL BE CHARITY.***

Munbaz's final comment:

אֲבוֹתַי גָּנְזוּ לָעוֹלָם הַזֶּה – **MY FATHERS HOARDED** wealth **FOR THIS WORLD,** וַאֲנִי גָּנַזְתִּי לָעוֹלָם הַבָּא – **AND I HAVE HOARDED** merits **FOR THE WORLD TO COME,** שֶׁנֶּאֱמַר: ,,וְהָלַךְ לְפָנֶיךָ צִדְקֶךָ כְּבוֹד ה' יַאַסְפֶךָ" – **AS IT IS STATED:**[17] ***AND YOUR CHARITY SHALL GO BEFORE YOU, AND THE GLORY OF GOD SHALL BE YOUR REWARD.***[18]

Thus concludes Munbaz's recital of the advantages of giving charity over the hoarding of wealth.

The Mishnah had stated:

וְאִם קָנָה בָּהּ בֵּית דִּירָה הֲרֵי הוּא כְּאַנְשֵׁי הָעִיר – **AND IF HE BOUGHT A HOUSE** in the city, **HE IS IMMEDIATELY** treated **LIKE** one of **THE CITIZENS OF THE CITY** and must help bear the municipal expenses mentioned in the Mishnah.

The Gemara cites a dissenting view:

מַתְנִיתִין – **Our Mishnah,** which states that only the purchase of a fully constructed house immediately accords the buyer the status of a citizen, דְּלָא כְּרַבָּן שִׁמְעוֹן בֶּן גַּמְלִיאֵל – **does not accord with** the view of **Rabban Shimon ben Gamliel,** דְּתַנְיָא – **for it was taught in a Baraisa:** רַבָּן שִׁמְעוֹן בֶּן גַּמְלִיאֵל אוֹמֵר – **RABBAN SHIMON BEN GAMLIEL SAYS:** אִם קָנָה בָּהּ קַרְקַע כָּל שֶׁהוּא – **IF ONE PURCHASED** even **THE SLIGHTEST** parcel of **LAND IN** [**THE CITY**],[19] הֲרֵי הוּא כְּאַנְשֵׁי הָעִיר – **HE IS** treated **LIKE** one of **THE CITIZENS OF THE CITY.** Rabban Shimon maintains that *any* purchase of real estate – no matter how small – indicates the buyer's intent to remain in the city – and that it is this intent that qualifies him for citizen status.

The Gemara quotes a conflicting Baraisa:

וְהָא תַּנְיָא רַבָּן שִׁמְעוֹן בֶּן גַּמְלִיאֵל אוֹמֵר – **But it was taught in** another **Baraisa: RABBAN SHIMON BEN GAMLIEL SAYS:** אִם קָנָה שָׁם קַרְקַע הָרְאוּיָה לְבֵית דִּירָה – **IF ONE PURCHASED THERE** in the city a parcel of **LAND SUITABLE FOR** constructing **A HOUSE** upon it, הֲרֵי הוּא כְּאַנְשֵׁי הָעִיר – **HE IS** treated **LIKE** one of **THE CITIZENS OF THE CITY.** In this Baraisa Rabban Shimon rules that the purchase of a minuscule parcel of land would not qualify the buyer for citizen status, for there is no indication that he actually intends to reside in the city.[20] Thus, there are two conflicting rulings, both attributed to Rabban Shimon ben Gamliel. – ? –

The Gemara explains:

תְּרֵי תַּנָּאֵי – The two Baraisos present the rulings of **two Tannaim,** וְאַלִּיבָּא דְּרַבָּן שִׁמְעוֹן בֶּן גַּמְלִיאֵל – **and** each Tanna taught **according to** the opinion of **Rabban Shimon ben Gamliel** as he understood it.

Mishnah

This Mishnah is the source of the ruling (discussed above, 3a) that prohibits the forced division of jointly owned property if each partner does not receive a share that performs the function of the whole. The Mishnah applies the ruling to various types of property:

אֵין חוֹלְקִין אֶת הֶחָצֵר – **We do not divide a** jointly owned **courtyard** against the will of one partner עַד שֶׁיְּהֵא אַרְבַּע אַמּוֹת לָזֶה וְאַרְבַּע אַמּוֹת לָזֶה – **unless there are four *amos* for this** partner **and four *amos* for that** partner.[21] וְלֹא אֶת הַשָּׂדֶה – **And** we do **not** divide **a grain field** עַד שֶׁיְּהֵא בָהּ תִּשְׁעָה קַבִּין לָזֶה וְתִשְׁעָה קַבִּין לָזֶה – **unless there are nine *kavs* for this** partner **and nine *kavs* for that** partner.[22] רַבִּי יְהוּדָה אוֹמֵר – **R' Yehudah says:** We do not divide a grain field עַד שֶׁיְּהֵא בָהּ תִּשְׁעַת חֲצָיֵי קַבִּין לָזֶה וְתִשְׁעַת חֲצָיֵי קַבִּין לָזֶה – **unless there are nine half-*kavs* for this** partner **and nine half-*kavs* for that** partner.[23] וְלֹא אֶת הַגִּינָּה – **Nor** do we divide **a** vegetable **garden** עַד שֶׁיְּהֵא בָהּ חֲצִי קַב לָזֶה וַחֲצִי קַב לָזֶה – **unless there is a half-*kav* for this** partner **and a half-*kav* for that** partner.[24] רַבִּי עֲקִיבָא אוֹמֵר בֵּית רוֹבַע – **R' Akiva says:** It is enough if each partner receives **a quarter-*kav*.**[25]

The Mishnah now mentions other divisible properties:

וְלֹא אֶת הַטְּרַקְלִין וְלֹא אֶת הַמּוֹרָן – **And** we divide **not a salon, nor a hall,**[26] וְלֹא אֶת הַשּׁוֹבָךְ וְלֹא אֶת הַטַּלִּית – **nor a**

NOTES

14. Charity and kind deeds are among the few mitzvos that produce "fruits" (i.e. blessings) to be enjoyed in this world, even as the principal reward for their performance remains intact in the World to Come (*Rashi;* see *Kiddushin* 39b).

15. *Proverbs* 11:30. Most commentators understand that the verse speaks of righteous men who inspire others by word and deed to follow the ways of God. Munbaz understands that it refers to those who, through their gifts of charity, *acquire* merit by preserving the lives of their fellow Jews (see note 13 above).

16. *Deuteronomy* 24:13. On the simple level, the verse teaches that returning collateral for a debtor's nocturnal use is considered a charitable act. Munbaz interprets homiletically that the reward for charitable acts in general will be reserved exclusively "for you" – the one who performs them.

17. *Isaiah* 58:8.

18. The verse mentions two of the six rewards of charity stated in the Gemara above (9b). "God's glory" refers to the Divine Presence, which is revealed in the World to Come.

19. I.e. even one unsuitable for building a house upon it.

20. Where, however, the tract is large enough to accommodate a house, there is a reasonable assumption that he plans to build and settle down.

21. Each partner must receive an area measuring four *amos* by four *amos.* This is the minimum area needed for basic courtyard uses. The Gemara below explains that additional space (of 4x4 *amos*) must be available for unloading animals.

22. I.e. each partner must be left with a plot of land large enough to plant nine *kavs* of seed in it. Any lesser area is too small to be worth the effort of plowing and sowing (*Tosafos*).

A *kav* is one-sixth of a *se'ah*, which is the amount of seed planted in an area 50 by 50 *amos.* Thus, nine *kavs* is 1.5 *se'ah*, and an area large enough for planting nine *kavs* is 3,750 square *amos* (*Yad Ramah, Tos. Yom Tov*).

23. Although R' Yehudah's minimum share is half that of the Tanna Kamma, the Gemara will explain that the two opinions do not conflict.

24. A vegetable garden requires less work and yields more per *kav* of seed than does a grain field. Thus, even a parcel for one half-*kav* of seed can be cultivated profitably.

A half-*kav* translates to 208 1/3 square *amos* (approx. 650 square feet).

25. A quarter-*kav* translates to 104 1/6 square *amos.* Rishonim dispute whether or not R' Akiva takes issue with the Tanna Kamma (see *Nimukei Yosef* and *Yad Ramah* to 12a).

26. Various types of chambers in a palace. From *Rashbam* below, 98b it appears that a *traklin* was used as a meeting place for officers.

דלא סיימוה קמיה. דר' אמי לעניי עובדי כוכבים חלקן רבא והנך דאמרן לעיל (דף ח.) דשדרה נמי איפרא הורמיז למלוה רבה משום שלום מלכות נמי קבלינהו ולא אפשר ליה לחלקן לעניי עובדי כוכבים דאסור לגנוב דעת הבריות ואפילו דעתו של עובד כוכבים אבל במעות המתחלקות לעניים אין גניבת דעת דאינהו נמי ידעי שישראל רגילים לפרנס עניי עובדי כוכבים כדאמרי' במס' גיטין (דף סא.) מפרנסין עניי עובדי כוכבים עם עניי ישראל מפני דרכי שלום: **אתה אמרת כו'.** מתורתך למדנו לפיכך נברא אדם יחידי לומר לך כל המקיים נפש אחת [מישראל] כאילו קיים העולם מלא וכתיב (בראשית ד) קול דמי אחיך דמו ודם זרעותיו אף כשאתה מקיים דמי אחיך עמך מעלה עליך חייו וחיי זרעותיו שמדה טובה מרובה ממדת פורעניות: **מונבז המלך.** בנה של הילני המלכה מזרע החשמונאים: **כשאמת מארץ תצמח.** אף משמים נשקף הצדק לשלם גמול: **נשקף.** מביט כמו ונשקפה (שופטים ה) כלומר זכות וחייב הצדקה מביט ומסתכל למטה: **מכון כסאך.** גנוזין תחת מכון הכסא: **(במקום) [דבר] שעושה פירות.** והקרן קיים לעוה"ב והפירות אוכל בחייו שנאמר כי פרי מעלליהם יאכלו: **אוצרות נפשות.** שנאמר ולוקח נפשות חכם בהאי קרא: **מתני' טרקלין ומורן.** מיני פלטין: **בית השלחין.** מתוך שיש לו מעיין ודלו להשקותו תדיר אם אין בו ט' קבין זורעין בו שאר זרעים לפיכך אפילו בפחות מכאן יש בו דין חלוקה: **אפילו בפחות מכאן יחלוקו.** משום דבעי למיתני וכתבי הקדש אע"פ ששניהם רוצים לא יחלוקו תני רישא (א): **כתבי הקדש.** כ"ד ספרים והיו רגילים לכותבן בגליון כס"ת שלנו לפיכך גנאי הדבר לחתכן: **גמ' חוץ משל פתחים.** חצר של שניהם שני בתים פתוחין לתוכה ולפני הפתח ארבע אמות לאורך הבית הן לפרק משאו מעל חמורו וחוץ מאותן ד' אמות צריך שיהא ארבע אמות לשאר תשמישין: **חצר מתחלקת לפתחי'.** היתה לו חצר וזה שני בתים ואחד מהן פתוחין לו שני פתחים לחצר ולבית השני אין פתוח לחצר אלא פתח אחד והולך נכסיו על פיו ונותן האחד לראובן בנו והשני לשמעון ואת החצר לא חילק אם באו לחלוק את החצר זה שיש לו שני פתחים נוטל שני חלקים בחצר ואחיו נוטל חלק אחד: **נותן לכל פתח** (ב) **ד' אמות.** כנגד החצר להלן מן הפתח כנגד הרוחב כפי רוחב הפתח: **נוטל שמונה אמות.** דהיינו כנגד רוחב הפתח ולארבע אמות ברוחב החצר להלן מן הפתח: **האי פירא דסופלי.** מי שיש לו חפירה בחצר שנותנין בה גרעיני תמרים למאכל בהמה יש לו ארבע אמות בחצר לכל סביבותיה: **דלא מייחד ליה פיתחא.** שלא היה לו פתח אבל חפירה אלא דרך פתח ביתו שהוא יוצא ונכנס בו היה לו דרך לצאת לחצר ולילך אחר החפירה שלפני סוף ביתו ומשתמש: אבל

דלא סיימוה קמיה תניא אמרו עליו על בנימין הצדיק שהיה ממונה על קופה של צדקה פעם אחת באתה אשה לפניו בשני בצורת אמרה לו רבי פרנסני אמר לה העבודה שאין בקופה של צדקה כלום אמרה לו רבי אם אין אתה מפרנסני הרי אשה ושבעה בניה מתים עמד ופרנסה משלו לימים חלה ונטה למות אמרו מלאכי השרת לפני הקב"ה רבש"ע אתה אמרת כל המקיים נפש אחת מישראל כאילו קיים עולם מלא ובנימין הצדיק שהחיה אשה ושבעה בניה ימות בשנים מועטות הללו מיד קרעו לו גזר דינו תנא הוסיפו לו עשרים ושתים שנה על שנותיו ת"ר מעשה במונבז המלך שבזבז אוצרותיו ואוצרות אבותיו בשני בצורת וחברו עליו אחיו ובית אביו ואמרו לו אבותיך גנזו והוסיפו על של אבותם ואתה מבזבזם אמר להם אבותי גנזו למטה ואני גנזתי למעלה שנאמר א) אמת מארץ תצמח וצדק משמים נשקף אבותי גנזו במקום שהיד שולטת בו ואני גנזתי במקום שאין היד שולטת בו שנאמר ב) צדק ומשפט מכון כסאך אבותי גנזו דבר שאין עושה פירות ואני גנזתי דבר שעושה פירות שנאמר ג) אמרו צדיק כי טוב כי פרי מעלליהם יאכלו אבותי גנזו [אוצרות] ממון ואני גנזתי אוצרות נפשות שנאמר ד) פרי צדיק עץ חיים ולוקח נפשות חכם אבותי גנזו לאחרים ואני גנזתי לעצמי שנאמר ה) ולך תהיה צדקה אבותי גנזו לעולם הזה ואני גנזתי לעולם הבא שנאמר ו) והלך לפניך צדקך כבוד ה' יאספך: ואם קנה בה בית דירה הרי הוא כאנשי העיר: מתניתין דלא כרשב"ג דתניא רבן שמעון ב"ג אומר אם קנה בה קרקע כל שהוא הרי הוא כאנשי העיר והא תניא רבן שמעון בן גמליאל אומר אם קנה שם קרקע הראויה לבית דירה הרי הוא כאנשי העיר תרי תנאי ואליבא דרבן שמעון בן גמליאל: **מתני'** אין חולקין את החצר עד שיהא ארבע אמות לזה וארבע אמות לזה ולא את השדה עד שיהא בה תשעה קבין לזה ותשעה קבין לזה ר' יהודה אומר עד שיהא בה תשעת חצאי קבין לזה ותשעת חצאי קבין לזה ולא את הגינה עד שיהא בה חצי קב לזה וחצי קב לזה ר' עקיבא אומר בית רובע ולא את הטרקלין ולא את המורן ולא את השובך ולא את הטלית ולא את המרחץ ולא את בית הבד ולא את בית השלחין עד שיהא בהן כדי לזה וכדי לזה זה הכלל כל שיחלק ושמו עליו חולקין ואם לאו אין חולקין אימתי בזמן שאין שניהם רוצים אבל בזמן ששניהם רוצים אפי' פחות מכאן יחלוקו וכתבי הקדש אע"פ ששניהם רוצים לא יחלוקו: **גמ'** א"ר אסי א"ר יוחנן ארבע אמות שאמרו חוץ משל פתחים תניא נמי הכי אין חולקים את החצר עד שיהא בה שמונה אמות לזה ושמונה אמות לזה והא אנן תנן ארבע אמות לזה וארבע אמות לזה אלא ש"מ כדרבי אסי שמע מינה ואיכא דרמי להו מירמא תנן אין חולקין את החצר עד שיהא בה ארבע אמות לזה וארבע אמות לזה והתניא שמונה אמות לזה ושמונה אמות לזה א"ר אסי אמר ר' יוחנן ארבע אמות שאמרו חוץ משל פתחים אמר רב הונא חצר מתחלקת לפי פתחיה ורב חסדא אמר נותנין ארבע אמות לכל פתח ופתח והשאר חולקין בשוה תניא כוותיה דרב חסדא פתחים שבחצר יש להן ארבע אמות היה לזה פתח אחד ולזה שני פתחים זה שיש לו פתח אחד נוטל ארבע אמות וזה שיש לו שני פתחים נוטל שמונה אמות והשאר חולקין בשוה היה לזה פתח רחב שמונה אמות נוטל שמונה אמות כנגד הפתח וארבע אמות בחצר ארבע אמות בחצר מאי עבידתייהו אמר אביי הכי קאמר נוטל שמונה אמות באורך החצר וארבע אמות ברוחב החצר אמר אמימר האי פירא דסופלי יש לו ארבע אמות לכל רוח ורוח ולא אמרן אלא דלא מייחד ליה פתחא אבל

ולא את השדה עד שיהיה בה ט' קבין וכו'. אף על גב דבכל דהו מקרי שדה כדאמרינן בפרק האומר בקידושין (דף סא.) אין לי (ג) אלא בית כור זרע חומר שעורים מנין לרבות סאה וחצי סאה תרקב וחצי תרקב ת"ל שדה מ"מ אינו חשוב לטרוח לחרוש ולזרוע בפחות מט' קבין והא דאמר בסוף כתובות (דף קיב.) אמר ההוא מינא לר' חנינא יתות משבחתיו (ד) בארעייכו בית סאה הניח לי אבא ממנה משח [ממנה חמר] ממנה עיבור ממנה קטנית כו' התם היה במקום שמתברך ביותר: הכל

מסורת הש"ס

א) [סנהדרין דף לז.], ב) [תוס' פאה פ"ד], ג) [לעיל ב:] סוכה ג., ד) [לקמן קב: כתובות קח.], ה) [עיין לעיל ג.], ו) [לקמן יג: לעיל ג.], ז) [סוכה ג:]

הגהות הב"ח

(א) רש"י ד"ה אפי' וכו' תני רישא יחלוקו הס"ד: (ב) ד"ה נותן לכל פתח ד' אמות להלן מן הפתח כנגדו ורוחבו כפי רוחב הפתח ומיהת ברוחב החצר נמחק ואח"כ מ"ה הכי קאמר נוטל ח' אמות באורך החצר דהיינו וכו' מן הפתח כנגדו הס"ד: (ג) תוס' ד"ה ולא וכו' אין לי אלא זרע חומר שעורים בחמשים מנין לרבות לתך סאה תרקב כצ"ל ותיבת בית כור ותיבת סאה נמחק: (ד) בא"ד משבחתיו לארעייכו:

תורה אור השלם

א) אֱמֶת מֵאֶרֶץ תִּצְמָח וְצֶדֶק מִשָּׁמַיִם נִשְׁקָף: [תהלים פה, יב]

ב) צֶדֶק וּמִשְׁפָּט מְכוֹן כִּסְאֶךָ חֶסֶד וֶאֱמֶת יְקַדְּמוּ פָנֶיךָ: [תהלים פט, טו]

ג) אִמְרוּ צַדִּיק כִּי טוֹב כִּי פְרִי מַעַלְלֵיהֶם יֹאכֵלוּ: [ישעיה ג, י]

ד) פְּרִי צַדִּיק עֵץ חַיִּים וְלֹקֵחַ נְפָשׁוֹת חָכָם: [משלי יא, ל]

ה) הָשֵׁב תָּשִׁיב לוֹ אֶת הָעֲבוֹט כְּבוֹא הַשֶּׁמֶשׁ וְשָׁכַב בְּשַׂלְמָתוֹ וּבֵרְכֶךָּ וּלְךָ תִּהְיֶה צְדָקָה לִפְנֵי יְיָ אֱלֹהֶיךָ: [דברים כד, יג]

ו) אָז יִבָּקַע כַּשַּׁחַר אוֹרֶךָ וַאֲרֻכָתְךָ מְהֵרָה תִצְמָח וְהָלַךְ לְפָנֶיךָ צִדְקֶךָ כְּבוֹד יְיָ יַאַסְפֶךָ: [ישעיה נח, ח]

ליקוטי רש"י

[תחילת לקוטי רש"י ששייך לכאן נדפס בדף י:] **וכתבי הקדש.** כגון תורה נביאים וכתובים [שבת קטז.]. ספר תורה שהוא בכרך אחד וכן נביאים וכתובים הכתובים בכרך אחד כס"ת [לעיל ג.]. **חצר מתחלקת לפי פתחיה.** חצר שהיו בתים פתוחים לה ולחלקו שני אחים ביניהם זה נטל שלשה בתים קטנים וזה נטל כנגדן בית גדול אחד אם באו לחלק חלוקת החצר זה שנטל שלשה בתים קטנים נוטל שלשה חלקים כמנין שלשה פתחים וזה נוטל רביע לפי שהחצר עשוי ליציאה וביאה שדרך החצר נכנסין ויוצאין מן הבתים לרשות הרבים ומכניסין משאויהן ופורקין לפני פתחיהם לפיכך חצר מתחלקת לפי הפתחים. **ורב חסדא אמר.** אין צריך ליתן לכל פתח אלא ד"א כנגדן מן הפתח והלאה ורחבן ברוחב הפתח ואפילו הוא רחב י' אמות נוטל ד' אמות במשך וכנגד כל רחבו לפרק משאו [סוכה ג:]. **פירא דסופלי.** חפירה העשויה להטיל שם גרעיני תמרים למאכל בהמות [קידושין עג:]. גומא עמוקה ושם היו מניחין גרעיני התמרים לאכול השוורים. **פירא.** גומא כמו פירא דכוורי במס' תענית (כד.) [עירובין כו.].

עין משפט נר מצוה

צד א מיי' פ"א מהל' רוצח ושמירת נפש הלכה טז:

צה ב ג ד מיי' פ"א מהל' שכנים הל' ד ופ"ב הלכה א סמג עשין פב טוש"ע ח"מ סי' קעא סעיף ג:

צו ה מיי' שם פ"א הל' ה סמג שם:

צז ו מיי' שם הל' ד סמג שם טוש"ע שם סעיף ג:

צח ז ח מיי' שם פ"ב הלכה ט סמג שם טוש"ע ח"מ סי' קעג סעיף א:

צט ט מיי' פ"א שם הל' א וסמג שם טוש"ע ח"מ סי' קעא סעיף ג:

ק י כ ל מיי' שם וסמג שם טוש"ע ח"מ סי' קעג סעיף א:

קא מ נ מיי' שם הל' ג טוש"ע שם ס"ג:

רבינו גרשום

לא סיימוה קמיה. דחילקו לעניי עובדי כוכבים דאין להם זכות בכך: **מונבז** ממלכי חשמונאים היה: **במקום שאין עושין פירות.** שהממון המונח באוצר אינו מייתר כלום: **אם קנה בה קרקע** הראוי לבית דירה אע"פ שלא עשה בה דירה: **פיס: ארבע אמות** לזה וד' אמות לזה שאמרו בחצר חוץ משל פתחים לכל פתח יש לו בחצר ד' אמות לפרק משאו. ועכשיו אם יהיה חצר ט"ז אמה דמטי לפתחים ח' ולחלוק ח' (חלקים) והיינו ח' אמות לכל אחד עם הפתח שלו: **אמר רב הונא חצר מתחלקת לפי פתחיה.** שאם הניח להם אביהן לזה בית אחד של ב' פתחים ולזה בית אחד של פתח אחד ולפני בתים הללו היתה חצר מתחלקת אותה חצר לפי פתחיה וזה שיש לו ב' פתחים נוטל ב' ידות מן החצר וזה שאין לו אלא פתח אחד נוטל שליש דלפי שיש חזקה לזה טפי: **ורב חסדא אמר ד' אמות לכל פתח ופתח.** ולא כל שתי ידות החצר דאי מייתר מד' ד' לכל פתח **חולקין בשוה.** נוטל ח' אמות באורך החצר כנגד ח' אמות של רוחב הפתח וד' אמות ברוחב החצר כנגד הפתח כלומר דלא שקיל אלא (על) ח' ברוחב ד': **פירא דסופלי** אם הגיעם חצר אחרת גדולה ובתוך אותה חצר היתה פירא דסופלי חפירה שמשימין גרעיני תמרים לצורך מאכל בהמה הגיע ליורש אחד אותה פירא דסופלי. **יש לו ד' אמות** בחצר זה הואיל דעדיין לא נעשה פתח ודרך לאותה חפירה אמרינן דיש לו ד' אמות לכל רוח ליכנס באיזה רוח שירצה ולהשתמש ד' אמות לכל רוח: **אלא שלא ייחד אביהן פתח.** לאותה חפירא דסופלי: **אבל וכו'.** ל"א אם יש לאחד מן השותפים פירות דסופלי חריץ שמשימין בו תבן ומספוא לשוורים בהאי חצר **נוטל ד' אמות לכל רוח** של חריץ זו כלומר כשיעור תשמיש ועבודת טלטול החריץ לבד החלוקה שחולקין בשווה דיש לו ליטול לפי חזקה דאית ליה בתוך החצר. למורי הרב: [מכאן שייך לע"ב:] **אכסדרה** גג מקורה הקבוע על ד' קונדסין ופתוחה מכל צדדיה ואינה עשויה אלא לצל בעלמא כשחולקין את החצר למי שיגיע לו האכסדרה **אין נוטל ד' אמות** חוץ לאכסדרה כמו לפתח **דטעמא מאי** אמרו דנוטל ד' אמות כנגד פתחו בחצר כדי עבודת הפתח **לפרק משאו** מעל גבי בהמתו בהני ד' אמות דאינו רוצה ללכלך ולטנף ביתו מזבל בהמתו אבל **הכא** באכסדרה זו הואיל שאין לה דפנות סביב **אפשר לו דעייל** באכסדרה זו (דבי בי רב שלומדין שם תלמידים שיש לה ג' דפנות) **ומפרק** דבלאו הכי נמי מטונפות מן הזבלים ומן הגשמים ולהכי אין צריכין ד' אמות: **באכסדרה דבי רב** שלומדין בה תלמידין שיש לה ג' דפנות עד הסכך (ופ') ודופן רביעית אינה מגעת לסכך משום שיהא אורה ופתח אותה אכסדרה יש לו ד' אמות **ומקשינן אכסדרה דבי רב אידרונא** חדר **מעליא הוא** ולא צריך למימר דיש לה ד' אמות: **באכסדרה רומייתא** דיש לה ג' מחיצות מגיעות לסכך ומחיצה רביעית נמוכה ובונין עליה על פני כולה חלונות גדולות על גבי פצימין כעין אותם שקורין קלושטי"ר ופתח באמצעיות אותה מחיצה נמוכה ולאותו פתח יש לו ד' אמות אף על גב דיש הרבה סביב חלונות גדולות אבל לא לאכסדר' העומדת על קונדסין. (כלומר) **בית שער** יש לו ד' אמות במבוי **מרפסת** היינו עלייה **שיש לה ד' פתחים או יותר** בשורה אחת ועושין לפניהם נסר ארוך שרופסין עליו ולסוף אותו נסר סולם שיורדין בו לארץ ולפני אותו סולם יש פתח שנועל בעד המרפסת כל אותן ד' פתחים של עלייה **אין להם** בחצר **אלא ד' אמות** שלפני פתח הסולם שכולם יוצאין באותו פתח: **לול של תרנגולים.** ארובה של עלייה שמשימין דרך אותה ארובה תרנגולין לעלייה כלומר אם אין לאותן היורשין שום פתח לשם אלא לול של תרנגולין משום חזקת אותו לול **אינו נוטל ד' אמות** בחצר כמו לפתח דליכא התם משום פריקת משוי שהתרנגול מטפס ועולה (ניסרין). יש לו לאחד מן היורשין בית שחציו מקורה וחציו אינו מקורה. מי אמרי' כיון דחציו אינו מקורה יכול לפרק משאו באותו צד שאינו מקורה **ואין לו ד' אמות** בחצר או דילמא כיון דיש לו ד' מחיצות ופתח כשאר בית אע"פ שחציו אינו מקורה **יש לו ד' אמות: לא מיבעיא.** היכא דהוה אותו חצי (קורה) **[קירוי] כלפי פנים** הבית כלומר לאחורי הבית והא דאינו מקורה סמוך לחצר דאע"ג דאיכא פתח בית הפתוח לחצר דאינו נוטל ד' אמות בחצר מתוך **דהכא מצי לפרק משאו** בהאי חצי דאינו מקורה שסמוך לחצר **אלא אע"פ** אי הוה אותו חצי קירוי לצד חרץ סמוך לחצר ושאינו מקורה לצד אחורי הבית אפי' הכי אינו נוטל ד' אמות בחצר כנגד פתח הבית משום דיכול להכניס באותו חצי שאחורי הכותל שאינו מקורה ומפרק שם לחצר: **פתחו למבוי אחר.** שאם היה פתחו פתוח למבוי זה ואחרי פתחו איכא מבוי אחר ורוצה לסתום פתחו מיכן ולפותחו למבוי שאחורי ביתו: **בני מבוי.** שעכשיו רוצה לפתוח פתחו לשם **יכולין לעכבו** לצאת ולבוא דרך מבואן הואיל ועד עתה לא הוחזק באותו מבוי או לא. ותו בעא מיניה **אכסניא.** אכסנאין של מלך שעוברין בעיר ומחלקין אותן בבתי העיר ליתן להם לינה ופרנסה השתא בעי **לפי בני מבוי** שיש להם בתים לכל בית מחלקים **או לפי פתחיה מחלקים** שאם יש בבית ב' פתחים שיתנו לו ב' חלקים מן האכסנאין שיעור שני בתים: **זבל שבחצר לפי פתחים מתחלק.** שאם היו בבית ב' פתחים ולבית אחר פתח א' שמוציאין זבל ובאו לחלקן זה של שני פתחים נוטל פי שנים וחלק שלישי [נוטל האחר] לפי שיעור הפתחים היו מוציאים הזבל: **לסתום כנגד פתחו.** שכשם שיש לו לפתח ד' אמות בחצר כך יש לו לכל פתח חצר ד' אמות במבוי וזה בקש לסתום אותן ד' אמות שלו ולהקיפן בגדר **בני מבוי** שכניו **מעכבין עליו שמרבה עליהן את הדרך** להקיף אותו סתום (מבוי): **ה' חצרות** זו בצד זו **הפתוחות למבוי** אותה הסמוכה לרשות הרבים קרויה חיצונה ואותה שבסוף המבוי מצד אחר קרויה פנימית **כולן** הד' **משתמשות עם חיצונית.** כלומר דיש לכולן רשות לעבור לפני פתח החיצונה **והחיצונה משתמשת לעצמה.** שרשאה לסתום כנגד פתחה הד' אמות ולהשתמש בתוכן. **והם.** הני השאר **משתמשות עם השניה** שעוברין לפני פתחיה **ושניה משתמשת לעצמה.** שרשאה לסתום ד' אמות נגד פתחה **ומשתמשת עם החיצונה** שמקפת ד' אמות ויוצאת לחוץ. **נמצאת הפנימית** שבמבוי שהיא **משתמש' עם כולן** שעוברת עליהן **ומשתמשת לעצמה** קשיא לרב הונא:

dovecote, nor a cloak, וְלֹא אֶת הַמֶּרְחָץ וְלֹא אֶת בֵּית הַבַּד וְלֹא אֶת בֵּית הַשְּׁלָחִין – **nor a bathhouse, nor the place that houses an olive press, nor an irrigated field**[27] against one partner's will עַד שֶׁיְּהֵא בָּהֶן כְּדֵי לָזֶה וּכְדֵי לָזֶה – **unless there will be enough for this** partner **and enough for that** partner.[28]

The Mishnah provides a guideline for determining if property is large enough to divide:

זֶה הַכְּלָל – **This is the general rule:** כָּל שֶׁיֵּחָלֵק וּשְׁמוֹ עָלָיו חולקין – **Anything that is divided and retains its name,**[29] **we divide.** וְאִם לָאו אֵין חולקין – **But if not, we do not divide** it, since each share does not perform the function of the whole.

The Mishnah qualifies the previous rulings:

אֵימָתַי – **When** does the general rule concerning the division of property apply? בִּזְמַן שֶׁאֵין שְׁנֵיהֶם רוֹצִים – **When they do not both consent** to divide. אֲבָל בִּזְמַן שֶׁשְּׁנֵיהֶם רוֹצִים – **But when both** partners **consent** to divide, אֲפִילּוּ פָּחוֹת מִכָּאן יַחֲלוֹקוּ – **they may divide even** property that is **smaller than [the minimum standards]** mentioned above.[30]

However, in one instance division is forbidden even when both partners consent:

וְכִתְבֵי הַקֹּדֶשׁ אַף עַל פִּי שֶׁשְּׁנֵיהֶם רוֹצִים לֹא יַחֲלוֹקוּ – **But [partners] may not divide** scrolls of **the Holy Scriptures**[31] **even if both consent** to do so, for cutting them is a disgraceful act.[32]

Gemara The Gemara elaborates on the Mishna's ruling on the division of a courtyard:

אָמַר רַבִּי אַסִּי אָמַר רַבִּי יוֹחָנָן – **R' Assi said in the name of R' Yochanan:** אַרְבַּע אַמּוֹת שֶׁאָמְרוּ – **The four** ***amos*** by four *amos* **that [the Mishnah] said** was the minimum size for each share of a divided courtyard חוּץ מִשֶּׁל פְּתָחִים – **excludes** the area **of the entrances.**[33] Each partner must receive an additional four *amos* in front of the width of entrance to serve as an unloading area.

The Gemara adduces support for R' Assi's ruling:

תַּנְיָא נַמִּי הָכִי – **A Baraisa also taught thus:** אֵין חולקים אֶת הֶחָצֵר – **WE DO NOT DIVIDE** a jointly owned **COURTYARD** against one partner's will עַד שֶׁיְּהֵא בָּהּ שְׁמוֹנֶה אַמּוֹת לָזֶה וּשְׁמוֹנֶה אַמּוֹת לָזֶה – **UNLESS THERE WILL BE EIGHT** ***AMOS*** **FOR THIS** partner **AND EIGHT** ***AMOS*** **FOR THAT** partner after the division.

Developing its corroboration, the Gemara asks rhetorically:

וְהָא אֲנַן תְּנַן – **But we learned in our Mishnah** that a courtyard may be divided even if there are only אַרְבַּע אַמּוֹת לָזֶה וְאַרְבַּע אַמּוֹת לָזֶה – **FOUR** ***AMOS*** **FOR THIS** partner **AND FOUR** ***AMOS*** **FOR THAT** other partner! אֶלָּא שְׁמַע מִינָּהּ – **Rather, deduce from [the Baraisa],** which stated that each partner must receive at least eight *amos* by four *amos,* that an additional four *amos* for unloading must be available to each partner, כְּדְרַבִּי אַסִּי – **in accordance with** the ruling **of R' Assi.**

The Gemara concludes:

שְׁמַע מִינָּהּ – Indeed, **deduce** R' Assi's ruling **from [the Baraisa]!**

The Gemara presents another version of the previous discussion:

וְאִיכָּא דְּרָמֵי לְהוּ מִירְמָא – **And there are those who point out** that the Baraisa is **a contradiction** to the Mishnah, rather than adducing the Baraisa to support R' Assi's dictum. Their version of the dialogue proceeds as follows: תְּנַן אֵין חולקין אֶת הֶחָצֵר – **We learned in** our **Mishnah: WE DO NOT DIVIDE A** jointly owned **COURTYARD** עַד שֶׁיְּהֵא בָּהּ אַרְבַּע אַמּוֹת לָזֶה וְאַרְבַּע אַמּוֹת לָזֶה – **UNLESS THERE WILL BE FOUR** ***AMOS*** **FOR THIS** partner **AND FOUR** ***AMOS*** **FOR THAT** partner.

The Baraisa is cited as a contradiction to the Mishnah:

וְהָתַנְיָא – **But was it not taught in a Baraisa:** שְׁמוֹנֶה אַמּוֹת לָזֶה וּשְׁמוֹנֶה אַמּוֹת לָזֶה – We divide a courtyard only if there will be **EIGHT** ***AMOS*** **FOR THIS** partner **AND EIGHT** ***AMOS*** **FOR THAT** partner?

R' Assi resolves the contradiction:

אָמַר רַבִּי אַסִּי אָמַר רַבִּי יוֹחָנָן – **R' Assi said in the name of R' Yochanan:** אַרְבַּע אַמּוֹת שֶׁאָמְרוּ חוּץ מִשֶּׁל פְּתָחִים – **The four** ***amos*** **that [the Mishnah] said** was the minimum size for each share of a divided courtyard **excludes** the area **of the entrances.** Thus, there is no contradiction. The Mishnah, as explained by R' Assi, speaks only of the four *amos* needed for basic courtyard usage. The Baraisa requires an additional four *amos* for unloading.

The Gemara discusses a unique case of dividing a courtyard:

אָמַר רַב הוּנָא חָצֵר מִתְחַלֶּקֶת לְפִי פִּתְחֶיהָ – **Rav Huna said: A courtyard is divided according to its entrances** (i.e. the entrances of the houses in the courtyard).[34]

Rav Chisda disagreed:

NOTES

27. Since the field is irrigated, it can be used to grow many different types of crops, and thus can be cultivated profitably even if it is very small (*Rashi*).

28. None of the properties listed above may be divided against the will of either partner unless the division will provide a proper share for each, as the Mishnah will now explain.

29. I.e. each share still performs the function of the whole property and therefore retains its "name." For example, if through division a "cloak" simply becomes two smaller "cloaks," the property may be forcibly divided. If, however, either share is too small to be worn as a cloak, the property does not qualify for a legally compelled division.

30. This qualification is obvious, for the partners can surely do as they wish. It is stated only to preface the following ruling of the Mishnah (*Rashi*).

31. This refers to all twenty-four books of the Torah — the five books of Moses, the Prophets (*Neviim*) and the Holy Writings (*Kesuvim*) — since it was the custom at that time to write all twenty-four books on scrolls (*Rashi*).

32. *Rashi*, who adds (below, 13b) that it is disgraceful to cut them *in court* to settle a dispute; however, under certain circumstances, Torah scrolls may be divided (see below, 14a).

33. Since the entrance to each house is from the courtyard, each dividing partner needs to receive — in addition to four *amos* by four *amos* for basic courtyard use — another four *amos* in front of his doorway, for the purpose of unloading his animals there (*Rashi*).

The Gemara below quotes a Baraisa which states that he receives an area four amos deep along the entire width of his entrance; thus, if his doorway is eight amos wide, he receives an area four amos by eight amos. [If, however, the doorway is less than four amos wide, he would nevertheless receive four amos squared, the minimun area needed for unloading an animal (Rosh, Yad Ramah; see, however, Maggid Mishneh and Kessef Mishneh, Hil. Shecheinim 2:1 for a discussion of *Rashi's* view).]

34. Rav Huna speaks specifically of the case of a man who owned a courtyard that contained two houses. One house had two entrances to the courtyard, while the other house had only one. Before his death the man orally bequeathed one house to one of his sons and the second house to his other son. He did not, however, allocate the courtyard between his two sons (*Rashi*; cf. *Ri Migash*).

Subsequently, the brothers decided to divide the courtyard. Rav Huna rules that the brother who received the house with two entrances is entitled to a two-thirds share of the courtyard, while his sibling — the owner of the house with only one entrance — is awarded the remaining one-third share (*Rashi*). For since the house with two entrances makes greater use of the courtyard, we presume that the father intended to grant its owner a proportionally larger share thereof (see *Ritva*).

Rav Huna's ruling does not apply in the case of heirs who work out the

דלא סיימוה קמיה. דר' אמי דלעניי עובדי כוכבים חלקן רבא והנך דאמרינן לעיל (דף ח.) דשדרה נמי איפרא הורמיז למלוה רבה משום שלום מלכות נמי קבלינהו ולא אפשר ליה לחלקן לעניי עובדי כוכבים לאסור לגנוב דעת הבריות ואפילו דעתו של עובד כוכבים אבל במעות המתחלקות לעניים אין גניבת דעת דלאו כולהו נמי ידעי דישראל רגילים לפרנס עניי עובדי כוכבים כדאמרי' במס' גיטין (דף סא.) מפרנסין עניי עובדי כוכבים עם עניי ישראל מפני דרכי שלום: **אתה אמרת כו'.** מתוך למדנו לפיכך נברא אדם יחידי לומר לך כל המקיים נפש אחת [מישראל] כאילו קיים העולם מלא וכתיב (בראשית ד) קול דמי אחיך דמו ודם זרעותיו אף כשאתה מקיים דמי אחיך עמך מעלה עליך חייו וחיי זרעותיו שמדה טובה מרובה ממדת פורענות: **מונבז המלך.** בנה של הילני המלכה מזרע החשמונאים: **כשאמת מארץ תצמח.** אף משמים נשקף הצדק לשלם גמול: **נשקף.** מביט כמו נשקפה ותיבב (שופטים ה) כלומר זכות הצדקה מביט ומסתכל למטה: **מכון כסאך.** גנזתן תחת מכון הכסא: **(במקום) [דבר] שעושה פירות.** והקרן קיים לעוה"ב והפירות אוכל בחייו שנאמר כי פרי מעלליהם יאכלו: **אוצרות נפשות.** שנאמר ולוקח נפשות חכם בהאי קרא: **מתני' טרקלין ומורן.** מיני פלטין: **בית השלחין.** מתוך שיש לו מעיין ודלו להשקותו תדיר אם אין בו ט' קבין זורעין בו שאר זרעים לפיכך אפילו בפחות מכאן יש בו דין חלוקה: **אפילו בפחות מכאן יחלוקו.** משום דבעי למיתני וכתבי הקדש אע"פ ששניהם רוצים לא יחלוקו תני רישא (א): **כתבי הקדש.** כ"ד ספרים והיו רגילים לכותבן בגליון כס"ת שלנו לפיכך גנאי הדבר לחתכן: **גמ' חוץ משל פתחים.** חצר שני בתים פתוחין לתוכה ולפני הפתח ארבע אמות לאורך הבית הן לפרק משאו מעל חמורו וחוץ מאותן ד' אמות צריך שיהא ארבע אמות לשאר תשמישין: **חצר מתחלקת לפתחי'.** היתה לו חצר ובה שני בתים ואחד מהן פתוחין לו שני פתחים לחצר ולבית השני אין פתוח לחצר אלא פתח אחד וחולק נכסיו על פיו ונותן האחד לראובן בנו והשני לשמעון וחצר לא חילק אם באו לחלוק את החצר זה שיש לו שני פתחים נוטל שני חלקים בחצר ואחיו נוטל חלק אחד: **נותן לכל פתח (ג) ד' אמות.** ברוחב החצר להלן מן הפתח כנגד הרוחב כפי רוחב הפתח: **נוטל שמונה אמות.** דהיינו כנגד רוחב הפתח וארבע אמות ברוחב החצר להלן מן הפתח: **האי פירא דסופלי.** מי שיש לו חפירה בחצר שנותנין בה גרעיני תמרים למאכל בהמה יש לו ארבע אמות בחצר לכל סביבותיה: **דלא מייחד ליה פיתחא.** שלא היה לו פתח אלא חפירה אלא לדרך פתח ביתו שהוא יוצא ונכנס בו היה לו דרך לצאת לחצר ולילך אחר החפירה שלפני סוף ביתו ומשתמש: אבל

דלא סיימוה קמיה תניא אמרו עליו על בנימין הצדיק שהיה ממונה על קופה של צדקה פעם אחת באתה אשה לפניו בשני בצורת אמרה לו רבי פרנסני אמר לה העבודה שאין בקופה של צדקה כלום אמרה לו רבי אם אין אתה מפרנסני הרי אשה ושבעה בניה מתים עמד ופרנסה משלו לימים חלה ונטה למות אמרו מלאכי השרת לפני הקב"ה רבש"ע אתה אמרת א) כל המקיים נפש אחת מישראל כאילו קיים עולם מלא ובנימין הצדיק שהחיה אשה ושבעה בניה ימות בשנים מועטות הללו מיד קרעו לו גזר דינו תנא הוסיפו לו עשרים ושתים שנה על שנותיו ת"ר ב) מעשה במונבז המלך שבזבז אוצרותיו ואוצרות אבותיו בשני בצורת וחברו עליו אחיו ובית אביו ואמרו לו אבותיך גנזו והוסיפו על של אבותם ואתה מבזבזם אמר להם אבותי גנזו למטה ואני גנזתי למעלה שנאמר א) אמת מארץ תצמח וצדק משמים נשקף אבותי גנזו במקום שהיד שולטת בו ואני גנזתי במקום שאין היד שולטת בו שנאמר ב) צדק ומשפט מכון כסאך אבותי גנזו דבר שאין עושה פירות ואני גנזתי דבר שעושה פירות שנאמר ג) אמרו צדיק כי טוב כי פרי מעלליהם יאכלו אבותי גנזו אוצרות ממון ואני גנזתי אוצרות נפשות שנאמר ד) פרי צדיק עץ חיים ולוקח נפשות חכם אבותי גנזו לאחרים ואני גנזתי לעצמי שנאמר ה) ולך תהיה צדקה אבותי גנזו לעולם הזה ואני גנזתי לעולם הבא שנאמר ו) והלך לפניך צדקך כבוד ה' יאספך: ואם קנה בה בית דירה הרי הוא כאנשי העיר: מתניתין דלא כרשב"ג דתניא רבן שמעון בן ג"א אומר אם קנה בה קרקע כל שהוא הרי הוא כאנשי העיר והא תניא רבן שמעון בן גמליאל אומר אם קנה שם קרקע הראויה לבית דירה הרי הוא כאנשי העיר תרי תנאי ואליבא דרבן שמעון בן גמליאל: **מתני'** ג) אין חולקין את החצר עד שיהא ארבע אמות לזה וארבע אמות לזה ולא את השדה עד שיהא בה ד) תשעה קבין לזה ותשעה קבין לזה ר' יהודה אומר עד שיהא בה תשעת חצאי קבין לזה ותשעת חצאי קבין לזה ולא את הגינה עד שיהא בה חצי קב לזה וחצי קב לזה ר' עקיבא אומר בית רובע ולא את הטרקלין ולא את המורן ולא את השובך ולא את הטלית ולא את המרחץ ולא את בית הבד ולא את בית השלחין עד שיהא בהן כדי לזה וכדי לזה זה הכלל כל שיחלק ושמו עליו חולקין ואם לאו אין חולקין אימתי בזמן שאין שניהם רוצים אבל בזמן ששניהם רוצים אפי' פחות מכאן יחלוקו וכתבי הקדש אע"פ ששניהם רוצים לא יחלוקו: **גמ'** א"ר אסי א"ר יוחנן ארבע אמות שאמרו חוץ משל פתחים תניא נמי הכי אין חולקים את החצר עד שיהא בה שמונה אמות לזה ושמונה אמות לזה והא אנן תנן ארבע אמות לזה וארבע אמות לזה אלא ש"מ כדרבי אסי שמע מינה ואיכא דרמי להו מירמא תנן אין חולקין את החצר עד שיהא בה ארבע אמות לזה וארבע אמות לזה והתניא שמונה אמות לזה ושמונה אמות לזה א"ר אסי אמר ר' יוחנן ארבע אמות שאמרו חוץ משל פתחים אמר רב הונא חצר מתחלקת לפי פתחיה ורב חסדא אמר נותנין ארבע אמות לכל פתח ופתח והשאר חולקין בשוה תניא כוותיה דרב חסדא פתחים שבחצר יש להן ארבע אמות היה לזה פתח אחד ולזה שני פתחים זה שיש לו פתח אחד נוטל ארבע אמות וזה שיש לו שני פתחים נוטל שמונה אמות והשאר חולקין בשוה היה לזה פתח רחב שמונה אמות נוטל שמונה אמות כנגד הפתח וארבע אמות בחצר מאי עבידתייהו אמר אביי הכי קאמר נוטל שמונה אמות באורך החצר וארבע אמות ברוחב החצר אמר אמימר האי פירא דסופלי יש לו ארבע אמות לכל רוח ורוח ולא אמרן אלא דלא מייחד ליה פתחא אבל

ולא את השדה עד שיהיה בה ט' קבין וכו'. אף על גב דבכל דהו מקרי שדה כדאמרינן בפרק האומר בקידושין (דף סא.) אין לי (ג) אלא בית כור זרע חומר שעורים מנין לרבות סאה וחצי סאה תרקב וחצי תרקב ת"ל שדה מ"מ אינו חשוב לטרוח לחרוש ולזרוע בפחות מט' קבין והא דאמר בסוף כתובות (דף קי.) אמר ההוא מילה לר' חנינא יתמות משבחיתו (ד) בארעייכו בית סאה הניח לי אבא ממנה משח [ממנה חמר] ממנה עיבור ממנה קטנית כו' התם היה במקום שמתברך ביותר: הכא

עין משפט נר מצוה

צד א מיי' פ"א מהל' רוצח ושמירת נפש הלכה טז:

צה ב ג ד מיי' פ"א מהל' שכנים הל' ד ופ"ב הלכה א סמג עשין פב טוש"ע ח"מ סי' קעא סעיף ג:

צו ה מיי' שם פ"א הל' ה סמג שם:

צז ו מיי' שם הל' ד סמג שם טוש"ע שם סעיף ג:

צח ז ח מיי' שם פ"ב הלכה ט סמג שם טוש"ע ח"מ סי' קעג סעיף א:

צט ט מיי' שם הל' א וסמג שם טוש"ע ח"מ סי' קעא סעיף ג:

ק י כ ל מיי' שם וסמג שם טוש"ע ח"מ סי' קעב סעיף א:

קא מ נ מיי' שם הל' ג טוש"ע שם ס"ג:

רבינו גרשום

לא סיימוה קמיה. דחילקו לעניי עובדי כוכבים דאין להם זכות בכך: **מונבז** ממלכי חשמונים היה: **במקום שאין עושין פירות.** שהממון המונח באוצר אינו מייתר כלום: **אם קנה בה קרקע הראוי לבית דירה** אע"פ שלא עשה בה דירה: **פיס':** **ארבע אמות** לזה וד' אמות לזה שאמרו בחצר **חוץ משל פתחים** דלכל פתח יש לו בחצר ד' אמות לפרק משאו. ועכשיו אם יהיה חצר ט"ז אמה דמטי לפתחים ח' ולחלוק ח' (חלקים) והיינו ח' אמות לכל אחד עם הפתח שלו: **אמר רב הונא חצר מתחלקת לפי פתחיה.** שאם הניח להם אביהן לזה בית אחד של ב' פתחים ולזה בית אחד של פתח אחד ולפני בתים הללו היתה חצר, **מתחלקת** אותה חצר **לפי פתחיה** וזה שיש לו ב' פתחים נוטל ב' ידות מן החצר וזה שאין לו אלא פתח אחד נוטל שליש דלפי שיש חזקה לזה טפי: **ורב חסדא אמר ד' אמות לכל פתח ופתח.** ולא כל שתי ידות החצר דאי מייתר מד' ד' לכל פתח **חולקין בשוה:** **נוטל ח' אמות** באורך החצר כנגד ח' אמות של רוחב הפתח **וד' אמות ברוחב החצר** כנגד הפתח כלומר דלא שקיל אלא (על) ח' ברוחב ד': **פירא דסופלי** אם הגיעם חצר אחרת גדולה ובתוך אותה חצר היתה פירא דסופלי חפירה שמשימין גרעיני תמרים לצורך מאכל בהמה והגיע ליורש אחד אותה פירא דסופלי. **יש לו ד' אמות בחצר** זה הואיל דעדיין לא נעשה פתח ודרך לאותה חפירה אמרינן דיש לו ד' אמות **לכל רוח** ליכנס באיזה רוח שירצה ולהשתמש ד' אמות לכל רוח: **אלא שלא ייחד אביהן פתח.** לאותה חפירא דסופלי: **אבל וכו'.** ל"א אם יש לאחד מן השותפים פירות דסופלי חריץ שמשימין בו תבן ומספוא לשוורים בהאי חצר **נוטל ד' אמות לכל רוח** של חריץ זו כלומר כשיעור תשמיש ועבודת טלטול החריץ לבד החלוקה שחולקין בשוה דיש לו ליטול לפי חזקה דאית ליה בתוך החצר. למורי הרב: [מכאן שייך לע"ב:] **אכסדרה** גג מקורה הקבוע על ד' קונדסין ופתוחה מכל צדדיה ואינה עשויה אלא לצל בעלמא כשחולקין את החצר למי שיגיע לו האכסדרה **אין נוטל ד' אמות** חוץ לאכסדרה כמו לפתח **דטעמא מאי** אמרו דנוטל ד' אמות כנגד פתחו בחצר כדי עבודת הפתח **לפרק משאו** מעל גבי בהמתו בהני ד' אמות דאינו רוצה ללכלך ולטנף ביתו מזבל בהמתו אבל **הכא** באכסדרה זו הואיל שאין לה דפנות סביב **אפשר לו דעייל** באכסדרה זו (דבי בי רב שלומדין שם תלמידים שיש לה ג' דפנות) **ומפרק** דבלאו הכי נמי מטונפות מן הזבלים ומן הגשמים ולהכי אין צריכין ד' אמות: **באכסדרה דבי רב** שלומדין בה תלמידין שיש לה ג' דפנות עד הסכך (ופ') ודופן רביעית אינה מגעת לסכך משום שיהא אורה ופתח אותה אכסדרה יש לו ד' אמות **ומקשינן אכסדרה דבי רב אידרונא** חדר **מעליא הוא** ולא צריך למימר דיש לה ד' אמות: **באכסדרה רומייתא** דיש לה ג' מחיצות מגיעות לסכך ומחיצה רביעית נמוכה ובונין עליה על פני כולה חלונות גדולות על גבי פצימין כעין אותם שקורין קלושטי"ר ופתח באמצעיות אותה מחיצה נמוכה ולאותו פתח יש לו ד' אמות אף על גב דיש הרבה סביב חלונות גדולות אבל לא לאכסדר' העומדת על קונדסין. (כלומר) **בית שער** יש לו ד' אמות במבוי **מרפסת** היינו עלייה **שיש לה ד' פתחים או יותר** בשורה אחת ועושין לפניהם נסר ארוך שרופסין עליו ולסוף אותו נסר סולם שיורדין בו לארץ ולפני אותו סולם יש פתח שנועל בעד המרפסת כל אותן ד' פתחים של עלייה **אין להם** בחצר **אלא ד' אמות** שלפני פתח הסולם שכולם יוצאין באותו פתח: **לול של תרנגולים.** ארובה של עלייה שמשימין דרך אותה ארובה תרנגולין לעלייה כלומר אם אין לאותן היורשין שום פתח לשם אלא לול של תרנגולין משום חזקת אותו לול **אינו נוטל ד' אמות** בחצר כמו לפתח דליכא התם משום פריקת משוי שהתרנגול מטפס ועולה (ניסרין). יש לו לאחד מן היורשין בית שחציו מקורה וחציו אינו מקורה. מי אמרי' כיון דחציו אינו מקורה יכול לפרק משאו באותו צד שאינו מקורה **ואין לו ד' אמות** בחצר או דילמא כיון דיש לו ד' מחיצות ופתח כשאר בית אע"פ שחציו אינו מקורה **יש לו ד' אמות: לא מיבעיא.** היכא דהוה אותו חצי (קורה) **[קירוי] כלפי פנים** הבית כלומר לאחורי הבית והא דאינו מקורה סמוך לחצר דאע"ג דאיכא פתח בית הפתוח לחצר דאינו נוטל ד' אמות בחצר מתוך **דהכא מצי לפרק משאו** בהאי חצי דאינו מקורה שסמוך לחצר **אלא אע"פ** אי הוה אותו חצי קירוי לצד חוץ סמוך לחצר ושאינו מקורה לצד אחורי הבית אפי' הכי אינו נוטל ד' אמות בחצר כנגד פתח הבית משום דיכול להכניס באותו חצי שאחורי הכותל שאינו מקורה ומפרק שם לחצר: **פתחו למבוי אחר.** שאם היה פתחו פתוח למבוי זה ואחרי פתחו איכא מבוי אחר ורוצה לסתום פתחו מיכן ולפותחו למבוי שאחורי ביתו: **בני מבוי.** שעכשיו רוצה לפתוח פתחו לשם **יכולין לעכבו** לצאת ולבוא דרך מבואן הואיל ועד עתה לא הוחזק באותו מבוי או לא. ותו בעא מיניה **אכסניא.** אכסנאין של מלך שעוברין בעיר ומחלקין אותן בבתי העיר ליתן להם לינה ופרנסה השתא בעי **לפי בני מבוי** שיש להם בתים לכל בית מחלקים **או לפי פתחיה מחלקים** שאם יש בבית ב' פתחים שיתנו לו ב' חלקים מן האכסנאין שיעור שני בתים: **זבל שבחצר לפי פתחים מתחלק.** שאם היו בבית ב' פתחים ולבית אחר פתח א' שמוציאין זבל ובאו לחלקן זה של שני פתחים נוטל פי שנים וחלק שלישי [נוטל האחר] לפי שיעור הפתחים היו מוציאים הזבל: **לסתום כנגד פתחו.** שכשם שיש לו לפתח ד' אמות בחצר כך יש לו לכל פתח חצר ד' אמות במבוי וזה בקש לסתום אותן ד' אמות שלו ולהקיפן בגדר **בני מבוי** שכניו **מעכבין עליו שמרבה עליהן את הדרך** להקיף אותו סתום (מבוי): **ה' חצרות** זו בצד זו **הפתוחות למבוי** אותה הסמוכה לרשות הרבים קרויה חיצונה ואותה שבסוף המבוי מצד אחר קרויה פנימית **כולן** הד' **משתמשות עם חיצונית.** כלומר דיש לכולן רשות לעבור לפני פתח החיצונה **והחיצונה משתמשת לעצמה.** שרשאה לסתום כנגד פתחה הד' אמות ולהשתמש בתוכן. **והם.** הני השאר **משתמשות עם השניה** שעוברין לפני פתחיה **ושניה משתמשת לעצמה.** שרשאה לסתום ד' אמות נגד פתחה **ומשתמשת עם החיצונה** שמקפת ד' אמות ויוצאת לחרן. **נמצאת הפנימית** שבמבוי שהיא **משתמש' עם כולן** שעוברת עליהן **ומשתמשת לעצמה** קשיא לרב הונא:

מסורת הש"ס

א) [סנהדרין דף לז.], ב) [תוס' פאה פ"ד], ג) [לעיל ג:] סוכה ג:, ד) [לקמן קג: כתובות קח.], ה) [לעיל ג.], ו) [לקמן יג: לעיל ג.], ז) [סוכה ג:]:

הגהות הב"ח

(א) רש"י ד"ה אפי' וכו' תני רישא יחלוקו הס"ד: (ב) ד"ה נותן לכל פתח ד' אמות להלן מן הפתח כנגדו והרוחב כפי רוחב הפתח כצ"ל ותיבת ברוחב החצר נמחק ואח"כ מ"ה הכי קאמר נוטל ח' אמות באורך החצר דהיינו וכו' מן הפתח כנגדו הס"ד: (ג) תוס' ד"ה ולא וכו' אין לי אלא זרע חומר שעורים בחמשים מנין לרבות לתך סאה תרקב כצ"ל ותיבת בית כור ותיבת וחצי סאה נמחק: (ד) בא"ד משבחיתו לארעייכו:

תורה אור השלם

א) אֱמֶת מֵאֶרֶץ תִּצְמָח וְצֶדֶק מִשָּׁמַיִם נִשְׁקָף: [תהלים פה, יב]

ב) צֶדֶק וּמִשְׁפָּט מְכוֹן כִּסְאֶךָ חֶסֶד וֶאֱמֶת יְקַדְּמוּ פָנֶיךָ: [תהלים פט, טו]

ג) אִמְרוּ צַדִּיק כִּי טוֹב כִּי פְרִי מַעַלְלֵיהֶם יֹאכֵלוּ: [ישעיה ג, י]

ד) פְּרִי צַדִּיק עֵץ חַיִּים וְלֹקֵחַ נְפָשׁוֹת חָכָם: [משלי יא, ל]

ה) הָשֵׁב תָּשִׁיב לוֹ אֶת הָעֲבוֹט כְּבוֹא הַשֶּׁמֶשׁ וְשָׁכַב בְּשַׂלְמָתוֹ וּבֵרֲכֶךָּ וּלְךָ תִּהְיֶה צְדָקָה לִפְנֵי יְיָ אֱלֹהֶיךָ: [דברים כד, יג]

ו) אָז יִבָּקַע כַּשַּׁחַר אוֹרֶךָ וַאֲרֻכָתְךָ מְהֵרָה תִצְמָח וְהָלַךְ לְפָנֶיךָ צִדְקֶךָ כְּבוֹד יְיָ יַאַסְפֶךָ: [ישעיה נח, ח]

ליקוטי רש"י

[תחילת לקוטי רש"י ששייך לכאן נדפס בדף י:] **וכתבי הקדש.** כגון תורה נביאים וכתובים [שבת קטו.]. ספר תורה שהוא בכרך אחד וכן נביאים וכתובים הכתובים בגליון כס"ת [לעיל ג.]. **חצר מתחלקת לפי פתחיה.** חצר שהיו בתים פתוחין לה ותלקוה שני אחין ביניהם זה נוטל שלשה בתים קטנים וזה נוטל כנגדן בית גדול אם באו לחלק את החצר זה שנטל שלשה בתים קטנים נוטל שלשה חלקים כמנין שלשה פתחים וזה נוטל רביע לפי שהחצר עשוי לגלגלה ולפי שדרך החצר נכנסין ויוצאין בה ומכניסין משלומיהן ופורקין לפני פתחיהם לפיכך חצר מתחלקת לפי הפתחים. **ורב חסדא אמר.** אין צריך ליתן לכל פתח אלא ד"א כנגדן מן הפתח והלאה ורחבן ברוחב הפתח ואפילו הוא רחב י' אמות נוטל ד' אמות במשך וכנגד כל רחבו לפרק משאו [סוכה ג:]. **פירא דסופלי.** חפירה העשויה להטיל שם גרעיני תמרים למאכל בהמות [קידושין עג:]. שוחה עמוקה ושם היו מניחין גרעיני התמרים לאכול השוורים. **פירא.** שוחה כמו פירא דכוורי במס' תענית (כד.) [עירובין כו.].

וְרַב חִסְדָּא אָמַר נוֹתְנִין אַרְבַּע אַמּוֹת לְכָל פֶּתַח וּפֶתַח – **And Rav Chisda said: We award four *amos* for each and every entrance,** וְהַשְּׁאָר חוֹלְקִין בְּשָׁוֶה – **and [the brothers] divide the remainder** of the courtyard **equally.** Rav Chisda maintains that the father did not intend for the owner of the house with two entrances to receive any advantage in the courtyard other than the extra four *amos* to which he was entitled in any event.

The Gemara adduces support for Rav Chisda's opinion:

תַּנְיָא כְּוָותֵיהּ דְּרַב חִסְדָּא – **A Baraisa was taught in accordance with Rav Chisda:** פְּתָחִים שֶׁבֶּחָצֵר יֵשׁ לָהֶן אַרְבַּע אַמּוֹת – For each of the ENTRANCES to the houses IN A COURTYARD THERE IS an allotment of FOUR *AMOS* as part of the division of the courtyard, as explained above. הָיָה לָזֶה פֶּתַח אֶחָד – IF THIS partner HAD ONE ENTRANCE to the courtyard וְלָזֶה שְׁנֵי פְתָחִים – AND THAT partner HAD TWO ENTRANCES,[35] זֶה שֶׁיֵּשׁ לוֹ פֶּתַח אֶחָד – THIS one WHO HAS ONE ENTRANCE נוֹטֵל אַרְבַּע אַמּוֹת – TAKES the FOUR *AMOS* of courtyard before the entire width of the entrance; וְזֶה שֶׁיֵּשׁ לוֹ שְׁנֵי פְתָחִים – AND THAT one WHO HAS TWO ENTRANCES נוֹטֵל שְׁמוֹנֶה אַמּוֹת – TAKES EIGHT *AMOS*, four *amos* of courtyard before the entire width of each entrance; וְהַשְּׁאָר חוֹלְקִין בְּשָׁוֶה – AND THEY DIVIDE THE REMAINDER of the courtyard EQUALLY. The Baraisa thus corroborates Rav Chisda's ruling.

The Gemara quotes the next section of the Baraisa:

הָיָה לָזֶה פֶּתַח רָחָב שְׁמוֹנֶה אַמּוֹת – IF THIS partner HAD AN ENTRANCE EIGHT *AMOS* WIDE, נוֹטֵל שְׁמוֹנֶה אַמּוֹת כְּנֶגֶד הַפֶּתַח וְאַרְבַּע אַמּוֹת בֶּחָצֵר – HE TAKES EIGHT *AMOS* OPPOSITE THE ENTRANCE AND FOUR *AMOS* IN THE COURTYARD.

The Gemara assumes that the "four *amos* in the courtyard" is *in addition to* the eight *amos* for the entrance. The Gemara therefore asks:

אַרְבַּע אַמּוֹת בֶּחָצֵר מַאי עֲבִידְתַּיְיהוּ – **What is the purpose of the "four *amos* in the courtyard"?**

The Gemara explains the meaning of the Baraisa:

אָמַר אַבַּיֵי הָכִי קָאָמַר – **Abaye said: This is what [the Baraisa] said:** נוֹטֵל שְׁמוֹנֶה אַמּוֹת בְּאוֹרֶךְ הֶחָצֵר – **[The owner] takes eight *amos* along the length of the courtyard** in front of his wide entrance וְאַרְבַּע אַמּוֹת בְּרוֹחַב הֶחָצֵר – **and four *amos* along the width of the courtyard.** That is, the owner receives an eight *amah* by four *amah* parcel of land in front of his entrance. Thus, "four *amos* in the courtyard" does not mean a *second* piece of land, but the *depth* that the eight-*amah* strip extends into the courtyard.

The Gemara discusses another case of an extra allocation to one son:[36]

אָמַר אַמֵּימָר הַאי פִּירָא דְסוּפְלֵי – **Ameimar said:** Regarding **that pit of date stones,**[37] יֵשׁ לוֹ אַרְבַּע אַמּוֹת לְכָל רוּחַ וְרוּחַ – [the owner] of the pit **is entitled to four *amos* on each side** of the pit.[38] We presume that the father intended him to have four *amos* on each side of the pit for the purpose of depositing the date stones into the pit.

Ameimar qualified his ruling:

וְלֹא אֲמָרָן אֶלָּא דְּלָא מְיַיחֵד לֵיהּ פִּתְחָא – **And [this ruling] is said only when [the father] had not designated an entrance** to use for depositing the date stones into the pit.[39] Only in this case is the son entitled to four *amos* on all sides of the pit, for the dumping was done from all directions.

NOTES

division of an estate themselves, or in the case of partners who agree to divide, for in each of those cases we presume that each party (i.e. even the one that takes the house with one entrance) agrees only to an equal share of the courtyard (see *Rosh*, *Ritva* and *Ran*).

35. Since the Baraisa does not particularize, it speaks of *all* cases — even one such as ours, where the allocation of the courtyard was made by someone other than the present owners and its details were not disclosed.

36. The Gemara's case is similar to the one above, where a father bequeathed houses in a courtyard to his children but did not specifically allocate the courtyard itself (*Ritva*).

37. The courtyard contained a pit where date pits were deposited for fodder (*Rashi*).

38. We follow *Rashi's* interpretation. *Raavad* (cited by *Rashba*) understands, however, that the owner is entitled to only *one* area of four *amos* squared, but he may select an area on any side of the pit hechooses.

39. I.e. where there was no special door at the side of the house next to the pit. Rather, he would exit with the date stones through the main doorway of his house and walk through the courtyard to reach the pit (*Rashi*).

דלא סיימוה קמיה. דר' אמי דלעניי עובדי כוכבים חלקן רבא והנך דאמרן לעיל (דף ח.) דשדרה נמי איפרא הורמיז למלוה רבה משום שלום מלכות נמי קבלינהו ולא אפשר ליה לחלקן לעניי עובדי כוכבים דאסור לגנוב דעת הבריות ואפילו דעתו של עובד כוכבים אבל במעות המתחלקות לעניים אין גניבת דעת דאינהו נמי ידעי שישראל רגילים לפרנס עניי עובדי כוכבים כדאמרי' במס' גיטין (דף סא.) מפרנסין עניי עובדי כוכבים עם עניי ישראל מפני דרכי שלום: אתה אמרת כו'. מתורתך למדנו לפיכך נברא אדם יחידי לומר לך כל המקיים נפש אחת [מישראל] כאילו קיים העולם מלא וכתיב (בראשית ד) קול דמי אחיך דמו ודם זרעיותיו אף כשאתה מקיים דמי אחיך עמך מעלה עליך חייו וחיי זרעיותיו שמדה טובה מרובה ממדת פורענות: מונבז המלך. בנה של הילני המלכה מזרע החשמונאים: כשאמת מארץ תצמח. אף משמים נשקף הצדק לשלם גמול: נשקף. מביט כמו נשקפה ותייבב (שופטים ה) כלומר זכות הצדקה מביט ומסתכל למטה: מכון כסאך. גניזתן תחת מכון הכסא: (במקום) [דבר] שעושה פירות. והקרן קיים לעוה"ב והפירות אוכל בחייו שנאמר כי פרי מעלליהם יאכלו: אוצרות נפשות. שנאמר ולוקח נפשות חכם בהאי קרא: מתני' טרקלין ומורן. מיני פלטין: בית השלחין. מתוך שיש לו מעיין ובידו להשקותו תדיר אם אין בו ט' קבין זורעין בו שאר זרעים לפיכך אפילו בפחות מכאן יש בו דין חלוקה: אפילו בפחות מכאן יחלוקו. משום דבעי למיתני ובכתבי הקדש אע"פ ששניהם רוצים לא יחלוקו תני רישא (א): כתבי הקדש. כ"ד ספרים והיו רגילים לכותבן בגליון כס"ת שלנו לפיכך גנאי הדבר לחתכן: גמ' חוץ משל פתחים. חצר של שניהם שני בתים פתוחין לתוכה ולפני הפתח ארבע אמות לורך הבית הן לפרק משאו מעל חמורו וחוץ מאותן ד' אמות צריך שיהא ארבע אמות לשאר תשמישין: חצר מתחלקת לפתחי'. היתה לו חצר ובה שני בתים ואחד מהן פתוחין לו שני פתחים לחצר ולבית השני אין פתוח לחצר אלא פתח אחד וחולק נכסיו על פיו ונותן האחד לראובן בנו והשני לשמעון וחצר לא חילק אם באו לחלוק את החצר זה שיש לו שני פתחים נוטל שני חלקים בחצר ואחיו נוטל חלק אחד: נותן לכל פתח (ב) ד' אמות. ברוחב החצר להלן מן הפתח כנגד הרוחב כפי רוחב הפתח: נוטל שמונה אמות. דהיינו כנגד רוחב הפתח וארבע אמות ברוחב החצר להלן מן הפתח: האי פירא דסופלי. מי שיש לו חפירה בחצר שנותנין בה גרעיני תמרים למאכל בהמה יש לו ארבע אמות בחצר לכל סביבותיה: דלא מייחד ליה פיתחא. שלא היה לו פתח אצל חפירה אלא דרך פתח ביתו שהוא יוצא ונכנס בו היה לו דרך לצאת לחצר ולילך אחר החפירה שלפני סוף ביתו ומשתמש: אבל

דלא סיימוה קמיה תניא אמרו עליו על בנימין הצדיק שהיה ממונה על קופה של צדקה פעם אחת באתה אשה לפניו בשני בצורת אמרה לו רבי פרנסני אמר לה העבודה שאין בקופה של צדקה כלום אמרה לו רבי אם אין אתה מפרנסני הרי אשה ושבעה בניה מתים עמד ופרנסה משלו לימים חלה ונטה למות אמרו מלאכי השרת לפני הקב"ה רבש"ע אתה אמרת כל המקיים נפש אחת מישראל כאילו קיים עולם מלא ובנימין הצדיק שהחיה אשה ושבעה בניה ימות בשנים מועטות הללו מיד קרעו לו גזר דינו תנא הוסיפו לו עשרים ושתים שנה על שנותיו ת"ר מעשה במונבז המלך שבזבז אוצרותיו ואוצרות אבותיו בשני בצורת וחברו עליו אחיו ובית אביו ואמרו לו אבותיך גנזו והוסיפו על של אבותם ואתה מבזבזם אמר להם אבותי גנזו למטה ואני גנזתי למעלה שנאמר א) אמת מארץ תצמח וצדק משמים נשקף אבותי גנזו במקום שהיד שולטת בו ואני גנזתי במקום שאין היד שולטת בו שנאמר ב) צדק ומשפט מכון כסאך אבותי גנזו דבר שאין עושה פירות ואני גנזתי דבר שעושה פירות שנאמר ג) אמרו צדיק כי טוב כי פרי מעלליהם יאכלו אבותי גנזו אוצרות ממון ואני גנזתי אוצרות נפשות שנאמר ד) פרי צדיק עץ חיים ולוקח נפשות חכם אבותי גנזו לאחרים ואני גנזתי לעצמי שנאמר ה) ולך תהיה צדקה אבותי גנזו לעולם הזה ואני גנזתי לעולם הבא שנאמר ו) והלך לפניך צדקך כבוד ה' יאספך: ואם קנה בה בית דירה הרי הוא כאנשי העיר: מתניתין דלא כרשב"ג דתניא רבן שמעון בן גמליאל אומר אם קנה בה קרקע כל שהוא הרי הוא כאנשי העיר והא תניא רבן שמעון בן גמליאל אומר אם קנה שם קרקע הראויה לבית דירה הרי הוא כאנשי העיר תרי תנאי ואליבא דרבן שמעון בן גמליאל: **מתני'** אין חולקין את החצר עד שיהא ארבע אמות לזה וארבע אמות לזה ולא את השדה עד שיהא בה תשעה קבין לזה ותשעה קבין לזה ר' יהודה אומר עד שיהא בה תשעת חצאי קבין לזה ותשעת חצאי קבין לזה ולא את הגינה עד שיהא בה חצי קב לזה וחצי קב לזה ר' עקיבא אומר בית רובע ולא את הטרקלין ולא את המורן ולא את השובך ולא את הטלית ולא את המרחץ ולא את בית הבד ולא את בית השלחין עד שיהא בהן כדי לזה וכדי לזה זה הכלל כל שיחלק ושמו עליו חולקין ואם לאו אין חולקין אימתי בזמן שאין שניהם רוצים אבל בזמן ששניהם רוצים אפי' פחות מכאן יחלוקו וכתבי הקדש אע"פ ששניהם רוצים לא יחלוקו: **גמ'** א"ר אסי א"ר יוחנן ארבע אמות שאמרו חוץ משל פתחים תניא נמי הכי אין חולקים את החצר עד שיהא בה שמונה אמות לזה ושמונה אמות לזה והא אנן תנן ארבע אמות לזה וארבע אמות לזה אלא ש"מ כדרבי אסי שמע מינה ואיכא דרמי להו מירמא תנן אין חולקין את החצר עד שיהא בה ארבע אמות לזה וארבע אמות לזה והתניא שמונה אמות לזה ושמונה אמות לזה א"ר אסי אמר ר' יוחנן ארבע אמות שאמרו חוץ משל פתחים אמר רב הונא חצר מתחלקת לפי פתחיה ורב חסדא אמר נותנין ארבע אמות לכל פתח ופתח והשאר חולקין בשוה תניא כוותיה דרב חסדא פתחים שבחצר יש להן ארבע אמות היה לזה פתח אחד ולזה שני פתחים זה שיש לו פתח אחד נוטל ארבע אמות וזה שיש לו שני פתחים נוטל שמונה אמות והשאר חולקין בשוה היה לזה פתח רחב שמונה אמות נוטל שמונה אמות כנגד הפתח וארבע אמות בחצר ארבע אמות בחצר מאי עבידתייהו אמר אביי הכי קאמר נוטל שמונה אמות באורך החצר וארבע אמות ברוחב החצר אמר אמימר האי פירא דסופלי יש לו ארבע אמות לכל רוח ורוח ולא אמרן אלא דלא מייחד ליה פתחא אבל

ולא את השדה עד שיהיה בה ט' קבין וכו'. אף על גב דבכל דהו מקרי שדה כדאמרינן בפרק האומר בקידושין (דף סא.) אין לי (ג) אלא בית כור זרע חומר שעורים מנין לרבות סאה וחצי סאה תרקב וחצי תרקב ת"ל שדה מ"מ אינו חשוב לטרוח לחרוש ולזרוע בפחות מט' קבין והא דאמר בסוף כתובות (דף קיב.) אמר ההוא מינא לר' חנינא יאות משבחיתו (ד) בארעייכו בית סאה הניח לי אבא ממנה משח [ממנה חמר] ממנה עיבור ממנה קטנית כו' התם היה במקום שמתברך ביותר: הכא

ד"א כנגדן מן הפתח והלאה ורחבן ברוחב הפתח ואפילו הוא רחב י' אמות נוטל ד' אמות במשך וכנגד כל רחבו לפרק משאו [סוכה ג:]. פירא דסופלי. חפירה העשויה להטיל שם גרעיני תמרים למאכל בהמות [קידושין עג.]. שוחה עמוקה ושם היו מניחין גרעיני התמרים לאכול השוורים. פירא. שוחה כמו פירא דכוורי במס' תענית (כז.) [עירובין כו.].

רבינו גרשום

לא סיימוה קמיה. דחילקו לעניי עובדי כוכבים דאין להם זכות בכך: מונבז מלכי חשמונים היה: במקום שאין עושין פירות. שהממון המונח באוצר אינו מיתר כלום: אם קנה בה קרקע הראוי לבית דירה אע"פ שלא עשה בה דירה: פיס' ארבע אמות לזה וד' אמות לזה שאמרו חוץ משל פתחים דלכל פתח יש לו בחצר ד' אמות לפרק משאו. ועכשיו אם יהיה חצר ט"ז אמה דמטי לפתחים ח' ולחלוק ח' (חלקים) והיינו ח' אמות לכל אחד עם הפתח שלו: אמר רב הונא חצר מתחלקת לפי פתחיה. שאם הניח להם אביהן לזה בית אחד של ב' פתחים ולזה בית אחד של פתח אחד ולפני בתים הללו היתה חצר, מתחלקת אותה חצר לפי פתחיה וזה שיש לו ב' פתחים נוטל ב' ידות מן החצר וזה שאין לו אלא פתח אחד נוטל שליש דלפי שיש חזקה לזה טפי: ורב חסדא אמר ד' אמות לכל פתח ופתח. ולא כל שתי ידות החצר דאי מייתר מד' ד' לכל פתח חולקין בשוה. נוטל ח' אמות באורך החצר כנגד ח' אמות של רוחב הפתח וד' אמות ברוחב החצר כנגד הפתח כלומר דלא שקיל אלא (על) ח' ברוחב ד': פירא דסופלי אם הגיעם חצר אחרת גדולה ובתוך אותה חצר היתה פירא דסופלי חפירה ששמימין גרעיני תמרים לצורך מאכל בהמה והגיע ליורש אחד אותה פירא דסופלי. יש לו ד' אמות בחצר זה הואיל דעדיין לא נעשה פתח ודרך לאותה חפירה אמרינן דיש לו ד' אמות לכל רוח ליכנס באיזה רוח שירצה ולהשתמש ד' אמות לכל רוח: אלא שלא ייחד אביהן פתח. לאותה חפירא דסופלי: אבל וכו'. ל"א אם יש לאחד מן השותפים פירות דסופלי חריץ שמשימין בו תבן ומספוא לשוורים

בהאי חצר נוטל ד' אמות לכל רוח של חריץ זו כלומר כשיעור תשמיש ועבודת טלטול החריץ לבד החלוקה שחולקין בשוה דיש לו ליטול לפי חזקה דאית ליה בתוך החצר. למורי הרב: [מכאן שייך לע"ב:] אכסדרה גג מקורה הקבוע על ד' קונדסין ופתוחה מכל צדדיה ואינה עשויה אלא לצל בעלמא כשחולקין את החצר למי שיגיע לו האכסדרה אין נוטל ד' אמות חוץ לאכסדרה כמו לפתח דטעמא מאי אמרו דנוטל ד' אמות כנגד פתחו בחצר כדי עבודת הפתח לפרק משאו מעל גבי בהמתו

בהני ד' אמות ואינו רוצה ללכלך ולטנף ביתו מזבל בהמתו אבל הכא באכסדרה זו הואיל שאין לה דפנות סביב אפשר לו דעייל באכסדרה זו (דבי בי רב שלומדין שם תלמידים שיש לה ג' דפנות) ומפרק דבלאו הכי נמי מטונפות מן הזבלים ומן הגשמים ולהכי אין צריכין ד' אמות: באכסדרה דבי רב שלומדין בה תלמידין שיש לה ג' דפנות עד הסכך (ופ') ודופן רביעית אינה מגעת לסכך משום שיהא אורה ופתח אותה אכסדרה יש לו ד' אמות ומקשינן אכסדרה דבי רב אידרונא חדר מעליא הוא ולא צריך [...]מות: באכסדרה רומיתא דיש לה ג' מחיצות מגיעות לסכך ומחיצה רביעית נמוכה ובונין עליה על פני כולה חלונות גדולות על גבי פצימין כעין אותם שקורין קלושטי"ר ופתח באמצעיות אותה מחיצה נמוכה ולאותו פתח יש לו ד' אמות [...] סביב חלונות גדולות אבל לא לאכסדר' העומדת על קונדסין. (כלומר) בית שער יש לו ד' אמות במבוי מרפסת היינו עלייה שיש לה ד' פתחים או יותר בשורה אחת ועושין לפניהם נסר ארוך שרופסין עליו ולסוף אותו נסר סולם שיורדין [...]סולם יש פתח שנועל בעד המרפסת כל אותן ד' פתחים של עלייה אין להם בחצר אלא ד' אמות שלפני פתח הסולם שכולם יוצאין באותו פתח: לול של תרנגולים. ארובה של עלייה שמשימין דרך אותה ארובה תרנגולין לעלייה כלומר [...]ן שום פתח לשם אלא לול של תרנגולין משום חזקת אותו לול אינו נוטל ד' אמות בחצר כמו לפתח דליכא התם משום פריקת משוי שהתרנגול מטפס ועולה (ניסרין). יש לו לאחד מן היורשין בית שחציו מקורה וחציו אינו מקורה. מי [...] מקורה יכול לפרק משאו באותו צד שאינו מקורה ואין לו ד' אמות בחצר או דילמא כיון דיש לו ד' מחיצות ופתח כשאר בית אע"פ שחציו אינו מקורה יש לו ד' אמות: לא מיבעיא. היכא דהוה אותו חצי (קורה) [קירוי] כלפי פנים [...]הבית והא דאינו מקורה סמוך לחצר דאע"ג דאיכא פתח בית הפתוח לחצר דאינו נוטל ד' אמות בחצר מתוך דהכא מצי לפרק משאו בהאי חצי דאינו מקורה שסמוך לחצר אלא אע"פ אי הוה אותו חצי קירוי לצד חרץ סמוך לחצר ושאינו [...] בית אפי' הכי אינו נוטל ד' אמות בחצר כנגד פתח הבית משום דיכול להכניס באותו חצי שאחורי הכותל שאינו מקורה ומפרק שם לחצר: פתחו למבוי אחר. שאם היה פתחו פתוח למבוי זה ואחרי פתחו איכא מבוי אחר ורוצה לסתום [...]למבוי שאחורי ביתו: בני מבוי. שעכשיו רוצה לפתוח פתחו לשם יכולין לעכבו לצאת ולבוא דרך מבואן הואיל ועד עתה לא הוחזק באותו מבוי או לא. ותו בעא מיניה אכסניא. אכסנאין של מלך שעוברין בעיר ומחלקין אותן בבתי העיר [...]ה השתא בעי לפי בני מבוי שיש להם בתים לכל בית מחלקים או לפי פתחיה מחלקים שאם יש בבית ב' פתחים שיתנו לו ב' חלקים מן האכסנאין שיעור שני בתים: זבל שבחצר לפי פתחים מתחלק. שאם היו בבית ב' פתחים ולבית [...]ין זבל ובאו לחלקן זה של שני פתחים נוטל פי שנים וחלק שלישי [נוטל האחר] לפי שיעור הפתחים היו מוציאים הזבל: לסתום כנגד פתחו. שכשם שיש לו לפתח ד' אמות בחצר כך יש לו לכל פתח חצר ד' אמות במבוי וזה בקש לסתום [...] הקיפן בגדר בני מבוי שכניו מעכבין עליו שמרבה עליהן את הדרך להקיף אותו סתום (מבוי): ה' חצרות זו בצד זו הפתוחות למבוי אותה הסמוכה לרשות הרבים קרויה חיצונה ואותה שבסוף המבוי מצד אחר קרויה פנימית כולן [...] חיצונית. כלומר דיש לכולן רשות לעבור לפני פתח החיצונה והחיצונה משתמשת לעצמה. שרשאה לסתום כנגד פתחה הד' אמות ולהשתמש בתוכן. הני השאר משתמשות עם השניה שעוברין לפני פתחיה ושניה משתמשת [...]מה. שרשאה לסתום ד' אמות נגד פתחה ומשתמשת עם החיצונה. נמצאת הפנימית שבמבוי שהיא משתמש' עם כולן שעוברת עליהן ומשתמשת לעצמה קשיא לרב הונא:

עין משפט נר מצוה

צד א מיי' פ"ט מהל' רוצח ושמירת נפש הלכה טו:

צה ב ג ד מיי' פ"ז מהל' שכנים הל' ד ופ"ב הלכה א סמג עשין פב טוש"ע ח"מ סי' קעא סעיף ג:

צו ה מיי' שם הל' א סמג שם:

צז ו מיי' שם הל' ד סמג שם טוש"ע שם סעיף ג:

צח ז ח מיי' שם פ"ב הלכה ט סמג שם טוש"ע ח"מ סי' קעא סעיף א:

צט ט מיי' שם הל' א וסמג שם טוש"ע ח"מ סי' קעא סעיף ג:

ק י כ ל מיי' שם וסמג שם טוש"ע ח"מ סי' קעב סעיף א:

קא מ נ מיי' שם הל' ג טוש"ע שם ס"ג:

מסורת הש"ס

א) [סנהדרין דף לז.], ב) [תוס' פאה פ"ד], ג) [לעיל ג:] סוכה ג:, ד) [לקמן קב.] כתובות, ה) [לקמן יג:], ו) [לעיל ג.], ז) [סוכה ג:]

הגהות הב"ח

(א) רש"י ד"ה אפי' וכו' תני רישא יחלוקו הס"ד: (ב) ד"ה נותן לכל פתח ד' אמות להלן מן הפתח כנגדו והרוחב כפי רוחב הפתח כל"ל ותיבת ברוחב החצר נמחק ואח"כ מ"ה הכי קאמר נוטל ח' אמות באורך החצר דהיינו וכו' מן הפתח כנגדו הס"ד: (ג) תוס' ד"ה ולא וכו' אין לי אלא זרע חומר שעורים מנין לרבות לתך סאה תרקב כל"ל ותיבת בית כור ותיבת וחצי סאה נמחק: (ד) בא"ד משבחיתו לארעייכו:

תורה אור השלם

א) אֱמֶת מֵאֶרֶץ תִּצְמָח וְצֶדֶק מִשָּׁמַיִם נִשְׁקָף: [תהלים פה, יב]

ב) צֶדֶק וּמִשְׁפָּט מְכוֹן כִּסְאֶךָ חֶסֶד וֶאֱמֶת יְקַדְּמוּ פָנֶיךָ: [תהלים פט, טו]

ג) אִמְרוּ צַדִּיק כִּי טוֹב כִּי פְרִי מַעַלְלֵיהֶם יֹאכֵלוּ: [ישעיה ג, י]

ד) פְּרִי צַדִּיק עֵץ חַיִּים וְלֹקֵחַ נְפָשׁוֹת חָכָם: [משלי יא, ל]

ה) הָשֵׁב תָּשִׁיב לוֹ אֶת הָעֲבוֹט כְּבוֹא הַשֶּׁמֶשׁ וְשָׁכַב בְּשַׂלְמָתוֹ וּבֵרְכֶךָּ וּלְךָ תִּהְיֶה צְדָקָה לִפְנֵי יְיָ אֱלֹהֶיךָ: [דברים כד, יג]

ו) אָז יִבָּקַע כַּשַּׁחַר אוֹרֶךָ וַאֲרֻכָתְךָ מְהֵרָה תִצְמָח וְהָלַךְ לְפָנֶיךָ צִדְקֶךָ כְּבוֹד יְיָ יַאַסְפֶךָ: [ישעיה נח, ח]

ליקוטי רש"י

[תחילת לקוטי רש"י ששייך לכאן נדפס בדף י:] וכתבי הקדש. כגון תורה נביאים וכתובים [שבת קטז.]. ספר תורה שהוא בכרך אחד וכן נביאים וכתובים הכתובים בגליון כס"ת [לעיל ג.]. חצר מתחלקת לפי פתחיה. [...] ורב חסדא אמר. אין [...] אלא

אבל מייחד ליה פיתחא אין לו אלא ארבע אמות לפני פתחו אמר רב הונא [א]אכסדרה אין לה ד' אמות טעמא מאי משום פירוק משאו הכא אפשר דעייל לגואי ומפרק מתיב רב ששת אחד שערי בתים ואחד שערי אכסדראות יש להן ד' אמות כי תניא ההיא (א) באכסדרה דבי רב אכסדרה דבי רב פשיטא (ב) אידרונ' מעליא הוא [ב]אלא באכסדרה רומייתא ת"ר [ג]בית שער אכסדרה ומרפסת יש להן ד' אמות [ד]היו (א) חמשה בתים פתוחין למרפסת אין להן אלא ד' אמות בלבד בעא מיניה ר' יוחנן מר' ינאי לול של תרנגולין יש לו ד' אמות או אין לו ד' אמות [ה]א"ל טעמא מאי משום פירוק משאו הכא מטפס ועולה מטפס ויורד בעא מיניה רבא מרב נחמן בית חציו מקורה וחציו אינו מקורה יש לו ד' אמות או אין לו ד"א א"ל [ו]אין לו ד' אמות לא מבעיא קירויו מלגיו דאפשר דעייל לגואי ומפרק אלא אפילו קירויו כלפי חוץ אפשר דעייל לגואי ומפרק בעא מיניה רב הונא (ג) מרבי אמי אחד מבני מבוי שבקש להחזיר פתחו למבוי אחר בני מבוי מעכבין עליו או אין מעכבין עליו א"ל [ז]בני מבוי מעכבין עליו אכסניא לפי בני אדם מתחלקת או לפי פתחים מתחלקת א"ל [ח]לפי בני אדם מתחלקת תניא נמי הכי [ט]זבל שבחצר מתחלקת לפי פתחים אכסניא לפי בני אדם אמר רב הונא אחד מבני מבוי שבקש לסתום כנגד פתחו בני מבוי מעכבין עליו שמרבה עליהן את הדרך מיתיבי [י]חמש חצרות פתוחות למבוי כולן משתמשות עם החיצונה והחיצונה משתמשת לעצמה והשאר משתמשות עם השניה והשניה משתמשת לעצמה ומשתמשת עם החיצונה נמצאת פנימית משתמשת לעצמה ומשתמשת עם כל אחת ואחת תנאי היא דתניא אחד מבני מבוי שבקש להחזיר פתחו למבוי אחר בני מבוי מעכבין עליו היה סתום ובקש לפותחו אין בני מבוי מעכבין עליו דברי רבי ר"ש בן אלעזר אומר חמש חצרות הפתוחות למבוי כולן משתמשות במבוי זו עם זו חצרות מאן דכר שמייהו חסורי מחסרא והכי קתני וכן חמש חצרות הפתוחות למבוי כולן משתמשות עם החיצונה והחיצונה משתמשת לעצמה וכו' דברי רבי ר' שמעון בן אלעזר אומר חמש חצרות הפתוחות למבוי כולן משתמשות במבוי: אמר מר [כ]היה סתום ובקש לפותחו אין בני מבוי מעכבין עליו אמר רבא [ל]לא שנו אלא שלא פרץ את פצימיו אבל פרץ את פצימיו בני מבוי מעכבין עליו א"ל אביי לרבא תניא דמסייע לך

בית

רש"י

אבל מייחד ליה פיתחא. שהיה לו פתח לסוף ביתו אלא החפירה ולכך אותו פתח היה רגיל להשליך הגרעינין וליטלן אין לו בחצר בשביל החפירה אלא ד' אמות שלפני אותו פתח: **אכסדרה.** (ג) שיש לו מן הפתח לחצר: **אין לו ד' אמות.** בחלוקת החצר: **טעמא מאי.** אמור רבנן שיש לפתח בית ד' אמות בחצר: **משום פירוק משאו.** שיפרק שם משאו מעל חמורו לפי שפתח בית אינו פנוי מכלים ואי אפשר להכניס חמור עם משאו בבית לפרק לשם: **הכא.** באכסדרה כיון (דלית) לה דפנות אפשר דמעייל לגאו ומפרק: **אכסדרה דבי רב.** דפנות סביב לה אלא שמוקפות חלונות: **אכסדרה רומייתא.** מוקפות דפנות נמוכות שאין מגיעות לתקרה: **בית שער.** בית קטן שלפני פתח טרקלין וקורין לו פורק"א בלע"ז: **מרפסת.** אלוי"ר והרבה פתחי עלייה פתוחין לו וכולן עולין דרך סולם אחד שקורין דגרי"ד: **אין להן אלא ארבע אמות.** בין כולן אצל רגלי הסולם: **לול של תרנגולין.** בית קטן שמגדלין בו תרנגולין ויש לו פתח לחצר: **יש לו ד' אמות.** בחצר או לא: **מטפס ועולה.** התרנגול מטפס וטורח ועולה דרך ראש הכותל לתוך הלול: **בית חציו מקורה כו'.** ופתוח לחצר יש לו ד' אמות בחצר או לא: **לא מבעיא קירויו מלגיו.** והחצי שאינו מקורה לצד החצר דאין לו ארבע אמות בחצר דהא אפשר למעייל חמור במשאו ומפרק שם שאין דרך לתת כלים (ד) בחצר שאינו מקורה: **אלא אפי' קירויו לצד החוץ.** וגילויו לצד פנים נמי אין לו ד' אמות דהא אפשר דמעייל חמור עד הגילוי ומפרק: **למבוי אחר.** **בני מבוי מעכבין.** אבני מבוי (ד) אחר שאינו רגיל אלא שני מבואות: **אכסניא.** חיל של מלך המוטל על בני העיר לתת להן אכסניא בבתים: **לפי בני אדם.** הדרים בבית: **מתחלקת לפי פתחים.** לגל שדות לפי שדרך הפתחים השליכו שם עד שנעשית אשפה: **שבקש לסתום כנגד פתחו.** להקיף מחיצה סביבות ד"א שיש לו במבוי כנגד פתחו: **שמרבה עליהם הדרך.** שההולך מראשו (ה) עד לצד סופו צריך להקיף סביב המחיצה: **חמש חצרות הפתוחות למבוי.** זו אצל זו לארכו וקתני מבואות שמונין הן בסופן ואחד מקצותיו פתוח לר"ה: **כולם משתמשות במבוי עם החיצונה.** כנגדה שהרי לכולם יש דרך במבוי לצאת לדרך ראשו לרה"ר וכל שיש לו דרך יש לו תשמיש שאינו מעכב דרך המבוי: **והחיצונה משתמשת לעצמה.** כנגדה ברוחב המבוי אבל לא כנגד חברותי' שאין לה עליהן דרך: **משתמש' לעצמה.** לבדה וקשיא לרב הונא דאמר כולן מעכבין ואפי' החיצונים מעכבין על הפנימיים: **היה סתום.** שהיה לו מקודם פתח פתוח לו וסתמו ולאחר זמן נמלך לפותחו: **כולם משתמשין במבוי.** בכל המבוי ואפי' חיצון על הפנימי: **שלא פרץ פצימיו.** כשנסתם פתחו לא סלק מזוזתו (ו) ומשקוף ומפתן דגלי דעתיה דלא סילק נפשיה וסופו לפותחו לאחר זמן:

תוספות

הכא אפשר דמעייל לגואי ומפרק. פרש"י דפתח אכסדרה אין לה דפנות כלל וגרס נמי בסוף פ' כל גגות (עירובין דף לד: ושם. ד"ה בשתי) כי לית ליה לשמואל פי תקרה בד' באכסדרה שאין לה דפנות כלל לית ליה פירוש וסותם בכל ארבע מחיצות ולכך קאמר שמואל באכסדרה בבקעה דאין מטלטלין בה אלא בד' אבל בשלש אית ליה דהיינו אם יש בו דופן אחד אמרי' בג' פי תקרה ולר"י נראה דסתם אכסדרה יש לה שלש מחיצות כדאמר בלא יחפור (לקמן דף כה:) דעולם הזה לאכסדרה הוא דומה דרוח צפונית אינה מסובבת ובסוף פרק כל גגות (עירובין דף לד:) גרסי' כי לית ליה בג' אבל בארבע אית ליה פי' בשלש כשאין כי אם שלש מחיצות לא אמרי' פי תקרה ברביעית אבל בד' כשיש קצת גם ממחיצה רביעית אמר פי תקרה ואכסדרה דבי רב יש לה נמי שלש מחיצות גמורות והרביעית גבוהה ד' אמות ואכסדרה רומייתא הרביעית אינה גבוהה רק עשרה טפחים אי נמי דבי רב גבוהה רביעית עשרה ורומייתא פחות מעשרה טפחים: **בעא** רב הונא מרב אמי. והא דאמר בפרק הניזקין (גיטין דף נט: ושם) גבי רב הונא קרי בכהני שאני רב הונא דאפי' ר' אמי ור' אסי כהני חשיבי דארעא דישראל מיכף כייפי לרב הונא והכא היכי בעא מיניה וי"ל דרבי אמי לחוד ורב אמי לחוד: **אכסניא** לפי פתחים כו'. פירש רבינו חננאל דמיבעיא ליה שיירא שחנתה במקום אחד הזבל איך חולקין: **אחד** מבני מבוי שבקש לסתום כנגד פתחו. פירש הקונטרס להקיף מחיצות סביבות הארבע אמות שיש לו במבוי כנגד פתחו וקשה לרבינו יצחק דלא מצינו שיהא לו ארבע אמות במבוי אלא בחצר ונראה לרבינו יצחק כפי' רבינו חננאל כגון שיושב בסוף המבוי אצל צד הסתום ורוצה לסתום כנגד פתחו כל רוחב המבוי והשתא קאמר רב הונא שמעכבין עליו בני המבוי אע"פ שהם חיצונים לפי שמרבה עליהם את הדרך פי' רגל בני אדם שיכולין לומר בני המבוי [אף] כשיש רבים במבוי יכולים ליכנס עד סוף המבוי וע"י הסתימה תרבה עלינו את הדרך ע"י בני אדם הדורכים עלינו במבוי ואף לחצרות יצטרכו ליכנס מרוב דוחק ומצינו לשון מרבה עליהם את הדרך בענין זה דתנן לקמן בחזקת הבתים (דף נט:) לקח בית בחצר אחרת לא יפתחנו לחצר השותפים ומפר' טעמא בגמרא (דף ס.) מפני שמרבה עליהם את הדרך דהיינו רגל בני אדם ובתוספתא דפ"ק דמכילתין תניא יש לו חנות ברשות הרבי' ומבקש לפותחו לחצר השותפים יכולים לעכב על ידו מפני שמרבה עליהם את הדרך: **והפנימית** משתמשת עם כולן ומשתמשת לעצמה. פי' לעצמה שאין (ה) אחרונה משתמשת עמה וחיצונה משתמשת לעצמה דלעיל אין פירושו כמו זה אלא לעצמה שאינה משתמשת עם אחרות:

עין משפט נר מצוה

קב א ב ג ד מיי' פ"ב מהלכות שכנים הל' ג ד סמג עשין פב טוש"ע ח"מ סימן קעב סעיף ז:
קג ה מיי' שם הל' ה טוש"ע שם סעיף ו:
קד ו מיי' שם הל' ו טוש"ע שם סעיף ו:
קה ז מיי' פ"ה מהל' שכנים הלכה ב סמג שם טוש"ע ח"מ סי' קסב סעיף ו:
קו ח ט מיי' שם פ"ב הלכה ב סמג שם טוש"ע ח"מ סי' קעג סעיף ח:
קז י מיי' שם פ"ה הל' ט סמג שם טוש"ע ח"מ סי' קסב סעיף ז:
קח כ ל מיי' שם הל' י טוש"ע שם סעי' ה:

רבינו גרשום

[תחילת הפירוש ששייך לכאן נדפס בעמוד הקודם]

חסורי מיחסרא והכי קתני דתנא קמא מיירי [נמי] בחצירות נמצאת הפנימית משתמשת לעצמה ומשתמשת עם כולן דברי ר' דסבר אין מעכב עליו לסתום ד' אמות שלו ורבי שמעון אומר וכן כולם משתמשות במבוי בכל המבוי שהוא בהדיא שלא לסתום כנגד פתחו כדי שלא ירבה על האחרים את הדרך שיכולין בני מבוי לעכב עליו ורב הונא סבירא ליה כר"ש בן אלעזר. א) כפ"ה. ואית דאמרי חיצונה משתמשת לעצמה דיש לכולן רשות לעבור דרך עליה אבל היא משמשת לעצמה דאין לה רשות לעבור דרך עליהן. ולהכי אם ביקשה החיצונה לסתום לפניהם מלעבור עליה אינה יכולה לסתום מתוך דרשות לכולן יש (לו) לעבור עליה. אבל אם בקשו כולן לסתום לפני החיצונה כדי שלא תעבור עליהן. יכולין לסתום משום שאין דרכה של חיצונה לעבור עליהן. וכיון דסתמי לה הוי שלא תעבור עליהן תהא החיצונה משמשת לעצמה וכן לשנייה וכן לשלישית וכן לרביעית עד לחמישית שהיא פנימית דהשתא נמצא שיש לה רשות לעבור על כולן ואין לכולן רשות לעבור עליה להכי יכולה פנימית להשתמש ולסתום בפני עצמה כדי שלא יעבור כולן עליה והן אין יכולין לסתום בפניה כדי שלא תעבור עליהן אלמא דהני יכולין לסתום זה על זה וקשיא למאן דאמר אחד מבני מבוי דהכי משמע דכי קאמר תנא אחד מבני מבוי בין לחיצונה על כולן בין לכולן על החיצונה אין להם רשות על זה לסתום מפני שמרבה עליהן את הדרך. לא תנאי היא וכן כו' עד החיצונה משתמשת לעצמה כדדייקינן לעיל דלכולם יש להן רשות לעבור ולסתום בפני החיצונה ואין לחיצונה רשות לעבור ולסתום בפניהם: ר' שמעון אומר כולם משתמשות במבוי אמטו להכי דאית לכולן תשמיש למבוי להכי יש רשות לכולן לעבור זו על זו בין לחיצונה על כולן בין לכולן על החיצונה וכי היכי דזו אינה יכולה לסתום בפני כולן כך כולן אינן יכולין לסתום בפניהם כ"ז ג) למ"ה אבל מסתבר הכי: **היה סתום ובקש לפותחו.** כעין אמר מר שאם היה פתח פתוח לכתחילה לאותו מבוי שעכשיו רוצה לחזור פתחו שם וסתמו הואיל דהוה תמן מעיקרא **אין יכולין לעכב עליו. אמר רבא לא שנו** דאין מעכבין אלא שלא פרץ את פצימיו הואיל שאין נפרצין חזקה יש לפותחו: [מכאן שייך לדף יב.] **אינו מטמא כל סביביו.** אם היה מת בבית אע"פ שסתום הוא הואיל ולא פרץ את פצימיו אינו מטמא כל סביביו דבית בד' אמות כקבר דאיכא למימר הואיל שלא עקר הפצימין ולא סתמו לגמרי באותו פתח יפתח ויוציאהו **אבל פרץ את פצימיו וסתמו** מהכל **מטמא כל סביביו** דיש לו דין קבר הואיל וסתום מכל צדדיו כקבר דטומאה בוקעת ויוצאה דליכא למימר מן הצד יוציאהו: **ענין אחר שלא פרץ את פצימיו** כלומר היה סותם הפתח ולא היה סותר צורת הפתח המשקופין והמזוזות אלא בנה בנין סתימה עלייהו דמתוך שלא עקרן ודאי היה דעתו לפתוח להכי **אין מעכבין בו** מלפתוח. ודיקא נמי **דתניא** גבי בית דאע"ג דסתום פתחו **יש לו ד' אמות** והיינו נמי טעמא [כיון] דלא פרץ פצימיו והיה דעתו לפתוח: **קבר** שיש לאדם בחצירו ועשה מחיצה דפנות כל סביביו וסיכוך. והשתא אע"ג דאיכא מחיצה סביב הקבר ואיכא פתח בההנהו מחיצות. אם **כשסתם** אותו פתח **לא פרץ פצימה** כיון דנראה מקום הפתח. כמאן דאיתא לפתח דמי ובוקעת בו את הטומאה **ומטמא סביביו.** אבל אם פרץ והוי כשאר כותל **לא.** למ"ה: **מבואות המפולשות** פתוחין **לעיר אחרת.** כלומר דנהיגו בני העיר אחרת לעבור דרך האי מבוי וליכנס לעיר זו ולצאת ממנה דרך מבוי זה: **[לקלקלו.** לסותמו]. **המפולשין לרשות הרבים. להעמיד להן דלתות** לעכב **בני רה"ר** ליכנס במבוי כל שעה שירצו: **סבור מינה הני מילי** דמעכבין למיעבד דלתות ליסתם לבני רה"ר (הני מילי) **בתוך ד' אמות** של מבוי אותן ד' אמות הסמוכות לר"ה **כדר' זירא: ולא היא דלענין טומאה** אמרי' ד' אמות ג) במבוי בר"ה דספיקו טהור באותן ד' אמות (מבוי דברשות הרבים) דגמרינן מסוטה. **אבל הכא** בכוליה מבוי מצו לעכב דלא מצו למיזל בני רה"ר אלא דרך אותו מבוי: **פיסקא. ואין חולקין את השדה עד שתהא גדולה.** דיכולין לזרוע בה **ט' קבין לזה וט' קבין לזה** דבציר מהכי לא חשיב שדה שהוא סאה וחצי שהוא ע"ה אמה אורך על רוחב נ' דגמרי לה מחצר המשכן דהוי ק' על נ' ואמרינן דהיינו בית זרע סאתים: **מר כי אתריה** דבהכי חשיב שדה בט' קבין בציר לא ובאתריה דר"י היו השדות ביוקר והוי חשיבי שדה בט' חצאי קבין: **בבבל** שלא היו שדות ביוקר כבא"י **מאי** בכמה חשוב התם שדה. **א"ר יוסף בי רדו יומא.** כלומר כי היכי דיש לאכה לפועל לחרוש בה יום שלם לפי שלא ימצא פועל שישכיר עצמו כי אם ליום אחד שלם ואם יחלקו פחות מכדי ספוק יום פעולת יום אחד כל חד וחד נמצא הפועל משלים פעולתו בחצי היום או בט' שעות והיה מבקש הפועל שכירות יום שלם: **היכי דמי.** הא בי רדו יומא כלומר באיזה חריש אמרת שב' פעמים חורש את השדה אחת תיכף לקצירה ולאותה חרישה קרי כרבא ובאותה חרישה שתיכף לקצירה חורש הפועל כל היום עד לערב ושוב חורשין אותה ביום זריעה ואותו היום אין חורש הפועל אלא ט' שעות ובג' שעות זורע בעל הבית מה שהפועל חורש בט' שעות והכי מנהג ועכשיו בעי בעל גמרא באיזו חרישת פעולת יום **יום זריעה** דאינו אלא ט' שעות **לא הוי יומא כרבא** כלומר כשחוזר ומשכיר ביום קציר לא הוה פעולת יום שלם בחרישה דלאחר קצירה דבט' שעות תשלים פעולתו ונמצא יושב ובטל ג' שעות ונמצא מפסיד בעל הבית. **ואם בי רדו יומא כרבא** כלומר אם מאותה חרישה אמרת דחורשין תיכף לקצירה כל היום **לא הוי תרי יומא דזרעא** כלומר אין שם פעולת חרישת ב' ימים של יום זריעה שביום חרישה תכף לקצירה חורש כל י"ב שעות ואם תאמר באותו יום חרישה אמרי דהיינו פעולת יום שלם כשיבא לאותה חרישה של זריעה לא ימצא שם פעולת ב' ימים כי ביום זריעה אינו חורש אלא ט' שעות ולא ישאר לפעולה מחרת אלא פעולת ג' שעות ונמצא פועל יושב ט' שעות ויפסיד בעה"ב שצריך לשוכרו ביום שלם שלא ירצה פועל להשכיר עצמו למחצית היום.

חשק שלמה על רבינו גרשום א) הוא ר"מ: ק פירש המורה: ב) הוא ר"מ: לא מפי המורה: ג) נ"ל במבוי הסמוך לרה"ר כרה"ר דמי.

מסורת הש"ס

א) [מנחות דף לג.], ב) [תרגום של התדרה אידרון], ג) [נ"ל לאון], ד) [בדפו' בתלי ועי' רש"ש], ה) נ"ל אחרת ועי' רש"ש.

הגהות הב"ח

(א) גמרא היו ארבעה או חמשה בתים פתוחים למרפסת: (ב) שם ר"ה מרב אמי כל"ל ואות ר' נמחק: (ג) רש"י ד"ה אכסדרה שיש לה פתח לחצר כל"ל ותי' מן ואות ה' נמחק: (ד) שם ד"ה בני מבוי מעכבין בני מבוי האחר כל"ל: (ה) ד"ה שמרבה כו' שההולך מראשו לצד סופו כל"ל ותי' עד נמחק: (ו) ד"ה שלא פרץ וכו' מזוזתו ומשקופו ומפתנו דגלי:

לעזי רש"י

פורק"א. פירוש בית שער (עיין רש"י מנחות דף לג ע"ב ד"ה בית שער). אלוייר. פירוש מרפסת (עיין רש"י עירובין דף נט ע"א ד"ה מרפסת), גזוזטרא (רש"י עירובין דף עח ע"ב ד"ה שתי גזוזטראות ועיין רש"י סוכה דף לב ע"ב ד"ה והקיפום גזוזטרא). דגרי"ד. פירוש סולם, מעלות (רש"י שמות כ, כג), מדרגות (רש"י יחזקאל לג, שה"ש ב, יד):

ליקוטי רש"י

אכסדרה. מקורה בגג אלא עליות שלנו ואינו משופע והיא קירוי שבכל התלמוד [עירובין כה.]. פרוצה מד' רוחותיה ועומד קירויה על ד' יתידות ונותנין ד' קורות מיתד ליתד ועליהן מסדרין הנסרים וכו' [שם]. אכסדראות סמוכות להקיף בית או חצר ולאיכא מחיצה מבחוץ [שם]. פרוזדור שלפני בתים [יומא יא.]. שלפני הבית שקורין פורטיק"ו [סוכה ג:]. אין עושין דפנות אלא אכסדרה אלא פעמים שעושין אותה לפני הבית ודופן הבית סותמה מאחריה [שם יח:]. באכסדרה דבי רב. שיש לה ד' דפנות אלא שאין מגיעות לסכך [מנחות לג.]. אידרונא. חדר [לעיל ז.]. באכסדרה רומייתא. עשויה חלונות חלונות וקורין לוי"א [מנחות לג:]. מרפסת. עליה ארוכה על פני החצר על פני דפנות הרבה ובה פתחים הרבה לפי מחיצותיה ודיורין בכל אחת ואחת ועושין שם הפתחים לפני עליה וכולן עולים בסולם אחד למרפסת ודרך המרפסת נכנסין ויוצאין כולן מרפסת אלוייר סולם אשקל"א [סוכה ג.]. אלוויי"ר בלעז דיורי עליות סמוכות זו לזו ופתוחות לחצר ועושין מרפסת על פני אורך עליות ופותחין לה פתחי כולן ועולין ויורדין דרך סולם של מרפסת לחצר [עירובין נט.]. אלור"ד והוא ארוך לפני פתחי עליות הרבה וכולן עולין דרך שם [יומא שם]. אלוויי"א [מנחות שם]. פצימיו. עמודים [מנחות שם]. תניא דמסייע לך. דלא פקע שם פתח מיניה אלא בסתימה מעלייתא [שבת קמו:].

אֲבָל מְיַיחֵד לֵיהּ פִּיתְחָא – **But if he had designated an entrance for this** purpose,[1] אֵין לוֹ אֶלָּא אַרְבַּע אַמּוֹת לִפְנֵי פִּתְחוֹ – **[the son] has only** an area of **four *amos*** by four *amos* **in front of his door** (i.e. the special door near the pit).[2]

The Gemara discusses the "four-*amos* entitlement" with regard to other types of courtyard structures:

אָמַר רַב הוּנָא אַכְסַדְרָה אֵין לָהּ אַרְבַּע אַמּוֹת – **Rav Huna said:** The owner of **a pavilion**[3] **is not entitled to four *amos*** in front of the pavilion when the courtyard is divided.

Rav Huna explains his reasoning:

טַעְמָא מַאי – **What is the reason** that the Rabbis awarded four *amos* in front of each entrance to a house in a courtyard? מִשּׁוּם פֵּירוּק מַשָּׂאוֹ – **For purposes of unloading one's** donkey's **burden** there.[4] הָכָא אֶפְשָׁר דְּעָיֵיל לְגַוַּאי וּמְפָרֵק – **Here** in the case of a pavilion, however, **it is possible to go inside** with the animal **and unload** it there.[5] Hence, there was no need for the Rabbis to designate a loading area in courtyards in front of pavilions.

The Gemara challenges Rav Huna's ruling:

מְתִיב רַב שֵׁשֶׁת – **Rav Sheishess retorted** to Rav Huna by citing a Baraisa: אֶחָד שַׁעֲרֵי בָתִּים וְאֶחָד שַׁעֲרֵי אַכְסַדְרָאוֹת יֵשׁ לָהֶן אַרְבַּע אַמּוֹת – THE GATES[6] OF HOUSES AND THE GATES[6] OF PAVILIONS ARE BOTH ACCORDED FOUR *AMOS* for unloading purposes when the courtyard is divided! This contradicts Rav Huna, who ruled that the owner of a pavilion is not granted four *amos*. – ? –

The Gemara attempts to resolve the contradiction:

כִּי תַּנְיָא הַהִיא – **When the Baraisa taught that [ruling],** בְּאַכְסַדְרָה דְּבֵי רַב – it was **with respect to the pavilion of an academy.**[7] Since this type of pavilion was completely enclosed, furniture was kept there on a permanent basis, thus rendering it impossible to unload an animal inside. For that reason the owner received four *amos* at the entrance. Rav Huna, on the other hand, spoke of a pavilion without walls.

The Gemara rejects this explanation:

אַכְסַדְרָה דְּבֵי רַב – Can the Baraisa be referring to **the pavilion of an academy?** פְּשִׁיטָא – **It is obvious** that the owner of such a pavilion is entitled to four *amos*, אִידְרוֹנָא מְעַלְּיָא הוּא – for since it has four walls, **it is a regular room!** Since it is unnecessary to state the law of an academic pavilion, the Baraisa must be referring to a *standard* pavilion – thus contradicting Rav Huna's ruling!

The Gemara offers another solution:

אֶלָּא בְּאַכְסַדְרָה רוֹמְיְיתָא – **Rather,** the Baraisa refers **to a Roman pavilion.**[8]

The "four-*amos* entitlement" is applied to other courtyard structures:

תָּנוּ רַבָּנָן – **The Rabbis taught in a Baraisa:** בֵּית שַׁעַר אַכְסַדְרָה וּמִרְפֶּסֶת יֵשׁ לָהֶן אַרְבַּע אַמּוֹת – A PORCH,[9] A PAVILION[10] AND the staircase that ascends to A GALLERY[11] ARE ALL ACCORDED FOUR *AMOS* for unloading purposes when a courtyard is divided. הָיוּ חֲמִשָּׁה בָתִּים פְּתוּחִין לְמִרְפֶּסֶת – IF, for example, FIVE APARTMENTS on the second floor of the building OPENED ONTO THE GALLERY, and the residents of all five apartments used the same staircase to ascend from the courtyard to the gallery, אֵין לָהֶן אֶלָּא אַרְבַּע אַמּוֹת בִּלְבַד – [THESE PEOPLE] ARE nonetheless ENTITLED TO ONLY FOUR *AMOS* at the foot of the staircase – that is, each resident does not receive his own loading area in the courtyard. Just as the residents of the upper floor must share the staircase, so must they share the unloading area at the foot of the staircase.

R' Yochanan posed a question:

בְּעָא מִינֵּיהּ רַבִּי יוֹחָנָן מֵרַבִּי יַנַּאי – **R' Yochanan inquired of R' Yannai:** לוּל שֶׁל תַּרְנְגוֹלִין יֵשׁ לוֹ אַרְבַּע אַמּוֹת אוֹ אֵין לוֹ אַרְבַּע אַמּוֹת – **Is a chicken coop** that opens into a courtyard **accorded four *amos*** in front of its entrance **or not?**[12]

R' Yannai replied:

אָמַר לֵיהּ טַעְמָא מַאי – **[R' Yannai] said to [R' Yochanan]: What is the reason** that the Rabbis awarded four *amos* for each entrance to a house in a courtyard? מִשּׁוּם פֵּירוּק מַשָּׂאוֹ – **For purposes of unloading one's** animal's **burden** there. הָכָא מְטַפֵּס וְעוֹלֶה מְטַפֵּס וְיוֹרֵד – **Here,** however, the owner of a chicken coop has no unloading to do; rather, **[the chickens] scramble up and down** over the walls of the coop to let themselves in and out.[13] Therefore, four *amos* are not awarded to the owner of the coop.

The Gemara considers another case:

בְּעָא מִינֵּיהּ רָבָא מֵרַב נַחְמָן – **Rava inquired of Rav Nachman:** בַּיִת חֶצְיוֹ מְקוֹרֶה וְחֶצְיוֹ אֵינוֹ מְקוֹרֶה – Regarding **a building, half of which is covered** with a roof **and half of which is not covered** with a roof, and whose entrance opens into a courtyard, יֵשׁ לוֹ אַרְבַּע אַמּוֹת אוֹ אֵין לוֹ אַרְבַּע אַמּוֹת – **is it accorded four *amos*** in the courtyard **or is it not accorded four *amos*?**

NOTES

1. I.e. if the father had a special door at the end of the house near the pit, and it was through this door that he would normally pass either to throw the date stones into the pit or to remove them (*Rashi*).

2. His four *amos* are located on the side of the pit opposite the door. Thus, if the pit was situated within four *amos* of the door, the owner is entitled to *no* extra space, since in any event he is entitled to an area of four *amos* squared in front of his door.

3. This structure consists of a roof supported by columns, but lacking walls (*Rashi*). According to *Tosafos,* it is a four-sided structure with only three walls.

Our text of *Rashi* (ד״ה אכסדרה) reads: "[A pavilion] that he owns from the entrance to the courtyard." This version implies that the pavilion served as a passage from the courtyard to the house, and that Rav Huna's ruling applies to the house. *Bach*, however, emends *Rashi* to read: "[A pavilion] that has an entrance into the courtyard." This version implies that the pavilion was a detached structure, and was itself the subject of Rav Huna's ruling.

4. Since most houses are crowded with furniture, it would be impossible to bring the animal into the house and unload it there (*Rashi*).

5. Since a pavilion has no walls (or, according to *Tosafos,* has one open side), its owner does not keep furniture or other items there on a regular basis. Hence, there is ample space to unload the animal inside (*Rashba, Ritva*).

6. I.e. the entrances.

7. This type of pavilion had four walls; since, however, there were windows on all sides, the Baraisa referred to it as a "pavilion" (*Rashi;* cf. *Tosafos*).

8. This type of pavilion was surrounded on all sides by low walls – i.e. they did not reach the ceiling (*Rashi ;* cf. *Tosafos*). Hence, the Baraisa's ruling is not obvious, for one might surmise that the walls did not provide enough protection to keep furniture or other items inside. If that were the case, unloading could take place within the pavilion. The Baraisa thus informs us that a Roman pavilion is regarded as a closed room, in which articles or furniture are kept and unloading is unfeasible. The Baraisa therefore awarded an area of four *amos* before the entrance of the pavilion for that purpose. Rav Huna, on the other hand, spoke of a pavilion that had no walls at all.

9. This was a small enclosed structure that stood before the entrance of a mansion [and opened into the courtyard] (*Rashi*).

10. As explained above, this is a Roman pavilion.

11. A type of balcony erected along the front of the second floor of a two-story building. Residents of the apartments on the second floor exited their apartments onto the gallery, and then descended by means of a staircase into the courtyard (*Rashi*).

12. In this coop the owner was raising chickens and other species of fowl (*Rashi, Meiri*). R' Yochanan therefore asked whether the owner receives four *amos* in front of the coop in order to tend properly to the coop (see *Ritva* and *Meiri*).

13. This is *Rashi's* interpretation; cf. *Yad Ramah* and *Ritva*.

קב א ב ג ד מיי' פ"ב מהלכות שכנים הל' ג ד סמג עשין פב טוש"ע ח"מ סימן קנב סעיף ד:
קג ה מיי' שם הל' ה טוש"ע שם סעי' ה:
קד ו מיי' שם הל' ו טוש"ע שם סעיף ו:
קה ז מיי' שם פ"ה הלכה טו סמג שם טוש"ע ח"מ סי' קסב סעיף ו:
קו ח ט מיי' שם פ"ב הלכה ח סמג שם טוש"ע ח"מ סי' קנב סעיף ט:
קז י מיי' שם פ"ה הל' טו סמג שם טוש"ע ח"מ סי' קסב סעיף ז:
קח כ ל מיי' שם הל' טו טוש"ע שם סעי' ה:

רבינו גרשום

[תחילת הפירוש ששייך לכאן נדפס בעמוד הקודם] חסורי מיחסרא והכי קתני דתנא קמא מיירי [נמי] בחצירות ובמצאת הפנימית משתמשת לעצמה ומשתמשת עם כולן דברי ר' דסבר אין מעכב עליו כולן המבוי לסתום ד' אמות שלו ורבי שמעון אומר וכן כולם משתמשות במבוי בין החיצונה בין הפנימית כנגד פתחו כדי שלא ירבה על האחרים את הדרך שיכולין בני מבוי לעכב עליו ורב הונא סבירא ליה כר"ש בן אלעזר. א) כפ"ה. ואית דאמרי חיצונה משתמשת לעצמה דיש לכולן רשות לעבור דרך עליה אבל היא משתמשת לעצמה דאין לה רשות לעבור דרך עליהן. והכי אם ביקשה החיצונה לסתום לפניהם מלעבור עליה אינה יכולה לסתום מתוך שאם ביקשו כולן יש (לו) לעבור עליה. אבל אם בקשו כולן לסתום לפני החיצונה כדי שלא תעבור עליהן. יכולין לסתום משום שאין דרכה של חיצונה לעבור עליהן. וכיון דסתמי לה הרי שלא תעבור עליהן תהא החיצונה משמשת לעצמה וכן לשניה וכן לשלישית וכן לרביעית עד לחמישית שהיא פנימית דהשתא נמצא שיש לה רשות לעבור על כולן ואין לכולן רשות לעבור עליה להכי יכולה פנימית לישתמשה ולסתום בפני עצמה כדי שלא יעבור כולן עליה והן אין יכולין לסתום בפניה כדי שלא תעבור עליהן אלמא דהני יכולין לסתום זה על זה וקשיא למאן דאמר אחד מבני מבוי דהכי משמע ולא משמע אחד מבני מבוי בין לחיצונה על כולן בין לכולן על החיצונה אין להם רשות זה על זה לסתום מפני שמרבה עליהן את הדרך. לא תנאי היא וכן כו' עד החיצונה משתמשת לעצמה כדדייקינן לעיל דלכולם יש להן רשות לעבור ולסתום בפני החיצונה ואין לחיצונה רשות לעבור ולסתום בפניהם: ר' שמעון אומר כולם משתמשות במבוי אמטו להכי דאית לכולן תשמיש אחד להכי יש רשות לכולן לעבור על זו זו בין לחיצונה על כולן בין לכולן על החיצונה וכי

הכא

הכא אפשר דמעייל לגואי ומפרק. פרש"י דהכא אכסדרה אין לה דפנות כלל וגרס נמי בסוף פ' כל גגות (עירובין דף לד: ושם. ד"ה בשתי) כי לית ליה לשמואל פי תקרה בד' אבל בג' אית ליה פירוש באכסדרה שאין לה דפנות כלל לית ליה לשמואל פי תקרה יורד וסותם בכל ארבע מחיצות ולכך קאמר שמואל באכסדרה בבקעה דאין מטלטלין בה אלא בד' אבל בשלש אית ליה דהיינו אם יש בו דופן אחד אמרי' בג' פי תקרה ולר"י נראה דהכא אכסדרה יש לה שלש מחיצות כדאמר בלא יחפור (לקמן דף כה:) דעולם הזה לאכסדרה הוא דומה דרוח צפונית אינה מסובבת ובסוף פרק כל גגות (עירובין דף לד:) גרסי' כי לית ליה בג' אבל בארבע אית ליה פי' בשלש כשאין כי אם שלש מחיצות לא אמרי' פי תקרה ברביעית אבל בד' כשיש קצת גם ממחיצה רביעית אמר פי תקרה ואכסדרה דבי רב יש לה נמי שלש מחיצות גמורות והרביעית גבוהה ד' אמות ואכסדרה רומיתא הרביעית אינה גבוהה רק עשרה טפחים אי נמי דבי רב גבוהה רביעית עשרה ורומיתא פחות מעשרה טפחים: **בעא** רב הונא מרב אמי. והא דאמר בפרק הניזקין (גיטין דף נט: ושם) גבי רב הונא קרי בכהני שאני רב הונא דאפי' ר' אמי ור' אסי כהני חשיבי דארעא דישראל מיכף כייפי לרב הונא והכא היכי בעא מיניה וי"ל דרבי אמי לחוד ורב אמי לחוד: **אכסניא** לפי פתחים כו'. פירש רבינו חננאל דמיבעיא ליה שיירא שחנתה במקום אחד הזבל איך חולקין: **אחד** מבני מבוי שבקש לסתום כנגד פתחו. פירש הקונטרס להקיף מחיצות סביבות הארבע אמות שיש לו במבוי כנגד פתחו וקשה לרבינו יצחק דלא מצינו שיהא לו ארבע אמות במבוי אלא בחצר ונראה לרבינו יצחק כפי' רבינו חננאל כגון שיושב בסוף המבוי אצל צד הסתום ורוצה לסתום כנגד פתחו כל רוחב המבוי והשתא קאמר רב הונא שמעכבין עליו בני המבוי אע"פ שהם חיצונים לפי שמרבה עליהם את הדרך פי' רגל בני אדם שיכולין לומר בני המבוי [אף] כשיש רבים במבוי יכולים ליכנס עד סוף המבוי וע"י הסתימה תרבה עלינו את הדרך ע"י בני אדם הדורכים עלינו במבוי ואף לחצרות יצטרכו ליכנס מרוב דוחק ומצינו לשון מרבה עליהם את הדרך בענין זה דתנן לקמן בחזקת הבתים (דף נט:) לקח בית בחצר אחרת לא יפתחנו לחצר השותפים ומפר' טעמא בגמרא (דף ס.) מפני שמרבה עליהם את הדרך דהיינו רגל בני אדם ובתוספתא דפ"ק דמכילתין תניא יש לו חנות ברשות הרבי' ומבקש לפותחו לחצר השותפים יכולים לעכב על ידו מפני שמרבה עליהם את הדרך: **והפנימית** משתמשת עם כולן ומשתמשת לעצמה. פי' לעצמה שאין ה) אחרונה משתמשת עמה וחיצונה משתמשת לעצמה דלעיל אין פירושו כמו זה אלא לעצמה שאינה משתמשת עם אחרות:

אבל מייחד ליה פיתחא אין לו אלא ארבע אמות לפני פתחו אמר רב הונא א אכסדרה אין לה ד' אמות טעמא מאי משום פירוק משאו הכא אפשר דעייל לגואי ומפרק מתיב רב ששת אחד שערי בתים ואחד שערי אכסדראות יש להן ד' אמות כי תניא ההיא (א) באכסדרה דבי רב אכסדרה דבי רב פשיטא ג אידרונ' מעליא הוא ב אלא באכסדרה רומייתא ת"ר ג בית שער אכסדרה ומרפסת יש להן ד' אמות ד היו (א) חמשה בתים פתוחין למרפסת אין להן אלא ד' אמות בלבד בעא מיניה ר' יוחנן מר' ינאי לול של תרנגולין יש לו ד' אמות או אין לו ד' אמות ה א"ל טעמא מאי משום פירוק משאו הכא מטפס ועולה מטפס ויורד בעא מיניה רבא מרב נחמן בית חציו מקורה וחציו אינו מקורה יש לו ד' אמות או אין לו ד"א א"ל ו אין לו ד' אמות לא מבעיא קירויו מלגיו דאפשר דעייל לגואי ומפרק אלא אפילו קירויו כלפי חוץ אפשר דעייל לגואי ומפרק בעא מיניה רב הונא (ג) מרבי אמי אחד מבני מבוי שבקש להחזיר פתחו למבוי אחר בני מבוי מעכבין עליו או אין מעכבין עליו א"ל ז בני מבוי מעכבין עליו אכסניא לפי בני אדם מתחלקת או לפי פתחים מתחלקת א"ל ח לפי בני אדם מתחלקת תניא נמי הכי ט זבל שבחצר מתחלקת לפי פתחים אכסניא לפי בני אדם אמר רב הונא אחד מבני מבוי שבקש לסתום כנגד פתחו בני מבוי מעכבין עליו שמרבה עליהן את הדרך מיתיבי י חמש חצרות פתוחות למבוי כולן משתמשות עם החיצונה והחיצונה משתמשת לעצמה והשאר משתמשות עם השניה והשניה משתמשת לעצמה ומשתמשת עם החיצונה נמצאת פנימית משתמשת לעצמה ומשתמשת עם כל אחת ואחת תנאי היא דתניא אחד מבני מבוי שבקש להחזיר פתחו למבוי אחר בני מבוי מעכבין עליו היה סתום ובקש לפותחו אין בני מבוי מעכבין עליו דברי רבי ר"ש בן אלעזר אומר חמש חצרות הפתוחות למבוי כולן משתמשות במבוי זו עם זו חצרות מאן דכר שמייהו חסורי מחסרא והכי קתני וכן חמש חצרות הפתוחות למבוי כולן משתמשות עם החיצונה והחיצונה משתמשת לעצמה וכו' דברי רבי ר' שמעון בן אלעזר אומר חמש חצרות הפתוחות למבוי כולן משתמשות במבוי: אמר מר כ היה סתום ובקש לפותחו אין בני מבוי מעכבין עליו אמר רבא ל לא שנו אלא שלא פרץ את פצימיו אבל פרץ את פצימיו בני מבוי מעכבין עליו א"ל אביי לרבא תניא דמסייע לך
בית

רש"י

אבל מייחד ליה פיתחא. שהיה לו פתח לסוף ביתו אצל החפירה ודרך אותו פתח היה רגיל להשליך הגרעינין וליטלן אין לו בחצר בשביל החפירה אלא ד' אמות שלפני אותו פתח: אכסדרה. (ג) שיש לו מן הפתח לחצר: אין לו ד' אמות. במחלוקת החצר: טעמא מאי. אמור רבנן שיש לפתח בית ד' אמות בחצר: משום פירוק משאו. שיפרק שם משאו מעל חמורו לפי שהבית אינו פנוי מכלים ואי אפשר להכניס חמור עם משאו בבית לפרק שם: הכא. באכסדרה כיון ג) (דאית) לה דפנות אפשר דמעייל לגאו ומפרק: אכסדרה דבי רב. דפנות סביב לה אלא שמוקפות חלונות: אכסדרה רומייתא. מוקפות דפנות נמוכות שאין מגיעות לתקרה: בית שער. בית קטן שלפני פתח טרקלין וקורין לו פורק"א בלע"ז: מרפסת. אלווי"ר והרבה פתחי עלייה פתוחין לו וכולן עולין דרך סולם אחד שקורין דגרי"ד: אין להן אלא ארבע אמות. בין כולן אצל רגלי הסולם: לול של תרנגולין. בית קטן שמגדלין בו תרנגולין ויש לו פתח לחצר: יש לו ד' אמות. בחצר או לא: מטפס ועולה. התרנגול מטפס וטורח ועולה דרך ראש הכותל לתוך הלול: בית חציו מקורה כו'. ופתוח לחצר יש לו ד' אמות בחצר או לא: לא מבעיא קירויו מלגיו. והחצי שאינו מקורה לצד החצר דאין לו ארבע אמות בחצר דהא אפשר דמעייל חמור במשאו ומפרק שם שאין דרך לתת כלים ד) בחצר שאינו מקורה: אלא אפי' קירויו לצד החוץ. וגילויו לצד פנים נמי אין לו ד' אמות דהא אפשר דמעייל חמור עד הגילוי ומפרק: למבוי אחר. כגון בית שבין שני מבואות: בני מבוי מעכבין. אבני מבוי (ד) אחר שאינו רגיל אצלם: אכסניא. חיל של מלך המוטל על בני העיר לתת להן אכסניא בבתיהם: לפי בני אדם. הדרים בבית: מתחלקת לפי פתחים. לזבל שדות לפי שדרך הפתחים השליכו שם עד שנעשית אשפה: שבקש לסתום כנגד פתחו. להקיף מחיצה סביבות ד"א שיש לו במבוי כנגד פתחו: שמרבה עליהם הדרך. שההולך מראשו (ה) עד צד סופו צריך להקיף סביב המחיצה: חמש חצרות הפתוחות למבוי. זו אצל זו לארכו וסתם מבואות סתומין הן בסופן ואחד מקצותיו פתוח לר"ה: כולם משתמשות במבוי עם החיצונה. כנגדה שהרי לכולם יש דרך במבוי לצאת דרך ראשו לרה"ר וכל שיש לו דרך יש לו תשמיש שאינו מעכב דרך המבוי: והחיצונה משתמשת לעצמה. כנגדה ברוחב המבוי אבל לא כנגד חברותי' שאין לה עליהן דרך: משתמש' לעצמה. לבדה וקשיא לרב הונא דאמר כולן מעכבין ואפי' החצונים מעכבין על הפנימיים: היה סתום. שהיה לו מקודם פתח פתוח לו וסתמו ולאחר זמן נמלך לפותחו: כולם משתמשין במבוי. בכל המבוי ואפי' חיצון על הפנימי: שלא פרץ פצימיו. כשנסתם פתחו לא סלק מזוזתו (ו) ומשקוף ומפתן דגלי דעתיה דלא סילק נפשיה וסופו לפותחו לאחר זמן:

ה) גמרא לפני ל' מנחות דף לג:], ג) [תרגום של אידרון], ג) [צ"ל דלית], ד) [בדפוס"י בחצר ועי' רש"ש], ה) צ"ל אחרת ועי' רש"ש.

הגהות הב"ח

(א) גמרא היו ארבעה או חמשה בתים פתוחים למרפסת: (ב) שם ר"ה מרב אמי כצ"ל ותיבת מרבי נמחק: (ג) רש"י ד"ה אכסדרה שיש לה פתח לחצר כצ"ל ותי' מן ותיבת ה' נמחק: (ד) שם ד"ה בני מבוי מעכבין בני מבוי האחר כצ"ל: (ה) ד"ה שמרבה כו' ההולך מראשו לצד סופו כצ"ל ותי' עד נמחק: (ו) ד"ה שלא פרץ וכו' מזוזתו ומשקופו ומפתנו דגלי:

לעזי רש"י

פורק"א. פירוש בית שער (עיין רש"י מנחות דף לג ע"ב ד"ה בית שער). אלוויי"ר. פירוש מרפסת (עיין רש"י עירובין דף נט ע"ב ד"ה ומוכה דף ג ע"ב ד"ה מרפסת), גזוזטרא (רש"י עירובין דף עח ע"א ד"ה שתי גזוזטראות ועיין רש"י סוכה דף לא ע"ב ד"ה והקיפוה גזוזטרא). דגרי"ד. פירוש סולם, מעלות (רש"י שמות כ, כג), מדרגות (רש"י יחזקאל מ, כו, ש"ש ב, יד):

ליקוטי רש"י

אכסדרה. מקורה בגג אלא כעליות שלנו ואינו משופע והיא קירוי שבכל התלמוד [עירובין כה.]. פרוזה מד' רוחותיה ועומד קירויה על ד' יתידות ועומדין ד' קורות מיזד ליזד ועליהן מסדרין הנסרין וכו' בעיר סמך לאכסדראות מתוקנות להקיף בית או חצר ואינה מחיצה אחת או שתים [שם צ.]. פרוזדור שלפני בתים [יומא יא.]. שלפני הבית וקורין פורטיק"ו [סוכה ג:]. אין עושין דפנות לפנים לאכסדרה אבל עמודים שעושין אותה לפני הבית ודומן הבית סומכת מאחריה [שם יח.]. באכסדרה דבי רב. שיש לה ד' דפנות אלא שאין מגיעות לסכך [מנחות לג:]. אידרונא. חדר [לעיל ז.]. באכסדרה רומייתא. עשויה חלונות חלונות [מנחות שם]. מרפסת. עליה ארוכה על פני החצר על פני רשות הרבים וכה פתחים הרבה לפי מחלוקתה ודיורין בכל אחת ואחת ועושין מרפסת כלוחך לפני הפתחים כלוחך עליה וכולן עולים בסולם אחד למרפסת ודלך המרפסת נכנסין ויוצאין כולן מרפסת אלווי"ר סולם אשקל"א [סוכה ג.]. אלווי"ר בלע"ז דיורי עליות סמוכות זו לזו ופתוחות לחצר ועושין מרפסת על פני אורך עליות ופותחין לה פתחיהן ויורדין דרך כולן ועולין דרך סולם של מרפסת לחצר [עירובין נט:]. אלוו"ד והוא ארוך לפני פתחי עליות הרבה וכולן עולין דרך שם [יומא שם]. אלואייר"א [מנחות שם]. פצימיו. עמודים [מנחות שם]. תנא דמסייע לך. לא פקע שם פתח מיניה אלא בסתימה מעלייתא [שבת קמו:].

רבינו גרשום

היכי דמי אינה יכולה לסתום בפני כולן כך כולן אינן יכולין לסתום בפניה כ"ז ג) מ"ה אבל מסתבר הכי: היה סתום ובקש לפותחו. [מכאן שייך לדף יב.] כעין אמר מר שאם היה פתח פתוח לכתחילה לאותו מבוי שבקשו רוצה לחזור פתחו שם וסתמו הואיל דהדה תמן [illegible]

Rav Nachman replied:

אָמַר לֵיהּ אֵין לוֹ אַרְבַּע אַמּוֹת – [Rav Nachman] said to [Rava]: It is not accorded four *amos.*

Rav Nachman explained his reasoning:

לֹא מִבַּעֲיָא קֵירוּיוֹ מִלְּגָיו – It is unnecessary to state that the building is not accorded four *amos* for unloading **if its covering was within,** and the exposed part of the structure abutted the courtyard, **דְּאֶפְשָׁר דְּעָיֵיל לְגַוַּאי וּמְפָרֵק – for** in that case **it is possible to come inside** the uncovered section **and unload** the animal there.[14] **אֶלָּא אֲפִילּוּ קֵירוּיוֹ כְּלַפֵּי חוּץ – But even** if **its covering was without,** abutting the courtyard, and the exposed section was within, the owner still does not receive four *amos* in the courtyard, **אֶפְשָׁר דְּעָיֵיל לְגַוַּאי וּמְפָרֵק –** for **it is possible** to **come into** the **inner,** uncovered section **and unload** the animal there.[15] Thus, the owner of a partially covered structure does not receive four *amos* in the courtyard, regardless of the location of the exposed section.

The Gemara poses two questions, the second of which involves the subject of entrances to houses:

בְּעָא מִינֵּיהּ רַב הוּנָא מֵרַבִּי אַמִּי – Rav Huna inquired of Rav[16] **Ami: אֶחָד מִבְּנֵי מָבוֹי שֶׁבִּקֵּשׁ לְהַחֲזִיר פִּתְחוֹ לְמָבוֹי אַחֵר – If one of the residents of a *mavoi*** (alleyway)[17] **sought to reverse his** house's **entrance** to open **into another *mavoi*,**[18] **בְּנֵי מָבוֹי מְעַכְּבִין עָלָיו – can the residents of the** other ***mavoi*** legally **prevent him** from doing so, **אוֹ אֵין מְעַכְּבִין עָלָיו – or can they not prevent him?**

Rav Ami replied:

אָמַר לֵיהּ בְּנֵי מָבוֹי מְעַכְּבִין עָלָיו – [Rav Ami] said to [Rav Huna]: The residents of the second ***mavoi*** **can** legally **prevent him** from creating the entrance, on the grounds that it would increase the traffic[19] in their *mavoi.*[20]

Rav Huna posed a second question:

אַכְסַנְיָא – When private citizens are required to provide **quartering** for soldiers of the king's army, **לְפִי בְּנֵי אָדָם מִתְחַלֶּקֶת – is** [the quartering] assignment **divided according to the** number of **people** that inhabit each building, **אוֹ לְפִי פְּתָחִים מִתְחַלֶּקֶת – or is it divided according to** the number of **entrances** that each building has?[21]

Rav Ami replied:

אָמַר לֵיהּ – [Rav Ami] said to [Rav Huna]: לְפִי בְּנֵי אָדָם מִתְחַלֶּקֶת – [The quartering] is divided according to the number of **people** (i.e. families) that inhabit each building.

The Gemara cites a Baraisa whose second ruling supports Rav Ami:

תַּנְיָא נַמִּי הָכִי – It was also taught thus in a Baraisa: זֶבֶל שֶׁבְּחָצֵר מִתְחַלֶּקֶת לְפִי פְּתָחִים – FERTILIZER THAT IS lying **IN A** jointly owned **COURTYARD IS DIVIDED ACCORDING TO THE** number of **ENTRANCES** that open into the courtyard.[22] **אַכְסַנְיָא לְפִי בְּנֵי אָדָם – THE QUARTERING** of soldiers, however, is assigned **ACCORDING TO THE** number of **PEOPLE** (i.e. families) residing in each apartment building.[23] This ruling of the Baraisa supports Rav Ami.

The Gemara previously established that each entrance to a house in a courtyard is awarded four *amos* for unloading purposes. The Gemara now assumes that, similarly, every en-

NOTES

14. It is unlikely that the owner would keep furniture or other items in the exposed section of the building. [Hence, he would have sufficient room to unload his animal there] (*Rashi*). Of course, the exposed section must itself comprise an area of four *amos* by four *amos,* which is the minimum space required for unloading. If it does not, the owner is entitled to four *amos* before the entrance of the building (*Rashba, Ritva*).

15. Having to lead the animal through the covered part of the building to reach the inner section presents no problem, for since the building is partially exposed to the elements, the covered section will be sparsely furnished. Hence, there will be room for the animal to pass through easily (*Meiri*).

16. *Tosafos* point out that Rav Huna was addressing *Rav* Ami, and not Rabbi Ami (as the text of our Gemara would indicate); see also *Bach.*

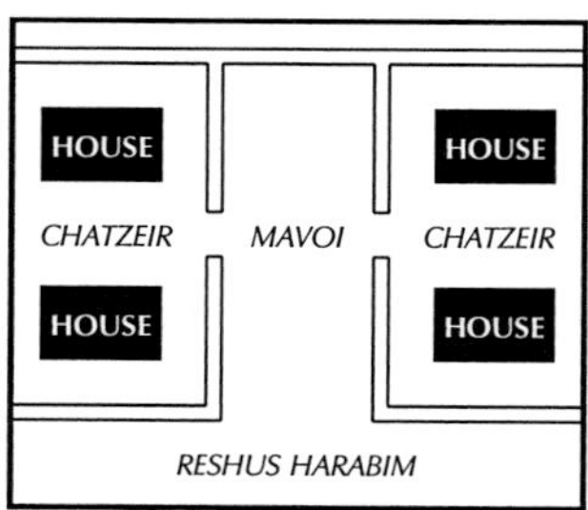

17. In Mishnaic times the layout of a town usually consisted of a network of houses, courtyards and alleyways that eventually led the *reshus harabim* (public thoroughfare). Normally, houses opened into courtyards (*chatzeiros),* which in turn opened into alleys (*mavois*) that led out to the *reshus harabim* (see diagram).

18. In the Gemara's case, this resident's house was situated between two *mavois* (*Rashi).* He wished to seal his old entrance (see *Rashba*), which led into mavoi A, and create a new entrance on the other side of his house so that he could exit to the *reshus harabim* through *mavoi* B (see diagram).

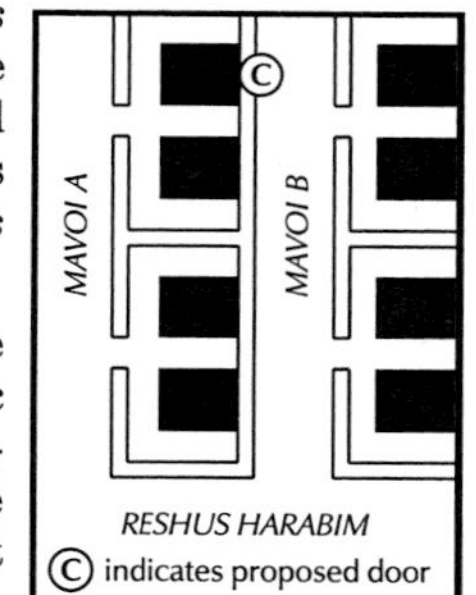

19. I.e. the traffic from this resident's house passing through their *mavoi* to the public thoroughfare (*Ramban;* cf. *Rashba*). *Meiri,* however, understands that the residents of the second *mavoi* may object on the grounds that they would be inconvenienced by having to detour around the four-*amos* area that the newcomer would receive in front of his entrance.

According to the first interpretation, if the entrance to the first *mavoi* was not sealed, then certainly the residents of the second *mavoi* could protest the opening of the second entrance, in order to prevent the several residents of the first *mavoi* from crossing into their *mavoi.* Rav Huna's query concerned only an increase of traffic from one household (*Rashba*).

Our elucidation of the Gemara has followed the interpretation of *Rashi* and other Rishonim, who understand that Rav Huna questions whether the residents of the *second mavoi* are empowered to prevent the creation of the new entrance. Still other Rishonim understand, however, that the question is whether the residents of the *first mavoi* have that power (see *Ran, Ritva*).

20. *Rashba* and *Yad Ramah* point out that Rav Huna's question applies only when the second *mavoi* is closed at one end (אֵינוֹ מְפוּלָּשׁ). If, however, public thoroughfares bounded the *mavoi* on both ends, the *mavoi's* residents could not protest the new entrance, since in any event their *mavoi* is inundated with traffic crossing from one *reshus harabim* to the other.

21. The Gemara speaks of multi-family apartment buildings with one or more entrances. Hence, the Gemara questions whether the number of soldiers assigned to each building is determined by the number of families in the building, or by the number of entrances to each building. According to the latter criterion, an apartment building housing several families but with only one entrance would be assigned only one unit of soldiers (*Rashi*; see *Meiri;* cf. interpretation of *Rabbeinu Chananel* cited by *Tosafos*).

22. The residents would throw their waste from their doorways into the courtyard. After a time they would create heaps of waste that eventually turned into manure, which they used to fertilize their fields. Since the waste was ejected through the entrances, the manure is divided according to the number of entrances in the courtyard [so that, for example, two or more families using the same entrance would divide one share of fertilizer] (*Rashi*). *Meiri* explains further: The conversion of waste to manure is stimulated by the interaction of the waste with the soil, upon which it rests. Hence, the manure is divided according to these plots of soil, and – of course – those buildings with more entrances have more plots of soil.

23. Thus, even if two families shared one entrance to their building, each family was counted for purposes of determining the number of soldiers to be quartered in the building.

אבל מייחד ליה פיתחא אין לו אלא ארבע אמות לפני פתחו אמר רב הונא א אכסדרה אין לה ד' אמות טעמא מאי משום פירוק משאו הכא אפשר דעייל לגואי ומפרק מתיב רב ששת אחד שערי בתים ואחד שערי אכסדראות יש להן ד' אמות כי תניא ההיא באכסדרה דבי רב אכסדרה דבי רב פשיטא ג) אידרונא מעליא הוא ב אלא באכסדרה רומייתא ת"ר ג בית שער אכסדרה ומרפסת יש להן ד' אמות ד היו (א) חמשה בתים פתוחין למרפסת אין להן אלא ד' אמות בלבד בעא מיניה ר' יוחנן מר' ינאי לול של תרנגולין יש לו ד' אמות או אין לו ד' אמות ה א"ל טעמא מאי משום פירוק משאו הכא מטפס ועולה מטפס ויורד בעא מיניה רבא מרב נחמן בית חציו מקורה וחציו אינו מקורה יש לו ד' אמות או אין לו ד"א א"ל ו אין לו ד' אמות לא מבעיא קירויו מלגיו דאפשר דעייל לגואי ומפרק אלא אפילו קירויו כלפי חוץ אפשר דעייל לגואי ומפרק בעא מיניה רב הונא (ב) מרבי אמי אחד מבני מבוי שבקש להחזיר פתחו למבוי אחר בני מבוי מעכבין עליו או אין מעכבין עליו א"ל ז בני מבוי מעכבין עליו אכסניא לפי בני אדם מתחלקת או לפי פתחים מתחלקת א"ל ח לפי בני אדם מתחלקת תניא נמי הכי ט זבל שבחצר מתחלקת לפי פתחים אכסניא לפי בני אדם אמר רב הונא אחד מבני מבוי שבקש לסתום כנגד פתחו בני מבוי מעכבין עליו שמרבה עליהן את הדרך מיתיבי י חמש חצרות פתוחות למבוי כולן משתמשות עם החיצונה והחיצונה משתמשת לעצמה והשאר משתמשות עם השניה והשניה משתמשת לעצמה ומשתמשת עם החיצונה נמצאת פנימית משתמשת לעצמה ומשתמשת עם כל אחת ואחת תנאי היא דתניא אחד מבני מבוי שבקש להחזיר פתחו למבוי אחר בני מבוי מעכבין עליו היה סתום ובקש לפותחו אין בני מבוי מעכבין עליו דברי רבי ר"ש בן אלעזר אומר חמש חצרות הפתוחות למבוי כולן משתמשות במבוי זו עם זו חצרות מאן דכר שמייהו חסורי מחסרא והכי קתני וכן חמש חצרות הפתוחות למבוי כולן משתמשות עם החיצונה והחיצונה משתמשת לעצמה וכו' דברי רבי ר' שמעון בן אלעזר אומר חמש חצרות הפתוחות למבוי כולן משתמשות במבוי: אמר מר כ היה סתום ובקש לפותחו אין בני מבוי מעכבין עליו אמר רבא ל לא שנו אלא שלא פרץ את פצימיו אבל פרץ את פצימיו בני מבוי מעכבין עליו א"ל אביי לרבא תניא דמסייע לך בית

רש"י

אבל מייחד ליה פיתחא. שהיה לו פתח לסוף ביתו אצל החפירה ולכך אותו פתח היה רגיל להשליך הגרעינין וליטלן אין לו בחצר בשביל החפירה אלא ד' אמות שלפני אותו פתח: אכסדרה. (ג) שיש לו מן הפתח לחצר: אין לו ד' אמות. בחלוקת החצר: טעמא מאי. אמור רבנן שיש לפתח בית ד' אמות בחצר: משום פירוק משאו. שיפרק שם משאו מעל חמורו לפי שסתם בית אינו פנוי מכלים ואי אפשר להכניס חמור עם משאו בבית לפרק לשם: הכא. באכסדרה כיון (דלית) לה דפנות אפשר דמעייל לגאו ומפרק: אכסדרה דבי רב. דפנות סביב לה אלא שמוקפות חלונות: אכסדרה רומייתא. מוקפות דפנות נמוכות שאין מגיעות לתקרה: בית שער. בית קטן שלפני פתח טרקלין וקורין לו פורק"א בלע"ז: מרפסת. אלוייר"ר והרבה פתחי עלייה פתוחין לו וכולן עולין דרך סולם אחד שקורין דגרי"ד: אין להן אלא ארבע אמות. בין כולן אצל רגלי הסולם: לול של תרנגולין. בית קטן שמגדלין בו תרנגולין ויש לו פתח לחצר: יש לו ד' אמות. בחצר או לא: מטפס ועולה. התרנגול מטפס וטורח ועולה דרך ראש הכותל לתוך הלול: בית חציו מקורה כו'. ופתוח לחצר יש לו ד' אמות בחצר או לא: לא מבעיא קירויו מלגיו. והחצי שאינו מקורה לצד החצר דאין לו ארבע אמות בחצר דהא אפשר למעייל חמור במשאו ומפרק שם שאין דרך לתת כלים ד) בחצר שאינו מקורה: אלא אפי' קירויו לצד החוץ. וגילוייו לצד פנים נמי אין לו ד' אמות דהא אפשר דמעייל חמור עד הגילוי ומפרק: למבוי אחר. כגון בית שבין שני מבואות: בני מבוי מעכבין. אבני מבוי (ד) אחר שאינו רגיל אצלם: אכסניא. חיל של מלך המוטל על בני העיר לתת להן אכסניא בבתיהם: לפי בני אדם. הדריס בבית: מתחלקת לפי פתחים. לזבל שדות לפי שדרך הפתחים השליכו שם עד שנעשית אשפה: שבקש לסתום כנגד פתחו. להקיף מחילה סביבות ד"א שיש לו במבוי כנגד פתחו: שמרבה עליהם הדרך. שההולך מראשו (ה) עד צד סופו צריך להקיף סביב המחילה: חמש חצרות הפתוחות למבוי. זו אצל זו לארכו וסתם מבואות סתומין הן בסופן ואחד מקצותיו פתוח לר"ה: כולם משתמשות במבוי עם החיצונה. כנגדה שהרי לכולם יש דרך במבוי לצאת דרך ראשו לרה"ר וכל שיש לו דרך יש לו תשמיש שאינו מעכב דרך המבוי: והחיצונה משתמשת לעצמה. כנגדה ברוחב המבוי אבל לא כנגד חברותי' שאין לה עליהן דרך: משתמש' לעצמה. לבדה וקשיא לרב הונא דאמר כולן מעכבין ואפי' החצונים מעכבין על הפנימיים: היה סתום. שהיה לו מקודם פתח פתוח לו וסתמו ולאחר זמן נמלך לפותחו: כולם משתמשין במבוי. בכל המבוי ואפי' חיצון על הפנימי: שלא פרץ פצימיו. כשנסתם פתחו לא סלק מזוזתו (ו) ומשקוף ומפתן דגלי דעתיה דלא סילק נפשיה וסופו לפותחו לאחר זמן:

תוספות

הכא אפשר דמעייל לגואי ומפרק. פרש"י דסתם אכסדרה אין לה דפנות כלל וגרס נמי בסוף פ' כל גגות (עירובין דף צד: ושם. ד"ה בשני) כי לית ליה לשמואל פי תקרה בד' אבל בג' אית ליה פירוש באכסדרה שאין לה דפנות כלל לית ליה לשמואל פי תקרה יורד וסותם בכל ארבע מחיצות ולכך קאמר שמואל באכסדרה בבקעה דלאין מטלטלין בה אלא בד' אבל בשלש אית ליה דהיינו אם יש בו דופן אחד אמרי' בג' פי תקרה ולר"י נראה דסתם אכסדרה יש לה שלש מחיצות כדאמר בלא יחפור (לקמן דף כה:) דעולם הזה לאכסדרה הוא דומה דרום לפונית אינה מסובבת ובסוף פרק כל גגות (עירובין דף צד:) גרסי' כי לית ליה בג' אבל בארבע אית ליה פי' בשלש כשאין כי אם שלש מחיצות לא אמרי' פי תקרה ברביעית אבל בד' כשיש קצת גם ממחיצה רביעית אמר פי תקרה ואכסדרה דבי רב יש לה נמי שלש מחיצות גמורות והרביעית גבוהה ד' אמות ואכסדרה רומאית הרביעית אינה גבוהה רק עשרה טפחים אי נמי דבי רב גבוהה רביעית עשרה ורומאית פחות מעשרה טפחים: בעא רב הונא מרב אמי. והא דאמר בפרק הניזקין (גיטין דף נט: ושם) גבי רב הונא קרי בכהני שאני רב הונא דאפי' ר' אמי ור' אסי כהני חשיבי דארעא דישראל מיכף כייפי לרב הונא והכא היכי בעא מיניה וי"ל דרבי אמי לחוד ורב אמי לחוד: אכסניא לפי פתחים כו'. פירש רבינו חננאל דמיבעיא ליה שיירא שחנתה במקום אחד הזבל איך חולקין: אחד מבני מבוי שבקש לסתום כנגד פתחו. פירש הקונטרס להקיף מחילות סביבות הארבע אמות שיש לו במבוי כנגד פתחו וקשה לרבינו יצחק דלא מצינו שיהא לו ארבע אמות במבוי אלא בחצר ונראה לרבינו יצחק כפי' רבינו חננאל כגון שיושב בסוף המבוי אצל צד הסתום ורוצה לסתום כנגד פתחו כל רוחב המבוי והשתא קאמר רב הונא שמעכבין עליו בני המבוי אע"פ שהם חיצונים לפי שמרבה עליהם את הדרך פי' רגל בני אדם שיכולין לומר בני המבוי [אף] כשיש רבים במבוי יכולים ליכנס עד סוף המבוי וע"י הסתימה תרבה עלינו את הדרך ע"י בני אדם הדורכים עלינו במבוי ואף לחצרות יצטרכו ליכנס מרוב דוחק ומצינו לשון מרבה עליהם את הדרך בענין זה דתנן לקמן בחזקת הבתים (דף נט:) לקח בית בחצר אחרת לא יפתחנו לחצר השותפים ומפר' טעמא בגמרא (דף ס.) מפני שמרבה עליהם את הדרך דהיינו רגל בני אדם ובתוספתא דפ"ק דמכילתין תניא יש לו חנות ברשות הרבי' ומבקש לפותחו לחצר השותפים יכולים לעכב על ידו מפני שמרבה עליהם את הדרך: והפנימית משתמשת עם כולן ומשתמשת לעצמה. פי' לעצמה שאין ה) אחרונה משתמשת עמה וחיצונה משתמשת לעצמה דלעיל אין פירושו כמו זה אלא לעצמה שאינה משתמשת עם אחרות:

עין משפט נר מצוה

קב א ב ג ד מיי' פ"ג מהלכות שכנים הל' ג ד סמג עשין פב טוש"ע ח"מ סימן קעג סעיף ד:
קג ה מיי' שם הל' ה טוש"ע שם סעי' ה:
קד ו מיי' שם הל' ו טוש"ע שם סעיף ו:
קה ז מיי' שם פ"ה הלכה טו סמג שם טוש"ע ח"מ סי' קסג סעיף ו:
קו ח ט מיי' שם פ"ג הלכה ח סמג שם טוש"ע ח"מ סי' קעג סעיף ט:
קז י מיי' שם פ"ה הל' טז סמג שם טוש"ע ח"מ סי' קסב סעיף ז:
קח כ ל מיי' שם הל' טו טוש"ע שם סעי' ה:

רבינו גרשום

[תחילת הפירוש ששייך לכאן נדפס בעמוד הקודם] **חסורי מיחסרא והכי קתני** דתנא קמא איירי [נמי] בחצירות **נמצאת הפנימית משתמשת לעצמה ומשתמשת עם כולן דברי ר'** דסבר אין מעכב עליו [בן] המבוי לסתום ד' אמות שלו **ורבי שמעון אומר וכן כולם משתמשות במבוי** כגון שהוא בהדיא שלא יסתום כנגד פתחו כדי שלא ירבה על האחרים את הדרך שיכולין בני מבוי לעכב עליו ורב הונא סבירא ליה כר"ש בן אלעזר. א) כפ"ה. **ואית דאמרי חיצונה משתמשת לעצמה** דיש לכולן רשות לעבור דרך עליה אבל היא משמשת לעצמה דאין לה רשות לעבור דרך עליהן. ולהכי אם ביקשה החיצונה לסתום לפניהם מלעבור עליה אינה יכולה לסתום מתוך דרשות כולן יש (לו) לעבור עליה. אבל אם בקשו כולן לסתום לפני החיצונה כדי שלא תעבור עליהן. יכולין לסתום משום שאין דרכה של חיצונה לעבור עליהן. וכיון דסתמי לה הני שלא תעבור עליהן תהא החיצונה משמשת לעצמה וכן לשניה וכן לשלישית וכן לרביעית עד לחמישית שהיא פנימית דהשתא נמצא שיש לה רשות לעבור על כולן ואין לכולן רשות לעבור עליה להכי יכולה פנימית לישתמיש ולסתום בפני עצמה כדי שלא יעבור כולן עליה והן אין יכולין לסתום פנימית כדי שלא תעבור עליהן אלמא דהני יכולין לסתום זה על זה וקשיא למאן דאמר אחד מבני מבוי דהכי משמע ותני דמשום **אחד מבני מבוי** בין לחיצונה על כולן בין לכולן על החיצונה אין להם רשות זה על זה לסתום **מפני שמרבה עליהן את הדרך.** לא תנאי היא וכן כו' עד **החיצונה משתמשת לעצמה** כדדייקינן לעיל דלכולם יש להן רשות לעבור ולסתום בפני החיצונה ואין לחיצונה רשות לעבור ולסתום בפניהם: **ר' שמעון אומר כולם משתמשות במבוי** אמטו להכי דאית לכולן תשמיש למבוי להכי יש רשות לכולן לעבור זו על זו בין לחיצונה על כולן בין לכולן על החיצונה וכי היכי דזו אינה יכולה לסתום בפני כולן כך כולן אינן יכולין לסתום בפניהם כ"ז ב) למ"ה אבל מסתבר הכי: **היה סתום ובקש לפותחו.** כעין אמר מר שאם היה פתח פתוח לכתחילה לאותו מבוי שעכשיו רוצה לחזור פתחו שם וסתמו הואיל דהוה תמן מעיקרא **אין יכולין לעכב עליו. אמר רבא לא שנו** דאין מעכבין אלא שלא פרץ את פצימיו הואיל שאין נפרצין חזקה יש לפותחו: [מכאן שייך לדף יב.] **אינו מטמא כל סביביו.** אם היה מת בבית אע"פ שסתום הוא הואיל ולא פרץ את פצימיו אינו מטמא כל סביביו דבית בד' אמות כקבר דאיכא למימר הואיל שלא עקר הפצימין ולא סתמו לגמרי באותו פתח יפתח ויוציאהו **אבל פרץ את פצימיו וסתמו** מהכל **מטמא כל סביביו** דיש לו דין קבר הואיל וסתום מכל צדדיו כקבר דטומאה בוקעת ויוצאה דליכא למימר מן הצד יוציאוהו: **ענין אחר שלא פרץ את פצימיו** כלומר היה סותם הפתח ולא היה סותר צורת הפתח המשקופין והמזוזות אלא בנה בנין סתימה עלייהו דמתוך שלא עקרן ודאי היה דעתו לפתוח להכי **אין מעכבין בו** מלפתוח. ודיקא נמי **דתניא** גבי בית דאע"ג דסתום פתחו **יש לו ד' אמות** והיינו נמי טעמא [כיון] דלא פרץ פצימיו והיה דעתו לפתוח: **קבר שיש** לאדם בחצירו ועשה מחיצה דפנות כל סביביו וסיכוך. והשתא אע"ג דאיכא מחיצה סביב הקבר ואיכא פתח בהנהו מחיצות. אם **כשסתם** אותו פתח **לא פרץ פצימה** כיון דנראה מקום הפתח. כמאן דאיתא לפתח דמי ובוקעת בו את הטומאה **ומטמא סביביו.** אבל אם פרץ והוי כשאר כותל **לא.** למ"ה: **מבואות המפולשות** פתוחין **לעיר אחרת.** כלומר דנהיגו בני העיר אחרת לעבור דרך האי מבוי וליכנס לעיר זו ולצאת ממנה דרך מבוי זה: **[לקלקלו.** לסותמו]. **המפולשין לרשות הרבים. להעמיד להן דלתות** לעכב בני רה"ר ליכנס במבוי כל שעה שירצו: **סבור מינה הני מילי** דמעכבין למיעבד דלתות ליסתם לבני רה"ר (הני מילי) **בתוך ד' אמות** של מבוי אותן ד' אמות הסמוכות לר"ה **כדר' זירא: ולא היא דלענין טומאה** אמרי' ד' אמות ג) במבוי בר"ה דספיקו טהור באותן ד' אמות (מבוי דברשות הרבים) דגמרינן מסוטה. **אבל הכא** בכוליה מבוי מצו לעכב דלא מצו למיזל בני רה"ר אלא דרך אותו מבוי: **פיסקא. ואין חולקין את השדה עד שתהא גדולה.** דיכולין לזרוע בה **ט' קבין לזה וט' קבין לזה** דבציר מהכי לא חשיב שדה שהוא סאה וחצי שהוא ע"ה אמה אורך על רוחב נ' דגמרי לה מחצר המשכן דהוי ק' על נ' ואמרינן דהיינו בית זרע סאתים: **מר כי אתריה** דבהכי חשיב שדה בט' קבין בציר לא ובאתריה דר"י היו השדות ביוקר והוי חשיבי שדה בט' חצאי קבין: **בבבל** שלא היו שדות ביוקר כבא"י **מאי** בכמה חשוב התם שדה. **א"ר יוסף בי רדו יומא.** כלומר כי היכי דיש מלאכה לפועל לחרוש בה יום שלם לפי שלא ימצא פועל שישכיר עצמו כי אם ליום אחד שלם ואם יחלקו פחות מכדי ספוק יום פעולת יום אחד כל חד וחד נמצא הפועל משלים פעולתו בחצי היום או בט' שעות והיה מבקש הפועל שכירות יום שלם: **היכי דמי.** הא בי רדו יומא כלומר באיזה חריש אמרת שב' פעמים חורש את השדה אחת תיכף לקצירה ולאותה חרישה קרי כרבא ובאותה חרישה שתיכף לקצירה חורש הפועל כל היום עד לערב ושוב חורשין אותה ביום זריעה ואותו היום אין חורש הפועל אלא ט' שעות ובג' שעות זורע בעל הבית מה שהפועל חורש בט' שעות והכי מנהג ועכשיו בעי בעל גמרא באיזו חרישת פעולת יום **יום זריעה** דאינו אלא ט' שעות **לא הוי יומא כרבא** כלומר כשחוזר ומשכיר ביום קציר לא הוה פעולת יום שלם בחרישה דלאחר קצירה דבט' שעות תשלים פעולתו ונמצא יושב ובטל ג' שעות ונמצא מפסיד בעל הבית. **ואם בי רדו יומא כרבא** כלומר אם מאותה חרישה אמרת דחורשין תיכף לקצירה כל היום **לא הוי תרי יומא דזרעא** כלומר אין שם פעולת חרישת ב' ימים של יום זריעה שביום חרישה תכף לקצירה חורש כל י"ב שעות ואם תאמר באותו יום חרישה אמרי דהיינו פעולת יום שלם כשיבא לאותה חרישה של זריעה לא ימצא שם פעולת ב' ימים כי ביום זריעה אינו חורש אלא ט' שעות ולא ישאר לפעולת מחרת אלא פעולת ג' שעות ונמצא פועל יושב ט' שעות ויפסיד בעה"ב שצריך לשוכרו ביום שלם שלא ירצה פועל להשכיר עצמו למחצית היום.

חשק שלמה על רבינו גרשום א) הוא ר"ח: כן פירש המורה: ב) הוא ר"ת: לא מפי המורה: ג) נ"ל במבוי הסמוך לרה"ר כרה"ר דמי.

מסורת הש"ס

א) [מנחות דף לג:], ב) [תרגום של התדרה אידרון], ג) [ל"ל דאין], ד) [בדפו"י בתלי וער' רש"ש], ה) ל"ל אתרת וער' רש"ש.

הגהות הב"ח

(א) גמרא היו ארבעה או חמשה בתים פתוחים למרפסת: (ב) שם ר"ה מרב אמי כל"ל ואות י' נמחק: (ג) רש"י ד"ה אכסדרה שיש לה פתח לחצר כל"ל ותי' מן ואות ה' נמחק: (ד) שם ד"ה בני מבוי מעכבין בני מבוי האחר כל"ל: (ה) ד"ה שמרבה כו' שההולך מראשו לצד סופו כל"ל ותי' עד נמחק: (ו) ד"ה שלא פרץ וכו' מזוזתו ומשקופו ומפתנו דגלי:

לעזי רש"י

פורק"א. פירוש בית שער (עיין רש"י מנחות דף לג ע"ב ד"ה בית שער). אלוייר"ר. פירוש מרפסת (עיין רש"י עירובין דף נט ע"ב ד"ה מרפסת, וסוכה דף ג ע"ב ד"ה מרפסת), גזוזטרה (רש"י עירובין דף עח ע"ב ד"ה שתי גזוזטראות ועיין רש"י סוכה דף כח ע"ב ד"ה והקיפוה גזוזטרא). דגרי"ד. פירוש סולם, מעלות (רש"י שמות כ, כג), מדרגות (רש"י יחזקאל לא, יח; שה"ש ב, יד):

ליקוטי רש"י

אכסדרה. מקורה בגג חלק כעליות שלנו ואינו משופע והיא קירוי שבכל התלמוד [עירובין כה.]. פרוצה מד' רוחותיה ועומד קירויה על ד' יתידות ונותנין ד' קורות מיתד ליתד ועליהן מסדרין הנסרין וכו' בעיר [שם]. אכסדרה. שתי אכסדראות מקומות להקיף בית או חצר ואינה מחיצה אלא אם פתוח [סוכה צ.]. פרוזדור שלפני בתים [יומא יא.]. שלפני הבית קורין פורטיק"ו [סוכה ג:]. אין עושין דפנות לאכסדראות אלא עמודים שעושין אותה לפני הבית ודופן הבית סומכת מאחריה [שם יח:]. באכסדרה דבי רב. שיש לה ד' דפנות אלא שאין מגיעות לגג [מנחות לג:]. אידרונא. חדר [לעיל ז.]. באכסדרה רומייתא. עשויה חלונות חלונות וקורין לה לויי"ר [מנחות לג:]. מרפסת. עלייה ארוכה על פני החצר על פני רשות הרבים והם ופתחים הרבה לפי מחלוקתה ודיורין בכל אחת ואחת ועושין מרפסת לפני הפתחים כלוכך אחד למרפסת ודרך המרפסת נכנסין ויוצאין כולן מרפסת ולויי"ר סולם אשקלי"ה [סוכה ג:]. אלדוי"ר בלעז דיורי עליות סמוכות זו לזו ופתוחות לחצר ועושין מרפסת על פני אורך עליות ופותחין לה פתחי כולן ועולין ויורדין דרך סולם של מרפסת לחצר [עירובין נט:]. אלרו"ד והוא ארוך לפני פתחי עליות הרבה וכולן עולין דרך שם [יומא שם]. אלואייר"א [מנחות שם]. פצימיו. עמודים [מנחות שם]. תניא דמסייע לך. דלא פקע שם פתח מיניה אלא בסתימה מעלייתא [שבת קמו:].

trance to a courtyard is awarded four *amos* in the *mavoi* to which it opens.[24] Rav Huna here decides whether the residents of the courtyard may enclose this loading area if they wish:

אָמַר רַב הוּנָא אֶחָד מִבְּנֵי מָבוֹי שֶׁבִּקֵּשׁ לִסְתּוֹם כְּנֶגֶד פִּתְחוֹ – **Rav Huna said:** If **one of the residents of a *mavoi* sought to enclose** the four-*amah* unloading area **opposite his** courtyard's **entrance** by erecting a wall around it, בְּנֵי מָבוֹי מְעַכְּבִין עָלָיו – **the** other **residents of the *mavoi* can** legally **prevent him** from doing so, שֶׁמַּרְבֶּה עֲלֵיהֶן אֶת הַדֶּרֶךְ – **because [the enclosure] will increase the way for them.**[25] Although the Rabbis awarded courtyard residents four *amos* in their *mavoi* for unloading, that space nonetheless belongs to all the residents of the *mavoi*,[26] and so use of the space may not unduly inconvenience these other residents.

Rav Huna ruled that "the residents of the *mavoi* can prevent" the erection of an enclosure that would impede traffic in the *mavoi*. This unqualified statement implies that *any* resident of the *mavoi* may assert that right. The Gemara now challenges this aspect of Rav Huna's ruling:

מֵיתִיבֵי חָמֵשׁ חֲצֵרוֹת פְּתוּחוֹת לְמָבוֹי – **They retorted** to Rav Huna from the evidence of a Baraisa: In the case of FIVE COURTYARDS THAT OPEN INTO A *MAVOI*,[27] כּוּלָּן מִשְׁתַּמְּשׁוֹת עִם הַחִיצוֹנָה – ALL the residents of the *mavoi* MAY USE the section of *mavoi* OPPOSITE THE OUTERMOST [COURTYARD], i.e. the courtyard closest to the public thoroughfare.[28] וְהַחִיצוֹנָה מִשְׁתַּמֶּשֶׁת לְעַצְמָהּ – AND the residents of THE OUTERMOST [COURTYARD] MAY USE only the section of *mavoi* OPPOSITE [THEIR OWN COURTYARD].[29]

The Baraisa continues:

וְהַשְּׁאָר מִשְׁתַּמְּשׁוֹת עִם הַשְּׁנִיָּה – AND THE REST of the residents of the *mavoi* (i.e. everyone but the residents of the outermost courtyard) MAY USE the section of *mavoi* OPPOSITE THE SECOND outermost [COURTYARD],[30] for they all must pass through it to reach the public thoroughfare. וְהַשְּׁנִיָּה מִשְׁתַּמֶּשֶׁת לְעַצְמָהּ – AND THE residents of the SECOND outermost [COURTYARD] MAY USE the section of *mavoi* OPPOSITE [THEIR OWN COURTYARD], וּמִשְׁתַּמֶּשֶׁת עִם הַחִיצוֹנָה – AND additionally MAY USE the section of *mavoi* OPPOSITE THE OUTERMOST [COURTYARD], since they have a right of passage through both sections.

The Baraisa concludes:

נִמְצֵאת פְּנִימִית – Thus, WE FIND that the residents of THE INNERMOST [COURTYARD][31] מִשְׁתַּמֶּשֶׁת לְעַצְמָהּ – MAY USE the section of *mavoi* opposite their own courtyard EXCLUSIVELY,[32] for no one else has reason to walk there, וּמִשְׁתַּמֶּשֶׁת עִם כָּל אַחַת וְאַחַת – AND THEY MAY also USE the sections of *mavoi* OPPOSITE EACH AND EVERY ONE of the other courtyards, for they must pass through the entire *mavoi* to reach the public thoroughfare. The Baraisa clearly indicates that residents of a *mavoi* have rights only in that part of the *mavoi* where they have a right of passage. The Baraisa thus contradicts Rav Huna, who ruled that *all* residents of a *mavoi* — even those from the courtyard closest to the public thoroughfare — have the right to protest the erection of an enclosure anywhere in the *mavoi*. — ? —

The Gemara answers:

תַּנָּאֵי הִיא – **[This matter] is** the subject of **a Tannaic dispute,** and Rav Huna takes the position of the Tanna, cited below, who disagreed with the ruling in the Baraisa just quoted, דְּתַנְיָא – **for it was taught in** another **Baraisa:** אֶחָד מִבְּנֵי מָבוֹי שֶׁבִּקֵּשׁ לְהַחֲזִיר פִּתְחוֹ לְמָבוֹי אַחֵר – If ONE OF THE RESIDENTS OF A *MAVOI* SOUGHT TO REVERSE HIS house's ENTRANCE to open INTO ANOTHER *MAVOI*,[33] בְּנֵי מָבוֹי מְעַכְּבִין עָלָיו – THE RESIDENTS OF THE other *MAVOI* CAN legally PREVENT HIM from doing so, on the grounds that the new entrance would increase traffic in their *mavoi*.[34] הָיָה סָתוּם – If, however, the original entrance of the house had opened into the second *mavoi* and WAS subsequently SEALED, וּבִקֵּשׁ לְפוֹתְחוֹ – AND afterward [THE OWNER] SOUGHT TO REOPEN IT, אֵין בְּנֵי מָבוֹי מְעַכְּבִין עָלָיו – THE RESIDENTS OF THE second *MAVOI* MAY NOT PREVENT HIM from restoring the entrance, inasmuch as he had previously acquired a right of passage in their *mavoi*. דִּבְרֵי רַבִּי – THESE ARE THE WORDS OF REBBI.[35] רַבִּי שִׁמְעוֹן בֶּן אֶלְעָזָר אוֹמֵר – R' SHIMON BEN ELAZAR SAYS: חָמֵשׁ חֲצֵרוֹת הַפְּתוּחוֹת לְמָבוֹי – In the case of FIVE COURTYARDS THAT OPEN INTO A *MAVOI*,[36] כּוּלָּן מִשְׁתַּמְּשׁוֹת בַּמָּבוֹי זוֹ עִם זוֹ – ALL the residents of the *mavoi* MAY USE THE entire *MAVOI* TOGETHER.

The Gemara is perplexed:

חֲצֵרוֹת מַאן דְּכַר שְׁמַיְיהוּ – **Courtyards?! Who mentioned them** previously, that R' Shimon ben Elazar would state his opinion on the issue?[37] Rebbi spoke only of restoring an entrance to a *mavoi*. — ? —

The Gemara explains:

חַסּוּרֵי מִחַסְּרָא – It is as if words **were missing** from the text of the Baraisa וְהָכִי קָתָנֵי – **and it teaches thus:** וְכֵן חָמֵשׁ חֲצֵרוֹת הַפְּתוּחוֹת לְמָבוֹי – AND ALSO[38] in the case of FIVE COURTYARDS THAT OPEN INTO A *MAVOI*, כּוּלָּן מִשְׁתַּמְּשׁוֹת עִם הַחִיצוֹנָה – ALL of

NOTES

24. This follows the commentary of *Rashi* and *Rabbeinu Gershom*. *Tosafos* and other Rishonim reject the notion of an unloading area in a *mavoi* for each courtyard, and therefore interpret the following passage of Gemara differently.

25. Anyone walking from one end of the *mavoi* to the other will have to detour around the enclosure (*Rashi*).

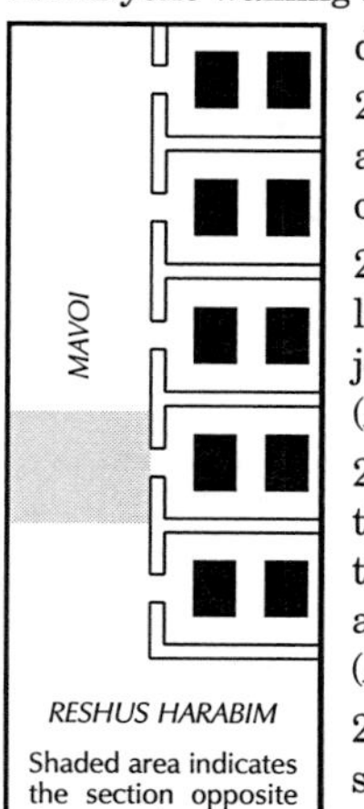

Shaded area indicates the section opposite the second outermost courtyard

26. Unlike the four-*amah* area before an entrance to a house in a courtyard (which belongs entirely to the owner of the house).

27. The five courtyards stood side by side along the length of a *mavoi* that was closed at one end and joined a public thoroughfare at its other end (*Rashi*). See diagram.

28. Since they all have the right to pass through this section of the *mavoi* to reach the public thoroughfare, they may make use of the section in any way that does not obstruct passage in the *mavoi* (*Rashi*).

29. They may not, however, use any of the inner sections of the *mavoi*, since they have no right of passage there (*Rashi*).

30. See shaded area in diagram.

31. I.e. the courtyard closest to the closed end of the *mavoi* (see note 27 above).

32. Here the word לְעַצְמָהּ means exclusively — i.e. the residents of the innermost courtyard have *exclusive* use of this space. When used previously with reference to the residents of the outermost courtyard, however, לְעַצְמָהּ connoted the idea of separateness — i.e. these residents could not use the other sections of the *mavoi* along with their neighbors from the other courtyards (*Tosafos*).

33. Although this part of the Baraisa is irrelevant to our discussion, it is nonetheless quoted because it concerns a subject previously treated (see note 18 above for an explanation of the case).

34. See notes 19 and 20 above.

35. Rabbi Yehudah HaNasi, the codifier of the Mishnah.

36. See note 27 above.

37. The language of the Baraisa (רַבִּי שִׁמְעוֹן בֶּן אֶלְעָזָר אוֹמֵר) indicates that R' Shimon was *replying* to a ruling by Rebbi on the subject of "five courtyards," for if he were introducing a new subject, the proper phrasing would be אָמַר רַבִּי שִׁמְעוֹן בֶּן אֶלְעָזָר.

38. This ruling is also issued by Rebbi, and follows his ruling on opening an entrance into another *mavoi*. The language "and also" indicates that this second ruling also empowers residents of a *mavoi* to restrict their neighbors' use of the *mavoi*.

הכא אפשר דמעייל לגואי ומפרק. פרש"י דפסקא אכסדרה אין לה דפנות כלל וגרס נמי בסוף פ' כל גגות (עירובין דף לד: ושם. ד"ה בשני) כי לית ליה לשמואל פי תקרה בד' אבל בג' אית ליה פירוש באכסדרה שאין לה דפנות כלל לית ליה לשמואל פי תקרה יורד וסותם בכל ארבע מחיצות ולכך קאמר שמואל באכסדרה בבקעה דאין מטלטלין בה אלא בד' אבל בשלש אית ליה דהיינו אם יש בו דופן אחד אמרי' בג' פי תקרה ולר"י נראה דסתם אכסדרה יש לה שלש מחיצות כדאמר בלא יחפור (לקמן דף כה:) דעולם הזה לאכסדרה הוא דומה דרום לפונית אינה מסובבת ובסוף פרק כל גגות (עירובין דף לד:) גרסי' כי לית ליה בג' אבל בארבע אית ליה פי' בשלש כשאין כי אם שלש מחיצות לא אמרי' פי תקרה ברביעית אבל בד' כשיש קצת גם ממחיצה רביעית אמר פי תקרה ואכסדרה דבי רב יש לה נמי שלש מחיצות גמורות והרביעית גבוהה ד' אמות ואכסדרה רומיתא הרביעית אינה גבוהה רק עשרה טפחים אי נמי דבי רב גבוהה רביעית עשרה ורומיתא פחות מעשרה טפחים: **בעא** רב הונא מרב אמי. והא דאמר בפרק הניזקין (גיטין דף נט: ושם) גבי רב הונא קרי בכהני שאני רב הונא דאפי' ר' אמי ור' אסי כהני חשיבי דארעא דישראל מיכף כייפי לרב הונא והכא היכי בעא מיניה וי"ל דרבי אמי לחוד ורב אמי לחוד: **אכסניא** לפי פתחים כו'. פירש רבינו חננאל דמיבעיא ליה שיירא שחנתה במקום אחד הזבל איך חולקין: **אחד** מבני מבוי שבקש לסתום כנגד פתחו. פירש הקונטרס להקיף מחיצות סביבות הארבע אמות שיש לו במבוי כנגד פתחו וקשה לרבינו יצחק דלא מצינו שיהא לו ארבע אמות במבוי אלא בחצר ונראה לרבינו יצחק כפי' רבינו חננאל כגון שיושב בסוף המבוי אצל צד הסתום ורוצה לסתום כנגד פתחו כל רוחב המבוי והשתא קאמר רב הונא שמעכבין עליו בני המבוי אע"פ שהם חיצונים לפי שמרבה עליהם את הדרך פי' רגל בני אדם שיכולין לומר בני המבוי [אף] כשיש רבים במבוי יכולים ליכנס עד סוף המבוי וע"י הסתימה מרבה עליו את הדרך ע"י בני אדם הדורכים עליו במבוי ואף לאחרות יצטרכו ליכנס מרוב דוחק ומליצו לשון מרבה עליהם את הדרך בענין זה דתנן לקמן בחזקת הבתים (דף נט:) לקח בית בחצר אחרת לא יפתחנו לחצר השותפים ומפר' טעמא בגמרא (דף ס.) מפני שמרבה עליהם את הדרך דהיינו רגל בני אדם ובתוספתא דפ"ק דמכלתין תניא יש לו חנות ברשות הרבים ומבקש לפותחו לחצר השותפים יכולים לעכב על ידו מפני שמרבה עליהם את הדרך: **והפנימית** משתמשת עם כולן ומשתמשת לעצמה. פי' לעצמה שאין (ז) אחרונה משתמשת עמה וחיצונה משתמשת לעצמה דלעיל אין פירושו כמו זה אלא לעצמה שאינה משתמשת עם אחרות:

אבל מייחד ליה פיתחא אין לו אלא ארבע אמות לפני פתחו אמר רב הונא אכסדרה אין לה ד' אמות טעמא מאי משום פירוק משאו הכא אפשר דעייל לגואי ומפרק מתיב רב ששת אחד שערי בתים ואחד שערי אכסדראות יש להן ד' אמות כי תניא ההיא באכסדרה דבי רב אכסדרה דבי רב פשיטא אידרונ' מעליא הוא אלא באכסדרה רומייתא ת"ר בית שער אכסדרה ומרפסת יש להן ד' אמות היו (א) חמשה בתים פתוחין למרפסת אין להן אלא ד' אמות בלבד בעא מיניה ר' יוחנן מר' ינאי לול של תרנגולין יש לו ד' אמות או אין לו ד' אמות א"ל טעמא מאי משום פירוק משאו הכא מטפס ועולה מטפס ויורד בעא מיניה רבא מרב נחמן בית חציו מקורה וחציו אינו מקורה יש לו ד' אמות או אין לו ד' אמות א"ל אין לו ד' אמות לא מבעיא קירויו מלגיו דאפשר דעייל לגואי ומפרק אלא אפילו קירויו כלפי חוץ אפשר דעייל לגואי ומפרק בעא מיניה רב הונא (ב) מרבי אמי אחד מבני מבוי שבקש להחזיר פתחו למבוי אחר בני מבוי מעכבין עליו או אין מעכבין עליו א"ל בני מבוי מעכבין עליו אכסניא לפי בני אדם מתחלקת או לפי פתחים מתחלקת א"ל לפי בני אדם מתחלקת תניא נמי הכי זבל שבחצר מתחלקת לפי פתחים אכסניא לפי בני אדם אמר רב הונא אחד מבני מבוי שבקש לסתום כנגד פתחו בני מבוי מעכבין עליו שמרבה עליהן את הדרך מיתיבי חמש חצרות פתוחות למבוי כולן משתמשות עם החיצונה והחיצונה משתמשת לעצמה והשאר משתמשות עם השניה והשניה משתמשת לעצמה ומשתמשת עם החיצונה נמצאת פנימית משתמשת לעצמה ומשתמשת עם כל אחת ואחת תנאי היא דתניא אחד מבני מבוי שבקש להחזיר פתחו למבוי אחר בני מבוי מעכבין עליו היה סתום ובקש לפותחו אין בני מבוי מעכבין עליו דברי רבי ר"ש בן אלעזר אומר חמש חצרות הפתוחות למבוי כולן משתמשות במבוי זו עם זו חצרות מאן דכר שמייהו חסורי מחסרא והכי קתני וכן חמש חצרות הפתוחות למבוי כולן משתמשות עם החיצונה והחיצונה משתמשת לעצמה וכו' דברי רבי רבי שמעון בן אלעזר אומר חמש חצרות הפתוחות למבוי כולן משתמשות במבוי: אמר מר [י]היה סתום ובקש לפותחו אין בני מבוי מעכבין עליו אמר רבא [כ]לא שנו אלא שלא פרץ את פצימיו אבל פרץ את פצימיו בני מבוי מעכבין עליו א"ל אביי לרבא תניא דמסייע לך בית

אבל מייחד ליה פיתחא. שהיה לו פתח לסוף ביתו אצל החפירה ודלכך אותו פתח היה רגיל להשליך הגרעינין וליטלן אין לו בחצר בשביל החפירה אלא ד' אמות שלפני אותו פתח: **אכסדרה.** (ג) שיש לו מן הפתח לחצר: **אין לו ד' אמות.** בחלוקת החצר: **טעמא מאי.** אמור רבנן שיש לפתח בית ד' אמות בחצר: **משום פירוק משאו.** שיפרק שם משאו מעל חמורו לפי שהשם בית אינו פנוי מכלים ואי אפשר להכניס חמור עם משאו בבית לפרק לשם: **הכא.** באכסדרה כיון ג) (דאית) לה דפנות אפשר דמעייל לגאו ומפרק: **אכסדרה דבי רב.** דפנות סביב לה אלא שמוקפות חלונות: **אכסדרה רומייתא.** מוקפות דפנות נמוכות שאין מגיעות לתקרה: **בית שער.** בית קטן שלפני פתח טרקלין וקורין לו פורק"א בלע"ז: **מרפסת.** אלויי"ר והרבה פתחי עלייה פתוחין לו וכולן עולין דרך סולם אחד שקורין דגרי"ד: **אין להן אלא ארבע אמות.** בין כולן אצל רגלי הסולם: **לול של תרנגולין.** בית קטן שמגדלין בו תרנגולין ויש לו פתח לחצר: **יש לו ד' אמות.** בחצר או לא: **מטפס ועולה.** התרנגול מטפס וטורח ועולה דרך ראש הכותל לתוך הלול: **בית חציו מקורה כו'.** ופתוח לחצר יש לו ד' אמות בחצר או לא: **לא מבעיא קירויו מלגיו.** והחצי שאינו מקורה לצד החצר דאין לו ארבע אמות בחצר דהא אפשר דמעייל חמור במשאו ומפרק שם שאין דרך לתת כלים ד) בחצר שאינו מקורה: **אלא אפי' קירויו לצד החוץ.** וגילויו לצד פנים נמי אין לו ד' אמות דהא אפשר דמעייל חמור עד הגילוי ומפרק: **למבוי אחר.** כגון בית שבין שני מבואות: **בני מבוי מעכבין.** אבני מבוי (ד) אחר שאינו רגיל אצלם: **אכסניא.** חיל של מלך המוטל על בני העיר לתת להן אכסניא בבתיהם: **לפי בני אדם.** הדרים בבית: **מתחלקת לפי פתחים.** לזבל שדות לפי שדרך הפתחים השליכו שם עד שנעשית אשפה: **שבקש לסתום כנגד פתחו.** להקיף מחילה סביבות ד"א שיש לו במבוי כנגד פתחו: **שמרבה עליהם הדרך.** שההולך מראשו (ה) עד לד סופו צריך להקיף סביב המחילה: **חמש חצרות הפתוחות למבוי.** זו אצל זו לארכו וסתם מבואות סתומין הן בסופן ואחד מקצותיו פתוח לר"ה: **כולם משתמשות במבוי עם החיצונה.** כנגדה שהרי לכולם יש דרך במבוי לצאת דרך ראשו לרה"ר וכל שיש לו דרך יש לו תשמיש שאינו מעכב דרך המבוי: **והחיצונה משתמשת לעצמה.** כנגדה ברוחב המבוי אבל לא כנגד חברותי' שאין לה עליהן דרך: **משתמש' לעצמה.** לבדה וקשיא לרב הונא דאמר כולן מעכבין ואפי' החצונים מעכבין על הפנימיים: **היה סתום.** שהיה לו מקודם פתח פתוח לו וסתמו ולאחר זמן נמלך לפותחו: **כולם משתמשין במבוי.** בכל המבוי ואפי' חיצון על הפנימי: **שלא פרץ פצימיו.** כשנסתם פתחו לא סלק מזוזתו (ו) ומשקוף ומפתן דגלי דעתיה דלא סילק נפשיה וסופו לפותחו לאחר זמן:

עין משפט נר מצוה

קב א ב ג ד מיי' פ"ב מהלכות שכנים הל' ג ד סמג עשין פב טוש"ע ח"מ סימן קנב סעיף ד:
קג ה מיי' שם הל' ה טוש"ע שם סעי' ה:
קד ו מיי' שם הל' ו טוש"ע שם סעיף ו:
קה ז מיי' שם פ"ה הלכה טו סמג שם טוש"ע ח"מ סי' קנב סעיף ו:
קו ח ט מיי' שם פ"ב הלכה ח סמג שם טוש"ע ח"מ סי' קנב סעיף ט:
קז י מיי' שם פ"ה הל' טו טוש"ע ח"מ סי' קסב סעיף ז:
קח כ ל מיי' שם הל' טו טוש"ע שם סעי' ה:

מסורת הש"ס

א) [מנחות דף לג:], ב) [תרגום של אדרונה אידרון], ג) [צ"ל לאין], ד) [בדפו' בצלר ועי' רש"ש], ה) צ"ל אחרת ועי' רש"ש.

הגהות הב"ח

(א) גמרא היו ארבעה או חמשה בתים פתוחים למרפסת: (ב) שם ר"ה מרב אמי כצ"ל ואות ר' נמחק: (ג) רש"י ד"ה אכסדרה שיש לה פתח לחצר כצ"ל ותי' מן ואות ה' נמחק: (ד) שם ד"ה בני מבוי מעכבין כו' מבוי האחר כצ"ל: (ה) ד"ה שמרבה כו' ההולך מראשו לצד סופו כצ"ל ותי' עד נמחק: (ו) ד"ה שלא פרץ וכו' מזוזתו ומשקופו ומפתנו דגלי:

לעזי רש"י

פורק"א. פירוש בית שער (עיין רש"י מנחות דף לג ע"ב ד"ה בית שער). אלוויי"ר. פירוש מרפסת (עיין רש"י עירובין דף נט ע"א ד"ה וסוכה דף ג ע"ב ד"ה מרפסת), גזוזטרא (רש"י עירובין דף עח ע"ב ד"ה שתי גזוזטראות ועיין רש"י סוכה דף נא ע"ב ד"ה והקיפוה גזוזטרא). דגרי"ד. פירוש סולם, מעלות (רש"י שמות כ, כג), מדרגות (רש"י יחזקאל מ, כ; שה"ש ב, יד):

ליקוטי רש"י

אכסדרה. מקורה בגג חלק כעליות שלנו ואינו משופע והיא קרויה שבכל התלמוד [עירובין כה.]. פרולא"ה מד' רוחותיה ועומד קירויה על ד' יתידות ונותנין ד' קורות מיתד ליתד ועליהן מסדרין הנסרין וכו' בעיר שהם אכסדראות סמוכות להקיף בית או חצר ואיכא מחילה אחת או שתים או [צ.]. פרוזדור שלפני בתים [יומא יא:]. שלפני הבית שקורין פורטק"ו [סוכה ג:]. אין עושין דפנות אלא אכסדרה שעושין פעמים שעושין אותה לפני הבית ודופן הבית מותמת מאחריה [שם יח:]. **באכסדרה דבי רב.** שיש לה ד' דפנות אלא שאין מגיעות לסכך [מנחות לג:]. **אידרונא.** חדר [לעיל ג.]. **באכסדרה רומייתא.** עשויה חלונות חלונות וקורין לייו"ר [מנחות לג:]. **מרפסת.** עלייה ארוכה על פני הבתים על פני רשות הרבים עליה לפני מחלותיהם ודיורין בכל אחת ואחת ועושין מרפסת ארוכה לפני הפתחים לכולן עלייה וכולן עולים בסולם אחד למרפסת ודרך המרפסת נכנסין ויוצאין כולן מרפסת אלוי"ר [סוכה ג:]. אלדויי"ר בלע"ז דיורי עליות סמוכות זו לזו ופתוחות לחצר ועושין מרפסת על פני אורך עליות ופותחין לה פתחי כולן עולין ויורדין דרך סולם של מרפסת לחצר [עירובין נט:]. אלרו"ר והוא ארוך לפני פתחי עליות הרבה וכולן עולין דרך שם [יומא שם]. אלואייר"א [מנחות שם]. **פצימיו.** עמודים [מנחות שם]. **תניא דמסייע לך.** דלא פקע שם פתח מיניה אלא בסתימה מעלייתא [שבת קמו:].

רבינו גרשום

[תחילת הפירוש ששייך לכאן נדפס בעמוד הקודם]

חסורי מיחסרא והכי קתני דתנא קמא מיירי [נמי] בחצירות נמצאת הפנימית משתמשת לעצמה ומשתמשת עם כולן דברי ר' דסבר אין מעכב עליו [בן] המבוי לסתום ד' אמות שלו ורבי שמעון אומר וכן כולם משתמשות במבוי כגון שהוא בהדיא שלא יסתום כנגד פתחו כדי שלא ירבה על האחרים את הדרך שיכולין בני מבוי לעכב עליו ורב הונא סבירא ליה כר"ש בן אלעזר. א) כפ"ה. ואית דאמרי חיצונה משתמשת לעצמה דיש לכולן רשות לעבור דרך עליה אבל היא משתמשת לעצמה דאין לה רשות לעבור דרך עליהן. ולהכי אם ביקשה החיצונה לסתום לפניהם מלעבור עליה אינה יכולה לסתום מתוך דרשות כולן יש (לו) לעבור עליה. אבל אם בקשו כולן לסתום לפני החיצונה כדי שלא תעבור עליהן. יכולין לסתום משום שאין דרכה של חיצונה לעבור עליהן. וכיון דסתמי להו הני שלא תעבור עליהן תהא החיצונה משמשת לעצמה וכן לשניה וכן לשלישית וכן לרביעית עד לחמישית שהיא פנימית דהשתא נמצא שיש לה רשות לעבור על כולן ואין לכולן רשות לעבור עליה להכי יכולה פנימית לישתמש ולסתום בפני עצמה כדי שלא יעברו כולן עליה והן אין יכולין לסתום בפניה כדי שלא תעבור עליהן אלמא דהני יכולין לסתום זה על זה וקשיא למאן דאמר אחד מבני מבוי דהכי משמע ותני דמשום אחד מבני מבוי בין לחיצונה על כולן בין לכולן על החיצונה אין להם רשות לסתום זה על זה לסתום מפני שמרבה עליהן את הדרך. תנאי היא ולכו' כו' עד החיצונה משתמשת לכולם דלדידיה יש להן רשות לעבור ולסתום בפני החיצונה ואין לחיצונה רשות לעבור ולסתום בפניהם: ר' שמעון אומר כולם משתמשות במבוי אמטו להכי דאית לכולן תשמיש למבוי להכי יש רשות לכולן לעבור זו על זו בין לחיצונה על כולן בין לכולן על החיצונה וכי היכי דזו אינה יכולה לסתום בפני כולן כך כולן אינן יכולין לסתום בפניהם כ"ז ב) למ"ה אבל מסתבר הכי: **היה סתום ובקש לפותחו.** כגון אמר מר שאם היה פתח פתוח לכתחילה לאותו מבוי שעכשיו רוצה לחזור פתחו שם וסתמו הואיל דהוה תמן מעיקרא **אין יכולין לעכב עליו. אמר רבא לא שנו** דאין מעכבין אלא שלא פרץ את פצימיו הואיל שאין נפרצין חזקה יש לפותחו: [מכאן שייך לדף יב.] **אינו מטמא כל סביביו.** אם היה מת בבית אע"פ שסתום הוא הואיל ולא פרץ את פצימיו אינו מטמא כל סביביו דבית בד' אמות כקבר דאיכא למימר הואיל שלא עקר הפצימין ולא סתמו לגמרי באותו פתח יפתח ויוציאהו **אבל פרץ את פצימיו וסתמו** מהכל **מטמא כל סביביו** דיש לו דין קבר הואיל וסתום מכל צדדיו כקבר דטומאה בוקעת ויוצאה דליכא למימר מן הצד יוציאוהו: **ענין אחר שלא פרץ את פצימיו** כלומר היה סותם הפתח ולא היה סותר צורת הפתח המשקוף והמזוזות אלא בנה בנין סתימה עליהו דמתוך שלא עקרן ודאי היה דעתו לפתוח להכי **אין מעכבין בו** מלפתוח. ודיקא נמי **דתניא** גבי בית דאע"ג דסתום פתחו **יש לו ד' אמות** והיינו נמי טעמא [כיון] דלא פרץ פצימיו והיה דעתו לפתוח: **קבר** שיש לו בחצירו ועשה מחיצה דפנות כל סביביו וסיכוך. והשתא אע"ג דאיכא מחיצה סביב הקבר ואיכא פתח בההוא מחיצות. אם **כשסתם** אותו פתח **לא פרץ פצימיה** כיון דנראה מקום הפתח. כמאן דאיתא לפתח דמי ובוקעת בו את הטומאה **ומטמא סביביו.** אבל פרץ והוי כשאר כותל **לא.** למ"ה: **מבואות המפולשות** פתוחין **לעיר אחרת.** כלומר דנהיגו בני העיר אחרת לעבור דרך האי מבוי וליכנס לעיר זו ולצאת ממנה דרך מבוי זה: **[לקלקלו.** לסותמו]. **המפולשין לרשות הרבים. להעמיד להן דלתות** לעכב בני **רה"ר** ליכנס במבוי כל שעה שירצו: **סבור מינה הני מילי** דמעכבין למיעבד דלתות ליסתם לבני רה"ר (הני מילי) **בתוך ד' אמות** הסמוכות לר"ה **כדר' זירא: ולא היא דלענין טומאה** אמרי' ד' אמות ג) במבוי בר"ה דספיקו טהור באותן ד' אמות (מבוי דברשות הרבים) דגמרינן מסוטה. **אבל הכא** בכוליה מבוי מצו לעכב דלא מצו למיזל בני רה"ר אלא דרך אותו מבוי: **פיסקא. ואין חולקין את השדה עד שתהא גדולה.** דיכולין לזורע בה ט' קבין לזה וט' קבין לזה דבציר מהכי לא חשיב שדה שהוא סאה וחצי שהוא ע"ה אמה אורך על רוחב נ' דגמרי לה מחצר המשכן דהוי ק' על נ' ואמרינן דהיינו בית זרע סאתים: **מר כי אתריה** דבהכי חשיב שדה בט' קבין בציר לא ובאתריה דר"י היו השדות ביוקר והוי חשיבי שדה בט' חצאי קבין **בבבל** שלא היו שדות ביוקר כבא"י **מאי** בכמה חשוב התם שדה. **א"ר יוסף בי רדו יומא.** כלומר כי היכי דיש מלאכה לפועל לחרוש בה יום שלם לפי שלא ימצא פועל שישכיר עצמו כי אם ליום אחד שלם ואם יחלקו פחות מכדי ספוק יום פעולת יום אחד לכל חד וחד נמצא הפועל משלים פעולתו בחצי היום או בט' שעות והיה מבקש הפועל שכירות יום שלם: **היכי דמי.** הא בי רדו יומא כלומר באיזה חריש אמרת שב' פעמים חורש את השדה אחת תיכף לקצירה ולאותה חרישה קרי כרבא ובאותה חרישה שחורשין לקצירה חורש הפועל כל היום עד לערב ושוב חורשין אותה ביום זריעה ואותו היום אין חורש הפועל אלא ט' שעות ובג' שעות זורע בעל הבית מה שהפועל חורש בט' שעות והכי מנהג ועכשיו בעי בעל גמרא באיזו חרישת פעולת יום **יום זריעה** דאינו אלא ט' שעות **לא הוי יומא כרבא** כלומר כשחוזר ומשכיר ביום קציר לא הוה פעולת יום שלם בחרישה דלאחר קצירה דבט' שעות תשלים פעולתו ונמצא יושב ובטל ג' שעות ונמצא מפסיד בעל הבית. **ואם בי רדו יומא כרבא** כלומר אם מאותה חרישה אחת דחורשין תיכף לקצירה כל היום **לא הוי תרי יומא דזרעא** כלומר אין שם פעולת חרישת ב' ימים של יום זריעה שביום חרישה תכף לקצירה חורש כל י"ב שעות ואם תאמר באותו יום חרישה אמרי דהיינו פעולת יום שלם כשיבא לאותה חרישה של זריעה לא ימצא שם פעולת ב' ימים כי ביום זריעה אינו חורש אלא ט' שעות ולא ישאר לפעולת מחרת אלא פעולת ג' שעות ונמצא פועל יושב ט' שעות ויפסיד בעה"ב שצריך לשוכרו ביום שלם שלא ירצה פועל להשכיר עצמו למחצית היום.

חשק שלמה על רבינו גרשום א) הוא ר"ת: כן פירש המורה: ב) הוא ר"ת: לא מפי המורה: ג) נ"ל במבוי הסמוך לרה"ר כרה"ר דמי.

the residents of the *mavoi* MAY USE the section of *mavoi* OPPOSITE THE OUTERMOST [COURTYARD], וְהַחִיצוֹנָה מִשְׁתַּמֶּשֶׁת לְעַצְמָהּ וכו׳ – AND the residents of THE OUTERMOST [COURTYARD] MAY USE only the section of *mavoi* OPPOSITE [THEIR OWN COURTYARD] **etc.**[39] דִּבְרֵי רַבִּי – THESE ARE THE WORDS OF REBBI. רַבִּי שִׁמְעוֹן בֶּן אֶלְעָזָר אוֹמֵר – R' SHIMON BEN ELAZAR SAYS: חָמֵשׁ חֲצֵרוֹת הַפְּתוּחוֹת לְמָבוֹי – In that case of FIVE COURTYARDS THAT OPEN INTO A *MAVOI,* כּוּלָּן מִשְׁתַּמְּשׁוֹת בְּמָבוֹי – ALL the residents of the *mavoi* MAY USE THE entire *MAVOI* together. That is, residents of the outermost courtyard have the right to use even the innermost portion of the *mavoi.* Thus, in ruling that *any* resident of a *mavoi* has the right to protest the erection of an enclosure anywhere in the *mavoi,* Rav Huna follows the expansive position of this Tanna – R' Shimon ben Elazar.[40]

The Gemara now turns its attention to a ruling mentioned previously in passing: אָמַר מַר הָיָה סָתוּם וּבִקֵּשׁ לְפוֹתְחוֹ – **Master had said** in the Baraisa: If the original entrance WAS SEALED AND subsequently [THE OWNER] of the house SOUGHT TO REOPEN IT, אֵין בְּנֵי מָבוֹי מְעַכְּבִין עָלָיו – THE RESIDENTS OF THE second *MAVOI* MAY NOT PREVENT HIM from doing so, for he had previously acquired a right of passage in their *mavoi.*

Rava qualified this ruling:

אָמַר רָבָא לֹא שָׁנוּ אֶלָּא שֶׁלֹּא פָּרַץ אֶת פַּצִּימָיו – **Rava said: They taught** this ruling **only where [the owner]** of the house **did not tear down the frame**[41] **[of the door]** when he sealed the entrance.[42] אֲבָל פָּרַץ אֶת פַּצִּימָיו – **But if he tore down [the door's] frame** when he sealed the entrance, בְּנֵי מָבוֹי מְעַכְּבִין עָלָיו – **the residents of the** second ***mavoi*** **can** legally **prevent him** from reopening the entrance. For by removing the frame he indicated that he has no intention of reopening the entrance, and so he relinquished his right of passage in the second *mavoi.*

Support is provided for Rava's qualification:

אָמַר לֵיהּ אַבַּיֵי לְרָבָא – **Abaye said to Rava:** תַּנְיָא דִּמְסַיַּיע לָךְ – **A Baraisa taught [a ruling] that supports you:**

NOTES

39. They may not, however, use any other part of the *mavoi.* Rebbi's restrictive view is that of the Baraisa quoted above. The rest of his statement ("etc.") follows the text of that Baraisa. Rav Huna's position conflicts with that of Rebbi.

40. It is apparent that Rav Huna was not actually cognizant of the Baraisa that presented the dispute between Rebbi and R' Shimon ben Elazar. If he were, he would have simply declared that the halachah follows the opinion of R' Shimon ben Elazar. Further, had he known of the Baraisa he would quite possibly have adopted Rebbi's position, in accordance with the general rule that in a dispute between Rebbi and a fellow Tanna the halachah follows Rebbi's opinion. Indeed, *Rabbeinu Chananel* and the *Rif* followed that rule in actually deciding the law (*Rabbeinu Yonah, Rashba*).

41. I.e. the doorposts, lintel and threshold (*Rashi*).

42. This omission indicated that he intended to reopen the entrance at a later date, and therefore did not relinquish his right of passage in the second *mavoi* (*Rashi*).

בַּיִת סָתוּם – The owner of **A HOUSE** whose entrance to a courtyard was **SEALED** יֵשׁ לוֹ אַרְבַּע אַמּוֹת – **IS ENTITLED TO FOUR *AMOS*** in front of the entrance when the courtyard is divided, as if the entrance were still open. פָּרַץ אֶת פְּצִימָיו – If, however, **HE TORE DOWN THE [DOOR'S] FRAME** when he sealed the entrance, אֵין לוֹ אַרְבַּע אַמּוֹת – **HE IS NOT ENTITLED TO FOUR *AMOS*,** for when the frame was removed the entrance ceased to exist, and the owner lost his right to an unloading area in the courtyard. Similarly, in Rava's case, when the frame is removed the entrance ceases to exist, and the owner loses his right of passage in the second *mavoi*. The Baraisa thus provides support for Rava's qualification.

The Baraisa continues:[1]

(קֶבֶר שֶׁפִּתְחוֹ סָתוּם – **A TOMB WHOSE ENTRANCE IS SEALED** אֵינוֹ מְטַמֵּא כָּל סְבִיבָיו – **DOES NOT RENDER *TAMEI***[2] one who approaches within four *amos* of it from **ALL SIDES.** פָּרַץ אֶת פְּצִימָיו וּסְתָמוֹ – If, however, **ONE TORE DOWN THE FRAME [OF THE DOOR] AND** thereby **SEALED [THE TOMB]** permanently, מְטַמֵּא כָּל סְבִיבָיו) – **[THE TOMB] RENDERS *TAMEI*** one who approaches within four *amos* of it from **ALL SIDES.**[3]

The Gemara continues to quote the Baraisa: בַּיִת סָתוּם – **A HOUSE** with a corpse inside whose entrance is **SEALED** אֵינוֹ מְטַמֵּא כָּל סְבִיבָיו – **DOES NOT RENDER *TAMEI*** one who approaches within four *amos* of it from **ALL SIDES.**[4] פָּרַץ אֶת פְּצִימָיו – If, however, **ONE TORE DOWN THE FRAME [OF THE DOOR]** and thereby sealed the house permanently, מְטַמֵּא כָּל סְבִיבָיו – **[THE HOUSE] RENDERS *TAMEI*** anyone who approaches within four *amos* of it from **ALL SIDES,** for the house is accorded the status of a closed grave. Just as removing the door frame affects the status of the house, so in Rava's case its removal affects the homeowner's right of passage in the second *mavoi*. Thus, the Baraisa again provides support for Rava's qualification.

The Gemara now discusses instances where people are empowered to restrain the actions of others to protect an established right:

אָמַר רַבָּה בַּר בַּר חָנָה אָמַר רַבִּי יוֹחָנָן – **Rabbah bar bar Chanah said in R' Yochanan's name:** מְבוֹאוֹת הַמְפוּלָּשׁוֹת לְעִיר אַחֶרֶת – If there are **alleyways** in a city that are **open** at one end and lead to roads **to another city,** וּבִקְּשׁוּ בְּנֵי הָעִיר לְסוֹתְמָן – **and the residents of the** first **city sought to close off [these alleyways]** to prevent residents of the other city from using them as a shortcut, בְּנֵי אוֹתָהּ הָעִיר מְעַכְּבִין עֲלֵיהֶן – **the residents of that** other **city can** legally **prevent them** from doing so, for the other city's residents have already established a right to use these alleyways as a shortcut.

Rabbah bar bar Chanah amplified his ruling:

לֹא מִיבַּעְיָא כִּי לֵיכָּא דַּרְכָּא אַחֲרִינָא דִּמְעַכְּבֵי – **It is not necessary** to state **that [the residents]** of the other city **may prevent** the closing of the alleyways **when there is no other route** between the two cities, for the alleyways are indeed the established route! אֶלָּא אֲפִילּוּ כִּי אִיכָּא דַּרְכָּא אַחֲרִינָא – **Rather, even when another route exists** and the alleyways are merely a shortcut, נַמִּי מְעַכְּבֵי – [the residents] of the other city **can also** legally **prevent** the closure of the alleyways. מִשּׁוּם דְּרַב יְהוּדָה אָמַר רַב דְּאָמַר – **For** that case is subject to the ruling **of Rav Yehudah in the name of Rav, who stated:**[5] מֵצַר שֶׁהֶחֱזִיקוּ בּוֹ רַבִּים – **A** private **boundary** strip **on which the public established** a right-of-way אָסוּר לְקַלְקְלוֹ – **may not be ruined** by its owner.[6] Similarly, in our case, once the residents of the other city established their right to use the alleyways as a shortcut, it is forbidden to close them off.

A similar ruling is noted:[7]

(כִּדְרַב גִּידֵּל דְּאָמַר רַב גִּידֵּל – It **accords with** the ruling **of Rav Gidal, for Rav Gidal stated:** רַבִּים שֶׁבָּרְרוּ דֶּרֶךְ לְעַצְמָן – **If the masses chose for themselves a path** through a field,[8] מַה שֶּׁבָּרְרוּ בָּרְרוּ) – **what they have chosen, they have chosen,** and they cannot be displaced. Thus, Rav adopted the reasoning of Rav Gidal.

The Gemara presents another ruling involving the closure of alleyways:

אָמַר רַב עָנָן אָמַר שְׁמוּאֵל – **Rav Anan said in the name of Shmuel:** מְבוֹאוֹת הַמְפוּלָּשִׁין לִרְשׁוּת הָרַבִּים – If the **alleyways** of a city **are** completely **open to a public thoroughfare** at one end,[9] וּבִקְּשׁוּ בְּנֵי מְבוֹאוֹת לְהַעֲמִיד לָהֶן דְּלָתוֹת – **and the residents of the alleyways sought to erect doors for [the entrances]** so that travelers on the public thoroughfare could not enter the alleyways, בְּנֵי רְשׁוּת הָרַבִּים מְעַכְּבִין עֲלֵיהֶן – **the users of the public thoroughfare** (i.e. the residents of the city) **can prevent [the residents]** of the alleyways from erecting these doors.[10]

The Gemara elucidates Rav Anan's ruling:

NOTES

1. This section of the Baraisa is deleted by *Maharshal* and ignored by *Rashi*. It is also omitted when the Baraisa is quoted in tractate *Shabbos* (146b).

2. Ritually unclean; see Glossary.

3. The Sages imposed *tumah* on anyone who approaches within four *amos* of a grave, so that people who handle food that they wished to maintain in a state of *taharah* (ritual purity) would not inadvertently stand over the grave itself and become *Scripturally* unclean. As long as a tomb has an entrance, even one that is sealed, it is not considered a grave, and so only someone standing opposite the entrance (within four *amos* thereof) is rendered *tamei*. If the tomb is sealed and the door frame removed, however, the tomb is considered a large, closed grave, and it renders *tamei* anyone who approaches within four *amos* of it on any side (see *Rashi*).

4. This case of a house that shelters a corpse is perfectly analogous to the previous case of the tomb. Note 3 above provides an explanation of this case as well.

5. *Bach* and *Maharshal* add: רַב יְהוּדָה אָמַר רַב, *for Rav Yehudah said in Rav's name.*

6. In the days of the Talmud, fields were generally separated by narrow strips of land that were higher or lower than the fields themselves (*Rashbam* below, 53b ד״ה או). These strips would occasionally be used by members of the public as shortcuts to their own fields. Rav Yehudah ruled that if a property owner stood by while the public established a right-of-way on his boundary strip and did not object, he could not afterward ruin their walkway and reclaim the strip for his own private use.

7. This next passage of Gemara is ignored by *Rashi* and deleted by *Maharam*. The Gemara below (100a) seems to indicate that Rav Gidal's law is predicated on Rav's boundary-strip ruling — and not the reverse, as this text implies, but see *Rashbam* there.

8. In this case the public had once established a right-of-way through a particular field, but its precise location had been forgotten. Hence, when the public chooses a new path, it cannot be displaced. The public may not, however, peremptorily create new paths through private property.

9. Although when applied to a *mavoi* the term מְפוּלָּשׁ, *open*, usually means open at *both* ends, here that is not the case (for reasons why, see *Ritva*). Rather, here the alleyways are open only at one end, but since the opening encompasses the *entire* width of the *mavoi* (i.e. the side of the *mavoi* adjoining the public thoroughfare is not partially walled), the term מְפוּלָּשׁ — which connotes a generous opening — is appropriate (*Rashba, Ritva;* cf. *Ramban*, above 11b citing the Rabbis of Spain. *Tur, Choshen Mishpat* 162 citing *R' Barceloni*; see also *Rashi* above, 11b ד״ה חמש חצירות).

10. For when the public road becomes congested, the traffic finds an outlet in the alleyways (*Rashi*). The flow of traffic into the *mavoi* cannot be restricted, for the *mavoi* is considered a *boundary that the public has established for a path,* and the right-of-way cannot be abrogated.

בית סתום יש לו ד' אמות פרץ את פצימיו אין לו ד' אמות (קבר שפתחו סתום אינו מטמא כל סביביו פרץ את פצימיו וסתמו מטמא כל סביביו) בית סתום אינו מטמא כל סביביו פרץ את פצימיו מטמא כל סביביו אמר רבה בר בר חנה א"ר יוחנן מבואות המפולשות לעיר אחרת ובקשו בני העיר לסותמן בני אותה העיר מעכבין עליהן לא מיבעי כי ליכא דרכא אחרינא דמעכבי אלא אפילו כי איכא דרכא אחרינא נמי מעכבי משום דרב יהודה אמר רב דאמר רב מצר שהחזיקו בו רבים אסור לקלקלו (כדרב גידל דא"ר גידל רבים שבררו דרך לעצמן מה שבררו בררו) אמר רב ענן אמר שמואל מבואות המפולשין לרה"ר ובקשו בני מבואות להעמיד להן דלתות בני רה"ר מעכבין עליהן סבור מינה הני מילי בד' אמות כדר' זירא אמר רב נחמן דאמר רבי זירא אמר רב נחמן ד' אמות הסמוכות לרה"ר כרה"ר דמיין ולא היא התם לענין טומאה אבל הכא זימנין דדחקי בני רה"ר ועיילי טובא: ולא את השדה עד שיהא בה תשעה קבין לזה ותשעה קבין לזה כו': ולא פליגי מר כי אתריה ומר כי אתריה בבבל מאי אמר רב יוסף בי רדו יומא מאי בי רדו יומא אי יומא זרעא תרי יומא כרבא לא הוי אי יומא כרבא יומא דזרעא לא הוי אי בעית אימא יומא דכרבא דכריב ותני ואי בעית אימא יומא דזרעא בהדורי דוולא אמר רב נחמן בי דאלו יומא פרדסא אמר אבוה דשמואל בת שלשת קבין תניא נמי הכי האומר לחבירו מנת בכרם אני מוכר לך סומכוס אומר לא יפחות מג' קבין א"ר יוסי אין אלו אלא דברי נביאות בבבל מאי אמר רבא בר קסנא תלת אציאתא בני תריסר גופני כי היכי דרפיק גברא ביומא אמר רבי אבדימי דמן חיפה מיום שחרב בית המקדש ניטלה נבואה מן הנביאים וניתנה לחכמים אטו חכם לאו נביא הוא הכי קאמר אע"פ שניטלה מן הנביאים מן החכמים לא ניטלה אמר אמימר וחכם עדיף מנביא שנאמר ונביא לבב חכמה מי נתלה במי הוי אומר קטן נתלה בגדול אמר אביי תדע דאמר גברא רבה מילתא ומתאמר' משמיה דגברא רבה אחרינא כוותי' אמר רבא ומאי קושיא ודילמא תרוייהו בני חד מזלא נינהו אלא אמר רבא תדע דאמר גברא רבה מילתא ומתאמרא

רש"י

בית סתום. שהיה לו פתח לחצר וסתמו: יש לו ד' אמות. בחלוקת החצר אם באו לחלוק כאילו הוא פתוח: אינו מטמא סביביו. אלא כנגד הפתח אם מת בתוכו: פרץ את פצימיו. הרי הוא כקבר וחכמים טימאו את סביבות הקבר ד' אמות כדי שלא יקרבו עושי טהרות עד הקבר ויאהילו ולאו אדעתייהו: לעיר אחרת. לדרך עיר אחרת: ובקשו בני העיר. שהמבואות בה לסותמן מאחריהם: בני אותה העיר. האחרת מעכבין עליהן שכבר הוחזקו לעבור דרכן לדרך אותן המבואות: בני רה"ר מעכבין עליהן. משום דכי דחקו בני רה"ר מסתלקי לתוך המבואות: הני מילי. תוך ד' אמות של (ב) ראש המבוי הסמוכות לרה"ר מעכבין מלהעמיד דלתות לשם: כרה"ר דמו. לענין ספק טומאה כרה"ר: ולא היא. שאפי' לא להעמידם לפנים מד' אמות מעכבין עליהן: בי רדו יומא. בית חרישת יום אחד לזה וכן לזה לא תחרוש מתרגמינן לא תרדי (דברים כב): ה"ג בי רדו יומא מאי אי יומא זרעא תרי יומא כרבא לא הוי ואי יומא כרבא יומא דזרעא לא הוי אי בעית אימא יומא דזרעא באתרא דכריב ותני ואי בעית אימא ביומא דכרבא ובאהדורי: אי יומא דזרעא. בשעת הזרע הוא נוח לחרוש שכבר נחרשת בשעת (ג) הניר: תרי יומי כרבא לא הוי. כלומר בשעת הניר היאך ישכור שוורים אין בו כדי מלאכת ב' ימים ויש בו יותר מכדי מלאכת יום אחד: ואי ביומא כרבא. של שעת הניר קאמרת לא הוי יומא דזרעא והיאך ישכור שוורים בשעת הזרע: אי בעית אימא יומא דזרעא. ודקא קשיא לך תרי יומי כרבא לא הוי באתרא דכרבי ותנו בשעת הניר איכא ביומא דזרעא תרי יומי כרבא: ואי בעית אימא יומא כרבא. ודקאמרת לא הוי יומא דזרעא בהדורי עסקינן שארץ קשה ויש בה מעלות ומורדות ויש טורח בשעת הזרע כשעת הניר: לישנא אחרינא איפכא גרסינן ואי בעית אימא יומא דכרבא ודקשי' לך יומא דזרעא לא הוי באתרא דכריב ותני בשעת הזרע אחת קודם לזריעה ואחת לאחר הזריעה לכסות הזרעי' ואי בעית אימא יומא זרעא ודקאמר' תרי יומי כרבא לא הוי בהדורי עסקינן שיש טורח גדול בשעת הניר ויומא זרעא הוי תרי יומי כרבא ולשון זה הגון: דוולא. אם יש להן בור שממנו משקין שדה: בי דלו יומא. עד שיהא בו כדי להשקות שדה כדי פעולת יום לזה וכדי פעולת יום לזה משום שכר פועל: פרדיסא. כרם: ג' קבין. לכל אחד לפי חשבון סאתים כחצר המשכן: אין אלו אלא דברי נביאות. בלא טעם: אוציתא. כל י"ב גפנים קרי אוציא: דרפיק. עודר: ניטלה נבואה כו'. משום דאמר ליה לעיל אין אלו אלא דברי נביאות שקרא דברי חכמים נבואה נקט לה להא מילתא: אטו חכם לאו נביא הוא. וכי אין חכם ראוי להיות נביא דקאמר מר ניטלה מן הנביאים וניתנה לחכמים מכלל דמעיקרא לא היתה נבואה לחכמים: הכי קאמר אע"פ שניטלה מן הנביאים. שאינם חכמים מן חכמים לא ניטלה (ד) ונביאים יש להן לבב חכמה: תדע. שלא ניטלה מן חכמים: משמיה

תוספות

פרץ פצימיו מטמא כל סביביו. פי' הקונטר' כל סביביו ד' אמות כקבר ואין נראה לר' שמשון כיון דמסיימי מחילות וליכא למיחש שמא יעלה על הבית ויאהיל עליו לית לן למימר שיטמא ד' אמות סביביו כדמוכח בפ' משוח מלחמה (סוטה דף מד.) גבי חצר הקבר העומד בתוכה טהור ה"מ חצר הקבר דמסיימי מחילו' אבל (ה) בעלמא תפיס לכך נראה לו לפרש כגון שיש זיזין הרבה בולטין מן הבית מכל צד ויש בהן פותח טפח (ו) לכל אחד ובשלא פרץ פצימיו אף על פי שסתמו אינו מטמא תחת השאר זיזין שסתמו של מת עומד לצאת דרך פתח אבל אם פרץ פצימיו וחזר ובנאו כשאר כותל ואין כאן פתח כלל מטמא כל סביביו דכל זיז וזיז איכא לספוקי דשמא דרך תחת אותו זיז יצא מן הבית ויש ליישב פי' הקונטרס דבית נמי לא מסיימי מחיצתא דאע"ג דליכא למיחש שמא יעלה על הבית מ"מ איכא למיחש שמא יגע בכתלי' דקבר מטמא במגע אפי' מן הצד כדמוכח בספרי בפרשת פרה אדומה (ז) בקבר זה קבר סתום או אינו אלא פתוח אמרת ק"ו ומה אהל שהוא מקבל טומאה אינו מטמא מכל הצדדין כשהוא פתוח הקבר שאינו מקבל טומאה אינו דין שלא יטמא מכל הצדדין כשהוא פתוח משמע דכשהוא סתום מטמא אף בנוגע בו מן הצד: מצר שהחזיקו בו רבים אסור לקלקלו. היינו כשהחזיקו ברשות אבל אם באין להחזיק שלא ברשות יש למחות בידם ולנקוט פיזרא וליתיב כדמוכח בהמניח (ב"ק דף כח. ושם): ולא פליגי מר כי אתריה ומר כי אתריה. פי' ר"י ב"ר מרדכי דבאתריה דרבי יהודה היה קרקע חשוב וטוב והיה חשוב לטרוח בתשעה חצאי קבין (ח) אבל באתריה דתנא קמא לא היה קרקע טוב כל כך שיהיה חשוב לטרוח בפחות מתשעה קבין ואף על פי שלא היה בו כדי חרישת יום ראוי היה לטרוח והשתא בעי בבבל מאי שאין הקרקע טוב כל כך ואינו ראוי כשיעור השנוי במשנתינו: ה"ג ר"ח (ט) ואי בעית אימא בכרבא וזרעא ובהדורי. פירוש בית חרישת יום ושפיר הוי יומא לזרעא דכשיבא לזורעה חורש ובחזירתו עוד מושך המחרישה על הקרקע וזורע וזה בהדורי: ואי בעית אימא יומא דזרעא. ודקאמרת לא הוי תרי יומי כרבא כריב יומא ופלגא והדר תני וכריב עד דשלים יומא: דוולא. פר"ח ארץ שמשקין אותה בדלי לכל אחד ארץ שדולין לה יום אחד וקשה לר"י דא"כ הוה ליה (י) למיתני בבבל מאי כדבעי באינך ע"כ נראה כפ"ה: א"ר יוסי אין אלו אלא דברי נביאות. לא לשבח קאמר אלא כלומר שאומר בלא טעם דכי האי גוונא בסוף (כ) (אלו) מומין (בכורות דף מה. ושם ד"ה עשו) גבי יתרת שאין בה ליפורן מטמא במגע ובמשא אבל לא באהל וקאמר עשו דבריהן כדברי נביאות מה נפשך אי אבר הוא ליטמא באהל ואי לא אבר הוא לא ליטמא כלל וכן י"ל בסוף פ' כילד מעברין (עירובין דף ס: ושם ד"ה אין): אטו חכם לאו נביא הוא. וא"ת בפ' בן סורר (סנהדרין דף עה.) דקאמר משחרב בהמ"ק ניטל טעם ביאה וניתן לעוברי עבירה תקשי ליה נמי אטו קודם שנחרב לא הוה להו טעם ביאה לעוברי עבירה הא מפיק ליה מדכתיב מים גנובים ימתקו (משלי ט) כדפריך הכא וי"ל דאיכא לשנויי התם כדמשני הכא ניטל טעם ביאה ומעוברי עבירה לא ניטלה ולא חש להקשות בכל מקום: [וע"ע תוס' גיטין עב. ד"ה ומשום וכו']:

מסורת הש"ס

א) שבת קמו:, ב) רש"ל מ"ז, ג) תוספתא דאהלות ספט"ו, ד) ב"ק [לקמן כו: ע"ש], ה) [נדף ק. ע"ש], ו) רש"ל מ"ז, ז) פסחים ג. וש"נ, ח) עירובין ס: בכורות מה., ט) [וכה"ג שבע"י איתא ונביא יש לו לבב חכמה], י) [צ"ל בעינן לכל כו']:

הגהות הב"ח

(א) גמ' משום דרב יהודה אמר רב דאמר רב יהודה אמר רב מצר: (ב) רש"י ד"ה הני מילי וכו' של ראשי המבואות הסמוכות לרה"ר: (ג) ד"ה אי יומא וכו' בשעת הניר: (ד) ד"ה הכי קאמר וכו' ואח"כ מ"ה ונביא יש לו לבב חכמה: (ה) תוס' ד"ה פרץ וכו' אבל בעלמא תפיס: (ו) בא"ד טפח לכל אחד ובשלא פרץ: (ז) בא"ד פרה אדומה או בקבר: (ח) ד"ה ולא פליגי וכו' חשוב לטרוח אבל באתריה דת"ק: (ט) ד"ה ואי בעית אימא וכו': (י) ד"ה דוולא וכו' הוה ליה למיתני בבבל כו': (כ) ד"ה אמר וכו' בסוף מומין אלו גבי:

גליון הש"ס

גמרא אמר ר"נ ד' אמות כו'. עיין תוס' פ"כ: וחכם עדיף מנביא. עי' ירושלמי פ"א דברכות:

תורה אור השלם

א) לִמְנוֹת יָמֵינוּ כֵּן הוֹדַע וְנָבִא לְבַב חָכְמָה: [תהלים צ, יב]

ליקוטי רש"י

בית סתום יש לו ארבע אמות.

עין משפט נר מצוה

קט א מיי' פ"ב מהל' שכנים הל' ז סמג עשין פב טוש"ע ח"מ סי' קעב סעיף ז:

קי ב מיי' פ"ז מהל' טומאת מת הל' א סמג עשין רלג:

קיא ג ד טוש"ע ח"מ סי' קסב סעיף ג:

קיב ה מיי' פי"ג מהל' נזקי ממון הל' כד סמג עשין עג טוש"ע ח"מ סי' שעז בהגה"ה וסי' תיז סעיף ב:

קיג ו ז מיי' פ"ב מהל' שכנים הל' יג סמג עשין פב טוש"ע ח"מ סי' קסב סעי' א:

קיד ח ט מיי' פ"א מהל' שכני' הל' ד סמג שם טוש"ע ח"מ סי' קעא סעיף ג:

רבינו גרשום

[תחילת הפירוש ששייך לכאן נדפס בעמוד הקודם] איבעית אימ' יומא זרעא. ודקא קשיא לך לא הוי יומא כרבא: דכריב ותני. שחורש באותו יום שתיכף לקצירה פעמים מה שחורש בט' שעות חוזר ושונה בג' שעות והוה שוה בשוה: איבעית אימא יומא כרבא. ודקא קשיא לך לא הוי תרי יומא זרעא. לעולם איכא תרי יומי זרעא: בהדורי. שהארץ קשה היא וארץ הרים סלעים וטרשין היא ומה שפועל חורש ביום אחד תיכף לקצירה חוזר ומתקשה וצריך לחרוש בה פעולת ב' ימים דזריעה מחמת הקשיות שמתקשה אחר חרישת קצירה. ול"א. מוגה בספרים הכי היכי דמי אי בי רדו יומי זריעה לא הוי תרי יומי כרבא. בהאי לישנא משמע דטפי חורש הפועל בהני ט' שעות דיום זריעה מבכולה יומא דכרבא דכבר רכיכא ארעא דחרושה כבר חדא זימנא והכי קאמר לא הוי [תרי] יומי כרבא דטפי מיומא הוי אבל לא הוי פעולת תרי יומי ואי בי רדו יומא כרבא להאי לישנא לא הוי יומא זרע דכל שחורש ביום כרבא יכול לחרוש ביום זריעה בפחות מט' שעות כדאמר בהאי לישנא דניחא לחרוש ביום זריעה מתיכף לקצירה. איבעית אימא בכרבא יומא דזרעא. ודקשיא לך לא הוי תרי יומי כרבא דזרעא דהוי דאע"ג דניחא לחרוש חורשה באותו יום ב' פעמים. ואיבעית אימא בזורעא ודקשיא לך לא הוי תרי יומי כרבא להאי לישנא. לעולם איכא תרי יומי בהדורי ארץ טרשים היא ובתחלה היא קשה הרבה דכל מה שחורש בב' ימים תיכף לקצירה יכול לחרוש ביום אחד דזורעא וכ"ך קבלתי אני מר' אב"ל חבירי' הבינונו בזה הענין. היכא דמי אי בי רדו יומא בזורעא שבין זריעה ובין חרישה שחורשין את השדה פעם אחרת בימות הגשמים לבד מכריבה ראשונה שכורבין בימות החמה חורשין אותה בימות הגשמים סמוך [לזריע'] לפי שתהא נוחה לזרוע ואם צריך יום אחד למלאכה לפועל אחד בין חרישה בין זריעה אפילו

מפסיד [דין] פתחו בכך פירץ את פצימיו ואחר כך סתמו פקע שם פתח מיניה. בית סתום. והמת בתוכו אינו מטמא סביביו. פרץ את פצימיו. וסתמו נעשה קבר ומטמא סביביו. מצר. שבין שתי שדות שהחזיקו בו רבים [רשב"ם לקמן ס.]. שהחזיקו בו רבים. אסור לקלקלו. כרבא. חרישה [ב"ק צו:]. אין אלו אלא דברי נביאות. כמתנבאת מפי הגבורה שאינו נותן טעם לדבריו [עירובין ס:].

חשק שלמה על רבינו גרשום א) נ"ל כשמתקרקע קשה. ב) אולי צ"ל ג' קבין לו ד' או ה'. ג) נראה דצ"ל אם מכר לו בכלל מנת בכרם וכו'.

סְבוּר מִינָּהּ הָנֵי מִילֵּי בְּאַרְבַּע אַמּוֹת – **It was originally thought**[11] that **these words** (i.e. Rav Anan's ruling) **concerned** only a door to be erected within **four** ***amos*** of the entrance to the *mavoi*,[12] כִּדְרַבִּי זֵירָא אָמַר רַב נַחְמָן – **in accord with** the ruling **of R' Zeira in the name of Rav Nachman,** דְּאָמַר רַבִּי זֵירָא אָמַר רַב נַחְמָן – **for R' Zeira said in the name of Rav Nachman:** אַרְבַּע אַמּוֹת הַסְּמוּכוֹת לִרְשׁוּת הָרַבִּים כִּרְשׁוּת הָרַבִּים דָּמְיָין – The **four** ***amos*** **adjoining the public domain are regarded like the public domain.**[13] Hence, it was initially assumed that the public could protest only those doors erected within four *amos* of where the *mavoi* joined the public thoroughfare, for its jurisdiction extended only that far.

The Gemara explains that such is not the case:

וְלֹא הִיא – **But it is not** so! The public can legally protest the erection of doors anywhere in the *mavoi* – even beyond four *amos* from the public thoroughfare. הָתָם לְעִנְיַן טוּמְאָה – For **there** R' Zeira established that the four adjoining *amos* are regarded as part of the public domain **for the law of** doubtful **impurity.** אֲבָל הָכָא – **But here** R' Zeira's designation of only the first four adjoining *amos* as *reshus harabim* is immaterial, for זִימְנִין דְּדָחֲקִי בְּנֵי רְשׁוּת הָרַבִּים וְעָיְילֵי טוּבָא – it **sometimes** happens **that the people in the public thoroughfare are crowded and penetrate considerably** into the *mavoi* – even further than four *amos* from the entrance. Hence, the public has gained a right-of-way in the entire *mavoi*, and this privilege cannot be abrogated by the actions of the *mavoi's* residents.[14]

The Gemara quotes a section of the Mishnah that discusses how large a jointly owned field must be in order for one partner to compel the other to dissolve the partnership:

וְלֹא אֶת הַשָּׂדֶה עַד שֶׁיְּהֵא בָּהּ תִּשְׁעָה קַבִּין לָזֶה וְתִשְׁעָה קַבִּין לָזֶה כו׳ – NOR do we divide A FIELD UNLESS IT CONTAINS [AN AREA LARGE ENOUGH TO GIVE] NINE *KAVS* TO THIS ONE AND NINE *KAVS* TO THAT ONE ETC.[15] R' Yehudah says: We divide a field even if it contains an area large enough to give nine half-*kavs* to each.

The Gemara explains:

וְלֹא פְּלִיגֵי – **And [the Tanna Kamma and R' Yehudah] do not disagree** over the minimum area of land that is profitable to cultivate. מָר כִּי אַתְרֵיהּ וּמָר כִּי אַתְרֵיהּ – Rather, **one master** rules **according to** the soil quality in **his place, and** the other **master** rules **according to** the soil quality in **his place.**[16] Both agree, though, that one partner can compel the other to divide only if each will be left with enough land to work profitably.

The Gemara inquires as to what the minimum area for division is in less fertile places:

בְּבָבֶל מַאי – **In Babylonia, what** is the smallest field that is **profitable to** cultivate?[17]

The Gemara provides a general formula:

אָמַר רַב יוֹסֵף – **Rav Yosef said:** בֵּי רְדוּ יוֹמָא – Each partner must receive at least **an area that takes a** full **day to plow;** a field must be at least that large to be cultivated profitably.[18]

The Gemara clarifies Rav Yosef's ruling:

מַאי בֵּי רְדוּ יוֹמָא – **What** does **"an area that takes a day to plow"** mean? Does it refer to an area that takes a day to plow during the plowing season or during the planting season?[19] אִי יוֹמָא זַרְעָא – **If** it refers to an area that takes **a day** to plow **during** the **planting** season, after the field was already softened by the first plowing, תְּרֵי יוֹמָא כַּרְבָא לָא הָוֵי – it will **not** take **two** full **days** to plow **during** the **plowing season,** since the first plowing does not take twice as long as the second plowing. Thus, on a parcel of land this size, one will lose money in the (first) plowing season. אִי יוֹמָא כַּרְבָא – Conversely, **if** it refers to an area that takes **a day** to plow **during** the **plowing season,** יוֹמָא דְּזַרְעָא לָא הָוֵי – **it will not** take **a** full **day** to plow it **during** the **planting season.** Thus, he will lose money in that season. How is it possible, then, to divide a field so that it can be plowed economically?[20]

The Gemara explains that it is possible in either of the following cases:[21]

אִי בָּעֵית אֵימָא יוֹמָא דְּכַרְבָא – **If you prefer, say** that Rav Yosef

NOTES

11. Literally: they understood from it.

12. Only in that case did Rav Anan empower the public to prevent the erection of a door (*Rashi*).

13. R' Zeira issued this dictum in the context of a general ruling on deciding doubtful cases of ritual impurity (*tumah*). That is, in the case of a person who may have contracted *tumah,* R' Zeira ruled that if the doubt arose in a private domain, the person is declared *tamei;* if, however, it arose in a public domain, he is *tahor* (ritually clean; see *Niddah* 3a). R' Zeira ruled further that if the doubt arose within four *amos* of a public domain, the person is nonetheless *tahor,* since the four *amos* adjoining a public domain have the status of a public domain. The Gemara therefore assumed that Rav Anan's ruling applied only to the portion of *mavoi* within four *amos* of the public thoroughfare, but that beyond that point the erection of doors was permitted.

14. *Rashba* notes that if the opening of the *mavoi* was partially walled and contained only a portal to the public thoroughfare, the public has no right-of-way in the *mavoi.* For by initially constructing the opening in this manner, the residents in essence voiced their objection to the public's establishing a right-of-way in their *mavoi.*

15. Any plot smaller than this is unprofitable to cultivate (*Tosafos* 11a).

16. Surely, one partner can compel the other to dissolve the partnership only if each will be left with enough land to work profitably. The minimum size of a profitable share, however, varies from place to place. In the Tanna Kamma's locale, the smallest profitable area was one large enough for nine *kavs* of seed to be planted in it. In R' Yehudah's locale, however, where the soil was more fertile, it was profitable to cultivate even an area half that size.

17. The Tanna Kamma and R' Yehudah, both of whom lived in Eretz Yisrael, discussed the minimum area of land profitable to cultivate there [and in other lands that were equally fertile (see *Rambam, Hil. Shecheinim* 1:4)]. In Babylonia, however, the land was less fertile than in Eretz Yisrael. It was thus unprofitable to cultivate even an area of land in which nine *kavs* of seed could be planted (*Tosafos;* cf. *Meiri*). The Gemara therefore inquires what the smallest profitable area is in Babylonia and similar locales.

18. Oxen had to be rented for a full day even if they were needed for only part of the day. It was thus unprofitable to rent them for less than a full day's work (*Rashi*; see *Rabbeinu Gershom*).

19. In the Gemara's time, fields were plowed twice every year. They were first plowed after the harvest to soften the ground somewhat. The fields then lay fallow for several months until the planting season arrived. At that time, they were plowed again before being planted. Hence, what took a day to plow during the first plowing season took less than a day to plow during the planting season. The Gemara now inquires: What is the minimum size land that is economical to plow? Must it be large enough to be plowed for a full day during the planting season or can it be just large enough to be plowed for a day during the (first) plowing season?

20. It takes longer to plow the first time (when the ground is still hard) than the second time but not twice as long. For example, if it takes a full day to plow the second time, it will take somewhat more than a day to do so the first time but not two full days. Conversely, if it takes one full day to plow the first time, it will take less than a day to do so the second time. Thus, even if it takes whole days to plow a field during one plowing season, the amount of time needed to plow during the other season will be measured in fractions of days. Any field, then, should be uneconomical to plow, since it will be necessary to rent oxen for a fraction of a day (see note 18).

21. *Rashi* offers two versions of the text of the Gemara's answer. The text printed in the standard edition of the Gemara follows *Rashi's* second version, for which *Rashi* himself indicates a preference.

בית סתום יש לו ד' אמות פרץ את פצימיו אין לו ד' אמות (קבר שפתחו סתום אינו מטמא כל סביביו פרץ את פצימיו וסתמו מטמא כל סביביו) בית סתום אינו מטמא כל סביביו פרץ את פצימיו מטמא כל סביביו אמר רבה בר בר חנה א"ר יוחנן מבואות המפולשות לעיר אחרת ובקשו בני העיר לסותמן בני אותה העיר מעכבין עליהן לא מיבעי כי ליכא דרכא אחרינא דמעכבי אלא אפילו כי איכא דרכא אחרינא נמי מעכבי משום דרב יהודה אמר רב דאמר (א) מצר שהחזיקו בו רבים אסור לקלקלו (כדרב גידל דא"ר גידל רבים שבררו דרך לעצמן מה שבררו בררו) אמר רב ענן אמר שמואל מבואות המפולשין לרה"ר ובקשו בני מבואות להעמיד להן דלתות בני רה"ר מעכבין עליהן סבור מינה הני מילי בד' אמות כדר' זירא דאמר רבי זירא אמר רב נחמן ד' אמות הסמוכות לרה"ר כרה"ר דמיין ולא היא התם לענין טומאה אבל הכא זימנין דדחקי בני רה"ר ועיילי טובא: ולא את השדה עד שיהא בה תשעה קבין לזה ותשעה קבין לזה כו': ולא פליגי מר כי אתריה ומר כי אתריה בבבל מאי אמר רב יוסף בי רדו יומא מאי בי רדו יומא אי יומא זרעא תרי יומא כרבא לא הוי אי יומא כרבא יומא דזרעא לא הוי אי בעית אימא יומא דכרבא דכריב ותני ואי בעית אימא יומא דזרעא בהדורי דוולא אמר רב נחמן בי דאלו יומא פרדסא אמר אבוה דשמואל בת שלשת קבין תניא נמי הכי האומר לחבירו מנת בכרם אני מוכר לך סומכוס אומר לא יפחות מג' קבין א"ר יוסי אין אלו אלא דברי נביאות בבבל מאי אמר רבא בר קסנא תלת אציאתה בני תריסר גופני כי היכי דרפיק גברא ביומא אמר רבי אבדימי דמן חיפה מיום שחרב בית המקדש ניטלה נבואה מן הנביאים וניתנה לחכמים אטו חכם לאו נביא הוא הכי קאמר אע"פ שניטלה מן הנביאים מן החכמים לא ניטלה אמר אמימר וחכם עדיף מנביא שנאמר א) ונביא לבב חכמה מי נתלה במי הוי אומר קטן נתלה בגדול אמר אביי תדע דאמר גברא רבה מילת' ומתאמר' משמיה דגברא רבה אחרינא כוותי' אמר רבא ומאי קושיא ודילמא תרוייהו בני חד מזלא נינהו אלא אמר רבא תדע דאמר גברא רבה מילתא ומתאמרא

רש"י

בית סתום. שהיה לו פתח לחצר וסתמו: **יש לו ד' אמות.** בחלוקת החצר אם באו לחלוק כאילו הוא פתוח: **אינו מטמא סביביו.** אלא כנגד הפתח אם מת בתוכו: **פרץ את פצימיו.** הרי הוא כקבר וחכמים טימאו את סביבות הקבר ד' אמות כדי שלא יקרבו עושי טהרות עד הקבר ויאהילו ולא אדעתייהו: **לעיר אחרת.** לדרך עיר אחרת: **ובקשו בני העיר.** שהמבואות בה לסותמן מאחריהם: **בני אותה העיר.** האחרת מעכבין עליהן שכבר הוחזקו לקצר דרכן לדרך אותן המבואות: **בני רה"ר מעכבין עליהן.** משום דכי דחקו בני רה"ר מסתלקי לתוך המבואות: **הני מילי.** תוך ד' אמות של (ג) ראש המבוי הסמוכות לרה"ר מעכבין מלהעמיד דלתות לשם: **כרה"ר דמו.** לענין ספק טומאה ברה"ר: **ולא היא.** שאפי' רצו להעמידם לפנים מד' אמות מעכבין עליהן: **בי רדו יומא.** בית חרישת יום אחד לזה ולזה לא תחרוש מתרגמינן לא תרדי (דברים כב): ה"ג בי רדו יומא מאי אי יומא זרעא תרי יומא כרבא לא הוי ואי יומא כרבא יומא דזרעא לא הוי אי בעית אימא יומא דזרעא באתרא דכריב ותני ואי בעית אימא ביומא דכרבא ובהדורי: **אי יומא דזרעא.** בשעת הזרע נוח לחרוש שכבר נחרשת בשעת (ג) הקיר: **תרי יומי כרבא לא הוי.** כלומר בשעת הקיר היאך ישכור שוורים אין בו כדי מלאכת ב' ימים ויש בו יותר מכדי מלאכת יום אחד: **ואי ביומא כרבא.** של שעת הקיר קאמרת שיש בו יומא דזרעא והיאך ישכור שוורים בשעת הזרע: **אי בעית אימא יומא דזרעא.** ודקא קשיא לך תרי יומי כרבא לא הוי באתרא דכריב ותנו בשעת הקיר איכא ביומא דזרעא תרי יומי כרבא: **ואי בעית אימא יומא כרבא.** ודקאמרת לא הוי יומא דזרעא בהדורי עסקינן שארץ קשה ויש בה מעלות ומורדות שיש טורח בשעת הזרע כבשעת הקיר: לישנא אחרינא איפכא גרסינן ואי בעית אימא יומא דכרבא ודקשי' לך יומא דזרעא לא הוי באתרא דכריב ותני בשעת הזרע אחת קודם לזריעה ואחת לאחר הזריעה לכסות הזרע: ואי בעית אימא יומא זרעא ודקאמר' תרי יומי כרבא לא הוי בהדורי עסקינן שיש טורח גדול בשעת הזרע תרי יומא וזרעא הוי תרי יומי כרבא ולשון זה הגון: **דוולא.** אם יש להן בור שממנו משקין שדה: **בי דלו יומא.** עד שיהא בו כדי להשקות שדה כדי פעולת יום לזה וכדי פעולת יום לזה משום שכר פועל: **פרדיסא.** כרם: **ג' קבין.** לכל אחד לפי חשבון סאתים כחצר המשכן: **אין אלו אלא דברי נביאות.** בלא טעם: **אוציתא.** כל י"ב גפנים קרי אוליא: **דרפיק.** עודר: **ניטלה נבואה כו'.** משום דאמר ליה לעיל אין אלו אלא דברי נביאות שקרא דברי חכמים נבואה נקט לה להא מילתא: **אטו חכם לאו נביא הוא.** וכי אין חכם ראוי להיות נביא דקאמר מר ניטלה מן הנביאים וניתנה לחכמים מכלל דמעיקרא לא היתה נבואה לחכמים: **הכי קאמר אע"פ שניטלה מן הנביאים.** שאינם חכמים מן חכמים לא ניטלה (ד) ונביאים יש להן לבב חכמה: **תדע.** שלא ניטלה מן חכמים: משמיה

תוספות

פרץ פצימיו מטמא כל סביביו. פי' הקונטר' כל סביביו ד' אמות כקבר ואין נראה לר' שמשון כיון דמסיימי מחילות וליכא למיחש שמא יעלה על הבית ויאהיל עליו לית לן למימר שיטמא ד' אמות סביביו כדמוכח בפ' משוח מלחמה (סוטה דף מד.) גבי חצר הקבר העומד בתוכה טהור ה"מ חצר הקבר דמסיימי מחיצו' אבל (ה) בעלמא תפיס לכך נראה לו לפרש כגון שיש זיזין הרבה בולטין מן הבית מכל צד ויש בהן פותח טפח (ו) לכל אחד ובשלא פרץ פצימיו אף על פי שסתמו אינו מטמא תחת השאר זיזין שסתמו של מת עומד לצאת דרך פתח אבל אם פרץ פצימיו וחזר ובנאן כשאר כותל ואין כאן פתח כלל מטמא כל סביביו דכל זיז וזיז איכא לספוקי דשמא דרך תחת אותו זיז יצא מן הבית ויש ליישב פי' הקונטרס דבית נמי לא מסיימי מחילתא דאע"ג דליכא למיחש שמא יעלה על הבית מ"מ איכא למיחש שמא יגע בכתלי' דקבר מטמא במגע אפי' מן הצד כדמוכח בספרי בפרשת פרה אדומה (ז) בקבר זה קבר סתום או אינו אלא פתוח אמרת ק"ו ומה אהל שהוא מקבל טומאה אינו מטמא מכל הצדדין כשהוא פתוח הקבר שאינו מקבל טומאה אינו דין שלא יטמא מכל הצדדין כשהוא פתוח משמע דכשהוא סתום מטמא אף בנוגע בו מן הצד:

מצר שהחזיקו בו רבים אסור לקלקלו. היינו כשהחזיקו ברשות אבל אם באין להחזיק שלא ברשות יש למחות בידם ולנקוט פיזרא וליתיב כדמוכח בהמניח (ב"ק דף כח. ושם): **ולא** פליגי מר כי אתריה ומר כי אתריה. פי' ר"י ב"ר מרדכי דבאתריה דרבי יהודה היה קרקע חשוב וטוב והיה חשוב לטרוח בתשעה חצאי קבין (ח) אבל באתריה דתנא קמא לא היה קרקע טוב כל כך שיהיה חשוב לטרוח בפחות מתשעה קבין ואף על פי שלא היה בו כדי חרישת יום ראוי היה לטרוח והשתא בעי בבבל מאי שאין הקרקע טוב כל כך ואינו ראוי כשיעור השנוי במשנתינו: ה"ג ר"ח (ט) **ואי** בעית אימא בכרבא וזרעא ובהדורי. פירוש בית חרישת יום ושפיר הוי יומא לזרעא דכשיבא לזורעה חורש ובחזירתו עוד מושך המחרישה על הקרקע וזורע וזה בהדורי: **ואי** בעית אימא יומא דזרעא. ודקאמרת לא הוי תרי יומי כרבא כריב יומא ופלגא והדר תני וכריב עד דשלים יומא:

דוולא. פר"ח ארץ שמשקין אותה ט) בדלי לכל אחד ארץ שדולין לה יום אחד וקשה לר"י דא"כ הוה ליה (י) למיתני בבבל מאי כדבעי באיך ע"כ נראה כפ"ה: **א"ר** יוסי אין אלו אלא דברי נביאות. לא לשבח קאמר אלא כלומר שאומר בלא טעם דכי האי גוונא בסוף (כ) (אלו) מומין (בכורות דף מה. ושם ד"ה עשו) גבי יתרת שאין בה ליפורן מטמאה במגע ובמשא אבל לא באהל וקאמר עשו דבריהן כדברי נביאות מה נפשך אי אבר הוא ליטמא באהל ואי לא אבר הוא לא ליטמא כלל וכן י"ל בסוף פ' כיצד מעברין (עירובין דף ס: ושם ד"ה אין): **אטו** חכם לאו נביא הוא. וא"ת בפ' בן סורר (סנהדרין דף עה.) דקאמר משחרב בהמ"ק ניטל טעם ביאה וניתן לעוברי עבירה תקשי ליה נמי אטו קודם שנחרב לא הוה להו טעם ביאה לעוברי עבירה הא מפיק ליה מדכתיב מים גנובים ימתקו (משלי ט) כדפריך הכא וי"ל דאיכא לשנויי התם כדמשני הכא ניטל טעם ביאה ומעוברי עבירה לא ניטלה ולא חש להקשות בכל מקום: [וע"ע תוס' גיטין עב. ד"ה ומשום וכו']:

עין משפט נר מצוה

קט א מיי' פ"ג מהל' שכנים הל' ו סמג עשין פב טוש"ע ח"מ סי' קעב סעיף ז:
קי ב מיי' פ"ג מהל' טומאת מת הל' א סמג עשין רלג:
קיא ג ד טוש"ע ח"מ סי' קסב סעיף ג:
קיב ה מיי' פי"ג מהל' נזקי ממון הל' כד סמג עשין סח טוש"ע ח"מ סי' שעז בהג"ה וסי' תח סעיף ב:
קיג ו ז מיי' פ"ה מהל' שכנים הל' יא סמג עשין פב טוש"ע ח"מ סי' קסב סעי' א:
קיד ח ט מיי' פ"א מהל' שכני' הל' ד סמג שם טוש"ע ח"מ סי' קעא סעיף ג:

מסורת הש"ס

א) שבת קמו:, ב) רש"ל מ"ז, ג) תוספתא דאהלות ספט"ו, ד) ב"ק כח. ע"ש לקמן כו: ע"ש [ודף ס: ע"ש ודף קנ: ע"ש], ה) רש"ל מ"ז, ו) פסחים ג. וש"נ, ז) עירובין ס:, ח) בכורות מה., ט) [וכרש"י שבע"י ובנוסח יש לו לבב חכמה], י) [צ"ל בעינן לכל כו']

תורה אור השלם

א) לִמְנוֹת יָמֵינוּ כֵּן הוֹדַע וְנָבִא לְבַב חָכְמָה: [תהלים צ, יב]

referred to a field that takes **a day** to plow **during** the first **plowing season,** דִּכְרִיב וְתָנֵי – but he speaks of places **where they plow twice** during planting season.[22] In such places, a field can take an even number of days to plow during both seasons. וְאִי בָּעֵית אֵימָא יוֹמָא דְּזַרְעָא – **And if you prefer, say** that Rav Yosef referred to a field that takes **a day** to plow **during** the **planting season,** בַּהֲדוּרֵי – but he speaks of **[fields] that are hilly.** Since hilly fields take longer to plow,[23] it will take two full days to plow these fields during the first plowing season. Thus, in either of the above cases, the amount of time necessary to plow the field amounts to an even number of days in both plowings. In either case, one partner can compel the other to dissolve the partnership.[24]

The Gemara discusses the minimum size for division of other types of property:

דְּוּוֹלָא – When dividing a **water hole,** אָמַר רַב נַחְמָן – **Rav Nachman said:** בֵּי דְּאָלוּ יוֹמָא – Each partner must receive **an amount** from which he can **draw** enough water daily to irrigate for a full **day.**[25] פַּרְדֵּסָא – When dividing **a vineyard,** אָמַר אֲבוּהַּ דִּשְׁמוּאֵל – **the father of Shmuel said:** בַּת שְׁלֹשֶׁת קַבִּין – Each partner must receive at least an area measuring **three *kavs*.**[26]

The Gemara quotes a Baraisa that supports this view:

תַּנְיָא נַמִּי הָכִי – **This was taught in a Baraisa as well:** הָאוֹמֵר לַחֲבֵירוֹ מְנַת בְּכֶרֶם אֲנִי מוֹכֵר לְךָ – IF SOMEONE SAYS TO HIS FRIEND, "I AM SELLING YOU A PORTION OF A VINEYARD," without specifying the size of the portion, סוּמְכוֹס אוֹמֵר לֹא יִפְחוֹת מִשְּׁלֹשָׁה קַבִּין – SUMCHOS SAYS: HE MAY NOT GIVE the buyer [AN AREA MEASURING] LESS THAN THREE *KAVS*. This supports the ruling of Shmuel's father.[27]

The Gemara comments on the ruling:

אָמַר רַבִּי יוֹסֵי אֵין אֵלוּ אֶלָּא דִּבְרֵי נְבִיאוּת – **R' Yose said: These words** [of Shmuel's father] **are nothing but prophecy**, i.e. there is no logical way of deriving the minimum size for division.[28]

The Gemara inquires as to what the minimum area for division is in another place:

בְּבָבֶל מַאי – **What** is the minimum-size vineyard **in Babylonia?**

The Gemara responds:

אָמַר רָבָא בַּר קִסְנָא – **Rava bar Kisna said:** תְּלַת אֲצִיאָתָה בְּנֵי תְּרֵיסַר גּוּפְנֵי – Each partner must receive an area in which **three rows** of vines can be planted, **each** row **consisting of twelve vines,** כִּי הֵיכִי דְּרָפִיק גַּבְרָא בְּיוֹמָא – **so that** each partner has a share large enough **for a person to hoe for a** full **day.** If the division would leave each with a smaller area, which would be unprofitable to hoe, the vineyard is not divided.

Having quoted R' Yose's comment equating the ruling of Shmuel's father with prophecy, the Gemara digresses to discuss prophecy:

אָמַר רַבִּי אַבְדִּימִי דְּמִן חֵיפָה – **R' Avdimi from Chaifah said:** מִיּוֹם שֶׁחָרַב בֵּית הַמִּקְדָּשׁ – **From the day that the** First **Temple was destroyed,** נִיטְּלָה נְבוּאָה מִן הַנְּבִיאִים וְנִיתְּנָה לַחֲכָמִים – the power of **prophecy was taken from the prophets and given to sages.**[29]

The Gemara asks:

אַטּוּ חָכָם לָאו נָבִיא הוּא – **Is it really true that no sage** before the Destruction **was a prophet?**[30]

The Gemara interprets R' Avdimi's statement:

הָכִי קָאָמַר – **This** is what R' Avdimi meant **to say:** אַף עַל פִּי שֶׁנִּיטְּלָה מִן הַנְּבִיאִים – When the Temple was destroyed, **although [prophecy] was taken from prophets** that were *not* sages, מִן הַחֲכָמִים לֹא נִיטְּלָה – **it was not taken from sages** – they *retained* their prophetic power even after the Temple's destruction.[31]

The Gemara adds:

אָמַר אַמֵּימַר וְחָכָם עָדִיף מִנָּבִיא – **Ameimar said: And a sage is** even **greater than a prophet,** שֶׁנֶּאֱמַר: "וְנָבִא לְבַב חָכְמָה" – **as [the verse] states:**[32] **"And a prophet** (*v'navi*) **has a heart of wisdom."** מִי נִתְלֶה בְּמִי – When we compare two things, **which one do we compare to the other?** הֱוֵי אוֹמֵר קָטָן נִתְלֶה בְּגָדוֹל – **I**

NOTES

22. [Literally: they plowed and repeated.] In addition to plowing before planting, they plowed again afterwards to cover the seeds with soil (*Rashi*). Plowing once during the first season (when the ground was hard) and twice during the second season (after the ground was already softened) takes the same amount of time.

23. Hilly fields are more difficult to plow than level ones. Thus, although plowing a level field the first time does not take twice as long as plowing it the second time, plowing a hilly field does take twice as long.

24. Accordingly, whenever a field is divided, each partner must be allocated a share that can be plowed in an even number of days. If a large field is divided, then, each partner is allocated only a portion that takes a full day (or multiples of full days) to plow during both plowing seasons. Any leftover land containing less than two such portions is not divided and they retain joint ownership of the parcel (*Taz, Choshen Mishpat* 171:3. See *Aruch HaShulchan* ibid. 171:4 who attributes this view to *Rashi*). *Sma* (ibid. 171:8) disagrees, maintaining that if a field is large enough to provide each partner with a portion that takes a full day to plow, the partners divide the entire field.

25. Rav Nachman's reasoning parallels that of Rav Yosef. Workers were paid by the day to irrigate fields. Thus, if the ditch provided less than enough water to irrigate for a full day, the worker would be paid a full day's wages anyway.

26. I.e. an area of 1,250 square *amos*. The calculation converting *kavs* to *amos* is based on the assumption that the size of a field in which two *se'ah* of barley are sown equals the area of the Tabernacle's courtyard. We know that the area of the Tabernacle's courtyard equaled 5,000 square *amos* (100x50). Thus, one *se'ah* of grain can be sown in 2,500 square *amos*. Now there are six *kavs* in a *se'ah*. Hence, three *kavs* (i.e. half a *se'ah*) can be sown in an area of 1,250 square *amos* (see *Rashi*).

27. According to Sumchos, the buyer is entitled only to the smallest area that can be cultivated profitably, because the seller never specified how much he was selling. Sumchos rules that he can demand 1,250 square *amos* (an area in which three *kavs* are planted). This proves that a vineyard must be at least that size to be cultivated profitably, as Shmuel's father maintained.

28. Shmuel's father relayed this to us just as a prophet relays information communicated to him by God: with no logical corroboration. Nevertheless, as is also true of prophecy, the information is definitely true despite our inability to prove it logically, for Shmuel's father would not have made such an arbitrary ruling unless he heard it from his teachers (see *Rashi* and *Ritva* here, and *Rashi* to *Eruvin* 60b).

29. That is, prophecy ceased at the beginning of the Second Temple era. During the seventy-year interval between the Temples, however, there were still several prophets (*Maharsha* 12b). The Gemara below will clarify R' Avdimi's statement.

30. R' Avdimi stated that sages received the power of prophecy *at the time of the destruction*. This implies that before then, no sage possessed this power (*Rashi*).

31. That is, their minds are able to perceive far more than humans are normally able to perceive.

Sages and prophets are both considered to have "prophetic power" in the sense that they transcend the natural limits of human knowledge and perception. The nature of their powers, however, is different. A prophet merely becomes aware of knowledge that is beyond a human's ability to ascertain. A sage, on the other hand, is accorded insight and understanding beyond anything that human intelligence could naturally perceive (see *Ritva* quoted in *Ein Yaakov*).

32. *Psalms* 90:12. The term וְנָבִא can be a noun or a verb. As a noun, it means *and a prophet*; as a verb, it means *and we will bring*. Contextually, the verse means: ***And we will bring** wisdom to our hearts* (see *Radak* ibid.). Ameimar, however, interprets it exegetically to mean: *And **a prophet** has a heart of wisdom.*

בית סתום ישׁ לו ד׳ אמות את פצימיו אין לו ד׳ אמות (קבר שפתחו סתום אינו מטמא כל סביביו פרץ את פצימיו וסתמו מטמא כל סביביו) בית סתום אינו מטמא כל סביביו פרץ את פצימיו מטמא כל סביביו אמר רבה בר בר חנה א״ר יוחנן מבואות המפולשות לעיר אחרת ובקשו בני העיר לסותמן בני אותה העיר מעכבין עליהן לא מיבעי כי ליכא דרכא אחרינא דמעכבי אלא אפילו כי איכא דרכא אחרינא נמי מעכבי משום דרב יהודה אמר רב דאמר רב יהודה (א) מצר שהחזיקו בו רבים אסור לקלקלו (כדרב גידל דא״ר גידל רבים שבררו דרך לעצמן מה שבררו בררו) אמר רב ענן אמר שמואל מבואות המפולשין לרה״ר ובקשו בני מבואות להעמיד להן דלתות בני רה״ר מעכבין עליהן סבור מינה הני מילי בד׳ אמות כדר׳ זירא אמר רב נחמן דאמר רבי זירא אמר רב נחמן ד׳ אמות הסמוכות לרה״ר כרה״ר דמיין ולא היא התם לענין טומאה אבל הכא זימנין דדחקי בני רה״ר ועיילי טובא: ולא את השדה עד שיהא בה תשעה קבין לזה ותשעה קבין לזה כו׳: ולא פליגי מר כי אתריה ומר כי אתריה בבבל מאי אמר רב יוסף בי רדו יומא מאי בי רדו יומא אי יומא זרעא תרי יומא כרבא לא הוי אי יומא כרבא יומא דזרעא לא הוי אי בעית אימא יומא דכרבא דכריב ותני ואי בעית אימא יומא דזרעא בהדורי דוולא אמר רב נחמן בי דאלו יומא פרדסא אמר אבוה דשמואל בת שלשת קבין תניא נמי הכי האומר לחבירו מנת בכרם אני מוכר לך סומכוס אומר לא יפחות מג׳ קבין א״ר יוסי אין אלו אלא דברי נביאות בבבל מאי אמר רבא בר קסנא תלת אציאתה בני תריסר גופני כי היכי דרפיק גברא ביומא אמר רבי אבדימי דמן חיפה מיום שחרב בית המקדש ניטלה נבואה מן הנביאים וניתנה לחכמים אטו חכם לאו נביא הוא הכי קאמר אע״פ שניטלה מן הנביאים מן החכמים לא ניטלה אמר אמימר וחכם עדיף מנביא שנאמר ונביא לבב חכמה מי נתלה במי הוי אומר קטן נתלה בגדול אמר אביי תדע דאמר גברא רבה מילתא ומתאמרא משמיה דגברא רבה אחרינא כוותי׳ אמר רבא ומאי קושיא ודילמא תרוייהו בני חד מזלא נינהו אלא אמר רבא תדע דאמר גברא רבה מילתא ומתאמרא

בית סתום. שהיה לו פתח לחצר וסתמו: **יש לו ד׳ אמות.** בחלוקת החצר אם בא לחלוק כאילו הוא פתוח: **אינו מטמא סביביו.** אלא כנגד הפתח אם מת בתוכו: **פרץ את פצימיו.** הרי הוא כקבר וחכמים טימאו את סביבות הקבר ד׳ אמות כדי שלא יקרבו עושי טהרות עד הקבר ויאהילו ולא ידעו: **לעיר אחרת.** לדרך עיר אחרת: **ובקשו בני העיר.** שהמבואות בה לסותמן מלהתריסם: **בני אותה העיר.** האחרת מעכבין עליהן שכבר הוחזקו לקצר דרכן לדרך אותן המבואות: **בני רה״ר מעכבין עליהן.** משום דכי דחקו בני רה״ר מסתלקי לתוך המבואות: **הני מילי.** תוך ד׳ אמות של (ג) ראש המבוי הסמוכות לרה״ר מעכבין מלהעמיד דלתות לשם: **כרה״ר דמו.** לענין ספק טומאה ברה״ר: **ולא היא.** שאפי׳ רצו להעמידם לפנים מד׳ אמות מעכבין עליהן: **בי רדו יומא.** בית חרישת יום אחד לזה וכן לזה לא תחרוש מתרגמינן לא תרדי (דברים כב): ה״ג בי רדו יומא מאי אי יומא זרעא תרי יומא כרבא לא הוי ואי יומא כרבא יומא דזרעא לא הוי אי בעית אימא יומא דזרעא באתרא דכריב ותני ואי בעית אימא ביומא דכרבא ובהדורי: **אי יומא דזרעא.** בשעת הזרע הוא נוח לחרוש שכבר נחרשת בשעת (ג) הניר: **תרי יומי כרבא לא הוי.** כלומר בשעת הניר היאך ישכור שוורים אין בו כדי מלאכת ב׳ ימים ויש בו יותר מכדי מלאכת יום אחד: **ואי ביומא כרבא.** של שעת הניר קאמרת לא הוי יומא דזרעא והיאך ישכור שוורים בשעת הזרע: **אי בעית אימא יומא דזרעא.** ודקא קשיא לך תרי יומי כרבא לא הוי באתרא דכרבי ותנו ובשעת הניר איכא ביומא דזרעא תרי יומי כרבא: **ואי בעית אימא יומא כרבא.** ודקאמרת לא הוי יומא דזרעא בהדורי עסקינן שארץ קשה ויש בה מעלות ומורדות ויש טורח בשעת הזרע כשעת הניר: לישנא אחרינא איפכא גרסינן ואי בעית אימא יומא דכרבא ודקשי׳ לך יומא דזרעא לא הוי באתרא דכריב ותני בשעת הזרע אחת קודם לזריעה ואחת לאחר הזריעה לכסות הזרע׳ ואי בעית אימא יומא זרעא ודקאמר׳ תרי יומי כרבא לא הוי בהדורי עסקינן שיש טורח גדול בשעת הזרע תרי יומא ולשון זה הגון: **דוולא.** אם יש להן בור שממנו משקין שדה: **בי דלו יומא.** עד שיהא בו כדי להשקות שדה כדי פעולת יום לזה וכדי פעולת יום לזה משום שכר פועל: **פרדיסא.** כרם: **ג׳ קבין.** לכל אחד לפי חשבון שאתים כחצר המשכן: **אין אלו אלא דברי נביאות.** בלא טעם: **אוציאתה.** כל י״ב גפנים קרי אוליה. **דפיק.** עודר: **ניטלה נבואה כו׳.** משום דאמר ליה לעיל אין אלו אלא דברי נביאות שקרא דברי חכמים נבואה נקט לה להא מילתא: **אטו חכם לאו נביא הוא.** וכי אין חכם ראוי להיות נביא דקאמר מר ניטלה מן הנביאים וניתנה לחכמים מכלל דמעיקרא לא היתה נבואה לחכמים: **הכי קאמר אע״פ שניטלה מן הנביאים.** שאינם חכמים מן חכמים לא ניטלה (ד) ונביאים יש להן לבב חכמה: **תדע.** שלא ניטלה מן חכמים: משמיה

פרץ פצימיו מטמא כל סביביו. פי׳ הקונטר׳ כל סביביו ד׳ אמות לקבר ואין נראה לר׳ שמשון כיון דמסיימי מחילות וליכא למיחש שמא יעלה על הבית ויאהיל עליו לית לן למימר שיטמא ד׳ אמות סביביו כדמוכח בפ׳ משוח מלחמה (סוטה דף מד.) גבי חצר הקבר העומד בתוכה טהור ה״מ חצר הקבר דמסיימי מחיצו׳ אבל (ה) בעלמא תפיס לכך נראה לו לפרש כגון שיש זיזין הרבה בולטין מן הבית מכל צד ויש בהן פותח טפח (ו) לכל אחד ובשלא פרץ פצימיו אף על פי שסתמו אינו מטמא תחת השאר זיזין שסתמו של מת עומד לצאת דרך פתח אבל אם פרץ פצימיו וחזר ובנאו כשאר כותל ואין כאן פתח כלל מטמא כל סביביו דכל זיז וזיז איכא לספוקי דשמא דרך תחת אותו זיז יצא מן הבית ויש ליישב פי׳ הקונטרס דבית נמי לא מסיימי מחיצתא דאע״ג דליכא למיחש שמא יעלה על הבית מ״מ איכא למיחש שמא יגע בכתלי׳ דקבר מטמא במגע אפי׳ מן הצד כדמוכח בספרי בפרשת פרה אדומה (ז) בקבר זה קבר סתום או אינו אלא פתוח אמרת ק״ו ומה אהל שהוא מקבל טומאה אינו מטמא מכל הצדדין כשהוא פתוח הקבר שאינו מקבל טומאה אינו דין שלא יטמא מכל הצדדין כשהוא פתוח משמע דכשהוא סתום מטמא אף בנוגע בו מן הצד:

מצר שהחזיקו בו רבים אסור לקלקלו. היינו כשהחזיקו ברשות אבל אם באין להחזיק שלא ברשות יש למחות בידם ולנקוט פיזרא וליתיב כדמוכח בהמניח (ב״ק דף כח. ושם): **ולא** פליגי מר כי אתריה ומר כי אתריה. פי׳ ר״י ב״ר מרדכי דבאתריה דרבי יהודה היה קרקע חשוב וטוב והיה חשוב לטרוח בתשעה חצאי קבין (ח) אבל באתריה דתנא קמא לא היה קרקע טוב כל כך שיהיה חשוב לטרוח בפחות מתשעה קבין ואף על פי שלא היה בו כדי חרישת יום ראוי היה לטרוח והשתא בעי בבבל מאי שאין הקרקע טוב כל כך ואינו ראוי כשיעור השנוי במשנתינו: ה״ג ר״ח (ט) **ואי** בעית אימא בכרבא וזרעא ובהדורי. פירוש בית חרישת יום ושפיר הוי יומא לזרעא דכשיבא לזורעה חורש ובחזירתו עוד מושך המחרישה על הקרקע וזורע וזה בהדורי: **ואי** בעית אימא יומא דזרעא. ודקאמרת לא הוי תרי יומי כרבא כריב יומא ופלגא והדר תני וכריב עד דשלים יומא:

דוולא. פר״ח ארץ שמשקין אותה (ט) בדלי לכל אחד ארץ שדולין לה יום אחד וקשה לר״י דא״כ הוה ליה (י) למיתני בבבל מאי כדבעי באיך ע״כ נראה כפ״ה: **א״ר** יוסי אין אלו אלא דברי נביאות. לא לשבח קאמר אלא כלומר שאומר בלא טעם דכי האי גוונא בסוף (כ) (אלו) מומין (בכורות דף מה. ושם ד״ה עשו) גבי יתרת שאין בה צפורן דברי נביאות במגע ובמשא אבל לא באהל וקאמר עשו דבריהן כדברי נביאות מה נפשך אי אבר הוא ליטמא באהל ואי לאו אבר הוא לא ליטמא כלל וכן י״ל בסוף פ׳ כיצד מעברין (עירובין דף ס: ושם ד״ה אין): **אטו** חכם לאו נביא הוא. ול״ת בפ׳ בן סורר (סנהדרין דף עה.) דקאמר משחרב בהמ״ק ניטל טעם ביאה וניתן לעוברי עבירה ונימא נמי אטו קודם שחרב לא הוה להו טעם ביאה לעוברי עבירה הא מפיק ליה מדכתיב מים גנובים ימתקו (משלי ט) דלפריך הכא וי״ל דאיכא לשנויי התם כדמשני הכא ניטל טעם ביאה ומעוברי עבירה לא ניטלה ולא חש להקשות בכל מקום: [וע״ע תוס׳ גיטין עב. ד״ה ומשום וכו׳]:

would say, we compare **the lesser to the greater!** Thus, since the verse attributes wisdom to prophets, it is evident sages are the greater of the two.[33]

To support R' Avdimi's statement, the Gemara cites evidence that sages retained the power of prophecy after the Temple's destruction:

אָמַר אַבַּיֵי תֵּדַע – Abaye said: Know that this is true, **דְּאָמַר גַּבְרָא רַבָּה מִילְּתָא וּמִתְאַמְרָא מִשְּׁמֵיהּ דְּגַבְרָא רַבָּה אַחֲרִינָא כְּוָותֵיהּ – for one great sage will state something and** later, **the very same thing will be quoted in the name of another great sage,** even though neither had been in contact with the other.

The Gemara explains that this proves nothing:

אָמַר רָבָא וּמַאי קוּשְׁיָא – Rava said: And what is the difficulty of explaining this phenomenon without prophecy? **וְדִילְמָא תַּרְוַיְיהוּ בְּנֵי חַד מַזָּלָא נִינְהוּ – Now, perhaps both** of the sages **were of one nature**[34] and that is why they made identical statements. This does not prove, however, that they were prophets. – ? –

Having rejected Abaye's proof, the Gemara suggests another:

אֶלָּא אָמַר רָבָא תֵּדַע – Rather, Rava said: Know that this is true, **דְּאָמַר גַּבְרָא רַבָּה מִילְּתָא – for** one **great sage will state something וּמִתְאַמְרָא – and** later **the very same thing will be quoted**

NOTES

33. When we seek to elevate the status of one thing by comparing it to another, we elevate the status of the lesser thing by attributing to it a quality possessed by the greater. Hence, if we find that a verse compares x to y, we may assume that y is in fact the greater of the two. In our case, the Gemara applies this principle to determine the relative status of sages and prophets. Since the verse attributes wisdom to prophets, it is evident that sages, who possess wisdom, are the greater of the two (see above, note 32).

34. Literally: fortune. מַזָּלָא (*mazala*) generally refers to one's fortune or destiny. In this context, however, it describes the sage's intellectual capability. In a similar vein, *Rashi* to *Bava Kamma* 2b ד״ה אדם דאית ליה interprets מַזָּלָא to refer to mental capacity.

עין משפט נר מצוה

קט א מיי' פ"כ מהל' שכנים הל' ז סמג עשין פב טוש"ע ח"מ סי' קעב סעיף ז:
קי ב מיי' פ"ז מהל' טומאת מת הל' א סמג עשין רלג:
קיא ג ד טוש"ע ח"מ סי' קסב סעיף ג:
קיב ה מיי' פ"ג מהל' זכי' ומתנ' הל' כ סמג עשין פב טוש"ע ח"מ סי' שנו בהג"ה וסי' קע סעיף כ:
קיג ו ז מיי' פ"א מהל' שכנים הל' יג סמג עשין פב טוש"ע ח"מ סי' קסב סעי' א:
קיד ח ט מיי' פ"א מהל' שכני' הל' ד סמג שם טוש"ע ח"מ סי' קעא סעיף ג:

רבינו גרשום

[תחילת הפירוש ששייך לכאן נדפס בעמוד הקודם]

גמרא

בית סתום יש לו ד' אמות פרץ את פצימיו אין לו ד' אמות (קבר שפתחו סתום אינו מטמא כל סביביו פרץ את פצימיו וסתמו מטמא כל סביביו) בית סתום אינו מטמא כל סביביו פרץ את פצימיו מטמא כל סביביו אמר רבה בר בר חנה א"ר יוחנן מבואות המפולשות לעיר אחרת ובקשו בני העיר לסותמן בני אותה העיר מעכבין עליהן לא מיבעי כי ליכא דרכא אחרינא דמעכבי אלא אפילו כי איכא דרכא אחרינא נמי מעכבי משום דרב יהודה אמר רב דאמר (א) מצר שהחזיקו בו רבים אסור לקלקלו (כדרב גידל דא"ר גידל רבים שבררו דרך לעצמן מה שבררו בררו) אמר רב ענן אמר שמואל מבואות המפולשין לרה"ר ובקשו בני מבואות להעמיד להן דלתות בני רה"ר מעכבין עליהן סבור מינה הני מילי בד' אמות כדר' זירא אמר רב נחמן דאמר רבי זירא אמר רב נחמן ד' אמות הסמוכות לרה"ר כרה"ר דמיין ולא היא התם לענין טומאה אבל הכא זימנין דדחקי בני רה"ר ועיילי טובא: ולא את השדה עד שיהא בה תשעה קבין לזה ותשעה קבין לזה כו': ולא פליגי מר כי אתריה ומר כי אתריה בבבל מאי אמר רב יוסף בי רדו יומא מאי בי רדו יומא אי יומא זרעא תרי יומא כרבא לא הוי אי יומא כרבא יומא דזרעא לא הוי אי בעית אימא יומא דכרבא דכריב ותני ואי בעית אימא יומא דזרעא בהדורי דוולא אמר רב נחמן בי דאלו יומא פרדסא אמר אבוה דשמואל בת שלשת קבין תניא נמי הכי האומר לחבירו מנת בכרם אני מוכר לך סומכוס אומר לא יפחות מג' קבין א"ר יוסי אין אלו אלא דברי נביאות בבבל מאי אמר רבא בר קסנא תלת אציאתה בני תריסר גופני כי היכי דרפיק גברא ביומא אמר רבי אבדימי דמן חיפה מיום שחרב בית המקדש ניטלה נבואה מן הנביאים וניתנה לחכמים אטו חכם לאו נביא הוא הכי קאמר אע"פ שניטלה מן הנביאים מן החכמים לא ניטלה אמר אמימר וחכם עדיף מנביא שנאמר א ונביא לבב חכמה מי נתלה במי הוי אומר קטן נתלה בגדול אמר אביי תדע דאמר גברא רבה מילת' ומתאמר' משמיה דגברא רבה אחרינא כוותי' אמר רבא ומאי קושיא ודילמא תרוייהו בני חד מזלא נינהו אלא אמר רבא תדע דאמר גברא רבה מילתא ומתאמרא

רש"י

בית סתום. שהיה לו פתח לחצר וסתמו: יש לו ד' אמות. בחלוקת החצר אם באו לחלוק כאילו הוא פתוח: אינו מטמא כל סביביו. אלא כנגד הפתח אם מת בתוכו: פרץ את פצימיו. הרי הוא כקבר ומכהנים טימאו את סביבות הקבר ד' אמות כדי שלא יקרבו עושי טהרות עד הקבר ויאהילו ולאו אדעתייהו: לעיר אחרת. לדרך עיר אחרת: ובקשו בני העיר. שהמבואות בה לסותמן מאחריהם: בני אותה העיר. האחרת מעכבין עליהן שכבר הוחזקו לקצר דרכן דרך אותן המבואות: בני רה"ר מעכבין עליהן. משום דכי דחקו בני רה"ר מסתלקי לתוך המבואות: הני מילי. תוך ד' אמות של (ב) ראש המבוי הסמוכות לרה"ר מעכבין מלהעמיד דלתות שם: כרה"ר דמו. לענין ספק טומאה ברה"ר: ולא היא. שאפי' רצו להעמידם לפנים מד' אמות מעכבין עליהן: בי רדו יומא. בית חרישת יום אחד לזה וכן לזה לא תחרוש מתרגמינן לא תרדי (דברים כב): ה"ג בי רדו יומא מאי אי יומא זרעא תרי יומא כרבא לא הוי ואי יומא כרבא יומא דזרעא לא הוי אי בעית אימא יומא דזרעא באתרא דכריב ותני ואי בעית אימא ביומא דכרבא ובאהדורי: אי יומא דזרעא. בשעת הזרע הוא נוח לחרוש שכבר נחרשת בשעת (ג) הניר: תרי יומי כרבא לא הוי. כלומר בשעת הניר היאך ישכור שוורים אין בו כדי מלאכת ב' ימים ויש בו יותר מכדי מלאכת יום אחד: ואי ביומא כרבא. של שעת הניר קאמרת לא הוי יומא דזרעא והיאך ישכור שוורים בשעת הזרע: אי בעית אימא יומא דזרעא. ודקא קשיא לך תרי יומי כרבא לא הוי באתרא דכרבי ותנו בשעת הניר איכא ביומא דזרעא תרי יומי כרבא: ואי בעית אימא יומא כרבא. ודקאמרת לא הוי יומא דזרעא בהדורי עסקינן שארץ קשה ויש בה מעלות ומורדות ויש טורח בשעת הזרע כשעת הניר: לישנא אחרינא איפכא גרסינן ואי בעית אימא יומא דכרבא ודקשי' לך יומא דזרעא לא הוי באתרא דכריב ותני בשעת הזרע אחת קודם לזריעה ואחת לאחר הזריעה לכסות הזרעי' ואי בעית אימא יומא זרעא ודקאמר' תרי יומי כרבא לא הוי בהדורי עסקינן שיש טורח גדול בשעת הניר ויומא זרעא הוי תרי יומי כרבא ולשון זה הגון: דוולא. אם יש להן בור שממנו משקין שדה: בי דלו יומא. עד שיהא בו כדי להשקות שדה כדי פעולת יום לזה וכדי פעולת יום לזה משום שכר פועל: פרדיסא. כרם: ג' קבין. לכל אחד לפי חשבון שאתים כחצר המשכן: אין אלו אלא דברי נביאות. בלא טעם: אוציאתא. כל י"ב גפנים קרי אוציא: דרפיק. עודר: ניטלה נבואה כו'. משום דאמר ליה לעיל אין אלו אלא דברי נביאות קאמר לה מילתא: אטו חכם לאו נביא הוא. וכי אין חכם ראוי להיות נביא דקאמר מר ניטלה מן הנביאים וניתנה לחכמים מכלל דמעיקרא לא היתה נבואה לחכמים: הכי קאמר אע"פ שניטלה מן הנביאים. שאינם חכמים מן חכמים לא ניטלה (ד) ונביאים יש להן לבב חכמה: תדע. שלא ניטלה מן חכמים:

משמיה

תוספות

פרץ פצימיו מטמא כל סביביו. פי' הקונטרס כל סביביו ד' אמות כקבר ואין נראה לר"י שמשון כיון דמסיימי מחיצות וליכא למיחש שמא יעלה על הבית ויאהיל עליו לית לן למימר שיטמא ד' אמות כדמוכח בפ' משוח מלחמה (סוטה דף מג.) גבי חצר הקבר העומד בתוכה טהור כ"מ חצר הקבר דמסיימי מחיצו' אבל (ה) בעלמא תפיס לכך נראה לו לפרש כגון שיש זיזין הרבה בולטין מן הבית מכל צד ויש בהן פותח טפח (ו) לכל אחד ובשלא פרץ פצימיו אף על פי שסתמו אינו מטמא תחת השאר זיזין שסתמו של מת עומד לצאת דרך פתח אבל כשפרץ פצימיו וחזר ובנאן כשאר כותל ואין כאן פתח כלל מטמא כל סביביו דכל זיז וזיז איכא לספוקי דשמא דרך תחת אותו זיז יוצא מן הבית ויש לישב פי' הקונטרס דבית נמי לא מסיימי מחיצתא דאע"ג דליכא למיחש שמא יעלה על הבית מ"מ איכא למיחש שמא יגע בכתלי' דקבר מטמא במגע אפי' מן הצד כדמוכח בספרי בפרשת פרה אדומה (ז) בקבר זה קבר סתום אהל שהוא מקבל טומאה מאמרת ק"ו ומה אהל שהוא מקבל טומאה אינו מטמא מכל הצדדין כשהוא פתוח מטמא ק"ו אהל שהוא מקבל טומאה אינו דין שלא יטמא מכל הצדדין כשהוא פתוח משמע דכשהוא סתום מטמא אף בנוגע בו מן הצד:

מצר שהחזיקו בו רבים אסור לקלקלו. היינו כשהחזיקו ברשות אבל אם באו להחזיק שלא ברשות יש למחות בידם ולנקוט פזרה וליחיב כדמוכח בהמניח (ב"ק דף כח. ושם):

ולא פליגי מר כי אתריה ומר כי אתריה. פי' ר"י ב"ר מרדכי דבאתריה דרבי יהודה היה קרקע חשוב וטוב והיה חשוב לטרוח בתשעה קבין (ח) אבל באתריה דתנא קמא לא היה קרקע טוב כל כך שיהיה חשוב לטרוח בפחות מתשעה קבין ואף על פי שלא היה בו כדי חרישת יום ראוי היה לטרוח והשתא בעי בבבל מאי שאין הקרקע טוב כל כך ואינו ראוי כשיעור השנוי במשנתינו: ה"ג ר"ח (ט) ואי בעית אימא בכרבא וזרעא ובהדורי. פירוש בית חרישת יום ושפיר הוי יומא לזרעא דכשיבא לזורעה חורש ובחזירתו עוד מושך המחרישה על הקרקע וזורע חה בהדורי: ואי בעית אימא יומא דזרעא. ודקאמרת לא הוי תרי יומי כרבא כריב יומא ופלגא והדר תני וכריב עד דשלים יומא:

דוולא. פר"ח ארץ שמשקין אותה בדלי לכל אחד ארץ שדולין לה יום אחד וקשה לר"י דא"כ הוה ליה (י) למיתני בבבל מאי כדבעי באיך ע"כ נראה כפ"ה:

א"ר יוסי אין אלו אלא דברי נביאות. לא לשבח קאמר אלא כלומר שאומר בלא טעם דכי האי גוונא בסוף (כ) (אלו) מומין (בכורות דף מה.) גבי יתרת שאין בה עצם מטמא במגע ובמשא אבל לא באהל וקאמר עשו דבריהם כדברי נביאות כלל נפשך אי אבר הוא ליטמא באהל ואי לאו אבר הוא לא ליטמא כלל וכן י"ל בסוף פ' מילד מעברין (עירובין דף ס: ושם ד"ה אין):

אטו חכם לאו נביא הוא. ול"ת בפ' בן סורר (סנהדרין דף עה.) דקאמר משחרב בהמ"ק ניטל טעם ביאה וניתן לעוברי עבירה תקשי ליה נמי אטו קודם שנחרב לא הוה להו טעם ביאה הא מפיק ליה מדכתיב מים גנובים ימתקו (משלי ט) לכדפריך הכא וי"ל דאיכא לשנויי התם כדמשני הכא ניטל טעם ביאה ומעוברי עבירה לא ניטלה ולא חש להקשות בכל מקום: [וע"ע תוס' גיטין עב. ד"ה ומשום וכו']:

הגהות הב"ח

גליון הש"ס

תורה אור השלם

א) לְמְנוֹת יָמֵינוּ כֵּן הוֹדַע וְנָבִא לְבַב חָכְמָה: [תהלים צ, יב]

ליקוטי רש"י

חשק שלמה על רבינו גרשום

עין משפט
נר מצוה

קטו א ב מיי' פי"ב מהל' שכנים הלכה ג סמג עשין פב טוש"ע ח"מ סי' קעד סעיף ג:

קטז ג ד ה מיי' שם הל"א טוש"ע שם ס"א:

גליון הש"ס

גמרא מעלי' ליה עלויא. עיין פ"ו משנה ה' דדמאי בפירוש הרמב"ם: תוס' ד"ה כגון כו' אבל הא פשיטא שיכול למחות בו. עיין לקמן דף לט ע"ב ברשב"ם ד"ה אמאי שלא לא הגיעו:

רבינו גרשום

מאי קושיה. מאי ראייה דמייתית דילמא תרוייהו הני גברי ברבייא בני חדא מזלא נינהו משום הכי אמר האי כגון האי אע"ג דלא שמעיה ליה ולאו נביאות הוא: **א) אלא דלא תדע.** דהכי איכא למימר דנביאות הוא וליכא למימר דחד מזלא הוא שהרי ר' עקיבא דקים לן דלא היה מעולם גברא כוותיה ואפ"ה כי אתי חד תנא ואמר מנפשיה כוותיה אע"ג דלאו בני חד מזלא נינהו דלית דהוי ליה מזלא בתורה ובעושר כוותיה דר' עקיבא: **ודלמא כסומא בארובה.** ולא משום דהוה עדיף ומשני לאו טעמא קאמר שמביא אמתלא לדבריו ראייה ומדקאמר טעמא ודאי מרוב חכמתו קאמר ולא כסומא בארובה: **בגישרא.** דעברי בה [בנין השוק]. למ"ה: **דמליך.** דליעבדי מיניה ראש ישיבה: **הכי שמיה.** דהכי חתום שמיה בשטר: **טביומי.** והכי מיקרי שמיה ושמיה דרב אשי טביומי והאי דקרי ליה רב אשי משום שם לווי: **בכלה.** קרי לה לההוא מסכתא דדריש ריש מתיבתא: **כל המטיבין לו.** הואיל והטוב לרב אשי דפתח בראש ישיבה **לא במהרה מריעין לו** שלא יסלקוהו רב אחא אינו יכול להריע לו: **בכנפיה.** בחיקו: **כמה לבבות.** כמה שאין לבו מיושב עליו: **איש נבוב.** חלול הוא שלא אכל: **ילבב.** כמה לבבות: **אפי' לבו אטום בכתולה.** זו שאינה בעולה ואטומה היא מתנובב: **[פשיטא]** אם בכור ופשוט באו לחלוק בשדות אביהם והבכור נוטל פי שנים ואמר [הבכור] אני נוטל חלק בבכורי' סמוך לחלק פשוט **בחד מיצר** אין יכול הפשוט לעכב עליו ולומר שקול חלק פשוט בהאי גיסא וחלק בכור לאידך גיסא ואינו יכול לעלות עילוי דמים אם יניחו ליטול שניהם במיצר אחד דודינו ליטול ירושתו במקום אחד: **יבם מאי** יבם שמת אחיו בלא בנים ויבם את אשת אחיו ונטל חלקו ושל אחיו במיצר אחד

כל המריעין לו לא במהרה מטיבין לו. ובשילהי מרובה (ב"ק דף פ: ושם ד"ה לעולם) דקאמר רב אחא גופיה לעולם אין מטיבין לו איכא למימר דמתחל' אמר לא במהרה מטיבין שהיה מצפה שיחזירוהו לגדולתו וכשראה שלא החזירוהו שוב אמר לעולם אין מטיבין לו: **חלק** בכור וחלק פשוט יהבינן ליה אחד מצרא. כדנפקא לן ביש נוחלין (לקמן דף קכב.) מדכתיב פי שנים מקיש חלק בכורה לחלק פשוט: **אמיצרא** דבי נשי. אית דגרס בתר הכי אמרי אחוותא א"כ בי נשיה היינו חמיו ולא היו לחמיו בנים כי אם בנות. ואית דגרס אמרי אחי א"כ בי נשיה היינו אביו [ועי' תוס' שבת כג: ד"ה דבי נשא]: **כגון** זה כופין על מדת סדום. תימה לר"י לרבה אמאי איצטריך קרא בבכור דיהבינן ליה אחד מצרא ואומר ר"י לפי שלא נתן לו (ב) כח הכתוב אלא כב' אחיו ואילו היו שני אחיו רוצים להשתתף לא כפינן לשלישי לתת להם חלק ביחד ועוד דבכור מתנה קרייה רחמנא כדאמר ביש נוחלין (שם) דכתיב לתת לו פי שנים ואין לכוף את הנותן ולאביי נמי אי לאו דקרייה רחמנא בכור ה"א יקום על שם אחיו כאילו הוא ואחיו קיימין וריצב"א מפרש דהא דאמר רבה כופין לא מדין תורה קאמר דבדין היה יכול למחות שכנגדו דאיכא קפידא ברוחות כדאמר בכמה דוכתין ועוד הא דכופין על מדת סדום בזה נהנה וזה לא חסר היינו בשכבר דר בחצר חבירו שאינו מעלה לו שכר ° אבל הא פשיטא שיכול למחות בו שלא יכנס לדור בביתו אפי' בחצר דלא קיימא לאגרא וגברא דלא עביד למיגר דהוה זה (ט) נהנה וזה לא חסר אלא מתקנת חכמים קאמר הכא דכופין והשתא אין להקשות כלל אמאי איצטריך קרא בבכור: **מעלינן** ליה כנכסי דבר מריון. פירש הקונטרס בשדה הבעל (ג) שיכולים לומר שפעמים מתברכת משאר שדות ובתרתי ארעתא אתרי נגרי לא שייך למימר מעלינן כיון שצריך להשקות ואין מתברכת זו יותר מזו ואין נראה דגם אותם שצריך להשקות מתברכת אחת מהם פעמים יותר שאחת לוקה בשדפון ואחת אינה לוקה ופר"ת מעלינן כנכסי דבר מריון לא ניתן לך זכות שיש לנו בשדה זו אם לא בדמים יקרים כמו בני מריון שהיו עשירים ולא היו מוכרים קרקעותיהם אלא בדמים יקרים ותרתי ארעתא אתרי נגרי לא קאי אעובדא דההוא גברא אלא מילתא באנפי נפשיה כלומר שתי שדות שיש לכל אחד נגר ורוצה האחד שיחלקו כל אחת לשתים שיקח חצי שדה זו וחצי שדה זו אמר רבה כופין על מדת סדום ויטול כל (מ) שדה שלם כדי שיהא לכל אחד חלק אחד מצרא וכן יש לפרש תרתי ארעתא אחד נגרא שהנגר מפסיק בין שתי השדות ואם יחלקו כל שדה לשתים לא יהיה חלקו אחד מצרא והשתא בהכי לא שייך למימר מעלינן כנכסי דבי בר מריון דאטו אם האחד רצה לחלוק לעשרים נאמר שיחלקו משום מעלינן ולשון מעלינן נמי אינו מתיישב לפ"ה:

משמיה דרבי עקיבא כוותיה. וליכא למימר בני חד מזלא נינהו שהרי ר"ע חכם ממנו הרבה: ולאו טעמא קאמר. במילתיה וכיון דאמר טעמא אין זה כסומא שמכוון לילך בארובה במקרה בעלמא אלא סברת הלב היא הבאה לו בנבואה וזכה להסכים להלכה למשה מסיני: **בריסתקא.** שוק רשות הרבים: **דמליך.** אי השתא במתא מחסיא שעתיד בו להיות ראש הישיבה עכשיו: **טביומי חתים.** כשחותם באיגרת חותם שמו טביומי: **קיימא לי שעתא.** מזל: **שדרו זוגא דרבנן לגביה.** דמר בר רב אשי: **לאימלוכי ביה.** ליטול עצה ורשות להמליך את רב אחא: **פתח ותנא.** דרשה ונעשה ראש הישיבה: **כל המריעין לו כו'.** כלומר הואיל ונדחה השעה לא ימליכוני עוד: **איש נבוב.** כשהוא חלול בלא כרס מלאה: **ילבב.** כמה לבבות שאינו מסכים לדעת שלמה: **ינובב בתולות.** לב אטום כבתולות עושה נבוב וחלול: **פשיטא חלק בכור וחלק פשוט.** שני חלקין שהבכור נוטל אחד משום בכורה ואחד משום פשיטות יהבינן ליה אחד מצרא זו אצל זו שהרי שניהן חלקו הן והרי הן כחלק אחד: **יבם מאי.** המייבם את אשת אחיו דקם תחתיו לנחלה ונוטל שני חלקים מאי מי מצו אמרי ליה הואיל ומכח אחרינא קאתי לא יהבי להו (ו) ניהליה אחד מצרא זו אצל זו אי לאו מעליותא גבן בדמי: **הבכור אשר תלד.** ביבם קמשתעי למלוה בגדול לייבם אשר תלד פרט לאילונית והכי מדרש קרא יבמה יבא עליה וגו' והיה הבכור איזה מן היבמין יבא עליה הבכור אשר תלד וכגון שהיבמה את שיולדת היא פרט לאילונית: **דזבן ארעא אמצרא דבי נשא.** קנה קרקע אצל שדה אביו: **כי מטא למיפלג.** עם אחיו בנכסי אביו: **על מדת סדום.** זה נהנה וזה לא חסר: **אמרו אחי מעלינן ליה עילויא.** לנו היא משובחת כקרקעותיו של בר מריון שהיו מעולות ומשתבחת הא דרב יוסף בשדה (ח) בעל שיכולין לומר פעמים שזו מתברכת משאר השדות: **תרי ארעתא אתרי נגרי.** אם בית השלחין היא ויש לשני אחין לחלוק שתי שדות לכל אחת ואחת יש לה יאור להשקות ממנו וזה קנה שדה אצל (ע) האחד מהן ורוצה שיתן אחיו זו הסמוכה לשלו: כגון זו כופין. דהא לקרקע השניה גם היא יש לה יאור להשקות ממנו: **האי מדויל והאי לא מדויל.** דרך היאורים לייבש כשנהר (פ) (שם) נמשכין ממנו מתמעט לפעמים שזה יבש וזה אינו יבש ואומר לו טול חלקך בשתיהם דלאו מדת סדום היא או תן לנו עילוי בדמי: **תרתי.** ארעתא יש להם לחלוק על חד נגרא ואחד מהן קנה קרקעו אצל האחת: **כופין על מדת סדום.** דכיון דאחד נגרא ניהו שתיהן שוות: **ניחא לי לאפושי אריסי.** טוב לי שיהא לך שתי שדות אחת מכאן ואחת מכאן (י) ואחת לי באמצע כדי שתרבה לך אריסין ותהא שדה שלי משתמרת יפה:

משמיה דר' עקיבא בר יוסף כוותיה אמר רב אשי ומאי קושיא דלמא להא מילתא בר מזליה הוא אלא אמר רב אשי תדע דאמר גברא רבה מילתא ומתאמרא הלכה למשה מסיני כוותיה (א) ודלמא כסומא בארובה ולאו טעם (א) יהיב א"ר יוחנן מיום שחרב בית המקדש ניטלה נבואה מן הנביאים וניתנה לשוטים ולתינוקות לשוטים מאי היא כי הא דמר בר רב אשי דהוה קאי ברסתקא דמחוזא שמעיה לההוא שוטה דקאמר ריש מתיבתא דמליך (ב) במתא מחסיא טביומי חתים אמר מאן חתים טביומי ברבנן אנא שמע מינה לדידי קיימא לי שעתא קם אתא אדאתא אימנו רבנן לאותביה לרב אחא מדפתי ברישא כיון דשמעי דאתא ג) שדור זוגא דרבנן לגביה לאימלוכי ביה (ג) עכביה הדר שדור זוגא דרבנן אחרינא עכביה גביה עד דמלו בי עשרה כיון דמלו בי עשרה פתח הוא ותנא ודרש לפי שאין פותחין בכלה פחות מעשרה קרי רב אחא אנפשיה ג) כל המריעין לו לא במהרה מטיבין לו וכל המטיבין לו לא במהרה מריעין לו תנוקת מאי היא כי הא דבת רב חסדא הוה יתבה בכנפיה דאבוה הוו יתבי קמיה רבא ורמי בר חמא אמר לה מאן מינייהו בעית אמרה ליה תרוייהו אמר רבא ואנא בתרא (ד) א"ר אבדימי דמן חיפה קודם ד) שיאכל אדם וישתה יש לו שתי לבבות לאחר שאוכל ושותה אין לו אלא לב אחד שנאמר א) איש נבוב ילבב וכתיב ב) נבוב לוחות ומתרגמינן חליל לוחין אמר רב הונא בריה דרב יהושע הרגיל ביין אפי' לבו אטום כבתולה יין מפקחו שנאמר ג) ותירוש ינובב בתולות: אמר רב הונא בריה דרב יהושע א) פשיטא חלק בכור וחלק פשוט יהבינן ליה ה) אחד מצרא יבם מאי אמר אביי היא היא מ"ט בכור קרייה רחמנא רבא אמר ב) אמר קרא ד) והיה הבכור הוייתו כבכור ואין חלוקתו כבכור ההוא דזבן ארעא אמצרא דבי ו) נשיה כי קא פלגו א"ל פלגו לי אמצראי ז) אמר רבה ג) כגון זה כופין על מדת סדום מתקיף לה רב יוסף ד) אמרי ליה אחי ° מעלינן ליה עלויא כי נכסי דבי בר מריון והלכתא כרב יוסף תרי ארעתא אתרי נגרי אמר רבה כגון זה כופין על מדת סדום מתקיף לה רב יוסף זמנין דהאי מדויל והאי לא מדויל והלכתא כרב יוסף תרתי (ה) אחד נגרא א"ר יוסף ה) כגון זה כופין על מדת סדום מתקיף לה אביי מצי אמר בעינא דאפיש אריסי והלכתא כרב יוסף אפושי (ו) לאו מילתא היא

מסורת הש"ס

א) [נדה כ:], ב) [ב"ל שדור], ג) ב"ק פ:, ד) פ"א שאכל בו' ושתה בו', ה) [לקמן קכב.], ו) [פי' סמוך לשדה של חמיו ולא היה לחמיו בנים כי אם בנות. ערוך וע' תוס' דהכא ד"ה אמיצרא], ז) [לקמן נט. קמח. עירובין מט. כתובות קג.], ח) [ב"ל שמם], ט) ב"ל לא נהנה רש"ש:

הגהות הב"ח

(א) גמ' ולאו טעם קאמר א"ר יוחנן: (ב) שם דמליך השתא במתא מחסיא: (ג) שם לאימלוכי ביה עכבוהו הדר שדור וכו' עכבוהו גביה עד: (ד) שם ולאנא בתרא וכן הוא א"ר אבדימי: (ה) שם תרתי ארעתא אחד נגרא: (ו) שם אפושי אריסי לאו מילתא היא: (ז) רש"י ד"ה יבם וכו' לא יהבי ליה ניהלך אחד וכו' ומעלית גבן בדמי: (ח) ד"ה אמרו וכו' בשדה בית הבעל: (ט) ד"ה תרי וכו' אצל אחת מהן ורוצה שיתן אחיו לו: (י) ד"ה ניחא וכו' ואחת מכאן כדי שתרבה בו' ותיבת ואחת באמצע נמחק: (כ) תוס' ד"ה כגון וכו' שלא נתן לו הכתוב כח אלא: (ל) ד"ה מעלינן וכו' בשדה הבעל ואיירי שיכולים: (מ) בא"ד ויטול כל אחד שדה שלם:

הגהות מהר"ב רנשבורג

א] רש"י ד"ה דמליך השתא במתא כו'. מלת השתא נמחק: ב] בא"ד להיות ראש הישיבה. כלו' הס"ד ואח"כ מה"ד טביומי חתים כו' [אלא בגמרא ע"ל להגיה כי י"ג בגמרא לנוסחת רש"י וכן היתה גירסת רש"י]:

תורה אור השלם

א) וְאִישׁ נָבוּב יִלָּבֵב וְעַיִר פֶּרֶא אָדָם יִוָּלֵד: [איוב יא, יב]

ב) נְבוּב לֻחֹת תַּעֲשֶׂה אֹתוֹ כַּאֲשֶׁר הֶרְאָה אֹתְךָ בָּהָר כֵּן יַעֲשׂוּ: [שמות כז, ח]

ג) כִּי מַה טּוּבוֹ וּמַה יָּפְיוֹ דָּגָן בַּחוּרִים וְתִירוֹשׁ יְנוֹבֵב בְּתֻלוֹת: [זכריה ט, יז]

ד) וְהָיָה הַבְּכוֹר אֲשֶׁר תֵּלֵד יָקוּם עַל שֵׁם אָחִיו הַמֵּת וְלֹא יִמָּחֶה שְׁמוֹ מִיִּשְׂרָאֵל: [דברים כה, ו]

ליקוטי רש"י

ברסתקא. בשוק [ברכות נד.]. לרחבה [ב"מ סג.]. לחוץ העיר רשות הרבים [עירובין מד:]. ותירוש ינובב בתולות. זה יין

טוב שהוא משכר את האדם לגלות סתרי לבו האטומים כבתולה [יומא עו:]. אחד מצרא. שני חלקים יטול במקום אחד כלומר שדה אחד ותפקח מינה לכל מקום שנפל לו הגורל חלק פשוט יטול בצדו חלק בכורה ואם כן הן חילוק בנכסים דהא לבכור כשהן שני חלקין שדות ולא יפלו לו שלשה גורלות שנים לבכור ואחד לפשוט שהרי יטול ולא יכול חלק הפשוט שלו שהוא סמוך יוכל לו להם כן כך מצרא בדיוק ישוו גורלות ויגיע זכות שהכל יהיו למטה שלו שיבחר ולא יהא להם ממנו זכות בהם הפשוט מבכור חייב לבכור [רשב"ם לקמן קכב.]. מדת סדום. שאפילו מידי דלא חסר מידי לא יהבי [כתובות קג.]. כופין. אותו אחד על מדת סדום ולית ליה דחסר [רשב"ם לקמן נט.]. (לקמן (לקמן ...)) ויש אומרים זו היא מדת סדום [שבת קי.]. נגרא. חריץ של מים.

אשתו ושוב מת אביהן דשקיל האי יבם ירושת אחיו שני חלקים אחד חלק אחיו המת וחלק של עצמו. מי יהבי ליה אחד מיצרא כי חלק בכור או לא. מי אמרינן דיניה הוא דשקיל פי שנים ויהבי' ליה גבי בחד מיצרא או לא משמע ממש מיצרא הנהו ב' חלקים אי לא: **אביי אמר היא היא.** דשקיל נמי בחד מיצר **דבכור קרייה רחמנא** והיה הבכור אשר תלד וגו' אליבא דרבנן דאמרי' לי' יבם הבכור ויהבינן ליה. **הוייתו כבכור.** ליטול ב' חלקים **ולא חלוקתו כבכור** ליטול שניהם בחד מצרא: **אמצרא דבי נשא.** סמוך לשדה של חמיו והיה לו חמיו נכסים בנות ולא היו לו בנים היינו דבי נשא. סמוך לאותה שדה שקנה **אמר רבא** ודאי יהבינן ליה סמוך למיצריה **וכגון זה כופין על מדת סדום** שלא יעשה מדת סדום שהיו מקפידים ואפ' שלא לא שלי ושלך שלך. כך אלו כופין אותם שלא יעכבו אותו ליתן לו אלא מצר סמוך לשדה: **מתקיף לה רב יוסף** מצי אמרי ליה אחי מעלינן לך ולא משום ידה שהיא משובחת ועדיפא מן האחרת כי נכסי דבי בר מריון דהוו עדיפי. כלומר כמו שהיו יקרים להם דהוי דעל טפי כי היכי. **והא אמרי' לך כנכסי דבר מריון** דהוי ליה מקרקע מעולין והוי אמיד ולא מזבן ארעתיה כי אם בדמים יקרים הכי נמי מעלי לן בהאי. **דקא אמרי לחלוק** אחיו היה ולית לי ביה הנאה שנטול שדה סמוך לשדה שקנה ליה **מעלינן ליה** האי ארעא וחשבי' ליה ביוקר **דמשי מעלי לי'** ביוקר. תרי ארעי תרי שותפי דהוי להו לחלוק **תרי ארעתא דקיימי חדא אהאי נגרא וחדא אהאי** נגרא דמים אע"ג דרבא האי ארעא דהאי אמצרא דידיה ואמאי כופין **והלכתא כרב יוסף** אמר ליה בסמוך ליה חד לא לא יהבי' ליה: **כגון זה** כופין על מדת סדום בשדה כיון **דמגיע לו** קרקע תרי ארעתא דאית לן לחלוק דהני תרי ארעתא אהאי נגרא ואמר האי דזבן ארעא לאחת מהן סמוך לאחת מהם וכו' אמר ליה אמה המים שמשקין אותה ממון הוא ולקרקע שקנה בחלקו אינו חולק כל שדה חולק כל שדה וכל נגר דב נגר לי אותה שדה שסמוכה לאותה שקניתי אמר (רבא) [רבה] **כגון זה ודאי כופין** דלא מצי טעין אידך לא בעינא אלא נחלוק כל שדה וכל נגר דהב לשנים דשמא זמנין **דהאי מדויל** והאי יבש מסתפינא דלפא יבשא נגרא דמיצרך לא יבשה נגרא שלי ונגרא דמיצרך דהאי מדול והאי לא מדול ולכך אמר ליה **תרי ארעתא אחד נגרא** שהיו שתיהן משקות מנהר אחד מצד זה ומצד זה וזה קנה סמוך לאחד מהן מדבר למימר נחלק כל אחד ונגר חד לצד אחר ואמר ליה הב לי שדה שסמוכה לשדה שלי ושמינה הכל שוה דמשקו תרוייהו מחד נגרא **מתקיף לה רב יוסף** אמר ליה **אבי** מצי אמר **בעינא דאפיש אריסי ניחא לי לאפושי אריסי** כלומר אם היה שדהו שקנה מצד אחד ושדה שלי שהוא מצד אחר מצד האחר וזה ואחד בחלקו בשדה שלי מצד שהוא מאריסים שלי משתמרת שדי יותר שאם יהיה אריס אחד לצד אחד ושני לצד אחר יוכל לומר לו הלה איני רוצה שתחלק חלקך כי אם מצד האחר כדי שתהא שדה שלי באמצע והם מרובים ושומרים אותם יותר מאויבים וכי האי גוונא מצי לעכבו ואפי' הכי דאיכא למימר הכי הלכתא כוותיה דרב יוסף. ל"א. אמאי כופין הא מצי אמר ליה מדהאי ארעא וחצי ארעא דאמיצרך שקול פלגא ואמיצרך ארעא אחריתי תשקול פלגא ואנא אשקול פלגא ואנא אשקול פלגא כי היכי דלהוו

חשק שלמה על רבינו גרשום א) נראה דצ"ל אלא אמר רבא תדע וכו' ומתאמרה משמיה דר"ע בר יוסף דכוותיה דהכי איכא למימר וכו'.

מִשְּׁמֵיהּ דְּרַבִּי עֲקִיבָא בַּר יוֹסֵף כְּוָותֵיהּ – **in the name of R' Akiva bar Yosef,** even though neither had been in contact with the other. Now, R' Akiva was the greatest genius of his time;[1] certainly, no other sage had his intellectual capability. This phenomenon, then, can be understood only if sages indeed exercise the power of prophecy.

The Gemara refutes this proof as well:

אָמַר רַב אַשִׁי – **Rav Ashi said:** וּמַאי קוּשְׁיָא – **And what is the difficulty** of explaining this phenomenon? דִּלְמָא לְהָא מִילְּתָא בַּר מַזָּלֵיהּ הוּא – **Perhaps concerning this** one **matter, [the first sage] had the same** mental **nature,** i.e. intellectual tendencies, **[as R' Akiva] had.** Thus, although he was not the genius R' Akiva was, his arriving at *one* of R' Akiva's conclusions does not prove that he exercised the power of prophecy.

Having rejected Rava's proof, the Gemara offers another:

אֶלָּא אָמַר רַב אַשִׁי – **Rather, Rav Ashi said:** תֵּדַע – **Know** that sages exercise the power of prophecy, דְּאָמַר גַּבְרָא רַבָּה מִילְּתָא – **for a great sage will state something,** וּמִתְאַמְרָא הֲלָכָה לְמֹשֶׁה מִסִּינַי כְּוָותֵיהּ – **and** later **the very same thing will be quoted as a law taught orally to Moses at Sinai.** Since such laws cannot be derived from the Written Torah, the law must have been revealed to him prophetically.

The Gemara objects:

וְדִלְמָא כְּסוּמָא בַּאֲרוּבָּה – **But perhaps** the sage stumbled upon the law **as a blind man** finds his way down **through a skylight,** i.e. by sheer luck. Why assume, then, that he prophesied?

The Gemara replies:

וְלַאו טַעַם יָהִיב – **But** did the sage **not give a reason** for his ruling? Certainly he did! Since he was able to give a *reason* for his ruling, the reason must have been revealed to him prophetically.

R' Yochanan tells of others that prophesy nowadays:

אָמַר רַבִּי יוֹחָנָן – **R' Yochanan said:** מִיּוֹם שֶׁחָרַב בֵּית הַמִּקְדָּשׁ – **From the day that the Holy Temple was destroyed,** נִיטְּלָה נְבוּאָה מִן הַנְּבִיאִים וְנִיתְּנָה לְשׁוֹטִים וּלְתִינוֹקוֹת – the power of **prophecy was taken from the prophets and given to deranged people and to children.**[2]

The Gemara inquires:

לְשׁוֹטִים מַאי הִיא – You have said that prophecy was given **to deranged people. What is** an example of **this?**

The Gemara illustrates the idea:

כִּי הָא דְּמָר בַּר רַב אַשִׁי – **It is like that** incident **involving Mar bar Rav Ashi,** דַּהֲוָה קָאֵי בְּרִסְתְּקָא דִּמְחוֹזָא – **who was standing in the marketplace** of the city **of Mechuza.** שַׁמְעֵיהּ לְהַהוּא שׁוֹטֶה דְּקָאָמַר – **He** (Mar bar Rav Ashi) **heard a deranged person who was saying,** רֵישׁ מְתִיבְתָּא דְּמָלִיךְ בְּמָתָא מְחַסְיָא – **"The head of the Talmudic academy that is** [now][3] **being appointed in the city of Mechasya** טַבְיוֹמֵי חָתִים – **signs** the name **'Tavyumi.'** אָמַר – Upon hearing this pronouncement, **[Mar bar Rav Ashi] said** to himself: מַאן חָתִים טַבְיוֹמֵי בְּרַבָּנַן – **Who among the Rabbis signs** his name **"Tavyumi?"** אֲנָא – I do![4] שְׁמַע מִינָּהּ לְדִידִי קַיְימָא לִי שַׁעְתָּא – **This** statement thus **informs me that now is a fortuitous time for me**[5] to claim the head position at the Mechasya academy. קָם אֲתָא – **[Mar bar Rav Ashi]** then **arose and went** to Mechasya. אַדְּאָתָא – **By the time he arrived,** אִימְנוּ רַבָּנַן לְאוֹתְבֵיהּ לְרַב אַחָא מִדִּפְתִּי בְּרֵישָׁא – the sages of the academy **had** already **voted to install Rav Acha from Difti as** the **head** of the academy; however, he had not yet been formally installed. כֵּיוָן דִּשְׁמְעֵי דְּאָתָא – **When [the sages] heard that** Mar bar Rav Ashi **had come,** שַׁדּוּר זוּגָא דְּרַבָּנַן לְגַבֵּיהּ לְאִימְּלוּכֵי בֵּיהּ – **they sent a pair of rabbis to him to consult with him** and to ask his permission to install Rav Acha. עַכְּבֵיהּ – **[Mar bar Rav Ashi] held [them]**[6] **back,** requesting that they stay. הֲדַר שַׁדּוּר זוּגָא דְּרַבָּנַן אַחֲרִינָא – The sages in the academy **then sent another pair of rabbis** to Mar bar Rav Ashi, assuming that the first pair never reached him. עַכְּבֵיהּ גַּבֵּיהּ עַד דְּמָלוּ בֵּי עֲשָׂרָה – **[Mar bar Rav Ashi] held [the second pair] back** as well. This continued **until a complement of ten was reached.** כֵּיוָן דְּמָלוּ בֵּי עֲשָׂרָה – **Once a complement of ten was reached,** פָּתַח הוּא וְתָנָא וְדָרַשׁ – **[Mar bar Rav Ashi] began** a discourse **and he taught and expounded** to the assembled sages. After hearing his discourse, they decided to install him as the head of the academy instead of Rav Acha. This fulfilled the prophecy of the deranged person from Mechuza.

The Gemara digresses to explain why Mar bar Rav Ashi waited to begin his discourse:

לְפִי שֶׁאֵין פּוֹתְחִין בְּכַלָּה פָּחוֹת מֵעֲשָׂרָה – **Because one does not commence a lecture**[7] **with** an audience **of less than ten** people.

The story concludes:

קָרֵי רַב אַחָא אַנַּפְשֵׁיהּ – Assessing the situation, **Rav Acha said of himself:** כָּל הַמְּרִיעִין לוֹ לֹא בִּמְהֵרָה מְטִיבִין לוֹ – **Anyone dealt with harshly will not soon have good fortune** visited upon him; וְכָל הַמְּטִיבִין לוֹ לֹא בִּמְהֵרָה מְרִיעִין לוֹ – **and anyone dealt with generously will not soon have misfortune** visited upon him.[8] Hence, once my appointment has been deferred, I will not soon be appointed.

The Gemara again asks:

תִּנּוֹקֶת מַאי הִיא – You have said that prophecy was given **to a young girl.**[9] **What is** a case of **this?**

The Gemara illustrates:

כִּי הָא דְּבַת רַב חִסְדָּא – **It is like that** incident **involving Rav Chisda's daughter,** הֲוָה יָתְבָה בְּכַנְפֵּיהּ דַּאֲבוּהָ – **who was** once **sitting on her father's lap** as a young child. הֲווּ יָתְבֵי קַמֵּיהּ רָבָא וְרָמֵי בַּר חָמָא – At that time, **Rava and Rami bar Chama were**

NOTES

1. According to the Gemara in *Menachos* (29b), R' Akiva was so brilliant that Moses considered him better suited to receive the Torah than he was.

2. *Maharsha* suggests that the nature of a deranged person's or child's prophecy is different than that of a true prophet. See there for further elaboration.

3. *Bach* adds the word הַשְׁתָּא, *now,* to the text.

4. *Sefer HaYuchsin* asserts that the name *Tavyumi* is formed from the words *tav* and *yumi*, which mean *good* and *days*. He therefore suggests that Mar bar Rav Ashi called himself *Tavyumi* because the Jews fared well throughout his lifetime. *Maharsha* objects, however, that he could not have known this to be true until the end of his life. See *Maharsha* and *Rabbeinu Gershom*.

5. Literally: the hour is established for me.

6. Our translation follows *Bach's* emendation of עַכְּבֵיהּ (singular) to עַכְּבִינְהוּ (plural).

7. כַּלָּה refers to the subject on which the head of the Talmudic academy lectured (*Rabbeinu Gershom*; cf. *Rashi* to 22a; see also note 19 there).

8. For it is easier for someone to avoid misfortune than to triumph over it. Rav Acha's thought is analogous to the idea expressed in *Shabbos* (32a): "A person should always pray that he not take ill, for once someone takes ill, the Heavenly Court decrees: Let him prove himself worthy of being healed" (*Iyun Yaakov* to *Bava Kamma* 80b).

The statement of both our Gemara and the one in *Shabbos* can be understood to mean that as long as a person has good fortune, this continues until he becomes unworthy of it. Once a misfortune befalls him, though, he must prove himself especially worthy before God helps him overcome it.

9. Actually, R' Yochanan stated that the power of prophecy was given to children; he never specified that it was given only to girls. Since the forthcoming incident happened to involve a young girl, however, the Gemara specifies that young girls exercise the power of prophecy even though this is true of young boys as well.

עין משפט נר מצוה

קטו א ב מיי' פ"ב מהל' שכנים הלכה ב סמג עשין פב טוש"ע ח"מ סי' קעד סעיף ב:

קטז ג ד ה מיי' שם הל"א טוש"ע שם ס"א:

גליון הש"ס

גמרא מעלי' ליה עלויא. עיין פ"ו משנה ח' דדמאי בפירוש הרמב"ם: תוס' ד"ה כגון כו' אבל הא פשיטא שיכול למחות בו. עיין לקמן דף לט ע"ב ברשב"ם ד"ה אמאי שלו לא הגיעו:

רבינו גרשום

מאי קושיה. מאי ראייה דמייתית דילמא תרווייהו הני גברי רברבייא בני חדא מזלא נינהו משום הכי אמר האי כגון האי אע"ג דלא שמיעא ליה ולאו נביאות הוא: א) אלא דלא תדע. דהכי איכא למימר דנביאות הוא וליכא למימר דחד מזלא הוא שהרי ר' עקיבא דקים לן דלא היה מעולם גברא כוותיה ואפ"ה כי אתי חד תנא ואמר מנפשיה כוותיה אע"ג דלאו בני חד מזלא נינהו דלית דהוי ליה מזלא בתורה ובעושר כוותיה דר' עקיבא: ודלמא כסומא בארובה. ולא משום דהוה עדיף ומשני לאו טעמא קאמר שמביא אמתלא לדבריו ראייה ומדקאמר טעמא ודאי מרוב חכמתו קאמר ולא כסומא בארובה: ברסתקא. בגישרא דעברי בה [בני] השוק. למ"ה: דמליך. דליעבדי מיניה ראש ישיבה: הכי שמיה. דהכי חתום שמיה בשטר: טביומי. והכי מיקרי שמיה ושמיה דרב אשי טביומי והאי דקרי ליה רב אשי משום שם לווי: בכלה. קרי לה לההוא מסכתא דדריש ריש מתיבתא: כל המטיבין לו. הואיל והוטב לרב אשי דפתח בראש ישיבה לא במהרה מריעין לו שלא יסלקוהו רב אחא אינו יכול להריע לו: בכנפיה. בחיקו: כמה לבבות. שאין לבו מיושב עליו: איש נבוב. חלול הוא שלא אכל: ילבב. כמה לבבות: אפי' לבו אטום כבתולה. זו שאינה בעולה ואטומה היא מתנובב: [פשיטא] אם בכור ופשוט באו לחלוק בשדות אביהם והבכור נוטל פי שנים ואמר [הבכור] אני נוטל חלק בבכור' סמוך לחלק פשוט בחד מיצר אין יכול הפשוט לעכב עליו ולומר שקול חלק פשוט בהאי גיסא וחלק בכור לאידך גיסא ואינו יכול לעלות עילוי דמים אם יניחו ליטול שניהם במיצר אחד דדינו ליטול ירושתו במקום אחד: יבם מאי יבם שמת אחיו בחיי אביהן וייבם זה את אשתו ושוב מת אביהן דשקיל האי יבם ירושת אחיו שני חלקים אחד חלק אחיו שמת וחלק של עצמו. מי יהבי ליה אחד מיצרא הנהו ב' חלקים אי לא. מי אמרינן דיניה הוא דשקל פי שנים ויהבי' ליה גבי הדדי בחד מיצרא או לא משמע ממש דבכור הוא ולא יהבי' ליה בחד מיצרא. אביי אמר היא היא. דשקיל נמי בחד מיצר דבכור קרייה רחמנא והיה הבכור אשר תלד ודרשי' לי' הבכור מצוה בגדול הלכך דיניה כבכור ואחד מיצר יהבינן ליה. הוייתו כבכור. ליטול ב' חלקים ולא חלוקתו כבכור ליטול שניהן במיצר אחד: אמצרא דבי נשא. סמוך לשדה אחר של חמיו ולא היו לו לחמיו בנים כי אם בנות ומת חמיו והניח קרקעותיו לבנותיו אמר האי הבו לאשתי חלקה סמוך לאותה שדה שקניתי אמר רבא ודאי יהבינן ליה סמוך למיצריה וכגון זה אי מעכב איניש כופין על מדת סדום שלא יעשה מדת סדום שהיו מקפידין ואו' שלי שלי ושלך שלך. כך אלו כופין אותם שלא יעכבו ליתן לה חלקה אצל שדה בעלה שזה נהנה וזה לא חסר: מתקיף לה רב יוסף והא מצי למימר אחותה הואיל ויש לו הנאה שנוטל שדה סמוך ליה מעלינן ליה האי ארעא וחשבי' ליה ביוקר כנכסי דבי בר מריון דהוי ליה מקרקע מעולין והוי אמיד ולא מזבן ארעתיה כי אם בדמים יקרים הכי נמי מעלי לן האי גברא דמים אי יהבינן ליה בסמוך לו ואי לא לא יהבי' ליה אמצרא דידיה ואמאי כופין והלכתא כרב יוסף דמצי מעלי לי' ביוקר. תרי אחי או תרי שותפי דהוי להו לחלוק תרי ארעתא דקיימן חדא אהאי נגרא וחדא אהאי נגרא דלכל אחת יש לה נגר שלה וזה אמת המים שמשקין אותה ממנו וזבן חד מהני אחי או שותפי חד ארעא אחריתא סמוך לאחת מאלו ואמר האי דזבן הואיל דהני תרי ארעתא דאית לן לחלוק שוין הן במדה ולכל חדא יש לה נגר הב לי אותה שדה שסמוכה לאותה שקניתי אמר (רבא) [רבה] כגון זה ודאי כופין דלא מצי לעכב עליו. מתקיף לה רב יוסף אמאי כופין הא מצי טעין אידך לא בעינא אלא נחלוק כל שדה וכל נגר לשנים דשמא זימנין דהאי נגרא מדול והאי יבש מסתפינא דלמא יבשא נגרא שלי ונגרא דמיצרך לא יבשה ומצית את להשקות שדך ואנא לא מצינא ומפסדנא הלכך בעינא למפלג תרווייהו או יעלה לי דמים וכי האי גוונא מצי מעכב ליה. תרי ארעתא אחד נגרא שהיו שניהן מסתפקות מנגר אחד וקנה אחד מהן קרקע חד סמוך לאחת משדות אלו ואמר ליה לחבירו הב לי אמצראי דהשתא ליכא למימר דהאי מדוול והאי לא מדוול דתרווייהו סמיכי אחד נגר. אמר רב יוסף בהאי מודינא דכופין ויהיב ליה. אמר ליה אביי והא מצי למימר ליה אידך ניחא לי לאפושי אריסי כלומר אם היה שדהו שקנה בצד אחד סמוך למיצר ואמר הבו לי אמיצראי יכול לומר לו הלה איני רוצה שתקח חלקך כי אם מצדי האחר כדי שתהא שדה שלי אמצעית ותשים אריס אחד מצד אחד על אותה שדה שקנית ואריס אחד על חלקך המגיעך מצד אחר ומהן משתמרת שדה שלי שהיא אמצעית וכי האי גונא מצי לעכבי ואפי' הכי דאיכא למימר הכי הלכתא כוותיה דרב יוסף. ל"א. אמאי כופין הא יכול למימר אנא בעינא הכי למפלג דמההיא ארעא וחצי נגרא דאמיצרך שקול פלגא ומאידך ארעא אחורי תשקול פלגא ואנא אשקול פלגא ואנא אשקול פלגא כי היכי דלהוו

גמרא

משמיה דר' עקיבא בר יוסף כוותיה אמר רב אשי ומאי קושיא דלמא להא מילתא בר מזליה הוא אלא אמר רב אשי תדע דאמר גברא רבה מילתא ומתאמרא הלכה למשה מסיני כוותיה ודלמא כסומא בארובה ולאו טעם (א) יהיב א"ר יוחנן מיום שחרב בית המקדש ניטלה נבואה מן הנביאים וניתנה לשוטים ולתינוקות לשוטים מאי היא כי הא דמר בר רב אשי דהוה קאי ברסתקא דמחוזא שמעיה לההוא שוטה דקאמר ריש מתיבתא דמליך (ב) במתא מחסיא טבומי חתים אמר מאן חתים טביומי ברבנן אנא שמע מינה לדידי קיימא לי שעתא קם אתא אדאתא אימנו רבנן לאותביה לרב אחא מדפתי ברישא כיון דשמעי דאתא שדור זוגא דרבנן לגביה לאימלוכי ביה (ג) עכביה הדר שדור זוגא דרבנן אחרינא עכביה גביה עד דמלו בי עשרה כיון דמלו בי עשרה פתח הוא ותנא ודרש לפי שאין פותחין בכלה פחות מעשרה קרי רב אחא אנפשיה כל המריעין לו לא במהרה מטיבין לו וכל המטיבין לו לא במהרה מריעין לו תנוקת מאי היא כי הא דבת רב חסדא הוה יתבה בכנפיה דאבוה הוו יתבי קמיה רבא ורמי בר חמא אמר לה מאן מינייהו בעית אמרה ליה תרוייהו אמר רבא ואנא בתרא (ד) א"ר אבדימי דמן חיפה קודם שיאכל אדם וישתה יש לו שתי לבבות לאחר שאוכל ושותה אין לו אלא לב אחד שנאמר איש נבוב ילבב וכתיב נבוב לוחות ומתרגמינן חליל לוחין אמר רב הונא בריה דרב יהושע הרגיל ביין אפי' לבו אטום כבתולה יין מפקחו שנאמר ותירוש ינובב בתולות: אמר רב הונא בריה דרב יהושע פשיטא חלק בכור וחלק פשוט יהבינן ליה אחד מצרא יבם מאי אמר אביי היא היא מ"ט בכור קרייה רחמנא רבא אמר קרא אמר והיה הבכור הוייתו כבכור ואין חלוקתו כבכור ההוא דזבן ארעא אמצרא דבי נשיה כי קא פלגו א"ל פליגו לי אמצראי אמר רבה כגון זה כופין על מדת סדום מתקיף לה רב יוסף אמרי ליה אחי מעלינן ליה עלויא כי נכסי דבי בר מריון והלכתא כרב יוסף תרי ארעתא אתרי נגרי אמר רבה כגון זה כופין על מדת סדום מתקיף לה רב יוסף זמנין דהאי מדויל והאי לא מדויל והלכתא כרב יוסף תרתי (ה) אחד נגרא א"ר יוסף כגון זה כופין על מדת סדום מתקיף לה אביי מצי אמר בעינא דאפיש אריסי והלכתא כרב יוסף אפושי (ו) לאו מילתא היא

רש"י

משמיה דרבי עקיבא כוותיה. וליכא למימר בני חד מזלא נינהו שהרי ר"ע חכם ממנו הרבה: ולאו טעמא קאמר. במילתיה וכיון דלא אמר טעמא אין זה כסומא שמכוון לילך בארובה במקרה בעלמא אלא סברת הלב היא הבאה לו בנבואה וזכה להסכים להלכה למשה מסיני: ברסתקא. שוק רשות הרבים: דמליך. השתא במתא מחסיא שעתיד בו להיות ראש הישיבה עכשיו: טביומי חתים. כשהוא מתחיל בחתימת חותם שמו טביומי: קיימא לי שעתא. מזל: שדרו זוגא דרבנן לגביה. דמר בר רב אשי: לאימלוכי ביה. ליטול עצה ורשות להמליך את רב אחא: פתח ותנא. דרשה ונעשה ראש הישיבה: כל המריעין לו כו'. כלומר הואיל ונדחה השעה לא ימליכוהו עוד: איש נבוב. כשהוא חלול בלא כרס מלאה: ילבב. כמה לבבות שאינו מסכים לדעת שלמה: ינובב בתולות. לב אטום כבתולות עושה נבוב וחלול: פשיטא חלק בכור וחלק פשוט. שני חלקים שהבכור נוטל אחד משום בכורה ואחד משום פשיטות יהבינן ליה אחד מצרא זו אצל זו שהרי שניהן חלקו הן והרי הן כחלק אחד: יבם מאי. המייבם את אשת אחיו דקם תחתיו לנחלה ונוטל שני חלקים מאי מי אמרי' ליה הואיל ומכח אחרינא קאתי לא יהבי להו (ז) ניהליה אחד מצרא זו אצל זו או לאו מעליותא גבן בדמי: הבכור אשר תלד. ביבם קמשתעי דמצוה בגדול לייבם אשר תלד פרט לאילונית והכי מדרש קרא יבמה יבא עליה וגו' והיה הבכור איזה מן היבמין יבא עליה הבכור אשר תלד וכגון שהיבמה בת שבולדות היא פרט לאילונית: דזבן ארעא אמצרא דבי נשא. קנה קרקע אצל שדה אביו: כי מטא למיפלג. עם אחיו בנכסי אביו: על מדת סדום. זה נהנה וזה לא חסר: אמרו אחי מעלינן ליה עילוי. לנו היא משובחת כקרקעותיו של בר מריון שהיו מעולות ומשתבחת הא דרב יוסף בשדה (ח) בעל שיכולין לומר פעמים שזו מתברכת משאר השדות: תרי ארעתא אתרי נגרי. אם בית השלחין היא ויש לשני אחין לחלוק שתי שדות לכל אחת יש לה יאור להשקות ממנו וזה קנה שדה אצל (ט) האחד מהן ורוצה שיתן אחיו זו הסמוכה לשלו: כגון זו כופין. דהא לקרקע השניה גם היא יש לה יאור להשקות ממנו: האי מדויל והאי לא מדויל. דרך היאורים ליבש כשנהר (שם) נמשכין ממנו מתמעט לפעמים שזה יבש וזה אינו יבש ואומר לו טול חלקך בשתיהם דלאו מדת סדום היא אלו חן לנו עילוי בדמי: תרתי. ארעתא יש להם לחלוק על חד נגרא ואחד מהן קנה קרקע אצל האחת: כופין על מדת סדום. דכיון לאחד נגרא נינהו שתיהן שוות: ניחא לי לאפושי אריסי. טוב לי שיהא לך שתי שדות אחת מכאן ואחת מכאן (י) ואחת לי באמצע כדי שתרבה לך אריסין ותהא שדה שלי משתמרת יפה: חד

תוספות

כל המריעין לו לא במהרה מטיבין לו. ובשילהי מרובה (ב"ק דף פ: ושם ד"ה לעולם) דקאמר רב אחא גופיה לעולם אין מטיבין לו איכא למימר דמתחלה אמר לא במהרה מטיבין שהיה מצפה שיחזירוהו לגדולתו וכשראה שלא החזירוהו שוב אמר לעולם אין מטיבין לו: חלק בכור וחלק פשוט יהבינן ליה אחד מצרא. כדנפקא לן בית נחלין (לקמן דף קכג.) מדכתיב פי שנים מקיש חלק בכורה לחלק פשוט: אמיצרא דבי נשי. אית דגרס בתר הכי אמרי אחוותא א"כ בי נשיה היינו חמיו ולא היו לחמיו בנים כי אם בנות. ואית דגרס אמרי אחי א"כ בי נשיה היינו אביו [ועי' תוס' שבת קנ: ד"ה דבי נשא]: כגון זה כופין על מדת סדום. תימה לר"י לרבה אמאי איצטריך קרא בבכור דיהבינן ליה אחד מצרא ואומר ר"י לפי שלא נתן לו (כ) כח הכתוב אלא כב' אחיו ואילו היו שני אחיו רוצים להשתתף לא כפינן לשלישי לתת להם חלק ביחד ועוד דבכור מתנה קרייה רחמנא כדאמר בית נחלין (שם) דכתיב לתת לו פי שנים ואין לכוף את הנותן ולאפוקי נמי אי לאו דקרייה רחמנא בכור ה"א יקום על שם אחיו כאילו הוא ואחיו קיימין וריב"א מפרש הא דאמר רבה כופין לא מדין תורה קאמר דבדין היה יכול למחות שכנגדו דאיכא קפידא ברווחות כדאמר בכמה דוכתין ועוד הא דכופין על מדת סדום זה נהנה וזה לא חסר היינו בדר בחצר חבירו שאינו מעלה לו שכר אבל הא פשיטא שיכול למחות בו שלא יכנס לדור בביתו אפי' בחצר דלא קיימא לאגרא וגברא דלא עביד למיגר דהוה זה נהנה וזה לא חסר אלא מתקנת חכמים קאמר הכא דכופין והשתא אין להקשות כלל אמאי איצטריך קרא בבכור:

מעלינן ליה כנכסי דבר מריון. פירש הקונטרס בשדה הבעל (ג) שיכולים לומר פעמים מתברכת משאר שדות ונתרתי ארעתא אתרי נגרי לא שייך למימר מעלינן כיון שצריך להשקות ואין מתברכת זו יותר מזו ואין נראה דגם אותם שצריך להשקות מתברכת אחת מהם פעמים יותר שאחת לוקה בשדפון ואחת אינה לוקה ופר"ת מעלינן כנכסי דבר מריון לא ניתן לך זכות שיש לנו בשדה זו אם לא בדמים יקרים כמו בני מריון שהיו עשירים ולא היו מוכרים קרקעותיהם אלא בדמים יקרים ותרתי ארעתא אתרי נגרי לא קאי אעובדא דההוא גברא אלא מילתא באנפי נפשיה כלומר שתי שדות שיש לכל אחד נגר ורוצה האחד שיחלקו כל אחת לשתים שיקח חצי שדה זו וחצי שדה זו ואמר רבה כופין על מדת סדום ויטול כל (מ) שדה שלם כדי שיהא לכל אחד חלק אחד מצרא וכן יש לפרש תרתי ארעתא אחד נגרא שהנגר מפסיק בין שתי השדות ואם יחלקו כל שדה לשתים לא יהיה חלקו אחד מצרא והשתא בהכי לא שייך למימר מעלינן כנכסי דבי בר מריון דלאו מילתא היא אם האחד רוצה לחלוק לעשרים נאמר שיחלקו משום מעלינן ולשון מעלינן נמי אינו מתיישב לפ"ה:

מסורת הש"ס

א) [נדה כ:], ב) [צ"ל שדור], ג) ב"ק פ:, ד) ס"א שאכל כו' ושתה כו', ה) [לקמן קכד.], ו) [פי' סמוך לשדה של חמיו ולא היה לחמיו בנים כי אם בנות. ערוך וע' תוס' דהכא ד"ה אמיצרא], ז) [לקמן נט. קסח. עירובין מט. כתובות קג.], ח) [צ"ל שהם], ט) צ"ל לא נהנה רש"ש:

הגהות הב"ח

(א) גמ' ולאו טעם קאמר א"ר יוחנן: (ב) שם דמליך השתא במתא מחסיא: (ג) שם לאימלוכי ביה עכבינהו הדר שדור וכו' עכבינהו גביה עד: (ד) שם ואנא בתרא וכן הוה א"ר אבדימי: (ה) שם תרתי ארעתא אחד נגרא: (ו) שם אפושי אריסי לאו מילתא היא: (ז) רש"י ד"ה יבם וכו' לא יהבי להו ניהלך אחד וכו' מעלית גבן בדמי: (ח) ד"ה אמרו וכו' בשדה בית הבעל: (ט) ד"ה תרי וכו' אצל אחת מהן ורוצה שיתן אחיו לו: (י) ד"ה ניחא וכו' ואחת מכאן כדי שתרבה כצ"ל ותיבת ואחת באמצע נמחק: (כ) תוס' ד"ה כגון וכו' שלא נתן לו הכתוב כח אלא: (ל) ד"ה מעלינן וכו' בשדה הבעל ואיירי שיכולים: (מ) בא"ד ויטול כל אחד שדה שלם:

הגהות מהר"ב רנשבורג

א] רש"י ד"ה דמליך השתא במתא כו'. מלת השתא נמחק: ב] בא"ד להיות ראש הישיבה. כאן הס"ד ואח"כ מה"ד עכשיו טביומי חתים כצ"ל [אבל באמת א"ל להגיה כי י"ג בגמרא כגירסת הב"ח וכן היתה גירסת רש"י]:

תורה אור השלם

א) וְאִישׁ נָבוּב יִלָּבֵב וְעַיִר פֶּרֶא אָדָם יִוָּלֵד: [איוב יא, יב]

ב) נְבוּב לֻחֹת תַּעֲשֶׂה אֹתוֹ כַּאֲשֶׁר הֶרְאָה אֹתְךָ בָּהָר כֵּן יַעֲשׂוּ: [שמות כז, ח]

ג) כִּי מַה טּוּבוֹ וּמַה יָּפְיוֹ דָּגָן בַּחוּרִים וְתִירוֹשׁ יְנוֹבֵב בְּתֻלוֹת: [זכריה ט, יז]

ד) וְהָיָה הַבְּכוֹר אֲשֶׁר תֵּלֵד יָקוּם עַל שֵׁם אָחִיו הַמֵּת וְלֹא יִמָּחֶה שְׁמוֹ מִיִּשְׂרָאֵל: [דברים כה, ו]

ליקוטי רש"י

ברסתקא. בשוק [ברכות נד.]. רחבה [ב"מ פג.]. רחוב העיר רשות הרבים [עירובין מד:]. ותירוש ינובב בתולות. זה יין טוב שהוא משכר את האדם לגלות סתרי לבו האטומים כבתולה [יומא עו:]. אחד מצרא. שני חלקים יטול במקום אחד כחלק פשוט שהוא חלק אחד ונוטל במקום אחד ונפקא מינה דכל מקום שנפל לו הגורל לחלק פשוט יטול שם בלא גורל חלק בכורה ואם הן שני אחין ושלש שדות לא יפילו שלשה גורלות שנים לבכור ואחד לפשוט שהרי אם יפול חלק הפשוט בשדה האמצעי לא יזכה בו דאם כן נמצא נוטל הבכור בשני מקומות אלא שני גורלות יפילו ויטילום על שני שדות החיצונות ואיזה שיעלה לבכור יקח ויטול גם האמצעי שאצלו עמו [רשב"ם לקמן קכד.]. מדת סדום. דאפילו מידי דלא חסר ביה לא מהני לחבריה. שלי שלי [עירובין מט.]. זה נהנה וזה לא חסר לא היו עושין טובה [כתובות קג.]. כדתנן (אבות פ"ה מ"י) האומר שלי שלי שלך שלך זו מדה בינונית ויש אומרים זו מדת סדום [רשב"ם לקמן קסח.]. נגרא. חריץ של מים [שבת קי.].

חשק שלמה על רבינו גרשום א) נראה דצ"ל אלא אמר רבא תדע וכו' ומתאמרה משמיה דר"ע בר יוסף דכוותיה דהכי איכא למימר וכו'.

sitting in front of [Rav Chisda]. אָמַר לָהּ – **[Rav Chisda] said to [his daughter]** jokingly: מַאן מִינַּיְיהוּ בָּעֵית – **Which of these two** (Rava or Rami bar Chama) **do you want** for a husband? אָמְרָה לֵיהּ תַּרְוַיְיהוּ – **She said to [her father]: Both of them.** אָמַר רָבָא – **Rava said:** וַאֲנָא בַּתְרָא – And I want to be **last.**[10] The child's (Rav Chisda's daughter's) remark indeed came true.[11] Rami bar Chama married her and later died. After his death, Rava married her.

Having quoted one of R' Avdimi's statements on 12a, the Gemara now quotes another:

אָמַר רַבִּי אַבְדִּימִי דְּמִן חֵיפָה – **R' Avdimi from Chaifah said:** קוֹדֶם שֶׁיֹּאכַל אָדָם וְיִשְׁתֶּה יֵשׁ לוֹ שְׁתֵּי לְבָבוֹת – **Before a person eats and drinks, he has two hearts,** i.e. he vacillates.[12] לְאַחַר שֶׁאוֹכֵל וְשׁוֹתֶה אֵין לוֹ אֶלָּא לֵב אֶחָד – **After he eats and drinks,** however, **he has only one heart,** i.e. he is decisive; שֶׁנֶּאֱמַר: ,,אִישׁ נָבוּב יִלָּבֵב" – **as [the verse] states:**[13] ***An empty** (navuv) **man,*** i.e. a man with an empty stomach, ***will have many hearts."***

R' Avdimi now proves that *navuv* in fact means "empty." וּכְתִיב: ,,נְבוּב לֻחֹת" – **And it is written**[14] that the altar in the Tabernacle must be constructed ***nevuv luchos.*** וּמְתַרְגְּמִינַן חֲלִיל לוּחִין – **And [Onkelos] translates this as *"hollow*,** made out of **boards."** This proves that *navuv* indeed means *empty.*[15]

The Gemara quotes another verse in which the word *navuv* appears:

אָמַר רַב הוּנָא בְּרֵיהּ דְּרַב יְהוֹשֻׁעַ – **Rav Huna the son of Rav Yehoshua said:** הָרָגִיל בְּיַיִן – **If one** drinks **wine regularly,** אֲפִילוּ לִבּוֹ אָטוּם כִּבְתוּלָה – **even if his heart was as closed as a virgin** is, יַיִן מְפַקְּחוֹ – still **wine will open it,**[16] שֶׁנֶּאֱמַר: ,,וְתִירוֹשׁ יְנוֹבֵב בְּתֻלוֹת" – **as [the verse] states:**[17] ***And old wine will open** (yenoveiv) **the*** mouths of the ***maidens*** in song.[18]

The Gemara now returns to its discussion about the division of jointly owned fields:

אָמַר רַב הוּנָא בְּרֵיהּ דְּרַב יְהוֹשֻׁעַ – **Rav Huna the son of Rav Yehoshua said:** פְּשִׁיטָא חֵלֶק בְּכוֹר וְחֵלֶק פָּשׁוּט – **It is obvious** that concerning the **"firstborn portion"** and **"ordinary portion"** of a firstborn son, יַהֲבִינַן לֵיהּ אַחַד מֶצְרָא – **we award him** two portions **that** share **one border,** just as any son is awarded all of his land in one tract.[19]

Rav Huna then inquired:

יָבָם מַאי – **What** is the law regarding the two portions awarded **a *yavam?***[20] Can he demand two contiguous portions as a firstborn can, or not?

The Gemara presents one view:

אָמַר אַבָּיֵי – **Abaye said:** הִיא הִיא – **He is exactly the same** as a firstborn; he too is entitled to contiguous fields. מַאי טַעְמָא – **What is the reason** that they are treated the same? בְּכוֹר קַרְיֵיהּ רַחֲמָנָא – **The Merciful One**[21] **called [the *yavam*] a firstborn;**[22] this teaches that the two are accorded the same privileges.

The Gemara now presents another view:

רָבָא אָמַר – **Rava said:** אָמַר קְרָא: ,,וְהָיָה הַבְּכוֹר" – When discussing a *yavam,* **the verse states: *And it will be, the firstborn . . ."*** This implies that with regard to his father's estate, הֲוָיָיתוֹ כִּבְכוֹר וְאֵין חֲלוּקָתוֹ כִּבְכוֹר – **his** essential **status**[23] **is that of a firstborn,** i.e. he too receives a double portion,[24] **but the distribution of his** portion **is not like that of a firstborn,** i.e. he cannot demand two contiguous portions.

NOTES

10. Believing the child's remark to be prophetic (i.e. that she would indeed eventually marry both), Rava realized that whoever married her first would either die first or divorce her. Therefore, he hoped that Rami bar Chama would marry her first, then divorce her; he (Rava) could then marry her and stay married. Rami bar Chama expressed no reciprocal wish, however, because he refused to marry divorcees on principle (see *Pesachim* 112a). The only way for him to have married the child after Rava, then, would have been if Rava married her first and then died. Not wishing to curse Rava with an early death, he said nothing (*Maharsha*).

11. According to *Bach*, the words וְכֵן הֲוָה, "and indeed this came true," are included in the text.

12. The Biblical idiom speaks of decisions as being made in the heart. Thus, the expression *two hearts* connotes indecisiveness [equivalent to the English expression, "of two minds"].

13. *Job* 11:12.

14. *Exodus* 27:8.

15. A hollow object is one that contains empty space within it.

16. Here, the heart symbolizes emotions and feelings. Rav Huna thus means: Even if a person is very inhibited, unable to express his feelings at all, still, wine will open him up.

17. *Zechariah* 9:17.

18. The verse foretells that the bountiful blessings at the time of redemption will cause maidens to open (literally: empty) their mouths in song.

19. Generally, a man's estate is divided equally among his sons. This changes, however, if one of the sons is a בְּכוֹר, *a firstborn*, in which case the firstborn's share is twice as large as the others (see *Deut.* 21:17 and Gemara below, 123a). For example, if two sons inherit three contiguous fields of equal value, the firstborn is allotted two fields: one as an ordinary heir and the other due to his special status as firstborn. Our Gemara refers to the former as his חֵלֶק פָּשׁוּט, his *ordinary portion,* and to the latter as the חֵלֶק בְּכוֹרָה, his *firstborn portion.*

The Gemara now discusses how to distribute an estate to the brothers. A premise of the discussion is that it is advantageous for a person to have one large tract of land rather than to have several smaller pieces of land scattered over a large area. This being the case, it is reasonable to assume that each brother can insist on receiving all of his land in one tract. Our Gemara sets forth that in this respect a firstborn is no different than an ordinary brother; he too can insist on receiving his entire allotment of land (i.e. his firstborn portion and his ordinary portion) in one tract. In the case mentioned above, then, where two sons inherited three contiguous fields, the firstborn is allotted the middle field and the two brothers then cast lots to determine which of the outer fields each receives (see *Rashi*).

20. If a man dies childless, the Torah commands that one of his brothers (called a *yavam*) marry his widow through a procedure called *yibum*. When he does so, he receives the dead brother's share of their father's estate. A *yavam* thus receives a double portion in his father's estate: his own and that of his dead brother.

A *yavam's* double portion, however, differs from that of a firstborn. A firstborn inherits a double portion; therefore, he is certainly entitled to two contiguous portions of land, as explained in the previous note. A *yavam*, on the other hand, inherits only one portion himself; the second portion is actually his dead brother's share. Hence, it can be argued that he has the standing of any two brothers; just as two brothers have no claim to contiguous fields, neither does a *yavam*. According to this reasoning, if the *yavam* desires contiguous portions, the other brothers can charge him for the privilege (*Rashi*).

21. רַחֲמָנָא generally refers to either God or His Torah.

22. See *Deuteronomy* 25:5-6. The verses there states: *When brothers live together and one of them dies childless, [the widow's] yavam shall cohabit with [her] and [thereby] take her for a wife and acquire her through yibum. And it will be,* ***the firstborn*** *whom she bears. . .* According to the simple meaning of the verse, "the firstborn" refers to the son born of a *yibum* union rather than to the *yavam* himself. The Gemara in *Yevamos* (24a), however, exegetically interprets the verse as follows: *Her yavam shall cohabit with her . . . and it will be the firstborn* — which *yavam* has the primary *yibum* obligation? The firstborn (i.e. eldest) *yavam. Whom she bears* — this teaches that a woman incapable of bearing children is exempt from *yibum*. According to the Gemara's interpretation, then, *firstborn* refers to a *yavam* rather than to his son (*Rashi*).

23. Literally: his state of being. הֲוָיָיתוֹ is a derivation of the word וְהָיָה, which the verse states.

24. His own and that of his dead brother.

משמיה דר' עקיבא בר יוסף כוותיה אמר רב אשי ומאי קושיא דלמא להא מילתא בר מזליה הוא אלא אמר רב אשי תדע דאמר גברא רבה מילתא ומתאמרא הלכה למשה מסיני כוותיה ודלמא כסומא בארובה ולאו טעם (א) יהיב א"ר יוחנן מיום שחרב בית המקדש ניטלה נבואה מן הנביאים וניתנה לשוטים ולתינוקות לשוטים מאי היא כי הא דמר בר רב אשי דהוה קאי ברסתקא דמחוזא שמעיה לההוא שוטה דקאמר ריש מתיבתא דמליך (ב) במתא מחסיא טביומי חתים מאן חתים טביומי ברבנן אנא שמע מינה לדידי קיימא לי שעתא קם אתא אדאתא אימנו רבנן לאותביה לרב אחא מדפתי ברישא כיון דשמעי דאתא שדור זוגא דרבנן לגביה לאימלוכי ביה (ג) עכביה הדר שדור זוגא דרבנן אחרינא עכביה גביה עד דמלו בי עשרה כיון דמלו בי עשרה פתח הוא ותנא ודרש לפי שאין פותחין בכלה פחות מעשרה קרי רב אחא אנפשיה כל המריעין לו לא במהרה מטיבין לו וכל המטיבין לו לא במהרה מריעין לו תנוקת מאי היא כי הא דבת רב חסדא הוה יתבה בכנפיה דאבוה הוו יתבי קמיה רבא ורמי בר חמא אמר לה מאן מינייהו בעית אמרה ליה תרוייהו אמר רבא ואנא בתרא (ד) א"ר אבדימי דמן חיפה קודם שיאכל אדם וישתה יש לו שתי לבבות לאחר שאוכל ושותה אין לו אלא לב אחד שנאמר א) איש נבוב ילבב וכתיב ב) נבוב לוחות ומתרגמינן חליל לוחין אמר רב הונא בריה דרב יהושע הרגיל ביין אפי' לבו אטום כבתולה יין מפקחו שנאמר ג) ותירוש ינובב בתולות: אמר רב הונא ברי' דרב יהושע פשיטא חלק בכור וחלק פשוט יהבינן ליה אחד מצרא יבם מאי אמר אביי היא היא מ"ט בכור קרייה רחמנא אמר רבא אמר קרא ד) והיה הבכור הוייתו כבכור ואין חלוקתו כבכור ההוא דזבן ארעא אמצרא דבי נשיה כי קא פלגו א"ל פלגינו לי אמצראי אמר רבה כגון זה כופין על מדת סדום מתקיף לה רב יוסף אמרי ליה אחי מעלינן ליה עלויא כי נכסי דבי בר מריון והלכתא כרב יוסף תרי ארעתא אתרי נגרי אמר רבה כגון זה כופין על מדת סדום מתקיף לה רב יוסף זמנין דהאי מדויל והאי לא מדויל והלכתא כרב יוסף תרתי (ה) אחד נגרא א"ר יוסף כגון זה כופין על מדת סדום מתקיף לה אביי מצי אמר בעינא דאפיש אריסי והלכתא כרב יוסף אפושי (ו) לאו מילתא היא

רש"י

משמיה דרבי עקיבא כוותיה. וליכא למימר בני חד מזלא נינהו שהרי ר"ע חכם ממנו הרבה: ולאו טעמא קאמר. במילתיה וכיון דאמר טעמא אין זה כסומא שמכוון לירד בארובה במקרה בעלמא אלא סברת הלב היא הבאה לו בנבואה וזכה להסכים להלכה למשה מסיני: ברסתקא. שוק רשות הרבים: דמליך. א] השתא במתא מחסיא שעתיד ב] להיות ראש הישיבה עכשיו: טביומי חתים. כשחותם באיגרת חותם שמו טביומי: קיימא לי שעתא. מזל: שדרו זוגא דרבנן לגביה. דמר בר רב אשי: לאימלוכי ביה. ליטול עצה ורשות להמליך את רב אחא: פתח ותנא. דרשה ונעשה ראש הישיבה: כל המריעין לו כו'. כלומר הואיל והוחלה השעה עכשיו לא ימלוכו עוד: איש נבוב. כשהוא חלול בלא כרס מלאה: ילבב. כמה לבבות שאינו מכסים לדעת שלמה: ינובב בתולות. לב אטום כבתולות עושה נבוב וחלול: פשיטא חלק בכור וחלק פשוט. שני חלקים שהבכור נוטל אחד משום בכורה ואחד משום פשיטות יהבינן ליה אחד מצרא זו אצל זו שהרי שניהם חלקו הן והרי הן כחלק אחד: יבם מאי. המייבם את אשת אחיו דקם תחתיו לנחלה ונוטל שני חלקים מאי מי מצו אמרי ליה הואיל ומכח אחרינא קאתי לא יהבי להו (ז) ניהליה אחד מצרא זו אצל זו אי לאו מעליתא גבן בדמי: הבכור אשר תלד. ביבם קמשתעי דמלוה בגדול לייבם אשר תלד פרט לאיילונית והכי מדרש קרא יבמה יבא עליה וגו' והיה הבכור איזה מן היבמין יבא עליה הבכור אשר תלד וכגון שהיבמה בת וולדות היא פרט לאיילונית: דזבן ארעא אמצרא דבי נשא. קנה קרקע אצל שדה אביו: כי מטא למיפלג. עם אחיו בנכסי אביו: על מדת סדום. זה נהנה וזה לא חסר: אמרו אחי מעלינן ליה עילואי. לנו היא משובחת כקרקעותיו של בר מריון שהיו מעולות ומסתברא הא דרב יוסף בשדה (ח) בעל שיכולין לומר פעמים שזו מתברכת משאר השדות: תרי ארעתא אתרי נגרי. אם בית השלחין היא ויש לשני אחין לחלוק שתי שדות לכל אחת יש לה יאור להשקות ממנו וזה קנה שדה אצל (ט) האחד מהן ורוצה שיתן אחיו זו הסמוכה לשלו: כגון זו כופין. דהא לקרקע השניה גם היא יש לה יאור להשקות ממנו: האי מדויל והאי לא מדויל. דרך היאורים לייבש כשנהר י) (שם) נמשכין ממנו מתמעט לפעמים שזה יבש וזה אינו יבש ואומר לו טול חלקך בשתיהם דלאו מדת סדום היא או תן לנו עילוי בדמי: תרתי. ארעתא יש להם לחלוק על חד נגרא ואחד מהן קנה קרקעו אצל האחת: כופין על מדת סדום. דכיון דלאחד נגרא נינהו שתיהן שוות: ניחא לי לאפושי אריסי. טוב לי שיהא לך שתי שדות אחת מכאן ואחת מכאן (י) ואחת לי באמצע כדי שתרבה לך אריסין ותהא שדה שלי משתמרת יפה:

חד

תוספות

כל המריעין לו לא במהרה מטיבין לו. ובשלהי מרובה (ב"ק דף פ: ושם ד"ה לעולם) דקאמר רב אחא גופיה לעולם אין מטיבין לו איכא למימר דמתחלה אמר לא במהרה מטיבין ובשעה שהחזירוהו לגדולתו ובשראה שלא החזירוהו שוב אמר לעולם אין מטיבין לו: חלק בכור וחלק פשוט יהבינן ליה אחד מצרא. כדנפקא לן בית נותלין (לקמן דף קכב.) מדכתיב פי שנים מקיש חלק בכורה לחלק פשוט: אמיצרא דבי נשי. אית דגרס בתר הכי אמרי אחוותא א"כ בי נשיה היינו חמיו ולא היו לחמיו בנים כי אם בנות. ואית דגרס אמרי אחי א"כ בי נשיה היינו אביו [ועי' תוס' שבת נג: ד"ה דבי נשא]: כגון זה כופין על מדת סדום. תימה לר"י לרבה אמאי איצטריך קרא בבכור דיהבינן ליה אחד מצרא ואומר ר"י לפי שלא נתן לו (כ) כח הכתוב אלא כב' אחיו ואילו היו שני אחיו רוצים להשתתף לא כפינן לשליש לתת להם חלק ביחד ועוד דבכור מתנה קרייה רחמנא כדאמר בית נותלין (שם) דכתיב לתת לו פי שנים ואין לכוף את הנותן ולאביי נמי אי לאו דקרייה רחמנא בכור הוה אמינא לא יקום על שם אחיו כאילו הוא ואחיו קיימין וריב"א מפרש הא דאמר רבה כופין לא מדין תורה קאמר דבדין היה יכול למחות שכנגדו דאיכא קפידא ברווחות כדאמר בכמה דוכתין ועוד הא דכופין על מדת סדום בזה נהנה וזה לא חסר היינו בשכבר דר בחצר חבירו שאינו מעלה לו שכר * אבל הא פשיטא שיכול למחות בו שלא יכנס לדור בביתו אפי' בחצר דלא קיימא לאגרא וגברא דלא עביד למיגר דהוה זה נהנה וזה לא חסר אלא מתקנת חכמים קאמר הכא דכופין והשתא אין להקשות כלל אמאי איצטריך קרא בבכור: מעלינן ליה כנכסי דבר מריון. פירש הקונטרס בשדה הבעל (ל) שיכולין לומר שפעמים מתברכת משאר שדות ובתרתי ארעתא אתרי נגרי לא שייך למימר מעלינן כיון שצריך להשקות ואין מתברכת זו יותר מזו ואין נראה דגם אותה שצריך להשקות מתברכת אחת מהם פעמים יותר שאחת לוקה בשדפון ואחת אינה לוקה ופר"ת מעלינן כנכסי דבר מריון לא ניתן לך זכות שיש לנו בשדה זו אם לא בדמים יקרים כמו בני מריון שהיו עשירים ולא היו מוכרים קרקעותיהם אלא בדמים יקרים ותרתי ארעתא אתרי נגרי לא קאי אעובדא דההוא גברא אלא מילתא באנפי נפשיה כלומר שתי שדות שיש לכל אחד נגר ורוצה האחד שיחלקו כל אחת לשתים שיקח חצי שדה זו וחצי שדה זו אמר רבה כופין על מדת סדום ויטול כל (מ) שדה שלם כדי שיהא לכל אחד חלק אחד מגרא וכן יש לפרש תרתי ארעתא אחד נגרא שהנגר מפסיק בין שתי השדות ואם יחלקו כל שדה לשתים לא יהיה חלקו אחד מגרא והשתא בהני לא שייך למימר מעלינן כנכסי דבי בר מריון דאטו אם האחד רוצה לחלוק לעשרים נאמר שיחלקו משום מעלינן ולשון מעלינן נמי אינו מתיישב לפ"ה:

עין משפט נר מצוה

קטו א ב מיי' פי"ב מהל' שכנים הלכה ג סמג עשין פב טוש"ע ח"מ סי' קעד סעיף ג:
קטז ג ד ה מיי' שם הל"א טוש"ע שם ס"א:

גליון הש"ס

גמרא מעלי' ליה עלויא. עיין פ"ו משנה מ' דדמאי בפירוש הרמב"ם: תוס' ד"ה כגון כו' אבל הא פשיטא כו' למחות בו. עיין לקמן דף נט ע"ב ברשב"ם ד"ה אמאי שלא לא הגיעו:

מסורת הש"ס

א) [נדה כ:], ב) [ג"ל שדור], ג) ב"ק פ:, ד) ס"א שאכל אדם ושתה כו', ה) [לקמן קכד.], ו) [פי' סמוך לשדה של חמיו ולא היה לחמיו בנים כי אם בנות. ערוך וע' תוס' שבת נג: ד"ה אמילרא], ז) [לקמן נט. קסח. עירובין מט. כתובות קג.], ח) [ג"ל שהם], ט) ל"ל לא נהגה רש"י.

הגהות הב"ח

(א) גמ' ולאו טעם קאמר א"ר יוחנן: (ב) שם להמליך השתא במתא מחסיא: (ג) שם לאימלוכי ביה עכבוהו הדר שדור וכו' עכבוהו גביה עד: (ד) שם ואנא בתרא וכן הוה א"ר אבדימי: (ה) שם תרתי ארעתא אחד נגרא: (ו) שם אפושי אריסי לאו מילתא היא: (ז) רש"י ד"ה יבם וכו' לא יהבו ניהלך אחד וכו' מעליתא גבן בדמי: (ח) ד"ה אמרו וכו' בשדה בית הבעל: (ט) ד"ה תרי וכו' אצל אחת מהן ורוצה שיתן אחיו לו: (י) ד"ה ניחא וכו' ואחת מכאן כדי שתרבה כל"ל ותיבת ואחת באמצע נמחק: (כ) תוס' ד"ה כגון וכו' שלא נתן לו הכתוב כח אלא: (ל) ד"ה מעלינן וכו' בשדה הבעל ואיירי שיכולים: (מ) בא"ד ויטול כל אחד שדה שלם:

הגהות מהר"ב רנשבורג

א] רש"י ד"ה דמליך השתא במתא כו'. מלת השתא נמחק: ב] בא"ד להיות ראש הישיבה. כאן הס"ד ואח"כ מה"ד עכשיו וכו' טביומי חתים כו' [אבל באמת א"צ להגיה כי י"ג בגמרא כגירסת הב"ח וכן היתה גירסת רש"י]:

תורה אור השלם

א) וְאִישׁ נָבוּב יִלָּבֵב וְעַיִר פֶּרֶא אָדָם יִוָּלֵד: [איוב יא, יב]

ב) נְבוּב לֻחֹת תַּעֲשֶׂה אֹתוֹ כַּאֲשֶׁר הֶרְאָה אֹתְךָ בָּהָר כֵּן יַעֲשׂוּ: [שמות כז, ח]

ג) כִּי מַה טּוּבוֹ וּמַה יָּפְיוֹ דָּגָן בַּחוּרִים וְתִירוֹשׁ יְנוֹבֵב בְּתֻלוֹת: [זכריה ט, יז]

ד) וְהָיָה הַבְּכוֹר אֲשֶׁר תֵּלֵד יָקוּם עַל שֵׁם אָחִיו הַמֵּת וְלֹא יִמָּחֶה שְׁמוֹ מִיִּשְׂרָאֵל: [דברים כה, ו]

ליקוטי רש"י

ברסתקא. בשוק [ברכות נד.]. רחבה [ב"מ פג.]. רחוב העיר רשות הרבים [עירובין מד:]. ותירוש ינובב בתולות. זה יין טוב שהוא משכר את האדם לגלות סתרי לבו האטומים כבתולה [יומא עו:]. אחד מצרא. שני חלקים יטול במקום אחד כחלק פשוט שהוא חלק אחד ונוטל במקום אחד ונפקא מינה דכל מקום שנפל לו הגורל לחלק פשוט יטול שם בלא גורל חלק בכורה ואם הן שני אחין ושלש שדות לא יפילו שלשה גורלות שנים לבכור ואחד לפשוט שהרי אם יפול חלק הפשוט בשדה האמצעי לא יזכה בו דאם כן נמצא נוטל הבכור בשני מקומות אלא שני גורלות יפילו ויטילום על שני שדות הסילונות ואיזה שיעלה לבכור יקח ויטול גם האמצעי שאצלו עמו [רשב"ם לקמן קכד.]. מדת סדום. דאפילו מידי דלא חסר ביה לא מהני לחבריה. שלי שלי [עירובין מט.]. זה נהנה וזה לא חסר לא היו עושין טובה [כתובות קג.]. כדתנן (אבות פ"ה מ"י) האומר שלי שלי שלך שלך זו מדה בינונית ויש אומרים זו מדת סדום [רשב"ם לקמן קסח.]. נגרא. חריץ של מים [שבת קי.].

רבינו גרשום

מאי קושיה. מאי ראיה דמייתית דילמא תרווייהו הני גברי רברבייא בני חדא מזלא נינהו משום הכי אמר האי כגון האי אע"ג דלא שמיעא ליה ולאו נביאות הוא: א) אלא דלא תדע. דהכי איכא למימר דנביאות הוא וליכא למימר דחד מזלא הוא שהרי ר' עקיבא רבה טובא דלא הוה ההיא מעולם גברא כוותיה ואפ"ה כי אתי חד תנא ואמר מנפשיה כוותיה אע"ג דלאו בני חד מזלא נינהו דלית דהוי ליה מזלא בתורה ובעושר כוותיה דר' עקיבא: ודלמא כסומא בארובה. ולא משום דהוה עדיף ומשני לאו טעמא קאמר שמביא אמתלא לדבריו ראייה ומדקאמר טעמא ודאי מרוב חכמתו קאמר ולא כסומא בארובה. ברסתקא. בגשרא דעברי בה [בנין] השוק. למ"ה: דמליך. דליעבדי מיניה ראש ישיבה: הכי שמיה. דהכי חתום שמיה בשטר: טביומי. והכי מיקרי שמיה ושמיה דרב אשי טביומי והאי דקרי ליה רב אשי משום שם לווי: בכלה. קרי לה לההוא מסכתא דדריש ריש מתיבתא: כל המטיבין לו. הואיל והוטב לרב אשי דפתח בראש ישיבה לא במהרה מריעין לו שלא יסלקוהו רב אחא אינו יכול להריע לו: בכנפיה. בחיקו: כמה לבבות. שאין לבו מיושב עליו: איש נבוב. חלול הוא שלא אכל: ילבב. כמה לבבות: אפי' לבו אטום כבתולה. זו שאינה בעולה ואטומה היא מתנובב: [פשיטא] אם בכור ופשוט באו לחלוק בשדות אביהם והבכור נוטל פי שנים ואמר [הבכור] אני נוטל חלק בכורי' סמוך לחלק פשוטי בחד מצר אין יכול הפשוט לעכב עליו ולומר שקול חלק פשוט בהאי גיסא וחלק בכור לאידך גיסא ואינו יכול לעלות עילוי דמים אם יניחו ליטול שניהם במצר אחד דדינו ליטול ירושתו במקום אחד: יבם מאי יבם שמת אחיו בחיי אביהן וייבם זה את אשתו ושוב מת אביהן דשקיל האי יבם ירושת אחיו שני חלקים אחד חלק אחיו שמת וחלק של עצמו. מי יהבי ליה אחד שני חלקים אי לא. מי אמרינן דיניה הוא דשקל פי שנים ויהבי' ליה גבי הדדי בחד מיצרא או לא משמע ממש דלא יהבי' ליה בחד מיצרא. אביי אמר היא היא. דשקיל נמי בחד מיצר דבכור קרייה רחמנא והיה הבכור אשר תלד ודרשי' לי' הבכור מצוה בגדול הלכך דיניה כבכור ואחד מיצר יהבינן ליה. הוייתו כבכור. ליטול ב' חלקים ולא חלוקתו כבכור ליטול שניהן במיצר אחד: אמצרא דבי נשא. סמוך לשדה אחר של חמיו ולא היו לו לחמיו בנים כי אם בנות ומת חמיו והניח קרקעותיו לבנותיו אמר האי הבו לאשתי חלקה סמוך לאותה שדה שקניתי אמר רבא ודאי יהבינן ליה סמוך למיצריה וכגון זה אי מעכב איניש כופין על מדת סדום שלא יעשה מדת סדום שהיו מקפידין ואו' שלי שלי ושלך שלך. כך אלו כופין אותם שלא יעכבו ליתן לה חלקה אצל שדה בעלה שזה נהנה וזה לא חסר: מתקיף לה רב יוסף והא מצי למימר אחותה הואיל ויש לו הנאה שנוטל שדה סמוך ליה מעלינן ליה האי ארעא וחשבי' ליה ביוקר כנכסי דבי בר מריון דהוי ליה מקרקע מעולין והוי אמיד ולא מזבן ארעתיה כי אם בדמים יקרים הכי נמי מעלי לן דמים אי יהבינן ליה בסמוך לו ואי לא לא יהבי' ליה אמצרא דידיה ואמאי כופין והלכתא כרב יוסף דמצי מעלי לי' ביוקר. תרי אחי או תרי שותפי דהוי להו לחלוק תרי ארעתא דקיימן חדא אהאי נגרא וחדא אהאי נגרא ולכל אחת ואחת יש לה נגר שלה וזה אמת המים שמשקין אותה ממנו וזבן חד מהני אחי או שותפי חד ארעא אחריתא סמוך לאחת מאלו ואמר האי דזבן הואיל דהני תרי ארעתא דאית לן לחלוק שוין הן במדה ולכל חדא יש לה נגר הב לי אותה שדה שסמוכה לאותה שקניתי אמר (רבא) [רבה] כגון זה ודאי כופין דלא מצי לעכב עליו. מתקיף לה רב יוסף אמאי כופין הא מצי טעין אידך לא בעינא אלא נחלוק כל שדה וכל נגר לשנים דשמא זימנין דהאי מדויל והאי יבש מסתפינא דלמא יבשא נגרא שלי ונגרא דמיצרך לא יבשה ומצית את להשקות שדך ואנא לא מצינא ומפסדנא הלכך בעינא למפלג תרווייהו או יעלה לי דמים וכי האי גוונא מצי מעכב ליה. תרי ארעתא אחד נגרא שהיו שניהן מסתפקות מנגר אחד וקנה אחד מהן קרקע חד סמוך לאחת משדות אלו ואמר ליה לחבירו הב לי אמצראי דהשתא ליכא למימר דהאי מדויל והאי לא מדויל דתרווייהו סמיכי אחד נגר. אמר רב יוסף בהאי כופין ויהיב ליה. אמר ליה אביי והא מצי למימר ליה אידך ניחא לי לאפושי אריסי כלומר אם היה שדהו שקנה בצד אחד סמוך למיצר ואמר הבו לי אמיצראי יכול לומר לו הלה איני רוצה שתקח חלקך בצד האחר כדי שתהא שדה שלי אמצעית ותשים אריס אחד מצד אחד ואריס אחד על אותה שדה שקנית ואריס אחד על חלקך המגיעך מצד אחר ומהן משתמרת שדה שלי שהיא אמצעית וכי האי גונא מצי לעכבי ואפי' הכי דאיכא למימר הכי הלכתא כוותיה דרב יוסף. ל"א. אמאי כופין הא יכול למימר אנא בעינא הכי למפלג דמההיא ארעא וחצי נגרא דאמיצרך שקול פלגא ואנא אשקול פלגא ומאידך ארעא אחורי תשקול פלגא ואנא אשקול פלגא כי היכי

דלהוו

חשק שלמה על רבינו גרשום א) נראה דצ"ל אלא אמר רבא תדע וכו' ומתאמרה משמיה דר"ע בר יוסף דכוותיה דהכי איכא למימר וכו'.

The Gemara now discusses a case in which a field in an estate adjoins another field belonging to an heir. It then considers whether the proximity of these fields affects the allocation of the fields: הַהוּא דִּזְבַן אַרְעָא אַמְּצְרָא דְבֵי נָשֵׁיהּ – **There was a certain person who bought land on the boundary of his father's property.**[25] כִּי קָא פָּלְגוּ – **When [he and his brothers] were dividing** their father's estate, אָמַר לְהוּ פְּלִיגוּ לִי אַמְּצְרָאִי – **he said to [his brothers], "Award me** a tract of land that borders **on my boundary."** His brothers, however, refused to do so. אָמַר רַבָּה – Rabbah said: כְּגוֹן זֶה כּוֹפִין עַל מִדַּת סְדוֹם – **In an instance such as this, we coerce** people not to emulate **the traits** of the inhabitants **of Sodom,** i.e. we compel people to benefit others when it involves no loss to themselves.[26] Since it costs the brothers nothing to honor the request, we compel them to do so.[27]

Rav Yosef questioned Rabbah's assumption that the brothers lose nothing by giving that brother the field he requested: מַתְקִיף לָהּ רַב יוֹסֵף – **Rav Yosef challenged [Rabbah's ruling]:** אָמְרֵי לֵיהּ אַחֵי – But his **brothers can say to him,** מַעַלִּינַן לֵיהּ עִלּוּיָא – **"[The field]** that you request **is as valuable to us** כִּי נִכְסֵי דְבֵי בַּר מְרְיוֹן – **as the property of the** wealthy **Bar Meryon household,** whose fields were of the highest quality.[28] Therefore, we refuse to allot you the entire field unless you compensate us." Since the brothers would thus incur a loss if they honored the request, we do not compel them to do so.

The Gemara concludes:

וְהִלְכְתָא כְּרַב יוֹסֵף – **And the halachah is in accordance with Rav Yosef.**

A similar question is posed concerning irrigated fields: תְּרֵי אַרְעָתָא אַתְּרֵי נִגְרֵי – If two brothers inherit an estate that includes **two tracts of land** situated **on two irrigation canals,** can one of them demand the tract that borders his property?[29]

Again, the Gemara quotes two views: אָמַר רַבָּה – **Rabbah said:** כְּגוֹן זֶה כּוֹפִין עַל מִדַּת סְדוֹם – In an instance such as this, we coerce the other brother not to emulate **the traits** of the inhabitants **of Sodom.** That is, since honoring the request benefits the first brother at no cost to himself,[30] we compel him to do so.

This is challenged:

מַתְקִיף לָהּ רַב יוֹסֵף זִמְנִין דְּהַאי מִדְוִיל וְהַאי לֹא מִדְוִיל – **Rav Yosef challenged [Rabbah's ruling]:** There might be **times that this** canal running through one field **will** have water to **draw and this** other canal **will** dry up and have **no** water to **draw!** One brother can therefore insist on dividing both fields so that if one canal dries up, he will still have access to the other.[31]

The Gemara again concludes:

וְהִלְכְתָא כְּרַב יוֹסֵף – **And the halachah is in accordance with Rav Yosef.**

The Gemara discusses a third case:

תַּרְתֵּי [אַרְעָתָא][32] אַחַד נִגְרָא – Let us suppose that an estate includes **two [tracts of land]** situated **on one irrigation canal** and the canal irrigates both of them. If one of the tracts adjoins a particular brother's property, what is the law? Can the brother demand that tract or not?

The Gemara again quotes two opinions. In this case, however, Rav Yosef takes a position opposite that which he took in the previous cases:

אָמַר רַב יוֹסֵף – **Rav Yosef said:** כְּגוֹן זֶה כּוֹפִין עַל מִדַּת סְדוֹם – In an instance such as this, we coerce the other brother not to emulate **the traits of Sodom** residents. Since it is unreasonable to deny the request, we compel the other brother to honor it.[33]

This is challenged:

מַתְקִיף לָהּ אַבַּיֵי – **Abaye challenged [Rav Yosef's ruling]:** מָצֵי אָמַר בְּעֵינָא דְאַפִּישׁ אֲרִיסֵי – **[The other brother] can say," I want** him **to increase** the number of **sharecroppers** he hires so that my field will be better protected. Therefore, I demand a share in both fields."[34]

Rejecting Abaye's argument, the Gemara concludes:

וְהִלְכְתָא כְּרַב יוֹסֵף – **And the halachah is in accordance with Rav Yosef,** i.e. the second brother must honor the first brother's request, because אַפּוּשֵׁי [אֲרִיסֵי] לָאו מִילְּתָא הִיא – the benefit that accrues by **adding [sharecroppers] is not a** relevant **consideration.**[35] This completes the Gemara's discussion of whether an heir can demand that he be allotted a particular irrigated field on the grounds that it adjoins his property.

NOTES

25. *Rashi;* see also *Tosafos* and *Mesoras HaShas*. Literally, בֵּי means "the house of." Here, it is used in a more general sense and refers to "the property of."

26. Sodomites would not allow a person to benefit from their property even when this entailed no cost whatsoever to them (see *Avos* 5:10).

27. The Gemara discusses a case in which the quality of the fields was the same. In such a case, if one brother requests a field adjoining his own, we compel the others to honor his request because it is unreasonable to deny it. If the quality of the fields were different, however, it would be reasonable for the other brothers to demand a portion of each field. In such a case, if one brother requests the adjoining field, the others may deny the request (*Rashba*).

28. According to *Rashi*, the Gemara discusses fields that subsist solely on rainfall. Thus, even if the soils of such fields are of equal quality, they will still produce different yields if they receive different amounts of rain. The brothers can therefore say, "We want a share of the field that you want because it might receive more rainfall and produce more." See *Tosafos,* who interpret the Gemara differently.

29. As a general rule, when brothers inherit a number of fields, each field is divided between them; no brother can demand that he be allotted an entire field in return for his relinquishing his share in the others (*Rosh*). In our Gemara's case, however, one brother indeed requests such an allotment. He argues as follows: "We two brothers have inherited two irrigated fields, each with a canal running through it. Only I, though, own land adjacent to one of these fields. Please allot me the field adjacent to my land so that I will own one large tract of land rather than two smaller ones scattered over the area" (*Rashi*). The Gemara now presents two views on whether the other brother must honor the request.

30. Because each field has a canal running through it. It thus makes no difference to him if he is allotted one of the two fields rather than half of each.

31. As explained in note 29, when two brothers inherit a number of fields, each is entitled to a portion of each field; we therefore allot an entire field to one only if a division is not detrimental to the other's interest. In this case, however, it is detrimental because the other brother would then have only one canal in his portion instead of two. He can therefore tell his brother, who requested such a division, "If you are allotted an entire field, I stand to lose. Therefore, I demand that we divide the field unless you pay me to relinquish my claim" (*Rashi*).

32. Emendation and translation follow *Bach.*

33. In this case, one canal irrigates both fields. Thus, the reason for refusing the request in the previous case does not apply here (see *Rashi*).

34. I.e. I refuse to allot you the field adjoining your tract of land, because it is advantageous to me that I be allotted that field, since if I am altotted that field, my field will lie between two of yours. As a result, you will feel compelled to hire more sharecroppers to cultivate the fields than you otherwise would have. This is advantageous to me, because it will make my field more secure *(Rashi).*

[*Bach's* emendation of *Rashi* is based on a version of *Rashi* which can be found in *Rashi* on the *Rif*; our version is already corrected.]

35. [Emendation and translation follow Bach.] That is, one brother can request to be allotted the entire field adjoining his property as long as the other brother incurs no loss through this (i.e. the field that he receives must be no less desirable than the one the first brother receives). Now, in this case, the other brother indeed incurs no loss if the fields are allocated in this manner; he merely foregoes the additional protection that his field would have received if it were divided otherwise. This is not a valid reason to deny the first brother's request.

Since the Gemara had been discussing the division of irrigated fields, it now explains how such a field with a certain configuration of canals and rivers ought to be divided:

חַד גִּיסָא נִגְרָא וְחַד גִּיסָא נַהֲרָא – If **one side** of the field borders **a canal and one side** borders **a river,** פַּלְגִין לֵהּ בְּקַרְנָא זוֹל – **they divide it from the corners,**[1] i.e. they divide the field into eight sections and each brother takes alternate sections.[2]

The Gemara quotes the next section of the Mishnah:

וְלֹא אֶת הַטְּרַקְלִין כו׳ – AND we do NOT divide THE MANSION ETC. unless the property is large enough so that the division will leave each partner with a proper share.

The Gemara discusses a case in which two people own one of the properties mentioned in the Mishnah and one of them wants to dissolve the partnership:

אֵין בָּהֶן כְּדֵי לָזֶה וּכְדֵי לָזֶה מַהוּ – If **[these properties] are not** large **enough for this one** to receive a proper share **and that one** to receive a proper share, **what is [the law]?** Can one partner compel the other to dissolve the partnership or not?

The Gemara quotes two opinions:

רַב יְהוּדָה אָמַר – **Rav Yehudah said:** אִית דִּינָא דְּגוּד אוֹ אֲגוּד – Yes, **there is a law that** one partner can insist, "Either **you set** a price for my portion, **or I will set** a price for yours."[3]

רַב נַחְמָן אָמַר – **Rav Nachman said:** לֵית דִּינָא דְּגוּד אוֹ אֲגוּד – No, **there is no law that** one partner can insist, "Either **you set** a price for my portion **or I will set** a price for yours." If one partner puts forth such a proposal, then the other can reply, "I wish neither to buy your portion nor to sell mine; I just want to retain the partnership."

The Gemara questions Rav Nachman's view:

אָמַר לֵיהּ רָבָא לְרַב נַחְמָן – **Rava said to Rav Nachman:** לְדִידָךְ דְּאָמְרַתְּ לֵית דִּינָא דְּגוּד אוֹ אֲגוּד – **According to you, who said** that **there is no law that** one partner may insist, "**You set** a price or **I will set** a price," I would ask as follows: בְּכוֹר וּפָשׁוּט שֶׁהִנִּיחַ לָהֶן אֲבִיהֶן עֶבֶד וּבְהֵמָה טְמֵאָה – In the case of **a firstborn son and an ordinary son whose father** died and **left them a slave or a non-kosher animal,** כֵּיצַד עוֹשִׂין – **what should [the sons] do** about sharing these things equitably?[4] It is obviously too much trouble for a firstborn and ordinary brother to take turns working with these things. – **?** – [5]

NOTES

1. בְּקַרְנָא זוֹל (or, as in some texts, בקרנזול or בקרנזיל) means *go* (זיל) *from the corners,* i.e. after dividing the field into quadrants, divide each quadrant again by drawing diagonals from the corners (see *Rashi* to *Bava Metzia* 108b and diagram).

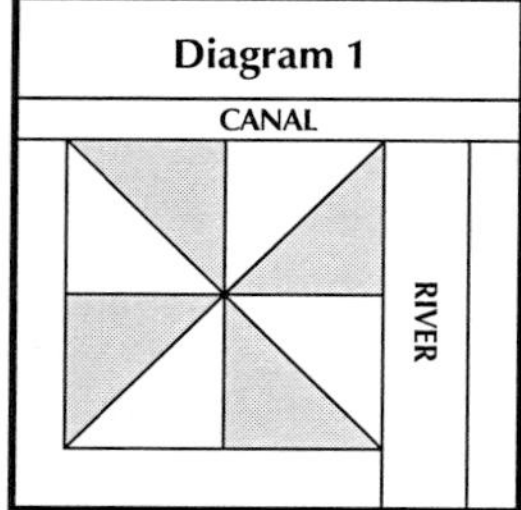

2. See diagram 1. This differs from a conventional division because generally, a field is divided in half either along a north-south line or an east-west line. Such divisions, however, would be inequitable in our Gemara's case, where one side of the field (e.g. the north) borders a canal and another (e.g. the east) borders a river. In this case, the northern and eastern portions are more desirable than the others because they adjoin a water source; the eastern portion, however, is the most desirable because it borders a river, which is a better source of water than a canal. Hence, if the field were divided along a north-south line, the brother allotted the eastern portion would receive the entire river and half the canal, whereas the other would receive nothing but half the canal (see diagram 2). Similarly, if the field were divided along an east-west line (see diagram 3), the brother allotted the northern portion would receive the canal and half the river, whereas the other would receive only half the river. To divide it equitably, then, the field is divided into eight sections and each brother then takes every other section (see diagram 1). This division is indeed equitable, because each brother then receives one section adjoining the river and one section adjoining the canal; the remaining sections adjoin neither (*Rashi;* see *Maharam*).

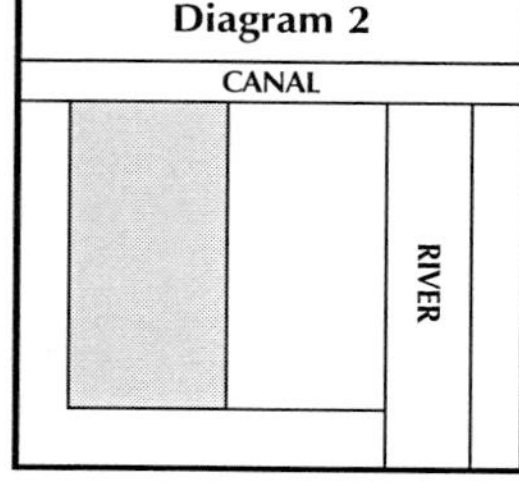

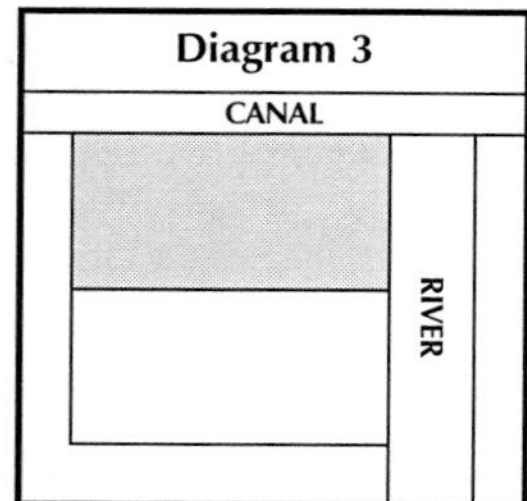

3. This translation follows *Rashi. Beis Yosef* (*Choshen Misphat* 171:5) explains that *Rashi* understands גוד to be a a derivation of גדד, *to cut,* as in גֹּדוּ אִילָנָא, *cut down the tree* (*Daniel* 4:11). In our Gemara's context, it means to set a price. (See below, 88a where a derivative of קצץ, which also means to cut, refers to setting a price as in קִיצֵי דָמֵיהּ, *its price was set.*) Thus, when a partner proposes גוד או אֲגוד, he means, "Either you set a price for my share and buy it or I will set a price for your share and buy it."

Beis Yosef develops *Rashi's* idea to show how an equitable settlement is reached. Of the two partners, one is given the right to set a price and the other is given the right of buying or selling at that price. The reluctant partner is given the choice of which right he wants and the other right goes to the other person. This assures that the ultimate purchaser will pay a reasonable price. The reason is that the person setting the price has no idea of whether he will eventually sell or buy. He will therefore set an equitable price so that either way he will not lose money on the deal (cf. *Dibros Moshe, Bava Basra* vol. I 14:61).

Tosafos (*Niddah* 36b) and *Aruch* present another interpretation of גוד או אֲגוד. They translate גוד as *pull,* as *Rashi* himself translates it elsewhere (see *Rashi* to *Eruvin* 89a, where he translates גוד אַסִּיק as *pull and elevate*). According to them, the partner proposing division sets a price and tells the reluctant partner, "גוד או אֲגוד – Either you pull (i.e. buy) my share or I will pull (i.e. buy) your share."

Tosafos here present two opinions as to whether the partner can set any price he wants. *Ri* maintains that he can do so; if the other partner refuses to pay, the first partner can then buy his share for that price. *Ritzva* objects, however, that if this were so, a rich partner could force his partner to sell by setting an exorbitant price for his share. *Rosh* (סימן נ׳) cites an opinion that the court therefore assesses the property's value and sets a fair selling price.

4. When two or more sons inherit their father's estate, they become partners in it and must either share the property of the estate or divide it. The Mishnah (11a) notes, however, that jointly held property is divided only if each partner will be left with a usable portion after the division; otherwise they must share it. Thus, if two brothers inherit a *kosher* animal, for example, it can be divided because after it is slaughtered, each brother will be left with a usable portion of meat. If they inherit a non-*kosher* animal, on the other hand, they obviously cannot physically divide it; they must share it instead by taking turns working with it. Rava therefore asked Rav Nachman: How can a firstborn and an ordinary brother share a non-*kosher* animal or a slave that they inherited?

Rava directed his question at Rav Nachman and not at Rav Yehudah because according to Rav Yehudah, the question is not difficult. According to Rav Yehudah, if jointly held property is not divisible, one partner can force the other to either sell his share or buy the other. Thus, the brothers, who are partners, need not share at all; one will simply take the entire slave (or animal) and compensate the other for his portion in it. According to Rav Nachman, however, a partner has the right to insist on retaining the partnership and sharing the property. How, though, asks the Gemara, can the firstborn and ordinary brother share these things fairly?

5. The Gemara inquires only how a firstborn and ordinary brother could share these things fairly and not how two ordinary brothers could do so. The reason for this, explains *Rashi,* is that a firstborn and ordinary brother have unequal shares in the animal or slave; it is thus more trouble for them to share than for two ordinary brothers, who have equal portions (see *Ramban* and *Pnei Shlomo*). *Tosafos* ד״ה בכור explains as follows: A firstborn is entitled to work with the animal or slave twice as much as the ordinary son. If a firstborn and ordinary son were to share a slave or an animal, then the firstborn would use it for two days

עין משפט נר מצוה

קיז א מיי' פ"ב מהל' שכנים הל' ג סמג עשין פב טוש"ע ח"מ סי' קעד סעיף ג:
קיח ב מיי' פ"א שם הלכה ג סמג שם טוש"ע ח"מ סי' קעא סעי' ו:
קיט ג ד מיי' פ"ז מהל' עבדים הל' ו סמג עשין פו טוש"ע י"ד סי' רסז סעי' סב:
קכ ה מיי' פ"א מהל' שכנים הל' ג ועיין בהשגות סמג עשין פב טוש"ע ח"מ סי' קעא סעיף ו:

גליון הש"ס

גמרא דינא דגוד. לשון משיכה כמו משכו וקחו (שמות יב) דמתרגמי' נגודו עיין תוס' נדה דף לו ע"ב ד"ה גדיים:

תורה אור השלם

א) כִּי כֹה אָמַר יְיָ בּוֹרֵא הַשָּׁמַיִם הוּא הָאֱלֹהִים יֹצֵר הָאָרֶץ וְעֹשָׂהּ הוּא כוֹנְנָהּ לֹא תֹהוּ בְרָאָהּ לָשֶׁבֶת יְצָרָהּ אֲנִי יְיָ וְאֵין עוֹד: [ישעיה מה, יח]

מסורת הש"ס

א) חגיגה ב. פסחים פח. ערכין ב: עדיות פ"א מ"ג [גיטין מא.], ב) לקמן קעב., ג) דא"כ כל עשיר יסלק עני שותפו בדבר שאין בו דין חלוקה כצ"ל מהרש"ל, ד) [יבמות סו.], ה) [וע"ע תוס' פסחים פח: ד"ה כופין]:

הגהות הב"ח

(א) גמ' לשבת יצרה אלא מפני תיקון העולם כופין את רבו: (ב) רש"י ד"ה פלגי לה בקרנזול וכו' מן הצפון לדרום נמצא כל הנהר לאחד והשני אין לו אלא נגר וכו' למערב יהיה לאחד חלי הנהר וכו' ולשני אין לו אלא חלי נהר במזרחו: (ג) ד"ה ה"ג וכו' העבד יכול לקנות עצמו ויוליך לחרות אבל העבד אינו יכול לומר לרבו קנה חלקי שאין דמים: (ד) תוס' ד"ה אית וכו' ע"י עילוי דמים בדבר שאין בו דין חלוקה: (ה) ד"ה לישא וכו' אור"י דלא כופין: (ו) ד"ה שנאמר וכו' דלא תהו בראה משום שהיא מצוה רבה: (ז) ד"ה כופין וכו' ועוד אפילו מפקדא אפשר לה באחר: (ח) בא"ד וכו' נמי דאפי' אין לו בנים ואשה רבו: (ט) בא"ד בלא קדושין וכו' ישאנה בלא קדושין וכו' מותר בשפחה לא הוה כופין: (י) בא"ד בפני עצמו הוא ומטעם:

גמרא

א חד גיסא נגרא וחד גיסא נהרא פלגין לה בקרנא זול: ולא את הטרקלין כו': אין בהן כדי לזה וכדי לזה מהו רב יהודה אמר ב איתא דינא דגוד או אגוד רב נחמן אמר לית דינא דגוד או אגוד א"ל רבא לרב נחמן לדידך דאמרת לית דינא דגוד או אגוד בכור ופשוט שהניח להן אביהן עבד ובהמה טמאה כיצד עושין א"ל שאני אומר עובד לזה יום אחד ולזה שני ימים מיתיבי א) מי שחציו עבד וחציו בן חורין עובד את רבו יום אחד ואת עצמו יום אחד דברי ב"ה אמרו להם ב"ש תקנתם את רבו ואת עצמו לא תקנתם לישא שפחה אינו יכול לישא בת חורין אינו יכול יבטל והלא לא נברא העולם אלא לפריה ורביה שנאמר א) לא תהו בראה לשבת יצרה אלא (א) ד כופין את רבו ועושין אותו בן חורין וכותבין שטר על חצי דמיו וחזרו ב"ה להורות כדברי ב"ש שאני הכא דאגוד איכא גוד ליכא ת"ש ב) ה שני אחין אחד עני ואחד עשיר והניח להן אביהן מרחץ ובית הבד עשאן לשכר השכר לאמצע עשאן לעצמן הרי עשיר אומר לעני קח

רש"י

חד גיסא ניגרא וחד גיסא נהרא. שדה של שני אחים שיש נהר על פני מזרח ונגר על פני צפונה: פלגי ליה בקרנא זול'. לפי שהנהר טוב מן הנגר והסמוך למים טוב מן הרחוק ואם תחלקנה מן הצפון (ב) לדרום (מן) כל הנהר לאחד והשני אין לו אלא נגר בצפונו ופעמים שהוא יבש ואם תחלקנה מן המזרח למערב יהיה לאחד הנהר על פני מזרחו ונגר על פני צפונו ולשני אין לו אלא נהר במזרחו לפיכך יחלקום לשמונה חלקים שיהא לשניהם בשוה סמוך לנהר ולנגר וכאשר ירחק מזה ירחק מזה כזה:

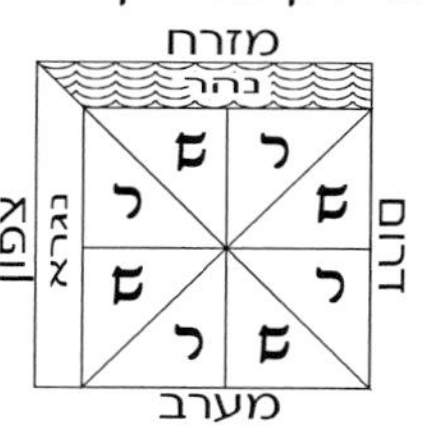

אית דינא דגוד או אגוד. זה שרוצה לחלוק אומר לזה שאינו רוצה לחלוק או קוץ לי דמים וקנה לך חלקי או אני אקוץ דמים ואתן לך בחלקך שאי אפשי בשותפותך: לית דינא. שזה יכול לומר לא שלך אקנה ולא שלי אמכור אלא שותפין נהיה בה: עבד או בהמה טמאה. שאי אפשר לחלקן כיצד יעשו לפיכך נקט בכור ופשוט דטריחא מילתא להיות שותפין בה: וחזרו בית הלל להורות כו'. טעמא דמפני תיקון העולם הא לאו משום פריה ורביה לא כייפינן ליה ולא מצי עבד למימר ליה אקוץ בדמים ואתן לך בחלקך: ה"ג שאני הכא דאגוד איכא גוד ליכא. העבד יכול לקנות (ג) אבל אינו אומר קנה חלקי שאין דמים לבן חורין שאין עבד עברי נמכר אלא לשש:

תוספות

חד גיסא ניגרא וחד גיסא נהרא. פירש רבינו חננאל שדה אשר מזרחה וצפונה נהרא ומערבה ודרומה מושך ניגרא חולקין אותה בקרנא זול פירוש חולקין אותה באלכסון מקרן מזרחית צפונית לקרן מערבית דרומית ויהיה לכל אחד צד אחד ניגרא וצד נהרא וכל היכא דמשיך נהרא או ניגרא קרוי חד גיסא: אית דינא דגוד או אגוד. נראה לר"י דאפילו בדמים יקרים הרבה יותר משוויו יכול לומר לו או גוד או אגוד ואין נראה לריב"א ג) דא"כ יוכל לסלק אחד את חבירו ע"י עילוי דמים (ד) בחלק שאין בו דין חלוקה: בכור ופשוט שהניח להן כו'. ותימה דאמאי נקט בכור ופשוט ולא נקט פשוט ופשוט ואומר ר"ת דפשוט ופשוט ניחא ליה שיעבוד לזה יום אחד ולזה יום אחד אבל בכור ופשוט קשיא ליה אם יעבוד לבכור ב' ימים הרי נטל הבכור יותר מפי שנים שאם יש עיר רחוקה מהלך יום אחד שמשתכרים בה הרבה שיש שם סחורה בזול ופשוט שאין לו שהות אלא יום אחד לא יוכל לילך שם והבכור שיש לו ב' ימים יכול לילך שם ומשתכר יותר הרבה מפשוט ומשני דמ"מ כך חולקין ור"י מפרש דלהכי נקט בכור ופשוט משום דאמר במי שהיה נשוי (כתובות דף פג.) דשור לחרישה ועומד לחרישה דכ"ע השכר לאמצע אע"פ שאין לזה כי אם מנה ולזה מאתים ולהכי פריך כיצד יעשו דעכשיו אין הבכור נוטל פי שנים ומשני דעובד לזה יום אחד ולזה ב' ימים ולא דמי לשור לחרישה ועומד לחרישה דהתם הוי השכר לאמצע משום דמעיקרא אדעתא דהכי נשתתפו אבל גבי בכור ופשוט דלא שייך האי טעמא כל אחד נוטל כפי חלקו:

לישא שפחה אינו יכול. ואע"ג דאמר בהבא על יבמתו (יבמות דף סב. ושם ד"ה הכל) דהכל מודים בעבד שאין לו חיים ולא קיים פריה ורביה והכא נמי אם ישא שפחה לא קיים כיון שהולד מתייחס אחריה ואפי' שבת לא קיים כדמשמע התם דשבת תלוי בפריה ורביה מ"מ אור"י (ה) לא כופין לרבו לעשותו בן חורין משום פריה ורביה אם היה יכול לקיים אפי' שבת כל דהו כיון שהוא אנוס: שנאמר לא תהו בראה וגו'. הא דלא מייתי קרא דפרו ורבו אור"י בר מרדכי משום דלשבת יצרה שייך אפי' בצד עבדות וחציה שפחה וחציה בת חורין ד) דלא כפו את רבה לשחררה אלא משום שנהגו בה מנהג הפקר הא דלא כפו אותו משום שבת דשמא אפילו כשתעשה בת חורין לא תקיים משום דלא מפקדא אפריה ורביה כדאמרינן בהבא על יבמתו (שם דף סה: ושם) דאיתתא לא מפקדא אפריה ורביה אבל עבד כשיהיה בן חורין ע"כ יקיים ור"י מפרש דלכך לא נקט קרא דפרו ורבו משום דפטור הוא מאותה מצוה כיון שהוא אנוס וכדי שיתחייב בה לא כפינן לרבו לעשותו בן חורין דא"כ בכל העבדים נכוף רבם לשחררם כדי שיתחייבו בכל המצות ולכך נקט קרא לא תהו בראה משום (ו) שהיא מצוה רבה ומשום הכי כפינן ובפ"ב דמגילה (דף כז.) נמי מייתי להאי קרא משום הכי גבי אין מוכרין ספר תורה אלא ללמוד תורה ולישא אשה דאמר מר גדול ת"ת שמביא לידי מעשה לישא אשה נמי לא תהו בראה אלא לשבת יצרה: כופין את רבו. וא"ת אמאי כופין ליתי עשה דפרו ורבו וידחה לא תעשה דלא יהיה קדש ואומר רבינו יצחק חדא דבעידנא דמיעקר לאו לא מקיים עשה דמשעת הערא' קא עקר ללאו ועשה דפרו ורבו לא מקיים עד גמר ביאה ועוד דהיא אסורה לינשא לו דלגבי דידה ליכא עשה ועוד אפי' מפקדא (ז) דאפשר לה באחר ועוד כיון דאפשר לקיים שניהם ע"י כפיה לא דחי וא"ת היכי כפינן לשחררו והא אמרי' בפ' השולח (גיטין דף לח: ושם) דכל המשחרר עבדו עובר בעשה וכי תימא מצוה שאני וכי אומרים לו לאדם חטא כדי שיזכה חבירך כדאמרי' בריש שבת (דף ד. ושם ד"ה וכי) והא דשחרר ר"א עבדו בהשולח (גיטין שם) שנכנס לבית הכנסת ולא מצא שם י' התם משום דר"א גופיה עשה מצוה בכך שהשלים המנין והא דאמר נמי בפ' בכל מערבין (עירובין דף לב: ושם ד"ה ולא) דניחא ליה לחבר למיעבד איסורא זוטרא ולא ליעבד עם הארץ איסורא רבה התם משום דקא עביד עם הארץ איסורא על ידו של חבר דקא מאכיל ליה טבל ואומר ר"י דמשום מצוה רבה שרי אע"ג דעובר בעשה כדאמרי' ריש תמיד נשחט (פסחים דף נט. ושם ד"ה אתי) אין לך דבר שמתעכב אחר תמיד של בין הערבים אלא קטרת ונרות ופסח ומחוסר כפורים דערבי פסחים ומפרש התם משום דאתי עשה דפסח שיש בו כרת ודחי עשה דהשלמה אלמא קעבר כהן אעשה דהשלמה כדי שיקיים מחוסר כפורים מצות פסח ה) וא"ת אמאי כופין וימכור עצמו בעבד עברי למ"ד בפ"ק דקדושין (דף יד: ושם) מוכר את עצמו רבו מוסר לו שפחה כנענית ולמ"ד נמי דאפי' אין לו בנים (ח) רבו מוסר לו שפחה כנענית ואע"ג דאין עבד עברי נוהג אלא בזמן שהיובל נוהג כדאמרי' בפ' האומר בקדושין (דף סט. ושם) הא בבית שני נהג יובל כדפי' ר"ת בהשולח (גיטין דף לו. ד"ה בזמן) גבי הלל תקן פרוזבול ואור"י דאין זה תקנה דאסור למכור עצמו בעבד עברי כדאמרינן בפ"ק דקדושין (דף כב:) אזן ששמעה על הר סיני כי לי בני ישראל עבדים וגו' וא"ת וישא חציה שפחה וחציה בת חורין ונהי דאינו יכול לקדשה דאתי צד עבדות ומשתמש בצד אשת איש (ט) ישאנה בלא קדושין כדאמר לישא שפחה כו' משמע דאי הוה מותר בשפחה לא כפינן לרבו אע"ג דאין קידושין תופסין בשפחה מ"מ היה נושאה בלא קידושין וי"ל דהשתא נמי אתי צד עבדות ומשתמש בצד חירות ולא דמי לפרדה דאמר בפרק אותו ואת בנו (חולין דף עט. ושם) דמרביעין עליה מינה ולא אמר דאתי צד חמור ומשתמש בצד סוס דהתם כלאים כתיב דמשמע שני מינים דומיא דשור וחמור דחרישה ופרדה מין אחד בפני עצמו (י) ומטעם זה מותר לרכוב עליה וא"ת וישא ממזרת דלצד עבדות מותר בממזרת כדתנן בהאומר בקדושין (דף סט.) יכולין ממזרין ליטהר כיצד ממזר נושא שפחה ובצד חירות נמי מותר כדתנן בפרק עשרה יוחסין (שם דף סט.) ממזרים וחרורים מותרין לבא זה בזה ואור"י דאין זה תקנה להרבות ממזרים בישראל וא"ת וישא נתינה דחרורי ונתיני מותרין לבא זה בזה כדתנן בפ' עשרה יוחסין (שם) וצד עבדות נמי מותר בנתינה דאמר בריש יש מותרות (יבמות דף פה:) ממזרת ונתינה לישראל איכא בינייהו למ"ד מפני שמרגילה הא [היא] מרגלה ליה פי' שיכול להכשיר זרעו ע"י בנו שישא שפחה וי"ל דלעולם אסור נתין בשפחה מ"מ מרגלה ליה כיון שיכול להכשיר אפי' ע"י איסור דהאי גברא לא איכפת ליה באיסור דהא נסיב ממזרת או נתינה וא"ת ומ"ש דאסור נתין בשפחה וממזר מותר הא נתין נמי הוי מפסולי קהל כמו ממזר דכתיב לא תתחתן בם ואור"ת משום דממזר קדש ועומד לפי שנולד מאיסור חמור דלא תפסי קידושין ולכך לא מיתסר בלאו דלא יהיה קדש ומיהו בזכור ובהמה אין להתירו אפי' למאן דמפיק להו בפרק ד' מיתות (סנהדרין דף נד:) מולא יהיה קדש דאין להתירו בקדישות אלא באותן שהוא בא ממנו ומקדישות דזכור ובהמה לא בא וא"ת ומ"ש דגירי וחרורי מותרים בנתינה ואסורים בשפחה ואע"ג דתרוייהו חייבי לאוין ואור"י דנתיני דתפסי בהו קדושין גמרינן משאר פסולי קהל כגון עמוני ומואבי מצרי ואדומי דמותרין בקהל גרים דלא איקרי קהל אבל שפחה דלא תפסי בה קדושין לא ילפא מינייהו:

שמע

ליקוטי רש"י

מי שחציו עבד כו'. כגון שהיה של ב' אחין או ב' שותפין ושחררו אחד מהם שאינו שותף בחלקו. תקנתם את רבו. שאינו חסר כלום [גיטין מא.]. את עצמו לא תקנתם. מה תקנה עליו [פסחים פח.]. כל תקנת רבו כאן היא אבל תקנת העבד אין כאן שלא נתקן כמשפט הממון אם לא נתקן בפריה ורביה [חגיגה ב:]. לישא שפחה אינו יכול. מפני צד חירות שבו [גיטין שם]. לצד חירות אסור בה דכתיב לא יהיה קדש [דברים כג] לא יהיה קדש לא יבא קהל [פסחים שם ובגיטין]. בת חורין אינו יכול. מפני צד עבדות שבו. לא תהו בראה. כרוך הוא את הארץ לא לתהו בראה ליושב אלא לשבת יצרה [חגיגה שם]. כי לשבת יצרה [ישעיה מה, יח]. יולד הארץ לא על תוהו ולא על ריקנית ברא אותה כי אם לשבת ולהיות בה יצרה [גיטין שם]. ובית הבד. בית שעוצרין שם זיתים [ב"מ קיז:].

רבינו גרשום

דליהוו נפישי אריסין מיכן ומיכן וישמרו זה את זה ואמאי כופין. למ"ה. שנים שיש להם שדה אחת לחלוק ולצד מזרח של שדה היה מושך נהר ולצד דרום של שדה יש שם נגר משוך לאורך השדה שמשקין ממנו השדה ומצד צפון ומערב של שדה יבישה והשתא אין יכולין לחלוק בשום ענין שלא יהא חלק אחד יפה מחבירו אלא א"כ צריכין לחלוק בקרנא זול כי עניין אותו ציור בד' חלקים מכלל רוח שיעשו ב' חלקים מן הנהר ב' מן הנגר וב' מן היבשה ב' ב' ויחלקו כי היא גונא כי היכי דלימטי לכל חד וחד שוה לחבירו מן הנהר ומן הנגר ומן צדי היבישה שם דנהר יפה מנגר ונגר יפה מיבשה ובחילוק ענין זה יחלוקו בקו השוה שלא יהא חלקו של אחד יפה משל חבירו ואין אחד מהם נוטל ב' חלקים בסמוך לו אלא כעין זה *

(הנהר המושך מצד מזרח): פיסקא אין חולקין את הטרקלין. פלטורין אא"כ יש בו כדי לזה וכדי לזה דהיינו י' על י' לזה וכן לזה דהיינו שיעור טרקלין. מורן. הוא מגדל. ולא את הטלית. אלא אם כן יכולין שניהן להתכסות בו זה בפני עצמו בטליתו. ולא את המרחץ עד שיכולין לרחוץ כל אחד בחלקו המגיעו. זה הכלל כל ששמו עליו כתחלה מקודם חלוקה שלאחר חלוקה אית לכל חלק שם אותו עצמו כמו שנקרא בתחלה חולקין. ואם לאו אין חולקין אלא מעלין זה לזה בדמים שיקנה אחד מהן חלק חבירו בדמים. ואי ליכא שיעור חלוקה מאי. רב יהודא אמר אית דינא דגוד או אגוד. דאם אחד רוצה שישתמשו בו שניהם בשותפות זה שבוע אחד וזה שבוע אחד והאחד אינו רוצה יכול לומר האי דאינו רוצה נישום אותו בדמים ותקנה אתה חלקי או אני חלקך. גוד. משוך תרגו' א). ורב נחמן אמר לית דינא דגוד או אגוד. כלומר אי האי אינו רוצה אינו יכול לכפותו ולומר לו כן אלא משתמשין בו בשותפות: בכור ופשוט. והוא הדין לפשוט ופשוט אלא להכי בעי בכור ופשוט קשה טפי לחלק בג' חלקים. ולהכי נקיט בהמה טמאה. דאי אפשר לשוחטה ולחלוק הבשר. אמר ליה עובד לפשוט יום אחד ולבכור ב' ימים וכן נמי בהמה טמאה זה ישתמש בה ב' ימים וזה יום אחד ואין כאן דין גוד או אגוד: וחציו בן חורין ששחררו אחד מן השותפין. לישא שפחה אינו יכול מפני צד חירות שבו וכותב שטר לרבו על חצי דמיו שיפרע לו ממה שירויח לאחר שיהיה כולו בן חורין מפני שכשהוא חצי עבד אין לו ממון כלום שכל מה שמרויח ביום שהוא עובד לעצמו סוף סוף למחר כשהוא עובד לרבו הרי הוא עבדו וכל מה שקנה עבד קנה רבו להכי צריך לכתוב שט"ח על חצי דמיו. וחזרו בית הילל כו' מפני תיקון העולם הא לאו מפני תיקון העולם אין כופין את רבו משום דאמרינן דלית דינא דגוד או אגוד דלא מצי עבד למימר לו שחררני ואתן לך דמי חצייך או תן אתה לי דמי חציי ואהא מהכל עבדך ותיובתא דרב יהודה. לעולם אמר לך רב יהודה בעלמא אית דינא דגוד או אגוד והכא גבי עבד שאני דגוד איכא אגוד ליכא. דעבד מצי למימר לרבו קצוב עלי דמים ואקנה חצי ממך אבל אינו יכול לומר לו אקצוב אני עליך דמי חציי ותקנה אותי מהכל דאינו יכול למכור צד שחרור שבו לישא שפחה. ואי"ת דמפרש"י אגוד ליכא לא מצי עבד למימר לרבו קנה חלקי המשוחרר שאם נותן לו הרב דמים עכשיו כשהוא רבו מהכל חוזר ונוטלן הימנו דמה שקנה עבד קנה רבו ונמצא שאין גופו קנוי כשהוא חוזר ונוטלן. למ"ה: אם עשאן אביהן לשכר שהיה רגיל להשכירן כדי שיהא משתכר בו הכי נמי ישכירום ויחלוקו השכר לאמצע: ואם לאו אינו יכול לומר עני לעשיר גוד והב לי דמי חלקי מן מרחץ ובית הבד דאין לי במה לישתמש בו כלום או תן לי דמים ממה שאתה משתמש בו יותר ממני דיכול העשיר לחזור ולומר לעני כו'. ומן שמיא קנסוהו לאותו עני ואין לו על העשיר כלום אלמא דלית דינא דגוד או אגוד. הכא נמי אגוד ליכא דאין לעני במה לפדות אבל בעלמא אמרינן אית דינא דגוד או אגוד:

חשק שלמה על רבינו גרשום א) [נ"ל תרגום משכו ונגידו].

The Gemara responds:

אָמַר לֵיהּ – **[Rav Nachman] said to [Rava]:** שֶׁאֲנִי אוֹמֵר עוֹבֵד לָזֶה יוֹם אֶחָד וְלָזֶה שְׁנֵי יָמִים – I would then say, **[the slave or animal] must work one day** out of three **for this** ordinary brother, **and two days** out of three **for this** firstborn. Although such an arrangement is inconvenient, it is the only possible solution according to Rav Nachman (who holds that one brother cannot force the other to dissolve the partnership).

The Gemara now questions Rav Yehudah's position:

מֵיתִיבֵי – **We challenged** Rav Yehudah's **ruling from a Mishnah,**[6] which states: מִי שֶׁחֶצְיוֹ עֶבֶד וְחֶצְיוֹ בֶּן חוֹרִין – ONE WHO IS HALF SLAVE AND HALF FREE[7] עוֹבֵד אֶת רַבּוֹ יוֹם אֶחָד וְאֶת עַצְמוֹ יוֹם אֶחָד – WORKS ONE DAY FOR HIS MASTER AND ONE DAY FOR HIMSELF.[8] דִּבְרֵי בֵּית הִלֵּל – These are THE WORDS OF BEIS HILLEL. בֵּית שַׁמַּאי אוֹמְרִים – BEIS SHAMMAI, however, SAY: תִּקַּנְתֶּם אֶת רַבּוֹ – YOU HAVE SOLVED the problem of HIS MASTER by awarding him the slave's service every other day[9] אֶת עַצְמוֹ לֹא תִקַּנְתֶּם – but YOU HAVE NOT SOLVED HIS OWN problem, i.e. whom to marry. לִישָּׂא שִׁפְחָה אֵינוֹ יָכוֹל – HE IS UNABLE TO MARRY A FEMALE SLAVE, because he is half free.[10] לִישָּׂא בַּת חוֹרִין אֵינוֹ יָכוֹל – HE IS UNABLE TO MARRY A FREE WOMAN, because he is half slave.[11] What, then, should he do? יִבָּטֵל – SHOULD HE REMAIN IDLE, not marrying at all? וַהֲלֹא לֹא נִבְרָא הָעוֹלָם אֶלָּא לִפְרִיָּה וְרִבְיָה – BUT IS IT NOT true that THE WORLD WAS CREATED ONLY FOR PROPAGATION, שֶׁנֶּאֱמַר: ,,לֹא־תֹהוּ בְרָאָהּ לָשֶׁבֶת יְצָרָהּ" – AS [THE VERSE] STATES:[12] "HE (GOD) DID NOT CREATE [THE WORLD] to be A VOID; HE FORMED IT TO BE INHABITED?[13] אֶלָּא – RATHER,[14] to enable the slave to marry, כּוֹפִין אֶת רַבּוֹ וְעוֹשִׂין אוֹתוֹ בֶּן חוֹרִין – WE COMPEL HIS MASTER to free him AND thereby MAKE HIM[15] A COMPLETELY FREE MAN so that he can marry a free woman; וְכוֹתְבִין שְׁטָר עַל חֲצִי דָמָיו – AND [THE SLAVE] MUST WRITE[16] A BOND to the master FOR HALF HIS VALUE.[17] וְחָזְרוּ בֵּית הִלֵּל לְהוֹרוֹת כְּדִבְרֵי בֵּית שַׁמַּאי – AND subsequently, BEIS HILLEL RETRACTED their ruling AND RULED IN ACCORDANCE WITH THE WORDS OF BEIS SHAMMAI. Both Beis Shammai and Beis Hillel agree, then, that if a half-slave were able to marry, his master could have insisted on retaining a share in him; the slave could not have declared, "I will set a price and buy your portion so that I will be completely free." This proves that one partner cannot compel the other to dissolve the partnership and thus refutes Rav Yehudah's view. – ? –

The Gemara answers:

שָׁאנִי הָכָא דְּאָגוּד אִיהָא גּוּד לֵיכָּא – **Here** (in the case of a half-slave) it **is different, for** such a slave **can** declare only, **"I will set** a price and redeem the half of me that is a slave," but **not, "You set** a price and buy my free half," because a free Jew cannot be sold.[18] Since the slave cannot offer his partner (in this case, his master) the option of buying or selling, even Rav Yehudah agrees that he cannot compel the other to dissolve the partnership.

The Gemara challenges Rav Yehudah's position from another Mishnah:

תָּא שְׁמַע – **Come, learn** a refutation from a Mishnah:[19] שְׁנֵי אַחִין אֶחָד עָנִי וְאֶחָד עָשִׁיר – If there were TWO BROTHERS, ONE POOR AND ONE RICH, וְהִנִּיחַ לָהֶן אֲבִיהֶן מֶרְחָץ וּבֵית הַבַּד – AND THEIR FATHER died and LEFT THEM A BATHHOUSE OR AN OLIVE PRESS,[20] עֲשָׂאָן לְשָׂכָר הַשָּׂכָר לָאֶמְצַע – IF HE MADE THEM FOR RENTING,[21] it is rented out AND THE RENT IS DIVIDED between the two brothers. עֲשָׂאָן לְעַצְמוֹ – IF, however, [THE FATHER] HAD MADE THEM FOR HIMSELF, i.e. for his personal use, הֲרֵי עָשִׁיר אוֹמֵר לְעָנִי – THEN THE RICH brother CAN SAY TO THE POOR one,

NOTES

out of three, whereas the ordinary son would use it for only one. This, notes the Gemara, gives the firstborn an unfair advantage. He gets the opportunity not only to work with it for twice as long as his brother, which he is entitled to do, but also to utilize it in ways that the ordinary brother cannot, e.g. traveling with the animal and sending the slave on business to places too far away for a profitable one-day trip.

[Rava asked only how brothers inheriting their father's property can divide these things fairly – not how any two partners (who entered their partnership voluntarily) can do so. Apparently, Rava assumed that if people voluntarily became partners in these things, there might indeed be no way for them to dissolve the partnership. He argues only that heirs, who never asked to be partners, must have a way to dissolve the partnership.]

6. *Gittin* 41a.

7. If a Jew acquires a gentile as a slave, the Jewish master may circumcise him (in the case of a male slave) and immerse him in a *mikveh* with the intent that he thereby become a slave (see *Leviticus* 25:44). The slave thereupon assumes the legal status of a "Canaanite slave," who is obligated to perform all the religious commandments binding on Jewish women. [These obligations are somewhat fewer than those binding on Jewish men – see Mishnah in *Kiddushin* 29a.]

A "half-slave, half-free man" refers to a Canaanite slave that belonged to two partners – one of whom freed him – or to a slave whose master freed half of him (see *Gittin* 41b). Such a slave owns himself jointly with his master.

8. The partnership of the master and slave is administered by dividing the rights to the slave according to time, each of them enjoying full monetary proprietorship on the day that the slave is in his possession. Thus, the half-slave serves the master one day and works for himself on the next day.

9. Thus precluding the slave from declaring, " I need not serve you at all, because I am half free" (*Tiferes Yaakov* to *Gittin* 41a).

10. A free Jew may not marry a female slave (*Deuteronomy* 23:18 with *Targum Onkelos*; see *Kiddushin* 68b and *Rambam Hil. Issurei Bi'ah* 12:11-14).

11. A slave may not marry a free Jewish woman (ibid.).

12. *Isaiah* 45:18.

13. A situation that negates the possibility of the slave being allowed to marry is unacceptable, because the charge to have children is a primary precept and may not be ignored. See *Tosafos* ד״ה שנאמר, who suggest several reasons why this verse is quoted rather than the Biblical commandment to be fruitful and multiply (*Genesis* 1:28).

14. *Bach* adds מִפְּנֵי תִּיקּוּן הָעוֹלָם, *for the sake of the general good,* as the Mishnah in *Gittin* (41b) states.

15. In *Gittin* 41b, the Mishnah reads וְעוֹשֶׂה, *and he* (singular – the master) *makes him*. This seems more correct than our text.

16. The translation follows the version of the Mishnah in *Gittin* 41a, which states וְכוֹתֵב שְׁטָר.

17. The Sages compel the master only to free his slave so that the slave can marry; they do not compel him to incur a financial loss by doing so. The newly freed slave thus becomes indebted to the master for the amount of market value that his master had owned and is now losing by freeing him.

18. [Whenever a Canaanite slave is freed, he becomes a full-fledged Jew.] A Jew cannot be sold as a Canaanite slave for any price; he can be sold only as a Hebrew servant for a period of six years. A freed Canaanite slave cannot be sold again as a Canaanite slave either, because a Canaanite slave becomes a full-fledged Jew once he is freed (*Rashi*). Thus, a half-slave cannot offer his master the option of buying his free half.

19. Below, 172a.

20. These things are of little use to a poor person, who has neither a household staff [to heat the bathhouse] nor olive holdings.

21. There is some question as to whether the Mishnah is to be interpreted literally. According to *Tosafos* (13b ד״ה אם), the father's intent is irrelevant. Rather, the Mishnah distinguishes between a [large] bathhouse or olive press which is suitable for rental to the public, and [a small] one which is not. Others, however, interpret the Mishnah literally; that is, the law depends on whether the father built the bathhouse and olive presses as rental properties or intended them for private use (*Rambam, Hil. Shechenim* 1:2, see *Rashbam* 172a ד״ה קח לך. See also *Rabbeinu Yonah,* who discusses both opinions).

מסורת הש"ס

א) חגיגה ב. פסחים פח. ערכין ב: עדיות פ"א מי"ג [גיטין מא.], ב) לקמן קעב., ג) דא"כ כל עשיר יסלק עני שותפו בדבר שאין בה דין חלוקה כצ"ל מהרש"ם, ד) [יבמות סו.], ה) [וע"ע תוס' פסחים פח: ד"ה כופין]:

עין משפט נר מצוה

קיז א מיי' פי"ב מהל' שכנים הל' ג סמג עשין פב טוש"ע ח"מ סי' קעד סעיף ג:

קיח ב מיי' פ"א שם הלכה ג סמג שם טוש"ע ח"מ סי' קעא סעי' ו:

קיט ג ד מיי' פ"ז מהל' עבדים הל' ו סמג עשין פו טוש"ע י"ד סי' רסז סעי' סב:

קכ ה מיי' פ"א מהל' שכנים הל' ג ועיין בהשגות סמג עשין פב טוש"ע ח"מ סי' קעא סעיף ו:

גמרא

אחד גיסא נגרא וחד גיסא נהרא פלגין לה בקרנא זול: ולא את הטרקלין כו': אין בהן כדי לזה וכדי לזה מהו רב יהודה אמר ב איתי דינא דגוד או אגוד רב נחמן אמר לית דינא דגוד או אגוד א"ל רבא לרב נחמן לדידך דאמרת לית דינא דגוד או אגוד בכור ופשוט שהניח להן אביהן עבד ובהמה טמאה כיצד עושין א"ל שאני אומר עובד לזה יום אחד ולזה שני ימים מיתיבי (א) מי שחציו עבד וחציו בן חורין עובד את רבו יום אחד ואת עצמו יום אחד דברי ב"ה ב"ש אומרים ג תקנתם את רבו את עצמו לא תקנתם לישא שפחה אינו יכול לישא בת חורין אינו יכול יבטל והלא לא נברא העולם אלא לפריה ורביה שנאמר א לא תהו בראה לשבת יצרה אלא (א) ד כופין את רבו ועושין אותו בן חורין וכותבין שטר על חצי דמיו וחזרו ב"ה להורות כדברי ב"ש שאני הכא דאגוד איכא גוד ליכא ת"ש ה שני אחין אחד עני ואחד עשיר והניח להן אביהן מרחץ ובית הבד עשאן לשכר השכר לאמצע עשאן לעצמו הרי עשיר אומר לעני קח

רש"י

חד גיסא נגרא וחד גיסא נהרא. שדה של שני אחים שיש נהר על פני מזרח ונגר על פני לפונה: פלגי ליה בקרנא זול. לפי שהנהר טוב מן הנגר והסמוך למים טוב מן הרחוק ואם תחלקנה מן הלפון (ב) נמלא (מן) כל הנהר לאחד והשני אין לו אלא נגר ללפונו ופעמים שהוא יבש ואם תחלקנה מן המזרח למערב יהיה לאחד הנהר על פני מזרחו ונגר על פני לפונו ולשני אין לו אלא נהר במזרחו לפיכך יחלקום לשמונה חלקים שיהא לשניהם בשוה סמוך לנהר ולנגר וכאשר ירחק מזה ירחק מזה כזה:

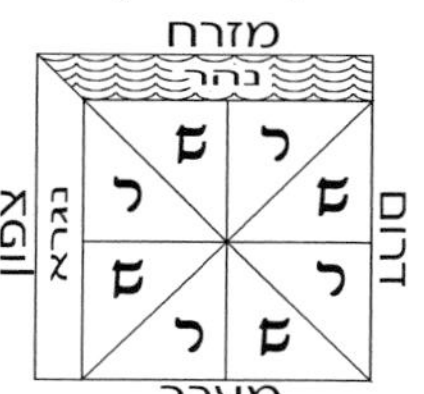

אית דינא דגוד או אגוד. זה שרוצה לחלוק אומר לזה שאינו רוצה לחלוק או קוץ לי דמים וקנה לך חלקי או אני אקוץ דמים ואתן לך בחלקך שאי אפשי בשותפותך: לית דינא. שזה יכול לומר לא שלך אקנה ולא שלי אמכור אלא שותפין נהיה בה: עבד או בהמה טמאה. שאי אפשר לחלקן כילד יעשו להכי נקט בכור ופשוט דטריחא מילתא להיות שותפין בה: וחזרו בית הלל להורות כו'. טעמא דמפני תיקון העולם הא לאו משום פריה ורביה לא כייפינן ליה ולא מלי עבד למימר ליה אקוץ בדמים ואתן לך בחלקך: ה"ג שאני הכא דאגוד איכא גוד ליכא. העבד יכול לקנות (ג) אבל אינו אומר קנה חלקי שאין דמים לבן חורין שאין עבד עברי נמכר אלא לשם: קח

תוספות

חד גיסא נגרא וחד גיסא נהרא. פירש רבינו חננאל שדה אשר מזרחה ולפונה נהרא ומערבה ודרומה מושך נגרא חולקין אותה בקרנא זול

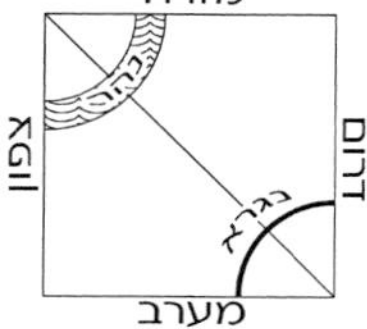

פירוש חולקין אותה באלכסון מקרן מזרחית לפונית לקרן מערבית דרומית ויהיה לכל אחד לד לאחד נגרא ולד נהרא וכל היכא דמשיך נהרא או נגרא קרוי חד גיסא: אית דינא דגוד או אגוד. נראה לר"י דאפילו בדמים יקרים הרבה יותר משוויו יכול לומר לו או גוד או אגוד ואין נראה לריב"א ב) דא"כ יוכל לסלק אחד את חבירו ע"י עילוי דמים (ד) בדבר שאין בה דין חלוקה: בכור ופשוט שהניח להן כו'. ותימה דלמאי נקט בכור ופשוט ולא נקט פשוט ופשוט ואומר ר"ת דפשוט ופשוט ניחא ליה שיעבוד לזה יום אחד ולזה יום אחד אבל בכור ופשוט קשיא ליה אם יעבוד לבכור ב' ימים הרי הבכור נוטל יותר מפי שנים שאם יש עיר רחוקה מהלך יום אחד שמשתכרים בה הרבה שיש שם סחורה בזול ופשוט שאין לו שהות אלא יום אחד לא יוכל לילך שם והבכור שיש לו ב' ימים יכול לילך שם ומשתכר יותר הרבה מפשוט ומשני דמ"מ כך חולקין ור"י מפרש דלהכי נקט בכור ופשוט משום דאמר במי שהיה נשוי (כתובות דף נג.) דשור לחרישה ועומד לחרישה דכ"ע השכר לאמצע אע"פ שאין לזה כי אם מנה ולזה מאתים ולהכי פריך כילד יעשו דעכשיו אין הבכור נוטל פי שנים ומשני דעובד לזה יום אחד ולזה ב' ימים ולא דמי לשור לחרישה ועומד לחרישה דהתם הוי השכר לאמצע משום דמעיקרא אדעתא דהכי נשתתפו אבל גבי בכור ופשוט דלא שייך האי טעמא כל אחד נוטל כפי חלקו: לישא שפחה אינו יכול. ואע"ג דאמר בהבא על יבמתו (יבמות דף סב. ושם ד"ה הכל) דהכל מודים בעבד שאין לו חיים ולא קיים פריה ורביה והכא נמי אם ישא שפחה לא קיים כיון שהולד מתייחס אחריה ואפי' שבת לא קיים כדמשמע התם דשבת תלוי בפריה ורביה מ"מ אור"י (ה) לא כופין לרבו לעשותו בן חורין משום פריה ורביה אם היה יכול לקיים אפי' שבת כל דהו כיון שהוא אנוס: שנאמר לא תהו בראה וגו'. הא דלא מייתי קרא דפרו ורבו אור"י בר מרדכי משום דלשבת יצרה שייך אפי' בלא עבדות וחליה שפחה וחליה בת חורין ד) דלא כפו את רבה לשחררה אלא משום שנהגו בה מנהג הפקר הא דלא כפו אותו משום שבת דשמא אפילו כשתעשה בת חורין לא תקיים משום דלא מפקדא אפריה ורביה כדאמרינן בהבא על יבמתו (שם דף סה: ושם) דאיתתא לא מפקדא אפריה ורביה אבל עבד כשיהיה בן חורין ע"כ יקיים ור"י מפרש דלכך לא נקט קרא דפרו ורבו משום דפטור הוא מאותה מלוה כיון שהוא אנוס וכדי שיתחייב בה לא כפינן לרבו לעשותו בן חורין דא"כ בכל העבדים נכוף רבם לשחררם כדי שיתחייבו בכל המלות ולכך נקט קרא לא תהו בראה משום (ו) שהיא מלוה רבה ומשום הכי כפינן ובפ"ב דמגילה (דף כ.) נמי מייתי להאי קרא משום הכי גבי אין מוכרין ספר תורה אלא ללמוד תורה ולישא אשה דאמר מר גדול ת"ת שמביא לידי מעשה לישא אשה נמי לא תהו בראה אלא לשבת יצרה: כופין את רבו. וא"ת אמאי כופין ליתי עשה דפרו ורבו וידחה לא תעשה דלא יהיה קדש ואומר רבינו יצחק חדא דבעידנא דמיעקר לאו לא מקיים עשה דמשעת הערארה קא עקר ללאו ועשה דפרו ורבו לא מקיים עד גמר ביאה ועוד דהיא אסורה לינשא לו דלגבי דידה ליכא עשה ועוד אפי' מפקדא (ז) דאפשר לה באחר ועוד כיון דאפשר לקיים שניהם ע"י כפיה לא דחי וא"ת היכי כפינן לשחררו והא אמרי' בפ' השולח (גיטין דף לח: ושם) דכל המשחרר עבדו עובר בעשה וכי תימא מלוה שאני וכי אומרים לו לאדם חטא כדי שיזכה חבירך כדאמרי' בריש שבת (דף ד. ושם ד"ה וכי) והא דשחרר ר"א עבדו בהשולח (גיטין שם) שנכנס לבית הכנסת ולא מלא שם י' התם משום דר"א גופיה עשה מלוה בכך שהשלים המנין והא דאמר נמי בפ' בכל מערבין (עירובין דף לב: ושם ד"ה ולא) דניחא ליה לחבר למיעבד איסורא זוטרא ולא ליעבד עם הארץ איסורא רבה התם משום דקא עביד עם הארץ איסורא על ידו של חבר דקא מאכיל ליה טבל ואומר ר"י דמשום מלוה רבה שרי אע"ג דעובר בעשה כדאמרי' ריש תמיד נשחט (פסחים דף נט. ושם ד"ה אתי) אין לך דבר שמתעכב אחר תמיד של בין הערבים אלא קטרת ונרות ופסח ומחוסר כפורים דערבי פסחים ומפרש התם משום דאתי עשה דפסח שיש בו כרת ודחי עשה דהשלמה אלמא קעבר כהן אעשה דהשלמה כדי שיקיים מחוסר כפורים מלות פסח ה) וא"ת אמאי כופין וימכור עצמו בעבד עברי למ"ד בפ"ק דקדושין (דף יד: ושם) מוכר את עצמו רבו מוסר לו שפחה כנענית ולמ"ד נמי דלאפי' אין לו בנים (ח) רבו מוסר לו שפחה כנענית ואע"ג דאין עבד עברי נוהג אלא בזמן שהיובל נוהג כדאמרי' בפ' האומר בקדושין (דף סט. ושם) הא בבית שני נהג יובל כדפי' ר"ת בהשולח (גיטין דף לו. ד"ה בזמן) גבי הלל תקן פרוזבול ואור"י דאין זה תקנה דאסור למכור עצמו בעבד עברי כדאמרינן בפ"ק דקדושין (דף כב:) אוזן ששמעה על הר סיני כי לי בני ישראל עבדים וגו' וא"ת וישא חליה שפחה וחליה בת חורין והי דלאינו יכול לקדשה דאתי לד עבדות ומשתמש בלד אשת איש (ט) ישאנה בלא קדושין כדאמר לישא שפחה כו' משמע דאי הוה מותר בשפחה לא כפינן לרבו אע"ג דאין קידושין תופסין בשפחה מ"מ היה נושאה בלא קידושין וי"ל דהשתא נמי אתי לד עבדות ומשתמש בלד חירות ולא דמי לפרדה דאמר בפרק אותו ואת בנו (חולין דף עט. ושם) דמרביעין עליה מינה ולא אמר דאתי לד חמור ומשתמש בלד סוס דהתם כלאים כתיב דמשמע שני מינים דומיא דשור וחמור דחרישה ופרדה מין אחד בפני עצמו (י) ומטעם זה מותר לרכוב עליה וא"ת וישא ממזרת דלד עבדות מותר בממזרת כדתנן בהאומר בקדושין (דף סט.) יכולין ממזרין ליטהר כילד ממזר נושא שפחה ובלד חירות נמי מותר כדתנן בפרק עשרה יוחסין (שם דף סט.) ממזרים וחרורים מותרין לבא זה בזה ואור"י דאין זה תקנה להרבות ממזרים בישראל וא"ת וישא נתינה דחרורי ונתיני מותרין לבא זה בזה כדתנן בפ' עשרה יוחסין (שם) ולד עבדות נמי מותר בנתינה דאמר בריש יש מותרות (יבמות דף פה:) ממזרת ונתינה לישראל איכא בינייהו למ"ד מפני שמרגילה הא [היא] מרגלה ליה פי' שיכול להכשיר זרעו ע"י בנו שישא שפחה וי"ל דלעולם אסור נתין בשפחה מ"מ מרגלה ליה כיון שיכול להכשיר אפי' ע"י איסור דהאי גברא לא איכפת ליה באיסור דהא נסיב ממזרת או נתינה וא"ת ומ"ש דאסור נתין בשפחה וממזר מותר הא נתין נמי הוי מפסולי קהל כמו ממזר דכתיב לא תתחתן בם ואור"ת משום דממזר קדש ועומד לפי שנולד מאיסור חמור דלא תפסי קדושין ולכך לא מיתסר בלאו דלא יהיה קדש ומיהו בזכור ובהמה אין להתירו אפי' למאן דמפיק להו בפרק ד' מיתות (סנהדרין דף נד:) מולא יהיה קדש דאין להתירו בקדישות אלא באותן שהוא בא ממנו ומקדישות דזכור ובהמה לא בא וא"ת ומ"ש דגירי וחרורי מותרים בנתינה ואסורים בשפחה ואע"ג דתרוייהו חייבי לאוין ואור"י דנתיני דתפסי בהו קדושין גמרינן משאר פסולי קהל כגון עמוני ומואבי מצרי ואדומי דמותרין בקהל גרים דלא איקרי קהל אבל שפחה דלא תפסי בה קדושין לא ילפא מינייהו: שמע

הגהות הב"ח

(א) גמ' לשבת יצרה אלא מפני תיקון העולם כופין את רבו: (ב) רש"י ד"ה פלגי לה בקרנזיל וכו' מן הלפון לדרום נמלא כל הנהר לאחד והשני אין לו אלא חלי נגר וכו' למערב יהיה לאחד חלי הנהר וכו' ולשני אין לו אלא חלי נהר במזרחו: (ג) ד"ה ה"ג וכו' העבד יכול לקנות עלמו וליללא לחרות אבל העבד אינו יכול לומר לרבו קנה חלקי שאין דמים: (ד) תוס' ד"ה אית וכו' ע"י עילוי דמים בדבר שאין בה דין חלוקה: (ה) ד"ה לישא וכו' אור"י דלא כופין: (ו) ד"ה שנאמר וכו' לא תוהו בראה משום שמשמע מלוה רבה: (ז) ד"ה כופין וכו' ועוד אפילו מפקדא אפרו ורבו אפשר לה באחר: (ח) בא"ד ולמ"ד נמי דלאפי' אין לו בנים ואשה רבו: (ט) בא"ד בלד אשת איש מכל מקום ישאנה בלא קידושין וכו' מותר בשפחה לא הוה כפינן: (י) בא"ד בפני עלמו הוא ומטעם:

ליקוטי רש"י

מי שחציו עבד כו'. כגון שהיו ב' אחין או ב' שותפין ושחרר א' את חלקו. תקנתם את רבו. שאינו חסר כלום [גיטין מא.]. שאינו מפסיד כלום מן הראוי לו. את עצמו לא תקנתם. מה תהא עליו [פסחים פח:]. כל תקנת רבו כאן היא אבל תקנת העבד אין כאן אם נתקן במשפט הממון לא נתקן בפריה ורביה [חגיגה ב:]. לישא שפחה אינו יכול. מפני לד חירות שבו [גיטין שם]. לצד חירות אסור בה דכתיב (דברים כג) לא יהיה קדש לא יקח איתתא אמה [פסחים שם וכעי"ז חגיגה שם]. בת חורין אינו יכול. מפני לד עבדות שבו. לא תהו בראה. לא ברא הקדוש ברוך הוא את הארץ להיות בלא יישוב אלא לשבת יצרה [חגיגה שם]. כי לשבת יצרה [ישעיה מה, יח]. יולר הארץ לא על תוהו להיות ריקנית ברא אותה כי אם לשבת להיות בה יישוב יצרה [גיטין שם]. ובית הבד. בית לעצור זיתים [ב"מ קיז:].

גליון הש"ס

גמרא דינא דגוד. לשון משיכה כמו משכו וקחו (שמות יב) דמתרגמי' נגודו ועיין תוס' נדה דף לו ע"ב ד"ה גדיים:

תורה אור השלם

א) כִּי כֹה אָמַר יְיָ בּוֹרֵא הַשָּׁמַיִם הוּא הָאֱלֹהִים יֹצֵר הָאָרֶץ וְעֹשָׂהּ הוּא כוֹנְנָהּ לֹא תֹהוּ בְרָאָהּ לָשֶׁבֶת יְצָרָהּ אֲנִי יְיָ וְאֵין עוֹד: [ישעיה מה, יח]

רבינו גרשום

דליהוו נפישי אריסין מיכן ומיכן וישמרו זה את זה ואמאי כופין. למ"ה. שנים שיש להם שדה אחת לחלוק ולצד מזרח של שדה היה מושך נהר ולצד דרום של שדה יש שם נגר משוך לאורך השדה שמשקין ממנו השדה ומצד צפון ומערב של שדה יבישה והשתא אין יכולין לחלוק בשום ענין שלא יהא חלק אחד יפה מחבירו אלא א"כ צריכין לחלוק בקרנא זול כי כעין אותו ציור בד' חלקים דמכל רוח יעשו ב' חלקים מן הנהר ב' ומן הנגר ב' ומן היבשה ב' ב' ויחלוקו כי האי גונא כי היכי דלימטי לכל חד וחד שוה לחבירו מן הנהר ומן הנגר ומן צדי היבשה משום דנהר יפה מנגר ונגר יפה מיבשה ובחילוק ענין זה יחלוקו בקו השוה שלא יהא חלקו של אחד יפה משל חבירו ואין אחד מהם נוטל ב' חלקים בסמוך לו אלא כעין זה *

(הנהר המושך מצד מזרח): פיסקא אין חולקין את הטרקלין. פלטורין אא"כ יש בו כדי לזה וכדי לזה דהיינו י' על י' לזה ולו לזה דהיינו שיעור טרקלין. מורן. הוא מגדל. ולא את הטלית. אלא אם כן יכולין שניהן להתכסות בו זה בפני עצמו בטליתו. ולא את המרחץ עד שיכולין לרחוץ כל אחד בחלקו המגיעו. זה הכלל כל ששמו עליו כתחלה מקודם חלוקה שלאחר חלוקה אית לכל אחד אותו עצמו כמו שנקרא בתחלה חולקין. ואם לאו אין חולקין אלא מעלין זה לזה בדמים שיקנה אחד מהן חלק חבירו בדמים. ואי ליכא שיעור חלוקה מאי. רב יהודא אמר אית דינא דגוד או אגוד. דאם אחד רוצה שישתמשו בו שניהם בשותפות זה שבוע אחד וזה שבוע אחד והאחד אינו רוצה יכול לומר האי דאינו רוצה נישום אותו בדמים ותקנה אתה חלקי או אני חלקך. גוד. משוך תרגו' א). ורב נחמן אמר לית דינא דגוד או אגוד. כלומר אי האי אינו רוצה אינו יכול לכפותו ולומר לו כן אלא משתמשין בו בשותפות: בכור ופשוט. והוא הדין לפשוט ופשוט אלא להכי בעי בכור ופשוט קשה טפי לחלק בג' חלקים. ולהכי נקיט בהמה טמאה. דאי אפשר לשוחטה ולחלוק הבשר. אמר ליה עובד לפשוט יום אחד ולבכור ב' ימים וכן נמי בהמה טמאה זה ישתמש בה ב' ימים וזה יום אחד ואין כאן דין גוד או אגוד: וחציו בן חורין ששחררו אחד מן השותפין. לישא שפחה אינו יכול מפני צד חירות שבו וכותב שטר לרבו על חצי דמיו שיפרע לו ממה שירויח לאחר שיהיה כולו בן חורין מפני שכשהוא חצי עבד אין לו ממון כלום שכל מה שמרויח ביום שהוא עובד לעצמו סוף סוף למחר כשהוא עובד לרבו הרי הוא עבדו וכל מה שקנה עבד קנה רבו להכי צריך לכתוב שט"ח על חצי דמיו. וחזרו בית הילל כו' מפני תיקון העולם הא לאו מפני תיקון העולם אין כופין את רבו משום דאמרינן דלית דינא דגוד או אגוד דלא מצי עבד למימר לו שחררני ואתן לך דמי חציי או תן אתה לי דמי חציי ואהא מהכל עבדך ותיובתא דרב יהודה. לעולם אמר לך רב יהודה בעלמא אית דינא דגוד או אגוד והכא גבי עבד שאני דגוד איכא אגוד ליכא. דעבד מצי למימר לרבו קצוב עלי דמים ואקנה חצי ממך אבל אינו יכול לומר לו אקצוב אני עליך דמי חציי ותקנה אותי מהכל דאינו יכול למכור צד שחרור שבו לישא שפחה. ואי"ת דמפרש"י אגוד ליכא לא מצי עבד למימר לרבו קנה חלקי המשוחרר שאם נותן לו הרב דמים עכשיו כשהוא רבו מהכל חוזר ונוטלן הימנו דמה שקנה עבד קנה רבו ונמצא שאין גופו קנוי כשהוא חוזר ונוטלן. למ"ה: אם עשאן אביהן לשכר שהיה רגיל להשכירן כדי שיהא משתכר בו הכי נמי ישכירום ויחלוקו השכר לאמצע: ואם לאו אינו יכול לומר עני לעשיר גוד והב לי דמי חלקי מן מרחץ ובית הבד דאין לי במה לישתמש בו כלום או תן לי דמים ממה שאתה משתמש בו יותר ממני דיכול העשיר לחזור ולומר לעני כו'. ומן שמיא קנסוהו לאותו עני ואין לו על העשיר כלום אלמא דלית דינא דגוד או אגוד. הכא נמי אגוד ליכא דאין לעני במה לפדות אבל בעלמא אמרינן אית דינא דגוד או אגוד:

חשק שלמה על רבינו גרשום א) [נ"ל תרגום משכו ונגידו].

קכא א מיי' פ"א מהל' שכנים הל' ז סמג עשין פב טוש"ע ח"מ סי' קעא סעיף ג:
קכב ב ג מיי' שם הל' ה טוש"ע שם סעיף ו:
קכג ד ה מיי' פ"ב מהל' שם הלכה ב סמג שם טוש"ע ח"מ סי' קעא סעיף ד:
קכד ו ז טוש"ע ח"מ סי' קעא סעי' יג:
קכה ח ט מיי' פ"ז מהל' ס"ת הל' טו סמג עשין כה טוש"ע י"ד סי' רעג סעיף א וסי' רפג סעיף א:

קח לך עבדים וירחצו במרחץ קח לך זיתים ובא ועשה בבית הבד התם נמי גוד איכא אגוד ליכא ת"ש (א) א כל שאילו יחלק ושמו עליו חולקין אם לאו מעלין אותו בדמים תנאי היא דתניא טול אתה שיעור ואני פחות שומעין לו רבן שמעון בן גמליאל אומר ב אין שומעין לו היכי דמי אילימא כדקתני מאי טעמא דרשב"ג אלא לאו חסורי מחסרא והכי קאמר טול אתה שיעור ואני פחות שומעין לו וגוד או אגוד נמי שומעין לו ואתא רשב"ג למימר אין שומעין לו לא לעולם כדקתני ודקאמרת מ"ט דרשב"ג משום דאמר ליה אי בדמי לית לי דמי למיתן לך (ב) ג במתנה לא ניחא לי דכתיב א) ושונא מתנות יחיה א"ל אביי לרב יוסף הא דרב יהודה דשמואל היא דתנן ה) וכתבי הקודש אע"פ ששניהם רוצים לא יחלוקו ואמר שמואל ד לא שנו אלא בכרך אחד אבל בשני כריכות חולקין ואי ס"ד לית דינא דגוד או אגוד מאי איריא בכרך אחד אפי' בשני כריכין נמי תרגמא רב שלמן ה בששניהן רוצין אמר אמימר הלכתא אית דינא דגוד או אגוד אמר ליה רב אשי לאמימר הא דרב נחמן מאי אמר ליה ו לא שמיעא לי כלומר לא סבירא לי ולא והא רב בר חיננא ורב דימי בר חיננא שבק להו אבוה תרתי אמהתא חדא ידעא אפיא ובשולי וחדא ידעא פילכא ונוולא ואתו לקמיה דרבא ואמר להו ז לית דינא דגוד או אגוד שאני התם דלמר מיבעי ליה תרווייהו ולמר מיבעי ליה תרווייהו כי קאמר ליה שקול את חדא ואנא חדא לאו גוד או אגוד הוא ח (וכי לא מצי למימר הכי) והא כתבי הקדש דתרווייהו מיבעי להו ואמר שמואל לא שנו אלא בכרך אחד אבל בשני כריכין חולקין הא תרגמא רב שלמן (ג) בשרצו ת"ר ח מדביק אדם תורה נביאים וכתובים כאחד דברי ר"מ ר' יהודה אומר תורה בפני עצמה נביאים בפני עצמן וכתובים בפני עצמן וחכ"א כל אחד ואחד בפני עצמו ואמר רב יהודה מעשה בביתוס בן זונין שהיו לו שמנה נביאים מדובקין כאחד על פי ר"א בן עזריה (ד) וי"א לא היו לו אלא אחד אחד בפני עצמו אמר רבי מעשה והביאו לפנינו תורה נביאים וכתובים מדובקים כאחד והכשרנום ט בין חומש לחומש של תורה ארבעה שיטין י וכן בין כל נביא לנביא ובנביא של שנים עשר ג' שיטין ומסיים מלמטה ומתחיל מלמעלה ת"ר הרוצה לדבק תורה נביאים וכתובים כאחד מדבק ועושה בראשו כדי לגול עמוד ובסופו כדי לגול היקף ומסיים מלמטה ומתחיל מלמעלה ואם

רש"י

קח לך עבדים. שיתממו אותו ורחוץ בו ולא מצי עני למימר ליה קנה חלקי: הכא נמי גוד איכא אגוד ליכא. שאין העני אומר לו (ה) אף אני אקנה חלקך שאין לו במה לקנות לפיכך אין יכול לכופו: ושמו עליו. כל דבר שיש בו שיעור שאם תחלקנו עדיין יהא עליו שמו הראשון: מעלין אותו בדמים. היינו גוד או אגוד: טול אתה שיעור ואני פחות. כגון חצר שאין בה שמנה אמות ואמר זה חלוק וטול לך ד' אמות ואני המותר: וגוד או אגוד נמי. שלא רצה למחול כלום אלא קנה חלקי או אקנה חלקך: הא דרב יהודה. דאמר גוד או אגוד משמיה דרביה קבלה: בכרך אחד. כל ספריהן עשויין בגליון ואם יפיאהו לצ"ד לחלקו בזיון הוא: אבל בשתי כריכות. כגון תורה בכרך אחד ונביאים בכרך אחד: חולקין. קס"ד דאפילו אין שניהם רוצים וע"כ אין דמיהן שוין ואי לית דינא דגוד או אגוד היאך הוא כופיהו זה יאמר אני לא אתן לך עודף הדמים וגם לא אתן לך היפה שאקבל ממך דמים. ולא גרסי' תרווייהו צריכין להאי: בששניהם רוצים. הא דשמואל אשניהם רוצים דמתניתין קאי דקתני לא יחלוקו ואמר שמואל בשתי כריכות אם שניהם רוצים יחלוקו: פילכא ונוולא. לטוות ולארוג. ל"א ביסתרקי תכשיטי ספסלים שקורין טפי"ד: לית דינא דגוד או אגוד. לכופו לתת דמי העודפים ביפה ולא למכור חלקו: לאו גוד או אגוד הוא. אי לא אמר ליה או קח שתיהם או אקח שתיהם דכל אחת אין בה כדי לאחד: אבל בב' כריכות חולקין. וקס"ד בע"כ של אחד מהן אלמא כי אמר ליה שקול חדא וגוד דמי היתירים או אגוד כייפינן ליה: כל אחד ואחד בפני עצמו. כל ספר וספר של נביאים ושל כתובים צריך להיות כרך לעצמו: בביתוס שמנה נביאים. כל ספרי נביאים שמנה הן: ה"ג וכן בין כל נביא ונביא ובנביא של שנים עשר שלש שיטין ומסיים מלמטה ומתחיל מלמעלה. אם נזדמן לו סיום הספר מלמטה בסוף הדף מתחיל ספרו האחר בראש הדף ואינו צריך להניח ריוח חלק ביניהם: כדי לגול עמוד. מניח קלף חלק לגלול על גבי עמוד של עץ שהספר נגלל עליו: ובסופו כדי לגול היקף. בסופו מניח חלק גדול כדי לגול בו כל הקיפו שאין עושה שני עמודים לגוללו לאמצעו כמו שאנו עושין לספר תורה אלא גוללו מתחלתו לסופו וכורך החלק על כל ההיקף: ואם

תוספות

שמע (לעיל) מינה דלית דינא דגוד או אגוד. וא"ת שאני הכא שאין העבד נותן לו דמים מיד אלא כותב לו שטר על דמיו וי"ל דמשמע משום דלא יבטל הוא דכופין הא לאו הכי אין כופין בכל ענין אפי' יתן דמים: ה) אם עשאן לשכר כו'. לאו דוקא עשאן לשכר דהוא הדין אפילו עשאן לעצמו אלא שמוצא להשכיר:

ואי ס"ד לית דינא דגוד או אגוד אפי' בשתי כריכות כו'. השתא ס"ד דחולקין כיון שאחד רוצה לחלוק וב' כריכות דומיא דכרך אחד שאין כתוב באחד מה שכתוב באחר כגון יהושע ושמואל ואמאי חולקין בע"כ והא אינם שוין אלא ודאי אית דינא דגוד או אגוד וא"ת אפילו אית דינא דגוד או אגוד אמאי חולקין כיון שכתוב בזה מה שאין בזה ותרווייהו צריכי להאי ולהאי וי"ל דהוי מצי למימר וליטעמיך ולא גרס הכא מה שכתוב במיעוט ספרים ואי ס"ד לית ליה דינא דגוד או אגוד כי היכי דתרווייהו צריכי להאי תרווייהו צריכי להאי דהא כל שכן דאי לא צריכי תרווייהו להאי ולהאי פריך טפי שפיר אי לית ליה דינא דגוד או אגוד אמאי חולקין: מדביק אדם תורה נביאים וכתובים כאחד. אע"פ שא"א שלא יתן נביאים וכתובים על גבי תורה ובמגילה בפ"ב (דף כז.) משמע דאסור להניח ה"מ בשתי כריכות אבל כשהן מדובקין יחד אינו גנאי: רבי יהודה אומר תורה בפני עצמה. לא מפני שאסור להניח זה על גב זה מצריך שיהא כל אחד בפני עצמו דלא אשכחן שיהא אסור להניח אלא נביאים וכתובים על גבי תורה אבל נביאים על גבי כתובים או איפכא לא אלא היינו טעמא שלא יראה הכל כמו תורה או הכל נביאים כי היכי דאמרי חכמים בתר הכי דבעו שיהא כל נביא ונביא בפני עצמו וע"כ טעמא שלא יהא נראה הכל כמו נביא אחד כן נראה לרשב"א: ומסיים מלמטה ומתחיל מלמעל'. פי' בקונטרס ואינו צריך להניח ד' שיטין ונראה לר"י דבין חומש לחומש של תורה צריך להניח ואנביאים דוקא קאמר דאין צריך כדמפרש טעמא לקמן שאם בא לחתוך חותך אבל בין חומש לחומש של תורה לא מידי דהוי אפרשה פתוחה שאם היה מסיים מלמטה היה צריך להניח שיטה אחת הכא נמי דין הוא להניח בסוף כל חומש פרשה של ד' שיטין וריצב"א מפרש ומסיים מלמטה ומתחיל מלמעלה ולעולם מניח ד' שיטין ודוקא בין נביא לנביא אבל בין חומש לחומש לא יסיים מלמטה ומתחיל מלמעלה אפי' בהנחת ד' שיטין כדאמר בירושלמי בפ"ק דמגילה וצריך שיהא גומר באמצע הדף ומתחיל באמצעיתו ובנביא מסיים בסופו ומתחיל בראשו כו' ונראה לי הטעם דאין לו לסיים בסוף הדף אפי' יניח ארבעה שיטין משום שמא יבוא לחתוך אבל בין נביא לנביא שאם בא לחתוך חותך מסיים מלמטה: ועושה בראשו כדי לגול עמוד ובסופו כדי היקף. כן כתוב בכל הספרים וקשה לר"י דתניא במס' סופרים כל הספרים נגללין לתחלתן ולקמן אמר נמי ספר עזרה לתחלתו הוא נגלל ומה שפי' הקונט' מתחלתו לסופו אין הלשון משמע כן וגבי מזוזה אמרינן נמי שכורכין אותה מאחד כלפי שמע דהיינו לתחלתה ובהדיא גרסי' בירושלמי בפ"ק דמגילה עושה אדם עמוד לספר תורה בסופו ע"כ נראה לר"י דגר' ועושה בראשו כדי היקף ובסופו כדי לגול עמוד ולרשב"א נראה לקיים גירסת הספרים והכא שאני דאיירי במדביק תורה נביאים וכתובים ואז אין נכון לעשות עמוד בסופו כמו בעלמא שגנאי הוא שתהא תורה נכרכת סביב נביאים וכתובים י ונראה כאילו נעשית להם שומר מלכלוך לכך עושה כאן עמוד בראשו כדי שתהא תורה מבפנים ונביאים וכתובים מבחוץ ולקמן דמשני לאדדין קתני לא גרס תחלת הספר כדי לגול עמוד וסופו כדי לגול היקף תורה נביאים וכתובים ואית לן למימר איפכא (ו) וברוב ספרים לא גרס אלא לאדדין קתני ותו לא ועוד אומר רשב"א דאפי' לספרים דגרסי לה לא קשיא כולי האי דניחא ליה לשנויי דומיא דהך ברייתא דקאי עלה: שאם

רבינו גרשום

כל שאילו יחלק כל הני דאמרינן במתני' ואם לאו מעלי' אותו בדמים דהיינו גוד או אגוד אלמא אית דינא דגוד או אגוד וקשיא לרב נחמן. תנאי היא דתניא כו' דהיכא דיש לשותפין חצר של ז' אמות לחלוק דלאו ראויה לחלוקה אלא אם כן יש בה ח' אמות ואמר אחד לחבירו נחלוק חצר זה וחבירו מעכב ואמר ליה האי אמאי מעכבת טול אתה שיעור דין חלוקה הד' אמות ואני אטול פחות הג' אמות שומעין לו דאין יכול לעכב עליו הואיל דנותן לו שיעור חלוקה. אי נימ' כדקתני כלומר דליכא שום דברים בהדיהו אלא כדקתני. וגוד או אגוד נמי. כלומר דהכי אמר ליה ברור לך אחד מב' דברים הללו או טול אתה שיעור ואני פחות או גוד או אגוד ואתא רשב"ג למימר מזה שומעין לו כשאמר לו טול אתה השיעור אבל מגוד או אגוד יכול לעכב עליו דקסבר דלית דינא דגוד או אגוד אלמא תנאי היא: ודקאמרת מאי טעמא דרשב"ג דבטול אתה שיעור נמי אין שומעין דמצי מעכב אידך משום דאמר ליה אותה אמה שאתה רוצה ליתן לי יותר איני מבקש אותה לא בדמים שאין לי דמים לקנותה וגם במתנה איני מבקשה ולא מצית מוקמת לה בתנאי: הא דר' יהודה דאמר לעיל אית דינא דגוד או אגוד דשמואל היא כלומר מינה דשמואל קבלה ולא מינה דרב דרב יהודה הוה תלמיד דרב ותלמיד דשמואל והא מילתא מינה דשמואל למדה ולא מינה דרב: אלא בכרך אחד. היו נכרכין בראשית ואלה שמות משום הכי אין חולקין משום בזיון והיינו כרך שהיו רגילין לכתוב ספריהן כעין ספר תורה והפטרות שאנו כותבין ולהכי קרי כרך שכרוך כעין מגילה אבל בשתי כריכות בראשית בכרך אחד ואלה שמות בכרך אחד חולקין דליכא בזיון דספר. ואי ס"ד דלגבי חצר היכא דליכא ד' לזה וד' לזה לית דינא דגוד או אגוד אלא תרווייהו ישתמשו ביה מאי אריא בכרך אחד דאין חולקין אפי' בב' כריכות נמי אין חולקין דשתיהן צריכי לתרווייהו כריכות והוי נמי שאין בחד כרך כדי לזה ולא יחלקו אפי' בב' כריכות אלא ליקום בשותפות אלא ש"מ מדחולקין להם משום דמצי למימר ליה

חבריה או חלוק או גוד עלי דמים ואסב תרווייהו או איגוד עליך ותיסב תרווייהו. תירגמא רב שלמן מהא ליכא למשמע מינה הא דינא דאגוד ודוקא קשיא א"כ אפילו שתי כריכות אמאי חולקין משום כשרצו שניהן לחלוק ובשתי כריכות מצי לחלוק אבל בכרך אחד לא משום בזיון אבל אי אחד מעכב וחד רוצה לא מצי למימר ליה גוד או אגוד. ודרב יהודה [לאו] דשמואל היא. הא דרב נחמן מאי. דאמר לית דינא דגוד. מיפא פת. ובשולי מיני תבשיל. ביסתרקי בל"ע שפיע. ואתו לקמיה דרבא...

חשק שלמה על רבינו גרשום א) ואפילו הכי חולקין לא אליבא דשמואל דסבר ככרך יהודה וכו'.

מסורת הש"ס

א) [לעיל יא.], ב) [ערכין קב: וש"נ], ג) מהרש"ע מ"ז, ד) [גיר' הרמב"ם והטור וכו' בש"ע סי' רפג סעיף א ובין כל נביא ונביא שלשה שיטין וכן בין כל נביא ונביא של תרי עשר וגם הוא מכוון כמס' סופרים פ"ב ה"ד אבל כרב אלפס איתא כמו הכא], ה) לעיל, ו) [עי' מג"א סי' כח ס"ק ד].

הגהות הב"ח

(א) גמ' מ"ש זה הכלל כל שאילו יחלק: (ב) שם למיתן לך ולאי במתנה: (ג) שם תרגמה רב שלמן בששניהם רוצים תנו רבנן: (ד) שם ר"א בן עזריה וחכמים אומרים לא היו לו אלא אחד: (ה) רש"י ד"ה הכא נמי וכו' אומר לו (אף) תז"מ ונ"ב ס"א לו: (ו) תוס' ד"ה ועושה וכו' למימר איפכא בראשו כדי היקף ובסופו כדי לגול עמוד וכרוב ספרים:

תורה אור השלם

א) עֹכֵר בֵּיתוֹ בּוֹצֵעַ בָּצַע וְשׂוֹנֵא מַתָּנֹת יִחְיֶה: [משלי טו, כז]

לעזי רש"י

טפי"ד. פירוש תכשיטי ספסלים, תכשיטי לכסא (רש"י תענית דף כה סוע"ב), שטיח (רש"י זבחים דף צד ע"ב ד"ה עולבת ועיין ערוך ערך אברזין ג' וערך טפיט).

ליקוטי רש"י

ושונא מתנות יחיה. מאחר שהוא שונא מתנות כל שכן שאינו אוהב את הגזל [משלי טו, כז]. וכתבי הקודש. כגון תורה נביאים וכתובים [שבת קטז.]. ספר תורה שהוא בכרך אחד וכן נביאים וכתובים הכתובים בגליון כס"ת [לעיל ג.]. כ"ד ספרים והיו רגילים לכותבן בגליון כס"ת שלנו לפיכך גנאי הדבר לחתכן [לעיל יא.].

קַח לְךָ עֲבָדִים וְיִרְחֲצוּ בַּמֶּרְחָץ – "ACQUIRE SLAVES FOR YOURSELF to heat the bathhouse AND LET [THE MEMBERS OF YOUR FAMILY] BATHE IN THE BATHHOUSE; קַח לְךָ זֵיתִים וּבֹא וַעֲשֵׂה בְּבֵית הַבַּד – ACQUIRE OLIVES FOR YOURSELF AND COME AND PROCESS THEM IN THE OLIVE PRESS." Although the poor brother has no use for a bathhouse or olive press, still he cannot force his wealthy brother to buy out these things. This, then, refutes Rav Yehudah's view that one partner can compel the other to dissolve the partnership. – ? –

The Gemara answers:

הָתָם נַמִּי גּוֹד אִיכָּא אָגוּד לֵיכָּא – **There** (in the Mishnah's case) **too,** the poor person, who cannot afford to buy his brother's share, can declare only, **"You set a price** and buy my portion," but not, "**I will set a price** and buy your portion." Since he cannot offer his brother a choice of either buying or selling, even Rav Yehudah agrees that he cannot compel him to dissolve the partnership, as explained above.

The Gemara challenges Rav Nachman's view from a Baraisa:

תָּא שְׁמַע – **Come, learn** a refutation: כָּל שֶׁאִילּוּ יֵחָלֵק וּשְׁמוֹ עָלָיו חוֹלְקִין – ANY shared object that is large enough so THAT, IF IT WERE DIVIDED, it WOULD RETAIN ITS NAME,[1] [THE PARTNERS] DIVIDE. אִם לָאו מַעֲלִין אוֹתוֹ בְּדָמִים – IF it would NOT retain its name, WE COMPENSATE HIM WITH MONEY. That is, one partner tells the other, "You set a price for my share or I will set a price for yours." This refutes Rav Nachman's position that one partner cannot make such a demand on the other.

To answer this question, the Gemara suggests that the above Baraisa reflects the view of only some Tannaim, whereas others indeed support Rav Nachman's position:

תַּנָּאֵי הִיא – **This** question **has** already **been disputed by Tannaim** in another Baraisa.

The Gemara now cites a Baraisa and suggests that it records such a dispute. The Baraisa discusses a jointly owned courtyard that is too small to be divisible:[2]

דְּתַנְיָא – **For it was taught in a Baraisa:** טוֹל אַתָּה שִׁיעוּר וַאֲנִי פָּחוֹת – If one partner told another, "YOU TAKE THE PRESCRIBED AMOUNT of property AND I WILL take LESS than that,"[3] שׁוֹמְעִין לוֹ – WE[4] LISTEN TO HIM. Since the reluctant partner will receive the prescribed amount of property, he can be compelled to dissolve the partnership. רַבָּן שִׁמְעוֹן בֶּן גַּמְלִיאֵל אוֹמֵר אֵין שׁוֹמְעִין לוֹ – RABBAN SHIMON BEN GAMLIEL SAID: WE DO NOT LISTEN TO HIM.

The Gemara analyzes Rabban Shimon ben Gamliel's ruling:

הֵיכִי דָמֵי – **How are we to construe the case** on which Rabban Shimon ben Gamliel ruled? אִילֵימָא כִּדְתָנֵי – **If you will say** that he rules on the case discussed by the Tanna Kamma, **as the Baraisa teaches,**[5] מַאי טַעְמָא דְּרַבָּן שִׁמְעוֹן בֶּן גַּמְלִיאֵל – **what** would be **the reasoning of Rabban Shimon ben Gamliel?** In that case, the partner's proposal seems reasonable. Why would Rabban Shimon ben Gamliel maintain that we reject it? אֶלָּא לָאו חַסּוּרֵי מִחַסְּרָא – **Rather, is it not that [the Baraisa]** must be understood as if it **were deficient,** וְהָכִי קָאָמַר – **and this** is what the Baraisa means to **say:** טוֹל אַתָּה שִׁיעוּר וַאֲנִי פָּחוֹת שׁוֹמְעִין לוֹ – According to the Tanna Kamma, if one partner said, "YOU TAKE THE PRESCRIBED AMOUNT AND I will take LESS," WE LISTEN TO HIM; וְגוֹד אוֹ אָגוּד נַמִּי שׁוֹמְעִין לוֹ – AND if one partner said, "YOU SET a price for my portion OR I WILL SET a price for yours,"[6] WE ALSO LISTEN TO HIM. וְאָתָא רַבָּן שִׁמְעוֹן בֶּן גַּמְלִיאֵל לְמֵימַר – **And,** directing his remark at the Tanna Kamma's *second* statement, **Rabban Shimon ben Gamliel came to say:** אֵין שׁוֹמְעִין לוֹ – **We do *not* listen to him,** because a partner has no right to say, "You set a price or I will set a price."[7] According to this interpretation, the Tanna Kamma of the Baraisa and Rabban Shimon ben Gamliel indeed dispute the same issue as did Rav Yehudah and Rav Nachman. In this dispute Rabban Shimon ben Gamliel supports Rav Nachman's view.

The Gemara objects that we need not interpret the Baraisa in this way:

לֹא – **No,** we need not adopt this interpretation. לְעוֹלָם כִּדְקָתָנֵי – **Really,** Rabban Shimon ben Gamliel ruled on the case in which one partner offered to allocate the prescribed amount of property to the other, **as the Baraisa taught.** וּדְקָאָמְרַתְּ מַאי טַעְמָא דְּרַבָּן שִׁמְעוֹן בֶּן גַּמְלִיאֵל – **And** concerning **that which you asked: What is the reasoning of Rabban Shimon ben Gamliel,** i.e. if a partner is offered a share of the prescribed size, why can he refuse to divide? The Gemara explains: מִשּׁוּם דְּאָמַר לֵיהּ – **Because he can say to [his partner]:** אִי בְּדָמֵי – **"If** you expect me to compensate you **with money** for allotting me the larger share, I refuse to do so, for לֵית לִי דָמֵי לְמִיתַּן לָךְ – **I have no money to give you.** בְּמַתָּנָה לֹא נִיחָא לִי – Moreover, if you expect me to accept the larger share **as a gift, I do not want** to do that either, דִּכְתִיב: ,,וְשׂוֹנֵא מַתָּנֹת יִחְיֶה" – **for it is written:**[8] **'And one who hates gifts will live.' "** Thus, the reluctant partner can indeed refuse to take more than his share, insisting instead on retaining the partnership. Given this possible interpretation, there is no proof that any Tanna supports Rav Nachman's position.[9]

NOTES

1. I.e. each portion would still provide the function of the original property and thereby retain its name.

2. [When two people own property jointly, one can compel the other to divide it only if each person's share would still provide the function of the original property. The Mishnah (11a) specifies how large the shares of different types of property must be. The minimum size of a share is called the "prescribed amount." For example, if two people own a courtyard together, one can compel the other to divide only if each would be left with an area of at least four *amos* by four *amos* (in addition to a unloading area). The prescribed amount of a courtyard, then, is four *amos* by four *amos.*] Our Baraisa discusses property that, if divided equally between the partners, would leave each with a portion lacking the prescribed amount, e.g. a courtyard that is only seven *amos* by four *amos.*

3. Because of the property's size, neither partner can insist that it be divided equally. What, though, if one partner tells the other, "You take an area of four *amos* by four *amos* and I will settle for the remaining three *amos* by four *amos*"? Can he compel his partner to dissolve the partnership on such terms? (*Rashi*).

4. *We* refers to the court deciding the case.

5. After recording the Tanna Kamma's ruling that we "listen to the partner" (i.e. accept his proposal) in a particular case, the Baraisa then quotes Rabban Shimon ben Gamliel's ruling that we do not listen to him. This clearly implies that Rabban Shimon ben Gamliel disputed the Tanna Kamma's ruling on the case cited in the Baraisa.

6. That is, the partner wanted to dissolve the partnership but refused to take a smaller portion than his partner. He therefore told his partner, "Either you take the larger portion and compensate me or I will take the larger portion and compensate you" (*Rashi,* according to *Ramban*).

7. That is, Rabban Shimon ben Gamliel did not rule on the case mentioned at the beginning of the Baraisa; he commented on a case in which one partner offered the other the choice of buying out or selling out. Presumably, then, the Tanna Kamma also ruled on that case, but his ruling is missing from the Baraisa.

8. *Proverbs* 15:27.

9. Previously, after citing a Baraisa refuting Rav Nachman's position, the Gemara suggested that Rabban Shimon ben Gamliel supports his view. The Gemara now asserts that this is not necessarily true; Rabban Shimon ben Gamliel might have been discussing another issue entirely. It thus remains unclear whether Rav Nachman's position is in fact supported by any Tanna.

קח לך עבדים וירחצו במרחץ קח לך זיתים ובא ועשה בבית הבד התם נמי גוד איכא אגוד ליכא ת"ש (א) א כל שאילו יחלק ושמו עליו חולקין אם לאו מעלין אותו בדמים תנאי היא דתניא טול אתה שיעור ואני פחות שומעין לו רבן שמעון בן גמליאל אומר ב אין שומעין לו היכי דמי אילימא כדקתני מאי טעמא דרשב"ג אלא לאו חסורי מחסרא והכי קאמר טול אתה שיעור ואני פחות שומעין לו וגוד או אגוד נמי שומעין לו ואתא רשב"ג למימר אין שומעין לו לא לעולם כדקתני ודקאמרת מ"ט דרשב"ג משום דאמר ליה אי בדמי לית לי דמי למיתן לך (ב) ג במתנה לא ניחא לי דכתיב א) ושונא מתנות יחיה א"ל אביי לרב יוסף הא דרב יהודה דשמואל היא דתנן א) וכתבי הקודש אע"פ ששניהם רוצים לא יחלוקו ואמר שמואל ד לא שנו אלא בכרך אחד אבל בשני כריכות חולקין ואי ס"ד לית דינא דגוד או אגוד מאי איריא בכרך אחד אפי' בשני כריכין נמי תרגמא רב שלמן ה בששניהן רוצין אמר אמימר הלכתא אית דינא דגוד או אגוד אמר ליה רב אשי לאמימר הא דרב נחמן מאי אמר ליה ו לא שמיעא לי כלומר לא סבירא לי ולא והא רב' בר חיננא ורב דימי בר חיננא שבק להו אבוה תרתי אמהתא חדא ידעא אפיא ובשולי וחדא ידעא פילכא ונוולא ואתו לקמיה דרבא ואמר להו ז דלמא לית דינא דגוד או אגוד שאני התם דלמר מיבעי ליה תרווייהו ולמר מיבעי ליה תרווייהו כי קאמר ליה שקול את חדא ואנא חדא לאו גוד או אגוד הוא ח (וכי לא מצי למימר הכי) והא כתבי הקדש דתרווייהו מיבעו להו ואמר שמואל לא שנו אלא בכרך אחד אבל בשני כריכין חולקין הא תרגמא רב שלמן (ג) בשרצו ת"ר ה מדביק אדם תורה נביאים וכתובים כאחד דברי ר"מ ר' יהודה אומר תורה בפני עצמה נביאים בפני עצמן וכתובים בפני עצמן וחכ"א כל אחד ואחד בפני עצמו ואמר רב יהודה מעשה בביתוס בן זונין שהיו לו שמונה נביאים מדובקין כאחד על פי ר"א בן עזריה (ד) וי"א לא היו לו אלא אחד אחד בפני עצמו אמר רבי מעשה והביאו לפנינו תורה נביאים וכתובים מדובקים כאחד והכשרנום ט בין חומש לחומש של תורה ארבעה שיטין י וכן בין כל נביא לנביא ובנביא של שנים עשר ג' שיטין ומסיים מלמטה ומתחיל מלמעלה ת"ר הרוצה לדבק תורה נביאים וכתובים כאחד מדבק ועושה בראשו כדי לגול עמוד ובסופו כדי לגול היקף ומסיים מלמטה ומתחיל מלמעלה ואם

רש"י

קח לך עבדים. שיחממו אותו ורחוץ בו ולא מצי עני למימר ליה קנה חלקי: הכא נמי גוד איכא אגוד ליכא. שאין העני אומר לו (ה) אף אני אקנה חלקך שאין לו במה לקנות לפיכך אין יכול לכופו: ושמו עליו. כל דבר שיש בו שיעור שאם תחלקנו עדיין יהא עליו שמו הראשון: מעלין אותו בדמים. היינו גוד או אגוד: טול אתה שיעור ואני פחות. כגון חצר שאין בה שמנה אמות ואמר זה חלוק ותטול לך ד' אמות ואני המותר: וגוד או אגוד נמי. שלא רצה למחול כלום אלא קנה חלקי או אקנה חלקך: הא דרב יהודה. דאמר גוד או אגוד משמיה דרביה קבלה: בכרך אחד. כל ספריהן עשוין בגליון ואם יחלקוהו לב"ד לחלקו בזיון הוא: אבל בשתי כריכות. כגון תורה בכרך אחד ונביאים בכרך אחד: חולקין. קס"ד דאפילו אין שניהם רוצים וע"כ אין דמיהן שוין ואי לית דינא דגוד או אגוד היאך הוא כופיהו זה יאמר אני לא אתן לך עודף הדמים וגם לא אתן לך היפה שאקבל ממך דמים. ולא גרסי' תרווייהו צריכין להאי: בששניהם רוצים. הא דשמואל כששניהם רוצים דמתניתין קאי דקתני לא יחלוקו ואמר שמואל בשתי כריכות אם שניהם רוצים יחלוקו: פילכא ונוולא. טוות ולארוג. ל"א ביסתרקי תכשיטי ספסלים שקורין טפי"ד: לית דינא דגוד או אגוד. לכופו לתת דמי העודפים ליפה או למכור חלקו: לאו גוד או אגוד הוא. אי לא אמר ליה או קח שתיהם או אקח שתיהם דכל אחת אין בה כדי לאחד: אבל בב' כריכות חולקין. וקס"ד בע"כ של אחד מהן אלמא כי אמר ליה שקול חדא וגוד דמי היתירים או אגוד כייפינן ליה: כל אחד ואחד בפני עצמו. כל ספר וספר של נביאים ושל כתובים צריך להיות כרך לעצמו: בביתוס שמנה נביאים. כל ספרי נביאים שמנה הן: ה"ג וכן בין כל נביא ונביא ובנביא של שנים עשר שלש שיטין ומסיים מלמטה ומתחיל מלמעלה. אם נזדמן לו סיום הספר מלמטה בסוף הדף מתחיל ספרו האחר בראש הדף ואינו צריך להניח ריוח חלק ביניהם: כדי לגול עמוד. מניח קלף חלק לגלול על גבי עמוד עד שהספר נגלל עליו: ובסופו כדי לגול היקף. בסופו מניח חלק גדול כדי לגול בו כל הקיפו שאין עושה שני עמודים וגוללו לאמצעו כמו שאנו עושין לספר תורה אלא גוללו מתחלתו לסופו וכורך החלק על כל ההיקף: ואם

תוספות

שמע מינה דלית דינא דגוד או אגוד. (לעיל) ול"ת שאני הכא שאין העבד נותן לו דמים מיד אלא כותב לו שטר על דמיו וי"ל דמשמע משום דלא יבטל הוא כופין בכל ענין אפי' יתן דמים: אם עשאן לשכר כו'. לאו דוקא עשאן לשכר דהוא הדין אפילו עשאן לעצמו אלא שמוצא להשכיר:

ואי ס"ד לית דינא דגוד או אגוד אפי' בשתי כריכות כו'. השתא ס"ד דחולקין כיון שאחד רוצה לחלוק וב' כריכות דומיא דכרך אחד שאין כתוב באחד מה שכתוב באחר כגון יהושע ושמואל ואמאי חולקין בע"כ והא אינם שוין אלא ודאי אית דינא דגוד או אגוד וא"ת אפילו אית דינא דגוד או אגוד אמאי חולקין כיון שכתוב בזה מה שאין בזה ותרוייהו צריכי להאי ולהאי וי"ל דהוי מצי למימר וליטעמיך ולא גרס הכא מה שכתוב במיעוט ספרים ואי ס"ד לית ליה דינא דגוד או אגוד כי היכי דתרוייהו צריכי להאי תרוייהו צריכי להאי דהא כל שכן דאי לא צריכי תרוייהו להאי ולהאי פריך טפי שפיר אי לית ליה דינא דגוד או אגוד אמאי חולקין: מדביק אדם תורה נביאים וכתובים כאחד. אע"פ שא"א שלא יתן נביאים וכתובים על גבי תורה ובמגילה בפ"ב (דף כז.) משמע דאסור להניח ה"מ בשתי כריכות אבל כשהן מדובקין יחד אינו גנאי: רבי יהודה אומר תורה בפני עצמה. לא מפני שאסור להניח זה על גב זה מצריך שיהא כל אחד בפני עצמו דלא אשכחן שיהא אסור להניח אלא נביאים וכתובים על גבי תורה אבל נביאים על גבי כתובים או איפכא לא אלא היינו טעמא שלא יראה הכל כמו תורה או הכל נביאים כי היכי דאמרי חכמים בתר הכי דבעו שיהא כל נביא ונביא בפני עצמו וע"כ טעמא שלא יהא נראה הכל כמו נביא אחד כן נראה לרשב"א: ומסיים מלמטה ומתחיל מלמעל'. פי' בקונטרס ואינו צריך להניח ד' שיטין ונראה לר"י דבין חומש לחומש של תורה צריך להניח ובנביאים דוקא קאמר דאין צריך כדמפרש טעמא לקמן שאם בא לחתוך חותך אבל בין חומש לחומש של תורה לא מידי דהוי אפרשה פתוחה שאם היה מסיים מלמטה היה צריך להניח שיטה אחת הכא נמי דין הוא להניח בסוף כל חומש פרשה של ד' שיטין וריצב"א מפרש ומסיים מלמטה ומתחיל מלמעלה ולעולם מניח ד' שיטין ודוקא בין נביא לנביא אבל בין חומש לחומש לא יסיים מלמטה ומתחיל מלמעלה אפי' בהנחת ד' שיטין כדאמר בירושלמי בפ"ק דמגילה וצריך שיהא גומר באמצע הדף ומתחיל באמצעיתו ובנביא מסיים בסופו ומתחיל בראשו כו' ונראה לי הטעם דאין לו לסיים בסוף הדף אפי' יניח ארבעה שיטין משום שמא יבוא לחתוך אבל בין נביא לנביא שאם בא לחתוך חותך מסיים מלמטה:

ועושה בראשו כדי לגול עמוד ובסופו כדי היקף. כן כתוב בכל הספרים וקשה לר"י דתניא במס' סופרים כל הספרים נגללין לתחלתן ולקמן אמר נמי ספר עזרה לתחלתו הוא נגלל ומה שפי' הקונט' מתחלתו לסופו אין הלשון משמע כן וגבי מזוזה אמרינן נמי שכורכין אותה מאחד כלפי שמע דהיינו לתחלתה והכי איתא גרסי' בירושלמי בפ"ק דמגילה עושה אדם עמוד לספר תורה בסופו ע"כ נראה לר"י דגר' ועושה בראשו כדי היקף ובסופו כדי לגול עמוד ולרשב"א נראה לקיים גירסת הספרים והכא שאני דאיירי במדביק תורה נביאים וכתובים ולא אין נכון לעשות עמוד בסופו כמו בעלמא שגנאי הוא שתהא תורה נכרכת סביב נביאים וכתובים י) ונראה כאילו נעשית להם שומר מלכלוך לכך עושה כאן עמוד בראשו כדי שתהא תורה מבפנים ונביאים וכתובים מבחוץ ולקמן דמשני לגדלין קתני לא גרס תחלת הספר כדי לגול עמוד וסופו כדי לגול היקף דהתם לא איירי במדביק תורה נביאים וכתובים ואית לן למימר איפכא (ו) וברוב ספרים לא גרס אלא לגדלין קתני ותו לא ועוד אומר רשב"א דאפי' לספרים דגרסי לה לא קשיא כולי האי דניחא ליה לשנויי דומיא דהך ברייתא דקאי עלה:

שאם

עין משפט נר מצוה

קכא א מיי' פ"א מהל' שכנים הל' ב סמג עשין פב טוש"ע ח"מ סי' קעא סעיף ג:

קכב ב ג מיי' שם הל' ה טוש"ע שם סעיף ב:

קכג ד ה מיי' פ"ז מהל' ס"ת הלכה ט סמג שם טוש"ע ח"מ סי' קעא סעיף ו:

קכד ו ז טוש"ע ח"מ סי' קעא סעי' יג:

קכה ח ט מיי' פ"ז מהל' ס"ת הל' טו סמג עשין כה טוש"ע י"ד סי' רעג סעיף א וסי' רפג סעיף א:

רבינו גרשום

כל שאילו יחלק כל הני דאמרינן במתני' ואם לאו מעלי' אותו בדמים דהיינו גוד או אגוד אלמא אית דינא דגוד או אגוד וקשיא לרב נחמן. תנאי היא דתניא כו' דהיכא דיש לשותפין חצר של ד' אמות לחלוק דלאו ראויה לחלוקה אלא אם כן יש בה ח' אמות ואמר אחד לחבירו נחלוק חצר זה וחבירו מעכב ואמר ליה האי אמאי מעכבת טול אתה שיעור דין חלוקה הד' אמות ואני אטול פחות הג' אמות שומעין לו דאין יכול לעכב עליו הואיל דנותן לו שיעור חלוקה. אי נימ' כדקתני כלומר דליכא שום דברים בהדיהו אלא כדקתני. וגוד או אגוד נמי. כלומר דהכי אמר ליה ברור לך אחד מב' דברים הללו או טול אתה שיעור ואני פחות או גוד או אגוד ואתא רשב"ג למימר מזה שומעין לו כשאמר לו טול אתה השיעור אבל מגוד או אגוד יכול לעכב עליו דקסבר דלית דינא דגוד או אגוד אלמא תנאי היא: ודקאמרת מאי טעמא דרשב"ג דבטול אתה שיעור נמי אין שומעין דמצי מעכב אידך משום דאמר ליה אותה אמה שאתה רוצה ליתן לי יותר איני מבקש אותה לא בדמים שאין לי דמים לקנותה וגם במתנה איני מבקשה ולא מצית מוקמת לה בתנאי: הא דר' יהודה דאמר לעיל אית דינא דגוד או אגוד דשמואל היא כלומר מינה דשמואל קבלה ולא מינה דרב דרב יהודה הוה תלמיד דרב ותלמיד דשמואל והא מילתא מינה דשמואל למדה ולא מינה דרב: אלא בכרך אחד. היו נכרכין בראשית ואלה שמות משום הכי אין חולקין משום בזיון והיינו כרך שהיו רגילין לכתוב ספריהן כעין ספר תורה והפטרות שאנו כותבין ולהכי קרי כרך שכרוך כעין מגילה אבל בשתי כריכות בראשית בכרך אחד ואלה שמות בכרך אחד חולקין דליכא בזיון דספר. ואי ס"ד דלגבי חצר היכא דליכא ד' לזה וד' לזה לית דינא דגוד או אגוד אלא תרווייהו ישתמשו ביה מאי אריא בכרך אחד דאין חולקין אפי' בב' כריכות נמי אין חולקין דשתיהן צריכי לתרווייהו כריכות והוי נמי שאין בחד כרך כדי לזה ולא יחלקו אפי' בב' כריכות אלא ליקום בשותפות אלא ש"מ מדחולקין להם משום דמצי למימר ליה חבריה או חלוק או גוד עלוי דמים ואסב תרווייהו או איגוד עליך ותיסב תרווייהו. תירגמא רב שלמן מהא ליכא למשמע מינה הא דינא דאגוד ודקא קשיא לך א"כ אפילו שתי כריכות אמאי חולקין משום כשרצו שניהן לחלוק ובשתי כריכות מצי לחלוק אבל בכרך אחד לא משום בזיון אבל אי חד מעכב וחד רוצה לא מצי למימר ליה גוד או אגוד. ודרב יהודה [לאו] דשמואל היא. (א"כ): הא דרב נחמן מאי. דאמר לית דינא דגוד. מיפא פת. ובשולי מיני תבשיל. ביסתרקי בל"ע שפיע. ואתו לקמיה דרבא אחד היה רוצה בשותפות השפחות ואחד לא היה רוצה והא קא טעין ההוא דלא היה רוצה גוד לעצמך הני תרתי שפחות או אנא איגוד ואמר להו הלכה למעשה לית דינא דגוד או אגוד. דליכא דין חלוקה בהני שפחות דכל חד מינייהו צריך לעבודת של הני תרתי שפחות אלא כדקיימי מעיקרא בשותפות לוקמו אלמא לית דינא דגוד כרב נחמן: לעולם אית דינא דגוד ושאני התם גבי הני שפחות לית דינא דגוד אלא לוקמי בשותפות משום דכל חד וחד צריך לעבודת דתרווייהו וכי אמר ליה חד לחבריה שקול את חדא ואנא חדא ואי לא גוד או איגוד לא מצי למימר הכי דמצי למימר ליה הכא לא גוד איכא ולא איגוד איכא דאת לא אפשר לך בלא תרוייהו ואנא לא אפשר לי בלא תרוייהו אבל בעלמא דאפשר בחלוקה אי מעכב חד מצי למימר אידך גוד או איגוד. והא כתבי הקדש דבשתי כריכות דהני תרי כריכות צריכי לכל חד ואפי' א) אוקמינן לה דלעולם אליבא דשמואל דסבר כר' יהודה דאית דינא דגוד כדדייקינן לעיל. ומתרגם כמתרגמינן דלעולם לית דינא דגוד ושאני הכא אמאי חולקין שתי כריכות כגון ששניהם רוצין: מדביק אדם כו' בחד כרך. תורה בפני עצמה משום דאי מדביקן אהדדי כי חוזרי הדפין של נביאים נמצא שנעשית התורה שימוש לנביאים. והכשרנום. ובלבד שיניח מן הקלף פנוי ד' שיטין בין חומש לחומש כגון בין סיום בראשית לאלה שמות. של שנים עשר. של ספר תרי עשר. מסיים מלמטה. כלומר כשיגיע לסיום ספרו מסיימו מלמטה מאותו דף ומתחיל הספר אחר מלמעלה מדף אחר שאע"פ שאין בסיום אותו ספר כדי השלמת כל אותו דף אפי' הכי מניח אותו דף

חשק שלמה על רבינו גרשום א) ואפילו הכי חלוקין לה אליבא דשמואל דסבר כרב יהודה וכו'.

מסורת הש"ס

א) [לעיל יא., ג) [עירובין קב: וש"נ], ג) מהרש"א, ד) [גירי' הרמב"ם והטור וכ"ה בש"ע סי' רפג סעיף א ובין כל נביא ונביא שלשה שיטין וכן בין כל נביא ונביא של תרי עשר וגם הוא מכוון במס' סופרים פ"ב ה"ד אבל ברב אלפס איתא כמו הכא], ה) לעיל, ו) [ער' מג"א סי' כח ס"ק ד].

הגהות הב"ח

(א) גמ' מ"ש זה הכלל כל שאילו יחלק: (ב) שם למיתן לך ולי במתנה: (ג) שם תרגמא רב שלמן בששניהם רוצים מנו רבנן: (ד) שם ר"א בן עזריה וחכמים אומרים לא היו לו אלא אחד: (ה) רש"י ד"ה הכא נמי וכו' אומר לו (אף) תוס' וכו' כ"ה ס"א לו: (ו) תוס' ד"ה ועושה וכו' למימר איפכא בראשו כדי היקף ובסופו כדי לגול עמוד וברוב ספרים:

תורה אור השלם

א) עֹכֵר בֵּיתוֹ בּוֹצֵעַ בָּצַע וְשׂוֹנֵא מַתָּנֹת יִחְיֶה: [משלי טו, כז]

לעזי רש"י

טפי"ד. פירוש תכשיטי ספסלים, תכשיטים לתך (רש"י תענית דף כט ע"ב), שטיח (רש"י זבחים דף לד ע"ב ד"ה עולבא ועיין ערוך ערך אברזין ב' וערך טפיטן).

ליקוטי רש"י

ושונא מתנות יחיה. מאחר שהוא שונא מתנות כל שכן שאינו את הגזל [משלי טו, כז]. וכתבי הקדש. כגון תורה נביאים וכתובים [שבת קטז.]. ספר תורה שהוא בכרך אחד וכן נביאים וכתובים הכתובים בגליון כס"ת [לעיל יא.]. כ"ד ספרים והיו רגילים לכותבן בגליון כס"ת שלנו שלא לפיסק גגלו הדבר למחכן [לעיל יא.].

Earlier, the Gemara cited one Baraisa that supports Rav Yehudah's view. The Gemara now cites another precedent for Rav Yehudah's ruling:

אָמַר לֵיהּ אַבַּיֵי לְרַב יוֹסֵף – Abaye said to Rav Yosef: הָא דְּרַב יְהוּדָה דִּשְׁמוּאֵל הִיא – **This** statement **of Rav Yehudah's** (that a partner may say, "You set a price or I will set one") reflects the view **of Shmuel**, his teacher.[10]

Abaye cites Shmuel's commentary on our Mishnah to prove his assertion:

דִּתְנַן – **For we learned in our Mishnah:**[11] וְכִתְבֵי הַקֹּודֶשׁ אַף עַל פִּי שֶׁשְּׁנֵיהֶם רוֹצִים לֹא יַחֲלוֹקוּ – AND regarding a manuscript of THE HOLY SCRIPTURES, EVEN IF BOTH [PARTNERS] AGREE to divide it, THEY MAY NOT DIVIDE it. וְאָמַר שְׁמוּאֵל – **And Shmuel said:** לֹא שָׁנוּ אֶלָּא בְּכֶרֶךְ אֶחָד – **This** ruling **was taught only with respect to** a manuscript written in **one scroll,** because dividing the scroll in court will disgrace it.[12] אֲבָל בִּשְׁנֵי כְּרִיכוֹת חוֹלְקִין – **But with respect to** a manuscript written **in two** separate **scrolls,**[13] the law is that **we divide them**, i.e. we award one scroll to each partner. Abaye assumed that according to Shmuel, one partner can even compel the other to divide two scrolls against his will.[14] Abaye therefore argues: וְאִי סָלְקָא דַעְתָּךְ לֵית דִּינָא דְּגוּד אוֹ אֲגוּד – **Now, if you would think** that according to Shmuel, **there is no law that** one partner can declare, "Either **you set** a price **or I will set** one," מַאי אִירְיָא בְּכֶרֶךְ אֶחָד – **what is the reason that** the Mishnah's ruling (that a manuscript cannot be divided) applies only to a manuscript written **in one scroll?** אֲפִילּוּ בִּשְׁנֵי כְּרִיכִין נַמִּי – **Even** if it was written **in two scrolls,** neither partner should be able to force the other to divide.[15] Apparently, then, Shmuel must hold that one partner can force the other either to sell his share or buy the other share. Shmuel's statement is thus a precedent for Rav Yehudah's ruling.

The Gemara reinterprets Shmuel's ruling, thereby refuting Abaye's proof:

תַּרְגְּמָא רַב שַׁלְמָן בְּשֶׁשְּׁנֵיהֶן רוֹצִין – **Rav Shalman construed [Shmuel's statement] as applying** only **when the two** partners **agree** to dissolve the partnership. Since Shmuel never taught that a partnership in two scrolls can be dissolved forcibly, his ruling is not a precedent for Rav Yehudah's position (that one partner *can compel* the other to dissolve a partnership).

The Gemara continues its discussion:

אָמַר אֲמֵימָר הִלְכְתָא אִית דִּינָא דְּגוּד אוֹ אֲגוּד – **Ameimar said:** According to **halachah, there is a law that** one partner can tell another, **"You set** a price **or I will set** a price."

The Gemara asks:

אָמַר לֵיהּ רַב אַשִׁי לַאֲמֵימָר הָא דְּרַב נַחְמָן מַאי – **Rav Ashi said to Ameimar:** And as to **this** opinion **of Rav Nachman** that one partner cannot tell another, "You set a price or I will set a price," **what** about that?

The Gemara replies:

אָמַר לֵיהּ לֹא שְׁמִיעָא לִי כְּלוֹמַר לֹא סְבִירָא לִי – **[Ameimar] said to [Rav Ashi]: I did not hear** it, **as if to say: I do not agree** with it. Believing Rav Nachman's view to be incorrect, Ameimar decided the halachah in favor of Rav Yehudah.

The Gemara questions why Ameimar rejected Rav Nachman's view:

וְלֹא – **Now,** does the halachah **not** follow Rav Nachman's view? וְהָא רַבָּה בַּר חִינָּנָא וְרַב דִּימִי בַּר חִינָּנָא – **But there was** an incident involving **Rabbah bar Chinena and** his brother **Rav Dimi bar Chinena,** שְׁבַק לְהוּ אֲבוּהָ תַּרְתֵּי אַמְהָתָא – whose **father** died and **left them two maidservants.** חֲדָא יָדְעָא אַפְיָא וּבַשּׁוּלֵי וַחֲדָא יָדְעָא פִּילְכָא וְנַוּוֹלָא – **One** maidservant **knew** how to **bake and cook and one knew** how to **spin** thread **and weave.**[16] The brothers disagreed over how to divide the estate[17] וְאָתוּ לְקַמֵּיהּ דְּרָבָא – **and they came before Rava** to settle the dispute. וְאָמַר לְהוּ לֵית דִּינָא דְּגוּד אוֹ אֲגוּד – **And [Rava] told them: There is no law that** one partner can tell the other, **"You set** a price **or I will set** one."[18] Hence, Rava apparently decided in favor of Rav Nachman's position. Why, then, did Ameimar reject this ruling in favor of Rav Yehudah's?[19]

The Gemara answers by distinguishing between Rava's ruling and that of Rav Nachman:

שָׁאנֵי הָתָם – **There** in the case on which Rava ruled (where the two maidservants had dissimilar skills), it **was different,** דְּלְמַר מִיבָּעֵי לֵיהּ תַּרְוַיְיהוּ וּלְמַר מִיבָּעֵי לֵיהּ תַּרְוַיְיהוּ – **for this master**

NOTES

10. After Rav's death, Rav Yehudah traveled to Shmuel's academy and studied under him (*Rashbam* 38b and 139b).

11. 11a.

12. Cutting the scroll in two for the purpose of dividing it between two partners disgraces it (*Rashi*; cf. *Nimukei Yosef*).

13. [Where each scroll contains a different section of Scripture, e.g.] the Torah was written in one scroll and the Prophets in another (*Rashi*). [A single scroll generally has different subject matters at the beginning and end. Thus since Shmuel contrasted two scrolls to one scroll, he presumably referred to two scrolls containing different subject matter.]

14. According to our Mishnah, when two people share property, either can force the other to divide it as long as each person's share will be large enough to be used for the same purpose for which the property had previously been used. Now if two people own two scrolls jointly and the partnership is dissolved, each partner can take one scroll and use it for the same purpose as before. It thus follows that one of the partners can force the other to dissolve the partnership.

15. According to Abaye's interpretation of Shmuel's statement, if two people jointly own two scrolls, one can compel the other to dissolve the partnership (see previous note). Abaye argues that this statement is the source for Rav Yehudah's position.

As noted above, Rav Yehudah ruled that if a jointly owned field is too small to divide, one partner can force the other to either sell his share or buy the other share. In other words, instead of physically dividing the property that *both* had owned, one of the partners uses his *own* money to pay the other for his share. Shmuel's ruling provides a precedent for dissolving a partnership in such a manner, for in his case too, one of the partners must use his personal assets to compensate the other. We can see that this is so through the following reasoning.

If Shmuel indeed said that two scrolls are forcibly divided (as Abaye now maintains), he obviously could not have meant that we split each in two, for this would disgrace them. He could not have meant that we simply award one scroll to each partner either, for since any two scrolls are presumably worth different amounts, a division along these lines would be inequitable. Thus, there is only one remaining possibility: Each partner takes a scroll, and the one receiving the more valuable manuscript compensates the other with his *own* money. Shmuel's ruling, then, serves as a precedent for Rav Yehudah's ruling, for the principle in the two cases is the same: When no other method of division is practicable, one partner can be forced to compensate the other with his own money (see *Rashi*).

16. According to another version, one knew how to ornament upholstery.

17. One brother wanted them each to take one maidservant and thereby dissolve the partnership. Since the maidservants were worth different amounts, the brother receiving the more valuable maidservant would compensate the brother receiving the less valuable one. The other brother refused to divide in this way and insisted that they retain the partnership.

18. I.e. one partner cannot force the other to either receive the more valuable maidservant and pay compensation or receive the less valuable maidservant and receive compensation (*Rashi*).

19. Rava, who lived one generation after Rav Yehudah and Rav Nachman, actually followed Rav Nachman's view in practice. The Gemara therefore questions why Ameimar rejected the ruling (see *Rabbeinu Gershom*).

קח לך עבדים וירחצו במרחץ קח לך זיתים ובא ועשה בבית הבד התם נמי גוד איכא אגוד ליכא ת"ש (א) א) כל שאילו יחלק ושמו עליו חולקין אם לאו מעלין אותו בדמים תנאי היא דתניא טול אתה שיעור ואני פחות שומעין לו רבן שמעון בן גמליאל אומר ב אין שומעין לו היכי דמי אילימא כדתני מאי טעמא דרשב"ג אלא לאו חסורי מחסרא והכי קאמר טול אתה שיעור ואני פחות שומעין לו וגוד או אגוד נמי שומעין לו ואתא רשב"ג למימר אין שומעין לו לא לעולם כדקתני ודקאמרת מ"ט דרשב"ג משום דאמר ליה אי בדמי לית לי דמי למיתן לך (ב) ג במתנה לא ניחא לי דכתיב א) ושונא מתנות יחיה א"ל אביי לרב יוסף הא דרב יהודה דשמואל היא דתנן ב) וכתבי הקודש אע"פ ששניהם רוצים לא יחלוקו ואמר שמואל ד לא שנו אלא בכרך אחד אבל בשני כריכות חולקין ואי ס"ד לית דינא דגוד או אגוד מאי איריא בכרך אחד אפי' בשני כריכין נמי תרגמא רב שלמן ה בששניהן רוצין אמר אמימר הלכתא אית דינא דגוד או אגוד אמר ליה רב אשי לאמימר הא דרב נחמן מאי אמר ליה ג) לא שמיעא לי כלומר לא סבירא לי ולא והא רב' בר חיננא ורב דימי בר חיננא שבק להו אבוה תרתי אמהתא חדא ידעא אפיא ובשולי וחדא ידעא פילכא ונוולא ואתו לקמיה דרבא ואמר להו ו לית דינא דגוד או אגוד שאני התם ז דלמר מיבעי ליה תרוייהו ולמר מיבעי ליה תרוייהו כי קאמר ליה שקול את חדא ואנא חדא לאו גוד או אגוד הוא ד) (וכי לא מצי למימר הכי) והא כתבי הקדש דתרוייהו מיבעי להו ואמר שמואל לא שנו אלא בכרך אחד אבל בשני כריכין חולקין הא תרגמא רב שלמן (ג) בשרצו ת"ר ח מדביק אדם תורה נביאים וכתובים כאחד דברי ר"מ ר' יהודה אומר תורה בפני עצמה נביאים בפני עצמן וכתובים בפני עצמן וחכ"א כל אחד ואחד בפני עצמו ואמר רב יהודה מעשה בביתוס בן זונין שהיו לו שמנה נביאים מדובקין כאחד על פי ר"א בן עזריה (ד) וי"א לא היו לו אלא אחד אחד בפני עצמו אמר רבי מעשה והביאו לפנינו תורה נביאים וכתובים מדובקים כאחד והכשרנום ט בין חומש לחומש של תורה ארבעה שיטין ה) וכן בין כל נביא לנביא ובנביא של שנים עשר ג' שיטין ומסיים מלמטה ומתחיל מלמעלה ת"ר הרוצה לדבק תורה נביאים וכתובים כאחד מדבק ועושה בראשו כדי לגול עמוד ובסופו כדי לגול היקף ומסיים מלמטה ומתחיל מלמעלה ואם

רש"י

קח לך עבדים. שיתממו אותו ורחוץ בו ולא מצי עני למימר ליה קנה חלקי: הכא נמי גוד איכא אגוד ליכא. שאין העני אומר לו (ה) אף אני אקנה חלקך שאין לו במה לקנות לפיכך אין יכול לכופו: ושמו עליו. כל דבר שיש בו שיעור שאם תחלקנו עדיין יהא עליו שמו הראשון: מעלין אותו בדמים. היינו גוד או אגוד: טול אתה שיעור ואני פחות. כגון חצר שאין בה שמנה אמות ואמר זה חלוק וטול לך ד' אמות ואני המותר: וגוד או אגוד נמי. שלא רצה למחול כלום אלא קנה חלקי או אקנה חלקך: הא דרב יהודה. דאמר גוד או אגוד משמיה דרביה קבלה: בכרך אחד. כל ספריהן עשויין בגליון ואם יבאוהו לצ"ד לחלקו בזיון הוא: אבל בשתי כריכות. כגון תורה בכרך אחד ונביאים בכרך אחד: חולקין. קס"ד דאפילו אין שניהם רוצים וע"כ אין דמיהן שוין ואי לית דינא דגוד או אגוד היאך הוא כופיהו זה יאמר אני לא אתן לך עודף הדמים וגם לא אתן לך היפה שאקבל ממך דמים. ולא גרסי' תרווייהו צריכין להאי: בששניהם רוצים. הא דשמואל אשניהם רוצים דמתניתין קאי דקתני לא יחלוקו ואמר שמואל בשתי כריכות אם שניהם רוצים יחלוקו: פילכא ונוולא. לטוות ולארוג. ל"א ביסתרקי תכשיטי ספסלים שקורין טפי"ד: לית דינא דגוד או אגוד. לכופו לתת דמי העודפים ביפה ולא למכור חלקו: לאו גוד או אגוד הוא. אי לא אמר ליה או קח שתיהם או אקח שתיהם דכל אחת אין בה כדי לאחד: אבל בב' כריכות חולקין. וקס"ד בע"כ של אחד מהן אלמא כי אמר ליה שקול חדא וגוד דמי היתירים או אגוד כייפינן ליה: כל אחד ואחד בפני עצמו. כל ספר וספר של נביאים ושל כתובים צריך להיות כרך לעצמו: בביתוס שמנה נביאים. כל ספרי נביאים שמנה הן: ה"ג וכן בין כל נביא ונביא ובנביא של שנים עשר שלש שיטין ומסיים מלמטה ומתחיל מלמעלה. אם נזדמן לו סיום הספר מלמטה בסוף הדף מתחיל ספרו האחר בראש הדף ואינו צריך להניח ריוח חלק ביניהם: כדי לגול עמוד. מניח קלף חלק לגלול על גבי עמוד של עץ שהספר נגלל עליו: וסופו כדי לגול היקף. בסופו מניח חלק גדול כדי לגול בו כל הקיפו שאין עושה שני עמודים לגוללו לאמצעו כמו שאנו עושין לספר תורה אלא גוללו מתחלתו לסופו וכורך החלק על כל ההיקף: ואם

תוספות

(לעיל) שמע מינה דלית דינא דגוד או אגוד. וא"ת שאני הכא שאין העבד נותן לו דמים מיד אלא כותב לו שטר על דמיו וי"ל דמשמע משום דלא יבטל הוא דכופין הא לאו הכי אין כופין בכל ענין אפי' יתן דמים: ה) אם עשאן לשכר כו'. לאו דוקא עשאן לשכר דהוא הדין אפילו עשאן לעצמו אלא שמואלא להשכיר:

ואי ס"ד לית דינא דגוד או אגוד אפי' בשתי כריכות כו'. השתא ס"ד דחולקין כיון שאחד רוצה לחלוק וב' כריכות דומיא דכרך אחד שאין כתוב באחד מה שכתוב באחר כגון יהושע ושמואל ואמאי חולקין בע"כ והא אינם שוין אלא ודאי אית דינא דגוד או אגוד וא"ת אפילו אית דינא דגוד או אגוד אמאי חולקין כיון שכתוב בזה מה שאין בזה ותרוייהו צריכי להאי ולהאי וי"ל דהוי מצי למימר וליטעמיך ולא גרס הכא מה שכתוב במיעוט ספרים ואי ס"ד לית ליה דינא דגוד או אגוד כי היכי דתרוייהו צריכי להאי תרוייהו צריכי להאי דהא כל שכן דלאי לא צריכי תרוייהו להאי ולהאי פריך טפי שפיר אי לית ליה דינא דגוד או אגוד אמאי חולקין: מדביק אדם תורה נביאים וכתובים כאחד. אע"פ שא"א שלא יתן נביאים וכתובים על גבי תורה ובמגילה בפ"ב (דף כז.) משמע דאסור להניח ה"מ בשתי כריכות אבל כשהן מדובקין יחד אינו גנאי: רבי יהודה אומר תורה בפני עצמה. לא מפני שאסור להניח זה על גב זה מצריך שיהא כל אחד בפני עצמו דלא אשכחן שיהא אסור להניח אלא נביאים וכתובים על גבי תורה אבל נביאים על גבי כתובים או איפכא לא אלא היינו טעמא שלא יראה הכל כמו תורה או הכל נביאים כי היכי דאמרי חכמים בתר הכי דבעו שיהא כל נביא ונביא בפני עצמו וע"כ טעמא שלא יהא נראה הכל כמו נביא אחד כן נראה לרשב"א:

ומסיים מלמטה ומתחיל מלמעל'. פי' בקונטרס ואינו צריך להניח ד' שיטין ונראה לר"י דבין חומש לחומש של תורה צריך להניח ואנביאים דוקא קאמר דאין צריך כדמפרש טעמא לקמן שאם בא לחתוך חותך אבל בין חומש לחומש של תורה לא מידי דהוי אפרשה פתוחה שאם היה מסיים מלמטה היה צריך להניח שיטה אחת הכא נמי דין הוא להניח בסוף כל חומש פרשה של ד' שיטין וריב"א מפרש ומסיים מלמטה ומתחיל מלמעלה ולעולם מניח ד' שיטין ודוקא בין נביא לנביא אבל בין חומש לחומש לא יסיים מלמטה ומתחיל מלמעלה אפי' בהנחת ד' שיטין כדאמר בירושלמי בפ"ק דמגילה וצריך שיהא גומר באמצע הדף ומתחיל באמצעיתו ובנביא מסיים בסופו ומתחיל בראשו כו' ונראה לי הטעם דאין לו לסיים בסוף הדף אפי' יניח ארבעה שיטין משום שמא יבוא לחתוך אבל בין נביא לנביא שאם בא לחתוך חותך מסיים מלמטה:

ועושה בראשו כדי לגול עמוד ובסופו כדי היקף. כן כתוב בכל הספרים וקשה לר"י דתניא במס' סופרים כל הספרים נגללין לתחלתן ולקמן אמר נמי ספר עזרה לתחלתו הוא נגלל ומה שפי' הקונט' מתחלתו לסופו אין הלשון משמע כן וגבי מזוזה אמרינן נמי שכורכין אותה מאחד כלפי שמע דהיינו לתחלתה והדיא גרסי' בירושלמי בפ"ק דמגילה עושה אדם עמוד לספר תורה בסופו ע"כ נראה לר"י דגר' ועושה בראשו כדי היקף ובסופו כדי לגול עמוד ולרשב"א נראה לקיים גירסת הספרים והכא שאני דאיירי במדביק תורה נביאים וכתובים ואז אין נכון לעשות עמוד בסופו כמו בעלמא שגנאי הוא שתהא תורה נכרכת סביב נביאים וכתובים י) ונראה כאילו נעשית להם שומר מלכלוך לכך עושה כאן עמוד בראשו כדי שתהא תורה מבפנים ונביאים וכתובים מבחוץ ולקמן דמשני לאידך קתני לא גרס תחלת הספר כדי לגול עמוד וסופו כדי לגול היקף דהתם לא איירי במדביק תורה נביאים וכתובים ואית לן למימר איפכא (ו) וברוב ספרים לא גרס אלא לאידך קתני ותו לא ועוד אומר רשב"א דאפי' לספרים דגרסי לה לא קשיא כולי האי דניחא ליה לשנויי דומיא דהך ברייתא דקאי עלה:

שאם

עין משפט נר מצוה

קכא א מיי' פ"א מהל' שכנים הל' ד סמג עשין פב טוש"ע ח"מ סי' קעא סעיף ג:

קכב ב ג מיי' שם הל' ה טוש"ע שם סעיף י:

קכג ד ה מיי' פ"ב שם הלכה ט סמג שם טוש"ע ח"מ סי' קעג סעיף א:

קכד ו ז טוש"ע ח"מ סי' קעא סעי' יג:

קכה ח ט מיי' פ"ז מהל' ס"ת הל' טו סמג עשין כה טוש"ע י"ד סי' רעג סעיף א וסי' רפג סעיף א:

רבינו גרשום

כל שאילו יחלק כל הני דאמרינן במתני' ואם לאו מעלי' אותו בדמים דהיינו גוד או אגוד אלמא אית דינא דגוד או אגוד וקשיא לרב נחמן. תנאי היא דתניא כו' דהיכא דיש לשותפין חצר של ד' אמות לחלוק דלאו ראויה לחלוקה אלא אם כן יש בה ח' אמות ואמר אחד לחבירו נחלוק חצר זה וחבירו מעכב ואמר ליה האי אמאי מעכבת טול אתה שיעור דין חלוקה הד' אמות ואני אטול פחות הג' אמות שומעין לו דאין יכול לעכב עליו הואיל דנותן לו שיעור חלוקה. אי נימ' כדקתני כלומר דליכא שום דברים בהדיהו אלא כדקתני. וגוד או אגוד נמי. כלומר דהכי אמר ליה ברוך לך אחד מב' דברים הללו או טול אתה שיעור ואני פחות או גוד או אגוד ואתא רשב"ג למימר מזה שומעין לו כשאמר לו טול אתה השיעור אבל מגוד או אגוד יכול לעכב עליו דקסבר דלית דינא דגוד או אגוד אלמא תנאי היא: ודקאמרת מאי טעמא דרשב"ג דבטול אתה שיעור נמי אין שומעין דמצי מעכב אידך משום דאמר ליה אותה אמה שאתה רוצה ליתן לי יותר איני מבקש אותה לא בדמים שאין לי דמים לקנותה וגם במתנה איני מבקשה ולא מצית מוקמת לה בתנאי: הא דר' יהודה דאמר לעיל אית דינא דגוד או אגוד דשמואל היא כלומר מינה דשמואל קבלה ולא מינה דרב דרב יהודה הוה תלמיד דרב ותלמיד דשמואל והא מילתא מינה דשמואל למדה ולא מינה דרב: אלא בכרך אחד. היו נכרכין בראשית ואלה שמות משום הכי אין חולקין משום בזיון והיינו כרך שהיו רגילין לכתוב ספריהן כעין ספר תורה והפטרות שאנו כותבין ולהכי קרי כרך שכרוך כעין מגילה אבל בשתי כריכות בראשית בכרך אחד ואלה שמות בכרך אחד חולקין דליכא בזיון דספר. ואי ס"ד דלגבי חצר היכא דליכא ד' לזה וד' לזה לית דינא דגוד או אגוד אלא תרוייהו ישתמשו ביה מאי אריא בכרך אחד דאין חולקין אפי' בב' כריכות נמי אין חולקין דשתיהן צריכי לתרוייהו כריכות והוי נמי שאין בחד כרך כדי לזה ולא יחלקו אפי' בב' כריכות אלא ליקום בשותפות אלא ש"מ מדחולקין להם משום דמצי למימר ליה חבריה או חלוק או גוד עלוי דמים ואסב תרוייהו או איגוד עליך ותיסב תרוייהו. תירגמא רב שלמן מהא ליכא למשמע מינה הא דינא דאגוד ודקא קשיא לך א"כ אפילו שתי כריכות אמאי חולקין משום כשרצו שניהן לחלוק ובשתי כריכות מצי לחלוק אבל בכרך אחד לא משום בזיון אבל אי חד מעכב וחד רוצה לא מצי למימר ליה גוד או אגוד. ודרב יהודה [לאו] דשמואל היא. (א"כ): הא דרב נחמן מאי. דאמר לית דינא דגוד. מיפא פת. ובשולי מיני תבשיל. ביסתרקי בל"ע שפיע. ואתו לקמיה דרבא אחד היה רוצה בשותפות השפחות ואחד לא היה רוצה והא קא טעין ההוא דלא היה רוצה גוד לעצמך הני תרתי שפחות או אנא איגוד ואמר להו הלכה למעשה לית דינא דגוד או אגוד. דליכא דין חלוקה בהני שפחות דכל חד מינייהו צריך לעבודת של הני תרתי שפחות אלא כדקיימי מעיקרא בשותפות לוקמו אלמא לית דינא דגוד כרב נחמן: לעולם אית דינא דגוד ושאני התם גבי הני שפחות לית דינא דגוד אלא לוקמי בשותפות משום דכל חד וחד צריך לעבודת דתרוייהו וכי אמר ליה חד לחבריה שקול את חדא ואנא חדא ואי לא גוד או איגוד לא מצי למימר הכי דמצי למימר ליה הכא לא גוד איכא ולא איגוד איכא דאת לא אפשר לך בלא תרוייהו ואנא לא אפשר לי בלא תרוייהו אבל בעלמא דאפשר בחלוקה אי מעכב חד מצי למימר אידך גוד או איגוד. והא כתבי הקדש דבשתי כריכות דהני תרי כריכות צריכי לכל חד ואפי' א) אוקמינן לה דלעולם אליבא דשמואל דסבר כר' יהודה דאית דינא דגוד כדדייקינן לעיל. ומתרגם כמתרגמינן דלעולם לית דינא דגוד ושאני הכא אמאי חולקין שתי כריכות כגון ששניהם רוצין: מדביק אדם כו' בחד כרך. תורה בפני עצמה משום דאי מדביקן אהדדי כי חזרי הדפין של נביאים נמצא שנעשית התורה שימוש לנביאים. כל אחד ואחד בפני עצמו. והכשרנום. ובלבד שיניח מן הקלף פנוי ד' שיטין בין חומש לחומש כגון בין סיום בראשית לאלה שמות. של שנים עשר. של ספר תרי עשר. מסיים מלמטה. כלומר כשיגיע לסיום ספרו מסיימו מלמטה מאותו דף ומתחיל הספר אחר מלמעלה מדף אחר שאע"פ שאין בסיום אותו ספר כדי השלמת כל אותו דף אפי' הכי מניח אותו דף

מסורת הש"ס

א) [לעיל יא.], ב) [ערכין קב: וש"נ], ג) מהרש"א מ"ז, ד) [גיר' הרמב"ם והטור וכ"ה בש"ע סי' רפג סעיף א ובין כל נביא ונביא שלשה שיטין וכן בין כל נביא ונביא של תרי עשר וגם הוא מכוון במס' סופרים פ"ב ה"ד אבל ברב אלפס איתא כמו הכא], ה) לעיל, ו) [ע' מג"א סי' כח ס"ק ד].

הגהות הב"ח

(א) גמ' מ"ש זה הכלל כל שאילו יחלק: (ב) שם למיתן לך ולי במתנה: (ג) שם תרגמא רב שלמן בששניהם רוצים תנו רבנן: (ד) שם ר"א בן עזריה וחכמים אומרים לא היו לו אלא אחד: (ה) רש"י ד"ה הכא נמי וכו' אומר לו (אף) תו"מ ונ"ב ס"א או: (ו) תוס' ד"ה ועושה וכו' למימר איפכא בראשו כדי היקף ובסופו כדי לגול עמוד וברוב ספרים.

תורה אור השלם

א) עֹכֵר בֵּיתוֹ בּוֹצֵעַ בָּצַע וְשׂוֹנֵא מַתָּנֹת יִחְיֶה: [משלי טו, כז]

לעזי רש"י

טפי"ד. פירוש תכשיטי ספסלים, תכשיטי לכר (רש"י תענית דף כט סוע"ב), שטיח (רש"י זבחים דף צד ע"ב ד"ה עולבא ועיין ערוך ערך אבר ג' וערך טפיט).

ליקוטי רש"י

ושונא מתנות יחיה. מאחר שהוא שונא מתנות כל שכן ששונא את הגזל [משלי טו, כז]. וכתבי הקדש. כגון תורה נביאים וכתובים [שבת קטו.]. ספר תורה שהוא בכרך אחד וכן נביאים וכתובים הכתובים בגליון כס"ת [לעיל ג.]. כ"ד ספרים והיו רגילים לכתובן בגליון כס"ת שלנו לפיכך גנאי הדבר לחתכן [לעיל יא.].

חשק שלמה על רבינו גרשום א) [ואפילו הכי חלקין לה אליבא דשמואל דסבר כרב יהודה וכו'].

(Rabbah) **needed both [maidservants] and this master** (Rav Dimi) **needed both [maidservants].** **כִּי קָאָמַר לֵיהּ שְׁקוֹל אַתְּ חֲדָא וַאֲנָא חֲדָא** – Thus, **when** one brother **told [the other], "You take one** maidservant **and I will take** the other **one," לָאו גּוּד אוֹ אָגוּד הוּא** – **it was not** tantamount to having said, **"You set** a price **or I will set** one." In such a case even Rav Yehudah would agree that one brother cannot force the other to divide.[20] Since Rava never rejected Rav Yehudah's view, Ameimar accepts it, because he believed it to be more correct.

The Gemara challenges Rava's ruling:

(וְכִי לָא מָצֵי לְמֵימַר הָכִי) – **And is it true that [a partner] cannot say ["You take one maidservant, I will take one maidservant"]** because each needed both maidservants?[21] **וְהָא כִּתְבֵי הַקֹּדֶשׁ דְּתַרְוַיְיהוּ מִיבָּעֵי לְהוּ** – **But** if a manuscript of **Holy Scriptures** was written in two scrolls, this too is a case **where both [partners] need [both scrolls],** **וְאָמַר שְׁמוּאֵל לֹא שָׁנוּ אֶלָּא בִּכְרֵךְ אֶחָד** – **and** yet **Shmuel said: [The Mishnah] taught** its ruling **only with respect to** a manuscript of Scriptures written in **a single scroll,** **אֲבָל בִּשְׁנֵי כְּרִיכִין חוֹלְקִין** – **but with respect to** a manuscript written in **two** separate **scrolls,** the Mishnah agrees that **we divide [the scrolls]** even against the will of one partner. This proves that according to Shmuel, if partners jointly own two things, one can compel the other to take one thing and either pay or receive compensation. – ? –

Citing the interpretation of Shmuel's statement mentioned above, the Gemara refutes the proof:

הָא תַּרְגְּמָא רַב שַׁלְמָן בְּשֶׁרָצוּ – **Rav Shalman** already **construed [Shmuel's statement] as applying** only **when** the partners **agreed** to dissolve the partnership. Since Shmuel never ruled that two scrolls can be divided forcibly, there is no precedent for maintaining that maidservants are divided forcibly either.

This passage about the division of scrolls of Scripture concludes the Gemara's discussion of "you set or I will set." The Gemara now takes up the question of whether individual scrolls of various parts of Scripture may be combined to form a single scroll:

תָּנוּ רַבָּנָן – **The Rabbis taught in a Baraisa:** **מַדְבִּיק אָדָם תּוֹרָה נְבִיאִים וּכְתוּבִים כְּאֶחָד** – **A PERSON MAY JOIN** scrolls of **THE PENTATEUCH, PROPHETS**[22] **AND WRITINGS**[23] **TOGETHER** to form a single scroll; **דִּבְרֵי רַבִּי מֵאִיר** – these are **THE WORDS OF R' MEIR.** **רַבִּי יְהוּדָה אוֹמֵר** – **R' YEHUDAH SAYS:** One who wishes to join books of Scripture together may do so provided that **תּוֹרָה בִּפְנֵי עַצְמָהּ** – **THE PENTATEUCH IS** in a scroll **BY ITSELF,** **נְבִיאִים בִּפְנֵי עַצְמָן** – **THE PROPHETS IS BY ITSELF** **וּכְתוּבִים בִּפְנֵי עַצְמָן** – **AND THE WRITINGS IS BY ITSELF.**[24] **וַחֲכָמִים אוֹמְרִים** – **BUT THE SAGES SAY:** **כָּל אֶחָד וְאֶחָד בִּפְנֵי עַצְמוֹ** – **EACH** book of the Prophets and Writings must be in a scroll **BY ITSELF.**[25]

R' Yehudah cites evidence for his position vis-a-vis that of the Sages:

וְאָמַר [רַבִּי] (רַב)[26] **יְהוּדָה** – **AND R' YEHUDAH SAID:** **מַעֲשֶׂה בְּבַיְתוֹס בֶּן זוֹנִין** – **IT HAPPENED WITH BEISSUS SON OF ZUNIN,** **שֶׁהָיוּ לוֹ שְׁמֹנָה נְבִיאִים מְדוּבָּקִין כְּאֶחָד** – **THAT HE HAD THE EIGHT BOOKS OF THE PROPHETS JOINED TOGETHER** in one scroll, **עַל פִּי רַבִּי אֶלְעָזָר בֶּן עֲזַרְיָה** – and this was **SANCTIONED**[27] **BY R' ELAZAR BEN AZARYAH.**

The Baraisa records a version of the preceding episode that accords with the Sages' position:

וְיֵשׁ אוֹמְרִים לֹא הָיוּ לוֹ אֶלָּא אֶחָד אֶחָד בִּפְנֵי עַצְמוֹ – **BUT SOME SAY**[28] that **[BEISSUS] HAD EACH** book of the Prophets in a scroll **BY ITSELF.**

Rebbi relates an incident in support of R' Meir's view:

אָמַר רַבִּי – **REBBI SAID:** **מַעֲשֶׂה וְהֵבִיאוּ לְפָנֵינוּ** – **IT HAPPENED THAT THEY BROUGHT BEFORE US** **תּוֹרָה נְבִיאִים וּכְתוּבִים מְדוּבָּקִים כְּאֶחָד** – the books of **THE PENTATEUCH, PROPHETS AND WRITINGS JOINED TOGETHER** in a single scroll, **וְהִכְשַׁרְנוּם** – **AND WE DECLARED THEM FIT FOR USE.**

The Baraisa continues with other laws that pertain to the combination of books of Scripture in a single scroll:

בֵּין חוּמָּשׁ לְחוּמָּשׁ שֶׁל תּוֹרָה אַרְבָּעָה שִׁיטִין – **BETWEEN ONE BOOK OF THE PENTATEUCH AND ANOTHER, FOUR LINES** must be left blank. **וְכֵן בֵּין כָּל נָבִיא לְנָבִיא** – **SIMILARLY, BETWEEN ONE BOOK OF THE PROPHETS AND ANOTHER,** four lines must be left blank.[29] **וּבְנָבִיא**

NOTES

20. Rav Yehudah ruled on a case in which two people owned property large enough to be used jointly but too small to be divided into two usable portions. In such a case, if one partner offers to either sell his entire share to the other or to buy the other share, whoever receives the land will be left with a usable portion. Rav Yehudah therefore maintains that one partner can force the other to accept such an offer. Similarly, Rav Yehudah would hold that if one of Chinena's sons had offered to sell or buy his share in *both* maidservants, that son could have compelled his brother to choose between the proposals (see *Rashi;* see, however, *Tur* §171 and *Derishah* there §21). In the case presented to Rava, though, neither brother made such an offer. Rather, one partner insisted that each take one maidservant and the one receiving the more valuable maidservant should compensate the other. Even Rav Yehudah might agree that the other partner can refuse such an offer, claiming, "I need the services of both maidservants. I therefore demand that we remain partners rather than each of us receiving one maidservant." [This is true even if the maidservants are of equal value (*Rosh*).]

The following distinction thus emerges. If one partner offers the other a choice that will afford him ownership of an entire thing, he can compel the other partner to accept the offer. If, however, he offers only to divide two things with different functions, the other partner can refuse the offer.

21. The *Vilna Shas* places these words in parentheses. However, the thrust of the Gemara's question is the same whether or not this phrase is included in the text.

22. נְבִיאִים, *Prophets,* consists of the following eight books: 1) יְהוֹשֻׁעַ, *Joshua;* 2) שׁוֹפְטִים, *Judges;* 3) שְׁמוּאֵל, *Samuel;* 4) מְלָכִים, *Kings;* 5) יִרְמְיָהוּ, *Jeremiah;* 6) יְחֶזְקֵאל, *Ezekiel;* 7) יְשַׁעְיָהוּ, *Isaiah;* 8) תְּרֵי עָשָׂר, *The Twelve Prophets.*

23. כְּתוּבִים, *Writings,* consists of eleven books: 1) תְּהִלִּים, *Psalms;* 2) מִשְׁלֵי, *Proverbs;* 3) אִיּוֹב, *Job;* 4) שִׁיר הַשִּׁירִים, *Song of Songs;* 5) רוּת, *Ruth;* 6) אֵיכָה, *Lamentations;* 7) קֹהֶלֶת, *Ecclesiastes;* 8) אֶסְתֵּר, *Esther;* 9) דָּנִיֵּאל, *Daniel;* 10) עֶזְרָא־נְחֶמְיָה, *Ezra-Nehemiah;* 11) דִּבְרֵי הַיָּמִים, *Chronicles.*

24. According to R' Yehudah, it is forbidden to combine one of the three parts of the Scriptures (the Pentateuch, Prophets and Writings) with another, because if they are combined, the impression might be given that all the books in the combined scroll belong to the Pentateuch or the Prophets [or the Writings] (*Tosafos*).

25. The individual books of the Prophets and Writings may not be joined together, because, if they are, the impression might be given that they were all written by the same prophet (*Tosafos*).

This ruling applies only to the books of the Prophets and Writings. As far as the five books of the Pentateuch are concerned, they may be combined into a single scroll, even according to the Sages (see *Rashi*). Indeed, *Shulchan Aruch* (*Yoreh Deah* 283:1) writes that scrolls of the five books of the Pentateuch, which are *not* joined together, are unfit for the communal Torah readings and it is disputed whether they are imbued with קְדֻשַּׁת סֵפֶר תּוֹרָה, *the sanctity of a Torah scroll.*

26. *Rashash* emends the text to read רַבִּי, *Rebbi* (abbreviated to R'). Since the following passage is a continuation of the Baraisa, the reference must be to R' Yehudah (the Tanna), not Rav Yehudah (the Amora).

27. Literally: by the mouth of.

28. *Bach* emends this to read: וַחֲכָמִים אוֹמְרִים, *But the Sages say.* [The Sages proceed to defend their position that each book of the Prophets (and Writings) must be in a scroll of its own.]

29. [This clause accords with the view of R' Meir and R' Yehudah that the books of the Prophets may be combined in a single scroll.]

Rambam (*Hil. Sefer Torah* 7:15) follows an alternative version of the Baraisa's text, according to which only *three* blank lines are required between each book of the Prophets. The halachah is in accordance with this view.

קח לך עבדים וירחצו במרחץ קח לך זיתים ובא ועשה בבית הבד התם נמי גוד איכא אגוד ליכא ת"ש (א) כל שאילו יחלק ושמו עליו חולקין אם לאו מעלין אותו בדמים תנאי היא דתניא טול אתה שיעור ואני פחות שומעין לו רבן שמעון בן גמליאל אומר אין שומעין לו היכי דמי אילימא כדתני מאי טעמא דרשב"ג אלא לאו חסורי מחסרא והכי קאמר טול אתה שיעור ואני פחות שומעין לו וגוד או אגוד נמי שומעין לו ואתא רשב"ג למימר אין שומעין לו לא לעולם כדקתני ודקאמרת מ"ט דרשב"ג משום דאמר ליה אי בדמי לית לי דמי למיתן לך (ב) במתנה לא ניחא לי דכתיב א) ושונא מתנות יחיה א"ל אביי לרב יוסף הא דרב יהודה דשמואל היא דתנן וכתבי הקודש אע"פ ששניהם רוצים לא יחלוקו ואמר שמואל לא שנו אלא בכרך אחד אבל בשני כריכות חולקין ואי ס"ד לית דינא דגוד או אגוד מאי איריא בכרך אחד אפי' בשני כריכין נמי תרגמא רב שלמן בששניהן רוצין אמר אמימר הלכתא אית דינא דגוד או אגוד אמר ליה רב אשי לאמימר הא דרב נחמן מאי אמר ליה לא שמיע לי כלומר לא סבירא לי ולא והא רב' בר חיננא ורב דימי בר חיננא שבק להו אבוה תרתי אמהתא חדא ידעא אפיא ובשולי וחדא ידעא פילכא ונוולא ואתו לקמיה דרבא ואמר להו לית דינא דגוד או אגוד שאני התם דלמר מיבעי ליה תרווייהו ולמר מיבעי ליה תרווייהו כי קאמר ליה שקול את חדא ואנא חדא לאו גוד או אגוד הוא (וכי לא מצי למימר הכי) והא כתבי הקדש דתרווייהו מיבעי להו ואמר שמואל לא שנו אלא בכרך אחד אבל בשני כריכין חולקין הא תרגמא רב שלמן (ג) בשרצו ת"ר מדביק אדם תורה נביאים וכתובים כאחד דברי ר"מ ר' יהודה אומר תורה בפני עצמה נביאים בפני עצמן וכתובים בפני עצמן וחכ"א כל אחד ואחד בפני עצמו ואמר רב יהודה מעשה בביתוס בן זונין שהיו לו שמונה נביאים מדובקין כאחד על פי ר"א בן עזריה (ד) וי"א לא היו לו אלא אחד אחד בפני עצמו אמר רבי מעשה והביאו לפנינו תורה נביאים וכתובים מדובקים כאחד והכשרנום בין חומש לחומש של תורה ארבעה שיטין וכן בין כל נביא לנביא ובנביא של שנים עשר ג' שיטין ומסיים מלמטה ומתחיל מלמעלה ת"ר הרוצה לדבק תורה נביאים וכתובים כאחד מדבק ועושה בראשו כדי לגול עמוד ובסופו כדי לגול היקף ומסיים מלמטה ומתחיל מלמעלה ואם

רש"י

קח לך עבדים. שיממנו אותו ורחוץ בו ולא מצי עני למימר ליה קנה חלקי: הכא נמי גוד איכא אגוד ליכא. שאין העני אומר לו (ה) אף אני אקנה חלקך שאין לו במה לקנות לפיכך אין יכול לכופו: ושמו עליו. כל דבר שיש בו שיעור שאם תחלקנו עדיין יהא עליו שמו הראשון: מעלין אותו בדמים. היינו גוד או אגוד: טול אתה שיעור ואני פחות. כגון חצר שאין בה שמונה אמות ואמר זה חלוק וטול לך ד' אמות ואני המותר: וגוד או אגוד נמי. שלא רצה למחול כלום אלא קנה חלקי או אקנה חלקך: הא דרב יהודה. דאמר גוד או אגוד משמיה דרביה קבלה: בכרך אחד. כל ספריהן עשוין בגליון ואם יביאהו לב"ד לחלקו בזיון הוא: אבל בשתי כריכות. כגון תורה בכרך אחד ונביאים בכרך אחד: חולקין. קס"ד דאפילו אין שניהם רוצים וע"כ אין דמיהן שוין ואי לית דינא דגוד או אגוד היאך הוא כופיהו זה יאמר אני לא אתן לך עודף הדמים וגם לא אתן לך היפה שאקבל ממך דמים. ולא גרסי' תרווייהו צריכין להאי: בששניהם רוצים. הא דשמואל אשניהם רוצים דמתניתין קאי דקתני לא יחלוקו ואמר שמואל בשתי כריכות אם שניהם רוצים יחלוקו: פילכא ונוולא. לטוות ולארוג. ל"א ביסתרקי תכשיטי ספסלים שקורין טפי"ד: לית דינא דגוד או אגוד. לכופו לתת דמי העודפים ביפה ולא למכור חלקו: לאו גוד או אגוד הוא. אי לא אמר ליה או קח שתיהם או אקח שתיהם דלכל אחת אין בה כדי לאחד: אבל בב' כריכות חולקין. וקס"ד בע"כ של אחד מהן אלמא כי אמר ליה שקול חדא וגוד דמי היתירים או אגוד כייפינן ליה: כל אחד ואחד בפני עצמו. כל ספר וספר של נביאים ושל כתובים צריך להיות כרך לעצמו: בביתוס שמנה נביאים. כל ספרי נביאים שמנה הן: ה"ג וכן בין כל נביא ונביא ובנביא של שנים עשר שלש שיטין ומסיים מלמטה ומתחיל מלמעלה. אם נזדמן לו סיום הספר מלמטה בסוף הדף מתחיל ספרו האחר בראש הדף ואינו צריך להניח ריוח חלק ביניהם: כדי לגול עמוד. מניח קלף חלק לגלול על גבי עמוד של עץ שהספר נגלל עליו: וסופו כדי לגול היקף. בסופו מניח חלק גדול כדי לגול בו כל הקיפו שאין עושה שני עמודים לגוללו לאמצעו כמו שאנו עושין לספר תורה אלא גוללו מתחלתו לסופו וכורך החלק על כל ההיקף: ואם

תוספות

(לעיל) שמע מינה דלית דינא דגוד או אגוד. ול"ת שאני הכא שאין העבד נותן לו דמים מיד אלא כותב לו שטר על דמיו וי"ל דמשמע משום דלא יבטל הוא דכופין הא לאו הכי אין כופין בכל ענין אפי' יתן דמים: (ה) אם עשאן לשכר כו'. לאו דוקא עשאן לשכר דהוא הדין אפילו עשאן לעצמו אלא שמוצא להשכיר:

ואי ס"ד לית דינא דגוד או אגוד אפי' בשתי כריכות כו'. השתא ס"ד דחולקין כיון שאחד רוצה לחלוק וב' כריכות דומיא דכרך אחד שאין כתוב באחד מה שכתוב באחר כגון יהושע ושמואל ואמאי חולקין בע"כ והא אינם שוין אלא ודאי אית דינא דגוד או אגוד וא"ת אפילו אית דינא דגוד או אגוד אמאי חולקין כיון שכתוב בזה מה שאין בזה ותרווייהו צריכי להאי ולהאי וי"ל דהוי מצי למימר וליטעמיך ולא גרס הכא מה שכתוב במיעוט ספרים ואי ס"ד לית ליה דינא דגוד או אגוד כי היכי דתרווייהו צריכי להאי תרווייהו צריכי להאי דהא כל שכן דאי לא צריכי תרווייהו להאי ולהאי פריך טפי שפיר אי לית ליה דינא דגוד או אגוד אמאי חולקין: מדביק אדם תורה נביאים וכתובים כאחד. אע"פ שא"א שלא יתן נביאים וכתובים על גבי תורה ובמגילה בפ"ב (דף כז.) משמע דאסור להניח ה"מ בשתי כריכות אבל כשהן מדובקין יחד אינו גנאי: רבי יהודה אומר תורה בפני עצמה. לא מפני שאסור להניח זה על גב זה מצריך שיהא כל אחד בפני עצמו דלא אשכחן שיהא אסור להניח אלא נביאים וכתובים על גבי תורה אבל נביאים על גבי כתובים או איפכא לא אלא היינו טעמא שלא יראה הכל כמו תורה או הכל נביאים כי היכי דאמרי חכמים בתר הכי דבעו שיהא כל נביא ונביא בפני עצמו וע"כ טעמא שלא יהא נראה הכל כמו נביא אחד כן נראה לרשב"א: ומסיים מלמטה ומתחיל מלמעל'. פי' בקונטרס ואינו צריך להניח ד' שיטין ונראה לר"י דבין חומש לחומש של תורה צריך להניח ואנביאים דוקא קאמר דאין צריך כדמפרש טעמא לקמן שאם בא לחתוך חותך אבל בין חומש לחומש של תורה לא מידי דהוי אפרשה פתוחה שאם היה מסיים מלמטה היה צריך להניח שיטה אחת הכא נמי דין הוא להניח בסוף כל חומש פרשה של ד' שיטין ורשב"א מפרש ומסיים מלמטה ומתחיל מלמעלה ולעולם מניח ד' שיטין ודוקא בין נביא לנביא אבל בין חומש לחומש לא יסיים מלמטה ומתחיל מלמעלה אפי' בהנחת ד' שיטין כדאמר בירושלמי בפ"ק דמגילה וצריך שיהא גומר באמצע הדף ומתחיל באמצעיתו ובנביא מסיים בסופו ומתחיל בראשו כו' ונראה לי הטעם דאין לו לסיים בסוף הדף אפי' יניח ארבעה שיטין משום שמא יבוא לחתוך אבל בין נביא לנביא שאם בא לחתוך חותך מסיים מלמטה:

ועושה בראשו כדי לגול עמוד ובסופו כדי היקף. כן כתוב בכל הספרים וקשה לר"י דתניא במס' סופרים כל הספרים נגללין לתחלתן ולקמן אמר נמי ספר עזרה לתחלתו הוא נגלל ומה שפי' הקונט' מתחלתו לסופו אין הלשון משמע כן וגבי מזוזה אמרינן נמי שכורכין אותה מאחד כלפי שמע דהיינו לתחלתה והדיא גרסי' בירושלמי בפ"ק דמגילה עושה אדם עמוד לספר תורה בסופו ע"כ נראה לר"י דגר' ועושה בראשו כדי היקף ובסופו כדי לגול עמוד ולרשב"א נראה לקיים גירסת הספרים והכא שאני דאיירי במדביק תורה נביאים וכתובים ואז אין נכון לעשות עמוד בסופו כמו בעלמא שגנאי הוא שתהא תורה נכרכת סביב נביאים וכתובים (י) ונראה כאילו נעשית להם שומר מלכלוך לכך עושה כאן עמוד בראשו כדי שתהא תורה מבפנים ונביאים וכתובים מבחוץ ולקמן דמשני לאדין קתני לא גרס תחלת הספר כדי לגול עמוד וסופו כדי לגול היקף דהתם לא איירי במדביק תורה נביאים וכתובים ואית לן למימר איפכא (ו) וברוב ספרים לא גרס אלא לאדין קתני ותו לא ועוד אומר רשב"א דאפי' לספרים דגרסי לה לא קשיא כולי האי דניחא ליה לשנויי דומיא דהך ברייתא דקאי עלה:

עין משפט נר מצוה

קכא א מיי' פ"א מהל' שכנים הל' ו סמג עשין פב טוש"ע ח"מ סי' קעא סעיף ג:

קכב ב ג מיי' שם הל' ה טוש"ע שם סעיף ה:

קכג ד ה מיי' פ"ב שם הלכה ט סמג שם טוש"ע ח"מ סי' קעא סעיף ו:

קכד ו ז טוש"ע ח"מ סי' קעה סעיף יג:

קכה ח ט מיי' פ"ז מהל' ס"ת הל' טו סמג עשין כה טוש"ע י"ד סי' רעג סעיף א וסי' רפג סעיף א:

רבינו גרשום

כל שאילו יחלק כל הני דאמרינן במתני' ואם לאו מעלי' אותו בדמים דהיינו דינא דגוד או אגוד וקשיא לרב נחמן. תנאי היא דתניא כו' דהכא דיש לשותפין חצר של ד' אמות לחלוק דלאו ראויה לחלוקה אלא אם כן יש בה ח' אמות ואמר אחד לחבירו נחלוק חצר זה וחבירו מעכב ואמר ליה האי אמאי מעכבת טול אתה שיעור דין חלוקה הד' אמות ואני אטול פחות הג' אמות שומעין לו דאין יכול לעכב עליו הואיל דנותן לו שיעור חלוקה. אי נימא כדקתני כלומר דליכא שום דברים בהדיהו אלא כדקתני. וגוד או אגוד נמי. כלומר דהכי אמר ליה ברור לך אחד מב' דברים הללו או טול אתה שיעור ואני פחות או גוד או אגוד ואתא רשב"ג למימר מזה שומעין לו כשאמר לו טול אתה השיעור אבל מגוד או אגוד אין יכול לעכב עליו דקסבר דלית דינא דגוד או אגוד אלמא תנאי היא: ודקאמרת מאי טעמא דרשב"ג דבטול נמי אין שומעין למה מעכב אידך משום דאמר ליה אותה אמה שאתה רוצה ליתן לי יותר איני מבקש אותה לא בדמים שאין לי דמים לקנותה וגם במתנה איני מבקשה לפי שאינה מקובלת לה בתנאי: הא דר' יהודה דאמר לעיל לית דינא דגוד או אגוד דשמואל היא כלומר מינה דשמואל קבלה ולא מינה דרב דהא רב יהודה תלמיד דרב ותלמיד דשמואל והא מילתא מינה דשמואל למדה ולא מינה דרב: אלא בכרך אחד. היו נכרכין בראשית ואלה שמות משום הכי אין חולקין משום דבזיון הוא כך שהיו רגילין לכתוב ספריהן כעין ספר תורה והפטרות שאנו כותבין ולהכי קרי כרך שכרוך כעין מגילה אבל בשתי כריכות בראשית בכרך אחד ואלה שמות בכרך אחד חולקין דליכא בזיון דספר. ואי ס"ד דלגבי דבר דלזה וד' לזה לית דינא דגוד או אגוד אלא תרווייהו דמשתמשו ביה מאי אריא בכרך אחד דאין חולקין אפי' בב' כריכות נמי אין חולקין דשתיהן צריכי לתרווייהו כריכות והוי כמו שאין בהד כרך כדי לזה וכדי לזה ולא יחלקו אפי' בב' כריכות אלא ליקום בשותפות אלא ש"מ מדחולקין להם משום דלא מצי למימר ליה

חבריה או חלוק או גוד עלוי דמים ואסב תרווייהו או אגוד עליך ותיסב תרווייהו. תרגמא רב שלמן מהא דליכא למשמע מינה הא דינא דגוד ודקא קשיא לך א"כ אפילו שתי כריכות אמאי חולקין משום כשרצו שניהן לחלוק ובשתי כריכות מצי לחלוק אבל בכרך אחד לא משום בזיון אבל אי לא מעכב חד מינייהו לא מצי למימר ליה גוד או אגוד. ודרב יהודה [לאו] דשמואל היא. (א"כ): הא דרב נחמן מאי. דאמר לית דינא דגוד. אפיא פת. ובשולי מיני תבשיל. ביסתרקי בל"ע שפיע. ואתו לקמיה דרבא אחד היה רוצה בשותפות השפחות ואחד לא היה רוצה והא קא טעין גוד הוא. ואמר להו הלכה למעשה לית דינא דגוד או אגוד. דליכא הכי חד מינייהו דמכל מקום לא אמר חד כדקיימי מעיקרא בשותפות דלוקמו אלא דינא לית דינא דגוד כרב נחמן: לעולם אית דינא דגוד ושאני התם בהני שפחות לית דינא דגוד אלא לוקי בשותפות משום דכל חד וחד צריך לעבודת תרווייהו וכי אמר ליה לחבריה שקול את חדא ואנא חדא ואי לא גוד או אגוד לא מצי למימר הכי דמצי למימר ליה הכא לא גוד איכא ולא אגוד איכא דאת לא אפשר לך בלא תרווייהו ואנא לא אפשר לי בלא תרווייהו אבל בעלמא דאפשר בחלוקה אי מעכב חד מצי אידך למימר גוד או אגוד. והא כתבי הקדש דתרווייהו מיבעי להו ואפ"ה בב' כריכות חולקין. ומתרגם כשרצו שניהם לחלוק. מדביק אדם כו'. תורה בפני עצמה ... של שנים עשר. של ספר תרי עשר. כלומר כשיגיע לסיום ספרו מסיים מלמטה מאותו דף: ומתחיל הספר אחר מלמעלה מדף אחר שאע"פ שאין בסיום אותו ספר כדי השלמת כל אותו דף אפי' הכי מניח אותו דף

חשק שלמה על רבינו גרשום א) ואפילו אינו חולקין לא אליבא דשמואל דסבר כרב יהודה וכו'].

מסורת הש"ס

א) [לעיל יא.], ב) [ערכין כב:], ג) [וש"נ], ג) מהרש"ל מ"ז, ד) [גי' הרמב"ם והטור וכ"ה בש"ע סי' רפג סעיף א ובין כל נביא ונביא שלשה שיטין וכן בין כל נביא ונביא של תרי עשר וגם הוא מכוון במס' סופרים פ"ב ה"ד אבל ברב אלפס איתא כמו הכא], ה) [לעיל], ו) [עי' מג"א סי' כח ס"ק ד].

הגהות הב"ח

(א) גמ' מ"ש זה הכלל כל שאילו יחלק: (ב) שם למיתן לך ואי במתנה: (ג) שם תרגמא רב שלמן בששניהם רוצים תנו רבנן: (ד) שם ר"א בן עזריה וחכמים אומרים לא היו לו אלא אחד: (ה) רש"י ד"ה הכא נמי וכו' אומר לו (אף) תו"מ ונ"ב ס"א או: (ו) תוס' ד"ה ועושה וכו' למימר איפכא בראשו כדי היקף ובסופו כדי לגול עמוד וברוב ספרים:

תורה אור השלם

א) עֹכֵר בֵּיתוֹ בּוֹצֵעַ בָּצַע וְשׂוֹנֵא מַתָּנֹת יִחְיֶה: [משלי טו, כז]

לעזי רש"י

טפי"ד. פירוש תכשיטי ספסלים, תכשיטים למעבר (רש"י תענית דף כט סוע"ב), שטיח (רש"י זבחים דף לב ע"א ד"ה עולבא ועיין ערוך ערך אבריז ג' וערך טפיט).

ליקוטי רש"י

ושונא מתנות יחיה. מאחר שהוא שונא מתנות כל שכן שאינו גוזל את הגזל [משלי טו, כז]. וכתבי הקדש. כגון תורה נביאים וכתובים [שבת קטו.]. ספר תורה שהוא בכרך אחד וכן נביאים וכתובים הכתובים בגליון כס"ת [לעיל ג.]. כ"ד ספרים והיו רגילין לכותבן בגליון כס"ת שלא לפיכך גנאי הדבר לחתכן [לעיל יא.].

שֶׁל שְׁנֵים עָשָׂר שָׁלֹשׁ שִׁיטִין – BUT between each PROPHETIC WORK OF THE TWELVE PROPHETS, only THREE LINES must be left blank.[30]

An exception to the rule that lines are left blank between one book and another:

וּמְסַיֵּים מִלְּמַטָּה – HOWEVER, if ONE FINISHES a book of Scripture AT THE BOTTOM of a column, וּמַתְחִיל מִלְמַעְלָה – ONE STARTS the next book AT THE TOP of the next column, without leaving any lines blank.[31]

A related Baraisa:

תָּנוּ רַבָּנָן – **The Rabbis taught in a Baraisa:** הָרוֹצֶה לְדַבֵּק תּוֹרָה נְבִיאִים וּכְתוּבִים כְּאֶחָד מְדַבֵּק – ONE WHO WISHES TO JOIN scrolls of THE PENTATEUCH, THE PROPHETS AND WRITINGS TOGETHER MAY DO SO.[32] וְעוֹשֶׂה בְּרֹאשׁוֹ כְּדֵי לָגוֹל עַמּוּד – AT THE BEGINNING [OF THIS SCROLL] ONE MUST LEAVE[33] ENOUGH blank parchment TO WIND AROUND its POLE.[34] וּבְסוֹפוֹ כְּדֵי לָגוֹל הֶיקֵּף – AT THE END of the scroll, one must leave ENOUGH blank parchment TO WIND AROUND THE CIRCUMFERENCE of the entire scroll. וּמְסַיֵּים מִלְּמַטָּה – If ONE FINISHES a book of Scriptures AT THE BOTTOM of a column, וּמַתְחִיל מִלְמַעְלָה – ONE BEGINS the next book AT THE TOP of the next column, without leaving any lines blank.

NOTES

30. The final book of the Prophets consists of twelve short prophetic works: 1) הוֹשֵׁעַ, *Hosea;* 2) יוֹאֵל, *Joel;* 3) עָמוֹס, *Amos;* 4) עֹבַדְיָה, *Obadiah,* 5) יוֹנָה, *Jonah;* 6) מִיכָה, *Micah;* 7) נַחוּם, *Nachum;* 8) חֲבַקּוּק, *Habakuk,* 9) צְפַנְיָה, *Zephaniah;* 10) חַגַּי, *Haggai,* 11) זְכַרְיָה, *Zechariah;* 12) מַלְאָכִי, *Malachi.* Because of their brevity, these works were combined into a single book – תְּרֵי עָשָׂר, *The Twelve Prophets* – for fear that otherwise they might become lost (Gemara 14b).

31. The reason for this is given below – Gemara 14a and note 3 there.

32. The opinion of R' Meir.

33. Literally: and he makes.

34. Scrolls of Scripture are wound around a single pole (with the exception of Torah scrolls which are wound around two poles) (see *Rashi*).

וְאִם בָּא לַחֲתוֹךְ חוֹתֵךְ – AND IF ONE WISHES TO CUT the scroll to separate the books of the Prophets or Writings from each other, ONE MAY DO SO.[1]

The Gemara questions the need for the Baraisa's last ruling:

מַאי קָאָמַר – **What** is **[the Baraisa] saying?** It is obvious that these books may be separated. No one disputes that preferably each book of the Prophets and Writings should be in a scroll of its own.[2] – ? –

The Gemara answers that the Baraisa's last sentence is not an independent ruling but an explanation of its previous ruling that if a book ends at the bottom of a column, the next book should begin at the top of the next column:

הָכִי קָאָמַר – **This is what [the Baraisa] is saying:** שֶׁאִם בָּא לַחֲתוֹךְ חוֹתֵךְ – *because* **if one wishes to cut** the scroll **one may do so,** and it would be unseemly for a book to begin with four blank lines.[3]

The preceding Baraisa taught that enough blank parchment must be left at the beginning of a scroll to wind around its pole and at the end of a scroll to wind around its circumference. The Gemara cites a Baraisa that apparently contradicts this:

וּרְמִינְהִי – **But contrast [the previous Baraisa]** with the following one: תְּחִלַּת סֵפֶר וְסוֹפוֹ כְּדֵי לָגוֹל – AT THE BEGINNING OF A SCROLL AND ITS END, ENOUGH parchment must be left blank TO WIND AROUND.

It is not clear from this Baraisa how much parchment must be left blank. However, it does imply that there is no difference in this regard between the beginning and end of a scroll. This Baraisa, therefore, contradicts the previous one.

The Gemara elaborates the contradiction:

כְּדֵי לָגוֹל מַאי – When the latter Baraisa says, "ENOUGH TO WIND AROUND," **what** does it mean? אִי כְּדֵי לָגוֹל עַמּוּד – **If** it means **enough to wind around a pole,** קַשְׁיָא הֶקֵּף – there is a **contradiction** between this Baraisa and the previous one which requires enough blank parchment at the *end* of a scroll to wind around the **circumference** of the scroll. אִי כְּדֵי לָגוֹל הֶקֵּף – **If** it means **enough to wind around the circumference** of the scroll, קַשְׁיָא עַמּוּד – there is a **contradiction** between this Baraisa and the previous one which ruled that at the *beginning* of a scroll enough blank parchment to wind around the **pole** is sufficient. – ? –

Rav Nachman resolves the problem:

אָמַר רַב נַחְמָן בַּר יִצְחָק – **Rav Nachman bar Yitzchak said:** לִצְדָדִין קָתָנֵי – **The Baraisa's term,** "enough to wind around," **has two meanings:** In reference to the beginning of a scroll, it means enough to wind around the pole; in reference to the end of a scroll, it means enough to wind around the circumference of the scroll.[4]

Rav Ashi offers a different solution:

רַב אַשִׁי אָמַר – **Rav Ashi says:** כִּי תַּנְיָא הַהִיא בְּסֵפֶר תּוֹרָה – **The [latter] Baraisa was taught** specifically **in regard to a Torah scroll.**[5] Unlike scrolls of other books of Scripture, which are wound around a single pole, a Torah scroll is attached to two poles, one at each of its ends. Hence, as far as a Torah scroll is concerned, the stretches of blank parchment at both ends of the scroll need be only long enough to be wound around a pole.

Rav Ashi quotes a Baraisa in support of this distinction between a Torah scroll and other sacred scrolls:

כִּדְתַנְיָא – **As it was taught in a Baraisa:** כָּל הַסְּפָרִים נִגְלָלִים מִתְּחִלָּתָן לְסוֹפָן – ALL sacred SCROLLS ARE ROLLED FROM BEGINNING TO END.[6] וְסֵפֶר תּוֹרָה נִגְלָל לְאֶמְצָעִיתוֹ – BUT A TORAH SCROLL IS ROLLED TOWARDS ITS MIDDLE from both ends, וְעוֹשֶׂה לוֹ עַמּוּד אֵילָךְ וְאֵילָךְ – AND A POLE SHOULD BE MADE FOR EACH OF ITS ENDS. אָמַר רַבִּי אֶלְ(י)עָזָר בְּרַבִּי צָדוֹק – R' ELAZAR SON OF R' TZADOK SAID: כָּךְ הָיוּ כּוֹתְבֵי סְפָרִים שֶׁבִּירוּשָׁלַיִם עוֹשִׂין סִפְרֵיהֶם – Indeed, THIS IS HOW THE SCRIBES OF JERUSALEM WOULD MAKE THEIR Torah SCROLLS.

Another Baraisa that pertains to the making of a Torah scroll:

תָּנוּ רַבָּנָן – **The Rabbis taught in a Baraisa:** אֵין עוֹשִׂין סֵפֶר תּוֹרָה לֹא אָרְכּוֹ יוֹתֵר עַל הֶקֵּיפוֹ – A TORAH SCROLL SHOULD NOT BE MADE WITH ITS LENGTH (i.e. height) EXCEEDING ITS CIRCUMFERENCE, וְלֹא הֶקֵּיפוֹ יוֹתֵר עַל אָרְכּוֹ – NOR WITH ITS CIRCUMFERENCE EXCEEDING ITS LENGTH (i.e. height).[7] שָׁאֲלוּ אֶת רַבִּי – THEY ASKED REBBI: שִׁיעוּר סֵפֶר תּוֹרָה בְּכַמָּה – WHAT IS THE PROPER SIZE OF A TORAH SCROLL? I.e. how high should one make a Torah scroll, whose lettering is of average size, so that its circumference will match its height? אָמַר לָהֶן – [REBBI] REPLIED TO THEM: בִּגְוִיל שִׁשָּׁה – A Torah scroll written ON *G'VIL* should be SIX

NOTES

1. Literally: and if he comes to cut, he cuts.

This is not a contradiction to the Gemara above (13b) which taught that inheritors may not divide a single scroll of Scripture (even if it includes several books — see *Rashi* there). That prohibition applies only to the cutting of a scroll for the sake of dividing an inheritance, which is considered abusive treatment of the scroll. Otherwise, cutting a scroll into its constituent books is permitted (*Tosafos*).

2. *Rashi.* The view of R' Meir and R' Yehudah that books of Scripture may be joined together is only a permit, not a requirement. Ideally, the books should be separate. That R' Meir's ruling is merely a permit is evidenced by the language of the second Baraisa: הָרוֹצֶה לְדַבֵּק וכו׳ מְדַבֵּק, *One who wishes to join etc. may do so.* (As mentioned above — see 13b note 25 — this does not apply to the five books of the Pentateuch which are not fit for the communal Torah readings unless they are combined.)

3. This Baraisa taught that if a book ends at the bottom of a column, one should start the next book at the top of the following column, without leaving any lines blank. The Gemara explains here that the reason for this ruling is contained in the Baraisa's very next clause: "because if one wishes to cut the scroll one may do so." If blank lines are left at the top of a column before the start of a book, then, should the scroll be cut and divided into its constituent books, the writing in the first column of one of the books will start lower than in the other columns (for no apparent reason) and that would appear unseemly (*Rashi*).

The above does not apply to a scroll of the Pentateuch. Since it is *forbidden* to cut and divide a scroll of the Pentateuch into its constituent books [for by doing so one lowers the sanctity of the scroll — *Nachalas Moshe,* based on *Megillah* 27a; see 13b note 25], there is no concern that one might do so. Therefore, when writing a scroll of the Pentateuch, a scribe leaves four lines blank between one book and another even at the top of a column (*Ritva,* 13b; see *Tosafos* to 13b ד״ה ומסיים).

4. [That is to say, the Tanna's intent was only to teach that some blank space must be left at the beginning and end of the scroll. He does not deal with the issue of how *much* space is required.]

5. I.e. a scroll of the Pentateuch.

6. [I.e. after use, the scroll should be rolled to its end.] This is *Rashi's* version of the text. Most commentators, however, have the following reading: כָּל הַסְּפָרִים נִגְלָלִין לִתְחִלָּתָן, *All [sacred] scrolls are rolled to their beginning* (see *Tosafos* to 13b ד״ה ועושה, *Shulchan Aruch Orach Chaim* 691:2 with *Beur HaGra, Maaseh Rav of the Gra* 36, *Rashash, Yesodei Yeshurun* vol. 4 p. 420).

7. The size of the lettering and the thickness of the parchment should correspond in such a way that when the finished scroll is rolled up, its circumference measures the same as its height (*Rashi*). Aesthetically, this is the ideal shape for a Torah scroll. It represents a fulfillment of the mitzvah — derived from *Exodus* 15:2, זֶה אֵלִי וְאַנְוֵהוּ, *this is my God and I shall glorify Him* — to beautify objects used in the Divine service (*Nimukei Yosef* to *Hilchos Sefer Torah* 3a; cf. *Ritva*). (However, as the Gemara reports below, making a Torah scroll in such a shape is most difficult and was rarely achieved in practice.)

ואם בא לחתוך חותך מאי קאמר הכי קאמר
א שאם בא לחתוך חותך ורמינהי ב תחלת ספר
וסופו כדי לגול מאי אי כדי לגול
עמוד קשיא הקף אי כדי לגול הקף קשי׳ עמוד
א״ר נחמן בר יצחק לצדדין קתני רב אשי אמר
ג כי תניא ההיא בספר תורה כדתניא ד כל
הספרים נגללים מתחלתן לסופן וס״ת נגלל
לאמצעיתו ועושה לו עמוד אילך ואילך א״ר
אליעזר בר׳ צדוק כך היו כותבי ספרים
שבירושלים עושין (א) ספריהם ת״ר ה אין עושין
ספר תורה לא ארכו יותר על הקיפו ולא הקיפו
יותר על ארכו שאלו את רבי שיעור ס״ת בכמה
אמר להן ו בגויל ששה ז בקלף בכמה איני יודע
רב הונא כתב שבעין ספרי דאורייתא ולא
איתרמי ליה אלא חד רב אחא בר יעקב כתב
חד אמשכיה דעיגלי ואיתרמי ליה ח יהבו ביה
רבנן עינייהו ונח נפשיה אמרו ליה רבנן לרב
המנונא כתב רבי אמי ד׳ מאה ספרי תורה
אמר להו דילמא א) תורה צוה לנו משה כתב
א״ל רבא לר׳ זירא נטע ר׳ ינאי ארבע מאה
כרמי א״ל דילמא שתים כנגד שתים ואחת
יוצא זנב מיתיבי ארון שעשה משה אמתים
וחצי ארכו ואמה וחצי רחבו ואמה וחצי
קומתו באמה בת ששה טפחים ט והלוחות
ארכן ששה ורחבן ששה ועביין שלשה
מונחות כנגד ארכו של ארון כמה לוחות
אוכלות בארון שנים עשר טפחים נשתיירו שם
שלשה טפחים צא מהן טפח חציו לכותל זה
וחציו לכותל זה נשתיירו שם שני טפחים
שבהן ספר תורה מונח שנאמ׳ ב) אין בארון רק
שני לוחות האבנים אשר הניח שם משה
[וגו׳] מאי אין בארון רק מיעוט אחר מיעוט
ג) ואין מיעוט אחר מיעוט אלא לרבות ס״ת
שמונח בארון פירנסת ארון לארכו צא ופרנס
ארון לרחבו כמה לוחות אוכלות בארון ששה
טפחים נשתיירו שם שלשה טפחים צא מהן
טפח חציו לכותל זה וחציו לכותל זה נשתיירו
שם שני טפחים שלא יהא ספר תורה נכנס
ויוצא כשהוא דחוק דברי ר״מ ר׳ יהודה אומר
באמה בת חמשה טפחים והלוחות ארכן
ששה ורחבן ששה ועביין שלשה מונחות
באורכו של ארון כמה לוחות אוכלות בארון
שנים עשר טפחים נשתייר שם חצי טפח
אצבע לכותל זה ואצבע לכותל זה פירנסת
ארון לארכו צא ופרנס ארון לרחבו כמה לוחות
י) אוגדות בארון ששה טפחים נשתייר שם
טפח ומחצה צא מהן חצי טפח אצבע (ב)
ומחצה לכותל זה ואצבע ומחצה לכותל זה נשתייר שם טפח שבו עמודין
עומדין שנאמר ג) אפריון עשה לו המלך שלמה מעצי הלבנון עמודיו עשה כסף
רפידתו זהב מרכבו ארגמן וגו׳ (ג) וארגז ששיגרו בו פלשתים דורון לאלהי ישראל
מונח מצדו שנאמר ד) ואת כלי הזהב אשר השבותם לו אשם תשימו בארגז
מצדו ושלחתם אותו והלך ועליו ס״ת מונח שנאמר ה) לקוח את ספר התורה
הזה ושמתם אותו מצד ארון ברית ה׳ מצד (ד) הוא מונח ולא בתוכו ומה אני מקיים אין בארון רק לרבות
שברי

רש״י

ואם בא לחתוך חותך מאי קאמר. מאי למימרא הכל מודים דאם כל אחד ואחד בפני עצמו טפי עדיף: הכי קאמר. ומתחיל מלמעלה ולא יניח חלק שהרי אם בא לחתוך חותך ונמלא זה ראש הכרך וגנאי הוא לו להיות דף זה משונה מחבירו על חנם: כדי לגול. קס״ד חד שיעורא יהיב ליה לתחילתו וסופו: לספריהן. לספרי תורה: לא ארכו יותר על הקיפו. לריך לנמלם הכתב לפי עובי הקלפי׳ לכשיגמור יהא חוט המקיף את עוביו כמדת ארכו: שיעור ספר תורה בכמה. ארכו מיבעיא להו: בגויל. שהוא עב והקיפו גדול לריך ששה טפחים זו היא מדה להיות נגמר בששה טפחים היקף בכתב בינוני: ולא איתרמי ליה. ארכו כהקיפו: איתרמי ליה. ארכו כהקיפו: דילמא תורה צוה לנו משה מורשה כתב. ארבע מאות פעמים אבל ארבע מאה (ה) ספרים אין פנאי לאדם אחד לכתוב: שתים כנגד שתים. שתי גפנים כנגד שתים וא׳ יוצא זנב בכך קרוי כרם לגבי לחזור עליו מעורכי המלחמה במסכת סוטה (דף מג.): באמה בת ששה טפחים. ר״מ לטעמיה דאמר (סוכה ה:) כל האמות היו בינוניות: לארכו של ארון. זו אצל זו: אוכלות. תופסות כך לשון המשנה (מדות פ״ג מ״א) אוכל בדרום אמה אחת גבי יסוד המזבח ואף בלשון מקרא כי יוכלו אתיקים מהנה בספר יחזקאל (מב): צא מהם טפח. לעובי הכתלים שהרי מבחוץ נמדד אמתי׳ וחצי ארכו: ס״ת. שכתב משה כמו שנאמר ויכתוב משה את ה) (התורה) וגו׳ (דברים לא): אין [מיעוט אחר מיעוט]. ו) אך ורק שני מיעוטין הן: שבהן ס״ת מונח. ארכו לרחבו של ארון: פירנסת ארון לארכו. כלומר מלאת כל חללו לארכו ופירשת צרכי מדתו: ששה טפחים. במדת רחבו: כדי שלא יהא ס״ת כו׳. כלומר לא היה צריך להיות רחבו כל כך אלא בשביל ס״ת המונח אורכו לרוחב הארון שלא יהא נכנס ויוצא בדוחק: ר״י אומר. מדת הארון באמה של ה׳ טפחים היתה רבי יהודה לטעמיה דקאמר אמת כלים באמה בת חמשה: מונחות לארכו של ארון. מוטלות על רוחבן ולא על חודן: אצבע לכותל זה. שהטפח ארבע אצבעות ולמאן דגריס אצבע ומחצה באצבע קטנה קאמר שהטפח ד׳ בגודל וחמש באצבע ושש בקטנה: שבו עמודים עומדים. ב׳ עמודי כסף כמין עמודי ספר תורה שוכבים לארכו והלוחות ביניהן שנאמר עמודיו עשה כסף: מונח שם בצדו. של ארון: ועליו ס״ת מונח. ולקמיה פריך מעיקרא היכי הוה מונח:
שברי

תוספות

שאם בא לחתוך חותך. תימה לרשב״א הא אמר לעיל בשתי כריכות חולקין ופ״ה כגון תורה בכרך אחד ונביאים בכרך א׳ משמע אבל תורה ונביאים בכרך א׳ אין חולקין אפי׳ שניהן רוצים וא״כ היכי אמר הכא דחותך ויש לומר דלא הוי בזיון הספר אלא כשחותך מחמת חלוקה: **בגויל** ששה טפחים בקלף בכמה. גויל הוא עור שלא ניתקן כלל אלא שהסירו את השער וכותבין בו במקום שער ולהכי קרי ליה גויל שאינו מתוקן כדאמר לעיל (דף ג.) גויל אבני דלא משפיין ופעמים חותכין אותו לשנים דרך עוביו ואותו שכלפי שער קרוי קלף ואותו שלצד בשר קרוי דוכסוסטוס ולשון דוכסוסטוס הוי פירושו מקום בשר דבלשון ז) מדי קורין לבשר סוסטוס ודוך היינו מקום כמו ח) דוך פלוני וכותבין על הקלף לצד בשר כדאמר בפ׳ המוציא (שבת דף עט:) ועל דוכסוסטוס לצד שער ובשניהם במקום חתך דשם הוא טוב לכתוב ושלנו דין קלף יש להם ולא דין דוכסוסטוס ולכך כותבין עליהם תפילין שאין כשרים על דוכסוסטוס אלא על הקלף כדאמר בהמוציא יין (שם): **דילמא** תורה צוה. ואומר ר״ת דאותו פסוק קרוי תורה כדאמר בפ׳ ג׳ דסוכה (דף מב.) קטן היודע לדבר אביו מלמדו תורה מאי תורה תורה צוה לנו משה: **שלא** יהא ספר תורה יוצא ונכנס כשהוא דחוק. וא״ת והלא לא היו מוציאין אותו מן הארון דהא אסור ליכנס בבית קדש הקדשים וביום הכפורים לא אשכחן בסדר יומא שהיה מוציאו וי״ל דלצורך כדי לתקן שרי ליכנס בבית קדש הקדשים כדאמרינן בעירובין (דף קה.) וה״נ יכולין ליכנס שם כדי לתקן ספר תורה כדי שלא יתעפש ויתקלקל וגם משחרב משכן שילה עד שבנה שלמה בית המקדש היו יכולין להוציאו מן הארון ולעיין בו: **אצבע** ומחצה לכותל זה. נראה לר״ת דלא גרס ומחצה אלא אצבע לכותל זה דאי גרס ומחצה תיקשי שנים עשר (ו) היכי יתבי כדפריך לקמן אלא אצבע גרס וזוטרתי דהויין ששה בטפח: **שבהן** עמודים עומדין. נראה לר״ת דסימן להעמדת ישראל היה ולא עשאום של זהב שלא להזכיר מעשה העגל דאין קטיגור נעשה סניגור וכן אמרינן [בר״ה] (דף כו.) דמשום הכי לא היה כהן משמש לפני ולפנים ביוה״כ בבגדי זהב משום דאין קטיגור נעשה סניגור והתם פריך והא הוה ארון שהיה של זהב והיה לפנים ומשני מכפר קאמרי׳ והני עמודים נמי היו כמו מכפר שהם עשוים סימן להעמדת ישראל והוא שיסד הפייט ט) תבנית אות יוסף עמודיו עשה כסף בשביל תבנית אות יוסף סימן של יוסף דהיינו עגל דיוסף נקרא שור שנאמר (דברים לג) בכור שורו הדר לו לכך עמודיו עשה כסף ולא זהב שלא להזכיר במעשה העגל:
תרי

מסורת הש״ס

א) [ברכות דף נח:], ב) [נדרים לח.], ג) [יומא עג. וש״נ], ד) נ״א אוכלות, ה) [צ״ל השירה], ו) [אין ורק], ז) [שבת עט: ד״ה קלף כתבו דבלשון יון], ח) [ברכות יח:], ט) ביום ראשון דפסח.

הגהות הב״ח

(א) גמ׳ עושין לספריהם: (ב) שם צא מהכן חצי טפח אצבע לכותל זה ואצבע לכותל זה כצ״ל ותיבת ומחצה נמחק ב׳ פעמים: (ג) שם מרכבו ארגמן וגו׳ תוכו רצוף אהבה וארגז: (ד) שם מצד היה מונח ולא: (ה) רש״י ד״ה דילמא וכו׳ ד׳ מאה ספרי תורות לא כתב דאין פנאי לאדם אחד לכתוב כולי האי הס״ד: (ו) תוס׳ ד״ה אצבע וכו׳ תקשה שנים עשר בי״ב היכי יתבי:

תורה אור השלם

א) תּוֹרָה צִוָּה לָנוּ מֹשֶׁה מוֹרָשָׁה קְהִלַּת יַעֲקֹב: [דברים לג, ד]

ב) אֵין בָּאָרוֹן רַק שְׁנֵי לֻחוֹת הָאֲבָנִים אֲשֶׁר הִנִּחַ שָׁם מֹשֶׁה בְּחֹרֵב אֲשֶׁר כָּרַת יְיָ עִם בְּנֵי יִשְׂרָאֵל בְּצֵאתָם מֵאֶרֶץ מִצְרָיִם: [מלכים א ח, ט]

ג) אַפִּרְיוֹן עָשָׂה לוֹ הַמֶּלֶךְ שְׁלֹמֹה מֵעֲצֵי הַלְּבָנוֹן: עַמּוּדָיו עָשָׂה כֶסֶף רְפִידָתוֹ זָהָב מֶרְכָּבוֹ אַרְגָּמָן תּוֹכוֹ רָצוּף אַהֲבָה מִבְּנוֹת יְרוּשָׁלָיִם: [שיר השירים ג, ט-י]

ד) וּלְקַחְתֶּם אֶת אֲרוֹן יְיָ וּנְתַתֶּם אֹתוֹ אֶל הָעֲגָלָה וְאֵת כְּלֵי הַזָּהָב אֲשֶׁר הֲשֵׁבֹתֶם לוֹ אָשָׁם תָּשִׂימוּ בָאַרְגַּז מִצִּדּוֹ וְשִׁלַּחְתֶּם אֹתוֹ וְהָלָךְ: [שמואל א ו, ח]

ה) לָקֹחַ אֵת סֵפֶר הַתּוֹרָה הַזֶּה וְשַׂמְתֶּם אֹתוֹ מִצַּד אֲרוֹן בְּרִית יְיָ אֱלֹהֵיכֶם וְהָיָה שָׁם בְּךָ לְעֵד: [דברים לא, כו]

ליקוטי רש״י

גויל. מעובד בעפצים [שבת עט.].

עין משפט נר מצוה

קכו א מיי׳ פ״ז מהל׳ ס״ת הל׳ ט סמג עשין כה (טוש״ע שם):

קכז ב ג מיי׳ פ״ט מהל׳ ס״ת הלכה ב סמג עשין כה טוש״ע י״ד סי׳ רעג סעיף ח:

קכח ד מיי׳ שם וסמג שם טוש״ע י״ד סי׳ רעה סעיף ג:

קכט ה ו ז מיי׳ שם פ״ט הלכה א וסמג שם טוש״ע י״ד סי׳ רעב סעיף א [וברב אלפס הלכות ספר תורה דף סו]:

רבינו גרשום

דף פנוי מלמטה ומתחיל באחר מלמעלה **שאם באו** לחלוק שיכולין **לחתוך** ולחלק יפה כבשתי כריכות. **שמונה נביאים** ח׳ ספרים של נביאים. **ועושה בראשו** של ספר תורה חלק **כשיעור לגול** עמוד בתחלתו והאי תחלה הוי סוף הספר לפי כי בסוף מתחילין לגלגל המגילה ומגלגל והולך עד ראש לפי שכל ספריהם נכתבין כעין מגילה ולא בקונטרסים (והם) והכי נמי מניח מן הקלף חלק **בסוף** כל הכרך שהוא תחלת הספר כשיעור שיכול לגול את כל ההיקף על אותו חלק כדי שיהא משמש הקלף פנוי לכתבי הקדש: **קשיא עמוד** דלעיל קתני בראשו כדי לגול עמוד והכא קתני תחלת הספר וסופו כדי לגול עמוד. **האי** כדי לגול דברייתא נמי **לצדדין קתני** כדאמרן דתחלה כדי לגול עמוד ובסוף כדי לגול היקף. **רב אשי אמר** לעולם לא קתני לצדדין אלא תחלתו וסופו כדי לגול עמוד **ובספר תורה** מיירי **דלאמצעיתו** נגלל על ב׳ עמודים אבל שאר ספרים היו נגללין הכל על עמוד אחד ואמטו להכי צריך להניח כדי היקף כדאמרן. **ולא אורכו יותר על הקיפו** שכשמושכין אותו בחוט של משיחה לאורכו של דף ומקיפין מן אותו חוט היקף הספר תורה שיהא שוים במדה. **בגויל ו׳ טפחים** אורך הדף שכך למד מגויל. אבל מן **קלף** לא אמר לפיכך אמר **איני יודע. ולא איתרמי ליה** שיהא אורכו שוה להקיפו. **יהבו ביה עינייהו** קינאו (אדון) בו שכך כיון. **תורה צוה לנו** כתב דדומה עליו גוזמא. **ורמינהו** מקשה על מאי דאמר שיהא ס״ת הקיפו כאורכו. **וארון שעשה משה** היה דומה כמין תיבה שאין לה כיסוי שבכפרת היה מכוסה. **באמת בת ו׳ טפחים. ואמתים וחצי אורכו** עולין לט״ו טפחי׳: **וכמה לוחות אוגדות בארון.** כלומר כמה מחזיקות בארון. **י״ב טפחי׳** שהיו מונחין הלוחות זו בצד זו. **ואין ורק** תרי מיעוטי **לרבות ספר תורה** שמונח בארון באותן ב׳ טפחים שנשתיירו מאורך הארון והיה אורכו של ספר תורה כרוחבו של לוחות ו׳ טפחים **נשתיירו ב׳ טפחים** פנוי טפח לצד כותל זה וטפח לצד כותל זה שבכל אותן ב׳ טפחים משימין ידיהן אחת מיכן ואחת מיכן ומגביהין ספר תורה בריוח ומוציאין אותו לחוץ **כדי שלא יהא נכנס ויוצא בדוחק: שבו** באותו טפח עמודיו של ארון עומדין שנאמר **אפריון עשה לו המלך שלמה.** המלך שהשלום שלו וכתב **עמודיו עשה כסף** של ארון. **בצידו מבחוץ.**
שברי

tefachim high.[8]

Rebbi was asked further:

בִּקְלָף בִּכְמָּה – If a Torah scroll is written ON *K'LAF,*[9] HOW [HIGH] should it be?

Rebbi replied:

אֵינִי יוֹדֵעַ – I DO NOT KNOW.[10]

The Gemara attests to the difficulty of equating the height and circumference of a Torah scroll:

רַב הוּנָא כָּתַב שִׁבְעִין סִפְרֵי דְאוֹרָיְיתָא – **Rav Huna wrote seventy Torah scrolls** in his lifetime, וְלֹא אִיתְרַמֵּי לֵיהּ אֶלָּא חַד – **and only one turned out** to be a scroll whose height and circumference were the same. רַב אַחָא בַּר יַעֲקֹב כָּתַב חַד אַמַּשְׁכֵיהּ דְּעֵיגְלֵי וְאִיתְרַמֵּי לֵיהּ – **Rav Acha bar Yaakov wrote one** Torah scroll, **on calfskin,**[11] **and it turned out** to be a scroll whose height and circumference were the same. יָהֲבוּ בֵּיהּ רַבָּנַן עֵינַיְיהוּ וְנָח נַפְשֵׁיהּ – **The Rabbis cast their eyes upon [Rav Acha bar Yaakov]** in disbelief **and he died.**[12]

Having mentioned that Rav Huna wrote seventy Torah scrolls, the Gemara cites a similar occurrence:

אָמְרוּ לֵיהּ רַבָּנַן לְרַב הַמְנוּנָא – **The Rabbis said to Rav Hamnuna:** כָּתַב רַבִּי אַמִי אַרְבַּע מֵאָה סִפְרֵי תוֹרָה – We heard that **R' Ami wrote four hundred Torah scrolls** in his lifetime! אָמַר לְהוּ – **[Rav Hamnuna,]** knowing that this was impossible, **said to them:** דִּילְמָא ,,תּוֹרָה צִוָּה לָנוּ מֹשֶׁה" כָּתַב – **Perhaps he wrote** the verse, ***Moses commanded us the Torah,***[13] four hundred times.[14]

A similar story:

אָמַר לֵיהּ רָבָא לְרַבִּי זֵירָא – **Rava said to R' Zeira:** נָטַע רַבִּי יַנַּאי אַרְבַּע מֵאָה כַּרְמֵי – **R' Yannai planted four hundred vineyards** in his lifetime. אָמַר לֵיהּ – **[R' Zeira,]** considering this highly unlikely, **said to him:** דִּילְמָא שְׁתַּיִם כְּנֶגֶד שְׁתַּיִם וְאַחַת יוֹצֵא זָנָב – **Perhaps** the vineyards he planted each consisted of only five vines, planted in the following configuration: **two** vines **opposite two** vines, **and one** vine **projecting** like **a tail** from the others.[15]

The Gemara quotes a lengthy Baraisa to challenge Rebbi's statement that a Torah scroll of average-size lettering written on *g'vil* whose height is six *tefachim* will have a circumference of six *tefachim*:

מֵיתִיבֵי – **They challenged** Rebbi's statement from the following Baraisa: אָרוֹן שֶׁעָשָׂה מֹשֶׁה – THE ARK THAT MOSES CONSTRUCTED: אַמָּתַיִם וָחֵצִי אָרְכּוֹ – TWO AND A HALF *AMOS* WAS ITS LENGTH, וְאַמָּה וָחֵצִי רָחְבּוֹ – ONE AND A HALF *AMOS* ITS WIDTH וְאַמָּה וָחֵצִי קוֹמָתוֹ – AND ONE AND A HALF *AMOS* ITS HEIGHT.[16] בְּאַמָּה בַּת שִׁשָּׁה טְפָחִים – THE *AMAH* REFERRED TO HERE MEASURES SIX *TEFACHIM.*[17] Hence, the Ark was fifteen *tefachim* long and nine *tefachim* wide. וְהַלּוּחוֹת אָרְכָּן שִׁשָּׁה וְרָחְבָּן שִׁשָּׁה וְעָבְיָין שְׁלֹשָׁה – THE two TABLETS of the Law,[18] WHOSE LENGTH WAS SIX *tefachim,* WIDTH SIX *tefachim,* AND THICKNESS THREE *tefachim,* מוּנָּחוֹת כְּנֶגֶד אָרְכּוֹ שֶׁל אָרוֹן – LAY side by side ALONG THE LENGTH OF THE ARK. כַּמָּה לוּחוֹת אוֹכְלוֹת בָּאָרוֹן – Consequently, HOW MUCH of the length OF THE ARK DID THE TABLETS TAKE UP? שְׁנֵים עָשָׂר טְפָחִים – TWELVE *TEFACHIM.* נִשְׁתַּיְּירוּ שָׁם שְׁלֹשָׁה טְפָחִים – THREE *TEFACHIM* REMAIN THERE [along the length of the ark] that are as yet unaccounted for. צֵא מֵהֶן טֶפַח – SUBTRACT FROM [THESE THREE *TEFACHIM*] one *TEFACH* for the walls of the Ark: חֶצְיוֹ לְכוֹתֶל זֶה וְחֶצְיוֹ לְכוֹתֶל זֶה – HALF [A *TEFACH*] FOR ONE WALL AND HALF FOR THE OTHER WALL.[19] נִשְׁתַּיְּירוּ שָׁם שְׁנֵי טְפָחִים – THERE REMAINS TWO *TEFACHIM* שֶׁבָּהֶן סֵפֶר תּוֹרָה מוּנָּח – IN WHICH THE TORAH SCROLL written by Moses LAY.[20] From where do we know that the Torah scroll of Moses was placed in the Ark? – שֶׁנֶּאֱמַר: ,,אֵין בָּאָרוֹן רַק שְׁנֵי לֻחוֹת הָאֲבָנִים אֲשֶׁר הִנִּחַ שָׁם מֹשֶׁה (וגו׳)"

NOTES

8. גְּוִיל, *g'vil,* is parchment prepared using the entire thickness of the hide, with just the hair removed. [It is the thickest type of parchment] (*Tosafos*).

Some authorities maintain that ideally a Torah scroll should be written on *g'vil*, rather than any other type of parchment (*R' Chananel,* cited by *Rashba*; *Ran* to *Shabbos* 79b; *Rashba* records a dispute on this matter; see *Kesef Mishnah* to *Hil. Tefillin* 1:8 and *Beur HaGra Yoreh Deah* 271:9).

A scroll six *tefachim* high written on *g'vil* in average-size lettering typically runs to a circumference of six *tefachim* (*Rashi*). Even a scroll that is more or less than six *tefachim* high is considered ideal provided that its circumference matches its height. The figure of six *tefachim* is given merely because that is the measurement for a scroll whose writing is of average size (*Rambam Hil. Sefer Torah* 9:1, *Ritva* and *Meiri*).

An alternative view: Some commentators maintain that six *tefachim* is the optimum height for a Torah scroll, because that was the height of the Tablets on which the Ten Commandments were engraved (*Levush,* cited by *Maadanei Yom Tov* on *Rosh* to *Hil. Sefer Torah* 8:5; *Eshkol, Sefer Torah* p. 37; *Maharsha*; see *Hagahos R' Yaakov Emden* and *Bnei Yonah, Hil. Sefer Torah* 272:1).

9. *G'vil* (see beginning of preceding note) can be divided into two layers. The layer that was on the outside of the animal is known as קְלָף, *k'laf* (*Tosafos*).

10. [It was impossible to ascertain the ideal height of a Torah scroll (i.e. the height that will match its circumference) except by means of trial and error. Therefore, Rebbi did not know the appropriate figure for *k'laf* since Torah scrolls were usually written on *g'vil* (see note 8, third paragraph).]

11. Calfskin, due to its thickness, cannot be rolled up snugly. Therefore, it is impossible to predict the height of a scroll of calfskin that will match its circumference. This made Rav Acha's achievement all the more remarkable (*Ben Yehoyada*).

12. [By wondering how Rav Acha had merited such an amazing accomplishment, the Sages inadvertently caused God to examine his deeds. See above (2b), where a similar explanation can be given for the phenomenon of עַיִן הָרָע, *the evil eye*.]

13. *Deuteronomy* 33:4. This verse is described as "Torah" by the Gemara (*Succah* 42a) which states: *When a child begins to talk his father must teach him Torah. What is meant by Torah?* [The verse:] תּוֹרָה צִוָּה־לָנוּ מֹשֶׁה, *Moses commanded us the Torah (Tosafos).*

14. Scribes wrote four hundred Torah scrolls for R' Ami. When they reached this verse, they told R' Ami and he wrote it in each of the scrolls (*Tosefos HaRosh*). It is thus considered as if he had written the four hundred scrolls (*Raavad,* cited by *Shitah Mekubetzes*, based on *Menachos* 30a).

Alternatively: R' Ami wrote this verse out four hundred times for children (*Maharsha*).

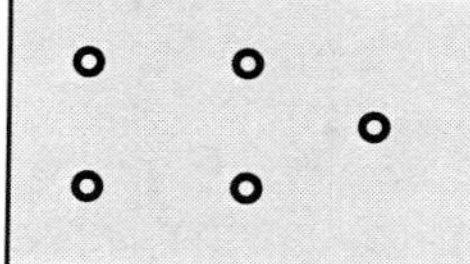

15. See diagram. The Gemara (*Sotah* 43a) defines this configuration as the legal minimum that can be classified as a vineyard (*Rashi*; see *Kilayim* 4:6 for elaboration).

He planted five vines, in such a configuration, in four hundred vineyards in Eretz Yisrael. It is thus considered as if he had planted the four hundred vineyards. He did this for the sake of יִשּׁוּב אֶרֶץ יִשְׂרָאֵל, *the settlement of Eretz Yisrael (Raavad*, cited by *Shitah Mekubetzes*).

16. *Exodus* 25:10.

17. As the Baraisa states below, this is the opinion of R' Meir, who holds that all the *amah* measurements given in reference to the Tabernacle and its appurtenances are in "standard" *amos* – i.e. lengths of 6 *tefachim* (as opposed to "small" *amos* which are 5 *tefachim* long, and "large" *amos* which measure 6⅛ *tefachim*) (*Rashi* here with *Rashi* to *Succah* 5b).

18. The two Tablets of sapphire brought down by Moses from Mt. Sinai, on which the Ten Commandments were engraved.

19. The Ark's measurements given in the Torah are for the *outside* of the Ark, including the thickness of its walls (*Rashi*).

20. Moses was commanded to write a Torah scroll for placement in the Tabernacle – see *Deuteronomy* 31:9,26.

ואם בא לחתוך חותך מאי קאמר הכי קאמר א) שאם בא לחתוך חותך ורמינהי ב) תחלת ספר וסופו כדי לגול מאי אי כדי לגול עמוד קשיא הקף אי כדי לגול הקף קשי' עמוד א"ר נחמן בר יצחק לצדדין קתני רב אשי אמר ג) כי תניא ההיא בספר תורה כדתניא ד) כל הספרים נגללים מתחלתן לסופן וס"ת נגלל לאמצעיתו ועושה לו עמוד אילך ואילך א"ר אליעזר בר' צדוק כך היו כותבי ספרים שבירושלים עושין (א) ספריהם ת"ר ה) אין עושין ספר תורה לא ארכו יותר על הקיפו ולא הקיפו יותר על ארכו שאלו את רבי שיעור ס"ת בכמה אמר להן ו) בגויל ששה ז) בקלף בכמה איני יודע רב הונא כתב שבעין ספרי דאורייתא ולא איתרמי ליה אלא חד רב אחא בר יעקב כתב חד אמשכיה דעיגלי ואיתרמי ליה ח) יהבו ביה רבנן עינייהו ונח נפשיה אמרו ליה רבנן לרב המנונא כתב רבי אמי ד' מאה ספרי תורה אמר להו דילמא א) תורה צוה לנו משה כתב א"ל רבא לר' זירא נטע ר' ינאי ארבע מאה כרמי א"ל דילמא שתים כנגד שתים ואחת יוצא זנב מיתיבי ארון שעשה משה אמתים וחצי ארכו ואמה וחצי רחבו ואמה וחצי קומתו באמה בת ששה טפחים ט) והלוחות ארכן ששה ורחבן ששה ועביין שלשה מונחות כנגד ארכו של ארון כמה לוחות אוכלות בארון שנים עשר טפחים נשתיירו שם שלשה טפחים צא מהן טפח חציו לכותל זה וחציו לכותל זה נשתיירו שם שני טפחים שבהן ספר תורה מונח שנאמ' ב) אין בארון רק שני לוחות האבנים אשר הניח שם משה [וגו'] מאי אין בארון רק מיעוט אחר מיעוט ואין מיעוט אחר מיעוט אלא לרבות ס"ת שמונח בארון פירנסת ארון לארכו צא ופרנס ארון לרחבו כמה לוחות אוכלות בארון ששה טפחים נשתיירו שם שלשה טפחים צא מהן טפח חציו לכותל זה וחציו לכותל זה נשתיירו שם שני טפחים שלא יהא ספר תורה נכנס ויוצא כשהוא דחוק דברי ר"מ ר' יהודה אומר באמה בת חמשה טפחים והלוחות ארכן ששה ורחבן ששה ועביין שלשה מונחות באורכו של ארון כמה לוחות אוכלות בארון שנים עשר טפחים נשתייר שם חצי טפח אצבע לכותל זה ואצבע לכותל זה פירנסת ארון לארכו צא ופרנס ארון לרחבו כמה לוחות אוכלות בארון ששה טפחים נשתייר שם אוגדות טפח ומחצה צא מהן חצי טפח אצבע (ב) ומחצה לכותל זה ואצבע ומחצה לכותל זה נשתייר שם טפח שבו עמודין עומדין שנאמר ג) אפריון עשה לו המלך שלמה מעצי הלבנון עמודיו עשה כסף רפידתו זהב מרכבו ארגמן וגו' (ג) וארגז ששיגרו בו פלשתים דורון לאלהי ישראל מונח מצדו שנאמר ד) ואת כלי הזהב אשר השבותם לו אשם תשימו בארגז מצדו ושלחתם אותו והלך ועליו ס"ת מונח שנאמר ה) לקוח את ספר התורה הזה ושמתם אותו מצד ארון ברית ה' מצד (ד) הוא מונח ולא בתוכו ומה אני מקיים אין בארון רק לרבות שברי

רש"י

ואם בא לחתוך חותך מאי קאמר. מאי למימרא הכל מודים דאם כל אחד ואחד בפני עצמו טפי עדיף: **הכי קאמר.** ומתחיל מלמעלה ולא יהיה חלק שהרי אם בא לחתוך חותך ונמצא זה ראש הכרך וגנאי הוא לו להיות דף זה משונה מחבירו על חנם: **כדי לגול.** קס"ד חד שיעורא יהיב ליה לתחילתו וסופו: **לספריהן:** לספרי תורה: **לא ארכו יותר על הקיפו.** צריך לצמצם הכתב לפי עובי הקלפי' כשיגמור יהא חוט המקיף את עוביו כמדת ארכו: **שיעור ספר תורה בכמה.** ארכו מיבעיא להו: **בגויל.** שהוא עב והקיפו גדול צריך ששה טפחים זו היא מדה להיות נגמר בששה טפחים היקף בכתב בינוני: **ולא איתרמי ליה.** ארכו כהקיפו: **איתרמי ליה.** ארכו כהקיפו: **דילמא תורה צוה לנו משה מורשה כתב.** ארבע מאות פעמים אבל ארבע מאה (ה) ספרים אין פנאי לאדם אחד לכתוב: **שתים כנגד שתים.** שתי גפנים כנגד שתים ואחת יוצא זנב בכך קרוי כרם לגבי לחזור עליו מעורכי המלחמה במסכת סוטה (דף מג.): **באמה בת ששה טפחים.** ר"מ לטעמיה דאמר (סוכה ה:) כל האמות היו בינוניות: **לארכו של ארון.** זו אצל זו: **אוכלות.** תופסות כך לשון המשנה (מדות פ"ג מ"א) אוכל בדרום אמה אחת גבי יסוד המזבח ואף בלשון מקרא כי יוכלו אתיקים מהנה בספר יחזקאל (מב): **צא מהם טפח.** לעובי הכתלים שהרי מכוון נמדד אמתי' וחצי ארכו: **ס"ת.** שכתב משה כמו שנאמר ויכתוב משה את (התורה) וגו' (דברים לא): **אין [מיעוט אחר מיעוט].** אך ורק שני מיעוטין הן: **שבהן ס"ת מונח.** ארכו לרחבו של ארון: **פירנסת ארון לארכו.** כלומר מלאת כל חללו לארכו ופירשת לרכי מדתו: **ששה טפחים.** במדת רחבו: **כדי שלא יהא ס"ת כו'.** כלומר לא היה צריך להיות רחבו כל כך אלא בשביל ס"ת המונח לרחבו לרוחב הארון שלא יהא נכנס ויוצא בדוחק: **ר"י אומר.** מדת הארון באמה של ה' טפחים היתה רבי יהודה לטעמיה דקאמר אמת כלים באמה בת חמשה: **מונחות לארכו של ארון.** מוטלות על רוחבן ולא על חודן: **אצבע לכותל זה.** שהטפח ארבע אצבעות ולמאן דגרים אצבע ומחצה באצבע קטנה קאמר שהטפח ד' בגודל וחמש באצבע ושש בקטנה: **שבו עמודים עומדים.** ב' עמודי כסף כמין עמודי ספר תורה שוכבים לארכו והלוחות ביניהן שנאמר עמודיו עשה כסף: **מונח שם בצדו.** של ארון: **ועליו ס"ת מונח.** ולקמיה פריך מעיקרא היכי הוה מונח: שברי

תוספות

שאם בא לחתוך חותך. תימה לרשב"א הא אמר לעיל בשתי כריכות חולקין ופ"ה כגון תורה בכרך אחד ונביאים בכרך א' משמע אבל תורה ונביאים בכרך א' אין חולקין אפי' שניהן רוצים וא"כ היכי אמר הכא דחותך ויש לומר דלא הוי בזיון הספר אלא כשחותך מחמת חלוקה: **בגויל** ששה טפחים בקלף בכמה. גויל הוא עור שלא ניתקן כלל אלא שהסירו את השער וכותבין בו במקום שער ולהכי קרי ליה גויל שאינו מתוקן כדאמר לעיל (דף ג.) גויל אבני דלא משפיין ופעמים חותכין אותו לשנים דרך עוביו ואותו שכלפי שער קרוי קלף ואותו שלצד בשר קרוי דוכסוסטוס ולשון דוכסוסטוס הוי פירושו מקום בשר דבלשון ז) מדי קורין לבשר סוסטוס ודוך היינו מקום כמו ח) דוך פלוני וכותבין על הקלף לצד בשר כדאמר בפ' המוציא (שבת דף עט:) ועל דוכסוסטוס לצד שער ובשניהם במקום אחך דשם הוא טוב לכתוב ושלנו דין קלף יש להם ולא דין דוכסוסטוס ולכך כותבין עליהם תפילין שאין כשרים על דוכסוסטוס אלא על הקלף כדאמר בהמוציא יין (שם): **דילמא** תורה צוה. ואומר ר"ת דאותו פסוק קרוי תורה כדאמר בפ' ג' דסוכה (דף מב.) קטן היודע לדבר אביו מלמדו תורה מאי תורה תורה צוה לנו משה: **שלא** יהא ספר תורה יוצא ונכנס כשהוא דחוק. וא"ת והלא לא היו מוציאין אותו מן הארון דהא אסור ליכנס בבית קדש הקדשים וביום הכפורים לא אשכחן בסדר יומא שהיה מוציאו וי"ל דלצורך כדי לתקן שרי ליכנס בבית קדש הקדשים כדאמרינן בעירובין (דף קה.) וה"נ יכולין ליכנס שם כדי לתקן ספר תורה כדי שלא יתעפש ויתקלקל וגם משחרב משכן שילה עד שבנה שלמה בית המקדש היו יכולין להוציאו מן הארון ולעיין בו: **אצבע** ומחצה לכותל זה. נראה לר"ת דלא גרס ומחצה אלא אצבע לכותל זה דאי גרס ומחצה תיקשי שנים עשר (ו) היכי יתבי כדפריך לקמן אלא אצבע גרס וזוטרתי דהויין ששה בטפח: **שבהן** עמודים עומדין. נראה לר"ת דסימן להעמדת ישראל היה ולא עשאום של זהב שלא להזכיר מעשה העגל דאין קטיגור נעשה סניגור וכן אמרינן [בר"ה] (דף כו.) דמשום הכי לא היה כהן משמש לפני ולפנים ביוה"כ בבגדי זהב משום דאין קטיגור נעשה סניגור והתם פריך והא הוה ארון שהיה של זהב והיה לפנים ומשני מכפר קאמרי' והני עמודים נמי היו כמו מכפר שהם עשוים סימן להעמדת ישראל והוא שיסד הפייט ט) תבנית אות יוסף עמודיו עשה כסף בשביל תבנית אות יוסף סימן של יוסף דהיינו עגל דיוסף נקרא שור שנאמר (דברים לג) בכור שורו הדר לו לכך עמודיו עשה כסף ולא זהב שלא להזכיר במעשה העגל: תרי

מסורת הש"ס

א) [ברכות דף נח:], ב) [נדרים לח.], ג) יומא מג. [ושם], ד) כ"ל אוכלות, ה) [נ"ל השירה], ו) [אין וקק], ז) [שבת עט: ד"ה קלף כתבו בלשון יון], ח) [ברכות יח:], ט) ביום ראשון דפסח.

הגהות הב"ח

(א) גמ' עושין לספריהם: (ב) שם לא מהן חצי טפח אצבע לכותל זה ואצבע לכותל זה כצ"ל ותיבת ומחצה נמחק בב' פעמים: (ג) שם מרכבו ארגמן וגו' תוכו רצוף אהבה וארגז: (ד) שם מלך היה מונח ולא: (ה) רש"י ד"ה דילמא וכו' ד' מאה ספרי תורות לא כתב דאין פנאי לאדם אחד לכתוב כולי האי הס"ד: (ו) תוס' ד"ה אצבע וכו' תקשה שנים עשר בי"ב היכי יתבי:

תורה אור השלם

א) תּוֹרָה צִוָּה לָנוּ מֹשֶׁה מוֹרָשָׁה קְהִלַּת יַעֲקֹב: [דברים לג, ד]
ב) אֵין בָּאָרוֹן רַק שְׁנֵי לֻחוֹת הָאֲבָנִים אֲשֶׁר הִנִּחַ שָׁם מֹשֶׁה בְּחֹרֵב אֲשֶׁר כָּרַת יְיָ עִם בְּנֵי יִשְׂרָאֵל בְּצֵאתָם מֵאֶרֶץ מִצְרָיִם: [מלכים א ח, ט]
ג) אַפִּרְיוֹן עָשָׂה לוֹ הַמֶּלֶךְ שְׁלֹמֹה מֵעֲצֵי הַלְּבָנוֹן: עַמּוּדָיו עָשָׂה כֶסֶף רְפִידָתוֹ זָהָב מֶרְכָּבוֹ אַרְגָּמָן תּוֹכוֹ רָצוּף אַהֲבָה מִבְּנוֹת יְרוּשָׁלָיִם: [שיר השירים ג, ט-י]
ד) וּלְקַחְתֶּם אֶת אֲרוֹן יְיָ וּנְתַתֶּם אֹתוֹ אֶל הָעֲגָלָה וְאֵת כְּלֵי הַזָּהָב אֲשֶׁר הֲשֵׁבֹתֶם לוֹ אָשָׁם תָּשִׂימוּ בָאַרְגַּז מִצִּדּוֹ וְשִׁלַּחְתֶּם אֹתוֹ וְהָלָךְ: [שמואל א ו, ח]
ה) לָקֹחַ אֵת סֵפֶר הַתּוֹרָה הַזֶּה וְשַׂמְתֶּם אֹתוֹ מִצַּד אֲרוֹן בְּרִית יְיָ אֱלֹהֵיכֶם וְהָיָה שָׁם בְּךָ לְעֵד: [דברים לא, כו]

ליקוטי רש"י

גויל. מעובד בעפצים [שבת עט.].

עין משפט נר מצוה

קכו א מיי' פ"ז מהל' ס"ת הל' טו סמג עשין כה (טוש"ע שם):
קכז ב ג מיי' פ"ט מהל' ס"ת הלכה ב סמג עשין כה טוש"ע י"ד סי' רעג סעיף א:
קכח ד מיי' שם וסמג שם טוש"ע י"ד סי' רעח סעיף ג:
קכט ה ו ז מיי' שם פ"ט הלכה א וסמג שם טוש"ע י"ד סי' רעג סעיף ז [וברב אלפס הלכות ספר תורה דף סו]:

רבינו גרשום

דף פנוי מלמטה ומתחיל באחר מלמעלה **שאם באו** לחלוק שיכולין **לחתוך** ולחלק יפה כבשתי כריכות. **שמונה נביאים** ח' ספרים של נביאים. **ועושה בראשו** של ספר תורה חלק **כשיעור לגול** עמוד בתחלתו והאי תחלה הוי סוף הספר לפי כי בסוף מתחילין לגלגל המגילה ומגלגל והולך עד ראש לפי שכל ספריהם נכתבין כעין מגילה ולא בקונטרסים (והם) והכי נמי מניח מן הקלף חלק **בסוף** כל הכרך שהוא תחלת הספר כשיעור שיכול לגול את כל ההיקף על אותו חלק כדי שיהא משמש הקלף פנוי לכתבי הקדש: **קשיא עמוד** דלעיל קתני בראשו כדי לגול עמוד והכא קתני תחלת הספר וסופו כדי לגול עמוד. **האי כדי לגול** דברייתא נמי **לצדדין קתני** כדאמרן דתחלה כדי לגול עמוד ובסוף כדי לגול היקף. **רב אשי אמר** לעולם לא קתני לצדדין אלא תחלתו וסופו כדי לגול עמוד **ובספר תורה** מיירי **דלאמצעיתו** נגלל על ב' עמודים אבל שאר ספרים היו נגללין הכל על עמוד אחד ואמטו להכי צריך להניח כדי היקף כדאמרן. **ולא אורכו יותר על הקיפו** שכשמושכין אותו בחוט של משיחה לאורכו של דף ומקיפין מן אותו חוט היקף הספר תורה שיהא שוים במדה. **בגויל ו' טפחים** אורך הדף שכך למד מגויל. אבל מן **קלף** לא אמר לפיכך אמר **איני יודע. ולא איתרמי ליה** שיהא אורכו שוה להקיפו. **יהבי ביה עינייהו** קינאו (אדון) בו שכך כיון. **תורה צוה לנו** כתב דדומה עליו גוזמא. **ורמינהו** מקשה על מאי דאמר שיהא ס"ת הקיפו כאורכו. **וארון שעשה משה** היה דומה כמין תיבה שאין לה כיסוי שבכפרת היה מכוסה. **באמת בת ו' טפחים. ואמתים וחצי אורכו** עולין לט"ו טפחי': **וכמה לוחות אוגדות בארון.** כלומר כמה מחזיקות בארון. **י"ב טפחי'** שהיו מונחין הלוחות זו בצד זו. **ואין ורק** תרי מיעוטי **לרבות ספר תורה** שמונח **בארון** באותן ב' טפחים שנשתיירו מאורך הארון והיה אורכו של ספר תורה כרוחבן של לוחות ו' טפחים **נשתיירו ב' טפחים** פנוי טפח לצד כותל זה וטפח לצד כותל זה שכל אותן ב' טפחים משימין ידיהן אחת מיכן ואחת מיכן ומגביהין ספר תורה בריוח ומוציאין אותו לחוץ **כדי שלא יהא נכנס ויוצא בדוחק: שבו** באותו טפח עמודיו של ארון **עומדין שנאמר אפריון עשה לו המלך שלמה.** המלך שהשלום שלו וכתב **עמודיו עשה כסף** של ארון. **בצידו מבחוץ.** שברי

AS IT IS SAID: *NOTHING WAS IN THE ARK — ONLY THE TWO TABLETS OF STONE WHICH MOSES PLACED THERE* [ETC.].[21] מַאי: ,,אֵין בָּאָרוֹן רַק" — WHAT IS meant by: *NOTHING WAS IN THE ARK — ONLY?* מִיעוּט אַחַר מִיעוּט — This is a case of ONE EXCLUSIONARY TERM ("only") FOLLOWING ANOTHER ("nothing"). וְאֵין מִיעוּט אַחַר מִיעוּט אֶלָּא לְרַבּוֹת סֵפֶר תּוֹרָה — AND the purpose here of ONE EXCLUSIONARY TERM FOLLOWING ANOTHER MUST BE TO INCLUDE[22] THE TORAH SCROLL written by Moses, שֶׁמּוּנָּח בָּאָרוֹן — THAT IT too LIES IN THE ARK.

The Baraisa continues:

פִּירְנַסְתָּ אָרוֹן לְאׇרְכּוֹ — Thus far, YOU HAVE ACCOUNTED FOR THE LENGTH OF THE ARK; צֵא וּפַרְנֵס אָרוֹן לְרׇחְבּוֹ — now GO AND ACCOUNT FOR THE WIDTH OF THE ARK. כַּמָּה לוּחוֹת אוֹכְלוֹת בָּאָרוֹן — HOW MUCH of the width OF THE ARK did THE TABLETS TAKE UP? שִׁשָּׁה טְפָחִים — SIX *TEFACHIM.* נִשְׁתַּיְּירוּ שָׁם שְׁלֹשָׁה טְפָחִים — Thus, THREE *TEFACHIM* REMAIN THERE across the width of the Ark that are as yet unaccounted for. צֵא מֵהֶן טֶפַח — SUBTRACT FROM [THESE THREE *TEFACHIM*] one *TEFACH* for the walls of the Ark: חֶצְיוֹ לְכוֹתֶל זֶה וְחֶצְיוֹ לְכוֹתֶל זֶה — HALF [A *TEFACH*] FOR ONE WALL AND HALF [A *TEFACH*] FOR THE OTHER WALL. נִשְׁתַּיְּירוּ שָׁם שְׁנֵי טְפָחִים — TWO *TEFACHIM* REMAIN THERE [across the width of the Ark], שֶׁלֹּא יְהֵא סֵפֶר תּוֹרָה נִכְנָס וְיוֹצֵא כְּשֶׁהוּא דָחוּק — the purpose of which was to ensure THAT WHEN THE TORAH SCROLL IS REMOVED AND INSERTED IT WOULD NOT BE PRESSED against the walls of the Ark.[23] דִּבְרֵי רַבִּי מֵאִיר — The preceding is THE OPINION OF R' MEIR.

The Baraisa presents an opposing view:

רַבִּי יְהוּדָה אוֹמֵר — R' YEHUDAH SAYS: בְּאַמָּה בַּת חֲמִשָּׁה טְפָחִים — THE *AMAH* of the Ark's dimensions given in the Torah MEASURES only FIVE *TEFACHIM.*[24] Accordingly, the Ark was 12 ½ *tefachim* long and 7 ½ *tefachim* wide. וְהַלּוּחוֹת אׇרְכָּן שִׁשָּׁה וְרׇחְבָּן שִׁשָּׁה וְעׇבְיָין שְׁלֹשָׁה — THE TABLETS, WHOSE LENGTH WAS SIX *tefachim*, WIDTH SIX *tefachim* AND THICKNESS THREE *tefachim*,[25] מוּנָּחוֹת בְּאוֹרְכּוֹ שֶׁל אָרוֹן — LAY side by side ALONG THE LENGTH OF THE ARK. כַּמָּה לוּחוֹת אוֹכְלוֹת בָּאָרוֹן — HOW MUCH of the length OF THE ARK DID THE TABLETS TAKE UP? שְׁנֵים עָשָׂר טְפָחִים — TWELVE *TEFACHIM.* נִשְׁתַּיֵּיר שָׁם חֲצִי טֶפַח — Hence, THERE REMAINS HALF A *TEFACH* along the length of the Ark which is as yet unaccounted for. אֶצְבַּע לְכוֹתֶל זֶה וְאֶצְבַּע לְכוֹתֶל זֶה — A FINGERBREADTH[26] is taken up BY ONE WALL AND A FINGERBREADTH BY THE OTHER WALL. פִּירְנַסְתָּ אָרוֹן לְאׇרְכּוֹ — Thus far, YOU HAVE ACCOUNTED FOR THE LENGTH OF THE ARK. צֵא וּפַרְנֵס אָרוֹן לְרׇחְבּוֹ — Now GO AND ACCOUNT FOR THE WIDTH OF THE ARK. כַּמָּה לוּחוֹת אוֹגְדוֹת[27] בָּאָרוֹן — HOW MUCH of the width OF THE ARK DID THE TABLETS TAKE UP? שִׁשָּׁה טְפָחִים — SIX *TEFACHIM.* נִשְׁתַּיֵּיר שָׁם טֶפַח וּמֶחֱצָה — ONE AND A HALF *TEFACHIM* REMAIN THERE [across the width of the Ark], צֵא מֵהֶן חֲצִי טֶפַח — SUBTRACT FROM THESE [ONE AND A HALF *TEFACHIM*] HALF A *TEFACH* for the walls: אֶצְבַּע וּמֶחֱצָה לְכוֹתֶל זֶה — ONE AND A HALF FINGERBREADTHS FOR ONE WALL וְאֶצְבַּע וּמֶחֱצָה לְכוֹתֶל זֶה — AND ONE AND A HALF FINGERBREADTHS FOR THE OTHER WALL.[28] נִשְׁתַּיֵּיר שָׁם טֶפַח שֶׁבּוֹ עַמּוּדִין עוֹמְדִין — one *TEFACH* REMAINS THERE, IN WHICH TWO silver RODS WERE POSITIONED, one on each side of the tablets; שֶׁנֶּאֱמַר — AS IT IS SAID: ,,אַפִּרְיוֹן עָשָׂה לוֹ הַמֶּלֶךְ שְׁלֹמֹה מֵעֲצֵי הַלְּבָנוֹן — *KING SHLOMO MADE HIMSELF A SEDAN-CHAIR OF THE WOOD OF LEBANON.* עַמּוּדָיו עָשָׂה כֶסֶף רְפִידָתוֹ זָהָב מֶרְכָּבוֹ אַרְגָּמָן וגו׳" — *HE MADE ITS PILLARS OF SILVER, ITS BACK OF GOLD, ITS SEAT OF PURPLE WOOL, ETC.*[29] Allegorically, this refers to the Tabernacle.[30] The "pillars of silver" denote the two silver rods placed in the Ark.

R' Yehudah continues:

וְאַרְגָּז שֶׁשִּׁיגְּרוּ בּוֹ פְּלִשְׁתִּים דּוֹרוֹן לֵאלֹהֵי יִשְׂרָאֵל — THE CHEST IN WHICH THE PHILISTINES SENT TRIBUTE TO THE GOD OF ISRAEL מוּנָּח מִצִּדּוֹ — WAS PLACED AT THE SIDE OF [THE ARK]; שֶׁנֶּאֱמַר — AS IT IS SAID: ,,וְאֵת כְּלֵי הַזָּהָב אֲשֶׁר הֲשֵׁבֹתֶם לוֹ אָשָׁם תָּשִׂימוּ בָאַרְגַּז מִצִּדּוֹ וְשִׁלַּחְתֶּם אֹתוֹ וְהָלָךְ" — The Philistine king instructed: *AND PUT THE GOLDEN UTENSILS, WHICH YOU ARE RETURNING TO HIM AS A GUILT OFFERING, IN A CHEST AT THE SIDE [OF THE ARK], AND SEND IT AWAY THAT IT MAY GO.*[31] This chest remained at the side of the

NOTES

21. *I Kings* 8:9.

22. This is one of the principles of Scriptural exegesis. When one exclusionary clause follows another the effect is similar to that of a double negative. One clause cancels out the other, and the overall effect is to indicate the *inclusion* of something not mentioned in the verse (see *Malbim* ad loc.).

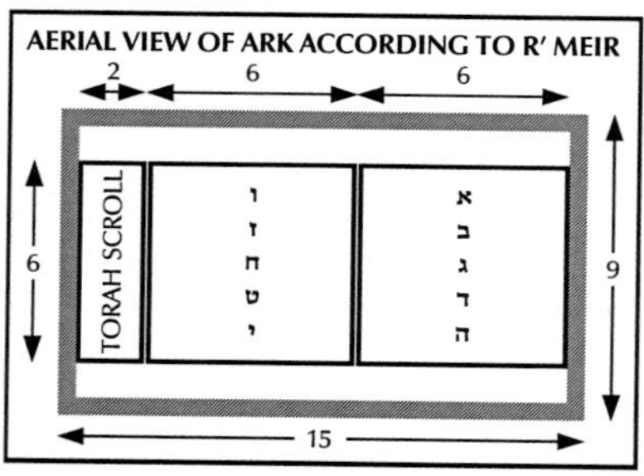

23. It is assumed that the height of Moses' Torah scroll was six *tefachim* (see end of note 8).

One *tefach* was left at the top of the Ark, and one *tefach* at the bottom, so that one could reach in and grasp the Torah scroll from both ends (*Rabbeinu Gershom*). See diagram.

[The scroll was removed from the Ark on the following occasions:] This was the scroll read by the king during the ceremony of *Hakhel*. The Kohen Gadol read from it on Yom Kippur (*Rashi* to 14b ד״ה ספר).

An alternative view: The Torah scroll was taken from the Ark only for the purposes of maintenance. [Although, as far as the service was concerned, no one entered the Holy of Holies (in which the Ark was situated) except the Kohen Gadol on Yom Kippur, even non-Kohanim are allowed to enter the Holy of Holies to make repairs — *Eruvin* 105a] (*Tosafos*).

24. The Gemara (*Succah* 5b) states that according to R' Yehudah, the *amah* measurements given in reference to the Tabernacle's appurtenances are "small" *amos* — i.e. lengths of 5 *tefachim* [see note 17] (*Rashi*).

25. R' Yehudah and R' Meir do not disagree about the size of the Tablets. They differ only in regard to the dimensions of the Ark and the other appurtenances of the Tabernacle.

26. There are three definitions of אֶצְבַּע, *fingerbreadth:* 1) thumb (¼ *tefach*); 2) index finger (⅕ *tefach*); 3) little finger (⅙ *tefach*) (*Rashi* below ד״ה אצבע). Here, the reference is to the "thumb" measurement.

27. Other texts read אוֹכְלוֹת [as in the statement of R' Meir] (*Mesoras HaShas*).

28. Here, the Gemara refers to the smallest size of fingerbreadth, which measures ⅙ *tefach* (see note 26). Thus, in this context, 1½ fingerbreadths is ¼ *tefach.*

There is an alternative version of the text which reads: אֶצְבַּע לְכוֹתֶל זֶה, *a fingerbreadth for this wall.* This version is preferred, for according to it the type of fingerbreadth referred to here is the same as the one mentioned above (see end of note 26); i.e. in both places the reference is to the "thumb" measurement — ¼ *tefach* (*Rashi;* cf. *Tosafos*).

29. *Song of Songs* 3:9,10.

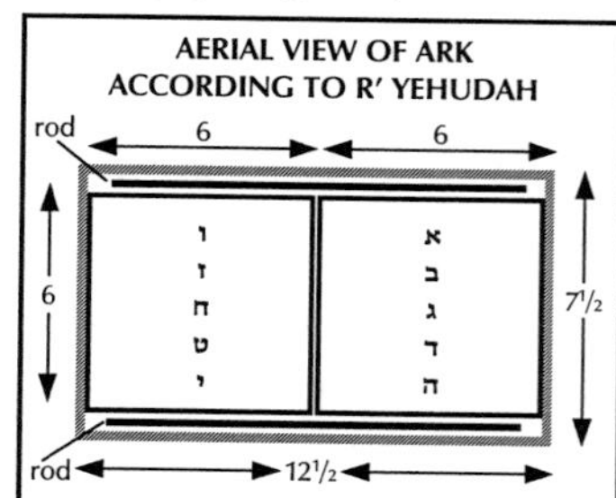

30. The verses are interpreted as follows: אַפִּרְיוֹן עָשָׂה לוֹ הַמֶּלֶךְ שְׁלֹמֹה, *The King to Whom peace belongs* (i.e. God) *made a Tabernacle for His presence,* מֵעֲצֵי הַלְּבָנוֹן, *of the wood of Lebanon.* עַמּוּדָיו עָשָׂה כֶסֶף, *Its rods He made of silver,* רְפִידָתוֹ זָהָב, *His resting place* [i.e. the cover of the Ark, on which the Divine Presence "rests"] *of gold,* מֶרְכָּבוֹ אַרְגָּמָן, *its suspended curtain* [i.e. the curtain between the Holy and the Holy of Holies] *of purple wool* (see *Rashi* and *Metzudos* ad loc.).

See diagram for the layout of the Ark's contents according to R' Yehudah.

31. *I Samuel* 6:8. During a battle against the Jews, the Ark was captured by the Philistines. When tragedies occurred wherever the Philistines kept the Ark, they decided to return it. They sent it in a wagon pulled by

ואם בא לחתוך חותך מאי קאמר הכי קאמר
א) שאם בא לחתוך חותך ורמינהי ב) תחלת ספר
וסופו כדי לגול מאי אי כדי לגול
עמוד קשיא הקף אי כדי לגול הקף קשי' עמוד
א"ר נחמן בר יצחק לצדדין קתני רב אשי אמר
ג) כי תניא ההיא בספר תורה כדתניא ד) כל
הספרים נגללים מתחלתן לסופן וס"ת נגלל
לאמצעיתו ועושה לו עמוד אילך ואילך א"ר
אליעזר בר' צדוק כך היו כותבי ספרים
שבירושלים עושין (א) ספריהם ת"ר ה) אין עושין
ספר תורה לא ארכו יותר על הקיפו ולא הקיפו
יותר על ארכו שאלו את רבי שיעור ס"ת בכמה
אמר להן ו) בגויל ששה ז) בקלף בכמה איני יודע
רב הונא כתב שבעין ספרי דאורייתא ולא
איתרמי ליה אלא חד רב אחא בר יעקב כתב
חד אמשכיה דעיגלי ואיתרמי ליה ח) יהבו ביה
רבנן עינייהו ונח נפשיה אמרו ליה רבנן לרב
המנונא כתב רבי אמי ד' מאה ספרי תורה
אמר להו דילמא א) תורה צוה לנו משה כתב
א"ל רבא לר' זירא נטע ר' ינאי ארבע מאה
כרמי א"ל דילמא שתים כנגד שתים ואחת
יוצא זנב מיתיבי ארון שעשה משה אמתים
וחצי ארכו ואמה וחצי רחבו ואמה וחצי
קומתו באמה בת ששה טפחים ט) והלוחות
ארכן ששה ורחבן ששה ועביין שלשה
מונחות כנגד ארכו של ארון כמה לוחות
אוכלות בארון שנים עשר טפחים נשתיירו שם
שלשה טפחים צא מהן טפח חציו לכותל זה
וחציו לכותל זה נשתיירו שם שני טפחים
שבהן ספר תורה מונח שנאמ' ב) אין בארון רק
שני לוחות האבנים אשר הניח שם משה
[וגו'] מאי אין בארון רק מיעוט אחר מיעוט
ואין מיעוט אחר מיעוט אלא לרבות ס"ת
שמונח בארון פירנסת ארון לארכו צא ופרנס
ארון לרחבו כמה לוחות אוכלות בארון ששה
טפחים נשתיירו שם שלשה טפחים צא מהן
טפח חציו לכותל זה וחציו לכותל זה נשתיירו
שם שני טפחים שלא יהא ספר תורה נכנס
ויוצא כשהוא דחוק דברי ר"מ ר' יהודה אומר
באמה בת חמשה טפחים והלוחות ארכן
ששה ורחבן ששה ועביין שלשה מונחות
בארכו של ארון כמה לוחות אוכלות בארון
שנים עשר טפחים נשתייר שם חצי טפח
אצבע לכותל זה ואצבע לכותל זה פירנסת
ארון לארכו צא ופרנס ארון לרחבו כמה לוחות
אוגדות בארון ששה טפחים נשתייר שם
טפח ומחצה צא מהן חצי טפח אצבע (ב)
ומחצה לכותל זה ואצבע ומחצה לכותל זה נשתייר שם טפח שבו עמודין
עומדין שנאמר ג) אפריון עשה לו המלך שלמה מעצי הלבנון עמודיו עשה כסף
רפידתו זהב מרכבו ארגמן וגו' (ג) וארגז ששיגרו בו פלשתים דורון לאלהי ישראל
מונח מצדו שנאמר ד) ואת כלי הזהב אשר השבותם לו אשם תשימו בארגז
מצדו ושלחתם אותו והלך ועליו ס"ת מונח שנאמר ה) לקוח את ספר התורה
הזה ושמתם אותו מצד ארון ברית ה' מצד (ד) הוא מונח ולא בתוכו ומה אני מקיים אין בארון רק לרבות
שברי

רש"י

ואם בא לחתוך חותך מאי קאמר. מאי למימרא הכל מודים דאם כל אחד ואחד בפני עצמו עדיף: הכי קאמר. ומתחיל מלמעלה ולא יניח חלק שהרי אם בא לחתוך חותך ונמצא זה ראש הכרך וגנאי הוא לו להיות דף זה משונה מחבירו על חנם: כדי לגול. קס"ד חד שיעורא יהיב ליה לתחילתו וסופו: לספריהם. לספרי תורה: לא ארכו יותר על הקיפו. צריך למלאת הכתב לפי עובי הקלפי' לכשיגמור יהא חוט המקיף את עוביו כמדת ארכו: שיעור ספר תורה בכמה. ארכו מיבעיא להו: בגויל. שהוא עב והקיפו גדול צריך ששה טפחים זו היא מדה להיות נגמר בששה טפחים היקף בכתב בינוני: ולא איתרמי ליה. ארכו כהקיפו: איתרמי ליה. ארכו כהקיפו: דילמא תורה צוה לנו משה מורשה כתב. ארבע מאות פעמים אבל ארבע מאה (ה) ספרים אין פנאי לאדם אחד לכתוב: שתים כנגד שתים. שתי גפנים כנגד שתים וא' יוצא זנב בכך קרוי כרם לגבי לחזור עליו מעורכי המלחמה במסכת סוטה (דף מג.): באמה בת ששה טפחים. ר"מ לטעמיה דאמר (סוכה ה:) כל האמות היו בינוניות: לארכו של ארון. זו אצל זו: אוכלות. תופסות כך לשון המשנה (מדות פ"ג מ"א) אוכל בדרום אמה אחת גבי יסוד המזבח ואף בלשון מקרא כי יוכלו אתיקים מהנה בספר יחזקאל (מב): צא מהם טפח. לעובי הכתלים שהרי מבחוץ נמדד אמתי' וחצי ארכו: ס"ת. שכתב משה כמו שנאמר ויכתוב משה את ט) (התורה) וגו' (דברים לא): אין [מיעוט אחר מיעוט]. י) אך ורק שני מיעוטין הן: שבהן ס"ת מונח. ארכו לרחבו של ארון: פירנסת ארון לארכו. כלומר מלאת כל חללו לארכו ופירשת צרכי מדתו: ששה טפחים. במדת רחבו: כדי שלא יהא ס"ת כו'. כלומר לא היה צריך להיות רחבו כל כך אלא בשביל ס"ת המונח אורכו לרוחב הארון שלא יהא נכנס ויוצא בדוחק: ר"י אומר. מדת הארון באמה של ה' טפחים היתה רבי יהודה לטעמיה דקאמר אמת כלים באמה בת חמשה: מונחות לארכו של ארון. מוטלות על רוחבן ולא על חודן: אצבע לכותל זה. שהטפח ארבע אצבעות ולמאן דגרים אצבע ומחצה באצבע קטנה קאמר שהטפח ד' בגודל וחמש באצבע ושש בקטנה: שבו עמודים עומדים. ג' עמודי כסף כמין עמודי ספר תורה שוכבים לארכו והלוחות ביניהן שנאמר עמודיו עשה כסף: מונח שם בצדו. של ארון: ועליו ס"ת מונח. ולקמיה פריך מעיקרא היכי הוה מונח:
שברי

תוספות

שאם בא לחתוך חותך. תימה לרשב"א הא אמר לעיל בשתי כריכות חולקין ופ"ה כגון תורה בכרך אחד ונביאים בכרך א' משמע אבל תורה ונביאים בכרך א' אין חולקין אפי' שניהן רוצים וא"כ היכי אמר הכא דחותך ויש לומר דלא הוי בזיון הספר אלא כשחותך מחמת חלוקה: בגויל ששה טפחים בקלף בכמה. גויל הוא עור שלא ניתקן כלל אלא שהסירו את השער וכותבין בו במקום שער ולהכי קרי ליה גויל שאינו מתוקן כדאמר לעיל (דף ג.) גויל אבני דלא משפיין ופעמים חותכין אותו לשנים דרך עוביו ואותו שכלפי שער קרוי קלף ואותו שלצד בשר קרוי דוכסוסטוס ולשון דוכסוסטוס הוי פירושו מקום בשר דבלשון ז) מדי קורין לבשר סוסטוס ודוך היינו מקום כמו ח) דוך פלוני וכותבין על הקלף לצד בשר כדאמר בפ' המוציא (שבת דף עט:) ועל דוכסוסטוס לצד שער ובשניהם במקום חתך דשם הוא טוב לכתוב ושלנו דין קלף יש להם ולא דין דוכסוסטוס ולכך כותבין עליהם תפילין שאין כשרים על דוכסוסטוס אלא על הקלף כדאמר בהמוציא יין (שם): דילמא תורה צוה. ואומר ר"ת דאותו פסוק קרוי תורה כדאמר בפ' ג' דסוכה (דף מב.) קטן היודע לדבר אביו מלמדו תורה מאי תורה תורה צוה לנו משה: שלא יהא ספר תורה יוצא ונכנס כשהוא דחוק. וא"ת והלא לא היו מוציאין אותו מן הארון דהא אסור ליכנס בבית קדש הקדשים וביום הכפורים לא אשכחן בסדר יומא שהיה מוציאו וי"ל דלצורך כדי לתקן שרי ליכנס בבית קדש הקדשים כדאמרינן בעירובין (דף קה.) וה"נ יכולין ליכנס שם כדי לתקן ספר תורה כדי שלא יתעפש ויתקלקל וגם משחרב משכן שילה עד שבנה שלמה בית המקדש היו יכולין להוציאו מן הארון ולעיין בו: אצבע ומחצה לכותל זה. נראה לר"ת דלא גרס ומחצה אלא אצבע לכותל זה דאי גרס ומחצה תיקשי שנים עשר (ו) היכי יתבי כדפריך לקמן אלא אצבע גרס וזוטרתי דהויין ששה בטפח: שבהן עמודים עומדין. נראה לר"ת דסימן להעמדת ישראל היה ולא עשאום של זהב שלא להזכיר מעשה העגל דאין קטיגור נעשה סניגור וכן אמרינן [בר"ה] (דף כו.) דמשום הכי לא היה כהן משמש לפני ולפנים ביוה"כ בבגדי זהב משום דאין קטיגור נעשה סניגור והתם פריך והא הוה ארון שהיה של זהב והיה לפנים ומשני מכפר קאמרי' והני עמודים נמי היו כמו מכפר שהם עשוים סימן להעמדת ישראל והוא שיסד הפייט ט) תבנית אות יוסף עמודיו עשה כסף בשביל תבנית אות יוסף סימן של יוסף דהיינו עגל דיוסף נקרא שור שנאמר (דברים לג) בכור שורו הדר לו לכך עמודיו עשה כסף ולא זהב שלא להזכיר במעשה העגל:
תרי

עין משפט נר מצוה

קכו א מיי' פ"ז מהל' ס"ת הל' טו סמג עשין כה (טוש"ע שם):
קכז ב ג מיי' פ"ט מהל' ס"ת הלכה ג סמג עשין כה טוש"ע י"ד סי' רעג סעיף א:
קכח ד מיי' שם וסמג שם טוש"ע י"ד סי' רעח סעיף ב:
קכט ה ו ז מיי' שם פ"ט הלכה א וסמג שם טוש"ע י"ד סי' רעב סעיף א [וברב אלפס הלכות ספר תורה דף סו]:

רבינו גרשום

דף פנוי מלמטה ומתחיל באחר מלמעלה **שאם באו** לחלוק שיכולין **לחתוך** ולחלק יפה כבשתי כריכות. **שמונה נביאים** ח' ספרים של נביאים. **ועושה בראשו** של ספר תורה חלק **כשיעור לגול** עמוד בתחלתו והאי תחלה הוי סוף הספר לפי כי בסוף מתחילין לגלגל המגילה ומגלגל והולך עד ראש לפי שכל ספריהם נכתבין כעין מגילה ולא בקונטרסים (והם) והכי נמי מניח מן הקלף חלק **בסוף** כל הכרך שהוא תחלת הספר כשיעור שיכול לגול את כל ההיקף על אותו חלק כדי שיהא משמש הקלף פנוי לכתבי הקדש: **קשיא עמוד** דלעיל קתני בראשו כדי לגול עמוד והכא קתני תחלת הספר וסופו כדי לגול עמוד. **האי** כדי לגול דברייתא נמי **לצדדין קתני** כדאמרן דתחלה כדי לגול עמוד ובסוף כדי לגול היקף. **רב אשי אמר** לעולם לא קתני לצדדין אלא תחלתו וסופו כדי לגול עמוד **ובספר תורה** מיירי **דלאמצעיתו** נגלל על ב' עמודים אבל שאר ספרים היו נגללין הכל על עמוד אחד ואמטו להכי צריך להניח כדי היקף כדאמרן. **ולא אורכו יותר על הקיפו** שכשמשכין אותו בחוט של מישחה לאורכו של דף ומקיפין מן אותו חוט היקף הספר תורה שיהא שוים במדה. **גויל** ו' **טפחים** אורך הדף שכך למד מגויל. אבל מן קלף לא אמר לפיכך **אמר איני יודע. ולא איתרמי ליה** שיהא אורכו שוה להקיפו. **יהבו ביה עינייהו** קינאו (אדון) בו שכך כיון. **תורה צוה לנו** כתב דדומה עליו גוזמא. **ורמינהו** מקשה על מאי דאמר שיהא ס"ת הקיפו כאורכו. **וארון שעשה** משה היה דומה כמין תיבה שאין לה כיסוי שבכפרת היה מכוסה. **באמה בת ו' טפחים. ואמתים וחצי אורכו** עולין לט"ו טפחי': **וכמה לוחות אוכלות בארון.** כלומר כמה מחזיקות בארון. **י"ב טפחי'** שהיו מונחין הלוחות זו בצד זו. **ואין ורק** תרי מיעוטי **לרבות ספר תורה שמונח בארון** באותן ב' טפחים שנשתיירו מאורך הארון והיה אורכו של ספר תורה כרוחבן של לוחות ו' טפחים **נשתיירו ב' טפחים** פנוי טפח לצד כותל זה וטפח לצד כותל זה שכל אותן ב' טפחים משימין ידיהן אחת מיכן ואחת מיכן ומגביהין ספר תורה בריוח ומוציאין אותו לחוץ **כדי שלא יהא נכנס ויוצא בדוחק: שבו** באותו טפח עמודיו של ארון עומדין **שנאמר אפריון עשה לו** זה ארון. **המלך שלמה.** המלך שהשלום שלו וכתב **עמודיו עשה כסף** של ארון. **בצידו מבחוץ.**
שברי

מסורת הש"ס

א) [ברכות דף נח:], ב) [נדרים לח.], ג) [יומא מג. וש"נ], ד) נ"א אוכלות, ה) [נ"ל הסירה], ו) [אין ורק], ז) [בשבת עט: ד"ה קלף כתבו דבלשון יון], ח) [ברכות יח:], ט) ביום ראשון דפסח:

הגהות הב"ח

(א) גמ' עושין לספריהם: (ב) שם לא מהן חצי טפח אצבע לכותל זה ואצבע לכותל זה כצ"ל ותיבת ומחצה נמחק ב' פעמים: (ג) שם מרכבו ארגמן וגו' תוכו רצוף אהבה וארגז: (ד) שם מצד היה מונח ולא: (ה) רש"י ד"ה דילמא וכו' ד' מאה ספרי תורות לא כתב דאין פנאי לאדם אחד לכתוב כולי האי הס"ד: (ו) תוס' ד"ה אצבע וכו' תקשה שנים עשר בי"ב היכי יתבי:

תורה אור השלם

א) תּוֹרָה צִוָּה לָנוּ מֹשֶׁה מוֹרָשָׁה קְהִלַּת יַעֲקֹב: [דברים לג, ד]

ב) אֵין בָּאָרוֹן רַק שְׁנֵי לֻחוֹת הָאֲבָנִים אֲשֶׁר הִנִּחַ שָׁם מֹשֶׁה בְּחֹרֵב אֲשֶׁר כָּרַת יְיָ עִם בְּנֵי יִשְׂרָאֵל בְּצֵאתָם מֵאֶרֶץ מִצְרָיִם: [מלכים א ח, ט]

ג) אַפִּרְיוֹן עָשָׂה לוֹ הַמֶּלֶךְ שְׁלֹמֹה מֵעֲצֵי הַלְּבָנוֹן: עַמּוּדָיו עָשָׂה כֶסֶף רְפִידָתוֹ זָהָב מֶרְכָּבוֹ אַרְגָּמָן תּוֹכוֹ רָצוּף אַהֲבָה מִבְּנוֹת יְרוּשָׁלָיִם: [שיר השירים ג, ט-י]

ד) וּלְקַחְתֶּם אֶת אֲרוֹן יְיָ וּנְתַתֶּם אֹתוֹ אֶל הָעֲגָלָה וְאֵת כְּלֵי הַזָּהָב אֲשֶׁר הֲשֵׁבֹתֶם לוֹ אָשָׁם תָּשִׂימוּ בָאַרְגַּז מִצִּדּוֹ וְשִׁלַּחְתֶּם אֹתוֹ וְהָלָךְ: [שמואל א ו, ח]

ה) לָקֹחַ אֵת סֵפֶר הַתּוֹרָה הַזֶּה וְשַׂמְתֶּם אֹתוֹ מִצַּד אֲרוֹן בְּרִית יְיָ אֱלֹהֵיכֶם וְהָיָה שָׁם בְּךָ לְעֵד: [דברים לא, כו]

ליקוטי רש"י

גויל. מעובד בעפצים [שבת עט.].

Ark when the Ark was replaced in the Holy of Holies, וְעָלָיו סֵפֶר תּוֹרָה מוּנָּח – AND UPON IT THE TORAH SCROLL of Moses WAS PLACED, שֶׁנֶּאֱמַר – AS IT IS SAID: ,,לָקֹחַ אֵת סֵפֶר הַתּוֹרָה הַזֶּה וְשַׂמְתֶּם אֹתוֹ מִצַּד אֲרוֹן בְּרִית־ה׳" – *TAKE THIS TORAH SCROLL AND YOU SHALL PLACE IT AT THE SIDE OF THE ARK OF THE COVENANT OF HASHEM.*[32] The verse specifies "at the side of the Ark," מִצַּד הוּא מוּנָּח וְלֹא בְּתוֹכוֹ – which implies that [THE TORAH SCROLL] WAS PLACED AT THE SIDE of the Ark, NOT INSIDE IT.[33]

R' Yehudah now explains the verse from which R' Meir derived that the Torah scroll of Moses was kept *inside* the Ark: וּמָה אֲנִי מְקַיֵּים: ,,אֵין בָּאָרוֹן רַק" – AND HOW DO I EXPLAIN the double exclusion: *THERE WAS NOTHING IN THE ARK – ONLY?* לְרַבּוֹת – It serves TO INCLUDE

NOTES

two cows, along with a chest full of gold as a penance. By a miracle, the cows, although they were not led, unerringly made their way to Eretz Yisrael (see *I Samuel* chs. 5,6).

32. *Deuteronomy* 31:26.

33. The Gemara below (14b) inquires where the Torah scroll was placed, according to R' Yehudah, *before* this chest was sent by the Philistines (*Rashi*).

מסורת הש"ס

א) [ברכות דף נח:], ב) [נדרים לח.], ג) [יומא מג. וש"נ], ד) נ"א אוכלות, ה) [נ"ל השירה], ו) [אין ורק], ז) [בשבת עט: ד"ה קלף כתבו דבלשון יון], ח) [ברכות יח:], ט) ביום ראשון דפסח:

הגהות הב"ח

(א) גמ' עושין לספריהם: (ב) שם לא מהן חצי טפח אצבע לכותל זה ואצבע לכותל זה כצ"ל ותיבת ומחצה נמחק ב' פעמים: (ג) שם מרכבו ארגמן וגו' תוכו רצוף אהבה וארגז: (ד) שם מצד היה מונח ולא: (ה) רש"י ד"ה דילמא וכו' ד' מאה ספרי תורות לא כתב דאין פנאי לאדם אחד לכתוב כולי האי הס"ד: (ו) תוס' ד"ה אצבע וכו' תקשה שנים עשר בי"ב היכי יתבי:

תורה אור השלם

א) תּוֹרָה צִוָּה לָנוּ מֹשֶׁה מוֹרָשָׁה קְהִלַּת יַעֲקֹב: [דברים לג, ד]

ב) אֵין בָּאָרוֹן רַק שְׁנֵי לֻחוֹת הָאֲבָנִים אֲשֶׁר הִנִּחַ שָׁם מֹשֶׁה בְּחֹרֵב אֲשֶׁר כָּרַת יְיָ עִם בְּנֵי יִשְׂרָאֵל בְּצֵאתָם מֵאֶרֶץ מִצְרָיִם: [מלכים א ח, ט]

ג) אַפִּרְיוֹן עָשָׂה לוֹ הַמֶּלֶךְ שְׁלֹמֹה מֵעֲצֵי הַלְּבָנוֹן: עַמּוּדָיו עָשָׂה כֶסֶף רְפִידָתוֹ זָהָב מֶרְכָּבוֹ אַרְגָּמָן תּוֹכוֹ רָצוּף אַהֲבָה מִבְּנוֹת יְרוּשָׁלָיִם: [שיר השירים ג, ט-י]

ד) וּלְקַחְתֶּם אֶת אֲרוֹן יְיָ וּנְתַתֶּם אֹתוֹ אֶל הָעֲגָלָה וְאֵת כְּלֵי הַזָּהָב אֲשֶׁר הֲשֵׁבֹתֶם לוֹ אָשָׁם תָּשִׂימוּ בָאַרְגַּז מִצִּדּוֹ וְשִׁלַּחְתֶּם אֹתוֹ וְהָלָךְ: [שמואל א ו, ח]

ה) לָקֹחַ אֵת סֵפֶר הַתּוֹרָה הַזֶּה וְשַׂמְתֶּם אֹתוֹ מִצַּד אֲרוֹן בְּרִית יְיָ אֱלֹהֵיכֶם וְהָיָה שָׁם בְּךָ לְעֵד: [דברים לא, כו]

ליקוטי רש"י

גויל. מעובד בעפצים [שבת עט.].

גמרא

ואם בא לחתוך חותך מאי קאמר הכי קאמר א שאם בא לחתוך חותך ורמינהי ב תחלת ספר וסופו כדי לגול כדי לגול מאי אי כדי לגול עמוד קשיא הקף אי כדי לגול הקף קשי' עמוד א"ר נחמן בר יצחק לצדדין קתני רב אשי אמר ג כי תניא ההיא בספר תורה כדתניא ד כל הספרים נגללים מתחלתן לסופן וס"ת נגלל לאמצעיתו ועושה לו עמוד אילך ואילך א"ר אליעזר בר' צדוק כך היו כותבי ספרים שבירושלים עושין (א) ספריהם ת"ר ה אין עושין ספר תורה לא ארכו יותר על הקיפו ולא הקיפו יותר על ארכו שאלו את רבי שיעור ס"ת בכמה אמר להן ו בגויל ששה ז בקלף בכמה איני יודע רב הונא כתב שבעין ספרי דאורייתא ולא איתרמי ליה אלא חד רב אחא בר יעקב כתב חד אמשכיה דעיגלי ואיתרמי ליה ח יהבו ביה רבנן עינייהו ונח נפשיה אמרו ליה רבנן לרב המנונא כתב רבי אמי ד' מאה ספרי תורה אמר להו דילמא א תורה צוה לנו משה כתב א"ל רבא לר' זירא נטע ר' ינאי ארבע מאה כרמי א"ל דילמא שתים כנגד שתים ואחת יוצא זנב מיתיבי ארון שעשה משה אמתים וחצי ארכו ואמה וחצי רחבו ואמה וחצי קומתו באמה בת ששה טפחים ט והלוחות ארכן ששה ורחבן ששה ועביין שלשה מונחות כנגד ארכו של ארון כמה לוחות אוכלות בארון שנים עשר טפחים נשתיירו שם שלשה טפחים צא מהן טפח חציו לכותל זה וחציו לכותל זה נשתיירו שם שני טפחים שבהן ספר תורה מונח שנאמ' ב אין בארון רק שני לוחות האבנים אשר הניח שם משה [וגו'] מאי אין בארון רק מיעוט אחר מיעוט ג ואין מיעוט אחר מיעוט אלא לרבות ס"ת שמונח בארון פירנסת ארון לארכו צא ופרנס ארון לרחבו כמה לוחות אוכלות בארון ששה טפחים נשתיירו שם שלשה טפחים צא מהן טפח חציו לכותל זה וחציו לכותל זה נשתיירו שם שני טפחים שלא יהא ספר תורה נכנס ויוצא כשהוא דחוק דברי ר"מ ר' יהודה אומר באמה בת חמשה טפחים והלוחות ארכן ששה ורחבן ששה ועביין שלשה מונחות באורכו של ארון כמה לוחות אוכלות בארון שנים עשר טפחים נשתייר שם חצי טפח אצבע לכותל זה ואצבע לכותל זה פירנסת ארון לארכו צא ופרנס ארון לרחבו כמה לוחות ד אוגדות בארון ששה טפחים נשתייר שם טפח ומחצה צא מהן חצי טפח אצבע (ב) ומחצה לכותל זה ואצבע ומחצה לכותל זה נשתייר שם טפח שבו עמודין עומדין שנאמר ג אפריון עשה לו המלך שלמה מעצי הלבנון עמודיו עשה כסף רפידתו זהב מרכבו ארגמן וגו' (ג) וארגז ששיגרו בו פלשתים דורון לאלהי ישראל מונח מצדו שנאמר ד ואת כלי הזהב אשר השבותם לו אשם תשימו בארגז מצדו ושלחתם אותו והלך ועליו ס"ת מונח שנאמר ה לקוח את ספר התורה הזה ושמתם אותו מצד ארון ברית ה' מצד (ד) הוא מונח ולא בתוכו ומה אני מקיים אין בארון רק לרבות שברי

רש"י

ואם בא לחתוך חותך מאי קאמר. מאי למימרא הכל מודים דאם כל אחד ואחד בפני עצמו טפי עדיף: הכי קאמר. ומתחיל מלמעלה ולא יניח חלק שהרי אם בא לחתוך חותך ונמצא זה ראש הכרך וגנאי הוא לו להיות דף זה משונה מחבירו על חנם: כדי לגול. קס"ד חד שיעורא יהיב ליה לתחילתו וסופו: לספריהן. לספרי תורה: לא ארכו יותר על הקיפו. צריך לעמוס הכתב לפי עובי הקלפי' לכשיגמור יהא חוט המקיף את עוביו כמדת ארכו: שיעור ספר תורה בכמה. ארכו מיבעיא להו: בגויל. שהוא עב והקיפו גדול צריך ששה טפחים זו היא מדה להיות נגמר בששה טפחים היקף בכתב בינוני: ולא איתרמי ליה. ארכו כהקיפו: איתרמי ליה. ארכו כהקיפו: דילמא תורה צוה לנו משה מורשה כתב. ארבע מאות פעמים אבל ארבע מאה (ה) ספרים אין פנאי לאדם אחד לכתוב: שתים כנגד שתים. שתי גפנים כנגד שתים ואחת יוצא זנב בכך קרוי כרם לגבי לחזור עליו מעורכי המלחמה במסכת סוטה (דף מג.): באמה בת ששה טפחים. ר"מ לטעמיה דאמר (סוכה ה:) כל האמות היו בינוניות: לארכו של ארון. זו אצל זו: אוכלות. תופסות כך לשון המשנה (מדות פ"ג מ"א) אוכל בדרום אמה אחת גבי יסוד המזבח ואף בלשון מקרא כי יוכלו אתיקים מהנה בספר יחזקאל (מב): צא מהם טפח. לעובי הכתלים שהרי מבחוץ נמדד אמתי' וחצי ארכו: ס"ת. שכתב משה כמו שנאמר ויכתוב משה את ו (התורה) וגו' (דברים לא): אין [מיעוט אחר מיעוט]. ז אך ורק שני מיעוטין הן: שבהן ס"ת מונח. ארכו לרחבו של ארון: פירנסת ארון לארכו. כלומר מלאת כל חללו לארכו ופירשת לרכי מדותו: ששה טפחים. במדת רחבו: כדי שלא יהא ס"ת כו'. כלומר לא היה צריך להיות רחבו כל כך אלא בשביל ס"ת המונח אורכו לרוחב הארון שלא יהא נכנס ויוצא בדוחק: ר"י אומר. מדת הארון באמה של ה' טפחים היתה ורבי יהודה לטעמיה דאמר אמת כלים באמה בת חמשה: מונחות לארכו של ארון. מוטלות על רוחבן ולא על חודן: אצבע לכותל זה. שהטפח ארבע אצבעות ולמאן דגרים אצבע ומחצה באצבע קטנה קאמר שהטפח ד' בגודל וחמש באצבע ושש בקטנה: שבו עמודים עומדים. ג' עמודי כסף כמין עמודי ספר תורה שוכבים לארכו והלוחות ביניהן שנאמר עמודיו עשה כסף: מונח שם בצדו. של ארון: ועליו ס"ת מונח. ולקמיה פריך מעיקרא היכי הוה מונח: שברי

תוספות

שאם בא לחתוך חותך. תימה לרשב"א הא אמר לעיל בשתי כריכות חולקין ופ"ה כגון תורה בכרך אחד ונביאים בכרך אחד משמע אבל תורה ונביאים בכרך א' אין חולקין אפי' שניהן רוצים וא"כ היכי אמר הכא דחותך ויש לומר דלא הוי בזיון הספר אלא כשחותך מחמת מחלוקה:

בגויל ששה טפחים בקלף בכמה. גויל הוא עור שלא ניתקן כלל אלא שהסירו את השער וכותבין בו במקום שער ולהכי קרי ליה גויל שאינו מתוקן כדאמר לעיל (דף ג.) גויל אבני דלא משפיין ופעמים חותכין אותו לשנים דרך עוביו ואותו שכלפי שער קרוי קלף ואותו שלצד בשר קרוי דוכסוסטוס ולשון דוכסוסטוס הוי פירושו מקום בשר דבלשון ז) מדי קורין לבשר סוסטוס ודוך היינו מקום כמו ח) דוך פלוני וכותבין על הקלף לצד בשר כדאמר בפ' המוציא (שבת דף עט:) ועל הדוכסוסטוס לצד שער ובשניהם במקום חתך דשם הוא טוב לכתוב ושלנו דין קלף יש להם ולא דין דוכסוסטוס ולכך כותבין עליהם תפילין שאין כשרים על דוכסוסטוס אלא על הקלף כדאמר בהמוציא יין (שם):

דילמא תורה צוה. ואומר ר"ת דאותו פסוק קרוי תורה כדאמר בפ' ג' דסוכה (דף מב.) קטן היודע לדבר אביו מלמדו תורה מאי תורה תורה צוה לנו משה:

שלא יהא ספר תורה יוצא ונכנס כשהוא דחוק. וא"ת והלא לא היו מוציאין אותו מן הארון דהא אסור ליכנס בבית קדש הקדשים וביום הכפורים לא אשכחן בסדר יומא שהיה מוציאו וי"ל דלצורך כדי לתקן שרי ליכנס בבית קדש הקדשים כדאמרינן בעירובין (דף קה.) וה"נ יכולין ליכנס שם כדי לתקן ספר תורה כדי שלא יתעפש ויתקלקל וגם משחרב משכן שילה עד שבנה שלמה בית המקדש היו יכולין להוציאו מן הארון ולעיין בו:

אצבע ומחצה לכותל זה. נראה לר"ת דלא גרס ומחצה אלא אצבע לכותל זה דאי גרס ומחצה תיקשי שנים עשר (ו) היכי יתבי כדפריך לקמן אלא אצבע גרס וזוטרתי דהויין שש בטפח:

שבהן עמודים עומדין. נראה לר"ת דסימן להעמדת ישראל היה ולא עשאום של זהב שלא להזכיר מעשה העגל דאין קטיגור נעשה סניגור וכן אמרינן [בר"ה] (דף כו.) דמשום הכי לא היה כהן משמש לפני ולפנים ביוה"כ בבגדי זהב משום דאין קטיגור נעשה סניגור והתם פריך והא הוה ארון שהיה של זהב והיה לפנים ומשני מכפר קאמרי' והני עמודים נמי היו כמו מכפר שהם עשוים סימן להעמדת ישראל והוא שיסד הפייט ט) תבנית אות יוסף עמודיו עשה כסף בשביל תבנית אות יוסף סימן של יוסף דהיינו עגל דיוסף נקרא שור שנאמר (דברים לג) בכור שורו הדר לו לכך עמודיו עשה כסף ולא זהב שלא להזכיר במעשה העגל:

תרי

עין משפט נר מצוה

קכו א מיי' פ"ז מהל' ס"ת הל' טו סמג עשין כה (טוש"ע יו"ד סי' רעג):

קכז ב ג מיי' פ"ט מהל' ס"ת הלכה ב סמג עשין כה טוש"ע י"ד סי' רעג סעיף א:

קכח ד מיי' שם וסמג שם טוש"ע י"ד סי' רעה סעיף ג:

קכט ה ו ז מיי' שם פ"ט הלכה א וסמג שם טוש"ע י"ד סי' רעג סעיף א [וברב אלפס הלכות ספר תורה דף סו]:

רבינו גרשום

דף פנוי מלמטה ומתחיל באחר מלמעלה שאם באו לחלוק שיכולין לחתוך ולחלק יפה כבשתי כריכות. שמונה נביאים ח' ספרים של נביאים. ועושה בראשו של ספר תורה חלק כשיעור לגול עמוד בתחלתו והאי תחלה הוי סוף הספר לפי כי בסוף מתחילין לגלגל המגילה ומגלגל והולך עד ראש לפי שכל ספריהם נכתבין כעין מגילה ולא בקונטרסים (והם) והכי נמי מניח מן הקלף חלק בסוף כל הכרך שהוא תחלת הספר כשיעור שיכול לגול את כל ההיקף על אותו חלק כדי שיהא משמש הקלף פנוי לכתבי הקדש: קשיא עמוד דלעיל קתני בראשו כדי לגול עמוד והכא קתני תחלת הספר וסופו כדי לגול עמוד. האי כדי לגול דברייתא נמי לצדדין קתני כדאמרן דתחלה כדי לגול עמוד ובסוף כדי לגול היקף. רב אשי אמר לעולם לא קתני לצדדין אלא תחלתו וסופו כדי לגול עמוד ובספר תורה מיירי דלאמצעיתו נגלל על ב' עמודים אבל שאר ספרים היו נגללין הכל על עמוד אחד ואמטו להכי צריך להניח כדי היקף כדאמרן. ולא אורכו יותר על הקיפו שכשמושכין אותו בחוט של משיחה לאורכו של דף ומקיפין מן אותו חוט היקף הספר תורה שיהא שוים במדה. בגויל ו' טפחים אורך הדף שכך למד מגויל. אבל מן קלף לא אמר לפיכך אמר איני יודע. ולא איתרמי ליה שיהא אורכו שוה להקיפו. יהבי ביה עינייהו קינאו (אדון) בו שכך כיון. תורה צוה לנו כתב דדומה עליו גוזמא. ורמינהו מקשה על מאי דאמר שיהא ס"ת הקיפו כאורכו. וארון שעשה משה היה דומה כמין תיבה שאין לה כיסוי שבכפרת היה מכוסה. באמת בת ו' טפחים. ואמתים וחצי אורכו עולין לט"ו טפחי': וכמה לוחות אוגדות בארון. כלומר כמה מחזיקות בארון. י"ב טפחי' שהיו מונחין הלוחות זו בצד זו. ואין ורק תרי מיעוטי לרבות ספר תורה שמונח בארון באותן ב' טפחים שנשתיירו מאורך הארון והיה אורכו של ספר תורה כרוחבו של לוחות ו' טפחים נשתיירו ב' טפחים פנוי טפח לצד כותל זה וטפח לצד כותל זה שכל אותן ב' טפחים משימין ידיהן אחת מיכן ואחת מיכן ומגביהין ספר תורה ברווח ומוציאין אותו לחוץ כדי שלא יהא נכנס ויוצא בדוחק: שבו באותו טפח עמודיו של ארון עומדין שנאמר אפריון עשה לו זה ארון. המלך שלמה. המלך שהשלום שלו וכתב עמודיו עשה כסף של ארון. בצידו מבחוץ.

שברי

עין משפט
נר מצוה

קל א ב מיי' פ"ז מהל' ס"ת הלכה טו סמג עשין כה טוש"ע י"ד סי' רפג סעיף ה:

תורה אור השלם

א) וַיָּקָם וַיֵּלֶךְ דָּוִד וְכָל הָעָם אֲשֶׁר אִתּוֹ מִבַּעֲלֵי יְהוּדָה לְהַעֲלוֹת מִשָּׁם אֵת אֲרוֹן הָאֱלֹהִים אֲשֶׁר נִקְרָא שֵׁם שֵׁם יְיָ צְבָאוֹת יֹשֵׁב הַכְּרֻבִים עָלָיו: [שמואל ב ו, ב]

ב) וְאֶכְתֹּב עַל הַלֻּחֹת אֶת הַדְּבָרִים אֲשֶׁר הָיוּ עַל הַלֻּחֹת הָרִאשֹׁנִים אֲשֶׁר שִׁבַּרְתָּ וְשַׂמְתָּם בָּאָרוֹן: [דברים י, ב]

ג) תְּחִלַּת דִּבֶּר יְיָ בְּהוֹשֵׁעַ וַיֹּאמֶר יְיָ אֶל הוֹשֵׁעַ לֵךְ קַח לְךָ אֵשֶׁת זְנוּנִים וְיַלְדֵי זְנוּנִים כִּי זָנֹה תִזְנֶה הָאָרֶץ מֵאַחֲרֵי יְיָ: [הושע א, ב]

רבינו גרשום

שברי לוחות מונחין בארון תחת השלימות. **מיכדי** הא א) (קרי) **לכל דבר שיש בהקיפו ג' טפחים יש בו רוחב טפח** וספר תורה ו' טפחים בהיקף וברוחב ב' טפחים. והני מילי כי נגלל כולו על עמוד אחד יש ברחבו ב' טפחים אבל כי הוי **נגלל לאמצעיתו** על ב' עמודין **נפיש ליה** שיעור בית מושבו יותר **על ב' טפחים** משום דאיכא **ריוח ביני ביני** של פתיחת חבור העמודין. **והשתא** אליבא דר' מאיר הואיל והוי רוחב הקיפו יותר מב' טפחים **בתרי פושכי** דפשו מארון על שיעור הלוחות **היכי הוי יתיב** ספר תורה. **ספר עזרה.** היינו ספר תורה המונח בארון **לתחלתו הוא נגלל.** הכל על עמוד אחד ולא הוי רוחב הקיפו אלא ב' טפחים. **ואכתי** אפי' הכי ספר תורה דהוי רוחב הקיפו **ב' טפחים. בתרי** טפח שבארון **היכי יתיב** אי לא הוי ביה רווחא פורתא **אמר רב אשי דכריך בה** בספר תורה **פורתא** לאחר שהיה כרוך כולו עמוד אחד היה חוזר וכורך מסופו לבדו כרך מעט כשיעור שיכנס האחד וישב בריוח באותן ב' טפחים ומנח ליה לאותו כרך קטן על הכרך הגדול וכי האי גוונא יתיב ברווחא. ואליבא דר' יהודה דספר תורה לא הוה יתיב בארון **מיקמי דליתי ארגז וכו'. ור' מאיר** דאמר דספר תורה בארון הוה יתיב **האי מצד ארון מאי עביד ליה** הא משמע מצדו ולא במתוכו: **האי מצד** כותל הארון ולעולם בתוכו. **שהשם הקודש** שאין מזכירין **וכל כינויו** כל שבעים שמות של הקב"ה מונחין בארון משמע כו'. והקשתי לר' מאי שנא דר' יהודה מרבה מאין רק שברי לוחות לידכר עמודין דקיימי לטעמיה באותו טפח הפנוי בארון כי היכי דמרבה ר' מאיר ספר תורה לטעמיה דקיימי בב' טפח פנוי והשיב לי משום הכי מרבה שברי לוחות הואיל וכתיבי בתורה ועמודיו לא כתיבי בתורה: **חגי זכריה ומלאכי לסוף אינביאו וזוטר נביאותייהו** כתבינן לה נמי גבייהו. **ונכתביה** באנפי נפשיה **ונקדמיה** מקמי [ישעיה] ומשני כיון **דזוטר מירכס** כלומר משום דכל הספרים נגללין מתחלתן אי כתבינן לה באפי נפשיה כשמגלגלין הספר מבליע נבואת הושע בהדי הספר ומירכס ומתעלם מן העין וליכא למיקם עלה היכא כתיבא משום הכי מוקמי' לה בהדי חגי זכריה דזוטר נבואתייהו: **מכדי ישעיה** הוה **קדים לירמיה (דיחוס) [ויחזקאל]** דישעיה הוי בימי מנשה וירמיה הוה בחורבן הבית בתר הכא טובא ויחזקאל הוה בגלות: **רות נמי פורענות.** דהוה רעב ומתו מחלון וכליון: ומשני **רות פורעניות דהוה ליה אחרית** טוב שלקחה בועז ומשום הכי מתחילין ברות [ואח"כ] בתהלים שיצא ממנה דוד שתקנו: **ופרשת בלעם.** אע"ג דבלעם גופיה הוה נביא. **שמונה פסוקים שבתורה** מן וימת משה. **על ידי עשרה זקנים ועל ידי אדם הראשון.** על ידי אדם הראשון היינו מזמור שיר

חשק שלמה על רבינו גרשום א) [אולי צ"ל הא קי"ל דכל שיש וכו'].

שברי לוחות שמונחים בארון ואי ס"ד ס"ת הקיפו ו' טפחים מכדי א) כל שיש בהקיפו שלשה טפחים יש בו רוחב טפח וכיון דלאמצעיתו נגלל ב) נפיש ליה מתרי טפחא רווחא דביני ביני היכי יתיב אמר רב אחא בר יעקב ספר עזרה לתחלתו הוא נגלל ואכתי ג) תרי בתרי היכי יתיב אמר רב אשי דכריך ביה פורתא וכרכיה לעיל ור' יהודה מקמי דליתי ארגז ספר תורה היכי הוה יתיב דפא הוה נפיק מיניה ויתיב עילוה ספר תורה ור"מ האי מצד ארון מאי עביד ליה ההוא מיבעי ליה דמתנח ליה מצד ולא מתנח ביני לוחי ולעולם בגויה מן הצד ור"מ עמודי היכא הוו קיימי מבראי ור"מ שברי לוחות דמונחין בארון מנ"ל נפקא ליה מדרב הונא דאמר רב הונא מאי דכתיב א) אשר נקרא שם שם ה' צבאות יושב הכרובים עליו ה) מלמד שלוחות ושברי לוחות מונחים בארון ואידך ההוא מבעי ליה לכדרבי יוחנן דא"ר יוחנן א"ר שמעון בן יוחאי מלמד ד) שהשם וכל כינויו מונחין בארון ואידך נמי מיבעי ליה להכי אין הכי נמי אלא שברי לוחות דמונחין בארון מנא ליה נפקא ליה מדתני רב יוסף ו) דתני רב יוסף ב) אשר שברת ושמתם מלמד שהלוחות ושברי לוחות מונחין בארון ואידך ההוא מיבעי ליה לכדריש לקיש ז) דאמר ר"ל אשר שברת אמר לו הקב"ה למשה יישר כחך ששברת: ת"ר א סדרן של נביאים יהושע ושופטים שמואל ומלכים ירמיה ויחזקאל ישעיה ושנים עשר מכדי הושע קדים דכתיב ג) תחלת דבר ה' בהושע ז) וכי עם הושע דבר תחלה והלא ממשה ועד הושע כמה נביאים היו וא"ר יוחנן שהיה תחלה לארבעה נביאים שנתנבאו באותו הפרק ואלו הן הושע וישעיה עמוס ומיכה וליקדמיה להושע ברישא כיון דכתיב נבואתיה גבי חגי זכריה ומלאכי וחגי זכריה ומלאכי סוף נביאים הוו חשיב ליה בהדייהו וליכתביה לחודיה וליקדמיה איידי דזוטר מירכס מכדי ישעיה קדים מירמיה ויחזקאל ליקדמיה לישעיה ברישא כיון דמלכים סופיה חורבנא וירמיה כוליה חורבנא ויחזקאל רישיה חורבנא וסיפיה נחמתא וישעיה כוליה נחמתא סמכינן חורבנא לחורבנא ונחמתא לנחמתא: ב סידרן של כתובים רות וספר תהלים ואיוב ומשלי קהלת שיר השירים וקינות דניאל ומגילת אסתר עזרא ודברי הימים ולמ"ד ח) איוב בימי משה היה ליקדמיה לאיוב ברישא ט) אתחולי בפורענותא לא מתחלינן רות נמי פורענות היא פורענות דאית ליה אחרית י) דאמר רבי יוחנן למה נקרא שמה רות שיצא ממנה דוד שריוהו להקב"ה בשירות ותושבחות ומי כתבן משה כתב ספרו כ) ופרשת בלעם ואיוב יהושע כתב ספרו ושמונה פסוקים שבתורה שמואל כתב ספרו ושופטים ורות דוד כתב ספר תהלים ע"י עשרה זקנים ע"י אדם הראשון על ידי מלכי צדק ועל ידי אברהם וע"י משה ועל ידי הימן וע"י ידותון ועל ידי אסף

תרי בתרי היכי יתיב. משמע שאם עמודין היה הקיפו ששה שאם היה הקיפו בלא עמודין אם כן נפיש ליה מששה טפחים בהדי עמודים: **ורבי** מאיר עמודין היכא הוו קיימי. אע"פ שיש ריוח הרבה לר"מ בכל האורך לבד מנגד ספר תורה פשוט היו לו שהיו מונחים בצד ראש הארון שספר תורה מונח: **ולמ"ד** איוב בימי משה היה. וא"ת מאי קאמר ולמ"ד (א) והאי תנא גופיה סבר דבימי משה היה דקתני סיפא משה כתב ספר איוב וי"ל דלאכי לא ידע סיפא דברייתא: **בפורענותא** לא מתחלינן. וא"ת וניכתביה מיד אחר רות ואומר ר"י משום שאחרית של רות היא אחרית שילא ממנה דוד שריוהו להקב"ה בשירות ותשבחות לכך כתב אחר כך מיד אותן שירות והוא אחרית שלה וא"ת ולמ"ד מעולי גולה היה לכתביה לאיוב לבסוף ואומר ר"י דמשום הכי כתבו בהדי תהלים ומשלי לפי שהוא מענין אחד כתובין מענין שירה ומקראות קלרים וניגון אחד דכדימיהם היה ניגון כדאמרינן (מגילה דף ג.) ויקראו בספר תורת אלהים מפורש והוא שכל מ) מאי והוא שכל פסוקי טעמי והא דלא כתבו אחר משלי משום שלא להפסיק בדברי שלמה ור"ת מפרש דלכן כתבו בהדי תהלים משום דאמר לקמן דוד כתב ספרו ע"י עשרה זקנים ואיוב נמי נכתב ע"י ד' זקנים לופר ובלדד ואליפז ואליהוא והשתא אתי שפיר שלא כתבו אחר משלי: **פורענות** דאית ביה אחרית. וא"ת איוב נמי אית ביה אחרית וי"ל דהאי אחרית דרות אחרית דכל ישראל ועוד דאיכא למ"ד י) דלא כפל הקב"ה שכרו אלא לטורדו מן העולם:

שברי לוחות שמונחין. תחת הלוחות: **יש בו רוחב טפח.** וזה שהקיפו ששה נמלא עובי רוחבו שני טפחים: **רווחא דביני וביני.** אויר שבין עמוד לעמוד: **ובתרי פושכי היכי יתיב.** דקתני נשתיירו שם ב' טפחים שם ס"ת מונח: **ספר עזרה.** ספר שכתב משה ובו קורין בעזרה פרשת המלך בהקהל וכהן גדול ביה"כ: **לתחלתו הוא נגלל.** אין לו אלא עמוד אחד ונגלל מתחלתו לסופו ו): **דכריך ביה פורתא.** שאינו גוללו כולו ומניח בו מקלת וכורכו לעצמו ומניח אותו הכרך על הספר מלמעלה: **וכרכיה לעיל.** וכורכו למעלה על ההיקף: **דמנח ליה מצד.** אצל הכותל ולא בין שני הלוחות: **היכא הוי קיימי.** כיון דמלריך טפח מכאן וטפח מכאן ברוחב הארון שלא יהא ס"ת יולא ונכנס בדוחק העמודים היכא מונחי הלא ימעטו את החלל: **שם שם.** תרי זימני כתיבי ללוחות ולשברי לוחות: **אשר שברת.** קרא יתירה הוא למסמכיה לושמתם לדרשה: **יישר כוחך.** ללמדך שהוא מן הדברים שעשה משה רבינו ע"ה מדעתו והסכימה דעתו לדעת המקום: **שנתנבאו באותו הפרק.** בימי אותם המלכים עוזיה יותם אחז יחזקיה בארבעה נביאים הללו כתיב כן חוץ ממיכה שלא היה בימי עוזיהו אבל היה בימי יותם אחז יחזקיה: **חגי זכריה ומלאכי סופם של נביאים.** שהן היו בבית שני בשנת שתים לדריוש האחרון: **ישעיה קדים לירמיה ויחזקאל.** שהרי ישעיה בימי עוזיה וירמיה בימי יאשיה ובניו נתנבא בירושלים ויחזקאל בגולה בימי צדקיה: **רות תהלים איוב כו'.** רות קדמה בימי שפוט השופטים תהלים דוד אמרן והוא קדם לאיוב כמ"ד בימי מלכת שבא היה ואחר כך שלשה ספרי שלמה: **משלי קהלת.** שניהם ספרי חכמה: **שיר השירים.** נראה בעיני שאמרו לעת זקנתו: **קינות.** ירמיה אמרן שהיה אחר שלמה: **דניאל.** אחר ירמיה בימי נבוכד נצר בגולה: **אסתר.** אחריו בימי אחשורוש: **עזרא.** אחריו בימי דריוש השני שעמד אחר אחשורוש: **למ"ד איוב בימי משה היה.** לקמן: **רות נמי פורענותא היא.** רעב וגלות ומיתת אלימלך ובניו: **דאית ליה אחרית.** סוף הפורענות נהפך לאחרית ותקוה שילא דוד מהם: **ופרשת בלעם.** נבואתו ומשליו אף על פי שאינן לורכי משה ותורתו וסדר מעשיו: **ושמונה פסוקים.** מן וימת משה עד סוף הספר: **שמואל כתב ספרו וספר שופטים.** שכולם קדמו לו ועמד וכתב ספרן ומה שעלתה לישראל בימיהם וכן רות שהיתה בימי השופטים: **על ידי עשרה זקנים.** כתב בו דברים שאמרו זקנים הללו שהיו לפניו ויש שהיו בימיו כגון אסף והימן וידותון מן הלוים המשוררים: **על ידי אדם הראשון.** כגון גלמי ראו עיניך ולי מה יקרו רעיך (תהלים קלט) אדם הראשון אמרן: **על ידי מלכי צדק.** נאם ה' לאדוני [שב לימיני] וכל המזמור (שם קי): **ועל ידי אברהם.** כדאמרינן לקמן איתן האזרחי זה אברהם: **ועל ידי משה.** תפלה למשה (שם צ) וכל אחד עשר מזמורים כסדרן: **ועל ידי הימן.** משכיל להימן: **ועל ידי ידותון.** למנצח לידותון:

חזקיה

מסורת הש"ס

א) [אהלות פי"ב מ"ו עירובין יג: עו. סוכה ז:], ב) [עיין מה שמקשה תוס' על זה בעירובין יד. ד"ה והאיכא], ג) [עיין תוס' עירובין שם], ד) [סוטה מב:], ה) [ברכות ח: מנחות צט:], ו) יבמות סב. שבת פז. [מנחות צט:], ז) [פסחים פז.], ח) [לקמן טו.], ט) [לקמן קח.], י) ברכות ז: ע"ש, כ) [עי' פי' הגון על זה בשל"ה דף שס"ב בפנים וגם בהג"ה ע"ש], ל) [עי' תוס' לעיל יג: ד"ה ועושה בראשון], מ) [במגילה שם ובנדרים לז: איתא ויבינו במקרא אלו פסקי טעמי'], נ) [לקמן טו:]:

הגהות הב"ח

(א) תוס' ד"ה ולמ"ד וכו' מאי קאמר ולמ"ד והא האי תנא:

גליון הש"ס

גמרא מלמד שהלוחות. עי' עירובין דף סג ע"ב תוס' ד"ה כל זמן:

ליקוטי רש"י

שהשם וכל כינויו מונחין בארון. היוצא עמהם במלחמה [סוטה מב:]. **מלמד שהלוחות ושברי לוחות מונחין בארון.** דכתיב (דברים י) אשר שברת ושמתם בארון אף השברים תשים בארון [ברכות ח:]. **אשר שברת** ושמתם בארון שישים השברים בארון. **יישר כחך ששברת.** שנאמר אשר שברת ולא אמר בלשון כעס שמע מינה הסכימה עמו דעת המקום [מנחות צט.]. **תחלת דבר ה' בהושע.** רבותינו אמרו תחלה לארבעה נביאים שנתנבאו (בימים הללו) הושע ישעיה עמוס ומיכה. ישעיה נתנבא שנאמר (ישעיה ו) וינועו אמות הספים וגומר והוא היה יום שנתנגע עוזיה שנכנס להיכל להקטיר ונחלקו העליונים לשורפו ומתחתונים לגולגו כשנגרש ... עמוס נאמר שנתים לפני הרעש. והושע אמרו לכולם שנאמר בו (מיכה א) בימי יותם אחז יחזקיה ולא נאמר בו עוזיה ופשוטו של מקרא תחלת דיבור שדבר הקב"ה עם הושע אמר לו לך קח וכו' [הושע א, ב].

שִׁבְרֵי לוּחוֹת — THE BROKEN PIECES OF THE first set of **TABLETS,**[1] **שֶׁמּוּנָּחִים בָּאָרוֹן — THAT THEY** too **LAY IN THE ARK,** underneath the complete Tablets.[2]

The Gemara now demonstrates how this Baraisa challenges Rebbi's ruling that the circumference of a standard Torah scroll should be six *tefachim:*[3]

וְאִי סַלְקָא דַּעְתָּךְ סֵפֶר תּוֹרָה הֶקֵּיפוֹ שִׁשָּׁה טְפָחִים — Now, if you should think that the circumference of a Torah scroll is six *tefachim,* מִכְּדִי — let us see: כָּל שֶׁיֵּשׁ בְּהֶקֵּיפוֹ שְׁלֹשָׁה טְפָחִים יֵשׁ בּוֹ רוֹחַב טֶפַח — Any circular object **whose circumference is three *tefachim* has a diameter of one *tefach*.**[4] Hence, a Torah scroll that has a circumference of six *tefachim* will be two *tefachim* wide. **וְכֵיוָן דִּלְאֶמְצָעִיתוֹ נִגְלָל — And since [a Torah scroll] is rolled** from both ends **to its middle,**[5] forming two smaller rolls, **נָפִישׁ לֵיהּ מִתְּרֵי טִפְחָא רַוְוחָא דְּבֵינֵי בֵּינֵי —** the total width of a Torah scroll actually **exceeds two *tefachim* by the space** that inevitably exists **between [the two rolls!]**[6] **בִּתְרֵי פּוּשְׁכֵי הֵיכִי יָתִיב — How,** then, **did [the Torah scroll of Moses] fit into** the **two-*tefach*** space in the Ark, which is all that is allotted to it according to R' Meir?[7]

The Gemara answers:

אָמַר רַב אַחָא בַּר יַעֲקֹב — Rav Acha bar Yaakov said: סֵפֶר עֲזָרָה לִתְחִלָּתוֹ הוּא נִגְלָל — The Torah **scroll of the Temple courtyard** [the scroll of Moses][8] **was rolled to its beginning,** i.e. it consisted of only one roll. Consequently, it was not more than two *tefachim* wide.

The Gemara considers this solution inadequate:

וְאַכַּתִּי — But there is **still** a difficulty. **תְּרֵי בִּתְרֵי הֵיכִי יָתִיב — How can** an object that is **two** *tefachim* wide **fit into** a space that is exactly **two** *tefachim* wide? The Torah scroll would have to be slightly narrower than two *tefachim* to fit into such a space.[9] — ? —

The Gemara answers:

אָמַר רַב אַשִׁי — Rav Ashi said: דְּכָרִיךְ בֵּיהּ פּוּרְתָּא וְכַרְכֵיהּ לְעֵיל — A small portion at the end of the scroll **was rolled** separately from the rest of the scroll, **and wound on top** of the main part of the scroll. In this way, the scroll was narrow enough to fit into a space that was two *tefachim* wide.[10]

The Gemara now probes the dispute between R' Meir and R' Yehudah recorded in the Baraisa:

וְרַבִּי יְהוּדָה — But according to **R' Yehudah,** who said that the Torah scroll of Moses lay on the chest sent by the Philistines, **מִקַּמֵּי דְּלֵיתֵי אַרְגָּז סֵפֶר תּוֹרָה הֵיכִי הֲוָה יָתִיב — where was the Torah scroll placed before the chest arrived?**

The Gemara answers:

דַּפָּא הֲוָה נָפִיק מִינֵּיהּ — A shelf protruded from [the Ark] וְיָתִיב עִילָוֵהּ סֵפֶר תּוֹרָה — on which the Torah scroll was placed.[11]

The Gemara now questions R' Meir's opinion that the Torah scroll of Moses was placed *inside* the Ark:

וְרַבִּי מֵאִיר — And R' Meir, הַאי ,,מִצַּד אֲרוֹן" מַאי עָבֵיד לֵיהּ — what interpretation does he give for[12] **this** verse, ***at the side of the Ark,***[13] which R' Yehudah adduced as proof that the scroll was placed *outside* the Ark?

The Gemara answers:

הַהוּא מִיבְּעֵי לֵיהּ דְּמִתְנַח לֵיהּ מִצַּד — According to R' Meir, **that** verse **is required** to teach **that [the scroll] was placed at the side** of the Tablets, **וְלֹא מִתְנַח בֵּינֵי לוּחֵי — and not placed between the Tablets. וּלְעוֹלָם בְּגַוֵּיהּ מִן הַצַּד — In fact,** it was placed **inside** the Ark, but **at the side,** next to the interior wall.[14]

The Gemara raises another problem with R' Meir's view:

וְרַבִּי מֵאִיר — And according to **R' Meir, עַמּוּדִים הֵיכָא הֲווּ קַיְימֵי — where were the** silver **rods positioned?** He allocates no space for them inside the Ark.[15] — ? —

The Gemara answers:

מִבַּרַאי — These rods were placed **outside** the Ark, at its side.

NOTES

1. When Moses descended from Mt. Sinai carrying the Tablets on which God had engraved the Ten Commandments, he saw the people worshiping the Golden Calf and threw the Tablets to the ground, and they shattered. At a later date, Moses returned to Mt. Sinai and received a second set of Tablets (*Exodus* 34:4).

2. *Rashi*. In their location beneath the intact Tablets, these pieces did not take up any of the length or width of the Ark; hence, they are not mentioned by the Baraisa (*Maharsha* to 14a; cf. *Tosafos* to *Menachos* 99a).

3. [Rebbi said that this is the ideal circumference of a Torah scroll written on *g'vil* in lettering of average size — see 14a note 8.] The following challenge is based on the assumption that Moses' scroll was written on *g'vil*. Either the Gemara had a tradition to this effect, or the halachah is that, ideally, a Torah scroll should be written on *g'vil* (see *Rashba* to 14a, *Maharsha*; see also 14a note 8).

4. See note 9.

5. Unlike other books of Scripture, which are wound around a single pole — see above, 14a.

6. *Rashi* (see following note). Since a Torah scroll is rolled to its middle, it is impossible to make it absolutely tight (*Ramban*).

7. This is *Rashi's* explanation of the Gemara. However, this explanation is difficult to understand, for it implies that were it not for the space between its two rolls, Moses' Torah scroll *would* fit into the allotted space. However, this is not so, for when a scroll whose diameter is two *tefachim* is rolled into two rolls, the total width of the two rolls is considerably more than two *tefachim.*

To avoid this problem, other commentators propose a different explanation of the Gemara: The words, רַוְוחָא דְּבֵינֵי בֵּינֵי, *the space between one and another,* refer to the difference between the width of a scroll rolled into a single roll and the width of the same scroll rolled into two rolls. It is because of this margin that Moses' Torah scroll cannot fit into the two *tefachim* allotted to it (*Pnei Shlomo, Rashash*).

In defense of *Rashi,* it may be argued that the measurement of six *tefachim* given by Rebbi applies to a Torah scroll that is already rolled to its middle (i.e. one that consists of two rolls). Rebbi teaches that the total of the circumferences of the two rolls is six *tefachim*. This means that each roll has a circumference of three *tefachim*. Consequently, the diameter of each roll is one *tefach,* yielding a total width of two *tefachim* (*Pnei Shlomo;* cf. *Ramban* and *Yad Remah* 183).

8. The Torah scroll written by Moses was called "the Scroll of the Courtyard" because it was read from in the Temple Courtyard by the Kohen Gadol on Yom Kippur, and by the king during the ceremony of *Hakhel* (*Rashi*; see *Rashash* to 14a תד"ה שלא).

9. This implies that the Gemara considers the ratio between a circle's circumference and its diameter to be exactly three. For if it were more than three, the width of Moses' Torah scroll would be less than two *tefachim,* and it would fit into a space of two *tefachim.* This is difficult in light of the fact that the ratio between a circle's circumference and its diameter is actually more than three (π — approximately $3^1/_7$) (*Tosafos* to *Eruvin* 14a). See the resolutions to this problem proposed by *Pnei Shlomo* and *Chasam Sofer*.

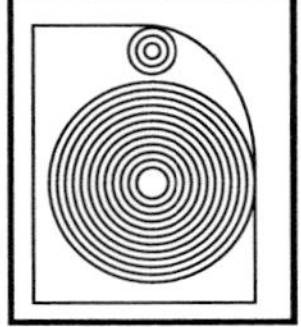

10. See diagram.

11. [This shelf was not an essential part of the Ark. It was added when God instructed Moses to put the Torah scroll at the side of the Ark. When the chest was received from the Philistines, it replaced the shelf.]

12. Literally: what does he do with it.

13. *Deuteronomy* 31:26. See end of 14a.

14. See diagram to 14a, note 23.

15. According to R' Meir, a *tefach* was left empty at each side of the Torah scroll to facilitate its removal and insertion (see diagram to 14a note 23). Filling that area with the silver rods would defeat this purpose (*Rashi*; see *Tosafos*).

שברי לוחות שמונחים בארון ואי ס"ד ס"ת הקיפו ו' טפחים מכדי א) כל שיש בהקיפו שלשה טפחים יש בו רוחב טפח וכיון דלאמצעיתו נגלל ב) נפיש ליה מתרי טפחא רווחא דביני ביני היכי יתיב אמר רב אחא בר יעקב ספר עזרה לתחלתו הוא נגלל ואכתי ג) תרי בתרי היכי יתיב אמר רב אשי דכריך ביה פורתא וכרכיה לעיל ור' יהודה מקמי דליתי ארגז ספר תורה היכי הוה יתיב דפא הוה נפיק מיניה ויתיב עילוה ספר תורה ור"מ האי מצד ארון מאי עביד ליה ההוא מיבעי ליה דמתנח ליה מצד ולא מתנח ביני לוחי ולעולם בגויה מן הצד ור"מ עמודי היכא הוו קיימי מבראי ור"מ שברי לוחות דמונחין בארון מנ"ל נפקא ליה מדרב הונא דאמר רב הונא מאי דכתיב א) אשר נקרא שם שם ה' צבאות יושב הכרובים עליו מלמד שלוחות ושברי לוחות מונחים בארון ואידך ההוא מבעי ליה לכדרבי יוחנן דא"ר יוחנן א"ר שמעון בן יוחאי מלמד ד) שהשם וכל כינויו מונחין בארון ואידך נמי מיבעי ליה להכי אין הכי נמי אלא שברי לוחות דמונחין בארון מנא ליה נפקא ליה מדרב יוסף ה) דתני רב יוסף ב) אשר שברת ושמתם מלמד שהלוחות ושברי לוחות מונחין בארון ואידך ההוא מיבעי ליה לכדריש לקיש ו) דאמר ר"ל אשר שברת אמר לו הקב"ה למשה יישר כחך ששברת: ת"ר סדרן של נביאים יהושע ושופטים שמואל ומלכים ירמיה ויחזקאל ישעיה ושנים עשר מכדי הושע קדים דכתיב ג) תחלת דבר ה' בהושע ז) וכי עם הושע דבר תחלה והלא ממשה ועד הושע כמה נביאים היו וא"ר יוחנן שהיה תחלה לארבעה נביאים שנתנבאו באותו הפרק ואלו הן הושע וישעיה עמוס ומיכה וליקדמיה להושע ברישא כיון דכתיב נבואתיה גבי חגי זכריה ומלאכי וחגי זכריה ומלאכי סוף נביאים הוו חשיב ליה בהדייהו וליכתביה לחודיה וליקדמיה איידי דזוטר מירכס מכדי ישעיה קדים מירמיה ויחזקאל ליקדמיה לישעיה ברישא כיון דמלכים סופיה חורבנא וירמיה כוליה חורבנא ויחזקאל רישיה חורבנא וסיפיה נחמתא וישעיה כוליה נחמתא סמכינן חורבנא לחורבנא ונחמתא לנחמתא: סידרן של כתובים רות וספר תהלים ואיוב ומשלי קהלת שיר השירים וקינות דניאל ומגילת אסתר עזרא ודברי הימים ולמ"ד ח) איוב בימי משה היה ליקדמיה לאיוב ברישא ט) אתחולי בפורענותא לא מתחלינן רות נמי פורענות היא פורענות דאית ליה אחרית י) דאמר רבי יוחנן למה נקרא שמה רות שיצא ממנה דוד שריוהו להקב"ה בשירות ותושבחות ומי כתבן משה כתב ספרו כ) ופרשת בלעם ואיוב יהושע כתב ספרו ושמונה פסוקים שבתורה שמואל כתב ספרו ושופטים ורות דוד כתב ספר תהלים ע"י עשרה זקנים ע"י אדם הראשון על ידי מלכי צדק ועל ידי אברהם וע"י משה ועל ידי הימן וע"י ידותון ועל ידי אסף

רש"י

שברי לוחות שמונחין. תחת הלוחות: יש בו רוחב טפח. וזה שהקיפו ששה נמלא עובי רוחבו שני טפחים: רווחא דביני וביני. אויר שבין עמוד לעמוד: ובתרי פושכי היכי יתיב. דקתני נשתיירו שם ב' טפחים ששם ס"ת מונח: ספר עזרה. ספר שכתב משה ובו קורין בעזרה פרשת המלך בהקהל וכהן גדול ביה"כ: לתחלתו הוא נגלל. אין לו אלא עמוד אחד ונגלל מתחלתו לסופו ל): דכריך ביה פורתא. שאינו גוללו כולו ומניח בו מקלת וכורכו לעצמו ומניח אותו הכרך על הספר מלמעלה: וכרכיה לעיל. וכורכו למעלה על ההיקף: דמנח ליה מצד. אצל הכותל ולא בין שני הלוחות: היכא הוי קיימי. כיון דמלריך טפח מכאן וטפח מכאן ברוחב הארון שלא יהא ס"ת יוצא ונכנס בדוחק העמודים היכא מנחי הלא ימעטו את החלל: שם שם. תרי זימני כתיבי ללוחות ולשברי לוחות: אשר שברת. קרא יתירה הוא למסמכיה לושמתם לדרשה: יישר כוחך. ללמדך שהוא מן הדברים שעשה משה רבינו ע"ה מדעתו והסכימה דעתו לדעת המקום: שנתנבאו באותו הפרק. בימי אותם המלכים עוזיה יותם אחז יחזקיה בארבעה נביאים הללו כתיב כן חוץ ממיכה שלא היה בימי עוזיהו אבל היה בימי יותם אחז יחזקיה: חגי זכריה ומלאכי סופם של נביאים. שהן היו בבית שני בשנת שתים לדריוש האחרון: ישעיה קדים לירמיה ויחזקאל. שהרי ישעיה בימי עוזיה וירמיה בימי יאשיה ובניו נתנבא בירושלים ויחזקאל בגולה בימי לדקיה: רות תהלים איוב כו'. רות קדמה בימי שפוט השופטים תהלים דוד אמרן והוא קדם לאיוב כמ"ד בימי מלכת שבא היה ואחר כך שלשה ספרי שלמה: משלי קהלת. שניהם ספרי חכמה: שיר השירים. נראה בעיני שאמרו לעת זקנתו: קינות. ירמיה אמרן שהיה אחר שלמה: דניאל. אחר ירמיה בימי נבוכד נלר בגולה: אסתר. אחריו בימי אחשורוש: עזרא. אחריו בימי דריוש השני שעמד אחר אחשורוש: למ"ד איוב בימי משה היה. לקמן: רות נמי פורענותא היא. רעב וגלות ומיתת אלימלך ובניו: דאית ליה אחרית. סוף הפורענות נהפך לאחרית ותקוה שילא דוד משם: ופרשת בלעם. נבואתו ומשליו אף על פי שאינן לורכי משה ותורתו וסדר מעשיו: ושמונה פסוקים. מן וימת משה עד סוף הספר: שמואל כתב ספרו וספר שופטים. שכולם קדמו לו ועמד וכתב ספרן ומה שעלתה לישראל בימיהם וכן רות שהיתה בימי השופטים: על ידי עשרה זקנים. כתב בו דברים שאמרו זקנים הללו שהיו לפניו ויש שהיו בימיו כגון אסף והימן וידותון מן הלוים המשוררים: על ידי אדם הראשון. כגון גלמי ראו עיניך ולי מה יקרו רעיך (תהלים קלט) אדם הראשון אמרן: על ידי מלכי צדק. נאם ה' לאדוני [שב לימיני] וכל המזמור (שם קי): ועל ידי אברהם. כדאמרינן לקמן איתן האזרחי זה אברהם: ועל ידי משה. תפלה למשה (שם צ) וכל אחד עשר מזמורים כסדרן: ועל ידי הימן. משכיל להימן: ועל ידי ידותון. למנצח לידותון:

חזקיה

תוספות

תרי בתרי היכי יתיב. משמע שעם עמודין היה הקיפו ששה שאם היה הקיפו בלא עמודין אם כן נפיש ליה משני טפחים בהדי עמודים: ורבי מאיר עמודין היכא הוו קיימי. אע"פ שיש ריוח הרבה לר"מ בכל האורך לבד מנגד ספר תורה פשוט היו לו שהיו מונחים בכל ראש הארון שספר תורה מונח: ולמ"ד איוב בימי משה היה. וא"ת מאי קאמר ולמ"ד (א) והאי תנא גופיה סבר דבימי משה היה דקתני סיפא משה כתב ספר איוב וי"ל דאכתי לא ידע סיפא דברייתא: בפורענותא לא מתחילינן. וא"ת ונכתביה מיד אחר רות ואומר ר"י משום שאחרית של רות היה אחרית שילא ממנה דוד שריוהו להקב"ה בשירות ותשבחות לכך כתב אחר כך מיד אותן שירות והוא אחרית שלה וא"ת ולמ"ד מעולי גולה היה לכתביה לאיוב לבסוף ואומר ר"י דמשום הכי כתבו בהדי תהלים ומשלי לפי שהוא מענין אחד כתובין מעין שירה ומקראות קלרים וניגון אחד דבימיהם היה ניגון כדאמרינן (מגילה דף ג.) ויקראו בספר תורת אלהים מפורש ושום שכל מ) מאי ושום שכל פסוקי טעמי והא דלא כתבו אחר משלי משום שלא להפסיק בדברי שלמה ור"ת מפרש דלכן כתבו בהדי תהלים משום דאמר לקמן דוד כתב ספרו ע"י עשרה זקנים ואיוב נמי נכתב ע"י ד' זקנים לופר ובלדד ואליפז ואליהוא והשתא אתי שפיר שלא כתבו אחר משלי: פורענות דאית ביה אחרית. וא"ת איוב נמי אית ביה אחרית וי"ל דהאי אחרית דרות אחרית דכל ישראל ועוד דאיכא למ"ד נ) דלא כפל הקב"ה שכרו אלא לטורדו מן העולם:

עין משפט נר מצוה

קל א ב מיי' פ"ז מהל' ס"ת הלכה טו סמג עשין כה טוש"ע י"ד סי' רפג סעיף ה:

תורה אור השלם

א) וַיָּקָם וַיֵּלֶךְ דָּוִד וְכָל הָעָם אֲשֶׁר אִתּוֹ מִבַּעֲלֵי יְהוּדָה לְהַעֲלוֹת מִשָּׁם אֵת אֲרוֹן הָאֱלֹהִים אֲשֶׁר נִקְרָא שֵׁם שֵׁם יְיָ צְבָאוֹת יֹשֵׁב הַכְּרֻבִים עָלָיו: [שמואל ב ו, ב]

ב) וְאֶכְתֹּב עַל הַלֻּחֹת אֶת הַדְּבָרִים אֲשֶׁר הָיוּ עַל הַלֻּחֹת הָרִאשֹׁנִים אֲשֶׁר שִׁבַּרְתָּ וְשַׂמְתָּם בָּאָרוֹן: [דברים י, ב]

ג) תְּחִלַּת דִּבֶּר יְיָ בְּהוֹשֵׁעַ וַיֹּאמֶר יְיָ אֶל הוֹשֵׁעַ לֵךְ קַח לְךָ אֵשֶׁת זְנוּנִים וְיַלְדֵי זְנוּנִים כִּי זָנֹה תִזְנֶה הָאָרֶץ מֵאַחֲרֵי יְיָ: [הושע א, ב]

רבינו גרשום

שברי לוחות מונחין בארון תחת השלימות. מיכדי הא א) (קרי) לכל דבר שיש בהקיפו ג' טפחים יש בו רוחב טפח וספר תורה ו' טפחים בהיקף וברוחב ב' טפחים. והני מילי כי נגלל כולו על עמוד אחד יש ברחבו ב' טפחים אבל כי הוי נגלל לאמצעיתו על ב' עמודין נפיש ליה שיעור בית מושבו יותר על ב' טפחים משום דאיכא ריוח ביני ביני של פתיחת חבור העמודין. והשתא אליבא דר' מאיר הואיל והוי רוחב הקיפו יותר מב' טפחים בתרי פושכי דפשו מארון על שיעור הלוחות היכי הוי יתיב ספר תורה. ספר עזרה. היינו ספר תורה המונח בארון לתחלתו הוא נגלל. הכל על עמוד אחד ולא הוי רוחב הקיפו אלא ב' טפחים. ואכתי אפי' הכי ספר תורה דהוי רוחב הקיפו ב' טפחים. בתרי טפח שבארון היכי יתיב אי לא הוי ביה רווחא פורתא אמר רב אשי דכריך בה בספר תורה פורתא לאחר שהיה כרוך כולו עמוד אחד היה חוזר וכורך מסופו לבדו כרך מעט כשיעור שיכנס האחד וישב בריוח באותן ב' טפחים ומנח ליה לאותו כרך קטן על הכרך הגדול וכי האי גוונא יתיב ברווחא. ואליבא דר' יהודה דספר תורה לא הוה יתיב בארון מיקמי דליתי ארגז וכו'. ור' מאיר דאמר דספר תורה בארון הוה יתיב האי מצד ארון מאי עביד ליה הא משמע מצדו ולא במתוכו: האי מצד כותל הארון ולעולם בתוכו. שהשם הקודש שאין מזכירין וכל כינויו כל שבעים שמות של הקב"ה מונחין בארון משמע כו'. והקשתי לר' מאי שנא דר' יהודה מרבה מאין רק שברי לוחות לידכר עמודין דקיימי לטעמיה באותו טפח הפנוי בארון כי היכי דמרבה ר' מאיר ספר תורה לטעמיה דקיימי בב' טפח פנוי והשיב לי משום הכי מרבה שברי לוחות הואיל וכתיבי בתורה ועמודיו לא כתיבי בתורה: חגי זכריה ומלאכי לסוף אינביאו וזוטר נביאותייהו כתבינן לה נמי גבייהו. ונכתביה באנפי נפשיה ונקדמיה מקמי [ישעיה] ומשני כיון דזוטר מירכס כלומר משום דכל הספרים נגללין מתחלתן אי כתבינן לה באפי נפשיה כשמגלגלין הספר מבליע נבואת הושע בהדי הספר ומתעלם מן העין וליכא למיקם עלה היכא כתיבא משום הכי מוקמי' לה בהדי חגי זכריה דזוטר נבואתייהו: מכדי ישעיה הוה קדים לירמיה (דיחוס) [ויחזקאל] דישעיה הוי בימי מנשה וירמיה הוה בחורבן הבית בתר הכא טובא ויחזקאל הוה בגלות: רות נמי פורענות. דהוה רעב ומתו מחלון וכליון: ומשני רות פורעניות דהוה ליה אחרית טוב שלקחה בועז ומשום הכי מתחילין ברות [ואח"כ] בתהלים שיצא ממנה דוד שתקנו: ופרשת בלעם. אע"ג דבלעם גופיה הוה נביא. שמונה פסוקים שבתורה מן וימת משה. על ידי עשרה זקנים ועל ידי אדם הראשון. על ידי אדם הראשון היינו מזמור שיר

חשק שלמה על רבינו גרשום א) [אולי צ"ל הא קיי"ל דכל שיש וכו'].

מסורת הש"ס

א) [אהלות פי"ב מ"ו עירובין יג: עו. סוכה ז:], ב) [עיין מה שמקשה תוס' על זה בעירובין יד. ד"ה והאיכא], ג) [עיין תוס' עירובין שם], ד) [סוטה מב:], ה) [ברכות ח: מנחות צט:], ו) יבמות סב. שבת פז. [מנחות צט:], ז) [פסחים פז.], ח) [לקמן טו.], ט) [לקמן קס.], י) ברכות ז: ע"ש, כ) [עי' פי' הגון על זה בשל"ה דף שמ"ב בפנים וגם בהג"ה ע"ש], ל) [עי' תוס' לעיל יג: ד"ה ועושה בראשון], מ) [במגילה שם ובנדרים לז: איתא וזינו במקרא אלו פסקי טעמי'], נ) [לקמן טו:]:

הגהות הב"ח

(א) תוס' ד"ה ולמ"ד וכו' מאי קאמר ולמ"ד והאי תנא:

גליון הש"ס

גמרא מלמד שהלוחות. עי' עירובין דף סג ע"ב תוס' ד"ה כל זמן:

ליקוטי רש"י

שהשם וכל כינויו מונחין בארון. ויולא עמהם במלחמה [סוטה מב:]. מלמד שהלוחות ושברי לוחות מונחין בארון. דכתיב (דברים י) אשר שברת ושמתם בארון אף השברים תשים בארון [ברכות ח:]. אשר שברת ושמתם בארון שישים השברים בארון. יישר כחך ששברת. שנאמר אשר שברת ולא אמר ליה בלשון כעס שמע מינה הסכימה עמו דעת השכינה כשביטל תורה ושיברן כיון דנתכוון לטובה [מנחות צט:]. תחלת דבר ה' בהושע. רבותינו אמרו תחילה לארבעה נביאים שנתנבאו (בימים הללו) הושע ישעיה עמוס ומיכה. ישעיה נתנבא שנאמר (ישעיה ו) וינועו אמות הספים וגומר והוא היה יום שנתנגע עוזיה שנכנס להיכל שרעשו העליונים לשורפו ותמהוהו לבולעו כעונשן של עדת קרח שהיו בהם בלועין ושרופים, בעמוס נאמר שנתים לפני הרעש. והושע קדם לכולם ומיכה היה אחרון לכולם שנאמר בו (מיכה א) בימי יותם אחז יחזקיה ולא נאמר בו עוזיה ופשוטו של מקרא תחילת דיבור שנדבר הקב"ה עם הושע אמר לו כן וכו' [הושע א, ב].

The Gemara asks yet another question regarding R' Meir's view:

וְרַבִּי מֵאִיר – **And R' Meir,** שִׁבְרֵי לוּחוֹת דְּמוּנָּחִין בָּאָרוֹן מְנָא לֵיהּ – **from where does he derive that the broken pieces of the** first set of **Tablets lay in the Ark?** He cannot infer this from the source adduced by R' Yehudah (viz. the double exclusion: *nothing was in the Ark – only*), for, according to R' Meir, the point of that phrase is to teach that the Ark must contain the Torah scroll of Moses. – ? –

The Gemara answers:

נַפְקָא לֵיהּ מִדְּרַב הוּנָא – **[R' Meir] derives it from** the same source **as Rav Huna** did, דְּאָמַר רַב הוּנָא – **for Rav Huna said:** מַאי דִּכְתִיב – **What** is meant by **that which is written:** ,,אֲשֶׁר־נִקְרָא שֵׁם שֵׁם ה׳ צְבָאוֹת יֹשֵׁב הַכְּרֻבִים עָלָיו" – [The Ark] ***which was called a name, the Name of Hashem,*** *Master of* ***Legions, Who is enthroned upon the Keruvim?***[16] מְלַמֵּד שֶׁלּוּחוֹת וְשִׁבְרֵי לוּחוֹת מוּנָּחִים בָּאָרוֹן – The apparently unnecessary repetition of the word "name" **teaches that the** second set of **Tablets *and* the broken pieces of** the first set of **Tablets lay in the Ark.**[17]

The Gemara now turns to R' Yehudah, who derived that the broken set of Tablets were placed in the Ark from a different source (viz. *nothing was in the Ark – only*):

וְאִידָךְ – **And the other one** [R' Yehudah], how does he explain the repetition of the word "name"? הַהוּא מִבְּעֵי לֵיהּ לִכְדְרַבִּי יוֹחָנָן – According to R' Yehudah, **that is required for** the exposition reported **by R' Yochanan** דְּאָמַר רַבִּי יוֹחָנָן אָמַר רַבִּי שִׁמְעוֹן בֶּן יוֹחָאי – **for R' Yochanan said in the name of R' Shimon ben Yochai:** מְלַמֵּד שֶׁהַשֵּׁם וְכָל כִּינּוּיָו מוּנָּחִין בָּאָרוֹן – The repetition of the word "name" **teaches that the** primary **Name of God and all His subordinate Names were** written down and **deposited in the Ark.**[18]

The Gemara now turns back to R' Meir:

וְאִידָךְ נַמִּי מִיבְּעֵי לֵיהּ לְהָכִי – **And the other one** [R' Meir] **too requires [this verse] for the aforementioned** teaching (viz. God's Names were deposited in the Ark). Therefore, he cannot derive from it that the broken Tablets were placed in the Ark. – ? –

The Gemara accepts this objection:

אִין הָכִי נַמִּי – **Indeed, this is so.** R' Meir agrees that the purpose of repeating the word "name" is to teach that God's Names were deposited in the Ark. אֶלָּא שִׁבְרֵי לוּחוֹת דְּמוּנָּחִין בָּאָרוֹן מְנָא לֵיהּ – **So from [where] does [R' Meir] derive that the broken pieces of the** first set of **Tablets were placed in the Ark?** נַפְקָא לֵיהּ מִדְּתָנֵי רַב יוֹסֵף – **He derives it from** the source recorded in **the Baraisa taught by Rav Yosef;** דְּתָנֵי רַב יוֹסֵף – **for Rav Yosef taught the following Baraisa:** ,,אֲשֶׁר שִׁבַּרְתָּ וְשַׂמְתָּם" – The juxtaposition of the apparently superfluous words, [the Tablets] ***WHICH YOU BROKE,*** to the words, ***AND YOU SHALL PUT THEM*** *in the Ark,*[19] מְלַמֵּד שֶׁהַלּוּחוֹת וְשִׁבְרֵי לוּחוֹת מוּנָּחִין בָּאָרוֹן – **TEACHES THAT THE** second set of **TABLETS AND THE BROKEN PIECES OF THE** first **TABLETS** were both **PUT IN THE ARK.**

The Gemara turns to R' Yehudah:

וְאִידָךְ – **And the other one** [R' Yehudah], what does he derive from these apparently superfluous words, *which you broke*? הַהוּא מִיבְּעֵי לֵיהּ לִכְדְרֵישׁ לָקִישׁ – According to R' Yehudah, **that** phrase **is required for [the teaching] of Reish Lakish.** דְּאָמַר רֵישׁ לָקִישׁ – **For Reish Lakish said:** ,,אֲשֶׁר שִׁבַּרְתָּ" – The phrase, ***which you broke***, is an allusion to God's approval of Moses' breaking of the Tablets. אָמַר לוֹ הַקָּדוֹשׁ בָּרוּךְ הוּא לְמֹשֶׁה – **The Holy One, Blessed is He, said to Moses:** יִישַׁר כֹּחֲךָ שֶׁשִּׁבַּרְתָּ – **Your strength shall be true to its mark, because you broke** the Tablets.[20]

The Gemara quotes a Baraisa that gives the order of the books of Prophets:[21]

תָּנוּ רַבָּנָן – **The Rabbis taught in a Baraisa:** סִדְרָן שֶׁל נְבִיאִים – **THE ORDER** of the books **OF THE PROPHETS** is as follows: יְהוֹשֻׁעַ – ***JOSHUA,*** וְשׁוֹפְטִים – ***JUDGES,*** שְׁמוּאֵל – ***SAMUEL,*** וּמְלָכִים – ***KINGS,*** יִרְמְיָה – ***JEREMIAH,*** וִיחֶזְקֵאל – ***EZEKIEL,*** יְשַׁעְיָה – ***ISAIAH*** וּשְׁנֵים עָשָׂר – ***AND THE TWELVE PROPHETS.***

The Gemara questions the position of the Book of *Hosea,* which is included in the *Twelve Prophets*:

מִכְּדִי – **Let us see.** הוֹשֵׁעַ קָדִים – **Hosea came first,** דִּכְתִיב: ,,תְּחִלַּת דִּבֶּר־ה׳ בְּהוֹשֵׁעַ" – **as it is written: *Hashem spoke first with Hosea.***[22] – ? –

Before concluding its question, the Gemara clarifies the verse:

וְכִי עִם הוֹשֵׁעַ דִּבֵּר תְּחִלָּה – **Was it with Hosea that [God] spoke first**, as the literal meaning of the verse implies? וַהֲלֹא מִמֹּשֶׁה וְעַד הוֹשֵׁעַ כַּמָּה נְבִיאִים הָיוּ – **Were there not many prophets between** the eras of **Moses and Hosea** to whom God spoke!? וְאָמַר רַבִּי יוֹחָנָן – **R' Yochanan explained** the verse as follows: שֶׁהָיָה תְּחִלָּה לְאַרְבָּעָה נְבִיאִים שֶׁנִּתְנַבְּאוּ בְּאוֹתוֹ הַפֶּרֶק – It teaches **that [Hosea] was the first of the four prophets who prophesied during that** particular **era.**[23] וְאֵלּוּ הֵן הוֹשֵׁעַ וִישַׁעְיָה עָמוֹס וּמִיכָה – **These** prophets **were: Hosea, Isaiah, Amos and Micah.**

The Gemara concludes its question:

וְלִיקַדְּמֵיהּ לְהוֹשֵׁעַ בְּרֵישָׁא – **So** the Book of ***Hosea*** **should be moved forwards to precede** the Book of *Isaiah.* – ? –

The Gemara answers:

כֵּיוָן דִּכְתִיב נְבוּאָתֵיהּ גַּבֵּי חַגַּי זְכַרְיָה וּמַלְאָכִי – **Since [Hosea's] prophecy was recorded at the same time as** the prophecies of

NOTES

16. *II Samuel* 6:2.

17. Each use of the word שֵׁם, *name,* signifies another of the sets of Tablets (*Rashi*).

18. The "primary" Name is either the four-letter Name of God (י־ה־ו־ה) or His forty-two-letter Name (see *Rambam, Hil. Yesodei HaTorah* 6:2 and *Hil. Tefillah* 14:10; *Rosh* to *Yoma* ch. 8 §19; see also *Sanhedrin* 60a and *Kiddushin* 71a with *Rashi*).

Rambam (Hil. Yesodei HaTorah ibid.) lists six subordinate names: א־ל, א־ל־ו־ה, א־ל־ה־ים, א־ל־ה־י, ש־ד־י, צ־ב־א־ו־ת.

19. *Deuteronomy* 10:2. The entire verse reads: וְאֶכְתֹּב עַל־הַלֻּחֹת אֶת־הַדְּבָרִים אֲשֶׁר הָיוּ עַל־הַלֻּחֹת הָרִאשֹׁנִים אֲשֶׁר שִׁבַּרְתָּ וְשַׂמְתָּם בָּאָרוֹן, *And I will write on the* [second] *Tablets the words that were on the first Tablets, which you broke, and you should put them in the Ark.* According to its plain meaning, this verse is an instruction to Moses to place the *second* set of Tablets in the Ark. However, the apparently superfluous phrase, אֲשֶׁר שִׁבַּרְתָּ, *which you broke,* prompts Rav Yosef to explain the instruction as referring to the broken Tablets as well (see *Maharsha*).

20. The juxtaposition of אֲשֶׁר שִׁבַּרְתָּ, *which you broke,* to the words וְשַׂמְתָּם בָּאָרוֹן, *and you shall put them in the Ark* (see previous note), indicates that God approved of the breaking of the Tablets. This prompts R' Yehudah to relate, on a homiletic level, the word אֲשֶׁר, *which,* to אַשְׁרֵי, *happy* (see *Ramban*).

This is one of the three decisions made independently by Moses to which God agreed (*Rashi,* from *Shabbos* 87a).

[R' Meir infers that God approved of Moses' breaking of the Tablets from the parallel verse, *Exodus* 34:1 (*Maharsha*).]

21. This Baraisa accords with the view of R' Meir and R' Yehudah that the books of Prophets may be combined into a single scroll (see 13b). It teaches the order that such a scroll must follow (*Chasam Sofer, Birkas Avraham*).

22. *Hosea* 1:2.

23. I.e. the era of the following four kings of Judah: Uziah, Yosam, Achaz and Chizkiyah. The prophets, Hosea, Isaiah and Amos, lived during the reigns of all these kings. Micah did not live during the reign of Uziah, but he was a contemporary of the other three kings (*Rashi*).

עין משפט נר מצוה

קל א ב מיי' פ"ז מהל' ס"ת הלכה טו סמג עשין כה טוש"ע י"ד סי' רפג סעיף ה:

תורה אור השלם

א) וַיָּקָם וַיֵּלֶךְ דָּוִד וְכָל הָעָם אֲשֶׁר אִתּוֹ מִבַּעֲלֵי יְהוּדָה לְהַעֲלוֹת מִשָּׁם אֵת אֲרוֹן הָאֱלֹהִים אֲשֶׁר נִקְרָא שֵׁם שֵׁם יְיָ צְבָאוֹת יֹשֵׁב הַכְּרֻבִים עָלָיו: [שמואל ב ו, ב]

ב) וְאֶכְתֹּב עַל הַלֻּחֹת אֶת הַדְּבָרִים אֲשֶׁר הָיוּ עַל הַלֻּחֹת הָרִאשֹׁנִים אֲשֶׁר שִׁבַּרְתָּ וְשַׂמְתָּם בָּאָרוֹן: [דברים י, ב]

ג) תְּחִלַּת דִּבֶּר יְיָ בְּהוֹשֵׁעַ וַיֹּאמֶר יְיָ אֶל הוֹשֵׁעַ לֵךְ קַח לְךָ אֵשֶׁת זְנוּנִים וְיַלְדֵי זְנוּנִים כִּי זָנֹה תִזְנֶה הָאָרֶץ מֵאַחֲרֵי יְיָ: [הושע א, ב]

שברי לוחות שמונחים בארון ואי ס"ד ס"ת הקיפו ו' טפחים מכדי (א) כל שיש בהקיפו שלשה טפחים יש בו רוחב טפח וכיון דלאמצעיתו נגלל (ב) נפיש ליה מתרי טפחא רווחא דביני ביני בתרי פושכי היכי יתיב אמר רב אחא בר יעקב ספר עזרה לתחלתו הוא נגלל ואכתי (ג) תרי בתרי היכי יתיב אמר רב אשי דכריך ביה פורתא וכרכיה לעיל ור' יהודה מקמי דליתי ארגז ספר תורה היכי הוה יתיב דפא הוה נפיק מיניה ויתיב עילוה ספר תורה ור"מ האי מצד ארון מאי עביד ליה ההוא מיבעי ליה דמתנח ליה מצד ולא מתנח ביני לוחי ולעולם בגויה מן הצד ור"מ עמודי' היכא הוו קיימי מבראי ור"מ שברי לוחות דמונחין בארון מנ"ל נפקא ליה מדרב הונא דאמר רב הונא מאי דכתיב א) אשר נקרא שם שם ה' צבאות יושב הכרובים עליו (ה) מלמד שלוחות ושברי לוחות מונחים בארון ואידך ההוא מבעי ליה לכדרבי יוחנן דא"ר יוחנן א"ר שמעון בן יוחאי מלמד (ו) שהשם וכל כינויו מונחין בארון ואידך נמי מיבעי ליה להכי אין הכי נמי אלא שברי לוחות דמונחין בארון מנא ליה נפקא ליה מדתני רב יוסף (ז) דתני רב יוסף ב) אשר שברת ושמתם מלמד שהלוחות ושברי לוחות מונחין בארון ואידך ההוא מיבעי ליה לכדריש לקיש (ח) דאמר ר"ל אשר שברת אמר לו הקב"ה למשה יישר כחך ששברת: ת"ר (ט) סדרן של נביאים יהושע ושופטים שמואל ומלכים ירמיה ויחזקאל ישעיה ושנים עשר מכדי הושע קדים דכתיב ג) תחלת דבר ה' בהושע (י) וכי עם הושע דבר תחלה והלא ממשה ועד הושע כמה נביאים היו וא"ר יוחנן שהיה תחלה לארבעה נביאים שנתנבאו באותו הפרק ואלו הן הושע וישעיה עמוס ומיכה וליקדמיה להושע ברישא כיון דכתיב נבואתיה גבי חגי זכריה ומלאכי וחגי זכריה ומלאכי סוף נביאים הוו חשיב ליה בהדייהו וליכתביה לחודיה וליקדמיה איידי דזוטר מירכס מכדי ישעיה קדים מירמיה ויחזקאל ליקדמיה לישעיה ברישא כיון דמלכים סופיה חורבנא וירמיה כוליה חורבנא ויחזקאל רישיה חורבנא וסיפיה נחמתא וישעיה כוליה נחמתא סמכינן חורבנא לחורבנא ונחמתא לנחמתא: (כ) סידרן של כתובים רות וספר תהלים ואיוב ומשלי קהלת שיר השירים וקינות דניאל ומגילת אסתר עזרא ודברי הימים ולמ"ד (ל) איוב בימי משה היה ליקדמיה לאיוב ברישא (מ) אתחולי בפורענותא לא מתחלינן רות נמי פורענות היא פורענות דאית ליה אחרית דאמר רבי יוחנן למה נקרא שמה רות שיצא ממנה דוד שריוהו להקב"ה בשירות ותושבחות ומי כתבן משה כתב ספרו (נ) ופרשת בלעם ואיוב יהושע כתב ספרו ושמונה פסוקים שבתורה שמואל כתב ספרו ושופטים ורות דוד כתב ספר תהלים ע"י עשרה זקנים ע"י אדם הראשון על ידי מלכי צדק ועל ידי אברהם וע"י משה ועל ידי הימן וע"י ידותון ועל ידי אסף

שברי לוחות שמונחין. תחת הלוחות: יש בו רוחב טפח. וזה שהקיפו ששה נמצא עובי רוחבו שני טפחים: רווחא דביני וביני. אויר שבין עמוד לעמוד: ובתרי פושכי היכי יתיב. דקתני נשתיירו שם ב' טפחים שבהם ס"ת מונח: ספר עזרה. ספר שכתב משה ובו קורין בעזרה פרשת המלך בהקהל וכהן גדול ביה"כ: לתחלתו הוא נגלל. אין לו אלא עמוד אחד ונגלל מתחלתו לסופו (ד): דכריך ביה פורתא. שאינו גוללו כולו ומניח בו מקלת וכורכו לעצמו ומניח אותו הכרך על הספר מלמעלה: וכרכיה לעיל. וכורכו למעלה על ההיקף: דמנח ליה מצד. אצל הכותל ולא בין שני הלוחות: היכא הוי קיימי. כיון דמצריך טפח מכאן וטפח מכאן ברוחב הארון שלא יהא ס"ת יוצא ונכנס בדוחק העמודים היכא מנחי הלא ימעטו את החלל: שם שם. תרי זימני כתיבי ללוחות ולשברי לוחות: אשר שברת. קרא יתירה הוא למסמכיה לושמתם לדרשה: יישר כוחך. ללמדך שהוא מן הדברים שעשה משה רבינו ע"ה מדעתו והסכימה דעתו לדעת המקום: שנתנבאו באותו הפרק. בימי אותם המלכים עוזיה יותם אחז יחזקיה בארבעה נביאים הללו כתיב כן חוץ ממיכה שלא היה בימי עוזיהו אבל היה בימי יותם אחז יחזקיה: חגי זכריה ומלאכי סופם של נביאים. שהן היו בבית שני בשנת שתים לדריוש האחרון: ישעיה קדים לירמיה ויחזקאל. שהרי ישעיה בימי עוזיה וירמיה בימי יאשיה ובניו נתנבא בירושלים ויחזקאל בגולה בימי צדקיה: רות תהלים איוב כו'. רות קדמה בימי שפוט השופטים תהלים דוד אמרן והוא קדם לאיוב כמ"ד בימי מלכת שבא היה ואחר כך שלשה ספרי שלמה: משלי קהלת. שניהם ספרי חכמה: שיר השירים. נראה בעיני שאמרו לעת זקנתו: קינות. ירמיה אמרן שהיה אחר שלמה: דניאל. אחר ירמיה בימי נבוכד נצר בגולה: אסתר. אחריו בימי אחשורוש: עזרא. אחריו בימי דריוש השני שעמד אחר אחשורוש: למ"ד איוב בימי משה היה. לקמן: רות נמי פורענותא היא. רעב וגלות ומיתת אלימלך ובניו: דאית ליה אחרית. סוף הפורענות נהפך לאחרית ותקוה שיצא דוד משם: ופרשת בלעם. נבואתו ומשליו אף על פי שאינן צורכי משה ותורתו וסדר מעשיו: ושמונה פסוקים. מן וימת משה עד סוף הספר: שמואל כתב ספרו וספר שופטים. שכולם קדמו לו ועמד וכתב ספרן ומה שעלתה לישראל בימיהם וכן רות שהיתה בימי השופטים: על ידי עשרה זקנים. כתב בו דברים שאמרו זקנים הללו שהיו לפניו ויש שהיו בימיו כגון אסף והימן וידותון מן הלוים המשוררים: על ידי אדם הראשון. כגון גלמי ראו עיניך ולי מה יקרו רעיך (תהלים קלט) אדם הראשון אמרן: על ידי מלכי צדק. נאם ה' לאדוני [שב לימיני] וכל המזמור (שם קי): ועל ידי אברהם. כדאמרינן לקמן איתן האזרחי זה אברהם: ועל ידי משה. תפלה למשה (שם צ) וכל אחד עשר מזמורים כסדרן: ועל ידי הימן. משכיל להימן: ועל ידי ידותון. למנצח לידותון:

חזקיה

תרי בתרי היכי יתיב. משמע שעם עמודין היה הקיפו ששה שאם היה הקיפו בלא עמודין אם כן נפיש ליה משני טפחים בהדי עמודים: ורבי מאיר עמודין היכא הוו קיימי. אע"פ שיש ריוח הרבה לר"מ בכל האורך לבד מנגד ספר תורה פשוט היו לו שהיו מונחים בצד ראש הארון שספר תורה מונח: ולמ"ד איוב בימי משה היה. וא"ת מאי קאמר ולמ"ד (א) והאי תנא גופיה סבר דבימי משה היה דקתני סיפא משה כתב ספר איוב וי"ל דאכתי לא ידע סיפא דברייתא: בפורענותא לא מתחילינן. וא"ת ונכתביה מיד אחר רות ואומר ר"י משום שאחרית של רות היה אחרית שיצא ממנה דוד שריוהו להקב"ה בשירות ותשבחות לכך כתב אחר כך מיד אותן שירות והוא אחרית שלה וא"ת ולמ"ד מעולי גולה היה לכתביה לאיוב לבסוף ואומר ר"י דמשום הכי כתבו בהדי תהלים ומשלי לפי שהוא מענין אחד כתובין מענין שירה ומקראות קצרים וניגון אחד דבימיהם היה ניגון כדאמרינן (מגילה דף ג.) ויקראו בספר תורת אלהים מפורש ושום שכל (מ) מאי ושום שכל פסוקי טעמי והא דלא כתבו אחר משלי משום שלא להפסיק בדברי שלמה ור"ת מפרש דלכן כתבו בהדי תהלים משום דאמר לקמן דוד כתב ספרו ע"י עשרה זקנים ואיוב נמי נכתב ע"י ד' זקנים צופר ובלדד ואליפז ואליהוא והשתא אתי שפיר שלא כתבו אחר משלי: פורענות דאית ביה אחרית. וא"ת איוב נמי אית ביה אחרית וי"ל דהאי אחרית דרות אחרית דכל ישראל ועוד דאיכא למ"ד (נ) דלא כפל הקב"ה שכרו אלא לטורדו מן העולם:

רבינו גרשום

שברי לוחות מונחין בארון תחת השלימות. מיכדי הא א) (קרי) לכל דבר שיש בהקיפו ג' טפחים יש בו רוחב טפח וספר תורה ו' טפחים בהיקף וברוחב ב' טפחים. והני מילי כי נגלל כולו על עמוד אחד יש ברחבו ב' טפחים אבל כי הוי נגלל לאמצעיתו על ב' עמודין נפיש ליה שיעור בית מושבו יותר על ב' טפחים משום דאיכא ריוח ביני ביני של פתיחת חבור העמודין. והשתא אליבא דר' מאיר הואיל והוי רוחב הקיפו יותר מב' טפחים בתרי פושכי דפשו מארון על שיעור הלוחות היכי הוי יתיב ספר תורה. ספר עזרה. היינו ספר תורה המונח בארון לתחלתו הוא נגלל. הכל על עמוד אחד ולא הוי רוחב הקיפו אלא ב' טפחים. ואכתי אפי' הכי ספר תורה דהוי רוחב הקיפו ב' טפחים. בתרי טפח שבארון היכי יתיב אי לא הוי ביה רווחא פורתא אמר רב אשי דכריך בה בספר תורה פורתא לאחר שהיה כרוך כולו עמוד אחד היה חוזר וכורך מסופו לבדו כרך מעט כשיעור שיכנס האחד וישב בריוח באותן ב' טפחים ומנח ליה לאותו כרך קטן על הכרך הגדול וכי האי גוונא יתיב ברווחא. ואליבא דר' יהודה דספר תורה לא הוה יתיב בארון מיקמי דליתי ארגז וכו'. ור' מאיר דאמר דספר תורה בארון הוה יתיב האי מצד ארון מאי עביד ליה הא משמע מצדו ולא במתוכו: האי מצד כותל הארון ולעולם בתוכו. שהשם הקודש שאין מזכירין וכל כינויו כל

שבעים שמות של הקב"ה מונחין בארון משמע כו'. והקשתי לר' מאי שנא דר' יהודה מרבה מאין רק שברי לוחות לידכר עמודין דקיימי לטעמיה באותו טפח הפנוי בארון כי היכי דמרבה ר' מאיר ספר תורה לטעמיה דקיימי בב' טפח פנוי והשיב לי משום הכי מרבה שברי לוחות הואיל וכתיבי בתורה ועמודיו לא כתיבי בתורה: חגי זכריה ומלאכי לסוף אינביאו וזוטר נביאותייהו כתבינן לה נמי גבייהו. ונכתביה באנפי נפשיה ונקדמיה מקמי [ישעיה] ומשני כיון דזוטר מירכס כלומר משום דכל הספרים נגללין מתחלתן אי כתבינן לה באפי נפשיה כשמגלגלין הספר מבליע נבואת הושע בהדי הספר ומירכס ומתעלם מן העין וליכא למיקם עלה היכא כתיבא משום הכי מוקמי' לה בהדי חגי זכריה דזוטר נבואתייהו: מכדי ישעיה הוה קדים לירמיה (דיחוס) [ויחזקאל] דישעיה הוי בימי מנשה וירמיה הוה בחורבן הבית בתר הכא טובא ויחזקאל הוה בגלות: רות נמי פורענות. דהוה רעב ומתו מחלון וכליון: ומשני רות פורענויות דהוה ליה אחרית טוב שלקחה בועז ומשום הכי מתחילין ברות [ואח"כ] בתהלים שיצא ממנה דוד שתקנו: ופרשת בלעם. אע"ג דבלעם גופיה הוה נביא. שמונה פסוקים שבתורה מן וימת משה. על ידי עשרה זקנים ועל ידי אדם הראשון. על ידי אדם הראשון היינו מזמור שיר

מסורת הש"ס

א) [אהלות פי"ב מ"ו עירובין יג: עו. סוכה ז:], ב) [עיין מה שמקשה תוס' על זה בעירובין יד. ד"ה והאיכא], ג) [עיין תוס' עירובין שם], ד) [סוטה מב:], ה) [ברכות ח: מנחות לט:], ו) יבמות סב. שבת פז. [מנחות לט:], ז) [פסחים פז.], ח) [לקמן טו.], ט) [לקמן קח.], י) ברכות ז: ע"ש, כ) [עי' פי' הגון על זה בשל"ה דף שס"ב בפנים וגם בהג"ה ע"ש], ל) [עי' תוס' לעיל יג: ד"ה ועושה בראשון], מ) [במגילה שם ובנדרים לז: איתא ודינו במקרא אלו פסקי טעמי'], נ) [לקמן טו:]:

הגהות הב"ח

(א) תוס' ד"ה ולמ"ד וכו' מאי קאמר ולמ"ד והא האי תנא:

גליון הש"ס

גמרא מלמד שהלוחות. עי' עירובין דף סג ע"ב תוס' ד"ה כל זמן:

ליקוטי רש"י

שהשם וכל כינויו מונחין בארון. היוצא עמהם במלחמה [סוטה מב:]. מלמד שהלוחות ושברי לוחות מונחין בארון. דכתיב (דברים י) אשר שברת ושמתם בארון אף השברים מונחים בארון [ברכות ח:]. אשר שברת ושמתם בארון שישים השברים בארון. יישר כחך ששברת. שנאמר אשר שברת ולא אמר ליה בלשון כעס שמע מינה הסכימה עמו דעת השכינה כשביטל תורה ושיברן כיון דנתכוין לטובה [מנחות צט:]. תחלת דבר ה' בהושע. רבותינו אמרו תחילה לארבעה נביאים שנתנבאו (בימים הללו) הושע ישעיה עמוס ומיכה. ישעיה נתנבא שנאמר (ישעיה ו) וינועו אמות הסיפים וגומר והוא היה יום שנתנגע עוזיה שנכנס להיכל שרעשו העליונים לשורפו והתחתונים לבולעו כעונשן של עדת קרח שהיו בהם בלועין ושרופים, בעמוס נאמר שנתים לפני הרעש. והושע קדם לכולם ומיכה היה אחרון לכולם שנאמר בו (מיכה א) בימי יותם אחז יחזקיה ולא נאמר בו עוזיה ופשוטו של מקרא תחילת דיבור שנדבר הקב"ה עם הושע אמר לו כן וכו' [הושע א, ב].

חשק שלמה על רבינו גרשום א) [אולי צ"ל הא קיי"ל דכל שיש וכו'].

Chaggai, Zechariah and Malachi,[24] **וְחַגַּי זְכַרְיָה וּמַלְאָכִי סוֹף נְבִיאִים הֲווּ – and Chaggai, Zechariah and Malachi were the last of the prophets,**[25] **חָשִׁיב לֵיהּ בַּהֲדַיְיהוּ – [Hosea's prophecy] is included with [their prophecies]** in the final book of the Prophets (viz. the *Twelve Prophets*).

The Gemara is dissatisfied with this answer:

וְלִיכְתְּבֵיהּ לְחוּדֵיהּ וְלִיקַדְּמֵיהּ – But [the Book of *Hosea*] should be written as a **separate** book, **and moved forwards** to its rightful position, before the Book of *Isaiah.* – ? –

The Gemara answers:

אַיְּידֵי דְּזוּטַר מִירְכַּס – Since [the Book of *Hosea*] is short, the Sages feared **it would be lost** if it were written as a separate book. Therefore, they included it in the Book of the *Twelve Prophets.*

The Gemara questions the position of the Book of *Isaiah* in the order of the books of the Prophets:

מִכְּדִי – Let us see. יְשַׁעְיָה קָדִים מִירְמְיָה וִיחֶזְקֵאל – Isaiah lived before Jeremiah and Ezekiel.[26] **לִיקַדְּמֵיהּ לִישַׁעְיָה בְּרֵישָׁא –** Therefore, the Book of ***Isaiah* should be moved forwards to precede** the Books of *Jeremiah* and *Ezekiel.* – ? –

The Gemara answers:

כֵּיוָן דִּמְלָכִים סוֹפֵיהּ חוּרְבָּנָא – Since the end of the Book of ***Kings*** **is** about **destruction, וְיִרְמְיָה כּוּלֵּיהּ חוּרְבָּנָא – and the entire** Book of ***Jeremiah*** **is** about **destruction, וִיחֶזְקֵאל רֵישֵׁיהּ חוּרְבָּנָא וְסֵיפֵיהּ נֶחָמְתָא – and the beginning of** the Book of ***Ezekiel*** **is** about **destruction and its end is** about **consolation, וִישַׁעְיָה כּוּלֵּיהּ נֶחָמְתָא – and the entire** Book of ***Isaiah*** **is** about **consolation, סָמְכִינַן חוּרְבָּנָא לְחוּרְבָּנָא – we juxtapose** prophecies of **destruction to** prophecies of **destruction, וְנֶחָמְתָא לְנֶחָמְתָא – and** prophecies of **consolation to** prophecies of **consolation.**[27]

The Baraisa continues by giving the order of the books of the Writings:

סִידְרָן שֶׁל כְּתוּבִים – THE ORDER OF THE books of **THE WRITINGS: רוּת – *RUTH,* וְסֵפֶר תְּהִלִּים – THE BOOK OF *PSALMS,* וְאִיּוֹב – *JOB,* וּמִשְׁלֵי – *PROVERBS,* קֹהֶלֶת – *ECCLESIASTES,* שִׁיר הַשִּׁירִים – *SONG OF SONGS,* וְקִינוֹת – *LAMENTATIONS,* דָּנִיֵּאל – *DANIEL,* וּמְגִילַּת אֶסְתֵּר – THE SCROLL OF *ESTHER,* עֶזְרָא – *EZRA,* וְדִבְרֵי הַיָּמִים – *CHRONICLES.*[28]**

The Gemara asks:

וּלְמַאן דְּאָמַר אִיּוֹב בִּימֵי מֹשֶׁה הָיָה – According to the one who said that Job lived in the days of Moses,[29] **לִיקַדְּמֵיהּ לְאִיּוֹב בְּרֵישָׁא –** the Book of ***Job* should be moved forwards to the beginning** of the Writings.

The Gemara answers:

אַתְחוּלֵי בְּפוּרְעֲנוּתָא לָא מַתְחֲלִינַן – We do not start with a depiction of **punishment** (such as that contained in the Book of *Job*).

The Gemara raises an objection to this answer:

רוּת נַמִּי פּוּרְעֲנוּת הִיא – The Book of ***Ruth* too is** a tale of **punishment.** It tells of famine, exile and the death of Elimelech and his sons. Yet, Writings begins with the Book of *Ruth.* – ? –

The Gemara answers:

פּוּרְעֲנוּת דְּאִית לֵיהּ אַחֲרִית – The Book of *Ruth* depicts **punishment with a** positive **end,** for King David descended from Ruth. **דְּאָמַר רַבִּי יוֹחָנָן – As R' Yochanan said: לָמָּה נִקְרָא שְׁמָהּ רוּת – Why was she called Ruth? שֶׁיָּצָא מִמֶּנָּה דָּוִד שֶׁרִיוָּהוּ לְהַקָּדוֹשׁ בָּרוּךְ הוּא בְּשִׁירוֹת וְתוּשְׁבָּחוֹת – Because David descended from her, who "sated" the Holy One, Blessed is He, with songs and praises.**[30]

The Baraisa now gives the authorship of the books of Scripture:[31] **וּמִי כְּתָבָן – WHO WROTE THEM? מֹשֶׁה כָּתַב סִפְרוֹ וּפָרָשַׁת בִּלְעָם וְאִיּוֹב – MOSES WROTE HIS BOOK** [the Pentateuch], **THE PASSAGE OF BILAM,**[32] **AND** the Book of ***JOB.*** **יְהוֹשֻׁעַ כָּתַב סִפְרוֹ וּשְׁמוֹנָה פְסוּקִים שֶׁבַּתּוֹרָה – JOSHUA WROTE HIS BOOK AND THE** last **EIGHT VERSES OF THE PENTATEUCH,** which describe events that took place after Moses' death. **שְׁמוּאֵל כָּתַב סִפְרוֹ וְשׁוֹפְטִים וְרוּת – SAMUEL WROTE HIS BOOK, AND** the Books of ***JUDGES* AND *RUTH.***[33] **דָּוִד כָּתַב סֵפֶר תְּהִלִּים עַל יְדֵי עֲשָׂרָה זְקֵנִים – DAVID WROTE THE BOOK OF *PSALMS* IN COLLABORATION WITH TEN ELDERS:**[34] **עַל יְדֵי אָדָם הָרִאשׁוֹן – WITH ADAM, THE FIRST MAN,** who contributed to psalm 139;[35]

NOTES

24. [Three of the *Twelve Prophets* — see 13b note 30.] Most of the prophets whose works comprise the *Twelve Prophets* did not transcribe their own prophecies. Instead, they were written at a later time by the Men of the Great Assembly (see 15a notes 6 and 8).

25. They were active during the Second Temple era, [notably] in the second year of the reign of [the Persian king] Darius II (*Rashi,* based on *Megillah* 15a).

26. Isaiah was a contemporary of King Uziah. Jeremiah lived many generations later, during the reigns of King Yoshiyah and his sons; he was based in Jerusalem [and lived through the destruction of the first Temple]. Ezekiel, a contemporary of King Zedekiah, was active during the period of exile that followed the Temple's destruction (*Rashi*).

27. The end of the Book of *Kings* describes the destruction of the First Temple. The Book of *Jeremiah* speaks of the exile that Jeremiah witnessed, which followed the destruction of the First Temple, as well as future exiles. The final portion of the Book of *Ezekiel* contains prophecies about the ultimate redemption. The theme of redemption recurs throughout the Book of *Isaiah.*

These descriptions are not absolute. There are some passages in the Book of *Jeremiah* that deal with consolation. However, its primary subject matter is destruction and exile. Similarly, with regard to the Book of *Isaiah,* although some passages foretell destruction and exile, its greater part is about hope and consolation (*Maharsha*).

28. This follows the chronological order. The story described in the Book of *Ruth* occurred during the rule of the judges, which preceded the rule of the kings. The Book of *Psalms* was written by King David. The Book of *Job* is next, for David preceded Job (according to the opinion that the story of Job took place during the era of the Sheba kingdom — see 15b notes 16 and 18). These books are followed by the works of David's son, Solomon: The Books of *Proverbs, Ecclesiastes* (Solomon's books of wisdom), and *Song of Songs* (which, apparently, was written in Solomon's later years). The Book of *Lamentations*, which is about the destruction of the First Temple, was written by Jeremiah many generations after Solomon. The Book of *Daniel* follows, for Daniel lived after Jeremiah, during the Babylonian exile. The Book of *Esther* describes events that happened towards the end of the Babylonian exile, during the reign of King Achashveirosh. Ezra, the author of the Book of *Ezra,* lived at the time of King Darius II, who ruled after Achashveirosh (*Rashi*; see *Rashash* ד״ה שיר). The Book of *Chronicles* gives the panorama of Jewish history from the Creation to the beginning of the Second Temple era.

29. This is one of the several opinions recorded below (15a-b) on the question of when Job lived.

30. The name רות (*Ruth*) is similar to the root רוה (*sate*).

31. [*Tosafos* maintain that the following is a continuation of the Baraisa. According to *Pnei Shlomo*, *Rashi* concurs with this view.]

32. Although it is part of the Pentateuch, the passage of Bilam (*Numbers* 23:7-24:24) is mentioned separately, because it contains his prophecies and parables, which are not directly related to Moses and his Torah (see *Rashi*; see also *Shelah* to *Parashas Balak,* end of *Maharal Diskin al haTorah* p. 148).

33. Samuel wrote about the Judges (all of whom preceded him) and what befell Israel in their times. He wrote the Book of *Ruth,* the events of which occurred during that period (*Rashi*).

34. David included in Psalms various chapters that had been composed by other writers. Some were his contemporaries (viz. Assaf, Heiman and Yedusun — members of the Levite choir, which sang in the Temple) and some lived before him (*Rashi*).

35. Adam composed the verses: גָּלְמִי רָאוּ עֵינֶיךָ, *Your eyes beheld my unshaped form* (v. 16) [a reference to Adam who was shaped by God]; and וְלִי מַה יָּקְרוּ רֵעֶיךָ, *To me, how precious are Your thoughts* (v. 17) [i.e. your purpose in the creation is beyond human comprehension — *Radak* ad loc.] (*Rashi*).

שברי לוחות שמונחים בארון ואי ס"ד ס"ת הקיפו ו' טפחים מכדי ^א כל שיש בהקיפו שלשה טפחים יש בו רוחב טפח וכיון דלאמצעיתו נגלל ^ב נפיש ליה מתרי טפחא רווחא דביני ביני בתרי פושכי היכי יתיב אמר רב אחא בר יעקב ספר עזרה לתחלתו הוא נגלל ואכתי ^ג תרי בתרי היכי יתיב אמר רב אשי דכריך ביה פורתא וכרכיה לעיל ור' יהודה מקמי דליתי ארגז ספר תורה היכי הוה יתיב דפא הוה נפיק מיניה ויתיב עילוה ספר תורה ור"מ האי מצד ארון מאי עביד ליה ההוא מיבעי ליה דמתנח ליה מצד ולא מתנח ביני לוחי ולעולם בגויה מן הצד ור"מ עמודי היכא הוו קיימי מבראי ור"מ שברי לוחות דמונחין בארון מנ"ל נפקא ליה מדרב הונא דאמר רב הונא מאי דכתיב ^א אשר נקרא שם שם ה' צבאות יושב הכרובים עליו ^ה מלמד שלוחות ושברי לוחות מונחים בארון ואידך ההוא מבעי ליה לכדרבי יוחנן דא"ר יוחנן א"ר שמעון בן יוחאי מלמד ^ד שהשם וכל כינויו מונחין בארון ואידך נמי מיבעי ליה להכי אין הכי נמי אלא שברי לוחות דמונחין בארון מנא ליה נפקא ליה מדתני רב יוסף ^ה דתני רב יוסף ^ב אשר שברת ושמתם מלמד שהלוחות ושברי לוחות מונחין בארון ואידך ההוא מיבעי ליה לכדריש לקיש ^ו דאמר ר"ל אשר שברת אמר לו הקב"ה למשה יישר כחך ששברת: ת"ר ^א סדרן של נביאים יהושע ושופטים שמואל ומלכים ירמיה ויחזקאל ישעיה ושנים עשר מכדי הושע קדים דכתיב ^ג תחלת דבר ה' בהושע ^ז וכי עם הושע דבר תחלה והלא ממשה ועד הושע כמה נביאים היו וא"ר יוחנן שהיה תחלה לארבעה נביאים שנתנבאו באותו הפרק ואלו הן הושע וישעיה עמוס ומיכה וליקדמיה להושע ברישא כיון דכתיב נבואתיה גבי חגי זכריה ומלאכי וחגי זכריה ומלאכי סוף נביאים הוו חשיב ליה בהדייהו וליכתביה לחודיה וליקדמיה איידי דזוטר מירכס מכדי ישעיה קדים מירמיה ויחזקאל ליקדמיה לישעיה ברישא כיון דמלכים סופיה חורבנא וירמיה כוליה חורבנא ויחזקאל רישיה חורבנא וסיפיה נחמתא וישעיה כוליה נחמתא סמכינן חורבנא לחורבנא ונחמתא לנחמתא: ^ב סידרן של כתובים רות וספר תהלים ואיוב ומשלי קהלת שיר השירים וקינות דניאל ומגילת אסתר עזרא ודברי הימים ולמ"ד ^ח איוב בימי משה היה ליקדמיה לאיוב ברישא ^ט אתחולי בפורענותא לא מתחלינן רות נמי פורענות היא פורענות דאית ליה אחרית ^י דאמר רבי יוחנן למה נקרא שמה רות שיצא ממנה דוד שריוהו להקב"ה בשירות ותושבחות ומי כתבן משה כתב ספרו ^כ ופרשת בלעם ואיוב יהושע כתב ספרו ושמונה פסוקים שבתורה שמואל כתב ספרו ושופטים ורות דוד כתב ספר תהלים ע"י עשרה זקנים ע"י אדם הראשון על ידי מלכי צדק ועל ידי אברהם וע"י משה ועל ידי הימן וע"י ידותון ועל ידי אסף

רש"י

שברי לוחות שמונחין. תחת הלוחות: יש בו רוחב טפח. וזה שהקיפו ששה נמלא עובי רוחבו שני טפחים: רווחא דביני ביני. אויר שבין עמוד לעמוד: ובתרי פושכי היכי יתיב. דקתני נשתיירו שם ב' טפחים שבהם ס"ת מונח: ספר עזרה. ספר שכתב משה ובו קורין בעזרה פרשת המלך בהקהל וכהן גדול ביה"כ: לתחלתו הוא נגלל. אין לו אלא עמוד אחד ונגלל מתחלתו לסופו ^ו: דכריך ביה פורתא. שאינו גוללו כולו ומניח בו מקלת וכורכו לעצמו ומניח אותו הכרך על הספר מלמעלה: וכרכיה לעיל. וכורכו למעלה על הסיקף: דמנח ליה מצד. אצל הכותל ולא בין שני הלוחות: היכא הוי קיימי. כיון דמלריך טפח מכאן וטפח מכאן ברוחב הארון שלא יהא ס"ת יוצא ונכנס בדוחק העמודים היכא מונחי הלא ימעטו את החלל: שם שם. תרי זימני כתיבי ללוחות ולשברי לוחות: אשר שברת. קרא יתירה הוא למסמכיה לושמתם לדרשה: יישר כוחך. ללמדך שהוא מן הדברים שעשה משה רבינו ע"ה מדעתו והסכימה דעתו לדעת המקום: שנתנבאו באותו הפרק. בימי אותם המלכים עוזיה יותם אחז יחזקיה בארבעה נביאים הללו כתיב כן חוץ ממיכה שלא היה בימי עוזיהו אבל היה בימי יותם אחז יחזקיה: חגי זכריה ומלאכי סופם של נביאים. שהן היו בבית שני בשנת שתים לדריוש המלך: ישעיה קדים לירמיה ויחזקאל. שהרי ישעיה בימי עוזיה וירמיה בימי יאשיה ובניו נתנבא בירושלים ויחזקאל בגולה בימי לדקיה: רות תהלים איוב כו'. רות קדמה בימי שפוט השופטים תהלים דוד אמרן והוא קדם לאיוב כמ"ד בימי מלכת שבא היה ואחר כך שלשה ספרי שלמה: משלי קהלת. שניהם ספרי חכמה: שיר השירים. נראה בעיני שאמרו לעת זקנתו: קינות. ירמיה אמרן שהיה אחר שלמה: דניאל. אחר ירמיה בימי נבוכד נלר בגולה: אסתר. אחריו בימי אחשורוש: עזרא. אחריו בימי דריוש השני שעמד אחר אחשורוש: למ"ד איוב בימי משה היה. לקמן: רות נמי פורענותא היא. רעב וגלות ומיתת אלימלך ובניו: דאית ליה אחרית. סוף הפורענות נהפך לאחרית ותקוה שילא דוד משם: ופרשת בלעם. נבואתו ומשליו אף על פי שאינן לורכי משה ותורתו וסדר מעשיו: ושמונה פסוקים. מן וימת משה עד סוף הספר: שמואל כתב ספרו וספר שופטים. שכולם קדמו לו ועמד וכתב ספרן ומה שעלתה לישראל בימיהם וכן רות שהיתה בימי השופטים: על ידי עשרה זקנים. כתב בו דברים שאמרו זקנים הללו שהיו לפניו ויש שהיו בימיו כגון אסף והימן וידותון מן הלוים המשוררים: על ידי אדם הראשון. כגון גלמי ראו עיניך ולי מה יקרו רעיך (תהלים קלט) אדם הראשון אמרן: על ידי מלכי צדק. נאם ה' לאדוני [שב לימיני] וכל המזמור (שם קי): ועל ידי אברהם. כדאמרינן לקמן איתן האזרחי זה אברהם: ועל ידי משה. תפלה למשה (שם צ) וכל אחד עשר מזמורים כסדרן: ועל ידי הימן. משכיל להימן: ועל ידי ידותון. למנלח לידותון:

חזקיה

תוספות

תרי בתרי היכי יתיב. משמע שעם עמודין היה הקיפו ששה שאם היה הקיפו בלא עמודין אם כן נפיש ליה משני טפחים בהדי עמודים: ורבי מאיר עמודין היכא הוו קיימי. אע"פ שיש ריוח הרבה לר"מ בכל האורך לבד מנגד ספר תורה פשוט היו לו שהיו מונחים בכל ראש הארון שספר תורה מונח: ולמ"ד איוב בימי משה היה. וא"ת מאי קאמר ולמ"ד ^(א) והאי תנא גופיה סבר דבימי משה היה דקתני סיפא משה כתב ספר איוב וי"ל דלהכי לא ידע סיפא דברייתא: בפורענותא לא מתחלינן. וא"ת ונכתביה מיד אחר רות ואומר ר"י משום שאחרית של רות היה אחרית שילא ממנה דוד שריוהו להקב"ה בשירות ותשבחות לכך כתב אחר כך מיד אותן שירות והוא אחרית שלה וא"ת ולמ"ד מעולי גולה היה לכתביה לאיוב בסוף ואומר ר"י דמשום הכי כתבו בהדי תהלים ומשלי לפי שהוא מענין אחד כתובין מענין שירה ומקראות קלרים וניגון אחד דמימאס היה ניגון כדאמרינן (מגילה דף ג.) ויקראו בספר תורת אלהים מפורש ושום שכל ^מ מאי ושום שכל פסוקי טעמי והא דלא כתבו אחר משלי משום שלא להפסיק בדברי שלמה ור"ת מפרש לכך כתבו בהדי תהלים משום דאמר לקמן דוד כתב ספרו ע"י ד' זקנים ואיוב נמי נכתב ע"י ד' זקנים לופר ובלדד ואליפז ואליהוא והשתא אתי שפיר שלא כתבו אחר משלי: פורענות דאית ביה אחרית. וא"ת איוב נמי אית ביה אחרית וי"ל דהאי אחרית לרות אחרית לכל ישראל ועוד דהיכא למ"ד ^נ דלא כפל הקב"ה שכרו אלא לטורדו מן העולם:

עין משפט נר מצוה

קל א ב מיי' פ"ז מהל' ס"ת הלכה טו סמג עשין כה טוש"ע י"ד סי' רפג סעיף ה:

תורה אור השלם

א) וַיָּקָם וַיֵּלֶךְ דָּוִד וְכָל הָעָם אֲשֶׁר אִתּוֹ מִבַּעֲלֵי יְהוּדָה לְהַעֲלוֹת מִשָּׁם אֵת אֲרוֹן הָאֱלֹהִים אֲשֶׁר נִקְרָא שֵׁם שֵׁם יְיָ צְבָאוֹת יֹשֵׁב הַכְּרֻבִים עָלָיו: [שמואל ב ו, ב]

ב) וְאֶכְתֹּב עַל הַלֻּחֹת אֶת הַדְּבָרִים אֲשֶׁר הָיוּ עַל הַלֻּחֹת הָרִאשֹׁנִים אֲשֶׁר שִׁבַּרְתָּ וְשַׂמְתָּם בָּאָרוֹן: [דברים י, ב]

ג) תְּחִלַּת דִּבֶּר יְיָ בְּהוֹשֵׁעַ וַיֹּאמֶר יְיָ אֶל הוֹשֵׁעַ לֵךְ קַח לְךָ אֵשֶׁת זְנוּנִים וְיַלְדֵי זְנוּנִים כִּי זָנֹה תִזְנֶה הָאָרֶץ מֵאַחֲרֵי יְיָ: [הושע א, ב]

רבינו גרשום

שברי לוחות מונחין בארון תחת השלימות. מיכדי הא א) (קרי) לכל דבר שיש בהקיפו ג' טפחים יש בו רוחב טפח וספר תורה ו' טפחים בהיקף וברוחב ב' טפחים. והני מילי כי נגלל כולו על עמוד אחד יש ברחבו ב' טפחים אבל כי הוי נגלל לאמצעיתו על ב' עמודין נפיש ליה שיעור בית מושבו יותר על ב' טפחים משום דאיכא ריוח ביני ביני של פתיחת חבור העמודין. והשתא אליבא דר' מאיר הואיל והוי רוחב הקיפו יותר מב' טפחים בתרי פושכי דפשו מארון על שיעור הלוחות היכי הוי יתיב ספר תורה. ספר עזרה. היינו ספר תורה המונח בארון לתחלתו הוא נגלל. הכל על עמוד אחד ולא הוי רוחב הקיפו אלא ב' טפחים. ואכתי אפי' הכי ספר תורה דהוי רוחב הקיפו ב' טפחים. בתרי טפח שבארון היכי יתיב אי לא הוי ביה רווחא פורתא אמר רב אשי דכריך בה בספר תורה פורתא לאחר שהיה כרוך כולו עמוד אחד היה חוזר וכורך מסופו לבדו כרך מעט כשיעור שיכנס האחד וישב בריוח באותן ב' טפחים ומנח ליה לאותו כרך קטן על הכרך הגדול וכי האי גוונא יתיב ברווחא. ואליבא דר' יהודה דספר תורה לא הוה יתיב בארון מיקמי דליתי ארגז וכו'. ור' מאיר דאמר דספר תורה בארון הוה יתיב האי מצד ארון מאי עביד ליה הא משמע מצדו ולא במתוכו: האי מצד כותל הארון ולעולם בתוכו. שהשם הקודש שאין מזכירין וכל כינויו כל שבעים שמות של הקב"ה מונחין בארון משמע כו'. והקשתי לר' מאי שנא דר' יהודה מרבה מאין רק שברי לוחות לידכר עמודין דקיימי לטעמיה באותו טפח הפנוי בארון כי היכי דמרבה ר' מאיר ספר תורה לטעמיה דקיימי בב' טפח פנוי והשיב לי משום הכי מרבה שברי לוחות הואיל וכתיבי בתורה ועמודיו לא כתיבי בתורה: חגי זכריה ומלאכי לסוף אינביאו וזוטר נביאותייהו כתבינן לה נמי גבייהו. ונכתביה באנפי נפשיה ונקדמיה מקמי [ישעיה] ומשני כיון דזוטר מירכס כלומר משום דכל הספרים נגללין מתחלתן אי כתבינן לה באפי נפשיה כשמגלגלין הספר מבליע נבואת הושע בהדי הספר ומירכס ומתעלם מן העין וליכא למיקם עלה היכא כתיבא משום הכי מוקמי' לה בהדי חגי זכריה דזוטר נבואתייהו: מכדי ישעיה הוה קדים לירמיה (דיחוס) [ויחזקאל] דישעיה הוי בימי מנשה וירמיה הוה בחורבן הבית בתר הכא טובא ויחזקאל הוה בגלות: רות נמי פורענות. דהוה רעב ומתו מחלון וכליון: ומשני רות פורעניות דהוה ליה אחרית טוב שלקחה בועז ומשום הכי מתחילין ברות [ואח"כ] בתהלים שיצא ממנה דוד שתקנו: ופרשת בלעם. אע"ג דבלעם גופיה הוה נביא. שמונה פסוקים שבתורה מן וימת משה. על ידי עשרה זקנים ועל ידי אדם הראשון. על ידי אדם הראשון היינו מזמור שיר

חשק שלמה על רבינו גרשום א) [אולי צ"ל הא קיי"ל דכל שיש וכו'].

מסורת הש"ס

א) [אהלות פי"ב מ"ו עירובין יג: עו. סוכה ז:], ב) [עיין מה שמקשה תוס' על זה בעירובין יד. ד"ה והאיכא], ג) [עיין תוס' עירובין שם], ד) [סוטה מג:], ה) [ברכות ח: מנחות לט:], ו) יבמות סב. שבת פז. [מנחות לט:], ז) [פסחים פז.], ח) [לקמן טו.], ט) [לקמן קח.], י) ברכות ז: ע"ש, כ) [עי' פי' הגון על זה בשל"ה דף שמ"ב בפנים וגם בהג"ה ע"ש], ל) [עי' תוס' לעיל יג: ד"ה ועושה בראשון], מ) [במגילה שם ובנדרים לז: איתא ויבינו במקרא אלו פסקי טעמי'], נ) [לקמן טו:]:

הגהות הב"ח

(א) תוס' ד"ה ולמ"ד וכו' מאי קאמר ולמ"ד והא האי תנא:

גליון הש"ס

גמרא מלמד שהלוחות. עי' עירובין דף סג ע"ב תוס' ד"ה כל זמן:

ליקוטי רש"י

שהשם וכל כינויו מונחין בארון. היולא עמהם במלחמה [סוטה מב:]. מלמד שהלוחות ושברי לוחות מונחין בארון. דכתיב (דברים י) אשר שברת ושמתם בארון אף השברים תשים בארון [ברכות ח:]. אשר שברת ושמתם בארון שיהיו השברים בארון. יישר כחך ששברת. שנאמר אשר שברת ולא אמר ליה בלשון כעס שמע מינה הסכימה עמו דעת השכינה כשביטל תורה ושיברן כיון דנתכוון לטובה [מנחות צט:]. תחלת דבר ה' בהושע. רבותינו אמרו תחלה לארבעה נביאים שנתנבאו [בימים ההם] הושע ישעיה עמוס ומיכה. ישעיה נתנבא שנאמר (ישעיה ו) וינועו אמות הספים וגומר ולכך היה יום שנתנגע עוזיה שנכנס להיכל שרעשו העליונים לשורפו ותחתונים לבלעו כענין של עדת קרח שהיו בהם בלועין ושרופים. בעמוס לפני הרעש. והושע קדם לכולם ומיכה היה אחרון לכולם שנאמר (מיכה א) בימי יותם אחז יחזקיה ולא נאמר בו עוזיה ופשוטו של מקרא תחלת דיבור שנדבר הקב"ה עם הושע שאמר לו לך קח וכו' [הושע א, ב].

עַל יְדֵי מַלְכִּי צֶדֶק – **WITH MALKI TZEDEK,** who composed psalm 110; וְעַל יְדֵי אַבְרָהָם – **WITH ABRAHAM,** who composed psalm 89;[36] וְעַל יְדֵי מֹשֶׁה – **WITH MOSES,** who composed psalms 90-100;[37] וְעַל יְדֵי הֵימָן – **WITH HEIMAN,** who composed psalm 88;[38] וְעַל יְדֵי יְדוּתוּן – **WITH YEDUSUN,** who composed psalm 39;[39] וְעַל יְדֵי אָסָף – **WITH ASSAF,** who composed psalms 73-83;[40]

NOTES

36. Psalm 89 begins מַשְׂכִּיל לְאֵיתָן, *A Maskil by Eisan the Ezrachite.* The Gemara below (15a) identifies Eisan the Ezrachite as Abraham.

37. [*Rashi,* from Midrash.] Psalm 90 is introduced by תְּפִלָּה לְמֹשֶׁה, *A prayer by Moses.*

38. The first verse of psalm 88 includes the words, מַשְׂכִּיל לְהֵימָן, *a Maskil by Heiman.*

39. Psalm 39 starts with the words לַמְנַצֵּחַ לידותון, *For the conductor, for Yedusun.*

40. Psalms 73-83 list Asaf as their composer. For example, psalm 83 begins שִׁיר מִזְמוֹר לְאָסָף, *A song, a psalm of Assaf.*

וְעַל יְדֵי שְׁלֹשָׁה בְּנֵי קֹרַח – WITH THE THREE SONS OF KORACH, who composed psalms 42-49.[1] יִרְמְיָה כָּתַב סִפְרוֹ וְסֵפֶר מְלָכִים וְקִינוֹת – JEREMIAH WROTE HIS BOOK, THE BOOK OF *KINGS*, AND the Book of *LAMENTATIONS*.[2] חִזְקִיָּה וְסִיעָתוֹ כָּתְבוּ – HEZEKIAH AND HIS ASSISTANTS[3] WROTE: (ימש״ק סִימָן) יְשַׁעְיָה מִשְׁלֵי שִׁיר הַשִּׁירִים וְקֹהֶלֶת – (MNEMONIC: Y'M'SH'K')[4] the Books of *ISAIAH, PROVERBS, SONG OF SONGS* AND *ECCLESIASTES*.[5] אַנְשֵׁי כְּנֶסֶת הַגְּדוֹלָה כָּתְבוּ – THE MEN OF THE GREAT ASSEMBLY[6] WROTE: (קנד״ג סִימָן) יְחֶזְקֵאל וּשְׁנֵים עָשָׂר דָּנִיֵּאל וּמְגִילַּת אֶסְתֵּר – (MNEMONIC: K'N'D'G')[7] the Books of *EZEKIEL, THE TWELVE PROPHETS, DANIEL* AND THE SCROLL OF *ESTHER*.[8] עֶזְרָא כָּתַב סִפְרוֹ וְיַחַס שֶׁל דִּבְרֵי הַיָּמִים עַד לוֹ – EZRA WROTE HIS OWN BOOK AND THE GENEALOGY [RECORDED IN] the Book of *CHRONICLES* TO the point of HIS OWN lineage.[9]

The Gemara notes:

מְסַיְּיעָא לֵיהּ לְרַב – **[This Baraisa] supports** a teaching by **Rav.** דְּאָמַר רַב יְהוּדָה אָמַר רַב – **For Rav Yehudah said in the name of Rav:** לֹא עָלָה עֶזְרָא מִבָּבֶל עַד שֶׁיִּחֵס עַצְמוֹ – **Ezra did not ascend from Babylonia** to Eretz Yisrael **until he traced his own genealogy.** וְעָלָה – It was only **then** that **he ascended.**

Since the Baraisa attributes only part of the Book of *Chronicles* to Ezra, the Gemara adds:

וּמַאן אַסְקֵיהּ – **Who finished it?** נְחֶמְיָה בֶּן חֲכַלְיָה – **Nechemiah son of Chachaliah.**

The Gemara quotes from the Baraisa:

אָמַר מַר – **The master taught** in the Baraisa: יְהוֹשֻׁעַ כָּתַב סִפְרוֹ וּשְׁמוֹנָה פְּסוּקִים שֶׁבַּתּוֹרָה – JOSHUA WROTE HIS BOOK, AND the final EIGHT VERSES IN THE TORAH, which describe events that took place after the death of Moses.

The Gemara aligns this view with one side of a Tannaic debate:

תַּנְיָא כְּמַאן דְּאָמַר – **This Baraisa was taught in accordance with the view** שְׁמוֹנָה פְּסוּקִים שֶׁבַּתּוֹרָה יְהוֹשֻׁעַ כְּתָבָן – **that the final eight verses of the Torah were written by Joshua.** דְּתַנְיָא – **For it was taught in a** different **Baraisa:** ,,וַיָּמָת שָׁם מֹשֶׁה עֶבֶד־ה׳״ – Scripture states: *AND MOSES, THE SERVANT OF HASHEM, DIED THERE*.[10] אֶפְשָׁר מֹשֶׁה (מֵת) וְכָתַב: ,,וַיָּמָת שָׁם מֹשֶׁה״ – IS IT POSSIBLE THAT AFTER MOSES DIED, HE WROTE: *AND MOSES DIED THERE?!*[11] אֶלָּא עַד כָּאן כָּתַב מֹשֶׁה – RATHER, MOSES WROTE UP TO THIS POINT מִכָּאן וְאֵילָךְ כָּתַב יְהוֹשֻׁעַ – and JOSHUA WROTE FROM THIS POINT ON; דִּבְרֵי רַבִּי יְהוּדָה וְאָמְרֵי לָהּ רַבִּי נְחֶמְיָה – these are THE WORDS OF R' YEHUDAH, OR, as SOME SAY, the words of R' NECHEMIAH. אָמַר לוֹ רַבִּי שִׁמְעוֹן – R' SHIMON SAID TO HIM:[12] אֶפְשָׁר סֵפֶר תּוֹרָה חָסֵר אוֹת אַחַת – IS IT POSSIBLE THAT THE TORAH SCROLL written by Moses WAS MISSING even ONE LETTER? וּכְתִיב – BUT IT IS WRITTEN in reference to Moses' scroll: ,,לָקֹחַ אֵת סֵפֶר הַתּוֹרָה הַזֶּה״ – *TAKE THIS TORAH SCROLL*,[13] which implies that it was complete! אֶלָּא עַד כָּאן הַקָּדוֹשׁ בָּרוּךְ הוּא אוֹמֵר – RATHER, R' Shimon explained, UP TO THIS POINT THE HOLY ONE, BLESSED IS HE, WOULD DICTATE what was to be written, וּמֹשֶׁה אוֹמֵר וְכוֹתֵב – MOSES WOULD SAY what God dictated[14] AND then WRITE it down. מִכָּאן וְאֵילָךְ הַקָּדוֹשׁ בָּרוּךְ הוּא אוֹמֵר וּמֹשֶׁה כּוֹתֵב בְּדֶמַע – But FROM THIS POINT ON, THE HOLY ONE, BLESSED IS HE, WOULD DICTATE AND MOSES WOULD WRITE WITH TEARS.[15]

R' Shimon continues by demonstrating that this method, of the master dictating to a scribe, was the standard practice:

כְּמוֹ שֶׁנֶּאֱמַר לְהַלָּן – AS IT IS STATED in a LATER verse: ,,וַיֹּאמֶר לָהֶם בָּרוּךְ מִפִּיו יִקְרָא אֵלַי אֵת כָּל־הַדְּבָרִים הָאֵלֶּה וַאֲנִי כֹּתֵב עַל־הַסֵּפֶר בַּדְּיוֹ״ – *AND BARUCH* [Jeremiah's scribe] SAID TO THEM, *"FROM HIS* [Jeremiah's] *MOUTH HE DICTATED TO ME ALL THESE WORDS, AND I WROTE THEM ON THE SCROLL WITH INK."*[16]

The Gemara quotes a halachic ruling that concerns the final eight verses of the Torah, and seeks to align it with one side of the preceding debate between R' Yehudah (or R' Nehemiah) and R' Shimon:

כְּמַאן אַזְלָא הָא דְּאָמַר רַבִּי יְהוֹשֻׁעַ בַּר אַבָּא אָמַר רַב גִּידֵּל אָמַר רַב – **With whose view does the following** ruling – **reported by R' Yehoshua bar Abba in the name of Rav Giddel who had said it**

NOTES

1. The introductory verses of psalms 42 and 44-49 make attribution to the sons of Korach. Psalm 43 is a continuation of psalm 42. They also composed psalms 84, 85, 87, 88.

2. Jeremiah, who lived through the Temple's destruction, wrote the Book of *Kings*, which recounts the history of the Jews preceding and during the destruction. He also wrote the Book of *Lamentations* about the destruction and the consequent exile.

3. Members of his generation who outlived him (*Rashi*).

4. The initial letters of יְשַׁעְיָה, *Yeshayah (Isaiah)*, מִשְׁלֵי, *Mishlei (Proverbs)*, שִׁיר הַשִּׁירִים, *Shir Hashirim (Song of Songs)*, and קֹהֶלֶת, *Koheles (Ecclesiastes)*.

5. The prophets generally composed their works [shortly] before their death. That is why Isaiah never put his own prophecies to writing, for [his life came to an unpredictable end when] he was murdered by Menashe (*Rashi*). And that is why King Solomon did not transcribe the books that contain his wisdom, *Proverbs, Ecclesiastes, Song of Songs*, for he was driven from the throne near the end of his life [see *Gittin* 68b] (*Maharsha*).

That Hezekiah's colleagues transcribed Solomon's works is evidenced by the verse (*Proverbs* 25:1): גַּם־אֵלֶּה מִשְׁלֵי שְׁלֹמֹה אֲשֶׁר הֶעְתִּיקוּ אַנְשֵׁי חִזְקִיָּה מֶלֶךְ־יְהוּדָה, *These also are proverbs of Solomon, which the men of Hezekiah, king of Judah, transcribed.* Since Hezekiah was instrumental in causing these men to study Torah (as related in *Sanhedrin* 94b), the Baraisa gives him the [primary] credit for the deed (*Rashi*).

6. Chaggai, Zechariah, Malachi, Zerubavel, Mordechai and their colleagues (*Rashi*).

The *Men of the Great Assembly* was a group of 120 Sages active at the end of the Babylonian exile and during the early years of the Second Temple (see *Pirkei Avos* 1:1,2 with commentaries).

7. The mnemonic is derived as follows: יְחֶזְקֵאל, *Yechezkel (Ezekiel)*, שְׁנֵים עָשָׂר, *Shnaim Asar (The Twelve Prophets)*, דָּנִיֵּאל, *Daniel*, מְגִילַּת אֶסְתֵּר, *Megillas Esther (The Scroll of Esther)*.

8. Ezekiel did not transcribe his own prophecies *possibly* because prophetic works may be written only in Eretz Yisrael and Ezekiel lived in the Diaspora. This suggested explanation is applicable to the Books of *Daniel* and *Esther* as well.

The [first nine] books of the *Twelve Prophets*, since they are short, were not written by the prophets whose names they bear. When Chaggai, Zechariah and Malachi – the last of the prophets – realized that the era of prophecy was ending, they transcribed their own prophecies and combined them with the other [nine] works into a single book, for fear that otherwise these works would be forgotten as a result of their brevity (*Rashi*).

9. I.e. he recorded the line of descent from Aaron to his father, Saryah (Ezra himself is not mentioned by name in *Chronicles*) (*Maharsha*; cf. *Tosafos*).

10. *Deuteronomy* 34:5.

11. In our editions of the Gemara the word מֵת, *died*, is parenthesized, for the text as it appears in *Menachos* 30a reads: אֶפְשָׁר מֹשֶׁה חַי וְכָתַב וַיָּמָת שָׁם מֹשֶׁה, *Is it possible that while Moses was alive he wrote: "and Moses died there"* [an apparent falsehood! – *Maharsha*].

12. R' Yehudah or R' Nechemiah.

13. *Deuteronomy* 31:26. (This is the Torah scroll of Moses discussed above, 14a-b.)

14. To avoid errors in the writing (*Rashi* to *Menachos* 30a).

15. I.e. Moses wrote these verses with tears in place of ink (see *Rashi* ד״ה הואיל). According to this view, Moses indeed wrote the verse, וַיָּמָת שָׁם מֹשֶׁה, *and Moses died there*, as well as the following verses, in his lifetime. However, to avoid the appearance of falsehood, two changes were made: Instead of using ink, Moses wrote with tears, which do not leave a permanent impression on the parchment. Furthermore, Moses did not repeat what God dictated to him before writing it down. Thus, Moses lied neither in writing nor in speech (*Maharsha*; cf. *Rashi* to *Menachos* 30a and *Gra* in *Divrei Eliyahu*).

16. *Jeremiah* 36:18.

ועל ידי שלשה בני קרח ירמיה כתב ספרו וספר מלכים וקינות חזקיה וסיעתו כתבו (ימש"ק סימן) ישעיה משלי שיר השירים וקהלת אנשי כנסת הגדולה כתבו (קנד"ג סימן) יחזקאל ושנים עשר דניאל ומגילת אסתר עזרא כתב ספרו ויחס של דברי הימים עד לו מסייעא ליה לרב דאמר רב יהודה אמר רב לא עלה עזרא מבבל עד שיחס עצמו ועלה ומאן אסקיה נחמיה בן חכליה אמר מר יהושע כתב ספרו ושמונה פסוקים שבתורה תניא כמאן דאמר שמונה פסוקים שבתורה יהושע כתבן [א] דתני' א) וימת שם משה עבד ה' אפשר משה ג) (מת) וכתב וימת שם משה אלא עד כאן כתב משה מכאן ואילך כתב יהושע דברי ר"י ואמרי לה ר' נחמיה אמר לו ר"ש אפשר ס"ת חסר אות אחת וכתיב ב) לקוח את ספר התורה הזה אלא עד כאן הקב"ה אומר (א) ומשה אומר וכותב מכאן ואילך הקב"ה אומר ומשה כותב בדמע כמו שנאמר להלן ג) ויאמר להם ברוך מפיו יקרא אלי את כל הדברים האלה ואני כותב על הספר בדיו כמאן אזלא הא דא"ר יהושע בר אבא אמר רב גידל אמר רב ד) שמונה פסוקים שבתורה יחיד קורא אותן ה) (ר"י היא) ודלא כר"ש אפילו תימא ר"ש הואיל ואשתנו אשתנו: יהושע כתב ספרו והכתיב ד) וימת יהושע בן נון עבד ה' דאסקיה אלעזר והכתיב ה) ואלעזר בן אהרן מת דאסקיה פנחס שמואל כתב ספרו והכתיב ו) ושמואל מת דאסקיה גד החוזה ונתן הנביא דוד כתב ספר תהלים על ידי עשרה זקנים וליחשוב נמי איתן האזרחי אמר רב איתן האזרחי זה הוא אברהם כתיב הכא ז) איתן האזרחי וכתיב התם ח) מי העיר ממזרח צדק [וגו'] ז) קא חשיב משה וקא חשיב הימן והאמר רב הימן זה משה כתיב הכא ט) הימן וכתיב התם י) בכל ביתי נאמן הוא תרי הימן הוו משה כתב ספרו ופרשת בלעם ואיוב מסייעא ליה לר' לוי בר לחמא דא"ר לוי בר לחמא ח) איוב בימי משה היה כתיב הכא כ) מי יתן אפוא ויכתבון מלי וכתיב התם ל) ובמה יודע אפוא ואימא בימי יצחק דכתיב מ) מי אפוא הוא הצד ציד ואימא בימי יעקב דכתיב נ) אם כן אפוא זאת עשו ואימא בימי יוסף דכתיב ס) איפה הם רועים לא ס"ד דכתיב כ) מי יתן בספר ויוחקו ומשה הוא דאיקרי מחוקק דכתיב ע) וירא ראשית לו כי שם חלקת מחוקק ספון רבא אמר איוב בימי מרגלים היה כתיב הכא פ) איש היה בארץ עוץ איוב שמו וכתיב התם צ) היש בה עץ מי דמי הכא עוץ התם עץ הכי קאמר להו משה לישראל ישנו לאותו אדם ששנותיו ארוכות כעץ ומגין על דורו כעץ יתיב ההוא מרבנן קמיה דר' שמואל בר נחמני ויתיב וקאמר איוב לא היה ולא נברא אלא משל היה א"ל עליך אמר קרא איש היה בארץ עוץ איוב שמו אלא מעתה ק) ולרש אין כל כי אם כבשה אחת קטנה אשר קנה ויחיה וגו' מי הוה אלא משל בעלמא הכא נמי משל בעלמא א"כ שמו ושם עירו למה רבי יוחנן ורבי אלעזר דאמרי תרוייהו איוב מעולי גולה היה ובית מדרשו בטבריא היה מיתיבי ימי שנותיו של איוב משעה שנכנסו ישראל למצרים ועד שיצאו
אימא

רש"י

חזקיה וסיעתו. בני דורו שהאריכו ימים אחריו: כתבו ישעיה. שהרגו מנשה ולא כתב ספרו שלא היו הנביאים כותבים ספריהן אלא לפני מותן: משלי קהלת. דכתיב בספר משלי (כה) אשר העתיקו אנשי חזקיה וגו' ועל שחזקיה גרם להן לעסוק בתורה כדאמרינן בחלק (סנהדרין דף צד:) נעץ חרב על פתח בית המדרש כו' נקרא הדבר על שמו: אנשי כנסת הגדולה. חגי זכריה ומלאכי זרובבל ומרדכי וחבריהם: כתבו יחזקאל. שנתנבא בגולה ואיני יודע למה לא כתבו יחזקאל בעצמו אם לא מפני שלא נתנה נבואה ליכתב בחוצה לארץ וכתבום אלו לאחר שבאו לארץ וכן ספר דניאל שהיה בגולה וכן מגילת אסתר ושנים עשר מתוך שהיו נבואותיהם קטנות לא כתבום הנביאים עצמם איש איש ספרו ובאו חגי זכריה ומלאכי וראו שרוח הקדש מסתלקת שהיו הם נביאים אחרונים ועמדו וכתבו נבואותיהם וצרפו נבואות קטנות עמהם ועשאום ספר גדול שלא יאבדו מחמת קטנם: עד לו. עד שייחס עצמו: מסייע לי' כו' עד שייחס עצמו. שכתב דברי הימים עד שייחס בו את עצמו: ומאן אסקיה. מי סיימו: תניא כמאן דאמר. כל הך דקתני לעיל יהושע כתב ספרו ושמונה פסוקים שבתורה אתיא כי האי תנא דלקמיה דאמר נמי יהושע כתבן: דתניא. פלוגתא דתנאי בהאי וימת שם משה כו': כמו שנאמר להלן כו'. אכולה מילתא קאי דקאמר הקב"ה אומר ומשה כותב כמה שמצינו שהנביאים כותבים מפי רבם: יחיד קורא אותן. כלומר אין מפסיקין בהן: לימא ר"י היא. דאמר לא כתבם משה לפיכך נשתנו משאר התורה ודלא כר"ש: הואיל ואישתנו. לכתוב בדמע אישתנו: ואימא יעקב כו'. לא גרסינן לה: ל"א (ג) גרסינן [למתניתא] דלעיל במניינא דעשרה זקנים קא חשיב אברהם ואיתן האזרחי ולא קא חשיב אסף דקסבר משלשה בני קרח הוא: והא אמר רב כו'. גבי ויחכם מכל האדם מאיתן האזרחי וגו' (מלכים א ה) איתמר וכן הך דהימן זה משה אהימן דההוא קרא איתמר דכתיב ביה והימן וכלכל וגו': תרי הימן הוו. משכיל להימן האזרחי הימן אחרינא הוא: ששנותיו כעץ. איוב שהאריך ימים רבים: משל היה. ללמוד ממנו תשובות למקטרגים על מדת הדין ושאין אדם נתפש על צערו: איש היה. אלמא הוא: אלא מעתה. ולרש אין כל וכו'. וקיפיה דקרא ותהי לו לבת: מי הוה. משום דכתיב ותהי:

תוספות

ועל ידי שלמה ועל ידי בני קרח. לפי הספרים דגרסי שלמה צ"ל לאסף הוא משלשה בני קרח והוא אביאסף ולספרים דל"ג שלמה לא הוי אסף אביאסף אלא אסף היה מן הלוים המשוררים וא"ת והנהו דלא גרסי ליה אמאי לא חשיב ליה הא כתיב (תהלים עב) לשלמה אלהים משפטיך וגו' וי"ל דדוד אמרו והתפלל על שלמה תדע דכתיב בסוף המזמור כלו תפלות דוד וא"ת לספרים דגרסי שלמה הכתיב כלו תפלות דוד וי"ל לפי שסיימו דוד והא דכתיב נמי שיר המעלות לשלמה דוד כמו כן אמרו לכל חמש עשרה מעלות דוד אמרן ויש ספרים דקא חשיב אברהם ואיתן האזרחי וגרים לקמן דקא חשיב אברהם וקא חשיב איתן והאמר רב איתן האזרחי הוא אברהם ומשני איתן האזרחי דקא חשיב הכא יעקב וקשה להאי גירסא דמגלה כן דדוד כתב ספרו על ידי אברהם כיון דלאיתן האזרחי לאו היינו אברהם: ירמיה כתב ספרו וספר מלכים. והא דלא כתב ישעיה דהיה קודם ירמיה ספר מלכים לפי שנהרג ולא היה בסוף מלכים ממנשה ואילך (לפי שנהרג) ואפילו ספרו לא כתב: חזקיה וסיעתו כתבו ישעיה. לפי שחזקיה גרם להם לעסוק בתורה נקרא הדבר על שמו אבל הוא לא כתבו שהרי מת קודם לישעיה דמנשה ח) בן בתו הרג לישעיה ט): עד לו. פירש ר"ח עד פסוק ולו אחים בני יהושפט (דה"ב כא) ומסייע לרב שייחס עצמו ועלה שייחוס עצמו כתב לפני זה הפסוק וקשה לפירושו דהל"ל עד ולו בוי"ו: פ"ה דיחזקאל לא כתב ספרו לפי שהיה בחוצה לארץ. וקשה ° דהא ירמיה נמי בחוצה לארץ היה שהלך למצרים ונתנבא שם כמה נבואות ולא מצינו שחזר יותר לארץ ישראל: שמונה פסוקים שבתורה. ה"ר משולם היה מצריך מכאן לקרות לאחד אותן ח' פסוקים שלא יקרא עמו שליח צבור ואין נראה לר"ת דהא כל התורה כולה נמי אחד קורא כדתנן במגילה (דף כא:) קראוה שנים יצאו ואמר בגמ' תנא מה שאין כן בתורה ואומר ר"ת י) דיחיד קורא בלא הפסקה שלא יקראו שנים זה ד' פסוקים וזה ד' ומה שנוהגים עתה לקרות שנים [בכל התורה] אומר ר"ת כדי שלא יתבייש מי שאינו יודע לקרות בעצמו כענין שמצינו במסכת ביכורים (פ"ג מ"ז) דתנן כל מי שיודע לקרות קורא בעצמו ושאינו יודע לקרות מקרין לפניו נמנעו מלהביא ביכורים התקינו שיהיו מקרין את מי שיודע לקרות ואת מי שאינו יודע לקרות והא דאמר בירושלמי במגילה רבי שמואל בר רב יצחק על לבי כנישתא וחזא חזנא דקאים וקורא ולא קאי בר איניש תחתיו א"ל אסור כשם שנתנה תורה על ידי סרסור כך אנו צריכין לנהוג בה על ידי סרסור אע"ג דמשמע שחזן עומד אצל הקורא לא שיקרא עמו אלא יעמוד ויקרא אותם שיש להם לקרות כדי שתנתן תורה על ידי סרסור ועוד אומר ר"י דיכול להיות שקלת מסייע לו בנחת והא דמשמע במגילה שלא יקראו שנים היינו שניהם שוין בקול רם:

איוב לא היה ולא נברא. האי לא סבר כריש לקיש דאמר בב"ר י) איוב לא היה שבאו עליו יסורין ולא אמר הכתוב שבאו עליו להודיעך כמו של איוב שאילו באו עליו היה יכול לעמוד בהן דאי סבר האי אמורא דאיוב היה בעולם א"כ מאי קאמר שמו ושם עירו למה טובא איצטריך לאשמועינן מי הוא אותו צדיק שהיה יכול לעמוד באותן יסורין:

מסורת הש"ס

א) מנחות ל. ב) [שם ליתא] ג) [שם ע"א] ד) [ס"א ואימא יעקב דכתיב ביה ויזרח לו השמש ההוא מיבעי ליה שמש שבאה בעבורו זרחה בעבורו קא זרח] ה) [לעיל יד:] ו) [יבמות מט:] ז) כבה, ח) [צ"ל נכו וכו"א בן בנו] ט) [כדאיתא יבמות מט:] י) [כן איתא בכ"י דהכא ובמנחות ל. אבל במגילה כא: ד"ה תנא מה שאין כן זה גם רש"י] כ) [סוף פ' וירא]

גליון הש"ס

גמרא מכאן ואילך כתב יהושע. ע' (מגילה) [מכות] דף יא ע"א תוס' ד"ה פ"ה כו' דהא ירמיה. עיין בתשובות נודע ביהודה מ"ת חא"ח סימן קו:

עין משפט נר מצוה

קל א מיי' פי"ג מהל' תפלה הלכה ז ועיין בהשגות סמג עשין יט טוש"ע א"ח סי' קמא סעיף ז [וברב אלפס פרק ד' דמגילה דף רע]:

הגהות הב"ח

(א) גמ' עד כאן הקב"ה אומר ומשה כותב כצ"ל ומיבת אומר נמחק: (ג) רש"י ד"ה ל"א הכי גרסינן למתניתא וכו' בני קרח הוא. וגרסינן כאן קא חשיב אברהם וקא חשיב איתן והאמר רב כו' ומשני איתן האזרחי דקא חשיב הכא יעקב דכתיב ביה ויזרח לו השמש הס"ד:

ליקוטי רש"י

שמונה פסוקים. וימות [שם] משה. אפשר ס"ת חסר. ומשה קורא לו ס"ת [דכתיב] לקוח את ספר התורה הזה. הקב"ה אומר. ומשה אומר אחריו כדי שלא יטעה בכתב וכותב. מכאן ואילך הקב"ה אומר ומשה כותב בדמע. ו(לא) [ולא] שלא היה אומר אחריו מרוב צערו. כמו שנאמר להלן וכו' מפיו יקרא וגו'. שלא היה אומר אחריו משום דקינות הוו. יחיד קורא אותן. אדם אחד קוראן ואין מפסיק ביניהם כדי לעמוד אחר ולקרות. ודלא כר"ש. דכיון דלאמר ר"ש משה כתבן הוו להו כשאר פסוקים ויפסיק ביניהם ויקרא אחר. הואיל ואשתנו. דנכתב בדמע אישתני משאר [פסוקי] [ד]ס"ת [מנחות ל. ע"פ שטמ"ק]. ולרש אין כל. באוריה משתעי משלו קרא. כבשה אחת. [זו] בת שבע [מגילה יג.].

רבינו גרשום

ליום השבת שנאמר בשביל אדם הראשון ועל ידי [י'] זקנים הני דקא חשיב א) לבר מאדם הראשון הוו י' והני י' כולהו קבוע בו מזמורים. תלמידיו. וסיעתו. וייחוס דברי הימים עד לו. כלומר הוא חשב היחס בדברי הימים מאדם הראשון עד עצמו: הואיל ואשתני. משאר תורה שהללו כת' משה בדמע: אשתני. נמי משאר תורה דיחיד יקרא אותו ולא שנים. ולמאן דאמר יהושע כתבו להכי יחיד קורא אותו והיינו דלא כר"ש שמעון דאיהו אמר דמשה כתבו: תרי הימן הוו. בן בנו של שמואל: (עד שעשאה כסולת נקיה). רבא אתי לסיועי למאן דאמר איוב בימי משה הוה. שדומה לעץ נקי מחטא: אלא משל היה. כמו שאמר שלמה יש צדיקים שמגיע אליהם כמעשה הרשעים ולא שממש הוה: שיצאו. מכלל דבימי משה הוה ולא מעולי גולה: לעולם מעולי גולה

חשק שלמה על רבינו גרשום

א) נראה דרבינו גרס גם וע"י שלמה וכמו שכתבו התוס' ולפיכך הוכחו לומר דקחשיב י' לבד מאדם הראשון:

תורה אור השלם

א) וַיָּמָת שָׁם מֹשֶׁה עֶבֶד יְיָ בְּאֶרֶץ מוֹאָב עַל פִּי יְיָ: [דברים לד, ה]

ב) לָקֹחַ אֵת סֵפֶר הַתּוֹרָה הַזֶּה וְשַׂמְתֶּם אֹתוֹ מִצַּד אֲרוֹן בְּרִית יְיָ אֱלֹהֵיכֶם וְהָיָה שָׁם בְּךָ לְעֵד: [דברים לא, כו]

ג) וַיֹּאמֶר לָהֶם בָּרוּךְ מִפִּיו יִקְרָא אֵלַי אֵת כָּל הַדְּבָרִים הָאֵלֶּה וַאֲנִי כֹּתֵב עַל הַסֵּפֶר בַּדְּיוֹ: [ירמיה לו, יח]

ד) וַיְהִי אַחֲרֵי הַדְּבָרִים הָאֵלֶּה וַיָּמָת יְהוֹשֻׁעַ בִּן נוּן עֶבֶד יְיָ בֶּן מֵאָה וָעֶשֶׂר שָׁנִים: [יהושע כד, כט]

ה) וְאֶלְעָזָר בֶּן אַהֲרֹן מֵת וַיִּקְבְּרוּ אֹתוֹ בְּגִבְעַת פִּינְחָס בְּנוֹ אֲשֶׁר נִתַּן לוֹ בְּהַר אֶפְרָיִם: [יהושע כד, לג]

ו) וּשְׁמוּאֵל מֵת וַיִּסְפְּדוּ לוֹ כָּל יִשְׂרָאֵל וַיִּקְבְּרֻהוּ בָרָמָה וּבְעִירוֹ וְשָׁאוּל הֵסִיר הָאֹבוֹת וְאֶת הַיִּדְּעֹנִים מֵהָאָרֶץ: [שמואל א כח, ג]

ז) מַשְׂכִּיל לְאֵיתָן הָאֶזְרָחִי: [תהלים פט, א]

ח) מִי הֵעִיר מִמִּזְרָח צֶדֶק יִקְרָאֵהוּ לְרַגְלוֹ יִתֵּן לְפָנָיו גּוֹיִם וּמְלָכִים יַרְדְּ יִתֵּן כֶּעָפָר חַרְבּוֹ כְּקַשׁ נִדָּף קַשְׁתּוֹ: [ישעיה מא, ב]

ט) שִׁיר מִזְמוֹר לִבְנֵי קֹרַח לַמְנַצֵּחַ עַל מָחֲלַת לְעַנּוֹת מַשְׂכִּיל לְהֵימָן הָאֶזְרָחִי: [תהלים פח, א]

י) לֹא כֵן עַבְדִּי מֹשֶׁה בְּכָל בֵּיתִי נֶאֱמָן הוּא: [במדבר יב, ז]

כ) מִי יִתֵּן אֵפוֹ וְיִכָּתְבוּן מִלָּי מִי יִתֵּן בַּסֵּפֶר וְיֻחָקוּ: [איוב יט, כג]

ל) וּבַמֶּה יִוָּדַע אֵפוֹא כִּי מָצָאתִי חֵן בְּעֵינֶיךָ אֲנִי וְעַמֶּךָ הֲלוֹא בְּלֶכְתְּךָ עִמָּנוּ וְנִפְלֵינוּ אֲנִי וְעַמְּךָ מִכָּל הָעָם אֲשֶׁר עַל פְּנֵי הָאֲדָמָה: [שמות לג, טז]

מ) וַיֶּחֱרַד יִצְחָק חֲרָדָה גְּדֹלָה עַד מְאֹד וַיֹּאמֶר מִי אֵפוֹא הוּא הַצָּד צַיִד וַיָּבֵא לִי וָאֹכַל מִכֹּל בְּטֶרֶם תָּבוֹא וָאֲבָרְכֵהוּ גַּם בָּרוּךְ יִהְיֶה: [בראשית כז, לג]

נ) וַיֹּאמֶר אֲלֵהֶם יִשְׂרָאֵל אֲבִיהֶם אִם כֵּן אֵפוֹא זֹאת עֲשׂוּ קְחוּ מִזִּמְרַת הָאָרֶץ בִּכְלֵיכֶם וְהוֹרִידוּ לָאִישׁ מִנְחָה מְעַט צֳרִי וּמְעַט דְּבַשׁ נְכֹאת וָלֹט בָּטְנִים וּשְׁקֵדִים: [בראשית מג, יא]

ס) וַיֹּאמֶר אֶת אַחַי אָנֹכִי מְבַקֵּשׁ הַגִּידָה נָּא לִי אֵיפֹה הֵם רֹעִים: [בראשית לז, טז]

ע) וַיַּרְא רֵאשִׁית לוֹ כִּי שָׁם חֶלְקַת מְחֹקֵק סָפוּן וַיֵּתֵא רָאשֵׁי עָם צִדְקַת יְיָ עָשָׂה וּמִשְׁפָּטָיו עִם יִשְׂרָאֵל: [דברים לג, כא]

פ) אִישׁ הָיָה בְאֶרֶץ עוּץ אִיּוֹב שְׁמוֹ וְהָיָה הָאִישׁ הַהוּא תָּם וְיָשָׁר וִירֵא אֱלֹהִים וְסָר מֵרָע: [איוב א, א]

צ) וּמָה הָאָרֶץ הַשְּׁמֵנָה הִוא אִם רָזָה הֲיֵשׁ בָּהּ עֵץ אִם אַיִן וְהִתְחַזַּקְתֶּם וּלְקַחְתֶּם מִפְּרִי הָאָרֶץ וְהַיָּמִים יְמֵי בִּכּוּרֵי עֲנָבִים: [במדבר יג, כ]

ק) וְלָרָשׁ אֵין כֹּל כִּי אִם כִּבְשָׂה אַחַת קְטַנָּה אֲשֶׁר קָנָה וַיְחַיֶּהָ וַתִּגְדַּל עִמּוֹ וְעִם בָּנָיו יַחְדָּו מִפִּתּוֹ תֹאכַל וּמִכֹּסוֹ תִשְׁתֶּה וּבְחֵיקוֹ תִשְׁכָּב וַתְּהִי לוֹ כְּבַת: [שמואל ב יב, ג]

in the name of Rav – conform? שְׁמוֹנָה פְּסוּקִים שֶׁבַּתּוֹרָה יָחִיד קוֹרֵא אוֹתָן – Regarding the communal reading of the Torah, the final **eight verses of the Torah must be read by a single person,** i.e. they may not be interrupted.[17] לֵימָא (רַבִּי יְהוּדָה הִיא) וּדְלָא כְּרַבִּי שִׁמְעוֹן – Are we **to say** that **it follows** the view of **R' Yehudah and not** the view of **R' Shimon?** For, in R' Shimon's view, the last eight verses were written by Moses, like the rest of the Torah, and thus should not be subject to any special regulations! – ? –

The Gemara replies:

אֲפִילּוּ תֵּימָא רַבִּי שִׁמְעוֹן – **You may even say** that Rav's ruling conforms with the view of **R' Shimon.** Although, according to R' Shimon, these eight verses were written by Moses, הוֹאִיל וְאִשְׁתַּנּוּ אִשְׁתַּנּוּ – **since they were** written in a **different** manner (i.e. with tears), **they are different** from the rest of the Torah and as such may be subject to special rules.

The Gemara returns to the Baraisa about the authorship of the books of Scripture:

יְהוֹשֻׁעַ כָּתַב סִפְרוֹ – JOSHUA WROTE HIS BOOK.

The Gemara asks:

וְהָכְתִיב: ,,וַיָּמָת יְהוֹשֻׁעַ בִּן־נוּן עֶבֶד ה׳ " – **But it is written** in the Book of *Joshua:* ***AND JOSHUA SON OF NUN, THE SERVANT OF HASHEM, DIED.***[18] Joshua could not have written this verse, or the following verses, which recount what happened after his passing. – ? –

The Gemara answers:

דְּאַסְקֵיהּ אֶלְעָזָר – **It was finished by Elazar** son of Aaron.

The Gemara asks:

וְהָכְתִיב: ,,וְאֶלְעָזָר בֶּן־אַהֲרֹן מֵת" – **But it is written** in the final verse of the Book of *Joshua:* ***AND ELAZAR SON OF AARON DIED*** etc. Who wrote this verse?

The Gemara answers:

דְּאַסְקֵיהּ פִּנְחָס – **It was finished by Pinchas** son of Elazar.[19]

The Gemara raises a similar difficulty with the Book of *Samuel:* שְׁמוּאֵל כָּתַב סִפְרוֹ – The Baraisa stated that SAMUEL WROTE HIS BOOK. וְהָכְתִיב: ,,וּשְׁמוּאֵל מֵת" – **But it is written** in the Book of *Samuel:* ***And Samuel died.***[20] – ? –

The Gemara answers:

דְּאַסְקֵיהּ גָּד הַחוֹזֶה וְנָתָן הַנָּבִיא – **It was finished by Gad the Seer and Nassan the Prophet.**

The Gemara quotes further from the Baraisa:

דָּוִד כָּתַב סֵפֶר תְּהִלִּים עַל יְדֵי עֲשָׂרָה זְקֵנִים – DAVID WROTE THE BOOK OF PSALMS IN COLLABORATION WITH TEN ELDERS.

The Gemara asks:

וְלִיחְשׁוֹב נַמִּי אֵיתָן הָאֶזְרָחִי – **Eisan the Ezrachite should also be included** among those who contributed to the Book of *Psalms,* for psalm 89 bears his name. – ? –

The Gemara answers:

אָמַר רַב – **Rav said:** אֵיתָן הָאֶזְרָחִי זֶה הוּא אַבְרָהָם – **Eisan the Ezrachite is** another name for **Abraham,** who *is* included among the ten Elders.

Rav provides a source for this identification:

כְּתִיב הָכָא: ,,אֵיתָן הָאֶזְרָחִי" – **Here,** in the Book of *Psalms,* **it is written:** ***Eisan the Ezrachite,***[21] וּכְתִיב הָתָם: ,,מִי הֵעִיר מִמִּזְרָח צֶדֶק [וגו׳]" – **and elsewhere,** in reference to Abraham, **it is written:** ***Who inspired** the one **from the east, righteousness [etc.].***[22] Abraham is referred to as "the one from the east." Thus, Ezrachite, which means "easterner," may be regarded as an appellation of Abraham.

The Gemara raises another difficulty with the Baraisa's list of ten Elders who contributed to the Book of *Psalms*:

קָא חָשִׁיב מֹשֶׁה וְקָא חָשִׁיב הֵימָן – **[This list] includes Moses and it** also **includes Heiman.** וְהָאָמַר רַב – **But Rav has said:** הֵימָן זֶה מֹשֶׁה – **Heiman is** another name for **Moses,** כְּתִיב הָכָא: ,,הֵימָן" – for **here,** in the Book of *Psalms,* the name ***Heiman* is written,**[23] וּכְתִיב הָתָם: ,,בְּכָל־בֵּיתִי נֶאֱמָן הוּא" – **and elsewhere,** in reference to Moses, **it is written:** ***In my entire house he*** [Moses] ***is trusted*** (*ne'eman*).[24] Why does the Baraisa list these names separately?

The Gemara answers:

תְּרֵי הֵימָן הֲווּ – **There were two people named Heiman:** Moses and the author of psalm 88.[25]

The Gemara quotes and comments on another section of the Baraisa. This introduces a lengthy passage about the authorship of the Book of *Job:*

מֹשֶׁה כָּתַב סִפְרוֹ וּפָרָשַׁת בִּלְעָם וְאִיּוֹב – MOSES WROTE HIS BOOK (the Pentateuch), THE PASSAGE OF BILAM AND the Book of *JOB.*[26] מְסַיְּיעָא לֵיהּ לְרַבִּי לֵוִי בַּר לַחְמָא – **[This Baraisa] supports** the view of **R' Levi bar Lachma:** דְּאָמַר רַבִּי לֵוִי בַּר לַחְמָא – **for R' Levi bar Lachma said:** אִיּוֹב בִּימֵי מֹשֶׁה הָיָה – **Job lived in the time of Moses.**[27]

R' Levi bar Lachma gives the source for his assertion:

כְּתִיב הָכָא: ,,מִי־יִתֵּן אֵפוֹ וְיִכָּתְבוּן מִלָּי" – **Here,** in the Book of *Job,* **it is written** that Job said: ***Oh, would that my words be written now*** (*eifo*)![28] On a homiletical level, Job is bemoaning his fate and saying: *Oh, would that my words be written, but where (eifo) [is the writer]?*[29] וּכְתִיב הָתָם: ,,וּבַמֶּה יִוָּדַע אֵפוֹא" – **And it is written** elsewhere that Moses said: ***For how will it then (eifo) be known?***[30] From Moses' use of the word *eifo,* it may be derived that he is the writer of the Book of *Job.*

The Gemara questions R' Levi's source:

וְאֵימָא בִּימֵי יִצְחָק – **But** on that basis **one could say** that Job lived

NOTES

17. *Rashi;* cf. *Rambam Hil. Tefillah* 13:6.

18. *Joshua* 24:29.

19. [Since Joshua wrote virtually the entire book, the Baraisa does not mention Elazar and Pinchas.]

20. *I Samuel* 28:3.

21. *Psalms* 89:1. (*Rashi's* reference to *I Kings* 5:11 applies to an alternative version of the Gemara's text.)

22. *Isaiah* 41:2. The subject of the verse is God, who instructed Abraham to leave his hometown in the east, and travel westward to Eretz Yisrael, as related in *Genesis* 12:1 (commentaries ad loc.).

23. *Psalms* 88:1. See note 25.

24. *Numbers* 12:7. [The Targum of נֶאֱמָן (trusted) is מְהֵימָן, *m'heiman.*]

25. Heiman, the author of מַשְׂכִּיל לְהֵימָן, *A Maskil by Heiman* (psalm 88), was a member of the Levite choir, which sang in the Temple (see 14b note 34). [In *I Chronicles* 6:18 mention is made of הֵימָן הַמְשׁוֹרֵר, *Heiman the singer.* The verse there states that he was a grandson of Samuel (see *Rabbeinu Gershom*).]

According to the Gemara's conclusion, Rav, who said that Heiman is Moses, refers not to the Heiman mentioned in *Psalms* (as had been thought originally) but to the Heiman mentioned in *I Kings* 5:11 (see *Rashi*).

26. Although this clause appears in the Baraisa *before* the sections already discussed, the Gemara saved this discussion for last because of its length (*Rashash*).

27. And Moses wrote the Book of *Job*, as the following exposition indicates.

28. *Job* 19:23.

29. *Maharsha.* [The word אֵפוֹא, *eifo*, a literary embellishment that is generally extraneous to the literal meaning of the verse – see *Rashi* to *Genesis* 43:11. Hence, it may be interpreted non-literally as if it said אֵיפֹה, *where.*]

30. *Exodus* 33:16.

ועל ידי שלשה בני קרח ירמיה כתב ספרו וספר מלכים וקינות חזקיה וסיעתו כתבו (ימש"ק סימן) ישעיה משלי שיר השירים וקהלת אנשי כנסת הגדולה כתבו (קנד"ג סימן) יחזקאל ושנים עשר דניאל ומגילת אסתר עזרא כתב ספרו ויחס של דברי הימים עד לו מסייעא ליה לרב דאמר רב יהודה אמר רב לא עלה עזרא מבבל עד שיחס עצמו ועלה ומאן אסקיה נחמיה בן חכליה אמר מר יהושע כתב ספרו ושמונה פסוקים שבתורה תניא כמאן דאמר שמונה פסוקים שבתורה יהושע כתבן (א) דתני' א וימת שם משה עבד ה' אפשר משה (ב) (מת) וכתב וימת שם משה אלא עד כאן כתב משה מכאן ואילך כתב יהושע דברי ר"י ואמרי לה ר' נחמיה אמר לו ר"ש אפשר ס"ת חסר אות אחת וכתיב ב לקוח את ספר התורה הזה אלא עד כאן הקב"ה אומר (א) ומשה אומר וכותב מכאן ואילך הקב"ה אומר ומשה כותב בדמע כמו שנאמר להלן ג ויאמר להם ברוך מפיו יקרא אלי את כל הדברים האלה ואני כותב על הספר בדיו כמאן אזלא הא דא"ר יהושע בר אבא אמר רב גידל אמר רב א שמונה פסוקים שבתורה יחיד קורא אותן לימא (ג) (ר"י היא) ודלא כר"ש אפילו תימא ר"ש הואיל ואשתנו אשתנו: יהושע כתב ספרו והכתיב ד וימת יהושע בן נון עבד ה' דאסקיה אלעזר והכתיב ה ואלעזר בן אהרן מת דאסקיה פנחס שמואל כתב ספרו והכתיב ו ושמואל מת דאסקיה גד החוזה ונתן הנביא דוד כתב ספר תהלים על ידי עשרה זקנים וליחשוב נמי איתן האזרחי אמר רב איתן האזרחי זה הוא אברהם כתיב הכא ז איתן האזרחי וכתיב התם ח מי העיר ממזרח צדק [וגו'] (ד) קא חשיב משה וקא חשיב הימן והאמר רב הימן זה משה כתיב הכא ט הימן וכתיב התם י בכל ביתי נאמן הוא תרי הימן הוו משה כתב ספרו ופרשת בלעם ואיוב מסייעא ליה לר' לוי בר לחמא דא"ר לוי בר לחמא כ איוב בימי משה היה כתיב הכא ל מי יתן אפוא ויכתבון מלי וכתיב התם (ה) ובמה יודע אפוא ואימא בימי יצחק דכתיב מ מי אפוא הוא הצד ציד ואימא בימי יעקב דכתיב נ אם כן אפוא זאת עשו ואימא בימי יוסף דכתיב ס איפה הם רועים לא ס"ד דכתיב ע מי יתן בספר ויוחקו ומשה הוא דאיקרי מחוקק דכתיב פ וירא ראשית לו כי שם חלקת מחוקק ספון רבא אמר איוב בימי מרגלים היה כתיב הכא צ איש היה בארץ עוץ איוב שמו וכתיב התם ק היש בה עץ אם אין מי דמי הכא עוץ והתם עץ הכי קאמר להו משה לישראל ישנו לאותו אדם ששנותיו ארוכות כעץ ומגין על דורו כעץ יתיב ההוא מרבנן קמיה דר' שמואל בר נחמני ויתיב וקאמר איוב לא היה ולא נברא אלא משל היה א"ל עליך אמר קרא איש היה בארץ עוץ איוב שמו אלא מעתה ר ולרש אין כל כי אם כבשה אחת קטנה אשר קנה ויחיה וגו' מי הוה אלא משל בעלמא הכא נמי משל בעלמא א"כ שמו ושם עירו למה רבי יוחנן ורבי אלעזר דאמרי תרוייהו איוב מעולי גולה היה ובית מדרשו בטבריא היה מיתיבי ימי שנותיו של איוב משעה שנכנסו ישראל למצרים ועד שיצאו אימא

רש"י

חזקיה וסיעתו. בני דורו שהאריכו ימים אחריו: כתבו ישעיה. שהרגו מנשה (ו) ולא כתב ספרו שלא היו הנביאים כותבים ספריהן אלא לפני מותן: משלי קהלת. דכתיב בספר משלי (כה) אשר העתיקו אנשי חזקיה וגו' ועל שחזקיה גרם להן לעסוק בתורה כדאמרינן בחלק (סנהדרין דף צד:) נעץ חרב על פתח בית המדרש כו' נקרא הדבר על שמו: אנשי כנסת הגדולה. חגי זכריה ומלאכי וזרובבל ומרדכי וחבריהם: כתבו יחזקאל. שנתנבא בגולה ואיני יודע למה לא כתבו יחזקאל בעצמו אם לא מפני שלא נתנה נבואה ליכתב בחוצה לארץ וכתבום אלו לאחר שבאו לארץ וכן ספר דניאל שהיה בגולה וכן מגילת אסתר ושנים עשר מתוך שהיו נבואותיהם קטנות לא כתבום הנביאים עצמם איש איש ספרו ובאו חגי זכריה ומלאכי וראו שרוח הקדש מסתלקת שהיו הם נביאים אחרונים ועמדו וכתבו נבואותיהם וצרפו נבואות קטנות עמם ועשאום ספר גדול שלא יאבדו מחמת קטנם: עד לו. עד שייחס עצמו: מסייע ליה כו' עד שייחס עצמו. שכתב דברי הימים עד שייחס בו את עצמו: ומאן אסקיה. מי סיימו: תניא כמאן דאמר. כל הך דקתני לעיל יהושע כתב ספרו ושמונה פסוקים שבתורה אתיא כי האי תנא דקמיה דלאמר נמי יהושע כתבן: דתניא. פלוגתא דתנאי בהאי וימת שם משה כו': כמו שנאמר להלן כו'. אכולה מילתא קאי דקאמר הקב"ה אומר ומשה כותב כמה שמצינו שהנביאים כותבים מפי רבם: יחיד קורא אותן. כלומר אין מפסיקין בהן: לימא ר"י היא. דאמר לא כתבם משה לפיכך נשתנו משאר התורה ולא כר"ש: הואיל ואשתנו. לכתוב בדמע אישתנו: ואימא יעקב כו'. לא גרסינן לה: ל"א (ג) גרסינן [למתניתא] דלעיל במניינא דעשרה זקנים דקא חשיב אברהם ואיתן האזרחי ולא קא חשיב אסף דקסבר משלשה בני קרח הוא: והא אמר רב כו'. גבי ויחכם מכל האדם מאיתן האזרחי וגו' (מלכים א ה) איתמר וכן הך דהימן זה משה אהימן דההוא קרא איתמר דכתיב ביה והימן וכלכל וגו': תרי הימן הוו. משכיל להימן האזרחי הימן אחרינא הוה: ששנותיו כעץ. איוב שהאריך ימים רבים: משל היה. ללמוד ממנו תשובות למקטרגים על מדת הדין ושאין אדם נתפס על צערו: איש היה. אלמא הוה: אלא מעתה ולרש אין כל וכו'. וסיפיה דקרא ותהי לו (ז) לבת: מי הוה. משום דכתיב ותהי: אימא

תוספות

ועל ידי שלמה ועל ידי בני קרח. לפי הספרים דגרסי שלמה צ"ל דאסף הוה משלשה בני קרח והוא אביאסף ולספרים דל"ג שלמה לא הוי אסף אביאסף אלא אסף היה מן הלוים המשוררים וא"ת ולהנהו דלא גרסי ליה אמאי לא חשיב ליה הא כתיב (תהלים עב) לשלמה אלהים משפטיך וגו' וי"ל דדוד אמרו והתפלל על שלמה תדע דכתיב בסוף המזמור כלו תפלות דוד וא"ת לספרים דגרסי שלמה הכתיב כלו תפלות דוד וי"ל לפי שסיימו דוד והא דכתיב נמי שיר המעלות לשלמה דוד כמו כן אמרו דכל חמש עשרה מעלות דוד אמרן ויש ספרים דקא חשיב אברהם ואיתן האזרחי וגרים לקמן דקא חשיב אברהם וקא חשיב איתן והאמר רב איתן האזרחי הוא אברהם ומשני איתן האזרחי דקא חשיב הכא יעקב וקשה להאי גירסא דמנא לן דדוד כתב ספרו על ידי אברהם כיון דאיתן האזרחי לאו היינו אברהם: ירמיה כתב ספרו וספר מלכים. והא דלא כתב ישעיה דהיה קודם ירמיה ספר מלכים לפי שנהרג ולא היה בסוף מלכים ממנשה ואילך (לפי שנהרג) ואפילו ספרו לא כתב: חזקיה וסיעתו כתבו ישעיה. לפי שחזקיה גרם להם לעסוק בתורה נקרא הדבר על שמו אבל הוא לא כתבו שהרי מת קודם לישעיה דמנשה (ח) בן בתו הרג לישעיה (ט): עד לו. פירש ר"ת עד פסוק ולו אחים בני יהושפט (דה"ב כא) ומסייע לרב שייחס עצמו ועלה שייחוס עצמו כתב לפני זה הפסוק וקשה לפירושו דהל"ל עד ולו בוי"ו: פ"ה דיחזקאל לא כתב ספרו לפי שהיה בחוצה לארץ. וקשה (ס) דהא ירמיה נמי בחוצה לארץ היה שהלך למצרים ונתנבא שם כמה נבואות ולא מצינו שחזר יותר לארץ ישראל: שמונה פסוקים שבתורה. ה"ר משולם היה מצריך מכאן לקרות לאחד אותן ח' פסוקים שלא יקרא עמו שליח צבור ואין נראה לר"ת דהא כל התורה כולה נמי אחד קורא כדתנן במגילה (דף כא:) קראוה שנים יצאו ואמר בגמ' תנא מה שאין כן בתורה ואומר ר"ת (י) דיחיד קורא בלא הפסקה שלא יקראו שנים זה ד' פסוקים וזה ד' ומה שנוהגים עתה לקרות שנים [בכל התורה] אומר ר"ת כדי שלא יתבייש מי שאינו יודע לקרות בעצמו כענין שמצינו במסכת ביכורים (פ"ג מ"ז) דתנן כל מי שיודע לקרות קורא בעצמו ושאינו יודע לקרות מקרין לפניו נמנעו מלהביא ביכורים התקינו שיהיו מקרין את מי שיודע לקרות ואת מי שאינו יודע לקרות והא דאמר בירושלמי במגילה רבי שמואל בר רב יצחק על לבי כנישתא וחזא חזנא דקאים וקורא ולא קאי בר אינש תחתיו א"ל אסור כשם שנתנה תורה על ידי סרסור כך אנו צריכין לנהוג בה על ידי סרסור אע"ג דמשמע שחזן עומד אצל הקורא לא שיקרא עמו אלא יעמוד ויקרא אותם שיש להם לקרות כדי שתתנו תורה על ידי סרסור ועוד אומר ר"י דיכול להיות שקצת מסייע לו בנחת והא דמשמע במגילה שלא יקראו שנים היינו שניהם שוין בקול רם:

איוב לא היה ולא נברא. האי לא סבר כריש לקיש דאמר בב"ר (ע) איוב לא היה שבאו עליו יסורין ולא אמר הכתוב להודיען כמו של איוב שאילו באו עליו יסורין היה יכול לעמוד בהן דאי סבר האי אמורא דאיוב לא היה בעולם (פ) כ"ש מאי קאמר מאי שמו ושם עירו למה טובא איצטריך לאשמועינן מי הוה אותו לדיק שהיה יכול לעמוד באותן יסורין:

עין משפט נר מצוה

קל א מיי' פי"ג מהל' תפלה הלכה ו ועיין בהשגות סמג עשין יט טוש"ע א"ח סי' קמא סעיף ז [וברב אלפס פרק ד' דמגילה דף רע]:

הגהות הב"ח

(א) גמ' עד כאן הקב"ה אומר ומשה כותב כצ"ל ותיבת אומר נמחק: (ב) רש"י ד"ה ל"א הכי גרסינן למתניתא וכו' בני קרח הוא. וגרסינן כאן קא חשיב איתן והאמר רב כו' ומשני איתן האזרחי דקא חשיב הכא יעקב דכתיב ביה ויזרח לו השמש הס"ד:

ליקוטי רש"י

שמונה פסוקים. מוימת [שם] משה. אפשר ס"ת חסר. ומשה קורא לו ס"ת [דכתיב] לקוח את ספר התורה הזה. הקב"ה אומר. ומשה אומר אחריו כדי שלא יטעה בכתב וכותב. מכאן ואילך הקב"ה אומר ומשה כותב בדמע. (ולא) [לא] שלא היה אומר אחריו מרוב צערו. כמו שנאמר להלן וכו' מפיו יקרא וגו'. שלא היה אומר אחריו משום דקינות הוו. יחיד קורא אותן. אדם אחד קורא ואין מפסיק בינתים כדי לעמוד אחר ולקרות. ודלא כר"ש. דכיון דלאמר ר"ש משה [כתבן] הוו להו כשאר פסוקים ויפסיק בינייהו ויקרא אחר. הואיל ואשתנו. דנכתב בדמע אישתני משאר [פסוקי] [ד]ס"ת [מנחות ל. ע"פ שטמ"ק]. ולרש אין כל. באוריה משתעי קרא. כבשה אחת. [זו] בת שבע [מגילה יג.].

רבינו גרשום

ליום השבת שנאמר בשביל אדם הראשון ועל ידי [י'] זקנים הני דקא חשיב א) לבר מאדם הראשון הוו י' והני י' כולהו קבוע בו מזמוריהן. וסיעתו. תלמידיו. ויחוס דברי הימים עד לו. כלומר הוא חשב היחס בדברי הימים מאדם הראשון עד עצמו: הואיל ואשתנו. משאר תורה שהללו כת' משה בדמע: אשתנו. נמי משאר תורה דיחיד יקרא אותו ולא שנים. ולמאן דאמר יהושע כתבו להכי יחיד קורא אותו והיינו דלא כר' שמעון דאיהו אמר דמשה כתבו: תרי הימן הוו. בן בנו של שמואל: (עד שעשאה כסולת נקיה). רבא אתי לסיועי למאן דאמר איוב בימי משה הוה. שדומה לעץ נקי מחטא: אלא משל היה. כמו שאמר שלמה יש צדיקים שמגיע אליהם כמעשה הרשעים ולא שממש הוה: שיצאו. מכלל דבימי משה הוה ולא מעולי גולה: לעולם מעולי גולה:

חשק שלמה על רבינו גרשום

א) נראה דרבינו גרס גם ועל ידי שלמה כו' ומשום הכי חשיב י' ולפיכך הוצרך לומר דקחשיב י' לבד מאדם הראשון:

מסורת הש"ס

א) מנחות ל., ב) [שם איתא חין], ג) [שם ליתא], ד) [ס"א ואימא יעקב דכתיב ביה ויזרח לו השמש ההוא מיבעי ליה שמש שבאה בעבורו זרחה בעבורו קא כו'], ה) [לעיל יד:], ו) [יבמות מט:], ז) [נ"ל בנו וכ"א גם], ח) [כדאיתא יבמות מט:], ט) [כך איתא ברש"י דהכא ובמנחות ל. וכ"ה בע"י], י) [כך איתא ברש"י דהכא ובמנחות ל.], כ) [סוף פ' ויגש].

גליון הש"ס

גמרא מכאן ואילך כתב יהושע. עי' (מגילה) [מכות] דף יא ע"א: תוס' ד"ה פ"ה כו' דהא ירמיה. עיין בתשובות נודע ביהודה מ"ת חא"ח סימן קו:

תורה אור השלם

א) וַיָּמָת שָׁם מֹשֶׁה עֶבֶד יְיָ בְּאֶרֶץ מוֹאָב עַל פִּי יְיָ: [דברים לד, ה]

ב) לָקֹחַ אֵת סֵפֶר הַתּוֹרָה הַזֶּה וְשַׂמְתֶּם אֹתוֹ מִצַּד אֲרוֹן בְּרִית יְיָ אֱלֹהֵיכֶם וְהָיָה שָׁם בְּךָ לְעֵד: [דברים לא, כו]

ג) וַיֹּאמֶר לָהֶם בָּרוּךְ מִפִּיו יִקְרָא אֵלַי אֵת כָּל הַדְּבָרִים הָאֵלֶּה וַאֲנִי כֹּתֵב עַל הַסֵּפֶר בַּדְּיוֹ: [ירמיה לו, יח]

ד) וַיְהִי אַחֲרֵי הַדְּבָרִים הָאֵלֶּה וַיָּמָת יְהוֹשֻׁעַ בִּן נוּן עֶבֶד יְיָ בֶּן מֵאָה וָעֶשֶׂר שָׁנִים: [יהושע כד, כט]

ה) וְאֶלְעָזָר בֶּן אַהֲרֹן מֵת וַיִּקְבְּרוּ אֹתוֹ בְּגִבְעַת פִּינְחָס בְּנוֹ אֲשֶׁר נִתַּן לוֹ בְּהַר אֶפְרָיִם: [יהושע כד, לג]

ו) וּשְׁמוּאֵל מֵת וַיִּסְפְּדוּ לוֹ כָּל יִשְׂרָאֵל וַיִּקְבְּרֻהוּ בָרָמָה וּבְעִירוֹ וְשָׁאוּל הֵסִיר הָאֹבוֹת וְאֶת הַיִּדְּעֹנִים מֵהָאָרֶץ: [שמואל א, ג]

ז) מַשְׂכִּיל לְאֵיתָן הָאֶזְרָחִי: [תהלים פט, א]

ח) מִי הֵעִיר מִמִּזְרָח צֶדֶק יִקְרָאֵהוּ לְרַגְלוֹ יִתֵּן לְפָנָיו גּוֹיִם וּמְלָכִים יַרְדְּ יִתֵּן כֶּעָפָר חַרְבּוֹ כְּקַשׁ נִדָּף קַשְׁתּוֹ: [ישעיה מא, ב]

ט) שִׁיר מִזְמוֹר לִבְנֵי קֹרַח לַמְנַצֵּחַ עַל מָחֲלַת לְעַנּוֹת מַשְׂכִּיל לְהֵימָן הָאֶזְרָחִי: [תהלים פח, א]

י) לֹא כֵן עַבְדִּי מֹשֶׁה בְּכָל בֵּיתִי נֶאֱמָן הוּא: [במדבר יב, ז]

כ) מִי יִתֵּן אֵפוֹא וְיִכָּתְבוּן מִלָּי מִי יִתֵּן בַּסֵּפֶר וְיֻחָקוּ: [איוב יט, כג]

ל) וּבַמֶּה יִוָּדַע אֵפוֹא כִּי מָצָאתִי חֵן בְּעֵינֶיךָ אֲנִי וְעַמֶּךָ הֲלוֹא בְּלֶכְתְּךָ עִמָּנוּ וְנִפְלֵינוּ אֲנִי וְעַמְּךָ מִכָּל הָעָם אֲשֶׁר עַל פְּנֵי הָאֲדָמָה: [שמות לג, טז]

מ) וַיֶּחֱרַד יִצְחָק חֲרָדָה גְּדֹלָה עַד מְאֹד וַיֹּאמֶר מִי אֵפוֹא הוּא הַצָּד צַיִד וַיָּבֵא לִי וָאֹכַל מִכֹּל בְּטֶרֶם תָּבוֹא וָאֲבָרְכֵהוּ גַּם בָּרוּךְ יִהְיֶה: [בראשית כז, לג]

נ) וַיֹּאמֶר אֲלֵהֶם יִשְׂרָאֵל אֲבִיהֶם אִם כֵּן אֵפוֹא זֹאת עֲשׂוּ קְחוּ מִזִּמְרַת הָאָרֶץ בִּכְלֵיכֶם וְהוֹרִידוּ לָאִישׁ מִנְחָה מְעַט צֳרִי וּמְעַט דְּבַשׁ נְכֹאת וָלֹט בָּטְנִים וּשְׁקֵדִים: [בראשית מג, יא]

ס) וַיֹּאמֶר אֶת אַחַי אָנֹכִי מְבַקֵּשׁ הַגִּידָה נָּא לִי אֵיפֹה הֵם רֹעִים: [בראשית לז, טז]

ע) וַיַּרְא רֵאשִׁית לוֹ כִּי שָׁם חֶלְקַת מְחֹקֵק סָפוּן וַיֵּתֵא רָאשֵׁי עָם צִדְקַת יְיָ עָשָׂה וּמִשְׁפָּטָיו עִם יִשְׂרָאֵל: [דברים לג, כא]

צ) אִישׁ הָיָה בְאֶרֶץ עוּץ אִיּוֹב שְׁמוֹ וְהָיָה הָאִישׁ הַהוּא תָּם וְיָשָׁר וִירֵא אֱלֹהִים וְסָר מֵרָע: [איוב א, א]

ק) וּמָה הָאָרֶץ הַשְּׁמֵנָה הִוא אִם רָזָה הֲיֵשׁ בָּהּ עֵץ אִם אַיִן וְהִתְחַזַּקְתֶּם וּלְקַחְתֶּם מִפְּרִי הָאָרֶץ וְהַיָּמִים יְמֵי בִּכּוּרֵי עֲנָבִים: [במדבר יג, כ]

ר) וְלָרָשׁ אֵין כֹּל כִּי אִם כִּבְשָׂה אַחַת קְטַנָּה אֲשֶׁר קָנָה וַיְחַיֶּהָ וַתִּגְדַּל עִמּוֹ וְעִם בָּנָיו יַחְדָּו מִפִּתּוֹ תֹאכַל וּמִכֹּסוֹ תִשְׁתֶּה וּבְחֵיקוֹ תִשְׁכָּב וַתְּהִי לוֹ כְּבַת: [שמואל ב יב, ג]

in the days of Isaac, for Isaac too used the word *eifo,* דִּכְתִיב: ,,מִי־אֵפוֹא הוּא הַצָּד צַיִד" – **as it is written:** ***Who then (eifo) was he that hunted game?***[31] וְאֵימָא בִּימֵי יַעֲקֹב – **Or one could say** that Job lived **in the days of Jacob** who also used the word *eifo,* דִּכְתִיב: ,,אִם־כֵּן אֵפוֹא זֹאת עֲשׂוּ" – **as it is written:** ***If so, then (eifo) do this!***[32] וְאֵימָא בִּימֵי יוֹסֵף – **Or one could say** that Job lived **in the days of Joseph** who also used this word, דִּכְתִיב: ,,אֵיפֹה הֵם רֹעִים" – **as it is written:** ***Where (eifoh) are they pasturing?***[33] Since all these people used the word *eifo*, or a similar word, what prompts R' Levi to specify Moses as having lived in the time of Job?

R' Levi replies:

לֹא סַלְקָא דַעְתָּךְ – **Do not think** that it was anyone other than Moses; דִּכְתִיב: ,,מִי־יִתֵּן בַּסֵּפֶר וְיֻחָקוּ" – **for it is written** at the end of that verse in *Job*: ***Oh, that they*** [the words of Job] ***were inscribed in a book!*** וּמֹשֶׁה הוּא דְּאִיקְּרִי מְחוֹקֵק – **and it is Moses who is described as "one who inscribes,"** דִּכְתִיב: ,,וַיַּרְא רֵאשִׁית לוֹ כִּי־שָׁם חֶלְקַת מְחֹקֵק סָפוּן" – **as it is written**: ***And he*** [Gad] ***saw fit to take the first part for himself, for there the*** burial ***portion of the "one who inscribes"*** [Moses] ***was hidden.***[34]

The Gemara records another opinion on the question of when Job lived:

רָבָא אָמַר – **Rava said:** אִיּוֹב בִּימֵי מְרַגְּלִים הָיָה – **Job lived in the time of the spies** who were sent by Moses to spy out Eretz Yisrael; כְּתִיב הָכָא: ,,אִישׁ הָיָה בְאֶרֶץ־עוּץ אִיּוֹב שְׁמוֹ" – **for here,** in the Book of *Job,* **it is written**: ***There was a man in the land of Utz whose name was Job,***[35] וּכְתִיב הָתָם: ,,הֲיֵשׁ־בָּהּ עֵץ" – **and elsewhere it is written** that Moses told the spies to see whether ***there are trees (eitz) in it*** [Eretz Yisrael].[36] Rava interprets the word *eitz* (tree) as a reference to Job, the man of *Utz.*

The Gemara challenges this derivation:

מִי דָּמֵי – **Is this a valid analogy?** הָכָא עוּץ הָתָם עֵץ – **Here** it says ***Utz,*** while **there** it says ***eitz***! – ? –

Rava explains that his derivation was not based on the similarity between *Utz* and *eitz,* but on the following interpretation of Moses' reference to a tree:

הָכִי קָאָמַר לְהוּ מֹשֶׁה לְיִשְׂרָאֵל – **This** is the meaning of what **Moses said to Israel** (i.e. the spies): יֶשְׁנוֹ לְאוֹתוֹ אָדָם שֶׁשְּׁנוֹתָיו אֲרוּכּוֹת כְּעֵץ – **There is a certain man** [Job] living among the non-Jews in Eretz Yisrael **whose years are as many as** those of **a tree** וּמֵגִין עַל דּוֹרוֹ כְּעֵץ – **and who protects his generation as a tree** protects with its shade. Go and find out whether this man is still alive.[37]

The Gemara records another opinion:

יָתִיב הַהוּא מֵרַבָּנָן קַמֵּיהּ דְּר' שְׁמוּאֵל בַּר נַחְמָנִי וְיָתִיב וְקָאָמַר – **While a certain scholar was** participating in a study session held **before R' Shmuel bar Nachmani, he said:** אִיּוֹב לֹא הָיָה וְלֹא נִבְרָא – **Job never lived; he was never created.** אֶלָּא מָשָׁל הָיָה – **Rather, it** [the story of Job] **is** merely **a parable.**[38]

R' Shmuel bar Nachmani responded:

עֲלָיךְ אָמַר קְרָא – אָמַר לֵיהּ – **[R' Shmuel] said to [the scholar]:** As a rebuttal **of** the view proposed by **you, the verse states:** ,,אִישׁ הָיָה בְאֶרֶץ־עוּץ אִיּוֹב שְׁמוֹ" – ***There was a man in the land of Utz whose name was Job.*** The word הָיָה, *he was,* indicates that Job did exist. – ? –

The scholar countered:

אֶלָּא מֵעַתָּה – **But if so,** that wherever the verb היה, *to be,* is used it must be taken literally, what does one make of the verse: ,,וְלָרָשׁ אֵין־כֹּל כִּי אִם־כִּבְשָׂה אַחַת קְטַנָּה אֲשֶׁר קָנָה וַיְחַיֶּהָ וגו'" – ***But the poor man had nothing except one small sheep which he had bought and reared, etc.?***[39] The verse concludes, *and it* [the sheep] *was* (וַתְּהִי) *like a daughter to him.* מִי הֲוָה – But **did [this sheep] exist?** It did not. אֶלָּא מָשָׁל בְּעָלְמָא – **Rather,** it is part of **a mere parable.** הָכָא נַמִּי מָשָׁל בְּעָלְמָא – Therefore, **here as well,** in regard to the story of Job, one may argue that **it is a mere parable**, despite the verse's use of the verb היה, *to be*.

R' Shmuel bar Nachmani replied:

אִם כֵּן – **If so,** that the story of Job is only a parable, שְׁמוֹ וְשֵׁם עִירוֹ לָמָּה – **why** does Scripture give **his name and the name of his town?** These points would be unnecessary in a parable. Evidently, Job did exist.

Another opinion on the question of when Job lived:

רַבִּי יוֹחָנָן וְרַבִּי אֶלְעָזָר דְּאָמְרֵי תַּרְוַיְיהוּ – **R' Yochanan and R' Elazar both said:** אִיּוֹב מֵעוֹלֵי גוֹלָה הָיָה – **Job was among those who ascended** to Eretz Yisrael **from** the Babylonian **exile,** וּבֵית מִדְרָשׁוֹ בִּטְבֶרְיָא הָיָה – **and his house of study was** located **in Tiberias.**

The Gemara asks:

מֵיתִיבֵי – **They challenged** this view from the following Baraisa: יְמֵי שְׁנוֹתָיו שֶׁל אִיּוֹב – THE DAYS OF JOB'S LIFE מִשָּׁעָה שֶׁנִּכְנְסוּ יִשְׂרָאֵל לְמִצְרַיִם וְעַד שֶׁיָּצְאוּ – WERE FROM THE TIME THE JEWS ENTERED EGYPT UNTIL THEY LEFT. According to this Baraisa, Job lived centuries before the ascension from Babylonia. – ? –

NOTES

31. *Genesis* 27:33.

32. Ibid. 43:11.

33. Ibid. 37:16.

34. *Deuteronomy* 33:21.

35. *Job* 1:1.

36. *Numbers* 13:20. [Since it was Moses who sent the spies, it is difficult to see what difference there is between this opinion (Job lived in the time of the spies) and the preceding one (Job was a contemporary of Moses). This problem may be resolved on the basis of *Tosafos'* assertion that according to the view which emphasizes that Job lived in the time of the spies, Job was definitely not a Jew (see below, 15b, and *Tosafos* there ד"ה בפירוש).]

37. Rava interprets Moses' instruction to the spies, ... וּרְאִיתֶם אֶת־הָאָרֶץ הֲיֵשׁ־בָּהּ עֵץ, *And you shall see the country...whether there is a tree in it* (ibid. vs. 18,20), as a request to find out whether Job is still alive and affords protection to his compatriots (see *Rashi* to *Numbers* 13:20 and 14:9). [This is the true basis of Rava's assertion that Job lived during the era of the spies. The analogy between *Utz* and *eitz* was intended merely as a mnemonic device – see also *Maharsha*.]

38. To provide arguments against those who question God's justice, and to teach that a person is not held accountable for what he says while under duress (*Rashi*).

39. *II Samuel* 12:3. This is from a parable used by Nassan the Prophet to illustrate King David's error in marrying Bathsheba.

מסורת הש"ס

א) מנחות ל., ב) [שם איתא חיי], ג) [שם ליתא], ד) [ס"א ואימא יעקב דכתיב ביה ויזרח לו השמש ההוא מיבעי ליה שמש שבאה בעבורו זרחה בעבורו קא פריך], ה) [לעיל יד:], ו) [יבמות מט:], ז) כנס, ח) [צ"ל בנו וכ"ה בס"י], ט) [כדאיתא יבמות מט:], י) [כן איתא בס"י דהכא ובמנחות ל. אבל במגילה כא: ה"א תנא כתבו דבר זה בשם רש"י], כ) [סוף פ' ויראה].

גליון הש"ס

גמרא מכאן ואילך כתב יהושע. ע' [מגילה] (מכות) דף יא ע"א: תוס' ד"ה פ"ה כו' דהא ירמיה. עיין בתשובות נודע ביהודה מ"ח חא"ח סימן קו:

עין משפט נר מצוה

קל א מיי' פי"ג מהל' תפלה הלכה ו ועיין בהשגות סמג עשין יט טוש"ע א"ח סי' תכח סעיף ז [וברב אלפס פרק ד' דמגילה דף רעג]:

ועל ידי שלשה בני קרח ירמיה כתב ספרו וספר מלכים וקינות חזקיה וסיעתו כתבו (ימש"ק סימן) ישעיה משלי שיר השירים וקהלת אנשי כנסת הגדולה כתבו (קנד"ג סימן) יחזקאל ושנים עשר דניאל ומגילת אסתר עזרא כתב ספרו ויחס של דברי הימים עד לו מסייעא ליה לרב דאמר רב יהודה אמר רב לא עלה עזרא מבבל עד שיחס עצמו ועלה ומאן אסקיה נחמיה בן חכליה אמר מר יהושע כתב ספרו ושמונה פסוקים שבתורה תניא כמאן דאמר שמונה פסוקים שבתורה יהושע כתבן [א] דתני' א) וימת שם משה עבד ה' אפשר משה [ב] (מת) וכתב וימת שם משה אלא עד כאן כתב משה ◦ מכאן ואילך כתב יהושע דברי ר' יהודה ואמרי לה ר' נחמיה אמר לו ר"ש אפשר ס"ת חסר אות אחת וכתיב ב) לקוח את ספר התורה הזה אלא עד כאן הקב"ה אומר (א) ומשה אומר וכותב מכאן ואילך הקב"ה אומר ומשה כותב בדמע כמו שנאמר להלן ג) ויאמר להם ברוך מפיו יקרא אלי את כל הדברים האלה ואני כותב על הספר בדיו כמאן אזלא הא דא"ר יהושע בר אבא אמר רב גידל אמר רב [א] שמונה פסוקים שבתורה יחיד קורא אותן לימא [ג] (ר' יהודה היא) ודלא כר"ש אפילו תימא ר"ש הואיל ואשתנו אשתנו: יהושע כתב ספרו והכתיב ד) וימת יהושע בן נון עבד ה' דאסקיה אלעזר והכתיב ה) ואלעזר בן אהרן מת דאסקיה פנחס שמואל כתב ספרו והכתיב ו) ושמואל מת דאסקיה גד החוזה ונתן הנביא דוד כתב ספר תהלים על ידי עשרה זקנים וליחשוב נמי איתן האזרחי אמר רב איתן האזרחי זה הוא אברהם כתיב הכא ז) איתן האזרחי וכתיב התם ח) מי העיר ממזרח צדק [וגו'] [ד] קא חשיב משה וקא חשיב הימן והאמר רב הימן זה משה כתיב הכא ט) הימן וכתיב התם י) בכל ביתי נאמן הוא תרי הימן הוו משה כתב ספרו ופרשת בלעם ואיוב מסייעא ליה לר' לוי בר לחמא דא"ר לוי בר לחמא [ה] איוב בימי משה היה כתיב הכא כ) מי יתן אפוא ויכתבון מלי וכתיב התם ל) ובמה יודע אפוא ואימא בימי יצחק דכתיב מ) מי אפוא הוא הצד ציד ואימא בימי יעקב דכתיב נ) אם כן אפוא זאת עשו ואימא בימי יוסף דכתיב ס) איפה הם רועים לא ס"ד דכתיב כ) מי יתן בספר ויוחקו ומשה הוא דאיקרי מחוקק דכתיב ע) וירא ראשית לו כי שם חלקת מחוקק ספון רבא אמר איוב בימי מרגלים היה כתיב הכא פ) איש היה בארץ עוץ איוב שמו וכתיב התם צ) היש בה עץ מי דמי הכא עוץ התם עץ הכי קאמר להו משה לישראל ישנו לאותו אדם ששנותיו ארוכות כעץ ומגין על דורו כעץ יתיב ההוא מרבנן קמיה דר' שמואל בר נחמני ויתיב וקאמר איוב לא היה ולא נברא אלא משל היה א"ל עליך אמר קרא איש היה בארץ עוץ איוב שמו אלא מעתה ק) ולרש אין כל כי אם כבשה אחת קטנה אשר קנה ויחיה וגו' מי הוה אלא משל בעלמא הכא נמי משל בעלמא א"כ שמו ושם עירו למה רבי יוחנן ורבי אלעזר דאמרי תרוייהו איוב מעולי גולה היה ובית מדרשו בטבריא היה מיתיבי ימי שנותיו של איוב משעה שנכנסו ישראל למצרים ועד שיצאו

אימא

רש"י

חזקיה וסיעתו. בני דורו שהאריכו ימים אחריו: כתבו ישעיה. שהרגו מנשה ולא כתב ספרו שלא היו הנביאים כותבים ספריהן אלא לפני מותן: משלי קהלת. דכתיב בספר משלי (כה) אשר העתיקו אנשי חזקיה וגו' ועל שחזקיה גרם להן לעסוק בתורה כדאמרינן בחלק (סנהדרין דף צד:) נעץ חרב על פתח בית המדרש נקרא הדבר על שמו: אנשי כנסת הגדולה. חגי זכריה ומלאכי וזרובבל ומרדכי וחבריהם: כתבו יחזקאל. שנתנבא בגולה ואיני יודע למה לא כתבו יחזקאל בעצמו אם לא מפני שלא נתנה נבואה ליכתב בחוצה לארץ וכתבום אלו לאחר שבאו לארץ וכן ספר דניאל שהיה בגולה וכן מגילת אסתר ושנים עשר מתוך שהיו נבואותיהם קטנות לא כתבום הנביאים עצמם איש איש ספרו ובאו חגי זכריה ומלאכי וראו שרוח הקדש מסתלקת שהיו הם נביאים אחרונים ועמדו וכתבו נבואותיהם וצרפו נבואות קטנות עמהם ועשאום ספר גדול שלא יאבדו מחמת קטנם: עד לו. עד שייחס עצמו: מסייע לי' כו' עד שייחס עצמו. שכתב דברי הימים עד שייחס בו את עצמו: ומאן אסקיה. מי סיימו: תניא כמאן דאמר. כל הך דקתני לעיל יהושע כתב ספרו ושמונה פסוקים שבתורה אתיא כי האי תנא דלקמיה דאמר נמי יהושע כתבן: דתניא. פלוגתא דתנאי בהאי וימת שם משה כו': כמו שנאמר להלן כו'. אכולה מילתא קאי דקאמר הקב"ה אומר ומשה כותב כמה שמצינו שהנביאים כותבים מפי רבם: יחיד קורא אותן. כלומר אין מפסיקין בהן: לימא ר' יהודה היא. דאמר לא כתבם משה לפיכך נשתנו משאר התורה ולא כר"ש: הואיל ואישתנו. לכתוב בדמע אישתנו: ואימא יעקב כו'. לא גרסינן לה: ל"א (ב) גרסינן [למתניתא] דלעיל במניינא דעשרה זקנים דקא חשיב אברהם ואיתן האזרחי ולא קא חשיב אסף דקסבר משלשה בני קרח הוא: והא אמר רב כו'. גבי ויחכם מכל האדם מאיתן האזרחי וגו' (מלכים א ה) איתמר וכן הך דהימן זה משה אהימן דהכא קאי דאיתמר דכתיב ביה והימן וכלכל וגו': תרי הימן הוו. משכיל להימן האזרחי הימן אחרינא הוא: ששנותיו כעץ. איוב שהאריך ימים רבים: משל היה. ללמוד ממנו תשובות למקטרגים על מדת הדין ושאין אדם נתפס על צערו: איש היה. אלמא הוה: אלא מעתה ולרש אין כל וכו'. וסיפיה דקרא ותהי לו [י] לבת: מי הוה. משום דכתיב ותהי:

אימא

תוספות

ועל ידי שלמה ועל ידי בני קרח. לפי הספרים דגרסי שלמה צ"ל דאסף הוה משלשה בני קרח והוא אביאסף ולספרים דל"ג שלמה לא הוי אסף אביאסף אלא אסף היה מן הלוים המשוררים וא"ת ולהנהו דלא גרסי ליה אמאי לא חשיב ליה הא כתיב (תהלים עב) לשלמה אלהים משפטיך וגו' וי"ל לדוד אמרו והתפלל על שלמה תדע דכתיב בסוף המזמור כלו תפלות דוד וא"ת לספרים דגרסי שלמה הכתיב כלו תפלות דוד וי"ל לפי שסיימו דוד והא דכתיב נמי שיר המעלות לשלמה דוד כמו כן אמרו דכל חמש עשרה מעלות דוד אמרן ויש ספרים דקא חשיב אברהם ואיתן האזרחי וגרים לקמן דקא חשיב אברהם וקא חשיב איתן והאמר רב איתן האזרחי הוא אברהם ומשני איתן האזרחי דקא חשיב הכא יעקב וקשה להאי גירסא דמנא לן דדוד כתב ספרו על ידי אברהם כיון דאיתן האזרחי לאו היינו אברהם: ירמיה כתב ספרו וספר מלכים. והא דלא כתב ישעיה דהיה קודם ירמיה ספר מלכים לפי שנהרג ולא היה בסוף מלכים ממנשה ואילך (לפי שנהרג) ואפילו ספרו לא כתב: חזקיה וסיעתו כתבו ישעיה. לפי שחזקיה גרם להם לעסוק בתורה נקרא הדבר על שמו אבל הוא לא כתבו שהרי מת קודם לישעיה דמנשה [ח] בן בתו הרג לישעיה [ט]: עד לו. פירש ר"ת עד פסוק ולו אחים בני יהושפט (דה"ב כא) ומסייע לרב שייחס עצמו ועלה שייחוס עצמו כתב לפני זה הפסוק וקשה לפירושו דהל"ל עד ולו בוי"ו: פ"ה דיחזקאל לא כתב ספרו לפי שהיה בחוצה לארץ. וקשה ◦ דהא ירמיה נמי בחוצה לארץ היה שהלך למצרים ונתנבא שם כמה נבואות ולא מצינו שחזר יותר לארץ ישראל: שמונה פסוקים שבתורה. ה"ר משולם היה מצריך מכאן לקרות לאחד אותן ח' פסוקים שלא יקרא עמו שליח צבור ואין נראה לר"ת דהא כל התורה כולה נמי אחד קורא כדתנן במגילה (דף כא:) קראוה שנים יצאו ואמר בגמ' תנא מה שאין כן בתורה ואומר ר"ת [י] דיחיד קורא בלא הפסקה שלא יקראו שנים זה ד' פסוקים וזה ד' ומה שנוהגים עתה לקרות שנים [בכל התורה] אומר ר"ת כדי שלא יתבייש מי שאינו יודע לקרות בעצמו כענין שמצינו במסכת ביכורים (פ"ג מ"ז) דתנן כל מי שיודע לקרות קורא בעצמו ושאינו יודע לקרות מקרין לפניו נמנעו מלהביא ביכורים התקינו שיהיו מקרין את מי שיודע לקרות ואת מי שאינו יודע לקרות והא דאמר בירושלמי במגילה רבי שמואל בר רב יצחק על לבי כנישתא וחזא חזנא דקאים וקורא ולא קאי בר איניש תחתיו א"ל אסור כשם שנתנה תורה על ידי סרסור כך אנו צריכין לנהוג בה על ידי סרסור אע"ג דמשמע שחזן עומד אצל הקורא לא שיקרא עמו אלא יעמוד ויקרא אותם שיש להם לקרות כדי שתנתן תורה על ידי סרסור ועוד אומר ר"י דיכול להיות שקלא מסייע לו בנחת והא דמשמע במגילה שלא יקראו שנים היינו שניהם שוין בקול רם:

איוב לא היה ולא נברא. האי לא סבר כריש לקיש דאמר בב"ר [ס] איוב לא היה שבאו עליו יסורין ולא אמר הכתוב שבאו עליו להודיעך כחו של איוב שאילו באו עליו היה יכול לעמוד בהן דאי סבר האי אמורא דאיוב היה בעולם א"כ מאי קאמר שמו ושם עירו למה טובא איצטריך לאשמועינן מי הוא אותו צדיק שהיה יכול לעמוד באותן יסורין:

הגהות הב"ח

(א) גמ' עד כאן הקב"ה אומר ומשה כותב כצ"ל ותיבת אומר נמחק: (ב) רש"י ד"ה ל"א הכי גרסינן למתניתא וכו' בני קרח הוא. וגרסינן כאן קא חשיב אברהם וקא חשיב איתן והאמר רב כו' ומשני איתן האזרחי דקא חשיב הכא יעקב דכתיב ביה ויזרח לו השמש הס"ד:

ליקוטי רש"י

שמונה פסוקים. מוימת [שם] משה. אפשר ס"ת חסר. ומשה קורא לו ס"ת [דכתיב] לקוח את ספר התורה הזה. הקב"ה אומר. ומשה אומר אחריו כדי שלא יטעה בכתב וכותב. מכאן ואילך הקב"ה אומר ומשה כותב בדמע. [ולא] שלא היה אומר אחריו מרוב צערו. כמו שנאמר להלן וכו' מפיו יקרא וגו'. שלא היה אומר אחריו משום דקינות הוו. יחיד קורא אותן. אדם אחד קורא ואין מפסיק בינתים כדי לעמוד אחר ולקרות. ודלא כר"ש. דכיון דאמר ר"ש משה כתבן] הוו להו כשאר פסוקים ויפסיק ביניהם ויקרא אחר. הואיל ואשתנו. דנכתבו בדמע. אישתני משאר [פסוקי] [ד]ס"ת [מנחות ל. ע"ש שטמ"ק]. ולרש אין כל. באוריה משתעי קרא. כבשה אחת. [זו] בת שבע [מגילה יג.].

רבינו גרשום

ליום השבת שנאמר בשביל אדם הראשון ועל ידי [י'] זקנים הני דקא חשיב [א] לבר מאדם הראשון הוו י' והני י' כולהו קבוע בו מזמוריהן. וסיעתו. תלמידיו. וייחוס דברי הימים עד לו. כלומר הוא חשב היחס בדברי הימים מאדם הראשון עד עצמו: הואיל ואשתנו. משאר תורה שהללו כת' משה בדמע: אשתני. נמי משאר תורה דיחיד יקרא אותו ולא שנים. ולמאן דאמר יהושע כתבנו להכי יחיד קורא אותו והיינו דלא כר' שמעון דאיהו אמר דמשה כתבו: תרי הימן הוו. בן בנו של שמואל: (עד שעשאה כסולת נקיה). רבא אתי לסיועי למאן דאמר איוב בימי משה הוה. שדומה לעץ נקי מחטא: אלא משל היה. כמו שאמר שלמה יש צדיקים שמגיע אליהם כמעשה הרשעים ולא שממש הוה: שיצאו. מכלל דבימי משה הוה ולא מעולי גולה: לעולם מעולי גולה:

חשק שלמה על רבינו גרשום

א) נראה דרבינו גרס גם וע"י שלמה וכמו שהובא בתוס' ולפיכך הוצרך לומר דקחשיב י' לבד מאדם הראשון:

תורה אור השלם

א) וַיָּמָת שָׁם מֹשֶׁה עֶבֶד יְיָ בְּאֶרֶץ מוֹאָב עַל פִּי יְיָ: [דברים לד, ה]

ב) לָקֹחַ אֵת סֵפֶר הַתּוֹרָה הַזֶּה וְשַׂמְתֶּם אֹתוֹ מִצַּד אֲרוֹן בְּרִית יְיָ אֱלֹהֵיכֶם וְהָיָה שָׁם בְּךָ לְעֵד: [דברים לא, כו]

ג) וַיֹּאמֶר לָהֶם בָּרוּךְ מִפִּיו יִקְרָא אֵלַי אֵת כָּל הַדְּבָרִים הָאֵלֶּה וַאֲנִי כֹּתֵב עַל הַסֵּפֶר בַּדְּיוֹ: [ירמיה לו, יח]

ד) וַיְהִי אַחֲרֵי הַדְּבָרִים הָאֵלֶּה וַיָּמָת יְהוֹשֻׁעַ בִּן נוּן עֶבֶד יְיָ בֶּן מֵאָה וָעֶשֶׂר שָׁנִים: [יהושע כד, כט]

ה) וְאֶלְעָזָר בֶּן אַהֲרֹן מֵת וַיִּקְבְּרוּ אֹתוֹ בְּגִבְעַת פִּינְחָס בְּנוֹ אֲשֶׁר נִתַּן לוֹ בְּהַר אֶפְרָיִם: [יהושע כד, לג]

ו) וּשְׁמוּאֵל מֵת וַיִּסְפְּדוּ לוֹ כָּל יִשְׂרָאֵל וַיִּקְבְּרֻהוּ בָרָמָה וּבְעִירוֹ וְשָׁאוּל הֵסִיר הָאֹבוֹת וְאֶת הַיִּדְּעֹנִים מֵהָאָרֶץ: [שמואל א כח, ג]

ז) מַשְׂכִּיל לְאֵיתָן הָאֶזְרָחִי: [תהלים פט, א]

ח) מִי הֵעִיר מִמִּזְרָח צֶדֶק יִקְרָאֵהוּ לְרַגְלוֹ יִתֵּן לְפָנָיו גּוֹיִם וּמְלָכִים יַרְדְּ יִתֵּן כֶּעָפָר חַרְבּוֹ כְּקַשׁ נִדָּף קַשְׁתּוֹ: [ישעיה מא, ב]

ט) שִׁיר מִזְמוֹר לִבְנֵי קֹרַח לַמְנַצֵּחַ עַל מָחֲלַת לְעַנּוֹת מַשְׂכִּיל לְהֵימָן הָאֶזְרָחִי: [תהלים פח, א]

י) לֹא כֵן עַבְדִּי מֹשֶׁה בְּכָל בֵּיתִי נֶאֱמָן הוּא: [במדבר יב, ז]

כ) מִי יִתֵּן אֵפוֹ וְיִכָּתְבוּן מִלָּי מִי יִתֵּן בַּסֵּפֶר וְיֻחָקוּ: [איוב יט, כג]

ל) וּבַמֶּה יִוָּדַע אֵפוֹא כִּי מָצָאתִי חֵן בְּעֵינֶיךָ אֲנִי וְעַמֶּךָ הֲלוֹא בְּלֶכְתְּךָ עִמָּנוּ וְנִפְלִינוּ אֲנִי וְעַמְּךָ מִכָּל הָעָם אֲשֶׁר עַל פְּנֵי הָאֲדָמָה: [שמות לג, טז]

מ) וַיֶּחֱרַד יִצְחָק חֲרָדָה גְּדֹלָה עַד מְאֹד וַיֹּאמֶר מִי אֵפוֹא הוּא הַצָּד צַיִד וַיָּבֵא לִי וָאֹכַל מִכֹּל בְּטֶרֶם תָּבוֹא וָאֲבָרְכֵהוּ גַּם בָּרוּךְ יִהְיֶה: [בראשית כז, לג]

נ) וַיֹּאמֶר אֲלֵהֶם יִשְׂרָאֵל אֲבִיהֶם אִם כֵּן אֵפוֹא זֹאת עֲשׂוּ קְחוּ מִזִּמְרַת הָאָרֶץ בִּכְלֵיכֶם וְהוֹרִידוּ לָאִישׁ מִנְחָה מְעַט צֳרִי וּמְעַט דְּבַשׁ נְכֹאת וָלֹט בָּטְנִים וּשְׁקֵדִים: [בראשית מג, יא]

ס) וַיֹּאמֶר אֶת אַחַי אָנֹכִי מְבַקֵּשׁ הַגִּידָה נָּא לִי אֵיפֹה הֵם רֹעִים: [בראשית לז, טז]

ע) וַיַּרְא רֵאשִׁית לוֹ כִּי שָׁם חֶלְקַת מְחֹקֵק סָפוּן וַיֵּתֵא רָאשֵׁי עָם צִדְקַת יְיָ עָשָׂה וּמִשְׁפָּטָיו עִם יִשְׂרָאֵל: [דברים לג, כא]

פ) אִישׁ הָיָה בְאֶרֶץ עוּץ אִיּוֹב שְׁמוֹ וְהָיָה הָאִישׁ הַהוּא תָּם וְיָשָׁר וִירֵא אֱלֹהִים וְסָר מֵרָע: [איוב א, א]

צ) וּמָה הָאָרֶץ הַשְּׁמֵנָה הִוא אִם רָזָה הֲיֵשׁ בָּהּ עֵץ אִם אַיִן וְהִתְחַזַּקְתֶּם וּלְקַחְתֶּם מִפְּרִי הָאָרֶץ וְהַיָּמִים יְמֵי בִּכּוּרֵי עֲנָבִים: [במדבר יג, כ]

ק) וְלָרָשׁ אֵין כֹּל כִּי אִם כִּבְשָׂה אַחַת קְטַנָּה אֲשֶׁר קָנָה וַיְחַיֶּהָ וַתִּגְדַּל עִמּוֹ וְעִם בָּנָיו יַחְדָּו מִפִּתּוֹ תֹאכַל וּמִכֹּסוֹ תִשְׁתֶּה וּבְחֵיקוֹ תִשְׁכָּב וַתְּהִי לוֹ כְּבַת: [שמואל ב יב, ג]

אימא כמשעה שנכנסו ישראל למצרים ועד [שעה] שיצאו מיתיבי שבעה נביאים נתנבאו לאומות העולם ואלו הן בלעם ואביו ואיוב אליפז התימני ובלדד השוחי וצופר הנעמתי ואליהוא בן ברכאל הבוזי (א"ל) וליטעמיך אליהוא בן ברכאל לאו מישראל הוה והא כתי' ממשפחת רם אלא אינבוי אינבי לאומות העולם ה"נ איוב אינבוי אינבי [לאומות העולם] אטו כולהו נביאי מי לא אינבוי לאומות העולם התם עיקר נביאותייהו לישראל הכא עיקר נביאותייהו לאומות העולם מיתיבי חסיד היה באומות העולם ואיוב שמו ולא בא לעולם אלא כדי לקבל שכרו הביא הקב"ה עליו יסורין התחיל מחרף ומגדף כפל לו הקב"ה שכרו בעוה"ז [כדי] לטרדו מן העולם הבא תנאי היא דתניא רבי אלעזר אומר איוב בימי שפוט השופטים היה שנאמר א) הן אתם כולכם חזיתם ולמה זה הבל תהבלו איזה דור שכולו הבל הוי אומר זה דורו של שפוט השופטים רבי יהושע בן קרחה אומר איוב בימי אחשורוש היה שנאמר ב) ולא נמצא נשים יפות כבנות איוב בכל הארץ איזהו דור שנתבקשו בו נשים יפות הוי אומר זה דורו של אחשורוש ואימא בימי דוד דכתיב ג) ויבקשו נערה יפה התם בכל גבול ישראל הכא בכל הארץ רבי נתן אומר איוב בימי מלכות שבא היה שנאמר ד) ותפל שבא ותקחם וחכ"א איוב בימי כשדים היה שנאמר ה) כשדים שמו שלשה ראשים ויש אומרים איוב בימי יעקב היה ודינה בת יעקב נשא כתיב הכא ו) כדבר אחת הנבלות תדברי וכתיב התם ז) כי נבלה עשה בישראל וכולהו (א) תנאי סבירא להו דאיוב מישראל הוה לבר מיש אומרים דאי ס"ד מאומות העולם הוה בתר דשכיב משה מי שריא שכינה על עובדי כוכבים והא אמר מר בקש משה שלא תשרה שכינה על עובדי כוכבים ונתן לו שנאמר ח) ונפלינו אני ועמך א"ר יוחנן דורו של איוב שטוף בזמה היה שנאמר הן אתם כולכם חזיתם ולמה זה הבל תהבלו וכתיב ט) שובי שובי השולמית שובי שובי ונחזה בך אימא בנבואה דכתיב י) חזון ישעיהו בן אמוץ א"כ למה זה הבל תהבלו למה לי וא"ר יוחנן מאי דכתיב כ) ויהי בימי שפוט השופטים דור ששופט את שופטיו אומר לו טול קיסם מבין (עיניך) אומר לו טול קורה מבין עיניך אמר לו ל) כספך היה לסיגים אמר לו סבאך מהול במים א"ר שמואל בר נחמני א"ר יונתן כל האומר מלכת שבא אשה היתה אינו אלא טועה מאי מלכת שבא מלכותא דשבא מ) ויהי היום ויבאו בני האלהים להתיצב על ה' ויבא גם השטן בתוכם ויאמר ה' אל השטן מאין תבא ויען השטן וגו' אמר לפניו רבש"ע שטתי בכל העולם כולו ולא מצאתי נאמן כעבדך אברהם שאמרת לו נ) קום התהלך בארץ לארכה ולרחבה כי לך אתננה ואפילו הכי בשעה שלא מצא מקום לקבור את שרה [עד שקנה בד' מאות שקל כסף] לא הרהר אחר מדותיך ס) ויאמר ה' אל השטן השמת לבך אל עבדי איוב כי אין כמוהו בארץ וגו' א"ר יוחנן גדול הנאמר באיוב יותר ממה שנאמר באברהם דאילו באברהם כתיב ע) כי עתה ידעתי כי ירא אלהים אתה ובאיוב כתיב איש תם וישר ירא אלהים [וסר מרע] מאי וסר מרע א"ר אבא בר שמואל איוב וותרן בממונו היה מנהגו של עולם נותן חצי פרוטה לחנוני איוב ויתרה משלו פ) ויען השטן את ה' ויאמר החנם ירא איוב אלהים צ) הלא אתה שכת בעדו ובעד ביתו וגו' מאי מעשה ידיו ברכת א"ר שמואל בר רב יצחק כל הנוטל פרוטה מאיוב מתברך מאי ומקנהו פרץ בארץ א"ר יוסי בר חנינא מקנהו של איוב פרצו גדרו של עולם מנהגו של עולם זאבים הורגים העזים מקנהו של איוב עזים הורגים את הזאבים ק) ואולם שלח נא ידך וגע בכל אשר לו אם לא על פניך יברכך ר) ויאמר ה' אל השטן הנה כל אשר לו בידך רק אליו אל תשלח ידך וגו' ש) ויהי היום ובניו ובנותיו אוכלים ושותים יין בבית אחיהם הבכור ומלאך בא אל איוב ויאמר הבקר היו חורשות וגו' מאי הבקר היו חורשות והאתונות רועות על ידיהם א"ר יוחנן מלמד שהטעימו הקב"ה לאיוב מעין

רשב"ם

אימא כמשעה שנכנסו כו'. מאתים ועשר דכתיב (איוב מב) ויוסף ה' את כל אשר לאיוב למשנה אף שנותיו הוכפלו דכתיב ויחי איוב אחר זאת מאה וארבעים שנה למדנו שהיה בן שבעים כשבאו יסורין עליו הרי מאתים ועשר ולעולם מעולי גולה היה: נתנבאו לאומות העולם. אלמא נכרי היה: אליהוא. על כרחך מדייחסיה קרא בשמו [ושם אביו] ושם משפחתו ישראל הוה ואית דאמרי ממשפחת רם היינו אברהם: שכולו הבל. הטובים שבהן לא היו כלום כדאמרינן לקמן שהנשפט היה לו פתחון פה לשפוט את שופטו ומוכיחו: בימי מלכות שבא היה. ובא (ב) גדוד מכשדים עליו: וחכ"א בימי מלכות כשדים. בימי נבוכדנצר היה ובא גם משבא גדוד עליו: וכולהו הני תנאי כו'. מסקנא דתירוצא הוא דתריך לעיל תנאי היא ההוא מתניתא דלעיל ס"ל עובד כוכבים הוה והני תנאי דהך מתניתא כולהו סבירא להו דישראל הוה בר מיש אומרים דאמרי בימי יעקב הוה: והא אמר מר. בפ"ק דברכות (דף ז.): ונפלינו. (ג) ונבדלנו בלכתך עמנו מכל האומות: ונחזה בך. לשון זימה [הוא זה] להסתכל בנשים שעובדי כוכבים אומרים לישראל שובי לתורתנו ותזני עמנו: ששופט את שופטיו. שהיו השופטין עצמן מקולקלים והיה פתחון פה לנשפט להוכיח את מוכיחו שאם אמר לו השופט טול קיסם מבין עיניך הסתלק ופרוש מעבירה קטנה שבידך יכול זה לומר טול קורה מבין עיניך פרוש מעבירה חמורה שבידך: סבאך. יינך כמו אל תהי בסבאי יין (משלי כג): מהול. מעורב וכן כל לשון הוללות שבתורה לשון ערבוב: קום התהלך. היינו דקאמר ומהתהלך בה מאותו שאמרת לו התהלך בארץ אני בא: ה"ג מנהג עולם נותן חצי פרוטה לחנוני. מי שיש לו מלאכה מועטת לעשות אומר לפועל חצי פרוטה אני נותן לך ולך אצל חנוני ונקנה בפרוטה ככר או בילים ונחלוק ואיוב ויתרה לחצי השני משלו ונותן לו כל הפרוטה שהיה רע בעיניו לדקדק בדבר קל שאינו ממון: והאתונות רועות [וגו']. ע"י הבקר דריש ליה לקרא שאוכלות חוזר מתלם המענה שהזרע צומח בשעתו: מעין

תוספות

בלעם ואביו. כדאמר במגילה (דף טו.) כל ששמו ושם אביו בנביאות בידוע שהוא נביא בן נביא:

ט) אימא כמשעה שנכנסו ישראל למצרים. וא"ת ומאי קמ"ל קרא כתיב ויוסף ה' את כל אשר לאיוב למשנה ואיוב אחרי אותו מעשה חיה ק"מ שנה וא"כ היה בן שבעים קודם וי"ל דס"ד דלא כפל אלא בעושר ויופי של בנות אבל בשנים לא:

אליהוא לאו מישראל הוה. משמע דפשיטא דאליהוא בן ברכאל מישראל הוה לכך נראה דפ"ק דע"ז (דף ג.) דאמר יבא בלדד השוחי וצופר הנעמתי ויעידו דכן בישראל שקיימו כל התורה כולה ל"ג התם ואליהוא בן ברכאל ונראה דשמעתא דהכא סברה כמ"ד איוב בימי יעקב הוה דהא אמר לקמן דממשה ואילך לא שרתה שכינה על עובדי כוכבים:

דור ששופט את שופטיו. תימה לר"י דאמר י) (בפ"ק) דתמורה (דף טו:) כל האשכולות שעמדו לישראל מימות משה עד שמת יוסף בן יועזר לא היה בהם שום דופי:

בפירוש רבינו חננאל גרס כולהו תנאי ואמוראי מודו לאיוב ישראל היה ולר"י נראה דל"ג ואמוראי דרבא ע"כ סבר לעיל דלאו מישראל הוה דקאמר לעיל הכי אמר להן משה למרגלים ישנו לאותו אדם ששנותיו כעץ כו': ויש אומרים איוב בימי יעקב הוה. הני יש אומרים לאו היינו ר' נתן דהא פליגי עליה כ) כדמוכח:

רבינו גרשום

אימא שהיה כשיעור שהיו ישראל במצרים והכי הוא חושבנא ישראל היו במצרים ר"י שנה ואיוב כשבאו עליו יסורין היה בן ע' שנה כדכתיב (איוב טו) גם שב גם ישיש בנו ואין שב פחות מע' שנה כדכתיב ימי שנותינו בהם שבעים שנה וכשהשיב הקב"ה שבותו נתן לו הכל למשנה ושנותיו הכפיל לו דכתיב ויחי איוב אחרי זאת ק"מ שנה והנהו ע' דמעיקרא הרי ר"י שנה: בלעם [ואביו] אינבויי אינבי לעובדי כוכבים על דור המבול ועל דור הפלגה. בלעם אינבי לעובדי כוכבים לעמלק [ולכתיים] וקשיא לר' יוחנן ולר' אלעזר דאמרי מעולי גולה היה: כדי לטורדו מן העולם. אלמא דאיוב מעובדי כוכבים הוה: תנאי היא כו' וכולהו הני תנאי מהא ברייתא דר' אלעזר ואילך מודו דאיוב מישראל הוה מדקא מיירי טעמייהו ממשה ואילך איכא למשמע מינה הואיל ושרתה עליו שכינה ממשה ואילך: לבד מיש אומרים דאמר בימי יעקב הוה שעדיין לא בא משה לעולם: דאי ס"ד דלשאר תנאי מאומות העולם היה וכי ממשה ואילך כו'. א) ואמוראי קרי לר' יוחנן ולר' אלעזר דאמרי תרוייהו איוב מעולי גולה היה ורבא נמי אמורא: מה תחזו בשולמית דכי היכי דהאי קרא משתעי בנקבה דהיינו זימה הכי נמי הן אתם כולכם חזיתם: ששופט. מי שהיה שפוט על פי בית דין הוא שופט את שופטיו שאם אמר לו השופט טול קיסם שלך גזילה מתחת ידיך היה משיב הוא לשופט טול קורה כלומר אני גזלתי קיסם שהוא מעט אתה גזלת קורה שהוא גדול מזה: אדם נותן חצי פרוטה לחנוני שאם היה חייב לפועל חצי פרוטה היה נותן לו איוב פרוטה שלימה ולא היה הולך לחנוני לחלוף לו חצי ליתן לו חצי לפועל [כמנהגם] היינו וסר מרע שלא היתה מדתו כמדת רעיו בני אדם: שהטעימו הקב"ה מעין

חשק שלמה על רבינו גרשום

א) נראה מזה שרבינו היה גורס וכולהו תנאי ואמוראי וכו' התוס' בשם ר"ח ע"ש:

ליקוטי רש"י

כולכם חזיתם. שזה חלק לאדם רשע. ולמה זה הבל תהבלו. להיות רשעים ומוכיחים [איוב כז, יב]. ולא נמצא נשים יפות כבנות איוב וגו'. ולא נמצאו מעשה של נשים יפות כמעשה יופי של בנות איוב ומקרא זה דוגמת ויהי אנשים אשר היו טמאים (במדבר ט) וכן הרבה [שם מב, טו]. ותפול שבא. נתקבלה ונקבצה מלכות שבא עליהם כמו (בראשית כה) על פני כל אחיו נפל [שם א, טו]. ונפלינו אני ועמך.

מסורת הש"ס

א) [בע"י ליתא], ב) כ"א שרתה, ג) ברכות ז., ד) [ערכין דף טו:], ה) [גירסת הע"י והילקוט שיניך], ו) [צ"ל משום בארץ ומהתהלך בה], ז) [מגילה דף כח.], ח) [פסחים דף קיב.], ט) [שייך לד"ה בלעם], י) צ"ל בפ"ב, כ) [ע' תוס' סוטה יב. ד"ה אחרי ותוס' ע"ז סד: ד"ה אחרים ותוס' לקמן נג: ד"ה מאן].

הגהות הב"ח

(א) גמ' וכולהו הני תנאי: (ב) רשב"ם ד"ה בימי וכו' ובא גם גדוד: (ג) ד"ה ונפלינו נ"ב וא"ג דבלכתך עמנו הוא תפלה אחרת שאלה ונתנו לו שתשרה שכינה על ישראל מ"מ שאלה ונתנו לו שכינה דבוקה עם בלכתך עמנו וכך אמר לו ועוד דבר אחר אני שואל ממך שנהיה נבדלים בלכתך עמנו מכל האומות:

תורה אור השלם

א) הֵן אַתֶּם כֻּלְּכֶם חֲזִיתֶם וְלָמָּה זֶּה הֶבֶל תֶּהְבָּלוּ: [איוב כז, יב]

ב) וְלֹא נִמְצָא נָשִׁים יָפוֹת כִּבְנוֹת אִיּוֹב בְּכָל הָאָרֶץ וַיִּתֵּן לָהֶם אֲבִיהֶם נַחֲלָה בְּתוֹךְ אֲחֵיהֶם: [איוב מב, טו]

ג) וַיְבַקְשׁוּ נַעֲרָה יָפָה בְּכֹל גְּבוּל יִשְׂרָאֵל וַיִּמְצְאוּ אֶת אֲבִישַׁג הַשּׁוּנַמִּית וַיָּבִאוּ אֹתָהּ לַמֶּלֶךְ: [מלכים א א, ג]

ד) וַתִּפֹּל שְׁבָא וַתִּקָּחֵם וְאֶת הַנְּעָרִים הִכּוּ לְפִי חָרֶב וָאִמָּלְטָה רַק אֲנִי לְבַדִּי לְהַגִּיד לָךְ: [איוב א, טו]

ה) עוֹד זֶה מְדַבֵּר וְזֶה בָּא וַיֹּאמַר כַּשְׂדִּים שָׂמוּ שְׁלֹשָׁה רָאשִׁים וַיִּפְשְׁטוּ עַל הַגְּמַלִּים וַיִּקָּחוּם וְאֶת הַנְּעָרִים הִכּוּ לְפִי חָרֶב וָאִמָּלְטָה רַק אֲנִי לְבַדִּי לְהַגִּיד לָךְ: [איוב א, יז]

ו) וַיֹּאמֶר אֵלֶיהָ כְּדַבֵּר אַחַת הַנְּבָלוֹת תְּדַבֵּרִי גַּם אֶת הַטּוֹב נְקַבֵּל מֵאֵת הָאֱלֹהִים וְאֶת הָרָע לֹא נְקַבֵּל בְּכָל זֹאת לֹא חָטָא אִיּוֹב בִּשְׂפָתָיו: [איוב ב, י]

ז) וּבְנֵי יַעֲקֹב בָּאוּ מִן הַשָּׂדֶה כְּשָׁמְעָם וַיִּתְעַצְּבוּ הָאֲנָשִׁים וַיִּחַר לָהֶם מְאֹד כִּי נְבָלָה עָשָׂה בְיִשְׂרָאֵל לִשְׁכַּב אֶת בַּת יַעֲקֹב וְכֵן לֹא יֵעָשֶׂה: [בראשית לד, ז]

ח) וּבַמֶּה יִוָּדַע אֵפוֹא כִּי מָצָאתִי חֵן בְּעֵינֶיךָ אֲנִי וְעַמֶּךָ הֲלוֹא בְּלֶכְתְּךָ עִמָּנוּ וְנִפְלֵינוּ אֲנִי וְעַמְּךָ מִכָּל הָעָם אֲשֶׁר עַל פְּנֵי הָאֲדָמָה: [שמות לג, טז]

ט) שׁוּבִי שׁוּבִי הַשּׁוּלַמִּית שׁוּבִי שׁוּבִי וְנֶחֱזֶה בָּךְ מַה תֶּחֱזוּ בַּשּׁוּלַמִּית כִּמְחֹלַת הַמַּחֲנָיִם: [שיר השירים ז, א]

י) חֲזוֹן יְשַׁעְיָהוּ בֶן אָמוֹץ אֲשֶׁר חָזָה עַל יְהוּדָה וִירוּשָׁלָםִ בִּימֵי עֻזִּיָּהוּ יוֹתָם אָחָז יְחִזְקִיָּהוּ מַלְכֵי יְהוּדָה: [ישעיה א, א] כ) וַיְהִי בִּימֵי שְׁפֹט הַשֹּׁפְטִים וַיְהִי רָעָב בָּאָרֶץ וַיֵּלֶךְ אִישׁ מִבֵּית לֶחֶם יְהוּדָה לָגוּר בִּשְׂדֵי מוֹאָב הוּא וְאִשְׁתּוֹ וּשְׁנֵי בָנָיו: [רות א, א] ל) כַּסְפֵּךְ הָיָה לְסִיגִים סָבְאֵךְ מָהוּל בַּמָּיִם: [ישעיה א, כב] מ) וַיְהִי הַיּוֹם וַיָּבֹאוּ בְּנֵי הָאֱלֹהִים לְהִתְיַצֵּב עַל יְיָ וַיָּבוֹא גַם הַשָּׂטָן בְּתוֹכָם: וַיֹּאמֶר יְיָ אֶל הַשָּׂטָן מֵאַיִן תָּבֹא וַיַּעַן הַשָּׂטָן אֶת יְיָ וַיֹּאמַר מִשּׁוּט בָּאָרֶץ וּמֵהִתְהַלֵּךְ בָּהּ: [איוב א, ו-ז] נ) קוּם הִתְהַלֵּךְ בָּאָרֶץ לְאָרְכָּהּ וּלְרָחְבָּהּ כִּי לְךָ אֶתְּנֶנָּה: [בראשית יג, יז] ס) וַיֹּאמֶר יְיָ אֶל הַשָּׂטָן הֲשַׂמְתָּ לִבְּךָ עַל עַבְדִּי אִיּוֹב כִּי אֵין כָּמֹהוּ בָּאָרֶץ אִישׁ תָּם וְיָשָׁר יְרֵא אֱלֹהִים וְסָר מֵרָע: [איוב א, ח] ע) וַיֹּאמֶר אַל תִּשְׁלַח יָדְךָ אֶל הַנַּעַר וְאַל תַּעַשׂ לוֹ מְאוּמָה כִּי עַתָּה יָדַעְתִּי כִּי יְרֵא אֱלֹהִים אַתָּה וְלֹא חָשַׂכְתָּ אֶת בִּנְךָ אֶת יְחִידְךָ מִמֶּנִּי: [בראשית כב, יב] פ) וַיַּעַן הַשָּׂטָן אֶת יְיָ וַיֹּאמַר הַחִנָּם יָרֵא אִיּוֹב אֱלֹהִים: [איוב א, ט] צ) הֲלֹא אַתָּה שַׂכְתָּ בַעֲדוֹ וּבְעַד בֵּיתוֹ וּבְעַד כָּל אֲשֶׁר לוֹ מִסָּבִיב מַעֲשֵׂה יָדָיו בֵּרַכְתָּ וּמִקְנֵהוּ פָּרַץ בָּאָרֶץ: [איוב א, י] ק) וְאוּלָם שְׁלַח נָא יָדְךָ וְגַע בְּכָל אֲשֶׁר לוֹ אִם לֹא עַל פָּנֶיךָ יְבָרְכֶךָּ: [איוב א, יא] ר) וַיֹּאמֶר יְיָ אֶל הַשָּׂטָן הִנֵּה כָל אֲשֶׁר לוֹ בְּיָדֶךָ רַק אֵלָיו אַל תִּשְׁלַח יָדֶךָ וַיֵּצֵא הַשָּׂטָן מֵעִם פְּנֵי יְיָ: [איוב א, יב] ש) וַיְהִי הַיּוֹם וּבָנָיו וּבְנֹתָיו אֹכְלִים וְשֹׁתִים יַיִן בְּבֵית אֲחִיהֶם הַבְּכוֹר: וּמַלְאָךְ בָּא אֶל אִיּוֹב וַיֹּאמַר הַבָּקָר הָיוּ חֹרְשׁוֹת וְהָאֲתֹנוֹת רֹעוֹת עַל יְדֵיהֶם: [איוב א, יג-יד]

ליקוטי רש"י (המשך)

ונהיה מובדלים בדבר הזה מכל העם כמו (שמות יא) והפלה ה' בין מקנה מצרים וגו' [שמות לג, טז]. כספך היה לסיגים. שהיו עושין מעות נחשת ומצפין אותן בכסף להונות בהם. סבאך מהול במים. ... אם לא על פניך יברכך. מיד כממיה [שם א, יא]. על ידיהם. כמו (במדבר ב) איש על ידו ואינו לשון מקום אלא על יד שהוא מוכן ומזומן לידו [שם א, יד].

The Gemara answers that the Baraisa does not refer to the era in which Job lived but to the length of his life:

אֵימָא – **Say** that the Baraisa means as follows: כְּמִשָּׁעָה שֶׁנִּכְנְסוּ יִשְׂרָאֵל לְמִצְרַיִם וְעַד [שָׁעָה] שֶׁיָּצְאוּ – Job lived AS LONG AS THE PERIOD BETWEEN THE JEWS' ARRIVAL IN EGYPT AND THEIR EXIT, i.e. two hundred and ten years.[1]

According to the opinion of R' Yochanan and R' Elazar, that Job was among the returnees from the Babylonian exile, it is evident that Job was a Jew. The Gemara, however, cites evidence to the contrary:

מֵיתִיבֵי – **They raised an objection** from the following Baraisa: שִׁבְעָה נְבִיאִים נִתְנַבְּאוּ לְאוּמּוֹת הָעוֹלָם – SEVEN PROPHETS PROPHESIED FOR THE NATIONS OF THE WORLD. וְאֵלּוּ הֵן – THESE prophets WERE: בִּלְעָם – BILAM, וְאָבִיו – AND HIS FATHER, וְאִיּוֹב – JOB, אֱלִיפַז הַתֵּימָנִי – ELIFAZ THE TEIMANITE, וּבִלְדַּד הַשּׁוּחִי – BILDAD THE SHUCHITE, וְצוֹפַר הַנַּעֲמָתִי – TZOFAR THE NA'AMASSITE, וֶאֱלִיהוּא בֶּן בַּרַכְאֵל הַבּוּזִי – AND ELIHU SON OF BARACHEL THE BUZITE.[2] Since this Baraisa describes Job as a prophet for the nations of the word, it seems that he was not a Jew. – ? –

The Gemara challenges the premise of the question:

(אמר ליה) וְלִיטַעֲמִיךְ אֱלִיהוּא בֶּן בַּרַכְאֵל לָאו מִיִּשְׂרָאֵל הֲוָה – **According to your premise,** that all the prophets listed in the Baraisa were gentiles, it would follow that **Elihu son of Barachel was not a Jew.** וְהָא כְּתִיב: ,,מִמִּשְׁפַּחַת רָם" – **But it is written** that Elihu was *of the family of Ram,*[3] which indicates that he was a Jew![4] אֶלָּא אִינַּבּוּי אִינַּבֵּי לְאוּמּוֹת הָעוֹלָם – **Rather,** the Baraisa must mean that **[Elihu] prophesied** ***to*** **the nations of the world.** הָכִי נַמִּי אִיּוֹב אִינַּבּוּי אִינַּבֵּי [לְאוּמּוֹת הָעוֹלָם] – **So too,** in reference to Job, the Baraisa means that **Job prophesied** ***to*** **the nations of the world.** According to this interpretation, it is possible that Job was a Jew, as R' Yochanan and R' Elazar maintain.

The Gemara questions this interpretation of the Baraisa:

אַטּוּ כּוּלְּהוּ נְבִיאֵי מִי לֹא אִינַּבּוּי לְאוּמּוֹת הָעוֹלָם – **But did not every prophet prophesy to the nations of the world?!** If this is the Baraisa's criterion, why does it specify these seven prophets?

The Gemara answers:

הָתָם עִיקַּר נְבִיאוּתַיְיהוּ לְיִשְׂרָאֵל – **There** [in the case of all other prophets], **their primary prophecies** were directed **to the Jewish people;** הָכָא עִיקַּר נְבִיאוּתַיְיהוּ לְאוּמּוֹת הָעוֹלָם – whereas **here** [in the case of the seven prophets listed by the Baraisa], **their primary prophecies** were directed **to the nations of the world.**

The Gemara continues to challenge the view of R' Yochanan and R' Elazar that Job was a Jew:

מֵיתִיבֵי – **They raised an objection** from the following Baraisa: חָסִיד הָיָה בְּאוּמּוֹת הָעוֹלָם וְאִיּוֹב שְׁמוֹ – THERE WAS A PIOUS MAN AMONG THE NATIONS OF THE WORLD WHOSE NAME WAS JOB. וְלֹא בָא לָעוֹלָם אֶלָּא כְּדֵי לְקַבֵּל שְׂכָרוֹ – HE CAME INTO THIS WORLD ONLY TO RECEIVE HIS REWARD.[5] הֵבִיא הַקָּדוֹשׁ בָּרוּךְ הוּא עָלָיו יִסּוּרִין הִתְחִיל מְחָרֵף וּמְגַדֵּף – THE HOLY ONE, BLESSED IS HE, INFLICTED HIM WITH SUFFERING and HE BEGAN TO BLASPHEME AND CURSE. כָּפַל לוֹ הַקָּדוֹשׁ בָּרוּךְ הוּא שְׂכָרוֹ בָּעוֹלָם הַזֶּה – THE HOLY ONE, BLESSED IS HE, thereupon DOUBLED HIS REWARD IN THIS WORLD, [כְּדֵי] לְטָרְדוֹ מִן הָעוֹלָם הַבָּא – IN ORDER TO BANISH HIM FROM THE WORLD TO COME.[6] This Baraisa states explicitly that Job was a gentile. – ? –

The Gemara answers that this Baraisa does not represent a refutation of the view of R' Yochanan and R' Elazar, because their view has alternative Tannaic support:

תַּנָּאֵי הִיא – **It** [the issue of Job's ethnicity] **is a** matter of **Tannaic dispute,** דְּתַנְיָא – **as it was taught in a Baraisa:** רַבִּי אֶלְעָזָר אוֹמֵר – R' ELAZAR SAYS: אִיּוֹב בִּימֵי שְׁפוֹט הַשּׁוֹפְטִים הָיָה – JOB LIVED IN THE TIME WHEN THE JUDGES JUDGED,[7] שֶׁנֶּאֱמַר – FOR IT IS STATED that Job told his friends: ,,הֵן אַתֶּם כֻּלְּכֶם חֲזִיתֶם וְלָמָּה־זֶּה הֶבֶל תֶּהְבָּלוּ" – ***BEHOLD, YOU HAVE ALL SEEN*** what befalls a wicked person, ***WHY THEN DO YOU ACT IN THIS FALSE MANNER?***[8] אֵיזֶה דוֹר שֶׁכּוּלּוֹ הֶבֶל – Now WHICH GENERATION WAS COMPLETELY FALSE, i.e. even the best of them were considered naught? הֱוֵי אוֹמֵר זֶה דּוֹרוֹ שֶׁל שְׁפוֹט הַשּׁוֹפְטִים – I WOULD SAY that THIS IS a reference to THE GENERATION WHEN THE JUDGES JUDGED.[9]

The Baraisa continues with another opinion:

רַבִּי יְהוֹשֻׁעַ בֶּן קָרְחָה אוֹמֵר – R' YEHOSHUA BEN KORCHAH SAYS: אִיּוֹב בִּימֵי אֲחַשְׁוֵרוֹשׁ הָיָה – JOB LIVED IN THE TIME OF ACHASHVEIROSH; שֶׁנֶּאֱמַר: ,,וְלֹא נִמְצָא נָשִׁים יָפוֹת כִּבְנוֹת אִיּוֹב בְּכָל־הָאָרֶץ" – FOR IT IS SAID: ***WOMEN AS BEAUTIFUL AS THE DAUGHTERS OF JOB WERE NOT TO BE FOUND IN THE ENTIRE WORLD.***[10] This implies that in Job's time a search was made for beautiful women. אֵיזֶהוּ דוֹר שֶׁנִּתְבַּקְּשׁוּ בּוֹ נָשִׁים יָפוֹת – Now, IN WHICH GENERATION WERE BEAUTIFUL WOMEN SOUGHT? הֱוֵי אוֹמֵר זֶה דּוֹרוֹ שֶׁל אֲחַשְׁוֵרוֹשׁ – I WOULD SAY that THIS IS a reference to THE GENERATION OF ACHASHVEIROSH, when a search was made to find a wife for Achashveirosh.[11]

NOTES

1. The length of Job's life can be deduced as follows: After Job was relieved of his suffering, he was blessed with twice as much as what he had originally (see *Job* 42:10-17). This blessing applied to the years of his life as well. Therefore, since Job lived 140 years after his afflictions ceased (ibid. v. 17), evidently he lived half that amount (70 years) before that time. This makes for a total of 210 years (*Rashi*).

2. The Gemara (*Megillah* 15a) teaches that wherever Scripture mentions a prophet together with his father in connection with a prophecy, it may be inferred that the father was also a prophet. [Hence, Bilam's father, Be'or, was a prophet, for it is stated (*Numbers* 24:3,15): נְאֻם בִּלְעָם בְּנוֹ בְעֹר, *So says Bilam son of Be'or*] (*Tosafos;* cf. *Maharsha*).

Elifaz, Bildad, Tzofar and Elihu were friends of Job, who came to comfort him in his time of suffering.

3. *Job* 32:2.

4. Scripture would not have recorded Elihu's genealogy were he not a Jew. Alternatively: "Ram" is an abbreviated form of "Abraham" [the first Jew] (*Rashi*).

5. [*R' Saadiah Gaon* writes that the purpose of Job's suffering was to afford him an opportunity to earn reward by accepting the suffering with faith *(Emunos VDe'os* 5:3). This is possibly the meaning of the present Baraisa: "He came into the world only to (suffer in faith and) receive his reward" (cf. *Maharsha).*]

6. Job was rewarded in this finite world for the good deeds he did perform, but he did not receive the unlimited reward of the World to Come which would have been his had he met the challenge that he was sent. [It seems that the Baraisa represents a minority opinion. The Gemara states below that Job was not held accountable for his apparently blasphemous statements (see 16b note 6, 16a end of note 5, *Rashi* to *Job* 42:7; cf. *Maharsha).*]

7. Scripture states (*Ruth* 1:1): וַיְהִי בִּימֵי שְׁפֹט הַשֹּׁפְטִים, *And it happened in the days when the Judges judged.* This refers to the period between Joshua's death and Saul's ascension to the throne, when the Jews were led by a succession of Judges.

8. *Job* 27:12.

9. This was a generation in which even the judges were corrupt. The literal translation of שְׁפֹט הַשֹּׁפְטִים is the judging of the judges, which can be taken to mean that the judges themselves were judged — see Gemara below.

According to this interpretation, the verse (*Job* 27:12) alludes to a retort made by Job to his friends. The friends had come to rebuke Job, who responds by saying that they are unfit to give rebuke, for the entire generation, including them, is corrupt (*Maharsha*).

10. *Job* 42:15.

11. *Esther* 2:1-4.

אימא כמשעה שנכנסו ישראל למצרים ועד [שעה] שיצאו מיתיבי שבעה נביאים נתנבאו לאומות העולם ואלו הן בלעם ואביו ואיוב אליפז התימני ובלדד השוחי וצופר הנעמתי ואליהוא בן ברכאל הבוזי (א) (א"ל) וליטעמיך אליהוא בן ברכאל לאו מישראל הוה והא כתי' ממשפחת רם אלא אינבוי אינבי לאומות העולם ה"נ איוב אינבוי אינבי [לאומות העולם] אטו כולהו נביאי מי לא אינבוי לאומות העולם התם עיקר נביאותיידהו לישראל הכא עיקר נביאותייהו לאומות העולם מיתיבי חסיד היה באומות העולם ואיוב שמו ולא בא לעולם אלא כדי לקבל שכרו הביא הקב"ה עליו יסורין התחיל מחרף ומגדף כפל לו הקב"ה שכרו בעוה"ז [כדי] לטרדו מן העולם הבא תנאי היא דתניא רבי אלעזר אומר איוב בימי שפוט השופטים היה שנאמר א) הן אתם כולכם חזיתם ולמה זה הבל תהבלו איזה דור שכולו הבל הוי אומר זה דורו של שפוט השופטים רבי יהושע בן קרחה אומר איוב בימי אחשורוש היה שנאמר ב) ולא נמצא נשים יפות כבנות איוב בכל הארץ איזהו דור שנתבקשו בו נשים יפות הוי אומר זה דורו של אחשורוש ואימא בימי דוד דכתיב ג) ויבקשו נערה יפה בכל גבול ישראל הכא בכל הארץ רבי נתן אומר איוב בימי מלכות שבא היה שנאמר ד) ותפל שבא ותקחם וחכ"א איוב בימי כשדים היה שנאמר ה) כשדים שמו שלשה ראשים ויש אומרים איוב בימי יעקב היה ודינה בת יעקב נשא כתיב הכא ו) כדבר אחת הנבלות תדברי וכתיב התם ז) כי נבלה עשה בישראל וכולהו (א) תנאי סבירא להו דאיוב מישראל הוה לבר מיש אומרים דאי ס"ד מאומות העולם הוה בתר דשכיב משה מי שריא שכינה על עובדי כוכבים והא ג) אמר מר בקש משה שלא תשרה שכינה על עובדי כוכבים ונתן לו שנאמר ח) ונפלינו אני ועמך א"ר יוחנן דורו של איוב שטוף בזמה היה שנאמר א) הן אתם כולכם חזיתם ולמה זה הבל תהבלו וכתיב ט) שובי שובי השולמית שובי שובי ונחזה בך אימא בנבואה דכתיב י) חזון ישעיהו בן אמוץ א"כ למה זה הבל תהבלו וא"ר יוחנן מאי דכתיב כ) ויהי בימי שפוט השופטים דור ששופט את שופטיו אומר לו ד) טול קיסם מבין ה) (עיניך) אומר לו טול קורה מבין עיניך אמר לו ל) כספך היה לסיגים אמר לו סבאך מהול במים א"ר שמואל בר נחמני א"ר יונתן כל האומר מלכת שבא אשה היתה אינו אלא טועה מאי מלכת שבא מלכותא דשבא מ) ויהי היום ויבאו בני האלהים להתיצב על ה' ויבא גם השטן בתוכם ויאמר ה' אל השטן מאין תבא ויען השטן וגו' ו) אמר לפניו רבש"ע שטתי בכל העולם כולו ולא מצאתי נאמן כעבדך אברהם שאמרת לו נ) קום התהלך בארץ לארכה ולרחבה כי לך אתננה ואפילו הכי בשעה שלא מצא מקום לקבור את שרה [עד שקנה בד' מאות שקל כסף] לא הרהר אחר מדותיך ס) ויאמר ה' אל השטן השמת לבך אל עבדי איוב כי אין כמוהו בארץ וגו' א"ר יוחנן גדול הנאמר באיוב יותר ממה שנאמר באברהם דאילו באברהם כתיב ע) כי עתה ידעתי כי ירא אלהים אתה ובאיוב כתיב ס) איש תם וישר ירא אלהים (וסר מרע) מאי וסר מרע א"ר אבא בר שמואל ז) איוב וותרן בממונו היה מנהגו של עולם נותן חצי פרוטה לחנוני איוב וותרה משלו פ) ויען השטן את ה' ויאמר החנם ירא איוב אלהים צ) הלא אתה סכת בעדו ובעד ביתו וגו' ח) מאי מעשה ידיו ברכת א"ר שמואל בר רב יצחק כל הנוטל פרוטה מאיוב מתברך מאי צ) ומקנהו פרץ בארץ א"ר יוסי בר חנינא מקנהו של איוב פרצו גדרו של עולם מנהגו של עולם זאבים הורגים העזים מקנהו של איוב עזים הורגים את הזאבים ק) ואולם שלח נא ידך וגע בכל אשר לו אם לא על פניך יברכך ר) ויאמר ה' אל השטן הנה כל אשר לו בידך רק אליו אל תשלח ידך וגו' ש) ויהי היום ובניו ובנותיו אוכלים ושותים יין בבית אחיהם הבכור ומלאך בא אל איוב ויאמר הבקר היו חורשות וגו' מאי הבקר היו חורשות והאתונות רועות על ידיהם א"ר יוחנן מלמד שהטעימו הקב"ה לאיוב

מעין

רש"י

אימא כמשעה שנכנסו כו'. מאתים ועשר דכתיב (איוב מב) ויוסף ה' את כל אשר לאיוב למשנה אף שנותיו הוכפלו דכתיב ויחי איוב אחר זאת מאה וארבעים שנה למדנו שהיה בן שבעים כשבאו יסורין עליו הרי מאתים ועשר ולעולם מעולי גולה היה: **נתנבאו לאומות העולם.** אלמא נכרי היה: **אליהוא.** על כרחך מדייחסיה קרא בשמו [ושם אביו] ושם משפחתו ישראל הוה ואית דאמרי ממשפחת רם היה היינו אברהם: **שכולו הבל.** הטובים שבהן לא היו כלום כדאמרינן לקמן שהנשפט היה לו פתחון פה לשפוט את שופטו ומוכיחו: **בימי מלכות שבא היה.** ובא (ב) גדול מכשדים עליו: **וחכ"א בימי מלכות כשדים.** בימי נבוכדנצר היה ובא גם משבא גדוד עליו: **וכולהו הני תנאי כו'.** מסקנא דתירוצא הוא דתריץ לעיל תנאי היא ההוא מתניתא דלעיל ס"ל עובד כוכבים הוה והני תנאי דהך מתניתא כולהו סבירא להו דישראל הוה בר מיש אומרים דאמרי בימי יעקב הוה: **והא אמר מר.** בפ"ק דברכות (דף ז.): **ונפלינו.** (ג) ונבדלנו בלכתך עמנו מכל האומות: **ונחזה בך.** לשון זימה [הוא זה] להסתכל בנשים שעובדי כוכבים אומרים לישראל שובי לתורתנו ותזני עמנו: **ששופט את שופטיו.** שהיו השופטין עצמן מקולקלים והיה פתחון פה לנשפט להוכיח את מוכיחו שאם אמר לו השופט טול קיסם מבין עיניך הסתלק ופרוש מעבירה קטנה שבידך יכול זה לומר טול קורה מבין עיניך פרוש מעבירה חמורה שבידך: **סבאך.** יינך כמו אל תהי בסבאי יין (משלי כג): **מהול.** מעורב וכן כל לשון הוללות שבתורה לשון ערבוב: **קום התהלך.** היינו דקאמר ומהתהלך בה מאותו שאמרת לו התהלך בארץ אני בא: **ה"ג מנהג עולם נותן חצי פרוטה לחנוני.** מי שיש לו מלאכה מועטת לעשות אומר לפועל חצי פרוטה אני נותן לך ונלך אצל חנוני ונקנה בפרוטה ככר או ביצים ונחלוק ואיוב ויתרה לחצי השני משלו ונותן לו כל הפרוטה שהיה רע בעיניו לדקדק בדבר קל שאינו ממון: **והאתונות רועות [וגו'].** ע"י הבקר דריש ליה לקרא שאוכלת חזיז מתלם המענה שהזרע צומח בשעתו:

מעין

תוספות

בלעם ואביו. כדאמר במגילה (דף טו.) כל ששמו ושם אביו בנביאות בידוע שהוא נביא בן נביא:

ט) **אימא** כמשעה שנכנסו ישראל למצרים. וא"ת ומאי קמ"ל קרא כתיב ויוסף ה' את כל אשר לאיוב למשנה ואיוב אחרי אותו מעשה חיה ק"מ שנה וא"כ היה בן שבעים קודם וי"ל דס"ד דלא כפל אלא בעושר ויופי של בנות אבל בשנים לא: **אליהוא** לא מישראל הוה. משמע דפשיטא דאליהוא בן ברכאל מישראל הוה לכך נראה דבפ"ק דע"ז (דף ג.) דאמר יבא בלדד השוחי וצופר הנעמתי ויעידו בהן בישראל שקיימו כל התורה כולה ל"ג התם ואליהוא בן ברכאל ונראה דשמעתא דהתם סברה כמ"ד איוב בימי יעקב הוה דהא אמר לקמן דממשה ואילך לא שרתה שכינה על עובדי כוכבים: **דור** ששופט את שופטיו. תימה לר"י דאמר י) (בפ"ק) דתמורה (דף טו:) כל האשכולות שעמדו לישראל מימות משה עד שמת יוסף בן יועזר לא היה בהם שום דופי: **בפירוש** רבינו חננאל גרס כולהו תנאי ואמוראי מודו דאיוב ישראל היה ולר"י נראה דל"ג ואמוראי דרבא ע"כ סבר לעיל דלאו מישראל הוה דקאמר לעיל הכי אמר להן משה למרגלים ישנו לאותו אדם ששנותיו כעץ כו': **ויש** אומרים איוב בימי יעקב הוה. הני יש אומרים לאו היינו ר' נתן דהא פליגי עליה כ):

ככותלא

רבינו גרשום

אימא שהיה כשיעור שהיו ישראל במצרים והכי הוא חושבנא ישראל היו במצרים ר"י שנה ואיוב כשבאו עליו יסורין היה בן ע' שנה כדכתיב (איוב טו) גם שב גם ישיש בנו ואין שב פחות מע' שנה כדכתיב ימי שנותינו בהם שבעים שנה וכשהשיב הקב"ה שבותו נתן לו הכל למשנה ושנותיו הכפיל לו דכתיב ויחי איוב אחרי זאת ק"מ שנה והנהו ע' דמעיקרא הרי ר"י שנה: **בלעם [ואביו] אינבויי אינבי** לעובדי כוכבים על דור המבול ועל דור הפלגה. בלעם אינבי לעובדי כוכבים לעמלק [ולכתיים] וקשיא לר' יוחנן ולר' אלעזר דאמרי מעולי גולה היה: **כדי לטורדו מן העולם.** אלמא דאיוב מעובדי כוכבים הוה: **תנאי היא כו'** וכולהו הני תנאי מהא ברייתא דר' אלעזר ואילך מודו דאיוב מישראל הוה מדקא מיירי טעמייהו ממשה ואילך איכא למשמע מינה הואיל ושרתה עליו שכינה ממשה ואילך: **לבר מיש אומרים** דאמר **בימי יעקב הוה** שעדיין לא בא משה לעולם: **דאי ס"ד** דלשאר תנאי **מאומות העולם היה וכי ממשה ואילך כו'.** א) ואמוראי קרי לר' יוחנן ולר' אלעזר דאמרי תרוייהו איוב מעולי גולה היה ורבא נמי אמורא: **מה תחזו בשולמית** דכי היכי דהאי קרא משתעי בנקבה דהיינו זימה הכי נמי **הן אתם כולכם חזיתם: ששופט.** מי שהיה שפוט על פי בית דין הוא שופט **את שופטיו** שאם אמר לו השופט **טול קיסם** שלך גזילה מתחת ידיך היה משיב הוא לשופט **טול קורה** כלומר אני גזלתי קיסם שהוא מעט אתה גזלת קורה שהוא גדול מזה: **אדם נותן חצי פרוטה לחנוני** שאם היה חייב לפועל חצי פרוטה היה נותן לו **איוב פרוטה שלימה** ולא היה הולך לחנוני לחלוף לו חצי ליתן לו חצי לפועל [כמנהגם] היינו **וסר מרע** שלא היתה מדתו כמדת רעיו בני אדם: **שהטעימו הקב"ה**

חשק שלמה על רבינו גרשום

א) נראה מזה שרבינו היה גורס וכולהו תנאי ואמוראי וכגי' התוס' בשם ר"ח ע"ש:

ליקוטי רש"י

כולכם חזיתם. שזה חלק אדם רשע. **ולמה זה הבל תהבלו.** להיות רשעים וחניפים [איוב כז, יב]. **ולא נמצא נשים יפות כבנות איוב וגו'.** ולא נמצא מעשה של נשים יפות כמעשה יופי של בנות איוב ומקרא זה דוגמת ויהי אנשים אשר היו טמאים (במדבר ט) וכן הרבה. [שם מב, טו]. **ותפול שבא.** נתנפלה ונתנה מלכות שבא עליהם כמו (בראשית כה) על פני כל אחיו נפל [שם א, טו]. **ונפלינו אני ועמך.** ונהיה מובדלים בדבר הזה מכל העם כמו (שמות ט) והפלה ה' בין מקנה מצרים וגו' [שמות לג טז]. **כספך היה לסיגים.** שהיו עושין מעות נחשת ומצפין אותן בכסף להונות בהם. **סבאך מהול במים.** משקים שלכם מעורבים במים כדאיתא בפסיקתא מהול מעורב ואין לו דמיון במקרא ומ"א פותר לשחוק אמרתי מהולל (קהלת ב ב) מעורבב [ישעיה א, כב]. **ויהי היום.** אותו יום שהיה ראש השנה (שהוא יום תרועה ולוה הקב"ה לשטן להביא זכות וחובה של כל הבריות הה"ד משוט בארץ). **ויבואו בני האלהים להתיצב על ה'.** לריב עמו שאין להתיצב אלא על דין שנאמר (ישעיה ג) נצב לריב ה'. (ד"א ויהי היום. אותו היום שחזרו חלילה לאכול בבית אחיהם הבכור. **בני האלהים.** בא השמים הקרובים לשכינה להיות בני ביתו ועל שם כך נקראו בניו. **להתיצב על ה'.** סביבותיו כמו (בראשי' מה) לכל הנצבים עליו) **ויבא גם השטן בתוכם.** לקטרג הבריות [איוב א, ו]. **מאין תבא.** דבר הכתוב דרך ארץ שהגדול מדבר תחילה ומרשה הקטן לענות. **ויען השטן וגו'.** משוט בארץ. לשוט ולראות רעים וטובים ושטתי בכל הארץ ולא מצאתי כאברהם שנא' בו קום התהלך בארץ (בראשית יג) ואמרו רז"ל שטן לשם שמים נתכוון כדי שלא יהא נשכח לפני אלהינו זכותו של אברהם [שם א, ז]. **השמת לבך על עבדי איוב.** שתרלה לקטרגו (ד"א. לשון תימה הוא. **תם וישר.** שלם במעשיו) [שם א, ח]. **החנם ירא איוב.** בתמיה. **הלא אתה סכת בעדו.** לפי שהוא יודע שאתה רגיל אללו לעשות לו נסים ופרה ורבה לפיכך עושה לדקות הללו אבל לא ניסית אותו (ד"א. הגנת בעדו כמחילה זו כמו הסר משוכתו (ישעיה ה) מחילתו וכל בעד האמור בלשון עברי אינו אלא לשון כנגדו ובפניו כמו וכפר בעדו (ויקרא טז) קנה העון כנגדך בפניך להיות הכפרה מגן בעדך וכן ה' מגן בעדי (תהלים ג) [שם א, ט]. **פרץ בארץ.** (נתחזקו כמו וכן יפרוץ (שמות א) ומתרגמינן יתקוף זהו פשוטו ורבותינו ז"ל אמרו בהגדה שהטעימו הקב"ה מעין עולם הבא שלאחר חרישה היו זורעים עם החרישה ורועות האתונות מיד חזיז מן התלם) [שם א, י]. **ואולם שלח נא ידך וגע.** לו **אם לא על פניך יברכך.** מיד בתמיה [שם א, יא]. **על ידיהם.** כמו (במדבר ב) איש על ידו ואינו לשון מקום אלא על שם שהוא מוכן ומזומן לידו [שם א, יד].

מסורת הש"ס

א) [בע"י ליתא], ב) נ"א שרתה, ג) ברכות ז., ד) [ערכין דף טז:], ה) [גירסת הע"י והילקוט שיניך], ו) [נ"ל משוט בארץ ומהתהלך בה], ז) [מגילה דף כח.], ח) [פסחים דף קיב.], ט) [שייך קודם לד"ה בלעם], י) נ"ל בפ"ב, כ) [ע' תוס' סוטה יב. ד"ה אחרי' ותוס' ע"ז סד: ד"ה אחרים ותוס' לקמן נג: ד"ה מאן]:

הגהות הב"ח

(א) גמ' וכולהו הני תנאי סבירא: (ב) רש"י ד"ה בימי וכו' ובא גם גדוד: (ג) ד"ה ונפלינו נ"ב אע"ג דבלכתך עמנו היא שאלה אחרת בקש שתשרה שכינה על ישראל מ"מ שאלת ונפלינו היא דבוקה עם בלכתך עמנו וכן אמר ועוד דבר אחר אני שואל ממך שנהיה נבדלים בלכתך עמנו מכל האומות:

תורה אור השלם

א) הֵן אַתֶּם כֻּלְּכֶם חֲזִיתֶם וְלָמָּה זֶּה הֶבֶל תֶּהְבָּלוּ: [איוב כז, יב]

ב) וְלֹא נִמְצָא נָשִׁים יָפוֹת כִּבְנוֹת אִיּוֹב בְּכָל הָאָרֶץ וַיִּתֵּן לָהֶם אֲבִיהֶם נַחֲלָה בְּתוֹךְ אֲחֵיהֶם: [איוב מב, טו]

ג) וַיְבַקְשׁוּ נַעֲרָה יָפָה בְּכֹל גְּבוּל יִשְׂרָאֵל וַיִּמְצְאוּ אֶת אֲבִישַׁג הַשּׁוּנַמִּית וַיָּבִאוּ אֹתָהּ לַמֶּלֶךְ: [מלכים א א, ג]

ד) וַתִּפֹּל שְׁבָא וַתִּקָּחֵם וְאֶת הַנְּעָרִים הִכּוּ לְפִי חָרֶב וָאִמָּלְטָה רַק אֲנִי לְבַדִּי לְהַגִּיד לָךְ: [איוב א, טו]

ה) עוֹד זֶה מְדַבֵּר וְזֶה בָּא וַיֹּאמַר כַּשְׂדִּים שָׂמוּ שְׁלֹשָׁה רָאשִׁים וַיִּפְשְׁטוּ עַל הַגְּמַלִּים וַיִּקָּחוּם וְאֶת הַנְּעָרִים הִכּוּ לְפִי חָרֶב וָאִמָּלְטָה רַק אֲנִי לְבַדִּי לְהַגִּיד לָךְ: [איוב א, יז]

ו) וַיֹּאמֶר אֵלֶיהָ כְּדַבֵּר אַחַת הַנְּבָלוֹת תְּדַבֵּרִי גַּם אֶת הַטּוֹב נְקַבֵּל מֵאֵת הָאֱלֹהִים וְאֶת הָרָע לֹא נְקַבֵּל בְּכָל זֹאת לֹא חָטָא אִיּוֹב בִּשְׂפָתָיו: [איוב ב, י]

ז) וּבְנֵי יַעֲקֹב בָּאוּ מִן הַשָּׂדֶה כְּשָׁמְעָם וַיִּתְעַצְּבוּ הָאֲנָשִׁים וַיִּחַר לָהֶם מְאֹד כִּי נְבָלָה עָשָׂה בְיִשְׂרָאֵל לִשְׁכַּב אֶת בַּת יַעֲקֹב וְכֵן לֹא יֵעָשֶׂה: [בראשית לד, ז]

ח) וּבַמֶּה יִוָּדַע אֵפוֹא כִּי מָצָאתִי חֵן בְּעֵינֶיךָ אֲנִי וְעַמֶּךָ הֲלוֹא בְּלֶכְתְּךָ עִמָּנוּ וְנִפְלִינוּ אֲנִי וְעַמְּךָ מִכָּל הָעָם אֲשֶׁר עַל פְּנֵי הָאֲדָמָה: [שמות לג, טז]

ט) שׁוּבִי שׁוּבִי הַשּׁוּלַמִּית שׁוּבִי שׁוּבִי וְנֶחֱזֶה בָּךְ מַה תֶּחֱזוּ בַּשּׁוּלַמִּית כִּמְחֹלַת הַמַּחֲנָיִם: [שיר השירים ז, א]

י) חֲזוֹן יְשַׁעְיָהוּ בֶן אָמוֹץ אֲשֶׁר חָזָה עַל יְהוּדָה וִירוּשָׁלִָם בִּימֵי עֻזִּיָּהוּ יוֹתָם אָחָז יְחִזְקִיָּהוּ מַלְכֵי יְהוּדָה: [ישעיה א, א]

כ) וַיְהִי בִּימֵי שְׁפֹט הַשֹּׁפְטִים וַיְהִי רָעָב בָּאָרֶץ וַיֵּלֶךְ אִישׁ מִבֵּית לֶחֶם יְהוּדָה לָגוּר בִּשְׂדֵי מוֹאָב הוּא וְאִשְׁתּוֹ וּשְׁנֵי בָנָיו: [רות א, א]

ל) כַּסְפֵּךְ הָיָה לְסִיגִים סָבְאֵךְ מָהוּל בַּמָּיִם: [ישעיה א, כב]

מ) וַיְהִי הַיּוֹם וַיָּבֹאוּ בְּנֵי הָאֱלֹהִים לְהִתְיַצֵּב עַל יְיָ וַיָּבוֹא גַם הַשָּׂטָן בְּתוֹכָם: וַיֹּאמֶר יְיָ אֶל הַשָּׂטָן מֵאַיִן תָּבֹא וַיַּעַן הַשָּׂטָן אֶת יְיָ וַיֹּאמַר מִשּׁוּט בָּאָרֶץ וּמֵהִתְהַלֵּךְ בָּהּ: [איוב א, ו-ז]

נ) קוּם הִתְהַלֵּךְ בָּאָרֶץ לְאָרְכָּהּ וּלְרָחְבָּהּ כִּי לְךָ אֶתְּנֶנָּה: [בראשית יג, יז]

ס) וַיֹּאמֶר יְיָ אֶל הַשָּׂטָן הֲשַׂמְתָּ לִבְּךָ עַל עַבְדִּי אִיּוֹב כִּי אֵין כָּמֹהוּ בָּאָרֶץ אִישׁ תָּם וְיָשָׁר יְרֵא אֱלֹהִים וְסָר מֵרָע: [איוב א, ח]

ע) וַיֹּאמֶר אַל תִּשְׁלַח יָדְךָ אֶל הַנַּעַר וְאַל תַּעַשׂ לוֹ מְאוּמָה כִּי עַתָּה יָדַעְתִּי כִּי יְרֵא אֱלֹהִים אַתָּה וְלֹא חָשַׂכְתָּ אֶת בִּנְךָ אֶת יְחִידְךָ מִמֶּנִּי: [בראשית כב, יב]

פ) וַיַּעַן הַשָּׂטָן אֶת יְיָ וַיֹּאמַר הַחִנָּם יָרֵא אִיּוֹב אֱלֹהִים: [איוב א, ט]

צ) הֲלֹא אַתָּה שַׂכְתָּ בַעֲדוֹ וּבְעַד בֵּיתוֹ וּבְעַד כָּל אֲשֶׁר לוֹ מִסָּבִיב מַעֲשֵׂה יָדָיו בֵּרַכְתָּ וּמִקְנֵהוּ פָּרַץ בָּאָרֶץ: [איוב א, י]

ק) וְאוּלָם שְׁלַח נָא יָדְךָ וְגַע בְּכָל אֲשֶׁר לוֹ אִם לֹא עַל פָּנֶיךָ יְבָרְכֶךָּ: [איוב א, יא]

ר) וַיֹּאמֶר יְיָ אֶל הַשָּׂטָן הִנֵּה כָל אֲשֶׁר לוֹ בְּיָדֶךָ רַק אֵלָיו אַל תִּשְׁלַח יָדֶךָ וַיֵּצֵא הַשָּׂטָן מֵעִם פְּנֵי יְיָ: [איוב א, יב]

ש) וַיְהִי הַיּוֹם וּבָנָיו וּבְנֹתָיו אֹכְלִים וְשֹׁתִים יַיִן בְּבֵית אֲחִיהֶם הַבְּכוֹר: וּמַלְאָךְ בָּא אֶל אִיּוֹב וַיֹּאמַר הַבָּקָר הָיוּ חֹרְשׁוֹת וְהָאֲתֹנוֹת רֹעוֹת עַל יְדֵיהֶם: [איוב א, יג-יד]

The Gemara interjects with a challenge to this derivation: וְאֵימָא בִּימֵי דָוִד – **But** on this basis **one could say** that Job lived **in the days of** King **David,** for in his time too a search was made for a beautiful woman; דִּכְתִיב: ,,וַיְבַקְשׁוּ נַעֲרָה יָפָה" – **as it is written:** ***They searched for a beautiful maiden.***[12] – ? –

The Gemara answers:

הָתָם ,,בְּכֹל גְּבוּל יִשְׂרָאֵל" – **There,** in the case of King David, the search was conducted only ***in all the boundaries of Israel;***[13] הָכָא ,,בְּכָל־הָאָרֶץ" – whereas **here,** in the case of Job, the verse describes the beauty of his daughters as unequaled ***in the entire world***, implying that a *worldwide* search was undertaken. Such a search took place only during the reign of Achashveirosh.[14]

The Gemara resumes its quotation of the Baraisa:

רַבִּי נָתָן אוֹמֵר – R' NASSAN SAYS: אִיּוֹב בִּימֵי מַלְכוּת שְׁבָא הָיָה – JOB LIVED IN THE TIME OF THE KINGDOM OF SHEBA;[15] שֶׁנֶּאֱמַר: ,,וַתִּפֹּל שְׁבָא וַתִּקָּחֵם" – AS IT IS STATED: *SHEBA ATTACKED AND TOOK [JOB'S CATTLE].*[16] וַחֲכָמִים אוֹמְרִים – BUT THE SAGES SAY: אִיּוֹב בִּימֵי כַשְׂדִּים הָיָה – JOB LIVED IN THE TIME OF THE CHALDEANS;[17] שֶׁנֶּאֱמַר: ,,כַּשְׂדִּים שָׂמוּ שְׁלֹשָׁה רָאשִׁים" – AS IT IS SAID: *THE CHALDEANS FIELDED THREE DIVISIONS that deployed themselves against [Job's] camels.*[18] וְיֵשׁ אוֹמְרִים – SOME [SCHOLARS] SAY: אִיּוֹב בִּימֵי יַעֲקֹב הָיָה – JOB LIVED IN THE TIME OF JACOB, וְדִינָה בַּת יַעֲקֹב נָשָׂא – AND HE MARRIED DINAH, THE DAUGHTER OF JACOB. כְּתִיב הָכָא – HERE, in the Book of *Job,* IT IS WRITTEN that Job said to his wife: ,,כְּדַבֵּר אַחַת הַנְּבָלוֹת תְּדַבֵּרִי" – *YOU TALK LIKE ONE OF THE LOATHSOME WOMEN (nevalos)!*[19] וּכְתִיב הָתָם – AND ELSEWHERE, in reference to Dinah, IT IS WRITTEN: ,,כִּי נְבָלָה עָשָׂה בְיִשְׂרָאֵל" – *FOR HE* [Shechem] *HAD COMMITTED A LOATHSOME ACT (nevalah) IN ISRAEL by lying with a daughter of Jacob* [Dinah].[20] The use of the word *nevalah* (loathsome) in both verses intimates a connection between Job's wife and Dinah.

The Gemara demonstrates how this Baraisa pertains to the question discussed above of whether Job was a Jew:

וְכוּלְהוּ תַּנָּאֵי סְבִירָא לְהוּ דְּאִיּוֹב מִיִּשְׂרָאֵל הֲוָה – **Now all the Tannaim** of this Baraisa **are of the opinion that Job was a Jew,** לְבַר מִיֵּשׁ אוֹמְרִים – **except for** the last opinion, which was introduced by the phrase, "SOME [SCHOLARS] SAY," according to which Job lived in the time of Jacob. דְּאִי סָלְקָא דַעְתָּךְ מֵאוּמּוֹת הָעוֹלָם הֲוָה – **For if you should think** that according to any of the former opinions **[Job] was from the nations of the world,** such a proposal is untenable, בָּתַר דִּשְׁכִיב מֹשֶׁה מִי שַׁרְיָא שְׁכִינָה עַל עוֹבְדֵי כוֹכָבִים – for **after Moses died, did the Divine Presence rest on idolaters?** וְהָא אָמַר מַר – **But the master has taught** in a Baraisa: בִּקֵּשׁ מֹשֶׁה שֶׁלֹּא תִשְׁרֶה שְׁכִינָה עַל עוֹבְדֵי כוֹכָבִים – MOSES REQUESTED of God THAT THE DIVINE PRESENCE NOT REST ON IDOLATERS וְנָתַן לוֹ – AND [GOD] GRANTED HIM this request; שֶׁנֶּאֱמַר: ,,וְנִפְלִינוּ אֲנִי וְעַמְּךָ" – AS IT IS SAID: *By Your going with us, I* [Moses] *AND YOUR PEOPLE SHALL BE DIFFERENT.*[21] Hence, according to all the Tannaim who maintain that Job lived after Moses, he must have been a Jew, for otherwise the Divine Presence would not have rested on him.[22] According to the last opinion, however, which places Job in the era of Jacob, Job was not a Jew.[23]

The Gemara elaborates on some of the verses quoted in the Baraisa:

אָמַר רַבִּי יוֹחָנָן – **R' Yochanan said:** דּוֹרוֹ שֶׁל אִיּוֹב שָׁטוּף בְּזִמָּה הָיָה – **The generation of Job was steeped in immorality;** שֶׁנֶּאֱמַר: ,,הֵן אַתֶּם כֻּלְּכֶם חֲזִיתֶם וְלָמָּה־זֶּה הֶבֶל תֶּהְבָּלוּ" – **as it is said:** ***Behold, you have all gazed*** (*chazisem*)***; why do you act in this false manner?***[24] The verb חזה, *chazah* (gaze), may be taken in the sense of immoral gazing at women, וּכְתִיב: ,,שׁוּבִי שׁוּבִי הַשּׁוּלַמִּית שׁוּבִי שׁוּבִי וְנֶחֱזֶה־בָּךְ" – as **it is written:** ***Turn, turn, O perfect one. Turn, turn that we may gaze*** (*nechezeh*) ***at you.***[25]

The Gemara questions this exposition:

אֵימָא בִּנְבוּאָה – But **one could say** that the root חזה, *chazah* (gaze), signifies gazing **at a prophetic vision,** דִּכְתִיב: ,,חֲזוֹן יְשַׁעְיָהוּ בֶן־אָמוֹץ" – **as it is written:** ***The prophetic vision*** (*chazon*) ***of Isaiah son of Amotz.***[26] It is possible, therefore, that

NOTES

12. *I Kings* 1:3.

13. Ibid.

14. A Baraisa, cited in *Megillah* 11a, teaches that Achashveirosh ruled from one end of the world to the other.

15. In the time of King Solomon (*Maharsha*; see note 18).

16. *Job* 1:15.

17. During the era of the Babylonian king, Nebuchadnezzar (*Rashi*, *Maharsha*; see note 18).

18. *Job* 1:17. See notes 15 and 17. Actually, the kingdom of Sheba was not chronologically limited to Solomon's reign, nor was the existence of the Chaldeans confined to the time of Nebuchadnezzar. Indeed, the fact that both Sheba and the Chaldeans played a role in Job's sudden downfall proves that they were contemporaneous. The dispute between R' Nassan and the Sages can be explained as follows: According to R' Nassan, the vital clue is the verse's mention of Sheba in the feminine construct, which indicates that Job lived when the kingdom of Sheba was referred to by Scripture in the feminine form, as it was in the days of Solomon (see note 33). That period coincides with the era in which Israel was ruled by Solomon. The Sages, on the other hand, place emphasis on the verse's description of the Chaldeans' raid against Job's servants and camels — *The Chaldeans fielded three divisions etc.* In their view, Job lived in the time of Nebuchadnezzar, when the Chaldeans first became a significant nation (*Maharsha,* based on *Isaiah* 23:13).

19. *Job* 2:10. This is Job's response to his wife's suggestion that he curse God and die.

20. *Genesis* 34:7. The verse speaks of the abduction and rape of Dinah committed by Shechem.

21. *Exodus* 33:16.

22. Job was a prophet as indicated by the Baraisa cited above: "Seven prophets prophesied for the nations of the world... Job." Prophecy requires reception of the Divine Spirit.

23. *Maharsha*. This resolves the Gemara's challenge to R' Yochanan and R' Elazar's opinion that Job was a returnee from the Babylonian exile, which meant that he was a Jew. Since their view finds Tannaic support in this Baraisa, it is not refuted by the Baraisa quoted above which taught that Job was not a Jew (*Rashi*).

An apparent difficulty: Why is there a dispute on the issue of when Job lived? Surely this question is a matter of tradition and historical fact.

The answer is possibly that the Book of *Job* was not a famous work; only a few individuals had access to it. As a result, much of its background information was forgotten over the course of time (*Ritva* to 15a).

If not historical recollection, what then underlies the dispute?

Maharal (Chidushei Aggada) explains the dispute as follows: All the discussants listed in the Baraisa and the preceding passage of Gemara base their views on a common premise: Under normal circumstances, it is hard to imagine Satan being granted the power he is depicted as having been given in the *Job* story. Only during a period of unmitigated מִדַּת הַדִּין, *propensity to uncompromising justice,* is such power conceivable. Hence, if a book has such a Satan as a protagonist, its historical setting must be one in which Satan might assume such authority. The discussion in the Baraisa and Gemara centers around the question of which historical periods were prone to the unbridled sway of מִדַּת הַדִּין, *propensity to uncompromising justice.*

24. *Job* 27:12.

25. *Song of Songs* 7:1. Idolaters call out to the Jews: "Turn to our ways; come and live immorally with us" (*Rashi*).

26. *Isaiah* 1:1.

בלעם ואביו. כדאמר במגילה (דף טו.) כל ששמו ושם אביו בנביאות בידוע שהוא נביא בן נביא:

ט) אימא כמשעה שנכנסו ישראל למצרים. וא"ת ומאי קמ"ל קרא כתיב ויוסף ה' את כל אשר לאיוב למשנה ואיוב אחרי אותו מעשה חיה ק"מ שנה וא"כ היה בן שבעים קודם וי"ל דס"ד דלא כפל אלא בעושר ויופי של בנות אבל בשנים לא: אליהוא לא מישראל הוה. משמע דפשיטא דאליהוא בן ברכאל מישראל הוה לכך נראה דבפ"ק דע"ז (דף ג.) דאמר יבא בלדד השוחי וצופר הנעמתי ויעידו בהן בישראל שקיימו כל התורה כולה ל"ג התם ואליהוא בן ברכאל ונראה דשמעתתא דהתם סברה כמ"ד איוב בימי יעקב הוה דהכא אמר לקמן דממשה ואילך לא שרתה שכינה על עובדי כוכבים: דור ששופט את שופטיו. תימה לר"י דאמר י) (בפ"ק) דתמורה (דף טו.) כל האשכולות שעמדו לישראל מימות משה עד שמת יוסף בן יועזר לא היה בהם שום דופי:

בפירוש רבינו חננאל גרס כולהו תנאי ואמוראי מודו דאיוב ישראל היה ולר"י נראה דל"ג ואמוראי דרבא ע"כ סבר לעיל דלאו מישראל הוה דקאמר לעיל הכי אמר להן משה למרגלים ישנו לאותו אדם ששנותיו כעץ כו': ויש אומרים איוב בימי יעקב הוה. הני יש אומרים לאו היינו ר' נתן דהא פליגי עליה ס):

אימא כמשעה שנכנסו ישראל למצרים ועד [שעה] שיצאו מיתיבי שבעה נביאים נתנבאו לאומות העולם ואלו הן בלעם ואביו ואיוב אליפז התימני ובלדד השוחי וצופר הנעמתי ואליהוא בן ברכאל הבוזי (א"ל) וליטעמיך אליהוא בן ברכאל לאו מישראל הוה והא כתי' ממשפחת רם אלא אינבוי אינבי לאומות העולם ה"נ איוב אינבוי אינבי [לאומות העולם] אטו כולהו נביאי מי לא אינבויי לאומות העולם התם עיקר נביאותייהו לישראל הכא עיקר נביאותייהו לאומות העולם מיתיבי חסיד היה באומות העולם ואיוב שמו ולא בא לעולם אלא כדי לקבל שכרו הביא הקב"ה עליו יסורין התחיל מחרף ומגדף כפל לו הקב"ה שכרו בעוה"ז [כדי] לטרדו מן העולם הבא תנאי היא דתניא רבי אלעזר אומר איוב בימי שפוט השופטים היה שנאמר א) הן אתם כולכם חזיתם ולמה זה הבל תהבלו איזה דור שכולו הבל הוי אומר זה דורו של שפוט השופטים רבי יהושע בן קרחה אומר איוב בימי אחשורוש היה שנאמר ב) ולא נמצא נשים יפות כבנות איוב בכל הארץ איזהו דור שנתבקשו בו נשים יפות הוי אומר זה דורו של אחשורוש ואימא בימי דוד דכתיב ג) ויבקשו נערה יפה בכל גבול ישראל הכא בכל הארץ התם בכל גבול ישראל רבי נתן אומר איוב בימי מלכות שבא היה שנאמר ד) ותפל שבא ותקחם וחכ"א איוב בימי כשדים היה שנאמר ה) כשדים שמו שלשה ראשים ויש אומרים איוב בימי יעקב היה ודינה בת יעקב נשא כתיב הכא ו) כדבר אחת הנבלות תדברי וכתיב התם ז) כי נבלה עשה בישראל וכולהו (א) תנאי סבירא להו דאיוב מישראל הוה לבר מיש אומרים דאי ס"ד מאומות העולם הוה בתר דשכיב משה מי שריא שכינה על עובדי כוכבים והא אמר מר בקש משה שלא תשרה שכינה על עובדי כוכבים ונתן לו שנאמר ח) ונפלינו אני ועמך א"ר יוחנן דורו של איוב שטוף בזמה היה שנאמר א) הן אתם כולכם חזיתם ולמה זה הבל תהבלו וכתיב ט) שובי שובי השולמית שובי שובי ונחזה בך אימא בנבואה דכתיב י) חזון ישעיהו בן אמוץ א"כ למה זה הבל תהבלו לי ואר"י מאי דכתיב כ) ויהי בימי שפוט השופטים דור ששופט את שופטיו אומר לו טול קיסם מבין (עיניך) אומר לו טול קורה מבין עיניך אמר לו ל) כספך היה לסיגים אמר לו סבאך מהול במים א"ר שמואל בר נחמני א"ר יונתן כל האומר מלכת שבא אשה היתה אינו אלא טועה מאי מלכת שבא מלכותא דשבא מ) ויהי היום ויבאו בני האלהים להתיצב על ה' ויבא גם השטן בתוכם ויאמר ה' אל השטן מאין תבא ויען השטן וגו' אמר לפניו רבש"ע שטתי בכל העולם כולו ולא מצאתי נאמן כעבדך אברהם שאמרת לו נ) קום התהלך בארץ לארכה ולרחבה כי לך אתננה ואפילו הכי בשעה שלא מצא מקום לקבור את שרה [עד שקנה בד' מאות שקל כסף] לא הרהר אחר מדותיך ס) ויאמר ה' אל השטן השמת לבך אל עבדי איוב כי אין כמוהו בארץ וגו' א"ר יוחנן גדול הנאמר באיוב יותר ממה שנאמר באברהם דאילו באברהם כתיב ע) כי עתה ידעתי כי ירא אלהים אתה ובאיוב כתיב ס) איש תם וישר ירא אלהים [וסר מרע] מאי וסר מרע א"ר אבא בר שמואל איוב וותרן בממונו היה מנהגו של עולם נותן חצי פרוטה לחנוני איוב ויתרה משלו פ) ויען השטן את ה' ויאמר החנם ירא איוב אלהים צ) הלא אתה סכת בעדו ובעד ביתו וגו' מאי מעשה ידיו ברכת א"ר שמואל בר רב יצחק כל הנוטל פרוטה מאיוב מתברך מאי ומקנהו פרץ בארץ א"ר יוסי בר חנינא מקנהו של איוב פרצו גדרו של עולם מנהגו של עולם זאבים הורגים העזים מקנהו של איוב עזים הורגים את הזאבים ק) ואולם שלח נא ידך וגע בכל אשר לו אם לא על פניך יברכך ר) ויאמר ה' אל השטן הנה כל אשר לו בידך רק אליו אל תשלח ידך וגו' ש) ויהי היום ובניו ובנותיו אוכלים ושותים יין בבית אחיהם הבכור ומלאך בא אל איוב ויאמר הבקר היו חורשות וגו' מאי הבקר היו חורשות והאתונות רועות על ידיהם א"ר יוחנן מלמד שהטעימו הקב"ה לאיוב מעין

אימא כמשעה שנכנסו כו'. מאתים ועשר דכתיב (איוב מב) ויוסף ה' את כל אשר לאיוב למשנה אף שנותיו הוכפלו דכתיב ויחי איוב אחר זאת מאה וארבעים שנה למדנו שהיה בן שבעים כשבאו יסורין עליו הרי מאתים ועשר ולעולם מעולי גולה היה: נתנבאו לאומות העולם. אלמא נכרי היה: אליהוא. על כרחך מדייחסיה קרא בשמו [ושם אביו] ושם משפחתו ישראל הוה ולאית דאמרי ממשפחת רם היינו אברהם: שכולו הבל. השופטים שבהן לא היו כלום דאמרינן לקמן שהנשפט היה לו פתחון פה לשפוט את שופטו ומוכיחו: בימי מלכות שבא היה. ובא (ג) גדוד משבא עליו: וחכ"א בימי מלכות כשדים. בימי נבוכדנצר היה ובא גם משבא גדוד עליו: וכולהו הני תנאי כו'. מסקנא דמילתא הוא דהדר לעיל תנאי היא ההוא מתניתא דלעיל ס"ל עובד כוכבים הוה והני תנאי דהכך מתניתא כולהו סבירא להו דישראל הוה בר מיש אומרים דאמרי בימי יעקב הוה: והא אמר מר. בפ"ק דברכות (דף ז.): ונפלינו. (ג) ונבדלנו בלכתך עמנו מכל האומות: ונחזה בך. לשון זימה [הוא זה] להסתכל בנשים שעובדי כוכבים אומרים לישראל שובי לתורתנו ותזני עמנו: ששופט את שופטיו. שהיו השופטין עצמן מקולקלים והיה פתחון פה לנשפט להוכיח את מוכיחו שאם אמר לו השופט טול קיסם מבין עיניך הסתלק ופרוש מעבירה קטנה שבידך יכול זה לומר טול קורה מבין עיניך פרוש מעבירה חמורה שבידך: סבאך. יינך כמו אל תהי בסבאי יין (משלי כג): מהול. מעורב וכן כל לשון הוללות שבתורה לשון ערבוב: קום התהלך. היינו דקאמר ומתהלך בה מאותו שאמרת לו התהלך בארץ לא היה לה: ה"ג מנהג עולם נותן חצי פרוטה לחנוני. מי שיש לו מלאכה מועטת לעשות אומר לפועל חצי פרוטה אני נותן לך ולך אל חנוני וקנה בפרוטה ככר או בילים ונחלוק ואיוב ויתרה לחצי השני משלו ונותן לו כל הפרוטה שהיה רע בעיניו לדקדק בדבר קל שאינו ממון: והאתונות רועות [וגו']. ע"י הבקר דריש ליה לקרא שאוכלות חזיז מתלם המענה שהזרע צומח בשעתו: מעין

אימא שהיה כשיעור שהיו ישראל במצרים והכי הוא חושבנא ישראל היו במצרים ר"ו שנה ואיוב כשבאו עליו יסורין היה בן ע' שנה כדכתיב (איוב טו) גם שב גם ישיש בנו ואין שב פחות מע' שנה כדכתיב ימי שנותינו בהם שבעים שנה וכשהשיב הקב"ה שבותו נתן לו הכל למשנה ושנותיו הכפיל לו דכתיב ויחי איוב אחרי זאת ק"מ שנה והנהו ע' דמעיקרא הרי ר"י שנה: בלעם [ואביו] אינבויי אינבי לעובדי כוכבים על דור המבול ועל דור הפלגה. בלעם אינבי לעובדי כוכבים לעמלק [ולכתים] וקשיא לר' יוחנן ולר' אלעזר דאמרי מעולי גולה היה: כדי לטורדו מן העולם. אלמא דאיוב מעובדי כוכבים הוה: תנאי היא כו'. וכולהו הני תנאי מהא ברייתא דר' אלעזר ואילך מודו דאיוב מישראל הוה מדקא מיירי טעמייהו ממשה ואילך איכא למשמע מינה הואיל ושרתה עליו שכינה ממשה ואילך: לבד מיש אומרים דאמר בימי יעקב הוה שעדיין לא בא משה לעולם: דאי ס"ד דלשאר תנאי מאומות העולם היה וכי ממשה ואילך כו'. א) ואמוראי קרי לר' יוחנן ולר' אלעזר דאמרי תרוייהו איוב מעולי גולה היה ורבא נמי אמורא: מה תחזו בשולמית דכי היכי דהאי קרא משתעי בנקבה דהיינו זימה הכי נמי הן אתם כולכם חזיתם: ששופט. מי שהיה שפוט על פי בית דין הוא שופט את שופטיו שאם אמר לו השופט טול קיסם שלך גזילה מתחת ידיך היה משיב הוא לשופט טול קורה כלומר אני גזלתי קיסם שהוא מעט אתה גזלת קורה שהוא גדול מזה: אדם נותן חצי פרוטה לחנוני שאם היה חייב לפועל חצי פרוטה היה נותן לו איוב פרוטה שלימה ולא היה הולך לחנוני לחלוף לו חצי ליתן לו חצי לפועל [כמנהגם] היינו וסר מרע שלא היתה מדתו כמדת רעיו בני אדם: שהטעימו הקב"ה

חשק שלמה על רבינו גרשום

א) נראה מזה שרבינו היה גורס וכולהו תנאי ואמוראי וכגי' התוס' בשם ר"ח ע"ש:

ליקוטי רש"י

כולכם חזיתם. שזה חלק אדם רשע. ולמה זה הבל תהבלו. להיות רשעים וחניפים [איוב כז, יב]. ולא נמצא נשים יפות כבנות איוב וגו'. ולא נמצא מעשה של נשים יפות כמעשה יופי של בנות איוב ומקרא זה דוגמת ויהי אנשים אשר היו טמאים (במדבר ט) וכן הרבה. [שם מב, טו]. ותפול שבא. נתנפלה וחנתה מלכות שבא עליהם כמו (בראשית כה) על פני כל אחיו נפל [שם א, טו]. ונפלינו אני ועמך. ונהיה מובדלים בדבר הזה מכל העם כמו (שמות ט) והפלה ה' בין מקנה מצרים וגו' [שמות לג טז]. כספך היה לסיגים. שהיו עושין מעות נחשת ומצפין אותן בכסף להיות כסף. סבאך מהול במים. משקים שלכם מעורבים במים כדאיתא בפסיקתא מהול מעורב ואין לו דמיון במקרא ומ"א פותר לשחוק אמרתי מהולל (קהלת ב ב) מעורבב [ישעיה א, כב]. ויהי היום. אותו יום שהיה ראש השנה (שהוא יום תרועה ולוה הקב"ה לשטן להביא זכות וחובה של כל הבריות הה"ד משוט בארץ). ויבואו בני האלהים להתיצב על ה'. לריב עמו שאין להתיצב אלא על דין שנאמר (ישעיה ג) נצב לריב ה'. (ד"א ויהי היום. אותו היום שחזרו חלילה לאכול בבית אחיהם הבכור. בני האלהים. לבא השמים הקרובים לשכינה להיות בני ביתו ועל שם כך נקראו בניו. להתיצב על ה'. סביבותיו כמו (בראשי' מה) לכל הנצבים עליו) ויבא גם השטן בתוכם. לקטרג הבריות [איוב א, ו]. מאין תבא. דבר הכתוב דרך ארץ שהגדול מדבר תחילה ומרשה הקטן לענות. ויען השטן וגו'. משוט בארץ ומהתהלך בה כן דרכי לשוט ולראות רעים וטובים ושטתי בכל הארץ ולא מצאתי כאברהם שנא' בו קום התהלך בארץ (בראשית יג) ואמרו רז"ל שטן לשם שמים נתכוון כדי שלא יהא נשכח לפני אלהינו זכותו של אברהם [שם א, ז]. השמת לבך על עבדי איוב. שתרלה לקטרגו (ד"א. לשון תימה הוא). תם וישר. שלם במעשיו) [שם א, ח]. החנם ירא איוב. בתמיה. הלא אתה סכת בעדו. לפי שהוא יודע שאתה רגיל אצלו לעשות לו נסים ופרה ורבה לפיכך עושה לדקות הללו אבל לא ניסית אותו (ד"א. הגנת בעדו כמחילה זו כמו הסר משוכתו (ישעיה ה) מחילתו וכל בעד האמור בלשון עברי אינו אלא לשון כנגדו ובפניו כמו וכפר בעדו (ויקרא טז) קנח העון כנגדך בפניך להיות הכפרה מגן בעדך וכן ה' מגן בעדי (תהלים ג) [שם א, ט]. פרץ בארץ. (נתחזקו כמו וכן יפרוץ (שמות א) ומתרגמינן יתקוף זהו פשוטו ורבותינו ז"ל אמרו בהגדה שהטעימו הקב"ה מעין עולם הבא שלאמר חרישת האתונות היו זורעים עם החרישה ורועות האתונות מיד חזיז מן התלם) [שם א, י]. ואולם שלח נא ידך וגע. לו היית נוגע בכל אשר לו. אם לא על פניך יברכך. מיד בתמיה [שם א, יא]. על ידיהם. כמו (במדבר ב) איש על ידו ואינו לשון מקום אלא על שם שהוא מוכן ומזומן לידו [שם א, יד].

מסורת הש"ס

א) [בע"י ליתא], ב) נ"א שרתה, ג) ברכות ז., ד) [ערכין דף טז:], ה) [גירסת הע"י והילקוט שיניך], ו) [נ"ל משוט בארץ ומהתהלך בה], ז) [מגילה דף כח.], ח) [פסחים דף קיב.], ט) [שייך קודם לד"ה בלעם], י) נ"ל בפ"ב, כ) [ע' תוס' סוטה יב. ד"ה אחרי' ותוס' ע"ז סד: ד"ה אחרים ותוס' לקמן לג: ד"ה מאן]:

הגהות הב"ח

(א) גמ' וכולהו הני תנאי סבירא: (ב) רש"י ד"ה בימי וכו' ובא גם גדוד: (ג) ד"ה ונפלינו נ"ב אע"ג דבלכתך עמנו היא שאלה אחרת בקש שתשרה שכינה על ישראל מ"מ שאלת ונפלינו היא דבוקה עם בלכתך עמנו וכך אמר ועוד דבר אחר אני שואל ממך שנהיה נבדלים בלכתך עמנו מכל האומות:

תורה אור השלם

א) הֵן אַתֶּם כֻּלְּכֶם חֲזִיתֶם וְלָמָּה זֶּה הֶבֶל תֶּהְבָּלוּ: [איוב כז, יב]

ב) וְלֹא נִמְצָא נָשִׁים יָפוֹת כִּבְנוֹת אִיּוֹב בְּכָל הָאָרֶץ וַיִּתֵּן לָהֶם אֲבִיהֶם נַחֲלָה בְּתוֹךְ אֲחֵיהֶם: [איוב מב, טו]

ג) וַיְבַקְשׁוּ נַעֲרָה יָפָה בְּכֹל גְּבוּל יִשְׂרָאֵל וַיִּמְצְאוּ אֶת אֲבִישַׁג הַשּׁוּנַמִּית וַיָּבִאוּ אֹתָהּ לַמֶּלֶךְ: [מלכים א א, ג]

ד) וַתִּפֹּל שְׁבָא וַתִּקָּחֵם וְאֶת הַנְּעָרִים הִכּוּ לְפִי חָרֶב וָאִמָּלְטָה רַק אֲנִי לְבַדִּי לְהַגִּיד לָךְ: [איוב א, טו]

ה) עוֹד זֶה מְדַבֵּר וְזֶה בָּא וַיֹּאמַר כַּשְׂדִּים שָׂמוּ שְׁלֹשָׁה רָאשִׁים וַיִּפְשְׁטוּ עַל הַגְּמַלִּים וַיִּקָּחוּם וְאֶת הַנְּעָרִים הִכּוּ לְפִי חָרֶב וָאִמָּלְטָה רַק אֲנִי לְבַדִּי לְהַגִּיד לָךְ: [איוב א, יז]

ו) וַיֹּאמֶר אֵלֶיהָ כְּדַבֵּר אַחַת הַנְּבָלוֹת תְּדַבֵּרִי גַּם אֶת הַטּוֹב נְקַבֵּל מֵאֵת הָאֱלֹהִים וְאֶת הָרָע לֹא נְקַבֵּל בְּכָל זֹאת לֹא חָטָא אִיּוֹב בִּשְׂפָתָיו: [איוב ב, י]

ז) וּבְנֵי יַעֲקֹב בָּאוּ מִן הַשָּׂדֶה כְּשָׁמְעָם וַיִּתְעַצְּבוּ הָאֲנָשִׁים וַיִּחַר לָהֶם מְאֹד כִּי נְבָלָה עָשָׂה בְיִשְׂרָאֵל לִשְׁכַּב אֶת בַּת יַעֲקֹב וְכֵן לֹא יֵעָשֶׂה: [בראשית לד, ז]

ח) וּבַמֶּה יִוָּדַע אֵפוֹא כִּי מָצָאתִי חֵן בְּעֵינֶיךָ אֲנִי וְעַמֶּךָ הֲלוֹא בְּלֶכְתְּךָ עִמָּנוּ וְנִפְלֵינוּ אֲנִי וְעַמְּךָ מִכָּל הָעָם אֲשֶׁר עַל פְּנֵי הָאֲדָמָה: [שמות לג, טז]

ט) שׁוּבִי שׁוּבִי הַשּׁוּלַמִּית שׁוּבִי שׁוּבִי וְנֶחֱזֶה בָּךְ מַה תֶּחֱזוּ בַּשּׁוּלַמִּית כִּמְחֹלַת הַמַּחֲנָיִם: [שיר השירים ז, א]

י) חֲזוֹן יְשַׁעְיָהוּ בֶן אָמוֹץ אֲשֶׁר חָזָה עַל יְהוּדָה וִירוּשָׁלָ‍ִם בִּימֵי עֻזִּיָּהוּ יוֹתָם אָחָז יְחִזְקִיָּהוּ מַלְכֵי יְהוּדָה: [ישעיה א, א] כ) וַיְהִי בִּימֵי שְׁפֹט הַשֹּׁפְטִים וַיְהִי רָעָב בָּאָרֶץ וַיֵּלֶךְ אִישׁ מִבֵּית לֶחֶם יְהוּדָה לָגוּר בִּשְׂדֵי מוֹאָב הוּא וְאִשְׁתּוֹ וּשְׁנֵי בָנָיו: [רות א, א] ל) כַּסְפֵּךְ הָיָה לְסִיגִים סָבְאֵךְ מָהוּל בַּמָּיִם: [ישעיה א, כב] מ) וַיְהִי הַיּוֹם וַיָּבֹאוּ בְּנֵי הָאֱלֹהִים לְהִתְיַצֵּב עַל יְיָ וַיָּבוֹא גַם הַשָּׂטָן בְּתוֹכָם: וַיֹּאמֶר יְיָ אֶל הַשָּׂטָן מֵאַיִן תָּבֹא וַיַּעַן הַשָּׂטָן אֶת יְיָ וַיֹּאמַר מִשּׁוּט בָּאָרֶץ וּמֵהִתְהַלֵּךְ בָּהּ: [איוב א, ו-ז] נ) קוּם הִתְהַלֵּךְ בָּאָרֶץ לְאָרְכָּהּ וּלְרָחְבָּהּ כִּי לְךָ אֶתְּנֶנָּה: [בראשית יג, יז] ס) וַיֹּאמֶר יְיָ אֶל הַשָּׂטָן הֲשַׂמְתָּ לִבְּךָ עַל עַבְדִּי אִיּוֹב כִּי אֵין כָּמֹהוּ בָּאָרֶץ אִישׁ תָּם וְיָשָׁר יְרֵא אֱלֹהִים וְסָר מֵרָע: [איוב א, ח] ע) וַיֹּאמֶר אַל תִּשְׁלַח יָדְךָ אֶל הַנַּעַר וְאַל תַּעַשׂ לוֹ מְאוּמָה כִּי עַתָּה יָדַעְתִּי כִּי יְרֵא אֱלֹהִים אַתָּה וְלֹא חָשַׂכְתָּ אֶת בִּנְךָ אֶת יְחִידְךָ מִמֶּנִּי: [בראשית כב, יב] פ) וַיַּעַן הַשָּׂטָן אֶת יְיָ וַיֹּאמַר הַחִנָּם יָרֵא אִיּוֹב אֱלֹהִים: [איוב א, ט] צ) הֲלֹא אַתָּה שַׂכְתָּ בַעֲדוֹ וּבְעַד בֵּיתוֹ וּבְעַד כָּל אֲשֶׁר לוֹ מִסָּבִיב מַעֲשֵׂה יָדָיו בֵּרַכְתָּ וּמִקְנֵהוּ פָּרַץ בָּאָרֶץ: [איוב א, י] ק) וְאוּלָם שְׁלַח נָא יָדְךָ וְגַע בְּכָל אֲשֶׁר לוֹ אִם לֹא עַל פָּנֶיךָ יְבָרְכֶךָּ: [איוב א, יא] ר) וַיֹּאמֶר יְיָ אֶל הַשָּׂטָן הִנֵּה כָל אֲשֶׁר לוֹ בְּיָדֶךָ רַק אֵלָיו אַל תִּשְׁלַח יָדֶךָ וַיֵּצֵא הַשָּׂטָן מֵעִם פְּנֵי יְיָ: [איוב א, יב] ש) וַיְהִי הַיּוֹם וּבָנָיו וּבְנֹתָיו אֹכְלִים וְשֹׁתִים יַיִן בְּבֵית אֲחִיהֶם הַבְּכוֹר: וּמַלְאָךְ בָּא אֶל אִיּוֹב וַיֹּאמַר הַבָּקָר הָיוּ חֹרְשׁוֹת וְהָאֲתֹנוֹת רֹעוֹת עַל יְדֵיהֶם: [איוב א, יג-יד]

Job was rebuking his friends for gazing at visions of false prophecy.[27] — ? —

The Gemara replies:

אִם כֵּן — **If so,** that Job refers to visions of false prophecy, "לָמָּה־זֶּה הֶבֶל תֶּהְבָּלוּ" לָמָּה לִי — **why was it necessary** for him to say: ***Why do you act in this false manner?*** To rebuke his friends for gazing at visions of false prophecy it would have sufficed to say: *You act in a false manner!*[28]

Another exposition by R' Yochanan on a verse quoted by the Baraisa:

וְאָמַר רַבִּי יוֹחָנָן — **And R' Yochanan** also **said:** מַאי דִּכְתִיב: "וַיְהִי בִּימֵי שְׁפֹט הַשֹּׁפְטִים" — **What is** the meaning of **that which is written: *And it happened in the days when the Judges judged?***[29] What is the point of this double expression? דּוֹר שֶׁשּׁוֹפֵט אֶת שׁוֹפְטָיו — It teaches that this was **a generation that judged its judges;**[30] i.e. the judges themselves were corrupt. אוֹמֵר לוֹ טוֹל קֵיסָם מִבֵּין (עיניך) שִׁנֶּיךָ[31] — **If [a judge] would say to [a defendant], "Remove the splinter from between your teeth** (i.e. refrain from a minor infraction)," אוֹמֵר לוֹ טוֹל קוֹרָה מִבֵּין עֵינֶיךָ — **[the defendant] would retort to [the judge], "Remove the beam from before your eyes** [i.e. refrain from a major trangression]**!"** אָמַר לוֹ, "כַּסְפֵּךְ הָיָה לְסִיגִים" — **If [a judge] said to [a defendant], "Your silver is dross,"**[32] אָמַר לוֹ, "סָבְאֵךְ מָהוּל בַּמָּיִם" — **[the defendant] would reply to him, "Your wine is mixed with water!"**

In connection with the Baraisa's mention of the kingdom of Sheba, the Gemara discusses the term found in Scripture, מַלְכַּת־שְׁבָא, *Malkas Sheba:*

אָמַר רַבִּי שְׁמוּאֵל בַּר נַחְמָנִי אָמַר רַבִּי יוֹנָתָן — **R' Shmuel bar Nachmani said in the name of R' Yonasan:** כָּל הָאוֹמֵר מַלְכַּת שְׁבָא אִשָּׁה הָיְתָה אֵינוֹ אֶלָּא טוֹעֶה — **Anyone who says that *Malkas Sheba* was a woman,** i.e. the Queen of Sheba, **is in error.** מַאי מַלְכַּת שְׁבָא — **What is** meant by ***Malkas Sheba?*** מַלְכוּתָא דִשְׁבָא — **The monarch of Sheba,** i.e. its king.[33]

The Gemara now proceeds through a passage of the Book of *Job* (1:6-2:7), giving expositions of some of its verses. It begins with verses 1:6,7:

"וַיְהִי הַיּוֹם וַיָּבֹאוּ בְּנֵי הָאֱלֹהִים לְהִתְיַצֵּב עַל־ה׳ וַיָּבוֹא גַם־הַשָּׂטָן בְּתוֹכָם" — ***On a certain day,***[34] ***the angels came to stand before Hashem and the Satan***[35] ***too came with them.*** וַיֹּאמֶר ה׳ אֶל־הַשָּׂטָן מֵאַיִן תָּבֹא וַיַּעַן הַשָּׂטָן וגו׳" — ***Hashem said to the Satan, "From where do you come?" Satan answered etc.*** *[Hashem, saying, "From exploring the earth, and wandering about (his'haleich) on it"].*[36]

The Gemara takes the word הִתְהַלֵּךְ, *his'haleich (wandering about),* as an allusion to Abraham:

אָמַר לְפָנָיו — **[The Satan] said before [God],** רִבּוֹנוֹ שֶׁל עוֹלָם שַׁטְתִּי בְּכָל הָעוֹלָם כּוּלוֹ — **"Master of the Universe! I have explored the entire world,** וְלֹא מָצָאתִי נֶאֱמָן כְּעַבְדְּךָ אַבְרָהָם — **and I have not found anyone as loyal as your servant Abraham,** שֶׁאָמַרְתָּ לוֹ — **to whom You said:** "קוּם הִתְהַלֵּךְ בָּאָרֶץ לְאָרְכָּהּ וּלְרָחְבָּהּ כִּי לְךָ אֶתְּנֶנָּה" — ***Arise, wander about*** *(his'haleich)* ***the land*** of Canaan, ***through its length and breadth! For to you I will give it.***[37] God promised the land of Canaan to Abraham, וַאֲפִילּוּ הָכִי בְּשָׁעָה שֶׁלֹּא מָצָא מָקוֹם — **and yet when [Abraham] was unable to find a place** לִקְבּוֹר אֶת שָׂרָה — **to bury** his wife **Sarah** [עַד שֶׁקָּנָה בד׳ מֵאוֹת שֶׁקֶל כֶּסֶף] — **[until he bought** the cave of Machpelah **for four hundred shekels of silver],**[38] לֹא הִרְהֵר אַחַר מִדּוֹתֶיךָ — **he did not ponder Your ways!"**

The Gemara resumes its quotation from the Book of *Job* (1:8):

"וַיֹּאמֶר ה׳ אֶל־הַשָּׂטָן הֲשַׂמְתָּ לִבְּךָ עַל־עַבְדִּי אִיּוֹב כִּי אֵין כָּמֹהוּ בָּאָרֶץ וגו׳" — ***Hashem said to the Satan, "Have you paid attention to My servant Job? For there is none like him on earth etc.*** *[a perfect and upright man, who fears God and eschews evil].*

The Gemara expounds:

אָמַר רַבִּי יוֹחָנָן — **R' Yochanan said:** גָּדוֹל הַנֶּאֱמָר בְּאִיּוֹב יוֹתֵר מִמַּה שֶּׁנֶּאֱמַר בְּאַבְרָהָם — **Greater are [the praises] stated regarding Job than those stated about Abraham.** דְּאִילּוּ בְּאַבְרָהָם כְּתִיב — **For regarding Abraham it is written:** "כִּי עַתָּה יָדַעְתִּי כִּי־יְרֵא אֱלֹהִים אַתָּה" — ***For now I*** [God] ***know that you are one who fears God;***[39] וּבְאִיּוֹב כְּתִיב — **whereas regarding Job it is written:** "אִישׁ תָּם וְיָשָׁר יְרֵא אֱלֹהִים [וְסָר מֵרָע]" — ***A perfect and upright man, who fears God and eschews evil.***

The Gemara explains the concluding phrase:

מַאי "וְסָר מֵרָע" — **What is** meant by ***and eschews evil?***[40] אָמַר רַבִּי אַבָּא בַּר שְׁמוּאֵל — **R' Abba bar Shmuel explained:** אִיּוֹב וַותְּרָן בְּמָמוֹנוֹ הָיָה — **Job was liberal with his money.** מִנְהָגוֹ שֶׁל עוֹלָם — **The universal practice** is that a person that owes his worker half a *perutah* נוֹתֵן חֲצִי פְּרוּטָה לְחֶנְוָנִי — **pays** him the **half-*perutah* by** buying a *perutah's* worth of merchandise from **a shopkeeper** and giving the worker half.[41] אִיּוֹב וִיתְּרָהּ מִשֶּׁלּוֹ —

NOTES

27. The inference from *Isaiah* 1:1 proves only that the verb חזה signifies gazing at a prophecy of some sort. In the case of Isaiah, it refers to Divine prophecy. But in the context of Job's rebuke to his friend, it refers to false prophecy (*Maharsha*).

28. The words לָמָּה־זֶּה, *why. . .this,* are superfluous. But if Job refers to gazing of a licentious nature, the words לָמָּה־זֶּה, *why. . .this,* are not superfluous, for the verse is then understood as follows: הֵן אַתֶּם כֻּלְּכֶם חֲזִיתֶם, *Behold, you have all gazed* [licentiously], וְלָמָּה־זֶּה הֶבֶל תֶּהְבָּלוּ, *so why do you act in this false manner* [i.e. why do you rebuke me]? The rebuke you give me is false, for by gazing licentiously you have rendered yourselves unfit to give rebuke (see note 9) (*Maharsha*).

29. *Ruth* 1:1.

30. See note 9.

31. The text as recorded by *Ein Yaakov* and *Yalkut* (*Mesoras HaShas*).

32. This expression and the one that follows are borrowed from *Isaiah* 1:22.

33. This would appear to be the plain meaning of the Gemara. *Maharsha*, however, points out that Scripture consistently treats מַלְכַּת־שְׁבָא, *Malkas Sheba,* as a feminine noun (see *I Kings* 10:1-13). On this basis, he suggests a different explanation of the Gemara: כָּל הָאוֹמֵר מַלְכַּת שְׁבָא אִשָּׁה הָיְתָה אֵינוֹ אֶלָּא טוֹעֶה, *Whoever says* [that] *the Queen of Sheba was a woman* [of common rank, who attained her title through marriage to the King of Sheba,] *is in error.* מַאי מַלְכַּת שְׁבָא, *What is* [meant by the title] *"Queen of Sheba"?* מַלְכוּתָא דִשְׁבָא, *The monarch of Sheba* [who ruled in her own right].

34. The Day of Judgment — Rosh Hashanah (*Rashi* ad loc.).

35. שָׂטָן, *Satan* (lit. adversary), is the angel whose duty it is to be the accuser in the Heavenly Court. [As the Gemara explains below, 16a, it is the same entity that entices people to sin (יֵצֶר הָרָע, *Evil Inclination*), accuses them in the Divine court (שָׂטָן, *Satan*) and is granted permission to kill them (מַלְאַךְ הַמָּוֶת, *the Angel of Death*).]

36. *Job* 1:6,7.

37. *Genesis* 13:17.

38. Ibid. ch. 23.

39. Ibid. 22:12.

40. Considering that Job was "perfect and upright," it is obvious that he "eschewed evil!"

41. A *perutah* is a coin of the smallest denomination ($^{1}/_{192}$ *zuz*). Hence, this was the only way to divide it.

אימא כמשעה שנכנסו ישראל למצרים ועד [שעה] שיצאו מיתיבי שבעה נביאים נתנבאו לאומות העולם ואלו הן בלעם ואביו ואיוב אליפז התימני ובלדד השוחי וצופר הנעמתי ואליהוא בן ברכאל הבוזי (א"ל) וליטעמיך אליהוא בן ברכאל לאו מישראל הוה והא כתי' ממשפחת רם אלא אינבוי אינבי לאומות העולם ה"נ איוב אינבוי אינבי [לאומות העולם] אטו כולהו נביאי מי לא אינבוי לאומות העולם התם עיקר נביאותייהו לישראל הכא עיקר נביאותיהו לאומות העולם מיתיבי חסיד היה באומות העולם ואיוב שמו ולא בא לעולם אלא כדי לקבל שכרו הביא הקב"ה עליו יסורין התחיל מחרף ומגדף כפל לו הקב"ה שכרו בעוה"ז [כדי] לטרדו מן העולם הבא תנאי היא דתניא רבי אלעזר אומר איוב בימי שפוט השופטים היה שנאמר א) הן אתם כולכם חזיתם ולמה זה הבל תהבלו איזה דור שכולו הבל הוי אומר זה דורו של שפוט השופטים רבי יהושע בן קרחה אומר איוב בימי אחשורוש היה שנאמר ב) ולא נמצא נשים יפות כבנות איוב בכל הארץ איזהו דור שנתבקשו בו נשים יפות הוי אומר זה דורו של אחשורוש ואימא בימי דוד דכתיב ג) ויבקשו נערה יפה התם בכל גבול ישראל הכא בכל הארץ רבי נתן אומר איוב בימי מלכות שבא היה שנאמר ד) ותפל שבא ותקחם וחכ"א איוב בימי כשדים היה שנאמר ה) כשדים שמו שלשה ראשים ויש אומרים איוב בימי יעקב היה ודינה בת יעקב נשא כתיב הכא ו) כדבר אחת הנבלות תדברי וכתיב התם ז) כי נבלה עשה בישראל וכולהו (א) תנאי סבירא להו דאיוב מישראל הוה לבר מיש אומרים דאי ס"ד מאומות העולם הוה בתר דשכיב משה מי ח) שריא שכינה על עובדי כוכבים והא ט) אמר מר בקש משה שלא תשרה שכינה על עובדי כוכבים ונתן לו שנאמר י) ונפלינו אני ועמך א"ר יוחנן דורו של איוב שטוף בזמה היה שנאמר א) הן אתם כולכם חזיתם ולמה זה הבל תהבלו וכתיב ב) שובי שובי השולמית שובי שובי ונחזה בך אימא בנבואה דכתיב ג) חזון ישעיהו בן אמוץ א"כ למה זה הבל תהבלו למה לי וא"ר יוחנן מאי דכתיב ד) ויהי בימי שפוט השופטים דור ששופט את שופטיו אומר לו ה) טול קיסם מבין (עיניך) אומר לו ו) טול קורה מבין עיניך אמר לו ז) כספך היה לסיגים אמר לו ח) סבאך מהול במים א"ר שמואל בר נחמני א"ר יונתן כל האומר מלכת שבא אשה היתה אינו אלא טועה מאי מלכת שבא מלכותא דשבא ט) ויהי היום ויבאו בני האלהים להתיצב על ה' ויבא גם השטן בתוכם ויאמר ה' אל השטן מאין תבא ויען השטן וגו' י) אמר לפניו רבש"ע שטתי בכל העולם כולו ולא מצאתי נאמן כעבדך אברהם שאמרת לו ג) קום התהלך בארץ לארכה ולרחבה כי לך אתננה ואפילו הכי בשעה שלא מצא מקום לקבור את שרה [עד שקנה בד' מאות שקל כסף] לא הרהר אחר מדותיך ויאמר ה' אל השטן השמת לבך אל עבדי איוב כי אין כמוהו בארץ וגו' א"ר יוחנן גדול הנאמר באיוב יותר ממה שנאמר באברהם דאילו באברהם כתיב מ) כי עתה ידעתי כי ירא אלהים אתה ובאיוב כתיב ס) איש תם וישר ירא אלהים [וסר מרע] מאי וסר מרע א"ר אבא בר שמואל ע) איוב וותרן בממונו היה מנהגו של עולם נותן חצי פרוטה לחנוני איוב ויתרה משלו פ) ויען השטן את ה' ויאמר החנם ירא איוב אלהים צ) הלא אתה סכת בעדו ובעד ביתו וגו' ק) מעשה ידיו ברכת א"ר שמואל בר רב יצחק כל הנוטל פרוטה מאיוב מתברך מאי צ) ומקנהו פרץ בארץ א"ר יוסי בר חנינא מקנהו של איוב פרצו גדרו של עולם מנהגו של עולם זאבים הורגים העזים מקנהו של איוב עזים הורגים את הזאבים ק) ואולם שלח נא ידך וגע בכל אשר לו אם לא על פניך יברכך ר) ויאמר ה' אל השטן הנה כל אשר לו בידך רק אליו אל תשלח ידך וגו' ש) ויהי היום ובניו ובנותיו אוכלים ושותים יין בבית אחיהם הבכור ומלאך בא אל איוב ויאמר הבקר היו חורשות והאתנות רועות על ידיהם א"ר יוחנן מלמד שהטעימו הקב"ה לאיוב מעין

רשב"ם

אימא כמשעה שנכנסו כו'. מאתים ועשר דכתיב (איוב מב) ויוסף ה' את כל אשר לאיוב למשנה אף שנותיו הוכפלו דכתיב ויחי איוב אחר זאת מאה וארבעים שנה למדנו שהיה בן שבעים כשבאו יסורין עליו הרי מאתים ועשר ולעולם מעולי גולה היה: נתנבאו לאומות העולם. אלמא נכרי היה: אליהוא. על כרחך מדייחסיה קרא בשמו [ושם אביו] ושם משפחתו ישראל הוה ואית דאמרי ממשפחת רם היה היינו אברהם: שכולו הבל. הטובים שבהן לא היו כלום כדאמרינן לקמן שהנשפט היה לו פתחון פה לשפוט את שופטו ומוכיחו: בימי מלכות שבא היה. ובא (ב) גדוד מכשדים עליו: וחכ"א בימי מלכות כשדים. בימי נבוכדנצר היה ובא גם משבא גדוד עליו: וכולהו הני תנאי כו'. מסקנא דתירוצא הוא דתריך לעיל תנאי היא ההוא מתניתא דלעיל ס"ל עובד כוכבים הוה והני תנאי דהך מתניתא כולהו סבירא להו דישראל הוה בר מיש אומרים דאמרי בימי יעקב הוה: והא אמר מר. בפ"ק דברכות (דף ז.): ונפלינו. (ג) ונבדלנו בלכתך עמנו מכל האומות: ונחזה בך. לשון זימה [הוא זה] להסתכל בנשים שעובדי כוכבים אומרים לישראל שובי לתורתנו ותזני עמנו: ששופט את שופטיו. שהיו השופטין עצמן מקולקלים והיה פתחון פה לנשפט להוכיח את מוכיחו שאם אמר לו השופט טול קיסם מבין עיניך הסתלק ופרוש מעבירה קטנה שבידך יכול זה לומר טול קורה מבין עיניך פרוש מעבירה חמורה שבידך: סבאך. יינך כמו אל תהי בסבאי יין (משלי כג): מהול. מעורב וכן כל לשון הוללות שבתורה לשון ערבוב: קום התהלך. היינו דקאמר ומהתהלך בה מאותו שאמרת לו התהלך בארץ אני בא: ה"ג מנהג עולם נותן חצי פרוטה לחנוני. מי שיש לו מלאכה מועטת לעשות אומר לפועל חצי פרוטה אני נותן לך ונלך אצל חנוני ונקנה בפרוטה ככר או ביצים ונחלוק ואיוב ויתרה לחצי השני משלו ונותן לו כל הפרוטה שהיה רע בעיניו לדקדק בדבר קל שאינו ממון: והאתונות רועות [וגו']. ע"י הבקר דריש ליה לקרא שאוכלת חזיז מתלם המענה שהזרע צומח בשעתו: מעין

תוספות

בלעם ואביו. דאמר במגילה (דף טו.) כל ששמו ושם אביו בנביאים בידוע שהוא נביא בן נביא:

אימא כמשעה שנכנסו ישראל למצרים. וא"ת ומאי קמ"ל קרא כתיב ויוסף ה' את כל אשר לאיוב למשנה ואיוב אחרי אותו מעשה חיה ק"מ שנה וא"כ היה בן שבעים קודם וי"ל דס"ד דלא כפל אלא בעושר ויופי של בנות אבל בשנים לא: **אליהוא** לא מישראל הוה. משמע דפשיטא דאליהוא בן ברכאל מישראל הוה לכך נראה דבפ"ק דע"ז (דף ג.) דאמר יבא בלדד השוחי וצופר הנעמתי ויעידו בהן בישראל שקיימו כל התורה כולה ל"ג התם ואליהוא בן ברכאל ונראה דשמעתא דהכא סברה כמ"ד איוב בימי יעקב הוה דהא אמר לקמן דממשה ואילך לא שרתה שכינה על עובדי כוכבים: **דור** ששופט את שופטיו. תימה לר"י דאמר י) (בפ"ק) דתמורה (דף טו:) כל האשכולות שעמדו לישראל מימות משה עד שמת יוסף בן יועזר לא היה בהם שום דופי:

בפירוש רבינו חננאל גרס כולהו תנאי ואמוראי מודו דאיוב ישראל היה ולר"י נראה דל"ג ואמוראי דרבא ע"כ סבר לעיל דלאו מישראל הוה דקאמר לעיל הכי אמר להן משה למרגלים ישנו לאותו אדם ששנותיו כעץ כו': **ויש** אומרים איוב בימי יעקב היה. הני יש אומרים לאו היינו ר' נתן דהא פליגי עליה כדמוכח:

רבינו גרשום

אימא שהיה כשיעור שהיו ישראל במצרים והכי הוא חושבנא ישראל היו במצרים ר"י שנה ואיוב כשבאו עליו יסורין היה בן ע' שנה כדכתיב (איוב טו) גם שב גם ישיש בנו ואין שב פחות מע' שנה כדכתיב ימי שנותינו בהם שבעים שנה וכשהשיב הקב"ה שבותו נתן לו הכל למשנה ושנותיו הכפיל לו דכתיב ויחי איוב אחרי זאת ק"מ שנה והנהו ע' דמעיקרא הרי ר"י שנה: **בלעם [ואביו] אינבויי אינבי** לעובדי כוכבים על דור המבול ועל דור הפלגה. בלעם אינבי לעובדי כוכבים לעמלק [ולכתיים] וקשיא לר' יוחנן ולר' אלעזר דאמרי מעולי גולה היה: **כדי לטורדו מן העולם.** אלמא דאיוב מעובדי כוכבים הוה: **תנאי היא כו'** וכולהו הני תנאי מהא ברייתא דר' אלעזר ואילך מודו דאיוב מישראל הוה מדקא מיירי טעמייהו ממשה ואילך איכא למשמע מינה הואיל ושרתה עליו שכינה ממשה ואילך: לבד **מיש אומרים** דאמר **בימי יעקב הוה** שעדיין לא בא משה לעולם: **דאי ס"ד** דלשאר תנאי **מאומות העולם היה וכי ממשה ואילך כו'.** א) ואמוראי קרי לר' יוחנן ולר' אלעזר דאמרי תרוייהו איוב מעולי גולה היה ורבא נמי אמורא: **מה תחזו בשולמית** דכי היכי דהאי קרא משתעי בנקבה דהיינו זימה הכי נמי **הן אתם כולכם חזיתם: ששופט.** מי שהיה שפוט על פי בית דין הוא שופט **את שופטיו** שאם אמר לו השופט **טול קיסם** שלך גזילה מתחת ידיך היה משיב הוא לשופט **טול קורה** כלומר אני גזלתי קיסם שהוא מעט אתה גזלת קורה שהוא גדול מזה: **אדם נותן חצי פרוטה לחנוני** שאם היה חייב לפועל חצי פרוטה היה נותן לו **איוב פרוטה שלימה** ולא היה הולך לחנווני לחלוף לו חצי ליתן לו חצי לפועל [כמנהגם] היינו **וסר מרע** שלא היתה מדתו כמדת רעיו בני אדם: **שהטעימו הקב"ה**

מסורת הש"ס

א) [בע"י ליתא], ב) ג"א שרתה, ג) ברכות ז., ד) [ערכין דף טו:], ה) [גירסת הע"י וילקוט שיניך], ו) [נ"א משום בארץ ומהתהלך בה], ז) [מגילה דף יא.], ח) [פסחים דף קיז.], ט) [שייך קודם לד"ה בלעם], י) נ"ל בפ"ג, כ) [ע' תוס' סוטה יב. ד"ה אחר ותוס' ע"ז כד: ד"ה אחרים ותוס' לקמן נג: ד"ה מאן].

הגהות הב"ח

(א) גמ' וכולהו הני תנאי סבירא: (ב) רשב"ם ד"ה בימי וכו' ובא גם גדוד: (ג) ד"ה ונפלינו נ"ב אע"ג דבלכתך עמנו לא שאלה אלא אחרת בקש שתשרה שכינה על ישראל מ"מ שאלת ונפלינו דהיינו דבוקה עם בלכתך עמנו וכן אמר ועוד דבר אחר אני שואל ממך שגם יהיו נבדלים בלכתך עמנו מכל האומות:

תורה אור השלם

א) הֵן אַתֶּם כֻּלְּכֶם חֲזִיתֶם וְלָמָּה זֶּה הֶבֶל תֶּהְבָּלוּ: [איוב כז, יב]

ב) וְלֹא נִמְצָא נָשִׁים יָפוֹת כִּבְנוֹת אִיּוֹב בְּכָל הָאָרֶץ וַיִּתֵּן לָהֶם אֲבִיהֶם נַחֲלָה בְּתוֹךְ אֲחֵיהֶם: [איוב מב, טו]

ג) וַיְבַקְשׁוּ נַעֲרָה יָפָה בְּכֹל גְּבוּל יִשְׂרָאֵל וַיִּמְצְאוּ אֶת אֲבִישַׁג הַשּׁוּנַמִּית וַיָּבִאוּ אֹתָהּ לַמֶּלֶךְ: [מלכים א א, ג]

ד) וַתִּפֹּל שְׁבָא וַתִּקָּחֵם וְאֶת הַנְּעָרִים הִכּוּ לְפִי חָרֶב וָאִמָּלְטָה רַק אֲנִי לְבַדִּי לְהַגִּיד לָךְ: [איוב א, טו]

ה) עוֹד זֶה מְדַבֵּר וְזֶה בָּא וַיֹּאמַר כַּשְׂדִּים שָׂמוּ שְׁלֹשָׁה רָאשִׁים וַיִּפְשְׁטוּ עַל הַגְּמַלִּים וַיִּקָּחוּם וְאֶת הַנְּעָרִים הִכּוּ לְפִי חָרֶב וָאִמָּלְטָה רַק אֲנִי לְבַדִּי לְהַגִּיד לָךְ: [איוב א, יז]

ו) וַיֹּאמֶר אֵלֶיהָ כְּדַבֵּר אַחַת הַנְּבָלוֹת תְּדַבֵּרִי גַּם אֶת הַטּוֹב נְקַבֵּל מֵאֵת הָאֱלֹהִים וְאֶת הָרָע לֹא נְקַבֵּל בְּכָל זֹאת לֹא חָטָא אִיּוֹב בִּשְׂפָתָיו: [איוב ב, י]

ז) וּבְנֵי יַעֲקֹב בָּאוּ מִן הַשָּׂדֶה כְּשָׁמְעָם וַיִּתְעַצְּבוּ הָאֲנָשִׁים וַיִּחַר לָהֶם מְאֹד כִּי נְבָלָה עָשָׂה בְיִשְׂרָאֵל לִשְׁכַּב אֶת בַּת יַעֲקֹב וְכֵן לֹא יֵעָשֶׂה: [בראשית לד, ז]

ח) וּבַמֶּה יִוָּדַע אֵפוֹא כִּי מָצָאתִי חֵן בְּעֵינֶיךָ אֲנִי וְעַמֶּךָ הֲלוֹא בְּלֶכְתְּךָ עִמָּנוּ וְנִפְלֵינוּ אֲנִי וְעַמְּךָ מִכָּל הָעָם אֲשֶׁר עַל פְּנֵי הָאֲדָמָה: [שמות לג, טז]

ט) שׁוּבִי שׁוּבִי הַשּׁוּלַמִּית שׁוּבִי שׁוּבִי וְנֶחֱזֶה בָּךְ מַה תֶּחֱזוּ בַּשּׁוּלַמִּית כִּמְחֹלַת הַמַּחֲנָיִם:

י) חֲזוֹן יְשַׁעְיָהוּ בֶן אָמוֹץ אֲשֶׁר חָזָה עַל יְהוּדָה וִירוּשָׁלָםִ בִּימֵי עֻזִּיָּהוּ יוֹתָם אָחָז יְחִזְקִיָּהוּ מַלְכֵי יְהוּדָה: [ישעיה א, א]

כ) וַיְהִי בִּימֵי שְׁפֹט הַשֹּׁפְטִים וַיְהִי רָעָב בָּאָרֶץ וַיֵּלֶךְ אִישׁ מִבֵּית לֶחֶם יְהוּדָה לָגוּר בִּשְׂדֵי מוֹאָב הוּא וְאִשְׁתּוֹ וּשְׁנֵי בָנָיו: [רות א, א]

ל) כַּסְפֵּךְ הָיָה לְסִיגִים סָבְאֵךְ מָהוּל בַּמָּיִם: [ישעיה א, כב]

מ) וַיְהִי הַיּוֹם וַיָּבֹאוּ בְּנֵי הָאֱלֹהִים לְהִתְיַצֵּב עַל יְיָ וַיָּבוֹא גַם הַשָּׂטָן בְּתוֹכָם: [איוב א, ו]

נ) וַיֹּאמֶר יְיָ אֶל הַשָּׂטָן מֵאַיִן תָּבֹא וַיַּעַן הַשָּׂטָן אֶת יְיָ וַיֹּאמַר מִשּׁוּט בָּאָרֶץ וּמֵהִתְהַלֵּךְ בָּהּ: [איוב א, ז]

ס) קוּם הִתְהַלֵּךְ בָּאָרֶץ לְאָרְכָּהּ וּלְרָחְבָּהּ כִּי לְךָ אֶתְּנֶנָּה: [בראשית יג, יז]

ע) וַיֹּאמֶר יְיָ אֶל הַשָּׂטָן הֲשַׂמְתָּ לִבְּךָ עַל עַבְדִּי אִיּוֹב כִּי אֵין כָּמֹהוּ בָּאָרֶץ אִישׁ תָּם וְיָשָׁר יְרֵא אֱלֹהִים וְסָר מֵרָע: [איוב א, ח]

פ) וַיֹּאמֶר אַל תִּשְׁלַח יָדְךָ אֶל הַנַּעַר וְאַל תַּעַשׂ לוֹ מְאוּמָה כִּי עַתָּה יָדַעְתִּי כִּי יְרֵא אֱלֹהִים אַתָּה וְלֹא חָשַׂכְתָּ אֶת בִּנְךָ אֶת יְחִידְךָ מִמֶּנִּי: [בראשית כב, יב]

צ) וַיַּעַן הַשָּׂטָן אֶת יְיָ וַיֹּאמַר הַחִנָּם יָרֵא אִיּוֹב אֱלֹהִים: [איוב א, ט]

ק) הֲלֹא אַתָּה שַׂכְתָּ בַעֲדוֹ וּבְעַד בֵּיתוֹ וּבְעַד כָּל אֲשֶׁר לוֹ מִסָּבִיב מַעֲשֵׂה יָדָיו בֵּרַכְתָּ וּמִקְנֵהוּ פָּרַץ בָּאָרֶץ: [איוב א, י]

ר) וְאוּלָם שְׁלַח נָא יָדְךָ וְגַע בְּכָל אֲשֶׁר לוֹ אִם לֹא עַל פָּנֶיךָ יְבָרְכֶךָּ: [איוב א, יא]

ש) וַיֹּאמֶר יְיָ אֶל הַשָּׂטָן הִנֵּה כָל אֲשֶׁר לוֹ בְּיָדֶךָ רַק אֵלָיו אַל תִּשְׁלַח יָדֶךָ וַיֵּצֵא הַשָּׂטָן מֵעִם פְּנֵי יְיָ:

ת) וַיְהִי הַיּוֹם וּבָנָיו וּבְנֹתָיו אֹכְלִים וְשֹׁתִים יַיִן בְּבֵית אֲחִיהֶם הַבְּכוֹר: וּמַלְאָךְ בָּא אֶל אִיּוֹב וַיֹּאמַר הַבָּקָר הָיוּ חֹרְשׁוֹת וְהָאֲתֹנוֹת רֹעוֹת עַל יְדֵיהֶם: [איוב א, יג-יד]

Job, however, **gave up his own** portion, i.e. he gave the entire *perutah* to the worker.[42]

The narrative is resumed with Satan's response to God's praise of Job (*Job* 1:9,10):

,,וַיַּעַן הַשָּׂטָן אֶת־ה׳ וַיֹּאמַר הַחִנָּם יָרֵא אִיּוֹב אֱלֹהִים – ***The Satan answered Hashem saying, "Is it for nothing that Job fears God?*** הֲלֹא־אַתְּ שַׂכְתָּ בַעֲדוֹ וּבְעַד־בֵּיתוֹ וגו׳ " – ***Have You not protected him, his household,* etc.** *[and all that he has? You have blessed whatever he has undertaken, and his possessions are spread throughout the land.]?* Job's righteousness is not surprising in view of the special blessings that you have bestowed upon him.

The Gemara elaborates on Job's blessings:

מַאי: ,,מַעֲשֵׂה יָדָיו בֵּרַכְתָּ" – **What is** meant by: ***You have blessed whatever he has undertaken?*** אָמַר רַב שְׁמוּאֵל בַּר רַב יִצְחָק – **Rav Shmuel bar Rav Yitzchak said:** כָּל הַנּוֹטֵל פְּרוּטָה מֵאִיּוֹב מִתְבָּרֵךְ – **Whoever took** even **a *perutah* from Job was blessed**; i.e. all who had dealings with Job prospered. מַאי: ,,וּמִקְנֵהוּ פָּרַץ בָּאָרֶץ" – **What is** meant by: ***And his possessions are spread (paratz) throughout the land?*** אָמַר רַבִּי יוֹסֵי בַּר חֲנִינָא – **R' Yose bar Chanina said:** מִקְנֵהוּ שֶׁל אִיּוֹב פָּרְצוּ גִּדְרוֹ שֶׁל עוֹלָם – **The flocks of Job breached** (*partzu*) **the natural order.** מִנְהָגוֹ שֶׁל עוֹלָם זְאֵבִים הוֹרְגִים הָעִזִּים – **According to the natural order, wolves kill sheep,** מִקְנֵהוּ שֶׁל אִיּוֹב עִזִּים הוֹרְגִים אֶת הַזְּאֵבִים – but in **the flocks of Job, the sheep killed the wolves.**

The narrative is resumed (*Job* 1:11-14):

,,וְאוּלָם שְׁלַח־נָא יָדְךָ וְגַע בְּכָל־אֲשֶׁר־לוֹ אִם־לֹא עַל־פָּנֶיךָ יְבָרְכֶךָּ" – [Satan continues:] ***But stretch out Your hand and afflict all that he has,*** and see ***if he does not bless*** (i.e. blaspheme)[43] ***You to Your face.*** וַיֹּאמֶר ה׳ אֶל־הַשָּׂטָן הִנֵּה כָל־אֲשֶׁר־לוֹ בְּיָדֶךָ רַק אֵלָיו אַל־תִּשְׁלַח יָדֶךָ וגו׳ – ***Hashem said to the Satan, "Behold, all that he has is in your hands, only do not lay a hand on him* etc.** You may attack his family and property, but not his person. וַיְהִי הַיּוֹם וּבָנָיו וּבְנֹתָיו אֹכְלִים וְשֹׁתִים יַיִן בְּבֵית אֲחִיהֶם הַבְּכוֹר – ***On a certain day, [Job's] sons and daughters were eating and drinking wine at the house of their brother, the firstborn.*** וּמַלְאָךְ בָּא אֶל־אִיּוֹב וַיֹּאמַר הַבָּקָר הָיוּ חֹרְשׁוֹת וגו׳ " – ***A messenger came to Job and said, "The oxen were plowing* etc.** *[and the she-asses were grazing nearby]."*

The Gemara interjects:

מַאי: ,,הַבָּקָר הָיוּ חֹרְשׁוֹת וְהָאֲתֹנוֹת רֹעוֹת עַל־יְדֵיהֶם" – **What is** meant by ***the oxen were plowing and the she-asses were grazing nearby?*** This implies that the seeds sprouted soon after they were planted and the she-asses grazed from the newly sprouted growths![44] אָמַר רַבִּי יוֹחָנָן – **R' Yochanan said:** מְלַמֵּד שֶׁהִטְעִימוֹ הַקָּדוֹשׁ בָּרוּךְ הוּא לְאִיּוֹב – This **teaches us that the Holy One, Blessed is He, gave Job a taste of**

NOTES

42. Job considered it wrong to be exacting over such a small amount, which does not even have legally recognized monetary value (*Rashi*).

This interpretation relates the word רַע *(bad)* to רֵעַ, *fellow man.* Hence, וְסָר מֵרָע means that Job departed from the general practice of his fellow men (*Rabbeinu Gershom*).

43. The verb ברך, *bless,* is often used as a euphemism for blasphemy.

44. This interpretation understands עַל־יְדֵיהֶם in the sense of "by their actions." The she-asses were enabled to graze *by the oxen's plowing*. As soon as the oxen drew the plow, the she-asses ate from the new growths in the furrow (*Rashi*). [The act of plowing referred to here is the one performed soon after planting or simultaneously with the planting.]

מֵעֵין הָעוֹלָם הַבָּא – **a semblance of the World to Come** (i.e. the Messianic era), when conception and birth will occur on the same day.[1]

The quotation from the Book of *Job* is resumed (1:16-2:2):

"עוֹד זֶה מְדַבֵּר וְזֶה בָּא וַיֹּאמַר אֵשׁ אֱלֹהִים וגו׳" – ***This one was still speaking when another came and said, "A fire of God etc.*** *[fell from heaven, raged among the sheep and the servants, and consumed them. Only I escaped, on my own, to tell you]."* "עוֹד זֶה מְדַבֵּר וְזֶה בָּא וַיֹּאמַר כַּשְׂדִּים שָׂמוּ שְׁלֹשָׁה רָאשִׁים וַיִּפְשְׁטוּ עַל־הַגְּמַלִּים וַיִּקָּחוּם וגו׳" – ***This one was still speaking when another came and said, "The Chaldeans fielded three divisions that deployed themselves against the camels and took them etc.*** *[and slew the servants by the sword. Only I escaped, on my own, to tell you]."* "עַד זֶה מְדַבֵּר וְזֶה בָּא וַיֹּאמַר בָּנֶיךָ וּבְנוֹתֶיךָ אֹכְלִים וְשֹׁתִים יַיִן בְּבֵית אֲחִיהֶם הַבְּכוֹר" – ***Once he had spoken, another came and said, "Your sons and daughters were eating and drinking wine in the house of their brother, the firstborn.*** "וְהִנֵּה רוּחַ גְּדוֹלָה בָּאָה מֵעֵבֶר הַמִּדְבָּר וַיִּגַּע בְּאַרְבַּע פִּנּוֹת הַבַּיִת וַיִּפֹּל עַל־הַנְּעָרִים וגו׳" – ***When, lo, a mighty wind came from across the wilderness. It struck the four corners of the house so that it collapsed upon the young men etc.*** *[and they died. Only I escaped, on my own, to tell you]."* "וַיָּקָם אִיּוֹב וַיִּקְרַע אֶת־מְעִלוֹ וַיָּגָז אֶת־רֹאשׁוֹ וגו׳" – ***Then Job arose, tore his shirt, plucked out [the hair of] his head, etc.*** *[threw himself upon the ground and prostrated himself].* "וַיֹּאמֶר עָרֹם יָצָתִי מִבֶּטֶן אִמִּי וְעָרֹם אָשׁוּב שָׁמָּה ה׳ נָתַן וַה׳ לָקָח יְהִי שֵׁם ה׳ מְבֹרָךְ" – ***He said, "Naked I came out of my mother's womb, and naked shall I return there.***[2] ***HASHEM has given, HASHEM has taken away; blessed be the Name of HASHEM."*** בְּכָל־זֹאת לֹא־חָטָא אִיּוֹב וְלֹא־נָתַן תִּפְלָה לֵאלֹהִים – ***Despite all this, Job did not sin or ascribe caprice to God.*** "וַיְהִי הַיּוֹם וַיָּבֹאוּ בְּנֵי הָאֱלֹהִים לְהִתְיַצֵּב וגו׳" – ***On a certain day,***[3] ***the angels came to stand, etc.*** *[before HASHEM, and the Satan too came with them to stand before HASHEM].* "וַיֹּאמֶר ה׳ אֶל־הַשָּׂטָן אֵי מִזֶּה תָּבֹא וַיַּעַן הַשָּׂטָן אֶת־ה׳ וַיֹּאמַר מִשֻּׁט בָּאָרֶץ [וגו׳]" – ***HASHEM asked the Satan, "From where do you come?" The Satan answered HASHEM, saying, "From exploring the earth*** **[etc.]** *[and wandering about (his'haleich) on it].*

As above, the Gemara takes the Satan's reply (which included the word *his'haleich*) as an allusion to Abraham:

אָמַר לְפָנָיו – **[The Satan] said before [God],** רִבּוֹנוֹ שֶׁל עוֹלָם שַׁטְתִּי בְּכָל הָעוֹלָם – **"Master of the Universe! I have explored the entire world,** וְלֹא מָצָאתִי כְּעַבְדְּךָ אַבְרָהָם – **and I have not found** anyone as loyal **as Your servant Abraham,** שֶׁאָמַרְתָּ לוֹ: "קוּם הִתְהַלֵּךְ בָּאָרֶץ לְאָרְכָּהּ וּלְרָחְבָּהּ כִּי לְךָ אֶתְּנֶנָּה" – **to whom You said,** ***"Arise, wander about*** *(his'haleich)* ***the land*** *of Canaan,* ***through its length and breadth, for to you I will give it",***[4] וּבְשָׁעָה שֶׁבִּקֵּשׁ לִקְבּוֹר שָׂרָה – **and yet when [Abraham] wanted to bury** his wife **Sarah,** לֹא מָצָא מָקוֹם לְקוֹבְרָהּ – and **could not find a place to bury her,** וְלֹא הִרְהֵר אַחַר מִדּוֹתֶיךָ – **he did not ponder Your ways!**

The Gemara returns to the narrative with God's reply to the Satan (*Job* 2:3):

"וַיֹּאמֶר ה׳ אֶל־הַשָּׂטָן הֲשַׂמְתָּ לִבְּךָ אֶל־עַבְדִּי אִיּוֹב כִּי אֵין כָּמֹהוּ בָּאָרֶץ וגו׳ וְעֹדֶנּוּ מַחֲזִיק בְּתֻמָּתוֹ וַתְּסִיתֵנִי בוֹ לְבַלְּעוֹ חִנָּם" – ***HASHEM said to the Satan, "Have you paid attention to My servant Job? For there is none like him in all the world etc.*** *[a perfect and upright man, one that fears God and avoids evil and still he maintains his integrity;]* ***and you turned Me against him, to destroy him for no reason!"***

The Gemara comments:

אָמַר רַבִּי יוֹחָנָן – **R' Yochanan said:** אִלְמָלֵא מִקְרָא כָּתוּב אִי אֶפְשָׁר לְאוֹמְרוֹ – **Were this verse not written, it would be impossible** for us **to say it** on our own. כְּאָדָם שֶׁמְּסִיתִין אוֹתוֹ וְנִיסָּת – It describes God **like a mortal, whom [others] urge and he is persuaded** by them![5]

A Baraisa elaborates on the machinations of the Satan:

בְּמַתְנִיתָא תָּנָא – **A Tanna taught in a Baraisa:** יוֹרֵד וּמַתְעֶה – **[THE SATAN] DESCENDS** to this world **AND LURES** people **INTO SIN:**[6] וְעוֹלֶה וּמַרְגִּיז – **HE** then **ASCENDS** to the Heavenly Court **AND INCITES** God's wrath by denouncing the sinner. נוֹטֵל רְשׁוּת וְנוֹטֵל נְשָׁמָה – **HE TAKES PERMISSION** to kill the sinner, **AND TAKES** his **SOUL.**[7]

The narrative is continued with the Satan's reply to God (*Job* 2:4-7):

"וַיַּעַן הַשָּׂטָן אֶת־ה׳ וַיֹּאמַר עוֹר בְּעַד־עוֹר וְכֹל אֲשֶׁר לָאִישׁ יִתֵּן בְּעַד נַפְשׁוֹ" – ***The Satan answered HASHEM saying, "Limb for limb – indeed all that a man has he will give up for his life.***[8] אוּלָם שְׁלַח־נָא יָדְךָ וְגַע אֶל־עַצְמוֹ וְאֶל־בְּשָׂרוֹ אִם־לֹא (עַל) [אֶל]־פָּנֶיךָ יְבָרְכֶךָּ" – ***But, stretch out Your Hand and strike his bones and his flesh,***

NOTES

1. In reference to the Messianic era, it is written (*Jeremiah* 31:7): וְקִבַּצְתִּים מִיַּרְכְּתֵי־אָרֶץ בָּם עִוֵּר וּפִסֵּחַ הָרָה וְיֹלֶדֶת יַחְדָּו, *I* [God] *will gather them* [Israel] *from the ends of the earth – with them, the blind and the lame, the woman carrying child and the woman that has given birth, together.* The Gemara (*Shabbos* 30b) homiletically interprets the phrase הָרָה וְיֹלֶדֶת יַחְדָּו, *the woman carrying child and the woman that has given birth together,* as meaning that a woman will conceive and give birth on the same day. [Similarly, the sprouting of vegetation will occur immediately after planting] (*Rashi* to *Shabbos* ibid.; cf. *Maharsha* here).

2. The word שָׁמָּה, *there*, signifies the place to which he is destined to return; namely, the earth in which he will be buried (*Rashi* ad loc.).

The thrust of Job's words is: How can I complain of the loss of my children and possessions? I was born without them, and I will die the same way (*Metzudos*).

3. The next appointed time for the Heavenly Court to convene in judgment (*Metzudos*) [possibly, Yom Kippur – see 15b note 34].

4. *Genesis* 13:17.

5. This anthromorphic expression, like similar expressions in the Torah, is used merely to make God's actions or attributes understandable to people. It should not be taken literally. God does not inflict punishment without reason for His justice is perfect. The reason for the suffering of the righteous is concealed from us. God's statement that He was persuaded to destroy Job "for no reason" is to be understood in the context of the Satan's rhetorical denunciation of Job (*Job* 1:9): הַחִנָּם יָרֵא אִיּוֹב אֱלֹהִים, *Does Job fear God for no reason?* [I.e. he serves God for ulterior motives – see above, 15a.] Our verse is interpreted as follows: וַתְּסִיתֵנִי בוֹ לְבַלְּעוֹ חִנָּם, *and you persuaded Me to destroy him* [on the basis of your argument, "Does Job fear God] *for no reason*" (*Maharsha*).

Ramban (ad loc.) gives a different perspective: The "destruction" which God wrought "for no reason" was really not a destruction at all. That which the Satan had hoped would break Job proved, on the contrary, to stimulate him to scale heights of spirituality hitherto beyond him. Where until now he had served God only out of fear, he would be in the end counted among those who are motivated by love.

6. [The Satan is also the יֵצֶר הָרָע, *Evil Inclination* (Gemara below).]

7. [The Satan is also the מַלְאַךְ הַמָּוֶת, *the Angel of Death* (Gemara below).] The Satan does not kill without permission from God, as evidenced by our verse: וַתְּסִיתֵנִי בוֹ לְבַלְּעוֹ, *And you persuaded Me* [God] *to destroy him* (*Rashi*).

8. A person will take a blow intended for one limb on another limb in order to save his life. One who sees a sword descending upon his head will raise his arm to ward off the blow, although it may be slashed as a result. Certainly, then, a man, knowing that he is deserving of capital punishment, would unbegrudgingly give his possessions to save his life (*Rashi* ad loc.). The Satan argued: Job possibly thinks that death has been decreed upon him, and the loss of everything he has is a substitute for his own death. Therefore, he accepts the loss gladly (*Metzudos*).

מסורת הש"ס

א) [סנהדרין דף קיא.], ב) [נ"א אלי], ג) [נ"א דרחמנותיה], ד) [קדושין ל:], ה) [נ"א ליתא], ו) נ"א רבא, ז) [בספרים שלפנינו כתיב לא כאלו], ח) נ"א רבא, ט) נ"א רבא, י) ע' תוס' ע"ז יז: ד"ה מעות:

הגהות הב"ח

(א) גמ' אמר רבא איהו באחרנייתא לא אסתכל אברהם אפי' בדידיה כצ"ל ומיבות עפרא לפומיה דאיוב נמחק: (ב) רש"י ד"ה להפוך קערה על פיה כלומר לעקור: (ג) בא"ד שברא להם יצה"ר וכו': (ד) ד"ה ברא לו תורה תבלין כצ"ל ותיבת הן נמחק:

הגהות מהר"ב רנשבורג

א] גמרא אלמא בדידיה קיימא מילתא כצ"ל:

רש"י

מעין העולם הבא. כדכתיב (ירמיה לא) הרה ויולדת יחדו הריון ולידה ביום אחד הכי דרשינן ליה במסכת שבת (דף ל:): **הכי גרסינן במתניתא תנא יורד ומתעה ועולה ומרגיז נוטל רשות ונוטל נשמה.** [וה"פ] יורד למטה ומתעה את הבריות לחטוא ועולה למעלה ומרגיז את חמת המלך בהסטנותו נוטל ממנו רשות להרוג את החוטא מכיון שנתנו רשות לשטן נוטל את נשמתו: **צערו של שטן.** שהחזקק לשמור את נפש איוב שלא תמות: **אלמא בדידיה קיימא.** ליטול את הנפש והזהירו שלא ליטלה: **בעבור הרעימה.** שמתרעם על שהיא עקרה ומתפללת: **להפוך קערה על פיה.** (ב) לעקור כל כבוד שמים וגידף: **לפטור את כל העולם כולו.** מדינו של הקב"ה לומר שאנוסין הן ע"י הקב"ה שברא (ג) יצה"ר והכי קאמר על דעתך כי לא ארשע אם היית חפץ לא הייתי רשע: **בראת שור בפרסות סדוקות וחמור בפרסות קלוטות.** את זה טהרת ואת זה טמאת הכל בא על ידך אתה בראת בו סימני הטומאה: **בראת צדיקים.** ע"י יצר טוב: **בראת רשעים.** על ידי יצר הרע לפיכך אין ניצול מידך כי מי יעכב אנוסין הן החוטאין: **ברא לו תורה.** (ד) הן תבלין שהיא מבטלת את הרהורי עבירה כדאמר בעלמא (קדושין דף ל:) אם פגע בך מנוול זה משכהו לבית המדרש אם אבן הוא נימוח כו' הלכך לאו אנוסין ניהו שהרי יכולין להציל עצמן: **ברכת אובד.** שהיה סבור שהיה אובד את שדהו: **שדי שמיה עלוה.** אומר שהיא קרובתו או מדבר בה להשיאה: **חברותא כלפי שמיא.** מדבר לפני השכינה כאדם המתווכח לחבירו בא ונשקול מי חייב לחבירו: **מן הסערה.** לשון שיער דקדוקי הרבה נימין בראתי באדם: **מטשטשות את הארץ.** עושות את הארץ כטיט:

גמרא

מעין העולם הבא א) עוד זה מדבר וזה בא ויאמר אש אלהים וגו' ב) עוד זה מדבר וזה בא ויאמר כשדים שמו שלשה ראשים ויפשטו על הגמלים ויקחום וגו' ג) עוד זה מדבר וזה בא ויאמר בניך ובנותיך אוכלים ושותים יין בבית אחיהם הבכור ד) והנה רוח גדולה באה מעבר המדבר ויגע בארבע פנות הבית ויפול על הנערים וגו' ה) ויקם איוב ויקרע את מעילו ויגז את ראשו וגו' ו) ויאמר ערום יצאתי מבטן אמי וערום אשוב שמה ה' נתן וה' לקח יהי שם ה' מבורך ז) בכל זאת לא חטא איוב ולא נתן תפלה לאלהים ח) ויהי היום ויבואו בני האלהים להתיצב וגו' ט) ויאמר ה' אל השטן אי מזה תבא ויען השטן את ה' ויאמר משוט בארץ [וגו'] אמר לפניו רבש"ע שטתי בכל העולם ולא מצאתי כעבדך אברהם שאמרת לו י) קום התהלך בארץ לארכה ולרחבה כי לך אתננה ובשעה שבקש לקבור שרה לא מצא מקום לקוברה ולא הרהר אחר מדותיך יא) ויאמר ה' אל השטן השמת לבך אל עבדי איוב כי אין כמוהו בארץ וגו' ועודנו מחזיק בתומתו ותסיתני בו לבלעו חנם אמר רבי יוחנן אלמלא מקרא כתוב אי אפשר לאומרו כאדם שמסיתין אותו וניסת במתניתא תנא יורד ומתעה ועולה ומרגיז נוטל רשות ונוטל נשמה יב) ויען השטן את ה' ויאמר עור בעד עור וכל אשר לאיש יתן בעד נפשו יג) אולם שלח נא ידך וגע אל עצמו ואל בשרו אם לא (על) פניך יברכך יד) ויאמר ה' אל השטן הנו בידך אך את נפשו שמור טו) ויצא השטן מאת פני ה' ויך את איוב וגו' אמר רבי יצחק קשה צערו של שטן יותר משל איוב משל לעבד שאמר לו רבו שבור חבית ושמור את יינה אמר ר"ל הוא שטן הוא יצר הרע הוא מלאך המות הוא שטן דכתיב טו) ויצא השטן מאת פני ה' הוא יצר הרע כתיב התם טז) רק רע כל היום וכתיב הכא (רק את נפשו שמור) [יז) רק אליו אל תשלח ידך] הוא מלאך המות דכתיב (רק) יד) [אך] את נפשו שמור א) אלמא בדידיה קיימא א"ר לוי שטן ופנינה לשם שמים נתכוונו שטן כיון דחזיא להקדוש ברוך הוא דנטיה דעתיה בתר איוב אמר חס ושלום מינשי ליה ג) לרחמנותיה דאברהם פנינה דכתיב יח) וכעסתה צרתה גם כעס בעבור הרעימה דרשה רב אחא בר יעקב בפפוניא אתא שטן נשקיה לכרעיה יט) בכל זאת לא חטא איוב בשפתיו אמר רבא בשפתיו לא חטא בלבו חטא מאי קאמר כ) ארץ נתנה ביד רשע פני שופטיה יכסה אם לא איפו מי הוא אמר רבא בקש איוב להפוך קערה על פיה אמר ליה אביי לא דבר איוב אלא כנגד השטן כתנאי ארץ נתנה ביד רשע רבי אליעזר אומר בקש איוב להפוך קערה על פיה אמר לו רבי יהושע לא דבר איוב אלא כלפי שטן כא) על דעתך כי לא ארשע ואין מידך מציל אמר רבא בקש איוב לפטור את כל העולם כולו מן הדין אמר לפניו רבונו של עולם בראת שור פרסותיו סדוקות בראת חמור פרסותיו קלוטות בראת גן עדן בראת גיהנם בראת צדיקים בראת רשעים מי מעכב על ידך ומאי אהדרו ליה חבריה [דאיוב] כב) אף אתה תפר יראה ותגרע שיחה לפני אל ברא הקדוש ברוך הוא יצר הרע ד) ברא לו תורה תבלין דרש רבא מאי דכתיב כג) ברכת אובד עלי תבא ולב אלמנה ארנין ברכת אובד עלי תבא מלמד שהיה גוזל שדה מיתומים ומשביחה ומחזירה להן ולב אלמנה ארנין דכל היכא דהוה ה) (איכא) אלמנה דלא הוו נסבי לה הוה אזיל שדי שמיה עילווה והוו אתו נסבי לה כד) לו שקול ישקל כעשי והותי במאזנים ישאו יחד אמר ו) רב עפרא לפומיה דאיוב חברותא כלפי שמיא ז) כה) לו יש בינינו מוכיח ישת ידו על שנינו אמר ח) רב עפרא לפומיה דאיוב כלום יש עבד שמוכיח את רבו כו) ברית כרתי לעיני ומה אתבונן על בתולה אמר רבא (א) עפרא לפומיה דאיוב איהו באחרניתא אברהם אפילו בדידיה לא איסתכל דכתיב כז) הנה נא ידעתי כי אשה יפת מראה את מכלל דמעיקרא לא הוה ידע לה כח) כלה ענן וילך כן יורד שאול לא יעלה אמר רבא מכאן שכפר איוב בתחיית המתים כט) אשר בשערה ישופני והרבה פצעי חנם ט) אמר רבה איוב בסערה חרף ובסערה השיבוהו בסערה חרף דכתיב אשר בשערה ישופני אמר לפניו רבונו של עולם שמא רוח סערה עברה לפניך ונתחלף לך בין איוב לאויב בסערה השיבוהו דכתיב ל) ויען ה' את איוב מן הסערה ויאמר [וגו'] לא) אזר נא כגבר חלציך ואשאלך והודיעני אמר לו הרבה נימין בראתי באדם וכל נימא ונימא בראתי לה גומא בפני עצמה שלא יהו שתים יונקות מגומא אחת שאלמלי שתים יונקות מגומא אחת מחשיכות מאור עיניו של אדם בין גומא לגומא לא נתחלף לי בין איוב לאויב נתחלף לי י) לב) מי פלג לשטף תעלה [וגו'] הרבה טיפין בראתי בעבים וכל טיפה וטיפה בראתי לה דפוס בפני עצמה כדי שלא יהו שתי טיפין יוצאות מדפוס אחד שאלמלי שתי טיפין יוצאות מדפוס אחד מטשטשות את הארץ ואינה מוציאה פירות בין טיפה לטיפה לא נתחלף לי בין איוב לאויב נתחלף לי מאי משמע דהאי תעלה לישנא דדפוס היא אמר רבה בר שילא דכתיב לג) ויעש תעלה כבית סאתים זרע לב) ודרך לחזיז קולות הרבה קולות בראתי בעבים וכל קול וקול בראתי לו שביל בפני עצמו כדי שלא יהו שתי קולות יוצאות משביל אחד שאלמלי שתי קולות יוצאות משביל אחד מחריבין את כל העולם בין קול לקול לא נתחלף לי בין איוב לאויב נתחלף לי לד) הידעת עת לדת יעלי סלע חולל אילות תשמור יעלה זו אכזרית על בניה בשעה שכורעת

רבינו גרשום

מעין העולם הבא. שלאלתר תיכף לחרישה היו רועות על ידיהן מיד והיה עשב יוצא וזורעות. וכן כתב לעולם הבא ונגש חורש בקוצר [עמוס ט]: **כאדם שמסיתין אותו.** אחרים וניסת על ידיהן: **בעבור הרעימה.** מה רעמים הללו לעולם אי אפשר בלא מטר כך היתה מתרעמת ומכעסת אותה כדי שתבקש רחמים עליה שיהיה לה ולדות: **אלא בלבו חטא.** שהיה מחשב בלבו על (פי) הבורא דברים אשר לא כן: **להפוך קערה על פיה.** להפוך יראת כל העולם. כלומר שאין דין אמת: **על דעתך כי לא ארשע.** כלומר בידך לבות בני אדם אם היה בדעתך להטותו לטובה לא היה רשע ובעבור שלא עשית כן אין מידך מציל: **מי מעכב על ידך.** שלא תתן לרשע לב צדיק: **אף אתה תפר יראת.** כשאמר כן תפר יראת חטא מבני אדם ותגרע תפלה מהם: **ברא לו תורה תבלין כנגדו.** מכלל שהכל בידי אדם יעסוק בתורה ויהיה צדיק: **כשמחזיר שדהו משובחת.** שהוא היה סבור שגזלה לו: **שדי שמיה עילויה.** שהיה מוציא שם שהוא קרובתו: **חברותא כלפי שמיא.** דקאמר ישאו יחד: **הנה נא ידעתי.** כשראה בבואה במים: **ויעש תעלה.** דפוס סילון לשטף המים:

ליקוטי רש"י

ויפשטו על הגמלים. זה לשון בזוז בו לפי מנהגם כל זמן שהם מהלכים נדבקים יחד והולכים במאסף שלא יעינו בהם ויבריחו את המקנה וכשמגיעים למקום המקנ' פושטים במרחב המקנה זה לכאן וזה לכאן לאסוף המקנה והמלאכים הללו שלוחי שטן היו וכדי להקניטו ולהחטיאו בישרוהו תחילה בהפסד מועט ואח"כ בגדול הימנו וכן כולם [איוב א, יז]. **מעבר המדבר.** מצד שני של מדבר והיה הבית מצד זה וזהו לשון עבר במקרא. **על הנערים.** בניו אבל אין צריך להזכיר הבנות [שם א, יט]. **ויגז.** תלש כמו (ירמיה ז) גזי נזרך ומתרגמינן תלישה וכמו (תהלים עא) ממעי אמי אתה גוזי מושכי [שם א, כ]. **מבטן אמי.** האדמה אשר לוקחתי משם או אמי ממש. **וערום אשוב שמה.** לא בבטן הוא מדבר ומה שמה אל מקום תשובתו ועל שהוא מוכן לכך ולא יחליף המוק לשוב כי אם אל העפר לפיכך לא הוצרך להזכירו [שם א, כא]. **לא נתן תפלה.** לא שום שמץ ותפלות נתן על הקב"ה כמו (ירמיה כג) ובנביאי שומרון ראיתי תפלה. ולא נתן. להטיל תפלה ועול אל הקב"ה כמו (שמואל א יח) נתנו לדוד הרבבות ולי נתנו האלפים [שם א, כב]. **אי מזה תבוא.** איה מקום שתוכל לומר מזה אני בא [שם ב, ב]. **ובשעה שבקש אברהם לקבור את שרה.** לא מצא קרקע עד שקנה בדמים מרובים [שמות ו, ט]. **ועודנו מחזיק.** אוחז כמו (שמות ד) וישלח ידו ויחזק בו מחזיק באזני כלב (משלי כו). **ותסיתני בו.** הסיתני לבולעו כל לשון הסתה אינו אלא לשון המשכה שממשיך את האדם לעצתו [שם ב, ג]. **עור בעד עור.** אבר בפני אבר כן דרך בני אדם כשרואה החרב באה על ראשו מגין בזרועו לפניו וכ"ש כל אשר לאיש בממון יתן. **בעד נפשו.** בפני נפשו להגין לפי שזה יודע בנפשו שנתחייב לפיכך אינו מצטער על ממונו [שם ב, ד]. **אולם.** אבל. **אם לא על פניך.** תראה בו מיד שעל פניך יברכך [שם ב, ה]. **את נפשו שמור.** מכות מות הכהו ולכך נלטוה לשמור נפשו [חולין מג.]. **שטן לשם שמים.** נתכוון כדי שלא יהא נשכח לפני אלהינו זכותו של אברהם [איוב א, ז]. **כעסתה צרתה.** אשת בעלה פנינה. **גם כעס.** כעס אחר כעס תמיד לכך נאמר גם כעס היתה אומרת לה כלום קנית היום מעפורת לבנך גדול או חלוק לבנך קטן. **בעבור הרעימה.** שתתאונן. ורבותינו אמרו (ב"ב טז.) בעבור הרעימה שתתפלל ולשם שמים נתכוונה [שמואל א א, ו]. **בפפוניא.** שהיה דר בפפונא [קידושין לה.]. **ביד רשע.** כלפי שטן. **פני שופטיה יכסה.** מהכמין כדבר אמת. ואם לא איפוא. דבר אמת דבר זה מי הוא המכלה את התמימים [איוב ט, כד]. **על דעתך.** יודע אתה [שם י, ז]. **אף אתה.** כל שכן אתה שמכס מאוד אתה תפר יראה במרבית דבריך ותגרע שיחה כמו כי יגרע נטפי מים (איוב לו) וכמו ותגרע אליך חכמה [שם טו, ד].

[המשך בעמוד ב']

תורה אור השלם

א) עוֹד זֶה מְדַבֵּר וְזֶה בָּא וַיֹּאמַר אֵשׁ אֱלֹהִים נָפְלָה מִן הַשָּׁמַיִם וַתִּבְעַר בַּצֹּאן וּבַנְּעָרִים וַתֹּאכְלֵם וָאִמָּלְטָה רַק אֲנִי לְבַדִּי לְהַגִּיד לָךְ: [איוב א, טז]

ב) עוֹד זֶה מְדַבֵּר וְזֶה בָּא וַיֹּאמַר כַּשְׂדִּים שָׂמוּ שְׁלֹשָׁה רָאשִׁים וַיִּפְשְׁטוּ עַל הַגְּמַלִּים וַיִּקָּחוּם וְאֶת הַנְּעָרִים הִכּוּ לְפִי חָרֶב וָאִמָּלְטָה רַק אֲנִי לְבַדִּי לְהַגִּיד לָךְ: [איוב א, יז]

ג) עַד זֶה מְדַבֵּר וְזֶה בָּא וַיֹּאמַר בָּנֶיךָ וּבְנוֹתֶיךָ אֹכְלִים וְשֹׁתִים יַיִן בְּבֵית אֲחִיהֶם הַבְּכוֹר: [איוב א, יח]

ד) וְהִנֵּה רוּחַ גְּדוֹלָה בָּאָה מֵעֵבֶר הַמִּדְבָּר וַיִּגַּע בְּאַרְבַּע פִּנּוֹת הַבַּיִת וַיִּפֹּל עַל הַנְּעָרִים וַיָּמוּתוּ וָאִמָּלְטָה רַק אֲנִי לְבַדִּי לְהַגִּיד לָךְ: [איוב א, יט]

ה) וַיָּקָם אִיּוֹב וַיִּקְרַע אֶת מְעִלוֹ וַיָּגָז אֶת רֹאשׁוֹ וַיִּפֹּל אַרְצָה וַיִּשְׁתָּחוּ: [איוב א, כ]

ו) וַיֹּאמֶר עָרֹם יָצָאתִי מִבֶּטֶן אִמִּי וְעָרֹם אָשׁוּב שָׁמָּה יְיָ נָתַן וַייָ לָקָח יְהִי שֵׁם יְיָ מְבֹרָךְ: [איוב א, כא]

ז) בְּכָל זֹאת לֹא חָטָא אִיּוֹב וְלֹא נָתַן תִּפְלָה לֵאלֹהִים: [איוב א, כב]

ח) וַיְהִי הַיּוֹם וַיָּבֹאוּ בְּנֵי הָאֱלֹהִים לְהִתְיַצֵּב עַל יְיָ וַיָּבוֹא גַם הַשָּׂטָן בְּתֹכָם לְהִתְיַצֵּב עַל יְיָ: [איוב ב, א]

ט) וַיֹּאמֶר יְיָ אֶל הַשָּׂטָן אֵי מִזֶּה תָּבֹא וַיַּעַן הַשָּׂטָן אֶת יְיָ וַיֹּאמַר מִשֻּׁט בָּאָרֶץ וּמֵהִתְהַלֵּךְ בָּהּ: [איוב ב, ב]

י) קוּם הִתְהַלֵּךְ בָּאָרֶץ לְאָרְכָּהּ וּלְרָחְבָּהּ כִּי לְךָ אֶתְּנֶנָּה: [בראשית יג, יז] יא) וַיֹּאמֶר יְיָ אֶל הַשָּׂטָן הֲשַׂמְתָּ לִבְּךָ אֶל עַבְדִּי אִיּוֹב כִּי אֵין כָּמֹהוּ בָּאָרֶץ אִישׁ תָּם וְיָשָׁר יְרֵא אֱלֹהִים וְסָר מֵרָע וְעֹדֶנּוּ מַחֲזִיק בְּתֻמָּתוֹ וַתְּסִיתֵנִי בוֹ לְבַלְּעוֹ חִנָּם: [איוב ב, ג] יב) וַיַּעַן הַשָּׂטָן אֶת יְיָ וַיֹּאמַר עוֹר בְּעַד עוֹר וְכֹל אֲשֶׁר לָאִישׁ יִתֵּן בְּעַד נַפְשׁוֹ: [איוב ב, ד] יג) אוּלָם שְׁלַח נָא יָדְךָ וְגַע אֶל עַצְמוֹ וְאֶל בְּשָׂרוֹ אִם לֹא אֶל פָּנֶיךָ יְבָרְכֶךָּ: [איוב ב, ה] יד) וַיֹּאמֶר יְיָ אֶל הַשָּׂטָן הִנּוֹ בְיָדֶךָ אַךְ אֶת נַפְשׁוֹ שְׁמֹר: [איוב ב, ו] טו) וַיֵּצֵא הַשָּׂטָן מֵאֵת פְּנֵי יְיָ וַיַּךְ אֶת אִיּוֹב בִּשְׁחִין רָע מִכַּף רַגְלוֹ וְעַד קָדְקֳדוֹ: [איוב ב, ז] טז) וַיַּרְא יְיָ כִּי רַבָּה רָעַת הָאָדָם בָּאָרֶץ וְכָל יֵצֶר מַחְשְׁבֹת לִבּוֹ רַק רַע כָּל הַיּוֹם: [בראשית ו, ה] יז) וַיֹּאמֶר יְיָ אֶל הַשָּׂטָן הִנֵּה כָל אֲשֶׁר לוֹ בְּיָדֶךָ רַק אֵלָיו אַל תִּשְׁלַח יָדֶךָ וַיֵּצֵא הַשָּׂטָן מֵעִם פְּנֵי יְיָ: [איוב א, יב] יח) וְכִעֲסַתָּה צָרָתָהּ גַּם כַּעַס בַּעֲבוּר הַרְּעִמָהּ כִּי סָגַר יְיָ בְּעַד רַחְמָהּ: [שמואל א א, ו] יט) וַיֹּאמֶר אֵלֶיהָ כְּדַבֵּר אַחַת הַנְּבָלוֹת תְּדַבֵּרִי גַּם אֶת הַטּוֹב נְקַבֵּל מֵאֵת הָאֱלֹהִים וְאֶת הָרָע לֹא נְקַבֵּל בְּכָל זֹאת לֹא חָטָא אִיּוֹב בִּשְׂפָתָיו: [איוב ב, י] כ) אֶרֶץ נִתְּנָה בְיַד רָשָׁע פְּנֵי שֹׁפְטֶיהָ יְכַסֶּה אִם לֹא אֵפוֹא מִי הוּא: [איוב ט, כד] כא) עַל דַּעְתְּךָ כִּי לֹא אֶרְשָׁע וְאֵין מִיָּדְךָ מַצִּיל: [איוב י, ז] כב) אַף אַתָּה תָּפֵר יִרְאָה וְתִגְרַע שִׂיחָה לִפְנֵי אֵל: [איוב טו, ד] כג) בִּרְכַּת אֹבֵד עָלַי תָּבֹא וְלֵב אַלְמָנָה אַרְנִן: [איוב כט, יג] כד) לוּ שָׁקוֹל יִשָּׁקֵל כַּעְשִׂי וְהַוָּתִי בְּמֹאזְנַיִם יִשְׂאוּ יָחַד: [איוב ו, ב] כה) לֹא יֵשׁ בֵּינֵינוּ מוֹכִיחַ יָשֵׁת יָדוֹ עַל שְׁנֵינוּ: [איוב ט, לג] כו) בְּרִית כָּרַתִּי לְעֵינָי וּמָה אֶתְבּוֹנֵן עַל בְּתוּלָה: [איוב לא, א] כז) וַיְהִי כַּאֲשֶׁר הִקְרִיב לָבוֹא מִצְרָיְמָה וַיֹּאמֶר אֶל שָׂרַי אִשְׁתּוֹ הִנֵּה נָא יָדַעְתִּי כִּי אִשָּׁה יְפַת מַרְאֶה אָתְּ: [בראשית יב, יא] כח) כָּלָה עָנָן וַיֵּלַךְ כֵּן יוֹרֵד שְׁאוֹל לֹא יַעֲלֶה: [איוב ז, ט] כט) אֲשֶׁר בִּשְׂעָרָה יְשׁוּפֵנִי וְהִרְבָּה פְצָעַי חִנָּם: [איוב ט, יז] ל) וַיַּעַן יְיָ אֶת אִיּוֹב מִן הַסְּעָרָה וַיֹּאמַר: [איוב לח, א] לא) אֱזָר נָא כְגֶבֶר חֲלָצֶיךָ וְאֶשְׁאָלְךָ וְהוֹדִיעֵנִי: [איוב לח, ג] לב) מִי פִלַּג לַשֶּׁטֶף תְּעָלָה וְדֶרֶךְ לַחֲזִיז קֹלוֹת: [איוב לח, כה] לג) וַיִּבְנֶה אֶת הָאֲבָנִים מִזְבֵּחַ בְּשֵׁם יְיָ וַיַּעַשׂ תְּעָלָה כְּבֵית סָאתַיִם זֶרַע סָבִיב לַמִּזְבֵּחַ: [מלכים א יח, לב] לד) הֲיָדַעְתָּ עֵת לֶדֶת יַעֲלֵי סָלַע חֹלֵל אַיָּלוֹת תִּשְׁמֹר: [איוב לט, א]

and he will surely bless (i.e. blaspheme)[9] ***You to Your Face!"*** וַיֹּאמֶר ה׳ אֶל־הַשָּׂטָן הִנּוֹ בְיָדֶךָ אַךְ אֶת־נַפְשׁוֹ שְׁמֹר – ***Hashem said to the Satan, "Behold, he is in your hands*** [to afflict as you wish]; ***only, spare his life."*** "וַיֵּצֵא הַשָּׂטָן מֵאֵת פְּנֵי ה׳ וַיַּךְ אֶת אִיּוֹב וגו׳" – ***The Satan departed from the presence of Hashem and inflicted Job etc.*** *[with a severe inflammation from the sole of his foot to the crown of his head].*

The Gemara notes that this challenge was very difficult for the Satan to meet:

אָמַר רַבִּי יִצְחָק – **R' Yitzchak said:** קָשֶׁה צַעֲרוֹ שֶׁל שָׂטָן יוֹתֵר מִשֶּׁל אִיּוֹב – **The suffering of the Satan exceeded** even **that of Job.** The Satan's task – to inflict extreme pain on Job without allowing him to die – was most difficult. מָשָׁל לְעֶבֶד שֶׁאָמַר לוֹ רַבּוֹ – **A** fitting **analogy** is that **of a servant who was told by his master,** שְׁבוֹר חָבִית וּשְׁמוֹר אֶת יֵינָהּ – **"Break a keg** of wine, **but save the wine within it."**[10]

Reish Lakish teaches that this entity, which our passage from *Job* refers to as the "Satan," has three identities:

אָמַר רֵישׁ לָקִישׁ – **Reish Lakish said:** הוּא שָׂטָן – **He is the Prosecutor,** who incites God's wrath against those who sin. הוּא יֵצֶר הָרָע – **He is the Evil Inclination,** which causes people to sin. הוּא מַלְאַךְ הַמָּוֶת – **He is the Angel of Death,** who executes sinners.[11]

Reish Lakish gives the Scriptural sources:

הוּא שָׂטָן דִּכְתִיב – We know that **he is the Prosecutor, for it is written:** "וַיֵּצֵא הַשָּׂטָן מֵאֵת פְּנֵי ה׳" – ***The Satan*** (after having prosecuted Job) ***departed from the presence of Hashem.*** הוּא יֵצֶר הָרָע – We know that **he is the Evil Inclination,** כְּתִיב הָתָם: "רַק רַע כָּל־הַיּוֹם" – **for elsewhere,** in reference to the Evil Inclination, **it is written,** ***only evil, all day long,***[12] וּכְתִיב הָכָא: [רַק אֵלָיו אַל־תִּשְׁלַח יָדֶךָ"] (רק את נפשו שמור"), – **and here,** in the first dialogue between God and the Satan, **it is written** that God told the Satan: ***only do not lay your hand on him.***[13] The connection between the two verses, established by their common use of the word "only," implies that the Satan and the Evil Inclination are one and the same. הוּא מַלְאַךְ הַמָּוֶת – We know **that he is the Angel of Death,** דִּכְתִיב "(רק) [אַךְ] אֶת־נַפְשׁוֹ שְׁמֹר" – **for it is written,** in the second dialogue, that God told the Satan: ***Only, spare his life.***[14] אַלְמָא בִּדִידֵיהּ קַיְימָא – **Evidently, it was within the purview of [the Satan]** to take Job's soul.

R' Levi reveals the Satan's motive in persecuting Job. He also discusses the motive of Peninah, wife of Elkanah, who taunted her co-wife Chanah for her childlessness:

אָמַר רַבִּי לֵוִי – **R' Levi said:** שָׂטָן וּפְנִינָּה לְשֵׁם שָׁמַיִם נִתְכַּוְּונוּ – **The intentions of the Satan and Peninah were for the sake of Heaven.** שָׂטָן כֵּיוָן דְּחַזְיָא לְהַקָּדוֹשׁ בָּרוּךְ הוּא דְּנָטְיָה דַּעְתֵּיהּ בָּתַר אִיּוֹב – **When the Satan saw that the Holy One, Blessed is He, was partial to Job,** אָמַר חַס וְשָׁלוֹם מִינְשֵׁי לֵיהּ לְרַחֲמָנוּתֵיהּ דְּאַבְרָהָם – **he said** to himself, **"God forbid that He will forget**[15] **the mercy of Abraham."**[16] Therefore, he set out to demonstrate Job's failings. פְּנִינָּה דִּכְתִיב – **Peninah** too had honorable motives, **as it is written:** "וְכִעֲסַתָּה צָרָתָהּ גַּם־כַּעַס בַּעֲבוּר הַרְּעִמָהּ" – ***And [Chanah's] co-wife*** [Peninah] ***angered her repeatedly, to make her fret*** [about her childlessness].[17] It was Peninah's intent to motivate Chanah to beseech God for a child.

דְּרַשָׁהּ רַב אַחָא בַּר יַעֲקֹב בְּפַפּוּנְיָא – **Rav Acha bar Yaakov taught it** [this teaching of R' Levi] **in** the town of **Papunia,** אֲתָא שָׂטָן נַשְׁקֵיהּ לְכַרְעֵיהּ – and **the Satan came and kissed his foot** in appreciation.

The Gemara records Job's reaction to the bodily suffering inflicted upon him:

"בְּכָל־זֹאת לֹא־חָטָא אִיּוֹב בִּשְׂפָתָיו" – ***Despite all this, Job did not sin with his lips.***[18] He did not complain against God for his suffering.

Rava draws an inference from the verse's expression, *with his lips:*

אָמַר רָבָא – **Rava said:** "בִּשְׂפָתָיו" לֹא חָטָא בְּלִבּוֹ חָטָא – ***With his lips*** **[Job] did not sin,** but **in his heart he did sin.** Job harbored improper thoughts in his mind, but did not voice them.

The Gemara quotes a verse that Rava understands as masking an unspoken blasphemy:

מַאי קָאָמַר – **What did [Job] mean** when he said: "אֶרֶץ נִתְּנָה בְיַד־רָשָׁע פְּנֵי־שֹׁפְטֶיהָ יְכַסֶּה אִם־לֹא אֵיפוֹא מִי־הוּא" – ***The land is delivered into the hand of the wicked one, he covers the faces of its judges. If not, then who is it*** (that inflicts suffering on the righteous)?[19] אָמַר רָבָא – **Rava explained:** בִּקֵּשׁ אִיּוֹב לַהֲפוֹךְ קְעָרָה עַל פִּיהָ – **Job sought to turn the plate upside down.**[20] He denied the mastery of God, believing that the world was controlled by forces of evil.[21]

Abaye disagrees with Rava's understanding of this verse:

אָמַר לֵיהּ אַבַּיֵי – **Abaye said to [Rava]:** לֹא דִבֵּר אִיּוֹב אֶלָּא כְּנֶגֶד הַשָּׂטָן – **Job was referring only to the Satan.** He castigates the Satan for his role in bringing suffering to the world.[22]

The Gemara notes that these views of Abaye and Rava have already been expressed by Tannaim:

כְּתַנָּאֵי – **This** dispute **corresponds to the dispute between Tannaim** that is recorded in the following Baraisa: "אֶרֶץ נִתְּנָה בְיַד־רָשָׁע" – [Job said:] ***THE LAND IS DELIVERED INTO THE HAND OF THE WICKED ONE.*** רַבִּי אֱלִיעֶזֶר אוֹמֵר – **R' ELIEZER SAYS:** בִּקֵּשׁ אִיּוֹב לַהֲפוֹךְ קְעָרָה עַל פִּיהָ – **JOB SOUGHT TO TURN THE PLATE UPSIDE DOWN;** i.e. he blasphemed. אָמַר לוֹ רַבִּי יְהוֹשֻׁעַ – **R' YEHOSHUA**

NOTES

9. See 15b note 43.

10. The physical body and the soul within it are compared to a barrel and its wine. The servant has the difficult task of making incisions in the side of the barrel that penetrate as far as possible without piercing the entire thickness. Similarly, the Satan had to inflict pain on Job's body, but not in such a way that it would cease to function. He therefore afflicted Job with an inflammation on the outside of his body, but did not damage any of the internal organs for that would put Job's very life at risk (*Maharsha*).

11. [This teaching echoes the Baraisa cited above which taught that the Satan lures people into sin, prosecutes them before God and then kills them. Reish Lakish adds the Scriptural sources.]

12. *Genesis* 6:5. The entire verse reads: וַיַּרְא ה׳ כִּי רַבָּה רָעַת הָאָדָם בָּאָרֶץ וְכָל־יֵצֶר מַחְשְׁבֹת לִבּוֹ רַק רַע כָּל־הַיּוֹם, *Hashem saw that the wickedness of man was great upon the earth, and that the entire inclination of the thoughts of his heart was only evil all day long.*

13. *Job* 1:12.

14. Ibid. 2:6.

15. A further example of anthromorphism (see note 5).

16. [I.e. the mercy that God bestows on the Jews in the merit of Abraham.]

17. *I Samuel* 1:6.

18. *Job* 2:10.

19. Ibid. 9:24.

20. I.e. he sought to overthrow every vestige of respect for God (*Rashi*; see *Gra* in *Divrei Eliyahu* p. 83).

21. This represents only what Job thought. The words he actually spoke are not to be understood in this blasphemous sense, for, as taught above, Job sinned only in his heart, not with his lips. His spoken words are a denunciation of the Satan (*Maharsha*).

22. [See previous note. According to Abaye, Job did not deny God's mastery even in his thoughts.]

מעין העולם הבא. כדכתיב (ירמיה לא) הרה ויולדת יחדו הריון ולידה ביום אחד הכי דרשינן ליה במסכת שבת (דף ל:): **הכי גרסינן במתניתא תנא יורד ומתעה ועולה ומרגיז נוטל רשות ונוטל נשמה.** [וה"פ] יורד למטה ומתעה את הבריות לחטוא ועולה למעלה ומרגיז את מדת המלך בהשטנותו נוטל ממנו רשות להרוג את החוטא מכיון שנתנו רשות דכתיב ותסיתני בו: **צערו של שטן.** שהחקק לשמור את נפש איוב שלא תמות והזהירו שלא ליטלה: **אלמא בדידיה קיימא.** ליטול את הנפש והכא לא מצי ליטלה: **בעבור הרעימה.** שתתרעם על שהיא עקרה ותתפלל: **להפוך קערה על פיה.** (ב) לעקור כל כבוד שחירף וגידף: **לפטור את כל העולם כולו.** מדינו של הקב"ה לומר שאנוסין הן ע"י הקב"ה שברא (ג) יצה"ר והכי קאמר על דעתך כי לא ארשע אם היית חפץ לא הייתי רשע: **בראת שור בפרסות סדוקות וחמור בפרסות קלוטות.** את זה טהרת ואת זה טמאת הכל בא על ידך אתה בראת בו סימני הטומאה: **בראת צדיקים.** ע"י יצר טוב: **בראת רשעים.** על ידי יצר הרע לפיכך אין ניצול מידך כי מי יעכב אנוסין הן החוטאין: **ברא לו תורה.** (ד) הן תבלין שהיא מבטלת את הרהורי עבירה כדאמר בעלמא (קדושין דף ל:) אם פגע בך מנוול זה משכהו לבית המדרש אם אבן הוא נימוח כו' הלכך לאו אנוסין נינהו שהרי יכולין להציל עצמן: **ברכת אובד.** שהיה סבור שהיה אובד את שדהו: **שדי שמיה עלוויה.** אומר שהיא קרובתו או מדבר בה להשיאה: **חברותא כלפי שמיא.** מדבר לפני השכינה כאדם המתווכח לחבירו בא ונשקול מי חייב לחבירו: **מן הסערה.** לשון שיער דקתני הרבה נימין בראתי באדם: **ממשמשות את הארץ.** עושות את הארץ כטיט:

מעין העולם הבא א) עוד זה מדבר וזה בא ויאמר אש אלהים וגו' ב) עוד זה מדבר וזה בא ויאמר כשדים שמו שלשה ראשים ויפשטו על הגמלים ויקחום וגו' ג) עוד זה מדבר וזה בא ויאמר בניך ובנותיך אוכלים ושותים יין בבית אחיהם הבכור ד) והנה רוח גדולה באה מעבר המדבר ויגע בארבע פנות הבית ויפול על הנערים וגו' ה) ויקם איוב ויקרע את מעילו ויגז את ראשו וגו' ו) ויאמר ערום יצאתי מבטן אמי וערום אשוב שמה ה' נתן וה' לקח יהי שם ה' מבורך ז) בכל זאת לא חטא איוב ולא נתן תפלה לאלהים ח) ויהי היום ויבואו בני האלהים להתיצב וגו' ט) ויאמר ה' אל השטן אי מזה תבא ויען השטן את ה' ויאמר משוט בארץ [וגו'] אמר לפניו רבש"ע שטתי בכל העולם ולא מצאתי כעבדך אברהם שאמרת לו י) קום התהלך בארץ לארכה ולרחבה כי לך אתננה א) ובשעה שבקש לקבור שרה לא מצא מקום לקוברה ולא הרהר אחר מדותיך יא) ויאמר ה' אל השטן השמת לבך אל עבדי איוב כי אין כמוהו בארץ וגו' ועודנו מחזיק בתומתו ותסיתני בו לבלעו חנם אמר רבי יוחנן אלמלא מקרא כתוב אי אפשר לאומרו כאדם שמסיתין אותו וניסת במתניתא תנא יורד ומתעה ועולה ומרגיז נוטל רשות ונוטל נשמה יב) ויען השטן את ה' ויאמר עור בעד עור וכל אשר לאיש יתן בעד נפשו יג) אולם שלח נא ידך וגע אל עצמו ואל בשרו אם לא ב) (על) פניך יברכך יד) ויאמר ה' אל השטן הנו בידך אך את נפשו שמור טו) ויצא השטן מאת פני ה' ויך את איוב וגו' אמר רבי יצחק קשה צערו של שטן יותר משל איוב משל לעבד שאמר לו רבו שבור חבית ושמור את יינה אמר ר"ל הוא שטן הוא יצר הרע הוא מלאך המות הוא שטן דכתיב טו) ויצא השטן מאת פני ה' הוא יצר הרע כתיב התם טז) רק רע כל היום וכתיב הכא (רק את נפשו שמור) [יז) רק אליו אל תשלח ידך] הוא מלאך המות דכתיב (רק) יד) [אך] את נפשו שמור א) אלמא בדידיה קיימא א"ר לוי שטן ופנינה לשם שמים נתכוונו שטן כיון דחזיא להקדוש ברוך הוא דנטיה דעתיה בתר איוב אמר חס ושלום מינשי ליה ג) לרחמנותיה דאברהם פנינה דכתיב יח) וכעסתה צרתה גם כעס בעבור הרעימה דרשה רב אחא בר יעקב בפפוניא אתא שטן נשקיה לכרעיה יט) בכל זאת לא חטא איוב בשפתיו אמר רבא בשפתיו לא חטא בלבו חטא מאי קאמר כ) ארץ נתנה ביד רשע פני שופטיה יכסה אם לא איפו מי הוא אמר רבא בקש איוב להפוך קערה על פיה אמר ליה אביי לא דבר איוב אלא כנגד השטן כתנאי ארץ נתנה ביד רשע רבי אליעזר אומר בקש איוב להפוך קערה על פיה אמר לו רבי יהושע לא דבר איוב אלא כלפי שטן כא) על דעתך כי לא ארשע ואין מידך מציל אמר רבא בקש איוב לפטור את כל העולם כולו מן הדין אמר לפניו רבונו של עולם בראת שור פרסותיו סדוקות בראת חמור פרסותיו קלוטות בראת גן עדן בראת גיהנם בראת צדיקים בראת רשעים מי מעכב על ידך ומאי אהדרו ליה חבריה [דאיוב] כב) אף אתה תפר יראה ותגרע שיחה לפני אל ברא הקדוש ברוך הוא יצר הרע ד) ברא לו תורה תבלין דרש רבא מאי דכתיב כג) ברכת אובד עלי תבא ולב אלמנה ארנין ברכת אובד עלי תבא מלמד שהיה גוזל שדה מיתומים ומשביחה ומחזירה להן ולב אלמנה ארנין דכל היכא דהוה ה) (איכא) אלמנה דלא הוו נסבי לה הוה אזיל שדי שמיה עילויה והוו אתו נסבי לה כד) לו שקול ישקל כעשי והותי במאזנים ישאו יחד ו) רב עפרא לפומיה דאיוב חברותא כלפי שמיא ז) כה) לו יש בינינו מוכיח ישת ידו על שנינו ח) רב עפרא לפומיה דאיוב כלום יש עבד שמוכיח את רבו כו) ברית כרתי לעיני ומה אתבונן על בתולה אמר רבא (א) עפרא לפומיה דאיוב באחרנייתא לא איסתכל אפילו בדידיה אברהם לא איסתכל דכתיב כז) הנה נא ידעתי כי אשה יפת מראה את מכלל דמעיקרא לא הוה ידע לה כח) כלה ענן וילך כן יורד שאול לא יעלה אמר רבא מכאן שכפר איוב בתחיית המתים כט) אשר בשערה ישופני והרבה פצעי חנם ט) אמר רבה בסערה חירף ובסערה השיבוהו בסערה חרף דכתיב אשר בשערה ישופני אמר לפניו רבונו של עולם שמא רוח סערה עברה לפניך ונתחלף לך בין איוב לאויב בסערה השיבוהו דכתיב ל) ויען ה' את איוב מן הסערה ויאמר [וגו'] לא) אזר נא כגבר חלציך ואשאלך והודיעני אמר לו הרבה נימין בראתי באדם וכל נימא ונימא בראתי לה גומא בפני עצמה שלא יהו שתים יונקות מגומא אחת שאלמלי שתים יונקות מגומא אחת מחשיכות מאור עיניו של אדם בין גומא לגומא לא נתחלף לי בין איוב לאויב נתחלף לי לב) מי פלג לשטף תעלה [וגו'] הרבה טיפין בראתי בעבים וכל טיפה וטיפה בראתי לה דפוס בפני עצמה כדי שלא יהו שתי טיפין יוצאות מדפוס אחד שאלמלי שתי טיפין יוצאות מדפוס אחד מטשטשות את הארץ ואינה מוציאה פירות בין טיפה לטיפה לא נתחלף לי בין איוב לאויב נתחלף לי מאי משמע דהאי תעלה לישנא דדפוס היא אמר רבה בר שילא דכתיב לג) ויעש תעלה כבית סאתים זרע לב) ודרך לחזיז קולות הרבה קולות בראתי בעבים וכל קול וקול בראתי לו שביל בפני עצמו כדי שלא יהו שתי קולות יוצאות משביל אחד שאלמלי שתי קולות יוצאות משביל אחד מחריבין את כל העולם בין קול לקול לא נתחלף לי בין איוב לאויב נתחלף לי לד) הידעת עת לדת יעלי סלע חולל אילות תשמור יעלה זו אכזרית על בניה בשעה שכורעת

מסורת הש"ס

א) [סנהדרין דף קיא.], ב) [צ"ל אל], ג) [ס"א לרחימותיה], ד) [קדושין ל:], ה) [בע"י ליתא], ו) נ"א רבא, ז) [בספרים שלפנינו כתיב לא באל"ף], ח) נ"א רבא, ט) [נדה נג.] [ושם איתא רבא], י) עי' תוס' ע"ז יז: ד"ה מעות:

הגהות הב"ח

(א) גמ' אמר רבא איהו באחרניתא לא אסתכל אברהם אפי' בדידיה כצ"ל ותיבות עפרא לפומיה דאיוב נמחק: (ב) רש"י ד"ה להפוך קערה על פיה כלומר לעקור: (ג) ד"ה לפטור וכו' שברא להם יצה"ר: (ד) ד"ה ברא לו תורה תבלין כצ"ל ותיבת הן נמחק:

הגהות מהר"ב רנשבורג

א] גמרא אלמא בדידיה קיימא מילתא כצ"ל:

תורה אור השלם

א) עוֹד זֶה מְדַבֵּר וְזֶה בָּא וַיֹּאמַר אֵשׁ אֱלֹהִים נָפְלָה מִן הַשָּׁמַיִם וַתִּבְעַר בַּצֹּאן וּבַנְּעָרִים וַתֹּאכְלֵם וָאִמָּלְטָה רַק אֲנִי לְבַדִּי לְהַגִּיד לָךְ: [איוב א, טז]

ב) עוֹד זֶה מְדַבֵּר וְזֶה בָּא וַיֹּאמַר כַּשְׂדִּים שָׂמוּ שְׁלֹשָׁה רָאשִׁים וַיִּפְשְׁטוּ עַל הַגְּמַלִּים וַיִּקָּחוּם וְאֶת הַנְּעָרִים הִכּוּ לְפִי חָרֶב וָאִמָּלְטָה רַק אֲנִי לְבַדִּי לְהַגִּיד לָךְ: [איוב א, יז]

ג) עַד זֶה מְדַבֵּר וְזֶה בָּא וַיֹּאמַר בָּנֶיךָ וּבְנוֹתֶיךָ אֹכְלִים וְשֹׁתִים יַיִן בְּבֵית אֲחִיהֶם הַבְּכוֹר: [איוב א, יח]

ד) וְהִנֵּה רוּחַ גְּדוֹלָה בָּאָה מֵעֵבֶר הַמִּדְבָּר וַיִּגַּע בְּאַרְבַּע פִּנּוֹת הַבַּיִת וַיִּפֹּל עַל הַנְּעָרִים וַיָּמוּתוּ וָאִמָּלְטָה רַק אֲנִי לְבַדִּי לְהַגִּיד לָךְ: [איוב א, יט]

ה) וַיָּקָם אִיּוֹב וַיִּקְרַע אֶת מְעִלוֹ וַיָּגָז אֶת רֹאשׁוֹ וַיִּפֹּל אַרְצָה וַיִּשְׁתָּחוּ: [איוב א, כ]

ו) וַיֹּאמֶר עָרֹם יָצָאתִי מִבֶּטֶן אִמִּי וְעָרֹם אָשׁוּב שָׁמָה יְיָ נָתַן וַייָ לָקָח יְהִי שֵׁם יְיָ מְבֹרָךְ: [איוב א, כא]

ז) בְּכָל זֹאת לֹא חָטָא אִיּוֹב וְלֹא נָתַן תִּפְלָה לֵאלֹהִים: [איוב א, כב]

ח) וַיְהִי הַיּוֹם וַיָּבֹאוּ בְּנֵי הָאֱלֹהִים לְהִתְיַצֵּב עַל יְיָ וַיָּבוֹא גַם הַשָּׂטָן בְּתֹכָם לְהִתְיַצֵּב עַל יְיָ: [איוב ב, א]

ט) וַיֹּאמֶר יְיָ אֶל הַשָּׂטָן אֵי מִזֶּה תָּבֹא וַיַּעַן הַשָּׂטָן אֶת יְיָ וַיֹּאמַר מִשֻּׁט בָּאָרֶץ וּמֵהִתְהַלֵּךְ בָּהּ: [איוב ב, ב]

י) קוּם הִתְהַלֵּךְ בָּאָרֶץ לְאָרְכָּהּ וּלְרָחְבָּהּ כִּי לְךָ אֶתְּנֶנָּה: [בראשית יג, יז] יא) וַיֹּאמֶר יְיָ אֶל הַשָּׂטָן הֲשַׂמְתָּ לִבְּךָ אֶל עַבְדִּי אִיּוֹב כִּי אֵין כָּמֹהוּ בָּאָרֶץ אִישׁ תָּם וְיָשָׁר יְרֵא אֱלֹהִים וְסָר מֵרָע וְעֹדֶנּוּ מַחֲזִיק בְּתֻמָּתוֹ וַתְּסִיתֵנִי בוֹ לְבַלְּעוֹ חִנָּם: [איוב ב, ג] יב) וַיַּעַן הַשָּׂטָן אֶת יְיָ וַיֹּאמַר עוֹר בְּעַד עוֹר וְכֹל אֲשֶׁר לָאִישׁ יִתֵּן בְּעַד נַפְשׁוֹ: [איוב ב, ד] יג) אוּלָם שְׁלַח נָא יָדְךָ וְגַע אֶל עַצְמוֹ וְאֶל בְּשָׂרוֹ אִם לֹא אֶל פָּנֶיךָ יְבָרְכֶךָּ: [איוב ב, ה] יד) וַיֹּאמֶר יְיָ אֶל הַשָּׂטָן הִנּוֹ בְיָדֶךָ אַךְ אֶת נַפְשׁוֹ שְׁמֹר: [איוב ב, ו] טו) וַיֵּצֵא הַשָּׂטָן מֵאֵת פְּנֵי יְיָ וַיַּךְ אֶת אִיּוֹב בִּשְׁחִין רָע מִכַּף רַגְלוֹ וְעַד קָדְקֳדוֹ: [איוב ב, ז] טז) וַיַּרְא יְיָ כִּי רַבָּה רָעַת הָאָדָם בָּאָרֶץ וְכָל יֵצֶר מַחְשְׁבֹת לִבּוֹ רַק רַע כָּל הַיּוֹם: [בראשית ו, ה] יז) וַיֹּאמֶר יְיָ אֶל הַשָּׂטָן הִנֵּה כָל אֲשֶׁר לוֹ בְּיָדֶךָ רַק אֵלָיו אַל תִּשְׁלַח יָדֶךָ וַיֵּצֵא הַשָּׂטָן מֵעִם פְּנֵי יְיָ: [איוב א, יב] יח) וְכִעֲסַתָּה צָרָתָהּ גַּם כַּעַס בַּעֲבוּר הַרְּעִמָהּ כִּי סָגַר יְיָ בְּעַד רַחְמָהּ: [שמואל א א, ו] יט) וַיֹּאמֶר אֵלֶיהָ כְּדַבֵּר אַחַת הַנְּבָלוֹת תְּדַבֵּרִי גַּם אֶת הַטּוֹב נְקַבֵּל מֵאֵת הָאֱלֹהִים וְאֶת הָרָע לֹא נְקַבֵּל בְּכָל זֹאת לֹא חָטָא אִיּוֹב בִּשְׂפָתָיו: [איוב ב, י] כ) אֶרֶץ נִתְּנָה בְיַד רָשָׁע פְּנֵי שֹׁפְטֶיהָ יְכַסֶּה אִם לֹא אֵפוֹא מִי הוּא: [איוב ט, כד] כא) עַל דַּעְתְּךָ כִּי לֹא אֶרְשָׁע וְאֵין מִיָּדְךָ מַצִּיל: [איוב י, ז] כב) אַף אַתָּה תָּפֵר יִרְאָה וְתִגְרַע שִׂיחָה לִפְנֵי אֵל: [איוב טו, ד] כג) בִּרְכַּת אֹבֵד עָלַי תָּבֹא וְלֵב אַלְמָנָה אַרְנִן: [איוב כט, יג] כד) לוּ שָׁקוֹל יִשָּׁקֵל כַּעְשִׂי וְהַוָּתִי בְּמֹאזְנַיִם יִשְׂאוּ יָחַד: [איוב ו, ב] כה) לֹא יֵשׁ בֵּינֵינוּ מוֹכִיחַ יָשֵׁת יָדוֹ עַל שְׁנֵינוּ: [איוב ט, לג] כו) בְּרִית כָּרַתִּי לְעֵינָי וּמָה אֶתְבּוֹנֵן עַל בְּתוּלָה: [איוב לא, א] כז) וַיְהִי כַּאֲשֶׁר הִקְרִיב לָבוֹא מִצְרָיְמָה וַיֹּאמֶר אֶל שָׂרַי אִשְׁתּוֹ הִנֵּה נָא יָדַעְתִּי כִּי אִשָּׁה יְפַת מַרְאֶה אָתְּ: [בראשית יב, יא] כח) כָּלָה עָנָן וַיֵּלַךְ כֵּן יוֹרֵד שְׁאוֹל לֹא יַעֲלֶה: [איוב ז, ט] כט) אֲשֶׁר בִּשְׂעָרָה יְשׁוּפֵנִי וְהִרְבָּה פְצָעַי חִנָּם: [איוב ט, יז] ל) וַיַּעַן יְיָ אֶת אִיּוֹב מִן הַסְּעָרָה וַיֹּאמַר: [איוב לח, א] לא) אֱזָר נָא כְגֶבֶר חֲלָצֶיךָ וְאֶשְׁאָלְךָ וְהוֹדִיעֵנִי: [איוב לח, ג] לב) מִי פִלַּג לַשֶּׁטֶף תְּעָלָה וְדֶרֶךְ לַחֲזִיז קֹלוֹת: [איוב לח, כה] לג) וַיִּבְנֶה אֶת הָאֲבָנִים מִזְבֵּחַ בְּשֵׁם יְיָ וַיַּעַשׂ תְּעָלָה כְּבֵית סָאתַיִם זֶרַע סָבִיב לַמִּזְבֵּחַ: [מלכים א יח, לב] לד) הֲיָדַעְתָּ עֵת לֶדֶת יַעֲלֵי סָלַע חֹלֵל אַיָּלוֹת תִּשְׁמֹר: [איוב לט, א]

רבינו גרשום

מעין העולם הבא. שלאלתר תיכף לחרישה היו רועות על ידיהן מיד והיה עשב יוצא ורועות. וכן כתב לעולם הבא ונגש חורש בקוצר [עמוס ט]: **כאדם שמסיתין אותו.** אחרים וניסת על ידיהן: **בעבור הרעימה.** מה רעמים הללו לעולם אי אפשר בלא מטר כך היתה מתרעמת ומכעסת אותה כדי שתבקש רחמים עליה שיהיו לה ולדות: **אלא בלבו חטא.** שהיה מחשב בלבו על (פי) הבורא דברים אשר לא כן: **להפוך קערה על פיה.** להפוך יראת כל העולם. כלומר שאין דין אמת: **על דעתך כי לא ארשע.** כלומר בידך לבות בני אדם אם היה בדעתך להטותו לטובה לא היה רשע ובעבור שלא עשית כן אין מידך מציל: **מי מעכב על ידך.** שלא תתן לרשע לב צדיק: **אף אתה תפר.** כשתאמר כן תפר **יראת** חטא מבני אדם ותגרע תפלה מהם: **ברא לו תבלין כנגדו.** מכלל שהכל בידי אדם יעסוק בתורה ויהיה צדיק: **כשמחזיר שדהו משובחת.** שהוא היה סבור שגזלה לו: **שדי שמיה עילויה.** שהיה מוציא שם שהיא קרובתו: **חברותא כלפי שמיא.** דקאמר ישאו יחד: **הנה נא ידעתי.** כשראה בבואה במים: **ויעש תעלה.** דפוס סילון לשטף המים:

ליקוטי רש"י

ויפשטו על הגמלים. זה לשון בזוז בו לפי מנהגם כל זמן שהם מהלכים נדבקים יחד והולכים במארב שלא יבינו בהם ויבריחו את המקנה וכשמגיעי' למקום המקנ' פושטים במרחב המקנה זה לכאן וזה לכאן לאסוף המקנה והמלאכים הללו שלוחי שטן היו וכדי להקניטו ולהחטיאו בישרוהו תחילה בהפסד מועט ואח"כ בגדול הימנו וכן כולם [איוב א, יז]. **מעבר המדבר.** מצד שני של מדבר והיה הבית מצד זה וזהו לשון עבר במקרא. **על הנערים.** בנים אבל אין צריך להזכיר הבנות [שם א, יט]. **ויגז.** תלש כמו (ירמיה ז) גזי נזרך ומתרגמינן תלישה וכמו (תהלים עא) ממעי אמי אתה גוזי מוצאי [שם א, כ]. **מבטן אמי.** האדמה אשר לוקחתי משם או אמי ממש. **וערום אשוב שמה.** לא בבטן הוא מדבר ומה שמה אל מקום תשובתו ועל שהוא מוכן לכך ולא יחליף החוק לשוב כי אם אל העפר לפיכך לא הוצרך להזכירו [שם א, כא]. **לא נתן תפלה.** לא שום שמץ ותפלות נתן על הקב"ה כמו (ירמיה כג) ובנביאי שומרון ראיתי תפלה. ולא נתן. להטיל תפלה ועול אל הקב"ה כמו (שמואל א יח) נתנו לדוד הרבבות ולי נתנו האלפים [שם א, כב]. **אי מזה תבוא.** אין מקום שתוכל לומר מזה אני בא [שם ב, ב]. **ובשעה שבקש אברהם לקבור את שרה.** לא מצא קרקע עד שקנה בדמים מרובים [שמות ו, ט]. **ועודנו מחזיק.** אוחז כמו (שמות ד) וישלח ידו ויחזק בו מחזיק באזני כלב (משלי כו). **ותסיתני בו.** הסיתני לבולעו כל לשון הסתה אינו אלא לשון המשכה שממשיך את האדם לעצתו [שם ב, ג]. **עור בעד עור.** אבר בפני אבר כן דרך בני אדם כשרואה החרב באה על ראשו מגין בזרועו לפניו וכ"ש כל אשר לאיש בממון יתן. **בעד נפשו.** בפני נפשו להגין לפי שזה יודע בנפשו שנתחייב לפיכך אינו מצטער על ממונו [שם ב, ד]. **אולם.** אבל. **אם לא על פניך.** תראה בו מיד שעל פניך יברכך [שם ב, ה]. **את נפשו שמור.** מכות מות הכהו ולכך נצטוה לשמור נפשו [חולין מג.]. **שטן לשם שמים.** נתכוון כדי שלא יהא נשכח לפני אלהינו זכותו של אברהם [איוב א, ז]. **כעסתה צרתה.** אשת בעלה פנינה. **גם כעס.** כעס אחר כעס תמיד לכך נאמר גם כעס קנית היום היתה אומרת לה כלום קנית היום מעפורת לבנך גדול או חלוק לבנך קטן. **בעבור הרעימה.** שתתאונן. ורבותינו אמרו (ב"ב טז.) בעבור הרעימה שתתפלל ולשם שמים נתכוונה [שמואל א, א, ו]. **בפפוניא.** שהיה דר בפפונא [קידושין לה.]. **ביד רשע.** כלפי שטן. **פני שופטיה יכסה.** מהכמין בדבר אמת. ואם לא איפוא. דבר אמת דבר זה מי הוא המכלה את התמימים [איוב ט, כד]. **על דעתך.** יודע אתה [שם י, ז]. **אף אתה.** כל שכן אתה שתכס מאוד אתה תפר יראה במרבית דבריך ותגרע שיחה כמו כי יגרע נטפי מים (איוב לו) וכמו ותגרע אליך חכמה [שם טו, ד].

[המשך בעמוד ב']

SAID TO [R' ELIEZER]: לֹא דִּבֵּר אִיּוֹב אֶלָּא כְּלַפֵּי שָׂטָן – **JOB WAS REFERRING ONLY TO THE SATAN.**

A statement by Job that is blasphemous:

"עַל־דַּעְתְּךָ כִּי־לֹא אֶרְשָׁע וְאֵין מִיָּדְךָ מַצִּיל", – [Job said to God:] ***Were it Your intention, I would not be wicked; none can save from Your hand.***[23] אָמַר רָבָא – **Rava said:** בִּקֵּשׁ אִיּוֹב לִפְטוֹר אֶת כָּל הָעוֹלָם כּוּלּוֹ מִן הַדִּין – **Job sought to exempt the entire world from** God's **judgment.** אָמַר לְפָנָיו – **[Job] said before [God],** רִבּוֹנוֹ שֶׁל עוֹלָם – **"Master of the Universe!** בָּרָאתָ שׁוֹר פַּרְסוֹתָיו סְדוּקוֹת – **You created an ox with split hooves.** בָּרָאתָ חֲמוֹר פַּרְסוֹתָיו קְלוּטוֹת – **You created an ass with closed hooves.**[24] I.e. you determine whether or not an animal is kosher. בָּרָאתָ גַּן עֵדֶן בָּרָאתָ גֵּיהִנֹּם – **You created** ***Gan Eden*** and **You created** ***Gehinnom.*** בָּרָאתָ צַדִּיקִים בָּרָאתָ רְשָׁעִים – **You created righteous people** and **You created wicked people.** מִי מְעַכֵּב עַל יָדְךָ – **Who can stop You?** Those who sin are compelled to do so by Divine decree; therefore, they should be exempt from punishment."[25]

The Gemara records the answer given by Job's friends to this argument:

וּמַאי אֲהַדְרוּ לֵיהּ חַבְרֵיהּ [דְּאִיּוֹב] – **What did Job's friends answer him?** "אַף־אַתָּה תָּפֵר יִרְאָה וְתִגְרַע שִׂיחָה לִפְנֵי־אֵל", – ***Certainly, you will mitigate fear*** of Heaven ***and diminish prayers to God.***[26] For, if all is preordained, of what use is fear or prayer? But your argument is false, because בָּרָא הַקָּדוֹשׁ בָּרוּךְ הוּא יֵצֶר הָרַע – granted that **the Holy One, Blessed is He, created the Evil Inclination,** בָּרָא לוֹ תּוֹרָה תַּבְלִין – **He created the Torah as its antidote.**[27] Hence, it is up to the individual whether he will be righteous or wicked.[28]

The Gemara digresses with an insight into Job's righteous character:

דָּרַשׁ רָבָא – **Rava expounded:** מַאי דִּכְתִיב – **What is** the meaning of **that which is written:**[29] "בִּרְכַּת אֹבֵד עָלַי תָּבֹא וְלֵב אַלְמָנָה אַרְנִן", – [Job said:] ***The blessing of the wretched was directed towards me and I brought joy to the widow's heart?*** "בִּרְכַּת אֹבֵד עָלַי תָּבֹא", – The phrase, ***The blessing of the wretched was directed towards me,*** מְלַמֵּד שֶׁהָיָה גּוֹזֵל שָׂדֶה מִיתוֹמִים – **teaches that [Job] would steal fields from orphans,** וּמַשְׁבִּיחָהּ וּמַחֲזִירָהּ לָהֶן – **improve them and** then **return them to [their owners],** thereby earning their blessings.[30] "וְלֵב אַלְמָנָה אַרְנִן", – The phrase, ***and I brought joy to the widow's heart,*** דְּכָל הֵיכָא דַּהֲוָה (אִיכָּא) אַלְמָנָה – teaches that **whenever there was a widow** דְּלָא הֲווּ נָסְבֵי לָהּ – **whom no one would marry,** הֲוָה אָזִיל שָׁדֵי שְׁמֵיהּ עִילָּוָהּ – **[Job] would go and associate his name with her,** claiming her as his relative.[31] וַהֲווּ אָתוּ נָסְבֵי לָהּ – **They would then come to marry her.**

The Gemara records several blasphemous statements made by Job:

"לוּ שָׁקוֹל יִשָּׁקֵל כַּעְשִׂי וְהַוָּתִי בְּמֹאזְנַיִם יִשְׂאוּ־יָחַד", – ***Would that my vexation be weighed, and my experience [placed] in the scale; let them be borne together.***[32] אָמַר רַב – **Rav**[33] **said:** עַפְרָא לְפוּמֵיהּ דְּאִיּוֹב – **Job's mouth** should be stuffed **with dirt!** חַבְרוּתָא כְּלַפֵּי שְׁמַיָּא – He talks as **a friend** would **to God.** He says to God: Let us decide which one of us is right![34]

Another blasphemous statement by Job:

"לֹא יֵשׁ־בֵּינֵינוּ מוֹכִיחַ יָשֵׁת יָדוֹ עַל־שְׁנֵינוּ", – [Job said to God:] ***There is no arbiter between us that might lay his hand on us both.***[35] אָמַר רַב – **Rav**[36] **said:** עַפְרָא לְפוּמֵיהּ דְּאִיּוֹב – **Job's mouth** should be stuffed **with dirt!** כְּלוּם יֵשׁ עֶבֶד שֶׁמּוֹכִיחַ אֶת רַבּוֹ – **Is there** such a thing as **a slave that calls his master to account?!** There is no agency that can act as arbiter of a dispute to which God is a party.

Another utterance by Job with which the Gemara finds fault:

"בְּרִית כָּרַתִּי לְעֵינָי וּמָה אֶתְבּוֹנֵן עַל־בְּתוּלָה", – ***I made a pact with my eyes; why would I contemplate a virgin?***[37] אָמַר רָבָא – **Rava said:** עַפְרָא לְפוּמֵיהּ דְּאִיּוֹב – **Job's mouth** should be stuffed **with dirt!** אִיהוּ בְּאַחֲרָנְיָתָא – He says that **he** did not gaze **at another woman** besides his wife, אַבְרָהָם אֲפִילוּ בְּדִידֵיהּ לֹא אִיסְתַּכֵּל – but **Abraham did not look even at his [wife].**[38] דִּכְתִיב: "הִנֵּה־נָא יָדַעְתִּי כִּי אִשָּׁה יְפַת־מַרְאֶה אָתְּ", – **As it is written** that Abraham told Sarah before they reached Egypt: ***Behold, now I know that you are a woman of beautiful appearance.***[39] מִכְּלַל דְּמֵעִיקָּרָא לֹא הֲוָה יָדַע לָהּ – The word *now* **implies that previously [Abraham] was unaware** of the beauty **of [Sarah].**

NOTES

23. *Job* 10:7. [This translation reflects Rava's teaching that follows.]

24. Split hooves is one of the distinguishing characteristics of a kosher animal (see *Leviticus* 11:3).

25. [As we learned above, the verse לֹא־חָטָא אִיּוֹב בִּשְׂפָתָיו, *Job did not sin with his lips,* teaches that Job's statement, אֶרֶץ נִתְּנָה בְיַד־רָשָׁע, *The land is delivered into the hand of the wicked one,* is not blasphemy, but a castigation of the Satan (see note 21). Later, however, Job made statements that were blasphemous (see *Ibn Ezra* to *Job* 2:10).]

26. *Job* 15:4.

27. Lit. spices. Study of the Torah drives away sinful thoughts, as the Gemara, *Kiddushin* 30b, teaches: *If this vile creature* [the Evil Inclination] *encounters you, draw it into a study hall: if it is stone, it will erode; if it is iron, it will shatter (Rashi).*

28. The principle that man has free will and can decide his own spiritual standing is alluded to by the verse's use of the second-person construct: *you will mitigate fear etc.* That is to say: *You* can do it, for it is within your power (*Maharsha*).

29. *Job* 29:13.

30. According to this interpretation, אוֹבֵד (lit. lost one) means one who thought he had lost his field (*Rashi*). It is clear that Job did not actually steal the fields for, as taught in *Bava Metzia* 61b, stealing is forbidden even where it is intended for the benefit of the owner. The orphans were merely under the impression that their fields had been stolen (*Rabbeinu Gershom;* cf. *Yad Ramah* and *Pnei Shlomo*).

31. *Rashi's* first explanation. Alternatively: Job would speak out [in praise of] the widow so that others would want to marry her (*Rashi*).

32. *Job* 6:2. According to the plain meaning of the verse, Job laments that if his sufferings would be placed in a weighing scale they would outweigh all the sand by all the seas in the world (see the following verse). Rava, however, interprets the verse as follows: If my sufferings were placed in one scale and my sins in the other, we would see which outweighs the other (see *Maharsha*).

33. According to an alternative version of the text, this statement is attributed to Rava (*Mesoras HaShas*).

34. Job talks to God like a person who contends with his [business] partner, saying, "Let us make a calculation and see which one of us owes the other" (*Rashi*; see note 25).

35. *Job* 9:33.

36. Alternative texts read "Rava" (see *Mesoras HaShas*).

37. Ibid. 31:1.

38. Presumably, Abraham saw Sarah before he married her, for the Gemara (*Kiddushin* 41a) teaches that it is forbidden to marry a woman without first looking at her, lest he see in her something objectionable. However, Abraham never gazed at Sarah during the intervening years and was unaware that she had retained her beauty (*Maharsha*).

[*Bach* deletes the expression עַפְרָא לְפוּמֵיהּ דְּאִיּוֹב, *Job's mouth should be stuffed with dirt,* for Job did not say anything improper. His statement merely indicated that he was not as great as Abraham. (See *Maharsha* for a justification of our text.)]

39. *Genesis* 12:11. Since they were descending to Egypt – a country steeped in immorality – God wished Abraham to realize the danger to Sarah. Therefore, he caused Abraham to notice her reflection (*Rabbeinu Gershom, Rashi* ad loc.).

מעין העולם הבא. כדכתיב (ירמיה לא) הרה ויולדת יחדו הריון ולידה ביום אחד הכי דרשינן ליה במסכת שבת (דף ל:): **הכי גרסינן במתניתא תנא יורד ומתעה ועולה ומרגיז נוטל רשות ונוטל נשמה.** [וה"פ] יורד למטה ומתעה את הבריות לחטוא ועולה למעלה ומרגיז את חמת המלך בהסטנותו נוטל ממנו רשות להרוג את החוטא מכיון שנתנו רשות כדכתיב ותסיתני בו: **צערו של שטן.** שהחקק לשמור את נפש איוב שלא תמות: **אלמא בדידיה קיימא.** ליטול את הנפש והזהירו שלא ליטלה: **בעבור הרעימה.** שתתרעם על שהיא עקרה ותתפלל: **להפוך קערה על פיה.** (ג) לעקור כל כבוד שחירף וגידף: **לפטור את כל העולם כולו.** מדינו של הקב"ה לומר שאנוסין הן ע"י הקב"ה שברא (ג) יצה"ר והכי קאמר על דעתך כי לא ארשע אם היית חפץ לא הייתי רשע: **בראת שור בפרסות סדוקות וחמור בפרסות קלוטות.** את זה טהרת ואת זה טמאת הכל בא על ידך אתה בראת כל סימני הטומאה: **בראת צדיקים.** ע"י יצר טוב: **בראת רשעים.** על ידי יצר הרע לפיכך אין ניצול מידך כי מי יעכב אנוסין הן החוטאין: **ברא לו תורה.** (ד) הן תבלין שהיא מבטלת את הרהורי עבירה כדאמר בעלמא (קדושין דף ל:) אם פגע בך מנוול זה משכהו לבית המדרש אם אבן הוא נימוח כו' הלכך לאו אנוסין נינהו שהרי יכולין להציל עצמן: **ברכת אובד.** שהיה סבור שהיה אובד את שדהו: **שדי שמיה עלוה.** אומר שהיא קרובתו או מדבר בה להשיאה: **חברותא כלפי שמיא.** מדבר לפני השכינה כאדם המתווכח לחבירו בא ונשקול מי חייב לחבירו: **מן הסערה.** לשון שיער כדקתני הרבה נימין בראתי באדם: **ממשמשות את הארץ.** עושות את הארץ כטיט:

מעין העולם הבא א) עוד זה מדבר וזה בא ויאמר אש אלהים וגו' ב) עוד זה מדבר וזה בא ויאמר כשדים שמו שלשה ראשים ויפשטו על הגמלים ויקחום וגו' ג) עוד זה מדבר וזה בא ויאמר בניך ובנותיך אוכלים ושותים יין בבית אחיהם הבכור ד) והנה רוח גדולה באה מעבר המדבר ויגע בארבע פנות הבית ויפול על הנערים וגו' ה) ויקם איוב ויקרע את מעילו ויגז את ראשו וגו' ו) ויאמר ערום יצאתי מבטן אמי וערום אשוב שמה ה' נתן וה' לקח יהי שם ה' מבורך ז) בכל זאת לא חטא איוב ולא נתן תפלה לאלהים ח) ויהי היום ויבואו בני האלהים להתיצב וגו' ט) ויאמר ה' אל השטן אי מזה תבא ויען השטן את ה' ויאמר משוט בארץ [וגו'] אמר לפניו רבש"ע שטתי בכל העולם ולא מצאתי כעבדך אברהם שאמרת לו י) קום התהלך בארץ לארכה ולרחבה כי לך אתננה א) ובשעה שבקש לקבור שרה לא מצא מקום לקוברה ולא הרהר אחר מדותיך יא) ויאמר ה' אל השטן השמת לבך אל עבדי איוב כי אין כמוהו בארץ וגו' ועודנו מחזיק בתומתו ותסיתני בו לבלעו חנם אמר רבי יוחנן אלמלא מקרא כתוב אי אפשר לאומרו כאדם שמסיתין אותו וניסת במתניתא תנא יורד ומתעה ועולה ומרגיז נוטל רשות ונוטל נשמה יב) ויען השטן את ה' ויאמר עור בעד עור וכל אשר לאיש יתן בעד נפשו יג) אולם שלח נא ידך וגע אל עצמו ואל בשרו אם לא ג) (על) פניך יברכך יד) ויאמר ה' אל השטן הנו בידך אך את נפשו שמור טו) ויצא השטן מאת פני ה' ויך את איוב וגו' אמר רבי יצחק קשה צערו של שטן יותר משל איוב משל לעבד שאמר לו רבו שבור חבית ושמור את יינה אמר ר"ל הוא שטן הוא יצר הרע הוא מלאך המות הוא שטן דכתיב טו) ויצא השטן מאת פני ה' הוא יצר הרע כתיב התם טז) רק רע כל היום וכתיב הכא (רק את נפשו שמור) [יז) רק אליו אל תשלח ידך] הוא מלאך המות דכתיב (רק) יד) [אך] את נפשו שמור א) אלמא בדידיה קיימא א"ר לוי שטן ופנינה לשם שמים נתכוונו שטן כיון דחזיא להקדוש ברוך הוא דנטיה דעתיה בתר איוב אמר חס ושלום מינשי ליה ג) לרחמנותיה דאברהם פנינה דכתיב יח) וכעסתה צרתה גם כעס בעבור הרעימה דרשה רב אחא בר יעקב בפפוניא אתא שטן נשקיה לכרעיה יט) בכל זאת לא חטא איוב בשפתיו אמר רבא בשפתיו לא חטא בלבו חטא מאי קאמר כ) ארץ נתנה ביד רשע פני שופטיה יכסה אם לא איפו מי הוא אמר רבא בקש איוב להפוך קערה על פיה אמר ליה אביי לא דבר איוב אלא כנגד השטן כתנאי ארץ נתנה ביד רשע רבי אליעזר אומר בקש איוב להפוך קערה על פיה אמר לו רבי יהושע לא דבר איוב אלא כלפי שטן כא) על דעתך כי לא ארשע ואין מידך מציל אמר רבא בקש איוב לפטור את כל העולם כולו מן הדין אמר לפניו רבונו של עולם בראת שור פרסותיו סדוקות בראת חמור פרסותיו קלוטות בראת גן עדן בראת גיהנם בראת צדיקים בראת רשעים מי מעכב על ידך ומאי אהדרו ליה חבריה [דאיוב] כב) אף אתה תפר יראה ותגרע שיחה לפני אל ברא הקדוש ברוך הוא יצר הרע ברא לו תורה תבלין ד) דרש רבא מאי דכתיב כג) ברכת אובד עלי תבא ולב אלמנה ארנין מלמד שהיה גוזל שדה מיתומים ומשביחה ומחזירה להן ולב אלמנה ארנין דכל היכא דהוה ה) (איכא) אלמנה דלא הוו נסבי לה הוה אזיל שדי שמיה עילווה והוו אתו נסבי לה כד) לו שקול ישקל כעשי והותי במאזנים ישאו יחד אמר ו) רב עפרא לפומיה דאיוב חברותא כלפי שמיא כה) לו יש בינינו מוכיח ישת ידו על שנינו אמר ז) רב עפרא לפומיה דאיוב כלום יש עבד שמוכיח את רבו כו) ברית כרתי לעיני ומה אתבונן על בתולה אמר רבא (א) עפרא לפומיה דאיוב איהו באחרניתא לא איסתכל אברהם אפילו בדידיה לא איסתכל דכתיב כז) הנה נא ידעתי כי אשה יפת מראה את מכלל דמעיקרא לא הוה ידע לה כח) כלה ענן וילך כן יורד שאול לא יעלה אמר רבא מכאן שכפר איוב בתחיית המתים כט) אשר בשערה ישופני והרבה פצעי חנם ח) אמר רבה איוב בסערה חרף ובסערה השיבוהו חרף דכתיב אשר בשערה ישופני אמר לפניו רבונו של עולם שמא רוח סערה עברה לפניך ונתחלף לך בין איוב לאויב בסערה השיבוהו דכתיב ל) ויען ה' את איוב מן הסערה ויאמר [וגו'] לא) אזר נא כגבר חלציך ואשאלך והודיעני אמר לו הרבה נימין בראתי באדם וכל נימא ונימא בראתי לה גומא בפני עצמה שלא יהו שתים יונקות מגומא אחת שאלמלי שתים יונקות מגומא אחת מחשיכות מאור עיניו של אדם בין גומא לגומא לא נתחלף לי בין איוב לאויב נתחלף לי לב) מי פלג לשטף תעלה [וגו'] הרבה טיפין בראתי בעבים וכל טיפה וטיפה בראתי לה דפוס בפני עצמה כדי שלא יהו שתי טיפין יוצאות מדפוס אחד שאלמלי שתי טיפין יוצאות מדפוס אחד מטשטשות את הארץ ואינה מוציאה פירות בין טיפה לטיפה לא נתחלף לי בין איוב לאויב נתחלף לי מאי משמע דהאי תעלה לישנא דדפוס היא אמר רבה בר שילא דכתיב לג) ויעש תעלה כבית סאתים זרע לב) ודרך לחזיז קולות הרבה קולות בראתי בעבים וכל קול וקול בראתי לו שביל בפני עצמו כדי שלא יהו שתי קולות יוצאות משביל אחד שאלמלי שתי קולות יוצאות משביל אחד מחריבין את כל העולם בין קול לקול לא נתחלף לי בין איוב לאויב נתחלף לי לד) הידעת עת לדת יעלי סלע חולל אילות תשמור יעלה זו אכזרית על בניה בשעה שכורעת

מלא קרקע עד שקנה בדמים מרובים [שמות ו, ט]. **ועודנו מחזיק.** אוחז כמו (שמות ד) וישלח ידו ויחזק בו מחזיק באזני כלב (משלי כו). **ותסיתני בו.** הסיתני לבולעו כל לשון הסתה אינו אלא לשון המשכה שממשיך את האדם לעצתו [שם ב, ג]. **עור בעד עור.** אבר בפני אבר כן דרך בני אדם כשרואה החרב באה על ראשו מגין בזרועו לפניו וכ"ש כל אשר לאיש בממון יתן. **בעד נפשו.** בפני נפשו להגין לפי שזה יודע בנפשו שנתחייב לפיכך אינו מצטער על ממונו [שם ב, ד]. **אולם.** אבל. **אם לא על פניך.** תראה בו מיד שעל פניך יברכך [שם ב, ה]. **את נפשו שמור.** מכות מות הכהו ולכך נצטוה לשמור נפשו [חולין מג.]. **שטן לשם שמים.** נתכוון כדי שלא יהא נשכח לפני אלהינו זכותו של אברהם [איוב א, ז]. **כעסתה צרתה.** אשת בעלה פנינה. **גם כעס.** כעס אחר כעס תמיד לכך נאמר גם כעס קנית היום אומרת לה כלום קנית היום מעפורת לבנך גדול או חלוק לבנך קטן. **בעבור הרעימה.** שתתאונן. ורבותינו אמרו (ב"ב טז.) בעבור הרעימה שתתפלל ולשם שמים נתכוונה [שמואל א, א, ו]. **בפפוניא.** שהיה דר בפפונא [קידושין לה.]. **ביד רשע.** כלפי שטן. **פני שופטיה יכסה.** מהבחין בדבר אמת. ואם לא איפוא. דבר אמת דבר זה מי הוא המכלה את התמימים [איוב ט, כד]. **על דעתך.** יודע אתה [שם י, ז]. **אף אתה.** כל שכן אתה שתכסה מאוד אתה תפר יראה במרבית דבריך ותגרע שיחה כמו כי יגרע נטפי מים (איוב לו) וכמו ותגרע אליך חכמה [שם טו, ד].

[המשך בעמוד ב']

רבינו גרשום

מעין העולם הבא. שלאלתר תיכף לחרישה היו רועות על ידיהן מיד והיה עשב יוצא ורועות. וכן כתב לעולם הבא ונגש חורש בקוצר [עמוס ט]: **כאדם שמסיתין אותו.** אחרים וניסת על ידיהן: **בעבור הרעימה.** מה רעמים הללו לעולם אי אפשר בלא מטר כך היתה מתרעמת ומכעסת אותה כדי שתבקש רחמים עליה שיהיו לה ולדות: **אלא בלבו חטא.** שהיה מחשב בלבו על (פי) הבורא דברים אשר לא כן: **להפוך קערה על פיה.** להפוך יראת כל העולם. כלומר שאין דין אמת: **על דעתך כי לא ארשע.** כלומר בידך לבות בני אדם אם היה בדעתך להטותו לטובה לא היה רשע ובעבור שלא עשית כן אין מידך מציל: **מי מעכב על ידך.** שלא תתן לרשע לב צדיק: **אף אתה תפר.** כשתאמר כן תפר יראת חטא מבני אדם ותגרע תפלה מהם: **ברא לו תבלין כנגדו.** מכלל שהכל בידי אדם יעסוק בתורה ויהיה צדיק: **כשמחזיר שדהו משובחת.** שהוא היה סבור שגזלה לו: **שדי שמיה עילויה.** שהיה מוציא שם שהיא קרובתו: **חברותא כלפי שמיא.** דקאמר ישאו יחד: **הנה נא ידעתי.** כשראה בבואה במים: **ויעש תעלה.** דפוס סילון לשטף המים:

ליקוטי רש"י

ויפשטו על הגמלים. זה לשון בזוז בו לפי מנהגם כל זמן שהם מהלכים נדבקים יחד והולכים במארב שלא יכירו בהם ויבריחו את המקנה וכשמגיעי' למקום המקנ' פושטים במרחב המקנה זה לכאן וזה לכאן לאסוף המקנה והמלאכים הללו שלוחי שטן היו וכדי להקניטו ולהחטיאו בישרוהו תחילה בהפסד מועט ואח"כ בגדול הימנו וכן כולם [איוב א, יז]. **מעבר המדבר.** מצד שני של מדבר והיה הבית מצד זה וזהו לשון עבר במקרא. **על הנערים.** בניו אבל אין צריך להזכיר הבנות [שם א, יט]. **ויגז.** תלש כמו (ירמיה ז) גזי נזרך ומתרגמינן תלישה וכמו (תהלים עא) ממעי אמי אתה גוזי מושכי [שם א, כ]. **מבטן אמי.** האדמה אשר לוקחתי משם או אמי ממש. **וערום אשוב שמה.** לא בבטן הוא מדבר ומה שמה אל מקום תשובתו ועל שהוא מוכן לכך ולא יחליף החוק לשוב כי אם אל העפר לפיכך לא הוצרך להזכירו [שם א, כא]. **לא נתן תפלה.** לא שום שמץ ותפלות נתן על הקב"ה כמו (ירמיה כג) ובנביאי שומרון ראיתי תפלה. ולא נתן. להטיל תפלה ועול אל הקב"ה כמו (שמואל א יח) נתנו לדוד הרבבות ולי נתנו האלפים [שם א, כב]. **אי מזה תבוא.** איה מקום שתוכל לומר מזה אני בא [שם ב, ב]. **ובשעה שבקש אברהם לקבור את שרה.** לא

מסורת הש"ס

א) [סנהדרין דף קיא.], ב) [נ"ל אל], ג) [ס"א לרחימותיה], ד) [קדושין ל:], ה) [בע"י ליתא], ו) נ"א רבא, ז) [בספרים שלפנינו כתיב לא בא"ל], ח) נ"א רבא, ט) [נדה נב.] [ושם איתא רבא], י) עי' תוס' ע"ז יז: ד"ה מעות:

הגהות הב"ח

(א) גמ' אמר רבא איהו באחרניתא לא אסתכל אברהם אפי' בדידיה כצ"ל ותיבות עפרא לפומיה דאיוב נמחק: (ב) רש"י ד"ה להפוך קערה על פיה כלומר לעקור: (ג) ד"ה לפטור וכו' שברא להם יצה"ר: (ד) ד"ה בראת לו תורה תבלין כצ"ל ותיבת הן נמחק:

הגהות מהר"ב רנשבורג

א] גמרא אלמא בדידיה קיימא מילתא כצ"ל:

תורה אור השלם

א) עוֹד זֶה מְדַבֵּר וְזֶה בָּא וַיֹּאמַר אֵשׁ אֱלֹהִים נָפְלָה מִן הַשָּׁמַיִם וַתִּבְעַר בַּצֹּאן וּבַנְּעָרִים וַתֹּאכְלֵם וָאִמָּלְטָה רַק אֲנִי לְבַדִּי לְהַגִּיד לָךְ: [איוב א, טז]

ב) עוֹד זֶה מְדַבֵּר וְזֶה בָּא וַיֹּאמַר כַּשְׂדִּים שָׂמוּ שְׁלֹשָׁה רָאשִׁים וַיִּפְשְׁטוּ עַל הַגְּמַלִּים וַיִּקָּחוּם וְאֶת הַנְּעָרִים הִכּוּ לְפִי חָרֶב וָאִמָּלְטָה רַק אֲנִי לְבַדִּי לְהַגִּיד לָךְ: [איוב א, יז]

ג) עַד זֶה מְדַבֵּר וְזֶה בָּא וַיֹּאמַר בָּנֶיךָ וּבְנוֹתֶיךָ אֹכְלִים וְשֹׁתִים יַיִן בְּבֵית אֲחִיהֶם הַבְּכוֹר: [איוב א, יח]

ד) וְהִנֵּה רוּחַ גְּדוֹלָה בָּאָה מֵעֵבֶר הַמִּדְבָּר וַיִּגַּע בְּאַרְבַּע פִּנּוֹת הַבַּיִת וַיִּפֹּל עַל הַנְּעָרִים וַיָּמוּתוּ וָאִמָּלְטָה רַק אֲנִי לְבַדִּי לְהַגִּיד לָךְ: [איוב א, יט]

ה) וַיָּקָם אִיּוֹב וַיִּקְרַע אֶת מְעִלוֹ וַיָּגָז אֶת רֹאשׁוֹ וַיִּפֹּל אַרְצָה וַיִּשְׁתָּחוּ: [איוב א, כ]

ו) וַיֹּאמֶר עָרֹם יָצָאתִי מִבֶּטֶן אִמִּי וְעָרֹם אָשׁוּב שָׁמָה יְיָ נָתַן וַייָ לָקָח יְהִי שֵׁם יְיָ מְבֹרָךְ: [איוב א, כא]

ז) בְּכָל זֹאת לֹא חָטָא אִיּוֹב וְלֹא נָתַן תִּפְלָה לֵאלֹהִים: [איוב א, כב]

ח) וַיְהִי הַיּוֹם וַיָּבֹאוּ בְּנֵי הָאֱלֹהִים לְהִתְיַצֵּב עַל יְיָ וַיָּבוֹא גַם הַשָּׂטָן בְּתֹכָם לְהִתְיַצֵּב עַל יְיָ: [איוב ב, א]

ט) וַיֹּאמֶר יְיָ אֶל הַשָּׂטָן אֵי מִזֶּה תָּבֹא וַיַּעַן הַשָּׂטָן אֶת יְיָ וַיֹּאמַר מִשֻּׁט בָּאָרֶץ וּמֵהִתְהַלֵּךְ בָּהּ: [איוב ב, ב]

י) קוּם הִתְהַלֵּךְ בָּאָרֶץ לְאָרְכָּהּ וּלְרָחְבָּהּ כִּי לְךָ אֶתְּנֶנָּה: [בראשית יג, יז] יא) וַיֹּאמֶר יְיָ אֶל הַשָּׂטָן הֲשַׂמְתָּ לִבְּךָ אֶל עַבְדִּי אִיּוֹב כִּי אֵין כָּמֹהוּ בָּאָרֶץ אִישׁ תָּם וְיָשָׁר יְרֵא אֱלֹהִים וְסָר מֵרָע וְעֹדֶנּוּ מַחֲזִיק בְּתֻמָּתוֹ וַתְּסִיתֵנִי בוֹ לְבַלְּעוֹ חִנָּם: [איוב ב, ג] יב) וַיַּעַן הַשָּׂטָן אֶת יְיָ וַיֹּאמַר עוֹר בְּעַד עוֹר וְכֹל אֲשֶׁר לָאִישׁ יִתֵּן בְּעַד נַפְשׁוֹ: [איוב ב, ד] יג) אוּלָם שְׁלַח נָא יָדְךָ וְגַע אֶל עַצְמוֹ וְאֶל בְּשָׂרוֹ אִם לֹא אֶל פָּנֶיךָ יְבָרְכֶךָּ: [איוב ב, ה] יד) וַיֹּאמֶר יְיָ אֶל הַשָּׂטָן הִנּוֹ בְיָדֶךָ אַךְ אֶת נַפְשׁוֹ שְׁמֹר: [איוב ב, ו] טו) וַיֵּצֵא הַשָּׂטָן מֵאֵת פְּנֵי יְיָ וַיַּךְ אֶת אִיּוֹב בִּשְׁחִין רָע מִכַּף רַגְלוֹ וְעַד קָדְקֳדוֹ: [איוב ב, ז] טז) וַיַּרְא יְיָ כִּי רַבָּה רָעַת הָאָדָם בָּאָרֶץ וְכָל יֵצֶר מַחְשְׁבֹת לִבּוֹ רַק רַע כָּל הַיּוֹם: [בראשית ו, ה] יז) וַיֹּאמֶר יְיָ אֶל הַשָּׂטָן הִנֵּה כָל אֲשֶׁר לוֹ בְּיָדֶךָ רַק אֵלָיו אַל תִּשְׁלַח יָדֶךָ וַיֵּצֵא הַשָּׂטָן מֵעִם פְּנֵי יְיָ: [איוב א, יב] יח) וְכִעֲסַתָּה צָרָתָהּ גַּם כַּעַס בַּעֲבוּר הַרְּעִמָהּ כִּי סָגַר יְיָ בְּעַד רַחְמָהּ: [שמואל א א, ו] יט) וַיֹּאמֶר אֵלֶיהָ כְּדַבֵּר אַחַת הַנְּבָלוֹת תְּדַבֵּרִי גַּם אֶת הַטּוֹב נְקַבֵּל מֵאֵת הָאֱלֹהִים וְאֶת הָרָע לֹא נְקַבֵּל בְּכָל זֹאת לֹא חָטָא אִיּוֹב בִּשְׂפָתָיו: [איוב ב, י] כ) אֶרֶץ נִתְּנָה בְיַד רָשָׁע פְּנֵי שֹׁפְטֶיהָ יְכַסֶּה אִם לֹא אֵפוֹא מִי הוּא: [איוב ט, כד] כא) עַל דַּעְתְּךָ כִּי לֹא אֶרְשָׁע וְאֵין מִיָּדְךָ מַצִּיל: [איוב י, ז] כב) אַף אַתָּה תָּפֵר יִרְאָה וְתִגְרַע שִׂיחָה לִפְנֵי אֵל: [איוב טו, ד] כג) בִּרְכַּת אֹבֵד עָלַי תָּבֹא וְלֵב אַלְמָנָה אַרְנִן: [איוב כט, יג] כד) לוּ שָׁקוֹל יִשָּׁקֵל כַּעְשִׂי וְהַוָּתִי בְּמֹאזְנַיִם יִשְׂאוּ יָחַד: [איוב ו, ב] כה) לֹא יֵשׁ בֵּינֵינוּ מוֹכִיחַ יָשֵׁת יָדוֹ עַל שְׁנֵינוּ: [איוב ט, לג] כו) בְּרִית כָּרַתִּי לְעֵינָי וּמָה אֶתְבּוֹנֵן עַל בְּתוּלָה: [איוב לא, א] כז) וַיְהִי כַּאֲשֶׁר הִקְרִיב לָבוֹא מִצְרָיְמָה וַיֹּאמֶר אֶל שָׂרַי אִשְׁתּוֹ הִנֵּה נָא יָדַעְתִּי כִּי אִשָּׁה יְפַת מַרְאֶה אָתְּ: [בראשית יב, יא] כח) כָּלָה עָנָן וַיֵּלַךְ כֵּן יוֹרֵד שְׁאוֹל לֹא יַעֲלֶה: [איוב ז, ט] כט) אֲשֶׁר בִּשְׂעָרָה יְשׁוּפֵנִי וְהִרְבָּה פְצָעַי חִנָּם: [איוב ט, יז] ל) וַיַּעַן יְיָ אֶת אִיּוֹב מִן הַסְּעָרָה וַיֹּאמַר: [איוב לח, א] לא) אֱזָר נָא כְגֶבֶר חֲלָצֶיךָ וְאֶשְׁאָלְךָ וְהוֹדִיעֵנִי: [איוב לח, ג] לב) מִי פִלַּג לַשֶּׁטֶף תְּעָלָה וְדֶרֶךְ לַחֲזִיז קֹלוֹת: [איוב לח, כה] לג) וַיִּבְנֶה אֶת הָאֲבָנִים מִזְבֵּחַ בְּשֵׁם יְיָ וַיַּעַשׂ תְּעָלָה כְּבֵית סָאתַיִם זֶרַע סָבִיב לַמִּזְבֵּחַ: [מלכים א יח, לב] לד) הֲיָדַעְתָּ עֵת לֶדֶת יַעֲלֵי סָלַע חֹלֵל אַיָּלוֹת תִּשְׁמֹר: [איוב לט, א]

Another blasphemous statement by Job: ,,כָּלָה עָנָן וַיֵּלַךְ כֵּן יוֹרֵד שְׁאוֹל לֹא יַעֲלֶה" – ***As a cloud dissipates and is gone, so one who goes down to the grave will not rise.***[40] אָמַר רָבָא – **Rava said:** מִכָּאן שֶׁכָּפַר אִיּוֹב בִּתְחִיַּית הַמֵּתִים – **From here** we see **that Job denied** the doctrine of **the Resurrection of the Dead.**

Another blasphemous utterance by Job: ,,אֲשֶׁר־בִּשְׂעָרָה יְשׁוּפֵנִי וְהִרְבָּה פְצָעַי חִנָּם" – ***For He has shattered me with a whirlwind (s'arah), multiplied my wounds for no reason.***[41] אָמַר רַבָּה – **Rabbah**[42] **said:** אִיּוֹב בִּסְעָרָה חֵרֵף וּבִסְעָרָה הֱשִׁיבוּהוּ – **Job angered** God **with** the word ***s'arah*** (whirlwind) **and he was answered with** the word ***s'arah.*** בִּסְעָרָה חֵרֵף – **He angered** God **with** the word ***s'arah,*** דִּכְתִיב: ,,אֲשֶׁר־בִּשְׂעָרָה יְשׁוּפֵנִי" – **as it is written:** ***For He has shattered me with a whirlwind*** (*s'arah*), which, on a homiletic level, alludes to the following: אָמַר לְפָנָיו – **[Job] said before [God],** רִבּוֹנוֹ שֶׁל עוֹלָם שֶׁמָּא רוּחַ סְעָרָה עָבְרָה לְפָנֶיךָ – **"Master of the Universe! Perhaps a whirlwind passed before You,** וְנִתְחַלֵּף לְךָ בֵּין אִיּוֹב לְאוֹיֵב – **and You confused** my name **Iyov** (Job) with the word ***oyev*** (enemy)."[43] Job suggested that God's punishment of him was a mistake! בִּסְעָרָה הֱשִׁיבוּהוּ דִּכְתִיב – **He was answered with** the word *s'arah,* **as it is written:**[44] ,,וַיַּעַן־ה' אֶת־אִיּוֹב מִן הַסְּעָרָה וַיֹּאמַר [וגו']" – ***Then God answered Job from out of the whirlwind (s'arah), saying* etc.** אֱזָר־נָא כְגֶבֶר חֲלָצֶיךָ וְאֶשְׁאָלְךָ וְהוֹדִיעֵנִי" – ***Gird up your loins like a warrior.** I will put questions to you, and you will enlighten Me.*

Basing himself on the similarity between the words סְעָרָה (whirlwind) and שְׂעָרָה (hair),[45] Rava interprets the phrase, God answered Job from out of the *whirlwind,* as an allusion to the following argument: אָמַר לוֹ – **[God] said to [Job],** הַרְבֵּה נִימִין בָּרָאתִי בָּאָדָם – **"I created many hairs on a person,** וְכָל נִימָא וְנִימָא בָּרָאתִי לָהּ גּוּמָא בִּפְנֵי עַצְמָהּ – **and for each and every hair I created its own hole,** שֶׁלֹּא יְהוּ שְׁתַּיִם יוֹנְקוֹת מִגּוּמָא אַחַת – **so that two hairs do not grow from one hole.** שֶׁאִלְמָלֵי שְׁתַּיִם יוֹנְקוֹת מִגּוּמָא אַחַת – **for if two hairs were to grow from one hole,** מַחֲשִׁיכוֹת מְאוֹר עֵינָיו שֶׁל אָדָם – **they would darken a person's eyesight.** בֵּין גּוּמָא לְגוּמָא לֹא נִתְחַלֵּף לִי – **I do not confuse one hole with another.** בֵּין אִיּוֹב לְאוֹיֵב נִתְחַלֵּף לִי – **Would I confuse *Iyov*** (Job) **with *oyev*** (enemy)?!"

God continues with a second example of His powers of precision: ,,מִי־פִלַּג לַשֶּׁטֶף תְּעָלָה [וגו']" – ***Who opened a channel for the rushing waters (t'alah)? [etc.]***[46] הַרְבֵּה טִיפִּין בָּרָאתִי בֶּעָבִים – God said, **"I created many drops of rain in the clouds,** וְכָל טִיפָּה וְטִיפָּה בָּרָאתִי לָהּ דְּפוּס בִּפְנֵי עַצְמָהּ – **and for each and every drop I created a channel of its own,** כְּדֵי שֶׁלֹּא יְהוּ שְׁתֵּי טִיפִּין יוֹצְאוֹת מִדְּפוּס אֶחָד – **so that two drops will not issue from a single channel.** שֶׁאִלְמָלֵי שְׁתֵּי טִיפִּין יוֹצְאוֹת מִדְּפוּס אֶחָד – **For if two drops would issue from a single channel,** מְטַשְׁטְשׁוֹת אֶת הָאָרֶץ – **[the resulting torrents] would turn** fertile **earth into clay** וְאֵינָהּ מוֹצִיאָה פֵּירוֹת – **and [the earth] would not yield produce.** בֵּין טִיפָּה לְטִיפָּה לֹא נִתְחַלֵּף לִי – **I do not confuse one drop with another.** בֵּין אִיּוֹב לְאוֹיֵב נִתְחַלֵּף לִי – **Would I confuse *Iyov*** (Job) **with *oyev*** (enemy)?!"

This interpretation is based on the translation of the word תְּעָלָה, *t'alah*, as channel: מַאי מַשְׁמַע דְּהַאי תְּעָלָה לִישָּׁנָא דִּדְפוּס הִיא – **How is it known that this** word, ***t'alah*,** signifies **"channel"?** אָמַר רַבָּה בַּר שִׁילָא – **Rabba bar Shila said:** דִּכְתִיב: ,,וַיַּעַשׂ תְּעָלָה כְּבֵית סָאתַיִם זֶרַע" – **For it is written:**[47] ***[Elijah] made a channel*** (*t'alah*) *whose area was* ***equivalent to the area required [to sow] two se'ahs of seed.***

A third example of God's powers of precision: ,,וְדֶרֶךְ לַחֲזִיז קֹלוֹת" – ***And*** who made ***a path for the clouds*** which carry ***the blasts of thunder?***[48] הַרְבֵּה קוֹלוֹת בָּרָאתִי בֶּעָבִים – God said, **"I created many thunderclaps in the clouds,** וְכָל קוֹל וְקוֹל בָּרָאתִי לוֹ שְׁבִיל בִּפְנֵי עַצְמוֹ – **and for each and every thunderclap I created its own path,** כְּדֵי שֶׁלֹּא יְהוּ שְׁתֵּי קוֹלוֹת יוֹצְאוֹת מִשְּׁבִיל אֶחָד – **so that two thunderclaps should not go forth on the same path.** שֶׁאִלְמָלֵי שְׁתֵּי קוֹלוֹת יוֹצְאוֹת מִשְּׁבִיל אֶחָד – **For if two thunderclaps would go forth on the same path,** מַחֲרִיבִין אֶת כָּל הָעוֹלָם – **they would destroy the entire world.**[49] בֵּין קוֹל לְקוֹל לֹא נִתְחַלֵּף לִי – **I do not confuse one thunderclap with another.** בֵּין אִיּוֹב לְאוֹיֵב נִתְחַלֵּף לִי – **Would I confuse *Iyov*** (Job) **with *oyev*** (enemy)?!"

A fourth example: ,,הֲיָדַעְתָּ עֵת לֶדֶת יַעֲלֵי־סָלַע חֹלֵל אַיָּלוֹת תִּשְׁמֹר" – ***Can you fathom when the mountain-goat will give birth? Can you anticipate the pangs of the gazelle?***[50] יְעֵלָה זוֹ אַכְזָרִית עַל בָּנֶיהָ – God said, **"This goat is cruel to its offspring.** בְּשָׁעָה שֶׁכּוֹרַעַת – **When it squats**

NOTES

40. *Job* 7:9.

41. Ibid. 9:17.

42. In *Niddah* 52a the Gemara attributes this teaching to Rava (see notes 33 and 36).

43. By the transposition of the two middle letters, אִיּוֹב (Job) becomes אוֹיֵב (enemy).

44. *Job* 38:1,3.

45. (In homiletic exposition, the letters שׂ and ס are interchangable.)

46. Ibid. v. 25.

47. *I Kings* 18:32. The verse refers to the trench which Elijah filled with water during his confrontation with the priests of Baal on Mt. Carmel.

48. *Job* 38:25.

49. No creature would withstand the tremendous sound that would result (*Rashi* ad loc.).

50. Ibid. 39:1.

מעין העולם הבא א) עוד זה מדבר וזה בא ויאמר אש אלהים וגו' ב) עוד זה מדבר וזה בא ויאמר כשדים שמו שלשה ראשים ויפשטו על הגמלים ויקחום וגו' ג) עוד זה מדבר וזה בא ויאמר בניך ובנותיך אוכלים ושותים יין בבית אחיהם הבכור ד) והנה רוח גדולה באה מעבר המדבר ויגע בארבע פנות הבית ויפול על הנערים וגו' ה) ויקם איוב ויקרע את מעילו ויגז את ראשו וגו' ו) ויאמר ערום יצאתי מבטן אמי וערום אשוב שמה ה' נתן וה' לקח יהי שם ה' מבורך ז) בכל זאת לא חטא איוב ולא נתן תפלה לאלהים ח) ויהי היום ויבואו בני האלהים להתיצב וגו' ט) ויאמר ה' אל השטן אי מזה תבא ויען השטן את ה' ויאמר משוט בארץ [וגו'] אמר לפניו רבש"ע שטתי בכל העולם ולא מצאתי כעבדך אברהם שאמרת לו י) קום התהלך בארץ לארכה ולרחבה כי לך אתננה ובשעה שבקש לקבור שרה לא מצא מקום לקוברה ולא הרהר אחר מדותיך יא) ויאמר ה' אל השטן השמת לבך אל עבדי איוב כי אין כמוהו בארץ וגו' ועודנו מחזיק בתומתו ותסיתני בו לבלעו חנם אמר רבי יוחנן אלמלא מקרא כתוב אי אפשר לאומרו כאדם שמסיתין אותו וניסת במתניתא תנא יורד ומתעה ועולה ומרגיז נוטל רשות ונוטל נשמה יב) ויען השטן את ה' ויאמר עור בעד עור וכל אשר לאיש יתן בעד נפשו יג) אולם שלח נא ידך וגע אל עצמו ואל בשרו אם לא (על) פניך יברכך יד) ויאמר ה' אל השטן הנו בידך אך את נפשו שמור טו) ויצא השטן מאת פני ה' ויך את איוב וגו' אמר רבי יצחק קשה צערו של שטן יותר משל איוב משל לעבד שאמר לו רבו שבור חבית ושמור את יינה אמר ר"ל הוא שטן הוא יצר הרע הוא מלאך המות הוא שטן דכתיב ויצא השטן מאת פני ה' הוא יצר הרע כתיב התם טז) רק רע כל היום וכתיב הכא (רק את נפשו שמור) [יז) רק אליו אל תשלח ידך] הוא מלאך המות דכתיב (רק) [אך] את נפשו שמור א) אלמא בדידיה קיימא א"ר לוי שטן ופנינה לשם שמים נתכוונו שטן כיון דחזיא להקדוש ברוך הוא דנטיה דעתיה בתר איוב אמר חס ושלום מינשי ליה לרחמנותיה דאברהם פנינה דכתיב יח) וכעסתה צרתה גם כעס בעבור הרעימה דרשה רב אחא בר יעקב בפפוניא אתא שטן נשקיה לכרעיה יט) בכל זאת לא חטא איוב בשפתיו אמר רבא בשפתיו לא חטא בלבו חטא מאי קאמר כ) ארץ נתנה ביד רשע פני שופטיה יכסה אם לא איפו מי הוא אמר רבא בקש איוב להפוך קערה על פיה אמר ליה אביי לא דבר איוב אלא כנגד השטן כתנאי ארץ נתנה ביד רשע רבי אליעזר אומר בקש איוב להפוך קערה על פיה אמר לו רבי יהושע לא דבר איוב אלא כלפי שטן כא) על דעתך כי לא ארשע ואין מידך מציל אמר רבא בקש איוב לפטור את כל העולם כולו מן הדין אמר לפניו רבונו של עולם בראת שור פרסותיו סדוקות בראת חמור פרסותיו קלוטות בראת גן עדן בראת גיהנם בראת צדיקים בראת רשעים מי מעכב על ידך ומאי אהדרו ליה חבריה [דאיוב] כב) אף אתה תפר יראה ותגרע שיחה לפני אל ברא הקדוש ברוך הוא יצר הרע ברא לו תורה תבלין דרש רבא מאי דכתיב כג) ברכת אובד עלי תבא ולב אלמנה ארנין ברכת אובד עלי תבא מלמד שהיה גוזל שדה מיתומים ומשביחה ומחזירה להן ולב אלמנה ארנין דכל היכא דהוה (איכא) אלמנה דלא הוו נסבי לה הוה אזיל שדי שמיה עילווה והוו אתו נסבי לה כד) לו שקול ישקל כעשי והותי במאזנים ישאו יחד אמר רב עפרא לפומיה דאיוב חברותא כלפי שמיא כה) לו יש בינינו מוכיח ישת ידו על שנינו אמר רב עפרא לפומיה דאיוב כלום יש עבד שמוכיח את רבו כו) ברית כרתי לעיני ומה אתבונן על בתולה אמר רבא (א) עפרא לפומיה דאיוב איהו באחרניתא לא איסתכל אברהם אפילו בדידיה לא איסתכל דכתיב כז) הנה נא ידעתי כי אשה יפת מראה את מכלל דמעיקרא לא הוה ידע לה כח) כלה ענן וילך כן יורד שאול לא יעלה אמר רבא מכאן שכפר איוב בתחיית המתים כט) אשר בשערה ישופני והרבה פצעי חנם אמר רבה איוב בסערה חרף ובסערה השיבוהו בסערה חרף דכתיב אשר בשערה ישופני אמר לפניו רבונו של עולם שמא רוח סערה עברה לפניך ונתחלף לך בין איוב לאויב בסערה השיבוהו דכתיב ל) ויען ה' את איוב מן הסערה ויאמר [וגו'] לא) אזר נא כגבר חלציך אשאלך והודיעני אמר לו הרבה נימין בראתי באדם וכל נימא ונימא בראתי לה גומא בפני עצמה שלא יהו שתים יונקות מגומא אחת שאלמלי שתים יונקות מגומא אחת מחשיכות מאור עיניו של אדם בין גומא לגומא לא נתחלף לי בין איוב לאויב נתחלף לי לב) מי פלג לשטף תעלה [וגו'] הרבה טיפין בראתי בעבים וכל טיפה וטיפה בראתי לה דפוס בפני עצמה כדי שלא יהו שתי טיפין יוצאות מדפוס אחד שאלמלי שתי טיפין יוצאות מדפוס אחד מטשטשות את הארץ ואינה מוציאה פירות בין טיפה לטיפה לא נתחלף לי בין איוב לאויב נתחלף לי מאי משמע דהאי תעלה לישנא דדפוס היא אמר רבה בר שילא דכתיב לג) ויעש תעלה כבית סאתים זרע ודרך לחזיז קולות הרבה קולות בראתי בעבים וכל קול וקול בראתי לו שביל בפני עצמו כדי שלא יהו שתי קולות יוצאות משביל אחד שאלמלי שתי קולות יוצאות משביל אחד מחריבין את כל העולם בין קול לקול לא נתחלף לי בין איוב לאויב נתחלף לי לד) הידעת עת לדת יעלי סלע חולל אילות תשמור יעלה זו אכזרית על בניה בשעה שכורעת

רש"י

מעין העולם הבא. כדכתיב (ירמיה לא) הרה ויולדת יחדו הריון ולידה ביום אחד הכי דרשינן ליה במסכת שבת (דף ל:): הכי גרסינן במתניתא תנא יורד ומתעה ועולה ומרגיז נוטל רשות ונוטל נשמה. [וה"פ] יורד למטה ומתעה את הבריות לחטוא ועולה למעלה ומרגיז את חמת המלך בהסטנותו נוטל ממנו רשות להרוג את החוטא מכיון שנתנו רשות דכתיב ותסיתני בו: צערו של שטן. שהוחקק לשמור את נפש איוב שלא תלא: אלמא בדידיה קיימא. ליטול את הנפש והזהירו שלא ליטלה: בעבור הרעימה. שתתרעם על שהיא עקרה ותתפלל: להפוך קערה על פיה. (ב) לעקור כל כבוד שחירף וגידף: לפטור את כל העולם כולו. מדינו של הקב"ה לומר שאנוסין הן ע"י הקב"ה שברא (ג) יצה"ר והכי קאמר על דעתך כי לא ארשע אם היית חפץ לא הייתי רשע: בראת שור בפרסות סדוקות וחמור בפרסות קלוטות. את זה טהרת ואת זה טמאת הכל בא על ידך אתה בראת בו סימני הטומאה: בראת צדיקים. ע"י יצר טוב: בראת רשעים. על ידי יצר הרע לפיכך אין ניצול מידך כי מי יעכב אנוסין הן החוטאין: ברא לו תורה. (ד) הן תבלין שהיא מבטלת את הרהורי עבירה כדאמר בעלמא (קדושין דף ל:) אם פגע בך מנוול זה משכהו לבית המדרש אם אבן הוא נימוח כו' הלכך לאו אנוסין ניהו שהרי יכולין להציל עצמן: ברכת אובד. שהיה סבור שהיה אובד את שדהו: שדי שמיה עלווה. אומר שהיא קרובתו או מדבר בה להשיאה: חברותא כלפי שמיא. מדבר לפני השכינה כאדם המתווכח לחבירו בא ונשקול מי חייב לחבירו: מן הסערה. לשון שיער כדקתני הרבה נימין בראתי באדם: מטשטשות את הארץ. עושות את הארץ כטיט:

רבינו גרשום

מעין העולם הבא. שלאלתר תיכף לחרישה היו רועות על ידיהן מיד והיה עשב יוצא ורועות. וכן כתב לעולם הבא ונגש חורש בקוצר [עמוס ט]: כאדם שמסיתין אותו. אחרים וניסת על ידיהן: בעבור הרעימה. מה רעמים הללו לעולם אי אפשר בלא מטר כך היתה מתרעמת ומכעסת אותה כדי שתבקש רחמים עליה שיהיו לה ולדות: אלא בלבו חטא. שהיה מחשב בלבו על (פי') הבורא דברים אשר לא כן: להפוך קערה על פיה. להפוך יראת כל העולם. כלומר שאין דין אמת: על דעתך כי לא ארשע. כלומר בידך לבות בני אדם אם היה בדעתך להטותו לטובה לא היה רשע ובעבור שלא עשית כן אין מידך מציל: מי מעכב על ידך. שלא תתן לרשע לב צדיק: אף אתה תפר. כשתאמר כן תפר יראת חטא מבני אדם ותגרע תפלה מהם: ברא לו תבלין כנגדו. מכלל שהכל בידי אדם יעסוק בתורה ויהיה צדיק: כשמחזיר שדהו משובחת. שהוא היה סבור שגזלה לו: שדי שמיה עילויה. שהיה מוציא שם שהיא קרובתו: חברותא כלפי שמיא. דקאמר ישאו יחד: הנה נא ידעתי. כשראה בבואה במים: ויעש תעלה. דפוס סילון לשטף המים:

ליקוטי רש"י

ויפשטו על הגמלים. זה לשון בזוז בז לפי מנהגם כל זמן שהם מהלכים נדבקים יחד והולכים במארב שלא יבינו בהם ויבריחו את המקנה וכשמגיעי' למקום המקנ' פושטים במרחב המקנה זה לכאן וזה לכאן לאסוף המקנה והמלאכים הללו שלוחי שטן היו וכדי להקניטו ולהחטיאו בישרוהו תחילה בהפסד מועט ואח"כ בגדול הימנו וכן כולם [איוב א, יז]. מעבר המדבר. מצד שני של מדבר והיה הבית מצד זה וזהו לשון עבר במקרא. על הנערים. בניס אבל אין צריך להזכיר הבנות [שם א, יט]. ויגז. תלש כמו (ירמיה ז) גזי נזרך ומתרגמינן תלישה וכמו (תהלים עא) ממעי אמי אתה גוזי מושכי [שם א, כ]. מבטן אמי. האדמה אשר לוקחתי משם או אמי ממש. וערום אשוב שמה. לא בבטן הוא מדבר ומה שמה אל מקום תשובתו ועל שהוא מוכן לכך ולא יחליף החוק לשוב כי אם אל העפר לפיכך לא הוצרך להזכירו [שם א, כא]. לא נתן תפלה. לא שום שמץ ותפלות נתן על הקב"ה כמו (ירמיה כג) ובנביאי שומרון ראיתי תפלה. ולא נתן. להטיל תפלה ועול אל הקב"ה כמו (שמואל א יח) נתנו לדוד הרבבות ולי נתנו האלפים [שם א, כב]. אי מזה תבוא. איה מקום שתוכל לומר מזה אני בא [שם ב, ב]. ובשעה שבקש אברהם לקבור את שרה. לא מצא קרקע עד שקנה בדמים מרובים [שמות ו, ט]. ועודנו מחזיק. אוחז כמו (שמות ד) וישלח ידו ויחזק בו מחזיק באזני כלב (משלי כו). ותסיתני בו. הסיתני לבולעו כל לשון הסתה אינו אלא לשון המשכה שממשיך את האדם לעצתו [שם ב, ג]. עור בעד עור. אבר בפני אבר כן דרך בני אדם כשרואה החרב באה על ראשו מגין בזרועו לפניו וכ"ש כל אשר לאיש בממון יתן. בעד נפשו. בפני נפשו להגין לפי שזה יודע בנפשו שנתחייב לפיכך אינו מצטער על ממונו [שם ב, ד]. אולם. אבל. אם לא על פניך. תראהו בו מיד שעל פניך יברכך [שם ב, ה]. את נפשו שמור. מכות מות הכהו ולכך נצטוה לשמור נפשו [חולין מג.]. שטן לשם שמים. נתכוון כדי שלא יהא נשכח לפני אלהינו זכותו של אברהם [איוב א, ז]. כעסתה צרתה. אשת בעלה פנינה. גם כעס. כעס אחר כעס תמיד לכך נאמר גם כעס היתה אומרת לה כלום קנית היום מעפורת לבנך גדול או חלוק לבנך קטן. בעבור הרעימה. שתתאונן. ורבותינו אמרו (ב"ב טז.) בעבור הרעימה שתתפלל ולשם שמים נתכוונה [שמואל א, א, ו]. בפפוניא. שהיה דר בפפונא [קידושין לה.]. ביד רשע. כלפי שטן. פני שופטיה יכסה. מהכחין בדבר אמת. ואם לא איפוא. דבר אמת דבר זה מי הוא המכלה את התמימים [איוב ט, כד]. על דעתך. יודע אתה [שם י, ז]. אף אתה. כל שכן אתה שתכסה מאוד אתה תפר יראה במריבת דבריך ותגרע שיחה כמו כי יגרע נטפי מים (איוב לו) וכמו ותגרע אליך חכמה [שם טו, ד].

[המשך בעמוד ב']

מסורת הש"ס

א) [סנהדרין דף קיא.], ב) [ל"ל אל], ג) [ס"א לרחימותיה], ד) [קדושין ל:], ה) [בע"י ליתא], ו) ל"א רבא, ז) [בספרים שלפנינו כתיב לא באל"ף], ח) ל"א רבא, ט) [נדה נב.] [ושם איתא רבא], י) ע"י תוס' ע"ז יז: ד"ה מעות:

הגהות הב"ח

(א) גמ' אמר רבא איהו באחרניתא לא אסתכל אברהם אפי' בדידיה כל"ל ותיבות עפרא לפומיה דאיוב נמחק: (ב) רש"י ד"ה להפוך קערה על פיה כלומר לעקור: (ג) ד"ה לפטור וכו' שברא להם יצה"ר: (ד) ד"ה ברא לו תורה תבלין כל"ל ותיבת הן נמחק:

הגהות מהר"ב רנשבורג

א] גמרא אלמא בדידיה קיימא מילתא כל"ל:

תורה אור השלם

א) עוד זה מדבר וזה בא ויאמר אש אלהים נפלה מן השמים ותבער בצאן ובנערים ותאכלם ואמלטה רק אני לבדי להגיד לך: [איוב א, טז]

ב) עוד זה מדבר וזה בא ויאמר כשדים שמו שלשה ראשים ויפשטו על הגמלים ויקחום ואת הנערים הכו לפי חרב ואמלטה רק אני לבדי להגיד לך: [איוב א, יז]

ג) עד זה מדבר וזה בא ויאמר בניך ובנותיך אכלים ושתים יין בבית אחיהם הבכור: [איוב א, יח]

ד) והנה רוח גדולה באה מעבר המדבר ויגע בארבע פנות הבית ויפל על הנערים וימותו ואמלטה רק אני לבדי להגיד לך: [איוב א, יט]

ה) ויקם איוב ויקרע את מעלו ויגז את ראשו ויפל ארצה וישתחו: [איוב א, כ]

ו) ויאמר ערם יצאתי מבטן אמי וערם אשוב שמה ה' נתן וה' לקח יהי שם ה' מברך: [איוב א, כא]

ז) בכל זאת לא חטא איוב ולא נתן תפלה לאלהים: [איוב א, כב]

ח) ויהי היום ויבאו בני האלהים להתיצב על ה' ויבוא גם השטן בתכם להתיצב על ה': [איוב ב, א]

ט) ויאמר ה' אל השטן אי מזה תבא ויען השטן את ה' ויאמר משט בארץ ומהתהלך בה: [איוב ב, ב]

י) קום התהלך בארץ לארכה ולרחבה כי לך אתננה: [בראשית יג, יז] יא) ויאמר ה' אל השטן השמת לבך אל עבדי איוב כי אין כמהו בארץ איש תם וישר ירא אלהים וסר מרע ועדנו מחזיק בתמתו ותסיתני בו לבלעו חנם: [איוב ב, ג] יב) ויען השטן את ה' ויאמר עור בעד עור וכל אשר לאיש יתן בעד נפשו: [איוב ב, ד] יג) אולם שלח נא ידך וגע אל עצמו ואל בשרו אם לא אל פניך יברכך: [איוב ב, ה] יד) ויאמר ה' אל השטן הנו בידך אך את נפשו שמר: [איוב ב, ו] טו) ויצא השטן מאת פני ה' ויך את איוב בשחין רע מכף רגלו ועד קדקדו: [איוב ב, ז] טז) וירא ה' כי רבה רעת האדם בארץ וכל יצר מחשבת לבו רק רע כל היום: [בראשית ו, ה] יז) ויאמר ה' אל השטן הנה כל אשר לו בידך רק אליו אל תשלח ידך ויצא השטן מעם פני ה': [איוב א, יב] יח) וכעסתה צרתה גם כעס בעבור הרעמה כי סגר ה' בעד רחמה: [שמואל א א, ו] יט) ויאמר אליה כדבר אחת הנבלות תדברי גם את הטוב נקבל מאת האלהים ואת הרע לא נקבל בכל זאת לא חטא איוב בשפתיו: [איוב ב, י] כ) ארץ נתנה ביד רשע פני שפטיה יכסה אם לא אפוא מי הוא: [איוב ט, כד] כא) על דעתך כי לא ארשע ואין מידך מציל: [איוב י, ז] כב) אף אתה תפר יראה ותגרע שיחה לפני אל: [איוב טו, ד] כג) ברכת אבד עלי תבא ולב אלמנה ארנן: [איוב כט, יג] כד) לו שקול ישקל כעשי והותי במאזנים ישאו יחד: [איוב ו, ב] כה) לא יש בינינו מוכיח ישת ידו על שנינו: [איוב ט, לג] כו) ברית כרתי לעיני ומה אתבונן על בתולה: [איוב לא, א] כז) ויהי כאשר הקריב לבוא מצרימה ויאמר אל שרי אשתו הנה נא ידעתי כי אשה יפת מראה את: [בראשית יב, יא] כח) כלה ענן וילך כן יורד שאול לא יעלה: [איוב ז, ט] כט) אשר בשערה ישופני והרבה פצעי חנם: [איוב ט, יז] ל) ויען ה' את איוב מן הסערה ויאמר: [איוב לח, א] לא) אזר נא כגבר חלציך ואשאלך והודיעני: [איוב לח, ג] לב) מי פלג לשטף תעלה ודרך לחזיז קלות: [איוב לח, כה] לג) ויבנה את האבנים מזבח בשם ה' ויעש תעלה כבית סאתים זרע סביב למזבח: [מלכים א יח, לב] לד) הידעת עת לדת יעלי סלע חלל אילות תשמר: [איוב לט, א]

כבוחלא דרישקא במינה. אע"ג דכחול הוא שחור כדפירש בה"ג אוכמא אוכמא [חולין מו:] היינו דמיא לכוחלא ה"פ כי היכי דכוחלא דרישקא מקרין ומאיר משאר כוחלא כך היא היתה נאה משאר נשים וקרן הפוך לשון כי קרן עור פני משה (שמות לד) והשתא אתי שפיר הא דמייתי ותקרעי בפוך עיניך דכחול דומה לפוך שנותנין כחול בעין אבל לפירוש רש"י דגרס כי כורכמא דרישקא קשה לרשב"א א"כ מאי מייתי ותקרעי בפוך עיניך ויונתן תרגם נרד וכרכום רשק ג) וכרכום כפרים עם נרדים עם רישקא (שיר ד): **שכל** חולה שרואה אותה מיד מתרפא. וא"ת והא בימי אברהם אכתי לא היה חולי בעולם כדאמרי' בהשוכר את הפועלים (ב"מ דף פז.) דעד יעקב לא הוה חולשא ועד אלישע לא הוה דאיחלש ואיתפח ומצינן למימר דהכא בחולה של מכה איירי ור"ת ור"י מפרשים דעד יעקב לא הוה דאיחלש היינו חולי של מיתה מכאן ואילך הוה דאיחלש חולי של מיתה ולא הוה דאיתפח עד אלישע: **בא** על נערה המאורסה. ואם תאמר והלא לא נצטוו בני נח על נערה המאורסה כדאמרי' בפ' ארבע מיתות (סנהדרין דף נז: ושם ד"ה לנערה) בעולת בעל יש להן נכנסת לחופה ולא נבעלה אין להן ואומר ר"י דאף על פי שלא נצטוו מכל מקום מכוער הדבר כמו ושט את הבכורה אף על פי שאינו מצווה על כך:
שלשה

ללדת עולה לראש ההר כדי שיפול ממנה וימות ואני מזמין לה נשר שמקבלו בכנפיו ומניחו לפניה ואלמלי מקדים רגע אחד או (א) מתאחר רגע אחד מיד מת בין רגע לרגע לא נתחלף לי בין איוב לאויב נתחלף לי א) חולל אילות תשמור א) אילה זו רחמה צר בשעה שכורעת ללדת אני מזמין לה דרקון שמכישה בבית הרחם (ב) ומתרפה ממולדה ואלמלי מקדים רגע אחד או מאחר רגע אחד מיד מתה בין רגע לרגע לא נתחלף לי בין איוב לאויב נתחלף לי ב) [איוב] לא בדעת ידבר ודבריו לא בהשכל ג) (וכתיב ג) כי לא דברתם אלי נכונה כעבדי איוב) אמר רבא מכאן שאין אדם נתפס בשעת צערו ד) וישמעו שלשת רעי איוב את כל הרעה הזאת הבאה עליו ויבאו איש ממקומו אליפז התימני ובלדד השוחי וצופר הנעמתי ויועדו יחדו לבוא לנוד לו ולנחמו מאי ויועדו יחדו אמר רב יהודה אמר רב מלמד שנכנסו כולן בשער אחד ותנא בין כל אחד ואחד שלש מאות פרסי מנא הוו ידעי איכא דאמרי כלילא הוה להו ואיכא דאמרי אילני הוה להו וכיון דכמשי הוו ידעי אמר רבא היינו דאמרי אינשי או חברא כחברי דאיוב או ג) מיתותא ה) ויהי כי החל האדם לרוב על פני האדמה ובנות יולדו להם רבי יוחנן אמר רביה באה לעולם ריש לקיש אמר מריבה באה לעולם אמר ליה ריש לקיש לרבי יוחנן לדידך דאמרת רבייה באה לעולם מפני מה לא נכפלו בנותיו של איוב אמר לו נהי דלא נכפלו בשמות אבל נכפלו ביופי דכתיב ו) ויהי לו שבענה בנים ושלש בנות ויקרא שם האחת ימימה ושם השנית קציעה ושם השלישית קרן הפוך ימימה שהיתה דומה ליום קציעה שהיה ריחה נודף כקציעה קרן הפוך אמרי דבי רבי שילא שדומה לקרנא דקרש מחייכו עלה במערבא קרנא דקרש לקותא היא אלא אמר רב חסדא ככורכמא דרישקא במיניה שנאמר ז) כי תקרעי בפוך ה) רבי שמעון ברבי איתילידא ליה ברתא הוה קא חלש דעתיה אמר ליה אבוה רביה באה לעולם אמר ליה בר קפרא תנחומין של הבל ניחמך אבוך ו) [דתניא] אי אפשר לעולם בלא זכרים ובלא נקבות אלא אשרי למי שבניו זכרים אוי לו למי שבניו נקבות אי אפשר לעולם בלא בסם ובלא בורסי אשרי מי שאומנותו בוסמי אוי לו מי שאומנותו בורסי כתנאי ח) וה' ברך את אברהם בכל ז) מאי בכל רבי מאיר אומר שלא היתה לו בת רבי יהודה אומר שהיתה לו בת ח) אחרים אומרים בת היתה לו לאברהם ובכל שמה ר"א המודעי אומר ט) איצטגנינות היתה בלבו של אברהם אבינו שכל מלכי מזרח ומערב משכימין לפתחו רבי שמעון בן יוחי אומר י) אבן טובה היתה תלויה בצוארו של אברהם אבינו שכל חולה הרואה אותו מיד מתרפא ובשעה שנפטר אברהם אבינו מן העולם תלאה הקדוש ברוך הוא בגלגל חמה אמר אביי היינו דאמרי אינשי כ) אידלי יומא אידלי קצירא דבר אחר שלא מרד עשו בימיו דבר אחר ל) שעשה ישמעאל תשובה בימיו שלא מרד עשו בימיו מנלן דכתיב ט) ויבא עשו מן השדה והוא עיף ותנא אותו היום נפטר אברהם אבינו ועשה יעקב אבינו תבשיל של עדשים לנחם את יצחק אביו [ומ"ש של עדשים] אמרי במערבא משמיה דרבה בר מרי מה עדשה זו אין לה פה אף אבל אין לו פה דבר אחר מה עדשה זו מגולגלת אף אבילות מגולגלת ומחזרת על באי העולם מאי בינייהו איכא בינייהו לנחומי בביעי אמר רבי יוחנן חמש עבירות עבר אותו רשע באותו היום בא על נערה מאורסה והרג את הנפש וכפר בעיקר וכפר בתחיית המתים ושט את הבכורה בא על נערה מאורסה כתיב הכא ט) ויבא עשו מן השדה וכתיב התם י) כי בשדה מצאה הרג את הנפש כתיב הכא עיף וכתיב התם כ) אוי נא לי כי עיפה נפשי להורגים וכפר בעיקר כתיב הכא ל) למה זה לי וכתיב התם מ) זה אלי ואנוהו וכפר בתחיית המתים דכתיב ל) הנה אנכי הולך למות ושט את הבכורה דכתיב נ) ויבז עשו את הבכורה ושעשה ישמעאל תשובה בימיו מנלן כי הא דרבינא ורב חמא בר בוזי הוו יתבי קמיה דרבא וקא מנמנם רבא א"ל רבינא לרב חמא בר בוזי ודאי דאמריתו (ג) ט) כל מיתה שיש בה גויעה זו היא מיתתן של צדיקים א"ל אין והא דור המבול א"ל אנן גויעה ואסיפה קאמרינן והא ישמעאל דכתיב ביה גויעה ואסיפה אדהכי איתער בהו רבא אמר להו י) דרדקי הכי א"ר יוחנן ישמעאל עשה תשובה בחיי אביו שנאמר ס) ויקברו אותו יצחק וישמעאל בניו (ד) ודילמא פ) דרך חכמתן קא חשיב להו אלא מעתה ע) ויקברו אותו עשו ויעקב בניו מאי טעמא לא חשיב להו דרך חכמתן אלא מדאקדמיה אדבוריה ומדאדבריה שמע מינה תשובה עבד בימיו ת"ר שלשה הטעימן הקב"ה בעולם הזה מעין

דרקון. נחש: מכישה. נושכה: ומתרפה. לשון רפיון: שאין אדם נתפס. להתחייב על שהוא מדבר קשה מחמת צער ויסורין דקאמר לא בדעת ידבר לא אמר לא ברשע ידבר אלא לא בדעת: כלילי הוו להו. כתרים ובכל כתר שלשה פרצופים ואיש את שמו מחוקק על פרצופו וכשבאין יסורין על אחד מהן פרצופו משתנה וכן אילני: דכמשי. פלטיי"א: או חברא כחברי דאיוב. אם אין לו לאדם אוהבים נוח לו שימות: לרוב על פני האדמה ובנות יולדו וגו': רביה באה לעולם. כשנולדה בת לפי שממהרת להיות לו זרע: הוכפלו ביופי. ואין לך כפל טוב ממנו: שדומה ליום. ברה כחמה: כקציעה. מין בושם הוא: קרנא דקרש. מין חיה וקרניה משחירין כמו צבע: כורכמא דרישקא. כרכום של גן הגדל בגינה: במיניה. שהוא מעולה (ה) ממין שאר בשמים: איצטגנינות. חוזה בכוכבים: משכימים לפתחו. ליטול עצה ממנו: אידלי יומא. הוגבה שמש כשהחמה זורחת: אידלי קצירא. מיקל החולי: אבל אין לו פה. שהוא יושב ודומם: עדשים אין להן פה. כמו שיש לפולין ולשאר מיני קיטנית כמין סדק: לנחומי בביעי. אין להם פה אבל אינם מגלגלים כגלגל: וישט את הבכורה. וביזה את העבודה שהיתה בבכורות שט תרגום של בזיון מדוע הקילתני (שמואל ב יט) תרגום יונתן אשטתני:
בכל

רבינו גרשום

ומתרפא. רחמה ומרויח: מכאן שאין אדם נתפס על צערו. על מה שמדבר מכובד צערו דכתיב לא בדעת ידבר כלומר שאין דעתו מיושבת עליו מחמת צער: כי לא דברתם אלי נכונה כעבדי איוב. דברים הגונים חשיב ושאינן הגונין לא חשיב [לא] תפסו מכל מה שדבר כנגדו: כלילא הוה להו. כתר וחקוקין עליו ג' פרצופין של ג' חביריו וכשרואין שאחת מהן נשתנה פניה מיד היו יודעין שחבירו אין שרוי בנחת. ויש אומרים ג' אילנות היו נטועין בפרדס שכל אחד היה קורא לכל א' על שם חבירו ואם היה מייבש אחד מן האילנות שבו היו יודעין שאין שרוי בטובה אותו שנקרא (העירה) [האילן] על שמו: רביה. כלומר פריה ורביה שהנקבה מגדלת בניה: ולדידך דאמרת רביה. דדבר טוב הוא: שבענה. היינו ב' פעמים ז': קציעה. קדה: בושם. שקורין קר"ש: דקרש. חיה ששמה קרש: לקותא היא. ואינה יפה מפני שיש בה כמה גוונין: כי כוחלא. שהוא שחור הרבה מבהיק מאד: רישקה. בלע"ז ארינטי"ל: במיניה. שהוא משובח במינו: כורכמא דרישקא. קרוק"ו. איינטי"ל. מה אותו צבע יפה הרבה במינו כך היתה יפה בין שאר נשים: איצטגנינות גדולה. שהיה בקי (אותו צבע) הרבה במזלות והיו שואלין מה יארע להן: אידלי יומא. [בשחרית] כשהשמש זורח שם מונחת אותה אבן: אידלי קצירא. מיקל חולה מחליו ולערב מכביד לו: ד"א. מאי בכל: מה עדשה שאין לה פה. שאין לה שום ביקוע: לנחומי בביעי. דלמאן דאמר פה עדשה אין לה פה ביצים [נמי] אין להם פה ומנחמין בהן אבלים כמו בעדשים ולמאן דאמר מה עדשה זו מגולגלת בביצים אין מנחמין מפני שאינם מגולגלים כל כך כעדשים: לאלתר כשמת אברהם עבר אותו רשע ה' עבירות: היינו בכל. דלא מרד בימיו: ש"מ דעבד תשובה. דנהג ביה כבוד ליצחק ואדבריה מקמיה:

לעזי רש"י

פלטיי"א. פירוש כמושים (רש"י סוכה דף לא סוע"א), נקמטים (מוסף הערוך ערך כמש), נובלים (עיין רש"י ישעיה א, ל).

ליקוטי רש"י

ברכת אובד. אדם מת בעונו ונעזר. עלי תבא. כי היתומים זן את בניו ואת אשתו ורכושו אמרו שהיה גוזל שדה יתומים ומחזירה להם ומשביחה [illegible]

מסורת הש"ס

א) [ערכין טז: יומא כט.], ב) רש"ל מ"ז, ג) [תענית כג. ע"ש ברש"י], ד) סנהדרין ק: קדושין פב: ע"ש [פסחים סה. ע"ש], ה) לקמן קמא. ע"ש [תוספתא דקדושין פ"ה], ו) [לעמ"ש תוס' ברכות ט: ובסוטה יב. ובע"ז סד: ד"ה אחרים יתישב גם הכא], ז) [יומא כח:], ח) נ"א מרגלית, ט) נ"א משמיה דר' יוחנן, י) [עי' פרש"י בשבת דף קמה:], כ) [סנהדרין דף סט:], ל) [נ"ל ותרגם. יעב"ץ]:

הגהות הב"ח

(א) גמ' או מאחר רגע אחד מיד נופל ומת בין: (ב) שם ומתרפא ויולדת ואלמלי מקדים רגע: (ג) שם ודאי דאמריתו משמיה דר' יוסי כל מיתה שיש בה גויעה: (ד) שם יצחק וישמעאל בניו מכדי ישמעאל קשיש מיצחק מ"ט דקחשיב ליה ליצחק מקמיה ש"מ תשובה עביד ואדבריה ליצחק מקמיה ודלמא דרך חכמתן: (ה) רש"י ד"ה במיניה שהוא מעולה משאר כרכומין כצ"ל:

גליון הש"ס

גמרא ר"ש ברבי אתילידא. עיין מדרש רבה בראשית פ' כו: שם אידלי יומא. עי' נדרים דף מ ע"א בהרא"ש ד"ה סירגא דיומא: שם ישמעאל עשה תשובה. עיין סנהדרין דף קד ע"א ובתורת חיים שם ובתוס' ישנים יומא דף לח ע"ב ד"ה מעשה:

תורה אור השלם

א) הֲיָדַעְתָּ עֵת לֶדֶת יַעֲלֵי סָלַע חֹלֵל אַיָּלוֹת תִּשְׁמֹר: [איוב לט, א]
ב) אִיּוֹב לֹא בְדַעַת יְדַבֵּר וּדְבָרָיו לֹא בְהַשְׂכֵּיל: [איוב לד, לה]
ג) וַיְהִי אַחַר דִּבֶּר יְיָ אֶת הַדְּבָרִים הָאֵלֶּה אֶל אִיּוֹב וַיֹּאמֶר יְהוָה אֶל אֱלִיפַז הַתֵּימָנִי חָרָה אַפִּי בְךָ וּבִשְׁנֵי רֵעֶיךָ כִּי לֹא דִבַּרְתֶּם אֵלַי נְכוֹנָה כְּעַבְדִּי אִיּוֹב: [איוב מב, ז]
ד) וַיִּשְׁמְעוּ שְׁלֹשֶׁת רֵעֵי אִיּוֹב אֵת כָּל הָרָעָה הַזֹּאת הַבָּאָה עָלָיו וַיָּבֹאוּ אִישׁ מִמְּקֹמוֹ אֱלִיפַז הַתֵּימָנִי וּבִלְדַּד הַשּׁוּחִי וְצוֹפַר הַנַּעֲמָתִי וַיִּוָּעֲדוּ יַחְדָּו לָבוֹא לָנוּד לוֹ וּלְנַחֲמוֹ: [איוב ב, יא]
ה) וַיְהִי כִּי הֵחֵל הָאָדָם לָרֹב עַל פְּנֵי הָאֲדָמָה וּבָנוֹת יֻלְּדוּ לָהֶם: [בראשית ו, א]
ו) וַיְהִי לוֹ שִׁבְעָנָה בָנִים וְשָׁלוֹשׁ בָּנוֹת: וַיִּקְרָא שֵׁם הָאַחַת יְמִימָה וְשֵׁם הַשֵּׁנִית קְצִיעָה וְשֵׁם הַשְּׁלִישִׁית קֶרֶן הַפּוּךְ: [איוב מב, יג-יד]
ז) וְאַתְּ שָׁדוּד מַה תַּעֲשִׂי כִּי תִלְבְּשִׁי שָׁנִי כִּי תַעְדִּי עֲדִי זָהָב כִּי תִקְרְעִי בַפּוּךְ עֵינַיִךְ לַשָּׁוְא תִּתְיַפִּי מָאֲסוּ בָךְ עֹגְבִים נַפְשֵׁךְ יְבַקֵּשׁוּ: [ירמיה ד, ל]
ח) וְאַבְרָהָם זָקֵן בָּא בַּיָּמִים וַייָ בֵּרַךְ אֶת אַבְרָהָם בַּכֹּל: [בראשית כד, א]
ט) וַיָּזֶד יַעֲקֹב נָזִיד וַיָּבֹא עֵשָׂו מִן הַשָּׂדֶה וְהוּא עָיֵף: [בראשית כה, כט]
י) כִּי בַשָּׂדֶה מְצָאָהּ צָעֲקָה הַנַּעֲרָה הַמְאֹרָשָׂה וְאֵין מוֹשִׁיעַ לָהּ: [דברים כב, כז]
כ) כִּי קוֹל כְּחוֹלָה שָׁמַעְתִּי צָרָה כְּמַבְכִּירָה קוֹל בַּת צִיּוֹן תִּתְיַפֵּחַ תְּפָרֵשׂ כַּפֶּיהָ אוֹי נָא לִי כִּי עָיְפָה נַפְשִׁי לְהֹרְגִים: [ירמיה ד, לא]
ל) וַיֹּאמֶר עֵשָׂו הִנֵּה אָנֹכִי הוֹלֵךְ לָמוּת וְלָמָּה זֶּה לִי בְּכֹרָה: [בראשית כה, לב]
מ) עָזִּי וְזִמְרָת יָהּ וַיְהִי לִי לִישׁוּעָה זֶה אֵלִי וְאַנְוֵהוּ אֱלֹהֵי אָבִי וַאֲרֹמְמֶנְהוּ: [שמות טו, ב]
נ) וְיַעֲקֹב נָתַן לְעֵשָׂו לֶחֶם וּנְזִיד עֲדָשִׁים וַיֹּאכַל וַיֵּשְׁתְּ וַיָּקָם וַיֵּלַךְ וַיִּבֶז עֵשָׂו אֶת הַבְּכֹרָה: [בראשית כה, לד]
ס) וַיִּקְבְּרוּ אֹתוֹ יִצְחָק וְיִשְׁמָעֵאל בָּנָיו אֶל מְעָרַת הַמַּכְפֵּלָה אֶל שְׂדֵה עֶפְרֹן בֶּן צֹחַר הַחִתִּי אֲשֶׁר עַל פְּנֵי מַמְרֵא: [בראשית כה, ט]
ע) וַיִּגְוַע יִצְחָק וַיָּמָת וַיֵּאָסֶף אֶל עַמָּיו זָקֵן וּשְׂבַע יָמִים וַיִּקְבְּרוּ אֹתוֹ עֵשָׂו וְיַעֲקֹב בָּנָיו: [בראשית לה, כט]

[illegible] (תהלים קיט) לאן אובדות (ירמיה כ). ולב אלמנה ארנין. שהיה מטיל שמו על אלמנות לאמר קרובתי [illegible] כדי שיקפצו עליה מוכעים [איוב כט, יג]. והותי. שברי. ישאו יחד. עם משקל שכנגדם ואפי' הם חול ימים [illegible] מוכיח. דרשב"ר בלע"ז מרא' לכל א' מוכתו וחכותו. ישת ידו. משטר אימתו ויגוש. על שנינו. שלא [illegible] [שם לג]. ברית כרתי לעיני. שלא להסתכל באשת איש. ומה אתבונן על בתולה. מה לי להתבונן בה כך [illegible] לתת עין אפילו בפנויה שמא לאחר ימים תנשא ונמצאתי כרוך אחריה כך מפורש באבות דרבי נתן [שם לא א]. [illegible] אשה יפת מראה. מדרש אגדה עד עכשיו לא הכיר בה מתוך צניעות שבשניהם ועכשיו הכיר בה ע"י [illegible] א]. אשר בשערה. נתחלפה לורתי (ס"א שורתי) לפניו. ישופני. יכתתני ואכות אותו טחון (דברים ט) [illegible] פצעי. מכה המוציאה דם וליחה [איוב ט יז]. מן הסערה. מנה שערות שלך ואשיבך דברים כנגדן. מן [illegible] בסערה ישופני (איוב ט) ממנה אשיב לך כאשר תשמע בסוף הענין מי פלג לשטף תעלה גומא לכל שער [illegible] בסערה רפאהו כדמפרש בספרי [שם לח א]. כלומר משער הראש אני משיבך תשובה הרבה נימין בראתי באדם [illegible] נא כגבר חלציך. רמז לו שיתעורר מן חליו ויסוריו [איוב לח ג]. מי פלג לשטף תעלה. בערביא קורין [illegible] ושיער שבראש פלגתי לו תעלה גומא לינק ממנה שאילו שנים יונקות מגומא אחת מחשיכות מאור עיניו [illegible] נתחלפו לי בין איוב לאויב נתחלף לי חזהו מן הסערה ד"א לשטף טיפת גשם שוטף פילגתי לכל טיפה גומא בעבים שאילו יורדות ב' טפות מגומא אחת מטשטשות את הארץ ונעשי' טיט. ודרך לחזיז קולות. מי פלג [illegible] אחד אין הבריות סובלות את הקול [שם לח כה]. יעלי סלע. אשטנבו"ק ושונאה את ולדה ועולה לראש סלע גבוה כשכורעת לילד כדי שיפול לארץ וימות והקב"ה מזמן לו נשר ומקבלו בכנפיו. חולל אילות תשמור [illegible] אין הוולד יכול לצאת ובשעת לידתה אני מזמן לה דרקון ומכישה ברחמה ונפתח ואם מקדים ומאחר רגע מיד מתה ובין אותם רגעים איני מחליף ובין איוב לאויב נתחלף לי [שם לט א]. [ע"כ שייך לדף טז.] כי לא דברתם
דברתם אלי טענה נכונה כעבדי איוב שהרי הוא לא פשע בי כי אם על אשר אמר (איוב ט) תם ורשע [המשך בדף יז.]

לֵלֵדֶת – **to give birth,** עוֹלָה לְרֹאשׁ הָהָר – **it ascends to the top of a mountain,** כְּדֵי שֶׁיִּפּוֹל מִמֶּנָּה וְיָמוּת – **so that [its offspring] will fall from her and die.** וַאֲנִי מַזְמִין לָהּ נֶשֶׁר – **But I** [God] **prepare an eagle for it** שֶׁמְּקַבְּלוֹ בִּכְנָפָיו וּמַנִּיחוֹ לְפָנֶיהָ – **that catches [the falling newborn] in its wings and sets it before [its mother].**[1] וְאִלְמָלֵי מַקְדִּים רֶגַע אֶחָד אוֹ מִתְאַחֵר רֶגַע אֶחָד – **Now, if [the eagle] would [fly by] one moment earlier or one moment later,** מִיָּד מֵת – **[the newborn] would die instantly.** בֵּין רֶגַע לְרֶגַע לֹא נִתְחַלֵּף לִי – **I do not confuse one moment with another!** בֵּין אִיּוֹב לְאוֹיֵב נִתְחַלֵּף לִי – **Would I confuse** ***Iyov*** (Job) **with** ***oyev*** (enemy)?

A fifth example of God's powers of precision:

״חֹלֵל אַיָּלוֹת תִּשְׁמֹר״ – ***Can you anticipate the pangs of the gazelle?***[2] אַיָּלָה זוֹ רַחְמָהּ צַר – **The birth canal of this gazelle is** too **narrow** for its young to pass through. בְּשָׁעָה שֶׁכּוֹרַעַת לָלֶדֶת – So **when she squats to give birth,** אֲנִי מַזְמִין לָהּ דְּרָקוֹן – **I prepare a snake for her** שֶׁמַּכִּישָׁהּ בְּבֵית הָרֶחֶם וּמִתְרַפָּה (ממולדה) [וְיוֹלֶדֶת][3] – **that bites her in the birth canal, which becomes loose** as a result, **and [the gazelle]** then **gives birth.** וְאִלְמָלֵי מַקְדִּים רֶגַע אֶחָד אוֹ מְאַחֵר רֶגַע אֶחָד מִיָּד מֵתָה – **Now, if [the snake] would [bite] one moment earlier or one moment later, [the mother] would instantly die.** בֵּין רֶגַע לְרֶגַע לֹא נִתְחַלֵּף לִי – **I do not confuse one moment with another!** בֵּין אִיּוֹב לְאוֹיֵב נִתְחַלֵּף לִי – **Would I confuse** ***Iyov*** (Job) **with** ***oyev*** (enemy)?

The Gemara concludes its discussion of Job's blasphemous remarks with the following exoneration:

״[אִיּוֹב] לֹא בְדַעַת יְדַבֵּר וּדְבָרָיו לֹא בְהַשְׂכֵּיל״ – Scripture states: ***Job speaks without thought, his words lack deliberation.***[4] (וּכְתִיב: ״כִּי לֹא דִבַּרְתֶּם אֵלַי נְכוֹנָה כְּעַבְדִּי אִיּוֹב״) – **(And** furthermore **it is written:** ***You did not speak to Me properly as My servant Job [did].)***[5] אָמַר רָבָא – **Rava said:** מִכָּאן שֶׁאֵין אָדָם נִתְפָּס בִּשְׁעַת צַעֲרוֹ – **From here** we learn **that a person is not held** accountable for harsh words uttered **while he is in pain.**[6]

The Gemara embarks on a discussion about the three friends of Job:

״וַיִּשְׁמְעוּ שְׁלֹשֶׁת רֵעֵי אִיּוֹב אֵת כָּל־הָרָעָה הַזֹּאת הַבָּאָה עָלָיו וַיָּבֹאוּ אִישׁ מִמְּקֹמוֹ אֱלִיפַז הַתֵּימָנִי וּבִלְדַּד הַשּׁוּחִי וְצוֹפַר הַנַּעֲמָתִי וַיִּוָּעֲדוּ יַחְדָּו לָבוֹא לָנוּד־לוֹ וּלְנַחֲמוֹ״ – ***The three friends of Job heard of all this harm that had befallen him, and each man came from his place – Elifaz the Teimanite, Bildad the Shuchite and Tzofar the Na'amassite. They met together to go to commiserate***[7] ***with him and comfort him.***[8]

The Gemara expounds on the words *they met together to go etc.,* which imply that the friends met each other before they went to Job:

מַאי ״וַיִּוָּעֲדוּ יַחְדָּו״ – **What is** the meaning of ***they met together?*** אָמַר רַב יְהוּדָה אָמַר רַב – **Rav Yehudah said in the name of Rav:** מְלַמֵּד שֶׁנִּכְנְסוּ כּוּלָּן בְּשַׁעַר אֶחָד – **[This] teaches that all of them** simultaneously[9] **entered** Job's town **through the same gate.** וְתָנָא – This feat was all the more remarkable because as **a Tanna taught in a Baraisa:** בֵּין כָּל אֶחָד וְאֶחָד שְׁלֹשׁ מֵאוֹת פַּרְסֵי – BETWEEN EACH of the places where the friends lived was a distance of THREE HUNDRED *PARSAHS.*[10]

The Gemara explains how the friends heard of Job's plight:

מְנָא הֲווּ יָדְעֵי – **How did they know?**[11] אִיכָּא דְּאָמְרֵי כְּלִילָא הֲוָה לְהוּ – **Some say** that **they** [Job and his friends] each **had a crown,** on which the faces and names of the other three were engraved. When suffering befell one of them, the appearance of his face on the crowns of his three comrades would change. וְאִיכָּא דְּאָמְרֵי אִילָנֵי הֲוָה לְהוּ – **Some say** that **they** each **had** three **trees** that were named for each of the other friends. וְכֵיוָן דְּכָמְשִׁי הֲווּ יָדְעֵי – **When [the trees]** which bore the name of one of the friends **withered, they knew** that affliction had come upon him. אָמַר רָבָא – **Rava said:** הַיְינוּ דְּאָמְרֵי אִינָשֵׁי – **This [bears out] what people say:** אוֹ חַבְרָא כְּחַבְרֵי דְּאִיּוֹב אוֹ מִיתוּתָא – **"Either friends like those of Job or death!"**[12]

The Gemara shifts to a different subject, introduced here because of its connection to the saga of Job:

״וַיְהִי כִּי־הֵחֵל הָאָדָם לָרֹב עַל־פְּנֵי הָאֲדָמָה וּבָנוֹת יֻלְּדוּ לָהֶם״ – Scripture states: ***And it came to pass when mankind began to propagate*** (*larov*) ***on the face of the earth, daughters were born to them.***[13]

This verse associates the birth of daughters with the root רבה, *ravah.* The Gemara presents two interpretations of this association:

רַבִּי יוֹחָנָן אָמַר – **R' Yochanan said:** רְבִיָּה בָּאָה לָעוֹלָם – With the birth of daughters, **propagation** (*reviah*) **came to the world.**[14] רֵישׁ לָקִישׁ אָמַר – **Reish Lakish said:** מְרִיבָה בָּאָה לָעוֹלָם – With the birth of daughters, **conflict** (*merivah*) **came to the world.**[15]

Reish Lakish challenges R' Yochanan's view:

אָמַר לֵיהּ רֵישׁ לָקִישׁ לְרַבִּי יוֹחָנָן – **Reish Lakish said to R' Yochanan:** לְדִידָךְ דְּאָמְרַת רְבִיָּה בָּאָה לָעוֹלָם – **According to you**

NOTES

1. [The goat's hatred of her young is a temporary phenomenon, prompted by the pain of labor. Later, when the eagle places the child before her, she accepts it.]

2. *Job* 39:1.

3. Emendation follows the text recorded in *Ein Yaakov;* see also *Rashi;* cf. *Rabbeinu Gershom; Bach.*

4. *Job* 34:35.

5. Ibid. 42:7. [These words are parenthesized for they are deleted by *Maharshal.* See, however, *Rabbeinu Gershom* and *Maharsha.*]

6. The verse says "without thought" rather than "without wickedness" (*Rashi*). Job's words were indeed wicked; however, since they were uttered under duress, he was not punished for them (see 15b note 6).

7. Literally: to shake. In this context, to shake one's head in commiseration (see *Metzudos* ad loc.).

8. *Job* 2:11.

9. *Maharsha.*

10. A *parsah* (parasang) is 8,000 *amos* (between 2.4 and 2.9 miles). Hence, three hundred *parsahs* is approximately 800 miles.

11. Since they arrived at the gate simultaneously, it would seem that they heard of Job's travail simultaneously. Hence, this information must have reached them through some unconventional means, for had they heard by word of mouth, the news would not have reached all of them at the same time (*Maharsha*).

12. A person without friends is better off dead (*Rashi*).

There was a popular saying: אוֹ חַבְרוּתָא אוֹ מִיתוּתָא, *Either companionship or death!* (*Taanis* 23a). Here, the Gemara teaches that this maxim applies only to the degree of comradeship displayed by friends as loyal as those of Job who traveled 300 *parsahs* to comfort him (*Maharsha*).

13. *Genesis* 6:1.

14. The reproductive system of women matures earlier than that of men (*Rashi,* from *Sanhedrin* 69b).

Alternatively: Women are more essential than men for the propagation of humanity, for only one man is required to cause several women to conceive (*Maharsha*).

15. This can be explained on the basis of the Gemara, *Yevamos* 63a, which teaches that men who are unworthy are punished with antagonistic wives (*Maharsha*).

ככוחלא דרישקא במינה. אע"ג דכחול הוא שחור כדפירש בה"ג אוכמא אוכמא [חולין מז:] היינו דמיא לכוחלא ה"פ כי היכי דכוחלא דרישקא מקרין ומאיר משאר כוחלא כך היא היתה נאה משאר נשים וקרן הפוך לשון כי קרן עור פני משה (שמות לד) והשתא אתי שפיר הא דמייתי ותקרעי בפוך עיניך דכחול דומה לפוך שנותנין כחול בעין אבל לפירוש רש"י דגרס כי כורכמא דרישקא קשה לרשב"א א"כ מאי מייתי ותקרעי בפוך עיניך ויונתן תרגם נרד וכרכום רשך [ל] וכרכום כפרים עם נרדים עם רישקא (שיר ד):

שכל חולה שרואה אותה מיד מתרפא. וא"ת והא בימי אברהם אכתי לא היה חולי בעולם כדאמרי' בהשוכר את הפועלים (ב"מ דף פז.) דעד יעקב לא הוה חולשא ועד אלישע לא הוה דאיחלש ואיתפח ומצינן למימר דהכא בחולה של מכה איירי ור"ת ור"י מפרשים דעד יעקב לא הוה דאיחלש היינו חולי של מיתה מכאן ואילך הוה דאיחלש חולי של מיתה ולא הוה דאיתפח עד אלישע:

בא על נערה המאורסה. ואם תאמר והלא לא נצטוו בני נח על נערה המאורסה כדאמרי' בפ' ארבע מיתות (סנהדרין דף מ: ושם ד"ה לנערה) בעולת בעל יש להן נכנסת לחופה ולא נבעלה אין להן ואומר ר"י דאף על פי שלא נצטוו מכל מקום מכוער הדבר כמו ושט את הבכורה אף על פי שאינו מצווה על כך:

שלשה

דרקון. נחש: מכישה. נושכה: ומתרפה. לשון רפיון: **שאין אדם נתפס.** להתחייב על שהוא מדבר קשה מחמת צער ויסורין דקאמר לא בדעת ידבר לא אמר לא ברשע ידבר אלא לא בדעת: **כלילי הוו להו.** כתרים ובכל כתר שלשה פרצופים ואיש את שמו מחוקק על פרצופו וכשבאין יסורין על אחד מהן פרצופו משתנה וכן אילני: **דכמשי.** פלטיי"א: **או חברא כחברי דאיוב.** אם אין לו לאדם אוהבים נוח לו מיתה: **לרוב על פני האדמה ובנות יולדו וגו':** **רביה באה לעולם.** כשנולדה בת לפי שממהרת להיות לו זרע: **הוכפלו ביופי.** ואין בכל טוב ממנו: **שדומה ליום.** ברה כחמה: **בקציעה.** מין בושם הוא: **קרנא דקרש.** מין חיה וקרניה משחירין כמו צבע: **כורכמא דרישקא.** כרכום של גן הגדל בגינה: **במיניה.** שהוא מעולה (ה) ממין אחר בשמים: **איצטגנינות.** חוזה בכוכבים: **משכימים לפתחו.** ליטול עצה ממנו: **אידלי יומא.** הוגבה שמש כשהחמה זורחת: **אידלי קצירא.** מיקל החולי: **אבל אין לו פה.** שהוא יושב ודומם: **עדשים אין להן פה.** כמו שיש לפולין ולשאר מיני קטניות כמין סדק: **לנחומי בביעי.** אין להם פה אבל אינם מגולגלים כגלגל: **ושט את הבכורה.** וביזה את העבודה שהיתה בבכורות שט תרגום של בזיון מדוע הקילתני תרגום יונתן אשטתני (שמואל א ב יט): כל

ללדת עולה לראש ההר כדי שיפול ממנה וימות ואני מזמין לה נשר שמקבלו בכנפיו ומניחו לפניה ואלמלי מקדים רגע אחד או (א) מתאחר רגע אחד מיד מת בין רגע לרגע לא נתחלף לי בין איוב לאויב נתחלף לי א) חולל אילות תשמור א) אילה זו רחמה צר בשעה שכורעת ללדת אני מזמין לה דרקון שמכישה בבית הרחם (ב) ומתרפה ממולדה ואלמלי מקדים רגע אחד או מאחר רגע אחד מיד מתה בין רגע לרגע לא נתחלף לי בין איוב לאויב נתחלף לי ב) [איוב] לא בדעת ידבר ודבריו לא בהשכל ג) (וכתיב ג) כי לא דברתם אלי נכונה כעבדי איוב) אמר רבא מכאן שאין אדם נתפס בשעת צערו ד) וישמעו שלשת רעי איוב את כל הרעה הזאת הבאה עליו ויבאו איש ממקומו אליפז התימני ובלדד השוחי וצופר הנעמתי ויועדו יחדו לבוא לנוד לו ולנחמו מאי ויועדו יחדו אמר רב יהודה אמר רב מלמד שנכנסו כולן בשער אחד ותנא בין כל אחד ואחד שלש מאות פרסי מנא הוו ידעי איכא דאמרי כלילא הוה להו ואיכא דאמרי אילני הוה להו וכיון דכמשי הוו ידעי אמר רבא היינו דאמרי אינשי או חברא כחברי דאיוב או ג) מיתותא ה) ויהי כי החל האדם לרוב על פני האדמה ובנות יולדו להם רבי יוחנן אמר רביה באה לעולם ריש לקיש אמר מריבה באה לעולם אמר ליה ריש לקיש לרבי יוחנן לדידך דאמרת רבייה באה לעולם מפני מה לא נכפלו בנותיו של איוב אמר לו נהי דלא נכפלו בשמות אבל נכפלו ביופי דכתיב ו) ויהי לו שבענה בנים ושלש בנות ויקרא שם האחת ימימה ושם השנית קציעה ושם השלישית קרן הפוך ימימה שהיתה דומה ליום קציעה שהיה ריחה נודף כקציעה קרן הפוך אמרי דבי רבי שילא שדומה לקרנא דקרש מחייכו עלה במערבא קרנא דקרש לקותא היא אלא אמר רב חסדא ככורכמא דרישקא במיניה שנאמר ז) כי תקרעי בפוך עיניך • רבי שמעון ברבי איתילידא ליה ברתא הוה קא חלש דעתיה אמר ליה אבוה רביה באה לעולם אמר ליה בר קפרא תנחומין של הבל ניחמך אבוך [דתניא] אי אפשר לעולם בלא זכרים ובלא נקבות אלא אשרי למי שבניו זכרים אוי לו למי שבניו נקבות אי אפשר לעולם בלא בסם ובלא בורסי אשרי מי שאומנותו בוסמי אוי מי שאומנותו בורסי כתנאי ח) וה' ברך את אברהם בכל ט) מאי בכל רבי מאיר אומר שלא היתה לו בת רבי יהודה אומר שהיתה לו בת י) אחרים אומרים בת היתה לו לאברהם ובכל שמה ר"א המודעי אומר כ) איצטגנינות היתה בלבו של אברהם אבינו שכל מלכי מזרח ומערב משכימין לפתחו רבי שמעון בן יוחי אומר ל) אבן טובה היתה תלויה בצוארו של אברהם אבינו שכל חולה הרואה אותו מיד מתרפא ובשעה שנפטר אברהם אבינו מן העולם תלאה הקדוש ברוך הוא בגלגל חמה אמר אביי היינו דאמרי אינשי • אידלי יומא אידלי קצירא דבר אחר שלא מרד עשו בימיו דבר אחר • שעשה ישמעאל תשובה בימיו מנלן דכתיב ט) ויבא עשו מן השדה והוא עיף ותנא אותו היום נפטר אברהם אבינו ועשה יעקב אבינו תבשיל של עדשים לנחם את יצחק אביו [ומ"ש של עדשים] אמרי במערבא משמיה דרבה בר מרי מה עדשה זו אין לה פה אף אבל אין לו פה דבר אחר מה עדשה זו מגולגלת אף אבילות מגולגלת ומחזרת על באי העולם מאי בינייהו איכא בינייהו לנחומי בביעי אמר רבי יוחנן חמש עבירות עבר אותו רשע באותו היום בא על נערה מאורסה והרג את הנפש וכפר בעיקר וכפר בתחיית המתים ושט את הבכורה בא על נערה מאורסה כתיב הכא ויבא עשו מן השדה וכתיב התם י) כי בשדה מצאה הרג את הנפש כתיב הכא עיף וכתיב התם כ) אוי נא לי כי עיפה נפשי להורגים וכפר בעיקר כתיב הכא ל) למה זה לי וכתיב התם מ) זה אלי ואנוהו וכפר בתחיית המתים דכתיב ל) הנה אנכי הולך למות ושט את הבכורה דכתיב נ) ויבז עשו את הבכורה ושעשה ישמעאל תשובה בימיו מנלן כי הא דרבינא ורב חמא בר בוזי הוו יתבי קמיה דרבא וקא מנמנם רבא א"ל רבינא לרב חמא בר בוזי ודאי דאמריתו (ג) מ) כל מיתה שיש בה גויעה זו היא מיתתן של צדיקים א"ל אין והא דור המבול א"ל אנן גויעה ואסיפה קאמרינן והא ישמעאל דכתיב ביה גויעה ואסיפה אדהכי איתער בהו רבא אמר להו דרדקי הכי א"ר יוחנן ישמעאל עשה תשובה בחיי אביו שנאמר ס) ויקברו אותו יצחק וישמעאל בניו (ד) ודילמא י) דרך חכמתן קא חשיב להו אלא מעתה ע) ויקברו אותו עשו ויעקב בניו מאי טעמא לא חשיב להו דרך חכמתן אלא מדאקדמיה אדבוריה אדבריה ומדאדבריה שמע מינה תשובה עבד בימיו ת"ר שלשה הטעימן הקב"ה בעולם הזה מעין

רבינו גרשום

ומתרפא. רחמה ומרויח: **מכאן שאין אדם נתפס על צערו.** על מה שמדבר מכובד צערו **דכתיב לא בדעת ידבר** כלומר שאין דעתו מיושבת עליו מחמת צער: **כי לא דברתם אלי נכונה כעבדי איוב.** דברים הגונים חישב ושאינן הגונין לא חישב [לא] תפסו מכל מה שדבר כנגדו: **כלילא הוה להו.** כתר וחקוקין עליו ג' פרצופין של ג' חביריו וכשרואין שאחת מהן נשתנה פניה מיד היו יודעין שחבירו אין שרוי בנחת. ויש אומרים ג' אילנות היו נטועין בפרדס שכל אחד היה קורא לכל א' על שם חבירו ואם היה מייבש אחד מן האילנות שבו היו יודעין שאין שרוי בטובה אותו שנקרא (העירה) [האילן] על שמו: **רבייה.** כלומר פריה ורביה שהנקבה מגדלת בניה: **ולדידך דאמרת רבייה.** דדבר טוב הוא: **שבענה.** היינו ב' פעמים ד': **קציעה.** קדה: **בושם.** שקורין קו"ש: **דקרש.** חיה ששמה קרש: **לקותא היא.** ואינה יפה מפני שיש בה כמה גוונין: **כי כוחלא.** שהוא שחור הרבה מבהיק מאד: **רישקה.** בלע"ז ארייניט"ל: **במיניה.** שהוא משובח במינו: **כורכמא דרישקא.** קרוק"ו. אינטי"ל. מה אותו צבע יפה הרבה במינו כך היתה יפה בין שאר נשים: **איצטגנינות גדולה.** שהיה בקי (אותו צבע) הרבה במזלות והיו שואלין מה יארע להן: **אידלי יומא.** [בשחרית] כשהשמש זורח שם מונחת אותה אבן: **אידלי קצירא.** מיקל חולה מחליו ולערב מכביד לו: **ד"א.** מאי בכל: **מה עדשה שאין לה פה.** שאין לה שום ביקוע: **לנחומי בביעי.** דלמאן דאמר פה עדשה אין לה פה ביצים [נמי] אין להם פה ומנחמין בהן אבלים כמו בעדשים ולמאן דאמר מה עדשה זו מגולגלת בביצים אין מנחמין מפני שאינם מגולגלים כל כך כעדשים: **לאלתר** כשמת אברהם **עבר אותו רשע ה' עבירות: היינו בכל.** דלא מרד בימיו: **ש"מ דעבד תשובה.** דנהג ביה כבוד ליצחק ואדבריה מקמיה:

לעזי רש"י

פלטיי"א. פירוש כמושים (רש"י סוכה דף לא סוע"א), נקמטים (מוסף הערוך ערך כמש), נובלים (עיין רש"י ישעיה א, ל):

ליקוטי רש"י

ברכת אובד. אדם מת בעונו ונטרד. **עלי תבא.** כי הייתי זן את בניו ואת אשתו ורבותינו אמרו שהיה גוזל שדה יתומים ומשביחה ומחזירה להם ופשטיה דקרא אינו נראה כך שאין קרוי אובד אלא דבר שהוא עצמו אובד כמו ככלי אובד (תהלים לא) וכן תעיתי כשה אובד (תהלים קיט) לאין אובדות (ירמיה כ). **ולב אלמנה ארנין.** שהיה מטיל שמו על אלמנות לאמר קרובתי היא או אני אשיאנה כדי שיקפלו עליה תובעים [איוב כט, יג]. **והותי.** שברי. **ישאו יחד.** עם משקל שכנגדם ואפי' הם חול ימים יכבד ממנו [שם ו ב]. **מוכיח.** דרשני"ר בלע"ז מרא' לכל א' תוכחו וזכותו. **ישת ידו.** משטר אימתו וניגושו. **על שנינו.** שלא יחזק את הרפה [שם ט לג]. **ברית כרתי לעיני.** שלא להסתכל באשת איש. **ומה אתבונן על בתולה.** מה לי להתבונן בה כך היתה חסידותי שלא לתת עין אפילו בפנויה שמא לאחר ימים תנשא ונמצאתי כרוך אחריה כך מפורש באבות דרבי נתן [שם לא א]. **הנה נא ידעתי כי אשה יפת מראה.** מדרש אגדה עד עכשיו לא הכיר בה מתוך צניעות שבשניהם ועכשיו הכיר בה ע"י מעשה [בראשית יב יא]. **אשר בשערה.** נתחלפה גורמי (ס"א שורמי) לפניו. **ישופני.** יכתתני ואכות אותו טחון (דברים ט) מתרגמינן ושפית יתיה. **פצעי.** מכה המוליאה דם וליחה [איוב ט יז]. **מן הסערה.** מנה שערות שלך ואשיבך דברים כנגדן. מן הסערה שתרפתני אשר בסערה ישופני (איוב ט) ממנה אשיב לך כאשר תשמע בסוף הענין מי פלג לשטף תעלה גומא לכל שער ד"א בסערה הכהו בסערה רפאהו כדמפרש בספרי [שם לח א]. כלומר משער הראש אני משיבך תשובה הרבה נימין בראתי באדם וכו' [נדה נב:]. **אזר נא כגבר חלציך.** רמז לו שיתעורר מן חליו ויסוריו [איוב לח ג]. **מי פלג לשטף תעלה.** בערביא קורין לשערה שיטפא כל שער ושער שבראש פלגתי לו תעלה גומא לינק ממנה שאלו שנים יונקות מגומא אחת מחשיכות מאור עיניו של אדם והם לא נתחלפו לי בין איוב לאויב נתחלף לי ויזהו מן הסערה ד"א לשטף טיפת גשם שוטף פילגתי לכל טיפה גומא בעבים שאילו יורדות ב' טפות מגומא אחת מטשטשות את הארץ ועושי' טיט. **ודרך לחזיז קולות.** מי פלג לכל קול וקול יש לו שביל ואם שנים הולכים בשביל אחד אין הבריות סובלות את הקול [שם לח כה]. **יעלי סלע.** אשטנבו"ק ושונאה את ולדה ועולה לראש סלע גבוה כשכורעת לילד כדי שיפול לארץ וימות והקב"ה מזמין לו נשר ומקבלו בכנפיו. **חולל אילות תשמור.** האילה רחמה צר ואין הוולד יכול לצאת ובשעת לידתה אני מזמין לה דרקון ומכישה ברחמה ונפתח ואם מקדים ומאחר רגע מיד מתה ובין אותם רגעים איני מחליף ובין איוב לאויב נתחלף לי [שם לט א]. [ע"כ שייך לדף טז.] **כי לא דברתם אלי נכונה כעבדי איוב** שהרי הוא לא פשע בי כי אם על אשר אמר (איוב ט) תם ורשע דברתם אלי טענה נכונה כעבדי איוב [המשך בדף יז.]

מסורת הש"ס

א) [ערובין נד: יומא כט.], ב) רש"ל מ"ז, ג) [תענית כג. ע"ש ברש"י], ד) סנהדרין ק: קדושין פב: ע"ש [פסחים סה. ע"ש], ה) לקמן קמא. ע"ש [תוספתא דקדושין פ"ה], ו) [לפמ"ש תוס' ברכות ט: ובסוטה יב. ובע"ז סד: ד"ה אחרים יחייבו גם הכא], ז) [יומא כח:], ח) נ"א מרגלית, ט) נ"א משמיה דר' יוחנן, י) [עי' פרש"י בשבת דף קמה:], כ) [סנהדרין דף סט:], ל) [נ"ל ותרגם. יעב"ץ]:

הגהות הב"ח

(א) גמ' או מאחר רגע אחד מיד נופל ומת בין: (ב) שם ומתרפא ויולדת ואלמלי מקדים רגע: (ג) שם ודאי דאמריתו משמיה דר' יוסי כל מיתה שיש בה גויעה: (ד) שם יצחק וישמעאל בניו מכדי ישמעאל קשיש מיצחק מ"ט דקחשיב ליה ליצחק מקמיה ש"מ תשובה עביד ואדבריה ליצחק מקמיה ודלמא דרך חכמתן: (ה) רש"י ד"ה במיניה שהוא מעולה משאר כרכומין כצ"ל:

גליון הש"ס

גמרא ר"ש ברבי אתילידא. עיין מדרש רבה בראשית פ' כו: שם אידלי יומא. עי' נדרים דף מ ע"א בהרא"ש ד"ה סירגא דיומא: שם ישמעאל עשה תשובה. עיין סנהדרין דף קד ע"א ובתורת חיים שם ובתוס' ישנים יומא דף לד ע"ב ד"ה מעשה:

תורה אור השלם

א) הֲיָדַעְתָּ עֵת לֶדֶת יַעֲלֵי סָלַע חֹלֵל אַיָּלוֹת תִּשְׁמֹר: [איוב לט, א]

ב) אִיּוֹב לֹא בְדַעַת יְדַבֵּר וּדְבָרָיו לֹא בְהַשְׂכֵּיל: [איוב לד, לה]

ג) וַיְהִי אַחַר דִּבֶּר יְיָ אֶת הַדְּבָרִים הָאֵלֶּה אֶל אִיּוֹב וַיֹּאמֶר יְהוָה אֶל אֱלִיפַז הַתֵּימָנִי חָרָה אַפִּי בְךָ וּבִשְׁנֵי רֵעֶיךָ כִּי לֹא דִבַּרְתֶּם אֵלַי נְכוֹנָה כְּעַבְדִּי אִיּוֹב: [איוב מב, ז]

ד) וַיִּשְׁמְעוּ שְׁלֹשֶׁת רֵעֵי אִיּוֹב אֵת כָּל הָרָעָה הַזֹּאת הַבָּאָה עָלָיו וַיָּבֹאוּ אִישׁ מִמְּקֹמוֹ אֱלִיפַז הַתֵּימָנִי וּבִלְדַּד הַשּׁוּחִי וְצוֹפַר הַנַּעֲמָתִי וַיִּוָּעֲדוּ יַחְדָּו לָבוֹא לָנוּד לוֹ וּלְנַחֲמוֹ: [איוב ב, יא]

ה) וַיְהִי כִּי הֵחֵל הָאָדָם לָרֹב עַל פְּנֵי הָאֲדָמָה וּבָנוֹת יֻלְּדוּ לָהֶם: [בראשית ו, א]

ו) וַיְהִי לוֹ שִׁבְעָנָה בָנִים וְשָׁלוֹשׁ בָּנוֹת: וַיִּקְרָא שֵׁם הָאַחַת יְמִימָה וְשֵׁם הַשֵּׁנִית קְצִיעָה וְשֵׁם הַשְּׁלִישִׁית קֶרֶן הַפּוּךְ: [איוב מב, יג-יד]

ז) וְאַתְּ שָׁדוּד מַה תַּעֲשִׂי כִּי תִלְבְּשִׁי שָׁנִי כִּי תַעְדִּי עֲדִי זָהָב כִּי תִקְרְעִי בַפּוּךְ עֵינַיִךְ לַשָּׁוְא תִּתְיַפִּי מָאֲסוּ בָךְ עֹגְבִים נַפְשֵׁךְ יְבַקֵּשׁוּ: [ירמיה ד, ל]

ח) וְאַבְרָהָם זָקֵן בָּא בַּיָּמִים וַיְיָ בֵּרַךְ אֶת אַבְרָהָם בַּכֹּל: [בראשית כד, א]

ט) וַיָּזֶד יַעֲקֹב נָזִיד וַיָּבֹא עֵשָׂו מִן הַשָּׂדֶה וְהוּא עָיֵף: [בראשית כה, כט]

י) כִּי בַשָּׂדֶה מְצָאָהּ צָעֲקָה הַנַּעֲרָ הַמְאֹרָשָׂה וְאֵין מוֹשִׁיעַ לָהּ: [דברים כב, כז]

כ) כִּי קוֹל כְּחוֹלָה שָׁמַעְתִּי צָרָה כְּמַבְכִּירָה קוֹל בַּת צִיּוֹן תִּתְיַפֵּחַ תְּפָרֵשׂ כַּפֶּיהָ אוֹי נָא לִי כִּי עָיְפָה נַפְשִׁי לְהֹרְגִים: [ירמיה ד, לא]

ל) וַיֹּאמֶר עֵשָׂו הִנֵּה אָנֹכִי הוֹלֵךְ לָמוּת וְלָמָּה זֶּה לִי בְּכֹרָה: [בראשית כה, לב]

מ) עָזִּי וְזִמְרָת יָהּ וַיְהִי לִי לִישׁוּעָה זֶה אֵלִי וְאַנְוֵהוּ אֱלֹהֵי אָבִי וַאֲרֹמְמֶנְהוּ: [שמות טו, ב]

נ) וְיַעֲקֹב נָתַן לְעֵשָׂו לֶחֶם וּנְזִיד עֲדָשִׁים וַיֹּאכַל וַיֵּשְׁתְּ וַיָּקָם וַיֵּלַךְ וַיִּבֶז עֵשָׂו אֶת הַבְּכֹרָה: [בראשית כה, לד]

ס) וַיִּקְבְּרוּ אֹתוֹ יִצְחָק וְיִשְׁמָעֵאל בָּנָיו אֶל מְעָרַת הַמַּכְפֵּלָה אֶל שְׂדֵה עֶפְרֹן בֶּן צֹחַר הַחִתִּי אֲשֶׁר עַל פְּנֵי מַמְרֵא: [בראשית כה, ט]

ע) וַיִּגְוַע יִצְחָק וַיָּמָת וַיֵּאָסֶף אֶל עַמָּיו זָקֵן וּשְׂבַע יָמִים וַיִּקְבְּרוּ אֹתוֹ עֵשָׂו וְיַעֲקֹב בָּנָיו: [בראשית לה, כט]

who says that with the birth of daughters **propagation came to the world,** מִפְּנֵי מָה לֹא נִכְפְּלוּ בְּנוֹתָיו שֶׁל אִיּוֹב – **why was** the number of **Job's daughters not doubled?**[16]

R' Yochanan responds:

אָמַר לוֹ – **[R' Yochanan] said to [Reish Lakish]:** נְהִי דְלֹא נִכְפְּלוּ בְּשֵׁמוֹת אֲבָל נִכְפְּלוּ בְּיוֹפִי – **Granted they were not doubled in number,**[17] **but they were doubled in beauty.**[18] דִּכְתִיב: ,,וַיְהִי־לוֹ שִׁבְעָנָה בָנִים וְשָׁלוֹשׁ בָּנוֹת – **As it is written:** ***And he*** [Job] ***had fourteen***[19] ***sons and three daughters.*** וַיִּקְרָא שֵׁם־הָאַחַת יְמִימָה וְשֵׁם הַשֵּׁנִית קְצִיעָה וְשֵׁם הַשְּׁלִישִׁית קֶרֶן הַפּוּךְ" – ***He gave one the name Yemimah, the second the name Ketziah and the third the name Keren Hapuch.***[20] Each of these names depicts its bearer's beauty. ,,יְמִימָה" שֶׁהָיְתָה דּוֹמָה לַיּוֹם – The first daughter was named ***Yemimah*** **for she** (i.e. her complexion) **was** as clear **as the** light of **day** (*yom*). ,,קְצִיעָה" שֶׁהָיָה רֵיחָהּ נוֹדֵף כִּקְצִיעָה – The second one was named ***Ketziah*** **for she emitted a fragrance like cassia.**[21] ,,קֶרֶן הַפּוּךְ" אָמְרֵי דְּבֵי רַבִּי שִׁילָא שֶׁדּוֹמָה לְקַרְנָא דְקֶרֶשׁ – The third was named ***Keren Hapuch*** **for, as taught in the school of R' Shila, she was like the horn** (*keren*) **of a** ***keresh***.[22] מְחַיְּיכוּ עֲלָהּ בְּמַעַרְבָא קַרְנָא דְקֶרֶשׁ לְקוּתָא הִיא – **In the West** (i.e. Eretz Yisrael), **they mocked [this interpretation],** for resemblance to **the horn of a** ***keresh*** is considered **a blemish.** אֶלָּא אָמַר רַב חִסְדָּא כְּכוּרְכְּמָא דְרִישְׁקָא בְּמִינֵיהּ – **Rather, Rav Chisda explained,** she was **like garden saffron,** which is **the best of its kind.**[23] שֶׁנֶּאֱמַר: ,,כִּי־תִקְרְעִי בַפּוּךְ" – **As it is said:** ***Though you enlarge*** your eyes ***with cosmetics*** (*puch*).[24]

The Gemara cites a related dialogue:

רַבִּי שִׁמְעוֹן בְּרַבִּי אִיתְיְלִידָא לֵיהּ בְּרַתָּא – When **a daughter was born to R' Shimon the son of Rebbi,** הֲוָה קָא חָלַשׁ דַּעְתֵּיהּ – **he was disappointed.**[25] אָמַר לֵיהּ אֲבוּהָ – **His father** [Rebbi] **said to him:** רְבִיָּה בָּאָה לָעוֹלָם – But **propagation has come to the world.**[26] אָמַר לֵיהּ בַּר קַפָּרָא – **Bar Kappara** thereupon **said to [R' Shimon]:** תַּנְחוּמִין שֶׁל הֶבֶל נִיחַמְךָ אֲבוּךְ – **The solace offered you by your father is worthless**[27] [דְּתַנְיָא] – **[for it was taught in a Baraisa]:** אִי אֶפְשָׁר לָעוֹלָם בְּלֹא זְכָרִים וּבְלֹא נְקֵבוֹת – IT IS IMPOSSIBLE FOR THE WORLD to function WITHOUT MALES AND FEMALES. אֶלָּא אַשְׁרֵי לְמִי שֶׁבָּנָיו זְכָרִים – YET HAPPY IS HE WHOSE CHILDREN ARE MALES אוֹי לוֹ לְמִי שֶׁבָּנָיו נְקֵבוֹת – and WOE TO HIM WHOSE CHILDREN ARE FEMALES.[28] אִי אֶפְשָׁר לָעוֹלָם בְּלֹא בַּסָּם וּבְלֹא בּוּרְסִי – Similarly, IT IS IMPOSSIBLE FOR THE WORLD to function WITHOUT PERFUME MERCHANTS AND TANNERS. אַשְׁרֵי מִי שֶׁאוּמָּנוּתוֹ בּוּסְמִי – Yet HAPPY IS HE WHOSE OCCUPATION IS THAT OF A PERFUME MERCHANT, אוֹי לְמִי שֶׁאוּמָּנוּתוֹ בּוּרְסִי – AND WOE TO HIM WHOSE OCCUPATION IS THAT OF A TANNER.

The Gemara notes:

כְּתַנָּאֵי – **This** discussion **is related to the dispute between Tannaim** recorded in the following Baraisa: ,,וַה' בֵּרַךְ אֶת־אַבְרָהָם בַּכֹּל" – Scripture states: *HASHEM BLESSED ABRAHAM WITH EVERYTHING* (*bakol*).[29] מַאי: ,,בַּכֹּל" – WHAT IS signified by the term ***with everything*** (*bakol*)? רַבִּי מֵאִיר אוֹמֵר – R' MEIR SAYS: שֶׁלֹּא הָיְתָה לוֹ בַּת – He was blessed in THAT HE DID NOT HAVE A DAUGHTER.[30] רַבִּי יְהוּדָה אוֹמֵר – R' YEHUDAH SAYS: שֶׁהָיְתָה לוֹ בַּת – His blessing was THAT HE HAD A DAUGHTER.[31] אֲחֵרִים אוֹמְרִים – OTHERS SAY: בַּת הָיְתָה לוֹ לְאַבְרָהָם וּבַכֹּל שְׁמָהּ – ABRAHAM was blessed in that he HAD A DAUGHTER, AND *BAKOL* WAS HER NAME. רַבִּי אֶלְעָזָר הַמּוֹדָעִי אוֹמֵר – R' ELAZAR OF MOUNT MODA'I SAYS: אִיצְטַגְנִינוּת הָיְתָה בְּלִבּוֹ שֶׁל אַבְרָהָם אָבִינוּ – ABRAHAM OUR FOREFATHER WAS so well VERSED IN ASTROLOGY[32] שֶׁכָּל מַלְכֵי מִזְרָח וּמַעֲרָב מַשְׁכִּימִין לְפִתְחוֹ – THAT ALL (*kol*) THE KINGS OF THE EAST AND WEST WOULD ARRIVE EARLY AT HIS DOOR to seek advice. רַבִּי שִׁמְעוֹן בֶּן יוֹחַי אוֹמֵר – R' SHIMON BEN YOCHAI SAYS:

NOTES

16. After his period of suffering, Job was blessed with twice as many sons and possessions as he had before. He merited having fourteen sons in place of the seven who died. However, the number of his daughters remained three, as before.

17. Literally: in names (see *Maharsha*).

18. No "doubling" is better than this (*Rashi*).

19. שִׁבְעָנָה means *twice seven,* or fourteen (*R' Gershom; Rashi* and *Metzudos* ad loc.; cf. *Maharsha* here).

20. *Job* 42:13,14.

21. קְצִיעָה, *cassia*, is one of the fragrant herbs that comprise the incense offered in the Temple.

22. A *keresh* is an animal with horns that blacken what comes into contact with them (*Rashi*).

23. I.e. it is superior to other kinds of cosmetics (*Rashi;* cf. *Rashi* in *Ein Yaakov;* see also *Hagahos HaBach*). [Similarly, she was more beautiful than other women (see *Tosafos*).]

24. *Jeremiah* 4:30. [This verse is adduced to show that פּוּךְ, *puch*, is a form of cosmetics. Thus, קֶרֶן הַפּוּךְ, *keren hapuch*, can be understood as "choicest of cosmetics" (see Mishnah *Niddah* 19a where קֶרֶן, *keren,* is used in the sense of choicest). This is taken as a reference to garden saffron which is superior (see previous note).]

25. A daughter is a gift from God! Furthermore, the mitzvah of פְּרוּ וּרְבוּ, *Be fruitful and multiply (Genesis* 1:28), obligates one to have at least one daughter. Consequently, it is difficult to understand how a righteous man such as R' Shimon the son of Rebbi could have been disappointed by the birth of a daughter. The explanation is possibly that this was his first child and thus had it been a son he would have been able to fulfill the mitzvah of פִּדְיוֹן הַבֵּן, *redemption of the [firstborn] son.* R' Shimon the son of Rebbi was disappointed over being denied the opportunity to fulfill this mitzvah (*Ben Yehoyada*).

26. The birth of a daughter is essential for your fulfillment of the mitzvah of פְּרוּ וּרְבוּ, *Be fruitful and multiply* (*Maharsha*).

27. Alternatively: The solace offered you by your father is the solace of Hevel [the son of Adam] (*Maharsha*; see following note).

28. [From the Gemara (*Sanhedrin* 100b) it is evident that this is because a daughter is a constant source of worry to her father.]

It was not Bar Kappara's intent to make R' Shimon the son of Rebbi more disappointed than he already was. His remarks were intended as follows:

When Adam lost his son, Hevel, he lost his fulfillment of the mitzvah of "be fruitful and multiply," for he was left with only a daughter — Hevel's twin sister. (One must have a son and a daughter to fulfill this mitzvah [*Yevamos* 61b].) Kayin was not considered a son of Adam in this regard [*Pirkei D'Rebbi Eliezer*; cf. *Yevamos* 62a]. Adam did not regain the mitzvah until Sheiss was born, and then he was consoled for the loss of Hevel; as it is said (*Genesis* 4:25): *God has provided me another child in place of Hevel.*

This is the meaning of Bar Kappara's statement to R' Shimon b' Rebbi: תַּנְחוּמִין שֶׁל הֶבֶל נִיחַמְךָ אֲבוּךְ, *The solace offered you by your father is* [similar to that received by Adam for the death] *of Hevel.* Just as the birth of Sheiss enabled Adam to fulfill the mitzvah of "be fruitful and multiply" (which was a comfort to him for the loss of Hevel), likewise, the birth of your daughter enables you to fulfill this mitzvah. It is only in the case of one who has a number of children, and *many* of them are daughters, that there are grounds for disappointment; as it is said, "Woe to him whose *children* are females" (*Maharsha*).

29. *Genesis* 24:1.

30. This was a blessing to Abraham. For if he had a daughter, whom could she have married? To avoid marrying a member of the local populace — the cursed Canaanite nation — she would have had to find a husband outside Eretz Yisrael who might have influenced her to worship idols. Abraham did not want any of his pure progeny, which issued from his wife Sarah, to leave Eretz Yisrael, and he certainly did not want them to worship idols (*Ramban* ad loc.).

31. With the birth of a daughter, Abraham was blessed "with everything." He now had everything that people want (*Ramban* ibid.).

32. Literally: astrology was in the heart (or mind) of Abraham our father.

כבוחלא דרישקא במינה. אע"ג דכחול הוא שחור כדפירש בה"ג אוכמא אוכמא [חולין מו:] היינו דמיא לכוחלא ה"פ כי היכי דכוחלא דרישקא מקרין ומאיר משאר כוחלא כך היא היתה נאה משאר נשים וקרן הפוך לשון כי קרן עור פני משה (שמות לד) והשתא אתי שפיר הא דמייתי ותקרעי בפוך עיניך דכחול דומה לפוך שנותנין כחול בעין אבל לפירוש רש"י דגרס כי כורכמא דרישקא קשה לרשב"א א"כ מאי מייתי ותקרעי בפוך עיניך ויונתן מתרגם נרד וכרכום רשק וכרכום כפרים עם נרדים עם רישקא (שיר ד): **שכל** חולה שרואה אותה מיד מתרפא. וא"ת והא בימי אברהם אכתי לא היה חולי בעולם כדאמרי' בהשוכר את הפועלים (ב"מ דף פז.) דעד יעקב לא הוה חולשא ועד אלישע לא הוה דאיחלש ואיתפח ומלינן למימר דהכא בחולה של מכה איירי ור"ת ור"י מפרשים דעד יעקב לא הוה דאיחלש היינו חולי של מיתה מכאן ואילך הוה דאיחלש חולי של מיתה ולא הוה דאיתפח עד אלישע: **בא** על נערה המאורסה. ואם תאמר והלא לא נצטוו בני נח על נערה המאורסה כדאמרי' בפ' ארבע מיתות (סנהדרין דף נז: ושם ד"ה לנערה) בעולת בעל יש להן נכנסת לחופה ולא נבעלה אין להן ואומר ר"י דאף על פי שלא נצטוו מכל מקום מכוער הדבר כמו ושט את הבכורה אף על פי שאינו מצווה על כך: שלשה

ללדת עולה לראש ההר כדי שיפול ממנה וימות ואני מזמין לה נשר שמקבלו בכנפיו ומניחו לפניה ואלמלי מקדים רגע אחד או (א) מתאחר רגע אחד מיד מת בין רגע לרגע לא נתחלף לי בין איוב לאויב נתחלף לי א) חולל אילות תשמור אילה זו רחמה צר בשעה שכורעת ללדת אני מזמין לה דרקון שמכישה בבית הרחם (ב) ומתרפה ממולדה ואלמלי מקדים רגע אחד או מאחר רגע אחד מיד מתה בין רגע לרגע לא נתחלף לי בין איוב לאויב נתחלף לי ב) [איוב] לא בדעת ידבר ודבריו לא בהשכל (וכתיב ג) כי לא דברתם אלי נכונה כעבדי איוב) אמר רבא מכאן שאין אדם נתפס בשעת צערו ד) וישמעו שלשת רעי איוב את כל הרעה הזאת הבאה עליו ויבאו איש ממקומו אליפז התימני ובלדד השוחי וצופר הנעמתי ויועדו יחדו לבוא לנוד לו ולנחמו מאי ויועדו יחדו אמר רב יהודה אמר רב מלמד שנכנסו כולן בשער אחד ותנא בין כל אחד ואחד שלש מאות פרסי מנא הוו ידעי איכא דאמרי כלילא הוה להו ואיכא דאמרי אילני הוה להו וכיון דכמשי הוו ידעי אמר רבא היינו דאמרי אינשי או חברא כחברי דאיוב או מיתותא ה) ויהי כי החל האדם לרוב על פני האדמה ובנות יולדו להם רבי יוחנן אמר רביה באה לעולם ריש לקיש אמר מריבה באה לעולם אמר ליה ריש לקיש לרבי יוחנן לדידך דאמרת רביה באה לעולם מפני מה לא נכפלו בנותיו של איוב אמר לו נהי דלא נכפלו בשמות אבל נכפלו ביופי דכתיב ו) ויהי לו שבענה בנים ושלש בנות ויקרא שם האחת ימימה ושם השנית קציעה ושם השלישית קרן הפוך ימימה שהיתה דומה ליום קציעה שהיה ריחה נודף כקציעה קרן הפוך אמרי דבי רבי שילא שדומה לקרנא דקרש מחייכו עלה במערבא קרנא דקרש לקותא היא אלא אמר רב חסדא ככורכמא דרישקא במיניה שנאמר ז) כי תקרעי בפוך רבי שמעון ברבי איתילידא ליה ברתא הוה קא חלש דעתיה אמר ליה אבוה רביה באה לעולם אמר ליה בר קפרא תנחומין של הבל ניחמך אבוך [דתניא] אי אפשר לעולם בלא זכרים ובלא נקבות אלא אשרי למי שבניו זכרים אוי לו למי שבניו נקבות אי אפשר לעולם בלא בסם ובלא בורסי אשרי מי שאומנותו בוסמי אוי למי שאומנותו בורסי כתנאי ח) וה' ברך את אברהם בכל מאי בכל רבי מאיר אומר שלא היתה לו בת רבי יהודה אומר שהיתה לו בת אחרים אומרים בת היתה לו לאברהם ובכל שמה ר"א המודעי אומר איצטגנינות היתה בלבו של אברהם אבינו שכל מלכי מזרח ומערב משכימין לפתחו רבי שמעון בן יוחי אומר אבן טובה היתה תלויה בצוארו של אברהם אבינו שכל חולה הרואה אותו מיד מתרפא ובשעה שנפטר אברהם אבינו מן העולם תלאה הקדוש ברוך הוא בגלגל חמה אמר אביי היינו דאמרי אינשי אידלי יומא אידלי קצירא דבר אחר שלא מרד עשו בימיו דבר אחר שעשה ישמעאל תשובה בימיו מנלן דכתיב ט) ויבא עשו מן השדה והוא עיף ותנא אותו היום נפטר אברהם אבינו ועשה יעקב אבינו תבשיל של עדשים לנחם את יצחק אביו [ומ"ש של עדשים] אמרי במערבא משמיה דרבה בר מרי מה עדשה זו אין לה פה אף אבל אין לו פה דבר אחר מה עדשה זו מגולגלת אף אבילות מגלגלת ומחזרת על באי העולם מאי בינייהו איכא בינייהו לנחומי בביעי אמר רבי יוחנן חמש עבירות עבר אותו רשע באותו היום בא על נערה מאורסה והרג את הנפש וכפר בעיקר וכפר בתחיית המתים ושט את הבכורה בא על נערה מאורסה כתיב הכא ט) ויבא עשו מן השדה וכתיב התם י) כי בשדה מצאה הרג את הנפש כתיב הכא עיף וכתיב התם כ) אוי נא לי כי עיפה נפשי להורגים וכפר בעיקר כתיב הכא ל) למה זה לי וכתיב התם מ) זה אלי ואנוהו וכפר בתחיית המתים דכתיב ל) הנה אנכי הולך למות ושט את הבכורה דכתיב נ) ויבז עשו את הבכורה ושעשה ישמעאל תשובה בימיו מנלן כי הא דרבינא ורב חמא בר בוזי הוו יתבי קמיה דרבא וקא מנמנם רבא א"ל רבינא לרב חמא בר בוזי ודאי דאמריתו (ג) ט) כל מיתה שיש בה גויעה זו היא מיתתן של צדיקים א"ל אין והא דור המבול א"ל אנן גויעה ואסיפה קאמרינן והא ישמעאל דכתיב ביה גויעה ואסיפה אדהכי איתער בהו רבא אמר להו י) דרדקי הכי א"ר יוחנן ישמעאל עשה תשובה בחיי אביו שנאמר ס) ויקברו אותו יצחק וישמעאל בניו (ד) ודילמא פ) דרך חכמתן קא חשיב להו אלא מעתה ע) ויקברו אותו עשו ויעקב בניו מאי טעמא לא חשיב להו דרך חכמתן אלא מדאקדמיה אדבוריה ומדאדבריה שמע מינה תשובה עבד בימיו ת"ר שלשה הטעימן הקב"ה בעולם הזה מעין

דרקון. נחש: מכישה. נושכה: ומתרפה. לשון רפיון: **שאין אדם נתפס.** להתחייב על שהוא מדבר קשה מחמת צער ויסורין דקאמר לא בדעת ידבר לא אמר לא ברשע ידבר אלא לא בדעת: **כלילי הוו להו.** כתרים ובכל כתר שלשה פרצופים ואיש את שמו מחוקק על פרצופו וכשבאין יסורין על אחד מהן פרצופו משתנה וכן אילני דכמשי. פלטיי"א: **או חברא כחברי דאיוב.** אם אין לו לאדם אוהבים נוח לו מיתות: **לרוב על פני האדמה ובנות יולדו וגו':** רביה באה לעולם. כשנולדה בת לפי שממהרת להיות לו זרע: הוכפלו ביופי. ואין לך כפל טוב ממנו: שדומה ליום. ברה כחמה: בקציעה. מין בושם הוא: **קרנא דקרש.** מין חיה וקרניה משחירין כמו צבע: **כורכמא דרישקא.** כרכום של גן הגדל בגינה: **במיניה.** שהוא מעולה (ה) ממין שאר בשמים: **איצטגנינות.** חוזה בכוכבים: **משכימים** לפתחו. ליטול עצה ממנו: **אידלי** יומא. הוגבה שמש כשהחמה זורחת: **אידלי קצירא.** מיקל החולי: **אבל אין** לו פה. שהוא יושב ודומם: **עדשים** אין להן פה. כמו שיש לפולין ולשאר מיני קיטנית כמין סדק: **לנחומי** בביעי. אין להם פה אבל אינם מגלגלים כגלגל: **ושט את הבכורה.** וביזה את העבודה שהיתה בבכורות שט תרגום של בזיון מדוע הקילתני (שמואל ב יט) תרגום יונתן אשטתני: בכל

רבינו גרשום

ומתרפא. רחמה ומרויח: מכאן שאין אדם נתפס על צערו. על מה שמדבר מכובד צערו דכתיב לא בדעת ידבר כלומר שאין דעתו מיושבת עליו מחמת צער: כי לא דברתם אלי נכונה כעבדי איוב. דברים הגונים חשיב ושאינן הגונין לא חשיב [לא] תתפס מכל מה שדבר כנגדי: כלילא הוה להו. כתר וחקוקין עליו ג' פרצופין של ג' חבירו וכשראו שאחת מהן נשתנה פניה מיד היו יודעין שחבירו אין שרוי בנחת. ויש אומרים ג' אילנות היו נוטעין בפרדס שכל אחד היה קורא לכל א' על שם חבירו ואם היה מייבש אחד מן האילנות שבו היו יודעין שאין חבירו בטובה אותו שנקרא (העירה) [האילן] על שמו: רביה באה לעולם. כלומר פריה ורביה שהנקבה מגדלת בנים: ולדידך דאמרת רביה. דבדבר טוב הוא: שבענה. היינו ב' פעמים ז': קציעה. קדה: בושם. שקורין קו"ש: דקרש. חיה ששמה קרש: לקותא היא. ואינה יפה מפני שיש בה כמה גוונין: כי כוחלא. שהוא שחור הרבה מבהיק מאד: רישקא. בלע"ז ארינטצי"ל: במינה. שהוא משובח במינו: כורכמא דרישקא. קרוק"ו. איינטצ"ל. מה אותו צבע יפה הרבה במינו כך היתה יפה בין שאר נשים: איצטגנינות גדולה. שהיה בקי (אותו צבע) הרבה במזלות והיו שואלין מה יארע להן: אידלי יומא. [בשחרית] כשהשמש זורח שם מונחת אותה אבן: אידלי קצירא. מיקל חולה מחליו ולערב מכביד לו: ד"א. מאי בכל: מה עדשה שאין לה פה. שאין שום בקיע: לנחומי בביעי. דלמאן דאמר מה עדשה אין לה פה ביצים [נמי] אין להן פה ומנחמין בהן אבלים כמו בעדשים ולמאן דאמר מה עדשה זו מגולגלת בביצים אין מנחמין שאין מגולגלים כל כך כעדשים: לאלתר כשמת אברהם עבר אותו רשע ה' עבירות: היינו בכל. דלא מרד בימיו: שמ"מ דעבד תשובה. דנהג ביה כבוד ליצחק ואדבריה מקמיה:

תורה אור השלם

א) הֲיָדַעְתָּ עֵת לֶדֶת יַעֲלֵי סָלַע חֹלֵל אַיָּלוֹת תִּשְׁמֹר: [איוב לט, א]
ב) אִיּוֹב לֹא בְדַעַת יְדַבֵּר וּדְבָרָיו לֹא בְהַשְׂכֵּיל: [איוב לד, לה]
ג) וַיְהִי אַחַר דִּבֶּר יְיָ אֶת הַדְּבָרִים הָאֵלֶּה אֶל אִיּוֹב וַיֹּאמֶר יְהוָה אֶל אֱלִיפַז הַתֵּימָנִי חָרָה אַפִּי בְךָ וּבִשְׁנֵי רֵעֶיךָ כִּי לֹא דִבַּרְתֶּם אֵלַי נְכוֹנָה כְּעַבְדִּי אִיּוֹב: [איוב מב, ז]
ד) וַיִּשְׁמְעוּ שְׁלֹשֶׁת רֵעֵי אִיּוֹב אֵת כָּל הָרָעָה הַזֹּאת הַבָּאָה עָלָיו וַיָּבֹאוּ אִישׁ מִמְּקֹמוֹ אֱלִיפַז הַתֵּימָנִי וּבִלְדַּד הַשּׁוּחִי וְצוֹפַר הַנַּעֲמָתִי וַיִּוָּעֲדוּ יַחְדָּו לָבוֹא לָנוּד לוֹ וּלְנַחֲמוֹ: [איוב ב, יא]
ה) וַיְהִי כִּי הֵחֵל הָאָדָם לָרֹב עַל פְּנֵי הָאֲדָמָה וּבָנוֹת יֻלְּדוּ לָהֶם: [בראשית ו, א]
ו) וַיְהִי לוֹ שִׁבְעָנָה בָנִים וְשָׁלוֹשׁ בָּנוֹת: וַיִּקְרָא שֵׁם הָאַחַת יְמִימָה וְשֵׁם הַשֵּׁנִית קְצִיעָה וְשֵׁם הַשְּׁלִישִׁית קֶרֶן הַפּוּךְ: [איוב מב, יג-יד]
ז) וְאַתְּ שָׁדוּד מַה תַּעֲשִׂי כִּי תִלְבְּשִׁי שָׁנִי כִּי תַעְדִּי עֲדִי זָהָב כִּי תִקְרְעִי בַפּוּךְ עֵינַיִךְ לַשָּׁוְא תִּתְיַפִּי מָאֲסוּ בָךְ עֹגְבִים נַפְשֵׁךְ יְבַקֵּשׁוּ: [ירמיה ד, ל]
ח) וְאַבְרָהָם זָקֵן בָּא בַּיָּמִים וַייָ בֵּרַךְ אֶת אַבְרָהָם בַּכֹּל: [בראשית כד, א]
ט) וַיָּזֶד יַעֲקֹב נָזִיד וַיָּבֹא עֵשָׂו מִן הַשָּׂדֶה וְהוּא עָיֵף: [בראשית כה, כט]
י) כִּי בַשָּׂדֶה מְצָאָהּ צָעֲקָה הַנַּעֲרָה הַמְאֹרָשָׂה וְאֵין מוֹשִׁיעַ לָהּ: [דברים כב, כז]
כ) כִּי קוֹל כְּחוֹלָה שָׁמַעְתִּי צָרָה כְּמַבְכִּירָה קוֹל בַּת צִיּוֹן תִּתְיַפֵּחַ תְּפָרֵשׂ כַּפֶּיהָ אוֹי נָא לִי כִּי עָיְפָה נַפְשִׁי לְהֹרְגִים: [ירמיה ד, לא]
ל) וַיֹּאמֶר עֵשָׂו הִנֵּה אָנֹכִי הוֹלֵךְ לָמוּת וְלָמָּה זֶּה לִי בְּכֹרָה: [בראשית כה, לב]
מ) עָזִּי וְזִמְרָת יָהּ וַיְהִי לִי לִישׁוּעָה זֶה אֵלִי וְאַנְוֵהוּ אֱלֹהֵי אָבִי וַאֲרֹמְמֶנְהוּ: [שמות טו, ב]
נ) וְיַעֲקֹב נָתַן לְעֵשָׂו לֶחֶם וּנְזִיד עֲדָשִׁים וַיֹּאכַל וַיֵּשְׁתְּ וַיָּקָם וַיֵּלַךְ וַיִּבֶז עֵשָׂו אֶת הַבְּכֹרָה: [בראשית כה, לד]
ס) וַיִּקְבְּרוּ אֹתוֹ יִצְחָק וְיִשְׁמָעֵאל בָּנָיו אֶל מְעָרַת הַמַּכְפֵּלָה אֶל שְׂדֵה עֶפְרֹן בֶּן צֹחַר הַחִתִּי אֲשֶׁר עַל פְּנֵי מַמְרֵא: [בראשית כה, ט]
ע) וַיִּגְוַע יִצְחָק וַיָּמָת וַיֵּאָסֶף אֶל עַמָּיו זָקֵן וּשְׂבַע יָמִים וַיִּקְבְּרוּ אֹתוֹ עֵשָׂו וְיַעֲקֹב בָּנָיו: [בראשית לה, כט]

אֶבֶן טוֹבָה הָיְתָה תְּלוּיָה בְּצַוָּארוֹ שֶׁל אַבְרָהָם אָבִינוּ – A PRECIOUS STONE HUNG FROM THE NECK OF ABRAHAM OUR FOREFATHER שֶׁכָּל חוֹלֶה הָרוֹאֶה אוֹתוֹ מִיָּד מִתְרַפֵּא – AND ANY (*kol*) SICK PERSON THAT LOOKED AT IT WAS INSTANTLY CURED. וּבְשָׁעָה שֶׁנִּפְטַר אַבְרָהָם אָבִינוּ מִן הָעוֹלָם – WHEN ABRAHAM OUR FOREFATHER PASSED FROM THE WORLD, תְּלָאָהּ הַקָּדוֹשׁ בָּרוּךְ הוּא בְּגַלְגַּל חַמָּה – THE HOLY ONE, BLESSED IS HE, HUNG [THIS STONE] IN THE ORB OF THE SUN.

The Gemara interjects:

אָמַר אַבַּיֵי – Abaye said: הַיְינוּ דְּאָמְרֵי אִינָשֵׁי – **This is** borne out by **the popular saying:** אִידְּלֵי יוֹמָא אִידְּלֵי קְצִירָא – **"When the sun**[33] **is lifted, sickness is lifted."** I.e., sunshine helps to alleviate sickness.[34]

The Baraisa continues with other versions of the blessing signified by בַּכֹּל, *with everything:*

דָּבָר אַחֵר – ANOTHER INTERPRETATION: שֶׁלֹּא מָרַד עֵשָׂו בְּיָמָיו – Abraham was blessed in THAT his grandson, ESAU, DID NOT REBEL DURING HIS LIFETIME.[35] דָּבָר אַחֵר – ANOTHER INTERPRETATION: שֶׁעָשָׂה יִשְׁמָעֵאל תְּשׁוּבָה בְּיָמָיו – Abraham was blessed in THAT his son, ISHMAEL, REPENTED DURING HIS LIFETIME.[36]

The Gemara gives the sources for these two opinions:

שֶׁלֹּא מָרַד עֵשָׂו בְּיָמָיו מְנָלַן – From where do we know **that Esau did not rebel during [Abraham's] lifetime?** דִּכְתִיב: ,,וַיָּבֹא עֵשָׂו מִן־הַשָּׂדֶה וְהוּא עָיֵף" – **For it is written:** ***Esau came in from the field, weary.***[37] וְתָנָא – **And a Tanna taught in a Baraisa:** אוֹתוֹ הַיּוֹם נִפְטַר אַבְרָהָם אָבִינוּ – It was on THAT DAY that ABRAHAM OUR FOREFATHER PASSED AWAY, וְעָשָׂה יַעֲקֹב אָבִינוּ תַּבְשִׁיל שֶׁל עֲדָשִׁים – AND OUR FOREFATHER JACOB MADE A STEW OF LENTILS לְנַחֵם אֶת יִצְחָק אָבִיו – with which TO COMFORT HIS FATHER ISAAC, the son of Abraham.[38]

Before proving that Esau rebelled on the day of Abraham's passing, the Gemara explains why Jacob chose lentils as an appropriate dish to offer a mourner:

[וּמַאי שְׁנָא שֶׁל עֲדָשִׁים] – **[Why** did Jacob choose a dish **of lentils?]** אָמְרֵי בְּמַעֲרְבָא מִשְּׁמֵיהּ דְּרַבָּה בַּר מָרִי – **In the West** (Eretz Yisrael) **they explained in the name of Rabbah bar Mari:** מָה עֲדָשָׁה זוֹ אֵין לָהּ פֶּה – **Just as a lentil has no "mouth"** (it is not fissured like other legumes), אַף אָבֵל אֵין לוֹ פֶּה – **so too, a mourner has no mouth** (he sits in silence). דָּבָר אַחֵר – **Another explanation:** מָה עֲדָשָׁה זוֹ מְגוּלְגֶּלֶת – **Just as a lentil is round,** אַף אֲבֵילוּת מְגַלְגֶּלֶת וּמְחַזֶּרֶת עַל בָּאֵי הָעוֹלָם – **so too, mourning goes around** in an inescapable cycle, **befalling the inhabitants of the world.**

The Gemara notes a practical difference between these two explanations:

אִיכָּא מַאי בֵּינַיְיהוּ – **What is** the difference **between them?** בֵּינַיְיהוּ לְנַחוּמֵי בְּבֵיעֵי – The difference **between them is** whether it is appropriate **to comfort** a mourner **with eggs.** According to the first explanation, eggs are also appropriate for this purpose, for they have no "mouth." According to the second explanation, eggs are not appropriate, for they are not round.

The Gemara now proves that Esau rebelled on the day of Abraham's passing:

אָמַר רַבִּי יוֹחָנָן – **R' Yochanan said:** חָמֵשׁ עֲבֵירוֹת עָבַר אוֹתוֹ רָשָׁע בְּאוֹתוֹ הַיּוֹם – **That scoundrel,** Esau, **committed five sins on that day:** בָּא עַל נַעֲרָה מְאוֹרָסָה – **He had relations with a betrothed maiden;** וְהָרַג אֶת הַנֶּפֶשׁ – **he murdered someone;** וְכָפַר בְּעִיקָּר – **he denied the fundamental belief** [the existence of God]; וְכָפַר בִּתְחִיַּית הַמֵּתִים – **he denied** the doctrine of **the Resurrection of the Dead** וְשָׁט אֶת הַבְּכוֹרָה – **and he belittled the birthright.**[39]

The Scriptural sources:

בָּא עַל נַעֲרָה מְאוֹרָסָה – We know that **he had relations with a betrothed maiden,** כְּתִיב הָכָא: ,,וַיָּבֹא עֵשָׂו מִן־הַשָּׂדֶה" – **for here it is written:** ***And Esau came in from "the field";*** וּכְתִיב הָתָם: ,,כִּי בַשָּׂדֶה מְצָאָהּ" – **and elsewhere,** in reference to the violation of a betrothed maiden, **it is written:** ***For he found her in "the field."***[40] הָרַג אֶת הַנֶּפֶשׁ – We know that **he murdered someone,** כְּתִיב הָכָא: ,,עָיֵף" – for **here it is written** that Esau was ***"weary"***; וּכְתִיב הָתָם: ,,אוֹי־נָא לִי כִּי־עָיְפָה נַפְשִׁי לְהֹרְגִים" – **and elsewhere,** in reference to murder, **it is written:** ***Woe to me for my soul is "weary" of those that murder.***[41] וְכָפַר בָּעִיקָּר – We know that **he denied the fundamental belief** (the existence of God), כְּתִיב הָכָא: ,,לָמָּה־זֶּה לִי" – for **here it is written** that Esau said: *What is "this" to me;*[42] וּכְתִיב הָתָם: ,,זֶה אֵלִי וְאַנְוֵהוּ" – **and elsewhere,** in reference to God, **it is written:** ***"This" is my God, and I will glorify Him.***[43] וְכָפַר בִּתְחִיַּית הַמֵּתִים – We know that **he denied the** doctrine of the **Resurrection of the Dead,** דִּכְתִיב: ,,הִנֵּה אָנֹכִי הוֹלֵךְ לָמוּת" – **for it is written** that Esau said to Jacob: ***Look, I am going to die!***[44] וְשָׁט אֶת הַבְּכוֹרָה – We know that **he belittled the birthright,** דִּכְתִיב: ,,וַיִּבֶז עֵשָׂו אֶת־הַבְּכֹרָה" – **for it is written:** ***And Esau belittled the birthright.***[45]

NOTES

33. Literally: the day.

34. Abraham possessed profound knowledge of all scientific and spiritual matters. (As stated above, he was an expert in astrology.) By teaching this wisdom to others, he drew them close to God. R' Shimon's statement may be understood in this light.

A precious stone hung from the neck of Abraham: In Scripture and the Talmud, a precious stone is used as a metaphor for wisdom. By means of his neck (where the sound-producing organs are located), Abraham verbalized his wisdom and imparted it to others. *Any sick person that looked at it was instantly cured:* Those who studied under Abraham came under the protection of the Divine Presence. *When Abraham our forefather passed from the world, the Holy One, Blessed is He, hung [this stone] in the orb of the sun:* After Abraham's death there was no one to fill his place, so it became necessary to observe for oneself the movement of the heavenly spheres, and other such sciences, as a first step in the ascent to knowledge of God. (Abaye's quotation of the popular saying, "When the sun is lifted, sickness is lifted," was intended only to reinforce the metaphor) (*Rashba* in *Ein Yaakov;* cf. *Maharsha*).

35. Esau did not commit blatant transgressions until the day of Abraham's death (see Gemara below).

According to this interpretation בַּכֹּל, *with everything,* teaches that *both* Esau and Jacob were righteous for the duration of Abraham's lifetime (*Iyun Yaakov*).

36. בַּכֹּל, *with everything,* signifies that *all* Abraham's children were virtuous at the time of his death (*Iyun Yaakov*).

37. *Genesis* 25:29.

38. Traditionally, a mourner's first meal is brought to him by others.

39. I.e. his right, as a firstborn, to perform the Divine service (which, even before the building of the Mishkan, included offering sacrifices [see *Rashi* to *Genesis* 25:31]). At first this privilege was enjoyed by the firstborn. After the sin of the Golden Calf, it was transferred to the Kohanim and Leviim.

40. *Deuteronomy* 22:27.

41. *Jeremiah* 4:31.

42. *Genesis* 25:32. [According to the plain meaning of the verse, Esau refers to the birthright.]

43. *Exodus* 15:2.

44. *Genesis* 25:32. The entire verse reads: וַיֹּאמֶר עֵשָׂו הִנֵּה אָנֹכִי הוֹלֵךְ לָמוּת וְלָמָּה־זֶּה לִי בְּכֹרָה, *Esau said, "Look, I am going to die, so of what use to me is a birthright."* Esau saw his death as the termination of the usefulness of the birthright. This proves that he denied the possibility of resurrection.

45. Ibid. v. 34.

ללדת עולה לראש ההר כדי שיפול ממנה וימות ואני מזמין לה נשר שמקבלו בכנפיו ומניחו לפניה ואלמלי מקדים רגע אחד או (א) מתאחר רגע אחד מיד מת בין רגע לרגע לא נתחלף לי בין איוב לאויב נתחלף לי א) חולל אילות תשמור אילה זו רחמה צר בשעה שכורעת ללדת אני מזמין לה דרקון שמכישה בבית הרחם (ב) ומתרפה ממולדה ואלמלי מקדים רגע אחד או מאחר רגע אחד מיד מתה בין רגע לרגע לא נתחלף לי בין איוב לאויב נתחלף לי ב) [איוב] לא בדעת ידבר ודבריו לא בהשכל (וכתיב ג) כי לא דברתם אלי נכונה כעבדי איוב) אמר רבא מכאן שאין אדם נתפס בשעת צערו ד) וישמעו שלשת רעי איוב את כל הרעה הזאת הבאה עליו ויבאו איש ממקומו אליפז התימני ובלדד השוחי וצופר הנעמתי ויועדו יחדו לבוא לנוד לו ולנחמו מאי ויועדו יחדו אמר רב יהודה אמר רב מלמד שנכנסו כולן בשער אחד ותנא בין כל אחד ואחד שלש מאות פרסי מנא הוו ידעי איכא דאמרי כלילא הוה להו ואיכא דאמרי אילני הוה להו וכיון דכמשי הוו ידעי אמר רבא היינו דאמרי אינשי או חברא כחברי דאיוב או מיתותא ה) ויהי כי החל האדם לרוב על פני האדמה ובנות יולדו להם רבי יוחנן אמר רביה באה לעולם ריש לקיש אמר מריבה באה לעולם אמר ליה ריש לקיש לרבי יוחנן לדידך דאמרת רביה באה לעולם מפני מה לא נכפלו בנותיו של איוב אמר לו נהי דלא נכפלו בשמות אבל נכפלו ביופי דכתיב ו) ויהי לו שבענה בנים ושלש בנות ויקרא שם האחת ימימה ושם השנית קציעה ושם השלישית קרן הפוך ימימה שהיתה דומה ליום קציעה שהיה ריחה נודף כקציעה קרן הפוך אמרי דבי רבי שילא שדומה לקרנא דקרש מחיכו עלה במערבא קרנא דקרש לקותא היא אלא אמר רב חסדא ככורכמא דרישקא במיניה שנאמר ז) כי תקרעי בפוך * רבי שמעון ברבי איתילידא ליה ברתא הוה קא חלש דעתיה אמר ליה אבוה רביה באה לעולם אמר ליה בר קפרא תנחומין של הבל ניחמך אבוך [דתניא] אי אפשר לעולם בלא זכרים ובלא נקבות אלא אשרי למי שבניו זכרים אוי לו למי שבניו נקבות אי אפשר לעולם בלא בסם ובלא בורסי אשרי מי שאומנותו בוסמי אוי למי שאומנותו בורסי כתנאי ח) וה' ברך את אברהם בכל מאי בכל רבי מאיר אומר שלא היתה לו בת רבי יהודה אומר שהיתה לו בת אחרים אומרים בת היתה לו לאברהם ובכל שמה ר"א המודעי אומר * איצטגנינות היתה בלבו של אברהם אבינו שכל מלכי מזרח ומערב משכימין לפתחו רבי שמעון בן יוחי אומר אבן טובה היתה תלויה בצוארו של אברהם אבינו שכל חולה הרואה אותו מיד מתרפא ובשעה שנפטר אברהם אבינו מן העולם תלאה הקדוש ברוך הוא בגלגל חמה אמר אביי היינו דאמרי אינשי * אידלי יומא אידלי קצירא דבר אחר שלא מרד עשו בימיו דבר אחר * שעשה ישמעאל תשובה בימיו דבר אחר שלא מרד עשו בימיו מנלן דכתיב ט) ויבא עשו מן השדה והוא עיף ותנא אותו היום נפטר אברהם אבינו ועשה יעקב אבינו תבשיל של עדשים לנחם את יצחק אביו [ומ"ש של עדשים] אמרי במערבא משמיה דרבה בר מרי מה עדשה זו אין לה פה אף אבל אין לו פה דבר אחר מה עדשה זו מגולגלת אף אבילות מגולגלת ומחזרת על באי העולם מאי בינייהו איכא בינייהו לנחומי בביעי אמר רבי יוחנן חמש עבירות עבר אותו רשע באותו היום בא על נערה מאורסה והרג את הנפש וכפר בעיקר וכפר בתחיית המתים ושט את הבכורה בא על נערה מאורסה כתיב הכא ט) ויבא עשו מן השדה וכתיב התם י) כי בשדה מצאה הרג את הנפש כתיב הכא עיף וכתיב התם כ) אוי נא לי כי עיפה נפשי להורגים וכפר בעיקר כתיב הכא ל) למה זה לי וכתיב התם מ) זה אלי ואנוהו וכפר בתחיית המתים דכתיב ל) הנה אנכי הולך למות ושט את הבכורה דכתיב נ) ויבז עשו את הבכורה ושעשה ישמעאל תשובה בימיו מנלן כי הא דרבינא ורב חמא בר בוזי הוו יתבי קמיה דרבא וקא מנמנם רבא א"ל רבינא לרב חמא בר בוזי ודאי דאמריתו (ג) כל מיתה שיש בה גויעה זו היא מיתתן של צדיקים א"ל אין והא דור המבול א"ל אנן גויעה ואסיפה קאמרינן והא ישמעאל דכתיב ביה גויעה ואסיפה אדהכי איתער בהו רבא אמר להו דרדקי הכי א"ר יוחנן ישמעאל עשה תשובה בחיי אביו שנאמר ס) ויקברו אותו יצחק וישמעאל בניו (ד) ודילמא דרך חכמתן קא חשיב להו אלא מעתה ע) ויקברו אותו עשו ויעקב בניו מאי טעמא לא חשיב להו דרך חכמתן אלא מדאקדמיה אדבורי אדבריה ומדאדבריה שמע מינה תשובה עבד בימיו ת"ר שלשה הטעימן הקב"ה בעולם הזה

מעין

רש"י

דרקון. נחש: **מכישה.** נושכה: **ומתרפה.** לשון רפיון: **שאין אדם נתפס.** להתחייב על שהוא מדבר קשה מחמת צער ויסורין דקאמר לא בדעת ידבר לא אמר לא ברשע ידבר אלא לא בדעת: **כלילי הוו להו.** כתרים ובכל כתר שלשה פרצופים ואיש את שמו מחוקק על פרצופו וכשבאין יסורין על אחד מהן פרצופו משתנה וכן אילני: **דכמשי.** פלטיי"א: **או חברא כחברי דאיוב.** אם אין לו לאדם אוהבים נוח לו שימות: **לרוב על פני האדמה ובנות יולדו וגו':** **רביה באה לעולם.** כשנולדה בת לפי שממהרת להיות לו זרע: **הוכפלו ביופי.** ואין לך כפל טוב ממנו: **שדומה ליום.** ברה כחמה: **בקציעה.** מין בושם הוא: **קרנא דקרש.** מין חיה וקרניה משחירין כמו צבע: **כורכמא דרישקא.** כרכום של גן הגדל בגינה: **במיניה.** שהוא מעולה (ה) ממין שאר בשמים: **איצטגנינות.** חוזה בכוכבים: **משכימים לפתחו.** ליטול עצה ממנו: **אידלי יומא.** הוגבה שמש כשהחמה זורחת: **אידלי קצירא.** מיקל החולי: **אבל אין לו פה.** שהוא יושב ודומם: **עדשים אין להן פה.** כמו שיש לפולין ולשאר מיני קיטנית כמין סדק: **לנחומי בביעי.** אין להם פה אבל אינם מגלגלים כגלגל: **ושט את הבכורה.** וביזה את העבודה שהיתה בבכורות שט תרגום של בזיון מדוע הקילתני (שמואל ב יט) תרגום יונתן אשטתני:

בכל

תוספות

כבוחלא דרישקא במינה. אע"ג דכחול הוא שחור כדפירש בה"ג אוכמא אוכמא [חולין מו:] היינו דמיא לכוחלא ה"פ כי היכי דכוחלא דרישקא מקרין ומאיר משאר כוחלא כך היא היתה נאה משאר נשים וקרן הפוך לשון כי קרן עור פני משה (שמות לד) והשתא אתי שפיר הא דמייתי ותקרעי בפוך עיניך דכחול דומה לפוך שנותנין בכחול בעין אבל לפירוש רש"י דגרס כי כורכמא דרישקא קשה לרשב"א א"כ מאי מייתי ותקרעי בפוך עיניך ויונתן תרגם נרד וכרכום רשק ו) וכרכום כפרים עם נרדים עם ריסקא (שיר ד):

שכל חולה שרואה אותה מיד מתרפא. וא"ת והא בימי אברהם אכתי לא היה חולי בעולם כדאמרי' בהשוכר את הפועלים (ב"מ דף פז.) דעד יעקב לא הוה חולשא ועד אלישע לא הוה דאיחלש ואיתפח ומלינן למימר דהכא בחולה של מכה איירי ור"ת ור"י מפרשים דעד יעקב לא הוה דאיחלש היינו חולי של מיתה מכאן ואילך הוה דאיחלש חולי של מיתה ולא הוה דאיתפח עד אלישע:

בא על נערה המאורסה. ואם תאמר והלא לא נצטוו בני נח על נערה המאורסה כדאמרי' בפ' ארבע מיתות (סנהדרין דף נז: ושם ד"ה לנערה) בעולת בעל יש להן נכנסת לחופה ולא נבעלה אין להן ואומר ר"י דאף על פי שלא נצטוו מכל מקום מכוער הדבר כמו ושט את הבכורה אף על פי שאינו מצווה על כך:

שלשה

רבינו גרשום

ומתרפא. רחמה ומרויח: **מכאן שאין אדם נתפס על צערו.** על מה שמדבר מכובד צערו **דכתיב לא בדעת ידבר** כלומר שאין דעתו מיושבת עליו מחמת צער: **כי לא דברתם אלי נכונה כעבדי איוב.** דברים הגונים חישב ושאינן הגונין לא חישב [לא] תפסו מכל מה שדבר כנגדו: **כלילא הוה להו.** כתר וחקוקין עליו ג' פרצופין של ג' חביריו וכשרואין שאחת מהן נשתנה פניה מיד היו יודעין שחבירו אין שרוי בנחת. ויש אומרים ג' אילנות היו נטועין בפרדס שכל אחד היה קורא לכל א' על שם חבירו ואם היה מייבש אחד מן האילנות שבו היו יודעין שאין שרוי בטובה אותו שנקרא (העירה) [האילן] על שמו: **רביה.** כלומר פריה ורביה שהנקבה מגדלת בניה: **ולדידך דאמרת רביה.** דדבר טוב הוא: **שבענה.** היינו ב' פעמים ז': **קציעה.** קדה: **בושם.** שקורין קר"ש: **דקרש.** חיה ששמה קרש: **לקותא היא.** ואינה יפה מפני שיש בה כמה גוונין: **כי כוחלא.** שהוא שחור הרבה מבהיק מאד: **רישקה.** בלע"ז ארייניטי"ל: **במיניה.** שהוא משובח במינו: **כורכמא דרישקא.** קרוק"ו. איינטי"ל. מה אותו צבע יפה הרבה במינו כך היתה יפה בין שאר נשים: **איצטגנינות גדולה.** שהיה בקי (אותו צבע) הרבה במזלות והיו שואלין מה יארע להן: **אידלי יומא.** [בשחרית] כשהשמש זורח שם מונחת אותה אבן: **אידלי קצירא.** מיקל חולה מחליו ולערב מכביד לו: **ד"א.** מאי בכל: **מה עדשה שאין לה פה.** שאין לה שום ביקוע: **לנחומי בביעי.** דלמאן דאמר פה עדשה אין לה פה ביצים [נמי] אין להם פה ומנחמין בהן אבלים כמו בעדשים ולמאן דאמר מה עדשה זו מגולגלת בביצים אין מנחמין מפני שאינם מגולגלים כל כך כעדשים: לאלתר כשמת אברהם **עבר אותו רשע ה' עבירות: היינו בכל.** דלא מרד בימיו: **ש"מ דעבד תשובה.** דנהג ביה כבוד ליצחק ואדבריה מקמיה:

לעזי רש"י

פלטיי"א. פירוש כמושים (רש"י סוכה דף לא סוע"א), נקמטים (מוסף הערוך ערך כמש), נובלים (עיין רש"י ישעיה א, ל):

ליקוטי רש"י

ברכת אובד. אדם מת בעונו ונטרד. **עלי תבא.** כי הייתי זן את בניו ואת אשתו ורבותינו אמרו שהיה גוזל שדה יתומים ומשביחה ומחזירה להם ופשטיה דקרא אינו נראה כך שאין קרוי אובד אלא דבר שהוא עצמו אובד כמו ככלי אובד (תהלים לא) וכן תעיתי כשה אובד (תהלים קיט) לאן אובדות (ירמיה כ). **ולב אלמנה ארנין.** שהיה מטיל שמו על אלמנות לאמר קרובתי היא או אני אשיאנה כדי שיקפצו עליה תובעים [איוב כט, יג]. **והותי.** שברי. **ישאו יחד.** עם משקל שכנגדם ואפי' הם חול ימים יכבד ממנו [שם ו ב]. **מוכיח.** לרשנ"ר בלע"ז מרא' לכל א' חובתו וזכותו. **ישת ידו.** משטר אימתו וניגושו. **על שנינו.** שלא יחזק את הרפה [שם ט לג]. **ברית כרתי לעיני.** שלא להסתכל באשת איש. **ומה אתבונן על בתולה.** מה לי להתבונן בה כך היתה חסידותי שלא לתת עין אפילו בפנויה שמא לאחר ימים תנשא ונמצאתי כרוך אחריה כך מפורש באבות דרבי נתן [שם לא א]. **הנה נא ידעתי כי אשה יפת מראה.** מדרש אגדה עד עכשיו לא הכיר בה מתוך צניעות שבשניהם ועכשיו הכיר בה ע"י מעשה [בראשית יב יא]. **אשר בשערה.** נתחלפה לורתי (ס"א שורתי) לפניו. **ישופני.** יכתתני ואכות אותו טחון (דברים ט) מתרגמינן ושפית יתיה. **פצעי.** מכה המוציאה דם וליחה [איוב ט יז]. **מן הסערה.** מנה שערות שלך ואשיבך דברים כנגדן. מן הסערה שחרפתני אשר בסערה ישופני (איוב ט) ממנה אשיב לך כאשר תשמע בסוף הענין מי פלג לשטף תעלה גומא לכל שער ד"א בסערה הכהו בסערה רפאהו כדמפרש בספרי [שם לח א]. כלומר משער הראש אני משיבך תשובה הרבה נימין בראתי באדם וכו' [נדה נב:]. **אזר נא כגבר חלציך.** רמז לו שיתעורר מן חליו ויסוריו [איוב לח ג]. **מי פלג לשטף תעלה.** בערביא קורין לשערה שיטפה כל שער ושער שבראש פלגתי לו תעלה גומא לינק ממנה שאילו שנים יונקות מגומא אחת מחשיכות מאור עיניו של אדם והם לא נתחלפו לי בין איוב לאויב נתחלף לי וזהו מן הסערה ד"א לשטף טיפת גשם שוטף פילגתי לכל טיפה גומא בעבים שאילו יורדות ב' טפות מגומא אחת מטשטשות את הארץ ועשי' טיט. **ודרך לחזיז קולות.** מי פלג כל קול וקול יש לו שביל ואם שנים הולכים בשביל אחד אין הבריות סובלות את הקול [שם לח כה]. **יעלי סלע.** אשטנבו"ק ושונאה את ולדה ועולה לראש סלע גבוה כשכורעת לילד כדי שיפול לארץ וימות והקב"ה מזמן לו נשר ומקבלו בכנפיו. **חולל אילות תשמור.** האילה רחמה צר ואין הוולד יכול לצאת ובשעת לידתה אני מזמין לה דרקון ומכישה ברחמה ונפתח ואם מקדים ומאחר רגע מיד מתה ובין אותם רגעים איני מחליף ובין איוב לאויב נתחלף לי [שם לט א]. [ע"כ שייך לדף טז.] **כי לא דברתם אלי נכונה כעבדי איוב** שהרי הוא לא פשע בי כי אם על אשר אמר (איוב ט) תם ורשע [המשך בדף יז.]

מסורת הש"ס

א) [עירובין נד: יומא כט.], ב) רש"ל מ"ז, ג) [תענית כג. ע"ש ברש"י], ד) סנהדרין ק: קדושין פב: ע"ש [פסחים סה. ע"ש], ה) לקמן קמא. ע"ש [תוספתא דקדושין פ"ה], ו) [לפמ"ש תוס' ברכות ט: וכסוטה יב. ובע"ז סד: ד"ה אחרים יתיישב גם הכא], ז) [יומא כח:], ח) נ"א מרגלית, ט) נ"א משמיה דר' יוחנן, י) [עי' פרש"י בשבת דף קמה:], כ) [סנהדרין דף סט:], ל) [נ"ל ותרגם. יעב"ץ]:

הגהות הב"ח

(א) גמ' או מאחר רגע אחד מיד נופל ומת בין: (ב) שם ומתרפא ויולדת ואלמלי מקדים רגע: (ג) שם ודאי דאמריתו משמיה דר' יוסי כל מיתה שיש בה גויעה: (ד) שם יצחק וישמעאל בניו מכדי ישמעאל קשיש מיצחק מ"ט דקחשיב ליה ליצחק מקמיה ש"מ תשובה עביד ואדבריה ליצחק מקמיה ודלמא דרך חכמתן: (ה) רש"י ד"ה במיניה שהוא מעולה משאר כרכומין כצ"ל:

גליון הש"ס

גמרא ר"ש ברבי אתילידא. עיין מדרש רבה בראשית פ' כו: **שם אידלי יומא.** עי' נדרים דף מ ע"א בהרא"ש ד"ה מירגא דיומא: **שם ישמעאל עשה תשובה.** עיין סנהדרין דף קד ע"א ובתורת חיים שם ובתוס' ישנים יומא דף לד ע"ב ד"ה מעשה:

תורה אור השלם

א) הֲיָדַעְתָּ עֵת לֶדֶת יַעֲלֵי סָלַע חֹלֵל אַיָּלוֹת תִּשְׁמֹר: [איוב לט, א]

ב) אִיּוֹב לֹא בְדַעַת יְדַבֵּר וּדְבָרָיו לֹא בְהַשְׂכֵּיל: [איוב לד, לה]

ג) וַיְהִי אַחַר דִּבֶּר יְיָ אֶת הַדְּבָרִים הָאֵלֶּה אֶל אִיּוֹב וַיֹּאמֶר יְהוָה אֶל אֱלִיפַז הַתֵּימָנִי חָרָה אַפִּי בְךָ וּבִשְׁנֵי רֵעֶיךָ כִּי לֹא דִבַּרְתֶּם אֵלַי נְכוֹנָה כְּעַבְדִּי אִיּוֹב: [איוב מב, ז]

ד) וַיִּשְׁמְעוּ שְׁלֹשֶׁת רֵעֵי אִיּוֹב אֵת כָּל הָרָעָה הַזֹּאת הַבָּאָה עָלָיו וַיָּבֹאוּ אִישׁ מִמְּקֹמוֹ אֱלִיפַז הַתֵּימָנִי וּבִלְדַּד הַשּׁוּחִי וְצוֹפַר הַנַּעֲמָתִי וַיִּוָּעֲדוּ יַחְדָּו לָבוֹא לָנוּד לוֹ וּלְנַחֲמוֹ: [איוב ב, יא]

ה) וַיְהִי כִּי הֵחֵל הָאָדָם לָרֹב עַל פְּנֵי הָאֲדָמָה וּבָנוֹת יֻלְּדוּ לָהֶם: [בראשית ו, א]

ו) וַיְהִי לוֹ שִׁבְעָנָה בָנִים וְשָׁלוֹשׁ בָּנוֹת: וַיִּקְרָא שֵׁם הָאַחַת יְמִימָה וְשֵׁם הַשֵּׁנִית קְצִיעָה וְשֵׁם הַשְּׁלִישִׁית קֶרֶן הַפּוּךְ: [איוב מב, יג-יד]

ז) וְאַתְּ שָׁדוּד מַה תַּעֲשִׂי כִּי תִלְבְּשִׁי שָׁנִי כִּי תַעְדִּי עֲדִי זָהָב כִּי תִקְרְעִי בַפּוּךְ עֵינַיִךְ לַשָּׁוְא תִּתְיַפִּי מָאֲסוּ בָךְ עֹגְבִים נַפְשֵׁךְ יְבַקֵּשׁוּ: [ירמיה ד, ל]

ח) וְאַבְרָהָם זָקֵן בָּא בַּיָּמִים וַיְיָ בֵּרַךְ אֶת אַבְרָהָם בַּכֹּל: [בראשית כד, א]

ט) וַיָּזֶד יַעֲקֹב נָזִיד וַיָּבֹא עֵשָׂו מִן הַשָּׂדֶה וְהוּא עָיֵף: [בראשית כה, כט]

י) כִּי בַשָּׂדֶה מְצָאָהּ צָעֲקָה הַנַּעֲרָ הַמְאֹרָשָׂה וְאֵין מוֹשִׁיעַ לָהּ: [דברים כב, כז]

כ) כִּי קוֹל כְּחוֹלָה שָׁמַעְתִּי צָרָה כְּמַבְכִּירָה קוֹל בַּת צִיּוֹן תִּתְיַפֵּחַ תְּפָרֵשׂ כַּפֶּיהָ אוֹי נָא לִי כִּי עָיְפָה נַפְשִׁי לְהֹרְגִים: [ירמיה ד, לא]

ל) וַיֹּאמֶר עֵשָׂו הִנֵּה אָנֹכִי הוֹלֵךְ לָמוּת וְלָמָּה זֶּה לִי בְּכֹרָה: [בראשית כה, לב]

מ) עָזִּי וְזִמְרָת יָהּ וַיְהִי לִי לִישׁוּעָה זֶה אֵלִי וְאַנְוֵהוּ אֱלֹהֵי אָבִי וַאֲרֹמְמֶנְהוּ: [שמות טו, ב]

נ) וְיַעֲקֹב נָתַן לְעֵשָׂו לֶחֶם וּנְזִיד עֲדָשִׁים וַיֹּאכַל וַיֵּשְׁתְּ וַיָּקָם וַיֵּלַךְ וַיִּבֶז עֵשָׂו אֶת הַבְּכֹרָה: [בראשית כה, לד]

ס) וַיִּקְבְּרוּ אֹתוֹ יִצְחָק וְיִשְׁמָעֵאל בָּנָיו אֶל מְעָרַת הַמַּכְפֵּלָה אֶל שְׂדֵה עֶפְרֹן בֶּן צֹחַר הַחִתִּי אֲשֶׁר עַל פְּנֵי מַמְרֵא: [בראשית כה, ט]

ע) וַיִּגְוַע יִצְחָק וַיָּמָת וַיֵּאָסֶף אֶל עַמָּיו זָקֵן וּשְׂבַע יָמִים וַיִּקְבְּרוּ אֹתוֹ עֵשָׂו וְיַעֲקֹב בָּנָיו: [בראשית לה, כט]

The Gemara now gives the source for the final opinion recorded in the Baraisa, that Ishmael repented in Abraham's lifetime: וְשֶׁעָשָׂה יִשְׁמָעֵאל תְּשׁוּבָה בְּיָמָיו מְנָלַן – **From where** do we know that **Ishmael repented in [Abraham's] lifetime?** כִּי הָא דְּרָבִינָא וְרַב חָמָא בַּר בּוּזִי – The answer to this is **as** mentioned in **the following** discussion **involving Ravina and Rav Chama bar Buzi,** הֲווּ יָתְבִי קַמֵּיהּ דְּרָבָא וְקָא מְנַמְנֵם רָבָא – **who were sitting before Rava while Rava was dozing.** אָמַר לֵיהּ רָבִינָא לְרַב חָמָא בַּר בּוּזִי – **Ravina said to Rav Chama bar Buzi:** וַדַּאי דְּאָמְרִיתּוּ כָּל מִיתָה שֶׁיֵּשׁ בָּהּ גְּוִיעָה – **"Are you sure of what you said that any** mention of **death** in Scripture **where the term** ***gvi'ah*** **is** used זוֹ הִיא מִיתָתָן שֶׁל צַדִּיקִים – **[describes] the death of a righteous person?"** אָמַר לֵיהּ – **[Rav Chama bar Buzi] replied to [Ravina]:** אִין – **"Yes."** וְהָא דּוֹר הַמַּבּוּל – Ravina asked: **"But** what of **the Generation of the Flood?"** Although they were evil, Scripture uses the term *gvi'ah* in reference to their deaths.[46] אָמַר לֵיהּ – **[Rav Chama] replied to [Ravina]:** אֲנַן גְּוִיעָה וַאֲסִיפָה קָאָמְרִינַן – **"We refer to** the use of the term ***gvi'ah*** **together with** the term ***asifah.***"[47] This compound term is used exclusively in reference to righteous people. וְהָא יִשְׁמָעֵאל דִּכְתִיב בֵּיהּ גְּוִיעָה וַאֲסִיפָה – Ravina questions even this: **"But what of Ishmael, concerning whom** ***gvi'ah*** **and** ***asifah*** **is written?"**[48] אַדְּהָכִי אִיתְּעַר בְּהוּ רָבָא – **At this point, Rava awoke** אָמַר לְהוּ – and **said to them:** דַּרְדְּקֵי הָכִי אָמַר רַבִּי יוֹחָנָן – **"Children! This is what R' Yochanan said:** יִשְׁמָעֵאל עָשָׂה תְּשׁוּבָה בְּחַיֵּי אָבִיו – **Ishmael repented in his father's lifetime,** שֶׁנֶּאֱמַר: "וַיִּקְבְּרוּ אֹתוֹ יִצְחָק וְיִשְׁמָעֵאל בָּנָיו" – **as it is said:** ***[Abraham's] sons, Isaac and Ishmael, buried him.***"[49] From the order in which they are mentioned it seems that Ishmael, the older brother, allowed Isaac to go first. This shows that Ishmael had repented.

An objection is raised to R' Yochanan's inference:

וְדִילְמָא דֶּרֶךְ חָכְמָתָן קָא חָשִׁיב לְהוּ – **But maybe [Scripture] lists them** [Isaac and Ishmael] **according to the order of their wisdom,** not according to the order of their participation in Abraham's burial. – ? –

The Gemara answers:

אֶלָּא מֵעַתָּה – **But if so,** that Scripture follows the order of wisdom, then in the case of Isaac's burial, concerning which it is written: "וַיִּקְבְּרוּ אֹתוֹ עֵשָׂו וְיַעֲקֹב בָּנָיו" – ***[Isaac's] sons, Esau and Jacob, buried him,***[50] מַאי טַעְמָא לֹא חָשִׁיב לְהוּ דֶּרֶךְ חָכְמָתָן – **why does [Scripture] not list them** [Esau and Jacob] **in the order of their wisdom?** Evidently, Scripture does not follow the order of wisdom in such a context. אֶלָּא מִדְּאַקְדְּמֵיהּ – **Therefore, since in** connection with Abraham's burial **[Scripture] mentions [Isaac] first,** אַדְבּוּרֵי אַדְבְּרֵיהּ – it is evident that **[Ishmael] persuaded [Isaac]** to go first. וּמִדְּאַדְבְּרֵיהּ שְׁמַע מִינָּהּ תְּשׁוּבָה עָבַד בְּיָמָיו – **And, from** the fact **that [Ishmael] had [Isaac]** go first, **one can infer that [Ishmael] repented in [Abraham's] lifetime.**

Another Baraisa that discusses the blessing of בַּכֹּל, *with everything,* bestowed upon Abraham:

תָּנוּ רַבָּנָן – **The Rabbis taught in a Baraisa:** שְׁלֹשָׁה הִטְעִימָן הַקָּדוֹשׁ בָּרוּךְ הוּא בָּעוֹלָם הַזֶּה – There were THREE PEOPLE WHOM THE HOLY ONE, BLESSED IS HE, GAVE A TASTE IN THIS WORLD

NOTES

46. Ibid. 7:21.

47. אֲסִיפָה literally means gathering. [When a righteous person dies, he is "gathered" in to his people.]

48. Ibid. 25:17.

49. Ibid. 25:9.

50. Ibid. 35:29.

מֵעֵין הָעוֹלָם הַבָּא – OF A SEMBLANCE OF THE WORLD TO COME. אֵלוּ הֵן אַבְרָהָם יִצְחָק וְיַעֲקֹב – THEY ARE: ABRAHAM, ISAAC AND JACOB.

The Scriptural sources:

אַבְרָהָם דִּכְתִיב בֵּיהּ: ,,בַּכֹּל" – We know that **Abraham** merited this blessing, **for it is written of him**: *HASHEM blessed Abraham with everything* (*bakol*);[1] יִצְחָק דִּכְתִיב בֵּיהּ: ,,מִכֹּל" – **Isaac, for it is written of him:** *I ate from everything* (*mikol*);[2] יַעֲקֹב דִּכְתִיב בֵּיהּ: ,,כֹּל" – **Jacob, for it is written of him:** *I have everything* (*kol*).[3] These expressions of כֹּל, *everything,* indicate that the Patriarchs enjoyed every possible blessing, even a taste of the World to Come.[4]

The Baraisa continues:

שְׁלֹשָׁה לֹא שָׁלַט בָּהֶן יֵצֶר הָרָע – There were THREE people OVER WHOM THE EVIL INCLINATION HAD NO POWER. אֵלוּ הֵן אַבְרָהָם יִצְחָק וְיַעֲקֹב – THEY WERE: ABRAHAM, ISAAC AND JACOB.[5]

The Scriptural sources:

דִּכְתִיב בְּהוּ: ,,בַּכֹּל" ,,מִכֹּל" ,,כֹּל" – **For it is written of them** respectively: ***With everything, from everything, everything.*** These expressions of כֹּל, *everything,* signify not only physical benefit but spiritual achievement as well.

The Baraisa continues with a dissenting view:

וְיֵשׁ אוֹמְרִים אַף דָּוִד – SOME [SCHOLARS] SAY that King DAVID AS WELL was immune from the wiles of the Evil Inclination.

The Scriptural source:

דִּכְתִיב: ,,וְלִבִּי חָלַל בְּקִרְבִּי" – **For it is written** that David said: ***my heart*** (i.e. the Evil Inclination) ***has died within me.***[6]

The Gemara asks:

וְאִידָךְ – **And the other** Tanna (i.e. the first opinion recorded in the Baraisa), why does he not include David?

The Gemara answers that according to the first Tanna, David's verse, *my heart has died within me,* does not refer to the Evil Inclination:

צַעֲרֵיהּ הוּא דְּקָא מַדְכַּר – In this verse, **[David] recalls his suffering.** As a result of his many troubles, his heart was bereft of feeling.

The Gemara quotes another Baraisa, which deals with a similar theme:

תָּנוּ רַבָּנָן – **The Rabbis taught in a Baraisa:** שִׁשָּׁה לֹא שָׁלַט בָּהֶן מַלְאַךְ הַמָּוֶת – There were SIX PEOPLE OVER WHOM THE ANGEL OF DEATH DID NOT HAVE DOMINION. Their souls were taken by God Himself. וְאֵלוּ הֵן – THEY ARE: אַבְרָהָם – ABRAHAM, יִצְחָק – ISAAC, וְיַעֲקֹב – JACOB, מֹשֶׁה – MOSES, אַהֲרֹן – AARON וּמִרְיָם – AND MIRIAM.

The Scriptural sources:

אַבְרָהָם יִצְחָק וְיַעֲקֹב – We know that **Abraham, Isaac and Jacob** were accorded this honor דִּכְתִיב בְּהוּ: ,,בַּכֹּל",,מִכֹּל",,כֹּל" – **for it is written of them** respectively: ***with everything, from everything, everything.***[7] מֹשֶׁה אַהֲרֹן וּמִרְיָם – And we know that **Moses, Aaron and Miriam** were accorded this honor, דִּכְתִיב בְּהוּ: ,,עַל־פִּי ה׳ " – **for it is written of them:** ***By the mouth of HASHEM;***[8] i.e. they died through a "kiss" from God,[9] not at the hands of the Angel of Death.

The Gemara asks:

וְהָא מִרְיָם לֹא כְּתִיב בָּהּ: ,,עַל־פִּי ה׳ " – **But** the phrase, *by the mouth* ***of God,*** **is not written in connection with Miriam.** So how do we know that Miriam's soul was taken by God Himself?

The Gemara answers:

אָמַר רַבִּי אֶלְעָזָר – **R' Elazar said:** מִרְיָם נַמִּי בִּנְשִׁיקָה מֵתָה – **Miriam also died through a "kiss"** from God. דְּאַתְיָא ,,שָׁם" ,,שָׁם" מִמֹּשֶׁה – **This emerges** from an analogy between the word ***there*** that is written in connection with the death of Miriam, and the same word ***there*** that is written in reference to the death of **Moses.**[10] וּמִפְּנֵי מָה לֹא נֶאֱמַר בָּהּ: ,,עַל־פִּי ה׳ " – **And why** is the phrase, ***by the mouth of HASHEM,*** **not stated** explicitly **in connection with [Miriam]?** שֶׁגְּנַאי הַדָּבָר לוֹמַר – **Because it would be indelicate to say** such a thing.

A third Baraisa on a similar theme:

תָּנוּ רַבָּנָן – **The Rabbis taught in a Baraisa:** שִׁבְעָה לֹא שָׁלַט בָּהֶן רִמָּה וְתוֹלֵעָה – There were SEVEN people whose corpses WERE NOT AFFECTED WITH WORMS OR MAGGOTS. וְאֵלוּ הֵן – THEY ARE: אַבְרָהָם – ABRAHAM, יִצְחָק – ISAAC, וְיַעֲקֹב – JACOB, מֹשֶׁה – MOSES, אַהֲרֹן – AARON, וּמִרְיָם – MIRIAM וּבִנְיָמִין בֶּן יַעֲקֹב – AND BENJAMIN SON OF JACOB.

The Scriptural sources:

אַבְרָהָם יִצְחָק וְיַעֲקֹב – **Abraham, Isaac and Jacob:** דִּכְתִיב [בְּהוּ]: ,,בַּכֹּל" ,,מִכֹּל" ,,כֹּל" – **for it is written of them** respectively: ***with everything, from everything, everything.***[11] מֹשֶׁה אַהֲרֹן וּמִרְיָם – **Moses, Aaron and Miriam:** דִּכְתִיב [בְּהוּ]: ,,עַל־פִּי ה׳ " – **for it is written of them** that they died ***by the mouth of HASHEM.***[12] בִּנְיָמִין בֶּן יַעֲקֹב – **Benjamin son of Jacob:** דִּכְתִיב: ,,(ו)לְבִנְיָמִן אָמַר יְדִיד ה׳ יִשְׁכֹּן לָבֶטַח עָלָיו" – **for it is written:** ***Of Benjamin he*** [Moses] ***said, "The beloved of God, He shall***

NOTES

1. *Genesis* 24:1.

2. *Genesis* 27:33. [The plain meaning of the verse refers to the meal that Jacob served Isaac, before he was blessed by Isaac.]

3. *Genesis* 33:11.

4. This is the source for the sentence in בִּרְכַּת הַמָּזוֹן, *Grace After Meals:* הָרַחֲמָן הוּא יְבָרֵךְ... אוֹתָנוּ וְאֶת כָּל אֲשֶׁר לָנוּ כְּמוֹ שֶׁנִּתְבָּרְכוּ אֲבוֹתֵינוּ אַבְרָהָם יִצְחָק וְיַעֲקֹב ,,בַּכֹּל" ,,מִכֹּל" ,,כֹּל" כֵּן יְבָרֵךְ אוֹתָנוּ כֻּלָּנוּ יַחַד בִּבְרָכָה שְׁלֵמָה – *The compassionate One! May He bless...us and all that is ours, just as our forefathers Abraham, Isaac and Jacob were blessed "with everything," "from everything" [and with] "everything"; so may He bless us all together with a perfect blessing.*

We learned above (15b) that Job too was blessed with an inkling of the World to Come. However, Job is not listed in this Baraisa because he received this special blessing in only one aspect of his life – namely, his crops. The Patriarchs, on the other hand, were accorded this treatment in כֹּל, *everything (Tosafos).*

5. This does not mean that the *Yetzer Hara* (Evil Inclination) was always powerless against the Patriarchs, for then they would not be deserving of reward. Rather, the meaning is that since for many years the Patriarchs fought fiercely against the *Yetzer Hara,* God aided them in their later years by protecting them from its wiles *(Tosafos).*

6. *Psalms* 109:22.

7. These verses teach that Abraham, Isaac and Jacob enjoyed every conceivable honor. Therefore, since we find that Moses, Aaron and Miriam were accorded this honor, evidently it was bestowed upon the Patriarchs as well (*Rashi*).

8. Moses – *Deuteronomy* 34:5; Aaron – *Numbers* 33:38; see note 10.

9. The proximity of God's presence causes the soul to leave the body and cling to God (see *Ohr HaChaim* to *Leviticus* 16:1 ד״ה אי and 26:11 ד״ה ונתתי).

10. Regarding Miriam, it is written: וַתָּמָת שָׁם מִרְיָם וַתִּקָּבֵר שָׁם, *Miriam died there and was buried there (Numbers* 20:1). In reference to Moses, it is written: וַיָּמָת שָׁם מֹשֶׁה, *Moses died there (Deuteronomy* 34:5). The appearance of the same word [שָׁם, *there*] in both verses establishes a connection between them, from which it is derived that just as Moses died through a kiss from God, so did Miriam. (This is a homiletic use of the exegetical device known as גְּזֵרָה שָׁוָה, *gezeirah shavah.*)

11. [The preceding Baraisa taught, on the basis of these expressions, that the Patriarchs died through the "kiss" of God. See following note.]

12. The Gemara, *Avodah Zarah* 20b, teaches that a drop of poison passes from the sword of the Angel of Death to his victim. It is this poison that causes death and the subsequent decay of the corpse. Since the people mentioned here were put to death by God Himself, not by the Angel of Death, their corpses were not subject to decay (*Rashi*).

מסורת הש"ס

א) [מו"ק כח.], ב) [נ"א אברהם יצחק יעקב משה אהרן ומרים כדאמרן בנימין בן יעקב וכו' וכזה תמצא פירש"י להלן ד"ה כדאמרן וכו'], ג) שבת נה:, ד) נ"א וסד.

מעין העולם הבא אלו הן אברהם יצחק ויעקב אברהם דכתיב ביה א) בכל יצחק דכתיב ביה ב) מכל יעקב דכתיב ביה ג) כל שלשה לא שלט בהן יצר הרע אלו הן אברהם יצחק ויעקב דכתיב בהו בכל מכל כל ויש אומרים אף דוד דכתיב ד) ולבי חלל בקרבי ואידך צעריה הוא דקא מדכר תנו רבנן ששה לא שלט בהן מלאך המות ואלו הן אברהם יצחק ויעקב משה אהרן ומרים אברהם יצחק ויעקב דכתיב בהו בכל מכל כל משה אהרן ומרים דכתיב בהו ה) על פי ה' והא מרים לא כתיב בה על פי ה' אמר ר"א א) מרים נמי בנשיקה מתה דאתיא ו) שם שם ממשה ומפני מה לא נאמר בה על פי ה' שגנאי הדבר לומר תנו רבנן שבעה לא שלט בהן רמה ותולעה ואלו הן אברהם יצחק ויעקב משה אהרן ומרים ובנימין בן יעקב ב) אברהם יצחק ויעקב דכתיב [בהו] בכל מכל כל משה אהרן ומרים דכתיב [בהו] ע"פ ה' בנימין בן יעקב דכתיב ז) ולבנימין אמר ידיד ה' ישכון לבטח עליו וי"א אף דוד דכתיב ח) אף בשרי ישכון לבטח ואידך ההוא רחמי הוא דקא בעי תנו רבנן ג) ארבעה מתו בעטיו של נחש ואלו הן בנימין בן יעקב ועמרם אבי משה וישי אבי דוד וכלאב בן דוד וכולהו גמרא לבר מישי אבי דוד דמפרש ביה [קרא] דכתיב ט) ואת עמשא שם אבשלום תחת יואב על הצבא ועמשא בן איש ושמו יתרא הישראלי אשר בא אל אביגיל בת נחש אחות צרויה אם יואב וכי בת נחש היא והלא בת ישי היא דכתיב י) ואחיותיהם צרויה ואביגיל אלא בת מי שמת בעטיו של נחש:

הדרן עלך השותפין

לא א יחפור אדם בור סמוך לבורו של חבירו ולא שיח ולא מערה ולא אמת המים ולא נברכת כובסין אא"כ הרחיק (א) מכותל חבירו שלשה טפחים וסד בסיד ב ומרחיקים את הגפת ואת הזבל ואת המלח ואת הסיד ואת הסלעים (ב) מכותלו של חבירו שלשה טפחים ד) (או) סד בסיד ג מרחיקין את הזרעים ואת המחרישה ואת מי רגלים מן הכותל שלשה טפחים ד ומרחיקין את הריחים שלשה מן השכב שהן ארבעה מן הרכב ה ואת התנור שלשה מן הכליא שהן ארבעה מן השפה: **גמ'**

פתח

רש"י

בכל מכל כל. באברהם כתיב (בראשית כד) וה' ברך את אברהם בכל ביצחק כתיב (שם כז) ואוכל מכל ביעקב כתיב (שם לג) וכי יש לי כל כלומר לא חסרו שום טובה: **חלל בקרבי.** יצר הרע מת בקרבי: **צעריה קא מדכר.** על לבו ממש הוא מתרעם ואומר שמת בקרבו מרוב צרות: **שלא שלט בהן מלאך המות.** אלא מתו בנשיקה על פי שכינה: **בכל מכל כל.** לא חסרו שום כבוד ומעלה כבוד זה במשה ואהרן שנאמר בהן על פי ה' ואם אלו מתו ע"י מלאך [המות] נמצא שחסרו כבוד: **כדאמרן.** שמתו ע"פ שכינה ואין ראויה רמה לשלוט במי שנשוק משכינה שהרי אין הרמה באה אלא מטפה מרה המטפטפת מסכינו של מלאך המות דאמר מר (ע"ז דף כ:) ממנה מת ממנה מסריח ממנה פניו מוריקות: **ישכון לבטח עליו.** הכי דריש (ג) ישכון לבטח בנימין על סמיכות ידידות השכינה: **בעטיו של נחש.** בעצתו של נחש כלומר לא היו ראוין למות אלא שנגזרה גזירת מיתה על כל תולדותיו של אדם הראשון בעצתו של נחש בעטיו תרגום של עצתו כדכתיב (דניאל ו) אתייעטו כל וגו' וכן התיב עטא וטעם (שם ב): **ואחיותיהם.** בבני ישי כתיב:

הדרן עלך השותפין

לא יחפור. **בור שיח ומערה.** מפורשים בבבא קמא בפרק שור שנגח את הפרה (דף נ:): **בור.** עגול: **שיח.** ארוך וקצר: **מערה.** מקורה בקירוי: **נברכת הכובסים.** חופר חפירה מרובעת בעומק אמה או יותר ומי גשמים מתכנסים בה לכבס בגדיהם והיו להם שתים אחת שורים את הבגדים יום או יומים בגומת כלבים והיא קרויה מחמלן בגמ' ואחת שמשפשפים בה והיא קרויה נדיין: **אא"כ כו'.** מפני שהחפירה הסמוכה לבור מחלשת כותלי הבור ומרפה אותן: **וסד בסיד.** את כותלי חפירתן: **גפת.** פסולת זיתים שנתעצרו בבית הבד: **הסלעים.** אבנים שהאור יוצא מהן שקורין קוליי"ש שכל אלו קשין לחומה שמוציאין הבל: **מן הכותל.** כותל לבנים של טיט הבנוי על גבי קרקע ולאו בבור קאי השתא: **זרעים.** קשין לכותל כדמפרש בגמ': **ומחרישה.** מרפה את יסודו ונופל: **מי רגלים.** ממסמסין את הלבנים שהן של טיט יבש: **ריחים.** קשין לכותל שמנידין את הקרקע בגלגול חבטתו: **מן השכב.** היא הריחים התחתונה: **הרכב.** היא העליונה הרוכבת על זו והיא קצרה טפח מן התחתונה: **ואת התנור שלשה מן הכליא.** תנור כלי חרס הוא שרוף בכבשן כשאר קדירות ופיו למעלה והבא לקובעו בארץ עושה בנין טיט ואבנים שיהיו לו לבסים ומושיבין אותו עליו שלא יפטנו שוליו מחמת קרקע ואותו בנין עשוי בשיפוע רחב מלמטה וקצר מלמעלה כמדת התנור תחתונה קרוי כליא ועליונו קרוי שפה כלומר שפת הכליא שפתה עליונה ולפי שהבלו של תנור קשה לכותל צריך להרחיקו: **גמ'**

פתח

תוספות

שלשה כו' מעין העולם הבא. תימה לרשב"א אמאי לא חשיב נמי איוב דאמר לעיל (דף טו:) והאתנות רועות על ידיהם מלמד שהטעימו הקב"ה מעין עולם הבא וי"ל דאיוב לא היה אלא בחד מילתא ואברהם ויצחק ויעקב נהנו מעין עוה"ב מכל וכל:

שבעה שלא שלטה בהן רמה. תימה לרשב"א דכולהו צדיקי נמי דאמר בשבת בפ' שואל (דף קנב:) ורקב עצמות קנאה מי שיש לו קנאה בלבו עצמותיו נרקבין ושאין קנאה בלבו אין עצמותיו מרקיבין וי"ל דיכול להיות שלא ירקב וישלטו בו רמה כדאמר במעשה דרבי (ד) אלעזר בן שמעון בהשוכר את הפועלים (ב"מ דף פד:) דנפיק ריחשא מאודניה:

שלשה לא שלט בהן יצר הרע. אין לפרש שלא שלט כלל דא"כ היכי קבלו עליה אגרא אלא כדאמר (יומא דף לח:) מאי דכתיב רגלי חסידיו ישמור כיון שעבר אדם רוב שנותיו ולא חטא שוב אינו חוטא וה"נ כיון שראה הקב"ה שהיו דוחקין עצמן כל כך להתרחק מן העבירה סייעם הקדוש ברוך הוא מכאן ואילך שלא שלט בהן יצר הרע:

הדרן עלך השותפין

לא יחפור. כל הני איירי דאית בהו מיא וטעמא משום מתונתא כדאמרינן בגמרא ותימה לר"י והא אמרי' בגמ' כל מרא ומרא דקא מחית כו' ואומר ר"י דלא קאמר אלא שמאותה שעה מתחיל ההיזק וכיון דבתחילת ההיזק הוו גירי דיליה מודה ר' יוסי ומיהו אי לאו משום מיא לא היה צריך הרחקה ג' טפחים:

לא שיח ולא מערה. וה"ה חרילין ונעילין והני נקט אגב בור דבכל מקום רגיל לשנות שיח ומערה בהדי בור ואמת המים ונברכת הכובסין דאין רגיל לשנותן גבי בור מפרש בגמ' דצריכי תרוייהו ומיהו הא לא מפרש אמאי לא הוה שמעינן להו מבור דמצי למימר דבור ושיח דעמוקין טפי בעי הרחקת שלשה אבל הנך דלא עמיקי כולי האי הוה אמינא דלא בעי הרחקת שלשה ואי תנא הני הוה אמינא דבור ושיח דעמיקי טפי בעי הרחקה יותר מג' ובפרק הפרה (ב"ק דף נ:) דתנן אחד החופר בור ושיח ומערות ומצריך להו לכולהו בגמרא התם ניחא דלא הוה ליה לתנא למינקטינהו אגב בור כיון דכתיב בור בקרא אלא הוה ליה למיתני בור לחודיה:

סלעים. אבנים שאש יוצא מהן ולא סלעי נחושת דאין דרך להניחן אצל הכתלים והא דאמר בירושלמי אית תנא תני טומנין בסלעים ואית (ה) תני דאין טומנין כאן בסלעים של כסף כאן בסלעים של נחושת הוה מצי לשנויי כאן בסלעים של אבנים כאן בשל כסף אלא ניחא ליה לשנויי כולהו במתכת:

וסד בסיד. נראה לר"י דבסיפא נמי גרס וסד בסיד ולא גרס או דאי גרסי' בסיפא או סד בסיד אם כן תפשוט דברישא וסד בסיד תנן מדלא קתני או סד ברישא כמו בסיפא אלא ודאי בסיפא נמי גרס וסד והא דפשיטא ליה בגמרא (לקמן דף יט.) דבסיפא הוי או סד בסיד היינו משום דאין ההיזק כל כך מרובה שלא יועיל לו סיד לחודיה:

כליא. פירש ר"ח בטן דתנור צר מלמטה ובאמצעיתו מרחיב ובולט ויוצא כשיעור טפח ומאמצעיתו מיצר ועולה:

פתח

הגהות הב"ח

(א) במשנה ולא נברכת כובסין אא"כ הרחיק מכותלו של חבירו: (ב) שם ואת הסלעים מן הכותל של: (ג) רש"י ד"ה ישכון וכו' הכי דריש ליה ישכון בנימין לבטח על סמיכות: (ד) תוס' ד"ה שבעה וכו' דר' אלעזר בר"ש: (ה) שם ד"ה סלעים כו' ואית תנא תני דאין טומנין:

תורה אור השלם

א) וְאַבְרָהָם זָקֵן בָּא בַּיָּמִים וַייָ בֵּרַךְ אֶת אַבְרָהָם בַּכֹּל: [בראשית כד, א]

ב) וַיֶּחֱרַד יִצְחָק חֲרָדָה גְּדֹלָה עַד מְאֹד וַיֹּאמֶר מִי אֵפוֹא הוּא הַצָּד צַיִד וַיָּבֵא לִי וָאֹכַל מִכֹּל בְּטֶרֶם תָּבוֹא וָאֲבָרְכֵהוּ גַּם בָּרוּךְ יִהְיֶה: [בראשית כז, לג]

ג) קַח נָא אֶת בִּרְכָתִי אֲשֶׁר הֻבָאת לָךְ כִּי חַנַּנִי אֱלֹהִים וְכִי יֶשׁ לִי כֹל וַיִּפְצַר בּוֹ וַיִּקָּח: [בראשית לג, יא]

ד) כִּי עָנִי וְאֶבְיוֹן אָנֹכִי וְלִבִּי חָלַל בְּקִרְבִּי: [תהלים קט, כב]

ה) וַיַּעַל אַהֲרֹן הַכֹּהֵן אֶל הֹר הָהָר עַל פִּי יְיָ וַיָּמָת שָׁם בִּשְׁנַת הָאַרְבָּעִים לְצֵאת בְּנֵי יִשְׂרָאֵל מֵאֶרֶץ מִצְרַיִם בַּחֹדֶשׁ הַחֲמִישִׁי בְּאֶחָד לַחֹדֶשׁ: [במדבר לג, לח]

וַיָּמָת שָׁם מֹשֶׁה עֶבֶד יְיָ בְּאֶרֶץ מוֹאָב עַל פִּי יְיָ: [דברים לד, ה]

ו) וַיָּבֹאוּ בְנֵי יִשְׂרָאֵל כָּל הָעֵדָה מִדְבַּר צִן בַּחֹדֶשׁ הָרִאשׁוֹן וַיֵּשֶׁב הָעָם בְּקָדֵשׁ וַתָּמָת שָׁם מִרְיָם וַתִּקָּבֵר שָׁם: [במדבר כ, א]

ז) לְבִנְיָמִן אָמַר יְדִיד יְיָ יִשְׁכֹּן לָבֶטַח עָלָיו חֹפֵף עָלָיו כָּל הַיּוֹם וּבֵין כְּתֵפָיו שָׁכֵן: [דברים לג, יב]

ח) לָכֵן שָׂמַח לִבִּי וַיָּגֶל כְּבוֹדִי אַף בְּשָׂרִי יִשְׁכֹּן לָבֶטַח: [תהלים טז, ט]

ט) וְאֶת עֲמָשָׂא שָׂם אַבְשָׁלֹם תַּחַת יוֹאָב עַל הַצָּבָא וַעֲמָשָׂא בֶן אִישׁ וּשְׁמוֹ יִתְרָא הַיִּשְׂרְאֵלִי אֲשֶׁר בָּא אֶל אֲבִיגַל בַּת נָחָשׁ אֲחוֹת צְרוּיָה אֵם יוֹאָב: [שמואל ב יז, כה]

י) וְאַחְיוֹתֵיהֶם צְרוּיָה וַאֲבִיגָיִל וּבְנֵי צְרוּיָה אַבְשַׁי וְיוֹאָב וַעֲשָׂה אֵל שְׁלֹשָׁה: [דברי הימים א ב, טז]

עין משפט נר מצוה

א א מיי' פ"ט מהלכות שכנים הלכה א סמג עשין פב טוש"ע ח"מ סי' קנה סעיף י:
ב ב מיי' שם הלכה ב טוש"ע שם סעיף ד:
ג ג מיי' שם טוש"ע שם סעיף ה:
ד ד מיי' שם הלכה ג טוש"ע שם סעיף ז:
ה ה מיי' שם הלכה ד טוש"ע שם סעיף ח:

רבינו גרשום

על פי ה'. דמי שמת ע"י מלאך המות שולט בו רמה ותולעה מפני כי ג' טיפין של מרה תלוין בו בסכינו ממנה מת ממנה מסריח ממנה פניו מוריקים ואותם שמתו על פי ה' **לא שלט בהן רמה ותולעה: חלל בקרבי.** שאין בו יצר הרע: **צעריה דמדכר.** כלומר זה בקרבו מפחד מאותו מעשה שאירע לו: **רחמי הוא דבעי** א) שוכן בו לבטח: **בעטיו של נחש.** בעצה שיעצה לחוה ולא מפני חטא אדם עטיו לשון עצה כמו (דניאל ב) עטא וטעם:

הדרן עלך השותפין

לא יחפור אדם בור כו'. משום דקא מרפיה ליה לארעיה ומקלקל לבורו: **ולא שיח.** זהו חפירה שחופרין להשקות שדותיהן ועשויה אריך וקטין: **לא מערה.** שהיא מרובעת: **נברכת הכובסין.** ששם רוחצין וכובסין את בגדיהן:

חשק שלמה על רבינו גרשום

א) [נראה דל"ל רחמי הוא דבעי שישכון בשרו לבטח].

לעזי רש"י

קוליי"ש. פירוש אבני חלמיש (עיין רש"י דברים לב, יג ותוספות ב"ב דף יט ע"א ד"ה משום).

ליקוטי רש"י

הוא מלכה וע"י השטן המקטרג את העולם שנאמר (שם) אם שוט ימית פתאום וגו' ואם הוסיף לדבר אותו מקשי יסורין אשר כבדו וחזקו עליו דבר אבל אם פשעתם עם אשר הרשעתם אותו לאמר (שם ד) הלא יראתך כסלתך והתחזקתם אותו בחזקת רשע ולבסוף הריהם משותקים ומנולגלים לפניו והיה לכם לנחמו כאשר עשה אליפז ולא די לאיוב בצרתו ויסורו כי גם הוספתם על חטאותיו פשע להקניטו [איוב מב, ז]. **רעי איוב.** אוהביו. **לנגד.** כמו מי ינוד לך (ישעיה נא) לא תנודו לו (ירמיה טו) [שם ב, יא]. **שבענה.** הם פעמים שבע שתי שביעיות כמו (ויקרא יב) שבועים שהם שתי שבועות [איוב מב, יג]. **ויקרא שם האחת ימימה.** ע"ש יופיהן נקראו שמותיהן ימימה. לחה ומלובנה כיום. **קציעה.** ריחה נודף ערב ומבושם כקציעה של בשם. **קרן הפוך.** על שם הקרן שטוחנין בו כחול ובורית שנאמר ותקרעי בפוך עיניך (ירמיה ד) [שם מב, יד]. **כורכמא דרישקא.** כרכום של גן קרו"ג אורינט"ל הגדל בגנים [שבת קי.]. כרכום של גן שקורין קרוג אודמינל"ט והוא משובח שבכורכמין [ב"מ קז:]. קרוג אורייניט"ל [רשב"ם לקמן לח.]. **איצטגנינות.** להיות בקי בהליכות המזלות ותחילות השעות [יומא כח:]. איצטגניות דכל התלמוד לשון מזלות וחוזים בכוכבים [סנהדרין מט.]. **משכימין לפתחו.** לשאול במזלות [יומא שם]. **ושט את הבכורה.** לשון בזיון ויבז מתרגמי' ושט [יחזקאל טז, נז, וירמיה מט, טו]. **ויבז עשו.** העיד הכתוב על רשעו שביזה עבודתו של מקום [בראשית כה, לד]. **דרדקי.** בחורים שלא הגיעו לסברא [שבת קמה:]. [ע"כ שייך לדף טז:]

ולבי חלל בקרבי. יצר הרע הרי הוא כמת בקרבי שיש בידי לכופו [ברכות סא:]. יצר הרע חלל בקרבי ואין לו כח לשלוט בקרבי [ע"ז ד:]. **מתו בעטיו של נחש.** בעצתו של נחש שהשיא לחוה ולא בחטא אחר שלא חטאו בעטיו כמו עטא וטעם (דניאל ב) [שבת נה:]. **שמת בעטיו של נחש.** הוא ישי אבי דוד רבותינו אמרו שמת בלא עון בעטיו של נחש [שמואל ב, יז, כה]. **מערה.** מרובעת ומכוסה בקרוי אלא שיש לה פה [ב"ק נ:]. **גפת.** פסולת של בית הבד של שמן שהוא כנוס יחד וחם מאד [שבת מז:].

dwell securely upon him."[13]

The Baraisa continues with a dissenting view:

וְיֵשׁ אוֹמְרִים אַף דָּוִד – SOME [SCHOLARS] SAY that the corpse of King DAVID AS WELL was not subject to decay.

The Scriptural source:

דִּכְתִיב: ,,אַף־בְּשָׂרִי יִשְׁכֹּן לָבֶטַח" – **For it is written** that David said: ***even my flesh will rest securely.***[14]

The Gemara asks:

וְאִידָךְ – **And the other** Tanna (i.e. the first opinion recorded in the Baraisa), why does he not include David?

The Gemara responds that the first Tanna has a variant interpretation of David's verse, *even my flesh will rest securely*:

הַהוּא רַחֲמֵי הוּא דְּקָא בָּעֵי – In this verse, **[David] requests mercy.** He prays that his body will not decompose in the grave.

A related Baraisa:

תָּנוּ רַבָּנָן – **The Rabbis taught in a Baraisa:** אַרְבָּעָה מֵתוּ בְּעֶטְיוֹ שֶׁל נָחָשׁ – FOUR people DIED AS A RESULT OF THE SERPENT'S COUNSEL.[15] וְאֵלּוּ הֵן – THEY ARE: בִּנְיָמִין בֶּן יַעֲקֹב – BENJAMIN SON OF JACOB, וְעַמְרָם אֲבִי מֹשֶׁה – AMRAM FATHER OF MOSES וְיִשַׁי אֲבִי דָוִד – YISHAI FATHER OF DAVID וְכִלְאָב בֶּן דָּוִד – AND KILAV SON OF DAVID.

The sources:

וְכוּלְּהוּ גְּמָרָא – **All of them** are known through **tradition,** לְבַר מִיִּשַׁי אֲבִי דָוִד דִּמְפָרֵשׁ בֵּיהּ [קְרָא] דִּכְתִיב – **except for Yishai father of David, concerning whom the verse is explicit, as it is written:** ,,וְאֶת־עֲמָשָׂא שָׂם אַבְשָׁלֹם תַּחַת יוֹאָב עַל־הַצָּבָא – ***Avshalom put Amassa in charge of the army instead of Yoav.*** וַעֲמָשָׂא בֶּן־אִישׁ וּשְׁמוֹ יִתְרָא הַיִּשְׂרְאֵלִי – ***Now Amassa was the son of a man whose name was Yisra the Israelite*** אֲשֶׁר־בָּא אֶל־אֲבִיגַל בַּת־נָחָשׁ אֲחוֹת צְרוּיָה אֵם יוֹאָב" – ***who had relations with Avigal*** *(Avigayil) who was* ***the daughter of Nachash*** *and* ***the sister of Tzeruyah mother of Yoav.***[16] Avigayil is described here as the daughter of Nachash. וְכִי בַּת נָחָשׁ הִיא – **But was she the daughter of Nachash?** וַהֲלֹא בַּת יִשַׁי הִיא – **Was she not the daughter of Yishai,** דִּכְתִיב: ,,וְאַחְיֹתֵיהֶם צְרוּיָה וַאֲבִיגָיִל" – **as it is written** in reference to the sons of Yishai: ***And their sisters were Tzeruyah and Avigayil!***[17] Why then does the preceding verse refer to Avigayil's father as Nachash (which literally means serpent)?

אֶלָּא בַּת מִי שֶׁמֵּת בְּעֶטְיוֹ שֶׁל נָחָשׁ – **Rather,** the verse must mean that Avigayil was **the daughter of someone** (viz. Yishai) **who died as a result of the serpent's counsel.**

הדרן עלך השותפין

WE SHALL RETURN TO YOU, HASHUTAFIN

NOTES

13. *Deuteronomy* 33:12. The plain meaning of the verse is that God will dwell in the Temple, which will be in the portion of Benjamin (see *Rashi* and Targum ad loc.).

In our context, the verse is interpreted as follows: *The beloved of God, [Benjamin,] will rest securely on account of Him.* I.e. because of God's closeness, Benjamin's body will rest securely [in the grave, without decomposing] (see *Rashi*).

14. *Psalms* 16:9.

15. As a result of the serpent's enticement of Eve, Adam and Eve partook of the forbidden fruit of the "Tree of Knowledge." For this sin, God decreed death on mankind. The four people listed here did not otherwise deserve to die; they were put to death only as a consequence of this decree. [All others deserved to die anyway, for their sins] (*Rashi*).

16. *II Samuel* 17:25.

17. *I Chronicles* 2:16.

מעין העולם הבא אלו הן אברהם יצחק ויעקב אברהם דכתיב ביה א) בכל יצחק דכתיב ביה ב) מכל יעקב דכתיב ביה ג) כל שלשה לא שלט בהן יצר הרע אלו הן אברהם יצחק ויעקב דכתיב בהו בכל מכל כל ויש אומרים אף דוד דכתיב ד) ולבי חלל בקרבי ואידך צעריה הוא דקא מדכר תנו רבנן ששה לא שלט בהן מלאך המות ואלו הן אברהם יצחק ויעקב משה אהרן ומרים אברהם יצחק ויעקב דכתיב בהו בכל מכל כל משה אהרן ומרים דכתיב בהו ה) על פי ה' והא מרים לא כתיב בה על פי ה' אמר ר"א א) מרים נמי בנשיקה מתה דאתיא ו) שם שם ממשה ומפני מה לא נאמר בה על פי ה' שגנאי הדבר לומר תנו רבנן שבעה לא שלט בהן רמה ותולעה ואלו הן אברהם יצחק ויעקב משה אהרן ומרים ובנימין בן יעקב ב) אברהם יצחק ויעקב דכתיב [בהו] בכל מכל כל משה אהרן ומרים דכתיב [בהו] ע"פ ה' בנימין בן יעקב דכתיב ז) ולבנימין אמר ידיד ה' ישכון לבטח עליו וי"א אף דוד דכתיב ח) אף בשרי ישכון לבטח ואידך ההוא רחמי הוא דקא בעי תנו רבנן ג) ארבעה מתו בעטיו של נחש ואלו הן בנימין בן יעקב ועמרם אבי משה וישי אבי דוד וכלאב בן דוד וכולהו גמרא לבר מישי אבי דוד דמפרש ביה [קרא] דכתיב ט) ואת עמשא שם אבשלום תחת יואב על הצבא ועמשא בן איש ושמו יתרא הישראלי אשר בא אל אביגיל בת נחש אחות צרויה אם יואב וכי בת נחש היא והלא בת ישי היא דכתיב י) ואחיותיהם צרויה ואביגיל אלא בת מי שמת בעטיו של נחש:

הדרן עלך השותפין

לא א) יחפור אדם בור סמוך לבורו של חבירו ולא שיח ולא מערה ולא אמת המים ולא נברכת כובסין אא"כ הרחיק (א) מכותל חבירו שלשה טפחים וסד בסיד ב) ומרחיקים את הגפת ואת הזבל ואת המלח ואת הסיד ואת הסלעים (ב) מכותלו של חבירו שלשה טפחים ז) (או) סד בסיד ג) מרחיקין את הזרעים ואת המחרישה ואת מי רגלים מן הכותל שלשה טפחים ד) ומרחיקין את הריחים שלשה מן השכב שהן ארבעה מן הרכב ה) ואת התנור שלשה מן הכליא שהן ארבעה מן השפה: **גמ'**

פתח

רש"י

בכל מכל כל. באברהם כתיב (בראשית כד) וה' ברך את אברהם בכל ביצחק כתיב (שם כז) ואוכל מכל ביעקב כתיב (שם לג) וכי יש לי כל כלומר לא חסרו שום טובה: חלל בקרבי. יצרי הרע מת בקרבי: צעריה קא מדכר. על לבו ממש הוא מתרעם ואומר שמת בקרבו מרוב לרות: שלא שלט בהן מלאך המות. אלא מתו בנשיקה על פי שכינה: בכל מכל כל. לא חסרו שום כבוד ומלינו כבוד זה במשה ואהרן שנאמר בהן על פי ה' ואם אלו מתו ע"י מלאך [המות] נמלא שחסרו כבוד: כדאמרן. שמתו ע"פ שכינה ואין ראויה רמה לשלוט במי שנשוק משכינה שהרי אין הרמה באה אלא מטפה מרה המטפטפת מסכינו של מלאך המות דאמר מר (ע"ז דף כ:) ממנה מת ממנה מסריח ממנה פניו מוריקות: ישכון לבטח עליו. הכי דריש (ג) ישכון לבטח בנימין על שמירות ידידות השכינה: בעטיו של נחש. בעלתו של נחש כלומר לא היו ראוין למות אלא שנגזרה גזירת מיתה על כל תולדותיו של אדם הראשון בעלתו של נחש בעטיו תרגום של עלתו כדכתיב (דניאל ו) אתייעטו כל וגו' וכן התיב עטא וטעם (שם ב): ואחיותיהם. בבני ישי כתיב:

הדרן עלך השותפין

לא יחפור. בור שיח ומערה. מפורשים בבבא קמא בפרק שור שנגח את הפרה (דף נ:): בור. עגול: שיח. ארוך וקלר: מערה. מקורה בקירוי: נברכת הכובסים. חופר חפירה מרובעת בעומק אמה או יותר ומי גשמים מתכנסים בה לכבס בגדיהם והיו להם שתים אחת שכורים את הבגדים יום או יומים בלוחת כלים והיא קרויה מתמלין בגמ' ואחת שמשפשפים בה והיא קרויה נדיין: אא"כ כו'. מפני שהחפירה הסמוכה לבור מחלשת כותלי הבור ומרפה אותן: וסד בסיד. את כותלי חפירתן: גפת. פסולת זיתים שנתעלרו בבית הבד: הסלעים. אבנים שהאור יולא מהן שקורין קויל"ש שכל אלו קשין לחומה שמוליאין הבל: מן הכותל. כותל לבנים של טיט הבנוי על גבי קרקע ולאו בבור קאי השתא: זרעים. קשין לכותל כדמפרש בגמ': ומחרישה. מרפה את יסודו ונופל: מי רגלים. ממסמסין את הלבנים שהן של טיט יבש: ריחים. קשין לכותל שמנידין את הקרקע בגלגול חבטתו: מן השכב. היא הריחים התחתונה: הרכב. היא העליונה הרוכבת על זו והיא קלרה טפח מן התחתונה: ואת התנור שלשה מן הכליא. תנור כלי חרס הוא שרוף בכבשן כשאר קדירות ופיו למעלה והבא לקובעו בארץ עושה בנין טיט ואבנים שיהיו לו לבסיס ומושיבין אותו עליו שלא יטנו שוליו מחמת קרקע ואותו בנין עשוי בשיפוע רחב מלמטה וקלר מלמעלה כמדת התנור תחתונה קרוי כליא ועליונו קרוי שפה כלומר שפת הכליא שפתה עליונה ולפי שהבלו של תנור קשה לכותל לריך להרחיקו: **גמ'**

פתח

תוספות

שלשה כו' מעין העולם הבא. תימה לרשב"א אמאי לא חשיב נמי איוב דאמר לעיל (דף טו:) והאלהות רוצות על ידיהם מלמד שהטעימו הקב"ה מעין עולם הבא וי"ל דאיוב לא היה אלא בחד מילתא ואברהם ויצחק ויעקב נהנו מעין עוה"ב מכל וכל:

שבעה שלא שלטה בהן רמה. תימה לרשב"א דכולהו לדיקי נמי דאמר בשבת בפ' שואל (דף קנב:) ורקב עלמות קנאה כל מי שיש לו קנאה בלבו עלמותיו נרקבין ושאין קנאה בלבו אין עלמותיו מרקיבין וי"ל דיכול להיות שלא ירקב וישלוט בו רמה כדאמר במעשה דרבי (ד) אלעזר בן שמעון בהשוכר את הפועלים (ב"מ דף פד:) דנפיק ריחשא מאודניה:

שלשה לא שלט בהן יצר הרע. אין לפרש שלא שלט כלל דא"כ היכי קבלו עליה אגרא אלא כדאמר (יומא דף לח:) מאי דכתיב רגלי חסידיו ישמור כיון שעבר אדם רוב שנותיו ולא חטא שוב אינו חוטא ה"נ כיון שראה הקב"ה שהיו דוחקין עלמן כל כך להתרחק מן העבירה סייעם הקדוש ברוך הוא מכאן ואילך שלא שלט בהן יצר הרע:

הדרן עלך השותפין

לא יחפור. כל הני איירי דאית בהו מים וטעמא משום מתונתא כדאמרינן בגמרא ותימה לר"י והא אמרי' בגמ' כל מרא ומרא דקא מחית כו' ואומר ר"י דלא קאמר אלא שמאותה שעה מתחיל ההיזק וכיון דבתחילת ההיזק הוו גירי דיליה מודה ר' יוסי ומיהו אי לאו משום מיא לא היה לריך הרחקה ג' טפחים:

לא שיח ולא מערה. וה"ה חרלין ונעילין והני נקט אגב בור דבכל מקום רגיל לשנות שיח ומערה בהדי בור ואמת המים ונברכת הכובסין דאין רגיל לשנותן גבי בור מפרש בגמ' דלריכי תרוייהו ומיהו הא לא מפרש אמאי לא הוה שמעינן להו מבור דמלי למימר דבור ושיח דעמוקין טפי בעי הרחקת שלשה אבל הנך דלא עמיקי כולי האי הוה אמינא דלא בעי הרחקת שלשה ואי תנא הני הוה אמינא דבור ושיח דעמיקי טפי בעי הרחקה יותר מג' ובפרק הפרה (ב"ק דף נ:) דתנן אחד החופר בור ושיח ומערות ומלריך להו לכולהו בגמרא התם ניחא דלא הוה ליה לתנא למינקטינהו אגב בור כיון דכתיב בור בקרא אלא הוה ליה למיתני בור לחודיה:

סלעים. אבנים שאש יולא מהן ולא סלעי נחושת דאין דרך להניחן אצל הכתלים והא דאמר בירושלמי אית תנא תני טומנין בסלעים ואית (ה) תני דאין טומנין כאן בסלעים של כסף כאן בסלעים של נחושת הוה מלי לשנויי כאן בסלעים של אבנים כאן בשל כסף אלא ניחא ליה לשנויי כולהו במתכת: **וסד** בסיד. נראה לר"י דבסיפא נמי גרס וסד בסיד ולא גרס או דאי גרסי' בסיפא או סד בסיד אם כן תפשוט דברישא וסד בסיד תנן מדלא קתני או סד ברישא כמו בסיפא אלא ודאי בסיפא נמי גרס וסד והא דפשיטא ליה בגמרא (לקמן דף יט.) דבסיפא הוי או סד בסיד היינו משום דאין ההיזק כל כך מרובה שלא יועיל לו סיד לחודיה:

כליא. פירש ר"ח בטן דתנור לר מלמטה ובאמלעיתו מרחיב וגולט ויולא כשיעור טפח ומאמלעיתו מילר ועולה:

פתח

מסורת הש"ס

א) [מו"ק כח.], ב) [נ"א אברהם יצחק יעקב משה אהרן ומרים כדאמרן בנימין בן יעקב וכו' וכזה תמצא פירש"י דהכא ד"ה כדאמרן וכו'], ג) שבת נה:, ד) נ"א וסד:

הגהות הב"ח

(א) במשנה ולא נברכת כובסין אא"כ הרחיק מכותלו של חבירו: (ב) שם ואת הסלעים מן הכותל של: (ג) רש"י ד"ה ישכון וכו' הכי דריש ליה ישכון בנימין לבטח על סמיכות: (ד) תוס' ד"ה שבעה וכו' דר' אלעזר בר"ש: (ה) שם ד"ה סלעים כו' ואית תנא תני לאין טומנין:

תורה אור השלם

א) וְאַבְרָהָם זָקֵן בָּא בַּיָּמִים וַיְיָ בֵּרַךְ אֶת אַבְרָהָם בַּכֹּל: [בראשית כד, א]

ב) וַיֶּחֱרַד יִצְחָק חֲרָדָה גְּדֹלָה עַד מְאֹד וַיֹּאמֶר מִי אֵפוֹא הוּא הַצָּד צַיִד וַיָּבֵא לִי וָאֹכַל מִכֹּל בְּטֶרֶם תָּבוֹא וָאֲבָרְכֵהוּ גַּם בָּרוּךְ יִהְיֶה: [בראשית כז, לג]

ג) קַח נָא אֶת בִּרְכָתִי אֲשֶׁר הֻבָאת לָךְ כִּי חַנַּנִי אֱלֹהִים וְכִי יֶשׁ לִי כֹל וַיִּפְצַר בּוֹ וַיִּקָּח: [בראשית לג, יא]

ד) כִּי עָנִי וְאֶבְיוֹן אָנֹכִי וְלִבִּי חָלַל בְּקִרְבִּי: [תהלים קט, כב]

ה) וַיַּעַל אַהֲרֹן הַכֹּהֵן אֶל הֹר הָהָר עַל פִּי יְיָ וַיָּמָת שָׁם בִּשְׁנַת הָאַרְבָּעִים לְצֵאת בְּנֵי יִשְׂרָאֵל מֵאֶרֶץ מִצְרַיִם בַּחֹדֶשׁ הַחֲמִישִׁי בְּאֶחָד לַחֹדֶשׁ: [במדבר לג, לח]

וַיָּמָת שָׁם מֹשֶׁה עֶבֶד יְיָ בְּאֶרֶץ מוֹאָב עַל פִּי יְיָ: [דברים לד, ה]

ו) וַיָּבֹאוּ בְנֵי יִשְׂרָאֵל כָּל הָעֵדָה מִדְבַּר צִן בַּחֹדֶשׁ הָרִאשׁוֹן וַיֵּשֶׁב הָעָם בְּקָדֵשׁ וַתָּמָת שָׁם מִרְיָם וַתִּקָּבֵר שָׁם: [במדבר כ, א]

ז) לְבִנְיָמִן אָמַר יְדִיד יְיָ יִשְׁכֹּן לָבֶטַח עָלָיו חֹפֵף עָלָיו כָּל הַיּוֹם וּבֵין כְּתֵפָיו שָׁכֵן: [דברים לג, יב]

ח) לָכֵן שָׂמַח לִבִּי וַיָּגֶל כְּבוֹדִי אַף בְּשָׂרִי יִשְׁכֹּן לָבֶטַח: [תהלים טז, ט]

ט) וְאֶת עֲמָשָׂא שָׂם אַבְשָׁלֹם תַּחַת יוֹאָב עַל הַצָּבָא וַעֲמָשָׂא בֶן אִישׁ וּשְׁמוֹ יִתְרָא הַיִּשְׂרְאֵלִי אֲשֶׁר בָּא אֶל אֲבִיגַל בַּת נָחָשׁ אֲחוֹת צְרוּיָה אֵם יוֹאָב: [שמואל ב יז, כה]

י) וְאַחְיוֹתֵיהֶם צְרוּיָה וַאֲבִיגָיִל וּבְנֵי צְרוּיָה אַבְשַׁי וְיוֹאָב וַעֲשָׂה־אֵל שְׁלשָׁה: [דברי הימים א ב, טז]

עין משפט נר מצוה

א א מיי' פ"ט מהלכות שכנים הלכה א סמג עשין פב טוש"ע ח"מ סי' קנה סעיף א:
ב ב מיי' שם הלכה ג טוש"ע שם סעיף ד:
ג ג מיי' שם טוש"ע שם סעיף ז:
ד ד מיי' שם הלכה ג טוש"ע שם סעיף ז:
ה ה מיי' שם הלכה ד טוש"ע שם סעיף ח:

רבינו גרשום

על פי ה'. דמי שמת ע"י מלאך המות שולט בו רמה ותולעה מפני כי ג' טיפין של מרה תלוין בו בסכינו ממנה מת ממנה מסריח ממנה פניו מוריקים ואותם שמתו על פי ה' לא שלט בהן רמה ותולעה: חלל בקרבי. שאין בו יצר הרע: צעריה דמדכר. כלומר זה בקרבו מפחד מאותו מעשה שאירע לו: רחמי הוא דבעי א) שוכן בו לבטח: בעטיו של נחש. בעצה שיעצה לחוה ולא מפני חטא אדם עטיו לשון עצה כמו (דניאל ב) עטא וטעם:

הדרן עלך השותפין

לא יחפור אדם בור כו'. משום דקא מרפיה ליה לארעיה ומקלקל לבורו: ולא שיח. זהו חפירה שחופרין להשקות שדותיהן ועשויה אריך וקטין: לא מערה. שהיא מרובעת: נברכת הכובסין. ששם רוחצין וכובסין את בגדיהן:

חשק שלמה על רבינו גרשום

א) נראה דצ"ל רחמי הוא דבעי שישכון בשרו לבטח.

לעזי רש"י

קוויל"ש. פירוש אבני חלמיש (עיין רש"י דברים לב, יג ותוספות ב"ב דף יט ע"א ד"ה משום).

ליקוטי רש"י

הוא מכלה וכו' השטן המקטרג את העולם שנאמר (שם) את שוט ימים פתאום וגו' ואם הוסיף לדבר מעשי קושי יסורין אשר כבדו וחזקו עליו דבר אבל אתם פשעתם שלא אשר הרשעתם אותו לאמר (שם ז) הלא ירשאתך ככלתך והמחזקתם אותו בחזקת רשע ולבסוף הייתם משומים ומנולמים לפניו והיה לכם לנחמו כאשר עשה אליהוא אלא די לאיוב בלרתו ויסוריו כי גם הוסיפתם על חטאתיכם פשע להקניטו [איוב מב, ז]. רעי איוב. אוהביו. לנגד. כמו מי יגוד לך (ישעיה נא) לא תנודו לו (ירמיה טו) [שם ב, יא]. שבוע. הם פעמים שבע של שביעיות כמו שבע (ויקרא יב) שבועים שהם שתי שבועות [איוב מב, יג]. ויקרא שם האחת ימימה. ע"ש יופין נקראו שמותיהן ימימה. לשה והלבנה כיום. קציעה. ריחה נודף כעין ומבושם כקליא של בשם. קרן הפוך. על שם הקרן

שנותכו כו כחול ובורית שנאמר ותקרעי בפוך עיניך (ירמיה ד) [שם מב, יד]. כורכמא דרישקא. כרכום של גן קרו"ג אורינט"ל הגדל בגנים [שבת קי.]. כרכום של גן שקורין קרוג אורמילי"ע והוא משובח שבכורכמין [ב"מ קז:]. קרוג אורינט"ל [רשב"ם לקמן לח.]. איצטגנינות. להיות בקי בהליכות המזלות ומחילות השעות [יומא כח:]. איצטגנינות לכל התלמוד לשון מזלות וחוזים בכוכבים [סנהדרין מט.]. משכימין לפתחו. לשאול במזלות [יומא שם]. ושם את הבכורה. לשון בזיון וכזו מתרגמי' ושט [יחזקאל טז, נז; וירמיה מט, ג]. ויבז עשו. העיד הכתוב על רשעו שביזה עבודתו של מקום [בראשית כה, לד]. דרדקי. כחורים שלא הגיעו לפרקן [שבת קמה.]. [ע"כ שייך לדף טז:]

ולבי חלל בקרבי. ילר הרע הרי הוא כמת בקרבי ואין לו כח שהמית אותו בתענית (תהלים קט, כב). ילר הרע כמת בקרבי שאין לו שליטה בי כמו ששליטה בבני אדם [ברכות סא:]. מתו בעטיו של נחש. בעלתו של נחש שהשיאו לחוה לאכול מן העץ ולא מחטא אחר [שבת נה:]. בעטיו. בעלתו [ע"ז ה.]. ולא חטא כשאר בני אדם כמו שאמרו מתו בעטיו של נחש ולא בחטאם [שמואל ב, ז, כה]. מערה. מרובעת ומכוסה בקירוי אלא שיש לה פה [ב"ק נ:]. גפת. פסולת של בית הבד של שמן שהוא כנוס יחד יותר מאד [שבת מז:].

Chapter Two

Introduction

The second chapter deals with the limitations imposed upon a person's use of his property because of the damage that his activities may cause to a neighbor's property or enterprises.

The Dispute Between the Sages and R' Yose

The extent of these limitations is the subject of a fundamental dispute between Tannaim, which runs through the entire chapter. The Sages hold that, generally speaking, the responsibility for preventing damage rests upon the one who is causing the damage. This position is referred to as עַל הַמַּזִּיק לְהַרְחִיק אֶת עַצְמוֹ, *it is the responsibility of the owner of the hazard to distance it [from the property liable to be damaged].* R' Yose, however, holds that one is generally entitled to use his own property as he pleases, and it is up to the threatened party to ensure that his property is not damaged. This position is known as עַל הַנִּיזָּק לְהַרְחִיק אֶת עַצְמוֹ, *it is the responsibility of the threatened party to distance his property [out of harm's reach].*

גִּירֵי דִּילֵיהּ (דִּידֵיהּ), *His Arrows*

However, where damage to a neighbor results *directly* from an activity performed within one's property, R' Yose agrees that it is the responsibility of the one engaging in such activity to prevent damage from occurring (see 22b). The technical term for this type of activity is גִּירֵי דִּידֵיהּ, *his arrows.*[1] The analogy is to a person standing in his property and shooting arrows into the courtyard of his neighbor, which he is obviously forbidden to do (*Rambam Hil. Shecheinim* 10:5).

TERMS RELEVANT TO THIS CHAPTER

גִּירֵי דִּילֵיהּ, *his arrows*	— direct damage.
מַזִּיק, *the owner of a hazard*	— the one who has or does something in his property that is detrimental to his neighbor's property or enterprise.
נִיזָּק, *the threatened party*	— the owner of property or the enterprise that is liable to be damaged.
מֵיצַר, *boundary*	— the boundary between the property in which the hazard is situated and the neighboring property.

NOTES

1. According to most Rishonim, virtually all the cases dealt with in the following Mishnahs are classified as גִּירֵי דִּילֵיהּ, *his arrows.* Hence, in their view, these Mishnahs represent the views of both the Sages and R' Yose, except where noted otherwise. *Rashi,* however, following a more limited definition of גִּירֵי דִּילֵיהּ, *his arrows,* writes that many of the Mishnahs in this chapter are not reflective of the view of R' Yose (see 22b note 25).

Chapter Two

Mishnah This chapter deals with restrictions against using one's property in a way that could result in damage to the property of a neighbor. This Mishnah begins by listing precautions required to prevent damage to a neighbor's pit:

לֹא יַחְפּוֹר אָדָם בּוֹר סָמוּךְ לְבוֹרוֹ שֶׁל חֲבֵירוֹ – **A person may not dig a pit** in his own property **near his neighbor's pit,** וְלֹא שִׁיחַ וְלֹא מְעָרָה וְלֹא אַמַּת הַמַּיִם וְלֹא נִבְרֶכֶת כּוֹבְסִין – **nor** may he dig **a ditch, vault,**[1] **irrigation channel, or launderer's pool,**[2] אֶלָּא אִם כֵּן הִרְחִיק מִכּוֹתֶל חֲבֵירוֹ שְׁלֹשָׁה טְפָחִים – **unless he distances** it at least **three *tefachim* from his neighbor's wall,**[3] וְסָד בְּסִיד – **and applies lime** to the walls of his pit, ditch, etc.[4]

The remainder of the Mishnah delineates various precautions that must be taken in order to avoid damaging a neighbor's brick wall:[5]

וּמַרְחִיקִים אֶת הַגֶּפֶת וְאֶת הַזֶּבֶל וְאֶת הַמֶּלַח וְאֶת הַסִּיד וְאֶת הַסְּלָעִים – **Olive refuse,**[6] **manure, salt, lime, and** flint **stones**[7] **must be distanced** מִכּוֹתְלוֹ שֶׁל חֲבֵירוֹ שְׁלֹשָׁה טְפָחִים – at least **three *tefachim* from the** brick **wall of one's neighbor,** (אוֹ) סָד בְּסִיד – **or one must apply lime** to the wall.[8]

מַרְחִיקִין אֶת הַזְּרָעִים וְאֶת הַמַּחֲרֵישָׁה וְאֶת מֵי רַגְלַיִם – **Seeds,** the use of **a plow, and urine must be distanced** מִן הַכּוֹתֶל שְׁלֹשָׁה טְפָחִים – at least **three *tefachim* from the wall** of one's neighbor.[9]

וּמַרְחִיקִין אֶת הָרֵיחַיִם שְׁלֹשָׁה מִן הַשֶּׁכֶב – **A mill must be distanced** at least **three** *tefachim* from the wall of one's neighbor, as measured **from the lower millstone,** שֶׁהֵן אַרְבָּעָה מִן הָרֶכֶב – **which is** equivalent to **four** *tefachim* from the wall as measured **from the upper millstone.**[10] וְאֶת הַתַּנּוּר שְׁלֹשָׁה מִן הַכַּלְיָא – **An oven** must be distanced at least **three** *tefachim* from the wall of one's neighbor, as measured **from** the lower rim of **the** oven's **base,** שֶׁהֵן אַרְבָּעָה מִן הַשָּׂפָה – **which is** equivalent to **four** *tefachim* as measured **from the** upper **rim** of the base.[11]

NOTES

1. A שִׁיחַ, *ditch,* is long and narrow, as opposed to a בּוֹר, *pit,* which is round. A מְעָרָה, *vault,* is covered (*Rashi,* from *Bava Kamma* 50b).

2. A square pit of at least one *amah* or more in depth in which rain water is collected for the purpose of laundering. The laundering process involved two such pools: one in which the clothing is left to soak in cleaning agents for a day or two, and one in which the clothing is scrubbed (*Rashi*). The Gemara (19a) specifies to which of these pools our Mishnah refers.

[The reason *Rashi* mentions that the depth of a laundering pool is one *amah* (six *tefachim*) is possibly to teach that a laundering pool is subject to this restriction even though it is not as deep as a pit (which is usually ten *tefachim* deep – see Mishnah *Bava Kamma* 50b) (see *Tosafos* ד״ה לא שיח).]

3. The Gemara (17b) explains that this refers to the wall of his neighbor's pit.

Some commentators maintain that it is the *digging* of the pit, ditch, etc. that causes damage. The very act of digging weakens the surrounding ground and could cause the walls of a nearby pit to cave in. According to this view, the three-*tefach* limit applies even to a pit, ditch, etc. that does *not* contain water (*Ramban, Ran, Nimukei Yosef;* see *Ritva*). [It appears that *Rashi* takes this approach – see *Maharam* and *Pnei Shlomo.*]

Other commentators, however, are of the opinion that the Mishnah's restriction applies only to a pit, ditch, etc. that contains water. In their view, the concern is that water might seep out and damage the neighbor's pit (*Tosafos, Rashba*).

This dispute pertains only to a pit, ditch and vault. As far as an irrigation channel and launderer's pool are concerned, all agree that they must be distanced only if they contain water (*Ramban;* see *Nachalas Moshe*).

4. This reinforces the walls and prevents the surrounding ground from crumbling (*Ritva*). Alternatively: the purpose of lining the pit with lime is to prevent seepage (*Rambam, Hil. Shecheinim* 9:1). [See previous note.]

The *vav* prefix, which usually means "and," indicates that both preventive measures – plastering and distancing – are required. The Gemara (19a), however, entertains the possibility that the correct version of the text is או סד וכו׳, *or he plastered etc.,* which means that either preventive measure is sufficient by itself (*Rashi* to 19a, as explained by *Chasam Sofer;* cf *Tosafos* here).

5. In fact, the hazards mentioned above (pit, ditch, etc.) are also damaging to a wall and must be distanced from a wall (*Rambam Hil. Shecheinim* 9:1, *Shulchan Aruch Choshen Mishpat* 155:10). [Possibly, the reason those hazards are mentioned specifically in reference to a pit is that in contrast to the following hazards which are harmful *only* to a wall (see end of note 9), those hazards are harmful to a pit as well.]

6. The pulp that remains after olives have been pressed (*Rashi*).

7. Stones from which fire is produced. These stones, and all the other substances mentioned in this clause, are damaging to a brick wall in that they generate heat (*Rashi*).

8. The application of lime to the wall is sufficient in itself to prevent these materials from damaging the wall. Therefore, only one preventive measure – either plastering or distancing – is required (*Tosafos*).

[When lime (calcium oxide) is mixed with water, a chemical reaction takes place in which a great deal of heat is released. The resulting substance is calcium hydroxide, which is used as plaster. Once it dries it no longer gives off heat, and in fact protects the wall.]

9. The act of plowing can cause a wall to fall by weakening its foundation. Urine dissolves the clay bricks of which the wall is made. The reason for the restriction against seeds is given in the Gemara [19b] (*Rashi*).

In this clause, the preventive measure of plastering the wall is not mentioned. Since seeds and plowing affect the ground beneath the wall, rather than the wall itself, plastering the wall would be of no avail (*Meiri*). Plastering is also ineffective against the corrosive properties of urine (*Beis Yosef Choshen Mishpat* 155).

Although a pit can be damaged by moisture and the agitation of the ground, these hazards need not be distanced from a neighbor's pit, because their damaging effects do not extend deeply enough into the ground to harm a pit (*Meiri*).

10. The lower millstone protrudes one *tefach* from the upper one.

A mill can be harmful to a nearby wall, for when it revolves it causes the surrounding ground to vibrate. The upper millstone is known as the רֶכֶב (from רכב, *ride*) because it "rides" on the lower one (*Rashi*). [The lower stone, which merely "lies" in position, is referred to as the שֶׁכֶב – from שכב, *lie.*]

11. A תַּנּוּר, *tanur,* is an earthenware oven whose opening is at the top. In order to insulate the oven from the cold ground, it was placed on a base of clay and stones. This base had sloping sides, with its lower edge protruding one *tefach* beyond the upper edge (*Rashi;* cf. *Tosafos*).

The heat generated by the oven is damaging to a wall (*Rashi*).

מעין העולם הבא אלו הן אברהם יצחק ויעקב אברהם דכתיב ביה א) בכל יצחק דכתיב ביה ב) מכל יעקב דכתיב ביה ג) כל שלשה לא שלט בהן יצר הרע אלו הן אברהם יצחק ויעקב דכתיב בהו בכל מכל כל ויש אומרים אף דוד דכתיב ד) ולבי חלל בקרבי ואידך צעריה הוא דקא מדכר תנו רבנן ששה לא שלט בהן מלאך המות ואלו הן אברהם יצחק ויעקב משה אהרן ומרים אברהם יצחק ויעקב דכתיב בהו בכל מכל כל משה אהרן ומרים דכתיב בהו ה) על פי ה' והא מרים לא כתיב בה על פי ה' אמר ר"א א) מרים נמי בנשיקה מתה דאתיא ו) שם שם ממשה ומפני מה לא נאמר בה על פי ה' שגנאי הדבר לומר תנו רבנן שבעה לא שלט בהן רמה ותולעה ואלו הן אברהם יצחק ויעקב משה אהרן ומרים ובנימין בן יעקב ב) אברהם יצחק ויעקב דכתיב [בהו] בכל מכל כל משה אהרן ומרים דכתיב [בהו] ע"פ ה' בנימין בן יעקב דכתיב ז) ולבנימין אמר ידיד ה' ישכון לבטח עליו וי"א אף דוד דכתיב ח) אף בשרי ישכון לבטח ואידך ההוא רחמי הוא דקא בעי תנו רבנן ג) ארבעה מתו בעטיו של נחש ואלו הן בנימין בן יעקב ועמרם אבי משה וישי אבי דוד וכלאב בן דוד וכולהו גמרא לבר מישי אבי דוד דמפרש ביה [קרא] דכתיב ט) ואת עמשא שם אבשלום תחת יואב על הצבא ועמשא בן איש ושמו יתרא הישראלי אשר בא אל אביגיל בת נחש אחות צרויה אם יואב וכי בת נחש היא והלא בת ישי היא דכתיב י) ואחיותיהם צרויה ואביגיל אלא בת מי שמת בעטיו של נחש:

הדרן עלך השותפין

לא א יחפור אדם בור סמוך לבורו של חבירו ולא שיח ולא מערה ולא אמת המים ולא נברכת כובסין אא"כ הרחיק (א) מכותל חבירו שלשה טפחים וסד בסיד ב ומרחיקים את הגפת ואת הזבל ואת המלח ואת הסיד ואת הסלעים (ב) מכותלו של חבירו שלשה טפחים ד) (או) סד בסיד ג מרחיקין את הזרעים ואת המחרישה ואת מי רגלים מן הכותל שלשה טפחים ד ומרחיקין את הריחים שלשה מן השכב שהן ארבעה מן הרכב ה ואת התנור שלשה מן הכליא שהן ארבעה מן השפה: **גמ'** פתח

רש"י

בכל מכל כל. באברהם כתיב (בראשית כד) וה' ברך את אברהם בכל ביצחק כתיב (שם כז) ואוכל מכל ביעקב כתיב (שם לג) וכי יש לי כל כלומר לא חסרו שום טובה: **חלל בקרבי.** יצרי הרע מת בקרבי: **צעריה קא מדכר.** על לבו ממש הוא מתרעם ואומר שמת בקרבו מרוב צרות: **שלא שלט בהן מלאך המות.** אלא מתו בנשיקה על פי שכינה: **בכל מכל כל.** לא חסרו שום כבוד ומלוי כבוד זה במשה ואהרן שנאמר בהן על פי ה' ואם אלו מתו ע"י מלאך [המות] נמצא שחסרו כבוד: **כדאמרן.** שמתו ע"פ שכינה ואין ראויה רמה לשלוט במי שנשוק משכינה שהרי אין הרמה באה אלא מטפה מרה המטפטפת מסכינו של מלאך המות דאמר מר (ע"ז דף כ:) ממנה מת ממנה מסריח ממנה פניו מוריקות: **ישכון לבטח עליו.** הכי דריש (ג) ישכון לבטח בנימין על סמיכות ידידות השכינה: **בעטיו של נחש.** בעצתו של נחש כלומר לא היו ראוין למות אלא שנגזרה גזירת מיתה על כל תולדותיו של אדם הראשון בעצתו של נחש בעטיו תרגום של עצתו כדכתיב (דניאל ו) אתייעטו כל וגו' וכן השיב עטא וטעם (שם ב): **ואחיותיהם.** בבני ישי כתיב:

הדרן עלך השותפין

לא יחפור. בור שיח ומערה. מפורשים בבבא קמא בפרק שור שנגח את הפרה (דף נ:): **בור.** עגול: **שיח.** ארוך וקצר: **מערה.** מקורה בקירוי: **נברכת הכובסים.** חופר חפירה מרובעת בעומק אמה או יותר ומי גשמים מתכנסים בה לכבס בגדיהם והיו להם שתים אחת שורים את הבגדים יום או יומים בלוחות כלים והיא קרויה ממחקן בגמ' ואחת שמשפשפים בה והיא קרויה נדיין: **אא"כ כו'.** מפני שהחפירה הסמוכה לבור מחלחלת כותלי הבור ומרפה אותן: **וסד בסיד.** את כותלי חפירתן: **גפת.** פסולת זיתים שנתעצרו בבית הבד: **הסלעים.** אבנים שהאור יוצא מהן שקורין קוליי"ש שכל אלו קשין לחומה שמוציאין הבל: **מן הכותל.** כותל לבנים של טיט הבנוי על גבי קרקע ולאו בבור קאי השתא: **זרעים.** קשין לכותל כדמפרש בגמ': **ומחרישה.** מרפה את יסודו ונופל: **מי רגלים.** ממסמסין את הלבנים שהן של טיט יבש: **ריחים.** קשין לכותל שמנידין את הקרקע בגלגול תבטתו: **מן השכב.** היא הריחים התחתונה: **הרכב.** היא העליונה הרוכבת על זו והיא קצרה טפח מן התחתונה: **ואת התנור שלשה מן הכליא.** תנור כלי חרס הוא שרוף בכבשן כשאר קדירות ופיו למעלה והבא לקובעו בארץ עושה בנין טיט ואבנים סביביו לבסים ומושיבין אותו עליו שלא יטלטלו שוליו מחמת קרקע ואותו בנין עשוי בשיפוע רחב מלמטה וקצר מלמעלה כמדת התנור תחתונה קרוי כליא ועליונו קרוי שפה כלומר שפת הכליא שפתה עליונה ולפי שהבלו של תנור קשה לכותל צריך להרחיקו: **גמ'**

תוספות

שלשה כו' **מעין העולם הבא.** תימה לרשב"א אמאי לא חשיב נמי איוב דאמר לעיל (דף טו:) והאתונות רועות על ידיהם מלמד שהטעימו הקב"ה מעין עולם הבא וי"ל דאיוב לא היה אלא בחד מילתא ואברהם ויצחק ויעקב נהנו מעין עוה"ב מכל וכל:

שבעה שלא שלטה בהן רמה. תימה לרשב"א דכולהו צדיקי נמי דאמר בשבת בפ' שואל (דף קנב:) ורקב עצמות קנאה מי שיש לו קנאה בלבו עצמותיו נרקבין ושאין קנאה בלבו אין עצמותיו מרקיבין וי"ל דיכול להיות שלא ירקב וישלוט בו רמה כדאמר במעשה דרבי (ד) אלעזר בן שמעון בהשוכר את הפועלים (ב"מ דף פד:) דנפיק ריחשא מאודניה:

שלשה לא שלט בהן יצר הרע. אין לפרש שלא שלט כלל דא"כ היכי קבלו עליה אגרא אלא כדאמר (יומא דף לח:) מאי דכתיב רגלי חסידיו ישמור כיון שעבר אדם רוב שנותיו ולא חטא שוב אינו חוטא ה"נ כיון שראה הקב"ה שהיו דוחקין עצמן כל כך להתרחק מן העבירה סייעם הקדוש ברוך הוא מכאן ואילך שלא שלט בהן יצר הרע:

הדרן עלך השותפין

לא יחפור. כל הני איירי דאית בהו מיא וטעמא משום מתונתא כדאמרינן בגמרא ותימה לר"י והא אמרי' בגמ' כל מרא ומרא דקא מחית כו' ואומר ר"י דלא קאמר אלא שמאותה שעה מתחיל ההיזק וכיון דבתחילת ההיזק הוו גירי דיליה מודה ר' יוסי ומיהו אי לאו משום מיא לא היה צריך הרחקה ג' טפחים:

לא שיח ולא מערה. וה"ה חרילין ונעילין והני נקט אגב בור דבכל מקום רגיל לשנות שיח ומערה בהדי בור ואמת המים ונברכת הכובסין דאין רגיל לשנותן גבי בור מפרש בגמ' דצריכי תרוייהו ומיהו הא לא מפרש אמאי לא הוה שמעינן להו מבור דמצי למימר דבור ושיח דעמוקין טפי בעי הרחקת שלשה אבל הנך דלא עמיקי כולי האי הוה אמינא דלא בעי הרחקת שלשה ואי תנא הני הוה אמינא דבור ושיח דעמיקי טפי בעי הרחקה יותר מג' ובפרק הפרה (ב"ק דף נ:) דתנן אחד החופר בור ושיח ומערות ומצריך להו לכולהו בגמרא התם ניחא דלא הוה ליה לתנא למינקטינהו אגב בור כיון דכתיב בור בקרא אלא הוה ליה למיתני בור לחודיה:

סלעים. אבנים שאש יוצא מהן ולא סלעי נחושת דאין דרך להניחן אצל הכתלים והא דאמר בירושלמי אית תנא תני טומנין בסלעים ואית (ה) תני דאין טומנין כאן בסלעים של כסף כאן בסלעים של נחושת הוה מצי לשנויי כאן בסלעים כאן באבנים כאן בשל כסף אלא ניחא ליה לשנויי כולהו במתכת: **וסד בסיד.** נראה לר"י דבסיפא נמי גרס וסד בסיד או לא גרס או דלא גרסי' בסיפא אם כן סד בסיד או לפסוק בסיד או דלא נקט בסיד ונקט תנן מדלא קתני סד בסיד בסיפא נמי גרס וסד והא דבסיפא ליה בגמרא (לקמן דף יט.) דבסיפא הוי או סד בסיד היינו משום דלאו היזק כל כך מרובה שלא יועיל לו סיד לחודיה:

כליא. פירש ר"ח בטן התנור צר מלמטה ובאמצעיתו מרחיב ובולט ויוצא לשיעור טפח ומאמצעיתו מיצר ועולה:

פתח

מסורת הש"ס

א) [מו"ק כח.], ב) [נ"א אברהם יצחק יעקב משה אהרן ומרים כדאמרן בנימין בן יעקב וכו' וכזה הבין פירש"י דהכלל ד"ה כדאמרן וכו'], ג) שבת נה:, ד) נ"א וסד:

הגהות הב"ח

(א) במשנה ולא נברכת כובסין אא"כ הרחיק מכותלו של חבירו: (ב) שם ואת הסלעים מן הכותל של: (ג) רש"י ד"ה ישכון וכו' הכי דריש ליה ישכון בנימין לבטח על סמיכות: (ד) תוס' ד"ה שבעה וכו' דר' אלעזר בר שמעון: (ה) בא"ד ד"ה סלעים כו' ואית תנא תני דאין טומנין:

תורה אור השלם

א) וְאַבְרָהָם זָקֵן בָּא בַּיָּמִים וַיי בֵּרַךְ אֶת אַבְרָהָם בַּכֹּל: [בראשית כד, א]

ב) וַיֶּחֱרַד יִצְחָק חֲרָדָה גְּדֹלָה עַד מְאֹד וַיֹּאמֶר מִי אֵפוֹא הוּא הַצָּד צַיִד וַיָּבֵא לִי וָאֹכַל מִכֹּל בְּטֶרֶם תָּבוֹא וָאֲבָרְכֵהוּ גַּם בָּרוּךְ יִהְיֶה: [בראשית כז, לג]

ג) קַח נָא אֶת בִּרְכָתִי אֲשֶׁר הֻבָאת לָךְ כִּי חַנַּנִי אֱלֹהִים וְכִי יֶשׁ לִי כֹל וַיִּפְצַר בּוֹ וַיִּקָּח: [בראשית לג, יא]

ד) כִּי עָנִי וְאֶבְיוֹן אָנֹכִי וְלִבִּי חָלַל בְּקִרְבִּי: [תהלים קט, כב]

ה) וַיַּעַל אַהֲרֹן הַכֹּהֵן אֶל הֹר הָהָר עַל פִּי יְיָ וַיָּמָת שָׁם בִּשְׁנַת הָאַרְבָּעִים לְצֵאת בְּנֵי יִשְׂרָאֵל מֵאֶרֶץ מִצְרַיִם בַּחֹדֶשׁ הַחֲמִישִׁי בְּאֶחָד לַחֹדֶשׁ: [במדבר לג, לח]

ו) וַיָּמָת שָׁם מֹשֶׁה עֶבֶד יְיָ בְּאֶרֶץ מוֹאָב עַל פִּי יְיָ: [דברים לד, ה]

ז) וַיָּבֹאוּ בְנֵי יִשְׂרָאֵל כָּל הָעֵדָה מִדְבַּר צִן בַּחֹדֶשׁ הָרִאשׁוֹן וַיֵּשֶׁב הָעָם בְּקָדֵשׁ וַתָּמָת שָׁם מִרְיָם וַתִּקָּבֵר שָׁם: [במדבר כ, א]

ז) לְבִנְיָמִן אָמַר יְדִיד יְיָ יִשְׁכֹּן לָבֶטַח עָלָיו חֹפֵף עָלָיו כָּל הַיּוֹם וּבֵין כְּתֵפָיו שָׁכֵן: [דברים לג, יב]

ח) לָכֵן שָׂמַח לִבִּי וַיָּגֶל כְּבוֹדִי אַף בְּשָׂרִי יִשְׁכֹּן לָבֶטַח: [תהלים טז, ט]

ט) וְאֶת עֲמָשָׂא שָׂם אַבְשָׁלֹם תַּחַת יוֹאָב עַל הַצָּבָא וַעֲמָשָׂא בֶן אִישׁ וּשְׁמוֹ יִתְרָא הַיִּשְׂרְאֵלִי אֲשֶׁר בָּא אֶל אֲבִיגַל בַּת נָחָשׁ אֲחוֹת צְרוּיָה אֵם יוֹאָב: [שמואל ב יז, כה]

י) וְאַחְיוֹתֵיהֶם צְרוּיָה וַאֲבִיגָיִל וּבְנֵי צְרוּיָה אַבְשַׁי וְיוֹאָב וַעֲשָׂה־אֵל שְׁלֹשָׁה: [דברי הימים א ב, טז]

עין משפט נר מצוה

א א מיי' פ"ט מהלכות שכנים הלכה א סמג עשין פב טוש"ע ח"מ סי' קנה סעיף יב:
ב ב מיי' שם הלכה ג טוש"ע שם סעיף ד:
ג ג מיי' שם טוש"ע שם סעיף ה:
ד ד מיי' שם הלכה ג טוש"ע שם סעיף ז:
ה ה מיי' שם הלכה ד טוש"ע שם סעיף ח:

רבינו גרשום

על פי ה'. דמי שמת ע"י מלאך המות שולט בו רמה ותולעה מפני כי ג' טיפין של מרה תלוין בו בסכינו ממנה מת ממנה מסריח ממנה פניו מוריקים ואותם שמתו על פי ה' לא שלט בהן רמה ותולעה: חלל בקרבי. שאין בו יצר הרע: צעריה דמדכר. כלומר זה בקרבו מפחד מאותו מעשה שאירע לו: רחמי הוא דבעי א) שוכן בו לבטח: בעטיו של נחש. בעצה שיעצה לחוה ולא מפני חטא אדם עטיו לשון עצה כמו (דניאל ב) עטא וטעם:

הדרן עלך השותפין

לא יחפור אדם בור כו'. משום דקא מרפיה ליה לארעיה ומקלקל לבורו: ולא שיח. זהו חפירה שחופרין להשקות שדותיהן ועשויה ארוך וקטן: לא מערה. שהיא מרובעת: נברכת הכובסין. ששם רוחצין וכובסין את בגדיהן:

חשק שלמה על רבינו גרשום

א) [נראה דל"ל רחמי הוא דבעי שישכון בשרו לבטח].

לעזי רש"י

קוליי"ש. פירוש אבני חלמיש (עיין רש"י דברים לב, יג ותוספות ב"ב דף יט ע"א ד"ה משום).

ליקוטי רש"י

הוא מלכה וע"י השטן המקטרג את העולם שנאמר (שם) אם שוט ימית פתאום וגו' ואם הוסיף לדבר מפני קושי יסורין אשר כבדו וחזקו עליו דבר אבל אתם פשעים על אשר הרשעתם אותו לאמר (שם ד) הלא יראתך כסלתך והתחזקתם אותו בחזקת רשע ולבסוף הייתם משוסקים ומנולסים לפניו והיה לכם לנחמו כאשר עשה אליהוא ולא די לאיוב בצרתו ויסוריו כי גם הוספתם על חטאותיו פשע להקניטו [איוב מב, ז]. רעי איוב. אוהביו. לנוד. כמו מי ינוד לך (ישעיה נא) לא תנודו לו (ירמיה טו) [שם ב, יא]. שבענה. הם פעמים שבע של שבועות כמו (ויקרא יב) שבועים שהם שתי שבועות [איוב מב, יג]. ויקרא שם האחת ימימה. ע"ש יופיין נקראו שמותיהן ימימה כיום. קציעה. ריחה נודף כבשם. ומנושם כקציעה של בשם. קרן הפוך. על שם הקקן

שנותנין בו כחול ובורית שנאמר ותקרעי בפוך עיניך (ירמיה ד) [שם מב, יד]. כורכמא דרישקא. כרכום של גן קרו"ג אורינט"ל הגדל בגנים [שבת קי.]. כרכום של גן קורין קרוג אורטולי"ל והוא משובח שבכורכמין [ב"מ קז:]. קרוג אוריינט"ל [רשב"ם לקמן לח.]. איצטגנינות. להיות בקי בהלכות המזלות ומחילות השעות [יומא כח:]. איצטגנינות לכל התלמוד לשון מזלות וחזיית כוכבים [סנהדרין סה:]. משכימין לפתחו. לשאול ממנו [יומא שם]. ושט את הבכורה. לשון בזיון וכן מתרגמי' ושט [יחזקאל טז, נז וירמיה מט, ג]. ויבז עשו. העיד הכתוב על רשעו שביזה עבודתו של מקום [בראשית כה, לד]. דרדקי. תנוקות שלא הגיעו לפרקם [שבת קמה:]. [ע"כ שייך לדף טז:]

ולבי חלל בקרבי. יצר הרע הרי הוא כמת בקרבי שלא יכולתי לכופו [ברכות סא:]. מתו בעטיו של נחש. בעצתו של נחש שהשיא לחוה ולא חטא ... עטא וטעם (דניאל ב) [שבת נה:]. שמת בעטיו של נחש. הוא ישי אבי דוד שמתו כולן [שבת נה:].

עין משפט נר מצוה

ו א מיי' פכ"א מהלכות מכירה הל' יג סמג עשין פב טוש"ע ח"מ סי' ריז סעיף ה:
ז ב ג מיי' פ"ט מהל' שכנים הל' י סמג עשין פב טוש"ע ח"מ סי' קנה סעיף יח:

מסורת הש"ס

א) רש"ל מ"ז, ב) [לקמן כה: כו: ב"מ קיז.], ג) [לקמן כב: כה:], ד) לקמן יט. ע"ש [תוספתא פ"א], ה) צ"ל סותר וכ"ה בע"י:

פתח בבור ומסיים בכותל (א) (ליתני אלא אם כן הרחיק מבורו של חבירו ג"ט) אמר אביי ואיתימא רב יהודה מכותל בורו שנינו וליתני אא"כ הרחיק מבורו של חבירו ג' טפחים הא קמ"ל דכותל בור שלשה טפחים נפקא מינה למקח וממכר כדתניא א האומר לחבירו בור וכותליה אני מוכר לך צריך שיהא הכותל שלשה טפחים איתמר הבא לסמוך בצד המצר אביי אמר סומך ורבא אמר אינו סומך בשדה העשויה לבורות דברי הכל אינו סומך כי פליגי בשדה שאינה עשויה לבורות אביי אמר סומך דהא אינה עשויה לבורות רבא אמר אינו סומך דאמר ליה כי היכי דאת אימלכת וחפרת אנא נמי ממלכנא וחפרנא איכא דאמרי ב בשדה שאינה עשויה לבורות דברי הכל סומך כי פליגי בשדה העשויה לבורות אביי אמר סומך אפילו לרבנן דאמרי ג מרחיקין את האילן מן הבור עשרים וחמש אמה התם הוא דבעידנא דקא נטע איתא לבור אבל הכא בעידנא דקא חפר ליתא לבור ורבא אמר ג אינו סומך ואפילו לר' יוסי דאמר ג זה חופר בתוך שלו וזה נוטע בתוך שלו הני מילי התם דבעידנא דקא נטע ליתנהו לשרשין דמזקי לה לבור אבל הכא אמר ליה כל מרא ומרא דקא מחיית קא מרפית לה לארעאי תנן לא יחפור אדם בור סמוך לבורו של חבירו טעמא דאיכא בור הא ליכא בור סומך בשלמא להך לישנא דאמרת בשדה שאינה עשויה לבורות דברי הכל סומך מתניתין בשדה שאינה עשויה לבורות אלא להך לישנא דאמרת בשדה שאינה עשויה לבורות פליגי בשלמא לאביי ניחא אלא לרבא קשיא אמר לך רבא הא איתמר עלה אמר אביי ואיתימא רב יהודה מכותל בורו שנינו איכא דאמרי (א) ואיתמר עלה אמר אביי ואיתימא רב יהודה מכותל בורו שנינו בשלמא להך לישנא דאמרת בשדה העשויה לבורות דברי הכל אינו סומך מתניתין בשדה העשויה לבורות אלא להך לישנא דאמרת בשדה העשויה לבורות פליגי בשלמא לרבא ניחא אלא לאביי קשיא אמר לך אביי מתני' שבאו לחפור בבת אחת תא שמע ד סלע הבא בידים זה חופר בורו מכאן וזה חופר בורו מכאן זה מרחיק שלשה טפחים וסד בסיד וזה מרחיק שלשה טפחים וסד בסיד בא בידים שאני ודקארי לה מאי קארי לה בא בידים איצטריכא ליה ס"ד אמינא כיון דבא בידים ליבעי נמי רווחא טפי קא משמע לן תא שמע מרחיקין את הגפת ואת הזבל ואת המלח

רש"י

פתח בבור. סמוך לבורו של חבירו והדר סיים אלא אם כן הרחיק מכותל הוה ליה למיתני אלא אם כן הרחיק מבורו דאילו מכותלו כותל הבור על גבי קרקע הוא: **מכותל בורו שנינו.** כלומר האי כותל דקתני מכותל בורו קאמר שאף הוא קרוי כותל: **וליתני מבורו של חבירו.** ואנא ידענא דמכותל קאמר דאי מחלל בורו קאמר אין זה כונס לתוך שלו כלום ופעמים שהוא סותר אף כותל חבירו אם הוא רחב משלשה: **הא קא משמע לן.** במאי (ב) דתניא מכותל בורו למדנו בה שהכותל בורו של ראשון מילא כל שלשה טפחים שהוחקק גם הוא להרחיק מן המיצר וממאי מדקתני שהחפירות חללו של זה אינה מופלגת מכותלו של זה אלא שלשה טפחים שהוא כונס לתוך שלו נמצא ששלשת הטפחים שכנס גם זה לתוך שלו הכותל מלאם ואשמועינן שיעור רוחב כותלי בור: **ונפקא מינה למקח וממכר.** וא"ת מנלן (ג) שהכותל הראשון הוא הוי שיעור הרחקה מן המיצר והלא לא היה לחבירו בור סמוך למיצר ופליגי בה אביי ורבא ושמעינן ליה לאביי דאמר ראשון אינו צריך להרחיק תריץ הא שמעינן ליה לאביי גופיה דאוקמה כשבאו לחפור בבת אחת שניהן הוחקקו להרחיק כל אחד ואחד שלשה טפחים: **הבא לסמוך.** בורו תחילה בצד המיצר ולחבירו אין שם בור: **העשוייה לבורות.** כגון בית השלחין שצריכה להשקות תדיר: **אפי' לרבנן דאמרי כו'.** דשמעינן מינה אדם צריך לכנוס לתוך שלו כדי שלא יזיק את חבירו ולא אמרינן זה חופר בתוך שלו וזה נוטע בתוך שלו: **ליתנהו לשרשים.** אלא סופן שיתפשטו עשרים וחמשה אמה ויזיקו את כותלי הבור: **מרפית לי.** שהיא מרעדת ונדה מחמת המכה: **הא איתמר עלה מכותל בורו שנינו.** ולמדנו בה שאף הראשון הוחקק להרחיק כדי כותל שהוא שלשה טפחים כדאמרן: **אלא לאביי קשיא.** דהוא גופיה אוקים דמכותל בורו שנינו ועל כרחך לא הוזכר שם כותל אלא ללמדנו ששיעור כותל כדי הרחקת המיצר הוא אלמא אף הראשון הוחקק להרחיק: **הבא בידים.** קרקע רך מתכתש מאליו: **זה וזה מרחיק.** אלמא אף על הראשון להרחיק: **ה"ג בא בידים שאני ודקארי לה מאי קארי לה בא בידים איצטריך סד"א כו'.** כלומר הוא הדין אע"ג דלא בא בידים והאי דנקט (ד) בידים רבותא אשמעינן דאף על גב דבא בידים אין צריך להרחיק אלא שלשה טפחים:

מתונתא

תוספות

פתח בבור וסיים בכותל. בקונטרס גרס בתר דשני מכותל בורו שנינו וליתני אלא אם כן הרחיק מבורו ואינו נראה כמו שפירש ולא גרס לה הכי גרס לה פתח בבור וסיים בכותל וליתני אלא אם כן הרחיק מבורו וכן משמע מתוך פירוש ר' חננאל ואע"ג דבריש המניח (בבא קמא דף כז.) כי פריך פתח בכד וסיים בחבית לא קא מסיים וליתני ולא החזק בעל הכד כו' אין לשון הגמרא שוה אלא פעמים מאריך ופעמים מקצר: **מכותל** בורו שנינו. כלומר לא מחלל בורו קאמר אלא מכותל שיש לבור שהראשון הניח כשחפר בורו ומהך מילתא דרב יהודה דייקא לקמן דאסור לסמוך מדהוחקק הראשון להניח כותל ופריך מינה לאביי והשתא לא אפשר למיגרס וליתני אלא אם כן הרחיק מבורו דא"כ הוה משמע מחלל בורו ומה שפירש הקונטרס דאי הוה תני מבורו הוה ידענא דמכותל בורו קאמר דאי מחלל בורו קאמר אין [זה] כונס לתוך שלו כלום כו' גרסת ספרו דחקתו אבל אין נראה דודאי אי תני מבורו הוה אמינא מחלל בורו קאמר ושרי לסמוך ואם הראשון הרחיק מאיליו מן המיצר ג' טפחים או יותר ה"א דהשני יכול לסמוך עד המיצר ואם כן צריך לשנות מכותלו לאשמועינן דאסור לסמוך לרבא ולאביי צריך הרחקה בין שני הבורות ששה טפחים ומיהו יש ליישב הגירסא ופריך אליבא דאביי דאליבא דידיה קיימא דליתני אלא אם כן הרחיק מבורו ששה טפחים: **למאי** נפקא מינה למקח וממכר. הך נפקותא לא איצטריך לרבא דהא קא משמע לן דאסור לסמוך אלא לאביי דקא סבר מותר לסמוך וקאמר למאי נפקא מינה אי לאשמועינן דבעי הרחקה ו' טפחים ליתני אלא אם כן הרחיק מבורו ו' טפחים: **אביי** אמר סומך דהא אינה עשויה לבורות. והואיל וכן אינו מזיק לו אם הוא סומך וקשה לרשב"א דהא מפסיד הוא שאם יטע אילן יצטרך להרחיקו יותר מחמת שסומך זה עד המיצר דמרחיקין האילן מן הבור חמש ועשרים אמה וי"ל דמכל מקום אינו עושה לו היזק דהא דמרחיק יותר לא מפני שלא יזיקנו הבור אלא מפני שלא יזיק הוא לבור ולהכי אין לזה להניח מלסמוך בשביל כך דאם לא כן ירחיק כל כ"ה אמה את בורו: **אביי** אמר סומך. אומר ר"י דלשתי הלשונות לאביי דאמר סומך אם בא אחד לחפור בור לאחר מכאן צריך הוא להרחיק כל ששה טפחים: **לאביי** ניחא. השתא ס"ד דמכותל בורו היינו מחלל בורו ולא דקדק בלשון: **ה"ג** בספרים ישנים סלע הבא בידים כו' וזה מרחיק ג' טפחים וסד בסיד (ה). וקשה לאביי ה"נ שבאו לחפור שניהם בבת אחת ובא בידים איצטריך ליה סד"א כיון דבא בידים ליבעי רווחא טפי קמ"ל והשתא לא היה צריך לאסוקי ובא בידים איצטריך ליה שהרי לא הקשה כלום מבא בידים אלא אגב דאייתי ברייתא מפרש לה ויש ספרים דגרסי טעמא דבא בידים הא לא בא בידים לא ופריך לרבא ומשני ה"ה אפי' לא בא בידים ובא בידים איצטריך ליה וכו' ואין נראה לר"ת לחלק לענין היתר לסמוך בין בא בידים ובין לא בא בידים ולר"י נראה לחלק שפיר דאע"ג דלא בא בידים שרי לסמוך בבא בידים אסור לסמוך לפי שהקרקע מתבקעת ונופלת קרקע של שדה חבירו: **מרחיקין** את הגפת כו' טעמא דאיכא כותל כו'. פירוש וקשה לרבא ותימה מאי קושיא הכא ודאי מותר לסמוך בשאין כותל שאין מזיק כלום וכשיחפוץ זה לעשות כותל יסיר את הגפת וי"ל דהני נמי מקלקלין את הקרקע ויזיק לכותל לכשיבנה אפי' שוב יסיר ועוד אומר ר"י דבכל אלו יש טורח בסילוקן ולכך מעתה יכול לעכב עליו כי יש לחוש שמא לא יזהר לסלקו כשירצה לעשות כותל וא"ת אכתי מאי פריך לרבא הא מפרש טעמא לעיל משום דכל מרא ומרא דקא מחית מרפית לארעאי וי"ל דההוא טעמא לא קאמר אלא אליבא דרבי יוסי והכא לא פריך אלא אליבא דרבנן:

דטירייא

רבינו גרשום

ומקשינן **פתח בבור** לא יחפור בור **וסיים בכותל** דקתני אא"כ הרחיק מכותל חבירו **ליתני מבורו של חבירו.** והא אכתי לא פריש מילי דבור: א) וג' טפחים הוי במחיצה של לבנים כדקתני באידך פירקין דלעיל בלבנים זה נותן טפח ומחצה וזה נותן טפח ומחצה: **אין ה"נ** קתני מתני' **אא"כ הרחיק מכותל בורו של חבירו ג' טפחים** דהיינו בין בור זה לבור חבירו ו' טפחים והא אתא לאשמועינן **דכותל בור ג' טפחים** הוי דאי חפיר סמוך לכותל בור חבירו צריך להרחיק ג' ואי עביד כותל לבורו לא צריך הרחקה כלל: **הבא לסמוך בצד המצר.** כלומר שאם רוצה אחד לחפור בורו סמוך לשדה חבירו הפנויה מבורות: **אביי אמר סומך.** בצד ממש בלא הרחקה הואיל דאינו מזיק לחבירו דלית ליה לחבירו השתא בור: **ורבא אמר אינו סומך.** אא"כ ירחיק כדין דאע"ג דלית ליה האידנא אימור אימלוך וחפיר נמי חבירו ואי לא ירחיק האי אתי לאזוקי ליה: **שדה העשויה לבורות.** שצריכה לבורות דבית השלחין היא (לחבירו) **ד"ה אינו סומך** האידנא בור דהואיל ולא סגי בלא בור ודאי עביד בה בור ואתי לאזוקי אי לא ירחיק: **כי פליגי בשדה שאינה עשויה לבורות.** דבית הבעל היא: **דבעידנא דקא נטע אילן איתא לבור.** משום הכי מרחיק כ"ה אמות כי היכי דלא ליזלו שרשיו ומזקי לבור אבל הכא ב) דתני מבצר במצר סמיך משום **דבעידנא דקא חפיר ליתיה לבור** דהיאך **ליתנהו לשרשיו.** בההיא שעתא: **מרפית לארעא.** וכי בעינא למיחפר בור יפול העפר לתוכו: **טעמא דאיכא בור.** סמוך ליה משה"ה אינו סומך בלא הרחקה **הא** דוק מיניה אי **ליכא בור** סומך למצר חבירו בלא הרחקה: **בשלמא להך לישנא.** בתראה **בשדה שאינה עשויה לבורות דברי הכל סומך** (מש"ה) [שפיר] מתוקמ' **מתני'** דקתני הא ליכא בור סמיך **בשדה שאינה עשויה לבורות** מש"ה אי ליכא בור סמיך ואתיא מתני' כד"ה: **אלא להיאך לישנא דאמרת בשדה שאינה עשויה לבורות פליגי.** אבל בשדה העשויה לבורות דברי הכל אינו סומך א"כ לא מיתוקמא מתני' אלא אליבא דאביי: **אלא לרבא** דאמר בין בשדה העשויה לבורות בין שאינה עשויה לבורות אינו סומך ומתני' **קשיא** ליה דמתני' דיקא הא ליכא בור סמיך: **אמר [לך] רבא.** לעולם אינו סומך לא בשדה העשויה לבורות ולא בשדה שאינה עשויה לבורות וממתני' לא מצי למידק הא ליכא בור סמיך **דהא איתמר**

עלה דמתני' לעיל **אמר אביי ואי תימא רב יהודה מכותל בורו** של חבירו **שנינו.** מדקתני מכותל בורו מכלל דההוא דחפר מעיקרא הרחיק בורו ג' טפחים כשיעור כותל ולא סמך בצד ממש בלא הרחקה: ג) מתני' מתוקמ' לד"ה **אלא להיאך לישנא דאמר בשדה העשויה לבורות פליגי בשלמא לרבא** דאמר אינו סומך **ניחא** ומתוקמא מתני' דתני לא יחפור אא"כ הרחיק לדעתיה ד): **אלא לאביי** דאמר בין בשדה העשויה לבורות ובין שאינה עשויה לבורות סומך [illegible] **קשיא** [illegible] **אמר לך אביי** מתני' [illegible] **כשבאו לחפור בבת אחת** [illegible] **סלע הבא בידים** [illegible] **ודקארי לה.** [illegible] **איכא** [illegible] בראשית דקיימא האי סלע בין המצרים הללו מצי סמיך אמיצריה משום דלא אתיא להתפוטט אלמא דסמיך וקשיא לרבא דלעיל פסיק ואמר לא סמיך. למ"ה: **גפת.** פסולת זיתים שמוציאין מבית הבד: **ואם הוא**

הגהות הב"ח

(א) גמ' איכא דאמרי תנן לא יחפור אדם בור סמוך לבורו של חבירו ואיתמר עלה אמר אביי: (ב) רש"י ד"ה הא קמ"ל במאי דקתני מכותל בורו למדנו בה שהכותל בורו וכו' מדקתני שחפירות חללו של זה אינה מופלגת. נ"ב כלומר אין הכותל קרויה הפלגה אלא בג"ט לאפוקי בפחות מג': (ג) ד"ה ונפקא וכו' מנלן שכותל הראשון: (ד) ד"ה הכי דנקט בא וכו' והאי דנקט בא בידים: (ה) תוס' ד"ה הכי גר' וכו' וסד בסיד פי' וקשה לאביי:

ליקוטי רש"י

מן הבור. שהשרשין מתפשטין ונוקבין בכותלי הבור ומקלקלין את הקרקע והכתלים נופלים [ב"מ קיז.]. **בא בידים איצטריכא.** למנקט ליה לתנא ולאע"ג דה"ה לא בא בידים [לקמן יט.]. **ואפילו לר' יוסי דאמר.** דפליג בסיפא דפירקין בנוטע אילן סמוך לבור [לקמן כה:]. **הגפת.** פסולת זיתים שנתעצרו בבית הבד [לעיל ע"א]. פסולת של בית הבד של שמן שהוא כונס יחד וחם מאד [שבת מז:].

חשק שלמה על רבינו גרשום

א) [מכאן ועד זה נותן טפח ומחצה נראה דשייך להלן בסמוך אחר תיבות לא צריך הרחקה כלל]: ב) [אולי כצ"ל דרוצה לחפור סמוך למיצר סמיך וכו']: ג) [אפשר כצ"ל אי אמתני' בשדה העשויה לבורות וד"ה אינו סמיך, לישנא וכו']: ד) אא"כ הרחיק לדעתיה בשדה העשויה לבורות: ה) [נראה דצ"ל ולעולם לא אמרו בא בידים אפי' בשאר קרקע שלא בא בידים ומיתוקמא לאביי קשי]: ו) [נראה דצ"ל שבאו לחפור בבת אחת]:

Gemara The Gemara notes an inconsistency in the first sentence of the Mishnah, which reads: "A person may not dig a pit near his neighbor's pit . . . unless he distances it three *tefachim* from his neighbor's wall":

פָּתַח בְּבוֹר וּמְסַיֵּים בְּכוֹתֶל – **[The Tanna] begins by** speaking **of a pit but ends by** speaking **of a wall!**[1] (לִיתְנֵי אֶלָּא אִם כֵּן הִרְחִיק מִבּוֹרוֹ שֶׁל חֲבֵירוֹ ג׳ טְפָחִים)[2] – **He should have said: ". . . unless he distances** it **three *tefachim* from his neighbor's *pit*."** – ? –

The Gemara answers:

אָמַר אַבַּיֵי וְאִיתֵּימָא רַב יְהוּדָה – **Abaye – or,** as **some say, Rav Yehudah – said:** מִכּוֹתֶל בּוֹרוֹ שָׁנִינוּ – When the Mishnah says "from his neighbor's wall," **it means**[3] **from the wall of his pit.**[4]

The Gemara now seeks the reason why the Mishnah changed its terminology:

וְלִיתְנֵי – **But let [the Mishnah] say:** אֶלָּא אִם כֵּן הִרְחִיק מִבּוֹרוֹ שֶׁל חֲבֵירוֹ שְׁלֹשָׁה טְפָחִים – **". . . unless he distances it three *tefachim* from his neighbor's *pit*."** Granted that "wall" signifies the wall of a pit; nevertheless, for the sake of consistency, the Tanna should have used the word pit.[5] – ? –

The Gemara answers:

הָא קָא מַשְׁמַע לָן – By using the word wall, **[the Tanna] teaches us the following:** דְּכוֹתֶל בּוֹר שְׁלֹשָׁה טְפָחִים – **The standard width of a pit's wall is three *tefachim*.**[6] נַפְקָא מִינָּהּ לְמִקָּח וּמִמְכָּר – The potential consequence that **emerges from this** pertains **to** the laws of **buying and selling.** כִּדְתַנְיָא – **As it was taught in a Baraisa:** הָאוֹמֵר לַחֲבֵירוֹ – If ONE SAYS TO HIS FELLOW, בּוֹר וְכוֹתָלֶיהָ אֲנִי מוֹכֵר לָךְ – "I AM SELLING YOU A PIT AND ITS WALLS," without specifying any dimensions, צָרִיךְ שֶׁיְּהֵא הַכּוֹתֶל שְׁלֹשָׁה טְפָחִים – THE WALL MUST BE THREE *TEFACHIM* wide; i.e. the buyer is entitled to a strip of land surrounding the pit that is three *tefachim* wide.

As the Mishnah taught, it is forbidden to dig a pit near the boundary of one's property lest it damage a pit in the neighboring property. The Gemara discusses whether this restriction applies only *after* a pit has been dug on the other side of the boundary or even *before* such a pit exists:

אִיתְּמַר – **It was stated:** הַבָּא לִסְמוֹךְ בְּצַד הַמֵּצַר – Regarding **one who wants to place** a pit **near the boundary** between his property and his neighbor's before there is a pit on the other side of the boundary: אַבַּיֵי אָמַר – **Abaye says:** סוֹמֵךְ – **He may place** it **near** the boundary, without any distancing. וְרָבָא אָמַר – **But Rava says:** אֵינוֹ סוֹמֵךְ – **He may not place** it **near** the boundary; he must distance it three *tefachim*.

The Gemara defines this dispute:

בְּשָׂדֶה הָעֲשׂוּיָה לְבוֹרוֹת – **Regarding land in which it is the practice to dig pits,**[7] דִּבְרֵי הַכֹּל אֵינוֹ סוֹמֵךְ – in **the opinion of all** (even Abaye), **one may not place** a pit **near** the boundary.[8] כִּי פְּלִיגֵי – **In which case do [Abaye and Rava] argue?** בְּשָׂדֶה שֶׁאֵינָהּ עֲשׂוּיָה לְבוֹרוֹת – They argue **with regard to land in which it is not the practice to dig pits.** אַבַּיֵי אָמַר – **Abaye says:** סוֹמֵךְ – **One may place** a pit **near** the boundary, דְּהָא אֵינָהּ עֲשׂוּיָה לְבוֹרוֹת – **for this is [land] in which it is not the practice to dig pits.**[9] רָבָא אָמַר – **Rava says:** אֵינוֹ סוֹמֵךְ – **One may not place** a pit **near** the boundary, דְּאָמַר לֵיהּ – **for [the neighbor] can say to him:** כִּי הֵיכִי דְּאַתְּ אִימְּלַכְתְּ וְחָפַרְתְּ – **"Just as you reconsidered and dug** a pit, even though it is not the practice to do so in this type of land, אֲנָא נַמִּי מִמְּלַכְנָא וְחָפַרְנָא – **I might also reconsider and dig** a pit, even though it is not the practice to do so."

The Gemara reports a variant definition of the dispute between Abaye and Rava:

אִיכָּא דְּאָמְרֵי – **There are those who report** the following version: בְּשָׂדֶה שֶׁאֵינָהּ עֲשׂוּיָה לְבוֹרוֹת – **Regarding land in which it is not the practice to dig pits,** דִּבְרֵי הַכֹּל סוֹמֵךְ – in **the opinion of all** (even Rava), **one may place** a pit **near** the boundary, for it can be assumed that the neighbor will not dig a pit. כִּי פְּלִיגֵי – **In which case do they argue?** בְּשָׂדֶה הָעֲשׂוּיָה לְבוֹרוֹת – They argue **with regard to land in which it is the practice to dig pits.**

The Gemara examines this version of the dispute in the light of a Tannaic dispute between R' Yose and the Sages as to whether

NOTES

1. The word כּוֹתֶל (wall) presumably refers to a wall that is above the ground (*Rashi*; cf. *Rashba, Ritva*).

2. These words are parenthesized for they do not appear in many versions of the text – see *Tosafos* ד״ה פתח.

3. Literally: we learned.

4. The Gemara answers that in this context the word כּוֹתֶל, *wall*, refers not to a wall built above ground, but to the subterranean walls of a pit (*Rashi*).

The "wall" of a pit is defined as the earth between the pit and the boundary of the property in which it is situated (*Ramban*; see *Rashi* ד״ה וליתני and *Maharam*). Hence, according to this interpretation of the Mishnah, the required three-*tefach* distancing is measured not from the pit itself, but from the boundary (which is the nearest point of the pit's "wall").

5. This question requires explanation. Surely it is necessary for the Mishnah to specify "wall," for had it said "pit," one would have been led to the erroneous conclusion that the three-*tefach* measurement is made from the pit itself. By specifying "wall," the Mishnah teaches that the three-*tefach* measurement is made from the boundary (see previous note).

Rashi explains that even if the Mishnah would have said "pit," we would know that the three-*tefach* measurement is made from the boundary. The reasoning behind this is as follows: [The Mishnah most probably speaks of a case where the neighbor's pit is at least three *tefachim* from the boundary, for people are generally not so foolish as to dig a pit near the boundary, where it could be damaged – see *Rashba* ד״ה ואתמר. Therefore,] if the three-*tefach* distancing is measured from the pit itself, it would result that the Mishnah's restriction is of no practical consequence, for every point in one's property is at least three *tefachim* from the neighbor's pit. (Indeed, if the neighbor's pit is *more* than three *tefachim* from the boundary, a distancing of three *tefachim* from the pit itself would place the second pit in the neighbor's property!) Hence, it is obvious that the three-*tefach* distancing is measured from the boundary, regardless of whether the Mishnah says "pit" or "wall."

6. In the Mishnah, the word "wall" refers to the gap between the neighbor's pit and the boundary (see note 4). The Tanna changed the terminology of the Mishnah and used the word "wall" in order to teach, by way of allusion, that the standard width of a pit's wall is the same as the width of this gap between the neighbor's pit and the boundary. (The definition of the standard width of a pit's wall is required for the laws of commerce, as the Gemara proceeds to explain.)

One difficulty remains to be addressed, however: How does the Gemara know that the width of this gap is three *tefachim* and not some other measurement?

The answer is that Abaye understands the Mishnah as referring to an instance in which the neighbor was *also* obligated to distance his pit three *tefachim* from the boundary (the Gemara below discusses the reason for this). Thus, the distance between his pit and the boundary is three *tefachim*. From the fact that the Mishnah refers to this three-*tefach* gap as the "wall" of a pit, it is derived that the standard width of a pit's wall is three *tefachim* (see *Rashi*).

7. For example, fields that require constant irrigation (*Rashi*).

8. [Since pits are customarily dug in such fields, it is likely that the neighbor will eventually dig one even though he has not yet done so.]

9. [It can be assumed that the neighbor will not dig a pit on his side of the boundary.]

ו א מיי' פכ"ח מהלכות מכירה הל' ו' סמג עשין פב טוש"ע ח"מ סי' ריז סעיף ה:

ז ב ג מיי' פ"ט מהל' שכנים הל' י' סמג עשין פב טוש"ע ח"מ סי' קנה סעיף יח:

פתח בבור ומסיים בכותל (א) (ליתני אלא אם כן הרחיק מבורו של חבירו ג"ט) אמר אביי ואיתימא רב יהודה מכותל בורו שנינו וליתני אא"כ הרחיק מבורו של חבירו ג' טפחים הא קמ"ל דכותל בור שלשה טפחים נפקא מינה למקח וממכר כדתניא א האומר לחבירו בור וכותליה אני מוכר לך צריך שיהא הכותל שלשה טפחים איתמר הבא לסמוך בצד המצר אביי אמר סומך ורבא אמר אינו סומך בשדה העשויה לבורות דברי הכל אינו סומך כי פליגי בשדה שאינה עשויה לבורות אביי אמר סומך דהא אינה עשויה לבורות רבא אמר אינו סומך דאמר ליה כי היכי דאת אימלכת וחפרת אנא נמי ממלכנא וחפרנא איכא דאמרי ב בשדה שאינה עשויה לבורות דברי הכל סומך כי פליגי בשדה העשויה לבורות אביי אמר סומך אפילו לרבנן דאמרי ג מרחיקין את האילן מן הבור עשרים וחמש אמה התם הוא דבעידנא דקא נטע איתא לבור אבל הכא בעידנא דקא חפר ליתא לבור ורבא אמר ג אינו סומך ואפילו לר' יוסי דאמר ד זה חופר בתוך שלו וזה נוטע בתוך שלו הני מילי התם דבעידנא דקא נטע ליתנהו לשרשין דמזיקי לה לבור אבל הכא אמר ליה כל מרא ומרא דקא מחיית קא מרפית לה לארעאי תנן לא יחפור אדם בור סמוך לבורו של חבירו טעמא דאיכא בור הא ליכא בור סומך בשלמא להך לישנא דאמרת בשדה שאינה עשויה לבורות דברי הכל סומך מתניתין בשדה העשויה לבורות אלא להך לישנא דאמרת בשדה שאינה עשויה לבורות פליגי בשלמא לאביי ניחא אלא לרבא קשיא אמר לך רבא הא איתמר עלה אמר אביי ואיתימא רב יהודה מכותל בורו שנינו איכא דאמרי (א) ואיתמר עלה אמר אביי ואיתימא רב יהודה מכותל בורו שנינו בשלמא להך לישנא דאמרת בשדה העשויה לבורות דברי הכל אינו סומך מתניתין בשדה העשויה לבורות אלא להך לישנא דאמרת בשדה העשויה לבורות פליגי בשלמא לרבא ניחא אלא לאביי קשיא אמר לך אביי מתני' שבאו לחפור בבת אחת תא שמע ד סלע הבא בידים זה חופר בורו מכאן וזה חופר בורו מכאן זה מרחיק שלשה טפחים וסד בסיד וזה מרחיק שלשה טפחים וסד בסיד בא בידים שאני ודקארי לה מאי קארי לה בא בידים איצטריכא ליה ס"ד אמינא כיון דבא בידים ליבעי נמי רווחא טפי קא משמע לן תא שמע מרחיקין את הגפת ואת הזבל ואת המלח

פתח בבור. סמוך לבורו של חבירו והדר סיים אלא אם כן הרחיק מכותל הוה ליה למיתני אלא אם כן הרחיק מבורו דאילו מכותלו כותל הבנוי על גבי קרקע הוא: מכותל בורו שנינו. כלומר האי כותל דקתני מכותל בורו קאמר שאף הוא קרוי כותל: וליתני מבורו של חבירו. ואנא ידענא דמכותל קאמר דאי מחלל בורו קאמר אין זה כונס לתוך שלו כלום ופעמים שהוא סותר אף כותל חבירו אם הוא רחב משלשה: הא קא משמע לן. במאי (ב) דתניא מכותל בורו למדנו בה שהכותל בורו של ראשון מילא כל שלשה טפחים שהוחקק גם הוא להרחיק מן המיצר וממאי מדקתני שהחפירות חללו של זה אינה מופלגת מכותלו של זה אלא שלשה טפחים שהוא כונס לתוך שלו נמצא שלשת הטפחים שכנס גם זה לתוך שלו הכותל מלאם ואשמועינן שיעור רוחב כותלי בור: ונפקא מינה למקח וממכר. וא"ת מנלן (ג) שהכותל הראשון הוא הוי שיעור הרחקה מן המיצר והלא לא היה לחבירו בור סמוך למיצר ופליגי בה אביי ורבא ושמעינן ליה לאביי דאמר ראשון אינו צריך להרחיק תריץ הא שמעינן ליה לאביי גופיה דאוקמה כשבאו לחפור בבת אחת שניהן הוחקקו להרחיק כל אחד ואחד שלשה טפחים: הבא לסמוך. בורו תחילה בצד המיצר ולחבירו אין שם בור: העשוייה לבורות. כגון בית השלחין שצריכה להשקות תדיר: אפי' לרבנן דאמרי כו'. דשמעינן מינה אדם צריך לכנוס לתוך שלו כדי שלא יזיק את חבירו ולא אמרינן זה חופר בתוך שלו וזה נוטע בתוך שלו: ליתנהו לשרשים. אלא סופן שיתפשטו עשרים וחמשה אמה ויזיקו את כותלי הבור: מרפית לי. שהיא מרעדת ונדה מחמת המכה: הא איתמר עלה מכותל בורו שנינו. ולמדנו בה שאף הראשון הוחקק להרחיק כדי כותל שהוא שלשה טפחים כדאמרן: אלא לאביי קשיא. דהוא גופיה אוקים דמכותל בורו שנינו ועל כרחך לא הוזכר שם כותל אלא ללמדנו שיעור כותל כדי הרחקת המיצר הוא אלמא אף הראשון הוחקק להרחיק: הבא בידים. קרקע רך מתכתש מאיליו: זה וזה מרחיק. אלמא אף על הראשון להרחיק: ה"ג בא בידים שאני ודקארי לה מאי קארי לה בא בידים איצטריך סד"א כו'. כלומר הוא הדין אע"ג דלא בא בידים והאי דנקט (ד) בידים רבותא אשמעינן דאף על גב דבא בידים אין צריך להרחיק אלא שלשה טפחים:

מתונתא

פתח בבור וסיים בכותל. בקונטרס גרס בתר דשני מכותל בורו שנינו וליתני אלא אם כן הרחיק מבורו ואינו נראה כמו שפירש ואי גרס לה הכי גרס לה פתח בבור וסיים בכותל וליתני אלא אם כן הרחיק מבורו וכן משמע מתוך פירוש ר' חננאל ואע"ג דבריש המניח (בבא קמא דף ט.) כי פריך פתח בכד וסיים בחבית לא קא מסיים וליתני ואם הוזק בעל הכד כו' אין לשון הגמרא שוה אלא פעמים מאריך ופעמים מקצר:

מכותל בורו שנינו. כלומר לא מחלל בורו קאמר אלא מכותל שיש לבור שהראשון הניח כשחפר בורו ומהך מילתא דרב יהודה דייקא לקמן דאסור לסמוך מדהוחקק הראשון להניח כותל ופריך מינה לאביי והשתא לא אפשר למיגרס וליתני אלא אם כן הרחיק מבורו דא"כ הוה משמע מחלל בורו ומה שפירש הקונטרס דאי הוה תני מבורו הוה ידעינא דמכותל בורו קאמר דאי מחלל בורו קאמר אין [זה] כונס לתוך שלו כלום כו' גרסת ספרו דחקתו אבל אין נראה דודאי אי תני מבורו הוה אמינא מחלל בורו קאמר ושרי לסמוך ואם הראשון הרחיק מאיליו מן המיצר ג' טפחים או יותר ה"א דהשני יכול לסמוך עד המיצר ואם כן צריך לשנות מכותלו לאשמועינן דאסור לסמוך לרבא ולאביי צריך הרחקה בין שני הבורות ששה טפחים ומיהו יש ליישב הגירסא ופריך אליבא דאביי דאליבא דידיה קיימא דליתני אלא אם כן הרחיק מבורו ששה טפחים:

למאי נפקא מינה למקח וממכר. הך נפקותא לא איצטריך לרבא דהא קא משמע לן דאסור לסמוך אלא לאביי דקא סבר מותר לסמוך וקאמר למאי נפקא מינה אי לאשמועינן דבעי הרחקה ו' טפחים ליתני אלא אם כן הרחיק מבורו ו' טפחים: **אביי** אמר סומך דהא אינה עשויה לבורות. והואיל וכן אינו מזיק לו אם הוא סומך וקשה לרשב"א דהא מפסיד הוא שאם יטע אילן יצטרך להרחיקו יותר מחמת שסומך זה עד המיצר דמרחיקין האילן מן הבור חמש ועשרים אמה וי"ל דמכל מקום אינו עושה לו היזק דהא דמרחיק יותר לא מפני שלא יזיקנו הבור אלא מפני שלא יזיק הוא לבור ולהכי אין לזה להניח מלסמוך בשביל כך דאם לא כן ירחיק כל כ"ה אמה את בורו:

אביי אמר סומך. אומר ר"י דלשתי הלשונות לאביי דאמר סומך אם בא אחד לחפור בור לאחר מכאן צריך הוא להרחיק כל ששה טפחים:

לאביי ניחא. השתא ס"ד דמכותל בורו היינו מחלל בורו ולא דקדק בלשון: **ה"ג** בספרים ישנים סלע הבא בידים כו' וזה מרחיק ג' טפחים וסד בסיד (ה). וקשה לאביי ה"נ שבאו לחפור שניהם בבת אחת ובא בידים אילטריך ליה סד"א כיון דבא בידים ליבעי רווחא טפי קמ"ל והשתא לא היה צריך לאסוקי ובא בידים אילטריך ליה שהרי לא הקשה כלום מבא בידים אלא אגב דאייתי ברייתא מפרש לה ויש ספרים דגרסי טעמא דבא בידים הא לא בא בידים לא ופריך לרבא ומשני ה"ה אפי' לא בא בידים ובא בידים אילטריך ליה וכו' ואין נראה לר"ת לחלק לענין היתר לסמוך בין בא בידים ובין לא בא בידים ולר"י נראה לחלק שפיר דאע"ג דלא בא בידים שרי לסמוך בבא בידים אסור לסמוך לפי שהקרקע מתבקעת ונופלת קרקע של שדה חבירו: **מרחיקין** את הגפת כו' טעמא דאיכא כותל כו'. פירוש וקשה לרבא ותימה מאי קושיא הכא ודאי מותר לסמוך בשאין כותל שאין מזיק כלום וכשיחפוץ זה לעשות כותל יסיר את הגפת וי"ל דהני נמי מקלקלין את הקרקע ויזיק לכותל לכשיבנה אפי' שוב יסיר ועוד אומר ר"י דבכל אלו יש טורח בסילוקן ולכך מעתה יכול לעכב עליו כי יש לחוש שמא לא יתחר לסלקן לכשירצה לעשות כותל וא"ת א"כ מאי פריך לרבא הא מפרש טעמא לעיל משום דכל מרא ומרא דקא מחית מרפית לארעאי וי"ל דהשתא טעמא לא קאמר אלא אליבא דרבי יוסי והכא לא פריך אלא אליבא דרבנן:

דטרייא

א) רש"ל מ"ז, ב) [לקמן כה: מ: ב"מ קח.], ג) [לקמן כב: כה:], ד) לקמן יט. ע"ש [תוספתא פ"א], ה) ס"ל סותר וכ"ה בע"י:

הגהות הב"ח

(א) גמ' איכא דאמרי תנן לא יחפור אדם בור סמוך לבורו של חבירו ואיתמר עלה אמר אביי: (ב) רש"י ד"ה הא קמ"ל במאי דקתני מכותל בורו למדנו בה שכותל בורו וכו' מדקתני שחפירות חללו של זה אינה מופלגת. נ"ב כלומר אין הכותל קרויה הפלגה אלא בנ"ע לאפוקי בפחות מג': (ג) ד"ה ונפקא וכו' מנלן שכותל הראשון: (ד) ד"ה ה"ג בא וכו' והאי דנקט בא בידים: (ה) תוס' ד"ה הכי גר' וכו' וסד בסיד פי' וקשה לאביי:

ליקוטי רש"י

מן הבור. שהשרשין מתפשטין ונוקבין בכותלי הבור וממלחלין את הקרקע והכתלים נופלים [ב"מ קיז.]. בא בידים איצטריכא. למתנא ואע"ג דה"ה דלא בא בידים [לקמן יט.]. ואפילו לר' יוסי דאמר. דפליג בסיפא דפירקין בנוטע אילן סמוך לבור [לקמן כה:]. הגפת. פסולת זיתים שנתעצרו בבית הבד [לעיל ע"א]. פסולת של בית הבד של שמן שהוא כונס יחד וחם מאד [שבת מז:].

חשק שלמה על רבינו גרשום

א) [מכאן ועד זה נותן טפח ומחצה נראה דשייך להכא בסמוך אחר תיבות לא צריך הרחקה כלל]: ב) [אבל הכא דרוצה לחפור סמוך למצר וכו']: ג) [חסר כאן ונ"ל מתני' בשדה העשויה לבורות וד"ה אלא להאך לישנא וכו']: ד) דא"כ הרחיק לדעתיה בשדה העשויה לבורות: ה) [נראה דצ"ל ולעולם לא מצי סמיך אפי' בשאר קרקע בא בידים ותיובתא דאביי וכו']: ו) [נראה דצ"ל שבאו לחפור בבת אחת]:

רבינו גרשום

ומקשינן פתח בבור לא יחפור בור וסיים בכותל דקתני אא"כ הרחיק מכותל חבירו ליתני מבורו של חבירו. והא אכתי לא פריש מילי דבור: א) וג' טפחים הוי במחיצה של לבנים כדקתני באידך פירקין דלעיל בלבנים זה נותן טפח ומחצה וזה נותן טפח ומחצה: אין ה"ג קתני מתני' אא"כ הרחיק מכותל בורו של חבירו ג' טפחים דהיינו בין בור זה לבור חבירו ו' טפחים והא אתא לאשמועינן דכותל בור ג' טפחים הוי דאי חפיר סמוך לכותל בור חבירו צריך להרחיק ג' ואי עביד כותל לבורו לא צריך הרחקה כלל: הבא לסמוך בצד המצר. כלומר שאם רוצה אחד לחפור בורו סמוך לשדה חבירו הפנויה מבורות: אביי אמר סומך. בצד ממש בלא הרחקה הואיל דאינו מזיק לחבירו דלית ליה לחבירו השתא בור: ורבא אמר אינו סומך. אא"כ ירחיק כדין דאע"ג דלית ליה האידנא אימור אימלוך וחפור נמי חבירו ואי לא ירחיק האי אתי לאזוקי ליה: שדה העשויה לבורות. שצריכה לבורות דבית השלחין היא (לחבירו) ד"ה אינו סומך דאיהו נמי עבדא בור דהואיל ולא סגי בלא בור ודאי עביד בה בור ואתי לאזוקי אי לא ירחיק: כי פליגי בשדה שאינה עשויה לבורות. דבית הבעל היא: דבעידנא דקא נטע איתא לבור. משום הכי מרחיק כ"ה אמות כי היכי דלא ליזלו שרשיו ומזיקי לבור אבל הכא ב) דחפר בצד המצר ליכא סמך משום דבעידנא דקא חפר ליתיה לבור דהיאך: ליתנהו לשרשיו. בההיא שעתא: מרפית לארעא. וכו' בעינא לא למיחפר בור יפול העפר לתוכו: טעמא דאיכא בור. סמוך ליה הרחקה הא דליכא בור סמוך למצר חבירו סומך בלא הרחקה: בשלמא להך לישנא. בתראה בשדה שאינה עשויה לבורות דברי הכל סומך (משנ"ה) [שפיר] מתוקם מתני' דקתני הא ליכא בור סמוך בשדה שאינה עשויה לבורות מש"ה אי ליכא בור סמוך ואתיא מתני' כד"ה: אלא להאך לישנא דאמרת בשדה שאינה עשויה לבורות פליגי. אבל בשדה העשויה לבורות דברי הכל אינו סומך א"כ לא מיתוקמא מתני' אלא אליבא דאביי. אלא לרבא דאמר בין בשדה העשויה לבורות בין שאינה עשויה לבורות אינו סומך מתני' קשיא ליה דמתני' דיקא הא ליכא בור סמיך: אמר [לך] רבא. אינו סומך לא בשדה העשויה לבורות ולא בשדה שאינה עשויה לבורות ומתני' לא מצי סמיך הא ליכא בור סמיך דהא איתמר

עלה דמתני' לעיל אמר אביי ואי תימא רב יהודה מכותל בורו של חבירו שנינו. מדקתני מכותל בורו מכלל דההוא דחפר מעיקרא הרחיק בורו ג' טפחים כשיעור כותל ולא סמיך בצד ממש בלא הרחקה: ג) מתני' מתוקמ' לד"ה אלא להאך לישנא דאמר בשדה העשויה לבורות פליגי בשלמא לרבא ניחא ומתוקמא מתני' דתני לא יחפור אא"כ הרחיק לדעתיה ד) אלא לאביי דאמר סומך קשיא: אמר לך אביי. מתני' שבאו לחפור בבת אחת תרווייהו ולהכי צריך כל אחד להרחיק: סלע הבא בידים. קרקע רך: בא בידים שאני. דמתרפית ארעא: ודקארי לה מאי קארי לה. בא בידים איצטריכא ליה סד"א כיון דבא בידים ליבעי רווחא טפי קמ"ל: מרחיקין את הגפת. פסולת זיתים:

one may plant a tree where it is liable to damage the pit of a neighbor:[10]

Abaye's view:

אַבַּיֵי אָמַר – **Abaye says:** סוֹמֵךְ – Even in land in which it is the practice to dig pits, **one may place** a pit **near** one's boundary. אֲפִילוּ לְרַבָּנַן דְּאָמְרֵי – And this is so **even according to the Sages who say:** מַרְחִיקִין אֶת הָאִילָן מִן הַבּוֹר עֶשְׂרִים וְחָמֵשׁ אַמָּה – ONE MUST DISTANCE A TREE TWENTY-FIVE *AMOS* FROM THE PIT of a neighbor. The difference between the two cases is as follows: הָתָם הוּא דִּבְעִידְנָא דְּקָא נָטַע אִיתָא לְבוֹר – **It is in that case** that the Sages require the owner of the tree to distance it, **for when he plants** the tree, **the** neighbor's **pit is** already **in existence.** אֲבָל הָכָא בְּעִידְנָא דְּקָא חָפַר לֵיתָא לְבוֹר – **But in the present case, when [the owner of the pit] digs** his pit, **there is no pit** in the neighboring property that is liable to be damaged.[11]

Rava's view:

וְרָבָא אָמַר – **Rava says:** אֵינוֹ סוֹמֵךְ – In land in which it is the practice to dig pits, **one may not place** a pit **near** one's boundary. וַאֲפִילוּ לְרַבִּי יוֹסֵי דְּאָמַר – **And** this is so **even according to R' Yose, who says:** זֶה חוֹפֵר בְּתוֹךְ שֶׁלּוֹ – Just as THIS [NEIGHBOR] MAY DIG a pit IN HIS [PROPERTY], וְזֶה נוֹטֵעַ בְּתוֹךְ שֶׁלּוֹ – THE OTHER ONE MAY PLANT a tree IN HIS [PROPERTY]. (I.e. there is no prohibition against planting a tree even where it is liable to damage the pit of one's neighbor.)[12] הָנֵי מִילֵּי הָתָם – For **that ruling** of R' Yose applies only **in that case,** דִּבְעִידְנָא דְּקָא נָטַע – **where at the time he plants** the tree, לֵיתְנְהוּ לְשָׁרָשָׁיו דְּמַזְּקֵי לָהּ לְבוֹר – **its roots, which** will eventually **damage the pit, are not** yet **in existence.** אֲבָל הָכָא – **But in the present case,** אָמַר לֵיהּ – **[the neighbor] can say to [the one who wishes to dig a pit]:** כָּל מָרָא וּמָרָא דְּקָא מַחְיַית – **"Every time you strike** the earth **with your spade,**[13] קָא מַרְפֵּית לָהּ לְאַרְעַאי – **you weaken my land!"**[14] [15]

The Gemara attempts to prove which opinion is correct:

תְּנַן – **We learned in our Mishnah:** לֹא יַחְפּוֹר אָדָם בּוֹר – A PERSON MAY NOT DIG A PIT סָמוּךְ לְבוֹרוֹ שֶׁל חֲבֵירוֹ – NEAR THE PIT OF HIS NEIGHBOR, unless he distances it at least three *tefachim* from the wall of his neighbor's pit. The Mishnah implies that the neighbor's pit is already in existence. This gives rise to the following inference: טַעְמָא דְּאִיכָּא בּוֹר – **The reason** distancing is required **is that there is a pit** on the neighbor's side of the boundary; הָא לֵיכָּא בּוֹר סוֹמֵךְ – **but** if **there is no pit** in harm's way, **one may place** a pit **near** the boundary! בִּשְׁלָמָא לְהַךְ לִישָּׁנָא דְּאָמַרְתְּ – Now, **[this] is in order according to that version** (i.e. the second version) of the dispute between Abaye and Rava **which stated:** בְּשָׂדֶה שֶׁאֵינָהּ עֲשׂוּיָה לְבוֹרוֹת – **"Regarding land in which it is not the practice to dig pits,** דִּבְרֵי הַכֹּל סוֹמֵךְ – in **the opinion of all, one may place** a pit **near** the boundary." מַתְנִיתִין בְּשָׂדֶה שֶׁאֵינָהּ עֲשׂוּיָה לְבוֹרוֹת – For, according to that version, **the Mishnah** can be explained as **referring to land** in which it is **not the practice to dig pits.** With regard to such land, even Rava agrees that one may dig a pit near the boundary. אֶלָּא לְהַךְ לִישָּׁנָא דְּאָמַרְתְּ – **However, according to the other version** (i.e. the first version) of the dispute, **which stated:** בְּשָׂדֶה שֶׁאֵינָהּ עֲשׂוּיָה לְבוֹרוֹת פְּלִיגֵי – **"Regarding land** in which it is **not the practice to dig pits, they disagree** as to whether one may dig a pit near the boundary," בִּשְׁלָמָא לְאַבַּיֵי נִיחָא – **[the law]** inferred from our Mishnah **is in order** only **according to Abaye,** who permits the digging of a pit under such circumstances.[16] אֶלָּא לְרָבָא – **But according to Rava,** who forbids the digging of a pit even under such circumstances, קַשְׁיָא – the Mishnah poses **a difficulty. – ? –**

The Gemara presents Rava's defense:

אָמַר לָךְ רָבָא – **Rava will say to you:** הָא אִיתְּמַר עֲלָהּ – **But it was stated in reference to [this Mishnah]:** אָמַר אַבַּיֵי וְאִיתֵּימָא רַב יְהוּדָה – **Abaye – or,** as **some say, Rav Yehudah – said:** מִכּוֹתֶל בּוֹרוֹ שָׁנִינוּ – When the Mishnah says "from his neighbor's wall," **it means "from the wall of his pit."** In fact, the Mishnah reflects Rava's view, for its use of the word "wall" indicates that the first neighbor to dig a pit near the boundary is also required to leave a gap (known as the pit's "wall") between his pit and the boundary.[17]

NOTES

10. This dispute is recorded in the Mishnah, 25b. The Sages rule that a tree must be distanced at least twenty-five *amos* from a neighbor's pit lest its roots damage the pit. R' Yose, however, permits one to plant a tree anywhere in one's property, even though it will eventually damage the neighbor's pit.

The view of the Sages is apparently incompatible with the view of Abaye as it is defined by the *second* version of the dispute between Abaye and Rava. The Sages forbid the performance of an action that is likely to cause damage to a neighbor's property even though the damage is not immediate. Abaye, on the other hand, permits even an action that is likely to cause damage (e.g. digging a pit near property in which it is the practice to dig pits) on the grounds that the damage is not immediate. The Gemara proceeds to reconcile these two views.

There is no contradiction, however, between the *first* version of Abaye's opinion and that of the Sages. Since, according to the first version, Abaye concedes that it is forbidden to dig a pit near property in which it is the practice to dig pits, evidently, Abaye agrees with the Sages' view that an action which is likely to cause damage in the future is forbidden even though the damage is not immediate. According to this version, the reason Abaye permits the digging of a pit near a field in which it is *not* the practice to dig pits is that, in such a case, damage is unlikely ever to occur (*Rashba*).

11. [Abaye argues that the Sages restrict the placement of a hazard only in a case where the object liable to be damaged is already in harm's way. Therefore, they would permit the digging of a pit near the boundary between two properties – provided there is no pit yet on the other side – even in land in which it is the practice to dig pits.]

12. R' Yose is of the opinion that one is not required to distance harmful agents from the property of a neighbor. In his view, it is up to the threatened party to take his property out of harm's way (see Chapter Introduction).

13. Literally: each and every spade that you strike.

14. The very action of digging loosens the surrounding soil. The neighbor's land is thereby damaged insofar as it is rendered unfit for the digging of pits (see *Rabbeinu Yonah* ד״ה רבא, *Rashba* ד״ה רבא, cf. *Meiri*). This is an activity that causes direct damage, which even R' Yose concedes is forbidden (see Chapter Introduction).

15. An apparent difficulty: The views of Rava and R' Yose seem to be contradictory according to either version of the dispute between Abaye and Rava. So why did the Gemara discuss this problem only in the context of the second version?

The answer is that the Gemara was concerned primarily with the difference between the views of the Sages (the majority opinion) and Abaye, which, as explained above, is a problem only according to the second version (see note 10). Once the Gemara discusses the difference between Abaye and the Sages, it deals with the difference between Rava and R' Yose as well.

Alternatively: The Gemara did not resolve the difference between R' Yose and the first version of Rava's view because it is impossible to do so. The reconciliation of the views of Rava and R' Yose is based on the reasoning that the very act of digging renders the neighbor's field unfit for the digging of pits (see note 14). But this reasoning is of no consequence with regard to the first version of Rava's view, according to which Rava's restriction applies even to land in which it is not the practice to dig pits anyway (*Rashba*).

16. [Abaye can explain the Mishnah as referring to land in which it is not the practice to dig pits.]

17. See notes 4 and 6.

ו א מיי' פכ"א מהלכות מכירה הל' יב סמג עשין פב טוש"ע ח"מ סי' רז סעיף ה:

ז ב ג מיי' פ"ט מהל' שכנים הל' י סמג עשין פב טוש"ע ח"מ סי' קנה סעיף יח:

פתח בבור ומסיים בכותל א) (ליתני אלא אם כן הרחיק מבורו של חבירו ג"ט) אמר אביי ואיתימא רב יהודה מכותל בורו שנינו וליתני אא"כ הרחיק מבורו של חבירו ג' טפחים הא קמ"ל דכותל בור שלשה טפחים ונפקא מינה למקח וממכר כדתניא [א] האומר לחבירו בור וכותליה אני מוכר לך צריך שיהא הכותל שלשה טפחים איתמר הבא לסמוך בצד המצר אביי אמר סומך ורבא אמר אינו סומך בשדה העשויה לבורות דברי הכל אינו סומך כי פליגי בשדה שאינה עשויה לבורות אביי אמר סומך דהא אינה עשויה לבורות רבא אמר אינו סומך דאמר ליה כי היכי דאת אימלכת וחפרת אנא נמי ממלכנא וחפרנא איכא דאמרי [ב] בשדה שאינה עשויה לבורות דברי הכל סומך כי פליגי בשדה העשויה לבורות אביי אמר סומך אפילו לרבנן דאמרי [ג] מרחיקין את האילן מן הבור עשרים וחמש אמה התם הוא דבעידנא דקא נטע איתא לבור אבל הכא בעידנא דקא חפר ליתא לבור ורבא אמר [ג] אינו סומך ואפילו לר' יוסי דאמר [ה] זה חופר בתוך שלו וזה נוטע בתוך שלו הני מילי התם דבעידנא דקא נטע ליתנהו לשרשיו דמזקי לה לבור אבל הכא אמר ליה כל מרא ומרא דקא מחיית קא מרפית לה לארעאי תנן לא יחפור אדם בור סמוך לבורו של חבירו טעמא דאיכא בור הא ליכא בור סומך בשלמא להך לישנא דאמרת בשדה שאינה עשויה לבורות דברי הכל סומך מתניתין בשדה שאינה עשויה לבורות אלא להך לישנא דאמרת בשדה שאינה עשויה לבורות פליגי בשלמא לאביי ניחא אלא לרבא קשיא אמר לך רבא הא איתמר עלה אמר אביי ואיתימא רב יהודה מכותל בורו שנינו איכא דאמרי (א) ואיתמר עלה אמר אביי ואיתימא רב יהודה מכותל בורו שנינו בשלמא להך לישנא דאמרת בשדה העשויה לבורות דברי הכל אינו סומך מתניתין בשדה העשויה לבורות אלא להך לישנא דאמרת בשדה העשויה לבורות פליגי בשלמא לרבא ניחא אלא לאביי קשיא אמר לך אביי מתני' שבאו לחפור בבת אחת תא שמע [ד] סלע הבא בידים זה חופר בורו מכאן וזה חופר בורו מכאן זה מרחיק שלשה טפחים וסד בסיד וזה מרחיק שלשה טפחים וסד בסיד בא בידים שאני ודקארי לה מאי קארי לה בא בידים איצטריכא ליה ס"ד אמינא כיון דבא בידים ליבעי נמי רווחא טפי קא משמע לן תא שמע מרחיקין את הגפת ואת הזבל ואת המלח

רש"י

פתח בבור. סמוך לבורו של חבירו והדר סיים אלא אם כן הרחיק מכותל בורו ליה למיתני אלא אם כן הרחיק מבורו דאילו מכותלו כותל הבנוי על גבי קרקע הוא: מכותל בורו שנינו. כלומר האי כותל דקתני מכותל בורו קאמר שאף הוא קרוי כותל: וליתני מבורו של חבירו. ואנא ידענא דמכותל קאמר דאי מחלל בורו קאמר אין זה כונס לתוך שלו כלום ופעמים שהוא סותר אף כותל חבירו אם הוא רחב משלשה: הא קא משמע לן. במאי (ב) דתניא מכותל בורו למדנו בה שהכותל בורו של ראשון מילא כל שלשה טפחים שהוזקק גם הוא להרחיק מן המיצר וממאי מדקתני שהחפירות חללו של זה אינה מופלגת מכותלו של זה אלא שלשה טפחים שהוא כונס לתוך שלו נמצא ששלשת הטפחים שכנס גם זה לתוך שלו הכותל מלאם ואשמועינן שיעור רוחב כותלי בור: ונפקא מינה למקח וממכר. וא"ת מנלן (ג) שהכותל הראשון הוא הוי שיעור הרחקה מן המיצר והלא לא היה לחבירו בור סמוך למיצר ופליגי בה אביי ורבא ושמעינן ליה לאביי דאמר ראשון אינו צריך להרחיק תריץ הא שמעינן ליה לאביי גופיה דאוקמה כשבאו לחפור בבת אחת שניהן הוזקקו להרחיק כל אחד ואחד שלשה טפחים: הבא לסמוך. בורו תחילה בצד המיצר ולחבירו אין שם בור: העשוייה לבורות. כגון בית השלחין שצריכה להשקות תדיר: אפי' לרבנן דאמרי כו'. דשמעינן מינה אדם צריך לכנוס לתוך שלו כדי שלא יזיק את חבירו ולא אמרינן זה חופר בתוך שלו וזה נוטע בתוך שלו: ליתנהו לשרשים. אלא סופן שיתפשטו עשרים וחמשה אמה ויזיקו את כותלי הבור: מרפית לי. שהיא מרעדת ונדה מחמת המכה: הא איתמר עלה מכותל בורו שנינו. ולמדנו בה שאף הראשון הוזקק להרחיק כדי כותל שהוא שלשה טפחים כדאמרן: אלא לאביי קשיא. דהוא גופיה אוקים דמכותל בורו שנינו ועל כרחך לא הוזכר שם כותל אלא ללמדנו ששיעור כותל כדי הרחקת המיצר הוא אלמא אף הראשון הוזקק להרחיק: הבא בידים. קרקע רך מתכתש מאליו: זה וזה מרחיק. אלמא אף על הראשון להרחיק: ה"ג בא בידים שאני ודקארי לה מאי קארי לה בא בידים איצטריך סד"א כו'. כלומר הוא הדין אע"ג דלא בא בידים והאי דנקט (ד) בידים רבותא אשמעינן דאף על גב דבא בידים אין צריך להרחיק אלא שלשה טפחים:

מתונתא

תוספות

פתח בבור וסיים בכותל. בקונטרס גרס בתר דשני מכותל בורו שנינו וליתני אלא אם כן הרחיק מבורו ואינו נראה כמו שאפרש ואי גרס לה הכי גרס לה פתח בבור וסיים בכותל וליתני אלא אם כן הרחיק מבורו וכן משמע מתוך פירוש ר' חננאל ולפ"ג דבריש המניח (בבא קמא דף כ.) כי פריך פתח בכד וסיים בחבית לא קא מסיים וליתני ואם הוזק בעל הכד כו' אין לשון הגמרא שוה אלא פעמים מאריך ופעמים מקצר:

מכותל בורו שנינו. כלומר לא מחלל בורו קאמר אלא מכותל שיש לבור שהראשון הניח כשחפר בורו ומהך מילתא דרב יהודה דייקא לקמן דאסור לסמוך מדהוזקק הראשון להניח כותל ופריך מינה לאביי והשתא לא אפשר למיגרס וליתני אלא אם כן הרחיק מבורו דא"כ הוה משמע מחלל בורו ומה שפירש הקונטרס דאי הוה תני מבורו הוה ידעינא דמכותל בורו קאמר דאי מחלל בורו קאמר אין [זה] כונס לתוך שלו כלום כו' גרסת ספרו דחקתו אבל אין נראה דודאי אי תני מבורו הוה אמינא מחלל בורו קאמר ושרי לסמוך ואם הראשון הרחיק מאליו מן המיצר ג' טפחים או יותר ה"א דהשני יכול לסמוך עד המיצר ואם כן צריך לשנות מכותלו לאשמועינן דאסור לסמוך לרבא ולאביי צריך הרחקה בין שני הבורות ששה טפחים ומיהו יש ליישב הגירסא ופריך אליבא דאביי דאליבא דידיה קיימא דליתני אלא אם כן הרחיק מבורו ששה טפחים:

למאי נפקא מינה למקח וממכר. הך נפקותא לא איצטריך לרבא דהא קא משמע לן דאסור לסמוך אלא לאביי דקא סבר מותר לסמוך וקאמר למאי נפקא מינה אי לאשמועינן דבעי הרחקה ו' טפחים ליתני אלא אם כן הרחיק מבורו ו' טפחים: אביי אמר סומך דהא אינה עשויה לבורות. והואיל וכן אינו מזיק לו אם הוא סומך וקשה לרשב"א דהא מפסיד הוא שאם יטע אילן יצטרך להרחיקו יותר מחמת שסומך זה עד המיצר דמרחיקין האילן מן הבור חמש ועשרים אמה וי"ל דמכל מקום אינו עושה לו היזק דהא דמרחיק יותר לא מפני שלא יזיקנו הבור אלא מפני שלא יזיק הוא לבור ולהכי אין לזה להניח מלסמוך בשביל כך דאם לא כן ירחיק כל כ"ה אמה את בורו:

אביי אמר סומך. אומר ר"י דלשתי הלשונות לאביי דאמר סומך אם בא אחד לחפור בור לאחר מכאן צריך הוא להרחיק כל ששה טפחים:

לאביי ניחא. השתא ס"ד דמכותל בורו היינו מחלל בורו ולא דקדק בלשון: ה"ג בספרים ישנים סלע הבא בידים כו' וזה מרחיק ג' טפחים וסד בסיד (ה). וקשה לאביי ה"נ שבאו לחפור שניהם בבת אחת ובא בידים איצטריך ליה סד"א כיון דבא בידים ליבעי רווחא טפי קמ"ל והשתא לא היה צריך לאוקמי ובא בידים איצטריך ליה שהרי לא הקשה כלום מבא בידים אלא אגב דאייתי ברייתא מפרש לה ויש ספרים דגרסי טעמא דבא בידים הא לא בא בידים לא ופריך לרבא ומשני ה"ה אפי' לא בא בידים ובא בידים איצטריך ליה וכו' ואין נראה לר"ת לחלק לענין היתר לסמוך בין בא בידים ובין לא בא בידים ולר"י נראה לחלק שפיר דאע"ג דלא בא בידים שרי לסמוך בבא בידים אסור לסמוך לפי שהקרקע מתבקעת ונופלת קרקע של שדה חבירו: **מרחיקין** את הגפת כו' טעמא דאיכא כותל כו'. פירוש וקשה לרבא ותימה מאי קושיא הכא ודאי מותר לסמוך בשאין כותל שאין מזיק כלום וכשיחפוץ זה לעשות כותל יסיר את הגפת וי"ל דהכי נמי מקלקלין את הקרקע ויזיק לכותל לכשיבנה אפי' שוב יסיר ועוד אומר ר"י דבכל אלו יש טורח בסילוקן ולכך מעתה יכול לעכב עליו כי יש לחוש שמא לא יזהר לסלקן כשירצה לעשות כותל ומ"ת הכא מאי פריך לרבא הא מפרש טעמא לעיל משום דכל מרא ומרא דקא מחית מרפית לארעאי וי"ל דהשתא טעמא לא קאמר אלא אליבא דר' יוסי והכא לא פריך אלא אליבא דרבנן:

דטויילא

רבינו גרשום

ומקשינן פתח בבור וסיים בכותל דקתני אא"כ הרחיק מכותל חבירו ליתני מבורו של חבירו. והא אכתי לא פריש מילי דבור: א) וגו' טפחים הוי במחיצה של לבנים כדקתני באידך פירקין דלעיל בלבנים זה נותן טפח ומחצה וזה נותן טפח ומחצה: אין ה"נ קתני מתני' אא"כ הרחיק מכותל בורו של חבירו ג' טפחים דהיינו בין בור זה לבור חבירו ו' טפחים והא אתא לאשמועינן דכותל בור ג' טפחים הוי דאי חפיר סמוך לכותל בור חבירו צריך להרחיק ג' ואי עביד כותל לבורו לא צריך הרחקה כלל: הבא לסמוך בצד המצר. כלומר שאם רוצה אחד לחפור בורו סמוך לשדה חבירו הפנויה מבורות: אביי אמר סומך. בצד ממש בלא הרחקה כלל דאינו מזיק לחבירו דלית ליה לחבירו השתא בור: ורבא אמר אינו סומך. אא"כ ירחיק כדין דאע"ג דלית ליה האידנא אימור אימלוך ואחפור גם אני ואי לא ירחיק האי אתי לאזוקי ליה: שדה העשויה לבורות. שצריכה לבורות דבית השלחין היא (לחבירו) ד"ה אינו סומך האידנא בור דהואיל ולא סגי בלא בור ודאי עביד בה בור ואתי לאזוקי אי לא ירחיק: כי פליגי בשדה שאינה עשויה לבורות. דבית הבעל היא: דבעידנא דקא נטע אילן איתא לבור. משום הכי מרחיק כ"ה אמות כי היכי דלא ליזלו שרשיו ומזקי לבור אבל הכא ג) דהוי במצר דאיכא משום דבעידנא דקא חפיר ליתיה לבור דהאי ליתנהו לשרשיו. בההיא שעתא: מרפית לארעא. וכי בעינא למיחפר בור יפול העפר לתוכו: טעמא דאיכא בור. דקתני ליה מש"ה אינו סומך בלא הרחקה הא דוק מיניה אי ליכא בור סומך למצר חבירו בלא הרחקה: בשלמא להך לישנא. בתראה בשדה שאינה עשויה לבורות דברי הכל סומך (מש"ה) [שפיר] מתוקמ' מתני' דקתני הא ליכא בור סומך בשדה שאינה עשויה לבורות מש"ה אי ליכא בור סמיך ואתיא מתני' כד"ה: אלא להאך לישנא דאמרת בשדה שאינה עשויה לבורות פליגי. אבל בשדה העשויה לבורות ד"ה אינו סומך א"כ לא מיתוקמא מתני' אלא אליבא דאביי. אלא לרבא דאמר בין בשדה העשויה לבורות בין שאינה עשויה לבורות אינו סומך מתני' קשיא ליה דמתני' דיקא הא ליכא בור סומך: הא איתמר [לך] רבא. לעולם אינו סומך לא בשדה העשויה לבורות ולא בשדה שאינה עשויה לבורות וממתני' לא מצי למידק הא ליכא בור סמיך דהא איתמר

עלה מתני' לעיל אמר אביי ואי תימא רב יהודה מכותל בורו של חבירו שנינו. מדקתני מכותל בורו מכלל דההוא בור [illegible] הרחיק [illegible] ג' טפחים כשיעור כותל ולא סמיך בצד ממש בלא הרחקה: ג) מתני' מתוקמ' לד"ה אלא להאך לישנא [illegible] אלא לאביי [illegible] [illegible] ואם הוא

א) רש"ל מ"ז, ב) [לקמן כה: ס: ב"מ קח.], ג) [לקמן כג: כה:], ד) לקמן יט. ע"ש [תוספתא פ"א], ה) נ"ל סותר וכ"ה בע"י:

הגהות הב"ח

(א) גמ' איכא דאמרי תנן לא יחפור אדם בור סמוך לבורו של חבירו ואיתמר עלה אמר אביי: (ב) רש"י ד"ה הא קמ"ל במאי דקתני מכותל בורו למדנו בה שהכותל בורו וכו' מדקתני שחפירות חללו של זה אינה מופלגת. נ"ב כלומר אין הכותל קרויה הפלגה אלא בג"ט לאפוקי בפחות מג': (ג) ד"ה ונפקא וכו' מנלן שהכותל הראשון: (ד) ד"ה ה"ג בא וכו' והאי דנקט בא בידים: (ה) תוס' ד"ה הכי גר' וכו' וסד בסיד פי' וקשה לאביי:

ליקוטי רש"י

מן הבור. שהשרשין מתפשטין ונוקבין כותלי הבור וממלחלין את הקרקע והכתלים נופלים [ב"מ קיח.]. בא בידים איצטריכא. למנקט ליה לתנא ואע"ג דה"ה לא בא בידים [לקמן יט.]. ואפילו לר' יוסי דאמר. דפליג בפירקין בנוטע אילן סמוך לבור [לקמן כה:]. הגפת. פסולת זיתים שנתעגלו בבית הבד [לעיל ע"א]. פסולת של בית הבד של שמן שהוא כונס יחד ועם מלד [שבת מז:].

חשק שלמה על רבינו גרשום

א) [מכאן ועד זה נותן טפח ומחצה נראה דשייך לכאן בסמוך אחר תיבות לא צריך הרחקה כלל]: ב) [אולי הכא דרוצה לחפור סמוך למצר סמיך וכו']: ג) [חסר כאן וצ"ל מתני' בשדה העשויה לבורות וד"ה לא סמיך לישנא וכו']: ד) אא"כ הרחיק לעמיד בשדה העשויה לבורות. ה) אולי דצ"ל ולעולם לא מצי סמיך אפי' בשאר קרקע שלא בא בידים ומיוכחא דלאביי וכו']: ו) [נראה דצ"ל שבאו לחפור בבת אחת].

The Gemara cites an alternative version of the proof inferred from our Mishnah:

אִיכָּא דְּאָמְרֵי – **There are those who report** the following version: The Mishnah taught that distancing is required from a neighbor's pit וְאִיתְּמַר עֲלָהּ – **and it was stated in reference to [this ruling]:** אָמַר אַבַּיֵי וְאִיתֵּימָא רַב יְהוּדָה – **Abaye – or,** as **some say, Rav Yehudah – said:** מִכּוֹתֶל בּוֹרוֹ שָׁנִינוּ – When the Mishnah says "from his neighbor's wall," **it means "from the wall of his pit."** Thus, the Mishnah implies that the first neighbor to dig a pit near the boundary is also required to leave a "wall" between his pit and the boundary. בִּשְׁלָמָא לְהַךְ לִישָּׁנָא דְּאָמְרַתְּ – **Now, [this] is in order according to that version** (i.e. the first version) of the dispute between Abaye and Rava **which stated:** בְּשָׂדֶה הָעֲשׂוּיָה לְבוֹרוֹת – **"Regarding land in which it is the practice to dig pits,** דִּבְרֵי הַכֹּל אֵינוֹ סוֹמֵךְ – in **the opinion of all, one may not place** a pit **near** the boundary." מַתְנִיתִין בְּשָׂדֶה הָעֲשׂוּיָה לְבוֹרוֹת – For, according to that version, **our Mishnah** can be explained as referring **to land in which it is the practice to dig pits.** With regard to such land, even Abaye concedes that one may not dig a pit near the boundary even before there is a pit on the other side. אֶלָּא לְהַךְ לִישָּׁנָא דְּאָמְרַתְּ – **However, according to the other version** (i.e. the second version) of the dispute, **which stated:** בְּשָׂדֶה הָעֲשׂוּיָה לְבוֹרוֹת פְּלִיגֵי – **"They disagree regarding land in which it is the practice to dig pits,"** בִּשְׁלָמָא לְרָבָא נִיחָא – **[the law]** inferred from our Mishnah **is in order according to Rava,** who rules that in such circumstances one may not dig a pit near the boundary.[18] אֶלָּא לְאַבַּיֵי – **But according to Abaye,** who permits the digging of a pit even under such circumstances, קַשְׁיָא – the Mishnah poses **a difficulty.**[19] – ? –

The Gemara presents Abaye's defense:

אָמַר לָךְ אַבַּיֵי – **Abaye will say to you:** מַתְנִיתִין שֶׁבָּאוּ לַחְפּוֹר בְּבַת אַחַת – **Our Mishnah** speaks of an instance **where [both neighbors] came to dig pits simultaneously.** In such a case, even Abaye holds that each neighbor is required to distance his pit from the boundary.[20]

The Gemara attempts to refute Abaye's position from a Baraisa:

תָּא שְׁמַע – **Come, learn** the following proof from a Baraisa: סֶלַע הַבָּא בְּיָדַיִם – In a field whose SOIL is so soft THAT it COMES away IN one's HANDS,[21] זֶה חוֹפֵר בּוֹרוֹ מִכָּאן – THIS [NEIGHBOR] MAY DIG HIS PIT ON THIS SIDE of the boundary וְזֶה חוֹפֵר בּוֹרוֹ מִכָּאן – AND THE OTHER [NEIGHBOR] MAY DIG HIS PIT ON THE OTHER SIDE only on condition that זֶה מַרְחִיק שְׁלֹשָׁה טְפָחִים וְסָד בְּסִיד – THIS ONE DISTANCES his pit THREE *TEFACHIM* from the boundary AND APPLIES LIME to its walls,[22] וְזֶה מַרְחִיק שְׁלֹשָׁה טְפָחִים וְסָד בְּסִיד – AND THE OTHER ONE also DISTANCES his pit THREE *TEFACHIM* from the boundary AND APPLIES LIME to its walls.

This Baraisa indicates that both the first neighbor to dig a pit near the boundary and the second one to do so are required to distance their pits three *tefachim* from the boundary. This refutes Abaye's view that the first one to dig a pit near the boundary is not required to distance it.[23] – ? –

The Gemara rejects the proof:

בָּא בְּיָדַיִם[24] שָׁאנֵי – **[Soil]** which is so soft that it **comes** away **in** one's **hands is different** from regular soil. Regarding soft soil, Abaye concedes that it is forbidden to dig a pit near the boundary even before there is a pit on the other side. His permit applies only to a field of regular soil.[25]

This answer is so obvious that the Gemara is prompted to ask:

וּדְקָאָרֵי לָהּ – **And the one who involved** himself with **this** Baraisa, i.e., who asked the question in the first place, מַאי קָאָרֵי לָהּ – **why did he involve it** in the discussion? The very fact that the Baraisa specifies soft soil surely indicates that the restriction it sets forth (viz. even the first pit must be distanced) applies *only* to soft soil![26] – ? –

The Gemara answers that the questioner understood the Baraisa's law as applying to both types of soil, and it specified soft soil for the following reason:

בָּא בְּיָדַיִם אִיצְטְרִיכָא לֵיהּ – **It was necessary for [the Tanna]** to mention **[soil] that comes away in** one's **hands,** סַלְקָא דַּעְתָּךְ אָמִינָא – for otherwise **it might have entered your mind to say** כֵּיוָן דְּבָא בְּיָדַיִם – that **since [such soil] comes away in** one's **hands,** לִיבְעֵי נַמִּי רְווּחָא טְפֵי – **a gap greater** than three *tefachim* **is required** between each pit and the boundary. קָא מַשְׁמַע לָן – **[The Tanna]** therefore **informs us,** by mentioning soft soil, that a distance of three *tefachim* is sufficient even in a field of soft soil.

The Gemara presents a series of challenges to Rava's view from our Mishnah:

תָּא שְׁמַע – **Come, learn** the following proof from our Mishnah: מַרְחִיקִין אֶת הַגֶּפֶת וְאֶת הַזֶּבֶל וְאֶת – ONE MUST DISTANCE OLIVE REFUSE, MANURE,

NOTES

18. [Rava can explain our Mishnah as referring to land in which it is the practice to dig pits.]

19. As the Gemara above imputed to Abaye, the use of the word "wall" in the Mishnah indicates that the distance between the neighbor's pit and the boundary is not some arbitrary amount, but an amount required by law (see note 6). If so, the Gemara asks, the Mishnah clearly indicates that Rava's view is correct – for, in Abaye's view, there is no requirement for the first pit to be distanced from the boundary!

20. Abaye's rationale for allowing one to dig a pit near the boundary is based on the consideration that the potential object of the damage (the neighbor's pit) is not yet in existence (see note 11). When both pits are dug simultaneously, however, each neighbor must take the other's pit into account, and so must distance his pit three *tefachim* from the boundary.

21. I.e. the soil can be dug using one's bare hands, without any tools (*Rabbeinu Gershom*).

22. See Mishnah 17a note 4.

23. This difficulty cannot be resolved by stating that the Baraisa refers to land in which it is the practice to dig pits, because it is not the practice to dig pits in soft soil. Furthermore, according to the second version of the dispute between Abaye and Rava, Abaye permits the placement of a pit even near a field in which it *is* the practice to dig pits.

24. [Many Rishonim follow a different version of the text. See *Tosafos, Ramban, Rashba* et al.]

25. With regard to regular soil, the digging of a pit near the boundary damages the neighboring field only insofar as it is rendered unfit for the digging of pits. Thus, for practical purposes, the neighbor suffers no harm until he decides to dig a pit. Since, on a *practical* level, the damage is not immediate, Abaye permits the digging of a pit under such circumstances. With regard to soft soil, however, even the *practical* damage is immediate, for the land itself caves in when a pit is dug nearby (*Ran*).

26. [If the restriction applies even to regular soil, the Baraisa should have stated this, since it would be the more novel ruling.] Did the questioner not know that the law pertaining to soft soil might be more stringent?! (*Rabbeinu Gershom*).

הַמֶּלַח – SALT, וְאֶת הַסִּיד – LIME וְאֶת הַסְּלָעִים – AND flint STONES, מִכּוֹתְלוֹ שֶׁל חֲבֵירוֹ שְׁלֹשָׁה טְפָחִים – at least THREE *TEFACHIM* FROM THE brick WALL OF ONE'S NEIGHBOR, אוֹ סָד בְּסִיד – OR ONE MUST APPLY LIME to the wall. The Mishnah implies that the neighbor's wall is already in existence. This gives rise to the following inference: טַעְמָא דְאִיכָּא כּוֹתֶל – **The reason** that such precautions are required **is that there is a wall** already standing; הָא לֵיכָּא כּוֹתֶל – **but where there is no wall,** סוֹמֵךְ – **one may place** these harmful materials **near** the boundary. This refutes Rava's position that one may not place a hazard near neighboring property even before the object liable to be damaged is in harm's way.[1] – ? –

The Gemara defends Rava's view:

לֹא – The inference from our Mishnah is **not** compelling. כִּי לֵיכָּא כּוֹתֶל נַמִּי לֹא סָמֵיךְ – One could argue that **even where there is no wall, one may not place** these materials **near** the boundary. וְאֶלָּא מַאי קָא מַשְׁמַע לָן – **And what then does [the Tanna]** mean to **inform us** by specifying a case in which there is a wall?[2] הָא קָא מַשְׁמַע לָן – **He informs us of the following:** דְּהָנֵי קָשׁוּ לְכוֹתֶל – **These** materials **are harmful to a wall.**[3]

The Gemara challenges Rava from the next clause of our Mishnah:

תָּא שְׁמַע – **Come, learn** the following proof from our Mishnah: מַרְחִיקִים אֶת הַזְּרָעִים וְאֶת הַמַּחֲרֵישָׁה וְאֶת מֵי רַגְלַיִם – SEEDS, the use of A PLOW, AND URINE MUST BE DISTANCED מִן הַכּוֹתֶל שְׁלֹשָׁה טְפָחִים – at least THREE *TEFACHIM* FROM THE WALL of one's neighbor. The Mishnah implies that the neighbor's wall is already in existence. This gives rise to the following inference: טַעְמָא דְאִיכָּא כּוֹתֶל – **The reason** distancing is required **is that there is a wall** already standing, הָא לֵיכָּא כּוֹתֶל – **but where there is no wall,** סָמֵיךְ – **one may place** these hazards **near** the boundary. – ? –

The Gemara defends Rava's view:

לֹא – This inference is **not** compelling. כִּי לֵיכָּא כּוֹתֶל נַמִּי לֹא סָמֵיךְ – One could argue that **even where there is no wall, one may not place** these hazards **near** the boundary. וְאֶלָּא מַאי קָא מַשְׁמַע לָן – **And what then does [the Tanna]** mean to **inform us** by specifying a case in which there is a wall? הָא קָא מַשְׁמַע לָן – **He informs us of the following:** דְּמִתּוּנְתָּא קָשָׁה לְכוֹתֶל – **Moisture**[4] **is harmful to a wall.**[5]

Again, the Gemara challenges Rava from our Mishnah:

תָּא שְׁמַע – **Come, learn** the following proof from our Mishnah: וְאֶת הָרֵיחַיִם שְׁלֹשָׁה מִן הַשֶּׁכֶב – AND A MILL must be distanced at least THREE *tefachim* from a neighbor's wall, as measured FROM THE LOWER MILLSTONE, שֶׁהֵן אַרְבָּעָה מִן הָרֶכֶב – WHICH IS equivalent to FOUR *tefachim* from the wall as measured FROM THE UPPER MILLSTONE. The Mishnah implies that the neighbor's wall is already in existence. This gives rise to the following inference: טַעְמָא דְאִיכָּא כּוֹתֶל – **The reason** distancing is required **is that there is a wall** already standing; הָא לֵיכָּא כּוֹתֶל – **but where there is no wall,** סָמֵיךְ – **one may place** this hazard **near** the boundary. – ? –

The Gemara defends Rava's view:

לֹא – This inference is **not** compelling. כִּי לֵיכָּא כּוֹתֶל נַמִּי לֹא סָמֵיךְ – One could argue that **even where there is no wall, one may not place** a mill **near** the boundary. וְאֶלָּא מַאי קָא מַשְׁמַע לָן – **And what then does [the Tanna]** mean to **inform us** by specifying a case in which there is a wall? הָא קָא מַשְׁמַע לָן – **He informs us of the following:** דְּטִירְיָיא קָשָׁה לְכוֹתֶל – **Vibrations are harmful to a wall.**[6]

The Gemara challenges Rava from our Mishnah's final ruling:

תָּא שְׁמַע – **Come, learn** the following proof from our Mishnah: וְאֶת הַתַּנּוּר שְׁלֹשָׁה מִן הַכַּלְיָא – AN OVEN must be distanced at least THREE *tefachim* from a neighbor's wall, as measured FROM THE lower rim of THE oven's BASE, שֶׁהֵן אַרְבָּעָה מִן הַשָּׂפָה – WHICH IS equivalent to FOUR *tefachim* from the wall as measured FROM THE upper RIM of the base. The Mishnah implies that the wall is already in existence. This gives rise to the following inference: טַעְמָא דְאִיכָּא כּוֹתֶל – **The reason** distancing **is** required is **that there is a wall** already standing; הָא לֵיכָּא כּוֹתֶל – **but where there is no wall,** סָמֵיךְ – **one may place** this hazard **near** the boundary.

The Gemara defends Rava's view:

לֹא – This inference is **not** compelling. כִּי לֵיכָּא כּוֹתֶל נַמִּי לֹא סָמֵיךְ – One could argue that **even** where **there is no wall, one may not place** an oven **near** the boundary. אֶלָּא מַאי קָא מַשְׁמַע לָן – And **what then does [the Tanna]** mean to **inform us** by specifying a case in which there is a wall? הָא קָא מַשְׁמַע לָן – **He**

NOTES

1. The Gemara's question requires explanation. Surely Rava concedes that it is permissible to place materials such as olive refuse etc. near the boundary when there is no wall there, for, as soon as the neighbor expresses a desire to build a wall, they can be removed!

Tosafos give two answers: (1) These substances harm the *ground,* rendering it unfit to support a wall. Hence, even if they are removed before the wall is built, the wall will be damaged. (2) Once these substances are in place it is difficult to remove them. Therefore, the neighbor can protest their placement near the boundary on the grounds that when he wants to build a wall they might not be removed in time.

A further difficulty: As stated above, Rava's restriction is based on the argument: "Every time you strike the earth with your spade, you weaken my land," which means that the damage is classified as גִּירֵי דִידֵיהּ, *his arrows,* even before a pit is present on the other side of the boundary. But regarding olive refuse etc. — even if we assume that the damage it causes to a wall is classified as *"his arrows"* (see 22b note 25), how can it be considered *"his arrows"* even before a wall is present? So on what basis does the Gemara assume that Rava's rule applies to cases such as olive refuse etc.?

The answer is that the Gemara adduced the aforementioned argument ("Every time etc.") only for the sake of aligning Rava's position with that of R' Yose. As far as the view of the Sages (R' Yose's disputants) is concerned, Rava's rule applies even where this argument is not applicable. The Gemara's question here assumes the view of the Sages (*Tosafos;* cf. *Ramban*).

2. The Tanna did not need to mention a wall. He could simply have said: "One may not place olive refuse etc. near the boundary."

3. [I.e. the Mishnah teaches that the reason why these materials must be distanced from the boundary is that they are harmful to a wall.]

An apparent difficulty: Since Rava forbids the placement of these substances near the property of a neighbor, regardless of whether or not a wall is there, what practical difference does it make that these substances are harmful to a wall?

The practical consequence is that in a case where it is unlikely that a wall will be built, one is allowed to place these substances near the boundary (*Ritva, Meiri;* see *Nachalas Moshe* who explains why this is true even according to the first version of Rava's view).

4. Plowing is forbidden because seeds are planted in the plow furrows, and seeds are harmful to a wall in that the water used in their irrigation is liable to cause it damage (see *Rabbeinu Gershom*). Thus, each of the hazards listed in this clause — urine, plow, seeds — causes damage, either directly or indirectly, through moisture. (This follows the initial assumption of the passage below, 19a-b, not its conclusion.)

5. See note 3.

6. See note 3. (See also 20b note 13.)

המלח ואת הסיד ואת הסלעים מכותלו של חבירו ג' טפחים (א) או סד בסיד טעמא דאיכא כותל הא ליכא כותל סומך לא כי ליכא כותל נמי לא סמיך ואלא מאי קא משמע לן הא קא משמע לן דהני קשו לכותל תא שמע מרחיקים את הזרעים ואת המחרישה ואת מי רגלים מן הכותל שלשה טפחים טעמא דאיכא כותל הא ליכא כותל סמיך לא כי ליכא כותל נמי לא סמיך ואלא מאי קמ"ל הא קא משמע לן דמתונתא קשה לכותל תא שמע ואת הריחים ג' מן השכב שהן ד' מן הרכב טעמא דאיכא כותל הא ליכא כותל סמיך לא כי ליכא כותל נמי לא סמיך ואלא מאי קא משמע לן הא קא משמע לן דטירייא קשה לכותל תא שמע ואת התנור שלשה מן הכליא שהן ד' מן השפה טעמא דאיכא כותל הא ליכא כותל סמיך לא כי ליכא כותל נמי לא סמיך אלא מאי קא משמע לן הא קא משמע לן דהבלא קשה לכותל תא שמע לא יפתח אדם חנות של נחתומין ושל צבעין תחת אוצרו של חבירו ולא רפת בקר טעמא דאיכא אוצר הא ליכא אוצר עביד דירה שאני דיקא נמי דתני עלה אם היתה רפת בקר קודמת לאוצר מותר ת"ש לא יטע אדם אילן סמוך לשדה אלא אם כן הרחיק ממנו ד' אמות ותני עלה ד' אמות שאמרו כדי עבודת הכרם טעמא דמשום כדי עבודת הכרם הא לאו משום כדי עבודת הכרם סמיך ואע"ג דאיכא שרשין דקא מזקי הכא במאי עסקינן דמפסיק צונמא (דיקא נמי דקתני) היה גדר בינתים זה סומך לגדר מכאן וזה סומך לגדר מכאן אי הכי אימא סיפא היו שרשיו יוצאין בתוך של חבירו מעמיק להן שלשה טפחים כדי שלא יעכב המחרישה ואי דמפסיק צונמא מאי בעו (א) התם ה"ק ואי לאו צונמא והיו שרשיו יוצאין לתוך של חבירו מעמיק שלשה טפחים כדי שלא יעכב המחרישה ת"ש מרחיקין את האילן מן הבור עשרים וחמש אמה טעמא דאיכא בור הא ליכא בור סמיך לא כי ליכא בור נמי לא סמיך והא קמ"ל דעד כ"ה אמה אזלי שרשים ומזקי לבור אי הכי אימא סיפא ואם אילן קדם לא יקוץ ואי דלא סמיך היכי משכחת לה כדא"ר פפא בלוקח ה"נ בלוקח ת"ש מרחיקין את המשרה מן הירק ואת הכרישין מן הבצלין ואת החרדל מן הדבורים טעמא דאיכא ירק הא ליכא ירק סמיך לא כי ליכא ירק נמי לא סמיך והא קמ"ל דהני קשו אהדדי א"ה אימא סיפא רבי יוסי מתיר בחרדל מפני שיכול לומר לו עד שאתה אומר לי הרחק חרדלך מן דבוראי הרחק דבורך מן חרדלאי שבאות ואוכלות לגלוגי חרדלאי ואי

רש"י

מתונתא. דבר לח: **טירייא.** איטוני"ר בלע"ז כמו דטריא לרישיה באלו טריפות (חולין דף מה:): **חנות של נחתומין.** מוכרי לחם שמסיקין שם אור תמיד: **אוצר.** עלייה שאוצרין בה תבואה ושמן ויין והעשן קשה להן: **ולא רפת בקר.** הריח קשה להן: **דירה שאני.** חנות ורפת בקר דירתן של אדם הן ואין לנו לאסור דירתו עליו אא"כ הניזק מוכן: **דיקא נמי.** דדירה שאני: **דקתני עלה.** דהסיפא אם היתה הרפת בקר קודמת לאוצר מותר ובכולהו שאר הרחקות דמתני' לא תנא הכי ש"מ הכא משום דדירה שאני אבל אינך אף הראשון צריך להרחיק: **אלא אם כן הרחיק ממנו ארבע אמות.** כדמפרש טעמא כדי עבודת הכרם שהיו חורשים הכרם במחרישה וכן בשעת הבציר בוצרין אותם בעגלות וצריך להן מקום פנוי ארבע אמות שלא תיכנס עגלת מחרישתו בקרקע חבירו: **טעמא משום עבודת הכרם.** שהוא מזיקו בידים הא לאו הכי סמיך ואע"ג (ב) שיתפשטו שרשיו ויזיקו בשדה בין לעכב המחרישה בין לחפירת הבור: **צונמא.** סלע חזק שלא יתפשטו שרשיו לשם: **גדר בינתים.** שאין מזיקו עוד לעבודת הכרם זה סומך אילנות לגדר מכאן וזה סומך אילנות לגדר מכאן ולא נמי אחד מהן שדה לבן אין כאן כלאים כדאמר בעירובין (דף יא.) אם גפנים מכאן מותר לזרוע כאן גבי נעץ ארבעה קונדיסין ומתח זמורה על גביהן דמהני לצורת הפתח קתני מיהא זה סומך ואע"ג דאזלי שרשים תחת הגדר ומתפשטין לתוך השדה: **מעמיק להן.** בעל השדה קוצץ את השרשין שיצאו בשדהו בעומק שלשה טפחים: **ואי לאו צונמא.** וזה נוטע שם שלא כדת מעמיק להו זה (ג) כשיזיקו הן: **עשרים וחמשה אמות.** כך שיעור שהשרשים נמשכין והולכין ומקלקלין את כותלי הבור: **הוא הדין כו'.** והא קמ"ל דעד כ"ה אמה אזלי שרשים ומזקי לבור: ה"ג **אי הכי אימא סיפא אם האילן קדם לא יקוץ אי לא סמיך היכי משכחת לה.** דהאילן קדם ואי שלא כדין סמך אמאי לא יקוץ מה לי בור קדם דקתני קוצץ ומאי שנא אילן קדם דתנא לא יקוץ: **כדאמר רב פפא.** לקמן בשמעתין: **הכא נמי בלוקח.** אדם שנטע אילן בתוך שדהו ואח"כ מכר חצי שדהו לאיש אחר ובא הלוקח וחפר בור אין זה צריך לקוץ אילן שנטעו ברשותו: **את המשרה.** מים ששורין בו את הפשתן: **מן הירק.** של מיני מאכל כרוב ושומין וכרישין: **ואת הכרישין.** כרתי פוריל"ש: **ואת החרדל מן הדבורים.** שאוכלין את החרדל ומחדד את פיהם ואוכלות את דבש שלהן: **כי ליכא ירק נמי לא סמיך.** והא קמ"ל דהנך קשו אהדדי: **עד שאתה אומר הרחק את חרדליך מדבוריי.** שבעל המזיק להרחיק עצמו הרחק אתה דבוריך מן חרדליי שאף אתה נקרא מזיק: ואי

תוספות

דטירייא קשה לכותל. אע"ג דלקמן (דף כ:) הדר ביה מטעמא דטירייא ומפרש אלא משום קלא מכל מקום נקט ליה הכא משום דמעיקרא הוה בעי לפרושי טעמא משום טירייא ולספרים דלא גרסי הכא אתי שפיר הכא דלההיא גירסא טירייא וקלא חד טעמא הוא: **לא** יפתח אדם חנות של נחתומין. פ"ה משום שהעשן קשה לאוצר וקשה לר"ת דלקמן אמר ביין התירו שמשביחו ועשן ודאי מזיק ליין דהא יין מעושן פסול לנסכים אלא נראה לר"ת דהיזק עשן ליכא כיון דאיכא שם תקרה ומעזיבה לא יכנס שם העשן אלא טעמא שההבל מזיק את האוצר אבל את היין משביח וגרסי' לקמן אמר רב יוסף והאי דידן אפילו שרגא קשיא ליה כלומר הבלא דשרגא ולא גרסי' קוטרא דשרגא: **הא** ליכא אוצר עביד. הוי מצי לשנויי ה"ה כי ליכא לא סמיך והא קמ"ל דהבלא (ד) קשיא לאוצר: **דיקא** נמי דקתני אם היתה רפת בקר קודמת כו'. ובכולהו הרחקות דמתני' לא תני הכי והוה ליה לאשמועינן בשאר וכ"ש בדירה ותימה דלעולם בשאר הרחקות נמי מותר לסמוך והא דנקטיה הכא לאשמועינן רבותא ° דאע"ג דהוי גירי דיליה אם היתה קודמת לאוצר מותר דהשתא הוי חידוש אפילו לרבי יוסי ואי אשמועינן בשאר לא הוי חידוש אלא לרבנן אבל לרבי יוסי דקסבר על הניזק להרחיק לא הוי שום חידוש: **דיקא** נמי דקתני כו'. ולאביי לא קשיא האי דיקא דלא משמע ליה שיהא חידוש בשאר טפי מבדירה: **ואם** היתה רפת בקר כו'. והוא הדין חנות של נחתומין ושל צבעין וחדא מינייהו נקט: **ותני** עלה ד' אמות שאמרו כדי עבודת הכרם. הוה ליה למינקט כדי עבודת האילן אלא נקט עבודת הכרם לפי שנזכר לשון זה במסכת כלאים גבי כרם שצריך הרחקה ד' אמות: **טעמא** משום עבודת הכרם כו'. בלאו האי דיוקא מצי למפרך בפשיטות דסגי בהרחקת ארבע אמות ואי אסור לסמוך היה צריך להרחיק כ"ה אמות כדתנן לקמן (דף כה:) שמרחיקין את האילן מן הבור אלא ניחא ליה למידק דאפילו תוך ארבע אמות מותר לסמוך: **דמפסיק** צונמא. וא"ת אמאי צריך ד' אמות פשיטא שחוץ לצונמא לא יחרוש שלא יועיל כלום לאילן וי"ל כשיחרוש עד הצונמא ירצה להפוך המחרישה לצד אחר המחרישה יכנס לשדה חבירו: **היו** שרשיו יוצאין כו'. וא"ת היאך סמך אי שלא ברשות א"כ יקוץ וצריך לאוקמי בלוקח ולריצב"א אין נראה להעמיד בלוקח מדלא מסיק לה כדבסמוך אלא נראה דמיירי בסמך שלא ברשות דאינו קוצץ האילן אלא בנתינת דמים וזה לא רצה להאריך ולהשמיענו: **הכא** נמי בלוקח. פ"ה שהאילן ביד מוכר ואין נראה לר"י בר' מרדכי דא"כ הול"ל במוכר אלא נראה לו לפרש שהאילן ביד לוקח ולשני הפירושים אלו אין להקשות מאי איריא שהאילן קדם אפילו קדם בור נמי כגון שאדם אחד עשה הבור ואח"כ נטע האילן ומכר הבור לפ"ה או אילן לפי' ר"י ברבי מרדכי לא יקוץ שהרי בהיתר עשאן דבכה"ג אילן קדם קרינא ביה שקדמה נטיעת האילן לערעור בעל הבור דערעור אינו בא אלא ע"י מכירת בור או מכירת האילן אבל לפר"ת שפי' בלוקח שלקח מאדם אחד את אילן וטוענין ללוקח קשה לר"י מאי איריא אילן קדם אפילו קדם בור נמי ועוד כיון דהחזיק באילן ג' שנים טוענין ללוקח לוקמה נמי בלא לוקח ובחזקה שיש עמה טענה:

רבינו גרשום

המלח. שחופרין להכניס לתוכן מים לעשות מלח ושיחות שעושין לשרוף בהן **הסיד ואת הסלעים** חפירה מלאה אבנים: **וסד בסיד.** החפירה דכל אלו מזיקין לכותל: **הא ליכא כותל.** הוי כשאר כותל **וסמיך** וקשיא לרבא דאמר גבי שדה דלא סמיך: **דמתונתא דהני.** זה לחלוחית המים שמשקין הזרעים בנגר ודאי **קשין לכותל** שמקלקלין המים יסוד הכותל: **מרחיקין את הריחים.** העשוין בקרקע מן הכותל חבירו: **ג' טפחים מן השכב.** זו אבן התחתונה שמו שכב. ורכב זו אבן עליונה שמורכבת עליה והתחתונה רחבה מן העליונה טפח לכל צד והיינו ג' מן השכב שהוא **ד' מן הרכב** מתוך דפחותה טפח: **טעמא דאיכא כותל.** וקשיא לרבא: **טירא קשה לכותל.** אותו ויעזוע שמזעזעין הקרקע בשעה שמתקנין שם הריחים. איכא דאמר טירא קול הברה שעושין הריחים: **מרחיקין את התנור מן הכותל.** אע"ג דלא תני כותל אפ"ה משמע דירחיק מן הכותל **ג' טפחים. מן הכיליא** איזהו כיליא כששעושין התנור מחרס שכל תנוריהן היו של חרס ועשוין כעין דלי פתוח מלמעלה והחרס קלוש ומדביקין סביב התנור מן הטיט בעובי טפח סביב כדי לחזק התנור מפני שהוא של חרס שלא ישבר ולאותו הדבק קרי כילייא והיינו דאמרי' במס' (פסחים) [חולין קכג:] וגורר את הטפילה **עד** שמגיע לארץ ואותה דאמרי' התם היינו כילייא **ושפה** זו שפת התנור עצמו שהוא **מרחיק מן הכותל ד' טפחים** כפ"ה. **איכא דאמרי** כילייא זה יסוד התנור דכל סביב התנור סמוך לקרקע יוצא בנין התנור טפח לחוץ וכי מעלה בנינו מקצר ועולה עד לשפה שלמעלה דפוחתת טפח. למ"ה: **הבלא.** חמימות התנור: **לא יפתח אדם חנות של נחתומין.** שאופה פתו למכור בכל עת תמיד אופה ומחמם התבואה או היין של חבירו שבאוצר שלמעלה הימנו בעלייה ומש"ה קרי לעלייה אוצר שכן דרך בני אדם שאוצרין פירותיהן בעליות. **וכן של צבעים** לא יפתח תחת האוצר מפני שתדיר עושה היסק גדול לצורך הצבע ומחמם התבואה: **ולא רפת בקר** נמי משום הבלא דזבל. **וטעמא** מאי לא יפתח **דאיכא אוצר** דקדם מעיקרא מש"ה אינו יכול לפתוח להפסידו. **הא לא הוי אוצר** מעיקרא אלא חנות קדם ברישא והשתא קא פתח (הוי) [האי] חנות של נחתומין אע"ג דיכול למימר האי בעל (האוצר) [המיצר] למחר אי עביד הכא לעיל אוצר שלי ומזקת לי כיון דעדיין לא מינכר היזקו **עביד** וסמיך הכי נמי סמיך א) למיצר וקשיא לרבא אמר לך רבא לעולם בעלמא לא סמיך [ודקא דייקי הא היכא] דליכא אוצר סמיך היינו טעמא **דדירתו** של אדם **שאני** שצריך לו לאדם לעשות צרכיו בדירתו משו"ה לא מצי מעכב ליה הואיל ואין לו שום אוצר עכשיו אבל גבי בור ושדה דעלמא דלא קבע תשמישתייהו כדירה לא סמיך משום דמזיק ליה בכך [דמרפי] ליה ארעיה ואי מימלך למיעבד בור לא מצי למיעבד בור: **דיקא נמי.** דדירה שאני: **דקתני אם היה רפת בקר קודם לאוצר מותר.** משום דדירה שאני: **כדי עבודת הכרם.** כדי איכר בקר וכליו דלא דייש ליה לשדהו דהתם היו חורשין את הכרמים בשוורים וכך נמי היו חורשין לשדה אילנות בשוורים: **דקא מפסיק צונמא.** בין שדה שלו לשל חבירו דלא קא עבדין בהני סלעים מש"ה מצי סמיך אי לאו מפני עבודת הכרם אבל בעלמא לא: **היה גדר בינתים.** בין הכרם לשדה **זה סומך** נטיעותיו **לגדר** [אע"ג] דעברין שרשין לשדה: **מעמיק לשרשיו בקרקע ג' טפחים כדי שלא יעכב את המחרישה. הכי קאמר אי לאו צונמא** והוה מרחיק ליה לאילנות כ"ה אמה כשיעור האילן. ולאחר כן הגדילו שרשין יותר מכ"ה והיו שרשין יוצאין לתוך של חבירו כנ"ל: **אית דמפרשי** האי שדה כרם הוא כדי להשתמש בהני ד' אמות עבודת תשמיש דצריך לכרם כגון בית הגת וגיגית שלועזין טיני. היינו בור שתחת הגת. אלמא דסמיך (ליה אלא) הכא במאי עסקינן דאי לאו משום עבודת הכרם סמיך דמפסיק צונמא כלומר דאיכא סלע חזק בין האילן לשדה דאינן יכולין השרשין לעבור ולהפסיד בשדה אבל גבי בור ושדה דעלמא דמפסיד לעולם לא סמיך. **זה סומך** אילנו **לגדר וזה** בורו אלמא דסמיך אע"ג דעברי שרשים תותי גדר לשדה חבירו וקא מזקי. לא הכא נמי דאיכא צונמא: **מעמיק** שרשי האילן בקרקע **ג' טפחים** ב) כי היכי דלא ליתזקו שרשין ואמאי צריך להעמיק בתמיה: **כדי שלא תעכב את המחרישה** ולא יפסיד. להכי צריך להעמיק וסמיך אבל גבי בור ושדה דעלמא דלעולם אי אפשר דליכא פסידא של רפיית הקרקע מבור לבור (אמאי) [אימא] לעולם לא סמיך. למ"ה: **אי הכי.** דכי ליכא בור [נמי] לא סמיך האילן **אימא סיפא אם האילן קדם** לבור דאם היה נטוע האילן קודם דנחפר הבור אע"ג דמזיק לה **לא יקוץ ואי לא סמיך** האילן על מצר שדה חבירו קודם חפירת הבור **היכי** מצי **משכחת לה** דמזיק לה השתא אלא לאו ש"מ דסמיך: לא לעולם לא סמיך. וכי תימא א"כ היכי הוה זה סומך אילנו אצל שדה חבירו: **כדאמר רב פפא** לקמן **בלוקח.** כגון דהוה מעיקרא האילן והשדה לאדם אחד ומכרו לשני בני אדם לא' מכר מקום האילן והאילן ולשני מכר כל שאר השדה משפת אילן ולהלן ובא זה שלקח שאר השדה וחפר בורו סמוך לאילן דהשתא קדם האילן לבור ולא סמכו זה לוקח אלא המוכר ברשות סמכו דהכל היה שלו ומשו"ה לא יקוץ ולעולם בעלמא לא סמיך: **מרחיקין את המשרה.** מים שמכבסין בהן פשתן וקשה הוא לירק. א"ד משרה שמכבסין שורין בהן את השדה וקשה לירק שמתקלקל: **מן הירק** ג) דאתרייהו ירקות דלא צריכי כל כך מים וניזוקין ביציאות המים הללו ומשו"ה מרחיקין הללו. למ"ה: **ולא כרתי אצל בצלים.** משום דמכחישי כרישין לבצלים וכן לחרדל מתוך דאכלי דבורים לחרדל: **דאכלי לגלוגי.** כלומר ענפי חרדלי:

מסורת הש"ס

א) כ"א וסד, ב) כ"א דהני, ג) לקמן כ:, ד) [שם], ה) לקמן כו. [ודף פג.], ו) לקמן כו., ז) כ"א ת"ש, ח) לקמן כו:, ט) כ"א ה"נ בצונמא, י) לקמן כה:, כ) ג"ז שם, ל) כ"א ותני עלה [לקמן כה:].

הגהות הב"ח

(א) גמ' מאי בעו שרשין התם: (ב) רש"י ד"ה טעמא וכו' ואע"ג דסופו שיתפשטו: (ג) ד"ה ואי לאו צונמא וכו' לזה זה (כשיזיקו הן) תא"מ ונ"ב ס"א כדי שלא יזיקו כשיזיקו הן: (ד) תוס' ד"ה הא ליכא וכו' דהבלא דהני קשה לאוצר:

גליון הש"ס

תוס' ד"ה דיקא כו' דאע"ג דהוי גירי. עיין לקמן דף כב ע"ב תוס' ד"ה ענין:

לעזי רש"י

איטוני"ר. פירוש להרעיד (רש"י ב"ב דף כ ע"ב ד"ה משום טירייא), לזעזע (רבינו גרשום ב"ב דף יח ע"א ודף כ ע"ב). פוריל"ש. פירוש כרישין, כרתי, קפלוטות (רש"י ביצה דף יח ע"ב, תליר (רש"י במדבר יא, ה).

ליקוטי רש"י

הסלעים. אבנים שהאור יוצא מהן שקורין קוילי"ש שכל אלו קשין לחומה שמוציאין הבל. [המשך בע"ב]

חשק שלמה על רבינו גרשום א) נראה דל"ל והכא נמי סמיך בור ממצר. ב) נראה דל"ל ג"ט כדי שלא תעכב את המחרישה ולא יפסיד אלא אי לאו צונמא וכו' ולהכי צריך להעמיק וכו'. ג) אולי צ"ל מתוך דהנהו ירקות לא צריכי כ"כ וכו'.

informs us of the following: דְּהַבְלָא קָשֶׁה לְכוֹתֶל – **Heat is harmful to a wall.**[7]

The Gemara attempts to refute Rava's view from the next Mishnah:

תָּא שְׁמַע – **Come, learn** the following proof from a Mishnah:[8] לֹא יִפְתַּח אָדָם חָנוּת שֶׁל נַחְתּוֹמִין וְשֶׁל צַבָּעִין – A PERSON MAY NOT OPEN A BAKERY OR A DYE SHOP תַּחַת אוֹצָרוֹ שֶׁל חֲבֵירוֹ – UNDER THE STOREROOM[9] OF HIS FELLOW, וְלֹא רֶפֶת בָּקָר – NOR may he open A CATTLE BARN under a storeroom. The Mishnah implies that the storeroom is already in existence. This gives rise to the following inference: טַעְמָא דְאִיכָּא אוֹצָר – **The reason** for these restrictions **is that there is a storeroom** in the upper story; הָא לֵיכָּא אוֹצָר – **but where there is no storeroom** in the upper story, עָבִיד – **one may open**[10] any of these establishments in the lower story. – ? –

The Gemara answers that this case is an exception:

דִּירָה שַׁאנֵי – **A** person's **residence is different.** A bakery, dye shop and cattle barn are industries that typically are operated in a person's own home. Rava concedes that restrictions are not placed on what a person does in his home except in a case where vulnerable property is already in harm's way.

The Gemara cites support for this distinction:

דַּיְקָא נַמֵי – One can **also infer this** from the following: דְּתָנֵי עֲלָהּ – **A Barisa was taught in reference to [this Mishnah]** which states: אִם הָיְתָה רֶפֶת בָּקָר קוֹדֶמֶת לָאוֹצָר מוּתָּר – IF the establishment of THE CATTLE BARN[11] PRECEDED that of the storeroom, IT IS PERMITTED to maintain the cattle barn. Since this qualification was taught *only* in reference to a cattle barn etc., evidently, it applies only in these cases and not in the other cases listed in our Mishnah. The reason for this exception must be, as explained above, that a person's residence is treated differently.

The Gemara makes another attempt to refute Rava's view:

תָּא שְׁמַע – **Come, learn** the following proof from a Mishnah:[12] לֹא יִטַּע אָדָם אִילָן סָמוּךְ לְשָׂדֶה – A PERSON MAY NOT PLANT A TREE or a vine NEAR THE FIELD of his neighbor אֶלָּא אִם כֵּן הִרְחִיק מִמֶּנּוּ אַרְבַּע אַמּוֹת – UNLESS HE DISTANCES it FOUR *AMOS* FROM [HIS NEIGHBOR'S FIELD]. וְתָנֵי עֲלָהּ – **And a Baraisa was taught in reference to [this Mishnah]:** אַרְבַּע אַמּוֹת שֶׁאָמְרוּ – THE FOUR *AMOS* THAT [THE SAGES] SAID must be maintained between a tree or vine and a neighboring field כְּדֵי עֲבוֹדַת הַכֶּרֶם – are required so that one will have ENOUGH room FOR THE CULTIVATION OF THE VINEYARD (or the orchard) without encroaching on the neighboring property.[13] The Gemara makes the following inference from this Baraisa: טַעְמָא דְמִשּׁוּם כְּדֵי עֲבוֹדַת הַכֶּרֶם – **The reason** the tree must be distanced **is that sufficient** space is required **for the cultivation of the vineyard.** הָא לָאו מִשּׁוּם כְּדֵי עֲבוֹדַת הַכֶּרֶם – **But were it not for** the necessity of allowing **sufficient** space **for the cultivation of the vineyard,** סָמִיךְ – **one may place** a tree **near** the boundary, וְאַף עַל גַּב דְּאִיכָּא שָׁרְשִׁין דְּקָא מַזְּקֵי – **even though there are roots** to the tree **that will** eventually grow and **cause damage!**[14] This refutes Rava's position that a hazard may not be placed near neighboring property even before the potential object of the damage is in harm's way. – ? –

The Gemara answers:

הָכָא בְּמַאי עַסְקִינַן – **What are we dealing with here?** דְּמַפְסִיק צוּנְמָא – The Mishnah refers to a case **where** a subterranean barrier of **rock separates** the two fields. The tree's roots cannot penetrate this rocky barrier and therefore cannot cause damage in the neighboring field.[15]

The Gemara proves that the Mishnah refers to such a case:

(דַּיְקָא נַמֵי דְּקָתָנֵי) – One can **also infer** this from the continuation of that Mishnah: הָיָה גָּדֵר בֵּינְתַיִם – IF THERE WAS A FENCE BETWEEN [THE TWO FIELDS], which prevents the entry of a plow into the neighboring field, זֶה סוֹמֵךְ לַגָּדֵר מִכָּאן – THIS [NEIGHBOR] MAY PLACE a tree NEAR THE FENCE [ON HIS SIDE] וְזֶה סוֹמֵךְ לַגָּדֵר מִכָּאן – AND THE OTHER [NEIGHBOR] MAY PLACE a tree NEAR THE FENCE [ON HIS SIDE].[16] Now this would not be permitted if there were not some form of impenetrable barrier (e.g. a section of rock) beneath the surface, for otherwise the roots would go under the fence and cause damage in the neighboring field.[17]

The Gemara asks:

אִי הָכִי – **If** this is **so,** that the Mishnah speaks of a case where a subterranean barrier of rock separates the two fields, אֵימָא סֵיפָא – **consider the latter clause** of that Mishnah: הָיוּ שָׁרָשָׁיו יוֹצְאִין בְּתוֹךְ שֶׁל חֲבֵירוֹ – If one planted a tree and ITS ROOTS EXTENDED INTO the property OF HIS NEIGHBOR, מַעֲמִיק לָהֶן שְׁלֹשָׁה טְפָחִים – [THE NEIGHBOR] MAY [CUT THEM OFF] TO A DEPTH OF THREE *TEFACHIM*,[18] כְּדֵי שֶׁלֹּא יְעַכֵּב הַמַּחֲרֵישָׁה – SO THAT THEY DO NOT IMPEDE THE progress of his PLOW. וְאִי דְּמַפְסִיק צוּנְמָא – Now **if** the Mishnah speaks of a case **where** a subterranean barrier of **rock separates** the fields, מַאי בָּעוּ הָתָם – **what are [the roots] doing there?** How could they have penetrated the rocky barrier?

The Gemara answers:

הָכִי קָאָמַר – **This is what [the latter clause of the Mishnah] means:** וְאִי לָאו צוּנְמָא – **But if** there is **no** barrier of

NOTES

7. See *Ritva,* and note 3.

8. Below, 20b.

9. The storeroom referred to here is an upper chamber in which grain, wine or oil is stored. The smoke produced by the constantly burning ovens of a bakery or dye shop (for boiling the dyes) is injurious to such items. Likewise, the odor emanating from a cattle barn is harmful to them (*Rashi;* see *Rashash*).

10. Literally: do.

11. The same applies to a bakery and dye shop (*Tosafos*).

12. Below, 26a.

13. Space is required between a tree (or vine) and neighboring property so that when the owner plows around his tree, or takes a wagon to collect its fruit, he will not enter his neighbor's field (*Rashi*).

14. By impeding the neighbor's plow or making it difficult for him to dig a pit (*Rashi;* see *Ramban* ד״ה הא דאמרינן דיקא). [To avoid this, the tree should be distanced 25 *amos* from the boundary (see Mishnah 25b).]

15. [Thus, were it not for the requirement that space must be allowed for "the cultivation of the vineyard," even Rava would concede that it is permitted to plant near the boundary.]

16. Furthermore, in a case where grain or greens are planted in one field and there is a vineyard in the other, the presence of the fence alleviates the prohibition of כִּלְאֵי הַכֶּרֶם, *mixtures of the vineyard.* The Torah prohibits the planting of grain or greens within four *amos* of a vineyard. But if a fence interposes, it is permitted to plant vines next to one side of the fence and grain or greens next to the other side. (The Gemara, *Eruvin* 11a, teaches that even a fence consisting merely of two vertical poles with a horizontal branch above them extending from one to the other [צוּרַת הַפֶּתַח, *the form of a doorway*] suffices for this purpose) (*Rashi*).

17. This clause of the Mishnah indicates that where a fence interposes, one is permitted to plant a tree even after his neighbor has already done so. Hence, even according to Abaye, the Mishnah must speak of a case where there is a rocky barrier beneath the surface, for otherwise it would be forbidden to plant a second tree near the boundary lest it damage the one that is already in place (*Ran;* see *Ramban, Rashba, Maharsha;* cf. *Maharam*).

18. He may cut off those roots that extend into his property where they are within three *tefachim* of the surface (*Rashi*).

המלח ואת הסיד ואת הסלעים מכותלו של חבירו ג' טפחים [א] או סד בסיד טעמא דאיכא כותל הא ליכא כותל סומך לא כי ליכא כותל נמי לא סמיך ואלא מאי קא משמע לן הא קא משמע לן דהני קשו לכותל תא שמע מרחיקים את הזרעים ואת המחרישה ואת מי רגלים מן הכותל שלשה טפחים טעמא דאיכא כותל הא ליכא כותל סמיך לא כי ליכא כותל נמי לא סמיך ואלא מאי קמ"ל הא קא משמע לן דמתונתא קשה לכותל תא שמע ואת הריחים ג' מן השכב שהן ד' מן הרכב טעמא דאיכא כותל הא ליכא כותל סמיך לא כי ליכא כותל נמי לא סמיך ואלא מאי קא משמע לן הא קא משמע לן דטירייא קשה לכותל תא שמע ואת התנור שלשה מן הכליא שהן ד' מן השפה טעמא דאיכא כותל הא ליכא כותל סמיך לא כי ליכא כותל נמי לא סמיך אלא מאי קא משמע לן הא קא משמע לן [ג] דהבלא קשה לכותל תא שמע [ד] לא יפתח אדם חנות של נחתומין ושל צבעין תחת אוצרו של חבירו ולא רפת בקר טעמא דאיכא אוצר הא ליכא אוצר עביד דירה שאני דיקא נמי דתני עלה [ה] אם היתה רפת בקר קודמת לאוצר מותר ת"ש [ו] לא יטע אדם אילן סמוך לשדה אלא אם כן הרחיק ממנו ד' אמות ותני עלה [ז] ד' אמות שאמרו כדי עבודת הכרם טעמא דמשום כדי עבודת הכרם הא לאו משום כדי עבודת הכרם סמיך ואע"ג דאיכא שרשין דקא מזקי הכא במאי עסקינן דמפסיק צונמא [ח] דיקא נמי דקתני [ט] היה גדר בינתים זה סומך לגדר מכאן וזה סומך לגדר מכאן [י] אי הכי אימא סיפא היו שרשיו יוצאין בתוך של חבירו מעמיק להן שלשה טפחים כדי שלא יעכב המחרישה ואי דמפסיק צונמא מאי בעו (א) התם ה"ק ואי לאו צונמא והיו שרשיו יוצאין לתוך של חבירו מעמיק שלשה טפחים כדי שלא יעכב המחרישה ת"ש [כ] מרחיקין את האילן מן הבור עשרים וחמש אמה טעמא דאיכא בור הא ליכא בור סמיך לא כי ליכא בור נמי לא סמיך והא קמ"ל דעד כ"ה אמה אזלי שרשים ומזקי לבור אי הכי אימא סיפא ואם אילן קדם לא יקוץ ואי דלא סמיך היכי משכחת לה כדא"ר פפא בלוקח ה"נ בלוקח ת"ש [ל] מרחיקין את המשרה מן הירק ואת הכרישין מן הבצלין ואת החרדל מן הדבורים טעמא דאיכא ירק הא ליכא ירק סמיך לא כי ליכא ירק נמי לא סמיך והא קמ"ל דהני קשו אהדדי א"ה אימא סיפא רבי יוסי מתיר בחרדל [מ] מפני שיכול לומר לו עד שאתה אומר לי הרחק חרדלך מן דבוראי הרחק דבורך מן חרדלאי שבאות ואוכלות לגלוגי חרדלאי ואי

רש"י

מתונתא. דבר לח: טירייא. איטוני"ר בלע"ז כמו דטרייא לרישיה באלו טריפות (חולין דף מה:): חנות של נחתומין. מוכרי לחם שמסיקין שם אור תמיד: אוצר. עלייה שאוצרין בה תבואה ושמן ויין והעשן קשה להן: ולא רפת בקר. הריח קשה להן: דירה שאני. חנות ורפת בקר דירתן של אדם הן ואין לנו לאסור דירתו עליו אא"כ ההיזק מוכן: דיקא נמי. דדירה שאני: דקתני עלה. דהיכא אם היתה הרפת בקר קודמת לאוצר מותר ובכולהו שאר הרחקות דמתני' לא תנא הכי ש"מ הכא משום דדירה שאני אבל איכך אף הראשון צריך להרחיק: אלא אם כן הרחיק ממנו ארבע אמות. כדמפרש טעמא כדי עבודת הכרם שהיו חורשים הכרם במחרישה וכן בשעת הבציר בוצרין אותם בעגלות וצריך להן מקום פנוי ארבע אמות שלא תיכנס עגלת מחרישתו בקרקע חבירו: טעמא משום עבודת הכרם. שהוא מזיקו בידים הא לאו הכי סמיך ואע"ג (ב) שיתפשטו שרשיו ויזיקו בשדה בין לעכב המחרישה בין לחפירת הבור: צונמא. סלע חזק שלא יתפשטו שרשיו לשם: גדר בינתים. שאין מזיקו עוד לעבודת הכרם זה סומך אילנות לגדר מכאן וזה סומך אילנות לגדר מכאן ואי נמי אחד מהן שדה לבן אין כאן כלאים כדאמר בעירובין (דף יא.) אם גפנים מכאן מותר לזרוע כאן גבי נעץ ארבעה קונדיסין ומתח זמורה על גביהן דמיא לצורת הפתח קתני מיהא זה סומך ואע"ג דאזלי שרשים תחת הגדר ומתפשטין לתוך השדה: מעמיק להן. בעל השדה קוצץ את השרשין שלא יזיקו בשדהו בעומק שלשה טפחים: ואי לאו צונמא. וזה נוטע שם שלא כדת מעמיק להו זה (ג) כשיזיקו הן: עשרים וחמשה אמות. כך שיערו שהשרשין נמשכין והולכין ומקלקלין את כותלי הבור: הוא הדין כו'. והא קמ"ל דעד כ"ה אמה אזלי שרשין ומזקי לבור: ה"ג אי הכי אימא סיפא אם האילן קדם לא יקוץ אי לא סמיך היכי משכחת לה. דהאילן קדם ואי שלא כדין סמך אמאי לא יקוץ מה לי בור קדם דקתני קוצץ ומאי שנא אילן קדם דתנא לא יקוץ: כדאמר רב פפא. לקמן בשמעתין: הכא נמי בלוקח. אדם שנטע אילן בתוך שדהו ואח"כ מכר חצי שדהו לאיש אחר ובא הלוקח וחפר בור אין זה צריך לקוץ אילן שנטעו ברשותו: את המשרה. מים ששורין בו את הפשתן: מן הירק. של מיני מאכל כרוב ושומין וכרישין: ואת הכרישין. כרתי פוריל"ש: ואת החרדל מן הדבורים. שאוכלין את החרדל ומחדד את פיהם ואוכלות את דבש שלהן: כי ליכא ירק נמי לא סמיך. והא קמ"ל דהנך קשו אהדדי: עד שאתה אומר הרחק את חרדליך מדבוריי. שעל המזיק להרחיק עצמו הרחק אתה דבוריך מן חרדליי שאף אתה נקרא מזיק: ואי

תוספות

דטירייא קשה לכותל. אע"ג דלקמן (דף כ:) הדר ביה מטעמא דטירייא ומפרש אלא משום קלא מכל מקום נקט ליה הכא משום דמעיקרא הוה בעי לפרושי טעמא משום טירייא ולספרים דלא גרסי אלא אתי שפיר הכא דלהאי גירסא טירייא וקלא חד טעמא הוא: לא יפתח אדם חנות של נחתומין. פ"ה משום שהעשן קשה לאוצר וקשה לר"ת דלקמן אמר ביין התירו שמשביחו ועשן ודאי מזיק ליין דהא יין מעושן פסול לנסכים אלא נראה לר"ת דהיזק עשן ליכא כיון דאיכא שם תקרה ומעזיבה לא יכנס שם העשן אלא טעמא שההבל מזיק את האוצר אבל את היין משביח וגרסי' לקמן אמר רב יוסף והאי דידן אפילו שרגא קשיא ליה כלומר הבלא דשרגא ולא גרסי' קוטרא דשרגא: הא ליכא אוצר עביד. הוי מצי לשנויי ה"ה כי ליכא לא סמיך והא קמ"ל דהבלא (ד) קשיא לאוצר: דיקא נמי דקתני אם היתה רפת בקר קודמת כו'. ובכולהו הרחקות דמתני' לא תני הכי והוה ליה לאשמועינן בשאר וכ"ש בדירה ותימה דלעולם בשאר הרחקות נמי מותר לסמוך והא דנקטיה הכא לאשמועינן רבותא ° דאע"ג דהוי גירי דיליה אם היתה קודמת לאוצר מותר דהשתא הוי חידוש אפילו לרבי יוסי ואי אשמועינן בשאר לא הוי חידוש אלא לרבנן אבל לרבי יוסי דקסבר על הניזק להרחיק לא הוי שום חידוש: דיקא נמי דקתני כו'. ולאביי לא קשיא האי דיקא דלא משמע ליה שיהא חידוש בשאר טפי מבדירה: ואם היתה רפת בקר כו'. והוא הדין חנות של נחתומין ושל צבעין וחדא מינייהו נקט: ותני עלה ד' אמות שאמרו כדי עבודת הכרם. הוה ליה למינקט כדי עבודת האילן אלא נקט עבודת הכרם לפי שנזכר לשון זה במסכת כלאים גבי כרם שצריך הרחקה ד' אמות: טעמא משום עבודת הכרם כו'. בלאו האי דיוקא מצי למפרך בפשיטות דסגי בהרחקת ארבע אמות ואי אסור לסמוך היה צריך להרחיק כ"ה אמות כדתנן לקמן (דף כה:) שמרחיקין את האילן מן הבור אלא ניחא ליה למידק דאפילו תוך ארבע אמות מותר לסמוך: דמפסיק צונמא. וא"ת אמאי צריך ד' אמות פשיטא שחוץ לצונמא לא יחרוש שלא יועיל כלום לאילן וי"ל כשיחרוש עד הצונמא ירצה להפוך המחרישה לצד אחר המחרישה יכנס לשדה חבירו: היו שרשיו יוצאין כו'. וא"ת היאך סמך אי שלא ברשות א"כ יקוץ וצריך לאוקמי בלוקח ולריצב"א אין נראה להעמיד בלוקח מדלא מסיק לה כדבסמוך אלא נראה דמיירי בסמך שלא ברשות דאינו קוצץ האילן אלא בנתינת דמים וזה לא רצה להאריך ולהשמיענו: הכא נמי בלוקח. פ"ה שהאילן ביד מוכר ואין נראה לר"י בר' מרדכי דא"כ הול"ל במוכר אלא נראה לו לפרש שהאילן ביד לוקח ולשני הפירושים אלו אין להקשות מאי איריא שהאילן קדם אפילו קדם בור נמי כגון שאדם אחד עשה הבור ואח"כ נטע האילן ומכר הבור לפ"ה או אילן לפי' ר"י ברבי מרדכי לא יקוץ שהרי בהיתר עשאן דבכה"ג אילן קדם קרינא ביה שקדמה נטיעת האילן לערעור בעל הבור דערעור אינו בא אלא ע"י מכירת בור או מכירת האילן אבל לפר"ת שפי' בלוקח שלקח מאדם אחד את אילן וטוענין ללוקח קשה לר"י מאי איריא אילן קדם אפילו קדם בור נמי ועוד כיון דהחזיק באילן ג' שנים איירי דבחזקת ג' שנים טוענין ללוקח לוקמה נמי בלא לוקח ובחזקה שיש עמה טענה:

רבינו גרשום

המלח. שחופרין להכניס לתוכן מים לעשות מלח ושיחות שעושין לשרוף בהן הסיד ואת הסלעים חפירה מלאה אבנים: וסד בסיד. החפירה דכל אלו מזיקין לכותל: הא ליכא כותל. הוי כשאר כותל וסמיך וקשיא לרבא דאמר גבי שדה דלא סמיך: דמתונתא דהני. זה לחלוחית המים שמשקין הזרעים בנגר ודאי קשין לכותל שמקלקלין המים יסוד הכותל: מרחיקין את הריחים. העשוין בקרקע מן הכותל חבירו: ג' טפחים מן השכב. זו אבן התחתונה שמו שכב. ורכב זו אבן עליונה שמורכבת עליה והתחתונה רחבה מן העליונה טפח לכל צד והיינו ג' מן השכב שהוא ד' מן הרכב מתוך דפחותה טפח: טעמא דאיכא כותל. וקשיא לרבא: טירא קשה לכותל. אותו זיעזוע שמזעזעין הקרקע בשעה שמתקנין שם הריחים. איכא דאמר טירא קול הברה שעושין הריחים: מרחיקין את התנור מן הכותל. אע"ג דלא תני כותל אפ"ה משמע דירחיק מן הכותל ג' טפחים. מן הכיליא איזהו כיליא שכשעושין התנור מחרס שכל תנוריהן היו של חרס ועשוין כעין דלי פתוח מלמעלה והחרס קלוש ומדביקין סביב התנור מן הטיט בעובי טפח סביב כדי לחזק התנור מפני שהוא של חרס שלא ישבר ולאותו הדבק קרי כילייא והיינו דאמרי' במס' (פסחים) [חולין קכג:] וגורר את הטפילה עד שמגיע לארץ ואותה דאמרי' התם היינו כילייא ושפה זו שפת התנור עצמו שהוא מרחיק מן הכותל ד' טפחים כפ"ה. איכא דאמרי כילייא זה יסוד התנור דכל סביב התנור סמוך לקרקע יוצא בנין התנור טפח לחוץ וכי מעלה בנינו מקצר ועולה עד לשפה שלמעלה דפוחת טפח. למ"ה: הבלא. חמימות התנור: לא יפתח אדם חנות של נחתומין. שאופה פתו למכור בכל עת תמיד אופה ומחמם התבואה או היין של חבירו שבאוצר שלמעלה הימנו בעלייה ומש"ה קרי לעלייה אוצר שכן דרך בני אדם שאוצרין פירותיהן בעליות. וכן של צבעים לא יפתח תחת האוצר מפני שתדיר עושה היסק גדול לצורך הצבע ומחמם התבואה: ולא רפת בקר נמי משום הבלא דזבל. וטעמא מאי לא יפתח דאיכא אוצר דקדם מעיקרא מש"ה אינו יכול לפתוח להפסידו. הא לא הוי אוצר מעיקרא אלא חנות קדם ברישא והשתא קא פתח (הוי) [האין] חנות של נחתומין אע"ג דיכול למימר האי בעל (האוצר) [המיצר] למחר אי עביד הכא לעיל אוצר שלי ומזקת לי כיון דעדיין לא מינכר היזקו עביד וסמיך הכי נמי סמיך (א) למיצר וקשיא לרבא אמר לך רבא לעולם בעלמא לא סמיך [ודקא דייקי הא היכא] דליכא אוצר סמיך היינו טעמא דדירתו של אדם שאני שצריך לו לאדם לעשות צרכיו בדירתו מש"ה לא מצי מעכב ליה הואיל ואין לו שום אוצר עכשיו אבל גבי בור ושדה דעלמא דלא קבע תשמישתייהו כדירה לא סמיך משום דמזיק ליה בכך [דמרפי] ליה ארעיה ואי מימלך למיעבד בור לא מצי למיעבד בור: דיקא נמי. דדירה שאני: דקתני אם היה רפת בקר קודם לאוצר מותר. משום דדירה שאני: כדי עבודת הכרם. כדי איכר בקר וכליו דלא דייש ליה לשדהו דהתם היו חורשין את הכרמים בשוורים וכך נמי היו חורשין לשדה אילנות בשוורים: דקא מפסיק צונמא. בין שדה שלו לשל חבירו דלא קא עברין בהני סלעים מש"ה מצי סמיך אי לאו מפני עבודת הכרם אבל בעלמא לא: היה גדר בינתים. בין הכרם לשדה זה סומך נטיעותיו לגדר [אע"ג] דעברין שרשין לשדה: מעמיק לשרשיו בקרקע ג' טפחים כדי שלא יעכב את המחרישה. הכי קאמר אי לאו צונמא והוה מרחיק ליה לאילנות כ"ה אמה כשיעור האילן. ולאחר כן הגדילו שרשין יותר מכ"ה והיו שרשין יוצאין לתוך של חבירו כנ"ל: אית דמפרשי האי שדה כרם הוא כדי להשתמש בהני ד' אמות עבודת תשמיש דצריך לכרם כגון בית הגת וגיגית שלועזין טיני. היינו בור שתחת הגת. אלמא דסמיך (ליה אלא) הכא במאי עסקינן דאי לאו משום עבודת הכרם סמיך דמפסיק צונמא כלומר דאיכא סלע חזק בין האילן לשדה דאינן יכולין השרשין לעבור ולהפסיד בשדה אבל גבי בור ושדה דעלמא דמפסיד לעולם לא סמיך. זה סומך אילנו לגדר וזה לגדר חה בורו אלמא דסמיך אע"ג דעברי שרשים תותי גדר לשדה חבירו וקא מזקי. לא הכא נמי דאיכא צונמא: מעמיק שרשי האילן בקרקע ג' טפחים ב) כי היכי דלא ליתזקו שרשין ואמאי צריך להעמיק בתמיה: כדי שלא תעכב את המחרישה ולא יפסיד. להכי צריך להעמיק וסמיך אבל גבי בור ושדה דעלמא דליכא פסידא של רפיית הקרקע מבור לבור (אמאי) [אימא] לעולם לא סמיך. למ"ה: אי הכי. דכי ליכא בור [נמי] לא סמיך האילן אימא סיפא אם האילן קדם לבור דאם היה נטוע האילן קודם דנחפר הבור אע"ג דמזיק לה לא יקוץ ואי לא סמיך האילן על מצר שדה חבירו קודם חפירת הבור היכי מצי משכחת לה דמזיק לה השתא אלא לאו ש"מ דסמיך: לא לעולם לא סמיך. וכי תימא א"כ היכי הוה זה סומך אילנו אצל שדה חבירו: כדאמר רב פפא לקמן בלוקח. כגון דהוה מעיקרא האילן והשדה לאדם אחד ומכרו לשני בני אדם לא' מכר מקום האילן והאילן ולשני מכר כל שאר השדה משפת אילן ולהלן ובא זה שלקח שאר השדה וחפר בורו סמוך לאילן דהשתא קדם האילן לבור ולא סמכו זה לוקח אלא המוכר דברשות סמכו דהכל היה שלו ומש"ה לא יקוץ ולעולם בעלמא לא סמיך: מרחיקין את המשרה. מים סרוחין ששורין בהן פשתן וקשה הוא לירק. א"ד משרה שמכבסין ושורין בהן את הבגדים: מן הירק מתוך ג) דאתנייהו ירקות דלא צריכי כל כך למים וניתזין ניצוצות הכביסה על הירק כל שעה ומזיק להו. למ"ה: ולא כרתי אצל בצלים. משום דמכחשי כרישין לבצלים וכן לחרדל מתוך דאכלי דבורים לחרדל: דאכלי לגלוגי. כלומר ענפי חרדלי:

חשק שלמה על רבינו גרשום א) נראה דצ"ל והכא נמי סמיך בור סמוך למיצר. ב) נראה דצ"ל ג"כ כדי שלא תעכב את המחרישה ולא יפסיד ואמאי צריך להעמיק בתמי': ה"ק ואי לאו צונמא וכו' ולהכי צריך להעמיק וכו'. ג) אולי צ"ל מתוך דהנהו ירקות לא צריכי כ"כ וכו'.

מסורת הש"ס

א) כ"מ וסה, ב) כ"מ דהני, ג) לקמן כ:, ד) לקמן כו. [וע"ש], ה) [שם], ו) לקמן כו. [ודף פג.], ז) כ"מ ת"ש, ח) לקמן כו, ט) כ"מ ה"ג בצונמא, י) לקמן כה:, כ) ג"ה שם, ל) כ"מ ותני עלה [לקמן כה:].

הגהות הב"ח

(א) גמ' מאי בעו שרשין התם: (ב) רש"י ד"ה טעמא וכו' ואע"ג דסופו שיתפשטו: (ג) ד"ה ואי לאו צונמא וכו' להו זה (כשיזיקו) תא"מ ונ"ב פ"א כדי שלא יזיקו כשיזיקו הן: (ד) תוס' ד"ה הא ליכא וכו' דהבלא דהני קשה לאוצר:

גליון הש"ס

תוס' ד"ה דיקא כו' דאע"ג דהוי גירי. עיין לקמן דף כב ע"ב תוס' ד"ה עני:

לעזי רש"י

איטוני"ר. פירוש להרעיד (רש"י ב"ב דף כ ע"ב ד"ה מאי טירייא), לזעזע (רבינו גרשום ב"ב דף יח ע"א ודף כ ע"ב). פוריל"ש. פירוש כרישין, כרתי, קפלוטות (רש"י ביצה דף יז ע"ב, תענית דף יח ע"ב, ועוד, רש"י במדבר יא, ה).

ליקוטי רש"י

הסלעים. אבנים שהאור יוצא מהן שקורין קוויל"ש שכל אלו קשין לכותל שמוציאין הבל. [המשך בע"ב]

rock separating the two fields,[19] וְהָיוּ שָׁרָשָׁיו יוֹצְאִין לְתוֹךְ שֶׁל חֲבֵירוֹ – **and its roots** (i.e. the roots of a tree one had planted near the boundary)[20] extend into the property **of his neighbor,** מַעֲמִיק שְׁלֹשָׁה טְפָחִים – **[the neighbor] may cut [them off] to a depth of three** ***tefachim,*** כְּדֵי שֶׁלֹּא יְעַכֵּב הַמַּחֲרֵישָׁה – **so that they do not impede the** progress of his **plow.**

The Gemara poses another challenge to Rava's view:

תָּא שְׁמַע – **Come, learn** the following proof from a Mishnah:[21] מַרְחִיקִין אֶת הָאִילָן מִן הַבּוֹר עֶשְׂרִים וְחָמֵשׁ אַמָּה – ONE MUST DISTANCE A TREE TWENTY-FIVE *AMOS* FROM THE PIT of a neighbor. The Mishnah implies that the pit is already in existence. This gives rise to the following inference: טַעְמָא דְּאִיכָּא בּוֹר – **The reason** the tree must be distanced **is that there is a pit** on the other side of the boundary; הָא לֵיכָּא בּוֹר – **but where there is no pit** on the other side of the boundary, סָמִיךְ – **one may place** a tree **near** the boundary. This refutes Rava's position that a hazard must be distanced from neighboring property even before the object liable to be damaged is in harm's way. – ? –

The Gemara defends Rava's view:

לֹא – This inference is **not** compelling. כִּי לֵיכָּא בּוֹר נַמִּי – One could argue that **even where there is no pit** on the other side of the boundary, לֹא סָמִיךְ – **one may not place** a tree **near** the boundary. וְהָא קָא מַשְׁמַע לָן – And this is what **the Mishnah informs us** by specifying a case in which there is a pit on the other side: דְּעַד עֶשְׂרִים וְחָמֵשׁ אַמָּה אָזְלֵי שָׁרָשִׁים וּמַזְּקֵי לַבּוֹר – The **roots** of a tree can **extend up to twenty-five** ***amos*** **and damage a pit.**[22]

The Gemara counters:

אִי הָכִי – But **if** this is **so,** that it is forbidden to plant a tree near the boundary even before a pit has been dug on the other side, אֵימָא סֵיפָא – **consider the latter clause** of that Mishnah: וְאִם אִילָן קָדַם – BUT IF THE planting of the TREE PRECEDED the digging of the pit, לֹא יָקוֹץ – [THE OWNER OF THE TREE] DOES NOT have to CUT down THE TREE.[23] וְאִי דְּלָא סָמִיךְ – Now **if** it is true **that one may not place** a tree **near** the boundary even before there is a pit on the other side, הֵיכִי מַשְׁכַּחַת לַהּ – **how can [such a situation] arise** that a tree is planted near the boundary between two fields? And if the tree was planted illegally, its owner should be required to cut it down.[24] – ? –

The Gemara answers that even if the law is that it is forbidden to plant a tree near the boundary, the Mishnah does not require the tree's removal because it refers to the following exceptional case:

כִּדְאָמַר רַב פַּפָּא – It is **as Rav Pappa said in** explanation of another Mishnah: בְּלוֹקֵחַ – "The Mishnah refers **to a buyer.**"[25] הָכָא נַמִּי – **Here too,** the same explanation is applicable. בְּלוֹקֵחַ – The Mishnah refers **to a buyer;** i.e. it refers to the following scenario: The owner of the tree planted it well within the boundaries of his property, but later he sold a portion of his property to another, who proceeded to dig a pit near the tree. In such a case, the tree was planted legally, and therefore its owner is not required to remove it.

The Gemara attempts to refute Rava's ruling from another Mishnah:

תָּא שְׁמַע – **Come, learn** the following proof from a Mishnah:[26] מַרְחִיקִין אֶת הַמִּשְׁרָה מִן הַיָּרָק – ONE MUST DISTANCE A FLAX POOL FROM THE VEGETABLES of his neighbor,[27] וְאֶת הַכְּרֵישִׁין מִן הַבְּצָלִין – LEEKS FROM THE ONIONS of his neighbor[28] וְאֶת הַחַרְדָּל מִן הַדְּבוֹרִים – AND MUSTARD plants FROM THE BEES of his neighbor.[29] The Mishnah implies that the vegetables[30] are already in place. This gives rise to the following inference: טַעְמָא דְּאִיכָּא יָרָק – **The reason** one is required to distance a flax pool **is that there are vegetables** in harm's way; הָא לֵיכָּא יָרָק – **but where there are no vegetables** in harm's way, סָמִיךְ – **one may place** a flax pool **near** the boundary. This refutes Rava's contention that a hazard must be distanced from neighboring property even before the object liable to be damaged is in harm's way. – ? –

The Gemara defends Rava's view:

לֹא – This inference is **not** compelling. כִּי לֵיכָּא יָרָק נַמִּי – One could argue that **even where there are no vegetables** in harm's way, לֹא סָמִיךְ – **one may not place** a flax pool **near** the boundary. וְהָא קָא מַשְׁמַע לָן – **And this** is what **the Mishnah informs us** by specifying a case in which the vegetables are already in place: דְּהָנֵי קָשׁוּ אַהֲדָדֵי – **These** (flax pool, leeks, mustard plants) **are harmful to these** (vegetables, onions and bees' honey respectively).[31]

The Gemara counters:

אִי הָכִי – But **if** this is **so,** that it is forbidden to place a hazard near the boundary even before the object liable to be damaged is in harm's way, אֵימָא סֵיפָא – **consider the latter clause** of that Mishnah: רַבִּי יוֹסֵי מַתִּיר בְּחַרְדָּל – R' YOSE PERMITS placing a hazard close to neighboring property IN THE CASE OF MUSTARD plants. And the following Baraisa was taught in explanation of R' Yose's ruling: מִפְּנֵי שֶׁיָּכוֹל לוֹמַר לוֹ – R' Yose permits the planting of mustard plants near neighboring property BECAUSE HE [the

NOTES

19. I.e. although the first clauses of the Mishnah speak of a case where a rocky barrier interposes between the fields, the latter clause speaks of a case where there is no such barrier.

20. This tree was planted illegally [for no subterranean barrier separates the two fields] (*Rashi*).

[A different Mishnah (25b) rules that one who plants a tree illegally can be forced to cut it down. The commentaries discuss why the present Mishnah does not mention this law — see *Tosafos, Rashba* et al.]

21. Below, 25b.

22. See note 3.

23. This is in contrast to the reverse case, where the tree was planted *after* the pit was dug. In such a case, the owner of the tree is indeed required to remove it (Mishnah 25b; see note 36 there).

24. Since the tree was planted illegally (according to Rava), the same law should apply as in the case where the tree was planted *after* the pit was dug, viz. the owner of the tree must cut it down [see previous note] (*Rashi*). The Mishnah, however, states that if the tree was there before the pit, it need not be removed.

25. Rav Pappa's comment, which is discussed in the Gemara below (18b), was made in reference to the Mishnah on 25a.

26. Below, 25a.

27. Before flax stems can be processed into linen thread, they must be retted (soaked) to break down their woody tissue and dissolve the substance binding their fibers together. The stems of flax plants would be soaked in a pool or pond for several days. The substances absorbed by the water during this process are toxic to growing plants, and they pass into the ground around the pool and damage the surrounding vegetation (see *Rambam, Hil. Shecheinim* 10:5). One must therefore distance these pools from the areas in which a neighbor grows vegetables.

28. Leeks diminish the sharpness of onions growing nearby (*Rambam Commentary to the Mishnah*).

29. The bees feed on the mustard plants, which leave a sharp taste in their mouths. The bees then consume the honey in their hives to relieve their discomfort (*Rashi*).

30. [The Gemara below mentions only the first case of the Mishnah (flax pool — vegetables), but the same applies to the second (leeks — onions) and third (mustard plants — bees) as well.]

31. Literally: these are harmful to each other. See note 3.

המלח ואת הסיד ואת הסלעים מכותלו של חבירו ג' טפחים א) או סד בסיד טעמא דאיכא כותל הא ליכא כותל סומך לא כי ליכא כותל נמי לא סמיך ואלא מאי קא משמע לן הא קא משמע לן דהני קשו לכותל תא שמע מרחיקים את הזרעים ואת המחרישה ואת מי רגלים מן הכותל שלשה טפחים טעמא דאיכא כותל הא ליכא כותל סמיך לא כי ליכא כותל נמי לא סמיך ואלא מאי קמ"ל הא קא משמע לן דמתונתא קשה לכותל תא שמע ואת הריחים ג' מן השכב שהן ד' מן הרכב טעמא דאיכא כותל הא ליכא כותל סמיך לא כי ליכא כותל נמי לא סמיך ואלא מאי קא משמע לן הא קא משמע לן דטירייא קשה לכותל תא שמע ואת התנור שלשה מן הכליא שהן ד' מן השפה טעמא דאיכא כותל הא ליכא כותל סמיך לא כי ליכא כותל נמי לא סמיך אלא מאי קא משמע לן הא קא משמע לן ג) דהבלא קשה לכותל תא שמע ד) לא יפתח אדם חנות של נחתומין ושל צבעין תחת אוצרו של חבירו ולא רפת בקר טעמא דאיכא אוצר הא ליכא אוצר עביד דירה שאני דיקא נמי דתני עלה ה) אם היתה רפת בקר קודמת לאוצר מותר ת"ש ו) לא יטע אדם אילן סמוך לשדה אלא אם כן הרחיק ממנו ד' אמות ותני עלה ז) ד' אמות שאמרו כדי עבודת הכרם טעמא דמשום כדי עבודת הכרם הא לאו משום כדי עבודת הכרם סמיך ואע"ג דאיכא שרשין דקא מזקי הכא במאי עסקינן דמפסיק צונמא ח) (דיקא נמי דקתני) ט) היה גדר בינתים זה סומך לגדר מכאן וזה סומך לגדר מכאן י) אי הכי אימא סיפא היו שרשיו יוצאין בתוך של חבירו מעמיק להן שלשה טפחים כדי שלא יעכב המחרישה ואי דמפסיק צונמא מאי בעו (א) התם ה"ק ואי לאו צונמא והיו שרשיו יוצאין לתוך של חבירו מעמיק שלשה טפחים כדי שלא יעכב המחרישה ת"ש כ) מרחיקין את האילן מן הבור עשרים וחמש אמה טעמא דאיכא בור הא ליכא בור סמיך לא כי ליכא בור נמי לא סמיך והא קמ"ל דעד כ"ה אמה אזלי שרשים ומזקי לבור אי הכי אימא סיפא ואם אילן קדם לא יקוץ ואי דלא סמיך היכי משכחת לה כדא"ר פפא בלוקח ה"נ בלוקח ת"ש ל) מרחיקין את המשרה מן הירק ואת הכרישין מן הבצלין ואת החרדל מן הדבורים טעמא דאיכא ירק הא ליכא ירק סמיך לא כי ליכא ירק נמי לא סמיך והא קמ"ל דהני קשו אהדדי א"ה אימא סיפא רבי יוסי מתיר בחרדל מ) מפני שיכול לומר לו עד שאתה אומר לי הרחק חרדלך מן דבוראי הרחק דבורך מן חרדלאי שבאות ואוכלות לגלוגי חרדלאי ואי

רש"י

מתונתא. דבר לח: טירייא. איטוני"ר בלע"ז כמו דטריא לריסה באלו טריפות (חולין דף מה:): חנות של נחתומין. מוכרי לחם שמסיקין שם תנור תמיד: אוצר. עליה שאוצרין בה תבואה ושמן ויין והעשן קשה להן: ולא רפת בקר. הריח קשה להן: דירה שאני. חנות ורפת בקר דירתן של אדם הן ואין לנו לאסור דירתו עליו אא"כ הסמיך מוקן: דיקא נמי. דדירה שאני: דקתני עלה. דההיא אם היתה הרפת בקר קודמת לאוצר מותר וכולהו שאר הרחקות דמתני' לא תנא הכי ש"מ הכא משום דדירה שאני אבל לא איירי אף הראשון צריך להרחיק: אלא אם כן הרחיק ממנו ארבע אמות. כדמפרש טעמא כדי עבודת הכרם שהיו חורשים הכרם במחרישה וכן בשעת הבציר בוצרין אותם בעגלות וצריך להן מקום פנוי ארבע אמות שלא תיכנס עגלת מחרישתו בקרקע חבירו: טעמא משום עבודת הכרם. שהוא מזיקו בידים הא לאו הכי סמיך ואע"ג (ב) שיתפשטו שרשיו ויזיקו בשדה בין לעכב המחרישה בין לחפירת הבור: צונמא. סלע חזק שלא יתפשטו שרשיו לשם: גדר בינתים. שאין מזיקו עוד לעבודת הכרם זה סומך אילנות לגדר מכאן וזה סומך אילנות לגדר מכאן ואי נמי אחד מהן שדה לבן אין כאן כלאים כדאמר בעירובין (דף יא.) אם גפנים מכאן מותר לזרוע כאן גבי נעץ ארבעה קונדיסין ומתח זמורה על גביהן דדמיא לצורת הפתח קתני מיהא זה סומך ואע"ג דאזלי שרשים תחת הגדר ומתפשטין לתוך השדה: מעמיק להן. בעל השדה קוצץ את השרשין שיצאו בשדהו בעומק שלשה טפחים: ואי לאו צונמא. וזה נוטע שם שלא כדת מעמיק להו זה (ג) כשיזיקו הן: עשרים וחמשה אמות. כך שיערו שהשרשין נמשכין והולכין ומקלקלין את כותלי הבור: הוא הדין כו'. והא קמ"ל דעד כ"ה אמה אזלי שרשין ומזקי לבור: ה"ג אי הכי אימא סיפא אם האילן קדם לא יקוץ אי לא סמיך היכי משכחת להו. דהאילן קדם ואי שלא כדין סמך אמאי לא יקוץ מה לי בור קדם דקתני קוצץ ומאי שנא אילן קדם דתנא לא יקוץ: כדאמר רב פפא. לקמן בשמעתין: הכא נמי בלוקח. אדם שנטע אילן בתוך שדהו ואח"כ מכר חצי שדהו לאיש אחר ובא הלוקח וחפר בור אין זה צריך לקוץ אילן שנטעו ברשותו: את המשרה. מים ששורין בו את הפשתן: מן הירק. של מיני מאכל כרוב ושומין וכרישין: ואת הכרישין. כרתי פוריל"ש: ואת החרדל מן הדבורים. שאוכלין את החרדל ומחדד את פיהם ואוכלות את דבש שלהן: כי ליכא ירק נמי לא סמיך. והא קמ"ל דהנך קשו אהדדי: עד שאתה אומר הרחק את חרדליך מדבוריי. שעל המזיק להרחיק עצמו הרחק אתה דבורייך מן חרדליי שאף אתה נקרא מזיק: ואי

תוספות

דטירייא קשה לכותל. אע"ג דלקמן (דף כ:) הדר ביה מטעמא דטירייא ומפרש אלא משום קלא מכל מקום נקט ליה הכא משום דמעיקרא הוה בעי לפרושי טעמא משום טירייא ולספרים דלא גרסי אלא אתי שפיר הכא דלהכיא גירסא טירייא וקלא חד טעמא הוא:

לא יפתח אדם חנות של נחתומין. פ"ה משום שהעשן קשה לאוצר וקשה לר"ת דלקמן אמר ביין התירו שמשביחו ועשן ודאי מזיק ליין דהא יין מעושן פסול לנסכים אלא נראה לר"ת דהיזק עשן ליכא כיון דאיכא שם תקרה ומעזיבה לא יכנס שם העשן אלא טעמא שההבל מזיק את האוצר אבל את היין משביח וגרסי' לקמן אמר רב יוסף והאי דידן אפילו שרגא קשיא ליה כלומר הבלא דשרגא ולא גרסי' קוטרא דשרגא:

הא ליכא אוצר עביד. הוי מצי לשנויי ה"ה כי ליכא לא סמיך והא קמ"ל דהבלא (ד) קשיא לאוצר:

דיקא נמי דקתני אם היתה רפת בקר קודמת כו'. וכולהו הרחקות דמתני' לא תני הכי והוה ליה לאשמועינן בשאר וכ"ש בדירה ותימה דלעולם בשאר הרחקות נמי מותר לסמוך והא דנקטיה הכא לאשמועינן רבותא ° דאע"ג דהוי גירי דיליה אם היתה קודמת לאוצר מותר דהשתא הוי חידוש אפילו לרבי יוסי ואי אשמועינן בשאר לא הוי חידוש אלא לרבנן אבל לרבי יוסי דקסבר על הניזק להרחיק לא הוי שום חידוש:

דיקא נמי דקתני כו'. ולאביי לא קשיא האי דיקא דלא משמע ליה שיהא חידוש בשאר טפי מבדירה:

ואם היתה רפת בקר כו'. והוא הדין חנות של נחתומין ושל צבעין וחדא מינייהו נקט:

ותני עלה ד' אמות שאמרו כדי עבודת הכרם. הוה ליה למינקט כדי עבודת האילן אלא נקט עבודת הכרם לפי שנזכר לשון זה במסכת כלאים גבי כרם שצריך הרחקה ד' אמות:

טעמא משום עבודת הכרם כו'. בלאו האי דיוקא מצי למפרך בפשיטות דסגי בהרחקת ארבע אמות ואי אסור לסמוך היה צריך להרחיק כ"ה אמות כדתנן לקמן (דף כה:) שמרחיקין את האילן מן הבור אלא ניחא ליה למידק דאפילו תוך ארבע אמות מותר לסמוך:

דמפסיק צונמא. וא"ת אמאי צריך ד' אמות פשיטא שחוץ לצונמא לא יחרוש שלא יועיל כלום לאילן וי"ל כשיחרוש עד הצונמא ירצה להפוך המחרישה לצד אחר המחרישה יכנס לשדה חבירו:

היו שרשיו יוצאין כו'. וא"ת היאך סמך אי שלא ברשות א"כ יקוץ וצריך לאוקמי בלוקח ולריצב"א אין נראה להעמיד בלוקח מדלא מסיק לה כדבסמוך אלא נראה דמיירי בסמך שלא ברשות דאינו קוצץ האילן אלא בנתינת דמים וזה לא רצה להאריך ולהשמיענו:

הכא נמי בלוקח. פ"ה שהאילן ביד מוכר ואין נראה לר"י בר' מרדכי דא"כ הול"ל במוכר אלא נראה לו לפרש שהאילן ביד לוקח ולשני הפירושים אלו אין להקשות מאי איריא שהאילן קדם אפילו קדם בור נמי כגון שאדם אחד עשה הבור ואח"כ נטע האילן ומכר הבור לפ"ה או אילן לפי' ר"י ברבי מרדכי לא יקוץ שהרי בהיתר עשאן דבכה"ג אילן קדם קרינא ביה שקדמה נטיעת האילן לערעור בעל הבור דערעור אינו בא אלא ע"י מכירת בור או מכירת האילן אבל לפר"ת שפי' בלוקח שלקח מאדם אחד את אילן וטוענין ללוקח קשה לר"י מאי איריא אילן קדם אפילו קדם בור נמי ועוד כיון דהחזיק באילן ג' שנים טוענין ללוקח לוקמה נמי בלא לוקח ובחזקה שיש עמה טענה:

מסורת הש"ס

א) נ"א וסד, ב) נ"א דהני, ג) לקמן כ:, ד) [שם], ה) לקמן כו. [ודף פג.], ו) [לקמן כו.], ז) נ"א ת"ש, ח) לקמן כו., ט) נ"א ה"נ בצונמא, י) לקמן כה:, כ) ג"ז שם, ל) נ"א ותני עלה [לקמן כה:]

הגהות הב"ח

(א) גמ' מאי בעו שרשין התם: (ב) רש"י ד"ה טעמא וכו' ואע"ג דסופו שיתפשטו: (ג) ד"ה ואי לאו צונמא וכו' לזה (כשיזיקו הן) תא"מ ונ"ב ס"א כדי שלא יזיקו כשיזיקו הן: (ד) תוס' ד"ה הא ליכא וכו' דהבלא דהכי קשה לאוצר:

גליון הש"ס

תוס' ד"ה דיקא כו' דאע"ג דהוי גירי. עיין לקמן דף כב ע"ב תוס' ד"ה ענין:

לעזי רש"י

איטוני"ר. פירוש להכתיש (רש"י ב"ב דף כ ע"ב ד"ה מאי טירייא), לטווש (רבינו גרשום ב"ב יח ע"א ודף כ ע"ב). פוריל"ש. פירוש כרישין, כרתי, קפלוטות (רש"י ביצה דף יח ע"ב, תלר (רש"י במדבר יא, ה)).

ליקוטי רש"י

הסלעים. אבנים שהאור יוצא מהן שקורין קוליי"ש שכל אלו קשין לחומה שמוליכין הבל. [המשך בע"ב]

owner of the mustard plants] **CAN SAY TO HIM** [the owner of the bees]: עַד שֶׁאַתָּה אוֹמֵר לִי הַרְחֵק חַרְדְּלָךְ מִן דְּבוֹרַאי – **"BEFORE YOU TELL ME, 'DISTANCE YOUR MUSTARD PLANTS FROM MY BEES,'** הַרְחֵק דְּבוֹרָךְ מִן חַרְדְּלָאי – I can tell you, **'DISTANCE YOUR BEES FROM MY MUSTARD** plants,' שֶׁבָּאוֹת וְאוֹכְלוֹת לְגְלוּגֵי חַרְדְּלָאי – **FOR THEY COME AND EAT THE FLOWERS OF MY MUSTARD** plants!"[32]

NOTES

32. That is to say: What is the basis for your claim that my mustard plants should be removed? The basis is that they are considered hazardous. But your bees are also hazardous (*Rashi*). Therefore, I have no greater obligation to remove my plants than you do to remove your bees. Just as you are not required to remove your bees, I am not required to distance my plants (see *Ran* to 18a ד״ה אי הכי).

With regard to two pits, however, although they are mutually injurious (see Mishnah 17a), even R' Yose concedes that once a pit has been dug near the boundary between two properties, it is forbidden to dig a pit on the other side. The distinction between these two cases is as follows:

A pit that has already been dug is not harmful. It is only the *digging* of a pit that causes damage. Therefore, one who digs a pit after one has been dug in neighboring property cannot claim that his obligation to prevent damage is no greater than his neighbor's; for, at this point, only he is causing damage while his neighbor is not. This is in contrast to the case of the bees and mustard plants, where each hazard continuously harms the other, and therefore the owner of the second hazard to be placed near the boundary can claim: "Your hazard is causing damage *now* and yet you do not have to remove it, so neither do I have to remove mine!" (*Ran* ibid. ד״ה וא״ת). [This approach is not viable according to *Tosafos'* position that a pit is prohibited because its water causes damage (see Mishnah 17a note 3). See *Tosafos* to 18b ד״ה ואי for a resolution to this difficulty that conforms with their approach.]

As mentioned above (17b note 14), R' Yose allows a person to do whatever he pleases within his own property provided his actions do not *directly* damage the property of another [גִּירֵי דִּידֵיהּ, *his arrows*]. The damage caused by bees and mustard plants to each other do not fall into this category. Hence, it is problematic that R' Yose adduced a different argument ("Before you tell me etc.") to support his permit in this case. This problem is dealt with in the course of the Gemara's discussion below (see 18b note 13).

המלח ואת הסיד ואת הסלעים מכותלו של חבירו ג' טפחים [א] או סד בסיד טעמא דאיכא כותל הא ליכא כותל סומך לא כי ליכא כותל נמי לא סמיך ואלא מאי קא משמע לן הא קא משמע לן דהני קשו לכותל תא שמע מרחיקים את הזרעים ואת המחרישה ואת מי רגלים מן הכותל שלשה טפחים טעמא דאיכא כותל הא ליכא כותל סמיך לא כי ליכא כותל נמי לא סמיך ואלא מאי קמ"ל הא קא משמע לן דמתונתא קשה לכותל תא שמע ואת הריחים ג' מן השכב שהן ד' מן הרכב טעמא דאיכא כותל הא ליכא כותל סמיך לא כי ליכא כותל נמי לא סמיך ואלא מאי קא משמע לן הא קא משמע לן דטירייא קשה לכותל תא שמע ואת התנור שלשה מן הכליא שהן ד' מן השפה טעמא דאיכא כותל הא ליכא כותל סמיך לא כי ליכא כותל נמי לא סמיך אלא מאי קא משמע לן הא קא משמע לן [ג] דהבלא קשה לכותל תא שמע [ה] לא יפתח אדם חנות של נחתומין ושל צבעין תחת אוצרו של חבירו ולא רפת בקר טעמא דאיכא אוצר הא ליכא אוצר עביד דירה שאני דיקא נמי דתני עלה [ז] אם היתה רפת בקר קודמת לאוצר מותר ת"ש [ה] לא יטע אדם אילן סמוך לשדה אלא אם כן הרחיק ממנו ד' אמות ותני עלה [י] ד' אמות שאמרו כדי עבודת הכרם טעמא דמשום כדי עבודת הכרם הא לאו משום כדי עבודת הכרם סמיך ואע"ג דאיכא שרשין דקא מזקי הכא במאי עסקינן דמפסיק צונמא [ט] (דיקא נמי דקתני) [ה] היה גדר בינתים זה סומך לגדר מכאן וזה סומך לגדר מכאן [ט] אי הכי אימא סיפא היו שרשיו יוצאין בתוך של חבירו מעמיק להן שלשה טפחים כדי שלא יעכב המחרישה ואי דמפסיק צונמא מאי בעו (א) התם ה"ק ואי לאו צונמא והיו שרשיו יוצאין לתוך של חבירו מעמיק שלשה טפחים כדי שלא יעכב המחרישה ת"ש [י] מרחיקין את האילן מן הבור עשרים וחמש אמה טעמא דאיכא בור הא ליכא בור סמיך לא כי ליכא בור נמי לא סמיך והא קמ"ל דעד כ"ה אמה אזלי שרשים ומזקי לבור אי הכי אימא סיפא ואם אילן קדם לא יקוץ ואי דלא סמיך היכי משכחת לה כדא"ר פפא בלוקח ה"נ בלוקח ת"ש [י] מרחיקין את המשרה מן הירק ואת הכרישין מן הבצלין ואת החרדל מן הדבורים טעמא דאיכא ירק הא ליכא ירק סמיך לא כי ליכא ירק נמי לא סמיך והא קמ"ל דהני קשו אהדדי א"ה אימא סיפא רבי יוסי מתיר בחרדל [ל] מפני שיכול לומר לו עד שאתה אומר לי הרחק חרדלך מן דבוראי הרחק דבורך מן חרדלאי שבאות ואוכלות לגלוגי חרדלאי ואי

מתונתא. דבר לח: **טירייא.** איטוני"ר בלע"ז כמו דטרייא לרישיה באלו טריפות (חולין דף מה:): **חנות של נחתומין.** מוכרי לחם שמסיקין שם אור תמיד: **אוצר.** עלייה שאוצרין בה תבואה ושמן ויין והעשן קשה להן: **ולא רפת בקר.** הריח קשה להן: **דירה שאני.** חנות ורפת בקר דירתן של אדם הן ואין לנו לאסור דירתו עליו אא"כ ההיזק מוכן: **דיקא נמי.** דדירה שאני: **דקתני עלה.** דהיא אם היתה הרפת בקר קודמת לאוצר מותר ובכולהו שאר הרחקות דמתני' לא תנא הכי ש"מ הכא משום דדירה שאני אבל אינך אף הראשון צריך להרחיק: **אלא אם כן הרחיק ממנו ארבע אמות.** כדמפרש טעמא כדי עבודת הכרם שהיו חורשים הכרם במחרישה וכן בשעת הבציר בוצרין אותם בעגלות וצריך להן מקום פנוי ארבע אמות שלא תיכנס עגלת מחרישתו בקרקע חבירו: **טעמא משום עבודת הכרם.** שהוא מזיקו בידים הא לאו הכי סמיך ואע"ג (ב) שיתפשטו שרשיו ויזיקו בשדה בין לעכב המחרישה בין לחפירת הבור: **צונמא.** סלע חזק שלא יתפשטו שרשיו לשם: **גדר בינתים.** שאין מזיקו עוד לעבודת הכרם זה סומך אילנות לגדר מכאן וזה סומך אילנות לגדר מכאן ואי נמי אחד מהן שדה לבן אין כאן כלאים כדאמר בעירובין (דף יא.) אם גפנים מכאן מותר לזרוע כאן גבי נעץ ארבעה קונדיסין ומתח זמורה על גביהן דדמיא לצורת הפתח קתני מיהא זה סומך ואע"ג דאזלי שרשים תחת הגדר ומתפשטין לתוך השדה: **מעמיק להן.** בעל השדה קוצץ את השרשין שיצאו בשדהו בעומק שלשה טפחים: **ואי לאו צונמא.** וזה נוטע שם שלא כדת מעמיק להו זה (ג) כשיזיקו הן: **עשרים וחמשה אמות.** כך שיערו שהשרשין נמשכין והולכין ומקלקלין את כותלי הבור: **הוא הדין כו'.** והא קמ"ל דעד כ"ה אמה אזלי שרשין ומזקי לבור: ה"ג **אי הכי אימא סיפא אם האילן קדם לא יקוץ אי לא סמיך היכי משכחת להו.** דהאילן קדם ואי שלא כדין סמך אמאי לא יקוץ מה לי בור קדם דקתני קוצץ ומאי שנא אילן קדם דתנא לא יקוץ: **כדאמר רב פפא.** לקמן בשמעתין: **הכא נמי בלוקח.** אדם שנטע אילן בתוך שדהו ואח"כ מכר חצי שדהו לאיש אחר ובא הלוקח וחפר בור אין זה צריך לקוץ אילן שנטעו ברשותו: **את המשרה.** מים ששורין בו את הפשתן: **מן הירק.** של מיני מאכל כרוב ושומין וכרישין: **ואת הכרישין.** כרתי פוריל"ש: **ואת החרדל מן הדבורים.** שאוכלין את החרדל ומחדד את פיהם ואוכלות את דבש שלהן: **כי ליכא ירק נמי לא סמיך.** והא קמ"ל דהנך קשו אהדדי: **עד שאתה אומר הרחק את חרדליך מדבוריי.** שבעל המזיק להרחיק עצמו הרחק אתה דבורייך מן חרדליי שאף אתה נקרא מזיק: ואי

דטירייא קשה לכותל. אע"ג דלקמן (דף כ:) הדר ביה מטעמא דטירייא ומפרש אלא משום קלא מכל מקום נקט ליה הכא משום דמעיקרא הוה בעי לפרושי טעמא משום טירייא ולספרים דלא גרסי אלא אתי שפיר הכא דלההיא גירסא טירייא וקלא חד טעמא הוא: **לא** יפתח אדם חנות של נחתומין. פ"ה משום שהעשן קשה לאוצר וקשה לר"ת דלקמן אמר ביין התירו שמשביחו ועשן ודאי מזיק ליין דהא יין מעושן פסול לנסכים אלא נראה לר"ת דהיזק עשן ליכא כיון דאיכא שם תקרה ומעזיבה לא יכנס שם העשן אלא טעמא שההבל מזיק את האוצר אבל את היין משביח וגרסי' לקמן אמר רב יוסף והאי דידן אפילו שרגא קשיא ליה כלומר הבלא דשרגא ולא גרסי' קוטרא דשרגא: **הא** ליכא אוצר עביד. הוי מצי לשנויי ה"ה כי ליכא לא סמיך והא קמ"ל דהבלא (ד) קשיא לאוצר: **דיקא** נמי דקתני אם היתה רפת בקר קודמת כו'. ובכולהו הרחקות דמתני' לא תני הכי והוה ליה לאשמועינן בשאר וכ"ש בדירה ותימה דלעולם בשאר הרחקות נמי מותר לסמוך והא דנקטיה הכא לאשמועינן רבותא [ס] דאע"ג דהוי גירי דיליה אם היתה קודמת לאוצר מותר דהשתא הוי חידוש אפילו לרבי יוסי ואי אשמועינן בשאר לא הוי חידוש אלא לרבנן אבל לרבי יוסי דקסבר על הניזק להרחיק לא הוי שום חידוש: **דיקא** נמי דקתני כו'. ולאביי לא קשיא האי דיקא דלא משמע ליה שיהא חידוש בשאר טפי מבדירה: **ואם** היתה רפת בקר כו'. והוא הדין חנות של נחתומין ושל צבעין וחדא מינייהו נקט: **ותני** עלה ד' אמות שאמרו כדי עבודת הכרם. הוה ליה למינקט כדי עבודת האילן אלא נקט עבודת הכרם לפי שנזכר לשון זה במסכת כלאים גבי כרם שצריך הרחקה ד' אמות: **טעמא** משום עבודת הכרם כו'. בלאו האי דיוקא מצי למפרך בפשיטות דסגי בהרחקת ארבע אמות ואי אסור לסמוך היה צריך להרחיק כ"ה אמות כדתנן לקמן (דף כה:) שמרחיקין את האילן מן הבור אלא ניחא ליה למידק דאפילו תוך ארבע אמות מותר לסמוך: **דמפסיק** צונמא. וא"ת אמאי צריך ד' אמות פשיטא שחוץ לצונמא לא יחרוש שלא יועיל כלום לאילן וי"ל כשיחרוש עד הצונמא וירצה להפוך המחרישה לצד אחר המחרישה יכנס לשדה חבירו: **היו** שרשיו יוצאין כו'. וא"ת היאך סמך אי שלא ברשות א"כ יקוץ וצריך לאוקמי בלוקח ולריצב"א אין נראה להעמיד בלוקח מדלא מסיק לה כדבסמוך אלא נראה דמיירי בסמך שלא ברשות דאינו קוצץ האילן אלא בנתינת דמים וזה לא רצה להאריך ולהשמיענו: **הכא** נמי בלוקח. פ"ה שהאילן ביד מוכר ואין נראה לר"י בר' מרדכי דא"כ הו"ל במוכר אלא נראה לו לפרש שהאילן ביד לוקח ולשני הפירושים אלו אין להקשות מאי איריא שהאילן קדם אפילו קדם בור נמי כגון שאדם אחד עשה הבור ואח"כ נטע האילן ומכר הבור לפ"ה או אילן לפי' ר"י ברבי מרדכי לא יקוץ שהרי בהיתר עשאן דבכה"ג אילן קדם קרינא ביה שקדמה נטיעת האילן לערעור בעל הבור דערעור אינו בא אלא ע"י מכירת בור או מכירת האילן אבל לפר"ת שפי' בלוקח שלקח מאדם אחד את אילן וטוענין ללוקח קשה לר"י מאי איריא אילן קדם אפילו קדם בור נמי ועוד כיון דהחזיק באילן ג' שנים איירי דבחזקת ג' שנים טוענין ללוקח לוקמה נמי בלא לוקח ובחזקה שיש עמה טענה:

מסורת הש"ס

א) כ"א וסד, ב) כ"א דהני, ג) לקמן כ:, ד) [שם], ה) לקמן כו. [ודף פג.], ו) [לקמן כו.], ז) כ"א ת"ש, ח) לקמן כו., ט) כ"א ה"ג בצונמא, י) לקמן כה:, כ) ג"ז שם., ל) כ"א ותני עלה [לקמן כה:]:

הגהות הב"ח

(א) גמ' מאי בעו שרשין התם: (ב) רש"י ד"ה טעמא וכו' ואע"ג דסופו שיתפשטו: (ג) ד"ה ואי לאו צונמא וכו' להו זה (כשיזיקו הן) תא"מ ונ"ב ס"א כדי שלא יזיקהו כשיזקינו הן: (ד) תוס' ד"ה הא ליכא וכו' דהבלא דהני קשה לאוצר:

גליון הש"ס

תוס' ד"ה דיקא כו' דאע"ג דהוי גירי. עיין לקמן דף כה ע"ב תוס' ד"ה עני:

לעזי רש"י

איטוני"ר. פירוש להרעיד (רש"י ב"ב דף כ ע"ב ד"ה מאי טירייא איכא), לזעזע (רבינו גרשום ב"ב דף יח ע"א ודף כ ע"ב). **פוריל"ש.** פירוש כרישין, כרתי, קפלוטות (רש"י ביצה דף יז ע"ב), חציר (רש"י במדבר יא, ה):

ליקוטי רש"י

הסלעים. אבנים שהאור יוצא מהן שקורין קוליי"ש שכל אלו קשין לחומה שמוציאין הבל. [המשך בע"ב]

רבינו גרשום

המלח. שחופרין להכניס לתוכן מים לעשות מלח ושיחות שעושין לשרוף בהן **הסיד ואת הסלעים** חפירה מלאה אבנים: **וסד בסיד.** החפירה דכל אלו מזיקין לכותל: **הא ליכא כותל.** הוי כשאר כותל **וסמיך** וקשיא לרבא דאמר גבי שדה דלא סמיך: **דמתונתא דהני.** זה לחלוחית המים שמשקין הזורעים בנגר ודאי **קשין לכותל** שמקלקלין המים יסוד הכותל: **מרחיקין את הריחים.** העשוין בקרקע מן הכותל חבירו: **ג' טפחים מן השכב.** זו אבן התחתונה שמו שכב. ורכב זו אבן עליונה שמורכבת עליה והתחתונה רחבה מן העליונה טפח לכל צד והיינו ג' מן השכב שהוא **ד' מן הרכב** מתוך דפחותה טפח: **טעמא דאיכא כותל.** וקשיא לרבא: **טירא קשה לכותל.** אותו זיעזוע שמזעזעין הקרקע בשעה שמתקנין שם הריחים. איכא דאמר טירא קול הברה שעושין הריחים: **מרחיקין את התנור מן הכותל.** אע"ג דלא תני כותל אפ"ה משמע דירחיק מן הכותל **ג'** טפחים. **מן הכיליא** איזהו כיליא שכשעושין התנור מחרס שכל תנוריהן היו של חרס ועשוין כעין דלי פתוח מלמעלה והחרס קלוש ומדביקין סביב התנור מן הטיט בעובי טפח סביב כדי לחזק התנור מפני שהוא של חרס שלא ישבר ולאותו הדבק קרי כיליא והיינו דאמרי' במס' (פסחים) [חולין קכג:] וגורר את הטפילה עד שמגיע לארץ ואותה דאמרי' התם היינו כיליא **ושפה** זו שפת התנור עצמו שהוא **מרחיק מן הכותל ד' טפחים** כפ"ה. **איכא דאמרי** כילייא זה יסוד התנור דכל סביב התנור סמוך לקרקע יוצא בנין התנור טפח לחוץ וכי מעלה בנינו מקצר ועולה עד לשפה שלמעלה דפוחת טפח. למ"ה: **הבלא.** חמימות התנור: **לא יפתח אדם חנות של נחתומין.** שאופה פתו למכור בכל עת תמיד אופה ומחמם התבואה או היין של חבירו שבאוצר שלמעלה הימנו בעלייה ומש"ה קרי לעלייה אוצר שכן דרך בני אדם שאוצרין פירותיהן בעליות. **וכן של צבעים** לא יפתח תחת האוצר מפני שתדיר עושה היסק גדול לצורך הצבע ומחמם התבואה: **ולא רפת בקר** נמי משום הבלא דזבל. **וטעמא** מאי לא יפתח **דאיכא אוצר** דקדם מעיקרא מש"ה אינו יכול לפתוח להפסידו. **הא לא הוי אוצר** מעיקרא אלא חנות קדם ברישא והשתא קא פתח (הוי) [האי] חנות של נחתומין אע"ג דיכול למימר האי בעל (האוצר) [המיצר] למחר אי עביד הכא לעיל אוצר שלי ומזקת לי כיון דעדיין לא מינכר היזקו **עביד** וסמיך הכי נמי סמיך א) למיצר וקשיא לרבא אמר לך רבא לעולם בעלמא לא סמיך [ודקא דייקי הא היכא] דליכא אוצר סמיך היינו טעמא **דדירתו** של אדם **שאני** שצריך לו לאדם לעשות צרכיו בדירתו מש"ה לא מצי מעכב ליה הואיל ואין לו שום אוצר עכשיו אבל גבי בור ושדה דעלמא דלא קבע תשמישתייהו כדירה לא סמיך משום דמזיק ליה בכך [דמרפי] ליה ארעיה ואי מימלך למיעבד בור לא מצי למיעבד בור: **דיקא נמי.** דדירה שאני: **דקתני אם היה רפת בקר קודם לאוצר מותר.** משום דדירה שאני: **כדי עבודת הכרם.** כדי איכר בקר וכליו דלא דייש ליה לשדהו דהתם היו חורשין את הכרמים בשוורים וכך נמי היו חורשין לשדה אילנות בשוורים: **דקא מפסיק צונמא.** בין שדה שלו לשל חבירו דלא קא עבדין בהני סלעים מש"ה מצי סמיך אי לאו מפני עבודת הכרם אבל בעלמא לא: **היה גדר בינתים.** בין הכרם לשדה **זה סומך** נטיעותיו **לגדר** [אע"ג] דעברין שרשין לשדה: **מעמיק** לשרשיו בקרקע **ג' טפחים כדי שלא יעכב את המחרישה. הכי קאמר אי לאו צונמא** והוה מרחיק ליה לאילנות כ"ה אמה כשיעור האילן. ולאחר כן הגדילו שרשין יותר מכ"ה והיו שרשין יוצאין לתוך של חבירו כנ"ל: **אית דמפרשי** האי שדה כרם הוא כדי להשתמש בהני ד' אמות עבודת תשמיש דצריך לכרם כגון בית הגת וגיגית שלועזין טיני. היינו בור שתחת הגת. אלמא דסמיך (ליה אלא) הכא במאי עסקינן דאי לאו משום עבודת הכרם סמיך דמפסיק צונמא כלומר דאיכא סלע חזק בין האילן לשדה דאינן יכולין השרשין לעבור ולהפסיד בשדה אבל גבי בור ושדה דעלמא דמפסיד לעולם לא סמיך. **זה סומך** אילנו **לגדר וזה** בורו אלמא דסמיך אע"ג דעברי שרשים תותי גדר לשדה חבירו וקא מזקי. לא הכא נמי דאיכא צונמא: **מעמיק** שרשי האילן בקרקע **ג' טפחים** ב) כי היכי דלא ליתזקו שרשין ואמאי צריך להעמיק בתמיה: **כדי שלא תעכב את המחרישה** ולא יפסיד. להכי צריך להעמיק וסמיך אבל גבי בור ושדה דעלמא דלעולם אי אפשר דליכא פסידא של רפיית הקרקע מבור לבור (אמאי) [אימא] לעולם לא סמיך. למ"ה: **אי הכי.** דכי ליכא בור [נמי] לא סמיך האילן **אימא סיפא אם האילן קדם** לבור דאם היה נטוע האילן קודם דנחפר הבור אע"ג דמזיק לה **לא יקוץ ואי לא סמיך** האילן על מצר שדה חבירו קודם חפירת הבור **היכי** מצי **משכחת לה** דמזיק לה השתא אלא לאו ש"מ דסמיך: לא לעולם לא סמיך. וכי תימא א"כ היכי הוה זה סומך אילנו אצל שדה חבירו: **כדאמר רב פפא** לקמן **בלוקח.** כגון דהוה מעיקרא האילן והשדה לאדם אחד ומכרו לשני בני אדם לא' מכר מקום האילן והאילן ולשני מכר כל שאר השדה משפת אילן ולהלן ובא זה שלקח שאר השדה וחפר בורו סמוך לאילן דהשתא קדם האילן לבור ולא סמכו זה לוקח אלא המוכר דברשות סמכו דהכל היה שלו ומש"ה לא יקוץ ולעולם בעלמא לא סמיך: **מרחיקין את המשרה.** מים סרוחין ששורין בהן פשתן וקשה הוא לירק. א"ד משרה שמכבסין ושורין בהן את הבגדים: **מן הירק** מתוך ג) דאתנייהו ירקות דלא צריכי כל כך למים ותיתזין ניצוצות הכביסה על הירק כל שעה ומזיק להו. למ"ה: **ולא כרתי אצל בצלים.** משום דמכחשי כרישין לבצלים וכן לחרדל מתוך דאכלי דבורים לחרדל: **דאכלי לגלוגי.** כלומר ענפי חרדלי:

חשק שלמה על רבינו גרשום א) נראה דל"ל והכא נמי סמיך בור סמוך למיצר. ב) נראה דל"ל ג"ט כדי שלא תעכב את המחרישה ולא יפסיד ואמאי צריך להעמיק בתמי': ה"ק ואי לאו צונמא וכו' ולהכי צריך להעמיק וכו': ג) אולי צ"ל מתוך דהנהו ירקות לא צריכי כ"כ וכו'.

ואי דלא סמיך היכי משכחת לה אמר רב פפא בלוקח אי בלוקח מאי טעמא דרבנן ועוד מאי טעמא דרבי יוסי אפילו משרה וירקא נמי אמר רבינא קא סברי רבנן על המזיק להרחיק את עצמו מכלל דר' יוסי סבר על הניזק להרחיק את עצמו אי על הניזק אפי' משרה וירקא נמי אלא לעולם ר' יוסי נמי על המזיק סבירא ליה והכי קאמר להו רבי יוסי לרבנן תינח משרה וירקא דהני מזקי הני והני לא מזקי הני אלא חרדל ודבורים תרווייהו מזקי אהדדי ורבנן דבורים לחרדל לא מזקי ליה אי בבינתא לא משכחא ליה אי בטרפא הדר פארי וסבר ר' יוסי על המזיק להרחיק את עצמו והתנן [א] רבי יוסי אומר אע"פ שהבור קודמת לאילן לא יקוץ שזה חופר בתוך שלו וזה נוטע בתוך שלו אלא לעולם ר' יוסי על הניזק ס"ל ולדבריהם דרבנן קאמר להו לדידי [א] על הניזק להרחיק את עצמו [ב] ואפי' משרה וירקא לא בעי רחוקי אלא לדידכו דאמריתו על המזיק תינח משרה וירקא דהני מזקי הני והני לא מזקי הני אלא חרדל ודבורים תרווייהו מזקי אהדדי ורבנן דבורים לחרדל לא מזקי ליה אי בבינתא לא

ואי לא סמיך. אינים הזיק למילר חבירו אפילו בשאין שם דבר הניזוק אית ליה לר' יוסי דאלו שניהן מזיקין הן היכי משכחת ליה ליסמוך חד מינייהו ברישא הרי חבירו מעכב עליו: בלוקח. אחר שעשה זה משרה בתוך שדהו או זרע שם חרדל מכר שדהו לאחר והלוקח זרע שם ירק או העמיד דבורים: אמאי מרחיק. הרי ברשות עשה: ועוד מאי טעמא דרבי יוסי. דלא פליג אלא בחרדל וטעמא משום דתרוייהו מזיקין הן וליפלוג נמי במשרה וירק: על המזיק להרחיק את עצמו. ואף על פי שמתחלה עשה ברשות: אי בבינתא. גרעין הזרע:

[3] לגלוגי חרדל. פי' הקונטרס פרחים ובערוך פירש גרעין ותרווייהו אין נראה לר"י דהא קאמרי רבנן דבורים לחרדל לא מזקי אי בבינתא כו' אי בטרפא כו' משמע דלא פירש רבי יוסי בדבריו מה הן מזיקין ולכך היו מסתפקין אי בבינתא כו' ונראה לר"י דלגלוגי הם ענפים והשתא לא פירש רבי יוסי מה הם מזיקות לכך אמרו ליה רבנן אי בבינתא כו' וא"ת מכל מקום הרי הן מזיקין לחרדל שיאכלו הפרחים וי"ל שהפרחים אינן כ"א מעט ויום או יומים שיעמדו אין יכולין להזיק: ואי לא סמיך היכי משכחת לה. פר"י בשלמא לאביי דאמר סמיך אתי שפיר דמיירי שסמך בעל דבורים תחילה ואע"ג דהשתא קס"ד דדבורים נמי מזקי לחרדל לכ"ע מכל מקום סברי רבנן דעל המזיק שני דהיינו בעל חרדל להרחיק את (א) כל ההרחקה כמו גבי בור דאם סמך הראשון על המיצר השני מרחיק כל ששה טפחים ורבי יוסי סבר כיון דדבורים מזקי חרדל ועשה קצת שלא כהוגן שסמך על המיצר שזה עתיד לסוף לזרוע חרדל אע"פ שבדין אינו יכול למונעו שלא יסמוך מ"מ קצת שלא כהוגן עושה וגם בעל חרדל יכול לסמוך ולא דמי לבור דהתם משום דמרפי ליה לארעיה ומזיק השני בידים לכותל בורו של ראשון לכך על השני להרחיק כל ההרחקה אבל הכא לא אלא לרבא דאמר לא סמיך היכי משכחת לה דבעל החרדל ירחיק כל ההרחקה לרבנן ולרבי יוסי לא ירחיק כלל דכיון דתרווייהו מזקי אהדדי על כל אחד ואחד להרחיק חצי ההרחקה ואפילו סמך בעל דבורים תחלה יש לו לסלקם הואיל ושלא כדין סמכם אמר רב פפא בלוקח שזרע חרדל ומכר חצי שדהו והלוקח העמיד דבורים וסברי רבנן כדמסיק דדבורים לא מזקי לחרדל ועל המזיק להרחיק את עצמו אף על פי שסמך בהיתר אע"ג דגבי אילן כשסמכו בהיתר אמרי דלא יקוץ הני מילי אילן שעשוי לעמוד שנים רבות ואיכא הפסד מרובה אבל משרה כרישין וחרדל לא דהכי נמי אמרינן גבי אילן אם הבור קדם קוצץ ונותן דמים אע"ג דסמך אילנו באיסור ובשאר דברים הנסמכים באיסור אינו נראה שיתנו דמים אלא טעמא דלהפסד מרובה חששו ורבי יוסי סבר דדבורים מזקי לחרדל וצריך בעל דבורים להרחיק כל ההרחקה כיון דבעל חרדל לא עשה כלל שלא כהוגן ומשום הכי נמי לא בעי לאוקמי כשסמך בעל דבורים תחלה ובלוקח ולא היה צריך לחוק ולומר דלרבנן על המזיק להרחיק אע"פ שעשה בהיתר מה שאינו גבי אילן ובור וגם לא יצטרך לומר דלרבנן דבורים לא מזקי לחרדל ופליגי ארבי יוסי דא"כ כיון דבעל דבורים סמך בהיתר ולא עשה שלא כהוגן לא היה מתיר רבי יוסי לבעל חרדל לסמוך ואם תאמר נוקי פלוגתייהו בלא לוקח דלרבנן דדבורים לא מזקי לחרדל צריך בעל חרדל להסיר ולהרחיק כל ההרחקה אע"פ שסמך תחלה ולרבי יוסי כיון דתרווייהו מזקי אהדדי אין לבעל החרדל להרחיק כל ההרחקה אלא החצי וי"ל דמתיר בחרדל משמע דמתיר לגמרי לסמוך אי הכי מאי טעמא דרבנן כיון דבהיתר נסמכו משרה וכרישין למה צריך להרחיקן כשבאו ירק ובצלים וכ"ש חרדל למה ירחיקוהו כשבאו דבורים כיון שגם הם מזקי דס"ד דדבורים נמי מזקי לחרדל לכ"ע ועוד מ"ט דרבי יוסי דלא פליג אלא בחרדל משום דדבורים נמי מזקי לחרדל אפילו משרה וירק כיון שנעשה המשרה בהיתר לא יצטרך להרחיקה כמו גבי אילן ובור ומשני רבינא לעולם בלוקח וקא סברי רבנן על המזיק להרחיק את עצמו אע"פ שעשה בהיתר ולהכי על בעל החרדל להרחיק שהוא [ג] הזיק ופריך כיון דשמעינן ממילתא דרבינא שהדבורים אינם מזיקים לחרדל דלכך נתנו רבנן הרחקה על בעל החרדל מכלל דרבי יוסי סבר על הניזק להרחיק עצמו מדשרי סמיכת חרדל אע"פ שהוא מזיק ולא ניזק א"כ אפילו משרה וירק נמי וה"ה דה"מ לאקשויי (ב) דברייתא בהדיא משמע שהדבורים מזקי נמי לחרדל דקתני ואוכלות לגלוגי חרדלי אלא ניחא ליה למינקט קושיא דאפי' משרה וירק נמי משום דהתחיל כבר להקשותה (ג): מכלל דסבר רבי יוסי על הניזק להרחיק וכו'. נ"ל לפירוש זה דזה המקשה אינו אותו שהקשה בתחלה ואי לא סמיך היכי משכחת לה דהא לדידיה הוה ניחא ליה לאביי דאמר סמיך ולא הוה קשה ליה מידי וסבר רבי יוסי על הניזק כו' וצ"ל שהמקשה הראשון הוה ידע שפיר המסקנא דדבורים לחרדל לא מזקי לרבנן אבל המקשה הזה לא ידע להכי פריך מכלל דסבר רבי יוסי כו' והקשה כיון דלרבנן חשיב בעל דבורים ניזק ולא מזיק שמצריכין לבעל חרדל להרחיק אף על גב שהם מזיקין לחרדל מכל מקום כיון דסמך בהיתר לא חשיב מזיק ועל בעל חרדל להרחיק א"כ גם לרבי יוסי חשיב ניזק ואפ"ה מותר לסמוך לבעל החרדל א"כ סבר דעל הניזק להרחיק את עצמו אי הכי אפילו משרה וירק נמי כן דאין סברא דלרבי יוסי חשיב בעל דבורים מזיק אע"פ שסמך בהיתר משום שעשה קצת שלא כהוגן ולרבנן לית להו האי סברא דאין סברא כלל דלפלוגינהו בהכי ומשני לעולם רבי יוסי על המזיק ס"ל וחשיב בעל דבורים מזיק אע"ג שסמך בהיתר כיון שעשה קצת שלא כהוגן בסמיכתו ורבנן נמי הוו מודו ליה בהך סברא אי הוו סברי דדבורים מזקי לחרדל אלא דס"ל דדבורים לא מזקי לחרדל ולכך מרחיק בעל החרדל וכמסקנא זו יש לפרש תחלת הסוגיא לדברי המקשה דפריך ואי לא סמיך היכי משכחת לה דבשלמא אי סמיך (ד) כדמסקינן השתא ולא כמו שפי' לפ"ה שיחלקו (ה) דלרבנן הוו דבורים כמו ירק כיון שנסמכו בהיתר אע"ג שגם הם מזיקין לחרדל כשיבא ור' יוסי מתיר לסמוך החרדל מפני שבעל הדבורים עשה קצת שלא כהוגן: וסבר ר' יוסי על המזיק כו'. (לעיל) לקמן על מקומה הוה ליה לאקשויי אלא משום דאיצטריך ליה לפרש הכא דסבר רבי יוסי דעל המזיק להרחיק את עצמו אסקוה לכולה מילתא הכא ובלוקח דהכא אי אפשר לפרשו כפירוש רבינו חננאל דפי' באדם שלוקח משרה וטוענין ללוקח דא"כ למה ירחיק המשרה כשיבא שם ירק כיון שטוענין לו שהמוכר קנה סמיכה זו אלא צריך לפרש בלוקח כמו שפירש בקונטרס או כר"י בר' מרדכי כך פי' ר"י כל הסוגיא לפי שיטת רש"י וקשה לו מה הוצרך לחלק בדוחק בין לוקח דאילן ללוקח דמשרה ועוד דלמה המתין להביא משנה זו דמשרה וירק באחרונה המוקדמין במשנתו ועוד דקתני בתוספתא (פ"א) רבי יוסי מתיר בחרדל שאומר לו כדרך שעשית בתוך שלך כך אני עושה בתוך שלי משמע דבעל דבורים סמך תחלה ומפרש רבינו תם ורבינו חננאל דהכי גרסינן אלא אמר רבינא קסברי רבנן על המזיק להרחיק את עצמו והשתא הדר ביה מכל שינויי דלעיל דודאי בכולהו מודה רבא דכי ליכא כותל או ירק דסמיך משום דקא סברי רבנן דדוקא על המזיק להרחיק את עצמו דהיינו כי איכא דבר הניזוק אבל כי ליכא דבר הניזוק לא מקרי הסומך מזיק ולא אסר רבא לסמוך אפי' לרבנן אלא דוקא בור משום טעמא דכל מרא ומרא דקא מחית מרפית לארעאי ולהכי חשוב הסומך מזיק אפילו כי ליכא בור וכיון דלרבנן נמי סמיך אתי שפיר פלוגתייהו כדפרישית לעיל אליבא דאביי ולכך הדר ביה ולא מוקי בלוקח וכגון שסמך בעל דבורים תחלה משום דא"כ לא היה מתיר ר"י לסמוך לבעל החרדל כיון דבעל הדבורים לא עשה כלל שלא כהוגן ודוקא בדסמיך בלא לוקח שעשה קצת שלא כהוגן בעל הדבורים מתיר רבי יוסי לבעל החרדל לסמוך כדפרישית לעיל ולפי זה אתי שפיר דלמסקנא זו לא נצטרך לחלק בין לוקח דאילן ללוקח משרה ולהכי המתין נמי כדי להביא מתניתין דמשרה משום דמינה צריך לחזור מכל שינויי דלעיל ואתי נמי שפיר דמיירי שסמך נמי בעל דבורים תחלה כמו שמוכח בתוספתא:

עין משפט
נר מצוה

ח א ב מיי' פ"י מהל' שכנים הל' ה סמג עשין פב טוש"ע ח"מ סי' קנה סעיף לג:

רבינו גרשום

ואי לא סמיך. היכי משכחת לה דיכולין אלו לטעון הכי זה כנגד זה אנא סמיכנא ואת הרחק והלא אין סומכין אפי' כי ליכא עדיין היזקא לחבריה אלא מדיכולין לטעון הכי ש"מ דסמיך. לא לעולם בעלמא לא סמיך והכא מאי טעמא סמיך בלוקח שלקח מן אחד מקום חרדל ושני לקח שאר מקום השדה והכניס שם דבורים ומש"ה לא מצי מעכבי זה לזה לטעמיה דר' יוסי דבעל חרדל טעין אנא לא מרחקנא דאתינא מכח דמוכר הסמך ברשות בתוך שלו. אבל את הרחק את דבורך דמזקי לחרדלאי. ובעל דבורים טעין את מזקת לי טפי מדאנא מזיקנא לך: אי הכי כדתרצת בלוקח מאי טעמא דפליגי רבנן עליה דר' יוסי דמחייבי להרחיק החרדל הואיל ולוקח הוא וברשות סמך. ועוד קושיא אחריתי כיון דאוקמת לה בלוקח מאי טעמא מתיר ר' יוסי בחרדל לחודיה ומודה לרבנן במשרה וירק ליפלוג נמי עלייהו במשרה וירק דלא צריך להרחיק הואיל דלוקח הוא וברשות סמך המוכר המשרה והירק והשומין. לעולם בלוקח ומאי דאמרת מאי טעמא דרבנן דאמרי מרחיקין חרדל ולא סמיך משום דסבירא להו דעל המזיק רמי להרחיק עצמו שלא יזיק אע"ג דברשות סמך דמתוך ששורין פיהם מחריפות החרדל חוזרות ואוכלות את דובשן. ומקשי' מכלל דר' יוסי דפליג עלייהו סבר על הניזק להרחיק דיכול לומר מזיק לניזק הרחק עצמך ממני שלא תזוק ולהכי מתיר בחרדל ודבורים א"כ מאי שנא ממשרה וירק דלא פליג על רבנן כי היכי דפליג בחרדל. אלא ודאי מסתברא ר' יוסי סבר דעל המזיק רמי להרחיק דלא סמיך כרבנן וכי תימא א"כ מאי טעמא דר' יוסי דמתיר גבי חרדל לחודיה לסמוך ופליג עלייהו אמשרה וירק משום דהכי קאמר להו ר' יוסי לרבנן בשלמא להנך תרתי במשרה ושומין מודינא לכו דעל המזיק להרחיק משום דהן מזיקין את הירק ואת הבצלים והם לא מזקי למשרה ושומין אבל גבי חרדל ודבורים דזה מזיק זה וזה מזיק זה פליגנא עלייכו דלא צריך חד מינייהו להרחיק טפי מחבריה ואמרי ליה רבנן לר' יוסי ל"ש בין חרדל למשרה וירק דכולן מזיקין ולא ניזוקין דחרדל מזיק לדבורים מתוך חריפות החרדל דאכלי דבורים מכחשו הדבש אבל דבורים לא מזקי לחרדל אמאי אמרת אי משום בינתא (בעתא בצתא) גרעינין דחרדל ליכא למיחש דאכלי ליה דבורים דכיון דהן דקין מאד לא משכחי להו דבורים ואי בטרפא כלומר אם תאמר שאוכלין העלין של חרדל מאי איכפת ליה הדר פארי. חוזר וגדל ולהכי סבירא להו גבי חרדל ודבורין כגון משרה וירק: וזה נוטע בתוך שלו. אע"ג דמזיק לבור של חבירו דאי בעי בעל הבור דהוי ניזק להרחיק ירחיק דהאי לא יניח שלא יטע בתוך שלו אע"ג דמזיק ליה אלמא דסבר ר' יוסי דעל הניזק רמי להרחיק את עצמו: אלא לעולם ר' יוסי ודאי [ס"ל] על הניזק להרחיק וכי תימא א"כ מאי טעמא דמודה לרבנן במשרה וירק דמסברי דעל המזיק רמי לא תימא דמודה להו אלא לדבריהן דרבנן קאמר לדידי אפי' משרה וירק נמי לא צריך להרחיק משום דסבירא לי דעל הניזק להרחיק אלא לדידכו וכו':

מסורת הש"ס

א) לקמן כה:, ב) שייך לע"א, ג) מזיק:

הגהות הב"ח

(א) תוס' ד"ה ואי לא וכו' להרחיק את עצמו כל הרחקות: (ב) בא"ד לאקשויי דבברייתא: (ג) אחר ד"ה ואי לא נ"ל ד"ה וסבר ואח"כ ד"ה מכלל וכו' וג' דבורים אלו הד"א ואח"כ נ"ל ד"ה לגלוגי: (ד) בא"ד אי סמיך פליגי כדמסקינן וכו': (ה) בא"ד שיחלקו בזה דלרבנן כנ"ל:

ליקוטי רש"י

מכותלו של חבירו. כותל לבנים של טיט הבנוי על גבי קרקע ולאו בכור קאי השתא. זרעים. קשין לכותל כדמפרש בגמ'. ואת המחרישה. מרפה את יסודו ונופל. מי רגלים. ממסמסין את הלבנים שהן של טיט יבש. ריחים. קשין לכותל שמנידין את הקרקע בגלגול חבטתו. מן השכב. היא הריחים התחתונה. הרכב. היא העליונה הרוכבת על זו והיא קצרה טפח מן התחתונה. ואת התנור שלשה מן הכליא. תנור כלי חרס הוא שרוף בכבשן כשאר קדירות ופיו למעלה והבא לקובעו בארץ עושה בנין טיט ואבנים שיהיו לו לבסים ומושיבין אותו עליו שלא יצטננו שוליו מחמת קרקע ואותו בנין עשוי בשיפוע רחב מלמטה וקצר מלמעלה כמדת התנור תחתונה קרוי כליא ועליונו קרוי שפה כלומר שפת הכליא שפתה עליונה ולפי שהבלו של תנור קשה לכותל צריך להרחיקו [לעיל יז.]. לא יטע אדם אילן סמוך לשדה. בקמה שדהו סמוך לשדה חבירו. כדי שלא תלך מחרישתו לחרוש אילן זה לרך שדה חבירו [רשב"ם לקמן פג.]. סמוך לשדה. בין שדה הלבן בין שדה האילן [לקמן כו.]. כדי עבודת הכרם. דבכדי הוי כלאים [לעיל ב.]. דמפסיק צונמא. שן סלע מבדיל [גיטין כב.]. צונמא. גלמין ארמי סלע [בראשית מא, כג ונדה ח.]. אבן [רשב"ם לקמן סט.]. מן הבור. שהשרשין מתפשטין ונוקבין בכותלי הבור ומקלקלין הכותלים טפלים [ב"מ קיז.]. לגלוגי חרדלאי. פרחי חרדלי [לקמן כה.].

The Gemara shows how this refutes Rava's view:

וְאִי דְּלָא סָמֵיךְ – Now if the law is, as Rava says, **that one may not place** a hazard **near** his neighbor's property even before the item liable to be damaged is in harm's way, **הֵיכִי מַשְׁכַּחַתְּ לָהּ – how can [such a situation] arise?** Since, according to R' Yose, both bees and mustard plants are classified as hazards, how could either have been placed near the boundary in the first place?[1]

The Gemara offers a solution:

אָמַר רַב פָּפָּא – Rav Pappa said: בְּלוֹקֵחַ – The Mishnah refers **to a buyer;** i.e. it refers to the following scenario: The owner of the hazard (flax pool, leeks, mustard plants) installed it well within the boundaries of his property, but later he sold a section of his property to another, who proceeded to install a vulnerable item (vegetables, onions, beehive) within range of the hazard. This is a situation in which a hazard can be found near the boundary between properties, even according to Rava.

The Gemara objects to this solution:

אִי בְּלוֹקֵחַ – But if the Mishnah refers **to a buyer** (i.e. the preceding scenario), **מַאי טַעְמָא דְּרַבָּנָן – what is the rationale of the Rabbis?** When the owner installed the hazardous agent, he did so legally. So why do the Rabbis require him to remove it? **וְעוֹד – Furthermore, מַאי טַעְמָא דְּרַבִּי יוֹסֵי – what is the rationale of R' Yose,** who permits the hazard to be left near the boundary only in the case of the bees and the mustard plants? **אֲפִילּוּ מִשְׁרָה וְיַרְקָא נַמִּי – Even** regarding the case of **a flax pool and vegetables,**[2] R' Yose should rule that the hazard may be left near the boundary, since it was placed there legally. — ? —

The Gemara answers the first objection:

אָמַר רָבִינָא – Ravina said:[3] **קָא סָבְרֵי רַבָּנָן – The Rabbis are of the opinion that עַל הַמַּזִּיק לְהַרְחִיק אֶת עַצְמוֹ – it is the responsibility of the owner of a hazard to distance it**[4] from the property liable to be damaged, even in a situation where it was installed legally.[5]

However, Ravina's approach does not solve the problem with R' Yose's opinion. In fact, it intensifies this problem:

מִכְּלָל – By specifying the Rabbis, Rava **implies דְּרַבִּי יוֹסֵי סָבַר עַל הַנִּיזָּק לְהַרְחִיק אֶת עַצְמוֹ – that R' Yose is of the opinion that it is the responsibility of the threatened party to distance his property**[6] from the hazard. **אִי עַל הַנִּיזָּק – But if** R' Yose is of the opinion that the responsibility for preventing damage rests **upon the threatened party, אֲפִילּוּ מִשְׁרָה וְיַרְקָא נַמִּי –** he should dispute the Rabbis' ruling in the case of **a flax pool and vegetables as well!**[7] Why does he argue only with regard to the case of bees and mustard plants?

The Gemara explains R' Yose's opinion:

אֶלָּא לְעוֹלָם – Rather, the truth is that **רַבִּי יוֹסֵי נַמִּי עַל הַמַּזִּיק סְבִירָא לֵיהּ – R' Yose too is of the opinion** that the responsibility for preventing damage rests **upon the hazard's owner. וְהָכִי קָאָמַר לְהוּ רַבִּי יוֹסֵי לְרַבָּנָן – And this is what R' Yose is saying to the Rabbis: תֵּינַח מִשְׁרָה וְיַרְקָא –** "Your view is **in order** with regard to the case of **a flax pool and vegetables, דְּהָנֵי מַזְּקֵי הָנֵי – for these** (flax pools) **damage these** (vegetables), **וְהָנֵי לָא מַזְּקֵי הָנֵי – while these** (vegetables) **do not damage these** (flax pools). Since the damage is only one way and the law is that it is the responsibility of the hazard's owner to prevent damage, I concur with your ruling that the hazard (the flax pool) must be removed. **אֶלָּא חַרְדָּל וּדְבוֹרִים – But** with regard to the case of **mustard** plants **and bees, תַּרְוַייהוּ מַזְּקֵי אַהֲדָדֵי –** where **each one damages the other,** I disagree with your ruling that the mustard plants must be removed!"[8]

The Gemara now gives the Rabbis' response to R' Yose's argument:

וְרַבָּנָן – And the Rabbis hold that **דְּבוֹרִים לְחַרְדָּל לָא מַזְּקֵי לֵיהּ – bees do not damage mustard** plants. **אִי בְּבִינִתָּא – As far as the** mustard **seeds are concerned, לָא מַשְׁכְּחָא לֵיהּ – [bees] cannot find them.**[9] **אִי בְּטַרְפָּא –** And **as far as the leaves are concerned,** even if the bees eat them the damage is not significant, **הָדַר פָּארֵי – for they grow back.**

The Gemara asserted that R' Yose agrees with the Rabbis' basic position that the responsibility to prevent damage rests upon the owner of the hazard. This assertion is now refuted:

וְסָבַר רַבִּי יוֹסֵי עַל הַמַּזִּיק לְהַרְחִיק אֶת עַצְמוֹ – But does R' Yose hold that it is the responsibility of the owner of a hazard to distance it from vulnerable property? **וְהָתְנַן – But we have**

NOTES

1. And if the owner of one of the hazards installed it near the boundary illegally, why does R' Yose say that his neighbor can only argue: "Before you tell me etc." (i.e. since I cannot force you to move your hazard, you cannnot force me to move mine)? R' Yose should have ruled that the neighbor can have the hazard removed! (See *Ran, Maharam*).

According to Abaye, however, this is not a difficulty, for even if both bees and mustard plants are hazards, one may be placed near the boundary *before* the other is present on the other side. Thus, the Mishnah speaks of a case where one neighbor placed one of these hazards near the boundary and then the other neighbor wished to put the other hazard on the opposite side.

[*Tosafos* stated above that the Gemara's challenges to Rava reflect the view of the Sages, not that of R' Yose (see 18a note 1). However, the Gemara's present challenge is clearly based on the view of R' Yose! *Rashba* answers this problem.]

2. And the Mishnah's second case involving leeks and onions as well. [For the sake of brevity, the Gemara mentions only the first case.]

3. [There is an alternative version of the text which reads: אֶלָּא אָמַר רָבִינָא, *Rather, Ravina said.* The word אֶלָּא, *rather*, signifies that the Gemara retracts its previous answer that the Mishnah refers to a buyer. *Rabbeinu Chananel*, *Rabbeinu Tam* (cited by *Tosafos* ד"ה וסבר) and other Rishonim follow this version, which necessitates a completely different explanation of the following passage of Gemara. Our elucidation, however, reflects the commentary of *Rashi* according to which the Gemara does not retract its previous answer (see *Rashi* ד"ה על המזיק).]

4. Literally: it is [incumbent] upon the one who damages to distance himself.

5. An apparent difficulty: This contradicts the ruling of the Mishnah (25b) that if someone planted a tree *before* a pit was dug in neighboring property, he is not required to remove the tree.

The answer is that the Rabbis made an exception in the case of a tree since its removal involves a substantial monetary loss (*Tosafos* ד"ה ואי לא). Alternatively: The Rabbis did not mandate the removal of the tree, because trees are essential for the habitation of the world (*Ramban, Ran,* from *Yerushalmi* 2:10).

6. Literally: it is [incumbent] upon the one who is damaged to distance himself. I.e. if the owner of the vulnerable property does not want it to be damaged, it is up to him to move it out of harm's way.

7. [Previously, R' Yose's acquiescence in the first two cases of the Mishnah was considered difficult for only one reason: viz. the hazard was placed legally. Now it is difficult for an additional reason: viz. R' Yose holds that it is up to the threatened party to prevent damage from occurring.]

8. See 18a, first paragraph of note 32.

9. The seed of the mustard plant is enclosed in a sheath (*Rashi* to 19a ד"ה לא; see *Rashba* here).

ח א ב מיי' פ"י מהל' שכנים הל' ה סמג עשין פב טוש"ע ח"מ סי' קנה סעיף לג:

ואי דלא סמיך היכי משכחת לה אמר רב פפא בלוקח אי בלוקח מאי טעמא דרבנן ועוד מאי טעמא דרבי יוסי אפילו משרה וירקא נמי אמר רבינא קא סברי רבנן על המזיק להרחיק את עצמו מכלל דר' יוסי סבר על הניזק להרחיק את עצמו אי על הניזק אפי' משרה וירקא נמי אלא לעולם ר' יוסי נמי על המזיק סבירא ליה והכי קאמר להו רבי יוסי לרבנן תינח משרה וירקא דהני מזקי הני והני לא מזקי הני אלא חרדל ודבורים תרווייהו מזקי אהדדי ורבנן דבורים לחרדל לא מזקי ליה אי בבינתא לא משכחא ליה אי בטרפא הדר פארי וסבר ר' יוסי על המזיק להרחיק את עצמו והתנן (א) רבי יוסי אומר אע"פ שהבור קודמת לאילן לא יקוץ שזה חופר בתוך שלו וזה נוטע בתוך שלו אלא לעולם ר' יוסי על הניזק ס"ל ולדבריהם דרבנן קאמר להו לדידי (א) על הניזק להרחיק את עצמו (ב) ואפי' משרה וירקא לא בעי רחוקי אלא לדידכו דאמריתו על המזיק תינח משרה וירקא דהני מזקי הני והני לא מזקי הני אלא חרדל ודבורים תרווייהו מזקי אהדדי ורבנן דבורים לחרדל לא מזקי ליה אי בבינתא לא

רש"י

ואי לא סמיך. אינו הזיק למיצר חבירו אפילו בשאין שם דבר הניזוק אין ליה לר' יוסי דאלו שניהן מזיקין הן היכי משכחת ליה דליסמוך חד מינייהו ברישא הרי חבירו מעכב עליו: **בלוקח.** אם עשה זה משרה בתוך שדהו או זרע שם חרדל מכר מחצה שדהו לאחר והלוקח זרע שם ירק או העמיד דבורים: **אמאי מרחיק.** הרי ברשות עשה: **ועוד מאי טעמא דרבי יוסי.** דלא פליג אלא בחרדל וטעמא משום דתרווייהו מזיקין הן וליפלוג נמי במשרה וירק: **על המזיק להרחיק את עצמו.** ואף על פי שמתחלה עשה ברשות: **אי בבינתא.** גרעין הזרע:

תוספות

לגלוגי חרדל. פי' הקונטרס פרחים ובערוך פירש גרעין ותרווייהו אין נראה לר"י דהא קאמרי רבנן דבורים לחרדל לא מזקי אי בבינתא כו' אי בטרפא כו' משמע דלא פירש רבי יוסי בדבריו מה הן מזיקין ולכך היו מסתפקין אי בבינתא כו' ונראה לר"י דלגלוגי הם ענפים והשתא לא פירש רבי יוסי מה הם מזיקות לכך אמרו ליה רבנן אי בבינתא כו' וא"ת מכל מקום הרי הן מזיקין לחרדל שיאכלו הפרחים ויש לומר שהפרחים אינן כ"א מעט וביום או יומים שיעמדו אין יכולין להזיק: **ואי לא סמיך היכי משכחת לה.** פר"י בשלמא לאביי דאמר סמיך אתי שפיר דמיירי שסמך בעל דבורים תחילה ואע"ג דהשתא קס"ד דדבורים נמי מזקי לחרדל לכ"ע מכל מקום סברי רבנן דעל המזיק שני דהיינו בעל חרדל להרחיק את (א) כל ההרחקה כמו גבי בור דאם סמך הראשון על המיצר השני מרחיק כל ששה טפחים ורבי יוסי סבר כיון דדבורים מזקי חרדל ועשה קצת שלא כהוגן שסמך על המיצר שזה עתיד לסוף לזרוע חרדל אע"פ שבדין אינו יכול למונעו שלא יסמוך מ"מ קצת שלא כהוגן עושה וגם בעל חרדל יכול לסמוך ולא דמי לבור דהתם משום דמרפי ליה לארעיה ומזיק השני בידים לכותל בורו של ראשון לכך על השני להרחיק כל ההרחקה אבל הכא לא אלא לרבא דאמר לא סמיך היכי משכחת לה דבעל החרדל ירחיק כל ההרחקה לרבנן ולרבי יוסי לא ירחיק כלל דכיון דתרווייהו מזקי אהדדי על כל אחד ואחד להרחיק חצי ההרחקה ואפילו סמך בעל דבורים תחלה יש לו לסלקם הואיל ושלא כדין סמכם אמר רב פפא בלוקח שזרע חרדל ומכר חצי שדהו והלוקח העמיד דבורים וסברי רבנן כדמסיק דדבורים לא מזקי לחרדל ועל המזיק להרחיק את עצמו אף על פי שסמך בהיתר אע"ג דגבי אילן כשסמכו בהיתר אמרי דלא יקוץ הני מילי אילן שעשוי לעמוד שנים רבות ואיכא הפסד מרובה אבל משרה כרישין וחרדל לא דהכי נמי אמרינן גבי אילן אם הבור קדם קוצץ ונותן דמים אע"ג דסמך אילנו באיסור ובשאר דברים הנסמכים באיסור אינו נראה שיתנו דמים אלא טעמא דלהפסד מרובה חששו ורבי יוסי סבר דדבורים מזקי לחרדל וצריך בעל דבורים להרחיק כל ההרחקה כיון דבעל חרדל לא עשה כלל שלא כהוגן ומשום הכי נמי לא בעי לאוקמי כשסמך בעל דבורים תחלה ובלוקח ולא היה צריך לדחוק ולומר דלרבנן על המזיק להרחיק אע"פ שעשה בהיתר מה שאינו גבי אילן ובור וגם לא יצטרך לומר דלרבנן דבורים לא מזקי לחרדל ופליגי אדרבי יוסי דא"כ כיון דבעל דבורים סמך בהיתר ולא עשה שלא כהוגן לא היה מתיר רבי יוסי לבעל חרדל לסמוך ואם תאמר נוקי פלוגתייהו בלא לוקח דלרבנן דדבורים לא מזקי לחרדל צריך בעל חרדל להסיר ולהרחיק כל ההרחקה אע"פ שסמך תחלה ולרבי יוסי כיון דתרווייהו מזקי אהדדי אין לבעל החרדל להרחיק כל ההרחקה אלא החצי וי"ל דמתיר בחרדל משמע דמתיר לגמרי לסמוך אי הכי מאי טעמא דרבנן כיון דבהיתר נסמכו משרה וכרישין למה צריך להרחיקן כשבאו ירק ובצלים וכ"ש חרדל למה ירחיקוהו כשבאו דבורים כיון שגם הם מזקי דס"ד דדבורים נמי מזקי לחרדל לכ"ע ועוד מ"ט דרבי יוסי דלא פליג אלא בחרדל משום דדבורים נמי מזקי לחרדל אפילו משרה וירק כיון שנעשה המשרה בהיתר לא יצטרך להרחיקה כמו גבי אילן ובור ומשני רבינא לעולם בלוקח וקא סברי רבנן על המזיק להרחיק את עצמו אע"פ שעשה בהיתר ולהכי על בעל החרדל להרחיק שהוא (ג) הזיק ופריך כיון דשמעינן ממילתא דרבינא שהדבורים אינם מזיקים לחרדל דלכך נתנו רבנן הרחקה על בעל החרדל מכלל דרבי יוסי סבר על הניזק להרחיק עצמו מדשרי סמיכת חרדל אע"פ שהוא מזיק ולא ניזק א"כ אפילו משרה וירק נמי וה"ה דה"מ לאקשויי (ג) דברייתא בהדיא משמע שהדבורים מזקי נמי לחרדל דקתני ואוכלות לגלוגי חרדלי אלא ניחא ליה למינקט קושיא דאפי' משרה וירק נמי משום דהתחיל כבר להקשותה (ג): **מכלל** דסבר רבי יוסי על הניזק להרחיק וכו'. נ"ל לפירוש זה דזה המקשה אינו אותו שהקשה בתחלה ואי לא סמיך היכי משכחת לה דהא לדידיה הוה ניחא ליה לאביי דאמר סמיך ולא הוה קשה ליה מידי וסבר רבי יוסי על הניזק כו' וצ"ל שהמקשה הראשון הוה ידע שפיר המסקנא דדבורים לחרדל לא מזקי לרבנן אבל המקשה הזה לא ידע להכי פריך מכלל דסבר רבי יוסי כו' והקשה כיון דלרבנן חשיב בעל דבורים ניזק ולא מזיק שמצריכין לבעל חרדל להרחיק אף על גב שהם מזיקין לחרדל מכל מקום כיון דסמך בהיתר לא חשיב מזיק ועל בעל חרדל להרחיק א"כ גם לרבי יוסי חשיב ניזק ואפ"ה מותר לסמוך לבעל החרדל א"כ סבר דעל הניזק להרחיק את עצמו אי הכי אפילו משרה וירק נמי כן דאין סברא לרבי יוסי חשיב בעל דבורים מזיק אע"פ שסמך בהיתר משום שעשה קצת שלא כהוגן ולרבנן לית להו האי סברא דאין סברא כלל לפלוגינהו בהכי ומשני לעולם רבי יוסי על המזיק ס"ל וחשיב בעל דבורים מזיק אע"ג שסמך בהיתר כיון שעשה קצת שלא כהוגן בסמיכתו ורבנן נמי הוו מודו ליה בהך סברא אי הוו סברי דדבורים מזקי לחרדל אלא דס"ל דדבורים לא מזקי לחרדל ולכך מרחיק בעל החרדל וכמסקנא זו יש לפרש תחלת הסוגיא לדברי המקשה דפריך ואי לא סמיך היכי משכחת לה דבשלמא אי סמיך (ד) כדמסקינן השתא ולא כמו שפי' לפ"ה שיחלקו (ה) דלרבנן הוו דבורים כמו ירק כיון שנסמכו בהיתר אע"ג שגם הם מזיקין לחרדל כשיבא ור' יוסי מתיר לסמוך החרדל מפני שבעל הדבורים עשה קצת שלא כהוגן: (לעיל) **וסבר** ר' יוסי על המזיק כו'. לקמן על מקומה הוה ליה לאקשויי אלא משום דאיצטריך ליה לפרש הכא דסבר רבי יוסי דעל המזיק להרחיק את עצמו אסקוה לכולה מילתא הכא ובלוקח דהכא אי אפשר לפרשו כפירוש רבינו חננאל דפי' באדם שלוקח משרה וטוענין ללוקח דא"כ למה ירחיק המשרה כשיבא שם ירק כיון שטוענין לו שהמוכר קנה סמיכה זו אלא צריך לפרש בלוקח כמו שפירש בקונטרס או כר"י בר' מרדכי כך פי' ר"י כל הסוגיא לפי שיטת רש"י וקשה לו מה הוצרך לחלק בדוחק בין לוקח דאילן ללוקח דמשרה ועוד דלמה המתין להביא משנה זו דמשרה וירק באחרונה המוקדמין במשנתנו ועוד דקתני בתוספתא (פ"א) רבי יוסי מתיר בחרדל שאומר לו כדרך שעשית בתוך שלך כך אני עושה בתוך שלי משמע דבעל דבורים סמך תחלה ומפרש רבינו תם ורבינו חננאל דהכי גרסינן אלא אמר רבינא קסברי רבנן על המזיק להרחיק את עצמו והשתא הדר ביה מכל שינויי דלעיל דודאי בכולהו מודה רבא דכי ליכא כותל או ירק דסמיך משום דקא סברי רבנן דדוקא על המזיק להרחיק את עצמו דהיינו כי איכא דבר הניזוק אבל כי ליכא דבר הניזוק לא מקרי הסומך מזיק ולא אסר רבא לסמוך אפי' לרבנן אלא דוקא בור משום טעמא דכל מרא ומרא דקא מחית מרפית לארעאי ולהכי חשוב הסומך מזיק אפילו כי ליכא בור וכיון דלרבנן נמי סמיך אתי שפיר פלוגתייהו כדפרישית לעיל אליבא דאביי ולכך הדר ביה ולא מוקי בלוקח וכגון שסמך בעל דבורים תחלה משום דא"כ לא היה מתיר ר"י לסמוך לבעל החרדל כיון דבעל הדבורים לא עשה כלל שלא כהוגן ודוקא דסמיך בלא לוקח שעשה קצת שלא כהוגן בעל הדבורים מתיר רבי יוסי לבעל החרדל לסמוך כדפרישית לעיל ולפי זה אתי שפיר דלמסקנא זו לא נצטרך לחלק בין לוקח האילן ללוקח משרה ולהכי המתין נמי כדי להביא מתניתין דמשרה משום דמינה צריך לחזור מכל שינויי דלעיל ואתי נמי שפיר דמיירי שסמך נמי בעל דבורים תחלה כמו שמוכח בתוספתא:

רבינו גרשום

ואי לא סמיך. היכי משכחת לה דיכולין אלו לטעון הכי זה כנגד זה אנא סמיכנא ואת הרחק והלא אין סומכין אפי' כי ליכא עדיין היזקא לחבריה אלא מדיכולין לטעון הכי ש"מ דסמיך. לא לעולם לא סמיך והכא מאי טעמא סמיך **בלוקח** שלקח מן אחד מקום שלקח מן השדה לקח שאר מקום השדה והכניס שם דבורים ומש"ה לא מצי מעכבי ליה לטעמיה דר' יוסי דבעל חרדל טעין אנא לא מרחקנא דאתינא מכח המוכר דסמך ברשות בתוך שלו. אבל את הרחק את דבורך דמזיקי לחרדלאי. ובעל דבורים טעין את מזקת לי טפי מדאנא מזיקנא לך: **אי** הכי כתרצת בלוקח **מאי טעמא דפליגי רבנן** עליה דר' יוסי דמחייבי להרחיק החרדל הואיל ולוקח הוא וברשות סמך. **ועוד** קושיא אחריתי כיון דאוקמת לה בלוקח מאי טעמא מתיר ר' יוסי בחרדל לחודיה ומודה לרבנן במשרה וירק נמי עלייהו **במשרה וירק** דלא צריך להרחיק הואיל דלוקח הוא וברשות סמך המוכר המשרה והירק והשומן. לעולם בלוקח ומאי טעמא דרבנן דאמרי מרחיקין חרדל ולא סמיך משום **דסבירא** להו דעל המזיק רמי **להרחיק עצמו** שלא יזיק אע"ג דברשות סמך דמתוך ששורין פיהם מחריפות החרדל חוזרות ואוכלות את הדובשן. ומקשי' **מכלל דר' יוסי** פליג עלייהו **סבר על הניזק להרחיק** דיכול לומר מזיק לניזק הרחק עצמך ממני שלא תזוק ולהכי מתיר בחרדל ודבורים א"כ **מאי שנא** משרה וירק דלא פליג על רבנן כי היכי דפליג בחרדל. **אלא** ודאי מסתברא **דר' יוסי סבר** דעל **המזיק** רמי **להרחיק** דלא סמיך כרבנן וכי תימא א"כ מאי טעמא דר' יוסי דמתיר גבי חרדל לחודיה לסמוך ופליג עלייהו אמשרה וירק משום **דהכי קאמר להו ר' יוסי לרבנן בשלמא** להנך תרתי **במשרה** ושומין מודינא לכו דעל המזיק להרחיק משום דהן מזיקין את הירק ואת הבצלים והם לא מזקי למשרה ושומין אבל גבי **חרדל ודבורים** דזה מזיק זה וזה מזיק זה פליגנא עלייכו דלא צריך חד מינייהו להרחיק טפי מחבריה ואמרי ליה **רבנן** לר' יוסי ל"ש בין חרדל למשרה וירק דכולן מזיקין ולא ניזוקין דחרדל מזיק לדבורים מתוך חריפות החרדל דאכלי דבורים מכחשו הדבש אבל **דבורים לא מזקי לחרדל** אמאי אמרת **אי משום בינתא** (בעתא בצתא) גרעינין דחרדל ליכא למיחש דאכלי ליה דבורים דכיון דהן דקין מאד **לא משכחי להו** דבורים **ואי בטרפא** כלומר אם תאמר שאוכלין העלין של חרדל מאי איכפת ליה **הדר פארי**. חוזר וגדל ולהכי סבירא להו גבי חרדל ודבורין כגון משרה וירק: **וזה נוטע בתוך שלו.** אע"ג דמזיק לבור של חבירו דאי בעי בעל הבור דהוי ניזק להרחיק ירחיק דהאי לא יטע בתוך שלו אע"ג דמזיק ליה אלמא דסבר ר' יוסי דעל הניזק להרחיק וכי תימא א"כ מאי טעמא מודה לרבנן במשרה וירק דמסברי דעל המזיק רמי לא תימא מודה להו אלא **אלא לעולם ר' יוסי** ודאי [ס"ל] **על הניזק** להרחיק את עצמו: **אלא לדבריהם דרבנן קאמר לדידי** אפי' משרה וירק נמי לא צריך להרחיק משום דסבירא לי דעל הניזק להרחיק **אלא לדידכו** וכו':

מסורת הש"ס

א) לקמן כה., ב) שייך לע"א, ג) מזיק.

הגהות הב"ח

(א) תוס' ד"ה ואי לא וכו' להרחיק את עצמו כל הרחקות: (ב) בא"ד לאקשויי דברייתא: (ג) בא"ד ד"ה וא"ל ד"ה וסבר ואח"כ ד"ה מכלל וכו' וג' דבורים אלו הד"א ואח"כ צ"ל ד"ה לגלוגי: (ד) בא"ד אי סמיך פליגי כדמסקינן וכו': (ה) בא"ד שיחלקו בזה דלרבנן כצ"ל:

ליקוטי רש"י

מכותלו של חבירו. כותל לבנים של טיט הבנוי על גבי קרקע ולא בכותל קאי השתא. **זרעים.** קשין לכותל כדמפרש בגמ'. **ואת המחרישה.** מרפה את יסודו ונופל. **מי רגלים.** ממסמסין את הלבנים שהן של טיט יבש. **ריחים.** קשין לכותל שמנידין את הקרקע בגלגול מכתשו. **מן השכב.** היא הריחים התחתונה. **הרכב.** היא העליונה הרוכבת על זו והיא קלה טפח מן התחתונה. **ואת התנור. שלשה מן הכליא.** תנור כלי חרס הוא שרוף בכבשן כשאר קדירות ופיו למעלה והוא לקובעו בארץ עושה בנין של טיט ואבנים שיהיו לו לבסיס ומושיבין אותו עליו שלא יטנפנו שוליו מחמת קרקע ואותו בנין עשוי בשיפוע רחב מלמטה וקצר מלמעלה מחמת התנור תחתונה קרוי כליא ועליונו קרוי שפה כלומר שפת הכליא שפה שלה ולפי שהבל של תנור קשה לכותל צריך להרחיקו [לעיל יז.]. **לא יטע אדם אילן סמוך לשדה.** בקלה שדהו סמוך לשדה חבירו. כדי שלא תלך מחרישתו בשדה חבירו. דרך שדה חבירו [רשב"ם לקמן פג.]. **סמוך לשדה.** בין שדה לבין שדה האילן [לקמן כו.]. **כדי עבודת הכרם.** דבכרם של ארבע אמות [לעיל ב.]. **דמפסיק צונמא.** שן סלע מבדיל [גיטין כב.]. **צונמא.** עומא גלגון ארמי סלע [בראשית מא, כג ונדה ח.]. אבן [רשב"ם לקמן פט.]. **מן הבור.** שהשרשין מתפשטין ונוקבין בכותלי הבור וממלאים את הקרקע והכותלים נופלים [לקמן קיז.]. **לגלוגי חרדלא.** פרחי חרדלי [לקמן כה.].

learned in a Mishnah:[10] אַף עַל – רַבִּי יוֹסֵי אוֹמֵר – R' YOSE SAYS: פִּי שֶׁהַבּוֹר קוֹדֶמֶת לָאִילָן לֹא יָקוֹץ – EVEN IF THE PIT WAS THERE BEFORE THE TREE, HE [the owner of the tree] DOES NOT have to CUT it down. שֶׁזֶּה חוֹפֵר בְּתוֹךְ שֶׁלּוֹ – FOR just as THIS ONE MAY DIG a pit IN HIS [PROPERTY], וְזֶה נוֹטֵעַ בְּתוֹךְ שֶׁלּוֹ – THE OTHER ONE MAY PLANT a tree IN HIS [PROPERTY] (there is no prohibition against planting a tree even where it is liable to damage the pit of one's neighbor). From this Mishnah it is evident that, according to R' Yose, the responsibility for preventing damage rests not upon the hazard's owner, but upon the threatened party.[11] – ? –

The Gemara therefore changes its explanation of R' Yose's view:

אֶלָּא לְעוֹלָם – **Rather, the truth is** that רַבִּי יוֹסֵי עַל הַנִּיזָּק סְבִירָא לֵיהּ – **R' Yose is of the opinion** that the responsibility for preventing damage rests **upon the threatened party.** Hence, in fact, R' Yose holds that it is permitted to place a flax pool near the vegetables of a neighbor. The reason he disputes the Rabbis' position only in the case of the mustard plants and bees is as follows: וּלְדִבְרֵיהֶם דְּרַבָּנָן קָאָמַר לְהוּ – **[R' Yose] is replying** to the Rabbis **in accordance with the Rabbis' own view** (viz. the responsibility for preventing damage rests upon the hazard's owner). לְדִידִי – R' Yose says to the Rabbis: **"In my opinion,** עַל הַנִּיזָּק לְהַרְחִיק אֶת עַצְמוֹ – **it is the responsibility of the threatened party to distance his property** from a hazard, וַאֲפִילוּ מִשְׁרָה וְיַרְקָא לֹא בָּעֵי רַחוּקֵי – **and** therefore **even** in the case of **a flax pool and vegetables, distancing** the hazard (the flax pool) **is not required.** אֶלָּא לְדִידְכוּ – **But according to you,** דְּאָמְרִיתוּ עַל הַמַּזִּיק – **who say** that the responsibility for preventing damage rests **upon the hazard's owner,** תֵּינַח מִשְׁרָה וְיַרְקָא – your ruling is **in order** with regard to the case of **a flax pool and vegetables,** דְּהָנֵי מַזְּקֵי הָנֵי – **for these** (flax pools) **damage these** (vegetables), וְהָנֵי לֹא מַזְּקֵי הָנֵי – **while these** (vegetables) **do not damage these** (flax pools);[12] אֶלָּא חַרְדָּל וּדְבוֹרִים – **but** regarding the case of **mustard** plants **and bees,** תַּרְוַויְהוּ מַזְּקֵי אַהֲדָדֵי – where **each is harmful to the other,** even you should concede that no distancing is required!"[13]

The Gemara gives the Rabbis' response:

וְרַבָּנָן – **And the Rabbis** hold that דְּבוֹרִים לְחַרְדָּל לֹא מַזְּקֵי לֵיהּ – **bees do not damage mustard** plants. אִי בְּבִינְתָא – **As far as the** mustard **seeds are concerned,**

NOTES

10. Below, 25b. The first part of this Mishnah records the view of the Rabbis that a tree must be distanced at least twenty-five *amos* from a neighbor's pit (lest its roots damage the pit), and if the tree was planted after the pit had been dug it must be cut down. The Gemara here cites the second part of the Mishnah, in which R' Yose's dissenting view is recorded.

11. As mentioned several times above, R' Yose holds that it is not the hazard owner's responsibility to prevent damage from occuring except where the damage is direct [גִּירֵי דִּידֵיהּ, *his arrows*]. The Gemara, therefore, can draw a parallel between the case of planting a tree near a pit and the three cases of the Mishnah under discussion insofar as none of them fall into the category of גִּירֵי דִּידֵיהּ, *his arrows.*

12. [Since the damage is one-sided, and we are assuming that it is the hazard owner's responsibility to prevent damage from occurring, you (the Rabbis) are right in saying that the flax pool must be distanced.]

13. [The problem raised above (18a end of note 32) is resolved with the present approach that the opinion of R' Yose, as it is recorded in the Mishnah, assumes the view of the Sages.]

לָא מַשְׁכַּחַת לֵיהּ – **[the bees] cannot find them.** אִי בְּטַרְפָּא – **And as far as the leaves are concerned,** even if the bees eat them the damage is not significant, הָדַר פָּארֵי – for **they grow back.**[1]

The Mishnah said:

וְלֹא נִבְרֶכֶת הַכּוֹבְסִין וכו׳ – NOR A LAUNDERER'S POOL **etc.** A person may not dig a launderer's pool within three *tefachim* of the wall of his neighbor's pit.

The Gemara qualifies this ruling:

אָמַר רַב נַחְמָן אָמַר רַבָּה בַּר אֲבוּהַ – **Rav Nachman said in the name of Rabbah bar Avuha:** לֹא שָׁנוּ אֶלָּא מִן הַמְּחַמְּצָן – **They did not teach** that a distance of three *tefachim* is sufficient **except from a soaking pool,** אֲבָל מִן הַנַּדְיָין אַרְבַּע אַמּוֹת – **but from a scrubbing pool** a distance of **four** ***amos*** is required.[2]

The Gemara adduces support for Rav Nachman's ruling by contrasting our Mishnah with a Baraisa:

תַּנְיָא נַמִּי הָכִי – **This was also taught in the** following **Baraisa:** נִבְרֶכֶת הַכּוֹבְסִין אַרְבַּע אַמּוֹת – A LAUNDERER'S POOL must be distanced at least FOUR *AMOS* from the wall of a neighbor's pit. וְהָא אֲנַן תְּנַן שְׁלֹשָׁה טְפָחִים – **But we have learned in** our **Mishnah** that the required distance is only **three** ***tefachim***?! אֶלָּא לָאו שְׁמַע מִינָּהּ כִּדְרַב נַחְמָן – **Surely,** one can **learn from this** that, **as Rav Nachman** stated, our Mishnah refers only to a soaking pool. The Baraisa, which requires a distance of four *amos,* refers to a scrubbing pool.

An alternative version of the previous discussion:

וְאִיכָּא דְּרָמֵי לְהוּ מִירְמֵי – **According to others,** at first **a contradiction was noted** between the Mishnah and the Baraisa as follows: תְּנַן – **We learned in our Mishnah** נִבְרֶכֶת הַכּוֹבְסִין שְׁלֹשָׁה טְפָחִים – that A LAUNDERER'S POOL must be distanced THREE *TEFACHIM* from the wall of a neighbor's pit. וְהָתַנְיָא אַרְבַּע אַמּוֹת – **But in a Baraisa it was taught** that FOUR *AMOS* are required! אָמַר רַב נַחְמָן אָמַר רַבָּה בַּר אֲבוּהַ – And in response to this problem, **Rav Nachman said in the name of Rabbah bar Avuha:** לָא קַשְׁיָא – **This poses no difficulty.** כָּאן מִן הַמְּחַמְּצָן – **Here** [our Mishnah] the reference is to distancing measured **from a soaking pool;** כָּאן מִן הַנַּדְיָין – whereas **here** [the Baraisa] the reference is to distancing measured **from a scrubbing pool.**

The Gemara quotes a Baraisa that explicitly supports Rav Nachman's contention that the distance of three *tefachim* applies only to a soaking pool:

רַב חִיָּיא בְּרֵיהּ דְּרַב אַוְיָא מַתְנֵי לָהּ בְּהֶדְיָא – **Rav Chiya the son of Rav Avya taught** a Baraisa that states **this** qualification **explicitly:** אֶלָּא אִם כֵּן הִרְחִיק מִשְּׂפַת מְחַמְּצָן וְלַכּוֹתֶל שְׁלֹשָׁה טְפָחִים – One may not dig [a launderer's pool] near the pit of a neighbor UNLESS ONE DISTANCES THE EDGE OF THE SOAKING POOL THREE *TEFACHIM* FROM THE WALL of the pit.

The Mishnah stated:

וְסָד בְּסִיד – A person may not dig a pit etc. unless he distances it three *tefachim* from the wall of his neighbor's pit AND APPLIES LIME to its walls.

The Gemara inquires as to the correct text of our Mishnah:

אִיבַּעְיָא לְהוּ – **They asked:** וְסָד בְּסִיד תְּנַן – **Do we learn** "*AND* HE APPLIES LIME," אוֹ דִילְמָא אוֹ סָד בְּסִיד תְּנַן – **or do we learn** "*OR* HE APPLIES LIME"? Is the application of lime required in addition to distancing the pit, or is it an alternative option?[3]

The Gemara attempts to decide this question:

פְּשִׁיטָא דְּוְסָד בְּסִיד תְּנַן – **It is obvious that we learn** "*AND* HE APPLIES LIME," דְּאִי סַלְקָא דַּעְתָּךְ דְּאוֹ סָד בְּסִיד תְּנַן – **for if you should think that we learn "*or* he applies lime,"** אִם כֵּן לִיעַרְבִינְהוּ וְלִיתְנִינְהוּ – **if so, they** [the first two clauses of the Mishnah] **should be combined and taught together,** for the text in the second clause is certainly "*or* he applies lime."[4] From the

NOTES

1. **In conclusion:**

A. The dispute between the Sages and R' Yose:

The Sages hold that it is the responsibility of the hazard's owner to prevent damage from occurring. Hence, in their view, in all the three cases of this Mishnah, the owner of the hazard (flax pool, leeks, mustard plants) is required to distance it from the threatened object (vegetables, onions and beehives respectively). According to **R' Yose** there is no obligation to distance any of the hazards mentioned in this Mishnah. His reasoning is that it is up to the threatened party to move his property out of harm's way. (In the case of the mustard plants and bees, R' Yose maintains that there is an additional basis for leniency: viz. bees and mustard plants are mutually injurious.)

[R' Yose agrees, however, that it is forbidden to cause *direct* damage, e.g. to dig a pit where it is liable to damage the pit of a neighbor.]

B. The dispute between Abaye and Rava:

Abaye and Rava disagree, regarding certain situations in which it is forbidden to place a hazard near the property of a neighbor (e.g. flax pool and vegetables, according to the Rabbis; two pits, according to both R' Yose and the Rabbis), as to whether the restriction applies even before the object liable to be damaged is present. **Abaye** rules that this is permitted while **Rava** rules that it is forbidden.

[According to the *first* version of the dispute between Abaye and Rava, Abaye's permit is limited to cases where it is unlikely that the object liable to be damaged will be installed on the other side of the boundary. According to the *second* version, Rava's restriction is limited to cases where it is likely that the object liable to be damaged will be installed.]

C. R' Yose's view according to Rava:

There are three instances of damage:

(1) Where the damage is not direct even to a vulnerable object already in place (e.g. planting a tree in proximity to a pit; installing a flax pool in proximity to vegetation): In such a case, R' Yose does not require distancing. Therefore, Rava's restriction certainly does not apply as far as R' Yose's view is concerned.

(2) Where the damage is direct to a vulnerable object that is in place, but does not otherwise damage the adjacent property (according to most views, an example of this is the introduction of olive refuse, which is damaging to a wall): Regarding such a case, even according to Rava, R' Yose requires distancing only *after* the vulnerable object is present (*Tosafos* et al; cf. *Meiri,* who holds that the installation of such a hazard, even before the vulnerable property is in place, is classified as *"his arrows"* according to Rava).

(3) Where the damage affects the adjacent property even in the absence of the vulnerable object (e.g. digging a pit, which weakens the surrounding ground rendering it unfit for the future introduction of pits): In such a case Rava's restriction certainly applies even with regard to R' Yose's view.

[It should be noted that, according to *Tosafos* (et al.), the Gemara concludes that Rava's restriction applies *only* in the case of digging a pit. This is based on their alternative version of the text to 18b — see ibid. note 3, *Tosafos* ibid. ד״ה וסבר.]

D. A hazard that was installed legally:

There is a dispute between Rishonim as to whether a hazard's owner is required to remove the hazard once vulnerable property is in harm's way even if the hazard was installed legally (e.g. the case of a buyer — see 18a and 18b). According to *Rashi's* understanding of the Gemara 18b, the hazard must be removed even in such circumstances (with the exception of a tree — see 18b note 5); whereas according to *Tosafos* et al., there is no such requirement.

2. Launderers used two pools: one in which the clothing is left to soak in cleaning agents for a day or two, and one in which the clothing is then scrubbed. A scrubbing pool must be kept at a greater distance than a soaking pool from a neighbor's pit, because water from a scrubbing pool splashes to considerable distances (*Rashi*).

3. See note 4 to Mishnah 17a.

4. In the second clause of our Mishnah, which begins "Olive refuse, manure, etc.," the ruling is that one must *either* distance the harmful substance *or* coat the wall with lime (see there, note 8). If the ruling of our clause, which begins "One may not dig a pit etc.," is the same, the Mishnah would have combined them into one clause, thereby obviating the need to repeat the same ruling (*Rashi*).

לא משכחת ליה אי בטרפא הדר פארי: ולא נברכת הכובסין וכו': אמר רב נחמן אמר רבה בר אבוה [א]לא שנו אלא מן המחמצן [ב]אבל מן הנדיין ד' אמות תניא נמי הכי נברכת הכובסין ד' אמות והא אנן תנן ג' טפחים אלא לאו ש"מ כדרב נחמן ש"מ ואיכא דרמי להו מירמי תנן נברכת הכובסין ג' טפחים והתניא ארבע אמות אמר רב נחמן אמר רבה בר אבוה לא קשיא כאן מן המחמצן כאן מן הנדיין רב חייא בריה דרב אויא מתני לה בהדיא אלא אם כן הרחיק משפת מחמצן ולכותל ג' טפחים: וסד בסיד: איבעיא להו וסד בסיד תנן או דילמא או סד בסיד תנן [ג]פשיטא דוסד בסיד תנן דאי סלקא דעתך דאו סד בסיד תנן אם כן ליערבינהו וליתנינהו דילמא משום דלא דמי האי היזיקא להאי היזיקא רישא היזיקא (א) דמתונא סיפא היזיקא דהבלא ת"ש רבי יהודה אומר סלע הבא בידים זה חופר בורו מכאן וזה חופר בורו מכאן זה מרחיק ג' טפחים וסד בסיד וזה מרחיק ג' טפחים וסד בסיד טעמא דבא בידים הא לא בא בידים לא ה"ה דאף על גב דלא בא בידים נמי סד בסיד ובא בידים איצטריכא ליה סד"א כיון דבא בידים ליבעי רווחא טפי קמ"ל: מרחיקין את הגפת ואת הזבל ואת המלח ואת (ב) הסלעים וכו': תנן התם [ד]במה טומנין ובמה אין טומנין אין טומנין לא בגפת ולא בזבל ולא במלח ולא בסיד ולא בחול בין לחין בין יבשין מאי שנא הכא דקתני סלעים ולא קתני חול ומאי שנא התם דקתני חול ולא קתני סלעים אמר רב יוסף לפי שאין דרכן של בני אדם להטמין בסלעים אמר ליה אביי וכי דרכן של בני אדם להטמין בגיזי צמר ולשונות של ארגמן דתניא [ה]טומנין בגיזי צמר ובציפי צמר ובלשונות של ארגמן ובמוכין ואין מטלטלין אותן [ו]אלא אמר אביי [א]יגיד עליו ריעו תנא הכא סלעים וה"ה לחול תנא התם חול והוא הדין לסלעים א"ל רבא אי יגיד עליו ריעו ליתנינהו לכולהו בחדא וליתני חדא מינייהו באידך (ג) וה"ה לאידך אלא אמר רבא הכא היינו טעמא דלא קתני סלעים משום דמשתכי לה לקדרה הכא היינו טעמא דלא קתני חול משום דמחממי חיים ומקררי קריר והא תני רבי אושעיא חול התם במתונא תנא דידן נמי ליתני ולוקמיה במתונא הא תנא ליה אמת המים אטו מי לא קתני אמת המים וקתני נברכת הכובסין הנהו צריכי דאי תנא אמת המים משום דקביעא אבל נברכת הכובסין דלא קביעא אימא לא ואי תנא נברכת הכובסין משום דקוו וקיימי אבל אמת המים לא צריכא: מרחיקין את הזרעים ואת המחרישה וכו': זרעים תיפוק ליה משום מחרישה במפולת יד מחרישה ותיפוק ליה משום זרעים בחורש לאילנות ותיפוק ליה משום מיא [ז]תנא בארץ ישראל קאי דכתיב [ב]למטר השמים תשתה מים למימרא דזרעים

רש"י

לא משכחת ליה. הדבורה לפי שהוא טמון בשרביטו: ואי בטרפא. ואם יאכל העלה: הדר פארי. חוזר ולומח: מן המחמצן. נברכת ששורין בו את הבגדים יום או יומים בלואת כלבים עד שמחמילין ומסריחין: אבל מן הנדיין. נברכת שכובסין ומשפשפין בה מתוך שהמים נתזין למרחוק לריך להרחיק ד' אמות: ה"ג או סד בסיד תנן. כלומר או ירחיק או סד: ליערבינהו. לתרתי בבי רישא ומליעתא דהתם או סד בסיד תנן אלא מדלא ערבינהו ש"מ דברישא וסד בסיד תנן דבעינן תרוייהו הרחקה וסיד: בא בידים אצטריך. למנקט ליה לתנא ואע"ג דה"ה ללא בא בידים: במה טומנין. את החמין בשבת דאמור רבנן דאסור להטמין בדבר המוסיף הבל והתם מפרש טעמא גזירה שמא יטמין ברמץ: לשונות של ארגמן. למר לבוע ואחר כך חזרו והחליקוהו במסרק ועשוי לשונות: וכי דרכן להטמין בהן. ואפ"ה איירי בהו רבנן: ציפי צמר. לאחר שסרקו ונפלו במסרק: ובמוכין. של שחקי בגדים שהסורק מוליא מבגדי הלמר בקולים: ואין מטלטלין אותם. שהן מוקלים למלאכת בגדים: ה"ג אי יגיד עליו ריעו ליתנינהו לכולהו בחדא וליתני חדא מינייהו באידך ולימא כו'. ליתנינהו לכולהו. כל הנך משום הבלא בחדא או כאן או אצל שבת: הנך משום דמשתכי לה לקדירה. שמשברין את הקדירה כך שמעתי כאן ובכל מקום שמעתיו שמעלה חלודה: דמחממי חיים. כשנותנין בו דבר חם הוא מתחמם וגבי הטמנה מחמימי הוא אבל גבי כותל קריר: והתנא רבי אושעיא. להרחקות דמתני' בתוספתא שלו (ד) וקאמר חול גבייהו: במתונא. אבל היזק לחלות שנאה ובחול לח ולא אבל היזק הבל: נברכת כובסין. לא קביעא כאמת המים שאמת המים (ה) עשויין להיות שם עולמית אבל זו הכובס פעמים שמשתנה לאומנות אחרת: דקוו וקיימי. וליחלוחן קשה יותר משל מים חיים: תיפוק ליה משום מחרישה. שהרי חרשו תחילה ואפי' לא זרע (ו) ליה תנא לי' מרחיקין: במפולת יד. שזרעו בלא חרישה חופר במרה ואינו מעמיק כעומק המחרישה: ותיפוק ליה משום זרעים. שפעמים חורשין ואין זורעים והא קתני זרעים: בחורש לאילנות. שיש שם אילנות מימים רבים ובא לחרוש תחתיהם להשביחן: ותיפוק ליה משום מיא. שצריך להשקותן תמיד וכיון דלאו אפשר לזרעים בלא מים למה ליה למתנינהו הא תנא ליה היזק דליחלות אצל כותל:

תוספות

בא בידים אין לא בא בידים לא. ה"ג ר"ש אלמא או סד בסיד תנן דדוקא בא בידים בעי הרחקה וסיד ומשני הוא הדין לא בא ובא בידים אילטריך ליה כו' ויש ספרים דלא גרסי האי דיוקא אלא משני בא בידים שאני ודקארי לה מאי קארי כו' ואין נראה דהיכי בעי למיפשט וסד בסיד תנן הא איכא למיבעי ההיא דרבי יהודה גופיה אי תרווייהו בעי אי לאו כיון דהשתא סבר דאין חילוק בין בא בידים ללא בא:

משום דמשתכי. פי' הקונטרס (ז) דמשברין הקדירה אין דרך להטמין בהן ואם תאמר אכתי תיקשי וכי דרך להטמין בגיזי למר כדפריך לעיל וי"ל דלעיל הוה בעי למימר דאין דרך להטמין בסלעים לפי שההבל יולא מבין הסלעים ואינו מתקיים ואעפ"כ לפעמים טומנין בהן להכי פריך שפיר מגיזי למר דתני לה משום דלפעמים טומנין בהן אבל הכא קאמר דאין דרך להטמין כלל בהן לפי שמשברין הקדירה והואיל ומילתא דלא שכיח היא כלל לא חש למיתנייה ועוד יש לפרש דכיון דלא שכיחא היא כלל שרי להטמין בהן דבמילתא דלא שכיחא לא גזרו בהו רבנן וכן מנהג שלנו שאנו נוהגין להטמין בסלעים שהאש יולא מהן שקורין קיילו"ש אבל מ"מ קשיא מה שהקשה בקונטר' דבכל מקום הוי שיתוך לשון חלודה כמו באלו מליאות (ב"מ דף כו.) דשתיך טפי ובפ' הבונה (שבת דף קג:) דכיון דמשתכי לא עבדי הכי ובפרק קמא דתענית (דף ח.) אם ראית דור שהשמים משתכין עליו כנחושת ומפרש ר"ת בענין אחר דמשתכי דהבל שלהן מקלקל המאכל ולר"י נראה כפירוש רבינו חננאל דמה שאמר להרחיקם משום דמשתכי שמלקין את הארץ ומאלידים אותה ומעלין עפר תיחוח כדאמרינן לקמן גבי זרעים ולא משום הבל דאין מוסיפין שום הבל וטומנין בהן ואפילו לפי הספרים דגרסי סלעים היינו טעמא דלא קתני להו התם יש לפרש דהכי קאמר דלהכי לא קתני להו התם משום דטעמא דהכא שלריך להרחיקם לא משום הבל אלא משום דמשתכי וה"ר מרדכי הביא ראיה מירושלמי דגרסי' [ח] התם איתמר (ח) שהסלעים מרתיחין [ז] והכא איתמר שאין הסלעים מרתיחין א"ר יוסי כאן וכאן אין הסלעים מרתיחין אלא מפני שעושים עפר תיחוח ומלקין ארעית הכותל:

דמחממי חיים. והא דאמר בפ' כירה (שבת דף לח: ושם ד"ה ולא) בילה אין טומנין אותה לא בחול ולא באבק דרכים התם בחול שהוחם (ט) מחמת השמש דומיא דאבק דרכים:

המבריך (שייך לע"ב) את הגפן. פירוש גפן יחידי שהוא מושרש בארץ וכופף את הגפן באמלעיתו ומכסהו בקרקע ונשרש שם וקאמר מותר לזרוע את הגלדין דאף על גב שאינו רחוק שלשה טפחים ויונק עם הגפן מתחת הקרקע כיון דמעל הקרקע ליכא עירבובי' שרי כדמוכח בעירובין (דף לג.) ובמסכת כלאים (פ"ז) דזה סומך לגדר מכאן וזה מכאן וא"ת והיכי דמי שזורע לגלדין אי כשהרחיק ג' טפחים מן הגלדין אפילו על גביו נמי ואי בלא הרחיק מן הגלדין נמי לא ואומר ר"י דמיירי כשזורע הגלדין ברחוק ג' (י) טפחים מגפן היולא מן הקרקע מכל לד דליכא ערבוביא למעלה מן הקרקע ומכל מקום אסור לזרוע על גביו מפני שהשרשין נכנסין בתוך הגפן והוי כמרכיב זרעים באילן דאסור ואם תאמר ומאי איריא דנקט גפן אפי' שאר אילן נמי אסור ואומר ר"י דשאר אילנות שהן קשין מותר לזרוע על גביו כנגד השורש דלא חיישינן שיכנס שורש הזרע בתוך האילן שהוא קשה אבל גפן שהוא רך חיישינן והאי [ט] (פירוקא) מלא ר"י בירושלמי בגמרא דהך משנה:

רבינו גרשום

פיסקא לא שנו דבג' טפחים סגי אלא מן המחמצן. אותו מקום ששורין בה בגדי כביסה עם צואת כלבים להכי קרי ליה מחמצן דכי היכי דמניחין את העיסה עד שתתחמץ דלא נגעי בה כך מניחין אלו בגדים דלא נגעו בהו עד שישורו יפה ולהכי סגי ברחוק ג' טפחים דלא אזלי טפי ולא מנתזו מן הכותל: אבל מן הנדיין. מקום שמכבסין הבגדים עצמן בתוך המים ומכין אותם ומנתזין על הכתלים מש"ה צריך להרחיק ד' אמות: איבעיא להו וסד בסיד תנן. דמשמע לבר מג' טפחים כלומר דתרווייהו צריך למיעבד להרחיק ג' טפחים ולסיידי שוב החפירה בסיד או דלמא או סד בסיד תנן דמשמע או ג' טפחים או אמר ליה פשיטא דאו סד בסיד תנן דא"כ דס"ד דוסד בסיד תנן הא בבא אחריתי דקתני מרחיקין את הגפת (כלומר) סד בסיד אי אתרווייהו בבי דסד בסיד ליערבינהו להנהו תרי בבי בחדא לא יחפור אדם כו' ומרחיקין את הגפת כו' וליתנינהו בתרווייהו חד וסד בסיד דמשמע אכולהו ותרי זמני וסד בסיד ל"ל דילמא לעולם אימא לך דתרווייהו וסד בסיד ניגהו והאי דלא עירב להו משום דתרווייהו צריכי דלא דמי היזיקא דרישא להזיקא דסיפא דהזיקא דרישא מחמת מתונא לחלוחית מים דשיח ובורות. והאי היזיקא דסיפא דהבלא הוא דגפת הבל וזבל ומלח כולהו מסקי הבלא ניגהו וקשי טפי ומש"ה צריך למיתנינהו תרווייהו דמחדא לא נפקא אידך ומיהא לא תפשוט. ת"ש זה מרחיק ג' טפחים מכאן כשיעור כותל בורו וסד בסיד הבור וכן נמי אידך וטעמא מאי בעי להרחיק ג' טפחים כל חד וחד ולסוד משום דבא בידים דארעא רפיא היא. אבל לאו בא בידים דהוה צונמא חזקה לעולם לא צריך לסוד בסיד אם ירחיק ג' טפחים אלמא תפשוט מהכא דאו סד בסיד תנן לא לעולם מהא לא תפשוט ה"ה דאפי' לא בא בידים בעי ג' טפחים וסד בסיד ובא בידים איצטריכא ליה כו'. רווחא טפי קמ"ל דלא. ולסוד בסיד קמ"ל דלא: מ"ש גבי מתני' דקתני סלעים משום הבלא ומ"ש גבי הטמנה דמשום הבלא נמי היא וקתני חול ולא סלעים: וא"ל אביי וכי דרכן של בני אדם להטמין בלשונות של ארגמן ואפ"ה קתני להו סלעים נמי אע"ג דאין דרכן

עין משפט נר מצוה

ט א מיי' פ"ט מהלכות שכנים הל' א סמג עשין פב טוש"ע ח"מ סי' קנה סעיף י:
י ב מיי' שם הלכה ה ועי' פי' במ"מ טוש"ע שם סעיף יא:
יא ג מיי' שם הל' א טוש"ע שם סעיף א:
יב ד מיי' פ"ד מהל' שבת הל' א סמג לאוין סה טוש"ע או"ח סי' רנז סעיף ג:
יג ה מיי' וסמג שם טוש"ע א"ח סי' רנט סעיף א:

מסורת הש"ס

א) לעיל יז: ע"ש [תוספתא פ"א], ב) שבת מז:, ג) שם מח., ד) [יבמות לג: וש"נ], ה) [שבת עג: וש"נ], ו) מהרש"ם והחס הכא, ז) מהרש"ם והחס, ח) ס"א פירכא.

הגהות הב"ח

(א) גמ' רישא היזקא דמתונא כצ"ל וכן בסמוך: (ב) שם ואת המלח ואת הסיד ואת הסלעים: (ג) שם וליתני חדא מינייהו באידך ולימא יגיד עליו ריעו אלא אמר רבא: (ד) רש"י ד"ה והתניא וכו' בתוספתא שלו וקתני חול: (ה) ד"ה נברכת וכו' שאמת המים עשוי להיות: (ו) ד"ה תיפוק וכו' לא זרע תנא כצ"ל ותיבת ליה נמחק: (ז) תוס' ד"ה משום וכו' הקונטרס כאן דמשברין את הקדרה ואין: (ח) בא"ד איתמר מפני שהסלעים: (ט) ד"ה דמחממי וכו' שהוא מחמת השמש: (י) ד"ה המבריך וכו' ברחוק ג' נ"ב עי' בפי' הר"ש מס' כלאים פ"ז:

גליון הש"ס

גמ' ואיכא דרמי להו מירמי. כעין זה סוכה [נו ע"א] לב ע"ב וש"נ:

תורה אור השלם

א) יַגִּיד עָלָיו רֵעוֹ מִקְנֶה אַף עַל עוֹלֶה: [איוב לו, לג]
ב) וְהָאָרֶץ אֲשֶׁר אַתֶּם עֹבְרִים שָׁמָּה לְרִשְׁתָּהּ אֶרֶץ הָרִים וּבְקָעֹת לִמְטַר הַשָּׁמַיִם תִּשְׁתֶּה מָּיִם: [דברים יא, יא]

ליקוטי רש"י

סלע הבא בידים. קרקע רך מתכתת מאליו. ובא בידים איצטריכא ליה סד"א וכו'. כלומר הוא הדין אע"ג דלא בא בידים והאי דנקט [בא] בידים רבותא דאשמעינן דאף על גב דבא בידים אין צריך להרחיק אלא שלשה טפחים [לעיל יז:]. במה טומנין. הבא לטמון קדירה ... גפת. פסולת של בית הבד ... גיזי צמר. ... ציפי צמר. ... לשונות. ... ובמוכין. ... יגיד עליו ריעו. ...

לעזי רש"י

קיילו"ש. פירוש אבני חלמיש (עיין רש"י ב"ב דף יח ע"א ד"ה סלעים ורש"י דברים לב, יג).

חשק שלמה על רבינו גרשום א) נ' טפחים או סד בסיד. ב) [מרחיקין את הגפת וכו' ולא כסיד ולא ... כעין דוסד בסיד וכו']:

fact that the Mishnah separates these two clauses, it is evident that the first clause reads *"and* he applies lime."

The Gemara rejects this proof by proposing that even if the ruling in both clauses is identical, they would be separated, for the following reason:

דִּילְמָא מִשּׁוּם דְּלָא דָּמֵי הַאי הֶיזֵּיקָא לְהַאי הֶיזֵּיקָא – **Perhaps** they are separated **because one** type of **damage** (i.e. that discussed in the first clause) **is dissimilar to the other** type of **damage** (i.e. that of the second clause): רֵישָׁא הֶיזֵּיקָא דִּמְתוּנָא – **The former clause** deals with **moisture damage,**[5] סֵיפָא הֶיזֵּיקָא דְּהַבְלָא – while **the latter clause** deals with **heat damage.**[6]

The Gemara makes another attempt to resolve its question: תָּא שְׁמַע – **Come, learn** from the following Baraisa: רַבִּי יְהוּדָה אוֹמֵר – **R' YEHUDAH SAYS:** סֶלַע הַבָּא בְּיָדַיִם – If the **SOIL** between neighboring properties is so soft **THAT** it **COMES** away **IN** one's **HANDS,**[7] the law is that זֶה חוֹפֵר בּוֹרוֹ מִכָּאן – **ONE** neighbor **MAY DIG HIS PIT ON ONE SIDE** וְזֶה חוֹפֵר בּוֹרוֹ מִכָּאן – **AND THE OTHER** neighbor **MAY DIG HIS PIT ON THE OTHER SIDE** provided that זֶה מַרְחִיק שְׁלֹשָׁה טְפָחִים וְסָד בְּסִיד – **THIS ONE DISTANCES** his pit **THREE** ***TEFACHIM*** from the boundary **AND APPLIES LIME** to its walls וְזֶה מַרְחִיק שְׁלֹשָׁה טְפָחִים וְסָד בְּסִיד – **AND THE OTHER ONE** also **DISTANCES** his pit **THREE *TEFACHIM*** from the boundary **AND APPLIES LIME** to its walls. From the fact that the Baraisa specifies soft as opposed to regular soil, the Gemara deduces: טַעְמָא דְּבָא בְּיָדַיִם – **The reason** the Baraisa requires both preventive measures (distancing and lime) **is that it** refers to **[soil]** that **comes** away **in** one's **hands;** הָא לָא בָּא בְּיָדַיִם לֹא – **but** in the case of **[soil] that does not come** away **in** one's **hands,** it is **not** necessary to effect both measures. This proves that the first clause of our Mishnah, which refers to regular soil, mentions the application of lime as an alternative option.

The Gemara rejects this proof as well:

הוּא הַדִּין דְּאַף עַל גַּב דְּלָא בָּא בְּיָדַיִם נַמִּי סָד בְּסִיד – It is possible that this **law** – namely, **one must apply lime** in addition to distancing the pit – **applies even** in the case of **[soil] that does *not* come** away **in** one's **hands.** וּבָא בְּיָדַיִם אִיצְטְרִיכָא לֵיהּ – Yet **it was necessary** for the Baraisa to specify **[soil] that does come** away **in** one's **hands,** for had it not done so סָלְקָא דַּעְתָּךְ אֲמִינָא כֵּיוָן דְּבָא בְּיָדַיִם – **I might have thought** that **since [the soil] comes** away **in** one's **hands,** לִיבָּעֵי רַוְוחָא טְפֵי – **a gap larger** than three *tefachim* **is required.** קָא מַשְׁמַע לָן – **[The Baraisa]** therefore **informs us** that a gap of three *tefachim* suffices even with regard to soil that comes away in one's hands.

The Gemara quotes the next section of the Mishnah:

מַרְחִיקִין אֶת הַגֶּפֶת וְאֶת הַזֶּבֶל וְאֶת הַמֶּלַח[8] וְאֶת הַסְּלָעִים וכו׳ – **OLIVE REFUSE, MANURE, SALT AND** flint **STONES, etc.** [must be kept at a distance of at least three *tefachim* from the brick wall of one's neighbor].

The Mishnah lists these materials together because they are all damaging to a wall in that they generate heat.[9] The Gemara notes discrepancies between this list of materials and a list found elsewhere whose criterion is also the capacity of materials to generate heat:

תְּנַן הָתָם – **We learned elsewhere in a Mishnah:**[10] בַּמֶּה טוֹמְנִין – **WITH WHAT** materials **MAY ONE WRAP** hot foods before the Sabbath, וּבַמֶּה אֵין טוֹמְנִין – **AND WITH WHAT** materials **MAY ONE NOT WRAP** hot foods before the Sabbath? אֵין טוֹמְנִין לֹא בְּגֶפֶת וְלֹא בְּזֶבֶל וְלֹא בְּמֶלַח וְלֹא בְּסִיד וְלֹא בְּחוֹל – **ONE MAY NOT WRAP WITH OLIVE REFUSE, MANURE, SALT, LIME, OR SAND,** בֵּין לַחִין בֵּין יְבֵשִׁין – **WHETHER THEY ARE WET OR DRY.** מַאי שְׁנָא הָכָא דְּקָתָנֵי סְלָעִים וְלָא קָתָנֵי חוֹל – **What is** the explanation for **the difference** between our Mishnah **here, which mentions** flint **stones but not sand,** וּמַאי שְׁנָא הָתָם דְּקָתָנֵי חוֹל וְלָא קָתָנֵי סְלָעִים – **and** the Mishnah **there, which mentions sand but not** flint **stones?**

Rav Yosef addresses the exclusion of flint stones from the Mishnah about wrapping foods:

אָמַר רַב יוֹסֵף – **Rav Yosef said:** לְפִי שֶׁאֵין דַּרְכָּן שֶׁל בְּנֵי אָדָם לְהַטְמִין בִּסְלָעִים – Flint stones are not mentioned in that Mishnah because **it is not the general practice to wrap** food **with** flint **stones.**[11]

Abaye does not accept this answer:

אָמַר לֵיהּ אַבָּיֵי – **Abaye said to [Rav Yosef]:** וְכִי דַּרְכָּן שֶׁל בְּנֵי אָדָם לְהַטְמִין בְּגִיזֵּי צֶמֶר וּלְשׁוֹנוֹת שֶׁל אַרְגָּמָן – **Is it the general practice to wrap** food **with wool shearings or strips**[12] **of purple wool?!** דְּתַנְיָא – Yet, **as it was taught in the** following **Baraisa,** these materials *are* mentioned in that very context: טוֹמְנִין בְּגִיזֵּי צֶמֶר וּבְצִיפֵי צֶמֶר וּבִלְשׁוֹנוֹת שֶׁל אַרְגָּמָן וּבְמוֹכִין – Before the Sabbath **ONE MAY WRAP** food **WITH WOOL SHEARINGS, COMBED WOOL,**[13] **STRIPS OF PURPLE WOOL, OR TUFTS** of wool,[14] וְאֵין מְטַלְטְלִין אוֹתָן – **BUT THEY MAY NOT BE MOVED** on the Sabbath.[15] Given that *these* rarely used materials are mentioned, why are flint stones not mentioned as well?

Having shown that Rav Yosef's answer is inadequate, Abaye advances his own:

אֶלָּא אָמַר אַבָּיֵי – **Rather, Abaye said,** יַגִּיד עָלָיו רֵיעוֹ – The Tanna applies the principle of **"one sheds light on the other."**[16]

NOTES

5. Actually, the prohibition against digging a pit, trench, or vault applies even to one that does not contain water, in which case the damage is caused not by moisture but by the loosening of the earth. Nevertheless, the Mishnah mentions them in an independent clause together with a water channel and launderer's pool (which do contain water), since even if they *were* to contain water a distance of three *tefachim* is sufficient. This is the basis for the Gemara's characterization of the damage referred to in this clause as that of moisture (*Ran* to 17a; cf. *Ritva* ibid., *Shitah Mekubetezes* [in the name of *Raavad*] and *Pnei Shlomo* here).

Of course, according to those commentators who maintain that the first clause applies only to excavations that do contain water, the Gemara's characterization is understood literally (see 17a note 3).

6. The substances listed in the second clause of the Mishnah – olive refuse, manure, etc. – cause damage by generating heat (see 17a note 7).

7. I.e. it can be dug out using bare hands, without any tools *(Rabbeinu Gershom* to 17b).

8. The words וְאֶת הַסִּיד, *and lime,* are inserted by *Bach*, in accordance with the Mishnah's text.

9. See 17a note 7.

10. *Shabbos* 47b. This Mishnah deals with the Rabbinic ban against wrapping foods before the Sabbath with materials that increase the heat of the food. The Gemara (ibid.) explains that this is prohibited so that people will not use glowing coals for this purpose [which could lead to the Biblical violation of stoking coals on the Sabbath] (*Rashi*).

11. For the heat escapes through the gaps between the stones (*Tosafos*).

12. Wool which is dyed purple and then formed into strips through combing (*Rashi*).

13. Wool that has been combed and disentangled (*Rashi*).

14. That are produced by combing worn-out woolen garments (*Rashi*).

15. Since these materials are designated for the manufacture of fabric [which is prohibited on the Sabbath, they are *muktzeh* and may not be moved on the Sabbath] (*Rashi*). [מוּקְצֶה, *muktzeh*, is the term used for a class of objects which in the normal course of events do not stand to be used on the Sabbath or Yom Tov. The Rabbis prohibited the moving of such objects on the Sabbath or Yom Tov. There are several different categories of *muktzeh*. (The Gemara, *Shabbos* 49a, explains how insulation that is *muktzeh* is removed from its position around a pot on the Sabbath.)]

16. Literally: his friend tells about him. This phrase is borrowed from *Job* 36:33.

לא משכחת ליה אי בטרפא הדר פארי: ולא נברכת הכובסין וכו': אמר רב נחמן אמר רבה בר אבוה א) לא שנו אלא מן המחמצן ב) אבל מן הנדיין ד' אמות תניא נמי הכי נברכת הכובסין ד' אמות והא אנן תנן ג' טפחים אלא לאו ש"מ כדרב נחמן ואיכא דרמי להו מירמי תנן נברכת הכובסין ג' טפחים והתניא ארבע אמות אמר רב נחמן אמר רבה בר אבוה לא קשיא כאן מן הנדיין כאן מן המחמצן רב חייא בריה דרב אויא מתני לה בהדיא אלא אם כן הרחיק משפת מחמצן ולכותל ג' טפחים: וסד בסיד: איבעיא להו וסד בסיד תנן או דילמא או סד בסיד תנן פשיטא דוסד בסיד תנן דאי סלקא דעתך דאו סד בסיד תנן אם כן ליערבינהו וליתנינהו דילמא משום דלא דמי האי היזיקא להאי היזיקא רישא היזיקא (א) דמתונא סיפא היזיקא דהבלא ת"ש רבי יהודה אומר סלע הבא בידים זה חופר בורו מכאן וזה חופר בורו מכאן זה מרחיק ג' טפחים וסד בסיד וזה מרחיק ג' טפחים וסד בסיד טעמא דבא בידים הא לא בא בידים לא ה"ה דאף על גב דלא בא בידים נמי סד בסיד ובא בידים איצטריכא ליה סד"א כיון דבא בידים ליבעי רווחא טפי קמ"ל: מרחיקין את הגפת ואת הזבל ואת המלח ואת (ב) הסלעים וכו': תנן התם ד) במה טומנין ובמה אין טומנין אין טומנין לא בגפת ולא בזבל ולא במלח ולא בסיד ולא בחול בין לחין בין יבשין מאי שנא הכא דקתני סלעים ולא קתני חול ומאי שנא התם דקתני חול ולא קתני סלעים אמר רב יוסף לפי שאין דרכן של בני אדם להטמין בסלעים אמר ליה אביי וכי דרכן של בני אדם להטמין בגיזי צמר ולשונות של ארגמן דתניא ה) טומנין בגיזי צמר ובציפי צמר ובלשונות של ארגמן ובמוכין ואין מטלטלין אותן ו) אלא אמר אביי א) יגיד עליו ריעו תנא הכא סלעים וה"ה לחול תנא התם חול והוא הדין לסלעים א"ל רבא אי יגיד עליו ריעו ליתנינהו לכולהו בחדא וליתני חדא מנייהו באידך (ג) וה"ה לאידך אלא אמר רבא התם היינו טעמא דלא קתני סלעים משום דמשתכי לה לקדרה הכא היינו טעמא דלא קתני חול משום דמחמימי חיים ומקרירי קריר והא תני רבי אושעיא חול התם במתונא תנא דידן נמי ליתני ולוקמיה במתונא הא תנא ליה אמת המים אטו מי לא קתני אמת המים וקתני נברכת הכובסין הנהו צריכי דאי תנא אמת המים משום דקביעא אבל נברכת הכובסין דלא קביעא אימא לא ואי תנא נברכת הכובסין משום דקוו וקיימי אבל אמת המים לא צריכא: מרחיקין את הזרעים ואת המחרישה וכו': זרעים תיפוק ליה משום מחרישה במפולת יד מחרישה ותיפוק ליה משום זרעים בחורש לאילנות ותיפוק ליה משום מיא ז) תנא בארץ ישראל קאי דכתיב ב) למטר השמים תשתה מים למימרא דזרעים

רש"י

לא משכחת ליה. הלכך לפי שהוא טמון בשרביטו: ואי בטרפא. ואם יאכל העלה: הדר פארי. חוזר ולומח: מן המחמצן. נברכת ששורין בו את הבגדים יום או יומים בלואת כלבים עד שמחמילין ומסריחין: אבל מן הנדיין. נברכת שכובסין ומשפשפין בה מתוך שהמים נתזין למרחוק לריך להרחיק ד' אמות: ה"ג או סד בסיד תנן. כלומר או ירחיק או סד: ליערבינהו. לתרתי בבי רישא ומליעתא דהתם או סד בסיד תנן אלא מדלא ערבינהו ש"מ דברישא וסד בסיד תנן דבעינן תרויהו הרחקה וסיד: בא בידים אצטריך. למנקט ליה לתנא ולא"ג דס"ד דלא בא בידים: במה טומנין. את החמין בשבת דאמור רבנן דאסור להטמין בדבר המוסיף הבל והתם מפרש טעמא גזירה שמא יטמין ברמץ: לשונות של ארגמן. למר לבוע ואחר כך חזרו והחליקוהו במסרק ועשו לשונות לשונות: וכי דרכן להטמין בהן. ואפ"ה איירי בהו רבנן: ציפי צמר. לאחר שסרקו ונפלו ממסרק: ובמוכין. של שחקי בגדים שהסורק מוליא מבגדי הלמר בקולים: ואין מטלטלין אותם. שהן מוקלים למלאכת בגדים: ה"ג אי יגיד עליו ריעו ליתנינהו לכולהו בחדא וליתני חדא מנייהו באידך וליתא כו'. ליתנינהו לכולהו. כל הנך משום הבלא בחדא או כאן או אלל שבת: הנך משום דמשתכי לה לקדירה. משברין את הקדירה כך שמעתי כאן ובכל מקום שמעתיו מעמלה מלודה: דמחממי חיים. כשטומנין בו דבר חם הוא מתחמם וגבי הטמנה מחממי הוא אבל גבי כותל קריר: והתניא רבי אושעיא. להרחקות דמתני' בתוספתא שלו (ד) וקאמר חול גבייהו: במתונא. אלל היזק לחלות שנאה ובחול לא ולא אלא היזק הבל: נברכת כובסין. לא קביעא כאמת המים שאמת המים (ה) עשויין להיות שם עולמית אבל זו הכובס פעמים משתנה לאומנות אחרת: דקוו וקיימי. וליחלוחן קשה יותר משל מים שוטפין: תיפוק ליה משום מחרישה. שהרי חרשו תחילה ואפי' לא זרע (ו) ליה תנא לי' מרחיקין: במפולת יד. שזרעו בלא חרישה חופר במרה ואינו מעמיק כעומק המחרישה: ותיפוק ליה משום זרעים. שהם חורשין סופן לזרוע והא קתני זרעים: בחורש לאילנות. שיש שם אילנות מימים רבים ובא לחרוש תחתיהם להשביחן: ותיפוק ליה משום מיא. שלריך להשקותן תמיד וכיון דאי אפשר לזרעים בלא מים למה ליה למתניינהו הא תנא ליה היזק דליחלות אלל כותל: לגדדין

תוספות

בא בידים אין לא בא בידים לא. אלמא או סד בסיד תנן ה"ג ר"ח דלדוקא בא בידים בעי הרחקה וסיד ומשני הוא הדין לא בא ובא בידים איצטריך ליה כו' ויש ספרים דלא גרסי האי דיוקא אלא משני בא בידים שאני ודקארי לה מאי קארי כו' ואין נראה להכי בעי למיפשט וסד בסיד תנן הא איכא למיבעי ההיא דרבי יהודה גופיה אי תרוייהו בעי אי לאו כיון דהשתא סבר דלאין חילוק בין בא בידים ללא בא:

משום דמשתכי. פי' הקונטרס (ז) דמשברין הקדירה אין דרך להטמין בהן ואם תאמר אמאי תיקשי וכי דרך להטמין בגיזי למר דפריך לעיל וי"ל דלעיל הוה בעי למימר דאין דרך להטמין בסלעים לפי שההבל יולא מבין הסלעים ואינו מתקיים ואעפ"כ לפעמים טומנין בהן להכי פריך שפיר מגיזי למר דאתי לה משום דלפעמים טומנין בהן אבל הכא קאמר דאין דרך להטמין כלל בהן לפי שמשברין הקדירה והוליל ומילתא דלא שכיחא היא כלל לא חש למיתנייה ועוד יש לפרש דכיון דלא שכיחא היא כלל שרי להטמין בהן דבמילתא דלא שכיחא לא גזרו בהו רבנן וכן מנהג שלנו שאנו נוהגין להטמין בסלעים שההבל יולא מהן שקורין קיילו"ש אבל מ"מ קשיא מה שהקשה הקונט' דבכל מקום הוי שיתוך לשון מלודה כמו בלאו מליאות (ב"מ דף כו.) דשתיך טפי ובפ' הבונה (שבת דף קג:) דכיון דמשתכי לא עבדי הכי ובפרק קמא דתענית (דף ח.) אם ראית דור שהשמים משתכין עליו כנחושת ומפרש ר"ח בענין אחר דמשתכי דהבל שלהן מקלקל המאכל ולר"י נראה כפירוש רבינו חננאל דמה שאמר להרחיקם משום דמשתכי שמלקין את הארץ ומתלחלחין אותה ומעלין עפר תיחות דלאמרינן לקמן גבי זרעים ולא משום הבל דאין מוסיפין הבל וטומנין בהן ואפילו לפי הספרים דגרסי סלעים היינו טעמא דלא קתני להו התם אע"ג דיש לפרש דהכי קאמר להכי לא קתני להו התם משום דטעמא דהכא שלריך להרחיקם לא משום הבל אלא משום דמשתכי וה"ר מנדכי הביא ראיה מירושלמי דגרסי' (ח) התם ליתמר שהסלעים מרתיחין (ט) והכא ליתמר שאין הסלעים מרתיחין א"ר יוסי כאן וכאן אין הסלעים מרתיחין אלא מפני שעושים עפר תיחות ומלקין ארעית הכותל:

דמחממי חיים. והא דאמר בפ' כירה (שבת דף לח: ושם ד"ה ולא) גבי לא יטמין אותה בחול ולא באבק דרכים לא שהוא (ט) מחממת השמש דומיא דאבק דרכים:

המבריך את הגפן. (שייך לע"ב) פירוש גפן יחידי שהוא מושרש בארץ וכופף את הגפן באמלעיתו ומכסהו בקרקע ונשרש שם וקאמר מותר לזרוע את הלדדין דאף על גב שאינו רחוק שלשה טפחים ויונק עם הגפן מתחת הקרקע כיון דמעל הקרקע ליכא עירבובי' שרי כדמוכח בעירובין (דף נג.) ובמסכת כלאים (פ"ד) דזה סומך לגדר מכאן וזה מכאן וא"ת והיכי דמי שזורע לצדדין אי כשהרחיק ג' טפחים מן הלדדין אפילו על גביו נמי ואי בלא הרחיק מן הלדדין נמי לא ואומר ר"י דמיירי כשזורע הלדדין ברחוק ג' (י) טפחים מגפן היולא מן הקרקע מכל לד דליכא ערבוביא למעלה מן הקרקע ומכל מקום אסור לזרוע על גביו מפני שהשרשין נכנסין בתוך הגפן והוי כמרכיב זרעים באילן דאסור ואם תאמר ומאי איריא דנקט גפן אפי' שאר אילן נמי אסור ואומר ר"י דשאר אילנות שהן קשין מותר לזרוע על גביו כנגד השורש דלא חיישינן שיכנס שורש הזרע בתוך האילן שהוא קשה אבל גפן שהוא רך חיישינן והאי כ) (פירוקא) מלא ר"י בירושלמי בגמרא דהך משנה:

רבינו גרשום

פיסקא לא שנו דבג' טפחים סגי אלא מן המחמצן. אותו מקום ששורין בה בגדי כביסה עם צואת כלבים להכי קרי ליה מחמצן דכי היכי דמניחין את העיסה עד שתתחמץ דלא נגעי בה כך מניחין אלו בגדים דלא נגעו בהו עד שישורו יפה ולהכי סגי ברחוק ג' טפחים דלא אזלי טפי ולא מנתזו מן הכותל: אבל מן הנדיין. מקום שמכבסין הבגדים עצמן בתוך המים ומכין אותם ומנתזין על הכתלים מש"ה צריך להרחיק ד' אמות: איבעיא להו וסד בסיד תנן. דמשמע לבר מג' טפחים כלומר דתרוייהו צריך למיעבד להרחיק ג' טפחים ולסייד שוב החפירה בסיד או דלמא או סד בסיד תנן דמשמע או ג' טפחים א) אמר ליה פשיטא דאו סד בסיד תנן דא"כ דס"ד דוסד בסיד תנן הא בבא אחריתי דקתני מרחיקין את הגפת ב) (כלומר) בבי בסיד אי אתרוייהו בבי דסד בסיד ליערבינהו להנהו תרי בבי כחדא כי יחפור אדם כו' ומרחיקין את הגפת כו' וליתנינהו בתרוייהו חד וסד בסיד וכו' דמשמע אכולהו ותרי זמני וסד בסיד ל"ל דילמא לעולם אימא לך דתרוייהו וסד בסיד נינהו והאי דלא עירב להו משום דתרוייהו צריכי דלא דמי היזקא דרישא להיזקא דסיפא היזק דרישא משום מתונא מחמת לחלוח מים דשיח ובורות. והאי היזקא דסיפא דהבלא הוא דגפת וזבל ומלח כולהו מסקי הבלא נינהו וקשי טפי ומש"ה צריך למיתנינהו תרוייהו דמהדא לא נפקא אידך ומיהא לא תפשוט. ת"ש זה מרחיק ג' טפחים מכאן כשיעור כותל בורו וסד בסיד הבור וכן נמי אידך וטעמא מאי צריך להרחיק ג' טפחים כל חד וחד ולסוד משום דבא בידים דארעא רפיא היא. אבל לאו בא בידים דהוה צונמא חזקה לעולם לא צריך לסוד בסיד אם ירחיק ג' טפחים אלמא תפשוט מהכא דאו סד בסיד תנן לא לעולם מהא לא תפשוט ה"ה דאפי' לא בא בידים בעי ג' טפחים וסד בסיד ובא בידים איצטריכא ליה כו'. רווחא טפי מג' טפחים ולסוד בסיד קמ"ל דלא: מ"ש גבי מתני' דקתני סלעים משום הבלא ומ"ש גבי הטמנה דמשום הבלא נמי היא וקתני חול ולא סלעים: וא"ל אביי וכי דרכן של בני אדם להטמין בלשונות של ארגמן ואפ"ה קתני להו סלעים נמי אע"ג דאין דרכן להטמין ליתנייהו: גיזי צמר והוא צמר הגדל מן הבהמה כמו שהוא. ציפי צמר זהו צמר סרוק ומלובן לצורך צביעה. וי"א ציפי צמר כריכות צמר גדול כדרך שמביאין הסוחרין ממדינתן. ולשונות של ארגמן צמר שאינו טורי שצובעין בארגמן כדי לנסות ורוב צביעתו היה ארגמן. ובמוכין צמר שמסרקין מן הבגדים לאחר שמכבסין אותן: ויגיד עליו רעו. יוכיח עליו כלומר תנא הכי במתני' [סלעים] דמסקא הבלא וה"ה לחול דמסיק הבלא טפי תנא התם גבי שבת חול דאין טומנין משום דקא מבשל בשבת ה"ה לסלעים דמבשלין טפי. ואי יגיד עליו רעו דמשמע תרוייהו ליתנינהו תרוייהו סלעים וחול גבי בור או בחדא מתני' ודיניהן שוין אע"ג דלא כתיבי באידך אלא בחד' מינייהו ודאי אמרי' יגיד עליו [רעו] ויוכיח על משנה זו דה"ה לתרוייהו אלא לאו ש"מ מדלא קתני לה הכי דלא אמרי' תני סלע וה"ה לחול תנא התם חול וה"ה לסלע ואכתי הדר קושין לדוכתא: דמשתבר לה לקדרה. שמשתברין בסלעים הקדרה ולהכי לא תנא אין טומנין בסלעין דלא אתי לאטמוני בגוייהו. וחול אמאי לא תנא הכא גבי כותל משום דזהו מנהג חול דמחמם חמים. כלומר אם מניחין אותם במקום שמתחמם מחמת דבר אחר או מחמת חמה או מחמת אור הכירה מתחמם ומוסיף הבלא להכי אין טומנין שמתחמם מחמת כן: אבל מקרירי קריר. כשהוא מונח במקום קור בגומא מתקרר

עין משפט נר מצוה

ט א מיי' פ"ט מהלכות שכנים הל' א סמג עשין פב טוש"ע ח"מ סי' קנה סעיף י:

י ב מיי' שם הלכה ה וע"פ בה"מ טוש"ע שם סעיף יא:

יא ג מיי' שם הל' א טוש"ע שם סעיף י:

יב ד מיי' פ"ד מהל' שבת הל' א סמג לאוין סה טוש"ע או"ח סי' רנז סעיף ג:

יג ה מיי' וסמג שם טוש"ע א"ח סי' רנט סעיף א:

מסורת הש"ס

א) לעיל יז: ע"ש [תוספתא פ"א], ב) שבת מז., ג) שם מח., ד) [יבמות לא: ושם], ה) [שבת עג: וש"נ], ו) מהרש"ם וכו', ז) מהרש"ם והס"ד, ח) ס"ד פירקא.

הגהות הב"ח

(א) גמ' רישא היזקא דמתונא כצ"ל וכן במשנה: (ב) שם ואת הסלעים: (ג) שם וליתני חדא מנייהו באידך ולימא יגיד עליו ריעו אלא אמר רבא: (ד) רש"י ד"ה והתניא וכו' בתוספתא שלו וקתני חול וכו': (ה) ד"ה נברכת וכו' שאמת המים עשוי להיות: (ו) ד"ה תיפוק וכו' לא זרע תנא כצ"ל ותיבת ליה נמחק: (ז) תוס' ד"ה משום וכו' הקונטרס כאן דמשברין את הקדרה ואין: (ח) בא"ד ליתמר מפני שהסלעים: (ט) ד"ה דמחממי וכו' מחממת השמש: (י) ד"ה המבריך וכו' ברחוק ג' כ"ב עי' בפי' הר"ש מס' כלאים פ"ז:

גליון הש"ס

גמ' ואיכא דרמי להו מירמי. כעין זה סוכה [נח ע"א] לב ע"ב וש"נ:

תורה אור השלם

א) יַגִּיד עָלָיו רֵעוֹ מִקְנֶה אַף עַל עוֹלֶה: [איוב לו, לג]

ב) וְהָאָרֶץ אֲשֶׁר אַתֶּם עֹבְרִים שָׁמָּה לְרִשְׁתָּהּ אֶרֶץ הָרִים וּבְקָעֹת לִמְטַר הַשָּׁמַיִם תִּשְׁתֶּה מָּיִם: [דברים יא, יא]

ליקוטי רש"י

סלע הבא בידים. קרקע רך מתפתת מאליו. ובא בידים איצטריכא ליה סד"א וכו'. כלומר הוא הדין אע"ג דלא בא בידים והאי דנקט [בא] בידים רבותא אשמעינן דאף על גב דבא בידים אין לריך להרחיק טפי משלשה טפחים [לעיל יז:]. במה טומנין. הבא לסלק קדירה מעל גבי כירה ולטומנה בדבר אחר ואמרו חכמים אין טומנין בדבר המוסיף הבל אלא בדבר המעמיד הבל מה הוא המוסיף והפור. גפת. פסולת של בית הבד של שמן שהוא כונס יחד ואם מלד [שבת מז:]. פסולת זיתים שנעלרו בבית הבד [לעיל יז.]. לחין. יש בהן הבל הרבה יותר מיבשין [שבת שם]. גיזי צמר. כמות שנגזזו. ציפי צמר. לאחר שנפלו ושטפוהו כמין מתללות משטיחין. לשונות. לאחר שלבען וסורקין אותן כמין לשונות ארוכין לטוותן [שם מח.]. ובמוכין. כל דבר רך קרוי מוכין כגון למר גפן ותלישי למר רך של בהמה וגרירת בגדים בלאים [שם מז:]. אין אלא לגפות ואסור לטלטלן אבל מוכין כגון למר גפן שקורין ממוכין ומוקלין הן למלאכה ואסור לטלטלן [שם מח.]. יגיד עליו ריעו. וגלמד משנה מחבירתה [ע"ז עו.].

לעזי רש"י

קיילו"ש. פירוש אבני חלמיש (עיין רש"י ב"ב דף יח ע"א ד"ה הסלעים ורש"ש דברים לב, יג).

The Tanna did not complete each list because he relied on us inferring the omitted items from the other list. תָּנָא הָכָא סְלָעִים וְהוּא הַדִּין לְחוֹל – **Here,** in our Mishnah, **the Tanna mentions** only flint **stones, but the same ruling applies to sand;** תָּנָא הָתָם חוֹל וְהוּא הַדִּין לִסְלָעִים – and **there,** in the Mishnah about wrapping food, **the Tanna mentions** only **sand but the same ruling applies to** flint **stones.**

Rava objects to this explanation:

אָמַר לֵיהּ רָבָא – **Rava said to [Abaye]:** אִי יַגִּיד עָלָיו רֵיעוֹ – **If** the Tanna is relying on the principle of **"one sheds light on the other,"** לִיתְנִינְהוּ לְכוּלְּהוּ בַּחֲדָא – **he would have mentioned all [the materials] in one** of the two Mishnahs, וְלִיתְנֵי חֲדָא מִנַּיְיהוּ בְּאִידָךְ – **and mentioned** only **one of them in the other Mishnah,** וְהוּא הַדִּין לְאִידָךְ – **and** it would be known through the principle of "one sheds light on the other" that **the same ruling applies to** all **the other** materials.

Having rejected Abaye's answer, Rava presents his own:

אֶלָּא אָמַר רָבָא – **Rather, Rava said,** הָתָם הַיְינוּ טַעְמָא דְּלֹא קָתָנֵי סְלָעִים – **The reason the Tanna does not mention** flint **stones there,** in the Mishnah about wrapping food, **is** מִשּׁוּם דְּמִשְׁתְּכֵי לָהּ לַקְּדֵרָה – **that they break**[17] **the pot** and therefore are never used for insulation. הָכָא הַיְינוּ טַעְמָא דְּלֹא קָתָנֵי חוֹל – **The reason the Tanna does not mention sand here,** in our Mishnah, **is** מִשּׁוּם דִּמְחַמֵּימֵי חַיֵּים – **that** [sand] **heats** only **items that are warm** to begin with; וּמְקָרִירֵי קָרִיר – **items that are cold it leaves cold.**[18] Hence, sand has no damaging effect on a cold wall.[19]

The Gemara asks:

וְהָא תָּנֵי רַבִּי אוֹשַׁעְיָא חוֹל – **But R' Oshaya taught a Baraisa** that includes **sand** among the substances that require distancing from a wall.[20] This contradicts Rava's assertion that sand is not damaging to a wall. – ? –

The Gemara answers:

הָתָם בִּמְתוּנָא – **There,** in R' Oshaya's Baraisa, the reference is **to wet [sand].** The Baraisa includes sand among those items that cause damage through moisture, not among those that damage through heat.[21]

The Gemara asks:

תָּנָא דִּידָן נַמִּי לִיתְנֵי – Then **our Tanna too should have mentioned** sand among those items that damage through moisture, וְלוֹקְמֵיהּ בִּמְתוּנָא – **and** it would be understood that **the reference is to wet [sand].** – ? –

The Gemara answers:

הָא תָּנָא לֵיהּ אַמַּת הַמַּיִם – **Since [our Tanna] has** already **taught** the requirement to distance items that damage through moisture by mentioning **an irrigation channel,** there is no need for him to mention (wet) sand as well.[22]

The Gemara objects to this answer:

אָטוּ מִי לֹא קָתָנֵי אַמַּת הַמַּיִם – **But did [the Tanna] not teach** the requirement to distance **an irrigation channel,** וְקָתָנֵי נִבְרֶכֶת הַכּוֹבְסִין – **and** yet in addition **he mentioned a launderer's pool,** even though it too causes damage through moisture? By the same token, he could have mentioned (wet) sand as well. – ? –

The Gemara answers:

הַנְהוּ צְרִיכֵי – Both of **these** items [irrigation channel and launderer's pool] **must be** mentioned. One cannot be inferred from the other. דְּאִי תָּנָא אַמַּת הַמַּיִם מִשּׁוּם דִּקְבִיעָא – **For if [the Tanna] had mentioned** only **an irrigation channel,** one might have thought that only an irrigation channel need be distanced from a neighbor's pit, **because [its usage] is permanent,** אֲבָל נִבְרֶכֶת הַכּוֹבְסִין דְּלֹא קְבִיעָא אֵימָא לֹא – **but a launderer's pool,** the usage of **which is not permanent** (for the launderer might take up a different occupation), need not be distanced. וְאִי תָּנָא נִבְרֶכֶת הַכּוֹבְסִין מִשּׁוּם דְּקָווּ וְקַיְימֵי – **And if [the Tanna] would have mentioned** only **a launderer's pool,** one might have thought that only a launderer's pool need be distanced **because [its water] is stagnant,** and thus it can cause severe water damage, אֲבָל אַמַּת הַמַּיִם לֹא – **but an irrigation channel,** which contains running water, need **not** be distanced. צְרִיכָא – Hence, **it is necessary** for the Tanna to mention both an irrigation channel *and* a launderer's pool.[23] Wet sand, however, is not included in the Mishnah, for its law can be inferred from those cases.

The Gemara discusses the next clause of our Mishnah:

מַרְחִיקִין אֶת הַזְּרָעִים וְאֶת הַמַּחֲרֵישָׁה וכו׳ – SEEDS AND the use of A PLOW MUST BE DISTANCED at least three *tefachim* from the wall of one's neighbor.

The Gemara asks:

זְרָעִים – Why does the Mishnah mention that **seeds** must be distanced three *tefachim* from a neighbor's wall? תֵּיפוֹק לֵיהּ מִשּׁוּם מַחֲרֵישָׁה – **This emerges** anyway **from** the restriction against **a plow,** for seeds are planted in plow furrows!

The Gemara answers:

בְּמַפּוֹלֶת יָד – The reference in our Mishnah is **to** seeds sown with

NOTES

17. In this context, מִשְׁתְּכֵי means break. Elsewhere, however, it is translated as rust or corrode (*Rashi*).

Alternatively: In order to make the meaning of this word consistent with its meaning elsewhere, *Rabbeinu Tam* translates מִשְׁתְּכֵי here as spoil. The heat from the flint stones spoils the food (*Tosafos*).

18. Literally: what is cold it makes cold.

19. An apparent difficulty: In the Gemara above, Abaye challenged Rav Yosef's approach by pointing out that although the Mishnah in tractate *Shabbos* does not mention flint stones, it does mention other infrequently used items such as wool shearings and strips of dyed wool. Why is this discrepancy a problem if we follow Rav Yosef's approach but not if we follow Rava's approach?

The answer is that according to Rav Yosef's approach, although flint stones are inefficient insulating material (see note 11), they are sometimes used for this purpose. Hence, it is truly a difficulty that the Mishnah fails to mention flint stones but does mention wool shearings etc., which are used with similar infrequency. According to Rava's approach, however, stones are *never* used to insulate food, because they can cause damage. That is why flint stones are not mentioned in that Mishnah (*Tosafos*).

20. In his corpus of Baraisos to *Bava Basra,* R' Oshaya included a Baraisa that lists the same substances as our Mishnah, with the addition of sand (*Rashi*).

21. The Gemara stated above that the items listed in the first clause of our Mishnah (pit, trench, etc.) cause damage through moisture and the items listed in the second clause (olive refuse, manure, etc.) cause damage through heat (see notes 5 and 6).

22. [The obligation to distance sand from a neighbor's wall can be inferred from that which the Mishnah *does* mention.]

23. An apparent difficulty: The Gemara has explained why it was necessary for the Mishnah to mention both an irrigation channel and a launderer's pool. But what is the reason for the Mishnah's inclusion of a pit, ditch and vault?

According to those commentators who maintain that a pit must be distanced three *tefachim* even if it does not contain water (see 17a note 3), the Mishnah mentions a pit to teach this very point (*Rashba* to 17a, *Ritva* here). See *Tosafos* and *Rashba* to 17a for an explanation why a pit is included according to the opinion that the Mishnah refers exclusively to a pit that contains water.

Once a pit is mentioned, the Tanna includes a ditch and vault too, because the phrase, בּוֹר שִׁיחַ וּמְעָרָה, *pit, ditch and vault,* is a composite expression that is commonly found throughout the Mishnah [see, for example, Mishnah *Bava Kamma* 50b, *Taanis* 18b] (*Tosafos, Ramban, Rashba* and *Ran* to 17a).

לא משכחת ליה אי בטרפא הדר פארי: ולא נברכת הכובסין וכו': אמר רב נחמן אמר רבה בר אבוה לא שנו אלא מן המחמצן אבל מן הנדיין ד' אמות תניא נמי הכי נברכת הכובסין ד' אמות והא אנן תנן ג' טפחים אלא לאו ש"מ כדרב נחמן ואיכא דרמי להו מירמי תנן נברכת הכובסין ג' טפחים והתניא ארבע אמות אמר רב נחמן אמר רבה בר אבוה לא קשיא כאן מן המחמצן כאן מן הנדיין רב חייא בריה דרב אויא מתני לה בהדיא אלא אם כן הרחיק משפת מחמצן ולכותל ג' טפחים: וסד בסיד: איבעיא להו וסד בסיד תנן או דילמא או סד בסיד תנן פשיטא דוסד בסיד תנן דאי סלקא דעתך דאו סד בסיד תנן אם כן ליערבינהו וליתנינהו דילמא משום דלא דמי האי היזיקא להאי היזיקא רישא היזיקא (א) דמתונא סיפא היזיקא דהבלא ת"ש רבי יהודה אומר סלע הבא בידים זה חופר בורו מכאן וזה חופר בורו מכאן זה מרחיק ג' טפחים וסד בסיד וזה מרחיק ג' טפחים וסד בסיד טעמא דבא בידים הא לא בא בידים לא ה"ה דאף על גב דלא בא בידים נמי סד בסיד ובא בידים איצטריכא ליה סד"א כיון דבא בידים ליבעי רווחא טפי קמ"ל: מרחיקין את הגפת ואת הזבל ואת המלח ואת (ג) הסלעים וכו': תנן התם במה טומנין ובמה אין טומנין אין טומנין לא בגפת ולא בזבל ולא במלח ולא בסיד ולא בחול בין לחין בין יבשין מאי שנא הכא דקתני סלעים ולא קתני חול ומאי שנא התם דקתני חול ולא קתני סלעים אמר רב יוסף לפי שאין דרכן של בני אדם להטמין בסלעים אמר ליה אביי וכי דרכן של בני אדם להטמין בגיזי צמר ולשונות של ארגמן דתניא טומנין בגיזי צמר ובציפי צמר ובלשונות של ארגמן ובמוכין ואין מטלטלין אותן אלא אמר אביי יגיד עליו ריעו תנא הכא סלעים וה"ה לחול תנא התם חול והוא הדין לסלעים א"ל רבא אי יגיד עליו ריעו ליתנינהו לכולהו בחדא וליתני חדא מנייהו באידך (ג) וה"ה לאידך אלא אמר רבא הכא היינו טעמא דלא קתני סלעים משום דמשתכי לה לקדרה הכא היינו טעמא דלא קתני חול משום דמחמימי חיים ומקרירי קריר והא תני רבי אושעיא חול התם במתונא תנא דידן נמי ליתני ולוקמיה במתונא הא תנא ליה אמת המים אטו מי לא קתני אמת המים וקתני נברכת הכובסין הנהו צריכי דאי תנא אמת המים משום דקביעא אבל נברכת הכובסין דלא קביעא אימא לא ואי תנא נברכת הכובסין משום דקוו וקיימי אבל אמת המים לא צריכא: מרחיקין את הזרעים ואת המחרישה וכו': זרעים תיפוק ליה משום מחרישה במפולת יד מחרישה ותיפוק ליה משום זרעים בחורש לאילנות ותיפוק ליה משום מיא תנא בארץ ישראל קאי דכתיב למטר השמים תשתה מים למימרא דזרעים

רש"י

לא משכחת ליה. הדבורה לפי שהוא טמון בשרביטו: ואי בטרפא. ואם יאכל העלה: הדר פארי. חוזר וצומח: מן המחמצן. נברכת ששורין בו את הבגדים יום או יומים בצואת כלבים עד שמחמילין ומסריחין: אבל מן הנדיין. נברכת שכובסין ומשפשפין בה מתוך שהמים נתזין למרחוק צריך להרחיק ד' אמות: ה"ג או סד בסיד תנן. כלומר או ירחיק או סד: ליערבינהו. לתרתי בבי רישא ומציעתא דהתם או סד בסיד תנן אלא מדלא ערבינהו ש"מ דברישא וסד בסיד תנן דבעינן תרוייהו הרחקה וסיד: בא בידים אצטריך. למנקט ליה לתנא ואע"ג דה"ה ללא בא בידים: במה טומנין. את החמין בשבת דאמור רבנן לאסור להטמין בדבר המוסיף הבל והתם מפרש טעמא גזירה שמא יטמין ברמץ: לשונות של ארגמן. צמר צבוע ואחר כך חזרו והחליקוהו במסרק ועשוי לשונות: וכי דרכן להטמין בהן. ואפ"ה איירי בהו רבנן: ציפי צמר. לאחר שסרקו ונפלו במסרק: ובמוכין. של שחקי בגדים שהסורק מוציא מבגדי הצמר בקוצים: ואין מטלטלין אותם. שהן מוקצים למלאכת בגדים: ה"ג אי יגיד עליו ריעו ליתנינהו לכולהו בחדא וליתני חדא מנייהו באידך ולימא כו'. ליתנינהו לכולהו. כל הנך משום הבלא בחדא או כאן או אצל שבת: הנך משום דמשתכי לה לקדירה. שמשברין את הקדירה כך שמעתי כאן ובכל מקום שמעתיו שמעלה חלודה: דמחממי חיים. כשנותנין בו דבר חם הוא מתחמם וגבי הטמנה מחמימי הוא אבל גבי כותל קריר: והתנא רבי אושעיא. להרחקות דמתני' בתוספתא שלו (ד) וקאמר חול גבייהו: במתונא. אבל היזק לחלוח שנאה ובחול לח ולא אבל היזק הבל: נברכת כובסין. לא קביעא כאמת המים שאמת המים (ה) עשויין להיות שם עולמית אבל זו הכובס פעמים שמשתנה לאומנות אחרת: דקוו וקיימי. וליחלוחן קשה יותר משל מים חיים: תיפוק ליה משום מחרישה. שהרי חרשו תחילה ואפי' לא זרע (ו) ליה תנא לי' מרחיקין: במפולת יד. שזורעו בלא חרישה חופר במרה ואינו מעמיק כעומק המחרישה: ותיפוק ליה משום זרעים. שסופן לזרוע והא קתני זרעים: בחורש לאילנות. שיש שם אילנות מימים רבים ובא לחרוש תחתיהם להשביחן: ותיפוק ליה משום מיא. שצריך להשקותן תמיד וכיון דאי אפשר לזרעים בלא מים למה ליה למתנייהו הא תנא ליה היזק דליחלוח אצל כותל:

תוספות

בא בידים אין לא בא בידים לא. ה"ג ר"ח אלמא או סד בסיד תנן דלדוקא בא בידים בעי הרחקה וסיד ומשני הוא הדין לא בא ובא בידים איצטריך ליה כו' ויש ספרים דלא גרסי האי דיוקא אלא משני בא בידים שאני ודקארי לה מאי קארי כו' ואין נראה להיכי בעי למיפשט וסד בסיד תנן הא איכא למיבעי ההיא דרבי יהודה גופיה אי תרוייהו בעי אי לאו כיון דהשתא סבר דאין חילוק בין בא בידים ללא בא:

משום דמשתכי. פי' הקונטרס (ז) דמשברין הקדירה אין דרך להטמין בהן ואם תאמר אכתי תיקשי וכי דרך להטמין בגיזי צמר כדפריך לעיל וי"ל דלעיל הוה בעי למימר דאין דרך להטמין בסלעים לפי שההבל יוצא מבין הסלעים ואינו מתקיים ואעפ"כ לפעמים טומנין בהן להכי פריך שפיר מגיזי צמר דתני לה משום דלפעמים טומנין בהן אבל הכא קאמר דאין דרך להטמין כלל בהן לפי שמשברין הקדירה והואיל ומילתא דלא שכיח היא כלל לא חש למיתנייה ועוד יש לפרש דכיון דלא שכיחא היא כלל שרי להטמין בהן דבמילתא דלא שכיחא לא גזרו בהו רבנן וכן מנהג שלנו שאנו נוהגין להטמין בסלעים שהאש יוצא מהן שקורין קיילו"ש אבל מ"מ קשיא מה שהקשה בקונטר' דבכל מקום הוי שיתוך לשון חלודה כמו באלו מציאות (ב"מ דף כו.) דשתיך טפי ובפ' הבונה (שבת דף קג:) דכיון דמשתכי לא עבדי הכי ובפרק קמא דתענית (דף ח.) אם ראית דור שהשמים משתכין עליו כנחושת ומפרש ר"ת בענין אחר דמשתכי דהבל שלהן מקלקל המאכל ולר"י נראה כפירוש רבינו חננאל דמה שאמר להרחיקם משום דמשתכי שמלקין את הארץ ומחלידים אותה ומעלין עפר תיחוח כדאמרינן לקמן גבי זרעים ולא משום הבל דאין מוסיפין שום הבל וטומנין בהן ואפילו לפי הספרים דגרסי סלעים היינו טעמא דלא קתני להו התם יש לפרש דהכי קאמר דלהכי לא קתני להו התם משום דטעמא דהכא שצריך להרחיקם לא משום הבל אלא משום דמשתכי וה"ר מרדכי הביא ראיה מירושלמי דגרסי' (ה) התם איתמר (ח) שהסלעים מרתיחין (ו) והכא איתמר שאין סלעים מרתיחין א"ר יוסי כאן וכאן אין הסלעים מרתיחין אלא מפני שעושים עפר תיחוח ומלקין ארעית הכותל:

דמחממי חיים. והא דאמר בפ' כירה (שבת דף לח: ושם ד"ה ולא) ביצה אין טומנין אותה לא בחול ולא באבק דרכים התם בחול שהוחם (ט) מחמת השמש דומיא דאבק דרכים:

המבריך את הגפן. (סוכה לט"ב) פירוש גפן יחידי שהוא מושרש בארץ וכופף את הגפן באמצעיתו ומכסהו בקרקע ונשרש שם וקאמר מותר לזרוע את הנלדין דאף על גב שאינו רחוק שלשה טפחים וינוק עם הגפן מתחת הקרקע כיון דמעל הקרקע ליכא עירבובי שרי כדמוכח בעירובין (דף ג.) ובמסכת כלאים (פ"ז) דזה סומך לגדר מכאן וזה מכאן וא"ת והיכי דמי שזורע לנלדין אי כשהרחיק ג' טפחים מן הנלדין אפילו על גביו נמי ואי בלא הרחיק מן הנלדין נמי לא ואומר ר"י דמיירי כשזורע הנלדין ברחוק ג' (י) טפחים מגפן היוצא מן הקרקע ומכל מקום אסור לזרוע על גביו מפני שהשרשים נכנסים בתוך הגפן והוי כמרכיב זרעים באילן דאסור ותימה דא"כ אמאי קאמר גפן אפי' שאר אילן נמי אסור ואומר ר"י דשאר אילנות שהן קשין מותר לזרוע על גביו כנגד השרש דלא חיישינן שיכנס שורש הזרע בתוך האילן אבל גפן שהוא רך חיישינן והאי (פירוקא) מלא ר"י בירושלמי בגמרא דהך משנה:

a casting of the hand into shallow holes dug with a trowel, not into plow furrows.

The Gemara asks the reverse question :

מַחֲרֵישָׁה – Why does the Mishnah mention that a **plow** must be distanced three *tefachim* from a neighbor's wall? **וְתֵיפּוּק לֵיהּ מִשּׁוּם זְרָעִים** – **This emerges** anyway **from** the restriction against **seeds,** for plow furrows are made for the planting of seeds.[24] – **?** –

The Gemara answers:

בְּחוֹרֵשׁ לְאִילָנוֹת – The Mishnah refers **to one who plows for** the benefit of **trees,**[25] not to plant seeds.

The Gemara again questions the need for the Mishnah to mention seeds:

וְתֵיפּוּק לֵיהּ מִשּׁוּם מַיָּא – The Mishnah's mention of a restriction against seeds is unnecessary, for **it emerges** anyway **from** the prohibition against putting **water** near a neighbor's wall.[26] Since seeds cannot grow without water, they would not be planted where one cannot irrigate them. – **?** –

The Gemara answers:

תַּנָּא בְּאֶרֶץ יִשְׂרָאֵל קָאֵי – **The Tanna's point of reference is Eretz Yisrael,** where irrigation is unnecessary, **דִּכְתִיב: ,,לִמְטַר הַשָּׁמַיִם תִּשְׁתֶּה־מָּיִם"** – **as it is written:**[27] ***It drinks the water of the rain of heaven.***

Having shown that the reason for the restriction against sowing seeds near the wall of a neighbor is *not* that water damage might ensue as a result, the Gemara now assumes that the reason seeds must be distanced from a wall is that their roots will spread sideways and loosen the earth beneath the wall. The Gemara therefore asks:

לְמֵימְרָא דִזְרָעִים – Are we **to say that seeds**

NOTES

24. Since seeds cannot be planted within three *tefachim* of the wall, one would not plow there.

25. He plows the ground around a tree to enhance its growth (see *Rashi*).

[In fact, a tree must also be distanced from a neighbor's wall (see Mishnah 25b). However, we refer here to a tree that was planted with permission. Although one is not obligated to remove such a tree, one may not plow the ground for its benefit (*Rashba*; see *Rashi*).]

26. As the Gemara stated above (18a), the reason for the Mishnah's restriction against urine is that moisture is harmful to a wall (see *Rashi*; see also 18a note 4).

27. *Deuteronomy* 11:11.

לא משכחת ליה אי בטרפא הדר פארי: ולא נברכת הכובסין וכו': אמר רב נחמן אמר רבה בר אבוה לא שנו אלא מן המחמצן אבל מן הנדיין ד' אמות תניא נמי הכי נברכת הכובסין ד' אמות והא אנן תנן ג' טפחים אלא לאו ש"מ כדרב נחמן ° ואיכא דרמי להו מירמי תנן נברכת הכובסין ג' טפחים והתניא ארבע אמות אמר רב נחמן אמר רבה בר אבוה לא קשיא כאן מן המחמצן כאן מן הנדיין רב חייא בריה דרב אויא מתני לה בהדיא אלא אם כן הרחיק משפת מחמצן ולכותל ג' טפחים: וסד בסיד: איבעיא להו וסד בסיד תנן או דילמא או סד בסיד תנן פשיטא דוסד בסיד תנן דאי סלקא דעתך דאו סד בסיד תנן אם כן ליערבינהו וליתנינהו דילמא משום דלא דמי האי היזיקא להאי היזיקא רישא היזיקא (א) דמתונא סיפא היזיקא דהבלא ת"ש רבי יהודה אומר סלע הבא בידים זה חופר בורו מכאן וזה חופר בורו מכאן זה מרחיק ג' טפחים וסד בסיד וזה מרחיק ג' טפחים וסד בסיד טעמא דבא בידים הא לא בא בידים לא ה"ה דאף על גב דלא בא בידים נמי סד בסיד ובא בידים איצטריכא ליה סד"א כיון דבא בידים ליבעי רווחא טפי קמ"ל: מרחיקין את הגפת ואת הזבל ואת המלח ואת (ב) הסלעים וכו': תנן התם במה טומנין ובמה אין טומנין אין טומנין לא בגפת ולא בזבל ולא במלח ולא בסיד ולא בחול בין לחין בין יבשין מאי שנא הכא דקתני סלעים ולא קתני חול ומאי שנא התם דקתני חול ולא קתני סלעים אמר רב יוסף לפי שאין דרכן של בני אדם להטמין בסלעים אמר ליה אביי וכי דרכן של בני אדם להטמין בגיזי צמר ולשונות של ארגמן דתניא טומנין בגיזי צמר ובציפי צמר ובלשונות של ארגמן ובמוכין ואין מטלטלין אותן אלא אמר אביי יגיד עליו ריעו תנא הכא סלעים והוא הדין לחול תנא התם חול והוא הדין לסלעים א"ל רבא אי יגיד עליו ריעו ליתנינהו לכולהו בחדא וליתני חדא מינייהו באידך (ג) וה"ה לאידך אלא אמר רבא התם היינו טעמא דלא קתני סלעים משום דמשתכי לה לקדרה הכא היינו טעמא דלא קתני חול משום דמחממי חיים ומקרירי קריר והא תני רבי אושעיא חול התם במתונא תנא דידן נמי ליתני ולוקמיה במתונא הא תנא ליה אמת המים אטו מי לא קתני אמת המים וקתני נברכת הכובסין הנהו צריכי דאי תנא אמת המים משום דקביעא אבל נברכת הכובסין דלא קביעא אימא לא ואי תנא נברכת הכובסין משום דקוו וקיימי אבל אמת המים לא צריכא: מרחיקין את הזרעים ואת המחרישה וכו': זרעים תיפוק ליה משום מחרישה במפולת יד מחרישה ותיפוק ליה משום זרעים בחורש לאילנות ותיפוק ליה משום מיא תנא בארץ ישראל קאי דכתיב למטר השמים תשתה מים למימרא דזרעים

רש"י

לא משכחת ליה. הדבורה לפי שהוא טמון בשרביטו: ואי בטרפא. ולא יאכל העלה: הדר פארי. חוזר ומוצא: מן המחמצן. נברכת שורין בו את הבגדים יום או יומים בצואת כלבים עד שמחמיצין ומסריחין: אבל מן הנדיין. נברכת שכובסין ומשפשפין בה מתוך שהמים נתזין למרחוק צריך להרחיק ד' אמות: ה"ג או סד בסיד תנן. כלומר או ירחיק או סד: ליערבינהו. לתרתי בבי רישא ומציעתא דהכא או סד בסיד תנן אלא מדלא ערבינהו ש"מ דברישא וסד בסיד תנן דבעינן תרוייהו הרחקה וסיד: בא בידים אצטריך. למנקט ליה לתנא ולאשמועינן דה"ה ללא בא בידים: במה טומנין. את החמין בשבת דאמור רבנן לאסור להטמין בדבר המוסיף הבל והתם מפרש טעמא גזירה שמא יטמין ברמץ: לשונות של ארגמן. צמר צבוע ואחר כך סרקו והליקוהו במסרק ועשוי לשונות: וכי דרכן להטמין בהן. ואפ"ה איירי בהו רבנן: ציפי צמר. לאחר שסרקו ונפצו במסרק: ובמוכין. של שחקי בגדים שהסורק מוציא מבגדי הצמר בקוצים: ואין מטלטלין אותם. שהן מוקצים למלאכת בגדים: ה"ג אי יגיד עליו ריעו ליתנינהו לכולהו בחדא וליתני חדא מינייהו באידך ולימא כו'. ליתנינהו לכולהו. כל הנך משום הבלא בחדא או כולן או אלא שבת: הנך משום דמשתכי לה לקדירה. שמשברין את הקדירה כך משתכי כאן ובכל מקום שמעתיו מעמלה חלודה: דמחממי חיים. כשטומנין בו דבר שם הוא מתחמם וגבי הטמנה מחממי הוא אבל גבי כותל קריר: והתנא רבי אושעיא. להרחקות דמתני' בתוספתא שלו (ד) וקאמר חול גבייהו: במתונא. אבל היזק לחלוח שבלה ובחול לא ולא אבל היזק הבל: נברכת כובסין. לא קביעא כאמת המים שאמת המים (ה) עשויין להיות שם עולמית אבל זו הכובס פעמים שמשתנה לאומנות אחרת: דקוו וקיימי. וליחלוחן קשה יותר משל מים חיים: תיפוק ליה משום מחרישה. שהרי חרשו תחילה ואפי' לא זרע (ו) ליה תנא לי' מרחיקין: במפולת יד. שזרעו בלא חרישה חופר במרה ואינו מעמיק כעומק המחרישה: ותיפוק ליה משום זרעים. שפעם חורשין סופן לזרוע והא קתני זרעים: בחורש לאילנות. שיש שם אילנות מימים רבים ובא לחרוש תחתיהם להשביחן: ותיפוק ליה משום מיא. שצריך להשקותן תמיד וכיון דאי אפשר לזרעים בלא מים למה ליה למתניינהו הא תנא ליה היזק דליחלוח אבל כותל: לגדלין

תוספות

ה"ג ר"ש בא בידים אין לא בא בידים לא. אלמא או סד בסיד תנן דלדוקא בא בידים בעי הרחקה וסיד ומשני הוא הדין לא בא ובא בידים איצטריך ליה כו' ויש ספרים דלא גרסי האי דיוקא אלא משני בא בידים שאני ודקארי לה מאי קארי כו' ואין נראה דהיכי בעי למיפשט וסד בסיד תנן הא איכא למיבעי ההיא דרבי יהודה גופיה אי תרוייהו בעי אי לאו כיון דהשתא סבר דאין חילוק בין בא בידים ללא בא:

משום דמשתכי. פי' הקונטרס (ז) דמשברין הקדירה אין דרך להטמין בהן ואם תאמר אכתי תיקשי וכי דרך להטמין בגיזי צמר כדפריך לעיל וי"ל דלעיל הוה בעי למימר דאין דרך להטמין בסלעים לפי שההבל יוצא מבין הסלעים ואינו מתקיים ואעפ"כ לפעמים טומנין בהן להכי פריך שפיר מגיזי צמר דתני לה משום דלפעמים טומנין בהן אבל הכא קאמר דאין דרך להטמין כלל בהן לפי שמשברין הקדירה והואיל ומילתא דלא שכיח היא כלל לא חש למיתנייה ועוד יש לפרש דכיון דלא שכיחא היא כלל שרי להטמין בהן דבמילתא דלא שכיחא לא גזרו בהו רבנן וכן מנהג שלנו שאנו נוהגין להטמין בסלעים שהאש יוצא מהן שקורין קיילו"ש אבל מ"מ קשיא מה שהקשה בקונטר' דבכל מקום הוי שיתוך לשון חלודה כמו באלו מציאות (ב"מ דף כו.) דשתיך טפי ובפ' הבונה (שבת דף קב:) דכיון דמשתכי לא עבדי הכי ובפרק קמא דתענית (דף ח.) אם ראית דור שהשמים משתכין עליו כנחושת ומפרש ר"ת בענין אחר דמשתכי דהבל שלהן מקלקל המאכל ולר"י נראה כפירוש רבינו חננאל דמה שאמר להרחיקם משום דמשתכי שמלקין את הארץ ומחלידים אותה ומעלין עפר תיחוח כדאמרינן לקמן גבי זרעים ולא משום הבל דאין מוסיפין שום הבל וטומנין בהן ואפילו לפי הספרים דגרסי סלעים היינו טעמא דלא קתני להו התם יש לפרש דהכי קאמר דלהכי לא קתני להו התם משום דטעמא דהכא שצריך להרחיקם לא משום הבל אלא משום דמשתכי וה"ר מרדכי הביא ראיה מירושלמי דגרסי' התם איתמר (ח) שהסלעים מרתיחין והכא איתמר שאין הסלעים מרתיחין א"ר יוסי כאן וכאן אין הסלעים מרתיחין אלא מפני שעושים עפר תיחוח ומלקין ארעית הכותל:

דמחממי חיים. והא דאמר בפ' כירה (שבת דף לח: ושם ד"ה ולא) ביצה אין טומנין אותה לא בחול ולא באבק דרכים התם בחול שהוחם (ט) מחמת השמש דומיא דאבק דרכים:

המבריך את הגפן. (שייך לע"ב) פירוש גפן יחידי שהוא מושרש בארץ וכופף את הגפן באמצעיתו ומכסהו בקרקע ונשרש שם וקאמר מותר לזרוע את האלדין דאף על גב שאינו רחוק שלשה טפחים ויונק עם הגפן מתחת הקרקע כיון דמעל הקרקע ליכא עירבובי' שרי כדמוכח בעירובין (דף לג.) ובמסכת כלאים (פ"ז) דזה סומך לגדר מכאן וזה מכאן וא"ת והיכי דמי שזורע לאלדין אי כשהרחיק ג' טפחים מן האלדין אפילו על גביו נמי ואי בלא הרחיק מן האלדין נמי לא ואומר ר"י דמיירי כשזורע האלדין ברחוק ג' (י) טפחים מגפן היוצא מן הקרקע מכל צד דליכא ערבוביא למעלה מן הקרקע ומכל מקום אסור לזרוע על גביו מפני שהשרשין נכנסין בתוך הגפן והוי כמרכיב זרעים באילן דאסור ואם תאמר ומאי איריא דנקט גפן אפי' שאר אילן נמי אסור ואומר ר"י דשאר אילנות שהן קשין מותר לזרוע על גביו כנגד השורש דלא חיישינן שיכנס שורש הזרע בתוך האילן שהוא קשה אבל גפן שהוא רך חיישינן והאי (פירוקא) מלא ר"י בירושלמי בגמרא דהך משנה:

רבינו גרשום

פיסקא לא שנו דבג' טפחים סגי אלא מן המחמצן. אותו מקום ששורין בה בגדי כביסה עם צואת כלבים להכי קרי ליה מחמצן דכי היכי דמניחין את העיסה עד שתתחמץ דלא נגעי בה כך מניחין אלו בגדים דלא נגעו בהו עד שישורו יפה ולהכי סגי ברחוק ג' טפחים דלא אזלי טפי ולא מנתזו מן הכותל: אבל מן הנדיין. מקום שמכבסין הבגדים עצמן בתוך המים ומכין אותם ומנתזין על הכתלים מש"ה צריך להרחיק ד' אמות: איבעיא להו וסד בסיד תנן. דמשמע לבר מג' טפחים כלומר דתרוייהו צריך למיעבד להרחיק ג' טפחים ולסייד שוב החפירה בסיד או דלמא או סד בסיד תנן דמשמע או ג' טפחים (א) אמר ליה פשיטא דאו סד בסיד תנן דא"כ דס"ד דוסד בסיד תנן הא בבא אחריתי דקתני מרחיקין את הגפת (ב) (כלומר) ד' בסיד אי אתרוייהו בבי דסד בסיד ליערבינהו להנהו תרי בבי כחדא לא יחפור אדם כו' ומרחיקין את הגפת כו' וליתנינהו בתרוייהו חד וסד בסיד דמשמע אכולהו ותרי זמני וסד בסיד ל"ל דילמא לעולם אימא לך דתרוייהו וסד בסיד נינהו והאי דלא עירב להו משום דתרוייהו צריכי דלא דמי היזקא דרישא להזיקא דסיפא דהיזק דרישא משום מתונא מחמת לחלוח מים דשיח ובורות. והאי היזקא דסיפא דהבלא הוא דגפת חבל ומלח כולהו מסקי הבלא נינהו וקשי טפי ומש"ה צריך למיתנינהו תרוייהו דמחדא לא נפקא אידך ומיהא לא תפשוט. ת"ש זה מרחיק ג' טפחים מכאן כשיעור כותל בורו וסד בסיד הבור וכן נמי אידך וטעמא מאי בעי להרחיק ג' טפחים כל חד וחד ולסוד משום דבא בידים דארעא רפיא היא. אבל לאו בא בידים דההוא צונמא חזקה לעולם לא צריך לסוד בסיד אם ירחיק ג' טפחים אלמא תפשוט מהכא דאו סד בסיד תנן לא לעולם מהא לא תפשוט ה"ה דאפי' לא בא בידים בעי ג' טפחים וסד בסיד ובא בידים איצטריכא ליה כו'. רווחא טפי מג' טפחים ולסוד בסיד קמ"ל דלא: מ"ש גבי מתני' דקתני סלעים משום הבלא ומ"ש גבי הטמנה דמשום הבלא נמי היא וקתני חול ולא סלעים: וא"ל אביי וכי דרכן של בני אדם להטמין בלשונות של ארגמן ואפ"ה קתני להו סלעים נמי אע"ג דאין דרכן להטמין ליתנייהו: גיזי צמר והוא צמר הגדל מן הבהמה כמו שהוא. ציפי צמר זהו צמר סרוק ומלובן לצורך צביעה. וי"א ציפי צמר כריכות צמר גדול כדרך שמביאין הסוחרין ממדינתן. ולשונות של ארגמן צמר שאינו טווי שצובעין בארגמן כדי לנסות ורוב צביעתו היה ארגמן. ובמוכין צמר שמסרקין מן הבגדים לאחר שמכבסין אותן: ויגיד עליו רעו. יוכיח עליו כלומר תנא הכי במתני' [סלעים] דמפסיק הבלא וה"ה לחול [illegible]

עין משפט נר מצוה

ט א מיי' פ"ט מהלכות שכנים הל' ה סמג עשין פב טוש"ע ח"מ סי' קנה סעיף י:
י ב מיי' שם הלכה ה ועי' פי' במ"מ טוש"ע שם סעיף יא:
יא ג מיי' שם הל' א טוש"ע שם סעיף א:
יב ד מיי' פ"ד מהל' שבת הל' א סמג לאוין סה טוש"ע או"ח סי' רנז סעיף ג:
יג ה מיי' וסמג שם טוש"ע או"ח סי' רנט סעיף א:

מסורת הש"ס

א) לעיל יז: ע"ש [תוספתא פ"א], ב) שבת מז:, ג) שם מח., ד) [יבמות לא: וש"נ], ה) [שבת עג: וש"נ], ו) מהר"ם ההם הכא, ז) מהר"ם והסם, ח) מ"י פירכא.

הגהות הב"ח

(א) גמ' רישא היזיקא דמתונא כל"ל וכן במתון: (ב) שם ואת המלח ואת הסלעים: (ג) שם ולימא חדא מינייהו באידך [illegible]: (ד) רש"י ד"ה והתנא ר' אושעיא וכו' שלו וקתני חול גבייהו: (ה) ד"ה נברכת וכו' שאמת המים עשוי להיות: (ו) ד"ה תיפוק וכו' זרע תנא כל"ל ותיבת ליה נמחק: (ז) תוס' ד"ה משום וכו' הקונטרס כאן דמשברין את הקדירה [illegible]: (ח) באד"ה איתמר מפני הסלעים: (ט) ד"ה דמחממי וכו' שהוחם מחמת: (י) ד"ה המבריך וכו' ברחוק ג' [illegible]

גליון הש"ס

גמ' ואיכא דרמי להו מירמי. כעין זה סוכה [נט ע"ב] לג ע"ב וש"נ:

תורה אור השלם

א) יַגִּיד עָלָיו רֵעוֹ מִקְנֶה אַף עַל עוֹלֶה: [איוב לו, לג]
ב) וְהָאָרֶץ אֲשֶׁר אַתֶּם עֹבְרִים שָׁמָּה לְרִשְׁתָּהּ אֶרֶץ הָרִים וּבְקָעֹת לִמְטַר הַשָּׁמַיִם תִּשְׁתֶּה מָּיִם: [דברים יא, יא]

ליקוטי רש"י

סלע הבא בידים. קרקע רך מתחתם מאליו. ובא בידים איצטריכא ליה סד"א וכו'. כלומר הוא הדין אע"ג דלא בא בידים [illegible] במה טומנין. [illegible]

לעזי רש"י

קיילו"ש. פירוש אבני חלמיש (עיין רש"י ב"ק דף ו ע"ב ד"ה לסלעים ורש"י דברים לב, יג).

חשק שלמה על רבינו גרשום א) [ג' טפחים או סד בסיד]. ב) [מרחיקין את הגפת וכו' וסד בסיד ואי בתרוייהו בבי כעין דוסד בסיד וכו']:

יד א ב מיי' פ"ו מהל' כלאים הל' ו טוש"ע י"ד סי' רצו סעיף ד:
טו ג מיי' פ"ט מהל' שכנים הל' ו סמג עשין פב טוש"ע ח"מ סי' קנה סעיף ו:
טז ד ה מיי' פט"ו מהל' טומאת מת הלכה ה:
יז ו ז ח ט מיי' שם הלכה ג:

לצדדין קא משתרשי והא תנן א המבריך את הגפן בארץ אם אין על גבה עפר שלשה טפחים לא יביא זרע עליה ותני עלה ב אבל זורע את הצדדין אילך ואילך אמר רבי חגא בשם רבי יוסי מפני שמחלידין ג את הקרקע ומעלין עפר תיחוח: ואת מי רגלים מן הכותל ג' טפחים וכו': אמר רבה בר בר חנה מותר לאדם להשתין מים בצד כותלו של חבירו דכתיב א והכרתי לאחאב משתין בקיר ועצור ועזוב בישראל והא אנן תנן ואת מי רגלים מן הכותל שלשה טפחים התם בשופכין (א) ג (ת"ש לא ישפוך אדם מים בצד כותלו של חבירו אלא אם כן הרחיק ממנו ג' טפחים התם נמי בשופכין) ת"ש ד לא ישתין אדם מים בצד כותלו של חבירו אלא אם כן הרחיק ממנו ג' טפחים בד"א בכותל לבינים אבל בכותל אבנים בכדי שלא יזיק וכמה טפח ושל צונמא מותר תיובתא דרבה בר בר חנה תיובתא והא רבה בר בר חנה קרא קאמר התם הכי קאמר אפילו מידי דדרכיה לאישתוני בקיר לא שביקנא ליה ומאי ניהו כלבא אמר ר' טובי בר קיסנא אמר שמואל ה רקיק אינו ממעט בחלון מאי איריא רקיק אפי' עבה נמי לא מיבעיא קאמר לא מיבעיא עבה (ב) כיון דאיחזי ליה לא מבטל ליה אבל רקיק דממאס אימא בטולי מבטיל ליה קמ"ל ותיפוק ליה דהוה ליה דבר שהוא מקבל טומאה וכל דבר שהוא מקבל טומאה אינו חוצץ בפני הטומאה ו שנילוש במי פירות מיתיבי ז קופה מלאה תבן וחבית מלאה גרוגרות המונחים בחלון רואין כל שאילו ינטלו ויכולין תבן וגרוגרות לעמוד בפני עצמן חוצצין ואם לאו אין חוצצין והא תבן חזי לבהמתו ז בסריא חזי לטינא ח דאית ביה קוצי חזי להסקה (ג) ט במתונא חזי להסק גדול לא שכיח גרוגרות הא חזו ליה אמר שמואל י בשהתריפו וכן תני רבה בר אבוה בשהתריפו האי חבית היכי דמיא אי דפומא לבר

רש"י

לצדדין קא משתרשי. ומחלידין מתחת לכותל ומקלקלים יסודו: המבריך את הגפן. גפן יחידי שאין בזרעים שאלא משום עירבוב דאין כרם בפחות מחמש גפנים שתים כנגד שתים ואחת יוצא זנב אלא שלא יינק הזרע מן הגפן: מבריך. כמו ויברך הגמלים (בראשית כד) כופף זמורת גפן מחוברת ומבריכה בקרקע בלדיה לכאן ולכאן וקורין בלע"ז פרובניי"ר: שמחלידין את הקרקע. אצל הכותל במקומן ומעלין עפר תיחוח ומתמוטט (ד) קרקע יסוד הכותל לצדדין: משתין בקיר. אלמא דרך בני אדם כן: בשופכין. עביט מלא ושופכו שם: לא ישתין. ליכא לאוקמי אלא במשתין ממש: בכותל לבינים. שהם של טיט שנתיבשו בחמה והם נימוקים מחמת המים: וכמה טפח. מפני שמטשטשת את הקרקע סמוך ליסוד הכותל: ובצונמא. אם כותל זה בנוי בסלע דליכא למיחש (ה) בטישטוש קרקע: מותר. סמוך ממש ואשיפה קאי בכותל אבנים: רקיק. סופגנין חררה דקה ורכה: אינו ממעט בחלון. שבין בית לבית ויש בו פותח טפח ומת מונח בחדא מהן וטומאה בוקעת לצד שני אין רקיק (ו) ממעט שיעורן מלהוליך טומאה דכיון דראוי לאכילה לא מבטל להתם דנהוי כסתימה: אבל רקיק דמאיס. מתוך שהוא דק ולחלוח הכותל מרטבו נמאס: שנילוש במי פירות. שאין מכשירין ואין אוכל מקבל טומאה בלא הכשר משקה הקרוי משקה כגון מים ויין וחלב: וחבית מלא גרוגרות. תאנים יבשים וכגון שלא הוכשרו: כל שאילו ינטלו. הקופה והחבית: ויכולין. התבן או הגרוגרות לעמוד בפני עצמן חוצצין בפני הטומאה: ואם לאו אין חוצצין. שהחבית והקופה אין חוצצין לפי שהן מקבלין טומאה: סריא. נרקב: והא חזי לטינא. ולא מבטל ליה: דאית ביה קוצי. (ז) והן היו רומסין ברגליהן בטיט: הא חזו. לאכילה. כולהו הנך תיובתא דשמואל דאמר מידי דחזי ליטלו משם לאחר זמן אין ממעט בחלון: בשהתריפו. התליעו: אי פומיה לבר. לצד הבית שאין המת בתוכו: שאין

תוספות

התם בשופכין. וא"ת בשלמא אי מיירי במשתין אע"ג דתנא ליה אמת המים תנא ליה נמי האי דס"ד משום לניעותא לישתרי אבל אי מיירי בשופכין מאי קמ"ל הא תנא ליה אמת המים דמהאי טעמא אמר לעיל דלא תני חול י"ל דשאני חול שהוא כל שעה אצל הכותל אבל הנך מי רגלים כלים כרגע:

ותיובתא דרבה בר בר חנה. ולא מצי לשנויי דכי קאמר רבה בר בר חנה בצונמא חדא דהוה ליה לפרושי בהדיא ועוד דדריש מקרא ש"מ דלא מפליג:

אמר רב טובי רקיק אינו ממעט. הך שמעתתא מייתי הכא אגב דפריך לקמן (ח) זרעים כיון דקשו לכותל שקיל להו:

רקיק אינו ממעט בחלון. דיני חלון פי' ר"י ב"ר מרדכי על פי המשניות דאם הוא חלון העשוי לתשמיש שיעורו להביא טומאה בפותח טפח וכשיתמעט מטפח אפילו במשהו אינו מביא ואם הוא חלון שעשוי לאורה ועשוי בידי אדם שיעורו כמלא מקדח גדול של לשכה שהוא כמלא פונדיון האיטלקי שהוא סלע נירונית והיא יתירה על סלע סתם דסלע סתם הוא פחות ממלא מקדח סתם וכל שכן ממקדח גדול כדאמרינן בבכורות (דף לח:) ואותו חלון שעשוי לאורה אינו מתמעט מסתימת משהו כיון שהיה בו כשיעור אלא עד שיתמעט שלא יהא בשיריים (ט) רום אצבעים על רוחב גודל ומאור שאינו עשוי בידי אדם אלא מעצמו כגון חררוהו מים או שרצים שיעורו מלא אגרוף חישב עליו לתשמיש שיעורו פותח טפח למאור שיעורו מלא מקדח ומלא אגרוף מפרש התם באגרופו של בן אבטיח ורבי יוסי אומר בראש כל אדם ושאינו עשוי (י) לאורה ולא לתשמיש אלא לאויר ולשמור גגות ופרדסים אותו שיעורו כמלא מקדח בינוני:

מאי איריא רקיק כו'. השתא ס"ד דנקט רקיק דוקא משום דאית ביה תרתי חדא (כ) דלא סתימה מעלייתא לפי שהוא רך ועשוי ליפול ועוד שאינו מבטלו משום הכי פריך אפי' עבה נמי שמתקיים הואיל ואינו מבטלו אינו ממעט:

ותיפוק ליה. (ל) אפי' אם יבטלו דלאו חוצץ משום דמקבל טומאה ותימה אם יבטל ליה תו לא מקבל טומאה וטהור כדמוכח בפרק העור והרוטב (חולין דף קכט. ושם) דאמר כיפת שאור שייחדה לישיבה בטלה ובית שסיכו בזרעים טהורים אלמא כיון דבטליה לא מקבל טומאה וי"ל דהתם מיירי כגון דעבד בהו שינוי מעשה דהא אמרי' (שבת דף נג:) כל הכלים יורדין לידי טומאה במחשבה ואין עולין מטומאה אלא ע"י שינוי מעשה וה"ה באוכלין דבעינן שינוי מעשה דאפילו בידות האוכלין מוכח בפרק קמא דסוכה (דף יד. ושם) דאיכא תנא דאית ליה דבעינן בהו שינוי מעשה:

שנילושה במי פירות. הו"מ לשנויי כגון שאין בו כביצה ובמסכת אהלות (פי"ג מ"ה) חשיב פחות מכביצה אוכלין בהדי הנך (מ) שאמר שממעטים את הטפח:

מי פירות. פי' ר"ח כגון שמן ולא דק דשמן מכשיר הוא כדמוכח בפרק קמא דשבת (דף ה:) ובריש פרק חבית (שם קמד.) דשמן חשיב משקה אלא דוקא מוהל היוצא מתחילה:

בתיבנא סריא. תימה אכתי חזיא לבהמתו ע"י פירוך כדמוכח בפרק בתרא דשבת (דף קנה:) דאמרינן תא שמע מפרכין את התבן כו' אלמא מיטרח באוכלא שרי ומשני בתיבנא סריא וי"ל דהכא מיירי שהוא מוסרח כל כך דאפי' ע"י שום תקון לא חזיא:

רואין כל שאילו ינטלו. אין לפרש דטעם משום דסופו ליטול חבית וקופה ולהכי בעינן שיהו גרוגרות ותבן יכולין לעמוד בפני עצמן דא"כ למאי דפריך תבן הא קא חזי ליה ורוצה להוכיח מכאן דאפילו סופו ליטלו חוצץ תיקשי ליה אמאי צריך שיכולין לעמוד בפני עצמן אלא אומר ר"י דכך הוא הדין דכל דבר החוצץ בעינן שיוכל לעמוד בפני עצמו דקתני לעיל מהך משנה במסכת אהלות (פי"ו מ"ב) קורות המת שהיו עוברין באכסדרה ובא אחד מהן והגיף את הדלת וסמכו במפתח אם יכולה דלת לעמוד בפני עצמה טהור ואם לאו טמא וכן חבית של גרוגרות וקופה של תבן שהן נתונין בחלון משמע דהכל חד טעמא הוא והיינו טעמא דסתימת ערלאי הוא דכיון שאינו יכול לעמוד בפני עצמו אי נמי משום דבעינן דבר החוצץ עומד על ידי דבר שאינו מקבל טומאה ומיהו בפירוש משניות מלא ר"י דמפרש אפילו במפתח שאינו מקבל טומאה איירי ומטמא דלא חשיב אהל לחוץ בפני הטומאה כיון שעמד על ידי כלי אף על פי שאינו מקבל טומאה ורבי אליעזר פליג עלה בתוספתא וקאמר דטהור כיון שהמפתח אינו מקבל טומאה ואולי לטעמייהו דפליגי במסכת אהלות (פט"ו מ"ט) בנדבך שהוא נתון על גבי כלים אפילו כלי גללים כלי אבנים כלי אדמה דלרבי אליעזר נעשה אהל לטהר ולרבנן אינו נעשה אהל אלא כשהוא נתון על גבי אבנים:

רבינו גרשום

יותר ולא מזיק כלל לכותל להכי לא תנא ליה והא קתני ר' הושעיא בתוספתא דידיה הני דמתני' וקתני חול. הני בהדי הדדי דרישא דמזיקי משום מתונתא לחלוה. ולא קתני לה בהדי הנך דסיפא דבפת ובזל דהנהו משום הבלא. ומקשי' מי לא תנן אמת המים וקתני נברכת הכובסין אע"ג דלא צריך הכא נמי ליתני חול ומשני אמת המים ונברכת הכובסין תרוייהו צריכי דאי תנא אמת המים דמרחיקין ג' טפחים הוה אמינא משום דקבועי כל הימים מרחיקין דמקלקל לכותל אבל ברכת הכובסין דלא קביעי דמים מכונסין ניהו אימא אין מרחיקין: דקוו וקימי ומחלידין בקרקע ואתיין על היסוד מש"ה מרחיקין אבל אמת המים דלא קוו וקימי דדרך היליכתן קא אזלי ואין מחלידין אימא דלא צריך לרחוקי קמ"ל דודאי צריך: פיסקא מרחיקין את הזרעים ואת המחרישה. משום דנכנסים שרשים של זרעים בכותל כדאמ' לקמן ומרעי לי'. הואיל דתני מחרישה למה לי למיתני זרעים שישוא דאין זרעים באים אלא ע"י מחרישה ומשני דאפי' בלא מחרישה מצי לזרוע במפולת יד דא"צ מחרישה בזורים משום כשזורעין בשוורים תולין שם שק מלא תבואה ומנקבין השק נקבים נקבים כשזורעין בכמה מקומות נופלת התבואה יותר ממקום אחד ולאחר כן חורשין כדי לכסות את התבואה ולהשוות את התבואה בשדה. אבל כשזורעין ביד משוה התבואה בשדה וא"צ מחרישה מש"ה איצטריך למתני במתני' זרעים ומחרישה דמזרעים לא מפקינן מחרישה. ומקשה ומחרישה מ"ט איצטריך למתני מאחר דתנא זרעים לא צריך למתני מחרישה דודאי אין חרישה בלי זרעים ומשני להרחיש לאילנות לצורך נטיעת אילנות דליכא זרעים ומש"ה איצטריך למתני מחרישה דמזרעים לא מפיק ליה מינה דמרחיקין: דמאחר דקתני מתני' מרחיקין אמת המים הכל הני ממילא איכא למשמע דמרחיקין זרעי' ומחרישה דהיינו משום מתונתא ותרתי דמיני למה לי משום מתונתא והא מש"ה מרחיקין הזרעים ומחרישה משום דמשקין הזרעים מן המים וקשה לכותל: תנא באי' קאי. דלא משקי זרעים אלא מטר אבל בבבל דצריכי להן מים להשקות שדותיהן מתוך שהיא יושבת במים אם

מסורת הש"ס

א) כלאים פרק ז מ"א, ב) [פי' רבינו חננאל יונקין כח הקרקע מתולדה שדרה בעיקרי הבתים. ערוך ערך תלד א'], ג) [ע"ש מ"ג], ד) [תוספתא פרק א], ה) אהלות פי"ג מ"ד ע"ש, ו) נ"א שאלה, ז) [ומטעמא כ"ל ועי' רש"ש]:

הגהות הב"ח

(א) גמ' התם בשופכין ת"ש לא יעיל אדם: (ב) שם לא מיבעיא עבה דכיון דחזי ליה: (ג) שם במתונא: (ד) רש"י ד"ה שמחלידין וכו' ומתמוטט הקרקע שתחת יסוד: (ה) ד"ה ובצונמא וכו' לטישטוש הקרקע: (ו) ד"ה אינו ממעט וכו' אין רקיק זה ממעט שיעורו וכו' לא מבטל ליה להתם: (ז) ד"ה דאית וכו' והם היו: (ח) תוס' ד"ה אמר וכו' לקמן אזרעים: (ט) ד"ה רקיק וכו' שלא יהא בשיריים כ"א אצבע על רוחב גודל: (י) בא"ד ושאינו עשוי לא לאורה: (כ) ד"ה מאי וכו' חדא דלאו סתימה מעלייתא היא לפי: (ל) ד"ה ותיפוק ליה פירוש אפי': (מ) ד"ה שנילושה וכו' בהדי הנך שממעטין כצ"ל ותיבת שאמר נמחק:

תורה אור השלם

א) הִנְנִי מֵבִיא אֵלֶיךָ רָעָה וּבִעַרְתִּי אַחֲרֶיךָ וְהִכְרַתִּי לְאַחְאָב מַשְׁתִּין בְּקִיר וְעָצוּר וְעָזוּב בְּיִשְׂרָאֵל: [מלכים א כא, כא]

לעזי רש"י

פרובניי"ר. פירוש להבריך, לכופף זמורת גפן מחוברת בקרקע, טומר בארץ ומבריך אותו לאחר החיבור וטומנו בעפר ומוציא ראש הזמורה ממקום אחר (עיין ערך ברך ב').

ליקוטי רש"י

המבריך. כופף את הזמורות בארץ שקורין פרופינ"א [ר"ה טו.]. [שכופף] הזמורה או היחור בארץ [סוטה מג.]. כופף אמצעית הגפן בקרקע ומכסהו בקרקע באמצעיתו וכשגדלו באמצעיתו מוציא עיקר הראשון ועושה שתי גפנים [רשב"ם לקמן פג.]. שמחלידין. לשון חולדה שחופרת (חולין דף לב.) שמקלקלת מתחת לקרקעית הכור [לקמן כה.]. צונמא. לאמת בלשון ארמי סלע [בראשית מא, כג] [רשב"ם לקמן פט.]. בסריא. נרקב ומסריח שאין ראוי למאכל בהמה. חזי לטינא. טיט לגבול לבנים [ביצה לו.].

חשק שלמה על רבינו גרשום א) נ"ל דזרעים לא מפקינן ממחרישה ומקשה מחרישה מ"ט וכו'

לְצְדָדִין קָא מִשְׁתָּרְשֵׁי – **spread their roots sideways?!** וְהָא תְּנַן – **But we have learned in a Mishnah:**[1] הַמַּבְרִיךְ אֶת הַגֶּפֶן בָּאָרֶץ – Concerning ONE WHO BENT a branch of A VINE and inserted it INTO THE GROUND,[2] the following law applies: אִם אֵין עַל גַּבָּה עָפָר שְׁלֹשָׁה טְפָחִים – IF the soil ABOVE IT [the buried part of the branch] IS NOT THREE *TEFACHIM* deep, לֹא יָבִיא זֶרַע עָלֶיהָ – HE MAY NOT PLANT[3] A SEED ON top of IT. Since there is a gap of less than three *tefachim* between the seed and the branch, the seed's roots might derive nourishment directly from the branch.[4] וְתָנֵי עֲלָהּ – **And the** following **Baraisa was taught in reference to [this ruling]:** אֲבָל זוֹרֵעַ אֶת הַצְּדָדִין אֵילָךְ וְאֵילָךְ – BUT HE MAY PLANT A SEED ON EITHER SIDE of the buried part of the branch.[5] The reason for this permit is that seeds do not take root sideways, only downwards. Therefore, the reason for our Mishnah's ruling (viz. seeds must be distanced from a neighbor's wall) cannot be, as previously assumed, that the seed's roots will spread sideways and damage the wall's foundation. – ? –

Its previous approach having been rejected, the Gemara offers a different explanation for the Mishnah's restriction against seeds: אָמַר רַבִּי חַגָּא בְּשֵׁם רַבִּי יוֹסֵי – **R' Chaga said in the name of R' Yose:** מִפְּנֵי שֶׁמַּחֲלִידִין אֶת הַקַּרְקַע וּמַעֲלִין עָפָר תִּיחוּחַ – One may not plant seeds near a wall **because [their roots] will break up the ground** directly beneath the seeds, **causing soft soil to rise** to the surface. This in turn causes a weakening of the soil upon which the wall stands.

The Mishnah said:
וְאֶת מֵי רַגְלַיִם מִן הַכּוֹתֶל שְׁלֹשָׁה טְפָחִים וכו׳ – URINE must be distanced THREE *TEFACHIM* FROM A WALL **etc.**

The Gemara quotes an Amoraic ruling that is apparently contradicted by our Mishnah:
אָמַר רַבָּה בַּר בַּר חָנָה – **Rabbah bar bar Chanah said:** מוּתָּר לְאָדָם לְהַשְׁתִּין מַיִם בְּצַד כּוֹתְלוֹ שֶׁל חֲבֵירוֹ – **A person is permitted to urinate at the side of his fellow's wall,** דִּכְתִיב – **for it is written:** "וְהִכְרַתִּי לְאַחְאָב מַשְׁתִּין בְּקִיר וְעָצוּר וְעָזוּב בְּיִשְׂרָאֵל" – ***I will cut off from** the house of **Achav** every **one that urinates against a wall*** (i.e. every male), *the wealth* ***stored*** *in the houses, and the livestock* ***left out*** *in the fields* ***in Israel.***[6] וְהָא אֲנַן תְּנַן – **But we have learned in our Mishnah:** וְאֶת מֵי רַגְלַיִם מִן הַכּוֹתֶל שְׁלֹשָׁה טְפָחִים – URINE must be distanced THREE *TEFACHIM* FROM THE WALL of a neighbor. – ? –

The Gemara answers:
הָתָם בְּשׁוֹפְכִין – **There,** in our Mishnah, the reference is **to [urine] poured** from a chamber pot, not to the act of urination.[7]

The Gemara raises another challenge to the view of Rabbah bar bar Chanah:
(תָּא שְׁמַע – **Come, learn** from the following Baraisa: לֹא יִשְׁפּוֹךְ אָדָם מַיִם בְּצַד כּוֹתְלוֹ שֶׁל חֲבֵירוֹ – A PERSON MAY NOT POUR WATER AT THE SIDE OF HIS FELLOW'S WALL אֶלָּא אִם כֵּן הִרְחִיק מִמֶּנּוּ שְׁלֹשָׁה טְפָחִים – UNLESS HE DISTANCES himself at least THREE *TEFACHIM* FROM [THE WALL]. This contradicts Rabbah bar bar Chanah's teaching that one is permitted to urinate against a wall. – ? –

The Gemara answers:
הָתָם נַמִּי בְּשׁוֹפְכִין – **There, too,** the reference is to **[water] poured** from a pot.[8]

The Gemara refutes the teaching of Rabbah bar bar Chanah:
תָּא שְׁמַע – **Come, learn** from the following Baraisa: לֹא יַשְׁתִּין אָדָם מַיִם בְּצַד כּוֹתְלוֹ שֶׁל חֲבֵירוֹ – A PERSON MAY NOT URINATE AT THE SIDE OF HIS FELLOW'S WALL אֶלָּא אִם כֵּן הִרְחִיק מִמֶּנּוּ שְׁלֹשָׁה טְפָחִים – UNLESS HE DISTANCES himself THREE *TEFACHIM* FROM [THE WALL]. בַּמֶּה דְּבָרִים אֲמוּרִים – IN WHAT circumstances DOES THIS RULING APPLY? בְּכוֹתֶל לְבֵינִים – It applies IN the case of A WALL made OF clay BRICKS, which can be dissolved by urine. אֲבָל בְּכוֹתֶל אֲבָנִים – BUT IN the case of A WALL made OF STONE, בִּכְדֵי שֶׁלֹּא יַזִּיק – he need distance himself only SO FAR AS is required NOT TO DAMAGE the wall. וְכַמָּה – AND HOW [FAR] is that? טֶפַח – A *TEFACH*.[9] וְשֶׁל צוּנְמָא – In the case OF a stone wall built on ROCKY GROUND, מוּתָּר – IT IS PERMISSIBLE to urinate right next to it.[10] תְּיוּבְתָּא דְּרַבָּה בַּר בַּר חָנָה – Surely this is **a refutation** of the ruling **of Rabbah bar bar Chanah,** who permitted urinating against any type of

NOTES

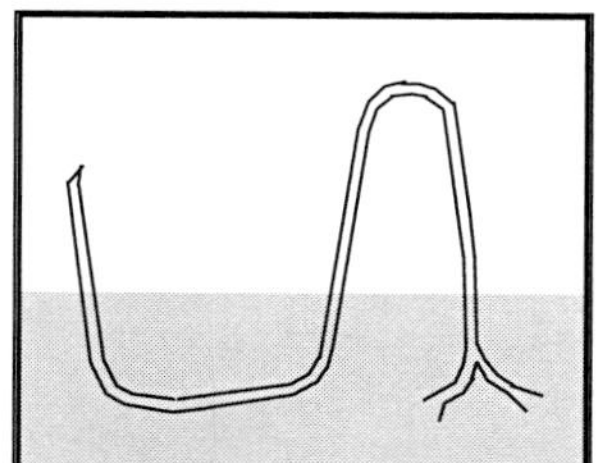

1. *Kilayim* 7:1.

2. See diagram.

3. Literally: bring.

4. This comes under the Torah's prohibition against הַרְכָּבָה, *grafting* [one species with another] (*Tosafos, Rashba* et al.).

5. However, this is permitted only if he does not plant the seed close to the vine where it breaches the surface. For there is a Biblical prohibition [כִּלְאֵי הַכֶּרֶם, *mixtures of the vineyard*] against planting grain or greens near vines (*Deuteronomy* 22:9). With regard to a vineyard (a minimum of five vines planted in a particular configuration – see 14a note 15), this means that one may not plant grain or greens within four *amos* of the vineyard. But in our case, which involves a solitary vine, it is not considered a forbidden "mixture" unless the grain or green is planted so close to the visible part of the vine that it derives nourishment from the same earth. [The exact distance is a matter of Tannaic dispute: According to the Sages, grain and greens must be distanced six *tefachim* from a solitary vine. In R' Akiva's view, a distance of three *tefachim* is sufficient – *Kilayim* 6:1] (see *Rashi* here and to *Shabbos* 85a). See diagram.

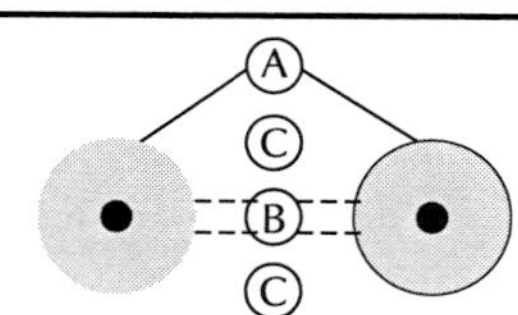

A. Perimeter around vine (3 or 6 *tefachim*) – forbidden as כִּלְאֵי הַכֶּרֶם.

B. Area directly above buried branch – forbidden where the buried branch is less than 3 *tefachim* below the surface (הַרְכָּבָה).

C. Permitted.

6. *I Kings* 21:21 (our translation follows that reported by *Radak* in the name of his father, and *Metzudos*).

Since the verse uses the expression "one that urinates against the wall" as a description of males, we may infer that men commonly conduct themselves in this manner (*Rashi*). Hence, it is evident that such behavior is permitted.

7. When urine is poured from a pot, it is deposited at a greater rate than by one who is urinating (*R' Yosef ibn Migash*, cited by *Shitah Mekubetzes*; see *Meiri*).

8. [Since the Baraisa stated "a person may not pour" (as opposed to "one may not urinate"), the Gemara's answer is obvious. For this reason, *Maharal* states that this passage should be deleted (see *Dikdukei Sofrim*), and therefore it appears in parentheses in our editions of the Gemara. *Bach* alleviates the problem by citing a version of the Baraisa which reads, לֹא יָטִיל אָדָם וכו׳, *A person may not deposit etc.*, which could refer either to urinating or to the emptying of a pot.]

9. One may not urinate within a *tefach* of a stone wall, lest the urine soften the ground adjacent to the base of the wall (*Rashi*). [The wall itself, however, since it is made of stone, is impervious to damage; therefore, one is not required to distance oneself more than a *tefach* from such a wall.]

From *Rashi* to the Mishnah (17a ד״ה מן הכותל), it seems that *all* the substances listed in the Mishnah need be distanced only from a wall of clay bricks, not from a stone wall. However, other commentators maintain that with regard to all the substances (except urine), the three-*tefach* limit applies even to a stone wall (see *R' Yonah, Rashba* et al.; see also *Choshen Mishpat* 155:9).

10. Since the wall is of stone *and* is built on rocky ground, urine cannot cause it any damage (see *Rashi* and preceding note).

לצדדין קא משתרשי והא [א] תנן [א]המבריך את הגפן בארץ אם אין על גבה עפר שלשה טפחים לא יביא זרע עליה ותני עלה [ב]אבל זורע את הצדדין אילך ואילך אמר רבי חגא בשם רבי יוסי מפני שמחלידין [ג]את הקרקע ומעלין עפר תיחוח: ואת מי רגלים מן הכותל ג' טפחים וכו': אמר רבה בר בר חנה מותר לאדם להשתין מים בצד כותלו של חבירו דכתיב [א]והכרתי לאחאב משתין בקיר ועצור ועזוב בישראל והא אנן תנן ואת מי רגלים מן הכותל שלשה טפחים התם בשופכין (א) [ג](ת"ש לא ישפוך אדם מים בצד כותלו של חבירו אלא אם כן הרחיק ממנו ג' טפחים התם נמי בשופכין) ת"ש [ד] [ג]לא ישתין אדם מים בצד כותלו של חבירו אלא אם כן הרחיק ממנו ג' טפחים בד"א בכותל לבינים אבל בכותל אבנים בכדי שלא יזיק וכמה טפח ושל צונמא מותר תיובתא דרבה בר בר חנה תיובתא והא רבה בר בר חנה קרא קאמר התם הכי קאמר אפילו מידי דדרכיה לאישתוני בקיר לא שביקנא ליה ומאי ניהו כלבא אמר ר' טובי בר קיסנא אמר שמואל [ד]רקיק אינו ממעט בחלון מאי איריא רקיק אפי' עבה נמי לא מיבעיא קאמר לא מיבעיא עבה (ב) כיון דאיחזי ליה לא מבטיל ליה אבל רקיק דממאיס אימא בטולי מבטיל ליה קמ"ל ותיפוק ליה דהוה ליה דבר שהוא מקבל טומאה וכל דבר שהוא מקבל טומאה אינו חוצץ בפני הטומאה [ה]שנילוש במי פירות מיתיבי [ו]קופה מלאה תבן וחבית מלאה גרוגרות המונחים בחלון רואין כל שאילו ינטלו ויכולין תבן וגרוגרות לעמוד בפני עצמן חוצצין ואם לאו אין חוצצין והא תבן חזי לבהמתו [ז]בסריא חזי לטינא [ח]דאית ביה קוצי חזי להסקה (ג) [ט]במתונא חזי להסק גדול הסק גדול לא שכיח גרוגרות הא חזו ליה אמר שמואל [י]בשהתריפו וכן תני רבה בר אבוה בשהתריפו האי חבית היכי דמיא אי דפומא לבר

רש"י

לצדדין קא משתרשי. ומחלידין מתחת לכותל ומקלקלים יסודו: **המבריך את הגפן.** גפן יחידי שאין בזורעים [י]שאלא משום עירבוב דאין כרם בפחות מחמש גפנים שתים כנגד שתים ואחת יוצאה זנב אלא שלא יינק הזרע מן הגפן: **מבריך.** כמו ויברך הגמלים (בראשית כד) כופף זמורת גפן מחוברת ומבריכה בקרקע בלידיה לכאן ולכאן וקורין בלע"ז פרובניי"ר: **שמחלידין את הקרקע.** אצל הכותל במקומן ומעלין עפר תיחוח ומתמוטט (ד) קרקע יסוד הכותל לצדדין: **משתין בקיר.** אלמא דרך בני אדם כן: **בשופכין.** עביט מלא ושופכו שם: **לא ישתין.** ליכא לאוקמי אלא במשתין ממש: **בכותל לבינים.** שהם של טיט שנתיבשו בחמה והם נימוקים מחמת המים: **וכמה טפח.** מפני שמטשטש את הקרקע סמוך ליסוד הכותל: **ובצונמא.** אם כותל זה בנוי בסלע דליכא למיחש (ה) בטישטוש קרקע: **מותר.** סמוך ממש ואסיפא קאי בכותל אבנים: **רקיק.** סופגנין חררה דקה ורכה: **אינו ממעט בחלון.** שבין בית לבית ויש בו פותח טפח ומת מונח באחת מהן וטומאה בוקעת לצד שני אין רקיק (ו) ממעט שיעורן מלהוציא טומאה דכיון דראוי לאכילה לא מבטיל להתם דנהוי כמחילה: **אבל רקיק דמאיס.** מתוך שהוא דק ולחלוח הכותל מרטבו נמאס: **שנילוש במי פירות.** שאין מכשירין ואין אוכל מקבל טומאה בלא הכשר משקה הקרוי משקה כגון מים ויין וחלב: **וחבית מלא גרוגרות.** תאנים יבשים וכגון שלא הוכשרו: **כל שאילו ינטלו.** הקופה וחבית: **ויכולין.** התבן או הגרוגרות לעמוד בפני עצמן חוצצין בפני הטומאה: **ואם לאו אין חוצצין.** שהחבית והקופה אין חוצצין לפי שהן מקבלין טומאה: **סריא.** נרקב: **והא חזי לטינא.** ולא מבטל ליה: **דאית ביה קוצי.** (ז) והן היו רומסין ברגליהן בטיט: **הא חזו.** לאכילה. כולהו הנך תיובתא דשמואל דאמר מידי דחזי ליטלו משם לאחר זמן אין ממעט בחלון: **בשהתריפו.** התליעו: **אי פומיה לבר.** לצד הבית שאין המת בתוכו: שאין

תוספות

התם בשופכין. וא"ת בשלמא אי מיירי במשתין אע"ג דתנא ליה אמת המים תנא ליה נמי הא דס"ד משום לניעותא לישתרי אבל אי מיירי בשופכין מאי קמ"ל הא תנא ליה אמת המים דמהאי טעמא אמר לעיל דלא תני חול וי"ל דשאני חול שהוא כל שעה אצל הכותל אבל הכא מי רגלים כלים כרגע:

ותיובתא דרבה בר בר חנה. ולא מצי לשנויי דכי קאמר רבה בר בר חנה בצונמא מדלא הוה ליה לפרושי בהדיא ועוד דדריש מקרא ש"מ דלא מפליג:

אמר רב טובי רקיק אינו ממעט. הך שמעתתא מייתי הכא אגב דפריך לקמן (ח) זרעים כיון דקשו לכותל שקיל להו:

רקיק אינו ממעט בחלון. דיני חלון פי' ר"י ב"ר מרדכי על פי המשניות דאם הוא חלון העשוי לתשמיש שיעורו להביא טומאה בפותח טפח וכשיתמעט מטפח אפילו במשהו אינו מביא ואם הוא חלון שעשוי לאורה ועשוי בידי אדם שיעורו כמלא מקדח גדול של לשכה שהוא כמלא פונדיון האיטלקי שהוא סלע נירונית והיא יתירה על סלע סתם דסלע סתם הוא פחות ממלא מקדח סתם וכל שכן ממקדח גדול כדאמרינן בבכורות (דף לז:) ואותו חלון שעשוי לאורה אינו מתמעט מסתימת משהו כיון שהיה בו כשיעור אלא עד שיתמעט שלא יהא בשיריים (ט) רוס אצבעים על רוחב גודל ומאור שאינו עשוי בידי אדם אלא מעצמו כגון חררוהו מים או שרצים שיעורו מלא אגרוף חישב עליו לתשמיש שיעורו פותח טפח למאור שיעורו מלא מקדח ומלא אגרוף מפרש התם באגרופו של בן אבטיח ורבי יוסי אומר בראש כל אדם ושאינו עשוי (י) לאורה ולא לתשמיש אלא לאויר ולשמור גגות ופרדסים אותו שיעורו כמלא מקדח בינוני: **מאי** אידיא רקיק כו'. השתא ס"ד דנקט רקיק דוקא משום דאית ביה תרתי חדא (כ) דלא סתימה מעלייתא לפי שהוא רך ועשוי ליפול ועוד שאינו מבטלו משום הכי פריך אפי' עבה נמי שמתקיים הואיל ואינו מבטלו אינו ממעט:

ותיפוק ליה. (ל) אפי' אם יבטלו דאינו חוצץ משום דמקבל טומאה ותימה אם יבטל ליה תו לא מקבל טומאה וטהור כדמוכח בפרק העור והרוטב (חולין דף קכט. ושם) דאמר כיפת שאור שייחדה לישיבה בטלה ובית שסיככו בזרעים טהורים אלמא כיון דבטליה לא מקבל טומאה וי"ל דהתם מיירי כגון דעבד בהו שינוי מעשה דהא אמרי' (שבת דף נב:) כל הכלים יורדין לידי טומאה במחשבה ואין עולין מטומאה אלא ע"י שינוי מעשה וה"ה באוכלין דבעינן שינוי מעשה דאפילו בידות האוכלין מוכח בפרק קמא דסוכה (דף יד. ושם) דאיכא תנא דאית ליה דבעינן בהו שינוי מעשה: **שנילושה** במי פירות. הו"מ לשנויי כגון שאין בו כביצה ובמסכת אהלות (פי"ג מ"ה) (מ) שאמר שממעטים את הטפח חשיב פחות מכביצה אוכלין בהדי הנך:

מי פירות. פי' ר"ח כגון שמן ולא דק דשמן מכשיר הוא כדמוכח בפרק קמא דשבת (דף ה:) ובריש פרק חבית (שם קמד.) דשמן חשיב משקה אלא דוקא מוהל היוצא מתחילה: **בתיבנא** סריא. תימה אכתי חזיא לבהמתו ע"י פירוך כדמוכח בפרק בתרא דשבת (דף קנה:) דאמרינן תא שמע מפרכין את התבן כו' אלמא מיטרח באוכלא שרי ומשני בתיבנא סריא וי"ל דהכא מיירי שהוא מוסרח כל כך דאפי' ע"י שום תקון לא חזיא: **רואין** כל שאילו ינטלו. אין לפרש דטעם משום דסופו ליטול חבית וקופה ולהכי בעינן שיהו גרוגרות ותבן יכולין לעמוד בפני עצמן דא"כ למאי דפריך תבן הא קא חזי ליה ורוצה להוכיח מכאן דאפילו סופו ליטלו חוצץ תיקשי ליה אמאי צריך שיכולין לעמוד בפני עצמן אלא אומר ר"י דכך הוא הדין דכל דבר החוצץ בעינן שיוכל לעמוד בפני עצמו דקתני לעיל מהך משנה במסכת אהלות (פ"ו מ"ג) קוברי המת שהיו עוברין באכסדרה ובא אחד מהן והגיף את הדלת וסמכו במפתח אם יכולה דלת לעמוד בפני עצמה טהור ואם לאו טמא וכן חבית של גרוגרות וקופה של תבן שהן נתונין בחלון משמע דהכל חד טעמא הוא והיינו טעמא דסתימת ערלי הוא דכיון שאינו יכול לעמוד בפני עצמו אי נמי משום דבעינן דבר החוצץ עומד על ידי דבר שאינו מקבל טומאה ומיהו בפירוש משניות מצא ר"י דמפרש אפילו במפתח שאינו מקבל טומאה ומטמא דלא חשיב אהל לחוץ בפני הטומאה כיון שעמד על ידי כלי אף על פי שאינו מקבל טומאה ורבי אליעזר פליג עלה בתוספתא וקאמר דטהור כיון שהמפתח אינו מקבל טומאה ואולי לטעמייהו דפליגי במסכת אהלות (בפ"ו מ"א) בנדבך שהוא נתון על גבי כלים אפילו כלי גללים כלי אבנים כלי אדמה דלרבי אליעזר נעשה אהל לטהר ולרבנן אינו נעשה אהל אלא כשהוא נתון על גבי אבנים:

עין משפט נר מצוה

יד א ב מיי' פ"ו מהל' כלאים הל' ז טוש"ע י"ד סי' רצו סעיף ד:

טו ג ד מיי' פ"ט מהל' שכנים הל' ו סמג עשין פב טוש"ע ח"מ סי' קנה סעיף ו:

טז ה ו מיי' פ"ה מהל' טומאת מת הלכה ה:

יז ו ז ח ט י מיי' שם הלכה ג:

רבינו גרשום

יותר ולא מזיק כלל לכותל להכי לא תנא ליה והא קתני ר' הושעיא בתוספתא דידיה הני דמתני' וקתני חול. דתני בהדי הני דרישא דמזיקי משום מתונתא לחלוה. ולא קתני לה בהדי הנך דסיפא דגפת וזבל והנהו משום הבלא. ומקשי' מי לא תנן אמת המים וקתני בברכת הכובסין אע"ג דלא צריך הכא נמי לא ליתני חול ומשני אמת המים והנך ברכת הכובסין תרוייהו צריכי דאי תנא אמת המים דמרחיקין הוה אמינא משום דקביעי כל היומים מרחיקין דמקלקל לכותל אבל ברכת הכובסין דלא קביעי דמים מכונסין ניהו אימא אין מרחיקין: דקוו וקיימי ומחלידין בקרקע ואתיין על היסוד קמ"ל: דאי תנא ברכת הכובסין דמרחיקין אבל אמת המים דלא קוו וקיימי דדרך הליכתן קא אזלי ואין מחלידין אימא דלא צריך לרחוקי קמ"ל דודאי צריך: פיסקא מרחיקין את הזרעים ואת המחרישה. משום דנכנסים שרשים של זרעים בכותל כדאמ' לקמן ומרעי לי'. הואיל דהני מחרישה למה לי למיתני זרעים פשיטא דאין זרעים באים אלא ע"י מחרישה ומשני דאפי' בלא מחרישה מצי לזרוע במפולת יד דא"צ מחרישה בזרעים משום כשזורעין בשוורים תולין שם שק מלא תבואה ומנוקב בהשק נקבים נקבים כשזורעין בבהמה מקומות נופלת התבואה יותר מקום אחד ולאחר כן חורשין כדי לכסות את התבואה ואת התבואה בשדה. אבל כשזורעין ביד משוה התבואה בשדה וא"צ מחרישה מש"ה איצטריך למתני במתני' זרעים [א] לא מפקינן מחרישה. ומקשה ומחרישה מ"ט איצטריך למתני מאחר דתנא זרעים לא צריך למתני מחרישה דודאי אין חרישה בלי זרעים ומשני לחרוש לאילנות לצורך נטיעת אילנות דהכא ליכא זרעים ומש"ה איצטריך למתני מחרישה דמזרעים לא מפיק מחרישה: ותיפוק ליה מינה דמרחיקין. דמאחר דקתני מתני' מרחיקין אמת המים וכל הני ממילא איכא למשמע דמרחיקין זרעי' ומחרישה דהיינו משום מתונתא ותרתי זימני למה לי משום מתונתא והא מש"ה מרחיקין זרעים ומחרישה משום דמשקין הזרעים מן המים וקשה לכותל: תנא בא"י קאי. לא משקי זרעים אלא מטר אבל בבבל דצריכי להן מים להשקות שדותיהן מתוך שהיא יושבת במים אם יבשו מים צריך להביא לשם מים כדי להשקות השדה שמתוך שהיא רגילה בכך צריך להשקות בכל שעה: [ע"כ שייך לעמוד א'] מדקתני מתני' מרחיקין את הזרעים ג' טפחים. מכלל דזרעים לצדדין עקמי ומשתרשי ואזלי ומש"ה מרחקין כי היכי דלא ליזקו בכותל ורמינהו המבריך את הגפן בארץ [illegible]

מסורת הש"ס

א) כלאים פרק ז מ"א, ב) [פי' רבינו חננאל יונקין [illegible]], ג) רש"ל מ"ז, ד) [תוספתא פרק א], ה) אהלות פ"ו מ"ג ע"ש, ו) נ"א שאלה, ז) [ומטעמא כל"ל ועי' רש"ש].

הגהות הב"ח

(א) גמ' התם בשופכין ת"ש לא ישפוך אדם וכו' עד בשופכין: (ב) שם לא מיבעיא עבה דכיון דאחזי ליה: (ג) שם במתונא: (ד) רש"י ד"ה שמחלידין וכו' ומתמוטט הקרקע מתחת יסוד: (ה) ד"ה ובצונמא וכו' לטשטוש הקרקע: (ו) ד"ה אינו ממעט וכו' אין רקיק זה ממעט שיעורו וכו' לא מבטל ליה להתם: (ז) ד"ה דאית וכו' והם היו: (ח) תוס' ד"ה אמר וכו' לקמן אזרעים: (ט) ד"ה רקיק וכו' שלא יהא בשיריים כ"א אצבע על רוחב גודל: (י) בא"ד ושאינו עשוי לא לאורה: (כ) ד"ה מאי וכו' חדא דלאו סתימה מעלייתא היא לפי: (ל) ד"ה ותיפוק ליה פירוש אפי': (מ) ד"ה שנילושה וכו' בהדי הנך שממעטין כל"ל ותיבת שאמר נמחק:

תורה אור השלם

א) הִנְנִי מֵבִיא אֵלֶיךָ רָעָה וּבִעַרְתִּי אַחֲרֶיךָ וְהִכְרַתִּי לְאַחְאָב מַשְׁתִּין בְּקִיר וְעָצוּר וְעָזוּב בְּיִשְׂרָאֵל: [מלכים א כא, כא]

לעזי רש"י

פרובניי"ר. פירוש להבריך, לכופף זמורת גפן מחוברת בקרקע, חופר באדמה ומבריך הזמור וטומנו בעפר ומוציא ראשו היסוד במקום אחר (ערוך ערך ברך ב'):

ליקוטי רש"י

המבריך. כופף את הזמורות בארץ שקורין פרופינ"א [ר"ה ט:]. [שכופף] הזמורה או היסוד בארץ [סוטה מג:]. כופף אמצעית הגפן בקרקע ומכסהו בקרקע באמצעיתו ובולטה באמצעיתו חוצפו עיקר הראשון ועשה שתי גפנים [רשב"ם לקמן פג.]. שמחלידין. לשון חלדה הולכת שחיטה (חולין דף לג.). שמהלכלת מתחת לקרקעות הבור (לקמן כה:). צונמא. טונמא בלשון ארמי סלע [בראשית מא, כג ונדה ח:]. אבן [רשב"ם לקמן סט:]. בסריא. נרקב ומסריח שאין ראוי לאכול בהמה. חזי לטינא. לטוח לגבנים [ביצה ל.].

חשק שלמה על רבינו גרשום א) [נ"ל דזרעים לא מפקינן ממחרישה ומקשה ממחרישה מ"ט וכו']:

wall?[11] תְּיוּבְתָּא – Indeed, it is **a refutation** of his view.

The Gemara, however, asks:

וְהָא רַבָּה בַּר בַּר חָנָה קְרָא קָאָמַר – **But Rabbah bar bar Chanah cited a verse** in support of his view. How is this verse to be explained?

The Gemara answers:

הָתָם הָכִי קָאָמַר – **There,** in the verse, **this is** what is **meant:** אֲפִילּוּ מִידִי דְּדַרְכֵּיהּ לְאִישְׁתּוּנֵי בְּקִיר – **"Even something whose practice it is to urinate against a wall,** לָא שְׁבִיקְנָא לֵיהּ – **I will not leave him** [Achav]." וּמַאי נִיהוּ – **And what is this?** כַּלְבָּא – **A dog.** The verse does not refer to a person, but to a dog.

The Gemara shifts to a different topic, which is tangentially related to our Mishnah.[12] The law of טוּמְאַת אֹהֶל, *tumas ohel* (roof *tumah*), states that a human corpse transmits *tumah* to people, utensils and foodstuffs that are under the same roof as it. But if a wall separates the corpse from the utensils etc., *tumah* is not transmitted to them unless there is an opening of at least one *tefach* by one *tefach*[13] in the wall. If the size of the opening is reduced to less than one *tefach* by one *tefach* by an object that has been abandoned there, the opening does not allow the passage of *tumah*.[14] The Gemara discusses whether an object that is in the opening but has *not* been abandoned there likewise obstructs the spread of *tumah:*

אָמַר רַבִּי טוּבִי בַּר קִיסְנָא אָמַר שְׁמוּאֵל – **R' Tuvi bar Kisna said in the name of Shmuel:** רָקִיק אֵינוֹ מְמַעֵט בְּחַלּוֹן – **A wafer** that is in an opening **does not reduce the size of the opening,**[15] for it will probably be removed to be eaten. Since it is not abandoned in the opening, it does not diminish the size of the opening.

The Gemara asks:

מַאי אִירְיָא רָקִיק – **Why** did Shmuel specifically **discuss a wafer,** which is thin? אֲפִילּוּ עָבֶה נַמִּי – According to his reasoning, **even a thick [cake]** does not reduce the size of an opening. – ? –

The Gemara answers:

לֹא מִיבַּעְיָא קָאָמַר – **[Shmuel] formulates his statement** according to the principle that there is **no need** to state the more obvious case. לֹא מִיבַּעְיָא עָבֶה – There is **no need** to discuss **a thick [cake].** כֵּיוָן דְּאִיחֲזֵי לֵיהּ לָא מְבַטֵּיל לֵיהּ – **Since [such a cake] is fit for one** to eat, **one** certainly **does not abandon**[16] it in the opening. אֲבָל רָקִיק דִּמְמְאִיס – In the case of **a** soft thin **wafer, however, which becomes** moldy and **repulsive** by absorbing moisture from the wall, אֵימָא בַּטּוּלֵי מְבַטֵּיל לֵיהּ – **I might have said** that **one surely abandons it** there. קָא מַשְׁמַע לָן – **[Shmuel]** therefore **informs us** that even a wafer is not abandoned, and thus does not reduce the dimensions of the opening.

The Gemara raises another difficulty with Shmuel's statement: וְתֵיפּוֹק לֵיהּ דְּהָוֵה לֵיהּ דָּבָר שֶׁהוּא מְקַבֵּל טוּמְאָה – **But let [Shmuel's ruling] emerge from** the fact that **[a wafer] is susceptible to** ***tumah*** contamination, וְכָל דָּבָר שֶׁהוּא מְקַבֵּל טוּמְאָה אֵינוֹ חוֹצֵץ בִּפְנֵי הַטּוּמְאָה – **and** it is a well-known rule that **any object susceptible to** ***tumah*** contamination **cannot obstruct** the passage of ***tumah***.[17] Therefore, even if the wafer were to be abandoned in the opening, it would not reduce the dimensions of the opening. – ? –

The Gemara answers:

שֶׁנִּילַּשׁ בְּמֵי פֵּירוֹת – Shmuel refers to a wafer made from a dough **that was kneaded with fruit juice,** instead of water. Such a wafer is not susceptible to *tumah* contamination.[18]

The Gemara challenges Shmuel's view that an object does not reduce the size of an opening unless it is abandoned there:

מֵיתִיבֵי – **They challenged** Shmuel's ruling from the following Mishnah:[19] קוּפָּה מְלֵאָה תֶּבֶן – Regarding A BOX FULL OF STRAW וְחָבִית מְלֵאָה גְּרוֹגְרוֹת – OR A KEG FULL OF DRIED FIGS הַמּוּנָּחִים בְּחַלּוֹן – THAT IS LYING IN AN OPENING between a room in which a corpse lies and an adjacent room under the same roof, רוֹאִין – WE CONSIDER the following: כָּל שֶׁאִילּוּ יִנָּטְלוּ – In EVERY case WHERE, IF [THE BOX OR BARREL] WERE TO BE REMOVED, וִיכוֹלִין תֶּבֶן וּגְרוֹגְרוֹת לַעֲמוֹד בִּפְנֵי עַצְמָן – THE STRAW OR DRIED FIGS WOULD BE ABLE TO STAY in the opening BY THEMSELVES, חוֹצְצִין – THEY [the straw or figs] OBSTRUCT the passage of *tumah* by reducing the size of the opening.[20] וְאִם לָאו – BUT IF the straw or figs would NOT be able to stay in the opening without the support of their containers, אֵין חוֹצְצִין – THEY DO NOT OBSTRUCT the passage of *tumah*.[21]

The Gemara shows how this Mishnah contradicts Shmuel's ruling:

וְהָא תֶּבֶן חָזֵי לִבְהֶמְתּוֹ – **But straw is fit** as fodder **for one's animal** and therefore it will probably be removed from the opening for this purpose. Yet, although the straw is not abandoned, the Mishnah rules that it reduces the size of the opening. This belies Shmuel's ruling that an item does not reduce the size of an opening unless it is abandoned there. – ? –

The Gemara answers:

בְּסַרְיָא – The Mishnah is dealing **with rotted [straw],** which is unfit for fodder.

The Gemara asks further:

חָזֵי לְטִינָא – **But** even **[rotted straw] is fit for** the reinforcement of **clay,** which is used to make bricks. It is likely to be removed from the opening for this purpose, and yet, contrary to Shmuel's ruling, it reduces the size of the opening. – ? –

The Gemara answers:

דְּאִית בֵּיהּ קוֹצֵי – The Mishnah refers to **[straw] that contains**

NOTES

11. The teaching of Rabbah bar bar Chanah cannot be explained as referring specifically to a stone wall built on rock, for his statement was made without any qualification. Furthermore, he adduced a Scriptural source [that makes no qualification] as proof (*Tosafos*).

12. *Tosafos* (see below, 20a notes 7 and 17).

13. These dimensions apply only to an opening that is used [to pass things from one room to the other]. Different rules apply to other types of opening, such as one whose purpose it is to provide light (*Tosafos*).

14. Since the object is permanently abandoned there, it is considered part of the wall (*Rashi*). Thus, the size of the opening is reduced.

15. חַלּוֹן is usually translated as window. See, however, note 13.

16. Literally: nullify. [Since he does not intend to abandon the cake, it does not lose its independent identity and does not merge with the wall – see note 14.]

17. See *Ohalos* 8:3.

18. From *Leviticus* 11:34,38 it is derived that foodstuffs cannot become *tamei* unless they had first come into contact – after they have been detached from the ground or tree where they grew – with one of the following seven liquids: wine, blood, oil, milk, dew, honey and water. Fruit juices (other than wine and olive oil) are not classified as liquids in this regard (see *Machshirin* 6:4).

19. *Ohalos* 6:2.

20. The figs had not come into contact with one of the seven liquids (*Rashi*; see note 18).

21. The keg and the box, since they are utensils, are susceptible to *tumah* contamination. Hence, when considering whether their contents obstruct the passage of *tumah*, the keg and box themselves are disregarded (*Rashi;* see 20a note 3; cf. *Tosafos*). [If, without their supporting containers, the figs and straw would fall, they certainly

עין משפט נר מצוה

יד א ב מיי' פ"ו מהל' כלאים הל' ז טוש"ע י"ד סי' רלה סעיף ד:
טו ג מיי' פ"ט מהל' שכנים הל' ו סמג עשין פב טוש"ע ח"מ סי' קנה סעיף ו:
טז ד ה מיי' פט"ו מהל' טומאת מת הלכה א:
יז ו ז ח ט י מיי' שם הלכה ב:

לצדדין קא משתרשי והא [א] תנן [א] המבריך את הגפן בארץ אם אין על גבה עפר שלשה טפחים לא יביא זרע עליה ותני עלה [ב] אבל זורע את הצדדין אילך ואילך אמר רבי חגא בשם רבי יוסי מפני שמחלידין [ג] את הקרקע ומעלין עפר תיחוח: ואת מי רגלים מן הכותל ג' טפחים וכו': אמר רבה בר בר חנה מותר לאדם להשתין מים בצד כותלו של חבירו דכתיב [א] והכרתי לאחאב משתין בקיר ועצור ועזוב בישראל והא אנן תנן ואת מי רגלים מן הכותל שלשה טפחים התם בשופכין (א) [ג] (ת"ש לא ישפוך אדם מים בצד כותלו של חבירו אלא אם כן הרחיק ממנו ג' טפחים התם נמי בשופכין) ת"ש [ד] לא ישתין אדם מים בצד כותלו של חבירו אלא אם כן הרחיק ממנו ג' טפחים בד"א בכותל לבינים אבל בכותל אבנים בכדי שלא יזיק וכמה טפח ושל צונמא מותר תיובתא דרבה בר בר חנה תיובתא והא רבה בר בר חנה קרא קאמר התם הכי קאמר אפילו מידי דדרכיה לאישתוני בקיר לא שביקנא ליה ומאי ניהו כלבא אמר ר' טובי בר קיסנא אמר שמואל [ד] רקיק אינו ממעט בחלון מאי איריא רקיק אפי' עבה נמי לא מיבעיא קאמר לא מיבעיא עבה (ב) כיון דאיחזי ליה לא מבטיל ליה אבל רקיק דממאיס אימא בטולי מבטיל ליה קמ"ל ותיפוק ליה דהוה ליה דבר שהוא מקבל טומאה וכל דבר שהוא מקבל טומאה אינו חוצץ בפני הטומאה [ה] שנילוש במי פירות מיתיבי [ו] קופה מלאה תבן וחבית מלאה גרוגרות המונחים בחלון רואין כל שאילו ינטלו ויכולין תבן וגרוגרות לעמוד בפני עצמן חוצצין ואם לאו אין חוצצין והא תבן חזי לבהמתו [ז] בסריא חזי לטינא [ח] דאית ביה קוצי להסקה (ג) [ט] במתונא חזי להסק גדול הסק גדול לא שכיח גרוגרות הא חזו ליה אמר שמואל [י] בשהתריפו וכן תני רבה בר אבוה בשהתריפו האי חבית היכי דמיא אי דפומא לבר

רש"י

לצדדין קא משתרשי. ומחלידין מתחת לכותל ומקלקלים יסודו: המבריך את הגפן. גפן יחידי שאין בזרעים [י] שאלא משום עירבוב דאין כרם בפחות מחמש גפנים שתים כנגד שתים ואחת יוצא זנב אלא שלא יינק הזרע מן הגפן: מבריך. כמו ויברך הגמלים (בראשית כד) כופף זמורת גפן מחוברת ומבריכה בקרקע בצידיה לכאן ולכאן וקורין בלע"ז פרובניי"ר: שמחלידין את הקרקע. אצל הכותל במקומן ומעלין עפר תיחוח ומתמוטט (ד) קרקע יסוד הכותל לצדדין: משתין בקיר. אלמא דרך בני אדם כן: בשופכין. עביט מלא ושופכו שם: לא ישתין. ליכא לאוקמי אלא במשתין ממש: בכותל לבינים. שהם של טיט שנתייבשו בחמה והם נימוקים מחמת המים: וכמה טפח. מפני שמטשטש את הקרקע סמוך ליסוד הכותל: ובצונמא. אם כותל זה בנוי בסלע דליכא למיחש (ה) בטישטוש קרקע: מותר. סמוך ממש ואסיפא קאי בכותל אבנים: רקיק. סופגנין חררה דקה ורכה: אינו ממעט בחלון. שבין בית לבית ויש בו פותח טפח ומת מונח באחת מהן וטומאה בוקעת לצד שני אין רקיק (ו) ממעט שיעורן מלהוציא טומאה דכיון דראוי לאכילה לא מבטיל להתם דנהוי כמחיצה: אבל רקיק דמאיס. מתוך שהוא דק ולחלוח הכותל מרטבו נמאס: שנילוש במי פירות. שאין מכשירין ואין אוכל מקבל טומאה בלא הכשר משקה הקרוי משקה כגון מים ויין וחלב: וחבית מלא גרוגרות. תאנים יבשים וכגון שלא הוכשרו: כל שאילו ינטלו. הקופה וחבית: ויכולין. התבן או הגרוגרות לעמוד בפני עצמן חוצצין בפני הטומאה: ואם לאו אין חוצצין. שהחבית והקופה אין חוצצין לפי שהן מקבלין טומאה: סריא. נרקב: והא חזי לטינא. ולא מבטל ליה: דאית ביה קוצי. (ז) והן היו רומסין ברגליהן בטיט: הא חזו. לאכילה. כולהו הנך תיובתא דשמואל דאמר מידי דחזי ליטלו משם לאחר זמן אין ממעט בחלון: בשהתריפו. התליעו: אי פומיה לבר. לצד הבית שאין המת בתוכו: שאין

תוספות

התם בשופכין. וא"ת בשלמא אי מיירי במשתין אע"ג דתנא ליה אמת המים תנא ליה נמי האי דס"ד משום צניעותא ליתסרי אבל אי מיירי בשופכין מאי קמ"ל הא תנא ליה אמת המים דמהאי טעמא אמר לעיל דלא תני חול י"ל דשאני חול שהוא כל שעה אצל הכותל אבל הנך מי רגלים כלים כרגע:

ותיובתא דרבה בר בר חנה. ולא מצי לשנויי דכי קאמר רבה בר בר חנה בצונמא חדא דהוה ליה לפרושי בהדיא ועוד דדריש מקרא ש"מ דלא מפליג:

אמר רב טובי רקיק אינו ממעט. הך שמעתתא מייתי הכא אגב דפריך לקמן (ח) זרעים כיון דקשו לכותל שקיל להו:

רקיק אינו ממעט בחלון. דיני חלון פי' ר"י ב"ר מרדכי על פי המשניות דאם הוא חלון העשוי לתשמיש שיעורו להביא טומאה בפותח טפח וכשיתמעט מטפח אפילו במשהו אינו מביא ואם הוא חלון שעשוי לאורה ועשוי בידי אדם שיעורו כמלא מקדח גדול של לשכה שהוא כמלא פונדיון האיטלקי שהוא סלע נירונית והיא יתירה על סלע סתם דסלע סתם הוא פחות ממלא מקדח סתם וכל שכן ממקדח גדול כדאמרינן בבכורות (דף לח:) ואותו חלון שעשוי לאורה אינו מתמעט מסתימת משהו כיון שהיה בו כשיעור אלא עד שיתמעט שלא יהא בשיריים (ט) רום אצבעים על רוחב גודל ומאור שאינו עשוי בידי אדם אלא מעצמו כגון חררוהו מים או שרצים שיעורו מלא אגרוף חישב עליו לתשמיש שיעורו פותח טפח למאור שיעורו מלא מקדח ומלא אגרוף מפרש התם באגרופו של בן אבטיח ורבי יוסי אומר בראש כל אדם ושאינו עשוי (י) לאורה ולא לתשמיש אלא לאויר ולשמור גגות ופרדסים אותו שיעורו כמלא מקדח בינוני: מאי איריא רקיק כו'. השתא ס"ד דנקט רקיק דוקא משום דאית ביה תרתי חדא (כ) דלא סתימה מעלייתא לפי שהוא רך ועשוי ליפול ועוד שאינו מבטלו משום הכי פריך אפי' עבה נמי שמתקיים הואיל ואינו מבטלו אינו ממעט:

ותיפוק ליה. (ל) אפי' אם יבטלו דאינו חוצץ משום דמקבל טומאה ותימה אם יבטל ליה תו לא מקבל טומאה וטהור כדמוכח בפרק העור והרוטב (חולין דף קכט. ושם) דאמר כיפת שאור שייחדה לישיבה בטלה ובית שסיככו בזרעים טהורים אלמא כיון דבטליה לא מקבל טומאה וי"ל דהתם מיירי כגון דעבד בהו שינוי מעשה דהא אמרי' (שבת דף נב:) כל הכלים יורדין לידי טומאה במחשבה ואין עולין מטומאה אלא ע"י שינוי מעשה וה"ה באוכלין דבעינן שינוי מעשה דאפילו בידות האוכלין מוכח בפרק קמא דסוכה (דף יד. ושם) דאיכא תנא דאית ליה דבעינן בהו שינוי מעשה: שנילושה במי פירות. הו"מ לשנויי כגון שאין בו כביצה ובמסכת אהלות (פי"ג מ"ה) חשיב פחות מכביצה אוכלין בהדי הנך (מ) שאמר שממעטים את הטפח:

מי פירות. פי' ר"ח כגון שמן ולא דק דשמן מכשיר הוא כדמוכח בפרק קמא דשבת (דף ה:) ובריש פרק חבית (שם קמד.) דשמן חשיב משקה אלא דוקא מוהל היוצא מתחילה: בתיבנא סריא. תימה אכתי חזיא לבהמתו ע"י פירוך כדמוכח בפרק בתרא דשבת (דף קנה:) דאמרינן תא שמע מפרכין את התבן כו' אלמא מיטרח באוכלא שרי ומשני בתיבנא סריא וי"ל דהכא מיירי שהוא מוסרח כל כך דאפי' ע"י שום תקון לא חזיא: רואין כל שאילו ינטלו. אין לפרש דטעם משום דסופו ליטול חבית וקופה ולהכי בעינן שיהו גרוגרות ותבן יכולין לעמוד בפני עצמן דא"כ למאי דפריך תבן הא קא חזי ליה ורוצה להוכיח מכאן דאפילו סופו ליטלו חוצץ תיקשי ליה אמאי צריך שיכולין לעמוד בפני עצמן אלא אומר ר"י דכך הוא הדין דכל דבר החוצץ בעינן שיוכל לעמוד בפני עצמו דקתני לעיל מהך משנה במסכת אהלות (פ"ו מ"ב) קוברי המת שהיו עוברין באכסדרה ובא אחד מהן והגיף את הדלת וסמכו במפתח אם יכולה דלת לעמוד בפני עצמה טהור ואם לאו טמא וכן חבית של גרוגרות וקופה של תבן שהן נתונין בחלון משמע דהכל חד טעמא הוא והיינו טעמא דסתימת עראי הוא דכיון שאינו יכול לעמוד בפני עצמו אי נמי משום דבעינן דבר החוצץ עומד על ידי דבר שאינו מקבל טומאה ומיהו בפירוש משניות מלא ר"י דמפרש אפילו במפתח שאינו מקבל טומאה איירי [ז] ומטמא דלא חשיב אהל לחוץ בפני הטומאה כיון שעמד על ידי כלי אף על פי שאינו מקבל טומאה ורבי אליעזר פליג עלה בתוספתא וקאמר דטהור כיון שהמפתח אינו מקבל טומאה ואזלי לטעמייהו דפליגי במסכת אהלות (בפ"ו מ"א) בנדבך שהוא נתון על גבי כלים אפילו כלי גללים כלי אבנים כלי אדמה דלרבי אליעזר נעשה אהל לטהר ולרבנן אינו נעשה אהל אלא כשהוא נתון על גבי אבנים:

רבינו גרשום

יותר ולא מזיק כלל לכותל להכי לא תנא ליה **והא קתני ר' הושעיא** בתוספתא דידיה הני דמתני' וקתני **חול.** דתני בהדי הני דרישא דמזקי **משום מתונתא** לחלות. ולא קתני לה בהדי הנך דסיפא דגפת וזבל דהנהו משום הבלא. **ומקשי' מי לא תנן אמת המים וקתני נברכת הכובסין** אע"ג דלא צריך הכא נמי ליתני חול ומשני אמת המים ונברכת הכובסין תרוייהו **צריכי דאי תנא אמת המים** דמרחיקין ג' טפחים הוה אמינא **משום דקביעי** כל הימים מרחיקין דמקלקל לכותל **אבל נברכת הכובסין דלא קביעי** דמים מכונסין נינהו **אימא** אין מרחיקין: **דקוו וקיימי** ומחלידין בקרקע ואתיין עד היסוד מש"ה מרחיקין **אבל אמת המים** דלא קוו וקיימי דדרך הליכתן קא אזלי ואין מחלידין **אימא דלא** צריך לרחוקי קמ"ל דודאי צריך: **פיסקא מרחיקין את הזרעים ואת המחרישה.** משום דנכנסים שרשים של זרעים בכותל כדאמ' לקמן ומרעי לי'. הואיל דתני מחרישה למה לי למיתני זרעים פשיטא דאין זרעים באים אלא ע"י מחרישה ומשני דאפי' בלא מחרישה מצי לזרוע **במפולת יד** דא"צ מחרישה בזרעים משום כשזורעין בשוורים תולין שם שק מלא תבואה ומנקבין השק נקבים נקבים כשזורעין בכמה מקומות נופלת התבואה יותר ממקום אחד ולאחר כן חורשין כדי לכסות את התבואה ולהשוות את התבואה בשדה. אבל כשזורעין ביד משוה התבואה בשדה וא"צ מחרישה מש"ה איצטריך למתני במתני' זרעים ומחרישה א) דמזורעים לא מפקינן מחרישה. **ומקשה** ומחרישה מ"ט איצטריך למתני מאחר דתנא זרעים לא צריך למתני מחרישה דודאי אין חרישה בלי זרעים ומשני **לחורש לאילנות** לצורך נטיעת אילנות דהכא ליכא זרעים ומש"ה איצטריך למתני מחרישה דמזורעים לא מפיק מחרישה: **ותיפוק ליה מינה** דמרחיקין. דמאחר דקתני מתני' מרחיקין אמת המים וכל הני ממילא איכא למשמע דמרחיקין זרעי' ומחרישה דהיינו משום מתונתא ותרתי זימני למה לי משום מתונתא והא מש"ה מרחיקין זרעים ומחרישה משום דמשקין הזרעים מן המים וקשה לכותל: **תנא בא"י קאי.** דלא משקי זרעים אלא מטר אבל בבבל דצריכי להן מים להשקות שדותיהן מתוך שהיא יושבת במים אם יבשו מים צריך להביא לשם מים כדי להשקות השדה שמתוך שהיא רגילה בכך צריך להשקות בכל שעה: (ע"כ שייך לעמוד א') מדקתני מתני' מרחיקין את הזרעים ג' טפחים. מכלל **דזרעים לצדדין** מעקמי **ומשתרשי** ואזלי ומש"ה מרחיקין כי היכי דלא ליזקו בכותל **ורמינהו המבריך את הגפן בארץ** [illegible] **אם אין על גבי הגפן** [illegible] **עפר** [illegible] **טפחים** ה"ז **לא יביא זרעים** לשם [illegible] [illegible] **אבל זורע את הצדדין אילך ואילך** [illegible] **שמחלידין** [illegible] **בכותל לבנים** [illegible] **בשופכין** [illegible] **ת"ש לא ישתין** [illegible] **רקיק אינו ממעט בחלון** [illegible] **אבל רקיק דממאיס** [illegible] **במי פירות** [illegible] **לעמוד בפני עצמן בחלון** [illegible] **והא תבן חזיא לבהמתו** [illegible] **דאית ביה קוצים** [illegible] היסק גדול לא שכיח. לא מיבעי ליה: **בשהתריפו.** שהתליעו: **אי פומיה לבר.** שפתחה של חבית. מחזרת מבחוץ:

חשק שלמה על רבינו גרשום א) [נ"ל דזרעים לא מפקינן ממחרישה ומקשה ממחרישה מ"ט וכו':]

מסורת הש"ס

א) כלאים פרק ז מ"א, ב) [פי' רבינו חננאל יונקין את הקרקע כחולדה שהלדה בעיקרי הכתלים. ערוך ערך חלד א'], ג) ב"ש מ"ג, ד) [תוספתא פרק א], ה) אהלות פ"ו מ"ב ע"ש, ו) נ"א שאלה, ז) [ומטמאה כל"ל וער' רש"ש].

הגהות הב"ח

(א) גמ' התם בשופכין ת"ש לא ישפוך אדם: (ב) שם לא מיבעיא עבה דכיון דאחזי ליה: (ג) שם במתונתא: (ד) רש"י ד"ה שמחלידין וכו' ומתמוטט הקרקע שתחת יסוד: (ה) ד"ה ובצונמא וכו' בטישטוש הקרקע: (ו) ד"ה אינו ממעט וכו' אין רקיק זה ממעט שיעורו וכו' מבטל ליה להתם: (ז) ד"ה דאית וכו' והם היו: (ח) תוס' ד"ה אמר וכו' לקמן זורעים: (ט) ד"ה רקיק וכו' שלא יהא בשיריים כ"א אצבע על רוחב גודל: (י) בא"ד ושאינו עשוי לא לאורה: (כ) ד"ה מאי וכו' חדא דלאו סתימה מעלייתא היא לפי: (ל) ד"ה ותיפוק ליה פירוש אפי': (מ) ד"ה שנילושה וכו' בהדי הנך שממעטין כל"ל ותיבת שאמר נמחק:

תורה אור השלם

א) הִנְנִי מֵבִיא אֵלֶיךָ רָעָה וּבִעַרְתִּי אַחֲרֶיךָ וְהִכְרַתִּי לְאַחְאָב מַשְׁתִּין בְּקִיר וְעָצוּר וְעָזוּב בְּיִשְׂרָאֵל: [מלכים א כא, כא]

לעזי רש"י

פרובניי"ר. פירוש להבריך, לכופף זמורת גפן מחוברת בקרקע, ומופר לארץ ומבריך היסוד ומוטמן בעפר ועולה לאה היסוד במקום אחר (ערוך ערך ברך ב'):

ליקוטי רש"י

המבריך. כופף את הזמורות לארץ שקורין פרובינ"א [ר"ה ט:]. [שכופף] הזמורה או היסוד לארץ [סוטה מג:]. כופף אמצעית הגפן בקרקע ומכסהו בקרקע באמצעיתו ובמאלעיתו מוציאין עיקר הראשון ונעשו שתי גפנים [רשב"ם לקמן פג.]. שמחלידין. לשון חולדה להלכות שחיטה [חולין דף נב.]. שמהלכלת מתחת לקרקעית הבור [לקמן כה:]. צונמא. סלע בלשון ארמי [בראשית מא, כג, ונדה ח:]. אבן [רשב"ם לקמן פט:]. בסריא. נרקב ומסריח שאין ראוי לאכול בהמה. חזי לטינא. לגבל לבנים [ביצה ל.].

thorns. Such straw is not used in the manufacture of bricks.[22]

The Gemara persists in its questioning:

חֲזֵי לְהַסָּקָה – But **[straw] is fit** for use as fuel **for a fire.** It is likely to be removed for this purpose. – ? –

The Gemara answers:

בִּמְתוּנָא – The Mishnah refers **to damp** straw, which is not useful as fuel.

The Gemara asks:

חֲזֵי לְהֶסֵּק גָּדוֹל – But even **[damp straw] is fit for a large fire.** – ? –

The Gemara answers:

הֶסֵּק גָּדוֹל לֹא שְׁכִיחַ – **A large fire is not common.** Therefore, it is unlikely that the straw will be removed for making a large fire.

Having failed to refute Shmuel's statement with the Mishnah's ruling concerning straw, the Gemara turns to the Mishnah's example of dried figs:

גְּרוֹגְרוֹת הָא חָזוּ לֵיהּ – **But dried figs are fit for one** to eat. They are likely to be removed to be eaten, and yet, while they are in the opening, they reduce its size. – ? –

The Gemara answers:

אָמַר שְׁמוּאֵל – **Shmuel said:** **בְּשֶׁהִתְרִיפוּ** – The Mishnah deals **with [figs] that are infested with worms.** Such figs serve no purpose and are abandoned. **וְכֵן תָּנֵי רַבָּה בַּר אֲבוּהּ** – **And so taught Rabbah bar Avuha in a Baraisa** that elaborates on this Mishnah: **בְּשֶׁהִתְרִיפוּ** – The reference is **to [figs] that are infested with worms.**

The Gemara raises a difficulty with the implication of the Mishnah that the keg itself does not obstruct the passage of *tumah*.[23]

הַאי חָבִית הֵיכִי דָּמְיָא – **What are the circumstances of this keg?** **אִי דְּפוּמָא לְבַר** – **If** its **opening is facing outward,** i.e. away from the room in which the corpse lies,

NOTES

cannot be viewed as part of the wall.]

22. The practice was to stamp on the clay with bare feet (*Rashi*). Hence, straw that contained thorns was unsuitable for this purpose.

23. See note 21; see also 20a, note 2.

הִיא גּוּפָהּ תֵּיחוּץ – **[the keg] itself should obstruct** the passage of *tumah,* דְּהָא כְּלִי חֶרֶשׂ אֵינוֹ מִטַּמֵּא מִגַּבּוֹ – **for an earthenware vessel** (such as a keg) **cannot contract *tumah* through its exterior,** only through its opening.[1] Since its opening is not facing the corpse, the keg cannot contract *tumah* from it. Therefore, the keg itself, contents notwithstanding, should reduce the size of the opening and thereby prevent the passage of *tumah* from one room to another.[2] – ? –

The Gemara gives two answers:

אֶלָּא דְּפוּמָא לְגָאו – **Rather,** the Mishnah refers to a keg **whose opening faces inward,** towards the corpse. In such a case, the keg *is* subject to *tumah* contamination from the corpse, and therefore does not block the passage of *tumah.* וְאִי בָּעֵית אֵימָא – **Or, if you prefer, say** לְעוֹלָם דְּפוּמָא לְבַר – that **in fact, the opening** of the keg **is facing outward,** away from the corpse. Yet it does not block the passage of *tumah,* הָכָא בְּמַאי עַסְקִינַן – for **what** type of keg **are we dealing with here?** בְּחָבִית שֶׁל מַתֶּכֶת – The Mishnah deals **with a metal keg,** which is susceptible to *tumah* contamination through both its exterior and its interior.[3]

The Gemara challenges Shmuel's ruling from a Baraisa that discusses the capacity of various items to block the transmission of *tumah* through an opening between one room and another:

מֵיתִיבֵי – **They challenged** Shmuel's ruling from the following Baraisa: עֲשָׂבִין שֶׁתְּלָשָׁן וְהִנִּיחָן בַּחַלּוֹן – **GRASS THAT WAS PLUCKED AND PLACED IN AN OPENING**[4] אוֹ שֶׁעָלוּ מֵאֲלֵיהֶן בַּחַלּוֹנוֹת – **OR [GRASS] THAT GREW BY ITSELF IN AN OPENING;** וּמַטְלוֹנִיּוֹת שֶׁאֵין בָּהֶן שָׁלֹשׁ עַל שָׁלֹשׁ – **SCRAPS OF FABRIC THAT DO NOT MEASURE THREE BY THREE** fingerbreadths; וְהָאֵבֶר וְהַבָּשָׂר הַמְּדוּלְדָּלִין בִּבְהֵמָה וּבְחַיָּה – **A** partially severed **LIMB OR** piece of **FLESH DANGLING FROM A FARM ANIMAL OR A WILD BEAST;** וְעוֹף שֶׁשָּׁכַן בַּחַלּוֹן – **A BIRD RESTING IN AN OPENING;** וְעוֹבֵד כּוֹכָבִים שֶׁיָּשַׁב בַּחַלּוֹן – **AN IDOLATER SITTING IN AN OPENING;** וּבֶן שְׁמוֹנָה הַמּוּנָּח בַּחַלּוֹן – **A BABY** born **OF** an **EIGHT**-month pregnancy **LYING IN AN OPENING;** וְהַמֶּלַח – **SALT;** וּכְלִי חֶרֶס – **AN EARTHENWARE VESSEL;** וְסֵפֶר תּוֹרָה – **A TORAH SCROLL:** כּוּלָם מְמַעֲטִין בַּחַלּוֹן – **ALL OF THESE REDUCE** the size of **THE OPENING** so that *tumah* cannot pass through it.[5] אֲבָל הַשֶּׁלֶג וְהַבָּרָד וְהַגְּלִיד וְהַכְּפוֹר וְהַמַּיִם – **BUT SNOW, HAIL, FROST, ICE AND WATER:** כּוּלָּן אֵין מְמַעֲטִין בַּחַלּוֹן – **ALL OF THESE DO NOT REDUCE** the size of **AN OPENING.**[6]

The Gemara contends that each of the items listed by the Baraisa as reducing the size of an opening is likely to be removed. Thus, starting with the first item, the Gemara poses a series of challenges to Shmuel, who maintains that an item does not reduce the size of an opening unless it is abandoned there:

וְהָא עֲשָׂבִין חֲזוּ לִבְהֶמְתּוֹ – **But GRASS is fit** for use as fodder **for one's animal.** It is likely to be removed for that purpose, and yet it reduces the size of the opening. – ? –

The Gemara answers:

בְּאַפְרַזְתָּא – The Baraisa is dealing **with *afrazta*** – a poisonous type of grass, which cannot be used as fodder.

The Gemara proceeds to the next case:

אוֹ שֶׁעָלוּ מֵאֲלֵיהֶן – **OR [GRASS] THAT GREW BY ITSELF.** כֵּיוָן דְּקָשׁוּ לְכוֹתֶל שָׁקִיל לְהוּ – **Since [grass]** planted near a wall **is harmful to a wall,**[7] **it will be removed. – ? –**

The Gemara presents two answers to this question:

אָמַר רַבָּה – **Rabbah said:** בְּכוֹתֶל חוּרְבָה – The Baraisa refers **to the wall of a ruined building,** in which case damage to the wall is of no concern. רַב פָּפָּא אָמַר – **Rav Pappa says:** אֲפִילוּ בְּכוֹתֶל יִישׁוּב – The Baraisa refers **even to the wall of a** building used as a **residence.** בְּבָאִין חוּץ לִשְׁלֹשָׁה לַחַלּוֹן – However, **the case is of [grass] that comes from beyond three** *tefachim* from the wall and extends **to the opening** in the wall. Since the grass was planted more than three *tefachim* away, it does not cause damage to the wall.[8]

NOTES

1. Generally, the means by which vessels become *tamei* is that *tumah* is conveyed to their exterior or interior. Vessels of earthenware are unique in that they contract *tumah* only through the entry of *tumah* into their interior (see *Leviticus* 11:33).

2. [The Mishnah, however, states that the question of whether or not *tumah* passes through the opening depends on whether the figs can stay there without the support of their containers. It implies thereby that it is only the figs, not the keg itself, that obstruct the passage of *tumah.*]

An apparent difficulty: Why does the Gemara assume that the keg should reduce the size of the opening? Since the keg is useful, surely it is not abandoned permanently in the opening.

The answer is that from the Baraisa's use of the word חוֹצְצִין (lit. interpose) it seems that the reference is to a case where the keg fills the *entire* opening. An earthenware vessel that fills the *entire* opening blocks the passage of *tumah,* even if it is not abandoned there permanently (*Tosafos*; see *Maharsha*).

3. [See note 1.] The Gemara could equally well have answered that the reference is to a vessel of wood. It mentions a metal vessel merely because such vessels were more common than those of wood (*Ritva*).

[*Rashi's* comment above (see 19b note 21), that the vessels mentioned in the Mishnah are susceptible to *tumah* contamination, assumes the answers given here.]

4. See 19b note 15.

5. As mentioned above, only an item that is immune to *tumah* contamination can block the passage of *tumah.* In the light of the basic rule that nothing except people, utensils and foodstuffs can contract *tumah*, it can be shown that each of the items listed here are immune to *tumah* contamination:

(1) *Grass* does not belong to any of the three categories that contract *tumah*: viz. a person, utensil or food.

(2) *Scraps of fabric:* A piece of fabric that measures less than three by three fingerbreadths is not considered a "utensil" (i.e. a useful item).

(3) *Partially severed limb or piece of flesh:* These have the status of food because they will eventually wither and fall off; however, as we learned above, food is not susceptible to *tumah* contamination unless it first came into contact with one of the seven liquids (Mishnah *Chullin* 127a; see 19a note 18).

(4) *Bird:* Only people contract *tumah*, not other living creatures.

(5) An *idolater* is not susceptible to *tumah* contamination, as derived from Scripture (see *Nazir* 61b).

(6) *A baby born of an eight-month pregnancy* is not considered viable. Hence, it is not classified as a person with regard to contracting *tumah* (see *Shabbos* 135a). [We do not assume that a baby is born of an eight-month pregnancy unless it shows physical symptoms of not having been completely formed. Otherwise, we assume that it is a baby of a seven-month pregnancy and its birth was delayed (*Tosafos* to *Shabbos* 135a).]

(7) *Salt,* on its own, is not considered a food (*Rashi*; see *Tosafos* to *Niddah* 50a ד״ה כל).

(8) *An earthenware vessel*: The Baraisa refers to an earthenware vessel whose opening faces away from the corpse and as such cannot be affected by the *tumah* of the corpse (see note 1).

(9) A *Torah scroll* is not considered a utensil (*Ramah;* cf. *Mishnah Acharonah* to *Keilim* 28:4).

6. Snow, hail, frost and ice do not reduce the opening's size for they eventually dissolve [and drip away]. This is true even of water held in a vessel, for the presence of the vessel is disregarded (see 19b note 21) and if the vessel were to be removed, the water would not remain in the opening (*Rashi*). [The vessel itself does not block the passage of *tumah* because it is susceptible to *tumah* contamination, e.g. it is earthenware with its opening towards the corpse, or it is metal.]

7. As evidenced by our Mishnah, which taught that seeds may not be planted within three *tefachim* of a neighbor's wall. This connection to our Mishnah explains why this passage about the laws of *tumah* is recorded here (*Tosafos* to 19b ד״ה אמר).

8. See previous note.

היא גופה תיחוץ דהא [א] כלי חרש אינו מטמא מגבו (א) [א]אלא דפומא לגאו ואי בעית אימא לעולם דפומא לבר הכא במאי עסקינן בחבית של מתכת מיתיבי [ב]עשבין שתלשן והניחן בחלון או שעלו מאליהן בחלונות ומטלוניות שאין בהן שלש על שלש והאבר והבשר המדולדלין בבהמה ובחיה ועוף ששכן בחלון ועובד כוכבים שישב בחלון ובן שמנה המונח בחלון והמלח וכלי חרס וספר תורה כולם ממעטין בחלון אבל השלג והברד והגליד והכפור והמים כולן אין ממעטין בחלון והא עשבין חזו לבהמתו [ג]באפרזתא (ב) או שעלו מאליהן כיון דקשו לכותל שקיל להו אמר רבה [ד]בכותל חורבה רב פפא אמר אפילו בכותל יישוב בבאין חוץ (ג) לשלשה לחלון מטלוניות חזו ליה לקריעה דלבושא [ה]בסמיכתא חזו לאומנא [ו]בריסקא אי בריסקא שאין בהן שלש על שלש שאין בהן ארבעה על ארבעה מיבעי ליה [ג]כעין ריסקא והאבר והבשר המדולדלין בבהמה ובחיה ערקא ואזלא [ז]בקשורה שחיט לה בטמאה מזבין לה לנכרי בכחושה פסיק שדי לה לכלבים כיון דאיכא צער בעלי חיים לא עביד ועוף ששכן בחלון פרח ואזיל [ח]בקשור שחיט ליה בטמא מזבין ליה לנכרי בקלניתא יהיב ליה לינוקא במסרט קלניתא לא מסרטא כעין קלניתא ועובד כוכבים שישב בחלון קאי ואזיל בכפות אתי חבריה שרי ליה במצורע אתי מצורע חבריה שרי ליה [ט]אלא בחבושי מלכות ובן שמנה המונח בחלון אתיא אמיה דריא ליה [י]בשבת [כ]דתניא [ל]בן שמנה הרי הוא כאבן ואסור לטלטלו בשבת אבל אמו שוחה עליו ומניקתו מפני הסכנה מלח חזיא ליה [מ]במרירתא חזיא לעורות [נ]דאית בה קוצי כיון דקשיא לכותל שקלא [ס]דיתבא אחספא חספא גופא תיחוץ

דלית

רש"י

שאין בה שלש על שלש. שאין מקבלין טומאה: המדולדלין. שתלושין ומעורין במקצת והבהמה עומדת אצל החלון והאבר מונח על החלון ותנן בהעור והרוטב (חולין קכט.) מטמאין טומאת אוכלין במקומן וצריכין הכשר ואלו לא הוכשרו: עובד כוכבים. אינו מקבל טומאה וכן בן שמנה שהרי הוא כאבן לא חי ולא מת: המלח. לא מקבל טומאה דלאו אוכל הוא באנפי נפשיה: וכלי חרס. שאחוריו לצד אהל הטומאה: והשלג והברד כו'. הוליא ונימוקים מאליהם אין ממעטים וכן מים שבכלי הוליא ואם יטול הכלי אין עומדים בפני עצמן אין ממעטין בחלון: הברד. גלא"ש: הכפור. גריישלא"ן: הגליד. קרח לבן שאינו שלג: ה"ג והא עשבים חזו לבהמתו. וסופו ליטלן ואפ"ה כל כמה דליתנהו התם ממעטי ותיובתא דשמואל: באפרזתא (ד). והוא סם המות לבהמה ומאן דגריס באפרזתא טועה [ה] שהוא קורנס של נפחים: כיון דקשו לכותל. שמאלידין אותו כדאמרי' במתני' שקיל להו ואפ"ה ממעט וקשה לשמואל: בבאין חוץ לשלשה. טפחים רחוק מן הכותל ועולין לתוך החלון ראשיהן: חזי לקריעה. לעשות טלאי: בסמיכתא. עב יותר מדאי: לאומנא. למקיז דם לקנח פי המכה: בריסקא. שהוא מסרט: אין בהן ארבעה על ארבעה מבעי ליה. שזו היא שיעור של שק: קלניתא. עוף כחוש מאד ואין ראוי לשום אדם: כעין קלניתא. כחוש כקלניתא והוא מסרט: דאית ביה קוצי. ויסרטו את ידיו: כיון דקשה לכותל. כדתנן במתניתין:

דלית

תוספות

היא גופה תיחוץ. ותימה היכי תיחוץ הא לא מבטל ליה התם ותירץ ר"י ב"ר מרדכי דכיון שהתריפו הגרוגרות [ט] גם החבית נתקלקל ומבטלו אבל קשה לר"י דבפ"ב דשבת (דף כז. ושם) דאמר שפקקו את המאור בטפיח כי פקקו מאי הוי הא לא מבטל ליה ואינו חוצץ וליכא למימר דביטלו הטפיח דא"כ היה בונה בשבת ונראה לר"ת ולר"י דלכלי חרס לא בעי ביטול אלא שפיר חוצץ אע"ג דלא מבטל ליה והא דקתני לקמן דכלי חרס ממעט בחלון ופריך כלי חרס הא חזי ליה התם מיירי בממעט חלון מכשיעור אבל אינו סותם כל החלון להכי בעי ביטול אבל היכא דסותם כל החלון כי הכא דקתני חוצלין דמשמע דסותם לגמרי וכן הכוה דפקקו את המאור התם ודאי [לא] בעי ביטול בכלי חרס ועוד אמר הר"ר שמואל דכלי עץ נמי שאינו מקבל טומאה כגון העשוי לנחת לא בעי ביטול דבפ"ב דמגילה (דף כו:) גבי ההוא בי כנישתא דיהודאי דהות פתיחא להיא אינדרונא דהוה בה מיתנא ובעו כהני לעיולי בה (ה) עד דאמר להו לכו תיבותא ואותבוה אבבא ולא בעי ביטול מאי מהני האי תיבה דמסתמא לא ביטלוה שם ועוד שלא היו יכולים לבטלה שהיה ספר תורה מונח בה ואסור לשוותה בדבר אחר דמעלין בקודש ולא מורידין: בחבית של מתכת. הקשה ר"ת דחבית גופה תביא טומאה לבית אחר דע"י אהל נעשית המתכת כחלל להיות אבי אבות הטומאה כדמוכח במסכת אהלות והוי כחלל נמי לטמא אחרים באהל דכוליה קרא דוכל אשר יגע על פני השדה בחלל חרב וגו' דריש לה בנזיר פרק כ"ג (דף נג: ושם) לענין אהל ונראה לרבינו תם דהכא מיירי כגון שהגרוגרות בולטות חוץ לפי חבית כל סביבותיו ומכסות אותו לגמרי שאין נראה כלל ודייק ר"ת מדנקט גרוגרות ולא נקט פירות לפי שהם מדובקות יחד אע"פ שיולאות חוץ לחבית אין נופלות וכי האי גוונא דייק בפרק חבית (שבת דף קמג.) ועוד אומר ר' יצחק דהכא מיירי בשאין חבית יוצאה חוץ לכותל דהשתא דרך החלון לא יבא טומאה לבית דטומאה רצוצה בוקעת ועולה ואינה מתפשטת לצדדין שהרי אין בו פותח טפח: שעלו מאליהן. תימה היאך ממעטין הטפח הא תנן במס' אהלות (פ"ח מ"ה) אלו לא מביאין ולא חוצלין הזרעים והירקות המחוברין לקרקע חוץ מן הירקות שמנו פירוש הנהו דמנו לעיל דמביאין וחוצלין האירוס והקיסוס וירקות חמור ולדעת יוונית וא"כ היכי קתני דעשבים שעלו מאליהן דחוצלין ותירץ רבינו תם דהתם איירי לענין אהל דאין נעשין אהל לחוץ בפני הטומאה על מה שתחתיהם או שעליהם או להביא טומאה מפני שהרוח מנשבו ואינו עומד במקום אחד והוי דומיא דעוף הפורח שאינו לא חוצץ ולא מביא והקשה ר"י דהכא בכולה שמעתין לא בעינן מירוח לא בעשבים ולא בחבית דפריך לעיל היא גופה תיחוץ והגוזל קמא (ב"ק דף קה.) אמר רבא הרי [י] חבית שניקבה וסתמוה שמרים הצילוה פקקה בזמורה עד שימרח מן הצדדין וי"ל דהתם (ו) בכלי בעינן מוקף למיד פתיל להכי צריך מירוח אבל הכא לא בעי למיד פתיל: ועוף ששכן בחלון. נראה דאתי אפילו לר"מ דאמר (עירובין דף טו:) כל דבר שיש בו רוח חיים אין עושין אותו לא דופן לסוכה ולא לחי למבוי כו' דהיינו לענין מחילת עשרה טפחים דוקא אבל הכא לענין ממעט בחלון ממעטו בכל דבר שיבטלנו: ועובד כוכבים שישב בחלון. דעובד כוכבים אינו מקבל טומאה כדנפקא לן מקרא בפ"ב דנזיר (דף סא: ושם) דכתיב ואיש אשר יטמא וגו' מתוך הקהל [ס] ילא עובד כוכבים שאין לו קהל ואע"ג דחכמים עשאום כזבים לכל דבריהם (שבת דף פג. נדה דף לד.) כיון דמדאורייתא לא מקבלי טומאה חוצלין מפני הטומאה וא"ת דבפרק יוצא דופן (נדה דף מג:) אמר חומר בשרץ מבשכבת זרע שהשרץ אין לו חלוקת טומאה ומסיק שכבת זרע דחלוקה טומאה מה היא אילימא בין ישראלים לנכרים ה"נ הא איכא עכבר דים ועכבר דיבשה משמע דשרץ אין חלוקה טומאתו בין ישראל לנכרי לאו פירכא היא דאע"ג דאין עובדי כוכבים טמאים בשרץ אין לו חלוקת טומאה דומיא דשכבת זרע דבשכבת זרע גופה איכא חילוק אבל בשרץ גופיה אין חילוק אלא בהנהו דמקבלי ממנו טומאה הילכך צריך למינקט עכבר דים ועכבר דיבשה והא דאיצטריך מיעוטא (שבת פג. נדה לד.) דעובד כוכבים אינו מטמא בזיבה משום דטומאת זיבה לאו טומאת מגע היא ומטומאה זו לא אשכחן דאימעטו ובן שמונה אינו מקבל טומאה כשהוא חי דלא איקרי אדם: והמלח. משמע מהכא דאין מלח מקבל טומאה אבל השלג מיירי שלא חישב עליו לאכילה דלא מקבל טומאה דאי חשב עליו תיפוק ליה דהוי דבר המקבל טומאה כדמוכח במסכת נדה [דף יז. וע"ש ולע"ג ואולי צ"ל אבל השלג מיירי שלא חישב עליו למשקה דלא מקבל טומאה וכו' וע"פ הגה"ה זו מובנים דברי התוספות על נכון]: כולן אין ממעטין בחלון. וטעמא משום דאין מתקיימין (ז) ונימסין במים דליכא למימר דטעמא משום דקשו לכותל ושקיל להו דהא מלח נמי קשה לכותל וקתני דממעט ומיירי כגון דמנחי בחספא והנך נמי ליתני דממעטי ודמנחי בחספא אלא אפילו דמנחי בחספא דלא קשו לכותל לא ממעטי: חזי לקריעה דלבושא. ואע"ג דאמר בפ"ק דסוכה (דף טז. ושם) ובשבת פרק כל הכלים (דף קכה.) דפחות משלש על שלש לא חזי לא לעניים ולא לעשירים ודאי לא מקבל טומאה כיון דלא מלנעו ליה אבל מ"מ לא ממעט דלא מבטל ליה דקא שקיל ליה כי [י] מלטרף לקריעה דלבושא: כיון דאיכא צער בעלי חיים כו'. וא"ת כולה בהמה שקיל ושדי לכלבים וי"ל דמיירי בקוף וכל דדמי ליה דמנח התם לטיולי ביה וניחא דנקט אבר ובשר ולא נקט בהמה גופה דאי חזיא לטיולי שקיל לה לטיולי בה ואי לא חזיא שדי לה לכלבים: אתיא אמיה ודריא ליה בשבת. ואיירי בגוסס שימות קודם שילא השבת ואמר דשם תהא קבורתו:

דלית

עין משפט נר מצוה

יח א ב ג ד ה ו ז ח ט י מיי' פט"ו מהלכות טומאת מת הלכה ג:

יט כ מיי' פ"א מהל' מילה הל' י, ועיין בכ"מ ופכ"ה מהל' שבת הל' ו טוש"ע א"ח סי' שח סעיף יא וטוש"ע י"ד סי' רסו סעיף יא בהג"ה:

כ ל מ נ מיי' פט"ו מהלכות טומאת מת הלכה ג:

רבינו גרשום

היא גופה תיחוץ בפני הטומאה. דהא קי"ל כלי חרס אינו מטמא מגבו: איבעית אימא דפומא לבר. (ומש"ה) אפ"ה אינה חוצצת: בחבית של מתכת. דמטמאה מגבה: או שעלו. שגדלו: ומטלניות שאין בהם ג' על ג'. דלא מקבלי טומאה. והאבר והבשר המדולדלין בבהמה ובחיה אבל עדיין סריכי בבהמה והן בחלון וכל הני מפרש לקמן למה ממעטין בחלון משום דלא הוי דבר חשוב ומבטלי להו אבל השלג וכול' אין ממעטין דמים הן: עשבים חזו לבהמה. ואמאי ממעטין הא לא מבטיל להו: באפרזתא. כלומר סם המות דבהמה דלא חזי לבהמה מש"ה מבטל ליה: כיון דקשי לכותל שקיל להו ולא מבטל להו ואמאי ממעטי בחלון. אמר רבא מש"ה ממעט דלא איכפת ליה מלקיית אותו כותל דחורבה היא ולא תליש להו בעוד שהטומאה בבית: בבאין חוץ מג' טפחים. חוץ מחלון דלא מזיק לכותל כלל וראשי ענפים מגיעין לכותל ליכא למיחש דילמא שקיל להו מש"ה ממעטין: ומטלניות. אמאי ממעט הא חזי לקריעה דלבושא לתקוני ומשני בסמיכתא דעב הוא ביותר ולא חזי: לאומנא. למקיז כלומר לקנח מן הדם ומשני בדשק דלא חזי לאומנא. אי הכי דמוקמת לה בדשק הא דתני שאין בהם ג' על ג' מש"ה לא מקבלי טומאה שאין בהן ד' על ד' מיבעי ליה דהכי דינא של שק. דעבה כעין שק ולא חזי שמחלדת כלי האומן כמו השק: בקלניתא. עוף הוא שכחש ביותר ואין ליה בשר וקא מבטל ליה ומקשה הא חזי לינוקא לשחק בו ולא מבטל ליה ואמאי ממעט ומשני במסרט דלא חזי לינוקא: והא קי"ל דקלניתא לא מסרט. ואמאי לא קמבטל ליה דחזיא לינוקא ומשני כעין קלניתא דכחוש הוא ביותר ומסרט: ועובד כוכבים ששכן בחלון. ה"ה נמי ישראל אלא מש"ה נקט עובד כוכבים א) לא שרי ליה דעובדי כוכבים נמי מבדלו מן המצורע מפני הסכנה שלא ימות קודם שעתו: במרריתא. שאין ראוי למאכל: דאית בה קוצי. וכשמתקנו בו העור יכנסו הקוצים בידים ולהכי מבטל ליה. ומקשי' כיון דקשי מלח לכותל כדתני במתני' אמאי ממעט הא שקל ליה שלא ילקה הכותל ומשני דמיתבא ההוא מלח בחספא דלא קשי לכותל. ומקשינן חספא גופא תיחוץ בלא מלח ואמאי נקט מלח:

מסורת הש"ס

א) [חולין דף כה.] ב) [תוספתא דאהלות פי"ד], ג) [עי' תוס' לקמן קיז. ד"ה דין], ד) שבת קכה. יבמות פ. [תוספתא שבת פט"ו], ה) [עי' רש"י ברכות לד. ובמגילה כה. ד"ה אפרזתא ובגיטין ע: ד"ה אפרזתא ומגלה לייסר וע"ע רש"י ב"ק מז: ד"ה באפרזתא], ו) [צ"ל הרי אמרו], ז) צ"ל מלטרף:

הגהות הב"ח

(א) גמ' אינו מטמא מגבו לא לריכא דפומא: (ב) שם באפרזתא חזיא או שעלו: (ג) שם חוץ משלשה לחלון: (ד) רש"י ד"ה באפרזתא גרסי' והוא סם: (ה) תוס' ד"ה מלא לכלו' בה כו' עד אמר להו וכו' לשותה לדבר: (ו) ד"ה שעלו וכו' וי"ל דהתם בעינן דבר בכלי נמחק: (ז) ד"ה כולן וכו' ונימוקין וליכא כצ"ל ותיבת במים נמחק:

גליון הש"ס

גמרא חזו ליה לקריעה. בערוך ערך רקע הגירסא למרקע לכותל ועיין מ"ק דף כח ע"א תוס' ד"ה מאן רקיע: תוס' ד"ה בחבית. גם החבית נתקלקל. כדאיתא בב"מ דף לא ע"ב: שם ד"ה לקנקנים: שם ד"ה ועכו"ם כו' יצא עכו"ם שאין לו קהל. בגמרא שם דפה זה דדלאת מכרת מטעמא ולא מטומאה ומסקינן דילפינן מקרא דאיש אשר יטמא ולא יתחטא כל שיש לו טהרה יש לו טומאה ועע"ג.

לעזי רש"י

גלש"א. פירוש ברד, קרח (רש"י ברכות דף יח ע"ב), כעין גרעינים המתהוים בחלל האויר מהמים הנקפאים ונופלים ארצה. גריישלא"ן. פירוש כפור, מה שיקפא מהמים היורדים כטל (רמב"ם אהלות פ"ח מ"ה ועיין רש"י שמות טז, יד).

ליקוטי רש"י

כלי חרש אינו מטמא מגבו. אפילו נגעה טומאה בגבו אינו מקבל טומאה בכך [חולין כד:]. באפרזתא. עשב והוא סם המות לבהמה [ב"ק מז:]. ומניקתו מפני הסכנה. מפני שחלב הכנס בדדיה ומביאה לידי חולי [שבת קלה.]. סכנת שניהם הבן והאם שאם שלא יכנס חלב הדדין ויחלנה ותמות [יבמות פ: ע"ש בב"ח].

חשק שלמה על רבינו גרשום

א) [נראה דצ"ל עובד כוכבים לרבותא דאפילו עובד כוכבים לא שרי ליה דעובדי כוכבים נמי וכו'].

The Gemara proceeds to the next case:

מַטְלוֹנִיּוֹת – SCRAPS OF FABRIC that do not measure three by three fingerbreadths. חָזוּ לֵיהּ לִקְרִיעָה דִּלְבוּשָׁא – But **they are fit for** one to use as a patch over **a tear in a garment!** They are likely to be removed from the opening for this purpose. – ? –

The Gemara answers:

בִּסְמִיכְתָּא – The Baraisa refers **to thick [fabric],** which is unsuitable for patching clothing.

The Gemara persists:

חָזוּ לְאוּמָּנָא – But even such **[scraps] are fit for** use by **a bloodletter** to clean the wound. – ? –

The Gemara answers:

בְּרִיסְקָא – The Baraisa refers **to** scraps of **sackcloth,** which are coarse and would irritate the wound.

The Gemara counters:

אִי בְּרִיסְקָא – **If** the Baraisa refers **to sackcloth,** שֶׁאֵין בָּהֶן שָׁלֹשׁ עַל שָׁלֹשׁ – why does it say, "THAT DO NOT MEASURE THREE BY THREE fingerbreadths"? שֶׁאֵין בָּהֶן אַרְבָּעָה עַל אַרְבָּעָה מִיבְּעֵי לֵיהּ – **It should be, "that do not measure four by four** *tefachim,"* for in regard to sackcloth that is the minimum size that can contract *tumah.*[9] – ? –

The Gemara answers:

כְּעֵין רִיסְקָא – The Baraisa refers to fabric that is **like sackcloth** only insofar as it is coarse. In other respects it has the properties of regular cloth, whose minimum size in regard to *tumah* contamination is three by three fingerbreadths.

The Gemara discusses the next case:

וְהָאֵבֶר וְהַבָּשָׂר הַמְדוּלְדָּלִין בִּבְהֵמָה וּבְחַיָּה – A partially severed LIMB OR piece of FLESH DANGLING FROM A FARM ANIMAL OR WILD BEAST. עָרְקָא וְאָזְלָא – But **[the animal] will run away.** – ? –

The Gemara answers:

בִּקְשׁוּרָה – The Baraisa refers **to [an animal] that is tied up** and cannot move away.

The Gemara asks:

שָׁחִיט לָהּ – But **[its owner] will** take the animal and **slaughter it** for food. – ? –

The Gemara answers:

בִּטְמֵאָה – The Baraisa refers **to a non-kosher [animal].**

Still, the Gemara persists:

מְזַבִּין לָהּ לְנָכְרִי – **He will sell it to a gentile** for food. – ? –

The Gemara answers:

בִּכְחוּשָׁה – The Baraisa refers **to a gaunt [animal],** which is not worth slaughtering for food.

The Gemara asks further:

פָּסֵיק שָׁדֵי לָהּ לִכְלָבִים – But **he will cut off** the partially severed limb and **throw it to the dogs.**[10] – ? –

The Gemara answers:

כֵּיוָן דְּאִיכָּא צַעַר בַּעֲלֵי חַיִּים – **Since,** were he to remove the limb, **there would be pain** caused **to a living creature,** לָא עָבִיד – **he would not do** it.[11]

The Gemara proceeds to the next case:

וְעוֹף שֶׁשָּׁכַן בַּחַלּוֹן – A BIRD RESTING IN AN OPENING. פָּרַח וְאָזִיל – But **it will fly away.** – ? –

The Gemara answers:

בְּקָשׁוּר – The Baraisa refers **to [a bird] that is tied up.**

The Gemara asks:

שָׁחִיט לֵיהּ – But **[the owner] will** take the bird and **slaughter it** for food. – ? –

The Gemara answers:

בְּטָמֵא – The Baraisa refers **to a non-kosher [bird].**

The Gemara persists:

מְזַבֵּין לֵיהּ לְנָכְרִי – **He will sell it to a gentile** for food. – ? –

The Gemara answers:

בִּקְלָנִיתָא – The Baraisa refers **to a *klanisa*** (a very thin bird, unsuitable for food).

The Gemara asks further:

יָהִיב לֵיהּ לִינוּקָא – But **he will give it** as a plaything **to a child.** – ? –

The Gemara answers:

בִּמְסָרֵט – The Baraisa refers **to [a bird] that scratches** and as such is unsuitable for a plaything.

The Gemara counters:

קְלָנִיתָא לָא מְסָרְטָא – But **a *klanisa* does not scratch.** – ? –

The Gemara answers:

כְּעֵין קְלָנִיתָא – The Baraisa refers to a bird that is **like a *klanisa*** in that it is thin and unsuitable for food, but it is unlike a *kalnisa* in that it scratches. There is no reason for such a bird to be removed from the opening.

The Gemara discusses the next case:

וְעוֹבֵד כּוֹכָבִים שֶׁיָּשַׁב בַּחַלּוֹן – OR A GENTILE SITTING IN THE OPENING. קָאֵי וְאָזִיל – But **he will get up and go** away. – ? –

The Gemara answers:

בִּכְפוּת – The Baraisa refers **to [a person] who is tied up** and cannot move away.

The Gemara asks:

אָתֵי חַבְרֵיהּ שָׁרֵי לֵיהּ – But **his fellow will come and untie him.** – ? –

The Gemara answers:

בִּמְצוֹרָע – The Baraisa refers **to someone afflicted with *tzaraas.***[12] No one will approach him for fear of contracting the disease.

The Gemara persists:

אָתֵי מְצוֹרָע חַבְרֵיהּ שָׁרֵי לֵיהּ – **A fellow victim of *tzaraas* will come** and **untie him.** – ? –

The Gemara modifies its explanation:

אֶלָּא בַּחֲבוּשֵׁי מַלְכוּת – **Rather,** we are dealing **with** someone who is tied up because he is **a prisoner of the king.** No one will dare untie him.

The Gemara proceeds to the next case:

וּבֶן שְׁמֹנָה הַמּוּנָּח בַּחַלּוֹן – A BABY born OF an EIGHT-month pregnancy LYING IN AN OPENING. אַתְיָא אִמֵּיהּ דָּרְיָא לֵיהּ – But **its mother will come and carry** it away. – ? –

The Gemara answers:

בְּשַׁבָּת – The Baraisa refers **to** the law as it applies on **the**

NOTES

9. The Mishnah (*Keilim* 27:2) teaches that the question of whether a piece of material is susceptible to *tumah* contamination depends on its type and size. In the case of regular cloth, a scrap three by three fingerbreadths or larger is considered of sufficient significance to contract *tumah.* With regard to sackcloth, the minimum size is four by four *tefachim.*

As mentioned above, an item susceptible to *tumah* contamination cannot obstruct the passage of *tumah.* That is why the Baraisa quoted here specifies scraps smaller than three by three fingerbreadths, for scraps of regular cloth larger than this can contract *tumah.* However, now that it has been established that the Baraisa refers to sackcloth, the size should be four by four *tefachim.*

10. [For the limb is useless to the animal anyway.]

11. The law of צַעַר בַּעֲלֵי חַיִּים, *tzaar baalei chaim,* states that one may not cause unnecessary pain to a living creature (see *Bava Metzia* 32a-b).

The option of killing the animal to throw all of it to the dogs is not considered, for that was not the general practice (*Rashba*).

12. צָרַעַת, *tzaraas,* is the malady described in *Leviticus* 13 (see 9b note 10).

היא גופה תיחוץ דהא [א] כלי חרש אינו מטמא מגבו (א) אלא דפומא לגאו ואי בעית אימא לעולם דפומא לבר הכא במאי עסקינן בחבית של מתכת מיתיבי [ב] עשבין שתלשן והניחן בחלון או שעלו מאליהן בחלונות ומטלניות שאין בהן שלש על שלש והאבר והבשר המדולדלין בבהמה ובחיה ועוף ששכן בחלון ועובד כוכבים שישב בחלון ובן שמונה המונח בחלון והמלח וכלי חרס וספר תורה כולם ממעטין בחלון אבל השלג והברד והגליד והכפור והמים כולן אין ממעטין בחלון והא עשבין חזו לבהמתו [ג] באפרזתא (ב) או שעלו מאליהן כיון דקשו לכותל שקיל להו אמר רבה [ד] בכותל חורבה רב פפא אמר אפילו בכותל יישוב בבאין חוץ (ג) לשלשה לחלון מטלניות ° חזו ליה לקריעה דלבושא [ה] בסמיכתא חזו לאומנא [ו] בריסקא אי בריסקא שאין בהן שלש על שלש אין בהן ארבעה על ארבעה מיבעי ליה [ג] בעין ריסקא והאבר והבשר המדולדלין בבהמה ובחיה ערקא ואזלא [ז] בקשורה שחיט לה בטמאה מזבין לה לנכרי בכחושה פסיק שדי לה לכלבים כיון דאיכא צער בעלי חיים לא עביד ועוף ששכן בחלון פרח ואזיל [ח] בקשור שחיט ליה בטמא מזבין ליה לנכרי בקלניתא יהיב ליה לינוקא במסרט קלניתא לא מסרטא בעין קלניתא ועובד כוכבים שישב בחלון קאי ואזיל בכפות אתי חבריה שרי ליה במצורע אתי מצורע חבריה שרי ליה [ט] אלא בחבושי מלכות ובן שמונה המונח בחלון אתיא אמיה דריא ליה [י] בשבת [כ] דתניא [ל] בן שמונה הרי הוא כאבן ואסור לטלטלו בשבת אבל אמו שוחה עליו ומניקתו מפני הסכנה מלח חזיא ליה [ל] במרירתא חזיא לעורות [מ] דאית בה קוצי כיון דקשיא לכותל שקלא [נ] דיתבא אחספא חספא גופא תיחוץ

דלית

רש"י

שאין בה שלש על שלש. שאין מקבלין טומאה: **המדולדלין.** שתלושין ומעורין במקצת והבהמה עומדת אצל החלון והאבר מונח על החלון ותנן בהעור והרוטב (חולין קכט.) מטמאין טומאת אוכלין במקומן וצריכין הכשר ואלו לא הוכשרו: **עובד כוכבים.** אינו מקבל טומאה וכן בן שמנה שהרי הוא כאבן לא חי ולא מת: **המלח.** לא מקבל טומאה דלאו אוכל הוא באנפי נפשיה: **וכלי חרס.** שאחוריו לצד אהל הטומאה: **והשלג והברד כו'.** הואיל ונימוקים מאליהם אין ממעטים וכן מים שבכלי הואיל ואם יטול הכלי אין עומדים בפני עצמן אין ממעטין בחלון: **הברד.** גלצ"א: **הכפור.** גריישלא"ן: **הגליד.** קרח לבן שאינו שלג: **ה"ג והא עשבים חזו לבהמתו.** וסופו ליטלן ואפ"ה כל כמה דליתנהו התם ממעטי ותיובתא דשמואל: **באפרזתא** (ד). והוא סם המות לבהמה ומאן דגריס בארופתא טועה ה) שהוא קורנס של נפחים: **כיון דקשו לכותל.** שמקלקלין אותו כדאמרי' במתני' שקיל להו ואפ"ה ממעט וקשה לשמואל: **בבאין חוץ לשלשה.** טפחים רחוק מן הכותל ועולין לתוך החלון לאשיכן: **חזי לקריעה.** לעשות טלאי: **בסמיכתא.** עב יותר מדאי: **לאומנא.** למקיז דם לקנות פי המכה: **בריסקא.** שהוא מסרט: **אין בהן ארבעה על ארבעה מבעי ליה.** שזו היא שיעור של שק: **קלניתא.** עוף כחוש מאד ואין ראוי לשום אדם: **כעין קלניתא.** כחוש כקלניתא והוא מסרט: **דאית ביה קוצי.** ויסרטו את ידיו: **כיון דקשה לכותל.** כדתנן במתניתין:

דלית

תוספות

היא גופה תיחוץ. ותימה היכי תיחוץ הא לא מבטל ליה התם ותירץ ר"י בר מרדכי דכיון שהתליפו הגרוגרות ° גם החבית נתקלקל ומבטלו אבל קשה לר"י דבפ"ב דשבת (דף כט. ושם) דאמר שפקקו את המאור בטפיח כי פקקו מאי הוי הא לא מבטל ליה ואינו חוצץ וליכא למימר דביטלו הטפיח דא"כ היה בונה בשבת ונראה לר"ת ולר"י דלכלי חרס לא בעי ביטול אלא שפיר חוצץ אע"ג דלא מבטל ליה והא דקתני לקמן דכלי חרס ממעט בחלון ופריך כלי חרס הא חזי ליה התם מיירי בממעט חלון מכשיעור אבל אינו סותם כל החלון דהכי בעי ביטול אבל היכא דסותם כל החלון כי הכא דקתני חוללין דמשמע דסותם לגמרי וכן ההוא דפקקו את המאור התם ודאי [לא] בעי ביטול בכלי חרס ועוד אמר הר"ר שמואל דכלי עץ נמי שאינו מקבל טומאה כגון העשוי לנחת לא בעי ביטול דבפ"ב דמגילה (דף כו:) גבי ההוא בי כנישתא דיהודאי דהוה פתיחא להוה אינדרונא דהוה בה מיתנא ובעו כהני לעיולי בה (ה) עד דאמר להו לכו תיבותא ואותבוה אבבא ואי לריך ביטול מאי מהני האי תיבה דמסתמא לא ביטלוה התם ועוד שלא היו יכולים לבטלה שהיה ספר תורה מונח בה ואסור לשנותה בדבר אחר דמעלין בקודש ולא מורידין: **בחבית** של מתכת. הקשה ר"ת דחבית גופה תביא טומאה לבית אחר דע"י אהל נעשית המתכת כחלל להיות כאבי אבות הטומאה כדמוכח במסכת אהלות והוי כחלל נמי לטמא אחרים באהל דכוליה קרא דוכל אשר יגע על פני השדה בחלל חרב וגו' דריש לה בנזיר פרק כ"ג (דף נד. ושם) לענין אהל ונראה לרבינו תם דהכא איירי כגון שהגרוגרות בולטות חוץ לפי חבית כל סביבותיו ומכסות אותו לגמרי שאין נראה כלל ודייק ר"ת מדנקט גרוגרות ולא נקט פירות לפי שהם מדובקות יחד אע"פ שיולאות חוץ לחבית אין נופלות וכי האי גוונא דייק בפרק חבית (שבת דף קמו.) ועוד אומר ר' יצחק דהכא מיירי בשאין חבית יוצאה חוץ לכותל דהשתא דרך החלון לא יבא טומאה לבית דטומאה רצוצה בוקעת ועולה ואינה מתפשטת לצדדין שהרי אין בו פותח טפח: **שעלו** מאליהן. תימה היאך ממעטין הטפח הא תנן במס' אהלות (פ"ח מ"ה) אלו לא מביאין ולא חוצצין הזרעים והירקות המחוברין לקרקע חוץ מן הירקות שמנו פירוש הנהו דמנו לעיל דמביאין וחוצצין האירוס והקיסוס וירקות חמור ודלעת יוונית וא"כ היכי קתני דעשבין שעלו מאליהן דחוצצין ותירץ רבינו תם דהתם איירי לענין אהל דאין נעשין אהל לחוץ בפני הטומאה על מה שתחתיהם או שעליהם או להביא טומאה מפני שהרוח מנשבו ואינו עומד במקום אחד והוי דומיא דעוף הפורח שאינו לא חוצץ ולא מביא הקשה ר"י דהכא בכולה שמעתין לא בעינן מירוח לא בעשבים ולא בחבית דפריך לעיל היא גופה תיחוץ ובהגוזל קמא (ב"ק דף קה.) אמר רבא הרי ו) חבית שניקבה וסתמוה שמרים הצילוה פקקה בזמורה עד שימרח מן הצדדין וי"ל דהתם (ו) בכלי בעינן מוקף צמיד פתיל להכי צריך מירוח אבל הכא לא בעי צמיד פתיל: **ועוף** ששכן בחלון. נראה דאתי אפילו לר"מ דאמר (עירובין דף טו:) כל דבר שיש בו רוח חיים אין עושין אותו לא דופן לסוכה ולא לחי למבוי כו' דהיינו לענין מחילת עשרה טפחים דוקא אבל הכא לענין ממעט בחלון ממעטו בכל דבר שיבטלנו: **ועובד** כוכבים שישב בחלון. דעובד כוכבים אינו מקבל טומאה כדנפקא לן מקרא בפ"ב דנזיר (דף סא: ושם) דכתיב ואיש אשר יטמא וגו' מתוך הקהל ° יצא עובד כוכבים שאין לו קהל ואע"ג דחכמים עשאום כזבים לכל דבריהם (שבת דף פג. נדה דף לד.) כיון דמדאורייתא לא מקבלי טומאה חוללין מפני הטומאה וא"ת דבפרק יוצא דופן (נדה דף מג:) אמר חומר בשרץ מבשכבת זרע שהשרץ אין לו חלוקת טומאה ומסיק שכבת זרע דחלוקה טומאה מה היא אילימא בין ישראלים לנכרים ה"נ הא איכא עכבר דים ועכבר דיבשה משמע דשרץ אין חלוקה טומאתו בין ישראל לנכרי לאו פירכא היא דלע"ג דאין עובדי כוכבים טמאים בשרץ אין לו חלוקת טומאה דומיא דשכבת זרע דבשכבת זרע גופה איכא חילוק אבל בשרץ גופיה אין חילוק אלא בהנהו דמקבלי ממנו טומאה הילכך לריך למינקט עכבר דים ועכבר דיבשה והא דאיצטריך מיעוטא (שבת פג. נדה לד.) דעובד כוכבים אינו מטמא בזיבה משום דטומאת זיבה לאו טומאת מגע היא ומטומאה זו לא אשכחן דאימעטו ובן שמונה אינו מקבל טומאה כשהוא חי דלא איקרי אדם: **והמלח.** משמע מהכא דאין מלח מקבל טומאה אבל השלג מיירי שלא חישב עליו לאכילה דלא מקבל טומאה דאי חשב עליו תיפוק ליה דהוי דבר המקבל טומאה כדמוכח במסכת נדה [דף יז. וע"ש ולע"ג ואולי צ"ל אבל השלג מיירי שלא חישב עליו למשקה דלא מקבל טומאה וכו' וע"פ הגה"ה זו מובנים דברי התוספות על נכון]: **כולן** אין ממעטין בחלון. וטעמא משום דאין מתקיימין (ז) ונימסין במים דליכא למימר דטעמא משום דקשו לכותל ושקיל להו דהא מלח נמי קשה לכותל וקתני דממעט ומיירי כגון דמנחי בחספא והנך נמי ליתני דממעטי דמנחי בחספא אלא אפילו דמנחי בחספא דלא קשו לכותל לא ממעטי: **חזי** לקריעה דלבושא. ואע"ג דאמר בפ"ק דסוכה (דף טז. ושם) ובשבת פרק כל הכלים (דף קכה.) דפחות משלש על שלש לא חזי לא לעניים ולא לעשירים ודאי לא מקבל טומאה כיון דלא מנלעו ליה אבל מ"מ לא ממעט דלא מבטל ליה דקא שקיל ליה כי ז) מלטרף לקריעה דלבושא: **כיון** דאיכא צער בעלי חיים כו'. וא"ת כולה בהמה שקיל ושדי לכלבים וי"ל דמיירי בקוף וכל דדמי ליה דמנח התם לטיולי ביה וניחא דנקט אבר ובשר ולא נקט בהמה גופה דאי חזיא לטיולי שקיל לה לטיולי בה ואי לא חזיא שדי לה לכלבים: **אתיא** אמיה ודריא ליה בשבת. ומיירי בנוסס שימות קודם שילא השבת ואמר דשם תהא קבורתו:

דלית

עין משפט נר מצוה

יח א ב ג ד ה ו ז ח ט י מיי' פט"ו מהלכות טומאת מת הלכה ג:

יט כ מיי' פ"א מהל' מילה הל' יג ועיין בכ"מ ופכ"ה מהל' שבת הל' ו טוש"ע א"ח סי' של סעיף ח וטוש"ע י"ד סי' רסו סעיף יא בהג"ה:

כ ל מ נ מיי' פט"ו מהלכות טומאת מת הלכה ג:

רבינו גרשום

היא גופה תיחוץ בפני הטומאה. **דהא** קי"ל **כלי חרס אינו מטמא מגבו: איבעית אימא דפומא לבר.** (ומש"ה) אפ"ה אינה חוצצת: **בחבית של מתכת.** דמטמאה מגבה: **או שעלו.** שגדלו: **ומטלניות שאין בהם ג' על ג'.** דלא מקבלי טומאה. **והאבר והבשר המדולדלין בבהמה ובחיה** אבל עדיין סריכי בבהמה והן בחלון וכל הני מפרש לקמן למה ממעטין בחלון משום דלא הוי דבר חשוב ומבטלי להו **אבל השלג וכול' אין ממעטין** דמים הן: **עשבים חזו לבהמה.** ואמאי ממעטין הא לא מבטיל להו: **באפרזתא.** כלומר סם המות דבהמה דלא חזי לבהמה מש"ה מבטל ליה: **כיון דקשי לכותל שקיל להו** ולא מבטל להו ואמאי ממעטי בחלון. **אמר רבא** מש"ה ממעט דלא איכפת ליה מלקיית אותו **כותל דחורבה** היא ולא תליש להו בעוד שהטומאה בבית: **בבאין חוץ מג' טפחים.** חוץ מחלון דלא מזיק לכותל כלל וראשי ענפים מגיעין לכותל ליכא למיחש דילמא שקיל להו מש"ה ממעטין: **ומטלניות.** אמאי ממעט הא **חזי לקריעה דלבושא** לתקוני ומשני **בסמיכתא** דעב הוא ביותר ולא חזי: **לאומנא.** למקיז כלומר לקנח מן הדם ומשני **בדשק** דלא חזי לאומנא. אי הכי דמוקמת לה בדשק הא דתני **שאין בהם ג' על ג'** מש"ה לא מקבלי טומאה **שאין בהם ד' על ד'** מיבעי ליה דהכי דינא של שק. דעבה **כעין שק** ולא חזי שמחללת כלי האומן כמו השק: **בקלניתא.** עוף הוא שכחש ביותר ואין ליה בשר וקא מבטל ליה ומקשה **הא חזי לינוקא** לשחק בו ולא מבטל ליה ואמאי ממעט ומשני **במסרט** דלא חזי לינוקא: והא קי"ל דקלניתא לא מסרט. ואמאי לא קמבטל ליה דחזיא לינוקא ומשני **כעין קלניתא** דכחוש הוא ביותר ומסרט: **ועובד כוכבים שישב בחלון.** ה"ה נמי ישראל אלא מש"ה נקט עובד כוכבים א) לא שרי ליה לעובדי כוכבים נמי מבדלו מן המצורע מפני הסכנה שלא ימות קודם שעתו: **במרירתא.** שאין ראוי למאכל: **דאית בה קוצי.** וכשמתקן בו העור יכנסו הקוצים בידים ולהכי מבטל ליה. **ומקשי'** כיון דקשי מלח לכותל כדתני במתני' אמאי ממעט הא שקיל ליה שלא יקלקל הכותל ומשני **דמיתבא** ההוא מלח **בחספא** דלא קשי לכותל. ומקשינן **חספא גופא תיחוץ** בלא מלח ואמאי נקט מלח:

מסורת הש"ס

א) [חולין דף כה.], ב) [תוספתא דאהלות פי"ד], ג) [עי' תוס' לקמן קיא. ד"ה דין], ד) שבת קלה. יבמות פ. [תוספתא שבת פט"ו], ה) [עי' רש"י ברכות לד. ובמגילה כה. ד"ה מרופתא ובגיטין עו: ד"ה ארופתא ומלוה לייסד וע"ע רש"י ב"ק מז: ד"ה באפרזתא], ו) [צ"ל הרי אמרו], ז) צ"ל מצטרף:

הגהות הב"ח

(א) גמ' אינו מטמא מגבו לא לריכא דפומא: (ב) שם באפרזתא חזיא להסקה בלחים או שעלו: (ג) שם חוץ משלשה לחלון: (ד) רש"י ד"ה באפרזתא גרסי' והוא סם: (ה) תוס' ד"ה היא וכו' לעיולי בה כו' עד אמר להו וכו' לשנותה לדבר: (ו) ד"ה שעלו וכו' וי"ל דהתם בעינן כצ"ל ותיבת בכלי נמחק: (ז) ד"ה כולן וכו' ונימוסין וליכא כצ"ל ותיבת במים נמחק:

גליון הש"ס

גמרא חזו ליה לקריעה. בערוך ערך רקע הגירסא למרקע לבושא ועיין מ"ק דף כח ע"א תוס' ד"ה מאן רקיע: תוס' ד"ה היא. גם החבית נתקלקל. כדאיתא בב"מ דף לח ע"ב וברש"י שם ד"ה לקנקנים: שם ד"ה ועובד כו' יצא עכו"ם שאין לו קהל. בגמרא שם דחה זה דדלמא מכרת אמעטא ולא מטומאה ומסקינן דילפינן מקרא ואיש אשר יטמא ולא יתחטא כל שיש לו טהרה יש לו טומאה ולע"ג:

לעזי רש"י

גלש"א. פירוש ברד, קרח (רש"י ברכות דף יח ע"ב), כעין גרעינים המתהוים בחלל האויר מהמים הנקפאים ונופלים ארצה. גריישלא"ן. פירוש כפור, מה שיקפה מהמים היורדים כטל (רמב"ם אהלות פ"ח מ"ה ועיין רש"י שמות טז, יד).

ליקוטי רש"י

כלי חרש אינו מטמא מגבו. אפילו נגעה טומאה בגבו אינו מקבל טומאה בכך [חולין כד:]. **באפרזתא.** עשב והוא סם המות לבהמה [ב"ק מז:]. **ומניקתו מפני הסכנה.** מפני שחלב נעכר בדדיה ומביאה לידי חולי [שבת קלה.]. סכנת שניהם הבן והאם שלא יכנס חלב הדדין ויחלום ותמות [יבמות פ. ע"ש בב"ח].

חשק שלמה על רבינו גרשום

א) נראה דצ"ל לרבינו דלפניו עובד כוכבים לא שרי ליה לעובדי כוכבים נמי וכו'.

Sabbath. Since the baby will certainly not live,[13] it is subject to the Sabbath prohibition of *muktzeh* and as such may not be moved.[14] דְּתַנְיָא – **As it was taught in a Baraisa:** בֶּן שְׁמֹנָה הֲרֵי הוּא כְּאֶבֶן וְאָסוּר לְטַלְטְלוֹ בַּשַּׁבָּת – A BABY born OF an EIGHT-month pregnancy IS treated LIKE A STONE; i.e. it is *muktzeh* and may not be moved on the Sabbath. אֲבָל אִמּוֹ שׁוֹחָה עָלָיו וּמְנִיקָתוֹ – HOWEVER, ITS MOTHER MAY BEND OVER IT AND without moving it NURSE IT מִפְּנֵי הַסַּכָּנָה – DUE TO THE DANGER posed to her by the excessive amount of milk she is carrying.[15]

The Gemara proceeds to the next case:

מֶלַח – SALT. חֲזְיָא לֵיהּ – But **[salt] is fit** for one to use as seasoning in one's food. It is likely to be removed from the opening for this purpose. – ? –

The Gemara answers:

בִּמְרִירְתָּא – The Baraisa refers **to bitter [salt],** which is unsuitable for seasoning.

The Gemara persists:

חֲזְיָא לְעוֹרוֹת – But even **[bitter salt] is fit for** tanning **hides.**[16] – ? –

The Gemara answers:

דְּאִית בָּהּ קוֹצֵי – The Baraisa refers to **[salt] in which there are thorns.** Such salt is unsuitable for use in the tanning process, because it scratches the hands.

The Gemara asks:

כֵּיוָן דְּקַשְׁיָא לְכוֹתֶל שָׁקְלָא – **Since [salt] is injurious to a wall,**[17] **he will remove** it for the sake of the wall's protection. – ? –

The Gemara answers:

דְּיָתְבָא אַחַסְפָּא – The Baraisa refers to **[salt] that rests on a shard of earthenware,** and thus is not in contact with the wall.

The Gemara counters:

חַסְפָּא גּוּפָא תֵּיחוּץ – Then **let the shard itself obstruct** the passage of *tumah!* Why does the Baraisa mention the salt? Even without the salt, the size of the opening is diminished by the shard. – ? –

NOTES

13. See note 5, paragraph (6).

14. מוּקְצֶה, *muktzeh,* is the term used for a class of objects which in the normal course of events do not stand to be used on the Sabbath or Yom Tov. The Rabbis prohibited the moving of such objects on the Sabbath or Yom Tov.

The reference here is to a baby already in the throes of death that will die before the Sabbath ends and will be buried where it is. [Therefore, it will not be removed from the opening, even after the Sabbath] (*Tosafos;* cf. *Ritva*).

15. It is unclear why the Baraisa uses the term סַכָּנָה, *danger*. Even the mere discomfort of the pressure in the mother's breasts should be sufficient grounds for allowing her to nurse the baby (*Tosafos* to *Shabbos* 135a).

16. As part of the tanning process, salt was rubbed into hides to soften them.

17. Our Mishnah (17a) teaches that salt must be distanced from a neighbor's wall (*Rashi*).

היא גופה תיחוץ דהא (א) כלי חרש אינו מטמא מגבו (א) אלא דפומא לגאו ואי בעית אימא לעולם דפומא לבר הכא במאי עסקינן בחבית של מתכת מיתיבי ג עשבין שתלשן והניחן בחלון או שעלו מאליהן בחלונות ומטלניות שאין בהן שלש על שלש והאבר והבשר המדולדלין בבהמה ובחיה ועוף ששכן בחלון ועובד כוכבים שישב בחלון ובן שמנה המונח בחלון והמלח וכלי חרס וספר תורה כולם ממעטין בחלון אבל השלג והברד והגליד והכפור והמים כולן אין ממעטין בחלון והא עשבין חזו לבהמתו ד באפרזתא (ג) או שעלו מאליהן כיון דקשו לכותל שקיל להו אמר רבה ה בכותל חורבה רב פפא אמר אפילו בכותל יישוב בבאין חוץ (ג) לשלשה לחלון מטלניות ו חזו ליה לקריעה דלבושא ה בסמיכתא חזו לאומנא י בריסקא אי בריסקא שאין בהן שלש על שלש שאין בהן ארבעה על ארבעה מיבעי ליה ג כעין ריסקא והאבר והבשר המדולדלין בבהמה ובחיה ערקא ואזלא ז בקשורה שחיט לה בטמאה מזבין לה לנכרי בכחושה פסיק שדי לה לכלבים כיון דאיכא צער בעלי חיים לא עביד ועוף ששכן בחלון פרח ואזיל ח בקשור שחיט ליה בטמא מזבין ליה לנכרי יהיב ליה לינוקא במסרט קלניתא לא מסרטא דלית כעין קלניתא ועובד כוכבים שישב בחלון קאי ואזיל בכפות אתי חבריה שרי ליה במצורע אתי מצורע חבריה שרי ליה ט אלא בחבושי מלכות ובן שמנה המונח בחלון אתיא אמיה דריא ליה י בשבת ד דתניא כ בן שמנה הרי הוא כאבן ואסור לטלטלו בשבת אבל אמו שוחה עליו ומניקתו מפני הסכנה מלח חזיא ליה ל במרירתא חזיא לעורות מ דאית בה קוצי כיון דקשיא לכותל שקלא נ דיתבא אחספא חספא גופא תיחוץ דלית

רש"י

שאין בה שלש על שלש. שאין מקבלין טומאה: **המדולדלין.** שתלושין ומעורין במקצת והבהמה עומדת אצל החלון והאבר מונח על החלון ותנן בהעור והרוטב (חולין קכט.) מטמאין טומאת אוכלין במקומן וצריכין הכשר ואלו לא הוכשרו: **עובד כוכבים.** אינו מקבל טומאה וכן בן שמנה שהרי הוא כאבן לא חי ולא מת: **המלח.** לא מקבל טומאה דלאו אוכל הוא באנפי נפשיה: **וכלי חרס.** שאחוריו לא הטומאה: **והשלג והברד כו'.** הואיל ונימוחים מאליהם אין ממעטים וכן מים שבכלי הואיל ואם ינטל הכלי אין עומדים בפני עצמן אין ממעטין בחלון: **הברד.** גלש"א: **הכפור.** גריישל"א: **הגליד.** קרח לבן שאינו שלג: **ה"ג והא עשבים חזו לבהמתו.** וסופו ליטלן ואפ"ה כל כמה דליתנהו התם ממעטי ומיותבא לשמואל: **באפרזתא (ד).** והוא סם המות לבהמה ומאן דגריס באחרפתא טועה שהוא קורנס של נפחים: **כיון דקשו לכותל.** שמקלקלין אותו כדאמרי' במתני' שקיל להו ואפ"ה ממעט וקשה לשמואל: **בבאין חוץ לשלשה.** טפחים רחוק מן הכותל ועולין לתוך החלון דאשיהן: **חזי לקריעה.** לעשות טלאי: **בסמיכתא.** עב יותר מדאי: **לאומנא.** למקיז דם לקנח פי המכה: **בריסקא.** שהוא מסרט. **ארבעה על ארבעה מבעי ליה.** שזו היא שיעור של שק: **קלניתא.** עוף כחוש מאד ואין ראוי לשום אדם: **כעין קלניתא.** כחוש כקלניתא והוא מסרט דאית ביה קוצי. ויסרטו את ידיו: **כיון דקשה לכותל.** כדתנן במתניתין: דלית

תוספות

היא גופה תיחוץ. ותימה היכי תיחוץ הא לא מבטל ליה התם ותירץ ר"י ב"ר מרדכי דכיון שהתריפו הגרוגרות ° גס החבית נתקלקל ומבטלו אבל קשה לר"י דבפ"ב דשבת (דף קכז. ושם) דאמר שפקקו את המאור בטפיח כי פקקו מאי הוי הא לא מבטל ליה ואינו חוצץ וליכא למימר דביטלו הטפיח דא"כ היה בונה בשבת ונראה לר"ת ולר"י דכלי חרס לא בעי ביטול אלא שפיר חוצץ אע"ג דלא מבטל ליה והא דקתני לקמן דכלי חרס ממעט בחלון ופריך כלי חרס הא חזי ליה התם מיירי בממעט חלון מכשיעור אבל אינו סותם כל החלון להכי בעי ביטול אבל היכא דסותם כל החלון כי הכא דקתני חוצצין דמשמע דסותם לגמרי וכן ההוא דפקקו את המאור התם ודאי [לא] בעי ביטול בכלי חרס ועוד אמר הר"ר שמואל דכלי עץ נמי שאינו מקבל טומאה כגון העשוי לנחת לא בעי ביטול דבפ"ב דמגילה (דף כו:) גבי ההוא בי כנישתא דיהודאי דהות פתיחא לההוא אינדרונא דהוה בה מיתנא ובעו כהני לצלויי בה (ה) עד דאמר להו דלו תיבותא ואותבוה אבבא ואי צריך ביטול מאי מהני האי תיבה דמסתמא לא ביטלוה שם ועוד שלא היו יכולים לבטלה שהיה ספר תורה מונח בה ואסור לשנותה בדבר אחר דמעלין בקודש ולא מורידין: **בחבית** של מתכת. הקשה ר"ת דחבית גופה תביא טומאה לבית אחר דע"י אהל נעשית המתכת כחלל להיות אבי אבות הטומאה כדמוכח במסכת אהלות והוי כחלל נמי לטמא אחרים באהל דכוליה קרא דוכל אשר יגע על פני השדה בחלל חרב וגו' דריש לה בנזיר פרק כ"ג (דף נד. ושם) לענין אהל ונראה לרבינו תם דהכא מיירי כגון שהגרוגרות בולטות חוץ לפי חבית כל סביבותיו ומכסות אותו לגמרי שאין נראה כלל ודייק ר"ת מדנקט גרוגרות ולא נקט פירות לפי שהם מדובקות יחד אע"פ שיוצאות חוץ לחבית אין נופלות וכי האי גוונא דייק בפרק חבית (שבת דף קמו.) ועוד אומר ר' יצחק דהכא מיירי בשאין חבית יוצאה חוץ לכותל דהשתא דרך החלון לא יצא טומאה לבית דטומאה רצוצה בוקעת ועולה ואינה מתפשטת לצדדין שהרי אין בו פותח טפח: **שעלו** מאיליהן. תימה היאך ממעטין הטפח הא תנן במס' אהלות (פ"ח מ"ה) אלו לא מביאין ולא חוצצין הזרעים והירקות המחוברין לקרקע חוץ מן הירקות שמנו פירוש הנהו דמנו לעיל דמביאין וחוצצין האירוס והקיסוס וירקות חמור ודלעת יוונית וא"כ היכי קתני דעשבין שעלו מאליהן דחוצצין ותירץ רבינו תם דהתם איירי לענין אהל דאין נעשין אהל לחוץ בפני הטומאה על מה שתחתיהם או שעליהם או להביא טומאה מפני שהרוח מנשבו ואינו עומד במקום אחד והוי דומיא דעוף הפורח שאינו לא חוצץ ולא מביא הקשה ר"י דהכא בכולה שמעתין לא בעינן מירוח לא בעשבים ולא בחבית דפריך לעיל היא גופה תיחוץ ובהגוזל קמא (ב"ק דף קה.) אמר רבא הרי ו) חבית שניקבה וסתמוה שמרים הצילוה פקקה בזמורה עד שימרח מן הצדדין וי"ל דהתם (ו) בכלי בעינן מוקף צמיד פתיל להכי צריך מירוח אבל הכא לא בעי צמיד פתיל: **ועוף** ששכן בחלון. נראה דאתי אפילו לר"מ דאמר (עירובין דף טו:) כל דבר שיש בו רוח חיים אין עושין אותו לא דופן לסוכה ולא לחי למבוי כו' דהיינו לענין מחיצת עשרה טפחים דוקא אבל הכא לענין ממעטו בחלון ממעטו בכל דבר שיבטלנו: **ועובד** כוכבים שישב בחלון. דעובד כוכבים אינו מקבל טומאה כדנפקא לן מקרא בפ"ב דנזיר (דף סא: ושם) דכתיב ואיש אשר יטמא וגו' מתוך הקהל ° יצא עובד כוכבים שאין לו קהל ואע"ג דחכמים עשאום כזבים לכל דבריהם (שבת דף פג. נדה דף לד.) כיון דמדאורייתא לא מקבלי טומאה חוצצין מפני הטומאה וא"ת דבפרק יוצא דופן (נדה דף מג:) אמר חומר בשרץ מבשכבת זרע שהשרץ אין לו חלוקת טומאה ומסיק שכבת זרע דחלוקה טומאה מה היא אילימא בין ישראלים לנכרים ה"נ הא איכא עכבר דים ועכבר דיבשה משמע דשרץ אין חלוקה טומאתו בין ישראל לנכרי לאו פירכא היא דאע"ג דאין עובדי כוכבים טמאים בשרץ אין לו חלוקת טומאה דומיא דשכבת זרע דשכבת זרע גופה איכא חילוק אבל בשרץ גופיה אין חילוק אלא בהנהו דמקבלי ממנו טומאה הילכך צריך למינקט עכבר דים ועכבר דיבשה והא דאיצטריך מיעוטא (שבת פג. נדה לד.) דעובד כוכבים אינו מטמא בזיבה משום דטומאת זיבה לאו טומאת מגע היא ומטומאה זו לא אשכחן דאימעטו ובן שמונה אינו מקבל טומאה כשהוא חי דלא איקרי אדם: **והמלח.** משמע מהכא דאין מלח מקבל טומאה אבל השלג מיירי שלא חישב עליו לאכילה דלא מקבל טומאה דאי חשב עליו תיפוק ליה דהוי דבר המקבל טומאה כדמוכח במסכת נדה [דף יז. וע"ש ולע"ג ואולי צ"ל אבל השלג מיירי שלא חישב עליו למשקה דלא מקבל טומאה וכו' וע"פ הג"ה זו מובנים דברי התוספות על נכון]: **כולן** אין ממעטין בחלון. וטעמא משום דאין מתקיימין (ז) ונימסין במים דליכא למימר דטעמא משום דקשו לכותל ושקיל להו דהא מלח נמי קשה לכותל וקתני דממעט ומיירי כגון דמנחי בחספא והנך נמי ליתני דממעטי ודמנחי בחספא אלא אפילו דמנחי בחספא דלא קשו לכותל לא ממעטי: **חזי** לקריעה דלבושא. ואע"ג דאמר בפ"ק דסוכה (דף טז. ושם) ובשבת פרק כל הכלים (דף קכה.) דפחות משלש על שלש לא חזי לא לעניים ולא לעשירים ודאי לא מקבל טומאה כיון דלא מלנעו ליה אבל מ"מ לא ממעט דלא מבטל ליה דקא שקיל ליה כי ׳) מצטרף לקריעה דלבושא: **כיון** דאיכא צער בעלי חיים כו'. וא"ת כולה בהמה שקיל ושדי לכלבים וי"ל דמיירי בקוף וכל דדמי ליה דמנח התם לטיולי ביה וניחא דנקט אבר ובשר ולא נקט בהמה גופה דאי חזיא לטיולי שקיל לה לטיולי בה ואי לא חזיא שדי לה לכלבים: **אתיא** אמיה ודריא ליה בשבת. ואיירי בגוסס שימות קודם שילא השבת ואמר דשם תהא קבורתו: דלית

מסורת הש"ס

א) [חולין דף כה.], ב) [תוספתא דאהלות פי"ד], ג) [עי' תוס' לקמן קיא. ד"ה דין], ד) שבת קלה. יבמות פ. [תוספתא שבת פט"ו], ה) [עי' רש"י ברכות לד. ובמגילה כה. ד"ה ארמפתא ובגיטין ע: ד"ה ארמפתא ומלוה ליסבד וע"ע רש"י ב"ק ע"ב ד"ה באפרזתא], ו) [צ"ל הרי אמרו], ז) צ"ל מלטרף.

הגהות הב"ח

(א) גמ' אינו מטמא מגבו לא לריכא דפומא: (ב) שם באפרזתא חזיא לסקסק בלאים או שעלו: (ג) שם חוץ משלשה לחלון: (ד) רש"י ד"ה באפרזתא גרסי' והוא סם: (ה) תוס' ד"ה היא וכו' ללויי בה כו' עד אמר להו וכו' לשנותה לדבר: (ו) ד"ה שעלו וכו' וי"ל דהתם בעינן כל"ל ותיבת בכלי נמחק: (ז) ד"ה כולן וכו' ונימסין כל"ל ותיבת במים נמחק:

גליון הש"ס

גמרא חזו ליה לקריעה. בערוך ערך רקע הגירסא למרקע לבושא ועיין מ"ק דף כו ע"א תוס' ד"ה מאן רקיע: תוס' ד"ה היא. גס החבית נתקלקל. כדאיתא בב"מ דף לח ע"ב ובר"ש פ"ח דטהרות משנה ח: שם ד"ה ועבכ"ם כו' יצא עבכ"ם שאין לו קהל. בגמרא שם דף סא ע"ב דלאו מכלל מעטינהו אלא מטומאה ומקנין דילפינן מקרא ואיש אשר יטמא ולא יתחטא כל שיש לו טהרה יש לו טומאה וכו' וע"ע בב"ח

לעזי רש"י

גלש"א. פירוש ברד, קרח (רש"י ברכות יח ע"ב), כעין גרעינים המתהווים בחלל האויר מהמים הנקפאים ונופלים ארצה. גריישל"א. פירוש כפור, מה שקופא מהמים היורדים כטל (רמב"ם אהלות פ"ח מ"ה ועיין רש"י שמות טז, יד):

ליקוטי רש"י

כלי חרש אינו מטמא מגבו. אפילו נגעה טומאה בגבו אינו מקבל טומאה בכך [חולין כד:]. באפרזתא. עשב והוא סם המות לבהמה [ב"ק מז:]. ומניקתו מפני הסכנה. מפני שחלב הרבה בדדיה ומביאה לידי חולי [שבת קלה.]. סכנת שניהם הבן והאם שלא ימשך חלב הדדין ותמות [יבמות פ. ע"ש בב"ח].

עין משפט נר מצוה

יח א ב ג ד ה ו ז ח ט י מיי' פט"ו מהלכות טומאת מת הלכה ב:
יט כ מיי' פ"א מהל' מילה הל' יג ועיין בכ"מ ופכ"ה מהל' שבת הל' ו טוש"ע א"ח סי' של סעיף ח וטוש"ע י"ד סי' רסו סעיף יא בהג"ה:
כ ל מ נ מיי' פט"ו מהלכות טומאת מת הלכה ב:

רבינו גרשום

היא גופה תיחוץ בפני הטומאה. דהא קי"ל כלי חרס אינו מטמא מגבו: איבעית אימא דפומא לבר. (ומש"ה) אפ"ה אינה חוצצת: בחבית של מתכת. דמטמאה מגבה: או שעלו. שגדלו: ומטלניות שאין בהם ג' על ג'. דלא מקבלי טומאה: והאבר והבשר המדולדלין בבהמה ובחיה אבל עדיין סריכי בבהמה והן בחלון וכל הני מפרש לקמן למה ממעטין בחלון משום דלא הוי דבר חשוב ומבטלי להו אבל השלג וכול' אין ממעטין דמים הן: עשבים חזו לבהמה. ואמאי ממעטין הא לא מבטיל להו: באפרזתא. כלומר סם המות דבהמה דלא חזי לבהמה מש"ה מבטל ליה: כיון דקשי לכותל שקיל להו ולא מבטל להו ואמאי ממעטי בחלון: אמר רבא מש"ה ממעט דלא איכפת ליה מלקיית אותו כותל דחורבה היא ולא חליש להו בעוד שהטומאה בבית: בבאין חוץ מג' טפחים. חוץ מחלון דלא מזיק לכותל כלל וראשי ענפים מגיעין לכותל ליכא למיחש דילמא שקיל להו מש"ה ממעטין: ומטלניות. אמאי ממעט הא חזי לקריעה דלבושא לתקוני ומשני בסמיכתא דעב הוא ביותר ולא חזי: לאומנא. למקיז כלומר לקנח מן הדם ומשני בדשק דלא חזי לאומנא: אי הכי מוקמת לה בדשק הא דתני שאין בהם ג' על ג' מש"ה לא מקבלי טומאה שאין בהן ד' על ד' מיבעי ליה דהכי דינא של שק: דעבה כעין שק ולא חזי שמחלת כלי האומן כמו השק: בקלניתא. עוף הוא שכחש ביותר ואין ליה בשר וקא מבטל ליה ומקשה הא חזי לינוקא לשחק בו ולא מבטל ליה ואמאי ממעט ומשני במסרט דלא חזי לינוקא: והא קי"ל דקלניתא לא מסרט. ואמאי לא קמבטל ליה דהא חזי ליה לינוקא ומשני כעין קלניתא דכחוש הוא ביותר ומסרט: ועובד כוכבים ששכן בחלון. ה"ה נמי ישראל אלא מש"ה נקט עובד כוכבים א) לא שרי ליה דעובדי כוכבים נמי מבדלו מן המצורע מפני הסכנה שלא ימות קודם שעתו: במרירתא. שאין ראוי למאכל: דאית בה קוצי. וכשמתקנו בו העור יכנסו הקוצים בידים ולהכי מבטל ליה. ומקשי' כיון דקשי מלח לכותל כדתנן במתני' אמאי ממעט הא שקיל ליה שלא ילקה הכותל ומשני דמותיבא ההוא מלח בחספא דלא קשי לכותל. ומקשינן חספא גופא תיחוץ בלא מלח ואמאי נקט מלח:

חשק שלמה על רבינו גרשום

א) נראה דצ"ל עובד כוכבים לרבותא דאפילו עובד כוכבים לא שרי ליה דעובדי כוכבים נמי וכו'.

דלית בה שיעורא (א) כדתנן חרס כדי ליתן בין פצים לחבירו כלי חרס חזי ליה דמיטנף חזי לאומנא דמנקב ספר תורה חזי למקרא בבלוי והא בעי גניזה דשם תהא גניזתה (ואמר) רב הבכל עושין מחיצה חוץ ממלח ורבב ושמואל אמר אפילו מלח אמר רב פפא ולא פליגי הא במלח סדומית הא במלח איסתרוקנית והשתא דאמר רבה עושה אדם שני צבורי מלח ומניח עליהם קורה שהמלח מעמדת את הקורה והקורה מעמדת את המלח אפי' מלח איסתרוקנית ולא פליגי הא דאיכא קורה הא דליכא קורה: מרחיקין את הריחים ג' מן השכב שהן ארבעה מן הרכב וכו': מאי טעמא משום טירא והא תניא ושל חמור שלשה מן האיסטרובל שהן ארבעה מן הקלת התם מאי טירא איכא אלא משום קלא: ואת התנור שלשה מן הכליא שהן ארבעה מן השפה: אמר אביי שמע מינה כליא דתנור טפח נפקא מינה למקח וממכר:

מתני' לא יעמיד אדם תנור בתוך הבית אלא אם כן יש על גביו גובה ארבע אמות היה מעמידו בעלייה צריך שיהא תחתיו מעזיבה שלשה טפחים ובכירה טפח ואם הזיק משלם מה שהזיק ר' שמעון אומר לא אמרו כל השיעורין האלו אלא שאם הזיק פטור מלשלם לא יפתח אדם חנות של נחתומין ושל צבעין תחת אוצרו של חבירו ולא רפת בקר באמת ביין התירו אבל לא רפת בקר:

גמ' והתניא בתנור ארבעה ובכירה שלשה אמר אביי כי תניא ההיא בדנחתומין דתנור דידן כי כירה דנחתומין (א): לא יפתח חנות וכו': תנא אם היתה רפת (ב) קודמת לאוצר מותר בעי אביי כיבד וריבץ קודמת לאוצר מהו ריבה בחלונות מהו (ג) אכסדרה תחת האוצר מהו בנה עלייה על גבי ביתו מהו תיקו בעי רב הונא בריה דרב יהושע תמרי ורמוני מאי תיקו: באמת ביין התירו וכו': תנא ביין התירו מפני שמשביחו ולא רפת בקר מפני שמסריחו אמר רב יוסף האי דידן אפילו קוטרא דשרגא נמי קשיא ליה א"ר ששת ואספסתא כרפת בקר דמיא:

מתני' חנות שבחצר יכול למחות בידו ולומר לו איני יכול לישן מקול הנכנסין ומקול היוצאין אבל עושה כלים יוצא ומוכר בתוך השוק ואינו יכול למחות בידו ולומר לו איני יכול לישן לא מקול הפטיש ולא מקול הריחים ולא מקול התינוקות: **גמ'** מ"ש רישא ומ"ש סיפא אמר אביי סיפא אתאן לחצר אחרת א"ל רבא אי הכי ליתני חצר אחרת מותר אלא אמר רבא סיפא

רש"י

דלית בה שיעורא. והוי כמאן דליתא: **חרס.** לענין הוצאת שבת: **כדי ליתן בין פצים לחבירו.** פצימי חלונות שבכותל מרחיקין זה מזה ברוחב החלון ליכנס האורה בין כל אחד ואחד ונותן בחומה למטה ולמעלה חרס רחב בין זה לזה וטח בטיט והחרס עב והוי שם כאבן: **והא בעי גניזה.** ומסלקו לגנזו: **חוץ ממלח ורבב.** מפני שהמלח מתפזר והרבב ניתך כשמתחמם: **מלח סדומית.** עבה וקשה כאבן: **שני צבורי מלח.** גבוהים עשרה אצל כותלי מבוי ומניח שני ראשי קורות המבוי עליהן שכובד הקורה מעמיד את המלח: **ושל חמור.** ריחים של חמור: **איצטרובלא.** הוא מושב הריחים שבתוך קליפת העץ שקורין לרק"א: **קלת.** היא אפרכסת שקורין טרויימוריי"ר: **מאי טירא איכא.** ריחים קטנים וקלים הן ואין הקרקע מרעיד בגילגולו: **משום קלא.** י"מ קול הנהגת החמור וי"מ קול הריחים: **מתני' אלא אם כן יש על גביו.** חלל גובה ארבע אמות מפי התנור עד התקרה כדי שלא יאחוז האור בתקרה: **עד שיהא תחתיו מעזיבה.** אשטרי"ך בלע"ז טיח קרקע ג' טפחי' שלא תבער תקרה התחתונה של עלייה ועל גביו ד' אמות: **ובכירה מעזיבה טפח.** אף היא כלי חרס שפותים קדירה על חללה ואין עושין בתוכה היסק גדול כמו שעושין בתנור: **ואם הזיק.** אחר (ד) שיהא שם כל השיעורין הללו משלם מה שהזיק ואעפ"כ מעכבין עליו השכנים להרחיק בכל השיעורים הללו שמא ידליק בתיהם ואין לו מה לשלם: **ביין התירו.** אם היה אוצר של יין התירו לפתוח תחתיו חנות של נחתומין ולצבעין שאין העשן קשה ליין: **אבל לא רפת בקר.** שהריח קשה ליין: **גמ' והתניא.** לענין מעמידה בעלייה בתנור ארבעה מעזיבה מתחתיו ובכירה שלשה: **בדנחתומין.** שמסיקין אותו תמיד וכן הכירה בכירת נחתומין: **תנור דידן.** דיהב ביה תנא דמתני' שיעור ג"ט כבירה דנחתומין דמי: **כיבד וריבץ.** גגו לצורך האוצר ולא הספיק להכניס לו תבואה עד שפתח זה חנות תחתיו מי הוי קקודם לאוצר או דילמא כיון דכיבד וריבץ הוי כקודם האוצר: **ריבה בחלונות.** בעלייתו דגלי דעתיה שלאוצר הוא עשוי שיכנס לו אויר שלא ירקב התבואה: **בנה עלייה על גבי ביתו.** על גגו ורגילין היו לבנות שם לאוצר מהו את"ל ריבה בחלונות לאו הקדמה הוא היכי דכולי בניינא להכי עביד מאי: **תמרי ורמוני.** הכניס שם תמרים ורמונים מי הויא התחלת אוצר או דילמא אין אוצר אלא בתבואה ויין ושמן: **והאי דידן.** יין שלנו אפילו עשן העולה מן הנר קשה לו: **אספסתא.** שחת של תבואה: **כרפת בקר דמיא.** מחמת שהוא לח (ה) ומתחמם ומעלה סרחון:

מתני' ולא מקול התינוקות. קא סלקא דעתך תינוקות הבאים לקנות יין ושמן וכל דבר הנמכר בחנות: **גמ' מאי שנא רישא.** דקתני יכול לומר איני יכול לישן מקול הנכנסין והיוצאין וסיפא קתני אינו יכול לומר לו איני יכול לישן מקול התינוקות: **סיפא**

תוספות

דלית בה שיעורא. פירוש דאין שיעור לחספא למעט מפותח טפח ולא גרסינן כדתנן דמה ענין זה לשיעורי שבת אלא וכדתנן בוי"ו וה"פ ואמאי מלח ממעט הא כי שקיל חספא כשיצטרך לו יסיר גם המלח כדי שלא יזיק את הכותל והאי מייתי וכדתנן כלומר דמיירי נמי דלית ביה כדי ליתן בין פצים לחבירו דאין ראוי לכלום ולא שקיל ליה ואית ספרים דלא גרסי חספא גופיה תימוך אלא גרסינן ותיפוק ליה משום חספא כלומר ותיפוק ליה שיסיר המלח כשיסיר חספא ומשני דלית בה שיעורא כדתנן כו' ולא שקיל ליה:

ושל חמור שלש מן האיצטרובלא. פי' ריב"א מגגלא דבשל חמור ליכא טירא לפי שאין חמור טוחן בה אלא חמור קורא לבנין פעמים הנושאים את הריחים כמו שמצינו דפעים הנושאים נקראים חמור כמו העץ שהמטה מוטלת עליו כדתנן (כלים פי"ח מ"ג) נקליטי המטה והחמור טהורים וכן העץ הסובל שידה תיבה ומגדל נקרא חמור דתנן חמור שתחת המלבן וספסלים שתחת הרגלים טהור וכן עץ שהנפה סומך עליו נקרא חמור דתנן (שם פט"ז מ"ג) חמור של נפחים (ו) טמאים וכן הריחים הבנין עשוי כמין כסא ועליו ריחים והוא אצטרובל ואדם יושב כנגד' במקום גבוה ורגליו (ז) מרווחות למטה ומסבב הגלגל ברגליו וטוחן ולית ביה טירא אלא קול בעלמא אבל בריחים שאדם טוחן בידיו או בגופו אית ביה נדנוד והיא טירא ולר"י נראה דשל חמור נמי טוחן ביד אלא (ח) כשהוא על גבי בנין כדתנן במס' זבים בפרק רביעי חמור של ריחים ושל יד והא דתניא בתוספת' בפ' קמא דמכילתין מרחיקין הריחים של יד שלשה מן השכב שהן ארבע מן הרכב ושל חמור שלשה מן האיצטרובל שהן ארבע מן הקלת לא משום דבשל חמור אין טוחנין ביד אלא סתם של יד אין בהן חמור אלא ע"ג קרקע ולכך קתני בתר הכי ושל חמור אבל תרוייהו טוחנין ביד:

שמע מינה כליא דתנור טפח. הא דלא קאמר נמי לעיל ש"מ שכב דריחים נמי טפח לפי שהיה פשוט להם איך היה:

תנור דידן כבירה דנחתומין דמי. כל אחד היה עושה תנור שלו כפי מה שהיה רוצה גדול או קטן אבל כירות של נחתומין היו כולן שוות והיו בקיאין בהן ונפקא מינה למקח וממכר:

מאי שנא רישא ומאי שנא סיפא. השתא ס"ד דתינוקות דסיפא היינו שבאין לקנות בחנות ומשום הכי פריך מ"ש אבל מפטיש וריחים לא פריך דאין שם נכנסין ויוצאין דמי שיש לו חטין לטחון נותן לבעל הריחים (ט) וכן פטיש:

עין משפט נר מצוה

כא א ב מיי' פט"ו מהל' טומאת מת הלכה ד:
כב ג ד מיי' פט"ו מהל' ... ב:
כג ה מיי' פט"ו מהל' שבת הל' כג סמג לאוין סה טוש"ע א"ח סי' שמה סעיף ה ...
כד ו ז מיי' פ"ט מהל' שכנים הל' ג סמג עשין פב טוש"ע ח"מ סי' קנה סעיף ז:
כה ח ט מיי' שם הל' יא סמג שם טוש"ע ח"מ סי' קנה סעיף ח:
כו י מיי' שם הל' יב טוש"ע שם סעיף ג:
כז כ מיי' שם הל' יא טוש"ע שם סעיף ח:
כח ל מיי' שם הל' יב טוש"ע שם סעיף ג:
כט מ נ ס מיי' שם הל' יג וטוש"ע שם סעיף ג:
ל ע פ צ מיי' שם הל' יג וטוש"ע שם סעיף ג:
לא ק מיי' שם פ"ו הל' יג סמג שם טוש"ע ח"מ סי' קנו סעיף ג:

רבינו גרשום

ומשני דלית ביה שיעור. משה"ה לא חיישן: בין פצים לחבירו. כעין שסומכין את הקורות המרוצעות על הקרקע כדי שלא יעקלו ומשימין תחת הקורה חתיכה של חרס לסומכן כמו שאנו רגילין לעשות באבנים: וכלי חרס נמי חזי ליה ושקיל ליה ואמאי ממעט בחלון דאגב דצריכי לכלי נקט ליה עם המלח. ומשני דמיטנף דלא חזי: חזי לאומנא. לקבל בו דם: שם תהא גניזתו ומבטל ליה ולא שקיל ליה: רבב. שומן: מחיצה. אי לענין שבת אי בפני הטומאה. מלח נמי לא מפסר כמים. מלח סדומית שעב הוא ואינו יפה ודאי עושין בו מחיצה לענין שבת משום דקא מבטל ליה התם אבל מלח אסתרוקנית שדק הוא לא מבטל ליה ואין עושין בו מחיצה: עושה אדם. לגבי מבוי. וקורה מעמדת את המלח שמכבשתו ומגנת עליו מן הגשמים. הא דאיכא קורה עושין בו מחיצה דאמר שהקורה מעמידתו: פיסקא משום טירא. שמזעזע הכותל מתוך הבנין הריחים הקבועין סמוך לכותל וי"א טירא המיית הריחים קשה לכותל. והני רחיים ג"מ שמחזיר ג"ט מן האצטרובל קרי התחתון שכב הרחיים של חמור והרכב קרי קלת: מאי טירא איכא הא לא קבע בבנינו בקרקע ולא מזעזע הקרקע ואמאי מרחיקין אלא משום קלא של רחיים שקשה לכותל מרחיקין הכא נמי משום קלא: לא יעמיד אדם תנור בתוך הבית. אם העלייה שעל גבי בית היא של חבירו אא"כ יש על גביו ועד העלייה ד' אמות מפני הלהב שלא ידליק העלייה: התנור בעלייה שלו ותחת העלייה בית של חבירו לא יעמידנו עד שיהא תחתיו מעזיבה ג' טפחים כדי שלא יזיק לבית של חבירו. ואפ"ה אם הזיק משלם מה שהזיק

מסורת הש"ס

א) שבת פב. ביצה לט., ב) [צ"ל אמר], ג) ב"ק סא: ב"מ קיח., ד) לעיל יח., ה) [בכלאים פ"ב מ"ב ובתרומות פ"ב מ"א ובב"מ נט: במשנה איתא באמת אמרו], ו) גי' ח"ח [לפי פי' תוס'] ותנור, ז) [לעיל יח.], ח) [בסהמ"ש ל"ג תי' אבל], ט) [בסהמ"ש אבל אינו יכול]:

הגהות הב"ח

(א) גמ' כי כירה דנחתומין דמי לא: (ב) שם רפת בקר קודמת: (ג) שם ריבה בחלונות מהו בנה כצ"ל ותיבות אכסדרה תחת אוצר מהו נמחק: (ד) רש"י ד"ה ואם הזיק אחר שהיו שם: (ה) ד"ה כרפת וכו' שהוא לח מתחמם כצ"ל ואות ו' נמחק: (ו) תוס' ד"ה ושל וכו' של נפחים טמא וכן: (ז) בא"ד ורגליו מתוחות למטה ומסבב: (ח) בא"ד טוחן ביד אלא שהוא כצ"ל ואות כ' נמחק: (ט) ד"ה מאי וכו' לבעל הריחים וטוחן וכן פטיש:

גליון הש"ס

רש"י ד"ה מלח סדומית עבה וקשה כאבן. עי' פרש"י ביצה לט ע"א ד"ה סדומית ולזה הכא ע"כ ט"ס והציון ברש"י הוא על מלח איסתרוקנית. וכן בסוגיין אפי' מלח איסתרוקנית ולא פליגי צ"ל אפי' מלח סדומית:

לעזי רש"י

צרק"א. פירוש האצטרובלא (זבים פ"ד מ"ג), מושב הריחים, עגול שסביב הריחים (רשב"ם ב"ב דף סה ע"א), מושב אמת הריחים (רש"י כתובות דף סט ע"א ועיין רש"י ברכות דף יח ע"ב ומו"ק דף י ע"ב ועירובין דף פט ע"א). טרוימוריי"ר. פירוש קלת, אפרכסת (רש"י חגיגה דף ג ע"ב). אשטריך. פירוש מעזיבה, לפסת טיט (שטוחין על התקרה).

ליקוטי רש"י

כדי ליתן בין פצים לחבירו. כשמגדלין פצימין ועמודין וקורות ועושין סולם של קורות על הארץ ויש חלל בין זה לזה סומכין במחמתיו שלא יתעקמו (שבת פב.).

The Gemara answers:

דְּלֵית בָּהּ שִׁיעוּרָא – **[The shard] is not of** sufficient **size** to be considered significant. Therefore, legally, it is regarded as if it was not there, and the diminution of the opening is accomplished only by the salt. That a piece of earthenware is not considered significant unless it is of a certain size can be proven כִּדְתְנַן – **as we learned in the** following **Mishnah:**[1] חֶרֶס – The minimum quantity of EARTHENWARE for which one is liable if one transferred it from one domain to another on the Sabbath כְּדֵי לִיתֵּן בֵּין פַּצִּים לַחֲבֵירוֹ – is a shard large ENOUGH TO PLACE BETWEEN ONE window SLAT AND ANOTHER.[2]

The Gemara discusses the next case:

כְּלִי חֶרֶס – AN EARTHENWARE VESSEL. חָזֵי לֵיהּ – But **it is fit for one** to use to hold food! It is likely to be removed for this purpose. – ? –

The Gemara answers:

דְּמִיטַּנֵּף – The Baraisa refers to a vessel **that is soiled.** Such a vessel is unfit to contain food.

The Gemara persists:

חָזֵי לְאוּמָּנָא – But **it is fit for** use by **a bloodletter** to catch the blood that emerges from the wound.[3] – ? –

The Gemara answers:

דְּמְנַקַּב – The Baraisa refers to a vessel **that is perforated.** Such a vessel cannot hold blood.

The Gemara discusses the final case of the Baraisa:

סֵפֶר תּוֹרָה – A TORAH SCROLL. חָזֵי לְמִקְרָא – But **it is fit for reading!** It is likely to be removed for this purpose. – ? –

The Gemara answers:

בִּבְלוּי – The Baraisa refers **to a worn-out [Torah scroll],** which cannot be used for reading.

The Gemara counters:

וְהָא בָּעֵי גְּנִיזָה – **But it must be** taken and **put into safekeeping.**[4] – ? –

The Gemara answers:

שָׁם תְּהֵא גְּנִיזָתָהּ – **Its safekeeping will be there,** in the opening.[5]

Having discussed the case of salt merging with an already formed wall, the Gemara discusses the legal status of a wall made entirely out of salt:[6]

(וְאָמַר)[7] רַב – **Rav said:** בַּכֹּל עוֹשִׂין מְחִיצָה חוּץ מִמֶּלַח וּרְבַב – A legally valid **partition may be made out of anything except salt and fat,** for a wall comprised of these substances will not endure.[8] וּשְׁמוּאֵל אָמַר – **And Shmuel said:** אֲפִילּוּ מֶלַח – A partition may be made **even** out of **salt.**

The statements of Rav and Shmuel are explained:

אָמַר רַב פָּפָּא – **Rav Pappa said** וְלָא פְּלִיגֵי – **[Rav and Shmuel] do not disagree** with each other. הָא בְּמֶלַח סְדוֹמִית – **This** ruling (Shmuel's ruling that a salt wall is valid) applies **to Sodomite salt,** which is thick and hard; הָא בְּמֶלַח אִיסְתְּרוּקָנִית – whereas **the other** ruling (Rav's ruling that a salt wall is not valid) applies **to Istrokian salt,**[9] which is loose.

The Gemara provides an alternative way to reconcile the rulings of Rav and Shmuel:

וְהַשְׁתָּא דְּאָמַר רַבָּה – **And now that Rabbah has said** עוֹשֶׂה אָדָם שְׁנֵי צִבּוּרֵי מֶלַח – that if **a person makes two piles of salt,** one at each side of the entrance to a *mavoi,*[10] וּמַנִּיחַ עֲלֵיהֶם קוֹרָה – **and places a crossbeam over them,** carrying is permitted in the *mavoi* on the Sabbath – שֶׁהַמֶּלַח מַעֲמֶדֶת אֶת הַקּוֹרָה – **for the salt supports the crossbeam,** וְהַקּוֹרָה מַעֲמֶדֶת אֶת הַמֶּלַח – **and** the weight of **the crossbeam keeps the salt in place** – אֲפִילּוּ מֶלַח אִיסְתְּרוּקָנִית – the statements of Rav and Shmuel may both be explained as referring **even** to **Istrokian salt.** וְלָא פְּלִיגֵי – **Yet they do not disagree,** הָא דְּאִיכָּא קוֹרָה – for **this** ruling (Shmuel's ruling that a salt wall is valid) applies to a wall of salt **with a crossbeam** over it that holds it in place, הָא דְּלֵיכָּא קוֹרָה – whereas **the other** ruling (Rav's ruling that a salt wall is not valid) applies to a wall of salt **without a crossbeam** over it.

The Gemara quotes the next section of the Mishnah:

מַרְחִיקִין אֶת הָרֵיחַיִם שְׁלֹשָׁה מִן הַשֶּׁכֶב – A MILL MUST BE DISTANCED at least THREE *tefachim* from a neighbor's wall, as measured FROM THE LOWER MILLSTONE, שֶׁהֵן אַרְבָּעָה מִן הָרֶכֶב וכו׳ – WHICH IS equivalent to FOUR *tefachim* from the wall as measured FROM THE UPPER MILLSTONE.

NOTES

1. *Shabbos* 82a. On the Sabbath, it is forbidden to transport an item from a *reshus harabim* (lit. public domain) to a *reshus hayachid* (lit. private domain) and vice versa, or four *amos* in a *reshus harabim.* As far as Scriptural law is concerned, one has not violated this prohibition unless the transferred item is one that people consider worth keeping.

2. This refers to a row of vertical slats in a window. These slats were positioned sufficiently apart from each other to allow light to enter. Two thick pieces of earthenware were plastered between adjacent slats [in order to prevent them from shifting], one at the top of the window and one at the bottom (*Rashi*).

3. [Since the blood is discarded, the state of the vessel in which it is collected is immaterial.]

4. An unusable Torah scroll must be put away in a safe place, where it will not be tampered with.

5. [Since it can remain there undisturbed, there is no need to remove it for storage elsewhere.]

6. The following passage applies both to the laws of *tumah* and to the laws of the Sabbath (*Rabbeinu Gershom*). [The definition of a wall is relevant to the laws of *tumah* in that only a halachically recognized wall blocks the passage of *tumas ohel* (roof *tumah*). It is relevant to the laws of the Sabbath in that a *reshus hayachid* (see note 1) is defined as an area enclosed by walls.]

7. [The word וְאָמַר, *and he said,* is in parentheses, for *Mesoras HaShas* emends the text to read אָמַר, *he said.* The *vav* prefix, which usually means "and," is inappropriate, for the following passage is a new discussion.]

8. Salt crumbles. Fat melts when it becomes warm (*Rashi*). [From *Rashi* (cf. *Rabbeinu Gershom*) it seems that the removal of the material that composes the wall is not at issue here. Since the owner used this material to build a wall, evidently it was not his intent to remove it for some other use.]

An apparent difficulty: Why is it that an entire wall made of salt is not recognized legally, but (as taught by the Baraisa above, 20a) a small amount of salt that is in an opening merges with the wall and reduces the size of the opening?

Since salt separates into individual grains over the course of time, a wall formed from salt cannot be considered a single solid entity. Therefore, such a wall is not halachically recognized. Regarding a solid wall with an opening, however, it is sufficient that the opening is diminished to the point where it no longer qualifies as a legal opening. To accomplish this, the diminishing agent must have permanency, but it is not necessary that its parts adhere to each other (*Tosefos Rid;* see *Meiri;* cf. *Rash* to *Ohalos* 13:5).

9. I.e. standard salt (see *Rashash* to *Beitzah* 39a).

10. The layout of residential areas in Mishnaic times was commonly one in which several houses would open into a courtyard *(chatzeir)* and several courtyards would, in turn, lead into an alley through which people would pass to get to the street (*reshus harabim*). Such an alley is known as a מָבוֹי, *mavoi.*

Typically, a *mavoi* does not have the status of a *reshus harabim* (see note 1), and therefore, Biblically speaking, it is permissible to carry in a *mavoi.* The Rabbis, however, legislated that carrying in a *mavoi* is prohibited unless a crossbeam *(korah)* is placed across its entrance, or a vertical pole *(lechi)* is put at the side of the entrance. Here, Rabbah rules that a crossbeam supported by two pillars of salt is acceptable for this purpose.

עין משפט
נר מצוה

כא א ב מיי' פט"ו מהל' טומאת מת הלכה ג:
כב ג ד מיי' שם הל' ג:
כג ה מיי' פט"ו מהל' שבת הל' יא סמג לאוין סה טוש"ע א"ח סי' שסג סעיף ח בהג"ה ושמעינן הא דמלח ורבב ע"ש:
כד ו ז מיי' פ"ט מהל' שכנים הל' יא סמג עשין פב טוש"ע ח"מ סי' קנה סעיף ז:
כה ח ט מיי' שם הל' יא סמג שם טוש"ע ח"מ סי' קנה סעיף יג:
כו י מיי' שם הל' יב טוש"ע שם סעיף ג:
כז כ מיי' שם טוש"ע שם סעיף ה:
כח ל מיי' שם הל' יב טוש"ע שם סעיף ה:
כט מ נ ס מיי' שם הל' יג טוש"ע שם סעיף ג:
ל ע פ צ מיי' שם הל' יב טוש"ע שם סעיף ב:
לא ק מיי' פ"ו מהל' שכנים הל' יב סמג שם טוש"ע ח"מ סי' קנו סעיף ב:

רבינו גרשום

ומשני דלית ביה שיעור. מש"ה לא חיישי: בין פצים לחבירו. כעין שסומכין את הקורות המוצעות על הקרקע כדי שלא יעקלו ושומכין תחת הקורה חתיכה של חרס לסומכן כמו שאנו רגילין לעשות באבנים. וכלי חרס נמי חזי ליה דשקיל ליה ואמאי ממעט בחלון דאבב דצריכי לכלי נקט ליה עם המלח. ומשני דמיטנף דלא חזי: חזי לאומנא. לקבל בו דם: שם תהא גניזתו ומבטל ליה ולא שקיל ליה: ורבב. שומן: מחיצה. אי לענין שבת אי בפני הטומאה: מלח נמי (א) משפר כמים. מלח סדומית שעב הוא ואינו יפה ודאי עושין בו מחיצה לענין שבת משום דקא מבטל ליה והא דאמר שמואל לא אבל מלח אסתרוקנית שדק הוא לא מבטל ליה ואין עושין בו מחיצה: עושה אדם. לגבי מבוי. וקורה מעמדת את המלח שמכבשתו ומגנת עליו מן הגשמים. הא דאיכא קורה עושין בו מחיצה דמבטל ליה: פיסקא משום טיריא. שמזעזע הכותל של ריחים שהן ריחים הקבועין סמוך לכותל וי"א טיריא המיית הריחים קשה לכותל. ואית רחיים (ב) שמחזיר חזור ג"ט מן האצטרובל קרי התחתון שבה הריחים של חמור והרכב קרי קלת: מאי טריא איכא הא לא קבוע בקרקע והא לא מזעזע את הקרקע ואמאי מרחיקין אלא משום קלא של רחיים שקשה לכותל מרחיקין הכא נמי משום קלא: לא יעמיד אדם תנור בתוך הבית. אם העלייה שעל גבי בית היא של חבירו א"כ יש על גביו ולא על גבי תנור ועד העלייה ד' אמות מפני הלהב שלא ידליק העלייה: התנור בעלייה שלו ותחת העלייה בית של חבירו לא יעמידנו עד שיהא תחתיו מעזיבה ג' טפחים כדי שלא יזיק לבית של חבירו. ואפ"ה אם הזיק

דלית בה שיעורא ^א כדתנן חרס כדי ליתן בין פצים לחבירו כלי חרס חזי ליה ^א דמיטנף חזי לאומנא ^ב דמנקב ספר תורה חזי למקרא ^ג בבלוי והא בעי גניזה ^ד שם תהא גניזתו ^ב (ואמר) רב ^ה בכל עושין מחיצה חוץ ממלח ורבב ושמואל אמר אפילו מלח אמר רב פפא ולא פליגי הא במלח סדומית הא במלח איסתרוקנית והשתא דאמר רבה עושה אדם שני צבורי מלח ומניח עליהם קורה שהמלח מעמדת את הקורה והקורה מעמדת את המלח אפי' מלח איסתרוקנית ולא פליגי הא דאיכא קורה הא דליכא קורה: מרחיקין את הריחים ג' מן השכב שהן ארבעה מן הרכב וכו': מאי טעמא ^ו משום טיריא והא תניא ושל חמור שלשה מן האיצטרוביל שהן ארבעה מן הקלת התם מאי טיריא איכא ^ז אלא משום קלא: ואת התנור שלשה מן הכליא שהן ארבעה מן השפה: אמר אביי שמע מינה כליא דתנור טפח נפקא מינה למקח וממכר: מתני' ^ח לא יעמיד אדם תנור בתוך הבית אלא אם כן יש על גביו גובה ארבע אמות היה מעמידו בעלייה צריך שיהא תחתיו מעזיבה שלשה טפחים ובכירה טפח ^ט ואם הזיק משלם מה שהזיק ר' שמעון אומר לא אמרו כל השיעורין האלו אלא שאם הזיק פטור מלשלם ^י לא יפתח אדם חנות של נחתומין ושל צבעין תחת אוצרו של חבירו ולא רפת בקר ^ו באמת ביין התירו אבל לא רפת בקר: גמ' והתניא בתנור ארבעה ובכירה שלשה אמר אביי כי תניא ההיא ^כ בדנחתומין ^י דתנור דידן כי כירה דנחתומין (א): לא יפתח חנות וכו': ^ז תנא ^ל אם היתה רפת (ב) קודמת לאוצר מותר ^מ בעי אביי כיבד וריבץ קודמת לאוצר מהו ריבה בחלונות מהו (ג) אכסדרה תחת האוצר מהו בנה עלייה על גבי ביתו מהו ^נ תיקו בעי רב הונא בריה דרב יהושע תמרי ורמוני מאי ^ס תיקו: באמת ביין התירו וכו': תנא ^ע ביין התירו מפני שמשביחו ולא רפת בקר מפני שמסריחו אמר רב יוסף ^פ האי דידן אפילו קוטרא דשרגא נמי קשיא ליה א"ר ששת ^צ ואספסתא כרפת בקר דמיא: מתני' ^ק חנות שבחצר יכול למחות בידו ולומר לו איני יכול לישן מקול הנכנסין ומקול היוצאין ^ח אבל עושה כלים יוצא ומוכר בתוך השוק ^ט ואינו יכול למחות בידו ולומר לו איני יכול לישן לא מקול הפטיש ולא מקול הריחים ולא מקול התינוקות: גמ' מ"ש רישא ומ"ש סיפא אמר אביי סיפא אתאן לחצר אחרת א"ל רבא אי הכי ליתני חצר אחרת מותר אלא אמר רבא סיפא

דלית בה שיעורא. פירוש דאין שיעור לחספא למעט מפותח טפח ולא גרסינן כדתנן דמה ענין זה לשיעורי שבת אלא וכדתנן בוי"ו וה"פ ואמאי מלח ממעט הא כי שקיל חספא כשיצטרך לו יסיר גם המלח כדי שלא יזיק את הכותל והאי מייתי וכדתנן כלומר דמיירי נמי דלית ביה כדי ליתן בין פצים לחבירו דאז ראוי לכלום ולא שקיל ליה ואית ספרים דלא גרסי חספא גופיה תיובתא אלא גרסינן ותיפוק ליה משום חספא כלומר ותיפוק ליה שיסיר המלח כשיסיר חספא ומשני דלית בה שיעורא כדתנן כו' ולא שקיל ליה:

ושל חמור שלש מן האיצטרובלא. פי' רבינו חננאל דבשל חמור ליכא טיריא דאין חמור טוחן בה אלא חמור קורא לבנין העצים הנושאים את הריחים כמו שמצינו דעצים הנושאים נקראים חמור כמו העץ שהמטה מוטלת עליו כדתנן (כלים פי"ח מ"ג) נקליטי המטה וחמור טהורים וכן העץ הסובל שידה תיבה ומגדל נקרא חמור כדתנן חמור שתחת המלבן וספסלים שתחת הרגלים טהור וכן עץ שהנפה סומך עליו נקרא חמור דתנן (שם פט"ז מ"ג) חמור של נפתים (ו) טמאים וכן הריחים הבנין עשוי כמין כסא ועליה ריחים והוא איצטרובל ואדם יושב כנגד' במקום גבוה ורגליו (ז) מרוחות למטה ומסבב הגלגל ברגליו וטוחן ולית ביה טיריא אלא קול בעלמא אבל בריחים שאדם טוחן בידיו או בגופו אית ביה נדנוד והיא טיריא ולר"י נראה דשל חמור נמי טוחן ביד אלא (ח) כשהוא על גבי בנין כדתנן במס' זבים בפרק רביעי חמור של ריחים ושל יד והא דתניא בתוספתא בפ' קמא דמכילתין מרחיקין הריחים של יד שלשה מן השכב שהן ארבע מן הרכב ושל חמור שלשה מן האיצטרובל שהן ארבע מן הקלת לא משום דבשל חמור אין טוחנין ביד אלא ההם של יד אין בהן חמור אלא ע"ג קרקע ולכך קתני בתר הכי ושל חמור כו' אבל תרוייהו טוחנין ביד:

שמע מינה כליא דתנור טפח. הא דלא קאמר נמי לעיל ש"מ שכב דריחים נמי טפח לפי שהיה פשוט להם איך היה:

תנור דידן ככירה דנחתומין דמי. כל אחד היה עושה תנור שלו כפי מה שהיה רוצה גדול או קטן אבל כירות של נחתומין היו כולן שוות והיו בקיאין בהן ונפקא מינה למקח וממכר:

מאי שנא רישא ומאי שנא סיפא. השתא ס"ד דתינוקות דסיפא היינו שבאין לקנות בחנות ומשום הכי פריך מ"ש אבל מפטיש וריחים לא פריך דאין שם נכנסין ויוצאין דמי שיש לו חטין לטחון נותן לבעל הריחים (ט) וכן פטיש:

דלית בה שיעורא. והוי כמאן דליתא: חרס. לענין הוצאת שבת: כדי ליתן בין פצים לחבירו. פלימי חלונות שבכותל מרחיקין זה מזה ברוחב החלון ליכנס האורה בין כל אחד ואחד ונותן בחומה למטה ולמעלה חרס רחב בין זה לזה וטח בטיט והחרס עב והוי שם כאבן: והא בעי גניזה. ומסלקו לגנזו: חוץ ממלח ורבב. מפני שהמלח מתפזר והרבב ניתך כשמתחמם: מלח סדומית. ° עבה וקשה כאבן: שני צבורי מלח. גבוהים עשרה אצל כותלי מבוי ומניח שני ראשי קורות המבוי עליהן שכובד הקורה מעמיד את המלח: ושל חמור. ריחים של חמור: איצטרובלא. הוא מושב הריחים שבתוך קליפת העץ שקורין ברק"א: קלת. היא אפרכסת שקורין טרוי"מוי"ר: מאי טיריא איכא. ריחים קטנים וקלים הן ואין הקרקע מרעיד בגילגולו: משום קלא. י"מ קול הנהגת החמור וי"מ קול הריחים: מתני' אלא אם כן יש על גביו. חלל גובה ארבע אמות מפי התנור עד התקרה כדי שלא יאחוז האור בתקרה: עד שיהא תחתיו מעזיבה. אשטרי"ך בלע"ז טיח קרקע ג' טפחי' שלא תבער תקרה התחתונה של עלייה ועל גביו ד' אמות: ובכירה מעזיבה טפח. אף היא כלי חרס שופתים קדירה על חללה ואין עושין בתוכה היסק גדול כמו שעושין בתנור: ואם הזיק. אחר (ד) שיהא שם כל השיעורין הללו משלם מה שהזיק ואעפ"כ מעכבין עליו השכנים להרחיק בכל השיעורים הללו שמא ידליק בתיהם ואין לו מה לשלם: ביין התירו. אם היה אוצר של יין התירו לפתוח תחתיו חנות של נחתומין ולצבעין שאין העשן קשה ליין: אבל לא רפת בקר. שהריח קשה ליין: גמ' והתניא. לענין מעמידה בעלייה בתנור ארבעה מעזיבה מתחתיו ובכירה שלשה: בדנחתומין. שמסיקין אותו תמיד וכן הכירה בכירת נחתומין: תנור דידן. דיהב ביה תנא דמתני' שיעור ג"ט ככירה דנחתומין דמי: כיבד וריבץ. גגו לצורך האוצר ולא הספיק להכניס לו תבואה עד שפתח זה חנות תחתיו מי הוי כקודם לאוצר או דילמא דכיון דכיבד וריבץ הוי כקידם האוצר: ריבה בחלונות. בעלייתו דגלי דעתיה שלאוצר הוא עשוי שיכנס לו אויר שלא ירקב התבואה: בנה עלייה על גבי ביתו. על גגו ורגילין היו לבנות שם לאוצר מהו את"ל ריבה בחלונות לאו הקדמה הוא היכי דכולי בניינא להכי עביד מאי: תמרי ורמוני. הכניס שם תמרים ורמונים מי הויא התחלת אוצר או דילמא אין אוצר אלא בתבואה ויין ושמן: והאי דידן. יין שלנו אפילו עשן העולה מן הנר קשה לו: אספסתא. שחת של תבואה: כרפת בקר דמיא. מחמת שהוא לח (ה) ומתחמם ומעלה סרחון:

מתני' ולא מקול התינוקות. קא סלקא דעתך תינוקות הבאים לקנות יין ושמן וכל דבר הנמכר בחנות: גמ' מאי שנא רישא. דקתני יכול לומר איני יכול לישן מקול הנכנסין והיוצאין וסיפא קתני אינו יכול לומר לו איני יכול לישן מקול התינוקות: סיפא

מסורת הש"ס

א) שבת פב. ביצה לב:, ב) [ל"ל אמר], ג) ב"ק פא. ב"מ קיז., ד) לעיל יח., ה) [בכלאים פ"ב מ"ג ובתרומות פ"ב מ"א ובב"מ נט: במשנה איתא באמת אמרו], ו) גי' ח"מ [לפי פי' תוס'] ותנור, ז) [לעיל יח.], ח) [בתוספתא ל"ג פי' אבל], ט) [בתוספ' אבל אינו יכול]:

הגהות הב"ח

(א) גמ' כי כירה דנחתומין דמי לה: (ב) שם רפת בקר קודמת: (ג) שם ריבה בחלונות מהו בנה כל"ל ותיבות אכסדרה תחת אוצר מהו נמחק: (ד) רש"י ד"ה ואם הזיק אחר שיהא שם: (ה) ד"ה כרפת וכו' שהוא לח מתחמם כל"ל ואות ו' נמחק: (ו) תוס' ד"ה ושל וכו' של נפתים טמא וכן: (ז) בא"ד ורגליו מתוחות למטה ומסבב: (ח) בא"ד טוחן ביד אלא שהוא על גבי ואות כ' נמחק: (ט) ד"ה מאי וכו' לבעל הריחים וטוחן וכן פטיש:

גליון הש"ס

רש"י ד"ה מלח סדומית עבה וקשה כאבן. עי' פרש"י ביצה לט ע"א ד"ה סדומית ולזה הכא ע"פ ע"ש והגיון ברש"י הוא על מלח איסתרוקנית. וכן בכוונין אפי' מלח איסתרוקנית ולא פליגי ב"ל אפי' מלח סדומית:

לעזי רש"י

ברק"א. פירוש האצטרובלא (זבים פ"ד מ"ב), מושב הריחים, עגול שסביב הריחים (רש"י ב"ב דף סח ע"א), מושב הריחים (רש"י כתובות דף סט ע"א ועיין רש"י ברכות דף יח ע"ב וד"ה ע"ב דף ב ע"א ועירובין דף סט ע"א). טרוימוי"ר. פירוש קלת, אפרכסת (רש"י חגיגה דף כ ע"ב), משפך (עיין חידושי ר"י מיגש). אשטרי"ך. פירוש מעזיבה, לפסת טיט (שטמנין על התקרה) (רש"י סוכה דף טו ע"א ועיין רש"י ד"ה מעזיבה ועיין רש"י ב"ק דף סא ע"ב וב"ב דף ג ע"ב ד"ה אגג).

ליקוטי רש"י

כדי ליתן בין פצים לחבירו. כשמדלדין פלימין ועמודים וקורות ועושין סולם של קורות על הארץ ויש חלל בין קורה לקורה סומכין אותם מתחתיו שלא יתעקמו [שבת פב.]. פצים כמו פלימי פתחים (סוכה יח.) ופלימי חלונות (לעיל יב.) הקבועים בחומה וכן של עץ ועודרין אותם למטה ולמעלה ומשני שפעמים שכן רוחות ברוחב ומושיבין קבראים

משלם מה שהזיק דפחות מן השיעור הזה ג) אין יכול לדוחקו אבל מן השיעור הזה אין יכול לדוחקו: והתניא בתנור. בענין ד' טפחים ובכירה ג' והיכי קתני מתני' היה מעמידו בעלייה צריך שיהא תחתיו מעזיבה ג' ובכירה טפח: דתנור דידן לא בעי אלא ג' טפחים ככירה של נחתומין: פיסקא בעי אביי כיבד וריבץ לאוצר. שהיה בדעתו לשום שם תבואה ולא הספיק להכניס עד שבא זה ופתח תחתיו חנות מהו: ריבה בחלונות. שעשה חלונות לאוצר: בנה עלייה על גבי ביתו. מהו: תמרי ורמוני. מהו:

חשק שלמה על רבינו גרשום א) נראה דל"ל דמחזיק כשמסתתמין הקרקע והוא ג"כ משום שכח וכן משום הפקר מים. ב) נראה דל"ל שמוחזר חזור ג' טפחים מן האצטרובל וד' מן הקלת: ג) נראה דל"ל דפחות מן השיעור הזה יכול לדוחקו ולעכב עליו.

The Gemara asks:

מַאי טַעְמָא – **What is the reason** for the law that a mill must be distanced from a neighbor's wall? מִשּׁוּם טִירְיָא – Presumably, a mill must be distanced **because of the vibrations** that it causes. וְהָא תַּנְיָא – **But it has been taught in a Baraisa:** וְשֶׁל חֲמוֹר שְׁלֹשָׁה מִן הָאִיסְטְרוּבִּיל – A DONKEY-POWERED [MILL] must be distanced at least THREE *tefachim* from a neighbor's wall, as measured FROM THE wooden FRAMEWORK THAT ENCIRCLES THE BASE OF THE MILL, שֶׁהֵן אַרְבָּעָה מִן הַקֶּלֶת – WHICH IS equivalent to FOUR *tefachim* from the wall as measured FROM THE HOPPER.[11] הָתָם מַאי טִירְיָא אִיכָּא – Now **there,** in the case of a donkey-powered mill, **what vibrations are there?** A donkey-powered mill is relatively small and light and does not cause vibrations.[12] – ? –

In the face of this objection, the Gemara gives a different explanation for the requirement to distance a mill.

אֶלָּא מִשּׁוּם קָלָא – **Rather,** a mill must be distanced **because of its noise,** which can damage a wall.[13]

The Gemara quotes the final section of the Mishnah:

וְאֶת הַתַּנּוּר שְׁלֹשָׁה מִן הַכַּלְיָא – AN OVEN must be distanced at least THREE *tefachim* from a neighbor's wall as measured FROM the lower rim of THE oven's BASE, שֶׁהֵן אַרְבָּעָה מִן הַשָּׂפָה – WHICH IS equivalent to FOUR *tefachim* from the wall as measured FROM THE upper RIM of the base.

The Gemara derives a law from the Mishnah:

אָמַר אַבַּיֵי – **Abaye said:** שְׁמַע מִינָּהּ כַּלְיָא דְּתַנּוּר טֶפַח – One can **learn from this** that the lower rim of **an oven's base** protrudes one ***tefach*** beyond its upper rim. נַפְקָא מִינָּהּ לְמִקָּח וּמִמְכָּר – The point that **emerges from this** is applicable **to** the laws of **buying and selling.** If a customer purchases an oven without specifying its dimensions, he is entitled to receive one whose base protrudes a *tefach.*

Mishnah

The Mishnah lists further restrictions against placing items in one's property where they pose a threat to the possessions of another:

לֹא יַעֲמִיד אָדָם תַּנּוּר בְּתוֹךְ הַבַּיִת – **A person may not set up an oven in a house** אֶלָּא אִם כֵּן יֵשׁ עַל גַּבָּיו גּוֹבַהּ אַרְבַּע אַמּוֹת – **unless there are four *amos*** of space **above it,** lest it set fire to the ceiling.[14] הָיָה מַעֲמִידוֹ בַּעֲלִיָּיה – If **one sets up [an oven] in an upper story,** צָרִיךְ שֶׁיְּהֵא תַּחְתָּיו מַעֲזִיבָה שְׁלֹשָׁה טְפָחִים – **there must be a layer of plaster beneath it three *tefachim*** thick, lest it set fire to the floor beams.[15] וּבְכִירָה טֶפַח – **But with regard to a stove** in an upper story, the layer of plaster beneath it need be only one ***tefach*** thick.[16] וְאִם הִזִּיק – **If,** despite the owner's observance of these precautions, **he damaged** the property of another (i.e. his oven or stove caused a fire), מְשַׁלֵּם מַה שֶּׁהִזִּיק – **he must pay for the damage.**[17] רַבִּי שִׁמְעוֹן אוֹמֵר – But **R' Shimon says:** לֹא אָמְרוּ כָּל הַשִּׁיעוּרִין הָאֵלּוּ – **[The Rabbis] did not state all these measurements** for distancing an oven or stove אֶלָּא שֶׁאִם הִזִּיק פָּטוּר מִלְּשַׁלֵּם – **except** to establish **that if it caused damage, [its owner] is exempt from paying.**[18]

The Mishnah lists other precautions that must be taken to prevent damage that can result from various items:

לֹא יִפְתַּח אָדָם חֲנוּת שֶׁל נַחְתּוֹמִין וְשֶׁל צַבָּעִין תַּחַת אוֹצָרוֹ שֶׁל חֲבֵירוֹ – **A person may not open a bakery or a dye shop under the storeroom of his fellow,** וְלֹא רֶפֶת בָּקָר – **nor** may he open **a cattle barn** under a storeroom.[19]

An exception to this ruling:

בֶּאֱמֶת בְּיַיִן הִתִּירוּ – **In truth,**[20] **in the case of** a storeroom that contains **wine, [the Rabbis] permitted** one to open a bakery or dye shop beneath it, אֲבָל לֹא רֶפֶת בָּקָר – **but not a cattle barn.**[21]

NOTES

11. [The wooden framework around the base of the mill protruded one *tefach* beyond the edge of the hopper.]

12. *Rashi;* cf. *Tosafos, Rashba* et al. [It is evident that, according to *Rashi,* the mill referred to by our Mishnah is larger and heavier than a donkey-powered mill. Perhaps, in *Rashi's* view, our Mishnah refers to a mill that is powered by the wind or water.]

13. Some authorities maintain that this refers to the noise of the mill itself, while others explain it as referring to the sound of the person urging the donkey to drive the mill (*Rashi*; see *Meiri*).

As indicated by the word אֶלָּא, *rather,* the Gemara rejects its previous position that a mill causes damage by causing the surrounding ground to shake and asserts instead that the damage is caused by its sound. According to this approach, the Gemara's statement above (18a) that a mill is harmful to a wall due to vibrations accords with the initial assumption of our Gemara, not its conclusion (*Tosafos* to 18a ד״ה דטירייא).

There is an alternative version of the Gemara's text that does not include the word אֶלָּא, *rather.* According to this version, the Gemara's answer — "because of noise" — is not a *replacement* of the previous explanation that the damage is caused by vibrations. It is an *explanation* as to how a donkey-powered mill causes vibrations; to wit, it causes vibrations through noise (*Rashba*; see *Tosafos* to 18a; it appears that *Rashi* followed this version of the text).

14. And the fire will spread to the neighboring houses (from *Rashi*; see *Rashi* to *Bava Kamma* 61b).

Other commentators explain the Mishnah as referring to a two-story house. The lower story, in which the oven is placed, is owned by one person and the upper story by another (*Rabbeinu Gershom, Rambam Hil. Shecheinim* 9:11, *Tosafos* to *Bava Kamma* 61b).

15. In addition, a gap of four *amos* is required above the oven [so that the ceiling will not catch fire] (*Rashi*).

16. The walls of a תַּנּוּר, *oven,* slope inwards. Therefore, its heat is more intense than that of a כִּירָה, *stove* (*Rashi* to *Shabbos* 38b ד״ה תנור). Accordingly, a thicker protective barrier is required beneath an oven than beneath a stove.

[The Mishnah does not state how much space must be left between a *stove* and the ceiling — see *Rashba* and *Tur Choshen Mishpat* 155.]

17. Although the owner is liable to compensate for any damage even if he took the proper precautions, his neighbors can insist that he take them, lest damage is done and the owner is unable to pay (*Rashi*).

[The Rishonim discuss whether this stringency applies in the cases listed by the previous Mishnah as well, or only in the case of an oven or stove, which cause damage in a more blatant manner (see *Meiri, Tur* 155:50 in the name of *Rosh*).]

18. Since the Sages formulated these precautions as law, one who observes them has done all that he can be expected to do. Consequently, if damage results despite his adherence to these codes, he is exempt (see *Rashba*).

19. The storeroom referred to here is an upper chamber in which grain, wine or oil is stored. The smoke produced by the constantly burning ovens of a bakery or dye shop (for boiling the dyes) is injurious to such items. Likewise, the odor emanating from a cattle barn is harmful to them (*Rashi* to 18a; cf. *Tosafos* ibid. ד״ה לא).

20. This term denotes that the halachah is in accordance with the following statement beyond any doubt (Gemara *Bava Metzia* 60a).

21. Smoke is not harmful to wine, but cattle odor is (*Rashi*).

דלית בה שיעורא כדתנן חרס כדי ליתן בין פצים לחבירו כלי חרס חזי ליה דמיטנף חזי לאומנא דמנקב ספר תורה חזי למקרא בבלוי והא בעי גניזה שם תהא גניזתה (ואמר) רב בכל עושין מחיצה חוץ ממלח ורבב ושמואל אמר אפילו מלח אמר רב פפא ולא פליגי הא במלח סדומית הא במלח איסתרוקנית והשתא דאמר רבה עושה אדם שני צבורי מלח ומניח עליהם קורה שהמלח מעמדת את הקורה והקורה מעמדת את המלח אפי' מלח איסתרוקנית ולא פליגי הא דאיכא קורה הא דליכא קורה: מרחיקין את הריחים ג' מן השכב שהן ארבעה מן הרכב וכו': מאי טעמא משום טיריא והא תניא ושל חמור שלשה מן האיסטרוביל שהן ארבעה מן הקלת התם מאי טיריא איכא אלא משום קלא: ואת התנור שלשה מן הכליא שהן ארבעה מן השפה: אמר אביי שמע מינה כליא דתנור טפח נפקא מינה למקח וממכר: **מתני'** לא יעמיד אדם תנור בתוך הבית אלא אם כן יש על גביו גובה ארבע אמות היה מעמידו בעלייה צריך שיהא תחתיו מעזיבה שלשה טפחים ובכירה טפח ואם הזיק משלם מה שהזיק ר' שמעון אומר לא אמרו כל השיעורין האלו אלא שאם הזיק פטור מלשלם לא יפתח אדם חנות של נחתומין ושל צבעין תחת אוצרו של חבירו ולא רפת בקר באמת ביין התירו אבל לא רפת בקר: **גמ'** והתניא בתנור ארבעה ובכירה שלשה אמר אביי כי תניא ההיא בדנחתומין דתנור דידן כי כירה דנחתומין (א): לא יפתח חנות וכו': תנא אם היתה רפת (ב) קודמת לאוצר מותר בעי אביי כיבד וריבץ לאוצר מהו ריבה בחלונות מהו (ג) אכסדרה תחת האוצר מהו בנה עלייה על גבי ביתו מהו תיקו בעי רב הונא בריה דרב יהושע תמרי ורמוני מאי תיקו: באמת ביין התירו וכו': תנא ביין התירו מפני שמשביחו ולא רפת בקר מפני שמסריחו אמר רב יוסף האי דידן אפילו קוטרא דשרגא נמי קשיא ליה א"ר ששת ואספסתא כרפת בקר דמיא: **מתני'** חנות שבחצר יכול למחות בידו ולומר לו איני יכול לישן מקול הנכנסין ומקול היוצאין אבל עושה כלים יוצא ומוכר בתוך השוק ואינו יכול למחות בידו ולומר לו איני יכול לישן לא מקול הפטיש ולא מקול הריחים ולא מקול התינוקות: **גמ'** מ"ש רישא ומ"ש סיפא אמר אביי סיפא אתאן לחצר אחרת א"ל רבא אי הכי ליתני חצר אחרת מותר אלא אמר רבא סיפא

רש"י

דלית בה שיעורא. והוי כמאן דליתא: **חרס.** לענין הוצאת שבת: **כדי ליתן בין פצים לחבירו.** פצימי חלונות שבכותל מרחיקין זה מזה ברוחב החלון ליכנס האורה בין כל אחד ואחד ונותן בחומה למטה ולמעלה חרס רחב בין זה לזה וטח בטיט והחרס עב והוי שם כאבן: **והא בעי גניזה.** ומסלקו לגמרי: **חוץ ממלח ורבב.** מפני שהמלח מתפזר והרבב ניתך כשמתחמם: **מלח סדומית.** עבה וקשה כאבן: **שני צבורי מלח.** גבוהים עשרה אלא כותלי מבוי ומניח שני ראשי קורות המבוי עליהן שכובד הקורה מעמיד את המלח: **ושל חמור.** ריחים של חמור: **איצטרובלא.** הוא מושב הריחים שבתוך קליפת העץ שקורין ברק"א: **קלת.** היא אפרכסת שקורין טרויימוי"ר: **מאי טיריא איכא.** ריחים קטנים וקלים הן ואין הקרקע מרעיד בגלגולו: **משום קלא.** י"מ קול הנהגת החמור וי"מ קול הריחים: **מתני' אלא אם כן יש על גביו.** חלל גובה ארבע אמות מפי התנור עד התקרה כדי שלא יאחוז האור בתקרה: **עד שיהא תחתיו מעזיבה.** אשטרי"ך בלע"ז טיח קרקע ג' טפחי' שלא תבער תקרה התחתונה של עלייה ועל גביו ד' אמות: **ובכירה** מעזיבה **טפח.** אף היא כלי חרס ששופתים קדירה על חללה ואין עושין בתוכה היסק גדול כמו שעושין בתנור: **ואם הזיק.** אחר (ד) שיהא שם כל השיעורין הללו משלם מה שהזיק ואעפ"כ מעכבין עליו השכנים להרחיק בכל השיעורים הללו שמא ידליק בתיהם ואין לו מה לשלם: **ביין התירו.** אם היה אוצר של יין התירו לפתוח תחתיו חנות של נחתומין ולצבעין שאין העשן קשה ליין: **אבל לא רפת בקר.** שהריח קשה ליין: **גמ' והתניא.** לענין מעמידה בעלייה בתנור ארבעה מעזיבה מתחתיו ובכירה שלשה: **בדנחתומין.** שמסיקין אותו תמיד וכן הכירה בכירת נחתומין: **תנור דידן.** דיהב ביה תנא דמתני' שיעור ג"ט ככירה דנחתומין דמי: **כיבד וריבץ.** גגו לצורך האוצר ולא הספיק להכניס לו תבואה עד שפתח זה חנות תחתיו מי הוי כקודם לאוצר או דילמא דכיון דכיבד וריבץ הוי כקודם האוצר: **ריבה בחלונות.** בעלייתו דגלי דעתיה שלאוצר הוא עשוי שיכנס לו אויר שלא ירקב התבואה: **בנה עלייה על גבי ביתו.** על גגו ורגילין היו לבנות שם לאוצר מהו את"ל ריבה בחלונות לאו הקדמה הוא היכי דכולי בניינא להכי עביד מאי: **תמרי ורמוני.** הכניס שם תמרים ורמונים מי הויא התחלת אוצר או דילמא אין אוצר אלא בתבואה ויין ושמן: **והאי דידן.** יין שלנו אפילו עשן העולה מן הנר קשה לו: **אספסתא.** שחת של תבואה: **כרפת בקר דמיא.** מחממת שהוא לח (ה) ומתחמם ומעלה סרחון: **מתני' ולא מקול התינוקות.** קא סלקא דעתך תינוקות הבאים לקנות יין ושמן וכל דבר הנמכר בחנות: **גמ' מאי שנא רישא.** דקתני יכול לומר איני יכול לישן מקול הנכנסין והיוצאין וסיפא קתני אינו יכול לומר לו איני יכול לישן מקול התינוקות: **סיפא**

תוספות

דלית בה שיעורא. פירוש דאין שיעור לחספא למעט מפותח טפח ולא גרסינן כדתנן דמה ענין זה לשיעורי שבת אלא וכדתנן גרסי' וה"פ ואמאי מלח ממעט הא כי שקיל חספא כשיצטרך לו יסיר גם המלח כדי שלא יזיק את הכותל והא מייתי וכדתנן כלומר דמיירי נמי דלית ביה כדי ליתן בין פצים לחבירו דאין ראוי לכלום ולא שקיל ליה ואית ספרים דלא גרסי חספא גופיה תיהוי אלא גרסינן ותיפוק ליה משום חספא כלומר ותיפוק ליה שיסיר המלח כשיסיר חספא ומשני דלית ביה שיעורא כדתנן כו' ולא שקיל ליה:

ושל חמור שלש מן האיצטרובלא. פי' רבינו חננאל דבשל חמור ליכא טיריא דאין חמור טוחן בה אלא חמור קורא לבנין העצים הנושאים את הריחים כמו שמצינו דעצים הנושאים נקראים חמור כמו העץ שהמטה מוטלת עליו כדתנן (כלים פי"ח מ"ג) נקליטי המטה וחמור טהורים וכן העץ הסובל שידה תיבה ומגדל נקרא חמור דתנן חמור שתחת המלבן וספסלים שתחת הרגלים טהור וכן עץ שהנפח סומך עליו נקרא חמור דתנן (שם פי"ד מ"ג) חמור של נפחים (ו) טמאים וכן הריחים הבנין עשוי כמין כסא ועליה ריחים וזהו איצטרובל ואדם יושב כנגד' במקום גבוה ורגליו (ז) מרווחת למטה ומסבב הגלגל ברגליו וטוחן ולית ביה טיריא אלא קול בעלמא אבל בריחים שאדם טוחן בידיו או בגופו אית ביה נדנוד והיא טיריא ולר"י נראה דשל חמור נמי טוחן ביד אלא (ח) כשהוא על גבי בנין כדתנן במס' זבים בפרק רביעי חמור של ריחים ושל יד והא דתניא בתוספת' בפ' קמא דמכילתין מרחיקין הריחים של יד שלשה מן השכב שהן ארבע מן הרכב ושל חמור שלשה מן האיצטרובל שהן ארבע מן הקלת לא משום דבשל חמור אין טוחנין ביד אלא סתם של יד אין בהן חמור אלא ע"ג קרקע ולכך קתני בתר הכי ושל חמור אבל תרוייהו טוחנין ביד:

שמע מינה כליא דתנור טפח. הא דלא קאמר נמי לעיל ש"מ שכב דריחים נמי טפח לפי שהיה פשוט להם איך היה:

תנור דידן כבירה דנחתומין דמי. כל אחד היה עושה תנור שלו כפי מה שהיה רוצה גדול או קטן אבל כירות של נחתומין היו כולן שוות והיו בקיאין בהן ונפקא מינה למקח וממכר:

מאי שנא רישא ומאי שנא סיפא. השתא ס"ד דתינוקות דסיפא היינו שבאין לקנות בחנות ומשום הכי פריך מ"ש אבל מפטיש וריחים לא פריך דאין שם נכנסין ויוצאין דמי שיש לו חטין לטחון נותן לבעל הריחים (ט) וכן פטיש:

עין משפט נר מצוה

כא א ב מיי' פט"ו מהל' טומאת מת הלכה ז:
כב ג ד מיי' שם הל' ג:
כג ה מיי' פט"ז מהל' שבת הל' כא סמג לאוין סה טוש"ע א"ח סי' שסב סעיף ה בהגה"ה הא דמלח ורבב ע"ש:
כד ו ז מיי' פ"ט מהל' שכנים הל' ג סמג עשין פב טוש"ע ח"מ סי' קנה סעיף ז:
כה ח ט מיי' שם הל' יא סמג שם טוש"ע ח"מ סי' קנה סעיף א:
כו י מיי' שם הל' יב טוש"ע שם סעיף ב:
כז כ מיי' שם הל' יא טוש"ע שם סעיף א:
כח ל מיי' שם הל' יב טוש"ע שם סעיף ב:
כט מ נ ס מיי' שם הל' יג וטוש"ע שם סעיף ג:
ל ע פ צ מיי' שם הל' יב וטוש"ע שם סעיף ב:
לא ק מיי' שם פ"ו הל' יב סמג שם טוש"ע ח"מ סי' קנו סעיף ב:

רבינו גרשום

ומשני דלית ביה שיעור. מש"ה לא חייץ: **בין פצים לחבירו.** כעין שסומכין את הקורות המוצעות על הקרקע כדי שלא יעקלו ומשימין תחת הקורה חתיכה של חרס לסומכן כמו שאנו רגילין לעשות באבנים: **וכלי חרס** נמי **חזי ליה** ושקל ליה ואמאי ממעט בחלון דאגב דצריכי לכלי נקט ליה עם המלח. ומשני **דמיטנף** דלא חזי: **חזי לאומנא.** לקבל בו דם: **שם תהא גניזתו** ומבטל ליה ולא שקל ליה: **רבב.** שומן: **מחיצה.** אי לענין שבת אי בפני הטומאה: **מלח** נמי א) מפשר כמים. **מלח סדומית** שעב הוא ואינו יפה ודאי עושין בו מחיצה לענין שבת משום דקא מבטל ליה ולא חזי אבל **מלח אסתרוקנית** שדק הוא לא מבטל ליה ואין עושין בו מחיצה: **עושה אדם.** לגבי מבוי. **וקורה מעמדת את המלח** שמכבשתו ומגנת עליו מן הגשמים. **הא דאיכא קורה** עושין בו מחיצה מפני שהקורה מעמידתו: **פיסקא משום טיריא.** שמזעזע הכותל מחמת בנין הרחיים הקבועין סמוך לכותל וי"א טיריא המיית הרחיים קשה לכותל. והני רחיים ב) שמחזיר מחזיר ג"ט מן האצטרוביל קרי התחתון שכב הרחיים של חמור ורכב קרי קלת: **מאי טריא איכא** הא לא קביע בנינו בקרקע ולא מזעזע הקרקע ואמאי מרחיקין **אלא משום קלא** של רחיים שקשה לכותל מרחיקין הכא נמי משום קלא: **לא יעמיד אדם תנור בתוך הבית.** אם העליה שעל גבי בית היא של חבירו **אא"כ יש על גביו** של תנור ועד העליה **ד' אמות** מפני הלהב שלא ידליק העליה: **היה מעמיד.** התנור **בעליה** שלו ותחת העליה בית של חבירו לא יעמידנו עד **שיהא תחתיו מעזיבה ג'** טפחים כדי שלא יזיק לבית של חבירו. ואפ"ה אם הזיק משלם מה שהזיק דפחות מן השיעור הזה אין יכול לדחוק: **והתניא בתנור.** בענין ד' טפחים ובכירה ג': **והיכי קתני מתני'** היה עושה בעליה צריך שיהא תחתיו מעזיבה ג' וכירה טפח: **תנא היא** ... **דתנור דידן** ... **פיסקא בעי אביי כיבד וריבץ לאוצר** ... **ריבה חלונות** ... **אם לא יפתח אדם רפת בקר** ... **באמת ביין התירו** ... **תמרי ורמוני** ... **אמר ליה** ... **האי יין דידן אפי' קוטרא** [דשרגא] ...

מסורת הש"ס

א) שבת פב. בילה לט., ב) [ל"ל אמר], ג) ב"ק סא: ב"מ קיח., ד) לעיל יח., ה) [בכלאים פ"ב מ"ב ובתרומות פ"ב מ"א ובב"מ נט: במשנה איתא באמת אמרו], ו) גי' ת"ח [לפי פי' תוס'] ותנור, ז) [לעיל יח.], ח) [בסהמ"ש ל"ג תי' אבל], ט) [בסהמ"ש אבל אינו יכול]:

הגהות הב"ח

(א) גמ' כי כירה דנחתומין דמי לא: (ב) שם רפת בקר קודמת: (ג) שם ריבה בחלונות מהו בנה כצ"ל ותיבות אכסדרה תחת אוצר מהו נמחק: (ד) רש"י ד"ה ואם הזיק אחר שהיו שם: (ה) ד"ה כרפת וכו' שהוא לח מתחמם כצ"ל ואות ו' נמחק: (ו) תוס' ד"ה ושל וכו' של נפחים טמא וכן: (ז) בא"ד ורגליו מתוחות למטה ומסבב: (ח) בא"ד טוחן ביד אלא שהוא כצ"ל ואות כ' נמחק: (ט) ד"ה מאי וכו' לבעל הריחים וטוחן וכן פטיש:

גליון הש"ס

רש"י ד"ה מלח סדומית עבה וקשה כאבן. עי' פרש"י בילה לט ע"א ד"ה סדומית ולזה הכא ע"כ ט"ס והגליון ברש"י הוא על מלח איסתרוקנית. וכן בסוגיין אפי' מלח איסתרוקנית ולא פליגי צ"ל אפי' מלח סדומית:

לעזי רש"י

צרק"א. פירוש האלטרובלא (זבים פ"ד מ"ג), מושב הריחים, עגול שסביב ...

טרויימוי"ר. פירוש קלת, אפרכסת ...

אשטרי"ך. פירוש מעזיבה, רצפה ...

ליקוטי רש"י

כדי ליתן בין פצים לחבירו. כשמסדרין פצימין ועמודים וקורות ועושין סותר של קורות על הארץ ויש חלל בין זה לזה סומכין אותו בחרס ...

א) [נראה דצ"ל תוך מרכב ומלח רכב משום שניכר כשמתחממים וכו'] ... ב) [אולי צ"ל וכי מרחיקין ג"ט ...] ג) [ונראה דצ"ל דפחות ...]

Gemara The Gemara notes a contradiction between our Mishnah and a Baraisa:

וְהָתַנְיָא – **But it has been taught in a Baraisa:** בְּתַנּוּר אַרְבָּעָה – REGARDING AN OVEN placed in an upper story, a layer of plaster FOUR *tefachim* thick is required beneath it; וּבְכִירָה שְׁלֹשָׁה – AND REGARDING A STOVE, a layer of THREE *tefachim* is required. This contradicts our Mishnah, which requires a layer of only three *tefachim* beneath an oven, and one *tefach* beneath a stove. – ? –

The Gemara resolves the contradiction:

אָמַר אַבַּיֵי – **Abaye said:** כִּי תַּנְיָא הַהִיא בְּדְנַחְתּוֹמִין – **That Baraisa was taught in reference to [the ovens and stoves] of bakers,** which are constantly lit, and thus require greater preventive measures. דְּתַנּוּר דִּידָן כִּי כִּירָה דְנַחְתּוֹמִין – **As our** type of **oven** (the type referred to by our Mishnah) **is equivalent to the stove of a baker;** both require a three-*tefach* layer beneath them.

The Mishnah stated:

לֹא יִפְתַּח חָנוּת וכו׳ – ONE MAY NOT OPEN A [BAKERY] **etc.** [or a cattle barn under someone else's storeroom].

The Gemara cites a related Baraisa:

תָּנָא – **A Tanna taught** the following Baraisa: אִם הָיְתָה רֶפֶת קוֹדֶמֶת לָאוֹצָר מוּתָּר – IF the establishment of THE CATTLE BARN[22] PRECEDED that of THE STOREROOM, IT IS PERMITTED to maintain the cattle barn.

In the light of the Baraisa's ruling, the Gemara seeks to define what constitutes the establishment of a storeroom:

בָּעֵי אַבַּיֵי – **Abaye asked** the following series of questions: כִּיבֵּד וְרִיבֵּץ לָאוֹצָר מַהוּ – If **he** [the owner of the upper story] **swept** his roof **and sprinkled** water to settle the dust in preparation **for** its use as **a storage place,** but before he stored anything there, a cattle barn was established below, **what is [the law]?** Is this considered the establishment of a storage place and therefore the cattle barn is illegal? Or is this not considered the establishment of a storage place, and therefore the cattle barn is permitted because it came first?

רִיבָּה בְּחַלּוֹנוֹת מַהוּ – Similarly, if **he increased the** number of **windows** in the upper story (which shows that he intends to use it as a storeroom),[23] but before he stored anything in it, a cattle barn was established below, **what is [the law]?** Is the cattle barn or the storeroom considered to have come first?

אַכְסַדְרָה תַּחַת הָאוֹצָר מַהוּ – If there is **a pavilion beneath the storeroom, what is [the law]?**[24]

בָּנָה עֲלִיָּיה עַל גַּבֵּי בֵּיתוֹ מַהוּ – Similarly, if **he built an upper room on top of his house**[25] (as people do for the purposes of storage), but before he stored anything in it, a cattle barn was established below, **what is [the law]?** Is the cattle barn or the storeroom considered to have come first?[26]

The Gemara concludes:

תֵּיקוּ – **Let [these questions] stand** unresolved.

Rav Huna raises a similar question:

בָּעֵי רַב הוּנָא בְּרֵיהּ דְּרַב יְהוֹשֻׁעַ – **Rav Huna son of Rav Yehoshua asked:** תְּמָרֵי וְרִמּוֹנֵי מַאי – If he began by storing only **dates and pomegranates** in the upper story, **what** is the law? The prohibition against opening a cattle barn under a storeroom was legislated specifically with regard to a storeroom of wine, grain or oil.[27] However, if the owner began by storing dates or pomegranates, perhaps it is forbidden to open a cattle barn below, because, having shown that he is using the room for storage, the owner might yet store wine, grain or oil in it.

The Gemara concludes:

תֵּיקוּ – **Let [the question] stand** unresolved.

The Gemara quotes the final section of the Mishnah:

בֶּאֱמֶת בְּיַיִן הִתִּירוּ וכו׳ – IN TRUTH, IN THE CASE OF a storeroom that contains WINE, ONE IS PERMITTED **etc.** [to open a bakery or dye shop beneath it].

The Gemara quotes an explanatory Baraisa:

תָּנָא – **A Tanna taught in a Baraisa:** בְּיַיִן הִתִּירוּ מִפְּנֵי שֶׁמַּשְׁבִּיחוֹ – IN THE CASE OF a storeroom of WINE, THE SAGES PERMITTED to open a bakery or dye shop beneath it, FOR [THE SMOKE] from the bakery or dye shop IMPROVES [THE WINE]. וְלֹא רֶפֶת בָּקָר מִפְּנֵי שֶׁמַּסְרִיחוֹ – BUT they did NOT permit one to open A CATTLE BARN beneath a storeroom of wine FOR IT IMPARTS A FOUL ODOR TO [THE WINE].

The Gemara qualifies the Mishnah's permit to open a bakery or dye shop beneath a storeroom of wine.

אָמַר רַב יוֹסֵף – **Rav Yosef said:** הַאי דִּידָן – As far as **our [wine]** is concerned, אֲפִילּוּ קוּטְרָא דִשְׁרָגָא נַמִּי קָשְׁיָא לֵיהּ – **even the smoke of a candle is harmful to it.** Therefore, this permit does not apply nowadays.

A ruling related to that of the Mishnah:

אָמַר רַב שֵׁשֶׁת – **Rav Sheishess said:** וְאַסְפַּסְתָּא כְּרֶפֶת בָּקָר דָּמְיָא – **And** *aspasta*[28] **is** as injurious **as a cattle barn.** The Mishnah's restriction against the placement of a cattle barn applies to the storage of *aspasta* as well.

NOTES

22. The same applies to a bakery and dye shop as well (*Tosafos* to 18a ד״ה ואם).

23. The extra windows increase the air circulation, which prevents the grain from rotting (*Rashi*).

24. *Bach* deletes this sentence. It does not appear in the versions of the text followed by most commentators, including *Rashi.* It does appear, however, in the text followed by *Ramah,* who explains it as follows:

If a pavilion interposes between the storeroom and the bottom story, is it permitted to use the bottom story as a cattle barn or not? Do we say that since air circulates all around the storeroom its contents are not liable to be damaged by the cattle barn, or perhaps we say that its contents are liable to be damaged nevertheless? [According to this explanation, the present inquiry is not relevant to the question of what constitutes the establishment of a storeroom. Assuming that the contents of a storehouse with a pavilion beneath it are not liable to be damaged, it is permitted to open a cattle barn in the bottom story even after the storeroom has definitely been established.]

25. [The owner of the upper story] built a room on top of his roof to serve as a storage place (*Rashi,* see *Rashba*). [It is evident that according to *Rashi* a bakery etc. is harmful to a storehouse even if a story interposes between them (*Rashba, Ritva*).]

26. Even if the addition of windows does not constitute the establishment of a storeroom, perhaps the building of an upper extension does (*Rashi*; cf. *Rabbeinu Gershom*).

27. Only a room in which wine, grain or oil is stored is legally recognized as a "storeroom" (*Nimukei Yosef;* see *Rashi*).

Alternatively: Only wine, grain and oil are harmed by a cattle barn, as opposed to other produce, such as dates and pomegranates, which are not (*Rabbeinu Gershom, Rashba* et al.).

28. אַסְפַּסְתָּא, *aspasta*, is a particular type of plant. Even in the early stages of its growth, it is fit for use as fodder (see *Rashi* here, *Rashi* to 28b ד״ה אספסתא and *Rashi* to *Kiddushin* 62b ד״ה אלא בשחת). [Cut *aspasta* is moist and warm, and it exudes a foul odor that can damage the contents of a storeroom above it.]

דלית בה שיעורא כדתנן חרס כדי ליתן בין פצים לחבירו כלי חרס חזי ליה דמיטנף חזי לאומנא דמנקב ספר תורה חזי למקרא בבלוי והא בעי גניזה שם תהא גניזתה (ואמר) רב בכל עושין מחיצה חוץ ממלח ורבב ושמואל אמר אפילו מלח אמר רב פפא ולא פליגי הא במלח סדומית הא במלח איסתרוקנית והשתא דאמר רבה עושה אדם שני צבורי מלח ומניח עליהם קורה שהמלח מעמדת את הקורה והקורה מעמדת את המלח אפי' מלח איסתרוקנית ולא פליגי הא דאיכא קורה הא דליכא קורה: מרחיקין את הריחים ג' מן השכב שהן ארבעה מן הרכב וכו': מאי טעמא משום טיריא והא תניא ושל חמור שלשה מן האיצטרוביל שהן ארבעה מן הקלת התם מאי טיריא איכא אלא משום קלא: ואת התנור שלשה מן הכליא שהן ארבעה מן השפה: אמר אביי שמע מינה כליא דתנור טפח נפקא מינה למקח וממכר: מתני' לא יעמיד אדם תנור בתוך הבית אלא אם כן יש על גביו גובה ארבע אמות היה מעמידו בעלייה צריך שיהא תחתיו מעזיבה שלשה טפחים ובכירה טפח ואם הזיק משלם מה שהזיק ר' שמעון אומר לא אמרו כל השיעורין האלו אלא שאם הזיק פטור מלשלם לא יפתח אדם חנות של נחתומין ושל צבעין תחת אוצרו של חבירו ולא רפת בקר באמת ביין התירו אבל לא רפת בקר: גמ' והתניא בתנור ארבעה ובכירה שלשה אמר אביי כי תניא ההיא בדנחתומין דתנור דידן כי כירה דנחתומין (א): לא יפתח חנות וכו': תנא אם היתה רפת (ב) קודמת לאוצר מותר בעי אביי כיבד וריבץ לאוצר מהו ריבה בחלונות מהו (ג) אכסדרה תחת האוצר מהו בנה עליה על גבי ביתו מהו תיקו בעי רב הונא בריה דרב יהושע תמרי ורמוני מאי תיקו: באמת ביין התירו וכו': תנא ביין התירו מפני שמשביחו ולא רפת בקר מפני שמסריחו אמר רב יוסף האי דידן אפילו קוטרא דשרגא נמי קשיא ליה א"ר ששת ואספסתא כרפת בקר דמיא: מתני' חנות שבחצר יכול למחות בידו ולומר לו איני יכול לישן מקול הנכנסין ומקול היוצאין אבל עושה כלים יוצא ומוכר בתוך השוק ואינו יכול למחות בידו ולומר לו איני יכול לישן לא מקול הפטיש ולא מקול הריחים ולא מקול התינוקות: גמ' מ"ש רישא ומ"ש סיפא אמר אביי סיפא אתאן לחצר אחרת א"ל רבא אי הכי ליתני חצר אחרת מותר אלא אמר רבא סיפא

תוספות

דלית בה שיעורא. פירוש דאין שיעור לחספא למעט מפותח טפח ולא גרסינן כדתנן דמה ענין זה לשיעורי שבת אלא וכדתנן בו"ו וה"פ ואמאי מלח ממעט הא כי שקיל חספא כשילטרך לו יסיר גס המלח כדי שלא יזיק את הכותל והאי מייתי וכדתנן כלומר דמיירי נמי דלית ביה כדי ליתן בין פצים לחבירו דאין ראוי לכלום ולא שקיל ליה ואית ספרים דלא גרסי חספא גופיה תיתוך אלא גרסינן ותיפוק ליה משום חספא כלומר ותיפוק ליה שיסיר המלח כשיסיר חספא ומשני דלית בה שיעורא כדתנן כו' ולא שקיל ליה:

ושל חמור שלש מן האיצטרובלא. פי' רבינו חננאל דבשל חמור ליכא טיריא דאין חמור טוחן בה אלא חמור קורא לבנין העצים הנושאים את הריחים כמו שמצינו דעצים הנושאים נקראים חמור כמו העץ שהמטה מוטלת עליו כדתנן (כלים פי"ח מ"ג) נקליטי המטה וחמור טהורים וכן העץ הסובל שידה תיבה ומגדל נקרא חמור דתנן חמור שתחת המלבן ופספלים שתחת הרגלים טהור וכן עץ שהנפה סומך עליו נקרא חמור דתנן (שם פט"ז מ"ג) חמור של נפחים (ו) טמאים וכן הריחים הבנין עשוי כמין כסא ועליה ריחים וזהו איצטרובל ואדם יושב כנגד' במקום גבוה ורגליו (ז) מרווחת למטה ומסבב הגלגל ברגליו וטוחן וליכא ביה טיריא אלא קול בעלמא אבל בריחים שאדם טוחן בידיו או בגופו איכא ביה נדנוד והוא טיריא ולר"י נראה דשל חמור נמי טוחן ביד אלא (ח) כשהוא על גבי בנין כדתנן במס' זבים בפרק רביעי חמור של ריחים ושל יד והא דתניא בתוספתא בפ' קמא דמכילתין מרחיקין הריחים של יד שלשה מן השכב שהן ארבע מן הרכב ושל חמור שלשה מן האיצטרובל שהן ארבעה מן הקלת לא משום דבשל חמור אין טוחנין ביד אלא פסק של יד אין בהן חמור אלא ע"ג קרקע ולכך קתני בתר הכי ושל חמור אבל תרוייהו טוחנין ביד:

שמע מינה כליא דתנור טפח. הא לא קאמר נמי לעיל ש"מ שכב דריחים נמי טפח לפי שהיה פשוט להם איך היה:

תנור דידן ככירה דנחתומין דמי. כל אחד היה עושה תנור שלו כפי מה שהיה רוצה גדול או קטן אבל כירות של נחתומין היו כולן שוות והיו בקיאין בהן ונפקא מינה למקח וממכר:

מאי שנא רישא ומאי שנא סיפא. השתא ס"ד דתינוקות דסיפא היינו שבאין לקנות בחנות ומשום הכי פריך מ"ש אבל מפטיש וריחים לא פריך דאין שם נכנסין ויוצאין דמי שיש לו חטין לטחון נותן לבעל הריחים (ט) וכן פטיש:

רש"י

דלית בה שיעורא. והוי כמאן דליתא: **חרס.** לענין הוצאת שבת: **כדי ליתן בין פצים לחבירו.** פלימי חלונות שבכותל מרחיקין זה מזה ברוחב החלון ליכנס האורה בין כל אחד ואחד ונותן בחומה למטה ולמעלה חרס רחב בין זה לזה וטח בטיט והחרס עב והוי שם כאבן: **והא בעי גניזה.** ומסלקו לגנזו: **חוץ ממלח ורבב.** מפני שהמלח מתפזר והרבב ניתך כשמתחמם: **מלח סדומית.** ° עבה וקשה כאבן: **שני צבורי מלח.** גבוהים עשרה אצל כותלי מבוי ומניח שני ראשי קורות המבוי עליהן שכובד הקורה מעמיד את המלח: **ושל חמור.** ריחים של חמור: **איצטרובלא.** הוא מושב הריחים שבתוך קליפת העץ שקורין ברק"א: **קלת.** היא אפרכסת שקורין טרווימויי"ר: **מאי טיריא איכא.** ריחים קטנים וקלים הן ואין הקרקע מרעיד בגילגולו: **משום קלא.** י"מ קול הנהגת החמור וי"מ קול הריחים: **מתני' אלא אם כן יש על גביו.** חלל גובה ארבע אמות מפי התנור עד התקרה כדי שלא יאחוז האור בתקרה: **עד שיהא תחתיו מעזיבה.** אשטרי"ך בלע"ז טיח קרקע ג' טפחי' שלא תבער תקרה תחתונה של עלייה ועל גביו ד' אמות: **ובכירה מעזיבה טפח.** אף היא כלי חרס שפותים קדירה על חללה ואין עושין בתוכה היסק גדול כמו שעושין בתנור: **ואם הזיק.** אחר (ד) שיהא שם כל השיעורין הללו משלם מה שהזיק ואעפ"כ מעכבין עליו השכנים להרחיק בכל השיעורים הללו שמא ידליק בתיהם ואין לו מה לשלם: **ביין התירו.** אם היה אוצר של יין התירו לפתוח תחתיו חנות של נחתומין ולצבעין שאין העשן קשה ליין: **אבל לא רפת בקר.** שהריח קשה ליין: **גמ' והתניא.** לענין מעמידה בעלייה בתנור ארבעה מעזיבה מתחתיו ובכירה שלשה: **בדנחתומין.** שמסיקין אותו תמיד וכן הכירה בכירת נחתומין: **תנור דידן.** דיהב ביה תנא דמתני' שיעור ג"ט ככירה דנחתומין דמי: **כיבד וריבץ.** גגו לצורך האוצר ולא הספיק להכניס לו תבואה עד שפתח זה חנות תחתיו מי הוי כקודם לאוצר או דילמא דכיון דכיבד וריבץ הוי כקידם האוצר: **ריבה בחלונות.** בעלייתו דגלי דעתיה שלאוצר הוא עשוי שיכנס לו אויר שלא ירקב התבואה: **בנה עלייה על גבי ביתו.** על גגו ורגילין היו לבנות שם לאוצר מהו את"ל ריבה בחלונות לאו הקדמה הוא היכי דכולי בניינא להכי עביד מאי: **תמרי ורמוני.** הכניס שם תמרים ורמונים מי הויא התחלת אוצר או דילמא אין אוצר אלא בתבואה ויין ושמן: **והאי דידן.** יין שלנו אפילו עשן העולה מן הנר קשה לו: **אספסתא.** שחת של תבואה: **כרפת בקר דמיא.** מחמת שהוא לח (ה) ומתחמם ומעלה סרחון:

מתני' ולא מקול התינוקות. קא סלקא דעתך תינוקות הבאים לקנות יין ושמן וכל דבר הנמכר בחנות: **גמ' מאי שנא רישא.** דקתני יכול לומר איני יכול לישן מקול הנכנסין והיוצאין וסיפא קתני אינו יכול לומר לו איני יכול לישן מקול התינוקות: סיפא

Mishnah In Mishnaic times, houses were grouped around courtyards. The following Mishnah discusses the rights of a courtyard resident to restrict commercial activities within his courtyard.

חָנוּת שֶׁבֶּחָצֵר – If a courtyard resident set up **a store in the courtyard,** יָכוֹל לִמְחוֹת בְּיָדוֹ וְלוֹמַר לוֹ – **one** of the other residents **can block him by claiming,** אֵינִי יָכוֹל לִישַׁן מִקּוֹל הַנִּכְנָסִין וּמִקּוֹל הַיּוֹצְאִין – **"I cannot sleep due to the noise of [your customers] who go in and out** of the courtyard." אֲבָל עוֹשֶׂה כֵּלִים יוֹצֵא וּמוֹכֵר בְּתוֹךְ הַשּׁוּק – **But [a courtyard resident] may manufacture utensils** in his home and **go out and sell** them **in the marketplace,** וְאֵינוֹ יָכוֹל לִמְחוֹת בְּיָדוֹ וְלוֹמַר לוֹ – **and one cannot block him by claiming,** אֵינִי יָכוֹל לִישַׁן לֹא מִקּוֹל הַפַּטִּישׁ – **"I cannot sleep due to the noise of the hammer,"** וְלֹא מִקּוֹל הָרֵיחַיִם – **or** "I cannot sleep **due to the noise of the mill,"** וְלֹא מִקּוֹל הַתִּינוֹקוֹת – **or** "I cannot sleep **due to the noise of the children."**[29]

Gemara The Gemara assumes that the children mentioned at the end of the Mishnah are customers who enter the courtyard to purchase items there. This gives rise to the following problem:

מַאי שְׁנָא רֵישָׁא וּמַאי שְׁנָא סֵיפָא – **What is** the explanation for **the difference between the first clause** of the Mishnah, which states that one can protest the entry of customers into a courtyard, **and the last clause,** which states that one cannot?

Abaye offers an explanation:

אָמַר אַבַּיֵי – **Abaye said:** סֵיפָא אֲתָאן לְחָצֵר אַחֶרֶת – **The latter clause refers to** one who protests the presence of customers in **another courtyard**. One cannot block the entry of customers into a neighboring courtyard; he has this right only with regard to his own courtyard.

Rava objects to this explanation:

אָמַר לֵיהּ רָבָא – **Rava said to [Abaye]:** אִי הָכִי – **If this** is what the Mishnah means, לִיתְנֵי חָצֵר אַחֶרֶת מוּתָּר – **let it state** explicitly: **"It is permitted** to open a store in **another courtyard** [i.e. one cannot block a business in a courtyard other than one's own]." – **?** –

Rava offers his own interpretation:

אֶלָּא אָמַר רָבָא – **Rather, Rava said,**

NOTES

29. [The Gemara discusses what is meant by "the noise of the children."]

The Mishnah's distinction requires explanation. Why is it that "the noise of those who go in and out [of the courtyard]" is grounds for blocking a business, while "the noise of the hammer etc." is not?

The explanation is possibly that one cannot protest "the noise of the hammer etc." because it is made by a member of the courtyard. This is in contrast to "the noise of those going in and out [of the courtyard]," which is made by people who do not reside in the courtyard (based on *Rashi* to 21a ד״ה סיפא, see *Tos. Yom Tov; cf. Meiri, S'ma Choshen Mishpat* 156:10).

An alternative approach: Noise, from any source, is insufficient grounds for preventing a courtyard resident from engaging in a business. The Mishnah's statement that one may claim, "I cannot sleep due to the noise of those who go in and out [of the courtyard]," is not to be taken literally as a reference to noise, but as a reference to the inconvenience of people crowding the courtyard (*Ramban, Rashba, Ran, Nimukei Yosef*).

סֵיפָא אֲתָאן לְתִינוֹקוֹת שֶׁל בֵּית רַבָּן – **The latter clause refers to** one who seeks to prevent **school children** who live elsewhere from entering his courtyard to study Torah. וּמִתַּקָּנַת יְהוֹשֻׁעַ בֶּן גַּמְלָא וְאֵילָךְ – **And** the Mishnah's ruling applies **after Yehoshua ben Gamla's**[1] **ordinance,** which mandated the installation of teachers in every town. After the enactment of that decree, a courtyard resident could not protest the teaching of children in his courtyard.[2]

The Gemara traces the development of our educational system, culminating with Yehoshua ben Gamla's ordinance:

דְּאָמַר רַב יְהוּדָה אָמַר רַב – **For Rav Yehudah said in the name of Rav:** בְּרַם זָכוּר אוֹתוֹ הָאִישׁ לְטוֹב וִיהוֹשֻׁעַ בֶּן גַּמְלָא שְׁמוֹ – **Indeed, that man is to be remembered – namely, Yehoshua ben Gamla – in a favorable way,** שֶׁאִלְמָלֵא הוּא נִשְׁתַּכַּח תּוֹרָה מִיִּשְׂרָאֵל – **for were it not for him, the Torah would have been forgotten by Israel.** שֶׁבַּתְּחִלָּה מִי שֶׁיֵּשׁ לוֹ אָב מְלַמְּדוֹ תּוֹרָה – **Originally,** if a **[child] had a father, [the father] would teach him Torah,** מִי שֶׁאֵין לוֹ אָב לֹא הָיָה לָמֵד תּוֹרָה – but **one who did not have a father would not learn Torah.** מַאי דְּרוּשׁ – **Which** verse **did they expound** as a source for this? "וְלִמַּדְתֶּם אֹתָם" – ***And you shall teach them*** [the words of Torah] *to your children.*[3] Since the word אֹתָם, *them,* is written without a *vav,* the verse can be read: וְלִמַּדְתֶּם אַתֶּם – ***and you yourselves shall teach*** [Torah to] *your children;* i.e. the father himself must teach his child.

Since many children were not receiving an education, the Sages established a school system:

הִתְקִינוּ שֶׁיְּהוּ מוֹשִׁיבִין מְלַמְּדֵי תִינוֹקוֹת בִּירוּשָׁלַיִם – **[The Sages] enacted that teachers of children should be installed in Jerusalem,** so that any youth could go there and be taught Torah. מַאי דְּרוּשׁ – **Which** verse **did they expound** as a source for this arrangement? "כִּי מִצִּיּוֹן תֵּצֵא תוֹרָה" – ***For Torah shall go forth from Zion*** *and the word of God from Jerusalem.*[4]

But this measure did not solve the problem:

וַעֲדַיִין מִי שֶׁיֵּשׁ לוֹ אָב הָיָה מַעֲלוֹ וּמְלַמְּדוֹ – **Even so,** if **[a child] had a father, [the father] would take him up** to Jerusalem **and have him taught** there. מִי שֶׁאֵין לוֹ אָב לֹא הָיָה עוֹלֶה וְלָמֵד – **Whoever did not have a father would not go up** to Jerusalem **and study.**

Therefore, the school system was expanded:

הִתְקִינוּ שֶׁיְּהוּ מוֹשִׁיבִין בְּכָל פֶּלֶךְ וּפֶלֶךְ – **[The Sages] enacted that [local authorities] should install teachers in every province,**[5] וּמַכְנִיסִין אוֹתָן כְּבֶן ט״ז כְּבֶן י״ז – **and they should bring in [youths] of ages sixteen or seventeen** who lacked an education to be taught by these teachers.

Even this measure, however, was not entirely effective:

וּמִי שֶׁהָיָה רַבּוֹ כּוֹעֵס עָלָיו – **[Any student] whose teacher became angry with him** מְבַעֵיט בּוֹ וְיָצָא – **would rebel against [the teacher] and leave.**[6] The matter was not resolved satisfactorily עַד שֶׁבָּא יְהוֹשֻׁעַ בֶּן גַּמְלָא וְתִיקֵּן – **until Yehoshua ben Gamla came and enacted** שֶׁיְּהוּ מוֹשִׁיבִין מְלַמְּדֵי תִינוֹקוֹת – **that [local authorities] should install teachers of children** בְּכָל מְדִינָה וּמְדִינָה וּבְכָל עִיר וָעִיר – **in every district and town,** וּמַכְנִיסִין אוֹתָן כְּבֶן שֵׁשׁ כְּבֶן שֶׁבַע – **and they should bring in [children] of ages six or seven** to be taught by these teachers.[7] With this ordinance, Yehoshua ben Gamla ensured that the Torah would not be forgotten by Israel.

Further teachings by Rav on the subject of education:

אֲמַר לֵיהּ רַב לְרַב שְׁמוּאֵל בַּר שִׁילַת – **Rav said to Rav Shmuel bar Shilas:**[8] עַד שִׁית לָא תְּקַבֵּיל – **Until** he reaches the age of **six, do not accept** a child as a student. מִכָּאן וְאֵילָךְ קַבֵּיל – **From that age and up accept** him, וְאַסְפֵּי לֵיהּ כְּתוֹרָא – **and stuff him** with Torah knowledge even against his will, just **as an ox** is harnessed by force to its yoke.[9]

וְאָמַר לֵיהּ רַב לְרַב שְׁמוּאֵל בַּר שִׁילַת – **And Rav said to Rav Shmuel bar Shilas:** כִּי מָחֵית לִינוּקָא – **When you hit a child** for disciplinary purposes, לָא תִּימְחֵי אֶלָּא בְּעַרְקְתָא דְּמְסָנָא – **hit** him **with only a shoelace,** i.e. hit him in such a way that he will not be injured.[10] דְּקָארֵי קָארֵי – If **he studies, he studies.** דְּלָא קָארֵי – And if **he does not study,** לֶיהֱוֵי צַוְותָא לְחַבְרֵיהּ – **let him remain in the company of his friends**[11] and eventually he will pay attention to the lesson.

The Gemara returns to the point made above by Rava, that a courtyard resident cannot block the teaching of children in his courtyard:

מֵיתִיבֵי – **They challenged** Rava's teaching from the following Baraisa: אֶחָד מִבְּנֵי חָצֵר שֶׁבִּיקֵּשׁ – If A COURTYARD RESIDENT לַעֲשׂוֹת רוֹפֵא אוּמָן וְגַרְדִּי וּמְלַמֵּד תִּינוֹקוֹת – WANTS TO BECOME A *MOHEL*, A BLOODLETTER, A WEAVER, OR A TEACHER OF CHILDREN, בְּנֵי חָצֵר מְעַכְּבִין עָלָיו – THE other COURTYARD RESIDENTS CAN PREVENT HIM from doing so, on the grounds that they are

NOTES

1. Yehoshua ben Gamla was one of the high priests that served in the Second Temple (*Rashi*; cf. *Tosefos Yeshanim* to *Yevamos* 61a; see *Tosafos* here).

2. An apparent difficulty: Yehoshua ben Gamla ordained that a teacher should be installed in every town. He did not decree the installation of a teacher in every courtyard. So why does a courtyard resident not have the right to demand that the teacher be shifted from the courtyard to a synagogue or study hall in the same town, which is indeed better suited for the purpose?

The answer is that if a teacher would have to travel from his courtyard, he might be deterred from the teaching profession. Hence, in order to ensure the availability of teachers for the implementation of Yehoshua ben Gamla's ordinance, the law is that a teacher is not required to leave his courtyard (*Nimukei Yosef*).

3. *Deuteronomy* 11:19.

4. *Isaiah* 2:3. The environment of Jerusalem was particulary conducive to Torah study. When a person beheld the tremendous sanctity [of the Temple in Jerusalem] and the Kohanim engaged in the Divine service, he was inspired to direct his heart to the awe of God and the study of Torah (*Tosafos*).

5. A פֶּלֶךְ, *province,* consists of many מְדִינוֹת, *[administrative] districts* (*Rashi*).

6. A youth of this age is not submissive to his teacher. If the teacher is angry with him, he will leave (*Maharam*).

7. The exact age – six or seven – depended on the health of the child (*Tosafos* ד״ה כבן). [The Mishnah in *Pirkei Avos* (5:25), which teaches that *five* is the age at which a child begins to study Scripture, means that a father introduces his son to Scripture at that age. A child does not begin intensive studies until he is at least six years old (*Tosefos HaRosh,* cited by *Shitah Mekubetzes; Ritva;* cf. *Tosafos*).]

When there was only one school in each province, children below the age of sixteen did not attend because it was often dangerous for them to travel to the nearest school. The establishment of schools in every town and district made it possible for even young children to attend (*Ritva, Maharsha*).

8. A [noted] teacher (*Rashi;* see above, 8b).

9. *Rashi.* Alternatively: Stuff him with Torah just as one stuffs an ox with food even against its will in order to fatten it (*Rabbeinu Gershom*; *Rashi* to *Kesubos* 50a).

10. Do not eject him from the class, or punish him excessively (*Rashi*).

11. Literally: let him be company for his friends.

We have interpreted the Gemara according to *Rashi's* understanding. *Maharsha,* however, explains the Gemara in its literal sense: The inattentive student should remain in class and provide company for his fellow students. Otherwise, the other students might be tempted to follow his example and idle away their time outside the class.

סיפא אתאן לתינוקות של בית רבן ומתקנת יהושע בן גמלא ואילך דאמר רב יהודה אמר רב ברם זכור אותו האיש לטוב ויהושע בן גמלא שמו שאלמלא הוא נשתכחה תורה מישראל שבתחלה מי שיש לו אב מלמדו תורה מי שאין לו אב לא היה למד תורה מאי דרוש [א] ולמדתם אותם ולמדתם אתם התקינו שיהו מושיבין מלמדי תינוקות בירושלים מאי דרוש [ב] כי מציון תצא תורה (א) ועדיין מי שיש לו אב היה מעלו ומלמדו מי שאין לו אב לא היה עולה ולמד התקינו שיהו מושיבין בכל פלך ופלך ומכניסין אותן כבן ט"ז כבן י"ז ומי שהיה רבו כועס עליו (ב) מבעיט בו ויצא עד שבא יהושע בן גמלא ותיקן [ב] שיהו מושיבין מלמדי תינוקות בכל מדינה ומדינה ובכל עיר ועיר [ג] ומכניסין אותן כבן שש כבן שבע [א] אמר ליה רב לרב שמואל בר שילת [ד] עד שית לא תקביל מכאן ואילך קביל ואספי ליה כתורא וא"ל רב לרב שמואל בר שילת [ה] כי מחית לינוקא לא תימחי אלא בערקתא דמסנא דקארי קארי דלא קארי [ו] ליהוי צוותא לחבריה מיתיבי [ז] אחד מבני חצר שביקש לעשות רופא אומן וגרדי ומלמד תינוקות בני חצר מעכבין עליו הכא במאי עסקינן [ח] בתינוקות דעכו"ם ת"ש [ט] שנים שיושבין בחצר וביקש אחד מהן לעשות רופא ואומן וגרדי ומלמד תינוקות חבירו מעכב עליו ה"נ בתינוקות דעכו"ם ת"ש [י] מי שיש לו בית בחצר השותפין ה"ז לא ישכירנו לא לרופא ולא לאומן ולא לגרדי ולא לסופר יהודי ולא לסופר ארמאי [כ] הכא במאי עסקינן בסופר מתא אמר רבא מתקנת יהושע בן גמלא ואילך [ל] לא ממטינן ינוקא ממתא למתא [מ] אבל מבי כנישתא לבי כנישתא ממטינן [נ] ואי מפסק נהרא לא ממטינן ואי [ס] איכא תיתורא ממטינן [ע] ואי איכא גמלא לא ממטינן (ג) ואמר רבא [צ] סך מקרי דרדקי עשרין וחמשה ינוקי ואי איכא חמשין מותבינן תרי [ק] ואי איכא ארבעין מוקמינן ריש [ג] דוכנא [ר] ומסייעין ליה ממתא ואמר רבא האי מקרי ינוקי דגרים ואיכא אחרינא דגרים טפי מיניה לא מסלקינן ליה דלמא אתי לאיתרשולי רב דימי מנהרדעא אמר [ש] כ"ש דגרים טפי [ד] קנאת סופרים תרבה חכמה ואמר רבא הני תרי מקרי דרדקי חד גרים ולא דייק וחד דייק ולא גרים מותבינן ההוא דגרים ולא דייק שבשתא ממילא נפקא רב דימי מנהרדעא אמר [ת] מותבינן דדייק ולא גרים [ה] שבשתא כיון דעל על דכתיב [ג] כי ששת חדשים ישב שם יואב וכל ישראל עד הכרית כל זכר באדום כי אתא לקמיה דדוד אמר ליה מאי

רש"י

סיפא אתאן לתינוקות של בית רבן. ואע"ג דקול הבא מחמת אחרים לא מצי מחויי: **משום תקנת יהושע בן גמלא.** אחד מן הכהנים הגדולים שעמדו בבית שני כדאמר ביבמות (דף סא.): **ולמדתם** (י) **אותם.** האב עצמו מצוה ללמדו: **פלך.** הרבה מדינות בפלך אחד והוא לשון אפרכיא: **רב שמואל בר שילת.** מלמד תינוקות היה (לעיל דף ח:): **ואספי ליה.** האכילהו והשקהו תורה בעל כרחו כשור שנותנין (ג) עליו עול על צוארו: **לא תמחייה אלא בערקתא דמסנא.** ברצועות של מנעלים כלומר מכה קלה שלא יוזק: **ליהוי צוותא לחבריה.** אינך זקוק לייסרו יותר מדאי ולא לסלקו מלפניך אלא ישב עם האחרים בצוותא וסופו לתת לב: **רופא.** מוהל: **אומן.** מקיז דם: **מעכבין עליו.** מפני שמרבה עליהן קול נכנסין ויוצאין: **לסופר יהודי.** מלמד תינוקות: **בסופר מתא.** מלמד תינוקות העיר ומושיב מלמדים תחתיו והוא מורה את כולם איך יעשו ויש שם קול גדול: **מתקנת יהושע בן גמלא ואילך.** שישבו מלמדי תינוקות בכל עיר: **לא ממטינן ינוקא ממתא למתא.** ללמוד מיום ליום שמא יוזק בדרכים שהשטן מקטרג בשעת הסכנה שנאמר פן יקראנו אסון (בראשית מב) אלא יוכל לכוף בני אותו מתא להושיב מלמדי תינוקות: **תיתורא.** גשר רחב וחבירו במנחות (דף לה.) תיתורא דתפילין מקום מושבם שדומה לגשר: **גמלא.** לוח קצרה: **סך מקרי דרדקי.** מנין תינוקות הראוין למלמד אחד: **ריש דוכנא.** שומע עם התינוקות מפי המלמד וחוזר ומשגירו בפי התינוקות ואותו ריש דוכנא נוטל שכר: **ומסייעין ליה ממתא.** לשכור לו אותו ריש דוכנא: **דילמא אתי לאיתרשולי.** יתפאר בלבו שאין כמותו ויתרשל מן התינוקות ולא יירא שמא יסלקוהו: **כל שכן.** כשמשבחוהו יתן לב להיות למד יפה שדואג מקנאת חבירו שסלקוהו מפניו שיביישנו בבני העיר: **דגרים ולא דייק.** שלומד הרבה ולא דייק בלימוד התינוקות שלא ישתבשו:

מאי

תוספות

זכור אותו האיש לטוב ויהושע בן גמלא שמו. הוא אותו (ד) האיש דאמר רב יוסף (יבמות דף סא.) תרקבא דדינרי עיילא ליה מרתא בת בייתוס לינאי המלך עד דאוקים ליהושע בן גמלא בכהני רברבי ולדיק גמור היה כדאשכחן הכא והא דקאמר התם (שם) קטיר קא חזינא הכא לפי שהיו אחרים חשובים ממנו:

ולמדתם אותם ולמדתם אתם. יש ספרים דלא גרסי ולמדתם אתם ודריש מדכתיב ולמדתם משמע (ה) מעצמכם: **כי** מציון תצא תורה. לפי שהיה רואה קדושה גדולה וכהנים עוסקים בעבודה היה מכוון לבו יותר ליראת שמים וללמוד תורה כדדרשי' בספרי למען תלמד ליראה וגו' גדול מעשר שני שמביא לידי תלמוד לפי שהיה עומד בירושלים עד שיאכל מעשר שני שלו והיה רואה שכולם עוסקים במלאכת שמים ובעבודה היה גם הוא מכוון ליראת שמים ועוסק בתורה: **כבן** שש כבן שבע. כבן שש בבריא כבן שבע בכחוש: **בבציר** מבר שית לא תקבל. והא דתנן במסכת אבות (פ"ה מכ"א) בן חמש שנים למקרא בבריא לגמרי כדאמר בכתובות (דף נ. ושם) הלומד בנו פחות מבן שש רץ אחריו ואינו מגיעו ואיכא דאמרי חבריו רצין אחריו ואין מגיעין אותו ותרוייהו איתנהו דחליש וגמיר ואיבעית אימא הא בכחוש והא בבריא:

אחד מבני מבוי כו'. פי' רשב"א דלא גרס מבוי אלא חצר דאי גרס מבוי תיקשי לאביי דשרי בחצר אחרת והיא דעושה אדם חנות בצד חנות של חבירו שרי (ו) לכל הפחות בחצר אחר ורבא נמי לא פליג עליה אלא דמוקי מתני' דשריא אף באותה חצר והכא אסר אפילו בחצר אחרת אלא אחד מבני חצר גרס:

וגרדי. וא"ת ומאי שנא גרדי מבעל ריחים דתנן במתני' דאין יכול למחות בידו ולומר איני יכול לישן מקול הריחים ומקול הפטיש וי"ל דמתני' בעושה לעצמו והכא בגרדי העושה לאחרים דאיכא נכנסין ויוצאין וא"ת הא אמרי' בסמוך האי בר מבואה דאוקי ריחיא כו' דינא הוא דמעכב עליה משום דאמר ליה קא פסקת לחיותי משמע דאי לאו משום דקא פסקת לחיותי היה יכול להעמיד שם הריחים אע"ג דעושה לאחרים ולקמן נמי תניא עושה אדם חנות בצד חנותו של חבירו כו' דאף על גב דאיכא נכנסין ויוצאין טובא ודוחק לחלק דהתם כבר יש יוצאין ונכנסין לריחים הראשון או לחנות הראשון וי"ל דהתם בחצר אחרת שרי א"נ מתני' נמי בעושה לאחרים ובריחים ובקול הפטיש אין נכנסין ויוצאין כל כך שנותנין לו פעם אחת וטוחן אבל בגרדי יש הרבה יוצאין ונכנסין שהרבה מביאין לו מטוה: **ולא** לסופר ארמאי. משמע דאם לא (ז) סופר הוה שרי להשכיר לארמאי וא"ת דאמרי' בהגוזל בתרא (ב"ק דף קיד.) האי בר ישראל דזבין ליה ארעא לעובד כוכבים אמיצרא דבר ישראל חבריה משמתינן ליה דא"ל אריא ארבעת אמיצראי ודוחק לחלק בין מכר לשכירות ונראה לר"י דהתם כשישראל רגה לקנות אבל אם אין ישראל רוצה לקנות מותר:

[ו] **בסופר** מתא. אין נראה לפרש כפ"ה דסופר מתא היינו מלמד תינוקות של כל העיר דאיכא קול גדול דהא לקמן אמר רבא מקרי דרדקי וסופר מתא כמותרין ועומדין כיון דאשמועינן דמקרי דרדקי הוי פסידא דלא הדר ה"ה מלמד כל תינוקות העיר ואמאי איצטריך תו למינקט סופר מתא ואין לפרש נמי כפ"ה [ח] בהמקבל (ב"מ דף קט:) סופר מתא מספר אנשי העיר דהא קרי (ח) הכא בברייתא סופר אלא נראה כמו שפי' ר"ח סופר מתא כותב שטרות העיר ולהכי חשיב ליה לקמן פסידא דלא הדר אם נכתב השטר שלא כדין:

מתקנת יהושע בן גמלא ואילך לא ממטינן ינוקא ממתא למתא. וכגון שיש כאן כ"ה ינוקי שראוין להשכיר להם מלמד ואם תאמר הא אי הוה ממטינן להו למתא אחריתי יצטרכו מלמד בפני עצמן כיון דאיכא כ"ה ינוקי וא"כ מאי נפקא מינה וי"ל דנפקא מינה דאי הוו ב' מלמדי תינוקות באידך מתא היו יכולין להושיב אצלם בפני זה ואצלם בפני זה:

סך מקרי דרדקי כ"ה ינוקי. אבל פחות מכאן אין בני העיר יכולין לכוף זה את זה להשכיר להם מלמד: פר"ח דרביה אקרייה זכר כדין והיינו רמייה דלא אשגח למידע היכי הוה קרי תלמידיה וכ"נ אבל אין נראה לפרש שגם רבו טעה ולימדו זכר דא"כ לאו רמייה הוא:

סופר

הגהות הב"ח

(א) גמ' תצא תורה וגו' ועדיין: (ב) שם מבעט בו ויצא ועד נמחק: (ג) רש"י ד"ה ואספי כו' שנותנין לו עול: (ד) תוס' ד"ה זכור וכו' הוא אותו דאמר כצ"ל ותיבת האיש נמחק: (ה) ד"ה ולמדתם וכו' משמע אתם מעצמכם: (ו) ד"ה אחד וכו' שרי לכל הפחות: (ז) ד"ה ולא וכו' דאם לא היה סופר וכו' וא"ת הא אמרי': (ח) ד"ה בסופר וכו' דהא קרי ליה סופר מתא:

מסורת הש"ס

א) כתובות דף נ., ב) [דימנין דנפלי תלמות ריש ולמתנין], ג) [פי' תינוקת נקרא דוכן שם יוסבין. ערוך ערך דכן], ד) [לקמן כב.], ה) פסחים קיב., ו) נ"ל אתם, ז) בדפוס ישן דפוס בכנסת כל אחד ספר בלא ו"ו רק מאחרון הכא בבריתא סופר הוא בר"י, ח) [לפנינו שם לא מגלא שום פי' בר"ן]

תורה אור השלם

א) וְלִמַּדְתֶּם אֹתָם אֶת בְּנֵיכֶם לְדַבֵּר בָּם בְּשִׁבְתְּךָ בְּבֵיתֶךָ וּבְלֶכְתְּךָ בַדֶּרֶךְ וּבְשָׁכְבְּךָ וּבְקוּמֶךָ: [דברים יא, יט]

ב) וְהָלְכוּ עַמִּים רַבִּים וְאָמְרוּ לְכוּ וְנַעֲלֶה אֶל הַר יְיָ אֶל בֵּית אֱלֹהֵי יַעֲקֹב וְיֹרֵנוּ מִדְּרָכָיו וְנֵלְכָה בְּאֹרְחֹתָיו כִּי מִצִּיּוֹן תֵּצֵא תוֹרָה וּדְבַר יְיָ מִירוּשָׁלָיִם: [ישעיה ב, ג]

ג) כִּי שֵׁשֶׁת חֳדָשִׁים יָשַׁב שָׁם יוֹאָב וְכָל יִשְׂרָאֵל עַד הִכְרִית כָּל זָכָר בֶּאֱדוֹם: [מלכים א יא, טז]

ליקוטי רש"י

ואספי ליה כתורא. אלעיטהו תורה כשור אתה מלעיטו ומכניס מאכל בית מגלא [כתובות נ.]. **גרדי.** אורג [פירש"י בכורות].

עין משפט נר מצוה

לב א מיי' פ"ב מהל' שכנים הל' יב ופ"ב מהל' ת"ת הל' ז סמג עשין יב טוש"ע ח"מ סי' קנו [קנו] סעיף ג וטוש"ע י"ד סי' רמה סעיף כג:

לג ב מיי' פ"ב מהלכות ת"ת הלכה א סמג עשין יב טוש"ע י"ד שם סעיף ז:

לד ג ד מיי' שם טוש"ע י"ד שם סעיף ה וסעיף ח:

לה ה מיי' שם טוש"ע י"ד שם סעיף י:

לו ו טוש"ע שם סעיף ע:

לז ז ח ט י כ מיי' פ"ו מהל' שכנים הל' יא סמג עשין פב טוש"ע ח"מ סי' קנו סעיף א:

לח ל מ נ ס ע פ מיי' פ"ב מהל' ת"ת הל' ו סמג עשין יב טוש"ע י"ד סי' רמה סעיף ח:

לט צ ק מיי' שם הל' ה טוש"ע י"ד שם סעיף טו:

מ ר מיי' שם טוש"ע יו"ד שם בהגה:

מא ש טוש"ע שם סעיף יח:

מב ת מיי' שם הל' ו טוש"ע י"ד שם סעיף יט:

רבינו גרשום

פיסקא חנות שבחצר השותפין. אם רוצה חבירו לפתוח שם חנות יכול חבירו לעכב עליו ולומר ליה איני יכול לישן מקול הנכנסין והיוצאין בחנות לקנות אבל ראשי לעשות כלים בתוך החצר ויוצא ומוכרן ולא מקול התינוקות. משמע ליה עכשיו תינוקות שבאין לקנות ממנו חפצים כעין שרגילין בני אדם לשלוח תינוקות בשליחותן מש"ה מקשה ליה בגמ' מ"ש רישא דקתני יכול חבירו למחות ולומר לו איני יכול לישן מפני הנכנסין והיוצאין ומ"ש סיפא דקתני אין יכול למחות בידו. לא מפני התינוקות של בית רבן שבאין ללמוד תורה זה אינו יכול לעכב עליו אבי' בחצר השותפין: מי שיש לו אב. שהיה חייב בלימודו מעלון: עד שית שנין לא תקבל ללומדו שאינו יכול לסבול עדיין טורח הלימוד: ואספי ליה כי תורא. כלומר תן עליו עול תורה כמו לשור זה שאובסין אותו בעל כרחו ומכניסין בו המאכל כדי שיהא שמן כך הכנס בו תורה: בערקתא דמסנא. ברצועה של מנעל ההוא ואל תכהו יותר מדאי שבשביל רוב הכאות אין מתפקח אא"כ קרי מנפשי' קרי ואי לא ליהוי צוותא לחבריה דקרי ואל תחוש להכותו יותר מדאי: בתינוקות דעובדי כוכבים. אם רוצה ללמוד ספר רפואה או מקרא יכול לעכב עליו דלא מצי עביד: ולא לסופר יהודי. מלמד תינוקות אלמא מצי מעכב. הכא במאי עסקינן בסופר מתא שהוא סופר העיר שכותב שטרות וספרים לכל מצי מעכב מחמת הנכנסין אצלו ואית דמפרשי בספר מתא שמגלגל כל בני העיר: לא ממטינן ינוקא ממתא למתא. מפני כן התקינו להושיב מלמדי תינוקות בכל פלך ופלך: ואי מפסק נהרא לא ממטינן. דאיכא למיחש

סופר

דלמא יהא רגיל למיזל לחודיה ונפיל לנהרא: **תיתורא.** גשר מרוחב: **גמלא.** גשר עשוי מנסר צר ומשני צדי הנהר קבועין ב' יתדות וקשור חבל א' מזה לזה ואותן העוברין על אותו נסר צר סומכין ידיהן בחבל ועוברין אבל התינוקות שאין בהן דעת לסמוך **לא ממטינן** דילמא אזיל לחודיה ונפיל: **סך מקרי דרדקי.** עד כ"ה תלמידים יכול ללמוד אחד: **ריש דוכנא.** ממונה תחתיו עד שיסייע לו ללמוד הנער. ואין מנכין לו לרב משכירותו אותו ריש דוכנא אלא **מסייעין ליה ממתא** הצבור שוכרין אותו וריש דוכנא. מאי טעמא לא מסלקי' ליה לההוא דלא גריס כל כך דאי מסלקינן ליה ומותבינן להו קמיה ההוא דגריס טפי **אתי לרשולי** למימר הואיל ולא מסלקי לי ואתי לרשולי. **כל שכן** דמותבינן להו קמיה ההוא **דגרס טפי** מימר אמר אי מרשילנא מסלקו להו מקמאי כי היכי דסלקי להו מקמיה דאידך ומעיין בהו שלא יבא אחר דגרס טפי מיניה ויסלקו מניה משום **קנאת סופרים תרבה חכמה** שזה מקנא לזה: **חד דגריס** הרבה ולא דייק כל כך:

disturbed by the noise of the extra traffic in the courtyard.[12] From this Baraisa we see that even the teaching of children can be precluded. — ? —

The Gemara deflects the challenge:

הָכָא בְּמַאי עַסְקִינַן — **With what are we dealing here?** בְּתִינוֹקוֹת דְּעַבְדֵי כּוֹכָבִים — We are dealing **with** the teaching of **the children of idolaters.** The teaching of idolaters' children was not addressed by Yehoshua ben Gamla's decree; hence, it can be protested.[13]

The Gemara makes another attempt to refute Rava's opinion: תָּא שְׁמַע — **Come, learn** the following proof from a Baraisa: שְׁנַיִם שֶׁיּוֹשְׁבִין בְּחָצֵר — IF TWO PEOPLE ARE LIVING IN A COURTYARD, וּבִיקֵּשׁ אֶחָד מֵהֶן לַעֲשׂוֹת רוֹפֵא וְאוּמָּן וְגַרְדִּי וּמְלַמֵּד תִּינוֹקוֹת — AND ONE OF THEM WANTS TO BECOME A *MOHEL*, A BLOODLETTER, A WEAVER, OR A TEACHER OF CHILDREN, חֲבֵירוֹ מְעַכֵּב עָלָיו — THE OTHER CAN PREVENT HIM from doing so on the grounds that he is disturbed by the noise of the extra traffic. This ruling contradicts Rava's view that the teaching of children cannot be blocked. — ? —

The Gemara deflects the challenge:

הָכָא נַמִי בְּתִינוֹקוֹת דְּעַבְדֵי כּוֹכָבִים — **Here too,** as in the previously quoted Baraisa, the reference is **to** the teaching of **the children of idolaters.**

The Gemara makes a third attempt to refute Rava's opinion: תָּא שְׁמַע — **Come, learn** a proof from the following Baraisa: מִי שֶׁיֵּשׁ לוֹ בַּיִת בְּחָצַר הַשּׁוּתָּפִין — ONE WHO OWNS A HOUSE IN A JOINTLY OWNED COURTYARD הֲרֵי זֶה לֹא יַשְׂכִּירֶנּוּ לֹא לְרוֹפֵא וְלֹא לְאוּמָּן וְלֹא לְגַרְדִּי — MAY NOT RENT IT TO A *MOHEL*, A BLOODLETTER, A WEAVER, וְלֹא לְסוֹפֵר יְהוּדִי וְלֹא לְסוֹפֵר אַרְמָאִי — A JEWISH TEACHER, OR A NON-JEWISH TEACHER! This Baraisa indicates that the use of a courtyard even for the education of Jewish children can be prevented. — ? —

The Gemara deflects the challenge:

הָכָא בְּמַאי עַסְקִינַן — **What are we dealing with here?** בְּסוֹפֵר מָתָא — We are dealing **with the** head **teacher of the town,** i.e. the individual who oversees the education of all the children of the town.[14] His work engenders an excessive amount of noise, and may therefore be blocked, even according to Rava.

The Gemara returns to its discussion of Yehoshua ben Gamla's ordinance, which mandated the establishment of local schools: אָמַר רָבָא — **Rava said:** מִתַּקָּנַת יְהוֹשֻׁעַ בֶּן גַּמְלָא וְאֵילָךְ — **From the** time **Yehoshua ben Gamla's ordinance** was enacted **and on,** לֹא מַמְטִינַן יָנוּקָא מִמָּתָא לְמָתָא — **one may not take** a child **from** his **town to** attend classes in another **town** on a daily basis, lest the child come to danger while on the road. Rather, the residents of the child's hometown are required to hire a teacher.[15] אֲבָל מִבֵּי כְּנִישְׁתָּא לְבֵי כְּנִישְׁתָּא מַמְטִינַן — **However, one may take** a child **from** the vicinity of one **synagogue to** the vicinity of another **synagogue,** within the same town.[16] וְאִי מַפְסֵק נַהֲרָא לֹא מַמְטִינַן — **But if a river separates** these two districts, a child should not be taken from one to the other.[17] וְאִי אִיכָּא תִּיתוּרָא מַמְטִינַן — **If there is a bridge** spanning the river, **one may take** a child across it. וְאִי אִיכָּא גַּמְלָא לֹא מַמְטִינַן — **But if there is a bridge that consists of** only **a narrow plank, one may not take** a child across it.

Another teaching by Rava on the subject of education: וְאָמַר רָבָא — **And Rava** also **said:** סַךְ מַקְרֵי דַּרְדְּקֵי עֶשְׂרִין וַחֲמִשָּׁה יָנוּקֵי — **The number** of students that **teachers** have in their classes **is twenty-five children.** וְאִי אִיכָּא חַמְשִׁין מוֹתְבִינַן תְּרֵי — **If there are fifty** students, **we install two** teachers. וְאִי אִיכָּא אַרְבְּעִין — **If there are forty** students, מוֹקְמִינַן רֵישׁ דּוּכְנָא — **we appoint an assistant** to the teacher, וּמְסַיְּיעִין לֵיהּ מִמָּתָא — **and [the teacher] is given** some financial **support from the** town to defray the cost of hiring the assistant.[18]

A third statement by Rava that pertains to education: וְאָמַר רָבָא — **And Rava** also **said:** הַאי מַקְרֵי יָנוּקֵי דְּגָרֵיס — **If the** current **teacher** of a class **of children teaches** at a certain pace וְאִיכָּא אַחֲרִינָא דְּגָרֵיס טְפֵי מִינֵּיהּ — **and there is another** teacher available **who teaches at a faster pace,**[19] לֹא מְסַלְּקִינַן לֵיהּ — **we do not remove [the first teacher]** and appoint the other one in his stead. For if the second teacher were to be appointed, דִּלְמָא אָתֵי לְאִיתְרַשּׁוּלֵי — **he might become lax** in his work, arrogantly believing that his teaching abilities are beyond compare and he will never be dismissed.

NOTES

12. The weaver mentioned in the Baraisa is one who works for others. People enter the courtyard to engage his services. But a weaver who makes cloth and sells it in the marketplace cannot be blocked, as the Mishnah taught: "but one may manufacture utensils and go out and sell [them] in the marketplace etc." (*Tosafos*).

13. The same applies to the teaching of secular subjects to Jewish children. The Gemara mentions children of idolaters only because Jewish children are generally taught Torah (*Rabbeinu Yonah, Rashba, Ritva*).

14. The town's teachers are appointed by him and are under his supervision — he teaches them proper methodology (*Rashi*).

15. According to some commentators, the Gemara refers to a single child. Even if only one child requires a teacher, the town must hire one for him. This appears to be the view of *Rashi* (see *Chidushei Anshei Shem;* see also *Rashba, Ritva*). Other commentators, however, understand the Gemara as referring to a group of twenty-five children. In their view, a town is not liable to hire a teacher unless at least twenty-five children require one (*Rosh, Tosafos*). [This dispute corresponds to the dispute presented in note 18.]

16. [Schools were often housed in synagogues — see note 2.]

17. The child might take the journey by himself and fall into the river (*Rabbeinu Gershom*).

[Where a river separates two districts in the same town, it is incumbent upon the local authorities to install a teacher in each district.]

18. The assistant hears the lesson from the teacher together with the students and then repeats it to them until they know it well (*Rashi*). Since he is learning [in addition to teaching], this assistant receives only a small stipend, not a full salary (*Ritva*).

There is a fundamental difference of opinion among the Rishonim as to how this passage of Gemara should be interpreted. According to some commentators, the numbers given here are maximums. Twenty-five is the maximum number of children to be assigned to one teacher. If there are more than twenty-five students, an assistant must be hired. If there are more than forty students, a second teacher must be hired [instead of an assistant]. If there are more than fifty students, an assistant must be hired [in addition to the two teachers] (*Rambam Hil. Talmud Torah* 2:5, *Rashba, Ritva, Nimukei Yosef* in the name of *Rabbeinu Yonah, Shulchan Aruch Yoreh Deah* 245:15; *Chidushei Anshei Shem* writes that *Rashi* takes this approach). (According to this view, the text of the Gemara is possibly understood as follows: סַךְ מַקְרֵי דַּרְדְּקֵי עֶשְׂרִין וַחֲמִשָּׁה יָנוּקֵי, *The* [maximum] *number of* [students that] *teachers* [should have in their classes] *is twenty-five.* וְאִי אִיכָּא חַמְשִׁין מוֹתְבִינַן תְּרֵי, *If there are* [more than forty but not more than] *fifty* [students], *we install two* [teachers]. וְאִי אִיכָּא אַרְבְּעִין מוֹקְמִינַן רֵישׁ דּוּכְנָא, *If there are* [more than twenty-five but not more than] *forty* [students], *we appoint an assistant.*)

An alternative approach: These numbers are minimums. A town is not obligated to hire a teacher unless there is a minimum of twenty-five children. It is not required to hire an assistant unless there are at least forty children. It is not required to hire two teachers unless there are at least fifty children (*Rosh, Tosafos*).

19. Literally: who reads more than him. In a given time the second teacher can cover more ground than the first one can (without sacrificing accuracy).

גמרא

ᵃסיפא אתאן לתינוקות של בית רבן ומתקנת יהושע בן גמלא ואילך דאמר רב יהודה אמר רב ברם זכור אותו האיש לטוב ויהושע בן גמלא שמו שאלמלא הוא נשתכח תורה מישראל שבתחלה מי שיש לו אב מלמדו תורה מי שאין לו אב לא היה למד תורה מאי דרוש ᵃ ולמדתם אותם ולמדתם אתם התקינו שיהו מושיבין מלמדי תינוקות בירושלים מאי דרוש ᵇ כי מציון תצא תורה (א) ועדיין מי שיש לו אב היה מעלו ומלמדו מי שאין לו אב לא היה עולה ולמד התקינו שיהו מושיבין בכל פלך ופלך ומכניסין אותן כבן ט"ז כבן י"ז ומי שהיה רבו כועס עליו (ג) מבעיט בו ויוצא עד שבא יהושע בן גמלא ותיקן ᵇשיהו מושיבין מלמדי תינוקות בכל מדינה ומדינה ובכל עיר ועיר ᵍומכניסין אותן כבן שש כבן שבע ᵒאמר ליה רב לרב שמואל בר שילת ᵈעד שית לא תקביל מכאן ואילך קביל ואספי ליה כתורא וא"ל רב לרב שמואל בר שילת ᵉכי מחית לינוקא לא תימחי אלא בערקתא דמסנא דקארי קארי דלא קארי ᶻליהוי צוותא לחבריה מיתיבי ᶻאחד מבני חצר שביקש לעשות רופא אומן וגרדי ומלמד תינוקות בני חצר מעכבין עליו הכא במאי עסקינן ᶜבתינוקות דעכו"ם ת"ש ᵗשנים שיושבין בחצר וביקש אחד מהן לעשות רופא ואומן וגרדי ומלמד תינוקות חבירו מעכב עליו ה"נ בתינוקות דעכו"ם ת"ש ᵗמי שיש לו בית בחצר השותפין ה"ז לא ישכירנו לא לרופא ולא לאומן ולא לגרדי ולא לסופר יהודי ולא לסופר ארמאי ᶜהכא במאי עסקינן בסופר מתא אמר רבא מתקנת יהושע בן גמלא ואילך ᵐלא ממטינן ינוקא ממתא למתא ᶻאבל מבי כנישתא לבי כנישתא ממטינן ᵒואי מפסק נהרא לא ממטינן ואי ᵉאיכא תיתורא ממטינן ᵖואי איכא גמלא לא ממטינן (ג) ואמר רבא ᶜסך מקרי דרדקי עשרין וחמשה ינוקי ואי איכא חמשין מותבינן תרי ᵖואי איכא ארבעין מוקמינן ריש (ג) דוכנא ᶜומסייעין ליה ממתא ואמר רבא האי מקרי ינוקי דגרים ואיכא אחרינא דגרים טפי מיניה לא מסלקינן ליה דלמא אתי לאיתרשולי רב דימי מנהרדעא אמר ᵚכ"ש דגרים טפי (ד) קנאת סופרים תרבה חכמה ואמר רבא הני תרי מקרי דרדקי חד גרים ולא דייק וחד דייק ולא גרים מותבינן ההוא דגרים ולא דייק שבשתא ממילא נפקא רב דימי מנהרדעא אמר ᵗמותבינן דדייק ולא גרים (ה) שבשתא כיון דעל על דכתיב (ג) כי ששת חדשים ישב שם יואב וכל ישראל עד הכרית כל זכר באדום כי אתא לקמיה דדוד אמר ליה מאי

רש"י

לשון אפרכיא: רב שמואל בר שילת. מלמד תינוקות היה (לעיל דף ח:): ואספי ליה. האכילהו והשקהו תורה כעל כרמו כשור שנותנין (ג) עליו עול על צוארו: לא תמחייה אלא בערקתא דמסנא. ברצועות של מנעלים כלומר מכה קלה שלא יוזק: ליהוי צוותא לחבריה. אינך זקוק לייסרו יותר מדאי ולא לסלקו מלפניך אלא ישב עם האחרים בצוותא וסופו לתת לב: רופא. מוהל: אומן. מקיז דם: מעכבין עליו. מפני שמרבה עליהן קול נכנסין ויוצאין: לסופר יהודי. מלמד תינוקות: בסופר מתא. מלמד תינוקות העיר ומושיב מלמדים מתחתיו והוא מורה את כולם איך יעשו ויש שם קול גדול: מתקנת יהושע בן גמלא ואילך. שישבו מלמדי תינוקות בכל עיר: לא ממטינן ינוקא ממתא למתא. ללמוד מיום ליום שמא יוזק בדרכים שהשטן מקטרג בשעת הסכנה שנאמר פן יקראנו אסון (בראשית מב) אלא יוכל לכוף בני אותו מתא להושיב מלמדי תינוקות: תיתורא. גשר רחב ומבירו במנחות (דף לה.) מיתורא דתפילין מקום מושבם שדומה לגשר: גמלא. לוח קלרה: סך מקרי דרדקי. מנין התינוקות הראויין למלמד אחד: ריש דוכנא. שומע עם התינוקות מפי המלמד וחוזר ומשגירו בפי התינוקות והוא ריש דוכנא נוטל שכר: ומסייעין ליה ממתא. לשכור לו אותו ריש דוכנא: דילמא אתי לאיתרשולי. יתפאר בלבו שאין כמותו ויתרשל מן התינוקות ולא יירא שמא יסלקוהו: כל שכן. כשמושיבוהו יתן לב להיות למד יפה שדואג מקנאת חבירו שלא יסלקוהו מפניו שיביישנו בבני העיר: דגרים ולא דייק. שלומד הרבה ולא דייק בלימוד התינוקות שלא ישתבשו: מאי

תוספות

זכור אותו האיש לטוב ויהושע בן גמלא שמו. הוא אותו (ד) האיש דאמר רב יוסף (יבמות דף סא.) תרקבא דדינרי עיילה ליה מרתא בת בייתוס לינאי המלך עד דאוקים ליהושע בן גמלא בכהני רברבי ולדיק גמור היה לדאשכחן הכא והא דקאמר התם (שם) קטיר קא חזינא הכא לפי שהיו אחרים חשובים ממנו:

ולמדתם אותם ולמדתם אתם. יש ספרים דלא גרסי ולמדתם אתם ודריש מדכתיב ולמדתם משמע (ה) מעלמכם: כי מציון תצא תורה. לפי שהיה רואה קדושה גדולה והכהנים עוסקים בעבודה היה מכוון לבו יותר ליראת שמים וללמוד תורה כדדרשי' בספרי למען תלמד ליראה וגו' גדול מעשר שני שמביא לידי תלמוד לפי שהיה עומד בירושלים עד שיאכל מעשר שני שלו והיה רואה שכולם עוסקים במלאכת שמים ובעבודה היה גם הוא מכוון ליראת שמים ועוסק בתורה: כבן שש כבן שבע. כבן שש בבריא כבן שבע בכחוש: בבציר מבר שית לא תקבל. והא דתנן במסכת אבות (פ"ה מכ"א) בן חמש שנים למקרא בבריא לגמרי כדאמר בכתובות (דף נ. ושם) הלומד בנו פחות מבן שש רץ אחריו ואינו מגיעו ואיכא דאמרי חבריו רצין אחריו ואין מגיעין אותו ותרווייהו איתנהו חלשים וגמיר ולאיבעית אימא הא בכחוש והא בבריא:

אחד מבני מבוי כו'. פי' רשב"א דלא גרס מבוי אלא חצר דאי גרס מבוי תיקשי לאביי דשרי בחצר אחרת והשתא דעושה אדם חנות בצד חנות של חבירו שרי (ו) לכל הפחות בחצר אחר ורבא נמי לא פליג עליה אלא למוקי מתני' דשריא אף באותה חצר והכא אסר אפילו בחצר אחרת אלא אחד מבני חצר גרס:

וגרדי. וא"ת ומאי שנא גרדי מבעל ריחים דלקמן דמתני' דאין יכול למחות בידו ולומר איני יכול לישן מקול הריחים ומקול הפטיש וי"ל למתני' בעושה לעצמו והכא בגרדי העושה לאחרים דאיכא נכנסין ויוצאין וא"ת הא אמרי' בסמוך האי בר מבואה דאוקי ריחיא כו' דינא הוא דמעכב עליה משום דאמר ליה קא פסקת לחיותי משמע דאי לאו משום דקא פסקת לחיותי היה יכול להעמיד שם הריחים אע"ג דעושה לאחרים ולקמן נמי תניא עושה אדם חנות בצד חנותו של חבירו כו' דאף על גב דאיכא נכנסין ויוצאין טובא ודוחק לחלק דהתם כבר יש יוצאין ונכנסין לריחים הראשון או לחנות הראשון וי"ל דהתם בחצר אחרת שרי א"נ מתני' נמי בעושה לאחרים ובריחים ובקול הפטיש אין נכנסין ויוצאין כל כך שנותנין לו פעם אחת וטוחן אבל בגרדי יש הרבה יוצאין ונכנסין שהרבה מביאין לו מטוה: ולא לסופר ארמאי. משמע דאסם לא (ז) סופר הוה שרי להשכיר לארמאי וא"ת דאמרי' בהגוזל בתרא (ב"ק דף קיד.) האי בר ישראל דזבין ליה ארעא לעובד כוכבים אמיצרא דבר ישראל חבריה משמתינן ליה דא"ל אריא ארבעת אמיצראי ודוחק לחלק בין מכר לשכירות ונראה לר"י דהתם כשישראל רצה לקנות אבל אם אין ישראל רוצה לקנות מותר:

ᶻבסופר מתא. אין נראה לפרש כפ"ה דסופר מתא היינו מלמד תינוקות של כל העיר דאיכא קול גדול דהא לקמן אמר רבא מקרי דרדקי וסופר מתא כמותרין ועומדין כיון דאשמועינן דמקרי דרדקי הוי פסידא דלא הדר ה"ה מלמד כל תינוקות העיר ואמאי איצטריך תו למינקט סופר מתא ואין לפרש נמי כפ"ה ᵖבהמקבל (ב"מ דף קט:) סופר מתא מספר אנשי העיר דהא קרי (ח) הכא בברייתא סופר אלא נראה כמו שפי' ר"ח סופר מתא כותב שטרות העיר ולהכי חשיב ליה לקמן פסידא דלא הדר אם נכתב השטר שלא כדין:

מתקנת יהושע בן גמלא ואילך לא ממטינן ינוקא ממתא למתא. וכגון שיש כאן כ"ה ינוקי שראויין להשכיר להם מלמד ואם תאמר הא אי הוה ממטינן להו למתא אחריתי יצטרכו מלמד בפני עצמן כיון דאיכא כ"ה ינוקי וא"כ מאי נפקא מינה וי"ל דנפקא מינה דאי הוו ב' מלמדי תינוקות באידך מתא היו יכולין להושיב חציים בפני זה וחציים בפני זה:

סך מקרי דרדקי כ"ה ינוקי. אבל פחות מכאן אין בני העיר יכולין לכוף זה את זה להשכיר להם מלמד: פר"ח דרביה אקרייה זכר כדין והיינו רמייה דלא אשגח למידע היכי הוה קרי תלמידיה וכ"נ אבל אין נראה לפרש שגם רבו טעה ולימדו זכר דא"כ לאו רמייה הוא:

סופר

דלמא יהא רגיל למיזל לחודיה ונפיל לנהרא: תיתורא. גשר מרוחב: גמלא. גשר עשוי מנסר צר ומשני צדי הנהר קבועין ב' יתדות וקשור חבל א' מזה לזה ואותן העוברין על אותו נסר צר סומכין ידיהן בחבל ועוברין אבל התינוקות שאין בהן דעת לסמוך לא ממטינן דילמא אזיל לחודיה ונפיל: סך מקרי דרדקי. עד כ"ה תלמידים יכול ללמוד אחד: ריש דוכנא. ממונה תחתיו עד שיסייע לו ללמוד הנער. ואין מנכין לו לרב משכירותו כדי לשכור אותו ריש דוכנא אלא מסייעין ליה ממתא הצבור שוכרין אותו ריש דוכנא. מאי טעמא לא מסלקי' ליה לההוא דלא גריס כל כך דאי מסלקינן ליה ומותבינן להו קמיה ההוא דגריס טפי אתי לרשולי למימר הואיל דליכא דגריס כוותי לא מסלקי לי ואתי לרשולי. כל שכן דמותבינן להו קמיה ההוא דגריס טפי מימר אמר אי מרשילנא מסלקו להו מקמאי כי היכי דסלקי להו מקמיה דאידך ומעיין בהו שלא יבא אחר דגרס טפי מיניה ויסלקו ממנו. ומתעסק בהן הרבה משום קנאת סופרים תרבה חכמה שזה מקנא לזה: חד דגריס הרבה ולא דייק כל כך:

רבינו גרשום

פיסקא חנות שבחצר השותפין. אם רוצה חבירו לפתוח שם חנות יכול חבירו לעכב עליו ולומר ליה איני יכול לישן מקול הנכנסין ויוצאין בחנות לקנות אבל רשאי לעשות כלים בתוך החצר ויוצא ומוכרן: ולא מקול התינוקות. משמע ליה עכשיו תינוקות שבאין לקנות ממנו חפצים כעין שרגילין בני אדם לשלוח תינוקות בשליחותן מש"ה מקשה ליה בגמ' מ"ש רישא דקתני יכול חבירו למחות ולומר לו איני יכול לישן מפני הנכנסין והיוצאין ומ"ש סיפא דקתני אין יכול למחות בידו. לא מפני התינוקות של בית רבן שבאין ללמוד תורה זה אינו יכול לעכב עליו אפי' בחצר השותפין: מי שיש לו אב. שהיה חייב בלימודו מעלן: עד שית שנין לא תקבל ללומדו שאינו יכול לסבול עדיין טורח הלימוד: ואספי ליה כי תורא. כלומר תן עליו עול תורה כמו לשור זה שאובסין אותו בעל כרחו ומכניסין בו המאכל כדי שיהא שמן כך הכנס בו תורה: בערקתא דמסנא. ברצוע' של מנעל הכהו ואל תכהו יותר מדאי שבשביל רוב הכאות אין מתפקח אא"כ קרי מנפשי' קרי ואי לא ליהוי צוותא לחבריה דקרי ואל תחוש להכותו יותר מדאי: בתינוקות דעובדי כוכבים. אם רוצה ללמוד ספר רפואה או מקרא יכול לעכב עליו דלא מצי עביד: ולא לסופר יהודי. מלמד תינוקות אלמא דמצי מעכב. הכא במאי עסקינן בסופר מתא שהוא סופר העיר שכותב שטרות וספרים לכל מצי מעכב מחמת הנכנסין אצלו ואית דמפרשי בספר מתא שמגלח כל בני העיר: לא ממטינן ינוקא ממתא למתא. מפני כן התקינו להושיב מלמדי תינוקות בכל פלך ופלך: ואי מפסיק נהרא לא ממטינן. דאיכא למיחש

תורה אור השלם

א) וְלִמַּדְתֶּם אֹתָם אֶת בְּנֵיכֶם לְדַבֵּר בָּם בְּשִׁבְתְּךָ בְּבֵיתֶךָ וּבְלֶכְתְּךָ בַדֶּרֶךְ וּבְשָׁכְבְּךָ וּבְקוּמֶךָ: [דברים יא, יט]

ב) וְהָלְכוּ עַמִּים רַבִּים וְאָמְרוּ לְכוּ וְנַעֲלֶה אֶל הַר יְיָ אֶל בֵּית אֱלֹהֵי יַעֲקֹב וְיֹרֵנוּ מִדְּרָכָיו וְנֵלְכָה בְּאֹרְחֹתָיו כִּי מִצִּיּוֹן תֵּצֵא תוֹרָה וּדְבַר יְיָ מִירוּשָׁלָיִם: [ישעיה ב, ג]

ג) כִּי שֵׁשֶׁת חֳדָשִׁים יָשַׁב שָׁם יוֹאָב וְכָל יִשְׂרָאֵל עַד הִכְרִית כָּל זָכָר בֶּאֱדוֹם: [מלכים א יא, טז]

ליקוטי רש"י

ואספי ליה כתורא. הלעיטהו תורה כשור שאתה מלעיטו ולוכסו מאכל [כתובות נ.]. גרדי. אורג [פירש"י בכורות כ.].

הגהות הב"ח

(א) גמ' מלא תורה וגו' ועדיין: (ב) שם מבעט בו וכו': (ג) רש"י ד"ה ואספי וכו' כשור שנותנין עליו עול: (ד) תוס' ד"ה זכור וכו' הוא אותו האיש דאמר: (ה) ד"ה ולמדתם וכו' משמע אתם בעצמכם: (ו) ד"ה אחד וכו' שרי לכל הפחות: (ז) ד"ה ולא וכו' דאם לא היה סופר וכו' וא"ת הא דאמרי': (ח) ד"ה בסופר וכו' דהא קרי ליה הכא:

עין משפט נר מצוה

לב א מיי' פ"ו מהל' שכנים הל' יב וע"ש מהל' מ"ת הל' ז סמג עשין פב טוש"ע ח"מ סי' קנו סעיף ג וטוש"ע י"ד סי' רמה סעיף כב:
לג ב מיי' פ"ב מהלכות ת"ת הלכה א סמג עשין יב טוש"ע שם סעיף ז:
לד ג ד מיי' שם טוש"ע י"ד שם סעיף ו וסעיף ח:
לה ה מיי' שם טוש"ע י"ד שם סעיף י:
לו ו טוש"ע שם סעיף ט:
לז ז ח ט י כ ל מיי' פ"ו מהל' שכנים הל' יא סמג עשין פב טוש"ע ח"מ סי' קנו סעיף ג:
לח מ נ ס ע פ צ מיי' פ"ב מהל' ת"ת הל' ו סמג עשין יב טוש"ע י"ד סי' רמה סעיף טו:
לט צ ק מיי' שם הל' ו טוש"ע י"ד שם סעיף טו:
מ ר מיי' שם טוש"ע י"ד שם סעיף יז:
מא ש טוש"ע שם סעיף יח:
מב ת מיי' שם הל' ו טוש"ע י"ד שם סעיף יט:

Rav Dimi, however, asserts that the current teacher *should* be replaced with the superior one:

רַב דִּימִי מִנְּהַרְדְּעָא אָמַר – Rav Dimi from Nehardea said: If the second teacher is given the position, **כָּל שֶׁכֵּן דְּגָרִיס טְפֵי – all the more so will he teach at a fast pace, קִנְאַת סוֹפְרִים תַּרְבֶּה חָכְמָה** – for **"jealousy between scholars increases wisdom."** The second teacher, wary of the jealousy felt toward him by the teacher he replaced, will exert himself all the more, lest the other teacher be afforded an opportunity to embarrass him by pointing out his shortcomings to the townsfolk.

Another dispute between Rava and Rav Dimi concerning the selection of teachers:

וְאָמַר רָבָא – And Rava also **said:** If a choice has to be made between **הָנֵי תְּרֵי מַקְרֵי דַּרְדְּקֵי – these two teachers of children, חַד גָּרִיס וְלָא דָּיֵיק – one** that **teaches** at a fast pace **but is not exact**[20] **וְחַד דָּיֵיק וְלָא גָּרִיס – and one** that **is exact but does not teach** at a fast pace, **מוֹתְבִינַן הַהוּא דְּגָרִיס וְלָא דָּיֵיק – we appoint the one that teaches** at a fast pace **but is not exact, שַׁבֶּשְׁתָּא מְמֵילָא נַפְקָא** – for any **mistake** that a child adopts as a result of learning from such a teacher **will, as a matter of course, be corrected** later in life.

Rav Dimi disagrees:

רַב דִּימִי מִנְּהַרְדְּעָא אָמַר – Rav Dimi from Nehardea said: מוֹתְבִינַן דְּדָיֵיק וְלָא גָּרִיס – We appoint [the teacher] that is exact but does not teach at a fast pace, **שַׁבֶּשְׁתָּא כֵּיוָן דְּעָל עָל** – for **once a mistake enters** a child's mind **it remains.**

Rav Dimi continues by citing an incident to illustrate his point:

דִּכְתִיב – As it is written: ,,כִּי שֵׁשֶׁת חֳדָשִׁים יָשַׁב־שָׁם יוֹאָב וְכָל־יִשְׂרָאֵל עַד־הִכְרִית כָּל־זָכָר בֶּאֱדוֹם" – ***For Yoav and all*** [the army of] ***Israel remained there for six months, until he had cut off every male in Edom.***[21] The females, however, were spared. **כִּי אֲתָא לְקַמֵּיהּ דְּדָוִד – When [Yoav] appeared before** King **David, אֲמַר לֵיהּ – [David] said to him:**

NOTES

20. This does not mean that the teacher himself reads the texts inaccurately. Such a teacher is certainly inferior. Rather, the reference is to one who does not check whether his students are reading accurately (*Ritva*; see *Rashi, Tosafos* ד״ה סך).

21. *I Kings* 11:16. This verse refers to the war described in *II Samuel* 8:13, which was fought by Yoav, the general of King David's army, against Edom (Amalek).

זכור אותו האיש לטוב ויהושע בן גמלא שמו. הוא אותו (ד) האיש דאמר רב יוסף (יבמות דף סא.) תרקבא דדינרי עיילא ליה מרתא בת בייתוס לינאי המלך עד דאוקים ליהושע בן גמלא בכהני רברבי ולדיק גמור היה כדאשכחן הכא והא דקאמר התם (שם) קטיר קא חזינא הכא לפי שהיו אחרים חשובים ממנו:

סיפא אתאן לתינוקות של בית רבן. ולע"ג דקול הבא מחמת אחרים לא מלי מחוי: **משום תקנת יהושע בן גמלא.** אחד מן הכהנים הגדולים שעמדו בבית שני כדאמר ביבמות (דף סא.): **ולמדתם** אותם. הרבה מדינות בפלך אחד והוא לשון אפרכיא: **רב שמואל בר שילת.** מלמד תינוקות היה (לעיל דף ח:): **ואספי ליה.** האכילהו והשקהו תורה כשור שנותנין (ג) עליו עול על צוארו: **לא תמחייה אלא בערקתא דמסנא.** ברצועות של מנעלים כלומר מכה קלה שלא יזוק: **ליהוי צוותא לחבריה.** אינך זקוק ליסרו יותר מדאי ולא לסלקו מלפניך אלא ישב עם האחרים בצוותא וסופו לתת לב: **רופא.** מוהל: **אומן.** מקיז דם: **מעכבין עליו.** מפני שמרבה עליהן קול נכנסין ויוצאין: **לסופר יהודי.** מלמד תינוקות: **בסופר מתא.** מלמד תינוקות העיר ומושיב מלמדים תחתיו והוא מורה את כולם איך יעשו ויש שם קול גדול: **מתקנת יהושע בן גמלא ואילך.** שישבו מלמדי תינוקות בכל עיר: **לא ממטינן ינוקא ממתא למתא.** ללמוד מיום ליום שמא יוזק בדרכים שהשטן מקטרג בשעת הסכנה שנאמר פן יקראנו אסון (בראשית מב) אלא יוכל לכוף בני אותו מתא להושיב מלמדי תינוקות: **תיתורא.** גשר רחב ובירו במנחות (דף לה.) תיתורא לתפלין מקום מושבם שדומה לגשר: **גמלא.** לוח קצרה: **סך מקרי דרדקי.** מנין תינוקות הראוין למלמד אחד: **ריש דוכנא.** שומע עם התינוקות מפי המלמד וחוזר ומשגירו בפי התינוקות ואותו ריש דוכנא נוטל שכר: **ומסייעין ליה ממתא.** לשכור לו אותו ריש דוכנא: **דילמא אתי לאיתרשולי.** יתפאר בלבו שאין כמותו ויתרשל מן התינוקות ולא יירא שמא יסלקוהו: **כל שכן.** כשמשכנוהו יתן לב להיות למד יפה שדואג מקנאת חבירו שסלקוהו מפניו שיושיבנו בבני העיר: **דגריס ולא דייק.** שלומד הרבה ולא דייק בלימוד התינוקות שלא ישתבשו: מאי

סיפא אתאן לתינוקות של בית רבן ומתקנת יהושע בן גמלא ואילך דאמר רב יהודה אמר רב ברם זכור אותו האיש לטוב ויהושע בן גמלא שמו שאלמלא הוא נשתכח תורה מישראל שבתחלה מי שיש לו אב מלמדו תורה מי שאין לו אב לא היה למד תורה מאי דרוש ולמדתם אותם ולמדתם אתם התקינו שיהו מושיבין מלמדי תינוקות בירושלים מאי דרוש כי מציון תצא תורה ועדיין מי שיש לו אב היה מעלו ומלמדו מי שאין לו אב לא היה עולה ולמד התקינו שיהו מושיבין בכל פלך ופלך ומכניסין אותן כבן ט"ז כבן י"ז ומי שהיה רבו כועס עליו מבעיט בו ויצא עד שבא יהושע בן גמלא ותיקן שיהו מושיבין מלמדי תינוקות בכל מדינה ומדינה ובכל עיר ועיר ומכניסין אותן כבן שש כבן שבע אמר ליה רב לרב שמואל בר שילת עד שית לא תקביל מכאן ואילך קביל ואספי ליה כתורא וא"ל רב לרב שמואל בר שילת כי מחית לינוקא לא תימחי אלא בערקתא דמסנא דקארי קארי דלא קארי ליהוי צוותא לחבריה מיתיבי אחד מבני חצר שביקש לעשות רופא ואומן וגרדי ומלמד תינוקות בני חצר מעכבין עליו הכא במאי עסקינן בתינוקות דעכו"ם ת"ש שנים שיושבין בחצר וביקש אחד מהן לעשות רופא ואומן וגרדי ומלמד תינוקות חבירו מעכב עליו ה"נ בתינוקות דעכו"ם ת"ש מי שיש לו בית בחצר השותפין ה"ז לא ישכירנו לא לרופא ולא לאומן ולא לגרדי ולא לסופר יהודי ולא לסופר ארמאי הכא במאי עסקינן בסופר מתא אמר רבא מתקנת יהושע בן גמלא ואילך לא ממטינן ינוקא ממתא למתא אבל מבי כנישתא לבי כנישתא ממטינן ואי מפסק נהרא לא ממטינן ואי איכא תיתורא ממטינן ואי איכא גמלא לא ממטינן ואמר רבא סך מקרי דרדקי עשרין וחמשה ינוקי ואי איכא חמשין מותבינן תרי ואי איכא ארבעין מוקמינן ריש דוכנא ומסייעין ליה ממתא ואמר רבא האי מקרי ינוקי דגריס ואיכא אחרינא דגריס טפי מיניה לא מסלקינן ליה דלמא אתי לאיתרשולי רב דימי מנהרדעא אמר כ"ש דגריס טפי קנאת סופרים תרבה חכמה ואמר רבא הני תרי מקרי דרדקי חד גריס ולא דייק וחד דייק ולא גריס מותבינן ההוא דגריס ולא דייק שבשתא ממילא נפקא רב דימי מנהרדעא אמר מותבינן דדייק ולא גריס שבשתא כיון דעל על דכתיב כי ששת חדשים ישב שם יואב וכל ישראל עד הכרית כל זכר באדום כי אתא לקמיה דדוד אמר ליה מאי

ולמדתם אותם ולמדתם אתם. יש ספרים דלא גרסי ולמדתם אתם ודריש מדכתיב ולמדתם משמע (ה) מעלמכם: **כי מציון תצא תורה.** לפי שהיה רואה קדושה גדולה והכהנים עוסקים בעבודה היה מכוון לבו יותר ליראת שמים וללמוד תורה כדדרשי' בספרי למען תלמד ליראה וגו' גדול מעשר שני שמביא לידי תלמוד לפי שהיה עומד בירושלים עד שיאכל מעשר שני שלו והיה רואה שכולם עוסקים במלאכת שמים ובעבודה היה גם הוא מכוון ליראת שמים ועוסק בתורה: **כבן** שש כבן שבע. כבן שש בבריא כבן שבע בכחוש: **בבציר** מבר שית לא תקבל. והא דתנן במסכת אבות (פ"ה מכ"א) בן חמש שנים למקרא בבריא לגמרי כדאמר בכתובות (דף נ. ושם) הלומד בנו פחות מבן שש רץ אחריו ואינו מגיעו ואיכא דאמרי חבריו רצין אחריו ואין מגיעין אותו ותרוייהו איתנהו דחליש וגמיר ואיבעית אימא הא בכחוש והא בבריא: **אחד** מבני מבוי כו'. פי' רשב"א דלא גרס מבוי אלא חצר דאי גרס מבוי תיקשי לאביי דשרי בחצר אחרת והיא דעושה אדם חנות בצד חנות של חבירו שרי (ו) לכל הפחות בחצר אחר ורבא נמי לא פליג עליה אלא דמוקי מתני' דשריא אף באותה חצר והכא אסר אפילו בחצר אחרת אלא אחד מבני חצר גרס: **וגרדי.** וא"ת ומאי שנא גרדי מבעל ריחים דתנן במתני' דאין יכול למחות בידו ולומר איני יכול לישן מקול הריחים ומקול הפטיש וי"ל דמתני' בעושה לעצמו והכא בגרדי העושה לאחרים דאיכא נכנסין ויוצאין וא"ת הא אמרי' בסמוך האי בר מבואה דאוקי ריחייא כו' דינא הוא דמעכב עליה משום דאמר ליה קא פסקת לחיותי משמע דאי לאו משום דקא פסקת לחיותי היה יכול להעמיד שם הריחים אע"ג דעושה לאחרים ולקמן נמי תניא עושה אדם חנות בצד חנותו של חבירו כו' דאף על גב דאיכא נכנסין ויוצאין טובא ודוחק לחלק דהתם כבר יש יוצאין ונכנסין לריחים הראשון או לחנות הראשון וי"ל דהתם בחצר אחרת שרי א"נ מתני' נמי בעושה לאחרים ובריחים ובקול הפטיש אין נכנסין ויוצאין כל כך שנותנין לו פעם אחת וטוחן אבל בגרדי יש הרבה יוצאין ונכנסין שהרבה מביאין לו מטוה: **ולא** לסופר ארמאי. משמע דאם לא (ז) סופר הוה שרי להשכיר לארמאי וא"ת דאמרי' בהגוזל בתרא (ב"ק דף קיד.) האי בר ישראל דזבין ליה ארעא לעובד כוכבים אמיצרא דבר ישראל חבריה משמתינן ליה דא"ל אריא ארבעת אמיצראי ודוחק לחלק בין מכר לשכירות ונראה לר"י דהתם כשישראל רצה לקנות אבל אם אין ישראל רוצה לקנות מותר:

בסופר מתא. אין נראה לפרש כפ"ה דסופר מתא היינו מלמד תינוקות של כל העיר דאיכא קול גדול דהא לקמן אמר רבא מקרי דרדקי וסופר מתא כמותרין ועומדין כיון דאשמועינן דמקרי דרדקי הוי פסידא דלא הדר ה"ה מלמד כל תינוקות העיר ואמאי איצטריך תו למינקט סופר מתא ואין לפרש נמי כפ"ה בהמקבל (ב"מ דף קט:) סופר מתא מספר אנשי העיר דהא קרי (ח) הכא בברייתא סופר אלא נראה כמו שפי' ר"ח סופר מתא כותב שטרות העיר ולהכי חשיב ליה לקמן פסידא דלא הדר אם נכתב השטר שלא כדין: **מתקנת** יהושע בן גמלא ואילך לא ממטינן ינוקא ממתא למתא. וכגון שיש כאן כ"ה ינוקי שראוין להשכיר להם מלמד ואם תאמר הא אי הוה ממטינן להו למתא אחריתי יצטרכו מלמד בפני עצמן כיון דאיכא כ"ה ינוקי וא"כ מאי נפקא מינה וי"ל דנפקא מינה דאי הוו ב' מלמדי תינוקות באידך מתא היו יכולין להושיב חציים בפני זה וחציים בפני זה: **סך** מקרי דרדקי כ"ה ינוקי. אבל פחות מכאן אין בני העיר יכולין לכוף זה את זה להשכיר להם מלמד: פר"ח דרביה אקרייה זכר כדין והיינו רמייה דלא אשגח למידע היכי הוה קרי תלמידיה וכ"נ אבל אין נראה לפרש שגם רבו טעה ולימדו זכר דא"כ לאו רמייה הוא: סופר

רבינו גרשום

פיסקא חנות שבחצר השותפין. אם רוצה חבירו לפתוח שם חנות יכול חבירו לעכב עליו ולומר ליה איני יכול לישן מקול הנכנסין ויוצאין בחנות לקנות **אבל רשאי לעשות כלים** בתוך החצר **ויוצא ומוכרן: ולא מקול התינוקות.** משמע ליה עכשיו תינוקות שבאין לקנות ממנו חפצים כעין שרגילין בני אדם לשלוח תינוקות בשליחותן מש"ה מקשה ליה בגמ' **מ"ש רישא** דקתני יכול חבירו למחות ולומר לו איני יכול לישן מפני הנכנסין והיוצאין **ומ"ש סיפא** דקתני אין יכול למחות בידו. לא מפני **התינוקות של בית רבן** שבאין ללמוד תורה זה אינו יכול לעכב עליו אפי' בחצר השותפין: **מי שיש לו אב.** שהיה חייב בלימודו מעלן: **עד שית שנין** לא תקבל ללומדו שאינו יכול לסבול עדיין טורח הלימוד: **ואספי ליה כי תורא.** כלומר תן עליו עול תורה כמו לשור זה שאובסין אותו בעל כרחו ומכניסין בו המאכל כדי שיהא שמן כך הכנס בו תורה: **בערקתא דמסנא.** ברצוע' של מנעל הכהו ואל תכהו יותר מדאי שבשביל רוב הכאות אין מתפקח אא"כ קרי מנפשי' **קרי ואי לא ליהוי צוותא לחבריה** דקרי ואל תחוש להכותו יותר מדאי: **בתינוקות דעובדי כוכבים.** אם רוצה ללמוד ספר רפואה או מקרא יכול לעכב עליו דלא מצי עביד: **ולא לסופר יהודי.** מלמד תינוקות אלמא דמצי מעכב. **הכא במאי עסקינן בסופר מתא** שהוא סופר העיר שכותב שטרות וספרים לכל מצי מעכב מחמת הנכנסין אצלו ואית דמפרשי בספר מתא שמגלח כל בני העיר: **לא ממטינן ינוקא ממתא למתא.** מפני כן התקינו להושיב מלמדי תינוקות בכל פלך ופלך: **ואי מפסק נהרא לא ממטינן.** דאיכא למיחש דלמא יהא רגיל למיזל לחודיה ונפיל לנהרא: **תיתורא.** גשר מרוחב: **גמלא.** גשר עשוי מנסר צר ומשני צדי הנהר קבועין ב' יתדות וקשור חבל א' מזה לזה ואותן העוברין על אותו נסר צר סומכין ידיהן בחבל ועוברין אבל התינוקות שאין בהן דעת לסמוך **לא ממטינן** דילמא אזיל לחודיה ונפיל: **סך מקרי דרדקי.** עד כ"ה תלמידים יכול ללמוד אחד: **ריש דוכנא.** ממונה תחתיו עד שיסייע לו ללמוד הנער. ואין מנכין לו לרב משכירותו כדי לשכור אותו ריש דוכנא אלא **מסייעין ליה ממתא** הצבור שוכרין אותו ריש דוכנא. מאי טעמא לא מסלקי' ליה לההוא דלא גריס כל כך דאי מסלקינן ליה ומותבינן להו קמיה ההוא דגריס טפי **אתי לרשולי** למימר הואיל דליכא דגריס כוותי לא מסלקי לי ואתי לרשולי. **כל שכן** דמותבינן להו קמיה ההוא **דגרס טפי** מימר אמר אי מרשילנא מסלקו להו מקמאי כי היכי דסלקי להו מקמיה דאידך ומעיין בהו שלא יבא אחר דגרס טפי מיניה ויסלקו ממנו. ומתעסק בהן הרבה משום **קנאת סופרים תרבה חכמה** שזה מקנא לזה: **חד דגריס** הרבה ולא דייק כל כך:

עין משפט נר מצוה

לב א מיי' פ"ו מהל' שכנים הל' יב וע"ש מהל' ת"ת הל' ז סמג עשין פב טוש"ע ח"מ סי' קנו סעיף ג וטוש"ע י"ד סי' רמה סעיף כג:
לג ב מיי' פ"ב מהלכות ת"ת הלכה א סמג עשין יב טוש"ע שם סעיף ז:
לד ג ד מיי' שם הל' ב טוש"ע י"ד שם סעיף ה וסעיף ח:
לה ה מיי' שם טוש"ע י"ד שם סעיף ט:
לו ו טוש"ע שם סעיף ט:
לז ז ח ט י כ ל מיי' פ"ו מהל' שכנים הל' יא סמג עשין פב טוש"ע ח"מ סי' קנו סעיף ה:
לח מ נ ס ע פ מיי' פ"ב מהל' ת"ת הל' ו סמג עשין יב טוש"ע י"ד סי' רמה סעיף יג:
לט צ ק מיי' שם הל' ה טוש"ע י"ד שם סעיף טו:
מ ר מיי' שם טוש"ע יו"ד שם בהג"ה:
מא ש טוש"ע שם סעיף יח:
מב ת מיי' שם הל' ו טוש"ע י"ד שם סעיף יט:

מסורת הש"ס

א) כתובות דף נ., ב) [דימונין דנפלי אלתות ריש ולחתכן], ג) [פי' אלטבח נקראת דוכן אלטבח שם יושבין גויר ערך דק], ד) [לקמן כב.], ה) פסחים קיב., ו) נ"ל אתם, ז) בדפוס ישן דפוס ונציאה בכל אתם' ספר בלא ו"ו רק אתמון הכא בבריתא סופר הוא בר"ן, ח) [לפנינו שם לא נמלא שום פי' בר"ח].

הגהות הב"ח

(א) גמ' תלא תורה וגו' עדיין: (ב) שם מבעט נ"ל ותוא י' נמחק: (ג) רש"י ד"ה ואספי כו' שנותנין עליו עול: (ד) תוס' ד"ה זכור וכו' הוא אותו דאמר כל"ל תיבת האיש נמחק: (ה) ד"ה ולמדתם וכו' משמע אתם בעצמכם: (ו) ד"ה אחד וכו' שרי לכל הפחות: (ז) ד"ה ולא וכו' דאם לא היה סופר וכו' ולא"ת הא אמרי': (ח) ד"ה בסופר וכו' דהא קרי ליה הכא:

תורה אור השלם

א) וְלִמַּדְתֶּם אֹתָם אֶת בְּנֵיכֶם לְדַבֵּר בָּם בְּשִׁבְתְּךָ בְּבֵיתֶךָ וּבְלֶכְתְּךָ בַדֶּרֶךְ וּבְשָׁכְבְּךָ וּבְקוּמֶךָ: [דברים יא, יט]
ב) וְהָלְכוּ עַמִּים רַבִּים וְאָמְרוּ לְכוּ וְנַעֲלֶה אֶל הַר יְיָ אֶל בֵּית אֱלֹהֵי יַעֲקֹב וְיֹרֵנוּ מִדְּרָכָיו וְנֵלְכָה בְּאֹרְחֹתָיו כִּי מִצִּיּוֹן תֵּצֵא תוֹרָה וּדְבַר יְיָ מִירוּשָׁלָיִם: [ישעיה ב, ג]
ג) כִּי שֵׁשֶׁת חֳדָשִׁים יָשַׁב שָׁם יוֹאָב וְכָל יִשְׂרָאֵל עַד הִכְרִית כָּל זָכָר בֶּאֱדוֹם: [מלכים א יא, טז]

ליקוטי רש"י

ואספי ליה כתורא. גלעיטהו תורה כשור שמלעיטו ואובסו מאכל [כתובות נ.]. **גרדי.** אורג [ע"ז פירש"י בכורות].

מג א מיי' פ"ב מהל' ת"ת הל' ג סמג שם טוש"ע י"ד סי' רמה סעיף יז:

מד ב ג מיי' פ"ו מהל' שכירות הל' ז ועי' בהשגות ובמ"מ סמג עשין פט טוש"ע ח"מ סי' שמ סעיף ח:

מה ד מיי' פ"ח מהל' מכירה הלכה ד סמג לאוין קע טוש"ע ח"מ סי' רכח סעיף יח:

מו ה ו ז ח ט מיי' פ"ו מהל' שכנים הל' יא סמג עשין פב טוש"ע ח"מ סי' קנו סעיף ז וע"ש בהג"ה:

מז י כ מיי' פ"ב מהל' ת"ת הל' ו ופ"ב מהל' ח"ת הל' ז סמג שם וסי' יב טוש"ע סי' רמה סעיף ו וטוש"ע י"ד סי' רמה סעיף כב:

רבינו גרשום

מאי טעמא עבדת הכי דמשיירת נשים: האי בר מבואה א) מההוא מבוי (בני אדם) ולא היה רגיל לכך וקא מוקים ריחים לבר סמוך לריחים של חבירו: דינא הוא כו'. מרחיקין מצודת הדג אחד לפרוש מצודתו בשכר שתיקן במים ובא חבירו ורצה לעשות מצודתו כמו כן מרחיקין אותה מן מצודת חבירו כמלוא ריצת הדג דמצי למימר ליה קא פסקת חיותאי ותסייע לרב הונא. מהא לא תסייע ליה דשאני דגים דיהבי סיירא דמשום הכי מרחיקין מפני כי מסיר לו דבר שבא כבר למצודתו במאכל שמשים במצודתו לפי שכשמעיינין ורואין מאכל במקום אחר בורחין ממצודתו של זה והולכין לשם וגזלו בידים דבר שכבר [בא] במצודתו אבל ברחוק פרסה אינו יכול להביא המאכל. אבל גבי ריחים דליכא למימר הכי דבר הבא לידי הסיר ממני שעדיין לא בא לידו כלום מודה דלא מצי לאוקמינהו במבוי: לימא דאמר כר' יהודה ולא כרבנן. מפני שמרגיל התינוקות לבוא אצלו ומצי למימר ליה שאר בעלי חנויות קא פסקת לחיותי: שוסקי. שקדים: ומרחץ. שהיו רגילין לשכור מרחץ כדי לרחוץ: אתה עושה בתוך שלך ואני עושה בתוך שלי. וקשיא לרב הונא: כופין בני מבוי זה את זה שלא להושיב בניהן לא חייט. כלומר אומנין של מבוי אחר אינן רשאין להושיב במבוי זה שלא לדעת כולן ולשכינו שבמבוי שלו אינו כופהו שלא יזקק מן אומנותו משום דאמר ליה אתה עושה בתוך שלך ואני בתוך שלי: רשב"ג אומר אף לשכנו כופהו. ורב הונא ס"ל כרשב"ג: בר מתא אבר מתא אחריתי מצי מעכב שאם היה אומן א' בעיר ובא אומן אחר מעיר אחרת כאותו ורצה לקבוע באותה מדינה יכול לעכב על ידו ולומר קא פסקת לחיותא ואי שייך אכרגא להתם שפורעין מס גולגלותם לאדון אחד דמי כמאן דהוה תרוייהו מאותה העיר ולא מצי מעכב ליה: דנפשיה. כלומר לשכינו לא מצי מעכב

תוספות

סופר מתא. לא כמו שפירש בקונטרס כותב ספר תורה בטעות דאין זה פסידא דלא הדר דיכולין להגיהו אלא כדפרישית לעיל כותב שטרות: **ומקרי** דרדקי. פי' בקונטרס בהמקבל (ב"מ דף קט. ושם) דהוי פסידא דלא הדרא משום דשבשתא כיון על וקשה לר"י דהא רבא גופיה אית ליה לעיל דשבשתא ממילא נפקא ואומר ר"י דהוה פסידא דלא הדר דאותה שעה שמלמד להם טעות הם מתבטלים ואותה שעה אין יכולין להחזיר לעולם: **שתלא.** וא"ת מאי פסידא איכא אי יפסיד ישלם וי"ל דאינו מפסיד אלא שפושע שאין הנטיעו' גדילות כמו שהיו ראויות ליגדל: **מרחיקין** מצודת הדג כו'. אע"ג דר"ת מפרש דבדבר של הפקר אפי' רשע לא מיקרי כדתנן (פאה פ"ד מ"ג) גבי פאה פירס טליתו עליה מעבירין אותו ממנה וכן תנן בפ"ק דב"מ (דף י.) ראה את המציאה ונפל עליה ובא אחר והחזיק בה זה שהחזיק בה זכה ולא מיקרי רשע אלא בעני המהפך בחררה ובא אחר ונטלה משום שאם לא ישתכר במקום זה ימצא להשתכר במקום אחר והך דשמעתא לא קשיא דאע"ג דהוי דבר של הפקר מ"מ בכמה מקומות ימצא שיוכל לפרוש מצודתו ועוד דהכא אומנותו בכך והא דאמרינן בפרק חזקת הבתים (לקמן דף נד:) נכסי כנענים הרי הן כמדבר כל המחזיק בהן זכה בהן מאי טעמא כנעני מכי מטא זוזי לידיה איסתלק ליה וישראל לא קני עד דמטי שטרא לידיה ופי' רשב"ם התם דישראל המחזיק רשע מיהא מיקרי ולפי' ר"ת אפי' רשע לא הוי כיון שלא ימצא במקום אחר וקשה לרשב"א מהא דאמר באיזהו נשך (ב"מ דף עג:) רב מרי בר רחל משכן ליה ההוא נכרי ביתא אזל רבא זבניה נטר תריסר ירחי שתא שקל אגר ביתא אמטייה לרבא א"ל האי דלא מטאי לה למר אגר ביתא עד השתא דאמר מר סתם משכנתא שתא ולא מצי נכרי לסלוקי והשתא כיון שקדמה חזקת רב מרי לחזקת רבא א"כ זכה בה רב מרי דנכסי הכנעני הרי הן כמדבר ואי מקרי רשע אתי שפיר דלא היה רוצה לזכות בה אבל לפירוש ר"ת דאפילו רשע לא מיקרי אמאי לא זכה בה רב מרי כיון דהיתר גמור הוא ושמא לפנים משורת הדין עבד ולריב"א נראה דחזקת רב מרי לא היתה אלא בתורת משכון ורבא קנה ממנו בשטר וזכה בה ואחר כך נתן מעות [וע"ע תוספות קדושין נט. ד"ה עני המהפך וכו' ותוס' ב"מ עג: סוף ד"ה נטר]: **תנאי** היא דתניא כו'. תימה לרשב"א דאמאי לא מייתי [ח] (הברייתא) דלעיל דממה נפשך רבי יהודה דאמר לא יחלק חנוני קליות ואגוזים לתינוקות פליג אהך ברייתא ושמא ניחא לאתויי תנאי דפליגי בהדיא בהכי: **כופין** בני מבוי זה את זה כו' ולא מלמד תינוקות. נראה לר"י דבמלמד תינוקות נכרים איירי ולא יתכן אי גרס לעיל אחד מבני מבוי דהא מוקמינן ליה (ז) בתינוקות נכרים ומעכבין עליו בני מבוי והכא קאמר דלשכינו אינו כופהו ואפילו רשב"ג לא פליג אלא משום דפסיק לחיותיה אבל משום קול תינוקות לא חייש ומיהו לפי מה שפירשתי [לעיל] דגרסינן אחד מבני חצר אתי שפיר ולר' שמשון בן אברהם נראה דהכא בתינוקות ישראל ואפילו אחר תקנת יהושע בן גמלא ושאני הכא דכבר יש שם מלמד תינוקות אחר ובסמוך דקאמר דמודה רב הונא במקרי דרדקי דלא מצי מעכב ואף על גב דאיהו סבר כרבנן שמעון בן גמליאל צריך לומר דרבן שמעון בן גמליאל לא פליג אמלמד תינוקות אלא אשארא: **פשיטא** לי דבר מתא אבר מתא [אחריתי מצין] מעכב. רב הונא בריה דרב יהושע כרבנן ס"ל ומיבעי ליה בר מבואה אבר מבואה דעלמא אי מצי מעכב אי הוי בכלל שכינו אי לאו כדפירש הקונטרס וכוותיה קיימא לן לגבי רב הונא דבתרא הוא: **ואי** שייך בכרגא דהכא לא מצי מעכב. פירוש בני העיר אבל בני מבוי מצי מעכבי שלא יכנס במבואם:

גמרא

מאי טעמא עבדת הכי אמר ליה דכתיב א) תמחה את זכר עמלק אמר ליה והא אנן (א) זכר קרינן א"ל אנא זכר אקריון אזל שייליה לרביה אמר ליה היאך אקריתן אמר ליה זכר שקל ספסירא למיקטליה אמר ליה אמאי א"ל דכתיב ב) ארור עושה מלאכת ה' רמיה א"ל שבקיה לההוא גברא דליקום בארור כתיב ב) וארור מונע חרבו מדם איכא דאמרי קטליה ואיכא דאמרי לא קטליה ואמר רבא מקרי ינוקא שתלא טבחא ואומנא וספר מתא כולן כמותרין ועומדין נינהו כללא דמילתא כל פסידא דלא הדר מותרה ועומד הוא אמר רב הונא האי בר מבואה דאוקי ריחיא ואתא בר מבואה חבריה וקמוקי גביה דינא הוא דמעכב עילויה דא"ל קא פסקת ליה לחיותי לימא מסייע ליה מרחיקים מצודת הדג מן הדג כמלא ריצת הדג וכמה אמר רבה בר רב הונא עד פרסה שאני דגים דיהבי סיירא א"ל רבינא לרבא לימא רב הונא דאמר כרבי יהודה דתנן רבי יהודה אומר לא יחלק חנוני קליות ואגוזין לתינוקות מפני שמרגילן (ג) אצלו וחכמים מתירין אפי' תימא רבנן עד כאן לא פליגי רבנן עליה דרבי יהודה התם אלא דאמר ליה אנא קמפלגינא אמגוזי את פלוג שיוסקי אבל הכא אפילו רבנן מודו דא"ל קא פסקת ליה לחיותי מיתיבי עושה אדם חנות בצד חנותו של חבירו ומרחץ בצד מרחצו של חבירו ואינו יכול למחות בידו מפני שיכול לומר לו אתה עושה בתוך שלך ואני עושה בתוך שלי תנאי היא דתניא כופין בני מבוי זה את זה שלא להושיב ביניהן לא חייט ולא בורסקי ולא מלמד תינוקות ולא אחד מבני אומניות ולשכנו אינו כופיהו רשב"ג אומר אף לשכנו כופיהו אמר רב הונא בריה דרב יהושע פשיטא לי בר מתא אבר מתא אחריתי מצי מעכב ואי שייך בכרגא דהכא לא מצי מעכב בר מבואה אבר מבואה דנפשיה לא מצי מעכב בעי רב הונא בריה דרב יהושע בר מבואה אבר מבואה אחרינא מאי תיקו אמר רב יוסף ומודי רב הונא במקרי דרדקי דלא מצי מעכב דאמר מר (עזרא תיקן להן לישראל שיהו מושיבין סופר בצד סופר וניחוש דילמא אתי לאיתרשולי א"ל) קנאת

רש"י

מאי טעמא עבדת הכי. שלא הרגת את הנקיבות: את זכר עמלק: ארור מונע חרבו. סיפיה דהאי קרא הוא: שתלא. נוטע כרמו למחצה: אומנא. מקיז דם: סופר מתא. לבלר: כמותרין ועומדין דמו. שלא יקלקלו ואם קלקלו מסלק להו בלא אתרייתא אע"פ שלא התרו בו קודם לכן: פסידא דלא הדר. כגון אלו שמשנתנבלה הבהמה או הרג המקיז והסופר כתב ספר תורה בטעות: דאוקי ריחיא. לטחון ולשכור: מרחיקין מצודת הדג מן הדג. צייד שנתן עיניו בדג עד שהכיר חורו מרחיקין שאר ציידין מצודתם משם אלמא אע"ג דלא זכה ביה ולא מטא לידיה מרחיקין משם דא"ל קא פסקת לחיותי: שאני דגים דיהבי סיירא. נותנין עין בהבטם להיות (ג) נוהגים לרוץ למקום שראו שם מזונות הילכך כיון שהכיר זה חורו ונתן מזונות בתוך מלא ריצתו בטוח הוא שילכדנו דה"ל כמאן דמטא לידיה ונמצא חבירו מזיקו אבל הכא מי שבא אצלי יבא ומי שבא אצלך יבא: שמרגילם. לבא אצלו כשאבותיהם שולחין אותן אל החנויות לקנות מן החנווים: שיוסקי. שקדים: אבל הכא. שזה העמיד תחילה והרגיל להשתכר בכך וזה בא לירד אצלו לאומנותו אומר לו פסקת לחיותאי: שלא להושיב ביניהן חייט ובורסקי. ממקום אחר להשכיר לו בית במבוי (ד) ויש כאן בני אותה אומנות: ולשכינו. הדר במבוי כמוהו: אינו כופהו. מלירד לאותו אומנות: רשב"ג אומר כו'. ורב הונא הוא דאמר כרשב"ג: מצי לעכב. מלעשות כאן אומנותם ולהביא כאן למכור ואפילו לרבנן דאמרי לשכינו אינו כופהו: ואי שייך בכרגא דהכא. שנותן מס גולגלתו למושל העיר הזאת כבר מתא (ה) לא מצי בר מתא לעכב עליו כל העיר ופשיטא לי דבר מבוי אבר מבוי דנפשיה לא מצי מעכב את המבוי מלירד לאומנותו כרבנן ולא כרב הונא מיהו איבעיא לי בר מבואה אבר מבואה אחרינא מאי מי מצי מעכב (ו) בן המבוי הזה או לא מי הוי שכינו ואינו כופיהו או דילמא שכינו דאמור רבנן בבר מבואה דההוא מבוי קאמרי אבל בר מבואה אחרינא לאו שכינו הוא: ומודה רב הונא. דאמר לעיל בר מבואה דאוקי ריחייא כו' דאית ליה כרשב"ג מודי הוא במקרי דרדקי דלא מצי מעכב לבר מבואה מללמד גם הוא התינוקות שמתוך כך יזהרו באומנותן שיראו זה מזה דאמר מר קנאת סופרים תרבה חכמה: ומודה

מסורת הש"ס

א) [עי' תוס' גיטין סח. ד"ה וכתיב], ב) [ב"מ קט.], ג) שם ס., ד) [שם], ה) [גי' רב אלפס והרא"ש מבעלי], ו) [תוספתא פ"א], ז) [מפי' רש"י סד"ה ומודה רב הונא נראה דלא גריס לכל זה וכ"כ תוס' ג"כ להדיא בסמוך ד"ה קנאת סופרים], ח) [צ"ל המשנה]:

הגהות הב"ח

(א) גמ' זכר קרינן א"ל לדידי זכר אקריון: (ב) שם מפני שמרגילן לבוא אצלו: (ג) רש"י ד"ה שאני דגים וכו' להיות רגילין לרוץ וכו' ונתן מלודה ומזונות וכו' וה"ל כמאן: (ד) ד"ה שלא וכו' במבוי זה ויש כאן: (ה) ד"ה ואי שייך וכו' כבר מתא הוא ולא וכו' לא מצי מעכב מלירד כל"ל ותיבות את המבוי נמחק: (ו) באד"ה מעכב עליה בן המבוי הזה או לא: (ז) תוס' ד"ה כופין וכו' מוקמינן ליה לעיל בתינוקות:

תורה אור השלם

א) וְהָיָה בְּהָנִיחַ יְיָ אֱלֹהֶיךָ לְךָ מִכָּל אֹיְבֶיךָ מִסָּבִיב בָּאָרֶץ אֲשֶׁר יְיָ אֱלֹהֶיךָ נֹתֵן לְךָ נַחֲלָה לְרִשְׁתָּהּ תִּמְחֶה אֶת זֵכֶר עֲמָלֵק מִתַּחַת הַשָּׁמָיִם לֹא תִּשְׁכָּח: [דברים כה, יט]

ב) אָרוּר עֹשֶׂה מְלֶאכֶת יְיָ רְמִיָּה וְאָרוּר מֹנֵעַ חַרְבּוֹ מִדָּם: [ירמיה מח, י]

ליקוטי רש"י

מקרי ינוקא. פסידא דלא הדר הוא דשבשתא כיון על על [ב"מ קט.]. ואומנא. מקיז דם [שם צז.]. מוהל תינוקות. כמותרין ועומדין נינהו. לסלקינהו [שם קט.].

חשק שלמה על רבינו גרשום

א) נראה דל"ל בר מבואה דאוקי ריחיא ואתא בר מבואה חבריה מההוא מבוי ולא היה כו': ב) [מד' רבינו ז"ל אלו נראה שהיה גורס בכאן ולא שייך בכרגא דהכא הא אמרת דלא מצי לעכב לא צריכא דלא שייך מאי עד כאן וכ"כ

לשכינו לא מצי מעכב ורב הונא בריה דר"י לא ס"ל הא דרב הונא דלעיל. ב) לא צריכא דלא שייך מאי. מי אמרי' הואיל דממתא חדא תרווייהו אע"ג דלא שייך כרגייהו בחדא לא מצי מעכב ליה. או דלמא כיון דלמבוי דידיה הוא מצי מעכב דלא ליקבע במבוי דידיה תיקו:

מַאי טַעְמָא עֲבַדְתְּ הָכִי – **Why did you do this?** Why did you spare the females? אָמַר לֵיהּ – **[Yoav] answered [David]:** דִּכְתִיב: "תִּמְחֶה אֶת־זְכַר עֲמָלֵק" – **For it is written:** ***You shall obliterate the male population of*** (*z'char*) ***Amalek.***[1] אָמַר לֵיהּ – **[David] said to [Yoav]:** וְהָא אֲנַן "זֵכֶר" קָרֵינַן – **But we read** the verse as follows: *You shall obliterate* ***the memory of*** (*zeicher*) *Amalek.* אָמַר לֵיהּ – **[Yoav] said to [David]:** אֲנָא "זְכַר" אַקְרְיוּן – **I was taught to read** ***z'char*** (the male population of). אָזַל שַׁיְילֵיהּ לְרַבֵּיהּ – **[Yoav]** then **went and asked his** childhood **teacher** which version the teacher had taught. אָמַר לֵיהּ – **[Yoav] said to [his teacher]:** הֵיאָךְ אַקְרִיתָן – **How did you read** the verse **to us?** אָמַר לֵיהּ – **[The teacher] said to [Yoav]:** "זֵכֶר" – I read ***zeicher*** (the memory of). The teacher's reading of the verse was correct. But Yoav had mistakenly read *z'char* (when he was a child) and, negligently, the teacher had failed to correct Yoav's faulty reading.[2] שְׁקַל סַפְסִירָא לְמִיקְטְלֵיהּ – **[Yoav] drew** his **sword to kill [the teacher].** אָמַר לֵיהּ – **[The teacher] said to [Yoav]:** אַמַּאי – **Why** do I deserve this? אָמַר לֵיהּ – **[Yoav] said to him:** דִּכְתִיב: "אָרוּר עֹשֶׂה מְלֶאכֶת ה' רְמִיָּה" – **For it is written:** ***Cursed is he that does the work of Hashem negligently.***[3] אָמַר לֵיהּ – **[The teacher] said to [Yoav]:** שַׁבְקֵיהּ לְהַהוּא גַּבְרָא דְּלֵיקוּם בְּאָרוּר – **Leave that man**[4] **to remain under the curse.** אָמַר לֵיהּ – **[Yoav] said to him:** כְּתִיב: "וְאָרוּר מֹנֵעַ חַרְבּוֹ מִדָּם" – But **it is written** in the continuation of that very verse: ***And cursed is he that withholds his sword from shedding blood.***[5] אִיכָּא דְּאָמְרֵי קַטְלֵיהּ – **Some say** that **[Yoav] killed [the teacher],** וְאִיכָּא דְּאָמְרֵי לֹא קַטְלֵיהּ – **and some say** that **he did not kill him.**

Another statement by Rava concerning one who teaches children incorrectly:

וְאָמַר רָבָא – **And Rava** also **said:** מַקְרֵי יְנוּקָא שַׁתָּלָא טַבָּחָא וְאוּמָּנָא וְסוֹפֵר מָתָא – **A teacher of children, a vine planter,**[6] **a butcher, a bloodletter and the town scribe** כּוּלָּן כְּמוּתְרִין וְעוֹמְדִין נִינְהוּ – **are all** considered **as having been forewarned.** That is to say, if they make a critical error, they may be dismissed without notice. כְּלָלָא דְּמִילְּתָא – **The general rule in this matter** is: כָּל פְּסֵידָא דְּלָא הָדַר – **Any** person whose occupation is such that he is in a position to cause an **irreversible loss** מוּתְרֶה וְעוֹמֵד הוּא – **is** considered **as forewarned** not to cause such a loss.[7]

The Mishnah (20b) taught that a person has the right to ban a business from his courtyard on the grounds that he is disturbed by the noise of the traffic it engenders. But the resident of one courtyard cannot ban a business from *another* courtyard on the basis of such an argument.[8]

The Gemara now discusses a claim that is effective even against a business in another courtyard:

אָמַר רַב הוּנָא – **Rav Huna said:** הַאי בַּר מְבוֹאָה דְּאוֹקֵי רֵיחְיָא – If **a resident of a** ***mavoi***[9] **set up a mill** for commercial purposes[10] וְאָתָא בַּר מְבוֹאָה חַבְרֵיהּ וְקָמוֹקֵי גַּבֵּיהּ – **and** then **a fellow resident of the** ***mavoi*** **comes and sets up** a mill **next to his** (i.e. in the same *mavoi,* but not necessarily in the same courtyard) for the same purpose, דִּינָא הוּא דִּמְעַכֵּב עִילָּוֵיהּ – **the law is that [the first one] can stop [the second one],** דְּאָמַר לֵיהּ – **for he can say to him:** קָא פָּסְקַתְּ לֵיהּ לְחַיּוּתִי – **You are cutting off my livelihood!** As a result of the presence of your business in the *mavoi,* I will lose patronage.

The Gemara attempts to support Rav Huna's ruling:

לֵימָא מְסַיֵּיעַ לֵיהּ – **Shall we say that [the following ruling] supports** that of **[Rav Huna]?** If a fisherman discovered the lair of a particular fish, and spread his net between that fish and its lair, מַרְחִיקִים מְצוּדַת הַדָּג מִן הַדָּג – **[other fishermen] must distance** their **fishing nets from the fish** כִּמְלֹא רִיצַת הַדָּג – **as far as the fish swims** in one spell. וְכַמָּה – **And how [far]** is that? אָמַר רַבָּה בַּר רַב הוּנָא – **Rabbah bar Rav Huna said:** עַד פַּרְסָה – **Up to a** ***parsah.***[11]

Even though the first fisherman has not yet acquired the fish, he can prevent other fishermen from taking it. This supports Rav Huna's contention that one who has set up a business in a *mavoi* can prevent another from taking potential customers.

The Gemara rejects the analogy by suggesting that the case of the fish is unique:

שָׁאנֵי דָּגִים דְּיָהֲבֵי סִיָּארָא – **Fish are different in that** once **they** have **set** their **sights** upon some food they will certainly swim to it.

NOTES

1. *Deuteronomy* 25:19. [This reading of the verse is incorrect, as the Gemara proceeds to explain. The correct version is תִּמְחֶה אֶת־זֵכֶר עֲמָלֵק, *You shall obliterate the memory of Amalek.*]

The Torah mandates the destruction of Amalek — the nation that is the very embodiment of evil on earth. Neither God's name nor His throne can be complete until the seed of Amalek is wiped from the face of the earth (*Midrash Tanchuma* to *Deuteronomy* 25; see *Rashi* to *Exodus* 17:16).

2. *Tosafos, Rashba* (see 21a note 20); cf. *Maharsha* . This incident illustrates Rav Dimi's point that a mistaken reading adopted in childhood remains ingrained.

3. *Jeremiah* 48:10. (See *Tosafos* to *Gittin* 68a ד"ה וכתיב.)

4. A euphemism for himself.

5. That is to say, I [Yoav] have a claim against you for you caused me to refrain from killing Amalek, thereby subjecting me to the curse mentioned in this verse, "And cursed is he that withholds his sword from shedding blood" (*Ritva*).

An alternative approach: The verse in its entirety reads, "Cursed is he that does the work of Hashem negligently, and cursed is he that withholds his sword from shedding blood." The juxtaposition of these two clauses implies that a person is cursed if he fails to kill one who does the work of God negligently. Thus, Yoav was dutybound to kill the teacher. (This is possibly the approach of *Rashi* — see ד"ה ארור. *Ritva,* however, rejects it. See *Netziv* in *Ha'ameik Sha'alah* 142:9.)

6. One who undertakes to plant and tend the vineyard of another, in return for a portion (usually half) of the crop (*Rashi*).

7. All of the professionals listed by Rava are in a position to cause an irreversible loss:

(1) *Teacher of children*: Although Rava himself holds that a mistake adopted in childhood will be corrected later in life (above, 21a), the time that was spent learning the wrong version is lost forever (*Tosafos*).

(2) *A vine planter*: If the crop grown by the sharecropper was not as large as it could have been, even if the deficiency occurred as a result of his negligence, he is not liable to compensate the owner. Thus, in such a case, the owner suffers an irreversible loss (*Tosafos*; see *S'ma* 306:20).

(3) *Butcher*: If a butcher slaughters an animal in a manner that is not in accordance with the laws of שְׁחִיטָה, *shechitah* (the method of slaughter prescribed by halachah), the meat may not be eaten (*Rashi*; see *Maggid Mishneh Hil. S'chirus* 10:7, *S'ma* 306:20).

(4) *Bloodletter*: A bloodletter could inadvertently kill his patient (*Rashi*).

(5) *Scribe*: A scribe who makes mistakes in the writing of a Torah scroll causes an irreversible loss (*Rashi*). The reference is to a situation where the mistakes may not be corrected; e.g. there are at least five mistakes in each column (*Rashba* in explanation of *Rashi*).

8. As Abaye said above (end of 20b): סֵיפָא אֲתָאן לְחָצֵר אַחֶרֶת, *the latter clause of the Mishnah* [which rules that one cannot ban a business activity from a courtyard on the grounds that he is disturbed by the traffic] *refers to* [one who lives in] *another courtyard*. Rava disagreed with Abaye's explanation only because, in his view, that is not the correct understanding of the Mishnah. He concedes, however, that the law itself is true (*Ramban* to the Mishnah 20b, *Tosafos* to 21a ד"ה אחד, *Ritva* to 20b ד"ה סיפא; see *Rashba* to the Mishnah 20b; cf. *Rambam Hil. Sh'cheinim* 6:8, *Choshen Mishpat* 156:5 with *Shach* and *Gra*).

9. For the definition of a *mavoi,* see 20b note 10.

10. To grind the grain of others or to rent the mill out for use by others (*Rashi*).

11. A *parsah* is equivalent to 8,000 *amos* (between 2.4 and 2.9 miles).

עין משפט נר מצוה

מג א מיי׳ פ״ג מהל׳ ת״ת הל׳ ג סמג שם טוש״ע י״ד סי׳ רמה סעיף ז:

מד ב ג מיי׳ פ״ו מהל׳ שכירות הל׳ ז ועי׳ בהשגות ובמ״מ סמג עשין פט טוש״ע ח״מ סי׳ שו סעיף ח:

מה ד מיי׳ פ״ח מהל׳ מכירה הלכה ד סמג לאוין קע טוש״ע ח״מ סי׳ רכח סעיף יח:

מו ה ו ז ח ט מיי׳ פ״ו מהל׳ שכנים הל׳ יב סמג עשין פב טוש״ע ח״מ סי׳ קנו סעיף ה וע״ש בהג״ה:

מז י כ מיי׳ פ״ב מהל׳ ת״ת הל׳ ז סמג שם טור וש״ע י״ד סי׳ רמה סעיף כב:

רבינו גרשום

מאי טעמא עבדת הכי דמשירות נשים: האי בר מבואה א) מההוא מבוי (בני אדם) ולא היה רגיל לכך וקא מוקים ריחים שלו סמוך לריחים של חבירו: דינא הוא כו׳. מרחיקין מצודת הדג מן הדג שאם היה רגיל אחד לפרוש מצודתו בְּשֶׁבֶר שתיקן במים ובא חבירו ורצה לעשות מצודתו כמו כן מרחיקין אותה מן מצודת חבירו כמלוא ריצת הדג דמצי למימר ליה קא פסקת חיותאי ותסייע לרב הונא. מהא לא תסייע ליה דשאני דגים דיהבי סיירא דמשום הכי מרחיקין מפני כי מסיר לו דבר שבא כבר למצודתו במאכל שמשים במצודתו לפי שכשמעיינין ורואין מאכל במקום אחר בורחין ממצודתו של זה והולכין לשם וגזלו בידים דבר שכבר [בא] במצודתו אבל ברחוק פרסה אינו יכול להביא המאכל. אבל גבי ריחים דליכא למימר הכי דבר הבא לידי הסיר ממני שעדיין לא בא לידו כלום מודה דמצי לאוקמינהו במבוי: לימא דאמר כרבי יהודה ולא כרבנן. מפני שמרגיל התינוקות לבוא אצלו ומצי למימר ליה שאר בעלי חנויות קא פסקת לחיותי: שושקי. קשקים: ומרחץ. שהיו רגילין לשכור מרחץ כדי לרחוץ: אתה עושה בתוך שלך ואני עושה בתוך שלי. וקשיא לרב הונא: כופין בני מבוי זה את זה שלא להושיב ביניהן לא חייט. כלומר אומנין של מבוי אחר אינן רשאין להושיב במבוי זה שלא לדעת כולן ולשכינו שבמבוי שלו אינו כופהו שלא יזקק מן אומנותו משום דאמר ליה אתה עושה בתוך שלך ואני בתוך שלי: רשב״ג אומר אף לשכינו כופהו. ורב הונא ס״ל כרשב״ג: בר מתא אבר מתא אחריתי מצי מעכב שאם היה אומן א׳ בעיר ובא אומן אחר מעיר אחרת כאותו ורצה לקבוע באותה מדינה יכול לעכב על ידו ולומר קא פסקת לחיותא ואי שייך אכרגא להתם שפורעין מס גולגלות לאדון אחד דמי כמאן דהוה תרווייהו מאותה העיר ולא מצי מעכב ליה: דנפשיה. כלומר לשכינו לא מצי מעכב

מסורת הש״ס

א) [ע׳ תוס׳ גיטין סח. ד״ה וכתיב], ב) [ב״מ קט.], ג) שם ס., ד) [סס], ה) [גי׳ רב אלפס והרא״ש מבעלי], ו) [תוספתא פ״א], ז) [תפי׳ רש״י סד״ה ומודה רב הונא נראה דלא גרים לכל זה וכ״כ תוס׳ ג״כ להדיא בסמוך ד״ה קנאת סופרים], ח) [ל״ע המשנה]:

הגהות הב״ח

(א) גמ׳ זכר קרינן א״ל לדידי זכר אקריון: (ב) שם מפני שמרגילן לבוא אצלו: (ג) רש״י ד״ה שאני דגים וכו׳ להיות לרוץ וכו׳ ונתן מלודה ומזונות וכו׳ וה״ל כמאן: (ד) ד״ה שלא וכו׳ במבוי זה ויש כאן: (ה) ד״ה ואי שייך וכו׳ כבר מתא הוא ולא וכו׳ לא מצי מעכב מליה כל״ל ותיבות את המבוי נמחק: (ו) באד״ה מעכב עליה בן המבוי הזה או לא: (ז) תוס׳ ד״ה כופין וכו׳ מוקמינן ליה לעיל בתינוקות:

תורה אור השלם

א) וְהָיָה בְּהָנִיחַ יְיָ אֱלֹהֶיךָ לְךָ מִכָּל אֹיְבֶיךָ מִסָּבִיב בָּאָרֶץ אֲשֶׁר יְיָ אֱלֹהֶיךָ נֹתֵן לְךָ נַחֲלָה לְרִשְׁתָּהּ תִּמְחֶה אֶת זֵכֶר עֲמָלֵק מִתַּחַת הַשָּׁמָיִם לֹא תִּשְׁכָּח: [דברים כה, יט]

ב) אָרוּר עֹשֶׂה מְלֶאכֶת יְיָ רְמִיָּה וְאָרוּר מֹנֵעַ חַרְבּוֹ מִדָּם: [ירמיה מח, י]

ליקוטי רש״י

מקרי ינוקא. פסולא דלא הדר הוא דשבשתא כיון דעל על [ב״מ קט.]. ואומנא. מקיז דם [שם צז.]. מוהל תינוקות. כמותרין ועומדין נינהו. לסלקינהו [שבועות].

מאי טעמא עבדת הכי אמר ליה דכתיב א) תמחה את זכר עמלק אמר ליה והא אנן (א) זכר קרינן א״ל אנא זכר אקריון אזל שייליה לרביה אמר ליה היאך אקריתן אמר ליה זכר שקל ספסירא למיקטליה אמר ליה אמאי א״ל דכתיב ב) ארור עושה מלאכת ה׳ רמיה א״ל שבקיה לההוא גברא דליקום בארור א״ל כתיב ב) וארור מונע חרבו מדם איכא דאמרי קטליה ואיכא דאמרי לא קטליה ג) ואמר רבא מקרי ינוקא שתלא טבחא ואומנא וספר מתא כולן כמותרין ועומדין נינהו ג כללא דמילתא כל פסידא דלא הדר מותרה ועומד הוא אמר רב הונא האי בר מבואה דאוקי ריחיא ואתא בר מבואה חבריה וקמוקי גביה דינא הוא דמעכב עילויה דא״ל קא פסקת ליה לחיותי לימא מסייע ליה מרחיקים מצודת הדג מן הדג כמלא ריצת הדג וכמה אמר רבה בר רב הונא עד פרסה שאני דגים דיהבי סיירא א״ל רבינא לרבא לימא רב הונא דאמר כרבי יהודה ג) דתנן רבי יהודה אומר לא יחלק חנוני קליות ואגוזין לתינוקות מפני שמרגילן (ב) אצלו וחכמים ד) מתירין אפי׳ תימא רבנן עד כאן לא פליגי רבנן עליה דרבי יהודה התם אלא דאמר ליה ז) אנא קמפלגינא אמגוזי את פלוג שושקי אבל הכא אפילו רבנן מודו דא״ל קא פסקת ליה לחיותי מיתיבי עושה אדם חנות בצד חנותו של חבירו ומרחץ בצד מרחצו של חבירו ואינו יכול למחות בידו מפני שיכול לומר לו אתה עושה בתוך שלך ואני עושה בתוך שלי תנאי היא דתניא ה) כופין בני מבואות זה את זה שלא להושיב ביניהן לא חייט ולא בורסקי ולא מלמד תינוקות ולא אחד ה) מבני בעלי אומניות ו) ולשכנו אינו כופיהו רשב״ג אומר אף לשכנו כופיהו אמר רב הונא בריה דרב יהושע ז) פשיטא לי בר מתא אבר מתא אחריתי מצי מעכב ח) ואי שייך בכרגא דהכא לא מצי מעכב בר מבואה אבר מבואה דנפשיה לא מצי מעכב ט) בעי רב הונא בריה דרב יהושע בר מבואה אבר מבואה אחרינא מאי תיקו אמר רב יוסף י) ומודי רב הונא במקרי דרדקי דלא מצי מעכב דאמר מר ז) כ) (עזרא תיקן להן לישראל שיהו מושיבין סופר בצד סופר וניחוש דילמא אתי לאיתרשולי א״ל) קנאת

סופר מתא. לא כמו שפירש בקונטרס כותב ספר תורה בטעות דאין זה פסידא דלא הדר דיכולין להגיהו אלא כדפרישית לעיל כותב שטרות: **ומקרי** דרדקי. פי׳ בקונטרס דהמקבל ר״ל דהוי פסידא דלא הדרא משום דשבשתא כיון דעל על (ב״מ דף קט. ושם) וקשה לר״י דהא רבה גופיה לית ליה לעיל דשבשתא ממילא נפקא ואומר ר״י דהוי פסידא דלא הדר דלאותה שעה שמלמד להם טעות הם מתבטלים ואותה שעה אין יכולין להחזיר לעולם: **שתלא**. ה״נ מאי פסידא איכא לי יפסיד ישלם וי״ל דאינו מפסיד אלא שפושע שאין הנטיעה גדילות כמו שהיו ראויות ליגדל: **מרחיקין** מצודת הדג כו׳. אע״ג דר״ת מפרש דבדבר של הפקר אפי׳ רשע לא מיקרי כדתנן (פאה פ״ד מ״ג) גבי פאה פירס טליתו עליה מעבירין אותו ממנה וכן תנן בפ״ק דב״מ (דף י.) ראה את המציאה ונפל עליה ובא אחר והחזיק בה זה שהחזיק בה זכה ולא מיקרי רשע אלא בעני המהפך בחררה ובא אחר ונטלה משום שאם לא ישתכר במקום זה ימצא להשתכר במקום אחר והכא דמשמעתא לא קשיא דלא אע״ג דהוי דבר של הפקר מ״מ בכמה מקומות ימצא שיוכל לפרוס מצודתו ועוד דהכא אומנותו בכך והא דאמרינן בפרק חזקת הבתים (לקמן דף נד:) נכסי כנענים הרי הן כמדבר כל המחזיק בהן זכה בהן מאי טעמא כנעני מכי מטא זוזי לידיה איסתלק ליה וישראל לא קני עד דמטי שטרא לידיה ופי׳ רשב״ם התם דישראל המחזיק רשע מיהא מיקרי ולפי׳ ר״ת אפי׳ רשע לא הוי כיון שלא ימצא במקום אחר וקשה לרשב״א מהא דאמר באיזהו נשך (ב״מ דף עג:) רב מרי בר רחל משכן ליה הוא נכרי ביתא אזל רבא וזבניה נטר תריסר ירחי שתא שקל אגר ביתא אמטייה לרבא א״ל האי דלא מטלי לה למר אגר ביתא עד השתא דאמר מר קאי משכנתא שתא ולא מצי נכרי לסלוקי והשתא כיון שקדמה חזקת רב מרי לחזקת רבא א״כ זכה בה רב מרי דנכסי הכנעני הרי הן כמדבר ואי מקרי רשע אתי שפיר דלא היה רוצה לזכות בה אבל לפירוש ר״ת דאפילו רשע לא מיקרי אמאי לא זכה בה רב מרי כיון דהיתר גמור הוא ושמא לפנים משורת הדין עבד ולריב״א נראה דחזקת רב מרי לא היתה אלא בתורת משכון ורבא קנה ממנו בשטר וזכה בה ואחר כך נתן מעות (וע״ע תוספות קדושין נט. ד״ה עני המהפך וכו׳ ותוס׳ ב״מ עג: סוף ד״ה נטר):

מאי טעמא עבדת הכי. שלא הרגת את הנקיבות: את זכר עמלק: ארור מונע חרבו. סיפיה דהאי קרא הוא: שתלא. נוטע כרמו למחצה: אומנא. מקיז דם: ספר מתא. לבלר: כמותרין ועומדין דמו. שלא יקלקלו ואם קלקלו מסלק להו בלא התראה אע״פ שלא התרו בו קודם לכן: פסידא דלא הדר. כגון אלו שמשתנתבלה הבהמה או הרג המקיז והסופר כתב ספר תורה בטעות: דאוקי ריחיא. לטחון ולשכור: מרחיקין מצודת הדג מן הדג. לייד שנתן עיניו בדג עד שהכיר מורו מרחיקין שאר ציידין מלודתם משם מלמא אע״ג דלא זכה ביה ולא מטא לידיה מרחיקין משם דה״ל קא פסקת לחיותי: שאני דגים דיהבי סיירא. נותנין עין בהבטם להיות (ג) נוהגים לרוץ למקום שראו שם מזונות הילכך כיון שהכיר זה מורו ונתן מזונות בתוך מלא רילתו בטוח הוא שילכדנו וה״ל כמאן דמטא לידיה ונמלא חבירו מזיקו אבל הכא מי שבא אללי יבא ומי שבא אלך יבא: שמרגילם. לבא אללו כשמתווים שולחין אותן אל החנויות לקנות מן החנוונים: שושקי. שקדים: אבל הכא. שזה העמיד תחילה והרגיל להשתכר בכך וזה בא לירד אללו לאומנותו אומר לו פוסקת לחיותי: שלא להושיב ביניהן חייט ובורסקי. ממקום אחר להשכיר לו בית במבוי (ד) ויש כאן בני אותה אומנות: ולשכינו. הדר במבוי כמוהו: אינו כופהו. מלירד לאותו אומנות: רשב״ג אומר כו׳. ורב הונא הוא דאמר כרשב״ג: מצי לעכב. מלעשות כאן אומנותם ולהביא כאן למכור ואפילו לרבנן דאמרי לשכינו אינו כופהו: ואי שייך בכרגא דהכא. שנותן מס גולגלתו למושל העיר הזאת כבר מתא (ה) לא מלי בר מתא לעכב עליו כל העיר ופשיטא לי דבר מבוי אבר מבוי דנפשיה לא מלי מעכב את המבוי מלירד לאומנותו כרבנן ולא כרב הונא מיהו איבעיא לי בר מבואה אבר מבואה אחרינא מאי מי מלי מעכב (ו) בן המבוי הזה או לא מי הוי שכינו ואינו כופיהו או דילמא שכינו דאמור רבנן בבר מבואה דההוא מבוי קאמרי אבל בר מבואה אחרינא לאו שכינו הוא: ומודה רב הונא. דאמר לעיל בר מבואה דאוקי ריחיא כו׳ דאית ליה כרשב״ג מודי הוא במקרי דרדקי דלא מלי מעכב לבר מבואה מללמד גם הוא התינוקות שמתוך כך יזהרו באומנותן שייראו זה מזה דאמר מר קנאת סופרים תרבה חכמה:

תנאי היא דתניא כו׳. תימה לרשב״א דאמאי לא מייתי ח) (הברייתא) דלעיל דממה נפשך רבי יהודה דאמר לא יחלק חנוני קליות ואגוזים לתינוקות פליג אהך ברייתא ושמא ניחא לאתויי תנאי דפליגי בהדיא בהכי: **כופין** בני מבוי זה את זה כו׳ ולא מלמד תינוקות. נראה לר״י דבמלמד תינוקות נכרים איירי ולא יתכן אי גרס לעיל אחד מבני מבוי דהא מוקמינן ליה (ז) בתינוקות נכרים ומעכבין עליו בני מבוי והכא קאמר דלשכינו אינו כופהו ואפילו רשב״ג לא פליג אלא משום דפסיק לחיותיה אבל משום קול תינוקות לא חיים ומיהו לפי מה שפירשתי [לעיל] דגרסינן אחד מבני חצר אתי שפיר ולר׳ שמעון בן אברהם נראה דהכא בתינוקות ישראל ואפילו אחר תקנת יהושע בן גמלא ושאני הכא דכבר יש שם מלמד תינוקות אחר ובסמוך דקאמר דמודה רב הונא במקרי דרדקי דלא מצי מעכב ואף על גב דלהיו סבר כרבן שמעון בן גמליאל צריך לומר דרבן שמעון בן גמליאל לא פליג אמלמד תינוקות אלא אשארא:

פשיטא לי דבר מתא אבר מתא [אחריתי מצין] מעכב. רב הונא בריה דרב יהושע כרבנן ס״ל ומיבעי ליה בר מבואה אבר מבואה דעלמא אי מצי מעכב אי הוי בכלל שכינו אי לאו כדפירש הקונטרס וכוותיה קיימא לן לגבי רב הונא דבתרא הוא: **ואי** שייך בכרגא דהכא לא מצי מעכב. פירוש בני העיר אבל בני מבוי מצי מעכבי שלא יכנס במבואם:

א״ל ה״נ מאי אמרי הואיל דממתא חדא תרוייהו מאי. מי אמרי הואיל דממתא חדא תרוייהו אע״ג דלא שייך כרגייהו בחדא לא מצי מעכב ליה. או דלמא כיון דלמבוי דידיה הוא לשכינו לא מצי מעכב ורב הונא בריה דר״י לא ס״ל הא דרב הונא דלעיל. ג) לא צריכא דלא שייך מאי. מי אמרי הואיל דממתא חדא תרוייהו אע״ג דלא שייך כרגייהו בחדא לא מצי מעכב ליה. או דלמא כיון דלמבוי דידיה הוא מצי מעכב דלא ליקבע במבוי דידיה תיקו:

חשק שלמה על רבינו גרשום א) נראה דל״ל בר מבואה דאוקי ריחיא ואתא בר מבואה חבריה מההוא מבוי ולא היה כו׳: ב) [מד׳ רבינו ז״ל אלו נראה שהיה גורס בכאן אבל בגמרא דהכא לא אמרת לי מאי לעכב לא לריכא דלא שייך מאי עד כאן וכ״ע מדברי הרמב״ם ז״ל בפ״ו מהל׳ שכנים שגרס כן ע״ש]:

Therefore, if a fisherman sets a trap with food in it near the lair of a fish, the fish is viewed as if it is already in his hands. If another fisherman would then take the fish, that would be tantamount to taking it directly from the first fisherman.[12]

Ravina suggests that Rav Huna's ruling corresponds to a minority Tannaic view:

לֵימָא רַב הוּנָא – אֲמַר לֵיהּ רָבִינָא לְרָבָא – **Ravina said to Rava:** דְּאָמַר כְּרַבִּי יְהוּדָה – Are we **to say that Rav Huna follows** the view of **R' Yehudah** in a dispute between R' Yehudah and the Sages? דִּתְנַן – **For we learned in a Mishnah:**[13] רַבִּי יְהוּדָה אוֹמֵר – **R' YEHUDAH SAYS:** לֹא יְחַלֵּק חֶנְוָנִי קְלָיוֹת וֶאֱגוֹזִין לְתִינוֹקוֹת – **A STOREKEEPER MAY NOT DISTRIBUTE PARCHED KERNELS**[14] **OR WALNUTS TO CHILDREN,** מִפְּנֵי שֶׁמַּרְגִּילָן אֶצְלוֹ – **FOR,** by doing so, **HE** accustoms **THEM** to come **TO HIM,**[15] and thereby deprives other storekeepers of the children's patronage. וַחֲכָמִים מַתִּירִין – **BUT THE SAGES PERMIT** this practice.

It would seem that Rav Huna, who does not allow one merchant to take the customers of another, follows the view of R' Yehudah.[16]

The Gemara replies that this is not necessarily so:

אֲפִילּוּ תֵּימָא רַבָּנָן – **You can say** that Rav Huna's ruling corresponds **even** to that of **the Sages.** עַד כָּאן לֹא פְּלִיגִי רַבָּנָן עֲלֵיהּ דְּרַבִּי יְהוּדָה הָתָם – **As far** as we know, **the Sages do not disagree with R' Yehudah there** אֶלָּא דְּאָמַר לֵיהּ – **except because** they reason that **he** [the storekeeper distributing sweets] **can say to [the other storekeeper],** אֲנָא קָמְפַלְּגִינָא אַמְגוֹזֵי – **"I am giving out walnuts,** אַתְּ פְּלוֹג שִׁיוּסְקֵי – **you give out almonds!"** That is to say, since both stores are already established, each is permitted to engage in activities that attract customers from the rival store.[17] אֲבָל הָכָא אֲפִילּוּ רַבָּנָן מוֹדוּ – **But here** [Rav Huna's case], where a merchant had already established a business in a courtyard and a rival came later, **even the Sages** possibly **concede** דְּאָמַר לֵיהּ – **that [the first merchant] can say to [the newcomer],** קָא פָּסְקַתְּ לֵיהּ לְחַיּוּתִי – **"You are cutting off my livelihood,"** and stop him from using the courtyard.

Rav Huna's ruling is challenged:

מֵיתִיבֵי – **They challenged [Rav Huna's ruling]** from the following Baraisa: עוֹשֶׂה אָדָם חֲנוּת בְּצַד חֲנוּתוֹ שֶׁל חֲבֵירוֹ – **A PERSON MAY OPEN A** rival **STORE NEXT TO THE STORE OF HIS FELLOW,** וּמֶרְחָץ בְּצַד מֶרְחָצוֹ שֶׁל חֲבֵירוֹ – **OR A** rival **BATHHOUSE NEXT TO THE BATHHOUSE OF HIS FELLOW,** וְאֵינוֹ יָכוֹל לִמְחוֹת בְּיָדוֹ – **AND [THE ESTABLISHED OPERATOR] CANNOT PREVENT HIM** from doing so, מִפְּנֵי שֶׁיָּכוֹל לוֹמַר לוֹ – **BECAUSE [THE RIVAL] CAN SAY TO [THE ESTABLISHED OPERATOR],** אַתָּה עוֹשֶׂה בְּתוֹךְ שֶׁלְּךָ – **"YOU DO** as you wish **INSIDE YOUR PROPERTY,** וַאֲנִי עוֹשֶׂה בְּתוֹךְ שֶׁלִּי – **AND I DO** as I wish **INSIDE MY [PROPERTY]!"** This Baraisa states clearly that, contrary to Rav Huna's view, an established merchant cannot prevent the opening of a rival store. – ? –

The Gemara responds that Rav Huna's ruling is not refuted by this Baraisa because there is an alternative Tannaic view that does take his position:

תַּנָּאֵי הִיא – **[Rav Huna's ruling] is a matter of dispute between Tannaim,** דְּתַנְיָא – **as it was taught in a** different **Baraisa:** כּוֹפִין בְּנֵי מְבוֹאוֹת זֶה אֶת זֶה – **RESIDENTS OF *MAVOIS* CAN COMPEL ONE ANOTHER** שֶׁלֹּא לְהוֹשִׁיב בֵּינֵיהֶן לֹא חַיָּיט וְלֹא בּוּרְסְקִי וְלֹא מְלַמֵּד תִּינוֹקוֹת וְלֹא אֶחָד מִבְּנֵי בַּעֲלֵי אוּמָנִיּוֹת – **NOT TO ALLOW THE RESIDENCE AMONG THEM OF A TAILOR, TANNER, TEACHER,**[18] **OR ANY OTHER TYPE OF CRAFTSMAN.** I.e. someone who has established a business in a *mavoi* can prevent the other *mavoi* residents from renting their property to someone from elsewhere who wishes to ply the same trade. וְלִשְׁכֵנוֹ אֵינוֹ כּוֹפֵיהוּ – **BUT HE CANNOT FORCE HIS NEIGHBOR**[19] to refrain from opening a competing business in the *mavoi.* רַבָּן שִׁמְעוֹן בֶּן גַּמְלִיאֵל אוֹמֵר – **RABBAN SHIMON BEN GAMLIEL SAYS:** אַף לִשְׁכֵנוֹ כּוֹפֵיהוּ – **HE CAN FORCE EVEN HIS NEIGHBOR**[20] to refrain from opening a competing business in the *mavoi.*

The Tanna Kamma differentiates between an outsider and a neighbor: one can block local competition if it is from an outsider, but not if it is from a neighbor. Rabban Shimon ben Gamliel, however, holds that even the rival business of a neighbor can be blocked. Rav Huna, who said that a *mavoi* resident can block the business of a member of his own *mavoi,* follows the view of Rabban Shimon ben Gamliel.

The Gemara defines the view of the Tanna Kamma:

אָמַר רַב הוּנָא בְּרֵיהּ דְּרַב יְהוֹשֻׁעַ – **Rav Huna son of Rav Yehoshua said:** פְּשִׁיטָא לִי – **It is obvious to me** בַּר מָתָא אַבַּר מָתָא אַחֲרִיתִי מָצֵי מְעַכֵּב – that **a resident of** one **town** who plies a certain trade **can prevent a resident of another town** from plying that trade anywhere in his town, even according to the Tanna Kamma.[21] וְאִי שַׁיָּיךְ בִּכְרָגָא דְּהָכָא – **But if he** [the tradesman from elsewhere] **pays the poll-tax of this town,**[22] he is viewed as one of its residents, לֹא מָצֵי מְעַכֵּב – and **one cannot prevent him** from plying his trade in the town.

Having discussed the Tanna Kamma's view with regard to banning an outsider from the town as a whole, Rav Huna son of Rav Yehoshua discusses the Tanna Kamma's view as it applies to a *mavoi*:

בַּר מְבוֹאָה אַבַּר מְבוֹאָה דְּנַפְשֵׁיהּ לֹא מָצֵי מְעַכֵּב – **A resident of a *mavoi* cannot prevent** another **resident of his own *mavoi*** from

NOTES

12. [With regard to a business, however, even a customer who frequents it cannot be said to have provided patronage on any particular occasion until he commits himself to do so. Therefore,] a newcoming rival can say to the established merchant: "Whoever wants to go to you will go to you, and whoever wants to come to me will come to me" (*Rashi;* cf *Ri MiGash*).

13. *Bava Metzia* 60a.

14. Kernels of wheat sweetened with honey and roasted. This was a popular children's treat.

15. When a child is sent to make purchases, he will go to that store (*Rashi*).

16. The implied difficulty is that Rav Huna follows the minority view [R' Yehudah], rather than the majority view [the Sages], which is generally adopted as halachah.

17. *Ritva;* see *Rashi* ד"ה אבל.

18. We learned above (21a) that a teacher of [Torah to] Jewish children cannot be barred from a courtyard on the grounds that the courtyard residents are disturbed by the noise. Likewise, a teacher of [Torah to] Jewish children cannot be barred from a *mavoi* on the grounds that he is depriving a teacher, who is already established there, of his livelihood. Therefore, this Baraisa, which rules that a teacher *can* be barred from a *mavoi*, must refer to a teacher of idolaters' children [or a teacher of secular subjects] (*Ri,* cited by *Tosafos;* see *Tosafos* for a dissenting view).

19. [It is unclear what the term "neighbor" means in this context. It certainly includes a member of the same *mavoi*. But it is questionable whether it also includes a member of the same town who lives in a different *mavoi* — see Gemara below and note 23.]

20. I.e. even a member of the same *mavoi.*

21. That is, he can ban the outsider not only from his *mavoi*, but also from the other *mavois* and streets in the town. This is true even according to the Tanna Kamma, for the Tanna Kamma concedes that competition from *elsewhere* can be blocked (see the beginning of the Baraisa).

22. Literally: he is involved with the tax of here.

סופר מתא. לא כמו שפירש בקונטרס כותב ספר תורה בטעות דאין זה פסידא דלא הדר דיכולין להגיהו אלא כדפירשית לעיל כותב שטרות: **ומקרי** דרדקי. פי' בקונטרס בהמקבל (ב"מ דף קט. ושם) דהוי פסידא דלא הדרא משום דשבשתא כיון דעל על וקשה לר"י דהא רבא גופיה אית ליה לעיל דשבשתא ממילא נפקא ואומר ר"י דהוה פסידא דלא הדר דאותה שעה שמלמד להם טעות הם מתבטלים ואותה שעה אין יכולין להחזיר לעולם: **שתלא.** וא"ת מאי פסידא איכא אי יפסיד ישלם וי"ל דאינו מפסיד אלא שפושע שאין הנטיעות גדילות כמו שהיו ראויות ליגדל: **מרחיקין** מצודת הדג כו'. אע"ג דר"ת מפרש דבדבר של הפקר אפי' רשע לא מיקרי כדתנן (פאה פ"ד מ"ג) גבי פאה פירס טליתו עליה מעבירין אותו ממנה וכן תנן בפ"ק דב"מ (דף י.) ראה את המציאה ונפל עליה ובא אחר והחזיק בה זה שהחזיק בה זכה ולא מיקרי רשע אלא בעני המהפך בחררה ובא אחר ונטלה משום שאם לא ישתכר במקום זה ימצא להשתכר במקום אחר והכן דשמעתא לא קשיא דאע"ג דהוי דבר של הפקר מ"מ בכמה מקומות ימצא שיוכל לפרוס מצודתו ועוד דהכא אומנותו בכך והא דאמרינן בפרק חזקת הבתים (לקמן דף נד:) נכסי כנעניים הרי הן כמדבר כל המחזיק בהן זכה בהן מאי טעמא כנעני מכי מטא זוזי לידיה איסתלק ליה וישראל לא קני עד דמטי שטרא לידיה ופי' רשב"ם התם דישראל המחזיק רשע מיהא מיקרי ולפי' ר"ת אפי' רשע לא הוי כיון שלא ימצא במקום אחר וקשה לרשב"א מהא דאמר באיזהו נשך (ב"מ דף עג:) רב מרי בר רחל משכן ליה ההוא נכרי ביתא אזל רבא וזבניה נטר תריסר ירחי שתא שקל אגר ביתא אמטייה לרבא א"ל האי דלא מטאי לה למר אגר ביתא עד השתא דאמר מר סתם משכנתא שתא ולא מצי נכרי לסלוקי והשתא כיון שקדמה חזקת רב מרי לחזקת רבא א"כ זכה בה רב מרי דנכסי הכנעני הרי הן כמדבר ואי מקרי רשע אתי שפיר דלא היה רוצה לזכות בה אבל לפירוש ר"ת דאפילו רשע לא מיקרי אמאי לא זכה בה רב מרי כיון דהיתר גמור הוא ושמא לפנים משורת הדין עבד ולריב"א נראה דחזקת רב מרי לא היתה אלא בתורת משכון ורבא קנה ממנו בשטר וזכה בה ואחר כך נתן מעות [וע"ע תוספות קדושין נט. ד"ה עני המהפך וכו' ותוס' ב"מ עג: סוף ד"ה נטר]:

מאי טעמא עבדת הכי אמר ליה דכתיב (א) תמחה את זכר עמלק אמר ליה והא אנן (א) זכר קרינן א"ל אנא זכר אקרון אזל שייליה לרביה אמר ליה היאך אקריתן אמר ליה זכר שקל ספסירא למיקטליה א"ל אמאי א"ל [א] דכתיב (ב) ארור עושה מלאכת ה' רמיה א"ל [א] שבקיה לההוא גברא דליקום בארור א"ל כתיב (ב) וארור מונע חרבו מדם איכא דאמרי קטליה ואיכא דאמרי לא קטליה [ג] ואמר רבא [ב] מקרי ינוקא שתלא טבחא ואומנא וספר מתא כולן כמותרין ועומדין נינהו [ג] כללא דמילתא כל פסידא דלא הדר מותרה ועומד הוא אמר רב הונא האי בר מבואה דאוקי ריחיא ואתא בר מבואה חבריה וקמוקי גביה דינא הוא דמעכב עילויה דא"ל קא פסקת ליה לחיותי לימא מסייע ליה מרחיקים מצודת הדג מן הדג כמלא ריצת הדג וכמה אמר רבה בר רב הונא עד פרסה שאני דגים דיהבי סייארא א"ל רבינא לרבא לימא רב הונא דאמר כרבי יהודה [ג] דתנן רבי יהודה אומר לא יחלק חנוני קליות ואגוזין לתינוקות מפני שמרגילן (ג) אצלו וחכמים [ד] מתירין אפי' תימא רבנן עד כאן לא פליגי רבנן עליה דרבי יהודה התם אלא דאמר ליה [ד] אנא קמפלגינא אמגוזי את פלוג שיוסקי אבל הכא אפילו רבנן מודו דא"ל קא פסקת ליה לחיותי מיתיבי עושה אדם חנות בצד חנותו של חבירו ומרחץ בצד מרחצו של חבירו ואינו יכול למחות בידו מפני שיכול לומר לו אתה עושה בתוך שלך ואני עושה בתוך שלי תנאי היא דתניא [ה] כופין בני מבואות זה את זה שלא להושיב ביניהן לא חייט ולא בורסקי ולא מלמד תינוקות ולא אחד [ו] מבני בעלי אומניות [ז] ולשכנו אינו כופיהו רשב"ג אומר אף לשכנו כופיהו אמר רב הונא בריה דרב יהושע [ז] פשיטא לי בר מתא אבר מתא אחריתי מצי מעכב [ח] ואי שייך בכרגא דהכא לא מצי מעכב בר מבואה אבר מבואה דנפשיה לא מצי מעכב [ט] בעי רב הונא בריה דרב יהושע בר מבואה אבר מבואה אחרינא מאי תיקו אמר רב יוסף [י] ומודי רב הונא במקרי דרדקי דלא מצי מעכב דאמר מר [כ] (עזרא) תיקן להן לישראל שיהו מושיבין סופר בצד סופר וניחוש דילמא אתי לאיתרשולי א"ל קנאת

מאי טעמא עבדת הכי. שלא הרגת את הנקיבות: את זכר עמלק. ארור מונע חרבו. סיפיה דהאי קרא הוא: שתלא. נוטע כרמו למחצה: אומנא. מקיז דם: סופר מתא. לבלר: כמותרין ועומדין דמו. שלא יקלקלו ואם קלקלו מסלק להו בלא אתרייתא אע"פ שלא התרו בו קודם לכן: פסידא דלא הדר. כגון אלו שמשתנקלה הבהמה או הרג המקיז והסופר כתב ספר תורה בטעות: דאוקי ריחיא. לטחון ולשכור: מרחיקין מצודת הדג מן הדג. צייד שנתן עיניו בדג עד שהכיר חורו מרחיקין שאר ציידין מלהצודו משם אלמא אע"ג דלא זכה ביה ולא מטא לידיה מרחיקין משם דא"ל קא פסקת לחיותי: שאני דגים דיהבי סיירא. נותנין עין בהבטט להיות (ג) ונוהגים לרוץ למקום שראו שם מזונות הילכך כיון שהכיר זה חורו ונתן מזונות בתוך מלא רילתו בטוח הוא שילכדו דהוה"ל כמאן דמטא לידיה ונמצא חבירו מזיקו אבל הכא כל מי שבא אצלי יבא ומי שבא אצלך יבא: שמרגילם. לבא אצלו כשלוחיהם שולחין אותם אל החנויות לקנות מן החנוונים: שיוסקי. שקדים: אבל הכא. שזה העמיד תחילה והרגיל להשתכר בכך וזה בא לירד אצלו לאומנותו אומר לו פוסקת לחיותי: שלא להושיב ביניהן חייט ובורסקי. ממקום אחר להשכיר לו בית במבוי (ד) ויש כאן בני אותה אומנות: ולשכנו. הדר במבוי כמוהו: אינו כופהו. מלירד לאותו אומנות: רשב"ג אומר כו'. ורב הונא הוא דאמר כרשב"ג: מצי לעכב. מלעשות כאן אומנותו ולהביא כאן למכור ואפילו לרבנן דאמרי לשכינו אינו כופהו: ואי שייך בכרגא דהכא. שנותן מס גולגלתו למושל העיר הזאת כבר מתא (ה) לא מצי בר מתא לעכב עליו כל העיר ופשיטא לי דבר מבוי אבר מבוי דנפשיה לא מצי מעכב את המבוי מלירד לאומנותו כרבנן ולא כרב הונא מיהו איבעיא לי בר מבואה אבר מבואה אחרינא מאי מי מצי מעכב (ו) בן המבוי הזה או לא מי הוי שכינו ואינו כופיהו או דילמא שכינו לאמור רבנן בבר מבואה דההוא מבוי קאמרי אבל בר מבואה אחרינא לאו שכינו הוא: ומודה רב הונא. דאמר לעיל בר מבואה דאוקי ריחייא כו' דאית ליה כרשב"ג מודי הוא במקרי דרדקי דלא מצי מעכב לבר מבואה מללמד גם הוא התינוקות שמתוך כך יזהרו באומנותן שייראו זה מזה דאמר מר קנאת סופרים תרבה חכמה: ומודה

תנאי היא דתניא כו'. תימה לרשב"א דאמאי לא מייתי (ח) (הברייתא) דלעיל דממה נפשך רבי יהודה דאמר לא יחלק חנוני קליות ואגוזים לתינוקות פליג אהך ברייתא ושמא ניחא לאתויי תנאי דפליגי בהדיא בהכי: **כופין** בני מבוי זה את זה כו' ולא מלמד תינוקות. נראה לר"י דבמלמד תינוקות נכרים איירי ולא יתכן אי גרס לעיל אחד מבני מבוי דהא מוקמינן ליה (ז) בתינוקות נכרים ומעכבין עליו בני מבוי והכא קאמר דלשכינו אינו כופהו ואפילו רשב"ג לא פליג אלא משום דפסיק לחיותיה אבל משום קול תינוקות לא חייש ומיהו לפי מה שפירשתי [לעיל] דגרסינן אחד מבני חצר אתי שפיר ולר' שמשון בן אברהם נראה דהכא בתינוקות ישראל ואפילו אחר תקנת יהושע בן גמלא ואשמי הכא לדבר יש שם מלמד תינוקות אחר ובסמוך דקאמר דמודה רב הונא במקרי דרדקי דלא מצי מעכב ואף על גב דלאיהו סבר כרבנן שמעון בן גמליאל צריך לומר דרבנן שמעון בן גמליאל לא פליג אלא במלמד תינוקות אלא אשמרא:

פשיטא לי דבר מתא אבר מתא [אחריתי מצי] מעכב. רב הונא בריה דרב יהושע כרבנן ס"ל ומיבעי ליה בר מבואה אבר מבואה דעלמא אי מצי מעכב אי הוי בכלל שכינו אי לאו כדפירש הקונטרס וכוותיה קיימא לן לגבי רב הונא דבתראה הוא: **ואי** שייך בכרגא דהכא לא מצי מעכב. פירוש בני העיר אבל בני מבוי מצי מעכבי שלא יכנס במבואם:

עין משפט נר מצוה

מג א מיי' פ"ב מהל' ת"ת הל' ו סמג שם טוש"ע י"ד סי' רמה סעיף יז:
מד ב ג מיי' פ"י מהל' שכירות הל' ז וע"ש בהשגות ובמ"מ סמג עשין פט טוש"ע ח"מ סי' שו סעיף ח:
מה ד מיי' פ"ה מהל' גזילה הלכה ד סמג לאוין קנ טוש"ע ח"מ סי' רכח:
מו ה ו ז ח ט מיי' פ"ו מהל' שכנים הל' ח סמג עשין פב טוש"ע ח"מ סי' קנו סעיף ה וע"ש בהג"ה:
מז י כ מיי' פ"ב מהל' ת"ת הל' ז סמג שם טוש"ע י"ד סי' רמה סעיף כב:

רבינו גרשום

מאי טעמא עבדת הכי דמשיירת נשים: האי בר מבואה (א) מההוא מבוי (בני אדם) ולא היה רגיל לכך וקא מוקים ריחים שלו סמוך לריחים של חבירו: דינא הוא כו'. מרחיקין מצודת הדג מן הדג שאם היה רגיל אחד לפרוש מצודתו בשבר שתיקן במים ובא חבירו ורצה לעשות מצודתו כמו כן מרחיקין אותה מן מצודת חבירו כמלוא ריצת הדג דמצי למימר ליה קא פסקת חיותאי ותסייע לרב הונא. מהא לא תסייע ליה דשאני דגים דיהבי סיירא דמשום הכי מרחיקין מפני כי מסיר לו דבר שבא כבר במצודתו במאכל שמשים במצודתו לפי שכשמעיינין ורואין מאכל במקום אחר בורחין ממצודתו של זה ההולכין לשם וגזלו בידים דבר שכבר [בא] במצודתו אבל ברחוק פרסה אינו יכול להביט המאכל. אבל גבי ריחים דליכא למימר הכי דבר הבא לידי הסיר ממני שעדיין לא בא לידו כלום מודה דמצי לאוקמינהו במבוי: לימא דאמר כר' יהודה ולא כרבנן. מפני שמרגיל התינוקות לבוא אצלו ומצי למימר ליה שאר בעלי חנויות קא פסקת לחיותי: שיוסקי. שקדים: ומרחץ. שהיו רגילין לשכור מרחץ כדי לרחוץ: אתה עושה בתוך שלך ואני עושה בתוך שלי. וקשיא לרב הונא: כופין בני מבוי זה את זה שלא להושיב ביניהן לא חייט. כלומר אומנין של מבוי אחר אינן רשאין להושיב במבוי זה שלא לדעת כולן ולשכינו שבמבוי שלו אינו כופהו שלא יזקק מן אומנותו משום דאמר ליה אתה עושה בתוך שלך ואני בתוך שלי: רשב"ג אומר אף לשכינו כופהו. ורב הונא ס"ל כרשב"ג: בר מתא אבר מתא אחריתי מצי מעכב שאם היה אומן א' בעיר ובא אומן אחר מעיר אחרת כאותו ורצה לקבוע באותה מדינה יכול לעכב על ידו ולומר קא פסקת לחיותא: ואי שייך אכרגא להתם שפורעין מס גולגלותם לאדון אחד דמי כמאן דהוה תרוייהו מאותה העיר ולא מצי מעכב ליה: דנפשיה. כלומר לשכינו לא מצי מעכב ורב הונא בריה דר"י לא ס"ל הא דרב הונא דלעיל. ב) לא צריכא דלא שייך מאי. מי אמרי' הואיל דממתא חדא תרווייהו אע"ג דלא שייך כרגייהו בחדא לא מצי מעכב ליה. או דלמא כיון דלמבוי דידיה הוא מצי מעכב דלא ליקבע במבוי דידיה תיקו:

חשק שלמה על רבינו גרשום א) נראה דל"ל בר מבואה דאוקי ריחיא ואתא בר מבואה חבריה מההוא מבוי וכו'. ב) [מד' רבינו ז"ל אלו נראה שהיה גורס כאן (כו') דהכא לא אמרת לא מצי לעכב רק בבר מבואה אחרינא ולא אמרו לא צריכא שייך מאי עד כאן וכ"ע מדברי הרמב"ם ז"ל בפ"ו מהל' שכנים שגרס כן ע"ש].

מסורת הש"ס

א) [עי' תוס' גיטין סח. ד"ה וכתיב], ב) [ב"מ קט.], ג) שם פ', ד) [שם], ה) [גי' רב אלפס והרא"ש מבעלי], ו) [תוספתא פ"א], ז) [תפי' רש"י סד"ה ומודה רב הונא נראה דלא גריס לכל זה וכ"כ תוס' ג"כ להדיא בסמוך ד"ה קנאת סופרים], ח) [נ"ל המשנה]:

הגהות הב"ח

(א) גמ' זכר קרינן א"ל לדידי זכר אקריון: (ב) שם מפני שמרגילן לבוא אצלו: (ג) רש"י ד"ה שאני דגים וכו' להיות רגילין לרוץ וכו' ונתן מלודה ומזונות וכו' וה"ל כמאן: (ד) ד"ה שלא וכו' במבוי זה ויש כאן: (ה) ד"ה ואי שייך וכו' כבר מתא הוא ולא וכו' לא מצי מעכב מלירד ומיבות את המבוי נמחק: (ו) באד"ה מצי מעכב עליו בן המבוי הזה או לא: (ז) תוס' ד"ה כופין וכו' מוקמינן ליה לעיל בתינוקות:

תורה אור השלם

א) וְהָיָה בְּהָנִיחַ יְיָ אֱלֹהֶיךָ לְךָ מִכָּל אֹיְבֶיךָ מִסָּבִיב בָּאָרֶץ אֲשֶׁר יְיָ אֱלֹהֶיךָ נֹתֵן לְךָ נַחֲלָה לְרִשְׁתָּהּ תִּמְחֶה אֶת זֵכֶר עֲמָלֵק מִתַּחַת הַשָּׁמָיִם לֹא תִּשְׁכָּח: [דברים כה, יט]

ב) אָרוּר עֹשֶׂה מְלֶאכֶת יְיָ רְמִיָּה וְאָרוּר מֹנֵעַ חַרְבּוֹ מִדָּם: [ירמיה מח, י]

ליקוטי רש"י

מקרי ינוקא. פסידא דלא הדר הוא דשבשתא כיון על על [ב"מ קט.]. ואומנא. מקיז דם [שם צז.]. מוהל תינוקות. כמותרין ועומדין נינהו. לסלקינהו [שבת קכט.].

opening a competing business. This is in accordance with the Tanna Kamma's statement that one's "neighbor" cannot be prevented from competing.

Rav Huna son of Rav Yehoshua concludes his analysis of the Tanna Kamma's view with the following inquiry:

בָּעֵי רַב הוּנָא בְּרֵיהּ דְּרַב יְהוֹשֻׁעַ – **Rav Huna son of Rav Yehoshua asked:** בַּר מְבוֹאָה אַבַּר מְבוֹאָה אַחֲרִינָא מַאי – But **what** is the law, according to the Tanna Kamma, regarding **the resident of a *mavoi*** who wishes to prevent **the resident of another *mavoi*** in the same town from entering his *mavoi* and setting up a rival business? When the Tanna Kamma said that a courtyard resident cannot block a "neighbor," was the reference only to residents of the same *mavoi*, or to any resident of that town?[23]

The Gemara responds:

תֵּיקוּ – **Let [the question] stand** unresolved.

The Gemara returns to its discussion of Rav Huna's opinion that a *mavoi* resident can prevent anyone, even a member of his own *mavoi*, from setting up a rival business. It notes an exception to his ruling:

אָמַר רַב יוֹסֵף – **Rav Yosef said:** וּמוֹדֵי רַב הוּנָא – **And Rav Huna** himself **concedes** בְּמַקְרֵי דַּרְדְּקֵי דְּלָא מָצֵי מְעַכֵּב – **that with regard to those who teach** Torah to **children, he** [a teacher who is established in a particular *mavoi*] **cannot prevent** another from teaching in that *mavoi*.[24] דְּאָמַר מַר – **For master said:** (עֶזְרָא תִּיקֵן לָהֶן לְיִשְׂרָאֵל[25] – **Ezra decreed for the Jewish nation** שֶׁיְּהוּ מוֹשִׁיבִין סוֹפֵר בְּצַד סוֹפֵר – **that one teacher should be installed next to another.**

And the following question was asked:

וְנֵיחוּשׁ דִּילְמָא אָתֵי לְאִיתְרַשּׁוּלֵי – **But it should be of concern that [a teacher] might become lax** in his work if he works next to another teacher. So what was the purpose of Ezra's decree?

And the following answer was given:

אָמַר לֵיהּ – **He** [the one who was asked the question] **said to [the questioner]:)**

NOTES

23. See note 19. The Tanna Kamma holds that a *mavoi* resident cannot bar the use of his *mavoi* to a "neighbor." Hence, according to the broad definition of "neighbor" (viz. a resident of that town), a *mavoi* resident cannot block a tradesman who lives anywhere in that town. But if we follow the narrow definition (viz. a resident of that *mavoi*), a *mavoi* resident can bar the use of his *mavoi* to anyone who does not reside in that *mavoi*.

An apparent difficulty: The first clause of the Baraisa teaches that even according to the Tanna Kamma a *mavoi* resident can bar the use of his *mavoi* to a tradesman from elsewhere. So according to the position that "neighbor" signifies a resident of the same *mavoi*, that clause refers to a tradesman from another *mavoi* in the same town. But according to the position that "neighbor" signifies anyone from the same town, to whom does that clause refer? It cannot refer to a tradesman from a different town, because such a tradesman can be barred from the entire town, whereas the Baraisa implies that he can be barred only from the *mavoi*.

The answer is that the first clause refers to a tradesman who does not actually live in that town, but pays the town's poll-tax. Although he is allowed to ply his trade in the town as a whole, he can be barred from doing so in a *mavoi* where a similar business has already been established (*Rashba*; see *Tosafos* ד״ה ואי).

In summary:

(1) *A tradesman who resides outside a town in which the type of business he practices has already been established:* He can be barred from plying his trade anywhere in that town.

(2) *A tradesman who resides outside the town but pays tax to the town:* He may ply his trade in the town as a whole, but not in the particular *mavoi* where the established business is located.

(3) *A tradesman who resides in the same town — but not in the same mavoi — as one in which a similar business has been established:* He is permitted to ply his trade in the town as a whole. The Gemara inquires as to whether he is allowed even in the *mavoi* where the established business is located.

(4) *A tradesman who resides in the same mavoi as one in which a similar business has already been established:* He is allowed to ply his trade even in that *mavoi*. [This follows the view of the Tanna Kamma. According to Rabban Shimon ben Gamliel, however, he is not allowed to ply his trade in that *mavoi*.]

24. Even if the rival is from a different town (*Shulchan Aruch Choshen Mishpat* 156:6).

25. The passage from here to the end of this page is parenthesized for it does not appear in most versions of the text. See *Tosafos* to 22a ד״ה קנאת and *Dikdukei Sofrim*.

קִנְאַת סוֹפְרִים תַּרְבֶּה חָכְמָה – **"Jealousy between scholars increases wisdom."** Each teacher, fearful of his rival, will perform his role with extra care.

Rav Huna son of Rav Yehoshua stated above that even according to the Tanna Kamma townsfolk may bar tradesmen who live elsewhere from trading in their town. The Gemara notes an exception to this ruling:

אָמַר רַב נַחְמָן בַּר יִצְחָק – **Rav Nachman son of Yitzchak said:** וּמוֹדֶה רַב הוּנָא בְּרֵיהּ דְּרַב יְהוֹשֻׁעַ – **But Rav Huna son of Rav Yehoshua agrees** בְּרוֹכְלִין הַמַּחֲזִירִין בָּעֲיָירוֹת – that, **with regard to peddlers who go from town to town** selling cosmetics, דְּלֹא מָצֵי מְעַכֵּב – **[a merchant]** already established in a particular town **cannot bar** them from his town. The reason for this exception is דְּאָמַר מַר – **as master has said:**[1] עֶזְרָא תִּקֵּן לָהֶן לְיִשְׂרָאֵל – **Ezra decreed for the Jewish nation** שֶׁיְּהוּ רוֹכְלִין מַחֲזִירִין בָּעֲיָירוֹת – **that peddlers should go from town to town** selling cosmetics כְּדֵי שֶׁיְּהוּ תַּכְשִׁיטִין מְצוּיִין לִבְנוֹת יִשְׂרָאֵל – **so that cosmetics would be readily available to the daughters of Israel.**[2]

The Gemara qualifies this license to sell cosmetics in a town other than one's own:

וְהָנֵי מִילֵּי לְאַהְדּוּרֵי – **This [ruling]** permits a peddler of cosmetics **to go around** from *mavoi* to *mavoi* and house to house selling his wares and then leave, אֲבָל לְאִקְּבוּעֵי לֹא – **but not to set up a permanent [shop].**

An exception to this point:

וְאִי צוּרְבָא מֵרַבָּנָן הוּא – **But if he** [the visiting peddler of cosmetics] **is a rabbinical student,** אֲפִילּוּ לְאִקְּבוּעֵי נַמֵּי – **he is allowed even to set up a permanent [shop].** כִּי הָא – **As** exemplified by **the case** דְּרָבָא שָׁרָא לְהוּ לְרַבִּי יֹאשִׁיָּה וּלְרַב עוֹבַדְיָה לְאִקְּבוּעֵי – **in which Rava allowed R' Yoshiah and Rav Ovadiah to set up a permanent shop** in a town other than their own דְּלֹא כְּהִילְכְתָא – although this is **not in accordance with** the strict letter of **the law.**[3] מַאי טַעְמָא – **What is the reason** for this special dispensation? כֵּיוָן דְּרַבָּנָן נִינְהוּ – **Since they are rabbinical students,** they are permitted to set up a permanent shop, אָתוּ לְטַרְדוּ מִגִּירְסַיְיהוּ – for otherwise **they might come to be diverted from their studies.**[4]

An incident that illustrates another exception to Rav Huna son of Rav Yehoshua's ruling that a tradesman can be barred from a town other than his own:

הַנְהוּ דִּיקוּלָאֵי דְּאַיְיתוּ דִּיקְלָאֵי לְבָבֶל – **There were these basket-sellers**[5] **who brought baskets to** the city of **Babylon**[6] on a market day. אָתוּ בְּנֵי מָתָא קָא מְעַכְּבֵי עִלַּוַיְיהוּ – **The residents of the city came to prevent them** from selling their baskets, claiming that only the local residents were entitled to sell in the city. אָתוּ לְקַמֵּיהּ דְּרָבִינָא – **They came before Ravina** for a judgment on the matter. אָמַר לְהוּ – **[Ravina] said to them:** מֵעָלְמָא אָתוּ וּלְעָלְמָא לִיזַבְּנוּ – Many **[people] have come from elsewhere** (i.e. outside the city) to buy here on this market day, so **let [the basket-sellers] sell to** those who have come from **elsewhere.**[7]

Ravina continues:

וְהָנֵי מִילֵּי בְּיוֹמָא דְשׁוּקָא – **This [permit]** applies **on a market day,** when customers from elsewhere come into the city, אֲבָל בְּלֹא וּבְיוֹמָא יוֹמָא דְשׁוּקָא לֹא – **but not** when it is **not a market day.** דְּשׁוּקָא נַמֵּי לֹא אָמְרִינַן – **And even on a market day, we do not say** that outside merchants are permitted אֶלָּא לְזַבּוּנֵי בְּשׁוּקָא – **except to sell in the marketplace** itself, where the customers from elsewhere are to be found, אֲבָל לְאַהְדּוּרֵי לֹא – **but not to go around** from house to house selling to the residents of the city.

Another exception to Rav Huna son of Rav Yehoshua's ruling that a town can be made off-limits to tradesmen from elsewhere:

הַנְהוּ עֲמוֹרָאֵי דְּאַיְיתוּ עַמְרָא לְפוּם נַהֲרָא – **There were these wool-sellers who brought wool to** the city of **Pum Nahara.** אָתוּ בְּנֵי מָתָא קָא מְעַכְּבֵי עִלַּוַיְיהוּ – **The residents of the city came to prevent them** from selling their wool. אָתוּ לְקַמֵּיהּ דְּרַב כַּהֲנָא – **[The quarreling parties] appeared before Rav Kahana** for a judgment on the matter. אָמַר לְהוּ – **[Rav Kahana] said to [the wool-sellers]:** דִּינָא הוּא דִּמְעַכְּבֵי עִלַּיְיכוּ – **The law is that [the local residents] can prevent you** from selling your wares here.[8] אָמְרוּ לֵיהּ – **They replied to [Rav Kahana]:** אִית לָן אַשְׁרָאֵי – **But we have debts** to collect from people in the city.[9] If we are not allowed to sell our wares while we remain here waiting for our payment, how will we support ourselves in the meantime? אָמַר לְהוּ – **[Rav Kahana] said to [the wool merchants]:** זִילוּ זַבְּנוּ שִׁיעוּר חִיּוּתַיְיכוּ – **Go** and **sell the amount** required **for your livelihood** עַד דְּעָקְרִיתוּ אַשְׁרָאֵי דִּידְכוּ – **until you have collected**[10] **your debts,** וְאַזְלִיתוּ – **and** then **you must go.**

A related incident:

רַב דִּימִי מִנְּהַרְדְּעָא אַיְיתֵי גְּרוֹגְרוֹת בִּסְפִינָה – **Rav Dimi from Nehardea brought dried figs by ship** to sell in the town where the Reish Gelusa[11] resided. אָמַר לֵיהּ רֵישׁ גָּלוּתָא לְרָבָא – **The Reish Galusa said to Rava:** פּוּק חֲזִי – **"Go** and **examine** him [Rav Dimi]. אִי צוּרְבָא מֵרַבָּנָן הוּא נְקִיט לֵיהּ שׁוּקָא – **If he is a rabbinic student, hold the marketplace for him** [i.e. announce that no one but he may sell dried figs in the town]." אָמַר לֵיהּ רָבָא לְרַב אַדָּא בַּר אַבָּא – **Rava** thereupon **said to** his disciple, **Rav Adda bar Abba:** פּוּק תְּהֵי לֵיהּ בְּקַנְקַנֵּיהּ – **"Go** and **smell his keg** to ascertain whether its contents are wine or vinegar [i.e. examine Rav Dimi with halachic questions to see whether or not he is a Torah scholar]." נְפַק [אַזַל] – **[Rav Adda bar Abba] left** and **went** to Rav Dimi. בְּעָא מִינֵּיהּ – **He asked [Rav Dimi]:** פִּיל שֶׁבָּלַע כְּפִיפָה מִצְרִית – "If **an elephant swallowed a willow-reed basket,** וְהֱקִיאָהּ דֶּרֶךְ בֵּית הָרְעִי – **and then ejected it through its rectum,** מַהוּ – **what is [the law]** regarding the capacity of the excreted basket to contract *tumah?*" Is it still considered a

NOTES

1. *Bava Kamma* 82a-b.

2. Ezra desired to promote family harmony by ensuring that women would have the means to make themselves attractive to their husbands (see *Bava Kamma* 82b).

3. Rather, it is לִפְנִים מִשּׁוּרַת הַדִּין, lit. within [i.e. beyond] the line of the law (*Rashi;* cf. *Yad Ramah*).

4. Since a rabbinical student is constantly engrossed in his studies, he does not make it a practice to peddle his wares from house to house [for this would divert him from his studies]. Therefore we permit him to set up a permanent shop (*Rashi*; see *Rabbeinu Gershom*).

5. Alternatively: sellers of vats (*Rashi*).

6. The term בָּבֶל, *Bavel,* usually signifies the country of Babylonia. In this context, however, it means the city of Babylon.

7. Since many customers have come from outside the town to buy at the market, merchants from outside the town cannot be barred from selling to the people gathered at the market (*Rashi*).

Provided the outside merchants limit their peddling to the marketplace, they may sell to whomever is there. It is not necessary for them to limit their trade to customers who are from outside the town (inferred by *Beis Yosef Choshen Mishpat* 156 from *Rambam Hil. Shecheinim* 6:10 and *Nimukei Yosef;* cf. *Tosafos;* see also *Prishah* ibid. §11 and *S'ma* §20).

8. In accordance with the ruling of Rav Huna son of Rav Yehoshua.

9. They had sold on credit (*Rashi*), before they knew that a protest had been lodged against them (*Ritva*).

10. Literally: uprooted.

11. The Exilarch — political leader of Babylonian Jewry.

ל) קנאת סופרים תרבה חכמה אמר רב נחמן בר יצחק ומודה רב הונא בריה דרב יהושע א ברוכלין המחזירין בעיירות דלא מצי מעכב ג) דאמר מר ב עזרא תקן להן לישראל שיהו רוכלין מחזירין בעיירות כדי שיהו תכשיטין מצויין לבנות ישראל ג והני מילי לאהדורי אבל לאקבועי לא ד ואי צורבא מרבנן הוא אפילו לאקבועי נמי כי הא דרבא שרא להו לר' יאשיה ולרב עובדיה לאקבועי דלא כהלכתא מאי טעמא כיון דרבנן נינהו אתו לטרדו מגירסייהו הנהו דיקולאי דאייתו דיקולאי לבבל אתו בני מתא קא מעכבי עלייהו אתו לקמיה דרבינא אמר להו ה מעלמא אתו ולעלמא ליזבנו ו והני מילי ביומא דשוקא אבל בלא יומא דשוקא לא וביומא דשוקא נמי לא אמרינן ז אלא לזבוני בשוקא אבל לאהדורי (א) לא הנהו עמוראי דאייתו עמרא לפום נהרא אתו בני מתא קא מעכבי עלייהו אתו לקמיה דרב כהנא אמר להו דינא הוא דמעכבי עלייכו אמרו ליה אית לן אשראי (ב) אמר להו ח זילו זבנו שיעור חיותייכו עד דעקריתו אשראי דידכו ואזליתו רב דימי מנהרדעא אייתי גרוגרות בספינה א"ל ריש גלותא לרבא פוק חזי אי צורבא מרבנן הוא נקיט ליה שוקא א"ל רבא לרב אדא בר אבא פוק תהי ליה בקנקניה נפק [אזל] בעא מיניה ט פיל שבלע כפיפה מצרית והקיאה דרך בית הרעי מהו לא הוה בידיה א"ל מר ניהו רבא י טפח ליה בסנדליה א"ל בין דידי לרבא איכא טובא מיהו על כרחך אנא רבך ורבא רבה דרבך לא נקטו ליה שוקא פסיד גרוגרות דידיה אתא לקמיה דרב יוסף א"ל חזי מר מאי עבדו לי א"ל מאן דלא שהייה לאוניתא דמלכא דאדום לא נשהייה לאוניתיך דכתיב א) כה אמר ה' על שלשה פשעי מואב ועל ארבעה לא אשיבנו על שרפו עצמות מלך אדום ט) לסיד נח נפשיה דרב אדא בר אבא רב יוסף אמר אנא ענישתיה דאנא לטייתיה רב דימי מנהרדעא אמר אנא ענישתיה דאפסיד גרוגרות דידי אביי אמר אנא ענישתיה דאמר להו לרבנן י) אדמגרמיתו גרמי בי אביי תו אכלו בישרא [שמינא] בי רבא ורבא אמר אנא ענישתיה [דכי הוה אזיל לבי טבחא למשקל אומצא] אמר להו לטבחי אנא שקילנא בישרא מיקמי שמעיה דרבא דאנא עדיפנא מיניה רב נחמן בר יצחק אמר אנא ענישתיה דרב נחמן בר יצחק ריש כלה הוה כל יומא מיקמי דניעול לכלה מרהיט בהדיה רב אדא בר אבא לשמעתיה והדר עייל לכלה ההוא יומא נקטוה רב פפא ורב הונא בריה דרב יהושע לרב אדא בר אבא משום דלא הוו בסיומא אמרו ליה אימא לן הני שמעתתא דמעשר בהמה היכי אמרינהו רבא אמר להו הכי אמר רבא והכי אמר רבא אדהכי נגה ליה [לרב נחמן בר יצחק] ז) (ולא אתי רב אדא בר אבא) אמרו ליה רבנן לרב נחמן בר יצחק קום דנגה לן למה יתיב מר אמר להו יתיבנא וקא (ג) מנטרא לערסיה דרב אדא בר אבא אדהכי נפק קלא דנח נפשיה דרב אדא בר אבא ומסתברא דרב נחמן בר יצחק ענשיה: **מתני'** ט מי שהיה כותלו סמוך לכותל חבירו לא יסמוך לו כותל אחר אא"כ הרחיק ממנו ארבע אמות ס) החלונות בין מלמעלן בין מלמטן בין כנגדן ארבע אמות: **גמ'** וקמא היכי סמיך אמר רב יהודה הכי קאמר

ומודה רב הונא בריה דרב יהושע. אע"ג דאמר בר מתא אבר מתא אחריתי מצי מעכב מלהביא כאן ולמכור מודה הוא ברוכלין מוכרי בשמים המחזירין בעיירות להביא בשמים לנשים להתקשט בהן דלא מצו לעכב עלייהו רוכלי העיר: **לאהדורי.** לחזור ולסבב במבואות העיר ובבתים על כל הרוצה לקנות ואחרי כן ישוב לעירו: **ואי צורבא מרבנן הוא.** דטריד בגירסא ולא אורחיה לאהדורי אפי' לאקבועי נמי: **דלא כהלכתא.** אלא לפנים משורת הדין: **דיקולאי.** מוכרי סלים ויש אומרים מוכרי יורות: **ולעלמא ליזבנו.** יומא דשוקא הוה והרבה באין ממקום אחר לקנות מן השוק לפיכך אין בני העיר מעכבין גם על המוכרים להביא אומנותם ולמכור לנקבלים לשוק: **עמוראי.** מוכרי צמר: **אית לן אשראי במתא.** מכרנו בהקפה ולריכים אנו לשהות כאן עד שנגבה חובות שלנו ואם אין אנו מוכרין סחורותינו במה נתפרנס: **עד דעקריתו.** שתעקרו חובותיכם מן הלוקחים מכם בהקפה: **נקיט ליה שוקא.** הכרז שלא ימכור איש בעיר גרוגרות אלא הוא: **תהי ליה בקנקניה.** הריח לו בקנקנו אם יין הוא אם חומץ כלומר בדקהו בהלכות אם תלמיד חכם הוא אם לאו. ריח היין כשמריחין אותו אם טוב הוא קרי תהי כדאמרינן במסכת ע"ז (דף סו:) וכן בכתובות (דף קה.) קרנא הוה תהי באמברא דחמרא: **כפיפה מצרית.** סל נצרים של ערבה: **מהו.** מי חשוב כמעוכל והויא ליה ככלי גללים ואין מקבל טומאה עוד: **א"ל.** רב דימי לרב אדא: **מר ניהו רבא.** אתה הוא רבא לפי ששמע על רבא שהוא גדול העיר וסבור שהוא זה: **טפח ליה בסנדליה.** הכהו על סנדלו במקל דרך שחוק כאדם שמכין למי שאינו חשוב: **דלא נשהייה.** שלא נמנע מלהפרע: **לאוניתא.** אונאת בושתו: **דמלכא דאדום.** אע"פ שהוא אדומי: **על שרפו.** מחמת בזיון: **דאמר להו לרבנן אדמגרמיתו גרמי בי אביי.** שהיה רגיל לומר לתלמידים עד שאתם הולכים אצל אביי לגרס עצמות כלומר ללמוד שלא לשובע: **תו אכלו כו'.** בואו ולמדו הלכות טובות מרווחות אצל רבא: **שמעיה דרבא.** שלוחו לקנות בשר: **ריש כלה.** דורש ברבים בשבתות: **דלא הוו בסיומא.** יש אומרים שלא היו בעלה כשנעשה רב נחמן ריש כלה ויש אומרים דלא הוו בסיומא דפירקא דרבא דדריש בשבת הרגל הלכות האמורות בפרק אחרון של בכורות: **שמעתתא דמעשר בהמה.** בפרק אחרון דבכורות ורבא אמרינהו בסיומא דפירקא: **אתו רבנן.** תלמידי הישיבה הבאים לשמוע: **נטרנא ערסיה דרב אדא.** אני מצפה כאן שיביאו את מטת רב אדא שמת: **מתני' לא יסמוך** לכותל חבירו כותל אחר אלא אם כן כו'. מפרש בגמ': **והחלונות.** מי שהיו לו חלונות פתוחים לחצר חבירו והוחזק בדבר זה שלש שנים ובא בעל החצר לבנות שם כותל צריך לשער ד' אמות: **בין מלמעלן.** אם בא להגביה יגביה כותלו ד' אמות מן החלונות: **בין מלמטן.** אם בא לבנותו נמוך צריך להשפילו מן החלונות ד' אמות וטעמא מפרש בגמ': **בין מכנגדן.** צריך להרחיקו מהן ד' אמות: **גמ' הבא**

קנאת סופרים תרבה חכמה. ולא גרסי' כמו שיש בספרים דאמר מר עזרא תיקן להם לישראל שיהו מושיבין סופר בצד סופר דהא לא חשיב ליה במרובה (ב"ק דף פב.) גבי עשר תקנות שתיקן: **מעלמא** אתו ולעלמא ליזבנו. מכאן משמע דביומא דשוקא היה מותר להלוות לבני אדם הבאים ממקומות שם לשוק לנכרים דאתו מעלמא אבל לבני המקום לא ודוקא בשוקא אבל לאהדורי לא: **אמר** ליה רבא לרב אדא בר אבא. כן גרים רבינו חננאל ולא גרסי' בר אהבה דאותו היה בימי רבי דאמרינן בקדושין (דף עב: ושם) היום ישב רב אדא בר אהבה בחיקו של אברהם אבינו: **פיל** שבלע כפיפה מצרית. בפ' ר' ישמעאל (מנחות דף סט. ושם ד"ה פיל) איתא להך בעיא דהכא ומסיק התם למאי אי למבטל טומאתו תנינא כל הכלים יורדין לידי טומאתן במחשבה ואין עולין מטומאתן אלא בשינוי מעשה וקאמר לא צריכא דבלע הוצין ועבדינהו כפיפה אי הוי עיכול והוי כלי גללים או לא והכא בלע הוצין בעא מיניה דאי כפיפה שלימה אמאי לא הוה בידיה מתני' היא וקשיא לר"ת א"כ אמאי לא נקיטו ליה שוקא הא בעיא זו לא איפשיטא התם וי"ל דמ"מ הוה ליה לאיתויי הך ראיות דמייתי התם ודחי להו: **אנא** ענישתיה. כל אחד מהן היה מתאונן שעל ידו מת רב אדא משום דאמרינן בשבת בפ' שואל (דף קמט:) כל מי שחבירו נענש על ידו אין מכניסין אותו במחיצתו של הקב"ה שנאמר (משלי יז) גם ענוש לצדיק לא טוב אלא רע וכתיב (תהלים ה) לא יגורך רע. ר"י: **וקמא** היכי סמיך. ס"ד דבנפל איירי מכן משמע הלשון דקתני מי שהיה כותלו סמוך לכותל חבירו ומשני רב יהודה הכי קאמר הבא לסמוך כו' ומתני' הכי פירוש' מי שהיה גבול כותלו סמוך לכותל חבירו והכא פריך דלכותל קתני ולא גבול וא"ת לרבא דאמר בריש פירקין דלסור לסמוך קמא היכי סמיך ואפילו לפי' ר"ת דלמסקנא שרי רבא לכולהו לסמוך לבד מבור מ"מ אמאי לא פריך מהכא דהוי רישא אלא ממשרה וירק דהוי סיפא וי"ל דלא אסר רבא לסמוך אלא מילתא דמגופיה אתי היזק אבל הכא הכותל אינו מזיק כלום אלא שגורם למעט הדוושא: **אלא**

עין משפט נר מצוה

מח א ב ג ד מיי' פ"ו מהל' שכנים הל' ט סמג עשין פב טוש"ע ח"מ סי' קנו סעיף ו:

מט ה ו ז ח מיי' שם הלכה י טוש"ע שם סעיף ז:

נ ט מיי' פ"ט שם הל' ט סמג שם טוש"ע ח"מ סי' קנה סעיף יג:

נא י מיי' שם פ"ז הל' א ב ג סמג שם טוש"ע ח"מ סי' קנד סעיף ג וסעיף כב:

רבינו גרשום

ברוכלין. שמוכרין תכשיטי נשים שרק וכחל אע"ג דלא שייכי בחד כרגא דלא מצי מעכב עליה האי רוכל דמתא: **והני מילי** דלא מצי מעכב **לאהדורי** לחזור ולילך משוק לשוק וממבוי למבוי ולמכור ולשוב לעירו אבל **לקבוע** חנותו בהני רוכלין למזבן תכשיטין **לא: דלא כהלכתא.** כלומר שלא ילמדו ממנו אחרים הלכה דלפנים משורת הדין עבד להו משום **דרבנן נינהו דלא ליבטלו מגירסייהו** לילך ולחזור בכל העיר ומשוק לשוק: **הנהו דקולאי.** שמוכרין סלים. **אתו דקולאי דמתא ומעכבי להו אמר להו** לא מציתו מעכבי עלייהו **דמעלמא אתי** ולהנהו דאתי **מעלמא** לשוק **לזבני אבל לאהדורי** בבתים לזבונינהו **לא** דודאי מצי למיעכב עלייהו: **אית לן אשראי במתא.** חוב שחייבין לנו ממון וצריכין לנו לעכובי הכא עד דפרעי לן והב לן רשותא דניזבין עד כפי חיותן עד דפרעי לן: **נקיט ליה שוקא.** שלא ימכור אדם עד שימכור כל גרוגרות שלו: **תהי ליה.** הוי מריח מה יש בו: **מצרית.** מצורי דקל מהו מי אמרי' הואיל דהוות במעיו **והקיאה [דרך] בית הרעי** כמאכל שנתעכל דמי ונתבטל' ואין מקבלת טומאה או דלמא הואיל ואכתי קיימת היא דבר חשוב הוי ואינה מבוטלת ומקבלת טומא': **אמר ליה.** רב דימי לרב אדא: **מאן ניהו מר רבא.** את הוא רבא: **טפח ליה.** רב אדא לרב דימי **בסנדליה** כלומר שלא היה חשוב בעיניו: **ורבא רביה דרבך.** שהוא רבי ואנא רבך: **מאן דלא שבקיה. לאוניתא** (דעמון) דמואב למלכא דאדום: **אדמגרמיתו גרמי בי אביי.** שהיה רגיל לומר לתלמידי אביי כל זמן שאתם מגררין עצמות שאין בהן לחלוח בי אביי יכולין אתם ללמוד תורה כשורה וכהלכתא בי רבא לפי שאביי לא למד כל כך ולפיכך אמר אביי אנא ענישתיה שהיה מבזיני: **ריש כלה הוה.** שהיה רגיל לדרוש בשבת שלפני החג ורב נחמן היה דורש אותן שבתות והיו מתקבצין שם מהרבה מקומו' תלמידין לשמוע: **עכבוהו רב פפא ורב הונא לרב אדא בר אהבה משום דלא הוי בסיומא** במס' בכורו' קמיה דרבא: **קום** והכנס לדרוש **דנגה לן** שכבר עבר מן היום הרבה: **קא נטרנא לערסיה.** כלומר שמת לפי שהיה מצערו כל כך שלא בא אליו לעיין עמו הדרשה: **פיסקא מי שהיה כותלו סמוך לכותל חבירו** ונפל **לא יסמוך כותל אחר.** שלא יבנה שם כותל אחר אלא אם כן הרחיק ממנו מכותל חבירו **ד' אמות** משום דוושא כדמפרש בגמ'. **החלונות** מלמעלן ומלמטן ומכנגדן ד' אמות כדמפרש בריש פ"ק: ומקשי' וכותל **קמא** דנפל דהוה מעיקרא היכי סמיך בקרוב מד' אמות: אמר רב יהודה. הכי תריץ מתני' **הבא לסמוך** תחלה **לא** יסמוך לכותל וכו':

מסורת הש"ם

א) [לעיל כא.], ב) ב"ק פב., ג) מנחות סט., ד) [מו"ק כה. ב"ק לב:], ה) [נ"ל לשיד], ו) [נ"ל אדמגרסיתו. ערוך גרס א'], ז) [רש"ל מ"ז וגרס רנב"י אתו רבנן א"ל לרב נב"י], ח) [לעיל ב:], ט) [ע"ש ד"ה היום וברש"י שם וע"ע תוס' תענית כ: ד"ה א"ל]:

הגהות הב"ח

(א) גמ' אבל לאהדורי במתא לא: (ב) שם אית לן אשראי במתא אמר: (ג) שם וקא נטרנא לערסיה:

גליון הש"ם

תוס' ד"ה וקמא כו' **אמאי לא פריך מהכא.** קשה לי על קושייתם הא מהכא לא היה ראיה לסתור ולחזור מכל שינויי דלעיל ולהוכיח דגם לרבנן דר"י מותר לסמוך לרבא דהא כמו דמשנינן על אילן קדם לבור דמיירי בלוקח ה"נ י"ל הכא דמיירי בלוקח המקום שאצל כותל חבירו. גם תמוה לי במה דנקטו קושייתם רק לס"ד דלעיל הא מבואר בסוגיא דחרדל למסקנא מה דקתני ר"י מתיר בחרדל היינו דאמר לדבריהם דרבנן התינח משרה וירק אבל חרדל יהיה מותר לסמוך אף דבעל דבורים סמך בהיתר מ"מ כיון דקנה עשה שלא כהוגן ומזיק להחרדל מותר לזה להעמיד אצלו חרדלו בלי הרחקה כיון דבעל דבורים מזיק גם אותו. ועלה אמרי' לעיל לרבנן היינו דרבנן לא היה להם לחלוק על סברא זו ומשני דס"ל דדבורים לא מזקי לחרדל עיי"ש היטב. א"כ הכא בדוושא דשניהם מזיקים זה לזה מה בכך שהראשון העמיד כותלו תחלה מ"מ יהא השני מותר לסמוך כותלו דאמר לו כמו שכותלי מזיק אותך כן כותלך מזיק אותי וביותר דזה לא יתורץ גם בתירוצם דדוושא לא הוי מזיק ממש דמ"מ יאמר השני מה שאני מזיקך בדוושא כמו כן אתה מזיקני בדוושא. ויהיה בהכרח לאוקמי הכא בלוקח דהראשון לא עשה אפילו קצת שלא כהוגן בזה השני צריך ליתן כל הרחקה כמ"ש תוס' בסוגיא דחרדל ולע"ג:

תורה אור השלם

א) כֹּה אָמַר יְיָ עַל שְׁלֹשָׁה פִּשְׁעֵי מוֹאָב וְעַל אַרְבָּעָה לֹא אֲשִׁיבֶנּוּ עַל שָׂרְפוֹ עַצְמוֹת מֶלֶךְ אֱדוֹם לַשִּׂיד: [עמוס ב, א]

ליקוטי רש"י

תהי ליה. לשון מריח כמו בת תיהא דמסכת עבודה זרה (סו:) [עירובין סו.]. לשון מריח בקנקן [ב"ק עו:]. **כפיפה מצרית.** סל העשוי מצורי דקל [שבת עח:]. סל של נצרי דקל זרדים שגדילין סביב הדקל [סוטה יד.]. קופה מצרית מצורי דקל [מנחות סט.]. **טפח ליה בסנדליה.** על סנדלו וכו' ע"א הכהו בסנדלו [מו"ק כה.]. הכהו על סנדלו ל"א בעט בסנדלו [ב"ק לב:]. **החלונות.** אחד מבני השותפים הבונה כותל בחצר כנגד חלונותיו של חבירו בין מלמעלה וכו' אם הכותל גבוה יותר מן החלונות צריך להגביה למעלה מהן ד"א כדמפרש ואזיל כדי שלא יעמוד על כותלו ויציץ ויראה בחלונותיו של חבירו. **בין מלמטן.** אם הכותל נמוך מן החלונות צריך להשפילו מהן ד"א כדי שלא יעמוד על עובי כותלו ויראה. **בין מכנגדן.** צריך להרחיק את הכותל מן החלונות ד' אמות כדי שלא יאפיל [לעיל ב:].

basket of reeds, which can contract *tumah?* Or, since it passed through the animal's digestive system, perhaps it is now reckoned as a utensil made of excrement, which cannot contract *tumah?*[12] לֹא הֲוָה בִּידֵיהּ – **[Rav Dimi] did not have an answer.**[13] אֲמַר לֵיהּ – **[Rav Dimi] said to [Rav Adda bar Abba]:** מַר נִיהוּ רָבָא – **"Are you, master, Rava?"**[14] טְפַח לֵיהּ בְּסַנְדְּלֵיהּ – **[Rav Adda bar Abba]** deprecatingly **tapped** his stick **on [Rav Dimi's] shoe,** אֲמַר לֵיהּ – **and said to him:** בֵּין דִּידִי לְרָבָא אִיכָּא טוּבָא – **"Between me and Rava there is a great gap,** מִיהוּ עַל כָּרְחָךְ אֲנָא רַבָּךְ – but, **at any rate, you are bound** to concede that **I am your teacher** (i.e. your superior), וְרָבָא רַבָּה דְּרַבָּךְ – **and Rava is the teacher of your teacher!"** לֹא נָקְטוּ לֵיהּ שׁוּקָא – **They did not hold the marketplace for [Rav Dimi].** פְּסִיד גְּרוֹגְרוֹת דִּידֵיהּ – As a result, **his dried figs spoiled.** אֲתָא לְקַמֵּיהּ דְּרַב יוֹסֵף אֲמַר לֵיהּ – **[Rav Dimi] came before Rav Yosef** and **said to him:** חֲזִי מַר מַאי עָבְדוּ לִי – **"Master, look what they did to me!"** אֲמַר לֵיהּ – **[Rav Yosef] said to [Rav Dimi]:** מַאן דְּלֹא שְׁהָיֵיהּ לְאוֹנִיתָא דְּמַלְכָּא דֶּאֱדוֹם – **"The One Who did not delay** avenging **the humiliation of the king of Edom** לֹא נַשְׁהֲיֵיהּ לְאוֹנִיתָיךְ – **will not delay** avenging **your humiliation.**[15] דִּכְתִיב – **For it is written:** ,,כֹּה אָמַר ה׳ עַל־שְׁלֹשָׁה פִּשְׁעֵי מוֹאָב וְעַל־אַרְבָּעָה לֹא אֲשִׁיבֶנּוּ עַל־שָׂרְפוֹ עַצְמוֹת מֶלֶךְ־אֱדוֹם לַשִּׂיד" – ***Thus says HASHEM: Regarding three sins of Moav*** I will grant pardon, ***but regarding a fourth*** – namely, ***that he burned the bones of the king of Edom into lime – I will not turn away from*** punishing ***him.***[16] נָח נַפְשֵׁיהּ דְּרַב אַדָּא בַּר אַבָּא – **Rav Adda bar Abba died.**

Each of several Sages lamented that he was responsible for the demise of Rav Adda bar Abba:[17]

רַב יוֹסֵף אָמַר – **Rav Yosef said:** אֲנָא עֲנִישְׁתֵּיהּ – **I punished him** (i.e. Rav Adda Bar Abba was punished on my account), דַּאֲנָא לְטַיִיתֵיהּ – **for I cursed him** by saying that God will not delay avenging the humiliation to which he subjected Rav Dimi. רַב דִּימִי מִנְּהַרְדְּעָא אָמַר – **Rav Dimi from Nehardea said:** אֲנָא עֲנִישְׁתֵּיהּ – **I punished him** (i.e. he was punished on my account), דְּאַפְסִיד גְּרוֹגְרוֹת דִּידִי – **for he caused my dried figs to spoil.** אַבַּיֵּי אָמַר – **Abaye said:** אֲנָא עֲנִישְׁתֵּיהּ – **I punished him** (i.e. he was punished on my account), דְּאָמַר לְהוּ לְרַבָּנַן – for **he** [Rav Adda bar Abba] **would say to the rabbinical students,** אַדְּמַגְרְמִיתוּ גַּרְמֵי בֵּי אַבַּיֵּי – **"Instead of chewing bones in the house of Abaye,** תּוּ אִכְלוּ בִּישְׂרָא [שְׁמֵינָא] בֵּי רָבָא – **come** and **eat juicy meat in the house of Rava** [i.e. you will derive more satisfaction from the teachings of Rava than from those of Abaye]." Abaye was afraid that it was because of this insult he had suffered that Rav Adda bar Abba was punished.

וְרָבָא אָמַר – **Rava said:** אֲנָא עֲנִישְׁתֵּיהּ – **I punished him** (i.e. he was punished on my account), [דְּכִי הֲוָה אָזִיל לְבֵי טַבָּחָא לְמִשְׁקַל אוּמְצָא] – **for when [Rav Adda bar Abba] would go to the butcher to buy meat,** אָמַר לְהוּ לְטַבָּחֵי – **he would say to the butcher:** אֲנָא שְׁקִילְנָא בִּישְׂרָא מִיקַּמֵּי שַׁמְעֵיהּ דְּרָבָא – **"I will take meat before the servant of Rava** [who had been sent by Rava to buy meat], דַּאֲנָא עֲדִיפְנָא מִינֵּיהּ – **for I am greater than him."**[18] Rava was afraid that it was because of this insult he had suffered that Rav Adda bar Abba was punished.

רַב נַחְמָן בַּר יִצְחָק אָמַר – **Rav Nachman bar Yitzchak said:** אֲנָא עֲנִישְׁתֵּיהּ – **I punished him** (i.e. he was punished on my account). דְּרַב נַחְמָן בַּר יִצְחָק רֵישׁ כַּלָּה הֲוָה – **For Rav Nachman bar Yitzchak was the lecturer of the *kallah*** discourses,[19] כָּל יוֹמָא מִיקַּמֵּי דְּנֵיעוּל לְכַלָּה – **and every day, before [Rav Nachman bar Yitzchak] entered** the area in which **the *kallah*** lecture was given, מַרְהִיט בַּהֲדֵיהּ רַב אַדָּא בַּר אַבָּא לִשְׁמַעְתֵּיהּ – **Rav Adda bar Abba quickly went through his lesson with him,** וַהֲדַר עָיֵיל לְכַלָּה – **and** it was only **then** that **[Rav Nachman] entered the *kallah*** lecture area to give the lecture. הַהוּא יוֹמָא – **That day** (i.e. the day on which Rav Adda bar Abba died), נַקְטוּהּ רַב פָּפָּא וְרַב הוּנָא בְּרֵיהּ דְּרַב יְהוֹשֻׁעַ לְרַב אַדָּא בַּר אַבָּא – **Rav Pappa and Rav Huna son of Rav Yehoshua took Rav Adda bar Abba** aside before he came to review the *kallah* lecture with Rav Nachman, מִשּׁוּם דְּלֹא הֲווּ בְּסִיּוּמָא – **for they had not been present at the** lecture given by Rava on the **final** chapter of tractate *Bechoros,* and they wished to find out what Rava had said.[20] אָמְרוּ לֵיהּ – **They said to [Rav Adda bar Abba]:** אֵימָא לָן – **"Tell us,** הָנֵי שְׁמַעְתָּתָא דְּמַעֲשַׂר בְּהֵמָה – **those halachic passages** in the chapter **of *Maaser Beheimah*** [the final chapter in tractate *Bechoros*], הֵיכִי אַמְרִינְהוּ רָבָא – **how did Rava explain them?"** אָמַר לְהוּ – **[Rav Adda bar Abba] said to them:** הָכִי אָמַר רָבָא וְהָכִי אָמַר רָבָא – **Rava said this and Rava said that** (i.e. he repeated Rava's discourse). [אַדְּהָכִי נָגַהּ לֵיהּ [לְרַב נַחְמָן בַּר יִצְחָק – **In the meantime, the hour had grown late for Rav Nachman bar Yitzchak** to start his lecture (וְלֹא אָתֵי רַב אַדָּא בַּר אַבָּא) – **and Rav Adda bar Abba had** still **not arrived** to review it with him.

NOTES

12. The Torah lists the types of utensils that can contract *tumah* contamination, and wooden vessels are among them (see *Leviticus* 11:32,33 and *Numbers* 31:20-24). Reed baskets are classified as wooden utensils and therefore are susceptible to *tumah* contamination. Utensils made of excrement, however, are not included in this list (see *Keilim* 10:1, *Menachos* 69b).

13. Literally: it was not in his hands. The correct answer is that the excreted basket can still contract *tumah.* The Mishnah (*Keilim* 25:9) states that a utensil which has the capacity to contract *tumah* does not lose that capacity unless its physical form is changed (*Rashba*; cf. *Tosafos*).

14. Rav Dimi thought that his questioner was Rava, for he had heard that Rava was the outstanding authority in that town (*Rashi*).

15. God, who did not delay avenging an Edomite, will certainly not delay avenging you (see *Rashi*).

Rava's intention was only that if Rav Dimi was not found to be a scholar, he should not be given the privilege of having the exclusive right to sell his wares in the marketplace. Rav Adda bar Abba went beyond this and embarrassed Rav Dimi by tapping him on the shoe and saying, "I am your teacher etc." (*Maharsha*).

16. *Amos* 2:1. The king of Moav burnt the heir to the Edomite throne, mixed his ashes with lime and smeared them on a wall (see *II Kings* 3:27 with *Radak* and *Malbim*).

17. The Gemara (*Shabbos* 149b) says that one who causes punishment to befall his fellow is not admitted to God's inner enclosure (*Tosafos*).

18. Although Rav Adda bar Abba recognized that Rava was the greater scholar ("Between me and Rava there is a great gap etc."), he thought that he should precede the *servant* of Rava. Rava, however, was concerned that perhaps this was nevertheless considered an insult to him since it was known that the servant was buying meat on his behalf (*Riaf* on *Ein Yaakov*).

19. The כַּלָּה, *kallah,* was a public lecture given on the Sabbath (*Rashi*). [*Rashi* here implies that the *kallah* discourse was delivered every Sabbath. However, *Rashi* indicates below (ד״ה דלא הוו בסיומא) that the discourse was held on "the Sabbath of the pilgrimage festival" (see *Hagahos Melo HaRo'im* and *R' Gershom*), and this is in harmony with his comments to *Yevamos* 122a ד״ה תלתא. In *Berachos* 6b ד״ה אגרא דכלה, *Rashi* writes that the discourse was held on the Sabbath preceding the festival. See *Rashi* to *Berachos* 57a ד״ה יער and *Sukkah* 26a ד״ה כדטעים where he gives a different interpretation to the term *kallah.*]

20. This is one of two explanations cited by *Rashi*. Alternatively, *Rashi* explains: מִשּׁוּם דְּלֹא הֲווּ בְּסִיּוּמָא, *for [Rav Pappa and Rav Huna] had not been present at the final meeting* at which Rav Nachman was appointed the lecturer of the *kallah* discourses. [According to this interpretation, the reason the Gemara mentions this point is possibly as follows: Rav Pappa and Rav Huna were unaware of Rav Nachman's appointment, and therefore did not realize that by conversing with Rav Adda bar Abba they were delaying the *kallah* lecture.]

א) קנאת סופרים תרבה חכמה אמר רב נחמן בר יצחק ומודה רב הונא בריה דרב יהושע א ברוכלין המחזירין בעיירות דלא מצי מעכב ב) דאמר מר ב עזרא תקן להן לישראל שיהו רוכלין מחזירין בעיירות כדי שיהו תכשיטין מצויין לבנות ישראל ג והני מילי לאהדורי אבל לאקבועי לא ד ואי צורבא מרבנן הוא אפילו לאקבועי נמי כי הא דרבא שרא להו לר' יאשיה ולרב עובדיה לאקבועי דלא כהלכתא מאי טעמא כיון דרבנן נינהו אתו לטרדו מגירסייהו הנהו דיקולאי דאייתו דיקלאי לבבל אתו בני מתא קא מעכבי עלויהו אתו לקמיה דרבינא אמר להו ה מעלמא אתו ולעלמא ליזבנו ו והני מילי ביומא דשוקא אבל בלא יומא דשוקא לא וביומא דשוקא נמי לא אמרינן ז אלא לזבוני בשוקא אבל לאהדורי (א) לא הנהו עמוראי דאייתו עמרא לפום נהרא אתו בני מתא קא מעכבי עלויהו אתו לקמיה דרב כהנא אמר להו דינא הוא דמעכבי עלייכו אמרו ליה אית לן אשראי (ב) אמר להו ח זילו זבנו שיעור חיותייכו עד דעקריתו אשראי דידכו ואזליתו רב דימי מנהרדעא אייתי גרוגרות בספינה א"ל ריש גלותא לרבא פוק חזי אי צורבא מרבנן הוא נקיט ליה שוקא א"ל רבא לרב אדא בר אבא פוק תהי ליה בקנקניה נפק [אזל] בעא מיניה ט פיל שבלע כפיפה מצרית והקיאה דרך בית הרעי מהו לא הוה בידיה א"ל מר ניהו רבא ד) טפח ליה בסנדליה א"ל בין דידי לרבא איכא טובא מיהו על כרחך אנא רבך ורבא רבה דרבך לא נקטו ליה שוקא פסיד גרוגרות דידיה אתא לקמיה דרב יוסף א"ל חזי מר מאי עבדו לי א"ל מאן דלא שהייה לאוניתא דמלכא דאדום לא נשהייה לאוניתיך דכתיב א) כה אמר ה' על שלשה פשעי מואב ועל ארבעה לא אשיבנו על שרפו עצמות מלך אדום ה) לסיד נח נפשיה דרב אדא בר אבא רב יוסף אמר אנא ענישתיה דאנא לטייתיה רב דימי מנהרדעא אמר אנא ענישתיה דאפסיד גרוגרות דידי אביי אמר אנא ענישתיה דאמר להו לרבנן ו) אדמגרמיתו גרמי בי אביי תו אכלו בישרא [שמינא] בי רבא ורבא אמר אנא ענישתיה [דכי הוה אזיל לבי טבחא למשקל אומצא] אמר להו לטבחי אנא שקילנא בישרא מיקמי שמעיה דרבא דאנא עדיפנא מיניה רב נחמן בר יצחק אמר אנא ענישתיה דרב נחמן בר יצחק ריש כלה הוה כל יומא מיקמי דניעול לכלה מרהיט בהדיה רב אדא בר אבא לשמעתיה והדר עייל לכלה ההוא יומא נקטוה רב פפא ורב הונא בריה דרב יהושע לרב אדא בר אבא משום דלא הוו בסיומא אמרו ליה אימא לן הני שמעתתא דמעשר בהמה היכי אמרינהו רבא אמר להו הכי אמר רבא והכי אמר רבא אדהכי נגה ליה [לרב נחמן בר יצחק] ז) (ולא אתי רב אדא בר אבא) אמרו ליה רבנן לרב נחמן בר יצחק קום דנגה לן למה יתיב מר אמר להו יתיבנא וקא (ג) מנטרנא לערסיה דרב אדא בר אבא אדהכי נפק קלא דנח נפשיה דרב אדא בר אבא ומסתברא דרב נחמן בר יצחק ענשיה:

מתני' ט מי שהיה כותלו סמוך לכותל חבירו לא יסמוך לו כותל אחר אא"כ הרחיק ממנו ארבע אמות ח) י החלונות בין מלמעלן בין מלמטן בין כנגדן ארבע אמות: גמ' וקמא היכי סמיך אמר רב יהודה הכי

רש"י

ומודה רב הונא בריה דרב יהושע. אע"ג דאמר בר מתא אבר מתא אחריתי מצי מעכב מלהביא כאן ולמכור מודה הוא ברוכלין מוכרי בשמים המחזירין בעיירות להביא בשמים לנשים להתקשט בהן דלא מצו לעכב עלייהו רוכלי העיר: לאהדורי. לחזור ולסבב במבואות העיר ובבתים על כל הרוצה לקנות ואחרי כן ישוב לעירו: ואי צורבא מרבנן הוא. דטריד בגירסא ולא אורחיה לאהדורי אפי' לאקבועי נמי: דלא כהלכתא. אלא לפנים משורת הדין: דיקולאי. מוכרי סלים ויש אומרים מוכרי יורות: ולעלמא ליזבנו. יומא דשוקא הוה והרבה באין ממקום אחר לקנות מן השוק לפיכך אין בני העיר מעכבין גם על המוכרים להביא אומנותם ולמכור לנכנסים לשוק: עמוראי. מוכרי צמר: אית לן אשראי במתא. מכרנו באמנה וצריכים אנו לשהות כאן עד שנגבה חובות שלנו ואם אין אנו מוכרין סחורותינו במה נתפרנס: עד דעקריתו. שתעקרו חובותיכם מן הלוקחים מכם באשראי: נקיט ליה שוקא. הכרז שלא ימכור איש בעיר גרוגרות אלא הוא: תהי ליה בקנקניה. הריח לו בקנקנו אם יין הוא אם חומץ כלומר בדקהו בהלכות אם תלמיד חכם הוא אם לאו. ריח היין כשמריחין אותו אם טוב הוא קרי תהי כדאמרינן בת תיהא במסכת ע"ז (דף סו:) וכן בכתובות (דף קה.) קרנא הוה תהי באמברא דחמרא: כפיפה מצרית. סל נצרים של ערבה: מהו. מי חשוב כמעוכל והוה ליה ככלי גללים ואין מקבל טומאה עוד: א"ל. רב דימי לרב אדא: מר ניהו רבא. אתה הוא רבא לפי ששמע על רבא שהוא גדול העיר וסבור שהוא זה: טפח ליה בסנדליה. הכהו על סנדלו במקל דרך שחוק כשם שמכין למי שאינו חשוב: דלא שהייה. שלא נמנע מלהפרע: לאוניתא. אונאת בושתו: דמלכא דאדום. אע"פ שהוא אדומי: על שרפו. מחמת בזיון: דאמר להו לרבנן אדמגרמיתו גרמי בי אביי. שהיה רגיל לומר לתלמידים עד שאתם הולכים אצל אביי לגרס עצמות כלומר ללמוד שלא לשובע: תו אכלו כו'. בואו ולמדו הלכות טובות מרווחות אצל רבא: שמעיה דרבא. שלוחו לקנות בשר: ריש כלה. דורש ברבים בשבתות: דלא הוו בסיומא. יש אומרים שלא היו בעלה כשנעשה רב נחמן ריש כלה ויש אומרים דלא הוו בסיומא דפירקא דרבא דדריש בשבת הרגל הלכות האמורות בפרק אחרון של בכורות: שמעתתא דמעשר בהמה. בפרק אחרון דבכורות ורבא אמרינהו בסופא דפירקא: אתו רבנן. תלמידי הישיבה הבאים לשמוע: נטרנא ערסיה דרב אדא. אני מצפה כאן שיביאו את מטת רב אדא שמת: מתני' לא יסמוך לכותל חבירו כותל אחר אלא אם כן כו'. מפרש בגמ': והחלונות. מי שהיו לו חלונות פתוחים לחצר חבירו והוחזק בדבר זה שלש שנים ובא בעל החצר לבנות שם כותל צריך לשער ד' אמות: בין מלמעלן. אם בא להגביה יגביה כותלו ד' אמות מן החלונות: בין מלמטן. אם בא לבנותו נמוך צריך להשפילו מן החלונות ד' אמות וטעמא מפרש בגמ': בין מכנגדן. צריך להרחיקו מהן ד' אמות:

תוספות

קנאת סופרים תרבה חכמה. ולא גרסי' כמו שיש בספרים דאמר מר עזרא תיקן להם לישראל שיהו מושיבין סופר בצד סופר דהא לא חשיב ליה במרובה (ב"ק דף פב.) גבי עשר תקנות שתיקן: מעלמא אתו ולעלמא ליזבנו. מכאן משמע דביומא דשוקא היה מותר להלוות לבני אדם הבאים ממקומות שם לשוק לנכרים דאתו מעלמא אבל לבני המקום לא ודוקא בשוקא אבל לאהדורי לא: אמר ליה רבא לרב אדא בר אבא. כן גריס רבינו חננאל ולא גרסי' בר אהבה דאותו היה בימי רבי כדאמרינן בקדושין (דף עב: ושם)(ט) היום ישב רב אדא בר אהבה בחיקו של אברהם אבינו: פיל שבלע כפיפה מצרית. בפ' ר' ישמעאל (מנחות דף סט. ושם ד"ה פיל) איתא להך בעיא דהכא ומסיק התם למאי אי למבטל טומאתו תנינא כל הכלים יורדין לידי טומאה במחשבה ואין עולין מטומאתן אלא בשינוי מעשה וקאמר לא צריכא דבלע הוצין ועבדינהו כפיפה אי הוי עיכול והוי ככלי גללים או לא והכא בלע הוצין בעא מיניה דאי כפיפה שלימה אמאי לא הוה בידיה מתני' היא וקשיא לר"ת א"כ אמאי לא נקיטו ליה שוקא הא בעיא זו לא איפשיטא התם וי"ל דמ"מ הוה ליה לאיתויי הנך ראיות דמייתי התם ודחי להו: אנא ענישתיה. כל אחד מהן היה מתאונן שעל ידו מת רב אדא משום דאמרינן בשבת בפ' שואל (דף קמט:) כל מי שחבירו נענש על ידו אין מכניסין אותו במחיצתו של הקב"ה שנאמר (משלי יז) גם ענוש לצדיק לא טוב אלא רע וכתיב (תהלים ה) לא יגורך רע. ר"י: וקמא היכי סמיך. ס"ד דבנפל איירי שכן משמע הלשון דקתני מי שהיה כותלו סמוך לכותל חבירו ומשני רב יהודה הכי קאמר הבא לסמוך כו' ומתני' הכי פירוש' מי שהיה גדול כותלו סמוך לכותל חבירו ורבא פריך דכותל קתני ולא גדול וא"ת לרבא דאמר בריש פירקין דאסור לסמוך קמא היכי סמך ואפילו לפי' ר"ת דלמסקנא שרי רבא לכולהו לסמוך לבד מבור מ"מ ט אמאי לא פריך מהכא דהוי רישא אלא ממשרה וירק דהוי סיפא וי"ל דלא אסר רבא לסמוך אלא מילתא דמגופיה אתי היזק אבל הכא הכותל אינו מזיק כלום אלא שגורם למעט הדושא: אלא

רבינו גרשום

ברוכלין. שמוכרין תכשיטי נשים שרק וכחל אע"ג דלא שייכי בחד כרגא דלא מצי מעכב עליה האי רוכל דמתא: והני מילי דלא מצי מעכב לאהדורי לחזור ולילך משוק לשוק וממבוי למבוי ולמכור ולשוב לעירו אבל לקבוע חנותו בבני רוכלין למזבן תכשיטין לא: דלא כהלכתא. כלומר שלא ילמדו ממנו אחרים הלכה לפנים משורת הדין עבד להו משום דרבנן נינהו דלא ליבטלו מגירסייהו לילך ולחזור בכל העיר ומשוק לשוק: הנהו דקולאי. שמוכרין סלים. אתו דקולאי דמתא ומעכבי להו אמר להו לא מציתו מעכבי עלייהו דמעלמא אתי ולהנהו דאתי מעלמא לשוק לזבוני אבל לאהדורי בבתים לזבונינהו לא דודאי מצי למיעבד עלייהו: אית לן אשראי במתא. חוב שחייבין לנו ממון וצריכין לנו לעכובי הכא עד דפרעי לן והב לן רשותא דניזבון עד כדי חיותן עד דפרעי לן: נקיט ליה שוקא. שלא ימכור אדם עד שימכור כל גרוגרות שלו: תהי ליה. הוי מריח מה יש בו: מצרית. מצורי דקל מהו מי אמרי' הואיל דהוות במעוין והקיאה [דרך] בית הרעי כמאכל שנתעכל דמי ונתבטל' ואין מקבלת טומאה או דלמא הואיל ואכתי קיימת היא דבר חשוב הוי ואינה מבוטלת ומקבלת טומ'. אמר ליה. רב דימי לרב אדא: מאן ניהו מר רבא. הוא רבא: טפח ליה. רב אדא לרב דימי בסנדליה כלומר שלא היה חשוב בעיניו: ורבא רביה דרבך. שהוא רבי ואנא רבך: מאן דלא שבקיה לאוניתא (דעמון) מואב למלכא דאדום: אדמגרמיתו גרמי בי אביי. שהיה רגיל לומר לתלמידי אביי כל זמן שאתם מגררין עצמות שאין בהן לחלוח בי אביי יכולין אתם ללמוד תורה כשורה וכהלכתא בי רבא לפי שאביי לא היה עשיר ולפיכך אמר אביי אנא ענישתיה שהיה מבזהו: ריש כלה הוה. שהיה רגיל לדרוש בשבת שלפני החג ורב נחמן היה דורש אותן שבתות והוו מתקבצין שם מהרבה מקומו' תלמידין לשמוע: נקטוה רב פפא ורב הונא לרב אדא בר אהבה משום דלא הוו בסיומא דמס' בהוכרו קמיה דרבא: קום דנגה לן לדרוש עבר מן היום הרבה: קא נטרנא לערסיה. כלומר שמת לפי שהיה מצער כל כך שלא בא אליו לעיין עמו הדרשה: פיסקא מי שהיה כותלו סמוך לכותל חבירו

עין משפט נר מצוה

מח א ב ג ד מיי' פ"ו מהל' שכנים הל' ט סמג עשין פב טוש"ע ח"מ סי' קנו סעיף ז:
מט ה ו ז ח מיי' שם הלכה י טוש"ע שם סעיף יב:
נ ט מיי' פ"ט שם הל' ט סמג שם טוש"ע ח"מ סי' קנה סעיף יב:
נא י מיי' שם פ"ז הל' ג סמג שם טוש"ע ח"מ סי' קנד סעיף ג וסעיף כב:

מסורת הש"ס

א) [לעיל כא.], ב) ב"ק פב., ג) מנחות סט., ד) [מו"ק כה. ב"ק לב:], ה) [צ"ל לשידך], ו) [צ"ל אדמגרסיתו. ערוך ערך גרם א'], ז) [רש"ל מ"ז וגרם רנב"י אתו רבנן א"ל לרב נב"י], ח) [לעיל ב:], ט) [ע"ש ד"ה היום ושם ד"ה ור"ש ועי' תוס' תענית כ: ד"ה א"ל].

הגהות הב"ח

(א) גמ' אבל לאהדורי נמצא לא: (ב) שם אית לן במתא אמר: (ג) שם וקא נטרנא לערסיה:

גליון הש"ס

תוס' ד"ה וקמא כו' אמאי לא פריך מהכא. קשה לי על קושייתם דהא מהכא לא היה ראיה לפסור ולחזור מכל שינוי דלעיל ולהוכיח דגם לרבנן דר"מ מותר לסמוך לרבה דהא כמו דמשנינן על אילן קדש לבור [illegible]

תורה אור השלם

א) כֹּה אָמַר יְיָ עַל שְׁלֹשָׁה פִּשְׁעֵי מוֹאָב וְעַל אַרְבָּעָה לֹא אֲשִׁיבֶנּוּ עַל שָׂרְפוֹ עַצְמוֹת מֶלֶךְ אֱדוֹם לַשִּׂיד: [עמוס ב, א]

ליקוטי רש"י

תהי ליה. לשון מריח כמו בת תיהא דמסכת עבודה זרה (סו.) [עירובין סו.]. לשון מרים קול [ב"ק עו:]. כפיפה מצרית. סל של נצרי דקל [שבת צח:]. סל של נצרי דקל וזרדים שגדילין סביב הדקל [סוטה יד.]. קופה מצרית מנצרי דקל [מנחות סט.]. טפח ליה בסנדליה. על סנדלו וכו' ע"ש הכהו בסנדלו [מו"ק כה.].

הכהו על סנדלו ל"ש בעט בסנדלו [ב"ק לב:]. החלונות. אחד מבני השותפים הבונה כותל בחצר כנגד חלונותיו של חבירו בין מלמעלה וכו' אם הכותל גבוה יותר מן החלונות צריך להגביה למעלה מהן ד"א כדמפרש ואזיל כדי שלא יסמוך על כותלו ויסתכל וילאה בין מלמטן. אם הכותל נמוך מן החלונות צריך להשפילו מהן ד"א כדי שלא יעמוד על גבי כותלו ויראה. בין מכנגדן. צריך להרחיק את הכותל מן החלונות ד' אמות כדי שלא יאפיל [לעיל ב:].

ונפל לא יסמוך כותל אחר. שלא יבנה שם כותל אחר אלא אם כן הרחיק ממנו משום דוושא כדמפרש בגמ'. החלונות מלמעלן ומלמטן ומכנגדן ד' אמות כדמפרש בריש פ"ק: ומקשי' וכותל קמא דנפל דהוה מעיקרא היכי סמיך בקרוב מד' אמות: אמר רב יהודה. הכי קאמר מתני' הבא לסמוך לכותל וכו':

אָמְרוּ לֵיהּ רַבָּנָן לְרַב נַחְמָן בַּר יִצְחָק – **The rabbis** who had assembled to hear the lecture **said to Rav Nachman bar Yitzchak:** קוּם דְּנַגְהָ לָן לָמָּה יָתִיב מַר – **"Arise** to give the lecture, **for it is late. Why is master sitting?"** אָמַר לְהוּ – **[Rav Nachman] said to them:** יָתֵיבְנָא וְקָא (מנטרא) [נָטַרְנָא] לְעַרְסֵיהּ דְּרַב אַדָּא בַּר אַבָּא – **"I am sitting and waiting for the bier**[21] **of Rav Adda bar Abba** to arrive."[22] אַדְּהָכִי נָפַק קָלָא דְּנָח נַפְשֵׁיהּ דְּרַב אַדָּא בַּר אַבָּא – **In the meantime, word came out that Rav Adda bar Abba had died.**[23]

The Gemara concludes:

וּמִסְתַּבְּרָא דְּרַב נַחְמָן בַּר יִצְחָק עַנְשֵׁיהּ – **And** the most **likely** explanation is **that** it was **Rav Nachman bar Yitzchak** who **punished him;** i.e. Rav Adda bar Abba died as a result of the remark made by Rav Nachman bar Yitzchak.

Mishnah The Mishnah sets forth restrictions against erecting a wall near the wall of a neighbor: מִי שֶׁהָיָה כּוֹתְלוֹ סָמוּךְ לְכוֹתֶל חֲבֵירוֹ – **One whose wall was near the wall of his neighbor** לֹא יִסְמוֹךְ לוֹ כּוֹתֶל אַחֵר – **may not place another wall near [his neighbor's wall]** אֶלָּא אִם כֵּן הִרְחִיק מִמֶּנּוּ אַרְבַּע אַמּוֹת – **unless he distances it** at least **four** ***amos*** **from [his neighbor's wall].**[24] הַחַלּוֹנוֹת – One who builds a wall opposite **the windows** of his neighbor's house בֵּין מִלְמַעְלָן בֵּין מִלְמַטָּן – must ensure that **either above or below [the windows],** בֵּין כְּנֶגְדָּן – **and** certainly **in front of them,** אַרְבַּע אַמּוֹת – there is a distance of at least **four** ***amos***. I.e. the top of the wall must be either four *amos* higher or four *amos* lower than the window; and, regardless of the wall's height, the horizontal distance between it and the window must be at least four *amos*.[25]

Gemara The first sentence of the Mishnah seems to mean that one who had a wall within four *amos* of his neighbor's wall and it collapsed[26] may not build another in its stead unless he distances it at least four *amos* from the neighbor's wall. The Gemara finds this to be an inherent contradiction:

וְקַמָּא הֵיכִי סָמִיךְ – **But how could he have put the first [wall] near** the wall of his neighbor? Why is it that only the second wall must be distanced and not the first one?

The Gemara answers:

אָמַר רַב יְהוּדָה – **Rav Yehudah said:** הָכִי קָאָמַר – **This is what [the Mishnah] means:**

NOTES

21. Literally: his bed. A stretcher was used for this purpose [Emendation follows *Bach*.]

22. [Rav Nachman said this jocularly: Since Rav Adda has not yet arrived, it would seem that he has died!]

23. Rav Nachman was afraid that it was his statement ("I am waiting for the bier of Rav Adda bar Abba") that had brought about Rav Adda bar Abba's death. A curse uttered by a righteous man, even if it is unintentional, is carried out immediately. The Gemara (*Moed Kattan* 18a, *Bava Metzia* 68a) compares this to a king who issues an order to execute someone. The king's order is carried out even if it was in error.

24. The Gemara (22b) explains what this means (*Rashi*).

25. The reasons for these restrictions are discussed by the Gemara (22b).

26. *Tosafos*.

קנאת סופרים תרבה חכמה אמר רב נחמן בר יצחק ומודה רב הונא בריה דרב יהושע ברוכלין המחזירין בעיירות דלא מצי מעכב דאמר מר עזרא תקן להן לישראל שיהו רוכלין מחזירין בעיירות כדי שיהו תכשיטין מצויין לבנות ישראל והני מילי לאהדורי אבל לאקבועי לא ואי צורבא מרבנן הוא אפילו לאקבועי נמי כי הא דרבא שרא להו לר' יאשיה ולרב עובדיה לאקבועי דלא כהלכתא מאי טעמא כיון דרבנן נינהו אתו לטרדו מגירסייהו הנהו דיקולאי דאייתו דיקלאי לבבל אתו בני מתא קא מעכבי עלויהו אתו לקמיה דרבינא אמר להו מעלמא אתו ולעלמא ליזבנו והני מילי ביומא דשוקא אבל בלא יומא דשוקא לא וביומא דשוקא נמי לא אמרינן אלא לזבוני בשוקא אבל לאהדורי לא הנהו עמוראי דאייתו עמרא לפום נהרא אתו בני מתא קא מעכבי עלויהו אתו לקמיה דרב כהנא אמר להו דינא הוא דמעכבי עלייכו אמרו ליה אית לן אשראי אמר להו זילו זבנו שיעור חיותייכו עד דעקריתו אשראי דידכו ואזליתו רב דימי מנהרדעא אייתי גרוגרות בספינה א"ל ריש גלותא לרבא פוק חזי אי צורבא מרבנן הוא נקיט ליה שוקא א"ל רבא לרב אדא בר אבא פוק תהי ליה בקנקניה נפק [אזל] בעא מיניה פיל שבלע כפיפה מצרית והקיאה דרך בית הרעי מהו לא הוה בידיה א"ל מר ניהו רבא טפח ליה בסנדליה א"ל בין דידי לרבא איכא טובא מיהו על כרחך אנא רבך ורבא רבה דרבך לא נקטו ליה שוקא פסיד גרוגרות דידיה אתא לקמיה דרב יוסף א"ל חזי מר מאי עבדו לי א"ל מאן דלא שהייה לאוניתא דמלכא דאדום לא נשהייה לאוניתך דכתיב כה אמר ה' על שלשה פשעי מואב ועל ארבעה לא אשיבנו על שרפו עצמות מלך אדום לסיד נח נפשיה דרב אדא בר אבא רב יוסף אמר אנא ענישתיה דאנא לטייתיה רב דימי מנהרדעא אמר אנא ענישתיה דאפסיד גרוגרות דידי אביי אמר אנא ענישתיה דאמר להו לרבנן אדמגרמיתו גרמי בי אביי תו אכלו בישרא [שמינא] בי רבא ורבא אמר אנא ענישתיה [דכי הוה אזיל לבי טבחא למשקל אומצא] אמר להו לטבחי אנא שקילנא בישרא מיקמי שמעיה דרבא דאנא עדיפנא מיניה רב נחמן בר יצחק אמר אנא ענישתיה דרב נחמן בר יצחק ריש כלה הוה כל יומא מיקמי דניעול לכלה מרהיט בהדיה רב אדא בר אבא והדר עייל לכלה ההוא יומא נקטוה רב פפא ורב הונא בריה דרב יהושע לרב אדא בר אבא משום דלא הוו בסיומא אמרו ליה אימא לן הני שמעתתא דמעשר בהמה היכי אמרינהו רבא אמר להו הכי אמר רבא והכי אמר רבא אדהכי נגה ליה [לרב נחמן בר יצחק] (ולא אתי רב אדא בר אבא) אמרו ליה רבנן לרב נחמן בר יצחק קום דנגה לן למה יתיב מר אמר להו יתיבנא וקא מנטרנא לערסיה דרב אדא בר אבא אדהכי נפק קלא דנח נפשיה דרב אדא בר אבא ומסתברא דרב נחמן בר יצחק ענשיה:

מתני' מי שהיה כותלו סמוך לכותל חבירו לא יסמוך לו כותל אחר אא"כ הרחיק ממנו ארבע אמות החלונות בין מלמעלן בין מלמטן בין כנגדן ארבע אמות: **גמ'** וקמא היכי סמיך אמר רב יהודה הכי קאמר הבא

רש"י

ומודה רב הונא בריה דרב יהושע. אע"ג דאמר בר מתא אבר מתא אחריתי מצי מעכב מלהביא כאן ולמכור מודה הוא ברוכלין מוכרי בשמים המחזירין בעיירות להביא בשמים לנשים להתקשט בהן דלא מצו לעכב עלייהו רוכלי העיר: **לאהדורי.** לחזור ולסבב במבואות העיר ובבתים על כל הרוצה לקנות ואחרי כן ישוב לעירו: **ואי צורבא מרבנן הוא.** דטריד בגירסא ולא אורחיה לאהדורי אפי' לאקבועי נמי: **דלא כהלכתא.** אלא לפנים משורת הדין: **דיקולאי.** מוכרי סלים ויש אומרים מוכרי יורות: **ולעלמא ליזבנו.** יומא דשוקא הוא והרבה באין ממקום אחר לקנות מן השוק לפיכך אין בני העיר מעכבין גם על המוכרים להביא אומנותם ולמכור לנקבלים לשוק: **עמוראי.** מוכרי צמר: **אית לן אשראי במתא.** מכרנו באמנה ולקוחים אנו לשהות כאן עד שנגבה חובות שלנו ואם אין אנו מוכרין סחורותינו במה נתפרנס: **עד דעקריתו.** שתעקרו חובותיכם מן הלוקחים מכם באשראי: **נקיט ליה שוקא.** הכרז שלא ימכור איש בעיר גרוגרות אלא הוא: **תהי ליה בקנקניה.** הריח לו בקנקנו אם יין הוא אם חומץ כלומר בדקהו בהלכות אם תלמיד חכם הוא אם לאו. ריח היין כשמריחין אותו אם טוב הוא קרי תהי כדאמרינן בת תיהא במסכת ע"ז (דף סו:) וכן בכתובות (דף קה.) קרנא הוה תהי באמברא דחמרא: **כפיפה מצרית.** של נצרים של ערבה. **מהו.** מי חשוב כמעוכל והוה ליה ככלי גללים ואין מקבל טומאה עוד: **א"ל.** רב דימי לרב אדא: **מר ניהו רבא.** אתה הוא רבא לפי שמשמע על רבא שהוא גדול העיר וסבור שהוא זה: **טפח ליה בסנדליה.** הכהו על סנדלו במקל דרך שחוק כשם שמכין למי שאינו חשוב: **דלא שהייה.** שלא נמנע מלהפרע: **לאוניתא.** אונאת בושתו: **דמלכא דאדום.** אע"פ שהוא אדומי: **על שרפו.** מחמת בזיון: **דאמר להו לרבנן אדמגרמיתו גרמי בי אביי.** שהיה רגיל לומר לתלמידים עד שאתם הולכים אצל אביי לגרס עצמות כלומר ללמוד שלא לשובע: **תו אכלו כו'.** כלומר ולמדו הלכות לשובע מרווחות אצל רבא: **שמעיה דרבא.** שלוחו לקנות בשר: **ריש כלה.** דורש ברבים בשבתות: **דלא הוו בסיומא.** יש אומרים שלא היו בעלה כשנעשה רב נחמן ריש כלה ויש אומרים דלא הוו בסיומא דפירקא דרבא דדריש בשבת הרגל הלכות האמורות בפרק אחרון של בכורות: **שמעתתא דמעשר בהמה.** בפרק אחרון דבכורות ורבא אמרינהו בסופה דפירקא: **אתו רבנן.** תלמידי הישיבה הבאים לשמוע: **נטרנא ערסיה דרב אדא.** אני מלפה כאן שיביאו את מטת רב אדא שמת: **מתני' לא יסמוך לכותל חבירו כותל אחר אלא אם כן כו'.** מפרש בגמ': **והחלונות.** מי שהיו לו חלונות פתוחים לחצר חבירו והוחזק בדבר זה שלש שנים ובא בעל החצר לבנות שם כותל צריך לשער ד' אמות: **בין מלמעלן.** אם בא להגביה יגביה כותלו ד' אמות מן החלונות: **בין מלמטן.** אם בא לבנותו נמוך צריך להשפילו מן החלונות ד' אמות וטעמא מפרש בגמ': **בין מכנגדן.** צריך להרחיקו מהן ד' אמות:

תוספות

קנאת סופרים תרבה חכמה. ולא גרסי' כמו שיש בספרים דאמר מר עזרא תיקן להם לישראל שיהו מושיבין סופר בצד סופר דהא לא חשיב ליה במרובה (ב"ק דף פב.) גבי עשר תקנות שתיקן: **מעלמא אתו ולעלמא ליזבנו.** מכאן משמע דביומא דשוקא היה מותר להלוות לבני אדם הבאים ממקומות שם לשוק לנכרים דאתו מעלמא אבל לבני המקום לא ודוקא בשוקא אבל לאהדורי לא: **אמר ליה רבא לרב אדא בר אבא.** כן גרים רבינו חננאל ולא גרסי' בר אהבה דאותו היה בימי רבי כדאמרינן בקדושין (דף עב: ושם) היום ישב רב אדא בר אהבה בחיקו של אברהם אבינו: **פיל שבלע כפיפה מצרית.** בפ' ר' ישמעאל (מנחות דף סט. ושם ד"ה פיל) איתא להך בעיא דהכא ומסיק התם למאי אי למבטל טומאתו תניא כל הכלים יורדין לידי טומאה במחשבה ואין עולין מטומאתן אלא בשינוי מעשה וקאמר לא צריכה דבלע הוצין ועבדינהו כפיפה אי הוי עיכול והוי ככלי גללים או לא והכא בלע הוצין בעא מיניה דאי כפיפה שלימה אמאי לא הוה בידיה מתני' היא וקשיא לר"ת א"כ אמאי לא נקטו ליה שוקא הא בעיא זו לא איפשיטא התם וי"ל דמ"מ הוה ליה לאיתויי הנך ראיות דמייתי התם ודחי להו: **אנא ענישתיה.** כל אחד מהן היה מתאונן שעל ידו מת רב אדא משום דאמרינן בשבת בפ' שואל (דף קמט:) כל מי שחבירו נענש על ידו אין מכניסין אותו במחיצתו של הקב"ה שנאמר (משלי יז) גם ענוש לצדיק לא טוב אלא רע וכתיב (תהלים ה) לא יגורך רע. ר"י: **וקמא היכי סמיך.** ס"ד דבנפל איירי שכן משמע הלשון דקתני מי שהיה כותלו סמוך לכותל חבירו ומשני רב יהודה הכי קאמר הבא לסמוך כו' ומתני' הכי פירוש' מי שהיה גבול כותלו סמוך לכותל חבירו ורבא פריך דכותל קתני ולא גבול וא"ת לרבא דאמר בריש פירקין דאסור לסמוך קמא היכי סמך ואפילו לפי' ר"ת דלמסקנא שרי רבא לכולהו לסמוך לבד מבור מ"מ אמאי לא פריך מהכא דהוי רישא אלא ממשרה וירק דהוי סיפא וי"ל דלא אסר רבא לסמוך אלא מילתא דמגופיה אתי היזק אבל הכא הכותל אינו מזיק כלום אלא שגורם למעט הדוושא: אלא

עין משפט נר מצוה

מח א ב ג ד מיי' פ"ו מהל' שכנים הל' ט סמג עשין פב טוש"ע ח"מ סי' קנו סעיף ו:
מט ה ו ז ח מיי' שם הלכה י טוש"ע שם סעיף ז:
נ ט מיי' פ"ט שם הל' ט סמג שם טוש"ע ח"מ סי' קנה סעיף יג:
נא י מיי' שם פ"ז הל' א ב ג סמג שם טוש"ע ח"מ סי' קנד סעיף ג וסעיף כב:

רבינו גרשום

ברוכלין. שמוכרין תכשיטי נשים שרק וכחל אע"ג דלא שייכי בחד כרגא דלא מצי מעכב עליה האי רוכל דמתא: **והני מילי** דלא מצי מעכב **לאהדורי** לחזור ולילך משוק לשוק וממבוי למבוי ולמכור ולשוב לעירו אבל **לקבוע** חנותו בהני רוכלין למזבן תכשיטין **לא**: **דלא כהלכתא.** כלומר שלא ילמדו ממנו אחרים הלכה דלפנים משורת הדין עבד להו משום **דרבנן נינהו דלא** ליבטלו **מגירסייהו** לילך ולחזור בכל העיר ומשוק לשוק: **הנהו דקולאי.** שמוכרין סלים. **אתו דקולאי דמתא ומעכבי להו אמר להו** לא מציתו מעכבי עלייהו **דמעלמא אתי** ולהנהו דאתי **מעלמא** לשוק **לזבני אבל לאהדורי** בבתים לזבונינהו **לא** דודאי מצי למיעכב עלייהו: **אית לן אשראי במתא.** חוב שחייבין לנו ממון וצריכין לנו לעכובי הכא עד דפרעי לן והב לן רשותא דניזבין עד כפי חיותן עד דפרעי לן: **נקיט ליה שוקא.** שלא ימכור אדם עד שימכור כל גרוגרות שלו: **תהי ליה.** הוי מריח מה יש בו: **מצרית.** מצורי דקל מהו מי אמרי' הואיל דהוות במעיו **והקיאה [דרך] בית הרעי** כמאכל שנתעכל דמי ונתבטל' ואין מקבלת טומאה או דלמא הואיל ואכתי קיימת היא דבר חשוב הוי ואינה מבוטלת ומקבלת טומא': **אמר ליה.** רב דימי לרב אדא: **מאן נינהו מר רבא.** את הוא רבא: **טפח ליה.** רב אדא לרב דימי **בסנדליה** כלומר שלא היה חשוב בעיניו: **ורבא רביה דרבך.** שהוא רבי ואנא רבך: **מאן דלא שבקיה. לאוניתא** (דעמון) דמואב למלכא דאדום: **אדמגרמיתו גרמי בי אביי.** שהיה רגיל לומר לתלמידי אביי כל זמן שאתם מגררין עצמות שאין בהן לחלוח בי אביי יכולין אתם ללמוד תורה כשורה וכהלכתא בי רבא לפי שאביי לא למד כל כך ולפיכך אמר אביי אנא ענישתיה שהיה מבזיני: **ריש כלה הוה.** שהיה רגיל לדרוש בשבת שלפני החג ורב נחמן היה דורש אותן שבתות והיו מתקבצין שם מהרבה מקומו' תלמידין לשמוע: **עכבוהו רב פפא ורב הונא לרב אדא בר אהבה משום דלא הוי בסיומא** במס' בכורו' קמיה דרבא: **קום** והכנס לדרוש **דנגה לן** שכבר עבר מן היום הרבה: **קא נטרנא לערסיה.** כלומר שמת לפי שהיה מצערו כל כך שלא בא אליו לעיין עמו הדרשה: **פיסקא מי שהיה כותלו סמוך לכותל חבירו** ונפל **לא יסמוך כותל אחר.** שלא יבנה שם כותל אחר **אלא אם כן הרחיק ממנו** מכותל חבירו **ד' אמות** משום דוושא כדמפרש בגמ'. **החלונות מלמעלן ומלמטן ומכנגדן ד' אמות** כדמפרש בריש פ"ק: ומקשי' וכותל **קמא** דנפל דהוה מעיקרא **היכי סמיך** בקרוב מד' אמות: **אמר רב יהודה.** הכי תריץ מתני' **הבא לסמוך** תחלה **לא יסמוך** לכותל וכו':

מסורת הש"ס

א) [לעיל כא.], ב) ב"ק פב., ג) מנחות סט., ד) [מו"ק כה. ב"ק לב:], ה) [נ"ל לשיד], ו) [נ"ל אדמגרסיתו. ערוך ערך גרם א'], ז) [רש"ל מ"ז וגרס רנב"י אתו רבנן א"ל לרב נב"י], ח) [לעיל ב:], ט) [ע"ש ד"ה היום וברש"י שם וע"ע תוס' תענית כ: ד"ה א"ל]:

הגהות הב"ח

(א) גמ' אבל לאהדורי במתא לא: (ב) שם אית לן אשראי במתא אמר: (ג) שם וקא נטרנא לערסיה:

גליון הש"ס

תוס' ד"ה וקמא כו' **אמאי לא פריך מהכא.** קשה לי על קושייתם הא מהכא לא היה ראיה לסתור ולחזור מכל שינויי דלעיל ולהוכיח דגם לרבנן דר"י מותר לסמוך לרבא דהא כמו דמשנינן על אילן קדם לבור דמיירי בלוקח ה"נ י"ל הכא דמיירי בלוקח המקום שאצל כותל חבירו. גם תמוה לי במה דנקטו קושייתם רק לס"ד דלעיל הא מבואר בסוגיא דחרדל דלמסקנא מה דקתני ר"י מתיר בחרדל היינו דאמר לדבריהם דרבנן הטינח משרה וירק אבל חרדל יהיה מותר לסמוך אף דבעל דבורים סמך בהיתר מ"מ כיון דקלא עשה שלא כהוגן ומזיק להחרדל מותר לזה להעמיד אצלו חרדלו בלי הרחקה כיון דבעל דבורים מזיק גם אותו. ועלה אמרי' לעיל לרבנן היינו דרבנן לא היה להם לחלוק על סברא זו ומשני דס"ל דדבורים לא מזקי לחרדל עיי"ש היטב. א"כ הכא בדוושא דשניהם מזיקים זה לזה מה בכך שהראשון העמיד כותלו תחלה מ"מ יהא השני מותר לסמוך כותלו דאמר לו כמו שכותלי מזיק אותך כן כותלך מזיק אותי ויעמוד דזה לא יתורץ בתירוצם דדוושא לא הוי מזיק ממש מ"מ יאמר השני מה שאני מזיק בדוושא כמו כן אתה מזיקני בדוושא. ויותר נראה דהכא בלוקח דהראשון לא עשה כלל שלא כהוגן הלוקח צריך לכן הרחקה כמ"ש תוס' בסוגיא דחרדל ולע"ג:

תורה אור השלם

א) כֹּה אָמַר יְיָ עַל שְׁלֹשָׁה פִּשְׁעֵי מוֹאָב וְעַל אַרְבָּעָה לֹא אֲשִׁיבֶנּוּ עַל שָׂרְפוֹ עַצְמוֹת מֶלֶךְ אֱדוֹם לַשִּׂיד: [עמוס ב, א]

ליקוטי רש"י

תהי ליה. לשון מריח כמו בת תיהא דמסכת עבודה זרה (סו:) [עירובין סו.]. לשון מריח בקנקן [ב"ק עו:]. **כפיפה מצרית.** סל העשוי מלולבי דקל [שבת צה:]. סל של נצרי דקל ודרים במגרדין אותו [סוטה יד.]. קופה מצרית מלולבי דקל [מנחות סט.]. **טפח ליה בסנדליה.** על סנדלו וכו' ע"ש הכהו בסנדלו [מו"ק כה.]. הכהו על סנדלו לא"ש כמו בעט בסנדלו [ב"ק לב:]. **החלונות.** אחד מבני השותפים הבונה כותל בחצר כנגד חלונותיו של חבירו בין מלמעלה וכו' אם הכותל גבוה יותר מן החלונות צריך להגביה למעלה מהן ד"א כדמפרש ואזיל כדי שלא יסמוך על כותלו ויצפה לתוך חלונותיו של חבירו. **בין מלמטן.** אם הכותל נמוך מן החלונות צריך להשפילו מהן ד"א כדי שלא יעמוד על גבי כותלו ויראה. **בין מכנגדן.** צריך להרחיק את הכותל מן החלונות ד' אמות כדי שלא יאפיל [לעיל ב:].

עין משפט נר מצוה

נב א מיי' פ"ט מהל' שכנים הל' ט סמג עשין פב טוש"ע ח"מ סי' קנה סעיף יג ובהג"ה ועיין בטור:

נג ב ג מיי' שם וע' בהשגות ובמ"מ טוש"ע שם סעיף יג:

נד ד מיי' שם פ"ז הל' א ב ג סמג שם טוש"ע ח"מ סי' קנד סעיף כב:

נה ה מיי' שם הל' ד וסמג שם טוש"ע שם סעיף כג וסי' קנה סעיף יד בהג"ה:

נו ו ז מיי' שם הל' ד וסמג שם טוש"ע ח"מ סי' קנד סעיף כב:

נז ח מיי' פ"ט שם הל' ה טוש"ע שם סעיף כד:

נח ט מיי' שם הל' ז סמג שם טוש"ע ח"מ סי' קנה סעיף כח:

נט י מיי' שם הל' ח טוש"ע שם סעיף לד:

ס כ מיי' שם פ"י הל' ה וסמג שם טוש"ע שם סעיף לא לב לג:

רבינו גרשום

והא מי שהיה כותלו סמוך לכותל חבירו קתני. כלומר להוסיף על המשנה ולתרצה את יכול אבל לחסר מינה אין אתה יכול: אלא אמר רבא הכי קאמר מי שהיה וכו' מאי טעמא דדוושא דהכא מהני התם. כלומר מש"ה צריכה להרחיק ד' אמות כדי שיהיו דשין שם בני אדם העוברין בינתים ומעלי ההיא דישה לכותל שניהם שמתחזקין היסודות: אמר רב לא שנו. צריך להרחיק ד' אמות אלא מכותל גינה שאין דשין שם בני אדם בשדה מחמת הירקות אבל בכותל חצר שנידושה היא מעיקרא שאינה צריכה חזוק הבא לסמוך סומך בפחות מד': בעיר ישנה. שנידושה היא מכבר שנים הא בא לסמוך סומך אבל בעיר חדשה אינו סומך בלא הרחקה מפני שצריכה דישה לחזק: מלמעלן. אם בנה כותל מן הצד סמוך לחלון חבירו צריך להגביה הכותל ד' אמות יותר מן החלון: כדי שלא יעמוד על כותלו וישוח ויציץ בחלון. ואם מגמיכו צריך להגמיכו מן החלון ד' אמות: שלא יעמוד. על כותלו זקוף ויראה בחלון ואם בנהו כנגדו צריך להרחיק ד' אמות שלא יאפיל חלונו: הכא במאי עסקינן. דקתני שלא יאפיל בבונהו מן הצד שלא מן החלון ולא כנגדו וצריך להרחיק מן החלון כדי שלא יאפיל השתא לא מצי למידק דטעמא שלא יאפיל אבל משום דוושא לא דהא ליכא מקום דוושא טובא אלא דוק מינה הכי ומכנגדו כלומר אם בנהו מכנגד חלון צריך להרחיק ד' אמות כדי שלא יאפיל אבל אם בונהו מן הצד סמוך לחלון אין צריך להרחיק כולי האי ד' אמות דבבציר מהכי סגי דמן צדי חלון לא מאפיל עליה כולי האי כמו מכנגדו ובבציר הרחקה סגי: וכמה. שיעור צריך להרחיק כותלו מן צד

 צריך להרחיק ולא מאפיל. ומקשי' הואיל ולא מרחיק כותלו משום היזק אורה אלא מלא רוחב החלון לא מגבי ליה נמי משום היזק ראיה למעלה מן החלון אלא כמלא רוחב חלון הא מציץ א"כ יכול להציץ בחלון: במדיר את כותלו. שעושהו חד למעלה כמדרון מכאן ומכאן שאינו יכול לעמוד עליו ולהציץ: והא אנן תנן ד' אמות צריך להרחיק. והיכי מצית למימר כמלא רוחב חלון. לא קשיא כאן מרוח אחת כלומר אם בנה כותל מצד אחד של חלון אינו צריך להרחיק אלא מלא רוחב חלון והא דקתני מתני' ד' אמות מן הצד נמי מיירי וכגון שבנה ב' כתלים מב' רוחות של חלון הואיל ואלו ב' כתלים מאפילים הרבה מש"ה צריך להרחיק מצד החלון ד' אמות. תנן ואת הכותל מרחיקין מן המזחילה של חבירו ד' אמות. שאם יש לחבירו חזקה בחצירו שהמזחילה של גגו שופכת בחצרו הואיל ויש לו כך חזקה יכול לזקוף סולם בחצר חבירו ואם רצה זה לבנות כותל סמוך לגגו צריך להרחיק ד' אמות ממנו כדי זקיפת סולם: הכא במאי עסקינן. דקתני זקיפת סולם ולאו משום דוושא צריך למיתני: דמצי אזלי תותי. ההיא שפוע היוצא חוץ לכותל ומצי למעביד דוושא אבל משום זקיפת סולם צריך להרחיק מן המזחילה ואילך ד' אמות: פיסקא כדי שלא תקפוץ הנמייה. חיה בסולם של שובך ואוכלת בשובך מיירי. דאם יש לזה שובך בצד כותלו של חבירו ולאידך סולם צריך להרחיק סולמו מן השובך ד' אמות: לימא מתני' דלא כר' יוסי דאמר זה חופר בתוך שלו וזה נוטע בתוך שלו הכא נמי זה זוקף סולמו בתוך שלו: מודה ר' יוסי בגירי דידיה. כלומר הכא שאני דהוי כעין שזורק אדם חץ ומזיק באותה זריקה דחייב: דהוי גירי דידיה ממש: זאת אומרת גרמא בניזקין אסור. ואע"ג דעביד בתוך שלו: דזימנין דבהדי דמנח ליה לסולם בתוך ד' אמות ממש יתבא בחור וקפצה דהואיל וקרוב לשובך הוא ואמאי חייב: תאלי. אילנות בחורים.

אלא אמר רבא ה"ק מי שהיה כותלו כו'. הקשה ריב"ס דלמה ליה למינקט בכי האי גוונא שהיה לו כותל ברחוק ארבע אמות ונפל ליתני שלא יסמוך כותלו לכותל חבירו אא"כ הרחיק ארבע אמות וליכא למימר דלדוקא בכי האי גוונא שהיה רחוק כבר ארבע אמות והרחיק הראשון קאמר דלא יסמוך א"כ מאי פריך בסמוך טעמא שלא יאפיל הא משום סולם אבל משום דוושא לא: אבל משום דוושא לא. וא"ת וליכא דאיירי בעיר ישנה ולומר ר"ת דבית הוי כגינה לפי שמוטתן מטה וכלים אצל הכותל ועוד י"ל דבהאי איכא דוושא דרבים מה שאין כן בבית ולר"י נראה דניחא ליה לשנויי בעיר חדשה דומיא דרישא וכן הסיפא דמרחיקין את הכותל מן המזחילה אע"ג דמפסקת בינתים הסיפא דמרחיקין את הסולם מן השובך: וכמה אמר רב ייבא כו'. ותימה דהשתא בעי וכמה ובתר הכי פריך והתנן ארבע אמות וי"ל דרב ייבא גופיה בעי וכמה ולא גמר' וכעניין זה יש בהלו מליאות (ב"מ דף כא. ושם ד"ה וכמה): במדיר את כותלו. ולא מצי לשנויי במגביה כותלו ד' אמות דליון דקאי מן הצד ואורך הכותל לרחבו של חלון יכול לעמוד בסוף הכותל ולשחות ולהציץ: והא אנן תנן ארבע אמות. למתני' איירי נמי מן הצד כיון דלא חיים לדוושא אלא משום חלונות: לימא תנן סתמא דלא כרבי יוסי. פר"ח מדקאמר הכא טפי לימא דלא כרבי יוסי ולא קאמר אמשניות דלעיל משמע דכולהו אתי כר"י והוי כולהו גירי דיליה דמהסיא שעתא משתכחת היזיקא ולא פליג רבי יוסי אלא באילן ול"נ לפי' דמתניתין דלעיל הוי נמי גירי דיליה דמיד כשסומך הכותל מונע הדוושא: כדי שיהא זוקף את הסולם. כשמכר ונתן לו זקיפת הסולם בחצירו איירי וקמ"ל דבעי ארבע אמות: והא גרמא הוא. תימה דלא פריך הכי לעיל גבי דוושא: זאת אומרת גרמא בנזקין אסור. ומעיקרא ס"ד כי היכי (ה) דמעיקרא פטור ה"נ דמותר הכא משמע דגרמא בנזקין דפטור וכן בפ' כילד הרגל (ב"ק דף כו:) זרק כלי מראש הגג והיו תחתיו כרים וכסתות וקדם וסילקן אפילו הוא פטור ובפרק הפרה (שם דף מז:) הכניס פירות לחצר בעל הבית שלא ברשות כו' וקאמר בגמרא דאם אכלה והוזקה פטור ונתן סם המות לפני בהמת חבירו דפטור (שם) ושולח בעירו ביד חרש שוטה וקטן (שם נט:) ופורץ גדר בפני בהמת חבירו וכופף קמת חבירו בפני הדליקה ועושה מלאכה במי חטאת (שם נו.) וליבה וליבתו הרוח דפטור בכל הנך כדאמר בפרק הכונס (שם דף נט:) ומבעית חבירו דהוי נמי גרמא כדאמר בפרק קמא דקדושין (דף כד:) דאיהו הוא דאבעית אנפשיה וכילד הרגל (ב"ק דף כג:) שיסה בו כלב שיסה בו נחש פטור ויש ליתן טעם מאי שנא כל הני מדינא דגרמי כגון אחוי דהגוזל בתרא (שם דף קטז: ושם) ומראה דינר לשולחני ונמצא רע ונפרעה אומר לו גדור ודן את הדין דחייב לר"מ אפילו לא נשא ונתן בידו והשורף שטרותיו של חבירו ומוכר שטר חוב לחבירו וחזר ומחלו וחילק רבינו יצחק לשון אח' דדינא דגרמי חייב היינו שעושה הוא עצמו היזק לממון חבירו ועוד חילק דדינא דגרמי דחייב היינו (ו) משעת מעשה שבא ההיזק ועל הכל קשה טיהר את הטמא ובעה"ב עצמו עירבן עם פירותיו ואמאי חייב דהוא עצמו אינו עושה היזק בממון חבירו וגם באותה שעה שמטהר אינו בא ההיזק ונראה לריצב"א דדינא דגרמי הוי מטעם קנס כדמוכח בירושלמי ולכך כל היזק המצוי ורגיל לבא קנסו חכמים וטעם דקנסו שלא יהא כל אחד הולך ומזיק לחבירו בעין והיינו טעמא דמאן דמחייב בהיזק שאינו ניכר ואפשר דבשוגג נמי קניס רבי מאיר כי היכי דקניס במטמא ומדמע אחד שוגג ואחד מזיד: אתו

הבא לסמוך לא יסמוך אלא אם כן הרחיק ממנו ארבע אמות מתקיף לה רבא והא מי שהיה כותלו סמוך לכותל חבירו קתני אלא אמר רבא הכי קתני מי שהיה כותלו סמוך לכותל חבירו ברחוק ארבע אמות ונפל לא יסמוך לו כותל אחר אלא אם כן הרחיק ממנו ד' אמות מ"ט דדוושא דהכא מעלי להתם אמר רב לא שנו אלא כותל גינה אבל כותל חצר אם בא לסמוך סומך רבי אושעיא אומר אחד כותל גינה ואחד כותל חצר אם בא לסמוך אינו סומך אמר רבי יוסי בר חנינא ולא פליגי הא בעיר ישנה הא בעיר חדשה תנן החלונות בין מלמעלן בין מלמטן בין מכנגדן ארבע אמות ותני עלה מלמעלן כדי שלא יציץ ויראה מלמטן שלא יעמוד ויראה ומכנגדן שלא יאפיל טעמא שלא יאפיל אבל משום דוושא לא הכא במאי עסקינן בבא מן הצד וכמה אמר (א) ייבא חמוה דאשיין בר נדבך משמיה דרב כמלא רחב חלון והלא מציץ א"ר זביד במדיר את כותלו והא אנן תנן ארבע אמות לא קשיא כאן מרוח אחת כאן משתי רוחות ת"ש ואת הכותל מן המזחילה ד' אמות כדי שיהא זוקף את הסולם טעמא משום סולם אבל משום דוושא לא הכא במאי עסקינן במזחילה משופעת דאי משום דוושא הוא הא קא אזיל ואתי תותיה:

מתני' מרחיקין את הסולם מן השובך ארבע אמות כדי שלא תקפוץ הנמייה ואת הכותל מן המזחילה ד' אמות כדי שיהא זוקף את הסולם: גמ' לימא מתניתין דלא כר' יוסי דאי ר' יוסי הא אמר זה חופר בתוך שלו וזה נוטע בתוך שלו אפילו תימא ר' יוסי הא אמר רב אשי כי הוינן בי רב כהנא הוה אמר מודי רבי יוסי בגירי דידיה ה"נ זמנין דבהדי דמנח ליה (ג) יתבא בחור וקפצה והא גרמא הוא א"ר טובי בר מתנה זאת אומרת גרמא בניזקין אסור רב יוסף הוה ליה הנהו תאלי דהוו אתו

הבא לסמוך. ממחילה כותל אצל כותל חבירו: והא מי שהיה קתני. אלמא כבר היה: ונפל לא יסמוך. לא יקרבנו לצד כותל חבירו: דדוושא דהכא מעלי להתם. מה שדשין ברגל בין שני הכתלים תמיד מועיל לשני הכתלים להקשות קרקעית יסודות הכתלים ולא ימוטו: אלא כותל גינה. מתוך שאין דשין אותה מכפנים צריכה דישה מבחוץ: עיר חדשה. שעדיין לא נידושה אף כותל חצר צריכה דוושא: מלמעלן. צריך להגביה שיעור שלא יוכל להשען על כותלו וישפיל ראשו ויראה דרך חלונות ויראה בבית חבירו: שלא יעמוד. על ראש עובי כותלו ויראה: ומכנגדן. צריך להרחיק כדי שלא יאפיל ולא יהיב תנא דברייתא שיעורא: טעמא שלא יאפיל. בשיש חלונות אבל משום דוושא בשאין שם חלונות לא אלמא לא חיישינן לדוושא: מן הצד. שאין הכותל (ג) האחרון מהלך לאורך כותל ראשון אלא מן הצד הוא בא אם זה ממזרח למערב זה בא מצפון לדרום וראש עוביו כנגד החלון ומאפיל דהכא ליכא למיחש לדוושא דההוא פורתא: וכמה. כדי שלא יאפיל לתנא דברייתא דלא יהיב שיעורא: והלא מציץ. כיון דסמוך הוא אע"פ שהוא מגביהו יכול להציץ: במדיר את כותלו. עושה ראש כותלו מדרון ומשפעו לצד החלונות עד שאינו ראוי לא לעמוד עליו ולא להשען עליו: משתי רוחות. שני כתלים זה כנגד זה משני צדי החלון: את הכותל מן המזחילה ד' אמות. מזחילה הוא צינור גדול כעין קנעל"א שלנו ומונחת לאורך הכותל על הכותל ומי הגג זבין לתוכה והיא מקלחתם לארץ ואם אורך כותלו מהלך על פני חצר חבירו ומזחילה עליו צריך זה להרחיק ממנה אם בא לבנות כותל בצדה ארבע אמות על פני ארכה כו' כדי שיהא זוקף שם סולם בשיפוע לעלות בו לתקן מזחילתו לנקותה מעפר וצרורות הנופלין בה ומעכבין קילוח המים: במזחילה משופעת. שתקרת הגג משופעת ויוצאת להלן מן הכותל לתוך החצר והמזחילה בסוף התקרה משוכה להלן מן הכותל לתוך החצר הלכך אי לאו משום זקיפת סולם לא היה צריך להתרחק מראשי התקרה: דאי משום דוושא הא אזיל ואתי תותיה. תחת השיפוע: מתני' מרחיקין את הסולם מן השובך. אם יש לזה שובך בחצירו סמוך לכותל שבין שתי החצירות וחבירו בא להעמיד סולם בחצירו אצל הכותל ירחיקנו מן השובך ארבע אמות: כדי שלא תקפוץ הנמייה. מן הסולם לשובך ותהרוג את היונים והיא חיה קטנה: גמ' לימא מתני' דלא כרבי יוסי. דפליג בסיפא דפירקין בנוטע אילן סמוך לבור. וטובא מילי איכא במתניתין דודאי לאו כרבי יוסי אלא לימא אף זו דסולם ושובך דלא כרבי יוסי: בגירי דיליה. בחצים הבאים לו מיד גופו של בעל הבית ממש: דבהדי דמנח ליה. בעוד שאוחז בסולם קפצה: גרמא בניזקין אסור. ואפי' (ד) למ"ד (ב"ק דף נה: ק.) דלא דאין דינא דגרמי ופטור מלשלם אסור לגרום וכשבא להעמיד גרמא להזיק חבירו מעכב: תאלי. דקלים קטנים: אומני

מסורת הש"ס

א) לעיל ג, ב) ג"ל וכמה טפח, ג) ג"ל במדרדר. רש"ל, ד) [לעיל יז: לקמן כה:], ה) [לקמן כה: ב"מ קיז.], ו) [במולין נג: כתב רש"י ד"ה שהיה מרטורי"א בלע"ז], ז) [וע"ע תוס' יומא עו. ד"ה הני ממחה ותוס' פסחים לג. ד"ה תתן ותוס' בכורות כט. סד"ה היכי אזיל ותוס' מיר ל. ד"ה פשיטא], ח) ג"ל הבערה.

הגהות הב"ח

(א) גמ' אמר רב ייבא: (ב) שם דמנח ליה (יתבא בחור) תא"מ ונ"ב רש"י ל"ג ליה: (ג) רש"י ד"ה מן הצד שאין הכותל האחר מהלך: (ד) ד"ה גרמא וכו' ואפי' לאמן דלא דאין וכו' מעכב עליו הס"ד: (ה) תוס' ד"ה זאת וכו' כי היכי דמעיקרא פטור ה"נ כצ"ל ותיבת דמעיקרא נמחק: (ו) בא"ד היינו דבשעת מעשה בא הזיק:

לעזי רש"י

קנעל"א. פירוש מזחילה, צנור גדול (רש"י ב"ב דף נח ע"ב ועיין רש"י עירובין דף נט ע"ב ד"ה קולט).

ליקוטי רש"י

מודי רבי יוסי בגירי דידיה. היכא דמטי ליה הזיקא מתוך ידיו של מזיק כההיא דאמרינן בהבית והעלייה (ב"מ קיז.) הכהו בי תרי חד דייר עילאי וחד דייר תתאי איפחית מעזיבה ולימא דמשי ידיה נפלי עליה דתתאי דכשנופלין מידו מים על התחתון קרי ליה גירי דיליה וכי פסקי והדר נפלי [כגון דמנגדרין] לא קרי ליה גירי דיליה [לקמן כה:]. אף גב דלמאר על הניזק להרחיק את עצמו ה"מ היכי דלאו אדם עצמו מזיקו כגון אילן וכור שבשעת נטיעתו וחפירתו אינו מזיק אלא השרשים גדלים ומשפשפין מאליהן לאחר זמן אבל היכא דלאו אדם מזיק חורך בו אליו ולמו מודה הוא דלא גרמא דניזקין להרחיק את עצמו מזיק ממש הוא ולאדם מועד לעולם עד ישן שוגג ומזיד [ב"מ קיז.].

הַבָּא לִסְמוֹךְ לֹא יִסְמוֹךְ – **one who comes to place** a wall **near** the wall of his neighbor **may not do so,** אֶלָּא אִם כֵּן הִרְחִיק מִמֶּנּוּ אַרְבַּע אַמּוֹת – **unless he distances** it at least **four** ***amos*** **from [his neighbor's wall].** The Mishnah makes no reference to a previously standing wall. It speaks only of a wall to be built where none had stood before.[1]

This explanation is rejected:

וְהָא מִי – מַתְקִיף לָהּ רָבָא **Rava challenged [this explanation:]** שֶׁהָיָה כּוֹתְלוֹ סָמוּךְ לְכוֹתֶל חֲבֵירוֹ קָתָנֵי – **But the Mishnah says: "ONE WHOSE WALL WAS NEAR THE WALL OF HIS NEIGHBOR."** The words, "one whose wall was," indicate that he had a wall previously. – ? –

Having rejected the preceding explanation, Rava advances his own:

אֶלָּא אָמַר רָבָא – **Rather, Rava said,** הָכִי קָתָנֵי – **this** is what **[the Mishnah] is saying:** מִי שֶׁהָיָה כּוֹתְלוֹ סָמוּךְ לְכוֹתֶל חֲבֵירוֹ בְּרִחוּק אַרְבַּע אַמּוֹת – **One who had a wall near his neighbor's wall, at a distance of four** ***amos,*** וְנָפַל – **and it collapsed,** לֹא יִסְמוֹךְ לוֹ כּוֹתֶל אַחֵר – **may not place another wall near [the neighbor's wall]** to replace the collapsed one אֶלָּא אִם כֵּן הִרְחִיק מִמֶּנּוּ אַרְבַּע אַמּוֹת – **unless he distances** it at least **four** ***amos*** **from [the neighbor's wall].**[2]

Rava gives the reason for this law that one may not build a wall within four *amos* of a neighbor's wall:

מַאי טַעְמָא – **What is the reason** for this restriction? דְּדִוּוּשָׁא דְּהָכָא מְעַלֵּי לְהָתָם – **Because treading** the ground **here** (i.e. between two walls) **is beneficial to** the ground **there** (i.e. at the base of each wall). Constant pedestrian traffic between two walls is beneficial for the walls in that it hardens the earth, thereby strengthening the walls' foundations. Accordingly, one must leave a gap of four *amos* between one's wall and a neighbor's, for if the gap is narrower, people will be unlikely to walk there and the neighbor's wall will not be reinforced.[3]

Rav qualifies the law that one may not build a wall within four *amos* of a neighbor's wall:

אָמַר רַב – **Rav said:** לֹא שָׁנוּ – **They did not teach** this ruling אֶלָּא כּוֹתֶל גִּינָּה – **except** in reference to a case where the neighbor's wall is the **wall of a garden.** People do not walk next to the inner side of a garden wall; therefore, it requires a passageway on its outer side through which people will pass and harden the ground. אֲבָל כּוֹתֶל חָצֵר – **But** in a case where the neighbor's wall is the **wall of a courtyard,** אִם בָּא לִסְמוֹךְ סוֹמֵךְ – **if one wants to build a wall near it** (i.e. within four *amos*), **one may do so.** Since people do walk next to the inner side of a courtyard wall, it does not require a passageway on its outer side to harden the ground.

A different ruling on this matter:

אֶחָד כּוֹתֶל גִּינָּה וְאֶחָד כּוֹתֶל חָצֵר – רַבִּי אוֹשַׁעְיָא אוֹמֵר – **R' Oshaya said:** – The law is **the same whether** the neighbor's wall is **the wall of a garden or the wall of a courtyard.** אִם בָּא לִסְמוֹךְ אֵינוֹ סוֹמֵךְ – In either case, **if one wants to build a wall near it** (i.e. within four *amos*), **one may not do so.**

The Gemara explains the difference between the teachings of Rav and R' Oshaya:

אָמַר רַבִּי יוֹסֵי בַּר חֲנִינָא – **R' Yose bar Chanina said:** וְלֹא פְּלִיגֵי – **They do not disagree** with each other. הָא בְּעִיר יְשָׁנָה – **This** [the statement of Rav, that distancing is required from a garden wall but not from a courtyard wall] refers **to an old town.** A courtyard wall in an old town does not require reinforcement, because the earth adjacent to it has been amply hardened by people passing alongside it through the years. הָא בְּעִיר חֲדָשָׁה – And **this** [the statement of R' Oshaya, that distancing is required even from a courtyard wall], refers **to a new town.** In a new town, both types of walls require reinforcement, for the earth has not yet been sufficiently hardened.[4]

Rava explained that the reason for our Mishnah's restriction against erecting a wall within four *amos* of a neighbor's is that a passageway is required through which people will pass and harden the ground. The Gemara challenges this explanation:

תְּנַן – **But we learned in the Mishnah:**[5] הַחַלּוֹנוֹת – One who builds a wall opposite **THE WINDOWS** of his neighbor's house בֵּין מִלְמַעְלָן בֵּין מִלְמַטָּן – must ensure that **EITHER ABOVE OR BELOW [THE WINDOWS],** בֵּין מִכְּנֶגְדָּן – **AND** certainly **IN FRONT OF THEM,** אַרְבַּע אַמּוֹת – there is a distance of at least **FOUR** ***AMOS.*** וְתָנֵי עֲלָהּ – **And the** following **Baraisa was taught in reference to [this Mishnah]:** מִלְמַעְלָן כְּדֵי שֶׁלֹּא יָצִיץ וְיִרְאֶה – If the wall is to be higher than the windows, it must be high enough **ABOVE THEM SO THAT ONE** who leans over the wall **WILL NOT** be able to **PEER AND LOOK** into the windows. מִלְמַטָּן שֶׁלֹּא יַעֲמוֹד וְיִרְאֶה – If the wall is to be lower than the windows, it must be low enough **BELOW THEM** so **THAT ONE CANNOT STAND** on top of the wall **AND LOOK** into the windows. וּמִכְּנֶגְדָּן שֶׁלֹּא יַאֲפִיל – **AND** a distance is required **OPPOSITE [THE WINDOWS],** between the windows and the wall, so **THAT [THE WALL] WILL NOT DARKEN** the neighbor's house by blocking the entry of sunlight.[6]

The Gemara makes the following inference from the Baraisa's last point:

טַעְמָא שֶׁלֹּא יַאֲפִיל – **The reason** why distancing is required in front of the windows **is that [the wall] should not darken** the neighbor's house, אֲבָל מִשּׁוּם דִּוּוּשָׁא לֹא – **but not** to provide space **for treading.**[7] This refutes Rava's explanation that the reason space must be left next to a wall is so that the ground will be trodden.[8] – ? –

NOTES

1. [According to this interpretation, the new wall is described by the Mishnah as כּוֹתֶל אַחֵר, *another wall,* in reference to the wall of the neighbor.]

2. According to this interpretation, there is no internal contradiction in the Mishnah. The first wall as well as the second one was distanced four *amos* from the neighbor's wall.

Although this law is taught in the context of a wall that had collapsed, the same applies to a wall that is built where none had stood before. Why then did the Mishnah choose to teach this law in this particular context? The Mishnah could simply have stated: "One may not build a wall within four *amos* of a neighbor's wall" (*Tosafos*). An answer to this question is given in the following note.

3. With this reasoning, it can be understood why the Mishnah specifies the case of a wall that had collapsed (see previous note). Before the wall collapsed, the traffic passing between the walls was confined to the relatively narrow space of four *amos* between the two walls. One might have thought, therefore, that the ground has been sufficiently hardened, and when the replacement wall is built, it need not be distanced four *amos* from the neighbor's wall. To reject this notion, the Mishnah teaches that even a wall built to replace one that had collapsed is subject to distancing (*Rosh;* see *Rashba* and other Rishonim who suggest other interpretations of the Gemara).

4. Our Mishnah [which does not differentiate between the wall of a garden and the wall of a courtyard] refers to a new town (*Tosafos, Rashba*).

The classification of a town as "new" or "old" is dependent upon the prevailing circumstances. This determination is made by the local *beis din* (*Rashba*).

5. The second half of our Mishnah, 22a.

6. The last clause applies to a wall that is higher than the window. If the wall is lower than the window, it will not block sunlight regardless of how close to the window it is (*Rambam Hil. Shecheinim* 7:3 with *Maggid Mishneh, Shulchan Aruch Choshen Mishpat* 154:21).

7. There is a practical difference between these two reasons: If the reason is to allow the entry of light, distancing is required only from a wall in which there is a window. But if the reason is to provide for the reinforcement of the wall, distancing is required even from walls that have no windows (see *Rashi*).

8. This difficulty cannot be resolved by saying that the Baraisa speaks of an old town (whose earth does not require hardening), for the Baraisa was stated in reference to our Mishnah, which speaks of a new town [see note 4] (*Tosafos*).

הבא לסמוך לא יסמוך אלא אם כן הרחיק ממנו ארבע אמות מתקיף לה רבא והא מי שהיה כותלו סמוך לכותל חבירו קתני אלא אמר רבא [א]הכי קתני מי שהיה כותלו סמוך לכותל חבירו ברחוק ארבע אמות ונפל לא יסמוך לו כותל אחר אלא אם כן הרחיק ממנו ד' אמות מ"ט דדוושא דהכא מעלי להתם אמר רב [ב]לא שנו אלא כותל גינה אבל כותל חצר אם בא לסמוך סומך רבי אושעיא אומר אחד כותל גינה ואחד כותל חצר אם בא לסמוך אינו סומך אמר רבי יוסי בר חנינא ולא פליגי [ג]הא בעיר ישנה הא בעיר חדשה תנן [א]החלונות בין מלמעלן בין מלמטן בין מכנגדן ארבע אמות [ד]ותני עלה מלמעלן כדי שלא יציץ ויראה מלמטן שלא יעמוד ויראה ומכנגדן שלא יאפיל טעמא שלא יאפיל אבל משום דוושא לא הכא במאי עסקינן [ה]בבא מן הצד [ו]וכמה אמר (א) ייבא חמוה דאשיין בר נדבך משמיה דרב [ז]כמלא רחב חלון והלא מציץ א"ר זביד [ח]במדיר את כותלו והא אנן תנן ארבע אמות לא קשיא כאן מרוח אחת [ט]כאן משתי רוחות ת"ש ואת הכותל מן המזחילה ד' אמות כדי שיהא זוקף את הסולם טעמא משום סולם אבל משום דוושא לא הכא במאי עסקינן במזחילה משופעת דאי משום דוושא הוא הא קא אזיל ואתי תותיה:

מתני' [י]מרחיקין את הסולם מן השובך ארבע אמות כדי שלא תקפוץ הנמייה ואת הכותל מן המזחילה ד' אמות כדי שיהא זוקף את הסולם: **גמ'** לימא מתניתין דלא כר' יוסי דאי ר"י הא אמר [ד]זה חופר בתוך שלו וזה נוטע בתוך שלו אפילו תימא ר' יוסי הא [ה]אמר רב אשי כי הוינן בי רב כהנא הוה אמר [כ]מודי רבי יוסי בגירי דידיה ה"נ זמנין דבהדי דמנח ליה (ב) יתבא בחור וקפצה והא גרמא הוא א"ר טובי בר מתנה זאת אומרת גרמא בניזקין אסור רב יוסף הוה ליה הנהו תאלי דהוו אתו

רש"י

הבא לסמוך. מתחילה כותל אלא כותל חבירו: והא מי שהיה קתני. אלמא כבר היה: ונפל לא יסמוך. לא יקרבנו אצל כותל חבירו: דוושא דהכא מעלי להתם. מה שדשין ברגל בין שני הכתלים תמיד מועיל לשני הכתלים להקשות קרקעית יסודות הכתלים ולא ימוטו: אלא כותל גינה. מתוך שאין דשין אותה מכניסין לריכה דישה מבחוץ: עיר חדשה. שעדיין לא נידושה אף כותל חצר לריכה דוושה: מלמעלן. צריך להגביה שיעור שלא יוכל להשענו על כותלו ויטה ויפיל ראשו ויראה דרך חלונות ויראה בבית חבירו: שלא יעמוד. על ראש עוביו כותלו ויראה: ומכנגדן. צריך להרחיק כדי שלא יאפיל ולא יהיב תנא לדברים שיעורא: טעמא שלא יאפיל. בשיש חלונות אבל משום דוושא בשאין שם חלונות לא אלמא לא חיישינן לדוושא: מן הצד. שאין הכותל (ג) האחרון מהלך לאורך כותל ראשון אלא מן הצד הוא בא אם זה ממזרח למערב זה בא מצפון לדרום וראש עוביו כנגד החלון ומאפיל דהכא ליכא למיחש לדוושא דהסוף פורתא: וכמה. כדי שלא יאפיל לתנא דבריתא דלא יהיב שיעורא: והלא מציץ. כיון שסמוך הוא אע"פ שהוא מגביהו יכול להלך: במדיר את כותלו. עושה ראש כותלו מדרון ומשפעו לצד החלונות עד שאינו ראוי לא לעמוד עליו ולא להשען עליו: משתי רוחות. שני כתלים זה כנגד זה משני לדי החלון: את הכותל מן המזחילה ד' אמות. מזחילה הוא ליזור גדול כעין קנאל"א שלנו ומונחת לאורך הכותל על הכותל ומי הגג זבין לתוכה והיא מקלחתם לארץ ואם אורך כותלו מהלך על פני חצר חבירו ומזחילה עליו צריך זה להרחיק ממנה אם בא לבנות כותל בלדה ארבע אמות על פני ארכה כו' כדי שיהא זוקף שם סולם בשיפוע לעלות בו לתקן מזחילתו לנקותה מעפר וצרורות הנופלין בה ומעכבין קילוח המים: במזחילה משופעת. שתקרת הגג משופעת ויוצאת להלן מן הכותל לתוך החצר והמזחילה בסוף התקרה משוכה להלן מן הכותל לתוך החצר הלכך אי לאו משום זקיפת סולם לא היה צריך להתרחק מראשי התקרה: דאי משום דוושא הא אזיל ואתי תותיה. תחת השיפוע: מתני' מרחיקין את הסולם מן השובך. אם יש לזה שובך בחצירו סמוך לכותל שבין שתי החצירות וחבירו בא להעמיד סולם בחצירו אצל הכותל ירחיקנו מן השובך ארבע אמות: כדי שלא תקפוץ הנמייה. מן הסולם לשובך ותהרוג את היונים והיא חיה קטנה [י]: גמ' לימא מתני' דלא כרבי יוסי. דפליג בסיפא דפירקין בנוטע אילן סמוך לבור. וטובא מילי איכא במתניתין דודאי לאו כרבי יוסי אלא לימא אף זו דסולם ושובך דלא כרבי יוסי: בגירי דיליה. בחלים הבאים לו מיד גופו של בעל הבית ממש: דבהדי דמנח ליה. בעוד שאוחז בסולם קפצה: גרמא בניזקין אסור. ואפי' (ד) למ"ד (ב"ק דף נג: ק.) דלא דאין דינא דגרמי ופטור מלשלם אסור לגרום וכשבא להעמיד גרמא להזיק חבירו מעכב: תאלי. דקלים קטנים: אומני

תוספות

אלא אמר רבא ה"ק מי שהיה כותלו כו'. הקשה ריב"ס דלמה ליה למינקט בכי האי גוונא שהיה לו כותל ברחוק ארבע אמות ונפל ליתני שלא יסמוך כותלו לכותל חבירו אא"כ הרחיק ארבע אמות וליכא למימר דדוקא בכי האי גוונא שהיה רחוק כבר ארבע אמות והרחיק הראשון קאמר דלא יסמוך א"כ מאי פריך בסמוך טעמא שלא יאפיל הא משום סולם אבל משום דוושא לא: **אבל** משום דוושא לא. וא"ת ולימא דלאיירי בעיר ישנה ואומר ר"ת דבית הוי כגינה לפי שמטלטלין מטה וכלים אלא הכותל ועוד י"ל דבחלר איכא דוושא לרבים מה שאין כן בבית ולר"י נראה דניחא ליה לשנויי בעיר חדשה דומיא דרישא וכן הסיפא דמרחיקין את הכותל מן המזחילה אע"ג דמפסקת בינתים הסיפא דמרחיקין את הסולם מן השובך: **וכמה** אמר רב ייבא כו'. ותימה דהשתא בעי וכמה ובתר הכי פריך והתנן ארבע אמות וי"ל דרב ייבא גופיה בעי וכמה ולא גמר' וכענין זה יש בהלו מליאות (ב"מ דף כא. ושם ד"ה וכמה)[ז]: **במדיר** את כותלו. ולא מצי לשנויי במגביה כותלו ד' אמות דכיון דקאי מן הצד ואורך הכותל לרחבו של חלון יכול לעמוד בסוף הכותל ולשחות ולהציץ: **והא** אנן תנן ארבע אמות. דמתני' איירי נמי מן הצד כיון דלא חייש לדוושא אלא משום חלונות: **לימא** תנן סתמא דלא כרבי יוסי. פר"ח מדקאמר הכא טפי לימא דלא כרבי יוסי ולא קאמר אמשניות דלעיל משמע דכולהו אתי כר"י והוי כולהו גירי דיליה דמההיא שעתא משתכחא היזקא ולא פליג רבי יוסי אלא באילן וי"ל לפי' דמתניתין דלעיל הוי נמי גירי דיליה דמיד כשסומך הכותל מונע הדוושא: **כדי** שיהא זוקף את הסולם. כשמכר ונתן לו זקיפת הסולם בחצירו איירי וקמ"ל דבעי ארבע אמות: **והא** גרמא הוא. תימה דלא פריך הכי לעיל גבי דוושא: **זאת** אומרת גרמא בנזקין אסור. ומעיקרא ס"ד כי היכי (ה) דמעיקרא פטור ה"נ דמותר הכא משמע דגרמא בנזקין דפטור וכן בפ' כילד הרגל (ב"ק דף כו:) זרק כלי מראש הגג והיו תחתיו כרים וכסתות וקדם וסילקן אפילו הוא פטור ובפרק הפרה (שם דף מז:) הכניס פירות לחצר בעל הבית שלא ברשות כו' וקאמר בגמרא דאם אכלה והוזקה פטור ונתן סם המות לפני בהמת חבירו פטור (שם) ושולח [ח]בעירו ביד חרש שוטה וקטן (שם נט:) ופורץ גדר בפני בהמת חבירו וכופף קמת חבירו בפני הדליקה ועושה מלאכה במי חטאת (שם נה: נו.) וליבה וליבתו הרוח דפטור בכל הנך כדאמר בפרק הכונס (שם דף נט:) ומבעית חבירו דהוי נמי גרמא כדאמר בפרק קמא דקדושין (דף כד:) דאיהו הוא דאבעית אנפשיה ובכילד הרגל (ב"ק דף כג:) שיסה בו כלב שיסה בו נחש פטור ויש ליתן טעם מאי שנא כל הני מדינא דגרמי כגון אחווי אחוויי דהגוזל בתרא (שם דף קטז: ושם) ומראה דינר לשולחני ונמצא רע ונפרעה אומר לו גדול ודן את הדין דחייב לר"מ אפילו לא נשא ונתן בידו והשורף שטרותיו של חבירו ומוכר שטר חוב לחבירו וחזר ומחלו וחילק רבינו יצחק לשון אח' דדינא דגרמי חייב היינו שעושה הוא עצמו היזק לממון חבירו ועוד חילק דדינא דגרמי דחייב היינו (ו) משעת מעשה שבא ההיזק ועל הכל קשה טיהר את הטמא ובעה"ב עצמו עירבן עם פירותיו ואמאי חייב דהוא עצמו אינו עושה היזק בממון חבירו וגם באותה שעה שמטהר אינו בא ההיזק ונראה לריב"א דדינא דגרמי הוי מטעם קנס כדמוכח בירושלמי ולכך כל היזק המצוי ורגיל לבא קנסו חכמים וטעם דקנסו שלא יהא כל אחד הולך ומזיק לחבירו בעין והיינו טעמא דמאן דמחייב בהיזק שאינו ניכר ואפשר דבשוגג נמי קניס רבי מאיר כי היכי דקניס במטמא ומדמע אחד שוגג ואחד מזיד: אתו

עין משפט נר מצוה

נב א מיי' פ"ט מהל' שכנים הל' ט סמג עשין פב טוש"ע ח"מ סי' קנה סעיף יב ובהגה"ה ועיין בטור:
נג ב ג מיי' שם הל' ועי' בהשגות ובמ"מ טוש"ע שם סעיף יג:
נד ד מיי' שם פ"ז הל' א ב ג סמג שם טוש"ע ח"מ סי' קנד סעיף כג:
נה ה מיי' שם פ"ט הל' ד וסמג שם טוש"ע שם סעיף כג וסי' קנה סעיף יד בהג"ה:
נו ו ז מיי' שם הל' ד וסמג שם טוש"ע ח"מ סי' קנד סעיף כג:
נז ח מיי' פ"ז שם הל' ה טוש"ע שם סעיף כד:
נח ט מיי' פ"ט שם הל' ז סמג שם טוש"ע ח"מ סי' קנה סעיף כה:
נט י מיי' שם פ"ט הל' ח טוש"ע שם סעיף כג:
ס כ מיי' שם פ"ט הל' ה וסמג שם טוש"ע שם סעיף לא לב לג:

רבינו גרשום

והא מי שהיה כותלו סמוך לכותל חבירו ד' אמות. כלומר להוסיף על המשנה ולתרצה את יכול אבל לחסר מינה אין אתה יכול: אלא אמר רבא הכי קאמר מי שהיה וכו' מאי טעמא דוושא דהכא מהני התם. כלומר מש"ה צריכה להרחיק ד' אמות כדי שיהיו דשין שם בני אדם העוברין בינתים ומעלי ההיא דישה לכותל שניהם שמתחזקין היסודות: אמר רב לא שנו. דצריך להרחיק ד' אמות אלא מכותל גינה שאין דשין שם בני אדם בשדה מחמת הירקות אבל בכותל חצר שנידושה היא מעיקרא שאינה צריכה חזוק הבא לסמוך סומך בפחות מד': בעיר ישנה. שנידושה היא מכמה שנים אם בא לסמוך סומך אבל בעיר חדשה אינו סומך בלא הרחקה מפני שצריכה דישה לחזק: מלמעלן. אם בנה כותלו מן הצד סמוך לחלון חבירו צריך להגביה הכותל ד' אמות יותר מן החלון: כדי שלא יעמוד על כותלו וישרה ויציץ בחלון. ואם מנמיכו מן החלון או מן החלון צריך להנמיכו מן החלון ד' אמות: שלא יעמוד. על כותלו זוקף ויראה בחלון ואם בנהו כנגדו צריך להרחיק ד' אמות שלא יאפיל חלונו: הכא במאי עסקינן. דקתני שלא יאפיל בבונהו מן הצד שלא חלון ולא כנגדו וצריך להרחיק מן החלון כדי שלא יאפיל הדשתא לא מצי למידק דטעמא שלא יאפיל אבל משום דוושא לא דהא ליכא מקום דוושא טובא אלא דוק מינה הכי ומכנגדן כלומר אם בונהו מכנגד חלון צריך להרחיק ד' אמות כדי שלא יאפיל אבל אם בונהו מן הצד סמוך לחלון אין צריך להרחיק כולי האי ד' אמות דבבציר מהכי סגי דמן צדי חלון לא מאפיל עליה כולי האי כמו מכנגדו ובבציר הרחקה סגי: וכמה. שיעור צריך להרחיק כותלו מן הצד החלון: כמלא רוחב חלון.

הגהות הב"ח

(א) גמ' אמר רב ייבא: (ב) שם דמנח ליה (יתבא בחור) תא"מ ונ"ב רש"ל ל"ג ליה: (ג) רש"י ד"ה מן הצד שאין הכותל האחר מהלך: (ד) ד"ה גרמא וכו' ואפי' למאן דלא דאין וכו' מעכב עליו הס"ד: (ה) תוס' ד"ה זאת וכו' כי היכי דפטור ה"נ כצ"ל ותיבת דמעיקרא נמחק: (ו) בא"ד היינו דבשעת מעשה בא ההיזק:

לעזי רש"י

קנאל"א. פירוש מזחילה, צנור גדול (רש"י ב"ב דף נח ע"ב ועיין רש"י עירובין דף נט ע"ב ד"ה קולט):

ליקוטי רש"י

מודי רבי יוסי בגירי דידיה. היכא דמטי ליה היזקא מתוך ידיו של מזיק כהשלח דאמרי' בהבית והעליה [ב"מ קיז.] הכהו בי תרי מד דייר עילאי וחד דייר תתאי איפחית מעזיבה וכל אימת דמשי ידיה נפלי עליה דתתאי דכשמשמש מרכו עד התתתון קרי ליה גירי דיליה וכי פסקי והדר נפלי [כגון דמנגדרין] לא קרי ליה גירי דיליה [לקמן כה.]. אף על גב דלאמר על הניזק להרחיק את עצמו ה"מ היכי דלאו אדם עצמו מזיקו כגון אילן וכור שבשעת נטיעתו וכרייתו אין מזיק אלא שרשים גדלים ומתפשטין מאליהן לאחר זמן אבל היכא דאדם עצמו מזיק חורך בו פלו וכו' מודה הוא דלא גרמא דגרמא דניזקין אסור מזיק ממש הוא ואדם מועד לעולם בין ער וישן שוגג ומזיד [ב"ק קיז.].

מסורת הש"ס

א) לעיל ג, ב) ג"א וכמה טפח, ג) ג"א במרדד. רש"ל, ד) [לעיל יח:] [לקמן כה.], ה) [לקמן כה: ב"מ קיז.], ו) [בתולין נג: כתב רש"י ד"ה מריס מרטורינ"א בלע"ז], ז) [וע"ע תוס' יומא עו. ד"ה הני ממשה ותוס' פסחים לג. ד"ה תנן ותוס' בכורות כט. סד"ה היכי אזיל ותוס' נזיר ל. ד"ה פשיטא], ח) ג"ל הבערה.

החלון: כמלא רוחב חלון. צריך להרחיק ולא מפאיל. ומקשי' הואיל ולא מרחיק כותלו משום היזק אורה אלא מלא רוחב החלון לא מגבי ליה נמי משום היזק ראיה למעלה מן החלון אלא כמלא רוחב חלון הא מציץ א"כ יכול להציץ בחלון: במדיר את כותלו. שעושהו חד למעלה כמדרון מכאן ומכאן שאינו יכול לעמוד עליו ולהציץ: והא אנן תנן ד' אמות צריך להרחיק. היכי מצית למימר כמלא רוחב חלון: לא קשיא כאן מרוח אחת כלומר אם בנה כותל מצידו אחד של חלון אינו צריך להרחיק אלא כמלא רוחב חלון והא דקתני מתני' ד' אמות מן הצד נמי מיירי וכגון שבנה ב' כתלים מב' רוחות של חלון הואיל ואלו ב' כתלים מאפילים הרבה מש"ה צריך להרחיק כל כותל וכותל מצד החלון ד' אמות: תנן ואת הכותל מרחיקין מן המזחילה של חבירו ד' אמות. כדי שיהא לו לחבירו חזקה בחצירו שהמזחילה של גגו שופכת בחצרו הואיל ויש לו כח חזקה יכול לזקוף סולם בחצר חבירו בעל כותלו ולעלות על גגו ואם רצה זה לבנות כותל סמוך לגגו צריך להרחיק ד' אמות ממנו כדי זקיפת סולם. דקתני זקיפת סולם לאו משום דוושא דלא צריך לה מתיחי: הכא במאי עסקינן. דקתני זקיפת סולם ולא משום דוושא במזחילה משופעת דאי משום דוושא דא מן הצד שהוא שפוע היוצא חוץ לכותל ומצי למעבד דוושא. היינו בחצרו בגגו מבחוץ בצד כותלו של שובך ואוכלת בשובך מיירי. דאם יש לזה שובך בצד כותלו של חבירו ולאידך בעל כותלו ולעלות על גגו ואם רצה זה לבנות כותל סמוך לגגו צריך להרחיק ד' אמות: מתני' מרחיקין את הסולם מן השובך. כתבונו מיהו דאין גירא שלו ולא ממש בחצירו: גמ' לימא מתני'. כר' יוסי דהכא הוי חמוה חיב דחטא דמשתמש כבר הוי דלבי איכא בידים ואין אדם מזיק ומיד לא אמר רב חייב מה"ט כדי מימרא. כלומר הכא שאני דהוי כעין שזורק אדם חץ ומזיק באותה זריקה חייב ה"נ כדמו דבשעה שמנח הסולם כבר קופצת ואוכלת שלפניו: מודה ר' יוסי בגירי דיליה ומשום הכי צריך להרחיק. דיליה: ר"ת ומיירי בגירי דיליה. כלומר הכא שאני דהוי מרחיק את הסולם מן השובך: מודה ר' יוסי בגרמא. כדאמרו: והא גרמא הוא. אבל הכא גרמא הוא ואפ"ה חייב. בגירא דיליה: זימנין בהדי דמנח ליה לסולם בתוך ד' אמות שלו זימנין דלא מיירי אגירי וכי אמר אביו דהוי איהו גרמא ואפ"ה חייב. ודא גרמא מקרי. והכא הוי דבהדי דמנח ליה דיתבא בחור וקפצה היינו גרמא דגרמא הוא: א"ר טובי בר מתנה דגרמא בניזקין אסור. כלומר הכא שאני דהוי מוגי אמר דלא ומגביל ומשתכחא דהוי מזיק וכי איגרמא בנזקין חייב ולא בשעת מעשה בידים לא דבר דבר בידי אדם ואמר דאין גרמא בניזקין אלא בעצמו: ומנול היכא דהוי ממש ולא נפיל מוקמי לה במאי דעבד דבידים אבל הכא הא גרמא היא ואמאי חייב: תאלי. אילנות בחורים:

The Gemara answers:

הָכָא בְּמַאי עָסְקִינַן — What are we dealing with here? בְּבָא מִן הַצַּד — The Baraisa refers **to [a wall] that is perpendicular** to the wall in which the window is situated. In such a case, hardening the ground is not a consideration, because only a small portion of the neighbor's wall is affected in this regard.[9]

The Baraisa did not specify how much space must be left so as not to darken the neighbor's window. It merely said: "And [a distance is required] opposite the windows so that the wall will not darken [the neighbor's house]." The Gemara now gives the specific distance required by the Baraisa:

וְכַמָּה — **And how much** distance is required by the Baraisa? אָמַר רַב יֵיבָא חֲמוּהָ דְּאַשְׁיָין בַּר נַדְבָּךְ מִשְּׁמֵיהּ דְּרַב — Rav **Yeiva, the father-in-law of Ashyan bar Nadbach, said in the name of Rav:** כִּמְלֹא רֹחַב חַלּוֹן — **The equivalent of the width of a** standard **window;** i.e. one *tefach.*[10]

The Gemara asks:

וַהֲלֹא מֵצִיץ — **But he will surely** be able to **look** into the window? Since the end of the wall is only one *tefach* away from the window, one who leans over the end of the wall will be able to look into the window even if the wall is considerably higher than the window.[11] — ? —

The Gemara answers:

אָמַר רַב זְבִיד — **Rav Zevid said:** בְּמַדִּיר אֶת כּוֹתְלוֹ — The Baraisa refers **to a sloping** wall.[12] The wall slopes towards the window and thus it is impossible to stand or lean on it.

It was explained above that the Baraisa, which requires distancing only for the sake of providing light, refers to a wall that is perpendicular to the wall in which the window is situated. From the fact that the second clause of our Mishnah specifies a wall with windows, it is evident that there too the only reason for distancing is the provision of light.[13] Hence, that part of our Mishnah must also speak of a wall that is perpendicular to the window. The Gemara now points out a contradiction between the Baraisa and the Mishnah.

וְהָא אֲנַן תְּנַן — **But we learned in our Mishnah:** אַרְבַּע אַמּוֹת — The required distance is FOUR *AMOS*. This contradicts Rav Yeiva's explanation of the Baraisa, according to which a gap of one *tefach* is sufficient. — ? —

The Gemara answers:

לֹא קַשְׁיָא — This is **not a difficulty:** כָּאן מֵרוּחַ אַחַת — **Here** [the Baraisa], the reference is to a single wall built **on one side** of the window. In such a case, the light blockage is minimal and therefore a distancing of one *tefach* is sufficient.[14] כָּאן מִשְּׁתֵּי רוּחוֹת — **Here** [the Mishnah], the reference is to two walls built **on** the **two sides** of the window. In such a case, the light blockage is substantial and therefore a distancing of four *amos* is required.[15]

Again, the Gemara challenges Rava's explanation that the reason why a gap is required between parallel walls is to provide space for treading the ground:

תָּא שְׁמַע — **Come, learn** the following proof from a Mishnah:[16] וְאֶת הַכּוֹתֶל מִן הַמַּזְחִילָה אַרְבַּע אַמּוֹת — A WALL must be distanced FOUR *AMOS* FROM THE GUTTER of a neighbor's house כְּדֵי שֶׁיְּהֵא זוֹקֵף אֶת הַסּוּלָּם — SO THAT the neighbor has space in which HE CAN PROP UP A LADDER against his house for the purpose of cleaning out his gutter.[17]

The Gemara infers from this Mishnah:

טַעְמָא מִשּׁוּם סוּלָּם — **The reason** distancing is required **is** to provide space **for a ladder,** אֲבָל מִשּׁוּם דַּוושָׁא לֹא — **but not** to provide space **for treading.** — ? —

The Gemara answers:

הָכָא בְּמַאי עָסְקִינַן — **What are we dealing with here?** בְּמַזְחִילָה מְשׁוּפַּעַת — That Mishnah refers **to a gutter** on a **slanted roof** which overhangs the area between the two walls.[18] In such a case, it is not necessary to distance one's wall four *amos* from the edge of the neighbor's roof for the purpose of having the ground trodden, דְּאִי מִשּׁוּם דַּוושָׁא הוּא — **because as far as treading is concerned,** הָא קָא אָזִיל וְאָתֵי תּוּתֵיהּ — **[people] go back and forth under [the overhang].**

Mishnah מַרְחִיקִין אֶת הַסּוּלָּם מִן הַשּׁוֹבָךְ אַרְבַּע אַמּוֹת — **One must distance a ladder four *amos* from a** neighbor's **dovecote,** כְּדֵי שֶׁלֹּא תִקְפּוֹץ הַנְּמִיָּה — **so that a marten should not** be able to climb up

NOTES

9. See diagram. Even if the gap between the two walls is too narrow for a passageway, only a small portion of the neighbor's wall (the shaded area in the diagram) will not be reinforced (*Rashi, Yad Ramah*).

10. The required distance is a *tefach,* regardless of the width of the window in question. The Gemara says חַלּוֹן, *a window* (i.e. a standard window), as opposed to הַחַלּוֹן, *the window* (i.e. the window in question) (*Yad Ramah*). There is an alternative version of the text which reads: וְכַמָּה טֶפַח, *And how much? A tefach* (see *Rif, Rosh, Rabbeinu Yonah*).

This one-*tefach* separation is to the side of the window, not in front of it (see diagram to note 14). [In this manner separating it from the window by a mere *tefach* allows sufficient light to enter] (see *Rashi* below ד״ה משתי רוחות).

11. *Rashi.* [*Ritva* rejects this understanding of the Gemara on account of the following difficulty: If one can see into a window (even though the wall is higher than that window, as required by the Baraisa) when the wall is only a *tefach* away from the window, certainly one will be able to see into the window when the wall is further away and the angle of the line of vision is less acute! See *Ritva* et al. for different explanations of the Gemara.]

12. Literally: one who slopes his wall.

13. *Tosafos.* If the reason for distancing is that the neighbor's wall requires reinforcement, the Mishnah would not have mentioned windows — see note 7.

In fact, instead of challenging Rava's explanation (viz. distancing is required for the sake of reinforcement) from the Baraisa, the Gemara could have challenged Rava from the second part of our Mishnah. The Baraisa was chosen only because it states *explicitly* that distancing is required for a reason other than that given by Rava (*Rashba, Maharsha*).

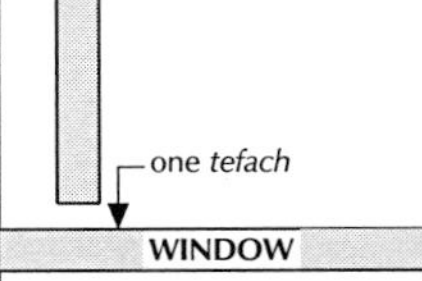

14. See diagram.

15. This means that the two new walls must be distanced four *amos* from *each other* (*Rambam Hil. Shecheinim* 7:5; see *Rosh;* cf. *Rashba*). See diagram.

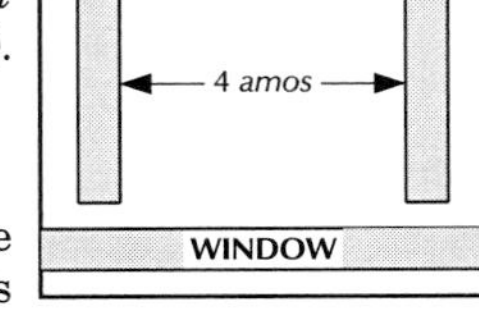

16. The next Mishnah on this *amud.*

17. The owner of the house purchased the right to place a ladder in his neighbor's property. The Mishnah teaches that although he did not specify any dimensions, he is entitled to a gap of four *amos* between the wall of his house and his neighbor's wall (*Tosafos*). An alternative approach: Once someone builds a house at the edge of his property without any protest from his neighbor, he automatically acquires the right to place a ladder in his neighbor's property for this purpose (*Rambam Hil. Shecheinim* 9:8; see *Maggid Mishneh* there).

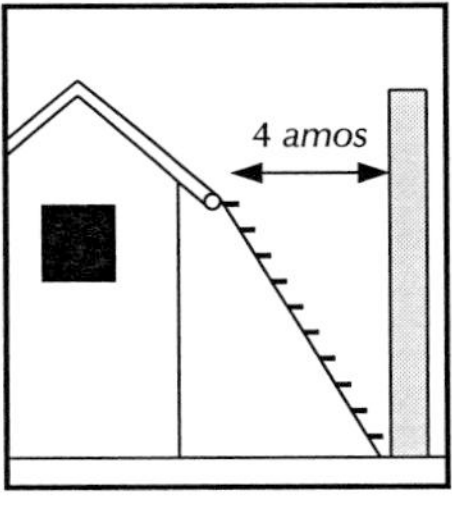

18. See diagram.

הבא לסמוך לא יסמוך אלא אם כן הרחיק ממנו ארבע אמות מתקיף לה רבא והא מי שהיה כותלו סמוך לכותל חבירו קתני אלא אמר רבא א הכי קתני מי שהיה כותלו סמוך לכותל חבירו ברחוק ארבע אמות ונפל לא יסמוך לו כותל אחר אלא אם כן הרחיק ממנו ד' אמות מ"ט דדוושא דהכא מעלי להתם אמר רב ב לא שנו אלא כותל גינה אבל כותל חצר אם בא לסמוך סומך רבי אושעיא אומר אחד כותל גינה ואחד כותל חצר אם בא לסמוך אינו סומך אמר רבי יוסי בר חנינא ולא פליגי ג הא בעיר ישנה הא בעיר חדשה תנן א) החלונות בין מלמעלן בין מלמטן בין מכנגדן ארבע אמות ד ותני עלה מלמעלה כדי שלא יציץ ויראה מלמטן שלא יעמוד ויראה ומכנגדן שלא יאפיל טעמא שלא יאפיל אבל משום דוושא לא הכא במאי עסקינן ה בבא מן הצד ב) וכמה אמר (א) ייבא חמוה דאשיין בר נדבך משמיה דרב ו כמלא רחב חלון והלא מציץ א"ר זביד ז במדיר את כותלו והא אנן תנן ארבע אמות לא קשיא כאן מרוח אחת ח כאן משתי רוחות ת"ש ואת הכותל מן המזחילה ד' אמות כדי שיהא זוקף את הסולם טעמא משום סולם אבל משום דוושא לא הכא במאי עסקינן במזחילה משופעת דאי משום דוושא הוא הא קא אזיל ואתי תותיה:

מתני' ט מרחיקין את הסולם מן השובך ארבע אמות כדי שלא תקפוץ הנמייה ואת י הכותל מן המזחילה ד' אמות כדי שיהא זוקף את הסולם: גמ' לימא מתניתין דלא כר' יוסי דאי ר"י הא אמר ד) זה חופר בתוך שלו וזה נוטע בתוך שלו אפילו תימא ר' יוסי הא ה) אמר רב אשי כי הוינן בי רב כהנא הוה אמר כ מודי רבי יוסי בגירי דידיה ה"נ זמנין דבהדי דמנח ליה (ב) יתבא בחור וקפצה והא גרמא הוא א"ר טובי בר מתנה זאת אומרת גרמא בניזקין אסור רב יוסף הוה ליה הנהו תאלי דהוו אתו

הבא לסמוך. מתחילה כותל אצל כותל חבירו: והא מי שהיה קתני. אלמא כבר היה: ונפל לא יסמוך. לא יקרבנו לצד כותל חבירו: דוושא דהכא מעלי להתם. מה שדשין ברגל בין שני הכתלים תמיד מועיל לשני הכתלים להקשות קרקעית יסודות הכתלים ולא ימוטו: אלא כותל גינה. מתוך שאין דשין אותה מכניסים צריכה דישה מבחוץ: עיר חדשה. שעדיין לא נידושה אף כותל חצר צריכה דוושא: מלמעלן. צריך להגביה שיעור שלא יציץ בהשענו על כותלו וישפיל ראשו ויראה דרך חלונות ויראה בבית חבירו: שלא יעמוד. על ראש עובי כותלו ויראה: ומכנגדן. צריך להרחיק כדי שלא יאפיל ולא יהיב תנא דברייתא שיעורא: טעמא שלא יאפיל. בשיש חלונות אבל משום דוושא בשאין שם חלונות לא אלמא לא חיישינן לדוושא: מן הצד. שאין הכותל (ג) האחרון מהלך לאורך כותל ראשון אלא מן הצד הוא בא אם זה ממזרח למערב זה בא מצפון לדרום וראש עוביו כנגד החלון ומאפיל דהכא ליכא למיחש לדוושא דההוא פורתא: וכמה. כדי שלא יאפיל לתנא דברייתא דלא יהיב שיעורא: והלא מציץ. כיון דסמוך הוא אע"פ שהוא מגביהו יכול להציץ: במדיר את כותלו. עושה ראש כותלו מדרון ומשפעו לצד החלונות עד שאינו ראוי לא לעמוד עליו ולא להשען עליו: משתי רוחות. שני כתלים זה כנגד זה משני צדי החלון: את הכותל מן המזחילה ד' אמות. מזחילה הוא צינור גדול כעין קנעל"א שלנו ומונחת לאורך הכותל על הכותל ומי הגג זבין לתוכה והיא מקלחתם לארץ ואם אורך כותלו מהלך על פני חצר חבירו ומזחילה עליו צריך זה להרחיק ממנה אם בא לבנות כותל בצדה ארבע אמות על פני ארכה כו' כדי שיהא זוקף שם סולם בשיפוע לעלות בו לתקן מזחילתו לנקותה מעפר וצרורות הנופלין בה ומעכבין קילוח המים: במזחילה משופעת. שתקרת הגג משופעת ויוצאת להלן מן הכותל לתוך החצר והמזחילה בסוף התקרה משוכה להלן מן הכותל לתוך החצר הלכך אי לאו משום זקיפת סולם לא היה צריך להתרחק מראשי התקרה: דאי משום דוושא הא אזיל ואתי תותיה. תחת השיפוע: מתני' מרחיקין את הסולם מן השובך. אם יש לזה שובך בחצירו סמוך לכותל שבין שתי החצירות וחבירו בא להעמיד סולם בחצירו אצל הכותל ירחיקנו מן השובך ארבע אמות: כדי שלא תקפוץ הנמייה. מן הסולם לשובך ותהרוג את היונים והיא חיה קטנה ו): גמ' לימא מתני' דלא כרבי יוסי. דפליג בסיפא דפירקין בנוטע אילן סמוך לבור. וטובא מילי איכא במתניתין דודאי לאו כרבי יוסי אלא לימא אף זו דסולם ושובך דלא כרבי יוסי: בגירי דיליה. בחצים הבאים לו מיד גופו של בעל הבית ממש: דבהדי דמנח ליה. בעוד שאוחז בסולם קפצה: גרמא בניזקין אסור. ואפי' (ד) למ"ד (ב"ק דף נה: ק.) דלא דאין דינא דגרמי ופטור מלשלם אסור לגרום וכשבא להעמיד גרמא להזיק חבירו מעכב: תאלי. דקלים קטנים: אומני

אלא אמר רבא ה"ק מי שהיה כותלו כו'. הקשה ריב"ם דלמה ליה למינקט בכי האי גוונא שהיה לו כותל ברחוק ארבע אמות ונפל ליתני שלא יסמוך כותלו לכותל חבירו אא"כ הרחיק ארבע אמות וליכא למימר דדוקא בכי האי גוונא שהיה רחוק כבר ארבע אמות והרחיק הראשון קאמר דלא יסמוך א"כ מאי פריך בסמוך טעמא שלא יאפיל אי משום סולם אבל משום דוושא לא. אבל משום דוושא לא. וא"ת וליעמא דאיירי בעיר ישנה ואומר ר"ת דבית הוי כגינה לפי שנותנין מטה וכלים אצל הכותל ועוד י"ל דבחצר איכא דוושא דרבים מה שאין כן בבית ולר"י נראה דניחא ליה לשנויי בעיר חדשה דומיא דרישא וכן הויא דמרחיקין את הכותל מן המזחילה אע"ג דמספקת בינתים היא דמרחיקין את הסולם מן השובך: וכמה אמר רב ייבא כו'. ותימה דהשתא בעי וכמה ובתר הכי פריך והתנן ארבע אמות וי"ל דרב ייבא גופיה בעי וכמה ולא גמר' וכענין זה יש באלו מציאות (ב"מ דף כה. ושם ד"ה וכמה): במדיר את כותלו. ולא מצי לשנויי במגביה כותלו ד' אמות דכיון דקאי מן הצד ואורך הכותל לרחבו של חלון יכול לעמוד בסוף הכותל ולשחות ולהציץ: והא אנן תנן ארבע אמות. מתני' איירי נמי מן הצד דכיון דלא חייש לדוושא אלא משום חלונות: לימא תנן סתמא דלא כרבי יוסי. פר"ח מדקאמר הכא טפי לימא דלא כרבי יוסי ולא קאמר אמשניות דלעיל משמע דכולהו אתי כר"י והוי כולהו גירי דיליה דמההיא שעתא משתכחא היזיקא ולא פליג רבי יוסי אלא באילן וי"ל לפי' דמתניתין דלעיל הוי נמי גירי דיליה דמיד כשסומך הכותל מונע הדוושא: כדי שיהא זוקף את הסולם. כשמכר ונתן לו זקיפת הסולם בחצירו איירי וקמ"ל דבעי ארבע אמות: והא גרמא הוא. תימה דלא פריך הכי לעיל גבי דוושא: זאת אומרת גרמא בנזקין אסור. ומעיקרא ס"ד כי היכי (ה) דמעיקרא פטור ה"נ דמותר הכא משמע דגרמא בנזקין דפטור וכן בפ' כילד הרגל (ב"ק דף כו:) זרק כלי מראש הגג והיו תחתיו כרים וכסתות וקדם וסילקן אפילו הוא פטור ובפרק הפרה (שם דף מז:) הכניס פירות לחצר בעל הבית שלא ברשות כו' וקאמר בגמרא דאם אכלה והוזקה פטור ונתן סם המות לפני בהמת חבירו דפטור (שם) ושולח ח) בעירו ביד חרש שוטה וקטן (שם נט:) ופורץ גדר בפני בהמת חבירו וכופף קמת חבירו בפני הדליקה ועושה מלאכה במי חטאת (שם נה: נו.) וליבה וליבתו הרוח דפטור בכל הנך כדאמר בפרק הכונס (שם דף נט:) ומבעית חבירו דהוי נמי גרמא כדאמר בפרק קמא דקדושין (דף כד:) דאיהו הוא דאבעית אנפשיה ובכילד הרגל (ב"ק דף כג:) שיסה בו כלב שיסה בו נחש פטור ויש ליתן טעם מאי שנא כל הני מדינא דגרמי כגון אחווי אחוויי דהגוזל בתרא (שם דף קטז: ושם) ומראה דינר לשולחני ונמצא רע ונפרעה אומר לו גדור ודן את הדין דחייב לר"מ אפילו לא נשא ונתן בידו והשורף שטרותיו של חבירו ומוכר שטר חוב לחבירו וחזר ומחלו וחילק רבינו יצחק לשון אח' דדינא דגרמי חייב היינו שעושה הוא עצמו היזק לממון חבירו ועוד חילק דדינא דגרמי דחייב היינו (ו) משעת מעשה שבא ההיזק ועל הכל קשה טיהר את הטמא ובעה"ב עצמו עירבן עם פירותיו ואמאי חייב דהוא עצמו אינו עושה היזק בממון חבירו וגם באותה שעה שמטהר אינו בא ההיזק ונראה לריצב"א דדינא דגרמי הוי מטעם קנס כדמוכח בירושלמי ולכך כל היזק המצוי ורגיל לבא קנסו חכמים וטעם דקנסו שלא יהא כל אחד הולך ומזיק לחבירו בעין והיינו טעמא דמאן דמחייב בהיזק שאינו ניכר ואפשר דבשוגג נמי קניס רבי מאיר כי היכי דקניס במטמא ומדמע אחד שוגג ואחד מזיד: אתו

עין משפט
נר מצוה

נב א מיי' פ"ט מהל' שכנים הל' ט סמג עשין פב טוש"ע ח"מ סי' קנה סעיף יג ובהג"ה ועיין בטור:
נג ב מיי' שם ועי' בהשגות ובמ"מ טוש"ע שם סעיף יג:
נד ג מיי' שם הל' ג ג סמג שם טוש"ע ח"מ סי' קנד סעיף כג:
נה ד מיי' שם הל' ד וסמג שם טוש"ע ח"מ סי' קנד סעיף כג וסי' קנה סעיף יד בהג"ה:
נו ה ו ז מיי' שם הל' ד וסמג שם טוש"ע ח"מ סי' קנד סעיף כג:
נז ח מיי' פ"ז שם הל' ה טוש"ע שם סעיף כד:
נח ט מיי' פ"ט שם הל' ג טוש"ע שם סעיף ו:
נט י מיי' שם הל' ח סמג שם טוש"ע ח"מ סי' קנה סעיף לו:
ס כ ל מיי' שם פ"י הל' [illegible] וסמג שם טוש"ע שם סעיף לה לג:

רבינו גרשום

והא מי שהיה כותלו סמוך לכותל חבירו קתני. כלומר להוסיף על המשנה ולתרצה אתה יכול אבל לחסר מינה אין אתה יכול: אלא אמר רבא הכי קאמר מי שהיה וכו' מאי טעמא דדוושא דהכא מהני התם. כלומר משה"ה צריכה להרחיק ד' אמות כדי שיהיו דשין שם בני אדם העוברים בינתים ומעלי ההיא דישה לכותל שניהם שמתחזקין היסודות: אמר רב לא שנו. דצריך להרחיק ד' אמות אלא מכותל גינה שאין דשין שם בני אדם בשדה מחמת הירקות אבל בכותל חצר שנידושה היא מעיקרא שאינה צריכה חיזוק הבא לסמוך סומך בפחות מד': בעיר ישנה. שנידושה היא מכמה שנים אם בא לסמוך סומך אבל בעיר חדשה אינו סומך בלא הרחקה מפני שצריכה דישה לחזק: מלמעלן. אם בנה כותלו מן הצד סמוך לחלון חבירו צריך להגביה הכותל ד' אמות יותר מן החלון: כדי שלא יעמוד על כותלו וישוח ויציץ בחלון. ואם מנמיכו כותלו מן החלון צריך להנמיכו מן החלון ד' אמות: שלא יעמוד. על כותלו זקוף ויראה בחלון ואם בונהו כנגדו צריך להרחיק ד' אמות שלא יאפיל חלונו: הכא במאי עסקינן. דקתני שלא יאפיל בבונהו מן הצד של חלון ולא כנגדו וצריך להרחיק מן החלון כדי שלא יאפיל דהשתא לא מצי למידק דטעמא שלא יאפיל אבל משום דוושא לא דהא איכא מקום דוושא טובא אלא דוק מינה הכי ומכנגדן כלומר אם בונהו מכנגד חלון צריך להרחיק ד' אמות כדי שלא יאפיל אבל אם בונהו מן הצד סמוך לחלון אין צריך להרחיק כולי האי ד' אמות דבבציר מהכי סגי דמן צדי חלון לא מאפיל עליה כולי האי כמו מכנגדו ובבציר הרחקה סגי: וכמה. שיעור צריך להרחיק כותלו מן צד החלון: כמלוא רוחב חלון. צריך להרחיק ולא מאפיל. ומקשי' הואיל ולא מרחיק כותלו משום היזק אורה אלא כמלא רוחב החלון לא מגבי ליה נמי משום היזק ראיה למעלה מן החלון אלא כמלא רוחב חלון הא מציץ א"כ יכול להציץ בחלון: [illegible] ידיה ונפל על תתאה דעבד בידים אבל הכא גרמא היא ואמאי חייב: תאלי. אילנות בחורים:

מסורת הש"ס

א) לעיל ג:, ב) ג"ל וכמה טפח, ג) ג"ל במרדד. רש"ל, ד) [לעיל יח:] [לקמן כה:], ה) [לקמן כה: ב"מ קיז.], ו) [בחולין נב: כתב רש"י ד"ה שהיה מרטוטי"א בלע"ז], ז) [וע"ע תוס' יומא עו. ד"ה הני מעשה ותוס' פסחים לג. ד"ה מתן ותוס' בכורות כט. סד"ה היכי אזיל ותוס' נזיר ג. ד"ה פשיטא], ח) ל"ל הבערה:

הגהות הב"ח

(א) גמ' אמר רב ייבא: (ב) שם דמנח ליה (יתבא בחור) תא"מ ונ"ב רש"ל ל"ג ליה: (ג) רש"י ד"ה מן הצד שאין הכותל האחר מהלך: (ד) ד"ה גרמא וכו' ואפי' למאן דלא דאין וכו' מעכב עליו הס"ד: (ה) תוס' ד"ה זאת וכו' כי היכי דפטור ה"נ כל"ל ותיבת דמעיקרא נמחק: (ו) בא"ד היינו דבשעת מעשה בא ההיזק:

לעזי רש"י

קנעל"א. פירוש מזחילה, צנור גדול (רשב"ם ב"ב דף נח ע"ב ועיין רש"י עירובין דף נט ע"ב ד"ה קולט).

ליקוטי רש"י

מודי רבי יוסי בגירי דידיה. היכא דמטי ליה היזקא מתוך ידיו של מזיק [illegible]

the ladder and **spring** into the dovecote.[19] וְאֶת הַכּוֹתֶל מִן הַמַּזְחִילָה אַרְבַּע אַמּוֹת – One must **also** distance **a wall four** ***amos*** **from the gutter** of his neighbor's house, כְּדֵי שֶׁיְּהֵא זוֹקֵף אֶת הַסּוּלָּם – **so that** [the neighbor] has space in which **he can prop up a ladder** against his house for the purpose of cleaning out his gutter.[20]

Gemara

The Gemara inquires whether the Mishnah's first rule is disputed:

לֵימָא מַתְנִיתִין דְּלָא כְּרַבִּי יוֹסֵי – **Shall we say** that **our Mishnah is not** in agreement **with** the view of **R' Yose?** דְּאִי רַבִּי יוֹסֵי – **For if** you will suggest that it agrees with the view of **R' Yose,** הָא אָמַר – **but [R' Yose] has said,** with regard to planting a tree near a boundary where its roots threaten to breach the walls of a neighbor's pit: זֶה חוֹפֵר בְּתוֹךְ שֶׁלּוֹ וְזֶה נוֹטֵעַ בְּתוֹךְ שֶׁלּוֹ – Just as THIS ONE MAY DIG a hole WITHIN HIS property, THAT ONE MAY PLANT a tree WITHIN HIS property.[21] In that instance, R' Yose holds that one is not required to distance a potentially harmful object from a neighbor's property. Does this not indicate he disagrees with our Mishnah?

The Gemara answers:

אֲפִילּוּ תֵּימָא רַבִּי יוֹסֵי – **You can even say** that the Mishnah concurs with **R' Yose,** הָא אָמַר רַב אַשִׁי – for **Rav Ashi has said:** כִּי הֲוֵינַן בֵּי רַב כַּהֲנָא הֲוָה אָמַר – **When we were** students **at Rav Kahana's academy, he** (Rav Kahana) **would** often **say:** מוֹדֵי רַבִּי יוֹסֵי בְּגִירֵי דִּידֵיהּ – **R' Yose agrees, with regard to "his arrows"** (i.e. actions that cause damage directly), that one must distance himself from a neighbor who may be harmed.[22] הָכָא נַמִּי – **Here too,** R' Yose agrees that one must distance his ladder from a neighbor's dovecote, זִמְנִין – because it may **sometimes** occur דְּבַהֲדֵי דְּמַנַּח לֵיהּ – **that as he places [the ladder]** against the wall, יָתְבָא בְּחוֹר וְקָפְצָה – **[a marten] will be resting in a hole** in the wall **and it will jump** onto the ladder and then immediately spring into the dovecote. Should this occur, the resulting damage to his neighbor will be a direct outgrowth of his action. Therefore, R' Yose agrees that one may not place the ladder near a dovecote.[23]

The Gemara raises a question:

וְהָא גְּרָמָא הוּא – **But** even if a marten springs onto the ladder as one places it against the wall, **it is** merely a **causative** act of damage that he commits by holding the ladder. Being that one is not liable for indirect damage, why must he distance his ladder from a dovecote?[24]

The Gemara answers:

אָמַר רַב טוּבִי בַּר מַתְנָה: – **Rav Tuvi bar Masnah said:** זֹאת אוֹמֶרֶת – **This** Mishnah **informs** us גְּרָמָא בְּנִיזָקִין אָסוּר – that a **causative** act of **damage**, i.e. an action that may cause damage indirectly, **is forbidden.** That is why the Mishnah rules that one is forbidden to place a ladder within four *amos* of a dovecote.[25]

The Gemara cites a related incident:

רַב יוֹסֵף הֲוָה לֵיהּ הַנְהוּ תַּאֲלֵי דַּהֲווּ – **Rav Yosef had these small** date **palms that**

NOTES

19. If one's neighbor has a dovecote near the wall that divides their properties, one may not prop up a ladder on his side of the wall within four *amos* of the dovecote, lest a marten [a small, weasel-like animal that has a tendency to climb and spring] jump into the dovecote and kill the doves (*Rashi*). This is consistent with the rule that one must refrain from performing within one's own property any activity that is potentially harmful to a neighbor.

20. See note 17.

21. Below, 25b. R' Yose maintains that one may plant a tree near the border of one's property even though its roots may damage a neighbor's pit. His opinion is that with regard to damages that arise from activities performed within one's own property, it is up to the one being damaged to protect himself by removing his vulnerable item from the proximity of the threatening object [עַל הַנִּיזָק לְהַרְחִיק אֶת עַצְמוֹ].

22. Although R' Yose permits planting a tree near a neighbor's pit, he agrees that one must refrain from performing within his property any activity that may cause damage to a neighbor *directly*.

23. If a marten jumps onto the ladder while he is in the process of placing it against the wall, his placement of the ladder will qualify as an "arrow," since by holding it in a position where it enables a marten to spring into the dovecote, he causes damage to his neighbor directly (*Rashi*). [Although there is usually no marten waiting to jump onto the ladder as one places it near a dovecote, one is nevertheless forbidden to place it there due to the possibility that such direct damage may occur. Moreover, one cannot argue that he will guard against a marten jumping onto the ladder as he places it against the wall, because any object that has the capability of acting as an "arrow" is forbidden according to R' Yose (*Ramban*).]

24. [Under the law of torts, one is liable only for damage that he commits with his own force, not for incidental damage that results from his actions.] The Gemara contends that any action that can result in nothing more than incidental damage should not qualify as "his arrow" (*Rabbeinu Yonah*).

25. I.e. although one is not required to *pay* for incidental damage that results from his actions, one is forbidden to perform any action that may result in damage to another person (*Rashi*). Accordingly, such action does qualify as "his arrows" (*Rabbeinu Yonah*).

What emerges from the Gemara's discussion is that the term "his arrows" does not merely refer to actual physical acts of damage, but includes also actions that *result* in damage. *Rashi* explains that any activity in which a damaging force emerges directly from one's action qualifies as an "arrow" and must be distanced from a neighbor's property, even if the force that inflicts the damage is not his own (as in the case of a marten that springs from his ladder). On the basis of this explanation, *Rashi* notes that although the Gemara has reconciled our Mishnah's ruling with R' Yose's opinion, numerous other Mishnahs in this chapter [such as the Mishnah (above, 17a) which ruled that one must distance olive refuse, salt, manure, lime and flint stones three *tefachim* from a neighbor's wall] cannot be reconciled with R' Yose's view. In those cases any resulting damage does not emerge directly from the physical act of placing the items near the wall. Accordingly, these items do not qualify as "his arrows."

Tosafos, however, deduce from the fact that the Gemara raised the question of whether the Mishnah agrees with R' Yose only in regard to our Mishnah, that all the other Mishnahs in the chapter can be readily reconciled with R' Yose's opinion. They therefore explain that the category "his arrows" includes any action that is *immediately,* albeit indirectly, detrimental to a neighbor's property. Thus, olive refuse, salt, manure and the like all qualify as "his arrows," because they begin to emit fumes that are detrimental to the neighbor's wall the moment one puts them down (cf. *Ramban, Rashba*).

אָתוּ אוּמָּנֵי וְיָתְבֵי תּוּתַיְיהוּ – bloodletters would come and sit under while they drew blood.[1] **וְאָתוּ עוֹרְבֵי אָכְלֵי דָּמָא – Now, crows would come** to **consume the blood, וְסָלְקֵי אַבֵּי תַאֲלֵי וּמַפְסְדֵי תַמְרֵי – and would** then **fly up onto the palms and ruin the dates** by smearing them with blood.[2]

Rav Yosef asked the bloodletters to move elsewhere:

אָמַר לְהוּ רַב יוֹסֵף – Rav Yosef said to [them]: אַפִּיקוּ לִי קוּרְקוּר מֵהָכָא – Rid me of this crowing! Draw blood elsewhere, so that crows will not come here and ruin my dates.

A claim was made in defense of the bloodletters:

אָמַר לֵיהּ אַבַּיֵי – Abaye said to [Rav Yosef]: וְהָא גְּרָמָא הוּא – But it is merely **causative** damage that the bloodletters are committing. Being that one is not liable for causative damage, why must they move away?[3]

Rav Yosef responded:

אָמַר לֵיהּ – [Rav Yosef] replied to him: הָכִי אָמַר רַב טוֹבִי בַּר מַתְנָה – This is what Rav Tuvi bar Masnah said, in reference to the Mishnah: **זֹאת אוֹמֶרֶת גְּרָמָא בְּנִיזָּקִין אָסוּר – This** Mishnah **informs** us that **causative** acts of **damage**, i.e. activities that cause damage indirectly, **are forbidden.** Accordingly, the bloodletters are required to move away.[4]

Abaye continued his defense of the bloodletters:

וְהָא אַחֲזִיק [לְהוּ] – But they have already **established a *chazakah,*** since you raised no objection to their bloodletting for the past three years.[5] – ? –

Rav Yosef rejected this contention:

הָא אָמַר רַב נַחְמָן אָמַר רַבָּה בַּר אֲבוּהַ – Rav Nachman has said in the name of Rabbah bar Avuha: אֵין חֲזָקָה לִנְזָקִין – There is no *chazakah* for damage.[6]

Abaye continued his argument:

וְלָאו אִיתְּמַר עֲלָהּ – But was it not said regarding this dictum of Rav Nachman: **רַב מָרִי אָמַר בְּקוּטְרָא – Rav Mari said:** It applies **to smoke; וְרַב זְבִיד אָמַר בְּבֵית הַכִּסֵּא – and Rav Zevid said:** It applies **to an outhouse?**[7] With regard to all other sources of damage, however, a *chazakah* can be established. – ? –

Rav Yosef replied:

אָמַר לֵיהּ – [He] said to [Abaye]: הָנֵי לְדִידִי דַּאֲנִינָא דַעְתָּאִי – To one **with a delicate nature,** such as **I,** the discomfort caused by **these** crows **כִּי קוּטְרָא וּבֵית הַכִּסֵּא דָּמוּ לִי – is comparable to smoke and an outhouse.**[8]

Mishnah **מַרְחִיקִין אֶת הַשּׁוֹבָךְ מִן הָעִיר חֲמִשִּׁים אַמָּה – One must distance a dovecote fifty *amos* from a city. וְלֹא יַעֲשֶׂה אָדָם שׁוֹבָךְ בְּתוֹךְ שֶׁלּוֹ – Similarly, a man should not build a dovecote within his** property **אֶלָּא אִם כֵּן יֵשׁ לוֹ חֲמִשִּׁים אַמָּה לְכָל רוּחַ – unless he owns fifty *amos*** of land bordering the dovecote **in each direction.**[9] **רַבִּי יְהוּדָה אוֹמֵר – R' Yehudah says: בֵּית אַרְבַּעַת כּוֹרִין –** One must have **an area of four *kor*** – one *beis kor* in each direction, **מְלֹא שֶׁגֶר הַיּוֹנָה – which is the extent of a dove's** single, uninterrupted **flight.**[10] **וְאִם לְקָחוֹ – However, if he purchased [the dovecote]** from the previous owner of the property, **אֲפִילּוּ בֵּית רוֹבַע – even** if the entire property is only **the area of a quarter-*kav,* הֲרֵי הוּא בְּחֶזְקָתוֹ – [the dovecote] retains its *chazakah.***[11]

NOTES

1. The bloodletters sat on their own property, in the shade of Rav Yosef's palms (*Tosafos*).

2. The bloodletters would shoo away the crows that were attracted by the blood, and the crows would then fly up onto the trees. The damage to the dates was thus attributable to their actions (*Rabbenu Yonah;* cf. *Tosafos,* 26a ד״ה זיקא).

3. See above, 22b note 24.

4. See 22b note 25.

5. One who engages in activity that is harmful to a neighbor for a period of three years without being challenged by the neighbor may claim that he purchased from his neighbor the right to engage in such activity, even though he is unable to produce evidence to substantiate the claim. His claim is presumed to be true, for had he not purchased that right, his neighbor would certainly have objected within the first three years. [The legal term for the establishment of presumptive ownership is חֲזָקָה, *chazakah.*] In this case, the bloodletters claimed that Rav Yosef had sold them the right to engage in this objectionable activity underneath his palms (*Tosafos; see Hagahos HaBach*). Abaye argued on their behalf that their claim was credible, since they had established a *chazakah*.

[According to *Rambam* (*Hil. Shecheinim* 11:4), a *chazakah* can be established by performing an objectionable activity in view of one's neighbor *even once,* if it goes unchallenged by the neighbor. Moreover, the one performing the harmful activity need not claim that he *acquired* the right to do so from his neighbor. If his activity is carried out on his own property and he is not laying claim to anything owned by his neighbor, the neighbor's silence in the face of his disturbing activity is tantamount to yielding him the right to engage in it (*Rambam* ibid., as explained by *Maggid Mishneh;* see also the opinion of *Ri bar R' Mordechai*, cited in *Tosafos* ד״ה והא).]

6. I.e. one cannot claim on the basis of three years of freedom of activity that his neighbor sold him [or yielded him] the right to engage in the harmful activity. The neighbor may have thought that his objection was self-evident and therefore did not deem it necessary to express it. Thus, his three-year silence does not lend credence to the damager's claim (*Rabbeinu Yonah*). [*Rabbeinu Tam,* cited in *Tosafos,* rules that even if the neighbor did sell this right he may nevertheless object if he claims that the discomfort is worse than he anticipated.]

7. *To smoke:* i.e. to install a kiln, which emits heavy clouds of smoke that drifts over a neighbor's property (*Tosafos*).

To an outhouse: i.e. to the type of outhouse common in Talmudic days in which the waste remains above ground (*Rashi*).

Only in regard to these highly disturbing items did Rav Nachman rule that there is no *chazakah,* because, barring concrete evidence, the claim that the neighbor relinquished his right to object to them is not credible. Accordingly, the neighbor need not publicize his objection, and his three-year silence lends no credence to the damager's claim (*Rabbeinu Yonah*). With respect to hazardous activity that is less objectionable, three years of silence on the part of the affected neighbor does support the claim that he sold the right to engage in that activity.

8. Rav Yosef was known to be a highly sensitive individual (*Tosafos* from *Pesachim* 113b), and as such, he could not bear the thought of using bloodstained dates (*Tosafos*). He therefore argued that just as there is no *chazakah* for smoke or an outhouse because the claim that a neighbor relinquished his right to object is not credible, there could be no *chazakah* for bloodletting under his palm trees because it was inconceivable that he had waived the right to object to this practice.

The same holds true for any individual who has an obvious intolerance toward a certain type of disturbing activity. A neighbor cannot establish a *chazakah* for engaging in that activity near his property (*Rosh*).

9. Doves generally feed on grain that they find within fifty *amos* of their roost. Accordingly, one who builds a dovecote on the outskirts of a city must distance it fifty *amos* from the city's edge to prevent the doves from feeding on produce growing in the city's gardens, and one who builds a dovecote on his own property must leave fifty *amos* between it and his boundary to protect the produce of his neighbor's field (*Rashi*).

10. A *beis kor* (i.e. the area suitable for sowing a *kor* – thirty *se'ah* – of barley grain) covers 75,000 square *amos.* This comes to a distance of 273.86 *amos* in each direction (*Tos. Yom Tov*).

11. [A *kav* is 1/6 of a *se'ah*, and there are thirty *se'ah* in a *kor.* Thus, a *kav* is 1/180 of a *kor,* and a quarter-*kav* is 1/720 of a *kor.* Since a *beis kor* covers 75,000 square *amos,* the area of a quarter-*kav* is approximately 104 square *amos.*] Thus, an area of a quarter-*kav* measures roughly 10.2 x 10.2 *amos* (*Rambam, Commentary to Mishnah*).

If one purchased a property this size on which a dovecote was located, he may keep the dovecote even if the neighbors object, provided that the previous owner had established a *chazakah* for the dovecote (*Rashi*). [See note 5.]

אתו אומני ויתבי תותייהו ואתו עורבי אכלי דמא וסלקי (א) אבי תאלי ומפסדי תמרי אמר להו רב יוסף אפיקו לי קורקור מהכא א"ל אביי והא גרמא הוא א"ל הכי אמר רב טובי בר מתנה זאת אומרת גרמא בניזקין אסור והא אחזיק [להו] הא אמר רב נחמן אמר רבה בר אבוה אין חזקה לנזקין ולאו איתמר עלה רב מרי אמר בקוטרא ורב זביד אמר בבית הכסא אמר ליה הני לדידי דאנינא דעתאי כי קוטרא ובית הכסא דמו לי: **מתני'** מרחיקין את השובך מן העיר חמשים אמה ולא יעשה אדם שובך בתוך שלו אלא אם כן יש לו חמשים אמה לכל רוח רבי יהודה אומר בית ארבעת כורין מלא שגר היונה ואם לקחו אפילו בית רובע הרי הוא בחזקתו: **גמ'** חמשים אמה ותו לא ורמינהי אין פורסין נשבין ליונים אלא אם כן היה רחוק מן הישוב שלשים ריס אמר אביי מישט שייטי טובא וכרסייהו בחמשים אמתא מליא ומישט שלשים ריס ותו לא והתניא ובישוב אפילו מאה מיל לא יפרוס רב יוסף אמר בישוב כרמים (ג) רבא אמר בישוב שובכין ותיפוק ליה משום שובכין גופייהו איבעית אימא דידיה ואיבעית אימא דכנעני ואיבעית אימא דהפקר: רבי יהודה אומר בית ארבעת כורין וכו': אמר רב פפא ואיתימא רב זביד זאת אומרת טוענין ללוקח וטוענין ליורש יורש תנינא הבא משום ירושה אינו צריך טענה לוקח איצטריכא ליה לוקח נמי תנינא לקח חצר ובה זיזין וגזוזטראות הרי (ג) זה בחזקתה צריכא דאי אשמעינן התם גבי רשות הרבים (ד) דאימור כונס לתוך שלו הוא אי נמי אחולי אחול בני רשות הרבים גביה אבל הכא לא ואי אשמעינן הכא דכיון דיחיד הוא אימא פיוסיה פייסיה (ה) אי נמי אחולי אחיל גביה אבל רבים מאן פייס ומאן שביק אימא לא צריכא: הרי הוא בחזקתו: והא אמר רב נחמן אמר רבה בר אבוה אין חזקה לנזקין רב מרי אמר בקוטרא רב זביד אמר בבית הכסא:

מתני'

רש"י

אומני. מקיזי דם: **קורקור.** עורבים שדומים בלעקתן כקורין קורקור: **אפיקו לי.** כלומר אל יקיזו לי עוד כאן שעל כן העורבים באין: **בקוטרא.** עשן: **בבית הכסא.** שעל גבי קרקע ונראה לעינים שכך היו בתי כסאות שלהן: **מתני'** מרחיקין השובך מן העיר. שהיונים מפסידין זרעוני גנות: **אא"כ יש לו כו'.** שלא יפסידו היונים בשדה חבירו: **מלא שגר היונה.** מרוצת פריחתה פעם אחת: **ואם לקחו.** כמו שהוא עם הקרקע אפילו אין לו כל סביביו אלא בית רובע הקב הרי הוא בחזקתו שהרי הוחזק בו הראשון כן: **גמ'** אין פורסין נשבין. שלא ילכדו בהם יוני הישוב: **שלשים ריס.** ארבע מילין: **וכרסייהו בחמשים אמה קמלייא.** במה שהן מלקטין בתוך חמשים אמה מתמלא כריסן ואין מפסידים בזרעים מכאן ולהלן: **לא יפרוס.** נשבין: **ביישוב כרמים.** שפורחין מכרם לכרם ושטים הרבה: **ביישוב שובכין.** שמדלג משובך לשובך: **ותיפוק ליה משום שובכין גופייהו.** מאי מאה מיל דקאמר דמשמע דבשביל יוני העיר מתרחק שבאין כאן דרך שובכין בלאו יוני העיר נמי לא יפרוס שהרי לוכד יוני שובכות של אחרים: **טוענין ליורש וטוענין ללוקח.** בית דין פותחים פה וטוענה ליורש וללוקח שערער אדם עליהן ויש לו עדים שהיתה שלו או של אבותיו וזה אומר ירשתיו מאבא או לקחתיו מפלוני שהוחזק בו ימים רבים והביא עדים שהוחזק בו אביו או המוכר לו שלש שנים אע"פ שלא טען והן לקחו ממך או מאבותיך טוענין לו בית דין (ו) ופותחים לו פה ואילו למי שלא ירשה ולא לקחה מאחר כשאמר לו המערער מה אתה עושה בתוך שלי והוא אומר החזקתי בה ג' שנים ולא אמרו לי דבר תנא במתני' (לקמן דף מא.) דאין לו חזקה ומתני' דקתני הרי הוא בחזקתו אשמועינן דהיכא דלקחה מאחר ובאו וערערו עליו אין צריך להרחיק אלא טענינן ליה ט) בשבילו שאותו שלקחה ממנו י) (וגימא) נתפייס עם סביביו במעות עד שנאותו: **אינו צריך טענה.** אינו צריך לומר אתה מכרת לאבי אלא ראיתי לאבי שהחזיק בה ולא ערער אדם עליו: **לקח חצר ובה זיזין.** (ז) במתני' בה"ה תנן אין מוציאין זיזין וגזוזטראות לרשות הרבים אדם הבונה בית לא יוציא ראשי קורות תקרתו לרה"ר אבל אם רוצה כונס בניינו לתוך שלו ובונה ומוציא ראשי קורותיו לחוץ ואם לקח חצר ובה זיזין וגזוזטראות יוצאים לרה"ר הרי הוא בחזקתה שבית דין טוענין לו שהראשון כנס לתוך שלו או נתפייס עם הרבים: (ח) **אימא לתוך שלו הוא כונס.** שאילמלא כן היו הרבים מעכבין עליו ולא היה יכול לעשות בזרוע אבל כנגד היחיד אימא עשה שהיה חזק ממנו: **מאן פייס.** מי היה ראשי לקבל מעות: **ומאן שביק.** מי הוא שבידו למחול ולסלוח:

מתני'

תוספות

אתו אומני ויתבי תותייהו. בקרקע שלהן היו יושבין ולא בקרקע של רב יוסף מדפריך בתר הכי והא גרמא הוא: **והא** אחזיקו להו. פי' ר"י ב"ר מרדכי כיון שלא בא להחזיק בקרקע של חבירו ולומר שלו הוא אלא לתשמיש בעלמא שנהנה ממנה מועלת חזקה שלא בטענה דמסתמא לא היו אומרים שמכר להם רב יוסף תשמיש זה והוו כי הנהו דלעיל (דף ו.) דאחזוק להורדי דמועלת חזקה שלא בטענה דמדלא מיחה ג' שנים מחל לו ואין נראה דאם לא הקנה לו כי החזיק להורדי אמאי החזיק לכשורי אלא על כרחך התם שטוען שהקנה לו ולהכי אחזיק לכשורי דאין אדם עושה קנין למחלה (ט): **אין** חזקה לנזקין. אומר ר"ת דאפי' הקנה (י) יכול לחזור בו דקנין בטעות הוא דסבור היה שיכול לקבל ועכשיו אין יכול לקבל ואין נראה דמדקאמר אין חזקה לנזקין איכא למידק הא ראיה יש כדדייקין בחזקת הבתים (לקמן דף מט:) גבי הא דתנן ולא כ) (לאשה חזקה בנכסי בעלה):

בקוטרא. נראה לר"י דדוקא בקוטרא דכבשן שהוא גדול ומזיק ביותר אין חזקה כדאמר במרובה (ב"ק דף פב:) אין עושין כבשונות בירושלים מ"ט משום קוטרא ודוקא נמי בית הכסא שלהן (כ) שהיה למעלה מן הקרקע והיה מסריח ביותר אבל בשלנו שהוא מכוסה יש חזקה: **לדידי** דאנינא דעתאי. פי' שהיה איסטניס כדאמרינן בערבי פסחים (פסחים דף קיג: ושם) שלשה חייהם אינן חיים הרחמנים והרתחנים ואניני הדעת אמר רב יוסף וכולהו איתנהו בי:

בקוטרא ובית הכסא דמו. והא דקאמר אפיקו קורקור מהכא משמע דמשום עורבים היה אומר ודאי אם לא היו עורבים היה סובל אף על גב דאנינא דעתיה אי נמי העורבים היו אוכלים הדם ופורחים ומקנחים בפירות:

מרחיקין השובך מן העיר חמשים אמה. מפני התבואה הנשטחת בגגות העיר כדי לייבש אבל לתבואה שבשדות ליכא למיחש בקרוב לעיר לפי שהשדות רחוקין מן העיר אלף אמה כדתנן (ערכין דף לג:) אין עושין מגרש שדה ולא שדה מגרש: **ולא** יעשה שובך תוך שלו. ברחוק מן העיר בין השדות ואצטריך למיתני תרוייהו דאי תנא רישא להרחיק מן העיר התם דוקא מרחיק מפני שתבואות העיר מגולות הן באלר הן בגג אבל תבואה הנזרעת בשדה ומכוסה אין צריך להרחיק ואי תנא סיפא משום דבשדות שכיחא תבואה אבל בעיר דלא שכיח כולי האי אימא לא: **בית** ארבעת כורין כמלא שגר היונה. ור' יהודה ורבנן לא פליגי בשגר היונה כמה הוי דמודו רבנן דבית ארבעה כורין הוי שגר היונה אלא רבנן סברי כיון דבחמשים אמה מליא כריסייהו כדאמרינן בגמ' תו לא מזקי טפי ור' יהודה סבר דכמלא שגר מזקי: **אלא** אם כן הרחיק שלשים ריס. היינו ד' מיל דהמיל ז' ריס ומחצה ופעמים שהגמרא נותן שיעור בריסין ופעמים במילין ופעמים בפרסה: **והתניא** ביישוב אפילו מאה מיל (ל). תימה דמאי ס"ד דהוי פי' וביישוב אי קרי העיר יישוב א"כ אפילו מאה מיל לאו דוקא כמו שמשמע אלא אפילו אלף מיל או יותר א"כ בשום מקום לא יפרוס אפילו במדבר ורחוק לאין סוף מן העיר ואפילו אם נאמר דמאה מיל דוקא מכל מקום היאך יפרש את הברייתא ל) דהכי תניא בתוספתא דמרובה אין פורסין נשבין ליונים אא"כ הרחיק מן היישוב שלשים ריס בד"א במדבר אבל ביישוב אפי' מאה מיל לא יפרוס כיון דעיר קרי יישוב ואי ס"ד דהכי פירושו בד"א במדבר פי' שאין זרעים אבל ביישוב פי' ביישוב זרעים אפילו מאה מיל לא יפרוס אם כן מאי קשיא ליה ואומר ריצב"א דודאי ס"ד דאיירי ביישוב זרעים ולהכי פריך ומישט שייטי שלשים ריס ותו לא אפי' ביישוב זרעים והא מוכח דביישוב זרעים שייטי טובא ואין זה אלא משום אכילה אלמא דלא מליא כריסייהו בחמשים אמה ומשני דלא איירי ביישוב זרעים אלא ביישוב שובכין ויישוב כרמים וקרי מדבר היכא דליכא שובכים וכרמים: **יורש** תנינא. וס"ד המקשה דמתני' אשמעינן ביורש וה"ה בלוקח ומיהו רב זביד דנקט נמי יורש אמתני' דלקמן סמיך אבל מתני' דהכא לא שמעינן מינה יורש מדאיצטריך מתני' דלקמן: **וצריכי.** וא"ת ביורש נמי ליתני תרתי וי"ל דאשמעינן בלוקח וה"ה ביורש: **אחולי** אחילו גביה. פי' ז' טובי העיר במעמד אנשי העיר שהרשות בידם כדאמר פרק בתרא דמגילה (דף כו.) וכיון דליכא לכל חד בדרך אלא פורתא מחלי טפי מיחיד:

עין משפט נר מצוה

סא א ב ג ד מיי' פי"א מהל' שכנים הל' ד ה סמג עשין פב טוש"ע ח"מ סי' קנה סעיף לו לט:
סב ה מיי' שם הל' ה טוש"ע שם סעיף לט:
סג ו ז מיי' פ"ו מהל' גזילה הל' ט סמג עשין עג טוש"ע ח"מ סי' קנה סעיף כד:
סד ח ט י כ ל מיי' שם הל' ט סמג שם טור ח"מ סי' שע:
סה מ נ טוש"ע ח"מ סי' קנה סעיף כד:

רבינו גרשום

אתו אומני. שהיו מקיזין והיו רגילין אנשים הרוצין להקיז באין שם להקיז ואגב שמתקבצין שם עורבים מחמת הדם עולין ומפסידין פירות האילנות: **אפיקו לי קורקור מהכא.** כלומר הוציאו עורבים הללו שקורין קורקור ומנקרין באילנות כלומר הוציאו האומנין משם ויכלו העורבים ולא יפסידו האילנות: **והא אחזיקו להו.** האומנין שרגילין להקיז תחת האילנות: **לא איתמר עלה.** היכא אמרי' אין חזקה לניזקין בקוטרא שאם היה חלון פתוחה לביתו של חבירו והיה עולה עשן ומזיק לו ודאי אין חזקה לניזקין דהאי נזקא גופא מחמת העשן הוא וכן נמי אם היה בית הכסא סמוך לביתו של חבירו והסרחון הולך אין חזקה משום אינות גופא אבל שאר היזקות אם החזיק יש חזקה: **דמו לי.** האי דמא: **פיסקא** מן העיר נ' אמה. כדי שלא יאכלו היונים זרעוני גינת העיר וכן נמי צריך להעמיד בתוך שלו א) שהיא לו נ' אמה לכל רוח שלא יאכלו זרעוני חבירו: **כמלא שגר היונה.** כמו שיכולה היונה לפרוח בפעם אחת: **ואם לקחו.** שנים מאחד והגיע לחלק אחד מקום השובך ולשני מקום הפנוי ואפי' אין בין שובך לגינת זה אלא הרחקת בית רובע הרי הוא בחזקתו [שלא] להרחיק יותר הואיל ומתחלה היה השובך והגינה של א': **נשבין.** מצודות: **אלא אם כן הרחיק מן הישוב ל' ריס.** דאתו יוני הישוב ונכנסין לתוך הנשבין ותפיס להו אלמא דשייטי טפי מן נ' אמה והיכי קתני דבנ' אמה סגי: **רב יוסף אמר.** הא דתני בישוב אפי' ק' מיל לא יפרוס ב) אפי' יהא ק' מיל לעיר משום דקאזלן יוני של עיר מכרם לכרם ואתו התם. והא דקתני אא"כ הרחיק ל' ריס דליכא ישוב כרמים בינתים. **ורבא אמר בישוב שובכין** דבהני ק' מיל איכא ישוב שובכין מש"ה לא יפרוס דהא אזלי יוני העיר משובך לשובך כעין שעושין היונים שאלו באין בשביל אלו: **ותיפוק ליה משום יוני שובכין גופן.** הללו אין פורסין: **איבעית אימא.** דהדנה שובכין שלהן ומש"ה לא יפרוס שבאין דרך שובכין הללו אבל משום יוני שובכין ליכא למיחש הואיל ושלו הן: **ואם לקחו.** שקנה (חצר מן) השובך אפי' בית רובע הרי הוא בחזקתו ולא צריך נ' אמה לכל רוח: **זאת אומרת.** דקתני הרי זה בחזקתו דטוענין ליורש וללוקח שאם אמר אדם לחבירו שדה זו גזלת ממני והלה אומר אני קניתיה ממך ושני חזקה אכלתיה אין זו ראיה אבל אם אמר אבא הניחה לי כלומר יורש הבא מחמת ירושה א"צ טענה שכשאמר אבא הניחה לי א"צ לו יותר לו הראני שטר מכירה שקנאה אביך ודאי א"צ לטעון לו יותר דב"ד טוענין בשבילו ואמרו שמא אבד שטרו ואי אתה יכול להוציאה מתחת ידו וה"ה ללוקח שאם אמר ד) לקחתיה וכבר החזקתי בה שני חזקה א"צ לטעון יותר שב"ד טוענין בשבילו שמא אבד לוקח שטרו: **הא נמי תנינא.** דאיצטריך לאשמועינן ללוקח מתני' דלקח חצר ובה זיזין וגזוזטראות הרי זה בחזקתו: **אחולי אחילו גביה בני רה"ר.** אבל גבי שובך לא אמרי' הרי הוא בחזקתו משום דיחיד לא מחיל לשדה של חבירו: **אבל רבים מאן פייס ומאן שביק.** דלא מצי למיתן ממון לכל העולם: **צריכא** דאפי' הכא הרי הוא בחזקתו: **והא אמר רב נחמן אין חזקה לניזקין.** ואמאי הרי הוא בחזקתו הא מזיק לשדות דאחריני: **רב מרי אמר** בקוטרא. היכא אמרי' אין חזקה בקוטרא דפרישית לעיל אבל בשאר מילי יש חזקה:

פיסקא

מסורת הש"ס

א) לקמן נ., ב) [שם], ג) ב"ק פג: [שם], ד) [שם פג.], ו) [גיטין נח.], ז) לקמן מח., ח) לקמן ס., ט) בכ"י בשביל אותו, י) כפ"י אין זה, כ) [צ"ל לאו חזקה בנכסי אשתו וכ"ה בכת"י], ל) פ"ה דהא קשה רישא לסיפא דרישא קתני לא ריס מן הישוב פורסין ובסיפא קתני אפי' מאה מיל לא יפרוס.

הגהות הב"ח

(א) גמ' וסלקי ויתבי באבאלי ומפסדי: שם רבה אמר בישוב שובכין: (ג) שם הרי זו בחזקתה: (ד) שם גבי רה"ר דאימור כונס לתוך שלו הוא אי נמי אחולי אחלי בני רה"ר גביה אבל יחיד אימא לא: (ה) שם פיוסיה פייסיה במעותיה אי נמי: (ו) רש"י ד"ה טוענין וכו' ב"ד לו ופותחין: (ז) ד"ה לקח חצר ובה זיזין במ"ה דף ס תנן כצ"ל ותיבת במתני' נמחק: (ח) ד"ה אימא לתוך שלו: (ט) תוס' ד"ה והא וכו' דאין אדם עושה קנין למחלה והכא נמי מיירי שהיו טוענים שהקנה להם והוי חזקה שיש עמה טענה: (י) ד"ה אין וכו' דאפילו הקנה יכול לחזור: (כ) ד"ה בקוטרא וכו' בית הכסא שלהן שהיו למעלה: (ל) ד"ה והתניא ביישוב אפי' מאה מיל לא יפרוס תימה וכו' א"כ אפי' מאה מיל:

גליון הש"ס

גמרא ומישט שלשים ריס. עי' חולין דף קכב ע"ב תוס' ד"ה עור: שם יורש תנינא. עיין גיטין דף נח ע"ב תוס' ד"ה כגון: שם צריכא. עי' בב"י חו"מ סי' קמ"ו בשם תשובת הרשב"א וכרמב"ן במלחמות פ"ד דב"ב בסוגיא דשער כיס שנפלו על הימים: תוס' ד"ה אלא כו' ז' ריס ומחצה. כלאיים ביומא דף סז ע"א:

ליקוטי רש"י

אין חזקה לנזקין. הא דקאמר רב נחמן אין חזקה לנזקין לאו בחזקת ג' שנים בקרקע חבירו איירי אלא בעושה היזק לחבירו [ב"ק כג.]. **מרחיקין את השובך.** שלא יפסידו תבואה ופירות שבעיר [ב"ק פג.]. **שובך.** שבונין לו מחילות הרבה קן אצל קן לכל זוג וזוג. **אין פורסין נשבין.** פחים שלא ילכדו בהן יוני בני הישוב. **שלשים ריס.** ארבע מילין [ביצה טו.]. **וכרסייהו בחמשים אמתא מליא.** כמה שהן מלקטות ומנקרות בקרקע מלאין כרסן ממזונות ולהלן משום יותר. **בישוב כרמים.** לכרם עד שמתרחק. **בדידיה.** שאותן שובכין [המשך בעמוד ב']

חשק שלמה על רבינו גרשום א) נ"ל אם יש לו נ' אמה וכו'. ב) נ"ל לא יפרוס מיירי דבהכי ק' מיל איכא ישוב כרמים משום דקאזלן וכו'. ג) נראה דט"ס נפל בכאן וצ"ל והלא אמרת שלא לקחתיה וכו'. ד) נראה דצ"ל שאם אמר לקחתיה מפלוני וכבר החזקתי בה.

Gemara The Gemara infers from the *Tanna Kamma* that the extent of a dove's flight is fifty *amos,* and asks: חֲמִשִּׁים אַמָּה וְתוּ לָא – Do doves fly **fifty *amos* and no further?** וּרְמִינְהִי – **But I will contrast this** with the following Mishnah:[12] אֵין פּוֹרְסִין נִשְׁבִּין לְיוֹנִים – ONE MAY NOT SET OUT TRAPS TO catch DOVES אֶלָּא אִם כֵּן הָיָה רָחוֹק מִן הַיִּשּׁוּב שְׁלֹשִׁים רִיס – UNLESS HE IS THIRTY *RISS* AWAY FROM THE nearest SETTLEMENT, because otherwise he might trap doves that belong to others. We learn from this Mishnah that doves travel up to thirty *riss* from their roost, a distance of 8,000 *amos*![13] – ? –

The Gemara answers:

אָמַר אַבַּיֵי – **Abaye said:** מֵישַׁט שָׁיְיטֵי טוּבָא – **They fly** a **great** distance, וּכְרֵסַיְיהוּ בַּחֲמִשִּׁים אַמְּתָא מַלְיָא – **but their stomach is filled** by the grain that they find **in** the first **fifty *amos*** of their flight and they are unable to eat afterward. Therefore, distancing a dovecote fifty *amos* from one's boundary suffices to protect his neighbor's grain.

The Gemara now raises a contradiction to the Mishnah it cited: וּמֵישַׁט שְׁלֹשִׁים רִיס וְתוּ לָא – **Do [doves] fly thirty *riss* and no further?** וְהָתַנְיָא – **But we have learned in a Baraisa,** regarding dove traps:[14] וּבְיִשּׁוּב – AND IN A SETTLED AREA, אֲפִילּוּ מֵאָה מִיל לֹא יִפְרוֹס – ONE MAY NOT SET OUT traps EVEN if there is no dovecote within A HUNDRED *MIL*! We learn from this Baraisa that doves are capable of traveling more than one hundred *mil* from their roost. – ? –

The Gemara offers two answers:

רַב יוֹסֵף אָמַר בְּיִשּׁוּב כְּרָמִים – **Rav Yosef said:** The Baraisa refers **to an area "settled" with vineyards.** רָבָא אָמַר בְּיִשּׁוּב שׁוֹבָכִין – **Rava said:** It refers **to an area "settled" with dovecotes.** When flying from vineyard to vineyard, or from one dovecote to the next, doves travel very great distances. However, when there are no vineyards or dovecotes along the way, they travel no more than thirty *riss.*

The Gemara challenges Rava's explanation of the Baraisa:

וְתֵיפוֹק לֵיהּ מִשּׁוּם שׁוֹבָכִין גּוּפַיְיהוּ – **But let it** (the prohibition to set traps) **emerge because of the** nearby **dovecotes themselves.** In an area settled with dovecotes, one is forbidden to set out traps on account of the nearby doves. Why must the Baraisa base its prohibition on the dovecotes that are a hundred *mil* away?

The Gemara offers three possible answers to this question: אִיבָּעֵית אֵימָא דִּידֵיהּ – **If you wish, I can say** that the nearby dovecotes are **his own,** i.e. they belong to the one setting out the traps; וְאִיבָּעֵית אֵימָא דִּכְנַעֲנִי – **or, if you wish, I can say** that they are owned **by a Canaanite;**[15] וְאִיבָּעֵית אֵימָא דְּהֶפְקֵר – **or, if you wish, I can say** that they are **ownerless.** In any of these instances, the nearby dovecotes are not a factor in forbidding one to set out traps.

The Mishnah states:

רַבִּי יְהוּדָה אוֹמֵר בֵּית אַרְבַּעַת כּוֹרִין וכו׳ – R' YEHUDAH SAYS: One must have AN AREA OF FOUR *KOR* etc. [However, if he purchased the dovecote from the previous owner of the property, even if the entire property is only the area of a quarter-*kav,* the dovecote retains it *chazakah.*]

The Gemara deduces a law from this ruling:

אָמַר רַב פָּפָּא וְאִיתֵּימָא רַב זְבִיד – **Rav Pappa, and some say Rav Zevid, said:** זֹאת אוֹמֶרֶת – **This** Mishnah **informs** us, טוֹעֲנִין לְלוֹקֵחַ – that **we** (the court) **plead on behalf of a purchaser** וְטוֹעֲנִין לְיוֹרֵשׁ – **and we** (the court) **plead on behalf of an heir.**[16]

The Gemara asks:

יוֹרֵשׁ תְּנֵינָא – With respect to **an heir, we have** already **been taught** this law **in** another **Mishnah,** which states:[17] הַבָּא מִשּׁוּם יְרוּשָּׁה – ONE [WHOSE CLAIM] to a property COMES BY VIRTUE OF INHERITANCE אֵינוֹ צָרִיךְ טַעֲנָה – NEEDS NO PLEA as to the source of his ownership, because the court pleads on his behalf. Why must our Mishnah repeat the identical law?

The Gemara answers:

לוֹקֵחַ אִיצְטְרִיכָא לֵיהּ – **[Our Mishnah] is necessary** because it teaches this law in regard to **a purchaser.** The other Mishnah merely stated it with respect to an heir.

The Gemara asks further:

לוֹקֵחַ נַמִּי תְּנֵינָא – With regard to **a purchaser as well, we have been taught** this law **in** another **Mishnah:**[18] לָקַח חָצֵר וּבָהּ זִיזִין וּגְזוֹזְטְרָאוֹת – if ONE PURCHASED A COURTYARD, WHICH HAS LEDGES AND BALCONIES that extend over the public domain, הֲרֵי (זה) [זוֹ] בְּחֶזְקָתָהּ – IT RETAINS ITS *CHAZAKAH,* for we plead on behalf of the purchaser that the seller built the projections legally.[19] Why must our Mishnah repeat this law?

NOTES

12. *Bava Kamma* 79b.

13. Thirty *riss* are equal to four *mil* (*Rashi,* from Mishnah, *Yoma* 67a). There are 2,000 *amos* in a *mil* and thus, four *mil* equal 8,000 *amos.*

14. This Baraisa is an elaboration of the previously cited Mishnah (see *Tosefta, Bava Kamma* 8:4).

15. Doves belonging to a Canaanite that fly into one's trap are considered the Canaanite's lost property, which the finder is permitted to keep (see *Bava Kamma* 113b).

16. [A *chazakah* for the ownership of real property is established by three years of continuous occupancy. After three years, if the occupant is challenged by a previous owner of the property who claims that it is still his, he is not required to produce proof of ownership, for he is presumed to have acquired the property from the previous owner. However, he is required to advance a valid claim as to how he came to own the property; i.e. that the previous owner sold it to him or granted it to him as a gift.] Three years of unchallenged occupancy with no valid claim to the property do not suffice to establish a *chazakah* (Mishnah, below 41a; see Introduction to Chapter Three). Nevertheless, there is a law that if one occupies a property for three years and then sells it, or dies and leaves it to an heir, the purchaser or the heir need not advance a claim as to the source of their ownership. All that they need do to retain possession of the property is prove that their benefactor enjoyed three years of unchallenged occupancy. Since they cannot be expected to know with certainty how their benefactor acquired the property, the court is obliged to consider ("to plead") on their behalf the claim that he purchased it from the original owner.

Our Mishnah teaches us this law, since it rules that one who purchases a dovecote on a small plot of land retains the *chazakah* that was established by the previous owner. Although he may not know what right the seller had to build the dovecote, the court pleads on his behalf that the seller negotiated a deal with the neighbors whereby they sold him the right to build the dovecote within fifty *amos* of their property (*Rashi*).

17. Below, 41a.

18. Below, 60a.

19. Emendation follows *Bach.* [זִיזִין, *ledges,* are small extensions; גְּזוֹזְטְרָאוֹת, *balconies,* are larger extensions (*Rashbam,* 60a).]

The preceding portion of this Mishnah (60a) teaches that one who builds a house may not construct ledges or balconies that extend over the public domain because passersby might bump into them. However, if he chooses to draw the wall of his house back from the edge of his property, he may build a ledge that extends until the boundary. The segment of the Mishnah cited here continues that one who purchased a courtyard from which a ledge or a balcony protrudes retains the *chazakah* that the previous owner enjoyed, because we plead on his behalf that the previous owner built the extension legally, either by recessing his wall and building it on his own property, which was then utilized by the public, or by acquiring permission from the public to build it over the public domain (*Rashi*).

אתו אומני ויתבי תותייהו ואתו עורבי אכלי דמא וסלקי (א) אבי תאלי ומפסדי תמרי אמר להו רב יוסף אפיקו לי קורקור מהכא א"ל אביי והא גרמא הוא א"ל הכי אמר רב טובי בר מתנה זאת אומרת גרמא בניזקין אסור והא אחזיק [להו] הא אמר רב נחמן אמר רבה בר אבוה אין חזקה לנזקין ולאו איתמר עלה רב מרי אמר בקוטרא ורב זביד אמר בבית הכסא אמר ליה הני לדידי דאנינא דעתאי כי קוטרא ובית הכסא דמו לי: **מתני'** מרחיקין את השובך מן העיר חמשים אמה ולא יעשה אדם שובך בתוך שלו אלא אם כן יש לו חמשים אמה לכל רוח רבי יהודה אומר בית ארבעת כורין מלא שגר היונה ואם לקחו אפילו בית רובע הרי הוא בחזקתו: **גמ'** חמשים אמה ותו לא ורמינהי אין פורסין נשבין ליונים אלא אם כן היה רחוק מן הישוב שלשים ריס אמר אביי מישט שייטי טובא וכרסייהו בחמשים אמתא מליא ומישט שלשים ריס ותו לא והתניא ובישוב אפילו מאה מיל לא יפרוס רב יוסף אמר בישוב כרמים (ב) רבא אמר בישוב שובכין ותיפוק ליה משום שובכין גופייהו איבעית אימא דידיה ואיבעית אימא דכנעני ואיבעית אימא דהפקר: רבי יהודה אומר בית ארבעת כורין וכו': אמר רב פפא ואיתימא רב זביד זאת אומרת טוענין ללוקח וטוענין ליורש יורש תנינא הבא משום ירושה אינו צריך טענה לוקח איצטריכא ליה לוקח נמי תנינא לקח חצר ובה זיזין וגזוזטראות הרי (ג) זה בחזקתה צריכא דאי אשמעינן התם גבי רשות הרבים (ד) דאימור כונס לתוך שלו הוא אי נמי אחולי אחול בני רשות הרבים גביה אבל הכא לא ואי אשמעינן הכא דכיון דיחיד הוא אימא פיוסה פייסיה (ה) אי נמי אחולי אחיל גביה אבל רבים מאן פייס ומאן שביק אימא לא צריכא: הרי הוא בחזקתו: והא אמר רב נחמן אמר רבה בר אבוה אין חזקה לנזקין רב מרי אמר בקוטרא רב זביד אמר בבית הכסא: מתני'

רש"י

אומני. מקיז דם: **קורקור.** עורבים שדומים בלעקתן כקורין קורקור: **אפיקו לי.** כלומר לא יקוצו לי עוד כאן שעל כן העורבים כאן: **בקוטרא.** עשן: **בבית הכסא.** שעל גבי קרקע ונראה לעיניים שכן היו בתי כסאות שלהן: **מתני' מרחיקין השובך מן העיר.** שהיונים מפסדין זרעוני גנות: **אא"כ יש לו כו'.** שלא יפסדו היונים בשדה חבירו: **מלא שגר היונה.** מרוצת פריחתה פעם אחת: **ואם לקחו.** כמו שהוא עם הקרקע אפילו אין לו כל סביביו אלא בית רובע הקב הרי הוא בחזקתו שהרי הוחזק בו הראשון כן: **גמ' אין פורסין נשבין.** שלא ילכדו בהם יוני היישוב: **שלשים ריס.** ארבע מילין: **וכרסייהו בחמשים אמה קמלייא.** במה שהן מלקטין בתוך חמשים אמה מתמלא כריסן ואין מפסידים זרעים מכאן ולהלן: **לא יפרוס.** נשבין: **ביישוב כרמים.** שפורחין מכרם לכרם וטעים הרבה: **ביישוב שובכין.** שמדלג משובך לשובך: **ותיפוק ליה משום שובכין גופייהו.** מאי מאה מיל דקאמר דמשמע דבשביל יוני העיר מתרחק שבאין כאן דרך שובכין בלאו יוני העיר נמי לא יפרוס שהרי לוכד יוני שובכות של אחרים: **טוענין ליורש וטוענין ללוקח.** בית דין פותחים פה וטוענין ליורש וללוקח שערער אדם עליהן ויש לו עדים שהיתה שלו או של אבותיו וזה אומר ירשתיה מאבא או לקחתיה מפלוני שהוחזק בה ימים רבים והביא עדים שהוחזק בו אביו או המוכר לו שלש שנים אע"פ שלא טען זה והן לקחו ממך או מאבותיך טוענין לו בית דין (ו) ופותחים לו פה ואילו למי שלא ירשה ולא לקחה מאחר כשאמר לו המערער מה אתה עושה בתוך שלי והוא אומר החזקתי בה ג' שנים ולא אמרו לי דבר תנא במתני' (לקמן דף מא.) דאין לו חזקה ומתני' דקתני הרי הוא בחזקתו אשמועינן דהיכא דלקחה מאחר ובאו וערערו עליו אין צריך להרחיק אלמא טענינן ליה (ט) בשבילו שאותו שלקחה ממנו (י) (ונימא) נתפייס עם סביביו במעות עד שנאותו: **אינו צריך טענה.** אינו צריך לומר אתה מכרת לאבי אלא ראיתי לאבי שהחזיק בה ולא ערער אדם עליו: **לקח חצר ובה זיזין.** (ז) במתני' בח"ה תנן אין מוציאין זיזין וגזוזטראות לרשות הרבים אדם הבונה בית לא יוציא ראשי קורות תקרתו לרה"ר אבל אם רוצה כונס בניינו לתוך שלו ובונה ומוציא ראשי קורותיו לחוץ ואם לקח חצר ובה זיזין וגזוזטראות יוצאים לרה"ר הרי הוא בחזקתה שבית דין טוענין לו שהראשון כנס לתוך שלו או נתפייס עם הרבים: (ח) **אימא לתוך שלו הוא כונס.** שאילמלא כן היו הרבים מעכבין עליו ולא היה יכול לעשות בזרוע אבל כנגד היחיד אימא בזרוע עשה שהיה חזק ממנו: **מאן פייס.** מי היה ראשי לקבל מעות: **ומאן שביק.** מי הוא שבידו למחול ולסלוח:

מתני'

תוספות

אתו אומני ויתבי תותייהו. בקרקע שלהן היו יושבין ולא בקרקע של רב יוסף מדפריך בתר הכי והא גרמא הוא: **והא אחזיקו להו.** פי' ר"י ב"ר מרדכי כיון שלא בא להחזיק בקרקע של חבירו ולומר שלו הוא אלא לתשמיש בעלמא שנהנה ממנה מועלת חזקה שלא בטענה דמסתמא לא היו אומרים שמכר להם רב יוסף תשמיש זה והוו כי הנהו דלעיל (דף ו.) דאחזוק להורדי דמועלת חזקה שלא בטענה דמדלא מיחה ג' שנים מחל לו ואין נראה דאם לא הקנה לו כי החזיק להורדי אמאי החזיק לכשורי אלא על כרחך התם שטוען שהקנה לו ולהכי אחזיק לכשורי דאין אדם עושה קנין למחלה (ט): **אין חזקה לנזקין.** אומר ר"ת דאפי' הקנה (י) יכול לחזור בו דקנין בטעות הוא דסבור היה שיכול לקבל ועכשיו אין יכול לקבל ואין נראה דמדקאמר אין חזקה לנזקין איכא למידק הא ראיה יש כדדייקינן בחזקת הבתים (לקמן דף מט:) גבי הא דתנן ולא (כ) (לאשה חזקה בנכסי בעלה): **בקוטרא.** נראה לר"י דדוקא בקוטרא דכבשן שהוא גדול ומזיק ביותר אין חזקה כדאמר במרובה (ב"ק דף פב:) אין עושין כבשונות בירושלים מ"ט משום קוטרא ודוקא נמי בית הכסא שלהן (כ) שהיה למעלה מן הקרקע והיה מסריח ביותר אבל בשלנו שהוא מכוסה יש חזקה: **לדידי דאנינא דעתאי.** פי' שהיה איסטניס כדאמרינן בערבי פסחים (פסחים דף קיג: ושם) שלשה חייהם אינן חיים הרחמנים והרתחנים ואניני הדעת אמר רב יוסף וכולהו איתנהו בי: **בקוטרא ובית הכסא דמו.** והא דקאמר אפיקו קורקור מהכא משמע דמשום עורבים היה אומר ודאי אם לא היו עורבים היה סובל אף על גב דאנינא דעתיה אי נמי העורבים היו אוכלים הדם ופורקים ומנקרים בפירות: **מרחיקין השובך מן העיר חמשים אמה.** מפני התבואה הנשטחת בגגות העיר כדי לייבש אבל לתבואה שבשדות ליכא למיחש בקרוב לעיר לפי שהשדות רחוקין מן העיר אלף אמה כדתנן (ערכין דף לג:) אין עושין מגרש שדה ולא שדה מגרש: **ולא יעשה שובך תוך שלו.** ברחוק מן העיר בין השדות ואצטריך למיתני תרוייהו דאי תנא רישא להרחיק מן העיר התם דוקא מרחיק מפני שתבואות העיר מגולות הן בחצר הן בגג אבל תבואה הנזרעת בשדה ומכוסה אין צריך להרחיק ואי תנא סיפא משום דבשדות שכיחא תבואה אבל בעיר דלא שכיח כולי האי אימא לא: **בית ארבעת כורין כמלא שגר היונה.** ור' יהודה ורבנן לא פליגי בשגר היונה כמה הוי דמודו רבנן דבית ארבעה כורין הוי שגר היונה אלא רבנן סברי כיון דבחמשים אמה מליא כריסייהו כדאמרינן בגמ' תו לא מזקי טפי ור' יהודה סבר דכמלא שגר מזקי: **אלא אם כן הרחיק שלשים ריס.** היינו ד' מיל דהמיל ° ז' ריס ומחצה ופעמים שהגמרא נותן שיעור בריסין ופעמים במילין ופעמים בפרסה: **והתניא ביישוב אפילו מאה מיל** (ל). תימה דמאי ס"ד דהוי פי' וביישוב אי קרי העיר יישוב א"כ אפילו מאה מיל לאו דוקא כמו שמשמע אלא אפילו אלף מיל או יותר א"כ בשום מקום לא יפרוס אפילו במדבר ורחוק לאין סוף מן העיר ואפילו אם נאמר דמאה מיל דוקא מכל מקום היאך יפרש את הברייתא (ל) דהכי תניא בתוספתא דמרובה אין פורסין נשבין ליונים אא"כ הרחיק מן היישוב שלשים ריס בד"א במדבר אבל ביישוב אפי' מאה מיל לא יפרוס כיון דעיר קרי יישוב ואי ס"ד דהכי פירושו בד"א במדבר פי' שאין זרעים אבל ביישוב פי' ביישוב זרעים אפילו מאה מיל לא יפרוס אם כן מאי קשיא ליה ואומר ריצב"א דודאי ס"ד דאיירי ביישוב זרעים ולהכי פריך ומישט שייטי שלשים ריס ותו לא אפי' ביישוב זרעים והא מוכח דביישוב זרעים שייטי טובא ואין זה אלא משום אכילה אלמא דלא מליא כריסייהו בחמשים אמה ומשני דלא איירי ביישוב זרעים אלא ביישוב שובכין ויישוב כרמים וקרי מדבר היכא דליכא שובכים וכרמים: **יורש תנינא.** וס"ד המקשה דמתני' אשמעינן ביורש וה"ה בלוקח ומיהו רב זביד דנקט נמי יורש אמתני' דלקמן סמיך אבל מתני' דהכא לא שמעינן מינה יורש מדאיצטריך מתני' דלקמן: **וצריכי.** וא"ת ביורש נמי ליתני תרתי וי"ל דלאשמעינן בלוקח וה"ה ביורש: **אחולי אחילו גביה.** פי' ז' טובי העיר במעמד אנשי העיר שהרשות בידם כדאמר פרק בתרא דמגילה (דף כו.) וכיון דליכא לכל חד בדרך אלא פורתא מחלי טפי מיחיד:

חוץ

עין משפט נר מצוה

סא א ב ג ד מיי' פי"א מהל' שכנים הל' ד ה סמג עשין פב טוש"ע ח"מ סי' קנה סעיף לו לט:
סב ה מיי' שם הל' ה טוש"ע שם סעיף לג:
סג ו ז מיי' פ"ו מהל' גזילה הל' ט סמג עשין עג טוש"ע ח"מ סי' קנה סעיף כד:
סד ח ט י כ ל מיי' שם הל' י סמג שם טור ח"מ סי' שע:
סה מ נ טוש"ע ח"מ סי' קנה סעיף כד:

רבינו גרשום

אתו אומני. שהיו מקיזין והיו רגילין אנשים הרוצין להקיז באין שם להקיז ואגב שמתקבצין שם עורבים מחמת הדם עולין ומפסידין פירות האילנות: **אפיקו לי קורקור מהכא.** כלומר הוציאו עורבים הללו שקורין קורקור ומנקרין באילנות כלומר הוציאו האומנין משם ויכלו העורבין ולא יפסידו האילנות: **והא אחזיקו להו.** האומנין שרגילין להקיז תחת האילנות: **לא איתמר עלה.** היכא אמרי' אין חזקה לניזקין בקוטרא שאם היה חלון פתוחה לביתו של חבירו והיה עולה עשן ומזיק לו ודאי אין חזקה לניזקין דהאי נזקא גופא מחמת העשן הוא וכן בית הכסא נמי אם היה בית הכסא סמוך לביתו של חבירו והסרחון הולך אין חזקה משום אניגות גופא אבל שאר היזקות אם החזיק יש לו חזקה: **דמו לי.** האי דמא: **פיסקא מן העיר נ' אמה.** כדי שלא יאכלו היונים זרעוני גינת העיר וכן נמי צריך להעמיד בתוך שלו (א) שהיא לו נ' אמה לכל רוח שלא יאכלו זרעוני חבירו: **כמלא שגר היונה.** כמו שיכולה היונה לפרוח בבת אחת: **ואם לקחו.** שנים שאחד הגיע לחלק אחד מקום השובך ולשני מקום הפנוי ואפי' אין בין שובך לגינת זה אלא הרחקת בית רובע הרי הוא השובך בחזקתו [שלא] להרחיק יותר הואיל ומתחלה היה בחזקה והגינה של א': **נשבין.** מצודות: **אלא אם כן** הרחיק הנשבין מן הישוב ל' ריס. דאתו יוני הישוב ונכנסין לתוך הנשבין ותפיס להו אלמא דשייטי טפי מן נ' אמה והיכי קתני דבנ' אמה סגי: **רב יוסף אמר.** הא דתני בישוב אפי' ק' מיל לא יפרוס ב) אפי' יהא ק' מיל לעיר משום דקאזלו יוני של עיר מכרם לכרם ואתו התם. והא דקתני אא"כ הרחיק ל' ריס דליכא ישוב כרמים בינתים. **ורבא אמר בישוב שובכין** דבהני ק' מיל איכא ישוב שובכין משה"ה לא יפרוס דהא אזלי יוני העיר משובך לשובך כעין שעושין היונים שאלו באין בשביל אלו: **ותיפוק** ליה משום יוני שובכין גופן. הללו אין פורסין: **איבעית אימא.** דהנהו שובכין שלהן ומשה"ה לא יפרוס משום יוני העיר שבאין דרך שובכין הללו אבל משום יוני שובכין ליכא למיחש הואיל ושלו הן: **ואם לקחו.** שקנה (חצר מן) השובך אפי' בית רובע הרי הוא בחזקתו ולא צריך נ' אמה לכל רוח: **זאת אומרת.** דקתני ה"ז בחזקתו **דטוענין ליורש וללוקח** שאם אמר אדם לחבירו שדה זו גזלת ממני ג) והלה אמר אני קניתיה ממך ושני חזקה אכלתיה אין זו ראיה אבל אם אמר אבא הניחה לי כלומר יורש הבא מחמת ירושה א"צ טענה שכשאמר אבא הניחה לי א"צ לו יותר לטעון שלא יכול הלה לחזור ולומר לו הראני שטר מכירה שקנאה אביך ודאי א"צ לטעון לו יותר דב"ד טוענין בשבילו ויאמרו שמא אבד שטרו ואי אתה יכול להוציא מתחת ידו וכן ה"נ לוקח שאם אמר ד) לקחתיה וכבר החזקתי בה שני חזקה אם טוען הלה ואמר הראה השטר א"צ ללוקח לטעון יותר שב"ד טוענין בשבילו [illegible] **אחיל גביה בני רה"ר.** [illegible] **אבל רבים מאן פייס ומאן שביק.** דלא מצי למיתן ממון לכל העולם **צריכא** דאפ"ה הכא הרי הוא בחזקתו. ואמאי הרי הוא בחזקתו: **אין חזקה לניזקין. רב מרי אמר.** היכא אמרי' אין חזקה בקוטרא כדפרישית לעיל אבל בשאר מילי יש חזקה:

פיסקא

מסורת הש"ס

א) לקמן נ., ב) [שם], ג) ב"ק פג., ד) [שם עג:], ה) [שם פג.], ו) גיטין נח:, ז) לקמן מח., ח) לקמן ס., ט) בשביל אותו, כ) צ"ל לאיש חזקה בנכסי אשתו וכו' ב"ח, ל) מ"ד והא קשה דרישא לסיפא דרישא קתני ל' ריס מן הישוב ובסיפא קתני אפי' מאה מיל לא יפרוס:

הגהות הב"ח

(א) גמ' וסלקי ויתבי בתאלי ומפסדי: (ב) שם רבה אמר ביישוב שובכין: (ג) שם הרי זו בחזקתה: (ד) שם גבי רה"ר דאימור כונס לתוך שלו הוא אי נמי אחולי אחלי בני רה"ר גביה אבל יחיד אימא לא: (ה) שם פיוסי פייסיה במעות או אחולי אחיל גביה אבל רבים: (ו) רש"י ד"ה טוענין וכו' טוענין וכו' ב"ד ופותחין: (ז) ד"ה לקח חצר וכו' זיזין בח"ה פ' תנן כצ"ל ותיבת במתני' נמחק: (ח) ד"ה אימא לתוך שלו: (ט) תוס' ד"ה והא וכו' דאין אדם עושה קנין למחלה והכא נמי מיירי שהיו טוענין שהקנה להם: (י) ד"ה אין וכו' דאפי' הקנה לו בעדים יכול לחזור: (כ) ד"ה בקוטרא וכו' בית הכסא שלהן שהיו למעלה: (ל) ד"ה והתניא ביישוב תימה וכו' לא יפרוס תימה וכו' א"כ אפי' מאה מיל:

גליון הש"ס

גמרא ומישט שלשים ריס. עי' חולין דף קכב ע"ב תוס' ד"ה לבגדו: שם יורש תנינא. עיין גיטין דף נח ע"ב תוס' ד"ה כגון: שם צריכא. עי' בב"י חו"מ סי' קי בשם תשובת הרשב"א והרמב"ן במלחמות פ"ד דב"ב בסוגיא דצריך כיס היוצא על היתומים: תוס' ד"ה אלא כו' ז' ריס ומחצה. כדאיתא ביומא דף סז ע"א:

ליקוטי רש"י

אין חזקה לנזקין. הא דקאמר רב נחמן אין חזקה לנזקין לא אמרו ג' שנים בקרקע חבירו איירי אלא בעושה בשלו ועושה בתוך שלו ואפי' בעושה בתוך שלו כגון עשן וריח בית הכסא וכה לאודויי שלו יזיק להם ואפי' החזיק בהן ימים רבים אין חזקה מועלת לו להזיק [רשב"ם לקמן נט.]. **מרחיקין את השובך.** שלא יאכלו תבואה ופירות שבגגים [ס"א שבחוץ] העיר [ב"ק פב.]. **שובך.** דכן שובך בו מחילות הרבה קן לכל זוג וזוג וחלון לכל קן וקן [ביצה ט.]. **אין פורסין נשבין.** פחים שלא ילכדו בהן יוני בני הישוב. **שלשים ריס.** ארבע מילין [ביצה עט:]. **וכרסייהו בחמשים אמתא מליא.** במה שהן מלקטות ומנקרות בקרקע מלאין בחמשין אמה הלכך לגבי אכילת תבואת עיר אין לחוש ביותר. **בישוב כרמים.** שהולך מכרם לכרם עד למרחוק. **בדידיה.** שאותן שובכין

[המשך בעמוד ב']

חשק שלמה על רבינו גרשום א) צ"ל אם יש לו נ' אמה וכו'. ב) צ"ל לא יפרוס מיירי דבכל ק' מיל איכא ישוב כרמים משום דקאזלו וכו'. ג) נ"ל דצ"ל והלה אומר אני לקחתיה ממך ושני חזקה אכלתיה וכו'. ד) נראה דצ"ל שאם אמר לו המערער [illegible]

The Gemara answers:

צְרִיכָא – Both Mishnahs are **necessary.** דְּאִי אַשְׁמְעִינַן הָתָם גַּבֵּי רְשׁוּת הָרַבִּים – **For if [the Mishnah] had taught** this ruling **there, in the case of** ledges that extend over **the public domain,** I might have said that only in that case do we plead on behalf of a purchaser, דְּאִימוּר כּוֹנֵס לְתוֹךְ שֶׁלּוֹ הוּא – **for** it is reasonable to **say that [the previous owner] recessed** the wall **into his** property and built the extension over his own land, אִי נַמִּי אַחוּלֵי אַחוּל בְּנֵי רְשׁוּת הָרַבִּים גַּבֵּיהּ – **or that the public**[20] **yielded him** the right to build an extension over their domain, since it is unlikely that anybody could have defied the public and built it illegally. Therefore, our claim on behalf of the purchaser is well grounded. אֲבָל הָכָא – **But here,** in the case of a dovecote that is harmful to an individual neighbor לֹא – we do **not** plead on the purchaser's behalf, because we must consider the possibility that the previous owner was a powerful person, whom the neighbors were unable to prevent from building the dovecote illegally. Our Mishnah therefore teaches us that in this case we also plead on behalf of the purchaser.[21]

The Gemara's answer continues:

וְאִי אַשְׁמְעִינַן הָכָא – **And if [the Mishnah] had taught** this rule **here,** in the case of a dovecote, I might have said that only in this case do we plead on the purchaser's behalf, דְּכֵיוָן דְּיָחִיד הוּא – **for since [the neighbor]** affected by the dovecote **is an individual,** אֵימָא פִּיּוּסֵי(ה) פַּיְיסֵיהּ – it is plausible to **say** that **[the previous owner] came to terms with him** and acquired the right to build the dovecote, אִי נַמִּי אַחוּלֵי אַחִיל גַּבֵּיהּ – **or** that **[the neighbor] yielded him** the right to build the dovecote. אֲבָל רַבִּים – **But** with regard to **a public** that is endangered by a protruding ledge, מַאן פַּיֵּיס – **with whom could he** possibly **have come to terms?** וּמַאן שָׁבִיק – **And who could have yielded** the public's right to object? Nobody is authorized to act on the public's behalf in this matter![22] אֵימָא לֹא – Accordingly, **I** might **say** that we do **not** plead on the purchaser's behalf. צְרִיכָא – Therefore, another Mishnah is **necessary,** to teach us that we plead on behalf of the purchaser, even in that case.[23]

The Mishnah concludes:

הֲרֵי הוּא בְּחֶזְקָתוֹ – [THE DOVECOTE] RETAINS ITS *CHAZAKAH.*

The Gemara raises a question:

וְהָא אָמַר רַב נַחְמָן אָמַר רַבָּה בַּר אֲבוּהַּ – **But Rav Nachman has said in the name of Rabbah bar Avuha:** אֵין חֲזָקָה לִנְזָקִין – **There is no *chazakah* for damage!** Accordingly, how can a *chazakah* have been established for a dovecote that is a source of damage to the neighbors?

The Gemara answers:

רַב מָרִי אָמַר בְּקוּטְרָא – **Rav Mari said:** Rav Nachman's ruling applies **to smoke.** רַב זְבִיד אָמַר בְּבֵית הַכִּסֵּא – **Rav Zevid said:** It applies **to an outhouse.** However, a *chazakah can* be established for less objectionable sources of damage.[24]

NOTES

20. Literally: members of the public domain.

21. Although we have no compelling reason to assume that the claim is true, it is nevertheless a plausible claim and we therefore plead it on behalf of the purchaser.

22. Earlier, the Gemara did consider the possibility that the public yielded him the right to build an extension over their domain, because the seven trustees of a city, acting in the presence of the townspeople, are authorized to yield public property (*Tosafos;* see *Megillah* 26a). Here, however, the Gemara rejects that consideration, because it is unlikely that they would do so (and had they indeed done so, it would most likely be common knowledge). Accordingly, the Gemara states that although the passersby may have yielded their objection to the extension, they are not authorized to act on behalf of the entire populace.

23. We plead on behalf of the purchaser that the seller recessed the wall of his house and built the protrusion over his own property, which was subsequently utilized by the public (*Ritva*).

24. See notes 5-7.

א) לקמן נ., ב) ב"ק פב., ג) [שם], ד) [שם פג.], ה) [שם עט.], ו) [גיטין נח:], ז) לקמן מא., ח) לקמן מב., ט) בס"א בשביל אותו, י) בס"י אין זה, כ) [נ"ל דלאו חזקה לנזקין היא דהא קשה רישא לסיפא דרישא קתני ריס מן הישוב פורסין וסיפא קתני אפי' מאה מיל לא יפרוס].

סא א ב ג ד מיי' פי"א מהל' שכנים הל' ד ה סמג עשין פב טוש"ע ח"מ סי' קנה סעיף לו לט: סב ה מיי' שם הל' ה טוש"ע שם סעיף לט: סג ו ז מיי' פי"ג מהל' גזילה הל' ט סמג עשין עג טוש"ע ח"מ סי' קנה סעיף כו: סד ח ט י כ ל מיי' שם הל' ח סמג שם טור ח"מ סי' שע: סה מ נ טוש"ע ח"מ סי' קנה סעיף כד:

אתו אומני ויתבי תותייהו ואתו עורבי אכלי דמא וסלקי (א) אבי תאלי ומפסדי תמרי אמר להו רב יוסף אפיקו לי קורקור מהכא א"ל אביי והא גרמא הוא א"ל הכי אמר רב טובי בר מתנה זאת אומרת גרמא בניזקין אסור והא אחזיק [להו] הא אמר רב נחמן אמר רבה בר אבוה אין חזקה לנזקין ולאו איתמר עלה רב מרי אמר בקוטרא ורב זביד אמר בבית הכסא אמר ליה הני לדידי דאנינא דעתאי כי קוטרא ובית הכסא דמו לי: **מתני'** מרחיקין את השובך מן העיר חמשים אמה ולא יעשה אדם שובך בתוך שלו אלא אם כן יש לו חמשים אמה לכל רוח רבי יהודה אומר בית ארבעת כורין מלא שגר היונה ואם לקחו אפילו בית רובע הרי הוא בחזקתו: **גמ'** חמשים אמה ותו לא ורמינהי אין פורסין נשבין ליונים אלא אם כן היה רחוק מן הישוב שלשים ריס אמר אביי מישט שייטי טובא וכרסייהו בחמשים אמתא מליא ומישט שלשים ריס ותו לא והתניא ובישוב אפילו מאה מיל לא יפרוס רב יוסף אמר בישוב כרמים (ב) רבא אמר בישוב שובכין ותיפוק ליה משום שובכין גופייהו איבעית אימא דידיה ואיבעית אימא דכנעני ואיבעית אימא דהפקר: רבי יהודה אומר בית ארבעת כורין מלא וכו': אמר רב פפא ואיתימא רב זביד זאת אומרת טוענין ללוקח וטוענין ליורש יורש תנינא הבא משום ירושה אינו צריך טענה לוקח איצטריכא ליה לוקח נמי תנינא לקח חצר ובה זיזין וגזוזטראות הרי (ג) זה בחזקתה צריכא דאי אשמעינן התם גבי רשות הרבים (ד) דאימור כונס לתוך שלו הוא אי נמי אחולי אחול בני רשות הרבים גביה אבל הכא לא ואי אשמעינן הכא דכיון דיחיד הוא אימא פיוסיה פייסיה (ה) אי נמי אחולי אחיל גביה אבל רבים מאן פיים ומאן שביק אימא לא צריכא: הרי הוא בחזקתו: והא אמר רב נחמן אמר רבה בר אבוה אין חזקה לנזקין רב מרי אמר בקוטרא רב זביד אמר בבית הכסא:
מתני'

רש"י

אתו אומני. מקיזי דם: **קורקור.** עורבים שדומים בצעקתן כקורין קורקור: **אפיקו לי.** כלומר אל יקיזו לי עוד כאן שעל כן העורבים באין: **בקוטרא.** עשן: **בבית הכסא.** שעל גבי קרקע ונראה לעיניים שכך היו בית כסאות שלהן: **מתני'** מרחיקין השובך מן העיר. שהיונים מפסידין זרעוני גנות: **אא"כ יש לו כו'.** שלא יפסידו היונים בשדה חבירו: **מלא שגר היונה.** מרוצת פריחתה פעם אחת: **ואם לקחו.** כמו שהוא עם הקרקע אפילו אין לו כל סביביו אלא בית רובע הקב הרי הוא בחזקתו שהרי הוחזק בו הראשון כן: **גמ' אין פורסין נשבין.** שלא ילכדו בהם יוני היישוב: **שלשים ריס.** ארבע מילין: **וכרסייהו בחמשים אמה קמליא.** כמה שהן מלקטין בתוך חמשים אמה מתמלא כריסן ואין מפסידים זרעים מכאן ולהלן: **לא יפרוס.** נשבין: **ביישוב כרמים.** שפורסין מכרם לכרם וטסים הרבה: **ביישוב שובכין.** שמדלג משובך לשובך: **ותיפוק ליה משום שובכין גופייהו.** מאי מאה מיל דקאמר דמשמע דבשביל יוני העיר מתרחק שאין כאן דרך שובכין בלאו יוני העיר נמי לא יפרוס שהרי לוכד יוני שובכות של אחרים: **טוענין ליורש וטוענין ללוקח.** בית דין פותחים פה וטוענה ליורש וללוקח שערער אדם עליהן ויש לו עדים שהיתה שלו או של אבותיו והוא אומר ירשתיה מאבא או לקחתיה מפלוני שהוחזק בו ימים רבים והביא עדים שהוחזק בו ג' שנים ואחר כך מכרו לו שלא שנים אע"פ שלא טען והן לקחו ממך או מאבותיך טוענין לו בית דין (ו) ופותחים לו פה ואילו למי שלא ירשה ולא לקחה מאחר כשאמר לו המערער מה אתה עושה בתוך שלי והוא אומר החזקתי בה ג' שנים ולא אמרו לי דבר תנא במתני' (לקמן דף מא.) דאין לו חזקה ומתני' דקתני הרי הוא בחזקתו אשמועינן דהיכא דלקחה מאחר ובאו וערערו עליו אין צריך להרחיק אלמא טענינן ליה (ט) בשבילו שאותו שלקחה ממנו (י) (וניחא) נתפייס עם סביביו במעות עד שנאותו: **אינו צריך טענה.** אינו צריך לומר אתה מכרת לאבי אלא ראיתי לאבי שהחזיק בה ולא ערער אדם עליו: **לקח חצר ובה זיזין.** (ז) במתני' בח"ה תנן אין מוציאין זיזין וגזוזטראות לרשות הרבים אדם הבונה בית לא יוציא ראשי קורות תקרתו לרה"ר אבל אם רוצה כונס בניינו לתוך שלו ובונה ומוציא ראשי קורותיו לחוץ ואם לקח חצר ובה זיזין וגזוזטראות יוצאים לרה"ר הרי הוא בחזקתה שבית דין טוענין לו שהראשון כנס לתוך שלו או נתפייס עם הרבים: (ח) **אימא לתוך שלו הוא כונס.** שאילמלא כן היו הרבים מעכבין עליו ולא היה יכול לעשות בזרוע אבל כנגד היחיד אימא בזרוע עשה שהיה חזק ממנו: **מאן פיים.** מי היה ראשי לקבל מעות: **ומאן שביק.** מי הוא שבידו למחול ולסלוח:
מתני'

תוספות

אתו אומני ויתבי תותיידו. בקרקע שלהן היו יושבין ולא בקרקע של רב יוסף מדפריך בתר הכי והא גרמא הוא: **והא** אחזיקו להו. פי' ר"י ב"ר מרדכי כיון שלא בא להחזיק בקרקע של חבירו ולומר שלו הוא אלא לתשמיש בעלמא שנהנה ממנה מועלת חזקה שלא בטענה דמסתמא לא היו אומרים שמכר להם רב יוסף תשמיש זה והוו כי הנהו דלעיל (דף ו.) דאחזוק להורדי דמועלת חזקה שלא בטענה דמדלא מיחה ג' שנים מחל לו ואין נראה דאם לא הקנה לו כי החזיק להורדי אמאי החזיק לכשורי אלא על כרחך התם שטוען שהקנה לו ולהכי אחזיק לכשורי דאין אדם עושה קנין למחלה (ט): **אין** חזקה לנזקין. אומר ר"ת דאפי' הקנה (י) יכול לחזור בו דקנין בטעות הוא דסבור היה שיכול לקבל ועכשיו אין יכול לקבל ואין נראה דמדקאמר אין חזקה לנזקין איכא למידק הא ראיה יש כדדייקינן בחזקת הבתים (לקמן דף מט:) גבי הא דתנן ולא (כ) (לאשה חזקה בנכסי בעלה):
בקוטרא. נראה לר"י דדוקא בקוטרא דכבשן שהוא גדול ומזיק ביותר אין חזקה כדאמר במרובה (ב"ק דף פב:) אין עושין כבשונות בירושלים מ"ט משום קוטרא ודוקא נמי בית הכסא שלהן (כ) שהיה למעלה מן הקרקע והיה מסריח ביותר אבל בשלנו שהוא מכוסה יש חזקה: **לדידי** דאנינא דעתאי. פי' שהיה איסטניס כדאמרינן בערבי פסחים (פסחים דף קיג: ושם) שלשה חייהם אינן חיים הרחמנים והרתחנים ואניני הדעת אמר רב יוסף וכולהו איתנהו בי:
בקוטרא ובית הכסא דמו. והא דקאמר אפיקו קורקור מהכא משמע דמשום עורבים היה אומר ודאי אם לא היו עורבים היה סובל אף על גב דאנינא דעתיה אי נמי העורבים היו אוכלים הדם ופורחים ומקנחים בפירות:
מרחיקין השובך מן העיר חמשים אמה. מפני התבואה הנשטחת בגגות העיר כדי לייבש אבל לתבואה שבשדות ליכא למיחש בקרוב לעיר לפי שהשדות רחוקין מן העיר אלף אמה כדתנן (ערכין דף לג:) אין עושין מגרש שדה ולא שדה מגרש: **ולא** יעשה שובך תוך שלו. ברחוק מן העיר בין השדות ואצטריך למיתני תרוייהו דאי תנא רישא להרחיק מן העיר התם דוקא מרחיק מפני שתבואות העיר מגולות הן בחצר הן בגג אבל תבואה המזרעת בשדה ומכוסה אין צריך להרחיק ואי תנא סיפא משום דבשדות שכיחא תבואה אבל בעיר דלא שכיח כולי האי אימא לא: **בית** ארבעת כורין כמלא שגר היונה. ור' יהודה ורבנן לא פליגי בשגר היונה כמה הוי דמודו רבנן דבית ארבעה כורין הוי שגר היונה אלא רבנן סברי כיון דבחמשים אמה מליא כריסייהו כדאמרינן בגמ' תו לא מזקי טפי ור' יהודה סבר דכמלא שגר מזקי: **אלא** אם כן הרחיק שלשים ריס. היינו ד' מיל דהמיל ° ז' ריס ומחצה ופעמים שהגמרא נותן שיעור בריסין ופעמים במילין ופעמים בפרסה: **והתניא** ביישוב אפילו מאה מיל (ג). תימה דמאי ס"ד דהוי פי' וביישוב אי קרי העיר יישוב א"כ אפילו מאה מיל לאו דוקא כמו שמשמע אלא אפילו אלף מיל או יותר א"כ בשום מקום לא יפרוס אפילו במדבר ורחוק לאין סוף מן העיר ואפילו אם נאמר דמאה מיל דוקא מכל מקום היאך יפרש את הברייתא ל) דהכי תניא בתוספתא דמרובה אין פורסין נשבין ליונים אא"כ הרחיק מן היישוב שלשים ריס בד"א במדבר אבל ביישוב אפי' מאה מיל לא יפרוס כיון דעיר קרי יישוב ואי ס"ד דהכי פירושו בד"א במדבר פי' שאין זרעים אבל ביישוב פי' ביישוב זרעים אפילו מאה מיל לא יפרוס אם כן מאי קשיא ליה ואומר ריצב"א דודאי ס"ד דאיירי ביישוב זרעים ולהכי פריך ומישט שייטי שלשים ריס ותו לא אפי' ביישוב זרעים והא מוכח דביישוב זרעים שייטי טובא ואין זה אלא משום אכילה אלמא דלא מליא כריסייהו בחמשים אמה ומשני דלא איירי ביישוב זרעים אלא ביישוב שובכין ויישוב כרמים וקרי מדבר היכא דליכא שובכים וכרמים: **יורש** תנינא. וס"ד המקשה דמתני' אשמעינן ביורש וה"ה בלוקח ומיהו רב זביד דנקט נמי יורש אמתני' דהכא לא שמעינן מינה יורש מדאיצטריך מתני' דלקמן: אבל מתני' לקמן סמיך **וצריכי.** וא"ת ביורש נמי ליתני תרתי וי"ל דאשמעינן בלוקח וה"ה ביורש: **אחולי** אחילו גביה. פי' ז' טובי העיר במעמד אנשי העיר שהרשות בידם כדאמר פרק בתרא דמגילה (דף כו.) וכיון דליכא לכל חד בדרך אלא פורתא מחלי טפי מיחיד:

חוץ

הגהות הב"ח

(א) גמ' וסלקי ויתבי באתלי ומפסדי: (ב) שם רבה אמר בישוב שובכין: (ג) שם הרי זו בחזקתה: (ד) שם גבי רה"ר דאימור כונס לתוך שלו הוא אי נמי אחולי אחול בני רה"ר גביה אבל יחיד אימא לא: (ה) שם פיוסיה פייסיה במאי דאי נמי: (ו) רש"י ד"ה טוענין וכו' ב"ד כן ופותחין: (ז) ד"ה לקח חצר וכו' זיזין בח"ה דף ס' תנן כו' וזיזה נמי במתני' נמחק: (ח) ד"ה אימא לתוך שלו: (ט) תוס' ד"ה והא וכו' דלאין אדם עושה קנין למחלה והכא נמי מיירי שהיו טוענים שהקנה להם והוי חזקה שיש עמה טענה הס"ד: (י) ד"ה אין וכו' דלאפילו הקנה יכול לחזור: (כ) ד"ה בקוטרא וכו' בית הכסא שלהן שהיה למעלה: (ל) ד"ה והתניא בישוב אפי' מאה מיל וכו' א"כ אפי' מאה מיל:

גליון הש"ס

גמרא ומישט שלשים ריס. עי' חולין דף קכב ע"ב תוס' ד"ה לגגל: שם יורש תנינא. עיין גיטין דף נח ע"ב תוס' ד"ה כגון: שם צריכא. עי' בב"י חו"מ סי' ק"נ בשם תשובת הרשב"א וברמב"ן במלחמות פ"ב דב"ב בסוגיא דשער חצר היוצאת על היתומים: תוס' ד"ה אלא כו' ד' ריס ומחצה. כדאיתא ביומא דף סז ע"א:

ליקוטי רש"י

אין חזקה לנזיקין. הא דקאמר רב נחמן אין חזקה לנזקין לא שנא חזקת ג' שנים בקרקע חבירו לאיירי אלא בעושה היזק לחבירו אפי' בבית שלו עצמו כגון עשן וריח רע ואמר לאחריו לא ימחה יזיק לחבירו ואפי' החזיק ימים רבים אין חזקה מועלת לו להזיק חבירו [ב"ק נג:]. מרחיקין את השובך. שלא יפסידו תבואה ופירות שסביבי [ס"א שבחוצה] העיר [ב"ק פב.]. שובך. לול שובך בו מחיצות הרבה קן לכל זוג וזוג ותולין לכל זוג וקן [ביצה ט.]. אין פורסין נשבין. פחים שלא ילכדו בהן יוני בני הישוב. שלשים ריס. ארבע מילין [ביצה שם]. וכרסייהו בחמשים אמתא מליא. כמה שהן מלקטות ומנקרות בקרקע מלאין בחמשין אמה הלכך לגבי אכילת תבואת עיר אין לחוש ביותר. בישוב כרמים. שהולך מכרם לכרם עד למרחוק. בדידיה. שאותן שובכין [המשך בעמוד ב']

רבינו גרשום

אתו אומני. שהיו מקיזין והיו רגילין אנשים הרוצין להקיז באין שם להקיז ואגב שמתקבצין שם עורבים מחמת הדם עולין ומפסידין פירות האילנות: אפיקו לי קורקור מהכא. כלומר הוציאו עורבים הללו שקורין קורקור ומנקרין באילנות כלומר הוציאו האומנין משם ויכלו העורבין ולא יפסידו האילנות: והוא אחזיקו להו. האומנין שרגילין להקיז תחת האילנות: לא איתמר עלה. היכא אמרי' אין חזקה לניזקין בקוטרא שאם היה חלון פתוחה לביתו של חבירו והיה עולה עשן ומזיק לו ודאי אין חזקה לניזקין דהאי נזקא גופא מחמת העשן הוא וכן הכי נמי אם היה בית הכסא סמוך לביתו של חבירו והסרחון הולך אין חזקה משום אנינות גופא אבל שאר היזיקות אם החזיק יש לו חזקה: דמו לי. האי דמא: פיסקא מן העיר נ' אמה. כדי שלא יאכלו היונים זרעוני גינת העיר וכן נמי צריך להעמיד בתוך שלו א) שהיא לו נ' אמה לכל רוח שלא יאכלו זרעוני חבירו: כמלא שגר היונה. כמו שיכולה היונה לפרוח בבת אחת: ואם לקחו. שנים שאחד הגיע לחלק אחד מקום השובך ולשני מקום הפנוי ואפי' אין בין שובך לגינת זה אלא הרחקה בית רובע הרי הוא השובך בחזקתו [שלא] להרחיק יותר הואיל ומתחלה היה השובך והגינה של א': נשבין. מצודות: אלא אם כן הרחיק הנשבין מן הישוב ל' ריס. דאתו יוני הישוב ונכנסין לתוך הנשבין ותפיס להו אלמא דשייטי טפי מן נ' אמה והיכי קתני דבנ' אמה סגי: רב יוסף אמר. הא דתני בישוב אפי' ק' מיל לא יפרוס ב) אפי' יהא ק' מיל לעיר משום דקאזלן יוני של עיר מכרם לכרם ואתו התם. והא דקתני אא"כ הרחיק ל' ריס דליכא ישוב כרמים בינתים. ורבא אמר בישוב שובכין דהכי ק' מיל איכא ישוב שובכין משו"ה לא יפרוס דהא אזלי יוני העיר משובך לשובך כעין שעושין היונים שאלו באין בשביל אלו: ותיפוק ליה משום יוני שובכין גופן. הללו אין פורסין: איבעית אימא. הנהו שובכין שלהן ומש"ה לא יפרוס משום יוני העיר שבאי דרך שובכין הללו אבל משום יוני שובכין ליכא למיחש הואיל ושלו הן: ואם לקחו. שקנה (חצר מן) השובך אפי' בית רובע הרי הוא בחזקתו ולא צריך נ' אמה לכל רוח: זאת אומרת. דקתני ה"ז בחזקתו דטוענין ליורש וללוקח שאם אמר אדם לחבירו שדה זו גזלת ממני ג) והלה אמר אני קניתיה ממך ושני חזקה אכלתיה אין זו ראיה אבל אם אמר אבא הניחה לי כלומר יורש הבא מחמת ירושה א"צ טענה שכשאמר אבא הניחה לי א"צ לו יותר לטעון שלא יכול הלה לחזור ולומר לו הראני שטר מכירה שקנאה אביך ודאי א"צ לטעון לו יותר דב"ד טוענין בשבילו ויאמרו שמא אבד שטרו ואי אתה יכול להוציאה מתחת ידו וכן ה"נ לוקח שאם אמר ד) לקחתיה וכבר החזקתי בה שני חזקה אם טוען הלה ואמר הראה השטר א"צ ללוקח לטעון יותר שב"ד טוענין בשבילו שמא אבד השטר הכי נמי בשחלקו הרי הוא בחזקתו וא"צ להרחיק יותר: הא נמי תנינא. באידך פירקין בחזקת הבתים אין מוציאין זיזין וגזוזטראות לרה"ר לקח חצר ובה זיזין וגזוזטראות הרי הן בחזקתן משום דכונס בתוך שלו היה אי נמי אחולי אחיל גביה בני רה"ר. אבל גבי שובך לא אמרי' הרי הוא בחזקתו משום דיחיד לא מחיל ליה שיכנסו יונים לתוך שדה שלו ולא אמרי' (דלא) הרי הוא בחזקתו קמ"ל דאפ"ה הרי הוא בחזקתו: אבל רבים מאן פייס ומאן שביק. דלא מצי למיתן ממון לכל העולם צריכא דאפי' הכא הרי הוא בחזקתו: אין חזקה לניזקין. ואמאי הרי הוא בחזקתו הא מזיק לשדות דאחריני: רב מרי אמר. היכא אמרי' אין חזקה בקוטרא כדפרישית לעיל אבל בשאר מילי יש חזקה:
פיסקא

חשק שלמה על רבינו גרשום א) נ"ל אם יש לו נ' אמה וכו'. ב) נ"ל לא יפרוס מיירי דבהני ק' מיל איכא ישוב כרמים משום דקאזלן וכו'. ג) נראה דט"ס נפל בכאן ונ"ל והלה אמר שלא אמרת לי דבר ושני חזקה אכלתיה וכו'. ד) נראה דל"ל שאם אמר לקחתיה מפלוני וכבר החזקתי בה.

עין משפט
נר מצוה

סו א מיי׳ פט״ו מהל׳ אבידה הל׳ יח סמג עשין עד טוש״ע ח״מ סי׳ רס סעיף ח:
סז ב מיי׳ שם ופ״ט מהל׳ רוצח הלכה ז סמג שם טוש״ע שם:
סח ג מיי׳ פ״ט מהל׳ רוצח הלכה ו:
סט ד הרמב״ם השמיט זה וע״ש בכ״מ:
ע ה ו ז ח ט מיי׳ פט״ו מהל׳ אבידה הל׳ יח סמג עשין עג טוש״ע ח״מ סי׳ רס סעיף ח:

רבינו גרשום

פיסקא ניפול הנמצא. גוזל שנפל מן השובך: חוץ מנ׳ אמה ה״ז של מוצאו. דאיכא למימר מעוברי דרכים נפל: אמר ר׳ חנינא. להיכא דאיכא רובא ואיכא קרוב הולכין אחר הרוב אע״ג דרובא דאורייתא דכתיב אחרי רבים להטות וקרוב דאורייתא דכתיב והיה העיר הקרובה אל החלל א) דאי איכא שובך ויש בו רוב הולכין אחריו דמיניה נפל: ואע״ג דאיכא. עיר רחוקה מינה דנפישי מינה דאיכא רובא דאינשי אלמא בתר קרוב אזלינן. ומשני בדליכא נפיש מינייהו מש״ה אזלינן בתר קרוב אבל היכא דהוי רוב וקרוב אזלינן בתר הרוב: וליזיל בתר רובא דעלמא. דאיכא למימר דקטליה עוברין ושבין: ביושבת בין ההרים. דלא קא עברי ואזלי אינשי להתם וליכא למימר ליזל בתר רובא דעלמא הואיל דליכא אינשי מש״ה אזלינן בתר קרוב אבל בעלמא לא אזלי׳ בתר קרוב: הכא במאי עסקינן. דהוי של מוצאו: במדדה. שאין יכול לברוח אלא מדדה עצמו מעט מעט: דאמר רב עוקבא כל המדדה אינו מדדה יותר מנ׳ אמה. והואיל דהאי נמצא חוץ מנ׳ אמה ודאי מעלמא נפל ומש״ה הרי הוא של מוצאו: רגלו אחת בתוך נ׳ אמה ורגלו אחת חוץ מנ׳. מי אזלינן בתר שובך או בתר רובא דעלמא: ועל דא אפקוהו לר׳ ירמי׳ מבי מדרשא. משום דמטריד להו בשאלות שאין בהן ממש:

חשק שלמה
על רבינו גרשום

א) נראה דצ״ל ואם איכא שובך אחר רחוק מזה ויש בו הרבה יותר מזה הולכין אחריו וכו׳.

תורה אור השלם
א) וְהָיָה הָעִיר הַקְּרֹבָה אֶל הֶחָלָל וְלָקְחוּ זִקְנֵי הָעִיר הַהִוא עֶגְלַת בָּקָר אֲשֶׁר לֹא עֻבַּד בָּהּ אֲשֶׁר לֹא מָשְׁכָה בְּעֹל: [דברים כא, ג]

מתני׳ [א] ניפול הנמצא בתוך חמשים אמה הרי הוא של בעל השובך חוץ מחמשים אמה הרי הוא של מוצאו נמצא בין שני שובכות קרוב לזה שלו קרוב לזה שלו מחצה על מחצה שניהם יחלוקו: **גמ׳** א) [א] אמר רבי חנינא [ב] רוב וקרוב הולכין אחר הרוב ואע״ג דרובא דאורייתא וקורבא דאורייתא אפילו הכי רובא עדיף מתיב רבי זירא א) והיה העיר הקרובה אל החלל ואע״ג דאיכא אחריתי דנפישא מינה [ג] בדליכא וליזיל בתר רובא דעלמא [ד] ביושבת בין ההרים תנן ניפול הנמצא בתוך חמשים אמה הרי הוא של בעל השובך ואף על גב דאיכא אחריתא דנפיש מיניה [ה] בדליכא אי הכי אימא סיפא חוץ מחמשים אמה הרי הוא של מוצאו ואי (א) דליכא ודאי מההוא נפל הכא במאי עסקינן [ו] במדדה [ז] דאמר רב עוקבא בר חמא [ז] כל המדדה אין מדדה יותר מנ׳ אמה (ב) בעי ר׳ ירמיה רגלו אחת בתוך נ׳ אמה ורגלו אחת חוץ מחמשים אמה מהו (ג) ועל דא אפקוהו לרבי ירמיה מבי מדרשא תא שמע נמצא בין שני שובכות קרוב לזה שלו וקרוב לזה שלו ואף על גב דחד מינייהו נפיש מחבריה [ח] הכא במאי עסקינן ששניהן שוין וליזיל בתר רובא דעלמא [ט] הכא במאי עסקינן

מתני׳ ניפול. גוזל: **הנמצא בתוך חמשים אמה.** של שובך: **נמצא בין שני שובכות.** בתוך חמשים לשניהן: **גמ׳ רוב וקרוב.** אם בא דבר לפנינו ויש בו להלך אחר הרוב והוא כך ואם תלך בו אחר הקרוב אינו כך הלך בו אחר הרוב ואע״ג דתרוייהו דאורייתא רובא דאורייתא דכתיב אחרי רבים להטות (שמות כג) וקורבא דאורייתא דכתיב והיה העיר הקרובה וגו׳: **ואע״ג דאיכא אחריתי.** שרחוקה ממנו שגדולה ממנה ברוב עם: **בדליכא.** רחוקה מזו שגדולה ממנה אלא כולן שוות: **בין ההרים.** שאין דרך רוצחים לבא ממקומו׳ אחרים לכאן: **לאו אע״ג דאיכא אחרינא.** חוץ לחמשים אמה דנפישי מהאי: **אימא סיפא כו׳.** הוא הדין דהוה מצי למיפרך נמי ליזיל בתר רובא דעלמא אלא דלית ליה פירכא לעדיפא (ד): **הכא במאי עסקינן.** כולה מתניתין מתרצא במדדה בגוזל שאינו יכול לעוף אלא בדידוי מעט מעט הלכך תוך חמשים אמה של בעל השובך ואף על גב דליכא אחריני (ה) דנפיש לכל המדדה אינו מדדה יותר מחמשים ותוך של חמשים של מוצאו דכיון דלאו מדדה יותר מחמשים וזה יצא חוץ לנ׳ נפק ליה מתורת מדדה וקם ליה בתורת מפריח ואיכא למיזל ביה בתר רובא דעלמא: **ועל דא אפקוהו.** שהיה מטריח עליהם: **וליזיל בתר רובא דעלמא.** וליהוי של מוצאו דקא ס״ד דנמצא בין שתי שובכות אחוץ לחמשים אמה נמי קאי דנפיק ליה מתורת מדדה: בשביל

חוץ לחמשים אמה הרי הוא של מוצאו. דאזלינן בתר רובא דעלמא ואפי׳ למ״ד אין הולכין בממון אחר הרוב היינו במקום (ו) שהוא מוחזק אבל הכא ליכא חזקה דממונא אזלינן בתר רובא וא״ת בפרק אלו מציאות (ב״מ דף כד. ושם) לרבנן דרבי שמעון בן אלעזר דאמרי אפילו בעיר שרובה כותים חייב להכריז בדבר שיש בו סימן ואמאי לא אזלינן בתר רובא כיון דליכא חזקה דממונא וי״ל דתקנת חכמים היא כדי לקיים מצות השבת אבידה כיון דיכול להתברר ע״י הכרזה אם היא של ישראל וישראל נמי לא מייאש דמסיק אדעתיה דלמא משכח ישראל ויכריז: **רוב** וקרוב הלך אחר הרוב. וא״ת מאי קא משמע לן מתניתא היא (כתובות דף טו. ט׳) תשע חנויות כולן מוכרות בשר שחוטה ואחת מוכרת בשר נבילה [וכו׳] ובנמצא הלך אחר הרוב משמע אפי׳ נמצא קרוב לחנות המוכרת נבילה ותירץ ר״י בר מרדכי דאי ממתניתא הוה אמינא כגון דאין דלתות מדינה נעולות דליכא תרי רובי וקמ״ל דר׳ חנינא דאפילו דלתות מדינה נעולות דליכא אלא חד רובא ור׳ זירא דפריך ליה בסמוך אע״ג דר׳ זירא נמי אית ליה לקמן אפילו דלתות מדינה נעולות היינו בתר דשני ליה דקיבלה מרבי חנינא ואין נראה לריב״א דאם כן מאי פריך ליה מקרא תיקשי ליה אמתניתא דתשע חנויות ואפילו תוקמה כשאין דלתות מדינה נעולות הא טעמא דבעינן תרי רובי אינו אלא מדרבנן משום גזירה כדאמר בסוף פ״ק דכתובות (דף טו.) ונראה לר״י דאי ממתני׳ ה״א בנמצא באמצע ועוד נראה לר״י דרבי חנינא אתא לאשמועינן דאפילו בקורבא דמוכח דאזלינן בתר רובא וכן משמע בסמוך גבי חבית שפה בנהר דבעי למימר דרב דאמר כנגד עיר שרובה ישראל מותרת לית ליה דרבי חנינא והיכי מתוקמא דהא משמע דמותרת אפילו נמצאת סמוך לבית נכרי וזהו מטעם דאזיל בתר רוב העיר ישראל וכרבי חנינא אלא ודאי לגבי קורבא דביתו של נכרי הוי קורבא דלא מוכח כיון שרוב ישראל באותה העיר ורב אזיל בתר רובא היכא דהקורבא לא מוכחא ודלא כרבי חנינא אבל אותה עיר כנגד ההיא דקירא הוי קורבא דמוכח ולכך אזיל בתרה וכל הלכה תתישב כמו שאפרש ולהכי לא מייתי בכוליה גמרא דרבי חנינא אלא לקמן גבי חצבא דאישתכח בפרדיסא של ערלה דקורבא דמוכח הוא שנמצא בפרדיסא דערלה גופיה ובפ״ק דביצה (דף י:) מייתי ליה נמי גבי הא דתנן זמן שחורים ומצא לבנים לבנים ומצא שחורים אסורים ומפרש בגמ׳ כגון שזימן שחורים ולבנים ומצא שחורים במקום לבנים ולבנים במקום שחורים מהו דתימא אינהו ניהנו ואיתהפוכי איתהפיך קמ״ל דהנך אזול לעלמא והני אחריני ניהנו ומעלמא אתו ומסיק עלה לימא מסייע ליה לרבי חנינא כו׳ והתם קורבא דמוכח הוא דהא שחורים ולבנים היו שם ומוכח דאינהו ניהנו: **מתיב** רבי זירא והיה העיר הקרובה כו׳ מאי לאו דאיכא אחריתי דנפישא מינה. אמתניתא דתשע חנויות נמי הוה ליה לאקשויי אלא דמתניתא איכא לשנויי בדליכא ותו ליכא לאקשויי ניזיל בתר רובא דעלמא דלגבי רובא דעלמא הוה קורבא דמוכח אבל לר׳ חנינא דאפילו בקורבא דמוכח הולך אחר הרוב פריך שפיר דכי נמי משנינן בדליכא אכתי תיקשי ניזיל בתר רובא דעלמא (ג): **בדליכא.** תימה דהכא משמע דטעמא דהעיר הקרובה מביאה עגלה ערופה משום דמתוך הקורבא מוכח שמשם בא ההורג ובסוטה (דף מה:) תניא מנין שאם נמצא סמוך לעיר שאין בה בית דין שמניחין אותה שאין בה בית דין והולכין לעיר אחרת שיש בה בית דין ואמאי והלא מתוך הקורבא נראה שמאותה שאין בה בית דין היה: **ביושבת** בין ההרים. ואם תאמר ואמאי איצטריך קרא בסוף פרק מרובה (ב״ק דף פב:) דאין ירושלים מביאה עגלה ערופה ואע״ג דכתיב (תהלים קכה) ירושלים הרים סביב לה מ״מ כל ישראל היו באין לרגל וגם בשאר ימות השנה להביא נדרים ונדבות וגם אומות העולם היו באין שם בסחורה שקרויה רוכלת עמים וי״ל שהיו מקומות שלא היו רגילים לבא רק בני ירושלים אי נמי בימי חזקיה שכל ישראל היו שם ולא היו באין לסחורה: **ניפול** הנמצא בתוך חמשים אמה כו׳. ומתניתא דתשע חנויות לא מצי למיפרך דהכא הוי קורבא דמוכח דהוי מתוך משובך זה דהוי תוך נ׳ ולעיל אמרינן דכרסייהו בחמשים אמה מלין: **בדליכא.** לא מצי למיפרך ניזיל בתר רובא דעלמא דמיירי דליכא שום שובך תוך שלשים ריס ותו לא: **ואי** דליכא אחריני ודאי מההוא נפל. דבשלמא אי איכא דנפיש מיניה אתי שפיר דהוי של מוצאו כגון דהוי ההוא דנפיש של הפקר או של כותים אבל השתא דליכא ודאי מההוא נפל ולא מצי לשנויי כגון דליכא דנפיש אלא שוין דמכל מקום אמאי הוי של מוצאו כיון שקרוב לזה דהכי משמע דמתוך לחמשים אמה הרי הוא של מוצאו אע״פ שקרוב לזה מזה דהא תנן מצאו בין שני שובכין קרוב לזה שלו דכשהן שוין אזלינן בתר קרוב: **ודאי** מההוא נפל. ואם תאמר ולמאי מעוברי דרכים נפל כדאמרינן לקמן גבי זיקי דחמרא דאישתכחן בי קופאי וי״ל דהיכא דודאי נפל ולא ידעינן ממי תלינן בעוברי דרכים אבל הכא מצי למימר דמשובך בא לית לן למיתלי ולאחזוקי בנפילה דבני אדם שהם מזהרין שלא יפלו מהם היונים: **ועל** דא אפקוהו לרבי ירמיה מבי מדרשא. אין לפרש משום דבעי מילתא דלא שכיחא דבכל הש״ס איתמרי דרגלו אחת תוך חמשים ורגלו אחת חוץ לחמשים בצמצום דהא אשכחנא דמתניתין נמי בכהאי גוונא איירי דקתני מחצה על מחצה ונראה לרבינו תם דמשום הכי אפקוהו משום דמדדה אינו מדדה כלל יותר מחמשים אמה אפילו רגלו אחת דהכי קבלו חכמים כן הוא: **מצאו** בין שני שובכין. ואע״ג דחד מינייהו נפיש אומר ר״י דהכך פירכא הוי מצי למיפרך אמתניתא דתשע חנויות דהתם קורבא דלא מוכח לא הוי תוך חמשים לזה ולזה הוי נמי תוך חמשים לזה ואי הוי תוך חמשים לזה הוי נמי תוך חמשים לזה ומיהו מלינן למימר דעיקר לא פריך אלא משום דבעי למיפרך וניזיל בתר רובא דעלמא אבל קשיא לרשב״א דהיכי מצי למימר אף על גב דחד מינייהו נפיש הא קתני מחצה על מחצה שניהם יחלוקו ואי חד מינייהו נפיש ניזל בתר רובא ואומר ר״י דהוי מצי למימר ולטעמיך:

וליזיל בתר רובא דעלמא. הוי מצי לשנויי דלאין לי אם שני שובכין תוך ל׳ ריס אלא בעי לשנויי דומיא דרישא דליש שובכין הרבה אע״ג דהשתא דמוקי לה בשביל של כרמים לא הוי דומיא דרישא דהא רישא לא מיירי בשביל של כרמים בהא לא קפיד במאי דלא הוי דומיא דרישא כיון שאין מזכיר במשנתינו שביל של כרמים בשום מקום ועוד הוה מצי לשנויי קרוב לזה שלו תוך חמשים אמה ובמדדה:

דכל

מסורת הש״ס

א) ביצה י:, ב) [שם יא.], ג) [וע״ע תוס׳ נדה יח. ד״ה הלך]:

הגהות הב״ח

(א) גמ׳ ואי בדליכא ודאי: (ב) שם יותר מנ׳ אמה בעי ר׳: (ג) שם על דא אפקוהו לר׳ ירמיה. נ״ב ע׳ בפ׳ גט פשוט סוף דף קס״ה דעל ידי מעשה עיילוהו לר׳ ירמיה: (ד) רש״י ד״ה אימא וכו׳ לעדיפא מינה הס״ד: (ה) ד״ה הכא במאי וכו׳ ואע״ג דליכא אחריני חוץ לחמשים אמה דנפיש: (ו) תוס׳ ד״ה חוץ וכו׳ היינו במקום שהאחר מוחזק:

הגהות מהר״ב רנשבורג

א] גמרא אמר ר׳ חנינא רוב וקרוב הולכין אחר הרוב. נ״ב עי׳ שו״ת מכתם לדוד בחלק אה״ע סימן ג׳ דף קמח ע״ב בד״ה אחר הדברים:

ליקוטי רש״י

שלו ומשום יוני שובכין שלא ילכדו בפחין אין לפוש דשלו הן אבל יש לחוש ליוני הישוב שבאין דרך השובכין למרחוק [ב״ק שם]. **הבא משום ירושה.** שאומר אכלתיה שני חזקה מכח ירושת אבי שהיה מוחזק בה ביום מותו [רשב״ם לקמן מא.]. והוא הדין משום לקיחה [שם מא:]. **אינו צריך טענה.** לומר היאך בא ליד אביו דאין אדם בקי בקרקעות אביו היאך באו לידו ומיהו ראיה בעדים בעי שראו את אביו הוחזק בה יום אחד והכי מפרש בגמרא [שם מא.]. **זיזין.** קורות קטנות. **גזוזטראות.** קורות גדולות הבולטות מן הבית לחוץ וליכא למיחש פן יכשלו בהם בני רה״ר והלכך אין מוליאין דהא כל בני רה״ר ליתנהו גביה דלימחלו. **ובה זיזין וגזוזטראות.** הבולטות לרשות הרבים. **הרי זו בחזקתה.** דטענינן ללוקח ואומרים אימר כונס לתוך שלו היה אבל המוכרה לו שהוליא הזיזין הוא היה לריך להביא עדים שכנס לתוך שלו או שיטעון שני חזקה החזקתי וכנסתי לתוך שלי דהוליא לה חזקה שיש עמה טענה אבל לוקח לא לריך למיטען מידי אלא כך לקחתיה וא״ל לטעון היאך הוליא המוכר את הזיזין לתוך לרה״ר דטוענין ליורש וטוענין ללוקח. **כונס.** לתוך קרקע שלו את כותלו ומניח מקרקעו לחוץ כשיעור הולאת זיזין ומוליא. [שם ס.]. [ע״כ שייך לע״א] **שובכות.** דלך שובכות להיות בו מחילות הרבה קן לכל זוג וזוג וחלון לכל קן וקן [ביצה ט.]. **רוב וקרוב הולכין אחר הרוב.** אם בא מעשה לפנינו ויש לתלותו בדבר הקרוב לו להתיר או לאסור ויש לתלותו אחר הרוב לענין אחר חלוף הקרוב הלך אחר הרוב [ביצה י:].

Mishnah Pursuant to the previous Mishnah which dealt with dovecotes, the following Mishnah discusses further laws that apply to a dovecote. Specifically, it deals with the status of a bird whose ownership is unknown that is found near a dovecote:[1]

נִיפּוּל הַנִּמְצָא בְּתוֹךְ חֲמִשִּׁים אַמָּה – If **a young dove was found within fifty** ***amos*** of a dovecote, הֲרֵי הוּא שֶׁל בַּעַל הַשּׁוֹבָךְ – **it belongs to the owner of the dovecote.** חוּץ מֵחֲמִשִּׁים אַמָּה – But if it was found **more than fifty** ***amos*** **away** from the dovecote, הֲרֵי הוּא שֶׁל מוֹצְאוֹ – **it belongs to the one who found it.**[2]

נִמְצָא בֵּין שְׁנֵי שׁוֹבָכוֹת – In the event that a bird was **found between two dovecotes,**[3] the law is as follows: קָרוֹב לָזֶה שֶׁלּוֹ – If it was found **closer to this [dovecote], it belongs to [the owner of this dovecote];** קָרוֹב לָזֶה שֶׁלּוֹ – if it was found **closer to [the other dovecote], it belongs to [the owner of that dovecote].** מֶחֱצָה עַל מֶחֱצָה שְׁנֵיהֶם יַחֲלוֹקוּ – If both dovecotes are **equal**[4] in distance from the bird, **the two [owners] divide** it.

Gemara Two principles can be used to determine the origin of a found object: (1) The principle of רוֹב, *majority,* stipulates that the object is from the same place as the *majority* of such objects. (2) The principle of קָרוֹב, *proximity,* stipulates that it is from the *nearest* location of such objects. The Gemara discusses what the law is when these two principles are in conflict:

אָמַר רַבִּי חֲנִינָא – **R' Chanina said:** רוֹב וְקָרוֹב הוֹלְכִין אַחַר הָרוֹב – When a conflict arises between the principles of **"majority" and "proximity," one follows the** principle of **"majority."** וְאַף עַל גַּב דְּרוּבָּא דְּאוֹרַיְיתָא וְקוּרְבָא דְּאוֹרַיְיתָא – **Although** the principles of **"majority" and "proximity" are** both of **Scriptural** origin,[5] אֲפִילּוּ הָכִי רוּבָּא עָדִיף – **nevertheless,** the principle of **"majority" is superior.**

R' Chanina's rule is challenged:

מְתִיב רַבִּי זֵירָא – **R' Zeira challenged** this rule: "וְהָיָה הָעִיר הַקְּרֹבָה אֶל־הֶחָלָל" – Scripture states: ***And it shall be that the town which is nearest to the slain person,*** *the elders of that town shall take a calf etc.*[6] The Torah rules that the obligation of the "decapitated calf" devolves upon the nearest town, וְאַף עַל גַּב דְּאִיכָּא אַחֲרִיתִי דִּנְפִישָׁא מִינָּהּ – **and,** since the Torah does not state otherwise, it would seem that this ruling applies **even** in a case **where there is another [town]** in the area **which is larger** (i.e. more populous) **than it** [the nearest town]. This indicates that, contrary to R' Chanina's ruling, the principle of "proximity" overrides that of "majority." – ? –

The Gemara rejects the assumption of the question:

בִּדְלֵיכָּא – The Torah obligates the nearest town only **in a case where there is no** town in the area larger than it.[7]

The Gemara persists:

וְלֵיזִיל בָּתַר רוּבָּא דְּעָלְמָא – **But we should follow the "majority of the world"!** I.e. since people from the world at large pass through the area in which the corpse was found, the murderer might have come from a town far from this area, which is larger than the nearest town.[8] Hence, the fact that the Torah obligates the *nearest* town proves that, contrary to R' Chanina's ruling, the principle of "proximity" overrides that of "majority." – ? –

The Gemara answers:

בְּיוֹשֶׁבֶת בֵּין הֶהָרִים – The Torah refers **to [a town] that is situated between mountains.** It is in an isolated area that is not frequented by people from elsewhere.[9]

The Gemara attempts to refute R' Chanina's ruling from our Mishnah:

תְּנַן – **We learned in our Mishnah:** נִיפּוּל הַנִּמְצָא בְּתוֹךְ חֲמִשִּׁים אַמָּה – If A YOUNG DOVE WAS FOUND WITHIN FIFTY *AMOS* of a dovecote, הֲרֵי הוּא שֶׁל בַּעַל הַשּׁוֹבָךְ – IT BELONGS TO THE OWNER OF THE DOVECOTE. The Mishnah rules that the bird is from the dovecote that is within fifty *amos,* וְאַף עַל גַּב דְּאִיכָּא אַחֲרִינָא דְּנָפִישׁ מִינֵּיהּ – **and,** since the Mishnah does not state otherwise, it would seem that this ruling applies **even** in a case **where there is another [dovecote]** in the area **which is larger than [this dovecote]** but is more than fifty *amos* from the bird. Since the Mishnah rules that the bird is from the nearer dovecote rather than the larger one, evidently, the law is that, contrary to R' Chanina's ruling, the principle of "proximity" overrides that of "majority." – ? –

The Gemara rejects the assumption of the question:

בִּדְלֵיכָּא – The Mishnah's ruling applies only **in a case where there is no** dovecote in the area that is larger than this one.[10]

The Gemara challenges this interpretation of the Mishnah:

אִי הָכִי – **If** this is **so,** that the Mishnah speaks of an instance where there is no dovecote in the area larger than this one,

NOTES

1. Were it not for its connection to the previous Mishnah, this Mishnah would have been included in the second chapter of *Bava Metzia,* which deals with the laws of found articles (*Ritva*).

2. These laws are explained in the Gemara.

3. But within fifty *amos* of each one (*Rashi*; see note 18).

4. Literally: half by half.

5. The principle of "majority" is derived from the verse (*Exodus* 23:2): אַחֲרֵי רַבִּים לְהַטֹּת, which is interpreted to mean, [follow] *after the majority to tilt* [the scales of judgment] (see *Chullin* 11a).

The principle of "proximity" is derived from the passage of עֶגְלָה עֲרוּפָה, *the decapitated calf* (*Deuteronomy* 21:1-9). The Torah commands that if the corpse of a murdered person is found and it is not known who killed him, a measurement must be made to ascertain which town is *nearest* to the corpse (the presumption being that the murderer came from there). The elders of that town bring a calf to an untilled valley and kill it there by breaking its neck. They then make a statement denying responsibility for the murder (*Rashi*).

6. *Deuteronomy* 21:3. See previous note.

7. All the towns [in the vicinity] are equally populous (*Rashi*). Since all of the towns have the same population, the principle of majority does not help to identify the town from which the murderer came. Therefore, we follow the principle of "proximity," which stipulates that the murderer came from the nearest town.

An apparent difficulty: Since most of the residents of the area do *not* live in the nearest town; the principle of "majority" stipulates that the murderer is *not* from that town! So why is the nearest town obligated? [*Ritva* answers this difficulty by stating that we speak of a case where there are only two towns in the vicinity. However, *Rashi* implies (see ד״ה בדליכא) that there are more than two towns in the area.]

Tosefos Rid answers that the various other towns cannot be combined to form a majority because each town is viewed as a separate entity. Therefore, since the murderer must have come from *one* of the towns, and no single town is larger than any of the others, we must assume that he came from the nearest town (see *Chidushei Chasam Sofer, Chidushei R' Shimon*).

8. *Tosefos Rid.*

9. Thus, the murderer must have come from one of the towns in the vicinity. (See first paragraph of note 7.)

In conclusion: The passage of עֶגְלָה עֲרוּפָה, *the decapitated calf,* refers to an area that is not frequented by people from elsewhere and in which each town in the area has the same population. It is only in such a case that a measurement is made (see note 5), and the obligation devolves upon the town *nearest* to the corpse.

10. I.e. all the dovecotes in the area are of the same size (see *Tosefos Rid,* note 7).

מתני' [א]ניפול הנמצא בתוך חמשים אמה הרי הוא של בעל השובך חוץ מחמשים אמה הרי הוא של מוצאו נמצא בין שני שובכות קרוב לזה שלו קרוב לזה שלו מחצה על מחצה שניהם יחלוקו: **גמ'** א] (א) אמר רבי חנינא [ב]רוב וקרוב הולכין אחר הרוב ואע"ג דרובא דאורייתא וקורבא דאורייתא אפילו הכי רובא עדיף מתיב רבי זירא [א] והיה העיר הקרובה אל החלל ואע"ג דאיכא אחריתי דנפישא מינה [ג]בדליכא וליזיל בתר רובא דעלמא [ד]ביושבת בין ההרים תנן ניפול הנמצא בתוך חמשים אמה הרי הוא של בעל השובך ואף על גב דאיכא אחרינא דנפיש מיניה [ה]בדליכא אי הכי אימא סיפא חוץ מחמשים אמה הרי הוא של מוצאו ואי (א) דליכא ודאי מההוא נפל הכא במאי עסקינן [ו]במדדה (ב) דאמר רב עוקבא בר חמא [ז]כל המדדה אין מדדה יותר מנ' (ב) בעי ר' ירמיה רגלו אחת בתוך נ' אמה ורגלו אחת חוץ מחמשים אמה מהו (ג) ועל דא אפקוהו לרבי ירמיה מבי מדרשא תא שמע נמצא בין שני שובכות קרוב לזה שלו וקרוב לזה שלו ואף על גב דחד מינייהו נפיש מחבריה [ח]הכא במאי עסקינן ששניהן שוין וליזיל בתר רובא דעלמא [ט]הכא במאי עסקינן

רש"י

מתני' ניפול. גוזל: הנמצא בתוך חמשים אמה. של שובך: נמצא בין שני שובכות. בתוך חמשים לשניהן: **גמ'** רוב וקרוב. אם בא דבר לפניו ויש בו להלך אחר הרוב והוא כך ואם תלך בו אחר הקרוב אינו כך הלך בו אחר הרוב ואע"ג דתרוייהו דאורייתא רובא דאורייתא דכתיב אחרי רבים להטות (שמות כג) וקורבא דאורייתא דכתיב והיה העיר הקרובה וגו': ואע"ג דאיכא אחריתי. שרחוקה ממנו שגדולה ממנה ברוב עם: בדליכא. רחוקה מזו שגדולה ממנה אלא כולן שוות: בין ההרים. שאין דרך רוצחים לבא ממקומו' אחרים לכאן: לאו אע"ג דאיכא אחרינא. חוץ לחמשים אמה דנפישי מהאי: אימא סיפא כו'. הוא הדין דהוה מצי למיפרך נמי ליזיל בתר רובא דעלמא אלא דלאית ליה פירכא דעדיפא (ד): הכא במאי עסקינן. כולה מתניתין מתרצא במדדה בגוזל שאינו יכול לעוף אלא בדידוי מעט מעט הלכך תוך חמשים אמה של בעל השובך ואף על גב דליכא אחריני (ה) דנפיש לכל המדדה אינו מדדה יותר מחמשים וחוץ של חמשים של מוצאו דכיון דאין מדדה יותר מחמשים וזה יצא חוץ לנ' נפק ליה מתורת מדדה וקם ליה בתורת מפריח ואיכא למיזל ביה בתר רובא דעלמא: ועל דא אפקוהו. שהיה מטריח עליהם: וליזיל בתר רובא דעלמא. וליהוי של מוצאו דקא ס"ד דנמצא בין שתי שובכות אחוץ לחמשים אמה נמי קאי דנפיק ליה מתורת מדדה: בשביל

תוספות

חוץ לחמשים אמה הרי הוא של מוצאו. דאזלינן בתר רובא דעלמא ואפי' למ"ד אין הולכין בממון אחר הרוב היינו במקום (ו) שהוא מוחזק אבל הכא דליכא חזקה דממונא אזלינן בתר רובא וא"ת בפרק אלו מציאות (ב"מ דף כד. ושם) לרבנן דרבי שמעון בן אלעזר דאמרי אפילו בעיר שרובה כותים חייב להכריז בדבר שיש בו סימן ואמאי לא אזלינן בתר רובא כיון דליכא חזקה דממונא וי"ל דתקנת חכמים היא כדי לקיים מצות השבת אבידה כיון דיכול להתברר ע"י הכרזה אם היא של ישראל וישראל נמי לא מייאש דמסיק אדעתיה דלמא משכח ישראל ויכריז: **רוב** וקרוב הלך אחר הרוב. וא"ת מאי קא משמע לן מתניתא היא (כתובות דף טו.) ט' חנויות כולן מוכרות בשר שחוטה ואחת מוכרת בשר נבילה [וכו'] ובנמצא הלך אחר הרוב משמע אפי' נמצא קרוב לחנות המוכרת נבילה ותירץ ר"י בר מרדכי דאי ממתניתא הוה אמינא כגון דאין דלתות מדינה נעולות דליכא תרי רובי קמ"ל דרבי חנינא דאפילו דלתות מדינה נעולות דליכא אלא חד רובא ור' זירא דפריך ליה בסמוך אע"ג דר' זירא נמי אית ליה לקמן אפילו דלתות מדינה נעולות היינו בתר דשני ליה דקיבלה מרבי חנינא ואין נראה לריב"א דאם כן מאי פריך ליה מקרא תיקשי ליה ממתניתא דתשע חנויות ואפילו תוקמה כשאין דלתות מדינה נעולות הא טעמא דבעינן תרי רובי איננו אלא מדרבנן משום גזירה כדאמר בסוף פ"ק דכתובות (דף טו.) ונראה לר"י דאי ממתני' ה"א בנמצא באמצע ועוד נראה לר"י דרבי חנינא אתא לאשמועינן דאפילו בקורבא דמוכח דאזלינן בתר רובא וכן משמע בסמוך גבי חבית שצפה בנהר דבעי למימר דרב דאמר כנגד עיר שרובה ישראל מותרת לית ליה דרבי חנינא והיכי מתוקמא דהא משמע דמותרת אפילו נמצאת סמוך לבית נכרי וזהו מטעם דאזיל בתר רוב העיר ישראל וכרבי חנינא אלא ודאי לגבי קורבא דביתו של נכרי הוי קורבא דלא מוכח כיון שדרים רוב ישראל באותה העיר ורב אזיל בתר רובא היכא דהקורבא לא מוכחא ודלא כרבי חנינא אבל אותה עיר כנגד האי דקירא הוי קורבא דמוכח ולכך אזיל בתרה וכל ההלכה תתיישב כמו שאפרש ולהכי לא מייתי בכוליה גמרא דרבי חנינא אלא לקמן גבי חצבא דאישתכח בפרדיסא של ערלה דקורבא דמוכח הוא שנמצא בפרדיסא דערלה גופיה ובפ"ק דבילה (דף י:) מייתי ליה נמי גבי הא דתנן זימן שחורים ומצא לבנים לבנים ומצא שחורים אסורים ומפרש בגמ' כגון שזימן שחורים ולבנים ומצא שחורים במקום לבנים ולבנים במקום שחורים מהו דתימא אינהו ניהו ואיתהפוכי איתהפיך קמ"ל דהנך אזול לעלמא והני אחריני ניהו ומעלמא אתו ומסיק עלה לימא מסייע ליה לרבי חנינא כו' והתם קורבא דמוכח הוא דהא שחורים ולבנים היו שם ומוכח דאינהו ניהו: **מתיב** רבי זירא והיה העיר הקרובה כו' מאי לאו דאיכא אחריתי דנפישא מינה. אמתניתא דתשע חנויות נמי הוה ליה לאקשויי אלא אמתניתא איכא לשנויי בדליכא ותו ליכא לאקשויי ניזיל בתר רובא דעלמא דלגבי רובא דעלמא הוה קורבא זו העיר קורבא דמוכח הלך אחר הרוב פריך שפיר דכי נמי משנינן בדליכא אכתי תיקשי ניזל בתר רובא דעלמא [ג]: דמוכח אבל לר' חנינא דאפילו בקורבא

בדליכא. תימה דהכא משמע דטעמא דהעיר הקרובה מביאה עגלה ערופה משום דמתוך הקורבא מוכח שמשם בא ההורג ובסוטה (דף מה:) תניא מנין שאם נמצא סמוך לעיר שאין בה בית דין שמניחין אותה שאין בה בית דין והולכין לעיר אחרת שיש בה בית דין ואמאי והלא מתוך הקורבא נראה שמאותה שאין בה בית דין היה: **ביושבת** בין ההרים. ואם תאמר ואמאי איצטריך קרא בסוף פרק מרובה (ב"ק דף פב:) דאין ירושלים מביאה עגלה ערופה ואע"ג דכתיב (תהלים קכה) ירושלים הרים סביב לה מ"מ כל ישראל היו באין לרגל וגם בשאר ימות השנה להביא נדרים ונדבות וגם אומות העולם היו באין שם בסחורה שקרויה רוכלת עמים וי"ל שהיו מקומות שלא היו רגילים לבא רק בני ירושלים אי נמי בימי חזקיה שכל ישראל היו שם ולא היו באין לסחורה: **ניפול** הנמצא בתוך חמשים אמה כו'. ואמתניתא דתשע חנויות לא מצי למיפרך דהכא הוי קורבא דמוכח דהוי משובך זה דהוי תוך חמשים והנך דנפישי הוי חוץ לנ' ולעיל אמרינן דכרסייהו בחמשים אמה מליין: **בדליכא.** לא מצי למיפרך דניזל בתר רובא דעלמא דמיירי דליכא שום שובך תוך שלשים ריס ואמר לעיל דלא שייטי אלא שלשים ריס ותו לא: **ואי** דליכא אחריני ודאי מההוא נפל. דבשלמא אי איכא דנפיש מיניה אתי שפיר דהוי של מוצאו כגון דהוי ההוא דנפיש של הפקר או של כותים אבל השתא דליכא ודאי מההוא נפל ולא מצי לשנויי כגון דליכא דנפיש אלא שוין דמכל מקום אמאי הוי של מוצאו כיון שקרוב לזה דהכי משמע דחוץ לחמשים אמה הרי הוא של מוצאו אע"פ שקרוב לזה מזה דהא תנן מצאו בין שני שובכין קרוב לזה שלו דכשהן שוין אזלינן בתר קרוב: **ודאי** מההוא נפל. ואם תאמר ודלמא מעוברי דרכים נפל כדאמרינן לקמן גבי זיקי דחמרא דאישתכחן בי קופאי וי"ל דהיכא דודאי נפל ולא ידעינן ממי תלינן בעוברי דרכים אבל הכא דמצי למימר דמשובך בא לית לן למיתלי ולאחזוקי בנפילה דבני אדם נזהרין שלא יפלו מהם היונים: **ועל** דא אפקוהו לרבי ירמיה מבי מדרשא. אין לפרש משום דבעי מילתא דלא שכיחא כלל דהיכי איתרמי דרגלו אחת תוך חמשים ורגלו אחת חוץ לחמשים בצמצום דהא אשכחנא דמתניתין נמי בכהאי גוונא איירי דקתני מחצה על מחצה יחלוקו ונראה לרבינו תם דמשום הכי אפקוהו משום דמדדה אינו מדדה כלל יותר מחמשים אמה אפילו רגלו אחת דכל מדות חכמים כן הוא: **מצאו** בין שני שובכין. ואע"ג דחד מינייהו נפיש אומר ר"י דהך פירכא הוי מצי למיפרך אמתניתא דתשע חנויות דהאי קורבא דלא מוכח הוא דלאי הוי תוך חמשים לזה הוי נמי תוך חמשים לזה ואי הוי חוץ חמשים לזה הוי נמי חוץ חמשים לזה אפילו הכי אזלינן בתר קורבא ומיהו מצינן למימר דעיקר לא פריך אלא משום דבעי למיפרך וניזל בתר רובא דעלמא אבל קשיא לרשב"א דהיכי מצי למימר אף על גב דחד מינייהו נפיש הא קתני מחצה על מחצה שניהם יחלוקו ואי חד מינייהו נפיש ניזל בתר רובא ואומר ר"י דהוי מצי למימר וליטעמיך:

וליזיל בתר רובא דעלמא. הוי מצי לשנויי דאין כי אם שני שובכין תוך ל' ריס אלא בעי לשנויי דומיא דרישא דיש שובכין הרבה אע"ג דהשתא דמוקי לה בשביל של כרמים לא הוי דומיא דרישא דהא רישא לא מיירי בשביל של כרמים בהא לא קפיד במאי דלא הוי דומיא דרישא כיון שאין מזכיר במשנתינו שביל של כרמים בשום מקום ועוד הוה מצי לשנויי קרוב לזה שלו תוך חמשים אמה ובמדדה:
דכל

עין משפט נר מצוה

סו א מיי' פט"ו מהל' גזילה ואבידה הל' יח סמג עשין עד טוש"ע ח"מ סי' רס סעיף ח:
סז ב מיי' שם ופ"ט מהל' רוצח הלכה ז סמג שם טוש"ע שם:
סח ג מיי' פ"ט מהל' רוצח הלכה ו:
סט ד הרמב"ם השמיט זה וע"ש בכ"מ:
ע ה ו ז ח ט מיי' פט"ו מהל' גזילה ואבידה הל' יח סמג עשין עד טוש"ע ח"מ סי' רס סעיף ח:

רבינו גרשום

פיסקא ניפול הנמצא. גוזל שנפל מן השובך: חוץ מנ' אמה ה"ז של מוצאו. דאיכא למימר מעוברי דרכים נפל: אמר ר' חנינא. להיכא דאיכא רובא ואיכא קרוב הולכין אחר הרוב אע"ג דרובא דאורייתא דכתיב אחרי רבים להטות וקרוב דאורייתא דכתיב והיה העיר הקרובה אל החלל (א) דאי איכא שובך ויש בו רוב הולכין אחריו דמיניה נפל: ואע"ג דאיכא. עיר רחוקה מינה דנפישי מינה דאיכא רובא דאינשי אלמא בתר קרוב אזלינן. ומשני בדליכא נפיש מינייהו מש"ה אזלינן בתר קרוב אבל היכא דאיכא רוב וקרוב אזלינן בתר הרוב: וליזיל בתר רובא דעלמא. דאיכא למימר דקטליה עוברין ושבקין: ביושבת בין ההרים. דלא קא עברי ואזלי אינשי להתם וליכא למימר ליזיל בתר רובא דעלמא הואיל דליכא אינשי מש"ה אזלינן בתר קרוב אבל בעלמא לא אזלי בתר קרוב: הכא במאי עסקינן. דהוי של מוצאו: במדדה. שאין יכול לפרוח אלא מדדה עצמו מעט מעט: דאמר רב עוקבא כל המדדה אינו מדדה יותר מנ' אמה. והואיל דהאי נמצא חוץ מנ' אמה ודאי מעלמא נפל ומש"ה הרי הוא של מוצאו: רגלו אחת בתוך נ' אמה ורגלו אחת חוץ מנ'. מי אזלינן בתר שובך או בתר רובא דעלמא: ועל דא אפקוהו לר' ירמי' מבי מדרשא. משום דמטריד להו בשאלות שאין בהן ממש:

חשק שלמה על רבינו גרשום

א) נראה דל"ל דאי איכא שובך אחר רחוק מזה ויש בו הרבה יותר מזה הולכין אחריו וכו'.

תורה אור השלם

א) וְהָיָה הָעִיר הַקְּרֹבָה אֶל הֶחָלָל וְלָקְחוּ זִקְנֵי הָעִיר הַהִוא עֶגְלַת בָּקָר אֲשֶׁר לֹא עֻבַּד בָּהּ אֲשֶׁר לֹא מָשְׁכָה בְּעֹל: [דברים כא, ג]

מסורת הש"ס

א) ביצה י., ב) [סס יא.], ג) [ועי' תוס' נדה יח. ד"ה הלך]:

הגהות הב"ח

(א) גמ' ואי בדליכא ודאי: (ב) שם יותר מנ' אמה בעי ר': (ג) שם על דא אפקוהו לר' ירמיה. נ"ב ע' בס' גט פשוט סוף דף קס"א דעל ידי מעשה עיילוהו לר' ירמיה: (ד) רש"י ד"ה אימא וכו' דעדיפא מינה הס"ד: (ה) ד"ה הכא במאי וכו' ואע"ג דליכא אחריני חוץ לחמשים אמה דנפיש: (ו) תוס' ד"ה חוץ וכו' היינו במקום שהאחר מוחזק:

הגהות מהר"ב רנשבורג

א] גמרא אמר ר' חנינא רוב וקרוב הולכין אחר הרוב. נ"ב עי' שו"ת מכתם לדוד בחלק אה"ע סימן ג' דף קמח ע"ב בד"ה אחר הדברים:

ליקוטי רש"י

שלו ומשום יוני שובכין שלא ילכדו בפחין אין לחוש דשלו הן אבל יש לחוש ליוני הישוב שבאין דרך השובכין למרחוק [ב"ק שם]. הבא משום ירושה. שאומר אכלתיה שני חזקה מכח ירושה אבי שהיה מוחזק בה ביום מותו [רשב"ם לקמן מא.]. והוא הדין משום לקיחה [שם מא.]. אינו צריך טענה. לומר היאך בא ליד אביו דאין אדם בקי בעסקי אביו היאך בא לידו ומיהו ראיה בעדים בעי שראו אביו מוחזק בה יום אחד והכי מפרש בגמרא [שם מא.]. זיזין. קורות קטנות. גזוזטראות. קורות גדולות הבולטות מן הכותל לחוץ ואיכא למיחש פן יכשלו בהם בני רה"ר והלכך אין מוציאין מן הכותל לרה"ר ליתנהו בגביה דלימתלו. ובה זיזין וגזוזטראות. הבולטות לרשות הרבים. הרי זו בחזקתה. דטוענין ללוקח ולומרים אימר כונס לתוך שלו היה אבל המוכר לה שלא הזיזין הוא היה לריך לעיין לתוך שכנס לתוך שלו או שיטענו שני מוחזק החזיקו ונכנסו לתוך שלו דהו"ל לה לתוך שיש עמה טענה אבל לנקוח לא לריך למיטען מידי אלא כך לקחתיה היא אלא היאך הוציא המוכר הזיזין לתוך לרה"ר דטוענין ליורש וטוענין ללוקח. כונס. לתוך קרקע שלו את כותלו ומניח מקרקעו לחוץ לתיבור זיזין וגזוזטראות [שם ס.]. [ע"כ שייך לע"א] שובכות. דרך שובכין להיות בו מחילות הרבה קן לזוג וזוג ומשום לכל קן וקן [ביצה ט.]. רוב וקרוב הולכין אחר הרוב. אם בא לפנינו ויש לו להלך בו לאסור ואם תלך אחר הקרוב להתיר או לאסור הלך אחר הרוב [ביצה י:].

אֵימָא סֵיפָא – **consider the latter clause** of the Mishnah: **חוּץ מֵחֲמִשִּׁים אַמָּה הֲרֵי הוּא שֶׁל מוֹצְאוֹ** – But if it was found MORE THAN FIFTY *AMOS* AWAY from the dovecote, IT BELONGS TO THE ONE WHO FOUND IT. **וְאִי דְּלֵיכָּא** – **Now if there is no** dovecote in the area larger than this one, **וַדַּאי מֵהַהוּא נָפַל** – **[the dove] certainly fell from this [dovecote]!**[11] Why then does the Mishnah rule that the finder can keep the dove?[12]

It is evident, therefore, that the Mishnah speaks of a case where there *is* a larger dovecote in the area. But if so, the original question falls back into place: Why, in the case where the bird was found within fifty *amos* of a dovecote, does the Mishnah award the bird to the owner of the dovecote?[13]

Its previous answer having been rejected, the Gemara advances a different answer:

הָכָא בְּמַאי עַסְקִינַן – **What are we dealing with here?** **בִּמְדַדֶּה** – The Mishnah refers **to a [bird] that** only **hops**, for it is too young to fly. If such a bird is found within fifty *amos* of a dovecote, it is awarded to the owner of that dovecote even if there is a larger dovecote more than fifty *amos* away, **דְּאָמַר רַב עוּקְבָא בַּר חָמָא** – **for Rav Ukva bar Chama said:** **כָּל הַמְדַדֶּה אֵין מְדַדֶּה יוֹתֵר מֵחֲמִשִּׁים** – **Any bird that hops** (for it is too young to fly) **does not hop more than fifty** *amos* from its nest. The bird could not have come from the larger dovecote for it is more than fifty *amos* away from it. Therefore, without resort to the principle of "proximity," the bird is awarded to the owner of the dovecote that is within fifty *amos*.[14]

R' Yirmiyah raised a question concerning the Mishnah's teaching:

בָּעֵי רַבִּי יִרְמְיָה – **R' Yirmiyah asked:** **רַגְלוֹ אַחַת בְּתוֹךְ חֲמִשִּׁים אַמָּה** – If a bird was found with **one of its legs within fifty** *amos* of a dovecote **וְרַגְלוֹ אַחַת חוּץ מֵחֲמִשִּׁים אַמָּה** – **and one of its legs more than fifty** *amos* **away** from the dovecote, **מַהוּ** – **what is [the law]?** Does the bird belong to the finder or the dovecote owner?[15]

The Gemara relates:

וְעַל דָּא אַפְּקוּהוּ לְרַבִּי יִרְמְיָה מִבֵּי מִדְרְשָׁא – **And for** asking **this** question, **[the Rabbis] ejected R' Yirmiyah from the house of study.**[16]

The Gemara now attempts to disprove R' Chanina's ruling from the second half of our Mishnah:

תָּא שְׁמַע – **Come, learn** the following proof from our Mishnah: **נִמְצָא בֵּין שְׁנֵי שׁוֹבָכוֹת** – In the event that a bird was FOUND BETWEEN TWO DOVECOTES, the law is determined as follows: **קָרוֹב לָזֶה שֶׁלּוֹ** – If it was found CLOSER TO THIS dovecote, IT BELONGS TO [THE OWNER OF THIS DOVECOTE]. **וְקָרוֹב לָזֶה שֶׁלּוֹ** – BUT if it was found CLOSER TO THE OTHER dovecote, IT BELONGS TO [THE OWNER OF THAT DOVECOTE]. The Mishnah rules that the bird is from the nearer dovecote, **וְאַף עַל גַּב דְּחַד מִינַּיְיהוּ נָפִישׁ מֵחַבְרֵיהּ** – **and,** since the Mishnah does not state otherwise, it would seem that this ruling applies **even** in a case **where one of [the two dovecotes] is larger than the other.** This proves that, contrary to R' Chanina's ruling, the principle of "proximity" overrides that of "majority." – ? –

The Gemara rejects the assumption of the question:

הָכָא בְּמַאי עַסְקִינַן – **What are we dealing with here?** **שֶׁשְּׁנֵיהֶן שָׁוִין** – The Mishnah refers to a case **where both [dovecotes] are equal** in size.[17]

The Gemara persists:

וְלֵיזִיל בָּתַר רוּבָּא דְּעָלְמָא – **But** we should **follow "the majority of the world!"** Since there are birds flying through this area that could have come from anywhere in the world at large, the finder of the bird should be allowed to keep it.[18] – ? –

The Gemara answers:

הָכָא בְּמַאי עַסְקִינַן – **What are we dealing with here?**

NOTES

11. [For it is the *nearest* dovecote and there is none larger than it.]

12. This is not a problem if we say, as the Gemara originally assumed, that there is a dovecote in the area larger than the nearest one. In such a case, the Mishnah's ruling is in order, for one could say that the largest dovecote is ownerless and therefore its birds become the property of whoever finds them (*Tosafos*).

The thrust of the Gemara's challenge to R' Chanina is as follows: What difference does it make whether the bird was found more or less than fifty *amos* away from the nearest dovecote? If there is a larger (ownerless) dovecote in the area, the finder should be allowed to keep the bird even if it was found within fifty *amos* of the nearest dovecote. And if there is no larger dovecote in the area, the bird should be awarded to the owner of the nearest dovecote even if it was found more than fifty *amos* away. Thus, whichever way the Mishnah is understood, it does not seem to conform to R' Chanina's ruling.

An apparent difficulty: But even if we take the opposite position, viz. the principle of "proximity" overrides that of "majority," the same difficulty applies: What is the reason for the Mishnah's distinction between more than and less than fifty *amos*? In either case, the bird should be awarded to the owner of the *nearest* dovecote. (See *Rabbeinu Yonah* for an answer to this question.)

13. [According to R' Chanina, the bird should be awarded to the one who found it, for in his view the principle of "majority" overrides that of "proximity" (see first paragraph of previous note).]

It should be noted that the Gemara could have asked a different question: Birds fly through this area that are not from any of the dovecotes in the area. So if R' Chanina's ruling is correct that the principle of "majority" overrides that of "proximity," the finder should be allowed to keep the bird even in the event that he finds it within fifty *amos* of a dovecote. Why does the Mishnah rule that in such a case the bird belongs to the owner of the dovecote?

Instead of asking this question, the Gemara asked a stronger one (*Rashi*).

14. In the Mishnah's latter case, however, where the bird was found more than fifty *amos* away from the nearest dovecote, [even if currently it is only hopping] it is assumed to have the capacity to fly, for otherwise it could not have come this far. Now, a bird that is capable of flying could have come from anywhere within flying range (*Rashi*). Therefore, the finder may keep it.

15. [Is such a bird deemed to have the capacity to fly and therefore is awarded to the finder? Or is it incapable of flying and therefore must have come from the nearest dovecote?]

16. They ejected him because he was burdening them (*Rashi*) with an absurd question (*Ritva's* understanding of *Rashi*).

Some say that the problem with R' Yirmiyah's inquiry was not that it was purely hypothetical. Indeed, our Mishnah speaks of a case where a bird was found equally distant from two dovecotes. (This must refer to a case where the bird had one foot on one side of the line that is equidistant from the two dovecotes and one foot on the other side of the line – *Rashba*.) Rather, R' Yirmiyah was ejected because he should have known that all Rabbinic measurements are absolute. If even only one of its legs is more than fifty *amos* from the dovecote, the bird cannot be classified as one that lacks the capacity to fly (*Tosafos* et al.). By raising this question, R' Yirmiyah displayed a lack of respect for Rabbinic law (*Ritva*).

[R' Yirmiyah's expulsion was only temporary. Later, when he displayed the proper respect, he was readmitted to the study hall (see below, 165b).]

17. [But where one is larger than the other, the bird would be deemed the property of the owner of the larger dovecote.]

18. Since the Mishnah does not state otherwise, it is assumed that it refers even to a bird found more than fifty *amos* from the dovecotes. Such a bird is deemed to have the capacity to fly (see note 14).

The Gemara could have resolved this difficulty by stating that the Mishnah refers specifically to a case where the bird was found within fifty *amos* of the dovecotes (*Tosafos*). [Indeed, this is how *Rashi* explained the Mishnah (see note 3).] The Gemara, however, proceeds to give a different answer.

בִּשְׁבִיל שֶׁל כְּרָמִים — The Mishnah refers **to** a case where the dovecotes between which the bird was found were situated at opposite ends of **a path between vineyards.** In such a case, even if the bird is found more than fifty *amos* from one of the dovecotes, there is no basis for assuming that it is capable of flying, for it could have hopped more than fifty *amos* by using the vines as a guide. Now, since it is incapable of flying, it could only have come from one of these two dovecotes, דְּאִם אִיתָא דְּמֵעָלְמָא אָתֵי — **for if** you will argue that **it came from elsewhere** (i.e. it hopped from other dovecotes that are on the other sides of the vineyards), one could retort: כֵּיוָן דִּמְדַדֵּי לָא מָצֵי אָתֵי — **Since it hops** (for it is incapable of flying), **it would not have been able to come** here, דְּכָל דִּמְדַדֵּי וְהָדַר חָזֵי לֵיהּ לְקִינֵּיהּ — **because as long as [such a bird] can hop and** still **turn around and see its nest,** מְדַדֵּי — **it will** continue to **hop,** וְאִי לָא לָא מְדַדֵּי — **but if** it is **not** able to see its nest, **it will not** continue to **hop.** Therefore, since the vineyards block the sight of the other dovecotes from the path, a young bird would not have hopped from those dovecotes to the path.[1]

Abaye adduces support for R' Chanina's ruling that the principle of "majority" overrides that of "proximity":

אָמַר אַבַּיֵּי — **Abaye said:** אַף אֲנַן נָמֵי תְּנֵינָא — **We have also learned** this **in a Mishnah:**[2] דָּם שֶׁנִּמְצָא בַּפְּרוֹזְדוֹר — If BLOOD WAS FOUND IN "THE CORRIDOR" (i.e. the vaginal canal),[3] סְפֵיקוֹ טָמֵא — even though IT IS of QUESTIONABLE origin, for it could have come from either the uterus (in which case it is *tamei*), or "the upper chamber"[4] (in which case it is *tahor*), IT IS deemed definitely *TAMEI,*[5] שֶׁחֶזְקָתוֹ מִן הַמָּקוֹר — BECAUSE IT IS ASSUMED to have come FROM THE UTERUS. וְאַף עַל גַּב דְּאִיכָּא עֲלִיָּיה דְּמִקַּרְבָא — **And** this is so **even though there is "the upper chamber"** above the vaginal canal, **which is** in fact **closer** to the vaginal canal than the uterus is and from which the blood might have come! Presumably, the reason for this ruling is that there is *more* blood coming from the uterus than from "the upper chamber." Thus, we see that the principle of "majority" overrides that of "proximity."

Rava rejects the proof:

אָמַר לֵיהּ רָבָא — **Rava said to [Abaye]:** רוֹב וּמָצוּי קָא אָמְרַתְּ — **You speak of** a case in which *two* factors —**"majority" and "frequency"**[6] — conflict with the principle of "proximity!" רוֹב וּמָצוּי לֵיכָּא לְמַאן דְּאָמַר — Regarding a case where the factors of both **"majority" and "frequency"** conflict with the principle of "proximity," **no one says** that we follow the principle of "proximity." Hence, this Mishnah does not prove R' Chanina's ruling that the principle of "majority" *alone* takes precedence over that of "proximity."

The Gemara cites a related Baraisa:

דְּתָנֵי רַבִּי חִיָּיא — **For**[7] **R' Chiya taught the** following **Baraisa:** דָּם הַנִּמְצָא בַּפְּרוֹזְדוֹר — If BLOOD WAS FOUND IN "THE CORRIDOR" (i.e. the vaginal canal) of a woman, it renders her *tamei* to the extent that חַיָּיבִין עָלָיו עַל בִּיאַת מִקְדָּשׁ — ON ACCOUNT OF IT, [SHE] IS LIABLE to bring a *chatas* offering FOR ENTERING THE TEMPLE,[8] וְשׂוֹרְפִין עָלָיו אֶת הַתְּרוּמָה — AND, ON ACCOUNT OF IT, *TERUMAH* touched by her IS BURNED.[9]

Evidently, R' Chiya holds that blood found in a woman's vaginal canal renders her *tamei* beyond any doubt.[10] This is the basis for the following statement by Rava:

וְאָמַר רָבָא — **And**[11] **Rava said:** שְׁמַע מִינָּהּ מִדְּרַבִּי חִיָּיא תְּלָת — One can **learn three** points **from this** statement **of R' Chiya:** שְׁמַע מִינָּהּ — Firstly, one can **learn from it** that where a רוֹב וְקָרוֹב הָלֵךְ אַחַר הָרוֹב — conflict arises between the principles of **"majority" and "proximity,"** we **follow** the principle of **"majority."**[12] וּשְׁמַע מִינָּהּ — Secondly, one can **learn from it** רוּבָּא דְּאוֹרַיְיתָא — that the principle of **"majority" is Scriptural** in origin.[13] וּשְׁמַע מִינָּהּ — **And** thirdly, one can **learn from it** אִיתָא לְדְרַבִּי זֵירָא — that **R' Zeira's** ruling **is correct.** דְּאָמַר רַבִּי זֵירָא — **For R' Zeira said** in reference to a Baraisa which permitted meat found in the street of a city the majority of whose butchers sell kosher meat: אַף עַל פִּי שֶׁדַּלְתוֹת מְדִינָה נְעוּלוֹת — "The Baraisa's ruling applies **even where the gates of the city are locked** (i.e.

NOTES

1. *Rashba;* see *Tosafos.*

2. *Niddah* 17b.

3. The Mishnah uses the layout of a building as a metaphor for the reproductive organs in a woman's body. The uterus, which is towards the back of the body, is described as "the room." The vaginal canal, which leads from the uterus, is called "the corridor." There is a cavity above these organs which is referred to as "the upper chamber" (*Rashi*). [As is consistent with our policy, our elucidation of the following passage reflects *Rashi's* approach. However, as noted by *Chasam Sofer,* it is difficult to reconcile *Rashi's* approach with current anatomical knowledge. See *Chasam Sofer* to *Niddah* 18a, *Rambam Commentary to Mishnah* ibid. 17b.]

4. See note 3.

5. The emission of menstrual blood renders a woman *tamei* (*Leviticus* 15:19). The blood itself is also *tamei* (Mishnah, *Niddah* 54b; see Gemara there).

6. Not only is the blood of the uterus more plentiful than any blood that might be found in "the upper chamber" but it is more likely to flow from the uterus than the blood of the upper cavity is (*Rashi*). [Only a wound would cause the presence of blood "in the upper chamber" and its emission into the uterus.]

7. The presence of the word "for" (the *daled* prefix of דְּתָנֵי) is difficult to explain, because the following does not support the immediately preceding statement. *Tosafos* suggest that the following Baraisa is cited by the Gemara to support Abaye's proof that was stated above. Since the Mishnah adduced by Abaye can be interpreted as meaning that the woman is only questionably *tamei,* the Gemara cites the following Baraisa to prove that the Mishnah means that the woman is definitely *tamei* (see the next two notes) and therefore Abaye's proof from the Mishnah is valid.

From *Tosafos* it seems that there is an alternative version of the text which lacks the *daled* prefix — תָּנֵי רַבִּי חִיָּיא, *R' Chiya taught.* According to this version, the following is a new point cited for the sake of pointing out a contradiction between two statements of Rava (see the continuation of the Gemara).

8. It is an offense to enter the Temple while in a state of *tumah.* One who does so unintentionally is liable to bring a *chatas* offering.

Since R' Chiya rules that this woman is liable to bring a *chatas* offering, evidently he holds that she is *tamei* beyond any doubt. For if her *tumah* status would be in question, her offering might not be consecrated and she would not be *allowed* to bring it to the Temple lest she violate the prohibition against bringing unconsecrated animals into the Temple [as an offering] (*Rashi*).

9. [*Terumah* is the portion of the crop (typically between 1/40 and 1/60) that must be given to a Kohen. *Terumah* that is *tamei* may not be eaten. If it is *tamei* beyond any doubt, it is burned.] If it is questionably *tamei,* it is neither eaten nor burned. From R' Chiya's ruling that *terumah* is burned if it was touched by a woman whose vaginal canal was found to contain blood, it is evident that he considers such a woman to be definitely *tamei* (*Rashi*).

10. See the two preceding notes.

11. *Bach* deletes the *vav* prefix, which usually means *and* (see note 7).

12. [Otherwise, the woman would not be definitely *tamei.*] This contradicts Rava's prior statement that no such inference can be drawn. The Gemara addresses this problem below.

13. If it were a Rabbinic principle, the woman's status of *tumah* would be only Rabbinic. One does not bring a *chatas* offering or burn *terumah* on account of Rabbinic *tumah.*

בשביל של כרמים דאם איתא דמעלמא אתי כיון דמידדי לא מצי אתי דכל דמידדי והדר חזי ליה לקיניה מידדי ואי לא לא מידדי אמר אביי אף אנן נמי תנינא [א]דם שנמצא בפרוזדור ספיקו טמא שחזקתו מן המקור ואע"ג דאיכא עלייה דמקרבא א"ל רבא רוב ומצוי ליכא למאן דאמר דתני ר' חייא [ב]דם הנמצא בפרוזדור חייבין עליו על ביאת מקדש ושורפין עליו את התרומה (א) ואמר רבא ש"מ מדרבי חייא תלת שמע מינה רוב וקרוב הלך אחר הרוב ושמע מינה רובא דאורייתא וש"מ איתא לדר' זירא [ג]דאמר רבי זירא אע"פ שדלתות מדינה נעולות דהא אשה דכי דלתות מדינה נעולות דמיא ואפי' הכי קא אזלינן בתר רובא והא רבא הוא דקאמר רוב ומצוי ליכא למ"ד הדר ביה רבא מההיא איתמר חבית שצפה בנהר אמר רב [ג]נמצאת כנגד עיר שרובה ישראל מותר כנגד עיר שרובה נכרים אסירא ושמואל אמר אפי' נמצאת כנגד עיר שרובה ישראל אסירא (ב) מהאי אימור מהאי דקרא אתאי לימא בדרבי חנינא קא מיפלגי דמר אית ליה דרבי חנינא ומר לית ליה דרבי חנינא לא דכולי עלמא אית להו דר' חנינא והכא בהא קמיפלגי דמ"ס אם איתא (ג) דמהאי דקרא אתאי [ד]עקולי ופשורי הוה מטבעי לה ומר סבר חריפא דנהרא נקט ואתאי [ה]ההוא חצבא דחמרא דאישתכח בפרדיסא דערלה שריא רבינא לימא משום דסבר לה (ד) דרבי חנינא [ו]שאני התם דאי מיגניב מינה אצנועי בגויה לא מצנעי והני מילי חמרא אבל עינבי מצנעי [ז]הנהו זיקי דחמרא דאשתכחן בי קופאי שרנהו רבא לימא לא סבר לה לדרבי חנינא [ח]שאני התם דרובא דשפוכאי

רש"י

בשביל של כרמים. דע"ז כרמים [ז] נדדה חוץ לחמשים (ה) ומיהו בתר רובא דעלמא ליכא למיזל דכל המדדה וחזי לקיניה כשמחזיר ראשו מדדה אי לא לא מדדה והאי אי מעלמא אתא לא מצי חזי לקיניה דכרמים מפסיקין לפניו: **אף אנן נמי תנינא.** כר' חנינא דרוב וקרוב הלך אחר הרוב: **נמצא בפרוזדור.** נמצא דם לאשה בין כותלי רחם מבחוץ הקרוי בית החיצון: **ספיקו טמא.** ספק זה (ו) טומאה ודאית מדקתני שחזקתו מן המקור ומה ספיקא יש כאן ויש דמתניתין במסכת נדה משל משלו באשה החדר והפרוזדור והעלייה דם החדר טמא והוא המקור ומפרש בגמרא החדר מבפנים בעובי גופה לצד אחוריה והפרוזדור מבחוץ לצד פניה והעלייה בנויה על גבי שניהם ודם העלייה טהור ולול פתוח מעלייה לפרוזדור וקתני נמצא בפרוזדור חזקתו מן המקור זב ויצא אל החוץ הואיל ורוב דמים מצויים בו ולא אמר מן העלייה נטף דרך הלול ואע"ג דעלייה קרוב לפרוזדור שעל גבו: **רוב ומצוי.** (ז) דמיו רבים יותר משל עלייה ועוד שהן תדירין לבוא ודמי העלייה אין תדירין לאתא בהא ליכא למאן דפליג על רבי חנינא: **חייבין עליו על ביאת מקדש.** דלא מספקינן לה כמביא חולין לעזרה דודאי דם נדה הוא: **ושורפין עליו תרומה.** ולא אמרי' ספק הוא ותולין לא אוכלין ולא שורפין: **שמע מינה.** מדמחזיק ליה כדם נדה ודאי תלת: **איתא לדר' זירא.** דאמר גבי תשע חנויות בשילהי פ"ק דכתובות ובנמצא הלך אחר הרוב ומותר דאע"פ שדלתות מדינה נעולות דליתא אלא חד רובא להכשירה רוב העיר שתשע חנויות שבה מוכרות בשר שחוטה והאחת מוכרת נבילה דאיכא מילתא דבעינן ביה (ח) תרתי רובי כדאמרי' התם כגון דלתות מדינות פתוחות ורוב טבחים סביבות המדינה ישראל דאיכא למיזל בתר תרי רובי להכשירה רוב העיר ורוב הבאין מחוצה לה: **דהא אשה כדלתות המדינה נעולות** (ט). כלומר דליכא למימר בה תרתי רובי אלא חד רובא שרוב דמים מן המקור וקא אזלי בה בתר רובא להביא קרבן לעזרה ולשרוף תרומה דמידי דאסור לעשותו מספק הוא: **והא רבא הוא דאמר.** לעיל רוב ומצוי ליכא למאן דאמר ולא תסייעין לר' חנינא מהא והכא מסייע ליה מינה דקאמר ש"מ תלת: **חבית.** של יין: (י) **מההיא דקרא.** שם מחוז הוא על נהר פרת כדאמר בקדושין (דף עב.) לענין יוחסין וגיטין ואין ישראל מצויין שם והוא למעלה מפרת ויכולה חבית לבוא משם אלינו: **רב לית ליה דרבי חנינא.** ואזיל בתר קורבא ושמואל אזל בתר רובא דאית ליה לדרבי חנינא: **עקולי ופשורי הוו טבעי ליה.** הרבה מקומות יש משם ועד כאן שהמים מתעקלין ומתגלגלין כגלגל במקום אחד מחמת כיפי סלעים ארוכים הבאים אל תוך הנהר והמים מכסין עליהם והספינות מתגלגלות שם וטובעות: **ופשורי.** הפשרות שלגים הנקוים אצל הנהר וקוו וקיימי ואם תבא החבית שם תעמוד שאין הנהר מוליכה: **חריפותא דנהרא נקט ואתאי.** שמא מתחלה נפלה באמצעית הנהר במקום חזקו ומרוצת המים הביאתה ולא הניחתה לנטות ימין ושמאל: **בפרדיסא דערלה.** בכרם של ערלה: **שרי רבינא.** ולא חש שמא מכרם זה גנב היין זה: (כ) **אי גניב מיניה אצנועי בגויה לא מצנעי.** אין דרך גנבים להצניע היין במקום שגנבוהו משם משום דמתיירא שמא ימצאהו דורך הענבים: **זיקי.** נודות: **בי קופאי.** טמונים בין גפנים שבכרם והיא של ישראל: **לימא לא סבר לה לדרבי חנינא.** לילך אחר הרוב אלא אחר הקרוב וכאן ישראל מצויים יותר מנכרים ולא אזלינן בתר רובא דעלמא:

דשפוכאי

תוספות

דכל דמידדי אי הדר חזי לקיניה מידדי. לא היה לריך למימר דקאמר אי הדר חזי לקיניה מידדי כיון דשוכבין דעלמא יותר מחמשים מן הכרמים (א) [א] ליכא למיחש לרובא דעלמא דכל המדדה אינו מדדה יותר מחמשים אבל הנך שני שוכבין שהכרמים בתוך חמשים אמה שלהם אתי שפיר דקרוב להו שלו אפילו נמצא חוץ לחמשים אמה דלא נפק מתורת מדדה דע"ז כרמים מידדי יותר מחמשים אלא איירי דאפילו אם יהו שוכבין דעלמא בין הכרמים ועוד מדנקט שביל משמע שאלו ב' השוכבין בתוך השביל והניפול כמו כן נמצא בתוך השביל דליכא למיחש שהן משוכבין דעלמא אפי' אינם רחוקים כלל כיון דלא מצי חזי לקיניה אבל אלו השוכבין הוא דאין דבר מפסיק בינו לבין השוכב: **אמר** אביי אף אנן נמי תנינא דם הנמצא בפרוזדור טמא כו'. בנמלא בגג פרוזדור מן הלול ולפנים איירי כדמוכח בפרק כל היד (נדה דף יח: ושם ד"ה מן) וסוגיא דהתם מפרש במקומה: **ואף** על גב דאיכא עלייה דמקרבא. וקרוב דמוכח הוא דקרוב לעלייה הוא ומן החדר אינו יכול לבא אא"כ שחתה ביותר כמו (ל) שפירש במסכת נדה (שם): **דתני** רבי חייא. אי גרסינן תני אתי שפיר אבל אי גרסינן דתני תימה היכי מייתי מהכא לרוב ומצוי הוא דלמא לאו משום דרוב ומצוי קאמר רבי חייא דשורפין את התרומה אלא משום דרוב וקרוב הלך אחר הרוב כרבי חנינא (מ) וי"ל דאפילו גרס' דתני לא מדברי רבא הוא אלא גמרא הוא דמייתי לה דשפיר הוה מוכח אביי ממתני' דנדה דרוב וקרוב הלך אחר הרוב דאף על גב דקתני ספיקו טמא על כרחך לאו ספיקא הוא מדתני רבי חייא דחייבין עליו על ביאת מקדש ושורפין עליו תרומה. (הג"ה) ומהר"ם אומר דרבא מייתי לה דרוב ומצוי הוא דאי אינו מצוי א"כ מאי קמ"ל רבי חנינא כיון דשמעינן לה מדתני רבי חייא אבל ממתני' דנדה לא היה יכול להוכיח דאפילו אם אינו רוב ומצוי הוצרך רבי חנינא לאשמועינן דלא נימא ספיקו טמא הוה ספק ממש ולמאי דהדר ביה רבא וקאמר דלא הוי רוב ומצוי איצטריך רבי חנינא לאשמועינן דאי מדתני רבי חייא ה"א דרוב ומצוי הוא קמ"ל ר' חנינא דלאו רוב ומצוי הוא (ע"כ הג"ה): **ושמע** מינה איתא לדר' זירא. נראה לריב"א דאע"ג דטעמא דבעינן תרי רובי הוי משום דגזרינן רוב סיעה אטו רוב העיר מ"מ איצטריך ליה למימר גבי חנות דלא בעינן תרי רובי דאע"ג דליכא למימר הכי מ"מ איכא למיגזר שמא יקח מן הקבוע אי לאו דאיכא רובא דעלמא וגבי אשה נמי אי גזרינן בעלמא הוה לן להחמיר שלא לשרוף מן הלול ולפנים אטו מן הלול ולחוץ (נ) ונראה לו דהלכה כרבי חנינא: [י]הג"ה וש"מ רובא דאורייתא. חשיב ליה רובא דליתיה קמן דברובא דאיתיה קמן לא לריך למידק ש"מ דקרא כתיב אחרי רבים להטות כדפריך פרק קמא דחולין (דף יא. ושם) גבי הא דבעי מנ"ל הא דאמרינן זיל בתר רובא ופריך מנ"ל דכתיב אחרי רבים להטות: **אימור** (ס) מהאי דקרא אתאי. ולאו דוקא נמצאת כנגד עיר שרובה ישראל אסר שמואל אלא אפי' עיר שכולה ישראל איכא למיחש להכי: **לימא** משום דסבר לה כר' חנינא. וליכא למימר דשריא משום דספק ערלה בחוצה לארץ מותרת דהא אי לית ליה כרבי חנינא אלא רוב וקרוב אזלינן בתר קרוב א"כ הויא ודאי ערלה: **ואצנועי** בגויה. ואם תאמר מכ"מ יהא אסור דרובא דעלמא נכרים נינהו והוי יין נסך וי"ל דרוב גנבי ישראל כדאמר בפרק בתרא דע"ז (דף ע.): **בי** קופאי. פי' בערוך [ז]מקום כדאמרי' (סוטה דף מו:) רב מרדכי אלויה לרב שימי בר אשי לבי קופאי ובכהאי גוונא היה דהוה קורבא דמוכח: **לימא** רבא לית ליה דר' חנינא. פי' והא רבא אית ליה לעיל דר' חנינא:

מרחיקין

רבינו גרשום

הכא במאי עסקינן דיחלוקו כגון דהוו הנהו שוכבין במאה אמה ואותן ק' אמה הן **שביל** שבין ב' **כרמים** ונמצא באמצע הדרך שבין הללו שוכבין דהשתא ליכא למיחש לרובא דעלמא וכיון דמדדה הוא ודאי מהנך שוכבין נפל **דאי מעלמא** לא מצי אתי דקי"ל **כל המדדה והדר חזי לקיניה מדדה ואי לא לא מדדי** והאי הואיל דהוי שביל של כרמים מפסיק ומחיצות של שביל מפסקי לא הוי חזי לקיניה ולא מצי אתי מעלמא משום הכי יחלוקו דמהנהו שוכבין נפלי: **אמר אביי אף אנן נמי תנינא.** דרוב וקרוב אזלי בתר רוב דתנן **דם הנמצא בפרוזדור ספיקו טמא שחזקתו מן המקור** בא שממנו רוב הדמים באין והמקור הוא פנימי מכולן והחדר סמוך למקור והפרוזדור הוא החיצוני ועליה בנויה על גבי שניהם על גבי החדר והפרוזדור ולול פתוח בין עליה ופרוזדור נמצא הדם מן הלול ולפנים ספיקו טמא מן הלול ולחוץ ספיקו טהור ודם הבא מן החדר טמא דמן המקור בא ומן העליה טהור מן הפרוזדור ספיקו טמא שחזקתו מן המקור בא **ואע"ג דאיכא עלייה** דדמה טהורה **דמקרבא** לגבי פרוזדור ממקור אזלינן בתר רוב דרוב דמים מן המקור באין: **אמר רבא.** מהא לא תסייע **דרוב ומצוי** שאני דדם המקור רוב הוא לכולהו ומצוי בו דם תדיר **דתני ר' חייא דם הנמצא בפרוזדור חייבין עליו** חטאת **על ביאת מקדש** אם נכנסה במקדש ואם נגעה בתרומה **שורפין עליו את התרומה** דלא אמרי' הכא כבשאר ספק טומאה אם נגעו בתרומ' דתולין לא אוכלין ולא שורפין אבל הכא ודאי שורפין דספיקו ודאי טמא הוא דדם מקור רוב ומצוי ודאי מן המקור בא וטמא: ש"מ מדקתני ושורפין עליו את התרומה מכלל **דרובא דאורייתא** דרוב דמים מן המקור **וש"מ** מדקאזיל בתר רוב אע"ג דאתרע רוב במקצת דהא יש דם עלייה דטהור הוא דמקרבא ואפ"ה אזיל **בתר רוב ש"מ דאיתא לדר' זירא דאמר** בפ"ק דכתובות בהנהו דאמר ר' יוסי מעשה בתינוקת שירדה מן המעיין ונאנסה ואמר ר"ע אם רוב העיר משיאין לכהונה ורוב סיעה של כשרין עוברין לשם הרי זו תינשא לכהונה. ור' זירא אמר **אע"ג שדלתות מדינה נעולות** דאיתרע לה רובא דליכא אלא חד רובא דלא קא עוברת סיעה של כשרין לשם אפ"ה משיאין לכהונה הואיל דרוב העיר משיאין לכהונה **דהא אשה** כיון דלית בה אלא חד רוב דרוב דמים מן המקור הן **כדלתות מדינה נעולות דמיין ואפ"ה אזלינן בתר רובא: והא רבא הוא דאמר ברוב ומצוי.** כגון דם דמקור **ליכא מאן** דפליג ודאי אזלינן בתר רוב מכלל דס"ל דבעלמא היכא דליכא אלא רוב וקרוב לא אזלינן בתר רוב והיכי אמר הכא ש"מ מדר' חייא דאזלינן בתר רוב דמשמע בכל דוכתא אזלי בתר רוב. **הדר ביה רבא מההיא** דלעיל דלא בעינן רוב ומצוי אלא דאזלינן בתר כל רוב: **חבית** של יין **שצפה בנהר.** ואין ידוע אם יין נכרים הוא אם יין ישראל: **אימור מההיא דקירא באה** כלומר מאותו עבר הקרייה של מעלה ממנה באה דרובא עיירות דנכרים נינהו. **דשמואל אית ליה דר' חנינא ורב לית ליה דר' חנינא: עקולי.** כעין שרגילין המים לעקול ולעקול סביב ובאותן מים שהתהום תחתיהן והולכין ומעגלין עד **שמטביעין** מה שצף על גבן. וכן הני **פשורי** לאותו מקום שהמים רפין ועומדין שאם היתה חבית זו צפה לשם הואיל שהמים רפין ואינן חריפין היתה **נטבעת** שם ומש"ה ליכא למיחש דמההיא דקירא אתאי: **ושמואל אמר** ודאי אסור דאיכא למיחש דמהההיא דקירא אתאי והאי דלא טבעי עקולי ופשורי **דחריפות' דנהרא** שכבר לקחה החבית המרוץ קודם שהגיעה לעקולי ופשורי **ונקט ואתאי** בשבולת המים והלכך אסירא. **לימא.** דמש"ה שריא דקסבר כר' חנינא דאמר רוב וקרוב הולכין אחר הרוב והכא האי פרדס דערלה מיעוט הוא לגבי שאר פרדסים דלא הוי ערלה וקרוב דבגויה אשתכח: **שאני התם.** דמש"ה שריא דליכא למימר דמיניה הוא ההיא חצבא **דאי מיגנב מיניה** לעולם **בגויה לא הוי מצנעי** אינשי ומש"ה איכא למימר דמשאר פרדסים דהיתרא הוי ולא משום דס"ל כר' חנינא: **והני מילי.** דשרי: **חמרא.** משום דלא מצנעי אינשי חמרא בפרדיסא דגנובי מיניה: **אבל ענבי מצנעי.** ואסורין: **זיקי.** נודות יין: **בי קופאי.** בין הגפנים: **שרינהו רבא.** משום דהנהו גפנים דישראל נינהו: **לימא.** מש"ה שרינהו **דלית ליה לר' חנינא** דאע"ג דרוב שאר גפנים דנכרים נינהו אזיל בתר קרוב הואיל דמשתכחן ביני גופני דישראל דהוה קרוב להנהו זיקי וקסבר רוב וקרוב הלך אחר קרוב: **שאני התם.** לעולם רבא סבר לה כר' חנינא דודאי אזלינן בתר רוב והתם נמי איכא רוב ישראל ומש"ה שרינהו **דרובא דשפוכאי** כלומר רובן של אותה העיר שדורכין ושופכין יין ישראל נינהו ועל ידן הולך הכל ואישתכח נמי בי גופני ישראל ודאי ישראל אצנעינהו ומותרין:

והני

עין משפט נר מצוה

עא א ב מיי' פ"ה מהל' איסורי ביאה הל' ה סמג לאוין קיא ועשין רמג:
עב ג ד מיי' פי"ג מהל' מאכלות אסורות הל' כח סמג לאוין קמח טוש"ע י"ד סי' קכט סעיף יח:
עג ה ו מיי' שם פי"א הל' יג סמג לאוין קמח טוש"ע י"ד סי' קלב סעיף יא וסי' קכט סעיף יט:
עד ז ח מיי' שם פי"ג הל' כג סמג לאוין קמח טוש"ע י"ד סי' קכט סעיף יט:

מסורת הש"ס

א) נדה יז., ב) [שם], ג) כתובות טו., ד) ל"ל מדדה. יעב"ץ, ה) רש"ל, ו) נ"א ה"ג, ז) [ערך קף ע"ז ע"ש שכתב בריש גמ' דפ' אין עומדין (דף לא.) רב מרדכי וכו']:

הגהות הב"ח

(א) גמ' אמר רבא ש"מ כצ"ל ואות ו' נמחק: (ב) שם אימור מאיסי דקירא אתאי: (ג) שם אם איתא דמאיסי דקירא אתאי: (ד) שם דסבר לה להא דר' חנינא: (ה) רש"י ד"ה בשביל וכו' חוץ לחמשים אמה ומיהו וכו' ואי לא לא וכו' בפניו הס"ד: (ו) ד"ה ספיקו טמא ספק זה טמא טומאה: (ז) ד"ה רוב ומצוי מקור דמיו: (ח) ד"ה איתא וכו' דבעינן ביה תרי רובי כדאמר התם כגון שהיו דלתות מדינה פתוחות: (ט) ד"ה דהא וכו' נעולות דמיא כלומר: (י) ד"ה מאיסי דקירא שם מחוז: (כ) ד"ה דאי מגניב מיניה וכו' ימלאהו דורכי הענבים: (ל) תוס' ד"ה ואע"ג וכו' כמו שפירשנו: (מ) ד"ה דתני כו' כר' חנינא (וכ"ל דאפי' גרסי' דתני) תא"מ וכ"ב ס"א וי"ל דהא דתני ר' חייא: (נ) ד"ה ושמע מינה וכו' מן הלול ולחוץ הגה"ה וכ"ל דהלכה כר' חנינא. ע"כ הגה"ה: (ס) ד"ה אימור מאיסי דקירא אתאי:

ליקוטי רש"י

דם שנמצא בפרוזדור ספיקו טמא. מספק טומאה ודאית. **שחזקתו כו'.** במקור מחזקינן ליה ולא אמרינן מעלייה אתא ודמים דעלייה טהורין דמפרוזדור לא אתי דם אלא דמי חדר ודמי עלייה פעמים שהן נכנסין לפרוזדור. **חייבין עליו על ביאת מקדש.** אם נכנסה למקדש דודאי טמאה [נדה יז:].

there is only one "majority")."[14] דְּהָא אִשָּׁה דְּכִי דַּלְתוֹת מְדִינָה נְעוּלוֹת דָּמְיָא – For the case of blood that was found in the vaginal canal of **a woman is analogous to** the case of meat found in **a city whose gates are locked,** for in the case of the woman as well there is only one "majority,"[15] וַאֲפִילּוּ הָכִי קָא אָזְלִינַן בָּתַר רוּבָּא – **and yet** R' Chiya ruled that **we follow** the principle of **"majority"** in that case.

The Gemara points out a contradiction in the statements of Rava:

וְהָא רָבָא הוּא דְּקָאָמַר – **But it was Rava who said** above: רוֹב וּמָצוּי לֵיכָּא לְמַאן דְּאָמַר – Regarding a case where the factors of both **"majority" and "frequency"** conflict with the principle of "proximity," **no one says** that we follow the principle of "proximity." With this reasoning, Rava rejected Abaye's attempt to prove from the case of blood found in the vaginal canal that the principle of "majority" overrides that of "proximity." But here, Rava himself adduces this very proof! – ? –

The Gemara answers:

הֲדַר בֵּיהּ רָבָא מֵהַהִיא – **Rava retracted [that statement].** That is, Rava retracted his rejection of Abaye's proof.[16]

The Gemara suggests that R' Chanina's ruling is a matter of dispute between Amoraim:

אִיתְּמַר – **It was stated** חָבִית שֶׁצָּפָה בַּנָּהָר – concerning **a keg** of wine whose origin is unknown that was found **floating in the River** Euphrates: אָמַר רַב – **Rav said:** נִמְצֵאת כְּנֶגֶד עִיר שֶׁרוּבָּהּ יִשְׂרָאֵל מוּתָּר – **If it was found** floating **parallel to a city the majority of [whose residents] are Jews, [the wine] is permitted.** כְּנֶגֶד עִיר שֶׁרוּבָּהּ נָכְרִים אֲסִירָא – If it was found floating **parallel to a city the majority of [whose residents] are non-Jews, [the wine] is forbidden.**[17] וּשְׁמוּאֵל אָמַר – **But Shmuel says:** אֲפִילּוּ נִמְצֵאת כְּנֶגֶד עִיר שֶׁרוּבָּהּ יִשְׂרָאֵל אֲסִירָא – **Even if [the keg] was found** floating **parallel to a city the majority of [whose residents] are Jews, [the wine] is forbidden,** אֵימוּר – for **I can say** מֵהַאי דְּקִרָא אֲתַאי – that **it came** down the river **from Hai Dekira** (a non-Jewish province situated on the banks of the Euphrates).[18]

The Gemara shows how this dispute between Rav and Shmuel corresponds to the ruling of R' Chanina:

לֵימָא בִּדְרַבִּי חֲנִינָא קָא מִיפַּלְגֵי – **Shall we say that they differ with regard to R' Chanina's** ruling that the principle of "majority" supersedes that of "proximity"? דְּמָר אִית לֵיהּ דְּרַבִּי חֲנִינָא – One **master** [Shmuel, who rules that the wine is forbidden, as is the majority of the wine in the entire region, even if it was found nearest to a Jewish town] **agrees with R' Chanina's ruling.** וּמָר לֵית לֵיהּ דְּרַבִּי חֲנִינָא – **And** the other **master** [Rav, who rules that if the wine is found nearest to a Jewish town, it is permitted, even though the majority of the wine in the region is forbidden] **disagrees with R' Chanina's** ruling.

The Gemara counters that this explanation of the dispute is not compelling:

לֹא – This is **not** necessarily the correct explanation of the dispute between Rav and Shmuel. דְּכוּלֵּי עָלְמָא אִית לְהוּ דְּרַבִּי חֲנִינָא – **For** it is possible that **all** [Rav and Shmuel] **agree with R' Chanina's** ruling that the principle of "majority" overrides that of "proximity." וְהָכָא בְּהָא קָמִיפַּלְגֵי – And here, they argue about the following: דְּמָר סָבַר – One **master** [Rav] **reasons** that the keg could not possibly have come from Hai Dekira אִם אִיתָא דְּמֵהַאי דְּקִרָא אֲתַאי – for **if it had come from Hai Dekira,** עֲקוּלֵי וּפְשׁוּרֵי הֲוָה מַטְבְּעֵי לָהּ – **the eddies and stagnant bodies of water** that are so commonplace in the river **would have prevented it**[19] from flowing downstream. וּמָר סָבַר – **And** the other **master** [Shmuel] **reasons** that it could have come from Hai Dekira, חֲרִיפָא דְּנַהֲרָא נָקֵט וַאֲתַאי – for **it** could have **caught the swift current** in the middle **of the river** and thus **come** downstream without being obstructed on the way. According to this explanation of their argument, Rav and Shmuel do not dispute the validity of R' Chanina's ruling; rather, they argue as to whether it is applicable in this case.

The Gemara cites an incident related to the ruling of R' Chanina:

הַהוּא חַצְבָּא דְּחַמְרָא דְּאִישְׁתְּכַח בְּפַרְדֵּיסָא דְּעָרְלָה – **There was this barrel of wine that was found in a vineyard of** ***orlah,***[20] and it was not known whether the wine had been stolen from this vineyard (in which case it would be forbidden as *orlah*) or whether it had come from some other vineyard.[21] שַׁרְיָא רָבִינָא – **Ravina permitted** the wine. He was not concerned that it might have been stolen from this vineyard.

The Gemara inquires:

לֵימָא מִשּׁוּם דְּסָבַר לָהּ דְּרַבִּי חֲנִינָא – **Shall we say** that Ravina permitted the wine **because he agrees with R' Chanina's** ruling? This would seem to be so, since Ravina assumed that the wine came not from the *nearest* vineyard, but from any one of the vineyards in the world at large, the *majority* of which are not *orlah.*

The Gemara responds that it is not evident from Ravina's decision that he agrees with R' Chanina's ruling, for his decision might have been based on a different consideration:

שָׁאנֵי הָתָם – **That case is different.** Perhaps, Ravina reasoned that the wine could not have been stolen from this particular vineyard, דְּאִי מִיגְּנִיב מִינָּהּ – **for if it had been stolen from [this vineyard],** אַצְנוּעֵי בְּגַוֵּיהּ לֹא מַצְנְעִי – **[the thieves] would not have hidden** it **[there],** lest it be discovered.[22]

NOTES

14. In some cases, the Rabbis legislated that a single "majority" is insufficient and two "majorities" are required (see *Kesubos* 15a). Therefore, one might have thought that this Baraisa's ruling applies only where butchers from elsewhere bring meat into the town and most of these visiting butchers sell kosher meat, in which case there are two "majorities" which dictate that the meat is kosher: (1) the majority of stores in the town; (2) the majority of butchers visiting the town. To reject this understanding of the Baraisa, R' Zeira states (ibid.) that even where the gates of the city are locked and no one brings in meat from outside, the found meat is nevertheless assumed to be kosher (*Rashi*).

15. Viz. most of the blood found in that part of her body will have come from the uterus.

16. Upon further reflection, Rava concluded that the case of blood found in the vaginal canal is indeed a valid proof for R' Chanina's ruling that the principle of "majority" overrides that of "proximity." [The Gemara does not explain why the phenomenon of "frequency" does not make a crucial difference. Possibly, the reason is that "frequency" is merely *due* to majority, rather than an independent factor.]

17. It is forbidden to derive benefit from wine that was used for idolatrous purposes [יֵין נֶסֶךְ, *libation wine*]. The Rabbis extended this prohibition to include any wine that was touched by a non-Jew [סְתָם יֵינָם, *their standard wine*].

18. [Hai Dekira is mentioned as an example of a non-Jewish province that was located upstream from the major Jewish centers of population (e.g. Nehardea, Pumbedisa) in the Euphrates region.]

19. Literally: would have sunk it.

20. עָרְלָה, *orlah,* is fruit that grows on a tree during its first three years. The Torah forbids the derivation of benefit from such fruit (see *Leviticus* 19:23).

21. Since the owner of the vineyard knows nothing about this barrel, it must have been brought there from another vineyard, or else it was stolen from this vineyard (see *Rabbeinu Yonah*).

22. By the workers who press the grapes (*Rashi;* see following note).

בשביל של כרמים דאם איתא דמעלמא אתי כיון דמידדי לא מצי אתי דכל דמידדי והדר חזי ליה לקיניה מידדי ואי לא לא מידדי אמר אביי אף אנן נמי תנינא [א]דם שנמצא בפרוזדור ספיקו טמא שחזקתו מן המקור ואע"ג דאיכא עלייה דמקרבא א"ל רבא רוב ומצוי ליכא למאן דאמר דתני ר' חייא [ב]דם הנמצא בפרוזדור חייבין עליו על ביאת מקדש ושורפין עליו את התרומה (א) ואמר רבא ש"מ מדרבי חייא תלת שמע מינה רוב וקרוב הלך אחר הרוב ושמע מינה רובא דאורייתא וש"מ איתא לדר' זירא [ג]דאמר רבי זירא אע"פ שדלתות מדינה נעולות דמיא ואפי' הכי קא אזלינן בתר רובא והא רבא הוא דקאמר רוב ומצוי ליכא למ"ד הדר ביה רבא מההיא איתמר חבית שצפה בנהר אמר רב [ג]נמצאת כנגד עיר שרובה ישראל מותר כנגד עיר שרובה נכרים אסירא ושמואל אמר אפי' נמצאת כנגד עיר שרובה ישראל אסירא אימור (ב) מהאי דקרא אתאי לימא בדרבי חנינא קא מיפלגי דמר אית ליה דרבי חנינא ומר לית ליה דרבי חנינא לא דכולי עלמא אית להו דר' חנינא והכא בהא קמיפלגי דמ"ס אם איתא (ג) דמהאי דקרא אתאי [ד]עקולי ופשורי הוה מטבעי לה ומר סבר חריפא דנהרא נקט ואתאי [ה]ההוא חצבא דחמרא דאישתכח בפרדיסא דערלה שריא רבינא לימא משום דסבר לה (ד) דרבי חנינא [ו]שאני התם דאי מיגניב מינה אצנועי בגויה לא מצנעי והני מילי חמרא אבל עינבי מצנעי [ז]הנהו זיקי דחמרא דאשתכחן בי קופאי שרנהו רבא לימא לא סבר לה לדרבי חנינא [ח]שאני התם דרובא דשפוכאי

רש"י

בשביל של כרמים. דע"י כרמים [ד] נדדה חוץ לחמשים (ה) ומיהו בתר רובא דעלמא ליכא למיזל דכל המדדה וחזי לקיניה כשמחזיר ראשו מדדה והאי דעלמא אתא לא מצי חזי לקיניה דכרמים מפסיקין לפניו: אף אנן נמי תנינא. כר' חנינא דרוב וקרוב הלך אחר הרוב: נמצא בפרוזדור. נמצא דם לאשה בין כותלי רחם מבחוץ הקרוי בית החיצון: ספיקו טמא. ספק זה (ו) טומאה ודאית מדקתני שחזקתו מן המקור ומה ספיקה יש כאן רישא דמתניתין במסכת נדה משל משלו באשה החדר והפרוזדור והעלייה דם החדר טמא והוא המקור ומפרש בגמרא החדר מבפנים בעובי גופה לצד אחוריה והפרוזדור מבחוץ לצד פניה והעלייה בנויה על גבי שניהם ודם העלייה טהור ולול פתוח מעלייה לפרוזדור וקתני נמצא בפרוזדור חזקתו מן המקור זב ויצא לחוץ הואיל ורוב דמים מצויים בו ולא אמר מן העלייה נטף דרך הלול ואע"ג דעלייה קרוב לפרוזדור שעל גגו: רוב ומצוי. (ז) דמיו רבים יותר משל עלייה ועוד שכן מדירין לזוב משם ודמי העלייה אין מדירין לצאת בהא ליכא למאן דפליג על רבי חנינא: חייבין עליו על ביאת מקדש. דלא מספקינן לה כמביא חולין לעזרה דודאי דם נדה הוא: ושורפין עליו תרומה. ולא אמרי' ספק הוא ותולין לא אוכלין ולא שורפין: שמע מינה. מדאחזיק ליה בדם נדה ודאי תלת: איתא לדר' זירא. דאמר גבי תשע חנויות בשילהי פ"ק דכתובות ובנמצא הלך אחר הרוב ומותר דאע"פ שדלתות מדינה נעולות דליכא אלא חד רובא להכשירה רוב העיר שתשע חנויות שבה מוכרות בשר שחוטה ואחת מוכרת נבילה דליכא מילתא דבעינן ביה (ח) תרתי רובי כדאמרי' התם כגון דלתות מדינות פתוחות ורוב טבחים סביבות המדינה ישראל דאיכא למיזל בתר תרי רובי להכשירה רוב העיר ורוב הבאין מחוצה לה: דהא אשה כדלתות המדינה נעולות (ט). כלומר דליכא למימר בה תרתי רובי אלא חד רובא שרוב דמים מן המקור וקא אזלי בה בתר רובא להביא קרבן לעזרה ולשרוף תרומה דמידי דאסור לעשותו מספק הוא: והא רבא הוא דאמר. לעיל רוב ומצוי ליכא למאן דאמר ולא תסייעין לר' חנינא מהא והכא מסייע ליה מינה דקאמר ש"מ תלת: חבית. של יין: (י) מהאי דקרא. שם מחוז הוא על נהר פרת כדאמר בקדושין (דף עב.) לענין יוחסין וגיטין ואין ישראל מצויין שם והוא למעלה מפרת ויכולה חבית לבוא משם אללנו: רב לית ליה דרבי חנינא. ואזיל בתר קורבא ושמואל אזל בתר רובא דאית ליה לדרבי חנינא: עקולי ופשורי הוו טבעי ליה. הרבה מקומות יש משם ועד כאן שהמים מתעקלין ומתגלגלין כגלגל במקום אחד מחמת כיפי סלעים ארוכים הבאים אל תוך הנהר והמים מכסין עליהם והספינות מתגלגלות שם וטובעות: ופשורי. הפשרות שלגים הנקוים אל הנהר וקוו וקיימי ואם תבא החבית שם תעמוד שאין הנהר מוליכה: חריפותא דנהרא נקט ואתאי. שמא מתחלה נפלה באמצעית הנהר במקום חזקו ומרוצת המים הביאתה ולא הניחתה לנטות ימין ושמאל: בפרדיסא דערלה. בכרם של ערלה: שרי רבינא. ולא חש שמא מכרם זה גנב היין זה: (כ) אי גניב מיניה אצנועי בגויה לא מצנעי. אין דרך גנבים להצניע היין במקום שגנבוהו משם משום דמתיירא שמא ימצאהו דורך הענבים: זיקי. נודות: בי קופאי. טמונים בין גפנים שבכרם והיא של ישראל: לימא לא סבר לה לדרבי חנינא. ליזיל אחר הרוב אלא אחר הקרוב וכאן ישראל מצויים יותר מנכרים ולא אזלינן בתר רובא דעלמא: דשפוכאי

תוספות

דכל דמידדי אי הדר חזי לקיניה מידדי. לא היה צריך למאי דקאמר אי הדר חזי לקיניה מידדי כיון דשובכין דעלמא יותר מחמשים מן הכרמים [ה] [אז] ליכא למיחש לרובא דעלמא דכל המדדה אינו מדדה יותר מחמשים אבל הנך שני שובכין שהכרמים בתוך חמשים אמה שלהם אתי שפיר דקרוב לזה שלו אפילו נמצא חוץ לחמשים אמה דלא נפק מתורת מדדה דע"י כרמים מידדי יותר מחמשים אלא איירי דאפילו אם יהו שובכין דעלמא בין הכרמים ועוד מדנקט שביל משמע שאלו ב' השובכין בתוך השביל והניפול כמו כן נמצא בתוך השביל דליכא למיחש שהן משובכין דעלמא אפי' אינם רחוקים כלל כיון דלא מצי חזי לקיניה אבל מאלו השובכין הוא דאין דבר מפסיק בינו לבין השובך: אמר אביי אף אנן נמי תנינא דם הנמצא בפרוזדור טמא כו'. בנמצא בגג פרוזדור מן הלול ולפנים איירי כדמוכח בפרק כל היד (נדה דף יז: ושם ד"ה מן) וסוגיא דהתם מפרש במקומה: ואף על גב דאיכא עלייה דמקרבא. וקרוב דמוכח הוא דקרוב לעלייה הוא ומן החדר אינו יכול לבא אא"כ שחתה ביותר כמו (ל) שפירש במסכת נדה (שם): דתני רבי חייא. אי גרסינן תני אתי שפיר אבל אי גרסינן דתני תימה היכי מייתי מהכא דרוב ומצוי הוא דלמא לאו משום דרוב ומצוי קאמר רבי חייא דשורפין עליו את התרומה אלא משום דרוב וקרוב הלך אחר הרוב כרבי חנינא (מ) וי"ל דאפילו גרסי' דתני לא מדברי רבא הוא אלא גמרא הוא דמייתי לה דשפיר הוה מוכח אביי ממתני' דנדה דרוב וקרוב הלך אחר הרוב דאף על גב דקתני ספיקו טמא על כרחך לאו ספיקא הוא מדתני רבי חייא דחייבין עליו על ביאת מקדש ושורפין עליו תרומה. (הג"ה) ומהר"ם אומר דרבא מייתי לה דרוב ומצוי הוא דאי אינו מצוי א"כ מאי קמ"ל רבי חנינא כיון דשמעינן לה מדתני רבי חייא אבל ממתני' דנדה לא היה יכול להוכיח דאפילו אם אינו רוב ומצוי הוצרך רבי חנינא לאשמועינן דלא נימא ספיקו טמא הוה ספק ממש ולמאי דהדר ביה רבא וקאמר דלא הוי רוב ומצוי איצטריך רבי חנינא לאשמועינן דאי מדתני רבי חייא ה"א דרוב ומצוי הוא קמ"ל ר' חנינא דלאו רוב ומצוי הוא (ע"כ הג"ה): ושמע מינה איתא לדר' זירא. נראה לריצב"א דאע"ג דטעמא דבעינן תרי רובי הוי משום דגזרינן רוב סיעה אטו רוב העיר מ"מ איצטריך ליה למימר גבי חנות דלא בעינן תרי רובי דאע"ג דליכא למימר הכי מ"מ איכא למיגזר שמא יקח מן הקבוע אי לאו דאיכא רובא דעלמא וגבי אשה נמי אי גזרינן בעלמא הוה לן להחמיר שלא לשרוף מן הלול ולפנים אטו מן הלול ולחוץ (נ) ונראה לו להלכה כרבי חנינא: [י]הג"ה וש"מ רובא דאורייתא. חשיב ליה רובא דליתיה קמן דברובא דאיתיה קמן לא צריך למידק ש"מ דקרא כתיב אחרי רבים להטות כדפריך פרק קמא דחולין (דף יא. ושם) גבי הא דבעי מנ"ל הא דאמרינן זיל בתר רובא ופריך מנ"ל דכתיב אחרי רבים להטות: אימור (ס) מהאי דקרא אתאי. ולאו דוקא נמצאת כנגד עיר שרובה ישראל אסר שמואל אלא אפי' עיר שכולה ישראל איכא למיחש להכי: לימא משום דסבר לה כר' חנינא. וליכא למימר דשריא משום דספק ערלה בחוצה לארץ מותרת דהא אי לית ליה כרבי חנינא אלא רוב וקרוב אזלינן בתר קרוב א"כ הוא ודאי ערלה: ואצנועי בגויה. ואם תאמר מכ"מ יהא אסור דרובא דעלמא נכרים נינהו והוי יין נסך וי"ל דרוב גנבי ישראל כדאמר בפרק בתרא דע"ז (דף ע.): בי קופאי. פי' בערוך [י]מקום כדאמרי' (סוטה דף מו:) רב מרדכי אלויה לרב שימי בר אשי לבי קופאי ובכהאי גוונא היה דהוה קורבא דמוכח: לימא רבא לית ליה דר' חנינא. פי' והא רבא אית ליה לעיל דר' חנינא: מרחיקין

עין משפט נר מצוה

עא א ב מיי' פ"ה מהל' איסורי ביאה הל' ה סמג לאוין קיא ועשין רמג:
עב ג ד מיי' פי"ב מהל' מאכלות אסורות הל' כח סמג לאוין קמח טוש"ע י"ד סי' קכט סעיף יז:
עג ה ו מיי' שם פי"א הל' יג סמג לאוין קמח טוש"ע י"ד סי' קלד סעיף יא וסי' קכט סעיף יח:
עד ז ח מיי' שם פי"ג הל' כט סמג לאוין קמח טוש"ע י"ד סי' קכט סעיף יט:

רבינו גרשום

הכא במאי עסקינן דיחלוקו כגון דהוו הנהו שובכין במאה אמה ואותן ק' אמה הן שביל שבין ב' כרמים ונמצא באמצע הדרך שבין הללו שובכין דהשתא ליכא למיחש לרובא דעלמא וכיון דמדדה הוא ודאי מהנך שובכין נפל דאי מעלמא לא מצי אתי דקי"ל כל המדדה והדר חזי לקיניה מדדה ואי לא לא מדדי והאי הואיל דהוי שביל של כרמים מפסיק ומחיצות של שביל מפסקי לא הוי חזי לקיניה ולא מצי אתי מעלמא משום הכי יחלוקו דמהנהו שובכין נפלי: אמר אביי אף אנן נמי תנינא. דרוב וקרוב אזלי בתר רוב דתנן דם הנמצא בפרוזדור ספיקו טמא שחזקתו מן המקור בא שממנו רוב הדמים באין והמקור הוא פנימי מכולן והחדר סמוך למקור והפרוזדור הוא החיצוני ועליה בנויה על גבי שניהם על גבי החדר והפרוזדור ולול פתוח בין עליה ופרוזדור נמצא הדם מן הלול ולפנים ספיקו טמא מן הלול ולחוץ ספיקו טהור ודם הבא מן החדר טמא דמן המקור בא ומן העליה טהור מן הפרוזדור ספיקו טמא שחזקתו מן המקור בא ואע"ג דאיכא עלייה דדמה טהורה דמקרבא לגבי פרוזדור ממקור אזלינן בתר רוב דרוב דמים מן המקור באין: אמר רבא. מהא לא תסייע דרוב ומצוי שאני דדם המקור רוב הוא לכולהו ומצוי בו דם תדיר דתני ר' חייא דם הנמצא בפרוזדור חייבין עליו חטאת על ביאת מקדש אם נכנסה במקדש ואם נגעה בתרומה שורפין עליו את התרומה דלא אמרי' הכא כבשאר ספק טומאו' אם נגעו בתרומ' דתולין לא אוכלין ולא שורפין אבל הכא ודאי שורפין דספיקו ודאי טמא הוא דדם מקור רוב ומצוי ודאי מן המקור בא וטמא: ש"מ מדקתני ושורפין עליו את התרומה מכלל דרובא דאורייתא דרוב דמים מן המקור וש"מ מדקאזיל בתר רוב אע"ג דאתרע רוב במקצת דהא יש דם עלייה דטהור הוא דמקרבא ואפ"ה אזיל בתר רוב ש"מ דאיתא לדר' זירא דאמר בפ"ק דכתובות בהנהו דאמר ר' יוסי מעשה בתינוקת שירדה מן המעיין ונאנסה ואמר ר"ע אם רוב העיר משיאין לכהונה ורוב סיעה של כשרין עוברין לשם הרי זו תנשא לכהונה. ור' זירא אמר אע"ג שדלתות מדינה נעולות דאיתרע לה רובא דליכא אלא חד רובא דלא קא עוברת סיעה של כשרין לשם אפ"ה משיאין לכהונה הואיל דרוב העיר משיאין לכהונה דהא אשה כיון דלית בה אלא חד רוב דרוב דמים מן המקור הן כדלתות מדינה נעולות דמיין ואפ"ה אזלינן בתר רובא: והא רבא הוא דאמר ברוב ומצוי. כגון דם דמקור ליכא מאן דפליג ודאי אזלינן בתר רוב והיכי אמר הכא ש"מ מדר' חייא דאזלינן בתר רוב דמשמע בכל דוכתא אזלי בתר רוב. הדר ביה רבא מההיא דלעיל דלא בעינן רוב ומצוי אלא דאזלינן בתר כל רוב: חבית של יין שצפה בנהר. ואין ידוע אם יין נכרים הוא אם יין ישראל: אימור מהאי דקירא באה כלומר מאותו עבר הקרייה של מעלה ממנה באה דרובא עיירות דנכרים נינהו. דשמואל אית ליה דר' חנינא ורב לית ליה דר' חנינא: עקולי. כיון שרגילין המים לעקול ולעקול סביב ובאותן מים שתהום תחתיהן והולכין ומעגלין עד שמטביעין מה שצף על גבן. וכן הני פשורי לאותו מקום שהמים רפין ועומדין שאם היתה חבית זו צפה לשם הואיל שהמים רפין ואינן חריפין היתה נטבעת שם ומש"ה ליכא למיחש דמההיא דקירא אתאי: ושמואל אמר ודאי אסור דאיכא למיחש דמההיא דקירא אתאי והאי דלא טבעי עקולי ופשורי דחריפות' דנהרא שכבר לקחה החבית המרוץ קודם שהגיעה לעקולי ופשורי ונקט ואתאי בשבולת המים והלכך אסירא. לימא. דמש"ה שריא דקסבר כר' חנינא דאמר רוב וקרוב הולכין אחר הרוב והכא האי פרדס דערלה מיעוט הוא לגבי שאר פרדסים דלא הוי ערלה וקרוב דבגויה אשתכח: שאני התם. דמש"ה שריא דליכא למימר דמיניה הוא וההיא חצבא דאי מיגנב מיניה בגויה לא הוי מצנעי אינשי ומש"ה איכא למימר דמשאר פרדסים דהיתרא הוי ולא משום דס"ל כר' חנינא: והני מילי. דשרי: חמרא. משום דלא מצנעי אינשי חמרא בפרדיסא דגנובי מיניה: אבל ענבי מצנעי. ואסורין: זיקי. נודות יין: בי קופאי. בין הגפנים: שרינהו רבא. משום דהנהו גפנים דישראל נינהו: לימא. מש"ה שרינהו דלית ליה לר' חנינא דאע"ג דרוב שאר גפנים דנכרים נינהו אזיל בתר קרוב הואיל דמשתכחן ביני גופני דישראל דהוה קרוב להנהו זיקי וקסבר רוב וקרוב הלך אחר קרוב: שאני התם. לעולם רבא סבר לה כר' חנינא דודאי אזלינן בתר רוב והתם נמי איכא רוב ישראל ומש"ה שרינהו דרובא דשפוכאי כלומר רובן של אותה העיר שדורכין ושופכין יין ישראל נינהו ועל ידן הולך הכל ואישתכח נמי בי גופני ישראל ודאי ישראל אצנעינהו ומותרין: והני

מסורת הש"ס

א) נדה יז, ב) [שם], ג) כתובות טו, ד) נ"ל מדלה. יעב"ץ, ה) כ"ל, ו) נ"א ה"ג, ז) [ערך קף ע"ש שכתב כרים גמ' דפ' אין עומדין (דף לא.) רב מרדכי וכו'].

הגהות הב"ח

(א) גמ' אמר רבא ש"מ כצ"ל ואות ו' נמחק: (ב) שם אימור מהאי דקירא אתאי: (ג) שם אם איתא מהאי דקירא אתאי: (ד) שם דסבר לה להא דר' חנינא: (ה) רש"י ד"ה בשביל וכו' חוץ לחמשים אמה ומיהו וכו' ואי לא לא וכו' בפניו הס"ד: (ו) ד"ה ספיקו טמא ספק זה אינו טומאה: (ז) ד"ה רוב ומצוי מקור דמיו: (ח) ד"ה איתא וכו' רובי כדאמר התם כגון שהיו דלתות מדינה וכו' פתוחות: (ט) ד"ה דהא אשה וכו' נעולות דמיא כלומר: (י) ד"ה מהאי דקירא מחוז: (כ) ד"ה דאי מגניב מיניה וכו' ימצאוהו דורכי הענבים: (ל) תוס' ד"ה ואע"ג וכו' כמו שפירשו: (מ) ד"ה דתני וכו' וי"ל דאפילו גרסינן דתני ל"ג מדברי: (נ) ד"ה וכו' מן הלול ולחוץ הג"ה וי"ל הלכה כר' חנינא. עיין בהג"ה: (ס) ד"ה אימור מהאי דקירא אתאי:

ליקוטי רש"י

דם שנמצא בפרוזדור ספיקו טמא. מספק טומאה ודאית. שחזקתו כו'. מקור מקומו ליה להו לאמרינן מעלייה אתא ודמים דעליה טהורין ומפרוזדור לא אתי דם אלא דמי חדר ודמי עליה פעמים שהן נכנסין לפרוזדור. חייבין עליו על ביאת מקדש. אם נכנסה למקדש דודאי טומאה [נדה יז:].

The Gemara adds:

וְהָנֵי מִילֵּי חַמְרָא – **This reasoning** applies to **wine.** אֲבָל עִינְבֵי מַצְנְעֵי – **But,** as far as **grapes** are concerned, **[thieves]** might **hide** them in the very vineyard from which the grapes had been stolen.[23]

The Gemara cites another incident related to the ruling of R' Chanina:

הַנְהוּ זִיקֵי דְחַמְרָא – **There were these leather bags of wine** דְּאִשְׁתַּכְּחָן בֵּי קוּפָאֵי – **that were found between the vines** of a vineyard that belonged to a Jew. Even though they might have fallen from a non-Jew, in which case they would be forbidden,[24] שְׁרַנְהוּ רָבָא – **Rava permitted them.**

The Gemara asks:

לֵימָא לֹא סָבַר לָהּ לְדְרַבִּי חֲנִינָא – Are we **to say that [Rava] disagrees with [the ruling] of R' Chanina?** In this case, it would seem that the principle of "majority" dictates that the bags of wine are forbidden, for most of the people from whom they could have fallen are non-Jews; whereas, the principle of "proximity" dictates that they are permitted, for the location in which they were found was frequented by Jews. Thus, Rava, who permitted the wine, apparently favors the principle of "proximity" over that of "majority." This runs contrary to R' Chanina's ruling which stipulates that the principle of "majority" is superior. **– ? –**

The Gemara responds that Rava could hold, as R' Chanina does, that the principle of "majority" overrides that of "proximity," and yet he permitted the wine for the following reason:

שָׁאנֵי הָתָם – **That case is different.** דְּרוּבָּא – **Since,** in the region under discussion, **most**

NOTES

23. For thieves could steal grapes before the harvest, at a time when there are no workers in the vineyard, and hide them there without fear of the grapes being discovered. But wine is present in a vineyard only when the grapes are pressed; hence, thieves would not leave wine in a vineyard lest it be discovered by the workers who press the grapes (*Taz Yoreh Deah* 294:17 as explained by *Nachalas Moshe;* see previous note; cf. *Rabbeinu Yonah*).

Therefore, if *grapes* are found in a vineyard of *orlah,* they would be forbidden were it not for R' Chanina's ruling that the principle of "majority" overrides that of "proximity" (*Rabbeinu Yonah;* cf. *Ramban, Ritva, Nimukei Yosef*).

24. See note 17.

מסורת הש"ס

א) נדה יז:, ב) [שם], ג) כתובות טו., ד) נ"ל מדדה. יעב"ץ, ה) רש"ל, ו) כ"א ה"ג, ז) [ערך קף ע"ז ע"ש שכתב בריש גמ' דפ' אין עומדין (דף לא.) רב מרדכי וכו']:

הגהות הב"ח

(א) גמ' אמר רבא ש"מ כצ"ל ואות ו' נמחק: (ב) שם אימור מהאי דקרא אתאי: (ג) שם אם איתא דמהאי דקרא אתאי: (ד) שם דסבר לה להא דר' חנינא: (ה) רש"י ד"ה בשביל וכו' חוץ לחמשים אמה ומיהו וכו' ואי לא לא וכו' בפניו הס"ד: (ו) ד"ה ספיקו טמא ספק זה טמא טומאה: (ז) ד"ה רוב ומצוי מקור דמיו: (ח) ד"ה איתא וכו' דבעינן ביה תרי רובי כדאמר התם כגון שהיו דלתות מדינה פתוחות: (ט) ד"ה דהא וכו' נעולות דמיא כלומר: (י) ד"ה מהאי דקרא שם מחוז: (כ) ד"ה דאי מגניב מיניה וכו' ימלאהו דורכי הענבים: (ל) תוס' ד"ה ואע"ג וכו' כמו שפירשנו: (מ) ד"ה דתני כו' כר' חנינא (ונ"ל דאפי' גרסי' דתני) תא"מ ונ"ב ס"א וי"ל דהא דתני ר' חייא: (נ) ד"ה ושמע מינה וכו' מן הלול ולחוץ הגה"ה ונ"ל דהלכה כר' חנינא. ע"כ הגה"ה: (ס) ד"ה אימור מהאי דקרא אתאי:

ליקוטי רש"י

דם שנמצא בפרוזדור ספיקו טמא. מספק טמא טומאה ודאית. שחזקתו כו'. במקור מחזקינן ליה ולא אמרינן מעלייה אתא ודמים דעלייה טהורין דמפרוזדור לא אתי דם אלא דמי חדר ודמי עליה פעמים שהן נכנסין לפרוזדור. חייבין עליו על ביאת מקדש. אם נכנסה למקדש דודאי טמאה [נדה יז:].

עין משפט נר מצוה

עא א ב מיי' פ"ה מהל' איסורי ביאה הל' ה סמג לאוין קיא ועשין רמג:
עב ג ד מיי' פי"ב מהל' מאכלות אסורות הל' כח סמג לאוין קמח טוש"ע י"ד סי' קכט סעיף יח:
עג ה ו מיי' שם פי"א הל' יג סמג לאוין קמד טוש"ע י"ד סי' קלד סעיף יא וסי' קכט סעיף יח:
עד ז ח מיי' שם פי"ב הל' כט סמג לאוין קמח טוש"ע י"ד סי' קכט סעיף יט:

גמרא

בשביל של כרמים דאם איתא דמעלמא אתי כיון דמידדי לא מצי אתי דכל דמידדי והדר חזי ליה לקיניה מידדי ואי לא לא מידדי אמר אביי אף אנן נמי תנינא [א]דם שנמצא בפרוזדור ספיקו טמא שחזקתו מן המקור ואע"ג דאיכא עליה דמקרבא א"ל רבא רוב ומצוי ליכא למאן דאמר דתני ר' חייא [ב]דם הנמצא בפרוזדור חייבין עליו על ביאת מקדש ושורפין עליו את התרומה (א) ואמר רבא ש"מ מדרבי חייא תלת שמע מינה רוב וקרוב הלך אחר הרוב ושמע מינה רובא דאורייתא וש"מ איתא לדר' זירא [ג]דאמר רבי זירא אע"פ שדלתות מדינה נעולות דהא אשה דכי דלתות מדינה נעולות דמיא ואפי' הכי קא אזלינן בתר רובא והא רבא הוא דקאמר רוב ומצוי ליכא למ"ד הדר ביה רבא מההיא איתמר חבית שצפה בנהר אמר רב [ג]נמצאת כנגד עיר שרובה ישראל מותר כנגד עיר שרובה נכרים אסירא ושמואל אמר אפי' נמצאת כנגד עיר שרובה ישראל אסירא אימור (ב) מהאי דקרא אתאי לימא בדרבי חנינא קא מיפלגי דמר אית ליה דרבי חנינא ומר לית ליה דרבי חנינא לא דכולי עלמא אית להו דר' חנינא והכא בהא קמיפלגי דמ"ס אם איתא (ג) דמהאי דקרא אתאי [ד]עקולי ופשורי הוה מטבעי לה ומר סבר חריפא דנהרא נקט ואתאי [ה]ההוא חצבא דחמרא דאישתכח בפרדיסא דערלה שריא רבינא לימא משום דסבר לה (ד) דרבי חנינא [ו]שאני התם דאי מיגנב מינה אצנועי בגויה לא מצנעי והני מילי חמרא אבל עינבי מצנעי [ז]הנהו זיקי דחמרא דאשתכחן בי קופאי שרנהו רבא לימא לא סבר לה לדרבי חנינא [ח]שאני התם דרובא דשפוכאי

רש"י

בשביל של כרמים. דע"י כרמים [ז]נלדה חוץ לחמשים (ה) ומיהו בתר רובא דעלמא ליכא למיזל דכל המדדה וחזי לקיניה כשמחזיר לאשו מדדה אי לא לא מדדה והאי מעלמא אתא לא מלי חזי לקיניה דכרמים מפסיקין לפניו: אף אנן נמי תנינא. כר' חנינא דרוב וקרוב הלך אחר הרוב: נמצא בפרוזדור. נמלא דם לאשה בין כותלי רחם מבחוץ הקרוי בית החיצון: ספיקו טמא. ספק זה (ו) טומאה ודאית מדקתני שחזקתו מן המקור ומה ספיקא יש כאן רישא דמתניתין במסכת נדה משל משלו באשה החדר והפרוזדור והעליה דם החדר טמא והוא המקור ומפרש בגמרא החדר מבפנים בעובי גופה לצד אחוריה והפרוזדור מבחוץ לצד פניה והעליה בנויה על גבי שניהם ודם העליה טהור ולול פתוח מעלייה לפרוזדור וקתני נמצא בפרוזדור חזקתו מן המקור זו ויצא אל החוץ הואיל ורוב דמים מצויים בו ולא אמר מן העליה נטף דרך הלול ואע"ג דעלייה קרוב לפרוזדור שעל גבו: רוב ומצוי. (ז) דמיו רבים יותר משל עליה ועוד שכן מדירין לזוב משם ודמי העלייה אין מדירין לאתא בהא ליכא למאן דפליג על רבי חנינא: חייבין עליו על ביאת מקדש. לא מספקינן לה כמביא חולין לעזרה דודאי דם נדה הוא: ושורפין עליו תרומה. ולא אמרי' ספק הוא ותולין לא אוכלין ולא שורפין: שמע מינה. מדמחזיק ליה כדם נדה ודאי תלת: איתא לדר' זירא. דאמר גבי תשע חנויות בשילהי פ"ק דכתובות ובנמלא הלך אחר הרוב ומותר דאע"פ שדלתות מדינה נעולות ליתא אלא חד רובא להכשירה רוב העיר שתשע חנויות שבה מוכרות בשר שחוטה והאחת מוכרת נבילה דליכא מילתא דבעינן ביה (ח) תרתי רובי כדאמרי' התם כגון דלתות מדינות פתוחות ורוב טבחים סביבות המדינה ישראל דליכא למיזל בתר תרי רובי להכשירה רוב העיר ורוב הבאין מחוצה לה: דהא אשה כדלתות המדינה נעולות (ט). כלומר דליכא למימר בה תרתי רובי אלא חד רובא שרוב דמים מן המקור וקא אזלי בה בתר רובא להביא קרבן לעזרה ולשרוף תרומה דמידי דאסור לעשותו מספק הוא: והא רבא הוא דאמר. לעיל רוב ומצוי ליכא למאן דאמר ולא תסייע לר' חנינא הכא מסייע ליה מינה דקאמר ש"מ תלת: (י) מההיא דקרא. של יין: חבית. שם מחוז הוא על נהר פרת כדאמר בקדושין (דף עב.) לענין יוחסין ובגיטין ואין ישראל מצויין שם והוא למעלה מפרת ויכולה חבית לבוא משם אללנו: רב לית ליה דרבי חנינא. ואזיל בתר קורבא ושמואל אזל בתר רובא דאית ליה לדרבי חנינא: עקולי ופשורי הוו טבעי ליה. הרבה מקומות יש משם ועד כאן שהמים מתעקלין ומתגלגלין כגלגל במקום אחד מחמת כיפי סלעים הבאים אל תוך הנהר והמים מכסין עליהם והספינות מתגלגלות שם וטובעות: ופשורי. הפשרות שלגים הנקוים אצל הנהר וקוו וקיימי ואם תבא החבית שם תעמוד שאין הנהר מוליכה: חריפותא דנהרא נקט ואתאי. שמא מתחלה נפלה באמצעית הנהר במקום חזקו ומרוצת המים הביאתה ולא הניחתה לנטות ימין ושמאל: בפרדיסא דערלה. בכרם של ערלה: שרי רבינא. ולא חש שמא מכרם זה גנב היין זה: (כ) אי גניב מיניה אצנועי בגויה לא מצנעי. אין דרך גנבים להצניע היין במקום שגנבוהו משם משום דמתיירא שמא ימלאהו דורכי העינבים: זיקי. נודות: בי קופאי. טמונים בין גפנים שבכרם והיא של ישראל: לימא לא סבר לה לדרבי חנינא. ליזיל אחר הרוב אלא אחר הקרוב וכאן ישראל מצויים יותר מנכרים ולא אזלינן בתר רובא דעלמא: דשפוכאי

תוספות

דכל דמידדי אי הדר חזי לקיניה מידדי. לא היה לריך למתני דקאמר אי הדר חזי לקיניה מידדי כיון דשובכין דעלמא יותר מחמשים מן הכרמים [ח] [לח] ליכא למיחש לרובא דעלמא דכל המדדה אינו מדדה יותר מחמשים אלא הכא שני שובכין שהכרמים בתוך חמשים אמה שלהם אתי שפיר דקרוב לזה שלו אפילו נמלא חוץ לחמשים אמה דלא נפק מתורת מדדה דע"י כרמים מידדי יותר מחמשים אלא איירי דאפילו אם יהו שובכין דעלמא בין הכרמים ועוד מדנקט שביל משמע שאלו ב' השובכין בתוך השביל והניפול כמו כן נמלא בתוך השביל דליכא למיחש שהן משובכין דעלמא אפי' אינם רחוקים כלל כיון דלא מלי חזי לקיניה אבל מאלו שובכין הוא דאין דבר מפסיק בינו לבין השובך: אמר אביי אף אנן נמי תנינא דם הנמצא בפרוזדור טמא כו'. בנמלא בגג פרוזדור מן הלול ולפנים איירי כדמוכח בפרק כל היד (נדה דף יז: ושם ד"ה מן) וסוגיא דהתם מפרש במקומה: ואף על גב דאיכא עלייה דמקרבא. וקרוב דמוכח הוא דקרוב לעלייה הוא ומן החדר אינו יכול לבא אא"כ שתתה ביותר כמו (ל) שפירש במסכת נדה (שם): דתני רבי חייא. אי גרסינן תני אתי שפיר אבל אי גרסינן דתני תימה היכי מייתי מהכא לרוב ומצוי הוא דלמא לאו משום דרוב ומצוי קאמר רבי חייא דשורפין עליו את התרומה אלא משום דרוב וקרוב הלך אחר הרוב כרבי חנינא (מ) וי"ל דאפילו גרס' דתני לא מדברי רבה הוא אלא גמרא הוא דמייתי לה לשפיר הוא מוכח אבי ממתני' דנדה דרוב וקרוב הלך אחר הרוב דאף על גב דקתני ספיקו טמא על כרחך לאו ספיקא הוא מדתני רבי חייא דחייבין עליו על ביאת מקדש ושורפין עליו תרומה. (הג"ה) ומהר"ם אומר דרבה מייתי לה דרוב ומצוי הוא דאי לאו אינו מצוי א"כ מאי קמ"ל רבי חנינא כיון דשמעינן לה מדתני רבי חייא אבל ממתני' דנדה לא היה יכול להוכיח דאפילו אם אינו רוב ומצוי הולכך רבי חנינא לא ימצא ספיקו טמא הוא ספק ממש ולמאי דבעי לה הוא דלא הוי רוב ומצוי אינטריך רבי חנינא לאשמועינן דלי מדתני רבי חייא ה"א דרוב ומצוי הוא קמ"ל ר' חנינא דלאו רוב ומצוי הוא (ע"כ הג"ה): ושמע מינה איתא לדר' זירא. נראה לר"י דאע"ג דטעמא דבעינן תרי רובי הוי משום דגזרינן רוב סיעה אטו רוב העיר מ"מ אינטריך ליה למימר גבי חנות דלא בעינן תרי רובי דאע"ג דליכא למימר הכי מ"מ איכא למיגזר שמא יקח מן הקבוע אי לאו דאיכא רובא דעלמא וגבי אשה נמי אי גזרינן בעלמא הוה לן להחמיר שלא לשרוף משום דם הלול ולפנים אטו מן הלול ולחוץ (נ) ונראה לו דהלכה כרבי חנינא: [ו] הג"ה וש"מ רובא דאורייתא. תשיב ליה רובא דליתיה קמן דברובא דליתיה קמן לא לריך למידק ש"מ דקרא כתיב אחרי רבים להטות כדפריך פרק קמא דחולין (דף יא. ושם) גבי הא דבעי מנ"ל הא דאמרינן זיל בתר רובא ופריך מנ"ל דכתיב אחרי רבים להטות: אימור (ס) מהאי דקרא אתאי. ולאו דוקא נמלאת כנגד עיר שרובה ישראל אסר שמואל אלא אפי' עיר שכולה ישראל איכא למיחש להכי: לימא משום דסבר לה כר' חנינא. וליכא למימר דשריא משום ספק ערלה בחולה לארץ מותרת דהא לא לית ליה כרבי חנינא אלא רוב וקרוב אזלינן בתר קרוב א"כ הוא ודאי ערלה: ואצנועי בגויה. ואם תאמר מ"מ יהא אסור דרובא דעלמא נכרים נינהו והוי יין נסך וי"ל דרוב גנבי ישראל כדאמר בפרק בתרא דע"ז (דף ע.): בי קופאי. פי' בערוך [ז] מקום כדאמרי' (סוטה דף מו:) רב מרדכי אלויה לרב שימי בר אשי לבי קופאי ובכהאי גוונא היה דהוה קורבא דמוכח: לימא רבא לית ליה דר' חנינא. פי' והא רבא אית ליה לעיל דר' חנינא:

מרקיקן

רבינו גרשום

הכא במאי עסקינן דיחלוקו כגון דהוו הנהו שובכין במאה אמה ואותן ק' אמה הן שביל שבין ב' כרמים ונמצא באמצע הדרך שבין הללו שובכין דהשתא ליכא למיחש לרובא דעלמא וכיון דמדדה הוא ודאי מהנך שובכין נפל דאי מעלמא לא מצי אתי דקי"ל כל המדדה והדר חזי לקיניה מדדה ואי לא לא מדדי והאי הואיל דהוי שביל של כרמים מפסיק ומחיצות של שביל מפסקי לא הוי חזי לקיניה ולא מצי אתי מעלמא משום הכי יחלוקו דמהנהו שובכין נפלי: אמר אביי אף אנן נמי תנינא. דרוב וקרוב אזלי בתר רוב דתנן דם הנמצא בפרוזדור ספיקו טמא שחזקתו מן המקור בא שממנו רוב הדמים באין והמקור הוא פנימי מכולן והחדר סמוך למקור והפרוזדור הוא החיצוני ועליה בנויה על גבי שניהם על גבי החדר והפרוזדור ולול פתוח בין עליה ופרוזדור נמצא הדם מן הלול ולפנים ספיקו טמא מן הלול ולחוץ ספיקו טהור ודם הבא מן החדר טמא דמן המקור בא ומן העליה טהור מן הפרוזדור ספיקו טמא שחזקתו מן המקור בא ואע"ג דאיכא עלייה דדמה טהורה דמקרבא לגבי פרוזדור ממקור אזלינן בתר רוב דרוב דמים מן המקור באין: אמר רבא. מהא לא תסייע דרוב ומצוי שאני דדם המקור רוב הוא לכולהו ומצוי בו דם תדיר דתני ר' חייא דם הנמצא בפרוזדור חייבין עליו חטאת על ביאת מקדש אם נכנסה במקדש ואם נגעה בתרומה שורפין עליו את התרומה דלא אמרי' הכא כבשאר ספק טומאר' אם נגעו בתרומ' דתולין לא אוכלין ולא שורפין אבל הכא ודאי שורפין דספיקו ודאי טמא הוא דדם מקור רוב ומצוי ודאי מן המקור בא וטמא: ש"מ מדקתני ושורפין עליו את התרומה מכלל דרובא דאורייתא דרוב דמים מן המקור וש"מ מדקאזיל בתר רוב אע"ג דאתרע רוב במקצת דהא יש דם עלייה דטהור הוא דמקרבא ואפ"ה אזיל בתר רוב ש"מ דאיתא לדר' זירא דאמר בפ"ק דכתובות בהנהו דאמר ר' יוסי מעשה בתינוקת שירדה מן המעיין ונאנסה ואמר ר"ע אם רוב העיר משיאין לכהונה ורוב סיעה של כשרין עוברין לשם הרי זו תינשא לכהונה. ור' זירא אמר אע"ג שדלתות מדינה נעולות דאיתרע לה רובא דליכא אלא חד רובא דלא קא עוברת סיעה של כשרין לשם אפ"ה משיאין לכהונה הואיל דרוב העיר משיאין לכהונה דהא אשה כיון דלית בה אלא חד רוב דרוב דמים מן המקור הן כדלתות מדינה נעולות דמיין ואפ"ה אזלינן בתר רובא: והא רבא הוא דאמר ברוב ומצוי. כגון דם דמקור ליכא מאן דפליג ודאי אזלינן בתר רוב מכלל דס"ל דבעלמא היכא דליכא אלא רוב וקרוב לא אזלינן בתר רוב והיכי אמר הכא ש"מ מדר' חייא דאזלינן בתר רוב דמשמע בכל דוכתא אזלי בתר רוב. הדר ביה רבא מההיא דלעיל דלא בעינן רוב ומצוי אלא דאזלינן בתר כל רוב: חבית של יין שצפה בנהר. ואין ידוע אם יין נכרים הוא אם יין ישראל: אימור מההיא דקירא באה כלומר מאותו עבר הקרייה של מעלה ממנה באה דרובא עיירות דנכרים נינהו. דשמואל אית ליה דר' חנינא ורב לית ליה דר' חנינא: עקולי. כעין שרגילין המים לעקול ולעקול סביב ובאותן מים שהתהום תחתיהן והולכין ומעגלין עד שמטביעין מה שצף על גבן. וכן הני פשורי לאותו מקום שהמים רפין ועומדין שאם היתה חבית זו צפה לשם הואיל שהמים רפין ואינן חריפין היתה נטבעת שם ומש"ה ליכא למיחש דמההיא דקירא אתאי: ושמואל אמר ודאי אסור דאיכא למיחש דמההיא דקירא אתאי והאי דלא טבעי עקולי ופשורי דחריפות' דנהרא שכבר לקחה החבית המרוץ קודם שהגיעה לעקולי ופשורי ונקט ואתאי בשבולת המים והלכך אסירא. לימא. דמש"ה שריא דקסבר כר' חנינא דאמר רוב וקרוב הולכין אחר הרוב והכא האי פרדס דערלה מיעוט הוא לגבי שאר פרדסים דלא הוי ערלה וקרוב דבגויה אשתכח: שאני התם. דמש"ה שריא דליכא למימר דמיניה הוא וההיא חצבא דאי מיגנב מיניה לעולם בגויה לא הוי מצנעי אינשי ומש"ה איכא למימר דמשאר פרדסים דהיתרא הוי ולא משום דס"ל כר' חנינא: והני מילי. דשרי: חמרא. משום דלא מצנעי אינשי חמרא בפרדיסא דגנובי מיניה: אבל ענבי מצנעי. ואסורין: זיקי. נודות יין: בי קופאי. בין הגפנים: שרינהו רבא. משום דהנהו גפנים דישראל נינהו: לימא. מש"ה שרינהו דלית ליה לר' חנינא דאע"ג דרוב שאר גפנים דנכרים נינהו אזיל בתר קרוב הואיל דמשתכחן ביני גופני דישראל דהוה קרוב להנהו זיקי וקסבר רוב וקרוב הלך אחר קרוב: לעולם רבא סבר לה כר' חנינא דודאי אזלינן בתר רוב והתם נמי איכא רוב ישראל ומש"ה שרינהו דרובא דשפוכאי כלומר רובן של אותה העיר שדורכין ושופכין יין ישראל נינהו ועל ידן הולך הכל ואישתכח נמי בי גופני ישראל ודאי ישראל אצנעינהו ומותרין:

והני

דשפובאי ישראל נינהו ^א וה"מ ברברבי אבל זוטרי אימור מעוברי דרכים נפול ^ב ואי איכא רברבי בהדייהו אימור באבורורי הוה מנחי: **מתני'** ^ג מרחיקין את האילן מן העיר עשרים וחמש אמה ובחרוב ובשקמה חמשים אמה אבא שאול אומר כל אילן סרק חמשים אמה (א) ^ד ואם העיר קדמה קוצץ ואינו נותן דמים ואם אילן קדם קוצץ ונותן דמים ^ו ספק זה קדם וספק זה קדם קוצץ ואינו נותן דמים: **גמ'** מאי טעמא אמר עולא ^ה משום נויי העיר ^ו ותיפוק ליה דאין עושין שדה מגרש ולא מגרש שדה לא צריכא לר"א דאמר ^ז עושין שדה מגרש ומגרש שדה הכא משום נויי העיר לא עבדינן ולרבנן נמי דאמרי אין עושין שדה מגרש ולא מגרש שדה ה"מ זרעים אבל אילנות עבדינן והכא משום נויי העיר לא (ב) ומנא תימרא דשאני בין זרעין לאילנות ^ח דתניא ^ז קרפף יותר מבית סאתים שהוקף לדירה נזרע רובו הרי הוא כגינה ואסור ניטע רובו הרי הוא כחצר ומותר: ואם העיר קדמה קוצץ ואינו נותן דמים וכו': מ"ש גבי בור דקתני ^י קוצץ ונותן דמים ומאי שנא הכא דקתני קוצץ ואינו נותן דמים אמר רב כהנא (ג) ^י קידרא דבי שותפי לא חמימא ולא קרירא ומאי קושיא דלמא שאני הזיקא דרבים מהזיקא דיחיד אלא אי איתמר דרב כהנא אסיפא איתמר אם האילן קדם קוצץ ונותן דמים ולימא להו הבו לי ברישא דמי והדר איקוץ אמר רב כהנא קידרא דבי שותפי לא חמימא ולא קרירא: ספק זה קדם וספק זה קדם קוצץ ואינו נותן דמים: מאי שנא מבור דאמרת לא יקוץ התם דודאי לאו למיקץ קאי ספיקו נמי לא אמרינן ליה קוץ הכא דודאי למיקץ קאי ספיקו נמי אמרינן ליה קוץ ואי משום דמי אמרינן ליה אייתי ראיה ושקול: **מתני'** ^ח מרחיקין את גורן קבוע מן העיר חמשים אמה ^ט לא יעשה אדם גורן קבוע בתוך שלו אא"כ יש לו חמשים אמה לכל רוח ומרחיק מנטיעותיו של חבירו ומנירו בכדי שלא יזיק: **גמ'** מ"ש רישא ומאי שנא סיפא אמר אביי סיפא אתאן לגורן שאינו קבוע היכי דמי גורן שאינו קבוע א"ר יוסי בר' חנינא כל שאינו זורה ברחת רב אשי אמר ^י מה טעם קאמר מאי טעמא מרחיקין גורן קבוע מן העיר חמשים אמה כדי שלא יזיק מיתיבי מרחיקין גורן קבוע מן העיר חמשים אמה וכשם שמרחיקין מן העיר חמשים אמה כך מרחיקין מדלועיו ומקשואיו ומנטיעותיו ומנירו של חבירו חמשים אמה כדי שלא יזיק בשלמא לרב אשי ניחא אלא לאביי קשיא קשיא בשלמא ממקשואיו ומדלועיו דאזיל אבקא ואתי בליביה ^ס ומצוי ליה אלא מנירו אמאי א"ר אבא בר זבדא ואיתימא ר' אבא בר זוטרא מפני

שעושה

רש"י

דשפובאי. שופכי יין מן החבית לנודות למכור לעוברי דרכים במדינה זאת כדמסיים ואזיל: **ברברבי.** דליכא למיחש ברוכא דעלמא למימר מעוברי דרכים נפול: **ואי איכא רברבי בהדייהו.** אף הקטנים מותרין דברברבי לאו אורחייהו דעוברי דרכים אלא כולהו (ד) מלוקחי יין של מדינה זו נינהו וישראל הן וקטנים שאין דרך לזוקן יין להביאם: **אימור באבורורי הוה מנחי.** להשוות משא החמור כשיש שתי נודות זה גדול מזה מעט ומכביד המשא לצד אחד מניחין נוד קטן אצלו להשוות המשא: **מתני' מרחיקין את האילן מן העיר.** בגמרא מפרש משום נויי העיר לפי שנוי לעיר כשיש מרחב פנוי לפניה: **חרוב ושקמה.** ענפיהם רבים: **ואילן סרק.** גנאי הוא לעיר: **ונותן דמים.** מי שהעיר שלו: **גמ' ותיפוק ליה דאין עושין שדה.** משנה היא בפ' אחרון של ערכין (דף לג:) ומגרש אלף אמה הוא לעיר וכל אלף אמה אסור לעשותו שדה וקס"ד לא שדה לבן ולא שדה אילן: **לא צריכא לר' אליעזר.** דפליג התם ואמר בד"א בערי הלוים אבל בערי ישראל כו': ה"ג **ולרבנן דאמרי אין עושין הני מילי בזרעים אבל באילנות עושין.** בתוך אלף אמה: **והכא.** בתוך עשרים וחמש אמה משום נויי העיר אין עושין: **קרפף יותר מבית סאתים שהוקף לדירה.** סאתים הוא שיעור חצר המשכן ונתנוהו חכמים שיעור לכל היקף שלא הוקף לדור בתוכו או להשתמש אלא שהוקף לשמור כגון קרפף שבבקעה אבל המוקף לדירה אפי' בית עשרה כורין מטלטלין בו וקאמר הכא יתר מבית סאתים שהוקף לדירה הוא מותר לטלטל בכולו: **נזרע רובו.** בטלו הזרעים שם דירה ממנו והרי הוא כגינה שאין הקפה לדירה הואיל ויותר מבית סאתים הוא אין מטלטלין בו עוד: **אבל ניטע רובו.** באילנות אין האילנות מבטלין תורת דירתו ממנו והרי הוא כחצר שלפני הבתים שהקיפוה לדירה ומותר: **מאי שנא (ה) בור.** דבעינן נמי הרחקה וקתני נמי אם הבור קדמה קוצץ ונותן דמי האילן לבעל האילן: **לא חמימא ולא קרירא.** שזה סומך על זה אף כאן דמי האילן מי יתנם אם באת להטילם על בני העיר כל אחד אומר ממני לא יתחילו ונמצא האילן עומד והעיר מגונה ואין זו תפארת ארץ ישראל: **ומאי קושיא.** מבור לעיר דאיצטריך לשנויי הכי דלמא שאני היזק דרבים מהזיקא דיחיד לא חייבו חכמים לקוץ אילנו בשביל בור היחיד בלא דמים אבל בשביל היזק רבים חייבוהו לקוץ: **לא חמימא כו'.** אם באת להמתין עד מתן מעות יעמוד (ו) זה לאורך ימים בני העיר סומכין זה על זה ובעל האילן רוצה בכך לפיכך יקוץ ואחרי כן יגבה מעותיו מהן בב"ד: **התם.** גבי בור דודאי של אילן אם ודאי קדם לאו למיקץ קאי כדקתני אם האילן קדם לא יקוץ ספיקו נמי לא אמר ליה קוץ שבעל הניזק להביא ראיה: **הכא דודאי.** נמי למיקץ קאי אלא שנוטל דמים כדקתני אם האילן קדם קוצץ ונותן דמים ספיקו נמי אמר ליה קוץ ממ"נ על כרחך וכשבא לגבות דמים אמר ליה אייתי ראיה דאת קדמת ושקול: **מתני' גורן קבוע.** בגמ' מפרש מאי קביעותא: **חמשים אמה.** מפני המוץ המזיק את בני העיר כשהוא זורה וגם הזרעים הוא מייבש: **ומנירו של חבירו.** ובגמרא מפרש מאי היזק דמוץ לניר. ניר היא חרישה שחורשין בימי הקיץ ואין זורעין בו עד ימות החורף כדי שימותו שרשי הקוצים והעשבים כדכתיב נירו לכם ניר ואל תזרעו אל קוצים (ירמיה ד): **בכדי שלא יזיק.** האי שיעורא משמע בציר מחמשים אמה ובגמרא פריך מ"ש מרישא דאמרת אלא אם כן יש לו חמשים אמה לכל רוח: **גמ' שאינו זורה ברחת.** שאין הכרי גדול וא"צ לזרות ברחת אלא הרוח מנשבת בכרי והמוץ נדף מאליו. רחת פל"ה בלע"ז כשהכרי גדול צריך להגביה התבואה ברחת וזורק כלפי מעלה והרוח מנשבת ודוחפת המוץ למרחוק: **רב אשי אמר.** שיעורא דסיפא כרישא ומה טעם קאמר: **מקשואיו ומדלועיו.** נטיעה שהקשואין והדלועין גדלין בה: **בשלמא לרב אשי ניחא.** דקתני בכולהו חמשים אמה: **אלא לאביי קשיא קשיא.** [הכי] גרסינן:

שעושה

תוספות

מרחיקין את האילן [מן העיר] כ"ה אמה. והכא צריך להרחיק מן העיר עד אלף אמה דאין עושין מגרש שדה:

מ"ש מבור דקוצץ ונותן דמים אמר רב כהנא קידרא דבי שותפי כו'. תימה לרשב"א א"כ כשהאילן קדם נמי אמאי נותן דמים מהאי טעמא וי"ל דכשהאילן קדם כיון דסמך בהיתר אין לחוש אם יתעצלו וישאר האילן עומד אבל עוד קשה לו דמאי שייך הכא קידרא דבי שותפי והלא קוצץ תחלה קודם שיתנו דמים ואומר ר"י דה"פ דמשום קידרא דבי שותפי לא חמימא ולא קרירא לא רצו לתקן שיתנו דמים דאע"ג דקוצץ תחלה פעמים שלא ישמע להם לקוץ תחלה אם לא ידע מי יתן לו הדמים וכל אחד ואחד יתרשל ולא יקוץ כדי שלא ליתן דמים כי בעל האילן ידרוש מעמו:

ולימא להו הבו לי ברישא והדר איקוץ. גבי בור לא שייך למיפרך הכי דניחא (ז) כיון שסמך באיסור שיקוץ תחלה:

קשיא לאביי. תימה מאי קשיא ליה הא ברייתא איירי בגורן קבוע ומתני' בגורן שאינו קבוע ויש לומר דאביי גופיה הוה מצי למימר דמה טעם קאמר אי לאו משום דקשיא ליה מה צריך לפרש טעמא כדי שלא יזיק והשתא דברייתא מפרש טעמא כדי שלא יזיק מתני' נמי איכא לפרושי הכי:

שעושה

עין משפט נר מצוה

עה א ב מיי' פי"ג מהל' מאכלות אסורות הל' כו סמג לאוין קמח טוש"ע י"ד סי' קכט סעיף יב:

עו ג מיי' פ"י מהלכות שכנים הל' א סמג עשין פב טוש"ע ח"מ סי' קנה סעיף כג:

עז ד מיי' וסמג שם טוש"ע ח"מ סי' קנה סעיף כב בהג"ה:

עח ה מיי' שם הל' ב סמג שם:

עט ו מיי' פי"ג מהל' שמיטה הל' ד סמג לאוין רעח ופסק כת"ק:

פ ז מיי' פט"ו מהלכות שבת הלכה ו סמג עשין מד"ס ה טוש"ע א"ח סי' שנח סעיף ט:

פא ח ט י מיי' פ"י מהל' שכנים הל' ג סמג עשין פב טוש"ע ח"מ סי' קנה סעיף כג:

מסורת הש"ס

א) [ב"מ קח.], ב) [שם קיב], ג) מכות יב. [ערכין לג:], ד) [ערכין שם], ה) עירובין כג:, ו) [לקמן כה:], ז) עירובין כג:, ח) [פי' שורף ומייבש לתלושים. ערוך].

הגהות הב"ח

(א) במשנה פרק ג' אמה אם כל"ל ואות ו' נמחק: (ב) גמ' לא עבדינן ומנא תימרא דשאני בין זרעים לאילנות: (ג) שם אמר רב כהנא היינו דאמרי אינשי קידרא דבי שותפי: (ד) רש"י ד"ה ואי איכא וכו' מלוקחי יין וכו' וישראל הן הקטנים וכו' מניחין עוד נוד קטן כל"ל והד"א: (ה) ד"ה מ"ש גבי בור וכו' וקתני ביה אם: (ו) ד"ה לא חמימא וכו' יעמוד לאורך כל"ל ותיבת זה נמחק: (ז) תוס' ד"ה ולימא וכו' דניחא ליה כיון:

לעזי רש"י

פל"ה. פירוש רחת, כלי עץ גדול כעין יעה לזרות בו את התבואה (עיין רש"י ישעיה ל, כד).

דִּשְׁפוֹכָאֵי יִשְׂרָאֵל נִינְהוּ — **of those who pour** wine into bags (in order to sell the wine) **are Jews,** if one finds *bags* of wine they most probably fell from a Jew.

The Gemara explains further:

וְהָנֵי מִילֵּי בְּרַבְרְבֵי — **Now, this presumption** is valid **with regard to large [bags],** which are used by wine merchants and not by travelers.[1] אֲבָל זוּטְרֵי — **But** if one finds **small [bags],** the wine in them is forbidden, אֵימוּר מֵעוֹבְרֵי דְרָכִים נָפוּל — for **I could say** that **they fell from travelers,** the majority of whom are non-Jews.

A qualification:

וְאִי אִיכָּא רַבְרְבֵי בַּהֲדַיְיהוּ — **But if there are large [bags]** found **together with [the small ones],** even the small ones are permitted. The large bags must have come from a wine merchant, for travelers do not carry large bags with them. And, as far as the small bags are concerned, אֵימוּר בְּאַבְרוּרֵי הֲוָה מַנְחֵי — **I could say** that **they were placed** on the wine merchant's animal (that was carrying the large bags) **for the sake of balancing** its load.

Mishnah

The Mishnah returns to the subject of items that must be distanced from a neighbor's property:

מַרְחִיקִין אֶת הָאִילָן מִן הָעִיר עֶשְׂרִים וְחָמֵשׁ אַמָּה — **One must distance a tree twenty-five *amos* from** the edge of **a city,** וּבְחָרוּב וּבְשִׁקְמָה — **and a carob or a sycamore** tree, חֲמִשִּׁים אַמָּה — **fifty *amos*.**[2] אַבָּא שָׁאוּל אוֹמֵר — **Abba Shaul says:** כָּל אִילָן סְרָק חֲמִשִּׁים אַמָּה — **All barren trees** must be distanced **fifty *amos*.**[3]

The Mishnah now turns to the law of a tree that has already been planted within the forbidden area:

וְאִם הָעִיר קָדְמָה — **If the city was** there **first** and one planted a tree afterward, קוֹצֵץ וְאֵינוֹ נוֹתֵן דָּמִים — **he must cut down** the tree, **and [the city] need not pay** compensation. וְאִם אִילָן קָדַם — **However, if the tree came first** and the city was built afterward, קוֹצֵץ וְנוֹתֵן דָּמִים — **he must** nevertheless **cut down** the tree, **and** in this case **[the city] pays** compensation.[4] סָפֵק זֶה קָדַם וְסָפֵק זֶה קָדַם — **If it is unclear whether [the tree] or [the city] came first,** קוֹצֵץ — **he must cut down** the tree, וְאֵינוֹ נוֹתֵן דָּמִים — **and [the city] need not pay** compensation.[5]

Gemara

The Gemara seeks the reason for the Mishnah's rule:

מַאי טַעְמָא — **What is the reason** that trees must be distanced from a city?

The Gemara explains:

אָמַר עוּלָּא — **Ulla said:** מִשּׁוּם נוֹיֵי הָעִיר — **For the sake of the city's beautification.**

The Gemara questions the need for the Mishnah to mandate a twenty-five-*amah* clearing:

וְתֵיפּוּק לֵיהּ — **But this** prohibition (to plant trees in the vicinity of a city) has already **emerged**[6] from another Mishnah, which states דְּאֵין עוֹשִׂין שָׂדֶה מִגְרָשׁ — **that** THEY (the inhabitants of a city) MAY NOT TURN FIELDS that are on the outskirts of a city INTO a *MIGRASH* וְלֹא מִגְרָשׁ שָׂדֶה — NOR may they turn a city's *MIGRASH* INTO FIELDS![7] Under that law, it is forbidden to plant anything within the one-thousand-*amah migrash* that borders a city. Why must our Mishnah forbid planting a tree within twenty-five *amos?*

The Gemara answers:

לֹא צְרִיכָא לְרַבִּי אֶלְעָזָר — **[Our Mishnah] is necessary** according **to** the view of **R' Elazar,** דְּאָמַר עוֹשִׂין שָׂדֶה מִגְרָשׁ וּמִגְרָשׁ שָׂדֶה — **who says** that ONE MAY TURN FIELDS INTO *MIGRASH* AND *MIGRASH* INTO FIELDS.[8] הָכָא — Nevertheless, our Mishnah teaches that **here,** within twenty-five *amos* of a city, מִשּׁוּם נוֹיֵי הָעִיר לֹא עַבְדִינַן — **for the sake of the city's beautification, trees may not [be planted].** וּלְרַבָּנַן נַמִּי — **And** according **to the Rabbis as well,** דְּאָמְרֵי אֵין עוֹשִׂין שָׂדֶה מִגְרָשׁ וְלֹא מִגְרָשׁ שָׂדֶה — **who say** that ONE MAY NOT TURN FIELDS INTO *MIGRASH* NOR *MIGRASH* INTO FIELDS, our Mishnah's ruling is necessary, because הָנֵי מִילֵּי זְרָעִים — **that** law against planting in a *migrash* **applies to grain,**[9] אֲבָל אִילָנוֹת עַבְדִינַן — **but trees may be [planted]** in a *migrash.*[10] וְהָכָא — **Nevertheless,** our Mishnah teaches that **here,** within twenty-five *amos* of a city, מִשּׁוּם נוֹיֵי הָעִיר לֹא — **for the sake of the city's beautification,** trees may **not** be planted.

The Gemara seeks a source for the distinction it made between trees and grain:

וּמְנָא תֵּימְרָא — **And how do we know**[11] דְּשָׁאנֵי בֵּין זְרָעִין לְאִילָנוֹת — **that there is a distinction between grain and trees,** with regard to planting in a *migrash?*

The Gemara answers:

דְּתַנְיָא — We know it **for we have been taught in a Baraisa:** קַרְפֵּף יוֹתֵר מִבֵּית סָאתַיִם — With regard to A *KARPAF* GREATER THAN TWO *BEIS SE'AH* שֶׁהוּקַף לְדִירָה — WHICH WAS ENCLOSED FOR RESIDENTIAL USE, thus making it permissible to carry in it on

NOTES

1. Therefore, if the bags that were found were large, there are no grounds for assuming that they fell from travelers (*Rashi*).

2. The Gemara explains that it is considered aesthetically pleasing for a city to be framed by an expanse of open land. Therefore, no tree may be planted in the immediate vicinity of a city's boundary. Carob and sycamore trees must be distanced further than other trees because their branches are more numerous (*Rashi*). This law applies only to cities in Eretz Yisrael (*Rashi* to Gemara ד״ה לא חמימא; *Tur Choshen Mishpat* 155:27) and only when the land is in the hands of the Jewish people (*Beis Yosef* ad loc.).

3. The presence of trees that do not bear fruit in the vicinity of a city is considered unbecoming to the city (*Rashi*). Such trees must therefore be distanced further than trees that bear fruit.

4. Although the tree was planted legally, it must be cut down because the public interest takes precedence over the rights of the individual. (Nevertheless, the tree's owner is compensated for his loss.) This stands in contrast to the law of a tree that was planted legally and afterward became a nuisance to an individual neighbor. In that case, the tree is not cut down (see Mishnah, 25b and *Ramban* here).

5. This ruling is explained in the Gemara.

6. Literally: but let this emerge.

7. (*Arachin* 33b). In earlier times, cities in Eretz Yisrael were bordered by an open expanse of land one thousand *amos* wide. This open expanse was known as a *migrash.* Another thousand *amos* around that expanse was reserved for fields which the cities' inhabitants would cultivate. The Mishnah cited here teaches that it is forbidden to convert either of these areas from its original use to a different function. The *migrash* immediately outside a city must be maintained as such in order to preserve the aesthetic quality of the city, and the fields must be maintained as such to ensure that the national food supply is not threatened (*Rashi* to *Arachin* ibid.).

8. R' Elazar maintains that only with respect to cities reserved for Levites is it forbidden to convert the *migrash* into fields and vice versa (*Rashi*), because the Torah mandates that the *migrash* and fields of the Levites' cities be preserved. With respect to other cities in Eretz Yisrael, R' Elazar's view is that the allocation of land surrounding the city is left to the choice of its owners (see *Arachin* 33b and *Tos. Yom Tov, Arachin* 9:8).

9. Or other types of plants.

10. The reason for this distinction will emerge from the Gemara's discussion.

11. Literally: from where do you [learn to] say.

עין משפט נר מצוה

עה א ב מיי׳ פי״ג מהל׳ מלוה ולוה הל׳ ... כמג לאוין קמא טוש״ע חו״מ סי׳ ...

עו ג מיי׳ פ״י מהלכות שכנים הל׳ ב סמג עשין פב טוש״ע ח״מ סי׳ קנה:

עז ד מיי׳ ... וסמג שם טוש״ע ח״מ סי׳ קנה סעיף כב בהג״ה:

עח ה מיי׳ שם הל׳ א סמג שם:

עט ו מיי׳ פי״ג מהל׳ שמיטה הל׳ ד סמג לאוין רעט ופסק כת״ק:

פ ז מיי׳ פט״ו מהלכות שבת הלכה ג סמג עשין מד״ס טוש״ע א״ח סי׳ שנח סעיף ט:

פא ח ט י מיי׳ פ״י מהל׳ שכנים הל׳ ג סמג עשין פב טוש״ע ח״מ סי׳ קנה סעיף כב:

רבינו גרשום

והני מילי. דמותרין היכא דהנהו זיקי רברבי נינהו אבל אי משתכחי זוטרי ודאי אסור דאימר מעוברי דרכים נפלו: ואי איכא רברבי ואשכח זוטרי בהדידהו אסירי. דחיישי׳ דמעוברי דרכים נפל דאימור באבורוי קא מנחי על גבי החמור כעין שקושרין עוברי דרכים נודותיהן על גבי חמוריהן וקושרין מצד החמור נוד גדול ומצד השני כמותו ומשימין בין שתי נודות הללו נוד אחד קטן והם נמצאו גדולים כה״ג וקטנים עמהן ודאי מעוברי דרכים נפול ומשאוי חמור ואסירי. ל״מ. ואי איכא רברבי בינייהו. אפי׳ דזוטרי מותרין דאימור באבוראי הונחו ושפוכי ישראל אנחינהו להתם כעין שרגילין לעשות כדפרישית לעיל באידך לישנא והכי עיקר: פיסקא מרחיקין את האילן מן העיר כ״ה [אמה]. מפרש בגמ׳ טעמ׳ מאי: בחרוב ובשקמה נ׳ אמה. משום דאיכא תרתי לריעותא חדא דאין פירותיהן שוין ועוד שענפיהן מרובין משאר אילנות: מ״ט. מרחיקין: אמר עולא משום נויי העיר. שיהיה משויר מישור יפה סמוך לעיר בלא שום עיכוב. ועולא למה ליה למימר משום נויי העיר מרחיקין תיפוק ליה דאין עושין שדה שיש בו זרע או אילנות אין עושין מגרש ולא מגרש שדה כדגרסי׳ בגמ׳ ה) מכות לגבי מגרש לוים [דכתיב] ומדותם מחוץ לעיר וגו׳ משום דהוי ג) להם לוים דכתיב ומגרשיהם יהיו לבהמתם וגו׳ להכי ג) צריכי אלפים אמה מגרש אבל שאר הערים בכ״ה אמה מגרש סגיא: לא צריכא לר״א דאמר עושין שדה מגרש ד) להיכא דזרע או נטע אילן בתוך כ״ה אמה סמוך לעיר: הני מילי דאין עושין להיכ׳ דזרע [דא״א] למיזל תחותיה בזרעים משום דקא מזקי זרעים לבני העיר דלא מצי למדרס בזרעים אבל אילן דמצי למיזל תחותיה ה) דאפי׳ אילנות

מרחיקין

מרחיקין את האילן [מן העיר] כ״ה אמה. וזרעים לריך להרחיק מן העיר עד אלף אמה דאין עושין מגרש שדה:

מ״ש מבור דקוצץ ונותן דמים אמר רב כהנא קידרא דבי שותפי כו׳. תימה לרשב״א א״כ כשהאילן קדם נמי אמאי נותן דמים מהאי טעמא וי״ל דכשהאילן קדם כיון דסמך בהיתר אין לחוש אם יתעצלו וישאר האילן עומד אבל עוד קשה לו דמאי שייך הכא קידרא דבי שותפי והלא קוצץ תחלה קודם שיתנו דמים ואומר ר״י דה״פ דמשום קידרא דבי שותפי לא חיימא ולא קרירא לא רצו לתקן שיתנו דמים לאע״ג דקוצץ תחלה פעמים שלא ישמע להם לקוץ תחלה אם לא ידע מי יתן לו הדמים וכל אחד ואחד יתרשל ולא יקוץ כדי שלא ליתן דמים כי בעל האילן ידרוש מעמו:

ולימא להו הבו לי ברישא והדר איקוץ. גבי בור לא שייך למיפרך הכי דניחא (ז) כיון שסמך באיסור שיקוץ תחלה:

קשיא לאביי. תימה מאי קשיא ליה הא ברייתא איירי בגורן קבוע ומתניתין בגורן שאינו קבוע וים לומר דלאביי גופיה הוה משני דמה טעם קאמר אי לאו משום דקשיא ליה מה לריך לפרש טעמא כדי שלא יזיק והשתא דברייתא מפרש טעמא כדי שלא יזיק מתני׳ נמי איכא לפרושי הכי:

דשפוכאי ישראל נינהו [א] וה״מ ברברבי אבל זוטרי אימור מעוברי דרכים נפול [ב] ואי איכא רברבי בהדייהו אימור באברורי הוה מנחי:

מתני׳ [א] [ג] מרחיקין את האילן מן העיר עשרים וחמש אמה ובחרוב ובשקמה חמשים אמה אבא שאול אומר כל אילן סרק חמשים אמה (א) [ד] ואם העיר קדמה קוצץ ואינו נותן דמים ואם אילן קדם קוצץ ונותן דמים [ה] ספק זה קדם וספק זה קדם קוצץ ואינו נותן דמים:

גמ׳ מאי טעמא אמר עולא [ו] משום נויי העיר [ז] ותיפוק ליה דאין עושין שדה מגרש ולא מגרש שדה לא צריכא לר״א דאמר [ח] [ט] עושין שדה מגרש ומגרש שדה הכא משום נויי העיר לא עבדינן ולרבנן נמי דאמרי אין עושין שדה מגרש ולא מגרש שדה ה״מ זרעים אבל אילנות עבדינן והכא משום נויי העיר לא (ב) ומנא תימרא דשאני בין זרעין לאילנות [ט] דתניא [י] קרפף יותר מבית סאתים שהוקף לדירה נזרע רובו הרי הוא כגינה ואסור ניטע רובו הרי הוא כחצר ומותר: ואם העיר קדמה קוצץ ואינו נותן דמים וכו׳: מ״ש גבי בור [י] דקתני [ז] קוצץ ונותן דמים ומאי שנא הכא דקתני קוצץ ואינו נותן דמים אמר רב כהנא (ג) [ב] קידרא דבי שותפי לא חמימא ולא קרירא ומאי קושיא דלמא שאני היזקא דרבים מהזיקא דיחיד אלא אי איתמר דרב כהנא אסיפא איתמר אם האילן קדם קוצץ ונותן דמים ולימא להו הבו לי ברישא דמי והדר איקוץ אמר רב כהנא קידרא דבי שותפי לא חמימא ולא קרירא: ספק זה קדם וספק זה קדם קוצץ ואינו נותן דמים: מאי שנא מבור דאמרת לא יקוץ התם הוא דודאי לאו למיקץ קאי ספיקו נמי לא אמרינן ליה קוץ הכא דודאי למיקץ קאי ספיקו נמי אמרינן ליה קוץ ואי משום דמי אמרינן ליה אייתי ראיה ושקול:

מתני׳ [ח] מרחיקין את גורן קבוע מן העיר חמשים אמה [ט] לא יעשה אדם גורן קבוע בתוך שלו אא״כ יש לו חמשים אמה לכל רוח ומרחיק מנטיעותיו של חבירו ומנירו בכדי שלא יזיק:

גמ׳ מ״ש רישא ומאי שנא סיפא אמר אביי סיפא אתאן לגורן שאינו קבוע היכי דמי גורן שאינו קבוע א״ר יוסי בר׳ חנינא כל שאינו זורה ברחת רב אשי אמר [י] מה טעם קאמר מאי טעמא מרחיקין גורן קבוע מן העיר חמשים אמה כדי שלא יזיק מיתיבי מרחיקין גורן קבוע מן העיר חמשים אמה וכשם שמרחיקין מן העיר חמשים אמה כך מרחיקין מדלועיו ומקשואיו ומנטיעותיו ומנירו של חבירו חמשים אמה כדי שלא יזיק בשלמא לרב אשי ניחא אלא לאביי קשיא קשיא בשלמא ממקשואיו ומדלועיו דאזיל אבקא ואתי בליביה [כ] ומצוי ליה אלא מנירו אמאי א״ר אבא בר זבדא ואיתימא ר׳ אבא בר זוטרא מפני

שעושה

דשפוכאי. שופכי יין מן החבית לנודות למכור לעוברי דרכים במדינה זאת כדמפרש ואזיל: ברברבי. דליכא למיחש לרובא דעלמא למימר מעוברי דרכים נפול: ואי איכא רברבי בהדייהו. אף הקטנים מותרין דברברבי לאו אורחייהו לעוברי דרכים אלא כולהו (ד) מלוקח יין של מדינה זו נינהו וישראל הן וקטנים שאין דרך ללוקח יין להביאם: אימור באברורי הוה מנחי. להשוות משא החמור כשיש שתי נודות זה גדול מזה מעט ומכביד המשא לצד אחד מניחין נוד קטן אצלו להשוות המשא: **מתני׳** מרחיקין את האילן מן העיר. בגמרא מפרש משום נוי העיר לפי שנוי לעיר כשיש מרחב פנוי לפניה: חרוב ושקמה. ענפיהם רבים: ואילן סרק. נמי: ואם העיר קדמה. כגון שנטעו בתוך כ״ה אמה סמוך לעיר: ונותן דמים. מי שהעיר שלו: **גמ׳** ותיפוק ליה דאין עושין מגרש שדה. משנה היא בפ׳ אחרון של ערכין (דף לג:) ומגרש אלף אמה הוא וכל תוך אלף אמה אסור לעשותו שדה וקס״ד לא שדה לבן ולא שדה אילן: לא צריכא לר׳ אליעזר. דפליג התם ואמר בד״א בערי הלוים אבל בערי ישראל כו׳: ה״ג ולרבנן דאמרי אין עושין הני מילי בזרעים אבל באילנות עושין. בתוך אלף אמה: והכא. בתוך עשרים וחמש אמה משום נוי העיר אין עושין: קרפף יותר מבית סאתים שהוקף לדירה. סאתים הוא שיעור חצר המשכן ונתנוהו חכמים שיעור לכל היקף שלא הוקף לדור בתוכו או להשתמש מן הבית לתוכו כגון קרפף שבבקעה אבל המוקף לדירה אפי׳ בית עשרה כורין מטלטלין בו וקאמר הכא יותר מבית סאתים שהוקף לדירה הוא מותר לטלטל בכולו: נזרע רובו. בטלו הזרעים שם דירה ממנו והרי הוא כגינה שאין הקפה לדירה הואיל ויותר מבית סאתים הוא אין מטלטלין בו עוד: אבל ניטע רובו. באילנות אין האילנות מבטלין תורת דירתו ממנו והרי הוא כחצר שלפני הבתים שהקיפום לדירה ומותר: מאי שנא (ה) בור. דבעינן נמי הרחקה וקתני נמי אם הבור קדמה קוצץ ונותן בעל הבור דמי האילן לבעל האילן: לא חמימא ולא קרירא. שזה סומך על זה אף כאן דמי האילן מי יתנם אם באת להטילם על בני העיר כל אחד אומר ממני לא יתחילו ונמלא האילן עומד והעיר מגונה ואין זו תפארת ארץ ישראל: ומאי קושיא. מבור לעיר דלאטרחיך לשנויי הכי דלמא שאני היזק דרבים מהזיקא דיחיד דלא חייבו חכמים לקוץ אילנו בשביל בור היחיד בלא דמים אבל בשביל היזק רבים חייבוהו לקוץ: לא חמימא כו׳. אם באת להמתין עד מתן מעות יעמוד (ו) זה לצורך ימים בני העיר סומכין זה על זה ובעל האילן רוצה בכך שיקוץ ואחרי כן יגבה מעותיו מהן בב״ד: התם. גבי בור דודאי של אילן קדם ודאי לאו למיקץ קאי שהרי לא קדם אלא אם הוא קדם לכדקתני אם האילן קדם לא יקוץ ספיקו נמי לא אמר ליה קוץ שעל הניזק להביא ראיה: הכא דודאי. נמי למיקץ קאי אלא שנוטל דמים כדקתני אם האילן קדם קוצץ ונותן דמים ספיקו נמי אמר ליה קוץ מ״מ על כרחך וכשבא לגבות דמים אמר ליה אייתי ראיה דאת קדמת ושקול: **מתני׳** גורן קבוע. בגמ׳ מפרש מאי קביעותא: חמשים אמה. מפני המוץ המזיק את בני העיר כשהוא זורה וגם הזרעים הוא מייבש: ומנירו של חבירו. ובגמרא מפרש מאי היזק דמוץ לניר. ניר היא חרישה שחורשין בימי הקיץ ואין זורעין בו עד ימות החורף כדי שימותו שרשי הקוצים והעשבים כדכתיב נירו לכם ניר ואל תזרעו אל קוצים (ירמיה ד): בכדי שלא יזיק. האי שיעורא משמע בציר מחמשים אמה ובגמרא פריך מ״ש מרישא דלאמרת אלא אם כן יש לו חמשים אמה לכל רוח: **גמ׳** שאינו זורה ברחת. שאין הכרי גדול וא״צ לזרות ברחת אלא הרוח מנשבת בכרי והמוץ נדף מאליו. רחת פל״ה בלע״ז כשהכרי גדול צריך להגביה התבואה ברחת וזורק כלפי מעלה והרוח מנשבת ודוחפת המוץ למרחוק: רב אשי אמר. שיעורא דסיפא כרישא ומה טעם קאמר: מקשואיו ומדלועיו. נטיעה שהקשואין והדלועין גדלין בה: בשלמא לרב אשי ניחא. דקתני בכולהו חמשים אמה: אלא לאביי קשיא קשיא. [הכי] גרסינן:

שעושה

מסורת הש״ס

א) [ב״מ קח.], ב) [שם קז:], ג) מכות יב. [ערכין לג.], ד) [ערכין שם], ה) עירובין כג., ו) [לקמן כה:], ז) עירובין כג., ח) [פי׳ שורף ומייבש לתלושים. ערוך]:

הגהות הב״ח

(א) במשנה סרק נ׳ אמה אם כו׳ צ״ל ותוס׳ ד׳ נמחק: (ב) גמ׳ לא עבדינן ומנא תימרא דשאני בין זרעים לאילנות: (ג) שם אמר רב כהנא היינו דאמרי אינשי קידרא דבי שותפי: (ד) רש״י ד״ה ואי איכא וכו׳ מלוקחי יין וכו׳ וישראל הן הקטנים וכו׳ מניחין עוד נוד קטן כצ״ל והד״א: (ה) ד״ה מ״ש גבי בור וכו׳ וקתני ביה אם: (ו) ד״ה לא חמימא וכו׳ יעמוד לצורך כצ״ל ותיבת זה נמחק: (ז) תוס׳ ד״ה ולימא וכו׳ דניחא ליה כיון:

לעזי רש״י

פל״ה. פירוש רחת, כלי עץ גדול כעין כף לזרות בו את התבואה (עיין רש״י ישעיה ל, כד).

ליקוטי רש״י

ספק זה קדם וספק זה קדם קוצץ. כיון דבין הכי ובין הכי קוצץ למיקץ קאי דכי קדם אילן נמי קוצץ כי מספקא לן אמרינן קוץ ומנא נפשך ... שהרי עליך לעשות נחלה הספק מוטל על הדמים ולא על קציצת האילן ... גבי אילן הסמוך לבור יחיד קתני בה גבי ודאי דקדים אם הבור קודם ... קוצץ ונותן דמים אם האילן קדם לא יקוץ תנן גבי ספק זה קדם וספק זה קדם לא יקוץ [ב״ק ...]. שדה מגרש. מגרש הוי אלף אמה סביב לעיר מלכתחילה (במדבר לה) מקיף העיר ותולה אלף אמה סביב וזה שאמרו לעשות אלף הוי להם ללוים אלף אמה לשדות וכרמים ... ומדותם מחוץ לעיר וגו׳ לא תהא אלף אמה מגרש והשאר שדות וכרמים מגרש פנוי מכלום ואין בו בית ואין זורעין אותן אלא נוי הוא לעיר אין עושין שדה מגרש. משום ישוב ארץ ישראל והיינו חורבן שממעט את הזריעה. ולא מגרש שדה. שמחריב את נוי העיר [ערכין לג:]. נזרע רובו. מרמעים ביטל דירתו דזרעונים לא לדירי אינשי והוא ליה גינה ואסור לטלטל בו שאינו מוזע. ניטע רובו. אילנות לא ביטל דירתו לאורחא להסתופף בצל אילנות תמיד [עירובין כג:]. דקתני קוצץ ונותן דמים. דכיון דברשות נטע שאינו מזיק עד זמן גדול לא חייבוהו חכמים לקוץ בלא דמים בשביל היזקא דיחיד [לקמן כה:].

קרפף שהוא יותר מבית סאתים. כחצר המשכן **שהוקף** לשום **דירה** אם **נזרע רובו הרי הוא כגינה** דזריעה היא **ואסור** ליליך בה בשבת משום דמדרסי זרעים ואיכא חלול שבת: **נטע רובו** מאילנות הרי הוא כחצר ומותר. משום אין נוטעין משום נויי העיר: **מ״ש גבי עיר דקתני** אם העיר קדמה **קוצצין ואין נותן דמים ומ״ש גבי בור דקתני** אם הבור קדמה **קוצץ ונותן דמים אמר רב (הונא) [כהנא]** מש״ה גבי עיר דמצי למיזל בין אילן לאילן. ואיכא דאמרי כשדה אסור לטלטל בו כחצר מותר לטלטל בו: **מ״ש גבי עיר** ... **דקידרה דבי שותפי לא חמימא ולא קרירא** שזה סומך על זה וזה על זה אבל גבי בור כיון דמיחיד אתי למגבי לא סמך אלא חד וידע אינו נותן דמים משום דליכא למיקם עלה דמלתא. למאן שאיל דמים הואיל ומרבים אתי למגבי סמכי אהדדי ולא יהבי כלום ... למאן שאיל דמים ומש״ה קוצצין ונותן דמים. ודלמא משום האי טעמא לא מצית למימר גבי עיר ... קדמה העיר לקדם הבור **דשני היזק דיחיד מהיזק דרבים** ... **והדר איקוץ אמר רב כהנא** ... **דקידרא דבי שותפי לא חמימא ולא קרירא** ... **ומ״ש מבור** דאמר ספק זה ... **פיסקא מרחיקין גורן קבוע מן העיר חמשים אמה.** משום דקא מזיק התבן שזורין מן קדם **לא יקוץ. התם** באילן דבור כיון **דודאי** דהיכא דידעי׳ דודאי דהאילן קדם **לא יקוץ ספיקו נמי לא יקוץ. קאי ז) זיל אייתי ראיה** דאילנך קדם **ושקול** דמיך: ... **רב אשי אמר.** סיפא ורישא חדא טעמא הוא **דמה טעם** מרחיק נ׳ אמה מן העיר כדי שלא יזיק נטיעות ולנירו: **בשלמא לרב אשי.** דמפרש התבואה לבני העיר: מ״ש דגורן מרחיק נ׳ אמה. ולגבי נטיעות מרחיקין בכדי שלא יזיק דהיינו בציר מחמשים אמה: **קשיא. בשלמא מקשואין ומדלועין** מש״ה צריך להרחיק חמשים אמה טעמא דמתני׳ **ניחא** דכן הכי נמי קתני בברייתא **אלא לאביי קשיא** דמתרץ סיפא לגורן שאינו קבוע והא קתני רישא דברייתא מרחיקין מן מקשואין ומדלועין דהיינו נטיעות נ׳ אמה: **קשיא.** ... **דאזיל התבן** ויתיב על פרח. **בליביה.** פרח. כמו ויצא פרח שתרגומו ואפיק לבלבין: **ומצבי ליה.** ומנפחו ומיבשו: **מפני שעושין אותו גלל.** התבואה הזריעה בקרקע תיעשה זבל ותירקב:

חשק שלמה על רבינו גרשום א) נ״ל כמש׳ ערכין דף לג. ב) אולי צ״ל משום דהוי לורך לוים וכו׳. ג) עי׳ סוטה כז במשנה ועירובין דף נו ע״ב ול״ע. ד) נראה דל״ל ומגרש שדה מ״מ להיכא וכו׳ סמוך לעיר אסור. ה) ר״ל עבדינן אבל בתוך כ״ה אפי׳ אילנות וכו׳. ו) עי׳ מד״ס ולימא ודו״ק. ז) נ״ל הכא דוודאי למיקץ קאי ספיקו נמי אמרינן ליה קוץ וזיל אייתי ראיה.

Shabbos despite its size:[12] נִזְרַע רוּבּוֹ – If A MAJORITY OF IT WAS then SOWN WITH SEED,[13] הֲרֵי הוּא כְּגִינָּה וְאָסוּר – [THE *KARPAF*] IS COMPARABLE TO A GARDEN AND [CARRYING] in it IS PROHIBITED. Since a garden is not suitable for dwelling, the *karpaf* has lost its residential designation.[14] נִיטַּע רוּבּוֹ – However, IF MOST OF [THE *KARPAF*] WAS PLANTED WITH TREES, הֲרֵי הוּא כְּחָצֵר וּמוּתָּר – IT IS COMPARABLE TO A COURTYARD, AND [CARRYING] in it IS PERMITTED. Since people stroll in the wooded area, it retains its status as a *karpaf* designated for residential use.[15] We learn from this Baraisa that sowing an open area with seed is considered a modification of the area's function, while planting it with trees is not. Accordingly, it is permissible to plant trees in a *migrash.*[16]

The Mishnah states:

וְאִם הָעִיר קָדְמָה קוֹצֵץ וְאֵינוֹ נוֹתֵן דָּמִים וכו׳ – IF THE CITY WAS there FIRST and the tree was planted afterward, HE MUST CUT DOWN the tree, AND [THE CITY] NEED NOT PAY compensation **etc.**

The Gemara contrasts this law with a law stated in another Mishnah:

מַאי שְׁנָא גַּבֵּי בּוֹר – **What is the difference between the case of** a tree that was planted illegally within twenty-five *amos* of **a** neighbor's **pit,** דְּקָתָנֵי – with regard to **which [the Mishnah] teaches:** קוֹצֵץ וְנוֹתֵן דָּמִים – HE (the tree's owner) MUST CUT DOWN the tree, AND [THE PIT'S OWNER] PAYS compensation,[17] וּמַאי שְׁנָא הָכָא – **and this** case (of a tree planted illegally within twenty-five *amos* of a city), דְּקָתָנֵי – with regard to **which [the Mishnah] teaches:** קוֹצֵץ וְאֵינוֹ נוֹתֵן דָּמִים – HE (the tree's owner) MUST CUT DOWN the tree, AND [THE CITY] NEED NOT PAY compensation? Why is a city not required to pay compensation just as the owner of a pit is?

The Gemara answers:

אָמַר רַב כַּהֲנָא – **Rav Kahana said:** קִידְרָא דְּבֵי שׁוּתְּפֵי לֹא חֲמִימָא וְלֹא קְרִירָא – **A pot** in the charge **of two** cooks **is neither hot nor cold,** because each one relies on the other to do the necessary work.[18] I.e. were he free from cutting down the tree unless the city paid compensation, it would never be cut down because none of the city's residents will consent to make the first contribution toward this cause.[19]

The Gemara challenges the premise of the original question:

וּמַאי קוּשְׁיָא – **But what difficulty** do these contrasting Mishnahs present? דִּלְמָא שָׁאנֵי הֶזֵּיקָא דְּרַבִּים מֵהֶזֵּיקָא דְּיָחִיד – **Perhaps damage** inflicted **on the public is different than damage** inflicted **on an individual.** Therefore, although one is compensated for cutting down a tree whose roots threaten an individual's pit, there is no compensation for cutting down a tree that mars public property.[20]

The Gemara accepts this rationale, and retracts its assertion that Rav Kahana's statement was made in regard to the previous question:

אֶלָּא אִי אִיתְּמַר דְּרַב כַּהֲנָא – **Rather, if Rav Kahana's** answer **was stated** in reference to our Mishnah, אַסֵּיפָא אִיתְּמַר – **it was stated in regard to** a difficulty presented by **the latter case** of the Mishnah, which states: אִם הָאִילָן קָדַם קוֹצֵץ וְנוֹתֵן דָּמִים – IF THE TREE CAME FIRST and the city was built afterward, HE MUST CUT DOWN the tree, AND [THE CITY] PAYS compensation.

The Gemara describes the difficulty presented by this ruling:

וְלֵימָא לְהוּ – **But let [the tree's owner] say to [the city's residents]:** הָבוּ לִי בְּרֵישָׁא דְּמֵי וַהֲדַר אִיקוּץ – "Pay **me first and I will then cut** down the tree." Why must he cut down the tree before he receives payment?[21]

Rav Kahana resolved this difficulty:

אָמַר רַב כַּהֲנָא – **Rav Kahana said:** קִידְרָא דְּבֵי שׁוּתְּפֵי לֹא חֲמִימָא וְלֹא קְרִירָא – **A pot** in the charge **of two** cooks **is neither hot nor cold.** I.e. were he entitled to let the tree remain until he was paid, it would never be cut down because none of the city's residents would consent to be the first to pay. Therefore, the Sages required him to cut it down first, and, if the city's residents do not pay, he may demand compensation in court.

The Mishnah states:

סָפֵק זֶה קָדַם וְסָפֵק זֶה קָדַם קוֹצֵץ וְאֵינוֹ נוֹתֵן דָּמִים – If it is UNCLEAR WHETHER [THE TREE] OR [THE CITY] CAME FIRST, HE MUST CUT DOWN the tree, AND [THE CITY] NEED NOT PAY compensation.

The Gemara contrasts this law with a law stated in another Mishnah:

מַאי שְׁנָא מִבּוֹר – **Why is** the law in this case **different than** the law of a tree that has been planted near **a** neighbor's **pit,** דְּאָמְרַתְּ לֹא יָקוּץ – **where [the Mishnah] states**[22] that if it is unclear

NOTES

12. [It is Biblically forbidden to transport an object four *amos* in a רְשׁוּת הָרַבִּים (*a public domain;* i.e. an unenclosed public area or thoroughfare) on Shabbos.] The Sages decreed that it also be forbidden to carry an object four *amos* within an enclosure that is larger than the Tabernacle courtyard, whose area was two *beis se'ah* (5,000 square *amos*). However, they applied this decree only to large enclosures (*karpafs*) that are designated for non-residential use. If a *karpaf* was enclosed for the purpose of residential use (i.e. to be lived in, or to serve as the courtyard of a house), it is permissible to carry within the *karpaf* regardless of its size. This Baraisa discusses the law of a *karpaf* greater than two *beis se'ah* that was originally enclosed for residential use and in which carrying was therefore permitted, but was later converted to a different function (*Rashi*).

13. The verb זרע refers to planting or sowing things other than trees. The verb for planting trees is נטע.

14. Accordingly, carrying for four *amos* is forbidden throughout the *karpaf,* since it is larger than two *beis se'ah* (*Rashi*).

15. This *karpaf* is similar to a courtyard in front of a house, which is considered an enclosure designated for residential use (*Rashi*).

16. The Gemara draws an analogy from the law of a *karpaf* to the law of a *migrash.* Just as planting trees does not effect a change in the status of a residential *karpaf* because the area remains suitable for strolling, so too it does not alter the status of a *migrash.* An area which can be used by a city's residents for leisure meets the criteria for *migrash* (*Ritva*).

17. The Mishnah below (25b) states that one may not plant a tree within twenty-five *amos* of a neighbor's pit because the tree's roots will eventually spread a great distance and may breach the walls of the pit. If a tree was planted illegally, its owner must cut it down but he is compensated for its loss by his neighbor (see 25b note 35).

18. This was a popular folk saying in Talmudic times (see *Eruvin* 3a).

19. Therefore, to ensure that the beauty of Eretz Yisrael is preserved, the Sages ruled that a tree planted outside a city is cut down without compensation (*Rashi*). On the other hand, in a case where the tree threatens an individual neighbor, it is up to the affected party to pay compensation if he wishes to have the tree removed.

20. [One who does actual monetary damage to property belonging to an individual is no less liable than one who damages public property. However, a tree planted within twenty-five *amos* of a neighbor's pit does not do any damage for which its owner is liable, because any damage that it might cause is merely an indirect result of planting the tree (*Ramban, Kuntres Dina DeGarmi*). Nevertheless, in both cases the Sages required the tree's owner to cut it down because it is a nuisance to others.] The Gemara reasons that while the Sages would not have required him to cut down the tree without compensation where it is merely disturbing to an individual neighbor, they may have required him to do so where his tree mars public property (*Rashi*).

21. Since the tree was planted legally before the city was built and he is being forced to cut it down with compensation for the sake of the city's beautification, he is in effect selling his tree to the city. As such, he should not be required to cut it down until he receives payment (*Ramban;* see also *Tosafos* ד״ה ולימא).

22. Below, 25b.

דשפוכאי ישראל נינהו [א] וה"מ ברברבי אבל זוטרי אימור מעוברי דרכים נפול [ב] ואי איכא רברבי בהדייהו אימור באברורי הוה מנחי:

מתני' [ג] מרחיקין את האילן מן העיר עשרים וחמש אמה ובחרוב ובשקמה חמשים אמה אבא שאול אומר כל אילן סרק חמשים אמה (א) ואם העיר קדמה קוצץ ואינו נותן דמים ואם אילן קדם קוצץ ונותן דמים ספק זה קדם וספק זה קדם קוצץ ואינו נותן דמים:

גמ' מאי טעמא אמר עולא משום נויי העיר ותיפוק ליה דאין עושין שדה מגרש ולא מגרש שדה לא צריכא לר"א דאמר עושין שדה מגרש ומגרש שדה הכא משום נויי העיר לא עבדינן ולרבנן נמי דאמרי אין עושין שדה מגרש ולא מגרש שדה ה"מ זרעים אבל אילנות עבדינן והכא משום נויי העיר לא (ב) ומנא תימרא דשאני בין זרעין לאילנות דתניא קרפף יותר מבית סאתים שהוקף לדירה נזרע רובו הרי הוא כגינה ואסור ניטע רובו הרי הוא כחצר ומותר: ואם העיר קדמה קוצץ ואינו נותן דמים וכו': מ"ש גבי בור דקתני קוצץ ונותן דמים ומאי שנא הכא דקתני קוצץ ואינו נותן דמים אמר רב כהנא (ג) קידרא דבי שותפי לא חמימא ולא קרירא ומאי קושיא דלמא שאני הזיקא דרבים מהזיקא דיחיד אלא אי איתמר דרב כהנא אסיפא איתמר אם האילן קדם קוצץ ונותן דמים ולימא להו הבו לי ברישא דמי והדר איקוץ אמר רב כהנא קידרא דבי שותפי לא חמימא ולא קרירא: ספק זה קדם וספק זה קדם קוצץ ואינו נותן דמים: מאי שנא מבור דאמרת לא יקוץ התם דודאי לאו למיקץ קאי ספיקו נמי לא אמרינן ליה קוץ הכא דודאי למיקץ קאי ספיקו נמי אמרינן ליה קוץ ואי משום דמי אמרינן ליה אייתי ראיה ושקול: **מתני'** מרחיקין את גורן קבוע מן העיר חמשים אמה לא יעשה אדם גורן קבוע בתוך שלו אא"כ יש לו חמשים אמה לכל רוח ומרחיק מנטיעותיו של חבירו ומנירו בכדי שלא יזיק: **גמ'** מ"ש רישא ומאי שנא סיפא אמר אביי סיפא אתאן לגורן שאינו קבוע היכי דמי גורן שאינו קבוע א"ר יוסי בר' חנינא כל שאינו זורה ברחת רב אשי אמר מה טעם קאמר מאי טעמא מרחיקין גורן קבוע מן העיר חמשים אמה כדי שלא יזיק מיתיבי מרחיקין גורן קבוע מן העיר חמשים אמה וכשם שמרחיקין מן העיר חמשים אמה כך מרחיקין מדלועיו ומקשואיו ומנטיעותיו ומנירו של חבירו חמשים אמה כדי שלא יזיק בשלמא לרב אשי ניחא אלא לאביי קשיא קשיא ממקשואיו ומדלועיו דאזיל אבקא ואתי בליביה ומצוי ליה אלא מנירו אמאי א"ר אבא בר זבדא ואיתימא ר' אבא בר זוטרא מפני שעושה

רש"י

דשפוכאי. שופכי יין מן החבית לנודות למכור לעוברי דרכים במדינה זאת כדמתמיס ואזיל: ברברבי. דליכא למיחש לרוצה דעלמא למימר מעוברי דרכים נפול: ואי איכא רברבי בהדייהו. אף הקטנים מותרין דברברבי לאו אורחייהו לעוברי דרכים אלא כולהו (ד) מלוקח יין של מדינה זו נינהו וישראל הן וקטנים שאין דרך ללוקח יין להבדיל אימור באברורי הוה מנחי. להשוות משא החמור כשיש שתי נודות זה גדול מזה מעט ומכביד המשא לצד אחד מניחין נוד קטן אצלו להשוות המשא: **מתני'** מרחיקין את האילן מן העיר. בגמרא מפרש משום נויי העיר לפי שנוי לעיר כשיש מרחב פנוי לפניה: חרוב ושקמה. ענפיהם רבים: ואילן סרק. גנאי הוא לעיר: ונותן דמים. מי שהעיר שלו: **גמ'** ותיפוק ליה דאין עושין מגרש שדה. משנה היא בפ' אחרון של ערכין (דף לג:) ומגרש אלף אמה הוא וכל אלף אמה אסור לעשותו שדה וקס"ד לא שדה לבן ולא שדה אילן: לא צריכא לר' אלעזר. דפליג התם ואמר בד"א בערי הלוים אבל בערי ישראל כו': ה"ג ולרבנן דאמרי אין עושין הני מילי בזרעים אבל באילנות עושין. בתוך אלף אמה: והכא. בתוך עשרים וחמש אמה משום נויי העיר אין עושין: קרפף יותר מבית סאתים שהוקף לדירה. סאתים הוא שיעור חצר המשכן ונתנוהו חכמים שיעור לכל היקף שלא הוקף לדור בתוכו או להשתמש מן הבית לתוכו כגון קרפף שבבקעה אבל המוקף לדירה אפי' בית עשרה כורין מטלטלין בו וקאמר הכא יתר מבית סאתים שהוקף לדירה הוא מותר לטלטל בכולו: נזרע רובו. בטלו הזרעים שם דירה ממנו והרי הוא כגינה שאין הקיפה לדירה הואיל ויתר מבית סאתים הוא אין מטלטלין בו: ועוד: אבל ניטע רובו. באילנות אין מבטלין תורת דירתו ממנו והרי הוא כחצר שלפני הבתים שהקיפוה לדירה ומותר: מאי שנא (ה) בור. דבעינן נמי הרחקה וקתני נמי אם הבור קדמה קוצץ ונותן בעל הבור דמי האילן לבעל האילן: לא חמימא ולא קרירא. שזה סומך על זה ואף כאן נמי האילן מי יתנם אם באת להטיל על בני העיר כל אחד אומר ממני לא יתחילו ונמצא האילן עומד והעיר מגונה ואין זו תפארת ארץ ישראל: ומאי קושיא. מבור לעיר דאיצטריך לשנויי הכי דלמא שאני היזק דרבים מהזיקא דיחיד לא חייבו חכמים לקוץ אילנו בשביל בור היחיד בלא דמים אבל בשביל היזק רבים חייבוהו לקוץ: לא חמימא כו'. אם באת להמתין עד מתן מעות יעמוד (ו) זה לאורך ימים בני העיר סומכין זה על זה ובעל האילן רוצה בכך לפיכך יקוץ ואחרי כן יגבה מעותיו מהן בב"ד: התם. גבי בור דודאי של אילן אם ודאי קדם לאו למיקץ קאי כדקתני אם האילן קדם לא יקוץ ספיקו נמי לא אמר ליה קוץ שעל הניזק להביא ראיה: הכא דודאי. נמי למיקץ קאי אלא שנוטל דמים כדקתני אם האילן קדם קוצץ ונותן דמים ספיקו נמי אמר ליה קוץ ממ"נ על כרחך וכשבא לגבות דמים אמר ליה אייתי ראיה דאת קדמת ושקול: **מתני'** גורן קבוע. בגמ' מפרש מאי קביעותא: חמשים אמה. מפני המוץ המזיק את בני העיר כשהוא זורה וגם הזרעים הוא מייבש: ומנירו של חבירו. ובגמרא מפרש מאי היזק דמוץ לניר. ניר היא חרישה שחורשין בימי הקיץ ואין זורעין בו עד ימות החורף כדי שימותו שרשי הקוצים והעשבים כדכתיב נירו לכם ניר ואל תזרעו אל קוצים (ירמיה ד): בכדי שלא יזיק. האי שיעורא משמע בציר מחמשים אמה ובגמרא פריך מ"ש מרישא דאמרת אלא אם כן יש לו חמשים אמה לכל רוח: **גמ'** שאינו זורה ברחת. שאין הכרי גדול וא"צ לזרות ברחת אלא הרוח מנשבת בכרי והמוץ נדף מאליו. רחת פל"ה בלע"ז כשהכרי גדול צריך להגביה התבואה ברחת וזורק כלפי מעלה והרוח מנשבת ודוחפת המוץ למרחוק: רב אשי אמר. שיעורא דסיפא כרישא ומה טעם קאמר: מקשואיו ומדלועיו. נטיעה שהקשואין והדלועין גדילין בה: בשלמא לרב אשי ניחא. דקתני בכולהו חמשים אמה: אלא לאביי קשיא קשיא. [הכי] גרסינן:

תוספות

מרחיקין את האילן [מן העיר] כ"ה אמה. וחוצה לכך להרחיק מן העיר עד אלף אמה דאין עושין מגרש שדה:

מ"ש מבור דקוצץ ונותן דמים אמר רב כהנא קידרא דבי שותפי כו'. תימה לרשב"א כשהאילן קדם נמי נותן דמים מהאי טעמא וי"ל דכשהאילן קדם כיון דסמך בהיתר אין לחוש אם יתעצלו ושאר האילן עומד אבל עוד קשה לו דמאי שייך הכא קידרא דבי שותפי והלא קוצץ תחלה קודם שיתנו דמים ואומר ר"י דה"פ דמשום קידרא דבי שותפי לא חמימא ולא קרירא לא רצו לתקן שיתנו דמים דאע"ג דקוצץ תחלה פעמים שלא ישמע להם לקוץ תחלה אם לא ידע מי יתן לו הדמים וכל אחד ואחד יתרשל ולא יקוץ כדי שלא ליתן דמים כי בעל האילן ידרוש מעמו:

ולימא להו הבו לי ברישא והדר איקוץ. גבי בור לא שייך למיפרך הכי דניחא (ז) כיון שסמך באיסור שיקוץ תחלה:

קשיא לאביי. תימה מאי קשיא ליה הא ברייתא איירי בגורן קבוע ומתניתין בגורן שאינו קבוע ויש לומר דלאביי גופיה הוה משני דמה טעם קאמר אי לאו משום דקשיא ליה מה צריך לפרש טעמא כדי שלא יזיק והשתא דבברייתא מפרש טעמא כדי שלא יזיק מתני' נמי איכא לפרושי הכי:

עין משפט נר מצוה

עה א ב מיי' פי"ג מהל' מאכלות אסורות הל' כט סמג לאוין קמח טוש"ע י"ד סי' קכט סעיף יט:

עו ג מיי' פ"י מהלכות שכנים הל' א סמג עשין פב טוש"מ סי' קנה:

עז ד מיי' וסמג שם טוש"ע ח"מ סי' קנה סעיף כב בהג"ה:

עח ה מיי' שם הל' א סמג שם:

עט ו מיי' פי"ג מהל' שמיטה הל' ד סמג לאוין רעח ופסק כת"ק:

פ ז מיי' פט"ז מהלכות שבת הלכה ו סמג עשין מד"ס א טוש"ע א"ח סי' שנח סעיף ט:

פא ח ט י מיי' פ"י מהל' שכנים הל' ב סמג עשין פב טוש"ע ח"מ סי' קנה סעיף כג:

רבינו גרשום

והני מילי. דמותרין: היכא דהנהו זיקי רברבי נינהו אבל אי משתכחי זוטרי ודאי אסור דאימר מעוברי דרכים נפלו: ואי איכא רברבי ואשכח זוטרי בהדייהו אסירי. דחיישי' דמעוברי דרכים נפל דאימור באברורי קא מנחי על גבי החמור כעין שקושרין עוברי דרכים נודותיהן על גבי חמוריהן וקושרין מצד החמור נוד גדול ומצד השני כמותו ומשימין בין שתי נודות הללו נוד אחד קטן ואם נמצאו גדולים כה"ג וקטנים עמהן ודאי מעוברי דרכים נפיל ומשואי חמור ואסירי. ל"מ. ואי איכא רברבי בינייהו. אפי' דזוטרי מותרין דאימור באברוארי הונחו ושפוכי ישראל אנחינהו להתם כעין שרגילין לעשות כדפרישית לעיל באידך לישנא והכי עיקר: פיסקא מרחיקין את האילן מן העיר כ"ה [אמה]. מפרש בגמ' טעמ' מאי: בחרוב ובשקמה נ' אמה. משום דאיכא תרתי לריעותא חדא דאין פירותיהן שוין כלום ועוד שענפיהן מרובין משאר אילנות: מ"ט. מרחיקין: אמר עולא משום נויי העיר. שיהיה מישור יפה סמוך לעיר בלא שום עיכוב. ועולא למה ליה למימר משום נויי העיר מרחיקין תיפוק ליה דאין עושין שדה שיש בו זרע או אילנות אין עושין מגרש ולא מגרש שדה כדגרסי' במס' א) מכות לגבי מגרש לוים [דכתיב] ומדותם מחוץ לעיר וגו' משום דהוי ב) להם לוים דכתיב ומגרשיהם יהיו לבהמתם

מסורת הש"ס

א) [ע"ז קיח.], ב) [שם קי:], ג) מכות יב. [ערכין לג:], ד) [ערכין שם], ה) עירובין כג., ו) [לקמן כה:], ז) עירובין ג'., ח) [פי' שורף ומייבש לתלומים. ערוך]:

הגהות הב"ח

(א) במשנה פרק ב' אמה אם כצ"ל ותוס ו' נמחק: (ב) גמ' לא עבדינן ומנא תימרא דשאני בין זרעים לאילנות: (ג) שם אמר רב כהנא היינו דאמרי אינשי קידרא דבי שותפי: (ד) רש"י ד"ה ואי איכא וכו' מלוקחי יין וכו' וישראל הן הקטנים וכו' מניחין עוד נוד קטן כצ"ל והד"א: (ה) ד"ה מ"ש גבי בור וכו' וקתני ביה אם: (ו) ד"ה לא חמימא וכו' יעמוד לאורך כצ"ל ותיבת זה נמחק: (ז) תוס' ד"ה ולימא וכו' דניחא ליה כיון:

לעזי רש"י

פל"ה. פירוש רחת, כלי עץ גדול לנער בו את התבואה (עיין רש"י ישעיה ל, כד).

ליקוטי רש"י

ספק זה קדם וספק זה קדם קוצץ. כיון דבין הכי ובין הכי למיקץ קאי דכי קדם אילן נמי קתני קוצץ כי מספקא לן אמרינן קוץ ממה נפשך [illegible]

whether the tree or the pit came first, **he need not cut down** the tree? Why is an instance of uncertainty decided in favor of the tree's owner in the case of a pit and against the tree's owner in the case of a city?

The Gemara answers:

הָתָם – There, in the case of a tree that has been planted near a pit, **דְּוַדַּאי – where** a tree that **definitely** came before a pit **לָאו לְמֵיקַץ קָאֵי – is not subject to cutting,**[23] **סְפֵיקוֹ נַמִּי** – in a case of **uncertainty as well, לֹא אַמְרִינַן לֵיהּ קוּץ – we do not tell [the tree's owner]** to **cut** it down. The burden of proof that the tree was planted illegally lies upon the owner of the pit.[24] **הָכָא – Here,** however, in the case of a tree that has been planted near a city, **דְּוַדַּאי – where** even a tree that **definitely** came before the city **לְמֵיקַץ קָאֵי – is subject to cutting,**[25] **סְפֵיקוֹ נַמִּי** – in a case of **uncertainty as well, אַמְרִינַן לֵיהּ קוּץ – we tell [the tree's owner]** to **cut** it down. **וְאִי מִשּׁוּם דְּמֵי – And as for compensation, אַמְרִינַן לֵיהּ – we tell him: אַיְיתֵי רְאָיָה וּשְׁקוֹל – "Prove** that your tree was here before the city **and** you may then **collect** compensation for cutting it down."[26]

Mishnah **מַרְחִיקִין אֶת גּוֹרֶן קָבוּעַ מִן הָעִיר חֲמִשִּׁים אַמָּה – One must distance a permanent granary fifty *amos* from a city.**[27] **לֹא יַעֲשֶׂה אָדָם גּוֹרֶן קָבוּעַ בְּתוֹךְ שֶׁלּוֹ** – Similarly, **a person may not make a permanent granary within his** property, **אֶלָּא אִם כֵּן יֵשׁ לוֹ חֲמִשִּׁים אַמָּה לְכָל רוּחַ – unless he owns fifty *amos*** of land bordering it **in each direction. וּמַרְחִיק מִנְּטִיעוֹתָיו שֶׁל חֲבֵירוֹ וּמִנִּירוֹ – One must also distance** a granary **from his neighbor's saplings, as well as from his plowed field,**[28] **בִּכְדֵי שֶׁלֹּא יַזִּיק** – far **enough that [the chaff]** that flies from the granary **not cause** them any **damage.**[29]

Gemara The Gemara examines the contradiction between the two cases of the Mishnah with regard to the distance required between a granary and neighboring property: **מַאי שְׁנָא רֵישָׁא וּמַאי שְׁנָא סֵיפָא – What is the difference between the first case** of the Mishnah, which mandates a distance of fifty *amos,* **and the latter case,** which implies that a lesser distance suffices?

The Gemara offers a solution:

אָמַר אַבָּיֵי – Abaye said: סֵיפָא אֲתָאן לְגוֹרֶן שֶׁאֵינוֹ קָבוּעַ – The latter case refers to a temporary granary. A temporary granary does not require as great a distance as a permanent granary.

The Gemara seeks a clarification:

הֵיכִי דָּמֵי גּוֹרֶן שֶׁאֵינוֹ קָבוּעַ – What is the definition of "a temporary granary"?

The Gemara answers:

אָמַר רַבִּי יוֹסֵי בְּרַבִּי חֲנִינָא – R' Yose the son of R' Chanina said: כָּל שֶׁאֵינוֹ זוֹרֶה בְּרַחַת – Any granary so small **that a shovel is not used for winnowing** its grain.[30]

The Gemara offers another interpretation of the Mishnah:

רַב אַשִׁי אָמַר – Rav Ashi said: מַה טַּעַם קָאָמַר – The second clause of **[the Mishnah] states the reason** that a distance of fifty *amos* is required: **מַאי טַעְמָא מַרְחִיקִין גּוֹרֶן קָבוּעַ מִן הָעִיר חֲמִשִּׁים אַמָּה – "What is the reason** that **one must distance a permanent granary fifty *amos* from a city? כְּדֵי שֶׁלֹּא יַזִּיק – In order that [the chaff]** that flies from the granary **not cause** any **damage."** Thus, the latter clause of the Mishnah is not an independent ruling that represents a contradiction to the first clause, but is rather an explanation of the Mishnah's first clause.[31]

The Gemara cites a challenge to Abaye's explanation of the Mishnah:

מֵיתִיבֵי – They challenged Abaye from the following Baraisa:

NOTES

23. Only a tree that has been planted illegally, after the neighbor's pit was in place, must be cut down (see Mishnah below, 25b).

24. The rule for any case of uncertainty regarding monetary matters is הַמּוֹצִיא מֵחֲבֵירוֹ עָלָיו הָרְאָיָה, *the* [*burden of*] *proof lies upon one who* [*wishes to*] *exact* [*money*] *from another.* Here too, since the owner of the pit wants to force the tree's owner to cut down his tree, he must prove that the tree was planted illegally.

25. A tree planted close to a city must be cut down regardless of whether it was there before the city or vice versa. The difference between a tree that was planted legally and one that was planted illegally is only in regard to compensation.

26. I.e. the burden of proof lies on the owner of the tree, who wishes to exact compensation from the city.

27. [The granary referred to here is an open-air storage area for grain. The grain in this place is winnowed by being shoveled and tossed in the air for the wind to separate the grain from its chaff.] Consequently, it must be located at least fifty *amos* away from the city so that the wind-swept chaff should not injure any townspeople or fall on their plants, causing them to dry out (*Rashi*). [The Gemara examines the significance of a permanent granary, as opposed to a temporary one.]

28. It was customary for farmers to plow furrows in their fields during the summer in preparation for the next winter's planting in order to destroy the roots of any weeds in the ground from the previous season. This practice is alluded to in Jeremiah's admonition (*Jeremiah* 4:3): נִירוּ לָכֶם נִיר וְאַל־תִּזְרְעוּ אֶל־קֹצִים – *Plow your furrow and [thereby] avoid sowing unto thistles.* [The message conveyed in this allegorical criticism is: Uproot your evil deeds in order that your prayers not go unanswered (*Rashi* ad loc.).] The Gemara explains how chaff is detrimental to a neighbor's plowed field (*Rashi*).

29. The implication of this rule is that a distance of less than fifty *amos* suffices to prevent the chaff from causing damage. The Gemara inquires why the law in this case is more lenient than in the previous case, where a distance of fifty *amos* is required (*Rashi*).

30. A granary that contains a large pile of grain can only be winnowed by shoveling the grain and tossing it in the air for the wind to separate the grain from the chaff. Since the wind blows the chaff a great distance, the granary may not be located within fifty *amos* of a city. Grain that is stored in a small pile can be winnowed without being tossed in the air. Since the grain is not heavily weighted, the wind blowing across the pile automatically separates the grain from the chaff. In such a case the chaff does not fly very far, and therefore a distance of less than fifty *amos* suffices between the granary and the city (*Rashi*).

[The Gemara presumes that a permanent granary contains a large volume of grain. Any pile of grain small enough to be winnowed without a shovel was most likely placed in its location temporarily.]

31. The Gemara originally understood the Mishnah as stating two laws: 1) A granary must be distanced fifty *amos* from a city or a neighboring property. 2) A granary must be distanced from a neighbor's saplings or plowed field *far enough* so that the chaff that blows from it will not cause any damage.

According to that interpretation, the second law seems to require a smaller distance than the first law. Therefore, Abaye explained that the second law refers to a temporary granary, i.e. a small pile of grain that is winnowed without shoveling.

Rav Ashi reinterprets the Mishnah – the second clause is not an independent ruling that implies a smaller measurement than the first ruling, but is actually an explanation of the first clause. Thus, the Mishnah states only one law: One must distance a granary fifty *amos* from a city or from a neighbor's property *in order* that the chaff not cause any damage. [The Mishnah's words in the second clause: בִּכְדֵי שֶׁלֹּא יַזִּיק, can either be interpreted as "*[far] enough* that (the chaff) not cause any damage," or as "*in order* that (the chaff) not cause any

מרחיקין את האילן [מן העיר] כ"ה אמה. וזרעים צריך להרחיק מן העיר עד אלף אמה דאין עושין מגרש שדה:

מ"ש מבור דקוצץ ונותן דמים אמר רב כהנא קידרא דבי שותפי כו'. תימה לרשב"א א"כ כשהאילן קדם נמי אמאי נותן דמים מהאי טעמא וי"ל דכשהאילן קדם כיון דסמך בהיתר אין לחוש אם יתעצלו וישאר האילן עומד אבל עוד קשה לו דמאי שייך הכא קידרא דבי שותפי והלא קוצץ תחלה קודם שיתנו דמים ואומר ר"י דה"פ דמשום קידרא דבי שותפי לא חיימא ולא קרירא לא רצו לתקן שיתנו דמים לאע"ג דקוצץ תחלה פעמים שלא ישמע להם לקוץ תחלה אם לא ידע מי יתן לו הדמים וכל אחד ואחד יתרשל ולא יקוץ כדי שלא ליתן דמים כי בעל האילן ידרוש מעמו:

ולימא להו הבו לי ברישא והדר איקוץ. גבי בור לא שייך למיפרך הכי דניחא (ז) כיון שסמך באיסור שיקוץ תחלה:

קשיא לאביי. תימה מאי קשיא ליה הא ברייתא איירי בגורן קבוע ומתניתין בגורן שאינו קבוע ויש לומר דאביי גופיה הוה משני דמה טעם קאמר אי לאו משום דקשיא ליה מה צריך לפרש טעמא כדי שלא יזיק והשתא דברייתא מפרש טעמא כדי שלא יזיק מתני' נמי איכא לפרושי הכי:

דשפוכאי ישראל נינהו [א] וה"מ ברברבי אבל זוטרי אימור מעוברי דרכים נפול [ב] ואי איכא רברבי בהדייהו אימור באברורי הוה מנחי:

מתני' (א) [ג] מרחיקין את האילן מן העיר עשרים וחמש אמה ובחרוב ובשקמה חמשים אמה אבא שאול אומר כל אילן סרק חמשים אמה (א) [ד] ואם העיר קדמה קוצץ ואינו נותן דמים ואם אילן קדם קוצץ ונותן דמים [ה] ספק זה קדם וספק זה קדם קוצץ ואינו נותן דמים:

גמ' מאי טעמא אמר עולא [ה] משום נויי העיר [ב] ותיפוק ליה דאין עושין שדה מגרש ולא מגרש שדה לא צריכא לר"א דאמר [ד] [ו] עושין שדה מגרש ומגרש שדה הכא משום נויי העיר לא עבדינן ולרבנן נמי דאמרי אין עושין שדה מגרש ולא מגרש שדה ה"מ זרעים אבל אילנות עבדינן והכא משום נויי העיר לא (ב) ומנא תימרא דשאני בין זרעין לאילנות [ה] דתניא [ז] קרפף יותר מבית סאתים שהוקף לדירה נזרע רובו הרי הוא כגינה ואסור ניטע רובו הרי הוא כחצר ומותר: ואם העיר קדמה קוצץ ואינו נותן דמים וכו': מ"ש גבי בור דקתני [ו] קוצץ ונותן דמים ומאי שנא הכא דקתני קוצץ ואינו נותן דמים אמר רב כהנא (ג) [ז] קידרא דבי שותפי לא חמימא ולא קרירא ומאי קושיא דלמא שאני היזקא דרבים מהזיקא דיחיד אלא אי איתמר דרב כהנא אסיפא איתמר אם האילן קדם קוצץ ונותן דמים ולימא להו הבו לי ברישא דמי והדר איקוץ אמר רב כהנא קידרא דבי שותפי לא חמימא ולא קרירא: ספק זה קדם וספק זה קדם קוצץ ואינו נותן דמים: מאי שנא מבור דאמרת לא יקוץ התם דודאי לאו למיקץ קאי ספיקו נמי לא אמרינן ליה קוץ הכא דודאי למיקץ קאי ספיקו נמי אמרינן ליה קוץ ואי משום דמי אמרינן ליה אייתי ראיה ושקול:

מתני' [ח] מרחיקין את גורן קבוע מן העיר חמשים אמה [ט] לא יעשה אדם גורן קבוע בתוך שלו אא"כ יש לו חמשים אמה לכל רוח ומרחיק מנטיעותיו של חבירו ומנירו בכדי שלא יזיק:

גמ' מ"ש רישא ומאי שנא סיפא אמר אביי סיפא אתאן לגורן שאינו קבוע היכי דמי גורן שאינו קבוע א"ר יוסי בר' חנינא כל שאינו זורה ברחת רב אשי אמר [י] מה טעם קאמר מאי טעמא מרחיקין גורן קבוע מן העיר חמשים אמה כדי שלא יזיק מיתיבי מרחיקין גורן קבוע מן העיר חמשים אמה וכשם שמרחיקין מן העיר חמשים אמה כך מרחיקין מדלועיו ומקשואיו ומנטיעותיו ומנירו של חבירו חמשים אמה כדי שלא יזיק בשלמא לרב אשי ניחא אלא לאביי קשיא קשיא בשלמא ממקשואיו ומדלועיו דאזיל אבקא ואתי בליביה [ח] ומצוי ליה אלא מנירו אמאי א"ר אבא בר זבדא ואיתימא ר' אבא בר זוטרא מפני שעושה

דשפוכאי. שופכי יין מן החבית זאת כדמסיים ואזיל: ברברבי. דליכא למיחש לרובא דעלמא למימר מעוברי דרכים נפול: ואי איכא רברבי בהדייהו. אף הקטנים מותרין דברברבי לאו אורחייהו דעוברי דרכים אלא כולהו (ד) מלוקח יין של מדינה זו נינהו וישראל הן וקטנים שאין דרך ללוקח יין להביאם: אימור באברורי הוה מנחי. להשוות משא החמור כשיש שתי נודות זה גדול מזה מעט ומכביד המשא לצד אחד מניחין נוד קטן אצלו להשוות המשא: מתני' מרחיקין את האילן מן העיר. בגמרא מפרש משום נויי העיר לפי שנוי לעיר כשיש מרחב פנוי לפניה: חרוב ושקמה. ענפיהם רבים: ואילן סרק. גנאי הוא לעיר: ונותן דמים. מי שהעיר שלו: גמ' ותיפוק ליה דאין עושין מגרש שדה. משנה היא בפ' אחרון של ערכין (דף לג:) ומגרש אלף אמה הוא וכל אלף אמה אסור לעשותו שדה וקס"ד לא שדה לבן ולא שדה אילן: לא צריכא לר' אלעזר. דפליג התם ואמר בד"א בערי הלוים אבל בערי ישראל כו': ה"ג ולרבנן דאמרי אין עושין הני מילי בזרעים אבל באילנות עושין. בתוך אלף אמה: והכא. בתוך עשרים וחמש אמה משום נויי העיר אין עושין: קרפף יותר מבית סאתים שהוקף לדירה. סאתים הוא שיעור חצר המשכן ונתנוהו חכמים שיעור לכל היקף שלא הוקף לדור בתוכו או להשתמש מן הבית לתוכו כגון קרפף שבבקעה אבל המוקף לדירה אפי' בית עשרה כורין מטלטלין בו וקאמר הכא יתר מבית סאתים שהוקף לדירה הוא מותר לטלטל בכולו: נזרע רובו. בטלו הזרעים שם דירה ממנו והרי הוא כגינה שאין הקפה לדירה הואיל ויתר מבית סאתים הוא אין מטלטלין בו עוד: אבל ניטע רובו. באילנות אין האילנות מבטלין תורת דירתו ממנו והרי הוא כחצר שלפני הבתים שהקיפוה לדירה ומותר: מאי שנא (ה) בור. דבעינן נמי הרחקה וקתני נמי אם הבור קדמה קוצץ ונותן בעל הבור דמי האילן לבעל האילן: לא חמימא ולא קרירא. שזה סומך על זה אף כאן דמי האילן מי יתנם אם באת להטילם על בני העיר כל אחד אומר ממני לא יתחילו ונמצא האילן עומד והעיר מגונה ואין זו תפארת ארץ ישראל: ומאי קושיא. מבור לעיר דאיצטריך לשנויי הכי דלמא שאני היזק דרבים מהזיקא דיחיד דיחיד לא חייבו חכמים לקוץ אילנו בשביל בור היחיד בלא דמים אבל בשביל היזק רבים חייבוהו לקוץ: לא חמימא כו'. אם באת להמתין עד מתן מעות יעמוד (ו) זה לאורך ימים בני העיר סומכין זה על זה ובעל האילן רוצה בכך לפיכך יקוץ ואחרי כן יגבה מעותיו מהן בב"ד: התם. גבי בור דודאי של אילן אם ודאי קדם לאו למיקץ קאי כדקתני אם האילן קדם לא יקוץ ספיקו נמי לא אמר ליה קוץ שעל הניזק להביא ראיה: הכא דודאי. נמי למיקץ קאי אלא שנוטל דמים כדקתני אם האילן קדם קוצץ ונותן דמים ספיקו נמי אמר ליה קוץ ממ"נ על כרחך וכשבא לגבות דמים אמר ליה אייתי ראיה דאת קדמת ושקול: מתני' גורן קבוע. בגמ' מפרש מאי קביעותא: חמשים אמה. מפני המוץ המזיק את בני העיר כשהוא זורה וגם הזרעים הוא מייבש: ומנירו של חבירו. ובגמרא מפרש מאי היזק דמוץ לניר. ניר היא חרישה שחורשין בימי הקיץ ואין זורעין בו עד ימות החורף כדי שימותו שרשי הקוצים והעשבים כדכתיב נירו לכם ניר ואל תזרעו אל קוצים (ירמיה ד): בכדי שלא יזיק. האי שיעורא משמע בציר מחמשים אמה ובגמרא פריך מ"ש מרישא דאמרת אלא אם כן יש לו חמשים אמה לכל רוח: גמ' שאינו זורה ברחת. שאין הכרי גדול וא"צ לזרות ברחת אלא הרוח מנשבת בכרי והמוץ נדף מאליו. רחת פל"ה בלע"ז כשהכרי גדול צריך להגביה התבואה ברחת חורק כלפי מעלה והרוח מנשבת ודוחפת המוץ למרחוק: רב אשי אמר. שיעורא דסיפא כרישא ומה טעם קאמר: מקשואיו ומדלועיו. נטיעה שהקשואין והדלועין גדלין בה: בשלמא לרב אשי ניחא. דקתני בכולהו חמשים אמה: אלא לאביי קשיא קשיא. [הכי] גרסינן:

שעושה

עין משפט נר מצוה

עה א ב מיי' פי"ג מהל' מאכלות אסורות הל' כט סמג לאוין קמח טוש"ע י"ד סי' קכט סעיף יט:

עו ג מיי' פ"י מהלכות שכנים הל' א סמג עשין פב טוש"ע ח"מ סי' קנה סעיף כו בהג"ה:

עז ד מיי' ומוג שם טוש"ע ח"מ סי' קנה סעיף כב בהג"ה:

עח ה מיי' שם הל' ב סמג שם:

עט ו מיי' פ"ב מהל' שמיטה הל' ד סמג לאוין עגם ופסק כת"ק:

פ ז מיי' פט"ז מהלכות שבת הלכה ג סמג עשין מד"ש א טוש"ע א"ח סי' שנח סעיף ט:

פא ח ט מיי' פי"א מהל' שכנים הל' ג סמג עשין פב טוש"ע ח"מ סי' קנה סעיף כג:

רבינו גרשום

והני מילי. דמותרין היכא דהנהו זיקי רברבי נינהו אבל אי משתכחי זוטרי ודאי אסור דאימור מעוברי דרכים נפלו: ואי איכא רברבי ואשכח זוטרי בהדייהו אסירי. דחיישי דאיכא מעוברי דרכים נפל דאימור באברורי קא מנחי על גבי החמור כעין שקושרין עוברי דרכים נודותיהן על גבי חמוריהן וקושרין מצד השני נוד גדול כמותו ומשימין בין שתי נודות הללו נוד אחד קטן ואם נמצאו גדולים כה"ג וקטנים עמהן ודאי מעוברי דרכים נפל ומשאוי חמור ואסורין. ל"מ. ואי איכא רברבי בינייהו. אפי' דזוטרי מותרין דאימור באברוארי הונחו ושפוכי ישראל אנחינהו כהם כעין שרגילין לעשות כדפרישית לעיל באידך לישנא והכי עיקר: פיסקא מרחיקין את האילן מן העיר כ"ה [אמה]. מפרש בגמ' טעמו: מאי. בחרוב ובשקמה נ' אמה. משום דאיכא תרתי לריעותא חדא דאין פירותיהן שוין כלום ועוד שנענפיהן מרובין משאר אילנות: מ"ש. מרחיקין. אמר עולא משום נויי העיר. שיהיה מרחב מישור יפה סמוך לעיר בלא שום עיכוב. ועולא למה ליה למימר משום נויי העיר מרחיקין תיפוק ליה דאין עושין שדה שיש בו זרע או אילנות אין עושין מגרש ולא מגרש שדה כדגרסי' במס' (א) מכות לגבי מגרש לוים במדבר ומגרשיהם יהיו להם ולכל חיתם ונותן מחוץ לעיר וגו' משום דהוי (ב) להם לוים דכתיב ומגרשיהם יהיו להם לבהמתם וגו' להכי (ג) צריכי אלפים אמה מגרש אבל שאר הערים לא כה"ג ממש סגיא: לא צריכא לר"א דאמר עושין שדה מגרש (ד) להכא דזרע או נטע אילן בתוך כ"ה אמה סמוך לעיר: הני מילי דאין עושין להכי: דזרע (דא"א) למיזל תחותיה בזרעים משום דהא מזיק זרעים לבני העיר דלא מצי למדרס בהו זרעים אבל אילן דמצי למיזל תחותיה (ה) דאפי' אילנות

מסורת הש"ס

א) [ב"מ קח.], ב) מכות יב. [ערכין לג:], ג) [ערכין שם], ד) עירובין כג:, ה) [לקמן כה:], ו) עירובין ג', ח) [פי' שורף ומייבש לתלושים. ערוך]:

הגהות הב"ח

(א) במשנה פרק ג' אמה אם כצ"ל ותות ו' נמחק: (ב) גמ' בגבי אלא עבדינן ומנא תימרא דשאני בין זרעים לאילנות: (ג) שם אמר רב כהנא היינו דאמרי אינשי קידרא דבי שותפי: (ד) רש"י ד"ה ואי איכא וכו' מלוקחי יין וכו' וישראל הן וכו' וקטנים וכו' מניחין עוד נוד קטן כצ"ל והד"א: (ה) ד"ה מ"ש גבי בור וכו' קדמה כצ"ל: (ו) ד"ה לא חמימא וכו' יעמוד לאורך כצ"ל ותיבת זה נמחק: (ז) תוס' ד"ה ולימא וכו' דניחא ליה כיון:

לעזי רש"י

פל"ה. פירוש רחת, כלי עץ גדול כעין את לזרות בו את התבואה (עיין רש"י ישעיה ל, כד).

ליקוטי רש"י

ספק זה קדם וספק זה קדם קוצץ. כיון דבין הכי ובין הכי למיקצץ קאי דכי האילן קדם נמי קתני קוצץ כי מספקא לן אמרינן קוץ ממה נפשך שהרי עליך לעשות ונמצא הספק מוטל על הדמים ולא אמרינן לבעל האילן לאלו גבי אילן הסמוך לבור של יחיד קתני בה ולגבי דידיה אם הבור קדמה קוצץ ונותן דמים אם האילן קדם לא יקוץ ומנן גבי ספק זה קדם וספק זה קדם לא יקוץ [ב"ב כה:]. שדה מגרש. מגרש הוי אלף אמה סביב לעיר כדכתיב (במדבר לה) מקיר העיר וחוצה אלף אמה סביב ותוך אלף לתוכו אלף היו להם לנוים אלף אמה לשדות וכרמים דכתיב (שם) ומדותם מחוץ לעיר וגו' לא מהם אלף אמה מגרש והשאר שדות וכרמים מגרש פנוי מכלום ואין בו בית ואין זורעין אותו אלא לנוי לעיר אין עושין שדה מגרש. משום ישוב ארץ ישראל והיינו חורבן שממעט את הזריעה. ולא מגרש שדה. שממעיט את נוי העיר [ערכין לג:]. נזרע רובו. כשהזרעים ביטול דירתו דזרעונים לא דיירי אינשי והוי גינה ואסור לטלטל בכולו שלא נזרע דבטיל ליה לגבי רובא. ניטע רובו. באילנות אינו בטל ביטול דירתו אילנות לא אורחא להשתמש בכל אילנות תמיד [עירובין כג:]. דקתני קוצץ ונותן דמים. דכיון דבכולה נטע שלא יזיק עד זמן גדול לא חייבו חכמים לקוץ בלא דמים בשביל היזק יחיד [לקמן כה:].

מַרְחִיקִין גּוֹרֶן קָבוּעַ מִן הָעִיר חֲמִשִּׁים אַמָּה – A PERMANENT GRANARY MUST BE DISTANCED FIFTY *AMOS* FROM A CITY, וּכְשֵׁם שֶׁמַּרְחִיקִין מִן הָעִיר חֲמִשִּׁים אַמָּה – AND JUST AS IT MUST BE DISTANCED FIFTY *AMOS* FROM A CITY, כָּךְ מַרְחִיקִין – SO TOO, IT MUST BE DISTANCED מִדִּלּוּעָיו וּמִקִּשּׁוּאָיו וּמִנְּטִיעוֹתָיו וּמִנִּירוֹ שֶׁל חֲבֵירוֹ חֲמִשִּׁים אַמָּה – FIFTY *AMOS* FROM A NEIGHBOR'S GOURDS, CUCUMBERS, SAPLINGS AND PLOWED FIELD, כְּדֵי שֶׁלֹּא יַזִּיק – IN ORDER THAT [THE CHAFF] NOT CAUSE them any DAMAGE. The Baraisa cites the possibility that the chaff may cause damage as the reason that the granary must be distanced fifty *amos.* It follows that the Mishnah should be interpreted the same way.[32] בִּשְׁלָמָא לְרַב אַשִׁי נִיחָא – **This is well** according **to Rav Ashi,** who indeed interpreted the Mishnah in that manner, אֶלָּא לְאַבַּיֵי קַשְׁיָא – **but** according **to Abaye** who interpreted the Mishnah differently, the Baraisa poses **a difficulty!**

The Gemara has no answer and concludes:

קַשְׁיָא – The **difficulty** stands.

The Gemara now explores in what way flying chaff can be harmful to the various items mentioned in the Baraisa:

בִּשְׁלָמָא מִמִּקְשׁוּאָיו וּמִדְּלוּעָיו – **It is well** that a granary must be distanced **from cucumber and gourd plants**[33] דְּאָזִיל אַבְקָא וְאָתֵי בְּלִיבֵּיהּ וּמְצַוֵּי לֵיהּ – **for the chaff**[34] **flies off and reaches the heart** of the plant **and dries it out,** אֶלָּא מִנִּירוֹ אַמַּאי – **but why** must a granary be distanced **from [a neighbor's] PLOWED FIELD?** How can flying chaff cause damage to the **FIELD?**

The Gemara answers:

אָמַר רַבִּי אַבָּא בַּר זַבְדָּא וְאִיתֵּימָא רַבִּי אַבָּא בַּר זוּטְרָא – **R' Abba bar Zavda, and some say R' Abba bar Zutra, said:** מִפְּנֵי – It must be distanced **because**

NOTES

damage."]

[See *Ritva,* who says that Rav Ashi actually argues with Abaye, and maintains that in the case of a temporary granary *no* distancing is necessary.]

32. The Baraisa paraphrases the Mishnah, and nevertheless clearly mandates a distance of fifty *amos* both in regard to a city (the first case of the Mishnah) and in regard to a neighbor's saplings and plowed field (the latter case of the Mishnah) (*Rashi*). It is thus clear that the phrase "that [the chaff] not cause damage" is not to be interpreted as "far enough that it not cause damage," i.e. a distance of less than fifty *amos,* but rather as "in order that it not cause damage," i.e. the reason for the fifty-*amah* rule (cf. *Ritva*).

33. The words for cucumbers and gourds are קִשּׁוּאִין וְדִלּוּעִין. The words for cucumber and gourd *plants* are מִקְשׁוּאִין וּמִדְלוּעִין (see *Rashi* ד״ה מקשואיו).

34. Literally: the dust.

שֶׁעוֹשֶׂה אוֹתוֹ גָּלָל – **[The chaff]** falling into the plowed fields and decomposing **makes [the soil] into manure;** i.e. it causes the field to be overfertilized, which ruins the next crop to be planted.[1]

Mishnah The Mishnah continues its discussion of the enterprises that must be kept at a distance from a town because of their adverse effects — in this case, due to foul odors. The Mishnah will also discuss the distance one must separate his crops from those of his neighbor because of the potential damage that might result to the neighbor's crops:

מַרְחִיקִין אֶת הַנְּבֵלוֹת – **One must distance** animal **carcasses,** וְאֶת הַקְּבָרוֹת – **graves** וְאֶת הַבּוּרְסְקִי – **and a tannery** מִן הָעִיר חֲמִשִּׁים אַמָּה – **fifty** ***amos*** **from a town,** so as not to disturb the town's residents with their foul odor. אֵין עוֹשִׂין בּוּרְסְקִי אֶלָּא לְמִזְרַח הָעִיר – Even at this distance, **one may not make a tannery except to the east of a town,** for the east wind is gentle and not usually strong enough to carry the odor to the town.[2] רַבִּי עֲקִיבָא אוֹמֵר – **R' Akiva,** however, **says:** לְכָל רוּחַ הוּא עוֹשֶׂה חוּץ מִמַּעֲרָבָהּ – **One may make** a tannery **on any side** of a town **except for its west** side;[3] וּמַרְחִיק חֲמִשִּׁים אַמָּה – **and one must distance** it **fifty** ***amos*** from the town. וּמַרְחִיקִין אֶת הַמִּשְׁרָה מִן הַיָּרָק – **One must distance a flax pool**[4] **from vegetables,** וְאֶת הַכְּרֵישִׁין מִן הַבְּצָלִים – **leeks from onions,**[5] וְאֶת הַחַרְדָּל מִן הַדְּבוֹרִים – **and mustard plants from** the **bees** of his neighbor;[6] וְרַבִּי יוֹסֵי מַתִּיר בְּחַרְדָּל – **R' Yose, however, permits** planting close by the threatened property **in** the case of **mustard plants.**[7]

Gemara The Gemara analyzes R' Akiva's ruling that one may locate a tannery on any side of a town except its west side, and that one must locate it at least fifty *amos* away:

אִיבַּעְיָא לְהוּ – **They inquired:** רַבִּי עֲקִיבָא הֵיכִי קָאָמַר – **How did R' Akiva mean** this? Did he mean that לְכָל רוּחַ הוּא עוֹשֶׂה וְסוֹמֵךְ – **one may make** it **on any side** of the town **and place it close by,** חוּץ מִמַּעֲרָבָהּ דְּמַרְחִיק חֲמִשִּׁים אַמָּה וְעוֹשֶׂה – **except for its west** side, **where one must** place it at a **distance** of **fifty** ***amos*** from the town **in order** to be allowed **to make it;** אוֹ דִּלְמָא – **or perhaps** R' Akiva meant that לְכָל רוּחַ הוּא עוֹשֶׂה וּמַרְחִיק חֲמִשִּׁים אַמָּה – **one may make** a tannery **on any side** of a town, **but he must** place it at a **distance of fifty** ***amos***; חוּץ מִמַּעֲרָבָהּ דְּאֵינוֹ עוֹשֶׂה כְּלָל – **except for its west** side, **where one may not make** a tannery **at all?**

The Gemara resolves the issue from a Baraisa:

תָּא שְׁמַע – **Come, learn** the proof from the following: דְּתַנְיָא – **For a Baraisa has taught:** רַבִּי עֲקִיבָא אוֹמֵר – R' AKIVA SAYS: לְכָל רוּחַ הוּא עוֹשֶׂה וּמַרְחִיק חֲמִשִּׁים אַמָּה – ONE MAY MAKE a tannery ON ANY SIDE of a town, BUT HE MUST place it at a DISTANCE of FIFTY *AMOS;* חוּץ מִמַּעֲרָבָהּ דְּאֵינוֹ עוֹשֶׂה כָּל עִיקָּר – EXCEPT FOR ITS WEST side, WHERE ONE MAY NOT MAKE a tannery AT ALL, מִפְּנֵי שֶׁהִיא תְּדִירָא – BECAUSE IT IS CONSTANT.

The Gemara investigates the meaning of the Baraisa's last statement:

אָמַר לֵיהּ רָבָא לְרַב נַחְמָן – **Rava said to Rav Nachman:** מַאי תְּדִירָא – **What is** the meaning of the Baraisa's statement that the west is **"constant"?** אִילֵימָא תְּדִירָא בְּרוּחוֹת – **If you will say** that it means that **the winds** from the west **are constant,** i.e. there is a constant breeze from the west which would carry the odors of the tannery to the town, וְהָא אָמַר רַב חָנָן בַּר אַבָּא אָמַר רַב – **but Rav Chanan bar Abba has said in the name of Rav:** אַרְבַּע רוּחוֹת מְנַשְּׁבוֹת בְּכָל יוֹם – **Four winds blow each day,** וְרוּחַ צְפוֹנִית עִם כּוּלָּן – **and the north wind blows with all of them;**[8] שֶׁאִילְמָלֵא כֵּן אֵין הָעוֹלָם מִתְקַיֵּים אֲפִילּוּ שָׁעָה אַחַת – **for if it were not so, the world would not survive even one hour.** וְרוּחַ דְּרוֹמִית קָשָׁה מִכּוּלָּן – **And the south wind is the harshest of them all;** וְאִילְמָלֵא בֶּן נֵץ שֶׁמַּעֲמִידָהּ – **and if it were not for the angel "Ben Neitz"**[9] **who blocks it,** מַחֲרֶבֶת אֶת הָעוֹלָם – **it would destroy the world.** שֶׁנֶּאֱמַר – **As [the verse] says:**[10] "הֲמִבִּינָתְךָ יַאֲבֶר־נֵץ יִפְרֹשׂ כְּנָפָו לְתֵימָן" – ***Is it from your wisdom that the "neitz" extends its limbs,*** *and* ***spreads its wings to the south?*** We see from the first part of Rav's statement that the wind which blows constantly is the *north* wind, not the west wind. Thus, R' Akiva, who speaks in the Baraisa of the west

NOTES

1. *Rashi.* Although manure is beneficial to grain, too much ruins the crop (*Tosafos* ד״ה שעושה).

2. The east wind is normally warm and gentle (*Rashi*), especially in the Land of Israel and surrounding areas (*Rambam, Commentary to Mishnah*). The east wind blows strongly only as a [Divinely sent] ill wind, bringing misfortune in its wake (*Rashi*).

3. The Gemara will explain the reason for this restriction.

4. Before flax stems may be processed into linen thread, the stems must be retted (soaked) to break down their woody tissue and dissolve the substance binding their fibers together. The stems of flax plants would be soaked in a pool or pond for several days. The substances absorbed by the water during this process are toxic to growing plants, and they pass into the ground around the pool and damage the surrounding vegetation (see *Rambam, Hil. Shecheinim* 10:5). One must therefore distance these pools from the areas in which a neighbor grows vegetables.

Whether this requirement applies generally or only along the border of a field in which the neighbor is actually growing vegetables is the subject of a dispute between Abaye and Rava, as we learned above (18a).

5. Leeks diminish the sharpness of onions growing nearby (*Rambam Commentary*). Thus, one may not grow leeks too close to his neighbor's onions.

6. The bees feed on the mustard plants, which leave a sharp taste in their mouths. The bees then consume the honey in their hives to relieve their discomfort (*Rashi* 18a). Others explain that the mustard consumed by the bees renders their honey pungent (*Rambam Commentary*).

The Mishnah does not specify in these last three cases how far one must distance the harmful agent. The Rishonim (see *Ramban, Rashba, Rabbeinu Yonah* and *Nimukei Yosef*) conclude that the distance required is the same as that in the beginning of the Mishnah — fifty *amos.*

7. R' Yose's opinion was discussed in depth in the Gemara above (18a-b). According to the Gemara's conclusion (18b), R' Yose permits placing the harmful agent close to the boundary of one's property in all three cases listed in this part of the Mishnah, because he holds that in such situations it is up to the injured party to remove his property from harm's way. The reason he speaks of mustard plants specifically was explained above in the Gemara on 18b; see also 25b note 33.

8. [I.e. the wind blows from each of the four directions every day, but no matter which direction the primary wind comes from, there is always a breeze accompanying it out of the north.] The north wind [in and around Eretz Yisrael (see *Hagahos Yavetz*)] is "soft, sweet and clear" [i.e. it blows gently, and its air is pleasant and clear], and it softens the impact of the winds blowing from the other directions (*Rashi*).

9. Literally: son of the hawk; i.e. an angel with a "resemblance" to a hawk. This angel spreads its wings to block the south wind (*Rashi*).

10. *Job* 39:26. This is from God's rebuke to Job, in which He asks Job whether it is by his wisdom and doing that the wonders of God's creation unfold each day.

שעושה אותו גלל: **מתני'** א מרחיקין את הנבלות ואת הקברות ואת הבורסקי מן העיר חמשים אמה ב אין עושין בורסקי אלא למזרח העיר רבי עקיבא אומר לכל רוח הוא עושה חוץ ממערבה ומרחיק חמשים אמה א) ומרחיקין את המשרה מן הירק ואת הכרישין מן הבצלים ואת החרדל מן הדבורים ג ורבי יוסי מתיר בחרדל: **גמ'** איבעיא להו ר' עקיבא היכי קאמר לכל רוח הוא עושה וסומך חוץ ממערבה דמרחיק נ' אמה ועושה או דלמא לכל רוח הוא עושה ומרחיק חמשים אמה חוץ ממערבה דאינו עושה כלל ת"ש דתניא ר"ע אומר לכל רוח הוא עושה ומרחיק חמשים אמה חוץ ממערבה דאינו עושה כל עיקר מפני שהיא תדירה מאי תדירא א"ל רבא לרב נחמן מאי תדירא אילימא תדירא ברוחות והא ב) אמר רב חנן בר אבא אמר רב ד' רוחות מנשבות בכל יום ורוח צפונית עם כולן שאילמלא כן אין העולם מתקיים אפילו שעה אחת ורוח דרומית קשה מכולן ואילמלא בן נץ שמעמידה מחרבת את העולם שנאמר א) המבינתך יאבר נץ יפרוש כנפיו לתימן אלא מאי תדירא תדירא בשכינה דאריב"ל בואו ונחזיק טובה לאבותינו (א) שהודיעו מקום תפלה דכתיב ב) וצבא השמים לך משתחוים מתקיף לה רב אחא בר יעקב ודלמא כעבד שנוטל פרס מרבו וחוזר לאחוריו ומשתחוה קשיא ורבי אושעיא סבר שכינה בכל מקום דאמר רבי אושעיא מאי דכתיב ב) אתה הוא ה' לבדך אתה עשית את השמים וגו' שלוחיך לא כשלוחי בשר ודם שלוחי בשר ודם ממקום שמשתלחים לשם מחזירים שליחותן אבל שלוחיך למקום שמשתלחין ג) משם מחזירין שליחותן שנאמר ג) התשלח ברקים וילכו ויאמרו לך הננו יבואו ויאמרו לא נאמר אלא וילכו ויאמרו מלמד שהשכינה בכל מקום ואף רבי ישמעאל סבר שכינה בכל מקום דתנא דבי רבי ישמעאל מנין ששכינה בכל מקום שנאמר ד) הנה המלאך הדובר בי יוצא ומלאך אחר יוצא לקראתו אחריו לא נאמר אלא לקראתו מלמד ששכינה בכל מקום ואף רב ששת סבר שכינה בכל מקום דא"ל רב ששת לשמעיה לכל רוחתא אוקמן לבר ממזרח ולאו משום דלית ביה שכינה אלא ד) משום דמורו בה מיני ורבי אבהו אמר שכינה במערב דא"ר אבהו מאי אוריה אויר יה אמר רב יהודה (ב) מאי דכתיב ה) יערוף כמטר לקחי זו רוח מערבית שבאה ז) מערפו של עולם תזל כטל אמרתי זו רוח צפונית שמזלת את הזהב וכן הוא אומר ו) הזלים זהב מכיס ה) כשעירים עלי דשא זו רוח מזרחית שמסערת את כל העולם כשעיר וכרביבים עלי עשב זו רוח דרומית שהיא מעלה רביבים ומגדלת עשבים תניא ר"א אומר עולם

רש"י

שעושה אותו גלל. מרבה לו זבל ושורף את הזרעים שמזרעו בו: **מתני'** את הנבלות ואת הקברות כו'. משום ריח רע: **אלא למזרח העיר.** שאין הרוח מזרחית קשה (ג) תדיר אא"כ באה לפורענות אבל כדרכה היא חמה ומנשבת בנחת דכתיב (יונה ד) רוח קדים חרישית ותך השמש וגו' לפיכך אינה מבאה הרוח לעיר: **חוץ מן מערבה.** בגמ' מפרש טעמא: **גמ' וסומך.** אינו צריך להרחיק נ' אמה: **שאינו עושה כלל.** ומרחיק נ' אמה דקאמר ר"ע אשאר רוחות דרישא קאי: **תדירא ברוחות.** אותו לד תדיר ברוח שרוח מערבית מנשבת תדיר משאר רוחות: **רוח צפונית מנשבת עם כל אחת.** מהרוחות לפי שהיא רכה וממוקה ולולא כדאמר ביבמות (דף עב.) וממתקתן: **בן נץ.** מלאך העשוי בדמות נץ: **מעמידה.** בכנפיו: **תדירא בשכינה.** במערב היא שוכנת: **לאבותינו.** אנשי כנה"ג שאמרו מקרא זה בספר עזרא: **וצבא השמים.** השמש והירח העומדים במזרח: **לך משתחוים.** למערב: **ודלמא.** הם למזרח משתחוים וכי תימא אין דרך להשתחוות סמוך לרב הם עושין כעבד שנוטל פרס מרבו וחוזר לאחוריו ומשתחוה כשהוא הולך לאחוריו משנוטל פרס מתרחק תמיד בהשתחויה: **פרס.** מתן: **אתה הוא ה' לבדך.** בתר וצבא השמים כתיב ועל עסקי שליחות צבא השמים הוא משבח ואומר אתה הוא לבדך במדה זו: **לשם מחזירין שליחות.** כשבאין לומר עשינו שליחותך צריכין לשוב אל מקום שהשולחם עומד שם: **למקום שמשתלחין.** פי' באותו מקום שנשתלחו שם אף שם השכינה מצויה ואומרים לו עשינו שליחותך: **והנה המלאך הדובר בי יוצא.** בנבואת זכריה כמו שאמר רוצה למוד את ירושלים כמה ארכה וגו' ומלאך אחר יוצא לספור שליחותו של ראשון שחזר בו המקום (ד) ולא ימן בה מדה ואומר פרזות תשב ירושלים והרי שניהם מאת השכינה באים ואחריו לא נאמר אלא לקראתו זה בא מכאן וזה בא מכאן: **רב ששת.** מאור עיניים הוה: **לכל רוחתא אוקמן.** העמידני להתפלל: **דמודו בה מיני.** תלמידי עובדי ע"ז מורים הוראה להתפלל במזרח: **אוריה.** אני שמעתי כך קורין למערב בלשון פרסי. ול"נ שכך קורין למזרח בלשון לעז והיינו דקאמר אויר יה שהשכינה במערב ופניו למזרח נמלא המזרח אוירו: **יערוף כמטר לקחי.** משה רבינו דימה את התורה לארבע רוחות כשם שאי אפשר בלא הם כך אי אפשר לעולם בלא תורה: **מערפו של עולם.** אני שמעתי מחזקו של עולם על שם שהשכינה במערב ס"ל ואני אומר מאחוריו של עולם שהמערב קרוי אחור שנאמר הן קדם אהלך ואיננו ואחור ולא אבין וגו' (איוב כג): **שמזלת את הזהב.** שמחממת ומביאה שרב ורעבון בא והזהב זל: **וכן הוא אומר.** דכתיב זילותא גבי זהב: **כשעיר.** שד: לאכסדרה

תוספות

שעושה אותו גלל. אע"ג דגלל משביח הקרקע כשהיא כולה גלל מזיק: **אין** עושין בורסקי אלא למזרח העיר. משום דרוח מערבי שהוא קשה ירחיק ויוליך הריח מן העיר כדאמרי' (ברכות מ.) הישן למזרח גרנו דמו בראשו מפני שרוח מערבית מביא הקש בחוטמו: **מפני** שהיא תדירה. לא גרסי' מ"ט דמן הברייתא היא דהכי איתא בתוספתא (פ"א ע"ש): **וצבא** השמים לך משתחוים. וא"ת בלילה נמי במזרח משתחוים וי"ל דאין לנו ללמוד אלא ממה שאנו רואין וא"ת ואמאי לא נדע מקום תפלה מבית המקדש שהיתה שם שכינה במערב וי"ל דמשם אין ללמוד דאע"ג דשכינה בכל מקום אי אפשר להשים ארון וכפורת אלא בצד אחד וריב"א אומר דמשם אין ללמוד דשכינה במערב דנהי דבית קדשי הקדשים היה במערב המקדש מ"מ הארון שהשכינה שם כדכתיב (שמות כה) ונועדתי לך שם היה במזרח בית קדשי הקדשים ה): **לכל** רוחתא אוקמן. כל הני אמוראי לית להו הא דתניא בברכות (דף ל.) שחייב אדם להתפלל נגד ירושלים משום דכתיב והתפללו אליך דרך ארצם אלא סברי כר' ישמעאל דאמר (ה) בכ"מ שכינה ומאן דאמר שכינה במערב סבר כר"ע דאמר מפני שהיא תדירה ור' חנינא דשמעתין דאמר כגון אתון דיתבון לצפונא דארעא דישראל אדרימו סבר לה כברייתא דברכות: **אוריה.** לשון שפ"ה דאוריה מערב נראה לר"ת ° ולר"ח עיקר: **רוח** מערבית שבא מערפו של עולם. כדפי' בקונט' מאחורו של עולם דמערב קרוי אחור דכתיב אחור וקדם צרתני ודרשינן [בחגיגה] (דף יב.) לענין מזרח ומערב וכתיב נמי ארם מקדם ופלשתים מאחור (ישעיה ט) וקרי נמי דרום ימין ולצפון שמאל כדאמרי' בשמעתין והיינו משום דשכינה במערב ופני השכינה למזרח לכך קרוי מערב אחור ומזרח קדם ודרום ימין וצפון שמאל ולמ"ד שכינה בכל מקום נ"ל דהאי דקרי מזרח קדם ומערב אחור ודרום ימין וצפון שמאל משום שכינה בבית המקדש שהיה במערב ופני השכינה כלפי ישראל שהיו במזרח ומשתחוים שם: **הגה"ה** ורבינו יצחק בר יהודה פירש דכשעמד אדם הראשון כשנברא היו פניו למזרח ואין נראה שהיה ערפו כלפי השכינה למאן דאמר שכינה במערב. ע"כ הגה"ה: **רוח** מזרחית שמסערת כל העולם כולו. והא דמשמע במתניתין שהיא נוחה מכל הרוחות היינו כשהיא באה כדרכה אבל כשבאה לפורענות היא מסערת ° כדפי' הקונט' במתניתין: וממזרים

מסורת הש"ס

א) לעיל יח., ב) גיטין לא:, ג) [ילקוט ובע"י איתא שם], ד) [ע' ערוך ערך ערך שמכתב בשם רבינו גרשום פירוש נכון על זה], ה) [וע' תוס' דכתוב סוף מ"ע ומ"ש עוד ביומא פ"ה מ"ב ע"ש], ו) וכ"ה הערוך ערך אסתנא ע' תוס' גיטין לא: ד"ה שהיא נשיב.

הגהות הב"ח

(א) גמ' שהודיעונו מקום תפלה: (ב) שם אמר רב יהודה אמר רב מאי דכתיב יערוף: (ג) רש"י ד"ה אלא וכו' קשה תמיד אא"כ: (ד) ד"ה והנה המלאך וכו' שחזר בו המקום מליתן בה מדה: (ה) תוס' ד"ה לכל וכו' דאמר שכינה בכ"מ ומאן דאמר:

גליון הש"ס

גמרא ומשתחוה קשיא. ע' סנהדרין דף לא ע"ב: תוס' ד"ה אוריה כו' ולר"ח עיקר. ע' קדושין דף יג ע"ב תוס' ד"ה והלכתא. ברש"י ד"ה רוח מזרחית. כדפי' הקונטרס במתני'. כל"ל ברש"י חבקוק א' ח':

תורה אור השלם

א) הַמִבִּינָתְךָ יַאֲבֶר נֵץ יִפְרֹשׂ כְּנָפָו לְתֵימָן: [איוב לט, כו]

ב) אַתָּה הוּא יְיָ לְבַדֶּךָ אַתָּה עָשִׂיתָ אֶת הַשָּׁמַיִם שְׁמֵי הַשָּׁמַיִם וְכָל צְבָאָם הָאָרֶץ וְכָל אֲשֶׁר עָלֶיהָ הַיַּמִּים וְכָל אֲשֶׁר בָּהֶם וְאַתָּה מְחַיֶּה אֶת כֻּלָּם וּצְבָא הַשָּׁמַיִם לְךָ מִשְׁתַּחֲוִים: [נחמיה ט, ו]

ג) הַתְשַׁלַּח בְּרָקִים וְיֵלֵכוּ וְיֹאמְרוּ לְךָ הִנֵּנוּ: [איוב לח, לה]

ד) וְהִנֵּה הַמַּלְאָךְ הַדֹּבֵר בִּי יֹצֵא וּמַלְאָךְ אַחֵר יֹצֵא לִקְרָאתוֹ: [זכריה ב, ז]

ה) יַעֲרֹף כַּמָּטָר לִקְחִי תִּזַּל כַּטַּל אִמְרָתִי כִּשְׂעִירִם עֲלֵי דֶשֶׁא וְכִרְבִיבִים עֲלֵי עֵשֶׂב: [דברים לב, ב]

ו) הַזָּלִים זָהָב מִכִּיס וְכֶסֶף בַּקָּנֶה יִשְׁקֹלוּ יִשְׂכְּרוּ צוֹרֵף וְיַעֲשֵׂהוּ אֵל יִסְגְּדוּ אַף יִשְׁתַּחֲווּ: [ישעיה מו, ו]

לעזי רש"י

אוריה. פירוש מזרח, המקום שמשם זורחת השמש.

ליקוטי רש"י

מרחיקין את המשרה. מים ששורין בו את הפשתן. מן הירק. של מיני מאכל כרוב ושומין וכרישין. כרתי פוריל"ש. ואת החרדל מן הדבורים. שאוכלין את החרדל ומחדד את פיהם ואוכלות את דבש שלהן [לעיל יח.]. ורוח צפונית. נוחה היא לא חמה ולא צוננת וממתקת את שאר הרוחות [גיטין לא.]. המבינתך יאבר נץ וגו'. יגדל הנץ כנף ומלאך הוא דמה לדמות נץ ומעמיד קושי רוח דרומית שלא תחריב את העולם [איוב לט, כו]. יאבר. לשון אברתו יגדיל כנף [גיטין שם]. ויאמרו לך הננו. במקום שנשתלחו שם הננו עשינו שליחותך שאין צריכין לחזור למקומן ולהשיב שלוחן [איוב לח, לה]. הנה המלאך הדובר בי וגו'. הוא אשר בידו חבל המדה [זכריה ב, ז]. הזלים זהב. ל' יזלו מים (תהלים קמז) [ישעיה מו, ו]. כשעירים. לשון רוח סערה כתרגומו כרוחי מטרא מה הרוחות הללו מחזקות את העשבים ומגדלין אותם אף דברי תורה מגדלין את לומדיהן. וכרביבים. טיפי מטר נראה לי על שם שיורה כחץ נקרא רביב כמה דאת אמר (בראשית מט) רובה קשת. דשא. ארברי"ץ עטיפת הארץ מכוסה בירק. עשב. קלח אחד קרוי עשב וכל מין ומין לעצמו קרוי עשב [דברים לב, ב]. לשון עשב ולא עשב לשון דשא וכו' שמיני דשאין מחולקין כל אחד לעצמו נקרא עשב פלוני ואין לשון למדבר לומר דשא פלוני שלשון דשא הוא לבישת הארץ בעשבים כשהיא מתמלאת בדשאים. בלשון לע"ז נקרא דשא ארברי"ץ (גראזיכט) כולן בערבוביא וכל שורש לעצמו נקרא עשב [בראשית א, יא].

עין משפט נר מצוה

פב א ב מיי' פ"י מהל' שכנים הל' ג סמג עשין פב טוש"ע ח"מ סי' קנה סעיף כג:

פג ג מיי' שם הלכה ה סמג שם טוש"ע שם סעיף לא:

פד ד טוש"ע א"ח סי' לד סעיף ג בהג"ה:

רבינו גרשום

פיסקא בורסקי. מקום שמעבדין בו העורות ומסריח: **אלא למזרח העי'.** מפני שרוח מערבי שהיא תדירא מנשבת בו ודוחה הסריחה שאינה באה לעיר: **חוץ ממערבה.** שהיא תדירא ודוחה את הסריחה לעיר א) מש"ה אין עושין: **שאלמלא כן.** שרוח צפונית מבלבלתן אין העולם מתקיים: **יפרוש כנפיו לתימן.** משום דמעמידה לאותו רוח תדיר: **בתפלה.** שהשכינ' במערב ומש"ה צריך להרחיק משם: **לך משתחוים.** [צבא] השמים היינו השמש והירח כשיוצאים במזרח לך משתחוים למערב ושם צריך להחזיר בשעת תפלה: **ואימא.** שהשכינה במזרח ודקאמר לך משתחוים עושים **כעבד שנוטל פרס מרבו ומשתחוה וחוזר לאחוריו.** כך בשעה שיוצאין ממזרח חוזרין פניהם לשכינה במזרח ומשתחוים ושוב יוצאין וזורחין. קשיא: **לבדך** משליחותך ומשנה מבשר ודם: **ויאמרו לך הננו.** בכ"מ שהן. [מלמד] שהשכינה בכל מקום: **והנה המלאך הדובר בי יוצא** מאת השכינה **ומלאך אחר יוצא לקראתו.** מן צד אחר יוצא ולפני שכינה: **דמודו בה מיני.** שמשתחוין לצבא השמים היוצאין מן המזרח: **אוריה.** קורין בלשונן לרוח מערבי: **יערוף כמטר לקחי.** זה העוסק בתורה לשמה ומרכין אזניו לשמוע לקחי עושה טובה לעולם כמטר זה שבא מן מערב: **שבאה מערפו של עולם.** מרוח מערבי ערפו של שכינה הוא. דכתיב צפון וימין אתה בראתם דמשמע דימינו של שכינה בדרום ושמאלו לצד צפון ופניו למזרח וערפו למערב אלמא דשכינה במערב: **ותזל כטל אמרתי.** היינו שמלמד תורה שעוסק שלא לשמה כרוח צפוני שמנשב ומביא רעה לעולם: **עד שמזלת את הזהב.** שנותנין בני אדם כספם וזהבם בזול בשביל התבואה: **כשעירים עלי דשא.** זהו העוסק בתורה שלא לשמה: **כשעירים.** כשד: וכל העוסק בתורה לשמה מביא טובה לעולם כרביבים הללו שיורדין בנחת:

חשק שלמה על רבינו גרשום

א) נראה דצ"ל משו"ה אין עושין כל עיקר.

as being constant, cannot be referring to the constancy of the wind. – ? –

The Gemara therefore advances another explanation:

אֶלָּא מַאי תְּדִירָא – Rather, what is meant by the Baraisa when it says that the west is **"constant"? תְּדִירָא בִּשְׁכִינָה –** That it is the **constant** direction **of the *Shechinah*.**[11] It is therefore improper to locate a tannery in that direction.

The Gemara quotes a statement of R' Yehoshua ben Levi to support the contention that the designated direction of the *Shechinah* is to the west:

דְּאָמַר רַבִּי יְהוֹשֻׁעַ בֶּן לֵוִי – For R' Yehoshua ben Levi said: בּוֹאוּ וְנַחֲזִיק טוֹבָה לַאֲבוֹתֵינוּ – Come, let us show gratitude to our forefathers, the Men of the Great Assembly, **שֶׁהוֹדִיעוּ מְקוֹם תְּפִלָּה – who,** by stating the following verse,[12] **made known** to us **the place,** i.e. the proper direction, **of prayer. דִּכְתִיב – For it is written: "וּצְבָא הַשָּׁמַיִם לְךָ מִשְׁתַּחֲוִים" – *And the heavenly legions bow to You*** – i.e. the sun, the moon and the stars rise in the east and then "bow" towards the west as they set.[13] Since they are bowing toward God, we see that the direction designated for the *Shechinah* is the west.

Rav Acha bar Yaakov takes issue with R' Yehoshua ben Levi's proof:

מַתְקִיף לָהּ רַב אַחָא בַּר יַעֲקֹב – Rav Acha bar Yaakov challenged this interpretation of the motion of the heavenly bodies: **וְדִלְמָא כְּעֶבֶד שֶׁנּוֹטֵל פְּרָס מֵרַבּוֹ – Perhaps** the motion of the sun and moon is **like** the motion of **a servant who receives a portion from his master וְחוֹזֵר לַאֲחוֹרָיו וּמִשְׁתַּחֲוֶה – and** then **backs away bowing!**[14] Thus, the "bowing" movements of the heavenly bodies while moving west would indicate that the *Shechinah* is in the east![15]

The Gemara concludes:

קַשְׁיָא – This is indeed **a difficulty.**

The Gemara now quotes other opinions as to the direction of the *Shechinah:*

וְרַבִּי אוֹשַׁעְיָא סָבַר שְׁכִינָה בְּכָל מָקוֹם – And R' Oshaya holds that the *Shechinah* is in all directions equally,[16] as we see from the following statement. **דְּאָמַר רַבִּי אוֹשַׁעְיָא – For R' Oshaya said: מַאי דִּכְתִיב – What is** the meaning **of that which is written: "אַתָּה־הוּא ה' לְבַדֶּךָ אַתְּ עָשִׂיתָ אֶת־הַשָּׁמַיִם וגו'" – *You are God, You alone; You have made the Heavens etc.?***[17] R' Oshaya explained: **שְׁלוּחֶיךָ לֹא כִּשְׁלוּחֵי בָּשָׂר וָדָם – Your messengers,**[18] God, **are not like the messengers of a** creature of **flesh and blood. שְׁלוּחֵי בָּשָׂר וָדָם – The messengers of flesh and blood, מִמָּקוֹם שֶׁמִּשְׁתַּלְּחִים לְשָׁם מַחֲזִירִים שְׁלִיחוּתָן – from the place from which they are sent, there they return** a report on **their mission** to the one who sent them. **אֲבָל שְׁלוּחֶיךָ – But Your messengers,** God, are unique, for **לַמָּקוֹם שֶׁמִּשְׁתַּלְּחִין – to the place to which they are sent, (מ)שָּׁם מַחֲזִירִין שְׁלִיחוּתָן – there**[19] **they return** a report on **their mission,** for the *Shechinah* is in all places.

R' Oshaya demonstrates this from the following verse:

שֶׁנֶּאֱמַר – As it states:[20] **"הַתְשַׁלַּח בְּרָקִים וְיֵלֵכוּ וְיֹאמְרוּ לְךָ הִנֵּנוּ" – *Can you send forth lightning bolts that they will go, and say to you, "Behold, we are here"?*** R' Oshaya explains: **יָבוֹאוּ וְיֹאמְרוּ לֹא נֶאֱמַר – It does not say** that **"they** (the bolts) **will *come* and say,"** which would have implied that they will return to their point of departure to report. **אֶלָּא "וְיֵלְכוּ וְיֹאמְרוּ" – Rather,** it says: **"and they will *go* and say,"** which implies that they will report at their destination! **מְלַמֵּד שֶׁהַשְּׁכִינָה בְּכָל מָקוֹם – This teaches that the *Shechinah* is in every place.**

The Gemara quotes a Tanna who concurs with R' Oshaya:

וְאַף רַבִּי יִשְׁמָעֵאל סָבַר שְׁכִינָה בְּכָל מָקוֹם – And R' Yishmael, too, holds that the *Shechinah* is in all directions. דְּתָנָא דְּבֵי רַבִּי יִשְׁמָעֵאל – For a Baraisa of the academy of R' Yishmael has taught: מִנַּיִן שֶׁשְּׁכִינָה בְּכָל מָקוֹם – FROM WHERE do we learn THAT THE *SHECHINAH* IS IN ALL PLACES? **שֶׁנֶּאֱמַר –** FOR [THE VERSE] STATES:[21] **"הִנֵּה הַמַּלְאָךְ הַדֹּבֵר בִּי יֹצֵא – *BEHOLD, THE ANGEL WHO SPOKE WITH ME CAME FORTH*** from God's presence **וּמַלְאָךְ אַחֵר יֹצֵא לִקְרָאתוֹ" – *AND ANOTHER ANGEL CAME FORTH*** from God's presence ***TOWARDS HIM.*** **אַחֲרָיו לֹא נֶאֱמַר – It does not say** in this verse that the second angel came forth **"following [the first],"** which is what would have happened had he emerged from the same place as the first. **אֶלָּא "לִקְרָאתוֹ" – Rather,** the verse says that the second angel came ***towards*** the first – i.e. from the opposite direction – although they were both coming from God's

NOTES

11. *Shechinah* – the manifestation of the Divine Presence. Although God's presence is everywhere, there are places where it is more manifest than others (such as in the Temple, for example). The discussion that follows addresses whether any specific direction possesses a greater presence. The Gemara explains the Baraisa by attributing to it the view of R' Yehoshua ben Levi, who says that it is proper to face west when praying, because the west is designated as the direction of the Divine Presence. [See note 15 below.] For this reason, it is improper to locate a tannery (which, due to its stench, is considered a base enterprise) to the west of a town.

12. *Nehemiah* 9:6. [Although Ezra wrote this book (Gemara 15a), this prayer was not authored by him, but by members of the Great Assembly; see *Rashi*.]

13. Bowing is the mark of submission to a greater authority. The setting of the sun and the other heavenly bodies is, metaphorically, the ultimate sign of their submission. Thus, the direction in which they set is the direction of their "bow" (*Maharal, Chidushei Aggados*).

14. A servant who receives a gift from his master does not turn his back on him as he departs, but backs away bowed, expressing his gratitude (see *Rashi*).

15. Bowing towards a master expresses the submission that results from one's sense of inconsequence relative to a superior. In the context of the heavenly bodies, this motion represents the realization that they are no more than the creations of God, to Whom they owe their very existence. Bowing while backing away from a master expresses the sense of gratitude that one feels for the favors he has received. In the context of the heavenly bodies, this motion represents the realization that they continue to shine and move about in their orbits only by the will of God. Since these movements are also appropriate to the heavenly bodies, Rav Acha bar Yaakov contends that the path of their motion cannot be used to prove that the west is the designated direction of the *Shechinah* (see *Maharal, Chidushei Aggados*).

Meiri suggests that the very point of designating the west as the direction of the *Shechinah* and praying in that direction is that the "bowing" of the heavenly bodies in that direction demonstrates the falseness of the widely held belief that the heavenly bodies were themselves deities possessed of an absolute existence. See also *Rambam, Moreh Nevuchim* 3:45.

16. [Thus, there is no preferred direction in which to pray, as the Gemara will state below in the name of Rav Sheishess.]

17. *Nehemiah* 9:6. This verse concludes with the passage cited above – *and the heavenly legions bow to You,* indicating that the unique quality to which the verse refers pertains to the relationship of the heavenly legions to God (*Rashi*; see *Rashash*).

18. I.e. the heavenly legions – the sun, the moon and the stars (*Rashi*).

19. I.e. at the site of their mission. (This translation follows the emendation of *Mesoras HaShas*.)

20. *Job* 38:35 (see note 10).

21. *Zechariah* 2:7. The two angels mentioned came with conflicting assignments: The first came to lay down boundaries for the city of Jerusalem. God then "reconsidered," and sent a second angel to instruct the first to desist, for Jerusalem was to be an open city, without boundaries (*Rashi*).

שעושה אותו גלל: **מתני'** א מרחיקין את הנבלות ואת הקברות ואת הבורסקי מן העיר חמשים אמה ב אין עושין בורסקי אלא למזרח העיר רבי עקיבא אומר לכל רוח הוא עושה חוץ ממערבה ומרחיק חמשים אמה ג ומרחיקין את המשרה מן הירק ואת הכרישין מן הבצלים ואת החרדל מן הדבורים ג ורבי יוסי מתיר בחרדל: **גמ'** איבעיא להו ר' עקיבא היכי קאמר לכל רוח הוא עושה וסומך חוץ ממערבה דמרחיק נ' אמה ועושה או דלמא לכל רוח הוא עושה ומרחיק חמשים אמה חוץ ממערבה דאינו עושה כלל ת"ש דתניא ר"ע אומר לכל רוח הוא עושה ומרחיק חמשים אמה חוץ ממערבה דאינו עושה כל עיקר מפני שהיא תדירה א"ל רבא לרב נחמן מאי תדירה אילימא תדירא ברוחות והא ג אמר רב חנן בר אבא אמר רב ד' רוחות מנשבות בכל יום ורוח צפונית עם כולן שאילמלא כן אין העולם מתקיים אפילו שעה אחת ורוח דרומית קשה מכולן ואילמלא בן נץ שמעמידה מחרבת את העולם שנאמר א) המבינתך יאבר נץ יפרוש כנפיו לתימן אלא מאי תדירא תדירא בשכינה דאריב"ל בואו ונחזיק טובה לאבותינו (א) שהודיעו מקום תפלה דכתיב ב) וצבא השמים לך משתחוים מתקיף לה רב אחא בר יעקב ודלמא כעבד שנוטל פרס מרבו וחוזר לאחוריו ו ומשתחוה קשיא ורבי אושעיא סבר שכינה בכל מקום דאמר רבי אושעיא מאי דכתיב ב) אתה הוא ה' לבדך אתה עשית את השמים וגו' שלוחיך לא כשלוחי בשר ודם שלוחי בשר ודם ממקום שמשתלחים לשם מחזירים שליחותן אבל שלוחיך למקום שמשתלחין ג משם מחזירין שליחותן שנאמר ג) התשלח ברקים וילכו ויאמרו לך הננו ויאמרו לא נאמר אלא וילכו ויאמרו מלמד שהשכינה בכל מקום ואף רבי ישמעאל סבר שכינה בכל מקום דתנא דבי רבי ישמעאל מנין ששכינה בכל מקום שנאמר ד) הנה המלאך הדובר בי יוצא ומלאך אחר יוצא לקראתו אחריו לא נאמר אלא לקראתו מלמד ששכינה בכל מקום ואף רב ששת סבר שכינה בכל מקום דא"ל רב ששת לשמעיה לכל רוחתא אוקמן לבר ממזרח ולאו משום דלית ביה שכינה אלא ד משום דמורו בה מיני ורבי אבהו אמר שכינה במערב דא"ר אבהו מאי אוריה אויר יה אמר רב יהודה (ב) מאי דכתיב ה) יערוף כמטר לקחי זו רוח מערבית שבאה ד מערפו של עולם תזל כטל אמרתי זו רוח צפונית שמזלת את הזהב וכן הוא אומר ו) הזלים זהב מכיס ה) כשעירים עלי דשא זו רוח מזרחית שמסערת את כל העולם כשעיר וכרביבים עלי עשב זו רוח דרומית שהיא מעלה רביבים ומגדלת עשבים תניא ר"א אומר עולם

רש"י

שעושה אותו גלל. מרבה לו זבל ושורף את הזרעים שמרעו בו: **מתני' את הנבלות ואת הקברות כו'.** משום ריח רע: **אלא למזרח העיר.** שאין הרוח מזרחית קשה (ג) תדיר אא"כ באה לפורענות אבל כדרכה היא חמה ומנשבת בנחת דכתיב (יונה ד) רוח קדים חרישית ותך השמש וגו' לפיכך אינה מביאה הרוח לעיר: **חוץ מן מערבה.** בגמ' מפרש טעמא: **גמ' וסומך.** אינו צריך להרחיק נ' אמה: **שאינו עושה כלל.** ומרחיק נ' אמה דקאמר ר"ע אשאר רוחות דרישא קאי: **תדירא ברוחות.** אותו לד תדיר ברוח שרוח מערבית מנשבת תדיר משאר רוחות: **רוח צפונית מנשבת עם כל אחת.** מהרוחות לפי שהיא רכה וממותקה ואלולה כדאמר ביבמות (דף עב.) וממתקתן: **בן נץ.** מלאך העשוי בדמות נץ: **מעמידה.** בכנפיו: **תדירא בשכינה.** במערב היא שוכנת: **לאבותינו.** אנשי כנה"ג שאמרו מקרא זה בספר עזרא: **וצבא השמים.** השמש והירח העומדים במזרח: **לך משתחוים.** למערב: **ודלמא.** הם למזרח משתחוים וכי תימא אין דרך להשתחוות סמוך לרב הם עושין כעבד שנוטל פרס מרבו וחוזר לאחוריו ומשתחוה כשהוא הולך לאחוריו משנטל פרס מתרחק תמיד בהשתחויה: **פרס.** מתן: **אתה הוא ה' לבדך.** בתר וצבא השמים כתיב ועל עסקי שליחות צבא השמים הוא משבח ואומר אתה הוא לבדך במדה זו: **לשם מחזירין שליחותן.** כשבאין לומר עשינו שליחותך צריכין לשוב אל מקום שהשולחם עומד שם: **למקום שמשתלחין.** פי' באותו מקום שנשתלחו שם אף שם השכינה מצויה ואומרים לו עשינו שליחותך: **והנה המלאך הדובר בי יוצא.** בנבואת זכריה למוד את ירושלים כמה ארכה וגו' ומלאך אחר יוצא לסתור שליחותו של ראשון שחזר בו המקום (ד) ולא יתן בה מדה ואומר פרזות תשב ירושלים והרי שניהם מאת השכינה באים ואחריו לא נאמר אלא לקראתו זה בא מכאן וזה בא מכאן: **רב ששת.** מאור עינים הוה: **לכל רוחתא אוקמן.** העמידני להתפלל: **דמורו בה מיני.** תלמידי עובדי ע"ז מורים הוראה להתפלל במזרח: **אוריה.** אני שמעתי כך קורין למערב בלשון פרסי. ול"נ שכך קורין למזרח בלשון לעז והיינו דקאמר אויר יה שהשכינה במערב ופניו למזרח נמצא המזרח אוירו: **יערוף כמטר לקחי.** משה רבינו דימה את התורה לארבע רוחות כשם שאי אפשר בלא הם כך אי אפשר לעולם בלא תורה: **מערפו של עולם.** אני שמעתי מחזקו של עולם על שם שהשכינה במערב ס"ל ואני אומר מאחוריו של עולם שהמערב קרוי אחור שנאמר הן קדם אהלך ואיננו ואחור ולא אבין וגו' (איוב כג): **שמזלת את הזהב.** שמחממת ומביאה שרב ורעבון בא והזהב זל: **וכן הוא אומר.** דכתיב זילותא גבי זהב: **כשעיר.** שד: לאכסדרה

תוספות

שעושה אותו גלל. הע"ג דגלל משביח הקרקע כשהיא כולה גלל מזיק: **אין עושין בורסקי אלא למזרח העיר.** משום דרוח מערבי שהוא קשה ירחיק ויוליך הריח מן העיר כדאמרי' (ברכות מ.) הישן למזרח גרנו דמו בראשו מפני שרוח מערבית מביא הקש בחוטמו: **מפני שהיא תדירה.** לא גרסי' מ"ט דמן הברייתא היא דהכי איתא בתוספתא (פ"א ע"ש): **וצבא השמים לך משתחוים.** וא"ת בלילה נמי במזרח משתחוים וי"ל דאין לנו ללמוד אלא ממה שאנו רואין וא"ת ואמאי לא נדע מקום תפלה מבית המקדש שהיתה שם שכינה במערב וי"ל דמשם אין ללמוד דאע"ג דשכינה בכל מקום אי אפשר להשים ארון וכפורת אלא בצד אחד וריצב"א אומר דמשם אין ללמוד דשכינה במערב דנהי דבית קדשי הקדשים היה במערב המקדש מ"מ הארון שהשכינה שם כדכתיב (שמות כה) ונועדתי לך שם היה במזרח בית קדשי הקדשים א): **לכל רוחתא אוקמן.** כל הני אמוראי לית להו הא דתניא בברכות (דף ל.) שחייב אדם להתפלל נגד ירושלים משום דכתיב והתפללו אליך דרך ארצם אלא סברי כר' ישמעאל דאמר (ה) בכ"מ שכינה ומאן דאמר שכינה במערב סבר כר"ע דאמר מפני שהיא תדירה ור' חנינא דשמעתין דאמר כגון אתון דיתבון לצפונא דארעא דישראל אדרימו סבר לה כברייתא דברכות: **אוריה.** לשון שפ"ה דאוריה מערב נראה לר"ת ° ולר"ת עיקר: **רוח מערבית שבא מערפו של עולם.** כדפי' בקונט' מאחורו של עולם דמערב קרוי אחור דכתיב אחור וקדם צרתני ודרשינן [בחגיגה] (דף יב.) לענין מזרח ומערב וכתיב נמי ארם מקדם ופלשתים מאחור (ישעיה ט) וקרי נמי דרום ימין ולצפון שמאל כדאמרי' בשמעתין והיינו משום דשכינה במערב ופני השכינה למזרח לכך קרוי מערב אחור ומזרח קדם ודרום ימין וצפון שמאל ולמ"ד שכינה בכל מקום צ"ל דהאי דקרי מזרח קדם ומערב אחור ודרום ימין וצפון שמאל משום שכינה בבית המקדש שהיה במערב ופני השכינה כלפי ישראל שהיו במזרח ומשתחוים שם: **הגה"ה** ורבינו יצחק בר יהודה פירש כשעמד אדם הראשון כשנברא היו פניו למזרח ואין נראה שהיה ערפו כלפי השכינה למאן דאמר שכינה במערב. ע"כ הגה"ה: **רוח מזרחית שמסערת כל העולם** כולו. והא דמשמע שהיא נוחה מכל הרוחות היינו כשהיא באה כדרכה אבל כשבאה לפורענות היא מסערת ° כדפי' הקונט' במתניתין: וממזריס

מסורת הש"ס

א) לעיל יח., ב) גיטין לא:, ג) [ילקוט ובע"י איתא שם], ד) [ע' ערוך ערך ערף שכתב בשם רבינו גרשום פירוש נכון על זה], ה) [וע' תו"ח דהכא סוף מ"ע ומ"ש עוד ביומא פ"ה מ"ב ע"ש], ו) וכ"ה הערוך ערך אסתנא ע' תוס' גיטין לא: ד"ה שדיא נשיב.

הגהות הב"ח

(א) גמ' שהודיעונו מקום תפלה: (ב) שם אמר רב יהודה אמר רב מאי דכתיב יערוף: (ג) רש"י ד"ה אלא וכו' קשה תמיד אא"כ: (ד) ד"ה והנה המלאך וכו' שחזר בו המקום מלימן בה מדה: (ה) תוס' ד"ה לכל וכו' דאמר שכינה בכ"מ ומאן דאמר:

גליון הש"ס

גמרא ומשתחוה קשיא. ע"י סנהדרין דף לא ע"ב: תוס' ד"ה אוריה כו' ולר"ת עיקר. ע' קדושין דף יב ע"ב תוס' ד"ה והאלהא: בא"ד רוח מזרחית. כדפי' הקונטרס במתני'. כצ"ל ברש"י חבקוק א' ט':

תורה אור השלם

א) הֲמִבִּינָתְךָ יַאֲבֶר נֵץ יִפְרֹשׂ כְּנָפָו לְתֵימָן: [איוב לט, כו]

ב) אַתָּה הוּא יְיָ לְבַדֶּךָ אַתָּה עָשִׂיתָ אֶת הַשָּׁמַיִם שְׁמֵי הַשָּׁמַיִם וְכָל צְבָאָם הָאָרֶץ וְכָל אֲשֶׁר עָלֶיהָ הַיַּמִּים וְכָל אֲשֶׁר בָּהֶם וְאַתָּה מְחַיֶּה אֶת כֻּלָּם וּצְבָא הַשָּׁמַיִם לְךָ מִשְׁתַּחֲוִים: [נחמיה ט, ו]

ג) הַתְשַׁלַּח בְּרָקִים וְיֵלֵכוּ וְיֹאמְרוּ לְךָ הִנֵּנוּ: [איוב לח, לה]

ד) וְהִנֵּה הַמַּלְאָךְ הַדֹּבֵר בִּי יֹצֵא וּמַלְאָךְ אַחֵר יֹצֵא לִקְרָאתוֹ: [זכריה ב, ז]

ה) יַעֲרֹף כַּמָּטָר לִקְחִי תִּזַּל כַּטַּל אִמְרָתִי כִּשְׂעִירִם עֲלֵי דֶשֶׁא וְכִרְבִיבִים עֲלֵי עֵשֶׂב: [דברים לב, ב]

ו) הַזָּלִים זָהָב מִכִּיס וְכֶסֶף בַּקָּנֶה יִשְׁקֹלוּ יִשְׂכְּרוּ צוֹרֵף וְיַעֲשֵׂהוּ אֵל יִסְגְּדוּ אַף יִשְׁתַּחֲווּ: [ישעיה מו, ו]

לעזי רש"י

אורי"ה. פירוש מזרח, המקום שמשם זורחת השמש.

ליקוטי רש"י

מרחיקין את המשרה. מים ששורין בו את הפשתן. מן הירק. של מיני מאכל כרוב ושומין וכרישין. ואת הכרישין. כרתי פורי"ש. ואת החרדל מן הדבורים. שאוכלין את החרדל ומחדד את פיהם ואוכלות את דבש שלהן [לעיל יח.]. ורוח צפונית. נוחה היא לא חמה ולא צוננת וממתקת את שאר הרוחות [גיטין לא.]. המבינתך יאבר נץ וגו'. יגדל הנץ כנף ומלאך הוא דמה לדמות נץ ומעמיד קושי רוח דרומית שלא תחריב את העולם [איוב לט, כו]. יאבר. לשון אברתו יגדיל כנף [גיטין שם]. ויאמרו לך הננו. במקום שנשתלחו שם הננו עשינו שליחותך שאין צריכין לחזור למקומן ולהשיב שלוחן שהשכינה בכל מקום [איוב לח, לה]. הנה המלאך הדובר בי וגו'. הוא אשר בידו חבל המדה [זכריה ב, ז]. הזלים זהב. ל' יזלו מים (תהלים קמז) [ישעיה מו, ו]. כשעירים. לשון רוח סערה כתרגומו כרוחי מטרא מה הרוחות הללו מחזיקות את העשבים ומגדלין אותם אף דברי תורה מגדלין את לומדיהן. וכרביבים. טיפי מטר נראה לי על שם שיורה כחץ נקרא רביב כמה דאת אמר (בראשית מט) רובה קשת. דשא. ארברי"ץ עטיפת הארץ מכוסה בירק. עשב. קלח אחד קרוי עשב וכל מין ומין לעצמו קרוי עשב [דברים לב, ב]. לא דשא לשון עשב ולא עשב לשון דשא וכו' שמיני דשאין מחולקין כל אחד לעצמו נקרא עשב פלוני ואין לשון למדבר לומר דשא פלוני שלשון דשא הוא לבישת הארץ בעשבים כשהיא מתמלאת בדשאים. בלשון לע"ז נקרא דשא ארברי"ץ (גראזיכט) כולן בערבוביא וכל שורש לעצמו נקרא עשב [בראשית א, יא].

עין משפט נר מצוה

פב א ב מיי' פ"י מהל' שכנים הל' ג סמג עשין פב טוש"ע ח"מ סי' קנה סעיף כג:
פג ג מיי' שם הלכה ה סמג שם טוש"ע שם סעיף לא:
פד ד טוש"ע א"ח סי' צד סעיף ג בהג"ה:

רבינו גרשום

פיסקא בורסקי. מקום שמעבדין בו העורות ומסריח: **אלא למזרח העי'.** מפני שרוח מערבי שהיא תדירא מנשבת בו ודוחה הסריחה שאינה באה לעיר: **חוץ ממערבה.** שהיא תדירא ודוחה את הסריחה לעיר א) מש"ה אין עושין: **שאלמלא כן.** שרוח צפונית מבלבלתן אין העולם מתקיים: **יפרוש כנפיו לתימן.** משום דמעמידה לאותו רוח תדיר: **בתפלה.** שהשכינ' במערב ומש"ה צריך להרחיק משם: **לך משתחוים.** [צבא] השמים היינו השמש והירח כשיוצאים במזרח לך משתחוים למערב ושם צריך להחזיר בשעת תפלה: **ואימא.** שהשכינה במזרח ודקאמר לך משתחוים עושים **כעבד שנוטל פרס מרבו ומשתחוה וחוזר לאחוריו.** כך בשעה שיוצאין ממזרח חוזרין פניהם לשכינה במזרח ומשתחוים ושוב יוצאין וזורחין. **קשיא: לבדך** משליחותך ומשנה מבשר ודם: **ויאמרו לך הננו.** בכ"מ שהן. [מלמד] **שהשכינה בכל מקום: והנה המלאך הדובר בי יוצא** מאת השכינה **ומלאך אחר יוצא לקראתו.** מן צד אחר יוצא ולפני שכינה: **דמודי בה מיני.** שמשתחוין לצבא השמים היוצאין מן המזרח: **אוריה.** קורין בלשונן לרוח מערבי: **יערוף כמטר לקחי.** זה העוסק בתורה לשמה ומרכין אזניו לשמוע לקחי עושה טובה לעולם כמטר זה שבא מן מערב: **שבאה מערפו של עולם.** מרוח מערבי ערפו של שכינה הוא. דכתיב צפון וימין אתה בראתם דמשמע דימינו של שכינה בדרום ושמאלו לצד צפון ופניו למזרח וערפו למערב אלמא דשכינה במערב: **ותזל כטל אמרתי.** היינו שמזלזל תורה שעוסק שלא לשמה מביא רעה לעולם כרוח צפוני שמנשב ומביא רעה לעולם: **את שמזלת את הזהב.** שנותנין בני אדם כספם וזהבם בזול בשביל התבואה: **כשעירים עלי דשא.** זהו העוסק בתורה שלא לשמה: כשד: והעוסק בתורה לשמה מביא טובה לעולם כרביבים הללו שיורדין בנחת:

חשק שלמה על רבינו גרשום

א) נראה דל"ל משו"ה אין עושין כל עיקר.

presence! מְלַמֵּד שֶׁשְּׁכִינָה בְּכָל מָקוֹם – **This teaches that the *Shechinah* is in all places.**[22]

The Gemara quotes yet another concurring opinion:

וְאַף רַב שֵׁשֶׁת סָבַר שְׁכִינָה בְּכָל מָקוֹם – **And Rav Sheishess, too, holds that the *Shechinah* is in all places.** דְּאָמַר לֵיהּ רַב שֵׁשֶׁת לְשַׁמָּעֵיהּ – **For Rav Sheishess,** who was blind,[23] **said to his attendant:** לְכָל רוּחֲתָא אוֹקְמָן לְבַר מִמִּזְרָח – **Stand me up** to pray **facing any direction except east.** וְלָאו מִשּׁוּם דְּלֵית בֵּיהּ שְׁכִינָה – **And** the reason I do not wish to face east is **not because the *Shechinah* is not present there,** אֶלָּא מִשּׁוּם דְּמוֹרוּ בָּהּ מִינֵי – **but rather, because the heretics instruct** that one pray **to that side** (east), and Rav Sheishess did not wish to lend credence to their heresy. From his lack of preference otherwise, we see that Rav Sheishess agrees that the *Shechinah* is manifest in all directions equally, so that there is no inherently preferred direction for prayer.[24]

The Gemara now quotes a differing view:

וְרַבִּי אַבָּהוּ אָמַר שְׁכִינָה בַּמַּעֲרָב – **But R' Abahu said** that **the *Shechinah* is in the west.** דְּאָמַר רַבִּי אַבָּהוּ – **For R' Abahu said:** מַאי אוֹרְיָה – **What is** the etymology of the word ***oryah,*** meaning "east"?[25] אֲוִיר יָהּ – It comes from two words ***avir Yah*** – the "air of God." Since the *Shechinah* is in the west, the east is the open "air" before the *Shechinah.*

The Gemara now returns to the discussion of winds, quoting a homiletical interpretation of *Deuteronomy* 32:2, in which the Torah is compared to the four winds:[26]

אָמַר רַב יְהוּדָה – **Rav Yehudah said:** מַאי דִּכְתִיב – **What is** the meaning of **that which is written:** "יַעֲרֹף כַּמָּטָר לִקְחִי" – ***Let My teaching drip*** (*ya'arof*) ***like the rain?*** זוֹ רוּחַ מַעֲרָבִית שֶׁבָּאָה מֵעָרְפּוֹ שֶׁל עוֹלָם – **This** (the word *ya'arof*) **refers to the west wind, which comes from the "back"** (*oref*) **of the world.**[27]

Rav Yehudah continues his exposition of the verse:

"תִּזַּל כַּטַּל אִמְרָתִי" – ***Let My words distill*** (*tizal*) ***like the dew.*** זוֹ רוּחַ צְפוֹנִית – **This** (the word *tizal*) **refers to the north wind,** שֶׁמְּזִלֶּת אֶת הַזָּהָב – **which devalues** the worth of **gold** (*zal*) by destroying the crops and bringing famine, thereby forcing people to spend money freely on food.[28] וְכֵן הוּא אוֹמֵר – **And so it states** in another verse which applies the word *zal* to spending gold freely: "הַזָּלִים זָהָב מִכִּיס" – ***Those who spend gold freely*** (*zalim*) ***from the purse.***[29]

The third phrase of the verse:

"כִּשְׂעִירִם עֲלֵי דֶשֶׁא" – ***Like winds*** (*se'erim*) ***which blow the vegetation.*** זוֹ רוּחַ מִזְרָחִית – **This** (*se'erim*) **refers to the east wind,** שֶׁמְּסַעֶרֶת אֶת כָּל הָעוֹלָם כְּשָׂעִיר – **which churns up the entire world like a demon** (*sa'ir*).[30]

The final phrase of the verse:

"וְכִרְבִיבִים עֲלֵי־עֵשֶׂב" – ***And like showers*** (*revivim*) ***upon the grasses.*** זוֹ רוּחַ דְּרוֹמִית – **This refers to the south wind,** שֶׁהִיא מַעֲלָה רְבִיבִים וּמְגַדֶּלֶת עֲשָׂבִים – **which brings up the showers and causes grasses to grow.**

The Gemara quotes a Baraisa concerning the path of the sun:[31]

תַּנְיָא – **A Baraisa has taught:** רַבִּי אֱלִיעֶזֶר אוֹמֵר – **R' ELIEZER SAYS:** עוֹלָם – **THE WORLD**

NOTES

22. [Scripture's reference to this unusual phenomenon is meant to teach us that we are not to associate the *Shechinah* – the manifestation of the Divine Presence – with one direction more than another. See note 11.]

23. *Rashi.* Thus, he could not tell which direction he was facing.

24. The Gemara has cited two opinions as to whether it is proper to pray specifically towards the west, or whether there is no directional preference. The Gemara in *Berachos* (30a) cites a Baraisa that the proper direction in which to pray is towards the Temple Mount in Jerusalem. [This opinion will also be cited by the Gemara below (25b) in the name of Rav Chanina.] Thus, there are in effect three Tannaic opinions regarding the direction in which one should pray: R' Akiva of our Mishnah, who prohibits placing a tannery to the west of a town, is of the opinion that one should pray towards the west. (In this he is followed by the Amora, R' Yehoshua ben Levi.) R' Yishmael (followed by the Amoraim, R' Oshaya and Rav Sheishess) holds that one may pray in any direction. The Tanna of the Baraisa quoted in *Berachos* (followed by the Amora, Rav Chanina, quoted below) rules that one should pray towards the Temple Mount (*Tosafos*). The halachah follows this last opinion. Therefore, those who live in Europe [and in the Americas], which are to the west of the Land of Israel, face east in prayer (*Tur* and *Rama, Orach Chaim* 94:2). However, since most of Europe [and North America] is not due west of the Land of Israel but somewhat north of it as well, it is best to face a bit to the southeast (*Levush* ibid.; *Mishnah Berurah* 94:11).

25. R' Abahu offers a homiletic etymology of a foreign word which means east (*Rashi,* in his preferred explanation). *Tosafos* prefer *Rashi's* other interpretation, that it is a Persian word meaning *west,* and is so called because the *Shechinah* is on the west side.

26. This verse is from the opening section of the song of *Haazinu,* in which God's words (specifically the Torah; see commentaries) are likened to the dew and the rain falling to earth. Rav Yehudah's interpretation sees in this verse a further comparison to the four winds. This is meant to convey that just as the world cannot long exist without the four winds (as stated above in the name of Rav), so too, the world cannot exist without Torah (*Rashi*).

27. The Biblical word for "east" – קֶדֶם – also means *front.* Thus, we see that Scripture depicts east as the "front" of the world, making "west" its *back.* This may be seen from the verse in *Job* (23:8): הֵן קֶדֶם אֶהֱלֹךְ וְאֵינֶנּוּ וְאָחוֹר וְלֹא־אָבִין לוֹ, *Behold, I go east, but He is not there; and west* [lit. backward], *but I cannot perceive Him* (*Rashi*).

28. The north wind warms [the Land of Israel] and dries out the land and its crops (*Rashi*). Although the north wind is a gentle wind (see note 8 above), it tends to disperse the clouds and thereby reduces the amount of rainfall (*Tosafos, Yevamos* 72a ד״ה דלא).

29. *Isaiah* 46:6.

30. As mentioned above (note 2), when the east wind blows strongly, it is catastrophic. The word שָׂעִיר is used in Scripture as a name for demons (see *Leviticus* 17:7).

31. [This is introduced here because it in turn introduces another Baraisa, which also speaks about the winds, and is therefore relevant to our discussion. It should be borne in mind that whenever the Gemara discusses the orbits of the astronomical bodies, it discusses them from the perspective of the observer, in which the sun and other heavenly bodies are seen to revolve around the earth.]

מסורת הש"ס

א) לעיל יח. ב) גיטין לא:, ג) [ילקוט ובע"י איתא תפלה], ד) [ע' בערוך ערך ערף שכתב בשם רבינו גרשום פירוש נכון על זה], ה) [וע' תוס' להלכה סוף מ"ע ומ"ש עוד ביומא פ"ה מ"ג ע"ש], ו) וכ"ה הערוך ערך אספקלר ע' תוס' גיטין לא: ד"ה שדיא נשיב:

עין משפט נר מצוה

פב א ב מיי' פ"י מהל' שכנים הל' ג סמג עשין פב טוש"ע ח"מ סי' קנה סעיף כ:
פג ג מיי' שם הלכה ה סמג שם טוש"ע שם סעיף לא:
פד ד טוש"ע א"ח סי' צד סעיף ג בהג"ה:

שעושה אותו גלל: **מתני'** מרחיקין את הנבלות ואת הקברות ואת הבורסקי מן העיר חמשים אמה אין עושין בורסקי אלא למזרח העיר רבי עקיבא אומר לכל רוח הוא עושה חוץ ממערבה ומרחיק חמשים אמה ומרחיקין את המשרה מן הירק ואת הכרישין מן הבצלים ואת החרדל מן הדבורים ורבי יוסי מתיר בחרדל: **גמ'** איבעיא להו ר' עקיבא היכי קאמר לכל רוח הוא עושה וסומך חוץ ממערבה דמרחיק נ' אמה ועושה או דלמא לכל רוח הוא עושה ומרחיק חמשים אמה חוץ ממערבה דאינו עושה כלל ת"ש דתניא ר"ע אומר לכל רוח הוא עושה ומרחיק חמשים אמה חוץ ממערבה דאינו עושה כל עיקר מפני שהיא תדירא א"ל רבא לרב נחמן מאי תדירא אילימא תדירא ברוחות והא אמר רב חנן בר אבא אמר רב ד' רוחות מנשבות בכל יום ורוח צפונית עם כולן שאילמלא כן אין העולם מתקיים אפילו שעה אחת ורוח דרומית קשה מכולן ואילמלא בן נץ שמעמידה מחרבת את העולם שנאמר המבינתך יאבר נץ יפרוש כנפיו לתימן אלא מאי תדירא תדירא בשכינה דאריב"ל בואו ונחזיק טובה לאבותינו שהודיעו מקום תפלה דכתיב וצבא השמים לך משתחוים מתקיף לה רב אחא בר יעקב ודלמא כעבד שנוטל פרס מרבו וחוזר לאחוריו ומשתחוה קשיא ורבי אושעיא סבר שכינה בכל מקום דאמר רבי אושעיא מאי דכתיב אתה הוא ה' לבדך אתה עשית את השמים וגו' שלוחיך לא כשלוחי בשר ודם שלוחי בשר ודם ממקום שמשתלחים לשם מחזירים שליחותן אבל שלוחיך למקום שמשתלחין משם מחזירין שליחותן שנאמר התשלח ברקים וילכו ויאמרו לך הננו יבואו ויאמרו לא נאמר אלא וילכו ויאמרו מלמד שהשכינה בכל מקום ואף רבי ישמעאל סבר שכינה בכל מקום דתנא דבי רבי ישמעאל מנין ששכינה בכל מקום שנאמר הנה המלאך הדובר בי יוצא ומלאך אחר יוצא לקראתו אחריו לא נאמר אלא לקראתו מלמד ששכינה בכל מקום ואף רב ששת סבר שכינה בכל מקום דא"ל רב ששת לשמעיה לכל רוחתא אוקמן לבר ממזרח ולאו משום דלית ביה שכינה אלא משום דמורו בה מיני ורבי אבהו אמר שכינה במערב דא"ר אבהו מאי אוריה אויר יה אמר רב יהודה מאי דכתיב יערוף כמטר לקחי זו רוח מערבית שבאה מערפו של עולם תזל כטל אמרתי זו רוח צפונית שמזלת את הזהב וכן הוא אומר הזלים זהב מכיס כשעירים עלי דשא זו רוח מזרחית שמסערת את כל העולם כשעיר וכרביבים עלי עשב זו רוח דרומית שהיא מעלה רביבים ומגדלת עשבים תניא ר"א אומר עולם

רש"י

שעושה אותו גלל. מרבה לו זבל ושורף את הזרעים שמזרעו בו: **מתני' את הנבלות ואת הקברות כו'.** משום ריח רע: **אלא למזרח העיר.** שאין הרוח מזרחית קשה (ג) תדיר אא"כ באה לפורענות אבל כדרכה היא חמה ומנשבת בנחת דכתיב (יונה ד) רוח קדים חרישית ותך השמש וגו' לפיכך אינה מביאה הרוח לעיר: **חוץ מן מערבה.** בגמ' מפרש טעמא: **גמ' וסומך.** אינו צריך להרחיק נ' אמה: **שאינו עושה כלל.** ומרחיק נ' אמה דקאמר ר"ע אשאר רוחות דלישא קאי: **תדירא ברוחות.** אותו לך תדיר ברוח שרוח מערבית מנשבת תדיר משאר רוחות: **רוח צפונית מנשבת עם כל אחת.** מהרוחות לפי שהיא רכה וממתקת ולולא כדאמר ביבמות (דף עב.) וממתקתן: **בן נץ.** מלאך העשוי בדמות נץ: **מעמידה.** בכנפיו: **תדירא בשכינה.** במערב היא שוכנת: **לאבותינו.** אנשי כנה"ג שאמרו מקרא זה בספר עזרא: **וצבא השמים.** השמש והירח העומדים במזרח: **לך משתחוים.** למערב: **ודלמא.** הם למזרח משתחוים וכי תימא אין דרך להשתחוות סמוך לרב הם עושין כעבד שנוטל פרס מרבו וחוזר לאחוריו ומשתחוה כשהוא הולך לאחוריו משנטל פרס מתרחק תמיד בהשתחויה: **פרס.** מתן: **אתה הוא ה' לבדך.** בתר וצבא השמים כתיב ועל עסקי שליחות לצבא השמים הוא משבח ואומר אתה הוא לבדך במדה זו: **לשם מחזירין שליחותן.** כשבאין לומר עשינו שליחותך צריכין לשוב אל מקום שהשולחם עומד שם: **למקום שמשתלחין.** פי' באותו מקום שנשתלחו שם אף שם השכינה מצויה ואומרים לו עשינו שליחותך: **והנה המלאך הדובר בי יוצא.** בנבואת זכריה למוד את ירושלים כמה ארכה וגו' ומלאך אחר יוצא לסתור שליחותו של ראשון שחזר בו המקום (ד) ולא יתן בה מדה ואומר פרזות תשב ירושלים והרי שניהם מאת השכינה באים ואחריו לא נאמר אלא לקראתו זה בא מכאן וזה בא מכאן: **רב ששת.** סגי נהור הוה: **לכל רוחתא אוקמן.** העמידני להתפלל: **דמורו בה מיני.** תלמידי עובדי ע"ז מורים הוראה להתפלל במזרח: **אוריה.** אני שמעתי כך קורין למערב בלשון פרסי. ול"נ שכך קורין למזרח בלשון לעז והיינו דקאמר אויר יה שהשכינה ופניו למזרח נמצא המזרח אוירו: **יערוף כמטר לקחי.** משה רבינו דימה את התורה לארבע רוחות כשם שאי אפשר בלא הם כך אי אפשר לעולם בלא תורה: **מערפו של עולם.** אני שמעתי מחזקו של עולם על שם שהשכינה במערב כ"ל ואני אומר מאחוריו של עולם שהמערב קרוי אחור שנאמר הן קדם אהלך ואיננו ואחור ולא אבין וגו' (איוב כג): **שמזלת את הזהב.** שמחממת ומביאה שרב ורעבון בא והזהב זל: **וכן הוא אומר.** דכתיב זילותא גבי זהב: **כשעיר.** שד: לאכסדרה

תוספות

שעושה אותו גלל. הע"ג דגלל משביח הקרקע כשהיא כולה גלל מזיק: **אין** עושין בורסקי אלא למזרח העיר. משום דרוח מערבי שהוא קשה ירחיק ויוליך הריח מן העיר כדאמרי' (ברכות מ.) הישן למזרח גרנו דמו בראשו מפני שרוח מערבית מביא הקש בחוטמו: **מפני** שהיא תדירה. לא גרסי' מ"ט דמן הברייתא היא דהכי איתא בתוספתא (פ"א ע"ש): **וצבא** השמים לך משתחוים. וא"ת בלילה נמי במזרח משתחוים וי"ל דאין לנו ללמוד אלא ממה שאנו רואין וא"ת ואמאי לא נדע מקום תפלה מבית המקדש שהיתה שם שכינה במערב וי"ל דמשם אין ללמוד דאע"ג דשכינה בכל מקום אי אפשר להשים ארון וכפורת אלא בצד אחד וריצב"א אומר דמשם אין ללמוד דשכינה במערב דנהי דבית קדשי הקדשים היה במערב המקדש מ"מ הארון שהשכינה שם כדכתיב (שמות כה) ונועדתי לך שם היה במזרח בית קדשי הקדשים ה): **לכל** רוחתא אוקמן. כל הני אמוראי לית להו הא דתניא בברכות (דף ל.) שחייב אדם להתפלל נגד ירושלים משום דכתיב והתפללו אליך דרך ארצם אלא סברי כר' ישמעאל דאמר (ה) בכ"מ שכינה ומאן דאמר שכינה במערב סבר כר"ע דאמר מפני שהיא תדירה ור' חנינא דשמעתין דאמר כגון אתון דיתבון לצפונא דארעא דישראל אדרימו סבר לה כברייתא דברכות: **אוריה.** לשון שפ"ה דאוריה מערב נראה לר"ת ° ולר"ח עיקר: **רוח** מערבית שבא מערפו של עולם. כדפי' בקונט' מאחורו של עולם דמערב קרוי אחור דכתיב אחור וקדם צרתני ודרשינן [בחגיגה] (דף יב.) לענין מזרח ומערב וכתיב נמי ארם מקדם ופלשתים מאחור (ישעיה ט) וקרי נמי דרום ימין ולצפון שמאל כדאמרי' בשמעתין והיינו משום דשכינה במערב ופני השכינה למזרח לכך קרוי מערב אחור ומזרח קדם ודרום ימין וצפון שמאל ולמ"ד שכינה בכל מקום צ"ל דהאי דקרי מזרח קדם ומערב אחור ודרום ימין וצפון שמאל משום שכינה בבית המקדש שהיה במערב ופני השכינה כלפי ישראל שהיו במזרח ומשתחוים שם: **הגה"ה** ורבינו יצחק בר יהודה פירש דכשעמד אדם הראשון כשנברא היו פניו למזרח ואין נראה שהיה ערפו כלפי השכינה למאן דאמר שכינה במערב. ע"כ הגה"ה: **רוח** מזרחית שמסערת כל העולם כולו. והא דמשמע במתניתין שהיא נוחה מכל הרוחות היינו כשהיא באה כדרכה אבל כשבאה לפורענות היא מסערת * כדפי' הקונט' במתניתין וממזרים

רבינו גרשום

פיסקא בורסקי. מקום שמעבדין בו העורות ומסריח: **אלא למזרח העי'.** מפני שרוח מערבי שהיא תדירא מנשבת בו ודוחה הסריחה שאינה באה לעיר: **חוץ ממערבה.** שהיא תדירא ודוחה את הסריחה לעיר א) מש"ה אין עושין: **שאלמלא כן.** שרוח צפונית מבלבלתן אין העולם מתקיים: **יפרוש כנפיו לתימן.** משום דמעמידה לאותו רוח תדיר: **בתפלה.** שהשכינ' במערב ומש"ה צריך להרחיק משם: **לך משתחוים.** [צבא השמים] היינו השמש והירח כשיוצאים במזרח לך משתחוים למערב ושם צריך להחזיר בשעת תפלה: **ואימא.** שהשכינה במזרח ודקאמר לך משתחוים עושים **כעבד שנוטל פרס מרבו ומשתחוה וחוזר לאחוריו.** כך בשעה שיוצאין ממזרח חוזרין פניהם לשכינה במזרח ומשתחוים ושוב יוצאין וזורחין. **קשיא: לבדך** משליחותך ומשנה מבשר ודם: **ויאמרו לך הננו.** בכ"מ שהן. **[מלמד] שהשכינה בכל מקום: והנה המלאך הדובר בי יוצא** מאת השכינה **ומלאך אחר יוצא לקראתו.** מן צד אחר יוצא ולפני שכינה: **דמודי בה מיני.** שמשתחוין לצבא השמים היוצאין מן המזרח: **אוריה.** קורין בלשונן לרוח מערבי: **יערוף כמטר לקחי.** זה העוסק בתורה לשמה ומרכין אזניו לשמוע לקחי עושה טובה לעולם כמטר זה שבא מן מערב: **שבאה מערפו של עולם.** מרוח מערבי ערפו של שכינה הוא. דכתיב צפון וימין אתה בראתם דמשמע דימינו של שכינה בדרום ושמאלו לצד צפון ופניו למזרח וערפו למערב אלמא דשכינה במערב: **ותזל כטל אמרתי.** היינו שמזלזל תורה שעוסק שלא לשמה מביא רעה לעולם כרוח צפוני שמנשב ומביא רעה לעולם: **עד שמזלת את הזהב.** שנותנין בני אדם כספם וזהבם בזול בשביל התבואה: **כשעירים עלי דשא.** זהו העוסק בתורה שלא לשמה: **כשעירים.** כשד: וכל העוסק בתורה לשמה מביא טובה לעולם כרביבים הללו שיורדין בנחת:

חשק שלמה על רבינו גרשום

א) נראה דצ"ל משו"ה אין עושין כל עיקר.

הגהות הב"ח

(א) גמ' שהודיעונו מקום תפלה: (ב) גמ' שם אמר רב יהודה אמר רב מאי דכתיב יערוף: (ג) רש"י ד"ה אלא וכו' קשה תמיד אא"כ: (ד) ד"ה והנה המלאך וכו' שחזר בו המקום מלומר בה מדה: (ה) תוס' ד"ה לכל וכו' דאמר שכינה בכ"מ ומאן דאמר:

גליון הש"ס

גמרא ומשתחוה קשיא. ע' סנהדרין דף לה ע"ב: תוס' ד"ה אוריה נראה לר"ת ולר"ח עיקר. ע' קדושין דף יג ע"ב תוס' ד"ה והלכתא: שם ד"ה רוח מזרחית. כדפי' הקונטרס במתני'. כצ"ל ברש"י מבקום א' מ':

תורה אור השלם

א) המבינתך יאבר נץ יפרש כנפו לתימן: [איוב לט, כו]
ב) אתה הוא יי לבדך אתה עשית את השמים שמי השמים וכל צבאם הארץ וכל אשר עליה הימים וכל אשר בהם ואתה מחיה את כלם וצבא השמים לך משתחוים: [נחמיה ט, ו]
ג) התשלח ברקים וילכו ויאמרו לך הננו: [איוב לח, לה]
ד) והנה המלאך הדבר בי יצא ומלאך אחר יצא לקראתו: [זכריה ב, ז]
ה) יערף כמטר לקחי תזל כטל אמרתי כשעירם עלי דשא וכרביבים עלי עשב: [דברים לב, ב]
ו) הזלים זהב מכיס וכסף בקנה ישקלו ישכרו צורף ויעשהו אל יסגדו אף ישתחוו: [ישעיה מו, ו]

לעזי רש"י

אוריי"ה. פירוש מזרח, המקום שמשם זורחת השמש.

ליקוטי רש"י

מרחיקין את המשרה. מים ששורין בו את הפשתן. **מן הירק.** של מיני מאכל כרוב ושומין וכרישין. **ואת הכרישין.** כרתי פוריל"ש. **ואת החרדל מן הדבורים.** שאוכלין את החרדל ומחדד את פיהם ואוכלות את דבש שלהן [לעיל יח.]. **ורוח צפונית.** נוחה היא לא חמה ולא צוננת וממתקת את שאר הרוחות [גיטין לא.]. **המבינתך יאבר נץ וגו'.** יגדל הנץ כנף ומלאך הוא דמה לדמות נץ ומעמיד קושי רוח דרומית שלא תחריב את העולם [איוב לט, כו]. **יאבר.** לשון אברתו יגדיל כנף [גיטין שם]. **ויאמרו לך הננו.** במקום שנשתלחו שם הננו עשינו שליחותך שאין צריכין לחזור למקומן ולהשיב שלוחן שהשכינה בכל מקום [איוב לח, לה]. **הנה המלאך הדובר בי וגו'.** הוא אשר בידו חבל המדה [זכריה ב, ז]. **הזלים זהב.** ל' יזלו מים (תהלים קמז) [ישעיה מו, ו]. **כשעירים.** לשון רוח סערה כתרגומו כרוחי מטרא מה הרוחות הללו מחזיקות את העשבים ומגדלין אותם אף דברי תורה מגדלין את לומדיהן. **וכרביבים.** טיפי מטר נראה לי על שם שיורה כחץ נקרא רביב כמה דאת אמר (בראשית מט) רובה קשת. **דשא.** אחריי"ף עטיפת הארץ מכוסה בירק. **עשב.** קלח אחד קרוי עשב וכל מין ומין לעצמו קרוי עשב [דברים לב, ב]. לא דשא לשון עשב ולא עשב לשון דשא וכו' שמיני דשאין מחולקין כל אחד לעצמו נקרא עשב פלוני ואין לשון למדבר לומר דשא פלוני שלשון דשא הוא לבישת הארץ בעשבים כשהיא מתמלאת בדשאים. בלשון לע"ז נקרא דשא אחריי"ף (גראזיכט) כולן בערבוביא וכל שורש לעצמו נקרא עשב [בראשית א, יא].

עין משפט
נר מצוה

פה א טוש"ע א"ח סי' צד סעיף ב בהג"ה:
פו ב מיי' פ"א מהל' בית הבחירה הל' ו סמג עשין קסו:
פז ג מיי' פ"י מהלכות שכנים הל' ז סמג עשין פב טוש"ע ח"מ סי' קנה סעיף לב:
פח ד מיי' שם הל' ה טוש"ע שם סעיף לא:
פט ה מיי' שם פי"א הלכה ג סמג שם טוש"ע שם סעיף טו:

ליקוטי רש"י

הולך אל דרום וגו'. לעולם ביום. וסובב אל צפון לעולם בלילה. סובב סובב הולך אל פני מזרח ומערב שפעמים מהלכתן ביום ופעמים מסבבתן בלילה בתמוז מהלכתן ובטבת סובבתן. הרוח רוחו של שמש טלנ"ט בלע"ז כמו אל אשר יהיה שם הרוח ללכת. ועל סביבותיו שב גם אחר כל היקף וסבוב שסבב אתמול הוא מקיף וסובב היום [קהלת א, ו]. לפי שהחמה לעולם ביום ממזרח לדרום מהלכת כדאמר קרא (קהלת א) הולך אל דרום והליכת החמה ביום היא אבל בלילה אינו הולך אלא סובב מחוץ לכיפה וביום הארוך עומדת בקרן מזרחית צפונית ומהלכת מזרח דרום [המשך בדף כו.]

רבינו גרשום

עולם לאכסדרה הוא דומה. מה אכסדרה זו שיש לה ג' דפנות ולא יותר ומסוככת כך העולם: ורוח צפונית. אין לה דופן ואינה מסוככת: וכשחמה מגעת. שהלכה כל היום ועכשיו כשמגעת בלילה בקרן מערבית צפונית נכפפת באותו רוח צפוני שאינו מסוכך ועולה למעלה מרקיע: ור' יהושע אומר עולם דומה לקובה. כאהל הוא דומה. מה אהל זה מסוככת לכל דפנותיה אף עולם מכל וכל מסוכך וכשחמה זורחת ביום ארוך זורחת ברוח צפונית מזרחית והולכת במזרח דרום עד שמגעת לקרן מערבית צפונית סמוך לחשיכה לקרן צפוני נכנסת בחלון א' בלילה ומקפת וחוזרת אחורי כיפה של עולם וסובב רוח צפונית כל הלילה שנאמר הולך אל דרום ביום בין בימות החמה בין בימות הגשמים. וכן הכי נמי וסובב אל צפון בלילה בין בימות החמה בין בימות הגשמים: סובב סובב הולך אלו פני מזרח ומערב. שפעמים מסבבתן ביום קצר ששוקעת החמה בקרן מזרחית דרומית והולך כל היום על פני דרום ולא יותר ובלילה נכנסת בקרן דרומית מערבית בחלון אחד וסובבת כל הלילה פני המערב ופני הצפון ופני המזרח עד קרן מזרחית דרומית. ופעמים מהלכתן ביום ארוך שזורחת חמה בקרן צפונית מזרחית והולכת כל המזרח ופני הדרום ופני המערב עד הלילה ובלילה נכנסת בקרן מערבית צפונית וסובבת כל הלילה לפני הצפון עד קרן צפונית מזרחית. מהלכתן בלילה: הוא היה אומר ר' אליעזר דהא ברייתא אתאן לטעמא דר"א דאמר עולם לאכסדרה הוא דומה: מן החדר תבוא סופה זו רוח דרומית. שדופן שלה אמצעי ופנימי ודומה לחדר: סופה. סערה: וממזרים קרה זו רוח צפונית. שכל העולם מזורים זרם מים לשם לפי שאין שם דופן והוא תוהו ובוהו ומים ואינה מסוככת: קרה. חורף אבל אינו קריר כל כך. קרח חורף ממש: זו רוח מזרחית. שמרחיבין שם הגשמים להצליח: צפון. יתפלל לרוח צפון: שולחן בצפון. שלא ירדו גשמים לשם: על ימין. זו רוח דרומית: ורעב. משמע פעמים רעב פעמים שבע: ויאכל ולא שבעו. בשפיכותא: לא הוגשמה רוח דרומית: ידרים. יתפלל לרוח דרומית: יצפין. היינו עושר שיצריך שולחנו מחמת עושרו: ומנורה בדרום. היינו חכמה כדכתיב כי נר מצוה ותורה אור: שנאמר אורך ימים וגו'. האי קרא לא אתי לאשמועינן אלא דתורה שהיא חכמה יש בה גם עושר וכבוד: דמצדד אצדודי. לא מכל וכל לרוח דרומית ולא מכל לרוח מערבית: אדרימו. כלומר כשתתפללו חזרו פניכם לצד דרום שנאמר והתפללו [אליך] דרך ארצם: פיסקא והחרוב והשקמה נ' אמה. ששרשיהן הולכין עמוק בקרקע: בין מלמעלה. שאם הבור עומד במקום גבוה צריך להרחיק האילן מן הבור כ"ה אמה ותנא בין שהבור למעלה במקום גבוה והאילן במקום נמוך והא לא קא מזיק ליה לבור כלל: ומלקין קרקעית של בור. ונעשה טיט: מודה ר' יוסי בגירי. כדפריש לעיל אע"פ שעושה בתוך שלו חייב: יונאה. שם מקום: הנך עצורי. שמכתשין שומשמין כדי להוציא שמן: וכמה נייד. דאמרי' דליהוי הני עצורי חייבין:

תוספות

וממזרים (ד) פי' רוח לפונית שכותל שלה מושלך כלומר שאינה מסובבת לרבי אליעזר: וכתיב צפון וימין וכו'. דויגזור על ימין (ה) ליכא למימר דבימין ושמאל של אדם מיירי (הג"ה. ועוד נראה שמא (ו) ממקרא קמא אין להוכיח שבדרום ימין ולא נאמר איפכא. ע"כ הג"ה): תנא בין שהבור למעלה ואילן למטה כו'. איצטריך לאיתויי הך אע"ג דבמתני' נמי תנן בין מלמעלן בין מלמטן מ"מ דאי ממתני' הוה אמינא דלאחרוב ושקמה קאי דעלה קאי קמ"ל ברייתא בכל אילן (הג"ה. ולספרים דלא גרסינן במתני' בין מלמטן אתי שפיר דאי ממתני' הוה אמינא בין מלמעלן דאילן קאי ולא אבור משום דלא תקשי אלא בור מלמעלה ואילן מלמטה אמאי כדפריך אברייתא. עד כאן הג"ה): עני והעשיר הוה. רבותא נקט שהיה עני ולא איבעי (ז) לאסוקי אדעתייהו שיבנה האפדנא אפי' הכי הוחקקו להרחיק משום דהוו גירי דידהו אף על גב דסמך בהיתר אין צריך להרחיק אפי' בגירי דיליה כדתניא (לעיל דף כ:) אם היה רפת בקר קודמת לאוצר מותר וה"ה חנות של נחתומים וצבעין ואין חילוק בין דירה לשאר לפי המסקנא אומר ר"ת דהכא היינו טעמא משום דלא קביעא תשמישייהו כל כך כי הנך דלעיל (הג"ה. ועוד דהכא (ח) משום דבאיסור סמך דכל מרא דמחי מרפי לארעא. ע"כ הג"ה): אפומא

גמרא

לאכסדרה הוא דומה ורוח צפונית אינה מסובבת וכיון שהגיעה חמה אצל קרן מערבית צפונית נכפפת ועולה למעלה מן הרקיע ורבי יהושע אומר עולם לקובה הוא דומה ורוח צפונית מסובבת וכיון שחמה מגעת לקרן מערבית צפונית מקפת וחוזרת אחורי כיפה שנאמר א) הולך אל דרום וסובב אל צפון וגו' הולך אל דרום ביום וסובב אל צפון בלילה א) סובב סובב הולך הרוח ועל סביבותיו שב הרוח אלו פני מזרח ופני מערב שפעמים מסבבתן ופעמים מהלכתן הוא היה אומר אתאן לר' אליעזר ב) מן החדר תבא סופה זו רוח דרומית וממזרים קרה זו רוח צפונית מנשמת אל יתן קרח זו רוח מערבית ורחב מים במוצק זו רוח מזרחית והאמר מר רוח דרומית מעלה רביבים ומגדלת עשבים לא קשיא הא דאתיא מטרא בניחותא הא בשפיכותא אמר רב חסדא מאי דכתיב ג) מצפון זהב יאתה זו רוח צפונית * שמזולת את הזהב וכן הוא אומר ד) הזלים זהב מכים אמר רפרם בר פפא אמר רב חסדא מיום שחרב בית המקדש לא הוגשמה רוח דרומית שנאמר ה) ויגזור על ימין ורעב ויאכל על שמאל ולא שבעו וכתיב ו) צפון וימין אתה בראתם ואמר רפרם בר פפא אמר רב חסדא מיום שחרב בית המקדש אין הגשמים יורדין מאוצר טוב שנאמר ז) יפתח ה' לך את אוצרו הטוב בזמן שישראל (א) עושין רצונו של מקום וישראל שרויין על אדמתם גשמים יורדין מאוצר טוב בזמן שאין ישראל שרויין על אדמתם אין גשמים יורדין מאוצר טוב אמר רבי יצחק א הרוצה שיחכים ידרים ושיעשיר יצפין ב וסימניך שלחן בצפון ומנורה בדרום ורבי יהושע בן לוי אמר לעולם ידרים שמתוך שמתחכם מתעשר שנאמר ח) אורך ימים בימינה בשמאלה עושר וכבוד והא רבי יהושע בן לוי אמר שכינה במערב ג דמצדד אצדודי אמר ליה רבי חנינא לרב אשי כגון אתון דיתביתו בצפונה דא"י אדרימו אדרומי ומנא לן ד דבבל לצפונה דארץ ישראל קיימא דכתיב ט) מצפון תפתח הרעה על כל יושבי הארץ: מרחיקין את המשרה מן הירק וכו': תנא רבי יוסי מתיר בחרדל ה שיכול לומר לו עד שאתה אומר לי הרחק חרדלך מן דבוריי הרחק דבורך מן חרדליי שבאות ואוכלות לגלוגי חרדליי: מתני' ו מרחיקין את האילן מן הבור עשרים וחמש אמה ובחרוב ובשקמה חמשים אמה בין מלמעלה בין מן הצד אם הבור קדמה ז קוצץ ונותן דמים ואם אילן קדם לא יקוץ ח ספק זה קדם וספק זה קדם לא יקוץ ט ר' יוסי אומר י אע"פ שהבור קודמת לאילן לא יקוץ י שזה חופר בתוך שלו וזה נוטע בתוך שלו: גמ' תנא בין שהבור למטה ואילן למעלה בין שהבור למעלה ואילן למטה בשלמא בור למטה ואילן למעלה קא אזלין שרשין מזקי לה לבור אלא בור למעלה ואילן למטה אמאי אמר רבי חגא בשם רבי יוסי מפני שמחלידין את הקרקע ומלקין קרקעיתה של בור: רבי יוסי אומר אע"פ שהבור קודמת לאילן לא יקוץ שזה חופר בתוך שלו וזה נוטע בתוך שלו: אמר רב יהודה אמר שמואל הלכה כרבי יוסי כ אמר רב אשי כי הוינן בי רב כהנא הוה אמרינן ל מודי ר' יוסי בגירי דידיה ההוא פאפי יונאה בנה אפדנא ה הוו הנך עצורי בשיבבותיה דכי הוו דייקי שומשמי הוה ניידא אפדניה אתא לקמיה דרב אשי א"ל כי הוינן בי רב כהנא הוה אמרינן מודי רבי יוסי בגירי דיליה וכמה כדנייד

רש"י

לאכסדרה. שאין לה דופן רביעית: אינה מסובבת. במחילה: למעלה מן הרקיע. ומהלכת את רוח לפון בגגו של רקיע: לקובה. אהל שכולו מוקף: לקרן מערבית צפונית. בלילה שהחמה לעולם מהלכת רוח לפונית בלילה ומן המערב היא פונה ללפון שכך הילוכה מן המזרח לדרום מן הדרום למערב וממערב ללפון: ומחזרת אחורי כיפה. דרך חלון: הולך אל דרום. היקף היום קרוי הילוך שהוא בתוך החלל ואת היקף הלילה קרוי סיבוב שהוא מקיף מחוץ וביום לעולם מהלכת בדרום אפילו ביום קצר אינו מהלך פחות מרוח דרומית: וסובב אל צפון בלילה. אף בלילה קצרה של תקופת תמוז אינו סובב פחות מרוח לפונית: פעמים מהלכתן. ביום ארוך של תקופת תמוז שהיא יוצאה בקרן לפונית מזרחית ושוקעת בקרן מערבית לפונית: פעמים סובבתן. ביום קצר שהיא יוצאה בקרן מזרחית דרומית ושוקעת בקרן מערבית דרומית ומהלכת בלילה ג' רוחות: אתאן לר' אליעזר. שאמר לאכסדרה דומה: וממזרים קרה זו רוח צפונית. שהדופן מוחזת ופרוצה: והאמרת רוח דרומית מעלה רביבים. וכאן אתה אומר רוח מזרחית מביאה מים: הא דאתיא מטרא בניחותא. בא מן הדרום וכי אתיא בשפיכותא בא מן המזרח דכתיב מים במולק: לא הוגשמה רוח דרומית. שהיתה רגילה להביא רביבים טובים: וכתיב צפון וימין. אלמא ימין הוא דרום וכתיב ביה רעב: את אוצרו הטוב. וסיפא לתת מטר ארצך: ידרים. בתפלתו יחזיר פניו לדרום: וסימניך. שלא תשכח: דמצדד אצדודי. (ב) מטנו לצד דרום: אדרימו. שתהיו פונים לצד ירושלים משום דכתיב והתפללו אליך דרך ארצם וגו' (מלכים א ח): עד שאתה אומר לי. שאני מזיק ועלי להרחיק את עצמי אני אומר לך שאתה מזיק: לגלוגי חרדלי. פרחי חרדלי: מתני' חרוב ושקמה. שרשיהם מרובים: בין מלמעלה. שאחד מהן מלמעלן בגובה שיפוע הר והשני בשפולו: בין מן הצד. בקרקע שוה: ונותן דמים. דכיון דברשות נטע שאינו מזיק עד זמן גדול לא חייבוהו חכמים לקוץ בלא דמים * בשביל הזיקא דיחיד: גמ' שמחלידין. לשון חלדה הלכות שחיטה (חולין דף לב.) שמהלכת מתחת לקרקעית הבור: הלכה כר' יוסי. שעל הניזק להרחיק את עצמו: בגירי דיליה. היכא דמטי ליה הזיקא מתוך ידיו של מזיק כהסיא דאמרי' בהבית והעלייה (ב"מ דף קיז.) הנהו בי תרי חד דייר עילאי וחד דייר תתאי איפחית מעזיבה וכל אימת דמשי ידיה נפלי עליה דתתאי דכשנופלין מידו ממש על התחתון קרי ליה גירי דיליה וכי פסקי והדר נפלי (ג) לא קרי ליה גירי דיליה: פאפי יונאה. כך שמו על שם מקומו: עצורי. עולרי שומשמין לעשות שמן: בגירי דיליה. והכא נמי מידיהם הוא בא לו שמכה מכותיהם הוא מרעיד: וכמה. תנוד אפדנא דבעי ארחוקי: כדנייד

מסורת הש"ס

א) עירובין נו., ב) [לקמן קמז. יומא כא: מנחות פו:], ג) נ"א ר' יאשיה, ד) [גיטין ו.], ה) [לעיל יח.], ו) ב"מ קיז. [לעיל יח. לקמן כז:], ז) [לעיל כד:], ח) (ב"מ קי:), ט) [לעיל יח:], י) [לעיל יז: כב:], כ) [לעיל כב: ב"מ קיז.], ל) נ"ל דהולכות:

הגהות הב"ח

(א) גמ' את אולרו הטוב בזמן שישראל שרוין על אדמתם כל"ל ותיבות עושים רלונו של מקום וישראל נמחק: (ב) רש"י ד"ה דמלדד אלדודי מטה ללד דרום: (ג) ד"ה בגירי דיליה וכו' והדר נפלי כגון דמגנדרי לא קרי ליה: (ד) תום' ד"ה וממזרים קרה זו רוח לפונית פי' שכותל שלה כל"ל: (ה) ד"ה וכתיב וכו' על ימין ליכא להוכיח דליכא למימר דבימין: (ו) בא"ד שמא דממקרא קמא אין להוכיח שדרום ימין: (ז) ד"ה עני וכו' ולא איבעי להו לאסוקי וכו' אע"ג דבסמך וכו' נחתומין ושל לבעין: (ח) בא"ד דהכא שאני משום דבאיסור וכו' מרא ומרא דמחי מרפי לארעא והוה דומיא דבור ע"כ הג"ה:

גליון הש"ם

גמרא שמזלת את הזהב. עי' יבמות עב ע"א תד"ה דלא: רש"י ד"ה ונותן כו' בשביל היזקא דיחיד. עיין לעיל דף יח ע"ב תוס' ד"ה ואי:

תורה אור השלם

א) הוֹלֵךְ אֶל דָּרוֹם וְסוֹבֵב אֶל צָפוֹן סוֹבֵב סֹבֵב הוֹלֵךְ הָרוּחַ וְעַל סְבִיבֹתָיו שָׁב הָרוּחַ: [קהלת א, ו]

ב) מִן הַחֶדֶר תָּבוֹא סוּפָה וּמִמְּזָרִים קָרָה: מִנִּשְׁמַת אֵל יִתֶּן קָרַח וְרֹחַב מַיִם בְּמוּצָק: [איוב לז, ט-י]

ג) מִצָּפוֹן זָהָב יֶאֱתֶה עַל אֱלוֹהַּ נוֹרָא הוֹד: [איוב לז, כב]

ד) הַזָּלִים זָהָב מִכִּיס וְכֶסֶף בַּקָּנֶה יִשְׁקֹלוּ יִשְׂכְּרוּ צוֹרֵף וְיַעֲשֵׂהוּ אֵל יִסְגְּדוּ אַף יִשְׁתַּחֲווּ: [ישעיה מו, ו]

ה) וַיִּגְזֹר עַל יָמִין וְרָעֵב וַיֹּאכַל עַל שְׂמֹאול וְלֹא שָׂבֵעוּ אִישׁ בְּשַׂר זְרֹעוֹ יֹאכֵלוּ: [ישעיה ט, יט]

ו) צָפוֹן וְיָמִין אַתָּה בְרָאתָם תָּבוֹר וְחֶרְמוֹן בְּשִׁמְךָ יְרַנֵּנוּ: [תהלים פט, יג]

ז) יִפְתַּח יְיָ לְךָ אֶת אוֹצָרוֹ הַטּוֹב אֶת הַשָּׁמַיִם לָתֵת מְטַר אַרְצְךָ בְּעִתּוֹ וּלְבָרֵךְ אֵת כָּל מַעֲשֵׂה יָדֶךָ וְהִלְוִיתָ גּוֹיִם רַבִּים וְאַתָּה לֹא תִלְוֶה: [דברים כח, יב]

ח) אֹרֶךְ יָמִים בִּימִינָהּ בִּשְׂמֹאולָהּ עֹשֶׁר וְכָבוֹד: [משלי ג, טז]

ט) וַיֹּאמֶר יְיָ אֵלָי מִצָּפוֹן תִּפָּתַח הָרָעָה עַל כָּל יֹשְׁבֵי הָאָרֶץ: [ירמיה א, יד]

לְאַכְסַדְרָה הוּא דוֹמֶה – RESEMBLES A PAVILION,[1] in that it is enclosed on three sides and open on the fourth; וְרוּחַ צְפוֹנִית אֵינָהּ מְסוּבֶּבֶת – AND THE NORTHERN SIDE IS NOT ENCLOSED.[2] וְכֵיוָן שֶׁהִגִּיעָה חַמָּה אֵצֶל קֶרֶן מַעֲרָבִית צְפוֹנִית – WHEN THE SUN REACHES THE NORTHWEST CORNER of the world,[3] נִכְפֶּפֶת – IT TURNS ABOUT וְעוֹלָה לְמַעְלָה מִן הָרָקִיעַ – AND ASCENDS ABOVE THE HEAVEN, where it travels back to the east to rise in the morning. וְרַבִּי יְהוֹשֻׁעַ אוֹמֵר – AND R' YEHOSHUA SAYS: עוֹלָם לְקוּבָּה הוּא דוֹמֶה – THE WORLD RESEMBLES A TENT, which is enclosed on all four sides, וְרוּחַ צְפוֹנִית מְסוּבֶּבֶת – AND THE NORTHERN SIDE IS also ENCLOSED. וְכֵיוָן שֶׁחַמָּה מַגַּעַת לְקֶרֶן מַעֲרָבִית צְפוֹנִית – WHEN THE SUN REACHES THE NORTHWEST CORNER of the world, מַקֶּפֶת וְחוֹזֶרֶת אֲחוֹרֵי כִּיפָּה – IT continues to CIRCLE AND PASSES BEHIND THE DOME of the sky.[4]

R' Yehoshua cites a verse in support of his position:

שֶׁנֶּאֱמַר – AS [THE VERSE] STATES[5] regarding the sun's path: "הוֹלֵךְ אֶל־דָּרוֹם וְסוֹבֵב אֶל־צָפוֹן" – *IT* [the sun] ***TRAVELS TOWARD THE SOUTH AND IT CIRCLES TO THE NORTH.*** "הוֹלֵךְ אֶל־דָּרוֹם" בַּיּוֹם – ***IT TRAVELS TOWARD THE SOUTH — DURING THE DAY,*** when the sun traverses the southern part of the sky.[6] "וְסוֹבֵב אֶל־צָפוֹן" בַּלַּיְלָה – ***AND IT CIRCLES TO THE NORTH — DURING THE NIGHT,*** when the sun passes behind the northern portion of the sky to return to its sunrise position.[7]

R' Yehoshua continues his exposition of the verse:

NOTES

1. An אַכְסַדְרָה, *pavilion,* is a structure walled on three sides and open on the fourth (*Rashi*). [Such structures were commonly used in Greek and Roman times as meeting places. The technical name for such a structure is an *exedra.*]

2. [The discussion that follows views the sky as a dome poised over the earth. This dome has substance and thickness to it, and the sun travels along it.] According to R' Eliezer, the dome does not extend completely around the world, but is open in the northern latitudes.

3. [The northwest corner of the world is the point along the horizon where the sun sets on the longest day of the year (see *Eruvin* 56a, and below, note 9).] According to R' Eliezer, the dome ends at a point opposite this spot. When the sun reaches this point, it slips out through the open side of the dome, curves around and over it, and then travels through the night across the outside of the dome from west to east, where it re-enters the dome and rises in the morning.

[*Maharal* (*Chidushei Aggados*) maintains that the Gemara here is not discussing the actual astronomical phenomena, but a metaphysical concept couched in astronomical language; see there for his detailed explanation (see also his *Be'er HaGolah, Be'er 6*). A similar view is expressed by *R' Moshe Chaim Luzzato* in his essay regarding Aggadah (*Maamar al HaAggados*), which is also printed in the introduction to *Ein Yaakov*. He makes the point that the non-halachic component of the Talmud includes ideas too esoteric to be presented to the general public, who would surely misunderstand and distort them. When compiling the Talmud, therefore, the Sages encapsulated these ideas in various cryptic statements and parables whose superficial meaning masked their true, esoteric content. These hidden meanings were divulged only to the few disciples in each generation deemed both worthy and capable of comprehending such sublime ideas. Occasionally, as in the Gemara here, the Sages even chose the commonly held notions of their day as a convenient metaphor for the secret knowledge they meant to convey. They did not concern themselves with the scientific accuracy of those notions because the superficial meaning was in any case meant only to obscure from public view the ultimately profound ideas being set down.

An exposition of some of the deeper meanings of this Gemara suggested by these two commentators is beyond the scope of this work. Our commentary will therefore restrict itself to explaining the simple meaning of this passage.]

4. According to R' Yehoshua, after the sun sets, it enters a "window" in the dome of the sky, passes through it (*Rashi*) and continues on behind it. It follows the path of its previous orbit, travels below the sphere of the Earth [along the outside of the dome] and circles completely around to the east, where it rises again the next morning (*Maharsha*). [There are a series of "windows" in the dome to accommodate the daily shift in the position of sunrise and sunset (see *Rabbeinu Chananel* to *Eruvin* 56a).]

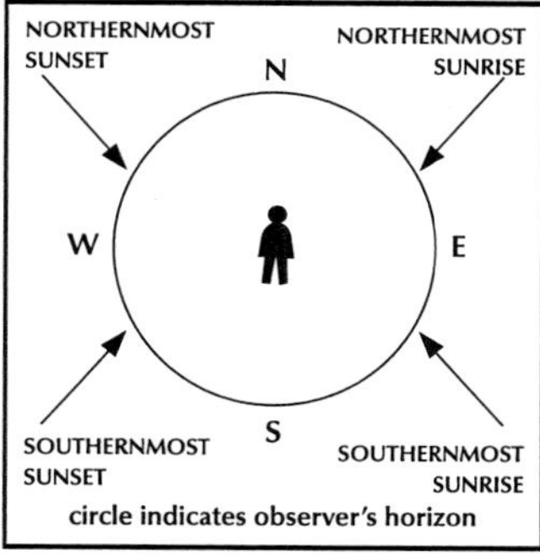

5. *Ecclesiastes* 1:6. The following Gemara makes reference to astronomical facts, which we will briefly introduce:

Though the sun rises each day in the east and sets in the west, it does not rise and set each day at the same points along the horizon. If one draws an imaginary line from himself to the horizon due east and due west, he will observe that in the summer the sun rises and sets north of this line, while in the winter it rises and sets south of this line. In the Northern Hemisphere, the sun rises and sets at its most northerly points on the longest day of the year (the summer solstice), and at its most southerly points on the shortest day of the year (the winter solstice). See diagram. Following the winter solstice, the sun rises and sets a bit further north each day until it reaches its most northerly point on the summer solstice, after which it begins rising and setting a bit further south each day until it again reaches its most southerly position on the winter solstice. The sun rises due east and sets due west only on the spring and autumn equinoxes.

Not only does the point of sunrise and sunset change through the seasons, but so does the entire daily path of the sun across the sky. Furthermore, the sun does not pass directly overhead in Eretz Yisrael (or anywhere on earth north of Eretz Yisrael). Rather, the arc of the sun's path is tilted at an angle to the earth, so that to an observer in the North Temperate Zone (from 23.5 degrees north latitude to the Arctic Circle), the noontime sun is never directly overhead, but remains to his south even in summer. [Although the sun reaches the zenith of its arc at noon, that point is still south of the point directly above the observer. See diagram below.] Since the entire arc of the sun moves further south each day from summer to winter, the noontime sun reaches its zenith further south each day until the winter solstice, when it reaches its most southerly extension. The process then reverses itself, with the arc of the sun's path and the noontime sun moving north (i.e. higher in the sky) each day, until it reaches its most northerly point on the summer solstice. However, even then, the noontime sun is still to the south of the observer in the North Temperate Zone. See diagram.

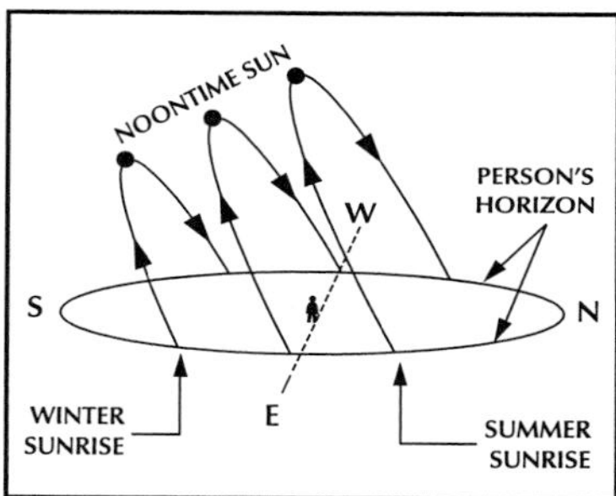

Thus, to an observer in Jerusalem (approximately 31.8 degrees north latitude), the noontime sun on the longest day of the year (the summer solstice) is still 8.3 degrees south of the point on the celestial sphere directly above the observer, while on December 21-22, it is 55.3 degrees to the south, as may be seen from the diagram. [The Gemara deals always with the Northern Hemisphere, the חֲצִי כַּדּוּר הַיִּשּׁוּב, *the settled hemisphere,* i.e. the part of the globe in which most of the civilized world resided. Virtually all the cities and countries mentioned in Scripture and the Talmud are within this zone. All references in the Gemara and the notes which follow are with respect to a person in this zone.]

6. I.e. the sun *always* traverses the southern part of the sky, from east to west, even during a winter day, when the sun's daytime path is at its shortest (*Rashi*). [As noted above, the daytime path of the sun goes through the southern portion of the sky at *all* times of the year and at an angle to the observer. In winter, it traverses only the southern sector of the sky, since it rises and sets at or near its most southerly position.]

7. The sun *always* passes behind the northern portion of the sky, even on short summer nights (*Rashi*). [As noted above, the sun is seen to complete a circle around the earth each twenty-four hours. Thus, its return path at night must circle the northern portion of the sky behind the earth (relative to the observer). See diagram.

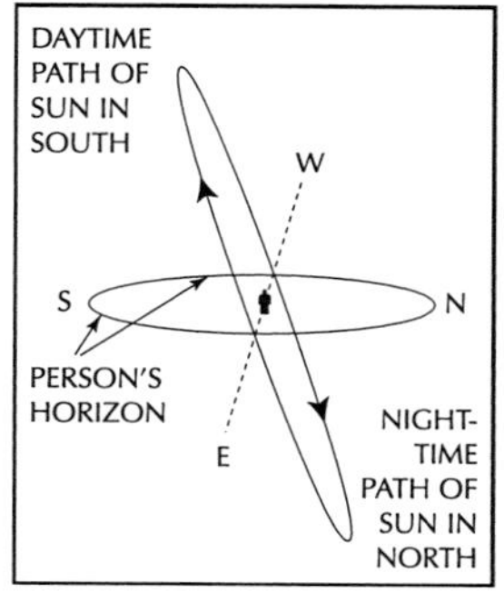

עין משפט נר מצוה

פה א טוש"ע ח"מ סי' לד סעיף ג בהג"ה:
פו ב מיי' פ"ז מהל' בית הבחירה הל' ז סמג עשין קסד:
פז ג מיי' פ"ה מהלכות שכנים הל' ז סמג עשין פב טוש"ע ח"מ סי' קנה סעיף לב:
פח ד מיי' שם הל' ה טוש"ע שם סעיף לא:
פט ה מיי' שם פי"א הלכה ג סמג שם טוש"ע שם סעיף טו:

גמרא

לאכסדרה הוא דומה ורוח צפונית אינה מסובבת וכיון שהגיעה חמה אצל קרן מערבית צפונית נכפפת ועולה למעלה מן הרקיע ורבי יהושע אומר עולם לקובה הוא דומה ורוח צפונית מסובבת וכיון שחמה מגעת לקרן מערבית צפונית מקפת וחוזרת אחורי כיפה שנאמר א) הולך אל דרום וסובב אל צפון וגו' א) הולך אל דרום ביום וסובב אל צפון בלילה א) סובב סובב הולך הרוח ועל סביבותיו שב הרוח אלו פני מזרח ופני מערב שפעמים מסבבתן ופעמים מהלכתן הוא היה אומר אתאן לר' אליעזר ב) מן החדר תבא סופה זו רוח דרומית וממזרים קרה זו רוח צפונית מנשמת אל יתן קרח זו רוח מערבית ורחב מים במוצק זו רוח מזרחית והאמר מר רוח דרומית מעלה רביבים ומגדלת עשבים לא קשיא הא דאתיא מטרא בניחותא הא בשפיכותא אמר רב חסדא מאי דכתיב ג) מצפון זהב יאתה זו רוח צפונית ° שמזלת את הזהב וכן הוא אומר ד) הזלים זהב מכיס אמר רפרם בר פפא אמר רב חסדא מיום שחרב בית המקדש לא הוגשמה רוח דרומית שנאמר ה) ויגזור על ימין ורעב ויאכל על שמאל ולא שבעו וכתיב ו) צפון וימין אתה בראתם ואמר רפרם בר פפא אמר רב חסדא מיום שחרב בית המקדש אין הגשמים יורדין מאוצר טוב שנאמר ז) יפתח ה' לך את אוצרו הטוב בזמן שישראל (א) עושין רצונו של מקום וישראל שרויין על אדמתם גשמים יורדין מאוצר טוב בזמן שאין ישראל שרויין על אדמתם אין גשמים יורדין מאוצר טוב אמר רבי יצחק הרוצה שיחכים ידרים ושיעשיר יצפין וסימניך שלחן בצפון ומנורה בדרום ורבי יהושע בן לוי אמר לעולם ידרים שמתוך שמתחכם מתעשר שנאמר ח) אורך ימים בימינה בשמאלה עושר וכבוד והא רבי יהושע בן לוי אמר שכינה במערב דמצדד אצדודי אמר ליה רבי חנינא לרב אשי כגון אתון דיתביתו בצפונה דא"י אדרימו ומנא לן דבבל לצפונה דארץ ישראל קיימא דכתיב ט) מצפון תפתח הרעה על כל יושבי הארץ: מרחיקין את המשרה מן הירק וכו': תנא רבי יוסי מתיר בחרדל שיכול לומר לו עד שאתה אומר לי הרחק חרדלך מן דבוריי הרחק דבורך מן חרדליי שבאות ואוכלות לגלוגי חרדליי: **מתני'** מרחיקין את האילן מן הבור עשרים וחמש אמה ובחרוב ובשקמה חמשים אמה בין מלמעלה בין מן הצד אם הבור קדמה קוצץ ונותן דמים ואם אילן קדם לא יקוץ ספק זה קדם וספק זה קדם לא יקוץ ר' יוסי אומר אע"פ שהבור קודמת לאילן לא יקוץ שזה חופר בתוך שלו וזה נוטע בתוך שלו: **גמ'** תנא בין שהבור למטה ואילן למעלה בין שהבור למעלה ואילן למטה בשלמא בור למטה ואילן למעלה קא אזלין שרשין מזקי לה לבור אלא בור למעלה ואילן למטה אמאי אמר רבי חגא בשם רבי יוסי מפני שמחלידין את הקרקע ומלקין קרקעיתה של בור: רבי יוסי אומר אע"פ שהבור קודמת לאילן לא יקוץ שזה חופר בתוך שלו וזה נוטע בתוך שלו: אמר רב יהודה אמר שמואל הלכה כרבי יוסי אמר רב אשי כי הואן בי רב כהנא הוה אמרינן מודי ר' יוסי בגירי דידיה פאפי יונאה עני והעשיר הוה בנה אפדנא הוו הנך עצורי בשיבבותיה דכי הוו דייקי שומשמי הוה נײדא אפדניה אתא לקמיה דרב אשי א"ל כי הואן בי רב כהנא הוה אמרינן מודי רבי יוסי בגירי דיליה וכמה כדנייד

תוספות

וממזרים (ד). פי' רוח צפונית שכותל שלה מושלך כלומר שאינה מסובבת לרבי אליעזר: **וכתיב** צפון וימין וכו'. דויגזור על ימין (ה) איכא למימר דבימין ושמאל של אדם איירי (הג"ה. ועוד נראה שמא (ו) מקרא קמא אין להוכיח שבדרום ימין ולא נאמר איפכא. ע"כ הג"ה): **תנא** בין שהבור למעלה ואילן למטה כו'. איצטריך לאיתויי הך אע"ג דבמתני' נמי תנן בין מלמעלן בין מלמטן מ"מ דאי ממתני' הוה אמינא דאחרוב ושקמה קאי דעלה קאי קמ"ל ברייתא בכל אילן (הגה"ה. ולספרים דלא גרסינן במתני' בין מלמטן אתי שפיר דאי ממתני' הוה אמינא בין מלמעלן אאילן קאי ולא אבור משום דלא תקשי אלא בור מלמעלה ואילן מלמטה אמאי כדפריך אברייתא. עד כאן הגה"ה): **עני** והעשיר הוה. רבותא נקט שהיה עני ולא איבעי (ז) לאסוקי אדעתייהו שיבנה האפדנא אפי' הכי הוזקקו להרחיק משום דהוו גירי דידהו אף על גב דסמך בהיתר אין צריך להרחיק אפי' בגירי דיליה כדתניא (לעיל דף כ:) אם היה רפת בקר קודמת לאוצר מותר וה"ה חנות של נחתומים ולבעין ואין חילוק בין דירה לשאר לפי המסקנא אומר ר"ת דהכא היינו טעמא משום דלא קביעא תשמישייהו כל כך כי הנך דלעיל (הג"ה. ועוד דהכא (ח) משום דבאיסור סמך דכל מרא דמחי מרפי לארעא. ע"כ הג"ה):
אפומא

רש"י

לאכסדרה. שאין לה דופן רביעית: אינה מסובבת. במחיצה: למעלה מן הרקיע. ומהלכת את רוח צפון בגגו של רקיע: לקובה. אהל שכולו מוקף: לקרן מערבית צפונית. בלילה שהחמה לעולם מהלכת רוח צפונית בלילה ומן המערב היא פונה לצפון שכך הילוכה מן המזרח לדרום מן הדרום למערב וממערב לצפון: ומחזרת אחורי כיפה. דרך חלון: הולך אל דרום. היקף היום קרוי הילוך שהוא בתוך החלל ואת היקף הלילה קרוי סיבוב שהוא מקיף בחוץ וביום לעולם מהלכת בדרום אפילו ביום קצר אינו מהלך פחות מרוח דרומית: וסובב אל צפון בלילה. אף בלילה קצרה של תקופת תמוז אינו סובב פחות מרוח צפונית: פעמים מהלכתן. ביום ארוך של תקופת תמוז שהיא יוצאה בקרן צפונית מזרחית ושוקעת בקרן מערבית צפונית: פעמים סובבתן. ביום קצר שהיא יוצאה בקרן מזרחית דרומית ושוקעת בקרן מערבית דרומית ומהלכת בלילה ג' רוחות: אתאן לר' אליעזר. שאמר לאכסדרה דומה: וממזרים קרה זו רוח צפונית. שהדופן מוזרת ופרוצה: והאמרת רוח דרומית מעלה רביבים. וכאן אתה אומר רוח מזרחית מביאה מים: הא דאתיא מטרא בניחותא. בא מן הדרום וכי אתיא בשפיכותא בא מן המזרח כדכתיב מים במוצק: לא הוגשמה רוח דרומית. שהיתה רגילה להביא רביבים טובים: וכתיב צפון וימין. אלמא ימין הוא דרום וכתיב ביה רעב: את אוצרו הטוב. וסיפא לתת מטר ארצך: ידרים. בתפלתו יחזיר פניו לדרום: וסימניך. שלא תחליף: דמצדד אצדודי. (ב) מעט לצד דרום: אדרימו. שתהיו פונים לצד ירושלים משום דכתיב והתפללו אליך דרך ארצם וגו' (מלכים א ח): עד שאתה אומר לי. שאני מזיק ועלי להרחיק את עצמי אני אומר לך שאתה מזיק: לגלוגי חרדליי. פרחי חרדליי: מתני' חרוב ושקמה. שרשיהם מרובים: בין מלמעלה. שאחד מהן מלמעלן בגובה שיפוע ההר והשני בשפולו: בין מן הצד. בקרקע שוה: ונותן דמים. דכיון דברשות נטע שאינו מזיק עד זמן גדול לא חייבוהו חכמים לקוץ בלא דמים ° בשביל היזקא דיחיד: גמ' שמחלידין. לשון חלדה דהלכות שחיטה (חולין דף לב.) ל) שמהלכת מתחת לקרקעית הבור: הלכה כר' יוסי. שעל הניזק להרחיק את עצמו: בגירי דיליה. היכא דמטי ליה הזיקא מתוך ידיו של מזיק כההיא דאמרי' בהבית והעלייה (ב"מ דף קיז.) הנהו בי תרי חד דייר עילאי וחד דייר תתאי איפחית מעזיבה וכל אימת דמשי ידיה נפלי עליה דתתאי דכשנופלין מידו ממש על התחתון קרי ליה גירי דיליה וכי פסקי והדר נפלי (ג) לא קרי ליה גירי דיליה: פאפי יונאה. כך שמו על שם מקומו: עצורי. עוצרי שומשמין לעשות שמן: בגירי דיליה. והכא נמי מידיהם הוא בא לו שמכת מכותיהם הוא מרעיד: וכמה. תנוד אפדנא דבעי ארחוקי: כדנייד

ליקוטי רש"י

הולך אל דרום וגו'. לעולם ביום. וסובב אל צפון לעולם בלילה. סובב סובב הולך אל פני מזרח ומערב שפעמים מהלכתן ביום ופעמים מסבבתן בלילה כשמה מהלכתן ובשעת סובבתן. הרוח רוחו של שמש קורא"ו בלע"ז כמו אל אשר יהיה שם הרוח ללכת. ועל סביבותיו שב גם מחר כל היקף וסבוב שסבב אתמול הוא חוזר וסובב היום [קהלת א, ו]. לפי שהחמה לעולם מהלכת ביום ממזרח לדרום מהלכת כדאמר קרא [קהלת א] הולך אל דרום והילוכת החמה ביום היא אבל בלילה אינו הולך אלא סובב מתוך לכיפה וביום הארוך עומדת בקרן מזרחית צפונית ומהלכת מזרח דרום [המשך בדף כו.].

רבינו גרשום

עולם לאכסדרה הוא דומה. מה אכסדרה זו שיש לה ג' דפנות ולא יותר ומסוככת כך העולם: ורוח צפונית. אין לה דופן ואינה מסוככת: וכשחמה מגעת. שהלכה כל היום ועכשיו שמגעת בלילה בקרן מערבית צפונית נכפפת באותו רוח צפוני שאינו מסוכך ועולה למעלה מרקיע: ור' יהושע אומר עולם דומה לקובה. כאהל הוא דומה. מה אהל זה מסוככת לכל דפנותיה אף עולם מכל וכל מסוכך וכשחמה זורחת ביום ארוך זורחת ברוח צפונית מזרחית והולכת במזרח דרום עד שמגעת לקרן מערבית צפונית סמוך לחשיכה לקרן צפוני נכנסת בחלון א' בלילה ומקפת וחוזרת אחורי כיפה של עולם וסובבת רוח צפונית כל הלילה שנאמר הולך אל דרום ביום בין בימות החמה בין בימות הגשמים. וכן הכי נמי וסובב אל צפון בלילה בין בימות החמה בין בימות הגשמים: סובב סובב הולך אלו פני מזרח ומערב. שפעמים מסבבתן ביום קצר שזורחת החמה בקרן מזרחית דרומית והולך כל היום על פני דרום ולא יותר ובלילה נכנסת בקרן דרומית מערבית בחלון אחד וסובבת כל הלילה פני המערב ופני הצפון ופני המזרח עד קרן מזרחית דרומית. ופעמים **מהלכתן** ביום ארוך שזורחת חמה בקרן צפונית מזרחית והולכת כל המזרח ופני הדרום ופני המערב עד הלילה ובלילה נכנסת בקרן מערבית צפונית וסובבת כל הלילה פני הצפון עד קרן צפונית. מהלכתן ביום ומסבבתן בלילה: **הוא היה אומר** ר' אליעזר דהא ברייתא **אתאן** לטעמא **דר"א** דאמר עולם לאכסדרה הוא דומה: **מן החדר תבוא סופה זו רוח דרומית.** שדופן שלה אמצעי ופנימי ודומה לחדר: **סופה.** סערה: **וממזרים קרה זו רוח צפונית.** שכל העולם ממזרים זרם מים לשם לפי שאין שם דופן והוא תהו ובהו ומים ואינה מסוככת: **קרה.** חורף אבל אינו קריר כל כך. **זו רוח מזרחית.** שמרחיבין שם הגשמים להציק. רוח של **ניחותא** מעלי. **בשפיכותא** שבא בקשיות ודאי קשה כסופה: **לא הוגשמה רוח צפונית.** שלא ירדו גשמים לשם: **על ימין.** זו רוח דרומית: **ורעב.** משמע פעמים רעב פעמים שבע: **ויאכל ולא שבעו.** משמע לא שבעו לפי שלא הוגשמה: **צפון.** הוא שמאל כדפרישית לעיל: **ידרים.** כלומר לרוח דרומית: **יצפין.** יתפלל לרוח צפון: **שולחן בצפון.** היינו עושר שיצריך שולחנו מחמת עושרו: **ומנורה בדרום.** היינו חכמה כדכתיב כי נר מצוה ותורה אור: **שנאמר ארך ימים וגו'.** האי קרא לא אתי לאשמועינן אלא דתורה שהיא חכמה יש בה נמי עושר וכבוד: **דמצדד אצדודי.** לא מכל וכל לרוח דרומית ולא מהכל לרוח מערבית: **אדרימו.** כלומר כשתתפללו חזרו פניכם לצד דרום שנאמר והתפללו [אליך] דרך ארצם: **פיסקא והחרוב והשקמה נ' אמה.** ששרשיהן הולכין הרבה: **בין מלמעלה.** שאם האילן עומד סמוך לבור והבור עמוק עד המים נ' אמה אינו מרחיק ואם לאו מרחיק **ובין מן הצד** שאם הבור אינו עמוק צריך להרחיק האילן מן הבור נ' אמה **ותנא בין שהבור מלמעלה** של אילן שהבור עומד במקום גבוה **והאילן** במקום נמוך **ובין שהבור במקום נמוך והאילן במקום גבוה** אם אין כ"ה אמה הרחקה מרחיק. והא לא קא מזיק ליה לבור כלל: **ומלקין קרקעית של בור.** ונעשה טיט: **מודה ר' יוסי בגירי.** כדפריש לעיל אע"פ שעושה בתוך שלו חייב: **יונאה.** שם מקום: **הנך עצורי.** שמכתשין ומעצרין את השומשמין כדי להוציא שמן: **וכמה** נייד. דאמרי' דליהוו הני עצורי חייבין:

מסורת הש"ס

א) עירובין נו., ב) [לקמן קמז. יומא כא: מנחות פו:], ג) ג"א ר' יאשיה, ד) [גיטין ו.], ה) [לעיל יח.], ו) ב"מ קז:, ז) [לעיל יח. לקמן כו:], ח) [לעיל כד:], ט) ב"מ קיז:, י) [לעיל יח:], כ) [לעיל יח: כב:], ל) [לעיל כב: ב"מ קיז.], מ) צ"ל דהולכות:

הגהות הב"ח

(א) גמ' את אוצרו הטוב בזמן שישראל שרוין על אדמתם כצ"ל ותיבות עושים רצונו של מקום וישראל נמחק: (ב) רש"י ד"ה דמצדד אצדודי מעט לצד דרום: (ג) ד"ה בגירי דיליה וכו' והדר נפלי כגון דמגנדרי לא קרי ליה: (ד) תוס' ד"ה וממזרים קרה זו רוח צפונית פי' שכותל שלה כצ"ל: (ה) ד"ה וכתיב וכו' על ימין ליכא להוכיח דליכא למימר דימין: (ו) בא"ד שמא דממקרא קמא אין להוכיח שבדרום ימין: (ז) ד"ה עני וכו' ולא איבעי להו לאסוקי וכו' אע"ג דסמך וכו' נחתומין ושל לבעין: (ח) בא"ד דהלכה שאני משום דלאיסור וכו' מרא דמחי מרפי לארעא והוה דומיא דבור ע"כ הג"ה:

גליון הש"ס

גמרא שמזלת את הזהב. עי' יבמות עב ע"א תד"ה דלא: רש"י ד"ה ונותן כו' בשביל היזקא דיחיד. עיין לעיל דף יח ע"ב תוס' ד"ה ולוי:

תורה אור השלם

א) הוֹלֵךְ אֶל דָּרוֹם וְסוֹבֵב אֶל צָפוֹן סוֹבֵב סֹבֵב הוֹלֵךְ הָרוּחַ וְעַל סְבִיבֹתָיו שָׁב הָרוּחַ: [קהלת א, ו]
ב) מִן הַחֶדֶר תָּבוֹא סוּפָה וּמִמְּזָרִים קָרָה: מִנִּשְׁמַת אֵל יִתֶּן קָרַח וְרֹחַב מַיִם בְּמוּצָק: [איוב לז, ט-י]
ג) מִצָּפוֹן זָהָב יֶאֱתֶה עַל אֱלוֹהַּ נוֹרָא הוֹד: [איוב לז, כב]
ד) הַזָּלִים זָהָב מִכִּיס וְכֶסֶף בַּקָּנֶה יִשְׁקֹלוּ יִשְׂכְּרוּ צוֹרֵף וְיַעֲשֵׂהוּ אֵל יִסְגְּדוּ אַף יִשְׁתַּחֲווּ: [ישעיה מו, ו]
ה) וַיִּגְזֹר עַל יָמִין וְרָעֵב וַיֹּאכַל עַל שְׂמֹאול וְלֹא שָׂבֵעוּ אִישׁ בְּשַׂר זְרֹעוֹ יֹאכֵלוּ: [ישעיה ט, יט]
ו) צָפוֹן וְיָמִין אַתָּה בְרָאתָם תָּבוֹר וְחֶרְמוֹן בְּשִׁמְךָ יְרַנֵּנוּ: [תהלים פט, יג]
ז) יִפְתַּח יְיָ לְךָ אֶת אוֹצָרוֹ הַטּוֹב אֶת הַשָּׁמַיִם לָתֵת מְטַר אַרְצְךָ בְּעִתּוֹ וּלְבָרֵךְ אֵת כָּל מַעֲשֵׂה יָדֶךָ וְהִלְוִיתָ גּוֹיִם רַבִּים וְאַתָּה לֹא תִלְוֶה: [דברים כח, יב]
ח) אֹרֶךְ יָמִים בִּימִינָהּ בִּשְׂמֹאולָהּ עֹשֶׁר וְכָבוֹד: [משלי ג, טז]
ט) וַיֹּאמֶר יְיָ אֵלָי מִצָּפוֹן תִּפָּתַח הָרָעָה עַל כָּל יֹשְׁבֵי הָאָרֶץ: [ירמיה א, יד]

"סוֹבֵב סֹבֵב הוֹלֵךְ הָרוּחַ" – It goes *AROUND, CIRCLING, TRAVERSING THE DIRECTIONS* of the horizon; "וְעַל־סְבִיבֹתָיו שָׁב הָרוּחַ" – *AND IN ITS CIRCLINGS IT RETRACES THE DIRECTIONS.*[8] אֵלּוּ פְּנֵי מִזְרָח וּפְנֵי מַעֲרָב – **THIS** section of the verse refers to **THE EASTERN FACE AND THE WESTERN FACE** of the horizon;[9] שֶׁפְּעָמִים מְסַבַּבְתָּן – **FOR SOMETIMES [THE SUN] CIRCLES THEM,** when it passes behind them during the night in winter, וּפְעָמִים מְהַלַּכְתָּן – **AND SOMETIMES IT TRAVERSES THEM,** when it passes over them during the day in summer.[10]

The Baraisa continues:

הוּא הָיָה אוֹמֵר – **HE WOULD SAY:**

The Gemara interrupts its quotation of the Baraisa to identify the author of this statement:

אֲתָאן לְרַבִּי אֱלִיעֶזֶר – **This brings us** back **to R' Eliezer.**[11]

The Baraisa resumes. What is the meaning of the verse which states:[12]

"מִן־הַחֶדֶר תָּבוֹא סוּפָה" – *FROM THE INNER CHAMBER COMES THE WHIRLWIND* – זוֹ רוּחַ דְּרוֹמִית – **THIS REFERS TO THE SOUTH WIND,** which comes from the innermost region of the world; "וּמִמְּזָרִים קָרָה" – *AND FROM THE DISPERSED PARTS,*[13] *THE COLD* – זוֹ רוּחַ צְפוֹנִית – **THIS REFERS TO THE NORTH WIND,** which comes from the open side of the world.[14] The Baraisa continues with an exposition of the next verse. "מִנִּשְׁמַת־אֵל יִתֶּן־קָרַח" – *BY THE BREATH OF GOD HE GIVES ICE* – זוֹ רוּחַ מַעֲרָבִית – **THIS REFERS TO THE WEST WIND;** "וְרֹחַב מַיִם בְּמוּצָק" – *AND AN EXPANSE OF WATER IN A TORRENT* –[15] זוֹ רוּחַ מִזְרָחִית – **THIS REFERS TO THE EAST WIND.**

The Gemara points out a contradiction between this Baraisa and the statement made above (25a) by Rav Yehudah:

וְהָאָמַר מַר – **But did the master** [Rav Yehudah] not **say** רוּחַ דְּרוֹמִית מַעֲלָה רְבִיבִים וּמְגַדֶּלֶת עֲשָׂבִים – that it is **the south wind that brings up showers and causes the grasses to grow,** while this Baraisa says that it is the east wind that brings rain ("water in torrents")! – ? –

The Gemara answers:

לָא קַשְׁיָא – This is **not a difficulty.** הָא – **This** (the statement of Rav Yehudah) דְּאַתְיָא מִטְרָא בְּנִיחוּתָא – **refers to when the rains come gently.** The gentle (i.e. normal) rains come from the south and cause the grasses to grow. הָא – **This** (the Baraisa's statement) בִּשְׁפִיכוּתָא – refers to **when** the rains come **in torrents;** as the verse states, the east wind brings torrents of rain.

The Gemara continues its discussion of winds:

אָמַר רַב חִסְדָּא – **Rav Chisda said:** מַאי דִּכְתִיב – **What is** the meaning of **that which [the verse] states:** "מִצָּפוֹן זָהָב יֶאֱתֶה" – *From the north, gold will come?*[16] זוֹ רוּחַ צְפוֹנִית שֶׁמְּזַלֶּלֶת אֶת הַזָּהָב – **This refers to the north wind, which devalues gold,** by bringing famine and forcing people to spend their gold freely on food. וְכֵן הוּא אוֹמֵר – **And so it states** in another verse, which applies the word *zal* to spending gold in this manner: "הַזָּלִים זָהָב מִכִּיס" – *Those who spend gold freely* (*zalim*) *from the purse.*[17]

The Gemara quotes another statement about winds:

אָמַר רַפְרָם בַּר פָּפָּא אָמַר רַב חִסְדָּא – **Rafram bar Pappa said in the name of Rav Chisda:** מִיּוֹם שֶׁחָרַב בֵּית הַמִּקְדָּשׁ – **From the day the Temple was destroyed,** לֹא הוּגְשְׁמָה רוּחַ דְּרוֹמִית – **the south wind has not been** filled **with rain;**[18] שֶׁנֶּאֱמַר – **as [the verse] states:** "וַיִּגְזֹר עַל־יָמִין וְרָעֵב" – *He decrees on the right*

NOTES

The verse's choice of words would seem to bear out R' Yehoshua's view that the dome of the sky is completely enclosed. The verse distinguishes between "traversing" [הוֹלֵךְ] in regard to the south, and "circling" [סוֹבֵב] in regard to the north. As the Gemara will explain below in regard to the eastern and western sides of the world, the difference between these two terms is that "circling" refers to passage *behind* the dome, whereas "traversing" refers to movement *inside* the dome [see note 10 below]. If so, when the verse uses the term "circling" to describe passage around the northern sector, it must refer to passage *behind* the dome, in which case the north side must be enclosed by the dome, as R' Yehoshua contends (*Maharsha*).

8. This translation is based on the Gemara's interpretation of the verse as referring to the sun's path around the horizon (see *Rashi* to *Ecclesiastes* 1:6).

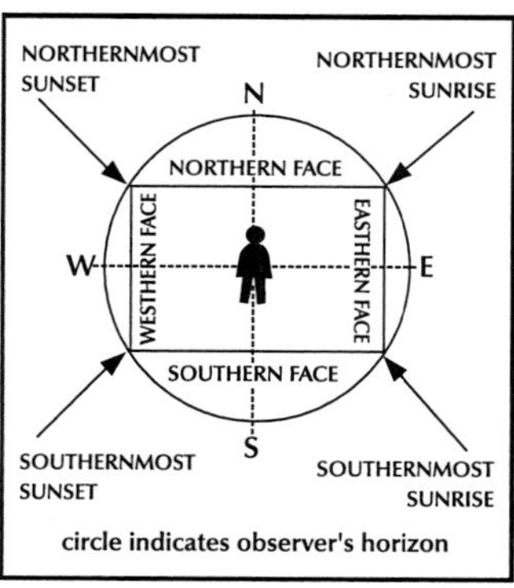

circle indicates observer's horizon

9. The horizon is always seen as a circle (360 degrees) around the observer. The farthest points of sunrise and sunset mark four points along this circle, roughly corresponding to the NE, SE, SW, NW. These four points may be connected to form a rectangle inside the circle. The four arcs formed by these four lines represent, in a general way, the four directions of the world; the areas of the horizon in front of these are the "faces" of these directions. See diagram.

10. The daytime path of the sun is referred to as "traversing," since it occurs inside the dome of the sky. The path of the sun during the night is referred to as "circling" because it takes place outside the dome of the sky (*Rashi*).

During the long summer days near the summer solstice, the sun rises and sets far to the north, and its path crosses over the areas at the eastern and western horizons during the day. Around the time of the winter solstice, however, the sun does not pass over these areas during the day, but circles (behind) them at night (*Rashi*).

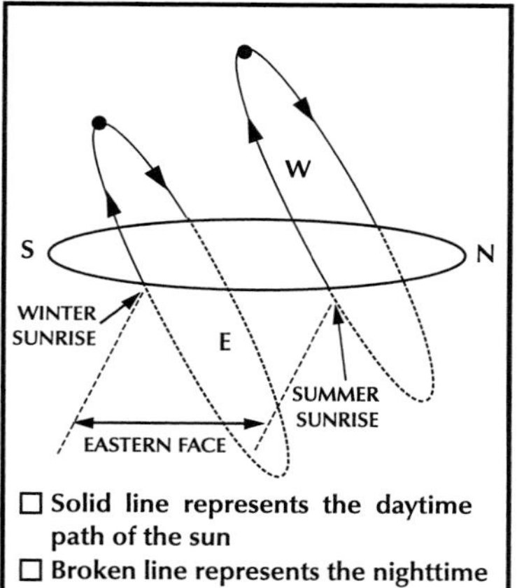

☐ Solid line represents the daytime path of the sun
☐ Broken line represents the nighttime path of the sun

See diagram. When the sun crosses over these areas during the day, it is said to *traverse* them [מְהַלַּכְתָּן]. When it does not cross over them during the day but passes behind them at night, it is said to *circle* them [מְסַבַּבְתָּן]. However, the sun always traverses to the south during the day, and always passes behind the north during the night.

11. [I.e the interpretation of the verse that follows expresses the view of R' Eliezer,] who says that the world is enclosed on only three sides and is open in the north (*Rashi*).

12. *Job* 37:9. This verse is part of a passage describing God's mastery over the climatic forces.

13. See *Radak*, *Shorashim* זרה; see also *Malbim* to verse.

14. Since in R' Eliezer's view the world is open in the north but closed on the other three sides, the south is the "innermost" region of the world. It is therefore identified as the "inner chamber" (*Rabbeinu Gershom*). The north, being open, is termed the "dispersed" section of the dome (*Rashi*).

15. The translation of this verse is based on Rashi's commentary to *Job* 37:10.

16. *Job* 37:22. The simple meaning of the verse is that the "gold" is sunshine, which is revealed when the clouds are dissipated by the winds. However, the dissipation of the clouds by the north wind also causes drought and, consequently, famine.

17. *Isaiah* 46:6. This was explained in the Gemara at the end of 25a.

18. I.e the beneficial rains, which bring forth the vegetation, have not been carried by the south wind (*Rashi*).

עין משפט נר מצוה

פה א טוש"ע ח"מ סי' קנה סעיף ג בהג"ה:
פו ב מיי' פ"א מהל' בית הבחירה הל' ז סמג עשין קסו:
פז ג מיי' פ"י מהלכות שכנים הל' ו סמג עשין פב טוש"ע ח"מ סי' קנה סעיף לב:
פח ד מיי' שם הל' ה טוש"ע שם סעיף ל:
פט ה מיי' שם פ"י הלכה ג סמג שם טוש"ע שם סעיף טו:

ליקוטי רש"י

הולך אל דרום וגו'. לעולם ביום. וסובב אל צפון לעולם בלילה. סובב סובב הולך אל פני מזרח ומערב שפעמים מסבבתן ביום ופעמים מסבבתן בלילה בתמוז מהלכתן ובטבת סובבתן. הרוח רוחו של שמש טלנ"ט בלע"ז כמו אל אשר יהיה שם הרוח ללכת. ועל סביבותיו שב גם מחר כל היקף וסבוב שסבב אתמול הוא מקיף וסובב והולך [קהלת א, ו]. לפי שהחמה לעולם ביום ממזרח לדרום מהלכת כדאמר קרא (קהלת א) הולך אל דרום והליכת החמה ביום היא אבל בלילה אינו הולך אלא סובב מחוץ לכיפה וביום הארוך עומדת בקרן מזרחית צפונית ומהלכת מזרח לדרום [המשך בדף כו.]

תוספות

וממזרים (ד). פי' רוח צפונית שכותל שלה מושלך כלומר שאינה מסובבת לרבי אליעזר: **וכתיב** צפון וימין וכו'. דויגזור על ימין (ה) איכא למימר דבימין ושמאל של אדם איירי (הג"ה. ועוד נראה שמא (ו) מקרא קמא אין להוכיח שבדרום ימין ולא נאמר איפכא. ע"כ הג"ה): **תנא** בין שהבור למעלה ואילן למטה כו'. איצטריך לאיתויי הך אע"ג דבמתני' נמי תנן בין מלמעלן בין מלמטן מ"מ דאי ממתני' הוה אמינא דאחרוב ושקמה קאי דעלה קאי קמ"ל ברייתא בכל אילן (הגה"ה. ולספרים דלא גרסינן במתני' בין מלמטן אתי שפיר דאי ממתני' הוה אמינא בין מלמעלן אאילן קאי ולא אבור משום דלא תקשי אלא בור מלמעלה ואילן מלמטה אמאי כדפריך אברייתא. עד כאן הגה"ה): **עני** והעשיר הוה. רבותא נקט שהיה עני ולא איבעי (ז) לאסוקי אדעתייהו שיבנה האפדנא אפי' הכי הוחקו להרחיק משום דהוו גירי דידהו אף על גב דסמך בהיתר אין צריך להרחיק אפי' בגירי דיליה כדתניא (לעיל דף כ:) אם היה רפת בקר קודמת לאוצר מותר וה"ה חנות של נחתומים וצבעין ואין חילוק בין דירה לשאר לפי המסקנא אומר ר"ת דהכא היינו טעמא משום דלא קביעא תשמישייהו כל כך כי הנך דלעיל (הג"ה. ועוד דהכא (ח) משום דבאיסור סמך דכל מרא ומרא דמחי מרפי לארעא. ע"כ הג"ה): אפומא

גמרא

לאכסדרה הוא דומה ורוח צפונית אינה מסובבת וכיון שהגיעה חמה אצל קרן מערבית צפונית נכפפת ועולה למעלה מן הרקיע ורבי יהושע אומר עולם לקובה הוא דומה ורוח צפונית מסובבת וכיון שחמה מגעת לקרן מערבית צפונית מקפת וחוזרת אחורי כיפה שנאמר א) הולך אל דרום וסובב אל צפון וגו' ה) הולך אל דרום ביום וסובב אל צפון בלילה א) סובב סובב הולך הרוח ועל סביבותיו שב הרוח אלו פני מזרח ופני מערב שפעמים מסבבתן ופעמים מהלכתן הוא היה אומר אתאן לר' אליעזר ב) מן החדר תבא סופה זו רוח דרומית וממזרים קרה זו רוח צפונית מנשמת אל יתן קרח זו רוח מערבית ורחב מים במוצק זו רוח מזרחית והאמר מר רוח דרומית מעלה רביבים ומגדלת עשבים לא קשיא הא דאתיא מטרא בניחותא הא בשפיכותא אמר רב חסדא מאי דכתיב ג) מצפון זהב יאתה זו רוח צפונית * שמוזלת את הזהב וכן הוא אומר ד) הזלים זהב מכיס אמר רפרם בר פפא אמר רב חסדא מיום שחרב בית המקדש לא הוגשמה רוח דרומית שנאמר ה) ויגזור על ימין ורעב ויאכל על שמאל ולא שבעו וכתיב ו) צפון וימין אתה בראתם ואמר רפרם בר פפא אמר רב חסדא מיום שחרב בית המקדש אין הגשמים יורדין מאוצר טוב שנאמר ז) יפתח ה' לך את אוצרו הטוב בזמן שישראל (א) עושין רצונו של מקום וישראל שרויין על אדמתם גשמים יורדין מאוצר טוב בזמן שאין ישראל שרויין על אדמתם אין גשמים יורדין מאוצר טוב אמר רבי יצחק א הרוצה שיחכים ידרים ושיעשיר יצפין ב וסימניך שלחן בצפון ומנורה בדרום ורבי יהושע בן לוי אמר לעולם ידרים שמתוך שמתחכם מתעשר שנאמר ח) אורך ימים בימינה בשמאלה עושר וכבוד והא רבי יהושע בן לוי אמר שכינה במערב אמר ליה רבי חנינא לרב ג אשי כגון אתון דיתביתו בצפונה דא"י אדרימו אדרומי ומנא לן ד דבבל לצפונה דארץ ישראל קיימא דכתיב ט) מצפון תפתח הרעה על כל יושבי הארץ: מרחיקין את המשרה מן הירק וכו': תנא רבי יוסי מתיר בחרדל י שיכול לומר לו עד שאתה אומר לי הרחק חרדלך מן דבוריי הרחק דבוריך מן חרדליי שבאות ואוכלות לגלוגי חרדליי: **מתני'** י מרחיקין את האילן מן הבור עשרים וחמש אמה ובחרוב ובשקמה חמשים אמה בין מלמעלה בין מן הצד אם הבור קדמה י קוצץ ונותן דמים ואם אילן קדם לא יקוץ ספק זה קדם וספק זה קדם לא יקוץ ר' יוסי אומר ג אע"פ שהבור קודמת לאילן לא יקוץ שזה חופר בתוך שלו וזה נוטע בתוך שלו: **גמ'** תנא בין שהבור למטה ואילן למעלה בין שהבור למעלה ואילן למטה בשלמא בור למטה ואילן למעלה קא אזלין שרשין מזקי לה לבור אלא בור למעלה ואילן למטה אמאי אמר רבי חגא בשם רבי יוסי מפני שמחלידין את הקרקע ומלקין קרקעיתה של בור: רבי יוסי אומר אע"פ שהבור קודמת לאילן לא יקוץ שזה חופר בתוך שלו וזה נוטע בתוך שלו: אמר רב יהודה אמר שמואל הלכה כרבי יוסי אמר רב אשי כי הואן בי רב כהנא הוה אמרינן ד מודי ר' יוסי בגירי דידיה פפי יונאה עני והעשיר הוה בנה אפדנא ה הוו הנך עצורי בשיבבותיה דכי הוו דייקי שומשמי הוה נייד אפדניה אתא לקמיה דרב אשי א"ל כי הואן בי רב כהנא הוה אמרינן מודי רבי יוסי בגירי דיליה וכמה כדנייד

רש"י

לאכסדרה. שאין לה דופן רביעית: **אינה מסובבת.** במחילה: **למעלה** מן הרקיע. ומהלכת את רוח צפון בגגו של רקיע: **לקובה.** אהל שכולו מוקף: **לקרן מערבית צפונית.** בלילה שהחמה לעולם מהלכת רוח צפונית בלילה ומן המערב היא פונה לצפון שכך הילוכה מן המזרח לדרום מן הדרום למערב וממערב לצפון: **ומחזרת אחורי כיפה.** דרך חלון: **הולך אל דרום.** היקף היום קרוי הילוך שהוא בתוך החלל ואת היקף הלילה קרוי סיבוב שהוא מקיף בחוץ וביום לעולם מהלכת בדרום אפילו ביום קצר אינו מהלך פחות מרוח דרומית: **וסובב אל צפון בלילה.** אף בלילה קצרה של תקופת תמוז אינו סובב פחות מרוח צפונית: **פעמים מהלכתן.** ביום ארוך של תקופת תמוז שהיא יוצאה בקרן צפונית מזרחית ושוקעת בקרן מערבית צפונית: **פעמים סובבתן.** ביום קצר שהיא יוצאה בקרן מזרחית דרומית ושוקעת בקרן מערבית דרומית ומהלכת בלילה ג' רוחות: **אתאן לר' אליעזר.** שאמר לאכסדרה דומה: **וממזרים קרה זו רוח צפונית.** שהדופן מוזרת ופרוצה: **והאמרת רוח דרומית מעלה רביבים.** וכאן אתה אומר רוח מזרחית מביאה מים: **הא דאתיא מטרא בניחותא.** בא מן הדרום וכי אתיא בשפיכותא בא מן המזרח כדכתיב מים במוצק: **לא הוגשמה רוח דרומית.** שהיתה רגילה להביא רביבים טובים: **וכתיב צפון וימין.** אלמא ימין הוא דרום וכתיב ביה רעב: **את אוצרו הטוב.** וסיפא לתת מטר ארצך: **ידרים.** בתפלתו יחזיר פניו לדרום: **וסימניך.** שלא תשכח: **דמצדד אצדודי.** (ב) מעט לצד דרום: **אדרימו.** שתהיו פונים לצד ירושלים משום דכתיב והתפללו אליך דרך ארצם וגו' (מלכים א ח): **עד שאתה אומר לי.** שאני מזיק ועלי להרחיק את עצמי אני אומר לך שאתה מזיק: **לגלוגי חרדליי.** פרחי חרדליי: **מתני' חרוב ושקמה.** שרשיהם מרובים: **בין מלמעלה.** שאחד מהן מלמעלן בגובה שיפוע הר והשני בשפולו: **בין מן הצד.** בקרקע שוה: **ונותן דמים.** דכיון דברשות נטע שאינו מזיק עד זמן גדול לא חייבוהו חכמים לקוץ בלא דמים * בשביל היזקא דיחיד: **גמ' שמחלידין.** לשון חולדה דהלכות שחיטה (חולין דף לב.) ל שמהלכת מתחת לקרקעית הבור: **הלכה כר' יוסי.** שעל הניזק להרחיק את עצמו: **בגירי דיליה.** היכא דמטי ליה היזקא מתוך ידיו של מזיק כהסיא דאמרי' בהבית והעלייה (ב"מ דף קיז.) הכהו בי תרי חד דייר עילאי וחד דייר תתאי איפחית מעזיבה וכל אימת דמשי ידיה נפלי עליה דתתאי דכשנופלין מידו ממש על התחתון קרי ליה גירי דיליה וכי פסקי והדר נפלי (ג) לא קרי ליה גירי דיליה: **פפי יונאה.** כך שמו על שם מקומו: **עצורי.** עוצרי שומשמין לעשות שמן: **בגירי דיליה.** והכא נמי מידיסס מכותיהם הוא בא לו שמכה מרעיד: **וכמה.** תנוד אפדנא דבעי ארחוקי: **כדנייד**

מסורת הש"ס

א) עירובין נו., ב) [לקמן קמז. יומא לא: מנחות פז:], ג) נ"א ר' יאשיה, ד) [גיטין ו.], ה) [לעיל יח.], ו) ב"מ קיז. לקמן כו:, ז) [לעיל כד:], ח) [ב"מ קי:], ט) [לעיל יח:], י) [לעיל יז: כב:], כ) [לעיל כב: ב"מ קיז.], ל) נ"א דהולכות:

הגהות הב"ח

(א) גמ' את אוצרו הטוב בזמן שישראל שרוין על אדמתם כצ"ל ותיבות עושים רצונו של מקום וישראל נמחק: (ב) רש"י ד"ה דמצדד אצדודי מטה לצד דרום: (ג) ד"ה בגירי דיליה וכו' והדר נפלי כגון דמגנדרי לא קרי ליה: (ד) תוס' ד"ה וממזרים קרה זו רוח צפונית פי' שכותל שלה כצ"ל: (ה) ד"ה וכתיב וכו' על ימין ליכא להוכיח דליכא למימר דבימין: (ו) בא"ד שמא דממקרא קמא אין להוכיח שדרום ימין: (ז) ד"ה עני וכו' ולא איבעי להו לאסוקי וכו' אע"ג דבסמך וכו' נחתומין ושל צבעין: (ח) בא"ד דהכא שאני משום דבאיסור וכו' מרא ומרא דמחי מרפי לארעא והוה דומיא דבור ע"כ הג"ה:

גליון הש"ס

גמרא **שמוזלת את הזהב.** עי' יבמות עב ע"א תד"ה דלא: רש"י ד"ה ונותן כו' **בשביל היזקא דיחיד.** עיין לעיל דף יח ע"ב תוס' ד"ה ואי:

תורה אור השלם

א) הוֹלֵךְ אֶל דָּרוֹם וְסוֹבֵב אֶל צָפוֹן סוֹבֵב סֹבֵב הוֹלֵךְ הָרוּחַ וְעַל סְבִיבֹתָיו שָׁב הָרוּחַ: [קהלת א, ו]

ב) מִן הַחֶדֶר תָּבוֹא סוּפָה וּמִמְּזָרִים קָרָה: מִנִּשְׁמַת אֵל יִתֶּן קָרַח וְרֹחַב מַיִם בְּמוּצָק: [איוב לז, ט-י]

ג) מִצָּפוֹן זָהָב יֶאֱתֶה עַל אֱלוֹהַּ נוֹרָא הוֹד: [איוב לז, כב]

ד) הַזָּלִים זָהָב מִכִּיס וְכֶסֶף בַּקָּנֶה יִשְׁקֹלוּ יִשְׂכְּרוּ צוֹרֵף וְיַעֲשֵׂהוּ אֵל יִסְגְּדוּ אַף יִשְׁתַּחֲווּ: [ישעיה מו, ו]

ה) וַיִּגְזֹר עַל יָמִין וְרָעֵב וַיֹּאכַל עַל שְׂמֹאול וְלֹא שָׂבֵעוּ אִישׁ בְּשַׂר זְרֹעוֹ יֹאכֵלוּ: [ישעיה ט, יט]

ו) צָפוֹן וְיָמִין אַתָּה בְרָאתָם תָּבוֹר וְחֶרְמוֹן בְּשִׁמְךָ יְרַנֵּנוּ: [תהלים פט, יג]

ז) יִפְתַּח יְיָ לְךָ אֶת אוֹצָרוֹ הַטּוֹב אֶת הַשָּׁמַיִם לָתֵת מְטַר אַרְצְךָ בְּעִתּוֹ וּלְבָרֵךְ אֵת כָּל מַעֲשֵׂה יָדֶךָ וְהִלְוִיתָ גּוֹיִם רַבִּים וְאַתָּה לֹא תִלְוֶה: [דברים כח, יב]

ח) אֹרֶךְ יָמִים בִּימִינָהּ בִּשְׂמֹאולָהּ עֹשֶׁר וְכָבוֹד: [משלי ג, טז]

ט) וַיֹּאמֶר יְיָ אֵלָי מִצָּפוֹן תִּפָּתַח הָרָעָה עַל כָּל יֹשְׁבֵי הָאָרֶץ: [ירמיה א, יד]

רבינו גרשום

עולם לאכסדרה הוא דומה. מה אכסדרה זו שיש לה ג' דפנות ולא יותר ומסוככת כך העולם: **ורוח צפונית.** אין לה דופן ואינה מסוככת: **וכשחמה מגעת.** שהלכה כל היום ועכשיו כשמגעת בלילה **בקרן מערבית צפונית** נכפפת באותו רוח צפוני שאינו מסוכך **ועולה למעלה מרקיע: ור' יהושע אומר עולם דומה לקובה.** כאהל הוא דומה. מה אהל זה מסוככת לכל דפנותיה אף עולם מכל וכל מסוכך וכשחמה זורחת ביום ארוך זורחת ברוח צפונית מזרחית והולכת במזרח דרום עד שמגעת **לקרן מערבית צפונית** סמוך לחשיכה לקרן צפוני נכנסת בחלון א' בלילה **ומקפת וחוזרת אחורי כיפה** של עולם וסובבת רוח צפונית כל הלילה **שנאמר הולך אל דרום ביום** בין בימות החמה בין בימות הגשמים. וכן הכי נמי וסובב אל צפון בלילה בין בימות החמה בין בימות הגשמים: **סובב סובב הולך אלו פני מזרח ומערב. שפעמים מסבבתן** ביום קצר ששוקעת החמה בקרן מזרחית דרומית והולך כל היום על פני דרום ולא יותר ובלילה נכנסת בקרן דרומית מערבית בחלון אחד וסובבת כל הלילה פני המערב ופני הצפון ופני המזרח עד קרן מזרחית דרומית. **ופעמים מהלכתן** ביום ארוך שזורחת חמה בקרן צפונית מזרחית והולכת כל המזרח ופני הדרום ופני המערב עד הלילה ובלילה נכנסת בקרן מערבית צפונית וסובבת כל הלילה פני הצפון עד קרן צפונית. מהלכתן ביום ומסבבתן בלילה: **הוא היה אומר** ר' אליעזר דהא ברייתא **אתאן** לטעמא **דר"א** דאמר עולם לאכסדרה הוא דומה: **מן החדר תבוא סופה זו רוח דרומית.** שדופן שלה אמצעי ופנימי ודומה לחדר: **סופה.** סערה: **וממזרים קרה זו רוח צפונית.** שכל העולם ממזרים זרם מים לשם לפי שאין שם דופן והוא תהו ובהו ומים ואינה מסוככת: **קרה.** חורף אבל אינו קריר כל כך. **קרח** חורף ממש: **זו רוח מזרחית.** שמרחיבין שם הגשמים להציק. רוח של **ניחותא** מעלי. **בשפיכותא** שבא בקשיות ודאי קשה כסופה: **לא הוגשמה רוח צפונית.** שלא ירדו גשמים לשם: **על ימין.** זו רוח דרומית: **ורעב.** משמע פעמים רעב פעמים שבע: **ויאכל ולא שבעו.** משמע לא שבעו לפי שלא הוגשמה: **צפון.** הוא שמאל כדפרישית לעיל: **ידרים.** כלומר לרוח דרומית: **יצפין.** יתפלל לרוח צפון: **שולחן בצפון.** היינו עושר שיצריך שולחנו מחמת עושרו: **ומנורה בדרום.** היינו חכמה כדכתיב כי נר מצוה ותורה אור: **שנאמר ארך ימים וגו'.** האי קרא לא אתי לאשמועינן אלא דתורה שהיא חכמה יש בה נמי עושר וכבוד: **דמצדד אצדודי.** לא מכל וכל לרוח דרומית ולא מהכל לרוח מערבית: **אדרימו.** כלומר כשתתפללו חזרו פניכם לצד דרום שנאמר והתפללו [אליך] דרך ארצם: **פיסקא והחרוב והשקמה נ' אמה.** ששרשיהן הולכין הרבה: **בין מלמעלה.** שאם האילן עומד סמוך לבור והבור עמוק עד המים נ' אמה אינו מרחיק ואם לאו מרחיק **ובין מן הצד** שאם הבור אין עמוק צריך להרחיק האילן מן הבור נ' אמה **ותנא בין שהבור מלמעלה** של אילן שהבור עומד במקום גבוה **והאילן** במקום נמוך **ובין שהבור במקום נמוך והאילן במקום גבוה** אם אין כ"ה אמה הרחקה מרחיק. והא לא קא מזיק ליה לבור כלל: **ומלקין קרקעית של בור.** ונעשה טיט: **מודה ר' יוסי בגירי.** כדפריש לעיל אע"פ שעושה בתוך שלו חייב: **יונאה.** שם מקום: **הנך עצורי.** שמכתשין ומעצרין את השומשמין כדי להוציא שמן: **וכמה** נייד. דאמרי' דליהוו הני עצירי חייבין:

and there is hunger, ויֹּאכַל עַל־שְׂמֹאול וְלֹא שָׂבֵעוּ״ – ***and consumes on the left and they will not be satisfied.***[19] וּכְתִיב – **And it is written** in another verse: ,,צָפוֹן וְיָמִין אַתָּה בְרָאתָם״ – ***North and right*** (i.e. south), ***You created them.***[20] We see from this latter verse that "right" can refer to "south." Accordingly, we may interpret the earlier verse to mean: He (God) decreed regarding the south that there will be hunger – because in the aftermath of the exile the south wind will no longer bring the beneficial rains.

The Gemara quotes a second statement by the same Amora:

וְאָמַר רַפְרָם בַּר פָּפָּא אָמַר רַב חִסְדָּא – **And Rafram bar Pappa** also **said in the name of Rav Chisda:** מִיּוֹם שֶׁחָרַב בֵּית הַמִּקְדָּשׁ – **From the day the Temple was destroyed** and the Jews went into exile, אֵין הַגְּשָׁמִים יוֹרְדִין מֵאוֹצָר טוֹב – **the rains have not descended from God's "good storehouse."**[21] שֶׁנֶּאֱמַר – **As [the verse] states** in regard to the blessings God promises to bestow on the Land of Israel:[22] ,,יִפְתַּח ה׳ לְךָ אֶת־אוֹצָרוֹ הַטּוֹב״ – ***God will open up for you His "good storehouse,"*** and the verse continues, *to give you rain for your land.* Thus, Rafram deduces: בִּזְמַן שֶׁיִּשְׂרָאֵל עוֹשִׂין רְצוֹנוֹ שֶׁל מָקוֹם – **In times when** the people of **Israel do the will of God**[23] וְיִשְׂרָאֵל שְׁרוּיִין עַל אַדְמָתָם – **and** the people of **Israel are present in their land,** גְּשָׁמִים יוֹרְדִין מֵאוֹצָר טוֹב – **the rains descend from the "good storehouse."** בִּזְמַן שֶׁאֵין יִשְׂרָאֵל שְׁרוּיִין עַל אַדְמָתָם – However, **in times when** the people of **Israel are not present in their land,** but are in exile, אֵין גְּשָׁמִים יוֹרְדִין מֵאוֹצָר טוֹב – **rains do not descend from the "good storehouse."**[24]

The Gemara now returns to a topic discussed above (25a) – the direction one should face during prayer:

אָמַר רַבִּי יִצְחָק – **R' Yitzchak said:** הָרוֹצֶה שֶׁיַּחְכִּים יַדְרִים – **One who wishes to become knowledgeable should face south** during his prayers; וְשֶׁיַּעֲשִׁיר יַצְפִּין – **while** one who wishes **to become wealthy should face north.** וְסִימָנֵיךְ – **And your mnemonic** for this rule, so that you not confuse the directions, is that in the Temple, שֻׁלְחָן בַּצָּפוֹן וּמְנוֹרָה בַּדָּרוֹם – **the table is** positioned **on the north** side of the Sanctuary, **while the menorah is on the south** side.[25]

Another view:

וְרַבִּי יְהוֹשֻׁעַ בֶּן לֵוִי אָמַר – **And R' Yehoshua ben Levi said:** לְעוֹלָם יַדְרִים – It is best that **one should always face south** during his prayers, שֶׁמִּתּוֹךְ שֶׁמִּתְחַכֵּם מִתְעַשֵּׁר – **for by becoming knowledgeable he will** be able to **become wealthy** as well, by applying his knowledge. שֶׁנֶּאֱמַר – **As [the verse] states:** ,,אֹרֶךְ יָמִים בִּימִינָהּ בִּשְׂמֹאולָהּ עֹשֶׁר וְכָבוֹד״ – ***Length of days*** (i.e. long life) ***is in its*** (the Torah's) ***right hand; in its left hand are wealth and honor.***[26]

The Gemara points out a contradiction:

וְהָא רַבִּי יְהוֹשֻׁעַ בֶּן לֵוִי אָמַר שְׁכִינָה בְּמַעֲרָב – **But R' Yehoshua ben Levi said**[27] that **the *Shechinah* is in the west** – which implies that one must face west while praying. How, then, can R' Yehoshua advise to pray facing the south?

The Gemara answers:

דִּמְצַדֵּד אַצְדּוּדֵי – R' Yehoshua's advice is **that one should turn** somewhat **toward the** south **side,** i.e pray in a somewhat southwesterly direction rather than due west.

The Gemara relates another statement regarding the direction one should face when praying:

אָמַר לֵיהּ רַבִּי חֲנִינָא לְרַב אַשִׁי – **R' Chanina said to Rav Ashi,** who lived in Babylonia: כְּגוֹן אַתּוּן דְּיָתְבִיתוּ בִּצְפוֹנָהּ דְּאֶרֶץ יִשְׂרָאֵל – People **such as yourself, who live to the north of Eretz Yisrael,** אַדְרִימוּ אַדְרוּמֵי – **should face south** and pray towards Jerusalem and the Holy Temple.[28]

The Gemara asks:

וּמְנָא לָן דְּבָבֶל לִצְפוֹנָהּ דְּאֶרֶץ יִשְׂרָאֵל קַיְימָא – **And from where do we know that Babylonia is to the north of Eretz Yisrael?**[29]

NOTES

19. *Isaiah* 9:19. The verse foretells the terrible famine that will prevail at the time of exile. The translation here follows the Gemara's exposition. According to its simple meaning, the verse states וַיִּגְזֹר עַל־יָמִין וְרָעֵב, *he* [the person living at the time of the exile] *snatches on the right* [from his fellow man] *and is* [still] *hungry,* וַיֹּאכַל עַל־שְׂמֹאול וְלֹא שָׂבֵעוּ, *and he eats from the left – and* [yet] *they are not satisfied.* The famine at the time of the exile will be so bitter that even those who are prepared to rob their neighbors at every turn will not be able to satisfy their hunger (*Rashi* to the verse).

20. *Psalms* 89:13. East is considered the "front" of the world (*Rashi* 25a ד״ה מערבו של עולם). When one is facing east, the south is to his right. Thus, "right" can refer to south.

21. I.e. truly blessed and bountiful rains have ceased to fall.

22. *Deuteronomy* 28:12.

23. This condition does not follow from Rafram's statement, nor does it find its parallel in the next line regarding the loss of bountiful rains. *Bach* deletes it from the text.

24. Indeed, following the destruction of the Second Temple, we find a significant number of droughts reported to have occurred in Eretz Yisrael [as evident from the names of the sages who were forced to decree public fasts because of the lack of rain (see *Taanis* 23b, 24a)]. In the centuries following the Crusades, during which the remaining Jewish community of Eretz Yisrael was almost completely eradicated, the fertility of the land declined precipitously and the country became a near wasteland. Although the Land of Israel had once supported a large populace, repeated attempts by foreign invaders to settle the land and rebuild it failed (see *Ramban* to *Lev.* 26:16). Only with the return of large numbers of Jews to the land in the last hundred years did the land begin to bloom again and become capable of sustaining a large population (taken from the *Arachim* lectures).

25. The Gemara offers a device for remembering which direction is appropriate for wealth and which for knowledge. The Sanctuary of the Temple contained the table (*shulchan*) on which the *lechem hapanim*, the twelve loaves of bread, were placed each week; it also contained the menorah. The table may be seen as symbolizing sustenance and prosperity; its position on the north side of the Sanctuary may therefore serve as a reminder that north is the appropriate direction for one who aspires to wealth. The menorah, with its burning lights, is symbolic of Torah knowledge, as the verse states (*Proverbs* 6:23): ,כִּי נֵר מִצְוָה וְתוֹרָה אוֹר, *For the commandment is a candle, and the Torah is a light* (*Rabbeinu Gershom*).

26. *Proverbs* 3:16. Thus we see that Torah can provide wealth as well (*Rabbeinu Gershom*).

27. Above (25a).

28. This is based on the verse stated by Solomon in his prayer at the consecration of the Temple (*I Kings* 8:48): *And they shall pray to You by way of their land, which You gave to their ancestors, [and] the city that You chose and the house that I have built to Your name.*

R' Chanina's position follows the view of a Baraisa quoted in *Berachos* 30a (see *Tosafos* 25a ד״ה לכל), and indeed this is the accepted halachah (*Orach Chaim* 94:2; see above, 25a note 28).

29. The geography of this is problematic, since Babylonia is more to the east of Eretz Yisrael than it is to the north. This is evident not only from a glance at a map but from the numerous references in the Babylonian Talmud to the scholars of Eretz Yisrael as בְּמַעֲרָבָא, *in the west* (see, for example: *Berachos* 47a with *Rashi* ד״ה ממערבא; *Shabbos* 65b, *Rashi* ד״ה מטרא במערבא; *Bava Metzia* 7a, *Rashi* ד״ה בר מערבא). *Tosafos* (*Bechoros* 55b ד״ה מטרא במערבא) note this problem and answer that Babylonia is actually to the northeast of Eretz Yisrael. [Accordingly, we may perhaps say that the meaning of R' Chanina's instruction אַדְרִימוּ אַדְרוּמֵי, *turn to the south,* is only that those living in Babylonia should turn at an angle to the south, and not face due west. (It was unnecessary for R' Chanina to mention that the people of Babylonia should face west, since it was well known that Eretz Yisrael was to the west. The only novelty of his

פה א טוש"ע ח"מ סי' קנ סעיף ב בהג"ה.
פו ב מיי' פ"ח מהל' בית הבחירה הל' ג סמג עשין קסו:
פז ג מיי' פי"א מהלכות שכנים הל' א סמג עשין פב טוש"ע ח"מ סי' קנה סעיף לב:
פח ד מיי' שם הל' ה טוש"ע שם סעיף לג:
פט ה מיי' שם פי"א הלכה ג סמג שם טוש"ע שם סעיף טו:

ליקוטי רש"י

הולך אל דרום וגו'. לעולם ביום. וסובב אל לפון לעולם בלילה. סובב סובב הולך אל פני מזרח ומערב שפעמים מהלכתן ביום ופעמים מסבבתן בלילה בתמוז מהלכתן ובטבת סובבתן. הרוח רוחו של שמש טלנ"ט בלע"ז כמו אל אשר יהיה שם הרוח ללכת. ועל סביבותיו שב גם מחר כל היקף וסבוב שסבב אתמול הוא מקיף וסובב היום [קהלת א, ו]. לפי שהחמה לעולם ביום ממזרח לדרום מהלכת כדאמר קרא (קהלת א) הולך אל דרום והליכת החמה ביום היא אבל בלילה אינו הולך אלא סובב מחוץ לכיפה וביום הארוך עומדת בקרן מזרחית לפונית ומהלכת מזרח לדרום [המשך בדף כו.]

רבינו גרשום

עולם לאכסדרה הוא דומה. מה אכסדרה זו שיש לה ג' דפנות ולא יותר ומסוככת כך העולם: **ורוח צפונית.** אין לה דופן ואינה מסוככת: **וכשחמה מגעת.** שהלכה כל היום ועכשיו כשמגעת בלילה **בקרן מערבית צפונית** נכפפת באותו רוח צפוני שאינו מסוכך **ועולה למעלה מרקיע: ור' יהושע אומר עולם דומה לקובה.** כאהל הוא דומה. מה אהל זה מסוככת לכל דפנותיה אף עולם מכל וכל מסוכך וכשחמה זורחת ביום ארוך זורחת ברוח צפונית מזרחית והולכת במזרח דרום עד שמגעת **לקרן מערבית צפונית** סמוך לחשיכה לקרן צפוני נכנסת בחלון א' בלילה **ומקפת וחוזרת אחורי כיפה** של עולם וסובב רוח צפונית כל הלילה **שנאמר הולך אל דרום ביום** בין בימות החמה בין בימות הגשמים. וכן הכי נמי וסובב אל צפון בלילה בין בימות החמה בין בימות הגשמים: **סובב סובב הולך אלו פני מזרח ומערב. שפעמים מסבבתן** ביום קצר ששוקעת החמה בקרן מזרחית דרומית והולך כל היום על פני דרום ולא יותר ובלילה נכנסת בקרן דרומית מערבית בחלון אחד וסובבת כל הלילה פני המערב ופני הצפון ופני המזרח עד קרן מזרחית דרומית. **ופעמים**

וממזרים (ד). פי' רוח לפונית שכותל שלה מושלך כלומר שאינה מסובבת לרבי אליעזר: **וכתיב צפון וימין וכו'.** דויגזור על ימין (ה) איכא למימר דימין ושמאל של אדם מיירי (הג"ה. ועוד נראה שמא (ו) מקרא קמא אין הוכיח שבדרום ימין ולא נאמר איפכא. ע"כ הג"ה): **תנא** בין שהבור למעלה ואילן למטה כו'. איצטריך לאיתויי הך אע"ג דבמתני' נמי תנן בין מלמעלן בין מן הצד מ"מ דאי ממתני' הוה אמינא דאחרוב ושקמה קאי דעלה קאי קמ"ל ברייתא בכל אילן (הגה"ה. ולספרים דלא גרסינן במתני' בין מלמטן אתי שפיר דאי ממתני' הוה אמינא בין מלמעלן אאילן קאי ולא אבור משום דלא תקשי אלא בור מלמעלה ואילן מלמטה אמאי לכך צריך אברייתא. עד כאן הגה"ה): **עני** והעשיר הוה. רבותא נקט שהיה עני ולא איבעי (ז) לאסוקי אדעתייהו שיבנה אפדנא אפי' הכי הוחזקו להרחיק משום דהוו גירי דידיה אף על גב דסמך בהיתר אין צריך להרחיק אפי' בגירי דיליה כדתניא (לעיל דף כ:) אם היה רפת בקר קודמת לאוצר מותר וה"ה חנות של נחתומים ולצבעין ואין חילוק בין גירי דיליה לשאר לפי המסקנא אומר ר"ת דהכא היינו טעמא משום דלא קביעא תשמישייהו כל כך כי הנך דלעיל (הג"ה. ועוד דהכא (ח) משום דבאיסור סמך דכל מרא ומרא דמחי מרפי לארעא. ע"כ הג"ה): אפומא

לאכסדרה הוא דומה ורוח צפונית אינה מסובבת וכיון שהגיעה חמה אצל קרן מערבית צפונית נכפפת ועולה למעלה מן הרקיע ורבי יהושע אומר עולם לקובה הוא דומה ורוח צפונית מסובבת וכיון שחמה מגעת לקרן מערבית צפונית מקפת וחוזרת אחורי כיפה שנאמר (א) הולך אל דרום וסובב אל צפון וגו' (ל) הולך אל דרום ביום וסובב אל צפון בלילה (א) סובב סובב הולך הרוח ועל סביבותיו שב הרוח אלו פני מזרח ופני מערב שפעמים מסבבתן ופעמים מהלכתן הוא היה אומר אתאן לר' אליעזר (ב) מן החדר תבא סופה זו רוח דרומית וממזרים קרה זו רוח צפונית מנשמת אל יתן קרח זו רוח מערבית ורחב מים במוצק זו רוח מזרחית והאמר מר רוח דרומית מעלה רביבים ומגדלת עשבים לא קשיא הא דאתיא מטרא בניחותא הא בשפיכותא אמר רב חסדא מאי דכתיב (ג) מצפון זהב יאתה זו רוח צפונית * שמזלת את הזהב וכן הוא אומר (ד) הזלים זהב מכיס אמר רפרם בר פפא אמר רב חסדא מיום שחרב בית המקדש לא הוגשמה רוח דרומית שנאמר (ה) ויגזור על ימין ורעב ויאכל על שמאל ולא שבעו וכתיב (ו) צפון וימין אתה בראתם ואמר רפרם בר פפא אמר רב חסדא מיום שחרב בית המקדש אין הגשמים יורדין מאוצר טוב שנאמר (ז) יפתח ה' לך את אוצרו הטוב בזמן שישראל (א) עושין רצונו של מקום וישראל שרויין על אדמתם גשמים יורדין מאוצר טוב בזמן שאין ישראל שרויין על אדמתם אין גשמים יורדין מאוצר טוב אמר רבי יצחק (א) הרוצה שיחכים ידרים ושיעשיר יצפין (ב) וסימניך שלחן בצפון ומנורה בדרום ורבי יהושע בן לוי אמר לעולם ידרים שמתוך שמתחכם מתעשר שנאמר (ח) אורך ימים בימינה בשמאלה עושר וכבוד והא רבי יהושע בן לוי אמר שכינה במערב דמצדד אצדודי אמר ליה רבי חנינא לרב (ג) אשי כגון אתון דיתביתו בצפונה דא"י אדרימו אדרומי ומנא לן (ד) דבבל לצפונה דארץ ישראל קיימא דכתיב (ט) מצפון תפתח הרעה על כל יושבי הארץ: מרחיקין את המשרה מן הירק וכו': תנא רבי יוסי מתיר בחרדל (י) שיכול לומר לו עד שאתה אומר לי הרחק חרדלך מן דבוריי הרחק דבורייך מן חרדליי שבאות ואוכלות לגלוגי חרדליי: **מתני'** (י) מרחיקין את האילן מן הבור עשרים וחמש אמה ובחרוב ובשקמה חמשים אמה בין מלמעלה בין מן הצד אם הבור קדמה (י) קוצץ ונותן דמים ואם אילן קדם לא יקוץ (מ) ספק זה קדם וספק זה קדם לא יקוץ (ר) ר' יוסי אומר (ג) אע"פ שהבור קודמת לאילן לא יקוץ (י) שזה חופר בתוך שלו וזה נוטע בתוך שלו: **גמ'** תנא בין שהבור למטה ואילן למעלה בין שהבור למעלה ואילן למטה בשלמא בור למטה ואילן למעלה קא אולין שרשין מזקי לה לבור אלא בור למעלה ואילן למטה אמאי אמר רבי חגא בשם רבי יוסי מפני שמחלידין את הקרקע ומלקין קרקעיתה של בור: רבי יוסי אומר אע"פ שהבור קודמת לאילן לא יקוץ שזה חופר בתוך שלו וזה נוטע בתוך שלו: אמר רב יהודה אמר שמואל הלכה כרבי יוסי (ס) אמר רב אשי כי הוינן בי רב כהנא הוה אמרינן (ד) מודי ר' יוסי בגירי דידיה פאפי יונאה עני והעשיר הוה בנה אפדנא (ה) הוו הנך עצורי בשיבבותיה דכי הוו דייקי שומשמי הוה נייד אפדניה אתא לקמיה דרב אשי א"ל כי הואן בי רב כהנא הוה אמרינן מודי רבי יוסי בגירי דיליה וכמה כדנייד

לאכסדרה. שאין לה דופן רביעית: **אינה מסובבת.** במחילה למעלה מן הרקיע. ומהלכת את רוח לפון בגגו של רקיע: **לקובה.** אהל שכולו מוקף: **לקרן מערבית צפונית.** בלילה שהחמה לעולם מהלכת רוח לפונית בלילה ומן המערב היא פונה לצפון שכן הילוכה מן המזרח לדרום מן הדרום למערב וממערב לצפון: **ומחזרת אחורי כיפה.** דרך חלון: **הולך אל דרום.** היקף היום קרוי הילוך שהוא בתוך החלל ואת היקף הלילה קרוי סיבוב שהוא מקיף בחוץ וביום לעולם מהלכת בדרום אפילו ביום קצר אינו מהלך פחות מרוח דרומית: **וסובב אל צפון בלילה.** אף בלילה קצרה של תקופת תמוז אינו סובב פחות מרוח לפונית: **פעמים מהלכתן.** ביום ארוך של תקופת תמוז שהיא יוצאה בקרן לפונית מזרחית ושוקעת בקרן מערבית לפונית: **פעמים סובבתן.** ביום קצר שהיא יוצאה בקרן מזרחית דרומית ושוקעת בקרן מערבית דרומית ומהלכת בלילה ג' רוחות: **אתאן לר' אליעזר.** שאמר לאכסדרה דומה: **וממזרים קרה זו רוח צפונית.** שהדופן מוזרת ופרוצה: **והאמרת רוח דרומית מעלה רביבים.** וכאן אתה אומר רוח מזרחית מביאה מים: **הא דאתיא מטרא בניחותא.** בא מן הדרום וכי אתיא בשפיכותא בא מן המזרח דכתיב מים במוצק: **לא הוגשמה רוח דרומית.** שהיא רגילה להביא רביבים טובים: **וכתיב צפון וימין.** אלמא ימין הוא דרום וכתיב ביה רעב: **את אוצרו הטוב.** וסיפא לתת מטר ארצך: **ידרים.** בתפלתו יחזיר פניו לדרום: **וסימניך.** שלא תחליף: **דמצדד אצדודי.** (ב) מעט ללד דרום: **אדרימו.** שתהיו פונים ללד ירושלים משום דכתיב והתפללו אליך דרך ארצם וגו' (מלכים א ח): **עד שאתה אומר לי.** שאני מזיק ועלי להרחיק את עלמי אני אומר לך שאתה מזיק: **לגלוגי חרדליי.** פרחי חרדליי: **מתני' חרוב ושקמה.** שרשיהם מרובים: **בין מלמעלה.** שאחד מהן מלמעלן בגובה שיפוע הר והשני בשפולו: **בין מן הצד.** בקרקע שוה: **ונותן דמים.** דלכיון דברשות נטע טעם שאינו מזיק עד זמן גדול לא חייבוהו חכמים לקוץ בלא דמים * בשביל היזקא דיחיד: **גמ' שמחלידין.** לשון חלדה דהלכות שחיטה (חולין דף נג.) (ל) שמהלכת מתחת לקרקעית הבור: **הלכה כר' יוסי.** שאין הניזק להרחיק את עלמו: **בגירי דיליה.** היכא דמטי ליה היזקא מתוך ידיו של מזיק כהסיא דאמרי' בהכית והטעליה (ב"מ דף קיז.) הנהו בי תרי חד דייר עילאי וחד דייר תתאי איפחית מעזיבה וכל אימת דמשי ידיה נפלי עליה דתתאי דלכשופלין מידו ממש על התחתון קרי ליה גירי דיליה וכי פסקי והדר נפלי (ג) לא קרי ליה גירי דיליה: **פאפי יונאה.** כך שמו על שם מקומו: **עצורי.** עולרי שומשמין לעשות שמן: **בגירי דיליה.** והכא נמי מידיסס הוא בא לו שמכה מכותיהם הוא מרעיד: **וכמה.** תנוד אפדנא דבעי ארחוקי: **כדנייד**

מסורת הש"ס

א) עירובין נו., ב) [לקמן קמז. יומא כא: מנחות פו:], ג) נ"א ר' **יאשיה**, ד) [גיטין ו.], ה) [לעיל יח.], ו) ב"מ קיז. [לעיל יח. לקמן כז:], ז) [לעיל כד:], ח) (ב"מ קי:), ט) [לעיל יח:], י) [לעיל יז: כב:], כ) [לעיל כב: ב"מ קיז.], ל) ל"ל דהולכות:

הגהות הב"ח

(א) **גמ'** את אוצרו הטוב בזמן שישראל שרוין על אדמתם כל"ל ותיבות עושים רצונו של מקום וישראל נמחק: (ב) **רש"י** ד"ה דמצדד אצדודי מעט ללד דרום: (ג) ד"ה בגירי דיליה וכו' והדר נפלי כגון דמגנדרי לא קרי ליה: (ד) **תוס'** ד"ה וממזרים קרה זו רוח לפונית פי' שכותל שלה כל"ל: (ה) ד"ה וכתיב וכו' על ימין ליכא להוכיח דליכא למימר דימין: (ו) **בא"ד** שמא דממקרא קמא אין להוכיח שדרום ימין: (ז) ד"ה עני וכו' ולא איבעי להו לאסוקי וכו' אע"ג דבסמך וכו' נחתומין ושל לבעין: (ח) **בא"ד** דהכא שאני משום דבאיסור וכו' מרא ומרא דמחי מרפי לארעא והוה דומיא דבור ע"כ הג"ה:

גליון הש"ס

גמרא שמזלת את הזהב. עי' יבמות עב ע"א תד"ה דלא: רש"י ד"ה ונותן כו' בשביל היזקא דיחיד. עיין לעיל דף יח ע"ב תוס' ד"ה ואי:

תורה אור השלם

א) הוֹלֵךְ אֶל דָּרוֹם וְסוֹבֵב אֶל צָפוֹן סוֹבֵב סֹבֵב הוֹלֵךְ הָרוּחַ וְעַל סְבִיבֹתָיו שָׁב הָרוּחַ: [קהלת א, ו]

ב) מִן הַחֶדֶר תָּבוֹא סוּפָה וּמִמְּזָרִים קָרָה: מִנִּשְׁמַת אֵל יִתֶּן קָרַח וְרֹחַב מַיִם בְּמוּצָק: [איוב לז, ט-י]

ג) מִצָּפוֹן זָהָב יֶאֱתֶה עַל אֱלוֹהַּ נוֹרָא הוֹד: [איוב לז, כב]

ד) הַזָּלִים זָהָב מִכִּיס וְכֶסֶף בַּקָּנֶה יִשְׁקֹלוּ יִשְׂכְּרוּ צוֹרֵף וְיַעֲשֵׂהוּ אֵל יִסְגְּדוּ אַף יִשְׁתַּחֲווּ: [ישעיה מו, ו]

ה) וַיִּגְזֹר עַל יָמִין וְרָעֵב וַיֹּאכַל עַל שְׂמֹאול וְלֹא שָׂבֵעוּ אִישׁ בְּשַׂר זְרֹעוֹ יֹאכֵלוּ: [ישעיה ט, יט]

ו) צָפוֹן וְיָמִין אַתָּה בְרָאתָם תָּבוֹר וְחֶרְמוֹן בְּשִׁמְךָ יְרַנֵּנוּ: [תהלים פט, יג]

ז) יִפְתַּח יְיָ לְךָ אֶת אוֹצָרוֹ הַטּוֹב אֶת הַשָּׁמַיִם לָתֵת מְטַר אַרְצְךָ בְּעִתּוֹ וּלְבָרֵךְ אֵת כָּל מַעֲשֵׂה יָדֶךָ וְהִלְוִיתָ גּוֹיִם רַבִּים וְאַתָּה לֹא תִלְוֶה: [דברים כח, יב]

ח) אֹרֶךְ יָמִים בִּימִינָהּ בִּשְׂמֹאולָהּ עֹשֶׁר וְכָבוֹד: [משלי ג, טז]

ט) וַיֹּאמֶר יְיָ אֵלָי מִצָּפוֹן תִּפָּתַח הָרָעָה עַל כָּל יֹשְׁבֵי הָאָרֶץ: [ירמיה א, יד]

מהלכתן ביום ארוך שזורחת חמה בקרן צפונית מזרחית והולכת כל המזרח ופני הדרום ופני המערב עד הלילה ובלילה נכנסת בקרן מערבית צפונית וסובבת כל הלילה פני צפון עד קרן צפונית. מהלכתן ביום ומסבבתן בלילה: **הוא היה אומר** ר' אליעזר דהא ברייתא **אתאן** לטעמא דר"א דאמר עולם לאכסדרה הוא דומה: **מן החדר תבוא סופה זו רוח דרומית.** שדופן שלה אמצעי ופנימי ודומה לחדר: **סופה.** סערה: **וממזרים קרה זו רוח צפונית.** שכל העולם ממזרים זרם מים לשם לפי שאין שם דופן והוא תהו ובהו ומים ואינה מסוככת: **קרה.** חורף אבל אינו קריר כל כך. **קרח** חורף ממש: **זו רוח מזרחית.** שמרחיבין שם הגשמים להצדיק. רוח של **ניחותא** מעלי. **בשפיכותא** שבא בקשיות ודאי קשה כסופה: **לא הוגשמה רוח דרומית.** שלא ירדו גשמים לשם: **על ימין.** זו רוח דרומית: **ורעב.** משמע פעמים רעב פעמים שבע: **ויאכל ולא שבעו.** משמע לא שבעו לפי שלא הוגשמה: **צפון.** הוא שמאל כדפרשית לעיל: **ידרים.** כלומר לרוח דרומית: **יצפין.** יתפלל לרוח צפון: **שולחן בצפון.** היינו עושר שיעריך שולחנו מחמת עושרו: **ומנורה בדרום.** היינו חכמה כדכתיב כי נר מצוה ותורה אור: **שנאמר ארך ימים וגו'.** הוא קרא לא אתי לאשמועינן אלא דתורה שנקראת חכמה יש בה כל מדרך עושר וכבוד: **דמצדד אצדודי.** כלומר כשתתפללו החזירו פניכם לצד דרום כדי שתפנו לצד ירושלים **אדרימו.** שנאמר והתפללו [אליך] דרך ארצם: **פיסקא והחרוב והשקמה נ' אמה.** שהאילן עומד סמוך לבור והבור עומד שאם הבור אין עמוק צריך להרחיק האילן מן הבור נ' אמה **ותנא בין שהבור מלמעלה** של אילן במקום גבוה והאילן במקום נמוך **ובין שהבור במקום נמוך והאילן במקום גבוה** אם אין כ"ה אמה הרחקה מרחיק. והא לא קא מזיק ליה לבור כלל: **ומלקין קרקעית של בור.** ונעשה טיט: **מודה ר' יוסי בגירי.** כדפרישית לעיל אע"פ שעשה בתוך שלו חייב: **יונאה.** שם מקום: **הנך עצורי.** שמכתשין ומעצרין את השומשמין כדי להוציא שמן: **וכמה נייד.** דאמרי' דליהוו הני עצירי חייבין:

דִּכְתִיב – **For it is written** in Scripture regarding the destruction of the land by the Babylonians:[30] "מִצָּפוֹן תִּפָּתַח הָרָעָה עַל כָּל־יוֹשְׁבֵי הָאָרֶץ" – ***Out of the north the evil shall open*** (i.e. come forth) ***upon all the inhabitants of the land.***

The Gemara quotes the next section of the Mishnah:

מַרְחִיקִין אֶת הַמִּשְׁרָה מִן הַיָּרָק וכו׳ – ONE MUST DISTANCE A FLAX POOL FROM VEGETABLES etc. [leeks from onions, and mustard plants from the bees of his neighbor. R' Yose permits in the case of the mustard plants].

The Gemara quotes a Baraisa that explains R' Yose's dissenting opinion:

תַּנְיָא – **It was taught in a Baraisa:** רַבִּי יוֹסֵי מַתִּיר בְּחַרְדָּל – R' YOSE PERMITS planting close to the neighbor's property IN the case of MUSTARD plants שֶׁיָּכוֹל לוֹמַר לוֹ – BECAUSE HE [the owner of the mustard] CAN SAY TO HIM [the owner of the bees]: עַד שֶׁאַתָּה אוֹמֵר לִי הַרְחֵק חַרְדָּלְךָ מִן דְּבוֹרָיי – JUST AS YOU SAY TO ME,[31] "DISTANCE YOUR MUSTARD plants FROM MY BEES," so that they not harm the honey,[32] הַרְחֵק דְּבוֹרָךְ מִן חַרְדָּלַיי – I reply to you, "DISTANCE YOUR BEES FROM MY MUSTARD plants שֶׁבָּאוֹת וְאוֹכְלוֹת לְגָלוּגֵי חַרְדָּלַיי – FOR THEY COME AND EAT THE FLOWERS OF MY MUSTARD plants." Thus, the owner of the mustard plants has no greater obligation to remove his plants than does the owner of the bees to remove his bees, and neither can evict the other.[33]

Mishnah

מַרְחִיקִין אֶת הָאִילָן מִן הַבּוֹר עֶשְׂרִים וְחָמֵשׁ אַמָּה – **One must distance a tree twenty-five *amos* from a** neighbor's **pit,** וּבְחָרוּב וּבְשִׁקְמָה חֲמִשִּׁים אַמָּה – **and a carob or a sycamore** tree, **fifty *amos*** from the pit,[34] בֵּין מִלְמַעְלָה בֵּין מִן הַצַּד – **whether** one is located **above** the other, on higher ground, **or beside** it, on level ground.

The Mishnah now turns to the law of a tree that has already been planted near a pit:

אִם הַבּוֹר קָדְמָה – **If the pit came first,** and one planted a tree within twenty-five *amos* afterward, קוֹצֵץ וְנוֹתֵן דָּמִים – **he must cut down** the tree, **and [the neighbor] pays** him compensation,[35] וְאִם אִילָן קָדַם – **but if the tree came first,** and the pit was dug afterward, לֹא יָקוֹץ – **he need not cut** it **down.** סָפֵק זֶה קָדַם וְסָפֵק זֶה קָדַם – **If it is unclear** whether **[the tree] or [the pit] came first,** לֹא יָקוֹץ – **he need not cut down** the tree.[36] רַבִּי יוֹסֵי אוֹמֵר – **R' Yose says:** אַף עַל פִּי שֶׁהַבּוֹר קוֹדֶמֶת לָאִילָן לֹא יָקוֹץ – **Even if the pit preceded the tree, he need not cut** it **down,** שֶׁזֶּה חוֹפֵר בְּתוֹךְ שֶׁלּוֹ וְזֶה נוֹטֵעַ בְּתוֹךְ שֶׁלּוֹ – because just as **this one may dig** a pit **within his** property, **that one may plant** a tree **within his** property.[37]

Gemara

The Gemara cites a Baraisa that elaborates on the rule that a tree must be distanced from a pit even if they are not on level ground:

תַּנְיָא – **It was taught in a Baraisa:** בֵּין שֶׁהַבּוֹר לְמַטָּה וְאִילָן לְמַעְלָה – The requirement to distance a tree applies WHETHER THE PIT IS BELOW AND THE TREE ABOVE it on higher ground, בֵּין שֶׁהַבּוֹר לְמַעְלָה וְאִילָן לְמַטָּה – OR THE PIT IS ABOVE AND THE TREE BELOW it on lower ground.

The Gemara explores the rationale for the Baraisa's ruling in each case:

בִּשְׁלָמָא בּוֹר לְמַטָּה וְאִילָן לְמַעְלָה – **It is understandable** that one must distance the tree in the case where the **pit** is **below and** the **tree above** it, קָא אָזְלִין שָׁרְשִׁין מַזְּקֵי לָהּ לְבוֹר – because the tree's **roots** will **travel** downward **and damage the pit,** אֶלָּא בּוֹר לְמַעְלָה וְאִילָן לְמַטָּה – **but** in the case where the **pit** is **above and** the **tree below** it, אַמַּאי – **why** must one distance the tree? Will its roots travel upward into the pit?

The Gemara answers:

אָמַר רַבִּי חַגָּא בְּשֵׁם רַבִּי יוֹסֵי – **R' Chagga said in R' Yose's name:** מִפְּנֵי שֶׁמַּחֲלִידִין אֶת הַקַּרְקַע וּמַלְקִין קַרְקָעִיתָהּ שֶׁל בּוֹר – The tree must

NOTES

statement was that they should also angle to the south.) Thus, R' Chanina's instruction to face south parallels R' Yehoshua ben Levi's earlier instruction that one who wishes to acquire knowledge should face south, which the Gemara above explained to mean: דְּמִצַּדֵּד אַצְדּוּדֵי, that he should *turn to the side* at somewhat of an angle to the south.

It follows from this that when the Gemara asks how we know that Babylonia is to the north of Eretz Yisrael, it does so not because the geographic facts were uncertain, but quite the contrary, because it was known that Babylonia was east of Eretz Yisrael. The Gemara's question therefore is how we know that it is also *somewhat* to the north. The Gemara cites the verse as proof that Babylonia is somewhat to the north of Eretz Yisrael.]

30. *Jeremiah* 1:14. God is telling the prophet Jeremiah about the impending destruction of Israel by an invasion from the north.

31. Literally: until you say to me.

32. See 25a note 7.

33. The Gemara above (18b) explained that the Rabbis (i.e. the Tanna Kamma) reject R' Yose's argument because they do not consider the damage inflicted by the bees to be significant. See also *Tosafos* 18b ד״ה לגלוגי.

The Gemara above (18b) explained that R' Yose actually disagrees with the Tanna Kamma in all three of the cases mentioned in the Mishnah. It is his view that as long as the owner of the harmful agent remains within his property and does not actively damage his neighbor, he has the right to make whatever use of his property he wishes, and it is up to the threatened party to protect himself by moving his objects out of harm's reach [עַל הַנִּיזָק לְהַרְחִיק אֶת עַצְמוֹ]. R' Yose states his objection in the case of mustard plants specifically only because he argues that planting them close to beehives should be permissible even according to the Tanna Kamma's view. Although the Tanna Kamma rules that it is the responsibility of the owner of the harmful agent to move it out of range [עַל הַמַּזִּיק לְהַרְחִיק אֶת עַצְמוֹ], since the bees are not only damaged by the mustard plants but damage them in turn, the owner of the beehive has no greater claim for protection than the owner of the mustard plants, as explained above on 18b.

34. The root systems of most trees extend up to twenty-five *amos* from the tree. Therefore, one must maintain that distance between a tree and a neighbor's pit to ensure that the tree's roots do not breach the walls of the pit (*Rashi,* 18a ד״ה עשרים וחמשה). Carob and sycamore trees, which have extensive root systems, necessitate a greater distance (*Rashi*).

35. Although the tree is potentially harmful to the neighbor's pit, its owner is compensated for cutting it down. The reason is that since the roots will not damage the pit until much later, when they reach the pit, one does not damage his neighbor's property at the time that he plants the tree. Therefore, the Rabbis did not require him to cut it down at a loss. However, compensation is awarded only where the party threatened by the tree is an individual neighbor. [A tree planted within twenty-five *amos* of a *city* is cut down without compensation (above, 24b).] (*Rashi*).

36. Since the requirement to cut down the tree is unclear, the owner of the tree cannot be made to suffer the loss of his tree out of doubt. This is consistent with the rule for any case of uncertainty regarding monetary issues, in which the ruling is made in favor of the defendant (*Rambam, Commentary to Mishnah*).

37. R' Yose maintains that with regard to damages that result from activities performed within one's own property, it is up to the one who is being damaged to protect himself by removing his vulnerable item from the proximity of the threatening object (see note 33).

לאכסדרה הוא דומה ורוח צפונית אינה מסובבת וכיון שהגיעה חמה אצל קרן מערבית צפונית נכפפת ועולה למעלה מן הרקיע ורבי יהושע אומר עולם לקובה הוא דומה ורוח צפונית מסובבת וכיון שחמה מגעת לקרן מערבית צפונית מקפת וחוזרת אחורי כיפה שנאמר הולך אל דרום וסובב אל צפון וגו' הולך אל דרום ביום וסובב אל צפון בלילה סובב סובב הולך הרוח ועל סביבותיו שב הרוח אלו פני מזרח ופני מערב שפעמים מסבבתן ופעמים מהלכתן הוא היה אומר אתאן לר' אליעזר מן החדר תבא סופה זו רוח דרומית וממזרים קרה זו רוח צפונית מנשמת אל יתן קרח זו רוח מערבית ורחב מים במוצק זו רוח מזרחית והאמר מר רוח דרומית מעלה רביבים ומגדלת עשבים לא קשיא הא דאתיא מטרא בניחותא הא בשפיכותא אמר רב חסדא מאי דכתיב מצפון זהב יאתה זו רוח צפונית שמוזלת את הזהב וכן הוא אומר הזלים זהב מכיס אמר רפרם בר פפא אמר רב חסדא מיום שחרב בית המקדש לא הוגשמה רוח דרומית שנאמר ויגזור על ימין ורעב ויאכל על שמאל ולא שבעו וכתיב צפון וימין אתה בראתם ואמר רפרם בר פפא אמר רב חסדא מיום שחרב בית המקדש אין הגשמים יורדין מאוצר טוב שנאמר יפתח ה' לך את אוצרו הטוב בזמן שישראל (א) עושין רצונו של מקום וישראל שרויין על אדמתם גשמים יורדין מאוצר טוב בזמן שאין ישראל שרויין על אדמתם אין גשמים יורדין מאוצר טוב אמר רבי יצחק הרוצה שיחכים ידרים ושיעשיר יצפין וסימניך שלחן בצפון ומנורה בדרום ורבי יהושע בן לוי אמר לעולם ידרים שמתוך שמתחכם מתעשר שנאמר אורך ימים בימינה בשמאלה עושר וכבוד והא רבי יהושע בן לוי הוא דאמר שכינה במערב דמצדד אצדודי אמר ליה רבי חנינא לרב אשי כגון אתון דיתביתו בצפונה דא"י אדרימו אדרומי ומנא לן דבבל לצפונה דארץ ישראל קיימא דכתיב מצפון תפתח הרעה על כל יושבי הארץ: מרחיקין את המשרה מן הירק וכו': תנא רבי יוסי מתיר בחרדל שיכול לומר לו עד שאתה אומר לי הרחק חרדלך מן דבוריי הרחק דבורייך מן חרדליי שבאות ואוכלות לגלוגי חרדליי: **מתני'** מרחיקין את האילן מן הבור עשרים וחמש אמה ובחרוב ובשקמה חמשים אמה בין מלמעלה בין מן הצד אם הבור קדמה קוצץ ונותן דמים ואם אילן קדם לא יקוץ ספק זה קדם וספק זה קדם לא יקוץ ר' יוסי אומר אע"פ שהבור קודמת לאילן לא יקוץ שזה חופר בתוך שלו וזה נוטע בתוך שלו: **גמ'** תנא בין שהבור למטה ואילן למעלה בין שהבור למעלה ואילן למטה בשלמא בור למטה ואילן למעלה קא אזלין שרשין מזקי לה לבור אלא בור למעלה ואילן למטה אמאי אמר רבי חגא בשם רבי יוסי מפני שמחלידין את הקרקע ומלקין קרקעיתה של בור: רבי יוסי אומר אע"פ שהבור קודמת לאילן לא יקוץ שזה חופר בתוך שלו וזה נוטע בתוך שלו: אמר רב יהודה אמר שמואל הלכה כרבי יוסי אמר רב אשי כי הואן בי רב כהנא הוה אמרינן מודי ר' יוסי בגירי דידיה פאפי יונאה עני והעשיר הוה בנה אפדנא הוו הנך עצורי בשיבבותיה דכי הוו דייקי שומשמי הוה נייד אפדניה אתא לקמיה דרב אשי א"ל כי הואן בי רב כהנא הוה אמרינן מודי רבי יוסי בגירי דיליה וכמה כדנייד

תוספות

וממזרים (ד). פי' רוח צפונית שכותל שלה מושלך כלומר שאינה מסובבת לרבי אליעזר: **וכתיב צפון וימין וכו'.** דויגזור על ימין (ה) איכא למימר דימין ושמאל של אדם מיירי (הג"ה. ועוד נראה שמא (ו) מקרא קמא אין להוכיח שבדרום ימין ולא נאמר איפכא. ע"כ הג"ה): **תנא** בין שהבור למעלה ואילן למטה כו'. אילטריך לאיתויי הך אע"ג דבמתני' נמי תנן בין מלמעלה בין מן הצד מ"מ דאי ממתני' הוה אמינא דאחרוב ושקמה קאי דלעלה קאי קמ"ל ברייתא בכל אילן (הג"ה. ולספרים דלא גרסינן בין מלמטה אתי שפיר דאי ממתני' הוה אמינא בין מלמעלה אאילן קאי ולא אבור משום דלא תקשי אלא בור מלמעלה ואילן מלמטה אמאי לפריך אברייתא. עד כאן הגה"ה): **עני** והעשיר הוה. רבותא נקט שהיה עני ולא איבעי (ז) לאסוקי לדעתייהו שיבנה האפדנא אפי' הכי החזיקו להרחיק משום דהוו גירי דידהו אף על גב דסמך בהיתר אין צריך להרחיק אפי' בגירי דיליה כדתניא (לעיל דף כ:) אם היה רפת בקר קודמת לאוצר מותר וה"ה תנות של נחתומים וצבעין ואין חילוק בין דירה לשאר לפי המסקנא אומר ר"ת דהכא היינו טעמא משום דלא קביעא תשמישייהו כל כך כי הנך דלעיל (הג"ה. ועוד דהכא (ח) משום דבאיסור סמך דכל מרא דמחי מרפי לארעא. ע"כ הג"ה): אפומא

רש"י

לאכסדרה. שאין לה דופן רביעית: **אינה מסובבת.** במחילה: **למעלה מן הרקיע.** ומהלכת את רוח לפון בגגו של רקיע: **לקובה.** אהל שכולו מוקף: **לקרן מערבית צפונית.** בלילה שהחמה לעולם מהלכת רוח לפונית בלילה ומן המערב היא פונה לצפון שכך הילוכה מן המזרח לדרום מן הדרום למערב וממערב לצפון: **ומחזרת אחורי כיפה.** דרך חלון: **הולך אל דרום.** היקף היום קרוי הילוך שהוא בתוך החלל ואת היקף הלילה קרוי סיבוב שהוא מקיף בחוץ וביום לעולם מהלכת בדרום אפילו ביום קלר אינו מהלך פחות מרוח דרומית: **וסובב אל צפון בלילה.** אף בלילה קלרה של תקופת תמוז אינו סובב פחות מרוח לפונית: **פעמים מהלכתן.** ביום ארוך של תקופת תמוז שהיא יולאה בקרן לפונית מזרחית ושוקעת בקרן מערבית לפונית: **פעמים סובבתן.** ביום קלר שהיא יולאה בקרן מזרחית דרומית ושוקעת בקרן מערבית דרומית ומהלכת בלילה ג' רוחות: **אתאן לר' אליעזר.** שאמר לאכסדרה דומה: **וממזרים קרה זו רוח צפונית.** שהדופן מוחרת ופרולה: **והאמרת רוח דרומית מעלה רביבים.** וכאן אתה אומר רוח מזרחית מביאה מים: **הא דאתיא מטרא בניחותא.** באה מן הדרום וכי אתיא בשפיכותא באה מן המזרח כדכתיב מים במולק: **לא הוגשמה רוח דרומית.** שהיתה רגילה להביא רביבים טובים: **וכתיב צפון וימין.** אלמא ימין הוא דרום וכתיב ביה רעב: **את אוצרו הטוב.** וסיפא לתת מטר ארלך: **ידרים.** בתפלתו יחזיר פניו לדרום: **וסימניך.** שלא תחליף: **דמצדד אצדודי.** (ב) מעט לצד דרום: **אדרימו.** שתהיו פונים לצד ירושלים משום דכתיב והתפללו אליך דרך ארלם וגו' (מלכים א ח): **עד שאתה אומר לי.** שאני מזיק ועלי להרחיק את עלמי אני אומר לך שאתה מזיק: **לגלוגי חרדליי.** פרחי חרדליי: **מתני'** חרוב ושקמה. שרשיהם מרובים: **בין מלמעלה.** שאחד מהן מלמעלן בגובה שיפוע הר והשני בשפולו: **בין מן הצד.** בקרקע שוה: **ונותן דמים.** דכיון דברשות נטע שאינו מזיק עד זמן גדול לא חייבוהו חכמים לקוץ בלא דמים ° בשביל הזיקא דיחיד: **גמ'** שמחלידין. לשון חלדה דהלכות שחיטה (חולין דף לב.) שמהלכת מתחת לקרקעית הבור: **הלכה כר' יוסי.** שעל הניזק להרחיק את עלמו: **בגירי דיליה.** היכא דמטי ליה היזקא מתוך ידיו של מזיק כההיא דאמרי' בהבית והעלייה (ב"מ דף קיז.) הנהו בי תרי חד דייר עילאי וחד דייר תתאי איפחית מעזיבה וכל אימת דמשי ידיה נפלי עליה דתתאי דכשנופלין מידו ממש על התחתון קרי ליה גירי דיליה וכי פסקי והדר נפלי (ג) לא קרי ליה גירי דיליה: **פאפי יונאה.** כך שמו על שם מקומו: **עצורי.** עולרי שומשמין לעשות שמן: **בגירי דיליה.** והכא נמי מידיסס הוא בא לו שמכת מכותיהם הוא מרעיד: **וכמה.** תנוד אפדנא דבעי ארחוקי: **כדנייד**

עין משפט נר מצוה

פה א טוש"ע א"ח סי' לד סעיף ג בהג"ה:
פו ב מיי' פ"א מהל' בית הבחירה הל' ג סמג עשין קסג:
פז ג מיי' פי"א מהלכות שכנים הל' ו סמג עשין פב טוש"ע ח"מ סי' קנה סעיף לב:
פח ד מיי' שם הל' ה טוש"ע שם:
פט ה מיי' שם פ"א הלכה ג סמג שם טוש"ע שם סעיף טו:

ליקוטי רש"י

הולך אל דרום וגו'. לעולם ביום, וסובב אל לפון לעולם בלילה. סובב סובב הולך אל פני מזרח ומערב שפעמים מהלכתן ביום ופעמים מסבבתן בלילה בתמוז מהלכתן ובטבת סובבתן. הרוח הוא של שמש כלו"ר בלע"ז כמו אל אשר יהיה שם הרוח ללכת. ועל סביבותיו שב גם אחר כל היקף וסבוב שסבב אמשול הוא חוזר מקיף וסובב. ולפי שהחמה היא מנהגת ביום ממזרח לדרום מהלכת כדאמר קרא (קהלת א, ו) הולך אל דרום. היום ביום ומהלכת החמה ביום היא אבל בלילה אינו הולך אלא סובב מחוץ לרקיע וביום הארוך עומדת בקרן מזרחית לפונית ומהלכת מזרח לדרום [המשך בדף כו.]

רבינו גרשום

עולם לאכסדרה הוא דומה. מה אכסדרה זו שיש לה ג' דפנות ולא יותר ומסוככת כך העולם: **ורוח צפונית.** אין לה דופן ואינה מסוככת: **וכשחמה מגעת.** שהלכה כל היום ועכשיו כשמגעת בלילה בקרן מערבית צפונית נכפפת באותו רוח צפוני שאינו מסוכך **ועולה למעלה מרקיע:** ור' יהושע אומר עולם דומה לקובה. כאהל הוא דומה. מה אהל זה מסוככת לכל דפנותיה אף עולם מכל וכל מסוכך וכשחמה זורחת ביום ארוך זורחת ברוח צפונית מזרחית והולכת במזרח דרום עד שמגעת **לקרן מערבית צפונית** סמוך לחשיכה לקרן צפוני נכנסת בחלון א' בלילה **ומקפת וחוזרת אחורי כיפה** של עולם וסובב רוח צפונית כל הלילה שנאמר **הולך אל דרום ביום** בין בימות החמה בין בימות הגשמים. וכן הכי נמי וסובב אל צפון בלילה בין בימות החמה בין בימות הגשמים: **סובב סובב הולך אלו פני מזרח ומערב. שפעמים מסבבתן** ביום קצר שזורחת החמה בקרן מזרחית דרומית והולך כל היום על פני דרום ולא יותר ובלילה נכנסת בקרן מערבית דרומית בחלון אחד וסובבת כל הלילה פני המערב ופני הצפון ופני המזרח עד קרן מזרחית דרומית. **ופעמים מהלכתן** ביום ארוך שזורחת חמה בקרן צפונית מזרחית והולכת כל המזרח ופני הדרום ופני המערב עד הלילה ובלילה נכנסת בקרן מערבית צפונית וסובבת כל הלילה פני הצפון עד קרן צפונית. מהלכתן ביום ומסבבתן בלילה: **הוא היה אומר** ר' אליעזר דהא ברייתא **אתאן** לטעמא **דר"א** דאמר עולם לאכסדרה הוא דומה: **מן החדר תבוא סופה זו רוח דרומית.** שדופן שלה אמצעי ופנימי ודומה לחדר: **סופה.** סערה: **וממזרים קרה זו רוח צפונית.** שכל העולם ממזרים זרם מים לשם לפי שאין שם דופן והוא תהו ובהו ומים ואינה מסוככת: **קרה.** חורף אבל אינו קריר כל כך: **רוח מזרחית.** שמרחיבין שם הגשמים להציק. רוח של **ניחותא** מעלי. **בשפיכותא** שבא בקשיות ודאי קשה כסופה: **לא הוגשמה רוח צפונית.** שלא ירדו גשמים לשם: **על ימין.** זו רוח דרומית: **ורעב.** משמע פעמים רעב פעמים שבע: **ויאכל ולא שבעו.** משמע לא שבעו לפי שלא הוגשמה: **צפון.** הוא שמאל כדפרישית לעיל: **ידרים.** כלומר לרוח דרומית: **יצפין.** יתפלל לרוח צפון: **שולחן בצפון.** היינו עושר שיעריך שולחנו מחמת עושרו: **ומנורה בדרום.** היינו חכמה כדכתיב כי נר מצוה ותורה אור: **שנאמר ארך ימים וגו'.** האי קרא לא אתי לאשמועינן אלא דתורה שהיא חכמה יש בה נמי עושר וכבוד: **דמצדד אצדודי.** לא מכל וכל לרוח דרומית ולא מהכל לרוח מערבית: **אדרימו.** כלומר כשתתפללו חזרו פניכם לדרום והתפללו [אליך] דרך ארצם: **פיסקא והחרוב והשקמה ג' אמה.** ששרשיהן הולכין הרבה: **בין מלמעלה.** שאם האילן עומד סמוך לבור והבור עמוק עד המים ג' אמה אינו מרחיק ואם לאו מרחיק **ובין מן הצד** שאם הבור אין עמוק צריך להרחיק האילן מן הבור נ' אמה **ותנא בין שהבור מלמעלה** של אילן שהבור עומד במקום גבוה **והאילן** במקום נמוך **ובין שהבור במקום נמוך והאילן במקום גבוה** אם אין כ"ה אמה הרחקה מרחיק. והא לא קא מזיק ליה לבור כלל: **ומלקין קרקעית של בור.** ונעשה טיט: **מודה ר' יוסי בגירי.** כדפריש לעיל אע"פ שעושה בתוך שלו חייב: **יונאה.** שם מקום: **הנך עצורי.** שמכתשין ומעצרין את השומשמין כדי להוציא שמן: **וכמה** נייד. דאמרי' דליהוו הני עצורי חייבין:

מסורת הש"ס

א) עירובין נו., ב) [לקמן קמז. יומא כא: מנחות פו:], ג) ג"א ראשית, ד) [גיטין ז.], ה) [לעיל יח.], ו) ב"מ קיז., ז) [לעיל יח. לקמן מג:], ח) [לעיל כד:], ט) [ב"מ קי:], י) [לעיל יז: כג:], כ) [לעיל כב: ב"מ קיז.], ל) ב"ל דהולכות:

הגהות הב"ח

(א) גמ' את אולרו הטוב בזמן שישראל שרוין על אדמתם כל"ל ותיבות עושים רלונו של מקום וישראל נמחק: (ב) רש"י ד"ה דמלדד אלדודי מטה ללד דרום: (ג) ד"ה בגירי דיליה וכו' והדר נפלי כגון דמגנדרי לא קרי ליה: (ד) תוס' ד"ה וממזרים קרה זו רוח לפונית פי' שכותל שלה כל"ל: (ה) ד"ה וכתיב וכו' על ימין ליכא להוכיח דאיכא למימר דימין: (ו) בא"ד שמא דממקרא קמא אין להוכיח שבדרום ימין: (ז) ד"ה עני וכו' ולא איבעי להו לאסוקי וכו' אע"ג דסמך וכו' נחתומין ושל לבעין: (ח) בא"ד דהכא שאני משום דבאיסור וכו' מרא ומרא דמחי מרפי וכו' לארעא והוה דומיא דבור ע"כ הג"ה:

גליון הש"ס

גמרא שמולת את הזהב. ע' יבמות עב ע"א תד"ה ולא: רש"י ד"ה ונותן כו' בשביל היזקא דיחיד. עיין לעיל דף יח ע"ב תוס' ד"ה ואי:

תורה אור השלם

א) הֹולֵךְ אֶל דָּרֹום וְסֹובֵב אֶל צָפֹון סֹובֵב סֹבֵב הֹולֵךְ הָרוּחַ וְעַל סְבִיבֹתָיו שָׁב הָרוּחַ: [קהלת א, ו]

ב) מִן הַחֶדֶר תָּבוֹא סוּפָה וּמִמְּזָרִים קָרָה: מִנִּשְׁמַת אֵל יִתֶּן קָרַח וְרֹחַב מַיִם בְּמוּצָק: [איוב לז, ט-י]

ג) מִצָּפוֹן זָהָב יֶאֱתֶה עַל אֱלוֹהַ נוֹרָא הוֹד: [איוב לז, כב]

ד) הַזָּלִים זָהָב מִכִּיס וְכֶסֶף בַּקָּנֶה יִשְׁקֹלוּ יִשְׂכְּרוּ צוֹרֵף וְיַעֲשֵׂהוּ אֵל יִסְגְּדוּ אַף יִשְׁתַּחֲווּ: [ישעיה מו, ו]

ה) וַיִּגְזֹר עַל יָמִין וְרָעֵב וַיֹּאכַל עַל שְׂמֹאול וְלֹא שָׂבֵעוּ אִישׁ בְּשַׂר זְרֹעוֹ יֹאכֵלוּ: [ישעיה ט, יט]

ו) צָפֹון וְיָמִין אַתָּה בְרָאתָם תָּבוֹר וְחֶרְמוֹן בְּשִׁמְךָ יְרַנֵּנוּ: [תהלים פט, יג]

ז) יִפְתַּח יְיָ לְךָ אֶת אוֹצָרוֹ הַטּוֹב אֶת הַשָּׁמַיִם לָתֵת מְטַר אַרְצְךָ בְּעִתּוֹ וּלְבָרֵךְ אֵת כָּל מַעֲשֵׂה יָדֶךָ וְהִלְוִיתָ גּוֹיִם רַבִּים וְאַתָּה לֹא תִלְוֶה: [דברים כח, יב]

ח) אֹרֶךְ יָמִים בִּימִינָהּ בִּשְׂמֹאולָהּ עֹשֶׁר וְכָבוֹד: [משלי ג, טז]

ט) וַיֹּאמֶר יְיָ אֵלָי מִצָּפוֹן תִּפָּתַח הָרָעָה עַל כָּל יֹשְׁבֵי הָאָרֶץ: [ירמיה א, יד]

be distanced **because [its roots] travel beneath the ground and damage the floor of the pit,** by loosening the earth beneath it.

The Mishnah states:

רַבִּי יוֹסֵי אוֹמֵר – **R' YOSE SAID:** אַף עַל פִּי שֶׁהַבּוֹר קוֹדֶמֶת לָאִילָן לֹא יָקוֹץ – **EVEN IF THE PIT PRECEDED THE TREE, HE NEED NOT CUT** it **DOWN,** שֶׁזֶּה חוֹפֵר בְּתוֹךְ שֶׁלּוֹ וְזֶה נוֹטֵעַ בְּתוֹךְ שֶׁלּוֹ – **BECAUSE** just as **THIS ONE MAY DIG** a pit **WITHIN HIS** property, **THAT ONE MAY PLANT** a tree **WITHIN HIS** property.

The Gemara sets down a ruling:

אָמַר רַב יְהוּדָה אָמַר שְׁמוּאֵל – **Rav Yehudah said in Shmuel's name:** הֲלָכָה כְּרַבִּי יוֹסֵי – **The halachah follows R' Yose.**

The Gemara elaborates on R' Yose's opinion:

אָמַר רַב אַשִׁי – **Rav Ashi said:** כִּי הֲוָאן בֵּי רַב כַּהֲנָא הֲוָה אָמְרִינַן – **When we were** students **at Rav Kahana's academy we would say:**[38] מוֹדֵי רַבִּי יוֹסֵי בְּגִירֵי דִּידֵיהּ – **R' Yose agrees, with regard to "his arrows"** (i.e. actions that cause damage directly), that one must distance himself from a neighbor who may be harmed.[39]

The Gemara cites an incident that illustrates this rule:

פַּאפִּי יוֹנָאָה עָנִי וְהֶעֱשִׁיר הֲוָה – **Papi the Yonaite**[40] **was a pauper who** one day **became wealthy,** בָּנָה אַפַּדְנָא – and **built a mansion** on his property. הֲווּ הָנָךְ עַצּוֹרֵי בְּשִׁיבָבוּתֵיהּ – Now, **there were these** sesame-seed **pressers in his neighborhood,**[41] דְּכִי הֲווּ דַּיְיקֵי שׁוּמְשְׁמֵי הֲוָה נַיְידָא אַפַּדְנֵיהּ – whose pressing caused such vibrations **that when they crushed** the **sesame** seeds, the walls of **his mansion would tremble.**

Papi demanded that they move elsewhere:

אָתָא לְקַמֵּיהּ דְּרַב אַשִׁי – **He came** with them **before Rav Ashi** for judgment. אָמַר לֵיהּ – **[Rav Ashi] said to him:** כִּי הֲוָאן בֵּי רַב כַּהֲנָא הֲוָה אָמְרִינַן – **When we were** students **at Rav Kahana's academy we would say:** מוֹדֵי רַבִּי יוֹסֵי בְּגִירֵי דִּילֵיהּ – **R' Yose agrees, with regard to "his arrows,"** that one must distance himself from a neighbor who may be harmed. Here too, the sesame pressers must move their press away, since the vibrations result directly from their operation of the sesame press, and are considered their "arrows."[42]

The Gemara inquires:

וְכַמָּה – **And how much** must the mansion tremble in order that they be forced to move away?[43]

NOTES

38. I.e. the consensus of Rav Kahana's academy was.

39. Although R' Yose permits planting a tree near a neighbor's pit, he agrees that one must refrain from performing within his property any activity that may cause damage to a neighbor *directly* (see above, 22b note 25).

The following incident (cited in *Bava Metzia* 117a) sheds light on what sort of activity qualifies as "his arrows": In a two-story house shared by neighbors, the ceiling of the lower floor decayed and wore away. Whenever the occupant of the upper floor washed his hands, water would drip on his neighbor below. The matter came to judgment, and the decision rendered was that since the water was at first absorbed in the ceiling and only dripped down afterward, it did not qualify as the "arrows" of the one residing above, and he was permitted to continue washing his hands. If, however, the water had begun to drip as he washed, it would have been considered "his arrows," and he would have been required to refrain from washing until the ceiling was repaired (*Rashi*).

40. I.e. from a place known as Yona. Alternatively: the Yevanite, i.e. the Greek.

41. They crushed the seeds to produce sesame oil (*Rashi*).

42. The press was operated by striking it to help crush the seeds. Thus, the vibrations were the direct result of their blows to the press (*Rashi*).

43. I.e. what degree of vibration is above the limit that can be tolerated?

The Gemara answers:

כְּדִנְיֵיד נַכְתְּמָא אַפּוּמֵיהּ דְּחַצְבָּא – Enough that the lid of a barrel resting on one of its walls **shakes** from the vibrations.[1]

The Gemara cites another incident that clarifies R' Yose's opinion:

דְּבֵי בַּר מְרְיוֹן בְּרֵיהּ דְּרָבִין כִּי הֲוָה נַפְצֵי כִּיתְּנָא – When members of **the household of Bar Meryon the son of Ravin would beat** their **flax,**[2] **הֲוָה אָזְלָא רַקְתָּא וּמַזְּקָא אִינָשֵׁי – the chaff would fly off and injure people. אָתוּ לְקַמֵּיהּ דְּרָבִינָא – [The injured parties] came before Ravina,** requesting that he order the flax-beaters to work elsewhere. **אָמַר לְהוּ – He told them: כִּי אָמְרִינַן מוֹדֶה רַבִּי יוֹסֵי בְּגִירֵי דִּילֵיהּ – When we say R' Yose agrees, with regard to "his arrows,"** that one must distance himself from a party that may be harmed, **הָנֵי מִילֵּי דְּקָא אָזְלָא מִכֹּחוֹ – we refer to** a case **where [the injurious article] is propelled by one's** own **force,** just as an arrow is. **הָכָא זִיקָא הוּא דְּקָא מַמְטֵי לָהּ – Here,** however, **it is the wind that carries** off **[the chaff]** and flings it forcefully upon people. Therefore, although the damage results directly from their flax-beating, it is not analogous to one's arrows, and the flax-beaters are not required to move away.

The Gemara challenges Ravina's ruling:

מַתְקִיף לָהּ מַר בַּר רַב אַשִׁי – Mar bar Rav Ashi challenged [this ruling]: מַאי שְׁנָא מִזּוֹרֶה וְרוּחַ מְסַיַּיעְתּוֹ – What is the difference between this law and the law of **winnowing** on Shabbos **with the wind's assistance?** By winnowing, one desecrates the Shabbos, even though the wind assists him by carrying off the chaff. Here, too, let the flax-beaters be held responsible, even though the wind assists in the damage.[3] **– ? –**

The Gemara records another opinion:

אַמְרוּהָ קַמֵּיהּ דְּמָרֵימָר – They stated the facts of **[this case] before Mereimar,** to hear his opinion, **אָמַר לְהוּ – and he said to them: הַיְינוּ זוֹרֶה וְרוּחַ מְסַיַּיעְתּוֹ – This is** analogous to the law of **winnowing** on Shabbos **with the wind's assistance.** Therefore, the flax-beaters are required to move to another location.

The Gemara presents another challenge to Ravina's ruling:

וּלְרָבִינָא – But according **to Ravina,** who ruled that the flax-beaters may continue their activity, even though the wind flings the chaff upon people, **מַאי שְׁנָא מִגֵּץ הַיּוֹצֵא מִתַּחַת הַפַּטִּישׁ וְהִזִּיק – what is the difference between** this case and the case of **a spark that shoots out of**[4] a blacksmith's **hammer and damages** another's property, **דְּחַיָּיב לְשַׁלֵּם – where [the blacksmith] is required to pay** for the damage, even though the spark is borne by the wind?

The Gemara answers:

הָתָם נִיחָא לֵיהּ דְּלֵיזִיל – There, [the blacksmith] prefers that [the sparks] fly off his property, for he fears that they may set his smithy afire. He therefore strikes the anvil with great force, so that the sparks fly off on their own without the wind's assistance. Accordingly, he is liable for damage caused by the flying sparks.[5] **הָכָא לָא נִיחָא לֵיהּ דְּלֵיזִיל – Here,** however, **[the flax-beaters] do not prefer that [the chaff] fly** off their property, for it poses them no threat. Accordingly, they do not beat the flax forcefully, and the chaff would not fly at all were it not for the wind. Therefore, they are not liable for damage caused by the flying chaff.

Mishnah

The previous Mishnah dealt with the issue of planting a tree in a location where its roots might damage a neighbor's pit. This Mishnah deals with a situation where the roots do not pose a threat to a neighbor's pit:[6]

לֹא יִטַּע אָדָם אִילָן סָמוּךְ לִשְׂדֵה חֲבֵירוֹ – One must not plant a tree near his neighbor's field אֶלָּא אִם כֵּן הִרְחִיק מִמֶּנּוּ אַרְבַּע אַמּוֹת – unless he distances the tree **four *amos* from [his neighbor's]** boundary, **אֶחָד גְּפָנִים וְאֶחָד כָּל אִילָן – whether** planting **grapevines or any** other **tree.**[7] **הָיָה גָּדֵר בֵּינְתַיִם – If there was a fence between** the two fields, **זֶה סוֹמֵךְ לַגָּדֵר מִכָּאן – this [neighbor] may bring** his tree **close to the fence on [one side]** of the boundary, **וְזֶה סוֹמֵךְ לַגָּדֵר מִכָּאן – and [the other neighbor] may bring** his tree **close to the fence on [the other side]** of the boundary.[8]

The Mishnah now addresses the issue of roots of a tree that was planted near a boundary:

הָיוּ שָׁרָשִׁים יוֹצְאִים לְתוֹךְ שֶׁל חֲבֵירוֹ – If one planted a tree and the **roots extended into his neighbor's** property,

---

NOTES

1. Literally: a lid on the mouth of a barrel moves. If the lid of a barrel resting on the mansion's outer wall shakes as a result of their pressing, the vibrations are deemed excessive and they are required to move away (*Rashi*). [*Ri* (quoted in *Tosafos* and *Ritva*) contends that the barrel's lid would not vibrate unless the walls shook so much that they were near collapse. Obviously, a lesser degree of vibration is sufficient to force the pressers to move away. He therefore interprets the Gemara's answer as an analogy: If the wall's trembling is comparable to the quivering of a barrel's lid that is occasioned when one carries the barrel (i.e. a very slight tremor), the pressers are required to move away.]

2. Flax is beaten to break up the fiber.

3. The force of the wind is normally employed in the winnowing process. Grain is tossed into the air and the wind carries away the chaff, while the heavier kernels fall back to earth. Although one who winnows does not separate the chaff from the kernels with his own hands, winnowing is counted among the thirty-nine *Avos Melachos* [Primary Categories of Labor] forbidden on Shabbos (see *Shabbos* 73a). The reason is that one who employs the force of the wind to carry out an action transgresses the prohibition against the performance of labor on Shabbos. We learn from this that performing an activity with the wind's assistance is akin to carrying out that action oneself. Therefore, Mar bar Rav Ashi argues that injury caused by the flying chaff is attributable to the flax-beaters, whose blows to the flax propel chaff into the air, to be carried off by the wind. Although the wind does the actual damage, the chaff may nevertheless be considered their "arrows." Therefore, they should be required to move away.

Ravina did not bother to respond to Mar bar Rav Ashi's challenge. He rejects the analogy to winnowing on Shabbos (see *Bava Kamma* 60a), because with regard to Shabbos, the Torah forbids מְלֶאכֶת מַחֲשֶׁבֶת, *purposeful labor,* a category that includes making purposeful use of an external force [such as the wind] to accomplish a desired objective. Monetary issues are subject to different guidelines, under which one is held responsible only for damages attributable to his own force, not for those caused by the force of the wind. Accordingly, he ruled that the flax-beaters need not move away (*Rashi*).

4. Literally: that goes out from underneath.

5. Even if the wind carries a spark a great distance, the blacksmith is liable for any damage it may cause. A spark sent flying into the street is apt to start a fire wherever it lands. Therefore, the blacksmith is liable whether the air is calm and the spark falls near the smith or it is windy and it lands farther away (*Tosafos*).

6. See Gemara above, 18a.

7. A space of four *amos* is required for maneuvering a plow around the tree when tilling the soil, without entering his neighbor's property and damaging its crops. The restriction applies whether one plants grapevines or other trees, and whether the neighbor's property is used as a grain field or an orchard, for in any case the plow might damage his neighbor's field (*Rashi*).

[The Mishnah specifies that this rule applies to trees as well as grapevines, because otherwise one might think that the four-*amah* distance applies only to grapevines, with regard to which the same distance is required under the laws of *kilayim* (the prohibition of planting vines together with other species) (*Tosafos*).]

8. The fence ensures that their plows will not cross the boundary.

כדנייד נכתמא אפומיה דחצבא דבי בר מריון בריה דרבין כי הוה נפצי כיתנא הוה אזלא רקתא ומזקא אינשי אתו לקמיה דרבינא אמר להו כי אמרינן מודה ר' יוסי בגירי דיליה הני מילי דקא אזלא מכחו הכא זיקא הוא דקא ממטי לה מתקיף לה מר בר רב אשי מאי שנא מזורה ורוח מסייעתו אמרוה קמיה דמרימר אמר להו היינו זורה ורוח מסייעתו ולרבינא מאי שנא מגץ היוצא מתחת הפטיש והזיק חייב לשלם התם ניחא ליה דליזיל הכא לא ניחא ליה דליזיל: **מתני'** לא יטע אדם אילן סמוך לשדה חבירו אלא אם כן הרחיק ממנו ארבע אמות אחד גפנים ואחד כל אילן היה גדר בינתים זה סומך לגדר מכאן וזה סומך לגדר מכאן היו שרשים יוצאים לתוך של חבירו מעמיק ג' טפחים כדי שלא יעכב את המחרישה היה חופר בור שיח ומערה קוצץ ויורד והעצים שלו: **גמ'** תנא ארבע אמות שאמרו כדי עבודת הכרם אמר שמואל לא שנו אלא בארץ ישראל אבל בבבל שתי אמות תניא נמי הכי לא יטע אדם אילן סמוך לשדה חבירו אלא אם כן הרחיק ממנו שתי אמות והא אנן תנן ארבע אמות אלא לאו כדשמואל שמע מינה ואיכא דרמי לה מירמא תנן לא יטע אדם אילן סמוך לשדה חבירו אלא אם כן הרחיק ממנו ארבע אמות והתניא שתי אמות אמר שמואל לא קשיא כאן בבבל כאן בארץ ישראל רבא בר רב חנן הוו ליה הנהו דיקלי אמיצרא דפרדיסא דרב יוסף הוו אתו צפורי יתבי בדיקלי ונחתי בפרדיסא ומפסדי ליה א"ל זיל קוץ א"ל והא ארחיקי לי א"ל ה"מ לאילנות אבל לגפנים בעינן טפי והא אנן תנן אחד גפנים ואחד כל אילן א"ל ה"מ אילן לאילן וגפנים לגפנים אבל אילן לגפנים בעינן טפי א"ל אנא לא קייצנא דאמר רב האי דיקלא דטעין קבא אסור למקצייה ואמר ר' חנינא לא שכיב שכחת ברי אלא דקץ תאנתא בלא זימניה מר אי ניחא ליה ליקוץ רב פפא הו"ל הנהו דיקלי אמיצרא דרב הונא בריה דרב יהושע אזל אשכחיה דהוה חפר וקא קאיץ שרשיו אמר ליה מאי האי אמר ליה תנן היו שרשים יוצאים לתוך של חבירו מעמיק שלשה כדי שלא יעכב המחרישה אמר ליה הני מילי שלשה מר קא חפר טפי אמר ליה אנא בורות שיחין ומערות קא חפרנא דתנן היה חופר בור שיח ומערה קוצץ ויורד והעצים שלו אמר רב פפא אמרי ליה (ג) כולהי ולא יכילי ליה עד

רש"י

כדנייד נכתמא אפומא דחצבא. שאם יניחו כד על החומה וכיסויה עליה ינוע הכיסוי מחמת הרעדה: רקתא. מה שמנערין מן הפשתן: מאי שנא מזורה. בשבת דחייב ואע"פ שהרוח מסייעתו חשיב ליה עושה מלאכה אלמא גירי דיליה נינהו: היינו זורה ורוח מסייעתו. כי היכי דלענין שבת הוי כמו לענין נזקין נמי כמו חשיב ליה: ולרבינא מאי שנא כו'. בשלמא זורה ורוח מסייעתו לא הויא ליה פירכא דקסבר ממונא מאיסור שבת לא ילפינן דהתם מלאכת מחשבת אסרה תורה וכה"ג מתרצינן ליה להא פירכא בב"ק בהכונס לאן לדיר (דף ס.) גץ. ענצינל"א היוצאה מן הברזל כשהפטיש מכה עליו: חייב. והרי הוליכו הרוח: ניחא ליה דליזיל. לחוץ שלא ידליק את ביתו: מתני' סמוך לשדה חבירו. בין שדה הלבן בין שדה האילן וטעמא כדי עבודת הכרם שכשיחרוש את אילנותיו לא יהא צריך להכנים מחרישתו לתוך שדה חבירו: מעמיק. לבעל השדה שילאו לתוכו: קוצץ. בעומק ג' טפחים: והעצים שלו. בגמרא מפרש של מי: גמ' אבל בבבל שתי אמות. שמחרישתן קלרה: פרדיסא. כרם: והא ארחיקי לי. ד' אמות: שכחת ברי. כך שמו: אשכחיה. רב פפא לרב הונא דקא חפר וקוץ שרשין: מאי האי. אמאי קייצת: אמרי ליה כולהו. הבאתי לו ראיות הרבה שלא יקוץ שהחזיקו

תוספות

אפומא דחצבא. על פי' הקונט' קשיא לר"י דאיך יהא האפדנא נייד כולי האי עד שתתנדנד הנכתמא דא"כ הבית קרוב ליפול ולפי הענין משמע שהיה בנין חזק שהרי מתוך העושר בנאה ובמס' שבת (דף עז.) נמי אמר מאי אפדנא אפיתחא דין שמאספין שם לדין משמע דדירה גדולה היא ונראה לר"י דכד נידא נכתמא כשאדם אוחז הכד בידו שזהו דבר מועט הרבה א"כ מתנדנד האפדנא חייב להרחיק ולריב"א נראה שאין פ"ה דחוק דבדבר מועט מתנדנד הנכתמא שהוא דבר קל אף על פי שהאפדנא אינו מתנדנד כל כך:

זיקא הוא דקא ממטי לה. קשיא לר"י דליחייב משום אש מידי דהוה אאבנו וסכינו ומשאו שהניחן בראש גגו ונפלו ברוח מצויה והזיקו דחייב משום אש כדאמר בפ"ק דב"ק (דף ו.) והכא דאמטי ליה ברוח מצויה איירי מדפריך עלה מזורה ורוח (ד) מסייעו דאיירי ברוח מצויה כדמשמע בהכונס (שם דף ס. ושם) גבי ליבה וליבתו הרוח ומדפריך מגץ היוצא מתחת הפטיש דהיינו ברוח מצויה דחייב משום אש דגבי אש קתני לה בהכונס ואומר ר"י דלא דמי לאש דאין חייב משום אש אלא כשעשה האדם את האש לבדו כדכתיב המבעיר את הבעירה בלא סיוע הרוח וא"כ הולכת על ידי רוח מצויה אבל הכא אין עושה לבדו כל עיקר אלא ע"י הרוח דאי לאו רוח לא הוה רקתא אזלא כל עיקר ודמי לליבה וליבתו הרוח דפטור והיינו דמשני כי פריך בסמוך מ"ש מגץ דהוה סלקא דעתך דדמי ממש לגן ומשני התם ניחא ליה דליזל ומתכוין להכות בכח עד שילא הגן (ה) ומתרחק בלא שום זיקא וחייב משום אש על מה שגומר והולך על ידי רוח מצויה אבל הכא לא ניחא ליה דתיזל כלומר ואינו מכה בכח ואי לאו (ו) רוח אין הרקתא הולכת כלל וא"ת מ"מ יהא חייב להרחיק מידי דהוה אגורן דמתניתין דחייב להרחיק אע"ג דזיקא ממטי ליה וי"ל דמתני' כרבנן והכא איירי אליבא דר' יוסי דלא מחייב אלא בגירי דיליה והא דפריך מגץ ולא מצי לאוקמי ההיא דגן כרבנן משום דלא פליגי רבי יוסי ורבנן לענין חיוב תשלומין אלא לענין הרחקה וא"ת מאי שנא מנמייה דאפילו לר' יוסי מרחיקין אע"ג דהיא גופה ממטיא נפשה (ז) כמר בר רב אשי ומיהו התם משום דזימנין דבהדי דנח כו' כדקאמר לעיל אבל קשה מעורבין לעיל (דף כג.) דאמר רב יוסף אפיקו לי קורקור מהכא וי"ל דגמרא לא סבר לה כרבינא דר"ת פוסק כמר בר רב אשי וכדאימר ועוד אומר ר"י דבעלי חיים שאני דחמירי טפי מרוח דכח אחר מעורב בהן כדאמרינן בבבא קמא (דף ו.):

מאי שנא מזורה ורוח מסייעתו. ורבינא לא חשיב לה פירכא דסבר כי היכי דלא גמרינן משבת לענין תשלומין כדמפרש רב אשי בהכונס (ב"ק דף ס. ושם) דגבי שבת מלאכת מחשבת אסרה תורה אבל הכא גרמא הוא וגרמא בנזקין פטור הכי נמי לא גמרינן מהתם שיהא חייב להרחיק ומר בר רב אשי סבר נהי דחיוב תשלומין לא גמרי' לענין הרחקה דליחשב גירי דיליה גמרינן שפיר כיון דגרמא בנזקין אסור: **ורבינא** מאי שנא מגץ. וא"ת ואמאי קאמר ורבינא לאימר נמי תיקשי לענין חיוב תשלומין מאי שנא מגץ וי"ל משום הכי נקט רבינא דלאימר הוי מצי לדחויי דה"נ (ח) חייב לדידיה בתשלומין דלגמרי מדמה לה לזורה ורוח מסייעתו:

אחד גפנים ואחד כל אילן. מתוך פ"ה לעיל (דף יח.) משמע דנקט אחד גפנים משום דשייך בהו כלאים דהביא ראיה מכאן דכשיש גדר ליכא איסור כלאים וזה סומך לגדר מכאן וזה מכאן ואין נראה דשדה חבירו דקתני לאו בשל זרעים איירי דהא מוקמי' בגמ' דמתני' אילנות לאילנות וגפנים לגפנים אבל אילנות לגפנים בעי טפי משום ליפרי ומאי טעמא גפנים לזרעים בעי טפי אלא דנראה דנקט אחד גפנים ואחד כל אילן דלא תיסוק אדעתי' למימר דשיעור ד' אמות דמתני' דוקא בגפנים שמלינו בהם שיעור זה במקום אחר לענין כלאים: **אבל** בבבל ב' אמות. תימה דבפרק המוכר את הספינה (לקמן דף פג.) גבי קנה ג' קנה קרקע דאמר רב יוסף עובדא הוה בדורא דרעותא כו' משמע מהתם דבבבל נמי בעינן ד' אמות דבבבל הוה היה להם מחרישה גדולה כמו בארץ ישראל: **אבל** בגפנים בעי טפי. והוא כשנטע דקלים [illegible] דממילא קא גדל ולא גירי דיליה הוא: **אנא** לא קייצנא דאמר רב כו'. וא"ת והתנן במתניתא דקוצץ ונותן דמים וי"ל דלאיכא באילן סרק אבל קשה דאמרינן בהחובל (ב"ק דף צא:) גבי הנהו דיקלי דמכחשי בגופני הוו דקאמר משום היזק גפנים מותר לקוץ דקלים ויש לפרש דשאני התם שיותר מדאי היו מכחישים בגפנים עד דהוה טעים בהו טעמא דחמרא:

מסורת הש"ס

א) [ב"ק ס.], ב) [שם סב. ושם], ג) [לעיל יח.], ד) [לעיל יח.], ה) [שם], ו) ב"ק צא:, ז) [שם ע"ש]

הגהות הב"ח

(א) במשנה זה סומך לגדר. נ"ב עי' לעיל דף י"ח: (ב) גמ' א"ל רב יוסף זיל קוץ: (ג) שם אמרי ליה כולהו ולא יכילי ליה: (ד) תוס' ד"ה זיקא וכו' ורוח מסייעתו: (ה) בא"ד ומתרחק: (ו) בא"ד ואי לאו הרוח: (ז) בא"ד אע"ג דהיא גופה ממטיא נפשה: (ח) ד"ה ורבינא וכו' דה"נ דחייב:

לעזי רש"י

אענצינל"א. פירוש גץ, ניצוץ (רש"י ישעיה א, לא).

עין משפט נר מצוה

צ א מיי' פי"א מהל' שכנים הלכה ג סמג עשין פב טוש"ע ח"מ סי' קנה סעיף כט:
צא ב מיי' שם הל' ו וסמג שם טוש"ע שם סעיף לד:
צב ג מיי' פ"ו מהל' חובל ומזיק הל' יא סמג עשין סח טוש"ע ח"מ סי' שפד סעיף ב:
צג ד ה מיי' פ"י מהל' שכנים הל' ח סמג עשין פב טוש"ע ח"מ סי' קנה סעיף כה:
צד ו ז מיי' שם הל' ז טוש"ע שם סעיף לו:
צה ח ט מיי' שם הל' ח טוש"ע שם סעי' כה:
צו י מיי' שם טוש"ע שם סעיף לא ועיין בהגה"ה ובמ"מ:
צז כ מיי' פ"ו מהל' מלכים הל' ט סמג לאוין רכט [וברב אלפס ב"ק סמוך לסוף פרק החובל דף לד: ועי' ע"ז יו"ד סי' קטז ס"ק ו]:

רבינו גרשום

כי היכי דנייד נכתמא אפומיה דחצבא. כלומר (א) היכסה שמכסין ממנו הקיקל: רקתא. שלועין אריש"א: אבל הכא גבי הנהו רקתא אינו חייב משום דהוי ליה גירי דידיה דזיקא הוא דקא ממטי ליה ואינו חייב: מ"ש. מהא דתנן גבי שבת באבות מלאכות דהיכא דזורה והרוח מסייעתו דהוי תבואות התבן דהוי חייב להכי היכא דרוח ממטי ליה אמאי אינו חייב: אמר ליה מרימר ודאי ברקתא חייב דהיינו כזורה ורוח מסייעתו דחייב משום שבת: ולרבינא מ"ש מגץ היוצא כו': התם בגץ ניחא ליה דליזיל מביתו אבל הכא גבי רקתא לא ניחא ליה דליזיל: פיסקא כדי עבודת הכרם: לא שנו בארץ ישראל שרגילין לחרוש בשוורים: אבל בבבל שחורשין בחמורים: אמות. דפרדיסא. גפנים: והא רחיקי ליה. ד' אמות: הני מילי באילנות: אסור למקצייה: שכחת. שמיה: אשכחיה לרב הונא: מר קא חפר טובא: אמרי ליה כולהו: ולא יכילי ליה:

חשק שלמה על רבינו גרשום

(א) נ"ל הכיסוי שמכסין בו וכו'.

ליקוטי רש"י

מן הצד. שניהם בקרקע השוה. ונותן דמים. בעל הבור לבעל האילן [ב"מ קיז.]. מודה ר' יוסי בגיריה דידיה. בחלים הבאים לו מיד גופו של בעל אילן ובור שבשעת נטיעתו אינו מזיקו אלא השרשים גדלין ומתפשטין מאליהן לאחר זמן אבל היכא דאדם עצמו מזיקו וזורק בו חליו מודה הוא. מאי שנא מזורה. ליהוי כזורה דחייב משום מלאכה בשבת אע"פ שהרוח מסייעתו כשהוא מגביה התבואה ברחת שקורין פליי"א [ב"ק ס.]. שדהו סמוך לשדה חבירו כדי שלא תלך מחרישתו לחרוש אילן זה דרך שדה חבירו [רשב"ם לקמן פג.]. היה גדר בינתים. שאין מזיקו עוד לעבודת הכרם. אמר בעירובין (יח.) אם גפנים מכאן מותר לזרוע כאן גבי נעץ ארבעה קונדיסין ומתח זמורה על גביהן דדמיא לצורת הפתח. מעמיק ג' טפחים. שיח ארוכה וקצרה מערה מרובעת ומכוסה בקרוי אלא שיש לה פה [ב"ק נ:]. כדי עבודת הכרם. שהיו חורשים הכרם במחרישה וכן בשעת הבציר בקרקע חבירו [לעיל יח.]. דבהכי הוי כלאים [לעיל ב.].

מַעֲמִיק שְׁלֹשָׁה טְפָחִים – **[the neighbor] may excavate three** ***tefachim*** of earth and remove the roots, כְּדֵי שֶׁלֹּא יְעַכֵּב אֶת הַמַּחֲרֵישָׁה – **so that they should not impede the** movement of his **plow.** הָיָה חוֹפֵר בּוֹר שִׁיחַ וּמְעָרָה – **If [the neighbor] was digging a pit, a ditch, or a vault,** and came upon the roots, קוֹצֵץ וְיוֹרֵד – **he may cut downward** to whatever depth he finds necessary, וְהָעֵצִים שֶׁלּוֹ – **and the wood** cuttings **are his.**[9]

Gemara

The Gemara cites a Baraisa that explains the reason for the Mishnah's first rule:

תַּנְיָא – **We learned in a Baraisa:** אַרְבַּע אַמּוֹת שֶׁאָמְרוּ – The FOUR *AMOS* THAT [THE SAGES] SAID must be maintained between vines and a neighboring field כְּדֵי עֲבוֹדַת הַכֶּרֶם – are needed to provide SUFFICIENT space FOR THE CULTIVATION OF THE VINEYARD without encroachment on a neighbor's property.[10]

The Gemara asserts that this rule does not apply universally:

אָמַר שְׁמוּאֵל – **Shmuel said:** לֹא שָׁנוּ אֶלָּא בְּאֶרֶץ יִשְׂרָאֵל – **They** (the Sages of the Mishnah) **taught this** law, mandating a distance of four *amos*, **only in** reference to **Eretz Yisrael,** where large plows are commonly used. אֲבָל בְּבָבֶל – **But in Babylonia,** where smaller plows are common,[11] שְׁתֵּי אַמּוֹת – **two** ***amos*** suffice.

The Gemara cites a Baraisa that supports Shmuel's ruling:

תַּנְיָא נַמִּי הָכִי – **It was taught similarly in a Baraisa:** לֹא יִטַּע אָדָם אִילָן סָמוּךְ לִשְׂדֵה חֲבֵירוֹ – ONE MUST NOT PLANT A TREE NEAR HIS NEIGHBOR'S FIELD אֶלָּא אִם כֵּן הִרְחִיק מִמֶּנּוּ שְׁתֵּי אַמּוֹת – UNLESS HE DISTANCES it TWO *AMOS* FROM [HIS NEIGHBOR'S] boundary.

The Gemara inquires:

וְהָא אֲנַן תְּנַן אַרְבַּע אַמּוֹת – **But we learned in our Mishnah:** FOUR *AMOS!* אֶלָּא לָאו כִּדְשְׁמוּאֵל – **Rather,** is it **not** clear that the Baraisa concurs **with Shmuel's** ruling that the Mishnah refers only to Eretz Yisrael, while in Babylonia a distance of two *amos* suffices? Therefore, referring to Babylonia, the Baraisa mandates a distance of only two *amos.* שְׁמַע מִינַּהּ – Indeed, we **learn from [this Baraisa]** that Shmuel's ruling is correct.

The Gemara now records another version of the preceding discussion:

וְאִיכָּא דְּרָמֵי לַהּ מִירְמָא – **There are those who contrasted [the Baraisa]** with our Mishnah, as follows: תְּנַן – **We learned in the Mishnah:** לֹא יִטַּע אָדָם אִילָן סָמוּךְ לִשְׂדֵה חֲבֵירוֹ – ONE MUST NOT PLANT A TREE NEAR HIS NEIGHBOR'S FIELD אֶלָּא אִם כֵּן הִרְחִיק מִמֶּנּוּ אַרְבַּע אַמּוֹת – UNLESS HE DISTANCES it FOUR *AMOS* FROM [HIS NEIGHBOR'S] boundary. וְהָתַנְיָא שְׁתֵּי אַמּוֹת – **But we were taught in a Baraisa:** TWO *AMOS!*

Shmuel resolves this apparent contradiction:[12]

אָמַר שְׁמוּאֵל לֹא קַשְׁיָא – **Shmuel said:** This is **not a difficulty.** כָּאן בְּבָבֶל – **Here,** in the Baraisa that mandates a distance of two *amos,* **we refer to Babylonia,** where small plows are commonly used, כָּאן בְּאֶרֶץ יִשְׂרָאֵל – while **here,** in the Mishnah, which mandates a distance of four *amos,* **we refer to Eretz Yisrael,** where larger plows are common.

The Gemara relates an incident which illustrates another exception to the Mishnah's rule:

רָבָא בַּר רַב חָנָן הֲווּ לֵיהּ הָנְהוּ דִּיקְלֵי – **Rava bar Rav Chanan had these palm trees** אַמֵּיצְרָא דְּפַרְדֵּיסָא דְּרַב יוֹסֵף – **along** his **boundary with Rav Yosef's vineyard.**[13] הֲווּ אָתוּ צִפּוֹרֵי יָתְבִי בְּדִיקְלֵי – Now, **birds would** occasionally **come to perch in the palms,** וְנָחֲתֵי בְּפַרְדֵּיסָא וּמַפְסְדֵי לֵיהּ – **and** from there **they would descend into the vineyard and damage [its crop].**

Rav Yosef sought to have the palms removed:

אָמַר לֵיהּ – **He said to [Rava bar Rav Chanan]:** זִיל קוֹץ – **Go cut down** your palms, since by providing a perch for the birds they cause damage to my vineyard. אָמַר לֵיהּ – **[Rava bar Rav Chanan] replied to him:** וְהָא אַרְחֵיקִי לִי – **But I have** already **distanced** the palms four *amos*[14] from your property, as prescribed by the Mishnah! אָמַר לֵיהּ – **[Rav Yosef] said to him:** הָנֵי מִילֵּי לְאִילָנוֹת – **Those words** of the Mishnah refer to the distance required **for trees** (i.e. where the neighbor had planted trees in his field), אֲבָל לְגְפָנִים בָּעֵינַן טְפֵי – **but for grapevines** (i.e. where the neighbor had planted a vineyard), a distance of **more** than four *amos* **is required.**[15]

Rava bar Rav Chanan protested:

וְהָא אֲנַן תְּנַן אֶחָד גְּפָנִים וְאֶחָד כָּל אִילָן – **But we learned in the Mishnah** that the four-*amah* distance applies to GRAPEVINES AS WELL AS ANY OTHER TREE! I am therefore permitted to maintain my trees at a distance of four *amos* from your vineyard.[16]

Rav Yosef reinterpreted the Mishnah:

אָמַר לֵיהּ – **He said to [Rava bar Rav Chanan]:** הָנֵי מִילֵּי אִילָן לְאִילָן וּגְפָנִים לִגְפָנִים – **Those words** of the Mishnah refer to the distance required between one **tree and** another **tree,** or between **grapevines and grapevines,** אֲבָל אִילָן לִגְפָנִים בָּעֵינַן טְפֵי – **but** between **a tree and grapevines,** a distance of **more** than four *amos* **is required.**[17]

Upon hearing this argument Rava bar Rav Chanan acquiesced:

אָמַר לֵיהּ – **He said to [Rav Yosef]:** אֲנָא לֹא קָיְיצְנָא – **I will not**

NOTES

9. The Gemara (26b) inquires whether the word *his* refers to the one who cut the roots or the one who planted the tree.

10. Although the Baraisa singles out the case of a vineyard, its reason applies equally to all trees. [See note 7.]

11. The hilly terrain of Eretz Yisrael necessitated larger, stronger plows than the flat ground of Babylonia (*Ramban*).

12. According to this version of the discussion, the Gemara did not cite the Baraisa to support Shmuel's ruling, but rather, Shmuel himself presented his ruling as a resolution to the apparent contradiction between the Mishnah and the Baraisa.

13. From the ensuing discussion, it is clear that he had distanced the trees four *amos* from the boundary, as mandated by the Mishnah.

14. (*Rashi*). *Rabbeinu Yonah* points out that Rava and Rav Yosef resided in Babylonia, where the distance required is only two *amos.* However, see *Tosafos* (ד״ה אבל), who prove that there were areas in Babylonia where large plows were used and the four-*amah* distance applied.

15. The Mishnah's four-*amah* distance serves only to ensure that one will not maneuver a plow onto his neighbor's property. However, if the neighbor had planted a vineyard, one must take into account the fact that birds which perch in his trees may damage his neighbor's grapes. Accordingly, he must distance the trees far enough from the vineyard that birds which perch in them cannot fly to the vineyard in one swoop (*Rosh*).

16. Rava bar Rav Chanan interpreted the Mishnah's clause "whether grapevines or any other tree" as referring to the item planted in the *neighbor's* field, not to the tree being planted now. According to his interpretation, the Mishnah reads: One must distance a tree four *amos* from his neighbor's field, whether *the neighbor* has planted a vineyard or trees (*Rosh*). [Rava bar Rav Chanan maintains that the owner of a tree is not held responsible for damage caused by birds that perch in his tree because that damage is not attributable to the tree itself.]

17. Rav Yosef interprets the Mishnah's clause "whether grapevines or any other tree" as referring to the tree being *planted.* Thus, the Mishnah reads: One must distance a tree four *amos* from his neighbor, whether *planting* vines [near a vineyard] or trees [near other trees]. The Mishnah does not refer to trees planted near a vineyard; in that case a greater distance is called for, since the trees provide a perch for birds that might cause damage to the vineyard.

אכדנייד נכתמא אפומיה דחצבא דבי בר מריון בריה דרבין כי הוה נפצי כיתנא הוה אזלא רקתא ומזקא אינשי אתו לקמיה דרבינא אמר להו כי אמרינן מודה ר' יוסי בגירי דיליה הני מילי דקא אזלא מכחו הכא זיקא הוא דקא ממטי לה מתקיף לה מר בר רב אשי מאי שנא מזורה ורוח מסייעתו אמרוה קמיה דמרימר אמר להו בהיינו זורה ורוח מסייעתו ולרבינא מאי שנא מגץ היוצא מתחת הפטיש והזיק דחייב לשלם התם ניחא ליה דליזיל הכא לא ניחא ליה דליזיל: **מתני'** דלא יטע אדם אילן סמוך לשדה חבירו אלא אם כן הרחיק ממנו ארבע אמות אחד גפנים ואחד כל אילן ההיה גדר בינתים (א) זה סומך לגדר מכאן וזה סומך לגדר מכאן והיו שרשים יוצאים לתוך של חבירו מעמיק ג' טפחים כדי שלא יעכב את המחרישה זהיה חופר בור שיח ומערה קוצץ ויורד והעצים שלו: **גמ'** תנא חארבע אמות שאמרו כדי עבודת הכרם אמר שמואל לא שנו טאלא בארץ ישראל אבל בבבל שתי אמות תניא נמי הכי לא יטע אדם אילן סמוך לשדה חבירו אלא אם כן הרחיק ממנו שתי אמות והא אנן תנן ארבע אמות אלא לאו כדשמואל שמע מינה ואיכא דרמי לה מירמא תנן לא יטע אדם אילן סמוך לשדה חבירו אלא אם כן הרחיק ממנו ארבע אמות והתניא שתי אמות אמר שמואל לא קשיא כאן בבבל כאן בארץ ישראל רבא בר רב חנן הוו ליה הנהו דיקלי אמיצרא דפרדיסא דרב יוסף הוו אתו צפורי יתבי בדיקלי ונחתי בפרדיסא ומפסדי ליה א"ל (ג) זיל קוץ א"ל והא ארחיקי לי א"ל ה"מ לאילנות אבל לגפנים בעינן טפי והא אנן תנן אחד גפנים ואחד כל אילן א"ל ה"מ אילן לאילן וגפנים לגפנים אבל אילן לגפנים בעינן טפי א"ל אנא לא קייצנא דאמר רב האי דיקלא דטעין קבא אסור למקצייה ואמר ר' חנינא לא שכיב שכחת ברי אלא דקץ תאנתא בלא זימניה מר אי ניחא ליה ליקוץ רב פפא הו"ל הנהו דיקלי אמיצרא דרב הונא בריה דרב יהושע אזל אשכחיה דהוה חפר וקא קאיץ שרשיו אמר ליה מאי האי אמר ליה תנן היו שרשים יוצאים לתוך של חבירו מעמיק שלשה כדי שלא יעכב המחרישה אמר ליה הני מילי שלשה מר קא חפר טפי אמר ליה אנא בורות שיחין ומערות קא חפרנא דתנן היה חופר בור שיח ומערה קוצץ ויורד והעצים שלו אמר רב פפא אמרי ליה (ג) כולהי ולא יכילי ליה

עד

כדנייד נכתמא אפומא דחצבא. שאם יניחו כד על החומה והכיסוי עליה יגוע הכיסוי מחמת הרעדה: **רקתא.** מה שמנערין מן הפשתן: **מאי שנא מזורה.** בשבת דחייב ואע"פ שהרוח מסייעתו חשיב ליה עושה מלאכה אלמא גירי דיליה נינהו: **היינו זורה ורוח מסייעתו.** כי היכי דלענין שבת הוי כמו לענין נזקין נמי כמו חשיב ליה: **ולרבינא מאי שנא גץ כו'.** בשלמא זורה ורוח מסייעתו לא הוי"א ליה פירכא דקסבר ממונא מאיסור שבת לא ילפינן דהתם מלאכת מחשבת אסרה תורה וכה"ג מתרצינן ליה להא פירכא בב"ק בהכונס לאן לדיר (דף ס.): **גץ.** אטנצייל"א היוצא מן הברזל כשהפטיש מכה עליו: **חייב.** והרי הוליכו הרוח: **ניחא ליה דליזיל.** לחוץ שלא ידליק את ביתו: **מתני' סמוך לשדה חבירו.** בין שדה הלבן בין שדה האילן וטעמא כדי עבודת הכרם שכשיחרוש את אילנותיו לא יהא צריך להכניס מחרישתו לתוך שדה חבירו: **מעמיק.** להן בעל השדה שיצאו לתוכו: **קוצץ.** בעומק ג' טפחים: **והעצים שלו.** בגמרא מפרש של מי: **גמ' אבל בבבל שתי אמות.** שמחרישתן קצרה: **פרדיסא.** כרם: **והא ארחיקי לי.** ד' אמות: **שכחת ברי.** כך שמו: **אשכחיה.** רב פפא לרב הונא דקא חפר וקייץ שרשין: **מאי האי.** מאי קייצת: **אמרי ליה כולהי.** הבאתי לו ראיות הרבה שלא יקוץ: **ולא יכילי ליה.** שהחזיקו

אפומא דחצבא. על פי' הקונט' קשיא לר"י דאיך יהא האפדנא נייד כולי האי עד שתתגלגל הכתמא דא"כ הבית קרוב ליפול ולפי הענין משמע שהיה בנין חזק שהרי מתוך העושר בנאה ובמס' שבת (דף עז.) נמי אמר מאי אפדנא אפיתחא דין שמאספין שם לדין משמע דבירה גדולה היא ונראה לר"י דכל נידא נכתמא כשאדם אוחז הכד בידו שזהו דבר מועט הרבה א"כ מתנדנד האפדנא חייב להרחיק ולריב"א נראה שאין פ"ה דחוק דבדבר מועט מתנדנד הנכתמא שהוא דבר קל אף על פי שהאפדנא אינו מתנדנד כל כך: **זיקא** הוא דקא ממטי לה. קשיא לר"י דליחייב משום אש מידי דהוה אאבנו סכינו ומשאו שהניחן בראש גגו ונפלו ברוח מצויה והזיקו דחייב משום אש כדאמר בפ"ק דב"ק (דף ו.) והכא דאמטי ליה ברוח מצויה איירי מדפריך עלה מזורה ורוח (ד) מסייעו דאיירי ברוח מצויה כדמשמע בהכונס (שם דף ס. ושם) גבי ליבה וליבתו הרוח ומדפריך מגץ היוצא מתחת הפטיש דהיינו ברוח מצויה דחייב משום אש דגבי אש קתני לה בהכונס ואומר ר"י דלא דמי לאש דאין חייב משום אש אלא כשעשה האדם את האש לבדו כדכתיב המבעיר את הבעירה בלא סיוע הרוח ואח"כ הולכת על ידי רוח מצויה אבל הכא אין עושה לבדו כל עיקר אלא ע"י הרוח דאי לאו רוח לא הוה רקתא אזלא כל עיקר ודמי לליבה וליבתו הרוח דפטור והיינו דמשני כי פריך בסמוך מ"ש מגץ דהוה סלקא דעתך דדמי ממש לגן ומשני התם ניחא ליה דליזיל ומתכוין להכות בכח עד שילא הגץ (ה) ומתרחק בלא שום זיקא וחייב משום אש על מה שגומר והולך על ידי רוח מצויה אבל הכא לא ניחא ליה דתיזל כלומר ואינו מכה בכח ואי לאו (ו) רוח אין הרקתא הולכת כלל וא"ת מ"מ יהא חייב להרחיק מידי דהוה אגורן דמתניתין דחייב להרחיק אע"ג דזיקא ממטי ליה וי"ל דמתני' כרבנן והכא איירי אליבא דר' יוסי דלא מחייב אלא בגירי דיליה והא דפריך מגן ולא מצי לאוקמי ההיא דגן כרבנן משום דלא פליגי רבי יוסי ורבנן לענין חיוב תשלומין אלא לענין הרחקה וא"ת מאי שנא מנמייה דאפילו לר' יוסי מרחיקין אע"ג דהיא גופה ממטיא נפשה (ז) כמר בר רב אשי ומיהו התם משום דזימנין דבהדי דנח כו' כדקאמר לעיל אבל קשה מעורבין לעיל (דף כג.) דאמר רב יוסף אפיקו לי קורקור מהכא וי"ל דגמרא לא סבר לה כרבינא דר"ת פוסק כמר בר רב אשי וכאמימר ועוד אומר ר"י דבעלי חיים שאני דאמירי טפי מרוח דכא אחר מעורב בהן כדאמרינן בבבא קמא (דף ו.):

מאי שנא מזורה ורוח מסייעתו. ורבינא לא חשיב לה פירכא דסבר כי היכי דלא גמרינן משבת לענין תשלומין כדמפרש רב אשי בהכונס (ב"ק דף ס. ושם) דגבי שבת מלאכת מחשבת אסרה תורה אבל הכא גרמא הוא וגרמא בנזקין פטור הכי נמי לא גמרינן מהתם שיהא חייב להרחיק ומר בר רב אשי סבר נהי דלחיוב תשלומין לא גמרי' לענין הרחקה דליחשב גירי דיליה גמרינן שפיר כיון דגרמא בנזקין אסור: **ורבינא** מאי שנא מגץ. וא"ת ואמאי קאמר ורבינא לאמימר נמי תיקשי לענין חיוב תשלומין מאי שנא מגץ וי"ל משום הכי נקט רבינא דלאמימר הוי מצי לחויי דה"נ (ח) חייב לדידיה בתשלומין דלגמרי מדמה לה לזורה ורוח מסייעתו:

אחד גפנים ואחד כל אילן. מתוך פ"ה לעיל (דף יח.) משמע דנקט אחד גפנים משום דשייך בהו כלאים דהביא ראיה מכאן דכשיש גדר ליכא איסור כלאים וזה סומך לגדר מכאן וזה מכאן ואין נראה דלשדה חבירו דקתני הכא על כרחך לאו בשל זרעים איירי דהא מוקמי' בגמ' דמתני' אילנות לאילנות וגפנים לגפנים אבל אילנות לגפנים בעי טפי משום ליפרי ומהאי טעמא גפנים לזרעים בעי טפי אלא דנראה דנקט אחד גפנים ואחד כל אילן דלא תיסוק אדעתי' למימר דשיעור ד' אמות דמתני' דוקא בגפנים שמצינו בהם שיעור זה במקום אחר לענין כלאים: **אבל** בבבל ב' אמות. תימה דבפרק המוכר את הספינה (לקמן דף פב: ושם דף פג.) גבי קנה ג' קנה קרקע דאמר רב יוסף עובדא הוה בדורא דרעותא כו' משמע מהתם דבבבל נמי בעינן ד' אמות דבבבל הוה מעשה וי"ל דבההיא דורא דרעותא היה להם מחרישה גדולה כמו בארץ ישראל: **אבל** בגפנים בעי טפי. והוא כשנטע דקלים כשהם גבוהים אבל אם נטע גרעין לא דממילא קא גדל ולא גירי דיליה הוא: **אנא** לא קייצנא דאמר רב כו'. וא"ת והתנן במתניתא דקוצץ ונותן דמים וי"ל דהיכא לאוקמי באילן סרק אבל קשה דאמרינן בהחובל (ב"ק דף צב.) גבי הנהו דיקלי דמכחשי בגופני הוו דקאמר למחר אייתי לי מקורייהו אלמא משום היזק גפנים מותר לקוץ דקלים ויש לפרש דשאני התם שיותר מדאי היו מכחישים בגפנים עד דהוה טעים בהו טעמא דחמרא:

עד

מסורת הש"ס

א) [ב"ק ס.], ב) [שם סב: וש"נ], ג) [לעיל יח.] לקמן פג., ד) [לעיל יח.], ה) [שם], ו) ב"ק לג., ז) [שם ע"ש]:

הגהות הב"ח

(א) במשנה זה סומך לגדר. נ"ב ע"ל דף י"ח דהיינו דוקא באפשוקי לנותא: (ב) גמ' א"ל רב יוסף זיל קוץ: (ג) שם אמרי ליה מכולהו ולא יכילנא ליה: (ד) תוס' ד"ה זיקא וכו' ורוח מסייעתו: (ה) בא"ד שילא הגץ ויתרחק: (ו) בא"ד ואי לאו הרוח: (ז) בא"ד אע"ג דהיא גופה ממטיא נפשה ומיהו התם משום דזימנין דבהדי דנמנם כו' כנ"ל ותיבות כמר בר רב אשי נמחק: (ח) ד"ה ורבינא וכו' דה"נ דחייב:

לעזי רש"י

אטנצייל"א. פירוש גץ, נילוץ (רש"י ישעיה א, לא):

ליקוטי רש"י

ומערב ושוקעת בקרן לפונית מערבית ובלילה סובבת פני צפון ולמחרת היום נקלר מעט ואינה יוצאה בקרן אלא נמשכת מן הקרן ולמזרח מעט ויוצאה ובערב שוקעת כמוך המערב משוך מן הקרן מעט ובלילה סובבת אותו מעט וכל הלפון ומעט במזרח יותר מליל של אמש וכן בכל יום עד שיולאה בתקופת תשרי באמלע המזרח ושוקעת באמלע המערב לפיכך היום והלילה שוין ועדיין בכל יום נמשכת לצד דרום ויולאה ובשקיעתה נמשכת לצד דרום ושוקעת עד שיולאה ביום בתקופת טבת בקרן מזרחית דרומית והולכת לדרום לבדו ושוקעת בקרן מערבית דרומית. **פני מזרח ופני מערב שפעמים מסבבתן.** בלילה בימי תקופת טבת. **ופעמים מהלכתן.** ביום בימים הארוכין [עירובין נו.]. **שולחן בצפון.** כדכתיב (שמות כו) והשלחן תתן על צלע צפון והמנורה בדרום כדכתיב (שם) ואת המנורה נכח השלחן [רשב"ם לקמן קמז.]. **עד שאתה אומר לי הרחק את חרדלך מן דבוריי.** שבעל המזיק להרחיק עלמו הרחק אתה דבוריך מן חרדלי שאף אתה נקרא מזיק. **מרחיקין את האילן מן הבור עשרים וחמש אמה.** כך שיעור שהשרשין נמשכין והולכין ומקלקלין את כותלי הבור [לעיל יח.]. **מן הבור.** שהשרשין מתפשטין ונוקבין בכותלי הבור ומקלקלין את הקרקע והכתלים נופלים. **ובחרוב ושקמה.** יש להן שרשין יתירין וארוכין משאר אילנות. **בין מלמעלה.** בין שהאילן נמוך מן הבור שקרקעית הבור למעלה משרשי האילן שהאילן נטוע בבקעה והבור בהר והתם מפרש מפני שמאלידין את הקרקע ומעלין עפר ומקלקלין קרקעיתו של בור. **מן הצד.** שניהם בקרקע השוה. **ונותן דמים.** בעל הבור לבעל האילן [ב"מ קיז.]. **מודה ר' יוסי בגיריה דידיה.** בחלים הבאים לו מיד גופו של בעל הבית ממש [לעיל כב:]. אע"ג דאמר על הניזק להרחיק את עלמו הני מילי היכי דלאו אדם עלמו מזיקו כגון אילן ובור שבשעת נטיעתו אינו מזיקו אלא השרשים גדילין ומתפשטין מאליהן לאחר זמן אבל היכא דאדם עלמו מזיקו וזורק בו חליו מודה הוא דלא גרמא דניזקין הוא דמיפטר אלא מזיק ממש הוא ואדם מועד לעולם ער וישן שוגג ומזיד [ב"מ שם]. [ע"כ שייך לדף כה:] **מאי שנא מזורה.** ליהוי כזורה דחייב משום מלאכה בשבת אע"פ שהרוח מסייעתו כשהוא מגביה התבואה ברחת שקורין פלוי"א [ב"ק ס.]. **מאי שנא מגץ.** גץ. נילוץ אישטינציל"ש. **פטיש.** קורנס גדול של נפחים [שבת כא:]. **לא יטע אדם אילן.** בקלה שדהו סמוך לשדה חבירו כדי שלא תלך מחרישתו לחרוש אילן זה לדרך שדה חבירו [רשב"ם לקמן פג.]. **היה גדר בינתים.** שאין מזיקו עוד לעבודת הכרם זה סומך אילנות לגדר מכאן וזה סומך אילנות לגדר מכאן ואי נמי אחד מהן שדה לבן אין כאן כלאים כדאמר בעירובין (יא.) אם גפנים מכאן מותר לזרוע כאן גבי נעץ ארבעה קונדיסין ומתח זמורה על גביהן דדמיא לצורת הפתח. **מעמיק ג' טפחים.** מעמיק להן בעל השדה קוצץ את השרשין שילאו בשדהו בעומק שלשה טפחים [לעיל יח.]. **בור שיח ומערה.** שיח ארוכה וקלרה מערה מרובעת ומכוסה בקרוי אלא שיש לה פה [ב"ק נ:]. **כדי עבודת הכרם.** שהיו חורשים הכרם במחרישה וכן בשעת הבציר בוצרין אותם בעגלות וצריך להן מקום פנוי ארבע אמות שלא תיכנס עגלת מחרישתו בקרקע חבירו [לעיל יח.]. דבהכי הוי כלאים [לעיל ב.].

עין משפט
נר מצוה

צ א מיי' פי"א מהל' שכנים הלכה ג סמג עשין פב טוש"ע ח"מ סי' קנה סעיף טו:
צא ב מיי' שם הל' א וסמג שם טוש"ע שם סעיף לד:
צב ג מיי' פ"ו מהל' חובל ומזיק הל' יא סמג עשין סח טוש"ע ח"מ סי' שפד סעיף ב:
צג ד ה מיי' פ"י מהל' שכנים הל' א סמג עשין פב טוש"ע ח"מ סי' קנה סעיף כה:
צד ו ז מיי' שם הל' ז טוש"ע שם סעיף ל:
צה ח ט מיי' שם הל' ח טוש"ע שם סעי' כה:
צו י מיי' שם טוש"ע שם ועיין בהג"ה ובמ"מ:
צז כ מיי' פ"ו מהלכות מלכים הל' ט סמג לאוין רכט [וברב אלפס ב"ק סמוך לסוף פרק החובל דף לד: ועי' ט"ז בי"ד סי' קטז ס"ק ו]:

רבינו גרשום

כי היכי דנייד נכתמא אפומיה דחצבא. כלומר א) היכסה שמכסין ממנו הקיקל: **רקתא.** שלועזין ארישת"א. **אבל הכא** גבי הנהו רקתא אינו חייב משום דהוי ליה גירי דידיה **דזיקא הוא דקא ממטי ליה ואינו חייב:** מ"ש. מהא דתנן גבי שבת באבות מלאכות דהיכא **דזורה** תבואתו **והרוח מסייעתו** לדחות התבן דהוי חייב הכא נמי היכא דרוח ממטי לה אמאי אינו חייב. **אמר ליה** מרימר ודאי ברקתא חייב **דהיינו כזורה ורוח מסייעתו** דחייב לענין שבת. **ולרבינא** מייתי תו קושיא **מ"ש מגץ היוצא כו'.** דלעולם אין דליקה בלא רוח ואפ"ה חייב הכא נמי מאי שנא (ומאי שנא). **התם** גבי גץ מש"ה חייב **דניחא ליה דליזיל** מביתו אבל **הכא** גבי רקתא **לא ניחא ליה דליזיל** דהוא צריך נמי לרקתא לצורך שום דבר מש"ה הואיל דלא קא אזיל מכוחו דזיקא קא ממטי ליה פטור: **פיסקא כדי עבודת הכרם.** כדי כלי בקר וצמדו שלא ידוש שדה חבירו. **לא שנו** דבעינן ד' אמות **אלא בארץ ישראל** שרגילין לחרוש שדה אילן בשוורים ומפני חוזק הקרקע **אבל בבבל** שחורשין בחמורים או חופרין **בב' אמות** הרחקה סגי: **דפרדיסא.** גפנים: **והא רחיקי ליה.** ד' אמות: **הני מילי באילנות.** משדה אילנות: **אחד** שדה **גפנים ואחד** שדה **אילן.** אין מרחיקין אלא ד' אמות: **אסור למקצייה.** דכתיב כי ממנו תאכל ואותו לא תכרות: **שכחת.** הכי שמיה דבריה: **תאלי.** אילנות: **אזל** רב פפא **אשכחיה** לרב הונא: **אמר ליה מאי האי.** דקצצת שרשי: שמעכבין לי. חרישתי: **מר קא חפר טובא.** וקא קציץ שרשין למטה מג' טפחים: **אמרי ליה מכולהו.** שהבאתי לו ראיות מכמה מקומות ולא יכלי ליה:

חשק שלמה
על רבינו גרשום

א) [נ"ל הכיסוי שמכסין בו וכו'].

cut down the palms **myself,** דְּאָמַר רַב – **for Rav said:** הַאי דִּיקְלָא דְּטָעִין קַבָּא אָסוּר לְמִקְצְיֵיהּ – **It is forbidden to cut down a palm that bears** even **a** ***kav*** of fruit per season.[18] וְאָמַר רַבִּי חֲנִינָא – **And** furthermore, **R' Chanina said:** לֹא שָׁכִיב שִׁכְחַת בְּרִי אֶלָּא דְּקָץ תְּאֵנְתָא בְּלֹא זִימְנֵיהּ – **"My son, Shikchas, died** prematurely **for no [reason] other than that he cut down a fig tree before its time** had arrived."[19] מַר אִי נִיחָא לֵיהּ לִיקוֹץ – However, **if the master** (Rav Yosef) **wishes to, he may cut them down** himself.[20]

The Gemara cites an incident related to the latter part of the Mishnah, which rules that a neighbor may remove roots that extend into his property:

רַב פָּפָּא הֲווּ לֵיהּ הָנְהוּ דִּיקְלֵי – **Rav Pappa had these palm trees** אַמֵּיצְרָא דְּרַב הוּנָא בְּרֵיהּ דְּרַב יְהוֹשֻׁעַ – **along** his **boundary with Rav Huna the son of Rav Yehoshua.** The roots of his palms extended into Rav Huna's property. אֲזַל אַשְׁכְּחֵיהּ דַּהֲוָה חָפַר – Now, **[Rav Pappa]** once **went** out and **came upon [Rav Huna the son of Rav Yehoshua] digging** holes in his property, וְקָא קָאִיץ שָׁרְשָׁיו – **and cutting [Rav Pappa's] roots.** אָמַר לֵיהּ מַאי הַאי – **[Rav Pappa] said to him: What is this?** Why are you cutting the roots of my palm trees? אָמַר לֵיהּ – **[Rav Huna the son of Rav Yehoshua] replied to him:** תְּנַן – **We learned in a Mishnah:** הָיוּ שָׁרָשִׁים יוֹצְאִים לְתוֹךְ שֶׁל חֲבֵירוֹ – IF the ROOTS EXTENDED INTO HIS NEIGHBOR'S property, מַעֲמִיק שְׁלֹשָׁה כְּדֵי שֶׁלֹּא יְעַכֵּב הַמַּחֲרֵישָׁה – [THE NEIGHBOR] MAY EXCAVATE THREE *tefachim* of earth and remove the roots, SO THAT THEY SHOULD NOT IMPEDE THE movement of his PLOW. I am merely following the Mishnah's ruling.

The argument continued:

אָמַר לֵיהּ – **[Rav Pappa] said to [Rav Huna the son of Rav Yehoshua]:** הָנֵי מִילֵּי שְׁלֹשָׁה – **Those words** of the Mishnah permit excavating **three** *tefachim* of earth, מַר קָא חָפַר טְפֵי – while **the master** (Rav Huna the son of Rav Yehoshua) **is digging beyond** three *tefachim* and cutting roots. אָמַר לֵיהּ – **[Rav Huna the son of Rav Yehoshua] replied to him:** אֲנָא בּוֹרוֹת שִׁיחִין וּמְעָרוֹת קָא חֲפַרְנָא – **I am digging pits, ditches and vaults.**[21] I am therefore entitled to cut downward to *any* depth, דִּתְנַן – **for we learned in the Mishnah:** הָיָה חוֹפֵר בּוֹר שִׁיחַ וּמְעָרָה קוֹצֵץ וְיוֹרֵד וְהָעֵצִים שֶׁלּוֹ – If [THE NEIGHBOR] WAS DIGGING A PIT, A DITCH, OR A VAULT, HE MAY CUT DOWNWARD to whatever depth he finds necessary, AND THE WOOD cuttings ARE HIS.

Rav Pappa later recounted the ensuing events:

אָמַר רַב פָּפָּא – **Rav Pappa said:** אֲמַרִי לֵיהּ כּוּלְּהִי – **I told him all** the proofs there are that he was forbidden to cut the roots,[22] וְלֹא יְכִילִי לֵיהּ – **but I could not win him over** with my arguments,

NOTES

18. The Torah forbids cutting down any tree that bears fruit (see *Deuteronomy* 20:19). Rav ruled that a palm which yields a *kav* of produce per season qualifies as a fruit-bearing tree and is subject to this prohibition. [A *kav* is a measure of volume. There are differing views regarding the conversion of this Talmudic measure into contemporary terms, with opinions ranging from approximately 1.5 quarts (*R' Avrohom Chaim Noeh*) to 2.65 quarts (*Chazon Ish*).]

19. I.e. the sin of cutting down a tree prematurely, while it still bore fruit, was the cause of his premature death. [R' Chanina's statement underscores the gravity of this sin.]

20. The prohibition against cutting down fruit trees does not apply to a tree that is a source of damage to others. Now, Rav Yosef held that these trees were harming his vineyard by providing a perch for birds that would fly across and damage its crop. He therefore demanded that they be cut down. Rava bar Rav Chanan was not fully convinced by Rav Yosef's argument that damage caused by birds is attributable to the tree in which they perch. Although he was willing to suffer the loss of his trees based on this contention, he refused to risk transgressing a prohibition by chopping them down. Accordingly, he told Rav Yosef: If you are confident in the validity of your argument – that the trees are considered a source of damage and are therefore not subject to this prohibition – you may cut them down yourself (*Rabbeinu Yonah;* cf. *Tosafos* ד״ה אנא).

21. He was probably digging only one of these, but borrowed the Mishnah's terminology to make his point. [See *Chasam Sofer*, who explains why Rav Huna phrased his reply in this manner, and also why he did not give this reply when first challenged by Rav Pappa.]

22. I.e. I cited many Mishnahs and Baraisas that support my point of view (see *Rashi*).

כדנייד נכתמא אפומיה דחצבא דבי בר מריון בריה דרבין כי הוה נפצי כיתנא הוה אזלא רקתא ומזקא אינשי אתו לקמיה דרבינא אמר להו כי אמרינן מודה ר' יוסי בגירי דיליה הני מילי דקא אזלא מכחו הכא זיקא הוא דקא ממטי לה מתקיף לה מר בר רב אשי מאי שנא מזורה ורוח מסייעתו אמרוה קמיה דמרימר אמר להו היינו זורה ורוח מסייעתו ולרבינא מאי שנא מגץ היוצא מתחת הפטיש והזיק דחייב לשלם התם ניחא ליה דליזל הכא לא ניחא ליה דליזל: **מתני'** לא יטע אדם אילן סמוך לשדה חבירו אלא אם כן הרחיק ממנו ארבע אמות אחד גפנים ואחד כל אילן היה גדר בינתים (א) זה סומך לגדר מכאן וזה סומך לגדר מכאן היו שרשים יוצאים לתוך של חבירו מעמיק ג' טפחים כדי שלא יעכב את המחרישה היה חופר בור שיח ומערה קוצץ ויורד והעצים שלו: **גמ'** תנא ארבע אמות שאמרו כדי עבודת הכרם אמר שמואל לא שנו אלא בארץ ישראל אבל בבבל שתי אמות תניא נמי הכי לא יטע אדם אילן סמוך לשדה חבירו אלא אם כן הרחיק ממנו שתי אמות והא אנן תנן ארבע אמות אלא לאו כדשמואל שמע מינה ואיכא דרמי לה מירמא תנן לא יטע אדם אילן סמוך לשדה חבירו אלא אם כן הרחיק ממנו ארבע אמות והתניא שתי אמות אמר שמואל לא קשיא כאן בבבל כאן בארץ ישראל רבא בר רב חנן הוו ליה הנהו דיקלי אמיצרא דפרדיסא דרב יוסף הוו אתו צפורי יתבי בדיקלי ונחתי בפרדיסא ומפסדי ליה א"ל (ב) זיל קוץ א"ל והא ארחיקי לי א"ל ה"מ לאילנות אבל לגפנים בעינן טפי והא אנן תנן אחד גפנים ואחד כל אילן א"ל ה"מ אילן לאילן וגפנים לגפנים אבל אילן לגפנים בעינן טפי א"ל אנא לא קייצנא דאמר רב האי דיקלא דטעין קבא אסור למקצייה ואמר ר' חנינא לא שכיב שכחת ברי אלא דקץ תאנתא בלא זימניה מר אי ניחא ליה ליקוץ רב פפא הו"ל הנהו דיקלי אמיצרא דרב הונא בריה דרב יהושע אזל אשכחיה דהוה חפר וקא קאיץ שרשיו אמר ליה מאי האי אמר ליה תנן היו שרשים יוצאים לתוך של חבירו מעמיק שלשה כדי שלא יעכב המחרישה אמר ליה הני מילי שלשה מר קא חפר טפי אמר ליה אנא בורות שיחין ומערות קא חפרנא דתנן היה חופר בור שיח ומערה קוצץ ויורד והעצים שלו אמר רב פפא אמרי ליה (ג) כולהו ולא יכילי ליה

עד

רש"י

כדנייד נכתמא אפומא דחצבא. שאם יניחו כד על החומה וכיסויה עליה ינוע הכיסוי מחמת הרעדה: **רקתא.** מה שמנערין מן הפשתן: **מאי שנא מזורה.** בשבת דחייב ואע"פ שהרוח מסייעתו חשיב ליה עושה מלאכה אלמא גירי דיליה נינהו: **היינו זורה ורוח מסייעתו.** כי היכי דלענין שבת הוי כחו לענין נזקין נמי כחו חשיב ליה: **ולרבינא מאי שנא כו'.** בשלמא זורה ורוח מסייעתו לא הויא ליה פירכא דקסבר ממונא מאיסור שבת לא ילפינן דהתם מלאכת מחשבת אסרה תורה וכה"ג מתרצינן ליה להא פירכא בב"ק בהכונס לאן לדיר (דף ס.): **גץ.** אטנצייל"א היוצאת מן הברזל כשהפטיש מכה עליו: **חייב.** והרי הוליכן הרוח: **ניחא ליה דליזיל.** לחוץ שלא ידליק את ביתו: **מתני' סמוך לשדה חבירו.** בין שדה הלבן בין שדה האילן וטעמא כדי עבודת הכרם שכשיחרוש את אילנותיו לא יהא צריך להכניס מחרישתו לתוך שדה חבירו: **מעמיק.** להן בעל השדה שיצאו לתוכו: **קוצץ.** בעומק ג' טפחים: **והעצים שלו.** בגמרא מפרש של מי: **גמ' אבל בבבל שתי אמות.** שמחרישתן קצרה: **פרדיסא.** כרם: **והא ארחיקי לי.** ד' אמות: **שכחת ברי.** כך שמו: **אשכחיה.** רב פפא לרב הונא דקא חפר וקייץ שרשין: **מאי האי.** אמאי קייצת: **אמרי ליה כולהו.** הבאתי לו ראיות הרבה שלא יקוץ:

תוספות

אפומא דחצבא. על פי' הקונט' קשיא לר"י דא"כ יהא האפלנא נייד כולי האי עד שמתגלגל הנכתמא דא"כ הבית קרוב ליפול ולפי הענין משמע שהיה בנין חזק שהרי מתוך העושר בנאה ובמס' שבת (דף עז:) נמי אמר מאי אפלנא אפיתחא אפיתחא דין שמאספין שם לדין משמע דבירה גדולה היא ונראה לר"י דכל נייד נכתמא כשאדם אוחז הכל בידו שזהו דבר מועט הרבה א"כ מתגלגל האפלנא חייב להרחיק ולריב"א נראה שאין פ"ה רחוק דבדבר מועט מתגלגל הנכתמא שהוא דבר קל אף על פי שהאפלנא אינו מתגלגל כל כך:

זיקא הוא דקא ממטי לה. קשיא לר"י לחייב משום אש מידי דהוה אאבנו וסכינו ומשאו שהניחן בראש גגו ונפלו ברוח מצויה והזיקו דחייב משום אש כדאמר בפ"ק דב"ק (דף ו.) והכא דאמטי ליה ברוח מצויה איירי מדפריך עלה מזורה ורוח (ד) מסייעו דאיירי ברוח מצויה כדמשמע בהכונס (שם דף ס. ושם) גבי ליבה וליבתו הרוח ומדפריך מגץ היוצא מתחת הפטיש דהיינו ברוח מצויה דחייב משום אש דגבי אש קתני לה בהכונס ואומר ר"י דלא דמי דהתם לא מיחייב משום אש אלא כשעשה האדם את האש לבדו דכתיב המבעיר את הבערה בלא סיוע הרוח ואח"כ הולכת על ידי רוח מצויה אבל הכא אין עושה לבדו כל שהוא אלא ע"י הרוח דאי לאו רוח לא הוה רקתא אזלא כלל עיקר ודמי לליבה וליבתו הרוח דפטור והיינו דמשני כי פריך מסמוך מ"ש מגץ דהוה סלקא דעתך דדמי ממש לגץ ומשני התם ניחא ליה דליזל ומתכוין להכות בכח עד שילך הגץ (ה) ומתרחק בלא שום זיקא וחייב משום אש על מה שגומר והולך על ידי רוח מצויה אבל הכא לא ניחא ליה דליזל כלומר ואינו מכה בכח ואי לאו (ו) רוח אין הרקתא הולכת כלל וא"ת מ"מ יהא חייב להרחיק מידי דהוה אגורן דמתניתין דחייב להרחיק אע"ג דזיקא ממטי ליה וי"ל דמתני' כרבנן והכא איירי אליבא דר' יוסי דלא מחייב אלא בגירי דיליה והא דפריך מגץ ולא מצי לאוקמי ההיא דגץ כרבנן משום דלא פליגי רבי יוסי ורבנן לענין חיוב תשלומין אלא לענין הרחקה וא"ת מאי שנא מנמייה דאפילו לר' יוסי מרחיקין אע"ג דהיא גופה ממטיא נפשה (ז) כמר בר רב אשי ומיהו התם משום דזימנין דבהדי דנח כו' כדקאמר לעיל אבל קשה מעורבין לעיל (דף כג.) דאמר רב יוסף אפיקו לי קורקור מהכא וי"ל דגמרא לא סבר לה כרבינא דר"ת פוסק כמר בר רב אשי וכאמימר ועוד אומר ר"י דבעלי חיים שאני דאמירי טפי מרוח דכח אחר מעורב בהן כדאמרינן בבבא קמא (דף ו.):

מאי שנא מזורה ורוח מסייעתו. ורבינא לא חשיב לה פירכא דסבר כי היכי דלא גמרינן משבת לענין תשלומין כדמפרש רב אשי בהכונס (ב"ק דף ס. ושם) דגבי שבת מלאכת מחשבת אסרה תורה אבל הכא גרמא הוא וגרמא בנזקין פטור הכי נמי לא גמרינן מהתם שיהא חייב להרחיק ומר בר רב אשי סבר נהי דלחיוב תשלומין לא גמרי' לענין הרחקה דליחשב גירי דיליה גמרינן שפיר כיון דגרמא בנזקין אסור: **ורבינא** מאי שנא מגץ. וא"ת ואמאי קאמר ורבינא לאמימר נמי תיקשי לענין חיוב תשלומין מאי שנא מגץ וי"ל משום הכי נקט רבינא דלאמימר הוי מצי לדחויי דה"נ (ח) חייב לדידיה בתשלומין דלגמרי מדמה לה לזורה ורוח מסייעתו:

אחד גפנים ואחד כל אילן. מתוך פ"ה לעיל (דף יח.) משמע דנקט אחד גפנים משום דשייך בהו כלאים דהביא ראיה מכאן דבשיש גדר ליכא איסור כלאים וזה סומך לגדר מכאן וזה מכאן ואין נראה דשדה חבירו דקתני הכא על כרחך לאו בשל זרעים איירי דהא מוקמי' בגמ' דמתני' אילנות לאילנות וגפנים לגפנים אבל אילנות לגפנים בעי טפי משום ליפרי ומהאי טעמא גפנים לזרעים בעי טפי אלא דנראה דנקט אחד גפנים ואחד כל אילן דלא תיסוק אדעתי' למימר דשיעור ד' אמות דמתני' דוקא בגפנים שמצינו בהם שיעור זה במקום אחר לענין כלאים: **אבל** בבבל ב' אמות. תימה דבפרק המוכר את הספינה (לקמן דף פב: ושם דף פג.) גבי קנה ג' קנה קרקע דאמר רב יוסף עובדא הוה בדורא דרעותא כו' משמע מהתם דבבבל נמי בעינן ד' אמות וי"ל דההיא דורא דרעותא היה להם מחרישה גדולה כמו בארץ ישראל: **אבל** בגפנים בעי טפי. והוא כשנטע דקלים כשהם גבוהים אבל אם נטע גרעין לא דממילא קא גדל ולא גירי דיליה הוא: **אנא** לא קייצנא דאמר רב כו'. וא"ת והתנן במתניתא דקוצץ ונותן דמים וי"ל דאיכא לאוקמי באילן סרק אבל קשה דאמרינן בהחובל (ב"ק דף צב.) גבי הנהו דיקלי דמכחשי בגופני הוו דקאמר למחר אייתי לי מקורייהו אלמא משום היזק גפנים מותר לקוץ דקלים ויש לפרש דשאני התם שיותר מדאי היו מכחישים בגפנים עד דהוה טעים בהו טעמא דחמרא:

עד

עין משפט נר מצוה

צ א מיי' פי"א מהל' שכנים הלכה ג סמג עשין פב טוש"ע ח"מ סי' קנה סעיף טו:
צא ב מיי' שם הל' א וסמג שם טוש"ע שם סעיף לד:
צב ג מיי' פ"ו מהל' חובל ומזיק הל' יא סמג עשין סח טוש"ע ח"מ סי' שפג סעיף ג:
צג ד ה מיי' פ"י מהל' שכנים הל' ח סמג עשין פב טוש"ע ח"מ סי' קנה סעיף כה:
צד ו ז מיי' שם הל' ז טוש"ע שם סעיף לג:
צה ח ט מיי' שם הל' ו טוש"ע שם סעי' כה:
צו י מיי' שם טוש"ע שם סעיף כה ועיין בהג"ה ובמ"מ:
צז כ מיי' פ"ו מהלכות מלכים הל' ט סמג לאוין רכט וע"ע תוספות ב"ק סמוך לסוף פרק החובל דף לד: ועי' ע"ז בי"ד סי' קטז ס"ק ו:

רבינו גרשום

כי היכי דנייד נכתמא אפומיה דחצבא. כלומר א) היכסה שמכסין ממנו הקיקל: רקתא. שלוצין ארעישא"ה. אבל הכא אינו חייב משום דהוי ליה גירי דידיה דזיקא הוא דקא ממטי ליה ואינו חייב. מ"ש. מהא דתנן גבי שבת באבות מלאכות דהזורה וזורה תבואתו והרוח מסייעתו לדחות התבן דהוי חייב הכא נמי היכא דרוח ממטי ליה אמאי אינו חייב. אמר ליה מרימר ודאי ברקתא חייב דהיינו כזורה ורוח מסייעתו דחייב לענין שבת. ולרבינא מאי שנא קושיא מ"ש מגץ היוצא כו'. דלעולם אין דליקה בלא רוח ואפ"ה חייב הכא נמי מאי שנא (ומאי שנא). התם גבי גץ מש"ה חייב דניחא ליה דליזל מביתו אבל הכא גבי רקתא לא ניחא ליה דליזל דהוא צריך להו לרקתא לצורך שום דבר מש"ה הואיל דלא קא אזיל מכוחו דזיקא קא ממטי ליה פטור: פיסקא כדי עבודת הכרם. כדי כלי בקר וצמדו שלא ידוש שדה חבירו. לא שנו דבעינן ד' אמות אלא בארץ ישראל שרגילין לחרוש שדה אילן בשוורים ומפני חוזק הקרקע אבל בבבל שחורשין בחמורים או חופרין בב' אמות הרחקה סגי: דפרדיסא. גפנים: והא רחיקו ליה. ד' אמות: הני מילי באילנות. משדה אילנות: אחד שדה גפנים ואחד שדה אילן. אין מרחיקין אלא ד' אמות: אסור למקצייה. דכתיב כי ממנו תאכל ואותו לא תכרות: שכחת. הכי שמיה דבריה: תאלי. אילנות: אזל רב פפא אשכחיה לרב הונא: אמר ליה מאי האי. דקצצת שרשי' שמעכבין לי. חרישתי: מר קא חפר טובא. וקא קציץ שרשין למטה ג' טפחים: אמרי ליה מכולהו. שהבאתי לו ראיות מכמה מקומות ולא יכלי ליה:

חשק שלמה על רבינו גרשום

א) [נ"ל הכיסוי שמכסין בו וכו'].

מסורת הש"ס

א) [ב"ק ס.], ב) [שם סב: וש"נ], ג) [לעיל יח.] לקמן פג., ד) [לעיל יח.], ה) [שם], ו) ב"ק לה., ז) [שם ע"ש].

הגהות הב"ח

(א) במשנה זה סומך לגדר. נ"ב ע"ל דף י"ח דהיינו דוקא באפסקי גומא: (ב) גמ' א"ל רב יוסף זיל קוץ: (ג) שם אמרי ליה מכולהו ולא יכילנא ליה: (ד) תוס' ד"ה זיקא וכו' ורוח מסייעתו: (ה) בא"ד שילך הגץ ומתרחק: (ו) בא"ד ואי לאו הרוח: (ז) בא"ד אע"ג דהיא גופה ממטיא נפשה ומיהו התם משום דזימנין דבהדי דנח כו' כל"ל ותיבות כמר בר רב אשי נמחק: (ח) ד"ה ורבינא וכו' דה"נ דחייב:

לעזי רש"י

אטנצייל"א. פירוש גץ, ניצוץ (רש"י ישעיה א, לא).

ליקוטי רש"י

ומערב ושוקעת בקרן מערבית צפונית ובלילה מסבבת פני צפון ולמחרת יוצאה מן הקרן שלא נכנסת מן הקרן ולמזרח מעט ובערב שוקעת מן הקרן המערבי משוך מעט ובלילה מסבבת אותו מעט וכל הצפון ומעט במזרח מעט יותר מליל של אמש וכן כל יום עד שיוצאה בתקופת תשרי באמצע המזרח ושוקעת באמצע המערב לפיכך היום והלילה שוין ועדיין כל יום נכנסת לצד דרום ויוצאה ובשקיעתה נכנסת לצד דרום ושוקעת עד שיוצאה ביום בתקופת טבת בקרן מזרחית דרומית ומהלכת דרום לבדו ושוקעת בקרן מערבית דרומית. **פני מזרח ופני מערב שפעמים מסבבתן.** בלילה בימי תקופת טבת. **ופעמים מהלכתן.** ביום בימים הארוכין [עירובין נו.]. **שולחן בצפון.** כדכתיב (שמות כו) והשלחן תתן על צלע צפון והמנורה לדרום כדכתיב (שם) ואת המנורה נכח השלחן [רשב"ם לקמן קמז.]. **עד שאתה אומר לי הרחק את חרדלך מן דבוריי.** שעל המזיק להרחיק עצמו הרחק אתה דבוריך מחרדלי שאף אתה נקרא מזיק. **מרחיקין את האילן מן הבור עשרים וחמש אמה.** כך שיעור שהשרשין מתפשטין והולכין ומקלקלין את כותלי הבור [לעיל יח.]. **מן הבור.** שהשרשין מתפשטין ומקלקלין את הקרקע והכותלים נופלים. **ובחרוב ושקמה.** יש להן שרשין יתירין ולרוכין מאחר אילנות. **בין מלמעלה.** בין שהאילן נמוך מן הבור שקרקעית הבור למעלה משרשי האילן שהאילן נטוע בבקעה והבור בהר והתם מפרש מפני שמחלידין את הקרקע ומעלין עפר ומקלקלין קרקעיתו של בור. **מן הצד.** שניהם בקרקע השוה. **ונותן דמים.** בעל הבור לבעל האילן [ב"מ קיז.]. **מודה ר' יוסי בגיריה דידיה.** בחלים הבאים לו מיד גופו של בעל הבית ממש [לעיל כב:]. אע"ג דאמר על הניזק להרחיק את עצמו הני מילי היכי דלאו אדם עצמו מזיקו כגון אילן ובור שבשעת נטיעתו אינו מזיקו אלא השרשים גדלין ומתפשטין מאליהן לאחר זמן אבל היכא דאדם עצמו מזיקו וזורק בו חציו מודה הוא דלא גרמא דניזקין הוא דמיפטר אלא מזיק ממש הוא ואדם מועד לעולם ער וישן שוגג ומזיד [ב"מ שם]. [ע"כ שייך לדף כה:] **מאי שנא מזורה.** ליהוי כזורה דחייב משום מלאכה בשבת אע"פ שהרוח מסייעתו כשהוא מגביה התבואה ברחת שקורין פליי"א [ב"ק ס.]. **מאי שנא מגץ.** נילוץ אישטינצל"ש. **פטיש.** קורנס גדול של נפחים [שבת כא:]. **לא יטע אדם אילן.** בקצה שדהו סמוך לשדה חבירו כדי שלא תלך מחרישתו לחרוש אילן זה דרך שדה חבירו [רשב"ם לקמן פג.]. **היה גדר בינתים.** שאין מזיקו עוד לעבודת הכרם זה סומך אילנות לגדר מכאן וזה סומך אילנות לגדר מכאן ואי נמי אחד מהן שדה לבן אין כאן כלאים כדאמר בעירובין (יח.) אם גפנים מכאן מותר לזרוע כאן גבי נעץ ארבעה קונדיסין ומתח זמורה על גביהן דדמיא לצורת הפתח. **מעמיק ג' טפחים.** מעמיק להן בעל השדה קוצץ את השרשין שיצאו בשדהו בעומק שלשה טפחים [לעיל יח.]. **בור שיח ומערה.** שיח ארוכה וקצרה מערה מרובעת ומכוסה בקרוי אלא שיש לה פה [ב"ק נ:]. **כדי עבודת הכרם.** שהיו חורשים הכרם במחרישה וכן בשעת הבציר בוצרין אותם בעגלות וצריך להן מקום פנוי ארבע אמות שלא תיכנס עגלת מחרישתו בקרקע חבירו [לעיל יח.]. דבהכי הוי כלאים [לעיל ב.].

עין משפט נר מצוה

צח א ב מיי' פ"ה מהל' מעילה הלכה ז:
צט ג מיי' שם ופ"ה מהל' שכנים הל' ו סמג עשין פב טוש"ע ח"מ סי' קנה סעיף לב:
ק ד מיי' פ"ג מהלכות שמיטה הל' ה סמג לאוין רסז:
קא ה מיי' שם הל' ג:

עד דאמרי ליה הא דאמר רב יהודה מצר שהחזיקו בו רבים אסור לקלקלו לבתר דנפק אמר אמאי לא אמרי ליה כאן חוץ לשש עשרה אמה כאן בתוך שש עשרה אמה: היה חופר בור שיח ומערה קוצץ ויורד והעצים שלו (וכו'): בעא מיניה יעקב הדייבא מרב חסדא עצים של מי אמר ליה תניתוה שרשי אילן של הדיוט הבאין בשל הקדש לא נהנין ולא מועלין אי אמרת בשלמא בתר אילן אזלינן משום הכי לא מועלין אלא אי אמרת בתר קרקע אזלינן אמאי לא מועלין אלא מאי בתר אילן אזלינן אימא סיפא של הקדש הבאים בשל הדיוט לא נהנין ולא מועלין ואי בתר אילן אזלינן אמאי לא מועלין מידי איריא בגידולין הבאין לאחר מכאן עסקינן וקא סבר אין מעילה בגידולין רבינא אמר לא קשיא כאן בתוך שש עשרה אמה כאן חוץ לשש עשרה אמה: אמר עולא אילן הסמוך למצר בתוך שש עשרה אמה גזלן הוא ואין מביאין ממנו בכורים מנא ליה לעולא הא אילימא מדתנן עשר נטיעות המפוזרות בתוך בית סאה חורשין כל בית סאה בשבילן עד ראש השנה כמה הוו להו תרי אלפין וחמש מאה גרמידי לכל חד וחד כמה מטי ליה מאתן וחמשין הא לא הוי דעולא ואלא מדתנן שלשה אילנות של ג' בני אדם הרי אלו מצטרפין וחורשין כל בית

רש"י

שהחזיקו בו רבים. לעשותו להן דרך אסור לקלקלו אע"פ שהוא של יחיד והנך נמי הא מחזיקי ליה: לבתר דנפק. רב פפא: אמר. רב הונא אמאי לא אמרי ליה: בתוך שש עשרה אמה. לאילן הוא מוחזק לאילן אבל חוץ לשש עשרה אמה אין מוחזקו חזקה שאע"פ שהשרשים מתפשטין כ"ה אמה אין יונקין אלא בתוך ט"ז אמה סמוך לאילן וכדאמרינן לקמן ואנא (א) הוא חוץ לט"ז אמה קיימנא: הדייבא. דמן הדייב: לא נהנין. מדרבנן: ולא מועלין. אם נהנה לא מעל אלמא לאו קדשי: מידי איריא. מסקנא דקושיא הוא כלומר מכולה לאו אירית היא לא למשמע מינה בתר אילן ולא למשמע מינה בתר קרקע דטעמא משום דהנך שרשים גידולים הבאים לאחר שהוקדש האילן הוא והיכא דאיכא למ"ד במס' מעילה אין מועלין בגידולין אפי' שרשי הקדש בשדה הקדש: לא נהנין מדאורייתא ליה: רבינא אמר ל"ק. רישא דקתני בתר אילן אזלינן היינו בתוך ט"ז אמה וסיפא דקתני של הקדש באין בתוך של הדיוט לא מועלין היינו חוץ לט"ז: גזלן הוא. שיונק משדה חבירו: ואין מביאין ממנו בכורים. אין לריך להביא ממנו בכורים דבעינן אשר תביא מארצך (דברים כו): עשר נטיעות מפוזרות בבית סאה. לארכו ולרחבו כולן בשוה יונקות מכל בית סאה וכולם לריך להם ומותר לחורשו ערב שביעית עד ראש השנה שהלכה למשה מסיני הוא ובית סאה חמשים אמה על חמשים אמה שאמר המשכן קרוי בית סאתים והוא מאה על חמשים: כמה הוי להו. בית סאה כי עבדת (ב) להו רלועה של אמה רוחב: תרי אלפים וחמש מאה גרמידי. שהרי יש כאן נ' רלועות של חמשים אמה ועולות לאלפים וחמש מאות אמה חלוק אותן לעשר אילנות תמלא לירוף קרקע יניקת כל אילן ואילן בין הכל מאתן וחמשין אמה אורך באמה רוחב: הא לא הוי כדעולא. דשיעור עולא נפיש דאמר דאילן יונק שש עשרה (ג) לכל לד הרי ל"ב על ל"ב עשה מהן רלועה אחת של אמה רוחב כאשר עשית מבית סאה תמלאנה של אלף וכ"ד אמה שהרי יש כאן שלשים ושתים רלועות כל אחת ואחת ל"ב אמה: ואלא מדתנן שלשה אילנות. גדולים שיונקים יותר מן הנטיעות ומפוזרין בבית סאה לארכו ולרחבו בשוה אע"פ שאינו של אדם אחד אלא של שלשה בני אדם מצטרפין להיות שדה אילן ולחרוש כל בית סאה בשבילן ערב שביעית עד עצרת כדין שדה אילן ואם לאו אין חורשין אלא כל אחד כדי צרכו דהיינו תחתיו וחוצה לו כמלא אורה וסלו והשאר הוי שדה הלבן ואין חורשין אותו אלא עד הפסח: בית

תוספות

עד דאמרי ליה הא דאמר רב יהודה מיצר שהחזיקו כו'. תימה מאי מייתי מרב יהודה דרבים שאני דלאו הכי קשיא מתני' דקתני קוצץ ויורד ופירש ר"ח וריב"ם דרבים החזיקו במגרופיא דרב הונא וברשותו דלאו הכי אין חזקתו מועלת כדמשמע בהמניח (ב"ק דף כח. ושם) ואתא רב הונא וקא חפר ברשות הרבים וקלץ שרשים לרב פפא ומשום הכי פריך מדרב יהודה דכיון שהחזיקו בו רבים אינו רשאי לחפור והא דקאמר אמאי לא אמרי ליה כאן בתוך שש עשרה אמה וכו' ה"פ כלומר כי קאמר רב יהודה מצר שהחזיקו בו רבים אסור לקלקלו ה"מ תוך ט"ז אמה אבל חוץ לט"ז אמה מותר לקלקלו כיון שמגיע ט"ז אמה כדין רשות הרבים וכסוף חזקת הבתים (לקמן דף נו:) דאסר רבי יוחנן לאדם שכנס תוך שלו להחזיר כתלים במקומן אע"ג דליכא רווחא כדמשמע התם אליבא דר"ל הכא איכא רווחא רווחא דקאמר התם (ד) שאינו סותם כל רשות הרבים אבל ליכא רווחא ט"ז אמה אבל אי איכא רווחא ט"ז אמה מודה רבי יוחנן דמותר לקלקלו ומחזיר כתלים למקומן כדאמר הכא ומיהו קשה מאי קאמר רב פפא אמרי ליה מכולהי מאי כולהי ומפרש ה"ר מנחם דמכולהי היינו מכל הני דתנן אם האילן קדם לא יקוץ ספק כו' ולא יכלי ליה שהיה דוחה אותו דמיירי דאילן עצמו אבל השרשים יקוץ ור"ח מפרש דרב הונא היה קולץ ולוקח השרשים לעצמו וא"ל רב פפא מאי האי כלומר למה אתה לוקח השרשים לעצמך א"ל דתנן קוצץ ויורד וכיון שבדין אני קוצץ כמו כן יהו העצים שלי ואמרי ליה מכולהי היינו הנהו דמייתי הכא והאיך דמייתי לקמן שרשי אילן הדיוט הבאים כו' דמינה מוכח לקמן דהעצים שלו דקתני במתני' היינו של בעל האילן ולא יכלי ליה שדחה לו כדדחי ליה לקמן עד דא"ל מרב יהודה כו' דנהי שלא תועיל חזקתי כחזקת רבים לענין שלא תהא רשאי לקוצצו לענין זה מיהא תועיל שיהו העצים שלי ומסיק אמאי לא אמרי ליה חוץ לשש עשרה יש להיות העצים שלי כדאמר רבינא לקמן כאן תוך שש עשרה כו':

אלא הכא בגידולין הבאין לאחר מכאן. ויש ספרים דגרסי מידי איריא הא בגידולין וכל זה מדברי המקשה כלומר על כרחך לא תוכל לפשוט מכאן דבגידולין הבאין לאחר מכאן איירי ואי בתר אילן אזלינן רישא אשמועינן דאין נהנין וסיפא אשמועינן דאין מועלין ואי בתר קרקע אזלינן רישא אשמועינן דאין מועלין וסיפא דאין נהנין בגידולין וא"ת ההיא בבא דאשמועינן דאין מעילה בגידולין לשמעינן של הקדש הבאין בשל הקדש דהוי רבותא טפי וי"ל דנקט הכי משום אידך בבא דאשמועינן דאין נהנין דהוי רבותא טפי שאין הכל של הקדש ור"ח לא גרים אלא והמתרץ הוא דקאמר הכי דמוקי סיפא דאין מעילה בגידולין והא דלא נקט דשל הקדש בשל הקדש משום דבעי למינקט דומיא דרישא דאין הכל דהקדש אלא חד דהקדש וחד דהדיוט אבל אי בתר קרקע אזלינן ורישא אשמועינן דאין מעילה בגידולין ליתני רישא של הקדש בשל הקדש דאין מיושב כל כך לומר תנא רישא אגב סיפא כמו תנא סיפא אגב רישא:

רבינא אמר לא קשיא כאן תוך ט"ז כו'. רישא בתוך ט"ז אמה דבתר אילן אזלינן וסיפא חוץ לט"ז אמה דבתר קרקע אזלינן ואם תאמר וליתני אידי ואידי תוך ט"ז וליתני סיפא מועלין אי נמי אידי ואידי אחר ט"ז וליתני ברישא מועלין וי"ל דתנא הכי לאשמועינן דבתרוייהו בין בתוך ט"ז אמה בין חוץ לט"ז אמה לא נהנין ולא מועלין:

גזלן הוא ואין מביאין ממנו בכורים. פי' ר"ח משום דאין מביאין גזל על גבי המזבח שנאמר אני ה' שונא גזל בעולה (ישעיה סא) וכתיב והבאתם גזול וגו' (מלאכי א) ולית לן דעולא דהא בהדיא פסקינן כרבי יוסי דאמר זה נוטע בתוך שלו כו' וא"ת לפירושו עולא כמאן סבר דכרבנן נמי לא הוי דרבנן לא בעו הרחקה אלא ד' אמות ולעולא שש עשרה אמה וי"ל דעולא הוי מוקי מתניתין בלונמא כדמוקי לה בריש פירקין ולהכי לא בעי אלא ד' אמות ומיהו קשיא לרבי יצחק דפריך לקמן לעולא מהקונה אילן וקרקעו מביא וקורא מאי לאו כל שהוא ומאי קושיא שאני התם שקנאו ולא הוה גזלן ונראה כפי' הקונטרס ° דאע"ג דמותר לסמוך אין מביאין ממנו בכורים דבעינן אשר תביא מארצך ולקמן דאמר אילן הסמוך מביא וקורא שעל מנת כן הנחיל יהושע את הארץ לא קאמר שעל מנת כן הנחיל שיהא מותר לסמוך דבלאו הכי שרי אלא על מנת כן הנחיל שיהא חשוב כמו מארצך ויכול לומר (ה) אשר נתת לי:

עשר נטיעות המפוזרות כו'. בסוכה (דף לד.) אמר עשר נטיעות וערבה וניסוך המים הלכה למשה מסיני ודוקא עשר לתוך בית סאה אבל פחות אין לריכין חרישה כל כך וכן נמי אם היו בבית סאה יותר מעשר נטיעות אין חורשין לפי שעומדין ליעקר: כמה

רבינו גרשום

מצר שהחזיקו בו רבים אסור לקלקלו. ואבותי ואבות אבותי החזיקו בו במכמה שנים: לבתר דנפק רב פפא אמר רב הונא אמאי לא אמרי ליה כאן בתוך שש עשרה. סמוך למיצר אם נטוע ויוצאין שרשין מתחת ונכנסין לשדה חבירו קוצץ ויורד וכאן חוץ לט"ז אמה שהרחיקו כדין ושוב נכנסו שרשיו מתחת לשדה חבירו אמר רב יהודה דאסור לקלקלו: פיסקא הבאין בשל הקדש בשדה הקדש לא נהנין מהן מן השרשין לכתחלה (א) אבל הנהנה מהן דין הקדש היינו דלא מועלין דבתר אילן אזלי דשל הדיוט הוא משו"ה מה שקוצצין מן השרשים יתן לבעל האילן. ושל הקדש: אילן הקדש: לעולם בתר אילן אזלי שרשים. ואמאי אין מועלין בסיפא משום דאותן השרשים של הקדש הבאין בשדה הדיוט בגדולין של הקדש הבאין לשדה הדיוט לאחר שהוקדש עסקינן ומש"ה אין מועלין דסבר אין מעילה בגידולין (ב) דאמר אבותי הקדישו קורות ואנו נתיר גמזיות: ורבינא אמר. לעולם בתר אילן אזלינן ומש"ה לא מועלין ודקא קשיא לך בסיפא אמאי לא מועלין בתר אילן ומועלין הא לא קשיא דרישא משום הכי אין מועלין דנטוע הוא בפחות מט"ז אמה סמוך למיצר אע"ג דאיכא למימר דמינך הוא משל הקדש הוא לא מועלין דשדינן עיקרו בתר אילן אבל סיפא בשדה הדיוט אילן של הקדש לא מועלין משום דרחוק מט"ז אמות הוא נטוע דליכא למימר משרשי ההקדש הן דהדאויל שהוא רחוק כל כך מי שקוצץ אותן שרשים שהן לסוף ט"ז אמה אין מכחיש כלום באילן משו"ה אין מועלין. ומתני' דקתני העצים של היה אם בתוך ט"ז אמה חופר וקוצץ הן של בעל האילן ואם חוץ לט"ז אמה חופר וקוצץ הן של בעל [הקרקע]: אמר עולא אילן הסמוך למצר של שדה חבירו בתוך לט"ז אמה. שרשיו יונקין משדה חבירו ואין מביא מפירותיו ביכורין דאין יכול לקרות את ראשית פרי האדמה אשר נתתה לפי שיונק משדה אחרים: מנא ליה לעולא הא. דאילן יונק מכל צדדיו עד שש עשרה אמה אילימא מדתנן במס' שביעית עשר נטיעות המפוזרות בתוך בית סאה [illegible]

מסורת הש"ס

א) ב"ק כח. לעיל יב. ע"ש ולקמן נו: ודף ק., ב) בס"י אימא הדייבא, ג) מעילה יג:, ד) שביעית פ"א מ"ו, ה) ג"ז שם מ"ה, ו) בס"י הדייבה, ז) נ"ל שאינו:

הגהות הב"ח

(א) רש"י ד"ה בתוך שש וכו' ואנא חוץ כל"ל ותיבת הוא נמחק: (ב) ד"ה כמה וכו' כי עבדת ליה רלועה אחת של אמה: (ג) ד"ה הא לא כו' יונק שש עשרה אמה לכל: (ד) תוס' ד"ה עד דאמרי ליה הא דאמר רב יהודה וכו' דקאמר התם היינו שאינו סותם: (ה) ד"ה גזלן וכו' ויכול לומר מן האדמה אשר נתת לי:

גליון הש"ס

תוס' ד"ה גזלן כו' דאע"ג דמותר לסמוך. עיין בר"ן ריש בכורים:

ליקוטי רש"י

מצר. שבין שתי שדות [רשב"ם לקמן ס:]. שהחזיקו בו רבים. שהשוהו וקנוהו להלוך ולעבור בו וכשהיו ידעו הבעלים אסור לקלקלו דודאי לרבים מחל [רשב"ם לקמן ק.]. שרשי אילן של הדיוט הבאין בשל הקדש לא נהנין ולא מועלין. דאזלינן בתר אילן ובשל הדיוט קאי. של הקדש הבאים בשל הדיוט. נמי לא מועלין ולא נהנין הואיל ועיקרו באו בשל הקדש [מעילה יג:]. [מכאן שייך לדף כז.] כמה מרובע יתר על העיגול רביע. [illegible]

[illegible]

עַד דְּאָמְרִי לֵיהּ הָא דְּאָמַר רַב יְהוּדָה – **until I told him the** following **statement of Rav Yehudah:** מֵצַר שֶׁהֶחֱזִיקוּ בּוֹ רַבִּים – A private **boundary divider on which the public established** a right of way אָסוּר לְקַלְקְלוֹ – **may not be ruined** by its owner.[1] I, too, had established the right to have my roots extend into his property and he was therefore forbidden to cut them.[2]

Although Rav Huna the son of Rav Yehoshua yielded to this argument, he later regretted having done so:

לְבָתַר דִּנְפַק אָמַר – **After [Rav Pappa] left** the field, **[Rav Huna the son of Rav Yehoshua] said** to himself: אַמַּאי לֹא אָמְרִי לֵיהּ – **Why did I not reply to [Rav Pappa]** as follows: כָּאן בְּתוֹךְ שֵׁשׁ עֶשְׂרֵה אַמָּה – **Here,** protected by the right that he had established in my property, are roots **within sixteen *amos*** of the tree, כָּאן חוּץ לְשֵׁשׁ עֶשְׂרֵה אַמָּה – while **here,** in the incident at issue, I was cutting roots that were **beyond sixteen *amos*.**[3]

The Mishnah states:

הָיָה חוֹפֵר בּוֹר שִׁיחַ וּמְעָרָה – IF [THE NEIGHBOR] WAS DIGGING A PIT, A DITCH, OR A VAULT, and came upon the roots, קוֹצֵץ וְיוֹרֵד – HE MAY CUT DOWNWARD to whatever depth he finds necessary, וְהָעֵצִים שֶׁלּוֹ (וכו׳) – AND THE WOOD cuttings ARE HIS.

The Gemara seeks a clarification of this ruling:

בְּעָא מִינֵּיהּ יַעֲקֹב הַדְיָיבָא מֵרַב חִסְדָּא – **Yaakov the Hadiyavian**[4] **inquired of Rav Chisda:** עֵצִים שֶׁל מִי – **To whom** do the **wood** cuttings belong – to the neighbor who cuts them or to the owner of the tree?[5]

אָמַר לֵיהּ תְּנִיתוּהָ – **[Rav Chisda] said to him: We learned [the answer]** to this question **in a Mishnah:**[6] שָׁרְשֵׁי אִילָן שֶׁל הֶדְיוֹט הַבָּאִין בְּשֶׁל הֶקְדֵּשׁ – The ROOTS OF A TREE THAT IS PRIVATELY OWNED[7] WHICH EXTEND INTO [LAND] OWNED BY THE TEMPLE TREASURY are subject to the following rule:[8] לֹא נֶהֱנִין – ONE MAY NOT DERIVE any BENEFIT from the roots, וְלֹא מוֹעֲלִין – BUT ONE DOES NOT COMMIT *ME'ILAH* by deriving benefit from them.[9]

Rav Chisda now explains the Mishnah's ruling and the proof that emerges from it:

אִי אָמְרַתְּ בִּשְׁלָמָא בָּתַר אִילָן אָזְלִינַן – **It is understandable if you say** that ownership of the roots **follows the tree** from which they grow;[10] מִשּׁוּם הָכִי לֹא מוֹעֲלִין – that is why one **does not commit *me'ilah*** by deriving benefit from these roots. Since roots growing in a neighboring property belong to the tree owner, these roots of a private tree are not Temple property and are therefore not subject to *me'ilah*.[11] אֶלָּא אִי אָמְרַתְּ בָּתַר קַרְקַע אָזְלִינַן – **But if you will say** that ownership of the roots **follows the ground** in which they grow, אַמַּאי לֹא מוֹעֲלִין – **why does one not commit *me'ilah*** by deriving benefit from the roots? If roots belong to the owner of the ground in which they grow, these roots that grew in Temple property belong to the Temple treasury and should be subject to *me'ilah!* We therefore learn from this Mishnah that roots belong to the tree owner, even if they grow in another person's property.

The Gemara challenges Rav Chisda's interpretation of the Mishnah:

אֶלָּא מַאי בָּתַר אִילָן אָזְלִינַן – **But what** is your conclusion – **that** ownership of the roots **follows the tree?** אֵימָא סֵיפָא – **I will cite the latter portion** of that same Mishnah, which contradicts your conclusion: שֶׁל הֶקְדֵּשׁ הַבָּאִים בְּשֶׁל הֶדְיוֹט – [ROOTS] OF a tree that is owned by THE TEMPLE TREASURY WHICH EXTEND INTO PRIVATELY HELD [PROPERTY][12] are subject to the following rule: לֹא נֶהֱנִין – ONE MAY NOT DERIVE any BENEFIT from the roots, וְלֹא מוֹעֲלִין – BUT ONE DOES NOT COMMIT *ME'ILAH* by deriving benefit from them. וְאִי בָּתַר אִילָן אָזְלִינַן – **Now, if** ownership of the roots **follows the tree,** אַמַּאי לֹא מוֹעֲלִין – **why does one not commit *me'ilah*** by deriving benefit from the roots? Since the tree is owned by the Temple treasury, its roots are also Temple property and should be subject to *me'ilah!* Thus, the latter part of the Mishnah contradicts Rav Chisda's conclusion that ownership of the roots follows the tree. – ? –

NOTES

1. In Talmudic days, fields were generally separated by narrow strips of land that were higher or lower than the fields themselves (*Rashbam* 53b ד״ה או). These strips would occasionally be used by the public as shortcuts to their own fields. Rav Yehudah ruled that if a property owner stood by while the public established a right of way on his boundary strip, and did not raise any objection, he could not afterward ruin their walkway and reclaim the strip for private use.

2. [Apparently, Rav Pappa's palm trees had been stationed on the boundary for some time before this incident occurred.] Rav Pappa claimed that since the trees had been there for so long with no objection raised by Rav Huna, he had established the right to let their root system develop on Rav Huna's property (*Rashi*). Accordingly, Rav Huna was now forbidden to destroy the roots, just as the owner of a boundary strip who stood by silently while the public established a walkway on his property cannot afterward ruin their walkway.

[*Tosafos* take issue with this explanation, noting that one is forbidden to take back only a right of way that was established by the *public*, not one that was established by an individual (such as Rav Pappa). They therefore offer alternative explanations for this passage.]

3. Although the root system of a tree extends for twenty-five *amos* (as indicated by the Mishnah on 25b), the tree is nourished chiefly by those roots that are within sixteen *amos*, as the Gemara will later prove. Therefore, establishing the right to develop a root system on a neighbor's property prohibits the neighbor from cutting only those roots that are within sixteen *amos* of the tree (*Rashi*). Roots that extend beyond sixteen *amos* are not essential to the tree's survival and are not protected by this right.

4. He was a native of the ancient nation of Adiabene, located in what is today northern Iraq (see *Aruch* ד״ה הדייב and ד״ה חדייב, with *Mossaf HaAruch*).

5. A simple reading of the Mishnah indicates that the roots belong to the neighbor who cuts them; presumably they are his because they grew in his property. However, one can argue that roots are a part of the tree and should belong to the owner of the tree. The wording of the Mishnah can be understood in this fashion as well. Thus, a clarification is necessary.

6. *Me'ilah* 13b.

7. Literally: that is a commoner's (property). [The term שֶׁל הֶדְיוֹט refers to property that is privately held, as opposed to שֶׁל הֶקְדֵּשׁ – property owned by the Temple treasury (*hekdesh*).]

8. While the Temple stood, it was common for people to consecrate property as a donation to the Temple treasury (*hekdesh*). (Such property would normally be sold by the Temple treasurers, who would then use the proceeds as necessary.) The Torah forbids private citizens to derive any benefit from property that belongs to *hekdesh*. If one inadvertently derived benefit from *hekdesh* property, one must pay *hekdesh* the value of that benefit plus a fine of one-fifth. Additionally, one is obligated to bring a sacrifice (see *Leviticus* 5:14-16; *Rashi* ad loc.). This transgression is known as *me'ilah*. The Mishnah now relates how the rule of *me'ilah* applies to roots of a privately held tree that grow in land belonging to *hekdesh*.

[*Me'ilah* does not apply to items that are attached to the ground [מְחוּבָּר לְקַרְקַע] (see *Me'ilah* 18b). The Mishnah's ruling applies after the roots are cut from the ground.]

9. I.e. he does not violate the Biblical prohibition of *me'ilah* and is not obligated to add a fifth to his payment, nor to bring a sacrifice. He must, however, pay for the benefit he has derived (*Rambam, Hil. Me'ilah* 1:6).

10. Literally: we follow the tree [in determining the owner of the roots].

11. Nevertheless, though the Biblical injunction of *me'ilah* does not apply, the Sages forbade one to derive any benefit from roots that grow in *hekdesh* property (*Rashi*). Accordingly, the Mishnah rules that one may not derive any benefit from these roots, but if he does, he has not committed *me'ilah*.

12. This is the inverse of the previously cited case.

עין משפט נר מצוה

צח א ב מיי' פ"ה מהל' מעילה הלכה ו:

צט ג מיי' שם ופ"י מהל' שכנים הל' ו סמג עשין פב טוש"ע ח"מ סי' קנה סעיף לב:

ק ד מיי' פ"ג מהלכות שמיטין הל' ו סמג לאוין רסו:

קא ה מיי' שם הל' ג:

רבינו גרשום

מצר שהחזיקו בו רבים אסור לקלקלו. ואבותי ואבות אבותי החזיקו בו מכמה שנים: לבתר דנפק רב פפא אמר רב הונא אמאי לא אמרי ליה כאן בתוך שש עשרה. סמוך למיצר אם נוטע ויוצאין שרשין מתחת ונכנסין לשדה חבירו קוצץ ויורד וכאן חוץ לט"ז אמה שהחזיקו כדין ושוב נכנסו שרשיו מתחת לשדה חבירו אמר רב יהודה דאסור לקלקלו: פיסקא הבאין בשל הקדש בשדה הקדש לא נהנין מהן מן השרשין לכתחלה א) אבל הנהנה מהן כדין הקדש היינו דלא מועלין דבתר אילן אזלי דשל הדיוט הוא מש"ה מה שקוצצין מן השרשים של האילן: ושל הקדש. אילן הקדש: לעולם בתר אילן אזלי שרשים. ואמאי אין מועלין בסיפא משום דאותן השרשים של הקדש שבאין בשדה הדיוט בגדולין של הקדש הבאין לשדה הדיוט לאחר שהוקדש עסקינן ומש"ה אין מועלין בגידולין דסבר אין מעילה בגידולין ב) דאמר אבותי הקדישו קורות ואנו נתיר גמזיות: ורבינא אמר. לעולם בתר אילן אזלינן ומש"ה לא מועלין ודקא קשיא לך בסיפא אמאי לא אזלינן בתר אילן ומועלין הא לא קשיא דרישא משום הכי אין מועלין דנוטע הוא בפחות מט"ז אמה סמוך למיצר אע"ג דאיכא למימר דיניק משל הקדש לא מועלין דשדינן עיקר בתר אילן אבל סיפא דקתני אילן של הקדש לא מועלין משום דנוטע חוץ לט"ז אמה הוא דליכא למימר דמשרשי הקדש הן הואיל שהוא רחוק כל כך מי שקוצץ אותן שרשים שהן לסוף ט"ז אמה אין מכחיש כלום באילן מש"ה אין מועלין. ומתני' דקתני העצים של מי אם בתוך ט"ז אמה חופר וקוצץ הן של בעל האילן ואם חוץ לט"ז אמה חופר וקוצץ הן של בעל [הקרקע]: אמר עולא אילן הסמוך למצר של שדה חבירו בתוך לט"ז אמה. שרשיו יונקין משדה חבירו ואין מביא מפירותיו ביכורין דאין יכול לקרות את ראשית פרי האדמה אשר נתתה לפי שיונק משדה אחרים: מנא ליה לעולא הא. דאילן יונק מכל צידיו עד שש עשרה אמה אילימא מדתנן במס' שביעית עשר נטיעות המפוזרין בתוך בית סאה

גמרא

עד דאמרי ליה הא א) דאמר רב יהודה מצר שהחזיקו בו רבים אסור לקלקלו לבתר דנפק אמר אמאי לא אמרי ליה כאן בתוך שש עשרה אמה כאן חוץ לשש עשרה אמה: היה חופר בור שיח ומערה קוצץ ויורד והעצים שלו (וכו'): בעא מיניה יעקב ב) הדריבא מרב חסדא עצים של מי אמר ליה תניתוה ג) א שרשי אילן של הדיוט הבאין בשל הקדש לא נהנין ולא מועלין אי אמרת בשלמא בתר אילן אזלינן משום הכי לא מועלין אלא אי אמרת בתר קרקע אזלינן אמאי לא מועלין אלא מאי בתר אילן אזלינן אימא סיפא ב של הקדש הבאים בשל הדיוט לא נהנין ולא מועלין ואי בתר אילן אזלינן אמאי לא מועלין מידי איריא בגידולין הבאין לאחר מכאן עסקינן וקא סבר אין מעילה בגידולין רבינא אמר לא קשיא ג כאן בתוך שש עשרה אמה כאן חוץ לשש עשרה אמה: אמר עולא אילן הסמוך למצר בתוך שש עשרה אמה גזלן הוא ואין מביאין ממנו בכורים מנא ליה לעולא הא אילימא ד) מדתנן ד עשר נטיעות המפוזרות בתוך בית סאה חורשין כל בית סאה בשבילן עד ראש השנה כמה הוו להו תרי אלפין וחמש מאה גרמידי לכל חד וחד כמה מטי ליה מאתן וחמשין הא לא הוי דעולא ואלא ה) מדתנן ה שלשה אילנות של ג' בני אדם הרי אלו מצטרפין וחורשין כל בית

רש"י

שהחזיקו בו רבים. לעשותו להן דרך אסור לקלקלו אע"פ שהוא של יחיד ולהכי נמי הא מחזיקי ליה: לבתר דנפק. רב פפא: אמר. רב הונא אמאי לא אמרי ליה: בתוך שש עשרה אמה. לאילן הויא חזקה דאילן אבל חוץ לשש עשרה אמה אין חזקתו חזקה שאע"פ ששרשיו מתפשטין כ"כ אמה אין יונקין אלא בתוך ט"ו אמה סמוך לאילן ולכי אמרינן לקמן ולעיל (א) הוא חוץ לט"ז אמה קיימא: הדריבא. למאן הדייק: לא נהנין. מדרבנן: ולא מועלין. אם נהנה לא מעל אלמא לאו קדשי: מידי איריא. מסקנא דקושיא הוא כלומר מכולה לאו מידי איריא ולא למשמע מינה בתר אילן ולא למשמע מינה בתר קרקע דטעמא משום דהנך שרשים גידולים הבאים לאחר שהוקדש האילן הוא ואיכא למ"ד במס' מעילה אין מועלין בגידולין אפי' שרשי הקדש בשדה הקדש: לא נהנין אלא מאיסורא ליה: רבינא אמר ל"ק. רישא דקתני בתר אילן אזלינן היינו בתוך ט"ז אמה וסיפא דקתני של הקדש הבאין בתוך של הדיוט לא מועלין היינו חוץ לט"ז: גזלן הוא. שיונק משדה חבירו: ואין מביאין ממנו בכורים. אין צריך להביא ממנו בכורים דבעינן אשר תביא מארצך (דברים כו): עשר נטיעות מפוזרות בבית סאה. לארכו ולרחבו כולן בשוה יונקות מכל בית סאה וכולם צריך להם ומותר לחורשו ערב שביעית עד ראש השנה שהלכה למשה מסיני הוא ובית סאה חמשים אמה על חמשים אמה שחצר המשכן קרוי בית סאתים והוא מאה על חמשים: כמה הוי להו. בית סאה כי עבדת (ב) להו רצועה של אמה רוחב: תרי אלפים וחמש מאה גרמידי. שהרי יש כאן נ' רצועות של חמשים אמה ועולות לאלפים וחמש מאות אמה חלוק אותן לעשר אילנות תמצא צירוף קרקע יניקת כל אילן ואילן בין הכל מאתן וחמשין אמה אורך באמה רוחב: הא לא הוי כדעולא. דשיעור עולא נפיש דאמר דאילן יונק שש עשרה (ג) לכל צד הרי ל"ב על ל"ב עשה מהן רצועה אחת של אמה רוחב כאשר עשית מבית סאה תמצאנה של אלף וכ"ד אמה שהרי יש כאן שלשים ושתים רצועות כל אחת ואחת ל"ב אמה: ואלא מדתנן שלשה אילנות. גדולים שיונקים יותר מן הנטיעות ומפוזרין בבית סאה לארכו ולרחבו בשוה אע"פ ו) שאינו של אדם אחד אלא של שלשה בני אדם מצטרפין להיות שדה אילן ולחרוש כל בית סאה בשבילן ערב שביעית עד עצרת כדין שדה אילן ואם לאו אין חורשין אלא כל אחד כדי צרכו דהיינו תחתיו וחוצה לו כמלא אורה וסלו והשאר הוי שדה הלבן ואין חורשין אותו אלא עד הפסח: בית

תוספות

עד דאמרי ליה הא דאמר רב יהודה מיצר שהחזיקו כו'. תימה מאי מייתי מרב יהודה דרבים שאני דלאו הכי קשיא מתני' דקתני קוצץ ויורד ופירש ר"ח וריב"ם דרבים החזיקו במצריה דרב הונא וברשותו דלאו הכי אין חזקתו מועלת כדמשמע בהמניח (ב"ק דף כח. ושם) ואתא רב הונא וקא חפר ברשות הרבים וקצץ שרשים דרב פפא ומשום הכי פריך מדרב יהודה דכיון שהחזיקו בו רבים אינו רשאי לחפור והא דקאמר אמאי לא אמרי ליה כאן בתוך שש עשרה אמה וכו' ה"פ כלומר כי קאמר רב יהודה מצר שהחזיקו בו רבים אסור לקלקלו ה"מ תוך ט"ז אמה אבל חוץ לט"ז אמה מותר לקלקלו כיון שמניח ט"ז אמה כדין רשות הרבים ובסוף חזקת הבתים (לקמן דף ס:) דאסר רבי יוחנן לאדם שכנס תוך שלו להחזיר כתלים במקומן אע"ג דליכא רווחא כדמשמע התם אליבא דר"ל הכא איכא רווחא רווחא דקאמר התם (ד) שאינו סותם כל רשות הרבים אבל ליכא רווחא ט"ז אמה אבל אי איכא רווחא ט"ז אמה מודה רבי יוחנן דמותר לקלקלו ומחזיר כתלים למקומן כדאמר הכא ומיהו קשה מאי קאמר רב פפא אמרי ליה מכולהי מאי כולהי ומפרש ה"ר מנחם דמכולהי היינו מכל הני דתנן אם האילן קדם לא יקוץ ספק כו' ולא יכלי ליה שהיה דוחה אותו דמיירי באילן עצמו אבל השרשים יקוץ ור"ח מפרש דרב הונא היה קוצץ ולוקח השרשים לעצמו וא"ל רב פפא מאי האי כלומר למה אתה לוקח השרשים לעצמך א"ל דתנן קוצץ ויורד וכיון שבדין אני קוצץ כמו כן יהו העצים שלי ואמרי ליה מכולהי היינו הנהו דמייתי הכא והיא דמייתי לקמן שרשי אילן הדיוט הבאים כו' דמינה מוכח לקמן דהעצים שלו דקתני במתני' היינו של בעל האילן ולא יכלי ליה שדחה לו כדדחי ליה לקמן עד דא"ל מרב יהודה כו' דנהי שלא תועיל חזקתי כחזקת רבים לענין שלא תהא רשאי לקוצצו לענין זה מיהא תועיל שיהו העצים שלי ומסיק אמאי לא אמרי ליה חוץ לשש עשרה יש להיות העצים שלי כדאמר רבינא לקמן כאן תוך שש עשרה כו':

אלא הכא בגידולין הבאין לאחר מכאן. ויש ספרים דגרסי מידי איריא הא בגידולין וכל זה מדברי המקשה כלומר על כרחך לא תוכל לפשוט מכאן דבגידולין הבאין לאחר מכאן איירי ואי בתר אילן אזלינן רישא אשמועינן דאין נהנין וסיפא אשמועינן דאין מועלין ואי בתר קרקע אזלינן רישא אשמועינן דאין מועלין וסיפא דאין נהנין בגידולין וא"ת ההיא בבא דאשמועינן דאין מעילה בגידולין לשמעינן של הקדש הבאין בשל הקדש דהוי רבותא טפי וי"ל דנקט הכי משום אידך בבא דאשמועינן דאין נהנין דהוי רבותא טפי שאין הכל של הקדש ור"ח לא גרים אלא והמתרץ הוא דקאמר הכי דמוקי סיפא דאין מעילה בגידולין והא דלא נקט דשל הקדש בשל הקדש משום דבעי למינקט דומיא דרישא דאין הכל דהקדש אלא חד דהקדש וחד דהדיוט אבל אי בתר קרקע אזלינן ורישא אשמועינן דאין מעילה בגידולין ליתני רישא של הקדש בשל הקדש דאין מיושב כל כך לומר תנא רישא אגב סיפא כמו תנא סיפא אגב רישא: **רבינא** אמר לא קשיא כאן תוך ט"ז כו'. רישא בתוך ט"ז אמה דבתר אילן אזלינן וסיפא חוץ לט"ז אמה דבתר קרקע אזלינן ואם תאמר וליתני אידי ואידי תוך ט"ז וליתני סיפא מועלין אי נמי אידי ואידי אחר ט"ז וליתני ברישא מועלין וי"ל דתנא הכי לאשמועינן דבתרוייהו בין בתוך ט"ז אמה בין חוץ לט"ז אמה לא נהנין ולא מועלין: **גזלן** הוא ואין מביאין ממנו בכורים. פי' ר"ח משום דאין מביאין גזל על גבי המזבח שנאמר אני ה' שונא גזל בעולה (ישעיה סא) וכתיב והבאתם גזול וגו' (מלאכי א) ולית לן דעולא דהא בהדיא פסקינן כרבי יוסי דאמר זה נוטע בתוך שלו כו' וא"ת לפירושו עולא כמאן סבר דכרבנן נמי לא הוי דרבנן לא בעו הרחקה אלא ד' אמות ולעולא שש עשרה אמה וי"ל דעולא הוי מוקי מתניתין בצונמא כדמוקי לה בריש פירקין ולהכי לא בעי אלא ד' אמות ומיהו קשיא לרבי יצחק דפריך לקמן לעולא מהקונה אילן וקרקעו מביא וקורא מאי לאו כל שהוא ומאי קושיא שאני התם שקנאו ולא הוה גזלן ונראה כפי' הקונטרס ° דאע"ג דמותר לסמוך אין מביאין ממנו בכורים דבעינן אשר תביא מארצך ולקמן דאמר אילן הסמוך מביא וקורא שעל מנת כן הנחיל יהושע את הארץ לא קאמר שעל מנת כן הנחיל שיהא מותר לסמוך דבלאו הכי שרי אלא על מנת כן הנחיל שיהא חשוב כמו מארצך ויכול לומר (ה) אשר נתת לי: **עשר** נטיעות המפוזרות כו'. בסוכה (דף לד.) אמר עשר נטיעות וערבה וניסוך המים הלכה למשה מסיני ודוקא עשר לתוך בית סאה אבל פחות אין צריכין חרישה כל כך וכן נמי אם היו בבית סאה יותר מעשר נטיעות אין חורשין לפי שעומדין ליעקר: כמה

מסורת הש"ס

א) ב"ק כח. לעיל יב. ע"ש ולקמן ס: וקף ק., ב) בס"י אימת הדריבא, ג) מעילה יג:, ד) שביעית פ"א מ"ה, ה) שם מ"ה, ו) בס"י מדריבא, ז) נ"ל שאין.

הגהות הב"ח

(א) רש"י ד"ה בתוך שש וכו' ולקמן חוץ לט"ז ומיהת הוא ולמקמן: (ב) ד"ה כמה וכו' כי עבדת ליה לרצועה אחת של אמה: (ג) ד"ה הא לא וכו' שש עשרה אמה לכל: (ד) תוס' ד"ה עד דאמרי ליה הא דאמר רב יהודה וכו' דקאמר התם היינו שאינו סותם: (ה) ד"ה גזלן וכו' ויכול לומר מן האדמה אשר נתת לי:

גליון הש"ס

תוס' ד"ה גזלן כו' דאע"ג דמותר לסמוך. עיין בר"ש ריש בכורים:

ליקוטי רש"י

מצר. שביל של שדות [רשב"ם לקמן ס:]. שהחזיקו בו רבים. שהשווהו ותקנוהו להלוך והבעלים ידעו ושתקו אסור לקלקלו דודאי לרבים מחל [רשב"ם לקמן ק.]. שרשי אילן של הדיוט הבאין בשל הקדש לא נהנין ולא מועלין. דאזלינן בתר אילן ואילן בשל הדיוט קאי. של הקדש הבאים בשל הדיוט. נמי לא מועלין ולא נהנין הואיל ועיקרו קאי של הקדש [מעילה יג:]. [מכאן שייך לדף כז.] כמה מרובע יתר על העיגול רביע. דהכל כל עיגול שרחבו אמה יש בו היקף שלש אמות כדאמרי' במתני' ואם היה מרובע אמה על אמה היה לו היקף ד' אמות אמה לכל רוח נמצא מרובע יתר על העגול רביע [עירובין יד:]. מתני' היא בא[הלות] ותשע מדות והדברים נראין לעינים דאילו עגולה חוט שלש אמות מקיפה ואמה מרובעת צריכה חוט ד' אמה לכל רוח [סוכה ח.] ועיי"ש במסורת הש"ס. ר"ע אומר קרקע כל שהוא חייב וכו'. ובוידוי לא גרסי' בסדר המשנה דבשלמא גבי פאה שדך כתיב קרקע כל שהוא גבי בכורים כתיב ראשית פרי האדמה אשר נתתה לי ולכתוב עליה פרוזבול הכי תקון רבנן אם יש לו ללוה קרקע כותבין פרוזבול למלוה לגבות חובו בשביעית דדמי כמאן דאית ליה משכון [illegible]

אע"ג דכתיב ביה (דברים כו) השקיפה ממעון קדשך וגו' ואת האדמה אשר נתתה לנו [וגו'] [illegible]

[illegible]

The Gemara continues its rebuttal of Rav Chisda's conclusion by providing an alternative explanation of the Mishnah:

מִידֵי אִירְיָא – In truth, **is [the Mishnah] at all relevant** to the question of to whom the roots belong? No, for the following reason: בְּגִידוּלִין הַבָּאִין לְאַחַר מִכָּאן עַסְקִינָן – In this Mishnah, **we are dealing with** a new **growth** of roots, **that came** into being **after [the property was consecrated].**[13] With new growth, the question of ownership is irrelevant, וְקָא סָבַר אֵין מְעִילָה בְּגִידוּלִין – because **[the Tanna]** of this Mishnah **holds** that new **growth is not subject to** ***me'ilah,*** even if produced by property that belongs to the Temple treasury.[14] Therefore, whether roots belong to the tree owner or to the landowner, they are not subject to *me'ilah* in this case. Thus, the Mishnah offers no indication as to the ownership of the roots.

The Gemara presents another interpretation of the Mishnah cited:

רָבִינָא אָמַר לֹא קַשְׁיָא – **Ravina said:** The contradiction between the first and latter case of the Mishnah presents **no difficulty,** for the following reason: כָּאן – **Here,** in the first case, which implies that roots belong to the tree owner, בְּתוֹךְ שֵׁשׁ עֶשְׂרֵה אַמָּה – we are dealing with roots that are **within sixteen** ***amos*** of the tree, כָּאן – while **here,** in the latter case, which implies that roots belong to the landowner, חוּץ לְשֵׁשׁ עֶשְׂרֵה אַמָּה – we are dealing with roots that extend **beyond sixteen** ***amos.***[15]

Having concluded that roots within sixteen *amos* nourish a tree, the Gemara cites a related law:

אָמַר עוּלָּא – **Ulla said:** אִילָן הַסָּמוּךְ לַמֵּצַר בְּתוֹךְ שֵׁשׁ עֶשְׂרֵה אַמָּה – **A tree that is within sixteen** ***amos*** **of a boundary** גַּזְלָן הוּא – **is a "thief,"** because it draws nutrients illegally from the neighboring field. וְאֵין מְבִיאִין מִמֶּנּוּ בִּכּוּרִים – **Accordingly, one does not bring** ***bikkurim*** (i.e. first-fruit offerings) **from [its fruits].**[16]

The Gemara seeks a source for the assertion that a tree draws nourishment from the area within sixteen *amos*:

מְנָא לֵיהּ לְעוּלָּא הָא – **From where does Ulla derive this** measurement? אִילֵימָא מִדְּתְנַן – **If you will say** that he derives it **from that which we learned in a Mishnah,** with regard to pre-*Shemittah* cultivation:[17] עֶשֶׂר נְטִיעוֹת הַמְפוּזָּרוֹת בְּתוֹךְ בֵּית סְאָה – TEN SAPLINGS THAT ARE evenly DISTRIBUTED THROUGHOUT A *BEIS SE'AH*[18] qualify for the following leniency: חוֹרְשִׁין כָּל בֵּית סְאָה בִּשְׁבִילָן עַד רֹאשׁ הַשָּׁנָה – ONE MAY PLOW THE ENTIRE *BEIS SE'AH* ON THEIR ACCOUNT UNTIL ROSH HASHANAH of the *Shemittah* year, because plowing the field contributes to the saplings' development and does not merely prepare the land for *Shemittah* growth.[19] We learn from this Mishnah that ten saplings draw nourishment from an entire *beis se'ah.*

The Gemara now calculates the area allotted for each sapling:

כַּמָּה הָווּ לְהוּ – **How many** square *amos* **are** in **[a** ***beis se'ah*****]?** תְּרֵי אַלְפִין וַחֲמֵשׁ מְאָה גַּרְמִידֵי – **Two thousand five hundred square** ***amos.*** לְכָל חַד וְחַד כַּמָּה מָטֵי לֵיהּ – **How much** does that **come to for each [sapling]?** מָאתָן וְחַמְשִׁין – **Two hundred fifty** square *amos.*[20]

The Gemara asks:

הָא לָא הָוֵי דְּעוּלָּא – **That is not** as great as **Ulla's** measurement! According to Ulla, a tree is nourished by sixteen *amos* of soil in each direction, an area of 1,024 square *amos*![21] –?–

NOTES

13. I.e. a person consecrated a field to the Temple treasury, and an adjoining tree later developed a root system in that field (in the first case of the Mishnah), or a person consecrated a tree to the Temple treasury and its roots later spread into an adjoining field (in the latter case of the Mishnah).

14. The Mishnah (*Me'ilah* 13a) records a dispute as to whether the law of *me'ilah* applies to new growth that accumulated on property owned by *hekdesh* (e.g. roots, tree branches, fruit). Although the new growth *belongs* to *hekdesh*, there is an opinion that it is not subject to *me'ilah* because it was not consecrated by a human donor, but merely accumulated naturally on *hekdesh* property (*Ramban* et al., below, 79a; see also *Tosefos R' Akiva* to *Me'ilah* 3:6 and *Ketzos HaChoshen* 200:1). Now, the Mishnah cited here rules that *me'ilah* does not apply to any roots, whether roots of a private tree that extend into *hekdesh* property, or roots of a *hekdesh* tree that extend into private property. Therefore, the Gemara reasons that this Mishnah must refer to roots that grew after the property was consecrated, and follows the opinion that new growth is not subject to *me'ilah* (*Rashi*). [Nevertheless, the Rabbis decreed that one is forbidden to derive any benefit from such new growth.]

15. As explained above (note 3), a tree draws nourishment chiefly from the area within sixteen *amos*. Therefore, Ravina explains, only the roots within sixteen *amos* are considered a part of the tree itself and belong to the tree owner. Roots beyond sixteen *amos* belong to the owner of the land in which they grow (just as one owns a new seedling that sprouts on his property). [The Mishnah cited is to be understood as follows: Roots of a private tree that extend into *hekdesh* property [within sixteen *amos* of the tree] are not subject to *me'ilah* (because they belong to the tree owner). Roots of a *hekdesh* tree that extend into private property [beyond sixteen *amos*] are not subject to *me'ilah* (because they belong to the landowner) (*Rashi*).]

Thus, the Gemara's original question — when a neighbor cuts roots that grew in his property, to whom do these roots belong — has now been resolved: Roots within sixteen *amos* of the tree belong to the tree owner, while roots beyond sixteen *amos* belong to the landowner.

16. The Torah obligates landowners in Eretz Yisrael to bring the first fruits of each year's crop of any of the seven species with which Eretz Yisrael is praised to the Temple and give them to a Kohen. However, the Torah qualifies this commandment as follows (*Deuteronomy* 26:2): וְלָקַחְתָּ מֵרֵאשִׁית כָּל־פְּרִי הָאֲדָמָה אֲשֶׁר תָּבִיא מֵאַרְצְךָ – *And you shall take from the first of all fruits of the earth that you bring* ***from your land...*** Thus, only fruit that grows from one's own land falls under this obligation. Fruit of a tree that draws nourishment from a neighbor's land is exempt from *bikkurim* (*Rashi*). [*Tosafos* offer another reason: Stolen produce is unfit for Temple service. Therefore, the fruit of this tree cannot be offered at the Temple.]

17. *Sheviis* 1:6. In the days of the Temple, it was forbidden to cultivate land in preparation for the *Shemittah* (Sabbatical) year (see *Rambam's Commentary* to *Sheviis* 1:1). For example, it was forbidden to plow a grain field after Pesach or an orchard after Shavuos of the year before *Shemittah*, because such plowing merely served to prepare the ground for *Shemittah* (*Sheviis* 1:1, 2:1). On the other hand, cultivation that provided an immediate benefit to the land was permitted until the very end of the pre-*Shemittah* year. This Mishnah describes a case in which plowing is permitted until the *Shemittah* year begins.

18. An area fifty *amos* square is known as a *beis se'ah* (literally: room for a *se'ah*) because it is suitable for sowing a *se'ah* of barley grain.

19. If the saplings are scattered over a larger area or condensed in a smaller area, one may not plow the entire *beis se'ah*, but only a small patch of land around each tree (see *Sheviis* ibid.).

20. As noted above, a *beis se'ah* is fifty *amos* square, and thus amounts to 2,500 square *amos*, or 250 square *amos* for each of the ten saplings.

Rashi's method for calculating square *amos* differs from the method commonly used today. *Rashi* explains the Gemara as follows: A *beis se'ah* (50x50) can be divided into fifty strips of land, each fifty *amos* long and an *amah* wide. Placed end to end, these would form a strip 2,500 *amos* long. Divide by ten and the result is that each sapling can be allotted a strip 250 *amos* long and an *amah* wide (i.e. 250 square *amos*).

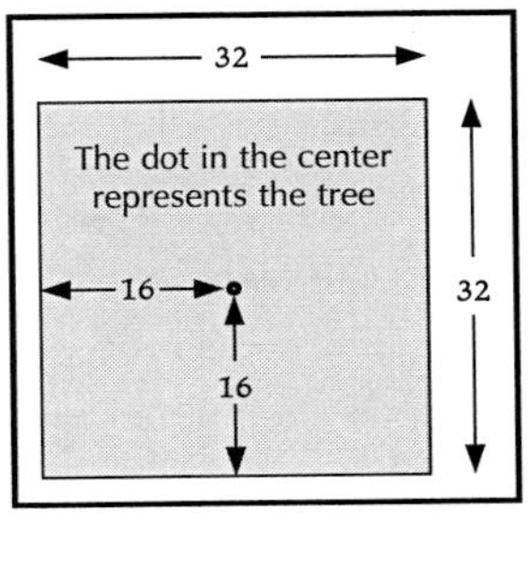

32

The dot in the center represents the tree

16

32

16

21. At this point, the Gemara assumes that the area from which a tree draws its sustenance forms a square, with the tree in the middle. Counting outward from the tree sixteen *amos* in each direction results in a square 32 *amos* across, or an area of 1,024 square *amos*. See diagram.

עין משפט נר מצוה

צח א ב מיי' פ"ט מהל' מעילה הלכה ו:
צט ג מיי' שם ופ"י מהל' שכנים הל' ו סמג עשין פב טוש"ע ח"מ סי' קנה סעיף לב:
ק ד מיי' פ"ג מהלכות שמיטין הל' ה סמג לאוין רסז:
קא ה מיי' שם הל' ג:

עד דאמרי ליה הא [א] דאמר רב יהודה מצר שהחזיקו בו רבים אסור לקלקלו לבתר דנפק אמר אמאי לא אמרי ליה כאן בתוך לשש עשרה אמה כאן חוץ לשש עשרה אמה: היה חופר בור שיח ומערה קוצץ ויורד והעצים שלו (וכו'): בעא מיניה יעקב [ג] הדייבא מרב חסדא עצים של מי אמר ליה תניתוה [ג] [א] שרשי אילן של הדיוט הבאין בשל הקדש לא נהנין ולא מועלין אי אמרת בשלמא בתר אילן אזלינן משום הכי לא מועלין אלא אי אמרת בתר קרקע אזלינן אמאי לא מועלין אלא מאי בתר אילן אזלינן אימא סיפא [ב] של הקדש הבאים בשל הדיוט לא נהנין ולא מועלין ואי בתר אילן אזלינן אמאי לא מועלין מידי איריא בגידולין הבאין לאחר מכאן עסקינן וקא סבר אין מעילה בגידולין רבינא אמר לא קשיא [ג] כאן בתוך שש עשרה אמה כאן חוץ לשש עשרה אמה: אמר עולא אילן הסמוך למצר בתוך שש עשרה אמה גוזלן הוא ואין מביאין ממנו בכורים מנא ליה לעולא הא אילימא [ז] מדתנן [ד] עשר נטיעות המפוזרות בתוך בית סאה חורשין כל בית סאה בשבילן עד ראש השנה כמה הוו להו תרי אלפין וחמש מאה גרמידי לכל חד וחד כמה מטי ליה מאתן וחמשין הא לא הוי דעולא ואלא [ה] מדתנן [ה] שלשה אילנות של ג' בני אדם הרי אלו מצטרפין וחורשין כל בית

רש"י

שהחזיקו בו רבים. לעשותו להן דרך אסור לקלקלו אע"פ שהוא של יחיד ולהא נמי הוה אחזיקו ליה: לבתר דנפק. רב פפא: אמר. רב הונא אמאי לא אמרי ליה: בתוך שש עשרה אמה. דאילן הוא מחזיק דאילן אבל חוץ לשש עשרה אמה אין חזקתו חזקה שאע"פ ששרשיו מתפשטין כ"ה אמה אין יונקין אלא בתוך ט"ז אמה סמוך לאילן וכדאמרינן לקמן ולהא (א) הוא חוץ לט"ז אמה קיימא: [י] הדייבא. דמן הדייב: לא נהנין. מדרבנן: ולא מועלין. אם נהנה לא מעל אלמא לא קדשי: מידי איריא. מסקנא דקושיא הוא כלומר מכולה לאו איריא היא לא למשמע מינה בתר אילן ולא למשמע מינה בתר קרקע לטעמא משום דהנך שרשים גידולים הבאים לאחר שהוקדש האילן הוא והיא למ"ד במס' מעילה אין מועלין בגידולין אפי' שרשי הקדש בשדה הקדש: לא נהנין לאיטריכא ליה: רבינא אמר ל"ק. רישא דקתני בתר אילן אזלינן היינו בתוך ט"ז אמה וסיפא דקתני של הקדש הבאין בתוך של הדיוט לא מועלין היינו חוץ לט"ז: גזלן הוא. שיונק משדה חבירו: ואין מביאין ממנו בכורים. אין לריך להביא ממנו בכורים דבעינן אשר תביא מארצך (דברים כו): עשר נטיעות מפוזרות בבית סאה. לארכו ולרחבו כולן בשוה יונקות מכל בית סאה וכולם לריך להם ומותר לחורשו ערב שביעית עד ראש השנה שהלכה למשה מסיני הוא ובית סאה חמשים אמה על חמשים אמה שאמר המשכן קרוי בית סאתים והוא מאה על חמשים: כמה הוי להו. בית סאה כי עבדת (ב) להו רלועה של אמה רוחב: תרי אלפים וחמש מאה גרמידי. שהרי יש כאן נ' רלועות של חמשים אמה ועולות לאלפים וחמש מאות אמה חלוק אותן לעשר אילנות תמלא לירוף קרקע יניקת כל אילן ואילן בין הכל מאתן וחמשין אמה אורך באמה רוחב: הא לא הוי כדעולא. דשיעור עולא נפיש דאמר דאילן יונק שש עשרה (ג) לכל לד הרי ל"ב על ל"ב עשה מהן רלועה אחת של אמה רוחב כאשר עשית מבית סאה תמלאנה של אלף וכ"ד אמה שהרי יש כאן שלשים ושתים רלועות כל אחת ואחת ל"ב אמה: ואלא מדתנן שלשה אילנות. גדולים שיונקים יותר מן הנטיעות ומפוזרין בבית סאה לארכו ולרחבו בשוה אע"פ [ו] שאינו של אדם אחד אלא של שלשה בני אדם מצטרפין להיות שדה אילן ולחרוש כל בית סאה בשבילן ערב שביעית עד עלרת כדין שדה אילן ואם לאו אין חורשין אלא כל אחד כדי לרכו דהיינו תחתיו וחוצה לו כמלא אורה וסלו והשאר הוי שדה הלבן ואין חורשין אותו אלא עד הפסח:
בית

תוספות

עד דאמרי ליה הא דאמר רב יהודה מיצר שהחזיקו כו'. תימה מאי מייתי מרב יהודה דרבים שאני דלאו הכי קשיא מתני' דקתני קוצץ ויורד ופירש ר"ח וריב"ם דרבים החזיקו במליאה דרב הונא וברשותו דלאו הכי אין חזקתו מועלת כדמשמע בהמניח (ב"ק דף כח. ושם) ואתא רב הונא וקא חפר ברשות הרבים וקלץ שרשים לרב פפא ומשום הכי פריך מדרב יהודה דכיון שהחזיקו בו רבים אינו רשאי לחפור והא דקאמר אמאי לא אמרי ליה כאן בתוך וכו' ה"פ כלומר כי קאמר רב יהודה מלר שהחזיקו בו רבים אסור לקלקלו ה"מ תוך ט"ז אמה אבל חוץ לט"ז אמה מותר לקלקלו כיון שמניח ט"ז אמה כדין רשות הרבים ובסוף חזקת הבתים (לקמן דף נ:) דאסר רבי יוחנן לאדם שכנס תוך שלו להחזיר כתלים במקומן אע"ג דליכא רווחא כדמשמע התם אליבא דר"ל הכא איכא רווחא דקאמר התם (ד) שאינו קונה כל רשות הרבים אבל ליכא רווחא ט"ז אמה אבל אי איכא רווחא ט"ז אמה מודה רבי יוחנן דמותר לקלקלו ומחזיר כתלים למקומן כדאמר הכלל ומיהו קשה מאי קאמר רב פפא אמרי ליה מכולהי מאי מכולהי ומפרש ה"ר מנחם דמכולהי היינו מכל הני דתנן אם האילן קדם לא יקוץ ספק כו' ולא יכלי ליה שהיה דוחה אותו דמיירי באילן עלמו אבל השרשים יקוץ ור"ח מפרש דרב הונא היה קולץ ולוקח השרשים לעלמו וא"ל רב פפא מאי האי כלומר למה אתה לוקח השרשים לעלמך א"ל דתנן קולץ ויורד וכיון שבדין אני קולץ כמו כן יהו העלים שלי ואמרי ליה מכולהי היינו הנהו דמייתי הכא והיא דמייתי לקמן שרשי אילן הדיוט הבאים כו' דמינה מוכח לקמן דהעלים שלו דקתני במתני' היינו של בעל האילן ולא יכלי ליה שדחה לו כדדחי ליה לקמן עד דא"ל מרב יהודה כו' דנהי שלא תועיל חזקתי כחזקת רבים לענין שלא תהא רשאי לקוללו לענין זה מיהא תועיל שיהו העלים שלי ומסיק אמאי לא אמרי ליה חוץ לשש עשרה יש להיות העלים שלי כדאמר רבינא לקמן כאן תוך שש עשרה כו':

אלא הכא בגידולין הבאין לאחר מכאן. ויש ספרים דגרסי מידי איריא הא בגידולין וכל זה מדברי המקשה כלומר על כרחך לא תוכל לפשוט מכאן דבגידולין הבאין לאחר מכאן איירי ואי בתר אילן אזלינן רישא אשמועינן דאין נהנין וסיפא אשמועינן דאין מועלין ואי בתר קרקע אזלינן רישא אשמועינן דאין מועלין וסיפא דאין נהנין בגידולין וא"ת ההיא בבא דאשמועינן דאין מעילה בגידולין לשמעינן של הקדש הבאין בשל הקדש דהוי רבותא טפי וי"ל דנקט הכי משום אידך בבא דאשמועינן דאין נהנין דהוי רבותא טפי שאין הכל של הקדש ור"ח לא גריס אלא והמתרץ הוא דקאמר הכי דמוקי סיפא דאין מעילה בגידולין והא דלא נקט דשל הקדש בשל הקדש משום דבעי למינקט דומיא דרישא דאין הכל דהקדש אלא חד דהקדש וחד דהדיוט אבל אי בתר קרקע אזלינן ורישא אשמועינן דאין מעילה בגידולין ליתני רישא של הקדש בשל הקדש דאין מיושב כל כך לומר תנא רישא אגב סיפא כמו תנא סיפא אגב רישא:

רבינא אמר לא קשיא כאן תוך ט"ז כו'. רישא בתוך ט"ז אמה דבתר אילן אזלינן וסיפא חוץ לט"ז אמה דבתר קרקע אזלינן ואם תאמר וליתני אידי ואידי תוך ט"ז וליתני סיפא מועלין אי נמי אידי ואידי אחר ט"ז וליתני ברישא מועלין וי"ל דתנא הכי לאשמועינן דבתרוייהו בין בתוך ט"ז אמה בין חוץ לט"ז אמה לא נהנין ולא מועלין:

גזלן הוא ואין מביאין ממנו בכורים. פי' ר"ח משום דאין מביאין גזל על גבי המזבח שנאמר אני ה' שונא גזל בעולה (ישעיה סא) וכתיב והבאתם גזול וגו' (מלאכי א) ולית לן דעולא דהא בהדיא פסקינן כרבי יוסי דאמר זה נוטע בתוך שלו כו' וא"ת לפירושו עולא כמאן סבר דכרבנן נמי לא הוי דרבנן לא בעו הרחקה אלא ד' אמות ולעולא שש עשרה אמה וי"ל דעולא הוי מוקי מתניתין בגוונא כדמוקי לה בריש פירקין והכי לא בעי אלא ד' אמות ומיהו קשיא לרבי יצחק דפריך לקמן לעולא מהקונה אילן וקרקעו מביא וקורא מאי לאו כל שהוא ומאי קושיא שאני התם שקנאו ולא הוה גזלן ונראה כפי' הקונטרס [ס] דאע"ג דמותר לסמוך אין מביאין ממנו בכורים דבעינן אשר תביא מארצך ולקמן דאמר אילן הסמוך מביא וקורא שעל מנת כן הנחיל יהושע את הארץ לא קאמר שעל מנת כן הנחיל שיהא מותר לסמוך דבלאו הכי שרי אלא על מנת כן הנחיל שיהא חשוב כמו מארצך ויכול לומר (ה) אשר נתת לי:

עשר נטיעות המפוזרות כו'. בסוכה (דף לד.) אמר עשר נטיעות וערבה וניסוך המים הלכה למשה מסיני ודוקא עשר לתוך בית סאה אבל פחות אין לריכין חרישה כל כך וכן נמי אם היו בבית סאה יותר מעשר נטיעות אין חורשין לפי שעומדין ליעקר:
כמה

רבינו גרשום

מצר שהחזיקו בו רבים אסור לקלקלו. ואבותי ואבות אבותי החזיקו בו מכמה שנים: לבתר דנפק רב פפא אמר רב הונא אמאי לא אמרי ליה כאן בתוך שש עשרה. סמוך למיצר אם נטוע ויוצאין שרשין מתחת ונכנסין לשדה חבירו קוצץ ויורד וכאן חוץ לט"ז אמה שהרחיק כדין ושוב נכנסו שרשיו מתחת לשדה חבירו אמר רב יהודה דאסור לקלקל: פיסקא הבאין בשל הקדש בשדה הקדש לא נהנין מן השרשים לכתחלה [א] אבל הנהנה מהן כדין הקדש היינו דלא מועלין דבתר אילן אזלי דשל הדיוט הוא משי"ה מה שקוצצין מן השרשים הן לבעל האילן: ושל הקדש. אילן הקדש: לעולם בתר אילן אזלינן. ואמאי אין מועלין בסיפא משום דאותן השרשים של הדיוט שבאין בשדה הקדש בגידולין של הקדש הבאין לשדה הדיוט לאחר שהוקדש עסקינן ומש"ה אין מועלין דסבר אין מועלין בגידולין [ב] דאמר אבותי הקדישו קורות ואנו נהיר גמזיות: ורבינא אמר. לעולם בתר אילן אזלינן ומש"ה לא מועלין ודקא קשיא לך בסיפא אמאי לא אזלינן בתר אילן ומועלין הא לא קשיא דרישא משום הכי אין מועלין דנטוע הוא בפחות מט"ז אמה סמוך למיצר אע"ג דאיכא למימר דמיניה הוא משל הקדש לא מועלין דשרשין עיקרו בתר אילן אבל סיפא דקתני דאילן של הקדש לא מועלין משום דהרחיק מט"ז אמות הוא נטוע דליכא למימר דמשרשי הקדש הוא דהואיל דהקדש הן רחוק כל כך מי שקוצץ אותן שרשים שהן לסוף ט"ז אמה אין מחשיב כלום באילן משי"ה אין מועלין. ומתני' דקתני העצים של מי אם בתוך ט"ז אמה חופר וקוצץ הן של בעל האילן ואם חוץ לט"ז אמה חופר וקוצץ הן של בעל הקרקע: אמר עולא אילן הסמוך למצר של שדה חבירו בתוך לט"ז אמה. שרשיו יונקין משדה חבירו ואין מביא מפירותיו ביכורין דאין יכול לקרות את ראשית פרי האדמה אשר נתתה לפי שיונק משדה אחרים: מנא ליה לעולא הא. דאילן יונק מכל צידיו עד שש עשרה אמה אילימא מדתנן במס' שביעית עשר נטיעות המפוזרות בתוך בית סאה

מסורת הש"ס

א) ב"ק כח. לעיל יב. ע"ש ולקמן נ: ודף ק., ב) בס"י איתא הדייבא, ג) מעילה יג:, ד) שביעית פ"א מ"ה, ה) ג"ז שם מ"ב, ו) [בס"י חדייבא], ז) [צ"ל שאינו:]

הגהות הב"ח

(א) רש"י ד"ה בתוך שש וכו' ולהא חוץ לט"ז ותיבת הוא נמחק: (ב) ד"ה כמה וכו' כי עבדת ליה רלועה אחת של אמה: (ג) ד"ה הא לא וכו' שש עשרה אמה לכל: (ד) תוס' ד"ה עד דאמרי ליה הא דאמר רב יהודה וכו' דקאמר התם היינו שאינו קונה: (ה) ד"ה גזלן וכו' ויכול לומר מן האדמה אשר נתת לי:

גליון הש"ס

תוס' ד"ה גזלן כו' דאע"ג דמותר לסמוך. עיין בר"ש ריש בכורים:

ליקוטי רש"י

מצר. שבין שתי שדות [רשב"ם לקמן ס:]. שהחזיקו בו רבים. שבשוהו ודקקוהו להלוך והעלים ידעו ושתקו אסור לקלקלו דודאי לרבים מחל [רשב"ם לקמן ק.]. שרשי אילן של הדיוט הבאין בשל הקדש לא נהנין ולא מועלין. דאזלינן בתר אילן ואילן בשל הדיוט קאי. של הקדש הבאים בשל הדיוט. נמי לא מועלין ולא נהנין הואיל ועיקרו קאי בשל הקדש [מעילה יג:]. כמה מרובע יתר על העיגול רביע. דהא כל עיגול שרבעו אמה יש בו היקף שלש אמות כדתנן במתני' ואם היה מרובע אמה על אמה היה לו היקף ד' אמות נמלא רוח מרובע יתר על העגול רביע [עירובין יד:]. מתני' היא בכורים. ושבעה מינין לעניים דאלו מהם וקורין הפסוק מקיפה וסמוכה לדרכה אמן. ר"ע אומר קרקע כל שהוא חייב וכו'.

The Gemara proposes another source for Ulla's measurement:

וְאֶלָּא מִדִּתְנַן – **But** perhaps Ulla derived his measurement **from that which we learned in** another **Mishnah:**[22] שְׁלֹשָׁה אִילָנוֹת שֶׁל שְׁלֹשָׁה בְּנֵי אָדָם – If THREE TREES BELONGING TO THREE different PEOPLE are planted within a *beis se'ah,* הֲרֵי אֵלּוּ מִצְטָרְפִין – THEY COMBINE to attain the status of an orchard,[23] וְחוֹרְשִׁין כָּל – AND ONE MAY therefore PLOW THE ENTIRE

NOTES

22. *Sheviis* 1:5. This Mishnah deals with cultivating fully grown trees prior to the *Shemittah* year. [Fully grown trees have extensive root systems, and therefore require more land than saplings (*Rashi*).]

23. The deadline for tilling the soil of a grain field in the year before *Shemittah* was Pesach. An orchard, however, could be tilled until Shavuos. The Mishnah rules that if three trees are evenly distributed within the area of a *beis se'ah*, they form an orchard and the entire area may be plowed until Shavuos, even if the trees are owned by three different people. [If the trees are scattered in a larger area, they do not form an orchard. In such a case, one may plow only a small patch of land around each tree after the Pesach deadline – a patch large enough for a harvester to circle the tree while holding his basket.] (*Rashi*).

בֵּית סְאָה בִּשְׁבִילָן – *BEIS SE'AH* **ON THEIR ACCOUNT** until Shavuos of the pre-*Shemittah* year. We learn from this Mishnah that three trees draw nourishment from an entire *beis se'ah.*

The Gemara now calculates the amount of land allotted for each tree:

כַּמָּה הֲווּ לְהוּ – **How many** square amos **are** in **[a *beis se'ah*]?** תְּרֵי אַלְפֵי וַחֲמֵשׁ מְאָה גַּרְמִידֵי – **Two thousand five hundred square *amos.*** לְכָל חַד כַּמָּה מָטֵי לֵיהּ – **How much** does that **come to for each** of the three trees? תַּמְנֵי מְאָה וּתְלָתִין וּתְלָתָא וְתִילְתָּא – **Eight hundred thirty-three and one-third** square *amos.*

The Gemara asks:

אַכַּתִּי נְפִישֵׁי לֵיהּ דְּעוּלָּא – **Still, Ulla's** total **is greater,** for Ulla allots a tree 1,024 square *amos.* – ? –

The Gemara answers:

לֹא דַּק – **[Ulla] was imprecise** in his measurement. He merely gave an approximation.[1]

The Gemara rejects this approach:

אֵימוּר דְּאָמְרִינַן לֹא דַּק – **When can we say** that an Amora **was imprecise** in a measurement? לְחוּמְרָא – Only where his approximation results **in a stringency.** לְקוּלָּא לֹא דַּק מִי אָמְרִינַן – **Can we say** that an Amora **was imprecise** where the approximation results **in a leniency?**[2] In our case, Ulla exempted from *bikkurim* any tree that is within sixteen *amos* of a neighboring field, while the Mishnah indicates that the true measurement is less than that.[3] – ? –

The Gemara reconciles the measurements:

מִי סָבְרַתְּ בְּרִיבּוּעָא קָא אָמְרִינַן – **Do you think we** mean to **say** that the area from which a tree is nourished is **a square?** בְּעִיגּוּלָא קָא אָמְרִינַן – No! **We** mean to **say** that it is **a circle.** The area of the circle, according to Ulla, closely parallels the Mishnah's measurement.[4]

The Gemara calculates the area of this circle:

מִכְּדִי – **Let us see.** כַּמָּה מְרוּבָּע יוֹתֵר עַל הָעִיגּוּל – **How much larger is a square than a circle** that is inscribed in it? רְבִיעַ – **One-fourth.**[5] Thus, the area of the circle from which a tree is nourished, according to Ulla, is one-fourth less than the 1,024 square *amos* that we calculated previously. If we deduct one-fourth of 1,024 (256), פָּשׁוּ לְהוּ שְׁבַע מְאָה וְשִׁתִּין וּתְמַנְיָא – **the remainder is seven hundred and sixty-eight** square *amos.*

The Gemara asks:

אַכַּתִּי פָּשׁ לֵיהּ פַּלְגָא דְּאַמְּתָא – **There still remains** a discrepancy of **one-half *amah*** between Ulla's measurement and the Mishnah's. According to the Mishnah, a tree draws nourishment from an area of 833⅓ square *amos.* A circle with that area has a radius of sixteen and one-half *amos.*[6] – ? –

The Gemara answers:

הַיְינוּ דְּלֹא דַּק – **This is where [Ulla] was imprecise** in his measurement, וּלְחוּמְרָא לֹא דַּק – **and his imprecision** results **in a stringency.** According to the Mishnah, a tree within 16½ *amos* of the boundary should be exempt from *bikkurim,* while Ulla gave the round figure of 16 *amos.* We may therefore conclude that Ulla's measurement was derived from this Mishnah.

Ulla ruled that a tree which draws nutrients from a neighbor's property is exempt from *bikkurim.* The Gemara now presents several Mishnahs from which it attempts to refute Ulla's ruling: תָּא שְׁמַע – **Come, learn** a proof from the following Mishnah:[7] הַקּוֹנֶה אִילָן וְקַרְקָעוֹ – One WHO PURCHASES A TREE AND ITS sur-

NOTES

1. An area of 833⅓ square *amos* forms a square with slightly less than 29 *amos* on each side. The distance from a tree in the center of this square to its perimeter is 14½ *amos.* Thus, according to the Mishnah, a tree draws nutrients from the area within 14½ *amos.* Ulla chose to give the approximate measurement of sixteen *amos.* [Amoraim occasionally laid down rulings based on approximate measurements, as the Gemara will shortly explain.]

2. When a ruling is based on a certain measurement, approximating the measurement will result in either a more stringent ruling or a more lenient one. We can postulate that an Amora's ruling reflects an approximate measurement if the approximation results in a more stringent ruling than the exact measurement would, but not if it results in a more lenient ruling.

3. According to the Mishnah, a tree draws nutrients from a distance of 14½ *amos* (see note 1). Applying this measurement to *bikkurim* would exempt only trees that are within 14½ *amos* of a boundary. Thus, Ulla's measurement is more lenient than that of the Mishnah.

4. Until this point, the Gemara had assumed that a tree's roots radiate to the four points of the compass and form a square. Therefore, if the roots that draw nutrition extend sixteen *amos* in each direction, their total area is a square of thirty-two *amos,* or 1,024 square *amos.* This is far greater than the Mishnah's calculation of 833⅓ square *amos.* The Gemara now recognizes its assumption as incorrect, for the diagonal of this square extends more than sixteen *amos* from its center (*Rashi*). Therefore, the Gemara concludes that the roots fan out in a circle whose radius is sixteen *amos.* Thus, the roots take up less area than originally thought.

5. I.e. the area of a circle is three-fourths the area of a square in which it can be inscribed. Thus, the square is larger than the circle by one-fourth the area of the square.

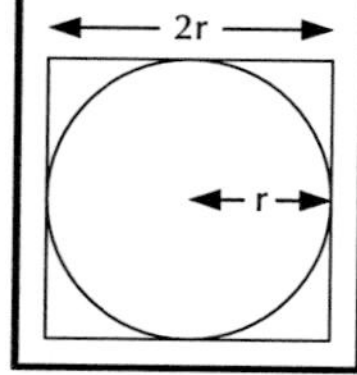

The Talmudic method for determining the area of a circle is to inscribe it inside a square and calculate the area of the square; the area of the circle is presumed to be three-quarters the area of the square.

This can be calculated as follows: When a circle is inscribed in a square, each side of the square is twice the length of the circle's radius. [See diagram.] Thus, the area of the square is 2r x 2r or $4r^2$. The area of the circle is $3r^2$ – three-quarters the area of the square. [The formula for calculating the area of a circle is πr^2, or mathematically, approximately $3^1/_7r^2$. However, in matters of Talmudic law the fraction is disregarded (see *Eruvin* 14a).]

In our case, a circle with a diameter of 32 *amos* (and a radius of 16) will have an area one-fourth less than that of a 32-*amah* square.

6. *Rashi* calculates this as follows: The Mishnah's figure (833⅓) exceeds Ulla's figure (768) by [approximately] 65 square *amos.* This can be made into a strip 65 *amos* long and one *amah* wide. Split the strip lengthwise and place the two halves end to end to form a strip 130 *amos* long and ½ *amah* wide. Apply this strip around the sides of a 32 *amah*×32 *amah* square (which is the area from which a tree is nourished, according to Ulla) as follows: Place 32×½ on top, and 32×½ on bottom. The resulting figure is a rectangle 33 *amos* long and 32 *amos* wide. From the original 130-*amah* strip (of which 64 *amos* have been accounted for), a strip of 66 *amos*×½ *amah* remains. Place 33×½ on one side of the rectangle and 33×½ on the other side, to form a square of 33×33 *amos.* Thus, the extra 65 square *amos* accorded by the Mishnah result in a square that is one *amah* larger than Ulla's. A tree placed in the center of this square has an extra half-*amah* of land in each direction. The Mishnah's measurement is thus one-half *amah* greater than Ulla's.

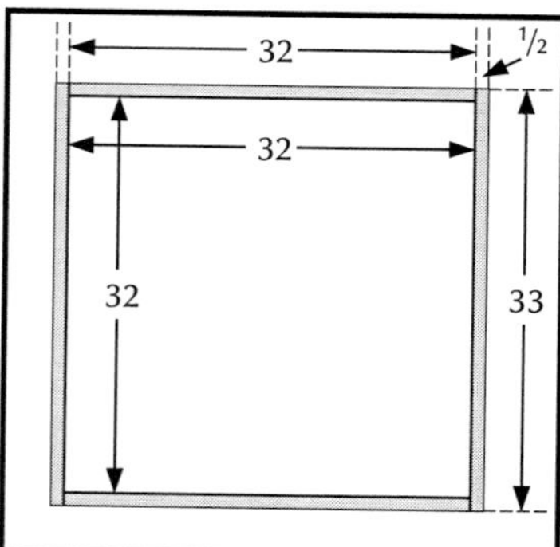

Rashi points out that this calculation is not accurate, for the Gemara has already discarded the notion that a tree's roots grow outward in a square, and has concluded that they form a circle. A circle with an area of 833⅓ square *amos* has a radius of 16⅔ *amos* [based on the formula: area=$3r^2$]. *Rashi* explains that the Gemara was not concerned with calculating the difference so precisely. However, there is a variant version of the text, which reads: *there remains* a discrepancy of *two-thirds of an amah.*

7. *Bikkurim* 1:11.

בית סאה בשבילן (א) כמה הוו להו תרי אלפי וה' מאה גרמידי לכל חד כמה מטי ליה תמני מאה ותלתין ותלתא ותילתא אכתי נפישי ליה דעולא לא דק אימור דאמרינן לא דק לחומרא לקולא לא דק מי אמרינן מי סברת בריבועא קא אמרינן בעיגולא קא אמרינן מכדי (א) כמה מרובע יותר על העיגול רביע (ב) פשו להו ז' מאה ושתין ותמניא אכתי פש ליה פלגא דאמתא היינו דלא דק ולחומרא לא דק תא שמע (ג) א הקונה אילן וקרקעו מביא וקורא מאי לאו ב כל שהוא לא י"ו אמה תא שמע (ג) ג קנה שני אילנות בתוך של חבירו מביא ואינו קורא הא ד שלשה מביא וקורא מאי לאו כל שהוא לא הכא נמי י"ו אמה ת"ש (ז) ר"ע אומר ה קרקע כל שהוא חייב בפאה ובבכורים ו וכותבין עליו פרוזבול

רש"י

בית סאה כמה הוו להו תרי אלפי ות"ק גרמידי. על אמה רוחב: כמה מטי. לכל חד מהנך אילנות תתל"ג ותילתא אכתי נפישין להו שש עשרה אמה דעולא דהוי אלף וכ"ד: לא דק. עולא לא דקדק כל כך הואיל וקרוב לשיעור זה קאמר ולא איכפת ליה: אימור דאמרינן לא דק. היכא דאזיל לחומרא הכא קא אזיל לקולא דאינו יונק כל כך וקאמר איהו דיונק ופטר ליה מביכורים: מי סברת. שש עשרה אמה דעולא בריבועא קאמר דליהוי שלשים ושתים על ל"ב כדקאמרינן: בעיגולא קאמר. שכל סביביו יונק שש עשרה והיינו בעיגולא דאילו ברבוע נמצא כנגד האלכסון יותר משש עשרה אמה: וכמה מרובע יותר על העיגול רביע. דל רביע מאלף וכ"ד פשו להו תשס"ח אמות ברוחב אמה אכתי לא שוי שיעורי דהשתא (ג) פשו להו שיעורי דמתני' אדעולא פלגא דאמתא ונמצא אילן יונק י"ו אמה ומחצה לכל צד דהיינו ל"ג על ל"ג דשיעורא דעולא תשס"ח ושיעורא דמתני' תתל"ג ונפיש שיעורא דמתניתין אדעולא ס"ה אמות באמה רוחב חלוק הרצועה לרוחב הרי ק"ל אמה אורך ברוחב חצי אמה הקף מהם האילן ל"ב אמה לצפון וכנגדו לדרום נמצא מהצפון לדרום ל"ג שהרי הוספת עליו חצי אמה לכאן וחצי אמה לכאן ובידך נשארו (ה) ס"ו ברוחב חצי אמה תן חציין למזרח וחציין למערב נמצא מוקף ברבוע ולא דקדק הגמרא כל כך דנקט פלגא אמתא דהא עולא בעיגול קאמר ואילו בעיגול הייתי יכול להוסיף עליו שני שליש אמה לכל צד אלא משום האי פורתא לא דק כולי האי. ואית דגרסי פש ליה תרי תילתי דאמתא: היינו דלא דק. עולא דהוה מצי למימר שיתסרי ופלגא ולחומרא לא דק ואזיל לחומרא ולא כמלא שיעורו: מאי לאו כל שהוא. חוץ לעביו של אילן לכל צד: הקונה שני אילנות בתוך של חבירו מביא ואינו קורא כו'. לקמן תנן בהמוכר את הספינה המוכר שתי אילנות לחבירו ולא פירש לו קרקע לא קנה קרקע אבל קנה שלשה קנה קרקע ואף על פי שלא פירש הלכך גבי ביכורים נמי שתי אילנות מביא ואינו קורא דלא מצי למימר פרי האדמה אשר נתתה לי (דברים כו): הא ג'. דקנה קרקע מביא וקורא: מאי לאו. משום דקנה קרקע מעט סביבם: לא. משום דקנה שש עשרה אמה סביב לכל אחד: ובוידוי. לא גרסינן ליה במתני' במסכת פאה דאין וידוי אלא במעשר והוא אינו תלוי בקרקע: פרוזבול. תנן במסכת גיטין (דף לו.) הלל תיקן פרוזבול שראה שנמנעו העם מלהלוות מפני השביעית המשמטת ועוברים על מה שכתוב השמר לך פן יהיה דבר וגו' עמד והתקין תקנה שלא תשמט שיהא מוסר שטרותיו לבית דין וכותב עליהן פרוזבול וזה גופו של פרוזבול מוסר אני לכם פלוני ופלוני הדיינים שבמקום פלוני שכל חוב שיש לי אצל פלוני שאגבנו כל זמן שארצה ותו לא משמטת ליה שביעית דלא קרינא ביה לא יגוש שאין תובע חובו אלא (י) מב"ד והתם מוקמינן לה בשביעית בזמן הזה דרבנן ואמרינן התם אין כותבין פרוזבול אלא על הקרקע אבל אין לו קרקע ללוה לא כתבינן ליה דהלואה דלא שכיחא היא דמסתמא אין אדם סומך אלא על קרקע הלוה וכשאין לו לא תיקן הלל פרוזבול:

תוספות

כמה מרובע יותר על העיגול רביע. הכי איתא בברייתא דמסכת מדות וכן בעירובין: הכי גרס ר"ת פש להו תרי תילתא אמתא. פי' כשתקיף אילן דעולא רצועה רחבה שני שלישי אמה יהא גדול כאילן המשנה שהי' יותר ס"ה אמות ושליש ברוחב אמה שהרי אם תקיף ל"ב על ל"ב מרובעים יצטרך קכ"ח ולד' קרנות ח' שלישים הרי ק"ל ושני שלישים אורך על שני שלישים רוחב תחסר הרביע שהעיגול פחות ישאר צ"ח וכן ס"ה אמה ושליש תחתוך לג' חלקים לאורך תהיה רצועה אחת של קכ"ו ברוחב שליש תחתוך לשנים ותשים זה בצד זה תהיה רצועה ארכה צ"ח על רוחב שני שלישי אמה עוד מלא ר"י בספר (ד) אחר מפורש בגמרת הספר להקיף בחוטים אילן דעולא שהוא ל"ב על ל"ב עד שיהא שני שלישי אמה סביב תחתוך החוטין ותפשטם יהיה העליון ארכו ק' שהוא מקיף ל"ג ושליש וכל שיש ברחבו טפח יש בהיקפו ג' והתחתון צ"ו שהוא מקיף ל"ב הרי (ה) התחתון פחות מן העליון מכל צד ב' אמות ותחתוך העודף מצד אחד ותמלא צד אחד האורך לצד הקצר תהיה רצועה צ"ח וכן הוא ס"ה ושליש דרך אחרת ל"ג ושליש על ל"ג ושליש מרובעים עולה אלף ומאה וי"א אמות ושליש של שליש שהיא תשיעית אמה תחסר הרביעית ישאר תתל"ג ושליש הרי אילן המשנה ל"ג ושליש על ל"ג ושליש (הג"ה. או כעין זה שליש סאה הוי י"ו וב' שלישים על חמשים תחתוך באמצע ותשים זה על זה יהיה עשרים וחמש על שלשים ושלש ושליש) דרך אחרת בית סאה היא מאה על כ"ה תקח השליש לאילן אחד יהיה ל"ג ושליש על כ"ה והם ל"ג ושליש על ל"ג ושליש עגולים שהרי מוסיף הרביע מלבד שהיא שליש מלגיו דהיינו ח' אמה ושליש באורך ל"ג ושליש יהיו ל"ג ושליש על ל"ג ושליש מרובעים (ולספרים דגרסינן פש להו פלגא דאמתא) ועשה אותו עגול שיחסר הרביע שהוספת ויהיה עגול ל"ג ושליש על ל"ג ושליש ולספרים דגרסי פש ליה פלגא דאמתא יש לפרש דחשיב עולא י"ו לכל צד לבד מקום האילן ומקום אילן שליש נמצא אילן דעולא ל"ג ושליש על ל"ג ושליש כשתקיף מכל צד פלגא דאמתא יהיה ל"ג ושליש ורביע על ל"ג ושליש ורביע ומקום האילן הוי אמה על אמה נמצא אילן דעולא ל"ג על ל"ג ואם היו מרובעים היה עולה אלף ופ"ט תחסר הרביע ישאר תתי"ו ושלשה רבעי אמה ול"ג (ח) (והוו) [פשו] להו ז' מאה ושתין ותמניא נמצא דאילן המשנה יתר על של עולא י"ו אמה ושליש ורביע ופלגא דאמתא קאי אבית סאה שהיא חמשים על חמשים כשתחסיר פלגא דאמתא לאורך וכן לרוחב יעלה החסרון חמשים אמה חסר רביע דהיינו לג' אילנות ולאילן אחד יעלה י"ו אמה ושליש ורביע וישאר כאילן דעולא: לחומרא לא דק. וא"ת והא נמי קולא הוא הא דמייתי ביכורים דמפקע להו מתרומה ומעשר כדאמרינן בהמוכר את הספינה (לקמן דף פא: ושם) ויש לומר דעולא לא איירי אלא במאי דאינו מביא בתוך י"ו אבל חוץ לי"ו פעמים מביא ופעמים אינו מביא: אילן וקרקעו כו'. למאי דמוקי לה בי"ו אמה צריך לפרש מאי אתא לאשמועינן ונראה לרשב"א דאתא לאשמועינן ונקנין ולמידק הא קנה אילן סתם אינו מביא וקורא ואם קנה ב' אפילו סתם מביא וקורא דקנה קרקע וכר"מ דאמר (לקמן פא.) הקונה ב' אילנות קנה קרקע: הא שלשה מביא וקורא. הוה מצי למיפרך מסיפא דקתני בהדיא במסכת ביכורים בסיפא דהך דמייתי הכא הקונה ג' אילנות תוך של חבירו מביא וקורא אלא דאורחא דגמ' בכמה מקומות שמדקדק מרישא מה שיכול [ועי' תוס' שבת לט: ד"ה אלא פניו]: לא שש עשרה אמה. וא"ת והא אמרינן בהמוכר את הספינה (לקמן דף פב. ושם) גבי שלשה קנה קרקע וכמה תחתיהן וביניהן וחוצה להן כמלא אורה וסלו וי"ל (ט) דהתם כשענפי האילן גדולים הרבה ויוצאין חוץ לשש עשרה אמה ואם תאמר קונה אילן אחד אמאי אינו מביא וקורא למ"ד קנין פירות כקנין הגוף דמי ומ"ש ממוכר שדהו לפירות דמביא וקורא לדידיה כדאמרינן בפרק השולח (גיטין דף מז: ושם) וליכא למימר דהאי תנא סבר דקנין פירות לאו כקנין הגוף דמי דהא ר"מ אית ליה דכקנין הגוף דמי בהשולח (שם דף מח.) ובהחובל (ב"ק דף ל. ושם) ואית ליה לקמן (דף פא.) דקונה אילן אחד (ט) (אינו מביא וקורא) וי"ל דשאני התם שהקרקע קנוי לו עד זמן קבוע אבל הכא אם יתייבש מיד האילן אין לו בקרקע כלום אי נמי התם קרקע קנויה לו לכל דבר למשטח בה פירי ולמיזרע בה סילקא וירקא אבל גבי אילן אין לו אלא יניקה לבדה: ובוידוי. פי' בקונטרס דלא גרסינן ובוידוי דלא כתיב במעשר שני (שיש) שום וידוי לא מארצך ולא מאדמה אשר נתת לי אע"ג דכתיב ביה וברך את עמך את ישראל ואת האדמה אשר נתתה לנו (דברים כו) לא שיהא לו לחלק אלא לכל ישראל ומיהו על כרחך אין וידוי בלא קרקע דתני עלה בירושלמי אף בוידוי ומכל מקום לא גרסינן ליה מדלא תני עלה בירושלמי מכלל דבמשנה ליתיה (י): ולכתוב עליה פרוזבול. אבל אמטלטלין אין כותבין פרוזבול מפני שיכול לכלותן והיא הלואה דלא שכיחא ועלין נקוב אע"פ שיכול לכלותו כותבין עליו פרוזבול דלא פלוג רבנן במקרקעי והא דכותבין אפילו על קרקע כל שהוא פי' רשב"ם בהשולח (גיטין דף לז. ד"ה אלא) משום דאין אונאה לקרקעות והוי כאילו יש לו משכון בכל ואין נראה דנהי דאין להן אונאה ביטול מקח ביתר מפלגא יש להן אלא היינו טעמא משום דגבי והדר גבי כמעשה דקטינא דאביי (כתובות דף צא:) דע"י כך ראוי לגבות כל חובו וכענין זה איכא סוף פרק כל הגט (גיטין דף ל:) גבי המלוה מעות את הכהן כו' הניח מלא מחט גובה מלא קורדום: [ועי' תוס' גיטין לז. ד"ה אלא ותוספות קדושין כו: ד"ה ולכתוב]:

בחטה

עין משפט נר מצוה

קב א ב מיי' פ"ב מהל' ביכורים הל' יג:

קג ג מיי' שם פ"ד הלכה ד:

קד ד מיי' שם פ"ב הלכה יג:

קה ה מיי' פ"ב מהל' מתנות עניים הל' ג:

קו ו מיי' פ"ט מהל' שמיטין הל' יט סמג לאוין רעא טוש"ע ח"מ סי' סז סעיף כב:

רבינו גרשום

כמה הוו להו לכל א' מהללו ג' אילנות ברצועות פשוטות תמני מאה ותלתין ותלתא ותילתא אמין שזהו השליש של חשבון בית סאה שחשבנו למעלה כ"ה מאות מישתכח דבין אילן לאילן תמני מאה ותלתין ותלתא ותילתא ואכתי נפיש ליה חשבון של עולא על האי חושבנא מאתן פחות ט'. ומשני עולא לא דק כלומר לא דקדק בדבר כל כך שהעמיד חשבון האילן על זה. ומקשי' אימור דאמרי' לא דק היכא דאיכא חומרא שאם היה מחמיר והיה מצריכו בפחות משיעור זה להביא ביכורין אמרי' ליה אימור לא דק א) אבל לחומרא אי לא דק ומי אמרי' דצריך ט"ז אמה לכל רוח כדפרישית איכא ליה קולא דפחות מט"ז אמה שעולה חשבון לאלף וכ"ד אם נטוע הוא אין מביאין ממנו ביכורין משום דקא יניק משדה חבירו והיינו קולא והוה ליה לעולא לעיין ולדקדק שלא יפטרנו מביכורין אלא כדינו ומאי לקולא לא דק: מי סברת. דהא דקחשיב עולא ט"ז אמה לכל רוח דאמות מרובעות קא בעי דאית להו מורשא דקרנתא בעגולא קא אמרי' דחשיב סביבות האילן ט"ז אמה בלא מורשא דקרנתא. ואכתי מקשה ליה למאי דבעי לתרוצי באמות עגולות מכדי כמה מרובע יותר על העיגול רביע וכשתוציא הרביע מן אלף וכ"ד אמות לא משתייר לך אלא תשס"ח כיצד מח' מאות תשליך מאתים נשתיירו שש מאות וממאתים תוציא ג' הרי הן ז' מאות וכ"ד אמות עגולות ומכ"ד תשליך הרביע נשתיירו י"ח ואותן י"ח מוסיף על ד' מאות וג' הרי תשס"ח. ואכתי אין מגיע חשבון של עולא לתמני מאה ותלתין ותלתא ותילתא לפי שחשבון של עולא שכשחושב בעיגול הוא פוחת חצי אמה מכלל ב) אמות האילן מחשבון של תמני מאה ותלתין ותלתא ותילתא וכשתרצה להשוות חשבונו של עולא לחשבון זה צריך אתה להביא ד' רצועות של רוחב חצי אמה ואורך כל אחת ל"ב אמה שהן ס"ד ותשימם מבחוץ לאלו תשס"ח אמה עגולות תשים אותן ד' רצועות בריבוע ולא בעיגול ויבא החשבון שוה ומהיכן אתה נוטל אותן ס"ד אמה שאתה מחלק לד' רצועות של אורך ל"ב (אורך ל"ב) אמה ורוחב חצי אמה שאתה משים בריבוע מחרץ לעיגול זה מכאן אתה נוטלן לפי שחשבון תמני מאה ותלתין ותלתא ותילתא הוא עודף על ד' מאות וס"ח ששים וה' אמות ושליש אמה ומחשבון זה אינו חושב אותו שליש אמה שאינו דבר חשוב אלא ס"ה אמות חושב מס"ד אמות נעשה אותן ד' רצועות שארכן ל"ב ורחבן חצי אמה ואותה אמה חמישית הנשארת חלוק אותה לד' רביעי אמה ויהיה כל רביע חצי אמה אורך וחצי אמה רוחב ותן אלו ד' רבעין לד' הקרנות של רצועות למלאות הזוית והיינו דקאמר אכתי פש ליה לעולא פלגא דאמתא דבציר חשבונו מחשבון ג' אילנות והיינו דלא דק עולא ולחומרא לא דק שמחייב להביא ביכורים בפחות משיעור ברייתא של ג' אילנות. והא דלא חשבינן ההוא שליש אמה משום דאי מרבעת לה להוסיפה על רצועות של חצי אמה לא היתה אפי' כחוט השער מש"ה לא חשיב ליה: מביא וקורא. מן הארץ אשר נתת לי: מאי לאו. דקני קרקע כל שהוא וקשיא לעולא דאמר דאילן הסמוך לתוך ט"ז אמה גזלן הוא: מביא ואינו קורא. משום דקי"ל דקנה [שני] אילנות בתוך שדה חבירו לא קנה קרקע אבל ג' אילנות דקנה קרקע מביא וקורא. מאי קנה קרקע לאו דקנה כל שהוא וקשיא לעולא. לא ט"ז אמה קנה מן האחרון ועד חבירו: ולכתוב עליה פרוזבול. היינו תקנת עשירים שהיו מלוים על משכון קרקע דלאו שמיטה משמט לא מלוה בשטר ולא מלוה על המשכון וכתוב הכי מוסרני לכם אגב קרקע ב"ד פלוני ופלוני חוב שיש לי על פלוני שאגבנו בכל שעה שארצה וחותמין עליו ב"ד אלמא דקרקע כל שהוא חייב בביכורים אע"ג דסמיך האי קרקע למצר אחר וקשיא לעולא:

בחטה

חשק שלמה על רבינו גרשום א) נראה דצ"ל אבל לקולא לא דק מי אמרינן כיון דמצריך וכו'. ב) אולי צ"ל מכל ד' צידי האילן.

מסורת הש"ס

א) [לקמן קא.] עירובין יד: ודף עו. מ. ע. סוכה ח. [אהלות פי"ב מ"ו], ב) בכורים פ"א מ"ו גיטין מח., ג) לקמן פא. בכורים פ"א מ"ו [גיטין מח.], ד) קדושין כו. פאה פ"ג מ"ח, ה) צ"ל פ"ה, ו) צ"ל ב"ה, ז) רש"ל מ"ז, ח) רש"ל, ט) [צ"ל מביא ואינו קורא], י) [עי' תוס' קדושין כו. ועי' תוס' ד"ה ובבכורים וכו' שהביאו תוס' ע"ש].

הגהות הב"ח

(א) גמ' בית סאה בשבילן עד עלמא כמה הוו: (ב) שם על העיגול רביע (פשו להו ז' מאה ושתין ותמניא) תא"מ ונ"ב ל' משולש לא גרס לה: (ג) רש"י ד"ה וכמה וכו' פשו ליה שיעורא דמתני': (ד) תוס' ד"ה הכי גרס ר"ת וכו' בספר אחר מפורש בגליון הספר וכו' עד שיהא רוחב החוט שני שלישי אמה: (ה) בא"ד הרי אורך התחתון פחות מן העליון:

גליון הש"ס

תוס' ד"ה לא כו' וי"ל דהתם כשענפי. עיין לקמן דף פא ע"ב תוס' ד"ה ואי:

ליקוטי רש"י

[תחילת לקוטי רש"י ששייך לכאן נדפס בדף כו:] פרוזבול. לפי שראה הלל שנמנעו העשירים מלהלוות לעניים מפני ירא השביעית שמשמטת והיו עוברים על מה שכתוב פן יהיה דבר עם לבבך בליעל וגו' עמד הלל והתקין פרוזבול. פרוזבול. פרוז בולי ובוטי כמו שפרשו במסכת נדה (דף ז:) בולאות שבהודה (גיטין לז.) כלומר ריוח לעשירים שלא יפסידו שלהם ותקון גופו של פרוזבול מוסרני לכם פלוני ופלוני הדיינים שבמקום פלוני שכל חוב שיש לי אצל פלוני שאגבנו כל זמן שארצה והדיינין חותמין עליו מלמטה או העדים והלכך לא משמטת שמוסר שטרותיו לב"ד גבינהו ואינו לא קנוי קרנין ביה לא יגוש הדיינין מגבוהו ליה ובקרקע ב"ד הפקר והפקר ב"ד הפקר וה"מ כשיש לו קרקע ללוה דדמי כאילו גבוי הוא דלא שייך לא יגוש גיזין דכתבו ליה אמ"כ יש לו קרקע להשתעבד למלוה ומילתא דשכיחא תקינו רבנן אבל כשאין לו קרקע מילתא דלא שכיחא היא ולא תקינו רבנן פרוזבול [רשב"ם לקמן סה:]. פרוז. תקנה [גיטין לו:]. בולי ובוטי. עשירים ועניים עשירים שלא יפסידו ועניים שלא תנעל דלת בפניהם [שם לז.].

rounding LAND מֵבִיא וְקוֹרֵא – MUST BRING *bikkurim* from the tree's fruit AND also RECITE the *bikkurim* verses.[8]

The Gemara asks:

מַאי לָאו כָּל שֶׁהוּא – Does this not include one who purchased **a minute measure** of land around the tree?[9] If so, the Mishnah contradicts Ulla's rule, because in such a case the roots obviously extend into a neighboring field. – ? –

The Gemara answers:

לֹא שֵׁשׁ עֶשְׂרֵה אַמָּה – No! The Mishnah refers to one who purchased at least **sixteen *amos*** of land around the tree. Thus, the Mishnah concurs with Ulla's ruling.[10]

The Gemara attempts once more to refute Ulla's ruling:

תָּא שְׁמַע – Come, learn a proof from the following Mishnah:[11] קָנָה שְׁנֵי אִילָנוֹת בְּתוֹךְ שֶׁל חֲבֵירוֹ – If one PURCHASED TWO TREES that are WITHIN HIS FELLOW'S PROPERTY, מֵבִיא וְאֵינוֹ קוֹרֵא – HE MUST BRING *bikkurim* from the trees' fruit, BUT HE DOES NOT RECITE the *bikkurim* verses, because he does not own the land from which the trees are nourished.[12]

הָא שְׁלֹשָׁה מֵבִיא וְקוֹרֵא – This implies that if, **however,** he purchased **three** trees, **he brings** *bikkurim* from the trees' fruit **and** also **recites** the *bikkurim* verses, for in that case he does acquire ownership of the land around the trees.[13]

The Gemara asks:

מַאי לָאו כָּל שֶׁהוּא – Is it not a minute measure of land around each tree that the purchaser acquires? If so, the roots extend into the neighboring property, and nevertheless, the Mishnah implies that the purchaser brings *bikkurim* and recites the *bikkurim* verses.[14] – ? –

The Gemara answers:

לֹא – No! The purchaser does not merely acquire a minute measure of land around each tree. הָכָא נַמִּי שֵׁשׁ עֶשְׂרֵה אַמָּה – **Here too,** as in the previously cited Mishnah, he acquires **sixteen *amos*** of land around each tree. Thus, the roots do not extend into a neighbor's property.

The Gemara again attempts to refute Ulla's ruling:

תָּא שְׁמַע – Come, learn a proof from the following Mishnah:[15] רַבִּי עֲקִיבָא אוֹמֵר – RABBI AKIVA SAYS: קַרְקַע כָּל שֶׁהוּא – Even A MINUTE MEASURE of LAND חַיָּיב בְּפֵאָה וּבְבִכּוּרִים – IS SUBJECT TO THE REQUIREMENTS OF *PE'AH*[16] AND *BIKKURIM,* וְכוֹתְבִין עָלָיו פְּרוֹזְבּוּל – AND is fit TO WRITE A *PROSBUL* ON ITS ACCOUNT,[17]

NOTES

8. When bringing *bikkurim* to the Temple, one would recite verses of praise to *Hashem* for having granted him a parcel of land and having blessed it with a crop. This recitation is composed of the verses in *Deuteronomy* 26:5-10.

9. Literally: *whatever* [amount of land] *it is.* Since the Mishnah does not state the amount of land that one must purchase to be subject to the *bikkurim* requirement, we deduce that it applies to any amount of land.

10. The Mishnah did not state explicitly that its ruling applies only to one who purchases sixteen *amos* of land around the tree, because it assumed that Ulla's rule was self-evident.

11. *Bikkurim* 1:6.

12. The *bikkurim* verses were recited only by one who owned the land from which the crops grew. This is because one of the verses is (*Deuteronomy* 26:10): וְעַתָּה הִנֵּה הֵבֵאתִי אֶת־רֵאשִׁית פְּרִי הָאֲדָמָה אֲשֶׁר־נָתַתָּ לִּי ה׳, *And now, I have brought the first fruit of the land that You, Hashem, have given me.* One who does not own the land that produced his fruit (e.g. a sharecropper) cannot recite this verse and is therefore excluded from the entire recitation. [Nevertheless, he is obligated to bring *bikkurim.*] Now, if one purchases two trees from his fellow, it is presumed that the land around the trees is not included in the sale. Therefore, although the purchaser is obligated to bring *bikkurim,* he does not recite the *bikkurim* verses (*Rashi*).

13. When one purchases three or more trees from his fellow, it is presumed that the sale is not limited to the trees, but also includes the land around the trees. Since the purchaser owns the land from which the trees are nourished, he recites the *bikkurim* verses (*Rashi*).

14. It would seem that the law stated explicitly in the Mishnah (one who purchased two trees brings *bikkurim,* even though he does not own the land around the trees) should suffice to refute Ulla's rule. See *Tos. Rid* and *Toras Chaim* who explain why the Gemara based its question on the Mishnah's implied ruling that one who purchased three trees brings *bikkurim* and recites the verses.

15. *Pe'ah* 3:6.

16. When harvesting a field, one may not take its entire crop, but must leave a corner (*pe'ah*) of the field uncut, for paupers to gather its produce (see *Leviticus* 19:9). This Mishnah teaches that even a minute parcel of land is subject to the *pe'ah* obligation. [However, there must be enough produce to allow for both harvesting and leaving for the poor (see *Tosafos* to *Kiddushin* 26a ד״ה קרקע).]

17. A *prosbul* is a document in which a creditor transfers to a court the authority to collect his debts. The Gemara in *Gittin* (36a) explains the need for this document: The Torah mandates that all outstanding debts be canceled every *Shemittah* year. Towards the end of the Second Temple era, Hillel noted that people would refrain from lending money close to the *Shemittah* year, in violation of the Torah's injunction (*Deuteronomy* 15:9): הִשָּׁמֶר לְךָ פֶּן־יִהְיֶה דָבָר עִם־לְבָבְךָ בְלִיַּעַל לֵאמֹר קָרְבָה שְׁנַת־הַשֶּׁבַע שְׁנַת הַשְּׁמִטָּה וְרָעָה עֵינְךָ בְּאָחִיךָ הָאֶבְיוֹן וְלֹא תִתֵּן לוֹ, *Take heed, lest your heart entertain a subversive thought, saying: "The seventh year, the Shemittah year, is approaching," and you will look unkindly upon your impoverished brother and not give him [a loan].* To alleviate this problem, Hillel ordained that before the *Shemittah,* one should draw up a *prosbul* document, thereby transferring his outstanding loans to a court. Loans owned by the court are not canceled by *Shemittah.* Therefore, the creditor can act as the court's agent, and collect the debt. [The legal basis for Hillel's enactment is further discussed in *Gittin* (ibid.).]

A *prosbul* may be written only for a debt which is secured by land. This is because Hillel instituted the *prosbul* only for ordinary instances of debt, and it was unusual to lend money without real property to secure the debt (*Rashi*). The Mishnah informs us that the value of the property he owns need not equal the full amount of the loan – even a minute parcel of land can serve as the basis for a *prosbul.*

בית סאה בשבילן (א) כמה הוו להו תרי אלפי וה' מאה גרמידי לכל חד כמה מטי ליה תמני מאה ותלתין ותלתא ותילתא אכתי נפישי ליה דעולא לא דק איזמור דאמרינן לא דק לחומרא לקולא לא דק מי אמרינן מי סברת בריבועא קא אמרינן בעיגולא קא אמרינן מכדי [א] כמה מרובע יותר על העיגול רביע (ג) פשו להו ז' מאה ושתין ותמניא אכתי פש ליה פלגא דאמתא היינו דלא דק ולחומרא לא דק תא שמע [ג] הקונה אילן וקרקעו מביא וקורא מאי לאו [ב] כל שהוא לא י"ו אמה תא שמע [ג] קנה שני אילנות בתוך של חבירו מביא ואינו קורא הא [ד] שלשה מביא וקורא מאי לאו כל שהוא לא הכא נמי י"ו אמה ת"ש [ז] ר"ע אומר [ה] קרקע כל שהוא חייב בפאה ובבכורים [ו] וכותבין עליו פרוזבול

רש"י

בית סאה כמה הוו להו תרי אלפי ות"ק גרמידי. על אמה רוחב: כמה מטי. לכל חד מהנך אילנות תמ"ג ותילתא אכתי נפישין להו שש עשרה אמה דעולא דהוי אלף וכ"ד: לא דק. עולא לא דקדק כל כך הוזיל וקרוב לשיעור זה קאמר ולא איכפת ליה: איזמור דאמרינן לא דק. היכא דאזיל לחומרא הכא קא אזיל לקולא דאינו יונק כל כך וקאמר איהו דיונק ופטור ליה מביכורים: מי סברת. שש עשרה אמה דעולא בריבועא קאמר דליהוי שלשים ושתים על ל"ב כדקאמרינן: בעיגולא קאמר. שכל סביביו יונק שש עשרה והיינו בעיגולא דאילו ברבוע נמלא כנגד האלכסון יותר משש עשרה אמה: וכמה מרובע יותר על העיגול רביע. דל רביע מאלף וכ"ד פשו להו תשס"ח אמות ברוחב אמה אכתי לא הוי שיעורי דהשתא (ג) פשו להו שיעורי דמתני' לדעולא פלגא דאמתא ונמלא אילן יונק י"ו אמה ומחצה לכל לד דהיינו ל"ג על ל"ג דשיעורא דעולא תשס"ח ושיעורא דמתני' תתל"ג ונפיש שיעורא דמתניתין לדעולא ס"ה אמות באמה רוחב חלוק הלרועה לרוחב הרי ק"ל אמה אורך ברוחב חצי אמה הקף מהם האילן ל"ב אמה לצפון וכנגדו לדרום נמלא מהלפון לדרום ל"ג שהרי הוספת עליו חצי אמה לכאן וחצי אמה לכאן ובידך נשארו (ז) ס"ו ברוחב חצי אמה תן חליין למזרח וחליין למערב נמלא מוקף ברבוע ולא דקדק הגמרא כל כך דנקט פלגא אמתא דהא עולא בעיגול קאמר ואילו בעיגול היית יכול להוסיף עליו שני שלישי אמה לכל לד אלא משום האי פורתא לא דק כולי האי. ולית דגרסי פש ליה תרי תילתי דאמתא: היינו דלא דק. עולא דהוה מלי למימר שיתסרי ופלגא ולחומרא לא דק ואזיל לחומרא ולא למעט שיעורו: מאי לאו כל שהוא. מוך לעביו של אילן לכל לד: הקונה שני אילנות בתוך של חבירו מביא ואינו קורא כו'. לקמן תנן בהמוכר את הספינה המוכר שתי אילנות לחבירו ולא פירש לו קרקע לא קנה קרקע אבל קנה שלשה קנה קרקע ואף על פי שלא פירש הלכך גבי ביכורים נמי שתי אילנות מביא ואינו קורא דלא מצי למימר פרי האדמה אשר נתת לי (דברים כו): הא ג'. דקנה קרקע מביא וקורא: מאי לאו. משום דקנה קרקע מעט סביבים: לא. משום דקנה שש עשרה אמה סביב כל אחד: ובוידוי. לא גרסינן ליה במתני' במסכת פאה דאין וידוי אלא במעשר והוא אינו תלוי בקרקע: פרוזבול. תנן במסכת גיטין (דף לו.) הלל תיקן פרוזבול שראה שנמנעו העם מלהלוות מפני השביעית המשמטת ועוברים על מה שכתוב השמר לך פן יהיה דבר וגו' עמד והתקין תקנה שלא תשמט שיהא מוסר שטרותיו לבית דין וכותב עליהן פרוזבול וזה גופו של פרוזבול מוסר אני לכם פלוני ופלוני הדיינים שבמקום פלוני שכל חוב שיש לי אצל פלוני שאגבנו כל זמן שארצה ותו לא משמטת ליה שביעית דלא קרינא ביה לא יגוש שאין תובע חובו אלא [י] מב"ד והתם מוקמינן לה בשביעית בזמן הזה דרבנן ואמרינן התם אין כותבין פרוזבול אלא על הקרקע אבל אין לו קרקע ללוה לא כתבינן ליה דהלואה דלא שכיחא היא דמסתמא אין אדם סומך אלא על קרקע הלוה וכשאין לו לא תיקן הלל פרוזבול:

ונקנין

תוספות

כמה מרובע יותר על העיגול רביע. הכי איתא בברייתא דמסכת מדות וכן בעירובין: הכי גרס ר"ת פש להו תרי תילתא אמתא. פי' כשתקיף אילן דעולא לרועה רחבה שני שלישי אמה יהא גדול כאילן המשנה שהרי יותר ס"ה אמות ושליש ברבוע אמה שהרי אם תקיף ל"ב על ל"ב מרובעים יעלו קכ"ח ולד' קרנות מ' שלישים הרי ק"ל ושני שלישים אורך על שני שלישים רוחב תחסר הרביע שהעיגול פחות ישאר ל"ח וכן ס"ה אמה ושליש מתחוך לג' חלקים לאורך תהיה לרועה אחת של קל"ו ברוחב שליש מתחוך לשנים ותשים זה בלד זה תהיה לרועה ארוכה ל"ח על רוחב שני שלישי אמה עוד מלא ר"ל בספר (ד) אחר מפורש בגמרת הספר להקיף בחוטים אילן דעולא שהוא ל"ב על ל"ב עד שיהא שני שלישי אמה סביב מתחוך החוטין ותפשטם יהיה העליון ארכו ק' שהוא מקיף ל"ג ושליש וכל שיש ברחבו טפח יש בהיקפו ג' והתחתון ל"ו שהוא מקיף ל"ב הרי (ה) התחתון פחות מן העליון מכל לד ב' אמות ותחתון העודף מלד אחד ומלא לד אחד האורך לבד הקלר תהיה לרועה ל"ח וכן הוא ס"ה ושליש לכך אחרת ל"ג ושליש על ל"ג ושליש מרובעים עולה אלף ומאה וי"א אמות ושליש של שליש שהיא תשיעית אמה תחסר הרביעית ישאר תתל"ג ושליש הרי אילן המשנה ל"ג ושליש על ל"ג ושליש (הג"ה. או כעין זה שליש סאה הוי י"ו וב' שלישים על חמשים מתוך בחמשים ושים זה על זה יהיה עשרים וחמש על שלשים ושלש ושליש) לכך אחרת בית סאה היא מאה על חמשים תקח השליש לאילן אחד יהיה ל"ג ושליש על חמשים ותקח מן החמשים ל"ג ושליש והם ל"ג ושליש על ל"ג ושליש שהרי מוסיף הרביע מלבד שהיא שליש מלגיו דהיינו ח' אמה ושליש ולכך אחרת לאורך יהיו ל"ג ושליש על ל"ג ושליש מרובעים [ז] ולספרים דגרסינן פש להו פלגא דאמתא ועשה אותו עגול שיחסר הרביע שהוספת ויהיה עגול ל"ג ושליש על ל"ג ושליש ולספרים דגרסי פש ליה פלגא דאמתא יש לפרש דחשיב עולא י"ו לכל לד מקום האילן ומקום אילן על שליש נמלא אילן דעולא ל"ג על ל"ג ושליש סביב מקום האילן ועל ל"ב ושליש ורביע ושליש ורביע שבתוך מכל לד ל"ב ושליש ומקום האילן הוי אמה על אמה נמלא דהוי אילן דעולא ל"ג על ל"ג ואם היו מרובעים היה עולה אלף ופ"ט תחסר הרביע ישאר תתי"ו ושלשה רבעי אמה ול"ג [ח] (והוו) [פשו] להו ז' מאה ושתין ותמניא נמלא דאילן המשנה יתר על של עולא י"ו אמה ושליש ורביע ופלגא דאמתא קאי אבית סאה שהיא חמשים על חמשים כשתסיר פלגא דאמתא לאורך וכן לרוחב יעלה החסרון חמשים אמה חסר רביע דהיינו לג' אילנות ולאילן אחד יעלה י"ו אמה ושליש ורביע וישאר כאילן דעולא:

לחומרא לא דק. וא"ת והא נמי קולא הוא הא דמייתי ביכורים דמפקע להו מתרומה ומעשר כדאמרינן בהמוכר את הספינה (לקמן דף פא: ושם) ויש לומר דעולא לא איירי אלא במאי דאינו מביא בתוך י"ו אבל חוץ לי"ו פעמים מביא ופעמים אינו מביא:

אילן וקרקעו כו'. למאי דמוקי לה בי"ו אמה לריך לפרש מאי אתא לאשמועינן ונראה לרשב"א דאתא לאשמועינן ולמידק הא קנה אילן סתם אינו מביא וקורא ואם קנה ב' אפילו סתם מביא וקורא דקנה קרקע וכר"מ דאמר (לקמן פא.) הקונה ב' אילנות קנה קרקע:

הא שלשה מביא וקורא. הוה מצי למיפרך מסיפא דקתני בהדיא במסכת ביכורים בסיפא דהך דמייתי הכא הקונה ג' אילנות תוך של חבירו מביא וקורא אלא דאורחא דגמ' בכמה מקומות שמדקדק מרישא מה שיכול [ועי' תוס' שבת לט: ד"ה אלא פניו]:

לא שש עשרה אמה. וא"ת והא אמרינן בהמוכר את הספינה (לקמן דף פב. ושם) גבי שלשה קנה קרקע וכמה תחתיהן וביניהן וחולה להן כמלא אורה וסלו וי"ל [ט] דהתם כשענפי האילן גדולים הרבה ויולאין חוץ לשש עשרה אמה ואם תאמר קונה אילן אחד אמאי אינו מביא וקורא למ"ד קנין פירות כקנין הגוף דמי ומ"ש ממוכר שדהו לפירות דמביא וקורא לדידיה כדאמרינן בפרק השולח (גיטין דף מז: ושם) וליכא למימר דהאי תנא סבר דקנין פירות לאו כקנין הגוף דמי דהא ר"מ אית ליה דכקנין הגוף דמי בהשולח (שם דף מח.) ובהחובל (ב"ק דף ל. ושם) ואית ליה לקמן (דף פא.) דקונה אילן אחד [ט] (אינו מביא וקורא) וי"ל דשאני התם שהקרקע קנוי לו עד זמן קבוע אבל הכא אם יתייבש מיד האילן אין לו בקרקע כלום אי נמי התם קרקע קנויה לו לכל דבר למשטח בה פירי ולמיזרע בה סילקא וירקא אבל גבי אילן אין לו אלא יניקה לבדה:

ובוידוי. פי' בקונטרס דלא גרסינן ובוידוי דלא כתיב במעשר שני (שם) שום וידוי לא מארצך ולא מאדמה אשר נתת לי אע"ג דכתיב ביה וברך את עמך את ישראל ואת האדמה אשר נתתה לנו (דברים כו) לא שיהא לו לחלק אלא לכל ישראל ומיהו על כרחך אין וידוי בלא קרקע דתני עלה בירושלמי אף בוידוי ומכל מקום לא גרסינן ליה מדתני עלה בירושלמי מכלל דבמשנה ליתיה [י]:

ולכתוב עליה פרוזבול. אבל אמטלטלין אין כותבין פרוזבול מפני שיכול לכלותן והיא הלואה דלא שכיחא ועליך נקוט אע"פ שיכול לכלותו כותבין עליו פרוזבול דלא פלוג רבנן במקרקעי והא דכותבין אפילו על קרקע כל שהוא פי' רשב"ם בהשולח (גיטין דף לז. ד"ה אלא) משום דאין אונאה לקרקעות והוי כאילו יש לו משכון בכל ואין נראה דנהי דאין להן אונאה ביטול מקח ביתר מפלגא יש להן אלא היינו טעמא משום דגבי והדר גבי כמעשה דקטינא דאביי (כתובות דף נא:) דע"י כך ראוי לגבות כל חובו וכענין זה איכא סוף פרק כל הגט (גיטין דף ל:) גבי המלוה מעות את הכהן כו' הניח מלא מחט גובה מלא קורדוס: [ועי' תוס' גיטין לז. ד"ה אלא ותוספות קדושין כו: ד"ה ולכתוב]:

בחטה

עין משפט נר מצוה

קב א ב מיי' פ"ב מהל' ביכורים הל' יג:
קג ג מיי' שם פ"ד הלכה ד:
קד ד מיי' שם פ"ב הלכה יג:
קה ה מיי' פ"ב מהל' מתנות עניים הל' ג:
קו ו מיי' פ"ט מהל' שמיטין הל' יט סמג לאוין רעב טוש"ע ח"מ סי' סז סעיף כב:

רבינו גרשום

כמה הוו להו לכל א' מהללו ג' אילנות ברצועות פשוטות תמני מאה ותלתין ותלתא ותילתא אמין שהוא השליש של חשבון בית סאה שחשבנו למעלה כ"ה מאות משכחת דבין אילאן תמני מאה ותלתין ותלתא ותילתא ואכתי נפיש ליה חשבון של עולא על האי חושבנא מאתן פחות ט'. ומשני עולא לא דק כלומר לא דקדק בדבר כל כך שהעמיד חשבון האילן על זה. ומקשי' איזמור דאמרי' לא דק היכא דאיכא חומרא שאם היה מחמיר והיה מצריכו בפחות משיעור זה להביא ביכורין אמרי' ליה איזמור לא דק [א] אבל לחומרא אי לא דק ומי אמרי' דצריך ט"ז אמה לכל רוח כדפרישית אית ליה קולא דפחות מט"ז אמה שעולה חשבון לאלף וכ"ד שהוא נטוע הוא אין מביאין ממנו ביכורין משום דקא יניק משדה חבירו והיינו קולא והוה ליה לעולא לעיין ולדקדק שלא יפטרו מביכורין אלא כדינו ומאי לקולא לא דק: מי סברת. דהא דקאמר עולא ט"ז אמה לכל רוח דאמות מרובעות קא בעי דאית להו מורשא דקרנתא בעגולא קא אמרי' דהשיב סביבות האילן ט"ז אמה בלא מורשא דקרנתא ואכתי מקשה ליה למאי דבעי לתרוצי באמות עגולות מכדי כמה מרובע יותר על העיגול רביע וכשתוציא הרביע מן אלף וכ"ד אלא תשס"ח משתייר לך כיצד מח' מאות תשליך מאתים נשתיירו שש מאות וממאתיים תרציא ג' הרי הן ד' מאות וג' אמות עגולות ומכ"ד תשליך הרביע נשתיירו י"ח ואותן י"ח מוסיף על ד' מאות הרי תשס"ח. ואכתי אין מגיע חשבון של עולא לתמני מאה ותלתין ותלתא ותילתא לפי שחשבון של עולא שכשחושב בעיגול הוא פוחת חצי אמה מכלל ב) אמות האילן מחשבון של תמני מאה ותלתין ותלתא ותילתא וכשתרצה להשוות חשבונו של עולא לחשבון זה צריך אתה להביא ד' רצועות של רוחב חצי אמה ואורך כל אחת של ל"ב אמה שהן ס"ד ותשימם מבחוץ לאלו תשס"ח אמה עגולות תשים אותן ד' רצועות בריבוע ולא בעיגול ויבא החשבון שוה ומהיכן אתה נוטל אותן ס"ד אמה שאתה מחלק לד' רצועות של אורך ל"ב (אורך ל"ב) אמה ורוחב חצי אמה שאתה משים בריבוע מחוץ לעיגול זה מכאן אתה נוטלן לפי שחשבון תמני מאה ותלתין ותלתא ותילתא הוא עודף על ד' מאות וס"ח ששים וה' אמות ושליש אמה ומחשבון זה אינו חושב אותו שליש אמה שאינו דבר חשוב אלא ס"ה אמות חושב מס"ד אמות נעשה אותן ד' רצועות שארכן ל"ב ורחבן חצי אמה ואותה אמה חמישית הנשארת חלוק אותה לד' רביעי אמה ויהיה כל רביע חצי אמה אורך וחצי אמה רוחב ותן אלו ד' רבעין לד' הקרנות של רצועות למלאות הזוית והיינו דקאמר אכתי פש ליה לעולא פלגא דאמתא דבציר חשבונו מחשבון ג' אילנות והיינו דלא דק ולחומרא לא דק שמחייב להביא ביכורים בפחות משיעור ברייתא של ג' אילנות. והא דלא חשבינן ההוא שליש אמה משום דאי מרבעת לה להוסיפה על רצועות של חצי אמה לא היתה אפי' כחוט השער משו"ה לא חשיב ליה: מביא וקורא. מן הארץ אשר נתת לי: מאי לאו. דקני קרקע כל שהוא וקשיא לעולא דאמר דאילן הסמוך לתוך ט"ז אמה גזלן הוא: מביא ואינו קורא. משום דקי"ל דקנה [שני] אילנות בתוך שדה חבירו לא קנה קרקע אבל ג' אילנות דקנה קרקע מביא וקורא. מאי קנה קרקע לאו דקנה כל שהוא וקשיא לעולא. לא ט"ז אמה קנה מן האחרון ועד חבירו: ולכתוב עליה פרוזבול. היינו תקנת עשירים שהיו מלוים על משכון קרקע דלאו שמיטה משמט לא מלוה בשטר ולא מלוה על המשכון וכתוב הכי מוסרני לכם אגב קרקע ב"ד פלוני ופלוני חוב שיש לי על פלוני שאגבנו בכל שעה שארצה וחותמין עליו ב"ד אלמא דקרקע כל שהוא חייב בביכורים אע"ג דסמיך האי קרקע למצר אחר וקשיא לעולא:

מסורת הש"ס

א) [לקמן קא:] עירובין יד: ודף עו. מ. עו: סוכה ח. [אהלות פי"ב מ"ו], ב) ביכורים פ"א מ"ו גיטין מח., ג) לקמן פא. ביכורים פ"א מ"ו [גיטין מח.], ד) קדושין כו. פאה פ"ג מ"ו לקמן קנ., ה) ל"ל פ"ה, ו) ל"ל ב"ד, ז) רש"ל מ"ו, ח) רש"ל, ט) [ל"ל מביא ואינו קורא], י) [עי' תוס' קדושין כו. ועי' תוי"ט ד"ה ובביכורים וכו' שמירת תוס' ע"ש].

הגהות הב"ח

(א) גמ' בית סאה בשבילן עד עלמא כמה הוו: (ב) שם על העיגול רביע (ג) פשו להו ז' מאה ושתין ותמניא) תא"מ ונ"ב ר' משולם לא גרס לה: (ג) רש"י ד"ה וכמה מרובע וכו' דהשתא פשה ליה שיעורא דמתני': (ד) תוס' ד"ה הכי גרס ר"ת וכו' בספר אחר מפורש בגלגון הספר וכו' עד שיהא רוחב החוט שני שלישי: (ה) בא"ד הרי אורך התחתון פחות מן העליון:

גליון הש"ס

תוס' ד"ה לא כו' וי"ל דהתם כשענפי. עיין לקמן דף פב ע"ב תוס' ד"ה ומלו:

ליקוטי רש"י

[תחילת לקוטי רש"י ששייך לכאן נדפס בדף כו:] פרוזבול. לפי שראה הלל שנמנעו העשירים מלהלוות לעניים מפני ירלת השביעית שמשמטת והיו עוברין על מה שכתוב פן יהיה דבר עם לבבך בליעל וגו' עמד הלל והתקין פרוזבול. פרוז בול ריום כמו שמפרשין על מדותיו כלומר בנדה (דף ז:) בול עשירים שביהודה ראשי בולאות כלומר ריוח לעשירים שלא יפסידו שלהם. ותנן גופו של פרוזבול מוסרני לכם פלוני ופלוני הדיינים שבמקום פלוני שכל חוב שיש לי אלל פלוני שאגבנו כל זמן שארלה והדיינין חותמין עליו מלמטה או העדים והלכך משמסר שטרותיו לב"ד לגבותן ואיהו לא קגבי לא קרינן ביה לא יגוש דדיינין קגבו ליה והפקר ב"ד הפקר וה"ם כשיש לו ללוה קרקע וגבי ליה הכי וסמכו מלוה בקרקע מלוה גבית דהכא לא שייך לא יגוש [כדכתב ועומד הוא] שלא יהא כל מה שיוכלו חכמים לתקן כדי שלא יגרמו עקירת דבר מן התורה התקינו כאן נראה הטעם עניי ומריבי זקני ז"ל שמעתי דהיינו טעמא דכל דבר שלא מן התורה תקנו ואע"פ שאין רגילין להלוותו אא"כ יש לו קרקע להשתעבד לעלמא ובמלותא דשכיחא תקינו רבנן אבל בשאין לו קרקע מילתא דלא שכיחא היא ולא תקינו רבנן פרוזבול [רשב"ם לקמן סה:]. פרוז. תקנה [גיטין לו:]. בולי ובוטי. עשירים ועניים עשירים שלא יפסידו ועניים שלא תנעל דלת בפניהם [שם לז.].

חשק שלמה על רבינו גרשום

א) נראה דל"ל אבל לקולא לא דק מי אמרינן כיון דמלריך וכו'. ב) אולי ל"ל מכל ד' לידי האילן.

קז א מיי׳ פ״ג מהל׳ מכירה הל׳ ח [ט] טוש״ע ח״מ סי׳ רב סעיף ז:
קח ב מיי׳ פ״א מהל׳ תרומות הל׳ כד:
קט ג מיי׳ פ״ב מהל׳ ביכורים הל׳ יא:
קי ד ה מיי׳ פ״י מהל׳ שכנים הל׳ ח סמג עשין פב טוש״ע ח״מ סי׳ קנה סעיף כו:
קיא ו מיי׳ פי״ג מהל׳ נזקי ממון הל׳ כו סמג עשין סח טוש״ע ח״מ סי׳ תח סעיף ז:

[א] ונקנין עמה נכסים שאין להם אחריות הכא במאי עסקינן בחיטי דיקא נמי דקתני כל שהוא ש״מ ת״ש [ב] אילן מקצתו בארץ ומקצתו בחו״ל טבל וחולין מעורבין זה בזה דברי רבי [ג] רבן שמעון בן גמליאל אומר הגדל בחיוב חייב הגדל בפטור פטור ע״כ לא פליגי אלא דמר סבר [ד] יש ברירה ומר סבר אין ברירה אבל גדל בפטור דברי הכל פטור (א) הכא במאי עסקינן דמפסיק צונמא אי הכי מאי טעמיה דרבי דהדרי ערבי (ב) ובמאי קא מיפלגי מר סבר אוירא מבלבל ומר סבר האי לחודיה קאי והאי לחודיה קאי ושש עשרה אמה ותו לא והא תנן [ה] מרחיקין את האילן מן הבור כ״ה אמה אמר אביי מיזל טובא אזלי אכחושי לא מכחשי אלא עד שש עשרה אמה טפי לא מכחשי כי אתא רב דימי אמר בעא מיניה ריש לקיש מרבי יוחנן אילן הסמוך למיצר בתוך י״ו אמה מהו אמר ליה גזלן הוא ואין מביאין ממנו בכורים [ו] כי אתא רבין אמר רבי יוחנן [ז] אחד אילן הסמוך למיצר ואחד אילן הנוטה מביא וקורא שעל מנת כן הנחיל יהושע לישראל את הארץ:

מתני׳ [ח] אילן שהוא נוטה לשדה חבירו קוצץ מלא [ט] המרדע על גבי המחרישה ובחרוב ובשקמה כנגד המשקולת [י] בית השלחין כל האילן כנגד המשקולת אבא שאול אומר כל אילן סרק כנגד המשקולת: גמ׳ איבעיא להו אבא שאול ארישא קאי או אסיפא קאי ת״ש דתניא בית השלחין אבא שאול אומר כל האילן כנגד המשקולת מפני שהצל רע לבית השלחין שמע מינה ארישא קאי אמר רב אשי מתניתין נמי דיקא דקתני כל אילן סרק אי אמרת בשלמא ארישא קאי היינו דקתני כל אילן אלא אי אמרת אסיפא קאי אילן סרק מיבעי ליה אלא לאו שמע מינה ארישא קאי שמע מינה: מתני׳ [י] אילן שהוא נוטה לרה״ר קוצץ כדי שיהא גמל עובר ורוכבו רבי יהודה אומר גמל טעון פשתן או חבילי זמורות רבי שמעון אומר כל האילן כנגד המשקולת מפני הטומאה: גמ׳ מאן תנא דבנזקין בתר אומדנא דהשתא אזלינן אמר ר״ל במחלוקת שנויה ורבי אליעזר היא דתנן [כ] אין עושין חלל תחת רשות הרבים בורות שיחין ומערות רבי אליעזר מתיר בכדי שתהא עגלה מהלכת וטעונה אבנים רבי יוחנן אמר אפילו תימא רבנן התם [ל] זימנין דמפחית ולאו אדעתיה אבל הכא קמא קמא קא קייץ ליה: ר׳ יהודה אומר גמל טעון פשתן או חבילי זמורות: איבעיא להו שיעורא דרבי יהודה נפיש או דלמא שיעורא דרבנן נפיש פשיטא דשיעורא דרבנן נפיש דאי ס״ד שיעורא דרבי יהודה נפיש רבנן בשיעורא דרבי יהודה היכי עבדי ואלא מאי שיעורא דרבנן נפיש רבי יהודה בשיעורא דרבנן מאי עביד אפשר דגחין וחליף תותיה: רבי שמעון אומר כל האילן כנגד המשקולת מפני הטומאה: תנא מפני אהל הטומאה פשיטא מפני הטומאה תנן אי ממתניתין הוה אמינא דלמא מייתי עורב טומאה ושדי התם (ג) וסגיא בדחלולי בעלמא קא משמע לן:

הדרן עלך לא יחפור

ונקנין עמה נכסים שאין להם אחריות. דתנן בקדושין (דף כו.) נכסים שאין להם אחריות נקנין עם נכסים שיש להם אחריות בכסף בשטר ובחזקה שהמטלטלין אין נקנין אלא במשיכה וקרקע נקנה בכסף ואם מכר לו קרקע ומטלטלין יחד כיון שנתן דמי הקרקע או מסר לו שטר מכירת קרקע או החזיק בקרקע מדעת מוכר נקנו המטלטלין בלא משיכה קתני מיהא קרקע כל שהוא חייב בביכורים וקס״ד ביכורי אילן קאמר: הכא במאי עסקינן בחטין. שכל ז׳ המינים חייבים בביכורים: מעורבין זה בזה. שאין סומכין על הברירה לחלקו לחלאים ולומר שלצד הארץ חייבין ושלצד החוץ פטורין: אבל דכ״ע הגדל בפטור פטור. שאם היו כל שרשיו בחו״ל פטור ואפילו עומד האילן בתוך שש עשרה אמה לארץ ולא אמרינן מן הארץ ינק: דמפסיק צונמא. באמצע שרשים ב) שאין שני לצדדין יכולין לינק זה מזה: דהדרי וערבי. האילן נעשה אחד למעלה בענפיו: אוירא מבלבל. אע״פ שבתוך הקרקע (ד) כשני אילנות הוא ולמעלה באויר העולם נעשה אחד מתערבין יונקותיו: כ״ה אמה. קשה לעולא דאמר י״ו אמה ותו לא: אכחושי לא מכחשי. בשדה חבירו אלא עד שיתסרי הלכך טפי מהכי לאו גזלן הוא: הנוטה. נופו לתוך שדה של חבירו: שעל מנת כן הנחיל יהושע. התנה עמהם שלא יקפידו על כך: מתני׳ מרדע. מלמד בקר: קוצץ. הענפים עד גובה מלא מרדע שלא יעכבוהו מלהוליך מחרשתו שם: החרוב והשקמה. אילנם מרובה וקשה לשדה: כנגד המשקולת. כל מה שנוטה לתוך שדהו: משקולת. חוט (ה) האמרכולין שבונין חומה ותולין בה משקולת של אבר: ואם בית השלחין היא כל האילן. אפי׳ אינו חרוב ושקמה קוצץ כנגד המשקולת שהצל רע לבית השלחין: אבא שאול אומר כו׳. בגמ׳ מפרש אהייא קאי: גמ׳ ארישא קאי. דקאמר ת״ק קוצץ מלא מרדע ואפי׳ אילן סרק חוץ מחרוב ושקמה ואמר ליה אבא שאול כל אילן סרק נמי כנגד המשקולת: או אסיפא קאי. דקאמר ת״ק (ו) כל האילן כנגד המשקולת ואפילו אילן העושה פירות ואמר ליה אבא שאול כל אילן סרק הוא דכנגד המשקולת אבל אילן העושה פירות נמי מלא מרדע ותו לא: כל האילן. כל האילנות: אי אמרת בשלמא ארישא קאי. ולטפויי אתא [מחרוב ושקמה דקאמר ת״ק] היינו דקאמר כל: אלא אי אמרת אסיפא קאי. מאי כל הא לגרועי אתא: מתני׳ אילן הנוטה לרשות הרבים קוצץ. מן הענפים התחתונות כדי שיהא גמל עובר תחת העליונות: מפני הטומאה. מפרש בגמ׳: גמ׳ בתר [אומדנא] דהשתא אזלינן. דקתני קוצץ מן הענפים כדי שיהא גמל עובר ורוכבו והרי חוזרין וגדלים לאחר זמן: כדי שתהא עגלה מהלכת. אם תקרתה חזקה כל כך מותר ואע״ג שסופה שתתליע ותפחת: קמא קמא קייץ ליה. כל ענף וענף שיקדים ויצמח יקצצנו: בשיעורא דרבי יהודה מאי עבדי ליה. כשיבא גמל טעון פשתן היאך יעבור: מפני אהל הטומאה. שמא יפול כזית מת אצל האילן והרי הענפים (ז) ארוכים מאהילין עליו ועל עוברי הדרכים ומביאים עליהם את הטומאה: ושדי התם. על האילן ומתוך שענפיו רבים הטומאה עומדת שם ואינה נופלת לארץ ובני אדם עוברים תחתיה ואי לא חיישינן אלא להכי בדחלולי בעלמא סגי ליה לקוץ אחד אחד מבינתים כדי להרחיק אויר ביניהם ולא תעמוד שם טומאה: קמ״ל מתניתא דאפילו לא נותר בו אלא ענף אחד מזיק הוא את הרבים: הדרן עלך לא יחפור

בחטה. וא״ת והא חטה יניקתה ג׳ טפחים כדמוכח בשבת פרק אמר ר״ע (דף פה.) ואין לומר דכל שהוא דהכא לאו דוקא דהא בפ״ק דקדושין (דף כו.) קא מיירי לה בשמעתא דלא בעי צבורין בה או לאו וקאמר כל שהוא לאמו חזי ומשני כגון שנעץ בה מחט וקאמר איכפל תנא לאשמועינן מחט מי לא עסקינן דתלי ביה מרגניתא משמע דכל שהוא דוקא וי״ל דנהי דיניקתה ג׳ מ״מ עיקר יניקתה אינו אלא כנגדה ואילן נמי יניקתו כ״ה אפ״ה עיקר יניקתו י״ו ט): ואחד אילן הנוטה מביא וקורא. בפרק המקבל (ב״מ דף קז. ושם) פליגי רב ושמואל באילן הנוטה על המיצר רב אמר הנוטה לכאן לכאן והנוטה לכאן לכאן ושמואל אמר חולקין ופירש בקונט׳ התם דבנטיעת שרשים איירי ולפיכך שמעתין דהכא כרב דאזיל בתר שרשין ורשב״א פירש שם בענין אחר: שעל מנת כן הנחיל יהושע וכו׳. במרובה (ב״ק דף פב.) פריך אמאי לא חשיב לה בהדי עשרה תנאין של יהושע ומשני לה: בדחלולי סגי. פי׳ ר״ח דחלולי לשון צורה שעושים צורה של עץ ונראין כבני אדם ואין העוף נראה לישאר שם קמ״ל דאע״פ שבורח העוף פעמים שמשאיר שם בשר המת שמביא בפיו ונשאר שם בענף הלכך אין לו תקנה אלא בקציצת ענפים כולם (ח):

רבינו גרשום

בחטה. זרוע בתוכו וממנה מביא בכורים דלא אזלי שרשין כלום וליכא למימר דקא ינקי ממצר אחר: דיקא נמי. דבחטה עסקי׳ דקתני קרקע כל שהוא דאי באילן עסקינן לא סגיא בקרקע כל שהוא כלל ש״מ: אילן הנטוע על שפת [ספר] של ארץ ישראל מקצתו נוטה בארץ ומקצתו נוטה בחו״ל טבל וחולין מעורבין זה בזה דאותו הנוטה בארץ הוה ליה טבל ואותו הנוטה בחו״ל הוה ליה חולין ולאו בר עישורי נינהו ולהכי טבל וחולין מעורבין זה בזה ואסורין רשב״ג סבר א) מש״ה אמר הגדל בחיוב חייב משום דיש ברירה דיכול לברור איזה ענף נוטה בחו״ל ואיזה בארץ ורבי סבר אין ברירה מש״ה טבל וחולין מעורבין זה בזה ואסור אבל גדל בחיוב דכולה אילן היה בא״י אע״ג דאזלי שרשין בחו״ל וקא ינקי מחו״ל דברי הכל חייב דשדיין עיקרו בתר נופו וקשיא לעולא: דמפסיק צונמא. דלא קאזלי שרשין כלל בחוצה לארץ מפני הצונמא דמפסיק מש״ה דברי הכל חייב אבל אי לא מפסיק צונמא פטור מפני השרשין דקא ינקי מחוץ לארץ: אי הכי. דמפסיק צונמא בהא לימא רבי טבל וחולין מעורבין זה בזה ב) דאותו הנוטה בארץ הוי ליה טבל ואותו הנוטה בחו״ל הוי ליה חולין ולאו בר עישורי אינן (והא גדל כולו בארץ) ומשני דהדרי ערבי נופין ולמעלה מקצתן בארץ ומקצתן בחו״ל רבי סבר אויר ארץ ואויר חו״ל מבלבלן ולהכי טבל וחולין מעורבין זה בזה: מרחיקין את האילן ט״ז אמה ותו לא ורמינהו וכו׳. מינק ינקי עד ט״ז אמה ואין מביא ממנו בכורים. ג) ור׳ יוחנן ס״ל כעולא אחד אילן הסמוך למצר חבירו וא׳ אילן הנוטה לתוך של חבירו מביא וקורא שעל מנת כן הנחיל יהושע לישראל את הארץ שזה חופר בתוך שלו וזה נוטע בתוך שלו: פיסקא קוצץ מלא מרדע על גבי המחרישה. שכשהוא עובר על גבי המחרישה והמרדע על כתיפו כל אותן הענפים שמעכבין לו קוצצין אותן שכנגד המחרישה: בחרוב ובשקמה. דאיכא תרתי לריעותא חדא דענפיו מרובים ומזיק לשדה ואין (שוין) פירותיהן חשובין: קוצץ כולו כנגד המשקולת. כל הענפים הנוטים לשדהו וקוצץ ממטה ועד למעלה כעין שיכול להוריד מלמעלה מן האילן ועד למטה קו המשקולת והולך שוה שאין שם עיכוב ענף: ואם בית השלחין היא. השדה הצריך לה מטר כל שעה להשקותה והצל רע לה קוצץ כל האילן בין עושה פרי בין אינו עושה כנגד המשקולת: אבא שאול אומר כל אילן סרק שאין בו פרי קוצץ כנגד המשקולת: איבעיא להו. הא דקתני אבא שאול כל אילן סרק כנגד המשקולת ארישא דמתני׳ קאי דקתני בחרוב ובשקמה כנגד המשקולת ואמר אבא שאול כל אילן סרק קוצץ כנגד המשקולת ולא חרוב ושקמה משום דקא טעני פירות כל שהוא או אסיפא קאי דקתני בית השלחין כל האילן כנגד המשקולת בין אילן סרק ובין אילן פירות ואתא אבא שאול למימר כל אילן סרק כנגד המשקולת אפי׳ חרוב ושקמה דדמי לאילן סרק משום דאיכא תרתי לריעותא אבל אילן פרי אינו קוצץ כל עיקר אפי׳ בבי׳ השלחין: ת״ש אבא שאול אומר כל האילן כנגד המשקולת מפני שהצל רע לבית השלחין דמזיקי ענפיו שאין יכול המטר לירד מש״ה קוצץ ש״מ הא דקתני במתני׳ כל אילן סרק כנגד המשקולת ארישא קאי דאתי לאפוקי חרוב ושקמה דאינו קוצץ משום דקא טעין פירא: אי אמרת בשלמא ארישא קאי היינו דקתני כל אילן סרק ולא חרוב ושקמה וקאמר אילן סרק קוצץ ולא אילן פירות א״כ ל״ל למיתני כל אילן סרק אילן סרק מיבעי ליה למיתני (הכי) אבא שאול אומר אילן סרק כנגד המשקולת ולא כל האילן שעושה פרי אלא ש״מ מדקתני כל אילן סרק ולא חרוב ושקמה ארישא קאי ולחומרא דאתי לאפוקי חרוב ושקמה דאינו קוצץ דהיינו חומרא: פיסקא אילן הנוטה (לשדה חבירו) [לרשות הרבים] כו׳. מאן תנא דלהיכא דאיכא נזק בתר אומדנא דהשתא אזלינן בתר נזק דעתיד למיתי: אמר ר״ל מחלוקת שנויה. במתני׳ אילן הנוטה ברה״ר קוצץ כדי שיהא הגמל עובר ברוכבו דאזלינן בתר היזק דהשתא ולא בתר דעתיד למיתי דאי אזלינן בתר העתיד מכל וכל צריך לקצצו דדלמא מגדלו וקא מזיק לרבים. ואליבא דר״א דאמר כדי שתהא עגלה מהלכת עליה וטעונה אבנים כלומר שתהא התקרה חזקה כדי שתהא יכולה לסבול עגלה טעונה אבנים אלמא דבנזקין אזלינן בתר אומדנא דהשתא ולא חייש דלמא היום או מחר מרקבת התקרה ונפלי בגווה אינשי דאזלי עלה.

מסורת הש"ס

א) גיטין כב., ב) נדרים נח:, ג) [עירובין לו: וש״נ], ד) [לעיל כה:], ה) ב״ק פב., ו) [לקמן פב:], ז) [פי׳ כשיבא לחרוש ומרים המרדע להכות הבהמה שחורש בה לא יהיו ענפי האילן מעכבין אותו. ערוך ערך מרדע], ח) לקמן ס., ט) [שם], י) פ״י שהלדדין אין יכולין, כ) רש״ל, ל) [וע״ע תוס׳ קדושין כו. ד״ה קרקע]:

הגהות הב"ח

(א) גמ׳ הכא במאי עסקינן. נ״ב מימה דס״ל להקשות ממשנה י׳ פ״ג דמעשרות להדיא דאילן העומד עיקרו בחו״ל פטור ממעשר וק״ל: (ב) שם דהדרי ערבי והכא קא מיפלגי: (ג) שם ושדי התם ובדחלולי בעלמא סגיא קמ״ל: (ד) רש״י ד״ה אוירא וכו׳ הקרקע הם כשני: (ה) ד״ה משקולת חוט האדרכלין שבונין: (ו) ד״ה או אסיפא וכו׳ ת״ק בית השלחין כל האילן: (ז) ד״ה מפני אהל וכו׳ הענפים המרובים מאהילין: (ח) תוס׳ ד״ה ובדחלולי וכו׳ ענפים כולם כנגד המשקולת הס״ד:

ליקוטי רש"י

טבל וחולין מעורבין זה בזה. אין לך פירי באילן זה שאין מקצתו מן הארץ שהוא טבל ומקצתו מחוצה לארץ שהוא חולין לפי שהיניקה מתערבת ונפקא מינה שאין מעשרין מטבל ודאי עליו להוי מן החיוב על הפטור ולא ממנו על טבל ודאי. הגדל בחיוב. מה שבתוך ארץ ישראל. דמפסיק צונמא. שן סלע מבדיל באמצע השרשים ומפסיקין עד הגזע הלכך לרבן שמעון לא ינקי מהדדי [גיטין כב.]. צונמא. צונמא בלשון ארמי סלע [בראשית מא, כג ונדה ח.]. אבן [רשב״ם לקמן פט:]. דהדרי ערבי. שטען מן הגזע ולמעלה שלם. מר סבר אוירא מבלבל. אע״פ שכל מה שיש מן השרשין בקרקע הוי מובדל הואיל וכשיבא לאויר הוא מעורב ומבלבל וינקי מהדדי. ומ״ס. אוירא לא מבלבל הואיל ובתוך הקרקע מובדל בסלע שאינו מלמים [גיטין כב.]. מרחיקין את האילן מן הבור. שהשרשין מתפשטין ונוקבין בכותלי הבור ומחלידין את הקרקע והכתלים נופלים [ב״מ קיז.]. כ״ה אמה. כך שיעור שהשרשין נמשכין והולכין ומקלקלין את כותלי הבור [לעיל יח.]. קוצץ מלא מרדע. בגבהו [רשב״ם לקמן פב:].

[המשך בדף כח.]

וְנִקְנִין עִמָּהּ נְכָסִים שֶׁאֵין לָהֶם אַחֲרָיוּת – AND MOVABLE PROPERTY[1] CAN BE ACQUIRED ALONG WITH IT.[2] Now, one of the laws taught in the Mishnah is that a minute measure of land is subject to *bikkurim.* This contradicts Ulla's ruling that a tree within sixteen *amos* of a neighboring property is exempt from *bikkurim.*[3]

The Gemara answers:

הָכָא בְּמַאי עָסְקִינַן – **With what are we dealing here,** in the Mishnah? בְּחִיטֵּי – **With** stalks of **wheat** growing on a minute piece of land. Wheat is subject to *bikkurim* even if it grows near a boundary.[4] It is only a *tree* within sixteen *amos* of a boundary that Ulla exempted from *bikkurim.*

The Gemara finds support for this interpretation of the Mishnah:

דַּיְקָא נַמִי – One can **also infer this from** a **precise** reading of the Mishnah, דְּקָתָנֵי כָּל שֶׁהוּא – **for the Mishnah states:** A MINUTE MEASURE of land. This implies that the Mishnah refers to wheat, which can indeed grow on a minuscule portion of land, and not to a tree, whose trunk surely takes up more than a "minute measure of land." שְׁמַע מִינָּהּ – Indeed, we **learn from [this wording]** that the Mishnah refers to wheat.

The Gemara attempts once again to refute Ulla's ruling:

תָּא שְׁמַע – **Come, learn** a proof from the following Baraisa: אִילָן מִקְצָתוֹ בָּאָרֶץ וּמִקְצָתוֹ בְּחוּצָה לָאָרֶץ – If A TREE is growing PARTLY INSIDE THE LAND of Israel AND PARTLY OUTSIDE THE LAND,[5] טֶבֶל וְחוּלִּין מְעוֹרָבִין זֶה בְּזֶה – its fruit is deemed to be *TEVEL* AND ORDINARY non-*tevel* produce INTERMINGLED WITH ONE ANOTHER.[6] דִּבְרֵי רַבִּי – These are THE WORDS OF REBBI. רַבָּן שִׁמְעוֹן בֶּן גַּמְלִיאֵל אוֹמֵר – RABBAN SHIMON BEN GAMLIEL SAYS: הַגָּדֵל בְּחִיּוּב חַיָּיב – [THE FRUIT] THAT GROWS IN [THE AREA] SUBJECT to *terumos* and tithes (i.e. inside the Land of Israel) IS SUBJECT to these requirements, הַגָּדֵל בִּפְטוּר פָּטוּר – while [THE FRUIT] THAT GROWS IN [THE AREA] EXEMPT from *terumos* and tithes (i.e. outside the Land) IS EXEMPT from these requirements.

The Gemara now presents the proof:

עַד כָּאן לֹא פְּלִיגֵי אֶלָּא – **They** (Rebbi and Rabban Shimon ben Gamliel) **do not disagree except insofar** דְּמַר סָבַר יֵשׁ בְּרֵירָה – **as** one **master** (Rabban Shimon ben Gamliel) **holds** that **a determination can be made** as to which part of the tree is growing inside the Land of Israel and which is not, וּמַר סָבַר אֵין בְּרֵירָה – **while the** other **master** (Rebbi) **holds** that **no** such **determination** can be made.[7] אֲבָל גָּדֵל בִּפְטוּר דִּבְרֵי הַכֹּל פָּטוּר – **However,** if the entire tree were **growing in [the area] exempt** from *terumos* and tithes (i.e. outside the Land), **all** would **agree** that its fruit would be **exempt** from these requirements, even if the tree were within sixteen *amos* of the Land of Israel. This contradicts Ulla's view that a tree's status is affected by the fact that it draws nourishment from the area within sixteen *amos*.[8] – **?** –

The Gemara answers:

הָכָא בְּמַאי עָסְקִינַן – **With what are we dealing here,** in the Baraisa? דְּמַפְסִיק צוּנְמָא – With a case **where** an underground section of **rock separates** the roots along the border. Thus, the roots on each side of the border are not nourished by soil on the other side. Similarly, if a tree were entirely outside the Land and a section of rock prevented its roots from crossing the border and drawing nutrients, its fruit would be exempt from *terumos* and tithes, because in that case, Ulla's rule would not apply.

NOTES

1. Literally: properties that have no responsibility. The Baraisa uses this term to describe movable property, in contrast to real property (land and houses), which is generally described as "properties that have responsibility."

When one incurs a debt and the debt is recorded in a document [מִלְוָה בִּשְׁטָר], a lien automatically takes effect on any real property owned by the debtor at that time. Even if the debtor subsequently sells the property, the lien is not voided. Should the debtor default on his obligation, the creditor can seize the real property from the buyer to satisfy the debt. For this reason, real property is said to have "responsibility." Since it will always be there, the lender relies on it for surety when he lends money (*Rashi* to *Kiddushin* 26a ד״ה שיש). In contrast, movable property has "no responsibility," i.e. the lender does not rely on it for surety.

The fact that movable property has "no responsibility" is not pertinent to the point of law discussed here. The term *properties that have no responsibility* is merely the Baraisa's idiom for "movable property," a way of characterizing the legal difference between real and movable property.

2. It is a basic principle of law that the ownership of an object cannot be transferred from one person to another unless the transaction is formalized by an *acquisitory act* (an *act of kinyan*). Torah law defines various *kinyanim* for acquisition of different types of property, and a *kinyan* effective for one category of property may not be effective for another. Movable property is generally acquired by מְשִׁיכָה (*meshichah*), i.e. the prospective owner *draws* the object *near* to himself. Real property is acquired בְּכֶסֶף בִּשְׁטָר וּבַחֲזָקָה, *by means of money* (i.e. payment), *a document, or a proprietary act* (i.e. an act of improving the property). Nevertheless, the Mishnah (*Kiddushin* 26a) teaches: נְכָסִים שֶׁאֵין לָהֶם אַחֲרָיוּת נִקְנִין עִם נְכָסִים שֶׁיֵּשׁ לָהֶם אַחֲרָיוּת בְּכֶסֶף וּבִשְׁטָר וּבַחֲזָקָה – *Movable property may be acquired together with real property by means of money, a document, or a proprietary act.* This means that if one sells movable property along with real property, the act of acquiring the real property by any method effective for its acquisition suffices to acquire the movable property as well. [The acquisition of movable property through the acquisition of real property is known as קִנְיַן אַגַּב – *acquisition by dint of*] (*Rashi*).

This Mishnah informs us that even the acquisition of a minute portion of land suffices to acquire movable property by dint of it.

3. The Gemara assumes that the Mishnah refers to a tree whose owner owns only a minute portion of land around it (*Rashi*). Thus, it stands in clear contradiction to Ulla's ruling.

4. The *bikkurim* obligation applies to all seven species of fruit for which the Land of Israel is distinguished [wheat, barley, grapes, figs, pomegranates, olives and dates] (*Rashi*). Although the roots of wheat stalks extend up to three *tefachim* in each direction, each stalk's main source of nourishment is the ground directly beneath it (*Tosafos*).

5. I.e. a tree was planted on the border of the Land of Israel, so that part of the trunk is on either side of the border.

6. Fruit grown in the Land of Israel may not be eaten until all *terumos* and tithes are separated from it. Untithed produce is known as *tevel.* Fruit grown outside the Land is exempt from these requirements. Thus, the fruit of a tree situated partly inside and partly outside the Land is a mixture of *tevel* and non-*tevel* produce, i.e. each individual fruit is partially subject to *terumos* and tithes and partially exempt from these requirements (*Ritva*).

7. According to Rabban Shimon ben Gamliel, we can determine which part of the tree is subject to *terumos* and tithes by splitting it along the border. Fruit growing inside the border is considered produce of the Land of Israel and is subject to these requirements, while fruit growing outside the border is considered foreign produce and is exempt from them. [The critical factor with regard to *terumos* and tithes is the *location* of the tree. In this case, each part of the tree is judged according to its own location (*Chazon Ish, Bava Basra, Likutim* 21; see also *Chidushei Maran Riz HaLevi, Hil. Terumos* 1:24).] Rebbi, on the other hand, holds that we may not look at each part of the tree individually, but must view it as a unit; the entire tree is growing both inside and outside the Land of Israel. Therefore, all of its fruit is a mixture of *tevel* and non-*tevel* produce (see *Rashi* and *Rabbeinu Gershom*).

8. The basis for Ulla's rule is that a tree's status with regard to *bikkurim* (as well as *terumos* and tithes) depends not only on its location, but also on its source of sustenance. Accordingly, a tree located within sixteen *amos* of the Land of Israel cannot be exempted from any requirements incumbent upon produce of the Land. Since it draws its nourishment from both inside and outside the Land, its fruit must be considered a mixture of *tevel* and non-*tevel* produce (*Chidushei Maran Riz HaLevi,* ibid.).

This view is contradicted by Rabban Shimon ben Gamliel, who ruled that the fruit growing on the side of the tree that is directly outside the border is exempt from tithes, and by Rebbi, who disagreed only in the case of a tree that is situated on both sides of the border.

עין משפט נר מצוה

קז א מיי' פ"ג מהל' מכירה הל' ח [ט] טוש"ע ח"מ סי' רב סעיף ז:

קח ב מיי' פ"א מהל' תרומות הל' כד:

קט ג מיי' פ"ב מהל' ביכורים הל' יא:

קי ד ה מיי' פ"י מהל' שכנים הל' ח סמג עשין פב טוש"ע ח"מ סי' קנה סעיף כו:

קיא ו מיי' פי"ג מהל' נזקי ממון הל' כו סמג עשין סח טור ש"ע ח"מ סי' תיז סעיף ד:

רבינו גרשום

בחטה. זרוע בתוכו וממנה מביא בכורים דלא אזלי שרשין כלום וליכא למימר דקא ינקי ממצר אחר: **דיקא נמי.** דבחטה עסקי' **דקתני** קרקע **כל שהוא** דאי באילן עסקינן לא סגיא בקרקע כל שהוא כלל ש"מ: **אילן הנטוע** על (שפת) [ספר] של ארץ ישראל **מקצתו** נוטה **בארץ ומקצתו** נוטה **בחו"ל טבל וחולין מעורבין זה בזה** דאותו הנוטה בארץ הוה ליה טבל ואותו הנוטה בחו"ל הוה ליה חולין ולאו בר עישורי נינהו ולהכי טבל וחולין מעורבין זה בזה ואסורין **רשב"ג סבר** א) מש"ה אמר **הגדל בחיוב חייב** משום דיש ברירה דיכול לברור איזה ענף נוטה בחו"ל ואיזה בארץ **ורבי סבר אין ברירה** מש"ה טבל וחולין מעורבין זה בזה ואסור אבל גדל בחיוב דכולה אילן היה בא"י אע"ג דאזלי שרשין בחו"ל וקא ינקי מחו"ל דברי הכל חייב דשדיין עיקרו בתר נופו וקשיא לעולא: **דמפסיק צונמא.** דלא קאזלי שרשין כלל בחוצה לארץ מפני הצונמא דמפסיק מש"ה דברי הכל חייב אבל אי לא מפסיק צונמא פטור מפני השרשין דקא ינקי מחוץ לארץ: **אי הכי.** דמפסיק צונמא בהא לימא רבי טבל וחולין מעורבין זה בזה ב) דאותו הנוטה בארץ הוי ליה טבל ואותו הנוטה בחו"ל הוי ליה חולין ולאו בר עישורי אינן (והא גדל כולו בארץ) ומשני **דהדרי ערבי** נופין ולמעלה מקצתן בארץ ומקצתן בחו"ל **רבי סבר אויר** ארץ ואויר חו"ל **מבלבלן** ולהכי טבל וחולין מעורבין זה בזה: מרחיקין את האילן **ט"ז אמה ותו לא ורמינהו וכו'.** מינק ינקי עד ט"ז אמה ואין מביא ממנו בכורים. ג) **ור' יוחנן** ס"ל כעולא **אחד אילן הסמוך למצר** חבירו **וא' אילן הנוטה** לתוך של חבירו **מביא וקורא שעל מנת כן הנחיל יהושע לישראל את הארץ** שזה חופר בתוך שלו וזה נוטע בתוך שלו: **פיסקא קוצץ מלא מרדע על גבי המחרישה.** שכשהוא עובר על גבי המחרישה והמרדע על כתיפו כל אותן הענפים שמעכבין לו קוצצין אותן שכנגד המחרישה: **בחרוב ובשקמה.** דאיכא תרתי לריעותא חדא דענפיו מרובים ומזיק לשדה ואין (שוין) פירותיהן חשובין: **קוצץ כולו כנגד המשקולת.** כל הענפים הנוטים לשדהו וקוצץ ממטה ועד למעלה כעין שיכול להוריד מלמעלה מן האילן ועד למטה קו המשקולת והולך שוה שאין שם עיכוב ענף: **ואם בית השלחין היא.** השדה דצריך לה מטר כל שעה להשקותה והצל רע לה קוצץ **כל האילן** בין עושה פרי בין אינו עושה **כנגד המשקולת: אבא שאול אומר כל אילן סרק** שאין בו פרי קוצץ **כנגד המשקולת: איבעיא להו.** הא דקתני אבא שאול כל אילן סרק כנגד המשקולת ארישא דמתני' **קאי** דקתני בחרוב ובשקמה כנגד המשקולת ואמר אבא שאול כל אילן סרק קוצץ כנגד המשקולת ולא חרוב ושקמה משום דקא טעני פירות כל שהוא **או אסיפא קאי** דקתני בית השלחין כל האילן כנגד המשקולת בין אילן סרק ובין אילן פירות ואתא אבא שאול למימר כל אילן סרק כנגד המשקולת אפי' חרוב ושקמה דדמי לאילן סרק משום דאיכא תרתי לריעותא אבל אילן פרי אינו קוצץ כל עיקר אפי' בבי' השלחין: **ת"ש אבא שאול** אומר כל האילן כנגד המשקולת מפני שהצל רע לבית השלחין דמזקי ענפיו שאין יכול המטר לירד מש"ה קוצץ **ש"מ** הא דקתני במתני' כל אילן סרק כנגד המשקולת **ארישא קאי** דאתי לאפוקי חרוב ושקמה דאינו קוצץ משום דקא טעין פירא: **אי אמרת** בשלמא ארישא קאי **היינו דקתני כל אילן** סרק ולא [illegible] **אלא אי אמרת אסיפא קאי** וקאמר אילן סרק קוצץ ולא אילן פירות א"כ ל"ל למיתני כל אילן סרק **אילן סרק מיבעי ליה** למיתני (הכי) אבא שאול אומר אילן סרק כנגד המשקולת ולא כל אילן פרי **אלא** ש"מ מדקתני כל אילן סרק ארישא קאי [illegible] חומרא דאתי לאפוקי חרוב ושקמה דאינו קוצץ דהיינו חומרא: **פיסקא** אילן הנוטה (לשדה חבירו) [לרשות הרבים] כו'. **מאן תנא דלהיכא דאיכא נזק בתר אומדנא דהשתא** אזלינן ולא בתר נזק דעתיד למיתי: **אמר ר"ל במחלוקת שנויה.** במתני' אילן הנוטה ברה"ר קוצץ כדי שיהא הגמל עובר ברוכבו דאזלינן בתר היזק דהשתא ולא בתר דעתיד למיתי דאי אזלינן בתר העתיד מכל וכל צריך לקצצו דדלמא מגדלו וקא מזיק לרבים. ואליבא דר"א דאמר **כדי שתהא עגלה מהלכת עליה וטעונה אבנים** כלומר שתהא התקרה חזקה כדי שתהא יכולה לסבול עגלה טעונה אבנים אלמא דבנזקין אזלינן בתר אומדנא דהשתא ולא חייש דלמא היום או מחר מרקבת התקרה ונפלי בגווה אינשי דאזלי עלה.

תוספות

בחטה. וא"ת והא חטה יניקתה ג' טפחים כדמוכח בשבת פרק אמר ר"ע בשמעתין דערוגה (דף פה.) ואין לומר דכל שהוא דהכא לאו דוקא דהא בפ"ק דקדושין (דף כו.) קא מייתי לה בשמעתא דלא בעי צבורין בה או לאו וקאמר כל שהוא למאי חזי ומשני כגון שנעץ בה מחט וקאמר איכפל תנא לאשמועינן מחט מי לא עסקינן דתלי ביה מרגניתא משמע דכל שהוא דוקא וי"ל דנהי דיניקתה ג' מ"מ עיקר יניקתה אינו אלא כנגדה ואילן נמי יניקתו כ"ה אפ"ה עיקר יניקתו י"ו ל):

ואחד אילן הנוטה מביא וקורא. בפרק המקבל (ב"מ דף קז. ושם) פליגי רב ושמואל באילן הנוטה על המיצר רב אמר הנוטה לכאן לכאן והנוטה לכאן לכאן ושמואל אמר חולקין ופירש בקונט' התם דבנטיית שרשים איירי ולפיכך שמעתין דהכא כרב דאזיל בתר שרשין ורשב"א פירש שם בענין אחר: **שעל** מנת כן הנחיל יהושע וכו'. במרובה (ב"ק דף פ:) פריך אמאי לא חשיב לה בהדי עשרה תנאין של יהושע ומשני לה: **בדחלולי** סגי. פי' ר"ח דחלולי לשון יראה שעושים צורה של עץ ונראין כמי אדם ואין העוף רשאי לישאר שם קמ"ל דאע"פ שברח העוף פעמים שמשאיר שם בשר המת שמביא בפיו ונשאר שם בענף הלכך אין לו תקנה אלא בקציצת ענפים כולם (ח):

הדרן עלך לא יחפור

גמרא

א ונקנין עמה נכסים שאין להם אחריות הכא במאי עסקינן בחיטי דיקא נמי דקתני כל שהוא ש"מ ת"ש א) ב אילן מקצתו בארץ ומקצתו בחו"ל טבל וחולין מעורבין זה בזה דברי רבי ג רבן שמעון בן גמליאל אומר הגדל בחיוב חייב הגדל בפטור פטור ע"כ לא פליגי אלא דמר סבר ג) יש ברירה ומר סבר אין ברירה אבל גדל בפטור דברי הכל פטור (א) הכא במאי עסקינן דמפסיק צונמא אי הכי מאי טעמיה דרבי דהדרי ערבי (ב) ובמאי קא מיפלגי מר סבר אוירא מבלבל ומר סבר האי לחודיה קאי והאי לחודיה קאי ושש עשרה אמה ותו לא והא תנן ד) מרחקין את האילן מן הבור כ"ה אמה אמר אביי מיזל טובא אזלי אכחושי לא מכחשי אלא עד שש עשרה אמה טפי לא מכחשי כי אתא רב דימי אמר בעא מיניה ריש לקיש מרבי יוחנן אילן הסמוך למיצר בתוך י"ו אמה מהו אמר ליה גזלן הוא ואין מביאין ממנו בכורים ה) כי אתא רבין אמר רבי יוחנן ד אחד אילן הסמוך למיצר ואחד אילן הנוטה מביא וקורא שעל מנת כן הנחיל יהושע לישראל את הארץ:

מתני' ו) ה אילן שהוא נוטה לשדה חבירו קוצץ מלא ז) המרדע על גבי המחרישה ובחרוב ובשקמה כנגד המשקולת ח) בית השלחין כל האילן כנגד המשקולת אבא שאול אומר כל אילן סרק כנגד המשקולת: **גמ'** איבעיא להו אבא שאול ארישא קאי או אסיפא קאי תא שמע דתניא בית השלחין אבא שאול אומר כל האילן כנגד המשקולת מפני שהצל רע לבית השלחין שמע מינה ארישא קאי שמע מינה אמר רב אשי מתניתין נמי דיקא דקתני כל אילן סרק אי אמרת בשלמא ארישא קאי היינו דקתני כל אילן אלא אי אמרת אסיפא קאי אילן סרק מיבעי ליה אלא לאו שמע מינה ארישא קאי שמע מינה:

מתני' ו אילן שהוא נוטה לרה"ר קוצץ כדי שיהא גמל עובר ורוכבו רבי יהודה אומר גמל טעון פשתן או חבילי זמורות רבי שמעון אומר כל האילן כנגד המשקולת מפני הטומאה: **גמ'** מאן תנא דבנזקין בתר אומדנא דהשתא אזלינן אמר ר"ל במחלוקת שנויה ורבי אליעזר היא דתנן ט) אין עושין חלל תחת רשות הרבים בורות שיחין ומערות רבי אליעזר מתיר בכדי שתהא עגלה מהלכת וטעונה אבנים רבי יוחנן אמר אפילו תימא רבנן התם י) זימנין דמפחית ולאו אדעתיה אבל הכא קמא קמא קא קייץ ליה: ר' יהודה אומר גמל טעון פשתן או חבילי זמורות: איבעיא להו שיעורא דרבי יהודה נפיש או דלמא שיעורא דרבנן נפיש פשיטא דשיעורא דרבנן נפיש דאי ס"ד שיעורא דרבי יהודה נפיש רבנן בשיעורא דרבי יהודה היכי עבדי ואלא מאי שיעורא דרבנן נפיש רבי יהודה בשיעורא דרבנן מאי עביד אפשר דגחין וחליף תותיה: רבי שמעון אומר כל האילן כנגד המשקולת מפני הטומאה: תנא מפני אהל הטומאה פשיטא תנן אי ממתניתין הוה אמינא דלמא מייתי עורב טומאה ושדי התם (ג) וסגיא בדחלולי בעלמא קא משמע לן:

הדרן עלך לא יחפור

רש"י

ונקנין עמה נכסים שאין להם אחריות. דתנן בקדושין (דף כו.) נכסים שאין להם אחריות נקנין עם נכסים שיש להם אחריות בכסף בשטר ובחזקה שהמטלטלין אין נקנין אלא במשיכה וקרקע נקנה בכסף ואם מכר לו קרקע ומטלטלין יחד כיון שנתן דמי הקרקע או מסר לו שטר מכירת קרקע או החזיק בקרקע מדעת מוכר נקנו המטלטלין בלא משיכה קתני מיהא קרקע כל שהוא חייב בביכורים וקס"ד ביכורי אילן קאמר: **הכא במאי עסקינן** בחטין. שכל ז' המינים חייבים בביכורים: מעורבין זה בזה. שאין סומכין על הברירה לחלקו לחצאים ולומר שלצד הארץ חייבין ושלצד החוץ פטורין: **אבל** דכ"ע הגדל בפטור פטור. שאם היו כל שרשיו בחו"ל פטור ואפילו עומד האילן בתוך שש עשרה אמה לארץ ולא אמרינן מן הארץ ינק: דמפסיק צונמא. באמצע שרשים י) שאין שני צדדין יכולין לינק זה מזה: דהדרי וערבי. האילן נעשה אחד למעלה בעביו: **אוירא מבלבל.** אע"פ שבתוך הקרקע (ד) כשני אילנות הוא ולמעלה באויר העולם נעשה אחד מתערבין יונקותיו: **כ"ה אמה.** קשה לעולא דאמר י"ו אמה ותו לא: **אכחושי לא מכחשי.** בשדה חבירו אלא עד שיתסרי הלכך טפי מהכי לאו גזלן הוא: הנוטה. נופו לתוך שדה של חבירו: שעל מנת כן הנחיל יהושע. התנה עמהם שלא יקפידו על כך: **מתני'** מרדע. מלמד בקר: קוצץ. הענפים עד גובה מלא מרדע שלא יעכבוהו מלהוליך מחרשתו שם: החרוב והשקמה. שצילם מרובה וקשה לשדה: כנגד המשקולת. כל מה שנוטה לתוך שדהו: משקולת. חוט (ה) האמרכולין שבונין חומה ותולין בה משקולת של אבר: **ואם בית השלחין היא כל האילן.** אפי' אינו חרוב ושקמה קוצץ כנגד המשקולת שהצל רע לבית השלחין: **אבא שאול אומר כו'.** בגמ' מפרש אהייא קאי: **גמ' ארישא קאי.** דקאמר ת"ק קוצץ מלא מרדע ואפי' אילן סרק חוץ מחרוב ושקמה ואמר ליה אבא שאול כל אילן סרק נמי כנגד המשקולת: **או אסיפא קאי.** דקאמר ת"ק (ו) כל האילן כנגד המשקולת ואפילו אילן העושה פירות ואמר ליה אבא שאול כל אילן סרק הוא דכנגד המשקולת אבל אילן העושה פירות נמי מלא מרדע ותו לא: **כל האילן.** כל האילנות: **אי אמרת בשלמא ארישא קאי.** ולטפויי אתא כ) [מחרוב ושקמה דקאמר ת"ק] היינו דקאמר כל: **אלא אי אמרת אסיפא קאי.** מאי כל הא לגרועי אתא: **מתני'** אילן הנוטה לרשות הרבים קוצץ. מן הענפים התחתונות כדי שיהא גמל עובר תחת העליונות: **מפני הטומאה.** מפרש בגמ': **גמ' בתר [אומדנא] דהשתא אזלינן.** דקתני קוצץ מן הענפים כדי שיהא גמל עובר ורוכבו והרי חוזרין וגדלים לאחר זמן: **כדי שתהא עגלה מהלכת.** אם תקרתה חזקה כל כך מותר ואע"ג שסופה שתתליע ותפחת: **קמא קמא קייץ ליה.** כל ענף וענף שיקדים ויצמח יקצצנו: **בשיעורא דרבי יהודה מאי עבדי ליה.** כשיבא גמל טעון פשתן היאך יעבור: **מפני אהל הטומאה.** שמא יפול כזית מת אצל האילן והרי הענפים (ז) ארוכים מאהילין עליו ועל עוברי הדרכים ומביאים עליהם את הטומאה: **ושדי התם.** על האילן ומתוך שענפיו רבים הטומאה עומדת שם ואינה נופלת לארץ ובני אדם עוברים תחתיה ואי לא חיישינן אלא להכי בדחלולי בעלמא סגי ליה לקוץ אחד אחד מבינתים כדי להרחיק אויר ביניהם ולא תעמוד שם טומאה: **קמ"ל.** מתניתא דאפילו לא נותר בו אלא ענף אחד מזיק הוא את הרבים: **הדרן עלך לא יחפור**

מסורת הש"ס

א) גיטין כב., ב) נדרים נח:, ג) [ערובין לו: וש"נ], ד) [לעיל כה:], ה) ב"ק פב., ו) [לקמן פב:], ז) [פי' כשיבא לחרוש ומריס המרדע להכות הבהמה שחורש בה לא יהיו ענפי האילן מעכבין אותו. ערוך ערך מרדע], ח) לקמן ס., ט) [שם], י) ס"י שהצדדין אין יכולין, כ) רש"ל, ל) [וע"ע תוס' קדושין כו. ד"ה קרקע]:

הגהות הב"ח

(א) גמ' הכא במאי עסקינן. נ"ב תימה דס"ל להקשות ממשנה י' פ"ג דמעשרות להדיא דאילן העומד עיקרו בחו"ל פטור ממעשר וק"ל: (ב) שם דהדרי ערבי והכא קא מיפלגי: (ג) שם ושדי התם ובדחלולי בעלמא סגיא קמ"ל: (ד) רש"י ד"ה אוירא וכו' הקרקע הם כשני: (ה) ד"ה משקולת חוט האדרכלין שבונין: (ו) ד"ה או אסיפא וכו' ת"ק בית השלחין כל האילן: (ז) ד"ה מפני אהל וכו' הענפים המרובים מאהילין: (ח) תוס' ד"ה ובדחלולי וכו' ענפים כולם כנגד המשקולת הס"ד:

ליקוטי רש"י

טבל וחולין מעורבין זה בזה. אין לך פירי באילן הזה שאין מקצתו מן הארץ שהוא טבל ומקצתו מחולה לארץ שהוא חולין לפי שהיניקה מתערבת ונפקא מינה שאין מעשרין מטבל ודאי עליו דהוי מן החיוב על הפטור ולא ממנו על טבל ודאי. **הגדל בחיוב.** מה שבתוך ארץ ישראל. **דמפסיק צונמא.** שן סלע מבדיל באמצע השרשים ומפסיקן עד הגזע הלכך לרבן שמעון לא ינקי מהדדי [גיטין כב.]. **צונמא.** צונמא בלשון ארמי סלע [בראשית מא, כג ונדה ח:]. **אבן** [רשב"ם לקמן פט:]. **דהדרי ערבי.** שהעץ מן הגזע ולמעלה שלם. **מר סבר אוירא מבלבל.** אע"פ שכל מה שיש מן השרשין בקרקע הוי מובדל הואיל וכשילא לאויר הוא מעורב ומבלבל ויינקי מהדדי. **ומ"ס.** אוירא לא מבלבל הואיל ובתוך הקרקע מובדל בסלע שאינו מלמיה [גיטין כב.]. **מרחיקין את האילן מן הבור.** שהשרשין מתפשטין ונוקבין בכותלי הבור ומחלידין את הקרקע והכתלים נופלים [ב"מ קיז.]. **כ"ה אמה.** כך שיעור שהשרשין נמשכין והולכין ומקלקלין את כותלי הבור [לעיל יח.]. **קוצץ מלא מרדע.** בגבהו [רשב"ם לקמן פב:].

[המשך בדף כח.]

The Gemara challenges this explanation:

אִי הָכִי – **If so,** that the roots are separated along the border, מַאי טַעְמֵיהּ דְּרַבִּי – **what is Rebbi's reasoning?** If the tree is divided underground, it stands to reason that we should view each section individually above the ground as well. – ? –

The Gemara answers:

דְּהַדְרֵי עָרְבֵי – **[The nutrients]** drawn by all the roots **mix** in the tree's trunk. We must therefore view the tree as a unit from the trunk upward.

The Gemara re-examines the dispute between Rebbi and Rabban Shimon ben Gamliel in light of its assertion that they are dealing with a tree whose roots are separated underground:

וּבְמַאי קָא מִיפַּלְגֵי – **Now, in what** point **do they disagree?** מַר סָבַר אֲוִירָא מְבַלְבֵּל – One **master** (Rebbi) **holds** that **the trunk**[9] **mixes** together all the nutrients. We therefore view the tree as a unit, all of whose fruit is the produce of soil on both sides of the border. וּמַר סָבַר הַאי לְחוּדֵיהּ קָאֵי וְהַאי לְחוּדֵיהּ קָאֵי – **The** other **master** (Rabban Shimon ben Gamliel) **holds that each** side of the tree **is independent of the other** side.[10]

The Gemara now challenges the accuracy of Ulla's measurement:

וְשֵׁשׁ עֶשְׂרֵה אַמָּה וְתוּ לֹא – Do roots extend **sixteen *amos*** from a tree **and no further?** וְהָא תְּנַן – **But we learned in a Mishnah:**[11] מַרְחִיקִין אֶת הָאִילָן מִן הַבּוֹר עֶשְׂרִים וְחָמֵשׁ אַמָּה – ONE MUST DISTANCE A TREE TWENTY-FIVE *AMOS* FROM A neighbor's PIT, so that its roots should not breach the walls of the pit. – ? –

The Gemara answers:

אָמַר אַבַּיֵי – **Abaye said:** מֵיזַל טוּבָא אָזְלֵי – **[The roots] travel a great** distance, up to twenty-five *amos* from the tree, אַכְחוּשֵׁי לֹא מַכְחֲשֵׁי אֶלָּא עַד שֵׁשׁ עֶשְׂרֵה אַמָּה – however, **they only drain** the earth of nutrients **within sixteen *amos*.** טְפֵי לֹא מַכְחֲשֵׁי – **Beyond** that distance **they do not drain** the earth of nutrients because a tree is not nourished by its outlying roots. Accordingly, a tree that is more than sixteen *amos* from a boundary is not considered a "thief."

The Gemara cites an opinion that concurs with Ulla:

כִּי אֲתָא רַב דִּימִי אָמַר – **When Rav Dimi arrived** in Babylonia from Israel, **he said:** בְּעָא מִינֵּיהּ רֵישׁ לָקִישׁ מֵרַבִּי יוֹחָנָן – **Reish Lakish inquired of R' Yochanan:** אִילָן הַסָּמוּךְ לְמֵיצַר בְּתוֹךְ שֵׁשׁ עֶשְׂרֵה אַמָּה מַהוּ – **What is** the law of *bikkurim* with regard to **a tree that is within sixteen *amos* of a** neighbor's **boundary?** אָמַר לֵיהּ – **[R' Yochanan] said to him:** גַּזְלָן הוּא וְאֵין מְבִיאִין מִמֶּנּוּ בִּכּוּרִים – **[The tree] is a "thief,"** because it draws nutrients from the neighboring field, **and one does not bring *bikkurim* from its** fruits.

The Gemara now cites another version of R' Yochanan's opinion:

כִּי אֲתָא רָבִין אָמַר רַבִּי יוֹחָנָן – **When Ravin arrived** in Babylonia from Israel, **he said in the name of R' Yochanan:** אֶחָד אִילָן הַסָּמוּךְ לְמֵיצַר וְאֶחָד אִילָן הַנּוֹטֶה – Whether **a tree is** planted **near a** neighbor's **boundary** (within sixteen *amos*) **or** the branches of **a tree extend** over a neighbor's property, מֵבִיא וְקוֹרֵא – **one brings** *bikkurim* from the tree's fruit, **and** also **recites** the *bikkurim* verses. The fact that the tree encroaches on another's property is irrelevant, שֶׁעַל מְנַת כֵּן הִנְחִיל יְהוֹשֻׁעַ לְיִשְׂרָאֵל אֶת הָאָרֶץ – **for it was on the condition [that this practice be tolerated] that Joshua apportioned the Jews** their **inheritance** in **the Land** of Israel.[12] Under Joshua's enactment, one is entitled to plant a tree near a boundary, and therefore, the tree is not considered a "thief."

Mishnah

אִילָן שֶׁהוּא נוֹטֶה לִשְׂדֵה חֲבֵירוֹ – If the branches of one's **tree extend over a neighbor's field,** קוֹצֵץ מְלֹא הַמַּרְדֵּעַ עַל גַּבֵּי הַמַּחֲרֵישָׁה – **[the neighbor] may cut off** enough of the lower branches to allow clearance for **the full** height **of an ox-goad** raised **over the plow.**[13] וּבֶחָרוּב וּבְשִׁקְמָה כְּנֶגֶד הַמִּשְׁקוֹלֶת – **In the case of a carob or a sycamore** tree, whose branches are very dense, he may cut *all* the protruding branches **along a plumb** line suspended over the boundary.[14] בֵּית הַשְּׁלָחִין – If the neighbor's property is **an irrigated field,** כָּל הָאִילָן כְּנֶגֶד הַמִּשְׁקוֹלֶת – he may cut the branches of **all trees along the plumb** line.[15] אַבָּא שָׁאוּל אוֹמֵר – **Abba Shaul says:** כָּל אִילָן סְרָק כְּנֶגֶד הַמִּשְׁקוֹלֶת – The branches of **all barren trees**[16] may be cut **along the plumb line.**

Gemara

The Gemara analyzes Abba Shaul's ruling:

אִיבַּעְיָא לְהוּ – **They inquired:** אַבָּא שָׁאוּל אַרֵישָׁא קָאֵי – **Did Abba Shaul address the first case** of the Mishnah, which deals with an ordinary field, אוֹ אַסֵּיפָא קָאֵי – **or did he address the latter case** of the Mishnah, which deals with an irrigated field?[17]

NOTES

9. Literally: the air (i.e. the trunk, which is above the ground).

10. [Literally: this (side) stands by itself and that (side) stands by itself.] According to Rabban Shimon ben Gamliel, location is the absolute criterion for determining whether a tree is subject to *terumos* and tithes. Therefore, although it is indisputable that nutrients from both sides of the border mix in the tree's trunk, we judge each side of the tree individually. The part that is inside the Land of Israel is subject to *terumos* and tithes even though some nutrients of foreign origin nourish its fruits. The part that is outside the Land is exempt from *terumos* and tithes even though it derives some nourishment from the Land (*Chazon Ish* ibid; cf. *Rashi* to *Gittin* 22a ד״ה מ״ס).

11. Above, 25b.

12. [The Land of Israel is known as the Jews' inheritance because it was originally promised to their forefathers by *Hashem.*]

When the Jews first entered Israel, the land was apportioned among them by Joshua. At that time, Joshua enacted a number of ordinances under which landowners were required to tolerate encroachments on their property in the public interest (*Rashi;* cf. *Tosafos* 26b ד״ה גזלן). One of the ordinances was that a landowner is permitted to plant a tree along his property line, even though its roots and branches may extend into his neighbor's property. [See *Bava Kamma* 81a-82a for a listing of Joshua's enactments.]

13. He may cut the branches off to the height necessary to allow clearance for a man driving a plow to pass under the tree and raise his ox-goad over the plow in order to prod the oxen (*Meiri*).

14. The owner of the affected field may cut away any branches that cross a plumb line hanging directly over the boundary, i.e. anything within the airspace of his property. This is because the branches of these two species of trees cast a great deal of shade, which is detrimental to produce growing in the field (*Rashi*).

15. The shade of any tree, even one whose branches are not as thick as a carob or a sycamore, is harmful to an irrigated field (*Rashi*). Sunlight assists in the proper absorption of the moisture provided by irrigation (*Nimukei Yosef*).

16. I.e. trees that do not bear fruit. It is unclear whether Abba Shaul is referring to trees that lean over an ordinary field or an irrigated field. This question is explored in the Gemara.

17. If Abba Shaul addressed the first case of the Mishnah (i.e. an ordinary field), his disagreement with the Tanna Kamma is this: The Tanna Kamma rules that all trees whose branches protrude may be cut enough to allow clearance for an ox-goad raised over a plow. Only carob and sycamore trees may be cut along the plumb line. Abba Shaul rules that all barren trees may also be cut along the plumb line.

If Abba Shaul addressed the latter case of the Mishnah (i.e. an irrigated field), the disagreement is as follows: The Tanna Kamma rules that *all* trees may be cut along the plumb line, while Abba Shaul holds

א ונקנין עמה נכסים שאין להם אחריות הכא במאי עסקינן בחיטי דיקא נמי דקתני כל שהוא ש"מ ת"ש ב אילן מקצתו בארץ ומקצתו בחו"ל טבל וחולין מעורבין זה בזה דברי רבי ג רבן שמעון בן גמליאל אומר הגדל בחיוב חייב הגדל בפטור פטור ע"כ לא פליגי אלא דמר סבר יש ברירה ומר סבר אין ברירה אבל גדל בפטור דברי הכל פטור הכא במאי עסקינן דמפסיק צונמא אי הכי מאי טעמיה דרבי דהדרי ערבי ובמאי קא מיפלגי מר סבר אוירא מבלבל ומר סבר האי לחודיה קאי והאי לחודיה קאי ושש עשרה אמה ותו לא והא תנן ד מרחיקין את האילן מן הבור כ"ה אמה אמר אביי מיזל טובא אזלי אכחושי לא מכחשי אלא עד שש עשרה אמה טפי לא מכחשי כי אתא רב דימי אמר בעא מיניה ריש לקיש מרבי יוחנן אילן הסמוך למיצר בתוך ט"ז אמה מהו אמר ליה גזלן הוא ואין מביאין ממנו בכורים ה כי אתא רבין אמר רבי יוחנן ג אחד אילן הסמוך למיצר ואחד אילן הנוטה מביא וקורא שעל מנת כן הנחיל יהושע לישראל את הארץ: **מתני'** ו אילן שהוא נוטה לשדה חבירו קוצץ מלא ז המרדע על גבי המחרישה ובחרוב ובשקמה כנגד המשקולת ה בית השלחין כל האילן כנגד המשקולת אבא שאול אומר כל אילן סרק כנגד המשקולת: **גמ'** איבעיא להו אבא שאול ארישא קאי או אסיפא קאי תא שמע דתניא בית השלחין אבא שאול אומר כל האילן כנגד המשקולת מפני שהצל רע לבית השלחין שמע מינה ארישא קאי שמע מינה אמר רב אשי מתניתין נמי דיקא דקתני כל אילן סרק אי אמרת בשלמא ארישא קאי היינו דקתני כל אילן אלא אי אמרת אסיפא קאי אילן סרק מיבעי ליה אלא לאו שמע מינה ארישא קאי שמע מינה: **מתני'** ו אילן שהוא נוטה לרה"ר קוצץ כדי שיהא גמל עובר ורוכבו רבי יהודה אומר גמל טעון פשתן או חבילי זמורות רבי שמעון אומר כל האילן כנגד המשקולת מפני הטומאה: **גמ'** מאן תנא דבנזקין בתר אומדנא דהשתא אזלינן אמר ר"ל במחלוקת שנויה ורבי אליעזר היא דתנן ח אין עושין חלל תחת רשות הרבים בורות שיחין ומערות רבי אליעזר מתיר בכדי שתהא עגלה מהלכת וטעונה אבנים רבי יוחנן אמר אפילו תימא רבנן התם ט זימנין דמפחית ולאו אדעתיה אבל הכא קמא קמא קא קייץ ליה: ר' יהודה אומר גמל טעון פשתן או חבילי זמורות: איבעיא להו שיעורא דרבי יהודה נפיש או דלמא שיעורא דרבנן נפיש פשיטא דשיעורא דרבנן נפיש דאי ס"ד שיעורא דרבי יהודה נפיש רבנן בשיעורא דרבי יהודה היכי עבדי ואלא מאי שיעורא דרבנן נפיש רבי יהודה בשיעורא דרבנן מאי עביד אפשר דגחין וחליף תותיה: רבי שמעון אומר כל האילן כנגד המשקולת מפני הטומאה: תנא מפני אהל הטומאה פשיטא מפני הטומאה תנן אי ממתניתין הוה אמינא דלמא מייתי עורב טומאה ושדי התם (ג) וסגיא בדחלולי בעלמא קא משמע לן:

הדרן עלך לא יחפור

רש"י

ונקנין עמה נכסים שאין להם אחריות. דתנן בקדושין (דף כו.) נכסים שאין להם אחריות נקנין עם נכסים שיש להם אחריות בכסף בשטר ובחזקה שהמטלטלין אין נקנין אלא במשיכה וקרקע נקנה בכסף ואם מכר לו קרקע ומטלטלין יחד כיון שנתן דמי הקרקע או מסר לו שטר מכירת קרקע או החזיק בקרקע מדעת מוכר נקנו המטלטלין בלא משיכה קתני מיהא קרקע כל שהוא חייב בביכורים וקס"ד ביכורי אילן קאמר: **הכא במאי עסקינן** בחטין. שכל ז' המינים חייבים בביכורים: **מעורבין זה בזה.** שאין סומכין על הברירה לחלקו לחצאים ולומר שלצד הארץ חייבין ושלצד החוץ פטורין: **אבל דכ"ע הגדל בפטור** פטור. שאם היו כל שרשיו בחו"ל פטור ואפילו עומד האילן בתוך שש עשרה אמה לארץ ולא אמרינן מן הארץ ינק: **דמפסיק צונמא.** באמצע שרשים ל שאין שני לדדין יכולין לינק זה מזה: **דהדרי וערבי.** האילן נעשה אחד למעלה בעביו: **אוירא מבלבל.** אע"פ שבתוך הקרקע (ד) כשני אילנות הואיל ולמעלה באויר העולם נעשה אחד מתערבין יונקותיו: **כ"ה אמה.** קשה לעולא דאמר י"ו אמה ותו לא: **אכחושי לא מכחשי.** בשדה חבירו אלא עד שיתסרי הלכך טפי מהכי לאו גזלן הוא: **הנוטה.** נופו לתוך שדה של חבירו: **שעל מנת כן הנחיל** יהושע. התנה עמהם שלא יקפידו על כך: **מתני'** מרדע. מלמד בקר: **קוצץ.** הענפים עד גובה מלא מרדע שלא יעכבוהו מלהוליך מחרשתו שם: **החרוב והשקמה.** שצלם מרובה וקשה לשדה: **כנגד המשקולת.** כל מה שנוטה לתוך שדהו: **משקולת.** חוט (ה) האמרכולין שבונין חומה ותולין בה משקולת של אבר: **ואם בית השלחין היא כל האילן.** אפי' אינו חרוב ושקמה קוצץ כנגד המשקולת שהצל רע לבית השלחין: **אבא שאול אומר כו'.** בגמ' מפרש אהייא קאי: **גמ' ארישא קאי.** דקאמר ת"ק קוצץ מלא מרדע ואפי' אילן סרק חוץ מחרוב ושקמה ואמר ליה אבא שאול כל אילן סרק נמי כנגד המשקולת: **או אסיפא קאי.** דקאמר ת"ק (ו) כל האילן כנגד המשקולת ואפילו אילן העושה פירות ואמר ליה אבא שאול כל אילן סרק הוא דכנגד המשקולת אבל אילן העושה פירות נמי מלא מרדע ותו לא: **כל האילן.** כל האילנות: **אי אמרת בשלמא ארישא קאי.** ולטפויי אתא ל [מחרוב ושקמה דקאמר ת"ק] היינו דקאמר כל: **אלא אי אמרת אסיפא קאי.** מאי כל הא לגרועי אתא: **מתני' אילן הנוטה לרשות הרבים קוצץ.** מן הענפים התחתונות כדי שיהא גמל עובר תחת העליונות: **מפני הטומאה.** מפרש בגמ': **גמ' בתר [אומדנא] דהשתא אזלינן.** דקתני קוצץ מן הענפים כדי שיהא גמל עובר ורוכבו והרי חוזרין וגדלים לאחר זמן: **כדי שתהא עגלה מהלכת.** אם תקרתה חזקה כל כך מותר ואע"ג שסופה שתתליע ותפחת: **קמא קמא קייץ ליה.** כל ענף וענף שיקדים ולמיח יקצצנו: **בשיעורא דרבי יהודה מאי עבדי ליה.** כשיבא גמל טעון פשתן היאך יעבור: **מפני אהל הטומאה.** שמא יפול כזית מת אלל האילן והרי הענפים (ז) סרוכים מאהילין עליו ועל עוברי הדרכים ומביאים עליהם את הטומאה: **ושדי התם.** על האילן ומתוך שענפיו רבים הטומאה עומדת שם ואינה נופלת לארץ ובני אדם עוברים תחתיה ואי לא חיישינן אלא להכי בדחלולי בעלמא סגי ליה לקוץ אחד אחד מבינתים כדי להרחיק אויר ביניהם ולא תעמוד שם טומאה: **קמ"ל.** מתניתא דאפילו לא נותר בו אלא ענף אחד מזיק הוא את הרבים: **הדרן עלך לא יחפור**

תוספות

בחטה. וא"ת והא חטה יניקתה ג' טפחים כדמוכח בשבת פרק אמר ר"ע בשמעתין דערוגה (דף פה.) ואין לומר דכל שהוא דהכא לאו דוקא דהא בפ"ק דקדושין (דף כו.) קא מייתי לה בשמעתא דלא בעי לבורין בה או לאו וקאמר כל שהוא למאי חזי ומשני כגון שנעץ בה מחט וקאמר איכפל תנא לאשמועינן מחט מי לא עסקינן דתלי ביה מרגניתא משמע דכל שהוא דוקא וי"ל דנהי דיניקתה ג' מ"מ עיקר יניקתה אינו אלא כנגדה ואילן נמי יניקתו כ"ה אפ"ה עיקר יניקתו י"ו (ל):

ואחד אילן הנוטה מביא וקורא. בפרק המקבל (ב"מ דף קז. ושם) פליגי רב ושמואל באילן הנוטה על המיצר רב אמר הנוטה לכאן לכאן והנוטה לכאן לכאן ושמואל אמר חולקין ופירש בקונט' התם דבנטיית שרשים איירי ולפיכך שמעתין דהכא כרב דאזיל בתר שרשין ורשב"א פירש שם בענין אחר: **שעל** מנת כן הנחיל יהושע וכו'. במרובה (ב"ק דף פא.) פריך אמאי לא חשיב לה בהדי עשרה תנאין של יהושע ומשני לה: **בדחלולי** סגי. פי' ר"ח דחלולי לשון יראה שעושים צורה של עץ ונראין כבני אדם ואין העוף רשאי לישאר שם קמ"ל דאע"פ שברח העוף פעמים שמשאיר שם בשר המת שמביא בפיו ונשאר שם בענף הלכך אין לו תקנה אלא בקציצת ענפים כולם (ח):

הדרן עלך לא יחפור

עין משפט נר מצוה

קז א מיי' פ"ג מהל' מכירה הל' ח [ט] טוש"ע ח"מ סי' רב סעיף ז:
קח ב מיי' פ"א מהל' תרומות הל' כד:
קט ג מיי' פ"ב מהל' ביכורים הל' יא:
קי ד ה מיי' פ"י מהל' שכנים הל' ח סמג עשין פב טוש"ע ח"מ סי' קנה סעיף כו:
קיא ו מיי' פי"ג מהל' נזקי ממון הל' כו סמג עשין סח טור ש"ע ח"מ סי' תיז סעיף ז:

רבינו גרשום

בחטה. זרוע בתוכו וממנה מביא בכורים דלא אזלי שרשין כלום וליכא למימר דקא ינקי ממצר אחר: **דיקא נמי.** דבחטה עסקי' **דקתני** קרקע **כל שהוא** דאי באילן עסקינן לא סגיא בקרקע כל שהוא כלל ש"מ: **אילן** הנטוע על (שפת) [ספר] של ארץ ישראל **מקצתו** נוטה בארץ **ומקצתו** נוטה בחו"ל **טבל וחולין מעורבין זה בזה** דאותו הנוטה בארץ הוה ליה טבל ואותו הנוטה בחו"ל הוה ליה חולין ולאו בר עישורי נינהו ולהכי טבל וחולין מעורבין זה בזה ואסורין **רשב"ג סבר** א) מש"ה אמר **הגדל בחיוב חייב** משום דיש ברירה דיכול לברור איזה ענף נוטה בחו"ל ואיזה בארץ **ורבי סבר אין ברירה** מש"ה טבל וחולין מעורבין זה בזה ואסור אבל גדל בחיוב דכולה אילן היה בא"י אע"ג דאזלי שרשין בחו"ל וקא ינקי מחו"ל דברי הכל חייב דשדיין עיקרו בתר נופו וקשיא לעולא: **דמפסיק צונמא.** דלא קאזלי שרשין כלל בחוצה לארץ מפני הצונמא דמפסיק מש"ה דברי הכל חייב אבל אי לא מפסיק צונמא פטור מפני השרשין דקא ינקי מחוץ לארץ: **אי הכי.** דמפסיק צונמא בהא לימא רבי טבל וחולין מעורבין זה בזה ג) דאותו הנוטה בארץ הוי ליה טבל ואותו הנוטה בחו"ל הוי ליה חולין ולאו בר עישורי אינן (והא גדל כולו בארץ) ומשני **דהדרי ערבי** נופין ולמעלה מקצתן בארץ ומקצתן בחו"ל **רבי סבר אויר** ארץ ואויר חו"ל **מבלבלן** ולהכי טבל וחולין מעורבין זה בזה: מרחיקין את האילן **ט"ז אמה ותו לא** ורמינהו וכו'. מינק ינקי עד ט"ו אמה ואין מביא ממנו בכורים. ג) **ור' יוחנן** ס"ל כעולא **אחד אילן הסמוך למצר חבירו וא' אילן הנוטה** לתוך של חבירו **מביא וקורא שעל מנת כן הנחיל** יהושע **לישראל את הארץ** שזה חופר בתוך שלו וזה נוטע בתוך שלו: **פיסקא קוצץ מלא מרדע על גבי המחרישה.** שכשהוא עובר על גבי המחרישה והמרדע על כתיפו כל אותן הענפים שמעכבין לו קוצצין אותן שכנגד המחרישה: **בחרוב ובשקמה.** דאיכא תרתי לריעותא חדא דענפיו מרובים ומזיק לשדה ואין (שוין) פירותיהן חשובין: **קוצץ כולו כנגד המשקולת.** כל הענפים הנוטים לשדהו וקוצץ ממטה ועד למעלה כעין שיכול להוריד מלמעלה מן האילן ועד למטה קו המשקולת והולך שוה שאין שם עיכוב ענף: **ואם בית השלחין היא.** השדה דצריך לה מטר כל שעה להשקותה והצל רע לה קוצץ **כל האילן** בין עושה פרי בין אינו עושה **כנגד המשקולת: אבא שאול אומר כל אילן סרק** שאין בו פרי קוצץ **כנגד המשקולת: איבעיא להו.** הא דקתני **אבא שאול** כל אילן סרק **כנגד המשקולת ארישא** דמתני' **קאי** דקתני בחרוב ובשקמה כנגד המשקולת ואמר אבא שאול כל אילן סרק קוצץ כנגד המשקולת ולא חרוב ושקמה משום דקא טעני פירות כל שהוא **או אסיפא קאי** דקתני בית השלחין כל האילן כנגד המשקולת בין אילן סרק ובין אילן פירות ואתא אבא שאול למימר כל אילן סרק כנגד המשקולת אפי' חרוב ושקמה דדמי לאילן סרק משום דאיכא תרתי לריעותא אבל אילן פרי אינו קוצץ כל עיקר אפי' בבי' השלחין: **ת"ש אבא שאול אומר כל האילן כנגד המשקולת מפני שהצל רע לבית השלחין** דמזיקי ענפיו שאין יכול המטר לירד מש"ה קוצץ **ש"מ** הא דקתני במתני' כל אילן סרק כנגד המשקולת **ארישא קאי** דאתי לאפוקי חרוב ושקמה דאינו קוצץ משום דקא טעין פירא: **אי אמרת בשלמא ארישא קאי היינו דקתני כל אילן** סרק ולא חרוב ושקמה אילן סרק קוצץ ולא אילן פירות א"כ ל"ל למיתני כל אילן סרק **אלא אי אמרת אסיפא קאי** וקאמר אילן סרק **אילן סרק מיבעי ליה** למיתני (הכי) אבא שאול אומר אילן סרק קוצץ כנגד המשקולת ולא כל האילן שעושה פרי **אלא ש"מ** מדקתני כל אילן סרק **ארישא קאי** ולחומרא דאתי לאפוקי חרוב ושקמה דאינו קוצץ דהיינו חומרא: **פיסקא אילן הנוטה (לשדה חבירו) [לרשות הרבים] כו'.** מאן תנא דלהיכא **דאיכא נזק בתר אומדנא דהשתא אזלינן** בתר נזק דשכיח ולא בתר נזק דעתיד למיתי: **אמר ר"ל מחלוקת שנויה.** במתני' אילן הנוטה ברה"ר קוצץ כדי שיהא הגמל עובר ברוכבו דאזלינן בתר היזק דהשתא ולא בתר דעתיד למיתי דאי אזלינן בתר העתיד מכל וכל צריך לקצצו דדלמא מגדלו וקא מזיק לרבים. **ואליבא דר"א דאמר כדי שתהא עגלה מהלכת עליה וטעונה אבנים** כלומר שתהא התקרה חזקה כדי שתהא יכולה לסבול עגלה טעונה אבנים אלמא דבנזקין אזלינן בתר אומדנא דהשתא ולא חייש דלמא היום או מחר מרקבת התקרה ונפלי בגווה אינשי דאזלי עלה.

מסורת הש"ס

א) גיטין כב., ב) נדרים נט:, ג) [עירובין לו: וש"נ], ד) [לעיל כה:], ה) ב"ק פב., ו) [לקמן פב:], ז) [פי' כשיבא לחרוש ומריס המרדע להכות הבהמה שחורש בה לא יהיו ענפי האילן מעכבין אותו. ערוך ערך מרדע], ח) לקמן ס., ט) [שם], י) ס"י שהלדדין אין יכולין, כ) רש"ל, ל) [וע"ע תוס' קדושין כו. ד"ה קרקע]:

הגהות הב"ח

(א) גמ' הכא במאי עסקינן. נ"ב תימה דה"ל להקשות ממשנה י' פ"ג דמעשרות להדיא דאילן העומד עיקרו בחו"ל פטור ממעשר וק"ל: (ב) שם דהדרי ערבי ובהא קא מיפלגי: (ג) שם ושדי התם ובדחלולי בעלמא סגיא קמ"ל: (ד) רש"י ד"ה אוירא וכו' הקרקע הם כשני: (ה) ד"ה משקולת חוט האדרכלין שבונין: (ו) ד"ה או אסיפא וכו' ת"ק בית השלחין כל האילן: (ז) ד"ה מפני אהל וכו' הענפים המרובים מאהילין: (ח) תוס' ד"ה ובדחלולי וכו' ענפים כולם כנגד המשקולת הס"ד:

ליקוטי רש"י

טבל וחולין מעורבין זה בזה. אין לך פירי באילן הזה שאין מקלתו מן הארץ שהוא טבל ומקלתו מחולה לארץ שהוא חולין לפי שהיניקה מתערבת ונפקא מינה שאין מעשרין מטבל ודאי עליו דהוי מן החיוב על הפטור ולא ממנו על טבל ודאי. **הגדל בחיוב.** מה שבתוך ארץ ישראל. **דמפסיק צונמא.** שן סלע מבדיל באמצע השרשים ומפסיקין עד הגזע הלכך לרבן שמעון לא ינקי מהדדי [גיטין כב.]. **צונמא.** לונמא בלשון ארמי סלע [בראשית מא, כג ונדה ח:]. אבן [רשב"ם לקמן פט:]. **דהדרי ערבי.** שהעץ מן הגזע ולמעלה שלם. **מר סבר אוירא מבלבל.** אע"פ שכל מה שיש מן השרשין בקרקע הוי מובדל הואיל וכשילא לאויר הוא מעורב ומבלבל וינקי מהדדי. **ומ"ס.** אוירא לא מבלבל הואיל ובתוך הקרקע מובדל בסלע שאינו מלמים [גיטין כב.]. **מרחיקין את האילן מן הבור.** שהשרשין מתפשטין ונוקבין בכותלי הבור וממלידין את הקרקע והכתלים נופלים [ב"מ קיז.]. **כ"ה אמה.** כך שיעור שהשרשין נמשכין והולכין ומקלקלין את כותלי הבור [לעיל יח.]. **קוצץ מלא מרדע.** בגבהו [רשב"ם לקמן פב:].

[המשך בדף כח.]

The Gemara cites a Baraisa to resolve this question:

תָּא שְׁמַע – **Come, learn** a proof, דְּתַנְיָא – **for it was taught in a Baraisa:** בֵּית הַשְּׁלָחִין – With regard to AN IRRIGATED FIELD, אַבָּא שָׁאוּל אוֹמֵר כָּל הָאִילָן כְּנֶגֶד הַמִּשְׁקוֹלֶת – ABBA SHAUL SAYS: The branches of ALL TREES that extend over the field may be cut ALONG THE PLUMB LINE, מִפְּנֵי שֶׁהַצֵּל רַע לְבֵית הַשְּׁלָחִין – BECAUSE SHADE IS HARMFUL TO AN IRRIGATED FIELD. The Baraisa states clearly that Abba Shaul agrees with the Tanna Kamma of our Mishnah with regard to an irrigated field. שְׁמַע מִינָּהּ אַרֵישָׁא קָאֵי – We **learn from [this Baraisa]** that in disagreeing with the Tanna Kamma, **[Abba Shaul] addressed the first case** of the Mishnah, which deals with an ordinary field. שְׁמַע מִינָּהּ – Indeed, we **learn** it **from [this Baraisa].**

The Gemara infers this interpretation of Abba Shaul's ruling from the Mishnah itself:

אָמַר רַב אַשִׁי – **Rav Ashi said:** מַתְנִיתִין נַמֵּי דַּיְקָא – A **precise** reading **of the Mishnah also yields this inference,** דְּקָתָנֵי כָּל אִילָן סְרָק – **for the Mishnah states** that Abba Shaul said: ALL BARREN TREES may be cut along the plumb line. אִי אָמְרַתְּ בִּשְׁלָמָא אַרֵישָׁא קָאֵי – **If you say** that **[Abba Shaul] addressed the first case** of the Mishnah, **it is well,** הַיְינוּ דְּקָתָנֵי כָּל אִילָן – for **that is why it states "**ALL BARREN TREES.**"** The word "all" implies that Abba Shaul is more permissive than the Tanna Kamma, who ruled that only a carob or sycamore may be cut along the plumb line. אֶלָּא אִי אָמְרַתְּ אַסֵּיפָא קָאֵי – **But if you will say** that **[Abba Shaul] addressed the latter case** of the Mishnah, אִילָן סְרָק מִיבְּעֵי לֵיהּ – **he should** merely **have** said **"barren trees"** may be cut along the plumb line, since he is less permissive than the Tanna Kamma, who permits cutting *all* trees along the plumb line. Why did he use the word "all"?

Rav Ashi concludes:

אֶלָּא לָאו שְׁמַע מִינָּהּ אַרֵישָׁא קָאֵי – **Rather,** do we **not learn from this** that **[Abba Shaul] addressed the first case** of the Mishnah? שְׁמַע מִינָּהּ – **Indeed,** we **learn** it **from this.**

Mishnah אִילָן שֶׁהוּא נוֹטֶה לִרְשׁוּת הָרַבִּים – If the branches of **a tree extend over the public domain,** קוֹצֵץ כְּדֵי שֶׁיְּהֵא גָמָל עוֹבֵר וְרוֹכְבוֹ – **one may cut off enough** of the lower branches to create clearance **for a camel and its rider to pass** underneath. רַבִּי יְהוּדָה אוֹמֵר – **R' Yehudah says:** גָּמָל טָעוּן פִּשְׁתָּן אוֹ חֲבִילֵי זְמוֹרוֹת – One may create sufficient clearance for **a camel laden with flax or bundles of twigs.**[18] רַבִּי שִׁמְעוֹן אוֹמֵר – **R' Shimon says:** כָּל הָאִילָן כְּנֶגֶד הַמִּשְׁקוֹלֶת – **Any tree** whose branches extend over the public domain may be cut **along the plumb** line, מִפְּנֵי הַטּוּמְאָה – **because of *tumah.***[19]

Gemara The Mishnah permits cutting branches so that they do not now interfere with traffic, but does not permit cutting off the limbs to ensure that they never grow back. The Gemara therefore asks:

מַאן תַּנָּא דִּבְנִזְקִין בָּתַר אוּמְדְּנָא דְּהַשְׁתָּא אַזְלִינַן – **Who is the Tanna** of our Mishnah, who holds **that with regard to** potential **damages, we follow** our **assessment of** the situation as it stands **now** and do not address future problems?

The Gemara answers:

אָמַר רֵישׁ לָקִישׁ – **Reish Lakish said:** בְּמַחֲלוֹקֶת שְׁנוּיָה – **[The law] taught** in our Mishnah **is** the subject **of a dispute,** וְרַבִּי אֱלִיעֶזֶר הִיא – **and** the Tanna of **[our Mishnah] is R' Eliezer.** דִּתְנַן – **As we learned in a Mishnah:**[20] אֵין עוֹשִׂין חָלָל תַּחַת רְשׁוּת הָרַבִּים בּוֹרוֹת שִׁיחִין וּמְעָרוֹת – ONE MAY NOT DIG A HOLE BENEATH THE PUBLIC DOMAIN, neither PITS, nor DITCHES, NOR VAULTS, for they may cause the street above them to collapse.[21] רַבִּי אֱלִיעֶזֶר מַתִּיר – R' ELIEZER PERMITS it, בִּכְדֵי שֶׁתְּהֵא עֲגָלָה מְהַלֶּכֶת וּטְעוּנָה אֲבָנִים – provided that one covers the hole with a roof STRONG ENOUGH FOR A WAGON LADEN WITH STONE TO TRAVEL over it. Although the roof may decay with time, we assess it at its current strength. Our Mishnah follows R' Eliezer's opinion.[22]

The Gemara deflects this analogy:

רַבִּי יוֹחָנָן אָמַר – **R' Yochanan said:** אֲפִילוּ תֵּימָא רַבָּנָן – **You can even say** that **the Rabbis** who argue with R' Eliezer taught our Mishnah, for the two cases are not analogous. הָתָם זִימְנִין דְּמִפְחִית וְלָאו אַדַּעְתֵּיהּ – **There,** in the case of an excavation beneath the street, **[the roof] can sometimes deteriorate and one will remain unaware** of it, since it is underground. Therefore, one must be concerned for future damages. אֲבָל הָכָא – **But here,** in the case of branches overhanging the street, קַמָּא קַמָּא קָא קָיֵיץ לֵיהּ – as **each one** grows back,[23] we **will cut it off.** Thus, future damages are not a concern.

The next section of the Mishnah is cited:

רַבִּי יְהוּדָה אוֹמֵר גָּמָל טָעוּן פִּשְׁתָּן אוֹ חֲבִילֵי זְמוֹרוֹת – R' YEHUDAH SAYS: A CAMEL LADEN WITH FLAX OR BUNDLES OF TWIGS.

The Gemara analyzes the conflicting opinions in the Mishnah:

אִיבַּעְיָא לְהוּ – **They inquired:** שִׁיעוּרָא דְּרַבִּי יְהוּדָה נְפִישׁ – **Is R' Yehudah's amount** (the height of a laden camel) **greater,** אוֹ דִּלְמָא שִׁיעוּרָא דְּרַבָּנָן נְפִישׁ – **or is, perhaps, the Rabbis' amount** (the height of a camel and its rider) **greater?**

The Gemara resolves the question:

פְּשִׁיטָא דְּשִׁיעוּרָא דְּרַבָּנָן נְפִישׁ – **It is obvious that the Rabbis' amount is greater,** דְּאִי סַלְקָא דַּעְתָּךְ שִׁיעוּרָא דְּרַבִּי יְהוּדָה נְפִישׁ – **for if you were to think** that **R' Yehudah's amount is greater,** רַבָּנָן בְּשִׁיעוּרָא דְּרַבִּי יְהוּדָה הֵיכִי עָבְדֵי – **what would the Rabbis do when R' Yehudah's amount** was required (i.e. when a laden camel passed underneath)?[24]

The Gemara reverses the question:

וְאֶלָּא מַאי – **But what** would you **rather** say? שִׁיעוּרָא דְּרַבָּנָן נְפִישׁ – That **the Rabbis' amount is greater.** רַבִּי יְהוּדָה בְּשִׁיעוּרָא דְּרַבָּנָן מַאי עָבִיד – If so, **what does R' Yehudah do when the Rabbis' amount** is required (i.e. when a man riding a camel passes underneath)?

NOTES

that only barren trees may be cut along the plumb line. Fruit-bearing trees may be cut only enough to allow clearance for an ox-goad raised over a plow (*Rashi*).

18. The Gemara inquires whether this height is greater or lesser than the height of a camel and its rider.

19. R' Shimon allows the entire overhanging portion to be cut away so that no branches protrude into public property. Otherwise, a person walking under the branches might become *tamei* (ritually impure). The Gemara explains how overhanging branches can cause *tumah* (ritual impurity).

20. Below, 60a.

21. Even one who intends to cover the hole with a very strong roof may not dig one, because the roof may decay and cave in at some future date.

22. R' Eliezer's view is that should the cover deteriorate, we will deal with it at that time. In our Mishnah as well, we will deal with the future growth of branches when it occurs. Now, however, we address only the problem immediately at hand.

23. Literally: the first [branch that grows back], the first [branch that grows back].

24. It is therefore obvious that the height of a camel and its rider is sufficient clearance for a laden camel as well.

ונקנין עמה נכסים שאין להם אחריות הכא במאי עסקינן בחיטי דיקא נמי דקתני כל שהוא ש"מ ת"ש אילן מקצתו בארץ ומקצתו בחו"ל טבל וחולין מעורבין זה בזה דברי רבי רבן שמעון בן גמליאל אומר הגדל בחיוב חייב הגדל בפטור פטור ע"כ לא פליגי אלא דמר סבר יש ברירה ומר סבר אין ברירה אבל גדל בפטור דברי הכל פטור הכא במאי עסקינן דמפסיק צונמא אי הכי מאי טעמיה דרבי דהדרי ערבי ובמאי קא מיפלגי מר סבר אוירא מבלבל ומר סבר האי לחודיה קאי והאי לחודיה קאי ושש עשרה אמה ותו לא והא תנן מרחיקין את האילן מן הבור כ"ה אמה אמר אביי מיזל טובא אזלי אכחושי לא מכחשי אלא עד שש עשרה אמה טפי לא מכחשי כי אתא רב דימי אמר בעא מיניה ריש לקיש מרבי יוחנן אילן הסמוך למיצר בתוך ט"ז אמה מהו אמר ליה גזלן הוא ואין מביאין ממנו בכורים כי אתא רבין אמר רבי יוחנן אחד אילן הסמוך למיצר ואחד אילן הנוטה מביא וקורא שעל מנת כן הנחיל יהושע לישראל את הארץ: מתני' אילן שהוא נוטה לשדה חבירו קוצץ מלא המרדע על גבי המחרישה ובחרוב ובשקמה כנגד המשקולת בית השלחין כל האילן כנגד המשקולת אבא שאול אומר כל אילן סרק כנגד המשקולת: גמ' איבעיא להו אבא שאול ארישא קאי או אסיפא קאי ת"ש דתניא בית השלחין אבא שאול אומר כל האילן כנגד המשקולת מפני שהצל רע לבית השלחין שמע מינה ארישא קאי שמע מינה אמר רב אשי מתניתין נמי דיקא דקתני כל אילן סרק אי אמרת בשלמא ארישא קאי היינו דקתני כל אילן אלא אי אמרת אסיפא קאי אילן סרק מיבעי ליה אלא לאו שמע מינה ארישא קאי שמע מינה: מתני' אילן שהוא נוטה לרה"ר קוצץ כדי שיהא גמל עובר ורוכבו רבי יהודה אומר גמל טעון פשתן או חבילי זמורות רבי שמעון אומר כל האילן כנגד המשקולת מפני הטומאה: גמ' מאן תנא דבנזקין בתר אומדנא דהשתא אזלינן אמר ר"ל במחלוקת שנויה ורבי אליעזר היא דתנן אין עושין חלל תחת רשות הרבים בורות שיחין ומערות רבי אליעזר מתיר בכדי שתהא עגלה מהלכת וטעונה אבנים רבי יוחנן אמר אפילו תימא רבנן התם זימנין דמפחית ולאו אדעתיה אבל הכא קמא קמא קא קייץ ליה: ר' יהודה אומר גמל טעון פשתן או חבילי זמורות: איבעיא להו שיעורא דרבי יהודה נפיש או דלמא שיעורא דרבנן נפיש פשיטא דשיעורא דרבנן נפיש דאי ס"ד שיעורא דרבי יהודה נפיש רבנן בשיעורא דרבי יהודה היכי עבדי ואלא מאי שיעורא דרבנן נפיש רבי יהודה בשיעורא דרבנן מאי עביד אפשר דגחין וחליף תותיה: רבי שמעון אומר כל האילן כנגד המשקולת מפני הטומאה: תנא מפני אהל הטומאה פשיטא מפני הטומאה תנן אי ממתניתין הוה אמינא דלמא מייתי עורב טומאה ושדי התם (ג) וסגיא בדחלולי בעלמא קא משמע לן:

הדרן עלך לא יחפור

ונקנין עמה נכסים שאין להם אחריות. דתנן בקדושין (דף כו.) נכסים שאין להם אחריות נקנין עם נכסים שיש להם אחריות בכסף בשטר ובחזקה שהמטלטלין אין נקנין אלא במשיכה וקרקע נקנה בכסף ואם מכר לו קרקע ומטלטלין יחד כיון שנתן דמי הקרקע או מסר לו שטר מכירת קרקע או החזיק בקרקע מדעת מוכר נקנו המטלטלין בלא משיכה קתני מיהא קרקע כל שהוא חייב בביכורים וקס"ד ביכורי אילן קאמר: הכא במאי עסקינן בחטין. שכל ז' המינים חייבים בבכורים: מעורבין זה בזה. שאין סומכין על הברירה לחלקו לחלאים ולומר שלצד הארץ חייבין ושלצד החוץ פטורין: אבל דכ"ע הגדל בפטור פטור. שאם היו כל שרשיו בחו"ל פטור ואפילו עומד האילן בתוך שש עשרה אמה לארץ ולא אמרינן מן הארץ ינק: דמפסיק צונמא. באמצע שרשים שאין שני לדדין יכולין לינק זה מזה: דהדרי וערבי. האילן נעשה אחד למעלה בעביו: אוירא מבלבל. אע"פ שבתוך הקרקע (ד) כשני אילנות הוא ולמעלה באויר העולם נעשה אחד מתערבין יונקותיו: כ"ה אמה. קשה לעולא דאמר י"ו אמה ותו לא: אכחושי לא מכחשי. בשדה חבירו אלא עד שיתסרי הלכך טפי מהכי לאו גזלן הוא: הנוטה. נופו לתוך שדה של חבירו: שעל מנת כן הנחיל יהושע. התנה עמהם שלא יקפידו על כך: מתני' מרדע. מלמד בקר: קוצץ. הענפים עד גובה מלא מרדע שלא יעכבוהו מלהוליך מחרשתו שם: החרוב והשקמה. שצילם מרובה וקשה לשדה: כנגד המשקולת. כל מה שנוטה לתוך שדהו: משקולת. חוט (ה) האמרכולין שבונין חומה ותולין בה משקולת של אבר: ואם בית השלחין היא כל האילן. אפי' אינו חרוב ושקמה קוצץ כנגד המשקולת שהצל רע לבית השלחין: אבא שאול אומר כו'. בגמ' מפרש אהייא קאי: גמ' ארישא קאי. דקאמר ת"ק קוצץ מלא מרדע ואפי' אילן סרק חוץ מחרוב ושקמה ואמר ליה אבא שאול כל אילן סרק נמי כנגד המשקולת: או אסיפא קאי. דקאמר ת"ק (ו) כל האילן כנגד המשקולת ואפילו אילן העושה פירות ואמר ליה אבא שאול כל אילן סרק הוא דכנגד המשקולת אבל אילן העושה פירות נמי מלא מרדע ותו לא: כל האילן. כל האילנות: אי אמרת בשלמא ארישא קאי. ולטפויי אתא [מחרוב ושקמה דקאמר ת"ק] היינו דקאמר כל: אלא אי אמרת אסיפא קאי. מאי כל הא לגרועי אתא: מתני' אילן הנוטה לרשות הרבים קוצץ. מן הענפים התחתונות כדי שיהא גמל עובר תחת העליונות: מפני הטומאה. מפרש בגמ': גמ' בתר [אומדנא] דהשתא אזלינן. דקתני קוצץ מן הענפים כדי שיהא גמל עובר ורוכבו והרי חוזרין וגדלים לאחר זמן: כדי שתהא עגלה מהלכת. אם תקרתה חזקה כל כך מותר ואע"ג שסופה שתתליע ותפחת: קמא קמא קייץ ליה. כל ענף וענף שיקדים ויצמיח יקצצנו: בשיעורא דרבי יהודה מאי עבדי ליה. כשיבא גמל טעון פשתן היאך יעבור: מפני אהל הטומאה. שמא יפול כזית מת אצל האילן והרי הענפים (ז) ארוכים מאהילין עליו ועל עוברי הדרכים ומביאים עליהם את הטומאה: ושדי התם. על האילן ומתוך שענפיו רבים הטומאה עומדת שם ואינה נופלת לארץ ובני אדם עוברים תחתיה ואי לא חיישינן אלא להכי בדחלולי בעלמא סגי ליה לקוץ אחד אחד מבינתים כדי להרחיק אויר ביניהם ולא תעמוד שם טומאה: קמ"ל. מתניתא דאפילו לא נותר בו אלא ענף אחד מזיק הוא את הרבים: הדרן עלך לא יחפור

בחטה. וא"ת והא חטה יניקתה ג' טפחים כדמוכח בשבת פרק אמר ר"ע בשמעתין דערוגה (דף פה.) ואין לומר דכל שהוא דהכא לאו דוקא דהא בפ"ק דקדושין (דף כו.) קא מייתי לה בשמעתא דלא בעי לצבורין בה או לאו וקאמר כל שהוא למאי חזי ומשני כגון שנעץ בה מחט וקאמר איכפל תנא לאשמועינן מחט מי לא עסקינן דתלי ביה מרגניתא משמע דכל שהוא דוקא וי"ל דנהי דיניקתה ג' מ"מ עיקר יניקתה אינו אלא כנגדה ואילן נמי יניקתו כ"ה אפ"ה עיקר יניקתו ט"ז:

ואחד אילן הנוטה מביא וקורא. בפרק המקבל (ב"מ דף קז. ושם) פליגי רב ושמואל באילן הנוטה על המיצר רב אמר הנוטה לכאן לכאן והנוטה לכאן לכאן ושמואל אמר חולקין ופירש בקונט' התם דבנטיית שרשים איירי ולפיכך שמעתין דהכא כרב דאזיל בתר שרשין ורשב"א פירש התם בענין אחר: שעל מנת כן הנחיל יהושע וכו'. במרובה (ב"ק דף פב.) פריך אמאי לא חשיב לה בהדי עשרה תנאין של יהושע ומשני לה: בדחלולי סגי. פי' ר"ח דחלולי לשון ילהא שעושים לורה של עץ ונראין כבני אדם ואין העוף רשאי ליפול שם קמ"ל דאע"פ שברח העוף פעמים שמשליך שם בשר המת שמגביה בפיו ונשאר שם בענף הלכך אין לו תקנה אלא בקציצת ענפים כולם (ח):

הדרן עלך לא יחפור

עין משפט נר מצוה

קז א מיי' פ"ג מהל' מכירה הל' ח [ט] טוש"ע ח"מ סי' רב סעיף ז:

קח ב מיי' פ"א מהל' תרומות הל' כד:

קט ג מיי' פ"ג מהל' ביכורים הל' יא:

קי ד ה מיי' פ"י מהל' שכנים הל' ה סמג עשין פב טוש"ע ח"מ סי' קנה סעיף כו:

קיא ו מיי' פי"ג מהל' נזקי ממון הל' כו סמג עשין סח טוש"ע ח"מ סי' תיז סעיף ד:

רבינו גרשום

בחטה. זרוע בתוכו וממנה מביא בכורים דלא אזלי שרשין כלום וליכא למימר דקא ינקי ממצר אחר: דיקא נמי. דבחטה עסקי' דקתני קרקע כל שהוא דאי באילן עסקינן לא סגיא בקרקע כל שהוא כלל ש"מ: אילן הנוטע על (שפת) [ספר] של ארץ ישראל מקצתו נוטה בארץ ומקצתו נוטה בחו"ל טבל וחולין מעורבין זה בזה דאותו הנוטה בארץ הוה ליה טבל ואותו הנוטה בחו"ל הוה ליה חולין ולאו בר עישורי נינהו והלכי טבל וחולין מעורבין זה בזה ואסורין רשב"ג סבר (א) משה"ה אומר הגדל בחיוב חייב משום דיש ברירה דיכול לברור איזה ענף נוטה בחו"ל ואיזה בארץ ורבי סבר אין ברירה מש"ה טבל וחולין מעורבין זה בזה ואסור אבל גדל בחיוב דכולה אילן היה בא"י אע"ג דאזלי שרשין בחו"ל וקא ינקי מחו"ל דברי הכל חייב דשדיין עיקרו בתר נופו וקשיא לעולא: דמפסיק צונמא. דלא קאזלי שרשין כלל בחוצה לארץ מפני הצונמא דמש"ה דברי הכל חייב אבל אי לא מפסיק צונמא פטור מפני השרשין דקא ינקי מחוץ לארץ: אי הכי. מפסיק צונמא בהא לימא רבי טבל וחולין מעורבין זה בזה ג) דאותו הנוטה בארץ הוי ליה טבל ואותו הנוטה בחו"ל הוי ליה חולין ולאו בר עישורי אינן (והא גדל כולו בארץ) ומשני דהדרי ערבי נופין ולמעלה מקצתן בארץ ומקצתן בחו"ל רבי סבר אויר ארץ ואויר חו"ל מבלבלן ולהכי טבל וחולין מעורבין זה בזה: מרחיקין את האילן ט"ז אמה ותו לא ורמינהו וכו'. מינק ינקי עד ט"ז אמה ואין מביא ממנו בכורים. ג) ור' יוחנן ס"ל כעולא אחד אילן הסמוך למצר חבירו וא' אילן הנוטה לתוך של חבירו מביא וקורא שעל מנת כן הנחיל יהושע לישראל את הארץ שזה חופר בתוך שלו וזה נוטע בתוך שלו: פיסקא קוצץ מלא מרדע על גבי המחרישה. שכשהוא עובר על גבי המחרישה והמרדע על כתיפו כל אותן הענפים שמעכבין לו קוצצין אותן שכנגד המחרישה: בחרוב ובשקמה. דאיכא תרתי לריעותא חדא דענפיו מרובים ומזיק לשדה ואין (שוין) פירותיהן חשובין: קוצץ כולו כנגד המשקולת. כל הענפים הנוטים לשדהו וקוצץ ממטה ועד למעלה כעין שיכול להוריד מלמעלה מן האילן ועד למטה קו המשקולת והולך שוה שאין שם עיכוב ענף: ואם בית השלחין היא. השדה דצריך לה מטר כל שעה להשקותה והצל רע לה קוצץ כל האילן בין עושה פרי בין אינו עושה כנגד המשקולת: אבא שאול אומר כל אילן סרק שאין בו פרי קוצץ כנגד המשקולת: איבעיא להו. הא דקתני אבא שאול כל אילן סרק כנגד המשקולת ארישא קאי דקתני חרוב ושקמה כנגד המשקולת ואמר אבא שאול כל אילן סרק [illegible] המשקולת בין אילן סרק ובין אילן פירות ואתא אבא שאול למימר כל אילן סרק כנגד המשקולת אפי' חרוב ושקמה [illegible] אבל אילן פרי אינו קוצץ כל עיקר אפי' בבי' השלחין: ת"ש אבא שאול אומר כל האילן כנגד המשקולת מפני שהצל רע לבית השלחין [illegible] היינו דקתני כל אילן [illegible] אילן סרק מיבעי ליה [illegible] פיסקא אילן הנוטה [לרשות הרבים] (לשדה חבירו) קוצץ כו'. מאן תנא [illegible] בתר אומדנא דהשתא אזלינן [illegible] אמר ר"ל מחלוקת שנויה. [illegible] ואליבא דר"א דאמר כדי שתהא עגלה מהלכת עליה וטעונה אבנים כלומר שתהא התקרה חזקה כדי שתהא יכולה לסבול עגלה טעונה אבנים [illegible] ונפלו בגווה אינשי דאזלי עלה.

מסורת הש"ס

א) גיטין כב., ב) נדרים נח:, ג) [ערכין ל: וש"נ], ד) [לעיל כה:], ה) ב"ק פב., ו) [לקמן פב:], ז) [פי' כשיפה לחרוש ומריס המרדע להכות הבהמה שחורש בה לא יהיו ענפי האילן מעכבין אותו. ערוך ערך מרדע], ח) לקמן פ., ט) [שם], י) ס"י שהלדדין אין יכולין, כ) רש"ל, ל) [וע"ע תוס' קדושין כו. ד"ה קרקע].

הגהות הב"ח

(א) גמ' הכא במאי עסקינן. נ"ב תימה הא"ל להקשות ממשנה דפ"ג דמעשרות להדיא האילן העומד עיקרו בחוץ ונופו בחוץ פטור ממעשר וק"ל: (ב) שם דהדרי ערבי והכא קא מיפלגי: (ג) שם ושדי התם ובדחלולי בעלמא סגיא קמ"ל: (ד) רש"י ד"ה אוירא וכו' הקרקע הם כשני: (ה) ד"ה משקולת חוט שהלבנאים בונין: (ו) ד"ה או אסיפא וכו' ת"ק בית השלחין כל האילן: (ז) ד"ה מפני אהל וכו' הענפים הארוכים מאהילין: (ח) תוס' ד"ה בדחלולי וכו' ענפים כולם כנגד המשקולת הס"ד:

ליקוטי רש"י

טבל וחולין מעורבין זה בזה. אין לך פירי באילן זה שאין מקצתו מן הארץ שהוא טבל ומקצתו מחולה לארץ שהוא חולין לפי שהיניקה מתערבת ונפקא מינה שאין מעשרין מטבל ודאי עליו דהוי מן החיוב על הפטור ולא ממנו על טבל ודאי. הגדל בחיוב. מה שכנגד ארץ ישראל. דמפסיק צונמא. כן סלע באמצע השרשים ומפסיקן מן הגזע הלכך לרבן שמעון לא ינקי מהדדי [גיטין כב.]. צונמא. צונמת סלע בלשון ארמי [בראשית מא, כג ותרגום ח:]. שם [רשב"ם לקמן פט:]. דהדרי ערבי. שהענף מן הגזע ולמעלה שם. מר סבר אוירא מבלבל. אע"פ שכל מה שיש מן השרשין בקרקע הוי מובדל הואיל וכשילא לאויר הוא מעורב ומבלבל וינקי מהדדי. ומ"ס. אוירא לא מבלבל הואיל ובתוך הקרקע מובדל בסלע שאינו מצמיח [גיטין כב.]. מרחיקין את האילן מן הבור. שהשרשין מתפשטין ונוקבין בכותלי הבור ומתלידין את הקרקע והכתלים נופלים [ב"מ קיז.]. כ"ה אמה. כך שיערו שהשרשין נמשכין והולכין ומקלקלין את כותלי הבור [לעיל יח.]. קוצץ מלא מרדע. בגבהו [רשב"ם לקמן פב:].

[המשך בדף כח.]

The Gemara answers:

אֶפְשָׁר דְּגָחִין וְחָלִיף תּוּתֵיהּ – **It is possible for [a rider] to bend over and pass beneath [the branches].** Therefore, a camel rider presents no difficulty, even if his height is greater than that of a laden camel.

The final segment of the Mishnah is cited:

רַבִּי שִׁמְעוֹן אוֹמֵר כָּל הָאִילָן כְּנֶגֶד הַמִּשְׁקוֹלֶת מִפְּנֵי הַטּוּמְאָה – **R' SHIMON SAYS: ANY TREE** may be cut **ALONG THE PLUMB** line, **BECAUSE OF *TUMAH.***

The Gemara cites a Baraisa that explains R' Shimon's statement:

תָּנָא – **We are taught in a Baraisa:** מִפְּנֵי אֹהֶל הַטּוּמְאָה – **BECAUSE** the branches may create **A TENT OF *TUMAH.***[25]

The Gemara asks:

פְּשִׁיטָא – **It is obvious** that this is the reason, מִפְּנֵי הַטּוּמְאָה תְּנַן – for **we learned in the Mishnah** that the branches are cut off **BECAUSE OF *TUMAH.*** What concern for *tumah* can the Mishnah refer to other than a tent of *tumah?*

The Gemara answers:

אִי מִמַּתְנִיתִין הֲוָה אָמִינָא – **Had** we merely learned the reason **from the Mishnah, I might have said** our concern is דִּלְמָא מַיְיתֵי עוֹרֵב טוּמְאָה וְשָׁדֵי הָתָם – that **perhaps a crow will bring** an article of ***tumah***[26] **and toss it [onto the branches],** where it might become lodged. One who passed underneath the article would be rendered *tamei.*[27] וְסַגְיָא בְּדַחְלוּלֵי בְּעָלְמָא – Were that our only concern, **it would be sufficient to merely thin out** the branches,[28] so that no article of *tumah* could remain lodged in them. קָא מַשְׁמַע לָן – **[The Baraisa]** therefore **informs us** that we must be concerned for the possibility that the branches will create a tent of *tumah.* Accordingly, all the branches must be cut along the plumb line.

הדרן עלך לא יחפור

WE SHALL RETURN TO YOU, LO YACHPOR

NOTES

25. A human corpse (or even an olive-sized piece [כְּזַיִת] of its flesh) can convey its *tumah* to an item merely by being present under the same roof as the susceptible item. This method of conveying *tumah* is referred to as אֹהֶל הַטּוּמְאָה – *a tent of tumah,* because the Biblical verse from which it is derived (*Numbers* 19:14) deals with a corpse that is located inside a tent.

Tree branches qualify as a "tent" (i.e. a roof) with regard to this law (see *Ohalos* 8:2). Accordingly, where branches lean over the public domain, there is room for concern that a small piece of flesh from a corpse may fall beneath the branches, and unknowing passersby who walk under them will be rendered *tamei* (*Rashi*). To preclude this occurrence, R' Shimon permits cutting off any branches that extend over the public domain.

26. I.e. an object that imparts *tumah,* such as a piece of flesh from a corpse.

27. One of the laws of *tumah* is that one who passes beneath a corpse (or a piece of its flesh) is rendered *tamei* (see *Ohalos* 3:1).

28. Literally: create spaces [between the branches]. According to this interpretation, the Mishnah would mean that *alternate branches* are to be cut along the plumb line.

Chapter Three

Introduction

⇐§ חֲזָקָה, Chazakah The main subject of this chapter is *chazakah.* The term *chazakah* has a wide range of meaning in the Talmud. It is used to refer to a type of formal transaction by which real property can be acquired (see Mishnah 42a, *Kiddushin* 26b), and, in its most common usage, to the legal presumption of the status quo for objects or people whose halachic status has come into question. In the context of this chapter, however, the term *chazakah* is used to refer to the uncontested occupancy of real property [i.e. land and houses] that creates the legal presumption that the occupant owns the occupied premises. As explained in the General Introduction, a basic principle of Torah law regarding monetary litigations is: הַמּוֹצִיא מֵחֲבֵרוֹ עָלָיו הָרְאָיָה, *the burden of proof is upon the one who seeks to exact property from another (Bava Kamma* 46b). That is, if one person is in possession of property and another claims it as his, the burden of proof is upon the claimant. However, in the case of real property, which is the primary subject of this chapter, physical "possession" of the property is impossible. Current occupancy of the property is also inconclusive, since it is impossible to prevent people from ever entering one's property. Rather, presumptive ownership is assigned to the last person known to have held the property (מָרָא קַמָּא). Thus, when a person known to have owned a property claims that the one presently occupying it is an illegal squatter, the burden of proof is on the occupant and he must prove that he acquired the property from the previous owner. However, if the current occupant has established a *chazakah* in the property, then he is the presumed owner and it is upon the previous owner to prove that the occupant has no legal claim to the property.

⇐§ Establishing a Chazakah To establish a *chazakah,* an occupant must have continuous occupancy of the premises for a prescribed period of time (generally, three years), during which he uses the property as an owner would. During this period of time, there must be no protest against the occupancy lodged by the previous owner. However, if during this time the previous owner protests the occupancy of his property before two witnesses, the occupant does not establish a *chazakah.* Rather, he must preserve his documentary or other proof of ownership in order to fend off the challenge of the previous owner.

As noted, the legal term for the occupancy that creates the presumption of ownership for the occupant is "*chazakah.*" Moreover, the presumption of ownership that derives from that occupancy is also called "*chazakah.*" The term *chazakah* will be used extensively throughout the commentary to this chapter in both senses. This chapter will discuss the various regulations governing the establishment of such a *chazakah* and its limits.

Chapter Three

Mishnah The first Mishnah discusses the length of occupancy necessary to establish the *chazakah*[1] of various types of real property. The time required depends on whether the property provides benefits throughout the year or seasonally, as explained below.

The first section of our Mishnah enumerates various types of real property that provide constant benefits, and then defines the extent of the three-year occupancy required to establish a *chazakah* for such properties.

חֶזְקַת הַבָּתִּים – Regarding **the *chazakah* of houses,** וְהַבּוֹרוֹת וְהַשִּׁיחִין וְהַמְּעָרוֹת – **pits, ditches, vaults,**[2] וְהַשּׁוֹבָכוֹת – **dovecotes** affixed to the ground, וְהַמֶּרְחֲצָאוֹת – **bathhouses,** וּבֵית הַבַּדִּין – **the place that houses olive presses,**[3] וּבֵית הַשְּׁלָחִין – **irrigated fields,**[4] וְהָעֲבָדִים – **slaves,**[5] וְכָל שֶׁהוּא עוֹשֶׂה פֵּירוֹת תָּדִיר – **or any** other property **that yields benefit continually –** חֶזְקָתָן שָׁלֹשׁ שָׁנִים מִיּוֹם לְיוֹם – **their *chazakah*** is established by an occupancy of **three years from day to day.**[6]

שְׂדֵה הַבַּעַל – Regarding **a rain-watered field –** חֶזְקָתָהּ שָׁלֹשׁ שָׁנִים וְאֵינָן מִיּוֹם לְיוֹם – **its *chazakah*** is established in **three years, but not from day to day.**[7] How long a *chazakah* is required? רַבִּי יִשְׁמָעֵאל אוֹמֵר – **R' Yishmael says:** שְׁלֹשָׁה חֳדָשִׁים בָּרִאשׁוֹנָה – **Three months in the first** year, שְׁלֹשָׁה בָּאַחֲרוֹנָה – **three months in the last** year וּשְׁנֵים עָשָׂר חֹדֶשׁ בָּאֶמְצַע – **and** a full **twelve months in the middle** year, הֲרֵי שְׁמוֹנָה עָשָׂר חֹדֶשׁ – **which is** a total of **eighteen months.**[8] רַבִּי עֲקִיבָא אוֹמֵר – **R' Akiva says:** חֹדֶשׁ בָּרִאשׁוֹנָה – **One month in the first** year, וְחֹדֶשׁ בָּאַחֲרוֹנָה – **one month in the last** year וּשְׁנֵים עָשָׂר חֹדֶשׁ בָּאֶמְצַע – **and** a full **twelve months in the middle** year, הֲרֵי אַרְבָּעָה עָשָׂר חֹדֶשׁ – **which is** a total of **fourteenth months.**[9]

R' Yishmael qualifies his ruling that a rain-watered field requires a *chazakah* of at least eighteen months: אָמַר רַבִּי יִשְׁמָעֵאל – **R' Yishmael said:** בַּמֶּה דְּבָרִים אֲמוּרִים – **In** regard to **what is this said?** בִּשְׂדֵה לָבָן – **In** regard to **a grain field.**[10] אֲבָל בִּשְׂדֵה אִילָן – **However, in** regard to **a field of trees,**[11] כָּנַס אֶת תְּבוּאָתוֹ – if **he gathered his** grape **produce,**[12] וּמָסַק אֶת זֵיתָיו – **picked his olives,** [וְ]כָנַס אֶת קֵייצוֹ – **and gathered in his dried figs,**[13] הֲרֵי אֵלּוּ שָׁלֹשׁ שָׁנִים – **these count as three years.**[14]

NOTES

1. The term *chazakah* has a wide range of meaning in the Talmud. As noted in the chapter introduction, *chazakah* in the context of our Mishnah is the term for the uncontested occupancy of real property [i.e. land and houses] that creates the legal presumption that the occupant owns the occupied premises. [Should the property's previous owner contest that he is still the owner and that the occupant is a squatter, the burden of proof rests on the contester once the occupant has established a *chazakah*. Thus, if the present occupant maintains that the previous owner sold the property to him but that he has since lost the deed, the burden of proof rests on the previous owner.] The term *chazakah* is also used here for the presumption of ownership that results from the requisite term of uncontested occupancy.

By "occupancy," we mean the *usage* of the particular property in the normal manner and with the normal frequency that an owner would use it [e.g. *dwelling* in a house, *cultivating* a field, *drawing water* from a reservoir].

2. (See above, 17a note 1.) All of these are used throughout the year as water reservoirs (*Yad Ramah*).

3. These, too, are used throughout the year. Although most people process all of their olives immediately after the harvest, there are those who store them and press them little by little throughout the year (*Tosafos*; cf. *Meiri, Ritva* and *Nimukei Yosef*).

4. I.e. a field that contains a spring. Since the field has a constant water source, it yields produce throughout the year (*Rashi*).

5. Though slaves are movable rather than fixed property, their *chazakah,* too, is established in three years (see *Rashba* and *Ritva*).

6. The three-year occupancy necessary to establish a *chazakah* is the occupant's use of *all* the benefits yielded by the property during that time period. Since the properties listed by the Mishnah until this point yield benefit *continually,* their occupancy must be continual; otherwise, the occupant has failed to utilize *all* the benefits potentially yielded by the property (*Rashi*).

Thus, the Mishnah here teaches that the term of occupancy necessary to establish a *chazakah* for these properties is *three full* years and that the occupancy during those three years must be *continual* (see *Ritva*).

[The constancy and extent of use necessary is that which would be normal for an actual owner (see *Baal HaItur* in the name of *Rabbeinu Tam,* cited by *Rashba* and *Ran*).]

7. [This section of the Mishnah discusses the length of occupancy required to establish a *chazakah* for properties that provide seasonal, rather than year-round, benefit.]

A non-irrigated field, which depends exclusively on rain for its water requirements, yields produce only once a year. [In Mediterranean climates, there is a specific rainy season; the rest of the year is invariably dry.] Consequently, the three-year *chazakah* need not consist of three complete years. The exact length of the required occupancy is debated by the two Tannaim that follow (*Rashi*). [Other Rishonim disagree with *Rashi,* maintaining that this statement represents the opinion of the Sages, who disagree with the two opinions that follow – see below, 36b (see *Rashba* et al.).]

8. That is, a *chazakah* can be established by occupying the field for the last three months of the first year, the entire second year and the first three months of the third year.

In the first year, the occupant can condense a full growing season (from planting to harvest) into the last three months of the year [i.e. the months of Tammuz, Av and Elul]. Similarly, in the last of the three years, he can condense a full growing season into the first three months of the year. After these eighteen months, we can assume that the original owner sold the field, because no one would allow a squatter to exploit the entire produce of his field for three years without issuing a protest (*Rashi,* as understood by *Tosafos;* see also *Rashbam* below 36b ד"ה פירא רבא). [See *Tosafos,* who object to the implication in *Rashi* that the occupant must plant *and* harvest the produce in both the first and third years.]

9. R' Akiva requires only a minimal crop in the first and last years. His dispute with R' Yishmael will be analyzed by the Gemara on 36a.

10. A grain field requires three years of occupancy [albeit two of them condensed] to establish a *chazakah* because its entire crop is harvested at one time each year (*Rashi*).

A grain field is known as a שְׂדֵה לָבָן [literally: white field], either because of the absence of any trees to provide shade (*Rash, Sheviis* 2:1) or because grain tends to whiten as it ripens (*Rash, Pe'ah* 3:1).

11. I.e. a field containing several varieties of fruit trees, each of whose fruits ripen at a different time of year (see *Rashi*). The Mishnah's present example deals with a field that contains grapes, olives and figs.

12. I.e. the wine produced by the field's vines (*Rashi*; see also *Tosafos*). [*Rashash* explains that the winepresses were generally in the vineyards (in contrast to olive presses, which were generally in the city). Consequently, the full use of the field in regard to its grapes is not complete until the wine is produced there.]

13. I.e. he picked the figs, left them in the field to dry, removed the stems and gathered them into the house (*Rashi*). [Our rendering of the word קְצִיעוֹת in *Rashi* follows his comments to *Beitzah* 3b; cf. *Rav* to *Maasros* 2:7 and *Aruch*.] [Emendation follows *Bach* and all manuscripts.]

14. The three distinct harvests of these three types of trees in a single year are the equivalent of three years of occupancy in a grain field and

חזקת [א] הבתים והבורות והשיחין והמערות והשובכות והמרחצאות ובית הבדין ובית השלחין והעבדים וכל (א) שהוא עושה פירות תדיר חזקתן שלש שנים מיום ליום [ב] שדה (ב) הבעל חזקתה שלש שנים ואינה מיום ליום [ה] ר' ישמעאל אומר ג' חדשים בראשונה ג' באחרונה ושנים עשר חדש באמצע הרי (ג) י"ח חדש ר"ע אומר חדש בראשונה וחדש באחרונה וי"ב חדש באמצע הרי י"ד חדש א"ר ישמעאל בד"א בשדה לבן אבל בשדה אילן כנס את תבואתו ומסק את זיתיו (ד) כנס את קייצו הרי אלו ג' שנים: גמ' אמר ר' יוחנן שמעתי מהולכי אושא שהיו אומרים מנין לחזקה (ה) ג' שנים משור המועד מה שור המועד כיון שנגח ג' נגיחות [ג] נפק לי' מחזקת תם וקם ליה בחזקת מועד ה"נ כיון דאכלה תלת שנין נפק לה מרשות מוכר וקיימא לה ברשות לוקח אי מה שור המועד [ד] עד נגיחה רביעית לא מיחייב ה"נ עד שנה רביעית לא קיימא ברשותיה הכי השתא התם מכי נגח שלש נגיחות הוי מועד ואידך

רשב"ם

בית השלחין. מתוך שהמעיין בתוכו שמשקים אותה ממנו תדיר עושה פירות תדיר וכל דבר שעושה פירות תדיר חזקתן ג' שנים מיום ליום אם החזיק בה שלש שנים שלימות אין צריך להביא שטר מכירה ואם ערערו עליה בעלים הראשונים וזה אומר מכרת לי ואבד שטרי חזקתו מועלת לו ואם לאו אין חזקתו מועלת לו לפי שכשאמרו ג' שנים לחזקה כל הראוי לאכול ממנה בג' שנים אמרו: שדה בית הבעל. המסתפקת במי גשמים אינה עושה פירות אלא פעם אחת בשנה חזקתה ג' שנים ואינה צריכה מיום ליום ומה היא חזקתה רבי ישמעאל אומר שלשה חדשים אחרונים של שנה ראשונה ושלשה חדשים ראשונים של שנה אחרונה ואמצעית שלימה שיש הממהרים לזרוע לפני ראש השנה וכיון שהחזיק בה סוף שנה ראשונה ג' חדשים ויש לו עדים שזורעה באותן ג' חדשים וכן בג' חדשים ראשונים של אחרונה הרי זו חזקת שלש שנים רצופות שאין לך אדם הרואה את חבירו שזורע את שדהו לאכול פרי העשוי לשנה ושותק: ר"ע אומר כו'. מפרש בגמרא במאי פליגי: בד"א. שצריך י"ח חדש לשדה בית הבעל: בשדה הלבן. שכל פירותיה נלקטין בפרק אחד לפיכך צריך ג' שנים: אבל בשדה האילן. שפירותיה נלקטים לפרקים ענבים בפרק אחד וזיתים בפרק אחר ותאנה בפרק אחר: כנס את תבואתו. יין של גפנים: ומסק את זיתיו וכנס את קייצו. תאנים ליקט וייבשן בה ועשה קציעות והכניסן לבית הרי זו חזקה כאילו הן ג' שנים: גמ' מהולכי אושא. שגלתה סנהדרין לאושא כדאמרינן בראש השנה (דף לא.) עשר גליות גלתה סנהדרין כו' מיבנה לאושא מאושא כו': לא מיחייב. לשלם אלא חצי נזק אף כאן עד גמר שנה רביעית לא הויא חזקה:

תוספות

חזקת הבתים ובית הבדים. פי' ר"י בר מרדכי דהא דתנן בפרק אומר בקדש (חגיגה כד:) עברו הגיתות והבדים דמשמע שיש להן זמן קבוע היינו שרוב העולם דורכים אז בזמן לקיטה אבל יש בני אדם שמאחרין כל השנה ודורכין במעט מעט: שלשה חדשים בראשונה. מתוך פ"ה משמע דבעי רבי ישמעאל שהוא יזרע ויקצור באותן שלשה חדשים ראשונים וכן באחרונים ואין תימה שתהא תבואה הנזרעת אחר ניסן גדילה בג' חדשים ואין זמנה עד ניסן הבא דמצינן כעין זה דאמרי' בר"ה (יג.) כל תבואה הנקצרת בחג בידוע שהביאה שליש לפני ר"ה אלמא גדלה פעמים באותו זמן אבל קשיא לר"י דא"כ אמאי צריך י"ח חדשים בט"ו חדשים סגי שיזרע ג' חדשים לפני ניסן ויקצור בניסן ושניה בסוף הקיץ ושלישית בניסן הבא וי"ל דצריך אכילה חשובה של י"ב כדמשמע בע"ג דאמרי' בגמ' אכל תלת פירי לתלתא ירחי כגון אספסתא לרבי ישמעאל הויא חזקה שאני התם לפי שהוא זמן שלה אבל קשה לר"י דאמרי' בגמ' (לקמן דף לו:) פירא רבה ופירא זוטא איכא בינייהו דר' ישמעאל ור"ע ופ"ה דר' ישמעאל סבר פירא רבה כגון שעורים ושבולת שועל שגדלים בג' חדשים ור"ע סבר פירא זוטא כגון ירק הגדל בחדש אחד והא אמרי' בגמרא (לקמן ע"ב) דאספסתא בחדש אחד הויא חזקה לרבי ישמעאל ונראה לר"י דלא בעי רבי ישמעאל שיזרע התבואה ויקצור אלא אפי' זרעה הראשון או הוא יזרענה בשלשה חדשים אחרונים אע"פ שלא קצרה ובהא פליגי דרבי ישמעאל סבר בעינן שיהא גדל הפרי ברשותו הרבה כגון ג' חדשים והיינו פירא רבה ור"ע סבר דאין צריך שיגדל ברשותו אלא חדש אחד והיינו פירא זוטא וא"ת היאך יהא ניכר שיחזיק בה כל ג' חדשים ראשונים או אחרונים כי ביום אחד או בב' יוכל לקצור או לזרוע וכי תימא שמנכש את השדה ומתקנו הא לא הויא חזקה מידי דהוה אניר דאמר לקמן (דף לו:) דלא הויא חזקה משום דמימר אמר כל שיבא דכרבא [ב] ניעול בה וי"ל כגון שאוכלה שחת והא דאמרי' (שם.) אכלה שחת לא הויא חזקה ה"מ כשאוכל בענין זה שאין התבואה חוזרת לבא דשייך לומר לאו אחזקת כדמחזקי אינשי לפיכך לא חש למחות אבל אם אכלה שחת בענין שאין התבואה מתקלקלת כדרך שבני אדם עושים בעוד שהוא ירק ולא בא עדיין גבעול שלה הויא חזקה ובשדה אילן דבעו רבנן דפליגי אר' ישמעאל בגמרא מיום ליום ג' שנים אע"ג דלא שייך התם אכלה שחת מ"מ איכא למימר כגון שזומר ומעכב העלים לעצמו ואע"ג דמתקן בכך והוי כמו ניר כיון [ג] (שמתקן) העלים לעצמו לא שייך למימר כל שיבא דכרבא ניעול בה ועוד אומר ר"י דאחזיק בה בכה"ג שנעל וגדר את השדה ונועל במפתח ואין מניח אדם ליכנס והא דאמר בגמרא (דף כט:) לונמא במאי קני לה ולא קאמר כגון שנעלה וגדרה איכא למימר דאין נעילה מועלת אא"כ איכא אכילה בהדה או זריעה אבל נעילה גרידא לא מהני מידי והשתא אתי שפיר נמי לרבנן דרבי ישמעאל: שהן י"ח חדש. תימה וכי מניינא אתא לאשמועינן וכה"ג פריך בכמה דוכתי וליכא למימר דרצופין אתי לאשמועינן דא"כ מאי קמ"ל רב הונא ובגמרא משמע דממתניתין לא הוה שמעינן דבעינן רצופים אי לא דאשמועינן רב הונא [עי' תוי"ט שתמה על זה]: כנס את תבואתו. להכי קרי ליה לכרם תבואה משום דכתיב (דברים כב) ותבואת הכרם וא"ת תינח הא דתנא תבואה קודם לשמן כדאמרינן באיזהו נשך (ב"מ סג.) הגיע זמן יין למכור ובתר הכי קאמר הגיע זמן למכור שמן אלא כנס את קייצו אמאי תני ליה בתר הכי הא תאנים קדמי דהא אמר בהמקבל (שם קו:) חצי ניסן ואייר וחצי סיון קציר חצי סיון ותמוז [ד] וחצי] אב קיץ ואילו בציר היה בתשרי כדאמרינן בברכות (דף לה:) דאמר להו רבא לרבנן במטותא מינייכו לא תיתחזיאו קמאי לא ביומי ניסן ולא ביומי תשרי ואמרינן נמי בסנהדרין (דף כו:) גנב ניסן וגנב תשרי לא שמיה גנב וה"מ באריסא ודבר מועט ואמרינן באיזהו נשך (ב"מ דף עג:) חזי מר להנהו רבנן דיהבי דמי אחמרא בתשרי ומבחרי להו בטבת מכל אלו משמע דבציר הוי בתשרי וכבר כלה הקיץ וי"ל דהא דקרי קיץ לחצי סיון ותמוז וחצי אב לפי שאז עיקר יובש של תאנים באילן ומיהו אין קוצלין אותו מן האילן עד לאחר הבציר א"נ לוקטין אותו קודם חצי סיון ומניחים אותו לייבש ולא (ו) זמן כניסתו לבית עד לאחר תבואת הכרם והא דלא הויא לקיטה חזקה כי שמא היו רגילין לייבשן באותו שדה שגדלו שם ולכך לא הויא חזקה עד שיביאם לביתו ור"ח מפרש כנס תבואתו בתשרי ומסק את זיתיו בשבט וכנס קייצו באב הרי זו חזקה נמצאת חזקה בשנה אחת ונקט כסדר זה משום דתשרי הוא תחלת השנה אבל יותר מיושב אי הוה תני להו כסדר גשמי שנה שהן גדלין עליהן: אי מה שור המועד עד נגיחה רביעית כו'. מכאן חזר בו רש"י ממה שהיה מפרש בב"ק (דף כג: ושם ד"ה ולא) גבי (ז) דפליגי אביי ורבא דאמר אביי תמול חד מתמול תרי שלשום תלת ולא אתאן בעליו ולא ישמרנו בעליו לנגיחה רביעית ורבא אמר תמול מתמול חד הוא כו' דאביי סבר דעד נגיחה רביעית לא מיחייב ורבא סבר דחייב בנגיחה שלישית דא"כ הוה מסיק הכא גמרא דלא כהלכתא דקי"ל כרבא לגבי אביי וחזר (ח) רש"י ופירש דמשמעות דורשין איכא בינייהו וה"ר עזרא מפרש דודאי לכ"ע לא מיחייב עד רביעית אבל בהא פליגי דלאביי דמפיק נגיחה רביעית מקרא דלא ישמרנו אם נגח נגיחה רביעית ביום ג' לא מיחייב עד שיגח ביום רביעי דלא ישמרנו קאי אימים דומיא דתמול שלשום אבל לרבא דנגיחה רביעית לא כתיבא בהדיא אפילו ביום שלישי אם נגח נגיחה רביעית מיחייב: עד נגיחה רביעית לא מיחייב. תימה לר"י דמאי פריך הא הכי יליף משור המועד מה התם הוחזק נגחן שלש פעמים ה"נ הוחזק שתקן בשלש שנים א"כ משלש שנים ואילך קמה ליה ברשותיה ואומר ר"י דס"ד דמקשה דהכי יליף מה התם מכי נגח ג' פעמים נפק ליה מחצי נזק לנזק שלם ה"נ כיון שאכלה שלש שנים ולא מיחה נפקא ליה מרשות מוכר לרשות לוקח אע"ג דמילתא בלא טעמא הוא:

אלא

מסורת הש"ס

א) [ועי' תוס' עירובין מח. ד"ה ר' יהודה וכו'], ב) נ"ל לעיל כז., ג) ס"א שמעתם, ד) מהרש"ל.

ליקוטי רש"י

בית השלחין. ארץ יבשה קרויה בית השלחין וצריך להשקותה תמיד ושדה בית הבעל יפה הימנו [שיר השירים ד, יג]. קרקע יבישה לא דייה במי הגשמים וממעיין שבה משקה אותה [ב"מ קג.]. שדה שהיא עומדת בכר וצריך להשקותה [מו"ק ב.]. אין עושין חלל תחת רשות הרבים. ואע"ג דמקבל עליה כל היזקא דאתי ממתמוטי שאין רצונם של בני אדם לזוק ולירד לדין על עסקי ממונו ומפרש ואזיל מה הוא אותו חלל בורות שיחין ומערות [רשב"ם לקמן ס.]. בורות שיחין ומערות. בור עגול הוא שיח ארוכה ומערה מרובעת ומכוסה בקירוי אלא שיש לה פה [ב"ק נ:]. רבי אליעזר מתיר. אלא שיכסנו כיסוי חזק כדי שתהא עגלה מהלכת עליה דר"א אזל בתר השתא ולא חייש שמא יתליע הכיסוי ויפול והכי אמרינן בבבא קמא (נב:). ואין זימנין דמפחית ולאו אדעתיה. משום דזימנין דמתליע מתוכו ומפחות ולא אדעתיה דעובר ברה"ר ועבור ויפול [רשב"ם לקמן ס.]. [ע"כ שייך לדף כז:]. הבורות שיחין ומערות. בור עגול הוא שיח ארוכה ומערה מרובעת ומכוסה בקירוי אלא שיש לה פה [ב"ק נ:]. והשובכות. דרך שובך להיות בו מחילות הרבה קן לכל זוג וזוג ולכל קן וקן [ביצה ט.]. בית הבדין. בית שעוצר זיתים [ב"מ קיז:]. בית השלחין. ארץ יבשה קרויה בית השלחין וצריך להשקותה תמיד ושדה בית הבעל יפה הימנו [שיר השירים ד, יג]. קרקע יבישה לא דייה במי הגשמים וממעיין שבה משקה אותה [ב"מ קג.]. שדה שהיא עומדת בכר וצריך להשקותה תמיד [מו"ק ב.]. שדה הבעל. מי יונתן אחר בית שקיא דמיא [שופטים א, טו]. שדה הוא בעמק ואינו צריך להשקותו [מו"ק שם]. שמעתי מהולכי אושא. שהיא אחת מעשר גליות שגלתה סנהדרין כדאמר בר"ה (לא.) [כתובות מט: ובכעי"ז ב"מ לה.]. אי מה שור המועד עד נגיחה רביעית לא מיחייב. שלא נעשה מועד עד שנגח ג' נגיחות ובנגיחה רביעית משלם נ"ש אבל באלישית פלגא נזקא הוא דמשלם [ב"ק כג:].

עין משפט נר מצוה

א א ב מיי' פי"ב מהל' טוען הלכה א סמג עשין צה טוש"ע ח"מ סי' קמא סעיף א:

ב ג ד מיי' פ"ו מהלכות נזקי ממון הל' א סמג עשין סח טוש"ע ח"מ סי' שפט סעיף ה:

רבינו גרשום

חזקת הבתי': והבורות זהו עגיל: שיחין. ארוך וקטן: המערות. מרובעות. וכל הני עושין כדי להשקות שדותיהן מהן: ובית הבדין. זהו בד של זיתים שלאחר דריסת הזיתים מניחין שם השמן ומסתפקין הימנו בכל יום ויום: ובית השלחין. צריך להשקותו בכל יום: והעבדים. שהוקשו לקרקעות שעובד בהן בכל יום: וכל דבר שהוא עושה פירות. כלומר כל דבר שמשתמשין בו בכל יום ויום תמיד: חזקתן ג' שנים מיום ליום. דכל הני עושין שמוש מיום ליום ואם החזיק בהן ג' שנים מיום ליום ואח"כ מערער עליהם שום אדם מחזיקין להו ביד המחזיק ומשו"ה בעינן מיום ליום כדי שלא יכול לטעון המערער אני באתי לשם ולא ראיתיו שהי' משתמש בו לפיכך לא מחיתי ולכך צריך שיביא עדים שראוהו משתמש בו בכל יום לפי שבאלו משתמשין בהן בכל יום: שדה בית הבעל חזקתו ג' שנים. ולא צריך שיהא משמש בו בכל יום שאם בא המערער ואמר אני באתי ולא ראיתיו משתמש בה לפיכך לא מחיתי יכול לומר לו אני הייתי משתמש בשעה שבני אדם רגילין להשתמש בשדה בית הבעל והואיל ולא מחית באותה שעה לא הוי מחאה: מהולכי אושא. מפרש לקמן דהיינו ר' ישמעאל: נפק ליה מחזקת תם. כדכתיב כי שור נגח הוא מתמול שלשום. וקם ליה בחזקת מועד. כדכתיב והועד בבעליו ולא ישמרנו: עד נגיחה רביעית לא מחייב. נזק שלם:

הגהות הב"ח

(א) במשנה וכל דבר שהוא עושה: (ב) שם שדה בית הבעל: (ג) שם הרי אלו י"ח וכו' הרי אלו י"ד: (ד) שם וכנס את קייצו: (ה) גמ' מנין לחזקה שהיא ג': (ו) תוס' ד"ה כנס וכו' ולא הוה זמן כניסתו וכו' שדה עצמה שגדלו וכו' יותר היה מיושב: (ז) ד"ה אי מה וכו' גבי הא דפליגי: (ח) בא"ד וחזר בו רש"י:

Gemara The Gemara examines the basis for the three-year *chazakah*:

אָמַר רַבִּי יוֹחָנָן – **R' Yochanan said:** שָׁמַעְתִּי מֵהוֹלְכֵי אוּשָׁא – **I heard from those** sages **who traveled to Usha,**[15] שֶׁהָיוּ אוֹמְרִים – **that they would say:** מִנַּיִן לַחֲזָקָה שָׁלֹשׁ שָׁנִים – **From where** do we derive the concept of **a three-year *chazakah*?** מִשּׁוֹר הַמּוּעָד – We derive it **from** the law of **the *muad* bull.**[16] מַה שּׁוֹר הַמּוּעָד – **Just as** with regard to **a *muad* bull,** כֵּיוָן שֶׁנָּגַח שָׁלֹשׁ נְגִיחוֹת – **once it has gored three times** נָפַק לֵיהּ מֵחֶזְקַת תָּם – **it leaves the** original **status of a *tam*** bull וְקָם לֵיהּ בְּחֶזְקַת מוּעָד – **and assumes the status of a *muad*** bull, הָכָא נַמִּי – **here, too,** with regard to *chazakah,* כֵּיוָן דַּאֲכָלָהּ תְּלָת שְׁנִין – **once [the occupant] has used [the property]**[17] for **three years,** נָפַק לָהּ מֵרְשׁוּת מוֹכֵר – **it leaves the possession of the seller** וְקַיְימָא לָהּ בִּרְשׁוּת לוֹקֵחַ – **and stands in the possession of the buyer.**[18]

The Gemara objects to R' Yochanan's derivation:

אִי מַה שּׁוֹר הַמּוּעָד עַד נְגִיחָה רְבִיעִית לֹא מִיחַיֵּיב – **If** so, say that **just as** in the case of **a *muad* bull, [the owner] is not liable** to pay full damages **until the fourth goring,** הָכָא נַמִּי עַד שָׁנָה רְבִיעִית לֹא קַיְימָא בִּרְשׁוּתֵיהּ – **here, too, the property should not stand in [the buyer's] possession until** the end of **the fourth year.**[19] – ? –

The Gemara defends R' Yochanan:

הָכִי הַשְׁתָּא – **Now,** is that **so?** הָתָם מִכִּי נָגַח שָׁלֹשׁ נְגִיחוֹת הֲוֵי מוּעָד – **There, once [the bull] gores three times, it is** already **a *muad;***

NOTES

suffice to establish a *chazakah* (*Rashi*). [According to R' Yishmael, the essential factor in establishing the *chazakah* of a field is the utilization of three entire *crops,* even if the time it takes to plant, raise and harvest them is essentially short – see Gemara 28b.]

15. The Gemara in *Rosh Hashanah* (31a) lists ten relocations that the Sanhedrin was forced to make in the period of the Destruction of the Second Temple; among them was a move from Yavneh to Usha (*Rashi*). R' Yochanan cites a statement he heard attributed to the sages after their move to Usha. [As the Gemara states on 28b, "those who traveled to Usha" is a reference to R' Yishmael, who lived considerably before R' Yochanan's time. Thus, R' Yochanan does not mean that he heard this teaching directly from "those who traveled to Usha," but rather that he heard it reported in their name (*Ritva*).]

16. The first three times a bull gores another animal, the bull's owner pays only half damages (*Exodus* 21:35). The Talmud refers to such a bull as a תָּם, *tam* (literally: ordinary). If the owner has been duly warned each time about his bull's violence, yet fails to take appropriate measures to guard his violent animal and it gores a fourth time, the owner must pay full damages for the fourth and subsequent attacks (ibid. v. 36). After the third warning, the bull is known as a מוּעָד, *muad* (literally: one [whose owner was] warned by witnesses [regarding its violent nature]). The bull is revealed to be a violent animal and its owner must take measures to protect the public from it.

17. Literally: eaten it [i.e. its yield].

18. [I.e. in the possession of the occupant, who claims to have bought the property from the original owner.]

In the case of the bull, it originally had a status of a *tam,* with the assumption being that it would not gore. The Torah teaches us that if it gores three times, it no longer has the status of *tam,* but rather has established itself to have a status of *muad,* with the assumption being, that it *is* likely to gore. The Sages of Usha derive from this that when an act which indicates a change of status is repeated three times, a new status is thus established.

The Sages of Usha applied this to the case of *chazakah* as follows: all real property is presumed to belong to the original occupant. If a second person occupies it and uses it as his own, each year that he does so is considered to be an act indicating that he has acquired it. Once he repeats this act three times, the property loses its status of presumably belonging to the original owner, and a new status of presumed ownership by the one making the *chazakah* is established. (According to this explanation, the establishment of the three-year *chazakah* has nothing to do with the length of *time* involved. Rather, the three years are considered to be three acts indicating that he has acquired the property, establishing a new status of presumed ownership by him.)

[According to this interpretation, which is based on the view of most Rishonim (see *Ramban, Rabbeinu Yonah, Ran, Ritva*), there is no *proof* that the occupier has indeed acquired property, but since the three years establish a status of presumed ownership by him, the burden of proof is no longer upon him. He now has a *"chazakah"* on the property, any anyone claiming that it is *not* his would have to bring proof to that claim. This would also seem to be the understanding of *Rashi* (see 28b ד״ה ומשני טעמא מאי and ד״ה תיהוי חזקה). (For alternate interpretations, see *Tosafos* ד״ה עד נגיחה and to 28b ד״ה אלא מעתה; cf. *Rashba* there ד״ה אלא מעתה).]

19. A bull that gores three times, does not pay full damages as a *muad* until it gores a fourth time. This would seem to indicate that although the bull no longer has a status of *tam* after three times, it does not attain a status of *muad* until it gores a fourth time. Therefore, in the case of *chazakah,* after three years, the property would indeed no longer have the status of presumed ownership by the one occupying it either. As a result, after three years, *neither* one would be considered the presumed owner, and it would have the legal status of a property whose ownership is unknown (see *Ramban* and *Ritva;* cf. *Tosafos*).

חזקת א הבתים והבורות והשיחין והמערות והשובכות והמרחצאות ובית הבדין ובית השלחין והעבדים וכל (א) שהוא עושה פירות תדיר חזקתן שלש שנים מיום ליום ב שדה (ב) הבעל חזקתה שלש שנים ואינן מיום ליום א) ר' ישמעאל אומר ג' חדשים בראשונה ג' באחרונה ושנים עשר חדש באמצע הרי (ג) י"ח חדש ר"ע אומר חדש בראשונה וחדש באחרונה וי"ב חדש באמצע הרי י"ד חדש א"ר ישמעאל בד"א בשדה לבן אבל בשדה אילן כנס את תבואתו ומסק את זיתיו (ד) כנס את קייצו הרי אלו ג' שנים: **גמ'** אמר ר' יוחנן שמעתי מהולכי אושא שהיו אומרים מנין לחזקה (ה) ג' שנים משור המועד מה שור המועד כיון שנגח ג' נגיחות ג נפק לי' מחזקת תם וקם ליה בחזקת מועד ה"נ כיון דאכלה תלת שנין נפק לה מרשות מוכר וקיימא לה ברשות לוקח אי מה שור המועד ד עד נגיחה רביעית לא מיחייב ה"נ עד שנה רביעית לא קיימא ברשותיה הכי השתא התם מכי נגח שלש נגיחות הוי מועד ואידך

רש"י

בית השלחין. מתוך שהמעיין בתוכו שמשקים אותה ממנו תדיר עושה פירות תדיר וכל דבר שעושה פירות תדיר חזקתן ג' שנים מיום ליום אם החזיק בה שלש שנים שלימות אין צריך להביא שטר מכירה ואם ערערו עליה בעלים הראשונים וזה אומר מכרת לי ואבד שטרי חזקתו מועלת לו ואם לאו אין חזקתו מועלת לו לפי שכשאמרו ג' שנים לחזקה כל הראוי לאכול ממנה בג' שנים אמרו: **שדה בית הבעל.** המסתפקת במי גשמים אינה עושה פירות אלא פעם אחת בשנה חזקתה ג' שנים ואינה צריכה מיום ליום ומה היא חזקתה רבי ישמעאל אומר שלשה חדשים אחרונים של שנה ראשונה ושלשה חדשים ראשונים של שנה אחרונה ואמצעית שלימה שיש שממהרים לזרוע לפני ראש השנה וכיון שהחזיק בה סוף שנה ראשונה ג' חדשים ויש לו עדים שזורעה באותן ג' חדשים וכן בג' חדשים ראשונים של אחרונה הרי זו חזקת שלש שנים רצופות שאין לך אדם הרואה את חבירו שזורע את שדהו לאכול פרי העשוי לשנה ושותק: **ר"ע אומר כו'.** מפרש בגמרא במאי פליגי: **בד"א.** שצריך י"ח חדש לשדה בית הבעל: **בשדה הלבן.** שכל פירותיה נלקטין בפרק אחד לפיכך צריך ג' שנים: **אבל בשדה האילן.** שפירותיה נלקטים לפרקים ענבים בפרק אחד וזיתים בפרק אחר ותאנה בפרק אחר: **כנס את תבואתו.** יין של גפנים: **ומסק את זיתיו וכנס את קייצו.** תאנים ליקט וייבשן בה ועשה קליעות והכניסן לבית הרי זו חזקה כאילו הן ג' שנים: **גמ' מהולכי אושא.** שגלתה סנהדרין לאושא כדאמרינן בראש השנה (דף לא.) עשר גליות גלתה סנהדרין כו' מיבנה לאושא מאושא כו': **לא מיחייב.** לשלם אלא חצי נזק אף כאן עד גמר שנה רביעית לא הויא חזקה: ואידך

תוספות

חזקת הבתים ובית הבדים. פי' ר"י בר מרדכי דהא דתנן בפרק חומר בקדש (חגיגה כד:) עברו הגיתות והבדים דמשמע שיש להן זמן קבוע היינו שרוב העולם דורכים אז בזמן לקיטה אבל יש בני אדם שמכניסין כל השנה ודורכין במעט מעט:

שלשה חדשים בראשונה. מתוך פ"ה משמע דבעי רבי ישמעאל שהוא יזרע ויקצור באותן שלשה חדשים ראשונים וכן באחרונים ואין תימה שתהא תבואה המזרעת אחר ניסן גדילה בג' חדשים ואין זמנה עד ניסן הבא דמלינן כענין זה דאמרי' בר"ה (יג.) כל תבואה הנקצרת בחג בידוע שהביאה שליש לפני ר"ה אלמא גדלה פעמים באותו זמן אבל קשיא לר"י דא"כ אמאי צריך י"ח חדשים בט"ו חדשים סגי שיזרע ג' חדשים לפני ניסן ויקצור בניסן ושניה בסוף הקיץ ושלישית בניסן הבא וי"ל דצריך אכילה חשובה של י"ב באמצע אע"ג דאמרי' בגמ' אכל תלת פירי לתלתא ירחי כגון אספסתא לרבי ישמעאל הויא חזקה שאני התם לפי שהוא זמן שלה אבל קשה לר"י דאמרי' בגמ' (לקמן דף לו:) פירא רבה ופירא זוטא איכא בינייהו דר' ישמעאל ור"ע ופ"ה דר' ישמעאל סבר פירא רבה כגון שעורים ושבולת שועל שגדלים בג' חדשים ור"ע סבר פירא זוטא כגון ירק הגדל בחדש אחד והא אמרי' בגמרא (לקמן ע"ב) דאספסתא בחדש אחד הויא חזקה לרבי ישמעאל ונראה לר"י דלא בעי רבי ישמעאל שיזרע התבואה ויקצור אלא אפי' זרעה הראשון או הוא יזרענה בשלשה חדשים אחרונים אע"פ שלא קצרה והא פליגי דרבי ישמעאל סבר בעינן שיהא גדל הפרי ברשותו הרבה כגון ג' חדשים והיינו פירא רבה ור"ע סבר דאין צריך שיגדל ברשותו אלא חדש אחד והיינו פירא זוטא וא"ת היאך יהא ניכר שיחזיק בה כל ג' חדשים ראשונים או אחרונים כי ביום אחד או בב' יוכל לקצור או לזרוע וכי תימא שמנכש את השדה ומתקנו הא לא הויא חזקה מידי דהוה אניר דאמר לקמן (דף לו:) דלא הויא חזקה משום דמימר אמר כל שיבא דכרבא ז) ניעול בה וי"ל כגון שאוכלה שחת והא דאמרי' (שם.) אכלה שחת לא הויא חזקה ה"מ כשאוכל בענין זה שאין התבואה חוזרת לבא דשייך לומר לאו אחזוקת כדמחזקי אינשי לפיכך לא חש למחות אבל אם אכלה שחת בענין שאין התבואה מתקלקלת כדרך שבני אדם עושים בעוד שהוא ירק ולא בא עדיין גבעול שלה הויא חזקה ובשדה אילן דבעו רבנן דפליגי אר' ישמעאל בגמרא מיום ליום ג' שנים אע"ג דלא שייך התם אכלה שחת מ"מ איכא למימר כגון שזומר ומעבד האילנות לעצמו ואע"ג דמתקן בכך והוי כמו ניר כיון ח) (שמתקן) האילנות לעצמו לא שייך למימר כל שיבא דכרבא ניעול בה ועוד אומר ר"י דאמחזיק בה בכה"ג שנעל וגדר את השדה ונועל במפתח ואין מניח אדם ליכנס והא דאמר בגמרא (דף כט.) לנעולה במאי קני לא קאמר כגון שנעלה וגדרה איכא למימר דאין נעילה בהדא או זריעה אבל נעילה גרידא לא מהני מידי והשתא אתי שפיר נמי לרבנן דרבי ישמעאל:

שהן י"ח חדש. תימה וכי מניינא אתא לאשמועינן וכה"ג פריך בכמה דוכתי וליכא למימר דרבותא אתי לאשמועינן דא"כ מאי קמ"ל רב הונא ובגמרא משמע דממתניתין לא הוה שמעינן דבעינן רצופים אי לא דאשמועינן רב הונא [עי' תוס' שמעתא על זה]:

כנס את תבואתו. להכי קרי ליה לכרם תבואה משום דכתיב (דברים כב) ותבואת הכרם וא"ת תימה הא דתנא תבואה קודם זיתים דיין קודם לשמן כדאמרינן באיזהו נשך (ב"מ סג.) הגיע זמן יין למכור וזמן שמן אלא כנס את קייצו. ומאי תני ליה בתר הכי הא תאנים קדמי דהא אמר המקבל (שם קו:) חצי ניסן ואייר וחצי סיון קציר חצי סיון ותמוז ו) ותלין אב קיץ ואלו בציר היה בתשרי כדאמרינן בברכות (דף לה:) דאמר להו רבא לרבנן במטותא מינייכו לא תיתחזו קמאי לא ביומי ניסן ולא ביומי תשרי ואמרינן נמי בסנהדרין (דף טו:) גנב ניסן וגנב תשרי לא שמיה גנב וה"מ באריסא ודבר מועט ואמרינן באיזהו נשך (ב"מ דף עג.) חזי מר להנהו רבנן דיהבי זוזי אחמרא בתשרי ומחברי להו בטבת מכל אלו משמע דבציר הוי בתשרי וכבר כלה הקיץ וי"ל דהא דקרי קיץ לתאני סיון ותמוז ואלו אב לפי שאז עיקר יובש של תאנים באילן ומיהו אין קוצצין אותו מן האילן עד לאחר הבציר א"נ לוקטין אותו קודם חצי סיון ומניחים אותו לייבש ולא ו) זמן כניסתו לבית עד לאחר תבואת הכרם והא דלא הויא לקיטה חזקה כי שמא היו רגילין לייבשן באותו שדה שגדלו שם ולכך לא הויא חזקה עד שיכניסם לבית כדמפרש כנס תבואתו ור"ח מפרש כנס תבואתו בתשרי ומסק את זיתיו בטבת וכנס קייצו באב הרי זו חזקה נמצאת חזקה בשנה אחת ונקט כסדר זה משום דמתשרי הוא תחלת השנה אבל יותר מיושב אי הוה תני להו כסדר גשמי שנה שהן גדלין עליהן:

אי מה שור המועד עד נגיחה רביעית כו'. מכאן חזר בו רש"י ממה שהיה מפרש בב"ק (דף כג: ושם ד"ה ולא) ז) דפליגי אביי ורבא דאמר אביי תמול חד מתמול חד שלשום תלת ולא ישמרנו בעליו אתאן לנגיחה רביעית ורבא אמר תמול ומתמול חד הוא כו' דלאביי סבר דעד נגיחה רביעית לא מיחייב ורבא סבר דחייב בנגיחה שלישית דא"כ הוה מסיק הכא גמרא דלא כהלכתא דקי"ל כרבא לגבי אביי וחזר ח) רש"י ופירש דמשמעות דורשין איכא בינייהו וה"ר עזרא מפרש דודאי לכ"ע לא מיחייב עד רביעית אבל בהא פליגי דלאביי דמפיק נגיחה רביעית מקרא דלא ישמרנו אם נגח ביום ג' לא מיחייב עד שיגח ביום רביעי דלא ישמרנו קאי אימים דומיא דתמול שלשום אבל לרבא דנגיחה רביעית לא כתיבה בהדיא אפילו ביום שלישי אם נגח נגיחה רביעית מיחייב:

עד נגיחה רביעית לא מיחייב. תימה לר"י דמאי פריך הא הכי יליף משור המועד מה התם הוחזק נגחן שלש פעמים ה"נ הוחזק שתקן בשלש שנים א"כ משלש שנים ואילך קמה ליה ברשותיה ואומר ר"י דס"ד דמקשה דהכי יליף מה התם מכי נגח ג' פעמים נפק ליה מחזקת תם אף כאן ה"נ כיון שאכלה שלש שנים ולא מיחה נפקא ליה מרשות מוכר לרשות לוקח אע"ג דמילתא בלא טעמא הוא: אלא

מסורת הש"ס

א) [ועי' תוס' עירובין מח. ד"ה ר' יהודה וכו'], ב) ל"ל לעיל ביה, ג) ס"א שמעכב, ד) מהרש"ל:

ליקוטי רש"י

בית השלחין. ארץ יבשה קרויה בית השלחין וצריך להשקותה תמיד ושדה בית הבעל יפה הימנו [שיר השירים ד, יג]. קרקע יבשה דלא דייה במי הגשמים וממעיין שבה משקה אותה [ב"מ קג:]. שדה שהיא עומדת בהר וצריך להשקותה תמיד [מו"ק ב.]. **אין עושין חלל תחת רשות הרבים.** ואע"ג דמקבל עליה כל היזקא דאתי מחמתיה שאין רצונם של בני אדם ליזוק ולירד לדין על עסקי ממונו ומפרש ואזיל מה הוא אותו חלל בורות שיחין ומערות [רשב"ם לקמן ס.]. **בורות שיחין ומערות.** בור עגול הוא שיח ארוכה וקצרה מערה מרובעת ומכוסה בקרוי אלא שיש לה פה [ב"ק נ:]. **רבי אליעזר מתיר.** אלא שיכסהו כיסוי חזק כדי שתהא עגלה מהלכת דר"א אזיל בתר השתא ולא חייש לשמא היום ולמחר יכלה הכיסוי ויפול והכי אמרינן בבבא קמא (נ:). **זימנין דמפחית ולאו אדעתיה.** משום דזימנין דמתליע מתוכו ויפחות ולאו אדעתיה דעובר ברה"ר ויעבור ויפול [רשב"ם לקמן ס.]. [ע"כ שייך לדף כז:]. **הבורות שיחין ומערות.** בור עגול הוא שיח ארוכה וקצרה מערה מרובעת ומכוסה בקרוי אלא שיש לה פה [ב"ק נ:]. **והשובכות.** דרך שובך להיות בו מחילות הרבה קן לכל זוג וזוג וחלון לכל קן וקן [ביצה ט.]. **בית הבדין.** בית לעצור זיתים [ב"מ קיז:]. **בית השלחין.** ארץ יבשה קרויה בית השלחין וצריך להשקותה תמיד ושדה בית הבעל יפה הימנו [שיר השירים ד, יג]. קרקע יבשה דלא דייה במי הגשמים וממעיין שבה משקה אותה [ב"מ קג.]. שדה שהיא עומדת בהר וצריך להשקותה תמיד [מו"ק ב.]. **שדה הבעל.** פי' יונתן אתר בית שקיא מטרא [שופטים א, טו]. שדה הוא בעמק ואינו צריך להשקותה [מו"ק שם]. **שמעתי מהולכי אושא.** שהיא אחת מעשר גליות שגלתה סנהדרין כדאמר בר"ה (לא.) [כתובות מט: וכעי"ז ב"מ לה.]. **אי מה שור המועד עד נגיחה רביעית לא מיחייב.** שאם לא שמרו ונגח נגיחה רביעית משלם נזק שלם מעליה נ"ש אבל מג' פעמים פלגא נזקא הוא דמשלם [ב"ק כג:].

עין משפט נר מצוה

א א ב מיי' פי"ב מהל' טוען ונטען הלכה א סמג עשין צה טוש"ע ח"מ סי' קמא סעיף א:

ב ג ד מיי' פ"ו מהלכות נזקי ממון הל' א סמג עשין סח טוש"ע ח"מ סי' שפט סעיף ה:

רבינו גרשום

חזקת הבתי': והבורות זהו עגיל: **שיחין.** ארוך וקטין: **המערות.** מרובעות. וכל הני עושין כדי להשקות שדותיהן מהן: **ובית הבדין.** זהו בד של זיתים שלאחר דריסת הזיתים מניחין שם השמן ומסתפקין הימנו בכל יום ויום: **ובית השלחין.** צריך להשקותו בכל יום: **והעבדים.** שהוקשו לקרקעות שעובד בהן בכל יום: **וכל דבר שהוא עושה פירות.** כלומר כל דבר שמשתמשין בו בכל יום ויום **תמיד: חזקתן ג' שנים מיום ליום.** דכל הני עושין שמוש מיום ליום ואם החזיק בהן ג' שנים מיום ליום ואח"כ מערער עליהם שום אדם מחזיקין להו ביד המחזיק ומשו"ה בעינן מיום ליום כדי שלא יכול לטעון המערער אני באתי לשם ולא ראיתיו שהי' משתמש בו לפיכך לא מחיתי ולכך צריך שיביא עדים שראוהו משתמש בו בכל יום לפי שבאלו משתמשין בהן בכל יום: **שדה בית הבעל חזקתו ג' שנים.** ולא צריך שיהא משמש בו בכל יום שאם בא המערער ואמר אני באתי ולא ראיתיו משתמש בה לפיכך לא מחיתי יכול לומר לו אני הייתי משתמש בשעה שבני אדם רגילין להשתמש בשדה בית הבעל והואיל ולא מחית באותה שעה לא הוי מחאה: **מהולכי אושא.** מפרש לקמן דהיינו ר' ישמעאל: **נפק ליה מחזקת תם.** כדכתיב כי שור נגח הוא מתמול שלשום: **וקם ליה בחזקת מועד.** כדכתיב והועד בבעליו ולא ישמרנו: **עד נגיחה רביעית לא מחייב.** נזק שלם:

הגהות הב"ח

(א) במשנה וכל דבר שהוא עושה: (ב) שם שדה בית הבעל: (ג) שם הרי אלו י"ח וכו' הרי אלו י"ד: (ד) שם וכנס את קייצו: (ה) גמ' מנין לחזקה שהיא ג': (ו) תוס' ד"ה כנס וכו' ולא הוה זמן כניסתו וכו' שדה עצמה שגדלו וכו' יותר היה מיושב: (ז) ד"ה אי מה וכו' גבי הא דפליגי: (ח) באד"ה וחזר בו רש"י:

ואידך כי לא נגח מאי לשלם הכא כיון דאכלה תלת שני קיימא לה ברשותיה אלא מעתה חזקה שאין עמה טענה תיהוי חזקה אלמה תנן א) כל חזקה שאין עמה טענה אינה חזקה טעמא מאי דאמרינן דלמא כדקאמר השתא איהו לא טעין אנן ליטעון ליה מתקיף לה רב עוירא אלא מעתה מחאה שלא בפניו לא תיהוי מחאה דומיא דשור מועד מה שור המועד בפניו בעינן אף הכא נמי בפניו בעינן התם א) והועד בבעליו כתיב הכא חברך חברא אית ליה וחברא דחברך חברא אית ליה ולר"מ ג) דאמר ריחק נגיחותיו חייב קירב נגיחותיו לא כ"ש אכלה תלתא פירי ד) בחד יומא כגון תאנה ליהוי חזקה דומיא דשור המועד מה שור המועד בעידנא (א) דאית ליה הא נגיחה ליתא להא נגיחה הכא נמי בעידנא דאיתא להאי פירא ליתא להאי פירא אכלה תלתא פרי ה) (בתלתא יומי) כגון צלף ליהוי חזקה התם פירא מיהא איתיה ומגמר הוא דקא גמר ואזיל אכלה תלתא פירי בתלתין יומי כגון אספסתא ליהוי חזקה היכי דמי דקדיח ואכלה דקדיח ואכלה התם משמט הוא דקא שמיט ואכיל אכלה תלתא פירי בתלתא ירחי כגון אספסתא ליהוי חזקה מאן הולכי אושא ר' ישמעאל לר' ישמעאל הכי נמי דתנן רבי ישמעאל אומר בד"א בשדה הלבן אבל בשדה אילן כנס את תבואתו ומסק את זיתיו וכנס את קייצו הרי אלו ג' שנים לרבנן מאי אמר רב יוסף קרא כתיב ב) שדות בכסף יקנו וכתוב בספר וחתום (ב) שהרי נביא עומד בעשר ומזהיר על אחת עשרה א"ל אביי דלמא התם י) עצה טובה קמ"ל דאי

רשב"ם

ואידך. כלומר ונגיחה רביעית דבעינן היינו משום דאי לא נגח לאמר שהוחזק מה ישלם: שאין עמה טענה. מפרש במתני' לקמן (דף מא.) אמר לו מה אתה עושה בתוך שלי אמר לו שלא אמר לי אדם דבר מעולם ולא אמר לו אתה מכרת לי: תיהוי חזקה. דהא אמרת שלש שנים מפקי ליה מרשות מוכר: ומשני טעמא מאי. אמרינן שלש שנים מפקי לה מחזקת מרה קמא דאמרינן דלמא כדאמר איהו זה אומר לקחתיה ממך וזה אומר גזלתיה ממני ואין אנו יודעין האמת עם מי אתיא חזקת שלש שנים ומוקי לה ברשותיה ואמרינן דלמא קושטא הוא כדקאמר אבל בלא טענה מהיכן קנאה בשביל אכילת שלש שנים: מחאה שלא בפניו לא תיהוי מחאה. אם מיחה המערער בתוך שלש שנים לפני עדים שלא בפני המחזיק ואמר דעו שפלוני מחזיק בקרקע שלי בגזילה לא תיהוי מחאה: דומיא דשור המועד. שמעידין שורו נגחן ובשלש פעמים שהעידו שלא בפניו אינו נעשה מועד אף התראת עדות של מחאה לא תיהוי עדות שלא בפניו דמחאה דומיא דהעדאה היא שהיא התראה לשמור שורו ואף המחאה התראה היא להזהר בראיית זכותו ושטר מכירתו: התם והועד בבעליו אמר רחמנא כו'. כלומר לא דמי נהי דגמרינן שלש שנים משלש נגיחות כי היכי (ג) דמפקי הני מחזקה הני נמי מפקי מחזקה אבל מחאה מהעדאה לית לן למיגמר דהתם כיון דהעדאה לחייבו ממון על נגיחותיו היא באה ולהעמיד שורו בחזקת מועד בעינן בפני בעלים שידעו לטעון ולהכחיש העדים ולהביא אחרים להזימן אבל טעמא דמחאה להתרות בו להיות זהיר בזכיותיו היא באה שזה טוען שבגזילה היא בידו הכא אפילו שלא בפניו נמי איתה: דחברך חברא אית ליה כו'. ויאמרו זה לזה והדבר בא לאזניו ואינו יכול לומר אילו שמעתי הייתי זהיר בראיית זכותי: ולר' מאיר דאמר כו'. כלומר לר"י דאמר בב"ק איזהו מועד כל שהעידו בו שלשה ימים איכא למימר הכא ג' שנים דומיא דג' ימים אלא לר"מ דאמר התם דאפי' נגח ג' פעמים ביום אחד הוי מועד מק"ו הכא נמי אכלה תלת פרי בחד יומא כגון תאנה שאינה מתבשלת יחד ויש שאינה מתבשלת שחרית ולערב היא ראויה הכי נמי דהויא חזקה ומשני דומיא דשור המועד כו': צלף. פרי שלא ניכר בו היום ונגמר לסוף ג' ימים: אספסתא. מין זרע הוא לעשב בהמות ולסוף ל' יום הוא נגמר ועוקרין אותו וזורעין אחר במקומו ובתוך שלשים יום גוזזין אותו שלש פעמים: דקדיח. גדל קלת: משמט הוא דקא שמיט ואכיל. ואין זו אכילת כל הפרי: בתלתא ירחי. שעקרה בסוף כל חדש וזרע אחרת: מאן הולכי אושא. דאמר רבי יוחנן לעיל להא מילתא משמייהו: רבי ישמעאל. לא פירש לי מהיכן אלא הכי גמירי שהוא היה באותו הזמן: לרבנן מאי. רבנן דלית להו הא דרבי ישמעאל מנא להו חזקה דשלש שנים: ה"ג שהרי נביא עומד בעשר ומזהיר על אחת עשרה. ירמיה בשנה העשירית לצדקיהו (ד) והיה כלוא בחצר המטרה כדכתי' בס' ירמיה ושם נאמר לו הנה חנמאל בן שלום וגו' וכתיב בההיא ענייגא שדות בכסף יקנו וכתוב בספר וגו' היה מזהיר (ה) לוקחי שדות לכתוב שטרות ולהעמיד עדים בחתימתם כי יגלו מן העיר בשנת אחת עשרה כשנלכדה העיר ולא יחזיקו במקח שלש שנים אלא עשירית ואחת עשרה דלמא בהני תרתי שנין לא הוי חזקה מכאן לחזקה שאינה פחותה משלש שנים: עצה טובה קמ"ל. כלומר לעולם חזקה הויא בשנה אחת ועצה טובה קא משמע לן שיהא שטרו בידו מוכן לראיה ולא יזקק לעדים לשיעורו עליו:

דאי

תוספות

אלא מעתה חזקה שאין עמה טענה כו'. תימה מאי ס"ד דמקשה דהיכי מצי לאוקמי בידיה כיון דלא טעין מידי וי"ל דהכי פריך כיון דילפת משור המועד מה התם בשלש נגיחות הוי בחזקת נגחן הכא נמי כיון דאכלה שלש שנים ולא מיחה הויא בחזקת שלו ימחה עוד ובלא טענה נמי תהא שלו דלית לן למימר שמא לו לא נמי הא דקא פריך למימרא דחזקה שלא בטענה תהא חזקה היינו כגון דאמר ליה מפלניא זבנתה דזבנה מינך אע"ג דלא אמר קמי דידי זבנה ולא דר בה אפי' חד יומא ולא ידע אי זבנה מיניה אי לא אלא דהכי א"ל תימה לרשב"א הא דמיבעיא לן בפ' כילד הרגל (ב"ק כד. ושם) אי לאיעודי גברא אי לאיעודי תורא גברא תפשוט מהכא דלאיעודי תורא הוא (ו) דקאמרי הולכי אושא מה שור המועד כיון שנגח ג' נגיחות נפקא ליה כו' ואי לאיעודי גברא לא מייעד עד נגיחה רביעית דלא הוא מועד לעבור בהתראות דכשנגח נגיחה שלישית והתרו בו עדיין לא עבר על שלש התראות עד שיגח פעם רביעית וי"ל דסוגיא דהכא כמאן דאמר לאיעודי תורא והולכי אושא לא אמרו אלא דגמרינן משור המועד ולא יותר וילפינן משלש התראות דגברא ולא משלש נגיחות דתורא ועוד דלמאן דאמר לאיעודי גברא אין צריך שיהו מוחזקות לעבור בהתראות דאם כן עד נגיחה חמישית לא יחייב אלא צריך שיודיעוהו בכל פעם כשיגח כדי שישמור שורו ומכל מקום חיובא דשור תליא במה שהוחזק ליגח: **אלא** מעתה מחאה שלא בפניו לא תהא מחאה. פירש ר"י כי היכי דילפת משור המועד דהוי חזקה בשלשה זימני הכי נמי נילף מה שור (ז) צריך העדאה בפניו ולא אמר קלא אית ליה ותועיל הכי נמי מחאה שלא בפניו אית לן למימר דלית ליה קלא ולא תהא חזקה אף על פי ששמע החזקה כיון דאין קול למחאה מה היה מועיל אם מוחה כיון שלא תגיע למחזיק מחאתו ואע"ג שמחאה באה לבטל החזקה והעדאה באה לקיים מ"מ פריך שפיר והא דנקט מחאה ולא נקט חזקה משום דחזקה נשמעת טפי מהעדאה אבל מחאה אינה נשמעת יותר ובלא שור המועד הוי מצי למיפרך דלא תהא מחאה כדפריך אליבא דרבנן אלא כיון דיליף משור המועד ניחא ליה למפרך מיניה ומשני חברך חברא אית ליה ויש קול בין למחאה בין להעדאה אבל בהעדאה גרידא גזירת הכתוב הוא דאין נעשה מועד אלא אם כן מעידים בפניו אפילו יתברר לו באלף עדים שהעידו על שורו בבית דין:

כגון צלף. (ח) בתר דשני ליה מתאנה פריך מצלף דתאנה גדולה היא בשעה שנוטלין חבירתה מן האילן אלא שלא נתבשלה עדיין אבל צלף קטן הפרי הרבה כשנוטלין האחת כדאמר בשבת (דף ל.) עתידין אילנות שיטענו פירות בכל יום לגלג עליו אותו תלמיד אין כל חדש תחת השמש אחוי ליה צלף ור"ח גריס ברישא תלתא פירי בחד יומא כגון צלף שיש לו שלשה פירות ביחד ובתר הכי גריס כגון תאנה והיא דשבת משמע כספרים שלנו:

ודלמא עצה טובה קא משמע לן. ה"נ מצי למיפרך ודלמא בתוך עשר הוה קאי ומזהיר על תחלת אחת עשרה דליכא אפילו שנה ולעולם בשנה אחת הויא חזקה ור"ח פירש דרב יוסף יליף הכי וגרים שהרי נביא עומד בתשע ומזהיר על י"א שתלכד העיר ויאבדו השטרות ויסמכו על חזקת שלש שנים ומביא ראיה מסדר עולם דבשנה תשיעית בחדש עשירי היה ומיהו בכל הספרים שלנו כתוב שהרי נביא עומד בעשירי וכן בסדר עולם שלנו תניא בשנה העשירית ועוד דלגירסתו נמי קשיא מנא ליה שלש שנים מיום ליום דלפי גירסת סדר עולם ליכא אלא שמנה עשר חודש שהרי בשנת אחת עשרה לחדש הרביעי בתשעה לחודש הובקעה העיר:

שתא

מסורת הש"ס

א) [לקמן מא.], ב) [לקמן כט. לט: כתובות קט: קי. ערכין כח.], ג) ב"ק כד. תענית כא., ד) [ע"ע הערוך ערך צלף בתלתא], ה) [גי' הערוך ביום אחד עמ"ש תוס' ד"ה כגון בשם ר"ח], ו) [עירובין נט: וש"נ וע"ע לקמן כט. קס:].

הגהות הב"ח

(א) גמ' בעידנא דאיתא להאי נגיחה ליתא להאי: (ב) שם בכסף וחתום וגו' שהרי: (ג) רשב"ם ד"ה התם והועד וכו' כי היכי דהני מפקי מחזקה: (ד) ד"ה ה"ג שהרי וכו' לצדקיהו היה כלוא היה ו' נמחק: (ה) בא"ד מזהיר את לוקחי וכו' עשירית ואחת עשרה וכשיחזרו מן הגלות אם יבואו המוכרים להוציא מידכם בשביל שלא מוחזקים ג' שנים תוציאו שטרותיכם ותקיימו בידכם אלמא בהני תרתי: (ו) תד"ה אלא מעתה חזקה וכו' דקאמרי הולכי: (ז) ד"ה אלא מעתה מחאה וכו' מה שור המועד צריך כו' למה היה מועיל אם היה מוחה: (ח) ד"ה כגון צלף אע"ג דשני ליה:

תורה אור השלם

א) וְאִם שׁוֹר נַגָּח הוּא מִתְּמֹל שִׁלְשֹׁם וְהוּעַד בִּבְעָלָיו וְלֹא יִשְׁמְרֶנּוּ וְהֵמִית אִישׁ אוֹ אִשָּׁה הַשּׁוֹר יִסָּקֵל וְגַם בְּעָלָיו יוּמָת: [שמות כא, כט]

ב) שָׂדוֹת בַּכֶּסֶף יִקְנוּ וְכָתוֹב בַּסֵּפֶר וְחָתוֹם וְהָעֵד עֵדִים בְּאֶרֶץ בִּנְיָמִן וּבִסְבִיבֵי יְרוּשָׁלַיִם וּבְעָרֵי יְהוּדָה וּבְעָרֵי הָהָר וּבְעָרֵי הַשְּׁפֵלָה וּבְעָרֵי הַנֶּגֶב כִּי אָשִׁיב אֶת שְׁבוּתָם נְאֻם יְיָ: [ירמיה לב, מד]

וְאִידָךְ – **and the other** [fourth] goring is necessary only because כִּי לֹא נָגַח מַאי לְשַׁלֵּם – **as long as it does not gore** again, **what** reason **is there to pay?** הָכָא כֵּיוָן דַּאֲכָלָהּ תְּלָת שְׁנֵי – **Here,** however, **as soon as [the occupant] uses [the property]** for **three years,** קַיְימָא לֵהּ בִּרְשׁוּתֵיהּ – **it stands in his possession.**[1]

The Gemara again challenges R' Yochanan:

אֶלָּא מֵעַתָּה – **But now,** if the laws of *chazakah* are derived from the *muad* bull, חֲזָקָה שֶׁאֵין עִמָּהּ טַעֲנָה תֶּיהֱוֵי חֲזָקָה – **then a** three-year ***chazakah*** **not accompanied by a claim should** also **be a** meaningful ***chazakah!*** אַלְמָּה תְּנַן – **Why,** then, **do we learn** otherwise **in a Mishnah,** which states: כָּל חֲזָקָה שֶׁאֵין עִמָּהּ טַעֲנָה אֵינָהּ חֲזָקָה – **ANY *CHAZAKAH* NOT ACCOMPANIED BY A CLAIM IS NOT A** meaningful ***CHAZAKAH?***[2]

The Gemara answers:

טַעְמָא מַאי – **What is the reason** for the effectiveness of a *chazakah?* דְּאָמְרִינַן דִּלְמָא כִּדְקָאָמַר – **Because we say: Perhaps** the facts are **as [the occupant] stated.**[3] הַשְׁתָּא אִיהוּ לֹא טָעִין – **Now, if [the occupant]** himself **does not advance a** legal **claim** to the property, אֲנַן לִיטְעוֹן לֵיהּ – **should we advance a claim for him?**[4]

The Gemara raises another objection:

מַתְקִיף לָהּ רַב עֵוִירָא – **Rav Avira challenged:** אֶלָּא מֵעַתָּה מְחָאָה שֶׁלֹּא בְּפָנָיו לֹא תֶּיהֱוֵי מְחָאָה – **But now, a protest** of the original owner **that is not** lodged **in [the occupant's] presence should not be a** meaningful **protest,**[5] דוּמְיָא דְשׁוֹר מוּעָד – **similar to** what we find in regard to **a *muad* bull** – מַה שּׁוֹר הַמּוּעָד בְּפָנָיו בְּעִינַן – **just as** with regard to **a *muad* bull, we require** that the testimony regarding his bull's violent activity be delivered **in [the owner's] presence,** אַף הָכָא נַמִּי בְּפָנָיו בְּעִינַן – **here, too, we** should **require** that the protest against the occupant's allegedly illegal occupancy of the property be lodged **in his presence!**[6] – ? –

The Gemara answers:

הָתָם "וְהוּעַד בִּבְעָלָיו" כְּתִיב – **There,** in the case of the *muad* bull, **it is written:**[7] ***Its owner was warned through testimony,*** which implies that the owner must be present,[8] and there is a specific reason for this requirement.[9] הָכָא חַבְרָךְ חַבְרָא אִית לֵיהּ – **Here,** with regard to *chazakah,* **your friend has a friend,** וְחַבְרָא דְחַבְרָךְ חַבְרָא אִית לֵיהּ – **and the friend of your friend has** yet another **friend.** Hence, the occupant will eventually hear about the protest, even when it is not lodged in his presence.[10]

The Gemara raises yet another objection to R' Yochanan's derivation of the law of *chazakah:*

וּלְרַבִּי מֵאִיר דְּאָמַר – **But according to R' Meir, who says,** רִיחֵק נְגִיחוֹתָיו חַיָּיב – "If in the case of **[a bull]** that **spread its** three **gorings** over a span of several days – one goring on each of three successive days – **[the owner] is liable** to pay full damages for any further attacks, קֵירֵב נְגִיחוֹתָיו לֹא כָּל שֶׁכֵּן – then **is it not certain** that the owner is liable **if it concentrated its gorings**

NOTES

1. [The fourth attack is necessary only to create a situation of indemnity. But the animal becomes established as violent immediately upon its third attack. Similarly, in the case of *chazakah,* the original owner becomes established as a non-protester immediately after the squatter's third unchallenged year in the property.]

2. The Mishnah below (41a) teaches that a three-year *chazakah* does not establish the occupant as the property owner unless he states the legal claim he has to it – e.g. that he bought it or received it as a gift from the original owner. But if he says that he has no claim to the property other than that no one ever protested his squatting there, then his three-year *chazakah* does not gain him ownership of the property (*Rashi*). The Gemara now asks that if, as derived from the law of the *muad* bull, a three-year *chazakah* establishes the original owner as a non-protester who has in effect abandoned his property to the squatter [see 28a note 18], then the occupant should not have to state a legal claim to the property other than his very occupancy of it (*Tosafos,* first approach; cf. *Tosafos's* second approach, *Ramban, Rashba* et al.).

3. [The Gemara rejects the questioner's premise that the three-year *chazakah* itself transfers the property from the original owner to the occupant. Rather,] the three-year *chazakah* serves only to *support* the occupant's claim that he acquired the property through one of the recognized means of transfer, though the original owner denies this (*Rashi*).

4. [I.e. the occupant himself admits that he has no legal claim to the property. What good, then, is his *chazakah?*]

5. An occupant's *chazakah* is voided if sometime during the three years of *chazakah* the original owner lodges a protest [מְחָאָה] in the presence of two witnesses that his property is being illegally occupied by the occupant. For although people who acquire property generally retain their deeds or other proof of ownership no longer than three years (see 29a), the original owner's protest serves notice on the occupant that the original owner means to lay claim to the property. If despite this notice the occupant fails to retain any proof of ownership beyond the usual three-year limit, then suspicion is cast on his claim to owning the property and it can no longer be substantiated merely on the basis of his *chazakah* (see *Rashi, Rashba*). The Gemara below (38b-39a) will rule that the original owner's protest need not be lodged in the occupant's presence.

6. For a habitually goring bull to become a *muad,* its owner must first be directly warned regarding each of his bull's three attacks [see 28a note 16]. These warnings take the form of witnesses to the attacks testifying about them in court in the presence of the bull's owner, as the Torah states (*Exodus* 21:29): וְהוּעַד בִּבְעָלָיו, *it was [so] testified "against" [the bull's] owner.* But if these warnings were not delivered *directly* to the owner, then his bull does not become a *muad.*

Now, warning the bull's owner and lodging a protest against a person's occupancy of a property serve analogous functions: both are meant to serve notice on the defendant and place him on guard – either to guard his bull or to guard his supposed proof of ownership [see previous note]. Thus, the Gemara asks that just as in the case of the *muad* bull the witnesses must serve notice in the presence of the defendant, so too should we require that the protester against occupancy lodge his protest in the presence of the occupant (*Rashi;* see *Tosafos*).

[As evidenced by the prefatory expression אֶלָּא מֵעַתָּה, *but now,* the Gemara's present question seems predicated on the fact that the very law of *chazakah* is derived from that of the *muad* bull. But had the source for *chazakah* been a different one, the question would not be so compelling, since there might be some fundamental difference between *muad* and *chazakah* that would account for the inability to derive the law of protest from that of warning regarding the requirement of the owner's presence. See an alternative approach in *Ramban* and *Ran.*]

7. *Exodus* 21:29.

8. [See *Bava Kamma* 24a and marginal emendation of *Maharam* there; see also *Bava Kamma* 112b.]

9. As will be explained in the following note.

10. In regard to *chazakah,* the sole purpose of the protest is to inform the occupant that the previous owner plans to press a claim to the property. This information is inevitably conveyed by word-of-mouth even if the protest is not made directly to the occupant. In the case of the *muad* bull, however, it is not sufficient that the owner merely be informed that his bull has attacked. For these attacks subject the owner to financial liability – not only must he pay half damages for the bull's first three attacks, but also the status of *muad* is conferred upon his bull, exposing the owner to full liability for any future attacks. Therefore, he must be given the opportunity to refute the charges in court (e.g. by producing witnesses who contradict the testimony of the prosecution's witnesses) and thereby absolve himself from financial liability. This opportunity is furnished only if he is present in court when the prosecution's witnesses testify about his bull's attacks (*Rashi;* see also *Ritva*).

ואידך כי לא נגח מאי לשלם הכא כיון דאכלה תלת שני קיימא לה ברשותיה אלא מעתה חזקה שאין עמה טענה תיהוי חזקה אלמה תנן א) כל חזקה שאין עמה טענה אינה חזקה טעמא מאי דאמרינן דלמא כדקאמר השתא איהו לא טעין אנן ליטעון ליה מתקיף לה רב עוירא אלא מעתה מחאה שלא בפניו לא תיהוי מחאה דומיא דשור מועד מה שור המועד בפניו בעינן אף הכא נמי בפניו בעינן התם א) והועד בבעליו כתיב הכא ג) חברך חברא אית ליה וחברא דחברך חברא אית ליה ולר"מ ג) דאמר ריחק נגיחותיו חייב קירב נגיחותיו לא כ"ש אכלה תלתא פירי ד) בחד יומא כגון תאנה ליהוי חזקה דומיא דשור המועד מה שור המועד בעידנא (א) דאית ליה הא נגיחה ליתא להא נגיחה הכא נמי בעידנא דאיתא להאי פירא ליתא להאי פירא אכלה תלתא פרי ה) (בתלתא יומי) כגון צלף ליהוי חזקה התם פירא מיהא איתיה ומגמר הוא דקא גמר ואזיל אכלה תלתא פירי בתלתין יומי כגון אספסתא ליהוי חזקה היכי דמי דקדיה ואכלה דקדיה ואכלה התם משמט הוא דקא שמיט ואכיל אכלה תלתא פירי בתלתא ירחי כגון אספסתא ליהוי חזקה מאן הולכי אושא ר' ישמעאל לר' ישמעאל הכי נמי דתנן רבי ישמעאל אומר בד"א בשדה הלבן אבל בשדה אילן כנס את תבואתו ומסק את זיתיו וכנס את קייצו הרי אלו ג' שנים לרבנן מאי אמר רב יוסף קרא כתיב ב) שדות בכסף יקנו וכתוב בספר וחתום (ב) שהרי נביא עומד בעשר ומזהיר על אחת עשרה א"ל אביי דלמא התם ו) עצה טובה קמ"ל דאי

רש"י

ואידך. כלומר ונגיחה רביעית דבעינן היינו משום דאי לא נגח לאחר שהוחזק מה ישלם: שאין עמה טענה. מפרש במתני' לקמן (דף מא.) אמר לו מה אתה עושה בתוך שלי אמר לו שלא אמר לי אדם דבר מעולם ולא אמר לו אתה מכרת לי: תיהוי חזקה. דהא אמרת שלש שנים מפקי ליה מרשות מוכר: ומשני טעמא מאי. אמרינן שלש שנים מפקי לה מחזקת מרה קמא דאמרינן דלמא כדאמר איהו זה אומר לקחתיה ממך וזה אומר גזלתיה ממני ואין אנו יודעין האמת עם מי אתיא חזקת שלש שנים ומוקי לה ברשותיה ואמרינן דלמא קושטא הוא כדקאמר אבל בלא טענה מהיכן קנאה בשביל אכילת שלש שנים: מחאה שלא בפניו לא תיהוי מחאה. אם מיחה המערער בתוך שלש שנים לפני עדים שלא בפני המחזיק ואמר דעו שפלוני מחזיק בקרקע שלי בגזילה לא תיהוי מחאה: דומיא דשור המועד. שמעידין ששורו נגחן ובשלש פעמים שהעידו שלא בפניו אינו נעשה מועד אף התראת עדות של מחאה לא תיהוי עדות שלא בפניו דמחאה דומיא דהעדאה היא שהיא התראה לשמור שורו ואף המחאה התראה היא להזהר בראיית זכותו ושטר מכירתו: התם והועד בבעליו אמר רחמנא כו'. כלומר לא דמי נהי דגמרינן שלש שנים משלש נגיחות כי היכי (ג) דמפקי הני מחזקה הני נמי מפקי מחזקה אבל מחאה מהעדאה לית לן למיגמר דהתם כיון דהעדאה לחייבו ממון על נגיחותיו היא באה ולהעמיד שורו בחזקת מועד בעינן בפני בעלים שידעו לטעון ולהכחיש העדים ולהביא אחרים להזימן אבל טעמא דמחאה להתרות בו להיות זהיר בזכיותיו היא באה שזה טוען שבגזילה היא בידו הכא אפילו שלא בפניו נמי איתה: דחברך חברא אית ליה כו'. ויאמרו זה לזה והדבר בא לאזניו ואינו יכול לומר אילו שמעתי הייתי זהיר בראיית זכותי: ולר' מאיר דאמר כו'. כלומר לר"י דאמר בב"ק איזהו מועד כל שהעידו בו שלשה ימים איכא למימר הכא ג' שנים דומיא דג' ימים אלא לר"מ דאמר התם דאפי' נגח ג' פעמים ביום אחד הוי מועד מק"ו הכא נמי אכלה תלת פרי בחד יומא כגון תאנה שאינה מתבשלת יחד ויש שאינה מתבשלת שחרית ולערב היא ראויה הכי נמי דהויא חזקה ומשני דומיא דשור המועד כו': צלף. פרי שלא ניכר בו היום ונגמר לסוף ג' ימים: אספסתא. מין זרע הוא לעשב בהמות ולסוף ל' יום הוא נגמר ועוקרין אותו וזורעין אחר במקומו ובתוך שלשים יום גוזזין אותו שלש פעמים: דקדיה. גדל קלת: משמט הוא דקא שמיט ואכיל. ואין זו אכילת כל הפרי: בתלתא ירחי. שעקרה בסוף כל חדש וזרע אחרת: מאן הולכי אושא. דאמר רבי יוחנן לעיל להא מילתא משמייהו: רבי ישמעאל. לא פירש לי מהיכן אלא הכי גמירי שהוא היה באותו הזמן: לרבנן מאי. רבנן דלית להו הא דרבי ישמעאל מנא להו חזקה דשלש שנים: ה"ג שהרי נביא עומד בעשר ומזהיר על אחת עשרה. ירמיה בשנה העשירית לצדקיהו (ד) והיה כלוא בחצר המטרה כדכתי' בס' ירמיה ושם נאמר לו הנה חנמאל בן שלום וגו' וכתיב בההיא ענינא שדות בכסף יקנו וכתוב בספר וגו' היה מזהיר (ה) לוקחי שדות לכתוב שטרות ולהעמיד עדים בחתימתם כי יגלו מן העיר בשנת אחת עשרה כשנלכדה העיר ולא יחזיקו במקח שלש שנים אלא עשירית ואחת עשרה אלמא בהני תרתי שנין לא הוי חזקה מכאן לחזקה שאינה פחותה משלש שנים: עצה טובה קמ"ל. כלומר לעולם חזקה הויא בשנה אחת ועצה טובה קא משמע לן שיהא שטרו בידו מוכן לראיה ולא יזקק לעדים כשיעוררו עליו:

תוספות

אלא מעתה חזקה שאין עמה טענה כו'. תימה מאי ס"ד דמקשה דהיכי מצי לאוקמי בידיה כיון דלא טעין מידי וי"ל דהכי פריך כיון דילפת משור המועד מה התם בשלש נגיחות הוי בחזקת נגחן הכא נמי כיון דאכלה שלש שנים ולא מיחה הויא בחזקת שלו ימחה עוד ובלא טענה נמי תהא שלו דלית לן למימר שמכל לו אי נמי הא דקא פריך למימרא דחזקה שלא בטענה תהא חזקה היינו כגון דאמר ליה מפלניא זבנתה דזבנה מינך אע"ג דלא אמר קמי דידי זבנה ולא דר בה אפי' חד יומא ולא ידע אי זבנה מיניה אי לא אלא דהכי ה"ל תימה לרשב"א הא דמיבעיא לן בפ' כיצד הרגל (ב"ק כד. ושם) אי לאיעודי תורא אי לאיעודי גברא תפשוט מהכא דלאיעודי תורא הוא (ו) דקאמרי הולכי אושא מה שור המועד כיון שנגח ג' נגיחות נפקא ליה כו' ואי לאיעודי גברא לא מייעד עד נגיחה רביעית דלא הוא מועד לעבור בהתראות דכשנגח נגיחה שלישית והתרו בו עדיין לא עבר על שלש התראות עד שיגח פעם רביעית וי"ל דסוגיא דהכא כמאן דאמר לאיעודי תורא והולכי אושא לא אמרו אלא דגמרינן משור המועד ולא יותר וילפינן משלש התראות דגברא ולא משלש נגיחות דתורא ועוד דלמאן דאמר לאיעודי גברא אין צריך שיהו מוחזקות לעבור בהתראות דהא כן עד נגיחה חמישית לא יחייב אלא צריך שיודיעוהו בכל פעם כשיגח כדי שישמור שורו ומכל מקום חובה לשור תלויה במה שהוחזק ליגח: אלא מעתה מחאה שלא בפניו לא תהא מחאה. פירש ר"י כי היכי דילפת משור המועד דהוי חזקה בשלשה זימני הכי נמי יליף מה שור (ז) צריך העדאה בפניו ולא אמר קלא אית ליה ותועיל הכי נמי מחאה שלא בפניו אית לן למימר דלית ליה קלא ולא תהא חזקה אף על פי שמשמע החזקה כיון דאין קול למחאה מה היה מועיל אם מוחה כיון שלא תגיע למחזיק מחאתו ואע"ג שמחאה באה לבטל החזקה וההעדאה באה לקיים מ"מ פריך שפיר והא דנקט מחאה ולא נקט חזקה משום דחזקה נשמעת טפי מהעדאה אבל מחאה אינה נשמעת יותר ובלא שור המועד הוי מצי למיפרך דלא תהא מחאה כדפריך אליבא דרבנן אלא כיון דיליף משור המועד ניחא ליה למפרך מיניה ומשני חברך חברא אית ליה ויש קול בין למחאה בין להעדאה אבל בהעדאה גרידא גזירת הכתוב הוא דאין נעשה מועד אלא אם כן מעידים בפניו אפילו יתברר לו באלף עדים שהעידו על שורו בבית דין:

כגון צלף. (ח) בתר דשני ליה מתאנה פריך מצלף דתאנה גדולה היא בשעה שנוטלין חבירתה מן האילן אלא שלא נתבשלה עדיין אבל צלף קטן הפרי הרבה כשנוטלין האחת כדאמר בשבת (דף ל.) עתידין אילנות שיטענו פירות בכל יום לגלג עליו אותו תלמיד אין כל חדש תחת השמש אחוי ליה צלף ור"ח גריס ברישא תלתא פירי בחד יומא כגון צלף שיש לו שלשה פירות ביחד ובתר הכי גריס כגון תאנה והיא דשבת משמע כספרים שלנו:

ודלמא עצה טובה קא משמע לן. ה"נ מצי למיפרך ודלמא בתוך עשר הוה קאי ומזהיר על תחלת אחת עשרה דליכא אפילו שנה ולעולם בשנה אחת הויא חזקה ור"ח פירש דרב יוסף יליף הכי וגריס שהרי נביא עומד בתשע ומזהיר על י"א שתלכד העיר ויאבדו השטרות ויסמכו על חזקת שלש שנים ומביא ראיה מסדר עולם דבשנה תשיעית בחדש עשירי היה ומיהו בכל הספרים שלנו כתוב שהרי נביא עומד בעשירי וכן בסדר עולם שלנו תניא בשנה העשירית ועוד דלגירסתו נמי קשיא מנא ליה שלש שנים מיום ליום דלפי גירסת סדר עולם ליכא אלא שמנה עשר חודש שהרי בשנת אחת עשרה לחדש הרביעי בתשעה לחודש הובקעה העיר:

רבינו גרשום

התם כי לא נגח. רביעית מאי לישלם: אלא מעתה. דאמרת כיון דאכלה ג' שנים קיימא ברשותיה אם כן כל חזקה שאין עמה טענה להיכא דקאמר ליה מערער מה אתה עושה בתוך שלי ואמר הלה אכלתיה שני חזקה ולא אמר לי אדם דבר תיהוי חזקה ואנן תנן דכל חזקה שאין עמה טענה שאינו טוען עם החזקה של אבא היתה וירתיה או שקניתיה ממך ואכלתיה שני חזקה אינה חזקה. ואי טעין הכי אע"ג דלית ליה שטרא טענינן ואמרינן הכי הוא כדקאמר ושטרא הוא דארכס ליה אבל אם אינו טוען אלא שאכלתיה שני חזקה אין זה טענה. ולדבריך דילפת משור מועד דלאחר ג' שנין קיימא ברשותיה תיהוי חזקה אע"ג דלית ליה טענה אחריתי ומשני טעמא מאי הוי חזקה שיש עמה טענה חזקה משום דאמרי' דלמא הכי כדקאמר ושטרא אירכס ליה. אבל להיכא דאין עמה טענה השתא איהו לא טען אנן טענינן ליה ולא הוה חזקה: מתקיף לה רב עויר' אלא מעתה. דמפקת ליה משור המועד להיכא דמיחה המערער שלא בפניו לא תיהוי מחאה דדומיא דשור המועד וכו' ומשני גבי שור המועד שאני משום דגזירת הכתוב הוא אבל מחאה שלא בפניו בדין הוא דהוי מחאה דאמרי' ליה למחזיק חברך כו' ומחברך שמעת המחאה: ולר' מאיר דאמר כו'. בשלמא אליבא דרבנן דפליגי עליה דר"מ דאמרי אינו חייב עד דנגח ג' נגיחות בג' ימים כדכתיב אם שור נגח הוא מתמול שלשום תמול [חד מתמול] תרי שלשום תלתא הכא נמי לא הוי חזקה עד דאכלה ג' שנים אלא לר' מאיר דאמר כיון דכי ריחק נגיחותיו דבג' ימים נגח ג' פעמים חייב קירב נגיחותיו בשנגח ג' פעמים ביום אחד לא כל שכן דהוי מועד הכא נמי לטעמי' למה לי תלת שנין לחזקה אפי' ביום אחד תהוי חזקה. והיכי דמי כגון דאכלה תלת פירי בחד יומא דומיא דג' שנים שאוכל ג' פירות כגון תאנה דבבקר מתבשלת תאנה זו ובחצי היום אידך ואידך לערב ותהוי חזקה: ומשני דומיא דשור המועד בעינן מה שור המועד בעידנא דעבד הא נגיחה אכתי ליכא לאידך נגיחה כלל. ה"נ גבי חזקה בעינן דבזמן דאיתא להאי פירא ליתא להאי כלל בעין דאכתי לא בא. והא לא מצית למישכח אלא בג' שנין אבל תאנה היום בשחרית היו שלשתן אלא שלא נתבשלו: כגון צלף. דבחד יומא מגדל חד פירא ועדיין אידך קטן הרבה ולמחר מתגדל ומתבשל [פירא אחריתא] ואידך ליום שלישי ואי אכלינהו בתלתא יומי תיהוי חזקה דומיא דשור המועד: ומשני התם נמי וכו' ומקשי' אכלה תלתא פירי בתלתין יומי כגון אספסתא שנוהגין בני אדם לקוצרה מי' ימים לי' ימים דהיינו ג' פעמים בל' יום ולבסוף ל' יום עוקרין אותה מכל וכל וחורשין השדה ליהוי חזקה דהשתא בעידנא דאיתא להאי ליתא להאי ומשני היכי דמי דתיהוי הכא חזקה א) כיון דבגין דקדמה כשמתגדלת אכלי מיד לסוף י' ימים ודאי בעידנא דאיתא להאי ליתא להאי אבל מ"מ דמי כאכילה גנובה שאין ממתין עד ל' עד שתתגדל כולה אלא משמט שמיט ואכל להכי לא הוי חזקה ומקשי' אכלה תלת פירי בתלתא ב) ירחי כגון אספסתא דסוף ל' עוקרין אותה מהקרקע מכל וזורעין אחרת תיהוי חזקה דהשתא ליכא למימר דשמיט ואכיל. ומשני מרא דשמעתא מאן הולכי אושא היינו ר' ישמעאל. ולר' ישמעאל הכי נמי. דהתנן [illegible] בשדה לבן. דהיינו שדה תבואה שאין בה אילנות ואינה עושה אלא תבואה אחת בשנה משום הכי בעינן ג' שנים: אבל בשדה אילן. [illegible] תבואותו וכו'. [illegible] כגון אספסתא. אספסתא מאכל בהמות היא שלועזין טריפ"א:

ורבנן דמתני' מנא להו [illegible] וחתום. שיהיו השטרות משומרין בידכם: שהרי נביא. ירמיה עומד ג) [illegible]

מסורת הש"ס

א) [לקמן מא.], ב) [לקמן כט. לח. לט. כתובות קט: קי. ערכין כח.], ג) ב"ק כד. תענית כט., ד) [גי' הערוך ערך צלף בתלתא], ה) [גי' הערוך ביום אחד עמ"ש תוס' ד"ה כגון בשם ר"ח], ו) [עירובין לב. וש"נ ועי' לקמן קמ. קס:].

הגהות הב"ח

(א) גמ' בעידנא דאיתא להאי נגיחה ליתא להאי: (ב) שם בספר וחתום וגו' שהרי: (ג) רש"י ד"ה התם והועד וכו' כי היכי דהני מפקי מחזקה: (ד) ד"ה ה"ג שהרי וכו' לצדקיהו היה כלוא וכו' ושם נאמר: (ה) באד"ה מזהיר את לוקחי וכו' עשירית ואחת עשרה וכשיחזרו מן הגלות לא יבואו המוכרים להוציא מידכם בשביל שלא החזקתם ג' שנים תוציאו שטרותיכם ותקיימו בידכם אלמא בהני תרתי: (ו) תד"ה אלא מעתה חזקה וכו' מדקאמרי הולכי: (ז) ד"ה אלא מעתה מחאה וכו' מה שור המועד וכו' דמה היה מועיל אם היה מוחה: (ח) ד"ה כגון צלף אע"ג דשני ליה:

תורה אור השלם

א) וְאִם שׁוֹר נַגָּח הוּא מִתְּמֹל שִׁלְשֹׁם וְהוּעַד בִּבְעָלָיו וְלֹא יִשְׁמְרֶנּוּ וְהֵמִית אִישׁ אוֹ אִשָּׁה הַשּׁוֹר יִסָּקֵל וְגַם בְּעָלָיו יוּמָת: [שמות כא, כט]

ב) שָׂדוֹת בַּכֶּסֶף יִקְנוּ וְכָתוֹב בַּסֵּפֶר וְחָתוֹם וְהָעֵד עֵדִים בְּאֶרֶץ בִּנְיָמִן וּבִסְבִיבֵי יְרוּשָׁלַיִם וּבְעָרֵי יְהוּדָה וּבְעָרֵי הָהָר וּבְעָרֵי הַשְּׁפֵלָה וּבְעָרֵי הַנֶּגֶב כִּי אָשִׁיב אֶת שְׁבוּתָם נְאֻם יְיָ: [ירמיה לב, מד]

ליקוטי רש"י

כל חזקה שאין עמה טענה. [illegible] מחאה שלא בפניו. כגון אם היה בעיר אחרת ומיחה שלא בפניו בפני שנים בעיר אחרת [כתובות יז:]. והועד בבעליו. לשון התראה בעדים כמו (בראשית מג) העד העיד בנו האיש [שמות כא, כט]. חברך חברא אית ליה וכו'. [illegible] קט:]. דהני דמתי באנפייהו מגלו לאחריני ובא הדבר לאזני המחזיק וה"ל לאזדהורי בשטריה [שם יז:]. [illegible] לחבירו עד שיודע [ערכין טז.]. ריחק נגיחותיו. ג' ימים. חייב. כדכתיב תמול שלשום [ב"ק כד.]. ריחק נגיחותיו לשור מועד קאי בבבא קמא בפרק כיצד הרגל מועדת (כד.) אי זהו תם ואי זהו מועד כל שהעידו בו ג' ימים דברי ר' יהודה ר' מאיר אומר כל שהעידו בו ג' פעמים ביום אחד רבי יהודה סבר כתיב או נודע כי שור נגח הוא מתמול שלשום שלשה ימים ורבי מאיר סבר ריחק נגיחותיו כשנגח בג' ימים זה אחר זה חייב קירב נגיחותיו [illegible] [תענית כא.]. צלף. [illegible]

חשק שלמה על רבינו גרשום א) נראה דצ"ל כיון דבגין דמקדים ואוכל מן כשמתגדל לסוף י' ימים וכו'. ב) נ"ל בתלתא ירחי. ג) גי' רבינו כגי' ר"ח שהובא בתוס' כאן דגרס שהרי נביא עומד בתשע.

into one day?"[11] אֲכָלָהּ תְּלָתָא פֵּירֵי בְּחַד יוֹמָא – **If [the occupant] used [the property]** by harvesting **three** separate **crops in one day,** כְּגוֹן תְּאֵנָה – **as** is possible **in the case of the fig** crop,[12] לֶיהֱוֵי חֲזָקָה – **let it be a** complete ***chazakah!***[13] **– ? –**

The Gemara answers:

דּוּמְיָא דְּשׁוֹר הַמּוּעָד – The one-day *chazakah* you describe is ineffective precisely because the law of *chazakah* must be **similar** to the law of **a *muad* bull:** מָה שׁוֹר הַמּוּעָד – **Just as** in the case of **the *muad* bull,** בְּעִידְנָא דְּאִית לֵיהּ הָא נְגִיחָה – **at the time that this goring exists,** לֵיתָא לְהָא נְגִיחָה – **this** other **goring does not** yet **exist,** הָכָא נַמִּי – **here, too,** with regard to *chazakah,* בְּעִידְנָא דְּאִיתָא לְהַאי פֵּירָא לֵיתָא לְהַאי פֵּירָא – we require that **at the time that this crop exists, this** next **crop does not** yet **exist.**[14]

The Gemara asks:

אֲכָלָהּ תְּלָתָא פֵּרֵי (בִּתְלָתָא יוֹמֵי) – But if **[the occupant] used [the property]** by harvesting **three crops in three days,** כְּגוֹן צְלָף – **as** is possible **in the case of a caperbush,** לֶיהֱוֵי חֲזָקָה – **let it be a** valid ***chazakah!***[15] **– ? –**

The Gemara answers:

הָתָם פֵּירָא מִיהָא אִיתֵיהּ – **There,** in the case of a caperbush as well, **the fruit** that will be picked on the third day **nevertheless exists** on the first day, וּמִגְמַר הוּא דְּקָא גָּמַר וְאָזִיל – **and it is but continuing to grow** to maturity, rather than developing initially.[16]

The Gemara persists and asks:

אֲכָלָהּ תְּלָתָא פֵּירֵי בִּתְלָתִין יוֹמֵי – But if **[the occupant] used [the property]** by harvesting **three crops in thirty days,** כְּגוֹן אַסְפַּסְתָּא – **as** is possible **in the case of *aspasta,***[17] לֶיהֱוֵי חֲזָקָה – **let it be a** valid ***chazakah!***[18] **– ? –**

The Gemara answers:

הֵיכִי דָּמֵי – **How is it** possible to harvest *aspasta* three times in thirty days? דְּקָדֵיחַ וַאֲכָלָהּ – Only if **it sprouts forth** a little **and he uses it,**[19] דְּקָדֵיחַ וַאֲכָלָהּ – **and it** again **sprouts forth** a little **and he eats it.** הָתָם מִשְׁמָט הוּא דְּקָא שָׁמִיט וְאָכִיל – **In that case,** he is merely **snatching and using,** which does not establish a *chazakah.*[20]

The Gemara modifies its previous question:

אֲכָלָהּ תְּלָתָא פֵּירֵי בִּתְלָתָא יַרְחֵי – But if **[the occupant] uses [the property]** by harvesting **three crops in three months,** כְּגוֹן אַסְפַּסְתָּא – **as** is possible **in the case of** three fully grown crops of ***aspasta,*** לֶיהֱוֵי חֲזָקָה – **let it be a** valid ***chazakah!***[21] **– ? –**

The Gemara concedes that this is indeed possible, according to R' Yochanan. Still, this poses no difficulty, because:

מַאן הוֹלְכֵי אוּשָׁא – **Who are "those who traveled to Usha,"** cited by R' Yochanan as deriving the law of *chazakah* from the law of the *muad* bull? רַבִּי יִשְׁמָעֵאל – They are none other than **R' Yishmael.**[22] לְרַבִּי יִשְׁמָעֵאל הָכִי נַמִּי – And **according to R' Yishmael it is indeed so** that a *chazakah* can be established in less than three years, דִּתְנַן – **for we learned in our Mishnah:** רַבִּי יִשְׁמָעֵאל אוֹמֵר – **R' YISHMAEL SAYS:** בַּמֶּה דְּבָרִים אֲמוּרִים – **IN** regard to **WHAT IS THIS SAID?** בִּשְׂדֵה הַלָּבָן – **IN** regard to **A GRAIN FIELD.** אֲבָל בִּשְׂדֵה אִילָן – **HOWEVER, IN** regard to **A FIELD OF TREES,** כָּנַס אֶת תְּבוּאָתוֹ – if **HE GATHERED HIS** grape **PRODUCE,** וּמָסַק אֶת זֵיתָיו – **PICKED HIS OLIVES** וְכָנַס אֶת קֵיִיצוֹ – **AND GATHERED IN HIS DRIED FIGS,** הֲרֵי אֵלּוּ שְׁלֹשָׁה שָׁנִים – **THESE**

NOTES

11. Scripture describes a *muad* as an animal that gored on three consecutive days (see *Exodus* 21:29). The Mishnah in *Bava Kamma* (23b) records a Tannaic dispute with regard to a bull that gored three times on the *same* day. R' Meir holds that if three gorings on three days reveal that an animal is a habitual gorer, then certainly three gorings on the same day demonstrate this fact and render the animal a *muad.* R' Yehudah disagrees, maintaining that the law of *muad* must be limited to the specifics of the Scriptural description – one goring on each of three successive days.

12. The fig crop does not ripen all at once. Rather, it is possible that some figs are ripe in the morning whereas others will not be edible until evening. In fact, it is possible to harvest three "separate" fig crops from the same field on the same day – each harvest collecting all the figs that are ripe at that time (*Rashi*).

13. The Gemara asks that if the law of *chazakah* is derived from the law of the *muad* bull, the three utilizations of a property that establish the *chazakah* should not always have to stretch over the span of three years – according to R' Meir, who holds that the Torah does not assign any minimum time frame to the gorings that render a bull a *muad.* Thus, in the case of a field that produces figs, for example, where three utilizations can take place in a single day, a *chazakah* should be established in one day. According to R' Yehudah, however, it is understandable that three years should be required for *chazakah,* just as three days are required for a *muad,* in his opinion (*Rashi*; cf. *Derishah, Orach Chaim* 114:3). [For just as the Torah assigns a minimum time frame to the goring that establishes a bull as a *muad,* so too must there be some minimum time frame to the utilization of a property that establishes a *chazakah.* Though it is not possible to derive from the law of *muad* exactly what time frame is needed in the case of *chazakah,* it is quite possible that the time frame is a year, since that is the usual period that completes a normal cycle of land utilization.]

14. I.e. although R' Meir considers three gorings on a single day cause to establish the bull as a *muad,* it is only if the bull gored the three animals on three separate occasions – that is, the three victims were not present simultaneously. However, if three animals are present in one place and a bull rampages and gores all three, even R' Meir does not construe that as three distinct gorings, but rather as one extended act of goring. Similarly, in regard to *chazakah,* since all three fig crops exist simultaneously in the field (although two of the crops have not yet ripened), harvesting all three on a single day is construed not as three distinct utilizations of the field, but as one extended utilization (see *Ritva* and *Rashash*).

15. The fruits of a caperbush complete their growth from visual emergence to ripening in three days (*Rashi*). Thus, the fruit that ripens one day is extremely small on the previous day, and should be considered inconsequential (*Tosafos*). Therefore, the Gemara asks that caperbush harvests conducted on three consecutive days – each harvest collecting the fruits that are ripe that day – should qualify as three distinct utilizations and establish a *chazakah* in the short period of three days (*Ritva*). [In the case of figs, on the other hand, the unripe fruits are quite substantial in size at the time the ripe ones are picked, and cannot be deemed as belonging to a "separate" harvest, as the Gemara has pointed out previously (see *Tosafos*).]

16. Thus, the three harvests are still deemed to be but one extended harvest, just as in the case of figs above (see *Ritva*).

17. *Aspasta,* a type of plant used for animal fodder, grows to completion in thirty days, during which it can be cut back three times. After the third cutting, the field is plowed under and a new *aspasta* crop is sown (*Rashi, Rabbeinu Gershom*).

18. Since it is possible to plant one *aspasta* crop, harvest it and repeat the process a second and third time in the span of thirty days, the three harvests should establish a *chazakah* in a single month.

19. I.e. he harvests it to feed to his animals.

20. Since he harvests the crop prematurely and has thus failed to utilize the entire potential yield of the property (*Rashi;* see 28a note 6). Moreover, by snatching the immature crop in this fashion, his use of the property suggests the furtive activity of a squatter rather than the open occupancy of an owner, and such furtive use cannot establish a *chazakah* (*Ritva; Rashbam* to 36a ד״ה אכלה שחת).

21. The occupant could plant a new crop after harvesting a fully grown crop at the end of the month (*Rashi*). This should be a valid *chazakah,* because each crop is distinct and three full utilizations of the field have taken place. Consequently, it should not always be necessary to utilize a property for the full three years to establish a *chazakah.*

22. The Gemara had a tradition that R' Yishmael, who lived during the Usha period, is the one referred to as הוֹלְכֵי אוּשָׁא, *those who traveled to Usha* (see *Rashi*).

ואידך כי לא נגח מאי לשלם הכא כיון דאכלה תלת שני קיימא לה ברשותיה אלא מעתה חזקה שאין עמה טענה תיהוי חזקה אלמה תנן א) כל חזקה שאין עמה טענה אינה חזקה טעמא מאי דאמרינן דלמא כדקאמר השתא איהו לא טעין אנן ליטעון ליה מתקיף לה רב עוירא אלא מעתה מחאה שלא בפניו לא תיהוי מחאה דומיא דשור מועד מה שור המועד בפניו בעינן אף הכא נמי בפניו בעינן התם א) והועד בבעליו כתיב הכא ב) חברך חברא אית ליה וחברא דחברך חברא אית ליה ולר"מ ג) דאמר ריחק נגיחותיו חייב קירב נגיחותיו לא כ"ש אכלה תלתא פירי ד) בחד יומא כגון תאנה ליהוי חזקה דומיא דשור המועד מה שור המועד בעידנא (א) דאית ליה הא נגיחה ליתא להא נגיחה הכא נמי בעידנא דאיתא להאי פירא ליתא להאי פירא אכלה תלתא פרי ה) (בתלתא יומי) כגון צלף ליהוי חזקה התם פירא מיהא איתיה ומגמר הוא דקא גמר ואזיל אכלה תלתא פירי בתלתין יומי כגון אספסתא ליהוי חזקה היכי דמי דקדיח ואכלה דקדיח ואכלה התם משמט הוא דקא שמיט ואכיל אכלה תלתא פירי בתלתא ירחי כגון אספסתא ליהוי חזקה מאן הולכי אושא ר' ישמעאל לר' ישמעאל הכי נמי דתנן רבי ישמעאל אומר בד"א בשדה הלבן אבל בשדה אילן כנס את תבואתו ומסק את זיתיו וכנס את קייצו הרי אלו ג' שנים לרבנן מאי אמר רב יוסף קרא כתיב ב) שדות בכסף יקנו וכתוב בספר וחתום (ב) שהרי נביא עומד בעשר ומזהיר על אחת עשרה א"ל אביי דלמא התם ו) עצה טובה קמ"ל דאי

רשב"ם

ואידך. כלומר ונגיחה רביעית דבעינן היינו משום דאי לא נגח לאמר שהוחזק מה ישלם: שאין עמה טענה. מפרש במתני' לקמן (דף מא.) אמר לו מה אתה עושה בתוך שלי אמר לו שלא אמר לי אדם דבר מעולם ולא אמר לו אתה מכרת לי: תיהוי חזקה. דהא אמרת שלש שנים מפקי ליה מרשות מוכר: ומשני טעמא מאי. אמרינן שלש שנים מפקי לה מחזקת מרה קמא דאמרינן דלמא כדקאמר איהו זה אומר לקחתיה ממך וזה אומר גזלתיה ממני ואין אנו יודעין האמת עם מי אלא מחזקת שלש שנים ומוקי לה ברשותיה ואמרינן דלמא קושטא הוא כדקאמר אבל בלא טענה מהיכן קנאה בשביל אכילת שלש שנים: מחאה שלא בפניו לא תיהוי מחאה. אם מיחה המערער בתוך שלש שנים לפני עדים שלא בפני המחזיק ואמר דעו שפלוני מחזיק בקרקע שלי בגזילה לא תיהוי מחאה: דומיא דשור המועד. שמעידין שורו נגחן ובשלש פעמים שהעידו שלא בפניו אינו נעשה מועד אף התראת עדות של מחאה לא תיהוי עדות שלא בפניו דמחאה דומיא דהעדאה היא שהיא התראה לשמור שורו ואף המחאה התראה היא להזהר בראיית זכותו ושטר מכירתו: התם והועד בבעליו אמר רחמנא כו'. כלומר לא דמי נהי דגמרינן שלש שנים משלש נגיחות כי היכי (ג) דמפקי הני מחזקה הני נמי מפקי מחזקה אבל מחאה מהעדאה לית לן למיגמר דהתם כיון דהעדאה לחייבו ממון על נגיחותיו היא באה ולהעמיד שורו בחזקת מועד בעינן בפני בעלים שידעו לטעון ולהכחיש העדים ולהביא אחרים להזימן אבל טעמא דמחאה להתרות בו להיות זהיר בזכיותיו היא באה שזה טוען שבגזילה היא בידו הכא אפילו שלא בפניו נמי איתה: דחברך חברא אית ליה כו'. ויאמרו זה לזה והדבר בא לאזניו ואינו יכול לומר אילו שמעתי הייתי זהיר בראיית זכותי: ולר' מאיר דאמר כו'. כלומר לר"י דאמר בב"ק איזהו מועד כל שהעידו בו שלשה ימים איכא למימר הכא ג' שנים דומיא דג' ימים אלא לר"מ דאמר התם דאפי' נגח ג' פעמים ביום אחד הוי מועד מק"ו הכא נמי אכלה תלת פרי בחד יומא כגון תאנה שאינה מתבשלת יחד ויש שאינה מתבשלת שחרית ולערב היא ראויה הכי נמי דהויא חזקה ומשני דומיא דשור המועד כו': צלף. פרי שלא ניכר בו היום ונגמר לסוף ג' ימים: אספסתא. מין זרע הוא לעשב בהמות ולסוף ל' יום הוא נגמר ועוקרין אותו וזורעין אחר במקומו ובתוך שלשים יום גוזזין אותו שלש פעמים: דקדיח. גדל קלת: משמט הוא דקא שמיט ואכיל. ואין זו אכילת כל הפרי: בתלתא ירחי. שעקרה בסוף כל חדש וזרע אחרת: מאן הולכי אושא. דאמר רבי יוחנן לעיל להא מילתא משמייהו: רבי ישמעאל. לא פירש לי מהיכן אלא הכי גמירי שהוא היה באותו הזמן: לרבנן מאי. רבנן דלית להו הא דרבי ישמעאל מנא להו חזקה דשלש שנים: ה"ג שהרי נביא עומד בעשר ומזהיר על אחת עשרה. ירמיה בשנה העשירית לצדקיהו (ד) והיה כלוא בחצר המטרה כדכתי' בס' ירמיה ושם נאמר לו הנה חנמאל בן שלום וגו' וכתיב בההיא ענינא שדות בכסף יקנו וכתוב בספר וגו' היה מזהיר (ה) לוקחי שדות לכתוב שטרות ולהעמיד עדים בחתימתם כי יגלו מן העיר בשנת אחת עשרה כשנלכדה העיר ולא יחזיקו במקח שלש שנים אלא עשירית ואחת עשרה אלמא בהני תרתי שנין לא הוי חזקה מכאן לחזקה שאינה פחותה משלש שנים: עצה טובה קמ"ל. כלומר לעולם חזקה הויא בשנה אחת ועצה טובה קא משמע לן שיהא שטרו בידו מוכן לראיה ולא יזקק לעדים כשיעוררו עליו:

דאי

תוספות

אלא מעתה חזקה שאין עמה טענה כו'. תימה מאי ס"ד דמקשה דהיכי מצי לאוקמי בידיה כיון דלא טעין מידי וי"ל דהכי פריך כיון דילפת משור המועד מה התם בשלש נגיחות הוי בחזקת נגחן הכא נמי כיון דאכלה שלש שנים ולא מיחה הוא בחזקת שלא ימחה עוד ולבלא טענה נמי תהא שלו דלית לן למימר שמחל לו אי נמי הא דקא פריך למימרא דמוקה בלא טענה תהא חזקה היינו כגון דאמר ליה מפלניא זבנתה דזבנה מינך אע"ג דלא אמר קמי דידי זבנה ולא דר בה אפי' חד יומא ולא ידע אי זבנה מיניה אי לא אלא דהכי א"ל תימה לרשב"א הא דמיבעיא לן בפ' כיצד הרגל (ב"ק כד. ושם) אי לאיעודי תורא אי לאיעודי גברא תפשוט מהכא דלאיעודי תורא הוא (ו) דקאמרי הולכי אושא מה שור המועד כיון שנגח ג' נגיחות נפקא ליה כו' ואי לאיעודי גברא לא מייעד עד נגיחה רביעית דאז הוא מועד לעבור בהתראות דכשנגח נגיחה שלישית והתרו בו עדיין לא עבר על שלש התראות עד שיגח פעם רביעית וי"ל דסוגיא דהכא כמאן דאמר לאיעודי תורא והולכי אושא לא אמרו אלא דגמרינן משור המועד ולא יותר וילפינן משלש התראות דגברא ולא משלש נגיחות דתורא ועוד דלמאן דאמר לאיעודי גברא אין צריך שיהו מוחזקות לעבור בהתראות דאם כן עד נגיחה חמישית לא יחייב אלא צריך שיודיעוהו בכל פעם כשיגח כדי שישמור שורו ומכל מקום חיובא דשור תליא במה שהוחזק ליגח: אלא מעתה מחאה שלא בפניו לא תהא מחאה. פירש ר"י כי היכי דילפת משור המועד דהוי חזקה בשלשה זימני הכי נמי נילף מה שור (ז) צריך העדאה בפניו ולא אמר קלא אית ליה ותועיל הכי נמי מחאה שלא בפניו אית לן למימר דלית ליה קלא ולא תהא חזקה אף על פי ששמע החזקה כיון דאין קול למחאה מה היה מועיל אם מוחה כיון שלא תגיע למחזיק מחאתו ואע"ג שמחאה באה לבטל החזקה וההעדאה באה לקיים מ"מ פריך שפיר והא דנקט מחאה ולא נקט חזקה משום דחזקה נשמעת טפי מהעדאה אבל מחאה אינה נשמעת יותר ובלא שור המועד הוי מצי למיפרך דלא תהא מחאה כדפריך אליבא דרבנן אלא כיון דיליף משור המועד ניחא ליה למפרך מיניה ומשני חברך חברא אית ליה ויש קול בין למחאה בין להעדאה אבל בהעדאה גרידא גזירת הכתוב הוא דאין נעשה מועד אלא אם כן מעידים בפניו אפילו יתברר לו באלף עדים שהעידו על שורו בבית דין:

כגון צלף. (ח) בתר דשני ליה מתאנה פריך מצלף דתאנה גדולה היא בשעה שנוטלין חבירתה מן האילן אלא שלא נתבשלה עדיין אבל צלף קטן הפרי הרבה כשנוטלין האחת כדאמר בשבת (דף ל.) עתידין אילנות שיטענו פירות בכל יום לגלג עליו אותו תלמיד אין כל חדש תחת השמש אחוי ליה צלף ור"ח גרים ברישא תלתא פירי בחד יומא כגון צלף שיש לו שלשה פירות ביחד ובתר הכי גרים כגון תאנה וההיא דשבת משמע כספרים שלנו:

ודלמא עצה טובה קא משמע לן. ה"נ מצי למיפרך ודלמא בתוך עשר הוה קאי ומזהיר על תחלת אחת עשרה דליכא אפילו שנה ולעולם בשנה אחת הויא חזקה ור"ח פירש דרב יוסף יליף הכי וגרים שהרי נביא עומד בתשע ומזהיר על י"א שתלכד העיר ויאבדו השטרות ויסמכו על חזקת שלש שנים ומביא ראיה מסדר עולם דבשנה תשיעית בחדש עשירי היה ומיהו בכל הספרים שלנו כתוב שהרי נביא עומד בעשירי וכן בסדר עולם שלנו תניא בשנה העשירית ועוד דלגירסתו נמי קשיא מנא ליה שלש שנים מיום ליום דלפי גירסת סדר עולם ליכא אלא שמנה עשר חודש שהרי בשנת אחת עשרה לחדש הרביעי בתשעה לחודש הובקעה העיר:

שתא

רבינו גרשום

התם כי לא נגח. רביעית מאי לישלם: אלא מעתה. דאמרת כיון דאכלה ג' שנים קיימא ברשותיה אם כן כל חזקה שאין עמה טענה להיכא דקאמר ליה מערער מה אתה עושה בתוך שלי ואמר הלה אכלתיה שני חזקה ולא אמר לי אדם דבר תיהוי חזקה ואנן תנן דכל חזקה שאין עמה טענה שאינו טוען עם החזקה של אבא היתה וירותיה או שקניתיה ממך ואכלתיה שני חזקה אינה חזקה. ואי טעין הכי אע"ג דלית ליה שטרא טענינן ואמרינן הכי הוא כדקאמר ושטרא הוא דארכס ליה אבל אם אינו טוען אלא שאכלתיה שני חזקה אין זה טענה. ולדבריך דילפת משור מועד דלאחר ג' שנין קיימא ברשותיה תיהוי חזקה אע"ג דלית ליה טענה אחריתי ומשני טעמא מאי הוי חזקה שיש עמה טענה חזקה משום דאמרי' דלמא הכי כדקאמר ושטרא איירכס ליה. אבל להיכא דאין עמה טענה השתא איהו לא טען אנן טענינן ליה ולא הוה חזקה: מתקיף לה רב עוירא אלא מעתה. דמפקת ליה משור המועד להיכא דמיחה המערער שלא בפניו לא תיהוי מחאה דדומיא דשור המועד וכו' ומשני גבי שור המועד בעינן בפניו משום דגזירת הכתוב הוא אבל מחאה שלא בפניו בדין הוא דהויא מחאה דאמרי' ליה למחזיק חברך כו' ומחברך שמעת מחאה: ולר' מאיר דאמר כו'. בשלמא אליבא דרבנן דאמרי אינו חייב עד דנגח ג' נגיחות בג' ימים כדכתיב אם שור נגח הוא מתמול שלשום [חד מתמול] תרי שלשום ותלת היום הכא נמי לא הוי חזקה עד דאכלה ג' שנים אלא לר' מאיר דאמר כיון דכי ריחק נגיחותיו חייב קירב נגיחותיו לא כל שכן דהוי מועד הכא נמי למה לי תלת שנין לחזקה אפי' ביום אחד תהוי דאכלה תלת פירי בחד יומא כגון תאנה ...

מסורת הש"ס

א) [לקמן מא.], ב) [לקמן כט. לח: לט. כתובות קט: קי. ערכין טז.], ג) ב"ק כד. תענית כא., ד) [גי' הערוך ערך צלף בתלתא], ה) [גי' הערוך ביום אחד עמ"ש תוס' ד"ה כגון בשם ר"ח], ו) [עירובין לג. וש"נ וע' לקמן כט. קט:].

הגהות הב"ח

(א) גמ' בעידנא דאיתא להאי נגיחה ליתא להאי: (ב) שם בספר וחתום וגו' שהרי: (ג) רשב"ם ד"ה התם והועד וכו' כי היכי דהני מפקי מחזקה: (ד) ד"ה ה"ג שהרי וכו' לצדקיהו היה כצ"ל ואות ו' נמחק: (ה) באד"ה מזהיר את לוקחי וכו' עשירית ואחת עשרה וכשיחזרו מן הגלות אם יבואו המוכרים להוציא מידכם בשביל שלא מוחזקים ג' שנים תוציאו שטרותיכם ותקיימו בידכם אלמא בהכי תרתי: (ו) תד"ה אלא מעתה חזקה וכו' מדקאמרי הולכי: (ז) ד"ה אלא מעתה מחאה וכו' מה שור המועד צריך וכו' למה היה מועיל אם היה מוחה: (ח) ד"ה כגון צלף אע"ג דשני ליה:

תורה אור השלם

א) וְאִם שׁוֹר נַגָּח הוּא מִתְּמֹל שִׁלְשֹׁם וְהוּעַד בִּבְעָלָיו וְלֹא יִשְׁמְרֶנּוּ וְהֵמִית אִישׁ אוֹ אִשָּׁה הַשּׁוֹר יִסָּקֵל וְגַם בְּעָלָיו יוּמָת: [שמות כא, כט]

ב) שָׂדוֹת בַּכֶּסֶף יִקְנוּ וְכָתוֹב בַּסֵּפֶר וְחָתוֹם וְהָעֵד עֵדִים בְּאֶרֶץ בִּנְיָמִן וּבִסְבִיבֵי יְרוּשָׁלַ‍ִם וּבְעָרֵי יְהוּדָה וּבְעָרֵי הָהָר וּבְעָרֵי הַשְּׁפֵלָה וּבְעָרֵי הַנֶּגֶב כִּי אָשִׁיב אֶת שְׁבוּתָם נְאֻם יְיָ: [ירמיה לב, מד]

ליקוטי רש"י

כל חזקה שאין עמה טענה. וככל חזקות מיירי לא שנא חזקה שלש שנים ל"ש חזקה יום אחד [לעיל ו.]. בין בחזקת יום אחד דקרקעות ובתים ואילנות בין בחזקת יום אחד כגון הנך דלמרינן לעיל (ו.) שהחזיק להודות כי מיירי וקאמר דלריך לטעון מחאה כה החזיק כה וכלכך כיון דטעין שנעשה מעולם שבידו...

חשק שלמה על רבינו גרשום א) נראה דצ"ל כיון דבעינן דמקדים ואוכל מיד כשמתגדל לסוף ל' ימים וכו'. ב) צ"ל בתלתא ירחי. ג) גי' רבינו כגי' ר"ח שהובא בתוס' כאן דגרים שהרי נביא עומד בתשע.

count as **THREE YEARS.** Thus, R' Yishmael, who derives the law of *chazakah* from the law of the *muad* bull, indeed does not require three years of occupancy, but rather three utilizations of the property. Similarly, he would agree that the *chazakah* of an *aspasta* field can be established in three months.

Since the Gemara has established that R' Yochanan's source for a three-year *chazakah* is appropriate only according to R' Yishmael's view, it now seeks the source of *chazakah* according to the Sages that dispute R' Yishmael and require occupancy for three full years for a *chazakah* to be established:[23]

לְרַבָּנָן מַאי – What is the source for *chazakah* **according to the Sages?**

Rav Yosef suggests a possible source:

אָמַר רַב יוֹסֵף – Rav Yosef said: קְרָא כְּתִיב – It is a written verse: "שָׂדוֹת בַּכֶּסֶף יִקְנוּ וְכָתוֹב בַּסֵּפֶר וְחָתוֹם" – *They shall buy fields for money, and record [the transaction] in a document and [have witnesses] sign [it].*[24] From this verse, it can be seen that at least three years are required for *chazakah,* **שֶׁהֲרֵי נָבִיא עוֹמֵד בְּעֶשֶׂר – for the prophet was standing in the tenth** year of King Tzidkiyahu's reign **וּמַזְהִיר עַל אַחַת עֶשְׂרֵה – and exhorting regarding the eleventh year.** I.e. Jeremiah was exhorting the people to retain valid bills of sale because the exile would take place in two years. This implies that the buyer's two-year occupancy of the field prior to the exile would not be a sufficient *chazakah* to establish his ownership of the bought field upon the return to Eretz Yisrael. Thus, we see that at least three years are necessary for a *chazakah* to be established.[25]

Abaye refutes this derivation:

אָמַר לֵיהּ אַבַּיֵי – Abaye said to [Rav Yosef]: דִּלְמָא הָתָם עֵצָה טוֹבָה קָא מַשְׁמַע לַן – Perhaps [the prophet] was merely **offering them good advice.**[26]

NOTES

23. Below, 36b. [Although the Gemara has not yet explicitly introduced this view, its existence has already been implied by the Gemara's statement that *according to R' Yishmael* three years are not necessary for a *chazakah* to be established – clearly implying that there is a dissenting Tannaic view that *does* require three full years (see *Rashba* to the Mishnah ד״ה שדה הבעל).]

24. *Jeremiah* 32:44. In the tenth year of King Tzidkiyahu's reign, the city of Jerusalem was under Babylonian siege. God instructed the prophet Jeremiah to prophesy that though the city and the rest of the land would fall to Nebuchadnezzar's armies and the populace exiled [in two years' time – the eleventh year of Tzidkiyahu's reign], God would eventually return them to their land. As an indication of their eventual return, the people were presently to buy fields and duly record the deeds, to be used as proof of ownership upon their return to the land (see *Rashi*). Since Jeremiah commanded them to buy fields *with money,* it is evident that the purpose of the documents was not to effect the transaction itself, but simply to provide the purchasers with evidence of ownership (*Rabbeinu Yonah; Ritva; Kiddushin* 26a).

25. The Rishonim point out an obvious difficulty. Granted that we can derive from here that a two-year occupancy does *not* establish a *chazakah,* how do we see that a three-year occupancy does? Some explain that Rav Yosef's derivation is also predicated upon the derivation from the *muad* bull. However, Rav Yosef derives from the verse in *Jeremiah* that a two-year *chazakah* is insufficient, which forces us to qualify the derivation from the *muad* bull: It is not merely three *utilizations* of a property (which in some fields could be accomplished in less than three years, as demonstrated by the Gemara above), but rather three *years* of utilization (*Rabbeinu Yonah; Rashba*). [The prophet urged the recording of deeds for *all* purchased fields, regardless of the crop that they produce. Thus, the two-year occupancy prior to the exile would have been insufficient even for fields producing fast-growing crops such as *aspasta* (*Ritva*).]

Alternatively, Rav Yosef's derivation is independent of the derivation from the *muad* bull. But he reasons that since the prophet waited until the *tenth* year to exhort the purchasers to record their deeds, the implication is that those who bought fields in the *ninth* did not require these measures, since their three-year occupancy prior to the exile would establish their *chazakah* (*Rashba*).

26. I.e. perhaps a *chazakah* can be established even in one year. Nevertheless, it was advisable for the purchasers to retain documentary evidence of ownership and thereby avoid the need to later find witnesses who could establish the purchasers' uninterrupted year-long occupancy of the field. Hence, no proof as to the length of time needed to establish a *chazakah* can be adduced from Jeremiah's exhortation, for he might have merely been offering the Jews sound advice in advance of their exile (*Rashi*).

דְּאִי לֹא תֵּימָא הָכִי – **For if you do not say this** [that the prophet's directives were sometimes motivated by practical rather than legal considerations], then when he sent word earlier to those already in exile: "בְּנוּ בָתִּים וְשֵׁבוּ וְנִטְעוּ גַנּוֹת וְאִכְלוּ אֶת־פִּרְיָן" – ***Build houses and settle, and plant gardens and eat their fruit,***[1] מַאי קָאָמַר – **what** law **was he telling** them? אֶלָּא עֵצָה טוֹבָה קָא מַשְׁמַע לָן – **Rather,** we must say that **he was** merely **offering them good advice.**[2] הָכָא נַמִּי עֵצָה טוֹבָה קָא מַשְׁמַע לָן – **Here, too,** in the directive to draw up valid deeds, we can say that **he was** merely **offering them good advice** not motivated by any legal considerations.

Abaye proves his point:

תֵּדַע – **You should know** that Jeremiah was devoted to giving them practical counsel, דִּכְתִיב – **for it is written** regarding a similar incident that Jeremiah instructed: "וּנְתַתָּם בִּכְלִי־חָרֶשׂ לְמַעַן יַעַמְדוּ יָמִים רַבִּים" – ***You shall place them into earthenware vessels so that they will keep for many days.***[3] Thus, the Gemara rejects Rav Yosef's explanation of the Sages' source for a three-year *chazakah.*

The Gemara proposes another possibility for the Sages' source of the three-year *chazakah*:

אֶלָּא אָמַר רָבָא – **Rather, Rava said:** שַׁתָּא קַמַּיְיתָא מָחֵיל אִינִישׁ – **The first** year that a squatter trespasses on a person's property, **the person** commonly **forgoes** his rights to the benefits that the squatter takes from his property. תַּרְתֵּי מָחֵיל – Even for **two** years, **he forgoes** those rights. תְּלָת לֹא מָחֵיל – But for **three years, he** certainly **does not forgo** his rights. Therefore, if the original owner allows the occupant's utilization of the property to continue for three years without protest, it can be assumed that he is indeed no longer the owner, but that the occupant legitimately acquired the property from him.

The Gemara objects:

אָמַר לֵיהּ אַבָּיֵי – **Abaye said to [Rava]:** אֶלָּא מֵעַתָּה כִּי הָדְרָא אַרְעָא – **Accordingly, when the land reverts** to the original owner as a result of a protest that he lodges at the end of two years of the newcomer's occupancy,[4] תֶּיהְדַּר לְבַר מִפֵּירֵי – **let it go back without the yield!** אַלְּמָה אָמַר רַב נַחְמָן – **Why, then, did Rav Nachman say:**[5] הָדְרָא אַרְעָא וְהָדְרֵי פֵּירֵי – **"The land goes back and the produce goes back** as well"?[6]

Rava, therefore, modifies his explanation:

אֶלָּא אָמַר רָבָא – **Rather, Rava said:** שַׁתָּא קַמַּיְיתָא לֹא קָפֵיד אִינִישׁ – **The first year** that a squatter trespasses on a person's property, **the person** commonly **does not protest.**[7] תַּרְתֵּי לֹא קָפֵיד – Even for **two** years, **he does not protest.** תְּלָת קָפֵיד – But **three** years of unauthorized use **he** certainly **protests.**[8] Therefore, if the original owner does not protest someone else's three-year occupancy of his property, it can be assumed that the occupant acquired the property legitimately.

Abaye objects to this explanation as well:

אָמַר לֵיהּ אַבָּיֵי – **Abaye said to [Rava]:** אֶלָּא מֵעַתָּה – **But now,** if establishment of a *chazakah* is based on when it can be assumed that the owner will protest unauthorized use of his property, כְּגוֹן הָנֵי דְּבֵי בַּר אֶלְיָשִׁיב – in cases involving people **such as those of the Bar Elyashiv family,** דְּקָפְדֵי אֲפִילּוּ אַמַּאן דְּחָלֵיף אַמֵּיצְרָא דִּידְהוּ – **who protest even** against **one who walks along their boundary divider,**[9] הָכִי נַמִּי דִּלְאַלְתַּר הָוֵי חֲזָקָה – **is it so that a *chazakah*** on their properties **would be established immediately?**[10] וְכִי תֵּימָא הָכִי נַמִּי – **And if you say** that **it is indeed so** that one can establish an immediate *chazakah* in the property of such an owner, אִם כֵּן נָתַתָּ דְּבָרֶיךָ לְשִׁיעוּרִין – **if so, you will have subjected your ruling to** constant **evaluation.**[11] – ? –

Rava therefore suggests his final explanation:

אֶלָּא אָמַר רָבָא – **Rather, Rava said:** שַׁתָּא קַמַּיְיתָא מִיזְדְּהַר אִינִישׁ בִּשְׁטָרֵיהּ – **The first year** after purchasing property, **a person is careful with his deed;** תַּרְתֵּי וּתְלָת מִיזְדְּהַר – for **two and three years, he is careful** with it. טְפֵי לֹא מִיזְדְּהַר – But **longer** than that, **he is not careful** to keep his deed unless his occupancy of the property has been challenged.[12] Therefore, after three years of unchallenged use of a property, we do not insist that the

NOTES

1. *Jeremiah* 29:5. This statement was issued by Jeremiah ten years earlier than the one cited previously by the Gemara. In it, Jeremiah informs the Jews who had already been exiled to Babylonia with King Yechonyah (Tzidkiyahu's nephew and predecessor) that they should build houses and settle there, since they would not return to Eretz Yisrael for another seventy years (*Rashi*).

2. That they should expect an extended stay in exile and make provisions accordingly.

3. *Jeremiah* 32:14. After Jeremiah bought a field from his cousin Chanamel, as God had commanded him to do, Jeremiah instructed his disciple, Baruch, to take the documents attesting to the purchase and place them in earthenware so that they would be preserved until the end of the Babylonian exile. Certainly, Jeremiah's advice as to where the documents would keep best was merely practical and nothing more (see *Rashi*; see also *Ritva*). [The previously cited statement (*Build houses and settle. . .*), however, might have not been so much advice as a dramatic way of informing the people of the length of the exile.]

4. [Since it takes three years to establish a *chazakah,* the land will be returned to the original owner if he protests after only two years of the newcomer's occupancy and the newcomer is unable to produce proof of purchase.]

5. Rav Nachman's ruling is stated below [33b] (*Rashi*).

[Note: *Rashi's* commentary to this tractate ends at this point. The commentary to the remainder of the tractate appearing in *Rashi* format is the work of his grandson, R' Shmuel ben Meir, commonly known by his acronym: *Rashbam.*]

6. Rav Nachman rules on a case in which the original owner of a property seeks to claim it from the current occupant. Though the occupant insists that he bought the property from the original owner and has established a *chazakah* in it by using it for three years, he is able to produce witnesses to substantiate only two years of use. Thus, the occupant has failed to establish a *chazakah.* Rav Nachman rules that the occupant must return to the original owner not only the property but also payment for the two-year yield that he took from it (*Rashbam* to 33b; perhaps, this is the intent of *Rashbam* here as well). Abaye challenges that if, as Rava asserts, a person forgoes his rights to the yield of his property for up to three years, he should not receive compensation for that yield when the squatter returns the property to him.

7. Although during the first or second year a property owner might not openly make an issue of a squatter's unauthorized use of his property, he does not forgo his rights to compensation for the yield that the squatter has taken from the property (*Rashbam*).

8. Since a person will not tolerate a squatter's violating his rights three times by occupying his property without authorization (*Rashbam*).

9. Boundaries of fields were usually raised above field level (see *Rashbam* 53b). [Since they were not planted they were often used by the public as shortcuts (see above, 12a, and below, 100a). But the family of Bar Elyashiv would object even to this practice.]

10. According to your reasoning, Rava, their silence in the face of even a momentary utilization of what was known to be their property should be proof that the user acquired it from them legitimately.

11. The Sages generally handed down rulings that should apply in all cases and not have to be adjusted according to the circumstances of the individual case. Thus, it is flawed to advance a rationale for *chazakah* according to which the duration necessary to establish it varies with the tolerance threshold of the individual property owner. [See *Rashba* and *Ritva.*]

12. Some Rishonim explain that people do not simply lose their documents after three years. Rather, after three years of silence on the part of the original owner, the occupants feel secure that the original

חזקת הבתים פרק שלישי בבא בתרא כט.

דאי לא תימא הכי א) בנו בתים ושבו ונטעו גנות ואכלו את פרין מאי קאמר אלא עצה טובה קמ"ל הכא נמי עצה טובה קמ"ל תדע דכתיב ב) ונתתם בכלי חרש למען יעמדו ימים רבים אלא אמר רבא שתא קמייתא מחיל איניש תרתי מחיל תלת לא מחיל אמר ליה אביי אלא מעתה כי הדרא ארעא תיהדר לבר מפירי אלמה (א) אמר רב נחמן הדרא ארעא והדרי פירי אלא אמר רבא שתא קמייתא לא קפיד איניש תרתי לא קפיד תלת קפיד א"ל אביי אלא מעתה כגון הני דבי בר אלישיב דקפדי אפילו אמאן דחליף אמיצרא דידהו הכי נמי דלאלתר הוי חזקה וכי תימא הכי נמי ג) אם כן נתת דבריך לשיעורין אלא אמר רבא א שתא קמייתא מיזדהר איניש בשטריה תרתי ותלת מיזדהר טפי לא מיזדהר אמר ליה אביי אלא מעתה מחאה שלא בפניו לא תיהוי מחאה דאמר ליה אי מחית (א) באפאי הוה מיזדהרנא בשטראי ב דאמר ליה ג) חברך חברא אית ליה וחברא דחברך חברא אית ליה אמר רב הונא ג שלש שנים שאמרו הוא שאכלן רצופות מאי קמ"ל תנינא חזקתן שלש שנים מיום ליום מהו דתימא מיום ליום לאפוקי מקוטעות ולעולם אפילו מפוזרות קמ"ל אמר רב חמא ד ומודי רב הונא באתרי דמוברי באגי פשיטא לא צריכא דאיכא דמובר ואיכא דלא מובר והאי גברא מוברה מהו דתימא (ב) א"ל אם איתא דדידך הואי איבעי לך למיזרעה קמ"ל דאמר ליה חדא ארעא בכוליה באגא לא מצינא לינטר ואי נמי ה בהכי ניחא לי דעבדא טפי תנן חזקת הבתים והא בתים דביממא ידעי בליליא לא ידעי אמר אביי מאן מסהיד אבתים שיבבי ו שיבבי מידע ידעי ביממא ובליליא רבא אמר ז כגון דאתו בי תרי ואמרי אנן אגרינן מיניה ודרינן ביה תלת שנין ביממא ובליליא אמר ליה רב ימר לרב אשי הני נוגעין בעדותן הן דאי לא אמרי הכי אמרינן להו זילו הבו ליה אגר ביתא להאי א"ל דייני דשפילי (ג) הכי דאיני מי לא עסקינן ח כגון דנקיטי אגר ביתא ואמרי למאן ליתביה אמר מר זוטרא ט ואי טעין ואמר ליתו תרי סהדי לאסהודי ליה דדר ביה תלת שני ביממא ובליליא טענה ומודי

רש"י

דאי לא תימא הכי. הרי שלח ירמיה לאותן שהיו בבבל שגלו עם יכניה י"א שנה קודם גלות צדקיהו בנו בתים ושבו כי לא תלאו משם עד מלאת לבבל שבעים שנה למה ליה להזהירם על זאת אלא עצה טובה (ד) קמ"ל דהוא משיא אותם הכא נמי עצה טובה בעלמא היא: תדע. דכל עלמו היה יגע ליעלם עלה טובה דקאמר להו נמי מקום גניזת שטרותיהם היכן הם מתקיימים יותר: מחיל איניש. על פירות קרקעו לאדם האוכלן: אלא מעתה. כיון דאתרי שנין מחיל תיהדר ארעא ממי שילא עליו ערעור לסוף שנתים תיהדר ארעא לבעלים לבר מפירי דהא מחיל ליה עלייהו: אלמה אמר רב נחמן. לקמן בשמעתין:

עד כאן פירוש רש"י זצ"ל ז)

מכאן ואילך פירוש רבינו שמואל ב"ר מאיר

אלמה אמר רב נחמן. לקמן בשמעתין גבי מחזיק בקרקע חבירו ואזיל אידך ואייתי סהדי דאכלן תרתין שנין ולא יותר ואמר רב נחמן הדרא ארעא והדרי פירי של שתי שנים: תרתי לא קפדי. על מה שזה יורד לתוך שדהו של חבירו בלא רשותו ומיהו פירי לא מחיל: תלת קפיד. הואיל ושילש באוולתו ליכנס בלא רשות הבעלים וזה ששתק ולא מיחה ודאי מכרו לו: ה"נ דלאלתר תיהוי חזקה. למי שירד לנכסי דבי בר אלישיב הואיל ולא מיחו (ה): אי מחית באפאי הוה מיזדהרנא בשטראי. יותר מג' שנים ומשני חברך חברא אית ליה ונודע לך שמחיתי ואם היתה לקוחה בידך כדבריך היה לך להזהר בשטרך יותר מג' שנים: שאכלן רצופות. אבל אם הניחה שנה שניה ואחר כך אכלה שתי שנים שלישית ורביעית מלי אמר בעל השדה האי דלא מחאי לך היינו משום דאוברת לה שנה שניה דגלית אדעתך דלאו דידך הואי והלכך לא זרעת אותה: חזקתן שלש שנים מיום ליום. שלא יהיה הפסק בינתים: מהו דתימא מיום ליום. דקתני מתניתין למעוטי מקוטעות דלא תימא שלש שנים מקוטעות קאמר כי היכי דקתני סיפא שדה הבעל חזקתה שלש שנים ואינה מיום ליום אלא ג' חדשים בראשונה וג' חדשים באחרונה וי"ב באמצע: קמ"ל. רב הונא לדוקא קתני להו למעוטי מפוזרות: ומודה רב הונא. דלי לו בחזקת אכילת שנים מפוזרות: באתרא דמוברי באגי. במקום שנוהגין לזרוע שנה ולהוביר שנה שלא להכחיש את הקרקע דהא אחזיק בה כדמחזקי אינשי ומיהו שנה שהובירה אינה עולה (ו) לחשבון שלש שני חזקה וצריך לשמור שטרו יותר משלש שנים עד שילקוט שלש שנים ואי טוען אידך לא אכלתי אלא שתים ובאתי שדה ריקם והלכך לא מחיתי מלי א"ל מ"מ היה לך למחות שאע"פ שלא זרעתה הייתי עושה בה ניר שאחר הקציר והיה לך להבין שבשביל שלא להכחיש כחה לא חפלתי לזרעה כמנהג שדות העיר: והאי גברא מוברה. ועומדת בין שדות זרועות כמותה: חדא ארעא בכולה באגא. שדה אחת זרועה בתוך בקעה גדולה איני יכול לשמור שם לבדו בשבילה אבל כשכולן זרועות שוכרין שומר בין כולם וגם (ז) כן אין מכניסין שם בהמות בשנה הבאה: בליליא לא ידעי. ואפילו הכי הויא חזקה דבשלמא גבי שדה וכל הנך אין דרכן לעשות מלאכה בלילה וכשמעמידין עדים על מלאכת ימי שלש שנים הרי זו חזקה אבל בתים שדרך לדור בהן בלילה והוא אין יכול להביא עדים שראוהו דר אף בלילות וכיון דלית ליה סהדי על הלילות הוו להו מפוזרות ואם איתא לדרב הונא הא מלי אידך למיטען אני ראיתי שלא היית דר בלילות ולכך לא חשתי למחות דגלית אדעתך דלאו דידך הואי ולמאי הויא חזקה: שיבבי. השכנים שלו שראוהו דר בו יום ולילה (ח) היו רגילין להעיד: שיבבי מידע ידעי. ואם יטעון ויאמר אייתי לי סהדי דדירת ביה בימים ובלילה יוכלו להעיד לו ומיהו אנן לא טענינן ליה כדמפרש בסמוך: דאי לא. שאם אין מעידין שהבית של משכיר: דייני דשפילי. שאין בקיאין בדין דייני הכי לקבל עדות אלו אם כבר נתנו שכר הבית למשכיר ומעולם בכי האי גוונא לא איירי רבא: אמר מר זוטרא אי טעין כו'. מילתא באנפי נפשה היא דפשיטא ליה למר זוטרא דאע"ג דבעו כל הנך אמוראי לעיל ג' שנים רצופות אפ"ה אין מחייבין את המחזיק להביא עדים שיעידו בפירוש על כל הימים והלילות אלא יעידו סתם שראוהו דר ג' שנים ומסתמא אם (ט) דר בבית אף בלילות דר בו וקאמר מר זוטרא דאי טעין מערער ואמר אייתי סהדי כו' טענתו טענה וצריך שיבואו עדים של לילות וימים דכיון דטעין טענת ברי דקאמר אני ראיתי שלא דר בלילות בבית וצריך חזקה ולכך לא אני אומר אייתי סהדי דדר ביה תלת שנין בין בימים בין בלילות ולכך צריך להביא עדים שראוהו דר בלילות ולכך לא מחיתי ואין חזקתו חזקה ולמה הוה לו שהיה לו למחות:
הכי

תוספות

שתא קמייתא לא קפיד וכו'. תימה (ט) מנא לן דר' ישמעאל דוקא יליף משור המועד ולא רבנן איהו נמי מלי גמרי משור המועד דהיינו טעמא נמי דלעיל דגמר משור המועד דכיון דקפיד בג' זמנין ולא מיחה א"כ ודאי מכרה או נתנה לו וי"ל דלא דמי דודאי דר' ישמעאל דאזיל בתר אכילות שפיר מלי למיגמר משור המועד דמה התם הוחזק נגחן בג' פעמים אף כאן בשלש אכילות אם לא שמכרה לו היה מקפיד ואין זה וזה תלויים בשהוי זמן אבל לרבנן דתלוי בשהוי זמן כמה ישהה ויקפיד לא שייך למגמר משור המועד:

אלא מעתה מחאה שלא בפניו כו'. אור"י דליכא לאוקמי פירכא דאביי אלא כשהן (י) בעיר אחת דאי בעיר אחרת היכי פריך דלא תהא מחאה ותהא חזקה אדרבה כיון דלא הויא מחאה לא הויא חזקה דהא אינו צריך לצאת בעיר אחרת לפני המחזיק ולמחות כדמוכח לקמן:

הני נוגעין בעדותן הן. ואם תאמר ואמאי הוו נוגעין בעדות הא איכא מיגו דה"מ אמרי פרענא לך אגר ואע"ג דבתר דתקון רבנן שבועת היסת לא מהימני לאסהודי בהאי מיגו כדאיתא בריש האיש מקדש (קדושין מג:) הכא דאמתני' קיימינן ואכתי לא ניתקנה שבועת היסת מאי פריך להימניה במיגו ויש לומר דהאי לאו מיגו הוא שיראים לומר פרענו לך כי שמא יזכה האחר (כ) ויתבע מהם פעם שנית [וע"ע תוס' שבועות מה: ד"ה בעדים]:

אמר מר זוטרא אי טעין ואמר כו'. הקשה ר"י בר מרדכי לפ"ה כי לא טעין נמי אמאי לא נשאל מהן כי שמא אין יודעין על הלילות שלא נוציא על פיהן שלא כדין דבכל עדיות אנו דורשין יפה וכאן נמי אמאי לא נחקור אותן מספק ולאו פירכא היא דכיון שהעידו על הימים אפי' יאמרו אין אנו

מסורת הש"ס

א) לקמן לג:, ב) שבת לה: מגילה יח: גיטין יז. חולין ע. לב:, ג) לעיל כח: וש"נ, ד) בדפוס פירנו הנוסח "באן מת רש"י ז"ל", ה) ל"ל הס:

עין משפט נר מצוה

א א מיי' פי"א מהלכות טוען הלכה ג [ד] סמג עשין לה טוש"ע ח"מ סי' קמ סעיף ז:
ב ב מיי' שם הל' ו סמג שם טוש"ע ח"מ סי' קמו סעיף א:
ג ג מיי' שם פי"ב הל' ד סמג שם טוש"ע ח"מ סי' קמ סעיף ח וסי' קמא סעיף ג:
ד ד ה מיי' שם וסמג שם טוש"ע ח"מ סימן קמא סעיף ג:
ה ו ז מיי' שם הלכה ה סמג שם טוש"ע ח"מ סי' קמ סעיף ח וע"ש בהג"ה:
ו ח [וע"ש בהגהות ובמ"מ] טוש"ע שם סעיף ט וסי' לו סעיף יג:
ז ט מיי' שם הלכה ג טוש"ע שם סי' קמ סעיף ח:

הגהות הב"ח

(א) גמ' אי מחית באנפאי הוה: (ב) שם מהו דתימא מלי א"ל אם איתא וכו' לא מנינא לאינטר ואי: (ג) שם דייני דשפילי דייני הכי מי לא: (ד) רש"י ד"ה דאי לא וכו' עלה טובה היא משיא כל"ל ותיבות קמ"ל דהוא נמחק: (ה) רשב"ם ד"ה ה"נ דלאלתר וכו' ולא מיחו הס"ד ואח"כ מ"ה טפי לא מודהר הלכך היה לבעלים הראשונים למחות בתוך שלש שלא יחזיק בקרקע שלו ואם לא מיחה הפסיד הס"ד ואח"כ מ"ה אי מחית: (ו) ד"ה באתרא וכו' עולה לו לחשבון וכו' עד שילקוט תבואות ג' שנים ולי טוען אידך ואומר לא: (ז) ד"ה חדא וכו' וגם אין מכניסין שם: (ח) ד"ה אמר מר זוטרא וכו' ומסתמא אם בימים וכו': (ט) תוס' ד"ה שתא וכו' תימה מנא לן: (י) ד"ה אלא וכו' כשהן דרין בעיר אחת וכו' לצאת לעיר אחרת: (כ) ד"ה הני וכו' יזכה האחר בדין ויתבע:

תורה אור השלם

א) בְּנוּ בָתִּים וְשֵׁבוּ וְנִטְעוּ גַנּוֹת וְאִכְלוּ אֶת פִּרְיָן: [ירמיה כט, ה]

ב) כֹּה אָמַר יְיָ צְבָאוֹת אֱלֹהֵי יִשְׂרָאֵל לָקוֹחַ אֶת הַסְּפָרִים הָאֵלֶּה אֵת סֵפֶר הַמִּקְנָה הַזֶּה וְאֵת הֶחָתוּם וְאֵת סֵפֶר הַגָּלוּי הַזֶּה וּנְתַתָּם בִּכְלִי חָרֶשׂ לְמַעַן יַעַמְדוּ יָמִים רַבִּים: [ירמיה לב, יד]

ליקוטי רש"י

אמר רב נחמן הדרא ארעא. דכשמתחזק שנין לא הויא חזקה. והדרי פירי. של ב' שנים שאכל שלא כדין דהא לא טוען מעיקרא אריס הייתי ולפירות ירדתי דמשתמיטנין ליה כדלקמן דלא עבדי אינשי [רשב"ם לקמן לג:]. כגון הני דבי בר אלישיב. אדם חזק [גיטין יז.]. מחאה שלא בפניו לא תיהוי מחאה. כגון אם היה בעיר אחת ומיחה שלא בפניו אם היה בעיר אחרת [כתובות יז:]. אם מיחה המערער בתוך שלש שנים לפני שנים או שלשה שלא בפני המחזיק ואמר דעו שפלוני מחזיק בקרקע שלי בגזולה לא יהיה מחאה [לעיל כח:]. חברך חברא אית ליה. ודומיהו [כתובות קט:]. דכיון דמחי באנפייהו מגלו באנפייהו וכה הדבר לאוזני המחזיק וה"ל לאזדהורי בשטריה [שם יז:]. חבר מגלה לחבירו וזה לחבירו עד שיודע [ערכין טז.].

רבינו גרשום

אלא אמר רבא. משום האי טעמא אמרו רבנן דבעינן ג' שנין חזקה: מחיל איניש ואינו חושש אם יעשה בה חבירו כלום תבואה אבל תלת לא מחיל והיכא דלא מיחה בג' שנין בודאי הוה חזקה: אם כן הואיל דאמרת דתרתי שנין מחיל ליה מאי דעביד בגוה: אם כן מיחה והדרא ארעא תיהדר לבר מפירי דעבד בה דקיימא השתא אלמה אמר רב נחמן וכו': לא קפיד אם שלא ברשותו ירד בה. תלת קפיד שלא יחזיק בה ומוחה: הכי נמי דתהוי לאלתר חזקה אם נשתמש אדם בנכסי דבר אלישיב: נתת דבריך לשיעורין דלמאן דלא קפיד יהבת ג' שנין לחזקה ולמאן דקפיד לאלתר הוי חזקה: [תרתי ותלת] מיזדהר איניש בשטריה. שיהא שמור שאם יערער אדם על מקחו שיהא לו לראיה ושוב מייאש לשומרו וכיון דג' שנים קים להו לרבנן דטפי לא מיזדהר מכלל שאם יבוא ויערער אדם לאחר ג' שנין אין בדבורו ממש אע"פ שאבד השטר משום דמוקמינן בידו בעדי חזקה שיש בידו ג' שנים: א"כ דטפי לא מיזדהר הואיל ולא שמע שום מערער. אם כן כי מיחה אדם בתוך ג' שנים במקום אחר שלא בפניו אמאי הוי מחאה הא מצי אמר ליה האי כיון דלא מחית באפאי לא מיזדהרנא בשטראי: ומשני דאמר ליה אידך חברך חברא אית ליה והוה לך לשמור שטרא: למעוטי מקוטעות שלא תהא סוף ראשונה ותחלת אחרונה ואמצעי' שלמה: (א) ולעולם שלמות בעינן ואפי' מפוזרות כגון שנה ראשונה ושלישית וחמישית קמ"ל רב הונא דרצופות בעינן ג' שנים והיינו מיום ליום דקאמר מתני': מודי רב הונא באתרא דמוברי באגי. שאותה שדה שזורעה שנה אחת. שנה שניה מניחין אותה בורה אם כך רגילין אפי' לא החזיק בה כי אם מפוזרות הוה חזקה דמצי למימר ליה למערער החזקתי בה בשעה שרגילין בני אדם לעבוד

שדותיהן: קמ"ל רב הונא. דמצי למימר לי' המחזיק איזרענא ארעאי הואיל דהני סביבותי אינן זורעין חדא ארעא בכולי באגי דאינן זורעין לא מצינא למינטר מקמיה דריסת רגל עוברין ושבין והמשו"ה לא זרענא לה. ואי נמי מצי למימר בהכי ניחא ליה דלא למיזרעה דעבדא טפי בשנה אחריתא: בליליא לא ידעי אינשי אי דייר בה אי לא ואע"ג דהני תלת שנין אינן רצופין משום ליליותא קשיא לרב הונא דאמר דבעינן רצופין: ומתרץ אביי דמאן מסהיד אבתים דהאי מחזיק דייר בהם שיבבי הבית בליליא ואכתי רצופות נינהו: ורבא מתרץ כגון דאתו וכו' אנן אגרנא מינה דהוה המחזיק: הני עדים נוגעין בעדותן הן משום דהוו ליה דמסייעי למחזיק דאי הוי אמרי דהוי המערער בימים ודהוו איתן שלהן דמסייעי למחזיק דאי הוי אמרי דהוי מחזיק דייר לא דיירינן ליה הוא חזקה ושלא כדין יהבינן ליה אגר ביתא מחייבינן להו ומאי מהימני: אמר ליה רב אשי חייבין אתון למיתן למערער דמחזיק נעבד ומשום הכי מסייעי למחזיק ואמרו בידי להו וכו' ומנו' מדיני הכי שיהוו מאמינים להם משום ששילמו שכר לו. דייני הכי דייני דשפילי מושפלים. דייני הכי שיהוו מאמינים להם מאחר שנתנו השכירות מי לא עסקינן דנקטי אכתי אגרי בידייהו ואמרי למאן ליתביה לא יהבינן להו מאן מחייב אי למחזיק אי למערער משום הכי מהימני דלא נגעי בעדותן: אמר מר זוטרא כשטען המחזיק כבר בידי שני חזקה ואמר המערער לייתי סהדי דלסהוד ביה דדייר בה תלת שנין בימי ובליליא ולא טעין ליה הכי אבל אי לא טעין הכי אנן לא ילפינן ליה למטען:

חשק שלמה על רבינו גרשום א) נראה דל"ל ולמלעיות שלמה בעינן ולעולם אפי' מפוזרות וכו'.

occupant produce documentary proof of ownership; rather, we rely on his very occupancy as proof.[13]

Abaye objects to this as well:

אָמַר לֵיהּ אַבָּיֵי – Abaye said to [Rava]: אֶלָּא מֵעַתָּה – But now, if establishment of a *chazakah* is based on how long a new owner keeps his deed, **מְחָאָה שֶׁלֹּא בְּפָנָיו לֹא תֶּיהֱוֵי מְחָאָה – then a protest** lodged by the original owner **not in [the occupant's] presence should not be a** valid **protest, דְּאָמַר לֵיהּ – for [the occupant] can say [to the original owner]** in court: **אִי מְחֵית בְּאַפַּאי הֲוָה מִיזְדַּהַרְנָא בִּשְׁטָרָאִי – "If you had protested in my presence, I would have been careful with my deed** and safeguarded it beyond the usual three-year limit."[14] – ? –

The Gemara answers that a protest in absentia is nonetheless valid:

דְּאָמַר לֵיהּ – For [the original owner] can say to him, חַבְרָךְ חַבְרָא אִית לֵיהּ – "Your friend has a friend, וְחַבְרָא דְּחַבְרָךְ חַבְרָא אִית לֵיהּ – and the friend of your friend has a friend." Thus, it was certain that word of the protest would get back to you and the protest, though made in your absence, was for all practical purposes as effective as if it had been made in your presence.

The Gemara elaborates on the law of the three-year *chazakah*:

אָמַר רַב הוּנָא – Rav Huna said: שָׁלֹשׁ שָׁנִים שֶׁאָמְרוּ – The three years of occupancy **that [the Sages] said** establish a *chazakah* **הוּא שֶׁאֲכָלָן רְצוּפוֹת – do so only if [the occupant] used** the property for **[the three years] consecutively.**[15]

The Gemara asks:

מַאי קָא מַשְׁמַע לָן – What is [Rav Huna] informing us? תְּנֵינָא – We learned this in **our Mishnah: חֶזְקָתָן שָׁלֹשׁ שָׁנִים מִיּוֹם לְיוֹם – THEIR *CHAZAKAH* IS** established **IN THREE YEARS FROM DAY TO DAY.**[16] – ? –

The Gemara answers:

מַהוּ דְּתֵימָא מִיּוֹם לְיוֹם לְאַפּוּקֵי מִקּוּטָּעוֹת – You might have said that the expression **"from day to day"** is meant only **to exclude partial years; וּלְעוֹלָם אֲפִילּוּ מְפוּזָּרוֹת – but, in reality, even** if the three full years of use **were scattered** over a longer period of time, **the** *chazakah* would still be effective.[17] **קָא מַשְׁמַע לָן – [Rav Huna]** therefore **informs us** that the three full years of occupancy must be consecutive.[18]

The Gemara qualifies Rav Huna's ruling:

אָמַר רַב חָמָא – Rav Chama said: וּמוֹדֵי רַב הוּנָא – But Rav Huna agrees that it is not necessary that the three *chazakah* years be consecutive **בְּאַתְרֵי דְּמוֹבְרֵי בָּאגֵי – in a place where they fallow fields** every other year.[19]

NOTES

owner has no intention of contesting their rights to the property and they have no further need for the documents (*Rashba, Ran* and *Nimukei Yosef;* see also *Rambam, Hil. To'en VeNitan* 11:4).

13. Some explain Rava to mean that the law of *chazakah* is simply a Rabbinic ordinance enacted for the protection of buyers. Since, as a general rule, people tend to lose track of their deeds after three years, the Sages legislated that after three years of uncontested occupancy, the occupant should no longer have to provide documentary proof of ownership. This enactment does not unduly compromise the original owner's rights, since he has the option of lodging a protest within the three years of occupancy, thereby making it incumbent on the occupant to retain his documentary evidence for three years following the protest (*Ketzos HaChoshen* 140:2, based on Rishonim; see *Rosh* here and *Rashi* to *Kesubos* 17b ד״ה שני חזקה).

Others explain that the institution of *chazakah* is predicated primarily on the evidence furnished by the original owner's inexplicable silence in face of the supposedly unauthorized use of his property. If he is indeed the true owner, why has he not protested this trespass? On the other hand, within the first three years the *occupant's* position is undermined by his inability to produce a bill of sale. If he has indeed obtained the property legitimately, why has he not retained documentary evidence? Once three years of uncontested occupancy have elapsed, however, the occupant cannot be faulted for having lost his document, and the original owner's inexplicable toleration of the alleged trespass proves to us that he lies when he insists that he never transferred the property to the occupant (*Ramban* to 42a, as explained by *Ketzos* loc. cit.; *Ritva* here; see also *Rambam, Hil. To'en VeNitan* 11:2-4).

Rashba advances a variation of this second approach: An owner might very well remain silent in face of up to three years of squatting on his property. Therefore, purchasers of property retain their documents for three years in case the original owner eventually contests their ownership. (These documents are retained for three years even if the seller is a person who would ordinarily protest immediately, since the purchaser does not want to have to prove the unusual temperament of the original owner in court.) Once three years have elapsed, however, purchasers no longer expect any challenge to their ownership and discard their documents. If the original owner delays his challenge until after the three years have elapsed, then he has fatally compromised his case, since it appears likely that he deliberately waited until the purchaser lost his document before contesting his ownership of the property.

14. The Gemara has already established above (28b) that word of a protest in absentia inevitably gets back to the occupant. Nevertheless, Abaye argues that the occupant could claim that the protest in absentia was not to be taken seriously, since a true owner would have confronted a trespasser directly. Therefore, he dismissed the protest as frivolous and did not hold on to his document (*Ritva*; see *Toras Chaim*).

15. But if he utilized a field one year, let it lie fallow one year and then utilized it during the third and fourth years, the original owner can claim that he did not lodge a protest because the occupant let the land lie fallow one year. By not planting the field on that year, the occupant indicated that he did not own the field; hence, there was no reason to protest (*Rashbam*).

16. The Gemara assumes that the Mishnah's expression "from day to day" means *consecutive* use (*Rashbam*). Accordingly, the requirement of consecutiveness is already stated in the Mishnah. What need is there for Rav Huna to reiterate it?

17. It would be possible to understand that the three years of occupancy do not have to be consecutive. Rather, by stating that the three years must be "from day to day," the Mishnah might mean to teach only that each of the three years must contain a full twelve months of occupancy, unlike the law in the case of a non-irrigated field, where the Mishnah later validates a *chazakah* based on only three months of occupancy in the first and third years (*Rashbam*).

18. I.e. Rav Huna teaches that the expression "from day to day" means that the three years must be both complete *and* consecutive (see *Rashbam, Ritva*).

19. In certain areas, it was the common farming practice for landowners to plant their fields only every other year. On the alternate years, the land would be plowed and left fallow so that the soil's nutrients not be depleted. As taught by Rav Chama, Rav Huna agrees that in such a locale an occupant could establish a *chazakah* even though he did not cultivate the field for three consecutive years, since he nevertheless occupied the property in the normal manner. Therefore, if the original owner claims that he did not protest the occupancy because he saw that the land was left fallow one year, the occupant could counter that he was indeed occupying the field in the manner customary for that locale. Although he did not plant the field one year, he nevertheless plowed it, and the original owner should have realized that the failure to plant was motivated by customary farming practice [rather than by a reluctance to display ownership]. Therefore, the original owner should have lodged a protest if he indeed had not sold the land (*Rashbam*).

Rashbam adds that although the fallow year does not invalidate the *chazakah,* it nevertheless cannot be counted as one of the three *chazakah* years. Rather, the occupant must guard his documents until he has actually harvested crops from the field for three years.

[As explained above (note 12), a buyer keeps his deed for three years because that is the time during which one would expect the original owner to contest the present occupancy if he had the mind to do so. For,

דאי לא תימא הכי (א) בנו בתים ושבו ונטעו גנות ואכלו את פרין מאי קאמר אלא עצה טובה קמ"ל הכא נמי עצה טובה קמ"ל תדע דכתיב (ב) ונתתם בכלי חרש למען יעמדו ימים רבים אלא אמר רבא שתא קמייתא מחיל איניש תרתי מחיל תלת לא מחיל אמר ליה אביי אלא מעתה כי הדרא ארעא תיהדר לבר מפירי אלמה (א) אמר רב נחמן הדרא ארעא והדרי פירי אלא אמר רבא שתא קמייתא לא קפיד איניש תרתי לא קפיד תלת קפיד א"ל אביי אלא מעתה כגון הני דבי בר אלישיב דקפדי אפילו אמאן דחליף אמיצרא דידהו הכי נמי דלאלתר הוי חזקה וכי תימא הכי נמי (ג) אם כן נתת דבריך לשיעורין אלא אמר רבא (א) שתא קמייתא מיזדהר איניש בשטריה תרתי ותלת מיזדהר טפי לא מיזדהר אמר ליה אביי אלא מעתה מחאה שלא בפניו לא תיהוי מחאה דאמר ליה אי מחית (ה) באפאי הוה מיזדהרנא בשטראי (ב) דאמר ליה (ג) חברך חברא אית ליה וחברא דחברך חברא אית ליה אמר רב הונא (ג) שלש שנים שאמרו הוא שאכלן רצופות מאי קמ"ל תנינא חזקתן שלש שנים מיום ליום מהו דתימא מיום ליום לאפוקי מקוטעות ולעולם אפילו מפוזרות קמ"ל אמר רב חמא (ד) ומודי רב הונא באתרי דמוברי באגי פשיטא לא צריכא דאיכא דמובר ואיכא דלא מובר והאי גברא מוברה מהו דתימא (ב) א"ל אם איתא דדידך הואי איבעי לך למיזרעה קמ"ל דאמר ליה חדא ארעא בכוליה באגא לא מצינא לינטר ואי נמי (ה) בהכי ניחא לי דעבדא טפי תנן חזקת הבתים והא בתים דביממא ידעי בליליא לא ידעי אמר אביי מאן מסהיד אבתים שיבבי (ו) שיבבי מידע ידעי ביממא ובליליא רבא אמר (ז) כגון דאתו בי תרי ואמרי אנן אגרינן מיניה ודרינן ביה תלת שנין ביממא ובליליא אמר ליה רב יימר לרב אשי הני נוגעין בעדותן הן דאי לא אמרי הכי אמרינן להו זילו הבו ליה אגר ביתא להאי א"ל דייני דשפילי (ג) הכי דאיני מי לא עסקינן (ח) כגון דנקיטי אגר ביתא ואמרי למאן ליתביה אמר מר זוטרא (ט) ואי טעין ואמר ליתו תרי סהדי לאסהודי ליה דדר ביה תלת שני ביממא ובליליא טענתיה טענה

ומודי

רש"י

דאי לא תימא הכי. הרי שלח ירמיה לאותן שהיו בבבל שגלו עם יכניה י"א שנה קודם גלות צדקיהו בנו בתים ושבו כי לא תצאו משם עד מלאת לבבל שבעים שנה למה ליה להזהירם על זאת אלא עצה טובה (ד) קמ"ל דהוא משיא אותם הכא נמי עצה טובה בעלמא היא: תדע. דכל עצמו היה יגע ליעצם עצה טובה דקאמר להו נמי מקום גניזת שטרותיהם היכן הם מתקיימים יותר: מחיל איניש. על פירות קרקעו לאדם האוכלן: אלא מעתה. כיון דאתרי שנין מחיל תיהדר ארעא ממי שיצא עליו ערעור לסוף שנתים תיהדר ארעא לבעלים לבר מפירי דהא מחיל ליה עלייהו: אלמה אמר רב נחמן. לקמן בשמעתין:

עד כאן פירוש רש"י זצ"ל (ד)

מכאן ואילך פירוש רבינו שמואל ב"ר מאיר

אלמה אמר רב נחמן. לקמן בשמעתין גבי מחזיק בקרקע חבירו ואזיל אידך ואייתי סהדי דאכלן תרתין שנין ולא יותר ואמר רב נחמן הדרא ארעא והדרי פירי של שתי שנים: תרתי לא קפדי. על מה שזה יורד לתוך שדהו של חבירו בלא רשותו ומיהו פירי לא מחיל: תלת קפיד. הואיל ושילש באוולתו ליכנס בלא רשות הבעלים וזה ששתק ולא מיחה ודאי מכרו לו: ה"נ דלאלתר תיהוי חזקה. למי שירד לנכסי דבי בר אלישיב הואיל ולא מיחו (ה): אי מחית באפאי הוה מיזדהרנא בשטראי. יותר מג' שנים ומשני חברך חברא אית ליה ונודע לך שמחיתי ואם היתה לקוחה בידך כדבריך היה לך להזהר בשטרך יותר מג' שנים: שאכלן רצופות. אבל אם הניחה שנה שניה ואחר כך אכלה שתי שנים שלישית ורביעית מצי אמר בעל השדה האי דלא מחאי לך היינו משום דאוברת לה שנה שניה דגלית אדעתך דלאו דידך הואי והלכך לא זרעת אותה: חזקתן שלש שנים מיום ליום. שלא יהיה הפסק בינתים: מהו דתימא מיום ליום. דקתני מתניתין למעוטי מקוטעות דלא תימא שלש שנים מקוטעות קאמר כי היכי דקתני סיפא שדה הבעל חזקתה שלש שנים ואינה מיום ליום אלא ג' חדשים בראשונה וג' חדשים באחרונה וי"ב באמצע: קמ"ל. רב הונא דדוקא קתני למעוטי מפוזרות: ומודה רב הונא. דדי לו בחזקת אכילת שנים מפוזרות: באתרא דמוברי באגי. במקום שנוהגין לזרוע שנה ולהוביר שנה שלא להכחיש את הקרקע דהא אחזיק בה כדמחזקי אינשי ומיהו שנה שהובירה אינה עולה (ו) לחשבון שלש שני חזקה וצריך לשמור שטרו יותר משלש שנים עד שילקוט שלש שנים ואי טוען אידך אני באתי בתוך שלש ומצאתי שדה ריקם ולכך לא מחיתי מצי א"ל מ"מ היה לך למחות שאע"פ שלא זרעתיה הייתי עושה בה ניר שאחר הקציר והיה לך להבין שבשביל שלא להכחיש כחה לא חפצתי לזרעה כמנהג שדות העיר: והאי גברא מוברה. ועומדת בין שדות בורות כמותה: חדא ארעא בכולה באגא. שדה אחת זרועה בתוך בקעה גדולה איני יכול להושיב שם שומר לבדו בשבילה אבל כשכולן זרועות שוכרין שומר בין כולם וגם (ז) כן אין מכניסין שם בהמות: דעבדה טפי. בשנה הבאה: בליליא לא ידעי. ואפילו הכי הויא חזקה דבשלמא גבי שדה וכל הנך אין דרכן לעשות מלאכה בלילה וכשמעמידין עדים על מלאכת ימי שלש שנים הרי זו חזקה אבל בתים שדרך לדור בהן בלילה והוא אין יכול להביא עדים שראוהו דר אף בלילות וכיון דלית ליה סהדי על הלילות הוו להו מפוזרות ואם איתא לדרב הונא הא מצי אידך למיטען אני ראיתי שלא היית דר בלילות ולכך לא חששתי למחות דגלית אדעתך דלאו דידך הואי ואמאי הויא חזקה: שיבבי. השכנים שלו ראוהו דר בו יום ולילה (ח) היו רגילין להעיד: שיבבי מידע ידעי. ואם יטעון ויאמר איתי לי סהדי דדירת ביה ביממא ובליליא יוכלו להעיד לו ומיהו אנן לא טענינן ליה כדמפרש בסמוך: דאי לא. שאם אין מעידין שהבית של משכיר: דייני דשפילי. דיינין בקיאין בדין דיינין דייני הכי לקבל עדות אלו אם כבר נתנו שכר הבית למשכיר ומעולם בכי האי גוונא לא איירי רבא: אמר מר זוטרא אי טעין כו'. מילתא באנפי נפשה היא דפשיטא ליה למר זוטרא דלא"ג דבעינן כל הנך אמוראי לעיל ג' שנים רצופות אפ"ה אין מחייבין את המחזיק להביא עדים שיעידו בפירוש על כל הימים והלילות אלא יעידו סתם שראוהו דר ג' שנים ומסתמא אם (ט) דר בבית אף בלילות דר בו וקאמר מר זוטרא דאי טוען מערער ואמר איתי סהדי כו' טענתו טענה וצריך שיבואו עדים של לילות וימים דכיון דטוען טענת ברי דקאמר אני ראיתי שלא היה דר בלילות בביתי ולכך לא מחיתי ואין חזקתו חזקה ולכך לא אמר איתי סהדי דדר ביה תלת שני ביממא ובליליא לכך צריך להביא עדים שיעידו בפירוש שנים בין ביממא בין בליליא דלא היה לו להכחישו ולומר לו שהיה לו למחות:

הכי

תוספות

שתא קמייתא לא קפיד וכו'. תימה (ט) מנא לן דר' ישמעאל דוקא יליף משור המועד ולא רבנן אינהו נמי מצי גמרי משור המועד דהיינו טעמא נמי דלעיל דגמר משור המועד דכיון דקפיד בג' זמנין ולא מיחה א"כ ודאי מכרה או נתנה לו וי"ל דלא דמי דודאי דר' ישמעאל דאזיל בתר אכילות שפיר מצי למיגמר משור המועד דמה התם הוחזק נגחן בג' פעמים אף כאן בשלש אכילות אם לא שמכרה לו היה מקפיד ואין זה וזה תלויים בשהוי זמן אבל לרבנן דתלוי בשהוי זמן כמה ישהה ויקפיד לא שייך למגמר משור המועד:

אלא מעתה מחאה שלא בפניו כו'. אור"י דליכא לאוקמי פירכא דאביי אלא כשהן (י) בעיר אחת דאי בעיר אחרת היכי פריך דלא תהא מחאה ותהא חזקה אדרבה כיון דלא הויא מחאה לא הויא חזקה דהא אינו צריך לבא בעיר אחרת לפני המחזיק ולמחות כדמוכח לקמן:

הני נוגעין בעדותן הן. ואם תאמר ואמאי הוו נוגעין בעדות הא איכא מיגו דה"מ אמרי פרענא לך אגר ואע"ג דבתר דתקון רבנן שבועת היסת לא מהימני לאסהודי בהאי מיגו כדאיתא בריש האיש מקדש (קדושין מג:) הכא דאמתני' קיימינן ואכתי לא ניתקנה שבועת היסת מאי פריך להימניה במיגו ויש לומר דהאי לאו מיגו הוא שיראים לומר פרענו לך כי שמא יזכה האחר (כ) ויתבע מהם פעם שנית [וע"ע תוס' שבועות מה: ד"ה בעדים]:

אמר מר זוטרא אי טעין ואמר כו'. הקשה ר"י בר מרדכי לפ"ה כי לא טעין נמי אמאי לא נשאל מהן כי שמא אין יודעין על הלילות שלא נוציא על פיהן שלא כדין דבכל עדיות אנו דורשין יפה וכאן נמי אמאי לא נחקור אותן מספק ולאו פירכא היא דכיון שהעידו על הימים אפי' יאמרו אין אנו

רבינו גרשום

אלא אמר רבא. משום האי טעמא אמרו רבנן דבעינן ג' שנין לחזקה: מחיל איניש ואינו חושש אם יעשה בה חבירו כלום תבואה אבל תלת לא מחיל והיכא דלא מיחה בג' שנין בודאי הוה חזקה: אם כן הואיל דאמרת דתרתי שנין מחיל א"כ מאי דעביד בגוה: אם כן מיחה והדרא ארעא תיהדר לבר מפירי דעבד בה דקיימא בשתא אלמה אמר רב נחמן וכו': לא קפיד אם שלא ברשותו ירד בה. תלת קפיד שלא יחזיק בה ומוחה: הכי נמי דתהוי לאלתר חזקה אם נשתמש אדם בנכסי דבר אלישיב. נתת דבריך לשיעורין דלמאן דלא קפיד יהבת ג' שנין לחזקה ולמאן דקפיד לאלתר הוי חזקה: [תרתי ותלת] מיזדהר איניש בשטריה. שיהא שמור שאם יערער אדם על מקחו שיהא לו לראיה ושוב מייאש לשומרו וכיון דג' קים להו לרבנן דטפי לא מיזדהר מכלל שאם יבוא ויערער אדם לאחר ג' שנין אין בדברו ממש אע"פ שאבד השטר משום דמוקמינן בידו בעדי חזקה שיש בידו ג' שנים: א"כ דטפי לא מיזדהר הואיל ולא שמע שום מערער: אם כן כי מיחה אדם בתוך ג' שנים במקום אחר שלא בפניו אמאי הוי מחאה הא מצי אמר ליה האי כיון דלא מחית באפאי לא מיזדהרנא בשטראי: ומשני דאמר ליה אידך חברך חברא אית ליה והוה לך לשמור שטרא: למעוטי מקוטעות שלא תהא סוף ראשונה ותחלת אחרונה ואמצעי' שלמה (א) ולעולם שלמות בעינן ואפי' מפוזרות כגון שנה ראשונה ושלישית וחמישית קמ"ל רב הונא דרצופות בעינן ג' שנים והיינו מיום ליום דקאמר מתני': מודי רב הונא באתרא דמוברי באגי. שאותה שדה שזורעה שנה אחת. שנה מניחין אותה בורה אם כך רגילין אפי' לא החזיק כי אם מפוזרות הוה חזקה דמצי למימר ליה למערער החזקתי בה בשעה שרגילין בני אדם לעבוד

עין משפט נר מצוה

ג א מיי' פי"א מהלכות טוען הלכה ג [ד] סמג עשין לה טוש"ע ח"מ סי' קמ סעיף ו:
ד ב מיי' שם פ"י הלכה ג וסמג שם טוש"ע ח"מ סי' קמו סעיף ח:
ה ג מיי' שם פי"ב הל' ד סמג שם טוש"ע ח"מ סי' קמ סעיף ט וסי' קמא סעיף ג:
ו ד ה מיי' שם טוש"ע ח"מ סימן קמא סעיף ג:
ז ו ז מיי' שם הלכה ב סמג שם טוש"ע ח"מ סי' קמ סעיף ח וע"ש בהג"ה:
ח ח [וע"ש בהגהות וכמ"מ] טוש"ע שם סעיף ט וסי' לז סעיף יב:
ט ט מיי' שם הלכה ג טוש"ע שם סי' קמ סעיף ט:

מסורת הש"ס

א) [לקמן לג.], ב) [שבת לה: מגילה יח. גיטין יד. חולין ט: לב.], ג) [לעיל כח: וש"נ], ד) בדפוס פיזרו הנוסח "כאן מת רש"י ז"ל", ה) נ"ל הס:

הגהות הב"ח

(א) גמ' אי מחית באנפאי הוה: (ב) שם מהו דתימא מצי א"ל אם איתא וכו' לא מצינא למינטר ואי נמי: (ג) שם דייני דשפילי דייני הכי מי לא: (ד) רש"י ד"ה דאי לא וכו' אלא עצה טובה היא משיא כצ"ל ותיבות קמ"ל דהוא נמחק: (ה) רשב"ם ד"ה ה"נ דלאלתר וכו' ולא מיחו הס"ד ואח"כ מ"ה טפי לא מזדהר הלכך היה לבעלים הראשונים למחות בתוך שלש שלא יחזיק קרקע שלו ואם לא מיחה הפסיד הס"ד ואח"כ מ"ה אי מחית: (ו) ד"ה באתרא וכו' עולה לו לחשבון וכו' עד שילקוט תבואות וכו' ואי טעין אידך ואומר אני: (ז) ד"ה חדא וכו' וגם אין מכניסין שם: (ח) ד"ה אמר מר זוטרא וכו' ומסתמא אם בימים כו': (ט) תוס' ד"ה שתא וכו' תימה א"כ מנא לן: (י) ד"ה אלא וכו' כשהן בעיר אחת וכו' לבוא לעיר אחרת: (כ) ד"ה הני וכו' יזכה האחר בדין ויתבע:

תורה אור השלם

א) בְּנוּ בָתִּים וְשֵׁבוּ וְנִטְעוּ גַנּוֹת וְאִכְלוּ אֶת פִּרְיָן: [ירמיה כט, ה]

ב) כֹּה אָמַר יְיָ צְבָאוֹת אֱלֹהֵי יִשְׂרָאֵל לָקוֹחַ אֶת הַסְּפָרִים הָאֵלֶּה אֵת סֵפֶר הַמִּקְנָה הַזֶּה וְאֵת הֶחָתוּם וְאֵת סֵפֶר הַגָּלוּי הַזֶּה וּנְתַתָּם בִּכְלִי חָרֶשׂ לְמַעַן יַעַמְדוּ יָמִים רַבִּים: [ירמיה לב, יד]

ליקוטי רש"י

אמר רב נחמן הדרא ארעא. דבתרתין שנין לא הויא חזקה. והדרי פירי. של ב' השנים שאכל שלא כדין לפי שלא טען מעיקרא אריס הייתי ולפירות ירדתי דמהימנינן ליה כדלקמן דשטרא לפירי לא עבדי אינשי [רשב"ם לקמן לג.]. כגון הני דבי בר אלישיב. [גיטין יד.]. מחאה שלא בפניו לא תיהוי מחאה. כגון שהיה בעיר אחת ומיחה שלא בפניו בפני שנים בעיר אחרת [כתובות יז:]. אם מיחה המערער בתוך שלש שנים לפני עדים שלא בפני המחזיק ואומר דעו שפלוני מחזיק בקרקע שלי בגזילה לא תיהוי מחאה [לעיל כח:]. חברך חברא אית ליה. ויודיעהו [כתובות קט:]. דהני דמחי באנפייהו מגלו לאחריני והדבר נודע למחזיק וה"ל לאזדהורי בשטריה [שם ח:]. זה מגלה לחבירו וזה לחבירו עד שיודע [ערכין טז.].

שדורהן: קמ"ל רב הונא. דמצי למימר לי' המחזיק אזורענא ארעאי הואיל דהני סביבותי אינן זורעין ... ומשו"ה לא זרענא לה. ואי נמי מצי למימר בהכי ניחא ליה דלא למיזרעה דעבדא טפי בשתא אחריתא: בליליא לא ידעי אינשי אי דייר ביה המחזיק אי לא ואע"ג דהני תלת שנין אינן רצופין משום לילותא אפ"ה הויא חזקה וקשיא לרב הונא דאמר בעינן רצופין: מתרץ אביי מאן מסהיד אבתים דהאי מחזיק דייר בה שיבבי הבית ואינהו מידע ידעי דדייר ביה בין ביממא בין בליליא ואכתי רצופות נינהו: ורבא מתרץ כגון דאתו וכו' אנן אגרינה מינה המחזיק: הני עדים נוגעין בעדותן ... דאי לא אמרי הכי אמרינן להו ... אגר ביתא מיניה: אמר ליה רב אשי דייני דשפילי ... מי לא עסקינן בדנקטי אכתי אגרי בידייהו ... למאן ניתביה ... אמר מר זוטרא כשטוען ... המערער לייתי סהדי דלסהדו ביה דדייר בה תלת שנין ביממא ובליליא טענתיה טענה אבל אי לא טעין הכי אנן לא ילפינן ליה למטען:

חשק שלמה על רבינו גרשום א) נראה דצ"ל ולעולם שלמה דשלמות בעינן ולעולם אפי' מפוזרות וכו'.

ומודי

The Gemara asks:

פְּשִׁיטָא – This is obvious![20] **– ? –**

The Gemara answers:

לֹא צְרִיכָא – No, [Rav Chama's clarification] is needed דְּאִיכָּא דְּמוֹבַר וְאִיכָּא דְּלָא מוֹבַר **–** in a region **where there are some** farmers **who fallow** their fields on alternate years **and some who do not fallow** them; וְהַאי גַּבְרָא מוֹבְרָהּ **– and this man** [the occupant in question] **fallowed [the field],** in keeping with the practice of those who farmed the fields immediately surrounding his own.[21] מַהוּ דְּתֵימָא אָמַר לֵיהּ **– You might have said** that **[the original owner] can say to [the occupant]:** אִם אִיתָא דְּדִידָךְ הֲוַאי **– "If it is true that [the land] is yours,** אִיבָּעֵי לָךְ לְמִיזְרְעָהּ **– you should have planted it** even during the year that the immediately surrounding fields were left fallow."[22] קָא מַשְׁמַע לָן **– [Rav Chama]** therefore **informs us** that the non-consecutive *chazakah* is nevertheless effective דְּאָמַר לֵיהּ **– for [the occupant] can reply to [the original owner]:** חֲדָא אַרְעָא בְּכוּלֵּיהּ בַּאגָא לָא מָצֵינָא לִינְטַר **– "I cannot guard one** piece of planted **land** situated **among an entire field** that has been left fallow!"[23] וְאִי נַמִּי **– Alternatively,** the occupant can reply: בְּהָכִי נִיחָא לִי **– "This way** [letting the land lie fallow every other year] **is preferable to me,** דְּעָבְדָא טְפֵי **– for [the field]** thereby **produces more** in the following year."[24]

The Gemara challenges Rav Huna's ruling:

תְּנַן – We learned in our Mishnah: חֶזְקַת הַבָּתִּים **– THE *CHAZAKAH* OF HOUSES** is established in three years. וְהָא בָּתִּים דְּבִימָמָא יָדְעֵי בְּלֵילְיָא לָא יָדְעֵי **– Now, houses** are properties **about which [witnesses] know** only about **daytime** occupancy, but **they do not know** about **nighttime** occupancy.[25] How, then, can one establish a *chazakah* on a house, if he must have proof that he used it consecutively – day and night – for three years?[26]

The Gemara answers:

אָמַר אַבָּיֵי – Abaye said: מַאן מַסְהִיד אַבָּתִּים **– Who** generally **testifies about** the occupancy of **houses?** שִׁיבָבֵי **– The neighbors!** שִׁיבָבֵי מֵידַע יָדְעֵי בִּימָמָא וּבְלֵילְיָא **– Neighbors certainly** are in a position to **know** whether the occupant was in the house **day and night.**[27]

The Gemara offers an alternative method of proving nighttime residency:

רָבָא אָמַר – Rava says: כְּגוֹן דְּאָתוּ בֵּי תְרֵי **–** A *chazakah* on a house can be established **in a case where two** men **come** forward וְאָמְרֵי אֲנַן אַגְרִינַן מִינֵּיהּ **– and say, "We rented** the house **from [the current holder],** וְדָרִינַן בֵּיהּ תְּלָת שְׁנִין בִּימָמָא וּבְלֵילְיָא **– and we lived in it for three years, day and night."**[28]

The Gemara points out a difficulty with Rava's explanation:

אָמַר לֵיהּ רַב יֵימַר לְרַב אַשִׁי – Rav Yeimar said to Rav Ashi: הָנֵי נוֹגְעִין בְּעֵדוּתָן הֵן **–** In Rava's case, **these** tenants should be disqualified as witnesses because **they have an interest in their testimony.** דְּאִי לָא אָמְרֵי הָכִי **– For if they do not testify so,** and the original owner is awarded the land retroactively, אָמְרִינַן לְהוּ **– we will say to them,** זִילוּ הָבוּ לֵיהּ אֲגַר בֵּיתָא לְהַאי **– "Go, give rent for the house to [the original owner]!"**[29] **– ? –**

NOTES

as Rava asserted above, an owner will certainly not tolerate three years of a squatter's use of his property in silence. In the present case, however, the three years of full occupancy that an owner would certainly not tolerate do not expire until after three years of *cultivation* have elapsed. Therefore, the occupant can be expected to preserve his deed until he has enjoyed three years of harvest, and no *chazakah* is established before then (*Rashba* above, ד״ה אלא אמר רבא).]

20. If this were not an effective *chazakah,* how then would a *chazakah* for fields be established in such regions? (*Ran*; *Nimukei Yosef*). [Certainly, an occupant cannot be expected to use a property in an abnormal manner.]

21. *Rashbam.*

22. I.e. in order to insure that you establish a *chazakah,* you should have been prudent and followed the practice of some of the other farmers in the region, who plant their fields every year (*Nimukei Yosef*).

23. The occupant can claim that he could not afford the expense of hiring a watchman to guard a lone piece of cultivated land among the open fields left fallow. However, when the surrounding fields are planted as well, the various owners share the expense of hiring the watchman. Furthermore, when all the fields are planted, animals are not brought in to graze there [thereby reducing the need to guard the field from foraging animals]. Thus, it is impractical to plant a single piece of land situated in the midst of fallow fields (*Rashbam*).

24. This second claim could be advanced even where his immediate neighbors did plant their fields [and could share the expense of a watchman with him]. The occupant could still claim that he wanted to fallow the field one year [in keeping with the practice of some of his more distant neighbors] in order to produce a better crop the following year (*Nimukei Yosef*).

25. [I.e. under normal circumstances, it is virtually impossible for witnesses to be able to know who is living in a house at night.]

26. According to Rav Huna, an occupant must produce witnesses that his occupancy of the property was continuous. Consequently, it should be impossible to establish a *chazakah* on a house, since it will be impossible to produce witnesses that the house was occupied during the nights. Testimony about occupancy during the days alone would not be sufficient, because the original owner could claim that he found the house unoccupied at night and therefore did not protest (*Rashbam*). [As explained above (note 15), the rationale for requiring consecutive use in order to establish a *chazakah* is that when the use is non-consecutive, the original owner can claim that he construed the breaks in use as evidence that the occupant did not consider the property his own.]

Were it not for Rav Huna's ruling, however, a *chazakah* on a house could be established through evidence of daytime usage alone. Although *chazakah* requires three *full* years of use and nighttime use cannot be documented, the Mishnah might mean that the occupant must substantiate *six* years of daytime use. If the three years of occupancy need not be consecutive, six years of daytime use would be the equivalent of three years of full-time use and establish a *chazakah* (*Rabbeinu Yonah, Rashba, Nimukei Yosef*).

The Gemara raises its question only from the law regarding a *chazakah* on houses, which are normally used day and night. However, the law regarding a *chazakah* on fields poses no problem. For in the case of a field, which is normally used only during the day, substantiating three consecutive years of daytime occupancy certainly serves to establish a *chazakah* (*Rashbam*). [The original owner cannot claim that he did not protest because he found the field vacant at night, since it is the nature of things for fields to be vacant at night. The occupant's nocturnal absence could certainly not be construed as an indication that he was not its legitimate owner.]

27. Therefore, if the original owner demands proof of three years of daytime and nighttime residence, the occupant can produce his neighbors as witnesses (*Rashbam*). [However, such testimony need not be produced unless *demanded* by the original owner, as emerges from the Gemara below (ibid.).]

As *Nimukei Yosef* explains, it cannot be necessary for the neighbors to testify that they saw him twenty-four hours a day for three years – how could they testify regarding the times that they were sleeping? Rather, it is sufficient that they testify that they did not notice the occupant move out with his belongings, something which they inevitably would have noticed (see also below, 44b).

28. One can establish a *chazakah* on a property not only by personally occupying it for three years, but also by leasing it to tenants for that time. In the case of a leased house, then, it would certainly be possible to establish round-the-clock utilization of the premises by producing the tenants themselves to testify to that effect.

29. The Gemara in *Bava Kamma* (21a) states that even if a tenant has paid rent to the one he *thought* was the landlord, he is still obligated to pay the real owner. Accordingly, in Rava's case, the two tenants would

מסורת הש"ס

א) [לקמן לג:], ב) [שבת י"ז: מגילה יח: גיטין יח. חולין ט. לב:], ג) [לעיל כח: וש"נ], ד) בדפוס פיזרו הגירסא "כאן מת רש"י ז"ל", ה) נ"ל הם.

הגהות הב"ח

(א) גמ' אי מחית באפאי הוה: (ב) שם מהו דתימא מאי אם איתא וכו' לא מצינא דאינטר ואי נמי: (ג) שם דייני דשפילי דייני הכי מי לא: (ד) רש"י ד"ה דאי לא וכו' עלה טובה היא משיא כל"ל ותיבות קמ"ל דהוא נמחק: (ה) רשב"ם ד"ה לאלתר וכו' ולא מיחה הס"ד ואח"כ מ"ה שפי לא מוזהר הלכך היה לבעלים להזהיר למחות בתוך שלש שלא יחזיק בקרקע שלו ואם לא מיחה מ"ה אי מחית: (ו) ד"ה באתרא וכו' עולה לו לחשבון וכו' עד שילקט תבואות ג' שנים ואי טעין אידך ואומר אני: (ז) ד"ה תלא וכו' וגם אין מכניסין שם: (ח) ד"ה אמר מר זוטרא וכו' ומסתמא אם בימים וכו': (ט) תוס' ד"ה שתא וכו' תימה א"כ מנא לן: (י) ד"ה לאלתר וכו' כשכן דלין בעיר אחרת וכו' לבא לעיר אחרת: (כ) ד"ה הני וכו' יוכה האחר בדין ויתבע:

תורה אור השלם

א) בְּנוּ בָתִּים וְשֵׁבוּ וְנִטְעוּ גַנּוֹת וְאִכְלוּ אֶת פִּרְיָן: [ירמיה כט, ה]

ב) כֹּה אָמַר יְיָ צְבָאוֹת אֱלֹהֵי יִשְׂרָאֵל לָקוֹחַ אֶת הַסְּפָרִים הָאֵלֶּה אֵת סֵפֶר הַמִּקְנָה הַזֶּה וְאֵת הֶחָתוּם וְאֵת סֵפֶר הַגָּלוּי הַזֶּה וּנְתַתָּם בִּכְלִי חָרֶשׂ לְמַעַן יַעַמְדוּ יָמִים רַבִּים: [ירמיה לב, יד]

ליקוטי רש"י

אמר רב נחמן הדרא ארעא. דבתרתין שנין לא הויא חזקה, והדרי פירי. אם לא ג' שנים שאכל שלא כדין דהא לא טעין מעיקרא ארים הייתי ולא עשרה ידעתי דמשמע ליה כלקמן לשלם דאחזיק לפירי לא עבדי אינשי [רשב"ם לקמן לג:]. כגון הני דבי בר אלישיב. דלא אכסו מוק [גיטין יז.]. מחאה שלא בפניו לא תיהוי מחאה. כגון אם היה בעיר אחת ומיחה שלא בפניו כפני שנים בעיר אחרת [כתובות יז:]. אם מיחה המערער בתוך שלש שנים לפני עדים שלא בפני המחזיק ואמר דעו שפלוני מחזיק בקרקע שלי בגזילה לא תיהוי מחאה [לעיל כח:]. חברך חברא אית ליה. וידיעוהו [כתובות קט:]. דהני דמחי באנפייהו מגלו לאחריני ובא הדבר לאזני המחזיק וה"ל לאזדהורי בשטריה [שם יז:]. וזה מגלה לחבירו וזה לחבירו עד שיודע [ערכין טז.].

עין משפט נר מצוה

ג א מיי' פי"א מהלכות טוען הלכה ג [ד] סמג עשין לה טוש"ע ח"מ סי' קמ סעיף ז:

ד ב מיי' שם הל' ה וסמג שם טוש"ע ח"מ סי' קמו סעיף ה:

ה ג מיי' שם פי"ב הל' ד סמג שם טוש"ע ח"מ סי' קמ סעיף ח וסי' קמא סעיף ג:

ו ד ה מיי' שם טוש"ע ח"מ סימן קמא סעיף ג:

ז ו ז מיי' שם הלכה ב סמג שם טוש"ע ח"מ סי' קמ סעיף ח וע"ש בהג"ה:

ח ח [וע"ש בהגהות ובמ"מ] טוש"ע שם סעיף ט וסי' לג סעיף יב:

ט ט מיי' שם הלכה ב טוש"ע שם סי' קמ סעיף ח:

גמרא

דאי לא תימא הכי א) בנו בתים ושבו ונטעו גנות ואכלו את פרין מאי קאמר אלא עצה טובה קמ"ל הכא נמי עצה טובה קמ"ל תדע דכתיב ב) ונתתם בכלי חרש למען יעמדו ימים רבים אלא אמר רבא שתא קמייתא מחיל איניש תרתי מחיל תלת לא מחיל אמר ליה אביי אלא מעתה כי הדרא ארעא תיהדר לבר מפירי אלמה א) אמר רב נחמן הדרא ארעא והדרי פירי אלא אמר רבא שתא קמייתא לא קפיד איניש תרתי לא קפיד תלת קפיד א"ל אביי אלא מעתה כגון הני דבי בר אלישיב דקפדי אפילו אמאן דחליף אמיצרא דידהו הכי נמי דלאלתר הוי חזקה וכי תימא הכי נמי ג) אם כן נתת דבריך לשיעורין אלא אמר רבא א שתא קמייתא מיזדהר איניש בשטריה תרתי ותלת מיזדהר טפי לא מיזדהר אמר ליה אביי אלא מעתה מחאה שלא בפניו לא תיהוי מחאה דאמר ליה אי מחית (א) באפאי הוה מיזדהרנא בשטראי ב דאמר ליה ג) חברך חברא אית ליה וחברא דחברך חברא אית ליה אמר רב הונא ג שלש שנים שאמרו הוא שאכלן רצופות מאי קמ"ל תנינא חזקתן שלש שנים מיום ליום מהו דתימא מיום ליום לאפוקי מקוטעות ולעולם אפילו מפוזרות קמ"ל אמר רב חמא ד ומודי רב הונא באתרא דמוברי באגי פשיטא לא צריכא דאיכא דמובר ואיכא דלא מובר והאי גברא מוברה מהו דתימא (ב) א"ל אם איתא דדידך הואי איבעי לך למיזרעה קמ"ל דאמר ליה חדא ארעא בכוליה באגא לא מצינא לינטר ואי נמי ה) בהכי ניחא לי דעבדא טפי תנן חזקת הבתים והא בתים דביממא ידעי בליליא לא ידעי אמר אביי מאן מסהיד אבתים שיבבי ו שיבבי מידע ידעי ביממא ובליליא רבא אמר ז כגון דאתו בי תרי ואמרי אנן אגרינן מיניה ודרינן ביה תלת שנין ביממא ובליליא אמר ליה רב ימר לרב אשי הני נוגעין בעדותן הן דאי לא אמרי הכי אמרינן להו זילו הבו ליה אגר ביתא להאי א"ל דייני דשפילי (ג) הכי דאיני מי לא עסקינן ח כגון דנקיטי אגר ביתא ואמרי למאן ליתביה אמר מר זוטרא ט ואי טעין ואמר ליתו תרי סהדי לאסהודי ליה דדר ביה תלת שני ביממא ובליליא טענתיה טענה ומודי

רש"י

דאי לא תימא הכי. הרי שלח ירמיה לאותן שהיו בבבל שגלו עם יכניה י"א שנה קודם גלות צדקיהו בנו בתים ושבו כי לא תלאו משם עד מלאת לבבל שבעים שנה למה ליה להזהירם על זאת אלא עצה טובה (ד) קמ"ל דהוה משיא אותם הכא נמי עצה טובה היא: תדע. דכל עלמו לא היה יגע ליעלם עצה טובה דקאמר להו נמי מקום גניזת שטרותיהם היכן הם מתקיימים יותר: מחיל איניש. על פירות קרקעו לאדם האוכלן: אלא מעתה. כיון דלאחרי שנין מחיל תיהדר ארעא ממי שילא עליו ערעור לסוף שנתים תיהדר ארעא לבעלים לבר מפירי דהא מחיל ליה עלייהו: אלמה אמר רב נחמן. לקמן בשמעתין:

עד כאן פירוש רש"י זצ"ל ד)

מכאן ואילך פירוש רבינו שמואל ב"ר מאיר

רשב"ם

אלמה אמר רב נחמן. לקמן בשמעתין גבי מחזיק בקרקע חבירו ואזיל אידך ואייתי סהדי דאכלן תרתין שנין ולא יותר ואמר רב נחמן הדרא ארעא והדרי פירי של שתי שנים: תרתי לא קפיד. על מה שזה יורד לתוך שדהו של חבירו בלא רשותו ומיהו פירי לא מחיל: תלת קפיד. הואיל ושילש באכילותו ליכנס בלא רשות הבעלים וזה ששתק ולא מיחה ודאי מכרו לו: ה"נ דלאלתר תיהוי חזקה. למי שירד לנכסי דבי בר אלישיב הואיל ולא מיחו (ה): אי מחית באפאי הוה מיזדהרנא בשטראי. יותר מג' שנים ומשני חברך חברא אית ליה ונודע לך שמחיתי ואם היתה לך קניה בידך כדבריך היה לך להזהר בשטרך יותר מג' שנים: שאכלן רצופות. אבל אם הניחה שנה שניה ואחר כך אכלה שתי שנים שלישית ורביעית מאי אמר בעל השדה האי דלא מחאי לך היינו משום דאוברת לה שנה שניה דגלית אדעתך דלאו דידך הואי והלכך לא זרעת אותה: חזקתן שלש שנים מיום ליום. שלא יהא הפסק בינתים: מהו דתימא מיום ליום. דקתני מתניתין למעוטי מקוטעות דלא תימא שלש שנים מקוטעות קאמר כי היכי דקתני סיפא שדה הבעל חזקתה שלש שנים ואינה מיום ליום אלא ג' חדשים בראשונה וג' חדשים באחרונה וי"ב באמצע: קמ"ל. רב הונא דדוקא קתני למעוטי מפוזרות: ומודה רב הונא. דדי לו בחזקת אכילת שנים מפוזרות: באתרא דמוברי באגי. במקום שנוהגין לזרוע שנה ולהוביר שנה שלא להכחיש את הקרקע דהא אחזיק בה כדמחזקי אינשי ומיהו שנה שהובירה אינה עולה (ו) לחשבון שלש שני חזקה וצריך לשמור שטרו יותר משלש שנים עד שילקוט שלש שנים ואי טעין אידך אני באתי בתוך שלש ומצאתי שדה ריקם ולכך לא מחיתי מאי הוי מ"מ היה לך למחות שאע"פ שלא זרעתיה הייתי עושה בה ניר שאחר הקציר והיה לך להבין שבשביל שלא להכחיש כחה לא חפצתי לזרעה כמנהג שדות העיר: והאי גברא מוברה. ועומדת בין שדות בורות כמותה: חדא ארעא בכולה באגא. שדה אחת זרועה בתוך בקעה גדולה איני יכול להושיב שם שומר לבדו בשבילה אבל כשכולן זרועות שוכרין שומר בין כולם וגם (ז) כן אין מכניסין שם בהמות: דעבדא טפי. בשנה הבאה: בליליא לא ידעי. ואפילו הכי הויא חזקה דבשלמא גבי שדה וכל הנך אין דרכן לעשות מלאכה בלילה וכשמעמידין עדים על מלאכת ימי שלש שנים הרי זו חזקה אבל בתים שדרך לדור בהן בלילה והוא אין יכול להביא עדים שראוהו דר אף בלילות וכיון דלית ליה סהדי על הלילות הוו להו מפוזרות ואם איתא לדרב הונא הא מצי אידך למיטען אני ראיתי שלא היית דר בלילות ולכך לא חשתי למחות דגלית אדעתך דלאו דידך הואי ולמאי הויא חזקה: שיבבי. השכנים שלו שראוהו דר בו יום ולילה ה) היו רגילין להעיד: שיבבי מידע ידעי. ואם יטעון ויאמר אייתי לי סהדי דדיירת ביה ביממא ובליליא יוכלו להעיד לו ומיהו אנן לא טענינן ליה כדמפרש בסמוך: דאי לא. שאם אין מעידין שהבית של משכיר: דייני דשפילי. שאין בקיאין בדין דייני הכי לקבל עדות אלו אם כבר נתנו שכר הבית למשכיר ומעולם בכי האי גוונא לא איירי רבא: אמר מר זוטרא אי טעין כו'. מילתא באנפי נפשה היא דפשיטא ליה למר זוטרא דאע"ג דבעו כל הנך אמוראי לעיל ג' שנים רצופות אפ"ה אין מחייבין את המחזיק להביא עדים שיעידו בפירוש על כל הימים והלילות אלא יעידו סתם שראוהו דר ג' שנים ומסתמא אם (ח) דר בבית אף בלילות דר בו וקאמר מר זוטרא דאי טעין מערער ואמר אייתי סהדי כו' טענתו טענה וצריך שיבואו עדים של לילות וימים דכיון דטעין טענת ברי דקאמר אני ראיתיו שלא דר בלילות בביתי ולכך לא מחיתי ואין חזקתו חזקה ולכך אני אומר אייתי סהדי דדר ביה תלת שנין בין ביממא בין בליליא הלכך צריך להביא עדים להכחישו ולומר לו שהיה לו למחות:

תוספות

שתא קמייתא לא קפיד וכו'. תימה (ט) מנא לן לר' ישמעאל דוקא יליף משור המועד ולא רבנן אינהו נמי מאי גמרי משור המועד דהיינו טעמא נמי דלעיל דגמר משור המועד דכיון דקפיד בג' זמנין ולא מיחה א"כ ודאי מכרה או נתנה לו וי"ל דלא דמי דודאי לר' ישמעאל דאזיל בתר אכילות שפיר מצי למיגמר משור המועד דמה התם הוחזק נגחן בג' פעמים אף כאן בשלש אכילות אם לא שמכרה לו היה מקפיד ואין זה וזה תלויים בשהוי זמן אבל לרבנן דתלוי בשהוי זמן כמה ישהה ויקפיד לא שייך למגמר משור המועד:

אלא מעתה מחאה שלא בפניו כו'. ור"י דליכא לאוקמי פירכא דאביי אלא כשכן (י) בעיר אחת דאי בעיר אחרת היכי פריך דלא תהא מחאה ותהא חזקה אדרבה כיון דלא הויא מחאה לא הויא חזקה דהא אינו צריך לבא בעיר אחרת לפני המחזיק ולמחות כדמוכח לקמן:

הני נוגעין בעדותן הן. ואם תאמר ולמאי הוו נוגעין בעדות הא איכא מיגו דה"מ אמרי פרענא לך אגר ואע"ג דבתר דתקון רבנן שבועת היסת לא מהימני לאסהודי בהאי מיגו כדאיתא בריש האיש מקדש (קדושין מג.) הכא לאמתמי' קיימינן ואכתי לא ליתקנה שבועת היסת מאי פריך להימניה במיגו ויש לומר דהאי לאו מיגו הוא שיראים לומר פרענו לך כי שמא יזכה האחר (כ) ויתבע מהם פעם שנית [וע"ע תוס' שבועות מה: ד"ה בעדים]:

אמר מר זוטרא אי טעין ואמר כו'. הקשה ר"י בר מרדכי לפ"ה כי לא טעין נמי מאי אמאי לא נשאל מהן כי שמא אין יודעין על הלילות שלא יועיל על פיהן שלא כדין דבכל עדיות אנו דורשין יפה וכאן נמי מאי אמאי לא נחקור אותן מספק ולאו פירכא היא דכיון שהעידו על הימים אפי' יאמרו אין אנו

רבינו גרשום

אלא אמר רבא. משום האי טעמא אמרו רבנן דבעינן ג' שנין לחזקה: מחיל איניש. ואינו חושש אם יעשה בה חבירו כלום תבואה אבל תלת לא מחיל והיכא דלא מיחה בג' שנין בודאי הוה חזקה: אם כן הואיל דאמרת דתרתי שנין מחיל ליה מאי דעביד בגוה: אם כן מיחה והדרא ארעא תיהדר לבר מפירי דעבד בה דקיימא השתא אלמה אמר רב נחמן וכו': לא קפיד אם שלא ברשותו ירד בה. תלת קפיד שלא יחזיק בה ומוחה: הכי נמי דתהוי לאלתר חזקה אם נשתמש אדם בנכסי דבר אלישיב. נתת דבריך לשיעורין דלמאן דלא קפיד יהבת ג' שנין לחזקה ולמאן דקפד לאלתר הוי חזקה: [תרתי ותלת] מיזדהר איניש בשטריה. שיהא שמור שאם יערער אדם על מקחו שיהא לו לראיה ושוב מייאש לשומרו וכיון לרבנן דקים להו דטפי לא מיזדהר מכלל שאם יבוא ויערער אדם לאחר ג' שנין אין בדבורו ממש אע"פ שאבד השטר משום דמוקמינן בידו בעדי חזקה שיש בידו ג' שנים: א"כ דטפי לא מיזדהר הואיל ולא שמע שום מערער: אם כן כי מיחה אדם בתוך ג' שנים במקום אחר שלא בפניו אמאי הוי מחאה הא מצי אמר ליה האי כיון דלא מחית באפאי לא מיזדהרנא בשטראי: ומשני דאמר ליה אידך חברך חברא אית ליה והוה לך לשמור שטרא: למעוטי מקוטעות שלא תהא סוף ראשונה ותחלת אחרונה ואמצעי' שלמה א) ולעולם שלמות בעינן ואפי' מפוזרות כגון שנה ראשונה ושלישית וחמישית קמ"ל רב הונא דרצופות בעינן ג' שנים והיינו מיום ליום דקאמר מתני': מודי רב הונא באתרא דמוברי באגי. שאותה שדה שזורעה שנה אחת. שניה מניחין אותה בורה אם כך רגילין אפי' לא החזיק כי אם מפוזרין הוה חזקה דמצי למימר ליה למערער החזקתי בה בשעה שרגילין בני אדם לעבוד שדותיהן: קמ"ל רב הונא. דמצי למימר לי' המחזיק איזרענא ארעאי הואיל דהני סביבותי אינן זורעין חדא ארעא בכולי באגי דאינן זרועין לא מצינא למינטר מקמיה דריסת רגל עוברין ושבין ומשו"ה לא זרענא לה. ואי נמי מצי למימר בהכי ניחא ליה דלא למיזרעה דעבדא טפי בשתא אחריתא: בליליא לא ידעי אינשי אי דייר בה המחזיק אי לא ואע"ג דהני תלת שנין אינן רצופין משום לילותא אפ"ה הויא חזקה וקשיא לרב הונא דאמר בעינן רצופין: ומתרץ אביי דמאן מסהיד אבתים דהאי מחזיק דייר בהם שיבבי הבית ואינהו מידע ידעי דהוה דייר ביה בין ביממא בין בלילה ואכתי רצופות נינהו: ורבא מתרץ כגון דאתו וכו' אנן אגרניה מינה דמחזיק: הני עדים נוגעין בעדותן דמשום ריוח שלהן מסייעי למחזיק דאי הוי אמרי ביממא דיירינן בלילה לא דיירינן לא הויא חזקה ושלא כדין יהביתו ליה ואכתי חייבין אתון למיתן למערער זימנא אחריתא אגריה ומשום הכי נוגעין בעדותן הן ואמאי מהימני. אמר ליה רב אשי דייני הכי דייני דשפילי מושפלים. דייני הכי שיהיו מאמינים להם מאחר שנתנו השכירות מי לא עסקינן דנקטי אכתי אגרי' בידי' ואמרי למאן ניתביה דאכתי לא יהבי דאינהו לא איכפת להו למאן מחייב להו למיתביה אי למחזיק אי למערער משום הכי מיהמני דלא נגעי בעדותן: אמר מר זוטרא כשטען המחזיק כבר היא בידי שני חזקה ואמר המערער לייתי סהדי דלסהוד ביה דדייר בה תלת שנין ביממא ובלילה טענתיה טענה אבל אי לא טעין הכי אנן לא ילפינן ליה למטען:

חשק שלמה על רבינו גרשום א) נראה דל"ל ולמעוטי שלמה דשלמות בעינן ולעולם אפי' מפחרות וכו'.

ומודי

The Gemara answers:

אָמַר לֵיהּ – [Rav Ashi] said to [Rav Yeimar]: דַּיָּינֵי דִּשְׁפִּילֵי הָכִי דָּאִינֵי – Only **ignorant judges would issue such a verdict.**[30] מִי לֹא עַסְקִינַן – **Are we not dealing** כְּגוֹן דִּנְקִיטֵי אֲגַר בֵּיתָא – with **a case in which [the tenants] are** still **holding the** unpaid **rent** for their three years of residence וְאָמְרֵי לְמַאן לִיתְבֵיהּ – **and are asking, "To whom should we give it?"** In this case, the renters have no interest in supporting the current holder's claim over that of the original owner. Their testimony can therefore be accepted. It was to such a case that Rava referred.

The Gemara elaborates on the need to substantiate continuous occupancy to establish a *chazakah*:

אָמַר מַר זוּטְרָא – **Mar Zutra said:** וְאִי טָעִין וְאָמַר – **But if [the original owner] claims,** לֵיתוּ תְּרֵי סַהֲדֵי לְאַסְהוּדֵי לֵיהּ – **"Let two witnesses come to testify on [the occupant's] behalf** דְּדָר בֵּיהּ תְּלַת שְׁנֵי בִּימָמָא וּבְלֵילְיָא – **that he lived in [the house] for three years, day and night,"** טַעֲנְתֵּיהּ טַעֲנָה – **his claim is a** legitimate **claim,** and the occupant must find witnesses who attest that he indeed lived in the house both day and night.[31]

NOTES

prefer to give testimony that would result in the house remaining in the possession of the current holder rather than allow it to return to the original owner, thereby subjecting them to new rent payments. Although they can recover their original payments from the dispossessed holder, they would prefer not to have to become involved in a court action (*Nimukei Yosef*).

[The disqualification of biased witnesses will be analyzed more fully in the Gemara below (43a-b).]

30. [Literally: *fallen* or *inferior judges.*] I.e. only unlearned judges would accept testimony from tenants who had already paid their rent to the current holder, and were consequently biased. Certainly, Rava did not refer to such a case (*Rashbam*)!

31. Mar Zutra takes it for granted that the rulings above mandating documentation of three full years of continuous occupancy do not mean, that under normal circumstances, the occupant of the house must produce witnesses who testify explicitly that he resided in the house day and night. Rather, as long as he produces witnesses who testify that he lived in the house for three years during the day, it can be assumed that he lived there at night as well [since it is highly unusual for a person to move out of a house at night and move back in the following morning (*Ritva*)]. Mar Zutra adds, however, that if the original owner claims that he did not protest because he *saw* that the occupant was absent from the house at night, the occupant must produce witnesses who explicitly contradict the original owner's assertion and attest to the fact that the occupant lived in the house all those nights as well (*Rashbam*; cf. *Tosafos* and *Ramban*).

דאי לא תימא הכי א) בנו בתים ושבו ונטעו גנות ואכלו את פרין מאי קאמר אלא עצה טובה קמ"ל הכא נמי עצה טובה קמ"ל תדע דכתיב ב) ונתתם בכלי חרש למען יעמדו ימים רבים אלא אמר רבא שתא קמייתא מחיל איניש תרתי מחיל תלת לא מחיל אמר ליה אביי אלא מעתה כי הדרא ארעא תיהדר לבר מפירי אלמה א) אמר רב נחמן הדרא ארעא והדרי פירי אלא אמר רבא שתא קמייתא לא קפיד איניש תרתי לא קפיד תלת קפיד א"ל אביי אלא מעתה כגון הני דבי בר אלישיב דקפדי אפילו אמאן דחליף אמיצרא דידהו הכי נמי דלאלתר הוי חזקה וכי תימא הכי נמי ג) אם כן נתת דבריך לשיעורין אלא אמר רבא ד) שתא קמייתא מיזדהר איניש בשטריה תרתי ותלת מיזדהר טפי לא מיזדהר אמר ליה אביי אלא מעתה מחאה שלא בפניו לא תיהוי מחאה דאמר ליה אי מחית (א) באפאי הוה מיזדהרנא בשטראי ה) דאמר ליה ו) חברך חברא אית ליה וחברא דחברך חברא אית ליה אמר רב הונא ז) שלש שנים שאמרו הוא שאכלן רצופות מאי קמ"ל תנינא חזקתן שלש שנים מיום ליום מהו דתימא מיום ליום לאפוקי מקוטעות ולעולם אפילו מפוזרות קמ"ל אמר רב חמא ח) ומודי רב הונא באתרי דמוברי באגי פשיטא לא צריכא דאיכא דמובר ואיכא דלא מובר והאי גברא מוברה מהו דתימא (ב) א"ל אם איתא דדידך הואי איבעי לך למיזרעה קמ"ל דאמר ליה חדא ארעא בכוליה באגא לא מצינא לינטר ואי נמי ה) בהכי ניחא לי דעבדא טפי תנן חזקת הבתים והא בתים דביממא ידעי בליליא לא ידעי אמר אביי מאן מסהיד אבתים שיבבי י) שיבבי מידע ידעי ביממא ובליליא רבא אמר ז) כגון דאתו בי תרי ואמרי אנן אגרינן מיניה ודרינן ביה תלת שנין ביממא ובליליא אמר ליה רב יימר לרב אשי הני נוגעין בעדותן הן דאי לא אמרי הכי אמרינן להו זילו הבו ליה אגר ביתא להאי א"ל דייני דשפילי (ג) הכי דאיני מי לא עסקינן ח) כגון דנקיטי אגר ביתא ואמרי למאן ליתביה אמר מר זוטרא ט) ואי טעין ואמר ליתו תרי סהדי לאסהודי ליה דדר ביה תלת שני ביממא ובליליא טענתיה טענה

ומודי

רש"י

דאי לא תימא הכי. הרי שלח ירמיה לאותן שהיו בבבל שגלו עם יכניה י"א שנה קודם גלות צדקיהו בנו בתים ושבו כי לא תלאו משם עד מלאת לבבל שבעים שנה למה ליה להזהירם על זאת אלא עלה טובה (ד) קמ"ל דהוא משיא אותם הכא נמי עלה טובה בעלמא היא: תדע. דכל עלמו היה יגע ליעלם עלה טובה דקאמר להו נמי מקום גניזת שטרותיהם היכן הם מתקיימים יותר: מחיל איניש. על פירות קרקעו לאדם האוכלן: אלא מעתה. כיון דלאחרי שנין מחיל תיהדר ארעא ממי שילא עליו ערעור לסוף שנתים תיהדר ארעא לבעלים לבר מפירי דהא מחיל ליה עלייהו: אלמה אמר רב נחמן. לקמן בשמעתין:

עד כאן פירוש רש"י זצ"ל ד)

מכאן ואילך פירוש רבינו שמואל ב"ר מאיר

אלמה אמר רב נחמן. לקמן בשמעתין גבי מחזיק בקרקע חבירו ואזיל אידך ואייתי סהדי דאכלן תרתין שנין ולא יותר ואמר רב נחמן הדרא ארעא והדרי פירי של שתי שנים: תרתי לא קפדי. על מה שזה יורד לתוך שדהו של חבירו בלא רשותו ומיהו פירי לא מחיל: תלת קפיד. הואיל ושילש באוולותו ליכנס בלא רשות הבעלים וזה שותק ולא מיחה ודאי מכרו לו: ה"נ דלאלתר תיהוי חזקה. למי שירד לנכסי דבי בר אלישיב הואיל ולא מיחו (ה): אי מחית באפאי הוה מיזדהרנא בשטראי. יותר מג' שנים ומשני חברך חברא אית ליה ואודע לך שמחיתי ואם היתה לקוחה בידך לכדריך היה לך להזהר בשטרך יותר מג' שנים: שאכלן רצופות. אבל אם הניחה שנה שניה ואחר כך אכלה שתי שנים שלישית ורביעית מלי אמר בעל השדה האי דלא מחאי לך היינו משום דאוברת לה שנה שניה דגלית אדעתך דלאו דידך הואי והלכך לא זרעת אותה: חזקתן שלש שנים מיום ליום. שלא יהיה הפסק בינתים: מהו דתימא מיום ליום. דקתני מתניתין למעוטי מקוטעות דלא תימא שלש שנים מקוטעות קאמר כי היכי דקתני סיפא שדה הבעל חזקתה שלש שנים ואינה מיום ליום אלא ג' חדשים בראשונה וג' חדשים באחרונה וי"ב באמצע:

קמ"ל. רב הונא דדוקא קתני למעוטי מפוזרות: ומודה רב הונא. דדי לו בחזקת אכילת שנים מפוזרות: באתרא דמוברי באגי. במקום שנוהגין לזרוע שנה ולהוביר שנה שלא להכחיש את הקרקע דהא אחזיק בה כדמחזקי אינשי ומיהו שנה שהובירה אינה עולה (ו) לחשבון שלש שני חזקה וצריך לשמור שטרו יותר משלש שנים עד שילקוט שלש שנים ואי טוען אידך אני באתי בתוך שלש ומצאתי שדה ריקם ולכך לא מחיתי מלי א"ל מ"מ היה לך למחות שאע"פ שלא זרעתיה הייתי עושה בה ניר שאחר הקציר והיה לך להבין שבשביל שלא להכחיש כחה לא חפצתי לזרעה כמנהג שדות העיר: והאי גברא מוברה. ועומדת בין שדות בורות כמותה: חדא ארעא בכולה באגא. שדה אחת זרועה בתוך בקעה גדולה איני יכול להושיב שם שומר לבדו בשבילה אבל כשכולן זרועות שוכרין שומר בין כולם וגם (ז) כן אין מכניסין שם בהמות: דעבדה טפי. בשנה הבאה: בליליא לא ידעי. ואפילו הכי הויא חזקה דבשלמא גבי שדה וכל הנך אין דרכן לעשות מלאכה בלילה וכשמעמידין עדים על מלאכת ימי שלש שנים הרי זו חזקה אבל בתים שדרך לדור בהן בלילה והוא אין יכול להביא עדים שראוהו דר אף בלילות וכיון דלית ליה סהדי על הלילות הוו להו מפוזרות ואם איתא לדרב הונא הא מצי אידך למיטען אני ראיתי שלא היית דר בלילות ולכך לא חשתי למחות דגלית אדעתך דלאו דידך הואי ואמאי הויא חזקה: שיבבי. השכנים שלו שראוהו דר בו יום ולילה ט) היו רגילין להעיד: שיבבי מידע ידעי. ואם יטעון ויאמר אייתי לי סהדי דדירת ביה ביממא ובליליא יוכלו להעיד לו ומיהו אנן לא טענינן ליה כדמפרש בסמוך: דאי לא. שאם אין מעידין שהבית של משכיר: דייני דשפילי. שאינן בקיאין בדין דייני הכי לקבל עדות אלו אם כבר נתנו שכר הבית למשכיר ומעולם בכי האי גוונא לא איירי רבא: אמר מר זוטרא אי טעין כו'. מילתא באנפי נפשה היא דפשיטא ליה למר זוטרא דאע"ג דבעו כל הנך אמוראי לעיל ג' שנים רצופות אפ"ה אין מחייבין את המחזיק להביא עדים שיעידו בפירוש על כל הימים והלילות אלא יעידו סתם שראוהו דר ג' שנים ומסתמא אם (ח) דר בבית אף בלילות דר בו וקאמר מר זוטרא דאי טוען מערער ואמר אייתי סהדי כו' טענתו טענה וצריך שיבואו עדים של לילות וימים דכיון דטוען טענת ברי דקאמר אני ראיתיו שלא דר בלילות בביתי ולכך לא מחיתי ואין חזקתו חזקה ולכך אני אומר אייתי סהדי דדר ביה תלת שנין בין ביממא בין בליליא הלכך צריך להביא עדים להכחישו ולומר לו שהיה לו למחות:

הכי

תוספות

שתא קמייתא לא קפיד וכו'. תימה (ט) מנא לן דר' ישמעאל דוקא יליף משור המועד ולא רבנן אינהו נמי מלי גמרי משור המועד דהיינו טעמא נמי דלעיל דגמר משור המועד דכיון דקפיד בג' זמנין ולא מיחה א"כ ודאי מכרה או נתנה לו וי"ל דלא דמי דודאי דר' ישמעאל דאזיל בתר אכילות שפיר מצי למיגמר משור המועד דמה התם הוחזק נגחן בג' פעמים אף כאן בשלש אכילות אם לא שמכרה לו היה מקפיד ואין זה וזה תלויים בשהוי זמן אבל לרבנן דתלוי בשהוי זמן כמה ישהה ויקפיד לא שייך למגמר משור המועד: אלא מעתה מחאה שלא בפניו כו'. אור"י דליכא לאוקמי פירכא דאביי אלא כשהן (י) בעיר אחת דאי בעיר אחרת היכי פריך דלא תהא מחאה ותהא חזקה אדרבה כיון דלא הויא מחאה לא הויא חזקה דהא אינו צריך לבא בעיר אחרת לפני המחזיק ולמחות כדמוכח לקמן: הני נוגעין בעדותן הן. ואם תאמר ואמאי הוו נוגעין בעדות הא איכא מיגו דה"מ אמרי פרענא לך אגר ואע"ג דבתר דתקון רבנן שבועת היסת לא מהימני לאסהודי בהאי מיגו כדאיתא בריש האיש מקדש (קדושין מג:) הכא דאמתני' קיימינן ואכתי לא ניתקנה שבועת היסת מאי פריך להימניה במיגו ויש לומר דהאי לאו מיגו הוא שיראים לומר פרענו לך כי שמא יזכה האחר (כ) ויתבע מהם פעם שנית [וע"ע תוס' שבועות מה: ד"ה בעדים]: אמר מר זוטרא אי טעין ואמר כו'. הקשה ר"י בר מרדכי לפ"ה כי לא טעין נמי אמאי לא נשאל מהן כי שמא אינן יודעין על הלילות שלא נוליא על פיהן שלא כדין דבכל עדיות אנו דורשין יפה וכאן נמי אמאי לא נחקור אותן מספק ולאו פירכא היא דכיון שהעידו על הימים אפי' יאמרו אין אנו

עין משפט נר מצוה

ג א מיי' פי"א מהלכות טוען הלכה ב [ד] סמג עשין לה טוש"ע ח"מ סי' קמ סעיף ו:
ד ב מיי' שם הל' ה וסמג שם טוש"ע ח"מ סי' קמו סעיף א:
ה ג מיי' שם פי"ב הל' ד סמג שם טוש"ע ח"מ סי' קמ סעיף ח וסי' קמא סעיף ג:
ו ד ה מיי' שם טוש"ע ח"מ סימן קמא סעיף ג:
ז ו ז מיי' שם הלכה ב סמג שם טוש"ע ח"מ סי' קמ סעיף ח וע"ש בהג"ה:
ח ח [וע"ש בהגהות וכמ"מ] טוש"ע שם סעיף ט וסי' לז סעיף יב:
ט ט מיי' שם הלכה ב טוש"ע שם סי' קמ סעיף ח:

רבינו גרשום

אלא אמר רבא. משום האי טעמא אמרו רבנן דבעינן ג' שנין לחזקה: מחיל איניש ואינו חושש אם יעשה בה חבירו כלום תבואה אבל תלת לא מחיל והיכא דלא מיחה בג' שנין בודאי הוה חזקה: אם כן הואיל דאמרת דתרתי שנין מחיל ליה מאי דעביד בגווה: אם כן מיחה והדרא ארעא תיהדר לבר מפירי דעבד בה דקיימא השתא אלמה אמר רב נחמן וכו': לא קפיד אם שלא ברשותו ירד בה. תלת קפיד שלא יחזיק בה ומוחה: הכי נמי דתהוי לאלתר חזקה אם נשתמש אדם בנכסי דבר אלישיב. נתת דבריך לשיעורין דלמאן דלא קפיד יהבת ג' שנין לחזקה ולמאן דקפדי לאלתר הוי חזקה: [תרתי ותלת] מיזדהר איניש בשטריה. שיהא שמור שאם יערער אדם על מקחו שיהא לו לראיה ושוב מייאש לשומרו וכיון דהכי קים להו לרבנן דטפי לא מיזדהר מכלל שאם יבוא ויערער אדם לאחר ג' שנין אין בדבורו ממש אע"פ שאבד השטר משום דמוקמינן בידו בעדי חזקה שיש בידו ג' שנים: א"כ דטפי לא מיזדהר הואיל ולא שמע שום מערער: אם כן כי מיחה אדם בתוך ג' שנים במקום אחר שלא בפניו אמאי הוי מחאה הא מצי אמר ליה האי כיון דלא מחית באפאי לא מיזדהרנא בשטראי: ומשני דאמר ליה אידך חברך חברא אית ליה והוה לך לשמור שטרא: למעוטי מקוטעות שלא ההא סוף ראשונה ותחלת אחרונה ואמצעי' שלמה א) ולעולם שלמות בעינן ואפי' מפוזרות כגון שנה ראשונה ושלישית וחמישית קמ"ל רב הונא דרצופות בעינן ג' שנים והיינו מיום ליום דקאמר מתני': מודי רב הונא באתרא דמוברי באגי. שאותה שדה שזורעה שנה אחת שנה מניחין אותה בורה אם כך רגילין אפי' לא החזיק כי אם מפוזרות הוה חזקה דמצי למימר ליה למערער החזקתי בה בשעה שרגילין בני אדם לעבוד

מסורת הש"ס

א) [לקמן לג.] ב) [שבת לה: מגילה יח: גיטין יז: חולין ט. לב:] ג) [לעיל כח: וש"נ] ד) בדפוס פיזרו הנוסח "כאן מת רש"י ז"ל" ה) נ"ל הס:

הגהות הב"ח

(א) גמ' אי מחית באנפאי הוה: (ב) שם מהו דתימא מהו א"ל אם איתא וכו' לא מצינא דלינטר ואי נמי: (ג) שם דייני דשפילי דייני הכי מי לא: (ד) רש"י ד"ה דאי לא וכו' עלה טובה היא משיא כל"ל ותיבות קמ"ל דהוא נמחק: (ה) רשב"ם ד"ה ה"נ דלאלתר וכו' ולא מיחו הס"ד ואח"כ מ"ה טפי לא מזדהר הלכך היה לבעלים הראשונים למחות בתוך שלש שלא יחזיק בקרקע שלו ואם לא מיחה מ"ה אי מחית: (ו) ד"ה באתרא וכו' עולה לו לחשבון וכו' אלא שילקוט תבואות של ג' שנים ואי טוען אידך ואומר אני: (ז) ד"ה חדא וכו' וגם אין מכניסין שם: (ח) ד"ה אמר מר זוטרא וכו' ומסתמא אם דר בימים דר וכו': (ט) תוס' ד"ה שתא וכו' תימה א"כ מנא לן: (י) ד"ה אלא כשהן דרין בעיר אחת וכו' לבוא לעיר אחרת: (כ) ד"ה הני וכו' יזכה האחר בדין ויתבע:

תורה אור השלם

א) בְּנוּ בָתִּים וְשֵׁבוּ וְנִטְעוּ גַנּוֹת וְאִכְלוּ אֶת פִּרְיָן: [ירמיה כט, ה]

ב) כֹּה אָמַר יְיָ צְבָאוֹת אֱלֹהֵי יִשְׂרָאֵל לָקוֹחַ אֶת הַסְּפָרִים הָאֵלֶּה אֵת סֵפֶר הַמִּקְנָה הַזֶּה וְאֵת הֶחָתוּם וְאֵת סֵפֶר הַגָּלוּי הַזֶּה וּנְתַתָּם בִּכְלִי חָרֶשׂ לְמַעַן יַעַמְדוּ יָמִים רַבִּים: [ירמיה לב, יד]

ליקוטי רש"י

אמר רב נחמן הדרא ארעא. דבתרתין שנין לא הויא חזקה. והדרי פירי. שאכל שלא כדין דהא לא עלו ליה מעיקרא אלא לפירות דלא עבדי אינשי [רשב"ם לקמן לג:]. כגון הני דבי בר אלישיב. אלים חזק [גיטין יד.]. מחאה שלא בפניו לא תיהוי מחאה. כגון שמיחה בעיר אחת ומיחה בפני עדים בעיר אחרת [כתובות יז:]. אם מיחה המערער בתוך שלש שנים לפני עדים שלא בפני המחזיק ואמר להם דעו שפלוני מחזיק בקרקע שלי שגזלה לא תיהוי מחאה [לעיל כח:]. חברך חברא אית ליה. וידיעתו [כתובות קט:]. דכולי דמאי באנפשיהו מגלו לאחריני והם מגלו לאחרים עד שיגיע לאוזני המחזיק וה"ל לאזדהורי בשטריה [שם יז:]. חס מגלה לחבירו וזה לחבירו עד שיודע [ערכין טז.].

שדותיהן: קמ"ל רב הונא. דמצי למימר לי' המחזיק איזרענא ארעאי הואיל דהני סביבותי אינן זורעין [illegible] **חדא ארעא בכולי באגי לא מצינא למינטר** [illegible] **ואי נמי מצי למימר בהכי ניחא ליה** [illegible] **בליליא לא ידעי** [illegible] **אביי דמאן מסהיד אבתים** [illegible] **שיבבי** [illegible] **מידע ידעי** [illegible] **הני עדים נוגעין בעדותן** [illegible] **אנן אגרינן מינה** [illegible] **דייני דשפילי** [illegible] **מי לא עסקינן דנקיטי אגר ביתא** [illegible] **אמר מר זוטרא כשטוען** [illegible] **ואמר** המערער לייתי סהדי לסהדו ביה דדייר בה תלת שנין ביממא ובליליה טענתיה טענה אבל אי לא טעין הכי אנן לא לפינן ליה למטען:

ומודי

חשק שלמה על רבינו גרשום א) נראה דל"ל ולאפוקי שלמה דשלמות בעינן ולעולם אפי' מפוזרות וכו'.

א ומודי מר זוטרא ברוכלין המחזירין בעיירות דאע"ג דלא טען טענינן ליה אנן ב ומודה רב הונא בחנותא דמחוזא דלימאמא עבידא לליליא לא עבידא רמי בר חמא ורב עוקבא בר חמא זבון ההיא אמתא בהדי הדדי מר אישתמש בה ראשונה שלישית וחמישית ומר אישתמש בה שניה רביעית וששית נפק ערער עילוה אתו לקמיה דרבא אמר להו מאי טעמא עבדיתו הכי כי היכי דלא תחזקו אהדדי ג כי היכי דלדידכו לא הוי חזקה לעלמא נמי לא הוי חזקה ולא אמרן אלא דלא כתוב עיטרא ד אבל כתוב עיטרא קלא אית ליה אמר רבא ה אכלה כולה חוץ מבית רובע קנה כולה חוץ מבית רובע אמר רב הונא בריה דרב יהושע ולא אמרן אלא (א) דבר זריעה היא אבל לאו בר זריעה היא אגב ארעא קני לה מתקיף לה רב ביבי בר אביי אלא מעתה צונמא במה יקנה ו אלא באוקומי בה חיותא ומשטחא בה פירי ה"נ איבעי ליה לאוקומי בה חיותא אי נמי משטחא בה פירי ז ההוא דאמר ליה לחבריה מאי בעית בהאי ביתא אמר ליה מינך זבינתיה ואכלית שני חזקה א"ל אנא בשכוני גוואי הואי (ב) אתא לקמיה דרב נחמן אמר ליה ח זיל ברור אכילתך אמר ליה רבא ט הכי דינא המוציא מחבירו עליו הראיה ורמי דרבא אדרבא ורמי דרב נחמן אדרב נחמן דההוא דא"ל

רשב"ם

הכי גרסינן ומודה מר זוטרא ברוכלין המחזירין בעיירות דאע"ג כו'. אע"ג דסבירא (ג) למר זוטרא דאי טעין טענתיה טענה אבל אנו לא נטעון בשבילו מודי הוא היכא דהוי מערער רוכל המחזר בעיירות למכור קישוטי נשים ואינו חוזר לעירו כי אם לזמן ארוך דאע"ג דלא טעין לייתי מחזיק סהדי דדר בה רצופות יומם ולילה אנן טענינן ליה דדילמא משום דלא קביע במתא החזיק זה בביתו וכי הוה אתי במתא הוי נפיק האי מחזיק מן ביתא ולא ידע ליה זה המערער מעולם שהחזיק זה בביתו ולכך שתק ולא מיחה הלכך יביא המחזיק עדים שלא יצא מן הבית כל שלש השנים אפילו לילה אחת. ול"ג ומודי רבא דהא לא איירי רבא לעיל אי טענינן ליה או טעין איהו לנפשיה וכל מאי דתריך רבא לעיל אליבא דרב הונא תריך ואי גרסינן הכי הוה לן למיגרס ומודה רב הונא: ומודה רב הונא. אע"ג דבעי רצופות יום ולילה בחנווניות דמחוזא חנויות שמוכרין בהן לחם ויין דאי טעין אין חוששין לטענתו דאע"ג דלא דר בו בלילות חזקה מעלייתא היא שאין דירתן אלא ביום: מר אישתמש ראשונה כו'. עובדת לזה שנה ולזה שנה שאין אחד מהן יכול להחזיק בה ג' שנים רצופות להפסיד חבירו: עיטרא. שטר חלוקה ובעדים שתעבוד לזה שנה ולזה שנה י"מ קלא אית ליה והיה לו למחות מיד ולא מיחה ולאלתר הויא חזקה דכמי שמכרה להם (ד) בפניו דמי שהרי הניחם להביא עדים ולכתוב עליו שטר חלוקה ושתק אי נמי כיון דאיכא תרתי שני חזקה מפוזרות ועיטרא איכא קלא וכחזקה גמורה דמי דהיה לו למחות ולא מיחה ואין נראה לי כלל אלא משלש שנים ראשונות הויא חזקה כיון דאיכא עדים ושטר בין זה לזה כדאמרינן לקמן בפירקין (דף מא:) שלש לקוחות מצטרפות אמר רב וכולן בשטר אלמא אמר רב אע"ג דכל אחד אין מחזיק אלא שנה אחת מצטרפים שלש השנים לחזקה משום דמכח שטר קאתו ה"נ לא שנא והיינו טעמא דהויא חזקה שהיה לו למערער למחות בתוך שלש שנים ואינו יכול לומר בשביל שראיתי' מחזיק בדילוג לא מחיתי שהייתי סבור לכך אתם עושים שאתם יראים להחזיק שנים רצופות שהשטר מוכיח שלא בשביל כן עושים אלא שע"מ כן חלקו שכן יהו משתמשין וכן עיקר: חוץ מבית רובע. באותו שדה שלא נעבד בו ולא נזרע: דבר זריעה היא. דאמר ליה אי דידך הואי אמאי לא זרעת והלכך לא מחיתי: אלא מעתה. הלוקח מחבירו צונמא (ה) במאי קני לה באיזו אכילה של שלש שנים הואיל ואינה בת זריעה וכי אינו קונה אותה בהעמדת שם בהמותיו לרבוץ ולרעות או לשטיחת פירותיו: הכא נמי כו'. ולא קני לה אגב ארעא: ואכלתיה שני חזקה. ואבדתי שטרי ואתה לא מחית לי שאזדהר בשטרי: אמר ליה. מערער: אנא בשכוני גוואי הואי. בחדרים הפנימים היתה עיקר דירתי והייתי עובר דרך עליך ומשתמש עמך בבית החיצון שדרת בו ברשותי ולכך לא מחיתי: אמר ליה. למחזיק: זיל ברור אכילתך. הבא עדים שדרת בבית לבדך ג' שנים בלא אותו שבא עמך (ו) כדין כל חזקת ג' שנים שצריך להביא עדים שהחזיק בה חזקה גמורה: המוציא מחבירו. דהיינו מוכר שהרי לוקח מוחזק: עליו. (ז) למערער להביא ראיה שנשתמש עמו וסבירא ליה לרבא דכיון שראו עדים לזה המוחזק שנשתמש בו שלש שנים אין לנו לחוש שמא גם זה היה עמו הואיל ולא שמענו בלתי היום. והאי עובדא לא מתוקם אלא כשהיה לו עדות למערער דבית זה שלו היה אבל בלא עדות אפילו רב נחמן מודי דהמחזיק נאמן בלא ראיה שהפה שאסר הוא הפה שהתיר דאי בעי אמר שלי הוא מעולם כי אמר נמי מינך זבינתה מהימן: כל

תוספות

אנו יודעים על הלילות מסתמא כיון שדר בימים דר נמי בלילות אם לא שטוען המערער שבודאי לא דר ור"ח פירש דמר זוטרא קאי אפירכא דרב יימר דפריך נוגעין בעדותן הן וקאמר מר זוטרא אי טעין ואמר המחזיק לייתו תרי סהדי דדרו ביה שלש שנים ביום ובלילה והבו לי אגרא ונפקו ואזלו להו והנהו דדיירי ביה אחריני ניתנו טענתו טענה ולא נוגעין בעדותן הן (ח) דלא דיירי בה השתא דמצי למימר להו הבו לי אגר ביתא אלא אינהו אמרו דיירנא ואינהו אמרו פרענו והפה שאסר הוא הפה שהתיר דאי בעו אמרי לא דיירנא ביה וליכא למימר דדילמא מכחיש להו שהוא לא היה יודע כלל שהיו דרים באותו בית ובסמוך לא גרסינן מודה מר זוטרא אלא ומודה רבא דבעי' שלש שנין ביממא ובליליא אם הנך עדים (ט) רוכלים המחזרים בעיירות אע"ג דלא אמרו דדרו ביה שלש שנין ביממא ובליליא אלא אמרי בידינו היה זה הבית שלש שנים רצופות אע"ג שימים רבים הם מחזרים בעיירות ולא היו (י) בזה הבית עדותן עדות ור"ח גרס דדיירנא ביה שלש שנין ופירש דאביי ורבא תרוייהו סבירא להו דאין צריך להביא עדים על הימים ועל הלילות ורבא לא אמר ביממא ובליליא אלא להוציא המקשה מסברתו ולא לפלוגי אאביי אתא וקאמר מר זוטרא אם אמר העידוני סתם שדרתי ג' שנים בחזקת ימים ולילות אע"פ שלא ראו ממש כל הימים והלילות אלא שבחזקת כן מחזקין אותו שכל שעה שהיו נכנסים פעמים ביום ופעמים בלילה היו רואין אותו בביתו טענתיה טענה והוה ליה למימר עדותן עדות אלא אגב דנקיט ברישא דמילתיה אי טעין אומר נמי טענתיה טענה ומודה רבא וה"ה מר זוטרא ואביי ברוכלין המחזרין בעיירות אף על גב דלא טען טענינן ליה דאין צריכים להעיד שראו ממש שהרי הם מחזרין בעיירות ואין יכולין להעיד על הראיה אלא יעידו שבחזקתו היה זה הבית שלש שנים ימים ולילות: **ומודה** רב הונא בחנותא דמחוזא דביממא עבדי ובליליא לא עבדי. פירוש ומועיל להם אם החזיקו ג' שנים ואע"ג דלאו שלש רצופות אלא מפוזרות כיון דאורחייהו בהכי דהוי כאתרי דמוברי באגי ואם תאמר א"כ פשיטא דמודה רב הונא כדפריך לעיל גבי באגי וי"ל לפי שבני אדם שאינם חנונים דרים בהן בין ביום ובלילה ואותן צריכים ג' שנים רצופות יום ולילה וס"ד דחנונים נמי יצטרכו כן קא משמע לן ומהאי טעמא אתי שפיר דבעינן להו שלש שנים שלימות דהיינו ו' שנים אע"ג דבשדות ובית הבדים לא בעינן אלא שלש שנים בין הכל (אלא) היינו משום דכמו שאר בני אדם הדרים שם שאין חנונים בעו ג' שנים ביום ובלילה ה"נ חנונים בעו ג' שנים שלימות דהיינו ו' שנים והא דלא אייתי להא לעיל גבי ומודה רב הונא אומר ר"ת משום דלא סלקא שמעתתא דבתי וכי האי גוונא איכא בסוף [הכונס] (ב"ק דף סא:) גבי ומודו חכמים לרבי יהודה: **דלא** תחזקו אהדדי. ואע"ג דתנן לקמן (דף מב.) השותפין אין להם חזקה זה על זה פרש"י דהכא הוזקקו לעשות כן לפי שלא היה להם עדי שותפות וקשיא לר"י דא"כ אותו שהחזיק שנה ראשונה יאמר שהוא שלו כיון שאין עדים שיש לחבירו חלק ונראה לר"י דלא היו רוצים שיחזיק האחד שלש שנים שלא תשתכח השותפות: **אבל** כתוב עיטרא קלא אית לה. והא דאמר בהמפקיד (ב"מ לט. ושם ד"ה לא) גבי אין מורידין לנכסי קטן ל"ש עביד עיטרא ל"ש לא עביד אין מורידין גבי יתמי החמירו [וע"ע תוס' גיטין כח. ד"ה והניחו]: **בשכוני** גוואי הואי. והואי לי (כ) אורח עלך ונראה לי שהיה לו עדים שהיה בשכוני גוואי אבל לא היו יודעים באיזה דרך היה יוצא דאי לא היה לו עדים כלל דהוה בשכוני גוואי היכי הוה קאמר רב נחמן זיל ברור אכילתך דאטו יש להם לעדי חזקה לידע שלא היה המערער באותו בית כל שלש שנים ואם יאמר המערער הייתי עמך שני ימים ואין לך שלש שנים שלימות והעדים אין יודעים יפסיד: לאו

עין משפט נר מצוה

י א מיי' פי"ב מהלכות טוען הלכה ג סמג עשין לה טוש"ע ח"מ סי' קמ סעיף ח:

יא ב מיי' שם ועי' בהשגות טוש"ע שם סעיף יד:

יב ג ד מיי' שם הלכה ה וסמג שם טוש"ע ח"מ סי' קמד סעיף א:

יג ה מיי' שם הלכה טז וסמג שם טוש"ע ח"מ סימן קמא סעיף יד:

יד ו מיי' פ"א מהלכות מכירה הלכה טו ועי' בהשגות ובמ"מ סמג עשין פב טוש"ע ח"מ סימן קצב סעיף ח וסימן קמא סעיף יג:

טו ז מיי' פי"ב מהלכות טוען הלכה יג סמג עשין לה טוש"ע ח"מ סי' קמא סעיף יב וסעיף יד:

טז ח ט מיי' שם פט"ו הלכה י' עי' מ"מ סמג שם טוש"ע ח"מ סי' קמו סעיף יא וסעיף יב:

רבינו גרשום

מודי מר זוטרא ברוכלין. דאי האי מחזיק הוי רוכל המחזר בעיירות דלא מצי למידר בה ביממא ובלילה מפני שהולך בסחורתו ואמר הרוכל החזקתי ג' שנים בלא ערעור והאי לא ידע לטעון כנגדו כיון דקים (ליה) [לן] דרוכל אינו שוהה תדיר בביתו שמא איתרמי דזה בא וכיון שלא ראהו שהיה דר שם שתיק ליה להכי ילפינן ליה למערער למיטען דליתי האי רוכל סהדי דדר בה בין ביממא בין בלילא ואי לא לא הוי חזקה: ומודי רב הונא. דאמר לעיל ג' שנים רצופות דמשמע בין בימאמא בין בלילה מודי דאי אחזיק חד בחנות דמיחזק בג' שנים ביממא אע"ג דלא דר בה בלילא הוה חזקה משום דלימאמא עבידי למיתב בהו ולא בלילה דמצי למימר המחזיק עבדי בה כדעבדי אינשי בימאמא: כי היכי דלדידכו לא הויא חזקה. משום דלית חד מיניה דאחזיק רצופין לעלמא נמי לא הויא חזקה ומשלמיתו לה למערער. והני מילי דלא הוי חזקה היכא דלא כתבי שטרא שטר חלוקה שתעבוד לזה שנה ולזה שנה אבל כתבו שטר חלוקה אע"ג דלא החזיקו בה ג' שנים רצופות הויא חזקה משום דעיטרא קלא אית להו ולאלתר איבעי ליה למיתי ולערער וכיון דלא ערער הויא חזקה: אמר רבא אכלה כולה קרקע שני חזקה חוץ מבית רובע בה: אבל לאו בת זריעה היא. אותו בית רובע: אלא מעתה הא צונמא דלאו בת זריעה היא ולא קני ליה אגב ארעא אי לא שטח בה פירי הכא נמי בהאי בית רובע אי לא יעביד בה מידי לא קני לה אגב ארעא: אנא בשכוני גואי. והחזקתי בה ולא שמשתה בה יותר ממני. אמר ליה ללוקח זיל ברור אכילתך כלומר הבא עדים שלא שימש עמך בבתי גואי ותחזיק בהו. ורב נחמן אוקמה השתא ביד מוכר ולהכי אמר ליה רבא דינא הכי ביד לוקח הוה לך לאוקמה ויהא המוכר המוציא מחבירו עליו הראיה דמוכר להוציא קאתי:

מסורת הש"ס

א) [לקמן דף קנט:], ב) נ"ל דינא הכי:

הגהות הב"ח

(א) גמ' דבת זריעה: (ב) שם אתו לקמיה דרב נחמן: (ג) רשב"ם ד"ה הכי גרסי' וכו' דסבירא ליה למר זוטרא וכו' ולא ידע זה כצ"ל ותיבת ליה נמחק: (ד) ד"ה עיטרא וכו' להם בפנינו דמי וכו' ולכתוב עליה שטר: (ה) ד"ה אלא וכו' צונמא טרשין במאי קני: (ו) ד"ה זיל ברור וכו' שבא עמך בדין כדין: (ז) ד"ה עליו להביא ראיה כצ"ל ותיבת למערער נמחק: (ח) תוס' ד"ה (בע"א) אמר וכו' בעדותן הן דהא לא דיירי: (ט) בא"ד עדים הם רוכלים: (י) בא"ד ולא היו לנים בזה הבית: (כ) ד"ה בשכוני גוואי הואי והואי לי דרך עליך:

ליקוטי רש"י

עיטרא. שטר חלוקה רק הבמות לא סרו (מלכים ב יב) מתרגם לא עטרא [גיטין פו.]. עיטרא. שטר חלוקה כשחלקו מתחילה (מלכים ב יב) רק הבמות לא סרו מתרגמינן במתא לא עטדו לא הפליגו מהם [ב"מ לט: ועי"ש במסורת הש"ס]. צונמא. צונמא בלשון ארמי סלע [בראשית מא, כג ונדה ח:]. סלע חזק [לעיל יח.]. אבן [רשב"ם לקמן פט:].

The Gemara qualifies this ruling:

וּמוֹדֵי מַר זוּטְרָא – And Mar Zutra agrees **בְּרוֹכְלִין הַמְּחֲזִירִין בָּעֲיָירוֹת** – **in** cases where the original owners are **peddlers who make** their **rounds of the cities** **דְּאַף עַל גַּב דְּלֹא טָעַן – that even though [the original owner] does not claim** that he saw the occupant absent from the premises at night, **טָעֲנִינַן לֵיהּ אֲנַן – we** advance **the claim on [the original owner's] behalf,** and the occupant must produce witnesses who substantiate his three years of nighttime occupancy as well.[1]

The Gemara now qualifies Rav Huna's requirement that the three years needed to establish a *chazakah* must be consecutive: **וּמוֹדֶה רַב הוּנָא – And Rav Huna agrees** **בְּחֶנְוָתָא דִּמְחוֹזָא – in** the case of **the stores of Mechuza** that the occupant need not produce proof that he was present at nighttime. **דְּלִימָמָא עֲבִידָא לְלֵילְיָא לֹא עֲבִידָא – For** such a store **is made for daytime** use, but **it is not made for nighttime** use.[2]

The Gemara cites an application of the requirement that the three-year utilization be continuous:

רָמִי בַּר חָמָא וְרַב עוּקְבָא בַּר חָמָא – Rami bar Chama and Rav Ukva bar Chama **זְבוּן הַהִיא אַמְתָא בַּהֲדֵי הֲדָדֵי – bought a certain maidservant jointly.** **מַר אִישְׁתַּמֵּשׁ בָּהּ רִאשׁוֹנָה שְׁלִישִׁית וַחֲמִישִׁית** – One **master utilized her** during the **first, third and fifth** years after their purchase, **וּמַר אִישְׁתַּמֵּשׁ בָּהּ שְׁנִיָּה רְבִיעִית וְשִׁשִּׁית – and the** other **master utilized her** during the **second, fourth and sixth** years.[3] **נְפַק עַרְעָר עִילָוָהּ – A challenge came out regarding** ownership of **[the maidservant],** her original owner claiming that he never sold her to the two partners. **אָתוּ לְקַמֵּיהּ דְּרָבָא – [The litigants] came before Rava** for judgment. **אָמַר לְהוּ – Rava said to [the partners]:** **מַאי טַעְמָא עֲבַדִיתוּ הָכִי – "What is the reason that you made this** arrangement? **כִּי הֵיכִי דְּלֹא תַּחְזְקוּ אַהֲדָדֵי – So that you would not establish a** ***chazakah*** **against each other** with three consecutive years of use. **כִּי הֵיכִי דִּלְדִידְכוּ לֹא הָוֵי חֲזָקָה** – Therefore, **just as with regard to** the two of **you no** ***chazakah*** **is established** with this interrupted use, **לְעָלְמָא נַמִּי לֹא הָוֵי חֲזָקָה – regarding others also no** ***chazakah*** is **established."**[4]

The Gemara qualifies Rava's ruling:

וְלֹא אֲמָרַן אֶלָּא דְּלֹא כְּתוּב עִיטְרָא – However, we say this ruling **only if no contract of apportionment has been written.**[5] **אֲבָל כְּתוּב עִיטְרָא – But if a contract of apportionment has been written,** **קָלָא אִית לֵיהּ – it becomes widely known.**[6] In that case, the combined use of the partners does succeed in establishing a *chazakah* vis-a-vis the original owner.[7]

The Gemara discusses another detail of the law of *chazakah*:

אָמַר רָבָא – Rava said: **אֲכָלָהּ כּוּלָּהּ חוּץ מִבֵּית רוֹבַע – If [the occupant] made use of the entire [field]** for three years **except for a quarter** ***beis kav*** of land[8] **קָנָה כּוּלָּהּ חוּץ מִבֵּית רוֹבַע – he acquires all of it except for** that **quarter beis kav** of land.[9]

The Gemara qualifies Rava's ruling:

אָמַר רַב הוּנָא בְּרֵיהּ דְּרַב יְהוֹשֻׁעַ – Rav Huna the son of Rav Yehoshua said: **וְלֹא אֲמָרַן אֶלָּא דְּבַר זְרִיעָה הִיא – However, we** say this ruling **only when [the unused piece of land] is suitable for planting;**[10] **אֲבָל לָאו בַּר זְרִיעָה הִיא – but if it is not suitable for planting,** **קָנֵי לָהּ אַגַּב אַרְעָא** – then **[the occupant] acquires [that piece] by dint of** the rest of **the land.**[11]

NOTES

1. In the case of a house owned by an itinerant peddler (who sells women's cosmetics [see above, 22a]) who returns home only rarely, an unscrupulous person can occupy the house during the peddler's long periods of absence, abandoning it only on those rare occasions that the peddler returns home from his route. It is thus possible that the peddler is not even aware that someone has occupied his house for three years and that is why the peddler has never lodged any protest. It is we, therefore, who advance the claim on the peddler's behalf; that is, we require the occupant to produce witnesses that he did not move out of the house for even a single night during his three years of occupancy. Only then will he have established a valid *chazakah* (*Rashbam's* preferred explanation; cf. *Tosafos* ד"ה אמר מר זוטרא and *Rashba*).

2. These stores sell bread and wine during the day and are not lived in at night. Therefore, the occupant establishes a *chazakah* with daytime use alone (*Rashbam*).

Tosafos explain as follows: [The occupant in question is a storekeeper.] Now, although storekeepers commonly do not live in their stores at night, these stores are nonetheless fit for use as nighttime residences and people indeed live in similar structures at night. Therefore, three full years of use are required to establish a *chazakah* on such a structure, and three years of daytime use alone constitute only half the use required. However, since it is common for storekeepers not to live in the stores at night, a storekeeper can establish his *chazakah* on the store with six years of daytime use, thereby spreading three full years of use over a period of six years. Although Rav Huna generally requires *consecutive* use, normal interruptions do not break the required continuity (as seen from the case of fields left fallow – see 29a and note 19 there). Thus, in the case of such stores, the original owner cannot claim that he was silent because the storekeeper's absence at night indicated a reluctance to act as an owner – the basis for Rav Huna's requirement of consecutiveness [see 29a note 15].

Nimukei Yosef, however, explains that these stores are no different than fields, which are generally unoccupied at night. Accordingly, the Gemara here means that a *chazakah* on these stores is established simply with three years of daytime use, just as is true in the case of ordinary fields. See also *Shach* 140:19.

3. The purpose of this staggered arrangement was so that neither partner would use the maidservant for three consecutive years and thereby be able to establish a *chazakah* on her to the detriment of the other partner (*Rashbam*; see *Tosafos*).

4. The three years of utilization of the property must be consecutive. Since neither partner made use of the maidservant for three consecutive years, the original owner regains control of his maidservant. [We do not view the partners as a single entity vis-a-vis the original owner.]

5. I.e. a document signed by witnesses attesting to the partners' staggered arrangement for use of their jointly owned property (*Rashbam*).

6. Literally: it has a voice.

7. In this case, the original owner surely knew of the partners' arrangement. He can no longer claim that he lodged no protest for three years because he construed the non-consecutive use of each user as evidence that each user was afraid to act as the maidservant's owner (which is the basis for the requirement of consecutiveness). Rather, the partners' alternating use of the maidservant was obviously the result of their terms of partnership clearly and publicly spelled out in the contract of apportionment (*Rashbam's* preferred explanation).

8. A *kav* is a unit of volume. A *rova* is a quarter *kav*. A *beis kav* is a unit of area – the area in which a *kav* of seed would normally be planted. Thus, a *beis rova* is the area of land large enough to plant a quarter *kav* of seed. This is approximately one hundred and four square *amos* (see above, 11a note 25).

9. In this case, the field's original owner asserts that the current occupant is a squatter. The occupant counters that he bought the entire field, and he has used all of it for three years except for an area the size of a quarter *beis kav*. Rava awards the occupant the bulk of the field, in which he has established a *chazakah,* but not the quarter *beis kav* of land, in which he has not established a *chazakah* (see *Rashbam*).

10. The original owner can claim that he remained silent regarding this arable piece of land because the occupant's failure to cultivate it indicated that he was not the owner (*Rashbam*).

11. [Since that small piece of the field is not arable, the original owner cannot excuse his silence regarding it on the basis of the occupant's failure to utilize it. Rather, because of the occupant's *chazakah* on the field in general, we award him the quarter *beis kav* section as well.]

א ומודי מר זוטרא ברוכלין המחזירין בעיירות דאע"ג דלא טען טענינן ליה אנן ב ומודה רב הונא בחנותא דמחוזא דליממא עבידא לליליא לא עבידא רמי בר חמא ורב עוקבא בר חמא זבון ההיא אמתא בהדי הדדי מר אישתמש בה ראשונה שלישית וחמישית ומר אישתמש בה שניה רביעית וששית נפק ערער עילוה אתו לקמיה דרבא אמר להו מאי טעמא עבדיתו הכי כי היכי דלא תחזקו אהדדי ג כי היכי דלדידכו לא הוי חזקה לעלמא נמי לא הוי חזקה ולא אמרן אלא דלא כתוב עיטרא ד אבל כתוב עיטרא קלא אית ליה אמר רבא ה אכלה כולה חוץ מבית רובע קנה כולה חוץ מבית רובע אמר רב הונא בריה דרב יהושע ולא אמרן אלא (א) דבר זריעה היא אבל לאו בר זריעה היא קני לה אגב ארעא מתקיף לה רב ביבי בר אביי אלא מעתה צונמא במה יקנה ו אלא באוקומי בה חיותא ומשטחא בה פירי ז ה"נ איבעי ליה לאוקומי בה חיותא אי נמי משטחא בה פירי ח ההוא דאמר ליה לחבריה מאי בעית בהאי ביתא אמר ליה מינך זבינתיה ואכלית שני חזקה א"ל אנא בשכוני גוואי הואי (ב) אתא לקמיה דרב נחמן אמר ליה ט זיל ברור אכילתך אמר ליה רבא י הכי דינא המוציא מחבירו עליו הראיה ורמי דרבא אדרבא ורמי דרב נחמן אדרב נחמן דההוא דא"ל

הכי גרסינן ומודה מר זוטרא ברוכלין המחזירין בעיירות דאע"ג כו'. אע"ג דסבירא (ג) למר זוטרא דאי טעין טענינן טענה אבל אנו לא נטעון בשבילו מודי הוא היכא דהוי מערער רוכל המחזר בעיירות למכור קישוטי נשים ואינו חוזר לעירו כי אם לזמן ארוך דאע"ג דלא טעין לייתי מחזיק סהדי דדר בה רצופות יומם ולילה אנן טענינן ליה דדילמא משום דלא קביע במתא החזיק זה בביתו וכי הוה אתי במתא הוי נפיק האי מחזיק מן ביתא ולא ידע ליה זה המערער מעולם שהחזיק זה בביתו ולכך שתק ולא מיחה הלכך יביא המחזיק עדים שלא יצא מן הבית כל שלש השנים אפילו לילה אחת. ול"ג ומודי רבא דהא לא איירי רבא לעיל אי טענינן ליה או טעין איהו לנפשיה וכל מאי דמתריץ רבא לעיל אליבא דרב הונא תריץ ואי גרסינן הכי הוה לן למיגרס ומודה רב הונא: ומודה רב הונא. אע"ג דבעי רצופות יום ולילה בחנוונותא דמחוזא חנויות שמוכרין בהן לחם ויין דאי טעין אין חוששין לטענתו דאע"ג דלא דר בו בלילות חזקה מעלייתא היא שאין דירתן אלא ביום: מר אישתמש ראשונה כו'. עובדת לזה שנה ולזה שנה שאין אחד מהן יכול להחזיק בה ג' שנים רצופות להפסיד חבירו: עיטרא. שטר חלוקה ובעדים שתעבוד לזה שנה ולזה שנה י"מ קלא אית ליה והיה לו למחות מיד ולא מיחה ולאלתר הויא חזקה דכמי שמכרה להם (ד) בפניו דמי שהרי הניחם להביא עדים ולכתוב עליו שטר חלוקה ושתק אי נמי כיון דאיכא תרתי שני חזקה מפוזרות ועיטרא איכא קלא וכחזקה גמורה דמי דהיה לו למחות ולא מיחה ואין נראה לי כלל אלא משלש שנים ראשונות הויא חזקה כיון דאיכא עדים ושטר בין זה לזה כדאמרינן לקמן בפירקין (דף מא:) שלש לקוחות מצטרפות אמר רב וכולן בשטר אלמא אמר רב אע"ג דכל אחד אין מחזיק אלא שנה אחת מצטרפים שלש השנים לחזקה משום דמכח שטר קאתו ה"נ לא שנא והיינו טעמא דהויא חזקה שהיה לו למערער למחות בתוך שלש שנים ואינו יכול לומר בשביל שראיתי' מחזיק בדילוג לא מחיתי שהייתי סבור לכך אתם עושים שאתם יראים להחזיק שנים רצופות שהשטר מוכיח שלא בשביל כן עושים אלא שע"מ כן חלקו שכן יהו משתמשין וכן עיקר: חוץ מבית רובע. באותו שדה שלא נעבד בו ולא נזרע: דבר זריעה היא. דאמר ליה אי דידך הואי אמאי לא זרעת והלכך לא מחיתי: אלא מעתה. הלוקח מחבירו צונמא (ה) במאי קני לה באיזו אכילה של שלש שנים הואיל ואינה בת זריעה וכי אינו קונה אותה בהעמדת שם בהמותיו לרבוץ ולרעות או לשטיחת פירותיו: הכא נמי כו'. ולא קני לה אגב ארעא: ואכלתיה שני חזקה. ואבדתי שטרי ואתה לא מחית לי שאזדהר בשטרי: אמר ליה. מערער: אנא בשכוני גוואי הואי. בחדרים הפנימים היתה עיקר דירתי והייתי עובר דרך עליך ומשתמש עמך בבית החיצון שדרת בו ברשותי ולכך לא מחיתי: אמר ליה. למחזיק: זיל ברור אכילתך. הבא עדים שדרת בבית לבדך ג' שנים בלא אותו שבא עמך (ו) כדין כל חזקת ג' שנים שצריך להביא עדים שהחזיק בה חזקה גמורה: המוציא מחבירו. דהיינו מוכר שהרי לוקח מוחזק: עליו. (ז) למערער להביא ראיה שנשתמש עמו וסבירא ליה לרבא דכיון שראו עדים לזה המוחזק שנשתמש בו שלש שנים אין לנו לחוש שמא גם זה היה עמו הואיל ולא שמענו בלתי היום. והאי עובדא לא מתוקם אלא כשהיה לו עדות למערער דבית זה שלו היה אבל בלא עדות אפילו רב נחמן מודי דהמחזיק נאמן בלא ראיה שהפה שאסר הוא הפה שהתיר דאי בעי אמר שלי הוא מעולם כי אמר נמי מינך זבינתה מהימן:

כל

אנו יודעים על הלילות מסתמא כיון שדר בימים דר נמי בלילות אם לא שטוען המערער שבודאי לא דר ור"ח פירש דמר זוטרא קאי אפירכא דרב ייבר דפריך נוגעין בעדותן הן וקאמר מר זוטרא אי טעין ואמר המחזיק לייתו תרי סהדי דדרו ביה שלש שנים ביום ובלילה והכי לי אגרא ונפקו ואזלו להו והנהו דדיירי ביה אחריני נינהו טענתו טענה ולא נוגעין בעדותן הן (ח) דלא דיירי בה השתא דמצי למימר להו הכי לי אגר ביתא אלא איהו אמרו דדיירנא ואיהו אמרו פרעוני והפה שאסר הוא הפה שהתיר דאי בעו אמרי לא דיירנא ביה וליכא למימר דדילמא מכחיש להו שהוא לא היה יודע כלל שהיו דרים באותו בית ובסמוך לא גרסינן מודה מר זוטרא אלא ומודה רבא דבעי' שלש שנים ביממא ובליליא אם הנך עדים (ט) רוכלים המחזרים בעיירות אע"ג דלא אמרו דדרו ביה שלש שנים ביממא ובליליא אלא אמרי דידעינו היה זה הבית שלש שנים רצופות אע"ג שימים רבים הם מחזרים בעיירות ולא היו (י) בזה הבית עדותן עדות ור"ת גרס דדיירנא ביה שלש שנין ופירש דאביי ורבא תרוייהו סבירא להו דאין צריך להביא עדים על הימים ועל הלילות ורבא לא אמר ביממא ובליליא אלא להוציא המקשה מסברתו ולא לפלוגי אאביי אתא וקאמר מר זוטרא אם אמר העידוני סתם שדרתי ג' שנים בחזקת ימים ולילות אע"פ שלא ראו ממש כל הימים והלילות אלא שבחזקת כן מחזיקין אותו שכל שעה שהיו נכנסים פעמים ביום ופעמים בלילה היו רואין אותו בביתו טענתיה טענה והוה ליה למימר עדותן עדות אלא אגב דנקיט ברישא דמילתיה אי טעין אומר נמי טענתיה טענה ומודה רבא וה"ה מר זוטרא ואביי ברוכלין המחזירין בעיירות אף על גב דלא טען טענינן ליה דאין צריכים להעיד שראו ממש שהרי הם מחזרין בעיירות ואין יכולין להעיד על הראיה אלא יעידו שבחזקתו היה זה הבית שלש שנים ימים ולילות:

ומודה רב הונא בחנותא דמחוזא דביממא עבדי ובליליא לא עבדי. פירוש ומועיל להם אם החזיקו ג' שנים ואע"ג דלאו שלש רצופות אלא מפוזרות כיון דלאורחייהו בהכי דהוי כאתרי דמוברי באגי ואם תאמר א"כ פשיטא דמודה רב הונא כדפריך לעיל גבי באגי וי"ל לפי שבני אדם שאינם חנוונים דרים בהן ביום ובלילה ואותן צריכים ג' שנים רצופות יום ולילה וס"ד דחנוונים נמי יצטרכו כן קא משמע לן ומהאי טעמא אתי שפיר דבעינן להו שלש שנים שלימות דהיינו ו' שנים אע"ג דבשדות ובית הבדים לא בעינן אלא שלש שנים בין הכל (אלא) היינו משום דכמו שאר בני אדם הדרים שם שאין חנוונים בעו ג' שנים ביום ובלילה ה"נ חנוונים בעו ג' שנים שלימות דהיינו ו' שנים והא דלא אייתי להא לעיל גבי באגי ומודה רב הונא אומר ר"ת משום דלא סלקא שמעתתא דבתי וכי האי גוונא איכא בסוף [הכונס] (ב"ק דף סא:) גבי ומודו חכמים לרבי יהודה: **דלא** תחזקו אהדדי. ואע"ג דתנן לקמן (דף מב.) השותפין אין להם חזקה זה על זה פרש"י דהכא הוחזקו לעשות שלא היה להם עדי שותפות וקשיא לר"י דא"כ אותו שהחזיק שנה ראשונה יאמר שהוא שלו כיון שאין עדים שיש לחבירו חלק ונראה לר"י דלא היו רוצים שיחזיק האחד שלש שנים שלא תשתכח השותפות: **אבל** כתוב עיטרא קלא אית לה. והא דאמר בהמפקיד (ב"מ לט. ושם ד"ה לא) גבי אין מורידין לנכסי קטן ל"ש עביד עיטרא ל"ש לא עביד אין מורידין גבי יתמי החמירו [וע"ע תוס' גיטין כח. ד"ה והניחו]: **בשכוני** גוואי הואי. והואי לי (כ) אורח עלך ונראה לי שהיה לו עדים שהיה בשכוני גוואי אבל לא היו יודעים באיזה דרך היה יוצא דאי לא היה לו עדים כלל דהוה בשכוני גוואי היכי הוה קאמר רב נחמן זיל ברור אכילתך דאטו יש להם לעדי חזקה לידע שלא היה המערער באותו בית כל שלש שנים ולא יאמר המערער הייתי עמך שני ימים ואין לך שלש שנים שלימות והעדים אין יודעים יפסיד:

לאו

עין משפט
נר מצוה

י א מיי' פי"ב מהלכות טוען הלכה ג סמג עשין צה טוש"ע ח"מ סי' קמ סעיף ח:

יא ב מיי' שם הלכה ה ועי' בהשגות טוש"ע שם סעיף יד:

יב ג ד מיי' שם הלכה ה וסמג שם טוש"ע ח"מ סי' קמד סעיף א:

יג ה מיי' שם הלכה טז וסמג שם טוש"ע ח"מ סימן קמא סעיף יד:

יד ו מיי' פ"א מהלכות מכירה הלכה טו ועי' בהשגות ובמ"מ סמג עשין פב טוש"ע ח"מ סימן קלב סעיף ח וסימן קמא סעיף יב:

טו ז מיי' פי"ב מהלכות טוען הלכה יג סמג עשין צה טוש"ע ח"מ סי' קמא סעיף יג וסעיף יד:

טז ח ט מיי' שם פט"ו הלכה י' עי' מ"מ סמג שם טוש"ע ח"מ סי' קמו סעיף יא וסעיף יב:

רבינו גרשום

מודי מר זוטרא ברוכלין. דאי האי מחזיק הוי רוכל המחזר בעיירות דלא מצי למידר בה ביממא ובלילה מפני שהולך בסחורתו ואמר הרוכל החזקתי ג' שנים בלא ערעור והאי לא ידע לטעון כנגדו כיון דקים (ליה) [לן] דרוכל אינו שוהה תדיר בביתו שמא איתרמי דזה בא וכיון שלא ראהו שהיה דר בה שתיק ליה להכי ילפינן ליה למערער דלימטען דליתי האי רוכל סהדי דדר בה ביממא בין בלילא ואי לא לא הוי חזקה: ומודי רב הונא. דאמר לעיל ג' שנים רצופות דמשמע בין ביממא בין בלילה מודי דאי אחזיק חד בחנות דמחזיק בג' שנים ביממא אע"ג דלא דר בה בלילא הוה חזקה משום דלימא עבידי למיתב בהו ולא בלילה דמצי למימר המחזיק עבדי בה כדעבדי אינשי בימא: כי היכי דלדידכו לא הויא חזקה. משום דלית חד מיניה דאחזיק רצופין לעלמא נמי לא הויא חזקה ומשלמותו לה למערער. והני מילי דלא הוי חזקה היכא דלא כתבי שטרא שטר חלוקה שתעבוד לזה שנה ולזה שנה אבל כתבו שטר חלוקה אע"ג דלא רצופות בה ג' שנים הויא חזקה משום דעיטרא קלא אית להו ולאלתר איבעי ליה למיחי ולערער וכיון דלא ערער הויא חזקה: אמר רבא אכלה כולה קרקע שני חזקה חוץ מבית רובע בה: אבל לאו בת זריעה היא. אותו בית רובע: אלא מעתה הא צונמא דלאו בת זריעה היא ולא קני ליה אגב ארעא אי לא שטח בה פירי הכא נמי בהאי בית רובע אי לא יעביד בה מידי לא קני לה: אנא בשכוני גואי. והחזקתי בה ולא שמשתה בה יותר ממני. אמר ליה ללוקח זיל ברור אכילתך כלומר הבא עדים שלא שימש עמך בבתי גואי ותחזיק בהו. רב נחמן אוקמה השתא ביד מוכר ולהכי אמר ליה רבא דינא הכי ביד לוקח הוה לך לאוקמה ויהא המוכר המוציא מחבירו עליו הראיה דמוכר להוציא קאתי:

מסורת הש"ס

א) [לקמן דף קנט:], ב) נ"ל דינא הכי:

הגהות הב"ח

(א) גמ' דבר זריעה: (ב) שם אתו לקמיה דרב נחמן: (ג) רשב"ם ד"ה הכי גרסי' וכו' דסבירא ליה למר זוטרא וכו' ולא ידע זה כל"ל ותיבת ליה נמחק: (ד) ד"ה עיטרא וכו' להם בפניו דמי וכו' ולכתוב עליו שטר: (ה) ד"ה אלא וכו' צונמא במאי קני: (ו) ד"ה זיל ברור וכו' שבא עמך כדין: (ז) ד"ה עליו להביא ראיה כל"ל ותיבת למערער נמחק: (ח) תוס' ד"ה (בע"א) אמר וכו' בעדותן הן דהא לא דיירי: (ט) בא"ד עדים הם רוכלים: (י) בא"ד ולא היו לנים בזה הבית: (כ) ד"ה בשכוני גוואי הואי והואי לי דרך עליך:

ליקוטי רש"י

עיטרא. שטר חלוקה רק הבמות לא סרו (מלכים ב יב) מתרגם לא עטרו [גיטין פו.]. עיטרא. שטר חלוקה כשחלקו ממלכות (מלכים ב יב) רק הבמות לא סרו מתרגמינן במתא לא עטרו דלא הסליקו מהם [ב"מ לט: ועי' במסורת הש"ס]. צונמא. צונמא בלשון ארמי סלע [בראשית מא, כג ונדה ח:]. סלע חזק [לעיל יח.]. אבן [רשב"ם לקמן פט:].

The Gemara objects to this qualification:
מַתְקִיף לָהּ רַב בִּיבִי בַּר אַבַּיֵי – Rav Bivi bar Abaye challenged: **אֶלָּא מֵעַתָּה – But now,** if you are to suggest that no utilization of a non-arable piece of land is possible, **צוּנְמָא בַּמֶּה יִקְנֶה – how does one acquire** [i.e. establish a *chazakah* in regard to] **a rocky field?** **אֶלָּא בְּאוֹקוּמֵי בָהּ חֵיוָתָא – Rather,** you must admit that he can establish a *chazakah* **by placing** his **animals there** to rest or graze **וּמִשְׁטְחָא בָהּ פֵּירֵי – or** by **spreading out fruits there** to dry. **הָכִי נַמִּי – So, too,** even when the non-arable piece of land is but a small portion of a larger, arable field, **אִיבְּעֵי לֵיהּ לְאוֹקוּמֵי בָהּ חֵיוָתָא – [the occupant] should have placed** his **animals in it** **אִי נַמִּי מִשְׁטְחָא בָהּ פֵּירֵי – or spread out fruits in it** in order to establish a *chazakah* there.[12]

The Gemara relates a case to illustrate a principle of *chazakah* law:[13]
הַהוּא דְּאָמַר לֵיהּ לְחַבְרֵיהּ – There was a person who said to his fellow, **מַאי בָּעֵית בְּהַאי בֵּיתָא – "What are you doing in this house?**[14] It belongs to me!" **אָמַר לֵיהּ – [The occupant] replied to him,** **מִינָךְ זְבִינְתֵּיהּ – "I bought it from you,** **וַאֲכַלִית שְׁנֵי חֲזָקָה – and I have used it** for **the three years** needed to establish a ***chazakah.***"[15] **אָמַר לֵיהּ – [The original owner] replied to him,** **אֲנָא בְּשְׁכוּנֵי גַּוָּואֵי הֲוַאי – "I was** residing **in the inner rooms** of the property in question during the entire period of your occupancy."[16] **(אתא) [אָתוּ] לְקַמֵּיהּ דְּרַב נַחְמָן – [The litigants] came**[17] **before Rav Nachman** for judgment. **אָמַר לֵיהּ – [Rav Nachman] said to the occupant:** **זִיל בְּרוֹר אֲכִילָתָךְ – "Go prove your** exclusive **use** of the house by producing witnesses that you lived alone there for three consecutive years, and you will then have established a *chazakah.*"[18]

Rava dissents:
אָמַר לֵיהּ רָבָא – Rava said to [Rav Nachman]: **הָכִי דִּינָא – Is this the law?** **הַמּוֹצִיא מֵחֲבֵירוֹ עָלָיו הָרְאָיָה –** But there is the legal principle that **the** burden of **proof rests upon the one who seeks to exact** payment **from his fellow!** Thus, the burden of proof should rest on the claimant, not on the occupant![19]

The Gemara points out apparent contradictions to both Rav Nachman's and Rava's positions in the matter, and asks:
וּרְמֵי דְּרָבָא אַדְּרָבָא – But contrast this ruling **of Rava with** another ruling **of Rava;** **וּרְמֵי דְּרַב נַחְמָן אַדְּרַב נַחְמָן –** and **contrast** this ruling **of Rav Nachman with** another ruling **of Rav Nachman.** **דְּהַהוּא – For there was a person**

NOTES

12. If he has failed to make some continuous use of the non-arable section, his *chazakah* in the larger field does not help him gain the upper hand in regard to the unused section (*Rashbam*).

[*Rosh* writes that the Gemara's choice of a piece of land the size of "a quarter *beis kav*" is specific. Anything smaller is considered insignificant in its own right and is awarded according to the *chazakah* established in the rest of the field.]

13. This incident is the first of many (spanning the next five pages of Gemara [until 34b]) cited to illustrate various aspects and principles of the law of *chazakah*.

14. Literally: what do you want in this house.

15. In addition, the occupant's position was that he lost his deed and that his occupancy was never contested so that he should have taken steps to insure the continued safety of his deed (*Rashbam*).

16. I.e. the original owner claims that his primary residence was in the inner rooms of that house and that he would often walk through the outer rooms and use them together with the occupant, who resided there with his permission as his guest. It was for this reason that he saw no need to protest the occupant's presence there (*Rashbam*; cf. *Tosafos* and *Ramban*).

17. [Emendation and translation follow *Bach* (as well as manuscripts), who emends the Gemara to read אָתוּ, *they came,* rather than אָתָא, *he* (or *it*) *came.*]

18. Rav Nachman ruled that this case is no different from any other case of *chazakah,* in which the burden of proof rests on the occupant to establish that he enjoyed an occupancy that yields him a *chazakah* (*Rashbam*). [Therefore, if the occupant cannot prove that the original owner did not share the premises during those three years, no *chazakah* is established.]

[*Rashbam* (ד״ה עליו) adds that the case must be one in which the claimant has proof (independent of the occupant's admission, "I bought the house from you") that he was the house's original owner. However, if the only proof he has is that the occupant admits this, then the occupant wins the case even without establishing his *chazakah.* For there is a legal principle that "the mouth that forbids is the mouth that permits"; i.e. if we are to rely on the occupant's admission that the claimant is the original owner, we must also rely on the occupant's statement that he subsequently bought the house from him.]

19. According to Rava, once the occupant establishes that he has lived in the house for three years, the presumption is that he lived there *alone,* since there has been no hint of joint residency until the original owner makes that claim in litigation. Accordingly, the occupant is presumed to have a *chazakah,* and the onus is on the original owner to overturn that presumption by proving that the occupant's *chazakah* is flawed (*Rashbam*).

כָּל נִכְסֵי דְּבֵי בַּר סִיסִין דְּאָמַר לֵיהּ לְחַבְרֵיהּ – who said to his fellow, מְזַבֵּינָא לָךְ – "I am selling you all of the property of the Bar Sissin estate."[1] הֲוַאי הַהִיא אַרְעָא – There was a certain piece of land owned by the seller דַּהֲוָה מִיקְרֵי דְּבֵי בַּר סִיסִין – that was called "a property of the Bar Sissin estate," but it was unknown whether it was so called because the seller had bought it from Bar Sissin or whether it was simply called that and was part of the seller's family estate.[2] אָמַר לֵיהּ – [The seller] said to [the buyer]: הָא לַאו דְּבֵי בַּר סִיסִין הִיא – "This land is not one that I purchased from the Bar Sissin estate; וְאִיקְרוּיֵי הוּא דְּמִיקַּרְיָא דְּבֵי בַּר סִיסִין – it is simply that it is called 'a property of the Bar Sissin estate.'" אָתוּ לְקַמֵּיהּ דְּרַב נַחְמָן – They came before Rav Nachman for judgment. אוֹקְמָא בִּידָא דְּלוֹקֵחַ – He placed the land in the buyer's possession.[3]

Rava dissents:

אָמַר לֵיהּ רָבָא – Rava said to [Rav Nachman]: דִּינָא הָכִי – Is this the law? הַמּוֹצִיא מֵחֲבֵירוֹ עָלָיו הָרְאָיָה – But there is the legal principle that the burden of proof rests upon the one who seeks to exact payment from his fellow! Thus, unless the buyer can prove his case, the land in question should remain the property of the seller, who currently holds it.[4]

The Gemara now explains its question:

קַשְׁיָא דְּרָבָא אַדְּרָבָא – The first ruling of Rava, which favors the new occupant, contradicts the second ruling of Rava, which favors the original owner. קַשְׁיָא דְּרַב נַחְמָן אַדְּרַב נַחְמָן – And the first ruling of Rav Nachman, which favors the original owner, contradicts the second ruling of Rav Nachman, which favors the buyer. – ? –

The Gemara answers that the two cases are not truly comparable:

דְּרָבָא אַדְּרָבָא לֹא קַשְׁיָא – The first ruling of Rava does not contradict the second ruling of Rava. הָתָם מוֹכֵר קָאֵי בְּנִכְסֵיהּ – There, in the Bar Sissin case, he favors the seller because it is the seller who occupies the property;[5] הָכָא לוֹקֵחַ קָאֵי בְּנִיכְסֵיהּ – but here, in the first case, he favors the buyer because it is the buyer who occupies the property.[6]

The Gemara continues:

דְּרַב נַחְמָן אַדְּרַב נַחְמָן נַמִּי לֹא קַשְׁיָא – Neither does the first ruling of Rav Nachman contradict the second ruling of Rav Nachman. כֵּיוָן דְּאָמַר לֵיהּ דְּבֵי בַּר סִיסִין – In the second case, since [the seller] told him that he was selling him all the properties of the Bar Sissin estate וּמִיקַּרְיָא דְּבֵי בַּר סִיסִין – and [the disputed property] is indeed called "a property of the Bar Sissin estate," עֲלֵיהּ דִּידֵיהּ רָמְיָא לְגַלּוּיֵי – Rav Nachman rules that it is incumbent upon [the seller] to show דְּלַאו דְּבֵי בַּר סִיסִין הִיא – that it is not a property that he bought from the Bar Sissin estate.[7] אֲבָל הָכָא לֹא יְהֵא אֶלָּא דְּנָקֵיט שְׁטָרָא – But here, in the first case, Rav Nachman reasons: Let it be no better than if [the occupant] was holding a contested deed! מִי לֹא אָמְרִינַן לֵיהּ – Would we not tell him: קַיֵּים שְׁטָרָךְ וְקוּם בְּנִיכְסֵי – "First validate your deed and only then stand in possession of the property"? Similarly, the current occupant must validate his contested three-year *chazakah* in order to be awarded title to the house.[8]

The Gemara cites a case to illustrate another aspect of the *chazakah* laws:

הַהוּא דְּאָמַר לֵיהּ לְחַבְרֵיהּ – There was a person who said to his fellow, מַאי בָּעֵית בְּהַאי בֵּיתָא – "What are you doing in this house, which is known to have belonged to me?" אָמַר לֵיהּ – [The occupant] replied to him, מִינָּךְ זְבַנְתֵּיהּ – "I bought it from you וַאֲכַלְתֵּיהּ שְׁנֵי חֲזָקָה – and I have used it for the three years needed to establish a *chazakah*." אָמַר לֵיהּ בְּשׁוּקֵי בָּרָאֵי הֲוַאי – [The original owner] said to [the occupant], "I was in faraway markets during those three years and did not know that you were occupying my property."[9] אָמַר לֵיהּ – [The occupant] thereupon said to [the original owner], וְהָא אִית לִי סַהֲדֵי – "But I have witnesses who can testify דְּכָל שַׁתָּא הֲוָה אָתֵית תְּלָתִין יוֹמֵי – that each year you would come to this city for thirty days."[10] אָמַר לֵיהּ – [The original owner] replied to him, תְּלָתִין יוֹמֵי – "All thirty days that I was in the city, בְּשׁוּקָאֵי הֲוָה טְרִידְנָא – I was preoccupied with my market activities, and did not know that you were living in my house."[11]

NOTES

1. I.e. I am selling to you all the properties that I have bought from the man named Bar Sissin (*Rashbam*). The buyer then made an act of acquisition to transfer all those properties from the domain of the seller to his own.

2. The purchase terms certainly covered only those lands that the seller had bought from Bar Sissin. Thus, if the seller had originally bought the land known as "a property of the Bar Sissin estate" from Bar Sissin, then it now belongs to the buyer. But if the land was simply called that, then it remains the property of the seller (*Rashbam* ד״ה כיון).

3. I.e. Rav Nachman ruled that the onus was on the seller to prove that this property was not one of the lands that he had acquired from Bar Sissin.

4. [Since the seller has never surrendered the land to the buyer and still occupies it (see *Rashbam*).]

5. Literally: [who] stands in his property.

6. Thus, Rava's rulings are consistent; in both cases he awards the property to the current occupant (*Rashbam*).

7. Since this land is called "a property of the Bar Sissin estate," it seems virtually certain that the land was indeed bought from Bar Sissin, as the buyer's claim asserts. Rav Nachman therefore rules that it is the seller's position that must be proven (*Rashbam*).

8. If a property's original owner contests that he never sold it and that the deed produced by the current occupant is a forgery, the occupant must certify his deed. [That is, he must produce the very witnesses who signed it or two other witnesses who recognize the handwriting of the signers.] Now, as explained in the Gemara above, a *chazakah* on a property simply stands in place of the deed that the occupant can justifiably claim to have lost after three years. Therefore, just as the original owner can demand certification of a deed, he can demand authentication of the *chazakah* that substitutes for the deed. Rav Nachman therefore ruled that the occupant had to certify his *chazakah* by producing witnesses who could testify that the original owner did not live in the house during the time that the *chazakah* was being established (*Rashbam*).

9. The Mishnah below (38a) states that one establishes a *chazakah* with a three-year occupancy only when the original owner must have been aware of that occupancy yet failed to lodge any protest. If, however, the original owner is abroad in a country that does not have regular communications with the place in which his property is located, no *chazakah* is established, since the original owner can claim that he lodged no protest simply because he never knew about the occupancy. Here, the challenger claimed to have been in such a place (*Rashbam*).

This is not to say that a *chazakah* can be established only if the original owner remains local. Just as the Gemara states above (28b, 29a) that knowledge of a protest lodged in the absence of the occupant invariably gets back to him by word of mouth ("your friend has a friend, and the friend of your friend has a friend"), so too will word of an occupancy invariably get back to the original owner even if he is not in town – as long as there are regular communications between the two locations (*Rashbam;* see Mishnah below, 38a).

10. Thus, you certainly became aware of my occupancy of this house during those thirty-day visits.

11. *Rashbam's* preferred explanation. In this case, the original owner had another house in the town, in which he lived during the month-long visits. Thus, he can reasonably claim that he was unaware that someone was occupying his second home (ibid.).

גמרא

א דא"ל (א) לחבריה כל נכסי דבי בר סיסין (א) מזבינא לך הואי ההיא ארעא דהוה מיקרי דבי בר סיסין אמר ליה הא לאו דבי בר סיסין היא ואיקרויי הוא דמיקריא דבי בר סיסין אתו לקמיה דרב נחמן (ב) ב אוקמא בידא דלוקח א"ל רבא דינא הכי המוציא מחבירו עליו הראיה קשיא דרבא אדרבא קשיא דרב נחמן אדרב נחמן דרבא אדרבא לא קשיא התם מוכר קאי בנכסיה הכא לוקח קאי בניכסיה דרב נחמן אדרב נחמן נמי לא קשיא (ג) כיון דאמר ליה דבי בר סיסין ומיקריא דבי בר סיסין עליה דידיה רמיא לגלויי דלאו דבי בר סיסין היא אבל הכא לא יהא אלא דנקיט שטרא מי לא אמרינן ליה קיים שטרך וקום בניכסיך: ג ההוא דאמר ליה לחבריה מאי בעית בהאי ביתא א"ל מינך זבנתיה ואכלתיה שני חזקה אמר ליה בשוקי בראי הואי אמר ליה והא אית לי סהדי דכל שתא הוה אתית תלתין יומי א"ל תלתין יומי בשוקאי הוה טרידנא אמר רבא ד עביד איניש דכל תלתין יומי טריד בשוקא ה ההוא דאמר ליה לחבריה מאי בעית בהאי ארעא אמר ליה מפלניא זבינתה (ד) דאמר לי דזבנה מינך אמר ליה את לאו קא מודית דהאי

רש"י

כל נכסי דבי בר סיסין. כלומר כל אותן קרקעות שקניתי מאותו אדם ששמו בר סיסין: דמקריא דבי בר סיסין. כך קורין לו ואין ידוע אם קנאה מבי בר סיסין ולפיכך נקראת כן או כך שמה מעולם וירושה היא לו מאבותיו: אוקמה בידא דלוקח. כדמפרש טעמא לקמיה דעליה דידיה רמיא לגלויי דלאו בר סיסין היא: אמר ליה רבא דינא הכי. להוציאה מספק מתחת יד המוכר שהוא מוחזק: המוציא מחבירו. דהיינו לוקח עליו להביא ראיית זכות ומאחר שאין לו ראיה יפסיד: קשיא דרבא אדרבא קשיא דרב נחמן אדרב נחמן. דלעיל מוקי לה רב נחמן ביד המוכר והכא ביד הלוקח והכא איפכא: דרבא אדרבא לא קשיא. דבכל דוכתי מוקי לה ביד המוחזק והתם מוכר כו': כיון. דכולי עלמא קרו ליה דבי בר סיסין ונראין הדברים שלפיכך נקראת כן שקנאה מבי בר סיסין והוא אומר לאו מבר סיסין לקחתיה עליה דידיה רמיא לגלויי ולהביא ראיה דלאו מבר סיסין לקחה ואם יביא עדים לאיקרויי הוא דמיקריא הכי ולא מהני שדות שלקח מבר סיסין היא מוקמינן לה בידיה דהא פשיטא לן דהאי דאמר ליה כל נכסי דבי בר סיסין מזבינא לך הכי קאמר ניכסי שקניתי ממנו ולא נכסי שלא קניתי ממנו אף על פי שנקראין כן. כך נראית השיטה: מי לא אמרינן ליה קיים שטרך. אחרי שהמוכר רוצה לפסלו והחזקה של שלש השנים במקום השטר היא באה ומאחר שהמוכר מערער על החזקה שאינה חזקה צריך זה להביא עדים שחזקתו גמורה שלא דר זה עמו. ובהני תרי עובדי סבירא לן כרב נחמן להלכתא כוותיה בדינא וכן פוסקין פירושי ר' חננאל איש רומי: מאי בעית בהאי ביתא. שהכל יודעין שלי היה: א"ל אנא בשוקי בראי הואי. בארץ מרחקים מקום שאין השיירות מצויות ולא ידעתי ולכך לא מחיתי ותנן בפרקין היה ביהודה והחזיק בגליל אינה חזקה עד שיהא עמו במדינה באותה מלכות דהוו שיירות מצויות. א"נ איכא לאוקמה בשעת חירום ואפילו באותה מדינה כדלקמן בהאי פירקין וכן פירשו הגאונים כפי' ר"ח אבל במקום שהשיירות מצויות וליכא חירום לא מצי טעין הכי דקי"ל בפירקין (דף לח:) מחזיקין בנכסי בורח דמחאה שלא בפניו הויא מחאה ואי טעין לא ידעתי שהחזיק איש פלוני בקרקע שלי ולכך לא מחיתי אינו נאמן דכי היכי דאמרינן מחאה שלא בפניו הויא מחאה דחברך חברא אית ליה ויאמרו לו למחזיק כמו כן אמרו לזה שאדם אחד מחזיק בקרקע שלו הואיל ושיירות מצויות וכן הלכה: בשוקאי הוה טרידנא. למכור סחורתי ולקנות אחרת ולא ידעתי שאתה דר בביתי וכגון שיש לו בית אחר באותה העיר שהיה מתאכסן שם כל ל' יום ויש מפרשים בשוקאי הוה טרידנא ולא היה לי פנאי למחות אע"פ שידעתי ואינו נראה בעיני:

אמר

תוספות

לאו קמודית דהא ארעא דידי הוא. פי' רבינו שמואל דאם מוחזק זה שלש שנים וטוען מפלניא זבנתיה דזבנה מינך קמי דידי דנאמן במיגו דלאי בעי אמר מינך זבנתיה ואכלתיה שני חזקה אי נמי אם יש לו עדים שהחזיק בה המוכר יום אחד והביא ראיה מההיא דדר בקשתא בעיליתא דלקמן ולדבריו כן הוא היכא דיש עדים למערער שהקרקע שלו היתה אבל בעובדא דהכא (ה) משמע שלא היה למערער עדים מדקאמר לאו קא מודית כו' אי הוה טעין קמי דידי זבנה מינך או דר בה חד יומא היה נאמן אף על פי שלא החזיק שלש שנים מיגו דלאי בעי אמר לא היתה שלך מעולם אבל ודאי השתא דאמר מפלניא זבינתה דזבנה מינך והודה שהיתה שלו תו לא מצי למיטען קמי דידי זבנה מינך או קמי דידי דר בה חד יומא (ו) מיגו דלאי בעי אמר בתחלה לא היתה שלך מעולם דמיגו למפרע לא אמרינן כדמוכח לקמן (דף מא:) גבי ההוא דדר בקשתא בעיליתא ארבע שנין ואמר מפלניא זבינתיה דזבנה מינך אתא לקמיה דר' חייא אמר ליה אייתי סהדי דדר ביה אפילו חד יומא ואוקמי' לה בידך משמע דאי לית ליה סהדי אין נאמן לומר קמי דידי דר בה חד יומא במיגו דלאי בעי אמר מינך זבינתיה כיון שכבר הודה דלאו מיניה זבנה לית ליה תו מיגו ואין לו להאמינו במאי דקאמר השתא (ז) מתוך שהיה יכול לשקר בתחילה קודם שהודה דלא הוה מסיק אדעתיה שהיה זקוק לטענה זו והא דקאמר התם רב וחזיתיה לדעתיה לתביעי דאי הוה א"ל קמי דידי זבנה מינך הוה מהימן ליה במיגו דאי בעי אמר מינך זבינתה לא קאמר שהיה עדיין נאמן בטענה זו אלא כלומר אי הוה טעין מעיקרא קודם שהודה וה"ה דאי הוה טעין מעיקרא קמי דידי דר בה חד יומא דהוה מהימן ועוד ראיה מסוף (ח) דזה בורר (סנהדרין דף לא.) גבי ההיא איתתא דנפק שטרא מתותי ידה אמרה ידענא ליה בהאי שטרא דפריע הוא כו' ולא הימנה רב נחמן א"ל רבא והא אי בעיא קלתיה כיון דאתחזק בבי דינא אי בעיא קלתיה לא אמרי' אלמא אע"ג דקודם שראיוהו בידה היתה נאמנת לומר דפרוע הוא במיגו דאי בעיא קלתי' השתא דאתחזק בבי דינא פי' שראיוהו בידה לא מהימנה דאין כאן עוד מיגו שעל כרחך צריכה עכשיו טענה זו שהיא אומרת אם רוצה לפטור את הלוה ובקונט' פי' שם אתחזק שהיה השטר מקוים ואין נראה לר"י דמה מועיל דמ"מ אי בעיא קלתיה ועוד ראיה דתנן בפ' שבועת הדיינין (שבועות דף לח:) מנה לי בידך אמר לו הן למחר א"ל תנהו לי נתתיו לך פטור ופריך מינה (שם מא.) למ"ד המלוה את חבירו בעדים צריך לפורעו בעדים והא הכא כיון דתבעיה בעדים כמאן דאוזפיה בעדים דמי וקתני פטור ומאי קושיא שאני הכא דפטור מיגו דאי בעי אמר אתמול לא היו דברים מעולם אלא ודאי כי האי גוונא לא אמרינן מיגו ומה שפ"ה בפ' בתרא דכתובות (דף קט: ושם) גבי עשאה סימן לאחר דאם טוען ואמר חזרתי ולקחתיה ממנו לאחר שעשיתיה סימן בשמו נאמן דהפה שאסר הוא הפה שהתיר דמאחר שיש עדים שהיתה שלו ונגזלה ממנו (ט) אין לו זכות אלא על פיו של זה שעשאה סימן לו והרי חזר ואמר לקחתיה ממך אין נראה לר"י דבכי האי גוונא לא אמרי' מיגו כדפרישית דע"י מה שהיה יכול לטעון תחילה אינו נאמן עכשיו אלא נראה לר"י דהתם נמי (י) חזר ואכלה שני חזקה אחר שעשאה סימן וכי תימא אי אכלה שני חזקה פשיטא ומאי קמ"ל ר' יוחנן דנאמן מתני' היא דחזקה שיש עמה טענה הרי זו חזקה וי"ל דס"ד דלא מהימן כיון שערער עליו קודם שאכלה שני חזקה לומר שהיא שלו לא עביד איניש דליזבנה בתר הכי קמ"ל וכן ההוא עובדא דמייתי בתר הכי איירי בשאכלה שני חזקה ובעובדא דידן אי הוה מייתי המחזיק סהדי דדר ביה חד יומא נראה לרשב"א דהוה (כ) לאוקומי לארעא בידיה אע"ג דליכא מיגו מ"מ טענינן ללוקח מאחר שהיה המוכר נאמן לומר זבינתה מינך במיגו דאי בעי אמר לא היתה שלך מעולם ואף על גב דהאי לוקח ידע שהיתה שלו והוי כחד סהדא מכל מקום הוי מיגו כדמשמע לקמן (דף לג:) גבי נסכא דר' אבא (ל) אי לא הוי מחויב שבועה ואינו יכול לישבע היה נאמן לומר דידי חטפי במיגו דאי בעי אמר לא חטפי והיה מכחיש את העד והכא לא הוי מחויב שבועה דאין נשבעין על הקרקעות וכה"ג מצינו בסוף המוכר (מ) (לקמן דף ע.) גבי מפקיד אצל חבירו בשטר דאע"ג דלא טענינן ליתמי נאנסו אפ"ה טענינן ליה החזרתיו לך כיון שאביהם היה נאמן בטענה זו במיגו דאי בעי אמר נאנסו ואור"י דלא דמי להאי דהמוכר את הבית דהכא אם היה רוצה המוכר לזכות בטענה זו דלא היתה שלך מעולם לא היה מעכבה הלוקח שהרי יודע היה שהיתה שלו. כתב ר"ח ראינו לרבותינו הגאונים ז"ל דהאי מחזיק לית ליה למיחת לדינא בהדי מריה דארעא אלא האי דזבין ליה מחית בהדיה ואין נראה לרשב"א דהא כל זכות שתבא לידו מכר ראשון לשני ולא יוכל לדחות ולומר לו לאו בעל דברים דידי את ולקמן אשכחן בהדיא גבי ההוא דדר בקשתא בעיליתא דלא מצי למימר ליה לאו בעל דברים דידי את אלא אי הוה משכח סהדי דדר ביה ההוא גברא חד יומא הוה מוקי לה ר' חייא בידיה:

מפלניא

מסורת הש"ס

א) לקמן דף קנט., ב) נ"ל דבי בר.

הגהות הב"ח

(א) גמ' בר סיסין מזבינא לך הוה ליה ההיא ארעא: (ב) שם אוקמה בידא: (ג) שם אדרב נחמן נמי לא קשיא כיון: (ד) שם מפלניא זבינתה דזבנה מינך כל"ל ותיבות דאמר לי נמחק: (ה) תוס' ד"ה לאו וכו' בעובדא דהכא משמע: (ו) בא"ד חד יומא במיגו: (ז) בא"ד דקאמר השתא מיגו שהיה יכול לשקר: (ח) בא"ד מסוף פרק זה בורר וכו' ידענא ביה בהאי שטרא וכו' אי בעיא קלתיה א"ל כיון דאיתחזק: (ט) בא"ד ונגזלה ממנו ואין לו זכות למחזיק אלא על פיו של זה המערער שעשאה: (י) בא"ד נראה לר"י דהתם נמי מיירי דחזר ואכלה: (כ) בא"ד לרשב"א דהוה ליה לאוקומי: (ל) בא"ד נסכא דר' אבא דאי לא הוי מחויב: (מ) בא"ד בסוף המוכר את הבית גבי וכו' טענינן להו החזרתיו:

ליקוטי רש"י

מינך זבנתיה ואכלתיה שני חזקה. ומאחר שלא מחית לי שלא אזהר בשטרי [רשב"ם לעיל כט.].

עין משפט נר מצוה

יז א ב מיי' פי"א מהל' מכירה הל' ב סמג עשין פב טוש"ע ח"מ סי' ריח סעיף כה:

יח ג ד מיי' פי"א מהל' טוען ונטען הל' ג סמג עשין צה טוש"ע ח"מ סי' קמג סעיף ג:

יט ה מיי' שם פי"ד הלכה יד סמג עשין צה טוש"ע ח"מ סי' קמו סעיף יג:

רבינו גרשום

נכסי דבי בר סיסין. כלומר אותן נכסים שקניתי מבר סיסין שהיה עשיר מזבינא לך: קשיא דרבא אדרבא. דלעיל סבירא ליה דביד הלוקח הוה ליה לאוקמי. והכא להיכא דרב נחמן אוקמה ביד לוקח ס"ל דביד מוכר הוה ליה לאוקמיה והוה ליה אידך המוציא מחבירו עליו הראיה: קשיא דרב נחמן אדרב נחמן. דלעיל אוקמא ביד מוכר והכא ביד לוקח: התם מוכר קאי בנכסיה שמוחזק הוא מההוא קרקע דמקרי בי בר סיסין ומש"ה (א) הוי ליה ללוקח להביא ראיה. וס"ל דביד מוכר: הכא הויא ליה למוכר להביא ראיה. דמוכר רמיא עליה. דמוכר רמיא לגלויי: מי לא אמרינן ליה לבעל שטרא להיכא דנפק עליה מערער קום קיים שטרך וקום בנכסי. ה"נ להיכא דאמר מוכר אנא בשכוני גוואי הוינא הוה ליה ללוקח להביא ראיה ולקום בנכסי והא מעשה דבר סיסין ודשכוני גוואי פרשתי היטב בסוף פרק מי שמת: אנא בשוקי בראי הואי. שהייתי הולך בסחורה במקום שווקים ולא הייתי יכול למחות מפני טרוד סחורתי: טרוד בשוקיה. ואינו יכול למחות: ב) הואיל ולא זבנתה מנאי דיל פוק מן ארעא דידי ולאו בעל דברים דידי את ותבע דמיך מאותו שקנית ממנו.

חשק שלמה על רבינו גרשום

א) נראה דצ"ל הוה ליה ללוקח להביא ראיה והוציאה מיד מוכר: הכא דלוקח קאי בנכסיה הוה ליה למוכר להביא ראיה: ב) נ"ל לאו קא מודית דהאי ארעא דידי היא ואת לא זבינתה מינאי. הואיל ולא זבינתה מינאי וכו'.

Rava rules:
אָמַר רָבָא – **Rava said:** עָבִיד אִינִישׁ דְּכָל תְּלָתִין יוֹמֵי טָרִיד בְּשׁוּקָא – **It is normal that a man would be preoccupied with market** activities **for the entire thirty days.** Therefore, the original owner is believed in his claim that he had never been apprised of the occupancy and he regains control of his house.

The Gemara cites another case:

הַהוּא דְּאָמַר לֵיהּ לְחַבְרֵיהּ – **There was a person who said to his fellow,** מַאי בָּעֵית בְּהַאי אַרְעָא – **"What are you doing in this land?"**[12] אָמַר לֵיהּ – **[The occupant] replied to the [challenger],** מִפְּלַנְיָא זְבִינְתָּהּ – **"I bought it from so-and-so,** דְּאָמַר לִי דְּזַבְנָהּ מִינָּךְ – **who said to me that he bought it from you."**[13] אָמַר לֵיהּ – **[The challenger] said to [the occupant],** אַתְּ לָאו קָא מוֹדֵית – **"Do you not admit**

NOTES

12. In this case, the challenger had no proof that he was the original owner [other than the occupant's admission, as emerges below] (*Rashbam* to 30b, see note 4 there).

13. The occupant had not utilized the land for the three years necessary to establish a *chazakah*. Nevertheless, he was still holding the deed that he received from the middle party from whom he had bought the land (*Rashbam* to 30b ד״ה אמר ליה מפלניא and ד״ה זיל). [The original owner, however, denies ever having sold the land to the middle party, who (he asserts) sold it to the current occupant under false pretenses.]

עין משפט נר מצוה

יז א ב מיי' פכ"ו מהל' מכירה הל' כא סמג עשין פב טוש"ע ח"מ סי' ריח סעיף כה:

יח ג ד מיי' פי"ג מהל' טוען ונטען הל' ג סמג עשין צה טוש"ע ח"מ סי' קמב סעיף א:

יט ה מיי' שם פי"ג הלכה יד סמג עשין צה טוש"ע ח"מ סי' קמו סעיף יג:

גמרא

א רא"ל (א) לחבריה כל נכסי דבי בר סיסין (א) מזבינא לך הואי ההיא ארעא דהוה מיקרי דבי בר סיסין אמר ליה הא לאו דבי בר סיסין היא ואיקרויי הוא דמיקריא דבי בר סיסין אתו לקמיה דרב נחמן (ב) ב אוקמא בידא דלוקח א"ל רבא דינא הכי המוציא מחבירו עליו הראיה קשיא דרבא אדרבא קשיא דרב נחמן אדרב נחמן דרבא אדרבא לא קשיא התם מוכר קאי בנכסיה הכא לוקח קאי בניכסיה דרב נחמן אדרב נחמן נמי לא קשיא (ג) כיון דאמר ליה דבי בר סיסין ומיקריא דבי בר סיסין עליה דידיה רמיא לגלויי דלאו דבי בר סיסין היא אבל הכא לא יהא אלא דנקיט שטרא מי לא אמרינן ליה קיים שטרך וקום בניכסי: ג ההוא דאמר ליה לחבריה מאי בעית בהאי ביתא א"ל מינך זבנתיה ואכלתיה שני חזקה אמר ליה בשוקי בראי הואי אמר ליה והא אית לי סהדי דכל שתא הוה אתית תלתין יומי א"ל תלתין יומי בשוקאי הוה טרידנא אמר רבא ד עביד איניש דכל תלתין יומי טריד בשוקא ה ההוא דאמר ליה לחבריה מאי בעית בהאי ארעא אמר ליה מפלניא זבינתה (ד) דאמר לי דזבנה מינך אמר ליה את לאו קא מודית

דהאי

רש"י

כל נכסי דבי בר סיסין. כלומר כל אותן קרקעות שקניתי מאותו אדם ששמו בר סיסין: דמקריא דבי בר סיסין. כך קורין לו ואין ידוע אם קנאה מבי בר סיסין ולפיכך נקראת כן או כך שמה מעולם וירושה היא לו מאבותיו: אוקמה בידא דלוקח. כלמפרש טעמא לקמיה דעליה דידיה רמיא לגלויי דלאו בר סיסין היא: אמר ליה רבא דינא הכי. להוציאה מספק מתחת יד המוכר שהוא מוחזק: המוציא מחבירו. דהיינו לוקח עליו להביא ראיה זכות ומאחר שאין לו ראיה יפסיד: קשיא דרבא אדרבא קשיא דרב נחמן אדרב נחמן. לדלעיל מוקי לה רב נחמן ביד המוכר ורבא ביד הלוקח והכא איפכא: דרבא אדרבא לא קשיא. דבכל דוכתי מוקי לה ביד המוחזק והתם מוכר כו': כיון. דכולי עלמא קרו ליה דבי בר סיסין ונראין הדברים שלפיכך נקראת כן שקנאה מבי בר סיסין והוא אמר לאו מבר סיסין לקחתיה עליה דידיה רמיא לגלויי ולהביא ראיה דלאו מבר סיסין לקחה ואם יביא עדים דלאיקרויי הוא דמיקריא הכי ולא מהני שדות שלקח מבר סיסין היא מוקמינן לה בידיה דהא פשיטא לן דהאי דאמר ליה נכסי דבי בר סיסין מזבינא לך הכי קאמר ניכסי שקניתי ממנו ולא נכסי שלא קניתי ממנו אף על פי שנקראין כן. כך נראית השיטה: מי לא אמרינן ליה קיים שטרך. אחרי שהמוכר רוצה לפסלו והחזקה של שלש השנים במקום השטר היא באה ומאחר שהמוכר מערער על החזקה שאינה חזקה צריך זה להביא עדים שחזקתו גמורה שלא דר זה עמו. ובהני תרי עובדי סבירא לן כרב נחמן דהלכתא כוותיה בדינא וכן פוסקין פירושי ר' חנינא איש רומי: מאי בעית בהאי ביתא. שהכל יודעין שלי היה: א"ל אנא בשוקי בראי הואי. בארץ מרחקים מקום שאין השיירות מצויות ולא ידעתי ולכך לא מחיתי ותנן בפרקין היה ביהודה והחזיק בגליל אינה חזקה עד שיהא עמו במדינה באותה מלכות דהוו שיירות מצויות. א"נ איכא לאוקמה בשעת חירום ואפילו באותה מדינה כדלקמן בהאי פירקין וכן פירשו הגאונים כפי' ר"ח אבל במקום שהשיירות מצויות וליכא חירום לא מצי טעין הכי דקי"ל בפירקין (דף לח:) מחזיקין בנכסי בורח דמחאה שלא בפניו הויא מחאה ואי טעין לא ידעתי שהחזיק איש פלוני בקרקע שלי ולכך לא מחיתי אינו נאמן דכי היכי דאמרינן מחאה שלא בפניו הויא מחאה דחברך חברא אית ליה ויאמרו לו למחזיק כמו כן אמרו לזה שאדם אחד מחזיק בקרקע שלו הואיל ושיירות מצויות וכן הלכה: בשוקאי הוה טרידנא. למכור סחורתי ולקנות אחרת ולא ידעתי שאתה דר בביתי וכגון שיש לו בית אחר באותה העיר שהיה מתאכסן שם כל ל' יום ויש מפרשים בשוקאי הוה טרידנא ולא היה לי פנאי למחות אע"פ שידעתי ואינו נראה בעיני:

אמר

תוספות

לאו קמודית דהא ארעא דידי הוא. פי' רבינו שמואל דאם מוחזק זה שלש שנים וטוען מפלניא זבנתיה דזבנה מינך קמי דידי דנאמן במיגו דאי בעי אמר מינך זבנתיה ואכלתיה שני חזקה אי נמי אם יש לו עדים שהחזיק בה המוכר יום אחד והביא ראיה מההיא דדר בקשתא בעיליתא דלקמן ודבריו כן הוא היכא דיש עדים למערער שהקרקע שלו היתה אבל בעובדא דהכא (ה) משמע שלא היה למערער עדים מדקאמר לאו קא מודית כו' אי הוה טעין קמי דידי זבנה מינך או דר בה חד יומא היה נאמן אף על פי שלא החזיק שלש שנים מיגו דאי בעי אמר לא היתה שלך מעולם אבל ודאי השתא דאמר מפלניא זבינתיה דזבנה מינך והודה שהיתה שלו תו לא מצי למיטען קמי דידי זבנה מינך או קמי דידי דר בה חד יומא (ו) מיגו דאי בעי אמר בתחלה לא היתה שלך מעולם דמיגו למפרע לא אמרינן כדמוכח לקמן (דף מא:) גבי ההוא דלעיל דדר בקשתא בעיליתא ארבע שנין ואמר מפלניא זבינתיה דזבנה מינך אתא לקמיה דר' חייא אמר ליה אייתי סהדי דדר ביה אפילו חד יומא ואוקמי' לה בידך משמע דאי לית ליה סהדי אין נאמן לומר קמי דידי דר בה חד יומא במיגו דאי בעי אמר מינך זבינתיה כיון שכבר הודה דלאו מיניה זבנה לית ליה תו מיגו ואין לו להאמינו במאי דקאמר השתא (ז) מתוך שהיה יכול לשקר בתחילה קודם שהודה דלא הוה מסיק אדעתיה שהיה זקוק לטענה זו והא דקאמר התם רב וחזיתיה לדעתיה דחביבי דאי הוה א"ל קמי דידי זבנה מינך הוה מהימן ליה במיגו דאי בעי אמר מינך זבינתה לא קאמר שהיה עדיין נאמן בטענה זו אלא כלומר אי הוה טעין מעיקרא קודם שהודה וה"ה דאי הוה טעין מעיקרא קמי דידי דר בה חד יומא דהוה מהימן ועוד ראיה מסוף (ח) דזה בורר (סנהדרין דף לא.) גבי ההיא איתתא דנפק שטרא מתותי ידה אמרה ידענא ליה בהאי שטרא דפריע הוא כו' ולא הימנה רב נחמן א"ל רבא והא אי בעיא קלתיה כיון דאתחזק בבי דינא אי בעיא קלתיה לא אמרי' אלמא אע"ג דקודם שראיוהו בידה היתה נאמנת לומר דפרוע הוא במיגו דאי בעיא קלתי' השתא דאתחזק בבי דינא פי' שראיוהו בידה לא מהימנה דאין כאן עוד מיגו שעל כרחך צריכה עכשיו טענה זו שהיא אומרת אם רוצה לפטור את הלוה ובקונט' פי' שם אתחזק שהיה השטר מקוים ואין נראה לר"י דמה מועיל דמ"מ אי בעיא קלתיה ועוד ראיה דתנן בפ' שבועת הדיינין (שבועות דף לח:) מנה לי בידך אמר לו הן למחר א"ל תנהו לי נתתיו לך פטור ופריך מינה (שם מא.) למ"ד המלוה את חבירו בעדים צריך לפורעו בעדים והא הכא כיון דתבעיה בעדים כמאן דאוזפיה בעדים דמי וקתני פטור ומאי קושיא שאני הכא דפטור מיגו דאי בעי אמר אתמול לא היו דברים מעולם אלא ודאי כי האי גוונא לא אמרינן מיגו ומה שפ"ה בפ' בתרא דכתובות (דף קט: ושם) גבי עשאה סימן לאחר דאם טען ואמר חזרתי ולקחתיה ממנו לאחר שעשיתיה סימן בשמו נאמן דהפה שאסר הוא הפה שהתיר דמאחר שיש עדים שהיתה שלו ונגזלה ממנו (ט) אין לו זכות אלא על פיו של זה שעשאה סימן לו והרי חזר ואמר לקחתיה ממך אין נראה לר"י דבכי האי גוונא לא אמרי' מיגו כדפרישית דע"י מה שהיה יכול לטעון תחילה אינו נאמן עכשיו אלא נראה לר"י דהתם נמי (י) חזר ואכלה שני חזקה אחר שעשאה סימן וכי תימא אי אכלה שני חזקה פשיטא ומאי קמ"ל ר' יוחנן דנאמן מתני' היא דחזקה שיש עמה טענה הרי זו חזקה וי"ל דס"ד דלא מהימן כיון שערער עליו קודם שאכלה שני חזקה לומר שהיא שלו לא עביד איניש דליזבנה בתר הכי קמ"ל וכן ההוא עובדא דמייתי בתר הכי איירי בשאכלה שני חזקה ובעובדא דידן אי הוה מייתי המחזיק סהדי דדר ביה חד יומא נראה לרשב"א דהוה (כ) לאוקומי לארעא בידיה אע"ג דליכא מיגו מ"מ טענינן ללוקח מאחר שהיה המוכר נאמן לומר זבינתה מינך במיגו דאי בעי אמר לא היתה שלך מעולם ואף על גב דהאי לוקח ידע שהיתה שלו והוי כחד סהדא מכל מקום הוי מיגו כדמשמע לקמן (דף לג:) גבי נסכא דר' אבא (ל) אי לא הוי מחויב שבועה ואינו יכול לישבע היה נאמן לומר דידי חטפי במיגו דאי בעי אמר לא חטפי והיה מכחיש את העד והכא לא הוי מחויב שבועה דאין נשבעין על הקרקעות וכה"ג מצינו בסוף המוכר (מ) (לקמן דף ע.) גבי מפקיד אצל חבירו בשטר דלא"ג דלא טעינן ליתמי נאנסו אפ"ה טענינן ליה החזרתיו לך כיון שאביהם היה נאמן בטענה זו במיגו דאי בעי אמר נאנסו ואור"י דלא דמי להאי דהמוכר את הבית דהכא אם היה רוצה המוכר לזכות בטענה זו דלא היתה שלך מעולם לא היה מעכבה הלוקח שהרי יודע היה שהיתה שלו. כתב ר"ח דאינו לרבותינו הגאונים ז"ל דהאי מחזיק לית ליה למיחת לדינא בהדי מריה דארעא אלא האי דזבין ליה מחית ליה לדינא ואין נראה לרשב"א דהא כל זכות שתבא לידו מכר ראשון לשני ולא יוכל לדחות ולומר לו לאו בעל דברים דידי את ולקמן אשכחן בהדיא גבי ההוא דדר בקשתא בעיליתא דלא מצי למימר ליה לאו בעל דברים דידי את אלא אי הוה משכח סהדי דדר ביה ההוא גברא חד יומא הוה מוקי לה ר' חייא בידיה:

מפלניא

רבינו גרשום

נכסי דבי בר סיסין. כלומר אותן נכסים שקניתי מבר סיסין שהיה עשיר מזבינא לך: קשיא דרבא אדרבא. דלעיל סבירא ליה דביד הלוקח הוה ליה לאוקמי. והכא להיכא דרב נחמן אוקמה ביד לוקח ס"ל דביד מוכר הוה ליה לאוקמיה והוה ליה אידך המוציא מחבירו עליו הראיה: קשיא דרב נחמן אדרב נחמן. דלעיל אוקמא ביד מוכר והכא ביד לוקח: התם מוכר קאי בנכסיה שמוחזק הוא מההוא קרקע דמקרי דבי בר סיסין ומש"ה (א) הוי על הלוקח להביא ראיה. וס"ל דביד מוכר: הכא הוא ליה למוכר להביא ראיה. דמוכר רמיא לגלויי: מי לא אמרינן ליה לבעל שטרא להיכא דנפק עליה מערער קום קיים שטרך וקום בנכסי ה"נ להיכא דאמר מוכר אנא בשכוני גוואי הרינא הוה ליה ללוקח להביא ראיה ולקום בנכסי והא מעשה דבר סיסין ודשכוני גוואי פרשתי היטב בסוף פרק מי שמת: אנא בשוקי בראי הואי. שהייתי הולך בסחורה במקום שווקים ולא הייתי יכול למחות מפני טרוד סחורתי: טרוד בשוקיה. ואינו יכול למחות: ב) הואיל ולא זבינתה מנאי זיל פוק מן ארעא דידי ולאו בעל דברים דידי את ותבע דמיך מאותו שקנית ממנו.

חשק שלמה על רבינו גרשום

א) נראה דצ"ל הוה ליה ללוקח להביא ראיה ולהוציא מיד מוכר: הכא דלוקח קאי בנכסיה הוי ליה למוכר להביא ראיה: ב) נ"ל את לאו קא מודית דהאי ארעא דידי היא ואת לא זבינתה מינאי. הואיל ולא זבינתה מינאי וכו':

מסורת הש"ס

א) לקמן דף קנט., ב) נ"ל דבי בר:

הגהות הב"ח

(א) גמ' בר סיסין מזבינא לך הוה ליה ההיא ארעא: (ב) שם אוקמה בידא: (ג) שם אדרב נחמן נמי לא קשיא השתא כיון: (ד) שם מפלניא זבינתה דזבנה מינך כצ"ל ותיבות דאמר לי נמחק: (ה) תוס' ד"ה לאו וכו' בעובדא דהכא למשמע: (ו) בא"ד חד יומא במיגו: (ז) בא"ד דקאמר השתא מיגו שהיה יכול לשקר: (ח) בא"ד מסוף פרק זה בורר וכו' ידענא ביה בהאי שטרא וכו' אי בעיא קלתיה א"ל כיון דאיתחזק: (ט) בא"ד ונגזלה ממנו ואין לו זכות למחזיק אלא על פיו של זה המערער שעשאה: (י) בא"ד נראה לר"י דהתם נמי איירי דחזר ואכלה: (כ) בא"ד לרשב"א דהוה ליה לאוקומי: (ל) בא"ד נסכא דר' אבא דאי לא הוה מחויב: (מ) בא"ד בסוף המוכר את הבית גבי וכו' טענינן להו החזרתיו:

ליקוטי רש"י

מינך זבנתיה ואכלתיה שני חזקה. ואבדתי שטרי ואתה לא מחית לי שאזהר בשטרי [רשב"ם לעיל כט:].

עין משפט
נר מצוה

כ א מיי' פי"ד מהל' טוען ונטען הלכה יד סמג עשין לד טוש"ע ח"מ סי' קמו סעיף יג:
כא ב ג מיי' פט"ז שם הלכה ג סמג עשין לה טוש"ע ח"מ סי' קמו סעיף יח וסי' קמז סעיף ה:
כב ד מיי' שם הלכה א סמג שם טוש"ע ח"מ סי' קמז סעיף א:
כג ה מיי' שם הלכה ד טוש"ע שם סעיף ה:
כד ו ז מיי' שם וסמג שם טוש"ע ח"מ סי' קמו סעיף יח:
כה ח ט י מיי' שם פט"ו הלכה ז סמג שם טוש"ע שם סעיף יט:

רבינו גרשום

דאמרי' **השני נוח לי** להוציאה מתחת ידו מש"ה אמרנא ליה זיל זבין **והראשון** שגזלה **קשה הימני** ולא הייתי יכול לטעון א) בעדו: **והוא** המערער **חתום עליה בעד אדמון אמר** יכול לומר המערער משום הכי חתמי על שטר מכירה **השני נוח לי והראשון קשה הימני** הכא נמי לא שנא: אבל **דבורא** דמשיא עצה **מיקרי ואמר** ליה: **אמינא איזבין דינאי.** כלומר אע"פ שהוא שלי מן הדין אמרתי אקנה אותה ממך שלא רציתי להקניט עמך ועכשיו הואיל ולא רצית למוכרה לי אוציאנה מידך בבית דין: **עביד איניש דזבין דיניה.** מי שאינו רוצה להתקוטט קונה דבר שבדין היה להיות שלו מפני קשיות בעל דינו: **ד' שנין.** כלומר שנה אחת היתה שלי קודם שהתחילו שני חזקה שלך: **והני מילי** דאמרי' עביד איניש דקרי לשני טובא שני חזקה להיכא **דאכלה שבע** שנים ג' שני חזקה קודם זמנו דשטרא דהאי. **אבל** אכליה המחזיק **שית** והאי אידך יש לו שטר שקנאה ד' שנים בתוך אותן ו' שנים דהאי לא אכלה כי אם ב' שנין קודם זמן שטרו יכול לומר לו האי בעל השטר למחזיק כיון דהמוכר מכרה לי לסוף ב' שנים שהיתה בידך אין לך מחאה גדולה מזה דגלי מוכר דעתיה דאותה חזקה שהחזיק בה אינה חזקה:

חשק שלמה
על רבינו גרשום

א) נראה דל"ל ולא הייתי יכול לטעון עמו:

מפלניא זבינתיה דזבנה מינך ואכלתיה שני חזקה אמר ליה פלניא גזלנא הוא. פי' יש לי עדים שהוא גזלן ולפי' דר ביה חד יומא הא קי"ל דגזלן אין לו חזקה ולא כפ"ה דפירש דאין לו עדים שהחזיק בה המוכר אפילו יום אחד דתו לא הוה מצי טוען פלניא גזלנא הוא משמע שרוצה לפרש גזלנא הוא לא שיש לו עדים שהוא גזלן אלא כלומר בגזל (ז) היא הקרקע בידו ואין נראה לר"י דהוה ליה לאסוקי כדמסיק לעיל לא קמודית לי דארעא דידי הוא ואת מינאי לא זבינתיה וכו':

עביד איניש דקרי לשני טובא שני חזקה. אבל אי לא עביד אף על גב דאית ליה סהדי דאכלה שבע שנין לא מהימנינן דהא איהו דמכחיש להו דמודה שלא אכלה אלא שני חזקה דהיינו שלש שנים: אבל

דהאי ארעא דידי היא ואת לא זבינתה מינאי זיל לאו בעל דברים דידי את אמר רבא אדינא קאמר ליה: בההוא דאמר ליה לחבריה מאי בעית בהאי ארעא אמר ליה מפלניא זבינא ואכלתיה שני חזקה אמר ליה פלניא גזלנא הוא אמר ליה והא אית לי סהדי דאתאי (א) אימלכי בך ואמרת לי זיל זבין אמר ליה השני נוח לי הראשון קשה הימנו אמר רבא גדינא קאמר ליה כמאן כאדמון דתנן דהעורר על השדה וחתום עליה בעד אדמון אומר השני נוח לי הראשון קשה הימנו וחכ"א איבד את זכותו האפילו תימא רבנן התם עבד ליה מעשה אבל הכא דבורא עביד איניש דמיקרי ואמר וההוא דאמר ליה לחבריה מאי בעית בהאי ארעא אמר ליה מפלניא זבינתה ואכלתיה שני חזקה אמר ליה פלניא גזלנא הוא אמר ליה והא אית לי סהדי דאתית באורתא ואמרת לי זבנה ניהלי א"ל אמינא איזבון דינאי אמר רבא זעביד איניש דזבין דיניה חההוא דאמר ליה לחבריה מאי בעית בהאי ארעא אמר ליה מפלניא זבינא ואכלתיה שני חזקה והא נקיטנא שטרא (ב) דזבני ליה מיניה הא ארבעי שני א"ל מי סברת שני חזקה תלת שני קא אמינא שני חזקה טובא קא אמינא אמר רבא טעבידי אינשי דקרו לשני טובא שני חזקה יוה"מ דאכלה שבע (ג) דקדים חזקה דהאי לשטרא דהך אבל

אמר ליה מפלניא זבינתה דזבנה מינך. כלומר שאמר לי בשעת מכירה שהוא לקחה ממך ומאחר שלא טוען ואכלתי' שני חזקה שטר מכירה שלו עודהו בידו ומסקנא דמילתא מוקמינן ליה ביד המערער והיינו טעמא דכיון דמודה דשלו היה הקרקע מתחלה לא מבעיא היכא דלא החזיק בה שלש שנים אלא אפילו החזיק בה שלש שנים נמי אינה חזקה ומפקינן ליה מיניה דהא חזקה שאין עמה טענה היא שהוא אינו יודע אם היתה של אותו שמכרה לו אם לאו והוה ליה להכיר בה בשדה שאינה שלו של מוכר ויחזירנה למערער והוא יגבה מעותיו מן המוכרו לו כדפסקינן בשנים אוחזין (ב"מ דף טו:) ואף על גב דליכא עדים למערער מדקאמר ולא מודית לי כו' ולא אמרינן מיגו דאי בעי אמר אנא זבינתה מינך ואכלתיה שני חזקה (ד) כדאמר מפלניא זבינתה דזבנה מינך נאמן שהוא עצמו אינו יודע אם לא זבנה המוכר מיניה למערער אם לאו הלכך כיון דהוא מודי למערער דשלו היתה הודאת בעל דין כמאה עדים דמי וגם הוא מודה שאינו יודע אם לקחה המוכרה לו מן הבעלים אם לאו דהא לא טוען דזבנה מינך קמאי דידי וגם אין לו עדים שהחזיק בה המוכר יום אחד הלכך הפסיד. אבל החזיק זה שלש שנים וטוען מפלניא זבינתה דזבנה מינך קמאי דידי כלומר שידעתי בברור שלקחה מינך נאמן מיגו דאי בעי אמר אנא זבינתה מינך ואכלתיה שני חזקה אי נמי יש לו עדים שהחזיק בה המוכר יום אחד והכי אמרינן לקמן בפירקין (דף מא:) גבי ההוא דדר בקטתא בעיליתא ארבע שנין. והכא בהאי עובדא אפילו אם באו עדים שהחזיק בה יום אחד אותו המוכר אבל אין יודע אם לקח אותה אם לאו אינו מועיל כלום מאחר שזה לא החזיק שלש שנים וגם הראשון אין לו שטר מכירה מן הבעלים: **ולא קא מודית לי כו'.** כמו שפירשתי: **ואת מינאי לא זבינתה.** שאפילו אם היית טוען דמינאי זבינתה הלא אין לך לא שטר ולא חזקה: **זיל.** מקרקע שלי לאו בעל דברים דידי את ואני מוחזק בה יותר ממך שאתה לא החזקת שלש שנים: **אמר רבא דינא קאמר ליה.** המערער ואפי' אם החזיק בה שלש שנים כמו שפירשתי וכן הלכה: **מפלניא זבינתה ואכלתיה שני חזקה.** ואין לו עדים שהחזיק בו אותו המוכר יום אחד דתו לא הוי מצי טוען פלניא גזלנא הוא דהא טוענין ללוקח והכי מפרש לקמן גבי ההוא דדר בקטתא בעיליתא ארבע שנין: **פלניא גזלנא הוא.** בשדה זו שממני גזלה: **ואימלכי.** נועלתי: **זיל זבין.** לך קנה: **השני נוח לי.** אתה נוח לי לריב עמך ולהוציאה ממך בדין: **אמר רבא דינא קא"ל.** המערער ויטול שדהו דאפילו אדמון ורבנן לא פליגי אלא בדעביד המערער מעשה לסייעו ללוקח לקנות שדהו אבל בדבורא בעלמא כולהו מודו כרבא כדמפרש ואזיל ואע"פ שהחזיק בה ג' שנים בלא מחאה יפסיד דהא חזקה שאין עמה טענה היא שמודה הוא שלא לקחה מיד הבעלים כי אם מיד איש נכרי שאין ידוע שהיה לו חלק בה אפילו יום אחד. ולא מצי טוען אמאי לא מיחה מערער בתוך שלש דהיכא אמרינן דמפסיד מערער בשתיקתו היינו היכא דטוען אידך מינך זבינתה ואכלתיה שני חזקה דעד שלש שנים מיזדהר איניש בשטריה טפי לא מיזדהר הלכך זה שלא מיחה והוא לא נזהר בשטרו הפסיד. אבל הכא דמודי מחזיק דלא מיניה דמערער זבניה שהוא בעל הקרקע ובעדים זבנה לא הורע כחו של מערער בשתיקתו שהחזקה במקום שטר מכירתו עומדת וכיון דאין שטרו מועיל לו שהרי מגזלן לקח אף חזקתו אינה כלום: **כמאן כאדמון.** ואנן קיימא לן כרבנן בפרק אחרון דכתובות: **דתנן.** ראובן העורר על שדה שמכר שמעון ללוי ואומר ראובן כי שמעון גזלו ממנו והוא ראובן המעורר חתום עליה בעד באותו שטר מכירה שכתב לו שמעון ללוי חתם ראובן ועד אחר עמו: **השני.** לוי נוח לי ולכך חתמתי: **מעשה.** שחתם עד: **דמקרי ואמר.** לשון ויקר מקרה (רות ב): **ואמרת לי זיל זבנה ניהלי.** ואם שלך היתה היה לך להוציא ממנו בדין חנם ולא לאבד מעותיך: **אמינא למיזבן דינא.** אמרתי בלבי טוב לי לקנות בדמים מועטים קרקע הראוי לי ולא לטרוח ולבא בדין: **עביד איניש דזבין דיניה.** אדם תם שאינו רוצה להתקוטט אפילו על שלו עשוי הוא להוציא מעותיו ליטול את שלו בלא דין ומחלוקת. ובפירוש ר"ח מפורש אמינא למיזבן דינאי לקנות המריבות כלומר אע"פ שהיא שלי איני מוציאה מידו בלא מריבות ודינין אקנה אותם הדינין והמריבות באלו המעות אע"פ שעיקר הארץ שלי: **ואכלתיה שני חזקה.** ולא נזהרתי בשטרי יותר: **אמר ליה והא נקיטנא שטרא.** שכתוב בה דזבנה לי כלומר שקניה אצלי מן המוכר הזה ארבע שנים ונמצא שקדם מקחי לחזקה שלך שנה אחת ואת מינאי לא זבינתה הלכך חזקה שאין עמה טענה היא שהמוכר לא יכול למוכרה לך שכבר מכרה לי קודם: **א"ל.** מחזיק למערער מי סברת דמאי דאמינא שני חזקה דהיינו תלת שני בלבלוס: **שני חזקה טובא קאמינא.** שקדמו לשטר שלך הרבה ויש לי עדים בכל החזקה כדמפרש (ה) לקמיה אבל לפיכך אמרתי שני חזקה סתם שלא הייתי יודע שהיה לך שטר של ארבע שנים שאצטרך לטעון ולפרש שני חזקה טובא: **אמר רבא עביד איניש דקרי שני טובא שני חזקה.** סתם ואם בא לטעון אחרי כן דשני חזקה טובא (ו) יותר מג' שנים אין זה חוזר וטוען טענות אחרות להכחיש טענות ראשונות ואנן קי"ל לקמן דאין אדם טוען בב"ד וחוזר וטוען טענות אחרות להכחיש הראשונות אלא אחר טענות הראשונות נפסוק הדין הלכך כי מייתי סהדי בהני שני חזקה טובא מהימנינן ליה שהרי לא חזר וטען: **והני מילי.** דמוקמינן לה בידיה דאייתי סהדי דאכלה ז' שנין שקדמו שני חזקה שלו למכירת השטר של מערער שהמוכר עצמו לא יכול למוכרה אחר שהחזיק בה ג' שנים בשופי אבל אי לית ליה סהדי אלא משית שני הדין עם בעל השטר דאין לך מחאה גדולה מזו שמיחה המוכר בזה המחזיק לסוף שתי שנים שמכר לאחר והיה לו לזה להזהר בשטרו לעולם עד שיוציא השטר מיד השני ויקרענו. ויש מפרשים דאין צריך עדי חזקת ז' שנים אלא של ג' אחרונים ואנן מהימנינן ליה על השאר מדאמר רבא עביד איניש דקרי לשני טובא שני חזקה למדו כן דאי איכא סהדי על כל השבע שנים אמאי איצטריך למימר עביד איניש כו'. ולאו מילתא הוא שהרי החזקה במקום השטר עומדת ולא יהא חזקת ג' שנים האחרונים שיש לו עדים עליהם אלא שטר של ג' שנים והרי שטר של ד' שנים הקודם לו פוסלו ומדברי רבא אין ללמוד דלא צריך עדים לז' שנים שהרי רבא להודיענו בא דאינו קרוי חוזר וטוען במאי דאמר לבסוף שני חזקה טובא קאמינא דעביד איניש כו' שאילו היה חוזר וטוען להכחיש דברים הראשונים אפי' כי מייתי סהדי בהני אחרונים אינו כלום דהודאת בעל דין כמאה עדים דמי ואחר טענות הראשונות נלך ובפי' ר"ח נמי מצריך עדים לכל הז' שנים:

זה

מסורת הש"ס

א) [לקמן דף מג:], ב) כתובות דף קט., ג) שייך לע"א:

הגהות הב"ח

(א) גמ' ואימלכי בך: (ב) שם דזבנא לי מיניה הא ארבע: (ג) שם דאכלה שבע שנין דקדים: (ד) רשב"ם ד"ה א"ל מפלניא וכו' שני חזקה כי אמר נמי מפלניא זבינתה דזבנה מינך נאמן וכו' יום אחד לכך הפסיד וכו' אם לקח אותה המוכר אם לאו: (ה) ד"ה שני חזקה טובא וכו' כדמפרש לקמן ולפיכך אמרתי כצ"ל ותיבת אבל נמחק: (ו) ד"ה אמר רבא וכו' טובא קאמר יותר מג' שנים: (ז) תוס' ד"ה מפלניא וכו' כלומר בגזל בא לו הקרקע בידו:

ליקוטי רש"י

השני נוח לי הראשון קשה הימנו. דקסבר שמעון לוי נוח לי ויהודה גברא אלמא הוא וקשה ממנו ולא אוכל לדון עמו [רשב"ם לקמן מג:]. **העורר על השדה כו'.** ראובן מערער על שדה שביד שמעון ואומר לוי שמכרה לך גזלה ממני. **וחתום עליה בעד.** על שטר המכירה שכתב לוי לשמעון כשמכרה לו. **אדמון אומר.** יכול הוא שיאמר מה שלא ערערתי בשעה שלקחת מלוי וחתמתי בתוך השטר עד לפי שלוי אדם חזק וקשה להוציאה מידו ונוח לי שתהא בידך שאוציאנה ממך בדין. **איבד את זכותו.** דהואיל וחתם הודה שאין לו עסק בה [כתובות קט.].

וְאַתְּ זִיל – דְּהַאי אַרְעָא דִּידִי הִיא – that this land was originally mine[1] לֹא זְבִינְתָּהּ מִינַּאי – and you have not bought it from me?[2] – Go out of the property; לָאו בַּעַל דְּבָרִים דִּידִי אַתְּ – you are not my litigant!"[3]

The Gemara presents the ruling:

אָמַר רָבָא – **Rava said:** דִּינָא קָאָמַר לֵיהּ – **[The challenger] is telling [the occupant] the** correct **law** and regains control of his property.[4]

The Gemara relates another incident:

הַהוּא דְּאָמַר לֵיהּ לְחַבְרֵיהּ – **There was a person who said to his fellow,** מַאי בָּעֵית בְּהַאי אַרְעָא – **"What are you doing in this land?"**[5] אָמַר לֵיהּ – **[The occupant] replied to him,** מִפְּלַנְיָא זְבִינָא – **"I bought** it **from so-and-so** וַאֲכַלְתִּיהּ שְׁנֵי חֲזָקָה – **and I made use of it for the** three **years** needed to establish a *chazakah.*" אָמַר לֵיהּ – **[The challenger] said to [the occupant]:** פְּלַנְיָא גַּזְלָנָא הוּא – **"So-and-so is a thief."**[6] אָמַר לֵיהּ – **[The occupant] replied to [the challenger],** וְהָא אִית לִי סַהֲדֵי – **"But I have witnesses** who will testify דַּאֲתַאי אִימְּלִכִי בָּךְ – **that I came and consulted with you** regarding my planned purchase of the field וְאָמַרְתְּ לִי זִיל זְבִין – **and** that **you told me, 'Go, buy** it.' This proves that you no longer owned the land at that point!" אָמַר לֵיהּ – **[The challenger] answered [the occupant],** הַשֵּׁנִי נוֹחַ לִי – **"The second one** [i.e. you] **is easy for me** to contend with in court; הָרִאשׁוֹן קָשֶׁה הֵימֶנּוּ – I find **the first one more difficult than he."**[7]

Rava rules:

אָמַר רָבָא – **Rava said:** דִּינָא קָאָמַר לֵיהּ – **[The challenger] is telling [the occupant] the** correct **law.**[8]

The Gemara asks:

כְּמַאן – **With whose** opinion does Rava's ruling accord? כְּאַדְמוֹן – **With** the minority opinion of **Admon!** דִּתְנַן – **For we learned in a Mishnah:**[9] הָעוֹרֵר עַל הַשָּׂדֶה – SOMEONE CHALLENGES an occupant's ownership of A FIELD, וְחָתוּם עָלֶיהָ בְּעֵד – BUT HE IS SIGNED AS A WITNESS ON the deed which records the sale of [THE FIELD] to the current occupant by a third person.[10] In that case, אַדְמוֹן אוֹמֵר – ADMON SAYS: הַשֵּׁנִי נוֹחַ לִי הָרִאשׁוֹן קָשֶׁה הֵימֶנּוּ – The challenger can say, "THE SECOND ONE IS EASY FOR ME

NOTES

1. Since the occupant stated that the seller told him that he had bought the land from the challenger, the occupant had tacitly admitted that his challenger had originally owned the land (*Rashbam;* see *Rosh;* cf. *Rabbeinu Yonah, Ritva;* see *Shach* 146:9).

2. I.e. [not only do you admit that you never bought it from me, but] even if you would assert that you bought it from me directly, you would have neither a bill of sale nor a *chazakah* to back such a claim (*Rashbam*).

3. [I.e. I do not have to litigate with you, since I, as the land's original owner, am currently its presumed owner (see *Rashbam;* see *Beis HaLevi* III:36:2).]

4. In the present case, the challenger had no witnesses to testify that he once owned the land. This can be seen from the fact that he was forced to claim to the occupant, "Do you not admit that I once owned the land?" If there were indeed witnesses to that effect, the challenger would not have had to rely on the occupant's admission. Nevertheless, Rava ruled in the original owner's favor, because of the principle: הוֹדָאַת בַּעַל דִּין כְּמֵאָה עֵדִים דָּמֵי, *the admission of a litigant is equivalent to one hundred witnesses*; in this case, the occupant's own admission that the challenger is the land's original owner establishes that fact beyond doubt (for purposes of their litigation). And since the occupant produces no evidence that he is now the rightful owner, he loses control of the land. [His deed proving his purchase of the land from the middle party is worthless, since there is no proof that the middle party ever bought the land from the original owner.] The occupant, however, can sue the middle party for the money that he paid him (*Rashbam*; cf. *Rashba* ד״ה ולענין האחריות, and other Rishonim, who argue that the occupant has no recourse to the middle party).

Although the Gemara discusses a case in which the occupant did not establish a three-year *chazakah,* the original owner would regain his land even if the current occupant had established a *chazakah.* For since the occupant has no proof that the middle party actually owned the land that he sold to him, his *chazakah* would not be accompanied by a defensible claim [see Mishnah below, 41a] and, hence, is meaningless (*Rashbam*).

Rashbam, however, adds that if the occupant *had* established a three-year *chazakah,* there would have been two sets of circumstances in which he would have retained control of the land:

1) If he initially replied to the challenger, "I bought the land from so-and-so who bought the land from you *in my presence.*" In that case, the occupant would be believed, for if he had wanted to retain the land illicitly by lying, he could have simply stated that he bought it directly from the original owner and had established a *chazakah.* He is therefore believed when he claims first-hand knowledge of the challenger's sale of the land to the middle party. [This is the principle of *migo* — see below, 31a note 3.]

2) Alternatively, the occupant would retain the land if he could produce valid testimony that the person who sold him the land had occupied it for even one day. [That would support the contention that the middle party indeed owned the land that he sold to the present occupant, causing the court to shift the burden to the challenger to prove that he in fact never sold the land (see *Ketzos HaChoshen* 146:9). [This is an application of the principle that the courts advance claims for buyers — see Gemara below, 41b, and note 13 there.]

[In the Gemara's actual case, however, where the occupant has *not* established a three-year *chazakah,* even if witnesses testify that the middle party occupied the land for a day, it would not be sufficient proof for the occupant, since the middle party had no contract proving that he had bought the land from the original owner (*Rashbam*; cf. *Tosafos*). See *Shach* (146:13), who writes that *Rashbam* would agree that if the occupant had made the other claim, "I bought the land from so-and-so who bought the land from you *in my presence,*" he would have won the case even though he did not have a *chazakah* (since the challenger has no witnesses that he is the original owner).]

5. The challenger had witnesses who could testify that he once owned the land (*Rashbam* ד״ה אמר רבא; *Nimukei Yosef;* cf. *Rashba*).

6. The one who sold the land to you was a thief who was squatting on my land and who had no right to sell it to you (see *Rashbam*; cf. *Tosafos*).

7. I.e. my advice to you to buy the land from the seller does not prove that I no longer owned the land. Rather, I cunningly misled you into buying the land because I find it easier to contend with you in a lawsuit than with the thief, who is a more difficult person (see *Rashbam* and *Ritva*).

8. [I.e. the challenger's assertion that he intentionally tricked the occupant into buying the land is credible. Thus, we have no proof that the challenger did not own the land at the time it was sold to the occupant, and the occupant is forced to return the land to the challenger.]

The occupant loses the land even though he has established a *chazakah* on it with three years of unchallenged utilization. Since by his own admission he did not purchase the land from the original owner, but rather from a stranger about whom it cannot be proven that he lived there for even one day, the *chazakah* is unaccompanied by a viable claim and, hence, meaningless (*Rashbam*; cf. *Tosafos*).

Normally, if an original owner remains silent for three years while someone is occupying his property, we can assume that he no longer owns the property (see above, 29a note 13). However, that evidence is strong enough to confer presumptive ownership upon the occupant only because his *chazakah* is equivalent to a contract (see above, 30a note 8). But in this case, since even his actual contract [from the middle party] is useless, proving only that the occupant bought the land from an alleged thief, the *chazakah* is not meaningful (*Rashbam*).

9. *Kesubos* 109a.

10. The challenger claims that the seller stole the field from him and sold it to the occupant, even though the challenger himself is one of the witnesses that signed the sale document. Does his participation in the sale by signing the sale document give the lie to his assertion that the seller stole the property from him and had no right to sell it? (see *Rashbam*).

דהאי ארעא דידי היא ואת לא זבינתה מינאי זיל לאו בעל דברים דידי את אמר רבא ^א דינא קאמר ליה: ^ב ההוא דאמר ליה לחבריה מאי בעית בהאי ארעא אמר ליה מפלניא זבינא ואכלתיה שני חזקה אמר ליה פלניא גזלנא הוא אמר ליה והא אית לי סהדי דאתאי (א) אימלכי בך ואמרת לי זיל זבין אמר ליה ^א השני נוח לי הראשון קשה הימנו אמר רבא ^ג דינא קאמר ליה כמאן כאדמון דתנן ^ג העורר על השדה וחתום עליה בעד אדמון אומר השני נוח לי הראשון קשה הימנו וחכ"א ^ד איבד את זכותו ^ה אפילו תימא רבנן התם עבד ליה מעשה אבל הכא דבורא עביד איניש דמיקרי ואמר ^ו ההוא דאמר ליה לחבריה מאי בעית בהאי ארעא אמר ליה מפלניא זבינתה ואכלתיה שני חזקה אמר ליה פלניא גזלנא הוא אמר ליה והא אית לי סהדי דאתית באורתא ואמרת לי זבנה ניהלי א"ל אמינא איזבון דינאי אמר רבא ^ז עביד איניש דזבין דיניה ^ח ההוא דאמר ליה לחבריה מאי בעית בהאי ארעא אמר ליה מפלניא זבינא ואכלתיה שני חזקה אמר ליה והא נקיטנא שטרא (ב) דזבני ליה מיניה הא ארבעי שני א"ל מי סברת שני חזקה תלת שני קא אמינא שני חזקה טובא קא אמינא אמר רבא ^ט עבידי אינשי דקרו לשני טובא שני חזקה ^י וה"מ דאכלה שבע (ג) דקדים חזקה דהאי לשטרא דהך אבל

^ג אמר ליה מפלניא זבינתה דזבנה מינך. כלומר שאמר לי בשעת מכירה שהוא לקחה ממך ומאחר שלא טוען ואכלתי שני חזקה שטר מכירה שלו עודנו בידו ומסקנא דמילתא מוקמינן ליה ביד המערער והיינו טעמא דכיון דמודה דשלו היה הקרקע מתחלה לא מבעיא היכא דלא החזיק בה שלש שנים אלא אפילו החזיק בה שלש שנים נמי אינה חזקה ומפקינן ליה מיניה דהא חזקה שאין עמה טענה היא שהוא אינו יודע אם היתה של אותו שמכרה לו אם לאו והוה ליה כהכיר בה בשדה שאינה שלו של מוכר ויחזירנה למערער והוא יגבה מעותיו מן המוכרו לו כדפסקינן בשנים אוחזין (ב"מ דף טו:) ואף על גב דליכא עדים למערער מדקאמר ולא מודית לי כו' ולא אמרינן מיגו דאי בעי אמר אנא זבינתה מינך ואכלתיה שני חזקה (ד) כדאמר מפלניא זבינתה דזבנה מינך נאמן שהוא עצמו אינו יודע אם זבנה המוכר מיניה דמערער אם לאו הלכך כיון דהוא מודי למערער דשלו היתה הודאת בעל דין כמאה עדים דמי וגם מודה הוא שאינו יודע אם לקחה המוכרה לו מן הבעלים אם לאו דהא לא טעין דזבנה מינך קמאי דידי וגם אין לו עדים שהחזיק בה המוכר יום אחד הלכך הפסיד. אבל החזיק זה שלש שנים וטוען מפלניא זבינתה דזבנה מינך קמאי דידי כלומר שידעתי בברור שלקחה מינך נאמן מיגו דאי בעי אמר אנא זבינתה מינך ואכלתיה שני חזקה אי נמי יש לו עדים שהחזיק בה המוכר יום אחד והכי אמרינן לקמן בפירקין (דף מא:) גבי ההוא דלר בקשתא בעיליתא ארבע שנין. והכא בהאי עובדא אפילו אם באו עדים שהחזיק בה יום אחד אותו המוכר אבל אין יודע אם לקח אותה אם לאו אינו מועיל כלום מאחר שזה לא החזיק שלש שנים וגם הראשון אין לו שטר מכירה מן הבעלים: ולא קא מודית לי כו'. כמו שפירשתי: ואת מינאי לא זבינתה. שאפילו אם היית טוען דמינאי זבינתה הלא אין לך לא שטר ולא חזקה: זיל. מקרקע שלי לאו בעל דברים דידי את ואני מוחזק בה יותר ממך שאתה לא החזקת שלש שנים: אמר רבא דינא קאמר ליה. המערער ואפי' אם החזיק בה שלש שנים כמו שפירשתי וכן הלכה: מפלניא זבינתה ואכלתיה שני חזקה. ואין לו עדים שהחזיק בו אותו המוכר יום אחד דאו לא הוי מצי טעין פלניא גזלנא הוא דהא טוענין ללוקח והכי מפרש לקמן גבי ההוא דלר בקשתא בעיליתא ארבע שנין: פלניא גזלנא הוא. בשדה זו שממני גזלה: ואימלכי. נועצתי: זיל זבין. לך קנה: השני נוח לי. אתה נוח לי לריב עמך ולהוציאה ממך בדין: אמר רבא דינא קא"ל. המערער ויטול שדהו דאפילו אדמון ורבנן לא פליגי אלא בדעביד המערער מעשה לסייעו ללוקח לקנות שדהו אבל בדבורא בעלמא כולהו מודו כרבא כדמפרש ואזיל ואע"פ שהחזיק בה ג' שנים בלא מחאה יפסיד דהא חזקה שאין עמה טענה היא שמודה הוא שלא לקחה מיד הבעלים כי אם מיד איש נכרי שאין ידוע שהיה לו חלק בה אפילו יום אחד. ולא מצי טעין אמאי לא מיחה מערער בתוך שלש דהיכא אמרינן דמפסיד מערער בשתיקתו היינו היכא דטעין אידך מינך זבינתה ואכלתיה שני חזקה דעד שלש שנים מיזדהר איניש בשטריה טפי לא מיזדהר הלכך זה שלא מיחה והוא לא נזהר בשטרו הפסיד. אבל הכא דמודי מחזיק דלא מיניה דמערער זבניה שהוא בעל הקרקע ובעדים זבנה לא הורע כחו של מערער בשתיקתו שהחזקה במקום שטר מכירתו עומדת וכיון דאין שטרו מועיל לו שהרי מגזלן לקח אף חזקתו אינה כלום: כמאן כאדמון. ואנן קיימא לן כרבנן בפרק אחרון דכתובות: דתנן. ראובן העורר על שדה שמכר שמעון ללוי ואומר ראובן כי שמעון גזלו ממנו והוא ראובן המעורר חתום עליה בעד באותו שטר מכירה שכתב לו שמעון ללוי חתם ראובן ועד אחר עמו: השני. לוי נוח לי ולכך חתמתי: מעשה. שחתם עד: דמקרי ואמר. לשון ויקר מקרה (רות ב): ואמרת לי זיל זבנה ניהלי. ואם שלך היתה היה לך להוציא ממנו בדין חנם ולא לאבד מעותיך: אמינא למיזבן דינא. אמרתי בלבי טוב לי לקנות בדמים מועטים קרקע הראוי לי ולא לטרוח ולבא בדין: עביד איניש דזבין דיניה. אדם תם שאינו רוצה להתקוטט אפילו על שלו עשוי הוא להוציא מעותיו ליטול את שלו בלא דין ומחלוקת. ובפירוש ר"ח מפורש אמינא למיזבן דינאי לקנות המריבות כלומר אע"פ שהיא שלי איני מוציאה מידו בלא מריבות ודינין אקנה אותם הדינין והמריבות באלו המעות אע"פ שעיקר הארץ שלי: ואכלתיה שני חזקה. ולא נזהרתי בשטרי יותר: אמר ליה והא נקיטנא שטרא. שכתוב בה דזבנה לי כלומר שקניה אצלי מן המוכר הזה ארבע שנים ונמצא שקדם מקחי לחזקה שלך שנה אחת ואת מינאי לא זבינתה הלכך חזקה שאין עמה טענה היא שהמוכר לא יכול למוכרה לך שכבר מכרה לי קודם: א"ל. מחזיק למערער מי סברת דמאי דאמינא שני חזקה דהיינו תלת שני בלמצום: שני חזקה טובא קאמינא. שקדמו לשטר שלך הרבה ויש לי עדים בכל החזקה כדמפרש (ה) לקמיה אבל לפיכך אמרתי שני חזקה סתם שלא הייתי יודע שהיה לך שטר של ארבע שנים שאצטרך לטעון ולפרש שני חזקה טובא: אמר רבא עביד איניש דקרי שני טובא שני חזקה. סתם ואם בא לטעון אחרי כן דשני חזקה טובא (ו) יותר מג' שנים אין זה חוזר וטוען טענות אחרות להכחיש טענות ראשונות ואנן קי"ל לקמן דאין אדם טוען בב"ד וחוזר וטוען טענות אחרות להכחיש הראשונות אלא אחר טענות הראשונות נפסוק הדין הלכך כי מייתי סהדי בהני שני חזקה טובא מהימנינן ליה שהרי לא חזר וטען: והני מילי. דמוקמינן לה בידיה דלייתי סהדי דאכלה ז' שנין שקדמו שני חזקה שלו למכירת השטר של מערער שהמוכר עצמו לא יכול למוכרה אחר שהחזיק בה ג' שנים בשופי אבל אי לית ליה סהדי אלא משית שני הדין עם בעל השטר דאין לך מחאה גדולה מזו שמיחה המוכר בזה המחזיק לסוף שתי שנים שמכר לאחר והיה לו לזה להזהר בשטרו לעולם עד שיוציא השטר מיד השני ויקרענו. ויש מפרשים דאין צריך עדי חזקת ז' שנים אלא של ג' אחרונים ואנן מהימנינן ליה על השאר מדאמר רבא עביד איניש דקרי לשני טובא שני חזקה למדו כן דלאי איכא סהדי על כל השבע שנים אמאי איצטריך למימר עביד איניש כו'. ולאו מילתא הוא שהרי החזקה במקום השטר עומדת ולא יהא חזקת ג' שנים האחרונים שיש לו עדים עליהם אלא שטר של ג' שנים והרי שטר של ד' שנים הקודם לו פוסלו ומדברי רבא אין ללמוד דלא צריך עדים לז' שנים שהרי רבא להודיענו בא דאינו קרוי חוזר וטוען במאי דאמר לבסוף שני חזקה טובא קאמינא דעביד איניש כו' שאילו היה חוזר וטוען להכחיש דברים הראשונים אפי' כי מייתי סהדי בהני אחרונים אינו כלום דהודאת בעל דין כמאה עדים דמי ואחר טענות הראשונות נלך ובפי' ר"ח נמי מצריך עדים לכל הז' שנים:

מפלניא זבינתיה דזבנה מינך ואכלתיה שני חזקה אמר ליה פלניא גזלנא הוא. פי' יש לי עדים שהוא גזלן ואפי' לר' ביה חד יומא הא קי"ל דגזלן אין לו חזקה ולא כפ"ה דפירש דאין לו עדים שהחזיק בה המוכר אפילו יום אחד דאו לא הוה מצי טעין פלניא גזלנא הוא משמע שרוצה לפרש גזלנא הוא לא שיש לו עדים שהוא גזלן אלא כלומר בגזל (ז) היא הקרקע בידו ואין נראה לר"י דהוה ליה לאסוקי כדמסיק לעיל לא קמודית לי דארעא דידי הוא ואת מינאי לא זבינתיה וכו': עביד איניש דקרי לשני טובא שני חזקה. אבל אי לא עביד אף על גב דאית ליה סהדי דאכלה שבע שנין לא מהימנינן דהא איהו דמכחיש להו דמודה שלא אכלה אלא שני חזקה דהיינו שלש שנים: אבל

כ א מיי' פי"ד מהל' טוען ונטען הלכה יד סמג עשין לד טוש"ע ח"מ סי' קמו סעיף יג:
כא ב ג מיי' פט"ו שם הלכה ג סמג עשין לה טוש"ע ח"מ סי' קמו סעיף יז וסי' קמו סעיף ה:
כב ד מיי' שם הלכה א סמג שם טוש"ע ח"מ סי' קמו סעיף ה:
כג ה מיי' שם הלכה ד טוש"ע שם סעיף ה:
כד ו ז מיי' שם וסמג שם טוש"ע ח"מ סי' קמו סעיף יז:
כה ח ט י מיי' שם פט"ו הלכה ז סמג שם טוש"ע שם סעיף יט:

רבינו גרשום

דאמרי' השני נוח לי להוציאה מתחת ידו מש"ה אמרנא ליה זיל זבין והראשון שגזלה קשה הימני ולא הייתי יכול לטעון (א) בעדו: והוא המערער חתום עליה בעד אדמון אומר יכול לומר המערער משום הכי חתמי על שטר מכירה השני נוח לי והראשון קשה הימני הכא נמי לא שנא: אבל דבורא דמשיא עצה מיקרי ואמר ליה: אמינא איזבון דינאי. כלומר אע"פ שהוא שלי מן הדין אמרתי אקנה אותה ממך שלא רציתי להקניט עמך ועכשיו הואיל ולא רצית למוכרה לי ארציאנה מידך בבית דין: עביד איניש דזבין דיניה. מי שאינו רוצה להתקוטט קונה דבר שבדין היה להיות שלו מפני קשיות בעל דינו: ד' שנין. כלומר שנה אחת היתה שלי קודם שהתחילו שני חזקה שלך: והני מילי דאמרי' עביד איניש דקרי לשני טובא שני חזקה להיכא דאכלה שבע שנים ג' שני חזקה קודם זמנו דשטרא דהאי. אבל אכליה המחזיק שית והאי אידך יש לו שטר שקנאה ד' שנים בתוך אותן ו' שנים דהאי לא אכלה כי אם ב' שנין קודם זמן שטרו יכול לומר לו האי בעל השטר למחזיק כיון דהמוכר מכרה לי לסוף ב' שנים שהיתה בידך אין לך מחאה גדולה מזה דגלי מוכר דעתיה דאותה חזקה שהחזיק בה אינה חזקה:

חשק שלמה על רבינו גרשום

(א) נראה דצ"ל ולא הייתי יכול לטעון עמו:

א) [לקמן דף מג:], ב) כתובות דף קט., ג) שייך לע"א:

הגהות הב"ח

(א) גמ' ואימלכי בך: (ב) שם דזבנה לי מיניה הא ארבע: (ג) שם דאכלה שבע שנין דקדים: (ד) רשב"ם ד"ה א"ל מפלניא וכו' שני חזקה כי אמר נמי מפלניא זבינתה דזבנה מינך נאמן וכו' יום אחד לכך הפסיד וכו' אם לקח אותה המוכר אם לאו: (ה) ד"ה שני חזקה טובא וכו' כדמפרש לקמן ולפיכך אמרתי כל"ל ותיבת אבל נמחק: (ו) ד"ה אמר רבא וכו' טובא קאמר יותר מג' שנים: (ז) תוס' ד"ה מפלניא וכו' כלומר בגזל בא לו הקרקע בידו:

ליקוטי רש"י

השני נוח לי הראשון קשה הימנו. דקסבר שמעון לוי נוח לי ויהודה גברא אלמא הוא ולקחה ממנו ולא אוכל לדון עמו [רשב"ם לקמן מג.]. העורר על השדה כו'. ראובן מערער על שדה שביד שמעון ואומר לוי שמכרה לך גזלה ממני. וחתום עליה בעד. על שטר המכירה שכתב לוי לשמעון כשמכרה לו. אדמון אומר. יכול הוא שיאמר לו שלא ערערתי בשעה שלקחת ונתמתי בתוך השטר עד לפי שלוי אדם חזק וקשה להוציא מידו ונוח לי שתהא בידך שאוציאנה ממך בדין. איבד את זכותו. דהודה ונתם הודה שאין לו עסק בה [כתובות קט.].

זה

to contend with in court; I find **THE FIRST ONE MORE DIFFICULT THAN HE."**[11] וַחֲכָמִים אוֹמְרִים — **BUT THE SAGES SAY:** אִיבֵּד אֶת זְכוּתוֹ — By signing on the deed, **HE HAS FORFEITED HIS RIGHT** to the field.[12] — ? —

The Gemara answers:

אֲפִילוּ תֵּימָא רַבָּנַן — **You can even say** that Rava's ruling follows the view of **the Rabbis** [i.e. the Sages of the Mishnah]. הָתָם עָבַד לֵיהּ מַעֲשֶׂה — For **there,** in the Mishnah's case, by signing on the deed **the person performed an *action*** that points to his non-ownership of the property. אֲבָל הָכָא דִּבּוּרָא — **Whereas here,** in Rava's case, he merely offered **spoken words** of advice. Words alone are not sufficient evidence because עָבִיד אִינִישׁ דְּמִיקְרֵי וְאָמַר — **a person will occasionally say** something that seems to undermine his rights.[13]

The Gemara cites an incident similar to the previous one:

הַהוּא דְּאָמַר לֵיהּ לְחַבְרֵיהּ — **There was a person who said to his fellow,** מַאי בָּעֵית בְּהַאי אַרְעָא — **"What are you doing in this land?"** אָמַר לֵיהּ — **[The occupant] replied to [the challenger],** מִפְּלַנְיָא זְבִינְתָּהּ — **"I bought it from so-and-so** וַאֲכַלְתִּיהָ שְׁנֵי חֲזָקָה — **and I have used it for the** three **years** needed to establish a *chazakah.*" אָמַר לֵיהּ — **[The challenger] said to [the occupant],** פְּלַנְיָא גַּזְלָנָא הוּא — **"So-and-so is a thief,** who had no right to sell you the property." אָמַר לֵיהּ — **[The occupant] replied to [the challenger],** וְהָא אִית לִי סַהֲדֵי — **"But I have witnesses** who will testify דְּאָתֵית בְּאוּרְתָּא — **that you came to me last night** וְאָמַרְתְּ לִי זַבְנָהּ נִיהֲלִי — **and you said to me, 'Sell me [the land].'** If the land was yours, why were you willing to pay me for it? You should have simply taken me to court!" אָמַר לֵיהּ — **[The challenger] said to [the occupant],** אֲמִינָא — **"I said** to myself, אֶיזְבּוֹן דִּינַאי — **I will buy what is mine by right** and thereby avoid litigation."[14]

The Gemara presents the ruling:

אָמַר רָבָא — **Rava said:** עָבִיד אִינִישׁ דְּזָבִין דִּינֵיהּ — **It is normal for a person to buy what is his by right** in order to avoid litigation.[15]

The Gemara records another incident:

הַהוּא דְּאָמַר לֵיהּ לְחַבְרֵיהּ — **There was a person who said to his fellow,** מַאי בָּעֵית בְּהַאי אַרְעָא — **"What are you doing in this land?** It belongs to me!" אָמַר לֵיהּ — **[The occupant] replied to [the challenger],** מִפְּלַנְיָא זְבִינָא וַאֲכַלְתִּיהָ שְׁנֵי חֲזָקָה — **"I bought** the land **from so-and-so, and I have used it for the years** needed to establish a *chazakah.*"[16] אָמַר לֵיהּ — **[The challenger] said to [the occupant],** וְהָא נְקִיטְנָא שְׁטָרָא — **"But I am holding a deed** to this property stating דְּזַבְנֵי לֵיהּ מִינֵּיהּ — **that I bought it from him** [the man that you claim sold it to you] הָא אַרְבְּעֵי שְׁנֵי — ***four* years ago!"**[17] אָמַר לֵיהּ — **[The occupant] said to [the challenger],** מִי סָבְרַתְּ שְׁנֵי חֲזָקָה — **"Do you think** that when I said that I used the field for **the years of *chazakah,*** תְּלָת שְׁנֵי קָא אֲמִינָא — **I meant** that I used it for only **three years?** שְׁנֵי חֲזָקָה טוּבָא קָא אֲמִינָא — **I meant** that I used the land for **many years of *chazakah*!**"[18]

The Gemara rules:

אָמַר רָבָא — **Rava said:** עֲבִידֵי אִינְשֵׁי דְּקָרוּ לִשְׁנֵי טוּבָא שְׁנֵי חֲזָקָה — **It is normal for people to refer to many years** of occupancy simply as **"years of *chazakah.*"** Therefore, the occupant retains control of the land.[19]

The Gemara qualifies this ruling:

וְהָנֵי מִילֵּי — **And this ruling** applies only דַּאֲכָלָהּ שֶׁבַע — **where [the occupant] has used [the land]** for **seven** years, דְּקָדִים חֲזָקָה דְּהַאי לִשְׁטָרָא דְּהַךְ — **so that [the occupant's]** three years of ***chazakah* preceded the document of [the challenger];**[20]

NOTES

11. I.e. the challenger's signing of the deed does not disprove his assertion of theft. Rather, he can claim that he participated in the supposed sale to make retrieving the land easier for himself, since he finds the thief a more difficult person to contend with than the hapless buyer.

12. According to the Sages, the challenger's signing on the deed indicates that he was indeed no longer the owner of the field. Why, then, does Rava here apparently follow Admon's view, when the halachah follows the Sages' opinion in this matter? (*Rashbam*).

13. It is true that a landowner might facilitate a transfer of his field from a thief to a third person by giving advice. However, he would not go so far as to take an action [such as signing a contract] that could be used as evidence that he no longer owns the land (*Nimukei Yosef*).

14. *Rashbam.* Alternatively, אֶיזְבּוֹן דִּינַאי is to be rendered: *I will buy my [potential] lawsuit;* i.e. I was willing to pay in order to avoid the stress and difficulty of litigation (*R' Chananel* cited by *Rashbam*).

[Our elucidation follows the version of the text before us. See, however, *Rashbam,* for a slightly different version of the text, which would indicate that the challenger had asked the occupant to purchase the property for him from the seller. See *Rashash, Rabbeinu Yonah.*]

15. A retiring person would rather pay to retrieve what is rightfully his than become embroiled in litigation (*Rashbam*).

16. Having established a *chazakah,* I was no longer careful to keep my deed and I lost it (*Rashbam*). [In this case, that other person was indeed known to be the original owner of the property.]

17. Since he sold me the land first, he could not later sell the land to you. Moreover you yourself admit that you did not buy the field from me. Therefore, your *chazakah* is meaningless, since it is not accompanied by a viable claim (*Rashbam*).

18. The occupant can produce witnesses to document those additional years of use. He explains that the reason he did not make the number of years clear in his original claim was that — unaware that the challenger had a deed dated four years earlier — he did not think the number of years beyond three were of any consequence (*Rashbam*). Now, there is a legal principle (see below, 31a) that a litigant cannot revise his initial claim [even if he can produce witnesses to support the revised version]. The question therefore arises whether, in the present case, the occupant's subsequent statement that he meant "many" years, not only three, represents a clarification of his initial claim (which is acceptable) or a revision of that claim (which is not) (*Rashbam*).

19. The occupant's second claim of "many years" is a reasonable clarification of his initial claim rather than a revision. Therefore, he retains the property if he can produce witnesses supporting a *chazakah* that predates the challenger's deed (*Rashbam*).

20. The current occupant must produce witnesses who testify that his occupancy began at least three years before the date of the deed held by the challenger. In that case, since the occupant had utilized the land unchallenged for those three years [he had established a *chazakah* prior to the land's sale to the challenger and] he can claim that the original owner had no right to sell the land afterwards to the challenger (*Rashbam's* preferred explanation). [See *Rashba* and *Yad Ramah,* who point out that it is not necessary to produce witnesses for all seven years, for as long as there are witnesses testifying that he made a *chazakah* the first three years, that would establish him as the new owner, and any sale of the field after that would be invalid.]

אֲבָל שִׁית – **But** if the occupant made use of the land for only **six** years, he must vacate the land, because אֵין לְךָ מְחָאָה גְּדוֹלָה מִזּוֹ – **there is no protest greater than this.**[1]

The Gemara cites an incident in which two litigants were disputing ownership of a property:[2]

זֶה אוֹמֵר שֶׁל אֲבוֹתַי – **This** one **claimed,** "It was the land **of my forefathers,"** וְזֶה אוֹמֵר שֶׁל אֲבוֹתַי – **and this** other one **claimed,** "It was the land **of my forefathers."** הַאי אַיְיתֵי סַהֲדֵי דְּאַבְהָתֵיהּ הִיא – **[The challenger] produced witnesses** who testified **that [the land]** had been **his forefathers'** וְהַאי אַיְיתֵי סַהֲדֵי דַּאֲכָלָהּ שְׁנֵי חֲזָקָה – **while [the current occupant] produced witnesses** who testified **that he had used it** for **the** three **years** needed to establish a ***chazakah;*** he did not, however, produce testimony that the land had belonged to his forefathers.

Rabbah, the judge in the case, handed down a ruling:

אָמַר רַבָּה – **Rabbah said:** מָה לוֹ לְשַׁקֵּר – **What** reason **is there for [the current occupant] to lie?** אִי בָּעֵי אָמַר לֵיהּ – **If he wanted** to gain possession of the land by lying, **he** could have **said to [the challenger],** מִינָּךְ זְבַנְתָּהּ – **"I bought [the land] from you,** וַאֲכַלְתִּיהָ שְׁנֵי חֲזָקָה – **and used it for the** three **years of *chazakah."*** Therefore, he is believed to claim that he inherited it.[3]

Rabbah's disciple objected:

אָמַר לֵיהּ אַבַּיֵי – **Abaye said to [Rabbah]:** מָה לִי לְשַׁקֵּר בִּמְקוֹם עֵדִים לָא אָמְרִינַן – **We do not say** that a litigant is believed by virtue of the principle of **"what** reason **is there for me to lie," in the face of witnesses** who contradict his claim![4]

Rabbah concurred with Abaye's objection and ruled in favor of the challenger, reversing his original ruling.[5] But the occupant persisted:

הֲדַר אָמַר לֵיהּ – **[The occupant] thereupon replied to [the challenger],** אִין דְּאַבְהָתָךְ הִיא – **"Yes, [the land]** indeed **belonged to your forefathers** at one time, וּזְבַנְתָּהּ (מינך) [מִנַּיְיהוּ] – **but I bought it from them.**[6] וְהַאי דְּאָמְרִי לָךְ דְּאַבְהָתִי – **And what** I meant when **I said to you that it was my forefathers'** was דְּסָמִיךְ לִי עֲלָהּ כִּדְאַבְהָתִי – **that I felt as secure in [its ownership] as** if it were **my forefathers'."**[7]

The Gemara discusses what the ruling should be, based on this latest development in the case:

טוֹעֵן וְחוֹזֵר וְטוֹעֵן – **May one** advance a **claim and return and** use another **claim** in such a case? אוֹ אֵין טוֹעֵן וְחוֹזֵר וְטוֹעֵן – **Or may one not** advance **a claim and return and use another claim?**[8]

The Gemara presents a dispute:

עוּלָּא אָמַר – **Ulla says:** טוֹעֵן וְחוֹזֵר וְטוֹעֵן – **He may claim and return and** use another **claim.** נְהַרְדָּעֵי אָמְרֵי – **The Nehardeans,** however, **say:** אֵינוֹ טוֹעֵן וְחוֹזֵר וְטוֹעֵן – **He may not claim and return and** use another **claim.**

The Gemara presents two qualifications to Ulla's ruling:

וּמוֹדֵי עוּלָּא – **But Ulla concedes** הֵיכָא דְּאָמַר לֵיהּ – that in a situation **where [the occupant]** originally **said to [the challenger],** שֶׁל אֲבוֹתַי וְלֹא שֶׁל אֲבוֹתֶיךָ – "It was the land **of my forefathers and not of your forefathers,"** דְּאֵינוֹ טוֹעֵן וְחוֹזֵר וְטוֹעֵן – **that [the occupant] may not claim and return and** use another **claim.**[9] וְהֵיכָא דַּהֲוָה קָאֵי בֵּי דִינָא וְלֹא טָעַן – **And** Ulla

NOTES

1. If the occupant can substantiate only the last six years of occupancy but not seven, then we must proceed on the premise that he began his occupancy only six years ago, which is only two years before the date recorded in the challenger's deed. It emerges, then, that the original owner sold this field to the challenger two years after the current occupant began his occupancy. In that case, the original owner's act of selling this field to a second buyer (within three years of the first "buyer's" occupancy) is as forceful a demonstration as any that the owner protests the current occupant's presence there. Hence, it would behoove the occupant [had he actually purchased the field] to guard his deed until the second buyer's supposed deed is destroyed (*Rashbam*). [The occupant's failure to retain his deed under such circumstances is inexcusable; thus, his years of *chazakah* are meaningless.]

2. Although this incident is not introduced, as the previous ones, by "There was a certain man etc.," it is nevertheless an actual account and not a hypothetical case, as will be seen in the Gemara below (*Rashbam*).

3. Rabbah ruled in favor of the current occupant because of the principle of *migo* (literally: since). This principle (which will come into play repeatedly in this chapter) applies to cases in which it is within a litigant's power to win a case with a strong claim, but instead he advances a weaker one. In such cases we reason: Although his claim is weak, he should be believed, since if he were lying, he could have won by advancing a stronger claim. In this particular case, where the occupant had established three years of *chazakah*, he could have retained control of the land by simply claiming that he bought it from his challenger. Therefore, now that he says it had originally belonged to his forefathers (a claim for which he does not produce witnesses), he is also believed (*Rashbam*).

4. [The testimony of two witnesses is given the ultimate credence in law, and supersedes any other type of proof that is advanced to contradict them, such as a *migo*.] Hence, Abaye objected to believing the occupant's claim with use of the *migo* principle, for that claim — that the land had belonged to his father — was contradicted by two valid witnesses who established that the land had actually belonged to the other litigant's father (*Rashbam*).

[The court did not interpret the occupant's claim to mean that his father had purchased it from the challenger's father, because his claim implied that the land had *always* belonged to his forefathers, not that they had purchased it (*Tosafos*).]

Although the occupant had utilized the land for three years [giving credence to the fact that the challenger did not own it], he still was obligated to relinquish the land, because the law is that a *chazakah* is effective only when the occupant concurrently advances a valid claim explaining how he obtained the land from the original owner (below, 41a). According to Abaye's logic, the occupant's *chazakah* was not considered to be accompanied by a valid claim, since the claim that he did advance was determined to be false as a result of the conflicting testimony of the witnesses (*Rashbam*).

5. Rabbah's deferral to his disciple can be seen from the Gemara that follows [in which it is apparent that the occupant was in danger of losing control of the land]. In addition, this can be inferred by the Gemara's words "Abaye said *to him*" (i.e. Rabbah), and not merely "Abaye said." [The latter is a statement of position; the former are Abaye's actual words to Rabbah. The fact that the comment was not formulated as a question but as a categorical statement indicates that there is no question that Abaye was correct.] (*Rashbam*).

6. The version found in the Vilna text, וּזְבַנְתָּה מִינָּךְ, *and I bought it from you,* is the version that was before *Ramah* (*Yad Ramah*), *Meiri*, *Rabbeinu Gershom* and (probably) *Ritva*. We have followed the version that seems to have been before *Rashbam* (see ד״ה דסמיך) וּזְבַנְתָּה מִינַּיְיהוּ, *and I bought it from them,* as indicated by *Bach* in his *Hagahos* (see *Dikdukei Sofrim* which states that this version is also found in some early prints and manuscripts. See also *Rambam Hil. To'ein VeNitan* 15:6).

7. The occupant now claimed that by his original statement he meant merely that he felt as secure in his possession of the land as if he had inherited it. That is, since he purchased it from the challenger's father, occupied it uncontestedly for three years and could produce witnesses to this effect, he could defend any challenge to his occupation (see *Rashbam*).

8. The law is that once someone has advanced a claim in court, he may not *retract* it and advance another claim; this point is not open to debate. The question is only whether one may advance a second claim that *reinterprets* an earlier one. In our case, the occupant first claimed that he should retain the land because he inherited it from his father. His new claim — that he had actually bought the land from the challenger's father — apparently contradicted his original claim. But he interpreted his original statement to have been only an expression of his security of ownership, not his actual claim to the land. The question now is whether such an interpretation is accepted by the court (*Rashbam*).

9. Ulla agrees that if the occupant had explicitly stated, "The land was my father's and not your father's," it is clear that his claim to the land was based on his position that he inherited it. In this case, he could not change his claim to state that he had bought the land from

אבל שית אין לך מחאה גדולה מזו: א) זה אומר של אבותי (א) וזה אומר של אבותי האי אייתי סהדי דאבהתיה היא והאי אייתי סהדי דאכלה שני חזקה ג) אמר רבה מה לו לשקר אי בעי א"ל מינך זבנתה ואכלתיה שני חזקה ג) א"ל אביי א) מה לי לשקר במקום עדים לא אמרינן הדר א"ל אין דאבהתך היא וזבנתה (ב) מינך והאי דאמרי לך דאבהתי דסמיך לי עלה כדאבהתי טוען וחוזר וטוען או אין טוען וחוזר וטוען עולא אמר ב) טוען וחוזר וטוען נהרדעי אמרי אינו טוען וחוזר וטוען ג) ומודי עולא היכא דא"ל של אבותי ולא של אבותיך דאינו טוען וחוזר וטוען ד) והיכא דהוה קאי בי דינא ולא טען ואתא מאבראי וטען אינו חוזר וטוען מאי טעמא טענתיה אגמריה ומודו נהרדעי היכא דאמר ליה ה) של אבותי שלקחוה מאבותיך דחוזר וטוען ה) והיכא דאישתעי מילי אבראי (ג) ולא טען ואתא לבי דינא וטען דחוזר וטוען מאי טעמא עביד איניש דלא מגלי טענתיה אלא לבי דינא אמר אמימר אנא נהרדעא אנא וסבירא לי דטוען וחוזר וטוען והלכתא טוען וחוזר וטוען: זה אומר של אבותי (ד) וזה אומר של אבותי האי אייתי סהדי דאבהתיה ואכלה שני חזקה והאי אייתי סהדי דאכלה שני חזקה אמר רב נחמן ו) אוקי אכילה לבהדי אכילה ואוקי ארעא בחזקת אבהתא א"ל רבא (ה) הא עדות מוכחשת היא אמר ליה נהי דאיתכחש באכילתה באבהתא

רשב"ם

זה אומר של אבותי. היה הקרקע והרי היא שלי וזה אומר כו' עובדא הוה כדמוכח לקמיה: אמר רבה מה לו לשקר. לזה המחזיק במאי דטוען דשל אבותיו וירשה מהם אי בעי אמר כו' והלכך בהאי מיגו מהימנינן ליה: אמר ליה. תלמידו אביי מה לי לשקר כו' כלומר על ידי האי מיגו דמה לי לשקר לא זכה בקרקע שהרי עדים מכחישים את דבריו שאומרים דשל אבותיו דאידך היא וגם החזקה אינה כלום שהרי אין עמה טענה כי אם טענת שקר. והלכה כאביי שהרי רבה הודה לו כדמוכח ואזיל: הדר א"ל אין כו'. דמשום שהיו מפסידין אותו כאביי הוצרך לחזור ולטעון כן דיקא נמי דקאמר גמרא אמר ליה אביי ולא קאמר אביי אמר: הדר א"ל. ההוא דאייתי עדי חזקה לאידך: דסמיך (ו) עלה כדאבהתי. הייתי סומך ומובטח על קרקע זו כאילו היא של אבותי לפי שהחזקתי בה בשופי ובעדים וקניתיה מאבותיך. ובעי גמרא טוען וחוזר וטוען יכול אדם לטעון בבית דין טוען בב"ד מה שהוא רוצה וחוזר וטוען לתקן דבריו הראשונים: עולא אמר טוען וחוזר וטוען. טוען בבית דין מה שהוא רוצה וחוזר אחרי כן לטעון דברים אחרים לתרץ דברים הראשונים אע"פ שמכחישם קצת בזה שחזר וטוען האי דאמר לאבהתי דסמיך עלה כדאבהתי: ומודי עולא. אף על גב דמהימנינן ליה להאי דטעין אין דאבהתך היא כו' שאם טען מתחילה ופירש של אבותי ולא של אבותיך דאינו חוזר וטוען טענה זו דסמיך עלה כדאבהתי שהרי עוקר לגמרי דברים הראשונים וכן הלכה דפסקינן לקמן כעולא: ומודי נמי עולא כל היכא דהוה קאי בי דינא ולא טען. תיקון דברים הראשונים אלא אחר שיצא מבית דין חזר לב"ד ותיקן דבריו הראשונים שאינו חוזר וטוען היכא דמכחישן קצת: טענתיה אגמריה. אוהביו וקרוביו: ומודו נהרדעי. בזה שטען מתחילה של אבותי וחזר וטען של אבותי שלקחוה מאבותיך דחוזר וטוען ומהימן דאינו עוקר דבריו הראשונים כלל אלא מוסיף עליהן וכיון דהחזיק בה שלש שנים מוקמינן לה בידיה דחזקה שיש עמה טענה היא דמה לו לשקר דאי בעי אמר מינך זבנתה ואכלתיה שני חזקה כי אמר נמי של אבותי שלקחוה מאבותיך מהימן. ואע"ג דגבי יורש קיימא לן לקמן בפירקין דאין צריך טענה מאחר שהחזיק בה שלש שנים היאך היתה של אביו אבל ראיה בעי שהחזיק בה אביו יום אחד הכא אין צריך להביא עדים שהחזיק בה אביו כלל שהרי זה טען טענה גמורה וחזקה שיש עמה טענה היא: ומודו נמי נהרדעי. כל היכא דאישתעי מילי מאבראי לבי דינא קודם שטען כלום בב"ד ולא טען מה שהוא טוען עכשיו בב"ד ואתא לבי דינא (ז) לטעון טענות שעוקרות לגמרי את הראשונות דחוזר וטוען: דלא מגלי טענתיה. שלא ילמד מהן מי שכנגדו ויתן לבו מתחלה קודם שיבאו לבית דין להשיב עליהם וכן הלכה. וה"מ (ח) טענות בעלמא אבל טען בפירוש בפני עדים חוץ לב"ד חייב אני מנה לפלוני הרי הודה לו ושוב אינו יכול לכפור בב"ד: וסבירא לי דחוזר וטוען. כלומר אנא נמי נהרדעי אנא ופליגנא עלייהו דנהרדעי: והלכתא חוזר וטוען. תיקון לשון הראשון אע"פ שמכחישם קצת הואיל ואינו עוקרן לגמרי כדלעיל: וזה אומר של אבותי. ואכלתיה שני חזקה אותן שלש שנים שאתה טוען אני אכלתיה ולא אתה: והאי אייתי סהדי דאכלה שני חזקה. אותן שלש שנים עצמן שהעידו אלו הראשונים עליהם ובאו אלו והכחישום: אמר רב נחמן. עדות דאכילה בטלה דאוקי עדות של אכילה כנגד עדות שניה של אכילה והרי מכחישים זה את זה אבל בעדות דאבהתא דלא אתכחשת עדותן קיימת ומוקמי' בידיה: הא עדות מוכחשת היא. כיון דהני ב' כתות מכחישות זו את זו אחת מהן פסולה לכל עדיות שבעולם ואחרי שאין לברר איזו הפסולה תיבטל עדותן לגמרי:

בדאבהתא

תוספות

אבל אכלה שית שנין כו'. הקשה ר"י בר מרדכי אפי' לא אייתי סהדי אלא דאכלה שלש שנין יהא נאמן לומר לקחתיה קודם מינך במיגו דאי בעי אמר מינך זבינתה ואומר ר"י דאין זה מיגו דמעיקרא לא יטעון כלל מינך זבינתה דאין יודע אם יש לזה שטר שקנאה ממנו: אמר רבה מה לו לשקר. רבא גרסינן דאביי ורבא אמרי לקמן (דף לג:) דלא סבירא להו הא דרב חסדא דמה לי לשקר במקום עדים לא אמרינן: מה לי לשקר במקום עדים לא אמרינן. תימה לרשב"א אמאי הוי במקום עדים נימא של אבותיו היתה יום אחד ונאמר שלקחה מאבותיו דהא טוענין ליורש ומהימנינן ליה בהא דקאמר שאבותיו דרו בו יום אחד במיגו דאי בעי אמר מינך זבנתיה ולקמן נמי (ט) דקאמרי נהרדעי היכא דאמר של אבותי שלקחוה מאבותיך דחוזר וטוען הא אפילו לא יטעון שלקחוה אלא שאמר אנן טענינן ליה ואומר רבינו יצחק דשל אבותי משמע שהיתה מעולם של אבותי ולא שלקחוה עד שיפרש בדבריו ולקמן דנקט שלקחוה לא שצריך שיטעון שידע שלקחוה אלא של אבותי שראיתי שדרו בה יום אחד על כן אני רוצה לזכות דשמא לקחוה (י) אבותי במשפט וטוענין ליורש: ומודו נהרדעי היכא דאמר שלקחוה כו'. מספקא לר"י היכא דנפיק לבראי וחזר ואתא לב"ד אי מצי למימר הכי: אמר ליה רבא והא עדות מוכחשת היא. תימה אמאי הוי עדות מוכחשת והא רבא אית לי' במרובה (ב"ק ד' עב: ושם ד"ה רבא) ובפ' זה בורר (סנהדרין דף כז. ושם ד"ה רבא) דעד זומם מכאן ולהבא הוא נפסל ולא מפסל אלא משעה דאתכחוש ואית לן למימר אאכילתה דאתכחוש אתכחוש אאבהתא דלא אתכחוש לא אתכחוש דהכי אמר במרובה (ב"ק דף עג. ושם) דהוזמו על הטביחה ועל הגניבה לא הוזמו אע"ג דתוך כדי דבור העידו על הגניבה ועל הטביחה לרבא כיון דמההיא שעתא דקא מיתזמי הוא דקא מיפסלי אטביחה דאיתזום איתזום על הגניבה דלא איתזום לא איתזום וללישנא דהוי טעמא דרבא (כ) משום דעד זומם חידוש ואין לך אלא משעת חידושו ניחא אלא ללישנא דמפרש טעמא דרבא משום פסידא דלקוחות ה"נ נהימנינהו ואפילו היכא דליכא פסידא דלקוחות לא מיפסל למפרע אפילו להאיך לישנא מדבעי התם מאי איכא בין האי לישנא להאי לישנא ולא קאמר איכא בינייהו להיכא דליכא פסידא דלקוחות ועוד קשיא דקאמר בסמוך אליבא דרב חסדא כולי עלמא לא פליגי משמע דרב נחמן לא מצי סבר בשום ענין כרב חסדא דחשיב להו סהדי שקרי ומנא ליה דלמא סבר רב נחמן דמכאן ולהבא הוא נפסל ומיהו הא איכא למימר משום דלא קיימא לן כרבא בהא ונראה דסוגיא דהכא כההיא לישנא דחידוש אבל ללישנא דפסידא דלקוחות סבר דלא אמר ליה רבא לרב נחמן מעולם הכי ולריב"א נראה דלא דמי הך דהכא להאיך דמרובה דהתם גניבה וטביחה תרי מילי נינהו ולהכי אגניבה דלא איתזום לא איתזום כיון דלהבא הוא נפסל אלא הכא כי איתכחוש אאכילה איתכחוש נמי אאבהתא דאבהתא בלא אכילתה לא מהני דהוי מוקמי' בידי' דאית ליה סהדי דאכלה שני חזקה דנאמן לומר היתה של אבותי יום אחד במיגו דאי בעי אמר מינך זבינתה ומיהו אכתי דחשיב לה גמרא כעדות אחרת לא אתי שפיר:

וזו

מסורת הש"ס

א) לקמן דף לג., ב) [לקמן לג:], ג) [קדושין סד: וש"נ].

הגהות הב"ח

(א) גמ' זה אומר של אבותי ואכלתיה שני חזקה וזה אומר של אבותי האי אייתי סהדי: (ב) שם אין דאבהתך היא וזבינתה מינייהו והאי דאמרי לך: (ג) שם אבראי לב"ד ולא טען: (ד) שם זה אומר של אבותי ואכלתיה שני חזקה וזה אומר של אבותי ואכלתיה שני חזקה האי אייתי סהדי דאבהתיה היא ואכלה: (ה) שם והא עדות: (ו) רשב"ם ד"ה דסמיך לי עלה וכו' ובעי תלמודא טוען וכו' ובעי יכול אדם לטעון בב"ד ולחזור אחרי כן ולטעון דברים אחרים לתרץ דברים וכו' עלה כדאבהתי הס"ד ואח"כ נ"ל ד"ה עולא אמר טוען וחוזר וטוען בב"ד מה שהוא רוצה וחוזר וטוען לתקן את דבריו קמא לאו דוקא דהא לא פליגי אלא בחוזר וטוען הס"ד ואח"כ נ"ל ד"ה אינו חוזר וטוען שהרי עוקר דברים הראשונים הס"ד ואח"כ מ"ה ומודה עולא אע"ג: (ז) ד"ה ומודו נמי נהרדעי וכו' לבי דינא וטען טענות: (ח) ד"ה דלא מגלי וכו' וה"מ היכא דטעין טענה בעלמא אבל טען: (ט) תוס' ד"ה מה לי וכו' דקאמר דמודו נהרדעי: (י) באד"ה דשמא לקחוה מאבותיך דטוענין ליורש: (כ) ד"ה אמר וכו' וללישנא דהוי טעמא דרבא דהתם משום חידוש הוא ואין לך בו אלא:

גליון הש"ס

גמ' של אבותי שלקחוה מאבותיך. עיין לקמן דף נב ע"ב תוספות ד"ה דברים:

ליקוטי רש"י

האי אייתי סהדי דאבהתיה היא. עד יום מותם ומעולם לא מכרו לאבותיו של זה הכא. אמר רבה מה לו לשקר. לזה שיש לו עדי חזקה במאי דטעין דשל אבותיו הוה א"ל שיש לו עדים זכות אבות מינך זבינתה ואכלתיה שני חזקה הלכך מיגו דמצי טעין הכי ויזכה בטענה זו ושוב לא חשש לטעון כך טוען נמי של אבותיו אע"ג דמכחשי להו לעדים מהימן [רשב"ם לקמן לג:]. מה לי לשקר אי בעי א"ל וכו'. והמימנא השתא נמי מהימנא [יבמות קטו.]. מה לי לשקר במקום עדים לא אמרינן. כלומר כל טענה שאדם טוען כנגד עדים ואתה באת לקיימה על ידי מה לי לשקר וטענה זו מכחשת עדים כי הכא לא מהימנינן ליה שהרי העדים מעידים שטענתו שקר והיאך מקיימנה על ידי מה לי לשקר הלא ודאי משקר הוא וחזקת השלש שנים אינה כלום דהויא לה חזקה שאין עמה טענה והכי הלכתא [רשב"ם לקמן לג:].

עין משפט נר מצוה

כו א ב ג מיי' פט"ו מהל' טוען הלכה ו סמג עשין לה טוש"ע ח"מ סי' קמו סעיף כד:

כז ד ה מיי' שם ופ"ז שם הלכה ח סמג שם טוש"ע שם וסי' פ סעיף ח:

כח ו מיי' שם פט"ו הלכה ה טוש"ע ח"מ סי' קמו סעיף כג:

רבינו גרשום

אמר רבא למה לו לשקר להאי מחזיק אי בעי למימר ליה מינך זבינתה ואכלתיה שני חזק' הואיל דיש לו עדים שאכלה שני חזקה ולא מצי איניש מכחיש ליה: מה לו לשקר במקום עדים. היכא דעדים מעידים דשל אבותיו דהאידך הוא תו לא אמרינן דליהוי נאמן. הדר אמר ליה ההוא דאייתי ראיה דאכלה שני חזקה אנא מודינא דאבהתך היא ומינך זבינתה והאי דאמרי דאבהתי הוה דסמיך עלה כדאבהתי כלומר מובטח וסומך הייתי עליה כמו שאם היתה של אבותי מאחר שקניתיה ממך: טוען חוזר וטוען אי לא. כלומר מאחר שטען תחלה טענה אחת ורואה שבית דין רוצין לחייבו באותה טענה וחוזר ורוצה לטעון טענה אחרת יכול או לא: עולא אמר. כל כי האי גוונא שטוען מעין טענה ראשונה ומתקנה ואינו מכחישה מהכל יכול לחזור ולטעון ולא אמרינן הואיל שטען שוב אינו טוען: ומודי עולא. לנהרדעי היכא דאמר מעיקרא של אבותי היה ולא של אבותיך ולבסוף הודה וחזר ואמר אין דאבהתך היא והא דאמרי של אבותי דסמיך לי עלה כדאבהתי דאינו טוען וחוזר וטוען משום דלא טעין מעין טענה ראשונה דמעיקרא אמר של אבותי היתה ולא של אבותיך: והיכא דקאי בבי דינא ולא טען טענה דמצי למיפטר נפשיה מבי דינא ונפק לבראי והדר אתי לבי דינא וטען טענה אחריתי דבעי למיפטר נפשיה דאינו חוזר וטוען: טענתיה אגמריה. של שקר: ומודו נהרדעי היכא דאמר ליה מעיקרא של אבותי שלקחוה מאבותיך ולסוף חזר אין דאבהתך וכו' דטוען וחוזר וטוען דמעין טענה ראשונה היא: מאבראי. חוץ לבית דין בפני שאר אנשים ולא טען בפניהם מה שהיה טוען בפני בית דין: אמר אמימר אנא נהרדעי אנא. ולא ס"ל כנהרדעי דלעיל אלא סבירא לי דטוען חוזר וטוען ובלבד שיהיה טוען מעין טענה ראשונה. אוקים עדי אכילתה בהדי עדי אכילתה דמכחישין אלו את אלו באכילה לא תסמוך על עדי חזקה: ואוקי ארעא בחזקת האי דאייתי עדים דאבותיו הוה: והא עדות מוכחשת היא. דכבר איתכחשא דאינך סהדי אמרי דהאי אכליה שני חזקה:

באבהתי

also concedes that **where [the occupant] was standing in the courtroom and did not** advance a new **claim** to reinterpret his first one, but left the room, וְאָתָא מֵאַבָּרַאי וְטָעַן – and when **he came** back to the courtroom **from outside he** advanced a new **claim,** אֵינוֹ חוֹזֵר וְטוֹעֵן – the law is that **he may not return and** use another **claim;** his reinterpretation is rejected. מַאי טַעְמָא – **What is the reason** for this second concession of Ulla? טַעֲנְתֵּיהּ אַגְמְרֵיהּ – Because we can assume that **[his friends] taught him his** new **claim.**[10]

The Gemara now presents two qualifications to the Nehardeans' ruling:

וּמוֹדוּ נְהַרְדָּעֵי – **And the Nehardeans concede** הֵיכָא דְּאָמַר לֵיהּ – that in a situation **where [the occupant]** modified his claim and **said to [the challenger],** שֶׁל אֲבוֹתַי שֶׁלְּקָחוּהָ מֵאֲבוֹתֶיךָ – "It was the property **of my forefathers, who bought it from your forefathers,"** דְּחוֹזֵר וְטוֹעֵן – **that he may return and** use this other **claim.**[11] וְהֵיכָא דְּאִישְׁתָּעֵי מִילֵּי אַבָּרַאי – **And** the Nehardeans also concede that in a situation **where [the litigants] were discussing their claims outside** the courtroom, וְלֹא טָעַן – **and [the occupant] did not** advance a certain **claim,** וְאָתָא לְבֵי דִּינָא וְטָעַן – **but** when **he came to court he** advanced that **claim,** דְּחוֹזֵר וְטוֹעֵן – **that he may return and** use that new **claim,** even if the new claim completely contradicts the claim he made outside of the courtroom.[12] מַאי טַעְמָא – **What is the reason** for this second concession? עֲבִיד אִינִישׁ דְּלֹא מְגַלֵּי טַעֲנָתֵיהּ אֶלָּא לְבֵי דִּינָא – **It is normal for a person to reveal his** intended **claims only to the court.**[13] אָמַר אַמֵּימַר – **Ameimar said:** אֲנָא נְהַרְדְּעָא אֲנָא – **I am a Nehardean,** וּסְבִירָא לִי דְּטוֹעֵן וְחוֹזֵר וְטוֹעֵן – **yet I hold that [a litigant] may claim and return and** use another **claim.**[14]

The Gemara concludes with a definitive ruling:

וְהִלְכְתָא – **And the halachah is:** טוֹעֵן וְחוֹזֵר וְטוֹעֵן – **[A litigant] may claim and return and** use another **claim.**[15]

The Gemara records another incident in which two men were disputing a certain property:

זֶה אוֹמֵר שֶׁל אֲבוֹתַי – **This one claimed,** "It was the land **of my forefathers,** and I used it for the three years needed to establish a *chazakah*"; וְזֶה אוֹמֵר שֶׁל אֲבוֹתַי – **while this** other **one claimed,** "It was the land **of *my* forefathers,** and *I* used the land during those three years!" הַאי אַיְיתֵי סַהֲדֵי דְּאַבְהָתֵיהּ – **This one produced witnesses who testified that [the land]** had been **his forefathers'** property, וַאֲכָלָהּ שְׁנֵי חֲזָקָה – **and** that **he had used it for the years of *chazakah*,** וְהַאי אַיְיתֵי סַהֲדֵי דַּאֲכָלָהּ שְׁנֵי חֲזָקָה – **while this** other **one produced witnesses** only to the effect **that he had used [the land] for the years of *chazakah*.**[16] However, he was unable to produce witnesses that the land had belonged to his forefathers.

A ruling:

אָמַר רַב נַחְמָן – **Rav Nachman said:** אוֹקֵי אֲכִילָה לְבַהֲדֵי אֲכִילָה – **Place** one testimony regarding the field's **use against** the other testimony regarding its **use,** and they offset each other; וְאוֹקֵי אַרְעָא בְּחֶזְקַת אַבְהָתָא – **and** then **establish the land in the possession of** the litigant who proved that the land has belonged to his **forefathers.**[17]

A dissenting opinion:

אָמַר לֵיהּ רָבָא – **Rava said to [Rav Nachman]:** הָא עֵדוּת מוּכְחֶשֶׁת הִיא – **But this is contradicted testimony!**[18] אָמַר לֵיהּ – **[Rav Nachman] replied to [Rava]:** נְהִי דְּאִיתְכַּחַשׁ בַּאֲכִילָתָהּ – **Although the testimony was contradicted with** regard to use of the land,

NOTES

the challenger's father because the new claim clearly contradicts his original claim (*Rashbam*). Thus, Ulla accepts a new claim only if the original claim can be reinterpreted to conform with the new one. If the original claim cannot be reinterpreted, the new claim is not accepted.

10. Since the occupant advanced this modified claim only after leaving the courtroom, it is probable that his friends or relatives advised him to return to court with a new, fictitious claim (*Rashbam*).

11. In this case, the occupant is not changing his original claim at all; he is merely adding to it. This enhanced claim – that he inherited it from his father who purchased it from the challenger's father – is not refuted by witnesses. (That is, they testify that the land *once* belonged to the challenger's father, and the occupant does not dispute that.) Hence, he retains the land, because his *chazakah* is accompanied by a valid claim. He is believed to assert that his father purchased the land from the challenger's father, because if he were lying, he could have claimed that he himself purchased it from the challenger (*Rashbam*).

[The Mishnah (below, 41a) rules that someone who claims to have inherited land from his father is not required to explain how his father came to own it, because a son cannot be expected to be knowledgable about his father's dealings. Rather, as long as the heir has used the land for three years, the court will step in and argue on his behalf that the land belonged to his father. However, the Gemara (below, 41b) states that before the court will argue for him, the heir must prove that his father had at least a minimal association with the land; specifically, that his father had used the land for at least one day. Why, then, does the Gemara not mention here that the occupant must prove that his father used the land for at least this small amount of time?

Rashbam explains that there is a basic difference between our Gemara and the case below. In that case, the heir does not claim to know that his father purchased the land. Consequently, the court must argue this point on his behalf, and to do this requires proof that his father was at least minimally associated with the land. In our case, however, the heir claims to know definitively that his father purchased it from the challenger's father. Since he has a bona fide claim, he does not need the court to argue for him. Therefore, he need not prove that his father used the land.]

12. That is, before he had entered the courtroom he advanced a certain claim. Later, when the trial began, he advanced a new claim. Even if this second claim totally contradicts the first claim, his second claim is accepted (*Rashbam*).

13. A litigant does not wish to divulge his claim before the trial begins so that his disputant will not have time to think of a way to refute it. [Therefore, any claim advanced outside of the court has no validity and may be contradicted at will] (*Rashbam*; see *Rabbeinu Yonah*).

Rashbam notes that this ruling applies only to *claims* advanced outside the court. But if someone explicitly *admits* in the presence of two witnesses that he owes a certain person money, he may not refute that admission in court.

14. Ameimar is stating that even though he is a Nehardean, he disagrees with the other Nehardeans in this matter (*Rashbam*).

15. As explained above, this ruling applies only where the new claim is merely a modification of the original claim. Since this new claim only partially conflicts with the original claim, and does not completely contradict it, it may be accepted by the court (*Rashbam*).

In summation: [1] If the second claim contradicts the first, all agree that this new claim is not valid. [2] If the second claim adds new information to the first, not contradicting it at all, all agree that it is valid. [3] The dispute between Ulla and the Nehardeans is in a case where the first claim can be reinterpreted to conform with the new claim. In that case, the Gemara rules in accordance with Ulla's view that the new claim is valid.

16. Thus, the two sets of witnesses contradicted each other in regard to who had used the field for those three years (*Rashbam*).

17. There is contradictory testimony regarding who utilized the field during the three *chazakah* years. Hence, the two *chazakah* testimonies offset each other and are eliminated. However, with regard to the identity of the original owner there is no conflicting testimony; only one pair of witnesses testifies about this fact. Therefore, the person producing that testimony becomes the presumed owner (*Rashbam*).

18. If a witness is found to be lying, he is disqualified from entering any testimony. In our case, it is impossible to ascertain which of the pairs of witnesses was lying with regard to who occupied the field for the *chazakah* years. Since one pair was definitely disqualified, Rava holds that *all* testimony originating from either pair should be inadmissible [even the testimony regarding the identity of the land's original owner] (*Rashbam*).

אבל שית אין לך מחאה גדולה מזו: (א) זה אומר של אבותי (א) וזה אומר של אבותי האי אייתי סהדי דאבהתיה היא והאי אייתי סהדי דאכלה שני חזקה ג אמר רבה מה לו לשקר אי בעי א"ל מינך זבנתה ואכלתיה שני חזקה ג א"ל אביי א מה לי לשקר במקום עדים לא אמרינן הדר א"ל אין דאבהתך היא וזבנתה (ב) מינך והאי דאמרי לך דאבהתי דסמיך לי עלה כדאבהתי טוען וחוזר וטוען או אין טוען וחוזר וטוען עולא אמר ב טוען וחוזר וטוען נהרדעי אמרי אינו טוען וחוזר וטוען ג ומודי עולא היכא דא"ל של אבותי ולא של אבותיך דאינו טוען וחוזר וטוען ד והיכא דהוה קאי בי דינא ולא טען ואתא מאבראי וטען אינו חוזר וטוען מאי טעמא טענתיה אגמריה ומודו נהרדעי היכא דאמר ליה ° של אבותי שלקחוה מאבותיך דחוזר וטוען ה והיכא דאישתעי מילי אבראי (ג) ולא טען ואתא לבי דינא וטען דחוזר וטוען מאי טעמא עביד איניש דלא מגלי טענתיה אלא לבי דינא אמר אמימר אנא נהרדעא אנא וסבירא לי דטוען וחוזר וטוען והלכתא טוען וחוזר וטוען: זה אומר של אבותי (ד) וזה אומר של אבותי האי אייתי סהדי דאבהתיה ואכלה שני חזקה והאי אייתי סהדי דאכלה שני חזקה אמר רב נחמן ו אוקי אכילה לבהדי אכילה ואוקי ארעא בחזקת אבהתא א"ל רבא (ה) הא עדות מוכחשת היא אמר ליה נהי דאיתכחש באכילתה באבהתא

רשב"ם

זה אומר של אבותי. היה הקרקע והרי היא שלי וזה אומר כו' עובדא הוה כדמוכח לקמיה: אמר רבה מה לו לשקר. לזה המחזיק במאי דטוען דשל אבותיו וירשה מהם אי בעי אמר כו' והלכך בהאי מיגו מהימנינן ליה: אמר ליה. תלמידו אביי מה לי לשקר כו' כלומר על ידי האי מיגו דמה לי לשקר לא יזכה בקרקע שהרי עדים מכחישים את דבריו שאומרים דשל אבותיו דלידך היא וגם החזקה אינה כלום שהרי אין עמה טענה כי אם טענת שקר. והלכה כאביי שהרי רבה הודה לו כדמוכח לקמן ואזיל: הדר א"ל אין כו'. דמשום שהיו מפסידין אותו כאביי הולך לחזור ולטעון כן דיקא נמי דקאמר גמרא אמר ליה אביי ולא קאמר אביי אמר: הדר א"ל. ההוא דאייתי עדי חזקה לאידך: דסמיך (ו) עלה כדאבהתי. הייתי סומך ומובטח על קרקע זו כאילו היא של אבותי לפי שהחזקתי בה בשופי ובעדים וקניתיה מאבותיך. ובעי גמרא טוען וחוזר וטוען יכול אדם לטעון בבית דין שטוען בב"ד מה שהוא רוצה וחוזר וטוען לתקן דבריו הראשונים: עולא אמר טוען וחוזר וטוען. טוען בבית דין מה שהוא רוצה וחוזר אחרי כן לטעון דברים אחרים לתרץ דברים הראשונים אע"פ שמכחישם קצת בזה שחוזר וטוען האי דאמר לאבהתי דסמיך עלה כדאבהתי: ומודי עולא. אף על גב דמהימנינן ליה להאי דטוען אין דאבהתך היא כו' שאם טען מתחילה ופירש של אבותי ולא של אבותיך דאינו חוזר וטוען טענה זו דסמיך עלה כדאבהתי שהרי עוקר לגמרי דברים הראשונים וכן הלכה דפסקינן לקמן כעולא: ומודי נמי עולא כל היכא דהוה קאי בי דינא ולא טען. תיקון דבריו הראשונים אלא אחר שיצא מבית דין חזר לב"ד ותיקן דבריו הראשונים שאינו חוזר וטוען היכא דמכחישן קצת: טענתיה אגמריה. אוהביו וקרוביו: ומודו נהרדעי. בזה שטוען מתחילה של אבותי וחוזר וטוען של אבותי שלקחוה מאבותיך דחוזר וטוען ומהימן דאינו עוקר דבריו הראשונים כלל אלא מוסיף עליהן וכיון דהחזיק בה שלש שנים מוקמינן לה בידיה דחזקה שיש עמה טענה היא דמה לו לשקר דאי בעי אמר מינך זבנתה ואכלתיה שני חזקה כי אמר נמי של אבותי שלקחוה מאבותיך מהימן. ואע"ג דגבי יורש קיימא לן לקמן בפירקין דאין צריך טענה מאחר שהחזיק בה שלש שנים היאך היתה של אביו אבל ראיה בעי שהחזיק בה אביו יום אחד הכא אין צריך להביא עדים שהחזיק בה אביו כלל שהרי זה טוען גמורה וחזקה שיש עמה טענה היא: ומודו נמי נהרדעי. כל היכא דאישתעי מילי מאבראי לבי דינא קודם שטוען כלום בב"ד ולא טען מה שהוא טוען עכשיו בב"ד ואתא לבי דינא (ז) לטעון טענות שעוקרות לגמרי את הראשונות דחוזר וטוען: דלא מגלי טענתיה. שלא ילמד מהן מי שכנגדו ויתן לבו מתחלה קודם שיבאו לבית דין להשיב עליהם וכן הלכה. וה"מ (ח) טענות בעלמא אבל טען בפירוש בפני עדים חוץ לב"ד חייב אני מנה לפלוני הרי הודה לו ושוב אינו יכול לכפור בב"ד: וסבירא לי דחוזר וטוען. כלומר אנא נמי נהרדעי אנא ופליגנא עלייהו דנהרדעי: והלכתא חוזר וטוען. תיקון לשון הראשון אע"פ שמכחישם קצת הואיל ואינו עוקרן לגמרי כדלעיל: וזה אומר של אבותי. ואכלתיה שני חזקה. אותן שלש שנים שאתה אומר של אבותי: והאי אייתי סהדי דאכלה שני חזקה. אותן שלש שנים עצמן שהעידו אלו הראשונים עליהם ובאו אלו והכחישום: אמר רב נחמן. עדות דאכילה בטלה דאוקי עדות של אכילה כנגד עדות שניה של אכילה והרי מכחישים זה את זה אבל בעדות דאבהתא דלא אתכחשת עדותן קיימת ומוקמי' בידיה: הא עדות מוכחשת היא. כיון דהני ב' כתות מכחישות זו את זו אחת מהן פסולה לכל עדיות שבעולם ואחרי שאין לברר איזו הפסולה תיבטל עדותן לגמרי:

תוספות

אבל אכלה שית שנין כו'. הקשה ר"י בר מרדכי אפי' לא אייתי סהדי אלא דאכלה שלש שנין יהא נאמן לומר לקחתיה קודם מינך במיגו דאי בעי אמר מינך זבינתה ואומר ר"י דאין זה מיגו דמעיקרא לא יטעון כלל מינך זבינתה דאין יודע אם יש לזה שטר שקנאה ממנו: אמר רבה מה לו לשקר. רבה גרסינן דאביי ורבא אמרי לקמן (דף לג.) דלא סבירא להו הא דרב חסדא דמה לי לשקר במקום עדים לא אמרינן: מה לי לשקר במקום עדים לא אמרינן. תימה לרשב"א מאי הוי במקום עדים נימא של אבותי היתה יום אחד ולקחה מאבותיו דהא טוענין ליורש ומהימנינן ליה בהא דקאמר שאבותיו דרו בו יום אחד במיגו דאי בעי אמר מינך זבנתה ולקמן נמי (ט) דקאמרי נהרדעי דהיכא דאמר של אבותי שלקחוה מאבותיך דחוזר וטוען הא אפילו לא יטעון שלקחוה אלא אמר שדרו בה יום אחד אנן טוענין ליה ואומר רבינו יצחק דשל אבותי משמע שהיתה מעולם של אבותי ולא שלקחוה עד שיפרש בדבריו ולקמן דנקט שלקחוה לא שצריך שיטעון שידע שלקחוה אלא של אבותי שראיתי שדרו בה יום אחד על כן אני רוצה לזכות דשמא לקחוה (י) אבותי במשפט וטוענין ליורש: ומודו נהרדעי היכא דאמר שלקחוה כו'. מספקא לר"י היכא דנפיק לבראי וחזר ואתא לב"ד אי מצי למימר הכי: אמר ליה רבא והא עדות מוכחשת היא. תימה אמאי הוי עדות מוכחשת והא רבא אית לי' במרובה (ב"ק ד' עב: ושם ד"ה רבא) ובפ' זה בורר (סנהדרין דף כז. ושם ד"ה רבא) דעד זומם מכאן ולהבא הוא נפסל ולא מפסל אלא משעה דאתכחוש ואית לן למימר אאכילתה דאתכחוש אתכחוש אאבהתא דלא אתכחוש לא אתכחוש דהכי אמר במרובה (ב"ק דף עג. ושם) דהוזמו על הטביחה ועל הגניבה לא הוזמו אע"ג דתוך כדי דבור העידו על הגניבה ועל הטביחה לרבא כיון דמההיא שעתא דקא מיתזמי הוא דקא מיפסלי אטביחה דאיתזום איתזום על הגניבה דלא איתזום לא איתזום וללישנא דהוי טעמא דרבא (כ) משום דעד זומם חידוש ואין לך אלא משעת חידושו ניחא אלא ללישנא דמפרש טעמא דרבא משום פסידא דלקוחות ה"נ נהימנינהו ואפילו היכא דליכא פסידא דלקוחות לא מיפסל למפרע אפילו להאי לישנא מדבעי התם מאי איכא בין האי לישנא להאי לישנא ולא קאמר איכא בינייהו להיכא דליכא פסידא דלקוחות ועוד קשיא דקאמר בסמוך אליבא דרב חסדא כולי עלמא לא פליגי משמע דרב נחמן לא מצי סבר בשום ענין כרב חסדא דחשיב להו סהדי שקרי ומנא ליה דלמא סבר רב נחמן דמכאן ולהבא הוא נפסל ומיהו הא איכא למימר משום דלא קיימא לן כרבא בהא ונראה דסוגיא דהכא כההיא לישנא דחידוש אבל ללישנא דפסידא דלקוחות סבר דלא אמר ליה רבא לרב נחמן מעולם הכי ולריב"א נראה דלא דמי הך דהכא לההיא דמרובה דהתם גניבה וטביחה תרי מילי נינהו ולהכי אגניבה דלא איתזום לא איתזום כיון דלהבא הוא נפסל אלא הכא כי איתכחוש אאכילה איתכחוש נמי אאבהתא דאבהתא בלא אכילתא לא מהני דהוי מוקמי' בידי' דאית ליה סהדי דאכלה שני חזקה דנאמן לומר היתה של אבותי יום אחד במיגו דאי בעי אמר מינך זבינתה ומיהו אכתי דחשיב לה גמרא כעדות אחרת לא אתי שפיר:

וזו

עין משפט נר מצוה

כו א ב ג מיי' פט"ו מהל' טוען הלכה ו סמג עשין לה טוש"ע ח"מ סי' קמו סעיף כד:

כז ד ה מיי' שם ופ"ז שם הלכה ח סמג שם טוש"ע שם וסי' פ ס"א:

כח ו מיי' שם פט"ו הלכה ה טוש"ע ח"מ סי' קמו סעיף כג:

רבינו גרשום

אמר רבא למה לו לשקר להאי מחזיק אי בעי למימר ליה מינך זבינתה ואכלתיה שני חזק' הואיל דיש לו עדים שאכלה שני חזקה ולא מצי איניש מכחש ליה: מה לו לשקר במקום עדים. היכא דעדים מעידים דשל אבותיו דהאיך הוא תו לא אמרינן דליהוי נאמן. הדר אמר ליה ההוא דאייתי ראיה דאכלה שני חזקה אנא מודינא דאבהתך היא ומינך זבינתה והאי דקאמרי דאבהתי הוה דסמיך עלה כדאבהתי כלומר מובטח וסומך הייתי עליה כמו שאם היתה של אבותי מאחר שקניתיה ממך: טוען חוזר וטוען אי לא. כלומר מאחר שטען תחלה טענה אחת ורואה שבית דין רוצין לחייבו באותה טענה וחוזר ורוצה לטעון טענה אחרת יכול או לא: עולא אמר. כל כי האי גוונא שטוען מעין טענה ראשונה ומתקנה ואינו מכחישה מהכל יכול לחזור ולטעון ולא אמרינן הואיל שטען שוב אינו טוען: ומודי עולא. לנהרדעי היכא דאמר מעיקרא של אבותי היה ולא של אבותיך ולבסוף הודה וחזר ואמר אין דאבהתך היא והא דאמרי של אבותי דסמיך לי עלה כדאבהתי דאינו טוען וחוזר וטוען משום דלא טעין מעין טענה ראשונה דמעיקרא אמר של אבותי היתה ולא של אבותיך: והיכא דקאי בבי דינא ולא טען טענה דמצי למיפטר נפשיה מבי דינא ונפק לבראי והדר אתי לבי דינא וטעין טענה אחריתי דבעי למיפטר נפשיה דאינו חוזר וטוען: טענתיה אגמריה. של שקר: ומודו נהרדעי היכא דאמר ליה מעיקרא של אבותי שלקחוה מאבותיך ולסוף חזר אין דאבהתך וכו' דטוען וחוזר וטוען דמעין טענה ראשונה היא: מאבראי. חוץ לבית דין בפני שאר אנשים ולא טען בפניהם מה שהיה טוען בפני בית דין: אמר אמימר אנא נהרדעי אנא. ולא ס"ל כנהרדעי דלעיל אלא סבירא לי דטוען חוזר וטוען ובלבד שיהיה טוען מעין טענה ראשונה. אוקים עדי אכילתה בהדי עדי אכילתה הואיל דמכחישין אלו את אלו באכילה לא תסמוך על עדי חזקה: ואוקי ארעא בחזקת האי דאייתי עדים דאבותיו הוה: והא עדות מוכחשת היא. דכבר איתכחשא דאינך סהדי אמרי דהאי אכליה שני חזקה:

באבהתי

מסורת הש"ס

א) לקמן דף לג., ב) [לקמן לב: לג.], ג) [קדושין סד: וש"נ].

הגהות הב"ח

(א) גמ' זה אומר של אבותי ואכלתיה שני חזקה וזה אומר של אבותי האי אייתי סהדי: (ב) שם אין דאבהתך היא וזבינתה מינייהו והאי דאמרי לך: (ג) שם אבראי לב"ד ולא טען: (ד) שם זה אומר של אבותי ואכלתיה שני חזקה וזה אומר של אבותי ואכלתיה שני חזקה האי אייתי סהדי דאבהתיה היא ואכלה: (ה) שם הא עדות: (ו) רשב"ם ד"ה דסמיך לי עלה וכו' ובעי תלמודא טוען וחוזר וטוען יכול אדם לטעון בב"ד ולחזור אחרי כן ולטעון דברים אחרים לתרץ דברים וכו' הס"ד ואח"כ מ"ה ד"ה עולא אמר טוען וחוזר וטוען הוא בב"ד מה שהוא רוצה וחוזר וטוען לתקן את דבריו טוען קמא לאו דוקא דהא לא פליגי אלא בחוזר וטוען הס"ד ואח"כ מ"ה ד"ה אינו חוזר וטוען שהרי עוקר את דבריו הראשונים הס"ד ואח"כ מ"ה ומודה עולא אע"ג: (ז) ד"ה ומודו נהרדעי וכו' לבי דינא דלא מגלי וכו' וה"מ דטוען טענה בעלמא אבל טוען: (ח) ד"ה ...: (ט) תוס' ד"ה מה לי וכו' דקאמר נהרדעי: (י) באד"ה דשמא לקחוה מאבותיך דטוענין ליורש: (כ) ד"ה אמר וכו' ולישנא דהוי טעמא דרבא הס"ד משום דעד זומם חידוש הוא ואין לך בו אלא משעת חידושו:

גליון הש"ס

גמ' של אבותי שלקחוה מאבותיך. עיין לקמן דף נב ע"ב תוספות ד"ה דברים:

ליקוטי רש"י

האי אייתי סהדי דאבהתיה היא. עד יום מותם ומעולם לא מכרו לאבותיו של זה המחזיק. אמר רבה מה לו לשקר. לזה שיש לו עדי חזקה במאי דטוען דשל אבותיו היה הוא אי בעי א"ל להאי מינך זבינתה ואכלתיה שני חזקה והלכך מיגו דמצי טעין זבינתה מהימן בה השתא נמי [רשב"ם לקמן לג:]. מה לו לשקר אי בעי וכו'. והמיגו נמי מהימנא [יבמות קטו.]. מה לי לשקר במקום עדים לא אמרינן. כלומר כל טענה שאדם טוען כנגד עדים והיאך נתן לך לטעון שאתה ... ואתה לקיימה על ידי מה לי לשקר וטענה זו מוכחשת עדים כי הכל לא מהימנינן ליה שהרי העדים מעידים שטענתו שקר והיאך מחזיקו על ידי מה לי לשקר הלא ודאי משקר הוא ומוחזק שלש שנים אינה כלום דהואיל ולא חזקה שאין עמה טענה והכי הלכתא [רשב"ם לקמן לג:].

באבהתא מי אתכחש לימא רבא ורב נחמן בפלוגתא דרב הונא ורב חסדא קמיפלגי [ו] דאיתמר ב' כתי עדים המכחישות זו את זו אמר רב הונא [א] זו באה בפני עצמה ומעידה וזו באה בפני עצמה ומעידה ורב חסדא אמר בהדי סהדי שקרי למה לי לימא רב נחמן דאמר כרב הונא ורבא כרב חסדא (א) אליבא דרב חסדא כולי עלמא לא פליגי כי פליגי אליבא דרב הונא רב נחמן כרב הונא ורבא עד כאן לא קאמר רב הונא אלא לעדות אחרת אבל לאותה עדות לא הדר אייתי סהדי דאבהתיה היא אמר רב נחמן [ב] אנן אחתיניה אנן מסקינן ליה לזילותא דבי דינא לא חיישינן מתיב רבא ואיתימא רבי זעירא [ג] שנים אומרים מת ושנים אומרים לא מת שנים אומרים נתגרשה ושנים אומרים לא נתגרשה הרי זו לא תנשא ואם נשאת לא תצא רבי מנחם ברבי יוסי אומר [ג] תצא אמר ר' מנחם בר' יוסי אימתי אני אומר תצא בזמן שבאו עדים ואח"כ נשאת אבל נשאת ואח"כ באו עדים הרי זו לא תצא א"ל אנא סברי למעבד עובדא השתא דאותיבתן את ואותבן רב המנונא בסוריא לא עבדינן בה עובדא נפק עבד עובדא מאן דחזא סבר טעותא היא בידיה ולא היא אלא משום [ג] דתליא באשלי רברבי [ד] דתנן רבי יהודה אומר [ד] אין מעלין לכהונה על פי עד אחד אמר ר' אלעזר אימתי (ב) במקום שיש עוררין אבל במקום שאין עוררין מעלין לכהונה על פי עד אחד רבן שמעון בן גמליאל אומר משום ר' שמעון בן הסגן מעלין לכהונה ע"פ עד אחד רשב"ג היינו ר' אלעזר וכי תימא ערער חד איכא בינייהו רבי אלעזר סבר ערער חד ורשב"ג

בדאבהתא מי איתכחש. עדות של אבהתא קיים הוא והכל מודים בו: **המכחישות זו את זו.** בעדות אחת כגון (ג) שנים אומרים פלוני לוה מפלוני מנה ושנים אחרים מכחישים ואמרו לא לוה ממנו כלום שהרי באותו היום שאתם אומרים שלוה ממנו היה עמנו הלוה כל אותו היום ולא לוה משום אדם כלום ובעדות כזה לא האמינה תורה האחרונים יותר מן הראשונים אלא בעדות הזמה כגון שמעידים על העדים עצמם עמנו הייתם במקום פלוני ולא ראיתם שלוה: **זו באה בפני עצמה ומעידה.** בשאר עדיות שבעולם דלא נחזיקה בפסולה מספק: **וזו באה כו'.** בעדות אחרת אבל לא בעדות אחת מכת זו ואחד מכת זו אין מצטרפין לעדות אחת דהא חד מהם פסול בודאי ואין כאן אלא חצי עדות וטעם דרב הונא משום דאוקי גברא אחזקיה ולא תפסלינהו מספק: [ה] (**א"ר חסדא**) **בהדי סהדי שקרי למה לי.** ולא יעידו (ד) בשום עדות בעולם דאוקי ממונא אחזקיה ולא מוציאו מספק את העדים פסולים: **לימא רב נחמן.** שמכשיר עדים מוכחשים לאבהתא דהיינו עדות אחרת שלא הוכחשו בו כדרב הונא שהכשירם בעדות אחרת שלא הוכחשו בה: **אליבא דרב חסדא כ"ע לא פליגי.** לומר כל אחד אלא סבירא כרב חסדא דודאי רב נחמן לא סבירא ליה כרב חסדא דהא רב חסדא פוסל אפילו בעדות אחרת בעלמא כל שכן בעדות לאבהתא שהוכחשו העדים מאכילה באותו עדות של אותו קרקע: **אבל באותו עדות.** דאותו קרקע עצמו לא [י] [והלכתא כר"נ שהרי נפסק הדין על פיו כדמוכח לקמן אנן אחתינן]: **הדר אייתי סהדי.** אותו שהפסידו רב נחמן: **דאבהתיה היא.** והרי לשניהם עדי חזקה ועדי אבות ואין כח לזה מזה וכל דאלים גבר כדאמר רב נחמן לקמן בשמעתין: **אנן מסקינן ליה.** כלומר לא נחזיק את זה יותר מזה הואיל ועדות שניהם שוה: **לזילותא דבי דינא.** שמא ילגלגו הבריות על ב"ד שסותרין את דיניהם ודמי לחוכא ואיטלולא: **שנים אומרים מת.** אשה שהלך בעלה למדינת הים ובאו שנים ואמרו לה מת בעליך ושנים אומרים לא מת א"נ שנים אומרים נתגרשה בחיי בעלה ואינה זקוקה ליבם ושנים אומרים לא נתגרשה וזקוקה ליבם א"נ כגון (ה) שהיה בעלה קיים ובאין להתירה לאחר הרי זו לא תנשא דאוקי תרי להדי תרי ואיתתא בחזקת איסור אשת איש קיימא: **ואם ניסת לא תצא.** דיעבד אין לכתחלה לא. ובפרק האשה שנתארמלה פרכינן מכדי תרי ותרי נינהו הבא עליה באשם תלוי קאי ומשני אמר רב ששת כגון שניסת לאחד מעדיה ותו פרכינן היא גופה באשם תלוי קיימא ומשני באומרת ברי לי שמת בעלי: **בזמן שבאו עדים.** האחרונים שאמרו לא מת ולאח"כ ניסת לפיכך תצא שהרי באיסור נשאת שאילו שאלה מב"ד היו אוסרין לה לינשא: **אבל אם נשאת.** על פי עדי מיתה שהתירוה בית דין לינשא ואחר כך באו עדים שהוא קיים לא תצא דחיישינן לזילותא דבי דינא וקשה לרב נחמן: **למעבד עובדא.** דמחתינן ליה ומסקינן ליה ולא ניחוש לזילותא דבי דינא: **דאותיבתן.** השיבותני מברייתא זו: **ואותבן רב המנונא.** השיב לו כמו כן מהא ברייתא דר' מנחם ורבנן: **נפק עבד.** רב נחמן עובדא ולא חש לזילותא דבי דינא: **טעותא היא בידיה.** שלא נזכר מהך ברייתא דלעיל ועוד דאמר לא עבדינן בה עובדא: **דתליא באשלי רברבי.** רבי יהודה ור' אלעזר ור' שמעון ב"ג כולהו סברי להו דלא חיישינן לזילותא דבי דינא כדמפרש רב אשי במסקנא: **אין מעלין לכהונה.** להחזיק אדם בכהן לאכול בתרומה ולעבוד עבודה ולישא את כפיו על פי עד אחד המעידו שהוא כהן כדמפרש ר' אלעזר לקמיה [בשמעתין]: **א"ר אלעזר אימתי.** אין מעלין ע"פ עד אחד בזמן שיש על הכהן עוררין עדים הפוסלים אותו כדמפרש בסמוך ולפרש דברי ר' יהודה בא ולא לחלוק עליו: **אבל אין עליו עוררים.** אלא קול פסול בעלמא כדמפרש לקמיה מעלין ע"פ עד אחד שמכחיש את הקול: **רשב"ג היינו ר' אלעזר.** דהא ודאי במקום שיש עוררין עליו לא אמר רשב"ג דליהוי חד נאמן וכי אמר מעלין במקום שאין עוררין קאמר: **ערער חד איכא בינייהו.** והא דקתני בזמן שיש עליו עוררין היינו עד אחד הפוסלו ומכחיש עד אחד המכשירו: **דרבי אלעזר סבר ערער חד.** הוי ערער ואין עד אחד נאמן עליו להכשירו: ורשב"ג

וזו באה בפני עצמה ומעידה. תימה בין לרב הונא בין לרב חסדא נהמניהו לבתראי במיגו דאי בעי פסלינהו לקמאי בגזלנותא ומיהו במיגו דאי בעי הוי מזימי להו ליכא להמניהו דיראים להזימן פן יוחמו גם הם ונראה לי דמיגו במקום עדים לא אמרינן [י] (ועוד דמיגו לא יוכל לסייעם יותר משני עדים ואפי' היו עמהן ק' עדים אין נאמנין לדברי כמאה ועוד אומר ר"י דלא שייך מיגו (ו) דאין דעת שניהם שוה ומה שירצה זה לטעון לא יטעון זה: **ורב נחמן כרב הונא.** תימה דבפרק ב' דכתובות (דף יט:) תניא שנים שהיו חתומין על השטר ומתו ובאו שנים ואמרו (ז) שכתב ידם הוא אבל קטנים או פסולי עדות או אנוסים היו אם כתב ידם יוצא ממקום אחר אין נאמנין ופריך ומגבי' ביה בשטרא תרי ותרי נינהו ומסיק התם (ח) כרב נחמן דלא מגבינן בשטרא ואוקי תרי להדי תרי ואוקי ממונא בחזקת מריה ואמאי לא מגבינן ביה והא סבירא ליה הכא כרב הונא דכשרים הם לעדות אחרת דמוקמינן להו אחזקת כשרות והתם (ח) כעדות אחרת דמי דהא אין מכחישים אלו את החתומים בזמן החתימה שהיו אומרים אין חייב לו כלום אלא שאמרו אינכם נאמנים בדבר זה דפסולים הייתם והוה לן למימר דנאמנים כמו הכא דכשרים אף על גב דאלו מכחישים אותם ופוסלים ומושבין אותן כשאר פסולים לכל דבר עדות ואומר ר"י דכי אמרו קטנים היו ליכא לאוקמינהו אחזקייהו וכן אנוסים נמי לא מפקי להו מחזקת כשרות דאמרינן אנוסים היו מחמת נפשות ופסולי עדות היו איכא למימר כגון שפוסלים אותן משנולדו שאומרים קרובים היו ועכשיו נתרחקו [ט]: **ורבא** כרב חסדא. ואם תאמר אם כן אמאי חשיב רבא במרובה (ב"ק דף עב: ושם ד"ה אין) ובפ' זה בורר (סנהדרין דף כז. ושם ד"ה אין) עד זומם חידוש הוא ואין לך בו אלא משעת חידושו והלא מה שהוא נפסל אינו חידוש דהא מן הדין היה להיות לשניהן פסולים כמו בשני כתי עדים המכחישות זו את זו א"כ לא הוי חידוש אלא מה שהמזימין כשרים ואומר ר"י דרבא דאמר חידוש הוא לא הוי אלא לפי המסקנא דאתי שפיר כרב הונא:

אנן אחתינן ליה אנן מסקינן ליה. ואם היה אותו דלית ליה חזקת אבהתיה מוחזק תחילה אתי שפיר אחתינן ומסקינן שנעמידה בידו כאשר היה בתחלה ואפילו לא היה מוחזק לא זה ולא זה מצי לפרש אחתינא ליה לתתה לזה ומסקינא ליה שנוציאנה מידו ויהא דין כל דאלים גבר. ר"י: **ואם** ניסת לא תצא. בפ"ב דכתובות (דף כב: ושם ד"ה כגון) מוקי כשניסת לאחד מעדיה ואומרת ברי לי וחשדא ליכא כדפי' התם: **אבל** ניסת ואח"כ באו עדים הרי זו לא תצא. וטעמא משום זילותא דבי דינא וקשה לרשב"א דעל כרחך לאו טעמא משום זילותא דבי דינא הוא דאם כן אפילו לא נשאת אלא התירוה לינשא תנשא כדמשמע בכל הסוגיא דאיכא זילותא אפילו לא נעשה מעשה וכ"ת דאין ה"נ ונשאת דקאמר היינו שהתירוה לינשא ושוב לא תצא מהיתרה הראשון דבאו עדים ואח"כ נשאת לא מצי לפרושי התירוה לינשא אלא נשאת ממש וע"כ טעמא דמספיקא לא מפקי לה מבעל ולא משום זילותא וי"ל לעולם טעמא משום זילותא ודוקא כשנשאת ואח"כ באו עדים איכא זילותא דבי דינא שכבר נאסרה לכל העולם כיון שנשאת נמצא מה שחוזרין לאסרה לבעל שנשאת לו אין חוזרין אלא בעבורו אבל אם באו עדים קודם שנשאת ליכא זילותא דעל כרחך צריכין לחזור מהיתרה הראשון כדי לאסרה לכל העולם הלכך ליכא זילותא אם אוסרים אותה נמי לעדיה. ר"י: והאמר

כט א מיי' פכ"ב מהל' עדות הלכה א סמג עשין קי טוש"ע ח"מ סי' לא סעיף א:
ל ב מיי' פט"ו מהל' טוען ונטען הל' ה סמג עשין צה טוש"ע ח"מ סי' קמו סעיף כג:
לא ג מיי' פי"ב מהל' גירושין הלכה כג סמג עשין נ טוש"ע אה"ע סי' קנב סעיף א וסי' יז סעיף נב וע"ש:
לב ד מיי' פ"כ מהלכות איסורי ביאה הלכה ד טוש"ע אה"ע סי' ג סעיף א ב ג:

א) שבועות דף מז, ב) כתובות דף כב. יבמות דף פח. ג) [גליון כו. ע"ז], ד) כתובות דף כג, ה) נ"ל רב חסדא אמר, ו) רש"ל, ז) רש"ל מ"ז, ח) [נ"ל רב], ט) [וע"ע תוס' כתובות כ. ד"ה אלא]:

הגהות הב"ח

(א) גמ' ורבא כרב חסדא לא אליבא דרב חסדא וכו' ורבא אמר לך עד כאן לא קאמר רב הונא התם אלא: (ב) שם אימתי בזמן שיש עליו עוררין אבל אין עליו עוררין מעלין כצ"ל: (ג) רשב"ם ד"ה המכחישות וכו' כגון שהעידו שנים פלוני לוה: (ד) ד"ה אמר רב חסדא וכו' ולא יעידו עוד בשום עדות: (ה) ד"ה שנים וכו' א"נ כגון שהיה בעלה קיים: (ו) תוס' ד"ה וזו באה וכו' דלא שייך מיגו אלא בדאדם אחד אבל בשנים לא שייך מיגו דאין דעת שניהם שוה: (ז) ד"ה ורב נחמן וכו' ואמרו ידענו שכתב ידם הוא אלא זה אבל קטנים היו או פסולי עדות היו או אנוסים: (ח) בא"ד והתם נמי כעדות אחרת דמי:

ליקוטי רש"י

שתי כתי עדים המכחישות זו את זו. שנים אומרים הרג ושנים אומרים לא הרג. זו באה בפני עצמה ומעידה. בעדות אחרת וכן זו ואע"פ שהאחת פסולה אין לך לפסול לא זו ולא זו הואיל ואינך יודע איזה מהן פסולה ולא לאחד מכת זו ואחד מכת זו אין נאמנין בעדות אחת דמה נפשך אחד מהן פסול והיינו דנקט ביה האי לישנא באה בפני עצמה ומעידה. בהדי סהדי שקרי למה לי. הואיל והאחת פסולה אין אחת מהן נאמנת לשום עדות [שבועות מז:]. ר' מנחם ב"ר יוסי וכו' בזמן שבאו עדים. שאמרו לא מת [כתובות כב:]. שבאו עדים ואמרו לא מת ולאח"כ נשאת הואיל והיתה בכתובות (כב:) כשאה שניסת לאחד מעדיה ואומרת ברי לי [יבמות פח:]. דתליא באשלי רברבי. בחבלים גדולים וגסים שקשין לינתק כלומר חכמים גדולים אמרוה ואין נותן לבעל דבריהם [ביצה כז:]. חבלים עבים וחזקים ויש אומרים באילנות גדולות כמו ויטע אשל (בראשית כא) [ע"ז ז:].

רבינו גרשום

באבהתי לא איתכחוש. להכי אוקמה נכסי בחזקת אבהתא דהאי: [ב' כתי עדי'] המכחישות זו את זו. בעדות אחת: אמר רב הונא. אע"ג דבהאי עדות מוכחשות הן זו באה בפני עצמה בעדות אחרת ומעידה וכשירה משום דלא ידעי איזו כת משקרא ולהכי אידך כת נמי באה בפני עצמה ומעידה וכשירה אבל תרוייהו כחדא לא מצי למיתי משום דאיכא למימר דחדא מינייהו מוכחשת היא ורב חסדא אמר בהדי סהדי שקרי למה לי הואיל דאתכחשא חדא מינייהו בחזקת מוכחשת נינהו תרוייהו ולא מצי לאסהודי נמי בעדות אחרת דמש"ה חדא מינייהו פסולה היא: נימא רב נחמן דאמר. נהי דאיתכחוש באכילה באבהתא מי מתכחש ומצי לאסהודי על אבהתא ס"ל כדרב הונא דהכי נמי אמר רב הונא אע"ג דאיתכחשו בהאי עדות זו באה בפני עצמה ומעידה משום דליכא למיקם עלה דמילתא מאן מכחשין וה"נ אידך: ורבא. דאמר שוו עדות מוכחשת ס"ל כרב חסדא: אליבא דרב חסדא כ"ע לא פליגי. דאפי' רב נחמן מודי דכיון דרב חסדא פוסלו לכל עדות אע"ג דבחד עדות מכחשי אהדדי בשאר עדיות דעלמא לא מכחשי כ"ש דס"ל לרב חסדא דהיכא דמכחשי באותו עדות במקצת באכילה בלבד דהם מוכחשין נמי לאבהתי ולא מוקמ' נכסי בחזקת אבהתא: כי פליגי. רב נחמן ורבא: אליבא דרב הונא. דאמר זו באה בפני עצמה ומעידה וזו באה בפני עצמה ומעידה רב נחמן דאמר נהי דאתכחוש באכילה באבהתא מי מכחשא ס"ל כרב הונא הואיל דליכא למיקם עלה דמילתא מאן מוכחשין: ורבא אמר לך כו' אבל באותה עדות לא מהימנא כלל: הדר איתי אידך סהדי נמי דשל אבהתי הוי השתא מיתכחשי כולה עדות אמר רב נחמן אנן אחתיניה לההוא דאייתי מעיקרא סהדי דהוו דאבהתי ונטלנו ניכסי מאה דהוי מוחזק בהו והנחנוה ליה וכיון דהדר אידך ואייתי סהדי דאבהתיה הוא סלקין להא דיהבינא ליה ומהדרי להו להאי ולזילותא דבי דינא דיהבינן לאידך בתחלה והדר יהבי לאידך לא חיישינן דודאי אנן אחתינן ליה ואנן מסקינן ליה: שנים אומרים מת בעל. במדינת הים: ושנים אומרים לא נתגרשה. ...שה. שאותן עדים עמנו היו באותה שעה: **בזמן שבאו עדים** נמי שאמרו שלא מת **ואחר כך נשאת** לבעל הואיל דהני מכחשי הני בדין הוא שתצא דמחמרי' גבי אשת איש **[אבל] נשאת** על פי שנים שאמרו ...ו עדים שלא מת **הרי זו לא תצא** דחיישינן לזילותא דבי דינא שהשיאוה על פי שנים שאמרו שמת וקשיא לרב נחמן: **א"ל.** רב נחמן: **נפק** ר' נחמן **ועבד עובדא** דלא חש לזילותא דבי דינא **מאן דחזא** דעבד ...ת הוא **בידיה** משום דמוקשה ועומד הוא: **באשלי רברבי.** דסברי דלא חיישינן לזילותא דבי דינא: **אין מעלין לכהונה על פי עד אחד.** לחלוק לו תרומה: **שיש עוררין** עליו. בקול ולא בעדות שהוא בן גרושה ובן חלוצה: **רשב"ג היינו ר' אלעזר.** דבמקום שיש עוררין לא קאמר רשב"ג דמעלין אלא במקום שאין עוררין. א) **דר' אלעזר סבר** מעלין ולהיכא דאיכא **עורר חד** אין מעלין **ורשב"ג סבר** עד דאיכא **ערער תרי**:

חשק שלמה על רבינו גרשום א) נ"ל ערער חד איכא בינייהו דר"א סבר דאף דליכא רק עורר חד ג"כ אין מעלין וכו'.

בְּאַבְהָתָא מִי אִתְכַּחַשׁ – **with** regard to **the forefathers'** ownership of the land **was it contradicted?** Since this part of the testimony was uncontested, Rav Nachman maintained that it remained admissible.

The Gemara seeks to relate the dispute between Rava and Rav Nachman to another known dispute:

לֵימָא רָבָא וְרַב נַחְמָן – **Are we to say** that **Rava and Rav Nachman** בִּפְלוּגְתָּא דְּרַב הוּנָא וְרַב חִסְדָּא קָמִיפַּלְגֵי – **disagree on a** matter that is the subject of a **dispute between Rav Huna and Rav Chisda?** דְּאִיתְּמַר – **For it was said** שְׁתֵּי כִּתֵּי עֵדִים הַמַּכְחִישׁוֹת זוֹ אֶת זוֹ – regarding **two pairs of witnesses that contradict one another** with their testimony,[1] אָמַר רַב הוּנָא – **Rav Huna says:** זוֹ בָּאָה בִּפְנֵי עַצְמָהּ וּמְעִידָה – **This** pair **may come alone**[2] **and testify** regarding other matters, וְזוֹ בָּאָה בִּפְנֵי עַצְמָהּ וּמְעִידָה – **and this** other pair **may come alone and testify** regarding other matters. Neither one is disqualified from testifying, although it might be the dishonest pair.[3] וְרַב חִסְדָּא אָמַר – **While Rav Chisda says:** בַּהֲדֵי סַהֲדֵי שִׁקְרֵי לָמָּה לִי – **What involvement should I have with lying witnesses?** Since either pair might be the dishonest one, neither pair may testify subsequently regarding any matter.[4]

The Gemara develops its comparison:

לֵימָא רַב נַחְמָן דְּאָמַר כְּרַב הוּנָא – **Shall we say that Rav Nachman,** who accepted the uncontested segment of the witnesses' testimony regarding ancestral possession of the field, **rules in accordance with Rav Huna,** וְרָבָא כְּרַב חִסְדָּא – **while Rava,** who disallowed all testimony by the contradicted witnesses, **rules in accordance with Rav Chisda?**[5]

The Gemara explains that this is not necessarily the case:

אַלִּיבָּא דְּרַב חִסְדָּא כּוּלֵּי עָלְמָא לֹא פְּלִיגֵי – Were we to rule **in accordance with Rav Chisda, no one**, even Rav Nachman, would **dispute** that in the instance discussed here we would disqualify the witnesses from testifying regarding ancestral ownership.[6] כִּי פְּלִיגֵי – **When** might **[Rava and Rav Nachman] disagree?** אַלִּיבָּא דְּרַב הוּנָא – They might disagree in what the ruling might be **according to Rav Huna**. How so? רַב נַחְמָן כְּרַב הוּנָא – **Rav Nachman** simply **followed Rav Huna's** position quoted above. Just as Rav Huna allows the witnesses to testify regarding other matters, Rav Nachman allowed the testimony regarding ancestral ownership. וְרָבָא – **While Rava** maintains that עַד כָּאן לֹא קָאָמַר רַב הוּנָא אֶלָּא לְעֵדוּת אַחֶרֶת – **thus far Rav Huna has said** his ruling that uncontested testimony could be accepted, **only with regard to other testimony,** unrelated to the original dispute. אֲבָל לְאוֹתָהּ עֵדוּת – **But in regard to this same testimony,** i.e. testimony related to the property about which they were contradicted, לֹא – Rav Huna would **not** say that it is accepted.[7]

This case was adjudicated in accordance with Rav Nachman's view, and the land was awarded to the litigant who had produced witnesses that the property had belonged to his forefathers. Later, however, there was a new development in the case:

הֲדַר אַיְיתֵי סַהֲדֵי דְּאַבְהָתֵיהּ הִיא – **[The litigant who lost the case] then brought witnesses** who testified **that [the land]** had **belonged to his forefathers,** thereby once again placing the two litigants on equal footing.

Rav Nachman handed down a verdict:

אָמַר רַב נַחְמָן – **Rav Nachman** thereupon **said:** אֲנַן אַחְתִּינֵיהּ – **We** (the court) originally **installed [the winner]** as occupant of the land, based on his then-unchallenged supporting testimony. אֲנַן מַסְקִינַן לֵיהּ – Now, **we remove him**[8] from the land and return it to its former indeterminate state, once again allowing both litigants a chance to vie for its possession.[9]

NOTES

1. E.g. one pair testifies that Reuven borrowed money from Shimon on a certain day, while the other pair testifies that Reuven was with them that entire day and did not borrow any money. Thus, the two testimonies offset each other.

[There are two ways in which a second pair of witnesses can refute an earlier pair. The second pair can claim that the first pair was elsewhere at the time of the alleged incident and could not possibly have witnessed it. In that case, the law is that the second pair is believed over the first (see *Makkos* 5a). However, our Gemara discusses a case in which the second pair contradicts the first about the testimony itself (such as, in our example, by claiming that Reuven did not borrow from Shimon). In this case, the second pair has no more credibility than the first and an offsetting situation is created (*Rashbam*).]

2. By "alone," Rav Huna means that each pair as a unit may testify in another case; however, a new pair composed of one witness from each group is invalid (*Rashi* to *Shevuos* 47b ד״ה זו. See following note for why this is so).

3. Generally, when the halachic status of a person or thing is known, and an event transpires that *may* have altered that status, we assume, lacking positive evidence to the contrary, that the person's or thing's status remains unchanged. In our case, each pair of witnesses was previously qualified to testify. After their contradictory testimonies, each individual pair's fitness is in doubt. Since it was previously qualified and its present disqualification is only doubtful, the status quo is maintained and it can testify in subsequent cases. However, Rav Huna concedes that one witness from the first pair may not join with one from the second pair to form a new pair of witnesses, because this new pair definitely contains one invalid witness (*Rashbam*).

4. Rav Chisda maintains that we follow the status quo of the property that stands to change hands as a result of their testimony, not the status quo of the witnesses' fitness. Thus, we do not take away property from one litigant and award it to another based on testimony of witnesses of questionable fitness (*Rashbam*).

5. Both disputes involve the question of the status of witnesses whose testimony was contradicted by others. Since Rav Nachman allowed the testimony regarding ancestral ownership to stand (although the witnesses were contradicted as far as the occupancy was concerned), he seems to dispute Rav Chisda's position that witnesses who may have lied are disqualified. Conversely, Rava, who rejected the testimony of ancestral ownership (since the witnesses may have been the ones who lied regarding the years of occupancy), appears to be at odds with Rav Huna who argues that qualified witnesses remain in a presumption of fitness even after being contradicted by another pair.

6. If Rav Chisda disqualified the witnesses from testifying even in unrelated cases, surely he would disqualify them with regard to the same property that their original problematic testimony had involved. Clearly, then, Rav Nachman cannot subscribe to Rav Chisda's view (*Rashbam*). We have no choice but to say that he follows Rav Huna's opinion.

7. The testimony regarding ancestral ownership and the testimony regarding use of the land for three years are considered to be two parts of one larger testimony, since the goal of both is to award the land to the same litigant. Consequently, the rule (cited in *Bava Kamma* 73a) applies that where one segment of a testimony is invalidated, the entire testimony (even that segment that is unrefuted) is similarly invalidated (*Rashba*). This is unlike Rav Huna's case in which the two testimonies are unrelated. Thus, although their first testimony is disqualified, they may testify in another case. Hence, it is possible that Rava might concur with Rav Huna's view.

8. Literally: we took him up, we put him down.

[The elucidation follows *Rabbeinu Gershom, Tosafos* and *Ritva*, who explain אַחְתִּינֵיהּ to refer to installing the winner in the land, and מַסְקִינַן to refer to his ouster from it. However, *Nimukei Yosef* has it in reverse: We took the loser out of the land, now we reinstate him to it.]

9. The elucidation follows *Rashbam*, who assumes that neither party had been in control of the land before the case began. Hence, the court restores the land to its original indeterminate status. As in any case in which the litigants' proofs are equal and offset each other, the court does not award the property to either party; rather, the court withdraws from the case, and allows the stronger litigant to take possession (see *Rashbam*; also see below, 34b, where the Gemara discusses this law at length; cf. *Ramban* here).

Alternatively, the case may have been that the loser was originally in control of the land, but lost it to his opponent when he produced

באבהתא מי אתכחש לימא רבא ורב נחמן בפלוגתא דרב הונא ורב חסדא קמיפלגי [א]דאיתמר ב' כתי עדים המכחישות זו את זו אמר רב הונא [א]זו באה בפני עצמה ומעידה וזו באה בפני עצמה ומעידה ורב חסדא אמר בהדי סהדי שקרי למה לי לימא רב נחמן דאמר כרב הונא ורבא כרב חסדא (א) אליבא דרב חסדא כולי עלמא לא פליגי כי פליגי אליבא דרב הונא רב נחמן כרב הונא ורבא עד כאן לא קאמר רב הונא אלא לעדות אחרת אבל לאותה עדות לא הדר אייתי סהדי דאבהתיה היא אמר רב נחמן [ב]אנן אחתיניה אנן מסקינן ליה לזילותא דבי דינא לא חיישינן מתיב רבא ואיתימא רבי זעירא [ג]שנים אומרים מת ושנים אומרים לא מת שנים אומרים נתגרשה ושנים אומרים לא נתגרשה הרי זו לא תנשא ואם נשאת לא תצא רבי מנחם ברבי יוסי אומר [ג]תצא אמר ר' מנחם בר' יוסי אימתי אני אומר תצא בזמן שבאו עדים ואח"כ נשאת אבל נשאת ואח"כ באו עדים הרי זו לא תצא א"ל אנא סברי למעבד עובדא השתא דאותיבתן את ואותבן רב המנונא בסוריא לא עבדינן בה עובדא נפק עבד עובדא מאן דחזא סבר טעותא היא בידיה ולא היא אלא משום [ג]דתליא באשלי רברבי [ד]דתנן רבי יהודה אומר [ד]אין מעלין לכהונה על פי עד אחד אמר ר' אלעזר אימתי (ב) במקום שיש עוררין אבל במקום שאין עוררין מעלין לכהונה על פי עד אחד רבן שמעון בן גמליאל אומר משום ר' שמעון בן הסגן מעלין לכהונה ע"פ עד אחד רשב"ג היינו ר' אלעזר וכי תימא ערער חד איכא בינייהו רבי אלעזר סבר ערער חד ורשב"ג

רשב"ם

בדאבהתא מי איתכחש. עדות של אבהתא קיים הוא והכל מודים בו: המכחישות זו את זו. בעדות אחת כגון (ג) שנים אומרים פלוני לוה מפלוני מנה ושנים אחרים הכחישום ואמרו לא לוה ממנו כלום שהרי באותו היום שאתם אומרים שלוה ממנו היה עמנו הלוה כל אותו היום ולא לוה משום אדם כלום ובעדות כזה לא האמינה תורה האחרונים יותר מן הראשונים אלא בעדות הזמה כגון שמעידים על העדים עצמם עמנו הייתם במקום פלוני ולא ראיתם שלוה: זו באה בפני עצמה ומעידה. כשאר עדיות שבעולם דלא נחזיקנה בפסולה מספק: וזו באה כו'. בעדות אחרת אבל אחד מכת זו ואחד מכת זו אין מצטרפין לעדות אחת דהא אחד מהם פסול בודאי ואין כאן אלא חצי עדות וטעם דרב הונא משום דאוקי גברא אחזקיה ולא תפסלינהו מספק: [ה](א"ר חסדא) בהדי סהדי שקרי למה לי. ולא יעידו (ד) בשום עדות בעולם דאוקי ממונא אחזקיה ולא תוליאנו מספק שמא העדים פסולים: לימא רב נחמן. שמכשיר עדות לאבהתא שהעידו עדים מוכחשים דהיינו עדות אחרת שלא הוכחשו בו כרב הונא שהכשירם בעדות אחרת שלא הוכחשו בה: אליבא דרב חסדא כ"ע לא פליגי. לומר כל אחד אנא סבירא כרב חסדא דודאי אף רב נחמן לא סבירא ליה כרב חסדא דהא רב חסדא אפילו בעדות אחרת בעלמא פוסל כל שכן בעדות לאבהתא שהוכחשו העדים מאליה באותו עדות של אותו קרקע: אבל באותו עדות. דאותו קרקע עצמו לא [ו][והלכתא כר"נ שהרי נפסק הדין על פיו כדמוכח לקמן אנן אחתינן]: הדר אייתי סהדי. אותו שהפסידו רב נחמן: דאבהתיה היא. והרי לשניהם עדי חזקה ועדי אבות ואין כח לזה מזה וכל דאלים גבר כדאמר רב נחמן לקמן בשמעתין: אנן מסקינן ליה. כלומר לא נחזיק את זה יותר מזה הואיל ועדות שניהם שוה: לזילותא דבי דינא. שמא ילגלגו הבריות על ב"ד על שסותרין את דיניהם ודמי לחוכא ואיטלולא: שנים אומרים מת. אשה שהלך בעלה למדינת הים ובאו שנים ואמרו לה מת בעליך ושנים אומרים לא מת א"נ שנים אומרים נתגרשה בחיי בעלה ואינה זקוקה ליבם ושנים אומרים לא נתגרשה וזקוקה ליבם א"נ כגון (ה) שהיה בעלה קיים ובאין להתירה לאחר הרי זו לא תנשא דאוקי תרי להדי תרי ואיתתא בחזקת איסור אשת איש קיימא: ואם ניסת לא תצא. דיעבד אין לכתחלה לא. ובפרק האשה שנתארמלה פרכינן מכדי תרי ותרי נינהו הבא עליה באשם תלוי קאי ומשני אמר רב ששת כגון שניסת לאחד מעדיה ותו פרכינן היא גופה באשם תלוי קיימא ומשני באומרת ברי לי שמת בעלי: בזמן שבאו עדים. האחרונים שאמרו לא מת ולאח"כ ניסת לפיכך תצא שהרי באיסור נשאת שאילו שאלה מב"ד היו אוסרין לה לינשא: אבל אם נשאת. על פי עדי מיתה שהתירוה בית דין לינשא ואחר כך באו עדים שהוא קיים לא תצא דחיישינן לזילותא דבי דינא וקשה לרב נחמן: למעבד עובדא. דמחתינן ליה ומסקינן ליה ולא ניחוש לזילותא דבי דינא: דאותיבתן. השיבותני מברייתא זו: ואותבן רב המנונא. השיב לו כמו כן מהא ברייתא דר' מנחם ורבנן: נפק עבד. רב נחמן עובדא ולא חש לזילותא דבי דינא: טעותא היא בידיה. שלא נזכר מהך ברייתא דלעיל ועוד דאמר לא עבדינן בה עובדא: דתליא באשלי רברבי. רבי יהודה ור' אלעזר ור' שמעון ב"ג כולהו סברי להו דלא חיישינן לזילותא דבי דינא כדמפרש רב אשי במסקנא: אין מעלין לכהונה. להחזיק אדם בכהן לאכול בתרומה ולעבוד עבודה ולישא את כפיו על פי עד אחד המעידו שהוא כהן כדמפרש ר' אלעזר לקמיה [בשמעתין]:

א"ר אלעזר אימתי. אין מעלין ע"פ עד אחד בזמן שיש על הכהן עוררין עדים הפוסלים אותו כדמפרש בסמוך ולפרש דברי ר' יהודה בא ולא לחלוק עליו: אבל אין עליו עוררים. אלא קול פסול בעלמא כדמפרש לקמיה מעלין ע"פ עד אחד שמכחיש את הקול: רשב"ג היינו ר' אלעזר. דהא ודאי במקום שיש עוררין עליו לא אמר רשב"ג ליהוי חד נאמן וכי אמר מעלין במקום שאין עוררין קאמר: ערער חד איכא בינייהו. והא דקתני בזמן שיש עליו עוררין היינו עד אחד הפוסלו ומכחיש עד אחד המכשירו: דרבי אלעזר סבר ערער חד. הוי ערער ואין עד אחד נאמן עליו להכשירו:

ורשב"ג

תוספות

וזו באה בפני עצמה ומעידה. תימה בין לרב הונא בין לרב חסדא נהמנינהו לבתראי במיגו דאי בעי פסלינהו לקמאי בגזלנותא ומיהו במיגו דאי בעי הוי מזמי להו ליכא להמנינהו דיראים להזמין פן יוזמו גם הם ונראה לי דמיגו במקום עדים לא אמרינן [ז](ועוד) דמיגו לא יוכל לסייעם יותר משני עדים ואפי' היו עמהן ק' עדים אין נאמנין דתרי כמאה ועוד אומר ר"י דלא שייך מיגו (ו) דאין דעת שניהם שוה ומה שירצה זה לטעון לא יטעון זה: ורב נחמן כרב הונא. תימה דבפרק ב' דכתובות (דף יט:) תניא שנים שהיו חתומין על השטר ומתו ובאו שנים ואמרו (ז) שכתב ידם הוא אבל קטנים או פסולי עדות או אנוסים היו אם כתב ידם יוצא ממקום אחר אין נאמנין ופריך ומגבי' ביה בשטרא תרי ותרי נינהו ומסיק התם ([ח]כרב) נחמן דלא מגבינן בשטרא ואוקי תרי להדי תרי ואוקי ממונא בחזקת מריה ואמאי לא מגבינן ביה והא סבירא ליה הכא כרב הונא דכשרים הם לעדות אחרת דמוקמינן להו אחזקת כשרות והתם (ח) כעדות אחרת דמי דהא אין מכחישים אלו את החתומים בזאת המלוה שהיו אומרים אין חייב לו כלום אלא שאמרו איכנס נאמנים בדבר זה דפסולים הייתם והוה לן למימר דנאמנים כמו הכא דכשרים אף על גב דאלו מכחישים אותם ופוסלים ומוציאין אותן כשאר פסולים לכל דבר עדות ואומר ר"י דכי אמרו קטנים היו ליכא לאוקמינהו אחזקייהו וכן אנוסים נמי לא מפקי להו מחזקת כשרות דלאמרינן אנוסים היו ממתת נפשות ופסולי עדות היו איכא למימר כגון שפוסלים אותן משנולדו שאומרים קרובים היו ועכשיו נתרחקו [ט]: ורבא כרב חסדא. ואם תאמר אם כן אמאי חשיב רבא במרובה (ב"ק דף עג: ושם ד"ה אין) ובפ' זה בורר (סנהדרין דף מ. ושם ד"ה אין) עד זומם חידוש הוא ואין לך בו אלא משעת חידושו והלא מה שהוא נפסל אינו חידוש דהא מן הדין היה להיות לשניהן פסולים כמו בשני כתי עדים המכחישות זו את זו א"כ לא הוי חידוש אלא מה שהמזימין כשרים ואומר ר"י דרבא דאמר חידוש הוא לא הוי אלא לפי המסקנא דאתי שפיר כרב הונא:

אנן אחתינן ליה אנן מסקינן ליה. ואם היה אותו דלית ליה חזקת אבהתיה מוחזק תחילה אתי שפיר אחתינן ומסקינן שנעמידה בידו כאשר היה בתחלה ואפילו לא היה מוחזק לא זה ולא זה מצי לפרש אחתינא ליה לתתה לזה ומסקינא ליה שנוציאנה מידו ויהא דין כל דאלים גבר. ר"י: ואם ניסת לא תצא. בפ"ב דכתובות (דף כב: ושם ד"ה כגון) מוקי כשניסת לאחד מעדיה ואומרת ברי לי וחשדא ליכא כדפי' התם: אבל ניסת ואח"כ באו עדים הרי זו לא תצא. וטעמא משום זילותא דבי דינא וקשה לרשב"א דעל כרחך לאו טעמא משום זילותא דבי דינא הוא דאם כן אפילו לא נשאת אלא התירוה לינשא תנשא כדמשמע בכל הסוגיא דאיכא זילותא אפילו לא נעשה מעשה וכ"ת דאין ה"נ ונשאת דקאמר היינו שהתירוה לינשא ושוב לא תנשא מהיתרה הראשון דבאו עדים ואח"כ נשאת לא מצי לפרושי התירוה לינשא אלא נשאת ממש וע"כ טעמא דמספיקא לא מפקי לה מבעל ולא משום זילותא וי"ל לעולם טעמא משום זילותא ודוקא כשנשאת ואח"כ באו עדים איכא זילותא דבי דינא שכבר נאסרה לכל העולם כיון שנשאת נמצא מה שחוזרין לאסרה לעד שנשאת לו אין חוזרין אלא בעבורו אבל אם באו עדים קודם שנשאת ליכא זילותא דעל כרחך צריכין לחזור מהיתרה הראשון כדי לאסרה לכל העולם הלכך ליכא זילותא אם אוסרים אותה נמי לעדיה. ר"י:

והאמר

עין משפט נר מצוה

כט א מיי' פט"ו מהל' עדות הלכה ב סמג עשין קי טוש"ע ח"מ סי' לא סעיף א:

ל ב מיי' פט"ו מהל' טוען ונטען הל' ה סמג עשין צה טוש"ע ח"מ סי' קמו סעיף ב:

לא ג מיי' פי"ב מהל' גירושין הלכה כב סמג עשין נ טוש"ע אה"ע סי' קנב סעיף א וסי' ז סעיף מב וע"ש:

לב ד מיי' פ"כ מהלכות איסורי ביאה הלכה ד טוש"ע אה"ע סי' ג סעיף א ג נ:

רבינו גרשום

באבהתי לא איתכחוש. להכי אוקמא נכסי בחזקת אבהתא דהאי: [ב' כתי עדי'] המכחישות זו את זו. בעדות אחת: אמר רב הונא. אע"ג דבהאי עדות מוכחשות הן זו באה בפני עצמה בעדות אחרת ומעידה וכשירה משום דלא ידעי איזו כת משקרא ולהכי אידך כת נמי באה בפני עצמה ומעידה וכשירה אבל תרוייהו כחדא לא מצי למיתי משום דאיכא למימר דחדא מינייהו מוכחשת היא ורב חסדא אמר בהדי סהדי שקרי למה לי הואיל דאתכחשא חדא מינייהו בחזקת מוכחשין נינהו תרוייהו ולא מצי לאסהודי נמי בעדות אחרת דממ"נ חדא מנייהו פסולה היא: נימא רב נחמן דאמר. נהי דאיתכחוש באכילה באבהתא מי מכחש ומצי לאסהודי על אבהתא דהוי ס"ל כדרב הונא דהכי נמי אמר רב הונא אע"ג דאיתכחשו עדות זו באה בפני עצמה ומעידה משום דליכא למיקם עלה דמילתא מאן מוכחשין הה"נ אידך: ורבא. דאמר שוו עדות מוכחשת ס"ל כרב חסדא: אליבא דרב חסדא כ"ע לא פליגי. דאפי' רב נחמן מודי דכיון דרב חסדא פוסלו לכל עדיות אע"ג דבחד עדות מכחשי אהדדי בשאר עדיות דעלמא לא מכחשי כ"ש דס"ל לרב חסדא דהיכא דמכחשי הני עדות במקצת באכילה באותו עדות דהם מוכחשין נמי לאבהתי ולא מוקמ' נכסי בחזקת אבהתא: כי פליגי. רב נחמן ורבא: אליבא דרב הונא. דאמר זו באה בפני עצמה ומעידה וזו באה בפני עצמה ומעידה רב נחמן דאמר נהי דאתכחוש באכילה באבהתא מי מכחש ס"ל כרב הונא הואיל דליכא למיקם עלה דמילתא מאן מוכחשין: ורבא אמר לך כו' אבל באותה עדות לא מהימנא כלל: הדר אייתי אידך סהדי נמי דשל אבהתי הוי השתא מיתכחשי כולה עדות אמר רב נחמן אנן אחתינה להאי דאייתי מעיקרא סהדי דהוי דאבהתי ונטלנו ניכסי מהאי דהוי מוחזק בהו ויהבינהו ליה וכיון דהדר אייתי ואייתי סהדי דאבהתיה הואי סלקין להא דיהבינא ליה ומהדרו להו להאי ולזילותא דבי דינא דיהבי להאי בתחלה והדר יהבי לאידך לא חיישינן דודאי אנן אחתינן ליה ואנן מסקינן ליה: שנים אומרים מת בעל. במדינת הים: ושנים אומרים לא נתגרשה. שאותן עדים עמנו היו באותה שעה: בזמן שבאו עדים נמי שאמרו שלא מת ואחר כך נשאת לבעל הואיל דהני מכחשי הני בדין הוא שתצא דמחמרי' גבי אשת איש [אבל] נשאת על פי שנים שאמרו מת ואחר כך באו עדים שלא מת הרי זו לא תצא דחיישינן לזילותא דבי דינא שהשיאוה על פי שנים שאמרו שמת וקשיא לרב נחמן: א"ל. רב נחמן: נפק ר' נחמן ועבד עובדא דלא חש לזילותא דבי דינא מאן דחזא דעבד עובדא סבר דטעות הוא בידיה משום דמוקשה ועומד הוא: באשלי רברבי. דסברי דלא חיישינן לזילותא דבי דינא: אין מעלין לכהונה על פי עד אחד. לחלוק לו תרומה: שיש עוררין עליו. בקול ולא בעדות שהוא בן גרושה ובן חלוצה: רשב"ג היינו ר' אלעזר. דבמקום שיש עוררין לא קאמר רשב"ג דמעלין אלא במקום שאין עוררין. א) דר' אלעזר סבר מעלין ולהיכא דאיכא עורר חד אין מעלין ורשב"ג סבר עד דאיכא ערער תרי:

חשק שלמה על רבינו גרשום א) נ"ל ערער חד איכא בינייהו דר"א סבר דאף דליכא רק עורר חד ג"כ אין מעלין וכו'.

מסורת הש"ס

א) שבועות דף מו:, ב) כתובות דף כב. יבמות דף פח., ג) [גיטין ס. ע"ז ז:], ד) כתובות דף כג., ה) נ"ל רב חסדא אמר, ו) רש"ל, ז) רש"א מ"ז, ח) [נ"ל רב], ט) [וע"ע תוס' כתובות כ. ד"ה אלא]:

הגהות הב"ח

(א) גמ' ורבא כרב חסדא לא אליבא דרב חסדא וכו' ורבא אמר לך עד כאן לא קאמר רב הונא התם אלא: (ב) שם אימתי בזמן שיש עליו עוררין אבל אין עליו עוררין מעלין כצ"ל: (ג) רשב"ם ד"ה המכחישות וכו' כגון שהעידו שנים פלוני לוה: (ד) ד"ה אמר רב חסדא וכו' ולא יעידו עוד בשום עדות: (ה) ד"ה שנים וכו' א"נ כגון שעדיין בעלה קיים: (ו) תוס' ד"ה וזו באה וכו' דלא שייך מיגו אלא באחד אבל בשנים לא שייך מיגו דאין דעת שניהם שוה: (ז) ד"ה ורב נחמן וכו' ואמרו יודעין שכתב ידם הוא זה אבל קטנים היו או פסולי עדות היו או אנוסים: (ח) בא"ד והתם נמי כעדות אחרת דמי:

ליקוטי רש"י

שתי כתי עדים המכחישות זו את זו. שנים אומרים הרג ושנים אומרים לא הרג: זו באה בפני עצמה ומעידה. בעדות אחרת וכן זו ואע"פ שאחת מהן פסולה אין לך בה לפסול לא זו ולא זו הואיל ואינך יודע איזה מהן פסולה אבל אחד מכת זו ואחד מכת זו אין נאמנין בעדות אחת דמה נפשך אחד מהן פסול [שבועות מז.]. ר' מנחם ב"ר יוסי וכו' בזמן שבאו עדים. שאמרו לא מת [כתובות כב:]. שבאו עדים ואמרו לא מת והוקמוה להיות בכתובות (כב:) באשה שניסת לאחד מעדיה ואומרת ברי לי [יבמות פח:]. דתליא באשלי רברבי. בחבלים גדולים וגסים שקשין ליינתק כלומר בחכמים גדולים אמרוה ואין נוחין לבטל דבריהם [ביצה כז.]. חבלים עבים וחזקים ויש אומרים באילנות גדולות כמו ויטע אשל [בראשית כא] (ע"ז ז.).

לְזִילוּתָא דְּבֵי דִינָא לֹא חָיְישִׁינַן – And **we are not concerned with** possible **disgrace of the court** which may result from such a reversal.[10]

Rava questions Rav Nachman's assertion that we are not concerned with the court's reputation:

מְתִיב רָבָא וְאִיתֵּימָא רַבִּי זְעִירָא – **Rava, and some say** it was **R' Ze'ira, challenged** Rav Nachman from a Baraisa.[11] שְׁנַיִם אוֹמְרִים מֵת – If TWO witnesses SAY that [THE HUSBAND] DIED, thereby permitting his wife to remarry,[12] וּשְׁנַיִם אוֹמְרִים לֹא מֵת – AND TWO other witnesses SAY THAT HE DID NOT DIE; שְׁנַיִם אוֹמְרִים נִתְגָּרְשָׁה – or if TWO witnesses SAY that [A WOMAN] WAS DIVORCED and may remarry,[13] וּשְׁנַיִם אוֹמְרִים לֹא נִתְגָּרְשָׁה – AND TWO other witnesses SAY THAT SHE WAS NOT DIVORCED, and may not remarry – הֲרֵי זוֹ לֹא תִּנָּשֵׂא – the law is that [SHE] MAY NOT MARRY. The two pairs of conflicting witnesses offset each other, and the woman retains her previous status of a married woman.[14] וְאִם נִשֵּׂאת לֹא תֵּצֵא – HOWEVER, IF SHE MARRIES without consulting the court, SHE DOES NOT have to LEAVE her new husband.[15] רַבִּי מְנַחֵם בְּרַבִּי יוֹסֵי אוֹמֵר – R' MENACHEM THE SON OF R' YOSE SAYS: תֵּצֵא – SHE MUST LEAVE her new husband. אָמַר רַבִּי מְנַחֵם בְּרַבִּי יוֹסֵי – But R' MENACHEM THE SON OF R' YOSE SAID: אֵימָתַי אֲנִי אוֹמֵר תֵּצֵא – WHEN DO I SAY that SHE MUST LEAVE her new husband? בִּזְמַן שֶׁבָּאוּ עֵדִים וְאַחַר כָּךְ נִשֵּׂאת – IN AN INSTANCE WHERE THE WITNESSES (who testified that she was forbidden to remarry) CAME first AND SHE MARRIED AFTERWARDS, for she married in a situation of doubt, where the court would have forbidden her to do so, had she asked. אֲבָל נִשֵּׂאת וְאַחַר כָּךְ בָּאוּ עֵדִים – BUT IF SHE MARRIED first, after the testimony of the supporting witnesses, AND THE WITNESSES who oppose the first pair CAME AFTERWARDS, הֲרֵי זוֹ לֹא תֵּצֵא – the law is that SHE DOES NOT have to LEAVE her new husband, for she married after the court permitted her to do so. Clearly, R' Menachem's rationale is that the court does not reverse its ruling and require her to leave, for we are concerned that the reversal will result in ridicule.[16] The Baraisa thus indicates that concern over possible ridicule is a valid reason not to reverse a ruling – contrary to Rav Nachman's statement. – ? –

Rav Nachman replied:

אָמַר לֵיהּ – **[Rav Nachman] said to [Rava]:** אֲנָא סָבְרִי לְמֶעְבַּד עוּבְדָא – **"I thought to take action** and reverse the original award (in the instance mentioned above), disregarding any resultant ridicule of the court. הַשְׁתָּא דְּאוֹתִיבְתַּן אַתְּ – **Now,** however, **that you have challenged us** from this Baraisa, וְאוֹתְבַן רַב הַמְנוּנָא בְּסוּרְיָא – **and Rav Hamnuna in Syria has** also **challenged us** from the same Baraisa, לֹא עָבְדִינַן בָּהּ עוּבְדָא – **we will not take action on it;** instead, we will allow the original ruling to stand."

Despite these words, however:

נְפַק עָבַד עוּבְדָא – **[Rav Nachman] went out and took action,** reversing his original award.[17] מַאן דַּחֲזָא – **Anyone who saw him** do so סָבַר טָעוּתָא הִיא בִּידֵיהּ – **thought that he had erred,** in light of his earlier declaration that he would take no action.[18] וְלֹא הִיא – **But this was not the case.** אֶלָּא מִשּׁוּם דְּתַלְיָא בְּאַשְׁלֵי רַבְרְבֵי – **Rather,** Rav Nachman acted as he did **because [his position] hangs on great ropes,** i.e. he subsequently found that great sages[19] concurred with his original view that the court does indeed reverse a decision, without concern for ridicule.

The Gemara analyzes a Mishnah and explains where Rav Nachman found support for his action:

דִּתְנַן – **For we have learned in a Mishnah:**[20] רַבִּי יְהוּדָה אוֹמֵר – R' YEHUDAH SAYS: אֵין מַעֲלִין לִכְהוּנָּה עַל פִּי עֵד אֶחָד – WE DO NOT

NOTES

witnesses that his father had owned it. Now that the loser produced witnesses that it was *his* father's, the testimonies offset each other and the court returns the land to the loser, who controlled it before the case began (*Tosafos*).

10. People may ridicule the court, because issuing a ruling one day and reversing it the next makes the judicial process seem farcical (*Rashbam*).

11. *Yevamos* 88b. The Baraisa discusses a case in which testimony is being introduced to allow a woman, known to have been married previously, to remarry.

12. The husband had traveled to a distant land and did not return. Now, two witnesses testify that he has died (*Rashbam*).

13. They testify that her husband divorced her before he died.

The Torah declares that when a man who dies childless is survived by one or more brothers, his widow may not marry someone from the general population. Instead, a brother of the deceased must take her as a wife in a process known as *yibum*. If he refuses to perform *yibum*, however, the Torah provides a mechanism known as *chalitzah* [taking off the shoe] by which the widow can be released from her restricted status (*Deuteronomy* 25:5-10). Since the witnesses testify that her husband divorced her before his death, his widow is not subject to *yibum* or *chalitzah*; she may marry anyone.

Alternatively, the Baraisa (in its second case) discusses a situation in which the husband is still alive. The witnesses testify that she is free to remarry because her husband divorced her (*Rashbam*).

14. This follows the principle explained above in note 3 that in cases of doubt the halachic status quo is maintained (*Rashbam*).

15. The Gemara in *Kesubos* (22b) explains that although the contradictory testimonies create a situation where marriage to the woman is forbidden due to the possibility that she is still married, this does not affect those who claim to know that she is not married. Thus, the Baraisa means that the couple may remain married if (a) the woman maintains that she is positive that her husband is dead [i.e. she is confident that if he were still alive, he would have returned to her (*Rashi* ibid. ד״ה באומרת)]; and (b) the new husband is one of the witnesses testifying to the woman's permitted status. Even in this case, they may not *initially* marry; rather, if they are already married we do not insist that they separate (see *Rashbam*).

16. Since we forbid her to marry, it is clear that we are concerned for the possibility that she is still wed to the first husband. Logically, then, we should insist that she leave her new husband even if she married him before the second pair testified that she is still married to the first husband. Yet R' Menachem rules that she may remain with the second husband. Clearly, the reason for this is that we are concerned for the ridicule that a reversal of the court's ruling might engender.

Although the Rabbis (the Tanna Kamma) disagree with R' Menachem's ruling, the Gemara can nevertheless adduce its proof from his ruling, because there is no indication that the Rabbis disagree with his concern about ridicule of the court. It is only that this concern never arises here according to the Rabbis, because they are altogether more lenient and always allow her to remain married to her new husband, even where she married him *after* the second pair of witnesses had already testified (*Ritva*).

It should be noted that the Gemara's debate about whether we refrain from reversing a previous decision out of concern for the court's reputation applies only where the reversal is due to doubt (such as in our case of contradictory testimony). However, where the court concludes that its original ruling was unquestionably wrong, it must reverse its ruling despite any resultant damage to its reputation (*Ritva*).

17. That is, he took back the property from the winner and withdrew the court from the case, leaving the land in its original indeterminate state and allowing the litigants to fight it out between themselves (see above, note 9).

According to the alternate explanation cited in note 9, he returned the land to the control of the loser.

18. In reversing the original ruling, he apparently forgot that this was contradicted by the Baraisa and that he himself had said that he would take no action (*Rashbam*).

19. R' Yehudah, R' Elazar and Rabban Shimon ben Gamliel all support this ruling, as will be seen below.

20. *Kesubos* 23b.

באבהתא מי אתחכש לימא רבא ורב נחמן בפלוגתא דרב הונא ורב חסדא קמיפלגי [א] דאיתמר ב' כתי עדים המכחישות זו את זו אמר רב הונא [א] זו באה בפני עצמה ומעידה וזו באה בפני עצמה ומעידה ורב חסדא אמר בהדי סהדי שקרי למה לי לימא רב נחמן דאמר כרב הונא ורבא כרב חסדא (א) אליבא דרב חסדא כולי עלמא לא פליגי כי פליגי אליבא דרב הונא רב נחמן כרב הונא ורבא עד כאן לא קאמר רב הונא אלא לעדות אחרת אבל לאותה עדות לא הדר אייתי סהדי דאבהתיה היא אמר רב נחמן [ב] אנן אחתיניה אנן מסקינן ליה לזילותא דבי דינא לא חיישינן מתיב רבא ואיתימא רבי זעירא [ג] שנים אומרים מת ושנים אומרים לא מת שנים אומרים נתגרשה ושנים אומרים לא נתגרשה הרי זו לא תנשא ואם נשאת לא תצא רבי מנחם ברבי יוסי אומר [ג] תצא אמר ר' מנחם בר' יוסי אימתי אני אומר תצא בזמן שבאו עדים ואח"כ נשאת אבל נשאת ואח"כ באו עדים הרי זו לא תצא א"ל אנא סברי למעבד עובדא השתא דאותיבתן את ואותבן רב המנונא בסוריא לא עבדינן בה עובדא נפק עבד עובדא מאן דחזא סבר טעותא היא בידיה ולא היא אלא משום [ג] דתליא באשלי רברבי [ד] דתנן רבי יהודה אומר [ד] אין מעלין לכהונה על פי עד אחד אמר ר' אלעזר אימתי (ב) במקום שיש עוררין אבל במקום שאין עוררין מעלין לכהונה על פי עד אחד רבן שמעון בן גמליאל אומר משום ר' שמעון בן הסגן מעלין לכהונה ע"פ עד אחד רשב"ג היינו ר' אלעזר וכי תימא ערער חד איכא בינייהו רבי אלעזר סבר ערער חד ורשב"ג

בדאבהתא מי איתחכש. עדות של אבהתא קיים הוא והכל מודים בו: **המכחישות זו את זו.** בעדות אחת כגון (ג) שנים אומרים פלוני לוה מפלוני מנה ושנים אחרים הכחישום ואמרו לא לוה ממנו כלום שהרי באותו היום שאתם אומרים שלוה ממנו היה עמנו הלוה כל אותו היום ולא לוה משום אדם כלום ובעדות כזה לא האמינה תורה האחרונים יותר מן הראשונים אלא בעדות הזמה כגון שמעידים על העדים עצמם עמנו הייתם במקום פלוני ולא ראיתם שלוה: **זו באה בפני עצמה ומעידה.** כשאר עדות שבעולם דלא נחזקינהו בפסולה מספק: **וזו באה כו'.** בעדות אחרת אבל לאחד מכת זו ולאחד מכת זו אין מצטרפין לעדות אחת דהא חד מהם פסול בודאי ואין כאן אלא חד עדות וטעם דרב הונא משום דאוקי גברא אחזקיה ולא תפסלינהו מספק: [ה] **(א"ר חסדא) בהדי סהדי שקרי למה לי.** ולא יעידו (ד) בשום עדות בעולם דאוקי ממונא אחזקיה ולא תוציאהו מספק שמא העדים פסולים: **לימא רב נחמן.** שמכשיר עדות דאבהתא שהעידו עדים מוכחשים דהיינו עדות אחרת שלא הוכחשו בו כדרב הונא שהכשירם בעדות אחרת שלא הוכחשו בה: **אליבא דרב חסדא כ"ע לא פליגי.** לומר כל אחד אלא סבירא כרב חסדא דודאי רב נחמן לא סבירא ליה כרב חסדא דהא רב חסדא אפילו בעדות אחרת בעלמא פוסל כל שכן בעדות דאבהתא שהוכחשו העדים מאכילה באותו עדות של אותו קרקע: **אבל באותו עדות.** לאותו קרקע עצמו לא [ו] (והלכתא כר"נ שהרי נפסק הדין על פיו למוכח לקמן אנן אחתינן): **הדר אייתי סהדי.** אותו שהפסידו רב נחמן: **דאבהתיה היא.** והרי לשניהם עדי חזקה ועדי אבות ואין כח לזה מזה וכל דאלים גבר כדאמר רב נחמן לקמן בשמעתין: **אנן מסקינן ליה.** כלומר לא נחזיק את זה יותר מזה הואיל ועדות שניהם שוה: **לזילותא דבי דינא.** שמא ילגלגו הבריות על ב"ד על שסותרין את דיניהם ודמי לחוכא ואיטלולא: **שנים אומרים מת.** אשה שהלך בעלה למדינת הים ובאו שנים ואמרו לה מת בעליך ושנים אומרים לא מת א"נ שנים אומרים נתגרשה בחיי בעלה ואינה זקוקה ליבם ושנים אומרים לא נתגרשה וזקוקה ליבם א"נ כגון (ה) שהיה בעלה קיים ובאין להתירה לאחר הרי זו לא תנשא דאוקי תרי להדי תרי ואיתתא בחזקת איסור אשת איש קיימא: **ואם ניסת לא תצא.** דיעבד אין לכתחלה לא. ובפרק האשה שנתארמלה פרכינן מכדי תרי ותרי נינהו הבא עליה באשם תלוי קאי ומשני אמר רב ששת כגון שניסת לאחד מעדיה ותו פרכינן היא גופה באשם תלוי קיימא ומשני באומרת ברי לי שמת בעלי: **בזמן שבאו עדים.** האחרונים שאמרו לא מת ולאח"כ ניסת לפיכך תצא שהרי באיסור נשאת שאילו שאלה מב"ד היו אוסרין לה לינשא: **אבל אם נשאת.** על פי עדי מיתה שהתירוה בית דין לינשא ואחר כך באו עדים שהוא קיים לא תצא דחיישינן לזילותא דבי דינא וקשה לרב נחמן: **למעבד עובדא.** דמחתינן ליה ומסקינן ליה ולא ניחוש לזילותא דבי דינא: **דאותיבתן.** השיבותני מברייתא זו: **ואותבן רב המנונא.** השיב לו כמו כן מהא ברייתא דר' מנחם ורבנן: **נפק עבד.** רב נחמן עובדא ולא חש לזילותא דבי דינא: **טעותא היא בידיה.** שלא נזכר מהך ברייתא דלעיל ועוד דאמר לא עבדינן בה עובדא: **דתליא באשלי רברבי.** רבי יהודה ור' אלעזר ור' שמעון ב"ג כולהו סברי להו דלא חיישינן לזילותא דבי דינא כדמפרש רב אשי במסקנא: **אין מעלין לכהונה.** להחזיק אדם בכהן לאכול בתרומה ולעבוד עבודה ולישא את כפיו על פי עד אחד המעידו שהוא כהן כדמפרש ר' אלעזר לקמיה [בשמעתין]: **א"ר אלעזר אימתי.** אין מעלין ע"פ עד אחד בזמן שיש על הכהן עוררין עדים הפוסלים אותו כדמפרש בסמוך ולפרש דברי ר' יהודה בא ולא לחלוק עליו: **אבל אין עליו עוררים.** אלא קול פסול בעלמא כדמפרש לקמיה מעלין ע"פ עד אחד שמכחיש את הקול: **רשב"ג היינו ר' אלעזר.** דהא ודאי במקום שיש עוררין עליו לא אמר רשב"ג דליהוי חד נאמן וכי אמר מעלין במקום שאין עוררין קאמר: **ערער חד איכא בינייהו.** והא דקתני בזמן שיש עליו עוררין היינו עד אחד הפוסלו ומכחיש עד אחד המכשירו: **דרבי אלעזר סבר ערער חד.** הוי ערער ואין עד אחד נאמן עליו להכשירו: ורשב"ג

וזו באה בפני עצמה ומעידה. תימה בין לרב הונא בין לרב חסדא נהמנינהו לבתראי במיגו דאי בעי פסלינהו לקמאי בגזלנותא ומיהו במיגו דאי בעי הוו זוממי להו ליכא להמנינהו דיראים להזימן פן יזומו גם הם ונראה לי דמיגו במקום עדים לא אמרינן [ז] (ועוד דמיגו לא יוכל לקיים יותר משני עדים ואפי' היו עמהן ק' עדים אין נאמנין דתרי כמאה ועוד אומר ר"י דלא שייך מיגו (ו) דאין דעת שניהם שוה ומה שירצה זה לטעון לא יטעון זה: **ורב נחמן כרב הונא.** תימה דבפרק ב' דכתובות (דף יט:) תנן שנים שהיו חתומין על השטר ומתו ובאו שנים ואמרו (ז) שכתב ידם הוא אבל קטנים או פסולי עדות או אנוסים היו אם כתב ידם יוצא ממקום אחר אין נאמנין ופריך ומגבי' ביה בשטרא תרי ותרי נינהו ומסיק התם (ח) (כרב) נחמן דלא מגבינן בשטרא ואוקי תרי להדי תרי ואוקי ממונא בחזקת מריה ואמאי לא מגבינן ביה והא סבירא ליה הכא כרב הונא דכשרים הם לעדות אחרת דמוקמינן להו אחזקת כשרות והתם (ט) כעדות אחרת דמי דהא אין מכחישים אלו את החתומים בזאת המלוה שהיו אומרים אין חייב לו כלום אלא שאמרו אינכם נאמנים בדבר זה דפסולים הייתם והוה לן למימר דנאמנים כמו הכא דכשרים אף על גב דאלו מכחישים אותם ופוסלים וחושבין אותן כשאר פסולים לכל דבר עדות ואומר ר"י דכי אמרו קטנים היו ליכא לאוקמינהו אחזקייהו וכן אנוסים נמי לא מפקי להו מחזקת כשרות דאמרינן אנוסים היו מחמת נפשות ופסולי עדות היו איכא למימר כגון שפסולים אותן משנולדו שאומרים קרובים היו ועכשיו נתרחקו [ט]: **ורבא** כרב חסדא. ואם תאמר אם כן אמאי חשיב רבא במרובה (ב"ק דף עב: ושם ד"ה אין) ובפ' זה בורר (סנהדרין דף כז. ושם ד"ה אין) על זוממם חידוש הוא ואין לך בו אלא משעת חידושו והלא מה שהוא נפסל אינו חידוש דהא מן הדין היה להיות לשניהן פסולים כמו בשני כתי עדים המכחישות זו את זו א"כ לא הוי חידוש אלא מה שהמזימין כשרים ואומר ר"י דרבא דאמר חידוש הוא לא הוי אלא לפי המסקנא דאתי שפיר כרב הונא: **אנן** אחתינן ליה אנן מסקינן ליה. ואם היה אותו דלית ליה חזקת אבהתיה מוחזק תחילה אתי שפיר אחתינן ומסקינן שנעמידה בידו כאשר היה בתחלה ואפילו לא היה מוחזק לא זה ולא זה מאי לפרש אחתינא ליה לזה ומסקינא ליה שנוציאנה מידו ויהא דין כל דאלים גבר. ר"י: **ואם** ניסת לא תצא. בפ"ב דכתובות (דף כב: ושם ד"ה כגון) מוקי כשניסת לאחד מעדיה ואומרת ברי לי וחשדא ליכא כדפי' התם: **אבל** ניסת ואח"כ באו עדים הרי זו לא תצא. וטעמא משום זילותא דבי דינא וקשה לרשב"א דעל כרחך לאו טעמא משום זילותא דבי דינא הוא דאם כן אפילו לא נשאת אלא התירוה לינשא תנשא כדמשמע בכל הסוגיא דאיכא זילותא אפילו לא נעשה מעשה וכ"ת דאין ה"נ ונשאת דקאמר היינו שהתירוה לינשא ושוב לא תצא מהיתרה הראשון דבאו עדים ואח"כ נשאת לא מצי לפרושי התירוה לינשא אלא נשאת ממש וע"כ טעמא דמספיקא לא מפקי לה מבעל ולא משום זילותא וי"ל לעולם טעמא משום זילותא ודוקא כשנשאת ואח"כ באו עדים איכא זילותא דבי דינא שכבר נאסרה לכל העולם כיון שנשאת נמצא מה שחוזרין לאסרה לעד שנשאת לו אין חוזרין אלא בעבורו אבל אם באו עדים קודם שנשאת ליכא זילותא דעל כרחך צריכין לחזור מהיתרה הראשון כדי לאסרה לכל העולם הלכך ליכא זילותא אם אוסרים אותה נמי לעדיה. ר"י: והאמר

עין משפט נר מצוה

כט א מיי' פכ"ב מהל' עדות הלכה ה סמג עשין קי טוש"ע ח"מ סי' לא סעיף א:

ל ב מיי' פט"ו מהל' טוען ונטען הל' ה סמג עשין צה טוש"ע ח"מ סי' קמו סעיף כג:

לא ג מיי' פי"ב מהל' גירושין הלכה כב סמג עשין נ טוש"ע אה"ע סי' יז סעיף מב קנב סעיף ג וסי' ה סעיף מב וע"ש:

לב ד מיי' פ"כ מהלכות איסורי ביאה הלכה ד טוש"ע אה"ע סי' ג סעיף א ב ג:

רבינו גרשום

באבהתי לא איתחכוש. להכי אוקמוה נכסי בחזקת אבהתא דהאי: [ב' כתי עדין] המכחישות זו את זו. בעדות אחת: אמר רב הונא. אע"ג דבהאי עדות מוכחשות הן זו באה בפני עצמה בעדות אחרת ומעידה וכשירה אבל משום דלא ידעי איזו כת משקרא ולהכי אידך כת נמי באה בפני עצמה ומעידה וכשירה אבל תרוייהו כחדא לא מצי למיתי משום דאיכא למימר חדא מינייהו מוכחשת היא ורב חסדא אמר בהדי סהדי שקרי למה לי הואיל דאתכחשא חדא מינייהו בחזקת מוכחשין נינהו תרוייהו ולא מצי לאסהודי נמי בעדות אחרת דממ"נ חדא מנייהו פסולה היא: נימא רב נחמן דאמר. נהי דאיתכחוש באכילה באבהתא מי אתכחוש ומצי לאסהודי על אבהתא ס"ל כדרב הונא דהכי נמי אמר רב הונא אע"ג דאיתכחוש בהאי עדות זו באה בפני עצמה ומעידה משום דליכא למיקם עלה דמילתא מאן מוכחשין הו"ה אידך: ורבא. דאמר שוו עדות מוכחשת כרב חסדא: אליבא דרב חסדא כ"ע לא פליגי. דאפי' רב נחמן מודי דכיון דרב חסדא פוסלו לכל עדות אע"ג דבחד מכחשי אהדדי בשאר עדות דעלמא לא מכחשי כ"ש דס"ל לרב חסדא דהיכא דמכחשי באותו עדות במקצת באכילתא בלבד דהם מוכחשין נמי לאבהתי ולא מוקי נכסי בחזקת אבהתא: כי פליגי. רב נחמן ורבא: אליבא דרב הונא. דאמר זו באה בפני עצמה ומעידה וזו באה בפני עצמה ומעידה רב נחמן דאמר נהי דאתכחוש באכילה באבהתא מי מכחשא ס"ל כרב הונא הואיל דליכא למיקם עלה דמילתא מאן מוכחשין: ורבא אמר לך כו' אבל באותה עדות לא מהימנא כלל: הדר אייתי אידך סהדי נמי דשל אבהתי הוי השתא מיתכחשי כולה עדות אמר רב נחמן אנן אחתינה להוא דאייתי מעיקרא סהדי דהוי דאבהתי ונטלנו ניכסי מהאי דהוי מוחזק בהו ויהבינהו ליה וכיון דהדר אידך ואייתי סהדי דאבהתיה הואי סלקין להא דיהיבנא ליה ומהדרי להו להאי ולזילותא דבי דינא דיהבי להאי בתחלה והדר יהבי לאידך לא חיישינן דודאי אנן אחתינן ליה ואנן מסקינן ליה: שנים אומרים מת בעל. במדינת הים: ושנים אומרים לא נתגרשה. שאותן עדים עמנו היו באותה שעה: בזמן שבאו עדים נמי שאמרו שלא מת ואחר כך נשאת לבעל הואיל דהני מכחשי הני בדין הוא שתצא דמחמרי' גבי אשת איש [אבל] נשאת על פי שנים שאמרו שמת ואחר כך באו עדים שלא מת הרי זו לא תצא דחיישינן לזילותא דבי דינא שהשיאוה על פי שנים שאמרו שמת וקשיא לרב נחמן: א"ל. רב נחמן: נפק ר' נחמן ועבד עובדא דלא חש לזילותא דבי דינא מאן דחזא דעבד עובדא סבר דטעות הוא בידיה משום דמוקשה ועומד הוא: באשלי רברבי. דסברי דלא חיישינן לזילותא דבי דינא: אין מעלין לכהונה על פי עד אחד. לחלוק לו תרומה: שיש עוררין עליו. בקול ולא בעדות שהוא בן גרושה ובן חלוצה: רשב"ג היינו ר' אלעזר. דבמקום שיש עוררין לא קאמר רשב"ג דמעלין אלא במקום שאין עוררין. א) דר' אלעזר סבר מעלין ולהיכא דאיכא עורר חד אין מעלין ורשב"ג סבר עד דאיכא ערער תרי:

חשק שלמה על רבינו גרשום א) נ"ל ערער חד איכא בינייהו דר"א סבר דאף דליכא רק עורר חד ג"כ אין מעלין וכו'.

מסורת הש"ס

א) שבועות דף מז, ב) כתובות דף כב. יבמות דף פח, ג) [גיטין כ. ע"ש], ד) כתובות דף כג, ה) צ"ל רב חסדא אמר, ו) רש"ל, ז) רש"א מ"ז, ח) [צ"ל רבא], ט) [ועי' תוס' כתובות כ. ד"ה אלא].

הגהות הב"ח

(א) גמ' ורבא כרב חסדא לא אליבא דרב חסדא וכו' ורבא אמר לך עד כאן לא קאמר רב הונא התם אלא: (ב) שם אימתי בזמן שיש עליו עוררין אבל אין עליו עוררין מעלין כו"ל: (ג) רשב"ם ד"ה המכחישות וכו' כגון שהעידו שנים פלוני לוה: (ד) ד"ה אמר רב חסדא וכו' ולא יעידו עוד בשום עדות: (ה) ד"ה שנים וכו' א"נ כגון שעדיין בעלה קיים: (ו) תוס' ד"ה וזו באה וכו' דלא שייך מיגו אלא כשאחד אבל בשנים לא שייך מיגו דאין דעת שניהם שוה: (ז) ד"ה ורב נחמן וכו' ואמרו ידענו שכתב ידם הוא אלא זה אבל קטנים היו או פסולי עדות היו או אנוסים: (ח) בא"ד והתם נמי כעדות אחרת דמי:

ליקוטי רש"י

שתי כתי עדים המכחישות זו את זו. שנים אומרים הרג ושנים אומרים לא הרג. זו באה בפני עצמה ומעידה. בעדות אחרת וכן זו ולא"ש שאחת מהן פסולה אין לך לפסול לזו ולא זו הואיל ואינך יודע איזה מהן פסולה אבל אחד מכת זו ואחד מכת זו אין נאמנין בעדות אחת דמה נפשך אחד מהן פסול [שבועות מז:]. ר' מנחם ב"ר יוסי וכו' בזמן שבאו עדים. שאמרו לא מת [כתובות כב:]. שבאו עדים ואמרו לא מת ואוקימנא להאי בכתובות (כב:) באשה שניסת לאחד מעדיה ואומרת ברי לי [יבמות פח:]. דתליא באשלי רברבי. בחבלים גדולים ובני קשין לינתק כלומר חכמים גדולים אמרום ואין נוחין לבטל דבריהם [ביצה כג:]. חבלים עבים וחזקים יש אומרים באילנות גדולות כמו ויטע אשל (בראשית כא) [ע"ז ז:].

RAISE a person TO the *KEHUNAH*[21] based ON THE TESTIMONY OF ONE WITNESS.

R' Elazar explains R' Yehudah's ruling:

אָמַר רַבִּי אֶלְעָזָר – R' ELAZAR SAID: אֵימָתַי – WHEN is one witness' testimony not believed? בְּמָקוֹם שֶׁיֵּשׁ עוֹרְרִין – IN A SITUATION WHERE THERE ARE CHALLENGERS who contest the person's fitness for the *Kehunah*.[22] אֲבָל בְּמָקוֹם שֶׁאֵין עוֹרְרִין – BUT IN A SITUATION WHERE THERE ARE NO CHALLENGERS,[23] מַעֲלִין לִכְהוּנָּה עַל פִּי עֵד אֶחָד – WE RAISE a person TO the *KEHUNAH* based ON THE TESTIMONY OF ONE WITNESS.

Another view:

רַבָּן שִׁמְעוֹן בֶּן גַּמְלִיאֵל אוֹמֵר – RABBAN SHIMON BEN GAMLIEL SAYS מִשּׁוּם רַבִּי שִׁמְעוֹן בֶּן הַסְּגָן – IN THE NAME OF R' SHIMON THE SON OF THE DEPUTY to the High Priest:[24] מַעֲלִין לִכְהוּנָּה עַל פִּי עֵד אֶחָד – WE RAISE a person TO the *KEHUNAH* based ON THE TESTIMONY OF ONE WITNESS.

Developing the proof, the Gemara asks:

רַבָּן שִׁמְעוֹן בֶּן גַּמְלִיאֵל הַיְינוּ רַבִּי אֶלְעָזָר – Is not **Rabban Shimon ben Gamliel** saying **the same** thing **as R' Elazar,** for Rabban Shimon could not possibly mean that one witness is believed against challengers?[25] וְכִי תֵּימָא עַרְעָר חַד אִיכָּא בֵּינַיְיהוּ – **And if you will say the difference between them is** in an instance where there is only **a single challenger,** רַבִּי אֶלְעָזָר סָבַר עַרְעָר חַד – **R' Elazar holding that a challenge** is valid even if raised **by** only **one** witness[26]

NOTES

21. I.e. to the status of Kohen, permitting him to eat *terumah,* serve in the Temple, or pronounce the priestly blessing. A person whose status as a Kohen is not known cannot be elevated to this status on the basis of a single witness' testimony (*Rashbam*).

22. *Kehunah* passes from father to son. However, a son begotten by a Kohen from a woman whom a Kohen may not marry does not have the status of a Kohen. Hence, the challengers assert that his mother was forbidden to his father, thus rendering him a non-Kohen.

23. But instead, merely a rumor that he is unfit (*Rashbam*).

24. He was the son of R' Chanina Segan HaKohanim (the Deputy of the Kohanim), mentioned in several places in the Six Orders of the Mishnah (*Rambam,* at the end of his introduction to his commentary on Mishnah, chapter 3).

25. At first glance, it would seem that Rabban Shimon ben Gamliel holds that we elevate a man to the *Kehunah* on the testimony of one witness, even where two witnesses assert that he is ineligible. However, this cannot be, because nobody can hold that one witness supersedes two. Rather, Rabban Shimon ben Gamliel probably means that one witness can effect the elevation when he is *unopposed* by challengers. If so, his opinion is identical with R' Elazar's! (*Rashbam*).

26. R' Elazar's statement would then be understood thusly: A single witness' testimony is sufficient to promote a man to the *Kehunah* if there are no challengers at all. Even a single challenger, however, is sufficient to negate that testimony.

וְרַבָּן שִׁמְעוֹן בֶּן גַּמְלִיאֵל סָבַר עַרְעָר תְּרֵי – while **Rabban Shimon ben Gamliel holds** that **a challenge** requires **two** witnesses to be effective,[1] this is not so. וְהָאָמַר רַבִּי יוֹחָנָן – **For R' Yochanan said:** דִּבְרֵי הַכֹּל אֵין עַרְעָר פָּחוֹת מִשְּׁנַיִם – **All agree that a challenge is not** effective if made **by fewer than two** witnesses![2]

The Gemara continues with an explanation of the Mishnah:

אֶלָּא עַרְעָר תְּרֵי – **Rather,** R' Elazar speaks of **a challenge by two;** וְהָכָא בְּמַאי עַסְקִינַן – **and here** in the Mishnah, **what are we discussing?** כְּגוֹן דְּמַחְזְקִינַן לֵיהּ בְּאֲבוּהַ דְּהַאי דְּכֹהֵן הוּא – We discuss **an instance where it had been established that [a certain person's] father was a Kohen,** thereby entitling his son to the privileges of the *Kehunah.* וְנָפַק עֲלֵיהּ קָלָא – Later **a rumor emerged regarding [the son]** דְּבֶן גְּרוּשָׁה וּבֶן חֲלוּצָה הוּא – **that he was the son of a divorcee or the son of a** ***chalutzah,***[3] וְאַחְתִּינֵיהּ – **and [the court] demoted him** from the *Kehunah* until the matter could be investigated.[4] וְאָתָא עֵד אֶחָד – **Then a single witness came** forward, וְאָמַר דְּכֹהֵן הוּא – **and said that [the man] was a Kohen** of untainted lineage, וְאַסְקִינֵיהּ – **and [the court] raised him** to his original status based on this testimony.[5] וְאָתוּ בֵּי תְּרֵי – **Subsequently, two witnesses came** forward, וְאָמְרֵי דְּבֶן גְּרוּשָׁה וַחֲלוּצָה הוּא – **and said that [the man] was the son of a divorcee or a** ***chalutzah,*** וְאַחְתִּינֵיהּ – **and [the court]** once again **demoted him** from the *Kehunah* based on their testimony.[6] וְאָתָא עֵד אֶחָד – **Then,** a *second* **single witness came** forward, וְאָמַר דְּכֹהֵן הוּא – **and** also **said that [the man] was a Kohen** of untainted lineage, corroborating the testimony of the first witness.

The Gemara now explains the reasoning behind the dispute:

וּדְכוּלֵּי עָלְמָא מִצְטָרְפִין עֵדוּת – **And all agree that** ordinarily **we combine the testimonies** of two witnesses, although they were offered separately.[7] וְהָכָא בְּמֵיחַשׁ לְזִילוּתָא דְּבֵי דִינָא קָא מִיפַּלְגֵי – **But here they dispute whether we are concerned for disgrace of the court** that may result if we promote him once again. רַבִּי אֶלְעָזָר סָבַר – **R' Elazar holds** כֵּיוָן דְּאַחְתִּינֵיהּ – that **since we** (the court) **demoted him,** לֹא מַסְקִינַן לֵיהּ – **we do not raise him** once again, חָיְישִׁינַן לְזִילוּתָא דְּבֵי דִינָא – because **we are concerned for disgrace of the court.**[8] וְרַבָּן שִׁמְעוֹן בֶּן גַּמְלִיאֵל סָבַר – **But Rabban Shimon ben Gamliel holds** אֲנַן אַחְתִּינֵיהּ וַאֲנַן מַסְקִינַן לֵיהּ – that although **we** originally **demoted him, we** now **raise him** based on the new evidence, וּלְזִילוּתָא דְּבֵי דִינָא לֹא חָיְישִׁינַן – **and we are not concerned for disgrace of the court.**

Rav Ashi objects to this interpretation of the dispute:

מַתְקִיף לָהּ רַב אַשִׁי – **Rav Ashi challenged [this explanation]:** אִי הָכִי – **If so,** that R' Elazar is concerned for disgrace of the court, מַאי אִירְיָא חַד – **why does [R' Elazar] speak of** a case in which the final testimony was that of only **one** witness? אֲפִילּוּ בִּתְרֵי נַמִי – **Even if two** witnesses come forward *simultaneously,* after two other witnesses had caused the man to be demoted, R' Elazar would **also** not re-elevate the man to the *Kehunah,* out of concern for the court's reputation![9]

Rav Ashi therefore advances another explanation:

אֶלָּא אָמַר רַב אַשִׁי – **Rather, Rav Ashi said:** דְּכוּלֵּי עָלְמָא לֹא חָיְישִׁינַן לְזִילוּתָא דְּבֵי דִינָא – Actually, ***everyone*** **agrees that we are not concerned for disgrace of the court.** וְהָכָא בִּלְצָרֵף עֵדוּת קָא מִיפַּלְגֵי – **But here, they dispute whether the testimonies** of the two single witnesses **can be combined.**[10] Rav Nachman thus was following the view of both R' Elazar and Rabban Shimon ben Gamliel. They are the "great ropes" mentioned above.

Rav Ashi introduces a Baraisa which records two disputes regarding the acceptance of testimony, the second of which parallels the dispute of R' Elazar and Rabban Shimon:

וּבִפְלוּגְתָּא דְּהָנֵי תַּנָּאֵי – **And** Rabban Shimon ben Gamliel and R'

NOTES

1. I.e. if only one challenger contests the man's status, we believe the single witness to promote him to the *Kehunah* (*Rashbam*). Thus, when Rabban Shimon ben Gamliel says, "We raise to the *Kehunah* by one witness," he means that we believe the witness over a single challenger's testimony.

2. It is not clear in what specific context R' Yochanan made his statement (*Rashbam*). Regardless, the Gemara assumes that it pertains to our discussion as well. Hence, R' Elazar must refer to a challenge raised by two.

[*Tosafos,* however, maintain that R' Yochanan made his declaration regarding this Mishnah; "all agree" means both R' Elazar and Rabban Shimon ben Gamliel.]

3. The Torah forbids a Kohen to wed a divorcee (*Leviticus* 21:7). The Rabbis additionally forbade him to marry a *chalutzah* (a woman who performed *chalitzah* — see above, 31b note 13), because she resembles a divorcee (in that a prescribed procedure released her from her attachment to a man). If a Kohen begets a son from one of these women, that son is divested of his *Kehunah* (see above, 31b note 22).

4. Although the Gemara mentioned above that a challenge raised by fewer than two witnesses is ineffective, this refers to a *permanent* removal. Even a rumor, however, can effect a *temporary* removal, which remains in force until the matter is clarified. This extra caution is exercised in an effort to keep the *Kehunah* free of blemished lineage (*Rashbam*).

5. Because even a single witness is believed to counter a rumor (*Rashbam*).

6. Because a single witness is ineffective when opposed by two (*Rashbam*).

7. In this case, combining the testimonies of the two individual witnesses would create a pair who testify to the man's status as a pedigreed Kohen, offsetting the testimony of the pair who testify that he is unfit for the *Kehunah.* As explained above on 31b note 3, in all cases of unresolvable doubt the status quo is maintained. Accordingly, we would reinstate the man as a legitimate Kohen based on his father's status as a Kohen of pure lineage, and also the status he was originally awarded by the court as a result of the testimony of the first witness (*Rashbam;* see *Ritva* and *Kovetz Shiurim* §132).

8. We are concerned that the court's reversal of its previous ruling might lead to ridicule. According to this interpretation of the dispute, R' Elazar's statement in the Mishnah is understood as follows: We do not raise a man to the *Kehunah* based on the testimony of a *second* single witness (as per the logic described in note 7) in an instance where two challengers have *already caused* his removal, due to concern for the ridicule that such a re-elevation might generate (*Rashbam*).

An apparent difficulty: The Gemara has explained that R' Elazar maintains that the court does not raise a man to the *Kehunah* after he was previously removed, due to concern for the court's reputation. But does not the Baraisa state that after removing the man because of a rumor, we reinstated him on the basis of a witness' testimony?

The answer is that only an elevation that follows a *full-fledged* demotion invites ridicule. However, a demotion following a rumor of the man's unfitness is not intended to be final; rather, it is a temporary measure, effective only while the court investigates the rumor. [The public realizes this and they will not ridicule the court for promoting the man after the investigation.] (*Rashbam;* cf. *Tosafos*).

9. The words in the Mishnah, "We do not raise on the basis of one witness," imply that it is the fact that he is unaccompanied by a second witness that renders him ineffective. But, Rav Ashi argues, according to the explanation just offered, the *number* of witnesses is irrelevant. Even *two* witnesses cannot effect the man's elevation when they follow an earlier court ruling that demoted him (*Rashbam*).

10. R' Elazar holds that since they did not testify as a unit, the first and last witnesses cannot be combined, so the Kohen remains in his deposed state due to the testimony of the two challengers. Rabban Shimon, on the other hand, maintains that the last witness combines with the first to oppose the incriminating testimony. Thus they create an impasse, which results in the elevation of the Kohen to his former status. Neither opinion, however, is concerned for possible ridicule of the court. Thus, if the two supporting witnesses had come forward simultaneously, all would agree that the Kohen's original status would be restored (*Rashbam*).

ורשב"ג סבר ערער תרי [א] והאמר רבי יוחנן דברי הכל אין ערער פחות משנים אלא ערער תרי והכא במאי עסקינן [א]כגון דמחזקינן ליה באבוה דהאי דכהן הוא ונפק עליה קלא דבן גרושה ובן חלוצה הוא ואחתיניה ואתא עד אחד ואמר דכהן (א) הוא ואסקיניה ואתו בי תרי ואמרי דבן גרושה וחלוצה הוא ואחתיניה ואתא עד אחד ואמר דכהן הוא ודכולי עלמא מצטרפין עדות והכא במיחש לזילותא דבי דינא קא מיפלגי ר' אלעזר סבר כיון דאחתיניה לא מסקינן ליה חיישינן לזילותא דבי דינא ורשב"ג סבר [ב]אנן אחתיניה ואנן מסקינן ליה ולזילותא דבי דינא לא חיישינן מתקיף לה רב אשי אי הכי מאי איריא חד אפי' בתרי נמי אלא אמר רב אשי דכולי עלמא לא חיישינן לזילותא דבי דינא והכא בלצרף עדות קא מיפלגי ובפלוגתא דהני תנאי [ג] דתניא לעולם אין עדותן מצטרפת עד שיראו שניהן כאחד ר' יהושע בן קרחה אומר [ג]אפי' בזה אחר זה אין עדותן מתקיימת בבית דין עד שיעידו שניהם כאחד ר' נתן אומר [ד]שומעין דבריו של זה היום ולכשיבא חבירו למחר שומעין דבריו: ההוא דאמר לחבריה מאי בעית בהאי ארעא א"ל מינך זבינתה והא שטרא אמר

ורשב"ג סבר ערער תרי. בעינן אבל במקום ערער אחד הוי עד אחד נאמן להכשירו: והא אמר ר' יוחנן. לא איתפרש היכא קאי: ונפק עליה קלא. קול בעלמא ולא עדות: ואחתיניה. מן הכהונה עד שיבדקו את הדבר שמעלה היא בכהונה וכל זה יותר לשון הוא בלא צורך דבלא קול נמי מיתוקמא שמעתתא שפיר בעד אחד מכשיר מעיקרא ועד אחד בסוף ושנים עדים עוררים בינתים כדמפרש ואזיל אלא משום הכי נקט ליה דבעי למימר ואתא עד אחד ואמר דכהן גמור הוא ואסקיניה דלמאי אתא עד אחד להכשירו אלא אם כן יצא עליו פסלות קודם לכן: ואסקיניה. דבמקום קול הוי עד אחד מהימן: ואחתיניה. דאחד במקום שנים אין דבריו כלום: ואתא עד אחד. לבסוף ואמר דכהן גמור הוא והוו להו שנים מכשירין: ודכולי עלמא. בין רבי אלעזר בין רשב"ג מצרפין עדים המעידים זה שלא בפני זה בשאר עדיות וה"נ יש לנו לצרף מן הדין עד ראשון ועד אחרון המכשירין ונכשירהו לזה אם לא מפני זילותא דבי דינא כדמפרש ואזיל: דרבי אלעזר סבר כיון דאחתיניה. על פי ב' עוררין ודין הורדנוהו דבכל מקום האמינה תורה שנים תו לא ליסקיה על פי עד אחד זה השני אף על פי שיש לצרפו עם הראשון ולהכשירו לזה דאוקי תרי לבהדי תרי ואוקי גברא אחזקיה דכשרות קמייתא דהוה מוחזק לן באבוה דכהן הוא וגם הכשרנוהו תחלה על פי עד אחד קודם שבאו עוררין: דחיישינן לזילותא דבי דינא. שהורידוהו על פי עוררין ועכשיו (ג) יעלו ויבטלו דבריהם והכי קאמר ר' אלעזר אימתי אין מעלין ע"פ עד אחד הבא לבסוף בזמן שיש עליו עוררין שנים הפוסלין אותו הלכך לא מהני עד שני הבא לבסוף להכשירו להצטרף עם הראשון המכשיר דאע"ג דאיכא למימר אוקי תרי מכשירין לבהדי תרי פוסלין ואוקי גברא אחזקיה ויהיה כשר אפי' הכי לא מסקינן ליה משום זילותא דבי דינא והאי דאסקוהו מעיקרא על פי עד אחד הבא לאו זילותא דבי דינא הוא דהשבית הקול לאו זילותא דבי דינא הוא למאי דאחתיניה בשביל קול בעלמא הוא ודבי לחזור ולהעלותו אחר שיבדקו הדבר הורדנוהו הלכך כי הדר מסקי ליה ליכא זילותא אבל כשהורדנוהו על פי עדים מן הדין הורדנוהו וכי הדר מסקי איכא זילותא: ואנן מסקינן ליה. ולא קשיא תרי ותרי נינהו ולמאי מסקינן ליה והא הוי ספק תריך אוקי תרי לבהדי תרי ואוקמיה אחזקיה קמייתא דאסקוהו על פי עד ראשון שהיה נאמן דהא הכי אין עוררין קול לאו עוררין הוא: דר' אלעזר חייש לזילותא דבי דינא: אי הכי. מאי איריא. עד הבא לבסוף דהכתם אין מעלין משום זילותא דקתני מתני' אין מעלין על פי עד אחד בזמן שיש עליו עוררין הא על פי שנים מעלין אפילו תרי אתו בהדי הדדי נמי בפעם שניה לרבי אלעזר לא מסקינן ליה: אלא אמר רב אשי דכולי עלמא כו'. והיינו אשלי רברבי לעיל: והכא בלצרף עדותן קא מיפלגי. לר' אלעזר אין מצרפין עד אחרון עם הראשון הואיל ולא העידו שניהם כאחד כרבנן דפליגי אדרבי נתן אבל אם באו שניהם ביחד הוה מסקינן ליה ומוקמינן ליה אחזקיה קמייתא דמוחזק לן באבוה דכהן הוא ולזילותא לא חיישינן ורשב"ג כר' נתן: דהני תנאי. ר' נתן ורבנן: דתניא אין עדותן מצטרפת. אין צריך כאן בהאי מחלוקת דרבי יהושע בן קרחה ורבנן אלא כך היא ברייתא שלימה בשילהי זה בורר ומשום גררא דסיפא נקט רישא: עד שיראו שניהם כאחד. את העדות לאפוקי אחד אומר בפני הלוהו ואחד אומר בפני הודה לו עליו: אפי' בזה אחר זה. אחד אומר ביום ראשון לוה פלוני מפלוני מנה ואחד אומר ביום שני ראיתיו גם אני שלוה ממנו דמ"מ אמנה קא מסהדי ות"ק סבר אמנה דקא מסהיד האי לא קא מסהיד האי וה"ל לגבי מנה חצי עדות וטעמייהו מפרש שפיר בסנהדרין מקרא ומסברא: אין עדותן מתקיימת. להתקבל בב"ד ואפי' ראו שניהם כאחד עד שיעידו שניהם כאחד בפני ב"ד ופלוגתא אחריתי היא ולאו ר' יהושע בן קרחה קאמר לה ור' אלעזר ורשב"ג בפלוגתא דר"נ ורבנן פליגי: ר' נתן אומר כו'. וטעמייהו מפרש התם שפיר מקרא ומסברא:
אמר

והאמר רבי יוחנן כו'. ונראה לר"י דר' יוחנן עיקר דבריו אהך משנה איתמר (ג) והיינו דקאמר דברי הכל היינו רשב"ג ור' אלעזר דאיירו בעוררין ולהכי לא קא משני הכא ה"מ היכא דאיכא חזקה לכשרות אבל היכא דליכא חזקה דכשרות לא אמר כדמשני בפ' עשרה יוחסין (קדושין דף עג:) גבי נאמנת חיה לומר זה כהן דאמתניתין דהכא קאי וא"ת כיון דאמתניתין דהכא קאי היכי פריך מיניה התם ובפ"ק דגיטין (דף ט. ושם) דלמא הא דקאמר ר' יוחנן אין ערער פחות משנים היינו משום דאיכא עד אחד דמכשיר וי"ל דהגמ' ידע דר' יוחנן מיירי כדמסיק דיצא עליו קול שהוא בן גרושה ואח"כ בא עד אחד דמכשיר להסיר הקול ואתו בי תרי כו' ובכה"ג אמר רבי יוחנן דאין (ד) פחות משנים ואע"ג דעד אחד שהכשיר והקול כליתנהו דמי שהרי העד גרוע מן הקול אם לא החזקה שהרי הקול פוסל והעד אינו פוסל [ג]:

אין ערער פחות משנים. לא בא לאפוקי אלא עד אחד אבל קול פוסל כדמסקינן:

ונפק עליה קלא ואחתיניה. לאו דוקא אחתיניה אלא כלומר ממילא ירד דאי דוקא אחתיניה ומאי אסקיניה והא איכא זילותא דב"ד וליכא למימר ליכא זילותא אלא כשהורידו ב' פעמים דבשמעתא מוכח דאפי' בחדא זימנא איכא זילותא א"נ הורדה גמורה קאמר וליכא זילותא דב"ד אלא היכא דהורידוהו על ידי עדות אבל בהורדה שע"י הקול ליכא זילותא:

ואתא חד סהדא ואסקיניה. ואע"ג דאמרינן בפרק המגרש (גיטין דף פא. ושם) דלא מבטלין קלא גבי גרושה לכהן משום דאית ליה תקנה אבל הכא דאי לא מסיקנא ליה פסול לעולם מבטלין אי נמי בתרומה דרבנן הקילו [ד]: אנן מסקינן ליה. דאוקי תרי בהדי תרי ואוקי גברא אחזקיה דמוחזק לן דאביו כהן הוא ותימה דאמרינן בפרק האומר בקדושין (דף סו.) גבי ינאי המלך ויבוקש ולא נמלא היכי דמי אילימא דתרי אמרי אישתבאי ותרי אמרי לא אישתבאי תרי ותרי נינהו מאי חזית דסמכת אהני סמוך אהני ואמאי לא נמלא והשתא מאי קא פריך אדרבה אית לן למימר אוקי תרי בהדי תרי ואוקי גברא אחזקיה ואוקי ינאי אחזקת אמו דלא אישתבאי ופירש התם בקונט' דחזקת האם לא מהניא להכשיר את ינאי לפי שאין עדים באין לפסול את האם לכהונה אלא להעיד על ינאי ואין נראה לר"י דלמה לא יועיל חזקת האם לבן הואיל ואינו יכול להיות שתהא האם כשרה אם לא יהיה הבן כשר ועוד דהכא אע"ג דעל הבן מעידים לפסלו מהניא ליה חזקת האב להכשירו ונראה לר"י דהיינו טעמא משום דמסקינן בפ' ד' אחין (יבמות דף לא. ושם ד"ה תרי) דכל תרי ותרי הויא ספיקא דרבנן והאם נמי הוי ספיקא דרבנן ולהכי פריך התם סמוך אהני דנהי דמדאורייתא אמרי' אוקי תרי בהדי תרי ואוקי איתתא אחזקה מ"מ מדרבנן יש לפוסלה והכא לענין תרומה דרבנן הקילו להתירו בה בתרי ותרי ולאוקמיה אחזקיה והא דאמר לעיל שנים אומרים מת וב' אומרים לא מת כו' אבל נשאת ואח"כ באו עדים לא תצא אע"ג דתרי ותרי ספיקא דרבנן היא ומדאורייתא אית לן לאוקמה אחזקה דהויא אשת איש והיה לה לצאת אע"פ שנשאת לאחד מעדיה אור"ת דאתיא חזקה דדייקא ומנסבא ומרעה חזקת אשת איש ואם תאמר כי איכא ב' עדים לא דייקא דליכא חומר בסופה כדאמר בהאשה רבה (שם דף פז: ושם) נשאת שלא ברשות מותרת לחזור לו ומפרש התם דהיינו שנשאת בעדים וי"ל הואיל ומכחישים זה את זה איכא חומרא אם תעמוד תחת בעלה בטענת ברי שלה וא"ת ב' אומרים נתגרשה וב' אומרים לא נתגרשה אמאי לא תנא בנשאת ואח"כ באו עדים הא לא דייקא דדוקא במת הוא דדייקא שירא שמא יבא וידעו הכל שלא מת ואינה נאמנת לומר נתגרשה דשלא בפני בעלה מעיזה ומעיזה ועוד היכא דאיכא עדים דקא מסייעי לה מעיזה ומעיזה וי"ל דלענין הכי דייקא ומרע' חזקת אשת איש דלעולם ירא שמא יוזמו או יפסלוס בגזלנות וא"ת אמאי דלא ידע דבאומר ברי לי איירי מאי קאמר היא גופא באשם תלוי קיימא ה"ל למימר בחטאת קיימא וי"ל דפריך אפילו נאמר דתרי ותרי הוה ספיקא דאורייתא כדפי' בפ' ד' אחין (שם דף לא. ד"ה אי) מ"מ באשם קיימא ואין להאריך ובכתובות (דף כו: ד"ה אנן) פירשתי: אמאי

עין משפט נר מצוה

לג א ב מיי' פ"כ מהל' איסורי ביאה הל' טו סמג לאוין קכב טוש"ע אה"ע סי' ג סעיף ז:

לד ג מיי' פ"ד מהלכות עדות הלכה ג סמג עשין קט טוש"ע ח"מ סי' ל סעיף ו:

לה ד מיי' שם הלכה ד ופ"כ מהל' איסורי ביאה הלכה טז סמג שם טוש"ע שם ס"ס טוש"ע אה"ע סי' ג' סעיף ז:

רבינו גרשום

והאמר ר' יוחנן אין ערער פחות משנים והיכי אמר ר' אלעזר דהיכא דאיכא ערער חד אין מעלין. לא הכא במאי עסקינן דמאי בינייהו כגון דמחזיק לן כו' דכולי עלמא מצטרף לעדותן דקמא ודבתרא דמכשרי ליה אע"ג דלא אתו בהדדי חיישינן לזילותא דבי דינא דהורידוהו מן הכהונה. והואיל דליכא אלא חד סהדא דאתי באפי נפשיה לא מסקינן ליה דהא דאין מעלין לכהונה על פי עד אחד הוא דאיכא עוררין ורשב"ג סבר דמסקינן ליה ולזילותא דבי דינא דאחתיה לא חיישינן הואיל דאיכא תרי סהדי אע"ג דלא אתו בהדדי. ורב נחמן משום הכי עבד עובדא דלא חיישינן לזילותא דבי דינא משום דס"ל כרשב"ג דאמר משום ר"ש הסגן. אי הכי דפליגי דחיישי' לזילותא דבי דינא מאי איריא עד אחד דאתי באפי נפשיה אפי' אתו תרי בהדא כיון דאחתיניה חיישי' לזילותא דבי דינא ולא מסקינן ליה. עד שיראו שניהם כאחד שאם העיד אחד אני ראיתי פלוני לוה מפלוני מנה ואח"כ העיד אחר אני ראיתי פלוני לוה מפלוני מנה אין עדותן מצטרפת עד שיראו ב' העדי' כאחד שלוה מנה דדלמא אמנה דקא מסהיד האי לא מסהיד האי דשמא פרע לו ושוב לוה ממנו. ר' יהושע בן קרחה אומר אפי' בזה אחר זה הואיל ועדות אחת הן מעידין וביום אחד ושעה אחת: ואין עדותן מתקיימת בבית דין. שאם אמר אחד אני ראיתי עדות זה וחבירו שם היה ולמחר בא חבירו והעיד כן אין מצטרפין עד שיעידו שניהם כאחד: ר' נתן אומר וכו'. דר' אלעזר סבירא ליה כרבנן דהואיל שלא באין שני עדים הללו בבת אחת להעיד על כהן זה אין עדותן מצטרפת ורשב"ג סבר כר' נתן דמצטרפין:
חספא

מסורת הש"ס

א) כתובות דף כו. קדושין דף עג: גיטין דף ט., ב) [לקמן דף קסה: גיטין דף ג.] סנהדרין דף ל. כתובות דף כו: [תוספתא סנהדרין פ"ה], ג) [וע"ע תוס' כתובות כו.], ד) [וע"ע תוס' כתובות כו: ד"ה ואסקיניה]:

הגהות הב"ח

(א) גמ' ואמר דכהן גמור הוא כצ"ל וכן בסמוך: (ב) רשב"ם ד"ה דחיישינן לזילותא וכו' ועכשיו יעלוהו ויבטלו וכו' להסבינן את הקול וכו' בשביל קול מעלה בעלמא כצ"ל והד"א עם ד"ה דר' אלעזר ובכל הענין צ"ל ר' אלעזר במקום ר' אליעזר: (ג) תוס' ד"ה והאמר וכו' איתמר והא דקאמר: (ד) בא"ד דאין ערער פחות משנים:

ליקוטי רש"י

והאמר ר' יוחנן דברי הכל אין ערער פחות משנים. לא איתפרש היכא [גיטין ט.]. ונפק עליה קלא. קול בעלמא ולא עדות. ואחתיניה. מן הכהונה עד שיבדקו את הדבר שמעלה הוא לכהונה [כתובות כו.]. ואסקיניה. דבמקום קול הוי עד מהימן. ודכולי עלמא. בין לר' אלעזר בין לר"ש. מצטרפין. שני עדים המעידים זה שלא בפני זה בשאר עדיות. חיישינן לזילותא דבי דינא. שהורידוהו על פי עוררין ועכשיו יעלוהו ויבטלו דבריהם והיינו דקאמר ר' אלעזר למאמר שהורידוהו ע"פ העוררין אין מעלין ע"פ עד זה השני אע"פ שיש לצרפו עם הראשון. ואנן מסקינן ליה. ולא קשיא תרי ותרי נינהו אוקי תרי לבהדי תרי ואוקמיה אחזקיה קמייתא דאסקיה ע"פ עד הראשון שהיה נאמן דהא לא היו אין עוררין דקול לאו עוררין הוא. אפילו בתרי. אתו בהדי הדדי לר' אלעזר לא מסקינן ליה. עד שיראו שניהן כאחד. את העדות לאפוקי אחד אומר בפני הלוהו ואחד אומר בפני הודה לו עליו [שם:]. אין עדותן מתקיימת. להתקבל בב"ד ואפי' ראו שניהן כאחד ופלוגתא דר' יהושע בן קרחה קאמר לה ורבי אלעזר ורבן שמעון בפלוגתא דרבי נתן ורבנן פליגי [כתובות שם]. לפסוק הדין על פיהם. עד שיעידו שניהם כאחד. ותמצא היא ולא ר' יהושע בן קרחה קאמר לה [סנהדרין ל.].

Elazar align themselves **with** the opinions in **the dispute of the following Tannaim.** דְּתַנְיָא – **For it was taught in a Baraisa:** לְעוֹלָם אֵין עֵדוּתָן מִצְטָרֶפֶת – [TWO WITNESSES'] TESTIMONIES CAN NEVER BE COMBINED, עַד שֶׁיִּרְאוּ שְׁנֵיהֶן כְּאֶחָד – UNLESS THEY BOTH SEE AS ONE, i.e. they must both testify to seeing the same thing at the same time.[11] רַבִּי יְהוֹשֻׁעַ בֶּן קָרְחָה אוֹמֵר – But R' YEHOSHUA BEN KORCHAH SAYS: אֲפִילוּ בְּזֶה אַחַר זֶה – Their testimonies may be combined EVEN if they testify that two separate events took place ONE FOLLOWING THE OTHER.[12]

The second dispute in the Baraisa: אֵין עֵדוּתָן מִתְקַיֶּימֶת בְּבֵית דִּין – And [WITNESSES'] TESTIMONY, even if they testify to the same event, CANNOT BE SUSTAINED IN COURT, עַד שֶׁיָּעִידוּ שְׁנֵיהֶם כְּאֶחָד – UNLESS THE TWO OF THEM TESTIFY AS ONE (i.e. together). רַבִּי נָתָן אוֹמֵר – R' NASSAN, however, SAYS: שׁוֹמְעִין דְּבָרָיו שֶׁל זֶה הַיּוֹם – WE LISTEN TO THE WORDS OF THIS [WITNESS] TODAY, וְלִכְשֶׁיָּבֹא חֲבֵירוֹ לְמָחָר – AND WHEN HIS FELLOW COMES to testify TOMORROW, שׁוֹמְעִין דְּבָרָיו – WE LISTEN TO HIS WORDS, and we combine their testimonies.[13] R' Elazar and Rabban Shimon ben Gamliel dispute this same point, R' Elazar siding with the Rabbis (i.e. the unnamed first opinion) and Rabban Shimon concurring with R' Nassan.[14]

The Gemara relates an incident in which the occupant of a property attempted to support his claim with a faulty document: הַהוּא דְּאָמַר לְחַבְרֵיהּ – There was **a certain man who said to his fellow:** מַאי בָּעֵית בְּהַאי אַרְעָא – **"What are you doing on this land?"**

אָמַר לֵיהּ – **[The occupant] said to [the challenger]:** מִינָּךְ זְבִינְתַּהּ – **"I bought it from you,** וְהָא שְׁטָרָא – **and here is the deed,** which proves my claim."[15]

NOTES

11. E.g. they must both testify that Reuven lent Shimon money on the same day (*Rabbeinu Gershom;* cf. *Rashbam* and *Rashash*).

12. Even if one witness testifies that Shimon borrowed a sum of money from Reuven on Sunday, and the other testifies that he borrowed a like sum on Monday, R' Yehoshua is of the opinion that the testimony is accepted, for both testify that Shimon owes Reuven the same sum of money. The Tanna Kamma, however, argues that since the witnesses testify about different loans, we lack the requisite two witnesses for any one loan. The dispute is discussed at length in tractate *Sanhedrin* (30a). Although this part of the Baraisa has no bearing on our Gemara, it is included here because the Gemara wishes to quote the Baraisa in its entirety (*Rashbam*).

13. [This dispute also is discussed at length in *Sanhedrin* (ibid.).]

14. See note 10.

15. The occupant did not claim to have occupied the land for the three years required to establish *chazakah.* He merely produced a bill of sale.

ורשב"ג סבר ערער תרי [א] והאמר רבי יוחנן דברי הכל אין ערער פחות משנים אלא ערער תרי והכא במאי עסקינן [א]כגון דמחזקינן ליה באבוה דהאי דכהן הוא ונפק עליה קלא דבן גרושה ובן חלוצה הוא ואחתיניה ואתא עד אחד ואמר דכהן (א) הוא ואסקיניה ואתו בי תרי ואמרי דבן גרושה וחלוצה הוא ואחתיניה ואתא עד אחד ואמר דכהן הוא ודכולי עלמא מצטרפין עדות והכא במיחש לזילותא דבי דינא קא מיפלגי ר' אלעזר סבר כיון דאחתיניה לא מסקינן ליה חיישינן לזילותא דבי דינא ורשב"ג סבר [ב]אנן אחתיניה ואנן מסקינן ליה ולזילותא דבי דינא לא חיישינן מתקיף לה רב אשי אי הכי מאי איריא חד אפי' בתרי נמי אלא אמר רב אשי דכולי עלמא לא חיישינן לזילותא דבי דינא והכא בלצרף עדות קא מיפלגי ובפלוגתא דהני תנאי [ג]דתניא לעולם אין עדותן מצטרפת עד שיראו שניהם כאחד ר' יהושע בן קרחה אומר [ג]אפי' בזה אחר זה אין עדותן מתקיימת בבית דין עד שיעידו שניהם כאחד ר' נתן אומר [ד]שומעין דבריו של זה היום ולכשיבא חבירו למחר שומעין דבריו: ההוא דאמר לחבריה מאי בעית בהאי ארעא א"ל מינך זבינתה והא שטרא אמר

ורשב"ג סבר ערער תרי. בעינן אבל במקום ערער אחד הוי עד אחד נאמן להכשירו: **והא אמר ר' יוחנן.** לא איתפרש היכא קאי: **ונפק עליה קלא.** קול בעלמא ולא עדות: **ואחתיניה.** מן הכהונה עד שיבדקו את הדבר שמעלה היא בכהונה וכל זה יותר לשון הוא בלא צורך דבלא קול נמי מיתוקמא שמעתתא שפיר בעד אחד מכשיר מעיקרא ועד אחד בסוף ושנים עדים עוררים בינתים כדמפרש ואזיל אלא משום הכי נקט ליה דבעי למימר ואתא עד אחד ואמר דכהן גמור הוא ואסקיניה דלמאי אתא עד אחד להכשירו אלא אם כן יצא עליו פסלות קודם לכן: **ואסקיניה.** דבמקום קול הוי עד אחד מהימן: **ואחתיניה.** דאחד במקום שנים אין דבריו כלום: **ואתא עד אחד.** לבסוף ואמר דכהן גמור הוא והוו להו שנים מכשירין: **ודכולי עלמא.** בין רבי אלעזר בין רשב"ג מצרפין עדים המעידים זה שלא בפני זה בשאר עדיות וה"נ יש לנו לצרף מן הדין עד ראשון ועד אחרון המכשירין ונכשירו לזה אם לא מפני זילותא דבי דינא כדמפרש ואזיל: **דרבי אלעזר סבר כיון דאחתיניה.** על פי ב' עוררין ובדין הורדנוהו דבכל מקום שהאמינה תורה שנים תו לא ליסקי ליה על פי עד אחד זה השני אף על פי שיש לצרפו עם הראשון ולהכשירו לזה דאוקי תרי לבהדי תרי ואוקי גברא אחזקיה דכשרות קמייתא דהוה מוחזק לן באבוה דכהן הוא וגם הכשרנוהו תחלה על פי עד אחד קודם שבאו עוררין: **דחיישינן לזילותא דבי דינא.** שהורידוהו על פי עוררין ועכשיו (ג) יעלו ויבטלו דבריהם והכי קאמר ר' אלעזר אימתי אין מעלין ע"פ עד אחד הבא לבסוף בזמן שיש עליו עוררים שנים הפוסלין אותו הלכך לא מהני עד שני הבא לבסוף להכשירו להצטרף עם הראשון המכשיר דאע"ג דאיכא למימר אוקי תרי מכשירין בהדי תרי פוסלין ואוקי גברא אחזקיה ויהיה כשר אפי' הכי לא מסקינן ליה משום זילותא דבי דינא והאי דאסקוהו מעיקרא על פי עד אחד הבא להשבית הקול לאו זילותא דבי דינא הוא דמאי דאחתיניה בשביל קול בעלמא הוא וכדי לחזור ולהעלותו אחר שיבדקו הדבר הורדנוהו הלכך כי הדר מסקי ליה ליכא זילותא אבל כשהורדנוהו על פי עדים מן הדין הורדנוהו וכי הדר מסקי איכא זילותא: **ואנן מסקינן ליה.** ולא קשיא תרי ותרי נינהו ואמאי מסקינן ליה והא הוי ספק דהוא תריך אוקי תרי לבהדי תרי ואוקמיה אחזקיה קמייתא דאסקוהו על פי עד ראשון שהיה נאמן דהא אכתי אין עוררין דקול לאו עוררין הוא: **אי הכי.** דר' אלעזר חייש לזילותא דבי דינא: **מאי איריא.** עד הבא לבסוף דהתם אין מעלין משום זילותא דקתני מתני' אין מעלין על פי עד אחד בזמן שיש עליו עוררין הא על פי שנים מעלין אפילו תרי אתו בהדי הדדי נמי בפעם שניה לרבי אלעזר לא מסקינן ליה: **אלא אמר רב אשי דכולי עלמא כו'.** והיינו אשלי רברבי דלעיל: **והכא בלצרף עדותן קא מיפלגי.** לר' אלעזר אין מצרפין עד אחרון עם הראשון הואיל ולא העידו שניהם כאחד כרבנן דפליגי אדרבי נתן אבל אם באו שניהם ביחד הוה מסקינן ליה ומוקמינן ליה אחזקיה קמייתא דמוחזק לן באבוה דכהן הוא ולזילותא לא חיישינן ורשב"ג כר' נתן: **דהני תנאי.** ר' נתן ורבנן: **דתניא אין עדותן מצטרפת.** אין צריך כאן בהאי מחלוקת דרבי יהושע בן קרחה ורבנן אלא כך היא ברייתא שלימה בשילהי זה בורר ומשום גררא דסיפא נקט רישא: **עד שיראו שניהם כאחד.** את העדות לאפוקי אחד אומר בפני הלוהו ואחד אומר בפני הודה לו עליו: **אפי' בזה אחר זה.** אחד אומר ביום ראשון לוה פלוני מפלוני מנה ואחד אומר ביום שני ראיתיו גם אני שלוה ממנו דמ"מ אמנה קא מסהדי ות"ק סבר אמנה דקא מסהיד האי לא קא מסהיד האי וה"ל לגבי מנה חלי עדות וטעמייהו מפרש שפיר בסנהדרין מקרא ומסברא: **אין עדותן מתקיימת.** להתקבל בב"ד ואפי' ראו שניהם כאחד עד שיעידו שניהם כאחד בפני ב"ד ופלוגתא אחריתי היא ולאו ר' יהושע בן קרחה קאמר לה ור' אלעזר ורשב"ג בפלוגתא דר"נ ורבנן פליגי: **ר' נתן אומר כו'.** וטעמייהו מפרש התם שפיר מקרא ומסברא: אמר

והאמר רבי יוחנן כו'. ונראה לר"י דר' יוחנן עיקר דבריו אהך משנה איתמר (ג) והיינו דקאמר דברי הכל היינו רשב"ג ור' אלעזר דאיירו בעוררין ולהכי לא קא משני הכא ה"מ היכא דליכא חזקה דכשרות אבל היכא דאיכא חזקה דכשרות לא אמר כדמשני בפ' עשרה יוחסין (קדושין דף עג:) גבי נאמנת חיה לומר זה כהן דלמתניתין דהכא קאי וא"ת כיון דלמתניתין דהכא קאי היכי פריך מיניה התם ובפ"ק דגיטין (דף ט. ושם) דלמא הא דקאמר ר' יוחנן אין ערער פחות משנים היינו משום דליכא עד אחד דמכשיר וי"ל דהגמ' ידע דר' יוחנן מיירי כדמסיק דילא עליו קול שהוא בן גרושה ואח"כ בא עד אחד דמכשיר להסיר הקול ואתו בי תרי כו' ובכה"ג אמר רבי יוחנן דאין (ד) פחות משנים ואע"ג דעד אחד שהכשיר והקול כליתנהו דמי שהרי העד גרוע מן הקול אם לא החזקה שהרי הקול פוסל והעד אינו פוסל [ג]:

אין ערער פחות משנים. לא בא לאפוקי אלא עד אחד אבל קול פוסל כדמסקינן:

ונפק עליה קלא ואחתיניה. לאו דוקא אחתיניה אלא כלומר ממילא ירד דאי דוקא אחתיניה אמאי אסקיניה והא איכא זילותא דב"ד וליכא למימר ליכא זילותא אלא כשהורידוהו ב' פעמים דבשמעתתא מוכח דאפי' בחדא זימנא איכא זילותא מ"מ הורדה גמורה קאמר וליכא זילותא דב"ד אלא היכא דהורידוהו על ידי עדות אבל בהורדה שע"י הקול ליכא זילותא:

ואתא חד סהדא ואסקיניה. ואע"ג דאמרינן בפרק המגרש (גיטין דף פא. ושם) דלא מבטלין קלא גבי גרושה לכהן משום דאית ליה תקנה אבל הכא דאי לא מסיקנא ליה פסול לעולם מבטלין אי נמי בתרומה דרבנן הקילו [ד]: **אנן** מסקינן ליה. דאוקי תרי בהדי תרי ואוקי גברא אחזקיה דמוחזק לן דאביו כהן הוא ותימה דאמרינן בפרק האומר בקדושין (דף סו.) גבי ינאי המלך ויבוקש ולא נמצא היכי דמי אילימא דתרי אמרי אישתבאי ותרי אמרי לא אישתבאי תרי ותרי נינהו מאי חזית דסמכת אהני סמוך אהני ואמאי לא נמצא והשתא מאי קא פריך אדרבה אית לן למימר אוקי תרי בהדי תרי ואוקי גברא אחזקיה ואוקי ינאי אחזקת אמו דלא אישתבאי ופירש התם בקונט' דחזקת האם לא מהניא להכשיר את ינאי לפי שאין עדים באין לפסול את האם לכהונה אלא להעיד על ינאי ואין נראה לר"י דלמה לא יועיל חזקת האם לבן הואיל ואינו יכול להיות שתהא האם כשרה אם לא יהיה הבן כשר ועוד דהכא אע"ג דעל הבן מעידים לפסלו מהניא ליה חזקת האב להכשירו ונראה לר"י דהיינו טעמא משום דמסקינן בפ' ד' אחין (יבמות דף לא. ושם ד"ה תרי) דכל תרי ותרי הויא ספיקא דרבנן והאם נמי הוי ספיקא דרבנן ולהכי פריך התם סמוך אהני דנהי דמדאורייתא אמרי' אוקי תרי בהדי תרי ואוקי איתתא אחזקה מ"מ מדרבנן יש לפוסלה והכא לענין תרומה דרבנן הקילו להתירו בה בתרי ותרי ולאוקמיה אחזקיה והא דאמר לעיל שנים אומרים מת וב' אומרים לא מת כו' אבל נשאת ואח"כ באו עדים לא תצא אע"ג דתרי ותרי ספיקא דרבנן היא ומדאורייתא אית לן לאוקמה אחזקה דהויא אשת איש והיה לה לצאת אע"פ שנשאת לאחד מעדיה אור"ת דאתיא חזקה דדייקא ומנסבא ומרעה חזקת אשת איש ואם תאמר כי איכא ב' עדים לא דייקא דליכא חוזר בסופה כדאמר בהאשה רבה (שם דף פז: ושם) נשאת שלא ברשות מותרת לחזור לו ומפרש התם דהיינו שנשאת בעדים וי"ל הואיל ומכחישים זה את זה איכא חומרא אם תעמוד תחת בעלה בטענת ברי שלה וא"ת ב' אומרים נתגרשה וב' אומרים לא נתגרשה אמאי לא תצא בנשאת ואח"כ באו עדים הא לא דייקא דדוקא במת הוא דדייקא שיראה שמא יבא וידעו הכל שלא מת ואינה נאמנת לומר נתגרשה דשלא בפני בעלה מעיזה ומעיזה ועוד היכא דאיכא עדים דקא מסייעי לה מעיזה ומעיזה וי"ל דלענין הכי דייקא ומרע' חזקת אשת איש דלעולם יראה שמא יוזמו או יפסלום בגזלנות וא"ת אמאי דלא ידע דבאומר ברי לי איירי מאי קאמר היא גופא באשם תלוי קיימא ה"ל למימר בחטאת קיימא וי"ל דפריך אפילו נאמר דתרי ותרי הוה ספיקא דאורייתא כדפי' בפ' ד' אחין (שם דף לא. ד"ה אי) מ"מ באשם קיימא ואין להאריך ובכתובות (דף כו: ד"ה אנן) פירשתי: אמאי

עין משפט נר מצוה

לג א ב מיי' פ"כ מהל' איסורי ביאה הל' טו סמג לאוין קכב טוש"ע אה"ע סי' ג סעיף ז:
לד ג מיי' פ"ד מהלכות עדות הלכה ג סמג עשין קט טוש"ע ח"מ סי' ל סעיף ו:
לה ד מיי' שם הלכה ד ופ"כ מהל' איסורי ביאה הלכה טו סמג שם טוש"ע שם ס"ט וטוש"ע אה"ע סי' ג' סעיף ז:

רבינו גרשום

והאמר ר' יוחנן אין ערער פחות משנים והיכי אמר ר' אלעזר דהיכא דאיכא ערער חד אין מעלין. לא **הכא במאי עסקינן** דמאי ביניהו **כגון דמחזיק לן** כו' **דכולי עלמא מצטרף** לעדותן דקמא ודבתרא דמכשרי ליה אע"ג דלא אתו בהדדי: **חיישינן לזילותא דבי דינא** דהורידוהו מן הכהונה. והואיל דליכא אלא חד סהדא דאתי באפי נפשיה **לא מסקינן ליה** דאין מעלין לכהונה על פי עד אחד הואיל דאיכא עוררין **ורשב"ג** סבר **דמסקינן ליה ולזילותא דבי דינא** דאחתיה **לא חיישינן** הואיל דאיכא תרי סהדי אע"ג דלא אתו בהדדי. ורב נחמן משום הכי עבד עובדא דלא חיישינן לזילותא דבי דינא משום דס"ל כרשב"ג דאמר משום ר"ש הסגן. **אי הכי** דפליגי דחיישי' לזילותא דבי דינא **מאי איריא עד אחד** דאתי באפי נפשיה **אפי'** אתו **תרי** בחדא כיון דאחתיניה חיישי' לזילותא דבי דינא ולא מסקינן ליה. **עד שיראו שניהם כאחד** שאם העיד אחד אני ראיתי פלוני לוה מפלוני מנה ואח"כ העיד אחר אני ראיתי פלוני לוה מפלוני מנה **אין עדותן מצטרפת עד שיראו** ב' העדים שלוה מנה דדלמא אמנה דקא מסהיד האי לא מסהיד האי דשמא פרע לו ושב ולוה לו ממנו. **ר' יהושע בן קרחה אומר אפי' בזה אחר זה** הואיל ועדות אחת הן מעידין וביום אחד ושעה אחת: **ואין עדותן מתקיימת בבית דין.** שאם אמר אחד אני ראיתי עדות זה וחברו שם היה ולמחר בא חבירו והעיד כן אין מצטרפין **עד שיעידו שניהם כאחד: ר' נתן אומר** וכו'. דר' אלעזר סבירא ליה כרבנן דהואיל שלא באין שני עדים הללו בבת אחת להעיד על כהן זה אין עדותן מצטרפת ורשב"ג סבר כר' נתן דמצטרפין: חספא

מסורת הש"ס

א) כתובות דף כו. קדושין דף עג: גיטין דף ט, ב) [לקמן דף קסה: גיטין דף לג:] סנהדרין דף ל. כתובות דף כו: [תוספתא סנהדרין פ"ה], ג) [וע"ע תוס' כתובות כו.], ד) [וע"ע תוס' כתובות כו: ד"ה ואסקיניה]:

הגהות הב"ח

(א) גמ' ואמר דכהן גמור הוא כצ"ל וכן בסמוך: (ב) רשב"ם ד"ה דחיישינן לזילותא וכו' ועכשיו יעלוהו ויבטלו וכו' להשבית את הקול וכו' בשביל קול מעלה בעלמא כצ"ל והד"א עם ד"ה דר' אלעזר ובכל הענין נ"ל ר' אלעזר במקום ר' אליעזר: (ג) תוס' ד"ה והאמר וכו' איתמר והא דקאמר: (ד) בא"ד דאין ערער פחות משנים:

ליקוטי רש"י

והאמר ר' יוחנן דברי הכל אין ערער פחות משנים. לא איתפרש היכא [גיטין ט.]. **ונפק עליה קלא.** קול בעלמא ולא עדות. **ואחתיניה.** מן הכהונה עד שיבדקו את הדבר שמעלה הוא לכהונה [כתובות כו.]. **ואסקיניה.** דבמקום קול הוי עד אחד מהימן. **ודכולי עלמא.** בין ר' אלעזר בין לר"ש. **מצטרפין.** שני עדים המעידים זה שלא בפני זה בשאר עדות. **חיישינן לזילותא דבי דינא.** שהורידוהו שני פעמים ועכשיו יעלוהו ויבטלו דבריהם והיינו דקאמר ר' אלעזר לאמר שהורידוהו ע"פ העוררין אין מעלין ע"פ עד זה השני אע"פ שיש לצרפו עם האחר. **ואנן מסקינן ליה.** ולא קשיא תרי ותרי נינהו אוקי תרי לבהדי תרי ואוקמינן אחזקיה קמייתא ע"פ עד הראשון שהוא נאמן דהא אכתי אין עוררין דקול לאו עוררין הוא. **אפילו בתרי.** אתו בהדי הדדי נמי בפעם שניה לרבי אלעזר לא מסקינן ליה. **עד שיראו שניהם כאחד.** את העדות לאפוקי אחד אומר בפני הלוהו ואחד אומר בפני הודה לו עליו [שם]. **אין עדותן מתקיימת.** להתקבל בב"ד ואפי' ראו שניהם כאחד עד שיעידו שניהם כאחד ופלוגתא אחריתי היא ולאו ר' יהושע בן קרחה קאמר לה ורבי אלעזר ורבן שמעון בן גמליאל בפלוגתא דרבי נתן ורבנן פליגי [כתובות שם]. לפסוק הדין על פיהם. **עד שיעידו שניהם כאחד.** ותמצא היא ולאו ר' יהושע בן קרחה קאמר לה [סנהדרין ל.].

עין משפט
נר מצוה

לז א מיי' פט"ו מהל' טוען ונטען הל' ט סמג עשין נה טוש"ע ח"מ סי' קמו סעיף כה:
לז ב מיי' פי"ד מהל' מלוה הלכה ו סמג שם טוש"ע ח"מ סי' פג סעיף ז:
לח ג ד מיי' שם הלכה ח וסמג שם טוש"ע שם סי' נז סעיף ג:

אמר ליה שטרא זייפא הוא גחין לחיש ליה לרבה אין שטרא זייפא הוא מיהו שטרא מעליא הוה לי ואירכס ואמינא אינקיט האי בידאי כל דהו ° אמר רבה (א) מה לו לשקר אי בעי אמר (א) ליה שטרא מעליא הוא אמר ליה רב יוסף אמאי (ב) סמכת אהאי שטרא האי שטרא חספא בעלמא הוא ההוא דאמר (ג) לחבריה הב לי מאה זוזי דמסיקנא בך והא שטרא א"ל שטרא זייפא הוא גחין לחיש ליה לרבה אין שטרא זייפא (ד) מיהו שטרא מעליא הוה לי ואירכס ואמינא אינקיט האי בידאי כל דהו אמר רבה מה לו לשקר אי בעי אמר ליה שטרא מעליא הוא א"ל רב יוסף אמאי קא סמכת אהאי שטרא האי שטרא חספא בעלמא הוא אמר רב אידי בר אבין הלכתא כוותיה דרבה בארעא והלכתא כוותיה דרב יוסף בזוזי הלכתא כרבה בארעא דהיכא דקיימא ארעא תיקום ב והלכתא כוותיה דרב יוסף בזוזי דהיכא דקיימי זוזי לוקמי: ההוא ערבא דאמר ליה ללוה הב לי מאה זוזי דפרעתי למלוה עילוך והא שטרא אמר ליה לאו פרעתיך אמר (ה) לאו הדרת שקלתינהו מינאי שלחה רב אידי בר אבין לקמיה דאביי כי האי גוונא מאי ג שלח ליה אביי מאי תיבעי ליה הא איהו דאמר הלכתא כוותיה דרבה בארעא והלכתא כוותיה דרב יוסף בזוזי דהיכא דאוקמו זוזי לוקמו ד והני מילי דא"ל הדרת אוזפתינהו מינאי אבל א"ל הדרתינהו ניהלך מחמת דהוו שייפי וסומקי אכתי איתיה לשעבודא דשטרא רבא בר שרשום נפק עליה קלא דקא אכיל ארעא דיתמי א"ל אביי אימא לי איזי גופא דעובדא היכי הוה אמר ליה ארעא במשכונתא הוה נקיטנא מאבוהון דיתמי והוה לי זוזי

אמאי קא סמכת אהאי שטרא האי שטרא חספא בעלמא הוא. תימה ליהמניה במיגו דאי בעי אמר שטרא מעליא הוה ותירץ ר"י בר' מרדכי דלא אמרי' מיגו להוציא ממון (כ) ומה שהוא מוחזק בקרקע אינו כלום דקרקע בחזקת בעליה קיימא כיון שאין לו שטר ולא חזקה אלא בדברים בעלמא שאומר שטרא מעליא הוה לי ואירכס ולא אמרי' מיגו אלא להחזיק ממון שיכול לפטור עצמו ע"י מיגו אי נמי אם יש לו שטר או חזקה וזה בא לפסול ראייתו אז זה יכול לקיימו ע"י מיגו כמו קמי דידי זבנה מינך מיגו דאי בעי אמר מינך זבינתיה ואכלתיה שני חזקה ואין נראה לר"י מדלא מפרש טעמא הכי בהדיא משמע דלאו משום הכי הוא ונראה לר"י דטעמא דרב יוסף דלא אמרי' מיגו הכא כיון דלית ליה הכא מיגו אא"כ שקר תחלה שהולך לשקר תחלה ולומר והא שטרא א"כ משום הכי לא אמרי' הכא מיגו משום דהוי חוזר וטוען דמעיקרא טען והא שטרא ועתה חוזר בו ומודה דחספא בעלמא הוא אלא שטרא מעליא הוה לי ג:

והלכתא כוותי' דרבה בארעא. רבינו שמואל פירש דמספקא ליה כמאן הלכתא וצריך לדחוק ולפרש ולחלק בין ספיקא דתרי ותרי לספיקא דדינא דהא דלא אוקמה בחזקת מרה קמא כמו בנכסי דבר שטיא דאמרי' (כתובות דף כ.) אוקי תרי בהדי תרי ואוקי נכסי בחזקת בר שטיא התם הוו תרי ותרי כמאן דליתנהו דמי ואוקמי' ארעא בחזקת מרה קמא אבל הכא דמספקא לן דינא כמאן התם לא שייך כולי האי למימר אוקמה אחזקת מרה קמא ° ונוציא מיד המוחזק ודוחק הוא ועוד דהילכתא משמע לגמרי פוסק כרבה ולא מספק אפי' עבד כרב יוסף בדיעבד לא עבד ונראה לר"י דהיינו טעמא דהלכתא בארעא כרבה וכרב יוסף בזוזי משום דאמרי' מיגו לאוקמי ממונא ולית לן לאוקמי ארעא בחזקת מרה דקיימא השתא ובהכותב (כתובות דף פה. ושם) דאמר מיגו דיכלי למימר לא היו דברים מעולם יכלי למימר הני סיטראי ניהו אף על גב דמיגו להוציא לא אמרינן שאני התם דליכא שטרא:

נפק עליה קלא דקא אכיל ארעא דיתמי. פירוש יצא הקול שהוא של יתומים אבל אין לפרש דיצא הקול דמתחלה היה של אביהם אבל עכשיו לא היו יודעין דא"כ הוה מצי למימר לקוחה היא בידי:
אמור

אמר ליה שטרא זייפא הוא. השטר מזויף וגם שני חזקה לא החזקת: **גחין.** בעל השטר: **לחיש לרבה.** בנחת שלא (ו) ישמע המערער: **אין שטרא זייפא הוא.** פי' ר"ח לאו שטרא זייפא ממש אלא כמו שטרא זייפא שלא נכתב על מכירה זו ומאי ניהו שטר אמנה דהוה בטל. מיהו אי לאו דאודי בטענתיה לתובע דשטרא זייפא הוא לאו כל כמיניה שהרי העדים מכירים חתימת ידיהם ומשום הכי אמר רבה מה לו לשקר ולומר שטרא מעליא הוה לי ואירכס לימא האי שטרא לאו זייפא הוא דאי הוה בעי לקיומיה מקיים ליה. א"נ איכא לפרושי זייפא שטר מזויף ממש שזייף חתימת העדים יפה וטועים העדים כסבורים חתימת ידיהם היא ומקיימים את השטר והלכך מצי לקיים את השטר ולומר שטרא מעליא הוא. א"נ מצי לקיימו בעדים שקרים שחתמו לו. ולשון עיקר: **לחיש ליה לרבה.** גרסינן דרבה מלך מקמי דרב יוסף כדאמרינן בשלהי דברכות (דף סד.) והיה רב יוסף חבירו מקשה לו: **אמאי קא סמכת אהאי שטרא.** דהא שני חזקה ליכא והאי שטרא חספא בעלמא הוא (ז) וכיון דאודי אודי ולא דמי לאמר מה לו לשקר שבגמרא ששתי טענות יכולות להיות אמת אותה שהוא טוען ואותה שהוא היה יכול לטעון ולא טען דאמרי' מיגו אבל הכא הכל דמי למה לו לשקר במקום עדים שהרי כל כחו וחזקתו בקרקע זו על ידי האי שטר הוא והיאך נאמר מה לו לשקר בשטר זה אי בעי אמר שטרא מעליא הוא והלא מודה שהשטר פסול והודאת בעל דין כמאה עדים ואילו באו שני עדים שאמרו שהוא פסול ליכא תו מה לו לשקר: **הב לי מאה זוזי כו'.** כפלוגתא דלעיל ובאותם הטעמים: **הלכתא כוותיה דרבה בארעא.** באותו דין ראשון דלעיל מספקא ליה לרב אידי בר אבין טעם של מי משניהם נראה יותר הלכך פוסק בראשון כרבה דאמרינן מה לו לשקר ויעמוד על מקומו דכיון דלא אתבריר טעמיהם של רבה ורב יוסף המוציא מחבירו עליו הראיה וגבי זוזי שהלוה מוחזק ולא בעל השטר אמרינן יביא בעל השטר ראיה ויטול דהיכא דקיימא ארעא תיקום ולא נוציא מספק וכן זוזי היכא דקיימי ליקום וכן הלכה. ואע"ג דפסקינן הלכה כרב יוסף בשדה ענין ומחצה (לקמן דף קיד:) מכלל דבכולי גמרא הלכה כרבה ולא כרב יוסף והכא פסקינן הלכה כרב יוסף לא קשיא דהא בהך פלוגתא נמי פסקינן כרבה: **דפרעתי למלוה עילוך.** כגון ערב קבלן א"נ כגון שאמר המלוה בשעת ההלואה ממי שארצה אפרע: **והא שטרא.** שטר שהיה לו למלוה עליך והחזירו לי לפי שפרעתי חובו והרי אתה משועבד לי בשטר זה כמו שהיית משועבד לו: **אמר.** לוה לערב וכי לא פרעתיך בתמיה: **לאו הדרת ושקלתינהו מינאי.** וכמי שלא פרעת דמי ולוה לא הודה לו בכך: **כה"ג מאי.** דלא דמי כל כך לשטר מלוה דלעיל דפסקינן כרב יוסף דהתם מודה היה בעל השטר ששטר אחר היה לו ונאבד ולקח את זה להיות בידו לזכות ואותו מזויף הוא ממש דלא נכתב על מלוה (ח) זה הלכך הפסיד דהיכא דקיימי זוזי תיקום אבל הכא לא היה לערב שטר אחר מעולם כי אם זה והלכך אע"ג דפרעינהו כיון דהדר שקלינהו כאילו לא פרעינהו דמי וחייב לפרעו. או דלמא מ"מ מודה הוא שפרעו וקיימא לן ג שטר שלוה בו ופרעו אינו חוזר ולוה בו שכבר נמחל שעבודו והאי שטרא חספא בעלמא הוא: **שלח ליה אביי והא את הוא דאמרת הלכתא כוותיה דרב יוסף בזוזי.** שמעינן מהכא דשטרא זייפא דאיירי בה רבה ורב יוסף לאו זייפא ממש דהוא שקר וכי זייף וכתב בכה"ג לדברי הכל ואפי' לרבה פסול הוא אלא כה"ג כגון שטר פרוע שנמחל שעבודו או כגון שטר אמנה שלא ניתן ליכתב וכיוצא בהן פליגי רבה ורב יוסף ואביי משוה ליה להאי שטרא כשטרא דאיירי ביה רבה ורב יוסף ואמר כיון דמודה הערב (ט) דפרע אלא הדר ושקלינהו להנהו זוזי אע"פ שהשטר ביד הערב לא מחייבינן ללוה לשלומי כן פי' ר"ח. ולי נראה דה"ה לזייפא ממש וקפסיק גמרא ואזיל: **וה"מ.** דאמרינן היכא דקיימי זוזי תיקום ולא מחייב לוה לפרוע לערב היכא דטעין ערב כדאמר לעיל דאמר פרעתינהו אבל הדר יזפתינהו מנאי דערב גופיה מודה שהשטר שבידו נמחל שעבודו: **אבל.** אי טעין ערב אני החזרתי לך אותם מעות עצמן משום דהוו שיפי ניסוף צורתן ולא היו יוצאין בהוצאה כמו הסף מטבע של חבירו (ב"ק דף נה.): **וסומקי.** האדים נחשתן יותר מדאי נמצא שעדיין לא פרעו: **אכתי איתיה לשעבודא דשטרא.** וכאילו טוען לא פרעתני דמי: (י) **שרשום נפיק עליה קלא דקאכיל ארעא דיתמי.** כדמפרש לקמיה דמשכון היתה אצלו עד עכשיו שכלו שני משכנתא והלכך נפק עליה קול של עדות אמת דמהשתא אכיל ארעא דיתמי: **משכנתא.** גבאי מאבוהון הוה במשכנתא דסורא דכתבי הכי במשלם שניא אלין תיפוק ארעא דא בלא כסף ובימי אביהם אכלתיה שני חזקה:
זוזי

מסורת הש"ס

א) [לעיל דף לא. וש"נ], ב) [כתובות דף פה.], ג) [ועי' תוספות ב"מ ג. ד"ה וחס]:

הגהות הב"ח

(א) גמ' אי בעי אמר שטרא כצ"ל ותיבת ליה נמחק: (ב) שם אמאי קא סמכת: (ג) שם ההוא דאמר ליה לחבריה: (ד) שם זייפא הוא מיהו: (ה) שם אמר ליה לאו הדרת: (ו) רשב"ם ד"ה לחיש וכו' שלא ישמע: (ז) ד"ה אמאי וכו' דכיון דאודי: (ח) ד"ה כה"ג מאי וכו' מלוה זו הלכך: (ט) ד"ה שלח וכו' דמודה הערב דאיפרע אלא: (י) ד"ה רבא בר שרשום נפיק: (כ) תום' ד"ה אמאי וכו' ממון מחזקתו דמה שהוא מוחזק:

גליון הש"ס

גמרא אמר רבה מה לי לשקר. עיין בב"מ דף ג ע"א תוס' ד"ה וחס ודף קטז ע"א תוס' ד"ה והא: תוס' ד"ה והלכתא כו' ונוציא מיד המוחזק. עיין לקמן דף מא ע"א ברשב"ם ד"ה סיישין:

רבינו גרשום

חספא בעלמא הוא. דהא איהו מודי דזייפא הוא. **הלכ' כוותי' דרב' בארעא** דאמרינן מה לי לשקר משום דכיון דמחזיק הוא בארעא **תיקום** ברשות מאן דמחזיק בה דאוקי ממונא בחזקת מריה ולא מפקינן מיניה עד דמייתי אידך ראיה דלא זבנה ניהליה. **והלכ' כוותיה דרב יוסף** דאמר האי שטרא חספא בעלמא הוא ואוקמי' זוזי ברשות דמחזיק בהון דאמרינן **היכא דקיימי זוזי** לוקמי ולא מפקי מיניה. **מאי תיבעי ליה** להאי רב אידי ב"ר אבין **והא איהו** גופיה **אמר הלכתא כותי' כו'. והני מילי** דאמרי' בזוזי היכי דקיימי לוקמן **היכי דאמר** האי ערב **הדר אוזיפתינהו** לך דמכל מקום מודי דפרע ליה לוה **אבל** אי **אמר הדרתינהו** לך **מחמת דהוו שיפי וסומקי** שנתגררו זה בזה ונתגלו נחושתן **אכתי איתא לשעבודא** דהאי שטרא ואית ליה לשטרא למגביה הואיל וזה אומר שלא קבלו בפרעון:

ליקוטי רש"י

מה לו לשקר אי בעי אמר ליה. ומהימנא השתא נמי מהימנא [יבמות קטו.]. **האי שטרא חספא בעלמא הוא.** שהוא אומר מזוייף הוא [ע"פ כתובות פז:].

אָמַר לֵיהּ – [The challenger] said to [the occupant]: שְׁטָרָא זַיְיפָא הוּא – "It is a forged deed and, as you do not claim to have a *chazakah,* you must vacate the property!" גְּחִין לְחִישׁ לֵיהּ לְרַבָּה – [The occupant] leaned over and whispered to Rabbah,[1] the judge of the case: אֵין שְׁטָרָא זַיְיפָא הוּא – "Yes, it is a forged deed.[2] מִיהוּ שְׁטָרָא מְעַלְיָא הֲוָה לִי – However, I originally had a valid deed, וְאִירְכַּס – and it was lost. וַאֲמִינָא – So I thought, אִינְקִיט הַאי בִּידַאי כָּל דְּהוּ – 'Let me take this forged deed in my hand to court so that I have at least some sort of document to support my claim.' "

Rabbah rendered judgment:

אָמַר רַבָּה – Rabbah said: מַה לוֹ לְשַׁקֵּר – Why would [the occupant] lie? אִי בָּעֵי אָמַר לֵיהּ – If he was prepared to lie in order to win the case, he could have denied the allegation of forgery and said to [the challenger]: שְׁטָרָא מְעַלְיָא הוּא – "The deed is valid," and he would have been believed![3] Therefore, we apply the principle of *migo,* and believe his present claim that he originally had a valid deed, and he retains the property.

Rabbah's colleague objects:

אָמַר לֵיהּ רַב יוֹסֵף – Rav Yosef said to [Rabbah]: אַמַּאי סָמְכַתְּ – On what could you base this verdict – אַהַאי שְׁטָרָא – on this deed, presented by the current occupant? הַאי שְׁטָרָא חַסְפָּא בְּעָלְמָא הוּא – But this deed is as worthless as a mere potsherd! Consequently, we must reject his claim to the land which is based on this worthless deed.[4]

A parallel dispute regarding a loan:

הַהוּא דְּאָמַר לְחַבְרֵיהּ – There was a certain man who said to his fellow: הַב לִי מְאָה זוּזֵי דְּמַסִּיקְנָא בָּךְ – "Give me the one hundred *zuzim* that you owe me, וְהָא שְׁטָרָא – and here is the loan document proving the debt." אָמַר לֵיהּ – [The second man] said to [the first]: שְׁטָרָא זַיְיפָא הוּא – "It is a forged document!" גְּחִין לְחִישׁ לֵיהּ לְרַבָּה – [The plaintiff] leaned over and whispered to Rabbah, the judge in the case: אֵין שְׁטָרָא זַיְיפָא – "Yes, it is indeed a forged document. מִיהוּ שְׁטָרָא מְעַלְיָא הֲוָה לִי – However, I originally had a valid document, וְאִירְכַּס – and it was lost. וַאֲמִינָא – So I thought, אִינְקִיט הַאי בִּידַאי כָּל דְּהוּ – 'Let me take this forged note in my hand to court so that I have at least some sort of document to support my claim.' "

Rabbah ruled as he had in the previous case:

אָמַר רַבָּה – Rabbah said: מַה לוֹ לְשַׁקֵּר – Why would [the plaintiff] lie? אִי בָּעֵי אָמַר לֵיהּ – If he was prepared to lie in order to win, he could have denied the allegation of forgery and said to [the defendant]: שְׁטָרָא מְעַלְיָא הוּא – "The document is genuine," and he would have been believed. Thus, we can assume that the plaintiff is being truthful, and he may collect the debt.

Rav Yosef demurred for the same reason as in the previous case:

אָמַר לֵיהּ רַב יוֹסֵף – Rav Yosef said to [Rabbah]: אַמַּאי קָא סָמְכַתְּ – On what could you base this verdict – אַהַאי שְׁטָרָא – on this document presented by the plaintiff? הַאי שְׁטָרָא חַסְפָּא בְּעָלְמָא הוּא – But this document is as worthless as a mere potsherd and the loan cannot be collected on its strength!

Rav Idi issued a ruling for both cases:

אָמַר רַב אִידִי בַּר אָבִין – Rav Idi bar Avin said: הִלְכְתָא כְּוָותֵיהּ דְּרַבָּה בְּאַרְעָא – The halachah is in agreement with Rabbah in such disputes regarding land, וְהִלְכְתָא כְּוָותֵיהּ דְּרַב יוֹסֵף בְּזוּזֵי – and the halachah is in agreement with Rav Yosef in disputes regarding money.

Rav Idi explained his logic:

הִלְכְתָא כְּרַבָּה בְּאַרְעָא – The halachah follows Rabbah in disputes regarding land, דְּהֵיכָא דְּקָיְימָא אַרְעָא תֵּיקוּם – for wherever the land is presently found, i.e. with whomever presently occupies it, it remains. וְהִלְכְתָא כְּוָותֵיהּ דְּרַב יוֹסֵף בְּזוּזֵי – And the halachah is in agreement with Rav Yosef in disputes regarding money, דְּהֵיכָא דְּקָיְימֵי זוּזֵי לוֹקְמֵי – for wherever the money is presently found, i.e. with whomever is presently in physical possession of it, it remains. Rav Idi was undecided whose opinion was the correct one. Therefore, he ruled that the opinion that maintained the status quo in each case should be followed.[5]

The Gemara relates an incident and attempts to compare it to the case just discussed:

הַהוּא עַרְבָא דְּאָמַר לֵיהּ לְלֹוֶה – There was a certain guarantor who said to the borrower for whom he had provided surety: הַב לִי מְאָה זוּזֵי – "Give me the one hundred *zuzim* דְּפָרַעְתִּי לְמַלְוֶה עִילָוָךְ – that I paid to the lender on your behalf, וְהָא שְׁטָרָא –

NOTES

1. So that the challenger could not hear (*Rashbam*).

2. *Rashbam* advances three possible explanations: (1) that the document was in fact a complete forgery, but one of such superior quality that the supposed signers themselves were fooled and attested that the signatures were genuine, not realizing that they had never signed the document; (2) that the deed was indeed false, but the signatures were genuine, having been affixed by dishonest witnesses; or (3) that honest witnesses had signed the deed — but, rather than being a valid deed, the document was actually a deed which had been prepared, signed and delivered to the intended purchaser in *anticipation* of a sale, which never actually took place. Such a document is known as a שְׁטַר אֲמָנָה, *a document [given] on trust;* the property's owner gives the document to the holder in good faith, trusting that he will not produce it unless the sale is actually consummated (see *Kesubos* 19a).

3. Since the witnesses testified that the signatures were theirs, the challenger's claim that the document was fraudulent or given on trust would not have been believed (*Rashbam*).

4. Rav Yosef maintains that the original claim, "I bought the land from you, and here is the deed," must be dealt with in its entirety. That is to say, we regard both assertions — that he purchased the land and that the document in his hand is the deed written for that purchase — as comprising one large claim, and as such we must either accept both assertions or reject them both. Clearly, we cannot accept the assertion that the document is the deed of sale, because he admits that it is forged. Consequently, we must also reject his assertion that he purchased the land even though his claim is supported by a *migo* (*Rashbam* as explained by *Rosh* §12). *Rosh* disputes *Rashbam's* explanation, wondering why we should link the occupant's claim to the land to our acceptance of the document he originally presented. Why can we now not accept his claim that he bought the land, based on the *migo,* as Rabbah maintains? See *Rosh* and other Rishonim who offer numerous variant explanations of Rav Yosef's objection.

5. A basic rule for civil law cases is that where there is doubt, property is left with the litigant in possession of it. Accordingly, since Rav Idi could not decide in favor of either Rabbah or Rav Yosef, he ruled that both the land and the money should remain with the current occupant and the litigant in possession of it, respectively (*Rashbam*).

[Rav Idi's ruling regarding the land seems at variance with what we have been assuming all along —that as far as land is concerned, the presumption is that it belongs to the original owner, not to the present occupant (see Chapter Introduction). Accordingly, it would seem that, being in doubt as to the proper ruling, Rav Idi should have followed Rav Yosef's opinion and allowed the original owner to return to the land.

The answer may lie in the nature of the doubt in this particular instance. While it is true that in most cases of doubt the court returns the land to the original owner, the course followed is different when the doubt hinges on an unresolved point of law (such as in our case). That is, when a doubt is created by the court's inability to decide a point of law, the court does not act. Hence, in disputes regarding ownership of land, instead of ousting the current occupant and allowing the original owner to return to the land, the court does nothing and allows the occupant to remain (see *Tosafos* in explanation of *Rashbam, Or Samei'ach Hil. To'ein VeNitan* 15:9 and *Kovetz Shiurim* §136. See also *Teshuvos of R' Akiva Eiger* I 37 באו"ד ויש לעשות.]

אמר ליה שטרא זייפא הוא גחין לחיש ליה לרבה אין שטרא זייפא הוא מיהו שטרא מעליא הוה לי ואירכס ואמינא אינקיט האי בידאי כל דהו ° אמר רבה [א] מה לו לשקר אי בעי אמר (א) ליה שטרא מעליא הוא אמר ליה רב יוסף אמאי (ב) סמכת אהאי שטרא האי שטרא חספא בעלמא הוא ההוא דאמר (ג) לחבריה הב לי מאה זוזי דמסיקנא בך והא שטרא א"ל שטרא זייפא הוא גחין לחיש ליה לרבה אין שטרא זייפא (ד) מיהו שטרא מעליא הוה לי ואירכס ואמינא אינקיט האי בידאי כל דהו אמר רבה מה לו לשקר אי בעי אמר ליה שטרא מעליא הוא א"ל רב יוסף אמאי קא סמכת אהאי שטרא האי שטרא חספא בעלמא הוא אמר רב אידי בר אבין הלכתא כוותיה דרבה בארעא והלכתא כוותיה דרב יוסף בזוזי הלכתא כרבה בארעא דהיכא דקיימא ארעא תיקום ב והלכתא כוותיה דרב יוסף בזוזי דהיכא דקיימי זוזי לוקמי: ההוא ערבא דאמר ליה ללוה הב לי מאה זוזי דפרעתי למלוה עילוך והא שטרא אמר ליה לאו פרעתיך אמר (ה) לאו הדרת שקלתינהו מינאי שלחה רב אידי בר אבין לקמיה דאביי כי האי גוונא מאי ג שלח ליה אביי מאי תיבעי ליה הא איהו דאמר הלכתא כוותיה דרבה בארעא והלכתא כוותיה דרב יוסף בזוזי דהיכא דאוקמו זוזי לוקמו ד והני מילי דא"ל הדרת אוזפתינהו מינאי אבל א"ל הדרתינהו ניהלך מחמת דהוו שייפי וסומקי אכתי איתיה לשעבודא דשטרא רבא בר שרשום נפק עליה קלא דקא אכיל ארעא דיתמי א"ל אביי אימא לי איזי גופא דעובדא היכי הוה אמר ליה ארעא במשכונתא הוה נקיטנא מאבוהון דיתמי והוה לי זוזי

אמאי קא סמכת אהאי שטרא האי שטרא חספא בעלמא הוא. תימה לליסמניה כמיגו דלוי בעי אמר שטרא מעליא הוה ותירץ ר"י בר' מרדכי דלא אמרי' מיגו להוציא ממון (כ) ומה שהוא מוחזק בקרקע אינו כלום דקרקע בחזקת בעליה קיימא כיון שאין לו שטר ולא חזקה אלא בדברים בעלמא שאומר שטרא מעליא הוה לי ואירכס ולא אמרי' מיגו אלא להחזיק ממון שיכול לפטור עצמו ע"י מיגו אי נמי אם יש לו שטר או חזקה וזה בא לפסול ראייתו אז זה יכול לקיימו ע"י מיגו כמו קמי דידי זבינתיה ואכלתיה שני חזקה ואין נראה לר"י מדלא מפרש טעמא הכי בהדיא משמע דלאו משום הכי הוא ונראה לר"י דטעמא דרב יוסף דלא אמרי' מיגו הכא כיון דלית ליה הכא מיגו אא"כ שקר תחלה שהולך לשקר תחלה ולומר והא שטרא א"נ משום הכי לא אמרי' הכא מיגו משום דהוי מחזר וטוען למעיקרא טען והא שטרא ועתה חוזר בו ומודה דחספא בעלמא הוא אלא אלא שטרא מעליא הוה לי ג:

והלכתא כוותי' דרבה בארעא. רבינו שמואל פירש דמספקא ליה כמאן הלכתא וצריך לדחוק ולפרש ולחלק בין ספיקא דתרי ותרי לספיקא דדינא דהא דלא אוקמה בחזקת מרה קמא כמו בנכסי דבר שטיא דאמרי' (כתובות דף כ.) אוקי תרי בהדי תרי ואוקי נכסי בחזקת בר שטיא התם הוו תרי ותרי כמאן דליתנהו דמי ואוקמי' ארעא בחזקת מרה קמא אבל הכא דמספקא לן דינא כמאן התם לא שייך כולי האי למימר אוקמה אחזקת מרה קמא ° ונוציא מיד המוחזק ודוחק הוא ועוד דהלכתא משמע לגמרי פוסק כרבה ולא מספק אפי' עבד כרב יוסף בדיעבד לא עבד ונראה לר"י דהיינו טעמא דהלכתא בארעא כרבה וכרב יוסף בזוזי משום דאמרי' מיגו לאוקמי ממונא ואית לן לאוקמי ארעא בחזקת מרה דקיימא השתא והכותב (כתובות דף פה. ושם) דאמר מיגו דיכלי למימר לא היו דברים מעולם יכלי למימר הני סיטראי ניהו אף על גב דמיגו להוציא לא אמרינן שאני התם דאיכא שטרא:

נפק עליה קלא דקא אכיל ארעא דיתמי. פירוש יצא הקול שהוא של יתומים אבל אין לפרש דיצא הקול דמתחלה היה של אביהם אבל עכשיו לא היו יודעין דא"כ הוה מצי למימר לקוחה היא בידי:

אמר ליה שטרא זייפא הוא. השטר מזויף וגם שני חזקה לא החזקת: **גחין.** בעל השטר: **לחיש לרבה.** בנחת שלא (ו) שמע המערער: **אין שטרא זייפא הוא.** פי' ר"ח לאו שטרא זייפא ממש אלא כמו שטרא זייפא שלא נכתב על מכירה זו ומאי ניהו שטר אמנה דהוא בטל. מיהו אי לאו דאודי בטענתיה דתובע דשטרא זייפא הוא לאו כל כמיניה שהרי העדים מכירים חתימת ידיהם ומשום הכי אמר רבה מה לו לשקר ולומר שטרא מעליא הוה לי ואירכס לימא האי שטרא לאו זייפא הוא דאי הוה בעי לקיומיה מקיים ליה. א"נ איכא לפרושי זייפא שטר מזויף ממש שזייף חתימת העדים יפה וטועים העדים כסבורים חתימת ידיהם היא ומקיימים את השטר והלכך מצי לקיים את השטר ולומר שטרא מעליא הוא. א"נ מצי לקיימו בעדים שקרים שחתמו לו. וראשון עיקר: **לחיש ליה לרבה.** גרסינן דרבה מלך מקמי דרב יוסף כדאמרינן בשלהי דברכות (דף סד.) והיה רב יוסף חבירו מקשה לו: **אמאי קא סמכת אהאי שטרא.** דהא שני חזקה ליכא והאי שטרא חספא בעלמא הוא (ז) וכיון דאודי אודי ולא דמי לשאר מה לו לשקר שבגמרא שבשתי טענות יכולות להיות אמת אותה שהוא טוען ואותה שהוא היה יכול לטעון ולא טען דאמרי' מיגו אבל הכא דמי למה לו לשקר במקום עדים שהרי כל כחו וחזקתו בקרקע זו על ידי האי שטר הוא והיאך נאמר מה לו לשקר בשטר זה אי בעי אמר שטרא מעליא הוא והלא מודה שהשטר פסול והודאת בעל דין כמאה עדים ואילו באו שני עדים שאמרו שהוא פסול ליכא תו מה לו לשקר: **הב לי מאה זוזי כו'.** כפלוגתא דלעיל ובאותם הטעמים: **הלכתא כוותיה דרבה בארעא.** באותו דין ראשון דלעיל מספקא ליה לרב אידי בר אבין טעם של מי משניהם נראה יותר הלכך פוסק בראשון כרבה דאמרינן מה לו לשקר ויעמוד על מקחו דכיון דלא אתברירו טעמיהם של רבה ורב יוסף המוציא מחבירו עליו הראיה וגבי זוזי שהלוה מוחזק ולא בעל השטר אמרינן יביא בעל השטר ראיה ויטול דהיכא דקיימא ארעא תיקום ולא נוציא מספק וכן זוזי היכא דקיימי ליקום וכן הלכה. ואע"ג דפסקינן הלכה כרב יוסף בשדה ענין ומחצה (לקמן דף קיד:) מכלל דבכולי גמרא הלכה כרבה ולא כרב יוסף והכא פסקינן הלכה כרב יוסף לא קשיא דהא בהך פלוגתא נמי פסקינן כרבה: **דפרעתי למלוה עילוך.** כגון ערב קבלן א"נ כגון שאמר המלוה בשעת ההלואה ממי שארצה אפרע: **והא שטרא.** שטר שהיה לו למלוה עליך והחזירו לי לפי שפרעתי חובו והרי אתה משועבד לי בשטר זה כמו שהיית משועבד לו: **אמר.** לוה לערב וכי לא פרעתיך בתמיה: **לאו הדרת ושקלתינהו מינאי.** וכמי שלא פרעת דמי ולוה לא הודה לו בכך: **כה"ג מאי.** דלא דמי כל כך לשטר מלוה דלעיל דפסקינן כרב יוסף דהתם מודה היה בעל השטר ששטר אחר היה לו ונאבד ולקח את זה להיות בידו לזכות ואותו מזויף הוא ממש דלא נכתב על מלוה (ח) זה הלכך הפסיד דהיכא דקיימי זוזי תיקום אבל הכא לא היה לערב שטר אחר מעולם כי אם זה והלכך אע"ג דפרעינהו כיון דהדר שקלינהו כאילו לא פרעינהו דמי וחייב לפרעו. או דלמא מ"מ מודה הוא שפרעו וקיימא לן ג שטר שלוה בו ופרעו אינו חוזר ולוה בו שכבר נמחל שעבודו והאי שטרא חספא בעלמא הוא: **שלח ליה אביי והא את הוא דאמרת הלכתא כוותיה דרב יוסף בזוזי.** שמעינן מהכא דשטרא זייפא דאיירי בה רבה ורב יוסף לאו זייפא ממש דהוא שקר וכי זייף וכתב בכה"ג לדברי הכל ואפי' לרבה פסול הוא אלא כה"ג כגון שטר פרוע שנמחל שעבודו או כגון שטר אמנה שלא ניתן ליכתב וכיוצא בהן פליגי רבה ורב יוסף ואביי משוה ליה להאי שטרא כשטרא דאיירי ביה רבה ורב יוסף ואמר כיון דמודה הערב (ט) דפרע אלא הדר ושקלינהו להנהו זוזי אע"פ שהשטר ביד הערב לא מחייבינן ללוה לשלומי כן פי' ר"ח. ולי נראה דה"ה לזייפא ממש וקפסיק גמרא ואזיל: **וה"מ.** דאמרינן היכא דקיימי זוזי תיקום ולא מיחייב לוה לפרוע לערב היכא דטוען ערב כדאמר לעיל דאמר פרעתינהו אבל הדר יזפתינהו מנאי דערב גופיה מודה שהשטר שבידו נמחל שעבודו: **אבל.** אי טוען ערב אני החזרתי לך אותם מעות עצמן משום דהוו שיפי נישוף צורתן ולא היו יוצאין בהוצאה כמו השף מטבע של חבירו (ב"ק דף צח.): **וסומקי.** האדים נחשתן יותר מדאי נמצא שעדיין לא פרעו: **אכתי איתיה לשעבודא דשטרא.** וכאילו טוען לא פרעתני דמי: (י) **שרשום נפיק עליה קלא דקאכיל ארעא דיתמי.** כדמפרש לקמיה דבמשכון היתה אצלו עד עכשיו שכלו שני משכנתא והלכך נפק עליה קול של עדות אמת דמהשתא אכיל ארעא דיתמי: **משכנתא.** גבאי מאבוהון הוה במשכנתא דסורא דכתבי הכי במשלם שניא אלין תיפוק ארעא דא בלא כסף ובימי אביהם אכלתיה שני חזקה:

זוזי

עין משפט נר מצוה

לו א מיי' פט"ו מהל' טוען ונטען הל' ט סמג עשין נה טוש"ע ח"מ סי' קמו סעיף כה:

לז ב מיי' פי"ד מהל' מלוה ולוה הלכה ו סמג שם טוש"ע ח"מ סי' קל סעיף ז:

לח ג ד מיי' שם הלכה ח וסמג שם טוש"ע שם סי' נז סעיף ג:

רבינו גרשום

חספא בעלמא הוא. דהא איהו מודי דזייפא הוא. הלכ' כוותי' דרב' בארעא דאמרינן מה לי לשקר משום דכיון דמחזיק הוא בארעא תיקום ברשות מאן דמחזיק בה דאוקי ממונא בחזקת מריה ולא מפקינן מיניה עד דמייתי אידך ראיה דלא זבנה ניהליה. והלכ' כוותיה דרב יוסף דאמר האי שטרא חספא בעלמא הוא ואוקמי' זוזי ברשות דמחזיק בהון דאמרינן היכא דקיימי זוזי לוקמי ולא מפקי מיניה. מאי תיבעי ליה להאי רב אידי בר אבין והא איהו גופיה אמר הלכתא כוות' כו'. והני מילי דאמרי' בזוזי היכי דאמר האי ערב הדר אוזפתינהו לך דמכל מקום מודי דפרע ליה להו אבל אי אמר הדרתינהו לך מחמת דהוו שיפי וסומקי שנתגררו זה בזה ונתגלו נחושתן אכתי איתא לשעבודא דהאי שטרא ואית ליה לשטרא למגביה הואיל וזה אומר שלא קבלו בפרעון:

ליקוטי רש"י

מה לו לשקר אי בעי אמר ליה. ומהימנא בשתא נמי מהימנא [יבמות קטו.]. האי שטרא חספא בעלמא הוא. שהוא אומר מזוייף הוא [ע"ש כתובות פז:].

מסורת הש"ס

א) [לעיל דף לא. וש"נ], ב) [כתובות דף פה.], ג) [ועי' תוספות ב"מ ז. ד"ה וזה]:

הגהות הב"ח

(א) גמ' אי בעי אמר שטרא כצ"ל ותיבת ליה נמחק: (ב) שם אמאי קא סמכת: (ג) שם ההוא דאמר ליה לחבריה: (ד) שם זייפא הוא מיהו: (ה) שם אמר ליה לאו הדרת: (ו) רשב"ם ד"ה לחיש וכו' שלא ישמע: (ז) ד"ה אמאי וכו' דכיון דאודי: (ח) ד"ה כה"ג מאי וכו' מלוה זו הלכך: (ט) ד"ה שלא וכו' דמודה הערב דאיפרע אלא: (י) ד"ה רבא בר שרשום נפיק: (כ) תום' ד"ה אמאי וכו' ממון ממזקתו דמה שהוא מוחזק:

גליון הש"ס

גמרא אמר רבה מה לי לשקר. עיין בב"מ דף ב ע"א תוס' ד"ה וזה ודף קטז ע"א תוס' ד"ה והא: תוס' ד"ה והלכתא כו' ונוציא מיד המוחזק. עיין לקמן דף מא ע"א ברשב"ם ד"ה חיישינן:

and here is the loan **document** that the lender gave to me when I paid him."[6] אָמַר לֵיהּ – **[The borrower] said to [the guarantor]:** לָאו פְּרַעְתִּיךְ – **"Did I not pay you back?"** אָמַר – **[The guarantor] replied:** לָאו הֲדַרְתְּ שְׁקַלְתִּינְהוּ מִינָּאי – "True, but **did you not** subsequently **take [the money] from me once more,** leaving me the document as my proof?"

The borrower disputed this claim, and the case came to Rav Idi for judgment:

שַׁלְחָהּ רַב אִידִי בַּר אָבִין לְקַמֵּיהּ דְּאַבַּיֵי – **Rav Idi bar Avin sent [the case]** to be presented **before Abaye** to inquire of him: כִּי הַאי גַּוְונָא מַאי – **What is the law in such a case?** Can it be compared to the case of a defense based on a faulty document, or not?[7] שְׁלַח לֵיהּ אַבַּיֵי – **Abaye sent** back **to [Rav Idi]:** מַאי תִּיבָּעֵי לֵיהּ – **What is [Rav Idi's] question?** הָא אִיהוּ דְּאָמַר – **Was it not he** himself **who said:** הִלְכְתָא כְּוָותֵיהּ דְּרַבָּה בְּאַרְעָא – **The halachah is in agreement with Rabbah in** disputes regarding **land,** וְהִלְכְתָא כְּוָותֵיהּ דְּרַב יוֹסֵף בְּזוּזֵי – **and the halachah is in agreement with Rav Yosef in** disputes regarding **money,** דְּהֵיכָא דְּאוֹקְמוּ זוּזֵי לוֹקְמוּ – **for wherever the money is found, it remains?!** Abaye felt that since the guarantor admitted that the original obligation had been repaid, the note was invalid for the alleged second loan. Consequently, the situation was similar to that of a lender using a forged document to support his claim. Therefore, the debtor would be believed to claim he never re-borrowed the money.

The Gemara qualifies the parallel drawn by Abaye:

וְהָנֵי מִילֵּי – **And this ruling** holds true only דְּאָמַר לֵיהּ הֲדַרְתְּ אוֹזַפְתִּינְהוּ מִינָּאי – **where [the guarantor] said to [the borrower], "You borrowed [the money] from me again,"** thus admitting that the original obligation had been satisfied and that the loan document was no longer valid. אֲבָל אָמַר לֵיהּ – **But if [the guarantor] said to [the borrower]:** הֲדַרְתִּינְהוּ נִיהֲלָךְ – **"I returned [the coins] to you,** מֵחֲמַת דַּהֲווּ שַׁיְיפֵי וְסוּמְקֵי – **because they were worn or reddened,"**[8] אַכַּתֵּי אִיתֵיהּ לְשִׁעְבּוּדָא דִשְׁטָרָא – **the document's obligation still remains,** for payment was never accepted. Thus, the document held by the guarantor is still valid, and he may use it to collect his debt.[9]

The Gemara moves on to another subject. In the instance discussed here, the occupant of the property, while admitting that he had not bought the property, nevertheless claimed that it was his by right:

רָבָא בַּר שַׁרְשׁוֹם נְפַק עֲלֵיהּ קָלָא – **A rumor emerged involving Rava bar Sharshum,** דְּקָא אָכִיל אַרְעָא דְיַתְמֵי – **that he was using land that belonged to orphans.**[10]

Abaye investigated the allegation:

אָמַר לֵיהּ אַבַּיֵי – **Abaye said to [Rava bar Sharshum]:** אֵימָא לִי אִיזִי – **"Tell me now,** גּוּפָא דְּעוּבְדָא הֵיכִי הֲוָה – **what were the** exact **facts of the case?"**[11] אָמַר לֵיהּ – **[Rava bar Sharshum] said to [Abaye]:** אַרְעָא בְּמַשְׁכּוֹנְתָּא הֲוָה נְקִיטְנָא מֵאֲבוּהוֹן דְּיַתְמֵי – **"I was holding the land as security from the father of the orphans,**[12] וַהֲוָה לִי – **and I was owed**

NOTES

6. I paid the creditor on your behalf and he in turn gave me the note he held against you. This note now evidences your obligation to me just as it formerly evidenced your obligation to the creditor.

Ordinarily, a creditor may not approach a guarantor for payment unless the creditor first fails in an attempt to collect from the debtor. Here, however, the guarantor had worded his pledge in a way that allowed the creditor to collect from him before approaching the borrower. Alternatively, the lender had stipulated at the time of the loan that he retained the prerogative to collect from either the borrower or the guarantor (*Rashbam*).

7. Once the debt is paid, the note composed for it may not be reused for a subsequent loan, even if the note is suitably worded for it (i.e. the same debtor borrows the same sum of money from the same creditor). Thus, in our case, if the guarantor's claim is true — that the debtor re-borrowed the money immediately after paying up the original debt — the old note should be invalid for the new loan. If so, this case would be comparable to the previous one in that the holder of the note admits that the note is faulty. As in the previous case, Rav Idi should rule that we follow Rav Yosef and do not allow the guarantor to collect, despite the *migo* that he need not have admitted that the original loan was repaid.

However, *Rashbam* explains, Rav Idi entertained the notion that since the borrower took back the money, we regard the original loan as having never been repaid (instead of considering that the old loan was paid and a new loan granted). Perhaps *Rashbam* means that the *very same money* that was used to repay was lent back to the borrower. It was this fact that gave rise to Rav Idi's doubt (cf. *Nachalas Moshe* who offers another explanation of *Rashbam*). However, as the Gemara will explain presently, Abaye disagreed with Rav Idi and saw no reason not to consider it a new loan.

8. Due to handling, the raised images stamped on the coins become rubbed out; likewise, the copper acquires a redder-than-normal tinge, rendering the coins unusable. Thus, the guarantor refused to accept them as payment (*Rashbam*).

9. For the guarantor is in essence saying, "You have not repaid me." Thus, the note is still valid (*Rashbam*).

10. Rava bar Sharshum had lent money to the orphans' father under the following arrangement: The loan would be paid by allowing Rava bar Sharshum to retain the debtor's land and consume its produce for a specified number of years. At the end of that time, the land would revert to the borrower and the debt would be considered paid. Rumor now had it that the specified time had expired and, rather than relinquishing the land as he had agreed, Rava bar Sharshum continued to use it (*Rashbam*).

11. Literally: how was the body of the case.

12. I was using the land for a specified term of years in payment of a loan to their father (as explained in note 10). Such an arrangement was common in Sura (a town in Babylonia), and property so designated was therefore known as a "Surean security" (see *Rashbam* and *Bava Metzia* 67b).

זוּזֵי אַחֲרִינֵי גַּבֵּיהּ – **other money by him**[1] as well, for which no special provisions for repayment had been made. וַאֲכַלְתָּהּ שְׁנֵי מַשְׁכַּנְתָּא – **And I had** already **used [the land about which there was a rumor] for the** term of **years** it was given to me as **security.** Thus, that particular loan had been fully repaid.

Rava bar Sharshum went on to explain why he had continued to consume the land's produce beyond the term stipulated for repayment:

אֲמִינָא – **I said** to myself: אִי מְהַדַּרְנָא לָהּ אַרְעָא לְיַתְמֵי – **If I return [the land] to the orphans,** וַאֲמִינָא – **and I say** afterwards גַּבֵּי דַּאֲבוּכוֹן דְּאִית לִי זוּזֵי אַחֲרִינֵי – **that your father owes me other money** which he had not yet repaid, I would be unable to collect without swearing. אָמוּר רַבָּנָן – For **the Rabbis say:** הַבָּא לִיפָּרַע מִנִּכְסֵי יְתוֹמִים – **One who comes to collect** a debt incurred by the father **from the property of orphans,** even if the creditor possesses incontrovertible proof (such as a valid loan document) that their father owed him money, לֹא יִפָּרַע אֶלָּא בִּשְׁבוּעָה – **may not collect without** taking **an oath** that he is owed the money. אֶלָּא אֶכְבְּשֵׁיהּ לִשְׁטַר מַשְׁכַּנְתָּא – I reasoned that **instead,** to circumvent the oath,[2] **I will conceal the document of security,** which states that my occupancy of the land was to collect a debt, וְאוֹכְלָהּ שִׁיעוּר זוּזֵי – **and I will** continue to **use [the land]** until I recover **the amount of money** that is owed to me from the other debt. In this way, I will be able to collect my other debt without swearing. How so? דְּמִיגּוֹ דְּאִי בָּעֵינָא – **For since, if I wished** to lie, אֲמִינָא לְקוּחָה הִיא בְּיָדִי – **I could say that I bought [the land]**[3] from the orphans' father, מְהֵימְנָא – **and I would be believed** without being required to swear, as I have already established *chazakah* during the father's lifetime.[4] כִּי אֲמִינָא דְּאִית לִי זוּזֵי גַּבַּיְיכוּ – Therefore, **if** instead **I say that you owe me money,** מְהֵימְנָנָא – **I will** likewise **be believed** without swearing! Thus, I concluded that the most judicious course was simply to say nothing and continue using the land until I consumed enough produce to cover the outstanding debt.[5]

Abaye replied by pointing out the fallacy of Rava bar Sharshum's reasoning:

אָמַר לֵיהּ – **[Abaye] said to [Rava bar Sharshum]:** לְקוּחָה בְּיָדִי לֹא מָצִית אָמְרַתְּ – **You are *not* able** (i.e. believed) **to say, "I bought [the land],"** even if you would wish to lie, דְּהָא אִיכָּא עֲלָהּ קָלָא – **for there** already **exists a rumor concerning it** דְּאַרְעָא דְּיַתְמֵי הִיא – **that it is the orphans' land.** This rumor functions as a protest and negates your *chazakah*. Thus, you would not have been believed to claim that you purchased the land.[6]

Accordingly, Abaye ruled:

אֶלָּא זִיל אַהְדְּרָהּ נִיהֲלַיְיהוּ – **Rather, go** now **and return [the property] to [the orphans],** וְכִי גָּדְלֵי יַתְמֵי – **and when the orphans mature,**[7] אִשְׁתַּעֵי דִּינָא בַּהֲדַיְיהוּ – you can **litigate with them** at that time and collect by taking an oath that you are owed the money. At this time, however, you have no recourse at all.[8]

NOTES

1. Literally: I had other money with him.

2. Although Rava bar Sharshum claimed that he was owed the money, he avoided taking even a truthful oath (*Ritva*). The Sages interpret a verse in the Torah (*Deuteronomy* 10:20) to teach that even swearing truthfully should be avoided except by the most God-fearing men (see *Rashi* ad loc. and to 6:13, whose source is *Midrash Tanchuma* to *Parashas Matos;* see also *Shulchan Aruch Orach Chaim* §156).

3. Literally: it is purchased in my hands.

4. Rava bar Sharshum had used the land for three years (in collection of the money owed to him) during the father's lifetime (*Rashbam*).

5. After consuming enough produce to cover the amount owed to him, Rava bar Sharshum planned to return the land, admitting that it was not his and that he had held it only to collect its produce to cover an outstanding debt. However, at that time, he reasoned, he would be believed without swearing, based on a *migo:* If he were lying, he could simply have retained the property on the strength of his *chazakah.*

[An apparent difficulty: Rava bar Sharshum's stated aim was to avoid having to take an oath that he was owed the money. To this end, he contrived a situation in which his claim would be supported by a *migo* that he could have won the land with proof of a *chazakah*. But the *migo* seems flawed, because even if he were to use a *chazakah* to prove his claim, he should be required to swear. This is because the Rabbis instituted that anyone who denies a claim against himself must swear to support his denial (*Shevuos* 40b); this oath is known as a *hesess* oath. Thus, if the orphans were to question his right to the land, it would seem that he would be required to swear. How, then, could Rava bar Sharshum have avoided an oath?

Rashbam answers that one whose claim to land is based on a *chazakah* is exempt from swearing on two counts. Firstly, as a general rule, an oath is not administered for a claim involving land (*Shevuos* 42b). Secondly, the function of *chazakah* is to replace a deed as proof of ownership; consequently, it is as effective as a deed. That is, just as one who produces a deed that evidences his ownership need not swear, so too one who uses *chazakah* as his proof is exempt from swearing. Thus, by using *chazakah* to support his claim he would have successfully evaded taking an oath. See, however, *Tosafos* and Rishonim who dispute *Rashbam* and maintain that one who uses a *chazakah* to support his claim ordinarily must swear. They suggest other resolutions to this difficulty.]

6. In explaining the logic of *chazakah,* the Gemara above (29a) stated that after three years pass without the original owner contesting his occupancy, the current occupant of real property is believed to claim that he purchased the field, but had been lax in guarding his deed. If, however, the original owner lodged a protest during the first three years, the court rejects the occupant's *chazakah,* saying: If you indeed purchased the land as you maintain, where is your deed? Since you were aware that the original owner contested your claim, how could you have carelessly misplaced or discarded your deed?

In reference to our case, Abaye contends that a rumor is certainly at least as effective as a challenger's protest. Thus, the court would have rejected Rava bar Sharshum's *chazakah,* saying: You were aware that the land was rumored to belong to the orphans' father and that people were saying you held it merely as security. If, as you claim, the rumor is unfounded and you indeed purchased the land, why do you not have a deed? Why were you not careful to retain it to refute the rumor? Your lack of a deed disproves your claim (*Rashbam*; cf. *Tosafos*). Hence, according to Abaye, Rava bar Sharshum's *migo* collapses.

7. I.e. when they reach thirteen years of age — see following note.

8. Rava's *migo* (had it not been dismissed by Abaye) would have benefited him in two ways: (1) He would have been able to collect *without swearing.* (2) He would have been able to collect *earlier* than he could have without a *migo.* To explain this last point: The law is that a debt may not be collected from heirs while they are minors. Since paying a debt is a *mitzvah*, and minors are exempt from *mitzvah*-performance, they cannot be forced to pay until they reach the age of thirteen — legal adulthood (see *Rashbam*). Alternatively, the court is concerned that the father may have in fact repaid, but that the young orphans, not being astute enough to refute the creditor's claim, will innocently assume that they are liable, and pay (see Gemara *Arachin* 22a and *Tosafos* here). Thus, without a *migo,* Rava bar Sharshum would be forced to wait until the orphans reached adulthood before he could collect his debt (even if he would swear that he was owed the money). With a *migo,* however, he could have collected his debt earlier, as follows: Since by virtue of his *chazakah* he would have been believed to claim the field as his, even before the orphans reached adulthood, he is likewise believed to claim that the father owed him money and to collect it, even while the orphans are still minors.

By dismissing Rava bar Sharshum's *migo,* then, Abaye deprived him of both benefits. Thus, Abaye told him that he must return the land to the orphans now, and could press his claim against them only when they turned thirteen. At that time, he could either present a note recording the debt or produce witnesses to the loan and thus collect — but only by additionally taking an oath that he was owed the money (*Rashbam*).

[In light of Abaye's ruling, *Tosafos* question why Rava bar Sharshum did not state that in addition to avoiding an oath, he hoped also to avoid being constrained to wait until the orphans reached adulthood before

זוזי אחריני גביה ואכלתה שני משכנתא אמינא אי מהדרנא (א) לה ארעא ליתמי ואמינא דאית לי זוזי אחריני גבי (ב) דאבוכון אמור רבנן [א] הבא ליפרע מנכסי יתומים לא יפרע אלא בשבועה (ג) אלא אכבשיה לשטר משכנתא ואוכלה שיעור זוזי [ב] דמיגו דאי בעינא אמינא לקוחה היא בידי מהימנא כי אמינא דאית לי זוזי גבייכו מהימננא א"ל לקוחה (ד) בידי לא מצית אמרת [ג] דהא איכא עלה קלא דארעא דיתמי היא אלא זיל אהדרה ניהליהו וכי גדלי יתמי אשתעי דינא בהדייהו: קריביה דרב אידי בר אבין שכיב ושבק דיקלא רב אידי בר אבין אמר אנא קריבנא טפי (ה) וההוא גברא אמר אנא קריבנא טפי [ג] לסוף אודי ליה דאיהו קריב טפי [ד] אוקמה רב חסדא בידיה א"ל [ה] ליהדר לי פירי דאכל מההוא יומא עד השתא אמר זה הוא שאומרים עליו אדם גדול הוא אמאן קא סמיך מר אהאי הא קאמר דאנא מקרבנא טפי אביי ורבא לא סבירא להו הא דרב חסדא

כיון

רש"י

זוזי אחריני גביה. שנתחייב לי שאין משכון עליהן ואמרי לאחר שכלו שני משכנתא אם אחזיר הקרקע ליתומים ואשאל להם חוב שיש לי על אביהם צריך אני לישבע דאמור רבנן הבא ליפרע כו' ואע"פ שיש בידי שטר חוב מחוייבי שבועה: **אכבשה.** אעלים אותה: **לקוחה היא בידי.** דהא אכלתיה שני חזקה בחיי אבוהון: **מהימננא.** בלא שבועה ° דאין נשבעין על הקרקעות ועוד לחזקת שלש שנים במקום שטר קיימא: **אמר ליה.** אביי הא דחשבת בדעתך דלאי בעינא טענינא לקוחה היא בידי כיון דידיעא מילתא דבמשכנתא (ו) איתנחית בה לא מצית למיטען לקוחה היא בידי דהא איכא קלא ועדות דלארעא דיתמי היא דהשתא שלימו שני משכנתא וכיון דידעת דאית קלא עלך דלארעא דא משכנתא היא גבך ולא לקוחה אין לך מחאה גדולה מזו והיה לך להזהר בשטרך הלכך זיל הדר ארעא ליתמי השתא וכי גדלי יתמי שיהו בני מיעבד מלוה דהיינו מבן שלש עשרה שנה ואילך דהוי חייב במלות אשתעי דינא בהדייהו על שטר חובך שיש לך על אביהם תשבע ותיטול כדין הבא ליפרע מנכסי היתומים דכל זמן שהם קטנים אין יורדין לנכסיהם לגבות מהן כדאמרינן בערכין בפרק שום היתומים (דף כב.) אין נזקקין לנכסי יתומים אא"כ רבית אוכלת בהן וכדפסיק התם רבא הלכתא אין נזקקין לנכסי יתומים ואם אמר תנו נותנין הלכך ממתינין להם עד דגדלי דהיינו מבן י"ג שנים ואילך כדמוכח התם. והא דאמרינן בפ' מי שמת (לקמן דף קנו.) ולמכור בנכסי אביו עד שיהא בן כ' ה"מ שמוכר לצורך הולאתו אבל לפרוע חוב אביו בית דין מוכרים מבן י"ג ואילך ואי נמי מלוה על פה היא כי גדלי לישתעי דינא בהדייהו וישבע ויטול כדאמר רב פפא בשמעתא בתרייתא דמכילתין הלכתא מלוה על פה גובה מן היורשין והני מילי שיש עדים שהלוהו וישבע שלא פרעו ויטול: **אתא ההוא גברא אמר אנא קריביה טפי.** ומתוך שלא נודע מי קרוב יותר החזיק אותו האיש בקרקע לפי שהיה אלם יותר כדאמר רב נחמן לקמיה גבי זה אומר של אבותי וזה אומר של אבותי כל דאלים גבר: **לסוף.** שנה או שנתים: **אודי ליה.** ההוא מחזיק לרב אידי בר אבין: **אוקמה רב חסדא בידיה.** דרב אידי: **א"ל.** רב אידי לרב חסדא: **להדר לי.** ההוא גברא פירי דאכל מההוא יומא עד האידנא מן היום שמת קרובי שאכלם שלא כדין: **אמאן קסמכת.** לזכות באילן: **אהאי.** אהודאת פיו שמודה עכשיו שאתה קרוב יותר והא איהו דאמר עד השתא אנא קריבנא טפי ואכל פירות בדין כל דאלים גבר וזה שמודה עכשיו הרי הוא כנותן לך (ז) את האילן מדעתו אף על פי שלא זכית בו מן הדין:

כיון

תוספות

אמור רבנן הבא ליפרע כו'. אע"פ שאף בשבועה לא היה יכול ליפרע מהם עד שיגדלו כדקאמרינן וכי גדלי אישתעי דינא בהדייהו לא היה מקפיד על ההמתנה אלא על השבועה ונראה דרבא בר שרשום סבר כרב הונא בריה דרב יהושע דמפרש (ח) טעמא בשילהי מכילתין (דף קעד.) טעמא דאין נזקקין לנכסי יתומים משום צררי דאי כרב פפא דמפרש משום דפריעת בעל חוב מצוה ויתמי לאו בני מיעבד מצוה נינהו א"כ אפילו יהא אמת כדבריו לא היה יכול לעכב להם הקרקע בחובו כיון דלאו בני מיעבד מצוה נינהו ולדרב הונא נמי פסקינן התם: **אכבשיה** לשטר משכנתא ואוכלה שיעור זוזי. דוקא משום דלכבש לשטר משכנתא מלי למימר לקוחה היא בידי דלא היה ידוע דבתורת משכנתא אתא לידיה דאי הוו ידעי דמעיקרא בתורת משכנתא אתא לידיה לא היה טוען רבא בר שרשום שיכול לומר לקוחה היא בידי מידי דהוה אאומן ואריס דאין לו חזקה בשדה אריסותו כיון דידוע דמעיקרא בתורת אריסותא אתו לידיה וכן לדברים העשויין להשאיל ולהשכיר וגזלן (ט) דמעיקרא ידעינן דגזל שדה זו דאין לו שום חזקה: **מיגו** דאי בעי למימר לקוחה היא. ותימה מאי דעתיה דרבא בר שרשום דאפילו אי טעין לקוחה היא בידי שבועת היסת לעולם צריך דנהי דאין נשבעין על קרקעות מדאורייתא מדרבנן נשבעים כמו שדקדק רב האי גאון מההיא דהכותב (כתובות דף פז.) הפוגמת כתובתה ועד אחד מעידה שהיא פרוע לא תפרע אלא בשבועה סבר רמי בר חמא למימר שבועה דאורייתא אמר רבא שתי תשובות בדבר כו' ועוד דאין נשבעין על כפירת שעבוד קרקעות אלמא דמדרבנן נשבעין וה"ה שבועת היסת דמ"מ ויש לומר דאין נשבעין שבועת היסת אלא היכא דטעין ברי אבל הכא לאו טענת ברי הוא שאין ודאי ליתומים שקרקע זו אינה לקוחה בידו הלכך אי הוה טעין לקוחה היא בידי לא הוה צריך שבועת היסת: **לקוחה** היא בידי לא מצית אמרת. אף על גב דאי הוה אמר לקוחה היא בידי הוה נאמן מ"מ לא הוי מיגו והכי פירושו דלא מצית אמרת לא היית יכול להעיז פניך ולומר כן כיון דנפק קלא ואין כאן מיגו וכענין זה יש בפרק שני דקדושין (דף נ.) ומה אם ירצה לומר מזיד הייתי לא משוי נפשיה רשיעא פי' אינו אומר ברצון מזיד הייתי ואין כאן מיגו אבל ודאי אם אמר מזיד הייתי פשיטא דמהימן: **קריביה** דרב אידי שבק דיקלא. אי לא גרסינן אלא שבק דיקלא צ"ל שלא היו לו בנים והקרוב יותר יורשו ואי גרס לקריביה יש לומר שהיו לו בנים להכי איצטריך ליה למימר דיקלא לקריביה: **ה"ג** לסוף אודי ליה. ולא גרים דאיהו קרוב טפי אלא לא היה רוצה לחלוק עם רב אידי ונתן לו הדקל בחנם ולא בשביל שהיה קרוב יותר ומשום הכי קאמר רב חסדא הא איהו דאמר אנא קריבנא טפי שמרצונו נתן לך ולא בשביל שאתה קרוב יותר ואביי ורבא סברי כיון דאודי אודי (י) ומסתמא לא היה מוחל לו אלא מפני שהוא יותר קרוב ולשון אודי דחוק הוא וכן סברת אביי ורבא ואין לפרש דגרסינן דאיהו קרוב טפי והיה טוען (כ) דלא אכל פירות ולרב אידי היו לו עדים שאכל והא דקאמר איהו קאמר אנא קריבנא טפי פירוש מעיקרא והואיל וכן השתא נמי מהימן במאי דאמר שלא אכלה במיגו שלא היה מודה וס"ל דאמרינן מיגו במקום עדים כדבסמוך דא"כ הוה ליה למימר הא איהו (ל) אמר לא אכלתי ואי בעי אמר אנא קריבנא טפי ועוד א"כ הוה ליה לאסוקי נמי הכא בהאי לישנא כדמסיק בסמוך אביי ורבא לא סבירא להו הא דרב חסדא [מה לי לשקר במקום עדים לא אמרינן] וגירסת ר"ח נראה לר"י עיקר דלא גרים לסוף אודי ליה אלא גרס לסוף אייתי סהדי דאיהו קריביה ולא גרס קרוב טפי שלא היו מעידים שרב אידי קרובו היה טפי מההוא גברא אלא היו מעידים שרב אידי קרובו היה וההוא גברא לא היו מכירים אם הוא היה קרובו או לאו ולא היה לו שום עדי קורבה ואפי' (מ) גרס טפי מלינו לפרש טפי מכל אותם שהיו העדים מכירים לכך אוקמה רב חסדא בידיה דרב אידי דהוי רב אידי ודאי וההוא גברא ספק והיה רב אידי תובע גם הפירות כיון שהודה שאכל ורב חסדא פטר ליה במיגו דאי בעי אמר לא אכלי כי אמר נמי אכלי ודידי אכלי מהימן (נ) ורבא ואביי סברי כיון שאכל פירות ואודי חייב לשלם ולא מהימן במיגו הואיל והקרקע יוצא מתחת ידו מן הדין דבקרקע ליכא מיגו וא"ת והא לקמן (דף לד.) אמרינן אי דמיא (ס) לרבי אבא לחד סהדא ולתרתין שנין ולפירי דכשמודה שאכל פירות ואיכא חד סהדא שחייב לשלם מתוך שאינו יכול לישבע אבל אי ליכא חד סהדא לא היה חייב לשלם ואמאי נימא כיון שהקרקע יוצא מתחת ידו גם הפירות ישלם וי"ל דהתם מיירי שאומר שאכלה שלש שנים והעד אינו מעיד אלא משתים דהתם ודאי אי לא הוה חד סהדא פשיטא דפטור אע"פ שהקרקע יוצא מתחת ידו דאי מהימן במאי דאמר דאכלה שלש שנים לא היה לנו להוציא הקרקע מידו כיון דאכלה שני חזקה וליכא למימר דנאמין לו שאכלה שלש שנים אבל לא נאמין שלקחה אלא בגזל אכלה כדאמרינן בהמזקין (גיטין דף נד: ושם) דנאמן אתה להפסיד שכרך ואין אתה נאמן להפסיד ספר תורה דלא דמי דהתם (ע) [ג] (אף על פי שספר תורה) כיון שהוא ביד לוקח כאילו יש עדים שנכתבו לשמן (פ) מ"מ מפסיד שכרו כיון שמודה שאין חייבין לו כלום:

ואי

מסורת הש"ס

א) כתובות דף פז. [לעיל ה: ע"ש תוס' ד"ה אע"ג גיטין לד:], ב) [ועי' נוסחת הרי"ף והרא"ש], ג) רש"ל מ"ז:

הגהות הב"ח

(א) גמ' מהדרנא ארעא כצ"ל ותיבת לה נמחק: (ב) שם גבי אבוכון כצ"ל ואות ד' נמחק: (ג) שם אלא בשבועה אכבשיה לשטר משכנתא בידי ואוכלה שיעור זוזי כצ"ל ותיבת אלא נמחק: (ד) שם לקוחה היא בידי: (ה) שם אנא קריבנא טפי אתא ההוא גברא: (ו) רשב"ם ד"ה א"ל אביי וכו' דבמשכנתא את נחית וכו' אין ב"ד יורדין וכו' כי גדלי יתמי לישתעי וכו' שיש עדים שהלוהו וישבע. נ"ב נראה מכאן דאפי' מת תוך הזמן לא גבי מיתומים קטנים בלא שבועה דכיון שהם קטנים חיישינן טפי לצררי וכך היא דעת ר"י בפ"ק סוף דף ה' בד"ה ואפי' מיתמי וכ"כ בהגהת אשירי שם אבל האשירי בפ"ק סימן ט' חולק על זה אלא דאפי' מיתומים קטנים גבי במת תוך הזמן דלא חיישינן לצררי תוך הזמן וכך היא דעת רוב הגאונים והכי נקטינן: (ז) ד"ה אהאי וכו' כנותן לך עכשיו את האילן: (ח) תוס' ד"ה אמור וכו' דמפרש בשילהי כצ"ל ותיבת טעמא נמחק: (ט) ד"ה אכבשיה וכו' וגזלן דידעי' דמעיקרא גזל שדה זו: (י) ד"ה ה"ג לסוף וכו' אודי דמסתמא: (כ) בא"ד שלא אכל פירות ולרב אידי היו לו עדים שאכל וקאמר רב חסדא הא איהו קאמר אנא קריבנא טפי: (ל) בא"ד הא איהו דאמר וכו' ועוד דהוה ליה למיפרך ולאסוקי נמי כצ"ל ותיבת א"כ נמחק: (מ) בא"ד ואפילו אי גרס' טפי: (נ) בא"ד מהימן ואביי ורבא סברי: (ס) בא"ד אי דמיא הא דרבי אבא לחד: (ע) בא"ד דלא דמי דהתם בספר תורה כיון כצ"ל ותיבת אע"פ נמחק: (פ) בא"ד ומכל מקום:

ליקוטי רש"י

הבא ליפרע מנכסי יתומים לא יפרע אלא בשבועה. וכל זמן שלא נשבעו אין להם רשות בהם [כתובות פז.]. ואפילו הוציא שטר דלאי הוה אבוהון דיתמי קיים דלמא הוה טוען ואמר אשתבע לי שלא פרעתיך ומשבעינן ליה כדאמרינן בשבועות (מא.) [גיטין ג.]. צריך שבועה שלא נתקבל מקבל חוב [שבועות מב:].

עין משפט נר מצוה

לט א מיי' פי"ד מהל' מלוה הלכה א סמג עשין פד טוש"ע ח"מ סי' קח סעיף יז:

מ ב מיי' פי"ד מהלכות טוען הלכה ח ועיין בהשגות ובמגיד משנה סמג עשין לה טוש"ע ח"מ סי' קמט סעיף כא:

מא ג מיי' שם סמג שם טוש"ע שם סעיף ג וסעיף כב וסי' קנ סעיף א ועי' שם:

מב ד ה מיי' שם פט"ו הלכה ג סמג שם טוש"ע ח"מ סי' קלט ס"ד:

רבינו גרשום

וכי גדלי יתמי אשתעי דינא בהדייהו. משום האי דקאמרת הבא ליפרע מנכסי יתומים (קטנים) לא יפרע אלא בשבועה מיתומים גדולים קאמר אבל מנכסי יתומים קטנים אפילו בשבועה לא יפרע דהכי קיי"ל אין מוציאין מנכסי יתומין אלא א) לאכילת רבית: **לסוף אודי ליה** ההוא גברא דתפיס דלא הוי קריב ליה כותיה. **א"ל** רב חסדא **זהו שאומרים וכו' אמאי קא סמך מר** אמלתיה **דהאי** דמודי ליה השתא. בזמן דהוי אכיל להו לפירי **הוה קאמר דאנא קריבנא טפי** ובדין אכל ולא מהדר לך דמי פירי. **ואביי ורבא לא סבירא להו דרב חסדא** אלא **כיון דאודי** אודי:

חשק שלמה על רבינו גרשום

א) נראה דל"ל אא"כ היתה רבית אוכלת בהן (והוא בערכין דף כב ע"א).

גליון הש"ס

רשב"ם ד"ה לקוחה היא בידי כו' דאין נשבעין על הקרקעות. עיין לקמן דף קכח ע"א ברשב"ם ד"ה לצורך:

The Gemara records an incident involving a disputed inheritance:

קְרִיבֵיהּ דְּרַב אִידִי בַּר אָבִין שְׁכִיב – **The relative of Rav Idi bar Avin died,** וְשָׁבַק דִּיקְלָא – **and left a date palm**[9] as his estate. רַב אִידִי בַּר אָבִין אָמַר אֲנָא קָרִיבְנָא טְפֵי – **Rav Idi bar Avin said: "I am the closest** living **relative** and the palm is mine," וְהַהוּא גַּבְרָא אָמַר – **while a certain** other **man said:** אֲנָא קָרִיבְנָא טְפֵי – ***"I* am the closest relative,** and the tree is *mine."* Neither party was able to prove his claim, and the second man took possession of the tree.[10] לְסוֹף אוֹדֵי לֵיהּ דְּאִיהוּ קָרִיב טְפֵי – **Ultimately,**[11] however, **[the man] admitted to [Rav Idi] that he** [Rav Idi] **was the closer relative.** אוֹקְמָהּ רַב חִסְדָּא בְּיָדֵיהּ – As a result of this admission, **Rav Chisda placed [the tree] in [Rav Idi's] possession.**

Rav Idi was not satisfied:

אָמַר לֵיהּ – **[Rav Idi] said to [Rav Chisda]:** לִיהֲדַר לִי פֵּירֵי – **"Let him** also **return to me** all **the produce** דְּאָכַל מֵהַהוּא יוֹמָא עַד הַשְׁתָּא – **which he consumed from that day** that he took possession of the tree **until now,** since he has admitted that he had no claim to the tree!"

Rav Chisda rejected this demand:

אָמַר – **[Rav Chisda]** disparagingly **said:** זֶה הוּא שֶׁאוֹמְרִים עָלָיו – **Is this** (referring to Rav Idi) **he of whom they say,** אָדָם גָּדוֹל הוּא – **that he is a great man** (i.e. scholar)?! How can he justifiably make such a demand?

Addressing Rav Idi, Rav Chisda explained his remark:

אַמַּאן קָא סָמֵיךְ מַר – **On whom does the master**[12] **base** his claim to the tree? אַהַאי – **On this man,** who has now admitted that the tree is the master's. הָא קָאָמַר דַּאֲנָא מְקָרַבְנָא טְפֵי – **But he has been claiming** until now, **"I am the closer relative!"** Thus, although he has now ceded the tree to you, this does not entitle you to the tree's past produce![13]

Abaye and Rava sided with Rav Idi:

אַבַּיֵי וְרָבָא לָא סְבִירָא לְהוּ הָא דְּרַב חִסְדָּא – **Abaye and Rava,** however, **do not agree with this** decision **of Rav Chisda.**

NOTES

collecting. *Tosafos* answer that apparently Rava bar Sharshum did not mind waiting a few years to collect his debt; his sole concern was to avoid an oath.]

9. Rav Idi's relative had no sons nor, indeed, any direct descendants. Thus, his inheritance passed to his closest surviving relative (*Tosafos*). *Tosafos* mention an alternate textual version according to which the deceased specifically bequeathed the palm to his "relative." This term excluded his sons from inheriting that particular palm (as sons are not referred to as "my relative" by a father), and the dispute centered around who was the man's relative.

10. In a case in which neither litigant advances proof to support his claim, and neither is in possession of the disputed property, the court (in certain cases, and when certain criteria exist – see below, 35a) withdraws and allows the stronger party to take possession. This is known as *kol d'alim g'var,* literally: "let he who is stronger prevail!" In this case, Rav Idi's opponent was the stronger, and he took possession of the tree.

11. I.e. after a year or two (*Rashbam*).

12. *Rashbam's* version of the text reads אַמַּאן קָסָמְכַתְּ, "on whom do *you* base . . .," omitting the honorific "master," which does not seem in line with the tone of Rav Chisda's belittling remark.

13. Until his admission, the man was legally in possession of the tree, having seized it when the court withdrew from the case and allowed the stronger litigant to prevail (see note 10). Since no new evidence was introduced, he could have persisted in his position and continued to harvest the tree's produce. Thus, his admission that you are the closer relative is viewed as if he gave you the tree as a gift. Hence, although you are now known to be the true heir to the tree, you are not entitled to the tree's past produce any more than had the man magnanimously given you the tree as a gift (see *Rashbam*).

זוזי אחריני גביה ואכלתה שני משכנתא אמינא אי מהדרנא (א) לה ארעא ליתמי ואמינא דאית לי זוזי אחריני גבי (ב) דאבוכון אמור רבנן [א] הבא ליפרע מנכסי יתומים לא יפרע אלא בשבועה (ג) אלא אכבשיה לשטר משכנתא ואוכלה שיעור זוזי [ב] דמיגו דאי בעינא אמינא לקוחה היא בידי מהימנא כי אמינא דאית לי זוזי גבייכו מהימננא א"ל לקוחה (ד) בידי לא מצית אמרת [ג] דהא איכא עלה קלא דארעא דיתמי היא אלא זיל אהדרה ניהליהו וכי גדלי יתמי אשתעי דינא בהדייהו: קריביה דרב אידי בר אבין שכיב ושבק דיקלא רב אידי בר אבין אמר אנא קריבנא טפי (ה) וההוא גברא אמר אנא קריבנא טפי [ג] לסוף אודי ליה דאיהו קריב טפי [ד] אוקמה רב חסדא בידיה א"ל [ה] ליהדר לי פירי דאכל מההוא יומא עד השתא אמר זה הוא שאומרים עליו אדם גדול הוא אמאן קא סמיך מר אהאי הא קאמר דאנא מקרבנא טפי אביי ורבא לא סבירא להו הא דרב חסדא כיון

רש"י

זוזי אחריני גביה. שנתחייב לי שאין משכון עליהן ואמרי לאחר שכלו שני משכנתא אם אחזיר הקרקע ליתומים ואשאל להם חוב שיש לי על אביהם צריך אני לישבע דאמור רבנן הבא ליפרע כו' ואע"פ שיש בידי שטר חוב מחוייבני שבועה: אכבשה. אעלים אותה: לקוחה היא בידי. דהא אכלתיה שני חזקה בחיי אבוהון: מהימננא. בלא שבועה ° דאין נשבעין על הקרקעות ועוד דחזקת שלש שנים במקום שטר קיימא: אמר ליה. אביי הא דמשבת בדעתך דלאי בעינא טענינא לקוחה היא בידי כיון דידיעא מילתא דמשכנתא (ו) ליתנהית בה לא מצית למיטען לקוחה היא בידי דהא איכא קלא ועדות דארעא דיתמי היא דהשתא שלימו שני משכונתא וכיון דידעת דאית קלא עלך דארעא דלא משכנתא היא גבך ולא לקוחה אין לך מחאה גדולה מזו והיה לך להזהר בשטרך הלכך זיל הדר ארעא ליתמי השתא וכי גדלי יתמי שיהו בני מיעבד מלוה דהיינו מבן שלש עשרה שנה ואילך דהוי חייב במצות אשתעי דינא בהדייהו על שטר חובך שיש לך על אביהם תשבע ותיטול כדין הבא ליפרע מנכסי היתומים דכל זמן שהם קטנים אין יורדין לנכסיהם לגבות מהן כדאמרינן בערכין בפרק שום היתומים (דף כב.) אין מזקקין לנכסי יתומים אא"כ רבית אוכלת בהן וכדפסיק התם רבא הלכתא אין מזקקין לנכסי יתומים ואם אמר תנו נותנין הלכך ממתינין להם עד דגדלי דהיינו מבן י"ג שנים ואילך כדמוכח התם. והא דאמרינן בפ' מי שמת (לקמן דף קנו.) ולמכור בנכסי אביו עד שיהא בן כ' ה"מ שמוכר לצורך הולאתו אבל לפרוע חוב אביו בית דין מוכרים מבן י"ג ואילך ואי נמי מלוה על פה היא כי גדלי ליתמי דינא בהדייהו וישבע ויטול כדאמר רב פפא בשמעתא בתרייתא דמכילתין הלכתא מלוה על פה גובה מן היורשין והני מילי שיש עדים שהלוהו וישבע שלא פרעו ויטול: אתא ההוא גברא אמר אנא קריבנא טפי. ומתוך שלא נודע מי קרוב יותר החזיק אותו האיש בקרקע לפי שהיה אלם יותר כדאמר רב נחמן לקמיה גבי זה אומר של אבותי וזה אומר של אבותי כל דאלים גבר: לסוף. שנה או שנתים: אודי ליה. ההוא מחזיק לרב אידי בר אבין: אוקמה רב חסדא בידיה. דרב אידי: א"ל. רב אידי לרב חסדא: להדר לי. ההוא גברא פירי דאכל מההוא יומא עד האידנא מן היום שמת קרובי שאכלם שלא כדין: אמאן קסמכת. לזכות לאילן: אהאי. אהודאת פיו שמודה עכשיו שאתה קרוב יותר והא איהו דאמר עד השתא אנא קריבנא טפי ואכל פירות כדין כל דאלים גבר וזה שמודה עכשיו הרי הוא כנותן לך (ז) את האילן מדעתו אף על פי שלא זכית בו מן הדין: כיון

תוספות

אמור רבנן הבא ליפרע כו'. אע"פ שאף בשבועה לא היה יכול ליפרע מהם עד שיגדלו כדקאמרינן ולכי גדלי אישתעי דינא בהדייהו לא היה מקפיד על ההמתנה אלא על השבועה ונראה דרבא בר שרשום סבר כרב הונא בריה דרב יהושע דמפרש (ח) טעמא בשילהי מכילתין (דף קעד.) טעמא דאין מזקקין לנכסי יתומים משום דגרי דאי כרב פפא דמפרש משום דפריעת בעל חוב מלוה ויתמי לאו בני מיעבד מצוה נינהו א"כ אפילו יהא אמת כדבריו לא היה יכול לעכב להם הקרקע בחובו כיון דלאו בני מיעבד מלוה נינהו וכדרב הונא נמי פסקינן התם: אכבשיה לשטר משכנתא ואוכלה שיעור זוזי. דוקא משום דכבש לשטר משכנתא מצי למימר לקוחה היא בידי דלא היה ידוע דבתורת משכנתא אתא לידיה דאי הוו ידעי דמעיקרא בתורת משכנתא אתא לידיה לא היה טוען רבא בר שרשום שיכול לומר לקוחה היא בידי מידי דהוה אאומן ואריס דאין לו חזקה בשדה אריסותו כיון דידוע דמעיקרא בתורת אריסותא אתו לידיה וכן דברים העשויין להשאיל ולהשכיר וגזלן (ט) דמעיקרא ידעינן דגזל שדה זו דאין לו שום חזקה: מיגו דאי בעי למימר לקוחה היא. ותימה מאי דעתיה דרבא בר שרשום דאפילו אי טעין לקוחה היא בידי שבועת היסת לעולם צריך דהני דאין נשבעין על קרקעות מדאורייתא מדרבנן נשבעים כמו שדקדק רב האי גאון מהאי דהכותב (כתובות דף פז.) הפוגמת כתובתה ועד אחד מעידה שהיא פרועה לא תפרע אלא בשבועה סבר רמי בר חמא למימר שבועה דאורייתא אמר רבא שתי תשובות בדבר כו' ועוד דאין נשבעין על כפירת שעבוד קרקעות אלמא למדרבנן נשבעין וה"ה שבועת היסת דמ"מ ויש לומר דאין נשבעין שבועת היסת אלא היכא דטעין ברי אבל הכא לאו טענת ברי הוא שאין ודאי ליתומים שקרקע זו אינה לקוחה בידו הלכך אי הוה טעין לקוחה היא בידי לא הוה צריך שבועת היסת:

לקוחה היא בידי לא מצית אמרת. אף על גב דאי הוה אמר לקוחה היא בידי הוה נאמן מ"מ לא הוי מיגו והכי פירושו דלא מצית אמרת לא היית יכול להעיז פניך ולומר כן כיון דנפק קלא ואין כאן מיגו וכעניין זה יש בפרק שני דקדושין (דף ס.) ומה אם ירלה לומר מזיד הייתי לא משוי נפשיה רשיעא פי' אינו אומר ברלון מזיד הייתי ואין כאן מיגו אבל ודאי אם אמר מזיד הייתי פשיטא דמהימן: קריביה דרב אידי שבק דיקלא. אי לא גרסינן אלא שבק דיקלא ל"ל שלא היו לו בנים והקרוב יותר יורשו ואי גרס לקריביה יש לומר שהיו לו בנים להכי איצטריך ליה למימר דיקלא לקריביה: ה"ג לסוף אודי ליה. ולא גרים דאיהו קרוב טפי אלא לא היה רוצה לחלוק עם רב אידי ונתן לו הדקל בחנם ולא בשביל שהיה קרוב יותר ומשום הכי קאמר רב חסדא הא איהו דאמר אנא קריבנא טפי שמרלונו נתן לך ולא בשביל שאתה קרוב יותר ואביי ורבא סברי כיון דאודי אודי (י) ומסתמא לא היה מוחל לו אלא מפני שהוא יותר קרוב ולשון אודי דחוק הוא וכן סברת אביי ורבא ואין לפרש דגרסינן דאיהו קרוב טפי והיה טוען (כ) דלא אכל פירות ולרב אידי היו לו עדים שאכל והא דקאמר איהו קאמר אנא קריבנא טפי היינו מפירות מעיקרא והואיל וכן השתא נמי מהימן במאי דאמר שלא אכלה במיגו שלא היה מודה וס"ל דאמרינן מיגו במקום עדים כדבסמוך דא"כ הוה ליה למימר הא איהו (ל) אמר לא אכלתי ואי בעי אמר אנא קריבנא טפי ועוד א"כ הוה ליה לאסוקי נמי הכא בהאי לישנא דמסיק בסמוך אביי ורבא לא סבירא להו הא דרב חסדא [מה לי לשקר במקום עדים לא אמרינן] וגירסת ר"ח נראה לר"י עיקר דלא גרים לסוף אודי ליה אלא גרס לסוף אייתי סהדי דאיהו קריביה ולא גרס קרוב טפי שלא היו מעידים שרב אידי קרובו היה טפי מההוא גברא אלא היו מעידים שרב אידי קרובו היה וההוא גברא לא היו מכירים אם הוא היה קרובו או לאו ולא היה לו שום עדי קורבה ואפי' (מ) גרס טפי מליני לפרש טפי מכל אותם שהיו העדים מכירים לכך אוקמה רב חסדא בידיה דרב אידי דהוי ספק וגברא והיה רב אידי תובע גם הפירות כיון שהודה שאכל ורב חסדא פטר ליה במיגו דאי בעי אמר לא אכלי כי אמר נמי אכלי ודידי אכלי מהימן (נ) ורבא ואביי סברי כיון שאכל פירות ואודי חייב לשלם ולא מהימן במיגו הואיל והקרקע יוצאת מתחת ידו מן הדין דבקרקע ליכא מיגו וא"ת והא לקמן (דף לד.) אמרינן אי דמיא (ס) לרבי אבא לחד סהדא ולתרתין שנין ולפירי דכשמודה שאכל פירות וליכא אלא חד סהדא שחייב לשלם מתוך שאינו יכול לישבע אבל אי ליכא חד סהדא לא היה חייב לשלם ולמאי ניחא כיון שהקרקע יוצאת מתחת ידו גם הפירות ישלם וי"ל דהתם מיירי שאומר שאכלה שלש שנים והעד אינו מעיד אלא משתים דהתם ודאי אי לא הוה חד סהדא פשיטא דפטור אע"פ שהקרקע יוצאת מתחת ידו דאי הימין במאי דאמר דאכלה שלש שנים לא היה לנו להוליא הקרקע מידו כיון דאכלה שני חזקה וליכא למימר דנאמן לו שאכלה שלש שנים אבל לא נאמין שלקחה אלא בגזל אכלה כדאמרינן בהמקין (גיטין דף נד: ושם) דנאמן אתה להפסיד שכרך ואין אתה נאמן להפסיד ספר תורה דלא דמי דהתם (ע) ג (אף על פי שספר תורה) (פ) מ"מ מפסיד שכרו לשמן כיון שהוא ביד לוקח כאילו יש עדים שנכתבו כיון שמודה שאין חייבין לו כלום: ואי

מסורת הש"ס

א) כתובות דף פז. [לעיל ה: ע"ש תוס' ד"ה אע"ג גיטין לד:], ב) [ועי' נוסחת הרי"ף והרא"ש], ג) רש"ל מ"ז:

הגהות הב"ח

(א) גמ' מהדרנא ארעא כל"ל ותיבת לה נמחק: (ב) שם גבי אבוכון כל"ל ואות ד' נמחק: (ג) שם אלא בשבועה אכבשיה לשטר משכנתא בידי ואוכלה שיעור זוזי כל"ל ותיבת אלא נמחק: (ד) שם לקוחה היא בידי: (ה) שם אנא קריבנא טפי אתא ההוא גברא: (ו) רשב"ם ד"ה א"ל אביי וכו' דבמשכנתא את נחית וכו' אין ב"ד יורדין וכו' כי גדלי יתמי לישתעי וכו' שיש עדים שהלוהו וישבע. נ"ב נראה מכאן דאפי' מת תוך הזמן לא גבי מיתומים קטנים בלא שבועה דכיון שהם קטנים חיישינן טפי לצררי וכך היא דעת ר"י בפ"ק סוף דף ה' בד"ה ואפי' מיתמי וכ"כ בהגהת אשירי שם אבל האשירי בפ"ק סימן ט' חולק על זה אלא דאפי' מיתומים קטנים גבי במת תוך הזמן דלא חיישינן לצררי תוך הזמן וכן היא דעת רוב הגאונים והכי נקטינן: (ז) ד"ה אהאי וכו' כנותן לך עכשיו את האילן: (ח) תוס' ד"ה אמור וכו' דמפרש בשילהי כל"ל ותיבת טעמא נמחק: (ט) ד"ה אכבשיה וכו' וגזלן דידעי' דמעיקרא גזל שדה זו: (י) ד"ה ה"ג לסוף וכו' אודי דמסתמא: (כ) בא"ד שלא אכל פירות ולרב אידי היו לו עדים שאכל וקאמר רב חסדא הא איהו קאמר אנא קריבנא טפי: (ל) בא"ד הא איהו דאמר וכו' ועוד דהוה ליה למיפרך ולאסוקי נמי כל"ל ותיבת א"כ נמחק: (מ) בא"ד ואפילו אי גרס' טפי: (נ) בא"ד מהימן ואביי ורבא סברי: (ס) בא"ד אי דמיא הא דרבי אבא לחד: (ע) בא"ד דלא דמי דהתם בספר תורה כיון כל"ל ותיבת אע"פ נמחק: (פ) בא"ד ומכל מקום:

ליקוטי רש"י

הבא ליפרע מנכסי יתומים לא יפרע אלא בשבועה. וכל זמן שלא נשבעו אין להם רשות בהם [כתובות פד.]. ואפילו הוליא שטר דאי הוה אבוהון דיתמי קיים דלמא הוה טעין ואמר אשתבע לי דלא פרעתיך ומשבעינן ליה כדאמרינן בשבועות (מא.) [גיטין ג.]. לריך שבועה שלא נתקבל חוב [שבועות מב:].

עין משפט נר מצוה

לט א מיי' פי"ד מהל' מלוה הלכה א סמג עשין פד טוש"ע ח"מ סי' קח סעיף יח:
מ ב מיי' פי"ד מהלכות טוען הלכה ח ועיין בהשגות ובמגיד משנה סמג עשין לה טוש"ע ח"מ סי' קמט סעיף כא:
מא ג מיי' שם סמג שם טוש"ע שם סעיף ב וסעיף כב וסי' קנ סעיף א ועי' שם:
מב ד ה מיי' שם פט"ו הלכה ג סמג שם טוש"ע ח"מ סי' קלט ס"ד:

רבינו גרשום

וכי גדלי יתמי אשתעי דינא בהדייהו. משום האי דקאמרת הבא ליפרע מנכסי יתומים (קטנים) לא יפרע אלא בשבועה מיתומים גדולים קאמר אבל מנכסי יתומים קטנים אפילו בשבועה לא יפרע דהכי קיי"ל אין מוציאין מנכסי יתומין אלא א) לאכילת רבית: לסוף אודי ליה ההוא גברא דתפיס דלא הוי קריב ליה כותיה. א"ל רב חסדא זהו שאומרים וכו' אמאי קא סמך מר אמלתיה דהאי דמודי ליה השתא. בזמן דהוי אכיל להו לפירי הוה קאמר דאנא קריבנא טפי ובדין אכל ולא מהדר לך דמי פירי. ואביי ורבא לא סבירא להו דרב חסדא אלא כיון דאודי אודי:

חשק שלמה על רבינו גרשום

א) נראה דל"ל אא"כ היתה רבית אוכלת בהן (והוא בערכין דף כב ע"א).

גליון הש"ס

רשב"ם ד"ה לקוחה היא בידי כו' דאין נשבעין על הקרקעות. עיין לקמן דף קכח ע"א ברשב"ם ד"ה רלונך:

כיון דאודי אודי: [א] זה אומר של אבותי וזה אומר של אבותי האי אייתי סהדי דאבהתיה הוא והאי אייתי סהדי דאכל שני חזקה אמר רב חסדא [ג] מה לו לשקר אי בעי א"ל מינך זבינתה ואכלתיה שני חזקה אביי ורבא לא סבירא להו הא דרב חסדא מה לי לשקר במקום עדים לא אמרינן ההוא דאמר ליה לחבריה מאי בעית בהאי ארעא אמר ליה מינך זבני ואכלתיה שני חזקה אזל אייתי סהדי דאכלה תרתי שני [ג] אמר רב נחמן [א] הדרא ארעא והדרי פירי אמר רב זביד [ב] אם טען ואמר לפירות ירדתי נאמן לאו מי [ד] אמר רב יהודה [ג] האי מאן דנקיט מגלא ותובלא (א) ואמר איזיל איגדריה לדיקלא דפלניא דזבניה ניהלי מהימן [ה] (אלמא) לא חציף איניש דגזר דיקלא דלאו דיליה הכא נמי לא חציף איניש למיכל פירי דלאו דיליה אי הכי ארעא נמי ארעא אמרינן ליה אחוי שטרך אי הכי פירי נמי שטרא לפירי לא עבדי אינשי ההוא דאמר (ב) לחבריה מאי בעית בהאי ארעא א"ל מינך זבנית ואכלתיה שני חזקה אייתי חד סהדא דאכלה תלת שני סבור רבנן קמיה דאביי למימר היינו נסכא דרבי אבא [ו] דההוא גברא דחטף נסכא מחבריה אתא לקמיה דרבי אמי הוה יתיב ר' אבא קמיה אייתי חד סהדא דמיחטף חטפא מיניה אמר ליה אין חטפי ודידי חטפי אמר רבי אמי היכי

כיון דאודי. דשלא כדין החזיק עד עתה: אודי. וישלם פירות שאכל וכן הלכה: ויש ספרים שכתוב בהם אייתי רב אידי בר אבין סהדי דהוה קריב אוקמה רב חסדא בידיה. וגם ר"ח פי' כן. א"ל רב חסדא אמאי קאמצת דאכלינהו לפירי אהודאת פיו הא עד השתא הוא טוען דאנא קריבנא טפי והני סהדי דאייתית לא מסהדי דאנת קרוב (ג) ולאו ליורשה והוא אינו ראוי ליורשה אלא אסהדי דאנת קרוב והאי לא ידעי ליה ומתוך שהוא יכול לומר לא אכלתי יכול לומר אין אכלי ודידי אכלי דאנא קריבנא טפי שאין עדים מכחישים אותו בכך הלכך לא מפקינן מיניה: (הג"ה. לא היא (אלא) שהודה שאכל הפירות אלא כדמפרש הרב לבסוף דלא נהירא ליה שהודה על אכילת הפירות אלא עדים היו שאכלו ולא היה יכול לכפור ושרא ליה מריה דמי זה שאמר שהודה על אכילת פירות הלא לא הודה אלא על הקרקע ומכל מקום מאי דאכל עד השתא לא מפקינן מיניה כיון דליכא עדים בדבר שרב אידי היה קרוב יותר אלא על פיו של זה ואביי ורבא סברי דכיון דלאודי אודי שהרי הודאת בעל דין כמאה עדים ופיו מחייבו ממון ואי הוה גרסינן הא אמאי לית ליה לרב חסדא הא סברא ויש לפרש בענין אחר ובדוחק ולכן לא כתבתיו. ע"כ) ולא נהירא לי דהא לא מוכח הא סוגיא דשמעתא שהודה על אכילת הפירות אלא עדים היו בדבר ולא היה יכול לכפור: האי אייתי סהדי דאבהתיה היא. עד יום מותם ומעולם לא מכרו לאבותיו של זה השני: אמר רב חסדא מה לו לשקר. לזה שיש לו עדי חזקה במאי דטעין דשל אבותיו היא אי בעי הוה א"ל להאי שיש לו עדות (ד) זכות אבות מינך זבינתה ואכלתיה שני חזקה הלכך מיגו דמצי טעין הכי ויזכה בטענה זו והוא לא חשש לטעון כי טעין נמי של אבותיו אע"ג דמכחיש להו לעדים מהימן: מה לי לשקר במקום עדים לא אמרינן. כלומר כל טענה שאדם טוען כגון זה שאמר של אבותי ואתה רוצה לקיימה על ידי מה לי לשקר וטענה זו מכחשת עדים כי הכא לא מהימנינן ליה שהרי העדים מעידים שטענתו שקר והיאך תקיימנה על ידי מה לי לשקר הלא ודאי משקר הוא וחזקת השלש שנים אינה כלום דהויא לה חזקה שאין עמה טענה והכי הלכתא: אזיל ואייתי סהדי דאכלה תרתין שנין. ועדיין היה מחזר לבקש עדות של שנה שלישית ולא מצא: אמר רב נחמן הדרא ארעא. דבתרתין שנין לא הויא חזקה: והדרי פירי. של ב' השנים שאכל שלא כדין דהא לא טעין מעיקרא ארים הייתי ולפירות ירדתי דמהימנינן ליה כדלקמן דשטרא לפירי לא עבדי אינשי והני מילי בדאיכא סהדי דאכלינהו לפירי (א) אבל אי ליכא סהדי דאכלינהו לפירי אלא בהודאת פיו והוא טוען דזבנתיה מינך ואכלתינהו לפירי דארעא ופירי דידי נינהו ארעא כיון דלית ליה ראיה בשטר ולא עדי חזקה הדרא למרה וחייב שבועת היסת על הפירות דזבינינהו מיניה דמיגו דמצי (ב) אמר לא אכלתי פירות כי אם מעט כגון עייל כורא ואפיק טפי מכורא דבהכי הוה חזקה כדלקמן כי אמר אכלי טובא ודידי אכלי מהימן דאין כאן מה לי לשקר במקום עדים שאין ידוע אם לקח קרקע זו מבעליה אם לא אלא לפי שאבד שטרו בתוך ג' שנים מפסיד ולא דמי להא דאביי ורבא דפליגי עליה דרב חסדא לעיל דהתם כיון דאיתבריר מילתא דרב אידי קרוב טפי הרי נודע שאין לו חלק בקרקע ופירות שאכל שלא כדין אכל ואפי' בהודאת פיו ליחייב: אמר רב זביד אי טעין כו'. מילתא באפי נפשה היא והכי קאמר אם מתחלה כשטענו בעל הקרקע מאי בעית בהאי ארעא אילו לא השיב לו מינך זבינתה אלא לפירות ירדתי כדין ארים למחצה לשליש ולרביע או שמכרת לי פירות עד עשר שנים: נאמן. במה שאכל למפרע ובשבועת היסת דזבינהו מיניה ואע"ג דאיכא סהדי דאכלינהו לפירי ושאין הקרקע קנוי לו דלא חציף איניש למיחת לארעא דחבריה ולמיכל פירי דחבריה בחנם כדמפרש ואזיל ומיהו מכאן ולהבא לא יאכל בלא עדים ושטר שקנה הפירות דא"כ כל אדם ירד לקרקע חבירו ויאכל פירותיו ויאמר לפירות ירדתי מאחר שלא נחוש לערעורו של בעל הקרקע: מגלא ותובלא. כלי גודרי תמרים המגל לגדור ותובלא חבל לעלות לדקל מרוב גובהו. וי"מ תובלא סל לקבל פירות: ואמר. בפניו: איזיל ואיגדריה לדיקלא דפלניא. כלומר אלקוט הפירות: מהימן. ושבקין ליה ב"ד ללקט הפירות בלא עדים ושטר אחרי שאין ידוע שהבעלים מוחין בדבר קודם לקיטה ואם אתא חבריה וטען להד"מ אחר שליקט האילן לית עליה אלא שבועת היסת אבל מקמי דליגדריה אתא מריה דדיקלא ואמר להד"מ לא מהימן מלקט עד דמייתי ראיה ודוקא בשטען מתחלה לפירות ירדתי נאמן במה שאכל כבר אבל אם מתחלה טען מינך זבינתה ואח"כ טען לפירות ירדתי שמכחיש דבריו הראשונים אינו טוען וחוזר וטוען: אי הכי אפי' ארעא נמי. כי טעין דזבינתה מינך ליהמנוהו בלא עדי חזקה דלא חציף איניש למיחת בארעא דלא דידיה היא ולמיכל פירותיה: פירי נמי. נימא אחוי שטרך: היינו נסכא דר' אבא. דין זה דומה לאותו דין של נסכא דר' אבא ולא ללמוד מדר' אבא היו צריכין דמילתא דפשיטא היא שישלם הקרקע אחרי שאין לו שני עדים ודומיא בעלמא מדמינן אותו אי נמי לכך היו מדמין האי דינא לנסכא דר' אבא כי היכי דלהדר פירי עם ארעא דהוי כמי שיש עדים דאכל פירות דבלא עדים לא מהדרי פירות כדלעיל דרב נחמן אלא קרקע לחוד:
היכי

ואי טעין ואמר לפירות ירדתי כו'. פי' מתחלה כי א"ל מאי בעית בהאי ארעא אע"ג דבשעה שאכל היה בעל השדה יכול לעכב ולא היה נאמן לומר לפירות הורדתני מיהו כיון שכבר אכלו וזה בא להוציא נאמן לומר לפירות ירדתי וא"ת מאי איריא משום דלא חציף תיפוק ליה משום דתפיס מידי דהוה אמטלטלין שאין עשויין להשאיל ולהשכיר דאי אמר לקוחין הן בידי נאמן וי"ל דאיצטריך טעמא דלא חציף אם לקטן והניח ברשות שאינו שלו דלא תפיס בהן וא"ת כי לא אמר נמי לפירות ירדתי אלא דאייתי סהדי דאכל ג' שנים כי הך דשמעתין יהא נאמן בטענתיה במיגו דאי בעי אמר לפירות ירדתי לאו פירכא היא דאין זה מיגו שהרי בא לתבוע גם הקרקע ודוקא פירי דתרתי שנין הדרי אבל פירי דשנה שלישית לא הדרי דאי מהימן במאי דאמר שאכלה שלש שנין גם הקרקע תהיה שלו: **איזיל** ואיגדריה לדיקלא. פי' לגדור תמרים שעל הדקל דגדירה שייכא בתמרים ולא איירי בקציצת הדקל דא"כ ה"ל למימר ואיקטליה כדאמרי' בפ' כל הנשבעין (שבועות דף מו. וסם) אר"י האי מאן דנקיט נרגא ואמר איזיל ואקטליה לדיקלא דפלניא כו' ונראה לר"י ולריב"א שאם היה בא לקוץ הדקל עצמו לא היה נאמן דדוקא פירות הוא דעבדי אינשי דמזבני אבל דקל אין דרך בני אדם למכור לקוץ תדע דאמרי' בפ' החובל (ב"ק דף צג. וסם) שורי הרגת נטיעותי קצצת אתה אמרת לי להרגו אתה אמרת לי לקצצו פטור ופריך א"כ לא שבקת חיי לכל בריה וכו' משמע דאינו נאמן במיגו דאי בעי אמר מכרת לי לקצצו: **לא** חציף איניש. לאו משום דקאמר בפרהסיא איזיל ואיגדריה קאמר דלא חציף דאפילו ליקט בצנעא נמי שייך לא חציף איניש אם לא שלקחם דרך גניבה: **אי** הכי אפילו ארעא נמי. למאי דפרישית לעיל דאינו נאמן אלא בפירות שלקט כבר אבל מכאן ואילך אינו נאמן אפילו בפירות אע"ג דשטרא (ה) בפירי לא עבדי אינשי צריך לפרש אפילו ארעא אם הוא טוען שהקרקע שלו שלקחה לא יחזיר פירות שככר אכל אבל קרקע פשיטא שיחזיר דאינו נאמן להבא: **היינו** נסכא דר' אבא. לא אקרקע קאי דפשיטא שמחזיר הקרקע אחר שאין לו שנים עדים אלא השתא נמי אפירי מסיק וסבר השתא כאילו חד סהדא לאורועי למחזיק קאתי על הפירות שאכל ואינו יכול לכפור ולימא לא אכלתי וכאילו בא לחייבו שבועה על הפירות אם יכפור ויאמר לא אכלתי ואע"פ שמעיד שהחזיק בה ג' שנים כיון דאין אחר עמו הרי כאילו אינו מעיד על החזקה אלא נעשה עד אחד לתובעו פירות הכי ס"ד וטועה עד דאמר (ו) אביי

עין משפט
נר מצוה

מג א מיי' פט"ו מהל' טוען ונטען הלכה ו סמג עשין לה טוש"ע ח"מ סי' קמה סעיף ג:
מד ב מיי' שם פי"ג הל' ו סמג עשין לה טוש"ע ח"מ סי' קמט סעיף א:
מה ג מיי' שם ועי' בהשגות ובמגיד משנה טוש"ע שם ס"ג:
מו ד מיי' שם פ"ד הל' ח ופ"ד מהל' גזילה הלכה יד סמג עשין לה טוש"ע ח"מ סי' עה סעיף יג וסי' שפד סעיף ג וסעיף ד:

רבינו גרשום

הדרא ארעא והדרי פרי. דאכל למפרע כיון דלא אסהידו אתלת שנין הדרא ארעא והדרא פירי: אמר רב זביד. אמאי הדרי פירי והא אי טעין ואמר לפירות ירדתי שנתמשכנה לו במשכנת' דסוריא או אריס אני בה נאמן: האי מאן דנקיט מגלא ותובלא ולפי שהדקלים הם גבוהין כשרוצין ללקוט התמרים (א) מביאין מגל ארוך ומשימין תובלא שהוא סל בראש עץ ארוך ומגביהין הסל כנגד התמרים וחותכין אותם במגל ונופלים התמרים בסל כדי שלא יפלו התמרים לארץ ויתבקעו ויתפלחו: אי הכי. להיכא דאחזיק בקרקע תרתין שנין אמאי לא אמרינן לא חציף איניש דאכל ארעא דלא דידיה ולא מסלקינן ליה ומשני ארעא אמרי' ליה אחוי שטרך:

חשק שלמה
על רבינו גרשום

(א) עי' בערוך ערך תבליא:

מסורת הש"ס

א) לעיל דף לא., ב) [שם וש"נ], ג) [לעיל כט.], ד) לקמן דף לג: ה) [שם ליתא אלא בכל דברי רב יהודה הן ובכרב אלפס בסוגיין דף קעא. קעב. גריס מאי טעמא לא חציף וכו' וכ"ה ברב אלפס עוד בשבועות פ"ז דף שיד:], ו) שבועות דף לג: ודף מו.:

הגהות חו"י

(א) נ"ב לפי פירושו ר"ל דיש עדים כמה אכל: (ב) נ"ב לפי זה ק"ל באין עדים וטוען קניתי ממך ועדיין לא החזיק ג"ש ג"כ לא משלם פירי מש"ה לטעם שכתב הרמב"ם הובא בש"ע סימן קמה ס"ג ובש"ע שם:

הגהות הב"ח

(א) גמ' ותובלי' בידיה ואמר: (ב) שם דאמר ליה לחבריה: (ג) רשב"ם ד"ה ויש ספרים וכו' ולאו ליורשו והוא אינו ראוי ליורשו: (ד) ד"ה אמר רב חסדא וכו' עדות אבות כל"ל ותיבת זכות נמחק: (ה) תוס' ד"ה אי הכי וכו' דשטרא לפירי וכו' אפי' ארעא אפי' אם הוא: (ו) ד"ה היינו וכו' דאמר להו אביי וכו':

ליקוטי רש"י

זה אומר של אבותי. היה הקרקע והרי היא שלי וזה אומר כו'. מה לי לשקר. לזה המחזיק במאי דטוען דשל אבותיו וירשה מהם אי בעי אמר כו' והלכך בהאי מיגו מהימנינן ליה. מה לי לשקר במקום עדים. כלומר על ידי האי מיגו דמה לי לשקר לא יזכה בקרקע שהרי עדים מכחישים את דבריו שאומרים דשל אבותיו דאידך היא וגם החזקה אינה כלום שהרי אין עמה טענה כי אם טענת שקר [רשב"ם לעיל לא.]. מינך זבני ואכלתיה שני חזקה. ואבדתי שטרי ואתה מחית לי שאדהכי בשטרי [שם כט:] ולא מהדרתי בשטרי יותר [שם ל:]. והדרי פירי. של שתי שנים [שם כט.]. נסכא. חתיכה של כסף [קידושין ח: ובכי"ז כתובות קי:]. פלטא של כסף [ב"ק צו: ובכי"ז ב"מ כו.]. חתיכת כסף או זהב [רשב"ם לקמן קכח.]. חתיכת כסף מותך לשון (ישעיה מ) הפסל נסך חרש [שבועות לב:]. חתיכה אחת של זהב שקורין פלנ"א [מנחות קז.]. אין חטפי ודידי חטפי. שלי חטפתי שאתה גזלתו ממני [שבועות שם].

כֵּיוָן דְּאוֹדֵי אוֹדֵי – They reason that **once [the man] admitted** that he had been holding the tree unlawfully, **he has** perforce also **admitted** that he was consuming its produce illegally. Therefore, he must compensate Rav Idi for that produce.[1]

The Gemara discusses a topic mentioned earlier (31a) – the effectiveness of a *migo* when it conflicts with witnesses' testimony:

זֶה אוֹמֵר שֶׁל אֲבוֹתַי וְזֶה אוֹמֵר שֶׁל אֲבוֹתַי – Ownership of a property is disputed by two claimants. **This** one **says,** "The land was **my forefathers'** and I inherited it," **and this** other one **says,** "It was **my forefathers'** and I inherited it."

הַאי אַיְיתֵי סַהֲדֵי דַּאֲבָהָתֵיהּ הוּא – **This** one **produces witnesses** who testify **that [the land] belonged to his forefathers,**[2] וְהַאי אַיְיתֵי סַהֲדֵי דְּאָכַל שְׁנֵי חֲזָקָה – **and this** other one **produces witnesses** who testify **that he used** it **for the** three **years** required for the establishment **of a *chazakah*.** Which litigant's claim of inheritance is accepted?

A ruling:

אָמַר רַב חִסְדָּא – **Rav Chisda said:** מַה לוֹ לְשַׁקֵּר – **Why should [the second man] lie?** אִי בָּעֵי אָמַר לֵיהּ – **If he wanted** to gain possession of the land by lying, **he** could have **said to [his opponent],** מִינָּךְ זְבִינְתָּהּ – **"I bought [the land] from you,** וַאֲכַלְתִּיהָ שְׁנֵי חֲזָקָה – **and used it for the years** required for establishment **of *chazakah*.**" Since he could have won the case with that other claim, we believe him with his present claim that he inherited the land, although this is contradicted by witnesses.

A dissenting opinion:

אַבַּיֵּי וְרָבָא לָא סְבִירָא לְהוּ הָא דְּרַב חִסְדָּא – **Abaye and Rava,** however, **do not concur with this** ruling **of Rav Chisda.** מַה לִי לְשַׁקֵּר בִּמְקוֹם עֵדִים לָא אָמְרִינַן – **We do not say** that a litigant is believed by virtue of the principle of **"what** reason **is there for me to lie," in the face of witnesses** who testify to the contrary.[3]

Another case:

הַהוּא דְּאָמַר לֵיהּ לְחַבְרֵיהּ – There was **a certain man who said to his fellow:** מַאי בָּעֵית בְּהַאי אַרְעָא – **"What are you doing on this land?"** אָמַר לֵיהּ – **[The occupant] replied to [his challenger]:** מִינָּךְ זַבְנִי וַאֲכַלְתִּיהָ שְׁנֵי חֲזָקָה – **"I bought it from you, and I have used** it **for the** three **years** required for establishment **of *chazakah*,** so I do not need to produce a deed as proof." אֲזַל אַיְיתֵי סַהֲדֵי דַּאֲכָלָהּ תַּרְתֵּי שְׁנֵי – **[The occupant] went** out and **brought witnesses that he had used [the land] for *two* years,** but was unable to provide proof for the third year. Thus, he could not establish *chazakah.*

A ruling is issued:

אָמַר רַב נַחְמָן – **Rav Nachman said:** הַדְרָא אַרְעָא – **The land returns** to the previous owner, as the occupant cannot substantiate his claim, וְהַדְרֵי פֵּירֵי – **and the produce returns** as well. Since the occupant lacks a *chazakah*, the land is presumed to belong to the original owner. Consequently, the occupant must pay for the produce he consumed.[4]

The Gemara notes that there is a particular claim an occupant can advance that allows him to retain the produce, although he relinquishes the land:

אָמַר רַב זְבִיד – **Rav Zevid said:** אִם טָעַן וְאָמַר לְפֵירוֹת יָרַדְתִּי – **If,** when challenged by the original owner, **[the occupant] advanced a claim, saying, "I entered** the field **to** consume its **produce,** which I am entitled to as per my agreement with you,"[5] נֶאֱמָן – **he is believed.** Although he must vacate the land, he need not pay for the produce consumed.[6]

NOTES

1. [Abaye and Rava maintain that we do not regard the man's admission as being akin to a gift of the tree. Rather, since we now know that he had been consuming the produce unlawfully, he must compensate the owner for it.]

Our commentary has followed *Rashbam's* textual reading, according to which the man ultimately admitted that Rav Idi was the closer relative. However, if so, Rav Chisda's rationale is difficult to comprehend. Although the court originally allowed the man to seize the tree and use its produce, this was only due to lack of evidence. Now that the man has confessed to lying, what rationale is there not to require him to compensate Rav Idi for the consumed produce? (*Tos. HaRosh* cited by *Shitah Mekubetzes*; see *Pnei Shlomo* for an explanation of Rav Chisda's position according to *Rashbam*).

Rabbeinu Chananel, however, possessed a variant text (cited by *Rashbam* and *Tosafos*) which reads: *Ultimately, [Rav Idi] brought witnesses* who testified *that he was a relative.* That is, while they did not testify one way or the other as far as his opponent's relationship to the deceased, they testified that Rav Idi was related (although not necessarily the closest relative). Since Rav Idi's relationship was definite and his opponent's was doubtful, Rav Chisda awarded the date palm to Rav Idi. Now, as far as its fruits, there were no witnesses that the man had consumed them; however, he admitted that he had. Rav Chisda absolved him from paying for them because of a *migo*: The man is believed (regarding those dates which he had eaten) to say that he is the closer relative and therefore entitled to those dates, since if he were lying, he could simply have denied eating any at all. Abaye and Rava disputed this ruling and maintained that since the dates belong to whoever owns the tree, and the tree was awarded to Rav Idi, the produce must perforce be awarded to him also; the tree cannot be awarded to one litigant and its produce to the other (*Tosafos*).

2. They testify that the first man's father owned it until the day he died and did not sell it to the second man's father (*Rashbam*; cf. *Tosafos* above, 31a ד״ה מה).

3. [One of the basic rules of evidence is that testimony of a pair of witnesses is categorically believed over any other type of evidence.] Hence, a claim made by a litigant (such as, in this case, the occupant's claim that he inherited the land from his father) that is disputed by witnesses is rejected, even if it is backed by a *migo.* Although the *migo* militates for saying that he is telling the truth, we have no choice but to assume that he is lying, since witnesses contradict him (*Rashbam*).

4. This ruling – that he must pay for the produce he consumed – applies only where witnesses testify how much produce he consumed. However, if they do not know how much but he admits to consuming a certain amount, he is not required to compensate the challenger for the produce, since he asserts that the land (and therefore the produce) was his. Although he forfeits the land because he lacks a *chazakah*, he retains the produce on the strength of a *migo*: If he were lying, he would not have admitted that he consumed more than the minimum amount needed to effect a *chazakah*. This does not conflict with the ruling of Abaye and Rava above (in the case of the disputed date palm) wherein the man's admission that he was not the closer relative obligated him to pay for the tree's produce. In that case, he admitted that he was not entitled to the fruit. In this case, however, he claims that the land was his and that he therefore was consuming his own produce. True, he loses the land, but that is not because we conclude *definitively* that the land is not his. Rather, since he lacks a *chazakah* (and he does not possess a deed), the land is returned to the challenger because he is the *presumptive* owner (*Rashbam*).

5. He claimed that he was a sharecropper (who customarily received between one-quarter and one-half of the crop). Alternatively, he claimed that he bought the entire yield of the field for a specified term of years. Accordingly, he claimed that the produce he was seen consuming was his by right.

This claim – that he is entitled to the produce – may not be advanced if the occupant had initially claimed ownership of the land itself, for he would then be altering his previous claim, which is not allowed (above, 31a). Rather, Rav Zevid means that if this is the occupant's *original* claim, he is believed, and need not return any produce (see *Rashbam*).

6. This applies only to the produce the occupant has *already* consumed. However, his claim to be a sharecropper or to have purchased the field's yield does not entitle him to *continue* to consume it. Rather, once the original owner challenges him, the court will restrain him from continuing to use the field, unless he can produce witnesses or a deed to prove his claim (*Rashbam;* see note 8).

מג א מיי' פט"ו מהל' טוען הלכה י סמג עשין צה טוש"ע ח"מ סי' קמה סעיף ג:

מד ב מיי' שם פ"ט הל' ו סמג עשין צה טוש"ע ח"מ סי' קמ סעיף א:

מה ג מיי' שם ועי' בהשגות ובמגיד משנה טוש"ע שם ס"ב:

מו ד מיי' שם פ"ד הל' ח ופ"ד מהל' גזילה הלכה יד סמג עשין צה טוש"ע ח"מ סי' צ סעיף יג וסי' שסד סעיף ג וסעיף ד:

כיון דאודי אודי: (א) זה אומר של אבותי וזה אומר של אבותי האי אייתי סהדי דאבהתיה הוא והאי אייתי סהדי דאכל שני חזקה אמר רב חסדא (ג) מה לו לשקר אי בעי א"ל מינך זבינתה ואכלתיה שני חזקה אביי ורבא לא סבירא להו הא דרב חסדא מה לי לשקר במקום עדים לא אמרינן ההוא דאמר ליה לחבריה מאי בעית בהאי ארעא אמר ליה מינך זבני ואכלתיה שני חזקה אזל אייתי סהדי דאכלה תרתי שני (ג) אמר רב נחמן (א) הדרא ארעא והדרי פירי אמר רב זביד (ב) אם טוען ואמר לפירות ירדתי נאמן לאו מי (ד) אמר רב יהודה (ג) האי מאן דנקיט מגלא ותובליא (א) ואמר איזיל איגדריה לדיקלא דפלניא דזבניה ניהלי מהימן (ה) (אלמא) לא חציף איניש דגזר דיקלא דלאו דיליה הכא נמי לא חציף איניש למיכל פירי דלאו דיליה אי הכי ארעא נמי ארעא אמרינן ליה אחוי שטרך אי הכי פירי נמי שטרא לפירי לא עבדי אינשי ההוא דאמר (ב) לחבריה מאי בעית בהאי ארעא א"ל מינך זבנית ואכלתיה שני חזקה אייתי חד סהדא דאכלה תלת שני סבור רבנן קמיה דאביי למימר היינו נסכא דרבי אבא (ו) דההוא גברא דחטף נסכא מחבריה אתא לקמיה דרבי אמי הוה יתיב ר' אבא קמיה אייתי חד סהדא דמיחטף חטפא מיניה אמר ליה אין חטפי ודידי חטפי אמר רבי אמי היכי

רשב"ם

כיון דאודי. דשלא כדין החזיק עד עתה: אודי. ושלש פירות שאכל וכן הלכה: ויש ספרים שכתוב בהם אייתי רב אידי בר אבין סהדי דהוה קריב אוקמה רב חסדא בידיה. וגרס ר"ח פי' כן. א"ל רב חסדא למאי קסמכת דאכליניהו לפירי אהודאת פיו הא עד השתא הוא טוען דאנא קריבנא טפי והני סהדי דאייתית לא מסהדי דאנת קרוב (ג) ולאו ליורשה הוא אלא אינו ראוי ליורשה אלא מסהדי דאנת קרוב והאי לא ידעי ליה ומתוך שהוא יכול לומר לא אכלתי יכול לומר אין אכלי ודידי אכלי דאנא קריבנא טפי שאין עדים מכחישים אותו בכך הלכך לא מפקינן מיניה: (הג"ה. לא היא (אלא) שהודה שאכל הפירות אלא כדמפרש הרב לבסוף דלא נהירא ליה שהודה על אכילת הפירות אלא עדים היו שאכלו ולא היה יכול לכפור ושרא ליה מריה דמי זה שאמר שהודה על אכילת פירות שלא הודה אלא על הקרקע ומכל מקום מאי דאכל עד השתא לא מפקינן מיניה כיון דליכא עדים בדבר שרב אידי היה קרוב יותר אלא על פיו של זה ואביי ורבא סברי דכיון דלודי אודי שהרי הודאת בעל דין כמאה עדים ופיו מחייבו ממון ואי הוה גרסינן הא למאי לית ליה לרב חסדא הא סברא ויש לפרש בענין אחר ובדוחק ולכן לא כתבתיו. ע"כ) ולא נהירא לי דהא לא מוכח הא סוגיא דשמעתא שהודה על אכילת הפירות אלא עדים היו בדבר ולא היה יכול לכפור: האי אייתי סהדי דאבהתיה היא. על יום מותם ומעולם לא מכרו לאבותיו של זה השני: אמר רב חסדא מה לו לשקר. לזה שיש לו עדי חזקה במאי דטעין דשל אבותיו היא אי בעי הוה א"ל להאי שיש לו עדות (ד) זכות אבות מינך זבינתה ואכלתיה שני חזקה הלכך מיגו דמצי טעין הכי ויזכה בטענה זו והוא לא חשש לטעון כי טעין נמי של אבותיו אע"ג דמכחיש להו לעדים מהימן: מה לי לשקר במקום עדים לא אמרינן. כלומר כל טענה שאדם טוען כגון זה שאמר של אבותי ואתה רוצה לקיימה על ידי מה לי לשקר וטענה זו מכחשת עדים כי הכא לא מהימנינן ליה שהרי העדים מעידים שטענתו שקר והיאך תקיימנה על ידי מה לי לשקר הלא ודאי משקר הוא וחזקת השלש שנים אינה כלום דהויא לה חזקה שאין עמה טענה והכי הלכתא: אזיל ואייתי סהדי דאכלה תרתין שנין. ועדיין היה מחזר לבקש עדות של שנה שלישית ולא מצא: אמר רב נחמן הדרא ארעא. דבתרתין שנין לא הויא חזקה: והדרי פירי. של ב' השנים שאכל שלא כדין דהא לא טעין מעיקרא אריס הייתי ולפירות ירדתי דמהימנינן ליה כדלקמן דשטרא לפירי לא עבדי אינשי והני מילי דאיכא סהדי דאכלינהו לפירי (א) אבל אי ליכא סהדי דאכלינהו לפירי אלא בהודאת פיו והוא טוען דזבנתיה מינך ואכלתינהו לפירי דארעא ופירי דידי נינהו ארעא כיון דלית ליה ראיה בשטר ולא עדי חזקה הדרא למרה וחייב שבועת היסת על הפירות דזבנינהו מיניה דמיגו דמצי (ב) אמר לא אכלתי פירות כי אם מעט כגון עייל כורא ואפיק טפי מכורא דבהכי הוה חזקה כדלקמן כי אמר אכלי טובא ודידי אכלי מהימן דאין כאן מה לי לשקר במקום עדים שאין ידוע אם לקח קרקע זו מבעליה אם לא אלא לפי שאבד שטרו בתוך ג' שנים מפסיד ולא דמי להא דאביי ורבא דפליגי עליה דרב חסדא לעיל דהתם כיון דאיתבריר מילתא דרב אידי קרוב טפי הרי נודע שאין לו חלק בקרקע ופירות שאכל שלא כדין אכל ואפי' בהודאת פיו ליחייב: אמר רב זביד אי טעין כו'. מילתא באפי נפשה היא והכי קאמר אם מתחילה כשטענו בעל הקרקע מאי בעית בהאי ארעא אילו לא השיב לו מינך זבינתה אלא לפירות ירדתי כדין אריס למחצה לשליש ולרביע או שמכרת לי פירות עד עשר שנים: נאמן. במה שאכל למפרע ובשבועת היסת דזבינהו מיניה ואע"ג דאיכא סהדי דאכלינהו לפירי ושאין הקרקע קנוי לו דלא חציף איניש למיחת לארעא דחבריה ולמיכל פירי דחבריה בחנם כדמפרש ואזיל ומיהו מכאן ולהבא לא יאכל בלא עדים ושטר שקנה הפירות דא"כ כל אדם ירד לקרקע חבירו ויאכל פירותיו ויאמר לפירות ירדתי מאחר שלא נחוש לערעורו של בעל הקרקע: מגלא ותובלא. כלי גודרי תמרים המגל לגדור ותובלא חבל לעלות לדקל מרוב גובהו. וי"מ תובלא סל לקבל פירות: ואמר. בפניו: איזיל ואיגדריה לדיקלא דפלניא. כלומר אלקוט הפירות: מהימן. ושבקין ליה ב"ד ללקט הפירות בלא עדים ושטר אחרי שאין ידוע שהבעלים מוחין בדבר קודם לקיטה ואם אתא חבריה וטען להד"מ אחר שליקט האילן לית עליה אלא שבועת היסת אבל מקמי דליגדריה אתא מריה דדיקלא ואמר להד"מ לא מהימן מלקט עד דמייתי ראיה ודוקא בשטען מתחילה לפירות ירדתי נאמן במה שאכל כבר אבל אם מתחילה טען מינך זבינתה ואח"כ טען לפירות ירדתי שמכחיש דבריו הראשונים אינו טוען וחוזר וטוען: אי הכי אפי' ארעא נמי. כי טעין דזבינתה מינך ליהמנוהו בלא עדי חזקה דלא חציף איניש למיחת בארעא דלא דידיה היא ולמיכל פירותיה: פירי נמי. נימא אחוי שטרך: היינו נסכא דר' אבא. דין זה דומה לאותו דין של נסכא דר' אבא ולא ללמוד מדר' אבא היו צריכין דמילתא דפשיטא היא שישלם הקרקע אחרי שאין לו שני עדים ודומיא בעלמא מדמינן אותו אי נמי לכך היו מדמין האי דינא לנסכא דר' אבא כי היכי דלהדר פירי עם ארעא דהוי כמי שיש עדים דאכל פירות דבלא עדים לא מהדרי פירות כדלעיל דרב נחמן אלא קרקע לחוד:

היכי

תוספות

ואי טעין ואמר לפירות ירדתי כו'. פי' תחלה כי א"ל מאי בעית בהאי ארעא אע"ג דבשעה שאכל היה בעל השדה יכול לעכב ולא היה נאמן לומר לפירות הורדתני מיהו כיון שכבר אכלו וזה לא להוציא נאמן לומר לפירות ירדתי וא"ת מאי איריא משום דלא חציף תיפוק ליה משום דתפיס מידי דהוה אמטלטלין שאין עשויין להשאיל ולהשכיר דאי אמר לקוחין הן בידי נאמן וי"ל דאיצטריך טעמא דלא חציף אם לקטן והניח ברשות שאינו שלו דלא תפיס בהן וא"ת כי לא אמר נמי לפירות ירדתי אלא דאייתי סהדי דאכל ג' שנים כי הך דשמעתין יהא נאמן בטענתיה במיגו דאי בעי אמר לפירות ירדתי לאו פירכא היא דאין זה מיגו שהרי בא לתבוע גם הקרקע ודוקא פירי דתרתי שנין הדרי אבל פירי דשנה שלישית לא הדרי דאי מהימן במאי דאמר שאכלה שלש שנין גם הקרקע תהיה שלו:

איזיל ואיגדריה לדיקלא. פי' לגדור תמרים שעל הדקל דגדירה שייכא בתמרים ולא איירי בקציצת הדקל דא"כ ה"ל למימר ואיקטליה כדאמרי' בפ' כל הנשבעין (שבועות דף מו. ושם) אר"נ האי מאן דנקיט נרגא ואמר איזיל ואקטליה לדיקלא דפלניא כו' ונראה לר"י ולריב"ס שאם היה בא לקצוץ הדקל עצמו לא היה נאמן דדוקא פירות הוא דעבדי אינשי דמזבני אבל דקל אין דרך בני אדם למכור לקוץ תדע דאמרי' בפ' החובל (ב"ק דף צג. ושם) שורי הרגת נטיעותי קצצת אתה אמרת לי להרגו אתה אמרת לי לקצצו פטור ופריך א"כ לא שבקת חיי לכל בריה וכו' משמע דאינו נאמן במיגו דאי בעי אמר מכרת לי לקצצו: לא חציף איניש. לאו משום דקאמר בפרהסיא איזיל ואיגדריה קאמר דלא חציף דאפילו ליקט בצנעא נמי שייך לא חציף איניש אם לא שלקחם דרך גניבה:

אי הכי אפילו ארעא נמי. למאי דפרישית לעיל דאינו נאמן אלא בפירות שלקט כבר אבל מכאן ואילך אינו נאמן אפילו בפירות אע"ג דשטרא (ה) בפירי לא עבדי אינשי צריך לפרש אפילו ארעא אם הוא טוען שהקרקע שלו שלקחה לא יחזיר פירות שכבר אכל אבל קרקע פשיטא שיחזיר דאינו נאמן להבא: היינו נסכא דר' אבא. לא אקרקע קאי דפשיטא שמחזיר הקרקע אחר שאין לו שנים עדים אלא השתא נמי אפירי מסיק וסבר השתא כאילו חד סהדא לאורועי למחזיק קאתי על הפירות שאכל ואינו יכול לכפור ולימא לא אכלתי וכאילו בא לחייבו שבועה על הפירות אם יכפור ויאמר לא אכלתי ואע"פ שמעיד שהחזיק בה ג' שנים כיון דאין אחר עמו הרי כאילו אינו מעיד על החזקה אלא נעשה עד אחד לתובעו פירות הכי ס"ד וטועה עד דאמר (ו) אביי

רבינו גרשום

הדרא ארעא והדרי פרי. דאכל למפרע כיון דלא אסהידו אתלת שנין הדרא ארעא והדרא פירי: אמר רב זביד. אמאי הדרי פירי והא אי טעין ואמר לפירות ירדתי שנתמשכנה לו במשכנתא דסורא או אריס אני בה נאמן: האי מאן דנקיט מגלא ותובליא ולפי שהדקלין הם גבוהין כשרוצין ללקוט התמרים (א) מביאין מגל ארוך ומשימין תובליא שהוא סל בראש עץ ארוך ומגביהין הסל כנגד התמרים וחותכין אותם במגל ונופלים התמרים בסל כדי שלא יפלו התמרים לארץ ויתבקעו ויתפלחו: אי הכי. להיכא דאחזיק בקרקע תרתין שנין אמאי לא אמרינן לא חציף איניש דאכל ארעא דלא דידיה ולא מסלקינן ליה ומשני ארעא אמרי' ליה אחוי שטרך:

חשק שלמה על רבינו גרשום

א) עי' בערוך ערך תבלא:

מסורת הש"ס

א) לעיל דף לא. ב) [שם וש"נ], ג) [לעיל כט.], ד) לקמן דף לו., ה) [שם ליתא אלא הכל דברי רב יהודה הן וכרב אלפס בסוגיין דף קעד. קעה. גרים מאי טעמא לא חציף וכו' וכ"כ רב אלפס עוד בשבועות פ"ז דף שיד:], ו) שבועות דף לב: ודף מז. :

הגהות חו"י

(א) נ"ב לפי פירושו ר"ל דיש עדים כמה אכל: (ב) נ"ב לפי זה כ"ה באין עדים וטוען קניתי ממך ועדיין לא החזיק ג"ש ג"כ לא משלם הרמב"ם מש"כ לטעם שכתב הרמב"ם הובא בש"ע סימן קמה ס"ג ובש"כ שם:

הגהות הב"ח

(א) גמ' ותובלי' בידיה ואמר: (ב) שם דאמר ליה לחבריה: (ג) רשב"ם ד"ה ויש ספרים וכו' ולאו ליורשו והוא אינו ראוי ליורשו: (ד) ד"ה אמר רב חסדא וכו' עדות אבות כצ"ל ותיבת זכות נמחק: (ה) תוס' ד"ה אי הכי וכו' דשטרא לפירי וכו' אפי' ארעא אם הוא: (ו) ד"ה היינו וכו' דאמר להו אביי וכו':

ליקוטי רש"י

זה אומר של אבותי. היה הקרקע והרי היא שלי וזה אומר כו'. מה לו לשקר. לזה המחזיק במאי דטוען דשל אבותיו וירשה מהם אי בעי אמר כו' והלכך בהאי מיגו מהימנינן ליה. מה לי לשקר במקום עדים. כלומר על ידי האי מיגו דמה לי לשקר לא יזכה בקרקע שהרי עדים מכחישים את דבריו שאומרים דשל אבותיו דאידך היא וגם החזקה אינה כלום שהרי אין עמה טענה כי אם טענת שקר [רשב"ם לעיל לא.]. מינך זבני ואכלתיה שני חזקה. ולאדני שטרי ואתה לא תחזיק בי לשאבד בשטרי [שם כט:]. ולא מחזקתי בשטרי יותר [שם ל:]. והדרי פירי. של שתי שנים [שם כט.]. נסכא. חתיכה של כסף [קידושין ח: וכעי"ז כתובות קי:]. פלטא של כסף [ב"ק צו: וכעי"ז ב"מ כו.]. חתיכת כסף או זהב [רשב"ם לקמן קכח.]. חתיכת כסף מותך לשון (ישעיה מ) הפסל נסך חרש [שבועות לב:]. חתיכה אחת של זהב שקורין פלט"א [מנחות קז.]. אין חטפי ודידי חטפי. שלי חטפתי שאתה גזלתו ממני [שבועות שם].

Rav Zevid explained the basis for his ruling: הַאי מַאן לָאו מִי אָמַר רַב יְהוּדָה – **Did not Rav Yehudah say:** דְּנָקִיט מַגְלָא וְתוּבַלְיָא – **Someone who takes a scythe and a rope** in his hands,[7] וְאָמַר – **saying,** אֵיזִיל אִיגְדְּרֵיהּ לְדִיקְלָא דִּפְלַנְיָא – **"I am going to harvest** the produce of **the palm tree belonging to so-and-so,** דִּזְבַנְיֵהּ נִיהֲלִי – **for he has sold [the produce] to me,"** מְהֵימַן – **is believed,** and the court allows him to do so, although he offers no proof that he in fact purchased it,[8] (אלמא) לֹא חָצִיף אִינִישׁ דְּגָזַר דִּיקְלָא דְּלָאו דִּילֵיהּ – because **a person is not so impudent as to harvest another's palm?** Since he is so bold, we assume that he must be telling the truth.[9] הָכָא נַמִּי – **Here as well,** regarding the occupant's claim that he was entitled to the produce, לֹא חָצִיף אִינִישׁ לְמֵיכַל פֵּירֵי דְּלָאו דִּילֵיהּ – we assume that **a person is not so impudent as to consume another's produce,** and he therefore must be telling the truth.

The Gemara asks:

אִי הָכִי – **If this is so,** that a person would not be so bold as to consume another's produce, אַרְעָא נַמִּי – even if the occupant claims **the land as well,** he should be believed, although he has no *chazakah!* The mere fact that he has consumed the land's produce should prove his claim. Why, then, is it ever necessary for an occupant to resort to *chazakah* to substantiate his claim?[10]

The Gemara answers:

אַרְעָא אָמְרִינַן לֵיהּ אַחְוֵי שְׁטָרָךְ – If he claims the **land, we say to him, "Show** us **your deed!"** The fact that he cannot produce a deed that records his purchase indicates that his claim is false, despite his bold consumption of the produce. Therefore, he must produce witnesses to his *chazakah* to prove his claim.

The Gemara asks:

אִי הָכִי – **If so,** פֵּירֵי נַמִּי – **also** in an instance where the occupant claims only **the produce** and not the land (as in Rav Zevid's ruling), his failure to produce a deed should disprove his claim. – ? –

The Gemara answers:

שְׁטָרָא לְפֵירֵי לֹא עָבְדֵי אִינְשֵׁי – **People do not** ordinarily **execute documents with regard to** purchase of **produce.** Thus, failure to produce a document in such an instance proves nothing. When purchasing land, however, a document is usually prepared, and, unless a *chazakah* is established, the occupant's failure to produce such a document disproves his claim.

Another case:

הַהוּא דְּאָמַר לְחַבְרֵיהּ – **A certain man** once **said to his fellow:** מַאי בָּעֵית בְּהַאי אַרְעָא – **"What are you doing on this land?"** אָמַר לֵיהּ – **[The occupant] said to [the challenger]:** מִינָּךְ זְבַנִית – **"I bought it from you,** וַאֲכַלְתִּיהָ שְׁנֵי חֲזָקָה – **and I have used it for the** three **years** required for establishment **of** ***chazakah."*** אַיְיתִי חַד סָהֲדָא דַּאֲכָלָהּ תְּלָת שְׁנֵי – **[The occupant] produced one witness that he had used [the land] for three years,** but could not find a second witness to corroborate the claim. Thus, he was forced to vacate the property.

A discussion ensued as to whether the occupant should be required to pay for produce he had consumed during the three years, as the single witness had testified. Some scholars drew a parallel between this case and a classic decision rendered by R' Abba:[11]

סְבוּר רַבָּנָן קַמֵּיהּ דְּאַבַּיֵי לְמֵימַר – **The Sages** who studied **before Abaye thought to say** הַיְינוּ נִסְכָּא דְּרַבִּי אַבָּא – **that this** case **is similar to** a famous decision rendered by R' Abba known as "the case of **R' Abba's silver** [12] **ingot."** What were the details of the case, and what was R' Abba's famous decision? דְּהַהוּא גַּבְרָא דַּחֲטַף נִסְכָּא מֵחַבְרֵיהּ – **For** there was **a certain man who snatched a silver ingot from his fellow.** אֲתָא לְקַמֵּיהּ דְּרַבִּי אַמֵּי – **[The case] came before R' Ami** for judgment, הֲוָה יָתֵיב רַבִּי אַבָּא קַמֵּיהּ – and **R' Abba was sitting before [R' Ami]** at the time.[13] אַיְיתִי חַד סָהֲדָא דְּמִיחְטַף חַטְפָא מִינֵּיהּ – **[The plaintiff] produced one witness that [the defendant] had snatched [the ingot] from him.** אָמַר לֵיהּ – **[The defendant] said to [the plaintiff]:** אִין חַטְפִי – **"Yes, I did** indeed **snatch it,** וְדִידִי חַטְפִי – **but it was my** ingot that **I snatched!"**[14]

R' Ami mentioned several possible decisions, but dismissed them one by one:

אָמַר רַבִּי אַמֵּי – **R' Ami said:**

NOTES

7. These are tools typically used to harvest dates. The scythe is for the actual cutting and the rope is used to scale the tall date palms (*Rashbam*).

8. That is, the court will allow him to harvest without proof as long as the tree's owner does not object (or is out of town). If the owner comes later and denies having made an agreement allowing the man to harvest the dates, he cannot force the harvester to pay for those he already consumed. However, he may not *continue* to reap the tree's produce without proving his claim. This is because a man would hesitate to illegally consume his fellow's produce only if he fears being stopped by the owner's protest. Since the court will remove him from the property if the owner protests, most people would not risk the disgrace of being ousted from the land. But if the law were to allow a man to continue harvesting a field's produce even after the land's owner protests, the harvester might brazenly enter his fellow's field and consume his produce, confident in the knowledge that the court will believe his false claim despite the owner's objection (see *Rashbam* and *Nimukei Yosef*).

9. *Tosafos* (ד״ה לא) maintain that although Rav Yehudah, in formulating his case, mentions that the man publicly stated that he was going to harvest the dates, the ruling holds true even if the harvester did so quietly and without fanfare, as the "impudence" refers to the taking of another's property, not the announcement of intent. Therefore, as long as the harvesting was not done in an overly secretive manner (which would suggest thievery), the harvester is assumed to have proceeded lawfully (cf. *Ramban*).

10. This explanation of the Gemara's question follows *Rashbam. Tosafos,* however, maintain that the Gemara cannot mean to ask that we should allow an occupant to continue occupying the land even in the face of the original owner's protest, because, as explained in notes 6 and 8, the logic of "a person is not so impudent etc." can only be used to permit the harvester to retain back produce, not to continue to harvest new produce. Accordingly, we cannot use this reasoning to allow the man to continue to occupy the land. Rather, the Gemara means to ask why it is that someone who claims to have purchased the land, but cannot prove his *chazakah,* must pay for the produce he consumed (as Rav Nachman ruled above). Why should the reasoning of Rav Zevid — that a man would not be so brazen as to consume his fellow's produce — not be sufficient proof to allow him to retain the produce, although he must relinquish the land? Others, however, maintain that continuing to remain on the land is not comparable to taking future yield. Rather, the occupant is *retaining* the land and this is analogous to retention of harvested produce. Thus, the Gemara asks that one should be believed to retain land that he already occupies (*Rashba,* see also *Ramban*).

11. There was no doubt about the law regarding the land itself — since the occupant could not produce two witnesses to his *chazakah,* he obviously could not retain the land. The question was only whether he was required to compensate the original owner for the produce consumed. It was this point that the scholars endeavored to clarify by their analogy to the case of R' Abba's silver bar (*Rashbam* in his second explanation, to which the other Rishonim subscribe; cf. *Rashbam's* first explanation).

12. *Rashi* to *Shevuos* 32b ד״ה נסבא.

13. The implication is that R' Abba was a disciple of R' Ami. However, see *Tosafos* below, 34a ד״ה הוה, who cite passages from elsewhere in the Talmud that seem to indicate otherwise.

14. I snatched it from you, because you had previously stolen it from me (*Rashi* to *Shevuos* 32b ד״ה חטפי).

הֵיכִי נִידַיְינוּהָ דַּיָּינֵי לְהַאי דִּינָא – How are judges to judge this case?[1] **לִישַׁלֵּם – Shall** they require that **he pay** for the ingot?[2] **לֵיכָּא תְּרֵי סַהֲדֵי** – But **there are not two witnesses** who testify that he snatched it, so his claim is buttressed by a *migo* that he could have denied doing so.[3] **לִיפְטְרֵיהּ** – Shall they then **exempt him** from paying, based on this *migo*? **אִיכָּא חַד סַהֲדָא – But there is one witness** who testifies that he did snatch the ingot, and if he were to contradict the witness, he would be required to swear.[4] Thus, his *migo* is weakened.[5] **לִישַׁתַּבַּע – Shall he swear** that he did not snatch it, to deflect the witness' testimony? **הָא אָמַר מִיחְטָף חַטְפָהּ – But he** himself **admits that he *did* snatch it, וְכֵיוָן דְּאָמַר דְּחַטְפָהּ – and since he admits that he snatched it, הֲוָה לֵיהּ כְּגַזְלָן** – he cannot possibly swear that he did not;[6] **he is as** unfit to take this oath as is **a robber** to take any oath.[7] Thus, concluded R' Ami, there is no simple adjudication to this litigation.[8]

R' Abba offered his opinion of what the decision should be: **אָמַר (להו) רַבִּי אַבָּא – R' Abba said to [R' Ami]: הָוֵי מְחוּיָּב שְׁבוּעָה שֶׁאֵינוֹ יָכוֹל לִישָּׁבַע – [The snatcher] is** in the position of a man who is **obligated to take an oath, but is unable to do so.**[9] **וְכָל הַמְחוּיָּב שְׁבוּעָה שֶׁאֵינוֹ יָכוֹל לִישָּׁבַע מְשַׁלֵּם – And** the law is that **anyone who is obligated to take an oath which he is unable to take must pay.** Thus, since the snatcher cannot swear that he did not snatch the ingot, he must return it.[10] The scholars of Abaye's academy drew an analogy from this case to the case before them. That is, since one witness testified that the occupant had used the land, he should be required to swear to refute the charge. However, since he did not deny the charge, he could not swear. Therefore, he should pay for the produce he consumed.[11]

NOTES

1. Three slightly different scenarios exist, all of which would have been relatively simple to judge: (a) If two witnesses had testified that the defendant had snatched the ingot, he would be forced to return it, for one may not simply snatch an item from his fellow and claim it to be his. This stems from the basic legal presumption that the owner of an object is the one in whose possession it is found. Thus, anyone who snatches it from him is deemed a robber, unless he can prove his claim. (b) If no witness had testified to the snatching, the ingot would remain in the possession of the snatcher, as his claim that he snatched back his own ingot would be bolstered by a *migo*: Had he wished to lie, he could have simply denied grabbing it and his possession of it would have led the court to presume it to be his. (c) If one witness had testified to the snatching, but the defendant had denied doing so, he would be required to take an oath to refute the witness' testimony, for although the testimony of a single witness is insufficient for the court to obligate the defendant to pay, it does require him to swear to refute the testimony. Any of the foregoing scenarios would therefore not have posed a problem. The complexity in this instance stemmed from the fact that there was one witness to the snatching, and that instead of denying the charge, the defendant sidestepped it by admitting that he had snatched the ingot and claiming that it was his by right (*Rashbam*).

2. Since he admits to snatching it, he may not legally retain it, because, as explained in the previous note, the holder of an object is presumed to be its owner (*Rashbam*).

3. Because, as explained in note 1, if the snatcher would have denied taking it, he would have been believed to retain it.

4. Because the law is that a single witness' testimony obligates the defendant to swear to support his claim. If he refuses to swear, he must pay.

5. [The logic of *migo* is predicated on the assumption that a liar would have opted for the strongest claim available to him. Accordingly, if there is any rationale whatsoever for which the defendant might have preferred his present claim, the basis of the *migo* is undermined.] In our case, had the defendant denied snatching the ingot, he would have had to swear to deflect the witness who testifies that he did. Thus, the defendant may well have chosen his present claim (that the ingot he snatched was his) in order to avoid the oath. Hence, his *migo* is weakened (*Rashbam*).

6. If he were to swear that he did not snatch the ingot he would be believed, as a solitary witness' testimony can be deflected by the defendant's oath to the contrary. But since he admits to the truth of the testimony, he cannot possibly swear to refute it. The only oath that the defendant could possibly take would be to affirm that the ingot was originally his. But this would be ineffective, because we do not simply concoct an oath to conform to the defendant's claim. To be effective, an oath must be imposed by law. Here, the only imposed oath is one that refutes the witness' testimony. No other oath will do (*Rashbam*).

7. [This explanation of the analogy to the robber follows *Rashbam's* elucidation and that of *Rashi* to *Shevuos* 32b ד״ה כיון and 47a ד״ה לישתבע. Others explain the Gemara to mean that once the defendant admits to snatching from another, he is presumed a robber and his oath is inadmissible (see *Mahadura Basra* of *Maharsha*). Still others altogether delete this analogy from the text (*Ritva*).]

8. Because on the one hand, we have the unrefuted testimony of one witness that he snatched the ingot, and there is nothing to support the snatcher's claim that he was entitled to do so. This militates for requiring him to pay. On the other hand, one could argue that a single witness' testimony is viable only where the defendant is able to take the oath that the witness imposes. But where he cannot, the witness serves no function and is ignored. Now, if we indeed ignore the witness, all we have to work with is the defendant's own admission that he snatched the ingot. But logically, if we believe him that he snatched it, we should also believe him that he was entitled to do so. This reasoning militates for exempting him from paying (*Kehilas Yaakov Bava Basra siman* 23; cf. *Rivam* cited in *Tosafos*). Thus, R' Ami was unsure of how to rule.

As explained in note 5, the snatcher's *migo* was undermined, because had he denied snatching, he would have been required to swear to support his claim. But, the Rishonim ask, why can the *migo* not be salvaged by his taking an oath to support his *present* claim that the ingot he snatched was his? By doing this, the defendant would demonstrate that he did not advance his present claim just to avoid swearing, because he obviously is not afraid to swear. This would effectively reinstate the *migo,* because now there is no logical reason for him to have admitted to snatching the ingot rather than deny it. We should therefore assume that he is telling the truth when he asserts that he was entitled to snatch it.

Some Rishonim answer that he might still prefer his present claim, because it does not involve contradicting anyone. Claiming that he did not snatch the ingot, on the other hand, necessitates denying the witness' charge that he did. Although he would be believed, he may not be bold enough to brazenly confront the witness. Thus, his *migo* is indeed weakened (see *Ri* quoted by *Tosafos*; cf. *Tosafos* themselves and other *Rishonim,* who question this answer and offer other solutions).

9. That is, the only way he can hope to retain the ingot is to take the oath imposed upon him by the witness (*Rashi* to *Shevuos* 32b ד״ה הוה). But he cannot possibly do this, because he concurs with the testimony.

10. As explained in note 8, one could argue that a solitary witness' testimony is meaningful only where he imposes an oath that the defendant is able to take. But where the defendant admits to the witness' charge, and is therefore unable to swear, the testimony is useless and is therefore disregarded. R' Abba states that this is not the case. Rather if, for any reason at all, the defendant does not swear to refute the witness, the witness' testimony is accepted as the absolute truth. In the case of the ingot, then, since the defendant cannot swear to refute the witness, the court fully accepts the witness' testimony that the defendant snatched the ingot. Thus, one cannot argue, as suggested in note 8, that the defendant's admission cannot be used against himself, because we need not rely on the defendant for our knowledge that he snatched; we know it from the unchallenged testimony of the witness! Hence, the snatcher is not believed to claim that he was entitled to snatch the ingot, and he must pay (*Kehilas Yaakov* ibid.).

11. Abaye's disciples likened the case before them to that of R' Abba. That is, three scenarios similar to those mentioned above (note 1) can be constructed here: Two witnesses to the occupant's *chazakah* would allow him to retain the land; no witnesses at all would result in the land reverting to the previous owner; one witness to the occupant's consumption coupled with the occupant's denial would allow the occupant to swear to refute the charge. Here, however, the occupant admitted to the witness' testimony that he had used the land. [Thus, he is in the category of one who is obligated to swear but cannot, with the result that he must pay for the produce] (*Rashbam*).

היכי נידיינוה דייני להאי דינא לישלם ליכא תרי סהדי ליפטריה איכא חד סהדא לישתבע הא אמר מיחטף חטפה וכיון דאמר דחטפה הוה ליה כגזלן אמר (א) להו רבי אבא [א] הוי מחויב שבועה שאינו יכול לישבע וכל המחויב שבועה שאינו יכול לישבע משלם א"ל אביי [ב] מי דמי התם סהדא לאורועי קאתי (א) כי אתי אחרינא בהדיה מפקינן לה מיניה הכא לסיועי קא אתי כי אתא אחרינא מוקמינן לה בידיה אלא אי דמיא הא דרבי אבא [ג] לחד סהדא ולתרתי שני ולפירי: ההוא

היכי לידיינוה דייני להאי דינא. שאילו היו שנים מעידים אותו שחטף היינו מחייבין אותו לשלם שאין אדם נאמן לחטוף דבר מיד חבירו ולומר שלי אני חוטף אא"כ יש לו עדים דהעמד ממון על חזקתו וזה המוחזק בו אין אדם יכול להוציאו ממנו בלא ראיה והחוטף ממנו גזלן גמור ואי נמי לא היה כאן עד אחד שחטף כי אמר נמי חטפי ודידי חטפי מהימן מיגו דאי הוה בעי הוה אמר לא חטפי שהרי אנו רואים אותו מוחזק בממון אי נמי כי איכא חד (ב) שחטף אילו היה זה מכחישו לומר לא חטפתי היה נשבע שלא חטף להכחיש העד דעד אחד קם הוא לשבועה ובג' דרכים הללו היה הדין פשוט אבל הכא דאיכא עד אחד שחטף וזה אינו מכחישו אלא מודה שודאי חטף ודידיה חטף היכי לידיינו דייני להאי דינא: **לישלם.** דהא מודי שחטף ולא כל הימנו של חוטף לומר שלי חטפתי דהעמד ממון על חזקתו: **ליכא תרי סהדי.** דחטף ובמיגו דאי בעי למימר לא חטפתי מהימן נמי למימר דידי חטפי: **ליפטריה.** (ג) משום האי מיגו איכא חד סהדא ואי אמר לא חטפי הוה בעי אישתבועי להכחיש את העד: **לישתבע.** את השבועה שהעד מחייבו אינו יכול דהא מודי דחטף והעד מחייבו לישבע שלא חטף להכחיש את העד דהכי משמע קרא (דברים יט) לא יקום עד אחד באיש לכל עון ולכל חטאת וגו' לשלם ממון שהוא כופר והעד מחייבו לא יקום אבל קם הוא לשבועה להכחיש את העד שלא חטף בממון זה וגבי הך שבועה פסול (ד) כגזלן אבל כל שבועות דהא לית ליה למימר לישתבע דדידיה חטף שאין זו שבועה המוטלת עליו ולמפטריה בלא כלום אי אפשר שהרי הורע כחו של מיגו: **א"ל רבי אבא הוה ליה.** האי חוטף כו' וה"נ איכא למימר כי האי גוונא כי הוו תרי סהדי דאכלה שני חזקה מוקמינן לה בידא דלוקח. ליכא סהדי דאכלה שני חזקה מפקינן לה מיניה ומהדרינן למרה. איכא חד סהדא דאכלה שלש שנים לישתבע דעד אחד לשבועה קם אפי' לא הוה קרקע לא משבעינן ליה על מאי דאסהיד סהדא דלא כפר ליה אלא מודי ליה דאכל וטוען אין אכלי ודידי אכלי: **א"ל אביי מי דמי.** לדרבי אבא: **התם.** בדר' אבא הוה חד סהדא לאורועי לחוטף קאתי דהא מסהיד ביה שחטף והורע כחו של מיגו דחוטף ומחייבו שבועה ומתוך שלא יכול לישבע משלם דאילו אתא חד סהדא שמעיד כמותו שראוהו שחטף מפקינן לה מיניה דחוטף ולא תועיל לו שבועה אפי' אם יוכל לישבע: **הכא.** בדין קרקע זה ההוא סהדא לסיועי (ה) ביה קאתי שמעיד שהחזיק בה שלש שנים וזכה בה דאי איכא חד סהדא אחרינא עם זה מוקמינן ליה בידא דמחזיק והיאך תאמר שעל יד עד זה יתחייב שבועה ומתוך שאינו יכול לישבע משלם והרי לא בא להורע כחו ומ"מ זה יפסיד הקרקע שהרי אין לו עדי חזקה: **אלא אי דמיא** (ו) **לנסכא דרבי אבא לחד סהדא ולתרתין שנין ולפירי.** כגון ראובן דתבעיה לשמעון וא"ל גזלתה לארעאי ואכלת פירותיה שנתים וא"ל שמעון זבנתה ניהלי ולית (ז) לשמעון עדי חזקה דדינא הוא לאהדורי ארעא למרה מכיון דלית ליה עדי חזקה ולפירי משתבע דבזביניה אכלתינון דקי"ל הפה שאסר הוא שהתיר ואע"ג דמהדר לה לארעא פירי לא מהדר דהא ליכא סהדי דאכיל הפירות ומיגו דיכול למימר לא אכלי כלל יכול למימר נמי אכלי בזביני ולית ליה עלה אלא שבועה אבל אי איכא סהדי דאכל פירי תרתין שנין מחייבין ליה להדורי אפי' פירי כרב נחמן דאמר הדרא ארעא והדרי פירי ואייתי ראובן חד סהדא דאכל פירי תרתין שנין וכגון שמעיד שלא אכל כי אם ב' שנים דלאו לסיועי לשמעון קאתי אמר שמעון אין אכלי ודידי אכלי שקניתי הקרקע והפירות אפס לא נזהרתי בשטרי הא הוא דאיכא לדמויי לדרבי אבא דאמרינן היכי לידיינו דייני להאי דינא ניחייביה להדורי פירי ליכא תרי סהדי דאכלינהו ואי משום דאודי הא טעין ואמר דידי אכלי וכה"ג ליכא הודאה לחיוביה ניפטריה במיגו הא איכא חד סהדא דאמר דאכלינהו לפירי תרתין שנין ואינו יכול לכפור בדברי העד לישבע לשקר ניחייביה שבועה בעד אחד דאי הוו תרוייהו מחייבי ליה ממונא וכ"מ ששנים מחייבין אותו ממון אחד מחייב אותו שבועה כי אמרי' עד אחד לשבועה אתי היכא דקא כפר במאי דמסהיד (ח) סהדא חד הוא דמשתבע דלא היו דברים מעולם אבל הכא הא קא מודי דאכל אלא טוען דידי אכלי:

אביי דלא דמי לדרבי אבא דהכא חד סהדא לסיועי קאתי בין לקרקע בין לפירות שהרי הוא מעיד שגם הקרקע שלו והא דאמרינן במסקנא אלא אי דמיא (ט) לדרבי אבא לחד סהדא לתרתין שנין ולפירי לא הוה צריך למינקט ולפירי כיון דעד השתא נמי לא איירי אלא בפירי אלא אגב תרתין שנין נקט נמי לחד סהדא ולפירי:

הוי מחויב שבועה ואינו יכול לישבע. שהרי מודה וא"ת וליהמניה בשבועה במאי דאמר דידי חטפי במיגו דאי בעי אמר לא חטפי וכי תימא דהא לא חשיב מיגו דהא אם אמר לא חטפי היה חייב שבועה דאורייתא לא היא דהא אמר בהמוכר את הבית (לקמן דף ע. ושם) המפקיד אצל חבירו בשטר נאמן לומר החזרתיו לך בשבועה מיגו דאי בעי אמר נאנסו דהוי נאמן בשבועה אע"ג דנאנסו איכא שבועה דאורייתא ומיהו לפי' ר"ת דפירש שבועה דנאנסו דהתם היא מדרבנן דלא מיחייב שבועה דאורייתא אפילו בנאנסו אלא היכא דאיכא הודאה במקצת אתי שפיר וליכא למימר נמי דהאי לא חשיב מיגו דלא הוה חציף למימר לא חטפי להכחיש את העד או משום שירא שלא יפסלוהו לעדות העד ובעל הנסכא כדאמר בפרק זה בורר (סנהדרין דף כה.) דבעל דבר מהימן למימר [לדידי אוחפן ברביתא] דהא משמע דאי לאו דעד מחייבו שבועה היה פטור והיינו על כרחך במיגו דאי לאו מיגו לאו כל כמיניה למימר דידי חטפי דהא כי איכא תרי סהדי משלם ואינו נאמן לומר דידי חטפי ואומר ר"י דודאי אם לא היה העד מחייבו שבועה היה נאמן במיגו דאי בעי אמר לא חטפי שיכול להעיז פניו להכחיש את העד בלא שבועה אבל השתא דמחייבו שבועה לא מהימן בשבועה ע"י מיגו (י) שהיה יכול להעיז פניו ולישבע בדבר שהעד מכחישו אבל קשה אי ליכא מיגו מאי טעמא דרב ושמואל דפליגי בפרק כל הנשבעין (שבועות דף מז. ושם) ארבי אבא ופטרי בנסכא דלית להו מתוך שאינו יכול לישבע משלם והשתא אמאי פטרי והא פשיטא דאינו נאמן לומר דידי חטפי בלא מיגו כדפרישי' לעיל לכך נראה כמו שפי' ריב"ם דודאי הוי מיגו ולהכי פטרי רב ושמואל דנאמן בשבועה במיגו דאי בעי אמר לא חטפי ור' אבא סבר אע"ג דאית ליה מגו חייב דכיון דאיכא אחד המחייבו שבועה מן התורה כן הוא הדין שישבע להכחיש את העד או ישלם ואין מועיל לו מיגו ליפטר וא"ת ור' אבא היכי מפיק לה בפ' כל הנשבעין (שם) מדכתיב שבועת ה' תהיה בין שניהם ולא בין היורשין דאמר ליה מנה לאבא ביד אביך ואמר חמשין ידענא וחמשין לא ידענא דדייק התם מדאיצטריך קרא למיפטר יורשים ש"מ באביו כה"ג מיחייב אלמא מחויב שבועה ואינו יכול לישבע משלם והיכי דייק מינה אנסכא התם ודאי משלם דליכא מיגו אבל הכא דאיכא מיגו מנא לן דמשלם ונראה לר"י דרבי אבא לא הוי טעמיה מקרא אלא מסברא בעלמא כדמפרש והא דקאמר התם כוותיה דר' אבא מסתברא מדתני ר' אמי שבועת ה' תהיה בין שניהם ולא בין היורשין קרא למיפטר יורשים אתא ולא לחייב האב והא דקאמר התם רב ושמואל האי שבועת ה' וגו' מאי דרשי ביה ה"ק כיון דבאב בכה"ג פטרי אמאי איצטריך קרא למיפטר יורשין וצ"ל דהא דאמרי' בהכותב (כתובות דף פה. ושם) גבי אבימי בריה דר' אבהו דהוו מסקי ביה זוזי בי חוזאי כו' מתוך דיכלי למימר להד"ם יכלי למימר סיטראי איירי בתר דתקון רבנן שבועת היסת דלא הוי השליש עד דנוגע בעדות הוא כיון דחייב שבועת היסת דאי קודם דתקינו רבנן שבועת היסת הוי השליש עד גמור דנאמן לומר למלוה פרעתי מיגו דאי בעי אמר אהדרתינהו ללוה כדאמר בריש האיש מקדש (קדושין דף מג:) וכיון דאיכא עד היכי מהימניה במיגו דלהד"ם דהוה ליה מחויב שבועה ומתוך שאין יכול לישבע משלם כדאמרינן הכא:

הוה יתיב רבי אבא קמיה. משמע דר' אבא היה תלמידו של ר' אמי וקשה דאמר בפ' כל הנשבעין (שבועות דף מז. ושם) א"ר אמי רבותינו שבא"י אמרו חזרה שבועה למחויב לה ואמר התם דרבותינו שבא"י היינו ר' אבא ואור"י דאשכחן בפ' חבית (שבת דף קמו:) דקרי רב לרב כהנא ולרב אסי רבותינו אף על גב שהיו תלמידיו אבל קשה לר"י דבאלו מציאות (ב"מ דף כד:) אמר דר' אמי אשכח פרגיות שחוטות אתא לקמיה דר' אבא א"ל זיל שקול לנפשך ולפי ספרים דגרסינן התם ר' אמי אתא לקמיה דר' אסי ניחא טפי אף על גב דרבי אמי היה גדול מר' אסי דבכ"מ מזכיר ר' אמי קודם ר' אסי ובהניזקין (גיטין דף נד:) אמר (כ) ההוא דאתא לקמיה דר' אמי כו' אמר לפניו רבי אסי רבי אתה אומר כן הכי א"ר יוחנן כו' ומ"מ חבירו היה ולפי שהיה גדול ממנו קורהו רבי ולפי שחבירו היה בא ר' אמי לפניו ליטול עצה ממנו וא"ל זיל שקול לנפשך: **וכל המחויב שבועה ואינו יכול לישבע משלם.** בפ' כל הנשבעין (שבועות דף מז. ושם) תנן חשודים שניהם על השבועה חזרה שבועה למקומה דברי ר"מ ורבי יוסי אומר יחלוקו ומפרש התם רבותינו שבא"י (ל) רבי אבא למקומה למחויב לה ומייתי התם מהך דשמעתין דרבותינו היינו רבי אבא והשתא רב נחמן דפסק התם כרבי יוסי (מ) ועובדא עבד כרבי יוסי יחלוקו לית ליה לר' אבא וקשה לר"י דאמרינן בפרק השואל (ב"מ דף צז: ושם) בגמ' דהשואל את הפרה לימא תיהוי תיובתיה דרב נחמן דאמר מנה לי בידך והלה אומר איני יודע פטור ומשני מתני' בשיש עסק שבועה ביניהן כדרבא דאמר רבא מנה

לי

מסורת הש"ס

א) [נ"ל ליה], ב) שייך לדף לג ע"ב.

הגהות הב"ח

(א) גמ' וכי אתי: (ב) רשב"ם ד"ה היכי וכו' חד עד שחטף: (ג) ד"ה ליפטריה מלשלם משום האי מיגו: (ד) ד"ה לישתבע וכו' פסול הוא כגזלן אבל כל שבועות דהא ליכא למימר לישתבע: (ה) ד"ה הכא וכו' לסיועי ליה קאתי: (ו) ד"ה אלא אי דמיא לנסכא וכו': (ז) בא"ד ולית לי' לשמעון וכו': (ח) בא"ד במאי דמסהיד חד סהדא התם הוא דמשתבע (כדף הקודם) היינו וכו': (ט) תוס' ד"ה אלא אי דמיא לדרבי כו' ולא לי נמקט: (י) ד"ה הוי מחויב וכו' ע"י מיגו שהיה יכול: (כ) ד"ה הוה יתיב וכו' ובהניזקין וכו' אמר נמי הכא: (ל) ד"ה וכל וכו' רבותינו שבא"י למקומה כצ"ל ותיבות ר' אבא נמחק: (מ) בא"ד כר' יוסי ועבד עובדא כר' יוסי:

ליקוטי רש"י

לישלם. שאין כל השותפין נאמנים לומר שלי גזלתי דא"כ אין לך גזלן משלם ואפילו יש עדים [שבועות לב:]. דהא מודה דחטף ולא כל הימנו של חוטף לומר שלי חטפתי [שבועות מז.]. **ליכא תרי סהדי.** דחטפה ואיכא למימר מיגו דאי בעי למימר לא חטפתי מהימן נמי למימר דידי חטפתי [שם מז.]. **ליפטריה.** מלהחזירו שהרי אין כאן שני עדים ומיגו דאי בעי למימר לא חטפתי כי אמר נמי דידי חטפתי נאמן [שם לב:]. **איכא חד סהדא.** דחטפה מיניה ואי הוה אמר לא חטפתי היה צריך לישבע להכחיש העד [שם לב: ומז.]. **לישתבע.** את השבועה שהעד מחייבו אינו יכול דהא מודה דחטף והעד מחייבו לישבע שלא חטף וגבי הך שבועה הוא פסול כגזלן אבל לא שבועה שבועות והא ליכא למימר לישתבע דדידיה חטף שאין זו שבועה המוטלת עליו [שם מז.]. **וכיון דאמר דחטפה.** הוה ליה כגזלן והמחייבו שבועה על פי עד אחד צריך לישבע על מה שהעד מעיד ולהכחיש את העד וזה אינו יכול לישבע לדברי העד שחטפה והוה ליה גזלן אצל שבועה זו כגזלן אצל כל שבועות שאינו יכול לישבע עליהן אף זה בשבועה זו אינו יכול לישבע שהרי מודה לו. **הוי מחויב שבועה שאינו יכול לישבע.** על כרחו אם לישבע בא ישבע ככה שחטף אם לישבע שאין לו הלוקח שלא עשה לא אחת ואינו יכול לישבע על מה שהעד מעיד ואינו יכול לישבע שהרי מודה לדבריו [שם לב:].

עין משפט נר מצוה

מז א מיי' פ"ד מהל' טוען ונטען הל' ט ופ"ד מהל' גזילה הל' יד סמג עשין צה טוש"ע ח"מ סי' עה סעיף יג וסי' שפב סעיף ג וסעיף ד:

מח ב ג מיי' פט"ו מה' טוען הל' ה סמג עשין צה טוש"ע ח"מ סי' קמו סעיף ג [ונרב אלפס שבועות פ"ז דף שטו:]:

רבינו גרשום

ליכא תרי סהדי. דמסהדי דחטפה מיניה. **לישתבע.** דדידיה הוה. הואיל דליכא אלא עד א'. לא מצי למישתבע דהא מודי דחטפה וה"ל כגזלן: **הוה ליה מחויב שבועה** ע"פ עד אחד **ואינו יכול לישבע משלם.** וכי היכי דהכא לא הוי אלא חד סהדא ואוקמוה בידא דחוטף ה"נ גבי ארעא דלית בה אלא חד סהדא נוקמה בידיה דתובע א"ל (ר' אמי) [אביי] מי דמי התם חד סהדא דאייתי תובע לאורועי להאי חוטף ולהכחישו קאתי דלא נאמן אלא בשבועה ואי הוה סהדא אחרינא בהדיה מפקינן ליה מיניה לגמרי והכא חד סהדא דאייתי נתבע לסיועיה אתי דמסהיד כוותיה דאכלה שני חזקה: **אלא אי בעית לדמינהו לדר' אבא לחד סהדא ולתרתי שנין ולפירא.** כגון דאמר ליה מאי בעית בהאי ארעא אמר ליה מינך זבינתה ואכלתיה שני חזקה ואזל ואייתי חד סהדא ואמר דאכלה תרתי שנין ולא יותר דהשתא האי סהדא מרע לחזקיה אי נמי דאמר אכלה תלת שנין אבל לא זבנה מיניה אלא לפירות יורד בה כדין אריס למחצה ולשליש ולרביע דמכחיש ומרע לדיבוריה והיינו דומיא דחד סהדא דנסכא דמרע לנתבע ומש"ה נמי האי סהדא דמכחיש ליה משוי ליה כגזלן ומתוך שאינו יכול לישבע שאין נשבעין על הקרקע מחזיר הקרקע:

Abaye disputed the analogy:

אָמַר לְהוּ אַבַּיֵי – Abaye said to [the Sages]: **מִי דָמֵי – Is [this instance]** truly **analogous** to R' Abba's case? **הָתָם סַהֲדָא לְאוֹרוּעֵי קָאָתֵי – There,** in R' Abba's case, **the** single **witness was introduced to oppose** the defendant.[12] **כִּי אָתֵי אַחֲרִינָא בַּהֲדֵיהּ** – This is evident from the fact that **had another** witness **come with him,** **מַפְּקִינַן לָהּ מִינֵּיהּ – [the court] would have taken away [the ingot] from [the defendant]** based on this testimony. Thus, the single witness requires him instead to take an oath, and since he is unable to do so, he must pay. **הָכָא – Here,** however, **לְסַיּוּעֵי קָא אָתֵי – [the single witness] was introduced to support [the occupant],** **כִּי אָתָא אַחֲרִינָא מוֹקְמִינַן לָהּ בִּידֵיהּ** – as is evident from the fact that **had another** witness **come** with him, **[the court] would have established [the land] in [the occupant's] possession.** Thus, although the occupant must vacate the property, for no second witness was forthcoming, the first witness does not obligate the occupant to take an oath to refute his testimony regarding consumption of produce.[13] Hence, no comparison can be drawn between this incident and R' Abba's case.

Abaye concluded his reply by citing a hypothetical case that would be analogous to R' Abba's case:

אֶלָּא אִי דָּמְיָא הָא דְּרַבִּי אַבָּא – Rather, continued Abaye, **if R' Abba's case is similar** to any, **לְחַד סַהֲדָא וּלְתַרְתֵּי שְׁנֵי – it is to** that of **one witness** introduced by the challenger, who testifies **to** ***two*** **years'** consumption of produce by the occupant, **וּלְפֵירֵי – and** where the purpose of the testimony was **to** require the occupant to pay for the **produce.**[14]

NOTES

12. Literally: do him ill.

13. The Torah declares: לֹא־יָקוּם עֵד אֶחָד בְּאִישׁ לְכָל־עָוֹן וּלְכָל־חַטָּאת, *One witness shall not arise against a man to* [impose] *any corporal punishment or monetary obligation (Deuteronomy* 19:15). The Sages expound this verse as follows: It is to impose corporal punishment or a monetary obligation that a solitary witness may not arise. However, he does arise to obligate the defendant to swear to refute the witness' testimony. Based on this exposition, the following rule may be formulated: Wherever two witnesses would obligate the defendant to pay, one witness obligates him to swear. If, however, two witnesses would not have required the defendant to pay, a single witness can likewise not obligate him to take an oath (*Kesubos* 87b). It is in this light that Abaye's objection is understood (see *Ritva*). Since two witnesses to the snatching would have required the snatcher to return the ingot, one witness requires him to swear (and since he cannot, for he admits to snatching, he must pay). But in the case of the field, if two witnesses were to testify that he used it for three years, he would *not* be required to yield it — on the contrary, they would be supportive of his *chazakah* and allow him to keep the field! Hence, one witness does not impose an oath upon him (see *Rashbam*).

Abaye does not mean to argue that the occupant should retain the land. Clearly, since he lacks two witnesses to his *chazakah*, he must relinquish the land. Rather, he means to dispute his disciples' ruling that the occupant must pay for the produce he consumed (*Rashbam*).

14. Abaye's hypothetical case is this: The challenger charges that the occupant had squatted on his land for two years and consumed its produce. The occupant, for his part, admits that he had consumed the produce, but claims that he had bought the land and lost his deed. Now, the same three scenarios as in the case of the silver ingot exist here as well. That is, if a pair of witnesses had supported the challenger's claim, the occupant would be required to pay for the produce. On the other hand, if the challenger had no witnesses to support his claim, he would be exempt from paying for the produce, based on a *migo*: He must be telling the truth, for if he were lying, he could have denied consuming any more than the minimum amount needed to effect *chazakah*. Now that one witness testifies that he consumed only two years' produce, he loses his *migo*, because he would have had to swear had he denied consumption. His sole remaining option is to swear that he did not consume the produce, but he cannot do this since he admits to the consumption. Thus, he must pay (*Rashbam*).

Abaye's case contrasts with the case discussed by his disciples in that by testifying that the occupant consumed produce for only two years, the witness is *opposing* the occupant. This can be seen from the fact that if two witnesses had testified to this effect, the occupant would be forced to pay for the produce. Thus, the single witness imposes an oath on the occupant. However, in the actual case before the scholars, the witness' testimony of three years' consumption was *supportive* of the occupant; had another witness corroborated his testimony, the occupant would have retained the produce. In that case, then, the witness does not obligate the occupant to swear.

היכי נידיינוה דייני להאי דינא לישלם ליכא תרי סהדי ליפטריה איכא חד סהדא לישתבע הא אמר מיחטף חטפה וכיון דאמר דחטפה הוה ליה כגזלן אמר (א) [להו] רבי אבא [א]הוי מחויב שבועה שאינו יכול לישבע וכל המחויב שבועה שאינו יכול לישבע משלם א"ל אביי [ב]מי דמי התם סהדא לאורועי קאתי (א) כי אתי אחרינא בהדיה מפקינן לה מיניה הכא לסיועי קא אתי כי אתא אחרינא מוקמינן לה בידיה אלא אי דמיא הא דרבי אבא [ג]לחד סהדא ולתרתי שני ולפירי: ההוא

היכי לידיינוה דייני להאי דינא. שאילו היו שנים מעידים אותו שחטף היינו מחייבין אותו לשלם שאין אדם נאמן לחטוף דבר מיד חבירו ולומר שלי אני חוטף אא"כ יש לו עדים דהעמד ממון על חזקתו וזה המוחזק בו אין אדם יכול להוציאו ממנו בלא ראיה והחוטף ממנו גזלן גמור ואי נמי לא היה כאן עד אחד שחטף כי אמר נמי חטפי ודידי חטפי מהימן מיגו דאי הוה בעי הוה אמר לא חטפי שהרי אנו רואים אותו מוחזק בממון אי נמי כי איכא חד (ג) שחטף אילו היה זה מכחישו לומר לא חטפתי היה נשבע שלא חטף להכחיש העד דעד אחד קם הוא לשבועה ובג' דרכים הללו היה הדין פשוט אבל הכא דאיכא עד אחד שחטף וזה אינו מכחישו אלא מודה שודאי חטף ודידיה חטף היכי לידיינו דייני להאי דינא: **לישלם.** דהא מודי שחטף ולא כל הימנו של חוטף לומר שלי חטפתי דהעמד ממון על חזקתו: **ליכא תרי סהדי.** דחטף ובמיגו דאי בעי למימר לא חטפי מהימן נמי למימר דידי חטפי: **ליפטריה.** (ג) משום האי מיגו איכא חד סהדא ואי אמר לא חטפי הוה בעי אישתבועי להכחיש את העד: **לישתבע.** את השבועה שהעד מחייבו אינו יכול דהא מודי דחטף והעד מחייבו לישבע שלא חטף להכחיש את העד דהכי משמע קרא (דברים יט) לא יקום עד אחד באיש לכל עון ולכל חטאת וגו' לשלם ממון שהוא כופר והעד מחייבו לא יקום אבל קם הוא לשבועה להכחיש את העד שלא חטף בממון זה וגבי הך שבועה פסול (ד) כגזלן אלא כל שבועות דהא לית ליה למימר לישתבע דדידיה חטף שאין זו שבועה המוטלת עליו ולמפטריה בלא כלום אי אפשר שהרי העד כמו של מיגו: **א"ל רבי אבא הוה ליה.** האי חוטף כו' וה"נ איכא למימר כי האי גוונא כי הוו תרי סהדי דאכלה שני חזקה מוקמינן לה בידא דלוקח. ליכא סהדי דאכלה שני חזקה מפקינן לה מיניה ומהדרינן למרה. איכא חד סהדא דאכלה שלש שנים ליתשבע דעד אחד לשבועה קם אפי' לא הוה קרקע לא משבעינן ליה על מאי דאסהיד סהדא דלא כפר ליה אלא מודי ליה דאכל וטוען אין אכלי ודידי אכלי: **א"ל אביי מי דמי.** לדרבי אבא: **התם.** בדר' אבא חד סהדא לאורועי קאתי דהא מסהיד ביה שחטף והרע כחו של מיגו דחוטף ומחייבו שבועה ומתוך שאינו יכול לישבע משלם דאילו אתא חד סהדא שמעיד כמותו שראוהו שחטף מפקינן לה מיניה דחוטף ולא תועיל לו שבועה אפי' אם יוכל לישבע: **הכא.** בדין קרקע זה ההוא סהדא לסיועי (ה) ביה קאתי שמעיד שהחזיק בה שלש שנים וזכה בה דאי איכא חד סהדא אחרינא עם זה מוקמינן ליה בידא דמחזיק והילך תאמר שעל יד עד זה יתחייב שבועה ומתוך שאינו יכול לישבע משלם והרי לא בא להורע כחו ומ"מ זה יפסיד הקרקע שהרי אין לו עדי חזקה: **אלא אי דמיא (ו) לנסכא דרבי אבא לחד סהדא ולתרתין שנין ולפירי.** כגון ראובן דמעיד לשמעון וא"ל גזלתה לארעאי ואכלת פירותיה שנתים וא"ל שמעון זבנתה ניהלי ולית (ז) לשמעון עדי חזקה דלא להדורי ארעא למרה מכיון דלית ליה עדי חזקה ולפירי משתבע דבזביניה אכלתינון דקי"ל הפה שאסר הוא שהתיר ואע"ג דמהדר לה לארעא פירי לא מהדר דהא ליכא סהדי דאכל הפירות ומיגו דיכול למימר לא אכלי כלל יכול למימר נמי אכלי בזביני ולית עלה אלא שבועה אבל אי איכא סהדי דאכל פירי תרתין שנין מחייבין ליה להדורי אפי' פירי כרב נחמן דאמר הדרא ארעא והדרי פירי ואייתי ראובן חד סהדא דאכל פירי תרתין שנין וכגון שמעיד שלא אכל כי אם ב' שנים דלאו לסיועי לשמעון קאתי ואמר שמעון אין אכלי ודידי אכלי שקניתי הקרקע והפירות אפס לא נזהרתי בשטרי הא הוא דאיכא לדמויי לדרבי אבא דאמרינן היכי לידיינו דייני להאי דינא ניחייביה להדורי פירי ליכא תרי סהדי דאכלינהו ואי משום דאודי הא טעין ואמר דידי אכלי וכה"ג ליכא הודאה לחיוביה ניפטריה במיגו הא איכא חד סהדא דאמר דאכלינהו לפירי תרתין שנין ואינו יכול לכפור בדברי העד לישבע לשקר ניחייביה שבועה בעד אחד דלאו הוו תרוייהו מחייבי ליה ממונא וכ"ש שאם שנים מחייבין אותו ממון אחד מחייב אותו שבועה כי אמרי' עד אחד לשבועה אתי היכא דקא כפר במאי דמסהיד (ח) סהדא חד הוא דמשתבע דלא היו דברים מעולם אבל הכא הא קא מודי דאכל אלא טוען דידי אכלי:

אביי דלא דמי לדרבי אבא דהכא חד סהדא לסיועי קאתי בין לקרקע בין לפירות שהרי הוא מעיד שגם הקרקע שלו והא דאמרינן במסקנא אלא אי דמיא (ט) לדרבי אבא לחד סהדא לתרתין שנין ולפירי לא הוה צריך למינקט ולפירי כיון דעד השתא נמי לא איירי אלא בפירי אלא אגב תרתין שנין נקט נמי לחד סהדא ולפירי:

הוי מחויב שבועה ואינו יכול לישבע. שהרי מודה וא"ת וליהמניה בשבועה במאי דאמר דידי חטפי במיגו דאי בעי אמר לא חטפי וכי תימא דהא לא חשיב מיגו דהא אם אמר לא חטפי היה חייב שבועה דאורייתא לא היא דהא אמר בהמוכר את הבית (לקמן דף ע. ושם) המפקיד אצל חבירו בשטר נאמן לומר החזרתיו לך בשבועה מיגו דאי בעי אמר נאנסו דהוי נאמן בשבועה אע"ג דבנאנסו איכא שבועה דאורייתא ומיהו לפי' ר"ת דפירש שבועה דנאנסו דהתם היא מדרבנן דלא מיחייב שבועה דאורייתא אפילו בנאנסו אלא היכא דאיכא הודאה במקצת אתי שפיר וליכא למימר נמי דהאי לא חשיב מיגו דלא הוה חציף למימר לא חטפי להכחיש את העד או משום שירא שלא יפסלוהו לעדות העד ובעל הנסכא כדאמר בפרק זה בורר (סנהדרין דף כה.) דבעל דבר מהימן למימר [לדידי אוזפן ברביתא] דהא משמע דאי לאו לעד מחייבו שבועה היה פטור והיינו על כרחך במיגו דאי לאו מיגו לאו כל כמיניה למימר דידי חטפי דהא כי איכא תרי סהדי משלם ואינו נאמן לומר דידי חטפי ואומר ר"י דודאי אם לא היה העד מחייבו שבועה היה נאמן במיגו דאי בעי אמר לא חטפי שיכול להעיז פניו להכחיש את העד בלא שבועה אבל השתא דמחייבו שבועה לא מהימן בשבועה ע"י מיגו (י) שהיה יכול להעיז פניו ולישבע בדבר שהעד מכחישו אבל קשה אי ליכא מיגו מאי טעמא דרב ושמואל דפליגי בפרק כל הנשבעין (שבועות דף מז. ושם) ארבי אבא ופטרי בנסכא דלית להו מתוך שאינו יכול לישבע משלם והשתא אמאי פטרי והא פשיטא דאינו נאמן לומר דידי חטפי בלא מיגו כדפרישי' לעיל לכך נראה כמו שפי' ריב"ם דודאי הוי מיגו ולהכי פטרי רב ושמואל דנאמן בשבועה במיגו דאי בעי אמר לא חטפי ור' אבא סבר אע"ג דלית ליה מגו חייב דכיון דליכא אחד המחייבו שבועה מן התורה כן הוא הדין שישבע להכחיש את העד או ישלם ואין מועיל לו מיגו ליפטר וא"ת ור' אבא היכי מפיק לה בפ' כל הנשבעין (שם) מדכתיב שבועת ה' תהיה בין שניהם ולא בין היורשין דאמר ליה מנה לאבא ביד אביך ואמר חמשין ידענא וחמשין לא ידענא דדייק התם מדאיצטריך קרא למיפטר יורשים ש"מ דאביו כה"ג מיחייב אלמא מחויב שבועה ואינו יכול לישבע משלם והיכי דייק מינה מסקנא התם ודאי משלם דליכא מיגו אבל הכא דליכא מיגו מנא לן דמשלם ונראה לר"י דרבי אבא לא הוי טעמיה מקרא אלא מסברא בעלמא כדמפרש והא דקאמר התם כוותיה דר' אבא מסתברא מדתני ר' חמי שבועת ה' תהיה בין שניהם ולא בין היורשין קרא למיפטר יורשים אתא ולא לחייב האב והא דקאמר התם רב ושמואל דאמרי תרווייהו שבועת ה' וגו' מאי דרשי ביה ה"ק כיון דבאב בכה"ג פטרי אמאי איצטריך קרא למיפטר יורשין וצ"ל דהא דאמרי' בהכותב (כתובות דף פה. ושם) גבי אבימי בריה דר' אבהו דהוו מסקי ביה זוזי בי חוזאי כו' מתוך דיכלי למימר להד"ס יכלי למימר סיטראי איירי בתר דתקון רבנן שבועת היסת דלא הוי השליח עד דטוען בעדות הוא כיון דלאו קודם דתקינו רבנן שבועת היסת הוי השליח עד גמור דנאמן לומר למלוה פרעתי מיגו דאי בעי אמר החזרתיהו ללוה כדאמר בריש האיש מקדש (קדושין דף מג.) וכיון דאיכא עד היכי מהימניה במיגו דלהד"ס דהוה ליה מחויב שבועה ומתוך שאין יכול לישבע משלם כדאמרינן הכא:

[ג]**הוה** יתיב רבי אבא קמיה. משמע דר' אבא היה תלמידו של ר' אמי וקשה דאמר בפ' כל הנשבעין (שבועות דף מז. ושם) א"ר אמי רבותינו שבא"י אמרו חזרה שבועה למחויב לה ואמר התם דרבותינו שבא"י היינו ר' אבא ואור"י דאשכחן בפ' חבית (שבת דף קמו:) דקרי רב לרב כהנא ולרב אסי רבותינו אף על גב שהיו תלמידיו אבל קשה לר"י דבלאו הכי מוכח (ב"מ דף כד:) אמר דר' אמי אשכח פרגיות שחוטות אתא לקמיה דר' אבא א"ל זיל שקול לנפשך ולפי ספרים דגרסי התם ר' אמי אתא לקמיה דר' אסי ניחא טפי אף על גב דרבי אמי היה גדול מר' אסי דבכ"מ מזכיר ר' אמי קודם ר' אסי ובהניזקין (גיטין דף סד:) אמר (כ) ההוא דאתא לקמיה דר' אמי כו' אמר לפניו רבי אסי רבי אתה אומר כן הכי א"ר יוחנן כו' ומ"מ חבירו היה ולפי שהיה גדול ממנו קורהו רבי ולפי שחבירו היה בא ר' אמי לפניו ליטול עצה ממנו וא"ל זיל שקול לנפשך: **וכל** המחויב שבועה ואינו יכול לישבע משלם. בפ' כל הנשבעין (שבועות דף מז. ושם) תנן חשודים שניהם על השבועה חזרה שבועה למקומה דברי ר"מ ורבי יוסי אומר יחלוקו ומפרש התם רבותינו שבא"י (ל) רבי אבא למקומה למחויב לה ומייתי התם מהך דשמעתין דרבותינו היינו רבי אבא והשתא רב נחמן דפסק התם כרבי יוסי (מ) ועובדא עבד כרבי יוסי יחלוקו לית ליה לר' אבא וקשה לר"י דאמרינן בפרק השואל (ב"מ דף צז: ושם) בגמ' דהשואל את הפרה לימא תיהוי תיובתיה דרב נחמן דאמר מנה לי בידך והלה אומר איני יודע פטור ומשני מתני' בשיש עסק שבועה ביניהן כדרבה דאמר רבה מנה לי

לי

עין משפט נר מצוה

מז א מיי' פ"ד מהל' טוען הל' ח ופ"ד מהל' גזילה הל' יד סמג עשין צה טוש"ע ח"מ סי' עה סעיף יג וסי' שפב סעיף ג וסעיף ד:

מח ב ג מיי' פט"ו מה' טוען הל' ה סמג עשין צה טוש"ע ח"מ סי' קמה סעיף ג [וברב אלפס שבועות פ"ו דף שנ:]:

רבינו גרשום

ליכא תרי סהדי. דמסהדי דחטפה מיניה: לישתבע. דדידיה הוה הואיל דליכא אלא עד א': לא מצי למישתבע דהא מודי דחטפה והו"ל כגזלן: הוה ליה מחויב שבועה ע"פ עד אחד ואינו יכול לישבע משלם. וכי היכי דהכא לא הוי אלא חד סהדא ואוקמה בידא דתובע ה"נ גבי ארעא דלית בה אלא חד סהדא נוקמה בידיה דתובע א"ל (ר' אמי) [אביי] מי דמי התם חד סהדא דאייתי תובע לאורועי להאי חוטף ולהכחישו קאתי דלא נאמן אלא בשבועה ואי הוה תרי סהדא אחרינא בהדיה מפקינן ליה מיניה לגמרי והכא חד סהדא דאייתי נתבע לסיועיה אתי דמסהיד כוותיה דאכלה שני חזקה: אלא אי בעית לדמינהו לדר' אבא לחד סהדא ולתרתי שנין ולפירא. כגון דאמר ליה מאי בעית בהאי ארעא אמר ליה מינך זבינתה ואכלתיה שני חזקה ואזל ואייתי חד סהדא ואמר דאכלה תרתי שנין ולא יותר דהשתא האי סהדא מרע לחזקה אי נמי דאמר אכלה תלת שנין אבל לא זבנה מיניה אלא לפירות ידך בה כדין אריס למחצה ולשליש ולרביע דמכחיש ומרע לדיבוריה והיינו דדומיא דחד סהדא דנסכא דמרע לנתבע ומש"ה נמי האי סהדא דמכחיש ליה משוי ליה כגזלן ומתוך שאינו יכול לישבע שאין נשבעין על הקרקע' מהדר הקרקע:

מסורת הש"ס

א) [צ"ל ליה], ב) שייך לדף לג ע"ב:

הגהות הב"ח

(א) גמ' וכו' אתי: (ב) רשב"ם ד"ה היכי וכו' חד עד שחטף: (ג) ד"ה ליפטריה מלשלם משום האי מיגו: (ד) ד"ה לישתבע וכו' פסול הוא כגזלן אלא כל שבועות דהא ליכא למימר לישתבע: (ה) ד"ה הכא לסיועי ליה קאתי: (ו) ד"ה אלא אי דמיא נסכא וכו': (ז) בא"ד ולית ל' לשמעון וכו': (ח) בא"ד במאי דמסהיד חד סהדא התם הוא דמשתבע: (ט) תוס' ד"ה (בדף הקודם) היינו וכו' אלא אי דמיא דרבי כל"ל ותיבת לא נמחק: (י) ד"ה הוי מחויב וכו' ע"י מיגו שלא היה יכול וכו': (כ) ד"ה הוה יתיב וכו' ובהניזקין אמר נמי ההוא: (ל) ד"ה וכל וכו' ומפרש התם רבותינו שבא"י למקומה כל"ל ותיבות ר' אבא נמחק: (מ) בא"ד כר' יוסי ועבד עובדא כר' יוסי:

ליקוטי רש"י

לישלם. שאין כל החוטפין נאמנים לומר שלי גזלתי דא"כ אין לך גזלן שמשלם ואפילו יש עדים [שבועות לב:]. דהא מודה דחטף ולא כל הימנו של חוטף לומר שלי חטפתי [שבועות מז.]. ליכא תרי סהדי. דחטפה ואיכא למימר מיגו [שם לב:]. ומיגו דאי בעי למימר לא חטפי מהימן נמי למימר דידי חטפי [שם מז.]. ליפטריה. מלשלומי שהרי אין כאן שני עדים ומיגו דאי בעי אמר לא חטפתי כי אמר נמי דידי חטפתי נאמן [שם לב:] משום האי מיגו [שם מז.]. איכא חד סהדא. דחטפה מיניה ואי הוה אמר לא חטפתי היה צריך לישבע להכחיש העד [שם לב: ומז.]. לישתבע. את השבועה שהעד מחייבו אינו יכול דהא מודה דחטף והעד מחייבו לישבע שלא חטף ובגזלן הך שבועה הוא דפסול כגזלן אבל כל שבועות והא ליכא למימר לישתבע דדידיה חטף שאין זו שבועה המוטלת עליו [שם מז.]. וכיון דאמר דחטפה. הוה ליה כגזלן והמחייבו שבועה על פי עד אחד צריך לישבע על מה שהעד מעיד ולהכחיש את העד וזה אינו יכול לישבע שכן שהרי מודה הוא לדברי העד שחטפה וזהו הא ליה אלא שבועה זו כגזלן אלא כל שבועות שאינו יכול לישבע עליהן אף זו השבועה זו אינו יכול לישבע שהרי מודה בה. הוי מחויב שבועה שאינו יכול לישבע. על כרחו אם בא להחזיק בה צריך הוא לישבע שהרי זה המוחזק וגזלן הוא שאין נאמן לומר שלי חטפתי והן השבועה מוטלת עליו מה שהעד מעיד ואינו יכול לישבע שהרי מודה לדבריו [שם לב:].

ההוא ארבא דהוו מינצו עלה בי תרי האי אמר דידי היא והאי אמר דידי היא אתא חד מינייהו לבי דינא ואמר תיפסוה (א) אדמייתינא סהדי דדידי היא תפסינן או לא תפסינן רב הונא אמר תפסינן רב יהודה אמר א לא תפסינן אזל ולא אשכח סהדי אמר להו אפקוה וכל דאלים גבר מפקינן או לא מפקינן רב יהודה אמר ב לא מפקינן רב פפא אמר מפקינן והלכתא לא תפסינן והיכא דתפס לא מפקינן: זה אומר של אבותי וזה אומר של אבותי א) אמר רב נחמן ג כל דאלים גבר ומאי שנא ב) משני שטרות היוצאין ביום אחד דרב

אלא הו״ל מחויב שבועה ואינו יכול לישבע ומשלם. כך נראה שיטה זו בעיני ושוב מצאתיה כן בפי׳ ר״ח ויש לשונות אחרים ואין בהם ממש וקי״ל בהא כרבי אבא מדיליף אביי מינה ואף על גב דפליגי עליה רב ושמואל בפרק כל הנשבעין (שבועות דף מז.) דאמרי חזרה שבועה לסיני והמוציא מחבירו עליו הראיה ותנן נמי התם וכן היתומים מן היתומים לא יפרעו אלא בשבועה ורב ושמואל דאמרי תרוייהו לא שנו אלא שמת מלוה בחיי הלוה אבל מת לוה בחיי מלוה כבר נתחייב מלוה לבני לוה שבועה ואין אדם מוריש שבועה לבניו ממון שהוא מחויב עליו שבועה אלמא הואיל ומחויב שבועה שלא התקבלתי חוב זה ויתומין אין יכולין לישבע כן אלא שלא פקדנו אבא ואין זו שבועה המוטלת על אביהם וגם יתומים של לוה אין יכולין לישבע שפרעו אביהם קא אמרי רב ושמואל שלא יפרע אלמא המחויב שבועה ואינו יכול לישבע לא זה ולא זה סבירא לרב ושמואל חזרה שבועה לסיני ואין כאן לא שבועה ולא פרעון ור״א פליג עלייהו ואמר יורשין נשבעין שבועת יורשים ונוטלין דלא ס״ל לדרב ושמואל ואמרי׳ התם האי דיינא דעבד כר״א עבד דעבד כרב ושמואל עבד אפ״ה הלכתא כר׳ אבא ולא כרב ושמואל דאמרינן התם הבו דלא להוסיף עלה עשו תקנה שלא להוסיף על דברי רב ושמואל ללמוד מדין זה ליתומים מן היתומים לשאר דינין ולומר חזרה שבועה לסיני דבדין זה לבדו דיתומים מן היתומים הוא דקי״ל כרב ושמואל דלדעבד משום תקנת יתומים בני לוה דחסינן עלייהו שלא לפרע מהן בלא שבועה מעלייתא אבל בשאר דינין קי״ל כר׳ אבא דהמחויב שבועה ואינו יכול לישבע משלם וגם ר״ח פסק הלכתא כרבי אבא: **ארבא.** ספינה שבנהר: **האי אמר דידי הוא** כו׳. ולא זה ולא זה מוחזקין בה מדלא רמי עלה ממתניתין דשנים אוחזין בטלית שזה נוטל עד מקום שידו מגעת וזה נוטל עד מקום שידו מגעת ולא אמרינן כל דאלים גבר כן פיר״ח: **תיפסוה.** פן ימכרנה אבל חזקה שהחזיק בה אחר שערער זה עליה אינה כלום דאנן סהדי שבתורת חטיפה באה לידו: **תפסינן או לא תפסינן.** מי לימא דתפסי לה ב״ד דהא אי לא משכח סהדי הדרינן ומפקינן לה כדמעיקרא ולא הפסיד בעל הספינה בתפיסת ב״ד כלום או דלמא לא תפסינן דדלמא לא משכח סהדי ולא הדרינן ומפקינן לה כדלקמן ונמצא שהפסיד בעל הספינה על ידינו דאי הוה שבקינן לה דלמא הוי אלים וגבר בעל הספינה ונמצא זוכה בשלו כן נ״ל טעם השאלה: **רב הונא אומר תפסינן.** ס״ל כרב פפא דאמר מפקינן רב יהודה אומר לא תפסינן משום דס״ל לא מפקינן כדלקמיה והלכך לא תפסינן דשמא זה אין לו עדים ושקרן הוא ומכל וכל רוצה להפסיד את חבירו דמאחר דתפסי׳ יודע הוא דתו לא מפקינן: **א״ל אפקוה.** וכגון דאיתרמי מילתא דתפסינן לה כרב הונא אי נמי שאמרו שניהם לב״ד לתפסה ודברי הכל: **וכל דאלים גבר.** בין בראיות בין בכח כמו שפוסק רב נחמן לפנינו כל דאלים גבר: **לא מפקינן.** דמאחר שבא ממון ישראל ביד ב״ד אין רשאין להפקירו אלא מעכבין אותו ממון עד שידעו למי ישיבו: **מפקינן.** כעין שמלאוהו מתחלה שלדעת כן תפסוהו שאם לא יביא עדים יחזירוהו וכל דאלים גבר: **והלכתא לא תפסינן והיכא דתפסינן לא מפקינן.** כרב יהודה: **זה אומר של אבותי וזה אומר של אבותי.** בין בספינה בין בקרקע ואין עדות וחזקה לזה יותר מזה: **ומ״ש משני שטרות היוצאין.** לפניו על שדה אחת של ראובן שכתב שטר מתנה לשמעון ושטר מתנה ללוי ושניהם ביום אחד ונמצא שאין זה מוחזק יותר מזה כלל ואפי׳ נתברר ששמעון בשחר ולוי אחריו בערב אין הקדמה

לי בידך והלה אומר אין לך בידי אלא חמשים וחמשים איני יודע מתוך שאינו יכול לישבע משלם והיינו כר׳ אבא ומיהו איכא למימר דר״נ דמוקי מתני׳ כר״מ וכמו שמפרש ר׳ אבא הוא סבר כר׳ יוסי אבל עוד קשה דבשמעתין משמע דהלכתא כר׳ אבא מדקאמרינן סבור רבנן קמיה דאביי למימר דהיינו נסכא דר׳ אבא וקאמר נמי אלא אי דמיא לרבי אבא כו׳ ובכ״מ קי״ל כרב נחמן בדיני ועוד תימה דהתם גבי יתומים מן היתומים קאמרי רב ושמואל דאם מת לוה בחיי מלוה כבר נתחייב מלוה לבני לוה שבועה ואין אדם מוריש שבועה לבניו ומתוך שאין התובעין יכולין לישבע פטור הנתבע ור״א פליג עליה (שם מח.) וקאמר יורשין נשבעין שבועת יורשים ונוטלין והיינו כרבי אבא דמתוך שאינו יכול לישבע או תובע או הנתבע משלם הנתבע ומסיק התם דעבד כרב ושמואל עבד דעבד כרבי אלעזר עבד ומפרש ר״ת דרב נחמן שפיר סבר כר׳ אבא בנסכא ובמנה יש לי בידך וא״ל אין לך בידי אלא חמשים וחמשים איני יודע ודוקא בשניהם חשודין פסיק רב נחמן כר׳ יוסי דאמר יחלוקו ורבי אבא בשניהם חשודין מודה לר״נ דהלכה כרבי יוסי וטעמא משום דקנסינן שכנגדו לפי שהוא חשוד הלכך מפסיד החצי אבל בעלמא מחויב שבועה ואינו יכול לישבע משלם והא דקאמר התם דרבותינו שבא״י ר׳ אבא לאו למימר דר׳ אבא סבר לה כר״מ אלא דדייק כיון דר׳ אבא בעלמא סבר דמתוך שאינו יכול לישבע משלם אית לן למימר דאיהו מפרש מילתיה דר״מ דחזרה שבועה למחויב לה והלכה כר״נ בשניהם חשודים וכר׳ אבא בנסכא ודוקא ביתומים מסקינן דעבד כרב ושמואל עבד ודעבד כר״א עבד כדאמר הבו דלא להוסיף עלה אבל אין לפרש (ב) טעמא דרב נחמן דאמר יחלוקו משום דר׳ אבא דכיון דשניהם חשודים ה״ל כאילו תרוייהו מחוייבים שבועה ואין יכולין והלכך כל אחד מפסיד חצי ורבי אבא סבר כיון דעיקר שבועה על הנתבע ואין יכול לישבע משלם הכל דא״כ ר׳ אבא ורב נחמן מאי סברי שפיר כרב ושמואל ביתומים מן היתומים כי מת לוה בחיי מלוה ומפסידין בני מלוה כיון דאין יכולין לישבע ואין נוטלין כמו שמפסיד שכנגדו חשוד על השבועה החצי שאינו נוטל כשגם הוא חשוד ובפ׳ כל הנשבעין (שבועות דף מז.) משמע כל הסוגיא דרב ושמואל פליגי אדרב נחמן ואדרבי אבא ג) וע״כ צ״ל דלרבי אבא וכן לרב נחמן מתוך שאינו יכול לישבע אפילו התובע משלם הנתבע כדפרי׳:

ההוא ארבא דהוו מינצו וכו׳. הדין כל דאלים גבר וא״ת מ״ש משנים אוחזין בטלית דאמר בריש ב״מ (דף ב. ושם ד״ה ויחלוקו) דיחלוקו ומפרש ר״ת דאוחזין שאני דכיון ששניהם מוחזקים אין לנו להניח שיגזול האחד לחבירו דחשיב כאילו אנו יודעין שיש לשניהן חלק בה שכל דבר יש להעמיד בחזקת מי שהוא בידו כדאמרי׳ גבי נסכא דר׳ אבא דאע״ג דאמר דידי חטפי חשבינן ליה גזלן וחייב לשלם כאילו הוא ברור שהיתה הנסכא של אותו שהיה מוחזק בה והא דמדמי ליה התם טלית לשאר [יהא מונח עד שיבא אליהו] אע״ג דבשאר דהתם אין שום אחד מוחזק צ״ל דשאר נמי חשיב להו כאילו שניהם מוחזקים בו כיון דמכח שניהם נפקד ולריב״א נראה דלאו דוקא אוחזין מדמדמי לה לשאר ולדשמעתין איכא לשנויי כדמשני התם אפי׳ תימא ר׳ יוסי התם ודאי איכא רמאי הכא איכא למימר תרוייהו בהדי הדדי אגבהוה הכי נמי בארבא כיון דליכא רמאי לא יחלוקו אלא הוי דינא כל דאלים גבר והא דלא אמרינן בשנים שהפקידו כל דאלים גבר משום דלא מפקינן כדאמרינן הכא אי תפסינן לא מפקינן אבל מ״ד מפקינן לא אתי שפיר ומאי פריך נמי בסמוך מב׳ שטרות וממחליף פרה בחמור והא התם ליכא רמאי ואין נראה (ג) דהא האי טעמא לא מסיק אלא לאוקומי מתני׳ כר׳ יוסי אבל לרבנן קאמר התם האי מנה ודאי דחד מינייהו הוא אבל טלית דאיכא למימר דתרוייהו הוא יחלוקו ולהאי טעמא ה״נ הוה לן למימר יחלוקו דאפשר להיות דהוה ארבא דתרוייהו ועוד פי׳ ריב״א דהיכא דאוחזין אפי׳ איכא רמאי יחלוקו כדתניא התם בפ״ק (דף ז.) גבי שנים אוחזין בשטר וקשיא לר״י דא״כ היכי פריך לפירושו (שם דף ג.) והא נמי כשאר דמיא דאיכא למימר אוחזין שאני דהא מהניא אפילו היכא דאיכא רמאי ועוד מאי פריך התם (דף ז.) ולית ליה לרבי מתני׳ דשנים אוחזין בטלית הא ע״כ יש חילוק בין דין שטר לדין טלית דבטלית אפי׳ אין אוחזין יחלוקו ובשטר כי אין אוחזין הוי דין כל דאלים גבר: **רב** הונא אמר תפסינן. פי׳ הקונט׳ משום דמפקינן ורב יהודה דאמר לא תפסינן משום דלא תפסינן לא מפקינן ואין נראה לר״י לתלות זה בזה מדלא פליגי הנהו אמוראי גופייהו במפקינן הנך דפליגי בתפסינן לכך נראה דר״ה דאמר דתפסינן אפי׳ למאן דאמר לא מפקינן דמהימנינא ליה שיביא עדים ורב יהודה דאמר לא תפסינן אפי׳ למ״ד מפקינן היינו היכא דתפסינן כבר אבל לכתחילה לא תפסינן דחיישינן דלמא לא מייתי עדים ולא נדע לברר של מי הוא ולמי להחזיר ולכך אין לנו ליכנס בדבר: **ומ״ש** משני שטרות כו׳. בשטרות מכר או מתנה איירי ולכך לשמואל דאמר שודא לא דמיא להא דתנן בפ׳ מי שהיה נשוי (כתובות דף צג.) היו כולן יוצאות ביום אחד ואין שם אלא מנה אחד כולן חולקות בשוה דהתם בשעבוד איירי דאין שעבוד חל אלא מאותה שעה שמוכיח מתוך שטר שמתחיל השעבוד דהיינו ממחרת יום שנכתבו דביום שנכתבו אין מוכיח מתוך השטר מתי התחיל אם בבקר אם בערב אבל מתנה או מכר כל הקודם באותו יום עצמו זכה:

רב

מט א ב מיי׳ פ״י מהל׳ טוען הל׳ ו סמג עשין צה טוש״ע ח״מ סי׳ קלט סעיף ג:
נ ג מיי׳ שם פט״ו הל׳ ד סמג שם טוש״ע ח״מ שם סעיף א וסי׳ קמו סעיף כב [וברב אלפס עוד בכתובות פ״ט דף קי:]:

רבינו גרשום

תפסוה. ברשותייכו בכח ב״ד לפי שאיני מאמינה לו דשמא ימכרנה: **אמר להו.** הואיל ולא מצאתי עדים **אפקוה** מרשותייכו ואותבוה בינינו כדמעיקרא **וכל דאלים** בכח יותר להוציא מיד חבירו **גבר** ותהא לו עד שיביאו עדים ואח״כ נותן למי שהעדים מעידין: **רב יהודה אמר.** הואיל דתפסוה בית דין מזה (חדא) **לא מפקינן** מידם עד דמייתי חד מינייהו סהדי. **והלכתא לא תפסי׳** לכתחלה דשמא מבדה ונתן עינו בה והיאך נוציאנה מיד זה בדבורו של זה **ואי תפסוה לא מפקינן: ומ״ש משני שטרות היוצאין ביום אחד.** שהיו שניהן באין שהלוו לכאחד ביום א׳ ולכל א׳ מהם משועבד קרקע ומכרו לא׳ והן באין לטורפן ואין שטר א׳ מהם מוקדם מחבירו:

א) [גיטין ס:], ב) כתובות לד., ג) צ״ל ואם כן:

הגהות הב״ח

(א) גמ׳ תיפסוה עד דמייתינא: (ב) תוס׳ ד״ה (בע״א) וכל וכו׳ דטעמא דרב נחמן דאמר יחלוקו משום דכיון כל״ל ותיבות דר׳ אבא נמחק: (ג) ד״ה ההוא וכו׳ ואין נראה לר״י דהא:

ליקוטי רש״י

כל דאלים גבר. וכגון שאין לו עדות וחזקה לזה יותר מזה ומשום דמספקא לן מי שרואה להחזיק יחזיק ולא נוציא מידו [רשב״ם לקמן מג: ע״ש:]. **משני שטרות היוצאין ביום אחד.** מכר שדה אחת לשני בני אדם ביום אחד [כתובות צד.].

Another incident:

דַּהֲווּ הַהוּא אַרְבָּא – There was **a certain boat** on the river מִינְצוּ עֲלָהּ בֵּי תְּרֵי – **that two men quarreled over,** הַאי אָמַר דִּידִי הִיא – **this one saying, "It is mine,"** וְהַאי אָמַר דִּידִי הִיא – **and the other saying, "It is mine."**[1] אָתָא חַד מִינַּיְיהוּ לְבֵי דִינָא – **One of [the litigants] came before the court** וְאָמַר – **and said,** תִּיפְסוּהָ – **"Seize [the boat],** אַדְמַיְיתִינָא סַהֲדֵי דְּדִידִי הִיא – **until I** can **produce witnesses that it belongs to me."**[2]

The question therefore presented itself:

תַּפְסִינַן אוֹ לֹא תַּפְסִינַן – **Does [the court] seize [the boat] or not?** רַב הוּנָא אָמַר תַּפְסִינַן – **Rav Huna says: We seize [the boat],** רַב יְהוּדָה אָמַר לֹא תַּפְסִינַן – **while Rav Yehudah says: We do not seize it.**[3]

The court did in fact seize the boat.[4] However:

אָזַל – **[The litigant who had requested the seizure] went forth,** וְלֹא אַשְׁכַּח סַהֲדֵי – **but did not find witnesses** to support his claim. אָמַר לְהוּ – **He** therefore **requested of [the court]:** אַפְקוּהָ – **"Release [the boat]** from escrow, וְכָל דְּאַלִּים גָּבַר – **and let the one who is stronger prevail!"**[5]

This raises a second question:

מַפְּקִינַן אוֹ לֹא מַפְּקִינַן – Having seized it, **does [the court] release it** from escrow **or not?** רַב יְהוּדָה אָמַר לֹא מַפְּקִינַן – **Rav Yehudah says: We do not release it,** רַב פָּפָּא אָמַר מַפְּקִינַן – while **Rav Pappa says: We release it.**[6]

A definitive ruling:

וְהִלְכְתָא – **And the halachah is:** לֹא תַּפְסִינַן – **We do not seize** disputed property, וְהֵיכָא דְּתָפַס – **but where we** already **seized** it[7] לֹא מַפְּקִינַן – **we do not release it.**[8]

The Gemara now discusses the ruling of "let he who is stronger prevail," cited above:

זֶה אוֹמֵר שֶׁל אֲבוֹתַי – Ownership of property is disputed by two men.[9] **This** one **says,** "It belonged **to my forefathers,"** וְזֶה אוֹמֵר שֶׁל אֲבוֹתַי – **and this** other one **says,** "It belonged **to my forefathers,"** and neither litigant can prove his claim. אָמַר רַב נַחְמָן – **Rav Nachman said:** כָּל דְּאַלִּים גָּבַר – **Let he who is stronger prevail!** I.e. the court withdraws and allows the litigants to fight over possession of the property.[10]

NOTES

1. Since neither litigant could prove his claim, and neither was in possession of the boat, the court was required to withdraw from the case and allow the stronger litigant to prevail. (The specific guidelines for when this ruling is applied will be discussed by the Gemara below.)

[It is only because the litigants were not in possession of the boat that the court was prepared to allow them to vie for seizure of it. However, had they both been holding on to it, the law requires the court to divide it between them (*Rashbam; cf. Tosafos* in the name of *Riva*).]

2. He claimed that he was able to produce witnesses that the boat was his, and the court granted him one month's time in which to do this (*Nimukei Yosef*). But he was concerned that in the interim, his opponent would sell the boat and pocket the proceeds. Therefore, he petitioned the court to impound the boat while he searched for witnesses (*Rashbam*).

3. Below, the Gemara will cite an Amoraic dispute concerning the following question: What is the law where the court seized a disputed item because one litigant promised to prove his claim, but that litigant ultimately was unable to do so? Does the court restore the item to the original "let the stronger one prevail" situation, allowing either litigant to seize it? Or, having already impounded it, does the court continue to hold it until one litigant can prove his claim?

It is on this disagreement that the present dispute hinges. Both Rav Huna and Rav Yehudah agree that the court may not impound the boat if this action could adversely affect its true owner. Thus, Rav Yehudah, who maintains (below) that the court does not release impounded property until it can determine its true owner, holds that the court should not initially impound it. This is because if the court impounds it, and the litigant who requested the impoundment is ultimately unable to prove his claim, the court would be forced to continue holding it. Specifically, we are concerned that the litigant who asked the court to impound it may be the impostor. Realizing that he will not succeed in his attempt to gain possession of the boat, he schemes to have the court seize it, because since they will not later release it, he will at least have deprived his fellow of it. This would be a detriment to the true owner, because had the court not impounded it, he might have been able to seize it under the "let the stronger one prevail" rule. Therefore, Rav Yehudah holds, the court may not initially seize it.

Rav Huna, on the other hand, rules that if the litigant who requested the impoundment was not able to prove his claim, the court would release the item to allow both litigants to vie for it. Thus, by initially impounding it, the court does no harm to the true owner. For if the litigant who petitioned for impoundment is able to prove his ownership, fine and well. If not, the court will release the item, which will allow the true owner a chance to seize it, just as he would have been able to do had the court not impounded it. Thus, Rav Huna maintains, there is no reason for the court to refrain from impounding it at the outset (*Rashbam; cf. Tosafos*).

4. It ruled in accordance with Rav Huna and impounded the boat. Alternatively, *both* litigants requested the impoundment. In this case, even Rav Yehudah agrees that the court impounds it [for even the boat's true owner requested the court to do so] (*Rashbam*).

5. [He requested that the court withdraw from the case (since there was no evidence to support either side) and allow the stronger one to prevail.] Specifically, this meant that the one who could muster either the physical power to seize it or the legal strength of evidence to prove ownership would gain control of the boat (*Rashbam*).

The legal decision of "let the stronger prevail" is discussed at length in the Gemara below.

6. Rav Yehudah maintains that once the court comes into possession of the boat, it may not release it to the indeterminate status it was in before it was impounded, because this may result in the impostor seizing it. Rather, the court is now duty bound to return the boat to its true owner, and if he has not yet been identified, to hold on to it until such time as his identity becomes known. Rav Pappa, on the other hand, argues that the court impounded the boat knowing full well that the litigant might not succeed in producing witnesses to his claim. Thus, their impoundment was made with the intention to release the boat to its previous indeterminate status if witnesses were not forthcoming. Therefore, if in fact the litigant does not produce witnesses, the court may release it and allow the stronger litigant to prevail (*Rashbam*).

7. Either through a unanimous request by both litigants or in error (*Nimukei Yosef, Ran*).

8. The halachah thus follows the view of Rav Yehudah on both questions (*Rashbam*).

9. The Gemara applies to both movable and real property, in an instance where neither litigant can prove his claim, and neither is in possession of the disputed property. Thus, neither has any ascendancy over the other (*Rashbam*).

10. Lacking evidence on which to base a ruling, the court withdraws and allows the stronger litigant to seize the disputed property.

Rosh (§22) maintains that once one litigant gains possession of it, the other may not take it back from him, because it is not logical to assume that the law would create a situation of perpetual feuding, wherein one litigant could seize the object one day and his opponent the next. See, however, *Shach* 139:2 that many *Poskim* (among them *Tosafos*) dispute *Rosh's* interpretation and rule that the other litigant may take the object back from the litigant who gained possession of it first.

Rosh further maintains that although the law of "let the stronger one prevail" is primarily a withdrawal by the court, in instituting it the Sages felt confident that the truth would ultimately triumph. Specifically, they reasoned that it is likely that the property's true owner would eventually come up with proof of his claim. Furthermore, the true owner will probably strive more vigorously to retain his property than the thief will to steal it, especially since the thief knows that even should he succeed in wresting control of it from the owner, his victory is likely to be short-lived, because the owner may be able to subsequently prove his claim.

ההוא ארבא דהוו מינצו עלה בי תרי האי אמר דידי היא והאי אמר דידי היא אתא חד מינייהו לבי דינא ואמר תיפסוה (א) אדמייתינא סהדי דדידי היא תפסינן או לא תפסינן רב הונא אמר תפסינן רב יהודה אמר [א] לא תפסינן אזל ולא אשכח סהדי אמר להו אפקוה וכל דאלים גבר מפקינן או לא מפקינן רב יהודה אמר [ב] לא מפקינן רב פפא אמר מפקינן והלכתא לא תפסינן והיכא דתפס לא מפקינן: זה אומר של אבותי וזה אומר של אבותי [א] אמר רב נחמן [ג] כל דאלים גבר ומאי שנא [ג] משני שטרות היוצאין ביום אחד דרב

אבלי הו"ל מחויב שבועה ואינו יכול לישבע ומשלם. כך נראה שיטה זו בעיני ושוב מצאתיה כן בפי' ר"ח ויש לשונות אחרים ואין בהם ממש וקי"ל בהא כרבי אבא מדליף אביי מינה ואף על גב דפליגי עליה רב ושמואל בפרק כל הנשבעין (שבועות דף מז.) דאמרי חזרה שבועה לסיני והמוציא מחבירו עליו הראיה ותנן נמי התם וכן היתומים מן היתומים לא יפרעו אלא בשבועה ורב ושמואל דאמרי תרוייהו לא שנו אלא שמת מלוה בחיי הלוה אבל מת לוה בחיי מלוה כבר נתחייב מלוה לבני לוה שבועה ואין אדם מוריש שבועה לבניו ממון שהוא מחויב עליו שבועה אלמא הואיל ומחויב שבועה שלא התקבלתי חוב זה ויתומין אין יכולין לישבע כן אלא שלא פקדנו אבא ואין זו שבועה המוטלת על אביהם וגם יתומים של לוה אין יכולין לישבע שפרעו אביהם קא אמרי רב ושמואל שלא יפרע אלמא המחויב שבועה ואינו יכול לישבע לא זה ולא זה סבירא לרב ושמואל חזרה שבועה לסיני ואין כאן לא שבועה ולא פרעון ור"א פליג עלייהו ואמר יורשין נשבעין שבועת יורשים ונוטלין דלא ס"ל לדרב ושמואל ואמרי' התם האי דיינא דעבד כר"א עבד דעבד כרב ושמואל עבד אפ"ה הלכתא כר' אבא ולא כרב ושמואל דאמרינן התם הכו דלא להוסיף עלה עשו תקנה שלא להוסיף על דברי רב ושמואל ללמוד מדין זה דיתומים מן היתומים לשאר דינין ולומר חזרה שבועה לסיני דדין זה לבדו דיתומים מן היתומים הוא דקי"ל כרב ושמואל בדיעבד משום תקנת יתומים בני לוה דחסינן עלייהו שלא לפרע מהן בלא שבועה מעלייתא אבל בשאר דינין קי"ל כר' אבא דהמחויב שבועה ואינו יכול לישבע משלם וגם ר"ח פסק דהלכתא כרבי אבא: **ארבא.** ספינה שבנהר: **האי אמר דידי הוא** כו'. ולא זה ולא זה מוחזקין בה מדלא רמי עלה ממתניתין דשנים אוחזין בטלית שזה נוטל עד מקום שידו מגעת וזה נוטל עד מקום שידו מגעת ולא אמרינן כל דאלים גבר כן פיר"ח: **תיפסוה.** פן ימכרנה אבל חזקה שהחזיק בה אחר שערער זה עליה אינה כלום דאנן סהדי שבתורת חטיפה באה לידו: **תפסינן או לא תפסינן.** מי לימא דתפסי לה ב"ד דהא אי לא משכח סהדי הדרינן ומפקינן לה כדמעיקרא ולא הפסיד בעל הספינה בתפיסת ב"ד כלום או דלמא לא תפסינן דדלמא לא משכח סהדי ולא הדרינן ומפקינן לה כדלקמן ונמצא שהפסיד בעל הספינה על ידינו דאי הוה שבקינן לה דלמא הוי אלים וגבר בעל הספינה ונמצא זוכה בשלו כן נ"ל טעם השאלה: **רב הונא אומר תפסינן.** ס"ל כרב פפא דאמר מפקינן רב יהודה אומר לא תפסינן משום דס"ל לא מפקינן כדלקמיה והלכך לא תפסינן דשמא זה אין לו עדים ושקרן הוא ומכל וכל רוצה להפסיד את חבירו דמאחר דתפסי' יודע הוא דתו לא מפקינן: **א"ל אפקוה.** וכגון דאיתרמי מילתא דתפסינן לה כרב הונא אי נמי שאמרו שניהם לב"ד לתפסה ודברי הכל: **וכל דאלים גבר.** בין בראיות בין בכח כמו שפוסק רב נחמן לפנינו כל דאלים גבר: **לא מפקינן.** דמאחר שבא ממון ישראל ביד ב"ד אין רשאין להפקירו אלא מעכבין אותו ממון עד שידעו למי ישיבו: **מפקינן.** כעין שמצאוהו מתחלה שלדעת כן תפסוהו שאם לא יביא עדים יחזירוהו וכל דאלים גבר: **והלכתא לא תפסינן והיכא דתפסינן לא מפקינן.** כרב יהודה: **זה אומר של אבותי וזה אומר של אבותי.** בין בספינה בין בקרקע ואין עדות וחזקה לזה יותר מזה: **ומ"ש משני שטרות היוצאין.** לפניו על שדה אחת של ראובן שכתב שטר מתנה לשמעון ושטר מתנה ללוי ושניהם ביום אחד ונמצא שאין זה מוחזק יותר מזה כלל ואפי' נתברר ששמעון בשחר ולוי אחריו בערב אין הקדמה

לי בידך והלה אומר אין לך בידי אלא חמשים וחמשים איני יודע מתוך שאינו יכול לישבע משלם והיינו כר' אבא ומיהו איכא למימר דר"נ דמוקי מתני' כר"מ וכמו שמפרש ר' אבא הוא סבר כר' יוסי אבל עוד קשה דבשמעתין משמע דהלכתא כר' אבא מדקאמרינן סבור רבנן קמיה דאביי למימר דהיינו נסכא דר' אבא וקאמר נמי אלא אי דמיא לרבי אבא כו' וכר"מ קי"ל כרב נחמן בדיני ועוד תימה דהתם גבי יתומים מן היתומים קאמרי רב ושמואל דאם מת לוה בחיי מלוה כבר נתחייב מלוה לבני לוה שבועה ואין אדם מוריש שבועה לבניו ומתוך שאין התובעין יכולין לישבע פטור הנתבע ור"א פליג עליה (שם מח.) וקאמר יורשין נשבעין שבועת יורשים ונוטלין והיינו כרבי אבא דמתוך שאינו יכול לישבע או תובע או הנתבע משלם הנתבע ומסיק התם דעבד כרב ושמואל עבד דעבד כרבי אלעזר עבד ומפרש ר"ת דרב נחמן שפיר סבר כר' אבא בנסכא ובמנה יש לי בידך וה"ל אין לך בידי אלא חמשים וחמשים איני יודע ודוקא בשניהם חשודין פסיק רב נחמן כר' יוסי דאמר יחלוקו ורבי אבא בשניהם חשודין מודה לר"נ דהלכה כרבי יוסי וטעמא משום דקנסינן שכנגדו לפי שהוא חשוד הלכך מפסיד החצי אבל בעלמא מחויב שבועה ואינו יכול לישבע משלם והא דקאמר התם דרבותינו שבא"י ר' אבא לאו למימר דר' אבא סבר לה כר"מ אלא דדייק כיון דר' אבא בעלמא סבר דמתוך שאינו יכול לישבע משלם אית לן למימר דאיהו מפרש מילתיה דר"מ דחזרה שבועה למחויב לה והלכה כר"נ בשניהם חשודים וכר' אבא בנסכא ודוקא ביתומים מסקינן דעבד כרב ושמואל עבד ודעבד כר"א עבד כדאמר הכו דלא להוסיף עלה אבל אין לפרש (ב) טעמא דרב נחמן דאמר יחלוקו משום דר' אבא דכיון דשניהם חשודים ה"ל כאילו תרוייהו מחויבים שבועה ואין יכולין והלכך כל אחד מפסיד חצי ורבי אבא סבר כיון דעיקר שבועה על הנתבע ואין יכול לישבע משלם הכל דא"כ ר' אבא ורב נחמן מאי סברי שפיר כרב ושמואל ביתומים מן היתומים כי מת לוה בחיי מלוה ומפסידין בני מלוה כיון דאין יכולין לישבע ואין נוטלין כמו שמפסיד שכנגדו חשוד על השבועה החצי שאינו נוטל כשגם הוא חשוד ובפ' כל הנשבעין (שבועות דף מז.) משמע כל הסוגיא דרב ושמואל פליגי אדרב נחמן ואדרבי אבא [ג] וע"כ צ"ל דלרבי אבא וכן לרב נחמן מתוך שאינו יכול לישבע אפילו התובע משלם הנתבע כדפרי':

ההוא ארבא דהוו מינצו וכו'. הדין כל דאלים גבר וא"ת מ"ש משנים אוחזין בטלית דאמר בריש ב"מ (דף ב. ושם ד"ה ויחלוקו) דיחלוקו ומפרש ר"ת דאוחזין שאני דכיון ששניהם מוחזקים אין לנו להניח שיגזול האחד לחבירו דחשיב כאילו אנו יודעין שיש לשניהן חלק בה שכל דבר יש להעמיד בחזקת מי שהוא בידו כדאמרי' גבי נסכא דר' אבא דאע"ג דאמר דידי חטפי חשבינן ליה גזלן וחייב לשלם כאילו הוא ברור שהיתה הנסכא של אותו שהיה מוחזק בה והא דמדמי ליה התם טלית לשאר [יהא מונח עד שיבא אליהו] אע"ג דבשאר דהתם אין שום אחד מוחזק צ"ל דשאר נמי חשיב להו כאילו שניהם מוחזקים בו כיון דמכח שניהם נפקד ולריב"א נראה דלאו דוקא אוחזין מדמדמי לה לשאר ואדשמעתין איכא לשנויי כדמשני התם אפי' תימא ר' יוסי התם ודאי איכא רמאי הכא איכא למימר תרוייהו בהדי הדדי אגבהוה הכי נמי בארבא כיון דאיכא רמאי לא יחלוקו אלא הוי דינא כל דאלים גבר והא דלא אמרינן בשנים שהפקידו כל דאלים גבר משום דלא מפקינן כדאמרינן הכא אי תפסינן לא מפקינן אבל מ"ד מפקינן לא אתי שפיר ומאי פריך נמי בסמוך מב' שטרות וממחליף פרה בחמור והא התם ליכא רמאי ואין נראה (ג) דהא האי טעמא לא מסיק אלא לאוקומי מתני' כר' יוסי אבל לרבנן קאמר התם האי מנה ודאי דחד מינייהו הוא אבל טלית דאיכא למימר דתרוייהו הוא יחלוקו ולהכי טעמא ה"נ הוה לן למימר יחלוקו דאפשר להיות דהוה ארבא דתרוייהו ועוד פי' ריב"א דהיכא דאוחזין אפי' איכא רמאי יחלוקו כדתניא התם בפ"ק (דף ז.) גבי שנים אוחזין בשטר וקשיא לר"י דא"כ היכי פריך לפירושו (שם דף ג.) והא נמי כשאר דמיא דאיכא למימר אוחזין שאני דהא מהניא אפילו היכא דאיכא רמאי ועוד מאי פריך התם (דף ז.) ולית ליה לרבי מתני' דשנים אוחזין בטלית הא ע"כ יש חילוק בין דין שטר לדין טלית דבטלית אפי' אין אוחזין יחלוקו ובשטר כי אין אוחזין הוי דין כל דאלים גבר: **רב** הונא אמר תפסינן. פי' הקונט' משום דמפקינן ורב יהודה דאמר לא תפסינן משום דלא תפסינן לא מפקינן ואין נראה לר"י לתלות זה בזה מדלא פליגי הנהו אמוראי גופייהו במפקינן הנך דפליגי בתפסינן לכך נראה דר"ה דאמר דתפסינן אפי' למאן דאמר לא מפקינן דמהימנינא ליה שיביא עדים ורב יהודה דאמר לא תפסינן אפי' למ"ד מפקינן היינו היכא דתפסינן כבר אבל לכתחילה לא תפסינן דחיישינן דלמא לא מייתי עדים ולא נדע לברר של מי הוא ולמי להחזיר ולכך אין לנו ליכנס בדבר: **ומ"ש** משני שטרות כו'. בשטרות מכר או מתנה איירי ולכך לשמואל דאמר שודא לא דמיא להא דתנן בפ' מי שהיה נשוי (כתובות דף צג:) היו כולן יוצאות ביום אחד ואין שם אלא מנה אחד כולן חולקות בשוה דהתם בשעבוד איירי דאין שעבוד חל אלא מאותה שעה שמוכיח מתוך שטר שמתחיל השעבוד דהיינו ממחרת יום שנכתבו דביום שנכתבו אין מוכיח מתוך השטר מתי התחיל אם בבקר אם בערב אבל מתנה או מכר כל הקודם באותו יום עצמו זכה:

רב

עין משפט נר מצוה

מט א ב מיי' פ"י מהל' טוען הל' ו סמג עשין צה טוש"ע ח"מ סי' קלט סעיף ג:

נ ג מיי' שם פט"ו הל' ד סמג שם טוש"ע ח"מ שם סעיף א וסי' קמו סעיף כב [וברב אלפס עוד בכתובות פ"ט דף קי:]:

רבינו גרשום

תפסוה. ברשותייכו בכח ב"ד לפי שאיני מאמינה לו דשמא ימכרנה: **אמר להו.** הואיל ולא מצאתי עדים **אפקוה** מרשותייכו ואותבוה בינינו כדמעיקרא **וכל דאלים** בכח יותר להוציא מיד חבירו **גבר** ותהא לו עד שיביאו עדים ואח"כ נותן למי שהעדים מעידין: **רב יהודה אמר.** הואיל דתפסוה בית דין מזה (חדא) **לא מפקינן** מידם עד דמייתי חד מינייהו סהדי. **והלכתא לא תפסי'** לכתחלה דשמא מבדה ונתן עינו בה והיאך נוציאנה מיד זה בדבורו של זה **ואי תפסוה לא מפקינן: ומ"ש משני שטרות היוצאין ביום אחד.** שהיו שניהן באין שהלוו לו כאחד ביום א' ולכל א' מהם משועבד קרקע ומכרו לא' והן באין לטורפן ואין שטר א' מהם מוקדם מחבירו:

מסורת הש"ס

א) [גיטין ס:], ב) כתובות לד., ג) נ"ל ואם כן:

הגהות הב"ח

(א) גמ' תיפסוה עד דמייתינא: (ב) תוס' ד"ה (בע"א) וכל וכו' דטעמא דרב נחמן דאמר יחלוקו משום דכיון כצ"ל ותיבות דר' אבא נמחק: (ג) ד"ה ההוא וכו' ואין נראה לר"י דהא:

ליקוטי רש"י

כל דאלים גבר. וכגון שאין לו עדות וחזקה לזה יותר מזה ומשום דמספקא לן מי שרולה להחזיק יחזיק ולא נוציא מידו [רשב"ם לקמן מג: ע"ש:]. **משני שטרות היוצאין ביום אחד.** מכר שדה אחת לשני בני אדם ביום אחד [כתובות צד.].

The Gemara asks:

וּמַאי שְׁנָא – **But why** is the ruling here **different** מִשְּׁנֵי שְׁטָרוֹת הַיּוֹצְאִין בְּיוֹם אֶחָד – **from** the case of **two deeds that are presented** before the court, each of which records a gift of the same property to a different individual and each of which was issued **on the same day**[11]

NOTES

11. Both deeds were written regarding a single property, one stating that the property was given to Shimon, the other stating that it was given to Levi. The dates on both documents are identical so that both Shimon and Levi have equal claim to the land. Even if witnesses testify that Shimon's document was delivered to him in the morning and Levi's in the afternoon, Shimon would nonetheless have no advantage over Levi, because the document does not transfer title till the final moment of the date inscribed therein. This is because since people customarily omit mention of a specific time of day from legal documents, they mean the document to effect the transaction only at the end of the day rather than at the moment it is delivered. Hence, since the date on Levi's document coincides with the one on Shimon's, Levi has an equal claim to the land (*Rashbam*).

דְּרַב אָמַר יַחֲלוֹקוּ – **regarding which Rav says: [The bearers of the deeds] divide** the disputed property, וּשְׁמוּאֵל אָמַר – **while Shmuel says:** שׁוּדָא דְדַיָּינֵי – It is up to **the judges' discretion,**[1] and they may award the property to whomever they see fit? Why does Rav Nachman disregard these two options, ruling instead that the court withdraws and allows the litigants to settle the matter?

The Gemara distinguishes between the two cases:

הָתָם – **There,** regarding the two identical deeds, לֵיכָּא לְמֵיקַם עֲלָהּ דְּמִילְּתָא – **it is not possible to ascertain** the truth of **the matter.**[2] Thus, the court arranges a settlement. הָכָא – **Here,** in Rav Nachman's case, אִיכָּא לְמֵיקַם עֲלָהּ דְּמִילְּתָא – **it is possible to ascertain** the truth of **the matter,** for further evidence may come to light. The court therefore withdraws rather than impose a settlement that they will quite possibly be forced to overturn.[3]

The Gemara questions this distinction, based on a Mishnah which mentions a court-imposed settlement even in a case where resolution of the uncertainty is possible:

וּמַאי שְׁנָא מֵהָא דִּתְנַן – **But why is [Rav Nachman's case] different from that which was learned in a Mishnah:**[4] הַמַּחֲלִיף פָּרָה בַּחֲמוֹר – If ONE EXCHANGES A COW FOR A DONKEY, וְיָלְדָה – AND IT CALVES;[5] וְכֵן הַמּוֹכֵר שִׁפְחָתוֹ וְיָלְדָה – AND, SIMILARLY, if ONE SELLS HIS MAIDSERVANT AND SHE GIVES BIRTH,[6] – זֶה אוֹמֵר עַד שֶׁלֹּא מָכַרְתִּי יָלְדָה – [THE SELLER] SAYS, "SHE GAVE BIRTH BEFORE I SOLD her, and the offspring is mine," וְזֶה אוֹמֵר מִשֶּׁלָּקַחְתִּי יָלְדָה – WHILE [THE BUYER] SAYS, "SHE GAVE BIRTH AFTER I BOUGHT her, and the offspring is mine,"[7] יַחֲלוֹקוּ – THEY DIVIDE.[8] Thus we see from the Mishnah that even in an instance where the uncertainty can be resolved,[9] the court will impose a settlement rather than withdraw, which contradicts Rav Nachman's ruling. – ? –

The Gemara explains the difference between these two cases:

הָתָם לְהַאי – **There** in the Mishnah's case **this litigant**

NOTES

1. Literally: toss of the judges. According to *Rashbam,* this means that the judges are required to analyze the situation and attempt to determine which of the two litigants the giver favored, for it is assumed that he meant to give the gift to this one. *Tosafos,* however, point out that this interpretation is not applicable to several instances in the Talmud where the decision of שׁוּדָא is mentioned. Therefore, they explain Shmuel's ruling to mean that the judges may give the land to whichever litigant they desire, without attempting to determine which one the giver favored.

While dividing the land seems to be an equitable compromise, it is certain that half the field has been awarded to the wrong party. Shmuel therefore rules that the judges should use their discretion and award it to one, for in this way there is at least a chance that the field has been awarded to its true owner (*Rashbam*).

2. Neither litigant can produce witnesses to support his claim, because both deeds bear identical dates. Thus, even if witnesses were to testify that one particular deed was transferred earlier in the day, it would not indicate that the man named in it was the true beneficiary, for a deed conveys title only at the end of the date written therein, as explained above, 34b note 11. Consequently, since the true owner will never be determined, the court imposes a settlement by either dividing the field between both litigants or discretionally awarding it to one of them (*Rashbam*).

3. If the court were to impose a settlement and witnesses were to subsequently come forth with testimony that is at odds with that settlement, the court would be forced to overturn its original decision. Therefore, rather than get involved, the court withdraws and allows possession to be determined by the litigants themselves. If new evidence emerges later, the court will step in at that time and adjudicate the case (*Rashbam*).

4. *Bava Metzia* 100a.

5. The Mishnah deals with a transaction effected by an act of acquisition known as *chalifin,* barter. In the form of *chalifin* discussed here, each object serves in place of payment of the other as well as its means of acquisition. Once it has been agreed that one object is to be exchanged for the other, the transfer of one object suffices to complete the transaction and the second object is then automatically acquired by its new owner as well.

In this particular case, Reuven has a cow and Shimon a donkey, which they agree to exchange. Reuven effects the exchange by drawing the donkey towards himself. This not only transfers ownership of the donkey to Reuven, but also causes Shimon to gain ownership of the cow, which in this case was elsewhere at the time. Later, it is discovered that the cow calved around the time of the *chalifin,* but it is unclear whether this happened before the acquisition took place (in which case the calf would belong to Reuven, having been born while the cow was still his), or following it (in which case it would belong to Shimon, having been born after he acquired the cow).

This doubt is possible only in the case of a barter. Should the cow be sold for money, the sale would not be final until the buyer drew the cow into his possession, because the law is that a transfer of money cannot effect the acquisition of movables. That being the case, it would be clear whether the cow had calved before or after the sale (*Rashbam*).

6. This case does not refer to *chalifin,* but to a straightforward sale. Non-Jewish slaves, the type to which the Mishnah refers, can be acquired with money, unlike other movables. Thus, it is possible to purchase a slave without the slave being physically present at the transaction. Consequently, as soon as Shimon, the buyer, gives the money to Reuven, the seller, the ownership of the slave is transferred to Shimon.

The slave in question was a pregnant woman who gave birth around the time of the sale, before entering Shimon's physical possession. It is therefore unclear whether she gave birth prior to the sale [which would leave the child the property of the seller], or following it [making the child the property of the buyer].

7. Reuven, the seller, claims that the cow or the maidservant gave birth before being exchanged or sold, and that the offspring therefore belongs to him. Shimon, the buyer, however, claims that the cow or the maidservant gave birth after the exchange or purchase, making the offspring his.

8. They divide the value of the calf or slave child. This is so, however, only if neither is in possession of the disputed article. Thus, the Mishnah must refer to a case in which the cow was in a public meadow and the slavewoman was in the street. Otherwise, the Gemara in *Bava Metzia* rules, the offspring would belong to the one in whose possession it was found, and it would be up to the other one to prove that it was his (*Rashbam*).

9. This uncertainty can be resolved if witnesses come forward who testify to the exact time of the birth. Thus, according to the distinction just made, no settlement should be imposed in such a case, for it may have to be overturned. Rather, the court should withdraw, and allow the stronger litigant to take possession! (*Rashbam*).

דרב אמר יחלוקו ושמואל אמר א שודא דדייני התם ליכא למיקם עלה דמילתא הכא איכא למיקם עלה דמילתא ומאי שנא מהא ג דתנן ב המחליף פרה בחמור וילדה וכן המוכר שפחתו וילדה זה אומר עד שלא מכרתי ילדה וזה אומר משלקחתי ילדה יחלוקו ד התם להאי

אית

הקדמה בשעות אלא בירושלים כדאמרי' בכתובות ג גבי ההוא עובדא דאימיה דרמי בר חמא בלפרא כתבתינהו לנכסי לרמי בר חמא ובאורתא כתבתינהו למר עוקבא בר חמא ואוקמיה ביד (א) רב עוקבא אע"פ שהוא אחרון ומשום האי טעמא אטו בירושלים יתבי דכותבין שעות וכיון שלא פירש לו ראובן לשמעון השעה נמצא שלא זכהו בכתב זה עד הערב הואיל ולא נתפרש בו שעת שחרית ונמצאו שניהם שוין: יחלוקו. דספיקא הוא וליכא למימר הכא המוציא מחבירו דלאין א' מוחזק (ב) מחבירו: שודא דדייני. לאותו שיראה נוטה לב הדיינים שהיה הנותן אוהבו או קרובו יותר דודאי להוהו גמר ולקני לו יתנו את הקרקע ושמא (ג) זכה בעל הקרקע בשלו אבל כשאתה אומר יחלוקו בודאי אחד נטל החצי שלא כדין: שודא. לשון השלכה ירה בים (שמות טו) [מתרגמינן] שדי בימא ולעיל נמי גימא רב נחמן חלוקה או שודא ואמאי אמר כל דאלים גבר: התם. בב' שטרות ליכא למיקם עלה דמילתא היום או למחר שיבא לאחד עדים ויבטל שטרי השטרות שוין בזמנן ואפילו אם יבאו עדים ויעידו זה נכתב ונמסר בבקר וזה בערב הלא אין הקדמה בשעות כמו שפירשנו למעלה וליכא למימר שמא זה נמסר תחלה יום או יומים או חדש ואחר כך נמסר השני לשני דמאחר שנכתבו ביום אחד מסתמא גם ביום אחד נמסרו כמו שמוכיח לשון הכתוב בשטר הלכך רב אמר חולקין ושמואל אמר שודא דדייני הואיל ואין לברר לעולם הדין עם מי משתלשין ב"ד בדין ודנין אותו. אבל הכא בהאי קרקע ליכא לא שטר ולא (ד) עדים וליכא למיקם עלה דמילתא אם יבאו ויעידו של מי הוא הלכך אין כאן לומר חלוקה ושודא דשמא יבאו עדים ויסתרו את הדין שדנו ב"ד הלכך אין ב"ד מזקקין להם לדון דין שסופו לבא לידי עיוות אלא מניחים אותן וכל דאלים גבר עד שיבאו עדים ויבררו הדבר: ומ"ש. הא דרב נחמן ממחליף פרה בחמור וכיון שמשך בעל הפרה את החמור נקנית הפרה לבעל החמור בכל מקום שהיא דמטלטלין נקנין בחליפין כדתנן בקדושין (דף כח.) כל הנעשה דמים באחר כיון שזכה זה נתחייב זה בחליפין ולכך אין הדבר ידוע הולד של מי הוא שהרי לא ראה עדיין את פרתו אבל במכירה בדמים לא מצי למינקט דאין מעות קונות ויחזרו בהן ואילו משכה לביתו אחר מתן מעות תו לא מצי מוכר למימר ברשותי ילדה דהא בביתא דלוקח קיימא הלכך נקט חליפין בחמור ופרה ולא דמים. ובפ' השואל פריך ונחזי ברשות דמאן קיימא וליהוי אידך המוציא מחבירו עליו הראיה ומשני דקיימא באגם. ומכירה נקט גבי שפחה דעבד נקנה בכסף בלא משיכה ומשנתן מעות נקנית לו השפחה בכ"מ שהיא והלכך אין ידוע ברשות מי ילדה שהרי לא ראה אותה הלוקח בשעת מתן מעות: יחלוקו. והא הכא דאיכא למיקם עלה דמלתא אם יבאו עדים ויעידו ברשות מי ילדה ואפילו הכי לא אמרינן כל דאלים גבר וקשיא לרב נחמן: התם. גבי המחליף פרה בחמור לתרוייהו אית להו דררא דממונא שהפרה והשפחה של שניהם היתה בזה אחר זה וכל אחד ואחד טוען פרתי ושפחתי ילדה בהיותה ברשותי אי נמי בשעת חליפין ילדה ואין לברר של מי הוי הולד הלכך יחלוקו ושודא דדייני ליכא למימר הכא אפי' לשמואל דלא שייך למימר אלא גבי מתנה לשנים שיראו ב"ד למי אוהב יותר דלדידיה גמר ומקני אבל הכא בדרב נחמן שזה אומר של אבותי כו': ז אי דמר לא דמר. לא היתה הקרקע של אידך מעולם. וי"מ האי ומאי שנא מהמחליף כו' דאדשמואל פריך דקאמר שודא והכא חזינן יחלוקו ואינה שיטת הגמרא דהא בכתובות בפרק מי שהיה נשוי איתא עיקר מילתייהו דרב ושמואל ופריך התם פירכי אחריני ומהכא לא פריך כל שכן הכא דלמרמי אדרב נחמן נקט לה הכא למילתייהו:

אם

רב אמר יחלוקו. להאי לישנא דמפרש בפרק מי שהיה נשוי (כתובות דף לד. ושם ד"ה לימא) דטעמא דרב משום דסבר כר"מ דאמר עדי חתימה כרתי ולכך יחלוקו אפילו איכא עדי מסירה שנמסר לאחד קודם כיון דמתוך החתימה אין ניכר מי קודם כדמוכח בריש כל הגט (גיטין דף כד:) דתנן כתב לגרש בו את הגדולה לא יגרש בו את הקטנה ודייק הא גדולה מצי מגרש ביה ומוקי לה בעדי מסירה ור"א אבל לר' מאיר אפי' גדולה לא מצי מגרש ביה אע"ג דאיכא עדי מסירה כיון דאין ניכר מתוך עדי החתימה ומיירי במתנה או במכר שקונה בשטר אבל אם קונה בכסף או בחזקה או בחליפין דאין השטר עומד אלא לראיה מודה רב דאמרינן שודא דאין צריך שיהא ניכר מתוך עדי החתימה כיון (ה) דאין אלא לראיה ולאותו לשון לא פריך מרב הכא דהכא דין הוא של שניהם כיון דביום אחד נחתמו אלא משמואל פריך ולפר"ח דפי' שודא דדייני מה שירצה הדיין יעשה אתי שפיר דהכא נמי בזה אומר של אבותי שייך שודא דדייני אבל לפ"ה שמפרש שודא למי שנראה לדיין שהיה אוהבו יותר קשה דבזה אומר של אבותי לא שייך שודא ויש לדחוק ולפרש שיטו הדיינים למי שנראה אמיתי בדבריו יותר (ו) ועוד להלהוי לישנא דמי שהיה נשוי (כתובות דף לד: ושם) דמוקי פלוגתא דרב ושמואל אליבא דר"א וס"ל לרב חלוקה עדיפא אתי שפיר דפריך (ז) מרב ולאותו לשון הוא עיקר כדמוכח התם מברייתא: ושמואל אמר שודא דדייני. היינו כר"א דאמר עדי מסירה כרתי דלר"מ לא הוה אמר שודא ונראה דהא דאמר (ח) בפרק מי שהיה נשוי (שם) כתב לאחד ומסר לאחר לזה שמסר לו קנה אע"פ שבשטר הא' נכתב קודם ונראה דהיינו דוקא שנכתבו ביום אחד הלכך הקודם במסירה זכה הואיל ואין ניכר מתוך השטר הא' שקדם אבל נכתב בב' ימים לזה שנכתב תחלה קנה שניכר מתוך החתימה שזה נכתב קודם אע"פ שמסר לזה מתחלה קנה דאח"כ כשמסר גם לזה זכה משעת חתימה דה"ק אביי בפ"ק דב"מ (דף יג.) עדיו בחתומיו זכין לו והשתא אתי שפיר דהא שמואל סבר הכא כר"א ובפ"ק דב"מ דחיק גמרא לאוקומי שמואל כאביי ועוד דבפ' זה בורר (סנהדרין דף כח:) גבי ההיא מתנתא דהוו חתימי עלה תרי גיסי משמע דסבר אביי כר' אלעזר דפריך ארב יוסף דקאמר זיל אקנייה בעדי מסירה כר"א ופריך אביי והא מודה ר"א במזויף מתוכו שהוא פסול וזהו דוחק (ט) דאליבא דרב יוסף קאמר וליה לא סבירא ליה: שודא דדייני. נראה לר"ת למי שירצה הדיין ליתן ולא כפ"ה שיאמדו דעתו של נותן דהא בסוף פ"ק דגיטין (דף יד: ושם ד"ה וכאן) גבי הולך מנה לפלוני (י) קאמר מה שירצה שליח יעשה וקרי ליה התם שודא ובפ' עשרה יוחסין (קדושין דף עד. ושם ד"ה שודא) נמי אמר נאמן הדיין לומר לזה זכיתי ולזה חייבתי בד"א כשבעלי דינין עומדים לפניו אבל אין בעלי דינין עומדים לפניו אינו נאמן ופריך ניהדר ונידייניה ומשני בשודא דדייני ואי כפ"ה אכתי ניהדר לאמוד דעתו של נותן ובהדיא בירושלמי אמר לאיזה מהן שירצו ב"ד להחליט מחליטים וא"ת א"כ יתן למי שיתן לו שכר וי"ל דכל דיינא דמקבל אגרא לאו דיינא הוא ומה שפר"ת דקבלה בידינו דלא אמרינן שודא אלא במקרקעי אין נראה לר"י דהא גבי הולך מנה לפלוני (כ) גבי שליח מייתי לה בספ"ק דגיטין (דף יד: ושם) עוד פירש דדוקא דיין מומחה עושה שודא דהא רב ששת גברא רבה הוה ואמר ליה רב נחמן מר לאו דיינא הוא גביה אימיה דרמי בר חמא (ל) ורב עוקבא בר חמא בפ' מי שהיה נשוי (כתובות דף לד:): ומאי שנא מהא דתנן המחליף פרה בחמור כו'. אין להוכיח מכאן דהלכה כסומכוס מדפריך מיניה דעד כאן לא פליגי עליה התם בהשואל (ב"מ דף ק.) אלא משום דאזלינן בתר חזקה דממונא ומוקמינן (מ) בחזקת מרה קמא הא לאו הכי מודו דיחלוקו ובהמוכר את הבית (לקמן דף סג. ושם) גבי האומר תנו חלק לפלוני מנכסי וכו' דמייתי מסומכוס ופ"ה דטעמא משום דחלק מספקא ליה אי הוי משהו או פלגא וממון המוטל בספק חולקין א"כ משמע דהלכה כסומכוס ויש לדחות דטעמא לאו משום ספיקא כדפירש הקונטרס אלא משום דחלק הוי רביע ונראה דאין הלכה כסומכוס אע"ג דבכמה מקומות סתם לן תנא כוותיה דהא סבר שמואל כרבנן כדאמרינן בריש הפרה (ב"ק דף מו. ושם) אמר שמואל זו דברי סומכוס אבל חכמים אומרים זה כלל גדול בדין כו' משמע זו ולא ס"ל אף על גב דמוכח בפרק בית כור (לקמן דף קה. ושם) דאיכא זו דס"ל מיהו סתם זו לא ס"ל ועוד דקאמרינן התם (ב"ק דף מו.) אי נמי זה כלל גדול בדין הוא לכי הא דהמוכר שור לחבירו ונמצא נגחן כו' משמע זה כלל גדול אפי' במוכר שור לחבירו אמרינן המוציא מחבירו עליו הראיה כ"ש בפלוגתא דסומכוס ורבנן דסבר שמואל המוציא מחבירו ע"ה וכן בפרק השואל (ב"מ דף קב: ושם ד"ה ובא) קאמר דשמואל מספקא ליה אי תפוס לשון ראשון או לשון אחרון ומתניתין (דף קב: ושם) דקתני באחד ששכר מרחץ בציפורי בי"ב זהובים לשנה מדינר זהב לחדש ובא מעשה לפני רשב"ג ור' יוסי ואמרו יחלוקו את חדש העבור ומוקי שמואל דבא באמצע החדש אבל בתחלת החדש כולו למשכיר בסוף חדש כולו לשוכר דאזלי בתר חזקה סבר כרבנן דאמר לסומכוס בכל ענין יחלוקו ורב נחמן סבר נמי כרבנן דקאמר התם דקרקע בחזקת בעליה קיימא ואפילו בא בסוף החדש כולו למשכיר ואפילו הכי מיפך ועל כרחך היינו טעמא דסבר כרבנן ומתניתין דהתם אוקי כסומכוס דלא תקשי ליה מתניתין וכרב נחמן קיימא לן כדיני והדליא פסקינן כוותיה בפ' המקבל (ב"מ דף קי.) גבי ההוא שטרא דהוה כתיב ביה ז שנים סתמא ואע"ג דקיימא לן כרשב"ג במשנתנו ה"מ בסתמא אבל (נ) הכא דפליג רב נחמן לא:

דררא

מסורת הש"ס
א) [קדושין עד. וש"נ], ב) ב"מ ק., ג) [דף לד ע"ב], ד) שייך לע"ב, ה) [ל"ל שנין].

הגהות הב"ח
(א) רשב"ם ד"ה ומ"ש משני וכו' ואוקמיה ביד מר עוקבא: (ב) ד"ה יחלוקו וכו' מוחזק יותר מחבירו: (ג) ד"ה שודא דדייני וכו' ושמא עתה זכה כל"ל והד"א עם ד"ה שודא: (ד) ד"ה התם וכו' לא שטר ולא עדי חזקה וליכא למיקם: (ה) תום' ד"ה רב כו' וכו' כיון דאינו אלא לראיה: (ו) בא"ד בדבריו יותר ולהוהוי לישנא כל"ל ותיבת ועוד נמחק: (ז) בא"ד אתי שפיר דפריך לפי' מרב: (ח) ד"ה ושמואל וכו' והא דאמר ר"א בפ' מי שהיה: (ט) בא"ד דאליבא דרב יוסף: (י) ד"ה שודא וכו' הולך מנה לפלוני ומת המשלח קאמר מה: (כ) בא"ד מנה לפלוני מייתי לה כל"ל ותיבות גבי שליח נמחק: (ל) בא"ד דרמי בר חמא ומר עוקבא: (מ) ד"ה ומאי וכו' ומוקמינן לה בחזקת: (נ) בא"ד אבל היכא דפליג רב נחמן לא:

ליקוטי רש"י
שודא. לשון השלכה כמו ירה בים שמתרגם שדי בימא (שמות טו). שודא דדייני. לפי ראות עיני הדיינים יטלו הזכות והטובה [כתובות צד.]. דין שאינו תלוי בטעם אלא לפי ראות עיני הדיין כי היכא דאמרינן (פה:) דאמר נכסי לטוביה ואתו שני טוביה שניהם שכנים ושניהם קרובים ותלמידי חכמים שודא דדייני למי שיתנדב לב הדיין לומר נראה לי שזה היה רגיל אצלו יותר לזה נתן [קידושין עד.]. המחליף פרה בחמור. להכי נקט המחליף ולא אמר המוכר פרה וילדה דאילו מוכר במעות לא קני לוקח עד דמשיך וכיון דמשך מידע ידיע אם ילדה כבר אי לא ילדה כבר וליכא לספוקי בעד שלא מכרתי ומשלקחתי אבל מחליף פרה בחמור לא היה צריך למשוך הפרה (או) [ו]החמור דלאחד מהן נקנין חליפין לחבירו במשיכתו של זה בכל מקום שהן כדאמרינן בהזהב (ב"מ מו.) כל הנעשה דמים באחר כיון שזכה זה נתחייב זה בחליפין לפי שכשמשך בעל הפרה את החמור נקנית הפרה לבעל החמור ואין ידוע אם ילדה או לא ילדה [ב"מ ק.]. להכי נקט מחליף גבי בהמה ולא תנא מוכר דנקט בשפחה דבהמה אינה נקנית בכסף עד שימשוך וכי משך דבר הנראה לעיניים הוא אם ילדה אם לאו ואין כאן ספק אבל בחליפין מתקנא כגון שלא משך בעל הפרה את החמור ונקנית הפרה אל בעל החמור במשיכה בכל מקום שהיא כדתנן קדושין (כח.) כל הנעשה דמים באחר כיון שזכה זה נתחייב זה בחליפין ולא ידעינן השתא אי כבר ילדה פרה בשעת משיכת החמור וברשות מוכר ילדה או לאחר משיכת החמור וברשות לוקח [ילדה] [ב"ק צז:]. קיימא לן עבד כנעני נקנה בכסף ובשטר ובחזקה. וכן המוכר שפחתו. ובשנתן מעות נקנית לו השפחה ואפילו היא בבית בעלים ואין ידוע אם עד שלא ילדה נתן הכסף והעובר שלו או לאחר שילדה והולד של בעלים זה אומר כן וזה אומר כן יחלוקו [ב"מ שם]. עבד כנעני נקנה בכסף ואע"ג שאין לפניו בשעת מתן מעות [ב"ק שם].

עין משפט נר מצוה
נא א מיי' פ"ה מהל' זכיה הל' ו ופ"ב מהל' מלוה הל' ג ועי' בהשגות סמג עשין פב טוש"ע ח"מ סי' רמ סעיף ג וסי' קד סעיף ח וסעיף י:
נב ב מיי' פ"כ מהל' מכירה הל' י סמג עשין פב טוש"ע ח"מ סי' רכג סעיף א ועל החלוקה לב"ח ראיה:
[ג רב אלפס כתובות פ"ט דף קיז:]

רבינו גרשום
דרב אמר יחלוקו. שניהן: ושמואל אמר שודא דדייני. כלומר להיכא שתינטה דעת ב"ד שדעת הלוה מחבב טפי להאי מלוה יהבי לפי שמחבבו יותר הקדימו אותו ולוה ממנו ושיעבד לו קודם לזה (שמוטב ליתנן) והא שלו ובתר ב"ד אזלי' והכא אמאי אמרי' כל דאלים גבר: התם ליכא למיקם עלה דמלתא. משום דההנהו תרי שטרי תרוייהו שוין בממון ובזמן ולא מצי לאחזוקי האי טפי מאידך מש"ה אמר מר יחלוקו ומר אמר שודא דדייני: אבל הכא איכא למיקם עלה דמלתא. דכל חד מינייהו מצי מייתי היום ומחר עדים דדידיה היא ולאו דחבריה משום הכי לא אמרי' דיחלוקו אלא כל דאלים גבר: המחליף פרה בחמור. דאורחא דפרה לחלוף ואורחא דשפחה לזבוני:

איתּ ליה דררא דממונא ולההוא אית ליה דררא דממונא הכא אי דמר לא דמר ואי דמר לא דמר אמרי נהרדעי (א) א אם בא אחד מן השוק והחזיק בה אין מוציאין אותה מידו דתני רבי חייא גזלן של רבים לאו שמיה גזלן רב אשי אמר ב לעולם שמיה גזלן ומאי לא שמיה גזלן ג שלא ניתן להשבון: חזקתן שלש שנים מיום ליום וכו': א"ר אבא ד אי דלי ליה איהו גופיה צנא דפירי לאלתר הוי חזקה אמר רב זביד ה ואם טען ואמר לפירות הורדתיו נאמן ו וה"מ בתוך שלש אבל לאחר שלש לא א"ל רב אשי לרב כהנא אי לפירא אחתיה מאי הוה ליה למעבד א"ל ז איבעי ליה למחויי דאי לא תימא הכי הני משכנתא דסורא א) דכתב בהו במשלם שניא אלין תיפוק ארעא דא בלא כסף אי כביש ליה לשטר משכנתא גביה ואמר לקוחה היא בידי הכי נמי דמהימן (ב) מתקני רבנן מידי דאתי ביה לידי פסידא ח אלא איבעי ליה למחויי הכא נמי איבעי ליה למחויי אמר רב יהודה אמר רב ישראל הבא מחמת עכו"ם הרי הוא כעכו"ם מה ט עכו"ם אין לו חזקה אלא בשטר י אף ישראל הבא מחמת עכו"ם אין לו חזקה אלא בשטר אמר רבא ואי אמר ישראל לדידי

אם בא אחד מן השוק והחזיק בה. בהך קרקע דאמר רב נחמן כל דאלים גבר ובא זה השלישי וחטפה מהשנים אלו הטוענין של אבותי: **אין מוציאין אותה.** בב"ד מידו של זה השלישי ואע"ג דלא טוען מידי דשמא גם לב' הראשונים אין להם חלק בה: **דתני רבי חייא גזלן של רבים כו'.** וסברי נהרדעי דבגזלן כי האי מיירי שגזל משנים החלוקים בדבר זה אומר שלי הוא וזה אומר שלי: **לאו שמיה גזלן.** לכופו בדיינים להוציא מידו מה שגזל: **רב אשי אמר לעולם** גזלן של רבים **שמיה גזלן.** הואיל ולא טוען מידי ומוציאים מידו ומעמידין אותה בפני שנים הראשונים שיש להם טענת אבות: **ומאי לא שמיה גזלן.** דקאמר רבי חייא לא להקל עליו בא לפטרו מלשלם אלא להחמיר עליו ולומר דלא ניתן להשבון לא (ג) מיכפר בהשבה דאינו יודע למי ישיב דמאחר שבא לידו אינו צריך להשיב לבעלים ולא להוציאה מתחת ידו ולהפקידה לשנים הראשונים וכל מאן דאלים (ד) גבר דספקינן לעיל ולאו תפסינן לא מפקינן כל שכן זה שבתורת גזל בא לידו והוא צריך להוציאה מתחת ידו והוא יודע למי ישיב והכי נמי אמרינן בהמוכר את הספינה (לקמן דף פט.) א"ר לוי קשה עונשן של מדות מעונשן של עריות ומפרש התם אפשר בתשובה והכא לא אפשר בתשובה דהמוכר במדה (ה) וגזל לרבים שאינו יודע למי ישיב ואליבא דרב אשי איירי נמי ר' חייא במוכר במדה שאינה ישרה לרבים כן נראה בעיני שיטה זו: **אי דלי ליה צנא דפירי לאלתר הוי חזקה.** אם יש עדים שהגביה המערער צנא דפירי מקרקע זו על כתפיו של זה המחזיק שטוען לקוחה היא בידי מאחר שסייע לו להוליך הפירות לביתו שוב אין יכול לטעון ולומר לא מכרתיה לו שלא היה לו לסייעו בלקיטת הפירות אלא היה לו למחות ומדסייע לו הפסיד וכמודה שמכר לו דמי. ור' חננאל פירש אי איכא סהדי דיהב ליה לוקח למריה ארעא צנא דפירי דורון להוליכה לביתו נתברר שאכילת הפירות של לוקח ומדידיה יהב ליה למוכר ואין נראה בעיני: **אמר רב זביד אי טעין.** המערער בתר דדלי ליה ללוקח צנא דפירי לפירות הורדתיו כדין אריס למחצה ושליש ולרביע וחלקו הוא דדלי ליה נאמן כלומר לא הפסיד במאי דדלי ליה: **והני מילי.** דנאמן: **בתוך שלש.** דאם איתא דזבנה מיניה אמאי לא מיזדהר בשטריה: **אבל לאחר שלש.** אי טעין לפירות הורדתיו אינו נאמן ואע"ג דלא דלי ליה צנא דפירי דעד תלת שנין מיזדהר איניש בשטריה טפי לא מיזדהר והוה ליה לזה למחות בתוך שלש כדמפרש ואזיל: **אי לפירא אחתיה.** כי משכנתא דסורא לעשר שנים או לעשרים: **מאי הוה ליה.** לבעל השדה למעבד נמצא שכל המוריד את חבירו לפירות של שלש שנים או יותר יפסיד קרקע שלו הואיל ולא יהא נאמן לאחר שלש לטעון לפירות הורדתיו: **א"ל איבעי [ליה] למחויי.** בתוך שלש ולומר לעדים דעו לכם שלפירות הורדתיו לכך וכך שנים וגוף הקרקע קנוי לי שאם אין לו שטר מכירה לזה המחזיק לא יוכל לטעון שטר היה לי ואבד כי לא נזהרתי בו אחר שלש דכיון דמיחה בו בעל השדה היה לו להזהר בשטרו: **דאי לא תימא הכי.** דמחאה לאלאין שמוחה על הקרקע ומודי בפירות לאו מחאה היא אלא כדאמרינן לקמן פלניא גזלנא הוא דקאכיל ארעא דידי בגזלנותא למחר תבענא ליה בדינא: **אם כן האי משכנתא דסורא כו'.** ותקנתא דרבנן הויא הך משכנתא משום דהמלוה לחבירו על שדהו אסור לאכול הפירות משום רבית אבל בנכייתא מותר כעין משכנתא דסורא שמלוה עשרה מנה על שדהו ולסוף עשר שנים חוזר הקרקע לבעלים בחנם ונמצא קונה פירות של כל שנה במנה ואין כאן צד רבית ואע"פ ששוין הפירות כפלים שהרי הוא קרוב לשכר וקרוב להפסד שמקבל פירות של כל שנה במנה ואפילו בשנת שדפון שלא יהו שוין פירות השנה דינר: **אי כביש.** טומן המלוה ואמר לאחר שלש לקוחה היא בידי הכי נמי דמהימן ולא יוכל זה לטעון לפירות הורדתיו ומחאה נמי לא תועיל לו: **דאתי ביה.** לוה לידי הפסד בתמיה: **אלא איבעי ליה למחויי.** בתוך כל שלש ומהניא ליה מחאה ומדלא מיחה הפסיד: **הכא נמי.** אם איתא דלפירא אחתיה איבעי ליה למחויי בתוך שלש קודם שיחזיק: **ישראל הבא מחמת עכו"ם הרי הוא כעכו"ם.** שדה שהכל יודעין שהיתה של ישראל ואכלה עכו"ם שלש שנים או יותר וטוען שלקחה מישראל ואזיל ישראל וקנה מההוא עכו"ם ואכלה גם הוא אחר העכו"ם שני חזקה או יותר לא הוי חזקה אלא אתי מריה דארעא ומפיק ליה מידיה דישראל וישראל ליזיל וליתבע לעכו"ם דזבן מיניה דאיהו הוא דאפסיד אנפשיה דלא הוה ליה למזבן ארעא דישראל מעכו"ם עד דלימא ליה הב לי שטר דזביני דזבנת לה מישראל דדין חזקה לית ליה לעכו"ם ולא כל מאן דאתי מחמתיה דסתם עכו"ם גזלנים הם וישראל ירא למחות והלכך לא תקנו בהם חזקה כדאמרינן לקמן בשמעתין הני דבי ריש גלותא לא מחזקי משום האי טעמא גופיה שיראים אנו למחות וישראל זה הבא מחמת עכו"ם אע"פ שהחזיק אין חזקתו כלום וחזקה שאין עמה טענה היא שהרי הוא טוען העכו"ם מכרה לי אבל איני יודע היאך באה לידי העכו"ם שיוכל למכרה אבל אי טען ישראל ואמר יהב לי ההוא עכו"ם שטר זביני דזבנה מינך וראיתי בו שלקחה ממך מהימן למאן דא"ל קמי דידי זבנה ההוא עכו"ם מינך דמסקי' לקמן דמהימן מיגו דאי בעי א"ל מינך זבנתה ואכלתה שני חזקה ודוקא בא מחמת עכו"ם דאילו בא מחמת ישראל אע"פ שלא דר בה אלא יום אחד אותו שמכרה לזה וזה החזיק שלש שנים חזקתו חזקה כדאמרי' לקמן (דף מא:) גבי ההוא דדר בקשתא בעיליתא ארבע שנין:

לדידי

דררא דממונא. פירוש דלא טענינהו מהכא יש ספק לב"ד דהי מינייהו הוה הולד אם נולד קודם שמכר או אחר שמכר וכן בשור שנגח את הפרה ונמצא עוברה בצדה (ב"ק דף מו.) בלא טענתם מסופקים ב"ד אם היה מעשה אם קודם שנגחה ילדה או לאחר שנגחה וכן בשור רודף אחר שור אחר והוזק (שם לה.) יש להסתפק אם בשורו הוזק או אם בסלע לקה וכן בכל מקום דפליגי רבנן וסומכוס אבל הכא בזה אומר של אבותי שעל פי טענותיהן בא הספק אמרינן כל דאלים גבר: **אין** מוציאים אותה מידו. ואפילו כתבו הרשאה זה לזה הואיל ורשעים הם (ו) אין זוקקים להם: **דתני** רבי חייא גזלן של רבים לא שמיה גזלן. שאין מוציאין מידו ומיירי בזה אומר של אבותי ולא בגזל מחמשה בני אדם דהתם אמאי אין מוציאין ורב אשי פליג אנהרדעי וסבר דרבי חייא לא להקל בא אלא להחמיר דלא סגי בהשבה אחת כמו לשאר גזלן עד שישלם גזלה לכל אחד ואחד כרבי עקיבא בהגוזל עצים (ב"ק קג.) ומיירי בגזל מחמשה וקונטרס פירש דמיירי בחנוני שמכר במדה שאינה ישרה דאינו יודע למי גזל ולכך לא ניתן להשבון ואף על פי שיכול לעשות בו צרכי צבור כדאמרינן בפרק אין צדין (ביצה דף כט.) האי לאו השבה מעלייתא היא: **ואי** דלי ליה צנא דפירי לאלתר הויא חזקה. וא"ת ולהימניה במיגו דאי בעי אמר לפירות הורדתיו וי"ל דהוי מיגו במקום עדים דאנן סהדי כיון דדלי ליה צנא דפירי מודה שהיו הפירות שלו ועוד דאינו רוצה לטעון לפירות הורדתיו אלא תובע הקרקע והפירות: **ואי** לפירא אחתיה מאי הוה ליה למעבד. אין לפרש דרב אשי סבר דלעולם נאמן לומר לפירות הורדתיך דאם כן קשה לרב אשי מאי טעמא דרבנן דבעו שלש שנים מיום ליום דהא לדידיה ליכא למימר כדמפרש רבא בריש פרקין דעד שלש שנים מיזדהר איניש בשטריה טפי לא מזדהר דהא לעולם צריך לשמרו פן יאמר לפירות הורדתיך ועוד דאם כן היכי קאמר דאי לא תימא הכי דאיבעי ליה למחויי אלא לא בעי למחויי דחזקתו אינה חזקה דיכול לומר לפירות הורדתיו ומייתי ממשכנתא דסורא ומאי מייתי אדרבה אם כדברי רב אשי תו ליכא פסידא שיכול לומר לפירות הורדתיך ונראה לרשב"א דרב אשי לא בא להאמינו אחר ג' אם אומר לפירות הורדתיך אלא שואל איזו תקנה יש לעשות מתחלה שלא יוכל לומר לאחר שלש שלי היא כשהורידו לפירות דסבר לא מהני מחאה אלא כשאמר פלניא גזלנא הוא דקא אכיל לארעאי בגזלנותא והיכא דאחתיה לפירות לא מצי למחויי הכי וכן פירש הקונטרס והשתא מייתי שפיר ממשכנתא דסורא דמהניא מחאה כי האי גוונא [ועי' תוס' ב"מ קי. ד"ה אמר ליה]:

הכי

נג א ב ג מיי' פט"ו מהל' טוען ונטען הלכה ד סמג עשין לה טוש"ע ח"מ סי' קלט סעיף ב וע"ש וסי' קמו סעיף ב:

נד ד מיי' פי"א מהל' טו ופ"א מהל' מכירה הל' יח סמג עשין לב טוש"ע ח"מ סי' קמב סעיף א וסי' קלב סעיף יא:

נה ה ו מיי' פי"ד מהל' טוען ונטען הל' ט סמג עשין לה טוש"ע ח"מ סי' קמב סעיף א:

נו ז ח טוש"ע ח"מ סי' קנ סעיף א:

נז ט מיי' פי"ד מהל' טוען ונטען הל' ה וע"ש בהשגות ובכ"מ וע"פ מהל' מכירה הל' ... טוש"ע ח"מ סי' קמט סעיף יד וסי' קלב סעיף א:

נח י מיי' שם סמג שם טוש"ע ח"מ סי' קמט סעיף טו וסי' קלב סש:

רבינו גרשום

התם להאי אית ליה דררא [דממונא] בגוה. דקודם מכירה הוה ממוניה דהאי ובתר מכירה דאידך ואין ידוע ממונו של מי ולדה משה"ה יחלוקו: גזלן של [רבים]. כלומר גזלן של שנים שעומדים במחלוקת ביניהם (א) בגונן כגון אלו שלא ניתן להשבון שאע"פ שמשיב קרוי גזלן שאין לדין ידוע של מי היתה שיחזירנה לו: פיסקא אמר ר' אבא אי דלי ליה. המערער כלומר שסייע למחזיק להגביה לו על כתפו (ב) או שהשליך אחריו לביתו צנא של פירות מאותה שדה שמערער עליה אע"פ שעדיין לא עמדה ברשותיה ג' שנין חזקה אלא כיון שיש לו עדים שהגביה לו צנא דפירי לאלתר הוי חזקה דאם איתא דשלו היא כיון שאמר לו המחזיק הגבה לי היה לו למחות ולומר והלא שלי הוא הקרקע ומה יש לך בפירות שדי: אמר רב זביד. אי דלי ליה צנא ושוב מערער על השדה דשלו הוא וטוען ואומר לפירות הורדתיו שיהא אריסי שיהא חצי הפירות שלו וזה שהגבהתי לו חלקו סייעתיו להגביה נאמן לומר כן: הני מילי. דנאמן לומר כן בתוך ג' כשלא החזיק בהן עדיין ג' שני חזקה אבל לאחר ג' [לא]: מאי הוה ליה למיעבד. מה היה יכול למחות הא לא מצי לסלקו קודם זמנו אם עשאו אריס לי' שנים עדיין לא הגיע זמנו: אפ"ה איבעי ליה למחויי. אע"ג דלא הוי עיקר מחאה דלא מצי למימר פלוני גזלנא הוא דאכיל ארעא דידי דהא ברשותיה אוכל דהורידו לפירות מ"מ צריך למחות בפני עדים בתוך ג' ולומר הוו עדים שפלוני [שעובד] [שאוכל] שדה שלי אני הורדתיו לפירות לכך שנים ואי לא אמר הכי לא מהימן למחות אחר ג': דאי לא תימא הכי. דצריך למחויי בתוך ג' ולהודיע לרבים שאינה שלו א"כ הני משכנתא דסורא דמשכן ליה לוה למלוה דליכול שדהו בנכייתא עד זמן שישתלם ממנו בפירות שיאכל מן השדה: אלא איבעי ליה למחויי. בתוך ג' להודיע לרבים שמשכנתא היא בידו ה"נ במוריד חבירו לשדהו לפירות בעי למחויי: ישראל הבא מחמת עכו"ם כעכו"ם. כגון שקנאה מן העכו"ם ג' שנים אינן חזקה מה עכו"ם אין לו חזקה מן ישראל אם קנה ממנו קרקע אא"כ יש לו שטר מכירה עליה לפי שבדיניהן אין חזקה בשנים אצל ישראל הבא מחמת עכו"ם נמי אין לו חזקה אא"כ יש לו אותו שטר שמכרה ישראל לעכו"ם ואע"פ שיש לו עדים לישראל שעמד בה עכו"ם אין חזקתו חזקה מה שאין כן בישראל שאם קנה ישראל קרקע מחבירו ישראל ועמד בה וערער עליה ואמר זה מישראל פלוני קניתיה אם יש לו עדים שעמד בה אותו ישראל אפי' יום אחד חזקתו חזקה: אמר רבא אי אתי ישראל ואמר. לדידי אמר אותו עכו"ם שמכרה לזה דההוא עכו"ם מהימן:

א) [לקמן לח. ב"מ סז: קי.]

הגהות הב"ח

(א) גמ' אמרי נהרדעי ואם: (ב) שם הכי נמי דמהימן וכי תימא הכי נמי מתקני רבנן מידי דאתי ביה: (ג) רשב"ם ד"ה ומאי לא וכו' לא מיכפר בהשבה וכו' להשיב לבעלים. נ"ב ודחי ממש להא דתנוי חייב על הגזלות שיכול דנעשה עליו גזלן ... לתינוק לקמן דף פ"ח ע"א: (ד) בא"ד וכל מאן דאלים משיעה גבר: (ה) בא"ד המוכר במדה לרבים אינו יודע: (ו) תוס' ד"ה אין מוציאים וכו' ורשעים הם. נ"ב וכן נראה לפרש לקמן בפ' מי שמת בני רוכל מקבלים אמן בדף קנ"ו:

ליקוטי רש"י

דררא דממונא. הפסד ממון [ב"מ ב:]. דאי לא תימא הכי. דמחאה כי האי גוונא לא הויא מחאה מאחר (שמודה) [שהמחזיק] בו (לאכול) [שהוא אוכל] עכשיו מן הקרקע מן הדין דלא הוי מחאה בטוען פלניא גזלנא הוא כדלקמן [לח.] [רשב"ם]. במשלם שניא. דלא יהיו כהלואה אלא כלוקח הימנו פירות השנים האלו במעות הללו [ב"מ סז:].

חשק שלמה על רבינו גרשום א) נראה דצ"ל שעומדים במחלוקת כגון אלו: שלא ניתן להשבון וכו'. ב) אולי צ"ל או שהלך אחריו לביתו וכו' ואפשר דכוונתו שהלך הלוקח אחריו של מריה דארעא וכמו שפי' הרשב"ם בשם הר"ח ז"ל.

אִית לֵיהּ דְּרָרָא דְּמָמוֹנָא – has a clear-cut claim to the disputed **money, וּלְהַהוּא אִית לֵיהּ דְּרָרָא דְּמָמוֹנָא – and that** litigant **has a clear-cut claim to the** disputed **money.**[1] Therefore, the court has no choice but to issue a ruling, and may not withdraw from the case. **הָכָא** – However, **here,** in Rav Nachman's case, **אִי דְּמַר לָא דְּמַר – if** the disputed property is associated **with [the first litigant],** then it is **not** at all associated **with [the second]. וְאִי דְּמַר לָא דְּמַר – And if** it is associated **with [the second],** it is **not** at all associated **with [the first].**[2] Therefore, the court is not obliged to rule and may withdraw from the case.

The Gemara discusses a ruling relevant to this situation, in which the court withdraws from a dispute in accordance with Rav Nachman's ruling:

אָמְרֵי נְהַרְדָּעֵי – The Nehardeans say: אִם בָּא אֶחָד מִן הַשּׁוּק – If someone from the street, (i.e. an outsider,) **comes וְהֶחֱזִיק בָּהּ – and takes possession of [the disputed property]** before either litigant can do so, **אֵין מוֹצִיאִין אוֹתָהּ מִיָּדוֹ – [the court] does not extract it from his possession.** Although he advances no claim to legitimize his occupancy, neither of the two original contestants may oust him from the property, because possibly it does not belong to any one of them either.[3]

The Nehardeans adduced support for their statement:

דְּתָנֵי רַבִּי חִיָּיא – For R' Chiya taught in a Baraisa: גַּזְלָן שֶׁל רַבִּים לָאו שְׁמֵיהּ גַּזְלָן – ONE WHO STEALS FROM THE PUBLIC IS NOT CONSIDERED A ROBBER; i.e. he cannot be forced to return the stolen item.[4]

A dissenting opinion:

רַב אַשִׁי אָמַר – Rav Ashi said: לְעוֹלָם שְׁמֵיהּ גַּזְלָן – Actually, [the outsider] ***is*** **considered a robber,** and he must vacate the property.[5] **וּמַאי לֹא שְׁמֵיהּ גַּזְלָן – Then what is** the meaning of the Baraisa's statement that **"he is not considered a robber"? שֶׁלֹּא נִיתַּן לְהִשָּׁבוֹן** – It means **that [the stolen property] cannot be restored** to its owner.[6]

The Gemara quotes a section of the Mishnah:

חֶזְקָתָן שָׁלֹשׁ שָׁנִים מִיּוֹם לְיוֹם וכו׳ – THEIR *CHAZAKAH* IS THREE YEARS FROM DAY TO DAY ETC.

R' Abba notes an exception to the three-year rule:

אָמַר רַבִּי אַבָּא – R' Abba said: אִי דְּלֵי לֵיהּ אִיהוּ גּוּפֵיהּ צַנָּא דְּפֵירֵי – **If** witnesses testify that **[the challenger] himself loaded a basket of** the field's **produce** from the field **onto [the occupant's]** shoulders, **לְאַלְתַּר הָוֵי חֲזָקָה** – the occupant's **ownership** of the land **is proven immediately,** and three years of use is unnecessary.[7]

However, the challenger is believed to explain his action in a different light:

אָמַר רַב זְבִיד – Rav Zevid said: וְאִם טָעַן וְאָמַר – But if [the challenger] counters and claims: לְפֵירוֹת הוֹרַדְתִּיו – "I installed [the occupant] in the land as a sharecropper, **to** grow **produce,** and the basket of fruit that I assisted him with was his

NOTES

1. That is, each litigant's claim to the offspring stems from the undisputed fact that he owned its mother at some time – the seller prior to the sale and the buyer after it. The question is only during whose term of ownership the mother gave birth. Since each one's ownership of the mother is undisputed, each is said to have a clear-cut claim to the disputed offspring. This fact compels the court to impose a settlement rather than withdraw from the case and allow one of them to seize the property by force (*Rashbam* as explained by *Ramban* to *Bava Metzia* 2b).

2. That is, the entire basis of each litigant's claim is disputed by his opponent; he asserts that the other has no grounds whatsoever for his claim. Therefore, since only one has a clear-cut claim to the disputed land, and the court cannot determine which one it is, the court is not compelled to rule on the case, and may withdraw (ibid.).

[This elucidation follows *Rashbam's* understanding of the term דְּרָרָא דְּמָמוֹנָא. *Tosafos,* however, explain the term to mean that the facts of the case themselves engender the uncertainty as to the object's ownership, even without the litigant's claims being advanced. As applied to the Baraisa's cases of the disputed calf and child, this means that the mere fact that the mother gave birth around the time of the transaction is sufficient to create the uncertainty in the court's mind as to who owns the offspring. The claims of the litigants are not needed to foster the uncertainty. Thus, although the disputants' claims cancel each other out, the court may not ignore the doubtful situation before it and must rule on the case; it may not withdraw. This contrasts with Rav Nachman's case in which it is only the two litigants' claims that give rise to the uncertainty as to who owns the property; had the litigants not advanced their claims, there would have been nothing about the property to cause the court to wonder who owned it. Consequently, since the litigants' claims cancel each other out, the court withdraws from the case and does not issue a ruling.]

3. The outsider does not advance any claim that would entitle him to the land; he simply occupies it. Nevertheless, since neither of the original two contestants offers any proof of his own claim, it is possible that the land does not belong to any one of them either. Therefore, they cannot oust the outsider from the land (*Rashbam*).

[*Tosafos,* however, appear to understand that we do in fact assume that the land belongs to one of the original contestants. However, only an owner may oust an unlawful squatter from his land. Since neither litigant can prove himself to be the land's owner to the exclusion of the other litigant, neither one can oust the squatter from it (*Kovetz Shiurim* §159).]

4. The Nehardeans do not take the word "public" in this Baraisa in its usual sense. Rather, "stealing from the public" here refers specifically to a case such as that discussed by Rav Nachman in which an item was left by the court to be seized by whichever of the litigants was stronger – "the public" being the litigants who are eligible to seize it. Hence, the Baraisa rules that if a third party seizes it without advancing a claim of ownership, he is not a robber and cannot be made to relinquish it – exactly as the Nehardeans ruled.

5. Rav Ashi maintains that although we do not know *which* of the two original litigants owns it, we assume that it definitely belongs to *one* of them. Thus, the outsider must relinquish it and allow one of the two contestants to occupy it (*Rashbam* – see *Rabbeinu Yonah*).

6. Literally: it is not given to return. The Baraisa means that this robber is unlike an ordinary robber in that he cannot atone for his sin by simply restoring the stolen object to its pre-robbery state, because he cannot be sure that its true owner will be the one who will gain possession of it. [It is only in this sense that the Baraisa's words "he is not considered a robber" are to be taken – they do *not* mean that he is not obligated to return the object, for in fact he must.] (*Rashbam*).

Now, upon analysis this seems difficult. It is true that by placing the object between the two litigants, the robber cannot be sure that the true owner will ultimately regain it, but this was the case even before the robber stole it! Why should the robber be obligated to do more than restore it to its pre-robbery state? *Rashbam* explains, though, that taking possession of an object belonging to another places a responsibility on the holder to see to it that it is returned to its owner. This is similar to the Gemara's ruling above, 34b, that where the court has impounded a disputed item, it may not later release it to its previous indeterminate state, but must retain it until it can identify its rightful owner (cf. *Ramban*).

Rashbam further states that according to Rav Ashi, the Baraisa is not limited to this case of the two litigants. Rather, the Baraisa would include any case where one stole from many people and has no way to return what he stole, e.g. a merchant who cheated his customers by using faulty measurements and has no record of all the transactions.

7. The fact that the challenger assisted the occupant in carrying away the field's produce is construed as an admission on the part of the challenger that the occupation was legal, because if the occupant was indeed a thief, the challenger should have protested his presence instead of helping him (*Rashbam;* see there for an alternate explanation from *Rabbeinu Chananel*). Therefore, the occupant's ownership is established immediately, for this admission obviates the need for a deed (see *Ketzos HaChoshen* 135:2).

אית ליה דררא דממונא ולהאי לית ליה דררא דממונא הכא אי דמר לא דמר ואי דמר לא דמר אמרי נהרדעי (א) אם בא אחד מן השוק והחזיק בה אין מוציאין אותה מידו דתני רבי חייא גזלן של רבים לאו שמיה גזלן רב אשי אמר לעולם שמיה גזלן ומאי לאו שמיה גזלן שלא ניתן להשבון: חזקתן שלש שנים מיום ליום וכו': א"ר אבא אי דלי ליה איהו גופיה צנא דפירי לאלתר הוי חזקה אמר רב זביד ואם טוען ואמר לפירות הורדתיו נאמן וה"מ בתוך שלש אבל לאחר שלש לא א"ל רב אשי לרב כהנא אי לפירא אחתיה מאי הוה ליה למעבד א"ל איבעי ליה למחויי דאי לא תימא הכי הני משכנתא דסורא דכתב בהו במשלם שניא אלין תיפוק ארעא דא בלא כסף אי כביש ליה לשטר משכנתא גביה ואמר לקוחה היא בידי הכי נמי דמהימן (ב) מתקני רבנן מידי דאתי ביה לידי פסידא אלא איבעי ליה למחויי הכא נמי איבעי ליה למחויי אמר רב יהודה אמר רב ישראל הבא מחמת עכו"ם הרי הוא כעכו"ם מה עכו"ם אין לו חזקה אלא בשטר אף ישראל הבא מחמת עכו"ם אין לו חזקה אלא בשטר אמר רבא ואי אמר ישראל לדידי

תוספות

דררא דממונא. פירוש דבלא טענתייהו מהלא יש ספק לב"ד דכי מינייהו הוה הולד אם נולד קודם שמכר או אחר שמכר וכן בשור שנגח את הפרה ונמצא עוברה בצדה (ב"ק דף מו.) בלא טענתם מסופקים ב"ד איך היה מעשה אם קודם שנגחה ילדה או לאחר שנגחה וכן בשור רודף אחר שור אחר והוזק (שם לה.) יש להסתפק אם בשורו הוזק או אי בסלע לקה וכן בכל מקום דפליגי רבנן וסומכוס אבל הכא דזה אומר של אבותי שעל פי טענותיהן בא הספק אמרינן כל דאלים גבר: **אין** מוציאים אותה מידו. ואפילו כתבו הרשאה זה לזה הואיל ורשעים הם (ו) אין מזקיקים להם: **דתני** רבי חייא גזלן של רבים לא שמיה גזלן. שאין מוציאין מידו ומיירי בזה אומר של אבותי ולא בגזל מחמשה בני אדם דהכא אמאי אין מוציאין ורב אשי פליג אנהרדעי וסבר דרבי חייא לא להקל בא אלא להחמיר דלא סגי בהשבה אחת כמו לשאר גזלן עד שישלם גזלה לכל אחד ואחד כרבי עקיבא בהגוזל עצים (ב"ק דף קג.) ומיירי בגזל מחמשה ובקונטרס פירש דמיירי בחנוני שמכר במדה שאינה ישרה דאינו יודע למי גזל ולכך לא ניתן להשבון ואף על פי שיכול לעשות בו צרכי צבור כדאמרינן בפרק אין צדין (ביצה דף כט.) האי לאו השבה מעלייתא היא: **ואי** דלי ליה צנא דפירי לאלתר הויא חזקה. וא"ת ולימנייה במיגו דאי בעי אמר לפירות הורדתיו וי"ל דהוי מיגו במקום עדים דאנן סהדי כיון דדלי ליה צנא דפירי מודה שהיו הפירות שלו ועוד דאינו רוצה לטעון לפירות הורדתיו אלא תובע הקרקע והפירות: **ואי** לפירא אחתיה מאי הוה ליה למעבד. אין לפרש דרב אשי סבר דלעולם נאמן לומר לפירות הורדתיך דאם כן קשה לרב אשי מאי טעמא דרבנן דבעו שלש שנים מיום ליום דהא לדידיה ליכא למימר כדמפרש רבא בריש פרקין דעד שלש שנים מיזדהר איניש בשטריה טפי לא מזדהר דהא לעולם צריך לשמרו פן יאמר לפירות הורדתיך ועוד דאם כן היכי קאמר דאי לא תימא הכי דאיבעי ליה למחויי אלא לא בעי למחויי דחזקתו אינה חזקה דיכול לומר לפירות הורדתיו ומייתי ממשכנתא דסורא ומאי מייתי אדרבה אם כדברי רב אשי תו ליכא פסידא שיכול לומר לפירות הורדתיך ונראה לרשב"א דרב אשי לא בא להאמינו אחר ג' אם אומר לפירות הורדתיך אלא שואל איזו תקנה יש לעשות מתחלה שלא יוכל לומר לאחר שלש שלי היא כשהורידו לפירות דסבר לא מהני מחאה אלא כשאמר פלניא גזלנא הוא דקא אכיל לארעאי בגזלנותא והיכא דאחתיה לפירות לא מצי למחויי הכי וכן פירש הקונטרס והשתא מייתי שפיר ממשכנתא דסורא דמהניא מחאה כי האי גוונא [ועי' תוס' ב"מ קי. ד"ה אמר ליה]: הכי

רשב"ם

אם בא אחד מן השוק והחזיק בה. בהך קרקע דאמר רב נחמן כל דאלים גבר ובא זה השלישי ותפסה מהשנים אלו הטוענין של אבותי: **אין מוציאין אותה.** בב"ד מידו של זה השלישי ואע"ג דלא טוען מידי דשמא גם לב' הראשונים אין להם חלק בה: **דתני רבי חייא** גזלן של רבים כו'. וסברי נהרדעי דבגזלן של רבים כי האי מיירי שגזל משנים החלוקים בדבר זה אומר שלי הוא וזה אומר שלי: **לאו שמיה גזלן.** לכופו בדיינים להוציא מידו מה שגזל: **רב אשי אמר לעולם** גזלן של רבים שמיה גזלן. הואיל ולא טוען מידי ומוציאים מידו ומעמידין אותה בפני שנים הראשונים שיש להם טענת אבות: **ומאי לא שמיה גזלן.** דקאמר רבי חייא לא להקל עליו בא לפטרו מלשלם אלא להחמיר עליו ולומר דלא ניתן להשבון לא (ג) מיכפר בהשבה דאינו יודע למי ישיב דמאחר שבא לידו צריך להשיב לבעלים ולא להוציאה מתחת ידו ולהפקירה לשנים הראשונים וכל מאן דאלים (ד) גבר דפסקינן לעיל ואי תפסינן לא מפקינן כל שכן זה שבתורת גזל בא לידו והוא צריך להוציאה מתחת ידו ואינו יודע למי ישיב והכי נמי אמרינן בהמוכר את הספינה (לקמן דף פח:) א"ר לוי קשה עונשן של מדות מעונשן של עריות ומפרש התם אפשר בתשובה והכא לא אפשר בתשובה דהמוכר במדה (ה) וגזל לרבים שאינו יודע למי ישיב ואליבא דרב אשי איירי נמי ר' חייא במוכר במדה שאינה ישרה לרבים כן נראה בעיני שיטה זו: **אי** דלי ליה צנא דפירי לאלתר הוי חזקה. אם יש עדים שהגביה המערער סלא דפירי מקרקע זו על כתפיו של זה המחזיק שטוען לקוחה היא בידי מאחר שסייע לו להוליך הפירות לביתו שוב אין יכול לטעון ולומר לא מכרתיה לו שלא היה לו לסייעו בלקיטת הפירות אלא היה לו למחות ומדסייע לו הפסיד וכמודה שמכר לו דמי. ור' חננאל פירש אי איכא סהדי דיהב ליה לוקח למריה ארעא סלא דפירי דורון להוליכה לביתו נתברר שאכילת הפירות של לוקח ומדידיה יהב ליה למוכר ואין נראה בעיני: **אמר רב זביד אי טעין.** המערער בתר דדלי ליה ללוקח סלא דפירי לפירות הורדתיו כדין אריס למחצה ושליש ולרביע וחלקו הוא דדלי ליה נאמן כלומר לא הפסיד במאי דדלי ליה: **והני מילי.** דנאמן: **בתוך שלש.** דאם איתא דזבנה מיניה אמאי לא מיזדהר בשטריה: **אבל לאחר שלש.** אי טעין לפירות הורדתיו אינו נאמן ואע"ג דלא דלי ליה סלא דפירי דעד תלת שנין מיזדהר איניש בשטריה טפי לא מיזדהר והוה ליה לזה למחות בתוך שלש כדמפרש ואזיל: **אי לפירא אחתיה.** כי משכנתא דסורא לעשר שנים או לעשרים: **מאי הוה ליה.** לבעל השדה למעבד נמצא שכל המוריד את חבירו לפירות של שלש שנים או יותר יפסיד קרקע שלו הואיל ולא יהא נאמן לאחר שלש לטעון לפירות הורדתיו: **א"ל איבעי [ליה] למחויי.** בתוך שלש ולומר לעדים דעו לכם שלפירות הורדתיו לכך וכך שנים וגוף הקרקע קנוי לי שאם אין לו שטר מכירה לזה המחזיק לא יוכל לטעון שטר היה לי ואבד כי לא נזהרתי בו אחר שלש דכיון דמיחה בו בעל השדה היה לו להזהר בשטרו: **דאי לא תימא הכי.** דמחאה לאלאין שמוחה על הקרקע ומודי בפירות לאו מחאה היא אלא כדאמרינן לקמן פלניא גזלנא הוא דקאכיל ארעא דידי בגזלנותא למחר תבענא ליה בדינא: **אם כן האי משכנתא דסורא כו'.** ותקנתא דרבנן הויא הך משכנתא משום דהמלוה לחבירו על שדהו אסור לאכול הפירות משום רבית אבל בנכייתא מותר כעין משכנתא דסורא שמלוה עשרה מנה על שדהו ולסוף עשר שנים חוזר הקרקע לבעלים בחנם ונמצא קונה פירות של כל שנה במנה ואין כאן צד רבית ואע"פ ששוין הפירות כפלים שהרי הוא קרוב לשכר וקרוב להפסד שמקבל פירות של כל שנה במנה ואפילו בשנת שדפון שלא יהו שוין פירות השנה דינר: **אי כביש.** טומן המלוה ואמר לאחר שלש לקוחה היא בידי הכי נמי דמהימן ולא יוכל זה לטעון לפירות הורדתיו ומחאה נמי לא תועיל לו: **דאתי ביה.** לוה לידי הפסד בתמיה: **אלא איבעי ליה למחויי.** בתוך כל שלש ומהניא ליה מחאה ומדלא מיחה הפסיד: **הכא נמי.** אם איתא דלפירא אחתיה איבעי ליה למחויי בתוך שלש קודם שיחזיק: **ישראל הבא מחמת עכו"ם הרי הוא כעכו"ם.** שדה שהכל יודעין שהיתה של ישראל ואכלה עכו"ם שלש שנים או יותר וטוען שלקחה מישראל ואזיל ישראל וקנה מההוא עכו"ם ואכלה גם הוא אחר העכו"ם שני חזקה או יותר לא הוי חזקה אלא אתי מריה דארעא ומפיק ליה מידיה דישראל וישראל ליזיל וליתבע לעכו"ם דזבן מיניה דאיהו הוא דאפסיד אנפשיה דלא הוה ליה למזבן ארעא דישראל מעכו"ם עד דלימא ליה הב לי שטר דזביני דזבנת לה מישראל דדין חזקה לית ליה לעכו"ם ולא כל מאן דאתי מחמתיה דסתם עכו"ם גזלנים הם וישראל ירא למחות והלכך לא תקנו בהם חזקה כדאמרינן לקמן בשמעתין הני דבי ריש גלותא לא מחזקי משום האי טעמא גופיה שיראים אנו למחות וישראל זה הבא מחמת עכו"ם אע"פ שהחזיק אין חזקתו כלום וחזקה שאין עמה טענה היא שהרי הוא טוען העכו"ם מכרה לי אבל איני יודע היאך באה לידי העכו"ם שיוכל למכרה אבל אי טען ישראל ואמר יהב לי ההוא עכו"ם שטר זביני דזבנה מינך ורמאי בו שלקחה ממך מהימן דדמי למאן דא"ל קמי דידי זבנה ההוא עכו"ם מינך דמסקי' לקמן דמהימן מיגו דאי בעי א"ל מינך זבנתה ואכלתה שני חזקה ודוקא בא מחמת עכו"ם דאילו בא מחמת ישראל אע"פ שלא דר בה אלא יום אחד אותו שמכרה לזה וזה החזיק שלש שנים חזקתו חזקה כדאמרי' לקמן (דף מא:) גבי ההוא דדר בקשתא בעיליתא ארבע שנין: לדידי

עין משפט נר מצוה

נג א ב ג מיי' פט"ו מהל' טוען ונטען הלכה ד סמג עשין לה טוש"ע ח"מ סי' קלט סעיף ג וע"ש ובסי' קמו סעיף כב:

נד ד מיי' פי"א שם הל' ט ופ"א מהל' מכירה הל' טו סמג עשין לד לה טוש"ע ח"מ סי' קמב סעיף א וסי' קלב סעיף יא:

נה ה ו מיי' פי"א מהל' טוען ונטען הל' ט סמג עשין לה טוש"ע ח"מ סי' קמב סעיף א:

נו ז ח טוש"ע ח"מ סי' קנ סעיף א:

נז ט מיי' פי"ד מהל' טוען ונטען הל' ה ועי' בהשגות ובמ"מ ופ"א מהל' מכירה הל' ח סמג עשין פד לה טוש"ע ח"מ סי' קמט סעיף יד וסי' קלד סעיף א:

נח י מיי' שם סמג שם טוש"ע ח"מ סי' קמט סעיף טו וסי' קלד שם:

רבינו גרשום

התם להאי אית ליה דררא [דממונא] בגוה. דקודם מכירה הות ממוניה דהאי ובתר מכירה דאידך ואין ידוע ממונו של מי ילדה מש"ה יחלוקו: **גזלן של [רבים].** כלומר גזלן של שנים שעומדים במחלוקת ביניהם א) כגון אלא **שלא ניתן להשבון** שאע"פ שמשיב קרוי גזלן שאין ידוע של מי היתה שיחזירנה לו: **פיסקא אמר ר' אבא אי דלי ליה.** המערער כלומר שסייע למחזיק להגביה לו על כתיפו ב) או שהשליך אחריו לביתו **צנא של פירות** מאותה שדה שמערער עליה אע"פ שעדיין לא עמדה ברשותיה ג' שנין חזקה אלא כיון שיש לו עדים שהגביה לו צנא דפירי **לאלתר הוי חזקה** דאם איתא דשלו היא כיון שאמר לו המחזיק הגבה לי היה לו למחות ולומר והלא שלי הוא הקרקע מה יש לך בפירות שדי: **אמר רב זביד.** אי דלי ליה צנא ושוב מערער על השדה דשלו הוא **וטוען ואומר לפירות הורדתיו** שיהא אריסי שיהא חצי הפירות שלו וזה שהגבהתי לו חלקו סיעתיו להגביה **נאמן** לומר כן: **הני מילי.** דנאמן לומר כן **בתוך ג'** כשלא החזיק בהן עדיין ג' שני חזקה **אבל לאחר ג' [לא]: מאי הוה ליה למיעבד.** מה היה יכול למחות הא לא מצי לסלקו קודם זמנו אם עשאו אריס לי' שנים עדיין לא הגיע זמנו: אפ"ה **איבעי ליה למחויי.** אע"ג דלא הוי עיקר מחאה דלא מצי למימר פלוני גזלנא הוא דאכיל ארעא דידי דהא ברשותיה אוכל דהורידו לפירות מ"מ צריך למחות בפני עדים בתוך ג' ולומר הוו עדים שפלוני (שעובד) [שאוכל] שדה שלי אני הורדתיו לפירות לכך שנים ואי לא אמר הכי לא מהימן למחות אחר ג': **דאי לא תימא הכי.** דצריך למחויי בתוך ג' ולהודיע לרבים שאינה שלו א"כ **הני משכנתא דסורא** דמשכן ליה לוה למלוה דליכול שדהו בנכייתא עד זמן שישתלם ממנו בפירות שיאכל מן השדה: **אלא איבעי ליה למחויי.** בתוך ג' להודיע לרבים שמשכנתא היא בידו ה"נ במוריד חבירו לשדהו לפירות **בעי למחויי: ישראל הבא מחמת עכו"ם כעכו"ם.** כגון שקנאה מן העכו"ם ג' שנים אינן חזקה מן ישראל אם קנה ממנו קרקע אא"כ יש לו שטר מכירה עליה לפי שבדיניהן אין חזקה בשנים אצל **ישראל הבא מחמת עכו"ם** נמי **אין לו חזקה אא"כ** יש לו אותו **שטר** שמכרה ישראל לעכו"ם ואע"פ שיש לו עדים לישראל שעמד בה עכו"ם אין חזקתו חזקה מה שאין כן בישראל שאם קנה ישראל קרקע מחבירו ישראל ועמד בה שני חזקה ובא אחר וערער עליה ואמר זה מישראל פלוני קניתיה אם יש לו עדים שעמד בה אותו ישראל אפי' יום אחד חזקתו חזקה: **אמר רבא אי אתי ישראל ואמר. לדידי אמר** אותו **עכו"ם** שמכרה לזה דההוא עכו"ם גופיה קנאה מישראל מהימן:

מסורת הש"ס

א) [לקמן לח.] ב"מ סז: קי:

הגהות הב"ח

(א) גמ' אמרי נהרדעי ואם: (ב) שם הכי נמי דמהימן וכי תימא הכי נמי מתקני רבנן מידי דאתי ביה: (ג) רשב"ם ד"ה ומאי לא וכו' לא מיתכפר בהשבה וכו' להשיב לבעלים. נ"ב ודמי ממש להא דמנוני חייב על הלוואות הלכה דנעשה עליו גזלן ולא יצא במה שמחזירו לאחיתוק לקמן דף פ"ח ע"א: (ד) בא"ד וכל מאן דאלים מחזיקים עליו גבר: (ה) בא"ד דהמוכר במדה לון לרבים אינו יודע: (ו) תוס' ד"ה אין מוציאים וכו' ורשעים הם. נ"ב וכן נראה לפרש לקמן בפ' מי שמת גבי רוכל מקבלים אמן כדף קנ"ו:

ליקוטי רש"י

דררא דממונא. חסרון ממון [ב"מ ב:]. **דאי לא תימא הכי.** דמחאה כי האי גוונא לא הויא מחאה מאחר (שמודה) [שמוחזקין] לו (ש)אוכל עכשיו מן הקרקע מן הדין דלא הויא מחאה בטוען פלניא גזלנא הוא כדלקמן [לקמן לח.] [רשב"ם לקמן לח.]. **שניא.** דלא מיחזי כמחאה אלא כמודה לפירות שלא הויא מחאה במעות הללו [ב"מ סז:].

חשק שלמה על רבינו גרשום א) נראה דצ"ל שעומדים במחלוקת כגון אלו: שלא ניתן להשבון וכו'. ב) אולי צ"ל או שתלה אחריו לביתו וכו' ואפשר דכוונתו שתלה הלוקח אחריו של מריה דארעא וכמו שפי' הרשב"ם בשם הר"ח ז"ל.

share of the crop," נֶאֱמָן – **[the challenger] is believed.**[8] וְהָנֵי מִילֵּי בְּתוֹךְ שָׁלֹשׁ – **But this applies** only **within** the first **three years** of occupancy, to effectively explain why he assisted the occupant in carrying away the field's produce.[9] אֲבָל לְאַחַר שָׁלֹשׁ לֹא – **But after three years** have passed, the challenger is **not** believed to use this as an explanation of why he did not protest the occupancy, and the occupant thus retains the land with his *chazakah*.[10]

Rav Ashi posed a practical problem:

אָמַר לֵיהּ רַב אַשִׁי לְרַב כַּהֲנָא – **Rav Ashi said to Rav Kahana:** אִי לְפֵירָא אַחְתֵּיהּ – **If [the challenger] did** in fact **install [the occupant]** as a sharecropper **to** grow the **produce,** מַאי הֲוָה לֵיהּ לְמֶעְבַּד – **what should [the challenger] have done** to protect himself against the sharecropper's using three years' occupation to falsely prove that he purchased the field?[11]

Rav Kahana replied:

אָמַר לֵיהּ – **Rav Kahana said to [Rav Ashi]:** אִיבָּעֵי לֵיהּ לְמַחוּיֵי – **He should have "protested"** within the three-year period by publicizing the fact that the occupant was merely a sharecropper and not the land's true owner.[12]

Rav Kahana adduced support for this reply:

דְּאִי לֹא תֵּימָא הָכִי – **For if you will not say so** – that such a "protest" suffices to prevent establishment of *chazakah*[13] – הָנֵי מַשְׁכַּנְתָּא דְסוּרָא – then a potentially dangerous situation is created by **these Surean securities**[14] דִּכְתַב בְּהוּ – **in [whose attendant bond] is written:** בְּמִשְׁלַם שְׁנַיָּא אִלֵּין – **"At the termination of these years,** תֵּיפּוּק אַרְעָא דָא בְּלָא כֶסֶף – **this property shall revert** to its original owner **without payment."**[15] אִי כָּבֵישׁ לֵיהּ לִשְׁטַר מַשְׁכַּנְתָּא גַּבֵּיהּ – For **if** after three years **[the lender] suppresses the security bond** וְאָמַר לְקוּחָה הִיא בְּיָדִי – **and says, "[The land] is mine because I purchased it,"** הָכִי נַמִּי דִּמְהֵימַן – **would he then be believed?**[16] מְתַקְּנֵי רַבָּנָן מִידֵי דְּאָתֵי בֵּיהּ לִידֵי פְּסֵידָא – Would **the Rabbis** then **enact [an arrangement] that can cause** the borrower **an** unfair **loss** of his land?[17] אֶלָּא – **Rather,** Rav Kahana continued, we are forced to conclude that אִיבָּעֵי לֵיהּ לְמַחוּיֵי – **[the borrower] should have**

NOTES

8. That is, the challenger is believed to explain away the seemingly incriminating evidence of his having helped the occupant carry off the field's produce, by asserting that the occupant was his sharecropper, and that he, the field's owner, was simply assisting the sharecropper take his share of the crop (*Rashbam*). Consequently, the occupant cannot prove his claim without producing witnesses of *chazakah*.

9. And the occupant's claim of ownership is dismissed, due to the fact that he has no deed (*Rashbam*).

10. If the occupant can prove that he used the field uncontestedly for three years, he wins possession of it, although he does not produce a deed (for a person is not careful to keep his deed after three years unless his occupancy is contested). The challenger is not believed to counter that the reason he did not protest was because the occupant was his sharecropper and, as such, was legally harvesting the field. Rather, the challenger's silence is inexcusable [and is taken as proof that he indeed sold the field] (*Rashbam*).

11. Since a challenger is not believed to assert that the occupant consumed the field's produce as a mere sharecropper, what is to stop an unscrupulous sharecropper from claiming that he purchased the field, once three years of sharecropping have passed? How can a landowner who employs a sharecropper possibly protect his field from being illegally wrested from him? (*Rashbam*).

[Rav Ashi is not disputing the previous ruling. Clearly, the challenger is not believed after three years to claim that the occupant is only a sharecropper. If such a claim would be believed, then no *chazakah* of three years would be viable, for the original owner could always make this claim and invalidate the *chazakah*! Obviously, then, he cannot make such a claim after three years. Rav Ashi was just questioning how an owner can prevent a sharecropper from falsely claiming ownership after three years (*Tosafos, Rashba, Ritva*).]

12. [Although he could not have protested by claiming that the occupant was on the field illegally,] he should have at least declared before witnesses that the land was his and the occupant was merely a sharecropper. This would effectively have blocked any attempt on the part of the sharecropper to use his three-year occupancy to prove ownership, because his lack of a deed would then be inexcusable – having been put on notice by the original owner's declaration, he should still be in possession of his deed (*Rashbam*).

13. Rav Kahana means to preclude the argument that a protest is effective only where the protester accuses the occupant of illegally consuming the produce and declares that he will sue the occupant. But where the challenger merely states that the field is his, while agreeing that the occupant's produce-consumption is legal, the protest is not forceful enough to be effective (*Rashbam*). [The force of this argument may be that in order to be effective, a protest must seem threatening enough to the occupant to motivate him to guard his deed, if in fact he has one. Here, since the challenger merely said that the occupant was his sharecropper, the occupant may argue as follows: When I heard that he told people that I was a sharecropper, I reasoned that he did not intend to sue me. For if he planned to take me to court and falsely claim that he did not sell the land to me, why did he now not protest that I was an out-and-out thief and am not entitled even to the produce? Apparently, he is not bold enough to falsely accuse me of doing something illegal! Consequently, I did not feel the need to guard my deed.] Rav Kahana now proceeds to show that this line of reasoning is perforce incorrect.

14. [The Torah forbids the charging of interest for a loan to a fellow Jew (*Leviticus* 25:36). This prohibition is violated no matter what form the interest charge takes.] Thus, if a borrower posts his field as security for a loan, and the lender harvests the field's crops during the time that the loan is outstanding, he violates this prohibition, because the crops harvested constitute an interest payment. However, the Sages permitted the lender to use the field if such usage is the agreed-upon method of repaying the loan. To illustrate: If the sum of the loan is one thousand *zuzim,* it may be repaid by allowing the lender to use the land for ten years and deducting one hundred *zuzim* per year from the outstanding balance. At the end of the ten-year term, the land reverts to the borrower and the loan is considered paid. This is permitted even if, for example, each year's crop turns out to be worth two hundred *zuzim,* because in agreeing to this arrangement, the lender takes the risk that the crops could fail and be worth little or nothing. Hence, rather than taking interest, the lender is, in essence, purchasing each year's crop for the set price of one hundred *zuzim.* [Such an arrangement was common in the Babylonian town of Sura and hence is known as a Surean security. Instead of the usual loan document, the lender is provided with a document of security stating that he is entitled to harvest the field's produce at the agreed-upon rate for the agreed-upon term of years.] (*Rashbam*).

15. If the bond were drawn up for the case illustrated above, it would state that at the end of ten years, the land would revert to the borrower and the debt would be considered fully satisfied.

16. The lender could conceal the document of security and falsely claim that he had purchased the land. [Since he had used the land for three years, his claim would be supported by a *chazakah* and he would be believed.] The borrower's assertion that the land was in the lender's control merely as a security would not be believed, just as a challenger is not believed to claim, after three years have passed, that the occupant is merely a sharecropper. Now, if the borrower's "protest" that the lender was holding the land merely as security is not regarded as valid, how can the borrower protect his property from being illegally wrested from him? (*Rashbam*).

17. It is unthinkable that the Rabbis would institute a practice that, while successfully avoiding the prohibition against taking interest, sets up a situation that is potentially damaging to the borrower.

[A solution to this problem would be for the Rabbis to enact that whenever a Surean security agreement was concluded, the borrower should be given a document attesting to this fact. In this way, the lender could not claim the land as his, because the borrower could produce the document to prove that the land was merely given as security. But since the Rabbis did *not* require that a document be written for the borrower, it is clear that there must be an alternate way for the borrower to protect himself (*Ramban*).]

אית ליה דררא דממונא ולההוא אית ליה דררא דממונא הכא אי דמר לא דמר ואי דמר לא דמר אמרי נהרדעי (א) אם בא אחד מן השוק והחזיק בה אין מוציאין אותה מידו דתני רבי חייא גזלן של רבים לאו שמיה גזלן רב אשי אמר לעולם שמיה גזלן ומאי לא שמיה גזלן שלא ניתן להשבון: חזקתן שלש שנים מיום ליום וכו': א"ר אבא דאי דלי ליה איהו גופיה צנא דפירי לאלתר הוי חזקה אמר רב זביד ואם טוען ואמר לפירות הורדתיו נאמן והו"מ בתוך שלש אבל לאחר שלש לא א"ל רב אשי לרב כהנא אי לפירא אחתיה מאי הוה ליה למעבד א"ל איבעי ליה למחויי דאי לא תימא הכי הני משכנתא דסורא דכתב בהו במשלם שניא אלין תיפוק ארעא דא בלא כסף אי כביש ליה לשטר משכנתא גביה ואמר לקוחה היא בידי הכי נמי דמהימן (ג) מתקני רבנן מידי דאתי ביה לידי פסידא אלא איבעי ליה למחויי הכא נמי איבעי ליה למחויי אמר רב יהודה אמר רב ישראל הבא מחמת עכו"ם הרי הוא כעכו"ם מה עכו"ם אין לו חזקה אלא בשטר אף ישראל הבא מחמת עכו"ם אין לו חזקה אלא בשטר אמר רבא ואי אמר ישראל לדידי

אם בא אחד מן השוק והחזיק בה. בהך קרקע דאמר רב נחמן כל דאלים גבר ובא זה וזה השלישי ותפסה מהשנים אלו הטוענין של אבותי: **אין מוציאין אותה.** בב"ד מידו של זה השלישי ואע"ג דלא טוען מידי דשמא גם לב' הראשונים אין להם חלק בה: **דתני רבי חייא** גזלן של רבים כו'. וסברי נהרדעי דבגזלן כי האי מיירי שגזל משנים החלוקים בדבר זה אומר שלי הוא וזה אומר שלי: **לאו שמיה גזלן.** לכופו בדיינים להוציא מידו מה שגזל: **רב אשי אמר לעולם** של רבים שמיה גזלן. הואיל ולא טוען מידי ומוציאים מידו ומעמידין אותה בפני שניהם הראשונים שיש להם טענת אבות: **ומאי לא שמיה גזלן.** דקאמר רבי חייא לא להקל עליו בא לפטרו מלשלם אלא להחמיר עליו ולומר דלא ניתן להשבון לא (ג) מיכפר בהשבה דאינו יודע למי ישיב דמאחר שבא לידו צריך להשיב לבעלים ולא להוציאה מתחת ידו ולהפקידה לשנים הראשונים וכל מאן דאלים (ד) גבר דלספקינן לעיל ואי תפסינן לא מפקינן כל שכן זה שבתורת גזל בא לידו והוא צריך להוציאה מתחת ידו ואינו יודע למי ישיב והכי נמי אמרינן בהמוכר את הספינה (לקמן דף פח.) א"ל לוי קשה עונשן של מדות מעונשן של עריות ומפרש התם אפשר בתשובה והכא לא אפשר בתשובה דהמוכר במדה (ה) וגזל לרבים שאינו יודע למי ישיב ואוקימנא דרב אשי איירי נמי ר' חייא במוכר במדה שאינה ישרה לרבים כן נראה בעיני שיטה זו: **אי דלי ליה צנא דפירי לאלתר הוי חזקה.** אם יש עדים שהגביה המערער צנא דפירי מקרקע זו על כתפיו של זה המחזיק שטוען לקוחה היא בידי מאחר שסייע לו להוליך הפירות לביתו שוב אין יכול לטעון ולומר לא מכרתיה לו שלא היה לו לסייעו בלקיטת הפירות אלא היה לו למחות ומדסייע לו הפסיד וכמודה שמכר לו דמי. ור' חננאל פירש אי איכא סהדי דיהב ליה לוקח למריה ארעא צנא דפירי דורון להוליכה לביתו נתברר שאכילת הפירות של לוקח ומדידיה יהב ליה למוכר ואין נראה בעיני: **אמר רב זביד אי טעין.** המערער בתר דדלי ליה ללוקח צנא דפירי לפירות הורדתיו כדין אריס למחצה ושליש ולרביע וחלקו הוא דדלי ליה נאמן כלומר לא הפסיד במאי דדלי ליה: **והני מילי.** דנאמן: **בתוך שלש.** דאם איתא דזבנה מיניה אמאי לא מיזדהר בשטריה: **אבל לאחר שלש.** אי טעין לפירות הורדתיו אינו נאמן ואע"ג דלא דלי ליה צנא דפירי דעד תלת שנין מיזדהר איניש בשטריה טפי לא מיזדהר והוה ליה לזה למחות בתוך שלש כדמפרש ואזיל: **אי לפירא אחתיה.** כי משכנתא דסורא לעשר שנים או לעשרים: **מאי הוה ליה.** לבעל השדה למעבד נמצא שכל המוריד את חבירו לפירות של שלש שנים או יותר יפסיד קרקע שלו הואיל ולא יהא נאמן לאחר שלש לטעון לפירות הורדתיו: **א"ל איבעי [ליה] למחויי.** בתוך שלש ולומר לעדים דעו לכם שלפירות הורדתיו לכך וכך שנים וגוף הקרקע קנוי לי שאם אין לו שטר מכירה לזה המחזיק לא יוכל לטעון שטר היה לי ואבד כי לא נזהרתי בו אחר שלש דכיון דמיחה בו בעל השדה היה לו להזהר בשטרו: **דאי לא תימא הכי.** דמחאה לאנאין שמוחה על הקרקע ומודי בפירות לאו מחאה היא אלא כדאמרינן לקמן פלניא גזלנא הוא דקאכיל ארעא דידי בגזלנותא למחר תבענא ליה בדינא: **אם כן האי משכנתא דסורא כו'.** ותקנתא דרבנן הויא הך משכנתא משום דהמלוה לחבירו על שדהו אסור לאכול הפירות משום רבית אבל בנכייתא מותר כעין משכנתא דסורא שמלוה עשרה מנה על שדהו ולסוף עשר שנים חוזר הקרקע לבעלים בחנם ונמצא קונה פירות של כל שנה במנה ואין כאן צד רבית ואע"פ ששוין הפירות כפלים שהרי הוא קרוב לשכר וקרוב להפסד שמקבל פירות של כל שנה במנה ואפילו בשנת שדפון שלא יהו שוין פירות השנה דינר: **אי כביש.** טומן המלוה ואמר לאחר שלש לקוחה היא בידי הכי נמי דמהימן ולא יוכל זה לטעון לפירות הורדתיו ומחאה נמי לא תועיל לו: **דאתי ביה.** לוה לידי הפסד בתמיה: **אלא איבעי ליה למחויי.** בתוך כל שלש ומהניא ליה מחאה ומדלא מיחה הפסיד: **הכא נמי.** אם איתא דלפירא אחתיה איבעי ליה למחויי בתוך שלש קודם שיחזיק: **ישראל הבא מחמת עכו"ם הרי הוא כעכו"ם.** שדה שהכל יודעין שהיתה של ישראל ואכלה עכו"ם שלש שנים או יותר וטוען שלקחה מישראל ואזיל ישראל וקנה מההוא עכו"ם ואכלה גם הוא אחר העכו"ם שני חזקה או יותר לא הוי חזקה אלא אתי מריה דארעא ומפיק ליה מידיה דישראל וישראל ליזיל וליתבע לעכו"ם דזבן מיניה דאיהו הוא דאפסיד אנפשיה דלא הוה ליה למזבן ארעא דישראל מעכו"ם עד דלימא ליה הב לי שטר דזביני דזבנת לה מישראל דדין חזקה לית ליה לעכו"ם ולא כל מאן דאתי מחמתיה דסתם עכו"ם גזלנים הם וישראל ירא למחות והלכך לא תקנו בהם חזקה כדאמרינן לקמן בשמעתין הני דבי ריש גלותא לא מחזקי משום האי טעמא גופיה שיראים אנו למחות וישראל זה הבא מחמת עכו"ם אע"פ שהחזיק אין חזקתו כלום וחזקה שאין עמה טענה היא שהרי הוא טוען העכו"ם מכרה לי אבל איני יודע היאך באה לידי העכו"ם שיוכל למכרה אבל אי טען ישראל ואמר יהב לי ההוא עכו"ם שטר זביני דזבנה מינך ורמיתי בו שלקחה ממך מהימן דדמי למאן דא"ל קמי דידי זבנה ההוא עכו"ם מינך דמסקי' לקמן דמהימן מיגו דאי בעי א"ל מינך זבנתה ואכלתה שני חזקה ודוקא בא מחמת עכו"ם דאילו בא מחמת ישראל אע"פ שלא דר בה אלא יום אחד אותו שמכרה לזה וזה החזיק שלש שנים חזקתו חזקה כדאמרי' לקמן (דף מא:) גבי ההוא דדר בקטתא בעיליתא ארבע שנין: לדידי

דררא דממונא. פירוש דלל טענתייהו מהכא יש ספק לב"ד דהי מינייהו הוא הולד אם נולד קודם שמכר או אחר שמכר וכן בשור שנגח את הפרה ונמצא עוברה בצדה (ב"ק דף מו.) בלא טענתם מסופקים ב"ד איך היה מעשה אם קודם שנגחה ילדה או לאחר שנגחה וכן בשור רודף אחר שור אחר והוזק (שם לה.) יש להסתפק אם בשורו הוזק או אי בסלע לקה וכן בכל מקום דפליגי רבנן וסומכוס אבל הכא בזה אומר של אבותי ובזה אומר של אבותי ליכא ספק אלא על פי טענותיהן בא הספק אמרינן כל דאלים גבר: **אין** מוציאים אותה מידו. ואפילו כתבו הרשאה זה לזה הואיל ושניהם (ו) אין מוחזקים להם: **דתני** רבי חייא גזלן של רבים לא שמיה גזלן. שאין מוציאין מידו ומיירי בזה אומר של אבותי ולא בגזל מחמשה בני אדם דהתם ודאי אין מוציאין ורב אשי פליג אנהרדעי וסבר דרבי חייא לא להקל בא אלא להחמיר דלא סגי בהשבה אחת כמו לשאר גזלן עד שישלם גזלה לכל אחד ואחד כרבי עקיבא בהגוזל עצים (ב"ק דף קג:) ומיירי בגזל מחמשה וקונטרס פירש דמיירי בחנוני שמכר במדה שאינה ישרה דאינו יודע למי גזל ולכך לא ניתן להשבון ואף על פי שיכול לעשות בו צרכי צבור כדאמרינן בפרק אין לדין (ב"ק דף צד.) הלא מאו השבה מעלייתא היא: **ואי** דלי ליה צנא דפירי לאלתר הויא חזקה. וא"ת ולהימניה במיגו דאי בעי אמר לפירות הורדתיו וי"ל דהוי מיגו במקום עדים דלאן סהדי כיון דדלי ליה צנא דפירי מודה שהיו הפירות שלו ועוד דאינו רוצה לטעון לפירות הורדתיו אלא תובע הקרקע והפירות: **ואי** לפירא אחתיה מאי הוה ליה למעבד. אין לפרש דרב אשי סבר דלעולם נאמן לומר לפירות הורדתיך דאם כן קשה לרב אשי מאי טעמא דרבנן דבעו שלש שנים מיום ליום דהא לדידיה ליכא למימר כדמפרש רבא בריש פרקין דעד שלש שנים מיזדהר איניש בשטריה טפי לא מזדהר דהא לעולם צריך לשמרו פן יאמר לפירות הורדתיך ועוד דאם כן היכי קאמר דאי לא תימא הכי דאיבעי ליה למחויי אלא לא בעי למחויי דחזקתו אינה חזקה דיכול לומר לפירות הורדתיו ומייתי ממשכנתא דסורא ומאי מייתי אדרבה אם כדברי רב אשי תו ליכא פסידא שיכול לומר לפירות הורדתיך ונראה לרשב"א דרב אשי לא בא להאמינו אחר ג' אם אומר לפירות הורדתיך אלא שואל איזו תקנה יש לעשות מתחלה שלא יוכל לומר לאחר שלש שלי היא כשהורידו לפירות דסבר לא מהני מחאה אלא כשאמר פלניא גזלנא הוא דקא אכיל לארעאי בגזלנותא והיכא דאחתיה לפירות לא מצי למחויי הכי וכן פירש הקונטרס והשתא מייתי שפיר ממשכנתא דסורא דמהניא מחאה כי האי גוונא [ועי' תוס' ב"מ קי. ד"ה אמר ליה]:

עין משפט נר מצוה

נג א ב ג מיי' פט"ו מהל' טוען ונטען הלכה ד סמג עשין לה טוש"ע ח"מ סי' קלט סעיף ב וטוש"ע וכסי' קמו סעיף כב:
נד ד מיי' פי"א שם הל' ט ופ"א מהל' מכירה הל' טז סמג עשין לד לה טוש"ע ח"מ סי' קמב סעיף א וסי' קלב סעיף יא:
נה ה ו מיי' פי"א מהל' טוען ונטען הל' ט סמג עשין לה טוש"ע ח"מ סי' קמב סעיף א:
נו ז ח טוש"ע ח"מ סי' קנ סעיף א:
נז ט מיי' פי"ד מהל' טוען ונטען הל' ה ועי' בהשגות ובכ"מ ופ"א מהל' מכירה הל' ח סמג עשין פב לה טוש"ע ח"מ סי' קמט סעיף יד וסי' קלד סעיף א:
נח י מיי' שם סמג שם טוש"ע ח"מ סי' קמט סעיף טו וסי' קלד שם:

רבינו גרשום

התם להאי אית ליה דררא [דממונא] בגוה. דקודם מכירה הות ממוניה דהאי ובתר מכירה דאידך ואין ידוע ממונו של מי ילדה מש"ה יחלוקו: **גזלן של [רבים].** כלומר גזלן של שנים שעומדים במחלוקת ביניהם א) כגון אלא **שלא ניתן להשבון** שאע"פ שמשיב קרוי גזלן שאין ידוע של מי היתה שיחזירנה לו: **פיסקא אמר ר' אבא אי דלי ליה.** המערער כלומר שסייע למחזיק להגביה לו על כתיפו ב) או שהשליך אחריו לביתו **צנא של פירות** מאותה שדה שמערער עליה אע"פ שעדיין לא עמדה ברשותיה ג' שנין חזקה אלא כיון שיש לו עדים שהגביה לו צנא דפירי **לאלתר הוי חזקה** דאם איתא דשלו היא כיון שאמר לו המחזיק הגבה לי היה לו למחות ולומר והלא שלי הוא הקרקע מה יש לך בפירות שדי: **אמר רב זביד.** אי דלי ליה צנא ושוב מערער על השדה דשלו הוא **וטוען ואומר לפירות הורדתיו** שיהא אריסי שיהא חצי הפירות שלו וזה שהגבהתי לו חלקו סיעתיו להגביה **נאמן** לומר כן: **הני מילי.** דנאמן לומר כן **בתוך ג'** כשלא החזיק בהן עדיין ג' שני חזקה **אבל לאחר ג' [לא]:** **מאי הוה ליה למיעבד.** מה היה יכול למחות הא לא מצי לסלקו קודם זמנו אם עשאו אריס לי' שנים עדיין לא הגיע זמנו: אפ"ה **איבעי ליה למחויי.** אע"ג דלא הוי עיקר מחאה דלא מצי למימר פלוני גזלנא הוא דאכיל ארעא דידי דהא ברשותיה אוכל דהורידו לפירות מ"מ צריך למחות בפני עדים בתוך ג' ולומר הוו עדים שפלוני (שעובד) [שאוכל] שדה שלי אני הורדתיו לפירות לכך שנים ואי לא אמר הכי לא מהימן למחות אחר ג': **דאי לא תימא הכי.** דצריך למחויי בתוך ג' ולהודיע לרבים שאינה שלו א"כ **הני משכנתא דסורא** דמשכן ליה לוה למלוה דליכול שדהו בנכייתא עד זמן שישתלם ממנו בפירות שיאכל מן השדה: **אלא איבעי ליה למחויי.** בתוך ג' להודיע לרבים שמשכנתא היא בידו ה"נ במוריד חבירו לשדהו לפירות **בעי למחויי: ישראל הבא מחמת עכו"ם כעכו"ם.** כגון שקנאה מן העכו"ם ג' שנים אינן חזקה מה עכו"ם אין לו חזקה מן ישראל אם קנה ממנו קרקע אא"כ יש לו שטר מכירה עליה לפי שבדיניהן אין חזקה בשנים אצל ישראל הבא מחמת עכו"ם נמי אין לו חזקה אא"כ יש לו אותו שטר שמכרה ישראל לעכו"ם ואע"פ שיש לו עדים לישראל שעמד בה עכו"ם אין חזקתו חזקה מה שאין כן בישראל שאם קנה ישראל קרקע מחבירו ישראל ועמד בה שני חזקה ובא אחר וערער עליה ואמר זה מישראל פלוני קניתיה אם יש לו עדים שעמד בה אותו ישראל אפי' יום אחד חזקתו חזקה: **אמר רבא אי אתי ישראל ואמר. לדידי** אמר אותו עכו"ם שמכרה לזה דההוא עכו"ם גופיה קנאה מישראל מהימן:

חשק שלמה על רבינו גרשום א) נראה דל"ל שעומדים במחלוקת כגון אלו: שלא ניתן להשבון וכו'. ב) אולי צ"ל או שנשא אחריו לביתו וכו' ואפשר דכוונתו ששלח הלוקח אחריו של מריה דארעא וכמו שפי' הרשב"ם בשם הר"ח ז"ל.

מסורת הש"ס

א) [לקמן מא.] ב"מ סז: קי.

הגהות הב"ח

(א) גמ' אמרי נהרדעי ואם: (ב) שם הכי נמי דמהימן וכי מיתא הכי נמי מתקני רבנן מידי דאתי ביה: (ג) רשב"ם ד"ה ומאי לא וכו' מיתכפר בהשבה וכו' להשיב לבעלים. נ"ב ודמי ממש להא דתנא חייב על הגלגולת היכא דנעשה עליו גזלן ולא ידע במאי שמחזירו כו לחיטתן לקמן דף פ"ח ע"א: (ד) בא"ד וכל מאן דאלים משמיהם גבר: (ה) בא"ד דהמוכר במדה אין לרבים אינו יודע: (ו) תוס' ד"ה אין מוציאים וכו' ושניהם הם. נ"ב וכן נראה לפרש לקמן בפ' מי שמת גבי רוכל מקדר למן דף קנ"ו:

ליקוטי רש"י

דררא דממונא. חסרון ממון [ב"מ ב:]. **דאי לא תימא הכי.** דמחאה כי האי גוונא לא הויא מחאה מאחר (שמודה) [שהמוחזק] כו (ש)אוכל עכשיו מן הדין הקרקע הוא ולא להוי מחאה כי גוונא פלניא גזלנא הוא כדלקמן [רשב"ם לקמן לח.]. **במשלם שניא.** דלא מיחזי כהלואה אלא כלוקח הימנו פירות השנים הללו במעות [ב"מ סז:].

"protested" before three years elapsed.[18] Thus, we see that such a "protest" is valid.[19] הָכָא נַמִּי – Then **here as well,** when a sharecropper is installed in a field, אִיבָּעֵי לֵיהּ לְמַחוּיֵי – **[thefield's owner] should have "protested"** before three years elapsed.[20]

Rav Yehudah discusses an instance in which even three years of occupancy are insufficient to prove ownership:

אָמַר רַב יְהוּדָה אָמַר רַב – Rav Yehudah said in the name of Rav: יִשְׂרָאֵל הַבָּא מֵחֲמַת עוֹבֵד כּוֹכָבִים – **A Jew who came** to occupy a property **through** acquisition from **an idolater**[21] הֲרֵי הוּא כְּעוֹבֵד כּוֹכָבִים – **is** on **the same** footing **as an idolater** in the following sense: מָה עוֹבֵד כּוֹכָבִים אֵין לוֹ חֲזָקָה אֶלָּא בִּשְׁטָר – **Just as an idolater cannot prove ownership** of property **except by** producing **a deed,**[22] אַף יִשְׂרָאֵל הַבָּא מֵחֲמַת עוֹבֵד כּוֹכָבִים – **so, too, a Jew who came** to occupy property **through** acquisition from **an idolater** אֵין לוֹ חֲזָקָה אֶלָּא בִּשְׁטָר – **cannot prove ownership** of it **except by** producing **a deed,** even though he has used the property for three years.[23]

Rava provides an exception to this rule:

אָמַר רָבָא – Rava said: וְאִי אָמַר יִשְׂרָאֵל – **But if the Jew says,**

NOTES

18. Since the Rabbis would not have created a situation in which the lender could defraud the borrower of his land, it is clear that the borrower could protect himself by declaring before witnesses that the land was his and that the man who occupied it was his creditor who merely held it as a security. Accordingly, the Rabbis were justified in promulgating the Surean security arrangement, because if the borrower does not make this declaration at least once every three years and thereby loses his land, he has only himself to blame (*Rashbam*).

19. Although by "protesting" in this fashion the borrower does not accuse the lender of unlawfully consuming the land's produce, it nevertheless constitutes a valid protest and negates the lender's *chazakah* (see note 13).

20. Hence, one who employs a sharecropper for three years or more is not doomed to lose his field, because he is able to block the sharecropper's *chazakah* by declaring before witnesses that the field is his and that the occupant is merely his sharecropper. Thus, Rav Ashi's problem is resolved.

21. A Jew purchased from an idolater a property that is known to have previously belonged to another Jew (*Rashbam*).

22. Unlike a Jew, an idolater cannot prove that he purchased land by producing witnesses that he occupied it uncontestedly for three years. The Rabbis did not enact *chazakah* for idolaters, because a Jew is generally reluctant to protest an idolater's occupation of his land, for fear of reprisal. Accordingly, the only way an idolater can prove that he indeed purchased land from a Jew is to produce his deed (*Rashbam*).

23. The Mishnah below, 41a, teaches that a *chazakah* is effective only where the occupant at the same time presents a clear claim that establishes his right to the land. Consequently, although the Jew who presently occupies the land can prove that he used it for three years, his *chazakah* is invalid, because he does not claim to know how the idolater who sold it to him came to possess it. Although witnesses testify that the idolater used the land for three years, this does not prove that he purchased it from the original owner, as explained in the previous note. Thus, the only way the present occupant is believed to retain the land is to produce a document that records the sale of the land by the original owner to the idolater. If he cannot produce that document, he must relinquish the land to the original owner, and attempt to recover his money from the idolater who sold the land to him (*Rashbam*).

[If the occupant used the property for three years, he would not have to actually produce the document. It would suffice for him to state that the idolater showed him the document providing proof of his purchase of the property from the original owner. For then, his *chazakah* comes together with a clear claim of ownership (*Rashbam*).]

Now, as explained above, in order for *chazakah* to be effective, the occupant must at the same time present a clear claim that establishes his right to the land. Thus, if he merely claims that he bought it from someone who said that he bought it from the original owner, his *chazakah* is ineffective, because he lacks a clear claim to the land. However, if there are witnesses who testify that the seller had at least some association with the land – i.e. that he lived there for even one day – the court will shift the presumption of ownership to the occupant. The logic behind this is that we cannot expect a buyer to know how a seller came to own the property he sells. Thus, although the occupant lacks a clear claim, the court will argue on his behalf that the seller did in fact buy the land from the original owner. Why, then, does the Gemara here state that if a Jew bought land from an idolater, he does not retain the land, even if the idolater lived in the land before selling it? Why does the court not argue on behalf of the present occupant that the idolater bought the land from the original owner?

It would seem that *Rashbam* resolves this question as follows: The court will argue on behalf of an occupant only where he need not have suspected that the seller was selling him stolen property. This is in fact the case when he purchased from a Jew. But where he purchased from an idolater, he should have demanded to see the deed that records the idolater's purchase from the original owner, because the average idolater is wont to steal. By not insisting on seeing the deed, the buyer acted irresponsibly, and the court will therefore not argue on his behalf. Since he lacks a clear claim, he must relinquish the land (cf. *Rabbeinu Yonah* and *Nesivos HaMishpat* 149:4).

לְדִידִי אָמַר לִי עוֹבֵד כּוֹכָבִים – "The idolater told me דְּמִינָּךְ זַבְנָהּ – that he bought [the land] from you," מְהֵימַן – he is believed, and he retains the land.[1]

The Gemara questions the logic behind this statement and asks:

מִי אִיכָּא מִידֵי – Is there then any [claim] דְּאִילוּ עוֹבֵד כּוֹכָבִים אָמַר לֹא מְהֵימַן – which, if an idolater advances it, he is not believed, וְאִילוּ אָמַר יִשְׂרָאֵל מִשְּׁמֵיהּ דְּעוֹבֵד כּוֹכָבִים – but if a Jew advances it in the idolater's name, מְהֵימַן – [the Jew] is believed? If the idolater's claim of ownership is not accepted even when supported by three years of unchallenged use, the fact that the Jew reports this claim in the idolater's name should not lend it greater validity.[2] – ? –

Rava therefore emended his statement:

אֶלָּא אָמַר רָבָא – Rather, Rava said: אִי אָמַר יִשְׂרָאֵל – If the Jew occupying the land says: קַמֵּי דִּידִי זַבְנָהּ עוֹבֵד כּוֹכָבִים מִינָּךְ – "The idolater bought [the land] from you in front of me, וְזַבְנָהּ נִיהֲלִי – and he subsequently sold it to me," מְהֵימַן – [the Jew] is believed, מִיגּוֹ דְּאִי בָּעֵי אָמַר לֵיהּ – since if he was lying he could just as well have said to [the original owner]: אֲנָא זְבִינְתָּהּ מִינָּךְ – "I myself bought the land directly from you," and he would have been believed.[3]

Another ruling of Rav Yehudah:

וְאָמַר רַב יְהוּדָה – And Rav Yehudah also said: הַאי מַאן דְּנָקִיט מַגְלָא וְתוּבַלְיָא – One who takes up a scythe and a rope,[4] וְאָמַר – and says: אֵיזִיל אֵיגְזְרֵהּ לְדִקְלָא דִּפְלַנְיָא – "I will go and cut down so-and-so's palm tree, דִּזְבַנְתֵּיהּ מִינֵּיהּ – for I have bought it from him," מְהֵימַן – is believed, and the court does not prevent him from proceeding. Why is this so? לֹא חָצִיף אִינִישׁ לְמִיגְזַר דִּקְלָא דְּלָאו דִּילֵיהּ – For a person is not so impudent as to cut down a palm tree that is not his. Thus, the very fact that he does so indicates that his claim is truthful.[5]

Now follow a series of rulings that define what types of usage constitute a *chazakah.*[6]

וְאָמַר רַב יְהוּדָה – And Rav Yehudah further said: הַאי מַאן דְּאַחֲזִיק מִגּוּדָא דַּעֲרוֹדֵי וּלְבַר – One who occupies that strip of field that is outside the "wild animal wall"[7] לָא הָוֵי חֲזָקָה – has not established a *chazakah,* although three years have passed without protest. מַאי טַעְמָא – What is the reason for this? מֵימַר אָמַר – For [the original owner] can say, כָּל דְּזָרַע נָמֵי עֲרוֹדֵי אָכְלֵי לֵיהּ – "Anything that he planted was eaten by the wild beasts, so I saw no need to protest."[8]

Another such ruling:

וְאָמַר רַב יְהוּדָה – And Rav Yehudah further said: אָכְלָהּ עָרְלָה אֵינָהּ חֲזָקָה – If [the occupant] used [the field] by harvesting *orlah* produce,[9] he has not established a *chazakah.*[10]

The Gemara quotes a Baraisa to support this ruling:

תַּנְיָא נָמֵי הָכִי – This was also taught in a Baraisa: אָכְלָהּ עָרְלָה שְׁבִיעִית וְכִלְאַיִם – If [THE OCCUPANT] USED [THE FIELD] by harvesting produce of *ORLAH, SHEVIIS*[11] OR *KILAYIM,*[12]

NOTES

1. [Rava understands, at this point, that Rav Yehudah's ruling applies only where the occupant merely says that he bought the land from an idolater. However, where the occupant additionally claims that the idolater told him that he bought the land from its owner, the occupant's *chazakah* is effective.] This is so because we assume that the occupant is being truthful when he says that the idolater told him this; if the occupant is lying, he would simply claim that he purchased the land directly from the original owner (*Rashbam*).

2. If the idolater himself had told the court that he bought the land, he would not be believed, in spite of his *chazakah.* Then of what use is it to believe the Jew that the idolater told him this? There is still no evidence that the idolater ever held legal title to the land! Thus, the occupant's *chazakah* is not accompanied by a valid claim and is therefore ineffective (*Rashbam*).

3. Had the current occupant claimed that he bought the property directly from the original owner, he would have won the case based on his *chazakah.* However, he does not claim this, but claims instead that he bought it from an idolater whom he saw buying it from the original owner. If he is not telling the truth, why would he concoct such an elaborate lie? It would be far simpler for him to claim that he bought it from the original owner. Thus, we assume that he is being truthful when he asserts that he witnessed the idolater buy the property from the original owner.

[The Gemara seems to say that a *migo* argument is needed to allow the occupant to retain the land. But this is not really so, because since his *chazakah* is now supported by a valid claim, he wins the case with his *chazakah* alone. See below, 41b note 13, for a fuller discussion of this.]

4. See above, 33b note 7.

5. Ibid. notes 8 and 9.

[This exact ruling was cited above, 33b, with the single exception that there Rav Yehudah is quoted as believing the man to cut the tree's *dates* while here he states that the man is believed to cut down the *tree.* However, *Tosafos* there ד"ה איזיל prove that the court does not in fact believe a man to cut down the tree itself. Presumably, then, the text here should be emended to conform to the Gemara above (*Rashash* and *R' Yaakov Emden;* cf. *Rashba* there).]

6. In order to establish a *chazakah,* an occupant must use the field for three years, and if the original owner does not protest during this time, his silence indicates that he indeed sold the field. It follows, then, that the occupant must use the land in a manner that would elicit protest from the original owner if in fact the occupant was acting illegally. The Gemara proceeds to discuss certain usages of the land that would not necessarily elicit such protest and are therefore ineffective for *chazakah.*

7. [Literally, עָרוֹד is a wild ass, i.e. an onager.] When enclosing his field, a landowner would sometimes intentionally place the fence a short distance before the border and leave a small strip of land unenclosed. This strip would not be planted in the usual manner; rather, the owner would strew seeds there and abandon to the wild animals whatever grain might take root and grow, in the hope that the animals would be content to feed there and would not seek to penetrate the field proper. In the case discussed by the Gemara, an occupant used this strip of land in the usual manner for three years (*Rashbam*).

8. A landowner is impelled to protest an illegal occupation of his land only if the occupant uses it as an owner would. This is because a landowner does not watch in silence while someone else acts in a manner that gives the impression to others that the field belongs to him, for the owner fears that his silence will be construed as an admission that he sold the field. But if the occupant uses the field in a manner that is inconsistent with normal usage, the owner does not feel the need to protest, since no false impression is being created. Accordingly, in this case, the owner may argue that he did not protest because it was clear to all that the land was not the occupant's; no owner would waste his efforts planting crops that would in the end be eaten by wild animals (see *Rashbam;* cf. *Nimukei Yosef*).

9. Fruit that grows on a tree during its first three years is called *orlah,* and the Torah forbids deriving any benefit from it (*Leviticus* 19:23-24).

10. Since the owner himself could not have benefited from the *orlah* produce, he is not impelled to protest if a thief consumes it. This applies if the occupant harvested *orlah* even for only one of the years, and certainly if he did so for all three (*Rashbam*).

11. The Torah declares that a farmer in Eretz Yisrael may not work his field during the Sabbatical year (*shemittah*), and must allow people and animals to enter at will and pick its fruit (*Leviticus* 25:1-7). In the Baraisa's case, an occupant harvests the produce of this seventh year (known as *sheviis* produce) and wants to reckon that year as one of the three needed for a *chazakah.*

12. When greens or grain is planted in a vineyard, the resultant produce (both of the seeds and the vine) is known as *kilei hakerem, mixtures of the vineyard,* or simply *kilayim, a mixture,* and is forbidden to be used. The Baraisa speaks of an occupant who harvests *kilei hakerem* for one or more of his *chazakah* years.

לדידי אמר לי עכו"ם דמינך זבנה מהימן מי איכא מידי דאילו (א) עכו"ם אמר לא מהימן ואילו אמר ישראל משמיה דעכו"ם מהימן אלא אמר רבא אי אמר ישראל קמי דידי זבנה עכו"ם מינך וזבנה ניהלי מהימן מיגו דאי בעי א"ל אנא זבינתה מינך ואמר רב יהודה האי מאן דנקיט מגלא ותובליא ואמר איזיל איגזרה לדקלא דפלניא דזבנתיה מיניה מהימן (ב) לא חציף איניש למיגזר דקלא דלאו דיליה ואמר רב יהודה האי מאן דאחזיק מגודא דערודי ולבר לא הוי חזקה מ"ט מימר אמר כל דזרע נמי ערודי אכלי ליה ואמר רב יהודה אכלה ערלה (ג) אינה חזקה תניא נמי הכי אכלה ערלה שביעית וכלאים אינה חזקה אמר רב יוסף אכלה שחת לא הוי חזקה אמר רבא ואי בצואר מחוזא קיימא הוי חזקה אמר רב נחמן תפתיחא לא הוי חזקה אפיק כורא ועייל כורא לא הוי חזקה והני דבי ריש גלותא לא מחזקי בן ולא מחזקינן בהו: והעבדים וכו': עבדים יש להם חזקה והאמר ר"ל הגודרות אין להן חזקה אמר רבא אין להן חזקה לאלתר אבל יש להן חזקה לאחר ג' שנים אמר רבא אם היה קטן מוטל בעריסה יש לו חזקה לאלתר פשיטא לא צריכא דאית ליה אימא מהו דתימא ניחוש דלמא אימיה עייליתיה להתם קמ"ל אימא לא מנשיא ברא הנהו עיזי דאכלו חושלא בנהרדעא אתא מרי חושלא תפסינהו והוה קא טעין טובא אמר אבוה דשמואל יכול לטעון עד כדי דמיהן דאי בעי אמר לקוחות הן בידי והאמר ר"ל הגודרות אין להן חזקה שאני עיזי דמסירה לרועה והא איכא צפרא ופניא בנהרדעא טייעי שכיחי ומידא לידא משלמי: ר' ישמעאל אומר שלשה חדשים וכו': לימא ניר איכא בינייהו דרבי ישמעאל סבר ניר לא הוי חזקה ורבי עקיבא סבר ניר הוי חזקה ותסברא לרבי עקיבא מאי איריא חודש אפילו

תוספות

הכי גרים ר"ח אכלה ערלה שביעית וכלאים הויא חזקה. וכן נראה לר"י עיקר ואיירי כשאכלה זמורות וכן מוכח בהאשה שנפלו (כתובות דף עט:) דתנן המוציא הוצאות על נכסי אשתו הוציא הרבה ואכל קימעא קימעא ואכל הרבה מה שהוציא הוציא ומה שאכל אכל ואמר בגמרא עבד רב יהודה עובדא בחבילי זמורות ורב יהודה לטעמיה דאמר רב יהודה אכלה ערלה שביעית וכלאים הויא חזקה ואין לומר דלעולם גרס הכא אינה חזקה והתם כשאכלה זמורות והכא כשאכלה פירות שהן אסורים ולכך לא הויא חזקה שלא אכל כדרך האוכלים דאם כן הוה ליה לאיתויי ההיא דהתם נמי הכא דאיירי בדיני חזקה וא"ת דהכא משמע דזמורות ועלי כלאים שרו ומ"ש מהא דאמרינן בפרק כל שעה (פסחים דף כו:) תנור שהסיקוהו בקליפי ערלה או בקשין של כלאי הכרם חדש יותץ מכלל דאסירי ואמרינן נמי התם (דף כה.) כלאי הכרם עיקרן נאסר ומיהו הא לא קשה דאיכא למימר דעיקרן נאסר משום דכתיב (דברים כב) הזרע וי"ל דהתם איירי בזרוע מעיקרן שנזרעו הזרעים עם נטיעות הכרם שגדלו הזמורות באיסור אבל הכא איירי בזמורות שהיו כבר גדולים קודם שנזרעו כלאים שאותן אין נאסרים אלא כשהוסיפו מאתים כדאמר בפרק כל שעה (שם דף כה.) ובפרק כל הבשר (חולין דף קטז.) זרוע ובא הוסיף מאתים אין לא הוסיף מאתים לא ומיירי הכא שזמורות לא הוסיפו מאתים והפירות הוסיפו ולכך לא הויא חזקה אלא בזמורות ואין זה דוחק דהכי הוי אורחא דמילתא שקודם מוסיפין הפירות מאתים מן הזמורות לפי שהזמורות כבר היו גדולות קודם זריעת כלאים: נרה

רשב"ם

לדידי אמר לי עכו"ם דמינך זבנה מהימן. דמלאסיק אדעתיה למיטען הכי ה"ל הוה מצי למיטען אנא זבינתה מינך ואכלתי' שני חזקה דמהימן הלכך מהימן נמי לשקר וקושטא קאמר: מי איכא מידי דאילו אמר עכו"ם לא מהימן כו'. השתא נמי חזקה שאין עמה טענה היא דאפי' אם טענתו אמת היא דאמר ליה עכו"ם דמישראל זבנה הלא אין בדבריו של עכו"ם כלום בלא שטר: קמאי דידי. כלומר שאני יודע בבירור היינו חזקה שיש עמה טענה: האי מאן דנקיט כו'. ככר פרשית לה לעיל: האי מאן דאחזיק מגודא דערודי ולבר לא הוי חזקה. חיות השדה שבאות ואוכלות הזרעים שבקצות השדה ויש שעושין קירות וגודרין השדה ומניחין קרקע חוץ לקיר מעט בשדות הסמוכות ליער ומשליכים שם זרע ומה שצומח באות החיות ואוכלות אותו ואינן נכנסות בשדה עכשיו ואם בא אדם והחזיק באותו הקרקע חוץ לגדר אינה חזקה דיכול לומר דכיון דכל מה דזרע בההוא קרקע ערודי אכלי ליה לא איכפת ליה למחות דלא אחזיק כדמחזקי אינשי לפיכך לא הויא חזקה: אכלה ערלה. אחת מן השלש שנים הויא שנת ערלה אינה חזקה דלא איכפת ליה לבעל השדה בשנת ערלה ולכך לא מיחה וכ"ש אם שלשתן שני ערלה. ערלה וכלאים אכילתן באיסור שביעית הפקר לכל לכך לא מיחה ולא הויא חזקה. ובפירוש ר"ח גרסינן הכי אכלה ערלה ושביעית וכלאים הרי זו חזקה ולא נהירא: אכלה שחת. שלא המתין עד שתגדל התבואה אלא ג' שנים קצרה כשהיא שחת ומאכיל לבהמתו אינה חזקה דשמיט ואכיל ולא היה אוכל כשאר בני אדם ולפיכך לא חשש זה למחות בו שיש רגלים לדבר שירא הוא להחזיק כשאר בני אדם לפי שבגזל ירד בה: ואמר רבא ואי. קאי האי שחת: בצואר מחוזא. בבקעת מחוזא הוי חזקה לפי שעשירים הם ובהמות להם הרבה ודרכם להאכיל השדות לבהמות כשהן שחת: תפתיחא. קרקע פתוחה ומלאה בקעים ואינה מוציאה פירותיה לא הויא חזקה דמפני רעתה לא הקפיד למחות. ורבי' חננאל פירש תפתיחא שדה שלא חרש אותה אלא הוגשמה וזרחה השמש ונשבה הרוח ונתבקעה כגון פתחי חרישה וזרע בה כגון זה אינה חזקה: אפיק כורא. זרע כור: ועייל כורא. וליקט בו כור והכניס לביתו דכיון דליכא הרווחה לא הוי חזקה דלא חשש זה למחות: לא מחזקי בן. אם החזיק אחד מהן בשדותינו אינה חזקה וצריך להזהר בשטרו דמחמת יראתן לא מיחו בהן: ולא מחזקינן בהו. שמתוך שהם עשירים ויש להם בתים ושדות הרבה מניחין בני אדם לדור בבתיהם ושותקים ושמחים כדי להשביח קרקע שלהם וימלאום מתוקנים וגם למחות אינן חוששים לפי שבזרוע יטלו את שלהם כל זמן שירצו וי"מ לפי שעסוקין בצרכי צבור אין יודעין מי מחזיק בשלהן ולא נהירא: הגודרות אין להן חזקה. גודרות צאן וכל דבר המהלך בדרכים ובשווקים שיכול לומר מעצמו נכנס או אתה הכנסתו לביתך והחזקת בו אינה חזקה ואין יכול לומר לקוח הוא בידי והעבדים מהלכים הם בכל מקום ותנן דיש להם חזקה: ומשני הא דאמר ר"ל אין להן חזקה ה"מ לאלתר. שהמחזיק בהן בביתו אין יכול לטעון לקוח הוא בידי בלא עדים ובלא ראיה כשאר מטלטלין שאין יכולין להלך ואין עשוין להשאיל ולהשכיר דנאמן בהן לומר לקוח הוא [בידי] הואיל וישנו בביתו דבשאר מטלטלין הוי חזקה לאלתר דהמוחזק בהן יכול לטעון שלי הוא שלקחתיו אבל יש [א] להן לעבדים ולגודרות חזקה לאחר ג' שנים שהיה לו לזה המערער למחות ולא מיחה: אמר רבא. עבד כנעני קטן המוטל בעריסה: יש לו חזקה לאלתר. אם החזיק בו אחד ואמר לקוח הוא בידי נאמן הואיל ואין יכול להלך ולא דמי לגודרות וגם אין עשוי להשאיל ולהשכיר: פשיטא. דודאי מעצמו לא הלך: דעיילא אימיה. דעבד בבית אותו המחזיק תדיר: אימיה עיילתיה. ושכחתיה שם דהשתא היינו גודרות: הני עיזי דאכלו חושלא. שעורים קלופים שנכנסו בשדה [ורמו] אותה תבואה השטוחה שם לשמש וקיימא לן שן מועדת היא לעולם וכי הויא ברשות הניזק נזק שלם משלמת ואין עדים מעידין מה אכלו מעט או הרבה וטוען בעל השדה כי הרבה אכלו יותר מכדי דמיהן של עזים הללו: יכול לטעון עד כדי דמיהן. של עזים מ"ט מיגו דיכול למימר בעל השדה לקוחין הן בידי דהא תפיס בהו ומהימן כי קאמר נמי כך וכך אכלו מהימן וקיימא לן האי מהימן בשבועה אבל בטפי מכדי דמיהן דליכא מיגו לא מהימן אלא בעדים: והאמר ר"ל כו'. ואמאי יכול לטעון עד כדי דמיהן הא ליכא מיגו דלא מצי למימר לקוחין הן בידי: שאני עיזי. דאע"ג דגודרות ניהו כיון דמסירי לרועה מתוך שמשונות הן יותר מאילים וכבשים ואין אדם יכול להחזיק בהן בדרך לפיכך יש להן חזקה: והאיכא צפרא. שהולכים יחידות מבית הבעלים עד בית הרועה: ופניא. שהרועה מביאן מן השדה עד תוך העיר וכל אחת הולכת מעצמה לבית הבעלים: טייעי. ישמעאלים גנבים: מידא לידא משלמי. מיד הבעלים ליד הרועה שחרית ומיד הרועה ליד הבעלים ערבית ואין הולכות יחידות כלל: ניר. חרישה כדכתיב נירו לכם ניר (הושע י): רבי ישמעאל סבר ניר לא הוי חזקה. אלא גמר פירי הלכך צריך ג' חדשים בראשונה וג' באחרונה דבהכי גדל פרי כל צרכו וי"ב חדשים באמצע דבעינן רצופין: ורבי עקיבא סבר ניר הוי חזקה. הלכך בחדש אחד סגי כדי לעשות ניר: אפי'

מסורת הש"ס

א) לעיל לג: ע"ש, ב) [כתובות פ. ע"ש], ג) [שם], ד) כתובות פד: גיטין כ:, ה) ב"מ קטו., ו) [צ"ל דמסירן, יעב"ץ], ז) [ועי' תוס' מנחות נח: ד"ה ואכלה דאמרי].

הגהות הב"ח

(א) גמ' דאילו אמר עכו"ם לא מהימן: (ב) שם מהימן מ"ט לא חציף: (ג) שם ואמר רב יהודה אכלה ערלה שביעית וכלאים אינה חזקה:

הגהות הגר"א

[א] רשב"ם ד"ה ומשני. אבל יש כו'. ש"ע סי' קנ וב"ה סי' קלה. ורמב"ם וש"ע סי' קלה כתבו עדים לבד (ועמ"ש רבינו שם בס"ק ה):

גליון הש"ס

גמרא עיזי דמסירי לרועה. עיין ב"ק דף עט ע"ב תוס' ד"ה אין:

ליקוטי רש"י

האי מאן דנקיט מגלא ותובליא. כלי גודרי תמרים המגל לגדור ותובליא חבל לעלות לדקל מרוב גובהו וי"מ תובליא סל לקבל פירות. ואמר. כפתו. איזיל איגזרה לדקלא דפלניא. כלומר מלקט הפירות. מהימן. [illegible]

עין משפט נר מצוה

נט א מיי' פי"ד מהל' טוען ונטען הלכה ו סמג עשין צה טוש"ע ח"מ סי' קמט סעיף נח:
ס ב מיי' שם הל' טו סמג עשין צה טוש"ע ח"מ סי' קמט סעיף יג:
סא ג מיי' שם הל' יב ועיין בהשגות ובמ"מ טוש"ע שם סעיף יא:
סב ד ה מיי' שם הל' יא טוש"ע שם סעיף י:
סג ו מיי' שם הל' ט טוש"ע שם סעיף ה:
סד ז מיי' שם הל' ט טוש"ע שם סעיף ו:
סה ח מיי' פי"ג שם הלכה ב סמג שם טור ח"מ סי' קמט:
[illegible]

רבינו גרשום

ומקשי' מי איכא מידי וכו'. אלא אמר רבא אי אמר ההוא ישראל דזבנה מעכו"ם קמי דידי זבנה ההוא עכו"ם מיניה דישראל ולבתר הכי זבנה (מיני') ניהלי מהימן מיגו וכו': האי מאן דאחזיק מגודא דערודי ולבר. כגון שרגילין בני אדם שיש להם שדות סמוך ליער משמרין מקצת משדה סמוך ליער וכונסין בשדה ועושין מחיצה בין השדה ליער בשביל שאם יצאו חיות ערודין מן היער כדי שירעו באותה הרחוקה שיש מן המחיצה ליער ולא יבואו לשבור המחיצה ולאכול התבואה ואם החזיק אדם באותו שיור שהניח בשביל הערודים אפילו לאחר שעמדה ברשותו ג' שנים אין חזקתו חזקה מאי טעם דאמרינן האי דלא מיחה זה בעל הקרקע בתוך ג' שנים דסבר הואיל וכל מאי דזרע האי ערודי אכלי ליה ומשום הכי שתק ולא איבד שדהו בשתיקתו: אכלה ג' שנים ערלה. היכי דמי כגון שהיו בה נטיעות ושנה ראשונה טען פירות מקצתן והיו ערלה ובשנה שניה טענו אחרים ובשלישית אחרים דכולהו הוי ערלה אינה חזקה דהאי דשתיק בעל השדה ולא ערער משום שלא היו ראוין לאכילה: אכלה שחת. ג' שנים שלא המתין עד שתגדל התבואה אלא היה קוצצה כשהיא שחת ומאכילה לבהמות אינה חזקה דשמיט ואכיל הוה ולא אכלה כאכילת בני אדם: אי בצואר מחוזא. כלומר אם אותה קרקע עומדת סמוך למחוזא שעשירים היו זורעין שדותיהן למאכל בהמתן אי לא מיחה הויא חזקה: תפתיחא. זוהי קרקע שפתוחה היא יותר מבית השלחין שפתוחה היא ובקועה ככברה זו שאינה מקבלת מים כך אין ניכרין בה המים ואין יכולין להשקותה ואינה מוציאה פירותיה אם החזיק בה אדם ג' שנים אינה חזקה הואיל שאין בה שום לחלוחית לא חשש למחות: אפיק כורא ועייל כורא. שאין מוציאה כי אם כעין שזורעין בה ולא יותר אינה חזקה דלא חשש למחות הואיל ואין מרווח בה: והני דבי ריש גלותא. אם מחזיקין בקרקעות שלנו ג' שנים אינה חזקה דבשביל כבודן שתקי אינשי: ולא מחזקינן בהו. בשדותם בג' שנים דמשום דעשירים נינהו שתקי אי נמי משום דטרידי בטורח צבור ולא ידעי ולא מחו: והעבדים יש להם חזקה. מי שמחזיק בהם ג' שנים: הגודרות אין להם חזקה. כגון צאן ובהמה שאם החזיק בהן אינה חזקה משום דיש בהם רוח חיים דאיכא למימר מאליהם הלכו אצלו והחזיק בהן גבי עבדים נמי איכא למימר מאליהן הלכו אצלו והחזיק בהן ואמאי יש להן חזקה: אמר רבא אין להם חזקה לאלתר אבל יש להן חזקה לאחר ג' שנים: א) כדקתני בהמה גבי עבדים וגבי גודרות בהמה דקה דאין להם שמירה כל כך אין להם חזקה אבל בהמה גסה דיש להן שמירה יש להם חזקה לאלתר דמצי אמר אתה מכרת לי: קטן עבד יש לו חזקה. משום דליכא למימר איהו אזיל לתמן: ב) אית ליה אימא לא מנשיא ברא ומדאיתא גבי האי ב' ימים או ג' ולא מיחה יש לו חזקה: חושלא. שעורין קלופות: דמסירי לרועה. ויש להן שמירה משום הכי כשהן ברשות של זה יש להן חזקה דליכא למימר דמאחריני נינהו: צפרא ופניא. דאזלי לחודייהו לרועה והדרי לביתייהו בלא שמירה ובדין הוא דלית להו חזקה דאיכא למימר מנפשייהו אזלי התם ואחזיק בהו. ומשני בנהרדעא שאני משום דשכיחי טייעי כלומר גנבים ישמעאלים לא שביק לגודרותיהו למיזל לחודייהו כי אם מידא דבעל הבהמות לידא דרועה ומידא דרועה לידא דבעל הבהמות משום הכי יש להן חזקה: פיס' ר' ישמעאל אומר שדה בית הבעל לא צריך לאחזוקי בה ג' שנים רצופות שלימות כי אם ג' חדשים בסוף שנה ראשונה וג' חדשים בתחלת שנה אחרונה וי"ב חדשים של אמצעית [illegible] לימא ניר איכא בינייהו דר' ישמעאל [illegible]

חשק שלמה על רבינו גרשום א) אולי צ"ל והא דלא קתני [illegible] ב) [illegible] ג) [illegible]

אֵינָהּ חֲזָקָה — IT DOES NOT CONSTITUTE A *CHAZAKAH*.[13]

A third ruling:

אָמַר רַב יוֹסֵף — **Rav Yosef said:** אֲכָלָהּ שַׁחַת — If **[the occupant] used [the land]** by harvesting **unripe grain,**[14] לֹא הָוֵי חֲזָקָה — **it does not constitute a *chazakah*,** for such use does not impel the owner to protest.[15]

Rava qualifies Rav Yosef's ruling:

אָמַר רָבָא — **Rava said:** וְאִי בְּצַוַּאר מְחוֹזָא קַיְימָא — **But if [the land] is situated in the vicinity of Mechuza,**[16] הָוֵי חֲזָקָה — **[such use] constitutes a *chazakah*,** since it is customary for farmers in that area to cut their grain while it is still unripe.[17]

A fourth such ruling:

אָמַר רַב נַחְמָן — **Rav Nachman said:** תַּפְתִּיחָא לֹא הָוֵי חֲזָקָה — Using **broken land**[18] **does not establish a *chazakah*** as the owner is not concerned with whatever meager crop it produces and thus will not protest.

A fifth such ruling:

אַפִּיק כּוֹרָא וְעַיֵּיל כּוֹרָא — If **[the occupant] planted a *kor*** of seed **and harvested** only **a *kor*** of produce,[19] i.e. the crop was so poor that it yielded no more than what he expended as seed, לֹא הָוֵי חֲזָקָה — **it does not establish a *chazakah*.**[20]

A sixth such ruling:

וְהָנֵי דְּבֵי רֵישׁ גָּלוּתָא — **And those** members **of the household of the Reish Galusa**[21] לֹא מַחְזְקֵי בָּן — **cannot establish *chazakah* in our** property,[22] וְלֹא מַחְזְקִינַן בְּהוּ — **nor can we establish a *chazakah* in theirs.**[23]

The Gemara quotes the next section of the Mishnah:

וְהָעֲבָדִים וכו׳ — AND SLAVES ETC.

The Mishnah includes slaves in its list of properties for which a full three-year *chazakah* is required. The Gemara questions this: עֲבָדִים יֵשׁ לָהֶם חֲזָקָה — And do **slaves** indeed **have *chazakah*** as proof of their ownership? וְהָאָמַר רֵישׁ לָקִישׁ — **But did not Reish Lakish say:** הַגּוֹרְדוֹת אֵין לָהֶן חֲזָקָה — **Animals,** which are mobile, **do not have *chazakah*** as proof of their ownership?[24] Since slaves are also mobile, *chazakah* should be ineffective for them as well. — ? —

The Gemara answers:

אָמַר רָבָא — **Rava said:** אֵין לָהֶן חֲזָקָה לְאַלְתַּר — Reish Lakish meant that **they do not have *chazakah* immediately,** i.e. merely possessing them does not prove their ownership, as it does for other movables. אֲבָל יֵשׁ לָהֶן חֲזָקָה לְאַחַר שָׁלֹשׁ שָׁנִים — **But they do have *chazakah* after** possessing them for **three years,** like land.[25] Thus, Reish Lakish's statement does not conflict

NOTES

13. Since one may not derive benefit from *orlah*, the original owner may argue that he did not protest, because he could not have used the produce in any event. Likewise, the occupant's forbidden use of *kilei hakerem* did not elicit his protest. Similarly, he did not protest when the occupant harvested the *shemittah* crops, because they were free for all to take. Hence, consumption of such produce cannot effect *chazakah* (see *Rashbam*).

14. Instead of allowing the grain to ripen [and become fit for human consumption], he cut it while it was still unripe and used it to feed his animals (*Rashbam*).

15. As explained in note 8, an owner is impelled to protest illegal occupation of his field only if the occupant acts in a manner that mimics true ownership. In such a case, the original owner's silence proves that he indeed sold the land. But where the occupant cuts the grain before it reaches its full height, he is not acting as an owner would, because a true owner allows the crop to mature so that he can realize the greatest possible profit. By cutting the grain early, the occupant seems willing to forgo a larger profit in order to avoid being spotted on the field; the sooner he cuts the grain the faster he can leave and the less chance he has of being detected. Thus, the original owner may argue that he saw no need to protest because the occupant's thieving conduct was apparent to all (see *Rashbam*).

16. A town situated on the Tigris.

17. The farmers of Mechuza were wealthy and owned large herds of animals. Thus, they would customarily cut their grain early and use it as animal fodder. [Accordingly, such conduct in this area is normal, and the original owner's failure to protest it is inexcusable. Hence, it establishes a *chazakah*.] (*Rashbam*).

18. I.e. land that is full of cracks and is therefore practically barren (*Rashbam*).

19. Literally: he takes out a *kor* and brings in a *kor*. A *kor* is a volume measure comprising thirty *se'ah*.

20. Since the occupant did not benefit by using the land, he does not give the impression of being its owner. Thus, the true owner did not feel compelled to protest (see note 8).

21. Head of the Exile, or Exilarch. He was the officially recognized leader of the Jewish community in Babylonia.

22. Because people are afraid to speak up against illegal occupation by these politically powerful men. Thus, silence on the part of the original owner does not constitute proof that he sold the land. Therefore, the only way a member of the Reish Galusa's household can prove he bought the land is to produce a deed (*Rashbam*).

23. Because they are purposely silent when someone cultivates their fields illegally, so that they will regain them in their improved state. They feel no need to protest because they rely on their political power to take back their fields whenever they please. Thus, their silence proves nothing, and *chazakah* on their fields is ineffective (*Rashbam*).

24. Literally: those of the pens do not have *chazakah*. [If a challenger can prove that he originally owned these animals,] the man presently in possession of them is not believed to claim that he purchased them, without bringing witnesses. His possession proves nothing, because they may have strayed into his property or he may have seized them while they wandered through the street. By logical extension, this is also true of slaves, since they too are mobile (*Rashbam*). Then how can Reish Lakish state that they do not have *chazakah*, in the face of the Mishnah that states that they do? (*Ritva*).

25. As explained in the General Introduction, the rules of *chazakah* for movables and non-movables differ. For the former, mere possession of them implies ownership, for "what a man holds is presumed to be his." Hence, no minimum amount of time is needed to effect this type of *chazakah*. For the latter (real property), ownership is assumed only after three years of occupancy. Now, animals should fall in the former category. But because they move about, Reish Lakish rules that their ownership — and, by extension, that of slaves — cannot be proven simply because they are in the holder's possession. However, even Reish Lakish agrees that their ownership can be established by the longer, three-year type of *chazakah*. Thus, Reish Lakish is not contradicted by the Mishnah.

A difficulty: Earlier, on 29a, the Gemara stated that *chazakah* is effective after three years for real property because people are wont to lose or discard their deed after this time. Therefore, until three years have elapsed, the court will demand to see the deed. After three years, the occupant's lack of a deed is excusable, and he retains the land merely on the strength of his *chazakah*. Now, this logic can be applied to slaves as well, because it is customary to draw up a deed for them. But it is not customary to draw up a deed when other movables are acquired. How, then, can Rava say that the three-year *chazakah* applies to animals?

Ritva (above, 28a) offers the following answer: Since an animal may have wandered into the holder's property, his possession of the animal does not prove he owns it. However, after a certain amount of time has passed, the original owner should have protested if indeed he did not sell it. Thus, his silence ought to be taken as proof that he sold it. But the amount of time after which an owner would protest varies with the temperament of each particular owner — some tend to protest earlier while others would not speak up until a longer time has passed. The result would be that there would be no fixed amount of time for *chazakah* of animals. Instead, to keep the laws uniform, the Rabbis declared that whenever immediate *chazakah* is not applicable, ownership cannot be proven until three years have passed, just as is the law with land. Consequently, although deeds are not drawn up for animals, their *chazakah* too is effected only after three years (Cf. *Rashba* there and *Rambam Hil. To'ein Ve'Nitan* 10:1 and *Shach, Choshen Mishpat* 135:3).

לדידי אמר לי עכו"ם דמינך זבנה מהימן מי איכא מידי דאילו (א) עכו"ם אמר לא מהימן ואילו אמר ישראל משמיה דעכו"ם מהימן אלא אמר רבא אי אמר ישראל קמי דידי זבנה עכו"ם מינך וזבנה ניהלי מהימן מיגו דאי בעי א"ל אנא זבינתה מינך ואמר רב יהודה האי מאן דנקיט מגלא ותובליא ואמר איזיל איגזרה לדקלא דפלניא דזבנתיה מיניה מהימן (ב) לא חציף איניש למיגזר דקלא דלאו דיליה ואמר רב יהודה האי מאן דאחזיק מגודא דערודי ולבר לא הוי חזקה מ"ט מימר אמר כל דזרע נמי ערודי אכלי ליה ואמר רב יהודה אכלה ערלה (ג) אינה חזקה תניא נמי הכי אכלה ערלה שביעית וכלאים אינה חזקה אמר רב יוסף אכלה שחת לא הוי חזקה אמר רבא ואי בצוער מחוזא קיימא הוי חזקה אמר רב נחמן תפתיחא לא הוי חזקה אפיק כורא ועייל כורא לא הוי חזקה והני דבי ריש גלותא לא מחזקי בן ולא מחזקינן בהו: והעבדים וכו': והאמר ר"ל הגודרות אין להן חזקה אמר רבא אין להן חזקה לאלתר אבל יש להן חזקה לאחר ג' שנים אמר רבא אם היה קטן מוטל בעריסה יש לו חזקה לאלתר פשיטא לא צריכא דאית ליה אימא מהו דתימא ניחוש דלמא אימיה עיילתיה להתם קמ"ל אימא לא מנשיא ברא הנהו עיזי דאכלו חושלא בנהרדעא אתא מרי חושלא תפסינהו והוה קא טעין טובא אמר אבוה דשמואל יכול לטעון עד כדי דמיהן דאי בעי אמר לקוחות הן בידי והאמר ר"ל הגודרות אין להן חזקה שאני עיזי דמסירה לרועה והא איכא צפרא ופניא בנהרדעא טייעי שכיחי ומידא לידא משלמי: ר' ישמעאל אומר שלשה חדשים וכו': לימא ניר איכא בינייהו דרבי ישמעאל סבר ניר לא הוי חזקה ורבי עקיבא סבר ניר הוי חזקה ותסברא לרבי עקיבא מאי איריא חודש אפילו

לדידי אמר לי עכו"ם דמינך זבנה מהימן. דמתפסיק אדעתיה למיטען הכי הא"נ הוה מצי למיטען אנא זבינתה מינך ואכלתי שני חזקה מהמיהן הלכך מה לו לשקר וקושטא קאמר: מי איכא מידי דאילו אמר עכו"ם לא מהימן כו'. השתא נמי חזקה שאין עמה טענה היא דאפי' אם טענתו אמת היא דאמר ליה עכו"ם דמישראל זבנה הלא אין בדבריו של עכו"ם כלום בלא שטר: קמאי דידי. כלומר שאני יודע בבירור היינו חזקה שיש עמה טענה: האי מאן דנקיט כו'. כבר פרישית לה לעיל: האי מאן דאחזיק מגודא דערודי ולבר לא הוי חזקה. חיות השדה שבאות ואוכלות הזרעים שבקצות השדה ויש שעושין קירות וגודרין השדה ומניחין קרקע חוץ לקיר מעט בשדות הסמוכות ליער ומשליכים שם זרע ומה שצומח באות החיות ואוכלות אותו ואין נכנסות בשדה עצמיו ואם בא אדם והחזיק באותו הקרקע חוץ לגדר אינה חזקה דיכול לומר דכיון דכל מה דזרע בההוא קרקע ערודי אכלי ליה לא איכפת ליה למחות דלא אחזיק כמחזיקי איניש לפיכך לא הויא חזקה: אכלה ערלה. אחת מן השלש שנים הויא שנת ערלה אינה חזקה דלא איכפת ליה לבעל השדה בשנת ערלה ולכך לא מיחה וכ"ש אם שלשתן שני ערלה. ערלה וכלאים אכילתן באיסור שביעית הפקר לכל לכך לא מיחה ולא הויא חזקה. ובפירוש ר"ח גרסינן הכי אכלה ערלה ושביעית וכלאים הרי זו חזקה ולא נהירא: אכלה שחת. שלא המתין עד שתגדל התבואה אלא ג' שנים קצרה כשהיא שחת ומאכיל לבהמתו אינה חזקה דשמיט ואכיל ולא היה אוכל כשאר בני אדם ולפיכך לא חשש זה למחות בו שיש רגלים לדבר שירא הוא להחזיק כשאר בני אדם לפי שבגזל ירד בה: ואמר רבא ואי. קאי האי שחת: בצוער מחוזא. בבקעת מחוזא הוי חזקה לפי שעשירים הם ובהמות להם הרבה ודרכם להאכיל השדות לבהמות כשהן שחת: תפתיחא. קרקע פתוחה ומלאה בקעים ואינה מוציאה פירותיה לא הויא חזקה דמפני רעתה לא הקפיד למחות. ורבי' חננאל פירש תפתיחא שדה שלא חרש אותה אלא הוגשמה ונשבה הרוח וזרחה השמש ונתבקעה כגון פתחי חרישה וזרע בה כגון זה אינה חזקה: אפיק כורא. זרע כור: ועייל כורא. וליקט בו כור והכניס לביתו דכיון דליכא הרווחה לא הוי חזקה דלא חשש זה למחות: לא מחזקי בן. אם החזיק אחד מהן בשדותינו אינה חזקה וצריך להזהר בשטרו דמחמת יראתן לא מיחו בהן: ולא מחזקינן בהו. שמתוך שהם עשירים ויש להם בתים ושדות הרבה מניחין בני אדם לדור בבתיהם ושותקים ושמחים כדי להשביח קרקע שלהם וימלאום מתוקנים וגם למחות אין חוששים לפי שבזרוע יטלו את שלהם כל זמן שירצו וי"מ לפי שעסוקין בצרכי צבור אין יודעין מי מחזיק בשלהן ולא נהירא: הגודרות אין להן חזקה. גודרות צאן וכל דבר המהלך בדרכים ובשווקים שיכול לומר מעצמו נכנס או אתה הכנסתו לביתך והחזקת בו אינה חזקה ואין יכול לומר לקוח הוא בידי והעבדים מהלכים הם בכל מקום ותנן דיש להם חזקה: ומשני הא דאמר ר"ל אין להן חזקה ה"מ לאלתר. שהמחזיק בהן בביתו אין יכול לטעון לקוח הוא בידי בלא עדים ובלא ראיה כשאר מטלטלין שאין יכולין להלך ואין עשוין להשאיל ולהשכיר דנאמן בהן לומר לקוח הוא [בידי] הואיל וישנו בביתו דבשאר מטלטלין הוי חזקה לאלתר דהמוחזק בהן יכול לטעון שלי הוא שלקחתיו אבל יש [א] להן לעבדים ולגודרות חזקה לאחר ג' שנים שהיה לו לזה המערער למחות ולא מיחה: אמר רבא. עבד כנעני קטן המוטל בעריסה: יש לו חזקה לאלתר. אם החזיק בו אחד ואמר לקוח הוא בידי נאמן הואיל ואין יכול להלך ולא דמי לגודרות וגם אין עשוי להשאיל ולהשכיר: פשיטא. דודאי מעצמו לא הלך: דעיילא אימיה. דעבד בבית אותו המחזיק תדיר: אימיה עיילתיה. ושכחתיה שם דהשתא היינו גודרות: הני עיזי דאכלו חושלא. שעורים קלופים שנכנסו בשדה [ורואו] אותה תבואה השטוחה שם לשמש וקיימא לן שן מועדת היא לעולם וכי הויא ברשות הניזק נזק שלם משלמת ואין עדים מעידין מה אכלו מעט או הרבה וטוען בעל השדה כי הרבה אכלו יותר מכדי דמיהן של עזים הללו: יכול לטעון עד כדי דמיהן. של עזים מ"ט מיגו דיכול למימר בעל השדה לקוחין הן בידי דהא תפיס בהו ומהימן כי קאמר נמי כך וכך אכלו מהימן וקיימא לן האי מהימן בשבועה אבל בטפי מכדי דמיהן דליכא מיגו לא מהימן אלא בעדים: והאמר ר"ל כו'. ואמאי יכול לטעון עד כדי דמיהן הא ליכא מיגו דלא מצי למימר לקוחין הן בידי: שאני עיזי. דאע"ג דגודרות נינהו כיון דמסירי לרועה מתוך שמשוות הן יותר מאילים וכבשים ואין אדם יכול להחזיק בהן בדרך לפיכך יש להן חזקה: והאיכא צפרא. שהולכים יחידות מבית הבעלים עד בית הרועה: ופניא. שהרועה מביאן מן השדה עד תוך העיר וכל אחת הולכת מעצמה לבית הבעלים: טייעי. ישמעאלים גנבים: מידא לידא משלמי. מיד הבעלים ליד הרועה שחרית ומיד הרועה ליד הבעלים ערבית ואין הולכות יחידות כלל: ניר. חרישה כדכתיב נירו לכם ניר (הושע י): רבי ישמעאל סבר ניר לא הוי חזקה. אלא גמר פירי הלכך צריך ג' חדשים בראשונה וג' באחרונה דבהכי גדל פרי כל צרכו וי"ב חדשים באמצע דבעינן רצופין: ורבי עקיבא סבר ניר הוי חזקה. הלכך בחדש אחד סגי כדי לעשות ניר: אפי'

הכי גרים ר"ח אכלה ערלה שביעית וכלאים הויא חזקה. וכן נראה לר"י עיקר ואיירי כשאכלה זמורות וכן מוכח בהאשה שנפלו (כתובות דף עט.) דתנן המוציא הוצאות על נכסי אשתו הוציא הרבה ואכל קימעא קימעא ואכל הרבה מה שהוציא הוציא ומה שאכל אכל ואמר בגמרא עבד רב יהודה עובדא בתבילי זמורות ורב יהודה לטעמיה דאמר רב יהודה אכלה ערלה שביעית וכלאים הויא חזקה ואין לומר דלעולם גרס הכא אינה חזקה והתם כשאכלה זמורות והכא כשאכלה פירות שהן אסורים ולכך לא הויא חזקה שלא אכל כדרך האוכלים דאם כן הוה ליה לאיתויי הסיא דהתם הכא נמי הכא דאיירי בדיני חזקה וה"ה דהכא משמע דבזמורות איירי ועוד כלאים שרו ומ"ש מהא דאמרינן בפרק כל שעה (פסחים דף כו:) תנור שהסיקוהו בקליפי ערלה או בקשין של כלאי הכרם חדש יותץ מכלל דאסירי ואמרינן נמי התם (דף כה.) כלאי הכרם עיקרן נאסר ומיהו הא לא קשה דאיכא למימר דעיקרן נאסר משום דכתיב (דברים כב) הזרע וי"ל דהתם איירי בזרוע מעיקרן שמרעו הזרעים עם נטיעות הכרם שגדלו הזמורות באיסור אבל הכא איירי בזמורות שהיו כבר גדולים קודם שנזרעו כלאים שאותן אין נאסרים אלא כשהוסיפו מאתים כדאמר בפרק כל שעה (שם דף כו.) ובפרק כל הבשר (חולין דף קטז.) זרוע ובא והוסיף מאתים אין לא הוסיף מאתים לא ומיירי הכא שזמורות לא הוסיפו מאתים והפירות הוסיפו ולכך לא הויא חזקה אלא בזמורות ואין זה דוחק דהכי הוי אורחא דמילתא שקודם שמוסיפין הפירות מאתים מן הזמורות לפי שהזמורות כבר היו גדולות קודם זריעת כלאים: נראה

מסורת הש"ס

א) לעיל לג: ע"ש, ב) [כתובות פ. ע"ש], ג) [שם], ד) כתובות פד: גיטין כ: ה) ב"מ קטז. ו) [נ"ל דמסירי, יעב"ץ], ז) [ועי' תוס' מנחות נח: ד"ה ואיבא דאמרי]

הגהות הב"ח

(א) גמ' דאילו אמר עכו"ם לא מהימן: (ב) שם מהימן מ"ט לא חציף: (ג) שם ואמר רב יהודה אכלה ערלה שביעית וכלאים אינה חזקה:

הגהות הגר"א

[א] רשב"ם ד"ה ומשני. אבל יש כו'. ש"ע סי' קלה וב"י שם. ורמב"ם וש"ע סי' קלה כתבו עבדים לבד (ועמ"ש רבינו שם בס"ק ה):

גליון הש"ס

גמרא עיזי דמסירי לרועה. עיין ב"ק דף קט ע"ב תוס' ד"ה אין:

ליקוטי רש"י

האי מאן דנקיט מגלא ותובליא. כלי גודרי תמרים להעלות לגדור ותובלא חבל לעלות לדקל מרוב גובהו וי"מ תובלא סל לקבל פירות. ואמר. כפניו. איזיל איגזרה לדקלא דפלניא. כלומר אלקוט הפירות. מהימן. כ"ד ללקט הפירות בלא עדים ושטר ואמרי שאין יודע שהבעלים מוחין בדבר קודם לקיטה ואם אתא מערער וטוען להד"מ אחר שליקט האלין לית עליה אלא שבועת היסת אבל מקמי דליגזריה אתא מריה דדקלא ואמר להד"מ מלקט עד דמייתי ראיה [רשב"ם לג:]. אמר רב יהודה אכלה ערלה [שביעית וכלאים] וכו'. הרי זו חזקה גרסינן הכא ובבבא בתרא. אכלה ערלה. לוקח שני ערלה שאין הנאתן אסור שהפירות שפירי אסור בהנאה או שביעית שהוא הפקר או שזורעה כלאים והזמורות לא נאסרו. [הרי זו חזקה]. עולין לו משלש שנים שלא אחת מאלו [כתובות פ.]. הגודרות. בהמות דקה על שם גדרות צאן (במדבר לב) [שם פד:]. בהמות על שם גדרות צאן [גיטין כ:]. אין להן חזקה. אין המחזיק בהם יכול לומר לקוחין הן בידי שאנו אומרים מעצמן באו לכך לגדור [כתובות שם]. אדם שתפסן אינו יכול לטעון לבעליהם מכרתם לי דלכך הלכו אלו [גיטין שם]. ניר לא הוי חזקה. לפי שכלל תלוי הפירות שאם יחרוש ולא יאכל אין בעל הקרקע מפסיד שהרי יזרע ולא יאכל [רשב"ם לקמן נז.].

עין משפט נר מצוה

נט א מיי' פי"ד מהל' טוען הלכה ו סמג עשין צה טוש"ע ח"מ סי' קמט סעיף טז:

ס ב מיי' שם פי"ב הל' טו סמג עשין צה טוש"ע ח"מ סי' קמא סעיף יג:

סא ג מיי' שם הל' יב ועיין בהשגות ובמ"מ טוש"ע שם סעיף יא:

סב ד ה מיי' שם הל' יא טוש"ע שם סעיף י:

סג ו מיי' שם הל' ט טוש"ע שם סעי' ה:

סד ז מיי' שם הל' י טוש"ע שם סעי' ו:

סה ח מיי' פי"ג שם הלכה ב סמג שם טוש"ע ח"מ סי' קמט:

סו ט מיי' שם טוש"ע ח"מ סי' קלה סעיף א:

סז י כ מיי' שם הלכה ד סמג שם טוש"ע ח"מ סי' קנה סעי' כ:

סח ל מיי' שם הל' ג סמג שם טוש"ע ח"מ סי' ע סעי' יז יח כא:

סט מ מיי' שם פ"ו הל' ג סמג שם טוש"ע ח"מ סי' קמט סעיף כט וסי' קלה סעיף ל [וברב אלפס עוד בכתובות פרק ט דף קח. ובשבועות פ"ז דף שיד:]:

רבינו גרשום

ומקשי' מי איכא מידי וכו'. אלא אמר רבא אי אמר ההוא ישראל דזבנה מעכו"ם קמי דידי זבנה ההוא עכו"ם מיניה דישראל ולבתר הכי זבנה [מיני] ניהלי מהימן מיגו וכו': האי מאן דאחזיק מגודא דערודי ולבר. כגון שרגילין בני אדם שיש להם שדות סמוך ליער משמרין מקצת משדה סמוך ליער וכונסין בשדה ועושין מחיצה בין השדה ליער בשביל שאם יצאו חיות ערודין מן היער כדי שירעו באותה הרחקה שיש מן המחיצה ליער ולא יבואו לשבור המחיצה ולאכול התבואה ואם החזיק אדם באותו שיור שהניח בשביל הערודים אפילו לאחר שעמדה ברשותו ג' שנים אין חזקתו חזקה מאי טעם דאמרינן האי דלא מיחה זה בעל הקרקע בתוך ג' שנים דקסבר הואיל וכל מאי דזרע האי ערודי אכלי ליה ומשום הכי שתק ולא איבד שדהו בשתיקתו: אכלה ג' שנים ערלה. היכי דמי כגון שהיו בה נטיעות ושנה ראשונה טען פירות מקצתן והוו ערלה ובשנה שניה טענו אחרים ובשלישית אחרים דכולהו הוו ערלה אינה חזקה דהאי דשתיק בעל השדה ולא ערער משום שלא היו ראוין לאכילה: אכלה שחת. ג' שנים שלא המתין עד שתגדל התבואה אלא היה קוצרה כשהיא שחת ומאכילה לבהמות אינה חזקה דשמיט ואכל הוה ולא אכלה כאכילת בני אדם: אי בצוער מחוזא. כלומר אם אותה קרקע עומדת סמוך למחוזא שעשירים היו וזורעין שדותיהן למאכל בהמתן אי לא מיחה בה הויא חזקה: תפתיחא. זוהי קרקע שפתוחה היא יותר מבית השלחין שנפתחה היא ובקועה ככברה זו שאינה מקבלת מים ואין ניכרין בה המים ואין יכולין להשקותה ואינה מוציאה פירותיה אם החזיק בה אדם ג' שנים אינה חזקה הואיל שאין

בה שום לחלוחית לא חשש למחות: אפיק כורא ועייל כורא. שאין מוציאה כי אם כעין שזורעין בה ולא יותר אינה חזקה דלא חשש למחות הואיל ואין מרויח בה: והני דבי ריש גלותא. שלנו ג' שנים אינה חזקה דבשביל כבודן שתקי אנשי: ולא מחזקינן בהו. בשדותם בג' שנים דמשום דעשירים נינהו שתקי אי נמי משום דטרידי בטורח צבור ולא ידעי ולא מחי: והעבדים יש להם חזקה. [illegible]

[illegible]

חשק שלמה על רבינו גרשום [illegible]

with the Mishnah.

Rava qualifies the Mishnah's ruling that slaves require three years for their *chazakah*:

אָמַר רָבָא – **Rava said:** אִם הָיָה קָטָן מוּטָל בַּעֲרִיסָה – **If [the slave] was an infant resting in a cradle,** יֵשׁ לוֹ חֲזָקָה לְאַלְתַּר – **he has *chazakah* immediately,** i.e. merely possessing him proves his ownership, just as it does for other non-mobile items.[26]

The Gemara asks:

פְּשִׁיטָא – But this is **self-evident!** Since a baby cannot move freely about, then clearly one who possesses him should be assumed to be his owner. – ? –

The Gemara answers:

לֹא צְרִיכָא דְּאִית לֵיהּ אִימָּא – **It was not necessary** to teach this ruling **except** for an instance **where [the infant] has a mother** who works in the house of the litigant currently holding the child. מַהוּ דְּתֵימָא נֵיחוּשׁ דִּלְמָא אִימֵּיהּ עַיְּילַתֵּיהּ לְהָתָם – For **you might argue** that **we should consider** that perhaps **his mother brought him there** and forgot him, which would invalidate the litigant's claim of *chazakah*.[27] קָא מַשְׁמַע לָן – **[Rava] therefore informs us** that this possibility is discounted, for אִימָּא לָא מַנְשְׁיָא בְּרָא – **a mother does not forget her son.**[28] Thus, the infant's presence in the litigant's house constitutes a valid *chazakah*.

The Gemara cites an incident in which an Amora ruled in a way that seemingly contradicts Reish Lakish's ruling:

הָנְהוּ עִיזֵּי דְּאָכְלוּ חוּשְׁלָא בִּנְהַרְדְּעָא – There were **these goats who ate** some **husked barley in** a field in **Nehardea.**[29] אֲתָא מָרֵי חוּשְׁלָא תְּפָסִינְהוּ – **The owner of the barley came and seized [the goats],** וַהֲוָה קָא טָעִין טוּבָא – **and claimed** that they had eaten **a great deal** of barley.[30] אֲמַר אֲבוּהּ דִּשְׁמוּאֵל – The case came before **the father of Shmuel** who **ruled:** יָכוֹל לִטְעוֹן עַד כְּדֵי דְמֵיהֶן – **[The barley's owner] is able** (i.e. believed) **to claim** damages **up to the value of [the goats],** דְּאִי בָּעֵי – **for if he had wished** to lie, אָמַר לְקוּחוֹת הֵן בְּיָדִי – **he** could have **said, "I purchased the goats,"** and he would have been believed. Therefore, he is likewise believed to claim damages up to their value.[31]

The Gemara asks:

וְהָאָמַר רֵישׁ לָקִישׁ – **But did Reish Lakish not say:** הַגּוֹדְרוֹת אֵין לָהֶן חֲזָקָה – **Animals do not have *chazakah*** as proof of their ownership? How, then, can Shmuel's father say that he would have been believed to claim the goats as his?

The Gemara answers:

שָׁאנֵי עִיזֵּי – **Goats are different** than other animals, דִּמְסִירָה לְרוֹעֶה – **for they are** customarily **entrusted to** the care of **a shepherd** and therefore do not roam about freely.[32]

The Gemara asks:

וְהָא אִיכָּא צַפְרָא וּפַנְיָא – **But there are** periods in the **morning and evening** when the goats are *not* supervised.[33] Thus, they should be governed by the same law that applies to other animals – ? –

The Gemara answers:

בִּנְהַרְדְּעָא טַיְיעֵי שְׁכִיחֵי – **In Nehardea Arab thieves abound** וּמִיָּדָא לְיָדָא מְשַׁלְמֵי – **and [the goats] are** therefore **delivered from hand to hand.**[34] Therefore, since they are always supervised, their possession proves their ownership.

The Gemara cites a section of the Mishnah:

רַבִּי יִשְׁמָעֵאל אוֹמֵר שְׁלֹשָׁה חֳדָשִׁים וכו' – **R' YISHMAEL SAYS: THREE MONTHS ETC.**

The Mishnah states that R' Yishmael requires the occupant to use a rain-watered field for three months in each of the first and third years in order to establish a *chazakah*, while R' Akiva requires only one month.[35] The Gemara now investigates the point on which this dispute hinges:

לֵימָא נִיר אִיכָּא בֵּינַיְיהוּ – **Shall we say that** the issue of whether **plowing** may be used as a part of the *chazakah* **is** the point **that divides them?**[36] How so? דְּרַבִּי יִשְׁמָעֵאל סָבַר נִיר לֹא הָוֵי חֲזָקָה – **R' Yishmael holds that plowing does not establish a**

NOTES

26. If someone is in possession of a slave infant and claims that he bought him from the original owner, he is believed. Since the infant cannot walk, he is in the same category as other non-movables for which possession is immediately taken as proof of ownership (*Rashbam*).

27. [Although he could not have come in on his own, his mother could have brought him there. The fact that the litigant is not also in possession of the mother can be explained by saying that she left the house and forgot him there.] Thus, the infant should be in the same category as animals and adult slaves whose possession is not taken as proof of ownership until three years have passed (*Rashbam*).

28. Therefore, since the mother is not also in the litigant's possession, we must assume that the original owner sold the infant to the man who presently holds him.

29. They entered a field and ate barley that had been left out in the sun to dry. The goat's owner was responsible to pay for the damage, but there were no witnesses as to how much barley the goats had eaten (*Rashbam*).

30. He claimed they had eaten an amount in excess of the goats' own value [and he seized the goats as security until their owner compensated him] (*Rashbam*).

31. [Since there were no witnesses who saw him seize the goats] he could have claimed that he bought them and he would have been believed, because, where movables are concerned, possession is taken as proof of ownership. Thus, his claim is bolstered by a *migo*. However, the *migo* is effective only for that portion of the claim that does not exceed the value of the goats. For the excess portion, though, there is no *migo*, because the plaintiff had no other claim available to him that would have allowed him to win the case. Thus, unless he produces witnesses, he is not believed regarding the excess amount (*Rashbam*).

32. Therefore, unlike other animals, it is unlikely that they [strayed into the holder's property or] were seized by him as they walked in the street. Therefore, they are like non-mobile objects and possession of them proves their ownership (*Rashbam*).

33. [In Talmudic times, it was common practice for a number of individual cattlemen to collectively hire one shepherd to graze their animals.] Each morning, the animals would, on their own, go from their owners' houses to the house of the shepherd, who would lead them out to pasture. In the evening, he would lead them back to town, and each would proceed, unaccompanied, to its owner's house (*Rashbam*). Thus, although goats are entrusted to a shepherd, there are still periods when they are left to themselves. If so, the holder could have seized them during those times, and possessing them should not be taken as proof of ownership.

34. They are delivered directly from owner to shepherd and from shepherd to owner and are never left unattended (*Rashbam*). Thus, in Nehardea, the fact that they are in the holder's possession proves they are his, for there was no time during which they could have strayed into his property or that he could have seized them illegally.

35. Since a rain-watered field does not produce crops on a constant basis, a farmer does not work it all twelve months of the year. To establish *chazakah,* therefore, it is sufficient to condense the year's work into a shorter period of time. Accordingly, one may work the field for a short period at the end of the first year and a short period at the beginning of the last year. These two abbreviated years, together with using the field for a full year in between (so that the use is consecutive), constitute a *chazakah* for a rain-watered field. Both R' Yishmael and R' Akiva agree to this. The question, though, is exactly how long a time the field must be used in the first and third years for the *chazakah* to be effective.

36. I.e. whether plowing the field without planting it is a sufficient show of ownership to effect a *chazakah*.

לדידי אמר לי עכו"ם דמינך זבנה מהימן מי איכא מידי דאילו (א) עכו"ם אמר לא מהימן ואילו אמר ישראל משמיה דעכו"ם מהימן אלא אמר רבא אי אמר ישראל קמי דידי זבנה עכו"ם מינך וזבנה ניהלי מהימן מיגו דאי בעי א"ל אנא זבינתה מינך ואמר רב יהודה האי מאן דנקיט מגלא ותובליא ואמר איזיל איגזרה לדקלא דפלניא דזבנתיה מיניה מהימן (ב) לא חציף איניש למיגזר דקלא דלאו דיליה ואמר רב יהודה האי מאן דאחזיק מגודא דערודי ולבר לא הוי חזקה מ"ט מימר אמר כל דזרע נמי ערודי אכלי ליה ואמר רב יהודה אכלה ערלה (ג) אינה חזקה תניא נמי הכי אכלה ערלה שביעית וכלאים אינה חזקה אמר רב יוסף אכלה שחת לא הוי חזקה אמר רבא ואי בצואר מחוזא קיימא הוי חזקה אמר רב נחמן תפתיחא לא הוי חזקה אפיק כורא ועייל כורא הוי חזקה והני דבי ריש גלותא לא מחזקי בן ולא מחזקינן בהו: והעבדים וכו': והאמר ר"ל הגודרות אין להן חזקה אמר רבא אין להן חזקה לאלתר אבל יש להן חזקה לאחר ג' שנים אמר רבא אם היה קטן מוטל בעריסה יש לו חזקה לאלתר פשיטא לא צריכא דאית ליה אימא מהו דתימא ניחוש דלמא אימיה עיילתיה להתם קמ"ל אימא לא מנשיא ברא הנהו עיזי דאכלו חושלא בנהרדעא אתא מרי חושלא תפסינהו והוה קא טעין טובא אמר אבוה דשמואל יכול לטעון עד כדי דמיהן דאי בעי אמר לקוחות הן בידי והאמר ר"ל הגודרות אין להן חזקה שאני עיזי דמסירי לרועה והא איכא צפרא ופניא בנהרדעא טייעי שכיחי ומידא לידא משלמי: ר' ישמעאל אומר שלשה חדשים וכו': לימא ניר איכא בינייהו דרבי ישמעאל סבר ניר לא הוי חזקה ורבי עקיבא סבר ניר הוי חזקה ותסברא לרבי עקיבא מאי איריא חודש אפילו

רשב"ם

לדידי אמר לי עכו"ם דמינך זבנה מהימן. דמדאפיק לדעמיה למיטען הכי ה"נ הוה מצי למיטען אנא זבינתה מינך ואכלתי שני חזקה דמהימן הלכך מה לו לשקר וקושטא קאמר: מי איכא מידי דאילו אמר עכו"ם לא מהימן כו'. השתא נמי חזקה שאין עמה טענה היא דאפי' אם טענתו אמת היא דאמר ליה עכו"ם דמישראל זבנה הלא אין בדבריו של עכו"ם כלום בלא שטר: קמאי דידי. כלומר שאני יודע בבירור היינו חזקה שיש עמה טענה: האי מאן דנקיט כו'. כבר פרישית לה לעיל: האי מאן דאחזיק מגודא דערודי ולבר לא הוי חזקה. חיות השדה שבאות ואוכלות הזרעים שבקצות השדה ויש שעושין קירות וגודרין השדה ומניחין קרקע חוץ לקיר מעט בשדות הסמוכות ליער ומשליכים שם זרע ומה שצומח באות החיות ואוכלות אותו ואינן נכנסות בשדה עכשיו ואם בא אדם והחזיק באותו הקרקע חוץ לגדר אינה חזקה דיכול לומר דכיון דכל מה דזרע בההוא קרקע ערודי אכלי ליה לא איכפת ליה למחות דלא אחזיק כדמחזקי אינשי לפיכך לא הויא חזקה: אכלה ערלה. אחת מן השלש שנים הויא שנת ערלה אינה חזקה דלא איכפת ליה לבעל השדה בשנת ערלה ולכך לא מיחה וכ"ש אם שלשתן שני ערלה. ערלה וכלאים אכילתן באיסור שביעית הפקר לכל לכך לא מיחה ולא הויא חזקה. ובפירוש ר"ח גרסינן הכי אכלה ערלה ושביעית וכלאים הרי זו חזקה ולא נהירא: אכלה שחת. שלא המתין עד שתגדל התבואה אלא ג' שנים קצרה כשהיא שחת ומאכיל לבהמתו אינה חזקה דשמיט ואכיל ולא היה אוכל כשאר בני אדם ולפיכך לא חשש זה למחות בו שיש רגלים לדבר שירא הוא להחזיק כשאר בני אדם לפי שבגזל ירד בה: ואמר רבא ואי. קאי האי שחת: בצואר מחוזא. בבקעת מחוזא הוי חזקה לפי שעשירים הם ובהמות להם הרבה ודרכם להאכיל השדות לבהמות כשהן שחת: תפתיחא. קרקע פתוחה ומלאה בקעים ואינה מוציאה פירותיה לא הויא חזקה דמפני רעתה לא הקפיד למחות. ורבי' חננאל פירש תפתיחא שדה שלא חרש אותה אלא הוגשמה ונשבה הרוח וזרחה השמש ונתבקעה כגון פתחי חרישה וזרע בה כגון זה אינה חזקה: אפיק כורא. זרע כור: ועייל כורא. וליקט בו כור והכניס לביתו דכיון דליכא הרווחה לא הוי חזקה דלא חשש זה למחות: לא מחזקי בן. אם החזיק אחד מהן בשדותינו אינה חזקה וצריך להזהר בשטרו דמחמת יראתן לא מיחו בהן: ולא מחזקינן בהו. שמתוך שהם עשירים ויש להם בתים ושדות הרבה מניחין בני אדם לדור בבתיהם ושותקים ושמחים כדי להשביח קרקע שלהם וימלאום מתוקנים וגם למחות אינן חוששים לפי שבזרוע יטלו את שלהם כל זמן שירצו וי"מ לפי שעסוקין בצרכי צבור אין יודעין מי מחזיק בשלהן ולא נהירא: הגודרות אין להן חזקה. גודרות לאן וכל דבר המהלך בדרכים ובשווקים שיכול לומר מעצמו נכנס או אתה הכנסתו לביתך והחזקת בו אינה חזקה ואין יכול לומר לקוח הוא בידי והעבדים מהלכים הם בכל מקום ותנן דיש להם חזקה: ומשני הא דאמר ר"ל אין להן חזקה ה"מ לאלתר. שהמחזיק בהן בביתו אין יכול לטעון לקוח הוא בידי בלא עדים ובלא ראיה כשאר מטלטלין שאין יכולין להלך ואין עשוין להשאיל ולהשכיר דנאמן בהן לומר לקוח הוא [בידי] הואיל וישנו בביתו דבשאר מטלטלין הוי חזקה לאלתר דהמוחזק בהן יכול לטעון שלי הוא שלקחתיו אבל יש [א] להן לעבדים ולגודרות חזקה לאחר ג' שנים שהיה לו לזה המערער למחות ולא מיחה: אמר רבא. עבד כנעני קטן המוטל בעריסה: יש לו חזקה לאלתר. אם החזיק בו אחד ואמר לקוח הוא בידי נאמן הואיל ואין יכול להלך ולא דמי לגודרות וגם אין עשוי להשאיל ולהשכיר: פשיטא. דודאי מעצמו לא הלך: דעיילא אימיה. דעבד בבית אותו המחזיק תדיר: אימיה עיילתיה. ושכחתיה שם דהשתא היינו גודרות: הני עיזי דאכלו חושלא. שעורים קלופים שנכנסו בשדה [ורצו] אותה תבואה השטוחה שם לשמש וקיימא לן שן מועדת היא לעולם וכי הויא ברשות הניזק נזק שלם משלמת ואין עדים מעידין מה אכלו מעט או הרבה וטוען בעל השדה כי הרבה אכלו יותר מכדי דמיהן של עזים הללו: יכול לטעון עד כדי דמיהן. של עזים מ"ט מיגו דיכול למימר בעל השדה לקוחין הן בידי דהא תפיס בהו ומהימן כי קאמר נמי כך וכך אכלו מהימן וקיימא לן האי מהימן בשבועה אבל בטפי מכדי דמיהן דליכא מיגו לא מהימן אלא בעדים: והאמר ר"ל כו'. ואמאי יכול לטעון עד כדי דמיהן הא ליכא מיגו דלא מצי למימר לקוחין הן בידי: שאני עיזי. דלא"ג דגודרות נינהו כיון דמסירי לרועה מתוך שמשומות הן יותר מאילים וכבשים ואין אדם יכול להחזיק בהן בדרך לפיכך יש להן חזקה: והאיכא צפרא. שהולכים יחידות מבית הבעלים עד בית הרועה: ופניא. שהרועה מביאן מן השדה עד תוך העיר וכל אחת הולכת מעצמה לבית הבעלים: טייעי. ישמעאלים גנבים: מידא לידא משלמי. מיד הבעלים ליד הרועה שחרית ומיד הרועה ליד הבעלים ערבית ואין הולכות יחידות כלל: ניר. חרישה כדכתיב נירו לכם ניר (הושע י): רבי ישמעאל סבר ניר לא הוי חזקה. אלא גמר פירי הלכך צריך ג' חדשים בראשונה וג' באחרונה דבהכי גדל פרי כל צרכו וי"ב חדשים באמצע דבעינן רצופין: ורבי עקיבא סבר ניר הוי חזקה. הלכך בחדש אחד סגי כדי לעשות ניר:

אפי'

תוספות

הכי גרים ר"ח אכלה ערלה שביעית וכלאים הויא חזקה. וכן נראה לר"י עיקר ואיירי כשאכלה זמורות וכן מוכח בהאשה שנפלו (כתובות דף עט:) דתנן המוציא הוצאות על נכסי אשתו הוציא הרבה ואכל קימעא קימעא ואכל הרבה מה שהוציא הוציא ומה שאכל אכל ואמר בגמרא עבד רב יהודה עובדא בחבילי זמורות ורב יהודה לטעמיה דאמר רב יהודה אכלה ערלה שביעית וכלאים הויא חזקה ואין לומר דלעולם גרס הכא אינה חזקה והתם כשאכלה זמורות והכא כשאכלה פירות שהן אסורים ולכך לא הויא חזקה שלא אכל כדרך האוכלים דאם כן הוה ליה לאיתויי ההיא דהתם נמי הכא דאיירי בדיני חזקה ואי"ת דהכא משמע דזמורות ועלי כלאים שרו ומ"ש מהא דאמרינן בפרק כל שעה (פסחים דף כו:) תנור שהסיקוהו בקליפי ערלה או בקשין של כלאי הכרם חדש יותץ מכלל דאסירי ואמרינן נמי התם (דף כה.) כלאי הכרם עיקרן נאסר ומיהו הא לא קשה דאיכא למימר דעיקרן נאסר משום דכתיב (דברים כב) הזרע וי"ל דהתם איירי בזרוע מעיקרן שנזרעו הזרעים עם נטיעות הכרם שגדלו הזמורות באיסור אבל הכא איירי בזמורות שהיו כבר גדולים קודם שנזרעו כלאים שאותן אינן נאסרים אלא כשהוסיפו מאתים כדאמר בפרק כל שעה (שם דף כה.) ובפרק כל הבשר (חולין דף קטז.) זרוע ובא הוסיף מאתים אין לא הוסיף מאתים לא ומיירי הכא שזמורות לא הוסיפו מאתים והפירות הוסיפו ולכך לא הויא חזקה אלא בזמורות ואין זה דוחק דהכי הוי אורחא דמילתא שקודם מוסיפין הפירות מאתים מן הזמורות לפי שהזמורות כבר היו גדולות קודם זריעת כלאים:

נרה

מסורת הש"ס

א) לעיל לג: ע"ש, ב) [כתובות פ. ע"ש], ג) [שם], ד) כתובות פד: גיטין כב. ה) ב"מ קטו, ו) [נ"ל דמסירין. יעב"ץ], ז) [ועי' תוס' מנחות נח: ד"ה ואכלה דאמרינן]:

הגהות הב"ח

(א) גמ' דאילו אמר עכו"ם לא מהימן: (ב) שם מהימן מ"ט לא חציף: (ג) שם ואמר רב יהודה אכלה ערלה שביעית וכלאים אינה חזקה:

הגהות הגר"א

[א] רשב"ם ד"ה ומשני. אבל יש כו'. ש"ע סי' עב ובס"ע סי' קלה, ורמב"ם ושו"ע סי' קלה כתבו עבדים לבד (ועמ"ש רבינו שם בס"ק ה):

גליון הש"ס

גמרא עיזי דמסירי לרועה. עיין ב"ק דף עט ע"ב תוס' ד"ה אין:

ליקוטי רש"י

האי מאן דנקיט מגלא ותובליא. כלי גודרי תמרים ומגל לגדור ותובליא חבל לעלות לדקל מרוב גובהו וי"מ תובליא סל לקבל פירות. ואמר. בפניו. איזיל איגזרה לדקלא דפלניא. כלומר ללקוט הפירות. מהימן. ובשקין ליה ב"ד ללקט הפירות בלא עדים ושטר דאמרי שאין יודע שזבנתה ממנו כדבר קודם לקיטה ואם אתא מכריה וטען להד"ם אחר שליקט האילן לית עליה אלא שבועת היסת [...] מקמי דליגזריה אתא מריה דדיקלא ואמר להד"ם לא מהימן מלקט עד דמייתי ראיה [רשב"ם לעיל לג:]. אמר רב יהודה אכלה ערלה [שביעית וכלאים] וכו'. הרי זו חזקה גרסינן הכא ובבבא בתרא. אכלה ערלה. לוקח שני ערלה שאין הנאתן אלא בזמורות שהפרי אסור או שביעית או הפקר או זמורות כלאים והזמורות לא נאסרו. [הרי זו] חזקה. שלש שנים לאו אחת מהשלש שנים אחת מאלו [כתובות פ.]. הגודרות. בהמות דקה על שם גדרות צאן (במדבר לב) [שם פד:]. בהמות על שם גדרות צאן [גיטין כב.]. אין להן חזקה. אין המחזיק בהם יכול לומר לקוחין הן בידי שמא מאליהן והכניסן בביתו לפי שדרכן להלך בשדות [כתובות שם]. אדם שתפסן אינו יכול לטעון לבעליהם מכרתם לי דליכא למימר מעצמן הלכו אצלו [גיטין שם]. ניר לא הוי חזקה. לפי שהכל תלוי באכילת הפירות שאם יחרוש ולא יאכל אין בעל הקרקע מפסיד שהרי יזרע ואחר יאכל [רשב"ם לקמן נז.].

עין משפט נר מצוה

נט א מיי' פי"ד מהל' טוען ונטען הלכה ו סמג עשין לה טוש"ע ח"מ סי' קמט סעיף טז:
ס ב מיי' שם פי"ב הל' טו סמג עשין לה טוש"ע ח"מ סי' קמא סעי' יג:
סא ג מיי' שם הל' יב ועיין בהשגות ובמ"מ טוש"ע שם סעיף יח:
סב ד ה מיי' שם הל' א טוש"ע שם סעיף י:
סג ו מיי' שם הל' ט טוש"ע שם סעי' ה:
סד ז מיי' שם הל' י טוש"ע שם סעי' ו:
סה ח מיי' פי"ג שם הלכה ב סמג שם טור ח"מ סי' קמט:
סו ט מיי' שם פ"ב הל' א סמג שם טוש"ע ח"מ סי' קלה ס"א וסי' עב סעי' כא:
סז י כ מיי' שם הלכה ד וסמג שם טוש"ע ח"מ סי' קנה סעי' ג:
סח ל מיי' שם הל' ג סמג שם טוש"ע ח"מ סי' עב סעי' ז יח כא:
סט מ מיי' שם פ"ו הל' ב סמג שם טוש"ע שם סעיף כא וסי' קלה סעיף א [וברב אלפס עוד בכתובות פרק ט דף קמ: ובשבועות פ"ז דף שיד:]:

רבינו גרשום

ומקשי' מי איכא מידי וכו'. אלא אמר רבא אי אמר ההוא ישראל דזבנה מעכו"ם קמי דידי זבנה ההוא עכו"ם מיניה דישראל ולבתר הכי זבנה (מיני') ניהלי מהימן מיגו וכו': האי מאן דאחזיק מגודא דערודי ולבר. כגון שרגילין בני אדם שיש להם שדות סמוך ליער משמרין מקצת משדה סמוך ליער וכונסין בשדה ועושין מחיצה בין השדה ליער בשביל שאם יצאו חיות ערודין מן היער כדי שירעו באותה הרחקה שיש מן המחיצה ליער ולא יבואו לשבור המחיצה ולאכול התבוא' ואם החזיק אדם באותו שיור שהניח בשביל הערודים אפילו לאחר שעמדה ברשותו ג' שנים אין חזקתו חזקה מאי טעם דאמרינן האי דלא מיחה זה בעל הקרקע בתוך ג' שנים דקסבר הואיל וכל מאי דזרע האי ערודי אכלי ליה ומשום הכי שתק ולא איבד שדהו בשתיקתו: אכלה ג' שנים ערלה. היכי דמי כגון שהיו בה נטיעות ושנה ראשונה טעון פירות מקצתן והיו ערלה ובשנה שניה טענו אחרים ובשלישית אחרים דכולהו הוי ערלה אינה חזקה דהאי דשתיק בעל השדה ולא ערער משום שלא היו ראוין לאכילה: אכלה שחת. ג' שנים שלא המתין עד שתגדיל התבואה אלא היה קוצרה כשהיא שחת ומאכילה לבהמות אינה חזקה דשמיט ואכל הוה ולא אכלה כאכילת בני אדם: אי בצואר מחוזא. כלומר אם אותה קרקע עומדת סמוך למחוזא שעשירים היו זורעין שדותיהן למאכל בהמתן אי לא מיחה הויא חזקה: תפתיחה. זוהי קרקע שפתוחה היא יותר מבית השלחין שפתוחה היא ובקועה ככברה זו שאינה מקבלת מים כך אין ניכרין בה המים ואין יכולין להשקותה ואינה מוציאה פירותיה אם החזיק בה אדם ג' שנים אינה חזקה הואיל שאין

בה שום לחלוחית לא חשש למחות: אפיק כורא ועייל כורא. שאין מוציאה כי אם כעין שזורעין בה ולא יותר אינה חזקה דלא חשש למחות הואיל ואין מרויח בה: והני דבי ריש גלותא. אם מחזיקין בקרקעות שלנו ג' שנים אינה חזקה דבשביל כבודן שתקי אנשי: ולא מחזקינן בהו. בשדותם בג' שנים דמשום דעשירים נינהו שתקי אי נמי משום דטרידי בטורח צבור ולא ידעי ולא מחו: והעבדים יש להם חזקה. מי שמחזיק בהם ג' שנים: הגודרות אין להם חזקה. כגון צאן ובהמה שאם החזיק בהן אינה חזקה משום דיש בהם רוח חיים דאיכא למימר מאליהם הלכו אצלו והחזיק בהן גבי עבדים נמי איכא למימר מאליהן הלכו אצלו והחזיק בהן ואמאי יש להן חזקה: אמר רבא אין להם חזקה לאלתר אבל יש להן חזקה לאחר ג' שנים: א) כדקתני בהמה גבי עבדים וגבי גודרות בהמה דקה דאין להם שמירה כל כך אין להם חזקה אבל בהמה גסה דיש להן שמירה יש להם חזקה לאלתר דמצי אמר אתה מכרת לי: קטן עבד יש לו חזקה. משום דליכא למימר איהו אזיל לתמן: ב) אית ליה אימא לא מנשיא ברא ומדאיתא גבי האי ב' ימים או ג' ולא מיחה יש לו חזקה: חושלא. שעורין קלופות: דמסירי לרועה. ויש להן שמירה משום הכי כשהן ברשות של זה יש להן חזקה דליכא למימר דמאחריני נינהו: צפרא ופניא. דאזלי לחודייהו לרועה והדרי לביתייהו בלא שמירה ובדין הוא דלית להו חזקה דאיכא למימר מנפשייהו אזלי התם ואחזיק בהו. ומשני בנהרדעא שאני משום דשכיחי טייעי כלומר גנבים ישמעאלים לא שביק לגודרותיהו למיזל לחודייהו כי אם מידא דבעל הבהמות לידא דרועה ומידא דרועה לידא דבעל הבהמות משום הכי יש להן חזקה: פיס' ר' ישמעאל אומר שדה בית הבעל לא צריך לאחזוקי בה ג' שנים רצופות שלימות כי אם ג' חדשים בסוף שנה ראשונה וג' חדשים בתחלת שנה אחרונה וי"ב חדשים של אמצעית דפחות מיכן לא חשיבי ג' שנים ולהכי נקט ג' חדשים דג' תבואות בעינן בג' שנים ובג' חדשים מתגדלות תבואה של שעורים ושל שבולת שועל ולכלן לועזין טרמיי"ש. לימא ניר איכא בינייהו דר' ישמעאל משום הכי בעי ג' חדשים ולא פחות דאם נייר לקרקע לא הוי חזקה: ור"ע סבר ניר הוי חזקה: ואמרי יום אחד סגיא. דבינו אחד

חשק שלמה על רבינו גרשום א) אולי צ"ל דלא חלק בין בהמה גסה לדקה וכו'. ב) צ"ל ל"ל דאית ליה אימא וכו'. ג) אולי צ"ל לא מנשיא ברא כ"ה.

chazakah, and thus requires a minimum of three months for the first and third segments, in order to be able to plant and harvest a crop,[37] וְרַבִּי עֲקִיבָא סָבַר נִיר הָוֵי חֲזָקָה – **while R' Akiva holds that plowing does establish a *chazakah*** and therefore only one month is required, since plowing can be completed in this short span of time.

The Gemara asks:

וְתִסְבְּרָא – **But is this logical?** לְרַבִּי עֲקִיבָא מַאי אִירְיָא חוֹדֶשׁ – If plowing can establish a *chazakah* **according to R' Akiva, why speak of an** entire **month**?

NOTES

37. Merely plowing is not enough. Rather, one must plant a crop and harvest it when it is ripe in order to effect a *chazakah*, and this takes a minimum of three months. Thus, the occupant must use the land for three months during each of the first and third years. [However, he must use the land during the second, middle year for a full twelve months to ensure that the *chazakah* term is consecutive (*Rashbam*).]

לדידי אמר לי עכו"ם דמינך זבנה מהימן מי איכא מידי דאילו (א) עכו"ם אמר לא מהימן ואילו אמר ישראל משמיה דעכו"ם מהימן אלא אמר רבא אי אמר ישראל קמי דידי זבנה עכו"ם מינך וזבנה ניהלי מהימן מיגו דאי בעי א"ל אנא זבינתה מינך ואמר רב יהודה האי מאן דנקיט מגלא ותובליא ואמר איזיל איגזרה לדקלא דפלניא דזבנתיה מיניה מהימן (ב) לא חציף איניש למיגזר דקלא דלאו דיליה ואמר רב יהודה האי מאן דאחזיק מגודא דערודי ולבר לא הוי חזקה מ"ט מימר אמר כל דזרע נמי ערודי אכלי ליה ואמר רב יהודה אכלה ערלה (ג) אינה חזקה תניא נמי הכי אכלה ערלה שביעית וכלאים אינה חזקה אמר רב יוסף אכלה שחת לא הוי חזקה אמר רבא ואי בצואר מחוזא קיימא הוי חזקה אמר רב נחמן תפתיחא לא הוי חזקה אפיק כורא ועייל כורא לא הוי חזקה והני דבי ריש גלותא לא מחזקי בן ולא מחזקינן בהו: והעבדים וכו': עבדים יש להם חזקה והאמר ר"ל הגודרות אין להן חזקה אמר רבא אין להן חזקה לאלתר אבל יש להן חזקה לאחר ג' שנים אמר רבא אם היה קטן מוטל בעריסה יש לו חזקה לאלתר פשיטא לא צריכא דאית ליה אימא מהו דתימא ניחוש דלמא אימיה עיילתיה להתם קמ"ל אימא לא מנשיא ברא הנהו עיזי דאכלו חושלא בנהרדעא אתא מרי חושלא תפסינהו והוה קא טעין טובא אמר אבוה דשמואל יכול לטעון עד כדי דמיהן דאי בעי אמר לקוחות הן בידי והאמר ר"ל הגודרות אין להן חזקה שאני עיזי דמסירה לרועה והא איכא צפרא ופניא בנהרדעא טייעי שכיחי ומידא לידא משלמי: ר' ישמעאל אומר שלשה חדשים וכו': לימא ניר איכא בינייהו דרבי ישמעאל סבר ניר לא הוי חזקה ורבי עקיבא סבר ניר הוי חזקה ותסברא לרבי עקיבא מאי איריא חודש אפילו

רש"י

לדידי אמר לי עכו"ם דמינך זבנה מהימן. דמלאסיק אדעתיה למיטען הכי ה"נ הוה מצי למיטען אנא זבינתה מינך ואכלתי' שני חזקה דמהימן הלכך מה לו לשקר וקושטא קאמר: מי איכא מידי דאילו אמר עכו"ם לא מהימן כו'. השתא נמי חזקה שאין עמה טענה היא דאפי' אם טענתו אמת היא דאמר ליה עכו"ם דמישראל זבנה הלא אין בדבריו של עכו"ם כלום בלא שטר: קמאי דידי. כלומר שאני יודע בבירור היינו חזקה שיש עמה טענה: האי מאן דנקיט כו'. כבר פרשית לה לעיל: האי מאן דאחזיק מגודא דערודי ולבר לא הוי חזקה. חיות השדה שבאות ואוכלות הזרעים שבקצות השדה ויש שעושין קירות וגודרין השדה ומניחין קרקע חוץ לקיר מעט בשדות הסמוכות ליער ומשליכים שם זרע ומה שצומח באות החיות ואוכלות אותו ואין נכנסות בשדה עכשיו ואם בא אדם והחזיק באותו הקרקע חוץ לגדר אינה חזקה דיכול לומר דכיון דכל מה דזרע בההוא קרקע ערודי אכלי ליה לא איכפת ליה למחות דלא אחזיק כדמחזקי אינשי לפיכך לא הויא חזקה: אכלה ערלה. אחת מן השלש שנים הוא שנת ערלה אינה חזקה דלא איכפת ליה לבעל השדה בשנת ערלה ולכך לא מיחה וכ"ש אם שלשתן שני ערלה. ערלה וכלאים אכילתן באיסור שביעית הפקר לכל לכך לא מיחה ולא הויא חזקה. ובפירוש ר"ח גרסינן הכי אכלה ערלה ושביעית וכלאים הרי זו חזקה ולא נהירא: אכלה שחת. שלא המתין עד שתגדל התבואה אלא ג' שנים קצרה כשהיא שחת ומאכיל לבהמתו אינה חזקה דשמיט ואכיל ולא היה אוכל כשאר בני אדם ולפיכך לא חשש זה למחות בו שיש רגלים לדבר שירא הוא להחזיק כשאר בני אדם לפי שבגזל ירד בה: ואמר רבא ואי. קאי האי שחת: בצואר מחוזא. בבקעת מחוזא הוי חזקה לפי שעשירים הם ובהמות להם הרבה ודרכם להאכיל השדות לבהמות כשהן שחת: תפתיחא. קרקע פתוחה ומלאה בקעים ואינה מוציאה פירותיה לא הויא חזקה דמפני רעתה לא הקפיד למחות. ורבי' חננאל פירש תפתיחא שדה שלא חרש אותה אלא הוגשמה ונשבה הרוח וזרחה השמש ונתבקעה כגון פתחי חרישה וזרע בה כגון זה אינה חזקה: אפיק כורא. זרע כור: ועייל כורא. וליקט בו כור והכניס לביתו דכיון דליכא הרווחה לא הוי חזקה דלא חשש זה למחות: לא מחזקי בן. אם החזיק אחד מהן בשדותינו אינה חזקה וצריך להזהר בשטרו דמחמת יראתן לא מיחו בהן: ולא מחזקינן בהו. שמתוך שהם עשירים ויש להם בתים ושדות הרבה מניחין בני אדם לדור בבתיהם ושותקים ושמחים כדי להשביח קרקע שלהם וימלאום מתוקנים וגם למחות אינן חוששים לפי שבזרוע יטלו את שלהם כל זמן שירצו וי"מ לפי שעסוקין בצרכי צבור אין יודעין מי מחזיק בשלהן ולא נהירא: הגודרות אין להן חזקה. גודרות צאן וכל דבר המהלך בדרכים ובשווקים שיכול לומר מעצמו נכנס או אתה הכנסתו לביתך והחזקת בו אינה חזקה ואין יכול לומר לקוח הוא בידי והעבדים מהלכים הם בכל מקום ותנן דיש להם חזקה: ומשני הא דאמר ר"ל אין להן חזקה ה"מ לאלתר. שהמחזיק בהן בביתו אין יכול לטעון לקוח הוא בידי בלא עדים ובלא ראיה כשאר מטלטלין שאין יכולין להלך ואין עשוין להשאיל ולהשכיר דנאמן בהן לומר לקוח הוא [בידי] הואיל וישנו בביתו דבשאר מטלטלין הוי חזקה לאלתר דהמוחזק בהן יכול לטעון שלי הוא שלקחתיו אבל יש [א] להן לעבדים ולגודרות חזקה לאחר ג' שנים שהיה לו לזה המערער למחות ולא מיחה: אמר רבא. עבד כנעני קטן המוטל בעריסה: יש לו חזקה לאלתר. אם החזיק בו אחד ואמר לקוח הוא בידי נאמן הואיל ואין יכול להלך ולא דמי לגודרות וגם אין עשוי להשאיל ולהשכיר: פשיטא. דודאי מעצמו לא הלך: דעיילא אימיה. לעבד בבית אותו המחזיק תדיר: אימיה עיילתיה. ושכחתיה שם דהשתא היינו גודרות: הני עיזי דאכלו חושלא. שעורים קלופים שנכנסו בשדה [ורלאו] אותה תבואה השטוחה שם לשמש וקיימא לן שן מועדת היא לעולם וכי הויא ברשות הניזק נזק שלם משלמת ואין עדים מעידין מה אכלו מעט או הרבה וטוען בעל השדה כי הרבה אכלו יותר מכדי דמיהן של עזים הללו: יכול לטעון עד כדי דמיהן. של עזים מ"ט מיגו דיכול למימר בעל השדה לקוחין הן בידי דהא תפיס בהו ומהימן כי קאמר נמי כך וכך אכלו מהימן וקיימא לן האי מהימן בשבועה אבל בטפי מכדי דמיהן דליכא מיגו לא מהימן אלא בעדים: והאמר ר"ל כו'. ואמאי יכול לטעון עד כדי דמיהן הא ליכא מיגו דלא מצי למימר לקוחין הן בידי: שאני עיזי. דאע"ג דגודרות נינהו כיון דמסירי לרועה מתוך שמשומרות הן יותר מאילים וכבשים ואין אדם יכול להחזיק בהן בדרך לפיכך יש להן חזקה: והאיכא צפרא. שהולכים יחידות מבית הבעלים עד בית הרועה: ופניא. שהרועה מביאן מן השדה עד תוך העיר וכל אחת הולכת מעצמה לבית הבעלים: טייעי. ישמעאלים גנבים: מידא לידא משלמי. מיד הבעלים ליד הרועה שחרית ומיד הרועה ליד הבעלים ערבית ואין הולכות יחידות כלל: ניר. חרישה דכתיב נירו לכם ניר (הושע י): רבי ישמעאל סבר ניר לא הוי חזקה. אלא אוכל פירי הלכך צריך ג' חדשים בראשונה וג' באחרונה דבהכי גדל פרי כל ערכו וי"ב חדשים באמצע דבעינן רצופין: ורבי עקיבא סבר ניר הוי חזקה. הלכך בחדש אחד סגי כדי לעשות ניר: אפי'

תוספות

הכי גרים ר"ח אכלה ערלה שביעית וכלאים הויא חזקה. וכן נראה לר"י עיקר ואיירי כשאכלה זמורות וכן מוכח בהאשה שנפלו (כתובות דף עט:) דתנן המוציא הוצאות על נכסי אשתו הוציא הרבה ואכל קימעא קימעא ואכל הרבה מה שהוציא הוציא ומה שאכל אכל ואמר בגמרא עבד רב יהודה עובדא בחבילי זמורות ורב יהודה לטעמיה דאמר רב יהודה אכלה ערלה שביעית וכלאים הויא חזקה ואין לומר דלעולם גרס הכא אינה חזקה והתם כשאכלה זמורות והכא כשאכלה פירות שהן אסורים ולכך לא הויא חזקה שלא אכל כדרך האוכלים דאם כן הוה ליה לאיתויי ההיא דהתם נמי הכא דאיירי בדיני חזקה וא"ת דהכא משמע דזמורות ועלי כלאים שרו ומ"ש מהא דאמרינן בפרק כל שעה (פסחים דף כו:) תנור שהסיקוהו בקליפי ערלה או בקשין של כלאי הכרם חדש יותץ מכלל דאסירי ואמרינן נמי התם (דף כה.) כלאי הכרם עיקרן נאסר ומיהו הא לא קשה דאיכא למימר דעיקרן נאסר משום דכתיב (דברים כב) הזרע וי"ל דהתם איירי בזרוע מעיקרן שנזרעו הזרעים עם נטיעות הכרם שגדלו הזמורות באיסור אבל הכא איירי בזמורות שהיו כבר גדולים קודם שנזרעו כלאים שאותן אינן נאסרים אלא כשהוסיפו מאתים כדאמר בפרק כל שעה (שם דף כה.) ובפרק כל הבשר (חולין דף קטז.) זרוע ובא הוסיף מאתים אין לא הוסיף מאתים לא ומיירי הכא שזמורות לא הוסיפו מאתים והפירות הוסיפו ולכך לא הויא חזקה אלא בזמורות ואין זה דוחק דהכי הוי אורחא דמילתא שקודם מוסיפין הפירות מאתים מן הזמורות לפי שהזמורות כבר היו גדולות קודם זריעת כלאים: נרה

מסורת הש"ס

א) לעיל לג: ע"ש, ב) [כתובות פ. ע"ש], ג) [שם], ד) כתובות סד: גיטין כ:, ה) ב"מ קטז., ו) [צ"ל דמסירין. יעב"ץ], ז) [וע' תוס' מנחות נח: ד"ה ואיבא דאמרי]

הגהות הב"ח

(א) גמ' דאילו אמר עכו"ם לא מהימן: (ב) שם מהימן מ"ט לא חציף: (ג) שם ואמר רב יהודה אכלה ערלה שביעית וכלאים אינה חזקה:

הגהות הגר"א

[א] רשב"ם ד"ה ומשני. אבל יש כו'. ע"ש סי' עב וב"י סי' קלה. ורמב"ם וש"ס סי' קלה כתבו עבדים לגד (ועמ"ש רבינו שם בס"ק ה).

גליון הש"ס

גמרא עיזי דמסירי לרועה. עיין ב"ק דף נט ע"ב תוס' ד"ה אין:

ליקוטי רש"י

עין משפט נר מצוה

נט א מיי' פי"ד מהל' טוען ונטען הלכה ו סמג עשין צה טוש"ע ח"מ סי' קמט סעיף טז:
ס ב מיי' שם פי"ב הל' טו סמג עשין צה טוש"ע ח"מ סי' קמא סעי' יג:
סא ג מיי' שם הל' יב ועיין בהשגות ובכ"מ טוש"ע שם סעיף יא:
סב ד ה מיי' שם הל' יא טוש"ע שם סעיף י:
סג ו מיי' שם הל' ט טוש"ע שם סעי' ה:
סד ז מיי' שם הל' י טוש"ע שם סעי' ו:
סה ח מיי' פ"י שם הלכה ב סמג שם טור ח"מ סי' קמט:
סו ט מיי' שם הל' א סמג שם טוש"ע ח"מ סי' קלה סעי' א:
סז י כ מיי' שם הלכה ד וסמג שם טוש"ע ח"מ סי' קנה סעי' ג:
סח ל מיי' שם הל' ג סמג שם טוש"ע ח"מ סי' צ סעיף יח:
סט מ מיי' שם הל' ב סמג שם טוש"ע שם סעיף כא וסי' קלה סעיף א [ובר"ג אלפס עוד בכתובות פרק ט דף קח: ובשבועות פ"ו דף שיד:]

רבינו גרשום

ומקשי' מי איכא מידי וכו'. אלא אמר רבא אי אמר ההוא ישראל דזבנה מעכו"ם קמי דידי זבנה ההוא עכו"ם מיניה דישראל ולבתר הכי זבנה (מיני') ניהלי מהימן מיגו וכו': האי מאן דאחזיק מגודא דערודי ולבר. כגון שרגילין בני אדם שיש להם שדות סמוך ליער משמרין מקצת משדה סמוך ליער וכונסין בשדה ועושין מחיצה בין השדה ליער בשביל שאם יצאו חיות ערודין מן היער כדי שירעו באותה הרחקה שיש מן המחיצה ליער ולא יבואו לשבור המחיצה ולאכול התבואה ואם החזיק אדם באותו שיור שהניחו בשביל הערודים אפילו לאחר שעמדה ברשותו ג' שנים אין חזקתו חזקה מאי טעם דאמרינן האי דלא מיחה זה בעל הקרקע בתוך ג' שנים דקסבר הואיל וכל מאי דזרע האי ערודי אכלי ליה ומשום הכי שתק ולא איבד שדהו בשתיקתו: אכלה ג' שנים ערלה. היכי דמי כגון שהיו בה נטיעות ושנה ראשונה טוען פירות מקצתן והיו ערלה ובשנה שניה טענו אחרים ובשלישית אחרים דכולהו הוי ערלה אינה חזקה דהאי דשתיק בעל השדה ולא ערער משום שלא היו ראוין לאכילה: אכלה שחת. ג' שנים שלא המתין עד שתגדיל התבואה אלא היה קוצרה כשהיא שחת ומאכילה לבהמות אינה חזקה דשמיט ואכל הוה ולא אכלה כאכילת בני אדם: אי בצואר מחוזא. כלומר אם אותה קרקע עומדת סמוך למחוזא שעשירים היו הורגין שדותיהן למאכל בהמתן אי לא מיחה הויא חזקה: תפתיחא. זוהי קרקע שפתוחה היא יותר מבית השלחין שפתוחה היא ובקועה כבכרה שאינה מקבלת מים כן אין ניכרין בה המים ואין יכולין להשקותה ואינה מוציאה פירותיה אם החזיק בה אדם אף ג' שנים אינה חזקה הואיל

ע א מיי' פי"ג מהל' טוען ונטען הל' ט סמג עשין צה טוש"ע ח"מ סי' קמא סעי' ה וסעי' ט:
עא ב מיי' שם הל' א טוש"ע שם ס"א:
עב ג טוש"ע שם סעיף טו:
עג ד מיי' שם הל' יט טוש"ע שם סעי' ח:

אפילו יום אחד נמי. אלא דכולי עלמא [א] ניר לא הוי חזקה והכא פירא רבא ופירא זוטא איכא בינייהו ת"ר ניר אינו חזקה וי"א הרי זה חזקה (א) [א] מאן י"א אמר רב חסדא ר' אחא היא דתניא נרה שנה וזרעה ב' נרה ב' וזרעה שנה אינה חזקה ר' אחא אומר הרי זו חזקה א"ר (ב) אשי שאלית כל גדולי הדור ואמרו לי ניר הרי זה חזקה א"ל רב ביבי לרב נחמן מאי טעמא דמ"ד ניר הוי חזקה לא עביד איניש דכריבו ליה לארעיה ושתיק ומ"ט דמ"ד ניר לא הוי חזקה מימר אמר כל שיבא ושיבא דכרבו לעייל ביה שלחו ליה לרב נחמן בר רב חסדא ילמדנו רבינו נירא הוי חזקה או לא הוי חזקה אמר להו ר' אחא וכל גדולי הדור אמרי ניר הרי זה חזקה אמר רב נחמן בר יצחק [ב] רבותא למיחשב גברי הא רב ושמואל בבבל ור' ישמעאל ור' עקיבא בא"י אמרי ניר לא הוי חזקה ר' ישמעאל ורבי עקיבא מתני' היא רב מאי היא דאמר רב יהודה אמר רב זו דברי ר' ישמעאל ורבי עקיבא אבל חכמים אומרים חזקתה ג' שנים מיום ליום מיום ליום למעוטי מאי לאו למעוטי ניר דלא שמואל מאי היא דאמר רב יהודה אמר שמואל זו דברי רבי ישמעאל ורבי עקיבא אבל חכמים אומרים עד [ב] [ג] שיגדור שלש גדירות ויבצור ג' בצירות וימסוק ג' מסיקות מאי בינייהו אמר אביי [ג]דקל נערה איכא בינייהו [ד](שעושה שלש פעמים בשנה): אמר רבי ישמעאל בד"א בשדה הלבן: אמר אביי מדרבי ישמעאל נשמע לרבנן [ד]היו לו שלשים אילנות ממטע עשרה לבית סאה אבל עשרה בשנה זו ועשרה בשנה זו ועשרה בשנה זו הרי זו חזקה
לאו

רש"י

אפי' יום אחד נמי. יכול לעשות בו ניר: פירא רבא ופירא זוטא איכא בינייהו. ר' ישמעאל ס"ל דלא הוי חזקה עד שילקט פירא רבא דהיינו כשנגמרה כל התבואה לפיכך צריך שלשה חדשים כגון שעורים ושבולת שועל ועדשים שגדלים בג' חדשים ור"ע סבר פירא זוטא דהיינו כגון שחת שגדל בשלשים יום הויא חזקה אע"פ שלא נגמרה התבואה אי נמי כגון ירק דגדלין הירקות בחדש אחד: נרה שנה. בלא זריעה: ושתיק. ולא מיחה ומדלא מיחה הפסיד: כל שיבא ושיבא דכרבו ליעול בה. כל קוסמים שבמחרישה יכנים בה כלומר הלואי וירבה הרבה עד שתכלה מחרשתו ותתרפה הקרקע ואח"כ אטלנה ואזרענה אני: ילמדנו רבינו ניר הוי חזקה. בשדה הבעל ודי בחזקת י"ב חדש ושני ימים: רבי ישמעאל ור' עקיבא דמתניתין. כדאוקמינן לר"ע ניר לא הוי חזקה כלומר יום א' בשנה שנר בו שהרי אינה חזקה להחשב כשנה שלמה לחשבון ג' שנים: זו דברי רבי ישמעאל ור"ע. דאמרי במתני' שדה הבעל חזקתו ג' שנים ואינה מיום ליום אלא י"ח חדשים לר' ישמעאל וי"ד לר"ע אבל חכמים אומרים חזקתן שלש שנים בכל דבר מיום ליום ואליבייהו דהני רבנן פרישנן בריש פירקין טעמא דחזקת ג' שנים דעד שלש שנים מיזדהר אינש בשטריה טפי לא מיזדהר וכוותייהו דהני רבנן אליבא דרב קיימי כדמוכח סוגיא דמכילתין דלא אזיל בתר לקיטת ג' פירות של ג' שנים אלא ג' שנים שלמות בעינן בכל דבר ומשום דאין אדם נזהר בשטרו יותר מג' שנים: לאו למעוטי ניר. דהא אפי' פירא רבא ופירא זוטא קא ממעט וכ"ש ניר דהא מיום ליום קתני למעוטי אפי' שנים מקוטעות אלמא ניר לא חשיב חזקת יום אחד דידיה כשנה שלמה דאם כן די בי"ב חדש ושני ימים ואנן שלש שנים מיום ליום בעינן: דאמר רב יהודה אמר שמואל זו דברי ר' ישמעאל ור"ע. דאמרי במתני' אבל בשדה אילן כנס את תבואתו ומסק את זיתיו וכנס את קייצו הרי אלו ג' שנים אלמא משליקט ג' פירות בשדה אחת בשנה אחת בג' זמנים זה אחר זה חשיב לה חזקה: אבל חכמים אומרים. פירות (ג) ג' שנים צריך עד שיגדור בתמרים ג' גדירות כו': מסיקות. בזיתים: מאי בינייהו. בין רב ושמואל בין למר ובין למר ג' שנים בעינן: דקל נערה איכא בינייהו. דקל ילדה ובחורה (ד) דפחות מג' שנים שלמות טוענת ג' פעמים לשמואל הויא חזקה בג' גדירות אע"ג דליכא ג' שנים שלמות ולרב בעינן ג' שנים מיום ליום. ורבינו חננאל פי' דקל נערה דקל המשיר פירותיו קודם גמרן מלשון גם חצני נערתי (נחמיה ה) לדברי שמואל דאמר בעינן ג' גדירות לא הוי חזקה דהא לא גדר לדברי רב דאמר בעינן ג' שנים והרי הוא מחזיק בו ג' שנים והויא חזקה ולפי הלשון הזה אפי' שמואל לא בא לגרוע מג' שנים והכי קי"ל. ל"א פירש עוד דקל נערה דקל דיופרין שעושה פעמיים בשנה לשמואל בשנה ומחצה הויא חזקה דהא איכא ג' גדירות ולרב לא הויא חזקה דליכא ג' שנים: אמר אביי מדברי ר' ישמעאל נשמע להו לרבנן היו לו שלשים כו'. ה"ג לה והכי פירושא דר' ישמעאל דבשנה אחת הוי חזקה בשדה אחת בשלש לקיטות בשלשה מקומות בשדה כדקתני כנס את תבואתו ומסק את זיתיו כו' מדבריו נשמע להו לרבנן דפליגי עליה כדאמר רב יהודה אמר שמואל לעיל ובעו ג' שנים דליכא פלוגתא בין ר' ישמעאל ובין רבנן אלא בשנה אחת וג' שנים אבל כל מאי דאמר ר' ישמעאל בשנה אחת אמרי רבנן בג' שנים: ממטע עשרה לבית סאה. דבית סאה צריך לעשר נטיעות כדאמר בלא יחפור (לעיל דף כו:) אבל אם פחות מבית סאה לי' אילנות הרי סמוכין ביותר והוי כיער ולא הוי חזקה דלא אחזיק כדמחזקי אינשי וביותר מבית סאה לי' נמי לא הויא חזקה בכל הקרקע אלא כנגד מה שצריך לאילנות: אבל י' בשנה זו כו' הרי זו חזקה. דכמי שהחזיק ג' שנים בכל השדה דמי שהיה אוכל בכל השנה מה שגדל בו:
לאו

תוספות

נרה שנה וזרע שתים כו'. נרה שתים וזרע שנה אחת לא נקט אלא משום רבותא דר' אחא דלאפי' הכי הויא חזקה ואומר ר"י (ה) דנראה דוקא כגון שנרה וזרע ונרה אבל נרה בזה אחר זה אפי' רבי אחא מודה דאינה חזקה דמה מועיל חרישה כל כך שמחרשה ג' שנים בלא זריעה: למעוטי מאי. תימה לרשב"א דהיכי מוכח מהכא דלמעוטי ניר קאתי דלמא קסברי רבנן ניר לא הוי חזקה והא דצריך ג' שנים מיום ליום משום דעד תלת שנין מיזדהר איניש בשטרא כדמפרש בריש פירקין ואפי' לא עשה באותן שלש אלא ניר הוי חזקה דלא עביד איניש דכרבי לארעיה ושתיק: מאי בינייהו. וא"ת טובא איכא בינייהו דשלש בצירות יכולין להיות בשתי שנים שבסוף שנה בצר וכו' ג' בצירות אחרי כן בשתי שנים ואומר ר"י דמשמע ליה דג' בצירות שלמות כל שנות הבצירות אבל תימה לר"י אמאי לא משני דאיכא בינייהו חרפי ואפלי כדאמרינן בפ"ב דע"ז (דף עה.) כמה מישכן י"ב חדש רשב"ג אומר מגת לגת מגד לגד היינו תנא קמא איכא בינייהו חרפי ואפלי: היו לו שלשים אילנות. (ו) ונראה דדוקא שלשים [ה] אבל ט' אילנות גדולים ממטע שלשה לבית סאה ואוכל אחת בשנה זו ואחת בשנה זו לא הויא חזקה מידי דהוה אשלשים היכא דלא באו בזויי והני אילנות לא בגדולים איירי דגדולים לא הוו אלא ג' לבית סאה כדאמרי' בפ' לא יחפור (לעיל דף כו:): ממטע [ו] לבית סאה. פ"ה דפחות מבית סאה לעשרה אילנות הוו סמוכי ביותר והוו כיער ולא הוי חזקה ואין נראה דהא מוכח בשמעתין דאכלכן לגופין הויא חזקה דפריך רבא אנהרדעי אלא מעתה האי אספסתא במאי קני ליה ולרשב"א נראה ליישב פ"ה דלקמן איירי שאוכל כל האילנו' (ז) אע"פ שהן רצופים הויא חזקה שהרי אכל העומדים ליעקר ואותן העומדים להתקיים אבל הכא שאינו אוכל כל אילנות אלא ג' בכל שנה אם היו ל"ג אילנות בג' סאין הרי יש בהן ג' אילנות העומדין ליעקר וכשהוא אוכל י"א אילנות בכל שנה שמא באותן י"א שאוכל אותן בשנה זו יש בהן ב' או ג' שעומדין ליעקר ובעינן בכל שנה שיאכל ג' מאותן העומדין להתקיים וביותר מבית סאה לעשרה נראה דלא קנה קרקע כל עיקר ולא כפ"ה דפי' דדוקא בכל הקרקע הוא דלא הוי חזקה אבל במה שצריך לאילנות הוי חזקה: ממטע עשרה לבית סאה. קשה לר"י דמאי שנא חזקה ממכר (ח) דגבי קנה ג' קנה קרקע ועשרה לבית סאה הוו מפוזרים ולא קנה קרקע דבעשר לבית סאה יש מאתן וחמשין לכל אילן ובהמוכר את הספינה (לקמן דף פג:) גבי קנה ג' כו' אמר כמה יהא ביניהן משמנה ועד שש עשרה אבל יותר מי"ו הוו מפוזרין וכשיש ביניהן י"ו הוי לכל אילן ח' (ט) מכל צד סביבותיו דהיינו טבלא של י"ו על י"ו עגולה שהאילן יונק סביבותיו בשוה וי"ו על י"ו מרובעים הוו מאתן וחמשין ושית דל רביע מינייהו דמרובע יתר על העיגול רביע לא ישאר אפי' מאתים אלמא לא הוי כשיעור י' לבית סאה ושמא יש לחלק בין מכר לחזקה דגבי מכר ודאי לא אמר דקנה קרקע אם אינן רצופין כדרך שבני אדם רגילין ליטע ודרך בני אדם אין להרחיק יותר מי"ו אמה אילן מאילן אע"פ שנכנסת יניקה של זה בתוך יניקה של זה שאילנות גדולים יונקין י"ו אמה מכל צד ולכך אין דרך להרחיק אילן מאילן כל שיעור יניקתם דהיינו ל"ב דא"כ לא יטע איש בשדה גדולה אלא ב' אילנות או ג' אבל גבי חזקה הויא חזקה כשיעור יניקה אע"פ שהן מרוחקין כשיעור יניקה אבל קשה לר"י דיפה כח הדיוט מכח הקדש דגבי הדיוט קנה שלשה קנה קרקע משמנה ועד י"ו וגבי הקדש תניא בסוף המוכר את הבית (לקמן דף עב.) הקדיש שלשה אילנות ממטע עשרה לבית סאה הרי זה הקדיש את הקרקע פחות מכאן או יותר על כן לא הקדיש את הקרקע מאי שנא הקדש ממכר ופי' הקונטרס בסוף המוכר את הבית (שם ד"ה ממטע) דהתם בדעת מוכר תליא מילתא אבל גבי הקדש ביניקה תליא מילתא ובהמוכר את הספינה (שם דף פג. ד"ה כמה) פירש גבי מכר והוא הדין למקדיש אילנות דהוי נמי האי שיעורא וברייתא דהמוכר את הבית (שם דף עב.) דקתני בהקדיש עשרה לבית סאה פליגא וראיה מתוספתא דמכילתין דקתני (י) כי קנה ג' קנה קרקע וכמה יהו קרובים זה לזה כדי שיהא הבקר עובר בכליו
וכמה

רבינו גרשום

מצי למעבד בה ניר: פירא רבא. דר' ישמעאל סבר בעינן שלשה חדשים דאיכא בהו פירא רבא וגמר פירי בעינן ור' עקיבא סבר בפירי זוטרא כגון אספסתא דבחדש אחד נגמר כולו פריו סגי והויא חזקה: נרה שנה וזרעה שתים. ושתיק דאם איתא דשלו הוא הוה מחי והואיל דלא מחי הוי חזקה: מימר אמר. המערער: כל שיבא דכרבא ליעילו בה. כלומר ולואי שיביאו כל אותן כלי אומנות שלהן דכרבי בהן וליכרבו לארעאי ולאחר כן שהיו מתקנים אותה הייתי מוחה. שיבא לועזין רישט"ל שמכסין בו את התבואה לאחר שיהא זרועה: אמר רב נחמן בר יצחק וכי מאי רבותא היא למיחשב גברי דסבירא להו דניר הוה חזקה. והא רב ושמואל ור' ישמעאל ור' עקיבא דמתני' דגברי דרברבי נינהו וסבירא להו כו'. כדאמרן לעיל. אלא דכולי עלמא ניר לא הוי חזקה. זו דברי ר' ישמעאל ור' עקיבא דבעי כל חד וחד שיעוריה כדקתני מתני' אבל חכמים אומ' כו' מאי לאו למעוטי ניר דלא הוי חזקה דהשתא מיום ליום ממעט מקוטעין דלא הוי חזקה כל שכן וכל שכן דניר לא הוי חזקה דבחד יומא מצי למעבדיה: ג' בצירות. דהיינו ג' שנים ולא ניר: מאי בינייהו. בין רב ובין לשמואל בין למר ובין למר ג' שנים אמרינן דבעינן חזקה: אמר אביי דקל נערה. דבחורה היא ובכחה עומדת וטוענת פרי ב' פעמים בשנה בב' שנים של חזקה סגיא משום דבדקל נערה מצי לגדור ג' גדירות בב' שנים: פיסקא אבל בשדה אילן שגדל שם התבואה נמי. קייצו תאנים. ה"ג אמר אביי מדר' ישמעאל נשמע היו לו ל' אילנות ממטע עשרה לבית סאה דה' אילנות צריכין בית סאה דבכך חשוב שדה אילן. מי לא אמר ר' ישמעאל במתני' להיכא דאכל חד פירא הוי חזקה לכולהו פרי דכל היכא דכנס את תבואתו דמי כמאן דמסק את זיתו וכנס קייצו בפעם אחת והיכא דמסק את זיתו דמי כמאן דכנס את תבואתו וכנס קייצו [בבת] אחת וכן הכי נמי כנס את קייצו דחד פירא הוי חזקה לכולהו ולא בעינן לכל פרי ופרי ג' שנים כי אם לכולהו פרי חד שתא. הכא נמי גבי אילנות היכא דאכל י' אילנות בשדה זו ולא אכל להני הוי חזקה והכי נמי לכולה [שדה] הוו י' חזקה הני להני אע"ג דלא אכל להו לכולהו אילנות בשתא חדא. אבל י' אילנות בשנה זו (וי' בשנה זו) וי' בשנה אחרת וי' בשנה שלישית שאם

מסורת הש"ס

א) [ע' תוס' לקמן נג: ד"ה מאן], ב) [יבמות מה.], ג) גי' רש"ל שיגדור ג' גדירות בדלי"ת והוא מלשון גודו אילנא, ד) רש"ל מ"ז, ה) אבל אילנות גדולות ממטע ט' ג' לבית סאה כ"ה במהרש"ל:

הגהות הב"ח

(א) גמ' מאן י"א. נ"ב אע"ג דבהוריות דף יג אמרו די"א היינו רבי נתן הכא קבלה היתה בידו וע"ל ר"פ המוכר פירות דף לג ע"ב במ"ש התוס' בד"ה מאן י"א: (ב) שם א"ר אחא שאלית כל גדולי וכו' הרי זו חזקה: (ג) רשב"ם ד"ה אבל וכו' פירות של ג': (ד) ד"ה דקל וכו' דפחות מג' וכו' דהא לא גדר דמה שליקט מן הארץ ולא מן האילן לדברי רב: (ה) תוס' ד"ה נרה וכו' ואומר ר"י דנרה דוקא כגון: (ו) ד"ה היו לו שלשים אילנות הני אילנות לא בגדולים איירי וכו' בפ' לא יחפור ונראה דדוקא שלשים אבל תשע אילנות ממטע שלש וכו' דלא בזויי הס"ד וה"ב פירוש אילנות גדולים וכן פירש בטור ח"מ בסי' קמ"א בשם ר"י: (ז) ד"ה ממטע וכו' דאע"פ שהן וכו' העומדים ליעקר והעומדים כצ"ל. ותיבת ואותן נמחק: (ח) ד"ה ממטע וכו' חזקה ממכר דהיכא דקנה שלשה: (ט) בא"ד ח' אמות מכל צד: (י) בא"ד מתוספתא דמכילתין דקתני גבי קנה:

ליקוטי רש"י

היו לו שלשים אילנות ממטע עשרה לבית סאה. עשר נטיעות מפוזרות בבית סאה לארכו ולרחבו כולן בשוה יונקות מכל בית סאה וכולם צריך להם וכו' ובית סאה חמשים אמה על חמשים אמה שהוא המשכן קרוי בית סאתים והוא מאה על חמשים. [לעיל כו:]. ממטע י' לבית סאה דהיינו מאתן וחמשין בצלא לכל חד כדאמרינן בלא יחפור (לעיל כו:) [רשב"ם לקמן עב.].

בא המערער וערער לאחר ג' שנים ואמר הואיל שלא היו טוענין כולן פירות לא הייתי מוחה שלא אכלתן כולן ג' שני חזקה. יכול לומר לו המחזיק אני אכלתים בזמן שהיו טוענין ולא מחית משום הכי הויא חזקה

אֲפִילוּ יוֹם אֶחָד נַמִּי – **Even one day also** would be sufficient, for a field can be plowed in a single day! Thus, R' Akiva should require only twelve months and two days to establish *chazakah*. – ? –

The Gemara therefore abandons this explanation and adopts another:

אֶלָּא דְּכוּלֵּי עָלְמָא נִיר לֹא הָוֵי חֲזָקָה – **Rather, all agree** that **plowing does not establish a *chazakah*,** וְהָכָא פֵּירָא רַבָּא וּפֵירָא זוּטָא אִיכָּא בֵּינַיְיהוּ – **and here the dispute between them is** whether a *chazakah* requires **a fully grown crop or a partially grown crop.**[1]

Having opened up the question of whether plowing can establish a segment of a *chazakah,* the Gemara quotes various opinions on this matter:

תָּנוּ רַבָּנָן – **The Rabbis taught in a Baraisa:** נִיר אֵינוֹ חֲזָקָה – PLOWING DOES NOT ESTABLISH A *CHAZAKAH.* וְיֵשׁ אוֹמְרִים הֲרֵי זֶה חֲזָקָה – BUT THERE ARE THOSE WHO SAY IT ESTABLISHES A *CHAZAKAH.*

The Gemara seeks to identify the author of the latter view:

מַאן יֵשׁ אוֹמְרִים – To **whom** does the Baraisa refer when it cites **"*those* who say"?**[2] אָמַר רַב חִסְדָּא – **Rav Chisda said:** רַבִּי אַחָא הִיא – **It is R' Acha.** דְּתַנְיָא – **For it was taught in a Baraisa:** נָרָה שָׁנָה וּזְרָעָה שְׁתַּיִם – If [THE OCCUPANT] PLOWED [THE FIELD] FOR ONE YEAR AND PLANTED IT FOR TWO years, נָרָה שְׁתַּיִם וּזְרָעָה שָׁנָה – or PLOWED IT FOR TWO years AND PLANTED IT FOR ONE, אֵינָהּ חֲזָקָה – THIS DOES NOT ESTABLISH A *CHAZAKAH.* רַבִּי אַחָא אוֹמֵר – R' ACHA SAYS: הֲרֵי זוֹ חֲזָקָה – THIS DOES ESTABLISH A *CHAZAKAH.*[3]

A supporting opinion:

אָמַר רַב אַשִׁי – **Rav Ashi said:** שַׁאֲלִית כָּל גְּדוֹלֵי הַדּוֹר – **I asked all the great** scholars **of the generation** וְאָמְרוּ לִי – **and they said to me,** נִיר הֲרֵי זֶה חֲזָקָה – **"Plowing establishes a *chazakah.*"**

The Gemara explains R' Acha's reasoning:

אָמַר לֵיהּ רַב בִּיבִי לְרַב נַחְמָן – **Rav Bivi said to Rav Nachman:** מַאי טַעְמָא דְּמַאן דְּאָמַר נִיר הָוֵי חֲזָקָה – **What is the reasoning of the one who says** that **plowing establishes a *chazakah?***

Rav Nachman replies:

לֹא עָבִיד אִינִישׁ דְּכָרִיבוּ לֵיהּ לְאַרְעֵיהּ וְשָׁתִיק – **A man would not see another plow his land and remain silent.** Thus, although the occupant does not harvest any produce, the fact that the previous owner does not protest indicates that he has indeed sold the land.

Rav Bivi inquires further:

וּמַאי טַעְמָא דְּמַאן דְּאָמַר נִיר לֹא הָוֵי חֲזָקָה – **And what is the reasoning of the one who says** that **plowing does not establish a *chazakah?***

Rav Nachman replied:

מֵימַר אָמַר – Because the owner is not motivated to protest. On the contrary, **he** is pleased and **says** to himself, כָּל שִׁיבָא וְשִׁיבָא דְּכָרְבוּ לְעַיֵּיל בֵּיהּ – **"Let him** only **put every last splinter of the plow into [the soil]!"**[4] Thus, his silence does not indicate his admission, and no *chazakah* is established.

A definitive ruling is sought:

שָׁלְחוּ לֵיהּ בְּנֵי פּוּם נַהֲרָא לְרַב נַחְמָן בַּר רַב חִסְדָּא – **The people of** the town **of Pum Nahara sent** the following inquiry **to Rav Nachman bar Rav Chisda:** יְלַמְּדֵנוּ רַבֵּינוּ – **Let our master teach us** the law: נִירָא הָוֵי חֲזָקָה אוֹ לֹא הָוֵי חֲזָקָה – **Does plowing establish a *chazakah* or not?**[5] אָמַר לְהוּ – **[Rav Nachman] said to [the people of Pum Nahara]:** רַבִּי אַחָא וְכָל גְּדוֹלֵי הַדּוֹר אָמְרֵי – **R' Acha and all the great** scholars **of the generation say** נִיר הֲרֵי זֶה חֲזָקָה – that **plowing establishes a *chazakah.***

Rav Nachman bar Yitzchak takes issue with this decision:

אָמַר רַב נַחְמָן בַּר יִצְחָק – **Rav Nachman bar Yitzchak said:** רְבוּתָא לְמִיחְשַׁב גַּבְרֵי – Is it **a great thing to enumerate authorities?** I.e. is it proper to rule that plowing establishes a *chazakah* simply because a number of sages maintain this view? I can cite authorities to the contrary, הָא רַב וּשְׁמוּאֵל בְּבָבֶל – **for** both **Rav and Shmuel in Babylonia** וְרַבִּי יִשְׁמָעֵאל וְרַבִּי עֲקִיבָא בְּאֶרֶץ יִשְׂרָאֵל – **and R' Yishmael and R' Akiva in Eretz Yisrael** אָמְרֵי נִיר לֹא הָוֵי חֲזָקָה – **say** that **plowing does *not* establish a *chazakah!***

The Gemara analyzes Rav Nachman bar Yitzchak's statement and asks:

רַבִּי יִשְׁמָעֵאל וְרַבִּי עֲקִיבָא מַתְנִיתִין הִיא – Now, as far as **R' Yishmael and R' Akiva,** their views can be found in **our Mishnah,** for since they require eighteen and fourteen months respectively, they obviously hold that plowing does not effect a *chazakah.*[6] רַב מַאי הִיא – But **Rav** – **what is [the source]** of his view?

The Gemara replies:

דְּאָמַר רַב יְהוּדָה אָמַר רַב – **For Rav Yehudah said in the name of Rav:** זוֹ דִּבְרֵי רַבִּי יִשְׁמָעֵאל וְרַבִּי עֲקִיבָא – **These** rulings in the Mishnah concerning the *chazakah* of a rain-watered field[7] **are the words of R' Yishmael and R' Akiva,** and they form only the minority opinion. אֲבָל חֲכָמִים אוֹמְרִים – **But the Sages say:** חֶזְקָתָהּ שָׁלֹשׁ שָׁנִים מִיּוֹם לְיוֹם – **[A rain-watered field's] *chazakah*** requires **three** full **years** of use **from day to day.** מִיּוֹם לְיוֹם לְמַעוּטֵי מַאי – Now, **what does** the term **"from day to day"** used by the Sages come **to exclude?** לָאו לְמַעוּטֵי נִיר דְּלָא – **Does it not** come **to exclude plowing,** implying **that** it does **not** effect

NOTES

1. R' Yishmael maintains that although the first and third segments of the *chazakah* of a rain-watered field may be abbreviated, the occupant must, as a minimum for each of these segments, use the field by planting a crop and harvesting it when it reaches full maturity. This can most quickly be accomplished with such fast-growing crops as barley, spelt or lentils. However, even these crops require three months to develop fully. Accordingly, R' Yishmael requires three months for the first and third segments of the *chazakah*. R' Akiva, on the other hand, holds that the occupant need not wait till the crop is fully developed before harvesting it. Rather, even cutting it early for use as animal fodder effects *chazakah*, and for this, one month's time suffices (*Rashbam*).

2. It is certainly neither R' Yishmael nor R' Akiva, as they require eighteen months and fourteen months respectively, and if plowing can establish *chazakah*, even twelve months and two days would suffice, as the Gemara noted above.

3. To point out the extent of R' Acha's view, the Baraisa says that not only one but even two of the *chazakah* years may consist of plowing. However, if the occupant plows all *three* years, he does not establish a *chazakah*. Additionally, the single year of planting must be the second, because only then are both plowings of any benefit. That is, by plowing one year, the crops of the following year prosper. Thus, by alternating years between plowing and planting, the occupant acts in a somewhat usual manner and thereby elicits protest from the original owner, if in fact the occupation is illegal. But if the occupant plows two years in a row and plants the third, he does not act at all as an owner would, because one year of plowing is of no benefit at all. Thus, the original owner is not motivated to protest, and the *chazakah* is ineffective (*Tosafos*).

4. [As long as the occupant derives no benefit from the field, the owner feels no need to protest.] On the contrary, he reasons that the more the occupant plows, the softer the soil becomes and the better crop he, the owner, will be able to produce from the field when he returns to it (*Rashbam*).

5. I.e. [since a field can be plowed in a single day,] does one year and two days suffice as a *chazakah* for a rain-watered field? (*Rashbam*).

6. For if plowing could be used as a segment of the *chazakah* for a rain-watered field, a year and two days would suffice, and R' Yishmael and R' Akiva require eighteen months or fourteen months respectively, as pointed out by the Gemara above (*Rashbam*).

7. I.e. the requirement of eighteen or fourteen months for establishing a *chazakah* (*Rashbam*).

אפילו יום אחד נמי אלא דכולי עלמא [א] ניר לא הוי חזקה והכא פירא רבא ופירא זוטא איכא בינייהו ת"ר ניר אינו חזקה וי"א הרי זה חזקה (א) [א] מאן י"א אמר רב חסדא ר' אחא היא דתניא נרה שנה וזרעה ב' נרה ב' וזרעה שנה אינה חזקה ר' אחא אומר הרי זו חזקה א"ר (ב) אשי שאלית כל גדולי הדור ואמרו לי ניר הרי זה חזקה א"ל רב ביבי לרב נחמן מאי טעמא דמ"ד ניר הוי חזקה לא עביד איניש דכריבו ליה לארעיה ושתיק ומ"ט דמ"ד ניר לא הוי חזקה מימר אמר כל שיבא ושיבא דכרבו לעייל ביה שלחו ליה לרב נחמן בר רב חסדא ילמדנו רבינו נירא הוי חזקה או לא הוי חזקה אמר להו ר' אחא וכל גדולי הדור אמרי ניר הרי זה חזקה אמר רב נחמן בר יצחק [ב] רבותא למיחשב גברי הא רב ושמואל בבבל ור' ישמעאל ור' עקיבא בא"י אמרי ניר לא הוי חזקה ר' ישמעאל ורבי עקיבא מתני' היא רב מאי היא דאמר רב יהודה אמר רב זו דברי ר' ישמעאל ורבי עקיבא אבל חכמים אומרים חזקתה ג' שנים מיום ליום למעוטי מאי לאו למעוטי ניר דלא שמואל מאי היא דאמר רב יהודה אמר שמואל זו דברי רבי ישמעאל ורבי עקיבא אבל חכמים אומרים עד [ג] שיגדור שלש גדירות ויבצור ג' בצירות וימסוק ג' מסיקות מאי בינייהו אמר אביי ג דקל נערה איכא בינייהו [ד] (שעושה שלש פעמים בשנה): אמר רבי ישמעאל בד"א בשדה הלבן: אמר אביי מדרבי ישמעאל נשמע לרבנן ד היו לו שלשים אילנות ממטע עשרה לבית סאה אכל עשרה בשנה זו ועשרה בשנה זו ועשרה בשנה זו הרי זו חזקה לאו

רש"י

אפי' יום אחד נמי. יכול לעשות בו ניר: פירא רבא ופירא זוטא איכא בינייהו. לר' ישמעאל ס"ל דלא הוי חזקה עד שילקט פירא רבה דהיינו כשנגמרה כל התבואה לפיכך לריך שלשה חדשים כגון שעורים ושבולת שועל ועדשים שגדלים בג' חדשים ור"ע סבר פירא זוטא דהיינו כגון שחת שגדל בשלשים יום הויא חזקה אע"פ שלא נגמרה התבואה א' נמי כגון ירק דגדלין הירקות בחדש אחד: נרה שנה. בלא זריעה: ושתיק. ולא מיחה ומדלא מיחה הפסיד: כל שיבא ושיבא דכרבו ליעול בה. כל קיסמים שבמחרישה יכנים בה כלומר הלואי ויחרוש הרבה עד שתהא מחרשתו ותתרפה הקרקע ואח"כ אטלנה ואזרענה אני: ילמדנו רבינו ניר הוי חזקה. בשדה הבעל ודי בחזקת י"ב חדש ושני ימים: רבי ישמעאל ור' עקיבא דמתניתין. כדאוקמינן דכ"ע ניר לא הוי חזקה כלומר יום א' בשנה שנר בו שדהו אינה חזקה להחשב כשנה שלמה לחשבון ג' שנים: זו דברי רבי ישמעאל ור"ע. דאמרי במתני' שדה הבעל חזקתו ג' שנים ואינה מיום ליום אלא י"ח חדשים לר' ישמעאל וי"ד לר"ע אבל חכמים אומרים חזקתן שלש שנים בכל דבר מיום ליום ואליבייהו דהני רבנן פרישנן בריש פירקין טעמא דחזקת ג' שנים דעד שלש שנים מיזדהר איניש בשטריה טפי לא מיזדהר וכוותייהו דהני רבנן אליבא דרב קיימי כדמוכח סוגיא דמכילתין דלא אזיל בתר לקיטת ג' פירות של ג' שנים אלא ג' שנים שלמות בעינן בכל דבר ומשום דאין אדם נזהר בשטרו יותר מג' שנים: לאו למעוטי ניר. דהא אפי' פירא רבא ופירא זוטא קא ממעט וכ"ש ניר דהא מיום ליום קתני למעוטי אפי' שנים מקוטעות אלמא ניר לא חשיב חזקת יום אחד דידיה כשנה שלמה דאם כן די בי"ב חדש ושני ימים ואנן שלש שנים מיום ליום בעינן: דאמר רב יהודה אמר שמואל זו דברי ר' ישמעאל ור"ע. דאמרי במתני' אבל בשדה אילן כנס את תבואתו ומסק את זיתיו וכנס את קייצו הרי אלו ג' שנים אלמא משליקט ג' פירות בשדה אחת בשנה אחת בג' זמנים זה אחר זה חשיב לה חזקה: אבל חכמים אומרים. פירות (ג) ג' שנים לריך עד שיגדור בתמרים ג' גדירות כו': מסיקות. בזיתים: מאי בינייהו. בין רב ושמואל בין למר ובין למר ג' שנים בעינן: דקל נערה איכא בינייהו. דקל ילדה ובחורה (ד) דפחות מג' שנים שלמות טוענת ג' פעמים לשמואל הויא חזקה בג' גדירות אע"ג דליכא ג' שנים שלמות ולרב בעינן ג' שנים מיום ליום. ורבינו חננאל פי' דקל נערה דקל המשיר פירותיו קודם גמרן מלשון גם אני נערתי (נחמיה ה) לדברי שמואל דאמר בעינן ג' גדירות לא הוי חזקה דהא לא גדר לדברי רב דאמר בעינן ג' שנים והרי הוא מחזיק בו ג' שנים והויא חזקה ולפי הלשון הזה אפי' שמואל לא בא לגרוע מג' שנים והכי קי"ל. ל"א פירש עוד דקל נערה דקל דיופרין שעושה פעמיים בשנה לשמואל בשנה ומחצה הויא חזקה דהא איכא ג' גדירות ולרב לא הויא חזקה דליכא ג' שנים: אמר אביי מדברי ר' ישמעאל נשמע להו לרבנן היו לו שלשים כו'. ה"ג לה והכי פירושא דר' ישמעאל דבשנה אחת הוי חזקה בשדה אחת בשלש לקיטות בשלשה מקומות בשדה כדקתני כנס את תבואתו ומסק את זיתיו כו' מדבריו נשמע להו לרבנן דפליגי עליה כדאמר רב יהודה אמר שמואל לעיל ובעו ג' שנים דליכא פלוגתא בין ר' ישמעאל ובין רבנן אלא בשנה אחת וג' שנים אבל כל מאי דאמר ר' ישמעאל בשנה אחת אמרי רבנן בג' שנים: ממטע עשרה לבית סאה. דבית סאה לריך לעשר נטיעות כדאמר בלא יחפור (לעיל דף כו:) אבל אם פחות מבית סאה לי' אילנות הרי סמוכין ביותר והוי כיער ולא הוי חזקה דלא אחזיק כדמחזקי אינשי וביותר מבית סאה לי' נמי לא הויא חזקה בכל הקרקע אלא כנגד מה שלריך לאילנות: אבל י' בשנה זו כו' הרי זו חזקה. דכמי שהחזיק ג' שנים בכל השדה דמי שהיה אוכל בכל השנה מה שגדל בו: לאו

תוספות

נרה שנה וזרע שתים כו'. נרה שתים וזרע שנה אחת לא נקט אלא משום רבותא דר' אחא דאפי' הכי הויא חזקה ואומר ר"י (ה) דנראה דוקא כגון שנרה וזרע ונרה אבל נרה בזה אחר זה אפי' רבי אחא מודה דאינה חזקה דמה מועיל חרישה כל כך שחורשה ב' שנים בלא זריעה: למעוטי מאי. תימה לרשב"א דהיכי מוכח מהכא דלמעוטי ניר קאתי דלמא קסברי רבנן ניר הוי חזקה והא דצריך ג' שנים מיום ליום משום דעד תלת שנין מיזדהר איניש בשטרא כדמפרש בריש פירקין ואפי' לא עשה באותן שלש אלא ניר הוי חזקה דלא עביד איניש דכרבי לארעיה ושתיק: מאי בינייהו. וא"ת טובא איכא בינייהו דשלש בצירות יכולין להיות בשתי שנים שבסוף שנה בצר וג' בצירות אחרי כן בשתי שנים ואומר ר"י דמשמע ליה דג' בצירות שלמות כל שנות הבצירות אבל תימה לר"י אמאי לא משני דאיכא בינייהו חרפי ואפלי כדאמרינן בפ"ב דע"ז (דף עז.) כמה מיישן י"ב חדש רשב"ג אומר מגת לגת מבד לבד היינו תנא קמא איכא בינייהו חרפי ואפלי: היו לו שלשים אילנות. (ו) ונראה דדוקא שלשים ה אבל כ' אילנות גדולים ממטע שלשה לבית סאה ואוכל אחת בשנה זו ואחת בשנה זו לא הויא חזקה מידי דהוה אשלשים היכא דלא באו זוזי והני אילנות לא בגדולים איירי דגדולים לא הוו אלא ג' לבית סאה כדאמרי' בפ' לא יחפור (לעיל דף כו:): ממטע ו לבית סאה. פ"ה דפחות מבית סאה לעשרה אילנות הוו סמוכי ביותר והוו כיער ולא הוי חזקה ולאו נראה דהא מוכח בשמעתין דאלכלן רצופין הויא חזקה דפריך רבה אנהרדעי אלא מעתה האי הספסתא במאי קני ליה ולרשב"א נראה לייש' פ"ה דלקמן איירי שאוכל כל האילנו' (ז) אע"פ שהן רצופים הויא חזקה שהרי אכל העומדים ליעקר ואותן העומדים להתקיים אבל הכא שאינו אוכל כל אילנות אלא ג' בכל שנה אם היו ל"ג אילנות בג' סאין הרי יש בהן ג' אילנות העומדין ליעקר וכשהוא אוכל י"א אילנות בכל שנה שמא באותן י"א שאוכל אותן בשנה זו יש בהן ב' או ג' שעומדין ליעקר ובעינן בכל שנה שיאכל ג' מאותן העומדין להתקיים וביותר מבית סאה לעשרה נראה דלא קנה קרקע כל עיקר ולא כפ"ה דפי' דדוקא בכל הקרקע הוא דלא הוי חזקה אבל במה שצריך לאילנות הוי חזקה: ממטע עשרה לבית סאה. קשה לר"י דמאי שנא חזקה ממכר (ח) דגבי קנה ג' קנה קרקע ועשרה לבית סאה הוו מפוזרים ולא קנה קרקע דבעשר לבית סאה יש מאתן וחמשין לכל אילן ובהמוכר את הספינה (לקמן דף פג:) גבי קנה ג' כו' אמר כמה יהא ביניהן משמנה ועד שש עשרה אבל יותר מי"ו הוו מפוזרין וכשיש ביניהן י"ו הוי לכל אילן ח' (ט) מכל לד סביבותיו דהיינו טבלא של י"ו על י"ו עגולה שהאילן יונק סביבותיו בשוה וי"ו על י"ו מרובעים הוו מאתן וחמשין ושית דל רביע מינייהו דמרובע יתר על העיגול רביע לא ישאר אפי' מאתים אלמא לא הוי כשיעור י' לבית סאה ושמא יש לחלק בין מכר לחזקה דגבי מכר ודאי לא אמר דקנה קרקע אם אינן רצופין כדרך שבני אדם רגילין ליטע ודרך בני אדם אין להרחיק יותר מי"ו אמה אילן מאילן אע"פ שנכנסת יניקה של זה בתוך יניקה של זה שאילנות גדולים יונקין י"ו אמה מכל לד ולכך אין דרך להרחיק אילן מאילן כל שיעור יניקתם דהיינו ל"ב דא"כ לא יטע איש בשדה גדולה אלא ד' אילנות או ג' אבל גבי חזקה הויא חזקה כשיעור יניקה אע"פ שהן מרוחקין כשיעור יניקה אבל קשה לר"י דיפה כח הדיוט מכח הקדש דגבי הדיוט קנה שלשה קרקע משמנה ועד י"ו וגבי הקדש תניא בסוף המוכר את הבית (לקמן דף עב.) הקדיש שלשה אילנות ממטע עשרה לבית סאה הרי זה הקדיש את הקרקע פחות מכאן או יותר על כן לא הקדיש את הקרקע מאי שנא הקדש ממכר ופי' הקונטרס בסוף המוכר את הבית (שם ד"ה ממטע) דהתם בדעת מוכר תליא מילתא אבל גבי הקדש ביניקה תליא מילתא ובהמוכר את הספינה (שם דף פג. ד"ה כמה) פירש גבי מכר והוא הדין למקדיש אילנות דהוי נמי האי שיעורא ובריית' דהמוכר את הבית (שם דף עב.) דקתני בהקדיש עשרה לבית סאה פליגא וראיה מתוספתא דמכילתין דקתני (י) כי קנה ג' קנה קרקע וכמה יהו קרובים זה לזה כדי שיהא הבקר עובר בכליו וכמה

עין משפט נר מצוה

ע א מיי' פי"א מהל' טוען ונטען הל' ט סמג עשין לה טוש"ע ח"מ סי' קמא סעי' ה וסעי' ט:

עא ב מיי' שם הל' ז טוש"ע שם ס"א:

עב ג טוש"ע שם סעיף טו:

עג ד מיי' שם הל' יט טוש"ע שם סעי' ח:

רבינו גרשום

מצי למעבד בה ניר: פירא רבא. דר' ישמעאל סבר בעינן שלשה חדשים דאיכא בהו פירא רבא וגמר פירי בעינן ור' עקיבא סבר בפירי זוטרא כגון אספסתא דבחדש אחד נגמר כולו פריו סגי והויא חזקה: נרה שנה וזרעה שתים. ושתיק דאם איתא דשלו הוא הוי מחי והואיל דלא מחי הוי חזקה: מימר אמר. המערער: כל שיבא דכרבא לעיילו בה. כלומר ולואי שיבאו כל אותן כלי אומנות שלהן דכרבי בהן וליכרבו לארעאי ולאחר כך שיהו מתקנים אותה הייתי מוחה. שיבא לועזין רישטי"ל שמכסין בו את התבואה לאחר שיהא זרועה: אמר רב נחמן בר יצחק וכי מאי רבותא היא למיחשב גברי דסבירא להו דניר הוה חזקה. והא רב ושמואל ור' ישמעאל ור' עקיבא דמתני' דגברי רברבי נינהו וסבירא להו כו'. כדאמרן לעיל. אלא דכולי עלמא ניר לא הוי חזקה. זו דברי ר' ישמעאל ור' עקיבא דבעי כל חד וחד שיעוריה כדקתני מתני' אבל חכמים אומ' כו' מאי לאו למעוטי ניר דלא הוי חזקה דהשתא מיום ליום ממעט מקוטעין דלא הוי חזקה כל שכן וכל שכן דניר דלא הוי חזקה דבחד יומא מצי למעבדיה: ג' בצירות. דהיינו ג' שנים ולא ניר: מאי בינייהו. בין רב ובין לשמואל בין למר ובין למר ג' שנים אמרינן דבעינן חזקה: אמר אביי דקל נערה. דבחורה היא ובכחה עומדת וטוענת פרי ב' פעמים בשנה בב' שנים של חזקה סגיא משום דבדקל נערה מצי לגדור ג' גדירות בב' שנים: פיסקא אבל בשדה אילן שגדל שם התבואה נמי. קייצו תאנים. ה"ג אמר אביי מדר' ישמעאל נשמע היו לו ל' אילנות ממטע עשרה לבית סאה דבי' אילנות צריכין בית סאה דבכך חשוב שדה אילן. מי לא אמר ר' ישמעאל במתני' להיכא דאכל חד פירא הוי חזקה לכולהו פרי דכל היכא דכנס את תבואתו דמי כמאן דמסק את זיתיו וכנס קייצו בפעם אחת והיכא דמסק את זיתיו דמי כמאן דכנס את תבואתו וכנס קייצו [בבת] אחת וכן הכי נמי כנס את קייצו דהוי דחד פירא הוי חזקה לכולהו ולא בעינן לכל פירי כולהו בעינן כי אם לכולהו פרי חד שתא. ה"נ גבי אילנות היכא דאכל י' אילנות בשדה זו ולא אכל להני הוי חזקה להני נמי לכולה [שדה] הוי י' חזקה הני להני אע"ג דלא אכל להו לכולהו אילנות בשתא חדא. אבל י' אילנות בשנה זו (וי' בשנה זו) וי' בשנה אחרת וי' בשנה שלישית שאם בא המערער וערער לאחר ג' שנים ואמר הואיל שלא היו טוענין כולן פירות לא הייתי מוחה שלא אכלתם כולן ג' שני חזקה. יכול לומר לו המחזיק אני אכלתים בזמן שהיו טוענין ולא מחית משום הכי הויא חזקה

מסורת הש"ס

א) [ע' תוס' לקמן נג: ד"ה מאן], ב) [יבמות מה.], ג) ג' רש"ל שיגדור ג' גדידות בדלי"ת והוא מלשון גודו אילנא, ד) רש"ל מ"ז, ה) אבל אילנות גדולות ממטע ט' לבית סאה כ"ה במהרש"ל:

הגהות הב"ח

(א) גמ' מאן י"א. נ"ב עא"ג דבכורות דף יג אמרו מד"א היינו רבי נתן הכל קבלה היתה בידו וע"ל ר"פ המוכר פירות דף צג ע"ב במ"ש התוס' בד"ה מאן י"א: (ב) שם א"ר אשי שאלית כל גדולי וכו' הרי זו חזקה: (ג) רשב"ם ד"ה אבל וכו' פירות של ג': (ד) ד"ה דקל וכו' דפחות מג' וכו' דהא לא גדר דמה שליקט מן הארץ ולא מן האילן לדברי רב: (ה) תוס' ד"ה נרה וכו' ואומר ר"י דנראה דוקא כגון: (ו) ד"ה היו לו שלשים אילנות הני אילנות לא בגדולים איירי וכו' כפ' לא יחפור ונראה דדוקא שלשים אבל אכל אילנות ממטע שלש וכו' דלא בזוי זוזי הס"ד ונ"ב פירוש אילנות גדולים וכן פירש בטור ח"מ בסי' קמ"א בשם ר"י: (ז) ד"ה ממטע וכו' דלא"פ שהן רצופים והעומדים כל"ל. ותיבת ואותן נמחק: (ח) ד"ה ממטע וכו' חזקה ממכר דהיכא דקנה שלשה: (ט) בא"ד מ' אמות מכל לד: (י) בא"ד מתוספתא דמכילתין דקתני גבי קנה:

ליקוטי רש"י

היו לו שלשים אילנות ממטע עשרה לבית סאה. עשר נטיעות מפוזרות בבית סאה לאורכו ולרחבו כולן בשוה יונקות מכל בית סאה וכולו צריך להן וכו' ובית סאה חמשים אמה על חמשים אמה כחצר המשכן קרוי בית סאתים והוא מאה על חמשים. [לעיל כו:] בית סאה דהיינו מאתן וחמשין לכל חד דאמרינן בלא יחפור (לעיל כו:) [רשב"ם לקמן עב.]

chazakah?[8] Thus, we see that Rav rules that plowing does not effect a *chazakah*.[9]

The Gemara continues analyzing Rav Nachman bar Yitzchak's statement and asks:

שְׁמוּאֵל מַאי הִיא – And **Shmuel, what is the** [**source**] of his view?

The Gemara replies:

דְּאָמַר רַב יְהוּדָה אָמַר שְׁמוּאֵל – **For Rav Yehudah said in the name of Shmuel:** זוּ דִבְרֵי רַבִּי יִשְׁמָעֵאל וְרַבִּי עֲקִיבָא – **These** words in the Mishnah regarding *chazakah* for a field of trees[10] **are the words of R' Yishmael and R' Akiva,**[11] and form only the minority opinion. אֲבָל חֲכָמִים אוֹמְרִים – **But the Sages say:** עַד שֶׁיִּגְדּוֹר שָׁלֹשׁ גְּדִירוֹת – A *chazakah* is not established **until** [**the occupant**] **harvests three crops of dates,** וְיִבְצוֹר שָׁלֹשׁ בְּצִירוֹת – **and reaps three crops of grapes** וְיִמְסוֹק שָׁלֹשׁ מְסִיקוֹת – **and picks three crops of olives,** which requires *three* years. We see, therefore, that Shmuel holds that plowing does not effect a *chazakah*.[12]

The Gemara asks:

מַאי בֵּינַיְיהוּ – **What is the** practical **difference between** [**Rav and Shmuel**] regarding their understanding of the Sages' view? Both seem to require three full years to establish *chazakah*![13]

The Gemara answers:

אָמַר אַבַּיֵי – **Abaye said:** דֶּקֶל נַעֲרָה אִיכָּא בֵּינַיְיהוּ (שעושה שלש פעמים בשנה) – The time required to establish a *chazakah* on **a young date palm is** the practical difference **between them.**[14]

The final section of the Mishnah:

אָמַר רַבִּי יִשְׁמָעֵאל – **R' YISHMAEL SAID:** בַּמֶּה דְבָרִים אֲמוּרִים בִּשְׂדֵה הַלָּבָן – **IN** regard to **WHAT IS THIS SAID? IN** regard to **A GRAIN FIELD** etc.

In the Gemara above, Shmuel quoted the view of the Sages who differ with R' Yishmael and require three harvests of *each* type of tree in order to establish a *chazakah*. Abaye addresses this:

אָמַר אַבַּיֵי – **Abaye said:** מִדְּרַבִּי יִשְׁמָעֵאל – **From** the words of **R' Yishmael** נִשְׁמַע לְרַבָּנָן – **we deduce** the opinion of **the Rabbis** in the following case:[15] הָיוּ לוֹ שְׁלֹשִׁים אִילָנוֹת – **If** [**the land**] **had thirty trees** מְמַטַּע עֲשָׂרָה לְבֵית סְאָה – **planted** in a density of **ten to a** ***beis se'ah*****,**[16] אָכַל עֲשָׂרָה בְּשָׁנָה זוֹ – and [**the occupant**] **harvested** the produce of **ten** trees [**the first**] **year,** וַעֲשָׂרָה בְּשָׁנָה זוֹ – **ten** [**the second year**] וַעֲשָׂרָה בְּשָׁנָה זוֹ – **and** the remaining **ten** [**the third**] **year,** הֲרֵי זוֹ חֲזָקָה – **this constitutes a** ***chazakah*** on the entire field.[17]

NOTES

8. Because since the Sages dispute even R' Yishmael's opinion, ruling that growing a crop in three months cannot be reckoned as a segment of a *chazakah,* they certainly rule that plowing the field in a single day is ineffective. (Actually, this is so obvious a conclusion from the view of the Sages that the Gemara's words indicating that it is a mere *inference* are puzzling. See *Rashba* who emends the text on this account.) Thus, no matter whether a property provides benefits continually or only seasonally, it requires three full calendar years for *chazakah*.

Now, this opinion of the Sages is not mentioned at all in the Mishnah on 28a. However, Rav indicates here that the law follows their view. Moreover, when Rava explained above, 29a, that the reason *chazakah* requires three years is that people cease to guard their deeds after this time, he perforce was following the view of the Sages. For according to our Mishnah that maintains that the length of the *chazakah*-term varies with the type of field, Rava's reason cannot apply, because people do not guard a deed of a rain-watered field any less than they do one of an irrigated field. Hence, the halachah is that a full three-year *chazakah* is required for *all* fields (*Rashbam; cf. Rif* and *Rambam*).

9. Since he cited the Sages as the majority view.

10. I.e. that by harvesting the crops of three separate types of trees, growing in one field, at three different times of the year, one establishes *chazakah* on the field in a single year (*Rashbam*).

11. [*Rashash* notes that the Mishnah, as we have it, quotes this only in the name of R' Yishmael, and not R' Akiva.]

12. The Sages maintain that it is not enough to harvest three types of tree *one* time each. Rather, each type of tree must be harvested *three* times. And since each type of tree produces only one crop per year, it would take three years to establish a *chazakah* even on a field of trees. Obviously, then, plowing does not effect a *chazakah,* for if it did, one could establish a *chazakah* in a year and two days (by plowing around the trees for a single day in each of the first and third years). And since Shmuel cites this opinion as the majority view, he obviously subscribes to it.

13. Because although Rav and Shmuel refer to different cases (Rav to a rain-watered grain field and Shmuel to a tree field), they both seem to agree that a *chazakah* requires three full years (see *Tosafos*).

14. A young date palm yields three crops in less than three years. Thus, since Shmuel insists only that one harvest the produce of the same trees three times, one could establish a *chazakah* on a field of young date palms in less than three years. Rav, on the other hand, requires three years in any case (*Rashbam*; see there for several alternative explanations as well).

15. The Gemara below, 37a, will explain exactly how this may be deduced.

16. An area fifty *amos* by fifty *amos*, or 2,500 square *amos.*

17. Although he harvested only one-third of the field's trees each year, he has established a *chazakah* on the entire field, because it is as if he had consumed the entire yield of the field each year, as the Gemara will explain below (*Rashbam*).

This is only so, though, if the trees were planted in a ratio of exactly ten per *beis se'ah*, because this much land is required to supply the nutrients needed to sustain ten saplings (as explained above, 26b). Thus, by maintaining this ratio, the occupant makes effective use of the entire field. However, if the trees are more sparsely planted, consuming their produce establishes a *chazakah* only on that portion of land needed for the trees' nutrition. Conversely, if more than ten trees were planted in a *beis se'ah*, no *chazakah* at all is established, for such overcrowding is detrimental to the trees. Thus, by so doing, the occupant does not use the land as an owner would and therefore does not elicit protest from the original owner. Hence, no *chazakah* is established (*Rashbam*; cf. *Tosafos*).

לָאו מִי אָמַר רַבִּי יִשְׁמָעֵאל – For did R' Yishmael not say חַד פֵּירָא הָוֵי חֲזָקָה לְכוּלְהוּ פֵּירֵי – an act of *chazakah* on one crop is tantamount to an act of *chazakah* in all the crops?[1] הָכָא נַמִּי – Then here, in the Sages' view as well, הָנֵי הָווּ חֲזָקָה לְהָנֵי – harvesting the produce of these ten trees in the first year is considered an act of *chazakah* even for those other twenty trees, וְהָנֵי הָווּ חֲזָקָה לְהָנֵי – and harvesting these ten trees in the second year is considered an act of *chazakah* even for those other twenty. Thus, it is as if produce of *all* the trees had been harvested in *each* of the three years.[2]

Abaye qualified his statement:

וְהָנֵי מִילֵּי – And these words apply only הֵיכָא דְּלֹא אַפִּיקוּ – in an instance where [the other twenty trees] did not bear fruit that year.[3] אֲבָל אַפִּיקוּ וְלֹא אָכַל – But if they did bear fruit and [the occupant] did not harvest it, לֹא הַוְיָא חֲזָקָה – it is not considered a *chazakah*, because he thereby indicates that he is not the field's true owner.[4]

Abaye adds a second qualification:

וְהוּא דְּבָאזֵי בְּאזוּזֵי – And this ruling (that harvesting ten trees each year establishes a *chazakah* for the entire field) applies only if [the ten trees] are scattered throughout the entire field.[5]

The Gemara shifts to a different subject: A man sold a field and the trees upon it to two different people. What are the rights that each of the buyers possess?[6]

זֶה הֶחֱזִיק בְּאִילָנוֹת וְזֶה הֶחֱזִיק בְּקַרְקַע – If this buyer performs a proprietary act on the trees, and the other buyer performs a proprietary act on the land, what is the law?[7] Does the buyer of the trees acquire any land together with his purchase of the trees? אָמַר רַב זְבִיד – Rav Zevid said: זֶה קָנָה אִילָנוֹת – "This buyer acquires only the trees and has no rights at all in the land, וְזֶה קָנָה קַרְקַע – and this buyer acquires all the land."[8]

Rav Pappa objects:

מַתְקִיף לָהּ רַב פָּפָּא – Rav Pappa challenged [this ruling], countering: אִם כֵּן – If this is so, אֵין לוֹ לְבַעַל אִילָנוֹת בְּקַרְקַע כְּלוּם – that the owner of the trees has no [rights] at all in the land, לֵימָא לֵיהּ בַּעַל קַרְקַע לְבַעַל אִילָנוֹת – then let the owner of the land say to the owner of the trees, when the trees eventually wither, עֲקוֹר אִילָנָךְ שְׁקוֹל וְזִיל – "Uproot your dead trees, take them and be gone!" It seems inequitable to rule that the tree owner acquires no rights at all, and that if his trees die, he can be forced off the land entirely.[9]

Rav Pappa therefore rules differently:

אֶלָּא אָמַר רַב פָּפָּא – Rather, Rav Pappa said: זֶה קָנָה אִילָנוֹת וַחֲצִי

NOTES

1. R' Yishmael rules that for fields that produce only seasonally, one effects a *chazakah* by harvesting three crops, although this may span less than three years. Additionally, he maintains that if an orchard grows three different types of fruit, one can establish a *chazakah* in the entire orchard in less than a year by harvesting each type only once. Actually, this last ruling contains an element of novelty, because by picking the fruit of one type, one does not use the land on which the other two types grow. Hence, any particular spot of land has been used only once! Nevertheless, R' Yishmael holds that since the field as a whole has been used three times, a *chazakah* has been established.

2. To explain — R' Yishmael's opinion regarding a tree field has two inherent novelties: (1) Its *chazakah* does not require three *years;* it can be effected by harvesting three *crops.* (2) Harvesting only *one-third* of the field's trees each time constitutes an act of *chazakah* for the *entire* field.

Now, the Sages clearly dispute the first point, because they require three *years* for *chazakah* for *any* field. But there is no reason to assume that they dispute the second point. Thus, if the occupant harvested the crop of ten of the field's thirty trees each year, he has effected a *chazakah* in the entire field, although he has used only one-third of the field each year (*Rashbam*).

3. Because R' Yishmael states his ruling regarding a tree field only where the fruit of the three types of tree ripen at different times of the year. Hence, when the occupant harvests grapes in the month of Tishrei, the olives and figs are not yet ready to be picked. Similarly, when he picks the olives in Shevat, the grapes and figs are not in season. Accordingly, the Sages, too, would consider harvesting ten trees a *chazakah* only if the other twenty did not yield fruit that year. This, *Rabbeinu Chananel* explains, is possible if the thirty trees were of a species of date tree known as *"bnos shuach,"* which yields fruit only once in three years (see *Sheviis* 5:1). Thus, if the planting of the trees was staggered, one-third of the trees would yield fruit each year (*Rashbam*).

4. By failing to harvest all the available produce, the occupant indicates that he fears to use the land in a normal manner, preferring instead to take a small amount of fruit at a time. Hence, he does not establish a *chazakah*, for the previous owner can claim he did not bother to protest such an obviously illegal occupation (*Rashbam*).

5. I.e. throughout the entire three *batei se'ah*. Only in such an instance does each year's harvest indicate possession of the entire tract. If, however, the occupant used ten trees in one section of the field one year, ten in the next section the second year and ten in the remaining section the third year, he has not effected a *chazakah,* for each *beis se'ah* is considered a separate field, and use of one field does not establish a *chazakah* for another. This second qualification of Abaye also derives from his parallel to the case of R' Yishmael, for the various trees in an orchard are generally not organized by type, but are scattered uniformly throughout the orchard (*Rashbam*).

6. If someone purchases trees from his fellow without specifying whether the purchase includes rights in the land, the law depends on the number of trees purchased. Specifically, three or more trees are deemed to constitute a tree field, and their sale automatically includes an amount of land around the trees (Mishnah below, 81a. The Gemara 82a defines this amount as the land underneath the trunk of the tree and its branches, the land under the spaces between the branches, plus a strip of land beyond the branches wide enough to allow a man to pick their fruit). However, if it is a sale of only two trees, the law is the subject of a dispute between Tannaim, as we will learn below.

Conversely, if someone purchases land without specifying if the sale includes the trees, the law is that the trees are secondary to the land and are automatically included in the sale (Mishnah below, 68b and Gemara 69b).

Our Gemara discusses a third case: A man sells his land and its trees, the land to one buyer and the trees to another. In this case, there is no question that the buyer of the land does not acquire the trees, for they were sold to his fellow. The question, though, is whether the buyer of the trees has acquired any rights in the land.

7. Land may be acquired by performing a symbolic act of proprietorship on the property. This is known as a *kinyan chazakah.* In this case, the land buyer dug up some of the land while the tree buyer pruned the trees (*Rashbam*).

8. The tree owner acquires no land at all, even if he purchased three trees. For although one who purchases three trees ordinarily acquires land with it, as explained in note 6, here he acquires no land, because the new landowner may argue, "Just as I acquired no rights in the trees [even though a purchase of land normally includes the trees], you acquire no rights in the land."

However, this does not mean that the landowner may demand that the tree owner remove his trees from the land, for clearly he purchased the trees with the right that they be allowed to continue to grow and bear fruit. Rather, it means that the tree owner owns none of the land and, should his trees wither and die, he is not entitled to plant others in their stead (*Rashbam*).

9. *Tosafos* explain that, specifically, Rav Pappa was unwilling to accept this ruling in a case in which the tree owner bought three trees, because, as explained in note 6, if he had purchased this amount from a seller who retained the land, the buyer would have acquired an actual section of land. Accordingly, in our case, the buyer should at least be entitled to replant new trees if the original trees die.

Despite Rav Pappa's objection, though, Rav Zevid maintains that since the tree owner does not acquire any actual land, he has no claim to entitle him to plant new trees if his should die.

לאו מי אמר ר' ישמעאל חד פירא הוי חזקה לכולהו פירי הכא נמי הני הוו חזקה להני והני הוו חזקה להני [א]והני מילי היכא דלא אפיקו (א) אבל אפיקו ולא אכל לא הויא חזקה [ב]והוא דבאזי באזוזי: זה החזיק באילנות וזה החזיק בקרקע אמר רב זביד זה קנה אילנות וזה קנה קרקע מתקיף לה רב פפא אם כן אין לו לבעל אילנות בקרקע כלום לימא ליה בעל קרקע לבעל אילנות עקור אילנך שקול וזיל אלא אמר רב פפא [ג]זה קנה אילנות וחצי קרקע וזה קנה חצי קרקע: [ד]פשיטא מכר קרקע ושייר אילנות לפניו יש לו קרקע ואפילו לר' עקיבא דאמר [א]מוכר בעין יפה מוכר [ג]ה"מ גבי בור ודות דלא מכחשו בארעא אבל אילנות דקמכחשי

לאו מי אמר רבי ישמעאל חדא פירא הוי חזקה לכולהו פירי. (ב) דבמקום הזיתים מהני למקום התבואה והקיץ וכאילו החזיק בשלשתן דמי וכן כשכנס את תבואתו כמי שהחזיק בשלשתן דמי שמן הטעם הזה הוי חזקת שלש שנים בכל השדה אע"פ שלא החזיק בו בכולהו פעם אחת הכי נמי חזקת מקום י' אילנות של שנה ראשונה זו חשובין כאילו החזיק נמי במקום העשרים וכן בשניה וכן בשלישית כאילו החזיק בכל שנה בג' אילנות: **וה"מ.** דהוי חזקה באכילת שלשים אילנות בג' שנים כה"ג היכא דלא אפיק אחריני כי העשרים לא עשו פירות כי אם עשרה לבד בכל שנה דומיא דרבי ישמעאל שמלקט כל מה שגדל בשדה ופירש ר"ח כגון בנות שוח שאין פירותיהם נגמרים עד ג' שנים: **אבל אי אפיק.** הני (ג) אילנות כולהו פירות בכל שנה ולא אכל אלא י' מינייהו לא הוי הני י' חזקה לכ' דכיון דלא אכל כל הפירות גילה על עצמו שהשדה אינה שלו וירא להחזיק חזקה גמורה ולפיכך לא חשש זה המערער למחות ולא הויא חזקה: **והוא דבזאי בזויי.** לשון בזיעה כלומר וה"מ דהוי חזקה כשאכל עשרה בכל שנה היינו ע"י פיזור שאכל ג' בכל בית סאה דנמצא מחזיק כל השדה אבל אכל י' אילנות ביחד בבית סאה (ד) זה ובשנה שניה כמו כן בבית סאה שני וכן בשלישית אינה חזקה דכל בית סאה חשוב שדה האילן בפני עצמו ושדה שלם לא הוי חזקה לשדה אחר והיינו נמי דומיא דרבי ישמעאל דכנס את תבואתו ומסק את זיתיו כו' שבכל השדה הוא אוכל דסתם שדה האילן על פני כולו מפוזרין הזיתים והדקלים: **זה החזיק באילנות וזה החזיק בקרקע.** שני לקוחות שלקחו שדה האילן מאדם אחד ביחד וכל הקרקע היה צריך לאילנות שהיו נטועים כדין שדה אילן והכי מתוקמא סוגיא דשמעתין לאחד מכר הקרקע ולאחד מכר האילנות והחזיק כל אחד בשלו כגון דרפק בה פורתא (ה) או עשה שום עבודת קרקע כל אחד בשלו דקרקע נקנה בכסף בשטר ובחזקה ולאו בחזקת ג' שנים מיירי ובהדיא מפרש לקמיה דבשני לקוחות מיירי: **אמר רב זביד זה קנה אילנות.** לפירותיהן בלא קרקע שאם יבשו האילנות לא יטע אחרים במקומן וזה קנה כל הקרקע אפי' אם יש שם ג' אילנות דתנן בהמוכר את הספינה (לקמן דף פא.) דקנה קרקע תחתיהם וביניהן וחוצה להן כמלא אורה וסלו ה"מ בלוקח אחד הקונה אילנות בתוך של חבירו דקנה קרקע אבל הכא בשני לקוחות שלוקחין ביחד זה אילנות וזה קרקע מאי אמר ליה בעל הקרקע לבעל האילנות כי היכי דלדידי לית לי באילנות לדידך נמי לית לך בקרקע והכי מפרש לקמיה: **לימא ליה.** כשייבש האילן עקור אילנך שקול וזיל ולא תטע אחר במקומו אבל כל זמן שהוא טוען פירות אינו יכול לומר כן ואע"ג דקרקע אין לו האילן (ו) כמות שהוא יונק מן הקרקע קנאו לפירותיו והכי נמי מוכח לקמן בשמעתא מדאמר ליה מר קשישא בריה דרב חסדא לרב אשי אי כורכמא ריסקא זבין ליה כו' ובהמוכר את הספינה (שם) נמי תנן הקונה ב' אילנות בתוך שדה חבירו הרי זה לא קנה קרקע כו' ואם מתו אין לו קרקע אלמא אע"ג דאין לו קרקע קתני ולא יעקרנו עד שימות וה"ה להא דרב זביד: **זה קנה אילנות וחצי קרקע.** לאו דוקא חצי קרקע אלא (ז) הצריך לאילנות תחתיהן וביניהן וחוצה להן כמלא אורה וסלו. אי נמי דוקא קאמר חצי וכגון שכל הקרקע צריך לאילנות אם לא מפני שמכר הקרקע לחבירו ואפילו לא הוו אלא ב' אילנות דקיימא לן בהמוכר את הספינה דאין להן קרקע הכא יש להן דכיון דשני לקוחות הן שקונין ביחד מאי אמר ליה בעל האילנות לבעל הקרקע כי היכי דלדידך בעין יפה זבין לידי נמי כו' והכי מפרש לקמיה: **מכר קרקע ושייר אילנות לפניו.** אפי' אינן אלא ב' יש לו קרקע כדי מחיית האילנות ולורכן ואם יבשו יטע אחרים במקומן דודאי מוכר לעצמו שייר קרקע והכי אמרינן בהדיא בהמוכר את הבית (לקמן דף עא.) אמר רב הונא אע"ג דאמור רבנן הקונה ב' אילנות בתוך של חבירו הרי זה לא קנה קרקע מכר קרקע ושייר ב' אילנות לפניו יש לו קרקע: **ואפי' לרבי עקיבא דאמר כו'.** פלוגתא דרבי עקיבא ורבנן לקמן בהמוכר את הבית (דף סד.) בשני מקומות גבי מוכר את הבית תנן לא מכר את היציע כו' ולא את הבור ולא את הדות אע"ג דכתב לו עומקא ורומא וצריך ליקח לו דרך דברי רבי עקיבא דמוכר בעין יפה מוכר ולא שייר במכירתו כלום וחכמים אומרים אינו צריך ליקח לו דרך דמוכר בעין רעה מוכר וגבי מוכר את השדה תנן [ג]נמי הכי דאמרינן מוכר בעין יפה מוכר ולא שייר אל עצמו דרך ללכת אל בורו: **ה"מ גבי בור ודות.** הוא דקאמר ר' עקיבא דלא עיכב דרך לעצמו סביבות הבור כלום דלא מכחשי בארעא שיכול הלוקח לזרוע על שפתו ולא יעכב עליו הלוקח לעקור בורו מכאן דהא אינו מזיקו כלל הלכך לא אסיק אדעתיה לעכב לעצמו כלום מן הקרקע והלכך צריך ליקח ממנו דרך בדמים לילך אל בורו:

וכמה יהו (ח) רחוקים ממטע עשרה לבית סאה פחות מכאן או יותר על כן או שקנה בזה אחר זה לא קנה את הקרקע ולא את האילן שביניהם ובתר הכי קתני במקדיש ההיא דמייתי בהמוכר את הבית (לקמן דף עב.) ונראה דפחות מכאן דקתני גבי הקדש קאי נמי אכדי שיעבור בקר וכליו ויותר מכאן קאי (ט) אלבית סאה כמו גבי מכר [ד] ולפי זה נמי ליכא למימר דאין חילוק בין חזקה למכר וסבר אביי כההיא ברייתא דתוספתא דהא אביי גופיה סבר כרב נחמן דאמר מח' ועד ששה עשר דא"ל אביי לרב יוסף לא תפלוג עליה דר"נ וא"ת ואי מדמינן מכר להקדש אם כן קשיא דר' שמעון אדר' שמעון דההיא דהמוכר את הבית מוקמינן לה כר' שמעון ובהמוכר את הספינה (לקמן דף פג.) אמר רבי מאיר ור' שמעון אומרים הנוטע את כרמו ח' על ח' מותר להביא זרע לשם אלמא חשיב ר' שמעון בח' אמות מפוזרים ומייתי התם ראיה מינה למכר אילנות ונראה לרשב"א דלא מוקי לה (י) בהמוכר את הבית (לקמן דף עב.) כרבי שמעון אלא במאי דקא סבר מקדיש בעין רעה הוא מקדיש אבל במאי דחשיב בח' אמות מפוזרים לא קיימא כוותיה:

היכא דלא אפיק. פי' ר"ח כגון בנות שוח שמשעה שנחנטו עד לקיטתן ג' שנים כדתנן (שביעית פ"ה מ"א) בנות שוח שביעית שלהן שנה שניה פי' בשנה ב' של שמיטה לפי שאותן פירות שנלקטים בשנה ב' של שמיטה נחנטו בשביעית ואסורין כדין שביעית ולכך אוקמה ר"ח בבנות שוח דבשאר אילנות באלף שנים לא יארע זה דבל' אילנות ילקו בשלפון ג' שנים ואותן שילקו בשנה זו לא ילקו בשנה זו ובזו בזויי [ה] וא"ת והיכי מלי מיירי בבנות שוח והא בריש פירקין אמרינן גבי חזקה בעינן דבעידנא דאיתיה להאי פירא ליתא להאי פירא והכא כשאכל פירות שנה ראשונה ושניה כבר נחנטו פירות שנת ג' וי"ל כיון שעדיין יש שנה עד גמר שלהן הוי שפיר בעידנא דאיתיה להאי פירא ליתא להאי פירא: **זה החזיק באילנות כו'.** פ"ה דלאו בחזקת ג' שנים איירי אלא שמכר לזה קרקע ולזה אילנות והחזיק כל אחד בשלו כגון דרפק בה פורתא ובעל אילנות פסחינהו כדאמר לקמן האי מאן דפסח דיקלא אדעתא דדיקלא קני וקשה לר"י דלא הוה ליה למיקבעיה אמתני' דהכא דאיירי בחזקת ג' שנים אלא לקמן גבי חזקות של קנין ועוד דאמאי נקט חזקה טפי משטר וכסף ואליפין הוה ליה למינקט מכר סתם כדנקט מכר בכולה סוגיא דבסמוך ונראה לר"י דאיירי בחזקת ג' שנים דלרב זביד זה קנה אילנות וזה קנה קרקע ואין לבעל אילנות בקרקע כלום ולכך כי יבשו לא יטע אחרים במקומן ורב פפא סבר דזה קנה אילנות וחצי קרקע פי' לא שיקנה בגוף הקרקע כלום שהרי זה החזיק בכל הקרקע אלא לענין שאם יתייבשו יטע אחרים במקומן. ומינה שמעי' בסמוך דמכר לזה אילנות ולזה קרקע דלרב זביד אין לבעל אילנות בקרקע כלום ליטע אחרים במקומן לכשיבשו ולרב פפא יש לו. דסברא הוא דאם מכר לזה אילנות ולזה קרקע בסתם קנה בעל אילנות הקרקע ליטע אחרים במקומן לכשייבשו גם חזקתו יש לו להועיל לענין זה:

לימא ליה בעל קרקע [לבעל אילנות] עקור אילנך שקול וזיל. פירוש לכשייבשו ואע"פ שכך הוא אמת לרב זביד מכל מקום פריך ליה רב פפא דאין סברא שידחוק אותו מיד לעקרו כשיבש כיון דג' אילנות מכר לו ועוד מצינו למימר עקור אילנך לאלתר קאמר והכי קשיא (כ) לרב פפא כיון דאפילו בג' אילנות אמרת דאין לו בקרקע כלום אע"ג דבעלמא בג' אילנות אית ליה קרקע משום דבשני לקוחות שאני (ל) וקאמר ליה כי היכי דלדידי לית לי באילנות הכי נמי לדידך לית לך בקרקע אי חשיב האי טעמא א"כ לאלתר נמי קודם שיבש לימא ליה עקור אילנך ואע"ג דבעלמא בחד לוקח בקנה שנים דלא קנה קרקע מ"מ יעמוד שם האילן עד שימות הכא גרע טפי מהאי טעמא דלית לך כי היכי דלדידי כו' אלא ודאי לית לך למימר האי טעמא הלכך כשמכר לזה קרקע ולזה אילנות בעל אילנות קנה מקום הגזע ליטע אחרים במקומן כשייבשו ומיירי בין בג' אילנות בין בב' כדפ"ה (מ) ואפילו בג' אין לו קרקע הצריך לאילנות [כיון] שפירש בהדיא לזה קרקע ואפי' בב' אילנות כשיבשו יטע אחרים במקומן משום כי היכי דלדידך בעין יפה זבין כו':

לאו

דקא

מסורת הש"ס

א) [לקמן סד: סה: עא. עב. פב:], ב) [לקמן עא.], ג) [לקמן עא.], ד) צ"ל ולפירושו רש"ע, ה) [וע' תוס' בכורות ח. ד"ה בנות].

הגהות הב"ח

(א) גמרא דלא אפיקו אחריני אבל אפיקו ולא אכל: (ב) רשב"ם ד"ה לאו מי וכו' דבמקום הזיתים וכו' שלא החזיק בו בכולהו כי אם פעם אחת וכו' בכל שנה בכל אילנות דמי הס"ד: (ג) ד"ה אבל אי אפיק הני שלשים אילנות: (ד) ד"ה והוא דבזאי וכו' בבית סאה זו ובשנה: (ה) ד"ה זה פורתא ובעל האילנות פסחינהו או עשה: (ו) ד"ה לימא וכו' האילן עצמו לו כמות שהוא יונק מן הקרקע שהרי קנאו לפירותיו: (ז) ד"ה זה קנה וכו' אלא קרקע הצריך לאילנות: (ח) תוס' ד"ה (בדף הקודם) וכמה יהו מרוחקים ממטע עשרה: (ט) בא"ד ויותר מכאן קאי אעבר לבית סאה כמו גבי מכר ולפי זה נמי: (י) בא"ד ונראה לרשב"א דלא מוקי לה ההיא דהמוכר את הבית לגמרי כר' שמעון אלא: (כ) ד"ה לימא וכו' והכי קשיא ליה לרב פפא: (ל) בא"ד שאני דקאמר ליה כי היכי: (מ) בא"ד כדפ"ה דאפילו בג':

ליקוטי רש"י

זה החזיק באילנות. זה קנה אילנות. שאם לא קנה קרקע סביביו כלל ואפי' מקום האילן והרי הוא כמי שקנאו לפירותיו שכשייבש יעקרנו וילך [רשב"ם לקמן פא.]. **מוכר בעין יפה מוכר.** כל דיני מכירות שבעולם [שם סד:]. **ה"מ גבי בור ודות.** גבי מכר את הבית שם דלית ליה שום היזק ללוקח דהא לא מכחשי בארעא ולא חשש לשייר כלום מן הקרקע סביב הבור ולא הדרך אבל האילנות שמכחישין את הקרקע שייר מקום האילנות לפניו [שם עא.]. **דלא מכחשו בארעא.** לא הבור ולא הדרך שאינו טוחנין לו הלכך בעין יפה זבין ליה: **אבל אילנות דקמכחשי.** דנהי נמי דאית ליה עין יפה בעין האילן במכר ושייר קרקע לפניו שיש לו קרקע לרבי עקיבא על מנת ליטע [אחרים] תחתיהן כדאמרן בחזקת הבתים (לעיל לו:) מיהו היזק גדול כל כך כגון [זה] שמכחיש לגמרי קרקע שלו לית ליה עין יפה [שם פב: ע"פ ב"ח].

עין משפט נר מצוה

עד א ב מיי' פי"ב מהל' טוען ונטען הל' יט ו ועיין בהשגות ובמ"מ סמג עשין לה טוש"ע ח"מ סי' קמא סעי' יז:

עה ג מיי' שם הל' ח ופכ"ד מהלכות מכירה הל' ט סמג שם טוש"ע שם סעיף יט וסי' רטו סעיף יג:

עו ד מיי' פכ"ד מהל' מכירה הלכה ח ועיין בהשגות ובמגיד משנה סמג עשין כב טוש"ע ח"מ סי' רטז סעי' יא יב [וכרב אלפס סוף פרק ר' דמכלתין דף קלג:]

רבינו גרשום

אבל אפיק ולא אכל. כי אם מעשרה לחודייהו לא הוי חזקה הני להם משום דמצי למימר ליה המערער הואיל שלא היית אוכל (א) לא הייתי מוחה: **והוא דבזאי בזויי.** כלומר היכא אמרינן כי לא אפיק דהני הוי חזקה להני היכא דלא אפיקו כל הני ל' בין כולהו אלא י' אילנות ולא בעינן ב) אותן שבבית סאה יחד אלא צריך דבזע בהו כגון דאפיק ג' בין עשרה בהאי בית סאה ובאידך בית סאה אפיק נמי ג' בתוך י' ובאידך שלישית אפיק ד' בין עשרה והיינו בזע בזויי שהוציא מתוך בית סאה זו לתוך בית סאה זו. ובאידך תרתי שנין ליפקי כי האי גוונא הנך דלא אפיק אשתכח דמצי למימר המחזיק אכלתי בכל שנה מכל בית סאה ואכלתים כולם בג' שנים ובדומיא דמתני' דקתני כנס את תבואתו ומסק את זיתיו וכנס את קייצו דמכולה אכל דהאי פירא הוי חזקה להאי ודמי כמאן דאכל מכולהו תלת זימני: **זה קנה אילנות וחצי קרקע.** מקום האילנות שאם מתייבשין האילן יכול לנטוע אחרים תחתיהן שאם לא היה לו כלום בקרקע היכא דייבשי היה יכול לומר לו עקור אילנך שקול וזיל אין לך שוב בקרקע כלום: **הא פשיטא לן מכר קרקע [ושייר אילנות לפניו] יש לו קרקע.** מקום האילנות: **ואפי' לר' עקיבא דאמר.** באידך פירקין דלקמן מכר את השדה לא מכר לו את הבור ולא את הדות וצריך ליקח לו דרך מן הלוקח לילך לבור ולדות משום דמוכר בעין יפה מוכר ומוכר לו כל השדה אפי' דרך של בורו: **הני מילי גבי בור ודות.** מש"ה מכר לו אפי' את הדרך דלא מכחשו בארעא דיכול לזרוע סמוך לבור ודות:

חשק שלמה על רבינו גרשום

א) נראה דל"ל שלא היית אוכל כל הפירות. ב) נ"ל ולא בעינן דלפיקו אותן י' שבבית סאה יחד אלא לריך וכו'.

וְזֶה קַרְקַע – **This** buyer **acquires the trees and half** of **the land,** קָנָה חֲצִי קַרְקַע – **and this** buyer **acquires half** of **the land.**[10] Thus, even if the trees die, their owner is entitled to plant others in their stead.[11]

The Gemara digresses to discuss instances where a man who owned a field with trees on it sold *either* the land *or* the trees and retained the other for himself:

פְּשִׁיטָא – The following law is **undisputed:** מָכַר קַרְקַע וְשִׁיֵּיר אִילָנוֹת לְפָנָיו – If **one sold** his **land and retained** the **trees** on it **for himself,**[12] יֵשׁ לוֹ קַרְקַע – the law is that **he has** a certain amount of **land** around the trees, and if the trees die, he is entitled to plant others.[13]

The Gemara defines the scope of this ruling:

וַאֲפִילוּ לְרַבִּי עֲקִיבָא – **And** this is so **even according to R' Akiva** דְּאָמַר מוֹכֵר בְּעַיִן יָפָה מוֹכֵר – **who says** that **a seller sells** property **generously.**[14] הָנֵי מִילֵּי גַּבֵּי בּוֹר וְדוּת – For **these words** of R' Akiva were said **regarding** a case in which the seller retains **a pit and a cistern,** דְּלָא מַכְחֲשׁוּ בְּאַרְעָא – **which do not impair the ground** around them.[15] In such a case, R' Akiva holds that the seller does not retain rights, for he is confident that the purchaser will not ask him to remove his pit.[16] אֲבָל אִילָנוֹת – **But** in the case discussed here, where he retains **trees,**

NOTES

10. "Half" in this context means merely a portion; namely, he acquires the ground under the trees and as much around them as is required for tending them [just as the law is when one purchases three trees from a seller who retains the land for himself]. Alternatively, the Gemara refers to a case in which the land sold was only as large as was needed to sustain the trees. In this case, the two buyers each receive half the land (*Rashbam*).

11. Rav Pappa holds that the tree owner acquires land even if he purchases only *two* trees, although the law is that one who purchases two trees from one seller who sells *only* the trees (but retains the land for himself) does not acquire any land at all. Below, the Gemara will explain that the logic of this is that the tree owner may tell the landowner, "Just as the seller sold you the land in a way that would allow you to retain it indefinitely, he likewise sold me the trees in a way that would allow me to retain them indefinitely. Thus, he meant to sell me the land surrounding the trees, so that if the trees die, I would be able to plant new ones to replace them" (*Rashbam*).

To summarize: Rav Zevid maintains that even if he purchases three trees, the tree owner does not acquire any land. Thus, if the trees die, he may not replant new ones. Rav Pappa, on the other hand, holds that even if he purchases only two trees, the tree owner acquires land around the trees. Consequently, he may replant new ones when the original ones die.

12. [Although the law is that one who purchases land automatically acquires the trees on it (as explained in note 6), this is only where no specific provisions for the trees were made at the time of the sale. Here, we discuss a case in which the seller states explicitly that he retains the trees for himself.]

13. This applies even if he retains only two trees, for even the Rabbis who hold (below) that one who *purchases* two trees does not acquire land with them agree that one who sells land and *retains* two trees retains enough land to allow himself to plant (and tend) new trees should the original ones die (*Rashbam*).

14. [Literally: with a good eye.] Below (64a, 71a), the Mishnah rules that a sale of a house or field does not include the pit or cistern located in its midst. Given this fact, R' Akiva and the Sages dispute whether the seller means to retain for himself a path to that pit. R' Akiva rules that one who sells does so generously; i.e. he means to sell the entire house or field, leaving himself no rights in it at all. Thus, the only way he can reach his pit is by purchasing a right-of-way from the new owner. The Sages, however, maintain that one who sells does so grudgingly, i.e. he retains for himself rights even if they impinge somewhat on the buyer's purchase. Hence, they hold that the seller retains a right-of-way through the buyer's property (*Rashbam*).

15. The pit or cistern do not in any way impinge upon the buyer's use of the field, since he can seed the ground around it (*Rashbam*).

16. Thus, as long as the buyers will not interfere with his use of the pit itself, he sells the field generously and does not retain even the right-of-way to the pit (*Rashbam*).

לאו מי אמר ר' ישמעאל חד פירא הוי חזקה לכולהו פירי הכא נמי הני הוו חזקה להני והני הוו חזקה להני [א] והני מילי היכא דלא אפיקו (א) אבל אפיקו ולא אכל לא הויא חזקה [ב] והוא דבאזי באזוזי: זה החזיק באילנות וזה החזיק בקרקע אמר רב זביד זה קנה אילנות וזה קנה קרקע מתקיף לה רב פפא אם כן אין לו לבעל אילנות בקרקע כלום לימא ליה בעל קרקע לבעל אילנות עקור אילנך שקול וזיל אלא אמר רב פפא [ג] זה קנה אילנות וחצי קרקע וזה קנה חצי קרקע: [ד] פשיטא מכר קרקע ושייר אילנות לפניו יש לו קרקע ואפילו לר' עקיבא דאמר [א] מוכר בעין יפה מוכר [ג] ה"מ גבי בור ודות דלא מכחשו בארעא אבל אילנות דקמכחשי

לאו מי אמר רבי ישמעאל חדא פירא הוי חזקה לכולהו פירי. (ג) דבמקום הזיתים מהני למקום התבואה והקיץ וכאילו החזיק בשלשתן דמי וכן כשכנס את תבואתו כמי שהחזיק בשלשתן דמי שמן הטעם הזה הוי חזקת שלש שנים בכל השדה אע"פ שלא החזיק בו בכולהו פעם אחת הכי נמי חזקת מקום י' אילנות של שנה ראשונה זו משוין כאילו החזיק נמי במקום העשרים וכן בשניה וכן בשלישית כאילו החזיק בכל שנה בג' אילנות: וה"מ. דהוי חזקה באכילת שלשים אילנות בג' שנים כה"ג היכא דלא אפיק אחריני כי העשרים לא עשו פירות כי אם עשרה לבד בכל שנה דומיא דרבי ישמעאל שמלקט כל מה שגדל בשדה ופירש ר"ח כגון בנות שוח שאין פירותיהם נגמרים עד ג' שנים: אבל אי אפיק. הני (ג) אילנות כולהו פירות בכל שנה ולא אכל אלא י' מינייהו לא הוי הני י' חזקה לכ' דכיון דלא אכל כל הפירות גילה על עצמו שהשדה אינה שלו וירא להחזיק חזקה גמורה ולפיכך לא חשש זה המערער למחות ולא הויא חזקה: והוא דבזאי בזויי. לשון בזיעה כלומר וה"מ דהוי חזקה כשאכל עשרה בכל שנה היינו ע"י פיזור שאכל ג' בכל בית סאה דנמצא מחזיק כל השדה אבל אכל י' אילנות ביחד בבית סאה (ד) זה ובשנה שניה כמו כן בבית סאה שני וכן בשלישית אינה חזקה דכל בית סאה חשוב שדה האילן בפני עצמו ושדה שלם לא הוי חזקה לשדה אחר והיינו נמי דומיא דרבי ישמעאל דכנס את תבואתו ומסק את זיתיו כו' שבכל השדה הוא אוכל דסתם שדה האילן על פני כולו מפוזרין הזיתים והדקלים: זה החזיק באילנות וזה החזיק בקרקע. שני לקוחות שלקחו שדה האילן מאדם אחד ביחד וכל הקרקע היה צריך לאילנות שהיו נטועים כדין שדה אילן והכי מתוקמא סוגיא דשמעתין לאחד מכר הקרקע ולאחד מכר האילנות והחזיק כל אחד בשלו כגון דרפק בה פורתא (ה) או עשה שום עבודת קרקע כל אחד בשלו דקרקע נקנה בכסף בשטר ובחזקה ולאו בחזקת ג' שנים מיירי והדיא מפרש לקמיה דבשני לקוחות מיירי: אמר רב זביד זה קנה אילנות. לפירותיהן בלא קרקע שאם יבשו האילנות לא יטע אחרים במקומן וזה קנה כל הקרקע אפי' אם יש שם ג' אילנות דתנן בהמוכר את הספינה (לקמן דף פא.) דקנה קרקע תחתיהם וביניהן וחוצה להן כמלא אורה וסלו ה"מ בלוקח אחד הקונה אילנות בתוך של חבירו דקנה קרקע אבל הכא בשני לקוחות שלוקחין ביחד זה אילנות וזה קרקע מצי אמר ליה בעל הקרקע לבעל האילנות כי היכי דלדידי לית לי באילנות לדידך נמי לית לך בקרקע והכי מפרש לקמיה: לימא ליה. כשייבש האילן עקור אילנך שקול וזיל ולא תטע אחר במקומו אבל כל זמן שהוא טוען פירות אינו יכול לומר כן ואע"ג דקרקע אין לו האילן (ו) כמות שהוא יונק מן הקרקע קנאו לפירותיו והכי נמי מוכח לקמן בשמעתא מדאמר ליה מר קשישא בריה דרב חסדא לרב אשי אי כורכמא ריסקא זבין ליה כו' ובהמוכר את הספינה (שם) נמי תנן הקונה ב' אילנות בתוך שדה חבירו הרי זה לא קנה קרקע כו' ואם מתו אין לו קרקע אלמא אע"ג דאין לו קרקע קתני ולא יעקרנו עד שימות וה"ה להא דרב זביד: זה קנה אילנות וחצי קרקע. לאו דוקא חצי קרקע אלא (ז) הצריך לאילנות תחתיהן וביניהן וחוצה להן כמלא אורה וסלו. אי נמי דוקא קאמר חצי וכגון שכל הקרקע צריך לאילנות אם לא מפני שמכר הקרקע לחבירו ואפילו לא הוו אלא ב' אילנות דקיימא לן בהמוכר את הספינה דאין להן קרקע הכא יש להן דכיון דשני לקוחות הן שקונין ביחד מצי אמר ליה בעל האילנות לבעל הקרקע כי היכי דלדידך בעין יפה זבין לדידי נמי כו' והכי מפרש לקמיה: מכר קרקע ושייר אילנות לפניו. אפי' אינן אלא ב' יש לו קרקע כדי מחיית האילנות וצורכן וגם אם יבשו יטע אחרים במקומן דודאי מוכר לעצמו שייר קרקע והכי אמרינן בהדיא בהמוכר את הבית (לקמן דף עא.) אמר רב הונא אע"ג דאמור רבנן הקונה ב' אילנות בתוך של חבירו הרי זה לא קנה קרקע מכר קרקע ושייר ב' אילנות לפניו יש לו קרקע: ואפי' לרבי עקיבא דאמר כו'. פלוגתא דרבי עקיבא ורבנן לקמן בהמוכר את הבית (דף סד.) בשני מקומות גבי מוכר את הבית תנן לא מכר את היציע כו' ולא את הבור ולא את הדות אע"ג דכתב לו עומקא ורומא וצריך ליקח לו דרך דברי רבי עקיבא דמוכר בעין יפה מוכר ולא שייר במכירתו כלום וחכמים אומרים אינו צריך ליקח לו דרך דמוכר בעין רעה מוכר וגבי מוכר את השדה תנן [ג] נמי הכי דאמרינן מוכר בעין יפה מוכר ולא שייר אל עצמו דרך ללכת אל בורו: ה"מ גבי בור ודות. הוא דקאמר ר' עקיבא דלא עיכב דרך לעצמו סביבות הבור כלום דלא מכחשי בארעא שיכול הלוקח לזרוע על שפתו ולא יעעק עליו הלוקח לעקור בורו מכאן דהא אינו מזיקו כלל הלכך לא אסיק מוכר אדעתיה לעכב לעצמו כלום מן הקרקע והלכך צריך ליקח ממנו דרך בדמים לילך אל בורו:

דקא

וכמה יהו (ט) לחוקים ממטע עשרה לבית סאה פחות מכאן או יותר על כן או שקנה בזה אחר זה לא קנה את הקרקע ולא את האילן שביניהם ובתר הכי קתני המקדיש הסיא דמייתי בהמוכר את הבית (לקמן דף עב.) ונראה דפחות מכאן דקתני גבי הקדש קאי נמי אכדי שיעבוד בקר וכליו ויותר מכאן קאי (ט) אלבית סאה כמו גבי מכר [ז] ולפי זה נמי ליכא למימר דאין חילוק בין חזקה למכר וסבר אביי כההיא ברייתא דתוספתא דהא אביי גופיה סבר כרב נחמן לקמן דאמר מח' ועד ששה עשר דא"ל אביי לרב יוסף לא תפלוג עליה דר"נ וא"ת ואי מדמינן מכר להקדש אם כן קשיא דר' שמעון אדר' שמעון דההיא דהמוכר את הבית מוקמינן לה כר' שמעון ובהמוכר את הספינה (לקמן דף פג.) אמר רבי מאיר ור' שמעון אומרים הנוטע את כרמו ח' על ח' מותר להביא זרע לשם אלמא חשיב ר' שמעון בח' אמות מפוזרים ומייתי התם ראיה מינה למכר אילנות ונראה לרשב"א דלא מוקי לה (י) בהמוכר את הבית (לקמן דף עב.) כרבי שמעון אלא במאי דקא סבר מקדיש בעין רעה הוא מקדיש אבל במאי דחשיב בח' אמות מפוזרים לא קיימא כוותיה:

היכא דלא אפיק. פי' ר"ח כגון בנות שוח שמשעה שנחנטו עד לקיטתן ג' שנים כדתנן (שביעית פ"ה מ"א) בנות שוח שביעית שלהן שניה פי' בשנה ב' של שמיטה לפי שאותן פירות שנלקטים בשנה ב' של שמיטה נחנטו בשביעית ואסורין כדין שביעית ולכך אוקמה ר"ח בבנות שוח דבשאר אילנות בחלף שנים לא יארע זה דבל' אילנות ילקו בשדפון ג' שנים ואותן שילקו בשנה זו לא ילקו בשנה זו ובזו בזויי [ה] וא"ת והיכי מצי מיירי בבנות שוח והא בריש פירקין אמרינן גבי חזקה בעינן דבעידנא דאיתיה להאי פירא ליתא להאי פירא והכא כשאכל פירות שנה ראשונה ושניה כבר נחנטו פירות שנת ג' וי"ל כיון שעדיין יש שנה עד גמר שלהן הוי שפיר בעידנא דאיתיה להאי פירא ליתא להאי פירא: זה החזיק באילנות כו'. פ"ה דלאו בחזקת ג' שנים איירי אלא שמכר לזה קרקע ולזה אילנות והחזיק כל אחד בשלו כגון דרפק בה פורתא ובעל אילנות פסחינהו כדאמר לקמן האי מאן דפסח דיקלא אדעתא דדיקלא קני וקשה לר"י דלא הוה ליה למיקבעיה אמתני' דהכא דאיירי בחזקת ג' שנים אלא לקמן גבי חזקות של קנין ועוד דלמאי נקט חזקה טפי משטר וכסף וחליפין הוה ליה למינקט מכר סתם כדנקט מכר בכולה סוגיא דבסמוך ונראה לר"י דאיירי בחזקת ג' שנים דלרב זביד זה קנה אילנות וזה קנה קרקע ואין לבעל אילנות בקרקע כלום ולכך כי יבשו לא יטע אחרים במקומן ורב פפא סבר דזה קנה אילנות וחצי קרקע פי' לא שיקנה בגוף הקרקע כלום שהרי זה החזיק בכל הקרקע אלא לענין שאם יתייבשו יטע אחרים במקומן. ומינה שמעי' בסמוך דמכר לזה אילנות ולזה קרקע דלרב זביד אין לבעל אילנות בקרקע כלום ליטע אחרים במקומן לכשיבשו ולרב פפא יש לו. דסברא הוא דאם מכר לזה אילנות ולזה קרקע בסתם קנה בעל אילנות הקרקע ליטע אחרים במקומן לכשיתייבשו גם חזקתו יש לו להועיל לענין זה:

לימא ליה בעל קרקע [לבעל אילנות] עקור אילנך שקול וזיל. פירוש לכשיתייבשו ואע"פ שכך הוא אמת לרב זביד מכל מקום פריך ליה רב פפא דאין סברא שידחוק אותו מיד לעקרו כשיבש כיון דג' אילנות מכר לו ועוד מאינו למימר עקור אילנך לאלתר קאמר והכי קשיא (כ) לרב פפא כיון דאפילו בג' אילנות אמרת דאין לו בקרקע כלום אע"ג דבעלמא בג' אילנות אית ליה קרקע משום דבשני לקוחות שאני (ל) וקאמר ליה כי היכי דלדידי לית לי באילנות הכי נמי לדידך לית לך בקרקע אי חשיב האי טעמא א"כ לאלתר נמי קודם שיבש לימא ליה עקור אילנך ואע"ג דבעלמא בחד לוקח בקנה שנים דלא קנה קרקע מ"מ יעמוד שם האילן עד שימות הכא גרע טפי מהאי טעמא דאית לך כי היכי דלדידי כו' אלא ודאי לית לך למימר האי טעמא הלכך כשמכר לזה קרקע ולזה אילנות בעל אילנות קנה מקום הגזע ליטע אחרים במקומן כשייבשו ומיירי בין בג' אילנות בין בב' כדפ"ה (מ) ואפילו בג' אין לו קרקע הצריך לאילנות [כיון] שפירש בהדיא לזה קרקע ואפי' בב' אילנות כשיבשו יטע אחרים במקומן משום כי היכי דלדידך בעין יפה זבין כו':

דלאי

עד א ב מיי' פי"ב מהל' טוען ונטען הל' יג ל ועיין בהשגות ובמ"מ סמג עשין לה טוש"ע ח"מ סי' קמא סעי' יז:
עה ג מיי' שם הל' יז ופכ"ד מהלכות מכירה הל' ט סמג שם טוש"ע שם סעיף יט וסי' רטז סעיף יג:
עו ד מיי' פכ"ד מהל' מכירה הלכה ח ועיין בהשגות ובמגיד משנה סמג עשין כב טוש"ע ח"מ סי' רטז סעי' יא יב [וברב אלפס סוף פרק ד' דמכילתין דף קלג:]:

רבינו גרשום

אבל אפיק ולא אכל. כי אם מעשרה לחודייהו **לא הוי חזקה** הני להם משום דמצי למימר ליה המערער הואיל שלא היית אוכל א) לא הייתי מוחה: **והוא דבזאי בזויי.** כלומר היכא אמרינן כי לא אפיקי דהני הוי חזקה להני היכא דלא אפיקו כל הני ל' בין כולהו אלא י' אילנות ולא בעינן ב) אותן שבבית סאה יחד אלא צריך דבזע בהו כגון דאפיק ג' בין עשרה בהאי בית סאה ובאידך בית סאה אפיק נמי ג' בתוך י' ובבית סאה שלישית אפיק ד' בין עשרה והיינו בזע בזועי שהוציא מתוך בית סאה זו לתוך בית סאה זו. ובאידך תרתין שנין ליפקי כי האי גוונא הנך דלא אפיקו אשתקד דמצי למימר המחזיק אכלתי בכל שנה מכל בית סאה ואכלתים כולם בג' שנים ובדומיא דמתני' דקתני כנס את תבואתו ומסק את זיתיו וכנס את קייצו דמכולה אכל דהאי פירא הוי חזקה להאי ודמי כמאן דאכל מכולהו תלת זימני: **זה קנה אילנות וחצי קרקע.** מקום האילנות שאם מתייבשין הללו יכול לנטוע אחרים תחתיהן שאם לא היה כלום בקרקע היכא דייבשי היה יכול לומר לו עקור אילנך שקול וזיל אין לך שוב בקרקע כלום: **הא פשיטא לן מכר קרקע [ושייר אילנות לפניו] יש לו קרקע.** מקום האילנות: **ואפי' לר' עקיבא דאמר.** באידך פירקין דלקמן מכר את השדה לא מכר לו את הבור ולא את הדות וצריך ליקח לו דרך מן הלוקח לילך לבור ולדות משום **דמוכר בעין יפה מוכר** ומוכר לו כל השדה אפי' דרך של בורו: **הני מילי גבי בור ודות.** משה"כ מכר לו אפי' את הדרך **דלא מכחשו בארעא** דיכול לזרוע סמוך לבור ודות:

חשק שלמה
על רבינו גרשום

א) נראה דצ"ל שלא היית אוכל כל הפירות. ב) צ"ל ולא בעינן דלאפיקו אותן י' שבבית סאה יחד אלא צריך וכו'.

א) [לקמן מד: סה: עא. עב. פב:], ב) [לקמן עא. פב:], ג) [לקמן עא.], ד) ולפירוש רש"ל, ה) [וע' תוס' בכורות ח. ד"ה בנות].

הגהות הב"ח

(א) גמרא דלא אפיקו אחריני אבל לא אפיקו אחריני ולא אכל: (ב) רשב"ם ד"ה לאו מי וכו' דבמקום הזיתים וכו' שלא החזיק בו בכולהו כי אם פעם אחת וכו' בכל שנה בכל אילנות דמי הס"ד: (ג) ד"ה אבל אי אפיק הני כל שלשים אילנות: (ד) ד"ה והוא דבזאי וכו' בבית סאה זה ובשנה: (ה) ד"ה זה החזיק וכו' דרפק בה פורתא וכו' ובעל האילנות פסחינהו או עשה: (ו) ד"ה לימא וכו' האילן יש לו כמות שהוא יונק מן הקרקע שהרי קנאו לפירותיו: (ז) ד"ה זה קנה וכו' לא קרקע הצריך לאילנות: (ח) תוס' ד"ה (בדף הקודם) ממטע וכמה יהו מרוחקים ממטע עשרה: (ט) בא"ד ויותר מכאן קאי אעשר לבית סאה כמו מכר ולפי זה נמי: (י) בא"ד ונראה לרשב"א דלא מוקי לה ההיא דהמוכר את הבית כרבי שמעון אלא: (כ) ד"ה לימא וכו' והכי קשיא ליה לרב פפא: (ל) בא"ד דקאמר ליה כי היכי: (מ) בא"ד כדפי' לפילו בג':

ליקוטי רש"י

זה החזיק באילנות. ממאלא לא קנה קרקע סביביו כלל ואפי' מקום האילן ונוף קנאו לפירותיו שכשייבש יעקרנו וילך [רשב"ם לקמן פא.]. **מוכר בעין יפה מוכר.** בכל דיני מכירות שבעולם [שם סד:]. **ה"מ גבי בור ודות.** גבי מכר את הבית ושייר בור ודות דלית ליה שום היזק ללוקח דלא מכחשי בארעא והלכך לא חשש לשייר כלום מן הקרקע סביב הבור ולא הלוקח אבל אילנות שמכחשין את הקרקע שייר מן הקרקע עם האילנות אף לחזור וליטע במקומן אם יקינו אלו משום דלא לימא ליה לוקח עקור אילנך כשימות [שם עא.]. **דלא מכחשו בארעא.** לא הבור ולא הדרך שאינו נוטע לו הלכך יכול למכור בעין יפה וזבין ניחא ליה לי דלך. **אבל אילנות דקמכחשי.** דנהי נמי דאית ליה עין יפה גבי אילן במכר אילנות ושייר קרקע לפניו שיש לו קרקע לרבי עקיבא על מנת ליטע [אחרים] מתחתיהן כדאמרן בחזקת הבתים (לעיל לז.) מיהו היזק גדול לו כגון [זה] שמאבדך לגמרי קרקע שלו לית ליה עין יפה [שם סב: ע"ש ב"ח].

עין משפט
נר מצוה

מסורת הש"ס

דקמכחשי בארעא שיורי שייר דאי לא שייר לימא ליה עקור (א) אילנא וזיל מכר אילנות ושייר קרקע לפניו פלוגתא דר"ע ורבנן לר"ע דאמר מוכר בעין יפה מוכר [א] אית ליה לרבנן לית ליה לר"ע אית ליה ואפילו לרב זביד דאמר אין לו ה"מ גבי שני לקוחות דא"ל כי היכי דלדידי לית לי באילנות לדידך נמי לית לך בקרקע אבל הכא מוכר בעין יפה מוכר לרבנן לית ליה ואפילו לרב פפא דאמר יש לו ה"מ גבי שני לקוחות דא"ל כי היכי דלדידך זבין בעין יפה לדידי נמי זבין בעין יפה אבל הכא מוכר בעין רעה מוכר אמרי נהרדעי אכלן רצופין אין לו חזקה [ב] מתקיף לה רבא אלא מעתה האי מישרא דאספסתא במאי קני לה אלא אמר רבא [ג] מכרן רצופין אין לו קרקע א"ר זירא כתנאי א) כרם שהוא נטוע על פחות מארבע אמות ר' שמעון אומר אינו כרם וחכ"א [ד] הרי זו כרם ורואין את האמצעיים כאילו אינן ב) אמרי נהרדעי האי מאן דזבין דקלא לחבריה קני ליה משפוליה עד תהומא מתקיף

דקא מכחשי. השרשים בקרקע וגם מעכבין את המחרישה ודאי אסיק אדעתיה לשייר לעצמו קרקע סביבות האילנות כדי שלא יוכל הלוקח לערער עליו ולומר כשיבשו אילנותיך עקור אילנותיך שקול וזיל דהא מזקי לארעאי: **לימא ליה.** כשייבש האילן: **מכר אילנות ושייר קרקע לפניו.** שפירש לו כן האילנות אני מוכר לך והקרקע אני מעכב לעצמי: **פלוגתא דר"ע ורבנן.** בין לרב זביד בין לרב פפא ובשני אילנות מיירי דבשלשה אילנות הכל מודים דקנה קרקע כדתנן סתמא בהמוכר את הספינה (לקמן דף פא.) ומוקמינן לה בגמ' כר"ע ומיהו רישא דקתני גבי שנים אין לו קרקע לאו ר"ע היא כדמוכח בשילהי המוכר את הבית (לקמן דף עב.) והתם פרשינן לה: **לר"ע דאמר מוכר בעין יפה מוכר אית לי'.** ללוקח מקום האילנות על הקרקע ליטע אחרים במקומן כשימותו: **לרבנן אין לו.** קרקע ואם ימותו לא יטע אחרים במקומן כדתנן סתמא הקונה שני אילנות לא קנה קרקע: **אפי' לרב זביד כו'.** כלומר לרב זביד נמי מצי למימר אליבא דר"ע ולא הויא מילתיה כתנאי אלא כדברי הכל: **ה"מ.** דקאמר רב זביד אין לו קרקע גבי ב' לקוחות כדפרישית לעיל: **לית לי באילנות.** לא בעצים ולא בפירות: **לית לך בקרקעות.** אפי' במקום האילן וכשייבש תעקרנו ותלך: **ה"מ.** דיש לו (ג) קרקעות: **גבי שני לקוחות דאמר.** בעל האילנות לבעל הקרקע כי היכי דלדידך זבין בעין יפה מה שמכר לך מן הקרקע על מנת להיות הקרקע שלך עולמית היא ופירותיה: **אף לדידי זבין בעין יפה.** שאוכל פירות אילנותי לעולם שאם ימותו אטע אחרים תחתיהן דאין אדם חוטא ולא לו למכור לזה בעין יפה ולזה בעין רעה: **אבל הכא.** שעיכב לעצמו כל לגבי עצמו בעין רעה מוכר כדי לשייר לעצמו: **אכלן רצופין.** להני שלשים אילנות כגון שנטועין ט"ו בבית סאה אינה חזקה ואפילו אכלן כולן כל שלש שנים דלא אחזיק כדמחזקי אינשי דאין ראוין לקיים (ג) אלא לעקור ולשרש: **מתקיף לה רבא אלא מעתה.** כיון דמשום דנטועין מחוברין לא הויא חזקה: **האי מישרא.** ערוגה דאספסתא במאי קני לה הרי (ד) זרועה רצופה ואפ"ה אמרי' בריש פירקין דהוי חזקה ומיהו לאו אתקפתא מעליתא היא דהאי אורחיה והאי לאו אורחיה האי מכחיש בארעא טפי והאי לא מכחיש טפי אלא רבא הוא דלית ליה האי סברא ובמילתא בעלמא הוא דמוקי להו לנהרדעי. ויש לפרש אכלן רצופין אינה חזקה שסופן לשרש אותן ולפזר נטיעתן שכן דרך אילנות לנטוע הרבה תחלה ביחד ואחר שגדלו מפזרים אותן הלכך לא הוי חזקה הואיל ולשרש קיימי ואין זו עיקר גידולן וראיה לדבר דגבי נטיעות אשכחן י' לבית סאה ובאילנות אמרו ג' לבית סאה ועל כרחך נטיעות היו מתחלה והיו י' לבית סאה ואח"כ מיעטום לג' בבית סאה וכן דרך אספסתא כמו כן לזרעה הרבה ביחד רצופין כמו שעושין לכרישין וכרוב ואח"כ עוקרין אותן וממלא מהן ערוגה גדולה והיינו דפריך רבא אלא מעתה האי מישרא דאספסתא כו' כן נראה בעיני: **אלא אמר רבא.** אי אית לן למימר מידי ברצופין הכי אמרינן: **מכרן רצופין אין לו קרקע.** כגון שנטועין יותר מי' בבית סאה דהכא לא אמרי' הקונה שלשה אילנות קנה קרקע דאין זה שדה האילן דלעקור ולשרש קיימא: **על פחות מד' אמות.** שאין בין שורה לשורה אלא ג' אמות אינו כרם והמביא זרע לשם אינו לוקה משום לא תזרע כרמך כלאים (דברים כב) ומותרין באכילה: **האמצעיים.** שורה בין שתי שורות רואין כאילו אינה והוו להו שש אמות בין שורה לשורה ולעיל נמי גבי מכרן רצופין לרבנן רואין את האמצעיים כאילו אינן ודינן כמפוזרין וגבי מכרן רצופין יש לו קרקע ולר"ש אין לו קרקע והיינו כתנאי דמילתא דרבא תנאי היא כר"ש ודלא כרבנן ובהמוכר את הספינה (לקמן פב:) מפרש כמה יהו מרוחקין יותר מד' אמות ואכתי הוי כרם: **קני ליה.** הלוקח לקרקע: **משיפולא עד תהומא.** שוליו (שמות כח) מתרגמינן שיפולוהי כלומר כל הקרקע (ה) בשולי האילן דהיינו שפת הקרקע עד תהום של קרקע שאע"פ שדקל יחידי הוא ותנן דאפי' ב' אין לו קרקע ה"מ סביבות האילן הוא דאין לו כלום כמו שיש לג' ביניהן וחוצה להן כמלא אורה וסלו אבל תחתיו דאילן מיהא אית ליה דכיון דאילן לפירותיו קונה להתקיים מקרקע זו גם אם ימות האילן יטע אחר במקומו ואשמעינן נמי דאין בעל השדה יכול לחפור תחת האילן אפילו למטה מאלף אמה:
מתקיף

דאי לא מצי למימר ליה עקור אילנך שקול וזיל. פירוש לכשייבש ובלאו טעמא דמכחשי ארעא אי לא משייר מצי א"ל עקור אילנך דעל כרחו לא יעכב האילן בשדהו ועוד שרוצה לזרוע מקום האילן: **מכר** אילנות ושייר קרקע. פ"ה דבב' אילנות איירי דבג' הכל מודין דקנה קרקע כדתנן בהמוכר את הספינה (לקמן דף פא.) ומוקי לה בגמ' כרבנן ודחי ומוקי לה אפי' כר"ע ולפי זה רישא דקתני שנים אין לו קרקע לא אתי כר"ע וכן מוכח בסוף המוכר את הבית (שם דף עב. ושם) דקתני הקדיש ג' אילנות ממטע י' לבית סאה כו' בזה אחר זה או שהקדיש את הקרקע ופריך (ו) מיניה אליבא דר' עקיבא דאמר מוכר בעין יפה מוכר וכ"ש מקדיש פי' ואמאי בזה אחר זה לא הקדיש את הקרקע אלמא משמע דקנה אילן אחד נמי קנה קרקע ואין נראה לר"י דהא כיון דהא דתנן בהמוכר את הספינה (שם דף פא.) קנה ג' קנה קרקע מוקי נמי כר"ע א"כ ע"כ לר"ע בשנים לא קנה קרקע דהכי משמע דוקא ג' קנה קרקע אבל ב' לא קנה קרקע לכך יש לפרש להא דשמעתין בג' אילנות ואע"ג דבעלמא בג' קנה קרקע שאני הכא דמיירי כגון שאין שם קרקע אלא לצורך האילנות ופירש בהדיא שמשייר הקרקע לעצמו (ז) או בשדה גדול ואומר בפירוש שכל הקרקע משייר ולכ"ע לא קנה בגוף הקרקע כלום אלא למ"ד מוכר בעין יפה מוכר יכול ליטע אחר במקומו כשייבש והיא דהמוכר את הבית ה"פ מני אילימא ר"ע ואליבא דרבנן דר"ש דסבירא להו מקדיש בעין יפה הוא מקדיש הא אמר מוכר בעין יפה הוא מוכר וכל שכן מקדיש ואלא רבנן ואליבא דרבנן דר' שמעון דאמרו במקדיש הקדיש את כולן הרי אומר מוכר בעין רעה מוכר אבל מקדיש בעין יפה מקדיש וכיון דסבירא להו דכולי האי מקדיש בעין יפה (ח) ממכר דאפי' בור ודות שאין הקרקע צריך להם הקדיש כ"ש במקדיש את האילן שהקדיש את הקרקע הצריכה לאילן ואע"ג דבמכר לא מכר את הקרקע ומיהו ההיא דבתר הכי אי אפשר לפרש כן [דקאמר] אלא פשיטא ר"ש ואליבא דמאן אילימא אליבא דר"ע הא אמר מוכר בעין יפה מוכר כ"ש מקדיש ומ"מ יש לפרש בדוחק דפריך מסברא כיון דמוכר בעין יפה מוכר אית לן למימר דמקדיש כל שכן דיותר מעט בעין יפה מקדיש ובאילן אחד נמי הקדיש המקדיש את הקרקע אע"ג דבמכר לא קנה ועוד יש לפרש דלא מכח הקדש זה אחר זה דייק התם דבעין רעה מקדיש אלא דייק מדקתני הקדיש שלשה אילנות ממטע י' לבית סאה הרי זה הקדיש את הקרקע כולה לפיכך כשהוא פודה פודה לפי בית זרע חומר שעורים כו' ואי ס"ל דבעין יפה מקדיש אע"פ שהקדיש את הקרקע ואת האילנות בבת אחת הו"ל למימר דפודה וחוזר ופודה תחלה את האילנות בשויין וחוזר ופודה את הקרקע לפי בית זרע חומר שעורים כדאמר רב הונא בפרק יש בערכין (ערכין דף יד.) הקדיש שדה מלאה אילנות כשהוא פודה פודה את האילן בשוויו וחוזר ופודה קרקע לפי בית זרע חומר שעורים בחמשים שקל כסף אלמא סבר רב הונא מקדיש כו' איתיביה ר"נ לרב הונא ופריך ליה מברייתא דהמוכר את הבית ומשני הא מני ר"ש היא דאמר בעין רעה הוא מקדיש והשתא מדקדק לקמן בפשיטות דכולה סוגיא דלקמן אליבא דרב הונא קיימא לטעמיה (ט) דאמרי' במס' ערכין (שם) בעין יפה הוא מקדיש: **אינו** כרם. ואין צריך להרחיק זרע ד' אמות אלא שלשה טפחים כעין (י) כרם יחידי ולענין מי שנטע כרם ולא חיללו דאינו חוזר מן המלחמה:
קני

עז א מיי' פכ"ד מהל' מכירה הל' ט סמג עשין פב טוש"ע ח"מ סי' רטז סעי' ו ובהג"ה:
עח ב מיי' פי"ג מהל' טוען הלכה א ועיין במ"מ סמג עשין לה טוש"ע ח"מ סי' קמא סעיף א וסעיף יח:
עט ג מיי' פכ"ד מהל' מכירה הלכה ג סמג עשין פב טוש"ע ח"מ סי' רטז סעיף ז:
פ ד מיי' פ"ז מהל' כלאים הלכה ג ע"ש בכ"מ סמג לאוין רפ טוש"ע י"ד סי' רצו סעיף לג:

רבינו גרשום

אבל אילנות דמכחשו בארעא. שרשים ואין יכול לזרוע תחתיהם מפני שענפין מעכבין מימי המטר שלא ירד עליהן כיון דקא מכחשי ודאי **שייר** לעצמו מקום האילנות: **לר' עקיבא.** מכר לו נמי מקום האילנות **ואפילו לרב זביד דאמר** לעיל להיכא דמכר לשנים שדהו זה החזיק באילנות וזה החזיק בקרקע **אין לו** לבעל האילנות כלל בקרקע. **הני מילי גבי שני לקוחות** דהאי טעין לי מכר הקרקע והאי טעין לי מכר האילנות משום הכי אין לו **דמצי למימר** לו בעל הקרקע לבעל האילנות **כי היכי דלדידי כו'. אבל הכא** להיכא דמכר אילנותיו לחד ושייר בקרקע לפניו ודאי מודה רב זביד דיש לו קרקע מקום אילנות **דמוכר בעין יפה מוכר. ורבנן** דמפלגי על ר' עקיבא סברי **לית ליה ואפי' לרב פפא דאמר** לעיל **יש לו הני מילי גבי שני לקוחות דמצי למימר ליה** בעל האילנות לבעל הקרקע **כי היכי דלדידך בעין יפה מכר** דלא שייר קרקע לפניו **לדידי נמי בעין יפה מכר** לי מקום האילנות. **אבל הכא** היכא דשייר קרקע לפניו **מוכר בעין רעה מוכר** ולא גמר ומקנה ליה מקום האילנות: **אכלן.** הני אילנות **רצופין.** כגון שהיו נטועין בבית סאה אחת ט"ו אילנות דדינייהו להיות י' ותו לא. **אינה חזקה** דמצי למימר ליה מערער לא החזקת כשאר חיזוקין של אחרים: **האי** שדה נטועה **מישרא דאספסתא.** ערוגה מלאה אספסתא שרצופין הן זה עם זה **במאי קני ליה: מכרן רצופין.** שהיו נטועין יותר ממטע עשרה לבית סאה **אין לו** ללוקח **קרקע** דחשוב הוא כיער מה יער לא מכר אלא לעצים האי נמי לא מכר אלא לעצים: **שדה כרם הנטוע על פחות מד' אמות** דבין גפנה לגפנה ליכא ד' אמות כדי עבודת הכרם **אינו כרם** ומותר להביא זרע אחר לשם ואינו עובר. **וחכ"א הרי זה כרם ודומין הגפנים אמצעים כאינן** הכא נמי סבירא להו לחכמים שרואין אותן שעודפין על מטע י' לבית סאה כאילו אינן ומכר לו את הקרקע ור' שמעון ס"ל כרבא והיינו כתנאי: **משיפולי** אילן. היינו מקום תפישת השרשין **ועד התהום** כל אותו קרקע מכר לו והיינו מדה בינונית של אילן דאי אמרינן קנה בקרקע ברוחב הענפים היינו יותר מדאי ואי אמרינן לא קנה אלא כנגד עובי קורות האילן היינו מעט יותר מדאי אבל משיפוליה היינו יותר מעובי קורת האילן ופחות מרוחב הענפים ובהכי סגי ליה בקרקע:

א) כלאים פ"ה מ"ג עירובין ג: לקמן פג. קב., ב) ערכין יד ע"ב:

הגהות הב"ח

(א) גמ' עקור אילנך שקול וזיל: (ב) רשב"ם ד"ה ה"מ דיש לו קרקע: (ג) ד"ה אכלן וכו' לקיים כן אלא: (ד) ד"ה האי מישרא וכו' הרי זו זרועה רצופה וכו' ואחר שגדלו קצת מפזרים: (ה) ד"ה משיפולא וכו' כל הקרקע משולי האילן: (ו) תום' ד"ה מכר וכו' ופריך מני אילימא ר"ע: (ז) בא"ד או בשדה גדול נ"ב פי' בשדה שיש בו שלשה אילנות דיש לו קרקע מ"מ כשאמר בהדיא דמשייר הקרקע ותנאי זה לא בעינן דבלא תנאי נמי אין לו יותר מתחתיהן לפיכך כשהתנה ושייר לעצמו לטפויי אתי ושייר לעצמו אף תחתיהן וכן אלל דרך ואלל ע"מ שהדיוטא עליונה שלי בפ' המוכר את הבית דף סג וסד איתא דתנאי שלא לצורך לטפויי מילתא אתי: (ח) בא"ד בעין יפה טפי ממכר דאפילו וכו' כ"ש במקדיש אילן כצ"ל ותיבת את נמחק: (ט) בא"ד לטעמיה דאמר במסכת ערכין: (י) ד"ה אינו וכו' כעין גפן יחידי וכו' מן מערכי המלחמה:

ליקוטי רש"י

אם איתא דלא שייר כו'. ואנן סהדי דלדעת כן עיכב את האילנות לעצמו שיהיו כאן לעולם אף לחזור וליטע אחרים במקומן כדרך שהיה לו כח זה באילנות הללו עד עכשיו אבל לוקח אילנות אין לומר לצורך כל הימים לקחו וליטע אחרים במקומן דעביד איניש דזבין ארעא ליומיה ולפירות קנאו [רשב"ם לקמן עא:]. **מכרן רצופין.** אם נטועין בפחות ממטע עשרה לבית סאה או ביותר מיכן אין זה סדר נטיעת אילנות [ערכין יד.]. **כרם שהוא נטוע על פחות מארבע אמות.** שאין בין שורה לשורה ארבע אמות אינו כרם ומותר לזרוע לשם [עירובין ג:]. **אינו כרם.** אלא יער ומותר בכלאים [רשב"ם שם]. **וחכ"א וכו' ורואין את האמצעיים.** הנטועין בתוך ריוח הראוי להיות בין שורה לשורה [עירובין שם]. דכל העומד ליעקר כעקור דמי ומותרא היא גבי כלאים [רשב"ם שם]. **קני ליה משיפוליה.** מקום מושב האילן עד תהומו [ערכין יד.].

דְּקַמְכַחְשֵׁי בְּאַרְעָא – which impair the ground,[1] שִׁיּוּרֵי שַׁיֵּיר – even R' Akiva agrees that **he leaves over** some land for himself.[2] דְּאִי לֹא שַׁיֵּיר – For the seller worries that **if he does not leave over** any land for himself, לֵימָא לֵיהּ – **[the buyer] might say to him,** should one of the trees die, עֲקוֹר אִילָנָא וְזִיל – **"Uproot** your **tree and be gone!"**[3] Thus, all agree that the seller reserves land around the trees for himself.

The Gemara now discusses the opposite case in which the owner of a field with trees on it sold the trees but kept the land:

מָכַר אִילָנוֹת – If **one sold trees,** וְשִׁייֵּר קַרְקַע לְפָנָיו – **but retained the land for himself,** פְּלוּגְתָּא דְּרַבִּי עֲקִיבָא וְרַבָּנָן – the law is the subject of **a dispute between R' Akiva and the Rabbis.**[4] לְרַבִּי עֲקִיבָא – **According to R' Akiva,** דְּאָמַר מוֹכֵר בְּעַיִן יָפָה מוֹכֵר – **who says that a seller sells** property **generously,** אִית לֵיהּ – **[the buyer] has** land under the trees, and therefore may replant new ones.[5] לְרַבָּנָן – **According to the Rabbis,** however, who maintain that a seller sells property grudgingly, לֵית לֵיהּ – **[the buyer] does not have** any land and therefore may not replant new ones.[6]

The Gemara explains that this dispute is unrelated to the dispute above between Rav Zevid and Rav Pappa:[7]

לְרַבִּי עֲקִיבָא אִית לֵיהּ – **According to R' Akiva, [the buyer] has** land under the trees. וַאֲפִילּוּ לְרַב זְבִיד – **And** this is true **even according to Rav Zevid,** דְּאָמַר אֵין לוֹ – **who says that** when one person buys the trees and another the land, **[the buyer of the trees] does not have** any land. הָנֵי מִילֵּי גַּבֵּי שְׁנֵי לְקוּחוֹת – For **[Rav Zevid's] ruling** was said only **with regard to** a case of **two buyers,** דְּאָמַר לֵיהּ – **for** in that case **[the buyer of the land] may say to [the buyer of the trees],** כִּי הֵיכִי דִּלְדִידִי לֵית לִי בְּאִילָנוֹת – **"Just as I have no share in the trees,**[8] לְדִידָךְ נַמִּי לֵית לָךְ בְּקַרְקַע – **so you have no share in the land."**[9] אֲבָל הָכָא – **But here** where a single purchaser buys trees situated on the seller's land, מוֹכֵר בְּעַיִן יָפָה מוֹכֵר – Rav Zevid could agree that **the seller sells generously,** and includes in the sale enough land to allow the buyer to plant new trees.[10]

The Gemara explains that the Rabbis' ruling, as well, is unrelated to the previous dispute:

לְרַבָּנָן לֵית לֵיהּ – **According to the Rabbis, [the buyer] does not have** land under the trees. וַאֲפִילּוּ לְרַב פָּפָּא – **And** this is true **even according to Rav Pappa,** דְּאָמַר יֵשׁ לוֹ – **who says** that when one person buys trees and another buys the land, **[the buyer of the trees] does have** land. הָנֵי מִילֵּי גַּבֵּי שְׁנֵי לְקוּחוֹת – For **[Rav Pappa's] ruling** was said only **with regard to** a case of **two buyers,** דְּאָמַר לֵיהּ – **for** in that case **[the buyer of the trees] may say to [the buyer of the land],** כִּי הֵיכִי דִּלְדִידָךְ זַבִּין בְּעַיִן יָפָה – **"Just as he sold** the land **to you generously,**[11] לְדִידִי נַמִּי זַבִּין בְּעַיִן יָפָה – **so he sold** the trees **to me generously."**[12] אֲבָל הָכָא – **But here** where a single purchaser buys trees situated on the seller's land, מוֹכֵר בְּעַיִן רָעָה מוֹכֵר – Rav Pappa might agree that **the seller sells grudgingly**[13] and does not include any land in the sale.

The Gemara cites a related ruling:

אָמְרֵי נְהַרְדְּעֵי – **The Nehardeans say:** אֲכָלָן רְצוּפִין – If **[the occupant] harvested [the thirty trees mentioned above],**[14] in a case in which they were planted too **densely,**[15] אֵין לוֹ חֲזָקָה – **he does not establish a** ***chazakah*** on the land. Since the trees will eventually have to be uprooted and replanted elsewhere, using them as they stand now is not considered a proper use of the land.[16]

NOTES

1. I.e. the roots weaken the surrounding soil and also impede the progress of a plow drawn through the field (*Rashbam*).

2. I.e. in this case even R' Akiva agrees that he sells only grudgingly (*Rashbam*).

3. Hence, although he is generous as far as what he sells, he does want the perpetual use of what he retains. Thus, he worries that should his trees die, the buyer would restrain him from planting new ones and he would be left with nothing! Consequently, he retains for himself the area around the trees, for in this way the buyer cannot stop him from replanting (*Rashbam*).

4. As explained above, 37a note 6, three or more trees legally constitute a tree field, and their sale automatically includes the land under and between them plus as much land around them as is needed to harvest their fruit. Two trees, however, do not constitute a tree field, and their sale is the subject of this dispute (*Rashbam;* cf. *Tosafos*).

5. Since according to R' Akiva a seller is understood to be generous in the transfer of property, we assume that he means to include in the sale the space that the trees occupy, so that the buyer will be entitled to plant new trees if the original ones die (*Rashbam*). [However, R' Akiva does not mean to equate the law for the sale of two trees with that of the sale of three. In the latter case, the entire area under, between and around the trees is included in the sale, because the seller is deemed to have sold a field of trees rather than merely three individual ones. In the former case, the seller sells no more land than is necessary to allow the buyer to replant the trees if they should die, for even R' Akiva concedes that two trees do not constitute a field of trees (see *Rashbam* here, and below, 71a ד״ה ה״ז and 72a ד״ה אילימא).]

6. As explained above on 37a note 6, a seller is assumed to sell his property only grudgingly, and therefore means to retain for himself all that he can. Thus, he does not sell any land along with the trees. Therefore, if the trees should die, the buyer may not replant new ones.

7. A superficial study of the two disputes would seem to indicate that they parallel each other. Rav Zevid, who holds that the tree owner acquires no land, seems to be following the view of the Rabbis, while Rav Pappa, who holds that the tree owner does receive a certain amount of land, seems to agree with R' Akiva. However, the Gemara will proceed to explain that Rav Zevid can concur even with R' Akiva, and Rav Pappa even with the Rabbis.

8. Although ordinarily one who purchases land automatically acquires the trees that are on it, as explained on 37a note 6 (see *Rashba* to 37a).

9. The force of the landowner's argument is this: I would ordinarily acquire the trees with my purchase of the land. Here, though, the fact that the seller sold them to you clearly shows that they were not included in my purchase. Likewise, then, the fact that the seller sold the land to *me* shows that no land was included in *your* purchase of the trees. Hence, even if the tree owner bought three trees (whose sale ordinarily includes some land), he acquires no land at all (ibid.).

10. However, in the case of the two buyers, we cannot assume that the seller was generous and included land along with his sale of the trees, for such "generosity" would be at the land buyer's expense! This is unlike R' Akiva's case in which the seller retains the field for himself. There, the seller can afford to sell generously, for his generosity is at his own expense (see *Rashbam* below, 65a ד״ה שניהם).

11. I.e. in a manner that allows you to retain the land and its yield forever (*Rashbam*).

12. I.e. in a manner that allows me to retain the use of my trees forever. Thus, the seller meant to include some land in the sale of the trees so that I could replant them if they die. The assumption that a seller sells grudgingly has application only where doing so allows the seller to retain property or rights for *himself.* Here, though, there is no reason to assume that the seller limited the scope of the tree owner's purchase just to benefit the landowner (*Rashbam*).

13. Literally: a seller sells with a bad eye.

14. 36b.

15. Instead of the normal ratio of ten saplings per *beis se'ah* (see above, 36b), the field contained, for example, fifteen (*Rashbam;* cf. *Rif*).

16. [Normally, a *chazakah* is established in a field by harvesting its fruits. This only applies, however, when the fruit is considered the *produce* of the field. If, however, a field was used merely to *store* grain on it, and that grain was consumed, no *chazakah* is established.] Now, trees were commonly planted in close proximity when young, and

דקמכחשי בארעא שיורי שייר דאי לא שייר לימא ליה עקור (א) אילנא וזיל מכר אילנות ושייר קרקע לפניו פלוגתא דר"ע ורבנן לר"ע דאמר מוכר בעין יפה מוכר [א]אית ליה לרבנן לית ליה לר"ע אית ליה ואפילו לרב זביד דאמר אין לו ה"מ גבי שני לקוחות דא"ל כי היכי דלדידי לית לי באילנות לדידך נמי לית לך בקרקע אבל הכא מוכר בעין יפה מוכר לרבנן לית ליה ואפילו לרב פפא דאמר יש לו ה"מ גבי שני לקוחות דא"ל כי היכי דלדידך זבין בעין יפה לדידי נמי זבין בעין יפה אבל הכא מוכר בעין רעה מוכר אמרי נהרדעי אכלן רצופין אין לו חזקה [ב]מתקיף לה רבא אלא מעתה האי מישרא דאספסתא במאי קני לה אלא אמר רבא [ג]מכרן רצופין אין לו קרקע א"ר זירא כתנאי [א] כרם שהוא נטוע על פחות מארבע אמות ר' שמעון אומר אינו כרם וחכ"א [ד]הרי זו כרם ורואין את האמצעיים כאילו אינן [ג] אמרי נהרדעי האי מאן דזבין דקלא לחבריה קני ליה משיפוליה עד תהומא מתקיף

דקא מכחשי. השרשים בקרקע וגם מעכבין את המחרישה ודאי אסיק אדעתיה לשייר לעצמו קרקע סביבות האילנות כדי שלא יוכל הלוקח לערער עליו ולומר כשיבשו אילנותיו עקור אילנותיך שקול זיל דהא מזקי לארעאי: לימא ליה. כשיבש האילן: מכר אילנות ושייר קרקע לפניו. שפירש לו כן האילנות אני מוכר לך והקרקע אני מעכב לעצמי: פלוגתא דר"ע ורבנן. בין לרב זביד בין לרב פפא ובשני אילנות מיירי דבשלשה אילנות הכל מודים דקנה קרקע כדתנן סתמא בהמוכר את הספינה (לקמן דף פא.) ומוקמינן לה בגמ' כר"ע ומיהו רישא דקתני גבי שנים אין לו קרקע לאו ר"ע היא כדמוכח בשילהי המוכר את הבית (לקמן דף עב.) והתם פרשינן לה: לר"ע דאמר מוכר בעין יפה מוכר אית ליה. ללוקח מקום האילנות על הקרקע ליטע אחרים במקומן כשימותו: לרבנן אין לו. קרקע ואם ימותו לא יטע אחרים במקומן כדתנן סתמא הקונה שני אילנות לא קנה קרקע: אפי' לרב זביד כו'. כלומר לרב זביד נמי מצי למימר אליבא דר"ע ולא הויא מילתא כתנאי אלא כדברי הכל: ה"מ. דקאמר רב זביד דאין לו קרקע גבי ב' לקוחות כדפרישית לעיל: לית לי באילנות. לא בעצים ולא בפירות: לית לך בקרקעות. אפי' במקום האילן וכשיבש תעקרנו ותלך: ה"מ. דיש לו (ב) קרקע: גבי שני לקוחות דאמר. בעל האילנות לבעל הקרקע כי היכי דלדידך זבין בעין יפה מה שמכר לך מן הקרקע על מנת להיות הקרקע שלך עולמית היא ופירותיה: אף לדידי זבין בעין יפה. שאוכל פירות אילנותי לעולם שאם ימותו אטע אחרים תחתיהן דאין אדם מוכר ולא לו למכור לזה בעין יפה ולזה בעין רעה: אבל הכא. שעיכב לעצמו כל לגבי עצמו בעין רעה מוכר כדי לשייר לעצמו: אכלן רצופין. להני שלשה אילנות כגון שנטועין ט"ו בבית סאה אינה חזקה ואפילו אכלן כולן כל שלש שנים דלא אחזיק כדמחזקי אינשי דאין רואין לקיים (ג) אלא לעקור ולשרש: מתקיף לה רבא אלא מעתה. כיון דמשום דנטועין מחוברין לא הויא חזקה: האי מישרא. ערוגה דאספסתא במאי קני לה הרי (ד) זרועה רצופה ואפי"ה אמרי' בריש פירקין דהוי חזקה ומיהו לאו אתקפתא מעליתא היא דהאי אורחיה והאי לאו אורחיה והאי מכחיש בארעא טפי והאי לא מכחיש טפי אלא רבא הוא דלית ליה האי סברא ובמילתא בעלמא הוא דמוקי להו לנהרדעי. ויש לפרש אכלן רצופין אינה חזקה שסופן לשרש אותן ולפזר נטיעתן שכן דרך אילנות לנטוע הרבה תחלה ביחד ואחר שגדלו מפזרים אותן הלכך לא הוי חזקה הואיל ולשרש קיימי ואין זו עיקר גידולן וראיה לדבר דגבי נטיעות אשכחן י' לבית סאה ובאילנות אמרו ג' לבית סאה ועל כרחך נטיעות היו מתחלה והיו י' לבית סאה ואח"כ מיעטום לג' בבית סאה וכן דרך אספסתא כמו כן לזרעה הרבה ביחד רצופין כמו שעושין לכרישין וכרוב ואח"כ עוקרין אותן וממלא מהן ערוגה גדולה והיינו דפריך רבא אלא מעתה האי מישרא דאספסתא כו' כן נראה בעיני: אלא אמר רבא. אי אית לן למימר מידי ברצופין הכי אמרינן: מכרן רצופין אין לו קרקע. כגון שנטועין יותר מי' בבית סאה דהכא לא אמרי' הקונה שלשה אילנות קנה קרקע דאין זה שדה האילן לעקור ולשרש קיימא: על פחות מד' אמות. שאין בין שורה לשורה אלא ג' אמות אינו כרם והמביא זרע לשם אינו לוקה משום לא תזרע כרמך כלאים (דברים כב) ומותרין באכילה: האמצעיים. שורה בין שתי שורות רואין כאילו אינה והוו להו שש אמות בין שורה לשורה ולעיל נמי גבי מכרן רצופין לרבנן רואין את האמצעיים כאילו אינן ודינן כמפוזרין וגבי מכרן רצופין יש לו קרקע ולר"ש אין לו קרקע והיינו כתנאי דמילתא דרבא תנאי היא כר"ש ודלא כרבנן ובהמוכר את הספינה (לקמן פב:) מפרש כמה יהו מרוחקין יותר מד' אמות ואכתי הוי כרם: קני ליה. הלוקח לקרקע: משיפולא עד תהומא. שוליו (שמות כח) מתרגמינן שיפולוהי כלומר כל הקרקע (ה) בשולי האילן דהיינו שפת הקרקע עד תהום של קרקע שאע"פ שדקל יחידי הוא ותנן דאפי' ב' אין לו קרקע ה"מ סביבות האילן הוא דאין לו כלום כמו שיש לג' ביניהן וחוצה להן כמלא אורה וסלו אבל תחתיו דאילן מיהא אית ליה דכיון דאילן לפירותיו קונה להתקיים מקרקע זו גם אם ימות האילן יטע אחר במקומו ואשמעינן נמי דאין בעל השדה יכול לחפור תחת האילן אפילו למטה מאלף אמה:

מתקיף

דאי לא מצי למימר ליה עקור אילנך שקול וזיל. פירוש לכשיבש ובלאו טעמא דמכחשי ארעא אי לא משייר מצי א"ל עקור אילנך דעל כרחו לא יעכב האילן בשדהו ועוד שרוצה לזרוע מקום האילן:

מכר אילנות ושייר קרקע. פ"ה דבג' אילנות איירי דבג' הכל מודין דקנה קרקע כדתנן בהמוכר את הספינה (לקמן דף פא.) ומוקי לה בגמ' כרבנן ודחי ומוקי לה אפי' כר"ע ולפי זה רישא דקתני שנים אין לו קרקע לא אתי כר"ע וכן מוכח בסוף המוכר את הבית (שם דף עב. ושם) דקתני הקדיש ג' אילנות ממטע י' לבית סאה כו' בזה אחר זה לא הקדיש את הקרקע ופריך (ו) מיניה אילימא רבי עקיבא האמר מוכר בעין יפה מוכר וכ"ש מקדיש פי' ומאי בזה אחר זה לא הקדיש את הקרקע אלמא משמע דקנה אילן אחד נמי קרקע ואין נראה לר"י דהא כיון דהא דתנן בהמוכר את הספינה (שם דף פא.) קנה ג' קנה קרקע מוקי נמי כר"ע א"כ ע"כ לר"ע בשנים לא קנה קרקע דהכי משמע דוקא ג' קנה קרקע אבל ב' לא קנה קרקע לכך יש לפרש להא דשמעתין בג' אילנות ואע"ג דבעלמא בג' קנה קרקע שאני הכא דמיירי כגון שאין שם קרקע אלא לצורך האילנות ופירש בהדיא שמשייר הקרקע לעצמו (ז) או בשדה גדול ולומר בפירוש שכל הקרקע משייר ולכ"ע לא קנה בגוף הקרקע כלום אלא למ"ד מוכר בעין יפה מוכר יכול ליטע אחר במקומו כשיבש והשתא ה"פ מני אילימא ר"ע ואליבא דרבנן דר"ש דסבירא להו מקדיש בעין יפה הוא מקדיש הא אמר מוכר בעין יפה הוא מוכר וכל שכן מקדיש ואלא רבנן ואליבא דרבנן דר' שמעון דאמרו במקדיש הקדיש את כולן הרי אומר מוכר בעין רעה מוכר אבל מקדיש בעין יפה מקדיש וכיון דסבירא להו דכולי האי מקדיש בעין יפה (ח) ממכר דאפי' בור ודות שאין הקרקע צריך להם הקדיש כ"ש במקדיש את האילן שהקדיש את הקרקע הצריכה לאילן ואע"ג דבמכר לא מכר את הקרקע ומיהו אההיא דבתר הכי אי אפשר לפרש כן [דקאמר] אלא פשיטא ר"ש ואליבא דמאן אילימא אליבא דר"ע הא אמר מוכר בעין יפה מוכר כ"ש מקדיש ומ"מ יש לפרש בדוחק דפריך מסברא כיון דמוכר בעין יפה מוכר אית לן למימר דמקדיש כל שכן דיותר מעט בעין יפה מקדיש ובאילן אחד נמי הקדיש המקדיש את הקרקע אע"ג דבמכר לא קנה ועוד יש לפרש דלא מכח מקדש זה אחר זה דייק התם דבעין רעה מקדיש אלא דייק מדקתני הקדיש שלשה אילנות ממטע י' לבית סאה הרי זה הקדיש את הקרקע כולה לפיכך כשהוא פודה פודה לפי בית זרע חומר שעורים כו' ואי ס"ל דבעין יפה מקדיש אע"פ שהקדיש את הקרקע ואת האילנות בבת אחת הו"ל למימר דפודה וחוזר ופודה תחלה את האילנות בשויין וחוזר ופודה את הקרקע לפי בית זרע חומר שעורים כדאמר רב הונא בפרק יש בערכין (ערכין דף יד.) הקדיש שדה מלאה אילנות כשהוא פודה פודה את האילן בשוויו וחוזר ופודה קרקע לפי בית זרע חומר שעורים בחמשים שקל כסף אלמא סבר רב הונא מקדיש כו' איתיביה ר"נ לרב הונא ופריך ליה מברייתא דהמוכר את הבית ומשני הא מני ר"ש היא דאמר בעין רעה הוא מקדיש והשתא מדקדק לקמן בפשיטות דכולה סוגיא דלקמן אליבא דרב הונא קיימא לטעמיה (ט) דאמרי' במס' ערכין (שם) בעין יפה הוא מקדיש: אינו כרם. ואין צריך להרחיק זרע ד' אמות אלא שלשה טפחים כעין (י) כרם יחידי ולענין מי שנטע כרם ולא חיללו דאינו חוזר מן המלחמה:

קני

עו א מיי' פכ"ד מהל' מכירה הל' ט סמג עשין פב טוש"ע ח"מ סי' רטו סעי' ו בהג"ה:
עח ב מיי' פי"ב מהל' טוען הלכה ג ועיין בכ"מ סמג עשין צה טוש"ע ח"מ סי' קמט סעיף א וסעיף יט:
עט ג מיי' פכ"ד מהל' מכירה הלכה ג סמג עשין פב טוש"ע ח"מ סי' רטו סעיף ו:
פ ד מיי' פ"ז מהל' כלאים הלכה ב ס"ס בכ"מ סמג לאוין רפ טוש"ע י"ד סי' רצו סעיף נג:

רבינו גרשום

אבל אילנות דמכחשו בארעא. שרשים ואין יכול לזרוע תחתיהם מפני שנופין מעכבין מימי המטר שלא ירד עליהן כיון דקא מכחשי ודאי שייר לעצמו מקום האילנות: לר' עקיבא. מכר לו נמי מקום האילנות ואפילו לרב זביד דאמר לעיל להיכא דמכר לשנים שהוא זה החזיק באילנות וזה החזיק בקרקע אין לו לבעל האילנות כלום בקרקע. הני מילי גבי שני לקוחות דהאי טוען לי מכר הקרקע והאי טוען לי מכר האילנות משום הכי אין לו דמצי למימר לו בעל הקרקע לבעל האילנות כי היכי דלדידי כו'. אבל הכא להיכא דמכר אילנות לחד ושייר קרקע לפניו ודאי מודה רב זביד דיש לו קרקע מקום אילנות דמוכר בעין יפה מוכר. ורבנן דמפלגי על ר' עקיבא סברי לית ליה ואפי' לרב פפא דאמר לעיל יש לו הני מילי גבי שני לקוחות דמצי למימר לו בעל האילנות לבעל הקרקע כי היכי דלדידך בעין יפה מכר דלא שייר קרקע לדידי נמי בעין יפה מכר לו מקום האילנות. אבל הכא היכא דשייר קרקע לפניו מוכר בעין רעה מוכר ולא גמר ומקנה ליה מקום האילנות: אכלן. הני אילנות רצופין. כגון שהיו נטועין בבית סאה אחת ט"ו אילנות דרגילין להיות י' ותו לא. אינה חזקה דמצי למימר ליה מערער לא אכלת הקרקע כשאר חיזוקין של אחרים: האי שדה נטועה מישרא דאספסתא. ערוגה מלאה אספסתא שרצופין הן זה עם זה במאי קני ליה: מכרן רצופין. שהיו נטועין יותר ממטע עשרה לבית סאה אין לו ללוקח קרקע דחשוב הוא כיער מה יער לא מכר אלא לעצים האי נמי לא מכר אלא לעצים: שדה כרם הנטוע על פחות מד' אמות דבין גפנה לגפנה ליכא ד' אמות כדי עבודת הכרם אינו כרם ומותר להביא זרע אחר לשם ואינו עובר. וחכ"א הרי זה כרם ודומין הגפנים מצעים כאינם והכא נמי סבירא להו לחכמים שרואין אותן שעודפים על מטע י' לבית סאה כאלו אינן ומכר לו את הקרקע ור' שמעון ס"ל כרבא והיינו כתנאי: משיפולי אילן. היינו מקום תפישת השרשין ועד התהום כל אותו קרקע מכר לו והיינו מדה בינונית של אילן דאי אמרינן קנה בקרקע ברוחב הענפים היינו יותר מדאי ואי אמרינן לא קנה אלא כנגד עובי קורות האילן היינו מעט יותר מדאי אבל משיפוליה היינו יותר מעובי קורת האילן ופחות מרוחב הענפים ובהכי סגי ליה בקרקע:

א) כלאים פ"ה מ"ב עירובין ג: לקמן פג. קב. ג) ערכין יד ע"ב:

הגהות הב"ח

(א) גמ' עקור אילנך שקול וזיל: (ב) רשב"ם ד"ה ה"מ דיש לו קרקע: (ג) ד"ה אכלן וכו' לקיים כן אלא: (ד) ד"ה האי מישרא וכו' הרי זו זרועה רצופה וכו' ואחר שגדלו קלח מפזרים: (ה) ד"ה משיפולא וכו' כל הקרקע משולי האילן: (ו) תוס' ד"ה מכר וכו' ופריך מני אילימא ר"ע: (ז) בא"ד או בשדה גדול נ"ב פי' בשדה שיש בו שלשה אילנות דיש לו קרקע מ"מ כשאמר בהדיא דמשייר הקרקע ותנאי זה לא בעינן דבלא תנאי נמי אין לו יותר מתחתיהן ולכך לא הצריך לומר משייר לעצמו שתחתם: (ח) בא"ד בעין יפה טפי ממכר דאפילו וכו' כ"ש מקדיש את הקרקע הצריכה לאילן: (ט) בא"ד לטעמיה דאמר במסכת ערכין: (י) ד"ה אינו וכו' כעין כרם יחידי וכו' מן מערכי המלחמה:

ליקוטי רש"י

אם איתא דלא שייר כו'. ואנן סהדי לדעתו כן עיכב את האילנות לעצמו שיהיו כאן לעולם אף לחזור וליטע אחרים במקומן כדרך שהיה לו כח זה באילנות הללו עד עכשיו אבל לוקח אילנות אין לומר לצורך כל הימים לקחו וליטע אחרים במקומן דעביד איניש דזבין ארעא ליומיה ולפירות קנאו [רשב"ם לקמן עא:]. מכרן רצופין. אם נטועין בפחות ממטע עשרה לבית סאה או ביותר מיכן אין זה סדר נטיעת אילנות [ערכין יד.]. כרם שהוא נטוע על פחות מארבע אמות. שאין בין שורה לשורה ארבע אמות אינו כרם ומותר לזרוע לשם [עירובין ג.]. אינו כרם. אלא יער ומותר בכלאים [רשב"ם שם]. וחכ"א וכו' ורואין את האמצעיים. הנטועין בתוך ריוח הכלוי הזה כאילו אינן בין שורה לשורה [עירובין שם]. דכל העומד ליעקר כעקור דמי ומותרת היא גבי כלאים [רשב"ם שם]. קני ליה משיפוליה. מקום מושב האילן עד תהומו [ערכין יד.].

The Gemara questions this ruling:

מַתְקִיף לָהּ רָבָא – **Rava challenged this:** אֶלָּא מֵעַתָּה – **But now,** if harvesting the produce of plants crowded too closely together cannot establish a *chazakah,* הַאי מִישְׁרָא דְּאַסְפַּסְתָּא בְּמַאי קָנֵי לָהּ – then **how is one to establish a *chazakah* in a bed of *aspasta,*** which is also initially planted densely and later transplanted?[17]

Rava therefore offered his own version of their ruling:

אֶלָּא אָמַר רָבָא – **Rather, Rava said:** מְכָרָן רְצוּפִין – If one ***sold* [trees]** that were planted too **densely,** אֵין לוֹ קַרְקַע – **[the buyer] does not receive** any **land.** Since the trees are destined to be uprooted, they do not constitute a field of trees and hence no land is included in their sale.[18]

But Rava's ruling is not uncontested:

אָמַר רַבִּי זֵירָא – **Rav Zeira said:** כְּתַנָּאֵי – Rava's ruling is **the subject of a Tannaic dispute,** for the Mishnah states:[19] כֶּרֶם שֶׁהוּא נָטוּעַ עַל פָּחוֹת מֵאַרְבַּע אַמּוֹת – If A VINEYARD IS PLANTED WITH LESS THAN FOUR *AMOS* between rows,[20] רַבִּי שִׁמְעוֹן אוֹמֵר אֵינוֹ כֶּרֶם – R' SHIMON SAYS: IT IS NOT A VINEYARD, and is regarded merely as a collection of individual vines.[21] וַחֲכָמִים אוֹמְרִים הֲרֵי זוֹ כֶּרֶם – BUT THE SAGES SAY: IT IS A VINEYARD, וְרוֹאִין אֶת הָאֶמְצָעִים כְּאִילּוּ אֵינָן – AND WE VIEW THE INTERIOR vines, i.e. those that encroach on the four-*amah* space that should be between rows, AS IF THEY ARE NOT present.[22] Thus, Rava's ruling accords only with that of R' Shimon.[23] The Sages, however, would rule that the buyer of densely planted trees acquires land together with them.[24]

Another related ruling:

אָמְרֵי נְהַרְדָּעֵי – **The Nehardeans say:** הַאי מַאן דְּזַבִּין דִּקְלָא לְחַבְרֵיהּ – **If one sells a palm tree to his fellow,** קָנֵי לֵיהּ מִשְׁפּוּלֵיהּ עַד תְּהוֹמָא – [the purchaser] acquires [the **soil under it**] **from [the tree's] base to the** furthest **depths** of the earth.[25]

NOTES

transplanted to other fields as they grew. Thus, often more than ten trees would be planted in a *beis se'ah,* with the excess being transplanted as necessary. [The Nehardeans regard the trees in such a field as being merely stored there temporarily, and therefore do not view their fruit as the field's produce. Thus,] consuming the produce of such trees does not establish a *chazakah* (*Rashbam's* preferred explanation; cf. *Ri Migash* cited in *Shitah Mekubetzes*).

[Conceivably this logic could be applied to ten saplings as well, for the Gemara above, 26b, states that only three mature trees can comfortably occupy a *beis se'ah.* Obviously, seven of the original ten saplings would eventually have to be transplanted. However, the Nehardeans only disallowed *chazakah* when the trees were planted so closely that some will have to be uprooted in the very near future. Ten saplings, however, can remain in a *beis se'ah* for many years until they mature. Thus, consuming their produce can confer *chazakah.*]

17. *Aspasta,* a type of plant grown for animal fodder, is commonly cultivated in closely crowded beds and then transplanted to other fields. If, as the Nehardeans suggest, harvesting the fruit of trees which are destined to be transplanted does not confer *chazakah,* it should be impossible to establish a *chazakah* on such an *aspasta* field, which cannot be, for this was the normal way to use an *aspasta* field! (*Rashbam*). Thus, this version of the Nehardeans' ruling is refuted.

18. [Earlier (37a note 6) we learned that three or more trees constitute a tree field and their sale automatically includes a certain amount of land under and around them. Rava now says that this is true only if the trees are properly planted. If, however, they are more closely planted than normal, they are destined to be uprooted and do not constitute a tree field. Accordingly, the buyer has purchased only a group of individual trees and their sale therefore does not include any land (*Rashbam*).

19. *Kilayim* 5:2. The Torah forbids planting grains or greens in the vicinity of a single grapevine, or in the vicinity of a vineyard (*Deuteronomy* 22:9). Not only is it forbidden to plant them there, but the resultant produce – both of the vines and the seeds – is forbidden to use. However, the area around a vineyard in which foreign planting is forbidden is much more extensive than the area forbidden around a single vine, and for this reason it is important to know what arrangement of vines constitute a vineyard. This Mishnah discusses one aspect of this arrangement.

20. I.e. instead of the usual four *amos* between rows of vines [to allow for plowing the vines with ox-drawn plows], only three *amos* of empty space was left between them (*Rashbam*).

21. R' Shimon says that since the rows are planted too closely together [to be plowed], the vines do not constitute a vineyard. Consequently, if one plants other kinds of seeds there, he does not violate the prohibition of planting foreign seeds in a vineyard, and the resultant growth is not forbidden to use (*Rashbam*). However, when planting foreign seeds there, one must still maintain a distance of six *tefachim* from any one vine, because even a single vine demands a certain separation (cf. *Tosafos* and *Rashash* to 82b).

22. Since they are destined to be uprooted, we view them as *having been* uprooted, and they can be ignored (*Rashbam* below, 83a ד״ה רואין). Thus, in the instance mentioned in note 20, we disregard every other row and view the vineyard as consisting of rows six *amos* apart.

23. Rava considers the extra trees in the field as robbing the group of its status as a tree field; he does not disregard them. Similarly, R' Shimon does not disregard the extra vines and their presence therefore deprives the group of its status as a vineyard.

24. The Rabbis disregard the extra vines in the vineyard. Similarly, then, they would disregard the extra trees planted in the field, and give it the status of a tree field. Hence, the trees would include land in their sale. Thus, Rava's statement that land is not included in the sale of closely planted trees is actually disputed by Tannaim (*Rashbam*).

25. *Rashbam* explains this to mean that the purchaser acquires enough land beneath the tree to enable him to plant a replacement tree if the purchased tree dies, and to prevent the seller from digging under the tree. Although the Mishnah (81a) clearly states that even the buyer of two trees (and certainly one) does not receive land, the Nehardeans interpret this to refer to land *around* the trees and under their foliage. The land *directly* beneath the tree's trunk, however, is included in the sale. They reason that since the buyer acquired not only the tree itself but also the right to have it grow in the seller's field, the buyer acquires this right for perpetuity. Thus, he is in actuality buying the land directly beneath the tree so that he can replant a new one after the original one dies.

Tosafos, however (38a ד״ה קני), point out that the Mishnah below, 81a, clearly states that if the tree dies, the buyer has no right to the land (presumably, to plant another tree). Thus, *Tosafos* explain that the Nehardeans mean that the buyer owns the land only insofar as preventing the seller from tunneling under the tree. However, even they agree that once the tree dies, the buyer may not plant another one (cf. *Ramban* and *Tos. HaRosh* cited in *Shitah Mekubetzes*).

Rava questions this ruling:
מַתְקִיף לָהּ רָבָא – Rava challenged [this ruling]: וְלֵימָא לֵיהּ – But **let [the seller] say to [the buyer],** כּוּרְכְּמָא דְּרִישְׁקָא זַבֵּינִי לָךְ – **"I sold you** the tree the way **garden saffron** is sold, i.e. without any land.[1] Therefore, since it died, עֲקוֹר כּוּרְכְּמָא דְּרִישְׁקָא וְזִיל – **I insist that you uproot** your **'garden saffron' and be gone!"** Why, then, do the Nehardeans maintain that the buyer acquires the land under the tree?[2]

Rava offers another version of the Nehardeans' ruling:
אֶלָּא אָמַר רָבָא – **Rather, Rava said:** בָּבָא מֵחֲמַת טַעֲנָה – The purchaser is awarded the land under the tree only **if he comes** forward **with a claim** that the seller specifically included the land under the tree in the sale.[3] Without such a claim, however, the purchaser does not receive the land.

The Gemara raises a practical problem:
אָמַר לֵיהּ מַר קְשִׁישָׁא בְּרֵיהּ דְּרַב חִסְדָּא לְרַב אַשִׁי – **Mar Keshisha**[4] **the son of Rav Chisda said to Rav Ashi:** וְאִי כּוּרְכְּמָא דְּרִישְׁקָא זַבִּין לֵיהּ – **But if [the seller] did** in fact **sell** the tree to **him** the way **garden saffron** is sold, i.e. without any land, מַאי הֲוָה לֵיהּ לְמֶעְבַּד – **what could [the seller] have done** to prevent the buyer from dishonestly claiming the land under the tree?[5]

Rav Ashi replies:[6]
אִיבָּעֵי לֵיהּ לְמַחוּיֵי – **[The seller] should have "protested"** within three years of the sale by declaring that the land under the tree was not included in the sale.[7] דְּאִי לֹא תֵּימָא הָכִי – **For if you will not say [that such a "protest" is valid],**[8] הָנֵי מַשְׁכַּנְתָּא דְסוּרָא – then a potentially dangerous situation is created by **these Surean securities,**[9] דִּכְתַב בְּהוּ הָכִי – **in [whose attendant bond] is written:** בְּמִישְׁלַם שְׁנַיָּא אִלֵּין – **"At the termination of these years,** תֵּיפּוֹק אַרְעָא דָא בְּלָא כֶסֶף – **this land shall revert** to its original owner **without payment."**[10] אִי כָּבֵישׁ לֵיהּ לִשְׁטַר מַשְׁכַּנְתָּא – For **if** after three years **[the lender] suppresses the security bond]** וְאָמַר לְקוּחָה הִיא בְּיָדִי – **and says, "[The land] is mine because I purchased it,"** הָכִי נַמֵּי דִּמְהֵימַן – **would he then be believed?**[11] מִיתַקְנֵי רַבָּנַן מִילְּתָא – Would **the Rabbis** then **enact [an arrangement]** דְּאָתֵי בָּהּ לִידֵי פְּסֵידָא – **that can cause** the borrower an unfair **loss** of his land?[12] אֶלָּא – **Rather,** Rav Ashi continued, we are forced to conclude that אִיבָּעֵי לֵיהּ לְמַחוּיֵי – **[the borrower] should have "protested"** before three years elapsed.[13] Thus, we see that such a "protest" is valid.[14] הָכָא נַמֵּי – Then **here, as well,** when a person sells a tree without the land underneath it, אִיבָּעֵי לֵיהּ לְמַחוּיֵי – **he should have "protested"** before three years elapsed.[15]

Mishnah The previous Mishnah discussed how long one must occupy land to establish a *chazakah.* The following Mishnah discusses whether establishment of *chazakah* depends upon whether the original owner lived in the same region as the field in question:[16]
שָׁלֹשׁ אֲרָצוֹת לַחֲזָקָה – There are **three lands** in Eretz Yisrael **with regard to *chazakah*:** יְהוּדָה וְעֵבֶר הַיַּרְדֵּן וְהַגָּלִיל – **Judea, Transjordan and the Galilee.**

NOTES

1. Garden saffron was commonly sold while it was still growing. The understanding was that the buyer obtained the right to retain the saffron in the seller's ground as long as the saffron grew. Once it ripened, however, the buyer was required to pluck it and could not replant in that spot, because his purchase did not include the ground under the saffron. Accordingly, Rava argues that a seller of a single tree may claim that he meant to sell it only as one does saffron – with the right to maintain it there as long as it grows, but without the land beneath it. Thus, when it dies, the seller could insist that the buyer remove it and not plant another (*Rashbam*).

2. As explained in note 25 to 37b, the Nehardeans' argument is that since the buyer acquires the right to maintain his tree in the seller's land, it is logical to assume that he has that right perpetually. Thus, he acquires the land beneath the tree to enable him to plant a new tree when this one dies. By citing the case of the garden saffron, Rava shows that there exists a sale under which terms the buyer obtains the right to leave his plant in the seller's land only as long as that plant lives. If so, there is no reason to assume that these are not also the terms for the sale of a tree (*Rashbam*).

3. I.e. the purchaser claims that he had purchased both the tree and the land beneath it, so that he could replant on that spot. He further claimed that he had possessed a deed attesting to this, but lost or discarded it after three years of harvesting the tree's produce. Such a claim, Rava rules, would be believed [because using the tree for three years constitutes a *chazakah* on the land] (*Rashbam*).

4. See 7b note 1.

5. Since Rava ruled that if the buyer uses the tree for three years he is believed to claim that he bought the ground beneath it, what is to prevent a buyer from falsely claiming this even if he in fact bought only the tree?

Now, ordinarily a landowner can block a squatter from establishing a *chazakah* on his land by protesting that the squatter is acting illegally. Here, however, the seller cannot do this, because the tree's owner is perfectly within his rights when he picks the tree's fruit. Thus, it seems that the seller is doomed to unjustly lose his land after three years elapse.

6. Above on 35b, Rav Ashi *received* this very reply (and the proof that follows) from Rav Kahana. Apparently, he accepted it as correct and now himself uses it to respond to Mar Keshisha's question (*Ritva*).

7. [Rav Ashi says that although he cannot protest by calling the buyer's use of the tree illegal, he can "protest" by declaring before witnesses that the sale of the tree did not include any land.] Consequently, the buyer would not be believed to claim he bought the land, for, having been put on notice by the seller's declaration, he should have retained his deed (if in fact he had one) to prove his claim. Thus, the seller is not doomed to unfairly lose his land (*Rashbam*).

8. Rav Ashi means to preclude the argument that a protest is effective only where the protester accuses the occupant of acting illegally. But where the challenger merely declares that the land is his, while agreeing that the occupant is entitled to use it, the protest is not forceful enough to be effective, and it does not motivate the occupant to guard his deed (*Rashbam*; see above, 35b note 13).

9. See above, 35b note 14.

10. Ibid. note 15.

11. Ibid. note 16.

12. Ibid. note 17.

13. Ibid. note 18.

14. Ibid. note 19.

15. Hence, a seller who sells a single tree but not the land beneath it is not doomed to lose his field to an unscrupulous buyer, because he can block the buyer's *chazakah* by declaring before witnesses that he sold the tree only in a garden saffron-type of sale, i.e. with no land included. Thus, Mar Keshisha's problem is resolved (*Rashbam*).

16. As discussed earlier, if a person occupies land for three continuous years during which his occupancy goes unchallenged, he establishes a *chazakah* (i.e. we assume him to be the rightful owner of the field until proven otherwise). The reason for this is that no true owner would tolerate someone's squatting on his land for three years; he would surely protest the unauthorized use and demand that the occupant vacate the land. His failure to protest thus indicates that the occupant is the rightful owner.

The above naturally applies only if news of a protest by the original owner would reach the occupant. In a case where it would not, however, absence of any objection by the owner is meaningless since the owner has no way of lodging an effective protest anyway. In such a case, his lack of objection does not prove that he ever relinquished ownership over the field and as a result, the occupant's three years of possession does not

מתקיף לה רבא [א] ולימא לי' כורכמא דרישקא זביני לך עקור כורכמא דרישקא וזיל אלא אמר רבא [ב] בבא מחמת טענה אמר ליה מר קשישא בריה דרב חסדא לרב אשי (א) ואי כורכמא דרישקא זבין ליה מאי ה"ל למעבד [ג] איבעי ליה למחויי דאי לא תימא הכי [א] הני משכנתא דסורא דכתב בה הכי במישלם שניא אלין תיפוק ארעא דא בלא כסף אי כביש ליה לשטר משכנתא ואמר לקוחה היא בידי הכי נמי דמהימן (ב) מיתקני רבנן מילתא דאתי בה לידי פסידא אלא איבעי ליה למחויי הכא נמי איבעי ליה למחויי: **מתני'** [ג] שלש ארצות לחזקה יהודה ועבר הירדן והגליל היה ביהודה והחזיק בגליל בגליל והחזיק ביהודה אינה חזקה עד שיהא עמו במדינה (ג) אמר רבי יהודה לא אמרו שלש שנים אלא כדי שיהא באספמיא ויחזיק שנה (ד) ילכו ויודיעוהו שנה ויבא לשנה אחרת: **גמ'** [ג] מאי קסבר ת"ק אי קסבר מחאה שלא בפניו הויא מחאה אפי' יהודה וגליל נמי אי קסבר מחאה שלא בפניו לא הויא מחאה אפילו יהודה ויהודה נמי לא א"ר אבא בר ממל אמר רב לעולם קסבר [ד] מחאה שלא בפניו הויא מחאה ומשנתינו [ה] בשעת חירום שנו ומ"ש יהודה וגליל דנקיט הא קא משמע לן דסתם

מתקיף לה רבא. אמאי קנה קרקע דכנגד האילן מאחר דמתן לא קנה קרקע כלל לא קנה ודקשיא לכו דכיון להתקיים בקרקע זו קנאו נמצא שקנה יניקת הקרקע גם ליטע אחר במקומו של זה אחר שייבש או יקלץ: **לימא ליה.** מוכר: **כורכמא דרישקא זביני לך.** קרוג אוריינטי"ל ורגילים למכרו בקרקע ומניחו עד שיגמור פריו ועוקרו אף האילן שמכרתי לך לפירותיו הקרקע לא מכרתי לך אלא להניח אילנך בקרקע שלי כל ימי שצריך לקרקע עד שייבש היינו דומיא דכרכום ומאחר שיבש לא תהא לו קרקע עוד: **עקור כורכמא דרישקא וזיל.** כמו שעוקרים את הכרכום אחר שנתבשל ואינו יכול ליטע כרכום אחר במקומו גם אתה לא תטע אילן אחר במקומו: **אלא אמר רבא.** הכא הוא דקני לקרקע שתחת האילן בבא מחמת הטענה שטוען למוכר בפירוש מכרת לי האילן והקרקע שתחתיו ליטע אחר במקומו ובשטר ואכלתיה שני חזקה ולא נזהרתי בשטרי יותר משלש שנים דהשתא לא דמי לכורכמא דרישקא: **א"ל מר קשישא בריה דרב חסדא לרב אשי.** מאחר שהקונה דקל יחידי נאמן בטענה זו ויטע אחר במקומו אי כורכמא דרישקא זבין ליה אם מכר לו סתם דקל לפירותיו ולא פירש לו קרקע דקיימא לן אין לו קרקע דאם יבש או נעקר לא יטע אחר במקומו: **מאי הוה ליה.** למוכר **למעבד** שלא יהא זה בא מחמת טענה ויטע אחר במקומו דכל אדם יטעון אחר שלש שנים שפירש לו קרקע מאחר שהוא נאמן בטענתו: **איבעי ליה למחויי.** בתוך כל שלש להודיע שלא מכר לו קרקע אלא כי כורכמא דרישקא ושוב לא יוכל לטעון אחר שלש שטר היה לי ואבד דכיון דמיחה בו זה היה לו להזהר בשטרו: **דאי לא תימא הכי.** דמחאה כי האי גוונא לא הויא מחאה מאחר (ה) שמודה בו שאוכל עכשיו מן הקרקע מן הדין דלא הויא מחאה אלא בטוען פלניא גזלנא הוא דלקמן: **מתני'** דסתם אמרינן בגמרא ארץ ישראל א"ר אלעזר אפי' שתי אכסניות כגון שלומי ונבורו והירדן מפסיק בינתים ועומד ורואה אחד מחזיק בשדה שלו אינה חזקה עד שיהא עמו באותה העיר ובאותה מדינה רב אמר עיקר חזקה הכנסת פירות דלאפי' ראהו חורש וקוצר ומעמר ודש וזורה ובורר ולא ראהו מכניס פירות אינה חזקה עד שיראהו מכניס פירות: **מתני' שלש ארצות.** בארץ ישראל: **לחזקה.** חלוקות זו מזו לענין חזקת שלש שנים כדמפרש ואזיל: **היה.** בעל הקרקע ביהודה והחזיק בה אדם שלש שנים בלא מחאה אינה חזקה כדמפרש טעמא בגמרא דסתם יהודה וגליל כשעת חירום דמי שאין שיירות מצויות מזו לזו ולא הויא מחאה בעל הקרקע מחאה שהרי אין מי שיגיד לו למחזיק שמיחה זה ויזהר בשטרו דהא אין שיירות מצויות הלכך כיון דלאינו יכול למחות אע"ג דלא מיחה לא הפסיד בשתיקתו והיה לו לזה המחזיק ליזהר בשטרו שהרי יודע שאין בעל הקרקע יכול למחות: **עד שיהא עמו במדינה.** כגון שהיה ביהודה בעיר אחת והחזיק ביהודה בעיר אחרת דכיון דשיירות מצויות הוה ליה למחויי ומדלא מיחה הפסיד: **א"ר יהודה לא אמרו שלש שנים כו'.** לחלוק בא ולומר דאין חלוקות לחזקה דהיה בגליל והחזיק ביהודה הויא חזקה ואפילו היה באספמיא שהוא רחוק מהלך שנה מארץ ישראל והחזיק בארץ ישראל הויא חזקה שהרי לכך האריכו שני חזקה זמן מרובה של שלש שנים כדי שיעור שאם היה באספמיא ואם יחזיק זה בקרקע שלו שנה ובתוך שנה ראשונה יצא הקול ילכו בשנה שניה ויודיעוהו לבעל הקרקע ולשנה שלישית יבא וימחה ובגמרא מפרש אי בעי ר' יהודה מחאה בפניו או לא ויותר ממהלך שנה אין דרך אדם להרחיק מביתו ולפי ההוה תקנו. וטעמא דר' יהודה לא משום דתלת שנין מיזדהר איניש בשטריה אלא כדמפרש כדי שיהא כו' וטעמא דחזקה לדידיה דלא שביק איניש דאכלוה לארעיה בלא רשותיה ואפילו שעה אחת ושתיק אלא לכך האריכו שלש שנים שפעמים היה המערער רחוק אבל אי הוי המערער בעיר הוי חזקה מיד כדאמרי' לקמן בפירקין: **גמ' מאי קסבר תנא קמא.** דר' יהודה: **אי קסבר מחאה.** שמוחה בעל הקרקע במחזיק אפי' שלא בפניו כגון שנייהם דרין בעיר אחת ומיחה בפני שנים מן השוק שלא בפניו של מחזיק אפי' הכי הויא מחאה דחברך חברא אית ליה ושמע המחזיק בדבר זה והיה לו להזהר בשטרו ומדלא נזהר הפסיד והלכך קתני עד שיהא עמו במדינה דכיון שנייהם במדינה אחת הויא מחאה אע"פ שאינם בעיר אחת: **אפי' יהודה וגליל נמי.** היה ביהודה והחזיק בגליל תיהוי מחאה: **ואי קסבר לא הויא מחאה.** כדקתני דהיה ביהודה והחזיק בגליל אינה חזקה: **אפי' היה ביהודה והחזיק ביהודה.** בעיר אחרת נמי לא תיהוי מחאה ואמאי קתני עד שיהא עמו במדינה: **לעולם קסבר מחאה שלא בפניו הויא מחאה.** ומשום הכי קתני עד שיהא עמו במדינה ודקשיא לך אפילו יהודה וגליל נמי תיהוי מחאה מתני' בשעת חירום תיגרות יש בין יהודה וגליל ואין שיירות מצויות מזו לזו ואם ימחה לא יבא הדבר לאזניו של מחזיק שיזהר בשטרו והלכך לא הויא מחאה וכיון דלא הויא מחאתו של מערער מחאה חזקתו של זה נמי לא הוי חזקה דטעמא דחזקה ג' שנים קונה משום דמצי טעין ליה מחזיק אמאי לא מחית בתוך שלש ואילו הכא לא מצי למטען הכי דהא לא יכול למחות דהא אינה מחאה: **ומ"ש יהודה וגליל דנקט.** דכיון דבשעת חירום מיירי הוא הדין לכל המלכיות שיש חירום בין זו לזו והכי הוה ליה למיתני כל הארצות חלוקות לחזקה בשעת חירום. ואית דמפרשי מ"ש יהודה וגליל דנקט כיון דבשעת חירום מוקמת לה מ"ש יהודה וגליל דלא הויא חזקה אפילו יהודה ויהודה לא תיהוי חזקה ואין נראה בעיני דאם כן הוה ליה למימר כדלעיל אי הכי אפילו יהודה ויהודה נמי לא ועוד דהכי מתרץ ר' אבא בשעת חירום שנו שיש תגרה בין המלכיות אבל עיירות של מדינה ומדינה אין ביניהם תגרה:

הא

קני ליה משיפוליה ועד תהומא. פירש הקונטרס שאם מת יטע אחר במקומו וקשיא לר"י דבהדיא קתני בהמוכר את הספינה (לקמן דף פא.) גבי קנה ב' אילנות דאם מתו אין לו קרקע ונראה לר"י דלא קני מקום האילן אלא לענין שלא יוכל (ו) לחפור זה חלל תחתיו דקני ליה עד תהומא ולכתי קשיא לרשב"א מהא דתנן בהמוכר את הבית (לקמן דף עב.) כשהקדיש ג' אילנות בזה אחר זה פודה את האילנות בשוויהן ואם היה מקום האילן קדוש כלל היה לו לפדות לפי חשבון בית זרע חומר שעורים בחמשים שקלים כסף דלכן הוא הדין כשמקדיש אפי' משהו קרקע עם האילן ואומר ר"י דבלאו הכי דחי רבא מילתייהו דנהרדעי שפיר ולרשב"א נראה דהכא כמ"ד בעין רעה מוכר ולפיכך אין קדוש אפי' מקום האילן אבל נהרדעי סברי מוכר בעין יפה הוא מוכר: **ואי** כורכמא דרישקא. לכך נקט כורכמא דרישקא שמתקיים בקרקע ג' שנים דהיינו שני חזקה ודרך להשהותו בקרקע כמו שיכול להתקיים: **אלא** כדי שיהא באספמיא. דעד שם יש מהלך שנה ויותר מכאן אין דרך להרחיק יותר מקרקעו ואם הרחיק יותר לא פלוג: **מחאה** שלא בפניו כו'. תימה דבכל דוכתי נקט מחאה ולמאי לא נקט חזקה שלא בפניו הויא חזקה ויש לומר לפי שהטעם תלוי במחאה ולא בחזקה שאדם המחזיק בקרקעותיו של חבירו אית ליה קלא שהוא חוקר ושואל על נכסיו אבל המחאה אין לה קול כל כך שאין המחזיק מחזר אם מוחה לו בעל קרקע לפיכך אין חזקתו חזקה כשאין יכול לשמוע מחאתו דמה יועיל שמיחה:

עין משפט נר מצוה

פא א מיי' פכ"ד מהל' מכירה הל' ו סמג עשין פב טוש"ע ח"מ סימן רטז סעיף ט:

פב ב ג מיי' פי"ב מהל' טוען ונטען הל' יח סמג עשין צה טוש"ע ח"מ סימן קמא סעי' כ:

פג ד מיי' שם פי"א הל' ה סמג שם טוש"ע ח"מ סימן קמו סעי' א:

פד ה מיי' שם הל' ג וסמג שם טוש"ע ח"מ סי' קמג סעי' א:

רבינו גרשום

מתקיף לה רבא אמאי קנה מקום האילן. **לימא ליה.** מוכר ללוקח **לכורכמא דרישקא זבינא לך.** דומיא הוא כעין שמוכר אדם לחבירו ירקות של צבע כורכמא דרישקא מעולה שקורין אריינט"ל שלא מכר לו כי אם הצבע עצמה ולא מקום הכורכמא הכי נמי מצי למימר ליה כי יבש האילן אנא הדקל זבינא לך **שקול אילנך ועקור וזיל. אלא אמר רבא.** משום הכי קני ליה משיפוליה ועד תהומא **בבא** הלוקח **מחמת טענה** שטוען ואמר אילן ומקומו מכר לי והחזקתי בו שני חזקה ולא מיחה במקומו אדם: **אי לכורכמא דרישקא.** כלומר האילן לבדו כל זמן שלא יתייבש **מאי הוה ליה למיעבד** מה מועיל לו מחאתו והא כששלמו שני חזקה עדיין לא הגיע זמן לקצור הכורכמא ועדיין ברשותו עומדת הקרקע שתחת הכורכמא וכן נמי האילן ומשום הכי לא מיחה ואמאי כשטוען הלוקח טענת חזקה אמאי הויא חזקה ומשני ודאי הויא חזקה הואיל ולא מיחה דאע"ג דעדיין היה לו לתפוש הקרקע לאחר ג' אפילו הכי **איבעי ליה** למוכר **למחויי** בתוך ג' שנים דלא מכר לו כי אם האילן לבדו והיכא דלא מיחה איהו דאפסיד אנפשיה: **פיסקא שלש ארצות לחזקה** שצריך שיהיו המחזיק והמערער במלכות אחת של הללו ג'. אבל **היה** העורר **ביהודה והמחזיק בגליל אינה חזקה** משום דאין שיירות מצויות דליזלו ולימרו ליה דהאי אחזיק בשדהו כדי שיבוא וימחה: **עד שיהא עמו במדינה.** באותו מלכות כמו ביהודה ויהודה דשיירות מצויות ומצי למימחי ולמשלח ליה על ידייהו דהני שיירות ואי לא מיחה הוי חזקה א) אי לא מיחה הואיל דמחאה שלא בפניו הויא מחאה: **אפי' יהודה וגליל נמי** (לא) הויא חזקה ואמאי קתני מתני' עד שיהא עמו במדינה.

חשק שלמה על רבינו גרשום

א) נראה דל"ל ואי לא מיחה הוי חזקה הואיל דמחאה וכו'.

מסורת הש"ס

א) [לעיל לה: וש"נ], ב) כתובות דף יז:, ג) [שם ע"ש], ד) [שייך לעמוד הקודם]:

הגהות הב"ח

(א) גמ' ואי לכורכמא: (ב) שם דמהימן וכי תימא הכי נמי מיתקני רבנן מילתא: (ג) שם במשנה עמו במדינה א"ר יהודה כצ"ל ותיבת אמר נמחק: (ד) שם וילכו ויודיעוהו: (ה) רשב"ם ד"ה דאי לא תימא וכו' מאחר שהמוחזק בו אוכל: (ו) תוס' ד"ה קני וכו' שלא יוכל זה לחפור חלל:

לעזי רש"י

קרו"ג אוריינט"ל. פירוש כרכום הגדל בארצות המזרח, כרכום של גן הגדל בגינה (רש"י ב"ב דף טז ע"ב ועיין רש"י ב"מ דף קז ע"ב וערוך ערך פון):

ליקוטי רש"י

כורכמא דרישקא. כרכום של גן קרו"ג אורינט"ל הגדל בגנים [שבת קי.]. כרכום של גן שקורין קרוג אודמילי"ט והוא משובח שבכורכמין [ב"מ קז:]. **הני משכנתא דסורא.** ותקנתא דרבנן הוא הך משכנתא משום דהמלוה למחבירו על שדהו אסור לאכול הפירות משום רבית אבל בנכייתא מותר כעין משכנתא דסורא שמלוה עשרה מנה על שדהו ולסוף עשר שנים חוזר הקרקע לבעלים בחנם ונמצא קונה פירות של כל שנה במנה ואין כאן צד רבית ואע"פ שעוין הפירות כפלים שהרי הוא קרוב לשכר וקרוב להפסד שמקבל פירות של כל שנה במנה ואפילו בשנת שדפון שלא יהו שוין פירות השנה דינר [רשב"ם לעיל לה:]. **במישלם שניא.** דלא מיחזי כהלואה אלא כלוקח הימנו פירות השנים האלו במעות הללו [ב"מ סז:]. **שלש ארצות לחזקה.** שלש ארצות של א"י חשובות חלוקות זו מזו לענין חזקה כאילו הן ארצות נכריות ואם היה בזו והחזיק אחר בקרקע שיש לו בחברתה אינה חזקה. **במדינה.** או שניהם בגליל או שניהם ביהודה ואפי' הן בשתי עיירות. **מחאה שלא בפניו.** כגון אם היה בעיר אחת ומיחה שלא בפניו בפני שנים בעיר אחרת [כתובות יז:]. אם מיחה המערער בתוך שלש שנים לפני עדים שלא בפני המחזיק ואמר דעו שפלוני מחזיק בקרקע שלי בגזלה [לעיל כח:]. **אפילו יהודה וגליל נמי.** הוה ליה למחויי היכא דהוי ומדלא מחי תיהוי חזקה. **אפילו יהודה ויהודה.** בשתי עיירות נמי לא תיהוי חזקה דלא הוה ליה למחויי שלא בפניו. **הויא מחאה.** דמחבר חברא אית ליה דהני דמחי באנפיהו מגלו לאחריני ובא הדבר לאזני המחזיק וה"ל לאזדהורי בשטריה. [כתובות שם]. ולא בעינן שיאמר שלותו למחות בפניו אלא מכיון שמיחה שלא בפניו הויא מחאה שהרי יכול הדבר לבא לאזניו ואפי' לא ידע המחזיק מחאתו של מערער לא חיישינן מאחר שמיחה זה כהוגן [רשב"ם לקמן לט.]. **ומשנתינו.** דקתני יהודה וגליל לא. **בשעת חירום שנו.** ומאי שנא יהודה וגליל דנקיט. דיכול לומר לא נגלית לי מחאתו שאשמור את שטרי. אם יש חירום נמי מעיר לעיר אפי' שתי עיירות באותה מדינה נמי לא [כתובות שם].

The Mishnah explains the significance of this division:

הָיָה בִיהוּדָה – **If [the original owner] was in Judea** וְהֶחֱזִיק בְּגָלִיל – and someone **assumed occupancy** of the owner's land **in the Galilee,** בְּגָלִיל – or if the original owner was **in the Galilee** וְהֶחֱזִיק בִּיהוּדָה – **and** someone **assumed occupancy** of land **in Judea,** אֵינָהּ חֲזָקָה – the occupant does **not establish a** ***chazakah***[17] עַד שֶׁיְּהֵא עִמּוֹ בִּמְדִינָה אַחַת – **until [the original owner] is with [the occupant] in the same province.**[18]

R' Yehudah offers a dissenting opinion:

אָמַר רַבִּי יְהוּדָה – **R' Yehudah said:** לֹא אָמְרוּ שָׁלֹשׁ שָׁנִים אֶלָּא – **[The Sages] stated** that **three years** of occupancy are required to establish a *chazakah* **only** כְּדֵי שֶׁיְּהֵא בְּאַסְפַּמְיָא – **so that if [the original owner] was in Spain**[19] וְיַחֲזִיק שָׁנָה – **and [someone] occupied** his field for **a year,** יֵלְכוּ וְיוֹדִיעוּהוּ שָׁנָה – observers can **go and notify him** of this during the second **year,** וְיָבֹא לְשָׁנָה אַחֶרֶת – **and he will come** to reclaim his field **in the following year.**[20]

Gemara The Gemara sees an apparent contradiction in the Mishnah's words:

מַאי קָסָבַר תַּנָּא קַמָּא – **What does the Tanna Kamma hold?** Is a protest lodged in the occupant's absence effective or not?[21] אִי קָסָבַר מְחָאָה שֶׁלֹּא בְּפָנָיו הָוְיָא מְחָאָה – **If he holds** that **a protest** lodged **not in [the occupant's] presence is an** effective **protest,** אֲפִילוּ יְהוּדָה וְגָלִיל נַמִּי – then **even** if the original owner protested in **Judea and** the occupied field was in **the Galilee,** the protest should be effective **as well.** The Mishnah, however, implies that this is not so.[22] אִי קָסָבַר מְחָאָה שֶׁלֹּא בְּפָנָיו לֹא הָוְיָא מְחָאָה – Conversely, **if he holds that a protest** lodged **not in [the occupant's] presence is not an** effective **protest,** אֲפִילוּ יְהוּדָה וִיהוּדָה נַמִּי לֹא – then **even** if the original owner was in one city located in **Judea and** the occupant in another city in **Judea,** the protest should **not** be effective and it should thus be impossible to establish a *chazakah* in such a case.[23] Why, then, does the Mishnah state that a *chazakah* can be established in that case?

The Gemara resolves the contradiction:

אָמַר רַבִּי אַבָּא בַּר מָמָל אָמַר רַב – **R' Abba bar Mammal said in Rav's name:** לְעוֹלָם קָסָבַר מְחָאָה שֶׁלֹּא בְּפָנָיו הָוְיָא מְחָאָה – **Actually, the [Tanna Kamma] holds that a protest** lodged **not in [the occupant's] presence is an** effective **protest.** וּמַתְנִיתִין בִּשְׁעַת חֵירוּם שְׁנוּ – **And** as to the ruling of **our Mishnah, it was taught regarding a time** of **hostility** during which travel between provinces was severely curtailed. During such times, if the owner lodges a protest while he and the occupant were in different provinces, it is indeed meaningless, because the hostilities prevent word of the protest from reaching the occupant. As a rule, though, the Mishnah holds that a protest lodged in the occupant's absence is effective.

The Gemara asks:

וּמַאי שְׁנָא יְהוּדָה וְגָלִיל דְּנָקִיט – **And what is different about Judea and Galilee that** explains why the Tanna Kamma **chose** to discuss them specifically?[24]

The Gemara answers:

הָא קָא מַשְׁמַע לָן – When the Mishnah discusses Judea and Galilee specifically, **this** is what **it teaches us:**

NOTES

establish a *chazakah.* The following Mishnah delineates the regions within which we assume that reports of the original owner's protest will reach the holder.

17. If the owner of a field located in the Galilee was living in Judea and someone occupied that field for three years, a *chazakah* is not established. Travel between these regions was generally so sparse that it could not be assumed that word of a protest lodged in one province would reach the other province. Accordingly, there was no point for the owner of the field to protest its occupation even if he knew about the situation, since word of his protest would not reach the occupant in any case. The latter, knowing that this is the situation, is clearly expected to preserve his deed. Therefore, if he cannot produce it when the case comes to court, he loses the property (*Rashbam*).

18. I.e. unless the owner of the field is in the same province as the field so that word of his protest is certain to reach the field's occupant. In such a case, the absence of a protest establishes a *chazakah* even if the original owner and current occupant are in different towns, because word of a protest can certainly travel from one town to another. Consequently, since there is no plausible rationale for the owner's failure to protest, the occupant is awarded presumptive title to the field (*Rashbam*).

19. Spain was one year's travel from Eretz Yisrael in Mishnaic times. The Rabbis based the length of *chazakah* on this limit because it was extremely rare for a person to travel further away from home than that (*Rashbam*).

20. After someone occupies the field in Eretz Yisrael, it can take up to a year for the occupation to become public knowledge. It can then take another year for someone to travel to Spain and notify the original owner of the occupation. The third year of the three-year *chazakah* period allows the owner of the field time after having learned about its illegal occupation to return to Eretz Yisrael and issue a protest (*Rashbam*).

R' Yehudah thus explains the three-year *chazakah* differently than does the Tanna Kamma. He maintains that if a person is silent about the occupation of his land for even one day, that is ample proof that he sold it to the person occupying it even if the latter cannot produce a deed. In R' Yehudah's opinion, a three-year *chazakah* is necessary only in certain cases, such as the one the Mishnah describes.

Given the above, R' Yehudah would disagree in practice with two of the Tanna Kamma's rulings. According to R' Yehudah, if the owner remains in the same district as his field — and is thus immediately aware of anyone occupying it — anyone can establish a *chazakah* immediately upon assuming occupancy of it unless the original owner lodges a protest at that point; he need not occupy the field for three years, as the Tanna Kamma requires (*Rashbam.* See, however, *Chavos Yair's* gloss to the *Rif*). Additionally, according to R' Yehudah, if the owner of a field located in the Galilee was living in Judea (or in any faraway place) and someone occupied the land for three years, a *chazakah* is established because according to him, the Sages designated a three-year *chazakah* for situations such as these in which spreading word of the occupation is difficult. He disputes the Tanna Kamma's assertion that in such a case, no *chazakah* can be established at all (see *Rashba*).

21. The legal significance of an owner's protest is that it challenges the occupant's claim to the field and alerts him to retain his deed. The Gemara now considers whether the original owner's protest in the occupant's absence is effective or not. Let us suppose, for example, that the field's occupant and original owner lived in two sections of the same city. The owner then protested the occupation of his field in the presence of witnesses but not in front of the occupant. Can it be assumed that the occupant will undoubtedly hear about it by word of mouth so that the protest is effective or not? (*Rashbam;* see *Tosafos*).

22. The Mishnah rules that the occupant does not establish a *chazakah* if he is in Judea and the original owner is in the Galilee. Presumably, the reason for this is that a protest lodged in the occupant's absence is ineffective. [That is, when the original owner and occupant are in different regions, word of the owner's protest would not reach the occupant. Realizing the impossibility of informing the occupant about a protest, the owner might not bother to lodge a protest at all. His lack of protest therefore does not prove the occupant's ownership.]

23. If the owner has no way of lodging an effective protest when he is away from the occupant, then the absence of any protest is meaningless (see note 16 above). Consequently, a *chazakah* cannot be established.

24. Let the Mishnah simply state, "When there are hostilities between *any* two lands, the lands are considered separate with regard to *chazakah*" (*Rashbam*).

מתקיף לה רבא [א] ולימא לי' כורכמא דרישקא זביני לך עקור כורכמא דרישקא וזיל אלא אמר רבא [ב] בבא מחמת טענה אמר ליה מר קשישא בריה דרב חסדא לרב אשי (א) ואי כורכמא דרישקא זבין ליה מאי ה"ל למעבד [ג] איבעי ליה למחויי דאי לא תימא הכי [ד] הני משכנתא דסורא דכתב בה הכי במישלם שניא אלין תיפוק ארעא דא בלא כסף אי כביש ליה לשטר משכנתא ואמר לקוחה היא בידי הכי נמי דמהימן (ג) מיתקני רבנן מילתא דאתי בה לידי פסידא אלא איבעי ליה למחויי הכא נמי איבעי ליה למחויי: **מתני'** [ג] שלש ארצות לחזקה יהודה ועבר הירדן והגליל היה ביהודה והחזיק בגליל בגליל והחזיק ביהודה אינה חזקה עד שיהא עמו במדינה (ג) אחת אמר רבי יהודה לא אמרו שלש שנים אלא כדי שיהא באספמיא ויחזיק שנה (ד) ילכו ויודיעוהו שנה ויבא לשנה אחרת: **גמ'** [ג] מאי קסבר ת"ק אי קסבר מחאה שלא בפניו הויא מחאה אפי' יהודה וגליל נמי אי קסבר מחאה שלא בפניו לא הויא מחאה אפילו יהודה ויהודה נמי לא א"ר אבא בר ממל אמר רב לעולם קסבר [ד] מחאה שלא בפניו הויא מחאה ומשנתינו [ה] בשעת חירום שנו ומ"ש יהודה וגליל דנקיט הא קא משמע לן דסתם

רש"י

[ז] **קני** ליה משיפוליה ועד תהומא. פירש הקונטרס אם מת יטע אחר במקומו וקשיא לר"י דבהדיא קתני בהמוכר את הספינה (לקמן דף פא.) גבי קנה ב' אילנות דאם מתו אין לו קרקע ונראה לר"י דלא קני מקום האילן אלא לענין שלא יוכל (ו) לחפור זה תחת תחתיו

מתקיף לה רבא. אמאי קנה קרקע דכנגד האילן מאחר דמתן לא קנה קרקע כלל לא קנה ודקשיא לכו דכיון להתקיים בקרקע זו קנאו נמצא שקנה יניקת הקרקע גם ליטע אחר במקומו של זה אחר שייבש או יקצץ: **לימא ליה.** מוכר: **כורכמא דרישקא זביני לך.** קרוג אורייטי"ל וגידלים למכרו בקרקע ומניחו עד שיגמור פריו ועוקרו אף האילן שמכרתי לך לפירותיו הקרקע לא מכרתי לך אלא להניח אילנך בקרקע שלי כל ימי שצריך לקרקע עד שייבש היינו דומיא דכרכום ומאחר שיבש לא תהני לו הקרקע עוד: **עקור כורכמא דרישקא וזיל.** כמו שעוקרים את הכרכום אחר שנתבשל ואינו יכול ליטע כרכום אחר במקומו גם אתה לא תטע אילן אחר במקומו: **אלא אמר רבא.** הכא הוא דקני לקרקע שתחת האילן בבא מחמת הטענה שטוען למוכר בפירות מכרת לי האילן והקרקע שתחתיו ליטע אחר במקומו ובשטר ואכלתיה שני חזקה ולא נזהרתי בשטרי יותר משלש שנים דהשתא לא דמי לכורכמא דרישקא: **א"ל מר קשישא בריה דרב חסדא לרב אשי.** מאחר שהקונה דקל יחידי נאמן בטענה זו ויטע אחר במקומו אי כורכמא דרישקא זבין ליה אם מכר לו סתם דקל לפירותיו ולא פירש לו קרקע דקיימא לן אין לו קרקע דאם יבש או נעקר לא יטע אחר במקומו: **מאי הוה ליה.** למוכר למעבד שלא יהא בא מחמת טענה ויטע אחר במקומו דכל אדם יטעון אחר שלש שנים שפירש לו קרקע מאחר שהוא נאמן בטענתו: **איבעי ליה למחויי.** בתוך כל שלש להודיע שלא מכר לו קרקע אלא כי כורכמא דרישקא ושוב לא יכול לטעון אחר שלש שטר היה לי ואבד דכיון דמיחה בו זה היה לו להזהר בשטרו: **דאי לא תימא הכי.** דמחאה כי האי גוונא לא הויא מחאה מאחר (ה) שמודה בו שאוכל עכשיו מן הקרקע מן הדין לא הויא מחאה אלא בטוען פלניא גזלנא הוא כדלקמן: **מתני'** אמרינן בגמרא ארץ ישראל א"ר אלעזר אפי' שתי אכסניות כגון שלומי ונבורו והירדן מפסיק ביניהם ועומד ורואה אחד מחזיק בשדה שלו אינה חזקה עד שיהא עמו באותה העיר ובאותה מדינה רב אמר עיקר חזקה הכנסת פירות דאפי' ראהו חורש וקוצר ומעמר ודש וזורה ובורר ולא ראהו מכניס פירות אינה חזקה עד שיראהו מכניס פירות: **מתני'** שלש ארצות. בארץ ישראל: לחזקה. חלוקות זו מזו לענין חזקת שלש שנים כדמפרש ואזיל: **היה.** בעל הקרקע ביהודה והחזיק בגליל שהיה הקרקע בגליל והחזיק בה אדם שלש שנים בלא מחאה אינה חזקה כדמפרש טעמא בגמרא דסתם יהודה וגליל בשעת חירום דמי שאין שיירות מצויות מזו לזו ולא הויא מחאה שהרי אין מי שיגיד לו למחזיק שמיחה זה ויזהר בשטרו דהא אין שיירות מצויות הלכך כיון דאינו יכול למחות אע"ג דלא מיחה לא הפסיד בשתיקתו והיה לו לזה המחזיק ליזהר בשטרו שהרי יודע שאין בעל הקרקע יכול למחות: **עד שיהא עמו במדינה.** כגון שהיה ביהודה בעיר אחרת דכיון דשיירות מצויות הוה ליה למחויי ומדלא מיחה הפסיד: **א"ר יהודה לא אמרו שלש שנים כו'.** לחלוק בא ולומר דאין חלוקות לחזקה דהיה בגליל והחזיק ביהודה הויא חזקה ואפילו היה באספמיא שהוא רחוק מהלך שנה מארץ ישראל והחזיק בארץ ישראל הויא חזקה שהרי לכך האריכו שני חזקה זמן מרובה של שלש שנים כדי שיעור שאם היה באספמיא ואם יחזיק זה בקרקע שלו שנה ובתוך שנה ראשונה ילכו הקול ילכו בשנה שניה ויודיעוהו לבעל הקרקע ולשנה שלישית יבא וימחה ובגמרא מפרש אי בעי ר' יהודה מחאה בפניו או לא ויותר ממהלך שנה אין דרך אדם להרחיק מביתו ולפי ההוה תקנו. וטעמא דר' יהודה לא משום דתלת שנין מיזדהר איניש בשטריה אלא כדמפרש כדי שיהא כו' וטעמא דחזקה לדידיה דלא שביק איניש דאכלוה לארעיה בלא רשותיה ואפילו שעה אחת ושתיק אלא לכך האריכו שלש שנים שפעמים היה המערער רחוק אבל אי הוי המערער בעיר הוי חזקה מיד כדאמרי' לקמן בפירקין: **גמ'** מאי קסבר תנא קמא. דר' יהודה: **אי קסבר מחאה.** שמוחה בעל הקרקע במחזיק אפי' שלא בפניו כגון שניהם דרין בעיר אחת ומיחה בפני שנים מן השוק שלא בפניו של מחזיק אפי' הכי הויא מחאה דחברך חברא אית ליה ושמע המחזיק בדבר זה והיה לו להזהר בשטרו ומדלא נזהר הפסיד והלכך קתני עד שיהא עמו במדינה אחת דכיון שניהם במדינה אחת הויא מחאה אע"פ שאינם בעיר אחת: **אפי' יהודה וגליל נמי.** היה ביהודה והחזיק בגליל תיהוי מחאה: **ואי קסבר לא הויא מחאה.** כדקתני דהיה ביהודה והחזיק בגליל אינה חזקה: **אפי' היה ביהודה והחזיק ביהודה.** בעיר אחרת נמי לא תיהוי מחאה ואמאי קתני עד שיהא עמו במדינה: **לעולם קסבר מחאה שלא בפניו הויא מחאה.** ומשום הכי קתני עד שיהא עמו במדינה ודקשיא לך אפילו יהודה וגליל נמי תיהוי מחאה מתני' בשעת חירום תיגרות יש בין יהודה וגליל ואין שיירות מצויות מזו לזו ואם ימחה לא יבא הדבר לאזניו של מחזיק שיזהר בשטרו והלכך לא הויא מחאה וכיון דלא הויא מחאתו של מערער מחאה חזקתו של זה נמי לא הוי חזקה דטעמא דחזקה ג' שנים קונה משום דמצי טעין ליה מחזיק אמאי לא מחית בתוך שלש ואילו הכא לא מצי למטען הכי דהא לא יכול למחות דהא אינה מחאה: **ומ"ש יהודה וגליל דנקט.** דכיון דבשעת חירום מיירי הוא הדין לכל המלכיות שיש חירום בין זו לזו והכי הוה ליה למיתני כל הארצות חלוקות לחזקה בשעת חירום. ואית דמפרשי מ"ש יהודה וגליל דנקט כיון דבשעת חירום מוקמת לה מ"ש יהודה וגליל דלא הויא חזקה אפילו יהודה ויהודה לא תיהוי חזקה ואין נראה בעיני דאם כן הוה ליה למימר כדלעיל אי הכי אפילו יהודה ויהודה נמי לא ועוד דהכי מתרץ ר' אבא בשעת חירום שנו שיש תגרה בין המלכיות אבל עיירות של מדינה ומדינה אין ביניהם תגרה:

הא

תוספות

לרשב"א מהא דתניא בהמוכר את הבית (לקמן דף עב.) כשהקדיש ג' אילנות בזה אחר זה היה פודה את האילנות בשווייהן ואם היה מקום האילן קדוש כלל היה לו לפדות לפי חשבון בית זרע חומר שעורים בחמשים שקלים כסף דכן הוא הדין כשמקדיש אפי' משהו קרקע עם האילן ואומר ר"י דבלאו הכי דמי רבא מילתייהו דנהרדעי שפיר ולרשב"א נראה דהתם כמ"ד בעין רעה מוכר לפיכך אין קדוש אפי' מקום האילן אבל נהרדעי סברי מוכר בעין יפה הוא מוכר: **ואי** כורכמא דרישקא. לכך נקט כורכמא דרישקא שמתקיים בקרקע ג' שנים דהיינו שני חזקה ולכך להשהותו בקרקע כמו שיכול להתקיים: **אלא** כדי שיהא באספמיא. דעד שם יש מהלך שנה ויותר מכאן אין דרך להרחיק יותר מקרקעו ואם הרחיק יותר לא פלוג: **מחאה** שלא בפניו כו'. תימה דבכל דוכתי נקט מחאה ואמאי לא נקט חזקה שלא בפניו הויא חזקה ויש לומר לפי שהטעם תלוי במחאה ולא בחזקה שאדם המחזיק בקרקעותיו של חבירו אין לו קול שהוא חוקר ושואל על נכסיו אבל המחאה אין לה קול כל כך שאין המחזיק מחזר אם מוחה לו בעל קרקע לפיכך אין חזקתו חזקה כשאין יכול לשמוע מחאתו דמה יועיל שמיחה:

דסתם

עין משפט נר מצוה

פא א מיי' פכ"ד מהל' מכירה הל' ו סמג עשין פב טוש"ע ח"מ סימן רטז סעיף ט:

פב ב ג מיי' פי"ג מהל' טוען ונטען הל' יח סמג עשין צה טוש"ע ח"מ סימן קמא סעי' כ:

פג ד מיי' שם פי"א הל' ה סמג שם טוש"ע ח"מ סימן קמו סעי' א:

פד ה מיי' שם הל' ג וסמג שם טוש"ע ח"מ סי' קמג סעי' א:

רבינו גרשום

מתקיף לה רבא אמאי קנה מקום האילן. לימא ליה. מוכר ללוקח לכורכמא דרישקא זבינא לך. דומיא הוא כעין שמוכר אדם לחבירו ירקות של צבע כורכמא דרישקא מעלה שקורין אריינט"ל שלא מכר לו כי אם הצבע עצמה ולא מקום הכורכמא הכי נמי מצי למימר ליה כי יבש האילן אנא הדקל זבינא לך שקול אילנך ועקור וזיל. אלא אמר רבא. משום הכי קני ליה משיפוליה ועד תהומא **בבא** הלוקח מחמת **טענה** שטוען ואמר אילן ומקומו מכר לי והחזקתי בו שני חזקה ולא מיחה במקומו אדם: **אי** לכורכמא דרישקא. כלומר האילן לבדו כל זמן שלא יתייבש **מאי הוה ליה למיעבד** מה מועיל לו מחאתו והא כשלשלם שני חזקה עדיין לא הגיע זמן לקצור הכורכמא ועדיין ברשותו עומדת הקרקע שתחת הכורכמא וכן נמי האילן ומשום הכי לא מיחה ואמאי כשטוען הלוקח טענת חזקה אמאי הויא חזקה ומשני ודאי הויא חזקה הואיל ולא מיחה דאע"ג דעדיין היה לו לתפוש הקרקע לאחר ג' אפילו הכי **איבעי ליה** למוכר **למחויי** בתוך ג' שנים דלא מכר לו כי אם האילן לבדו והיכא דלא מיחה איהו דאפסיד אנפשיה: **פיסקא שלש ארצות לחזקה** שצריך שיהיו המחזיק והמערער במלכות אחת של הללו ג'. אבל היה העורר ביהודה והמחזיק בגליל **אינה חזקה** משום דאין שיירות מצויות לדילדו ולימרו ליה דהאי אחזיק בשדהו כדי שיבוא וימחה: **עד שיהא עמו במדינה.** באותו מלכות כמו ביהודה ויהודה דשיירות מצויות ומצי למימחי ולמשלח ליה על ידייהו דהני שיירות ואי לא מיחה הוי חזקה (א) אי לא מיחה הואיל דמחאה שלא בפניו הויא מחאה: **אפי' יהודה** וגליל נמי (לא) הויא חזקה ואמאי קתני מתני' עד שיהא עמו במדינה.

חשק שלמה על רבינו גרשום

א) נראה דל"ל ואי לא מיחה הוי חזקה הואיל דמחאה וכו'.

מסורת הש"ס

א) [לעיל לה: וש"נ], ב) כתובות דף יז., ג) [שם ע"ש], ד) [שייך לעמוד הקודם].

הגהות הב"ח

(א) גמ' ואי לכורכמא: (ב) שם דמהימן וכי תימא הכי נמי מיתקני רבנן מילתא: (ג) שם במדינה עמו במדינה א"ר יהודה כל"ל ותיבת אחת נמחק: (ד) שם ילכו ויודיעוהו: (ה) רשב"ם ד"ה דאי לא תימא וכו' מאחר שהמחזיק בו אוכל: (ו) תוס' ד"ה קני וכו' שלא יוכל זה לחפור תחת:

לעזי רש"י

קרו"ג אורינט"ל. פירוש כרכום הגדל בארצות המזרח, כרכום של גן הגדל בגינה (רש"י ב"ב דף טז ע"ב ועיין רש"י ב"מ דף קז ע"ב וערוך ערך פוך).

ליקוטי רש"י

כורכמא דרישקא. כרכום של גן קרו"ג אורינט"ל הגדל בגנים [שבת קי.]. כרכום של גן שקורין קרוג אורמינל"ש והוא משובח שבכרכומין [ב"מ קז:]. **הני משכנתא דסורא.** ותקנתא דרבנן הויא הך משכנתא משום שהמלוה לחבירו על שדהו אסור לאכול הפירות משום רבית אבל בנכייתא מותר כעין משכנתא דסורא שמלוה עשרה מנה על שדהו ונותן עשר שנים ואחר הקרקע לבעלים בחנם ונמצא קונה פירות של כל שנה בחנם ואין כאן של רבית ואע"פ שאין הפירות כפלים שהרי הוא קרוב לשכר וקרוב להפסד שמקבל הקרקע בכל שנה במנה ואפילו בשנת שדפון שלא יהיו שוין פירות השנה דינר [רשב"ם לעיל לה:]. **במישלם שניא.** בלא מיחזי כהלואה אלא כלוקח הימנו פירות השנים האלו במעות הללו [ב"מ סז:]. **שלש ארצות לחזקה.** שלש ארצות של א"י משונות חלוקות זו מזו לענין חזקה כאילו הן ארצות נכריות ואם היה בזו והחזיק אחר בקרקע שיש לו בחברתה אינה חזקה. **במדינה.** או שניהם בגליל ואפי' הן בשתי עיירות. **מחאה שלא בפניו.** כגון אם היה בעיר אחת ומיחה שלא בפניו בפני שנים [כתובות יז:]. אם מיחה המערער בתוך שלש שנים לפני עדים שלא בפני המחזיק ואמר דעו שפלוני מחזיק בקרקע שלי בגזילה [לעיל כח:]. **אפילו יהודה וגליל נמי.** הוה ליה למחויי היכא דהוי ומדלא מחי תיהוי חזקה. **אפילו יהודה ויהודה.** בשתי עיירות נמי לא תיהוי חזקה דלא הוה ליה למחויי שלא בפניו. **הויא מחאה.** דהמכרך חברא אית ליה דהכי מגלו לאחריני.

וכל הדבר לאזני המחזיק והו"ל לאזדהורי בשטריה. ולא בעינן שישלח שלוחו לומר למחזיק מחאתו שהרי אם מוחה שלא בפניו אלא מכוין שמיחה אע"פ שהרי יכול הדבר לבא לאזניו ואפילו לא ידע המחזיק מחאתו אם לא מיישינן מאחר שמיחה זה כהוגן [רשב"ם לקמן לט.]. **ומשנתינו.** דקתני יהודה וגליל לא. **בשעת חירום שנו.** דיכול לומר לא נגלית לי מחאתו שאשמור את שטרי. **ומאי שנא יהודה וגליל דנקיט.** אם יש חירום נמי מעיל לעיר אפי' שתי עיירות באותה מדינה נמי לא [כתובות שם].

דסתם יהודה וגליל כשעת חירום דמו: אמר
רב יהודה אמר רב אין מחזיקין בנכסי בורח כי
אמריתה קמיה דשמואל אמר לי וכי למחות
בפניו הוא צריך ורב מאי קמ"ל מחאה שלא
בפניו לא הויא מחאה והאמר רב מחאה שלא
בפניו הויא מחאה רב טעמא דתנא דידן
קמפרש וליה לא סבירא ליה ואיכא דאמרי
אמר רב יהודה אמר רב מחזיקים בנכסי בורח
כי אמריתה קמיה דשמואל אמר לי פשיטא וכי
למחות בפניו הוא צריך ורב מאי קמ"ל מחאה
שלא בפניו הויא מחאה והא אמרה רב חדא
זימנא אלא הא קמ"ל [א]דאפי' מיחה בפני ב'
שאין יכולין לומר לו הויא מחאה (א) דאמר רב
ענן לדידי מפרשא לי מיניה דמר שמואל מיחה
בפני שני בני אדם שיכולים לומר לו הויא
מחאה מיחה בפני שני בני אדם שאין יכולין
לומר לו לא הויא מחאה ורב [ב]חברך
חברא אית ליה וחברא דחברך חברא אית
ליה אמר רבא הלכתא [ג]אין מחזיקין בנכסי
בורח (ג) ומחאה שלא בפניו הויא מחאה תרתי
לא קשיא [ד]כאן בורח מחמת ממון כאן בורח
מחמת מרדין: היכי דמי מחאה אמר רב זביד
[ה]פלניא גזלנא הוא לא הויא מחאה [ו]פלניא
גזלנא (ב) הוא דנקיט לה לארעאי בגזלנותא
ולמחר

רש"י

הא קמ"ל. ר' אבא: דסתם יהודה וגליל. אפי' בשעת שלום: כשעת חירום דמי. שאין שיירות מצויות מזו לזו אבל בשאר מלכיות אי איכא חירום לא הויא חזקה אבל בשעת שלום הויא חזקה דהא שיירות מצויות והאי דקאמר רבי אבא בשעת חירום שנו הכי קאמר יהודה וגליל הרי הן כשעת חירום של שאר מלכיות: אין מחזיקין בנכסי בורח. כלומר אם החזיק אינה חזקה כדמפרש ואזיל דקסבר מחאה שלא בפניו לא הויא מחאה וכיון דלא יכול למחות גם זה לא יכול להחזיק וכר' יהודה סבירא ליה דאמר במתניתין ילכו ויודיעוהו שנה ויבא לשנה אחרת דמשמע דצריך למחות בפניו: כי אמריתה. להא דרב קמיה דשמואל אחר פטירתו של רב שבא ללמוד לפני שמואל. רב מת מקמי שמואל כדאיתא בשחיטת חולין (דף צה:) דכל זמן שהיה רב קיים הוה שלח לי' ר' יוחנן לקדם רבינו שבבבל כי נח נפשיה דרב שלח לי' לשמואל לקדם חבירנו כו': א"ל. שמואל: וכי למחות בפניו הוא צריך. בתמיה אלא לא צריך למחות בפניו דמחאה שלא בפניו הויא מחאה והלכך מחזיקים נמי שלא בפניו דליבעי ליה למחויי: ומקשה גמ' והאמר רב מחאה שלא בפניו הויא מחאה. כדאמר ר' אבא אמר רב לעיל לעולם קסבר מחאה שלא בפניו כו' (ג) (ומדפריך) למילתיה דמ"ק איכא למימר דסבירא ליה הכי: לטעמא. דתנא קמא פירש רב משום דקשיא רישא לסיפא וליכא לתרצה אלא בכי האי גוונא: וליה לא סבירא ליה. אלא כרבי יהודה סבירא ליה: מחזיקין בנכסי בורח. דמחאה שלא בפניו הויא מחאה ואיבעי ליה למחויי ומדלא מיחה הפסיד דכיון דשיירות מצויות אנן סהדי שנודע לו שאחרים החזיקו בקרקע שלו ולא מצי טעין לא ידעתי ולפיכך לא מחיתי דכי היכי דמחאה שלא בפניו הויא מחאה משום דחברך חברא אית ליה ושמע המחזיק מחאתו של זה המערער הכי נמי נודע לו שהחזיק זה בקרקע שלו והוא לא מיחה ולפיכך הפסיד והאי דנקט בורח לאו דוקא דהוא הדין לכל מרחיקי ארצם אלא אורחא דמילתא נקט שאין דרך בני אדם להחזיק בקרקע של אחרים בגזל אלא בקרקע בורח: א"ל פשיטא. דמחזיקין דהא ממתניתין דקתני שלש ארצות לחזקה שמעינן דמחאה שלא בפניו הויא מחאה ואיבעי ליה למחויי ומדלא מיחה הפסיד. בגמרא ירושלמי רב אמר אין חזקה לבורח ולא מארץ לארץ ושמואל אמר יש להן חזקה אמר רב נחמן קרא מסייע ליה למר ויתן לה המלך סרים אחד לאמר השב את כל אשר לה ואת כל תבואת השדה מיום עזבה את הארץ ועד עתה (מלכים ב ח): ורב מאי קמ"ל. דקאמר מחזיקים בנכסי בורח הא ודאי קמ"ל מחאה שלא בפניו הויא מחאה והיה לו למחות הלכך חזקה נמי שלא בפניו בלא מחאה הויא חזקה: והא אמרה רב חדא זימנא. דאמר ר' אבא בר ממל אמר רב לעיל לעולם מחאה שלא בפניו הויא מחאה כו' ומסתמא הוה שמעינן דכסתם מתני' סבירא ליה מדמפרש לה הכי: אפי' מיחה בפני ב' שאין יכולין לומר לו. כגון איגרין או שהולכין למדינת הים ומרחיקין מאותו המלכות שדר בה המחזיק [ז](אפי') הכי מחזיקין בנכסי בורח דתיהני ליה מחאה כי הך ואע"ג דהנך לא יאמרו לו למחזיק דחברך חברא אית ליה והלכך כיון דהויא מחאה חזקה נמי הויא חזקה ושמואל שהיה מקשה על דברי רב ואומר פשיטא וכי למחות לפניו הוא צריך להך רבותא דקאמר רב לא אסיק אדעתיה והלכך פריך שפיר מאי אתא רב לאשמועינן: אמר רב ענן לדידי מיפרשא לי כו'. אשינוייא דשנינן אליבא דרב אתא [ח]לאשמועינן ולמימר דהך רבותא לא סבירא ליה לשמואל כדמפרש ואזיל והוה מתמה פשיטא: הלכתא אין מחזיקין בנכסי בורח. דמחאה שלא בפניו לא הויא מחאה וכיון דלא מצי מערער למחויי מחזיק נמי לא מצי אחזוקי: ומחאה שלא בפניו הויא מחאה. והלכך חזקה שלא בפניו הויא חזקה ומשום הכי מחזיקין בנכסי בורח דהא מצי למחויי ומדלא מיחה הפסיד והיינו דקפריך גמרא תרתי בתמיה משום דקשיא רישא לסיפא ומשני לא קשיא כאן בבורח מחמת ממון פסיק רבא הלכתא (ג) שלא בפניו הויא מחאה משום דמצי למחויי וכל מקום שזה יכול למחות חזקתו של חבירו בנכסיו הויא חזקה הואיל ולא מיחה דכיון דמחמת חוב ממון הוא בורח אין זה בורח אלא לאישתמוטי בעלמא עד דהוה ליה ופרע ואינו ירא למחות דכיון דאנוס הוא ואין לו מה לפרוע אין רודפין אחריו ואם נודע מקומו שברח שם אינו חושש: כאן בבורח מחמת מרדין. מחמת רציחת נפשות ירא למחות פן יודע מקום תחנותו וירדוף גואל הדם אחריו כי יחם לבבו והשיגו והרגו ובדידיה קפסיק רבא דאין מחזיקין בנכסי בורח והכי הלכתא: מרדין. לשון רציחה בלשון פרס כדאמרינן בהגוזל ומאכיל (ב"ק דף קיז.) השתא פרסאי דקפדי אשפיכות דמים ואמרי מרדין מרדין: היכי דמי מחאה. אמחאה שלא בפניו קאי דפסיקנא לעיל דהויא מחאה: אמר רב זביד. אמר לסהדי פלניא גזלנא הוא לא הויא מחאה שאפילו אם יאמרו עדים לשון זה למחזיק לא אתי לאזדהורי בשטריה דהא לא ידע אמאי קרי ליה גזלן שיזהר בשטרו: אבל אמר לו פלניא גזלנא הוא דקאכיל לארעאי בגזלנותא. שהרי לא מכרתיה לו דהשתא הוה ליה לאיזדהורי בשטר מכירת שדה (ד) זה מאחר שערער זה עליו והלכך הויא מחאה: ולמחר תבענא ליה בדינא הרי זה מחאה.

ואי

תוספות

דסתם יהודה וגליל כשעת חירום דמי. ואם תאמר ומאי שנא דגבי גט אמר בריש גיטין (ד' ז: ושם ד"ה כיון) המביא גט ממדינה למדינה בארץ ישראל אין צריך לומר בפני נכתב ובפני נחתם משום כיון דאיכא עולי רגלים משכח שכיחי לקיימו ואפי' בזמן שאין בהמ"ק (ה) כיון דאיכא בתי דינים דקביעי משכח שכיחי וי"ל דודאי גבי גט עדים מצויין לקיימו אפי' מיהודה לגליל לפי שהאשה רגילה לחזור אחר עדי קיום אבל הכא אי לאו דשכיחי טובא לעולם לא ישמע מחאתו שאין המחזיק רגיל לחזור אם מוחה לו ואם לאו הלכך בשיירות דעולי רגלים ובתי דינין לא סגי וא"ת והא דאמרי' התם (דף ו.) רב ששת מצריך אפי' [ו](ממעברא לעברא) ורבא מצריך אפי' באותה שכונה ופריך והא רבא הוא דאמר לפי שאין עדים מצויין לקיימו ומשני בני מחוזא דניידי אטו מי נימא דבמחוזא מחאה שלא בפניו לא הוי מחאה ויצטרך לבא לפניו למחות וי"ל דלא דמי דכשמותמים על הגט במחוזא והולכין להן אין דרך שיעסקו בעיר אנחנו חתמנו על גט פלוני אבל במחאה דרך הליכתם רגילות לומר פלוני מיחה ושומעין אחרים עד שנשמע בבית המחזיק: אין מחזיקין בנכסי בורח. בבורח מחמת ממון איירי דאי מחמת מרדין בהא לא פליג שמואל כדמוכח בסמוך ודוקא בבורח אבל באינש דעלמא הוי חזקה שיכול לבא למקום שמחזיק שם ולמחות אבל בורח אינו רשאי לבא במקום שעומד לא הויא מחאה שלא בפניו וסבר לה כר' יהודה דקתני ויבא לשנה אחרת וימחה משמע שצריך למחות בפניו וא"ת ודלמא ר' יהודה נמי לא בעי מחאה בפניו וה"ק ויבא במדינה שהמחזיק בה וימחה כגון אם הוא ביהודה יבא ביהודה וימחה שאז תשמע מחאתו וכי תימא (ו) וכיון שחזקה נשמעת עד אספמיא גם המחאה תשמע עד אספמיא ואי מחאה שלא בפניו הוי מחאה ליתיב אדוכתיה ולימחי הא ליתא דאי כל מקום שחזקה נשמעת גם המחאה נשמעת אם כן היכי מוכח לעיל לרבנן מחאה שלא בפניו הויא מחאה אימא דלעולם (ז) דלא הוי מחאה והיה ביהודה והחזיק ביהודה הוי חזקה לפי שהיא נשמעת ויבא וימחה לפני המחזיק אבל מיהודה לגליל אין החזקה נשמעת ומשום הכי לא הויא חזקה אלא ודאי פשיטא ליה לגמרא דהחזקה נשמעת מרחוק אבל מחאה לא ולהכי מוכח לעיל שפיר דסברי רבנן דהויא מחאה שלא בפניו דאי לא הויא מחאה אלא צריך לבא לפני המחזיק א"כ מיהודה לגליל תהא חזקה כמו שביהודה יש לו לילך ולמחות מיהודה לגליל נמי ילך לפניו וימחה וי"ל מדלא תני ר' יהודה אומר ויבא לשנה אחרת וימחה ויודיעהו שמע מינה שצריך למחות לפניו. ר"י:

ולמחר נקיטנא ליה. נראה לר"י דלא צריך למימר נקיטנא ליה אלא אורחא דמילתא נקט מדלא קאמר רב זביד פלוני גזלנא הוא דאכיל לארעאי בגזלנותא לא הויא מחאה פלוני גזלנא הוא דאכיל לארעאי בגזלנותא ולמחר נקיטנא ליה בדינא הויא מחאה:

רב

עין משפט נר מצוה

פה א ב מיי' פי"א מהל' טוען ונטען הל' ו סמג עשין לה טוש"ע ח"מ סי' קמו סעיף א:
פו ג ד מיי' פי"ד שם הל' י סמג שם טוש"ע ח"מ סי' קמג סעיף ג:
פז ה ו מיי' פי"א שם הלכה ז סמג שם טוש"ע ח"מ סי' קמו סעיף ד:

רבינו גרשום

ומשני האי דקתני יהודה וגליל לא הויא מחאה משום דבשעת חירום הדרכים שנו ומשום הכי לא הויא חזקה דאי טעין ליה מחזיק אלמלא היית מוחה בתוך ג' הייתי מזהר בשטרא דלא מירכס מצי למימר ליה המערער משום דחרם הדרכים הוא לא הוו שיירות מצויות דאזלי ולימחו לך ולהכי לא מחיתי. ומקשה אי הכי מאי שנא יהודה וגליל דנקיט דלא הויא חזקה אפי' יהודה ויהודה נמי לא הויא חזקה הואיל דבשעת חירום הוא ומשני משום הכי נקט [יהודה וגליל] דכשעת חירום דמי דלאו שיירות מצויות: אין מחזיקין בנכסי בורח. דאי ברח אינש ממלכות ואתא אחר והחזיק בנכסיו לא הויא חזקה. א) והא אמר ליה לרב דמ"ש הכי אין מחזיקין דמחאה שלא בפניו לא הויא מחאה. והא אמר ר' אבא בר ממל אמר רב לעיל כדמתרץ מתני' דמחאה שלא בפניו הויא מחאה ואמאי אין מחזיקין: רב לטעמיה דתנא דמתני' קאמר. איכא דאמרי כו' ה"ג כי אמריתה קמיה דשמואל אמר לי פשיטא וכי למחויי בפניו הוא צריך וכיון שהוא יכול למחות בכל מקום שהוא ולא מיחה פשיטא דמחזיקין. ורב מאי קמ"ל דמחזיקין אי משום דקסבר מחאה שלא בפניו הויא מחאה והאי לא מיחה להכי מחזיקין והא אמרה רב חדא זימנא כדאמרינן לעיל. אלא הא קמ"ל רב דאע"ג דמיחה בפני שנים שאינן יכולין לומר לו שאינן עוברי דרכים אפי' הכי הויא מחאה שאם אין יכולין לומר לו לימרו למאן דלימא ליה משום דחברך וכו' אבל אי לא מיח' כלל (אין) מחזיקין: תרתי. בתמי' קאמר כלומר דהני תרי מילי לא מצי קיימי דחדא קשיא לאידך משום דאי אמרינן אין מחזיקין בנכסי בורח משמע משום דמחאה שלא בפניו לא הויא מחאה והדר תני דהויא מחאה: כאן בבורח מחמת ממון שמחויב לאנשי העיר אין צריך לו להחביא עצמו כל כך והיה יכול למחות שלא בפניו והויא מחאה ואי לא מיחה והחזיק אחר בנכסיו הוי חזקה אבל בורח מחמת מרדין שהיה מורד ומחויב למלכות אין מחזיקין בנכסיו משום דאי הוה מוחה יוודע למלכות היכן הוא ויבקשוהו עד שימצאוהו ויהא מסוכן בגופו ומשום הכי

מסורת הש"ס

א) [לעיל כח: וש"נ], ב) [לקמן לט.], ג) צ"ל ומדמפרש, ד) גי' רש"א משום, ה) נ"א לאיפלוגי, ו) [צ"ל משכונה לשכונה]:

הגהות הב"ח

(א) גמ' דאמר רב ענן נ"ב גירסת רשב"ם אמר רב ענן: (ב) שם פלניא גזלנא הוא דקאכיל לה לארעאי: (ג) רשב"ם ד"ה ומחאה וכו' רבא הלכתא מחאה שלא בפניו וכו' דאנוס הוא דאין לו: (ד) ד"ה אבל וכו' שדה זו מאחר: (ה) תוס' ד"ה דסתם וכו' בית המקדש קיים כיון וכו' וי"ל דודאי גט עדים מצויין לקיימו וכו' אם מוחה לו אם לאו הלכך בשכיחות דעולי רגלים: (ו) ד"ה אין וכו' וכי תימא כיון כצ"ל ואות ו' נמחק: (ז) בא"ד אימא דלעולם לא כצ"ל ואות ד' נמחק:

ליקוטי רש"י

מחאה שלא בפניו הויא מחאה. לא הוי מחאה. עיין ליקוטי רש"י בע"א. חברך חברא אית ליה. ויודיעוהו [כתובות קט:]. דהני דמחי באנפייהו מגלו לאחריני ובא הדבר לאזני המחזיק וה"ל לאזדהורי בשטריה [שם יז:]. ויאמרו זה לזה והדבר בא לאזניו ואינו יכול לומר אילו שמעתי הייתי זהיר ברא"ית זכותי [לעיל כח:]. וזה מגלה לחבירו וזה לחבירו עד שיודע [ערכין טז.]. מחמת מרדין. שהרג את הנפש ופרסאי הורגין על שפיכות דמים כדאמרינן בבבא קמא (קיז.) מרדין היא רציחה בלשון פרסי וכן מפורש בשערים דרב האי גאון (שער מ) [ב"מ לט.].

חשק שלמה על רבינו גרשום

א) נראה דצ"ל ופריכין דרב מאי קמ"ל דאין מחזיקין משום דמחאה שלא בפניו.

דִּסְתָם יְהוּדָה וְגָלִיל בִּשְׁעַת חֵירוּם דָּמוּ – That as a **general** rule, **Judea and Galilee have the same status** concerning *chazakah* **as** that of other lands during **times of hostility.** That is, if the original owner and occupant are in different provinces, one in Judea and the other in Galilee, the owner cannot lodge an effective protest even during peacetime.[1]

Having discussed whether a protest must be lodged in the occupant's presence, the Gemara now cites a ruling related to that question:

אָמַר רַב יְהוּדָה אָמַר רַב – Rav Yehudah said in the name of Rav: **אֵין מַחֲזִיקִין בְּנִכְסֵי בּוֹרֵחַ – One cannot establish** an effective ***chazakah* upon the property of a fugitive,**[2] because according to Rav, an owner's protest that is not registered in the occupant's presence is meaningless.[3] Hence, since a fugitive owner cannot possibly lodge an effective protest, a *chazakah* cannot be established upon his property.[4]

Rav Yehudah now cites a dissenting view:

כִּי אַמְרִיתָהּ קַמֵּיהּ דִּשְׁמוּאֵל – When I repeated [the ruling] in Shmuel's presence,[5] **אָמַר לִי – he said to me:** **וְכִי לִמְחוֹת בְּפָנָיו הוּא צָרִיךְ – Now must [an owner] in fact protest in [the occupant's] presence?** Surely not! Even if a protest is lodged in the occupant's absence, it is effective anyway. Hence, one can indeed establish a *chazakah* upon a fugitive's property.[6]

The Gemara now challenges Rav's ruling from one of his own statements:

וְרַב מַאי קָא מַשְׁמַע לָן – Now as for **Rav, what does he teach us?** **מְחָאָה שֶׁלֹּא בְּפָנָיו לֹא הָוְיָא מְחָאָה – That a protest** lodged **not in [the occupant's] presence is not an** effective **protest?** **וְהָאָמַר רַב מְחָאָה שֶׁלֹּא בְּפָנָיו הָוְיָא מְחָאָה – But** that is difficult to say, for **did Rav not** previously **state** that according to our Mishnah, **a protest** lodged **not in [the occupant's] presence is an** effective **protest?**[7] Why, then, would he rule that the opposite is true?

To deflect the challenge, the Gemara explains that Rav's previous statement did not reflect his own opinion:

רַב טַעֲמָא דְּתַנָּא דִּידַן קָמְפָרֵשׁ – Rav was merely **explaining the reasoning of our [Mishnah's] Tanna** **וְלֵיהּ לֹא סְבִירָא לֵיהּ – but [Rav] himself does not agree with this** view; rather, he holds that a protest lodged in the occupant's absence is meaningless, as Rav Yehudah reported.[8]

The Gemara presents another version of the preceding discussion according to which Rav agrees with Shmuel:

וְאִיכָּא דְּאָמְרֵי – And there are those who relate Rav Yehudah's report as follows: **אָמַר רַב יְהוּדָה אָמַר רַב – Rav Yehudah said in the name of Rav:** **מַחֲזִיקִים בְּנִכְסֵי בּוֹרֵחַ – One can establish a *chazakah* upon the property of a fugitive.**[9] **כִּי אַמְרִיתָהּ קַמֵּיהּ דִּשְׁמוּאֵל – When I** (Rav Yehudah) **repeated [the ruling] in Shmuel's presence,** however, **אָמַר לִי – he said to me:** **פְּשִׁיטָא – The** ruling is **obvious!** **וְכִי לִמְחוֹת בְּפָנָיו הוּא צָרִיךְ – Must [the original owner] then protest in [the occupant's] presence?** Obviously not. Since the fugitive owner can protest even from a distance, the occupant can obviously establish a *chazakah* upon his land.[10] Thus, Shmuel argues that Rav's ruling teaches us nothing new.

The Gemara questions the necessity for Rav's ruling:

וְרַב מַאי קָא מַשְׁמַע לָן – Now as for **Rav – what** indeed **does he teach us** by ruling that one can establish a *chazakah* upon a fugitive's property? **מְחָאָה שֶׁלֹּא בְּפָנָיו הָוְיָא מְחָאָה – That a protest** lodged **not in [the occupant's] presence is an** effective **protest?** **וְהָא אֲמָרָהּ רַב חֲדָא זִימְנָא – But Rav** already **stated this once** before![7]

The Gemara answers that Rav's statement teaches an additional law:

אֶלָּא הָא קָא מַשְׁמַע לָן – Rather, this is what Rav teaches us: **דַּאֲפִילּוּ מִיחָה בִּפְנֵי ב׳ שֶׁאֵין יְכוֹלִין לוֹמַר לוֹ – That even if [the original owner] protested in the presence of two** witnesses

NOTES

1. The Mishnah thus differentiates between a case in which the original owner of a field was in Judea and the occupant was in the Galilee (or vice versa) and a case in which the owner and occupant were in two provinces outside Eretz Yisrael. In the latter case, we assume that people traveling between the provinces will spread word of the protest until it reaches the occupant. Only if the border between two provinces is closed as a result of hostilities is such a protest meaningless, because travel between the provinces ceases and the occupant will thus never hear about the protest. In the former case (i.e. when the owner was in Judea and the occupant was in the Galilee or vice versa), however, we cannot assume that travelers will spread word of the protest, because travel between Judea and Galilee was always sparse. R' Abba therefore teaches that even in times of peace, these provinces have the same status as countries at war: The original owner cannot effectively protest the occupation of a field located in one province while he is in another, because the occupant will never hear about it (*Rashbam*).

2. The Gemara below will explain who qualifies as a fugitive for the purposes of this law.

3. Rav's source for this view is R' Yehudah's position quoted in our Mishnah. According to R' Yehudah, if a resident of Spain owns a field in Eretz Yisrael, someone must occupy the field for three years to establish a *chazakah*: one year for the occupation to become public knowledge, one year for news of the occupation to reach the owner *and one year for the owner to return and lodge a protest.* Since R' Yehudah requires the owner to return to Eretz Yisrael, where the present occupant lives, and lodge his protest there, this indicates that a protest must be lodged in the occupant's presence (*Rashbam;* see Gemara 39a, which challenges this reasoning).

4. When a man flees his country, he obviously will not return to protest the occupation of his land located there; he will lodge his protest from a distance. Since, according to Rav, such a protest is meaningless, a *chazakah* cannot be established on that land (see 38a note 16).

5. Rav Yehudah was originally Rav's disciple. After Rav's death, he studied under Shmuel and reported many of Rav's teachings to him (*Rashbam*).

6. According to Shmuel, a protest not lodged in the occupant's presence is effective since reports of the protest will reach the occupant. Thus, even a fugitive owner, who cannot protest in the occupant's presence, can lodge an effective protest from wherever he is. If he fails to do so for three years, the occupant establishes a *chazakah.*

7. See 38a. The Gemara now assumes that since Rav explained our Mishnah's ruling, he also accepts it (*Rashbam*).

8. Although Rav's first statement (38a) explains the Tanna Kamma's ruling, this does not imply that he accepts it. Rav merely noted that the Mishnah's beginning and final clauses contradict each other and then interpreted the Mishnah in a way that resolves the contradiction (i.e. that according to the Tanna Kamma, an effective protest can be lodged even if the occupant is not present). Rav himself, however, follows R' Yehudah's view that the owner must lodge his protest in the occupant's presence (*Rashbam*).

9. According to this version, Rav holds that a protest may be lodged even if the occupant is not present because news of protests (and occupations) travels by word of mouth. Accordingly, if someone assumes occupancy of a fugitive's land and the fugitive fails to protest for three years, his silence is inexplicable: He undoubtedly heard about the occupation and he could have lodged an effective protest from afar. His failure to protest thus compromises his case and a *chazakah* is established.

Rav's ruling actually pertains not only to a fugitive's land but also to land belonging to anyone who left the country. Rav specifically discussed a fugitive's land, however, because it is a more common case. People would more readily seize the land of a fugitive, who cannot return, than the land of someone who left the country temporarily (*Rashbam*).

10. On 38a, the Gemara proved from our Mishnah that an owner need not protest in the occupant's presence. According to our Mishnah, if the owner of a field in Galilee lodged a protest while he was in Judea, the protest is meaningless (for since news does not travel between these

דסתם יהודה וגליל כשעת חירום דמו: אמר רב יהודה אמר רב אין מחזיקין בנכסי בורח כי אמריתה קמיה דשמואל אמר לי וכי למחות בפניו הוא צריך ורב מאי קמ"ל מחאה שלא בפניו לא הויא מחאה והאמר רב מחאה שלא בפניו הויא מחאה רב טעמא דתנא דידן קמפרש וליה לא סבירא ליה ואיכא דאמרי אמר רב יהודה אמר רב מחזיקים בנכסי בורח כי אמריתה קמיה דשמואל אמר לי פשיטא וכי למחות בפניו הוא צריך ורב מאי קמ"ל מחאה שלא בפניו הויא מחאה והא אמרה רב חדא זימנא אלא הא קמ"ל [א]דאפי' מיחה בפני ב' שאין יכולין לומר לו הויא מחאה (א) דאמר רב ענן לדידי מפרשא לי מיניה דמר שמואל מיחה בפני שני בני אדם שיכולים לומר לו הויא מחאה מיחה בפני שני בני אדם שאין יכולין לומר לו לא הויא מחאה ורב [ב]חברך חברא אית ליה וחברא דחברך חברא אית ליה אמר רבא הלכתא [ג]אין מחזיקין בנכסי בורח [ג]ומחאה שלא בפניו הויא מחאה תרתי לא קשיא [ד]כאן בבורח מחמת ממון כאן בורח מחמת מרדין: היכי דמי מחאה אמר רב זביד [ה]פלניא גזלנא הוא לא הויא מחאה [ו]פלניא גזלנא (ב) הוא דנקיט לה לארעאי בגזלנותא ולמחר

הא קמ"ל. ר' אבא: דסתם יהודה וגליל. אפי' בשעת שלום: כשעת חירום דמי. שאין שיירות מצויות מזו לזו אבל בשאר מלכיות אי איכא חירום לא הויא חזקה אבל בשעת שלום הויא חזקה דהא שיירות מצויות והאי דקאמר רבי אבא בשעת חירום שנו הכי קאמר יהודה וגליל הרי הן כשעת חירום של שאר מלכיות: אין מחזיקין בנכסי בורח. כלומר אם החזיק אינה חזקה כדמפרש ואזיל דקסבר מחאה שלא בפניו לא הויא מחאה וכיון דלא יכול למחות גם זה לא יכול להחזיק וכר' יהודה סבירא ליה דאמר במתניתין ילכו ויודיעוהו שנה ויבא לשנה אחרת למשמע דצריך למחות בפניו: כי אמריתה. להא דרב קמיה דשמואל אחר פטירתו של רב שבא ללמוד לפני שמואל. רב מת מקמי שמואל כדאמרינן בשחיטת חולין (דף קנ:) דכל זמן שהיה רב קיים הוה שלח לי' ר' יוחנן לקדם רבינו שבבבל כי נח נפשיה דרב שלח לי' לשמואל לקדם חבירנו כו': א"ל. שמואל: וכי למחות בפניו הוא צריך. בתמיה אלא לא צריך למחות בפניו דמחאה שלא בפניו הויא מחאה והלכך מחזיקים נמי שלא בפניו דלאיבעי ליה למחויי: ומקשה גמר' והאמר רב מחאה שלא בפניו הויא מחאה. כדאמר ר' אבא אמר רב לעיל לעולם קסבר מחאה שלא בפניו כו' [ג](ומדפריך) למילתיה דת"ק איכא למימר דסבירא ליה הכי: לטעמא. דתנא קמא פירש רב משום דקשיא רישא לסיפא וליכא לתרוצה אלא בכי האי גוונא: וליה לא סבירא ליה. אלא כרבי יהודה סבירא ליה: מחזיקין בנכסי בורח. דמחאה שלא בפניו הויא מחאה ואיבעי ליה למחויי ומדלא מיחה הפסיד דכיון דשיירות מצויות אנן סהדי שנודע לו שאחרים החזיקו בקרקע שלו ולא מצי טעין לא ידעתי ולפיכך לא מחיתי דכי היכי דמחאה שלא בפניו הויא מחאה משום דחברך חברא אית ליה ושמע המחזיק מחאתו של זה המערער הכי נמי נודע לו שהחזיק זה בקרקע שלו והוא לא מיחה ולפיכך הפסיד והאי דנקט בורח לאו דוקא דהוא הדין לכל מרחיקי ארצם אלא אורחא דמילתא נקט שאין דרך בני אדם להחזיק בקרקע של אחרים בגזל אלא בקרקע בורח: א"ל פשיטא. דמחזיקין דהא ממתניתין דקתני שלש ארצות לחזקה שמעינן דמחאה שלא בפניו הויא מחאה ואיבעי ליה למחויי ומדלא מיחה הפסיד. בגמרת ירושלמי רב אמר אין חזקה לבורח ולא מארץ לארץ ושמואל אמר יש להן חזקה אמר רב נחמן קרא מסייע ליה למר ויתן לה המלך סרים אחד לאמר השב את כל אשר לה ואת כל תבואת השדה מיום עזבה את הארץ ועד עתה (מלכים ב ח): ורב מאי קמ"ל. דקאמר מחזיקים בנכסי בורח הא ודאי קמ"ל מחאה שלא בפניו הויא מחאה והיה לו למחות הלכך חזקה נמי שלא בפניו בלא מחאה הויא חזקה: והא אמרה רב חדא זימנא. דאמר ר' אבא בר ממל אמר רב לעיל לעולם מחאה שלא בפניו הויא מחאה כו' ומסתמא הוה שמעינן דכסתם מתני' סבירא ליה מדמפרש לה הכי: אפי' מיחה בפני ב' שאין יכולין לומר לו. כגון חיגרין או שהולכין למדינת הים ומרחיקין מאותו המלכות שדר בה המחזיק [ד](אפי') הכי מחזיקין בנכסי בורח דתיהני ליה מחאה כי הך ואע"ג דהנך לא יאמרו לו למחזיק דחברך חברא אית ליה והלכך כיון דהויא מחאה חזקה נמי הויא חזקה ושמואל שהיה מקשה על דברי רב ואומר פשיטא וכי למחות לפניו הוא צריך להך רבותא דקאמר רב לא אסיק אדעתיה והלכך פריך שפיר מאי אתא רב לאשמועינן: אמר רב ענן לדידי מיפרשא לי כו'. אשינויא דשנינן אליבא דרב אתא [ה]לאשמועינן ולמימר דהך רבותא לא סבירא ליה לשמואל כדמפרש ואזיל והוה מתמה פשיטא: הלכתא אין מחזיקין בנכסי בורח. דמחאה שלא בפניו לא הויא מחאה וכיון דלא מצי מערער למחויי מחזיק נמי לא מצי אחזוקי: ומחאה שלא בפניו הויא מחאה. והלכך חזקה שלא בפניו הויא חזקה ומשום הכי מחזיקין בנכסי בורח דהא מצי למחויי ומדלא מיחה הפסיד והיינו דקפריך גמרא תרתי בתמיה משום דקשיא רישא לסיפא ומשני לא קשיא כאן בבורח מחמת ממון פסיק רבא הלכתא (ג) שלא בפניו הויא מחאה משום דמצי למחויי וכל מקום שזה יכול למחות חזקתו של חבירו בנכסיו הויא חזקה הואיל ולא מיחה דכיון דמחמת חוב ממון הוא בורח אין זה בורח אלא לאישתמוטי בעלמא עד דהוה ליה ופרע ואינו ירא למחות דכיון דאנוס הוא ואין לו מה לפרוע אין רודפין אחריו ואם נודע מקומו שברח שם אינו חושש: כאן בבורח מחמת מרדין. מחמת רציחת נפשות ירא למחות פן יודע מקום תחנותו וירדוף גואל הדם אחריו כי יחם לבבו והשיגו והרגו ובדידיה קפסיק רבא דאין מחזיקין בנכסי בורח והכי הלכתא: מרדין. לשון רציחה בלשון פרס כדאמרינן בהגוזל ומאכיל (ב"ק דף קיז.) השתא פרסאי דקפדי אשפיכות דמים ואמרי מרדין מרדין: היכי דמי מחאה. אמחאה שלא בפניו קאי דפסיקנא לעיל דהויא מחאה: אמר רב זביד. אמר לסהדי פלניא גזלנא הוא לא הויא מחאה שאפילו אם יאמרו עדים לשון זה למחזיק לא אתי לאזדהורי בשטריה דהא לא ידע אמאי קרי ליה גזלן שיזהר בשטרו: אבל אמר לו פלניא גזלנא הוא דקאכיל לארעאי בגזלנותא. שהרי לא מכרתיה לו דהשתא הוה ליה לאיזדהורי בשטר מכירת שדה (ד) זה מאחר שערער זה עליו והלכך הויא מחאה: ולמחר תבענא ליה בדינא הרי זה מחאה.

ואי

דסתם יהודה וגליל כשעת חירום דמי. ואם תאמר ומאי שנא דגבי גט אמר בריש גיטין (ד' ד: ושם ד"ה כיון) המביא גט ממדינה למדינה בארץ ישראל אין צריך לומר בפני נכתב ובפני נחתם משום כיון דאיכא עולי רגלים משכח שכיחי לקיימו ואפי' בזמן שאין בהמ"ק (ה) כיון דאיכא בתי דינים דקביעי משכח שכיחי וי"ל דלדלי גבי גט מצוין לקיימו אפי' מיהודה לגליל לפי שהשאלה רגילה לחזור אחר עדי קיום אבל הכא אי לאו דשכיחי טובא לעולם לא ישמע מחאתו שאין המחזיק רגיל לחזור אם מוחה לו ואם לאו הלכך בשיירות דעולי רגלים ובתי דינין לא סגי וא"ת והא דאמרי' התם (דף ו.) רב ששת מצריך [ו](מעסקא לערסקא) ורבא מצריך אפי' באותה שכונה ופריך והא רבא הוא דאמר לפי שאין עדים מצוין לקיימו ומשני התם בני מחוזא דניידי אטו מי נימא דבמחוזא מחאה שלא בפניו לא הוי מחאה ויצטרך לבא לפניו למחות וי"ל דלא דמי דכשהחותמים על הגט במחוזא והולכין להן אין דרך שיצעקו בעיר אנחנו חתמנו על גט פלוני אבל במחאה דרך הליכתם רגילות לומר פלוני מיחה ושומעין אחרים עד שנשמע בבית המחזיק: אין מחזיקין בנכסי בורח. בבורח מחמת ממון איירי דאי מחמת מרדין בהא לא פליג שמואל כדמוכח בסמוך ודוקא בבורח אבל באינים דעלמא הויא חזקה שיכול לבא למקום שהמחזיק שם ולמחות אבל בורח אינו רשאי לבא במקום שעומד לא הויא מחאה שלא בפניו וסבר לה כר' יהודה דקתני ויבא לשנה אחרת וימחה משמע שצריך למחות בפניו וא"ת ודלמא ר' יהודה נמי לא בעי מחאה בפניו וה"ק ויבא במדינה שהמחזיק בה וימחה כגון אם הוא ביהודה יבא ביהודה וימחה שאז תשמע מחאתו וכי תימא (ו) וכיון שחזקה נשמעת עד אספמיא גם המחאה תשמע עד אספמיא ואי מחאה שלא בפניו הוי מחאה ליתיב אדוכתיה ולימחי הא ליתא דאי כל מקום שחזקה נשמעת גם המחאה נשמעת אם כן היכי מוכח לעיל לרבנן מחאה שלא בפניו הויא מחאה אימא דלעולם (ז) דלא הוי מחאה והיה ביהודה והחזיק ביהודה הוי חזקה לפי שהיא נשמעת ויבא וימחה לפני המחזיק אבל מיהודה לגליל אין החזקה נשמעת ומשום הכי לא הויא חזקה אלא ודאי פשיטא ליה לגמרא דהחזקה נשמעת מרחוק אבל מחאה לא ולהכי מוכח לעיל שפיר דסברי רבנן דהויא מחאה שלא בפניו דאי לא הויא מחאה אלא צריך לבא לפני המחזיק א"כ מיהודה לגליל תהא חזקה כמו שביהודה יש לו לילך ולמחות מיהודה לגליל נמי ילך לפניו וימחה וי"ל מדלא תני ר' יהודה אומר ויבא לשנה אחרת וימחה ויודיעהו שמע מינה שצריך למחות לפניו. ר"י:

ולמחר נקיטנא ליה. נראה לר"י דלא צריך למימר נקיטנא ליה אלא אורחא דמילתא נקט מדלא קאמר רב זביד פלוני גזלנא הוא דאכיל לארעאי בגזלנותא לא הויא מחאה פלוני גזלנא הוא דאכיל לארעאי בגזלנותא ולמחר נקיטנא ליה בדינא הויא מחאה:

רב

עין משפט נר מצוה

פה א ב מיי' פי"א מהל' טוען ונטען הל' ו סמג עשין צה טוש"ע ח"מ סי' קמו סעיף ח:

פו ג ד מיי' פי"א שם הל' ה סמג שם טוש"ע ח"מ סי' קמו סעיף ג:

פז ה ו מיי' פי"א שם הלכה ז סמג שם טוש"ע ח"מ סי' קמו סעיף ד:

רבינו גרשום

ומשני האי דקתני יהודה וגליל לא הויא מחאה משום דבשעת חירום הדרכים שנו ומשום הכי לא הויא חזקה דאי טעין ליה מחזיק אלמלא היית מוחה בתוך ג' הייתי מזהר בשטרא דלא מירכס מצי למימר ליה המערער משום דחרום הדרכים הוא לא הוו שיירות מצויות דאזלי ולימחו לך ולהכי לא מחיתי. ומקשה אי הכי מאי שנא יהודה וגליל דנקיט דלא הויא חזקה אפי' יהודה ויהודה נמי לא הויא חזקה הואיל ובשעת חירום הוא ומשני משום הכי נקט [יהודה וגליל] דבשעת חירום דמי דלאו שיירות מצויות: אין מחזיקין בנכסי בורח. דאי ברח אינש ממלכות ואתא אחר והחזיק בנכסיו לא הויא חזקה. א) והא אמר ליה לרב דמ"ש הכי אין מחזיקין דקסבר מחאה שלא בפניו לא הויא מחאה. והא אמר ר' אבא בר ממל אמר רב לעיל כדמתרץ מתני' דמחאה שלא בפניו הויא מחאה ואמאי אין מחזיקין: רב לטעמיה דתנא דמתני' קאמר. איכא דאמרי כו' ה"ג כי אמריתה קמיה דשמואל אמר לי פשיטא וכי למחויי בפניו הוא צריך וכיון שהוא יכול למחות בכל מקום שהוא ולא מיחה פשיטא דמחזיקין. ורב מאי קמ"ל דמחזיקין אי משום דקסבר מחאה שלא בפניו הויא מחאה והאי לא מיחה להכי מחזיקין והא אמרה רב חדא זימנא כדאמרינן לעיל. אלא הא קמ"ל רב דאע"ג דמיחה בפני שנים שאינן יכולין לומר לו שאינן עוברי דרכים אפי' הכי הויא מחאה שאם אין יכולין לומר לו לימרו לו אחרים דלימא ליה משום דחברך וכו' אבל אי לא מיחה כלל (א) מחזיקין. תרתי. בתמי' קאמר כלומר דהני תרי מילי לא מצי קיימי דהדדי קשיא לאידך משום דאי אמרינן אין מחזיקין בנכסי בורח משמע משום דמחאה שלא בפניו לא הויא מחאה והדר תני דהויא מחאה: כאן בבורח מחמת ממון שמחויב לאנשי העיר אין צריך להבריח עצמו כל כך והיה יכול למחות שלא בפניו והויא מחאה ואי לא מיחה והחזיק אחר בנכסיו הרי חזקה אבל בורח מחמת מרדין שהיה מורד ומחויב למלכות אין מחזיקין בנכסיו שאינו יכול למחות דאי מחה מודע למלכות היכן הוא ויבקשוהו עד שימצאוהו ויהא מסוכן בגופו ומשום הכי

מסורת הש"ס

א) [לעיל כח: וש"נ], ב) [לקמן לט.], ג) צ"ל ומדמפרש, ד) גי' רש"ש משום, ה) נ"א לאשמועינ', ו) [צ"ל מפטונא לפטונא]

הגהות הב"ח

(א) גמ' דאמר רב ענן נ"ב גירסת רשב"ם אמר רב ענן: (ב) שם פלניא גזלנא הוא דקאכיל לה לארעאי: (ג) רשב"ם ד"ה ומחאה וכו' רבא הלכתא מחאה שלא בפניו וכו' דלמא הוא דאין לו: (ד) ד"ה אבל אמר שדה זו מאחר: (ה) תוס' ד"ה דסתם וכו' בית המקדש קיים כיון וכו' וי"ל דודאי גט עדים מצויין לקיימו וכו' אם מוחה לו אם לאו הלכך בשכיחות דעולי רגלים: (ו) ד"ה אין וכו' וכי תימא כיון כל"ל ואות ו' נמחק: (ז) באד"ה אימא דלעולם לא כל"ל ואות ח' נמחק:

ליקוטי רש"י

מחאה שלא בפניו הויא מחאה. לא הוי מחאה. עיין ליקוטי רש"י בע"ב. חברך חברא אית ליה. וודיעוהו [כתובות קט:]. דהני דמחי באנפייהו מגלו לאחריני ובא הדבר לאזני המחזיק וה"ל לאזדהורי בשטריה [שם יז.]. ויאמרו זה לזה והדבר בא לאזני ואינו יכול לומר אילו שמעתי הייתי זכיר בראיותיה זכותי [לעיל כח:]. חזו מגלה לחבירו וזה לחבירו עד שיודע [ערכין טז:]. מחמת מרדין. שהרג את הנפש ופרסאי הורגין על שפיכות דמים כדאמרינן בבבא קמא (קיז.) מרדין היא לישנא בלשון פרסי וכן מפורש בתשובת רב האי גאון [שער מ] (ב"מ לט.).

חשק שלמה על רבינו גרשום

א) נראה דצ"ל ופריכן דרב מאי קמ"ל דאין מחזיקין משום דמחאה שלא בפניו.

that cannot report the protest **to [the occupant],**[11] הָוְיָא מְחָאָה – still **this is an** effective **protest.**[12]

Having explained what Rav added with his second ruling, the Gemara now explains why Shmuel considered the ruling unnecessary:

דְּאָמַר רַב עָנָן – **Rav Anan said:**[13] לְדִידִי מְפָרְשָׁא לִי מִינֵּיהּ דְּמַר שְׁמוּאֵל – The following **was explained to me by master Shmuel:** מִיחָה בִּפְנֵי שְׁנֵי בְנֵי אָדָם שֶׁיְּכוֹלִים לוֹמַר לוֹ – If [the original owner] **protested in the presence of two people capable of telling [the occupant]** about the protest, הָוְיָא מְחָאָה – this **is an** effective **protest.** מִיחָה בִּפְנֵי שְׁנֵי בְנֵי אָדָם שֶׁאֵין יְכוֹלִין לוֹמַר לוֹ – If **he protested in the presence of two men who were incapable of telling [the occupant],** however, לֹא הָוְיָא מְחָאָה – this **is not an** effective **protest.** Never realizing that Rav disputed his ruling, Shmuel could not understand what Rav meant to teach.[14]

After explaining Shmuel's position, the Gemara now analyzes Rav's view:

וְרַב – **But** what does **Rav** hold? Why does he consider a protest effective even if none of the witnesses can tell the occupant about it?

The Gemara explains:

חַבְרָךְ חַבְרָא אִית לֵיהּ – **"Your friend** (i.e. the witnesses to the protest) **has a friend** וְחַבְרָא דְּחַבְרָךְ חַבְרָא אִית לֵיהּ – **and your friend's friend has a friend."** That is, although the witnesses cannot personally tell the occupant about the protest, they will discuss it with their own friends. The friends will then spread the word until the occupant hears about it.

The Gemara issues a definitive ruling:

אָמַר רָבָא – **Rava ruled:** הִלְכְתָא אֵין מַחֲזִיקִין בְּנִכְסֵי בּוֹרֵחַ – The **halachah** is that **one cannot establish a *chazakah* upon the property of a fugitive**[15] וּמְחָאָה שֶׁלֹּא בְּפָנָיו הָוְיָא מְחָאָה – **and a protest** lodged **not in [the occupant's] presence is an** effective **protest.**

The Gemara objects:

תַּרְתֵּי – Can **both** these rulings be true? Impossible! The first ruling states that a *chazakah* cannot be established in the owner's absence whereas the second ruling implies that the opposite is true.[16] – ? –

The Gemara resolves the contradiction:

לֹא קַשְׁיָא – There is **no difficulty,** for Rava's two rulings deal with two different situations. כָּאן – **Here,** Rava's second ruling deals with בּוֹרֵחַ מֵחֲמַת מָמוֹן – **one who flees because of** unpaid **monetary** obligations;[17] that is why a *chazakah* can be established. כָּאן – **Here,** Rava's first ruling deals with בּוֹרֵחַ מֵחֲמַת מַרְדִּין – **one who flees because of** a **murder** charge.[18]

Having discussed a protest lodged in the occupant's absence, the Gemara discusses how such a protest should be worded:

הֵיכִי דָּמֵי מְחָאָה – **How is such a protest to be stated?** אָמַר רַב זְבִיד – **Rav Zevid said:** פְּלָנְיָא גַּזְלָנָא הוּא לֹא הָוְיָא מְחָאָה – If the original owner merely tells two witnesses, **"So-and-so is a thief,"** this **is not an** effective **protest.**[19] פְּלָנְיָא גַּזְלָנָא הוּא דְּנָקִיט לָהּ לְאַרְעַאי בִּגְזֵלָנוּתָא – If, however, he tells two witnesses, **"So-and--so is a thief, for he has taken** possession of **my land through** an act of **theft**

NOTES

provinces, the occupant will never hear about the protest). This, however, implies that if the owner was in the same province as his field (or if they were in different provinces outside Eretz Yisrael), a protest lodged in the occupant's absence is effective. Shmuel therefore argues that our Mishnah implicitly taught Rav's ruling and it was thus unnecessary for Rav to teach it.

11. E.g. lame witnesses, who cannot travel at all, or witnesses who are leaving the occupant's country to go a faraway place (*Rashbam*).

12. Rav's first ruling (that a *chazakah* can be established upon a fugitive's property) indeed implied that a fugitive's protest is effective because word of it will reach the occupant. Rav explicitly ruled concerning a fugitive owner, though, to teach the following: Even if the fugitive fled to a place where he can find only lame witnesses, who cannot travel to the occupant, (or if he is afraid to protest in front of witnesses who can travel,) still the protest is effective (*Rashbam,* as explained by *Maharsha*). The reason for this is that although the witnesses will never personally notify the occupant about the protest, still they will discuss it with their friends. The occupant will then eventually learn of the protest by word of mouth.

Earlier, Rav Yehudah reported that when he related Rav's ruling to Shmuel, the latter asserted that it was obvious. The Gemara now assumes that when Shmuel raised his objection, he failed to realize that Rav meant to teach the above law (*Rashbam*).

13. Our translation follows *Rashbam's* text, which reads אָמַר רַב עָנָן, *Rav Anan said,* rather than our text, which reads דְּאָמַר רַב עָנָן, *for Rav Anan said*. According to *Rashbam's* version of the text, Rav Anan explains why Shmuel considered Rav's second ruling unnecessary and never realized, as the Gemara above did, that it teaches an additional law (that a protest lodged in the presence of witnesses who cannot travel to the occupant is effective).

14. Rav Anan explains that Rav and Shmuel disagreed over whether a protest lodged in the presence of witnesses who will not travel to the occupant is effective: Rav considered it effective whereas Shmuel considered it meaningless. Shmuel, though, had not heard that Rav disputed his ruling. In his view, then, Rav could not have taught that a protest lodged in the presence of these witnesses is effective because this is untrue; he must simply have been repeating his previous ruling (that a protest must be lodged in the occupant's presence). This, Shmuel asserted, was unnecessary.

15. The reason for Rava's ruling, our Gemara initially assumes, is that a protest lodged when the occupant is not present is meaningless. Accordingly, since a fugitive, who has fled his land, cannot possibly lodge an effective protest, a *chazakah* cannot be established upon his property (*Rashbam;* see 38a note 16).

16. If a protest lodged when the occupant is not present is effective, then even a fugitive can be expected to protest if someone occupies his field illegally. Thus, if a fugitive owner tolerates the unauthorized use of his property in silence for the three years, a *chazakah* should be established (*Rashbam*).

17. If someone flees to evade his creditors, he has no reason to hide his location from them, for they have really no reason to pursue him; even if they discover his whereabouts, they know that he cannot pay. Such a person therefore has no excuse for remaining silent for three years in the face of a supposedly unauthorized use of his property. If he does so, a *chazakah* is established (*Rashbam*).

18. Anyone facing a murder charge must hide from the victim's relatives to protect his life, for if they discover his whereabouts, they might pursue him and kill him. Such a person is obviously precluded from protesting the unauthorized use of his land, for doing so might reveal his location and thus endanger his life. Rava ruled that since he has a valid reason for remaining silent, a *chazakah* cannot be established upon his property (*Rashbam*).

19. To lodge an effective protest, a protester must assert that he is the true owner of the land. If, however, he merely asserts that the occupant is a thief (or even that he has stolen a particular tract of land), he does not advance *his own* claim to the land. In short, the focus of the claim is that the present occupant holds the land illegally, not that the protester is the true owner. Such a claim can be construed as an attempt to defame the occupant rather than to seriously contest his ownership. Therefore it is a meaningless protest (*Rashbam,* according to his preferred explanation).

וּלְמָחָר תְּבַעְנָא לֵיהּ בְּדִינָא – **and tomorrow I shall claim it from him in court,"** הַוְיָא מְחָאָה – this **is an** effective **protest.**[1]

The Gemara previously established that generally, a protest lodged in the occupant's absence is effective. It now presents four cases in which the people witnessing the protest will not personally tell the occupant about it and rules on whether such protests are valid. The first case is:

אָמַר לָא תֵּימְרוּ לֵיהּ – If **[the protester] said** to the witnesses, **"Do not tell [the occupant]** that I lodged a protest," מַאי – **what is** the law? Is such a protest effective or not?

The Gemara presents two views:

אָמַר רַב זְבִיד – **Rav Zevid said:** הָא קָאָמַר לָא תֵּימְרוּ לֵיהּ – The owner himself **is saying, "Do not tell [the occupant]** about my protest!" Since the witnesses will surely respect the owner's wishes and not inform the occupant, the protest is meaningless. רַב פָּפָּא אָמַר – **Rav Pappa,** however, **said:** The protester meant only, לְדִידֵיהּ לָא תֵּימְרוּ לֵיהּ – **"Do not tell [the occupant] himself** about the protest, לְאַחֲרִינֵי אֵימְרוּ לְהוּ – but **you may tell others** about it." The occupant will thus eventually hear about the protest for, as the saying goes, חַבְרָךְ חַבְרָא אִית לֵיהּ – **"Your friend has a friend** וְחַבְרָא דְחַבְרָךְ חַבְרָא אִית לֵיהּ – and **your friend's friend has a friend."** Therefore, the protest is effective.[2]

The Gemara now presents the second case:

אָמְרוּ לֵיהּ לָא אָמְרִינַן לֵיהּ – If **[the witnesses] said to [the protester], "We will not tell [the occupant]** about the protest," what is the law?

The Gemara cites two views:

אָמַר רַב זְבִיד – **Rav Zevid said:** הָא קָא אָמְרוּ לֵיהּ לָא אָמְרִינַן לֵיהּ – **[The witnesses] told [the protester], "We will not tell [the occupant]** about the protest!" Surely, then, the protest is meaningless.[3] רַב פָּפָּא אָמַר – **Rav Pappa,** however, **said:** The witnesses meant only, לְדִידֵיהּ לָא אָמְרִינַן לֵיהּ – **"We will not tell [the occupant] himself** about the protest לְאַחֲרִינֵי אָמְרֵי לְהוּ – but **we will tell others** about it."[4] The occupant will thus eventually hear about the protest for, as the saying goes, חַבְרָךְ חַבְרָא אִית לֵיהּ – **"Your friend has a friend** וְחַבְרָא דְחַבְרָךְ חַבְרָא אִית לֵיהּ – **and your friend's friend has a friend."** Therefore, the protest is effective.

The Gemara now rules on the third case:

אָמַר לְהוּ לָא תִּיפּוֹק לְכוּ שׁוּתָא – If **[the protester] said to [the witnesses], "Let no word** about my protest **leave your** mouths," אָמַר רַב זְבִיד – **Rav Zevid said:** הָא קָאָמַר לָא תִּיפּוֹק לְכוּ שׁוּתָא – **[The protester]** himself **said, "Let no word leave your** mouths." Since the witnesses will surely respect the charge, the occupant will never find out about the protest. Consequently, it is meaningless.[5]

The Gemara presents its fourth and final case:

אָמְרוּ לֵיהּ לָא מַפְקִינַן שׁוּתָא – If **[the witnesses] said to [the protester], "Not a word** about your protest **will leave** our mouths," אָמַר רַב פָּפָּא – **Rav Pappa said:** הָא קָאָמְרֵי לֵיהּ לָא מַפְקִינַן שׁוּתָא – **They have told [the protester], "Word** of the protest **will not leave** our mouths!" Surely, then, the occupant will never hear about the protest and it is therefore meaningless. רַב הוּנָא בְּרֵיהּ דְּרַב יְהוֹשֻׁעַ אָמַר – **Rav Huna the son of Rav Yehoshua,** however, **said:** The protest is effective because כָּל מִילְּתָא דְּלָא רָמְיָא עֲלֵיהּ דְּאִינִישׁ – **"Any matter that was not entrusted to a person** to keep confidential, אָמַר לָהּ וְלָאו אַדַּעְתֵּיהּ – a person **will** eventually **discuss inadvertently."** Here, too, then, the witnesses will eventually tell someone about the protest and word of it will then reach the occupant. Consequently, the protest is effective.

The Gemara returns to its previous discussion about a protest lodged in the occupant's absence:

אָמַר רָבָא אָמַר רַב נַחְמָן – **Rava said in the name of Rav Nachman:** מְחָאָה שֶׁלֹּא בְּפָנָיו הַוְיָא מְחָאָה – A **protest** lodged **not in [the occupant's] presence is an** effective **protest.**

Rava questioned his teacher's statement:

אֵיתִיבֵיהּ רָבָא לְרַב נַחְמָן – **Rava challenged Rav Nachman's ruling from the Mishnah:** אָמַר ר׳ יְהוּדָה – **R' Yehudah said:** לֹא אָמְרוּ שָׁלֹשׁ שָׁנִים אֶלָּא – **[The Sages] stated** that **three years** of occupancy establishes a *chazakah* **only** כְּדֵי שֶׁיְּהֵא בְּאַסְפַּמְיָא – **so that** if **[the original owner] was in Spain** וְיַחֲזִיק שָׁנָה – **and** someone **occupied** his field for **a year,** וְיֵלְכוּ וְיוֹדִיעוּהוּ שָׁנָה – **[observers] can go and notify [the original owner] during [the second year]** וְיָבֹא לְשָׁנָה אַחֶרֶת – **and he can come** to claim his field **in the following** (third) **year.** וְאִי סָלְקָא דַעְתָּךְ מְחָאָה שֶׁלֹּא

NOTES

1. Once the original owner accuses the occupant of stealing the field from him and holding it illegally, he advances his own claim to the land and his protest is therefore effective. Although the Gemara adds that the protester threatened to sue the occupant for the land, the protest is just as effective without the threat. The Gemara mentions it only because a protester would typically conclude his protest this way (*Rashbam,* according to his preferred explanation; cf. *Rambam, Hil. To'ein VeNitan* 11:7).

2. That is, once the witnesses inform their friends of the protest, the information will pass from friend to friend until it eventually reaches the occupant (*Rashbam*). The protest is therefore valid even if the witnesses never personally inform the occupant about the protest.

According to Rav Pappa's reasoning, it should follow that a protest is effective even if the witnesses who observe it are incapable of traveling to the occupant and notifying him. This apparently contradicts Shmuel's ruling on 38b that such a protest is in fact meaningless.

To resolve the contradiction, *Tosafos* suggest that Shmuel and Rav Pappa discussed different cases. Shmuel discussed a case in which the witnesses would never travel to the occupant's locale (due to age or infirmity for example) and spread word of the protest there. In such a case, since the occupant will indeed never hear about the protest, all agree it is meaningless. Rav Pappa, on the other hand, discussed a case in which the witnesses will eventually travel to the occupant's locale and inform people there about the protest. Since these people will in turn inform the occupant, the protest is valid. *Rosh,* however, rejects this distinction, maintaining instead that Rav Pappa and Shmuel disagree over whether a protest is effective if it was lodged in the presence of witnesses who will not travel to the occupant's locale. *Rashbam* concurs with *Rosh* (see below, note 4).

3. If the protester were indeed the true owner, he would have lodged another protest in front of other witnesses as soon as these refused to inform the occupant about the protest. His failure to do so thus undermined his position and the field is therefore awarded to the occupant (*Rashbam*).

4. Having emphasized that they will not tell *him* (the occupant), the witnesses obviously mean only to communicate their refusal to travel to the occupant's town and inform him. They are perfectly willing, however, to discuss the protest with others. Thus, the occupant will eventually hear about the protest by word of mouth, and it is therefore effective (*Rashbam*). [*Rashbam* thus disputes *Tosafos'* contention above (note 2), that an occupant is assured of hearing about a protest only if the witnesses travel to his locale.]

5. This case, where all agree that the protest is meaningless, differs from the first case, where Rav Pappa considered the protest effective. In that case, the protester never forbade the witnesses from publicizing the protest; he requested only that they conceal it from the occupant. Therefore, Rav Pappa considers the protest effective because the occupant will learn about it by word of mouth. In this case, on the other hand, the protester explicitly charged the witnesses with keeping the protest secret. Even Rav Pappa agrees that in such a case, the protest is meaningless (*Rashbam*).

ולמחר תבענא ליה (א) בדינא הויא מחאה אמר לא תימרו ליה מאי אמר רב זביד הא קאמר לא תימרו ליה רב פפא אמר [א]לדידיה לא תימרו ליה לאחריני אימרו להו [א] חברך חברא אית ליה וחברא דחברך חברא אית ליה אמרו ליה לא אמרינן ליה אמר רב זביד הא קא אמרו ליה לא אמרי' ליה רב פפא אמר [ב]לדידיה לא אמרי' ליה לאחריני אמרי להו חברך חברא אית ליה וחברא דחברך חברא אית ליה אמר להו לא תיפוק לכו שותא אמר רב זביד [ג]הא קאמר לא תיפוק לכו שותא אמרו ליה לא מפקינן שותא אמר רב פפא הא קאמרי ליה לא מפקינן שותא רב הונא בריה דרב יהושע אמר [ב] [ד]כל מילתא דלא רמיא עליה דאיניש אמר לה ולאו אדעתיה: אמר רבא אמר רב נחמן מחאה שלא בפניו הויא מחאה איתיביה רבא לרב נחמן אמר ר' יהודה לא אמרו שלש שנים אלא כדי שיהא באספמיא ויחזיק שנה וילכו ויודיעוהו שנה ויבא לשנה אחרת ואי ס"ד מחאה שלא בפניו הויא מחאה למה לי למיתי ליתיב התם אדוכתיה ולימחי התם [ג] עצה טובה קמ"ל דניתי ונשקול ארעא ופירי מדקא מותיב ליה רבא לרב נחמן מכלל דלא סבירא ליה דמחאה שלא בפניו הויא מחאה [ו] והאמר רבא מחאה שלא בפניו הויא מחאה בתר דשמעה מרב נחמן סברה אשכחינהו ר' יוסי בר' חנינא לתלמידיו דר' יוחנן אמר להו מי אמר (ב) ר' יוחנן מחאה בכמה ר' חייא בר אבא אמר ר' יוחנן מחאה [ה]בפני שנים ר' אבהו אמר ר' יוחנן מחאה בפני שלשה לימא בדרבה בר רב הונא קא מיפלגי [ו] דאמר רבה בר רב הונא [ז]כל מילתא דמתאמרא באפי תלתא לית

רשב"ם

ואי לא אמר למחר תבענא ליה בדינא ומפיקנא מיניה אלא פלוני גזלן דקאכיל לארעאי בגזלנותא בלבד הרי הוא כנותן פגם בחבירו ולא כמוסר עדות ואינה מחאה כן פר"ח. ל"א שמעתי משמועת רבי יעקב בר יקר ועיקר פלניא גזלנא הוא ואפי' הזכיר על קרקע זה שמחזיק לאו מחאה היא שהרי לא מיחה מחמת עצמו והרי הוא כמי שאמר פלוני מחזיק בקרקעות של אחרים ולפוגמו מתכוין ולא לערער שהרי אינו מזכיר שהוא שלו אבל אם פירש דקאכיל לארעאי בגזלנותא הרי מיחה מחמת עצמו והודיע שהקרקע שלו ומחזיק בעולה והויא מחאה ואע"ג דלא סיים למחר תבענא ליה בדינא ופירוש הוא למאי דקאמר דקאכיל לארעאי בגזלנותא: **אמר.** לעדים לא תימרו ליה מחאה זו: **אמר רב זביד הא קאמר כו'.** ולא הויא מחאה דהא לא אמרו ליה עדים תו: **רב פפא אמר.** לעולם מחאה הויא דהכי קאמר להו לעדים לדידיה לא תימרו אבל לאחרים תימרו וכיון שיאמרו לאחרים יחזרו אותן אחרים ויאמרו לו דחבריך חברא אית ליה כו': **אמרו ליה לא אמרינן ליה.** לא קאי אהיכא דאמר להו לא תימרו ליה דהא לרב זביד אפי' שתקו לא הויא מחאה וכל שכן הכא שהשיבו לדבריו אלא מילתא באפי נפשיה היא וקאי אהיכא דאמר להו מחאה גמורה ויוס לומר לו והם ענוהו לא אמרי' ליה ולא חזר ומיחה אחרי כן בפני עדים אחרים: **אמר רב זביד הא קאמרי ליה לא אמרינן ליה.** וכיון שלא יאמרו לו היה לו לזה למחות עוד בפני אחרים שיאמרו לו ואם לא מיחה אחרי כן הפסיד: **רב פפא אמר.** אין צריך למחות עוד בפני אחרים דמחאה מעלייתא היא דהכי קאמרו ליה לדידי' לא אמרינן שלא נלך עד מקומו: **לאחריני אמרינן כו'.** רב פפא קא דייק לא תימרו ליה לא אמרינן ליה דמשמע (ג) לא אמרי' ליה אבל לאחריני אמרי מדלא אמר לא תימרו: **לא תיפוק לכו שותא.** לא יצא דבר מפיכם דמשמע לא לו ולא לאחרים: **שותא.** דיבור כמו שותא דינוקא בשוקא או דאבוה או דאמא (סוכה דף נו:): **אמר רב זביד הא קאמר כו'.** ואינה מחאה: **אמרו ליה לא מפקי' שותא.** לא קאי אהיכא דאמר להו לא תפיק לכו שותא דהתם כ"ע לא פליגי דלא הויא מחאה בין אהדרו ליה בין לא אהדרו ליה שום דיבור ומילתא באפי נפשיה הוא (א) וכגון שלוה אותם לאמר לו והם אמרו לא מפקינן שותא אמר רב פפא הכא ודאי מודינא דלא הויא מחאה דהא קאמרי כו' דמשמע לא לו ולא לאחרים: **אמר רב הונא בריה דרב יהושע.** האי נמי מחאה הויא דכל מילתא דלא רמיא עליה דאינש שאינה מוטלת עליו (ד) לגרר וגם אינו מפסיד אם אומר אם לא אומרה אמר לה לבני אדם ולאו אדעתיה כלומר אינו נותן אל לבו שקיבל (ה) הדבר עליו לכסותו והלכך אינו צריך למחות בפני אחרים שהרי מיחה בפני בני אדם שיכולין לומר לו והלכתא בין אמר הממחה לא תימרו ליה מידי מהני מילי למחזיק ובין אמרו לא מפקינן שותא בכולהו הויא מחאה בר מדאמר להו הממחה דלא תיפוק לכו שותא דלא הויא מחאה וכן פסק ר"ח: ה"ג **אמר רבא אמר רב נחמן מחאה כו'.** ואע"ג דאותביה רבא לרב נחמן שיטת גמרא היא בהרבה מקומות כן והכי פי' כי שמעה רבא מרב נחמן להך מילתא דאמרינן בה אמר רבא אמר רב נחמן איתיביה הך תיובתא ורב אשי שסידר גמרא הוא דקאמר אמר רבא אמר רב נחמן וגם מפרש הקושיא אחרי כן שהקשהו: **מחאה שלא בפניו הויא מחאה.** ולא בעינן שישלח שלוחו למחות בפניו אלא מכיון שמיחה שלא בפניו הויא מחאה שהרי יכול הדבר לבא לאזניו ואפי' לא ידע המחזיק מחאתו של מערער לא חיישינן מאחר שמיחה זה כהוגן: **איתיביה רבא לר"נ אמר רבי יהודה כו'.** ואי קשיא אדפריך מסיפא לסייע מרישא דהא אוקימנא מחאה שלא בפניו הויא מחאה איכא למימר דרבא מוקי לה לרישא במילי אוחרי: **אלא כדי שיהא כו'.** טעמא דרבי יהודה לאו משום דתלת שנין מיזדהר איניש בשטריה אלא כדמפרש כדי שיהא כו' וטעמא דחזקה לדידיה משום דלא שביק איניש דאכלי ארעיה בלא רשותו אפי' שעה אחת ושתיק אלא לכך האריכו שלש שנים שפעמים שהמערער רחוק מהלך שנה ולא יבא ערעור שלו לאזניו עד ג' שנים ולאיפלוגי את"ק אתא דלא חיישינן לשעת חירום וחזקה בפניו מיד הויא חזקה הואיל ולא מיחה מיד מדתלי טעמא באספמיא (ו) לקמן בפרקין: **ויבא לשנה אחרת.** קס"ד דרבא דוקא קאמר (ז) שיבא המערער עצמו וימחה בסוף ג' בפניו של מחזיק אלמא מחאה שלא בפניו לא הויא מחאה והלכך חזקה שלא בפניו לא תיהוי חזקה ואע"ג דלרבי יהודה הויא חזקה בהכי לא סבירא ליה כרבי יהודה דר' יהודה מצריכו לילך ולערער ולרבא לא נצריכו אלא מתוך שאינו יכול למחות באספמיא גם המחזיק לא יכול להחזיק: **ואי ס"ד.** דאין צריך לשלוח שליח ולמחות בפניו בעדים אלא ימחה במקום שהוא שם ואם יבא הדבר לאזניו יבא למה ליה למיתי עד מקום המחזיק או לשלח שלוחו למחות בפניו: **ליתיב אדוכתיה.** באספמיא ולימחי בפני עדים שהרי יכולין לבא ולומר לו (ח) בסוף ג' אם ירצו: **ומשני עצה טובה קמ"ל.** דנייתי הוא עצמו ונשקול קרקע ופירותיו מיד המחזיק שאם ימחה במקומו ולא ילך ויוציא עכשיו מידו הפירות שאכל המחזיק יוציא ממנו בטורח דקשה גזל הנאכל ומיהו לאו דוקא מצריך ליה רבי יהודה לבא אלא הכי קאמר לא אמרו דצריך ג' שנים אלא כדי שאם יהיה המערער באספמיא ומשהחזיק זה יצא הקול ויודיעוהו בשנה שניה וימחה בתחלת שלש ויוכל הדבר לבא לאזניו של מחזיק בסוף שנה שלישית ואז יש הנאה למערער שאם ירצה הוא עצמו לבא בסוף שלש ויקח קרקע ופירות מעכשיו בלא דין ודברים: **והא אמר רבא מחאה שלא בפניו הויא מחאה.** לעיל פסק רבא הלכתא הכי: **ומשני בתר דשמעיה מרב נחמן.** ותירץ לו תשובה שהשיבהו פסק רבא הכי: ה"ג **מי שמיע לכו מרבי יוחנן מחאה בכמה.** בפני כמה בני אדם: **כל מילתא.** של גנאי: **דמתאמרא באפי תלתא לית בה משום לישנא בישא.** אם יחזרו ויאמרו לזה כך אמר פלוני עליך וטעמא כדמפרש בערכין ביש בערכין מ"ט חברך חברא אית ליה ואמר אביי התם דכל מילתא דעבידא לאיגלויי לית בה משום לישנא בישא והלכך גבי מחאה נמי מילתא דעבידא לאיגלויי בעינן כדי שיזהר המחזיק בשטרו ולהכי פליגי מ"ד בפני שנים לית ליה דרבה בר רב הונא דבעי תלתא דהא אפי' בתרי עבידא לאיגלויי והויא מחאה בפני שנים ולענין

תוספות

רב פפא אמר לדידיה לא תימרון לאחריני תימרון. נראה לר"י דרב פפא אית ליה שפיר דשמואל דאמר לעיל מיחה בפני בני אדם שאין יכולין לומר לו לא הויא מחאה דהתם מיירי בחולה וזקן שלעולם לא ילך למקום שמחזיק שם אבל הכא ילכו למקום המחזיק ויגידו לבני העיר ויאמרו לו והויא מחאה: **ליתיב** אדוכתיה ולימחי. תימה אדפריך מר' יהודה לסייעיה מרבנן דמוכח לעיל דסברי מחאה שלא בפניו הויא מחאה ואור"י דרבא היה טועה וס"ד דבכל מקום שהחזקה נשמעת גם המחאה נשמעת וכמו שהחזקה (ט) מיהודה לאספמיא ה"נ מחאה ואפילו הכי א"ר יהודה שיבא בפניו וימחה ורבנן סברי אפי' מיהודה לגליל אין החזקה נשמעת לכך לא הוי חזקה אבל מיהודה ליהודה נשמעת והוי חזקה עד שיבא בפניו וימחה ולכ"ע שלא בפניו לא הוי מחאה ורב נחמן דאיצטריך לשנויי עצה טובה קמ"ל ולא שני ליה דלא מצי למיתב אדוכתיה לפי שהמחאה אינה נשמעת אלא באותה מדינה משום דהכתי תקשי ליה אמאי מצריך רבי יהודה לבא לפניו ילך עד המדינה שהמחזיק שם וימחה דמדלא קתני ויבא לשנה אחרת וימחה ויודיעוהו משמע שצריך לבא לפניו כדפרישית: **ה"ג** מכלל דלא סבירא ליה הא אמר רבא מחאה שלא בפניו. ולא גר' והא אמר רבא אמר ר"נ:

מסורת הש"ס

א) [לעיל כח: וש"נ], ב) [שבועות לד: מח: מב.], ג) [לעיל כח: וש"נ], ד) [לעיל לח:], ה) ערכין טז:.

הגהות הב"ח

(א) גמ' תבענא ליה לדינא: (ב) שם מי אמר לכו ר' יוחנן: (ג) רשב"ם ד"ה לאחריני וכו' דמשמע ליה לא אמרינן אבל: (ד) ד"ה מוטלת עליו (לכחד) תא"מ ונ"ב ס"א לכסות: (ה) בא"ד אינו נותן אל לבו שקיבל עליו לכסות הדבר והלכך וכו' מהני מילי למחזיק ובין אמרו ליה ובין אמרו לא מפקינן שותא: (ו) ד"ה אלא וכו' באספמיא כדאמרינן לקמן: (ז) ד"ה ויבא לשנה וכו' דוקא קאמר רבי יהודה שיבא: (ח) ד"ה ליתיב וכו' ולומר לו בתוך ג': (ט) תוס' ד"ה ליתיב וכו' וכמו שהחזקה נשמעת מיהודה:

הגהות חו"י

(א) רשב"ם ד"ה אמרו ליה כו' והכא איירי שלוה אותם כצ"ל:

ליקוטי רש"י

לא תיפוק לכו שותא. שותא דיבור כמו לא תיפוק לכו שותא [ב"ב לט.] וקדושין (ע.) שותא דמר לא ידענא [סוכה נו:]. דמתאמרא באפי תלתא. שהשלשים אמרוה בפני ג' המגלה אותה אינו לשון הרע שזה גילה מתחלה אותו שאם מגלה אותו אינו חושש למידע יודע דסופה לגוגות דחברך חברא אית ליה וזה מגלה לחבירו וזה לחבירו עד שיודע [ערכין טז.].

עין משפט נר מצוה

פח א ב ג ד מיי' פי"א מהל' טוען ונטען הל' ו ופ"ו הלכה ד סמג עשין צה טוש"ע ח"מ סי' קמו סעיף ג וסי' עט סעיף א [ילף]:

פט ה מיי' שם הל' ח טוש"ע שם סעי' ח:

צ ו מיי' פ"ז מהל' דעות הלכה ה סמג לאוין ט:

רבינו גרשום

הכי לא מיחה ואין מחזיקין בנכסיו: לא הויא מחאה דמילי בעלמא קאמר אבל כי אמר להו למחר אתבעיה בדינא הויא מחאה דקאמר להו דאין דעתו למחול: אי אמר להו לא תימרו ליה דמחיתי אמר רב זביד הא קאמר לא תימרו ליה ולא הויא מחאה ומחזיקין. אמר רב פפא ודאי הוי מחאה דהכי אמר ליה המערער לעדים לדידיה לא תימרו ליה הא לאחריני אימרו: אמרו ליה העדים למערער לא אמרינן ליה לפלוני דמחית. אמר רב זביד הא קאמרו לא אמרינן ליה ולא הויא מחאה: אמר לעדים לא תיפוק לכו שותא כלומר לא תוציאו דבר מפיכם לשום אדם שמחיתי. אמר רב זביד הא קא מזהיר דלא תפיקו שותא ולא הויא מחאה. הא דקא מזהיר המערער הכי לעדים משום דחשב בדעתיה אמחה ואזהיר להו דלא לימרו ליה היום ולמחר אוציא עדי מחאה ואגבה הפירות ותיקון הקרקע. ואי אמרי לא מפקינן שותא. הא אמרי וכו' ולא הויא מחאה. אמר רב הונא אפי' הכי הויא מחאה משום דכל מלתא דלא רמיא עליה דאינש שאינו מוזהר שלא יאמר אומרה ולאו אדעתיה. אמר ר' יהודה לא אמרו א) משום שמקום של ר' יהודה הוא רחוק מאספמיא מהלך שנה להכי משער בהאי גוונא: מכלל דלא ס"ל כרב נחמן והא אמר רבא לעיל הלכתא מחאה שלא בפניו הויא מחאה. ומשני בתר דשמעה מרב נחמן הא דקא מתרץ מתני' הכי סברה כוותיה דרב נחמן דשלא בפניו הויא מחאה אבל מעיקרא ס"ל דלא הויא מחאה ומש"ה הוה מותיב ליה הכי: בכמה. בני אדם. כל מלתא של גנאי דמתאמרא באפי תלתא ואולי הני תלתא ומשתעי לה לאחריני לית בה משום לישנא בישא והא נמי דבר גנאי הוה דקאמר להו פלוני גזלנא הוא ב) מתאמרא באפי תרי והני תרי אמרי לה לאחרינא אית ביה משום לישנא בישא:

חשק שלמה על רבינו גרשום

א) נ"ל לא אמרו וכו' אלא כדי שיהא באספמיא וכו' משום שמקום וכו'. ב) נראה דל"ל ולי מתאמרא וכו'.

בְּפָנָיו הַוְיָא מְחָאָה – **Now, if you would think that a protest** lodged **not in the presence of [the occupant] is an** effective **protest,** לָמָּה לִי לְמֵיתֵי – **why must [the protester] come** back from Spain to lodge his protest? לֵיתִיב הָתָם אַדּוּכְתֵּיהּ וְלִימְחֵי – **Let him remain there in his place and protest** from there. Why, then, does R' Yehudah require the protester to return? Obviously, he must hold that a protest lodged in the occupant's absence is meaningless. This contradicts Rav Nachman's position.[6] – ? –

The Gemara deflects the challenge:

הָתָם עֵצָה טוֹבָה קָא מַשְׁמַע לַן – **There** in our Mishnah, **[R' Yehudah] is** merely **giving** the original owner **sound advice,** דְּנֵיתֵי וְנִשְׁקוֹל אַרְעָא וּפֵירֵי – viz. **that he should come** from Spain **and claim** both his **land and** his **produce** before the occupant consumes the produce. R' Yehudah might well agree with Rav Nachman, however, that protesting from afar voids the occupant's *chazakah*.[7]

The Gemara questions the premise of Rava's challenge:

מִדְּקָא מוֹתִיב לֵיהּ רָבָא לְרַב נַחְמָן – **From** the fact **that Rava challenged Rav Nachman,** מִכְּלַל דְּלָא סְבִירָא לֵיהּ דִּמְחָאָה שֶׁלֹּא בְּפָנָיו הַוְיָא מְחָאָה – **we can deduce that [Rava]** himself **does not hold that a protest** lodged **not in [the occupant's] presence is a** valid **protest.** וְהָאָמַר רָבָא מְחָאָה שֶׁלֹּא בְּפָנָיו הַוְיָא מְחָאָה – **But did Rava not rule**[8] **that a protest** lodged **not in [the occupant's] presence *is* an** effective **protest?**

The Gemara explains that Rava retracted his previously held opinion:

בָּתַר דִּשְׁמָעָהּ מֵרַב נַחְמָן סְבָרָהּ – **After** Rava **heard** the answer to his question **from Rav Nachman,** his teacher, **he accepted [Rav Nachman's ruling].** Rava's ruling reflects his position after the retraction.

The Gemara discusses one of the legal requirements for an effective protest:

אַשְׁכְּחִינְהוּ ר׳ יוֹסֵי בְּר׳ חֲנִינָא לְתַלְמִידָיו דְּר׳ יוֹחָנָן – **R' Yose the son of R' Chanina met** some **disciples of R' Yochanan.** אָמַר לְהוּ – **He inquired of them:** מִי אָמַר ר׳ יוֹחָנָן מְחָאָה בְּכַמָּה – **Did R' Yochanan** ever **state** an opinion regarding **how many** people must witness the original owner **protest** his field's occupation?

The Gemara quotes two views in R' Yochanan's name:

ר׳ חִיָּיא בַּר אַבָּא אָמַר ר׳ יוֹחָנָן – **R' Chiya bar Abba said in R' Yochanan's name:** מְחָאָה בִּפְנֵי שְׁנַיִם – **A protest** must be lodged **in the presence of two** witnesses. ר׳ אַבָּהוּ אָמַר ר׳ יוֹחָנָן מְחָאָה בִּפְנֵי שְׁלֹשָׁה – **R' Abahu said in R' Yochanan's name: A protest** must be lodged **in the presence of three** witnesses.

The Gemara attempts to link the dispute to an Amoraic ruling:

לֵימָא בִּדְרַבָּה בַּר רַב הוּנָא קָא מִיפַּלְגֵי – **Shall we say that [R' Chiya and R' Abahu] disagree** over the ruling **of Rabbah bar Rav Huna?** דְּאָמַר רַבָּה בַּר רַב הוּנָא – **For Rabbah bar Rav Huna said:**[9] כָּל מִילְּתָא דְּמִתְאַמְרָא בְּאַפֵּי תְּלָתָא – **Any tale that was related in front of three people**[10] can be assumed to have become public knowledge and therefore

NOTES

6. *Rashbam* notes that the Gemara could have defended Rav Nachman's position easily. According to Rav's interpretation of the Tanna Kamma, a protest lodged in the occupant's absence is indeed effective (see 38a). Thus, the Gemara could have explained that Rav Nachman follows the Tanna Kamma's ruling rather than that of R' Yehudah. The reason it did not advance this defense, suggests *Rashbam,* is that Rava might have interpreted the Tanna Kamma differently than Rav did (see *Tosafos*, who suggest a different interpretation).

Although Rava proves from R' Yehudah's ruling that a protest lodged in the occupant's absence is meaningless, he does not fully accept the ruling. According to R' Yehudah, if someone assumes occupancy of a field in Eretz Yisrael while its owner is in Spain, he establishes a *chazakah* unless the owner returns to protest within three years. Rava, however, does not accept R' Yehudah's view on this point, maintaining that since the owner cannot lodge a meaningful protest from Spain, the occupant can never establish a *chazakah*. Thus, although he accepts R' Yehudah's opinion that a protest lodged in the occupant's absence is meaningless, he rejects his view that a *chazakah* can be established in such a case (*Rashbam*; see *Rabbeinu Yonah*, *Ritva* and *Maharsha*).

7. That is, the protester voids the *chazakah* whether he protests from Spain or returns to Eretz Yisrael. To protect his produce, however, he must return to Eretz Yisrael. There, he can summon the occupant to court and demand that he either produce the deed or vacate the land. When the occupant fails to produce the deed, he is prevented from consuming any of the field's produce. If the owner lodges the protest in Spain, on the other hand, he cannot evict the occupant, and the occupant will continue consuming the produce. Although the owner can theoretically exact payment for the consumed produce when he later evicts him, it is difficult to do this in practice for he must first prove how much was consumed. R' Yehudah therefore advises the owner to return as soon as possible to evict and thus prevent him from consuming more produce (*Ri Migash* cited in *Shitah Mekubetzes*; see *Rashbam*).

8. 38b.

9. *Arachin* 16a.

10. I.e. if one person spoke disparagingly about another in front of three people and someone then relates this to the object of the discussion (*Rashbam*; see *Chofetz Chaim Be'er Mayim Chaim* 2:2).

מסורת הש"ס

א) [לעיל כח: וש"נ], ב) [שבועות לד: מא: מב.], ג) [לעיל כח: וש"נ], ד) [לעיל לח:], ה) ערכין טז.:

הגהות הב"ח

(א) גמ' תבענא ליה לדינא: (ב) שם מי אמר לכו ר' יוחנן: (ג) רשב"ם ד"ה לאחריני וכו' דמשמע ליה לא אמרינן אבל: (ד) ד"ה אמר רב הונא וכו' שאינה מוטלת עליו (לכחד) תז"מ ונ"ב ס"א לכסויא: (ה) בא"ד אינו נותן אל לבו שקיבל עליו לכסות הדבר והלכך וכו' מהני מילי למחזיק ובין א"ל לא אמרי' ליה ובין אמרו לא מפקינן שותא: (ו) ד"ה אלא וכו' באספמיא כדאמרינן לקמן: (ז) ד"ה ויבא לשנה וכו' דוקא קאמר רבי יהודה שיבא: (ח) ד"ה ליתיב וכו' ולומר לו בתוך ג': (ט) תוס' ד"ה ליתיב וכו' וכמו שהחזקה נשמעת מיהודה:

הגהות חו"י

(א) רשב"ם ד"ה אמרו ליה כו' והכא איירי שלוה אותם כצ"ל:

ליקוטי רש"י

לא תיפוק לכו שותא. שותא דיבור כמו לא תיפוק לכו שותא (ב"ב לט.) ובקדושין (ע.) שותא דמר לא ידענא [סוכה נו:]. **דמתאמרא באפי תלתא.** שהבעלים אמרוה בפני ג' המגלה אותה לאו לשון הרע הוא שזה גילה מחלה שלו שכן דעתו שאם מגלה אותו אינו חושש דמידע ידע דקושיא להגלות דמחברך חברא אית ליה וזה מגלה לחבירו וזה לחבירו עד שיודע [ערכין טז.].

גמרא

ולמחר תבענא ליה (א) בדינא הויא מחאה אמר לא תימרו ליה מאי אמר רב זביד הא קאמר לא תימרו ליה רב פפא אמר א לדידיה לא תימרו ליה לאחריני אימרו להו ב חברך חברא אית ליה וחברא דחברך חברא אית ליה אמרו ליה לא אמרינן ליה אמר רב זביד הא קא אמרו ליה לא אמרי' ליה רב פפא אמר ג לדידיה לא אמרי' ליה לאחריני אמרי להו חברך חברא אית ליה וחברא דחברך חברא אית ליה אמר להו לא תיפוק לכו שותא אמר רב זביד ד הא קאמר לא תיפוק לכו שותא אמרו ליה לא מפקינן שותא אמר רב פפא הא קאמרי ליה לא מפקינן שותא רב הונא בריה דרב יהושע אמר ה כל מילתא דלא רמיא עליה דאיניש אמר לה ולאו אדעתיה: אמר רבא אמר רב נחמן מחאה שלא בפניו הויא מחאה איתיביה רבא לרב נחמן אמר ר' יהודה לא אמרו שלש שנים אלא כדי שיהא באספמיא ויחזיק שנה וילכו ויודיעוהו שנה ויבא לשנה אחרת ואי ס"ד מחאה שלא בפניו הויא מחאה למה לי למיתי ליתיב התם אדוכתיה ולימחי התם ו עצה טובה קמ"ל דניתי ונשקול ארעא ופירי מדקא מותיב ליה רבא לרב נחמן מכלל דלא סבירא ליה דמחאה שלא בפניו הויא מחאה ז והאמר רבא מחאה שלא בפניו הויא מחאה בתר דשמעה מרב נחמן סברה אשכחינהו ר' יוסי בר' חנינא לתלמידיו דר' יוחנן אמר להו מי אמר (ב) ר' יוחנן מחאה בכמה ר' חייא בר אבא אמר ר' יוחנן מחאה ח בפני שנים ר' אבהו אמר ר' יוחנן מחאה בפני שלשה לימא בדרבה בר רב הונא קא מיפלגי ט דאמר רבה בר רב הונא י כל מילתא דמתאמרא באפי תלתא לית

רשב"ם

ואי לא אמר למחר תבענא ליה בדינא ומפיקנא מיניה אלא פלוני גזלן דקאכיל לארעאי בגזלנותא בלבד הרי הוא כנותן פגם בחבירו ולא כמוסר עדות ואינה מחאה כן פר"ח. ל"א שמעתי משמועת רבי יעקב בר יקר ועיקר פלניא גזלנא הוא ואפי' הזכיר על קרקע זה שמחזיק לאו מחאה היא שהרי לא מיחה מחמת עצמו והרי הוא כמי שאמר פלוני מחזיק בקרקעות של אחרים ולפוגמו מתכוין ולא לערער שהרי אינו מזכיר שהוא שלו אבל אם פירש דקאכיל לארעאי בגזלנותא הרי מיחה מחמת עצמו והודיע שהקרקע שלו מחזיק בעולה והויא מחאה ואע"ג דלא סיים למחר תבענא ליה בדינא ופירוש הוא למאי דקאמר דקאכיל לארעאי בגזלנותא: **אמר.** לעדים לא תימרו ליה מחאה זו: **אמר רב זביד הא קאמר כו'.** ולא הויא מחאה דהא לא אמרו ליה עדים תו: **רב פפא אמר.** לעולם מחאה הויא דהכי קאמר להו לעדים לדידיה לא תימרו אבל לאחרים תימרו וכיון שיאמרו לאחרים יחזרו אותן אחרים ויאמרו לו דחברך חברא אית ליה כו': **אמרו ליה לא אמרינן ליה.** לא קאי אהיכא דאמר להו לא תימרו ליה דהא לרב זביד אפי' שתקו לא הויא מחאה וכל שכן הכא היכא שהשיבו כדבריו אלא מילתא באפי נפשיה היא וקאי אהיכא דאמר להו מחאה גמורה וליום לומר לו והם ענוהו לא אמרי' ליה ולא חזר ומיחה אחרי כן בפני עדים אחרים: **אמר רב זביד הא קאמרי ליה לא אמרינן ליה.** וכיון שלא יאמרו לו היה לו לזה למחות עוד בפני אחרים שיאמרו לו ואם לא מיחה אחרי כן הפסיד: **רב פפא אמר.** אין צריך למחות עוד בפני אחרים דמחאה מעלייתא היא דהכי קאמרו ליה לדידי' לא אמרינן שלא נלך עד מקומו: **לאחריני אמרינן כו'.** רב פפא קא דייק לא תימרו ליה לא אמרינן ליה דמשמע (ג) לא אמרי' ליה אבל לאחריני אמרי מדלא אמר לא תימרו: **לא תיפוק לכו שותא.** לא יצא דבר מפיכם דמשמע לא לו ולא לאחרים: **שותא.** דיבור כמו שותא דינוקא בשוקא או דאבוה או דאמא (סוכה דף נו:): **אמר רב זביד הא קאמר כו'.** ואינה מחאה: **אמרו ליה לא מפקי' שותא.** לא קאי אהיכא דאמר להו לא תפיק לכו שותא דהתם כ"ע לא פליגי דלא הויא מחאה בין אהדרו ליה שום דיבור בין לא אהדרו ליה ומילתא באפי נפשיה הוא (א) וכגון שלוה אותם לאמר לו והם אמרו לא מפקינן שותא אמר רב פפא הכא ודאי מודינא דלא הויא מחאה דהא קאמרי כו' דמשמע לא לו ולא לאחרים: **אמר רב הונא בריה דרב יהושע.** האי נמי מחאה הויא דכל מילתא דלא רמיא עליה דאינש שאינה מוטלת עליו (ד) לבדר וגם אינו מפסיד אם אומר אם לא אומרה אמר לה לבני אדם ולאו אדעתיה כלומר אינו נותן אל לבו שקיבל (ה) הדבר עליו לכסותו והלכך אינו צריך למחות בפני אחרים שהרי מיחה בפני בני אדם שיכולין לומר לו והלכתא בין אמר הממחה לא תימרו ליה מידי מהני מילי למחזיק ובין אמרו לא מפקינן שותא בכולהו הויא מחאה בר מדאמר להו הממחה דלא תיפוק לכו שותא דלא הויא מחאה וכן פסק ר"ח: ה"ג **אמר רבא אמר רב נחמן מחאה כו'.** ואע"ג דאותביה רבא לרב נחמן שיטת גמרא היא בהרבה מקומות כן והכי פי' כי שמעה רבא מרב נחמן להך מילתא דאמרינן בה אמר רבא אמר רב נחמן איתיביה הך תיובתא ורב אשי שסידר גמרא הוא דקאמר אמר רבא אמר רב נחמן וגם מפרש הקושיא אחרי כן שהקשהו: **מחאה שלא בפניו הויא מחאה.** ולא בעינן שישלח שלוחו למחות בפניו אלא מכיון שמיחה שלא בפניו הויא מחאה שהרי יכול הדבר לבא לאזניו ואפי' לא ידע המחזיק מחאתו של מערער לא חיישינן מאחר שמיחה זה כהוגן: **איתיביה רבא לר"נ אמר רבי יהודה כו'.** ואי קשיא אדפריך מסיפא לסייע מרישא דהא אוקימנא מחאה שלא בפניו הויא מחאה איכא למימר דרבא מוקי לה לרישא במילי אוחרי: **אלא כדי שיהא כו'.** טעמא דרבי יהודה לאו משום דתלת שנין מיזדהר איניש בשטריה אלא כדמפרש כדי שיהא כו' וטעמא דחזקה לדידיה משום דלא שביק איניש דאכלי ארעיה בלא רשותו אפי' שעה אחת ושתיק אלא לכך הצריכו שלש שנים שפעמים שהמערער רחוק מהלך שנה ולא יבא ערעור שלו לאזניו עד ג' שנים ולאיפלוגי את"ק אתא דלא חיישינן לשעת חירום וחזקה בפניו מיד הויא חזקה הואיל ולא מיחה מיד מדתלי טעמא באספמיא (ו) לקמן בפרקין: **ויבא לשנה אחרת.** קס"ד דרבא דוקא קאמר (ז) שיבא המערער עצמו וימחה בסוף ג' בפניו של מחזיק אלמא מחאה שלא בפניו לא הויא מחאה והלכך חזקה שלא בפניו לא תיהוי חזקה ואע"ג דלרבי יהודה הויא חזקה בהכי לא סבירא ליה כרבי יהודה דר' יהודה מצריכו לילך ולערער ולרבא לא נצריכו אלא מתוך שאינו יכול למחות באספמיא גם המחזיק לא יכול להחזיק: **ואי ס"ד.** דאין צריך לשלוח שליח ולמחות בפניו בעדים אלא ימחה במקום שהוא שם ואם יבא הדבר לאזניו יבא למה ליה למיתי עד מקום המחזיק או לשלח שלוחו למחות בפניו: **ליתיב אדוכתיה.** באספמיא ולימחי בפני עדים שהרי יכולין לבא ולומר לו (ח) בסוף ג' אם ירצו: **ומשני עצה טובה קמ"ל.** דנייתי הוא עצמו ונשקול קרקע ופירותיו מיד המחזיק שאם ימחה במקומו ולא ילך ויוציא עכשיו מידו הפירות שאכל המחזיק יוציא ממנו בטורח דקשה גזל הנאכל ומיהו לאו דוקא מצריך ליה רבי יהודה לבא אלא הכי קאמר לא אמרו דצריך ג' שנים אלא כדי שאם יהיה המערער באספמיא ומשהחזיק זה יצא הקול ויודיעוהו בשנה שניה וימחה בתחלת שלש ויוכל הדבר לבא לאזניו של מחזיק בסוף שנה שלישית ואז יש הנאה למערער שאם ירצה הוא עצמו לבא בסוף שלש ויקח קרקע ופירות מעכשיו בלא דין ודברים: **והא אמר רבא מחאה שלא בפניו הויא מחאה.** לעיל פסק רבא הלכתא הכי: **ומשני בתר דשמעיה מרב נחמן.** ותירץ לו תשובה שהשיבהו פסק רבא הכי: ה"ג **מי שמיע לכו מרבי יוחנן מחאה בכמה.** בפני כמה בני אדם: **כל מילתא.** של גנאי: **דמתאמרא באפי תלתא לית בה משום לישנא בישא.** אם יחזרו ויאמרו לזה כך אמר פלוני עליך וטעמא כדמפרש בערכין דיש בערכין מ"ט חברך חברא אית ליה ואמר אביי התם דכל מילתא דעבידא לאיגלויי לית בה משום לישנא בישא והלכך גבי מחאה נמי מילתא דעבידא לאיגלויי בעינן כדי שיזהר המחזיק בשטרו ולהכי פליגי מ"ד בפני שנים לית ליה דרבה בר רב הונא דבעי תלתא דהא אפי' בתרי עבידא לאיגלויי והויא מחאה בפני שנים

ולענין

תוספות

רב פפא אמר לדידיה לא תימרון לאחריני תימרון. נראה לר"י דרב פפא אית ליה שפיר דשמואל דאמר לעיל מיחה בפני בני אדם שאין יכולין לומר לו לא הויא מחאה דהכא מיירי בחולה וזקן שלעולם לא ילך למקום שמחזיק שם אבל הכא ילכו למקום המחזיק ויגידו לבני העיר ויאמרו לו והויא מחאה: **ליתיב אדוכתיה ולימחי.** תימה אדפריך מר' יהודה לסייעיה מרבנן דמוכח לעיל דסברי מחאה שלא בפניו הויא מחאה ואור"י דרבה היה טועה וס"ד דבכל מקום שהחזקה נשמעת גם המחאה נשמעת וכמו שהחזקה (ט) מיהודה לאספמיא ה"נ מחאה ואפילו הכי א"ר יהודה שיבא בפניו וימחה ורבנן סברי אפי' מיהודה לגליל אין החזקה נשמעת לכך לא הוי חזקה אבל מיהודה ליהודה נשמעת והוי חזקה עד שיבא בפניו וימחה ולכ"ע שלא בפניו לא הוי מחאה ורב נחמן דלאלתר לשנויי עלה טובה קמ"ל ולא שני ליה דלא מצי למיתב אדוכתיה לפי שהמחאה אינה נשמעת אלא באותה מדינה משום דהכי תקשי ליה אמאי מצריך רבי יהודה לבא לפניו ילך עד המדינה שהמחזיק שם וימחה דמדלא קתני ויבא לשנה אחרת וימחה ויודיעוהו משמע שצריך לבא לפניו כדפרישית: **ה"ג מכלל דלא סבירא ליה הא אמר רבא מחאה שלא בפניו.** ולא גרס' והא אמר רבא אמר ר"נ:

עין משפט נר מצוה

פח א ב ג ד מיי' פי"א מהל' טוען ונטען הל' ו ופי"ו הלכה ד סמג עשין צה טוש"ע ח"מ סי' קמו סעיף ג וסי' קמט סעיף א [יא]:

פט ה מיי' שם הל' ח טוש"ע שם סעי' א:

צ ו מיי' פ"ז מהל' דעות הלכה ה סמג לאוין ט:

רבינו גרשום

הכי לא מיחה ואין מחזיקין בנכסיו: **לא הויא מחאה** דמילי בעלמ' קאמר אבל כי אמר להו **למחר אתבעיה בדינא הויא מחאה** דקאמר להו דאין דעתו למחול: אי **אמר** להו **לא תימרו ליה** דמחיתי **אמר רב זביד הא קאמר לא תימרו ליה** ולא הויא מחאה ומחזיקין. **אמר רב פפא** ודאי הוי מחאה דהכי אמר ליה המערער לעדים **לדידיה לא תימרו ליה הא לאחריני אימרו: אמרו ליה** העדים למערער **לא אמרינן ליה** לפלוני דמחית. **אמר רב זביד הא קאמרו לא אמרינן ליה** ולא הויא מחאה: **אמר** לעדים **לא תיפוק לכו שותא** כלומר לא תוציאו דבר מפיכם לשום אדם שמחיתי. **אמר רב זביד הא קא** מזהיר **דלא תפיקו שותא** ולא הויא מחאה. הא דקא מזהיר המערער הכי לעדים משום דחשב בדעתיה אמחה ואזהיר להו דלא לימרו היום ולמחר אוציא עדי מחאה ואגבה הפירות ותיקון הקרקע. ואי **אמרי לא מפקינן שותא.** הא אמרי וכו' ולא הויא מחאה. **אמר רב הונא** אפי' הכי הויא מחאה משום דכל מלתא דלא רמיא עליה דאיניש שאינו מוזהר שלא יאמר אומרה ולאו אדעתיה. **אמר ר' יהודה לא אמרו** א) משום שמקום של ר' יהודה הוא רחוק מאספמיא מהלך שנה להכי משער בהאי גוונא: **אמר** מכלל דלא ס"ל כרב נחמן **והא אמר רבא** לעיל הלכתא **מחאה שלא בפניו הויא מחאה.** ומשני **בתר דשמעה מרב נחמן** הא דקא מתרץ מתני' הכי סברה כוותיה דרב נחמן דשלא בפניו הויא מחאה אבל מעיקרא ס"ל דלא הויא מחאה ומש"ה הוה מותיב ליה הכי: **בכמה.** בני אדם. **כל מלתא** של גנאי **דמתאמרא באפי תלתא** ואולי הני תלתא ומשתעי לה לאחריני **לית בה משום לישנא בישא:** והא נמי דבר גנאי הוה דקאמר להו פלוני גזלנא הוא ב) מתאמרא באפי תרי והני תרי אמרי לה לאחרינא אית ביה משום לישנא בישא:

חשק שלמה על רבינו גרשום

א) נ"ל לא אמרו וכו' אלא כדי שיהא באספמיא וכו' משום שמקום וכו'. ב) נראה דצ"ל ואי מתאמרא וכו'.

עין משפט
נר מצוה

צא א מיי' פי"א מהל' טוען ונטען הלכה ח סמג עשין לה טוש"ע ח"מ סי' קמו סעי' ה:
צב ב טוש"ע שם סעיף ז:

רבינו גרשום

מאן דאמר בפני שנים הויא מחאה **לית ליה דרבה בר רב הונא** דודאי אם מספרין הני שנים למחזיק דמיחה המערער אין לשון הרע בכך. **ומאן דאמר בפני ג' אית ליה דרבה** דודאי ג' אין בהם משום לשון הרע אבל שנים אם מיחה בפניהם אין מספרים בשמו משום דלשון הרע הן מספרין: **מאן דאמר בפני שנים הויא מחאה** א) ודאי בפניו דמחזיק עצמו סגי בשנים משום **דמחאה שלא בפניו לא הויא מחאה** ובפניו בעינן מחאה אבל אי אמרינן דמחאה שלא בפניו (לא) הויא מחאה לא סגי בשנים משום דאית בה לישנא בישא ולא משתעו **ומאן דאמר בפני ג'** צריך למחות **קסבר** דאפי' **מחאה שלא בפניו הויא מחאה** ומשום הכי צריך ג' דכל מלתא דמתאמרא באפי תלתא לית בה משום לישנא בישא הא בתרי אית בה [לישנא בישא]: **סהדותא בעינן** ובתרי סגי במקבלי עדות. **גלויי מלתא בעינן** לפרסם וגלוי מלתא לא סגי בפחות מג': **גידל בר מניומי הוה ליה מחיתא למחויי** שהיה אחד מחזיק בנכסיו והיה מוחה: **צריך למחות** למחזיק **בסוף כל ג' וג'** שנים שאם לא ימחה בסוף כל ג' יכול המחזיק לומר אחרי שמחית מכרת לי וכבר החזקתי בה ג' שנין: **תהי בה ר' יוחנן** אמאי צריך למחות בסוף כל ג' **וכי גזלן יש לו חזקה.** כלומר מאחר שאמר אני קניתיה ממך אחר שמחיתה מכלל דמודי דקודם לכן באת לידו בגזלנות וכי גזלן יש לו חזקה כיון שגזלן הוא אע"פ שהחזיק בה כמה שנים אין חזקתו חזקה, ומקשי' **גזלן ס"ד** והא לאו גזלן הוא דהא קא טעין דזבנה ניהליה ובתורת מכירה אתאי לידיה ולאו גזלן הוא אלא פריך הכי וכי **כגזלן יש לו חזקה** האי דכגזלן דמי דטוען שיש לו חזקה שקנאה ממנו אחרי מחאתו ולא קודם וכי מי שהוא כגזלן יש לו חזקה ב) בתר דקאמר אלא ודאי אין לו חזקה ואמאי צריך למחות בסוף כל שלש: **ערער** בשנה ראשונה **וחזר וערער** בשניה **וחזר וערער** בשלישית **אם מחמת טענה ראשונה** היו כל ג' **ערעורין** שלא שנה דברו **אין לו חזקה** למחזיק **ואם לאו** ששנה המערער דבריו שאמר פעם אחת שלי היתה אני קניתיה ושוב אמר של אבותי היתה אין בדבריו כלום **ויש לו חזקה** למחזיק.

לית בה משום לישנא בישא מ"ד בפני שנים לית ליה דרבה בר רב הונא ומ"ד בפני ג' אית ליה דרבה בר רב הונא לא דכולי עלמא אית להו דרבה בר רב הונא והכא בהא קא מיפלגי מ"ד בפני שנים קסבר מחאה שלא בפניו לא הויא מחאה ומ"ד בפני ג' קסבר מחאה שלא בפניו הויא מחאה אי בעית אימא דכ"ע מחאה שלא בפניו הויא מחאה והכא בהא קמיפלגי מ"ד בפני ב' סבר סהדותא בעינן ומאן דאמר בפני ג' קסבר גלויי מילתא בעינן גידל בר מניומי הוה ליה (א) מחויאתא למחויי אשכחינהו לרב הונא ולחייא בר רב ולרב חלקיה בר טובי דהוו יתבי ומחה קמייהו לשנה הדר אתא למחויי אמרו ליה לא צריכת הכי אמר רב כיון שמיחה שנה ראשונה שוב אינו צריך למחות ואיכא דאמרי אמר ליה חייא בר רב כיון שמיחה שנה ראשונה שוב אין צריך למחות אר"ל משום בר קפרא וצריך למחות בסוף כל ג' וג' תהי בה רבי יוחנן וכי גזלן יש לו חזקה גזלן ס"ד אלא כגזלן יש לו חזקה אמר רבא [א] הלכתא צריך למחות בסוף כל ג' וג' תני בר קפרא [ב] ערער חזר וערער אם מחמת טענה ראשונה ערער אין לו חזקה ואם לאו יש לו חזקה אמר רבא א"ר נחמן מחאה בפני שנים ואין

לית בה משום לישנא בישא. דקלא אית לה וסופו שידע אע"ג דמלוה ע"פ אפי' בכמה עדים אינו גובה מן הלקוחות וטעמא משום דלית ליה קלא כדאמר לקמן (דף מב.) דהתם הוי טעמא משום דמאן דזיזף בצינעא יזיף ועוד דהתם אין יודעין מי יקח שיגידו לו פלוני חייב אבל מאן דידע מחאה יאמר למחזיק:

ולענין לשון הרע לית בה משום לישנא בישא היכא דמתאמרא קמי תרי: **ומ"ד בפני ג' אית ליה דרבה בר רב הונא.** דבג' הוי גלויי מילתא ולא בתרי הלכך בפני ב' לא הויא מחאה דלא עבידא לאיגלויי כן נראה שיטה זו בעיני ועיקר. (הגה"ה. תמיה לי אמאי לא אמר נמי לימא בדאביי קמיפלגי ושמא משום דלא מצי גמרא לאוקמי כדברי הכל כדמוקי דרבה בר רב הונא כדמסיק למילתיה לא דכ"ע אית להו דרבה בר רב הונא כו'. ע"כ) ולקמן נמי מוכח דמאן דבעי גלויי מילתא במחאה בעי שלשה והכי הויא מסקנא דשמעתא וכל רבותינו מפרשים דגבי מחאה נמי לשון הרע איכא דקאמר פלניא גזלנא הוא והלכך לרבה בר רב הונא אי מתאמרא קמי תרי לא הוי מחאה משום דלית בה משום לישנא בישא ולא יאמרו לו למחזיק ולאו מילתא היא דלא דמי ללשון הרע כלל דעיקר מחאה היינו משום דבעינן שיבא הדבר לאזניו של מחזיק ומלוה היא לומר לו כדי שיזהר בשטרו ולכך תקנו למערער שימחה בפני עדים כדי שיוציאו את הקול תדע דהיכא דאמר להו לא תפיקו לכו שותא לא הויא מחאה: **לא דכ"ע אית להו דרבה בר רב הונא.** דכל גלויי מילתא לא הוי בפחות מג' ואי הוה בעינא גלויי מילתא במחאה היה צריך למחות בפני שלשה אבל בהכי פליגי דמ"ד בפני שנים קסבר (ב) שלא בפניו לא הויא מחאה דכיון דאין מחאה אלא בפניו די לו בשני עדים שיעידו שמיחה בו וכיון דמיחה בפניו אין לך גלויי מילתא גדול מזה שהרי ודאי ידע המחזיק שמיחה בו זה ויזהר בשטרו ומ"ד בפני ג' קסבר מחאה שלא בפניו הויא מחאה והלכך היכא דמיחה שלא בפניו צריך ג' משום גלויי מילתא דכיון דידעי ג' כאילו כל העולם יודעין: **איבעית אימא דכ"ע מחאה שלא בפניו הויא מחאה.** (ג) כדאוקי מתני' וכדפסק הלכתא וכ"ע כרבה בר רב הונא סבירא להו דאין גלויי מילתא במחאה שלא בפניו אלא בג': **והכא בהא קמיפלגי מ"ד בפני שנים קסבר סהדותא בעינן.** ודי לנו בשני עדים שיעידו שמיחה זה בתוך ג' ואם יבא הדבר לאזניו יבא דמאחר שיוכל לבא לאזניו של מחזיק בשום ענין בעולם הויא מחאה דלא חייש אלא שלא יתרה בהם לכסות הדבר דכיון דלישנא בישא ליכא במחאה שמא אלו (ד) עצמן ילכו ויגידו למחזיק או יאמרו לאחרים שיאמרו לו: **גלויי מילתא בעינן.** שידע כל העולם וכיון דנודע לג' כאילו נודע כבר למחזיק דמי דמסתמא ידע במחאה זו אבל בשנים מסתמא לא ידע: **מחויאתא למחויי.** שהיה אחד מחזיק בנכסיו והיה רוצה למחות ומיחה קמייהו בפני שלשתן וה"ה לפני שנים כדאמר רבא לקמן מחאה בפני ב' ואין צריך לומר כתובו אלא הכי הוה עובדא וכן פסק ר"ח דמחאה בפני שנים: **לשנה אחרת אתא.** פעם שניה ומיחה קמייהו ס"ל דכל שנה ושנה צריך למחות ואם מיחה (ה) פעם ראשונה ושניה ולא מיחה בשנה שלישית איגלאי מילתא דשלא כדין מיחה ראשונה ושניה ולסוף שנה שלישית זו הויא חזקה ולא צריך להזהר בשטרו: **לא צריכת.** למחות כל שנה ושנה אבל פעם אחת מיהא צריך למחות בכל ג' וג' כדלקמן שלא יהו ג' שנים רצופים בלא מחאה ומיהו איהו לא איירי בהכי מידי אלא למעוטי ג' מחאות בתוך ג' שנים באו דדי בשנה ראשונה ושוב אין צריך למחות בכל הג' שנים: **ה"ג אמר ר"ל משום בר קפרא וצריך למחות בסוף כל ג' וג'.** דאע"ג דמשמיחה שנה ראשונה שוב אין צריך למחות ה"מ בהנהו ג' אבל בסוף ג' צריך למחות עדיין דלא נהוי תלת שנין בלא מחאה דתלת שנין מיזדהר איניש בשטריה אחר המחאה טפי לא מיזדהר והכי הלכתא ואע"ג דתהי בה רבי יוחנן תמיה היה אבל ירא היה לחלוק על בר קפרא וגם ר"ח פסק כן וי"מ טעמא דצריך למחות בסוף (ו) ג' כדי שלא יטעון לאחר המחאה מכרת לי ולא נהירא דכיון דעל כרחו מודי דמעיקרא לאו בתורת מכירה נחת בה אינו נאמן לומר אחרי כן החזקתי בה בתורת מכירה: **תהי.** מחשב ומקשה בה: **וכי גזלן יש לו חזקה.** כלומר אמאי צריך למחות בסוף כל ג' והלא משמיחה המערער שנה ראשונה והוציא קול על זה שהוא גזלן היה לו להזהר בשטרו כל הימים עד שירד עם זה לדין או עד שיראה את שטרו אחר המחאה לב"ד ומדלא נזהר בשטרו יפסיד דאיכא למימר גזלן הוא והיינו דקפריך גזלן ס"ד הא קטעין שטר היה לי קודם המחאה ואבד ומספיקא הוא דאנן מפסידין אותו את הקרקע לפי שלא נזהר בשטרו אלא אימא כגזלן וכדפרישית: **ערער וחזר וערער.** בסוף כל ג' וג' בר קפרא לטעמיה דאמר צריך למחות בסוף כל ג' וג' הילכך מנהג הוא לערער הרבה פעמים: **ערער.** מיחה בפני עדים: **אם מחמת טענה ראשונה ערער.** דבכולהו מחאות טעין קאכיל לארעאי בגזלנותא הרי זו מחאה והלכך אין לו חזקה למחזיק אבל אם במחאה ראשונה הזכיר שבגזלנות ירד אל שדה זו ובמחאה שניה הזכיר כי משכנתא בידו ואני מוסר לכם עדות זו כדי שלא יחזיק בה ויאמר מכורה היא בידי כיון ששינה בטענתו אינה מחאה ונתקיימה החזקה ביד המחזיק וה"ה למוחה ג' מחאות בתוך שלש שנים משני טענות המכחישות זו את זו דאין כאן מחאה כלל לא ראשונה ולא אחרונה והויא חזקה לסוף ג' דכיון דמיחה מחאה אחרת בשנה שניה שמכחשת מחאה של שנה ראשונה מודה הוא דההיא מחאה שלא כדין הוה והודאת בעל דין כמאה עדים דמי ובטלה לה לההיא מחאה קמייתא וכ"ש זו שניה דהוחזק כפרן וכמי שלא מיחה בתוך ג' כלל דמי: **ה"ג בפי' ר"ח מחאה בפני שנים ואין צריך לומר כתובו.** אלא כותבים לו העדים שטר מחאה למערער להיות בידו לעדות שמיחה בתוך ג' ואע"פ שלא נוח אותם דזכין לו לאדם שלא בפניו ושלא ברשותו דמסתמא ניחא ליה:

וכן

לית בה משום לישנא בישא. פירוש לאותו שאומר לפני ג' דבפרק יש בערכין (ערכין דף טו:) מייתי עלה הא דא"ר יוסי מעולם לא אמרתי דבר וחזרתי לאחורי פי' שלא היה חושש אם ישמעו בעלים: **מ"ד** בפני ב' קסבר מחאה שלא בפניו לא הוי מחאה. תימה להאי לישנא לרבה דקאמר לקמן מחאה בפני ב' ולעיל פסק רבא מחאה שלא בפניו הויא מחאה: **סהדותא** בעינן. ולאו משום סהדותא הוה סגי בחד דלהכך חברא אית ליה ואע"פ שלשון הרע אין נשמע היינו לפי שמעלימין אותו מבני אדם ומ"ד בפני ג' בעי גלויי מילתא כמו בלה"ר: **כיון** שמיחה שנה ראשונה שוב אין צריך למחות. פ"ה עד סוף (ז) ג' שנים וא"ת מתני' היא דקתני עד כדי שיחזיק שנה ויודיעוהו שנה ויבא לשנה אחרת וימחה אלמא דאין צריך למחות רק פעם אחת תוך ג' שנים וי"ל דאי ממתניתין ה"א דאין צריך כי אם מחאה אחת בסוף ג' אבל אם מיחה בתחלת ג' ושוב לא מיחה בכל אותן ג' ס"ד דמודה שהיא שלו ואין לפרש דאין צריך למחות עד עולם דא"כ פליגי אדר"ל והוה ליה למימר ר"ל אמר: **וצריך** למחות בסוף כל ג'. אין לפרש דטעמא שלא יאמר לקחתי אחר המחאה כדפ"ה כיון דעל כרחו מודה דמעיקרא קודם מחאה לא בתורת מכירה נחת בה אין נאמן לומר אחרי כן קניתי ועוד דא"כ שפיר קרי ליה גזלן אלא טעמא כדפ"ה משום דתלת שנין מזדהר איניש בשטריה אחר המחאה ותו לא ולהאי טעמא הא דאמר לעיל (דף לח.) אבל אכלה שית שנין אין לך מחאה גדולה מזו פליגא אהך דהכא דקאמר דצריך למחות כל ג' (ח) ונראה דכההיא הלכתא דסתמא דגמרא קאמר לה ולא כמו שפסק ר"ח דהלכה כבר קפרא: **מחאה** בפני שנים ואין צריך לומר כתובו. ואם תאמר ומה מועיל הכתיבה והא לא חשיב שטר אם לא נעשה מדעת מי שהוא חובתו כגון שטר מכר

מדעת

הגהות הב"ח

(א) גמ' הויא ליה מחיתא למחויי: (ב) רשב"ם ד"ה לא דכ"ע וכו' קסבר מחאה שלא בפניו לא הויא מחאה וכיון: (ג) ד"ה איבעית אימא וכו' כדאוקימנא מתני' וכדפסקינן הלכתא וכו': (ד) ד"ה והכא כו' שמא אלו מעצמן: (ה) ד"ה לשנה וכו' ואם מיחה שנה ראשונה וכו' להזהר עוד בשטרו: (ו) ד"ה ה"ג אמר ר"ל כו' בסוף כל ג' כדי: (ז) תום' ד"ה כיון וכו' פ"ה עד סוף כל ג' וג' שנים: (ח) ד"ה וצריך וכו' ונראה דכההיא הלכתא. נ"ב ובאשר"י פ"ג סימן מ' חולק על זה ומתרץ דל"ק מידי מההיא דלעיל:

ליקוטי רש"י

תהי בה. לשון מריח כמו בת תיהא דמסכת עבודה זרה (סו:) כלומר מעיין ומחשב לדעת טעמו של דבר [עירובין סו.]. לשון מריח בקנקן כמו תהי ליה אקנקניה (לעיל כב.) [ב"ק עו:].

חשק שלמה
על רבינו גרשום

א) נ"ל הוי מחאה ס"ל דבפניו דמחזיק עצמו בעינן מחאה ושלא בפניו לא הויא מחאה ולפיכך סגי בשנים אבל אי אמרינן דמחאה שלא בפניו הויא מחאה לא סגי בשנים וכו'. ב) נראה דצ"ל יש לו חזקה לטעון דקנאה בתר המחאה אלא ודאי וכו'.

לֵית בָּהּ מִשּׁוּם לִישָּׁנָא בִּישָׁא – **there is no** prohibition of **"disparaging talk" involved** in repeating it once more.[1] This indicates that at least three people must hear something to assure that word of it spreads. Accordingly, מַאן דְּאָמַר בִּפְנֵי שְׁנַיִם – **the one that says,** "A protest may be lodged **in the presence of two** people," לֵית לֵיהּ דְּרַבָּה בַּר רַב הוּנָא – **does not subscribe to** the view **of Rabbah bar Rav Huna,**[2] וּמַאן דְּאָמַר בִּפְנֵי ג׳ – **whereas the one that says,** "A protest must be lodged **in the presence of three** witnesses," אִית לֵיהּ דְּרַבָּה בַּר רַב הוּנָא – **subscribes to** the view **of Rabbah bar Rav Huna.**

The Gemara shows that the dispute is not necessarily related to Rabbah's principle; there are in fact other ways to explain the disagreement:

לֹא – **No,** this is not necessarily so, דְּכוּלֵּי עָלְמָא אִית לְהוּ דְּרַבָּה בַּר רַב הוּנָא – **for** it is possible that **all subscribe to** the view **of Rabbah bar Rav Huna** (that at least three people must hear something to assure that word of it spreads), וְהָכָא – **but here** (concerning the question of how many people must witness a protest), בְּהָא קָא מִיפַּלְגֵי – **they disagree over this** point: Must a protest be lodged in the occupant's presence, or not? מַאן דְּאָמַר בִּפְנֵי שְׁנַיִם – **The one that says,** "A protest may be lodged **in the presence of two** witnesses," קָסָבַר מְחָאָה שֶׁלֹּא בְּפָנָיו לֹא הָוְיָא מְחָאָה – **holds that a protest** lodged **not in [the occupant's] presence is not an** effective **protest;** it must be lodged in the occupant's presence to be effective. According to this, it is obviously unnecessary to ensure that the occupant hears about the protest, for he will have received it in person. Thus, the owner may lodge the protest in front of two witnesses.[3] וּמַאן דְּאָמַר בִּפְנֵי ג׳ – **But the one that says,** "A protest must be lodged **in the presence of three** witnesses," קָסָבַר מְחָאָה שֶׁלֹּא בְּפָנָיו הָוְיָא מְחָאָה – **holds that a protest** lodged **not in [the occupant's] presence is an** effective **protest.** If the owner indeed lodged his protest not in the occupant's presence, it must be witnessed by three people to assure that word spreads to the occupant.[4]

The Gemara suggests another way to explain the disagreement:

אִי בָּעֵית אֵימָא – **If you prefer, say** דְּכוּלֵּי עָלְמָא מְחָאָה שֶׁלֹּא בְּפָנָיו הָוְיָא מְחָאָה – **that** according to **both** views, **a protest** lodged **not in [the occupant's] presence is an** effective **protest,**[5] וְהָכָא – **but here** (concerning the question of how many people must witness a protest), בְּהָא קָמִיפַּלְגֵי – **they disagree over this point.** מַאן דְּאָמַר בִּפְנֵי ב׳ סָבַר – **The one that says,** "A protest may be lodged **in the presence of two** witnesses," **holds** סָהֲדוּתָא בְּעִינַן – that **we require** only **testimony** that the protest was lodged; therefore, it suffices for two to observe the protest.[6] וּמַאן דְּאָמַר בִּפְנֵי ג׳ קָסָבַר – **But the one that says,** "A protest must be lodged **in the presence of three," holds** גַּלוּיֵי מִילְּתָא בְּעִינַן – that **we require** enough witnesses to assure that **[the protest] becomes known;** therefore, at least three people must observe it.[7]

Having discussed one legal requirement for an effective protest (the minimum number of people that must witness it), the Gemara now discusses another:

גִּידֵּל בַּר מַנְיוּמֵי הֲוָה לֵיהּ מְחוּאָתָה לְמִחוּיֵי – **Gidal bar Manyumi had a protest to lodge.**[8] אַשְׁכְּחִינְהוּ לְרַב הוּנָא וּלְחִיָּיא בַּר רַב וּלְרַב חִלְקִיָּה בַּר טוֹבִי – **He came upon Rav Huna, Chiya bar Rav and Rav Chilkiyah bar Tuvi** דַּהֲווּ יָתְבֵי – **as they were sitting** together וּמְחָה קַמַּיְיהוּ – **and he lodged** his **protest in their presence.**[9] לְשָׁנָה – **The following year,** הֲדַר אָתָא לְמִחוּיֵי – **he came** before them **once again to** lodge a **protest** even though he had already lodged one a year before.[10] אָמְרוּ לֵיהּ לֹא צְרִיכַת – **They said to him, "You need not** lodge another protest,

NOTES

1. לִישָּׁנָא בִּישָׁא, *disparaging talk,* is a general term that refers to two Biblical prohibitions: לָשׁוֹן הָרַע, *talking disparagingly* about another, and רְכִילוּת, *talebearing* (eg. relating to a person that he was the object of another person's gossip). The latter prohibition applies only if the person hearing the tale would not have heard it otherwise. If he was virtually assured of hearing it by word of mouth anyway (i.e. if so many people heard the gossip that word of it would inevitably have reached him), however, it is not forbidden to repeat the gossip to him even if the gossip defames him. (The original talebearer, though, did transgress the prohibition of לָשׁוֹן הָרַע). This, then, is comparable to the law governing protests in one sense. An owner must lodge his protest in front of enough people to ensure that it will become public knowledge (so that the occupant will hear about it). Likewise, a tale may be repeated only if enough people heard it initially to assure that it would have been publicized anyway.

This being the case, Rabbah bar Rav Huna's ruling relates to protests as well as to talebearing. Rabbah bar Rav Huna's ruling (that the רְכִילוּת prohibition does not apply to a tale originally told to at least three people) implies that at least three people must hear something to ensure that it will eventually become public knowledge. It follows from this that for an owner to register an effective protest, he must lodge it in the presence of three people (*Rashbam;* cf. *Tosafos* and *Rashi* to *Arachin* 16a. See also *Chofetz Chaim, Be'er Mayim Chaim* 2:1-4, who elaborates on these and other possible interpretations of our Gemara).

Rashbam notes that although one generally transgresses the prohibition of לָשׁוֹן הָרַע whenever he speaks disparagingly about another, still an owner may protest an illegal occupation of his field and accuse the occupant of stealing it in the presence of witnesses. Such a protest does not violate the prohibition against לָשׁוֹן הָרַע since the protest has a purpose: It alerts the occupant to preserve his deed to the property.

2. I.e. that at least three people must hear something to ensure that it becomes public knowledge. If a protest may be lodged in front of even two, on the other hand, this implies that even two people will publicize whatever they hear.

3. After witnesses observe a protest, they can serve two functions: They can publicize the protest (and thus ensure that the occupant hears about it) and they can attest to having observed it, thus proving that the owner in fact lodged a protest (in case the occupant denies this). Accordingly, if the occupant must be present when the protest is lodged and thus hear the protest himself, as this opinion maintains, then the witnesses' only function is to testify later that the protest was indeed lodged. For this, two witnesses suffice (*Rashbam*).

4. If the protest happens to be lodged in the occupant's presence, however, even this opinion agrees that two witnesses suffice (*Rashbam*).

5. According to this, both disputants follow the Mishnah's opinion (as interpreted by Rav on 38a) and accord with the halachah (*Rashbam;* see *Tosafos*).

6. When people hear news, they generally spread it unless it is forbidden for them to do so. Accordingly, since it is permitted to publicize news of a protest (see note 1), it is quite possible that this news will reach the occupant even if only two witnesses observed the protest. A protest lodged in front of two witnesses is therefore effective (see *Rashbam*).

7. If a protest is lodged in front of at least three people, it will presumably become generally known. Accordingly, lodging a protest in front of three is tantamount to protesting to the occupant himself and is therefore effective. If a protest was lodged in front of only two, however, the occupant will not necessarily hear about it and the protest is therefore meaningless (*Rashbam*).

8. When someone occupied one of Gidal's properties, Gidal wished to lodge a protest to prevent the occupant from establishing a *chazakah* (*Rashbam*).

9. This does not mean that a protest *must* be lodged in the presence of three, for that is not true; the Gemara below rules that it may in fact be lodged even in the presence of two. Gidal lodged his protest in front of the three Sages only because all three happened to be sitting together at the time (*Rashbam*).

10. Gidal assumed that the original owner must lodge a protest each year during the three-year *chazakah* period. If he remains silent for one full year (even for the third year), this can be construed as an admission that he lied when he previously claimed ownership of the field. The occupant would then not be faulted for having lost his document after the third year and a *chazakah* would be established (*Rashbam*).

צא א מיי' פי"א מהל' טוען ונטען הלכה ח סמג עשין צה טוש"ע ח"מ סי' קמו סעי' ס:
צב ב טוש"ע שם סעיף ז:

לית בה משום לישנא בישא מ"ד בפני שנים לית ליה דרבה בר רב הונא ומ"ד בפני ג' אית ליה דרבה בר רב הונא לא דכולי עלמא אית להו דרבה בר רב הונא והכא בהא קא מיפלגי מ"ד בפני שנים קסבר מחאה שלא בפניו לא הויא מחאה ומ"ד בפני ג' קסבר מחאה שלא בפניו הויא מחאה אי בעית אימא דכ"ע מחאה שלא בפניו הויא מחאה והכא בהא קמיפלגי מ"ד בפני ב' סבר סהדותא בעינן ומאן דאמר בפני ג' קסבר גלויי מילתא בעינן גידל בר מניומי הוה ליה (א) מחויאתא למחויי אשכחינהו לרב הונא ולחייא בר רב ולרב חלקיה בר טובי דהוו יתבי ומחה קמייהו לשנה הדר אתא למחויי אמרו ליה לא צריכת הכי אמר רב כיון שמיחה שנה ראשונה שוב אינו צריך למחות ואיכא דאמרי אמר ליה חייא בר רב כיון שמיחה שנה ראשונה שוב אין צריך למחות אר"ל משום בר קפרא וצריך למחות בסוף כל ג' וג' תהי בה רבי יוחנן וכי גזלן יש לו חזקה גזלן ס"ד אלא כגזלן יש לו חזקה אמר רבא א הלכתא צריך למחות בסוף כל ג' וג' תני בר קפרא ב ערער חזר וערער אם מחמת טענה ראשונה ערער אין לו חזקה ואם לאו יש לו חזקה אמר רבא א"ר נחמן מחאה בפני שנים ואין

רשב"ם

לית בה משום לישנא בישא. דקלא אית לה וסופו שידע אע"ג דמלוה ע"פ אפי' בכמה עדים אינו גובה מן הלקוחות וטעמא משום דלית ליה קלא כדאמר לקמן (דף מב.) דהתם הוי טעמא משום דמאן דזיף בלינעא זיף ועוד דהתם אין יודעין מי יקח שיגידו לו פלוני חייב אבל מאן דידע מחאה יאמר למחזיק: ולענין לשון הרע לית בה משום לישנא בישא היכא דמתאמרא קמי תרי: ומ"ד בפני ג' אית ליה דרבה בר רב הונא. דבג' הוי גלויי מילתא ולא בתרי הלכך בפני ב' לא הויא מחאה דלא עבידא לאיגלויי כן נראה שיטה זו בעיני ועיקר. (הגה"ה. תמיה לי אמאי לא אמר נמי לימא דבהכי קמיפלגי ושמא משום דלא מלי גמרא לאוקמי כדברי הכל למוקי דרבה בר רב הונא כדמסיק למילתיה לא דכ"ע אית להו לדרבה בר רב הונא כו'. ע"כ) ולקמן נמי מוכח למאן דבעי גלויי מילתא במחאה בעי שלשה והכי הויא מסקנא דשמעתא וכל רבותינו מפרשים דגבי מחאה נמי לשון הרע איכא דקאמר פלניא גזלנא הוא והלכך לרבה בר רב הונא אי מתאמרא קמי תרי לא הוי מחאה משום דלית בה משום לישנא בישא ולא יאמרו לו למחזיק ולאו מילתא היא דלא דמי ללשון הרע כלל דעיקר מחאה היינו משום דבעינן שיבא הדבר לאזניו של מחזיק ומלוה היא לומר לו כדי שיזהר בשטרו ולכך תקנו למערער שימחה בפני עדים כדי שיוציאו את הקול תדע דהיכא דאמר להו לא תפיקו לכו שותא לא הויא מחאה: לא דכ"ע אית להו דרבה בר רב הונא. דכל גלויי מילתא לא הוי בפחות מג' ואי הוה בעינא גלויי מילתא במחאה היה צריך למחות בפני שלשה אבל בהכי פליגי דמ"ד בפני שנים קסבר (ב) שלא בפניו לא הויא מחאה דכיון דאין מחאה אלא בפניו די לו בשני עדים שיעידו שמיחה בו וכיון דמיחה בפניו אין לך גלויי מילתא גדול מזה שהרי ודאי ידע המחזיק שמיחה בו זה ויזהר בשטרו ומ"ד בפני ג' קסבר מחאה שלא בפניו הויא מחאה והלכך היכא דמיחה שלא בפניו צריך ג' משום גלויי מילתא דכיון דידעי ג' כאילו כל העולם יודעין: איבעית אימא דכ"ע מחאה שלא בפניו הויא מחאה. (ג) כדאוקי מתני' ודפסק הלכתא וכ"ע כרבה בר רב הונא סבירא להו דאין גלויי מילתא במחאה שלא בפניו אלא בג': והכא בהא קמיפלגי מ"ד בפני שנים קסבר סהדותא בעינן. ודי לנו בשני עדים שיעידו שמיחה זה בתוך ג' ואם יבא הדבר לאזניו יבא דמאחר שיוכל לבא לאזניו של מחזיק בשום ענין בעולם הויא מחאה דלא חייש אלא שלא יתרה בהם לכסות הדבר דכיון דלישנא בישא ליכא במחאה שמא אלו (ד) עצמן ילכו ויגידו למחזיק או יאמרו לאחרים שיאמרו לו: גלויי מילתא בעינן. שידע כל העולם וכיון דנודע לג' כאילו נודע כבר למחזיק דמי דמסתמא ידע במחאה זו אבל בשנים מסתמא לא ידע: מחויאתא למחויי. שהיה אחד מחזיק בנכסיו והיה רוצה למחות ומיחה קמייהו בפני שלשתן וה"ה לפני שנים כדאמר רבא לקמן מחאה בפני ב' ואין צריך לומר כתובו אלא הכי הוה עובדא וכן פסק ר"ח דמחאה בפני שנים: לשנה אחרת אתא. פעם שניה ומיחה קמייהו ס"ל דכל שנה ושנה צריך למחות ואם מיחה (ה) פעם ראשונה ושניה ולא מיחה בשנה שלישית איגלאי מילתא דשלא כדין מיחה ראשונה ושניה ולסוף שנה שלישית זו הויא חזקה ולא צריך להזהר בשטרו: לא צריכת. למחות כל שנה ושנה אבל פעם אחת מיהא צריך למחות בכל ג' וג' כדלקמן שלא יהו ג' שנים רצופים בלא מחאה ומיהו איניהו לא איירי בהכי מידי אלא למעוטי ג' מחאות בתוך ג' שנים באו דדי בשנה ראשונה ושוב אין צריך למחות בכל הג' שנים: ה"ג אמר ר"ל משום בר קפרא וצריך למחות בסוף כל ג' וג'. דאע"ג דמשמיחה שנה ראשונה שוב אין צריך למחות ה"מ בהנהו ג' אבל בסוף ג' צריך למחות עדיין דלא נהוי תלת שנין בלא מחאה דתלת שנין מיזדהר איניש בשטריה אחר המחאה טפי לא מיזדהר והכי הלכתא ואע"ג דתהי בה רבי יוחנן תמיה היה אבל ירא היה לחלוק על בר קפרא וגם ר"ח פסק כן וי"מ טעמא דצריך למחות בסוף (ו) ג' כדי שלא יטעון לאחר המחאה מכרת לי ולא נהירא דכיון דעל כרחו מודי דמעיקרא לאו בתורת מכירה באת בה אינו נאמן לומר אחרי כן החזקתי בה בתורת מכירה: תהי. מחשב ומקשה בה: וכי גזלן יש לו חזקה. כלומר אמאי צריך למחות בסוף כל ג' והלא משמיחה המערער שנה ראשונה והוציא קול על זה שהוא גזלן היה לו להזהר בשטרו כל הימים עד שירד עם זה לדין או עד שירצה את שטרו אחר המחאה לב"ד ומדלא נזהר בשטרו יפסיד דאיכא למימר גזלן הוא והיינו דקפריך גזלן ס"ד הא קטעין שטר היה לי קודס המחאה ואבד ומספיקא הוא דאנן מפסידין אותו את הקרקע לפי שלא נזהר בשטרו אלא אימא כגזלן וכדפרישית: ערער וחזר וערער. בסוף כל ג' וג' בר קפרא לטעמיה דאמר צריך למחות בסוף כל ג' וג' הילכך מנהג הוא לערער הרבה פעמים: ערער. מיחה בפני עדים: אם מחמת טענה ראשונה ערער. דבכולהו מחאות טעין קאכיל לארעאי בגזלנותא הרי זו מחאה והלכך אין לו חזקה למחזיק אבל אם במחאה ראשונה הזכיר שבגזלנות ירד אל שדה זו ובמחאה שניה הזכיר כי משכנתא בידו ואני מוסר לכם עדות זו כדי שלא יחזיק בה ויאמר מכורה היא בידי כיון ששינה בטענתו אינה מחאה ונתקיימה החזקה ביד המחזיק וה"ה למוחה ג' מחאות בתוך שלש שנים משני טענות המכחישות זו את זו דאין כאן מחאה כלל לא ראשונה ולא אחרונה והויא חזקה לסוף ג' דכיון דמיחה מחאה אחרת בשנה שניה שמכחשת מחאה של שנה ראשונה מודה הוא דההיא מחאה שלא כדין הוה והודאת בעל דין כמאה עדים דמי ובטלה לה לההיא מחאה קמייתא וכ"ש זו שניה דהוחזק כפרן וכמי שלא מיחה בתוך ג' כלל דמי: ה"ג בפי' ר"ח מחאה בפני שנים ואין צריך לומר כתובו. אלא כותבים לו העדים שטר מחאה למערער להיות בידו לעדות שמיחה בתוך ג' ואע"פ שלא נוח אותם דזכין לו לאדם שלא בפניו ושלא ברשותו דמסתמא ניחא ליה:

תוספות

ליה בה משום לישנא בישא. פירוש לאותו שאומר לפני ג' דבפרק יש בערכין (ערכין דף טו:) מייתי עלה הא דא"ר יוסי מעולם לא אמרתי דבר וחזרתי לאחורי פי' שלא היה חושש אם ישמעו בעלים: מ"ד בפני ב' קסבר מחאה שלא בפניו לא הוי מחאה. תימה להאי לישנא דרבא דקאמר לקמן מחאה בפני ב' ולעיל פסק רבא מחאה שלא בפניו הויא מחאה: סהדותא בעינן. ואי לאו משום סהדותא הוה סגי בחד דחברך חברא אית ליה ואע"פ שלשון הרע אין נשמע היינו לפי שמעלימין אותו מבני אדם ומ"ד בפני ג' בעי גלויי מילתא כמו בלה"ר: כיון שמיחה שנה ראשונה שוב אין צריך למחות. פ"ה עד סוף (ז) ג' שנים וא"ת מתני' היא דקתני עד כדי שיחזיק שנה ויודיעוהו שנה ויבא לשנה אחרת וימחה אלמא דאין צריך למחות רק פעם אחת תוך ג' שנים וי"ל דאי ממתניתין ה"א דאין צריך כי אם מחאה אחת בסוף ג' אבל אם מיחה בתחלת ג' ושוב לא מיחה בכל אותן ג' ס"ד דמודה שהיא שלו ואין לפרש דאין צריך למחות עד עולם דא"כ פליגי אדר"ל והוה ליה למימר ר"ל אמר: וצריך למחות בסוף כל ג'. אין לפרש דטעמא שלא יאמר לקחתי אחר המחאה כדפ"ה כיון דעל כרחו מודה דמעיקרא קודם מחאה לא בתורת מכירה באת בה אין נאמן לומר אחרי כן קניתי ועוד דא"כ שפיר קרי ליה גזלן אלא טעמא כדפ"ה משום דתלת שנין מזדהר איניש בשטריה אחר המחאה ותו לא ולהאי טעמא הא דאמר לעיל (דף לח.) אבל אכלה שית שנין אין לך מחאה גדולה מזו פליגא אהך דהכא דקאמר דצריך למחות כל ג' (ח) ונראה דכההיא הלכתא דסתמא דגמרא קאמר לה ולא כמו שפסק ר"ח דהלכה כבר קפרא: מחאה בפני שנים ואין צריך לומר כתובו. ואם תאמר ומה מועיל הכתיבה והא לא חשיב שטר אם לא נעשה מדעת מי שהוא חובתו כגון שטר מכר מדעת

רבינו גרשום

מאן דאמר בפני שנים הויא מחאה לית ליה דרבה בר רב הונא דודאי אם מספרין הני שנים למחזיק דמיחה המערער אין לשון הרע בכך. ומאן דאמר בפני ג' אית ליה דרבה דודאי ג' אין בהם משום לשון הרע אבל שנים אם מיחה בפניהם אין מספרים בשמו משום דלשון הרע הן מספרין: מאן דאמר בפני שנים הויא מחאה (א) ודאי בפניו דמחזיק עצמו סגי בשנים משום דמחאה שלא בפניו לא הויא מחאה ובפניו בעינן מחאה אבל אי אמרינן דמחאה שלא בפניו (לא) הויא מחאה לא סגי בשנים משום דאית בה לישנא בישא ולא משתעו ומאן דאמר בפני ג' צריך למחות קסבר דאפי' מחאה שלא בפניו הויא מחאה ומשום הכי צריך ג' דכל מלתא דמתאמרא באפי תלתא לית בה משום לישנא בישא [הא בתרי אית בה]: סהדותא בעינן ובתרי סגי במקבלי עדות. גלויי מלתא בעינן וגלויי מלתא לא סגי בפחות מג': גידל בר מניומי הוה ליה מחויתא למחויי שהיה אחד מחזיק בנכסיו והיה מוחה: צריך למחות בסוף כל ג' וג' שנים שאם לא ימחה בסוף כל ג' יכול המחזיק לומר אחרי שמחית מכרת לי וכבר החזקתי בה ג' שנין: תהי בה ר' יוחנן אמאי צריך למחות בסוף כל ג' וכי גזלן יש לו חזקה. כלומר מאחר שאמר אני קניתיה ממך אחר שמחיתה מכלל דמודי דקודם לכן באת לידו בגזלנות וכי גזלן יש לו חזקה כיון שגזלן הוא אע"פ שהחזיק בה כמה שנים אין חזקתו חזקה, ומקשי' גזלן ס"ד והא לאו גזלן הוא דהא קא טעין דזבנה ניהלה ובתורת מכירה אתאי לידיה ולאו גזלן הוא אלא פריך הכי וכי כגזלן יש לו חזקה האי דכגזלן דמי דטוען שיש לו חזקה שקנאה ממנו אחר מחאתו ולא קודם וכי מי שהוא כגזלן יש לו חזקה ב) בתר דקאמר אלא ודאי אין לו חזקה ואמאי צריך למחות בסוף כל שלש: ערער בשנה ראשונה וחזר וערער בשניה וחזר וערער בשלישית אם מחמת טענה ראשונה היו כל ג' ערעורין שלא שנה דבריו אין לו חזקה למחזיק ואם לאו ששנה המערער דבריו שאמר פעם אחת שלי היתה אני קניתיה ושוב אמר של אבותי היתה אין בדבריו כלום ויש לו חזקה למחזיק.

הגהות הב"ח

(א) גמ' הוה ליה מחויאתא למחויי: (ב) רשב"ם ד"ה לא דכ"ע וכו' קסבר מחאה שלא בפניו לא הויא מחאה וכיון: (ג) ד"ה איבעית אימא וכו' כדאוקימנא מתני' ודפסקינן הלכתא וכו': (ד) ד"ה והכא כו' שמא אלו עצמן: (ה) ד"ה לשנה וכו' ואם מיחה שנה ראשונה וכו' להזהר עוד בשטרו: (ו) ד"ה ה"ג אמר ר"ל כו' בסוף כל ג' כדי: (ז) תוס' ד"ה כיון וכו' פ"ה עד סוף כל ג' וג' שנים: (ח) ד"ה וצריך וכו' ונראה דכהיא הלכתא. נ"ב ובהפרש"י פ"ג סימן מ' חולק על זה ומתרץ דל"ק מידי מההיא דלעיל:

ליקוטי רש"י

תהי בה. לשון מריח כמו בת היתה דמסכת עבודה זרה (סו:) כלומר מעיין ומחשב לדעת טעמו של דבר [עירובין סו.]. לשון מריח בקנקן כמו תהי ליה אקנקניה (לעיל כב.) [ב"ק עו:].

חשק שלמה על רבינו גרשום

א) נ"ל הוי מחאה ס"ל דבפניו דמחזיק עצמו סגי מחאה ושלא בפניו לא הויא מחאה ולפיכך בשנים סגי אבל לאי אמרינן מחאה שלא בפניו הויא מחאה לא סגי בשנים משום דלית בה משום לשון הרע וכו'. ב) נראה דל"ל יש לו חזקה וטוען דקנאה בתר המחאה אלא ודאי וכו'.

וכן

הָכִי אָמַר רַב – **for so said Rav:** כֵּיוָן שֶׁמִּיחָה שָׁנָה רִאשׁוֹנָה – **Once [the original owner] has protested** during **the first year** of another's occupation, שׁוּב אֵינוֹ צָרִיךְ לִמְחוֹת – **he need not protest again** during that three-year period."[11] וְאִיכָּא דְּאָמְרִי – **And some say** אָמַר לֵיהּ חִיָּיא בַּר רַב – that **Chiya bar Rav said to Gidal:**[12] כֵּיוָן שֶׁמִּיחָה שָׁנָה רִאשׁוֹנָה – **"Once [the original owner] has lodged a protest** during **the first year** of another's occupation, שׁוּב אֵין צָרִיךְ לִמְחוֹת – **he need not protest again** during that three-year period."

The Gemara qualifies the ruling:

אָמַר רֵישׁ לָקִישׁ מִשּׁוּם בַּר קַפָּרָא – **Reish Lakish said in Bar Kappara's name:** וְצָרִיךְ לִמְחוֹת בְּסוֹף כָּל ג׳ וג׳ – **However,** the owner **must** indeed **protest at the end of every three** years, for if he remains silent for three continuous years, the occupant does establish a *chazakah*.[13]

A dissenting view:

תָּהֵי בָּהּ רַבִּי יוֹחָנָן – **R' Yochanan questioned [Bar Kappara's ruling]:**[14] וְכִי גַּזְלָן יֵשׁ לוֹ חֲזָקָה – **But can a robber indeed establish a *chazakah*?** Impossible! Why, then, must the owner lodge another protest every three years?[15]

Digressing from its discussion, the Gemara objects to the wording of R' Yochanan's question:

גַּזְלָן סָלְקָא דַּעְתָּךְ – **Do you** really **think** that Bar Kappara ruled on a case in which the occupant was **a** convicted **robber?** In Bar Kappara's case, the original owner only accused him of stealing the field; he never proved him guilty![16] Why, then, does R' Yochanan call the occupant a robber?

The Gemara therefore amends R' Yochanan's question:

אֶלָּא – **Rather,** R' Yochanan undoubtedly meant to ask: בְּגַזְלָן יֵשׁ לוֹ חֲזָקָה – When there is reason to believe that the occupant acted **as a robber** and stole the field, **can he establish a *chazakah*** upon it? Obviously not. It should thus be unnecessary for the owner to lodge additional protests every three years. – ? –

The Gemara concludes:

אָמַר רָבָא – **Rava said:** הִלְכְתָא צָרִיךְ לִמְחוֹת בְּסוֹף כָּל ג׳ וג׳ – **The halachah is that [the original owner] must** indeed lodge a **protest at the end of every three** years, in accordance with Bar Kappara's view.[17]

The Gemara expounds upon Bar Kappara's ruling:

תָּנֵי בַּר קַפָּרָא – **Bar Kappara taught:** עִרְעֵר חָזַר וְעִרְעֵר חָזַר וְעִרְעֵר – When a field's **[original owner] challenged** the occupant's ownership of it, then **challenged** it **again** and **challenged** it yet **again,**[18] אִם מֵחֲמַת טַעֲנָה רִאשׁוֹנָה עִרְעֵר – **if he mounted** each **challenge on account of his original claim,**[19] the protests are effective and אֵין לוֹ חֲזָקָה – **[the occupant] has not established a *chazakah*.** וְאִם לָאו – **But if not,** the protests are meaningless and יֵשׁ לוֹ חֲזָקָה – **[the occupant] has established a *chazakah*.**[20]

Having previously discussed how many people must witness a protest, the Gemara now discusses how many must witness other legal procedures:

אָמַר רָבָא אָמַר רַב נַחְמָן – **Rava said in Rav Nachman's name:** מְחָאָה בִּפְנֵי שְׁנַיִם – **A protest** must be lodged in the presence of two witnesses for it to be effective

NOTES

11. He is required to protest, however, once every three years, as the Gemara will state below (*Rashbam*).

12. In this version, only Chiya bar Rav himself propounded the ruling (viz. that the owner need lodge only one protest every three years) and he did so in his own name rather than having quoted it in Rav's name.

13. Once three years of uncontested occupancy have elapsed, the occupant can no longer be faulted for having lost his deed. Accordingly, the owner must lodge a protest every three years to alert the occupant that he must still retain his deed (*Rashbam,* preferred explanation).

14. R' Yochanan did not dispute Bar Kappara's ruling; he merely questioned it (*Rashbam*).

15. The only reason for an owner to lodge a protest is to prevent the occupant from establishing a *chazakah*. However, once a protest has been lodged, argues R' Yochanan, a *chazakah* cannot be established anyway and it should be unnecessary to lodge additional protests. R' Yochanan's argument is as follows: When an owner lodges his first protest, he accuses the occupant of having stolen his field (see 39a). This forewarns the occupant to preserve his deed either until he proves that he has one or until the matter is settled in court. If he claims to have lost his deed before this, his position is undermined and we suspect him of indeed having stolen the field. Why, then, should it be necessary for the original owner to lodge additional protests every three years? (*Rashbam*).

16. The occupant is denied the land only because we are in doubt whether he in fact bought it as he claims, not because we *know* that he has stolen it (*Rashbam*).

17. If the owner never protests again, this indicates that his original protest was not serious (*Ritva,* see also note 13).

18. That is, every three years, the original owner of a field protested in front of witnesses that the occupant is trespassing on his land (*Rashbam*).

19. That is, his story never changed. Every three years, he protested (for example) that the occupant robbed him of his land. Such protests are effective and prevent the holder from establishing a *chazakah* (*Rashbam*).

20. I.e. if the two protests contradict each other, neither is accepted and the occupant therefore establishes a *chazakah* [e.g. if the owner first protested that the occupant robbed him of his land and then (three years later) protested that the occupant was holding the land as a security for a debt]. When the owner lodges one protest that contradicts the previous one, he retracts the previous claim and it is thus meaningless. Moreover, he in effect admits that he is a liar (for one of the two claims is surely false). Accordingly, his second protest is meaningless as well, because a liar's claim is not believed (*Rashbam*).

וְאֵין צָרִיךְ לוֹמַר כְּתוֹבוּ – **and [the protester] need not tell** them, **"Write** a document that records the protest"; they may do so without his instruction.[1] מוֹדָעָא בִּפְנֵי שְׁנַיִם – **Notification** of coercion[2] must be given **in the presence of two** witnesses וְאֵין צָרִיךְ לוֹמַר כְּתוֹבוּ – **and [the one who serves notice] need not tell** them, **"Write** a document that records the notification."[3] הוֹדָאָה בִּפְנֵי שְׁנַיִם – **An admission** of indebtedness must be made **in the presence of two** witnesses[4] וְצָרִיךְ לוֹמַר כְּתוֹבוּ – **but [the one who admits] must tell** them explicitly, **"Write** a document that records the admission"; otherwise, they cannot write such a document.[5] קִנְיָן בִּפְנֵי שְׁנַיִם – The **act of acquisition** called *chalifin* must be carried out in the presence of **two** witnesses[6] וְאֵינוֹ צָרִיךְ לוֹמַר כְּתוֹבוּ – **and [the one conferring ownership] need not tell** them, **"Write** a document that records the act."[7] וְקִיּוּם שְׁטָרוֹת בִּשְׁלֹשָׁה – **But certification of documents** must be performed **by three** judges.[8]

The Gemara suggests a way to remember the aforementioned rulings.

(סִימָן ממהק – **mnemonic** ***m' m' h' k'***)[9]

The Gemara sees a contradiction in one of the above rulings:

אָמַר רָבָא – **Rava said:** אִי קַשְׁיָא לִי – **If** any of these rulings is **difficult for me** to understand, הָא קַשְׁיָא לִי – **this** is the ruling that is **difficult for me** to understand: הַאי קִנְיָן הֵיכִי דָּמֵי – **This** ***kinyan*** *chalifin* that Rav Nachman discussed, **how is it** classified? אִי כְּמַעֲשֵׂה בֵּית דִּין דָּמֵי – **If** it is classified **as a court proceeding,** it is understandable why it may be recorded in a document,[10] but לִיבָּעֵי תְּלָתָא – **it should** then **be necessary**

NOTES

1. Generally, witnesses lack the authority to write a legal document unless the principal (e.g. in our case the protester) authorized them to do so. Nevertheless, the Gemara rules that such authorization is unnecessary in our case, because the protester benefits when the protest is recorded; once it is recorded, he can prove that the occupant's chazakah was voided. Thus, since the protester is presumably amenable to having the document written, we employ the principle: *One may benefit a person without his knowledge or prior consent* (*Rashbam*).

Tosafos question why the document is valid even if the protester does consent for it to be written. A document is an instrument that records transactions or makes them binding. As such, the party that incurs an obligation, i.e. stands to lose, as a result of the transaction (e.g. the seller in a sales transaction) must authorize the drafting of the document. In our case, then, it should be the occupant's consent — not the protester's approval — that is necessary, for it is the occupant who must cede the property as a result of the document. In response to the question, *Tosafos* suggest that under Biblical law, the document might indeed be worthless since it lacks the occupant's consent. Subsequently, however, the Rabbis enacted that such a document should serve as evidence that the protest took place (see *Tosafos*, who suggest another solution as well; cf. *Nimukei Yosef* here and *Ketzos HaChoshen* 146:3).

2. The Sages instituted a procedure called מוֹדָעָא, *notification of coercion,* by which someone can void a transaction (e.g. a sale or gift transfer) performed under duress. To issue a מוֹדָעָא, the coerced party tells two witnesses, "Let it be known that if I perform such and such a transaction and record it in a document, I do it only because so-and-so is forcing me, but the transaction and document are actually meaningless. I have every intention of summoning him to court and calling upon you to corroborate my story." Rav Nachman teaches that witnesses to the declaration may record it in a document.

A מוֹדָעָא is effective only if the coerced party makes the declaration before he actually carries out the transaction; only then does it prove coercion. If he makes the declaration after he performed the transaction, however, it proves nothing because he might be misrepresenting the facts, attempting to reverse a valid transaction that he now regrets having completed (*Rashbam*). The Gemara below (40b, 48b-49a) will discuss the laws of *moda'a* in greater detail.

3. For the one serving notice clearly benefits if the document is written (see note 1).

4. When a person admits to owing money in the presence of two witnesses, the admission legally obligates him to repay the money (*Rashbam*).

5. As discussed above in note 1, witnesses can write a document without authorization only if this benefits the principal. Recording an admission of indebtedness, however, does not benefit the principal (i.e. the one who makes the admission); it actually weakens his position. If the admission had remained unrecorded and he later claimed to have repaid the debt, he would have been believed. Once the admission is recorded in a document and deposited with the creditor, though, such a claim lacks credibility until the debtor retrieves the document. Since writing such a document is thus detrimental to the debtor, it cannot be written without his authorization.

The Gemara records Rav Nachman's rulings concerning the above procedures separately (a protest must be lodged in front of two, a notification must be made in front of two, an admission must be made in front of two, etc.) rather than combining them (two witnesses must observe a protest, a notification, an admission, etc.). The reason for this is that Rava heard Rav Nachman's rulings over a period of time and later compiled a list of them. The Gemara therefore presents the list as Rava recorded it (*Rashbam*).

6. Under Biblical law, the transfer of ownership (save in the case of inheritance) must be accomplished through a formal act of acquisition (called *kinyan*). *Chalifin,* which literally means "exchange," is one such *kinyan* whereby two parties exchange an object as a means of effecting a given transaction. Rav Nachman ruled that such a *kinyan* must be performed in the presence of two witnesses.

There is some dispute over how to interpret Rav Nachman's ruling. Some maintain that even according to Rav Nachman, if a *kinyan chalifin* was performed in private, still it is valid. According to this opinion, Rav Nachman only suggests that two witnesses observe the *kinyan* to provide confirmation that the transaction took place (*Rabbeinu Yonah; see Tosafos*). Others maintain that if *chalifin* is performed with a handkerchief (as it frequently is), it is valid only if performed in the presence of witnesses. If it was performed in private, however, the transaction lacks seriousness; it does not appear to be a real *kinyan* and is therefore void (*Raavad,* cited in *Shitah Mekubetzes*).

7. [The Gemara below will explain the reason for this ruling.]

However, the witnesses may not write a document if the one conferring ownership explicitly orders them not to do so (*Tosafos*).

8. If a person holding a document wishes to establish a document's validity, he can take it to a court to have it certified. The court then examines it, confirms the authenticity of its signatures and appends a *henpeik* (statement of certification) to it.

Rav Nachman teaches that a document must be certified by a court consisting of at least three judges. *Rashbam* explains that this is true even according to Shmuel, who maintains that a two-judge panel can adjudicate most other monetary cases (although he admits that a three-court panel is preferable — see *Sanhedrin* 3a). The reason for this distinction is that most monetary cases involve a dispute. Thus, when litigants submit a dispute to a two-judge panel, it is clear that the judges are deciding a case and thus functioning as a court. When a document is certified, on the other hand, the judges do not decide a case; they merely confirm the authenticity of the document's signatures. It is thus not as apparent that they are serving as a court, adjudicating the signatures authentic. They can easily be seen as witnesses, simply testifying that the signatures were in fact signed. [If that were indeed true, their testimony would be meaningless because it is hearsay (i.e. they attest to what others testified and not to what occurred).] The Sages therefore required that documents be certified by a three-judge panel, which is clearly identified as a court (*Rashbam, Rabbeinu Yonah*).

9. This mnemonic is composed of the first Hebrew letter of each item upon which Rav Nachman ruled: **M** – ***Macha'ah,*** (protest), **M** – ***Moda'a*** (notification of coercion), **H** – ***Hoda'ah*** (admission), **K** – ***Kinyan.***

10. The Gemara suggests that a *kinyan* might be classified as a court proceeding for in a sense, the act of witnessing a *kinyan* is analogous to adjudicating a court case. When judges adjudicate a case, they can award one litigant's property to the other. Similarly, when people witness a *kinyan,* the resulting transaction transfers property from one person to another (see above, note 6).

If a *kinyan* is indeed classified as a court proceeding, this explains why

[א] ואין צריך לומר כתובו [ב] מודעא בפני שנים ואין צריך לומר כתובו [ג] הודאה בפני שנים וצריך לומר כתובו [ד] קנין בפני שנים ואינו צריך לומר כתובו [ה] וקיום שטרות בשלשה (סימן ממה"ק) אמר רבא אי קשיא לי הא קשיא לי האי קנין היכי דמי אי כמעשה בית דין דמי ליבעי תלתא אי לא כמעשה בית דין דמי אמאי אינו צריך לומר כתובו בתר דבעי הדר פשטא לעולם לאו כמעשה בית דין דמי והכא טעמא מאי דאינו צריך לומר כתובו משום [ו] דסתם קנין לכתיבה עומד רבה ורב יוסף דאמרי תרוייהו לא כתבינן מודעא אלא אמאן דלא ציית דינא אביי ורבא דאמרי תרוייהו [ז] אפי' עלי ועליך אמרי נהרדעי כל מודעא דלא

וכן מודעא בפני שנים. מי שאנסוהו למכור וליתן את שלו בעל כרחו ולכתוב שטר מכירה או מתנה בפני עדים צריך להודיע קודם לכן לשני עדים ולומר דעו לכם שמכירה (א) זו או מתנה של שדה זו שאני רוצה לעשות לפלוני שלא ברצון נפשי אעשה כי אונסני ומכריחני בעל כרחי ולא יהיה ממש באותו שטר שאעשה והיום או למחר תבענא ליה בדינא ומרענא לשטרא אפומייכו שמסרתי מודעא לפניכם קודם שנעשה השטר ודוקא קודם כתיבת השטר אבל אחרי כן אין המודעא שוה כלום דאם כן כל השטרות שבעולם כשיתחרט אחר שנעשו ונמסרו בכשרות יבא לפוסלן: ואין צריך לומר כתובו. שטר מודעא כללא דמילתא כל מידי דזכות הוא לו אין העדים צריכין ליטול הימנו רשות והא דלא כייל ותני להו ולימא מחאה ומודעא וקנין בפני ב' ואין צריך לומר כתובו היינו משום דרבא קאמר להו משמיה דר"נ ולאו בחד יומא שמעינהו אלא כל מילתא שמעה באפי נפשיה והדר חברינהו רבא כחדא כסדר כמו שמען והיינו דכתבינן ביטול מודעי בשטרי מכירה ומתנה דמעתה לא תועיל המודעא כדמוכח בערכין בפרק האומר בסופו (דף כא:) גבי גט דמהני ביטול המודעות והוא הדין לכל השטרות: הודאה בפני ב'. אדם שמודה לחבירו בפני ב' שחייב לו מנה צ"ל כתובו שילוה הלוה לכתוב לו שטר למלוה לעדות דכל שעה שירצה לגבות חובו יוציא שטרו על הלוה אבל שלא ברשות לוה אין כותבין דחוב הוא לו וכיון דבעל הלוה לכתוב והוא לא לוה איכא למימר דלא ניחא ליה לעשות חוב שחייב מלוה בשטר דבעד השתא הוא מלוה על פה ואע"ג דהודה בפני עדים נאמן הוא לומר כל שעה שירצה פרעתי דקיי"ל (לקמן קע.) המלוה לחבירו בעדים א"צ לפרעו בעדים ועכשיו כשיש בידו שטר אין הלוה נאמן לומר פרעתי אלא א"כ יביא עדים שפרע בפניהם אפילו הוציא המלוה על הלוה כתב ידו של לוה שהוא חייב לו גובה מנכסים בני חורין ואינו נאמן לומר פרעתי כ"ש בשטר שיש בו עדים: קנין. סודר על כל דבר בפני ב' ולא בעי תלתא ומשום דגבי קיום שטרות אמר ג' הוצרך לפרש בכל הני דדי בשנים: ואין צ"ל כתובו. כדמפרש טעמא לקמן: קיום שטרות בג'. מי שיש לו שטר על חבירו וחושש שמא ילכו העדים למדינת הים או ימותו וכשיבא לגבות חוב הכתוב בשטר יטעון הלוה כי פרוע הוא או מזויף הוא ויצטרך לקיים שטרו בעדים המכירים חתימת ידי עדים שבשטר ולא ימצא כיצד יעשה הולך לב"ד ומביא העדים עצמן ומעידין על חתימת ידיהן בפני ב"ד והם כותבים בסוף השטר למטה מחתימת העדים במותב תלתא כחדא הוינא ונפק שטרא דא קדמנא ואתו פלוני ופלוני ואסהידו אחתימות ידייהו ואשרנוהו וקיימנוהו כדחזי ומותמים בו ג' הדיינים והוא הנפק וגם אשרתא דדייני ולכך צריך ג' דשנים שדנו דיניהן דין אלא שנקראין ב"ד חצוף בסנהדרין (דף ג.) והכא אפי' דיעבד נמי לא דא"כ מה יש בין הנפק לשטר שלמעלה הימנו הכא תרי חתימי והכא תרי חתימי ודומה לב' עדים שמעידים מפי עדים שלמעלה שהשטר כשר ועד מפי עד פסול אבל כשהן ג' והן ב"ד זו עדות גמורה שהעידו על חתימת ידן לפני ב"ד והכשירו ב"ד את השטר ועכשיו חותמין ב"ד שטר זה כשר הוא ודומה לפסק דין: אמר רבא אי קשיא לי. בכל הנך דיניה דאמר לי רב נחמן גבי קנין לחוד הוא דקשיא לי האי קנין למאי מדמי ליה רב נחמן אי כמעשה ב"ד דמי ומשום דדומה לדין של דיינין שמוציאים מזה ונותנין לזה ואף עדי קנין ע"י עדותן שרואין בקנין יוצא ממון זה בשעת הקנין מיד המקנה ליד הקונה ומשום דדמי למעשה ב"ד קאמר ר"נ אין צ"ל כתובו אלמא אע"ג דחוב הוא למקנה לכתוב שטר וליפות זכותו של קונה אפ"ה כותבים העדים בלא רשותו כדין כל מעשה ב"ד שכח ב"ד יפה והפקירן הפקר לכתוב כל הנעשה בפניהן וא"כ ליבעי ג' כקיום שטרות: ואי לאו כמעשה ב"ד דמי. ומשום הכי קאמר דסגי בב' אמאי אינו צ"ל כתובו והלא חוב לו לכתוב בלא רשותו: לעולם לאו כמעשה ב"ד. דהא ודאי סהדותא בעלמא הוא ומשום הכי סגי בב': דסתם קנין לכתיבה עומד. משום דאין לאחר קנין כלום דכיון דמקנה ליה בסודר בפני עדים וממהר להקנותו מיד ואינו מדחהו עד שילך וימשוך במטלטלין או ילך ויחזיק בקרקעות מתכוין הוא להקנותו בעין יפה ומסתמא רוצה שיכתבו לו כדאמר בכתובות בפ' אע"פ (דף נה.) אמר לעדים כתובו וחתמו והבו ליה קנו מיניה לא צריך לאימלוכי ביה כשירצו לכתוב השטר שמא חוזר דסתם קנין לכתיבה עומד אבל לא קנו מיניה איכא למ"ד התם צריך לאימלוכי ביה ואע"ג דלוים בהדיא לכתוב לו: אמאן דלא ציית דינא. סרבן בדין דלא ציית דינא לימא ליה לא אניסת דלא קאים לך מאי דלא תבעת ליה בדינא: אפי' עלי ועליך. דאיימינן דינא ראוי לכתוב עליו מודעא דזימנין דאין ב"ד מזומן מיד:

דלא

מדעת מוכר ושטר מתנה מדעת נותן ושטר מלוה מדעת לוה ועדות נמי לא חשיב דמפיהם ולא מפי כתבם ופירש"י בפי' החומש שלא יכתבו עדותן באיגרת וישלחו לב"ד וי"ל דתקנת חכמים היא שיהא חשוב עדות כדי לבטל החזקה בעדות כל דהו שבדבר מועט מבטלים החזקה דהא אפילו יתברר לנו שלא שמע המחזיק מחאה מהני לבטל החזקה וגם במודעא תקנת חכמים היא להציל הנאנס וקיום שטרות נמי משום דמעשה ב"ד הוא וכל מעשה ב"ד נכתב שלא מרצון החייב ועוד אומר ר"י ששמע מן ר"ת שנוהגים לשלח העדים עדותם באיגרת לב"ד וחשיב עדות והא דדרשינן בספרי (א) מפיהם ולא מפי כתבם לא אתא אלא למעוטי דוקא אלם שאינו בר הגדה אבל ראוי להגדה אין הגדה מעכבת בו והא דאמרינן בפ"ב דכתובות (דף כ.) כותב אדם עדותו על השטר ומעיד עליה אחר כמה שנים והוא שזוכר מעצמו אבל אין זוכר מעצמו לא היינו כשאינו מוציא כתב ידו בב"ד ועוד שמא עד אחד בכתב אין חשוב עדות שאין שטר אלא בב' להכי לא מהני בההיא דכתובות אפי' יוצא כתב ידו אלא א"כ זוכר בראיית עדות ול"ע בההיא דעד אחד בכתב בגט פשוט (לקמן דף קסה. ושם ד"ה אמר [ג]) וא"ת מאי קמ"ל דאין צ"ל כתובו פשיטא כיון דזכותו הוא ובמחאה איכא למימר דנקיט ביה ואין צ"ל כתובו אגב אחריני ולא אתא לאשמועינן במחאה אלא שהיא בפני ב' אבל במודעא קשה למאי איצטריך וי"ל דאתא לאשמועינן דאע"פ שלא נוח להם לכתוב והם כתבו שלוה כשרה ולא מיחזי כשקרא דמסתמא לפיכך מחה או מסר מודעא בפניהם כדי שיכתבו: **קנין** בפני ב' ואין צריך כו'. אומר ר"ת דלא אתא למעוטי שלא יהא חשוב קנין כשנעשה שלא בפני שנים דהא אמרינן בקדושין (דף סה:) דלא איברו סהדי אלא לשקרי ואמרי' בפ' הזהב (ב"מ דף מו.) גבי היה עומד בגורן כו' ואי אמרינן מטבע נקנה בחליפין ניקנינהו ניהליה אגב סודר ומפרק דלית ליה סודר ולקניהו אגב קרקע דלית לי' והא עומד בגורן קתני כשאינו שלו איכפל תנא לאשמועינן בגברא ערטילאי דלית ליה כלום אלא ש"מ דאין מטבע נקנה בחליפין ואי לא חשיב קנין בלא עדים לישנינן דליכא עדים ועוד דבפ"ק דסנהדרין (דף ו.) אמרו רבנן פשרה ביחיד אע"ג דפשרה בעיא קנין כדמסיק התם: **ואין** צריך לומר כתובו. וכותבין בלא רשותו כל זמן שלא חזר בו ומיהו יכול לחזור בו כדאמרינן לקמן בפ' המוכר את הספינה (דף עז.) זכו בשדה זו לפלוני וכתבו לו את השטר חוזר בשטר ואינו חוזר בשדה והא דאמרינן בריש אע"פ (כתובות דף נה. ושם ד"ה כתובו) כתובו וחתמו והבו ליה קנו מיניה לא צריך לאימלוכי ביה לאו דוקא משום דאמר להו כתובו דאפי' לא אמר להו נמי כדאמרינן הכא אלא משום דבעי למימר לא קנו מיניה צריך לאימלוכי ביה אע"ג דאמר להו כתובו: **קיום** שטרות בשלשה. אע"ג דר"נ גופיה ס"ל בסנהדרין (דף ה:) ב' שדנו דיניהם דין קיום שטרות שאני כדפ"ה דאי ליכא אלא ב' מה יש בין קיום שטר לשטר שלמעלה הימנו הכא תרי חתימי והכא תרי חתימי ודומה לב' עדים ששמעו מפי עדים שלמעלה שהשטר כשר ועד מפי עד פסול אבל כשהם ג' ניכר שהם ב"ד שהעידו עדים לפניהם על כתב ידם והכשירו השטר ודומה לפסק דין והא דאמרינן בפ' ב' דכתובות (דף כב. ושם ד"ה ולמא) ג' שישבו לקיים את השטר ומת אחד מהן צריכי למיכתב במותב תלתא הוינא וחד ליתוהי ואמר ר"נ ואי כתב ביה בי דינא תו לא צריך ולמא ב"ד חצוף הוא דאמר שמואל ב' שדנו דיניהן דין דכתב ביה בי דינא דרבנן דבי רב אשי ולמא רבנן דבי רב אשי כשמואל סבירא להו לא ששמואל סובר דקיום שטרות בשנים אלא ה"פ ולמא רבנן דבי רב אשי סבירא להו בקיום שטרות כדשמואל בעלמא אבל שמואל מצי סבר שפיר דקיום שטרות בג' אע"ג דבעלמא ב' שדנו דיניהן דין כמו ר"נ וא"ת [ג] דרב נחמן גופיה קאמר בב"מ (דף לא:) גבי עובדא דאיסור גיורא ורב ספרא עבוד עסקא וכו' משמע התם דתרי לאו ב"ד מדקאמר ליה זיל אייתי לי תלתא דפלגת קמייהו א"נ תרי מגו תלתא וי"ל דהתם מיירי דלא עשאן ב"ד בפירוש אלא פלג קמייהו בסתם הלכך אי קמי תרי פלג נראה דלעשותן עדים נתכוין ואי קמי תלת פלג נראה דלעשותן ב"ד נתכוין אבל במקום שעשאן ב"ד בפירוש בשנים סגי [וע"ע תוס' גיטין לב: ד"ה ורב נחמן]:

אמאן דלא ציית דינא כו'. תימה מודעא דמאי אי דגיטין ודמתנה גלוי מילתא הוא דודאי הוא אנוס בשום ענין שאין יכול לבא לבית דין ואי דזביני והא אמר רבא לא כתבינן מודעא אזביני וכ"ת רבה ורב יוסף לית להו דרבא מ"מ הוה ליה למיפרך ולשנויי כדפריך בסמוך אנהרדעי ועוד והא אביי ורבא גופייהו דאמרי תרוייהו אפי' עלי ועליך א"כ לא איירי במודעא דזביני וכי ההוא מעשה דפרדיסא לא שייך הכא דאפי' ציית דינא פשיטא דכתבינן:

איכא

מסורת הש"ס
א) [וכן הוא ביבמות לא: גיטין עא.], ב) [וע"ע תוס' יבמות לא: ד"ה דחזו וכו'], ג) [בגמ' שלפנינו לא מוכר רב נחמן אלא רבה בר רב הונא הוא דקאמר זיל לאייתי תלתא וכו' וע"ל דגרס' תוס' היה כך בסוגי' דהתם מיהו סוף הסוגיא לב. דא"ל לאו מי איתמר עלה וכו' אמר רב נחמן וכו' קלת קשה].

הגהות הב"ח
(א) רשב"ם ד"ה וכן מודעא וכו' דעו לכם שמכירה או כצ"ל ותיבת זו נמחק:

ליקוטי רש"י
קנין בפני שנים ואין צריך לומר כתובו. לא צריך לאימלוכי ביה שיכתבו לו דכיון דקנו ממנו סתם קנין לכתיבה עומד [כתובות נה.].

עין משפט נר מצוה
צג א מיי' פי"א מהל' טוען הלכה ח סמג עשין לה טוש"ע ח"מ סי' קמו סעיף ה:
צד ב מיי' פי"י מהל' מכירה הל' א סמג עשין פב טוש"ע ח"מ סי' רה סעיף א:
צה ג מיי' פי"א מהל' מלוה הל' א ופ"ז מהל' טוען הל' ב סמג עשין לב טוש"ע ח"מ סי' לט סעיף ב ז וסי' פא ס"ח וסעי' י ועיין מה שכתב המ"מ בפ"ה מהל' מכירה הלכה ט:
צו ד מיי' פי"א מהל' מלוה הלכה א סמג שם טוש"ע ח"מ סי' לט סעי' ג ועיין במיי' פ"ה מהל' מכירה הלכה ט ובמ"מ שם ובטוש"ע ח"מ סי' קפט וסי' קנה סעיף א:
צז ה מיי' פ"ו מהל' עדות הלכה א סמג עשין קט טוש"ע ח"מ סי' מו סעי' ג וסעי' ד:
צח ו מיי' פי"א מהל' מלוה הלכה א סמג עשין לד טוש"ע ח"מ סי' לט סעיף ג:
צט ז מיי' פ"י מהל' מכירה הל' ב סמג עשין פב טוש"ע ח"מ סי' רה סעיף א:

רבינו גרשום
אין צריך לומר. לעדים **כתבו** שבלא ציוויו יכולין לכתוב שמיחה משום דזכות הוא לו שכותבין: **הודה בפני שנים.** ואמר אני מחויב מנה לפלוני. זה אין כותבין אלא אם כן **אמר** להו **כתובו** משום דחוב הוא לו: תפש **קנין** משום דבר בעולם **בפני שנים אין צריך לומר** להם **כתובו** ומפרש לקמן: **קיום שטרות.** צריכים להעיד שנים **בפני** ג' בית דין על חתימת עדים: **הא קשיא לי.** [**הא**] דאמר רב נחמן בקנין **אי כמעשה בית** דין דמי דמה בית דין אין נמלכין וכותבין אף קנין נמי אין צריך לימלך בו העדים אם כן ליבעי ג': דומיא דב"ד **ואי לאו** מעשה בית דין אלא כהודאה דמי **אמאי אין צריך** וכו': **דסתם קנין לכתיבה עומד.** דאין לאחר קנין כלום: **אלא אמאן דלא ציית דינא.** אבל אי גברא דציית הוא לא כתבי' עליה:

for **three** people to witness it.[11] אִי לֹא כְּמַעֲשֵׂה בֵּית דִּין דָּמֵי – **If** it is **not** classified **as a court proceeding,** on the other hand, it is understandable that two witnesses suffice but אַמַּאי אֵינוֹ צָרִיךְ לוֹמַר כְּתוֹבוּ – **why** does the principal **not have to tell** the witnesses, **"Write** a document that records the transfer"?[12]

Rava resolves the contradiction that he himself had noted: בָּתַר דִּבְעֵי הֲדַר פַּשְׁטָא – **After he asked** the question, **he** himself **answered it:** לְעוֹלָם לָאו כְּמַעֲשֵׂה בֵּית דִּין דָּמֵי – **Actually, [a *kinyan chalifin*] is not** classified as **a court proceeding** וְהָכָא טַעְמָא מַאי דְּאֵינוֹ צָרִיךְ לוֹמַר כְּתוֹבוּ – **but here, what is the reason that [the principal] need not tell** the witnesses to **write** a document? מִשּׁוּם דִּסְתָם קִנְיָן לִכְתִיבָה עוֹמֵד – **Because usually, *kinyan chalifin* is meant to be written.**[13]

The Gemara now discusses another one of the aforementioned legal procedures:

רַבָּה וְרַב יוֹסֵף דְּאָמְרֵי תַּרְוַיְיהוּ – **Rabbah and Rav Yosef both said:** לֹא כָּתְבִינַן מוֹדָעָא – **[Witnesses]** may **not write a notification** of coercion אֶלָּא אַמַּאן דְּלָא צַיְית דִּינָא – **except about [a coercer] who does not heed court rulings.**[14]

A dissenting opinion:

אַבַּיֵי וְרָבָא דְּאָמְרֵי תַּרְוַיְיהוּ – **Abaye and Rava both said:** אֲפִילוּ עֲלַי וְעָלֶיךָ – Witnesses may record the notification **even about** law-abiding people such as **me or you.**[15]

Another ruling regarding notification:

אָמְרֵי נְהַרְדָּעֵי – **The Nehardeans said:** כָּל מוֹדָעָא – **Any** written **notification** of coercion

NOTES

witnesses can record it in a document without having been instructed to do so. When a court renders a decision, it is recorded without the authorization of the party it obligates, for a court can even confiscate property outright; it certainly does not need a litigant's consent to record its decision. If a *kinyan* is classified as a court proceeding, then, it follows that it too may be recorded in a document without the principal's consent (*Rashbam*).

11. That is, if a *kinyan chalifin* is classified as a court proceeding, why can it be effected in the presence of only two witnesses? It should be necessary to carry it out in the presence of three people, just as a document must be certified by three (*Rashbam;* however, see note 8 above).

12. As noted above, witnesses generally lack the authority to write a document without authorization from the principal except to record a court proceeding (see notes 1 and 10). If a *kinyan chalifin* is not classified as a court proceeding, then, why can witnesses record it without authorization from the person who conferred ownership through it?

13. Whenever someone conveys ownership of his property through a *kinyan,* the transfer is final. In practical terms, some *kinyanim* are easier to carry out than others. *Chalifin*, specifically, is especially easy to carry out, for it can be completed through exchanging a handkerchief; it is unnecessary for the acquiring party to take physical possession of the property. Hence, if someone conveys ownership of his property by means of a *kinyan chalifin,* this indicates that he is eager to transfer the property and that he wholeheartedly endorses the transfer. Thus, he presumably intends for it to be recorded as well (*Rashbam*).

14. As noted above, if someone fears that another person will force him to perform a *kinyan*, he may notify two witnesses of his fear and call upon them in court. Rav Nachman ruled that the witnesses are to write the notification in a document. Rabbah and Rav Yosef now qualify this ruling, maintaining that the witnesses are to record the notification only if the alleged coercer refuses to respect court rulings. Otherwise, the notification seems suspicious: If the notifier is really being coerced as he claims, why does he not summon the alleged coercer to court? Therefore, Rabbah and Rav Yosef maintain, such notifications are not recorded (*Rashbam*).

15. For the coerced party might have no access to a court when he is forced to perform the *kinyan* (*Rashbam*).

[א]ואין צריך לומר כתובו [ב]מודעא בפני שנים ואין צריך לומר כתובו [ג]הודאה בפני שנים וצריך לומר כתובו [ד]קנין בפני שנים ואינו צריך לומר כתובו [ה]וקיום שטרות בשלשה (סימן ממה"ק) אמר רבא אי קשיא לי הא קשיא לי האי קנין היכי דמי אי כמעשה בית דין דמי ליבעי תלתא אי לא כמעשה בית דין דמי אמאי אינו צריך לומר כתובו בתר דבעי הדר פשטא לעולם לאו כמעשה בית דין דמי והכא טעמא מאי דאינו צריך לומר כתובו משום [ו]דסתם קנין לכתיבה עומד רבה ורב יוסף דאמרי תרוייהו לא כתבינן מודעא אלא אמאן דלא ציית דינא אביי ורבא דאמרי תרוייהו [ז]אפי' עלי ועליך אמרי נהרדעי כל מודעא דלא

וכן מודעא בפני שנים. מי שאנסוהו למכור וליתן את שלו בעל כרחו ולכתוב שטר מכירה או מתנה בפני עדים צריך להודיע קודם לכן לשני עדים ולומר דעו לכם שמכירה (א) זו או מתנה של שדה זו שאני רוצה לעשות לפלוני שלא ברצון נפשי אעשה כי אונסני ומכריחני בעל כרחי ולא יהיה ממש באותו שטר שאעשה והיום או למחר תבענא ליה בדינא ומרענא לשטרא אפומייכו שמסרתי מודעא לפניכם קודם שנעשה השטר ודוקא קודם כתיבת השטר אבל אחרי כן אין המודעא שוה כלום דאם כן כל השטרות שבעולם כשיתחרט אחר שנעשו ונמסרו בכשרות יבא לפוסלן: **ואין צריך לומר כתובו.** שטר מודעא כללא דמילתא כל מידי דזכות הוא לו אין העדים צריכין ליטול הימנו רשות והא דלא כייל ותני להו ולימא מחאה ומודעא וקנין בפני ב' ואין צריך לומר כתובו היינו משום דרבא קאמר להו משמיה דר"נ ולאו בחד יומא שמעינהו אלא כל מילתא שמעה באפי נפשיה והדר חברינהו רבא כחדא כסדר כמו ששמען והיינו דכתבינן ביטול מודעי בשטרי מכירה ומתנה דמעתה לא תועיל המודעא כדמוכח בערכין בפרק האומר בסופו (דף כא:) גבי גט דמהני ביטול המודעות והוא הדין לכל השטרות: **הודאה בפני ב'.** אדם שמודה לחבירו בפני ב' שחייב לו מנה צ"ל כתובו שילווה הלוה לכתוב לו שטר למלוה לעדות דכל שעה שירצה לגבות חובו יוציא שטרו על הלוה אבל שלא ברשות לוה אין כותבין דחוב הוא לו וכיון דעל הלוה לכתוב והוא לא צוה איכא למימר דלא ניחא ליה לעשות חוב שחייב מלוה בשטר דעד השתא הוה מלוה על פה ואע"ג דהודה בפני עדים נאמן הוא לומר כל שעה שירצה פרעתי דקיי"ל (לקמן קעה.) המלוה לחבירו בעדים א"צ לפרעו בעדים ועכשיו כשיש בידו שטר אין הלוה נאמן לומר פרעתי אלא א"כ יביא עדים שפרע בפניהם אפילו הוציא המלוה על הלוה כתב ידו של לוה שהוא חייב לו גובה מנכסים בני חורין ואינו נאמן לומר פרעתי כ"ש בשטר שיש בו עדים: **קנין.** סודר על כל דבר בפני ב' ולא בעי תלתא ומשום דגבי קיום שטרות אמר ג' הוצרך לפרש בכל הני דדי בשנים: **ואין צ"ל כתובו.** כדמפרש טעמא לקמן: **קיום שטרות בג'.** מי שיש לו שטר על חבירו וחושש שמא ילכו העדים למדינת הים או ימותו וכשיבא לגבות חוב הכתוב בשטר יטעון הלוה כי פרוע הוא או מזויף הוא ויצטרך לקיים שטרו בעדים המכירים חתימת ידי עדים שבשטר ולא ימצא כילד יעשה הולך לב"ד ומביא העדים עצמן ומעידין על חתימת ידיהן בפני ב"ד והם כותבים בסוף השטר למטה מחתימת העדים במותב תלתא כחדא הוינא ונפק שטרא דא קדמנא ואתו פלוני ופלוני ואסהידו אחתימות ידייהו ואישרנוהי וקיימנוהי כדחזי וחותמים בו ג' הדיינים והוא הנפק וגם אשרתא דדייני ולכך צריך ג' דשנים שדנו דיניהן דין אלא שנקראין ב"ד חצוף בסנהדרין (דף ג.) והכא אפי' דיעבד נמי לא דא"כ מה יש בין הנפק לשטר שלמעלה הימנו הכא תרי חתימי והכא תרי חתימי ודומה לב' עדים שמעידים ששמעו מפי עדים שלמעלה שהשטר כשר ועד מפי עד פסול אבל כשהן ג' והן ב"ד זו עדות גמורה שהעידו על חתימת ידן לפני ב"ד והכשירו ב"ד את השטר ועכשיו חותמין ב"ד שטר זה כשר הוא ודומה לפסק דין: **אמר רבא אי קשיא לי.** בכל הנך דינים דאמר לי רב נחמן גבי קנין לחוד הוא דקשיא לי האי קנין למאי מדמי ליה רב נחמן אי כמעשה ב"ד דמי ומשום דדומה לדין של דיינין שמוציאים מזה ונותנין לזה ואף עדי קנין ע"י עדותן שרואין בקנין יוצא ממון זה בשעת הקנין מיד המקנה ליד הקונה ומשום דדמי למעשה ב"ד קאמר ר"נ אין צ"ל כתובו אלמא אע"ג דחוב הוא למקנה לכתוב שטר וליפות זכותו של קונה אפ"ה כותבים העדים בלא רשותו כדין כל מעשה ב"ד שכח ב"ד יפה והפקירן הפקר לכתוב כל הנעשה בפניהן וא"כ ליבעי ג' כקיום שטרות: **ואי לאו כמעשה ב"ד דמי.** ומשום הכי קאמר דסגי בב' אמאי אינו צ"ל כתובו והלא חוב לו לכתוב בלא רשותו: **לעולם לאו כמעשה ב"ד.** דהא ודאי סהדותא בעלמא הוא ומשום הכי סגי בב': **דסתם קנין לכתיבה עומד.** משום דאין לאחר קנין כלום דכיון דמקנה ליה בסודר בפני עדים וממהר להקנותו מיד ואינו מדחהו עד שילך וימשוך במטלטלין או ילך ויחזיק בקרקעות מתכוין הוא להקנותו בעין יפה ומסתמא רוצה שיכתבו לו כדאמר בכתובות בפ' אע"פ (דף נה.) אמר לעדים כתובו וחתמו והבו ליה קנו מיניה לא צריך לאימלוכי ביה כשירצו לכתוב השטר שמא חזר דסתם קנין לכתיבה עומד אבל לא קנו מיניה איכא למ"ד התם צריך לאימלוכי ביה ואע"ג דליום בהדיא לכתוב לו: **אמאן דלא צייית דינא.** סרבן בדין דאי ציית דינא לימא ליה לא איניסת דאי קאנים לך אמאי לא תבעת ליה בדינא: **אפי' עלי ועליך.** דצייתינן דינא ראוי לכתוב עלינו מודעא דזימנין דאין ב"ד מזומן מיד:

דלא

מדעת מוכר ושטר מתנה מדעת נותן ושטר מלוה מדעת לוה ועדות נמי לא חשיב דמפיהם ולא מפי כתבם ופירש"י בפי' החומש שלא יכתבו עדותן באיגרת וישלחו לב"ד וי"ל דתקנת חכמים היא שיהא חשוב עדות כדי לבטל החזקה בעדות כל דהו שבדבר מועט מבטלים החזקה דהא אפילו יתברר לנו שלא שמע המחזיק מחאה מהני לבטל החזקה וגם במודעא תקנת חכמים היא להציל הנאנס וקיום שטרות נמי משום דמעשה ב"ד הוא וכל מעשה ב"ד נכתב שלא מרצון החייב ועוד אומר ר"י ששמע מן ר"ת שנוהגים לשלח העדים עדותם באיגרת לב"ד וחשיב עדות והא דדרשינן בספרי (א) מפיהם ולא מפי כתבם לא אתא אלא למעוטי דוקא אלם שאינו בר הגדה אבל ראוי להגדה אין הגדה מעכבת בו והא דאמרינן בפ"ב דכתובות (דף כ.) כותב אדם עדותו על השטר ומעיד עליה אחר כמה שנים והוא שזוכר מעצמו אבל אין זוכר מעצמו לא היינו כשאינו מוציא כתב ידו בב"ד ועוד שמא עד אחד בכתב אין חשוב עדות שאין שטר אלא בב' להכי לא מהני בההיא דכתובות אפי' יוצא כתב ידו אלא א"כ זוכר בראיית עדות וצ"ע בההיא דעד אחד בכתב בגט פשוט (לקמן דף קסה. ושם ד"ה אמר [ג]) וא"ת מאי קמ"ל דאין צ"ל כתובו פשיטא כיון דזכותו הוא ובמחאה איכא למימר דנקיט ביה ואין צ"ל כתובו אגב אחריני ולא אתא לאשמועינן במחאה אלא שהיא בפני ב' אבל במודעא קשה למאי איצטריך וי"ל דאתא לאשמועינן דאע"פ שלא צוה להם לכתוב והם כתבו שלוה כשרה ולא מיחזי כשקרא דמסתמא לפיכך מחה או מסר מודעא בפניהם כדי שיכתבו: **קנין בפני ב' ואין צריך כו'.** אומר ר"ת דלא אתא למעוטי שלא יהא חשוב קנין כשנעשה שלא בפני שנים דהא אמרינן בקדושין (דף סה:) דלא איברו סהדי אלא לשקרי ואמרי' בפ' הזהב (ב"מ דף מו.) גבי היה עומד בגורן כו' ואי אמרינן מטבע נקנה בחליפין ניקנינהו ניהליה אגב סודר ומפרק דלית ליה סודר ולקנינהו אגב קרקע דלית לי' והא עומד בגורן קתני כשאינו שלו איכפל תנא לאשמועינן בגברא ערטילאי דלית ליה כלום אלא ש"מ דאין מטבע נקנה בחליפין ואי לא חשיב קנין בלא עדים לישנין דליכא עדים ועוד דבפ"ק דסנהדרין (דף ו.) אמרו רבנן פשרה ביחיד אע"ג דפשרה בעיא קנין כדמסיק התם: **ואין צריך לומר כתובו.** וכותבין בלא רשותו כל זמן שלא חזר בו ומיהו יכול לחזור בו כדאמרינן לקמן בפ' המוכר את הספינה (דף עז.) זכו בשדה זו לפלוני וכתבו לו את השטר חוזר בשטר ואינו חוזר בשדה והא דאמרינן בריש אע"פ (כתובות דף נה. ושם ד"ה כתובו) כתובו וחתמו והבו ליה קנו מיניה לא צריך לאימלוכי ביה לאו דוקא משום דאמר להו כתובו דאפי' לא אמר להו נמי כדאמרינן הכא אלא משום דבעי למימר לא קנו מיניה צריך לאימלוכי ביה אע"ג דאמר להו כתובו: **קיום שטרות בשלשה.** אע"ג דר"נ גופיה ס"ל בסנהדרין (דף ה:) ב' שדנו דיניהם דין קיום שטרות שאני כדפי' דאי ליכא אלא ב' מה יש בין קיום שטר לשטר שלמעלה הימנו הכא תרי חתימי והכא תרי חתימי ודומה לב' עדים ששמעו מפי עדים שלמעלה שהשטר כשר ועד מפי עד פסול אבל כשהם ג' ניכר שהם ב"ד שהעידו לפניהם על כתב ידם והכשירו השטר ודומה לפסק דין והא דאמרינן בפ' ב' דכתובות (דף כב. ושם ד"ה ולמא) ג' שישבו לקיים את השטר ומת אחד מהן צריכי למיכתב במותב תלתא הוינא וחד ליתוהי ואמר ר"נ ואי כתב ביה בי דינא תו לא צריך ודלמא ב"ד חצוף הוא דאמר שמואל ב' שדנו דיניהן דין דלכתב ביה בי דינא דרבנן דבי רב אשי ודלמא רבנן דבי רב אשי כשמואל סבירא להו לא לא שמואל סובר דקיום שטרות בשנים אלא ה"פ ודלמא רבנן דבי רב אשי סבירא להו בקיום שטרות כדשמואל בעלמא אבל שמואל מצי סבר שפיר דקיום שטרות בג' אע"ג דבעלמא ב' שדנו דיניהן דין כמו ר"נ וא"ת [ח] דרב נחמן גופיה קאמר בב"מ (דף לג:) גבי עובדא דאיסור גיורא ורב ספרא עבוד עסקא וכו' משמע התם דתרי לאו ב"ד מדקאמר ליה זיל איתי לי תלתא דלפלגת קמייהו א"נ תרי מגו תלתא וי"ל דהתם מיירי דלא עשאן ב"ד בפירוש אלא פלג קמייהו בסתם הלכך אי קמי תרי פלג נראה לעשותן עדים נתכוין ואי קמי תלת פלג נראה לעשותן ב"ד נתכוין אבל במקום שעשאן ב"ד בפירוש בשנים סגי [וע"ע תוס' גיטין לג: ד"ה רב נחמן]: **אמאן דלא ציית דינא כו'.** תימה מודעא דמאי אי לגיטין ודמתנה גלוי מילתא הוא דודאי הוא אנוס בשום ענין שאין יכול לבא לבית דין ואי דזביני והא אמר רבא לא כתבינן מודעא אזביני וכ"ת רבה ורב יוסף לית להו דרבא מ"מ הוה ליה למיפרך ולשנויי כדפריך בסמוך אנהרדעי ועוד והא אביי ורבא גופייהו דאמרי תרוייהו אפי' עלי ועליך א"כ לא איירי במודעא דזביני וכי הוית מעשה דפרדיסא לא שייך הכא דאפי' ציית דינא פשיטא דכתבינן:

איכא

מסורת הש"ס

א) [וכן הוא ביבמות לג: גיטין עא.], ב) [וע"ע תוס' יבמות לג: ד"ה דהוו וכו'], ג) [בגמ' שלפנינו לא נזכר רב נחמן אלא רבה בר רב הונא הוא דקאמר זיל איתי תלתא וכו' וע"ל דגרס' תוס' היה כך בגמרא' דהתם מיהו סוף הסוגיא לב. דא"ל לאו מי איתמר עלה וכו' אמר רב נחמן וכו' קלת קשה]:

הגהות הב"ח

(א) רשב"ם ד"ה וכן מודעא וכו' דעו לכם שמכירה או כו"ל ותיבת זו נמחק:

ליקוטי רש"י

קנין בפני שנים ואין צריך לומר כתובו. לא צריך לאימלוכי ביה שיכתבו לו דכיון דקנו מיניה סתם קנין לכתיבה עומד [כתובות נה.].

עין משפט נר מצוה

צג א מיי' פי"א מהל' טוען הלכה ח סמג עשין לה טוש"ע ח"מ סי' קמו סעיף ה:

צד ב מיי' פ"י מהל' מכירה הל' א סמג עשין פב טוש"ע ח"מ סי' רה סעיף א:

צה ג מיי' פי"א מהל' מלוה הל' א ופ"ו מהל' טוען הל' ג סמג עשין לד טוש"ע ח"מ סי' לט סעיף ג וסי' פא סעי' ז וסעי' יו ועיין מה שכתב המ"מ בפ"ה מהל' מכירה הלכה ט:

צו ד מיי' פי"א מהל' מלוה הלכה א סמג שם טוש"ע ח"מ סי' לט סעי' ג ועיין במיי' פ"ה מהל' מכירה הלכה טו ובמ"מ שם ובטוש"ע ח"מ סי' קצה וסי' קלא סעיף א:

צז ה מיי' פי"א מהל' עדות הלכה א סמג עשין קט טוש"ע ח"מ סי' מו סעי' ג וסעי' ד:

צח ו מיי' פי"א מהל' מלוה הלכה א סמג עשין לד טוש"ע ח"מ סי' לט סעיף ג:

צט ז מיי' פי"א מהל' מכירה הל' א סמג עשין פב טוש"ע ח"מ סי' רה סעיף א:

רבינו גרשום

אין צריך לומר. לעדים כתבו שבלא צוויו יכולין לכתוב שמיחה משום דזכות הוא לו שכותבין: הודאה בפני שנים. ואמר אני מחויב מנה לפלוני. זה אין כותבין אלא אם כן אמר להן כתובו משום דחוב הוא לו: תפש קנין משום דבר בעולם בפני שנים אין צריך לומר להם כתובו ומפרש לקמן: קיום שטרות. צריכים להעיד שנים בפני ג' בית דין על חתימת עדים: הא קשיא לי. [הא] דאמר רב נחמן בקנין אי כמעשה בית דין דמי דהא בית דין אין נמלכין וכותבין אף קנין נמי אין צריך לימלך בו העדים אם כן ליבעי ג' דומיא דב"ד ואי לאו מעשה בית דין אלא כהודאה דמי אמאי אין צריך וכו': דסתם קנין לכתיבה עומד. דאין לאחר קנין כלום: אלא אמאן דלא ציית דינא. אבל אי גברא דציית הוא לא כתבי' עליה.

א דלא כתיב בה אנן ידעינן ביה באונסא דפלניא לאו מודעא היא מודעא דמאי ב אי דגיטא ודמתנתא גלויי מילתא בעלמא היא ואי דזביני והאמר רבא לא כתבינן מודעא אזביני ג מודי רבא היכא דאנים וכמעשה דפרדיסא א) ד דההוא גברא דמשכין פרדיסא לחבריה לתלת שנין בתר דאכלה תלת שני חזקה אמר (א) אי מזבנת לי מוטב ואי לא כבישנא לשטר משכנתא ואמינא לקוחה היא בידי כה"ג כתבינן מודעא: אמר רב יהודה האי מתנתא טמירתא לא מגבינן בה היכי דמי מתנתא טמירתא אמר רב יוסף דאמר להו לסהדי זילו אטמורו וכתבו ליה ואיכא דאמרי אמר רב יוסף דלא ה אמר להו תיתבו בשוקא ובבריתא ותכתבו ליה מאי בינייהו איכא בינייהו סתמא אמר רבא והויא מודעא לחברתה אמר רב פפא הא דרבא ו לאו בפירוש איתמר אלא מכללא איתמר ז דההוא גברא דאזל לקדושי אתתא אמרה ליה אי כתבת לי כולהו נכסיך הוינא לך (ב) ואי לא לא הוינא לך אזל כתביה לה לכולהו נכסי אתא בריה קשישא א"ל וההוא גברא מה תהוי עליה אמר להו לסהדי זילו אטמורו בעבר ימינא וכתבו ליה אתו לקמיה דרבא אמר להו ז לא מר קנה ולא מר קנה מאן דחזא סבר משום דהויא מודעא לחברתה ח ולא היא התם מוכחא מילתא דמחמת אונסא הוא דכתב לה ט אבל הכא מר ניחא ליה דליקני ומר לא ניחא ליה דליקני איבעיא להו סתמא

דלא כתיב בה אנן עדים ידעינן באונסא דפלניא. שאונס גמור יש לו ומכירין אנו איזה אונס אי לא כתב בה הכי אלא שאמר כתבו פלוני אמר לנו שנאנס: מודעא דמאי אי. במודעא דמסר אגיטא ומתנה לא צריך כולי האי אלא כיון דמודע לסהדי דהאי גיטא שאני נותן לאשתי אנוס אני בו ולא ברצון נפשי (ג) עשיתי לפיכך דעו שאני מבטלו בפניכם וכן המתנה שאני מקנה לפלוני אנוס אני ואיני מקנה אותה ברצוני תהא מבוטלת אע"ג דלא ידעי סהדי אונסא דיליה הרי גט והמתנה בטלין: גלוי מילתא בעלמא היא. כלומר הרבה בני אדם יוכלו לידע אונסו דכיון דאינו מקבל ממון במתנה ובגט זה שנותן אם איתא דניחא ליה ליתנה מדעתו למה לו למסור מודעא ואי לא ניחא לו ליתן למה לו ליתן גט ומתנה אלא ודאי נאנס בגט ובמתנה זו והלכך אין צריך לפרש אונסו דלא דמי לזביני דהתם צריך לפרש דאיכא למימר סתם מוכר לא ברצונו מוכר אלא משום חסרון מעות והלכך איכא למימר מסר מודעא דקסבר היום ולמחר כשיהיו לי מעות מפיקנא מודעא ותבענא ליה לדינא ויחזור קרקע שלי ואני אשלם מעותיו אבל הכא אם ברצון נפשו נותן גט ומתנה בלא אונס למה כותב מודעא בחנם כיון דלא יתן גט ולא איצטריך לכתוב מודעא אלא ודאי אנוס הוא ומשום הכי תקינו בגיטין דלא למיכתב גיטא עד שיבטל הבעל כל מודעות שמסר וכך הוא מפורש בערכין בפרק האומר משקלי עלי (דף כא.) אמר רב ששת האי מאן דמסר מודעא אגיטא מודעיה מודעא פשיטא לא צריכא דעשייה ואראיה מהו דתימא כיון דארציה בטולי בטליה למודעיה קמ"ל עד דאמר בטלתיה ואימא כיון דארצי בטליה ולא צריך לפרושי דבטליה ואמרינן א"כ נתני וכן אתה אומר בגיטי נשים כופין אותו עד שיתן אמאי קתני עד שיאמר רוצה אני אלא קמ"ל עד דמפרש דבטליה ודוקא מודעא שיש בה אונס אי טעין ואמר גט שמעשה לא יהא גט אין זה ביטול דכיון דלא נאנס כלל אנן סהדי דגמר בלבו בשעת מעשה לעשותו גט גמור ולא מהני ביה ביטול דקודם כתיבה ° אלא א"כ ביטלו אחר כתיבה: (ד) דגלויי מילתא בעלמא היא. כלומר די לנו בגלוי מילתא דלא חיישינן אם תתגלה מילתא או לא דסברא היא דאנים כדפרישית: ואי דזביני. שמוסר מודעא שנאנס ולפיכך לא הויא מודעא עד שיעידו העדים שמכירין באונסו משום דאיכא למימר דלא אנים אלא השתא למעות צריך והיום ולמחר ליבעי למיהדר בההיא מכירה כשיזדמנו לו מעות ולפיכך מסר השתא מודעא לבטל מכירתו: לא כתבינן מודעא אזביני. נראה לי טעמא דרבא משום דאמרינן לקמן בפירקין (דף מח.) (ה) הלכתא תליוה וזבין זביניה זביני ולא אמרן אלא בשדה סתם שכפאוהו למכור אחת משדותיו והוא בירר מעצמו אחת מהן ומכרה דלא הוי אונס אבל בשדה זו לא כו' והלכך לא כתבינן מודעא דאי בשדה זו הא לא הוי זביניה זביני ולא צריך מודעא אלא יביא עדים שאנסוהו ותיבטל שטר מכירה בלא שום מודעא ואי בשדה סתם הא הוי זביניה זביני ואין אונס בזה השדה שהרי מדעתיה בירר ומכר את זה השדה ומודעא זו שיכתוב פסולה היא דמודעא בלא אונס לאו כלום היא ומיהו רב הונא דאמר לקמן ג) תליוה וזבין זביניה זביני חזינן דאכשר מודעא אזביני דלית ליה הך סברא דרבא: ומשני מודי רבא דכתבינן מודעא היכא דאנים. (ו) כה"ג דמעשה דפרדס דלקמן דמתוך פחד שמפחידין אותו להפסיד הפרדס לגמרי בלא דמים קמזבין ליה אין בלבו למכור לגמרי אלא עד שינצל מן הפחד הכא ודאי כתבי' מודעא דהא אונס גמור הוא דאי לא מזבין ליה מערער למחזיק יפסיד אותו המחזיק למערער בטענותיו דהכא הוא דאמרי נהרדעי דצריך למיכתב אנו יודעים ביה כו': האי עובדא דפרדסא פר"ח היאך ידעו העדים באונס של בעל הפרדס דאם בפני עדים אמר לו המחזיק טענות דלקמן אין צריך מודעא אלא יעידו ששמעו לזה המחזיק שבא בעקיפין על בעל הפרדס ויטול בעל הפרדס את שלו וכך פירש אתא מריה דפרדיסא גבי סהדי ואודעינהו הני מילי שרוצה זה לגוזלו פרדס (ז) בטענותיו ואמר להו אנא תבענא ליה קמייכו ושמעו מיניה דטעין זבינתא ניהלי ולית לך עלי ולא מידי ובתר הכי א"ל בחשאי אנא מזביננא לך ואמר ליה כתוב לי שטר מכירה שלא בפני כדתנן כותבין שטר למוכר אע"פ שאין לוקח עמו והביאהו לי ואתן לך הדמים והלך זה וסיפר לעדים מה שאמר לו זה לכתוב לו שטר מכירה וכן עשה וקודם שכתב ומסר השטר מכירה אמר לעדים אתם שמעתם שטען לקוחה היא בידי זה ג' שנים ואנא כתבנא ליה שטר מכירה כמו שאמר שלא בפניו ואקבל הדמים השתא מסר אנא מודעא קמייכו דלאו ברעות נפשי מזבינא להאי פרדיסא אלא משום דכפר במשכנתא ובתר הכי תבענא ליה לדינא ומפקינא לה מיניה על ידי שיראה שטר מכירה זה שמהיום ואני אוציא המודעא לפניו המבטלתו והוא לא יתן לבו לטעון ולומר שג' שנים היתה לקוחה לו הקודמין לשטר זה: כה"ג. שמפסיד הכל אם לא ימכור מודי רבא דכתבי מודעא: מתנתא טמירתא. מתנה טמונה לקמיה מפרש: לא מגבינן בה. דשמא נתנה לאחר כבר או לעשותה מודעא לחברתה נתכוין כדלקמן: אטמורו. הטמינו עצמכם: ה"ג ואיכא דאמרי אמר רב יוסף דלא אמר להו תיתבו בשוקי ובבריתא. לא ליום לכתוב בשווקים וברחובות אלא סתם אמר להו כתובו: איכא בינייהו סתמא. שאמר להו כתובו סתם ולא אמר להם איטמורו וגם לא ליום לכתוב בשוקי ובבריתא ללישנא קמא דרב יוסף כשרה וללישנא בתרא פסולה דצריך לומר להם כתובו בשוקא ותחתמוה בברא. ובפירוש ר"ח גרסינן דאמר להו לא תיתבו בשוקא ובבריתא ואי אפשר לומר כן דלשני לשונות דרב יוסף משמע סתמא כשרה: בשוקא ובבריתא. לעין כל כתובו לו: אמר רבא והויא. הך מתנתא טמירתא מודעא לבטל חברתה שטר מתנה או מכירה גלויה וכשרה שנכתבה אחרי כן על שדה זו לאדם אחר דלכך כתבה להך טמירתא דלא לחזיק בהאי שדה האיך בתרא: אלא מכללא איתמר. וטעות הוא: אתא בריה קשישא. קודם כתיבת השטר לאשה: אמר להו לסהדי. קודם שנכתב שטר האשה: זילו איטמורו בעבר ימינא. באותו מקום: וכתבו ליה. לבני ויקדש שטרו ויגבה הכל: לא מר קנה. הבן משום דהויא טמירתא: ולא מר קנה. האשה משום דטמירתא הויא לה מודעא לבטלה: ולא היא. דמתנה טמירתא כמאן דליתיה היא ולא הויא מודעא: דמחמת אונסא. שאינה חפילה בו אא"כ יכתוב לה הלכך לא גמר בלבו להקנות לה אלא עד שישאנה ויחזור בו והלכך התם הוא דהויא במקום מודעא: אבל הכא. דליכא טענת אונס בבתרייתא לא הויא מתנה טמירתא קמייתא מודעא לבתרייתא שהיא עשויה כתקנה לבטלה דבקמייתא לא ניחא ליה דליקני הואיל ועבדה טמירתא אבל אחרון שנעשה לו שטר ראוי ניחא ליה דליקני שמעינן מהכא דמתנתא טמירתא לא הויא מודעא לחברתה אלא היכא דאיכא אונס בבתרייתא אבל בלא אונס ניחא ליה דליקני:

סתמא

איכא דאמרי אמר רב יוסף דלא אמר להו תיתבו כו'. הכי גירסא קשה לר"י מאי קבעי מאי בינייהו הא בהדיא חולקין בסתמא ועוד דפסקינן לקמן הלכתא דחיישינן בסתמא וא"כ היכי מגבינן כולהו מתנתא כיון דאינו אומר לסהדי כתבו בשוקי (ח) ברייתא ומיהו לפי שנוהגים עתה לכתוב בשטרי מתנה ואמר לנו מתנה זו כתבו בשוקא ותחתמו בברא הלכך כי אמר להו נמי סתמא דעתו לומר כמו שכותבים בשטרות ובימי האמוראים לא היו נוהגים לכתוב כך לכך היה צריך לומר להם בפירוש כתבו בשוקא כו'. ור"ח גריס דאמר להו לא תיתבו בשוקא ברא וקרי ליה סתמא שאינו אומר להם להטמין עצמו ואומר שלא לפרסם והיינו סתמא (ט) כלומר לא פרסם ולא הטמינם אבל כתובו לא חשיב סתמא וכשר לפר"ח ולפיכך מה שנהגו לכתוב בשטרות מתנה זו כתבו בשוקא ותחתמו בברא אינו אלא לשופרא דשטרא ומיהו לישנא דסתמא לא משמע הכי:

שלא

עין משפט נר מצוה

ק א מיי' פ"י מהל' מכירה הל' ב סמג עשין פב טוש"ע ח"מ סי' רה סעיף א:
קא ב מיי' שם הל' ג ופ"ו מהל' גירושין הל' כ ופ"ה מהל' זכייה הלכה ד סמג שם וסי' נ טוש"ע שם סעי' ב וסי' רמב סעי' א וטוש"ע אה"ע סי' קלד סעי' א:
קב ג ד מיי' פ"י מהל' מכירה הל' ד סמג עשין פב טוש"ע ח"מ סי' רה סעיף ז:
קג ה מיי' פ"ה מהל' זכייה הל' א ב ופ"ט שם הל' ב סמג עשין פב טוש"ע ח"מ סי' רמב סעי' ג ד ה:
קד ו ז מיי' שם פ"ה הלכה ה סמג שם טוש"ע שם סעי' ט וס"י:
קה ח ט מיי' שם והל' ג טוש"ע שם ובסעיף ח:

גליון הש"ס

רשב"ם ד"ה גילוי מלתא בסה"ד אא"כ ביטל אחר כתיבה. עי' גיטין דף לג ע"ב ובתוס' שם ד"ה (הכא) [התם]:

רבינו גרשום

דלא כתיב בה. עדים גופייהו ידעו באונסיה לא מודעא היא: מודעא דמאי. צריכה למכתב בה ידעינן באונסיה אי דגט או דמתנה שמכריחין אותו ליתן הכא לא צריך למכתב ידעינן באונסיה דהאי גלוי מלתא בעלמא דכיון שכפאוהו ועל כרחו נתן משום דאינו מקבל כלום אלא נותן: ואי מודעא דזביני. שכפאוהו למכור אמרת דצריכי למיכתב ידעי' באונסיה: והאמר רבא לא כתבי' מודעא לזביני. שמאחר שמקבל הוא דמים מיד גמר ומכר לו. ומודי רבא בזביני היכא דאניס דומיא דהאי מעשה דפרדיסא אע"ג דמקבל זוזי דכתבי' ליה מודעא וצריך למכתב ידענא באונסה: האי מתנה טמירתא. שאמר כתבו לי בהחבא לא מגבינן בה דשמא כבר נתנה לאחר: בשוקי בריתא. כלומר בגלוי לעיני הכל לא יכתבו: איכא בינייהו סתמא. ללישנא קמא אי אמר להו סתמא זילו כתובו הואיל דלא אמר להו זילו איטמרו הויא מתנה וללישנא בתרא אמר להו זילו כתובו לא הויא מתנה עד דאמר להו לסהדי תיתבו בשוקי ברייתא ותכתבו ליה: אמר רבא והויא מודעא לחברתה. שאם כתב מתנה טובה לחד כתובה וחתומה בשוק או בברא והדר אותה מתנה עצמה כתבה לאחר בטמירתה אינה מתנה לא זו ולא זו דשניה הוה מודעא לחברתה ראשונה דהא לא ניחא ליה דראשון קונה הואיל וכתב לשני ושניה טמונה היא כגון האי מעשה: בעבר ימינא. באותו מקום: דמחמת אונס הוא דכתב לה. דלא מיקדשה ליה אי לא כתב לה כל נכסיה: אבל הכא. דהיכא דכתב לראשון מתנה גלויה ולבתר הכי כתב ליה לאידך בטמירתא להאי אמרינן דניחא ליה דליקני [ולא] הוי מודעא

מסורת הש"ס

א) ב"מ עב., ב) [ברכות ט. וש"נ], ג) [דף מז: מח: וע"ש בפי' הרשב"ם]:

הגהות הב"ח

(א) גמ' אמר ליה אי מזבנת: (ב) שם הוינא לך לאיתתא ואי לא: (ג) רשב"ם ד"ה מודעא וכו' ולא ברצון נפשי אני נותן לה זה הגט לפיכך דעו וכו' בטלין דגלויי מילתא וכו' בגט זה ובמתנה זו וכו' אשלם לו מעותיו וכו' ולא יצטרך לכתוב כצ"ל והד"א: (ד) ד"ה גלויי מילתא כצ"ל ואות ד' נמחק: (ה) ד"ה לא כתבינן וכו' לקמן בפירקין אמר רבא הלכתא וכו' ואין כאן אונס בזה השדה שהרי מדעתו בירר: (ו) ד"ה ומשני מודה וכו' דאניס בכה"ג וכו' ואין בלבו וכו' והכא הוא דאמרי: (ז) ד"ה האי עובדא וכו' לגוזלו פרדס שלו בטענותיו וכו' המודעא שלפניו המבטלתו והוא לא יתן אל לבו: (ח) תום' ד"ה איכא וכו' בשוקי ובברייתא ומיהו יש לומר לפי שנוהגים וכו' ואמר לנו שטר מתנה: (ט) בא"ד והיינו סתמא דלא פי' לא פרסום ולא הטמנה אבל וכו' וכשר לפר"ח ולפי זה מה שנהגו:

ליקוטי רש"י

ההוא גברא דמשכין פרדיסא לחבריה. שיאכלנה ותחזור לבעלים בלא מעות דכתב ליה במשלם שניא אילין תיפוק ארעא דין בלא כסף [כתובות צה:]. משכן לו כרם במשכנתא דסורא אי נמי בנכייתא [ב"מ קט:]. פרדיסא. כרם [כתובות שם וב"מ עב.]. כבישנא. אטמין. ואמינא לקוחה היא בידי. ואבד שטר המכירה ואבא מכח חזקה של שלש שנים דכולי האי לא מצינא למיזהר בשטרא [ב"מ שם].

דְּלֹא כְּתִיב בָּהּ – **that does not include the clause,**[1] אֲנַן יָדְעִינָן בֵּיהּ בְּאוֹנְסָא דִּפְלַנְיָא – **"We** (the witnesses) **know about the coercion to** which **So-and-so** was subjected," לַאו מוֹדָעָא הִיא – **it is not an** effective **notification.**[2]

The Gemara questions when the above ruling applies:

מוֹדָעָא דְּמַאי – **Notification concerning what** type of transaction must contain this clause? אִי דְּגִיטָּא וּדְמַתַּנְתָּא – **If** you think that notification **concerning a bill of divorce or a gift** must contain it, that is impossible, for to void these transactions, גִּלּוּיֵי מִילְּתָא בְּעָלְמָא הִיא – the coerced party need **only disclose [that he is being forced]** to carry them out; the notification need not describe the form of coercion.[3] וְאִי דִּזְבִינֵי – **And if** you think that it applies to a notification **concerning a sale,** such a notification is not written at all, וְהָאָמַר רָבָא לֹא כַּתְבִינָן מוֹדָעָא אַזְּבִינֵי – for **did Rava not say: [Witnesses] should not write a notification** of coercion **to** void **a sale?**[4]

The Gemara answers:

לְעוֹלָם דִּזְבִינֵי – **Actually,** the requirement does apply to a notification **concerning a sale,** מוֹדֵי רָבָא – for **Rava agrees** that witnesses should record a notification הֵיכָא דְּאָנִיס – in a case **where [the seller] was coerced** וּכְמַעֲשֶׂה דְּפַרְדֵּיסָא – **as** he was in **"the incident of the orchard."**

The Gemara recounts the incident:

דְּהַהוּא גַּבְרָא – **For there was a certain man** דְּמַשְׁכֵּין פַּרְדֵּיסָא לְחַבְרֵיהּ לִתְלַת שְׁנִין – **who "mortgaged"**[5] **an orchard to his fellow for three years.** בָּתַר דַּאֲכָלָהּ תְּלַת שְׁנֵי חֲזָקָה – **After [the mortgage holder] used [the orchard] for three years,** אָמַר – **he said** to the owner of the orchard, אִי מְזַבַּנְתְּ לִי מוּטָב – **"If you sell** the orchard **to me, fine.** וְאִי לֹא – **But if not,** I will take it from you illegally. כְּבִישְׁנָא לִשְׁטַר מַשְׁכַּנְתָּא – **I will hide the mortgage contract,** וְאַמִינָא לְקוּחָה הִיא בְּיָדִי – **and I will claim** that **[the orchard] was purchased by me."**[6]

The Gemara concludes:

כְּהַאי גַּוְונָא כַּתְבִינָן מוֹדָעָא – **In such an instance,** Rava agrees that **[witnesses] should write a notification** to void the sale, because they cannot observe the coercion themselves.[7] When witnesses write a notification in such a case, they must, according to the Nehardeans, include a description of the coercion.

The Gemara now discusses a case tangentially related to the previous discussion:

אָמַר רַב יְהוּדָה – **Rav Yehudah said:** הַאי מַתַּנְתָּא טְמִירְתָּא – If someone holds a **secret gift document**[8] (i.e. a document written secretly), לֹא מַגְבִינָן בָּהּ – **he cannot collect** the gift **with it,** because the giver might not have intended to transfer ownership

NOTES

1. Literally: in which it was not written.

2. To void a transaction, the principal must actually have been coerced. Therefore, the witnesses must write that they have personal knowledge of coercion and describe it in the document. If they merely recorded that the principal claimed to have been coerced, this proves nothing because he might have been lying, as the Gemara below will explain (see *Rashbam*).

3. The Nehardeans require that the witnesses describe the coercion only to prove that the principal was in fact coerced (see previous note). It is thus sensible to require such a description if the one giving notice might have been motivated to lie about being coerced. A seller, for example, could indeed have been motivated to lie. He might well have been in need of money and reluctantly decided to sell something. If he falsely notifies witnesses that he is acting under duress (even though this is untrue), he will be able to reverse the sale later when he has enough money to return to the purchaser. Therefore, for a notification to be effective, the witnesses must actually observe the coercion and describe it in the document that they write. When someone gives a divorce or a gift, on the other hand, he has no reason to fabricate a story about coercion, because these transactions involve no money. If he is reluctant to carry out these transactions, he can simply not do so. Therefore, if the giver claims to be coerced, there is no reason for witnesses to describe the coercion when they write the document (*Rashbam;* cf. *Rabbeinu Yonah*).

4. *Rashbam* cites the Gemara below (48a) to explain Rava's ruling. The Gemara there states that if someone is coerced to sell a specific tract of land, the sale is void. If, however, he is forced only to sell one of his fields but is allowed to choose which one to sell, the sale is valid; for after choosing the field himself, he presumably reconciled himself to selling it. According to this, Rava reasoned, it is never permissible to record a notification of coercion because it is either unnecessary or untrue (see *Nesivos Hamishpat*, Introduction to *Choshen Mishpat* 205). If the seller was coerced to sell a specific field, the witnesses to the sale will see this and report the coercion to the court. It is thus unnecessary to record a notification, because the court will void the transaction on the basis of this testimony alone. If the seller was given a choice of which field to sell, he is considered to have sold it willingly and he is not considered to have been coerced (cf. *Ramban* and *Rashba*).

5. This refers to an arrangement known as a Surean security (see above, 35b note 14). This allows the creditor use of the debtor's property for a predetermined amount of time as payment for a loan.

6. If someone occupies land for three years during which his occupancy goes unchallenged, he establishes a *chazakah* (see 38, note 16); he is then believed if he claims to own the land. Hence, if the mortgage holder in our case falsely claimed to own the land after having used it for three years, we would believe him and award him the field.

7. This case differs from most other cases of coercion. In most other cases, a notification of coercion is either untrue or unnecessary (see note 4); in this case, however, the notification is both true and necessary. It is true that the owner is being coerced because the mortgage holder is forcing him to sell a specific orchard (see Gemara 48a and note 4 above). It is also necessary to record the notification because the mortgage holder made his threat in private (secretly threatening to lie in court and thereby take the field); the witnesses could not have observed him making the threat. The owner must therefore prove that he was coerced to sell. Rava enables him to do this by giving witnesses the authority to record the notification of coercion in a document, which the owner can later use as evidence of coercion (*Rashbam*, see *Nesivos Hamishpat,* Introduction to ch. 205; cf. *Ramban, Rishonim* et al.).

Rabbeinu Chananel (cited by *Rashbam*) explains how the owner is able to use the document as evidence of coercion. To prove that he is being coerced, he must substantiate his claim that (a) he is the current owner of the orchard (contrary to the mortgage holder's claim that it was sold three years earlier) and (b) that he is being coerced to sell it. To do so, he approaches witnesses and tells them that the mortgage holder is coercing him, threatening to take his field unless he sells it. He then confronts the mortgage holder (in front of the witnesses) and demands his land back. The mortgage holder will presumably carry out his threat and claim to have purchased the land three years earlier and to have subsequently lost his deed. The owner can now employ the following scheme to prove that the mortgage holder is lying and that his claim is meant only as a form of coercion. He approaches the mortgage owner in private and offers to sell him the orchard in private (see *Rashash*). If he indeed purchased it three years ago, as he claims, he will obviously refuse to buy it again. If he is lying, however, he will accept the offer and agree to pay for the field when the owner gives him a bill of sale. The owner then returns to the witnesses and tells them what happened. He then writes a deed but tells the witnesses, "I have just told you why I am writing this deed. I hereby notify you that I am about to make the sale against my will and it is therefore meaningless." The witnesses then write a document recording the mortgage owner's claim and the owner's assertion that he is being coerced. If the mortgage holder indeed buys the orchard and takes the deed, the owner can summon him to court and demand his land back. The mortgage holder will then presumably produce the deed as proof of ownership. The deed, however, will have a recent date. The owner can then produce the document containing the notification of coercion to prove that the mortgage owner had previously claimed to have bought the orchard three years before. This will corroborate the owner's story that he was being forced to sell the orchard and it will be awarded to him.

8. Literally: a hidden gift. The Gemara below will explain what this means.

[א] דלא כתיב בה אנן ידעינן ביה באונסא דפלניא לאו מודעא היא מודעא דמאי [ב] אי דגיטא ודמתנתא גלויי מילתא בעלמא היא ואי דזביני והאמר רבא לא כתבינן מודעא אזביני לעולם דזביני [ג] מודי רבא היכא דאנים וכמעשה דפרדיסא [ד] דההוא גברא דמשכין פרדיסא לחבריה לתלת שנין בתר דאכלה תלת שני חזקה אמר (א) אי מזבנת לי מוטב ואי לא כבישנא לשטר משכנתא ואמינא לקוחה היא בידי כה"ג כתבינן מודעא: אמר רב יהודה האי מתנתא טמירתא לא מגבינן בה היכי דמי מתנתא טמירתא אמר רב יוסף דאמר להו לסהדי זילו אטמורו וכתבו ליה ואיכא דאמרי אמר רב יוסף דלא [ה] אמר להו תיתבו בשוקא ובבריתא ותכתבו ליה מאי בינייהו איכא בינייהו סתמא אמר רבא והויא מודעא לחברתה אמר רב פפא הא דרבא [ג] לאו בפירוש איתמר אלא מכללא איתמר [ו] דההוא גברא דאזל לקדושי אתתא אמרה ליה אי כתבת לי כולהו נכסיך הוינא לך (ב) ואי לא לא הוינא לך אזל כתביה לה לכולהו נכסי אתא בריה קשישא א"ל וההוא גברא מה תהוי עליה אמר להו לסהדי זילו אטמורו בעבר ימינא וכתבו ליה אתו לקמיה דרבא אמר להו [ז] לא מר קנה ולא מר קנה מאן דחזא סבר משום דהויא מודעא לחברתה [ח] ולא היא התם מוכחא מילתא דמחמת אונסא הוא דכתב לה [ט] אבל הכא מר ניחא ליה ומר לא ניחא ליה דליקני איבעיא להו סתמא

רשב"ם

דלא כתיב בה אנן עדים ידעינן באונסא דפלניא. שאונס גמור יש לו ומכירין אנו איזה אונס אי לא כתב בה הכי אלא סתמא כתבו פלוני אמר לנו שנאנס: מודעא דמאי אי. במודעא דמסר אגיטא ומתנה לא צריך כולי האי אלא כיון דמודע לסהדי דהאי גיטא שאני נותן לאשתי אנוס אני בו ולא ברצון נפשי (ג) עשיתי לפיכך דעו שאני מבטלו בפניכם וכן המתנה שאני מקנה לפלוני אנוס אני ואיני מקנה אותה ברצוני תהא מבוטלת אע"ג דלא ידעי סהדי אונסא דיליה הרי גט והמתנה בטלין: גלוי מילתא בעלמא היא. כלומר הרבה בני אדם יוכלו לידע אונסו דכיון דאינו מקבל ממון במתנה ובגט זה שנותן אם איתא דניחא ליה ליתנה מדעתו למה לו למסור מודעא ואי לא ניחא לו ליתן למה לו ליתן גט ומתנה אלא ודאי נאנס בגט ובמתנה זו הלכך אין צריך לפרש אונסו דלא דמי לזביני דהתם צריך לפרש דאיכא למימר סתם מוכר לא ברצונו מוכר אלא משום חסרון מעות והלכך איכא למימר דמסר מודעא דקסבר היום ולמחר כשיהיו לי מעות מפיקנא מודעא ומבטלנא ליה לדינא ויחזור קרקע שלי ואני אשלם מעותיו אבל הכא אם ברצון נפשו נותן גט ומתנה בלא אונס למה כותב מודעא בחנם לא יתן גט ולא איצטריך לכתוב מודעא אלא ודאי אנוס הוא ומשום הכי תקינו בגיטין דלא למיכתב גיטא עד שיבטל הבעל כל מודעות שמסר וכך הוא מפורש בערכין בפרק האומר משקלי עלי (דף כא:) אמר רב ששת האי מאן דמסר מודעא אגיטא מודעיה פשיטא לא צריכא דעשייה וארליה מהו דתימא כיון דארליה בטולי בטליה למודעיה קמ"ל עד דאמר בטלתיה ואימא כיון דארלי בטליה ולא צריך לפרושי דבטליה ואמרינן א"כ נתני וכן אתה אומר בגיטי נשים כופין אותו עד שיתן אמאי קתני עד שיאמר רוצה אני אלא קמ"ל עד דמפרש דבטליה ודוקא מודעא שיש בה אונס אי טעין ואמר גט שאעשה לא יהא גט אין זה ביטול דכיון דלא נאנס כלל אנן סהדי דגמר בלבו בשעת מעשה לעשותו גט גמור ולא מהני ביה ביטול דקודם כתיבה (ט) אלא א"כ ביטלו אחר כתיבה: (ד) דגלויי מילתא בעלמא היא. כלומר די לנו בגלויי מילתא בעלמא דלא חיישינן אם תתגלה מילתא או לא דסברא היא דאנים לפרדיסיה: ואי דזביני. שמוסר מודעא שנאנס ולפיכך לא הויא מודעא עד שיעידו העדים שמכירין באונסו משום דאיכא למימר דלא אנים אלא השתא למעות צריך והיום ולמחר ליבעי למיהדר בההיא מכירה כשיזדמנו לו מעות ולפיכך מסר השתא מודעא לבטל מכירתו: לא כתבינן מודעא אזביני. נראה לי טעמא דרבא משום דאמרינן לקמן בפירקין (דף מח.) (ה) הלכתא תליוה וזבין זביניה זביני ולא אמרן אלא בשדה סתם שכפאוהו למכור אחת משדותיו והוא בירר מעצמו אחת מהן ומכרה דלא הוי אונס אבל בשדה זו לא כו' והלכך לא כתבינן מודעא דאי בשדה זו הא לא הוי זביניה זביני ולא צריך מודעא אלא יביא עדים שכפאוהו ויתבטל שטר מכירה בלא שום מודעא ואי בשדה סתם הא הוי זביניה זביני ואין אונס בזה השדה שהרי מדעתיה בירר ומכר את זה השדה ומודעא זו שיכתוב פסולה היא דמודעא בלא אונס לאו כלום היא ומיהו רב הונא דאמר לקמן [ה] תליוה וזבין זביניה זביני חזינן דלאכשר מודעא אזביני דלית ליה הך סברא דרבא: ומשני מודי רבא דכתבינן מודעא היכא דאניס. (ו) כה"ג כמעשה דפרדס לקמן דמתוך פחד שמפחידין אותו להפסיד הפרדס לגמרי בלא דמים קמזבין ליה אין בלבו למכור לגמרי אלא עד שיגלו מן הפחד הכל ודאי כתבי' מודעא דהא אונס גמור הוא דאי לא מזבין ליה מערער למחזיק יפסיד אותו המחזיק למערער בטענותיו דהכא הוא דאמרי להדעי דצריך למיכתב אנו יודעים ביה כו': האי עובדא דפרדסא פר"ח היאך ידעו העדים באונס של בעל הפרדס דאם בפני עדים אמר לו המחזיק טענות דלקמן אין צריך מודעא אלא יעידו ששמעו לזה המחזיק שבא בעקיפין על בעל הפרדס ויטול בעל הפרדס את שלו וכך פירש אתא מריה דפרדיסא גבי סהדי ואודעינהו הני מילי שרוצה זה לגוזלו פרדס (ז) בטענותיו ואמר להו אנא תבענא ליה קמייהו ושמעו מיניה דטעין זבינתא ניהלי וליה לך עלי ולא מידי ובתר הכי א"ל בחשאי אנא מזבינלך ואמר ליה כתוב לי שטר מכירה שלא בפני כדמתן כותבין שטר למוכר אע"פ שאין לוקח עמו והביאהו לי ואתן לך הדמים והלך זה וסיפר לעדים מה שאמר לו זה לכתוב לו שטר מכירה וכן עשה וקודם שכתב ומסר השטר מכירה אמר לעדים אתם שמעתם שטוען לקוחה היא בידי זה ג' שנים ואנא כתבנא ליה שטר מכירה כמו שאמר שלא בפניו ואקבל הדמים השתא מסר אנא מודעא קמייכו דלאו ברעות נפשי מזביננא להאי פרדיסא אלא משום דכפר במשכנתא ובתר הכי תבענא ליה לדינא ומפקינא לה מיניה על ידי שיראה שטר מכירה זה שמהיום ואני אוציא המודעא לפניו המבטלתו והוא לא יתן לבו לטעון ולומר שג' שנים היתה לקוחה לו הקודמין לשטר זה: כה"ג. שמפסיד הכל אם לא ימכור מודי רבא דכתבי' מודעא: מתנתא טמירתא. מתנה טמונה לקמיה מפרש: לא מגבינן בה. דשמא נתנה לאחר כבר או לעשותה מודעא לחברתה נתכוין כדלקמן: איטמורו. הטמינו עצמכם: ה"ג ואיכא דאמרי אמר רב יוסף דלא אמר להו תיתבו בשוקי ובבריתא. לא ליזיל לכתוב בשווקים וברחובות אלא סתם אמר להו כתובו: איכא בינייהו סתמא. שאמר להו כתובו סתם ולא אמר להם איטמורו וגם לא ליזיל לכתוב בשוקי ובבריתא ללישנא קמא דרב יוסף כשרה וללישנא בתרא פסולה דצריך לומר להם כתובו בשוקא ותחתמוה בברא. ובפירוש ר"ח גרסינן דאמר להו לא תיתבו בשוקא ובברייתא ואי אפשר לומר כן דלשני לשונות לרב יוסף משמע סתמא כשרה: בשוקא ובבריתא. לעיני כל כתובו לו: אמר רבא והויא. הך מתנתא טמירתא מודעא לבטל חברתה שטר מתנה או מכירה גלויה וכשרה שנכתבה אחרי כן על שדה זו לאדם אחר דלכך כתבה להך טמירתא דלא לחזיק בהאי שדה האיך בתרא: אלא מכללא איתמר. וטעות הוא: אתא בריה קשישא. קודם כתיבת השטר לאשה: אמר להו לסהדי. קודם שנכתב שטר האשה: זילו אטמורו בעבר ימינא. באותו מקום: וכתבו ליה. לבני ויקדם שטרו ויגבה הכל: לא מר קנה. הבן משום דהויא טמירתא: ולא מר קנה. האשה משום דטמירתא הויא לה מודעא לבטלה: ולא היא. דמתנה טמירתא כמאן דליתיה היא ולא הויא מודעא: דמחמת אונסא. שאינה חפיצה בו אא"כ יכתוב לה הלכך לא גמר בלבו להקנות לה אלא עד שישאנה ויחזור בו והלכך התם הוא דהויא במקום מודעא: אבל הכא. דליכא טענת אונס בבתרייתא לא הויא מתנה טמירתא קמייתא מודעא לבתרייתא שהיא עשויה כתקנה לבטלה דבקמייתא לא ניחא ליה דליקני הואיל ועבדה טמירתא אבל אחרון שנעשה כתקון שטר ראוי ניחא ליה דליקני שמעינן מהכא דמתנתא טמירתא לא הויא מודעא לחברתה אלא היכא דליכא אלא אונס בבתרייתא אונס דמוכח אבל בלא אונס ניחא ליה דליקני:

סתמא

תוספות

איכא דאמרי אמר רב יוסף דלא אמר להו תיתבו כו'. גירסא קשה לר"י מאי קבעי מאי בינייהו הא בהדיא חולקין בסתמא ועוד דפסקינן לקמן הלכתא דחיישינן בסתמא וא"כ היכי מגבינן כולהו מתנתא כיון דאינו אומר לסהדי כתבו בשוקי (א) ברייתא ומיהו לפי שנוהגים עתה לכתוב בשטרי מתנה ואמר לנו מתנה זו כתבוה בשוקא ותחתמוה בברא הלכך כי אמר להו נמי סתמא דעתו לומר כמו שכותבים בשטרות ובימי האמוראים לא היו נוהגים לכתוב כך לכך היה צריך לומר להם בפירוש כתבו בשוקא כו'. ור"ח גריס דאמר להו לא תיתבו בשוקא ברא וקרי ליה סתמא שאינו אומר להם להטמין עצמו ואומר שלא לפרסם והיינו סתמא (ט) כלומר לא פרסם ולא הטמינם אבל כתובו לא חשיב סתמא וכשר לפר"ח ולפיכך מה שנהגו לכתוב בשטרות מתנה זו כתבוה בשוקא ותחתמוה בברא אינו אלא לשופרא דשטרא ומיהו לישנא דסתמא לא משמע הכי:

שלא

עין משפט נר מצוה

ק א מיי' פ"י מהל' מכירה הל' ב סמג עשין פב טוש"ע ח"מ סי' רה סעיף א:

קא ב מיי' שם הל' ג ופ"ו מהל' גירושין הל' כ ופ"ה מהל' זכיה הלכה ד סמג שם וסי' נ טוש"ע שם סעי' ב וסי' רמב סעי' א וטוש"ע אה"ע סי' קלד סעי' א:

קב ג ד מיי' פ"י מהל' מכירה הל' ד סמג עשין פב טוש"ע ח"מ סי' רה סעיף ז:

קג ה מיי' פ"ה מהל' זכייה הל' א ב ופ"ט שם הל' ב סמג עשין פב טוש"ע ח"מ סי' רמב סעי' ג ד ה:

קד ו ז מיי' שם פ"ה הלכה ה סמג שם טוש"ע שם סעי' ט וס"י:

קה ח ט מיי' שם והל' ג טוש"ע שם ובסעיף ח:

גליון הש"ס

רשב"ם ד"ה גילוי מלתא בסה"ד אא"כ ביטל אחר כתיבה. עי' גיטין דף לב ע"ב ובתוס' שם ד"ה (הכא) [התם]:

רבינו גרשום

דלא כתיב בה. עדים גופייהו ידעו באונסיה לא מודעא היא: מודעא דמאי. צריכה למכתב בה ידעינן באונסיה אי דגט או דמתנה שמכריחין אותו ליתן הכא לא צריך למכתב ידעינן באונסיה דהאי גלוי מלתא בעלמא דכיון שכפאוהו ועל כרחו נתן משום דאינו מקבל כלום אלא נותן: ואי מודעא דזביני. שכפאוהו למכור אמרת דצריכי למיכתב ידעי' באונסיה: והאמר רבא לא כתבי' מודעא לזביני. שמאחר שמקבל הוא דמים מיד גמר ומכר לו. ומודי רבא בזביני היכא דאניס דומיא דהאי מעשה דפרדיסא אע"ג דמקבל זוזי דכתבי' ליה מודעא וצריך למכתב ידענא באונסה: האי מתנה טמירתא. שאמר כתבו לי בהחבא לא מגבינן בה דשמא כבר נתנה לאחר: בשוקי בריתא. כלומר בגלוי לעיני הכל לא יכתבו: איכא בינייהו סתמא. ללישנא קמא אי אמר להו סתמא זילו כתובו הואיל דלא אמר להו זילו איטמרו הויא מתנה וללישנא בתרא אמר להו זילו כתובו לא הויא מתנה עד דאמר להו לסהדי תיתבו בשוקי ברייתא ותכתבו ליה: אמר רבא והויא מודעא לחברתה. שאם כתב מתנה טובה לחד כתובה וחתומה בשוק או בברא והדר אותה מתנה עצמה כתבה לאחר בטמירתה אינה מתנה לא זו ולא זו דשניה הוה מודעא לחברתה ראשונה דהא לא ניחא ליה דראשון קונה הואיל וכתב לשני ושניה טמונה היא כגון האי מעשה: בעבר ימינא. באותו מקום: דמחמת אונס הוא דכתב לה. דלא מיקדשה ליה אי לא כתב לה כל נכסיה: אבל הכא. דהיכא דכתב לראשון מתנה גלויה ולבתר הכי כתב ליה לאידך בטמירתא להאי אמרינן דניחא ליה דליקני [ולא] הוי מודעא

מסורת הש"ס

א) ב"מ עב., ב) [ברכות ט. וש"נ], ג) [דף מז: מח: וע"ש בפי' הרשב"ם]:

הגהות הב"ח

(א) גמ' אמר ליה אי מזבנת: (ב) שם הוינא לך לאיתתא ואי לא: (ג) רשב"ם ד"ה מודעא וכו' ולא ברצון נפשי אני נותן לה זה הגט לפיכך דעו וכו' בטלין דגלויי מילתא וכו' בגט זה ובמתנה זו וכו' אשלם לו מעותיו וכו' ולא יצטרך לכתוב כצ"ל והד"א: (ד) ד"ה גלויי מילתא כצ"ל ואות ד' נמחק: (ה) ד"ה לא כתבינן וכו' לקמן בפירקין אמר רבא הלכתא וכו' ואין כאן אונס בזה השדה שהרי מדעתו בירר: (ו) ד"ה ומשני מודה וכו' דאניס בכה"ג וכו' ואין בלבו וכו' והכא הוא דאמרי: (ז) ד"ה האי עובדא וכו' לגוזלו פרדס שלו בטענותיו וכו' המודעא שלפניו המבטלתו והוא לא יתן אל לבו: (ח) תום' ד"ה איכא וכו' בשוקי וברייתא ומיהו יש לומר לפי שנוהגים וכו' ואמר לנו שטר מתנה: (ט) בא"ד והיינו סתמא דלא פי' לא פרסום ולא הטמנה אבל וכו' וכשר לפר"ח ולפי זה מה שנהגו:

ליקוטי רש"י

ההוא גברא דמשכין פרדיסא לחבריה. שיאכלנה ותחזור לבעלים בלא מעות דכתב ליה במשלם שניא אילין תיפוק ארעא דין בלא כסף [כתובות צה:]. משכן לו כרם במשכנתא דסורא אי נמי בנכייתא [ב"מ קט:]. פרדיסא. כרם [כתובות שם וב"מ עב.]. כבישנא. אטמין. ואמינא לקוחה היא בידי. ואבד שטר המכירה ואבא מכח חזקה של שלש שנים דכולי האי לא מלינא למיזהר בשטרא [ב"מ שם].

of his property with the document.[9]

The Gemara present two interpretations of a secret gift document:

הֵיכִי דָּמֵי מַתְּנְתָּא טְמִירְתָּא – **How is** the term **"secret gift" to be understood?** אָמַר רַב יוֹסֵף – **Rav Yosef said:** דְּאָמַר לְהוּ לְסַהֲדֵי – It refers to a gift document **concerning which** the giver **told witnesses,** זִילוּ אִטְמוֹרוּ וּכְתֻבוּ לֵיהּ – **"Go hide and** only then **write [the gift document]."** וְאִיכָּא דְּאָמְרֵי אָמַר רַב יוֹסֵף – **And some say that Rav Yosef said** דְּלָא אָמַר לְהוּ – **that** whenever **[the giver] did not say to [the witnesses],** תִּיתְבוּ בְּשׁוּקָא וּבִבְרַיְתָא וְתִכְתְּבוּ לֵיהּ – **"Sit in the marketplace** or **in the street**[10] **and write [the document],"** it is considered a secret gift.

The Gemara asks:

מַאי בֵּינַיְיהוּ – **What is the** practical **difference between [the two versions]?**

The Gemara responds:

אִיכָּא בֵּינַיְיהוּ סְתָמָא – The practical **difference between them emerges** in a case where the giver left the writing instructions **unspecified.** According to the first version, the document is valid because he never specified that it be kept secret. According to the second version, however, it is void because he never specified that it be written publicly.

The Gemara presents a view that a secret gift document does serve some purpose:

אָמַר רָבָא – **Rava said:** וְהָוְיָא מוֹדָעָא לַחֲבֶרְתָּהּ – **But** it **does constitute notification of its counterpart's** invalidity.[11]

The Gemara investigates the source of the attribution of this ruling to Rava:

אָמַר רַב פָּפָּא – **Rav Pappa said:** הָא דְּרָבָא – **This** ruling **of Rava's** לָאו בְּפֵירוּשׁ אִיתְּמַר – **was not specifically stated;** אֶלָּא מִכְּלָלָא אִיתְּמַר – **rather, it was deduced** from another statement of his.

The Gemara now cites the decision from which our ruling was deduced and explains why the deduction was mistaken: דְּהַהוּא גַּבְרָא דַּאֲזַל לְקַדּוּשֵׁי אִתְּתָא – **For there was a certain man who went to betroth a woman.** אָמְרָה לֵיהּ – **She said to him,** אִי כָּתְבַתְּ לִי כּוּלְּהוּ נִכְסָךְ הָוֵינָא לָךְ – **"If you deed all your property to me, I will** consent to **become your [wife],** וְאִי לָא לָא הָוֵינָא לָךְ – **but if not, I will not become your [wife]."** אֲזַל כַּתְבִיהּ לַהּ לְכוּלְּהוּ נִכְסֵי – **[The man]** then **went to deed all his property to her.** אֲתָא בְּרֵיהּ קַשִּׁישָׁא – Before he had done so, however, **his eldest son came** אָמַר לֵיהּ – and **said to him,** וְהַהוּא גַּבְרָא מָה תֶּהֱוֵי עֲלֵיהּ – **"But this man** (referring to himself), **what will happen to him?** What will be left for me if you give all your property to the woman?" אָמַר לְהוּ לְסַהֲדֵי – **[The father]** thereupon **said to witnesses,** זִילוּ אִטְמוֹרוּ בְּעֵבֶר יְמִינָא – **"Go hide in Eiver Yemina**[12] before you write a deed for the woman וּכְתֻבוּ לֵיהּ – **and write** a document giving my property **to [my son].** After that, you can write a deed for the woman."[13] The witnesses executed both documents. Later, both the son and the woman claimed the property. אֲתוֹ לְקַמֵּיהּ דְּרָבָא – **They came before Rava** and asked him to decide the case. אָמַר לְהוּ – **[Rava] said to them:** לֹא מָר קָנָה – **Neither this master** (the son) **acquired** the property וְלֹא מָר קָנָה – **nor did this master** (the woman) **acquire** the property.

The Gemara suggests an interpretation of the ruling:

מַאן דַּחֲזָא סָבַר – **The one who saw** Rava render the decision **assumed** מִשּׁוּם דְּהָוְיָא מוֹדָעָא לַחֲבֶרְתָּהּ – that he invalidated the woman's deed **because** the secret gift document written for the son **constituted notification of its counterpart**['s] (i.e. the woman's document's) invalidity. This explains the Gemara's earlier attribution of such a view to Rava.

The Gemara now rejects the deduction:

וְלָא הִיא – **But this is not so.** הָתָם מוּכְחָא מִילְּתָא – **There** (in Rava's case), **it was clear** דְּמֵחֲמַת אוּנְסָא הוּא דִּכְתַב לַהּ – **that [the man]** deeded his property **to [the woman] only under duress**[14] but he did not really want her to acquire it. Given the man's attitude, Rava ruled that the secret gift document was intended to nullify the subsequent document written for the woman.[15] אֲבָל הָכָא – **But here** (i.e. in most other cases), מַר נִיחָא לֵיהּ דְּלִיקְנֵי – when a person deeds a gift to someone, **[the giver] wants** the **master** holding the ordinary gift document **to acquire** his property וּמַר לֹא נִיחָא לֵיהּ דְּלִיקְנֵי – **and he does not**

NOTES

9. Someone who honestly wants to give property away would have no reason to write the gift document secretly. If someone avoids writing a document in public, then, he might well be trying to hide dishonest behavior. We can advance several explanations for what he is doing. Perhaps he is writing the document in secret because he has already given the property to someone else and does not want that recipient to hear about the second gift document. If so, the secret document is void because the giver no longer owned the property. On the other hand, perhaps he is keeping it secret because he never actually intended to give the property away; he wrote the document only to enable himself to dishonestly void documents that he will write in the future. (That is, if he later writes a gift document and that recipient tries to collect the gift property from him, he will produce the secret document, which was written earlier, and claim that it voids the later document — see note 13 below.) Because of these suspicions, a secret gift document is considered void (see *Rashbam*).

10. Literally: outside.

11. When someone writes a gift document, he gives a gift to the recipient named in the document and he also deprives anybody else of a potential claim to the property. Thus, even though a secret document does not convey a gift to the named recipient, still it deprives anybody else of a claim to the property and thus nullifies any future documents, be they bills of sale or gift documents (*Rashbam; cf. Rabbeinu Gershom*). The notion that a secret gift document can nullify any future bills of sale contradicts the Gemara's earlier assumption. The Gemara above assumed that a notification of coercion can nullify only sales performed under duress. The Gemara could thus have objected that even if someone wrote a secret gift document intending to nullify future bills of sale, this is meaningless unless he writes the bills of sale under duress. (It is understandable, however, that it would nullify future gift documents.) The Gemara apparently did not raise this objection because the Gemara had another objection anyway.

12. This was the name of a place.

13. Once someone gives his property away to one person, that person acquires the property; the previous owner obviously can no longer give it to anyone else. Hence, if two people hold gift documents, each conferring ownership of a given property upon its bearer, the property is awarded to the one holding the document with the earlier date (since that document was written first). Knowing this, the man in our case charged the witnesses with deeding the land to his son first so that he — not the woman — would actually acquire the land (*Rashbam*).

14. That is, he felt compelled to deed his property to the woman, because she refused to marry him until he did so.

15. In Rava's case, the man never wanted to deed his property to the woman but felt compelled to do so to induce her to marry him. Accordingly, he presumably wrote his secret gift document in advance to give notice that he is writing the woman's gift document under duress and it is thus meaningless. [Although this is not a clear case of coercion, if the man writes the secret gift document, this indicates he feels compelled to deed the property to the woman (see *Nimukei Yosef*).]

[In Rava's case, the woman apparently never stipulated that the validity of her marriage be contingent upon her receiving the man's property; had she done so, the marriage would obviously be invalid if the gift were voided. Rather, the woman refused to consider marriage until the man deeded all his property to her. Once he did so, however, she agreed to marry him unconditionally.]

[א]דלא כתיב בה אנן ידעינן ביה באונסא דפלניא לאו מודעא היא מודעא דמאי [ב]אי דגיטא ודמתנתא גלויי מילתא בעלמא היא ואי דזביני והאמר רבא לא כתבינן מודעא אזביני לעולם דזביני [ג]מודי רבא היכא דאנים וכמעשה דפרדיסא [ד]דההוא גברא דמשכין פרדיסא לחבריה לתלת שנין בתר דאכלה תלת שני חזקה אמר (א) אי מזבנת לי מוטב ואי לא כבישנא לשטר משכנתא ואמינא לקוחה היא בידי כה"ג כתבינן מודעא: אמר רב יהודה האי מתנתא טמירתא לא מגבינן בה היכי דמי מתנתא טמירתא אמר רב יוסף דאמר להו לסהדי זילו אטמורו וכתבו ליה ואיכא דאמרי אמר רב יוסף דלא [ה]אמר להו תיתבו בשוקא ובבריתא ותכתבו ליה מאי בינייהו איכא בינייהו סתמא אמר רבא והויא מודעא לחברתה אמר רב פפא הא דרבא [ג]לאו בפירוש איתמר אלא מכללא איתמר [ו]דההוא גברא דאזל לקדושי אתתא אמרה ליה אי כתבת לי כולהו נכסיך הוינא לך (ב) ואי לא לא הוינא לך אזל כתביה לה לכולהו נכסי אתא בריה קשישא א"ל וההוא גברא מה תהוי עליה אמר להו לסהדי זילו אטמורו בעבר ימינא וכתבו ליה אתו לקמיה דרבא אמר להו [ז]לא מר קנה ולא מר קנה מאן דחזא סבר משום דהויא מודעא לחברתה [ח]ולא היא התם מוכחא מילתא דמחמת אונסא הוא דכתב לה [ט]אבל הכא מר ניחא ליה דליקני ומר לא ניחא ליה דליקני איבעיא להו סתמא

רשב"ם

דלא כתיב בה אנן ידעינן באונסא דפלניא. שאונס גמור יש לו ומכריחין אותו ליתן אותו אי לא כתב בה הכי אלא סתמא כתבו פלוני אמר לנו שנאנס: מודעא דמאי אי. במודעא דמסר אגיטא ואמתנה לא צריך כולי האי אלא כיון דמודע לסהדי דהאי גיטא שאני נותן לאשתי אנוס אני בו ולא ברצון נפשי (ג) עשיתי לפיכך דעו שאני מבטלו בפניכם וכן המתנה שאני מקנה לפלוני אנוס אני ואיני מקנה אותה ברצוני תהא מבוטלת אע"ג דלא ידעי סהדי אונסא דיליה הרי גט והמתנה בטלין: גלוי מילתא בעלמא היא. כלומר הרבה בני אדם יוכלו לידע אונסו דכיון דאינו מקבל ממון במתנה ובגט זה שנותן אם איתא דניחא ליה ליתנה מדעתו למה לו למסור מודעא ואי לא ניחא לו ליתן למה לו ליתן גט ומתנה אלא ודאי נאנס בגט ובמתנה זו הלכך אין צריך לפרש אונסו דלא דמי לזביני דהתם צריך לפרש דאיכא למימר סתם מוכר לא ברצונו מוכר אלא משום חסרון מעות והלכך איכא למימר דמסר מודעא דקסבר היום ולמחר כשיהיו לי מעות מפיקנא מודעא ותבענא ליה לדינא ויחזור קרקע שלי ואני אשלם מעותיו אבל הכא אם ברצון נפשו נותן גט ומתנה בלא אונס למה כותב מודעא בחנם לא יתן גט ולא איצטריך לכתוב מודעא אלא ודאי אנוס הוא ומשום הכי תקינו בגיטין דלא למיכתב גיטא עד שיבטל הבעל כל מודעות שמסר וכן הוא מפורש בערכין בפרק האומר משקלי עלי (דף כא:) אמר רב ששת האי מאן דמסר מודעא אגיטא מודעיה מודעא פשיטא לא צריכא דעשייה וארציה מהו דתימא כיון דארציה בטולי בטליה למודעיה קמ"ל עד דאמר בטלתיה ואימא כיון דארצי בטליה ולא צריך לפרושי דבטליה ואמרינן א"כ נתני וכן אתה אומר בגיטי נשים כופין אותו עד שיתן אמאי קתני עד שיאמר רוצה אני אלא קמ"ל עד דמפרש דבטליה ודוקא מודעא שיש בה אונס אבל בלא אונס אי טעין ואמר גט שאעשה לא יהא גט אין זה ביטול דכיון דלא נאנס כלל אנן סהדי דגמר בלבו בשעת מעשה לעשותו גט גמור ולא מהני ביה ביטול דקודם כתיבה ° אלא א"כ ביטלו אחר כתיבה: (ד) דגלויי מילתא בעלמא היא. כלומר די לנו בגלויי מילתא בעלמא דלא חיישינן אם תתגלה מילתא או לא דסברא היא דאנים כדפרישית: ואי דזביני. שמוסר מודעא שנאנס ולפיכך לא הויא מודעא עד שיעידו העדים שמכירין באונסו משום דאיכא למימר דלא אנים אלא השתא למעות צריך והיום ולמחר ליבעי למיהדר בההיא מכירה כשיזדמנו לו מעות ולפיכך מסר השתא מודעא לבטל מכירתו: לא כתבינן מודעא אזביני. נראה לי טעמא דרבא משום דאמרינן לקמן בפירקין (דף מח.) (ה) הלכתא תליוה וזבין זביניה זביני ולא אמרן אלא בשדה סתם שכפאוהו למכור אחת משדותיו והוא בירר מעצמו אחת מהן ומכרה דלא הוי אונס אבל בשדה זו לא כו' והלכך לא כתבינן מודעא דאי בשדה זו הא לא הוי זביניה זביני ולא צריך מודעא אלא יביא עדים שאנסוהו ויתבטל שטר מכירה בלא שום מודעא ואי בשדה סתם הא הוי זביניה זביני ואין אונס בזה השדה שהרי מדעתיה בירר ומכר את זה השדה ומודעא זו שיכתוב פסולה היא דמודעא בלא אונס לאו כלום היא ומיהו רב הונא דאמר לקמן [ג] תליוה וזבין זביניה זביני חזינן דאכשר מודעא אזביני דלית ליה הך סברא דרבא: ומשני מודי רבא דכתבינן מודעא היכא דאנים. (ו) כה"ג דמעשה דפרדס דלקמן דמתוך פחד שמפחידין אותו להפסיד הפרדס לגמרי בלא דמים קמזבין ליה אין בלבו למכור לגמרי אלא עד שינצל מן הפחד הכא ודאי כתבי' מודעא דהא אונס גמור הוא דאי לא מזבין ליה מערער למחזיק יפסיד אותו המחזיק למערער בטענותיו דהכא הוא דאמרי נהרדעי דצריך למיכתב אנו יודעים ביה כו': האי עובדא דפרדסא פר"ח היאך ידעו העדים באונס של בעל הפרדס דאם בפני עדים אמר לו המחזיק טענות דלקמן אין צריך מודעא אלא יעידו ששמעו לזה המחזיק שבא בעקיפין על בעל הפרדס ויטול בעל הפרדס את שלו וכך פירש אתא מריה דפרדיסא גבי סהדי ואודעינהו הני מילי שרוצה זה לגוזלו פרדס (ז) בטענותיו ואמר להו אנא תבענא ליה קמייכו ושמעו מיניה דטעין זבינתא ניהלי ולית לך עלי ולא מידי ובתר הכי א"ל בחשאי אנא מזביננא לך ואמר ליה כתוב לי שטר מכירה שלא בפני כדתנן כותבין שטר למוכר אע"פ שאין לוקח עמו והביאהו לי ואתן לך הדמים והלך זה וסיפר לעדים מה שאמר לו זה לכתוב לו שטר מכירה וכן עשה וקודם שכתב ומסר השטר מכירה אמר לעדים אתם שמעתם שטען לקוחה היא בידי זה ג' שנים ואנא כתבנא ליה שטר מכירה כמו שאמר שלא בפניו ואקבל הדמים השתא מסר אנא מודעא קמייכו דלאו ברעות נפשי מזבינגא להאי פרדיסא אלא משום דכפר במשכנתא ובתר הכי תבענא ליה לדינא ומפקינא לה מיניה על ידי שיראה שטר מכירה זה שמהיום ואני אוציא המודעא לפניו המבטלתו והוא לא יתן לבו לטעון ולומר שג' שנים היתה לקוחה לו הקודמין לשטר זה: כה"ג. שמפסיד הכל אם לא ימכור מודי רבא דכתבי מודעא: מתנתא טמירתא. מתנה טמונה לקמיה מפרש: לא מגבינן בה. דשמא נתנה לאחר כבר או לעשותה מודעא לחברתה נתכוון כדלקמן: איטמורו. הטמינו עצמכם: ה"ג ואיכא דאמרי אמר רב יוסף דלא אמר להו תיתבו בשוקי ובבריתא. לא לישב לכתוב בשווקים וברחובות אלא סתם אמר להו כתובו: איכא בינייהו סתמא. שאמר להו כתובו סתם ולא אמר להם איטמורו וגם לא לישב לכתוב בשוקי ובבריתא ללישנא קמא דרב יוסף כשרה וללישנא בתרא פסולה דצריך לומר להם כתובו בשוקא וחתמוה בברא. ובפירוש ר"ח גרסינן דאמר להו לא תיתבו בשוקא ובבריתא ואי אפשר לומר כן דלשני לשונות דרב יוסף משמע סתמא כשרה: בשוקא ובבריתא. לעין כל כתובו לו: אמר רבא והויא. הך מתנתא טמירתא מודעא לבטל חברתה שטר מתנה או מכירה גלויה וכשרה שנכתבה אחרי כן על שדה זו לאדם אחר דלכך כתבה להך טמירתא דלא לחזיק בהאי שדה האיך בתרא: אלא מכללא איתמר. וטעות הוא: אתא בריה קשישא. קודם כתיבת השטר לאשה: אמר להו לסהדי. קודם שנכתב שטר האשה: זילו איטמורו בעבר ימינא. באותו מקום: וכתבו ליה. לבני ויקדם שטרו ויגבה הכל: לא מר קנה. הבן משום דהויא טמירתא: ולא מר קנה. האשה משום דטמירתא הויא לה מודעא לבטלה: ולא היא. דמתנה טמירתא כמאן דליתיה היא ולא הויא מודעא: דמחמת אונסא. שאינה חפיצה בו אא"כ יכתוב לה הלכך לא גמר בלבו להקנות לה אלא עד שישאנה ויחזור בו והלכך התם הוא דהויא במקום מודעא: אבל הכא. דליכא טענת אונס בבתרייתא לא הויא מתנה טמירתא קמייתא מודעא לבתרייתא שהיא עשויה כתקנה לבטלה דבקמייתא לא ניחא ליה דליקני הואיל ועבדה טמירתא אבל אחרון שנעשה לו שטר ראוי ניחא ליה דליקני שמעינן מהכא דמתנתא טמירתא לא הויא מודעא לחברתה אלא היכא דאיכא אונס בבתרייתא אבל בלא אונס דמוכח ניחא ליה דליקני:

סתמא

תוספות

איכא דאמרי אמר רב יוסף דלא אמר להו תיתבו כו'. אהך גירסא קשה לר"י מאי קבעי מאי בינייהו הא בהדיא חולקין בסתמא ועוד דפסקינן לקמן הלכתא דחיישינן בסתמא וא"כ היכי מגבינן כולהו מתנתא כיון דאינו אומר לסהדי כתבו בשוקי (ח) ובבריתא ומיהו לפי שנוהגים עתה לכתוב בשטרי מתנה ואמר לנו מתנה זו כתבוה בשוקא וחתמוה בברא הלכך כי אמר להו נמי סתמא דעתו לומר כמו שכותבים בשטרות ובימי האמוראים לא היו נוהגים לכתוב כך לכך היה צריך לומר להם בפירוש כתבו בשוקא כו'. ור"ח גריס דאמר להו לא תיתבו בשוקא ברא וקרי ליה סתמא שאינו אומר להם להטמין עצמו ואומר שלא לפרסם והיינו סתמא (ט) כלומר לא פרסם ולא הטמינם אבל כתובו לא חשיב סתמא וכשר לפר"ח ולפיכך מה שנהגו לכתוב בשטרות מתנה זו כתבוה בשוקא וחתמוה בברא אינו אלא לשופרא דשטרא ומיהו לישנא דסתמא לא משמע הכי: שלא

עין משפט נר מצוה

ק א מיי' פ"י מהל' מכירה הל' ג סמג עשין פב טוש"ע ח"מ סי' רה סעיף ח:

קא ב מיי' שם הל' ג ופ"ו מהל' גירושין הל' כ ופ"ה מהל' זכיה הלכה ד סמג שם ועשין נ טוש"ע אה"ע סי' קלד סעי' א וטוש"ע ח"מ סי' רמב סעי' א:

קב ג ד מיי' פ"י מהל' מכירה הל' ד סמג עשין פב טוש"ע ח"מ סי' רה סעיף ז:

קג ה מיי' פ"ה מהל' זכיה הל' ד ופ"ו הל' ב סמג עשין פב טוש"ע ח"מ סי' רמב סעי' ג ד ה:

קד ו ז מיי' שם הלכה ה סמג עשין פב טוש"ע שם סעי' ט וס"י:

קה ח ט מיי' שם ופ"ו שם הל' ג טוש"ע שם ובסעיף ח:

גליון הש"ס

רשב"ם ד"ה גלוי מלתא בבעה"ד אא"כ ביטלו אחר כתיבה. ע' גיטין דף לב ע"ב ובתוס' שם ד"ה (הכא) [התם]:

רבינו גרשום

דלא כתיב בה. עדים גופייהו ידעו באונסיה לא מודעא היא: מודעא דמאי. צריכה למכתב בה ידעינן באונסיה אי דגט או דמתנה שמכריחין אותו ליתן הכא לא צריך למכתב ידעינן באונסיה דהאי גלוי מלתא בעלמא דכיון שכפאוהו ועל כרחו נתן משום דאינו מקבל כלום אלא נותן: ואי מודעא דזביני. שכפאוהו למכור אמרת דצריכי למיכתב ידעי' באונסיה: והאמר רבא לא כתבי' מודעא לזביני. שמאחר שמקבל הוא דמים מיד גמר ומכר לו. ומודי רבא בזביני היכא דאניס דומיא דהאי מעשה דפרדיסא אע"ג דמקבל זוזי דכתבי' ליה מודעא וצריך למכתב ידענא באונסה: האי מתנה טמירתא. שאמר כתבו לי בהחבא לא מגבינן בה דשמא כבר נתנה לאחר: בשוקי בריתא. כלומר בגלוי לעיני הכל לא יכתבו: איכא בינייהו סתמא. ללישנא קמא אי אמר להו סתמא זילו כתובו הואיל דלא אמר להו זילו איטמרו הויא מתנה וללישנא בתרא אמר להו זילו כתובו לא הויא מתנה עד דאמר להו לסהדי תיתבו בשוקי ברייתא ותכתבו ליה: אמר רבא והויא מודעא לחברתה. שאם כתב מתנה טובה לחד כתובה וחתומה בשוק או בברא והדר אותה מתנה עצמה כתבה לאחר בטמירתה אינה מתנה לא זו ולא זו דשניה הוה מודעא לחברתה ראשונה דהא לא ניחא ליה דראשון קונה הואיל וכתב לשני ושניה טמונה היא כגון האי מעשה: בעבר ימינא. באותו מקום: דמחמת אונס הוא דכתב לה. דלא מיקדשה ליה אי לא כתב לה כל נכסיה: אבל הכא. דהיכא דכתב לראשון מתנה גלויה ולבתר הכי כתב ליה לאידך בטמירתא להאי אמרינן דניחא ליה דליקני [ולא] הוי מודעא

מסורת הש"ס

א) ב"מ עב., ב) [ברכות ט. וש"נ], ג) [דף מז: מח: וע"ש בפי' הרשב"ם],

הגהות הב"ח

(א) גמ' אמר ליה אי מזבנת: (ב) שם הוינא לך לאיתתא ואי לא: (ג) רשב"ם ד"ה מודעא וכו' ולא ברצון נפשי אני נותן לה זה הגט על כן לפיכך דעו וכו': בטלין דגלויי מילתא וכו' (ד) ד"ה גלויי מילתא כצ"ל ואות ד' נמחק: (ה) ד"ה לא כתבינן וכו' לקמן בפירקין אמר רבה הלכתא וכו' ואין כאן אונס בזה השדה שהרי מדעתו בירר: (ו) ד"ה ומשני מודה וכו' דאנים כה"ג וכו' ואין בלבו וכו' והכא ודאי כתבי: (ז) ד"ה האי עובדא וכו' לגוזלו פרדס שלו בטענותיו וכו' המודעא שלפניו המבטלתו והוא לא יתן אל לבו: (ח) תוס' ד"ה ואיכא וכו' בשוקי ובריתא ומיהו יש לומר לפי שנוהגים וכו' ואמר לנו שטר מתנה: (ט) בא"ד והיינו סתמא דלא פי' לא פרסום ולא הטמנה אבל וכו' וכשר לפר"ח ולפי זה מה שנהגו:

ליקוטי רש"י

ההוא גברא דמשכין פרדיסא לחבריה. שאלגלגה ותחזור לבעלים בלא מעות שכך דכתב ליה במשכנתא סניא אלימן תיפוק ארעא דין בלא כסף [כתובות צה:]. משכין לו כרם במשכנתא לפירות אי נמי בנכייתא [ב"מ קט:]. פרדיסא. כרם [כתובות שם וב"מ עב.]. כבישנא. אטמין. ואמינא לקוחה היא בידי. ואבד שטר המכירה ואבלא מכח חזקה של שלש שנים דשוב לא מלינא לו לאיזהר בשטרא [ב"מ שם].

want the **master** holding the secret gift document **to acquire the property.**[16] Rava, too, would agree that in such cases, the ordinary gift document is valid even if a secret document had been written earlier.

Earlier the Gemara presented two interpretations of "a secret gift document." The Gemara now decides which to accept:[17]

אִיבַּעְיָא לְהוּ – They inquired:

NOTES

16. Generally, when someone writes a secret gift document, we cannot assume that he actually wants to give his property away (see note 9); whenever someone writes an ordinary gift document, however, we assume that he does. Accordingly, even if someone wrote a secret document to one person before writing an ordinary document to another, we do not assume that he meant to nullify the ordinary document (unless he is being coerced, such as in Rava's case). Rather, we assume that the secret gift document is void and the ordinary one is valid (*Rashbam*).

17. As the Gemara above notes, a practical difference emerges between the interpretations in a case where the giver never told witnesses where to write a document. According to one interpretation, the document is valid and according to the other, it is void.

סְתָמָא מַאי – **What is** the law if the giver left it **unspecified** where the document should be written?

The Gemara records two opinions:

רָבִינָא אָמַר – **Ravina said:** לֹא חָיְישִׁינַן – **We are not concerned** that this might be considered a secret gift document. It is definitely a valid gift document. רַב אַשִׁי אָמַר – **Rav Ashi said:** חָיְישִׁינַן – **We are concerned** that it might be considered a secret gift document. Therefore, the status of the document is in doubt.[1] וְהִלְכְתָא חָיְישִׁינַן – **And the halachah** follows the opinion **that we are concerned** that such a secret gift document might be void.[2]

Mishnah כָּל חֲזָקָה שֶׁאֵין עִמָּהּ טַעֲנָה – **Any** ***chazakah***[3] **not accompanied by a claim** אֵינָהּ חֲזָקָה – **is not a** meaningful ***chazakah***; i.e. it does not entitle the occupant to keep the property.[4] כֵּיצַד – **How so?** אָמַר לוֹ – **If [the previous owner] said to [the occupant],** מָה אַתָּה עוֹשֶׂה בְּתוֹךְ שֶׁלִּי – **"What are you doing in my** property?" וְהוּא אָמַר לוֹ – **and he replied,** שֶׁלֹּא אָמַר לִי אָדָם דָּבָר מֵעוֹלָם – "I am here **because no one ever said anything to me,"**[5] אֵינָהּ חֲזָקָה – **[his *chazakah*] is not a** meaningful ***chazakah,*** and he must vacate the land.[6] If, however, the occupant replied: שֶׁמָּכַרְתָּ לִי – "I am here **because you sold [this land] to me,"** שֶׁנְּתַתָּהּ לִי בְּמַתָּנָה – or **"because you gave it to me as a gift,"** אָבִיךְ מְכָרָהּ לִי – or "because **your father sold it me,"** אָבִיךְ נְתָנָהּ לִי בְּמַתָּנָה – or **"your father gave it to me as a gift,"** הֲרֵי זוֹ חֲזָקָה – then **this is a** meaningful ***chazakah***, and the occupant keeps the property.[7] וְהַבָּא מִשּׁוּם יְרוּשָּׁה – **And one who comes into** a property **by way of inheritance** אֵינוֹ צָרִיךְ טַעֲנָה – **does not require a** supporting **claim.**[8]

Gemara The Gemara questions the necessity of teaching the Mishnah's opening ruling:

פְּשִׁיטָא – **This** law **is obvious!** If the occupant advances no claim of ownership, how can his occupancy demonstrate his right to it?

The Gemara responds:

מַהוּ דְּתֵימָא – **You might have said** had this law not been taught הַאי גַּבְרָא מִיזְבַּן זְבַנָּהּ לֵיהּ הַאי אַרְעָא – that perhaps **this man** [the occupant] **did** in fact **buy this property** from the challenger, וּשְׁטָרָא הֲוָה לֵיהּ וְאִירְכַּס – **and he** once **had a deed but it was lost,** וְהַאי דְּקָאָמַר הָכִי – **and the reason he** now **states this** other claim (that no one ever said anything to him) rather than declaring that he purchased the land, סָבַר – is because **he thinks** to himself, אִי אָמִינָא מִיזְבַּן זְבַנָּהּ לִי הַאי אַרְעָא – **"If I say that I purchased this land** from the challenger, אָמְרֵי לִי אַחְוֵי שְׁטָרָךְ – **they will say to me, 'Show us your deed,'** and I no longer have it!"[9] הִלְכָּךְ לֵימָא לֵיהּ אֲנַן – **Accordingly,** you might think that **we** [the court] **should say to [the occupant],** דִּלְמָא שְׁטָרָא הֲוָה לָךְ וְאִירְכַּס – **"Perhaps you had a deed and it was lost?"** כְּגוֹן זֶה: ,,פְּתַח־פִּיךָ לְאִלֵּם" הוּא – For in **such** an instance we should apply the principle of ***"Open your mouth on behalf of the mute."***[10] קָא מַשְׁמַע לָן – **[The Mishnah]** therefore **informs us** that it is not the court's place to suggest such a claim to the occupant.[11]

NOTES

1. According to Rav Ashi, we cannot conclusively determine whether such a document is valid and therefore preserve the status quo. We do not award the property to the recipient mentioned in the document. If the property was already awarded to the recipient (e.g. if the document's validity was not questioned until the property had been awarded to the recipient), however, we allow him to retain the property (*Rashbam*; cf. *Choshen Mishpat* 242:3 and *Rama* there).

2. Thus, when witnesses write a gift document, they must include a clause stating, "The giver charged us with writing the document publicly"; otherwise, the document's validity will be in doubt. *Rashbam* adds that when someone charges witnesses with writing a gift document, he presumably intends for them to write one that is valid under Rabbinic law. Thus, even if he never explicitly stipulated that the document be written publicly, the witnesses may assume this to have been his intent and they may include the above clause in the document.

3. The Mishnah speaks here not only of the three-year *chazakah* on real estate, but also of the immediate *chazakah* that can be established for a right in even a single day [of uncontested use], such as the right to lay beams on a neighbor's roof [see Gemara 6a] (*Rashbam*; see gloss in *Rashi* there ד"ה אחזיק).

4. In order for an occupant to retain a property based on his *chazakah,* he must advance an acceptable claim for his right to it. [A three-year *chazakah* does not *transfer* ownership of a property to the occupant; it merely serves to prove his claim of ownership.] Therefore, if the occupant claims that he acquired the property properly, his use of it for the time necessary to establish a *chazakah* discredits the previous owner's counter-claim. We assume that the previous owner would surely not have remained silent about the illegal use of his property for so long unless he had actually transferred it to the occupant (*Rashbam*). [However, if the occupant does not claim to have acquired the property legally, the *chazakah* itself can prove nothing.]

5. I.e. I do not know to whom this land belongs, but since [it was empty and] no one ever told me to leave it, I settled in it (*Rambam, Hil. To'ein VeNitan* 14:12). The Gemara will explain the necessity of stating the invalidity of such a claim.

6. Before he can reclaim it, however, the challenger must at least produce witnesses that the property once belonged to him (*Rambam, Hil. To'ein VeNitan* 14:12; *Choshen Mishpat* 146:9).

7. His uncontested occupancy supports the legitimacy of his claim (see note 4).

8. If the occupant claims he inherited the property from his father, and he proves that he used the land for three years following his father's death, he does not have to prove his father's title to the land. A son is not expected to be privy to his father's affairs. However, the Gemara below (41b) will state that he is required to produce witnesses that his father occupied the field for at least one day (*Rashbam*).

9. He is not aware of the law that once a person has used a property without challenge for three years, his *chazakah* stands in place of his deed (*Rashbam*). Being ignorant of the law, he is afraid that if he claims he bought the land and then fails to produce the deed, he will be branded a liar and be accused of stealing the land. He therefore thinks that it is better for him not to claim that he bought the land, but to claim instead that the owner's silence in the face of his prolonged use of it demonstrates that the owner yielded it to the user of the land (*Tosafos* דה אמרי לי).

10. *Proverbs* 31:8; i.e. speak up on behalf of someone who cannot do so for himself – either because he is physically disabled, or because he is legally disabled by his ignorance of the law or the circumstances of a case. [This verse serves as the basis for the court's advancing certain claims on behalf of orphans; see 23a.] This rule might be thought to apply in the case of one who advances no justification at all for his occupation of a property [since his response, taken at face value, seems unlikely and therefore quite possibly the product of ignorance]. Thus, perhaps it is the court's duty to question whether this is indeed the case.

11. Nevertheless, we may learn from this that if the occupant were to reverse his claim and assert that he bought the property and then lost the deed, he would be believed, and this would not be considered putting forth an entirely new claim (טוֹעֵן וְחוֹזֵר וְטוֹעֵן). [We learned above (31a) that though a litigant cannot repudiate his earlier claim and advance an entirely new claim, he can, according to the opinion of Ulla (which is the accepted view), explain his earlier claim in ways that modify its import. According to this view, if the occupant should later explain that he had actually bought the property and lost the deed, we would accept this revision, because these facts are consistent with his earlier reluctance to claim this openly.] It is only that the court cannot *suggest* such a claim to a defendant, but if he advances it himself, it is accepted (*Rashbam*). However, he must reverse himself before leaving the court, to preclude the possibility that the revision was suggested to him by someone else [as we learned in the Gemara on 31a] (*Nimukei Yosef*; *Tos. Rid*).

סתמא מאי רבינא אמר לא חיישינן רב אשי אמר חיישינן [א]והלכתא חיישינן: **מתני'** [א] [ב]כל חזקה שאין עמה טענה אינה חזקה כיצד אמר לו מה אתה עושה בתוך שלי והוא אמר לו שלא אמר לי אדם דבר מעולם אינה חזקה שמכרת לי שנתת לי במתנה אביך מכרה לי אביך נתנה לי במתנה הרי זו חזקה [ג]והבא משום ירושה אינו צריך טענה: **גמ'** פשיטא מהו דתימא האי גברא מיזבן זבנה ליה והאי ארעא ושטרא הוה ליה ואירכס והאי דקאמר הכי סבר אי אמינא מיזבן זבנה לי האי ארעא אמרי לי אחוי שטרך הלכך לימא ליה אנן דלמא שטרא הוה לך ואירכס [ג] כגון זה [א] פתח פיך לאלם הוא קמ"ל (ענ"ב סימן) [ד]רב ענן שקל בידקא בארעיה אזל (א) הדר גודא בארעיה דחבריה אתא לקמיה דרב נחמן א"ל זיל הדר והא אחזיקי לי אמר ליה כמאן כר' יהודה ור' ישמעאל דאמרי כל בפניו לאלתר הוי חזקה לית הלכתא כוותייהו א"ל והא אחיל דאתא וסייע בגודא בהדאי אמר ליה [ד]מחילה בטעות היא את גופך אי הוה ידעת (ג) לא עבדת כי היכי דאת לא הוה ידעת הוא נמי לא הוה ידע רב כהנא שקל בידקא בארעיה אזל הדר גודא בארעא דלא דידיה אתא

רש"י

סתמא מאי. משום דתרי לישני אמר רב יוסף לעיל ואיכא בינייהו סתמא חד פסל וחד מכשר הלכך קבעי הכא אמאי סמכינן אי אמר להן סתמא כתובו ולא אמר להו תיתבו בשוקא ובבריייתא ולא אמר להו נמי איטמרו מי הוי מתנתא טמירתא או לא. ויש מפרשים דאמודעא קאי דאוקימנא דלא הוי מתנתא טמירתא מודעא לחבירתה אבל סתמא מי הויא מודעא ולא נהירא כלל דלהאי לישנא דאמרי' סתמא פסולה ודאי לא הויא מודעא דהיינו טמירתא: **לא חיישינן.** דאינה טמירתא אלא כשרה: **חיישינן.** לטמירתא ולא מגבינן בה ואי מגבינן לא מהדרינן עובדא והיינו דלא קאמר רב אשי דלא מגבינן אלא חיישינן דספק הוא [ה]והיכא דקיימא ארעא תיקום: **והלכתא חיישינן.** דלא מגבינן בה והלכך צריך לכתוב בתוך השטר וכך אמר לנו כתבוה בשוקא וחתמוה בגלא ועל"ג דלא אמר אלא כתבוה לו סתם שטר מתנה כמו שתקנו חכמים קאמר: **מתני'** כל חזקה שאין עמה טענה אינה חזקה. בין בחזקת ג' שנים דקרקעות ובתים ואילנות בין בחזקת יום אחד כגון הנך דאמרינן לעיל (דף ו.) אחזיק להורדי כו' מיירי וקאמר דצריך לטעון מאיזה כח החזיק בה והלכך כיון דטוען טענתא מעליא שבדין ירד לקרקע זה ומתוך כך החזיק בה כשיעור חזקה שאמרו חכמים וזה שתק ולא מיחה הויא חזקה ואין המערער נאמן לומר לא על ידי ירד לקרקע שלי אלא בלא רשותי דאם כן למה הניחו להחזיק: **שלא אמר לי אדם דבר מעולם אינה חזקה.** בגמרא פריך פשיטא: **משום ירושה.** שאומר אכלתיה שני חזקה מכח ירושת אבי שהיה מוחזק בה ביום מותו: **אינו צריך טענה.** לומר היאך בא ליד אביו דאין אדם בקי בקרקעות אביו היאך באו לידו ומיהו ראיה בעדים בעי שראו את אביו הוחזק בה יום אחד והכי מפרש בגמרא: **גמ' פשיטא.** דכיון דאין לו טענה אינה חזקה: **מיזבן זבנה ליה.** האי ארעא מזה המערער לקחה ואבד שטרו: **אמרי לי אחוי שטרך.** שאינו בקי בדינין לידע שחזקה במקום שטר עומדת: **קמ"ל.** דאי טעין טענינן ליה ואי לא טעין אנו לא ילפינן ליה למיטען שמעינן מהכא דאי הוה טעין הכי מהמנינן ליה דכה"ג אינו קרוי חוזר וטוען דאין זה מכחיש טענות ראשונות: **שקל בידקא בארעיה.** שטף מים נכנס בשדהו ונטל את המחילות ולא נודע מקומן: **הדר גודא כו'.** עשה כותל חדש בינו לבין שכנו והרחיב קרקע שלו ועשה הכותל בשדה חבירו: **והא אחזיקי.** שבניתי כותל על פיו ובצואתו כדאמר לקמיה דאתא וסייע גודא בהדאי וכמאן דאמר לי חזוק וקני דמי וכיון שעל פיו עשיתי וגם החזקתי יום או יומים שהיה כותל שלי בקרקע שלו והוא ידע ולא מיחה אלא שתק הרי חזקתי חזקה שיש עמה טענה ואידך הוה טעין לא נתתיה ושני חזקה לא החזיק: **א"ל כמאן.** טענת והא אחזיקי דסבירא לך חזקת יום אחד הויא חזקה היכא דידע מערער ולא מיחה: **כר"י.** דמתני' דתלי טעם דג' שנים כדי שילך לאספמיא שנה כו' הא אם קרוב בתוך מהלך יום שיוכל לידע מיד כשידע ולא ימחה תהיה חזקה וכר' ישמעאל בר' יוסי נמי בשלהי פרקין (דף נו:) ת"ר מעשה באדם אחד שפתח חלונותיו לחצר השותפין בא לפני ר' ישמעאל א"ל החזקת משום דס"ל בפניו לאלתר הויא חזקה: **אין הלכה כו'.** אלא כרבנן דאמרי דלא חזקה ג' שנים מיום ליום שנים של"ש חזקה יום אחד: **והא אחיל כו'.** (ג) והא יש לי טענה ולאית שהקנה לי קרקע דיש לי עדים שראו שהיה מסייע לי לבנות הכותל וכמאן דאמר לך חזוק וקני דמי: **מחילה בטעות היא.** שלא היה יודע שאתה בונה בתוך שלו: **מי הוה עבדת.** בתמי' אלא גם אתה טעית וכסבור היית שאתה בונה בתוך שלך:

תוספות

שלא אמר לי אדם דבר מעולם. והוא הדין דאפי' אם אמר זבינתיה מפלוני דזבנה מינך דלא הויא חזקה עד שיאמר אתה מכרת לי דלכדקתני סיפא אלא הא עדיפא ליה למינקט שלא אמר לי אדם דבר מעולם לאשמועי' דלא הוי פתח פיך לאלם כדאמר בגמ': **אמרי** לי אחוי (לי) שטרך. וכשלא אוכל להראות שטרי שהפסדתיו יאמרו שגזלתיה אבל כשאומר לא אמר לי אדם [דבר] מעולם לא יאמרו שגזלתיה אלא ראיתי שלא מיחו בידי והחזקתי בה ונמלא שמחל לי: **והא** אחזיקי לי. פירש הקונטרס בניתי כותל על פיו והוא סייע לי וכיון שבצואתו (ד) עשה הוי חזקה שיש עמה טענה וקשה דמדקאמר בתר הכי והא אחיל משמע דעד השתא לא הוה מחזיק בה מטעם מחילה ועוד דלאלתר הוה ליה לרב נחמן למימר מחילה בטעות הואי ונראה לפרש דרב ענן טעין שלקח ממנו ולא הי' לו עדים שלקחה והיה רוצה להיות נאמן מתורת חזקה וכי א"ל רב נחמן דלאו חזקה היא השיב לו רב ענן והא אחיל דאע"פ שאינו נאמן לומר לקחתיה תהא שלי מטעם מחילה דסייע בגודא בהדאי והיה לו עדים או היה מודה בסיועו ואין הסוגיא מוכחת כן:

שלא אמר לי אדם דבר מעולם פשיטא. קשה למהר"ם דמאי פריך פשיטא הא לעיל (דף כט:) פריך גמרא אלא מעתה חזקה שאין עמה טענה כו' ופירש שם בתוספות פירוש (ה) א' דאפי' אמר [שלא אמר] לי אדם דבר מעולם פריך ונראה לומר דמכח סיפא דמשמע דאפי' מפלוני דזבנה מינך זבינתה לא הויא חזקה פריך פשיטא ונראה כי זה דוחק דמנא ליה למיפרך ארישא טפי מאסיפא דהא מרישא איכא למידק איפכא וליפרוך טפי מסיפא לרישא ונראה לי דמקשה לא מסיק אדעתיה דנטעון ליה אנן ולהכי פריך פשיטא דטענה גרידא אינה מועלת דאינה טענה ומשני דס"ד דנטעון ליה אנן דכיון דלא מיחה שלש שנים ודאי מכר לו או מחל ועוד יש לומר דלרבנן דרבי ישמעאל דלא ילפי משור (ו) פריך פשיטא אבל קשה דבמתניתין לא הוזכרו רבנן ומתני' כר' ישמעאל ונראה דפריך אחזקה דיום אחד דמתני' נמי איירי בה מדקתני כל חזקה כדפ"ה:

כמאן כר"י. קשה לרשב"א דהאמר רב ענן לעיל (דף לח:) לדידי מפרשא לי מיניה דמר שמואל מחאה בפני עדים שאין יכולין לומר לו כו' משמע דלא בעי (ז) בפניו מחאה ° והיינו דלא כר"י ושמא סבר כוותיה בחדא ופליג עליה בחדא: **אמר** ליה מחילה בטעות הואי. וקשה דבפ' איזהו נשך (ב"מ דף סו: ושם ד"ה התם) אמר רב נחמן השתא דאמור רבנן אסמכתא לא קני הדרא ארעא והדרי פירי למימרא דסבר רב נחמן מחילה בטעות לא הויא מחילה והא איתמר המוכר פירות דקל לחבירו כו' ואמר רב נחמן ומודינא דאי שמיט ואכיל לא מפקינן מיניה ומשני התם זביני והכא הלואה ופירש הקונטרס הכא הלואה (ח) ומיחזי כרבית שמתחלה בהלואה באו לידו וכרבית קצוצה דמו ואין אבק רבית אלא במכר כגון לקח ממנו פירות דריש מתניתין דהתם משמע דבכ"מ לרב נחמן מחילה בטעות הויא מחילה ומיהו בלאו הכי קשה על פירושו דהא אמר רבינא התם בריש פירקא (דף סג.) דמשכנתא בלא נכייתא לדידיה דליתיה אין מחזירין ממלוה לגוה דלא חשיב רבית קצוצה ומסתמא דלא פליג עליה רב נחמן ונראה לרבינו תם דה"פ דבכ"מ סבר רב נחמן דלא הויא מחילה מחילה כדאמר הכא ובריש המפקיד (ב"מ דף לה.) קאמר נמי רב נחמן התם שומא בטעות הוא וכספ"ק דגיטין (דף יד.) נמי אמר דקנין בטעות חוזר אלא היינו טעמא דרב נחמן דהתם זביני ולא הויא מחילה בטעות שאפי' היה המוכר יודע שיוכל לחזור לא היה חוזר דניחא ליה דליקו בהימנותיה וגמר ומקני אבל הכא הויא הלואה והלוה אינו מקני ליה אלא בתורת מכר והמכר אינו כלום דאסמכתא היא ולא גמר ומקני וכיון דהדרא ארעא הדרי נמי פירי אבל אם היה נותן בתורת רבית היה קונה דאבק רבית אין יוצא בדיינים ורבא דהוה בעי לאוקמי אונאה לא היה יודע זה הפירוש שאם היה יודע לא היה מקשה כלום מאונאה דהכא לא הויא מחילה בטעות כדפרי' גמר ומקני ור"נ היה משיב מאיילונית לפי סברת רבא כלומר אדמותבת לי מאונאה תסייען מאיילונית אלא על כרחך צריך אתה לחלק כדפרישית:

אתא

עין משפט נר מצוה

קו א מיי' פ"ה מהלכות זכיה הלכה כ סמג עשין פב טוש"ע ח"מ סי' רמב סעיף ג:

קז ב מיי' פי"ד מהל' טוען הל' יג סמג עשין לה טוש"ע ח"מ סי' קמו סעיף ט:

קח ג מיי' שם הל' יג טוש"ע שם סעי' י:

קט ד טוש"ע ח"מ סי' קמב סעי' ב:

תורה אור השלם

א) פְּתַח פִּיךָ לְאִלֵּם אֶל דִּין כָּל בְּנֵי חֲלוֹף: [משלי לא, ח]

רבינו גרשום

לראשון: **איבעיא להו.** להיכא דאמר לעדים זילו **סתם** כתיבו ליה חיישינן דלהוי מתנה טמירתא אי לא חיישינן: **פיסקא כל חזקה שאין עמה** למחזיק **טענה** אחרת של זכותו **אינה חזקה:** **והבא מחמת ירושה.** מי שהחזיק ג' שנים וערער אחד ואמר לו מה אתה עושה בשלי שירשתיה מאבי ואמר זה מהיכן באת לאביך אין צריך לזה לטעון היכן לקחה אביו או שום טענה אחרת: **פשיטא.** דהיכא דאין שום טענה מעליא דאינה חזקה. איצטרכין **דמהו דתימא** אם לא טעין אמרינן משום הכי לא טעין דהאי מיזבן הוא **דזבנה ליה** כו' קמ"ל דלא טענינן בשבילו דכיון דאיהו לא טעין אנן לא טענינן ליה: **שקל בדקא בארעיה.** שבא שטף ושטף לכותל ארעיה **ואהדר גודא בארעא דחבריה** שקבע כתליו בקרקע חבירו: **א"ל.** לרב ענן: **זיל אהדר** לו קרקעו וקבע מחיצתך בתוך שלך למקום שהיה מתחלה: **אמר ליה רב ענן והא אחזיקי לי.** שקבעתי בקרקע שלו בפניו ולא מיחה לי: **אמר ליה כמאן.** אמרת דבפניו הוי חזקה לאלתר: **כר' יהודה.** דקתני במתני' לא אמרו ג' שנים אלא שיהא באספמיא כו' הא אם מחזיק **בפניו** כו' **לאלתר הויא חזקה** (א"ל) **וכר' ישמעאל** דקתני בסיומא דהאי פירקין ת"ר מעשה באדם אחד שפתח חלונותיו לחצר השותפין בא לפני ר' ישמעאל ואמר לו החזקת בני החזקת משום דסבירא ליה **לאלתר בפניו הוה חזקה:** **אמר ליה מחילה בטעות הואי.** דאיהו לא ידע דעבדת בתוך שלו דאתה בונה כותלך כי היית בונה מדעתך בתוך שלו אלא **כי היכי דאת לא ידעת** משום דשטף המים סימני המיצר איהו נמי **לא הוי ידע** דעבדת בתוך שלו ואמטו להכי סייע לך לבנות וכשידע לא מחל:

מסורת הש"ס

א) [לעיל כח:], ב) [לעיל כב.], ג) [כתובות לו. גיטין לז:], ד) [גירסת הערוך בערך בדק ג' רב חנן ומיושב בזה קושית הרשב"א בתוס' ד"ה כמאן]:

הגהות הב"ח

(א) גמ' אזל אהדר גודא כו' זיל אהדר וכו' ור' ישמעאל בר' יוסי דאמרי כל בפניו: (ב) שם אי הוה ידעת מי הוה עבדת: (ג) רשב"ם ד"ה והא אחיל כו' והלא יש לי וכו' דאמר לי לך חזק: (ד) תוס' ד"ה והא וכו' שבצואתו עשיתי הוי חזקה: (ה) ד"ה שלא וכו' ופירש שם בתוספות פי' ראשון דאפי' לא אמר שלא אמר לי אדם דבר מעולם פריך ונראה לי דמכח סיפא דמשמע דאפי' אם אמר מפלוני דזבנה מינך וכו' ונראה דזה דוחק וכו' איכא למידק איפכא ולפרוך אסיפא מרישא ונראה לי דמקשה לא אסיק אדעתיה דנטעונן ליה אנן ולהכי פריך פשיטא דחזקה גרידא אינה מועלת בלא טענה ומשני דסלקא דעתך דנטעונן ליה אנן ולעיל פריך חזקה שאין עמה טענה תיהוי חזקה היינו דנטעונן ליה אנן דכיון דלא מיחה: (ו) באד משור המועד פריך פשיטא כצ"ל ונ"ב דיבור זה הוא גליון: (ז) ד"ה כמאן וכו' דלא בעי מחאה בפניו והיינו: (ח) ד"ה אמר וכו' ופי' הקונטרס הכא הלואה דמיחזי כרבית וכו' ומיחזי כרבית נמחק:

גליון הש"ס

רשב"ם ד"ה חיישינן כו' והיכא דקיימא ארעא תיקום. עיין לעיל דף לב ע"ב תוס' ד"ה והלכתא: תוס' ד"ה כמאן כו' והיינו דלא כר"י. עיין לקמן דף נו ע"א תוס' ד"ה אמרינן לעיל דגם ר"י מלי סבר דמחאה שלא בפניו הוי מחאה דלא בעינן טובא קמ"ל וביותר הא ר"י אמר כן לעיל ובפירוש אמר כאן לרב ענן כמאן כר"י וצ"ע:

ליקוטי רש"י

שאין עמה טענה. מפרש במתני' לקמן (מא.) אמר לו מה אתה עושה בתוך שלי אמר לו שלא אמר לי אדם דבר מעולם ולא אמר לו אתה מכרת לי [לעיל כח:]. וכלל חזקות מיירי בין שלש שנים ל"ש חזקת יום אחד [לעיל ו.]. **אינו צריך טענה.** אין צריך לומר אתה מכרת לאבי אלא ראיתי לאבי שהחזיק בה ואתה ערער אדם עליו [לעיל כג.]

The Gemara relates an incident in which possession of a property was invalidated because its supporting claim was deemed inadequate:

(ענ״ב סִימָן) – (*Anav*, a mnemonic)[12]

רַב עָנָן שְׁקַל בִּידְקָא בְּאַרְעֵיהּ – **A flood swept through Rav Anan's land,** washing away the boundary fences. אֲזַל הֲדַר גּוּדָא בְּאַרְעֵיהּ דְּחַבְרֵיהּ – **[Rav Anan] went** to repair the damage, and **he** inadvertently **replaced the fence inside his neighbor's land.**[13] Subsequently, the neighbor realized the error and demanded that the fence be moved back to its original position between the two properties. אָתָא לְקַמֵּיהּ דְּרַב נַחְמָן – **[Rav Anan] came before Rav Nachman** for judgment. אָמַר לֵיהּ – **[Rav Nachman] said to [Rav Anan]:** זִיל הֲדַר – **Go** and **return** the fence to its former position.

Rav Anan questioned the ruling:

וְהָא אַחֲזִיקִי לִי – **But I have established a *chazakah*** on the land, inasmuch as my neighbor was aware that I had built the fence there and he did not protest.[14] – ? –

Rav Nachman replied:

אָמַר לֵיהּ – **[Rav Nachman] said to [Rav Anan]:** כְּמַאן – **According to whose** view do you consider yourself to have established a *chazakah*? כְּר׳ יְהוּדָה וְר׳ יִשְׁמָעֵאל – Seemingly, **according to** the view of **R' Yehudah and R' Yishmael,** דְּאָמְרֵי כָּל בְּפָנָיו לְאַלְתַּר הָוֵי חֲזָקָה – **who say that any** occupation of property that takes place **in the presence of [the previous owner]** without his protest **establishes a *chazakah* immediately.**[15] On this basis you wish to claim a *chazakah* after only one day of silence. לֵית הִלְכְתָא כְּוָותַיְיהוּ – But **the halachah is not in accordance with their** view![16]

Rav Anan persisted:

אָמַר לֵיהּ – **[Rav Anan] replied to [Rav Nachman]:** וְהָא אַחִיל – **But [the neighbor] relinquished** his right to the annexed land, דְּאָתָא וְסַיֵּיע בְּגוּדָא בַּהֲדַאי – **for he came and assisted me in** rebuilding **the fence.** This was tantamount to offering me the land and telling me to acquire it![17]

This claim was rejected as well:

אָמַר לֵיהּ – **[Rav Nachman] replied to [Rav Anan]:** מְחִילָה בְּטָעוּת הִיא – **The relinquishment was made in error,** and proves nothing; אַתְּ גּוּפָךְ אִי הֲוָה יָדְעַתְּ לָא עָבְדַתְּ – for **you yourself, had you known** that the fence was placed improperly, **would not have done** what you did, to build your fence on his land. כִּי הֵיכִי דְּאַתְּ לָא הֲוָה יָדְעַתְּ – **Just as you did not realize** the error, הוּא נַמִּי לָא הֲוָה יָדַע – so too **[your neighbor] did not realize** it. Thus, his assistance does not constitute a relinquishment of any right to the land, and the fence must be restored to its original position.

The Gemara records a similar incident:

רַב כַּהֲנָא שְׁקַל בִּידְקָא בְּאַרְעֵיהּ – **A flood swept through Rav Kahana's land,** destroying the boundary fences. אֲזַל הֲדַר גּוּדָא בְּאַרְעָא דְּלָא דִּידֵיהּ – **[Rav Kahana] went** and inadvertently **replaced the fence on land that was not his.** His neighbor sued to have the land returned.

NOTES

12. This mnemonic refers to the chief figures in the following two incidents in the Gemara:
ע = עָנָן, *Anan*
נ = כַּהֲנָא, *Kahana*
ב = בִּידְקָא, *Flood*

13. The flood had obliterated all traces of the original boundary, leaving no sign as to where the fence had originally been. Consequently, when building a new fence, Rav Anan inadvertently placed it inside his neighbor's property instead of on the boundary, thereby enlarging his field at the expense of his neighbor (*Rashbam*).

14. The neighbor assisted in rebuilding the fence, as the Gemara will state below. Thus, Rav Anan claimed that his neighbor's agreement to Rav Anan's placement of the fence inside his land should constitute an agreement to allow Rav Anan to keep the portion of land which he had inadvertently annexed. [Rav Anan's construction of the fence would then constitute a *kinyan chazakah* (act of acquisition).] The neighbor's subsequent silence for a day or two before protesting should thus constitute a *chazakah*. (The Gemara will discuss why such a *chazakah* should not take three years to establish.) Thus, Rav Anan supported his *chazakah* with a claim of acquisition (*Rashbam*).

15. R' Yehudah's position regarding *chazakah* has been explained above (see 38a note 20 and 39a note 6). A similar position is held by R' Yishmael in the Gemara below (59b). Both of these Sages hold that *chazakah* is not linked to the loss of a deed. Rather, if it can be proven that the owner was aware of the occupant's use of his property and did not protest, *chazakah* can be established immediately. Rav Anan's claim that the neighbor's silence should confer an immediate *chazakah* would seem to accord with the view of these Sages.

16. Rather, the halachah follows the opinion of the Sages, who require three years of continuous use to establish a *chazakah* on land. Thus, Rav Anan's claim is invalid.

17. Rav Anan offered to produce witnesses to the fact that his neighbor had helped him build the fence. Thus, although Rav Anan agreed that a *chazakah* could not be established, he claimed that he did not need it since he could produce witnesses that he acquired the property from his neighbor (*Rashbam*).

סתמא מאי רבינא אמר לא חיישינן רב אשי אמר חיישינן א והלכתא חיישינן: מתני' ב) ב כל חזקה שאין עמה טענה אינה חזקה כיצד אמר לו מה אתה עושה בתוך שלי והוא אמר לו שלא אמר לי אדם דבר מעולם אינה חזקה שמכרת לי שנתת לי במתנה אביך מכרה לי אביך נתנה לי במתנה הרי זו חזקה ג והבא משום ירושה אינו צריך טענה: גמ' פשיטא מהו דתימא האי גברא מיזבן זבנה ליה האי ארעא ושטרא הוה ליה ואירכס והאי דקאמר הכי סבר אי אמינא מיזבן זבנה לי האי ארעא אמרי לי אחוי שטרך הלכך לימא ליה אנן דלמא שטרא הוה לך ואירכס ג) כגון זה א) פתח פיך לאלם הוא קמ"ל (ענ"ב סימן) ד) רב ענן שקל בידקא בארעיה אזל (א) הדר גודא בארעיה דחבריה אתא לקמיה דרב נחמן א"ל זיל הדר והא אחזיקי לי אמר ליה כמאן כר' יהודה ור' ישמעאל דאמרי כל בפניו לאלתר הוי חזקה לית הלכתא כוותייהו א"ל והא אחיל דאתא וסייע בגודא בהדאי אמר ליה ד מחילה בטעות היא את גופך אי הוה ידעת (ב) לא עבדת כי היכי דאת לא הוה ידעת הוא נמי לא הוה ידע רב כהנא שקל בידקא בארעיה אזל הדר גודא בארעא דלא דידיה אתא

רש"י

סתמא מאי. משום דתרי לישני אמר רב יוסף לעיל ואיכא בינייהו סתמא חד פסל וחד מכשר הלכך קבעי הכא אמאי סמכינן אי אמר להן סתמא כתובו ולא אמר להו תיתבו בשוקא ובברייתא ולא אמר להו נמי איטמרו מי הוי מתנתא טמירתא או לא. ויש מפרשין למודעא קאי דלוקימנה דלא הויא מתנתא טמירתא מודעא לחבירתה אבל סתמא מי הויא מודעא ולא נסירה כלל דלההוא לישנא דאמרי' סתמא פסולה ודאי לא הויא מודעא דהיינו טמירתא: לא חיישינן. דליהוי טמירתא אלא כשרה: חיישינן. לטמירתא ולא מגבינן בה ואי מגבינן לא מהדרינן עובדא והיינו דלא קאמר רב אשי דלא מגבינן אלא חיישינן דספק הוא (ב) והיכא דקיימא ארעא תיקום: והלכתא חיישינן. דלא מגבינן בה והלכך צריך לכתוב בתוך השטר וקא אמר לנו כתובו בשוקא ותיתבו בברא ואע"ג דלא אמר אלא כתובו לו סתם שטר מתנה כמו שתקנו חכמים קאמר: מתני' כל חזקה שאין עמה טענה אינה חזקה. בין בחזקת ג' שנים לקרקעות ובתים ואילנות בין בחזקת יום אחד כגון הנך דאמרינן לעיל (דף ו.) אחזיק להורדי כו' מיירי וקאמר דצריך לטעון מאיזה כח החזיק בה והלכך כיון דטוען טענתא מעליא שבדין ירד לקרקע זה ומתוך כך החזיק בה כשיעור חזקה שאמרו חכמים וזה שתק ולא מיחה הויא חזקה ואין המערער נאמן לומר לא על ידי ירד לקרקע שלי אלא בלא רשותי דאם כן למה הניחו להחזיק: שלא אמר לי אדם דבר מעולם אינה חזקה. בגמרא פריך פשיטא: משום ירושה. שאומר אבותיי שני חזקה מכח ירושת אבי שהיה מוחזק בה ביום מותו: אינו צריך טענה. לומר היאך בא ליד אביו דאין אדם בקי בקרקעות אביו היאך באו לידו ומיהו ראיה בעדים בעי שראו את אביו הוחזק בה יום אחד והכי מפרש בגמרא: גמ' פשיטא. כיון דאין לו טענה אינה חזקה: מיזבן זבנה ליה. האי ארעא מזה המערער לקחה ואבד שטרו: אמרי לי אחוי שטרך. שאינו בקי בדינין לידע שחזקה במקום שטר עומדת: קמ"ל. דאי טעין טענינן ליה ואי לא טעין אנו לא ילפינן ליה למיטען שמעינן מהכא דאי הוה טעין הכי מהמנינן ליה דהא"ג אינו קרוי חוזר וטוען דאין זה מכחיש טענות ראשונות: שקל בידקא בארעיה. שטף מים נכנס בשדהו ונטל את המחיצות ולא נודע מקומן: הדר גודא כו'. עשה כותל חדש ביני שכנו והרחיב קרקע שלו ועשה הכותל בשדה חבירו: והא אחזקי. שבניתי כותל על פיו ובעזותו כלומר לקמיה דאתא וסייע גודא בהדאי וכמאן דאמר לי חזוק וקני דמי וכיון שעל פיו עשיתי וגם החזקתי יום או יומים שהיה כותל שלי בקרקע שלו והוא ידע ולא מיחה אלא שתק הרי חזקתי חזקה שיש עמה טענה והיאך הוה טעין לא נתתיה ושני חזקה לא החזיק: א"ל כמאן. טענת והא אחזיקי דסבירא לך חזקת יום אחד הויא חזקה היכא דידע מערער ולא מיחה: כר"י. דמתני' דלתי טעם דג' שנים כדי שיהא באספמיא שנה כו' הא אם קרוב בתוך מהלך יום שיוכל לידע מיד כשידע ולא ימחה תהיה חזקה וכר' ישמעאל בר' יוסי נמי בשלהי פרקין (דף נט:) ת"ר מעשה באדם אחד שפתח חלונותיו לחצר השותפין בא לפני ר' ישמעאל א"ל החזקת משום דס"ל בפניו לאלתר הויא חזקה: אין הלכה כו'. אלא כרבנן דאמרי דכל דבר חזקה ג' שנים מיום ליום בעינן: והא אחיל כו'. (ג) והא יש לי טענה ודאית שהקנה לי קרקע דיש לי עדים שראו שהיה מסייע לי לבנות הכותל וכמאן דאמר לך חזק וקני דמי: מחילה בטעות היא. שלא היה יודע שאתה בונה בתוך שלו: מי הוה עבדת. בתמי' אלא גם אתה טעית וכסבור היית שאתה בונה בתוך שלך:

חד

תוספות

שלא אמר לי אדם דבר מעולם. והוא הדין דאפי' אם אמר זבינתיה מפלוני דזבנה מינך דלא הויא חזקה עד שיאמר אתה מכרת לי כדקתני סיפא אלא הא עדיפא ליה למינקט שלא אמר לי אדם דבר מעולם לאשמועי' דלא הוי פתח פיך לאלם כדאמר בגמ':

אמרי לי אחוי (ל') שטרך. וכשלא אוכל להראות שטרי שהפסדתיו יאמרו שגזלתיה אבל כשאומר לא אמר לי אדם [דבר] מעולם לא יאמרו שגזלתיה אלא ראיתי שלא מיחו בידי והחזקתי בה ונמצא שמחל לי:

והא אחזקי לי. פירש הקונטרס בניתי כותל על פיו והוא סייע לי וכיון שבמלותו (ד) עשה הוי חזקה שיש עמה טענה וקשה דמדקאמר בתר הכי והא אחיל משמע דעד השתא לא הוה מחזיק בה מטעם מחילה ועוד דלאלתר הוה ליה לרב נחמן למימר מחילה בטעות הואי ונראה לפרש דרב ענן הוה טעין שלקח ממנו ולא הי' לו עדים שלקחה והיה רוצה להיות נאמן מתורת חזקה וכי א"ל רב נחמן דלאו חזקה היא השיב לו רב ענן והא אחיל לפע"פ שאינו נאמן לומר לקחתיה תהא שלי מטעם מחילה דסייע בגודא בהדאי והיה לו עדים או היה מודה בסיועו ואין הסוגיא מוכחת כן:

שלא אמר לי אדם דבר מעולם פשיטא. קשה למהר"ס דמאי פריך פשיטא הא לעיל (דף כח:) פריך גמרא אלא מעתה חזקה שאין עמה טענה כו' ופירש שם בתוספות פירוש (ה) א' דלפי' אמר [שלא אמר] לי אדם דבר מעולם פריך ונראה לומר דמכח סיפא דמשמע דלפי' אם אמר מפלוני דזבנה מינך לא הויא חזקה פריך פשיטא ונראה כי זה דוחק דמנא ליה למיפרך ארישא טפי מאסיפא דהא מרישא איכא למידק איפכא וליפרוך טפי מסיפא לרישא ונראה לי דמקשה לא מסיק אדעתיה דנטעון ליה אנן ולהכי פריך פשיטא דטענה גרידא אינה מועלת לאינה טענה ומשני דס"ד דנטעון ליה אנן דכיון דלא מיחה שלש שנים ודאי מכר לו או מחל ועוד יש לומר דלרבנן דרבי ישמעאל דלא לפי מסור (ו) פריך פשיטא אבל קשה דבמתניתין לא הוזכרו רבנן ומתני' כר' ישמעאל ונראה דפריך אחזקה דיום אחד דמתני' נמי איירי בה מדקתני כל חזקה כדפי"ה:

כמאן כר"י. קשה לרשב"א דהאמר רב ענן לעיל (דף לח:) לדידי מפרשא לי מיניה דמר שמואל מחאה בפני עדים שאין יכולין לומר לו כו' משמע דלא בעי (ז) בפניו מחאה * והיינו דלא כר"י ושמא סבר כוותיה בחדא ופליג עליה בחדא: אמר ליה מחילה בטעות הואי. וקשה דבפ' איזהו נשך (ב"מ דף סו: ושם ד"ה התם) אמר רב נחמן השתא דאמור רבנן אסמכתא לא קני הדרא ארעא והדרי פירי למימרא דסבר רב נחמן מחילה בטעות לא הויא מחילה והא איתמר המוכר פירות דקל לחבירו כו' ואמר רב נחמן ומודינא דאי שמיט ואכיל לא מפקינן מיניה ומשני התם זביני והכא הלואה ופירש הקונטרס הכא הלואה (ח) ומיחזי כרבית שמתחלה בהלואה באו לידו וכרבית קצוצה דמו ואין אבק רבית אלא במכר כגון לקח ממנו פירות דריש מתניתין דהתם משמע דבכ"מ לרב נחמן מחילה בטעות הויא מחילה בר מהתם בהלואה דמיחזי כרבית והכא סבר רב נחמן דלא הויא מחילה ומיהו בלאו הכי קשה על פירושו דהא אמר רבינא התם בריש פירקא (דף סג.) דמשכנתא בלא נכייתא בדינינו אין מחזירין ממלוה ללוה דלא חשיב רבית קצוצה ומסתמא דלא פליג עליה רב נחמן ונראה לרבינו תם דה"פ דבכ"מ סבר רב נחמן דלא הויא מחילה כדאמר הכא ובריש המפקיד (ב"מ דף לה.) קאמר נמי רב נחמן התם שומא בטעות הוא ובספ"ק דגיטין (דף יד.) נמי אמר דקנין בטעות חוזר אלא היינו טעמא דרב נחמן דהתם זביני ולא הויא מחילה בטעות שאפי' היה המוכר יודע שיוכל לחזור לא היה חוזר דניחא ליה דליקו בהימנותיה וגמר ומקני אבל הכא הויא הלואה והלוה אינו מקני ליה אלא בתורת מכר והמכר אינו כלום דאסמכתא היא ולא גמר ומקני וכיון דהדרא ארעא הדרי נמי פירי אבל אם היה נותן בתורת רבית היה קונה דאבק רבית אין יוצא בדיינים ורבא דהוה בעי לאותובי אונאה לא היה יודע זה הפירוש שאם היה יודע לא היה מקשה כלום מאונאה דהכא לא הויא מחילה בטעות כדפרי' גמר ומקני ור"נ היה משיב מאיילונית לפי סברא רבא כלומר אדמותבת לי מאונאה תסייען מאיילונית אלא על כרחך צריך אתה לחלק כדפרישית:

אתא

מסורת הש"ס

א) [לעיל כח:], ב) [לעיל כב.], ג) [כתובות לו. גיטין לז:], ד) [גירסת הערוך בערך בדק ג' רב חנן ומיושב בזה קושית הרשב"א בתוס' ד"ה כמאן]:

הגהות הב"ח

(א) גמ' אזל אהדר גודא וכו' זיל אהדר וכו' ור' ישמעאל בר' יוסי דאמרי כל בפניו: (ב) שם אי הוה ידעת מי הוה עבדת: (ג) רשב"ם ד"ה והא אחיל כו' והלא יש לי וכו' דאמר לי לך חזק: (ד) תוס' ד"ה והא וכו' שבמלותו עשיתי הוי חזקה: (ה) ד"ה שלא וכו' ופירש שם בתוספות פי' ראשון דלפי' לא אמר שלא אמר לי אדם דבר מעולם פריך ונראה לי דמכח סיפא דמשמע דלפי' אם אמר מפלוני דזבנה מינך וכו' ונראה דזה דוחק וכו' איכא למידק איפכא ולפרוך טפי מרישא לסיפא ונראה לי דמקשה לא אסיק אדעתיה דנטעון ליה אנן ולהכי פריך פשיטא דחזקה גרידא אינה מועלת בלא טענה ומשני דסלקא דעתך דנטעון ליה אנן ולעיל פריך חזקה שאין עמה טענה מיהו חזקה היינו דנטעון ליה אנן דכיון שלא מיחה: (ו) בא"ד משור המועד פריך פשיטא כצ"ל וג"ב דיבור זה הוא גליון: (ז) ד"ה כמאן וכו' דלא בעי מחאה בפניו והיינו: (ח) ד"ה אמר וכו' ופי' הקונטרס הכא הלואה שמתחלה כצ"ל ותיבות ומיחזי כרבית נמחק:

גליון הש"ס

רשב"ם ד"ה חיישינן כו' והיכא דקיימא ארעא תיקום. עיין לעיל דף לב ע"ב תוס' ד"ה והלכתא: תוס' ד"ה כמאן כו' והיינו דלא כר"י. קשה לי הא אמרינן לעיל דגם ר"י מלי סבר דמחאה שלב"פ הוי מחאה אלא דעלה טובה קמ"ל וביותר הא ר"נ אמר כן לעיל ושפיר אמר כאן לרב ענן כמאן כר"י וצ"ע:

ליקוטי רש"י

שאין עמה טענה. מפרש במתני' לקמן (מא.) אמר לו מה אתה עושה בתוך שלי אמר לו שלא אמר לי אדם דבר מעולם ולא אמר לו אתה מכרת לי [לעיל כח:]. וככל חזקות מיירי לא שנא חזקת שלש שנים לא שנא חזקת יום אחד [לעיל ו.]. אינו צריך טענה. אינו צריך לומר אתה מכרת לאבי אלא ראיתי לאבי שהחזיק בה ולא ערער אדם עליו [לעיל כג.].

עין משפט נר מצוה

קו א מיי' פ"ה מהלכות זכייה הלכה ב סמג עשין פב טוש"ע ח"מ סי' רמב סעיף ג:

קז ב מיי' פי"ד מהל' טוען הל' יב סמג עשין לה טוש"ע ח"מ סי' קמו סעיף ט:

קח ג מיי' שם הל' יג טוש"ע שם סעי' י:

קט ד טוש"ע ח"מ סי' קמב סעי' ג:

תורה אור השלם

א) פְּתַח פִּיךָ לְאִלֵּם אֶל דִּין כָּל בְּנֵי חֲלוֹף: [משלי לא, ח]

רבינו גרשום

לראשון: איבעיא להו. להיכא דאמר לעדים זילו סתם כתיבו ליה חיישינן דלהוי מתנה טמירתא אי לא חיישינן: פיסקא כל חזקה שאין עמה למחזיק טענה אחרת של זכותו אינה חזקה: והבא מחמת ירושה. מי שהחזיק ג' שנים וערער אחד ואמר לו מה אתה עושה בשלי שירשתיה מאבי ואמר זה מהיכן באת לאביך אין צריך לזה לטעון היכן לקחה אביו או שום טענה אחרת: פשיטא. דהיכא דאין עמה טענה מעליא דאינה חזקה. איצטרכין דמהו דתימא אם לא טעין אמרינן משום הכי לא טעין דהאי מיזבן הוא דזבנה ליה כו' קמ"ל דלא טענינן בשבילו דכיון דאיהו לא טעין אנן לא טענינן ליה: שקל בדקא בארעיה. שבא שטף מים ושטף לכותלה ארעיה ואהדר גודא בארעא דחבריה שקבע כתליו בקרקע חבירו: א"ל. לרב ענן: זיל אהדר לו קרקעו וקבע מחיצתך בתוך שלך למקום שהיה מתחלה: אמר ליה רב ענן והא אחזיקי לי. שקבעתי בקרקע שלו בפניו ולא מיחה לי: אמר ליה כמאן. אמרת דבפניו הוי חזקה לאלתר: כר' יהודה. דקתני במתני' לא אמרו ג' שנים אלא שיהא באספמיא כו' הא אם מחזיק בפניו ולא מיחה לאלתר הויא חזקה (א"ל) וכר' ישמעאל דקתני בסיומא דהאי פירקין ת"ר מעשה באדם אחד שפתח חלונותיו לחצר השותפין בא לפני ר' ישמעאל ואמר לו החזקת בני החזקת משום דסבירא ליה לאלתר בפניו הוה חזקה: אמר ליה מחילה בטעות הואי. דאיהו לא ידע דעבדת בתוך שלו דאת גופך אי הוה ידעת דבתוך שלו אתה בונה כותלך מי היית בונה מדעתך בתוך שלו אלא כי היכי דאת לא ידעת משום דשטף המים סימני המיצר איהו נמי לא הוי ידע דעבדת בתוך שלו ואמטו להכי סייע לך לבנות וכשידע לא מחל:

אתא לקמיה דרב יהודה אזיל אייתי תרי סהדי חד אמר תרתי אוצייתא עאל וחד אמר תלת אוצייתא עאל א"ל זיל שלים תרתי מגו תלת א"ל כמאן כרבי שמעון בן אלעזר דתניא [א] אמר ר' שמעון בן אלעזר לא נחלקו בית שמאי ובית הלל על שתי כיתי עדים שאחת אומרת מנה ואחת אומרת מאתים שיש בכלל מאתים מנה על מה נחלקו על כת אחת שאחד אומר מנה ואחד אומר מאתים שבית שמאי אומרים נחלקה עדותן ובית הלל אומרים [ב] יש בכלל מאתים מנה א"ל והא [ג] מייתינא לך איגרתא ממערבא דאין הלכה כר' שמעון בן אלעזר א"ל לכי תיתי ההוא גברא דדר בקשתא בעיליתא ארבע שני אתא מארי דביתא אשכחיה א"ל מאי בעית בהאי ביתא א"ל מפלניא זבינתה דזבנה מינך אתא לקמיה דר' חייא א"ל אי אית לך סהדי דדר בה איהו דזבנת מיניה ואפי' חד יומא אוקימנא לה בידך ואי לא לא אמר רב הוה יתיבנא קמיה דחביבי ואמרי ליה וכי אין אדם עשוי ליקח ולמכור בלילה וחזיתיה לדעתיה דאי א"ל קמאי דידי זבנה מינך מהימן מיגו דאי בעי א"ל אנא זבנתה מינך אמר רבא כוותיה דר' חייא מסתברא דקתני [ד] הבא משום ירושה אינו צריך טענה טעמא דלא בעי [ה] הא ראיה בעי ודלמא לא ראיה בעי ולא טענה בעי ואיבעית אימא שאני לוקח דלא שדי זוזי בכדי איבעיא להו נראה בו מאי אמר אביי היא היא אמר רבא [ו] עביד איניש [ז] דסייר ארעיה ולא זבין [ח] שלשה לקוחות מצטרפין אמר רב [ט] וכולם בשטר למימרא דסבר רב שטר אית ליה קלא ועדים לית להו קלא והאמר רב [י] המוכר שדה בעדים גובה מנכסים משועבדים התם לקוחות אינהו

חד אמר. רב כהנא עייל כותלו בתוך של חבירו: תרתי אוצייתא. שתי שורות קרקע על פני השדה כדגרסינן בהשותפין (לעיל דף יב.) תלת אולייתא בי"ב גופני: תרתי מגו תלת. תרתי אולייתא מן השלש שמעיד האחד דתרווייהו מיהא מודו דתרתי אולייתא עייל דבכלל תלת איכא תרי: א"ל. רב כהנא לרב יהודה: כמאן. דיינת לי דהא תרווייהו מכחשי האי להאי ותבטל עדותן: א"ל כר"ש בן אלעזר. שהלכה כמותו ואליבא דב"ה: ואחת אומרת מאתים. היו באותו היום באותה שעה באותו מקום: שיש בכלל מאתים מנה. דהיינו מאה זוז ואין כת שניה מכחשת על מנה שכת ראשונה מעידה אלא מוסיפין הן מנה אחת אבל כת ראשונה מכחשת לשניה על אותו מנה שמוסיפין ובאותו מנה שני אוקי תרי לבהדי תרי ואוקי ממונא בחזקת מריה ולא ישלם: נחלקה עדותן. דמאי דקמסהיד מר לא קמסהיד מר: ב"ה אומרים יש בכלל מאתים מנה. ונוטל מנה הכא נמי יש בכלל תלת אולייתא תרתי ומיהדר ליה: א"ל. רב כהנא לרב יהודה: והא מייתינא איגרתא כו'. דאפי' ב"ה מודו דנחלקה עדותן: א"ל. אהדר מיד עד דמייתית איגרתא וכרב יהודה קיימא לן שכן נעשה הדין: בקשתא. מקום: בעיליתא. בעליה: דזבנה מינך. בחזקת שהייתי סבור דזבנה מינך לקחתיה ממנו: דדר בה. ההוא דאמרת דזבנה לך: אפי' חד יומא. כדי לאמת דבריך ואוקמה בידך הואיל והחזקת שני חזקה ושוב לא תצטרך להביא עדים שלקחה מבעליו אותו שמכרה לך משום דטוענין ליורש וטוענין ללוקח דהבא משום ירושה ומשום מקח אינו צריך טענה אלא ראיה שדר בה המוכרה לו יום אחד בעי: חביבי. ר' חייא דודו של רב כדאמרינן בסנהדרין (דף ה.) דרב בר אחוה דר"ח ובר אחתיה דר"ח: ואמרי ליה. לחביבי אמאי צריך להביא עדים שראוהו (א) בבית יום אחד: וכי אין אדם עשוי ליקח בלילה. ולמכור לאחר שיתן לו ריוח באותו לילה עצמו והוה לך לאוקומי להאי אנכסיה בטענה זו דהא טוענין ללוקח ומיהו כר"ח קיי"ל כדמוכח מסקנא: וחזיתיה לדעתיה. דר' חייא: דאי טעין ליה. האי מחזיק קמאי דידי זבנה מינך ההוא דזבנה ניהלי מהימן: מיגו דאי בעי אמר כו'. הלכך כיון דטוען נמי טענה מעלייתא אני יודע שממך לקחה מהימן דהשתא הויא ליה חזקה שיש עמה טענה אבל כי טעין מפלניא זבינתה בחזקת דאמר לי דזבנה מינך אבל איני יודע אם לקחה ממך אם לאו היינו חזקה שאין עמה טענה הואיל ואפי' יום אחד לא נראה דדר בה: כוותיה דר' חייא. דצריך להביא עדים שדר בה המוכרה לו יום אחד: הבא משום ירושה. והוא הדין משום לקיחה: אין צריך טענה. הך טענה דלעיל דקתני מתניתין אתה מכרת לי אתה נתת לי במתנה אין צריך יורש לטעון ולומר אתה מכרת לאבי: אבל ראיה. בעדים שדר בה אבי יום אחד מיהא קתני דבעי מלתא קתני הבא משום ירושה אינו צריך (ב) כלום דייקינן הכי: ודילמא לא ראיה כו'. והכי קאמר הבא משום ירושה אין צריך שום טענה בעולם אלא זו בלבד מאבי אני יורשה אבל לא עדי דירת יום אחד ולא עדי מכירה ומתנה שנותנה לאביו בעי: ה"ג ואי בעית אימא שאני לוקח כו'. אפילו אם תאמר כי היורש צריך ראיה לדר ביה מורישו יום אחד לוקח עדיף טפי מיורש דלוקח אילו לא בריר ליה מילתא דודאי זבנה המוכרה לו מבעל הקרקע לא הוה שדי זוזי בכדי הלכך ודאי קם אמילתא שפיר כשלקחה ואין צריך לא ראיה ולא טענה: איבעיא להו נראה בו. המוכרה ללוקח זה באותו קרקע למוד כמה ארכו וכמה רחבו מאי מי חשיבא עדות ראיה כעדות דירה ומשום דכר' חייא קיימא לן קבעי לה: שלשה לקוחות מצטרפין. שדה שיש עדים שהיתה של ראובן כל הימים והחזיק בה שמעון שנה כי טוען שקנאה מראובן שלא בשטר והחזיק לוי שנה ואח"כ מכרה שמעון ללוי בשטר והחזיק לוי שנה ואח"כ מכרה לוי ליהודה וכתב לו שטר מכירה כדלקמן והחזיק בה שנה הרי שלש שנים ואתא ראובן וקמערער ואומר כי לא מכרה לשמעון ויהודה טוען הרי החזקנו בין שלשתינו שלש שנים ולא מחית ושמעון שלקחה ממך שלא בלא עדים מכרו לא היה לו ליזהר בשטרו יותר מג' שנים וראובן משיב לפי שכל אחד מכם לא החזיק שלש שנים אלא שנה לא חששתי למחות שהייתי רואה שאתם יראים להחזיק כדמחזקי אינשי ולא הייתי יודע שבשביל שהייתם מוכרין זה לזה לסוף שנה לפיכך לא החזקתם כל אחד כי אם שנה: מצטרפין. הלקוחות ויפסיד ראובן דכיון דבשטר לקחו זה מזה כדמפרש רב בסמוך עדים שבשטר אפקו קלא וידע ראובן ומדלא מיחה הפסיד אבל בלא שטר מצי טוען האי דלא מחאי שלא החזיק אחד מכם שלש שנים ולא אחזקיתו כדמחזקי אינשי כדאמרינן לעיל (דף כח:) במלמתא: וכולן בשטר. אפי' לקוחות אחרונים קאי אבל לוקח ראשון שלקח מן המערער מה לנו ולשטרו [דאם יש לו שטר פשיטא דאין יכול לערער]: שטר אית ליה קלא. שמתאספין לכותבו ולחותמו והכל שומעין: ועדים לית להו קלא. מכירה בעדים בלא שטר: המוכר שדהו בפני עדים. וקבל עליו אחריותו: גובה. הלוקח מן המוכר אפי' מנכסים שמשעבד ומשכן או מכר קרקעותיו אחרי מכירה זו שקבל עליו אחריותה וטעם משום דעדים מפקי לקלא וידעו הלקוחות שמכר זה קרקע באחריות והיה להם להניח למוכר בני חורין כשיעור האחריות אלמא עדים בלא שטר אית להו קלא: שאני לקוחות. אע"ג דמכירה בעדים בלא שטר לית ליה קלא ממילא אלא אם כן יפשפשו ויחקרו הדבר: אינהו

אתא לקמיה דרב יהודה כו'. ומסיק דרב יהודה כר"ש בן אלעזר ס"ל ותימה דבפ' זה בורר (סנהדרין דף ל: ושם לא. ד"ה הוא) אמר רב יהודה עדות המכחשת זה את זה בבדיקות כשרה בדיני ממונות ומוקי לה באחד אומר ארנקי לבנה ואחד אומר ארנקי שחורה אבל אחד אומר מנה שחור ואחד אומר מנה לבן אין מצטרפין נהרדעי אמרי אפי' א' אומר מנה לבן ואחד אומר מנה שחור ומסיק דאינהו דאמור כר"ש בן אלעזר דהכא משמע דרב יהודה דפליג אנהרדעי פליג (ג) אר"ש בן אלעזר דהכא וי"ל דרב יהודה נמי כרשב"א ובהא פליגי דנהרדעי סברי דאחד אומר מנה שחור ואחד אומר מנה לבן דמי למילתיה דר"ש בן אלעזר דלא דייקי ביה סהדי ודמי לארנקי ורב יהודה סבר דלא דמי כלל לארנקי דהתם (ד) דאין זה גוף המעשה לא היה להן לבדוק אבל מנה דגוף הדבר הוא שמעידין עליו דייקי וקסבר דמודה ר"ש בן אלעזר במנה שחור דבטלה עדותן אפי' לב"ה ולא דמי למנה ומאתים דעבידי דטעו טפי אלא מדמה מנה שחור ומנה לבן לאחד אומר חבית של יין וא' אומר של שמן דהא מודו כולי עלמא דנחלקה עדותן כדאיתא התם:

נחלקה עדותן. הקשה ריב"א לב"ש דאמרי בכת אחת נחלקה עדותן דחשיבי להו עדות מוכחשת ואפי' בב' כיתי עדים נמי תבטל עדותן דהוי נמצא אחד מהן קרוב או פסול עדותן בטלה אפילו הן מאה כדאמר בפ"ק דמכות (דף ה:) ואומר ר"י דלאו פירכא היא דמצינו למימר דב"ש כר' יוסי סבירא להו דאמר התם במה דברי' אמורים בדיני נפשות אבל בדיני ממונות תתקיים העדות בשאר והכי הלכתא דפסיק רב נחמן [ז] כוותיה ואפי' לרבי נמי מצי למימר דהכא (ה) מצי מיירי כגון דאתו למיחזי ואפי' אתי לאסהודי הני מילי כי מסייעי אהדדי הוא דאמר נמצא אחד מהן קרוב או פסול עדותן בטלה אבל הכא דהא מכחשי אהדדי לא [ח]:

קי א מיי' פ"ג מהל' עדות הלכה ג סמג עשין קח טוש"ע ח"מ סי' ל סעיף ג:

קיא ב ג מיי' פי"ד מהל' טוען ונטען הלכה יד סמג עשין לה טוש"ע ח"מ סי' קמו סעיף יד:

קיב ד מיי' שם הל' יג טוש"ע שם סעיף ו:

קיג ו ז מיי' שם פי"ג הלכה ו סמג שם טוש"ע ח"מ סי' קמד סעיף ג:

קיד ח מיי' פי"א מהל' מלוה הלכה ה סמג עשין לד טוש"ע ח"מ סי' קנג סעיף א:

רבינו גרשום

חד אמר. עייל כותלו בשדה חבירו תרתי אוצייתא ברוחב ב' שורו' על פני כל השדה: אמר ליה זיל אהדר תרתי אוצייתא מגו תלת. דתרווייהו הני עדים מסהדי דתרתי אוצייתא עיילת בתוך שדהו ובכל תלתא איכא תרתי: אחת אומרת מנה. לזה פלוני מפלוני ואחת אומרת מאתים א) מנה ונוטל מנה הכי נמי יש בכלל ג' אוצייתא תרתי ומהדר לי' [תרתין]: א"ל. רב כהנא לר' יהודה והא מייתינא איגרתא ממערבא דלית הלכת' כר' שמעון בן אלעזר. דאפילו בית הלל מודו להיכא דאחד אומר מנה ואחד אומר מאתים דנחלקה עדותן ולא קא משלם אפילו מנה הכי נמי נחלקה עדותן: אמר ליה. אהדר מיד עד דתיתי איגרתא: בקשתא. שם מקום: בעיליתא. בעלייה: דדר בה ההוא דזבניה אפי' חד יומא כדי לאמת דבריך ואוקמה בידך הואיל דאחזקת בה ד' שנין: חביבי. ר' חייא דודו: ואמרי ליה. ואי לא מייתי סהדי דדר בה ההוא דזבניה ליה חד יומא אמאי לא מוקמי' בידיה וכי אין אדם עשוי לקנות מאחד בלילה ולמכור באותו הלילה ואמאי לא מוקמי' בידיה הא הכא איכא למימר דבלילה זבנה מאחר ולאלתר מכרה ליה: וחזיתיה לדעתי'. שהבנתי מתוך דבריו דאי אמר ליה המחזיק קמיה דידי זבנה מינך ההוא שקניתיה ממנו מהימן: כוותיה דר' חייא. דאמר לעיל דצריך לאתויי סהדי דדר בה ההוא אפי' חד יומא הכי מסתברא דקתני הבא מחמת ירושה והוא הדין מחמת לקיחה: הא ראיה. כל דהו בעי כהאי גוונא: ולא ראיה בעי. דהואיל ובא מחמת ירושה אנן טענינן ליה: איבעית אימא. משום הכי בעי ר' חייא ראיה גבי לוקח משום דלוקח שאני מיורש דלוקח לא שדי זוזי בכדי דהואיל ויהיב דמי מדקדק יפה דההוא דזבניה ניהליה דדייר ביה חד יומא והואיל שטוען מפלניא זבינתיה דזבנה מינך צריך למיתי ראיה דדר בה חד יומא ההוא דזבנה ניהליה אי לא מייתי ראיה לא מוקמינן לה בידיה: איבעיא להו נראה בו מהו. כלומר אית ליה סהדי דההוא דזבנה ליה הוה איתחזי בההוא ביתא והוה אזיל לעיוני במצרי הבית כמה ארכו וכמה רחבו הוי מי אמרינן הואיל וקא מעיין הכי ודאי קני מהאי מערער לאוקמי' ליה בידא דלוקח ודמי כמאן דדר בה חד יומא: אמר אביי היא היא. ודאי דמי כמאן דדר בה: רבא אמר. לא קנה לוקח דהואיל דלית ליה סהדי דדר בה ממש דעבד אינש דסייר ביתא דחבריה ולא זבין: ג' לקוחות מצטרפין. כגון שמכר שדה לאחד והחזיק בה שנה והלך זה שקנאה ומכר לשני ומכרה לשלישי והחזיק בה שנה מצטרפין אלו ג' שנים ודמי כאילו שהתה ביד לוקח שלישי ג' שנים והחזיק בה: אמר רב וכולן בשטר. כלומר אם אלו לקוחות מכרוה זה לזה בשטר בשעת מכירה אין יכול שוב למחות משום השטר: קלא אית ליה. ואם איתא דשלו היא היה מוחה בשעת מכירה: עדים לית להו קלא. שאם מכרו זה לזה בעדים שלא בשטר ולא מיחה יכול למימר לא ידעתי במכירתם: והאמר רב המוכר שדהו שלא בשטר גובה מנכסים משועבדים. שאם מכר שדהו בפני עדים לאחד באחריות ובא בעל חוב של מוכר וטרפה מן הלוקח גובה מנכסין משועבדין שמכר לאחרים בשיעור הקרקע שטרפה ממנו אלמא כיון דגובה מנכסין משועבדין ש"מ דקסבר רב בעדים אית

א) סנהדרין לא. מיר כ. ע"ש, ב) [סנהדרין כט.], ג) [שבועות מב:], ד) [לעיל כג., ה) [נ"ל דסייר ארעא], ו) מהרש"ל, ז) [עי' מכות ו. פסק רב נחמן הלכה כר' ומש"ע פסקו כל הפוסקים כרבי ובכן מלוה לתקן], ח) [וע"ע תוס' סנהדרין לא. ד"ה שב"ש אומרים]:

הגהות הב"ח

(א) רשב"ם ד"ה ואמרי ליה וכו' שראוהו שדר בבית: (ב) ד"ה אבל ראיה וכו' אינו צריך לטעון כלום: (ג) תוס' ד"ה אתא וכו' אר"ש בן אלעזר הכא: (ד) בא"ד דהתם כיון דאין זה גוף וכו' לגוף הדבר שמעידין עליו הוא דייקי: (ה) ד"ה נחלקה וכו' דהכא מיירי כל"ל ותיבת מלי נמחק:

ליקוטי רש"י

על כת אחת. זה אומר מנה וזה אומר מאתים דמכחישין זה את זה. נחלקה עדותן. שכיון שהאחד שקרן שוב אין כאן עדות [סנהדרין לא.]. דנחלקה עדותן דהא קא מכחשי אהדדי [נזיר כ.]. יש בכלל מאתים מנה. שניהם מעידין על מנה ומצטרפין ואין זה מכחישין זה את זה אין מצטרפין למנה שיש בכלל מאתים מנה ולא אמרינן שמיהן שקרו אלא הלך אחר הפחות שבהם [סנהדרין שם]. הבא משום ירושה אינו צריך טענה. אינו צריך לומר אתה מכרת לאבי אלא ראוי לאבי שהחזיק בה ולא ערער אדם עליו [לעיל כג.]. דסייר ארעא. סייר. מעיין [תענית ט:]. בודק תרגום פוקד (שמות לד) מסער כמו האי עבחא דלא סר סכינא קמיה מכס [שם כ: וכעי"ז גיטין סח.].

חשק שלמה על רבינו גרשום א) נ"ל שיש בכלל מאתים מנה ונוטל מנה וכו'.

אָתָא לְקַמֵּיהּ דְּרַב יְהוּדָה – [Rav Kahana] came before Rav Yehudah to judge the case. **אָזִיל אַיְיתִי תְּרֵי סָהֲדֵי – [The neighbor] went and produced two witnesses, חַד אָמַר תַּרְתֵּי אוּצְיָיתָא עָאל – one** of whom **said that [Rav Kahana] had encroached two rows** into his neighbor's land,[1] **וְחַד אָמַר תְּלָת אוּצְיָיתָא עָאל – and one** of whom **said that he had encroached three rows. אָמַר לֵיהּ – [Rav Yehudah] said to [Rav Kahana]: זִיל שְׁלִים תַּרְתֵּי מִגּוֹ תְּלָת – Go and restore two out of the three** rows mentioned by the witnesses.[2]

Rav Kahana objected to this ruling:

אָמַר לֵיהּ – [Rav Kahana] said to [Rav Yehudah]: כְּמַאן – In accordance **with whose** opinion do you issue this ruling?[3]

Rav Yehudah replied:

כְּרַבִּי שִׁמְעוֹן בֶּן אֶלְעָזָר – In accordance **with** the ruling of **R' Shimon ben Elazar. דְּתַנְיָא – For it was taught in a Baraisa: אָמַר ר׳ שִׁמְעוֹן בֶּן אֶלְעָזָר – R' SHIMON BEN ELAZAR SAID:**[4] **לֹא נֶחֶלְקוּ בֵּית שַׁמַּאי וּבֵית הִלֵּל – BEIS SHAMMAI AND BEIS HILLEL DID NOT DISAGREE עַל שְׁתֵּי כִיתֵּי עֵדִים – IN REGARD TO TWO SETS OF WITNESSES** to a loan, **שֶׁאַחַת אוֹמֶרֶת מָנֶה וְאַחַת אוֹמֶרֶת מָאתַיִם – ONE** of which **SAYS** the loan was **A** ***MANEH*** (a hundred *zuz*), **AND ONE** of which **SAYS** it was **TWO HUNDRED** ***zuz,*** **שֶׁיֵּשׁ בִּכְלַל מָאתַיִם מָנֶה – THAT INCLUDED IN** the testimony of **TWO HUNDRED IS** testimony regarding **A** ***MANEH.*** Thus, both sets of witnesses are testifying that he borrowed a *maneh* (one hundred *zuz*), and one *maneh* can therefore be collected.[5] **עַל מַה נֶּחֶלְקוּ – IN REGARD TO WHAT DID THEY DISAGREE? עַל כַּת אַחַת – IN REGARD TO A SINGLE SET** of witnesses, **שֶׁאֶחָד אוֹמֵר מָנֶה וְאֶחָד אוֹמֵר מָאתַיִם – ONE** of whom **SAYS** that the loan was **A** ***MANEH,*** **AND ONE** of whom **SAYS** it was **TWO HUNDRED** ***ZUZ.*** **שֶׁבֵּית שַׁמַּאי אוֹמְרִים נֶחֶלְקָה עֵדוּתָן – IN THIS, BEIS SHAMMAI SAY** that **THEIR TESTIMONY IS DIVIDED,** and the loan cannot be collected; **וּבֵית הִלֵּל אוֹמְרִים יֵשׁ בִּכְלַל מָאתַיִם מָנֶה – WHEREAS BEIS HILLEL SAY** that **INCLUDED IN** the testimony of **TWO HUNDRED IS** testimony regarding **A** ***MANEH*** (one hundred). Since there are two witnesses testifying that he borrowed a *maneh,* one *maneh* can be collected.[6] According to R' Shimon ben Elazar, Beis Hillel accept the common aspects of the testimony of two individual witnesses even when they do not agree entirely. Rav Yehudah follows this view.[7]

Rav Kahana protests Rav Yehudah's acceptance of R' Shimon ben Elazar's version of the dispute:

אָמַר לֵיהּ – [Rav Kahana] said to [Rav Yehudah]: וְהָא מַיְיתִינָא לָךְ אִיגַּרְתָּא מִמַּעֲרָבָא – But I will bring you a letter from the West (Eretz Yisrael),[8] **דְּאֵין הֲלָכָה כְּר׳ שִׁמְעוֹן בֶּן אֶלְעָזָר – that the halachah is not** in accordance with the view **of R' Shimon ben Elazar!**

Rav Yehudah was unimpressed:

אָמַר לֵיהּ – [Rav Yehudah] replied to [Rav Kahana]: לְכִי תֵּיתֵי – When you will produce such a letter I will reconsider.

The Gemara relates another incident in which a *chazakah* was ruled inadequate because of the lack of a proper supporting claim:

הַהוּא גַּבְרָא – There was a certain person דְּדָר בְּקַשְׁתָּא בְּעִילִיתָא אַרְבַּע שְׁנֵי – who lived in an upper story in a house **in Kashta** for **four years. אָתָא מָארֵי דְּבֵיתָא אַשְׁכְּחֵיהּ – The owner of the house came and found him there אָמַר לֵיהּ** – and **said to [the occupant]: מַאי בָּעֵית בְּהַאי בֵּיתָא – "What are you doing in this house?" אָמַר לֵיהּ – [The occupant] said to him: מִפְּלַנְיָא זְבִינְתָּה דִּזְבַנְהּ מִינָּךְ – "I bought it** [the upper story] **from so-and-so who,** I assume, **bought it from you."**[9] **אָתָא לְקַמֵּיהּ דְּר׳ חִיָּיא – He came before R' Chiya** for judgment. **אָמַר לֵיהּ – [R' Chiya] said to [the occupant]: אִי אִית לָךְ סָהֲדֵי – "If you have witnesses דְּדָר בַּהּ אִיהוּ דִּזְבַנְתְּ מִינֵּיהּ – that the person from whom you bought [the upper story] lived in it וַאֲפִילּוּ חַד יוֹמָא – for even one day, אוֹקִימְנָא לָהּ בִּיְדָךְ – I will establish it in your possession; וְאִי לָא לָא** – but if you **cannot** produce such testimony, I **cannot** award you the property."[10]

NOTES

1. I.e. the strip of land inadvertently annexed by Rav Kahana was two rows deep (*Rashbam*).

2. Since both witnesses testify that at least two rows of land were annexed (*Rashbam*). Although the two witnesses actually offered contradictory testimony, Rav Yehudah ruled that each bit of information is regarded as a separate facet of the testimony. Thus, the contradiction can be seen as occurring only in regard to the third row of land. Concerning the first two rows, however, there is no contradiction, and therefore Rav Kahana was required to return them.

3. Rav Kahana objected to Rav Yehudah's ruling on the grounds that the witnesses' testimony was contradictory and therefore inadmissible (*Rashbam*).

4. The Mishnah in *Nazir* (20a) records a dispute between Beis Shammai and Beis Hillel regarding the acceptability of conflicting testimony which is nevertheless in agreement on some facts. According to that Mishnah, the dispute concerns a contradiction between two sets of witnesses. R' Shimon ben Elazar, however, has a different version of that dispute, which he applies to the case of a loan, as recorded in this Baraisa. He begins by rejecting that Mishnah's version, and maintains that the dispute concerned the conflicting testimony of two single witnesses.

5. Both sets of witnesses testify to a loan made on the same date, at the same time and in the same place. [Therefore, it is obvious that they refer to the same loan.] With regard to the first *maneh*, both sets agree that it was borrowed; thus, it can be collected. It is concerning the second *maneh* that they clash, one set maintaining that it was borrowed and the other contesting this. Thus, the contradictory testimonies offset each other, and the second *maneh* cannot be collected (*Rashbam*).

6. Beis Shammai hold that when there is a contradiction between two witnesses concerning the amount of a loan, we must assume that one of the witnesses is lying. Thus, there are no longer two credible witnesses to the loan, and it cannot be collected. [This is unlike a contradiction between two *sets* of witnesses, in which case regardless of which set is lying, there is still one set testifying that he owes at least a *maneh.*]

Beis Hillel, however, do not assume that one of the witnesses is necessarily dishonest. Rather, they view the discrepancy as an inaccuracy on the part of one of the witnesses, leaving his credibility as a witness intact. Thus, since both witnesses concur that at least one *maneh* was borrowed, that *maneh* can be collected (see *Ritva*).

7. I.e. Rav Yehudah accepted R' Shimon ben Elazar's version of the dispute and ruled according to Beis Hillel (*Rashbam*). He therefore required Rav Kahana to restore two rows of land.

8. [In Babylonia they referred to Eretz Yisrael as "the West" (see above, 25b note 29). Rav Kahana protested that in the academy of Eretz Yisrael they had ruled against R' Shimon ben Elazar, and that he would obtain a letter to this effect.] This would mean that the halachah follows the view of Beis Hillel as given by the Mishnah in *Nazir.* According to that view even Beis Hillel dismiss the testimony of two contradictory witnesses (*Rashbam*) and accept this kind of testimony only in the case of two contradictory *sets* of witnesses, for the reason given in note 6.

9. [The occupant, however, did not claim to have personal knowledge of the purchase of the upper story from the original owner.] He merely stated that he bought it on the assumption that the seller had previously bought it from the original owner (*Rashbam*).

10. [Since the occupant admits that he did not buy the upper story from the original owner, it can only be awarded to him if it can be established that the person from whom he did buy it had previously bought it from the original owner. The occupant himself admits that he has no proof of this but merely assumed it to be true. Thus, he has no definite claim of ownership to support his *chazakah* and it is therefore of no avail.]

Nevertheless, there is a law that the court argues on behalf of a litigant who cannot be expected to know the facts of a case with certainty, such as an orphan (i.e. heir) or a purchaser [טָעֲנִינָן לְיַתְמֵי וְלִלְקוֹחוֹת]. (This is the law we learned in our Mishnah [41a]: "One who comes into a property by way of inheritance does not require a supporting claim.") Since the current occupant of the property cannot be expected to know how

קי א מיי' פ"ג מהל' עדות הלכה ג סמג עשין קח טוש"ע ח"מ סי' ל סעיף ג:

קיא ב ג מיי' פי"ד מהל' טוען הלכה יד סמג עשין לה טוש"ע ח"מ סי' קמו סעיף יד:

קיב ד ה מיי' שם הל' יג טוש"ע שם סעיף י:

קיג ו ז מיי' שם פי"ב הלכה ו סמג שם טוש"ע ח"מ סי' קמד סעיף ב:

קיד ח מיי' פי"א מהל' מלוה הלכה ה סמג עשין לד טוש"ע ח"מ סי' קנז סעיף א:

אתא לקמיה דרב יהודה אזיל אייתי תרי סהדי חד אמר תרתי אוצייתא עאל וחד אמר תלת אוצייתא עאל א"ל זיל שלים תרתי מגו תלת א"ל כמאן כרבי שמעון בן אלעזר דתניא [א] אמר ר' שמעון בן אלעזר לא נחלקו בית שמאי ובית הלל על שתי כיתי עדים שאחת אומרת מנה ואחת אומרת מאתים שיש בכלל מאתים מנה על מה נחלקו על כת אחת שאחד אומר מנה ואחד אומר מאתים שבית שמאי אומרים נחלקה עדותן ובית הלל אומרים א יש בכלל מאתים מנה א"ל והא [ב] מייתינא לך איגרתא ממערבא דאין הלכה כר' שמעון בן אלעזר א"ל [ג] לכי תיתי ההוא גברא דדר בקשתא בעיליתא ארבע שני אתא מארי דביתא אשכחיה א"ל מאי בעית בהאי ביתא א"ל מפלניא זבינתה דזבנה מינך אתא לקמיה דר' חייא א"ל ב אי אית לך סהדי דדר בה איהו דזבנת מיניה ואפי' חד יומא אוקימנא לה בידך ואי לא לא אמר רב הוה יתיבנא קמיה דחביבי ואמרי ליה וכי אין אדם עשוי ליקח ולמכור בלילה וחזיתיה לדעתיה ג אי א"ל קמאי דידי זבנה מינך מהימן מיגו דאי בעי א"ל אנא זבנתה מינך אמר רבא כוותיה דר' חייא מסתברא דקתני [ד] הבא משום ירושה אינו צריך טענה טענה הוא דלא בעי ד הא ראיה בעי ודלמא לא ראיה בעי ולא טענה בעי ואיבעית אימא שאני לוקח דלא שדי זוזי בכדי איבעיא להו נראה בו מאי אמר אביי היא היא רבא אמר ה עביד איניש [ה] דסיאר ארעיה ולא זבין: ו שלשה לקוחות מצטרפין אמר רב ז וכולם בשטר למימרא דסבר רב שטר אית ליה קלא ועדים לית להו קלא והאמר רב ח המוכר שדה בעדים גובה מנכסים משועבדים התם לקוחות אינהו

רש"י

חד אמר. רב כהנא עייל כותלו בתוך של חבירו: תרתי אוצייתא. שתי שורות קרקע על פני השדה כדגרסינן בהשותפין (לעיל דף יג.) תלת אולייתא בי"ב גופני: תרתי מגו תלת. תרתי אולייתא מן השלש שמעיד האחד למחזיקו מיהא מודו לתרתי אולייתא עייל דבכלל תלת איכא תרי: א"ל. רב כהנא לרב יהודה: כמאן. דיינת לי דהא תרוייהו מכחשי האי להאי ותבטל עדותן: א"ל כר"ש בן אלעזר. שהלכה כמותו ואליבא דב"ה: ואחת אומרת מאתים. היו באותו היום באותה שעה באותו מקום: שיש בכלל מאתים מנה. דהיינו מאה זוז ואין כת שניה מכחשת על מנה שכת ראשונה מעידה אלא מוסיפין הן מנה אחת אבל כת ראשונה מכחשת לשניה על אותו מנה שמוסיפין ובאותו מנה שני אוקי תרי לבהדי תרי ואוקי ממונא בחזקת מריה ולא ישלם: נחלקה עדותן. דמאי דקמסהיד מר לא קמסהיד מר: ב"ה אומרים יש בכלל מאתים מנה. ונוטל מנה הכא נמי יש בכלל תלת אולייתא תרתי ומיהדר ליה: א"ל. רב כהנא לרב יהודה: והא מייתינא איגרתא כו'. דאפי' ב"ה מודו דנחלקה עדותן: א"ל. אהדר מיד עד דמייתית איגרתא וכרב יהודה קיימא לן שכן עשה הדין: בקשתא. מקום: בעיליתא. בעליה: דזבנה מינך. בחזקת שסיתי סבור דזבנה מינך לקחתיה ממנו: דדר בה. ההוא דאמרת דזבנה לך: אפי' חד יומא. כדי לאמת דבריך ואוקמה בידך הואיל והחזקת שני חזקה ושוב לא תצטרך להביא עדים שלקחה מבעליו אותו שמכרה לך משום דטוענין ליורש וטוענין ללוקח דהבא משום ירושה ומשום מקח אינו צריך טענה אלא ראיה שדר בה המוכרה לו יום אחד בעי: חביבי. ר' חייא דודו של רב כדאמרינן בסנהדרין (דף ה.) דרב בר אחוה דר"ח ובר אחתיה דר"ח: ואמרי ליה. לחביבי אמאי צריך להביא עדים שראוהו (א) בבית יום אחד: וכי אין אדם עשוי ליקח בלילה. ולמכור לאחר שיתן לו ריוח באותו לילה עצמו והוה לך לאוקומי להאי אנכסיה בטענה זו דהא טוענין ללוקח ומיהו כר"ח קיי"ל כדמוכח מסקנא: וחזיתיה לדעתיה. דרבי חייא: דאי טעין ליה. האי מחזיק קמאי דידי זבנה מינך ההוא דזבנה ניהלי מהימן: מיגו דאי בעי אמר כו'. הלכך כיון דטעין נמי טענה מעלייתא אני יודע שממך לקחה מהימן דהשתא הויא ליה חזקה שיש עמה טענה אבל כי טעין מפלניא זבנתה בחזקת דאמר לי דזבנה מינך אבל איני יודע אם לקחה ממך אם לאו היינו חזקה שאין עמה טענה הואיל ואפי' יום אחד לא נראה לדר בה: כוותיה דר' חייא. דצריך להביא עדים שדר בה המוכרה לו יום אחד: הבא משום ירושה. והוא הדין משום לקיחה: אין צריך טענה. הך טענה דלעיל דקתני מתניתין אתה מכרת לי אתה נתת לי במתנה אין צריך יורש לטעון ולומר אתה מכרת לאבי: אבל ראיה. בעדים שדר בה יום אחד מיהא בעי מדלא קתני הבא משום ירושה אינו צריך (ב) כלום דייקינן הכי: ודילמא לא ראיה כו'. והכי קאמר הבא משום ירושה אין צריך שום טענה בעולם אלא זו בלבד מאבי אני יורשה אבל לא עדי דירת יום אחד ולא טענת מכירה ומתנה שניתנה לאביו בעי: ה"ג ואי בעית אימא שאני לוקח כו'. אפילו אם תאמר כי היורש צריך ראיה דדר ביה מורישו יום אחד לוקח עדיף טפי מיורש דלוקח אילו לא ברירא ליה מילתא דודאי זבנה המוכרה לו מבעל הקרקע לא הוי שדי זוזי בכדי הלכך ודאי קם אמילתא שפיר כשלקחה ואין צריך לא ראיה ולא טענה: איבעיא להו נראה בו. המוכרה ללוקח זה באותו קרקע למוד כמה ארכו וכמה רחבו מאי מי חשיבא עדות ראיה כעדות דירה ומשום דכר' חייא קיימא לן קבעי לה: שלשה לקוחות מצטרפין. שדה שיש עדים שהיתה של ראובן כל הימים והחזיק בה שמעון שנה כי טוען שקנאה מראובן ואח"כ מכרה שמעון ללוי בשטר והחזיק לוי שנה ואח"כ מכרה לוי ליהודה וכתב לו שטר מכירה כדלקמן והחזיק בה שנה הרי שלש שנים ואתא ראובן וקמערער ואומר כי לא מכרה לשמעון ויהודה טוען הרי החזקנו בין שלשתינו שלש שנים ולא מחית ושמעון שלקחה ממך שאנו באין מכחו לא היה לו ליזהר בשטרו יותר מג' שנים וראובן משיב לפי שכל אחד מכם לא החזיק שלש שנים אלא שנה לא חששתי למחות שהייתי רואה שאתם יראים להחזיק כדמחזקי אינשי ולא הייתי יודע שבשביל שהייתם מוכרין זה לזה לסוף שנה לפיכך לא החזקתם כל אחד כי אם שנה: מצטרפין. הלקוחות ויפסיד ראובן דכיון דבשטר לקחו זה מזה כדמפרש רב בסמוך עדים שבשטר אפקו לקלא וידע ראובן ומדלא מיחה הפסיד אבל בלא שטר מצי טעין האי דלא מחאי שלא החזיק אחד מכם שלש שנים ולא אחזקיתו כדמחזקי אינשי כדאמרינן לעיל (דף כט:) באמתא: וכולן בשטר. אשני לקוחות אחרונים קאי אבל לוקח ראשון שלקח מן המערער מה לנו ולשטרו [י] [דאם יש לו שטר פשיטא דאין יכול לערער]: שטר אית ליה קלא. שמתאספין לכותבו ולחותמו והכל שומעין: ועדים לית להו קלא. מכירה בעדים בלא שטר: המוכר שדהו בפני עדים. וקבל עליו אחריותו: גובה. הלוקח מן המוכר אפי' מנכסים שעבד ומשכן או מכר קרקעותיו אחרי מכירה זו שקבל עליו אחריותה וטעם משום דעדים מפקי לקלא וידעו הלקוחות שמכר זה קרקע באחריות והיה להם להניח למוכר בני חורין כשיעור האחריות אלמא עדים בלא שטר אית להו קלא: שאני לקוחות. אע"ג דמכירה בעדים בלא שטר לית ליה קלא ממילא אלא אם כן יפשפשו ויחקרו הדבר: אינהו

תוספות

אתא לקמיה דרב יהודה כו'. ומסיק דרב יהודה כר"ש בן אלעזר ס"ל ותימה דבפ' זה בורר (סנהדרין דף ל: ושם לא. ד"ה הוא) אמר רב יהודה עדות המכחשת זו את זו בבדיקות כשרה בדיני ממונות ומוקי לה באחד אומר ארנקי לבנה ואחד אומר ארנקי שחורה אבל אחד אומר מנה שחור ואחד אומר מנה לבן אין מצטרפין ונהרדעי אמרי אפי' א' אומר מנה לבן ואחד אומר מנה שחור ומסיק דאיהו דאמר כר"ש בן אלעזר דהכא משמע דרב יהודה דפליג אנהרדעי פליג (ג) אר"ש בן אלעזר דהכא וי"ל דרב יהודה נמי כרשב"א והכא פליגי נהרדעי סברי דאחד אומר מנה שחור ואחד אומר מנה לבן דמי למילתיה דר"ש בן אלעזר דלא דייקי ביה סהדי ודמי לארנקי ורב יהודה סבר דלא דמי כלל לארנקי דהתם (ד) דאין זה גוף המעשה לא היה להן לבדוק אבל מנה דגוף הדבר הוא שמעידין עליו דייקי וקסבר דמודה ר"ש בן אלעזר במנה שחור דבטלה עדותן אפי' לב"ה ולא דמי למנה ומאתים דעבידי דטעו טפי אלא מדמה מנה שחור ומנה לבן לאחד אומר חבית של יין וא' אומר של שמן דהכא מודו כולי עלמא דנחלקה עדותן כדאיתא התם:

נחלקה עדותן. הקשה ריב"א לב"ש דאמרי בכת אחת נחלקה עדותן דחשיבי להו עדות מוכחשת ואפי' בב' כיתי עדים נמי תבטל עדותן דהוי נמצא אחד מהן קרוב או פסול עדותן בטלה אפילו לכולהו כדאמר בפ"ק דמכות (דף ה:) ואומר ר"י דלא פירכא היא דמצינו למימר דב"ש כר' יוסי סבירא להו דאמר התם במה דברים אמורים בדיני נפשות אבל בדיני ממונות תתקיים העדות בשאר והכי הלכתא דפסיק רב נחמן ז) כוותיה ואפי' לרבי נמי מצי למימר דהכא (ה) מלי מיירי כגון דאתו למיחזי ואפי' אתי לאסהודי הני מילי כי מסייעי אהדדי הוא דאמר נמצא אחד מהן קרוב או פסול עדותן בטלה אבל הכא דהא מכחשי אהדדי לא ח):

רבינו גרשום

חד אמר. עייל כותלו בשדה חבירו תרתי אוצייתא ברוחב ב' שורו' על פני כל השדה: אמר ליה זיל אהדר תרתי אוצייתא מגו תלת. דתרווייהו הני עדים מסהדי דתרתי אוצייתא עיילת בתוך שדהו ובכל תלתא איכא תרתי: אחת אומרת מנה. לוה פלוני מפלוני ואחת אומרת מאתים א) מנה ונוטל מנה הכי נמי יש בכלל ג' אוצייתא תרתי ומהדר לי' [תרתין]: א"ל. רב כהנא לר' יהודה והא מייתינא איגרתא ממערבא דלית הלכת' כר' שמעון בן אלעזר. דאפילו בית הלל מודו להיכא דאחד אומר מנה ואחד אומר מאתים דנחלקה עדותן ולא קא משלם אפילו מנה הכי נמי נחלקה עדותן: אמר ליה. אהדר מיד עד דתיתי איגרתא: בקשתא. שם מקום: בעיליתא. בעלייה: דדר בה ההוא דזבניה אפי' חד יומא כדי לאמת דבריך ואוקמה בידך הואיל דאחזקת בה ד' שנין: חביבי. ר' חייא דודו: ואמרי ליה. ואי לא מייתי סהדי דדר בה ההוא דזבניה ליה חד יומא אמאי לא מוקמי' בידיה וכי אין אדם עשוי לקנות מאחד בלילה ולמכור באותו הלילה ואמאי לא מוקמי' בידיה הא הכא איכא למימר דבלילה זבנה מאחר ולאלתר מכרה ליה: וחזיתיה לדעתי'. שהבנתי מתוך דבריו דאי אמר ליה המחזיק קמיה דידי זבנה מינך ההוא שקניתיה ממנו מהימן: כוותיה דר' חייא. דאמר לעיל דצריך לאתויי סהדי דדר בה ההוא אפי' חד יומא הכי מסתברא דקתני הבא מחמת ירושה והוא הדין מחמת לקיחה: הא ראיה. כל דהו בעי כהאי גוונא: ולא ראיה בעי. דהואיל ובא מחמת ירושה אנן טענינן ליה: איבעית אימא. משום הכי בעי ר' חייא ראיה גבי לוקח משום דלוקח שאני מיורש דלוקח לא שדי זוזי בכדי דהואיל ויהיב דמי מדקדק יפה דההוא דזבניה ניהליה דדייר ביה חד יומא והואיל שטוען מפלניא זבינתיה דזבנה מינך צריך למיתי ראיה דדר בה חד יומא ההוא דזבנה ניהליה אי לא מייתי ראיה לא מוקמינן לה בידיה: איבעיא להו נראה בו מהו. כלומר אית ליה סהדי דההוא דזבנה ליה הוה איתחזי בההוא ביתא והוה אזיל לעיוני במצרי הבית כמה ארכו וכמה רחבו הוי מי אמרינן הואיל וקא מעיין הכי ודאי קני מהאי מערער לאוקמי' ליה בידא דלוקח ודמי כמאן דדר בה חד יומא: אמר אביי היא היא. ודאי דמי כמאן דדר בה חד יומא: רבא אמר. לא קנה לוקח דהואיל דלית ליה סהדי דדר בה ממש דעבד איניש דסייר ארעיה ולא זבין: ג' לקוחות מצטרפין. כגון שמכר שדה לאחד והחזיק בה שנה והלך זה שקנאה ומכר לשני והחזיק בה שנה והלך שני ומכרה לשלישי והחזיק בה שנה: אמר רב וכולן בשטר. כלומר אם אלו לקוחות מכרה זה לזה בשטר ולא מיחה אינו יכול שוב למחות משום השטר: קלא אית ליה. ואם איתא דשלו היא היה מוחה בשעת מכירה: עדים לית להו קלא. שאם מכר שדהו בפני עדים ולא מיחה יכול לומר לא ידעתי במכירתם: והאמר רב המוכר שדהו שלא בשטר גובה מנכסים משועבדים. שאם מכר שדהו בפני עדים לאחד וקיבל עליו אחריות ואח"כ בא ב"ח של מוכר וטרפה מן הלוקח גובה מנכסין משועבדים שאם מכר לאחרי כן שדה לאחר אחר שקבל לזה אחריות שמשועבד לפצותו גובה אותן משועבדין שמכר לאחרים בשיעור הקרקע שטרפה ממנו אלמא כיון דגובה מנכסין משועבדין ש"מ דסבר רב בעדים אית

חשק שלמה על רבינו גרשום א) נ"ל שיש בכלל מאתים מנה ונוטל מנה וכו'.

מסורת הש"ס

א) סנהדרין לא. נזיר כ. ע"ש, ב) [סנהדרין כט.], ג) [שבועות מח:], ד) לעיל כג., ה) [צ"ל דסייר ארעא], ו) סנהדרין לא:, ז) [עי' מכות ו. פסק רב נחמן הלכה כר' ומהרש"א פסקו כל הפוסקים כרבי וכבן עזאי לקמן], ח) [וע"ע תוס' סנהדרין לא. ד"ה שב"ש אומרים].

הגהות הב"ח

(א) רשב"ם ד"ה ואמרי ליה וכו' שראוהו שדר בבית: (ב) ד"ה אבל ראיה וכו' אינו צריך שמעון כלום: (ג) תוס' ד"ה אתא וכו' ור"י פליג נמי אר"ש בן אלעזר הכא: (ד) בא"ד דהתם כיון דאין זה גוף וכו' דגוף הדבר שמעידין עליו הוא דייקי: (ה) ד"ה נחלקה וכו' דהכא מיירי כל"ל ותיבת מלי נמחק:

ליקוטי רש"י

על כת אחת. זה אומר מנה וזה אומר מאתים דמכחישין זה את זה. נחלקה עדותן. שכיון שהאחד שקר הוא אין כאן עדות [סנהדרין לא.]. דנחלקה עדותן דהא קא מכחשי אהדדי [נזיר כ.]. יש בכלל מאתים מנה. שניהם מעידין על מנה. ובאותו מנה אין מכחישין זה את זה הלכך מצטרפין זה שיש בכלל מאתים מנה ולא אמרינן שמיהן שקרן אלא הלך אחר הספות [סנהדרין שם]. הבא משום ירושה אינו צריך טענה. אינו צריך לומר אתה מכרת לאבי אלא שאבי החזיק בה ולא אמר לו דבר לא טענה [לעיל כג.]. דסייר ארעא. סייר. מעיין [תענית ט:]. בודק ופוקד כמו ואני פוקד אתכם (שמות ג) מתרגם כמו האי ענינא דלא סר סכינא קמיה תכם [שם כ:] ובעי"ו גיטין סח.].

Rav, who had witnessed this exchange, commented:
אָמַר רַב – Rav said: הֲוָה יָתִיבְנָא קַמֵּיהּ דַּחֲבִיבִי – I was sitting before my uncle, R' Chiya,[11] when he rendered this decision, **וְאָמְרִי לֵיהּ – and I said to him, וְכִי אֵין אָדָם עָשׂוּי לִיקַּח וְלִמְכּוֹר בְּלַיְלָה – "Does a man not occasionally buy and sell** a property **in a** single **night** without ever living in it?" Thus, it should not be necessary to prove that the seller ever occupied the property at all.[12]

R' Chiya did not accept Rav's argument. Rav now elaborates R' Chiya's view:
וַחֲזִיתִיהּ לְדַעְתֵּיהּ – Although R' Chiya required some proof of occupancy, **I perceived that it was his opinion אִי אָמַר לֵיהּ** – that **if [the occupant] had said to [the original owner]: קַמָּאִי דִּידִי זַבְנָהּ מִינָּךְ – "He** [the man from whom I bought the house] **bought it from you in front of me," מְהֵימַן – he would be believed,** even without witnesses, **מִיגּוֹ דְּאִי בָּעֵי אָמַר לֵיהּ – since** if he were lying, **he could** just as well **have said to [the original owner]: אֲנָא זְבַנְתָּה מִינָּךְ** – "I bought [the upper story] directly **from you."**[13]

Rava commented on the dispute between R' Chiya and Rav:
אָמַר רָבָא – Rava said: כְּוָותֵיהּ דְּר׳ חִיָּיא מִסְתַּבְּרָא – The view of R' Chiya, requiring proof that the seller lived there at least one day, **seems more probable דְּקָתָנֵי** – inasmuch **as the Mishnah teaches: הַבָּא מִשּׁוּם יְרוּשָּׁה אֵינוֹ צָרִיךְ טַעֲנָה – "ONE WHO COMES INTO** a property **BY WAY OF INHERITANCE DOES NOT REQUIRE A** supporting **CLAIM." טַעֲנָה הוּא דְּלָא בָּעֵי** – This implies that **he does not require a *claim*, הָא רְאָיָה בָּעֵי – but he does require** some sort of **proof!**[14]

The Gemara rejects Rava's inference:
וְדִלְמָא לֹא רְאָיָה בָּעֵי וְלֹא טַעֲנָה בָּעֵי – But perhaps the Mishnah means that **he requires neither a proof nor a claim?**[15]

The Gemara suggests another way around Rava's proof:
וְאִיבָּעֵית אֵימָא – Or, if you prefer, say that the Mishnah is no proof to R' Chiya's ruling because **שָׁאנֵי לוֹקֵחַ – a purchaser is different** than an heir, **דְּלָא שָׁדֵי זוּזֵי בִּכְדִי – since** it can be assumed that **[a purchaser] would not throw his money away.**[16]

A question relating to R' Chiya's ruling is raised:
אִיבַּעְיָא לְהוּ – They inquired: נִרְאָה בּוֹ מַאי – If [the seller] was seen in [the property], but was not actually seen using it,[17] **what** is the law? Would this sighting be considered sufficient to satisfy R' Chiya's requirement?

The Gemara presents a dispute:
אָמַר אַבָּיֵי – Abaye said: הִיא הִיא – It is the same[18] as proof of occupancy. **רָבָא אָמַר – Rava,** however, **said: עָבִיד אִינִישׁ דְּסַיֵּיר [אַרְעָא] (ארעיה) וְלָא זָבֵין – It often happens that a person measures land and does not buy it** afterwards.[19]

The Gemara cites another ruling with respect to property that went through a succession of buyers:
שְׁלֹשָׁה לְקוֹחוֹת מִצְטָרְפִין – Three successive **purchasers** of a field, each of whom occupied it for a time, **combine** to establish a *chazakah* with regard to the original owner of the field.[20]

NOTES

the person who sold it to him obtained it from the original owner, the court should argue on his behalf that the seller obtained it legally, either by purchase or as a gift. Thus, since the occupant has a *chazakah* of more than three years, he should be allowed to retain the property. R' Chiya rules that indeed we do argue this on his behalf. However, it is necessary for the occupant to lend some credence to this claim by proving that the seller occupied the property for at least one day before selling it (*Rashbam* as explained by *Ketzos HaChoshen* 146:9; cf. *Ramban, Nimukei Yosef*).

11. R' Chiya was the brother of both Rav's father and mother. R' Chiya's half-brother [on his father's side] had married R' Chiya's half-sister [on his mother's side] (*Rashbam* from *Sanhedrin* 5a).

12. A person will occasionally resell a property immediately after buying it, if he can realize a quick profit. Thus, his failure to occupy it for even a single day is not necessarily remarkable, and should not prevent the court from arguing on behalf of the current occupant. R' Chiya, however, did not accept this argument, as is evident from the conclusion of this discussion (*Rashbam*).

13. Had the current occupant claimed that he bought the property directly from the original owner, he would have won the case based on his *chazakah*. However, he does not claim this, but claims instead that he bought it from a third person whom he saw buying it from the original owner. If he is not telling the truth about this, what is his purpose in concocting such an elaborate lie? It would be far simpler for him to claim that he bought it directly from the original owner! Thus, we must assume that he is telling the truth and we must therefore also believe him when he says that he *witnessed* this other person buying the property from the original owner.

This *migo* argument can only aid him, however, if he claims such definite knowledge. If he simply says, "I assumed my seller bought it from you," of what use is it to know that he is being truthful? He still has no evidence that the man who sold him the property ever held legal title to it. Therefore, unless he can prove at least a single day's occupancy, we cannot award him the property (*Rashbam*).

Ketzos HaChoshen (146:12) points out that it is not really necessary to resort to a *migo* proof in this case. Since the occupant claims to know with certainty that the person from whom he bought the property had bought it from the original owner, he is putting forth a definite claim of ownership. His *chazakah* alone should therefore suffice to demonstrate his right to the property, since it is now supported by a proper claim. The Gemara mentions the *migo* argument here not because it is necessary to prove his claim but only as a way of illustrating the acceptability of the occupant's claim to have witnessed the sale by the original owner and then to have bought it from the purchaser. The Gemara is stating in effect that this is no less a claim than stating that one bought it directly from the original owner (see also *Teshuvos R' Akiva Eiger* vol. 3, §29; cf. *Chidushei R' Shimon* §12).

14. This is implied by the fact that the Mishnah did not simply state, "one who comes into a property by way of inheritance needs nothing at all" (*Rashbam*). [Since the Mishnah does not make this more categorical statement, the implication is that the heir is exempted only from explaining how his father obtained the property. He is nonetheless required to show some evidence that his father at least held the property.] Although the Mishnah speaks only of an heir and R' Chiya ruled regarding a purchaser, the Gemara now assumes that a purchaser and an heir are identical with regard to this ruling.

15. I.e. perhaps when the Mishnah says that an heir does not require a claim, what it means is that he is not required to say anything more to the court than that he inherited the property (*Rashbam*).

16. I.e. even if we were to concede that Rava's inference from the Mishnah is valid, and an heir must prove that his father occupied the land for one day, this would not prove that a purchaser must also do so. A person does not generally spend money on a property unless he ascertains the validity of the seller's title. We may therefore assume that the occupant of this upper floor did indeed ascertain that the seller was its rightful owner before he paid him for it and there is no reason to require him to prove it once again (*Rashbam*).

Despite these rejections of Rava's proof, the halachah follows the view of R' Chiya, that both an heir and a purchaser must prove that the person from whom they received the property occupied it for at least one day. Only then does their *chazakah* establish the property as theirs (*Rashbam; Choshen Mishpat* 146:10,14).

17. He was seen measuring the property (*Rashbam*).

18. Literally: this [is] this.

19. Thus, seeing someone measure the boundaries of a property does not attest to his occupancy of it. It therefore does not satisfy R' Chiya's requirement.

20. For example, a field (which witnesses testify originally belonged to Reuven) was occupied by Shimon for one year. Shimon then sold it to Levi, who occupied the land for a second year, and he in turn sold it to Yehudah, who occupied the field for a third year. At that point, Reuven sought to repossess the field, claiming that Shimon had stolen it from him, and that Yehudah's title was therefore invalid. Yehudah counters

עין משפט
נר מצוה

קי א מיי' פ"ג מהל' עדות הלכה ג סמג עשין קט טוש"ע ח"מ סי' ל סעיף ג:
קיא ב ג מיי' פי"ד מהל' טוען ונטען הלכה יד סמג עשין צה טוש"ע ח"מ סי' קמו סעיף יד:
קיב ד ה מיי' שם הל' יג טוש"ע שם סעיף י:
קיג ו ז מיי' שם פי"ב הלכה ו סמג שם טוש"ע ח"מ סי' קמד סעיף ג:
קיד ח מיי' פי"ח מהל' מלוה הלכה ה סמג עשין צה טוש"ע ח"מ סי' קנה סעיף א:

אתא לקמיה דרב יהודה אזיל אייתי תרי סהדי חד אמר תרתי אוצייתא עאל וחד אמר תלת אוצייתא עאל א"ל זיל שלים תרתי מגו תלת א"ל כמאן כרבי שמעון בן אלעזר דתניא (א) אמר ר' שמעון בן אלעזר לא נחלקו בית שמאי ובית הלל על שתי כיתי עדים שאחת אומרת מנה ואחת אומרת מאתים שיש בכלל מאתים מנה על מה נחלקו על כת אחת שאחד אומר מנה ואחד אומר מאתים שבית שמאי אומרים נחלקה עדותן ובית הלל אומרים (א) יש בכלל מאתים מנה א"ל והא (ב) מייתינא לך איגרתא ממערבא דאין הלכה כר' שמעון בן אלעזר א"ל (ג) לכי תיתי ההוא גברא דדר בקשתא בעיליתא ארבע שני אתא מארי דביתא אשכחיה א"ל מאי בעית בהאי ביתא א"ל מפלניא זבינתה דזבנה מינך אתא לקמיה דר' חייא א"ל (ב) אי אית לך סהדי דדר בה איהו דזבנת מיניה ואפי' חד יומא אוקימנא לה בידך ואי לא לא אמר רב הוה יתיבנא קמיה דחביבי ואמרי ליה וכי אין אדם עשוי ליקח ולמכור בלילה וחזיתיה לדעתיה (ג) אי א"ל קמאי דידי זבנה מינך מהימן מיגו דאי בעי א"ל אנא זבנתה מינך אמר רבא כוותיה דר' חייא מסתברא דקתני (ד) הבא משום ירושה אינו צריך טענה טענה הוא דלא בעי (ה) הא ראיה בעי ודלמא לא ראיה בעי ולא טענה בעי ואיבעית אימא שאני לוקח דלא שדי זוזי בכדי איבעיא להו נראה בו מאי אמר אביי היא היא רבא אמר (ה) עביד איניש (ו) דסייר ארעיה ולא זבין: (ז) שלשה לקוחות מצטרפין אמר רב (ז) וכולם בשטר למימרא דסבר רב שטר אית ליה קלא ועדים לית להו קלא והאמר רב (ח) המוכר שדה בעדים גובה מנכסים משועבדים התם לקוחות אינהו

אתא לקמיה דרב יהודה כו'. ומסיק דרב יהודה כר"ש בן אלעזר ס"ל ותימה דבפ' זה בורר (סנהדרין דף ל: ושם לא. ד"ה הוא) אמר רב יהודה עדות המכחשת זה את זה בבדיקות כשרה בדיני ממונות ומוקי לה באחד אומר ארנקי לבנה ואחד אומר ארנקי שחורה אבל אחד אומר מנה שחור ואחד אומר מנה לבן אין מצטרפין ונהרדעי אמרי אפי' א' אומר מנה לבן ואחד אומר מנה שחור ומסיק דאיהו דאמור כר"ש בן אלעזר דהכא משמע דרב יהודה דפליג אנהרדעי פליג (ג) אר"ש בן אלעזר דהכא וי"ל דרב יהודה נמי כרשב"א ובהא פליגי דנהרדעי סברי דלאחד אומר מנה שחור ואחד אומר מנה לבן דמי למילתיה דר"ש בן אלעזר דלא דייקי ביה סהדי ודמי לארנקי ורב יהודה סבר דלא דמי כלל לארנקי דהתם (ד) דאין זה גוף המעשה לא היה להן לבדוק אבל מנה דגוף הדבר הוא שמעידין עליו דייקי וקסבר דמודה ר"ש בן אלעזר במנה שחור דבטלה עדותן אפי' לב"ה ולא דמי למנה ומאתים דעבידי דטעו טפי אלא מדמה מנה שחור ומנה לבן לאחד אומר חבית של יין וא' אומר של שמן דבהא מודו כולי עלמא דנחלקה עדותן כדאיתא התם:

נחלקה עדותן. הקשה ריב"א לב"ש דאמרי בכת אחת נחלקה עדותן דחשיבי להו עדות מוכחשת ואפי' בב' כיתי עדים נמי תבטל עדותן דהוי נמצא אחד מהן קרוב או פסול עדותן בטלה אפילו הן מאה כדאמר בפ"ק דמכות (דף ה:) ואומר ר"י דלאו פירכא היא דמצינו למימר דב"ש כר' יוסי סבירא להו דאמר התם במה דברים אמורים בדיני נפשות אבל בדיני ממונות תתקיים העדות בשאר והכי הלכתא דפסיק רב נחמן (ז) כוותיה ואפי' לרבי נמי מצי למימר דהכא (ה) מלי מיירי כגון דלאתו למיחזי ואפי' אתו לאסהודי הני מילי כי מסייעי אהדדי הוא דאמר נמצא אחד מהן קרוב או פסול עדותן בטלה אבל הכא דהא מכחשי אהדדי לא (ט):

חד אמר. רב כהנא עייל כותלו בתוך של חבירו: **תרתי אוצייתא.** שתי שורות קרקע על פני השדה לגרגסין בהשותפין (לעיל דף יב.) תלת אוצייתא ב"ב גופני: **תרתי מגו תלת.** תרתי אוצייתא מן השלש שמעיד האחד למחזיקו מיהא מודו לתרתי אוצייתא עייל דבכלל תלת איכא תרי: **א"ל.** רב כהנא לרב יהודה: **כמאן.** דיינת לי דהא תרווייהו מכחשי האי להאי ותבטל עדותן: **א"ל כר"ש בן אלעזר.** שהלכה כמותו ואליבא דב"ה: **ואחת אומרת מאתים.** היו בלותו היום בלותה שעה בלותו מקום: **שיש בכלל מאתים מנה.** דהשתא מאה זוז ואין כת שניה מכחשת על מנה שכת ראשונה מעידה אלא מוסיפין הן מנה אחת אבל כת ראשונה מכחשת לשניה על אותו מנה שמוסיפין ובאותו מנה שני אוקי תרי לבהדי תרי ואוקי ממונא בחזקת מריה ולא ישלם: **נחלקה עדותן.** דמאי דקמסהיד מר לא קמסהיד מר: **ב"ה אומרים יש בכלל מאתים מנה.** ונוטל מנה הכא נמי יש בכלל תלת אוצייתא תרתי ומיהדר ליה: **א"ל.** רב כהנא לרב יהודה: **והא מייתינא איגרתא כו'.** דלפני ב"ה מודו דנחלקה עדותן: **א"ל.** אהדר מיד עד דמייתית איגרתא וכרב יהודה קיימא לן שכן נעשה הדין: **בקשתא.** מקום: **בעיליתא.** עליה: **דזבנה מינך.** בחזקת שהייתי סבור דזבנה מינך לקחתיה ממנו: **דדר בה.** ההוא דאמרת דזבנה לך: **אפי' חד יומא.** כדי לאמת דבריך ואוקמה בידך הואיל והחזקת שני חזקה ושוב לא תצטרך להביא עדים שלקחה מבעליו אותו שמכרה לך משום דטוענין ליורש וטוענין ללוקח דהבא משום ירושה ומשום מקח אינו צריך טענה אלא ראיה שדר בה המוכרה לו יום אחד בעי: **חביבי.** ר' חייא דודו של רב כדאמרינן בסנהדרין (דף ה.) דרב בר אחוה דר"ח ובר אחתיה דר"ח: **ואמרי ליה.** לחביבי אמאי צריך להביא עדים שראוהו (א) בבית יום אחד: **וכי אין אדם עשוי ליקח בלילה.** ולמכור לאחר שיתן לו ריוח באותו לילה עצמו והוה לך לאוקומי להאי אנכסיה בטענה זו דהא טוענין ללוקח ומיהו כר"ח קיי"ל כדמוכח מסקנא: **וחזיתיה לדעתיה.** דרבי חייא: **דאי טעין ליה.** האי מחזיק קמאי דידי זבנה מינך ההוא דזבנה ניהלי מהימן: **מיגו דאי בעי אמר כו'.** הלכך כיון דטעין נמי טענה מעלייתא אני יודע שממך לקחה מהימן דהשתא הויא ליה חזקה שיש עמה טענה אבל כי טעין מפלניא זבנתה בחזקת דאמר לי דזבנה מינך אבל איני יודע אם לקחה ממך אם לאו היינו חזקה שאין עמה טענה הואיל ואפי' יום אחד לא נראה דדר בה: **כוותיה דר' חייא.** דצריך להביא עדים שדר בה המוכרה לו יום אחד: **הבא משום ירושה.** והוא הדין משום לקיחה: **אין צריך טענה.** הך טענה דלעיל דקתני מתניתין אתה מכרת לי אתה נתת לי במתנה אין צריך יורש לטעון ולומר אתה מכרת לאבי: **אבל ראיה.** בעדים שדר בה יום אחד מיהא בעי מדלא קתני הבא משום ירושה אינו צריך (ג) כלום דייקינן הכי: **ודילמא לא ראיה כו'.** והכי קאמר הבא משום ירושה אין צריך שום טענה בעולם אלא זו בלבד מאבי אני יורשה אבל לא עדי דירת יום אחד ולא טענת מכירה ומתנה שניתנה לאביו בעי: ה"ג **ואי בעית אימא שאני לוקח כו'.** אפילו אם תאמר כי היורש צריך ראיה דדר ביה מורישו יום אחד לוקח עדיף טפי מיורש דלוקח אילו לא ברירא ליה מילתא דודאי זבנה המוכרה לו מבעל הקרקע לא הוי שדי זוזי בכדי הלכך ודאי קם אמילתא שפיר כשלקחה ואין צריך לא ראיה ולא טענה: **איבעיא להו נראה בו.** המוכרה ללוקח זה באותו קרקע למוד כמה ארכו וכמה רחבו מאי מי חשיבא עדות ראיה כעדות דירה ומשום דכר' חייא קיימא לן קבעי לה: **שלשה לקוחות מצטרפין.** שדה שיש עדים שהיתה של ראובן כל הימים והחזיק בה שמעון שנה כי טוען שקנאה מראובן ואח"כ מכרה שמעון ללוי בשטר והחזיק לוי שנה ואח"כ מכרה לוי ליהודה וכתב לו שטר מכירה כדלקמן והחזיק בה שנה הרי שלש שנים ואתא ראובן וקמערער ואומר כי לא מכרה לשמעון ויהודה טוען הרי החזקנו בין שלשתינו שלש שנים ולא מחית ושמעון שלקחה ממך שאנו באין מכחו לא היה לו ליזהר בשטרו יותר מג' שנים וראובן משיב לפי שכל אחד מכם לא החזיק שלש שנים אלא שנה לא חששתי למחות שהייתי רואה שאתם יראים להחזיק כדמחזקי אינשי ולא הייתי יודע שבשביל שהייתם מוכרין זה לזה לסוף שנה לפיכך לא החזקתם כל אחד כי אם שנה: **מצטרפין.** הלקוחות ויפסיד ראובן דכיון דבשטר לקחו זה מזה כדמפרש רב בסמוך עדים שבשטר אפקו לקלא וידע ראובן ומדלא מיחה הפסיד אבל בלא שטר מצי טעין האי דלא מחאי שלא החזיק אחד מכם שלש שנים ולא אחזיקתו כדמחזקי אינשי כדאמרינן לעיל (דף כט:) באמתא: **וכולן בשטר.** אשני לקוחות אחרונים קאי אבל לוקח ראשון שלקח מן המערער מה לנו ולשטרו (י) [דאם יש לו שטר פשיטא דאין יכול לערער]: **שטר אית ליה קלא.** שמתפספין לכותבו ולחותמו והכל שומעין: **ועדים לית להו קלא.** מכירה בעדים בלא שטר: **המוכר שדהו בפני עדים.** וקבל עליו אחריותו: **גובה.** הלוקח מן המוכר אפי' מנכסים שמשועבד ומשכן או מכר קרקעותיו אחרי מכירה זו שקבל עליו אחריותה וטעם משום דעדים מפקי לקלא וידעו הלקוחות שמכר זה קרקע באחריות והיה להם להניח למוכר בני חורין כשיעור האחריות אלמא עדים בלא שטר אית להו קלא: **שאני לקוחות.** אע"ג דמכירה בעדים בלא שטר לית ליה קלא ממילא אלא אם כן יפספסו ויחקרו הדבר: אינהו

מסורת הש"ס

א) סנהדרין לא. מיר כ. ע"ש, ב) [סנהדרין כט.], ג) [שבועות מח:], ד) לעיל כג., ה) [צ"ל דסייר ארעא], ו) מהרש"ל, ז) [ער' מכות ו. פסק רב נחמן הלכה כר' יוסי ומה"ט פסקו כל הפוסקים כרבי ובכן מלוה לתקן], ח) [וע"ע תוס' סנהדרין לא. ד"ה סב"ה אומרים].

הגהות הב"ח

(א) רשב"ם ד"ה ואמרי ליה וכו' שראוהו שדר בבית: (ב) ד"ה אבל ראיה וכו' אינו צריך לטעון כלום: (ג) תוס' ד"ה אתא וכו' פליג נמי אר"ש בן אלעזר דהכא: (ד) בא"ד דהתם כיון דאין זה גוף וכו' דגוף הדבר שמעידין עליו הוא דייקי: (ה) ד"ה נחלקה וכו' דהכא מיירי כל"ל ותיבת מלי נמחק:

ליקוטי רש"י

ע"י כת אחת. זה אומר מנה וזה אומר מאתים דמכחישין זה את זה. נחלקה עדותן. שכיון שהאחד שקר שוב אין כאן עדות [סנהדרין לא.]. דנחלקה עדותן דהא קא מכחשי אהדדי [נזיר כ.]. יש בכלל מאתים מנה. שניהם מעידין על מנה ובאותו מנה אין מכחישין זה את זה ולא מצטרפין למנה שיש בכלל מאתים מנה ולא אמרינן שמיהן שקרו אלא הלך אחר הפחות [סנהדרין שם]. הבא משום ירושה אינו צריך טענה. אינו צריך לומר אתה מכרת לאבי אלא ראיתי לאבי שהחזיק בה ולא ערער אדם עליו [לעיל כג.]. [דסייר ארעא]. סייר. מעיין [תענית ט:]. מתרגם פוקד (שמות לד) מסער כמו האי עבדא דלא סר סכינא קמיה סכיא [שם כ: וכעי"ז גיטין סח.].

רבינו גרשום

חד אמר. עייל כותלו בשדה חבירו **תרתי אוצייתא** ברוחב ב' שורו' על פני כל השדה: **אמר ליה זיל אהדר תרתי** אוצייתא **מגו תלת.** דתרווייהו הני עדים מסהדי דתרתי אוצייתא עיילת בתוך שדהו ובכלל תלתא איכא תרתי: **אחת אומרת מנה.** לוה פלוני מפלוני **ואחת אומרת מאתים** א) מנה **ונוטל מנה** הכי נמי יש בכלל ג' אוצייתא תרתי ומהדר לי' [תרתי]: א"ל. רב כהנא לר' יהודה **והא מייתינא איגרתא ממערבא דלית הלכת' כר' שמעון בן אלעזר.** דאפילו בית הלל מודו להיכא דאחד אומר מנה ואחד אומר מאתים דנחלקה עדותן ולא קא משלם אפילו מנה הכי נמי נחלקה עדותן: **אמר ליה.** אהדר מיד **עד דתיתי** איגרתא: **בקשתא.** שם מקום: **בעיליתא.** בעלייה: **דדר בה ההוא דזבניה אפי' חד יומא** כדי לאמת דבריך **ואוקמה בידך** הואיל דאחזקת בה ד' שנין: **חביבי.** ר' חייא דודו: **ואמרי ליה.** ואי לא מייתי סהדי דדר בה ההוא דזבניה ליה חד יומא אמאי לא מוקמי' בידיה **וכי אין אדם עשוי לקנות** מאחד **בלילה ולמכור** באותו הלילה ואמאי לא מוקמי' בידיה הא הכא איכא למימר דבלילה זבנה מאחר ולאלתר מכרה ליה: **וחזיתיה לדעתי'.** שהבנתי מתוך דבריו **דאי אמר ליה** המחזיק **קמיה דידי זבנה מינך** ההוא שקניתיה ממנו **מהימן: כוותיה דר' חייא.** דאמר לעיל דצריך לאתויי סהדי דדר בה ההוא אפי' חד יומא הכי **מסתברא דקתני הבא מחמת ירושה** והוא הדין מחמת לקיחה: **הא ראיה.** כל דהו **בעי** כהאי גוונא: **ולא ראיה בעי.** דהואיל ובא מחמת ירושה אנן טענינן ליה: **איבעית אימא.** משום הכי בעי ר' חייא ראיה גבי לוקח משום **דלוקח שאני** מיורש דלוקח **לא שדי זוזי בכדי** דהואיל ויהיב דמי מדקדק יפה דההוא דזבניה ניהליה דדייר ביה חד יומא והואיל שטוען מפלניא זבינתיה דזבנה מינך צריך למיתי ראיה דדר בה חד יומא ההוא דזבנה ניהליה אי לא מייתי ראיה לא מוקמינן לה בידיה: **איבעיא להו נראה בו מהו.** כלומר אית ליה סהדי דההוא דזבנה ליה הוה איתחזי בההוא ביתא והוה אזיל לעיוני במצרי הבית כמה ארכו וכמה רחבו הוי מי אמרינן הואיל וקא מעיין הכי ודאי קני מהאי מערער לאוקמי' ליה בידא דלוקח ודמי כמאן דדר בה חד יומא: **אמר אביי היא היא.** ודאי דמי כמאן דדר בה: **רבא אמר.** לא קנה לוקח דהואיל דלית ליה סהדי דדר בה ממש **דעבד אינש דסייר ביתא** דחבריה **ולא זבין: ג' לקוחות מצטרפין.** כגון שמכר שדה לאחד והחזיק בה שנה והלך זה שקנאה ומכר לשני והחזיק בה שנה והלך זה שני ומכרה לשלישי והחזיק בה שנה מצטרפין אלו ג' שנים ודמי כאילו שהתה ביד לוקח שלישי ג' שנים והחזיק בה: **אמר רב וכולן בשטר.** כלומר אם אלו לקוחות מכרוה זה לזה בשטר ולא מיחה זה בשעת מכירה אין יכול שוב למחות משום השטר: **קלא אית ליה.** ואם איתא דשלו היא היה מוחה בשעת מכירה: **עדים לית להו קלא.** שאם מכרו זה לזה בעדים שלא בשטר ולא מיחה יכול שוב למחות דיכול למימר לא ידעתי במכירתם: **והאמר רב המוכר שדהו** שלא בשטר **גובה מנכסים משועבדים.** שאם מכר שדהו בפני עדים לאחד בא באחריות ובא בעל חוב של מוכר וטרפה מן הלוקח גובה מנכסין משועבדים שאם מכר לאחרי כן שדה לאחר אחר שקבל לזה אחריות שמשועבד לפצותו גובה אותן משועבדין שמכר לאחרים בשיעור הקרקע שטרפה ממנו אלמא כיון דגובה מנכסין משועבדין ש"מ דקסבר רב בעדים אית

חשק שלמה על רבינו גרשום א) נ"ל שיש בכלל מאתים מנה ונוטל מנה וכו'.

Rav qualifies this ruling:

אָמַר רַב – Rav said: וְכוּלָּם בִּשְׁטָר – This is only **if all [the purchases] were** recorded **in deeds.**[21]

The Gemara deduces from Rav's statement that purchases can only be assumed to be public knowledge if they were recorded in deeds; unrecorded purchases made in the presence of witnesses, however, may not become public knowledge.[22] The Gemara questions this:

לְמֵימְרָא דְּסָבַר רַב – Is this to say that Rav holds שְׁטָר אִית לֵיהּ קָלָא – that a sale recorded in **a deed becomes public knowledge,** וְעֵדִים לֵית לְהוּ קָלָא – **whereas** a sale in the presence of **witnesses does not become public knowledge** if it is not recorded?[23] וְהָאָמַר רַב – **But Rav has said:** הַמּוֹכֵר שָׂדֶה בְּעֵדִים – If **one sells a field in the presence of witnesses** without writing a deed, and he guarantees the purchase,[24] and the field is later seized by one of the seller's creditors, גּוֹבֶה מִנְּכָסִים מְשׁוּעְבָּדִים – **[the purchaser] can collect** even **from encumbered property;** i.e. he can collect from any other property owned by the seller at the time of the sale, even if it has since been sold.[25] This indicates that a sale made before witnesses becomes public knowledge even without a deed.[26] – ? –

The Gemara makes a distinction:

הָתָם – **There,** in the case of the guaranteed field, לְקוּחוֹת – **the** subsequent **purchasers**

NOTES

that Shimon had purchased the field, and, since three years passed without challenge, Shimon can no longer be expected to produce a deed. Reuven replies that he did not bother to contest the occupancy because no single occupant held the land for more than a year. This indicated to him that they were each afraid to hold the land long enough to establish a *chazakah*! Reuven claims to have been unaware that the reason for the change of occupants was because the field had been sold twice (*Rashbam*). [Rather, he thought that the rapid turnover of occupants betrayed their guilty knowledge that the field was not theirs, and it was therefore unnecessary for him to protest.]

The Gemara rules that the three years of occupancy do combine to establish a *chazakah,* Reuven's claim notwithstanding. The court does not find credible the original owner's claim to have been unaware of the sales, since they were each recorded in deeds (see next note). He should therefore have protested the occupancies and his failure to do so establishes the *chazakah* (*Rashbam*).

[This situation satisfies R' Chiya's requirement in the previous Gemara, since there are witnesses that Shimon occupied the land for a year. The Gemara's novel point is only that three separate occupancies combine to form a *chazakah.*]

21. It can be assumed that the original owner knew of the sales from the first occupant to the second, and from him to the third, only if they were sold with deeds. The recording of such documents inevitably spreads the news of the sales, insuring that the original owner hears of them. Thus, to establish a *chazakah* the current occupant must prove that those sales were recorded in deeds. [The first occupant obviously does not have his deed, since if he did, no dispute would exist. His deed is not needed, however, because the only issue is whether the original owner is likely to have heard of the sales to the second and third occupants.] (*Rashbam*).

22. For this reason Rav ruled that if it cannot be proved that the sales of the first and second occupants were recorded in deeds, the *chazakah* will be invalid, even though there are witnesses to the sales.

23. Literally: a deed has a voice but witnesses do not have a voice. A sale recorded in a deed is more likely to become public knowledge because a larger number of people gather to record and affix witnesses to a legal document, and they spread the news of it (*Rashbam*).

24. I.e. he guaranteed to refund the purchaser's money if the field is subsequently seized by a creditor of the seller. [Under Torah law, when a person incurs a debt, all his real property becomes subject to an automatic lien (see next note). This property may be sold, but the lien remains in force. Should the seller be unable to meet his obligation, the creditor may later seize the property from the buyer to satisfy the debt. (Such property is known as נְכָסִים מְשׁוּעְבָּדִים, *encumbered property.*) To protect the buyer, the seller in this case guaranteed the sale; i.e. he obligated himself to repay the buyer should the property be seized by a creditor.]

25. [For example, if Reuven sold a field to Shimon on the first of the month, and he then sold another field to Levi on the second, Shimon, if he loses his field to Reuven's creditor, may take Levi's field to satisfy his guarantee.]

26. [The law that an obligation creates an automatic lien on the debtor's property is only for obligations whose existence are assumed to become public knowledge, such as those recorded in a document. In such cases, it is up to the buyer to protect himself by making sure that he does not buy unless enough property remains in the hands of the seller to cover his outstanding obligations. Obligations that cannot be assumed to become public knowledge are excluded from this rule because buyers do not hear about them and therefore cannot protect themselves.] Since Rav says that the buyer who bought a field in the presence of witnesses – but without a deed – may later collect on his guarantee by seizing the property of those who bought after him, we see that Rav holds that the sale of the guaranteed property becomes well publicized even without a deed, merely because of the presence of witnesses. Thus, it was possible for the subsequent buyers to protect themselves by not buying from the seller unless he retained enough property to cover the guarantee (*Rashbam*).

אִינְהוּ אַפְסִידוּ אַנַּפְשַׁיְיהוּ – **have brought the loss upon themselves,** by not inquiring whether the seller had previously sold any land with a guarantee.[1]

The Gemara questions Rav's ruling that a guarantee can be collected from "encumbered property" even if the sale was not recorded in a deed:

וּמִי אָמַר רַב הָכִי – **Did Rav indeed say this?** וְהָתְנַן – **But we have learned in a Mishnah:**[2] הַמַּלְוֶה אֶת חֲבֵירוֹ בִּשְׁטָר – ONE WHO LENDS money TO HIS FELLOW ON the basis of A DOCUMENT attesting to the loan גּוֹבֶה מִנְּכָסִים מְשׁוּעְבָּדִים – MAY COLLECT the loan even FROM ENCUMBERED PROPERTIES;[3] עַל יְדֵי עֵדִים – if he made the loan ON THE BASIS OF WITNESSES, without drawing up a document, גּוֹבֶה מִנְּכָסִים בְּנֵי חוֹרִין – HE MAY COLLECT only FROM AVAILABLE PROPERTIES, i.e. property still in the hands of the borrower. We see from the Mishnah's ruling that an unrecorded loan *cannot* be collected from subsequent purchasers, because they are not expected to have inquired about previous liens.[4] This contradicts our explanation of Rav's view. – ? –

The Gemara considers and rejects a possible solution:

וְכִי תֵּימָא – **And if you will** perhaps **say** רַב תַּנָּא הוּא וּפְלִיג – that **Rav is** considered **a Tanna and he disagrees** with the Mishnah,[5] this cannot be the answer. וְהָא רַב וּשְׁמוּאֵל דְּאָמְרֵי תַּרְוַיְיהוּ – **For Rav and Shmuel have both stated:** מִלְוָה עַל פֶּה – In the case of **a loan undertaken orally,** i.e. without a document to record it, אֵינוֹ גּוֹבֶה לֹא מִן הַיּוֹרְשִׁים – **[a lender] cannot collect** it **either from the heirs** of the debtor's estate, וְלֹא מִן הַלָּקוֹחוֹת – **or from the purchasers** of his property.[6] Thus, Rav *himself* stated that unrecorded loans cannot be collected from encumbered property – indicating that purchasers are not expected to discover the existence of unrecorded liens![7]

The Gemara answers both questions by making a distinction:

מִלְוָה אַזְבִינֵי קָא רָמֵית – **Are you contrasting loans with sales?** The two cannot be compared! מִלְוָה – In the case of **a loan,** כִּי קָא יָזֵיף – **when [someone] borrows,** בְּצִנְעָא קָא יָזֵיף – **he borrows privately,** כִּי הֵיכִי דְּלָא לִיתְזְלוּ נִכְסֵיהּ עֲלֵיהּ – **so that his property should not lose its value for him.**[8] Therefore, we cannot assume that buyers will discover the existence of the lien.[9] זְבִינֵי – In the case of **sales,** however, מַאן דְּזַבִּין אַרְעָא – **one who sells land** בְּפַרְהֶסְיָא זַבִּין – **does so publicly,** כִּי הֵיכִי דְּלֵיפּוּק לָהּ קָלָא – **in order that word** of the impending sale **should spread** and cause more people to bid on it. Therefore, we assume that subsequent buyers will discover the existence of an earlier guaranteed sale if only they will investigate.[10]

The Gemara now returns to Rav's original ruling – that a *chazakah* can be established by three successive purchasers of a property – and cites a Baraisa in support of it:

תָּנוּ רַבָּנָן – **The Rabbis taught in a Baraisa:** אֲכָלָהּ הָאָב שָׁנָה – If A FATHER USED [A PROPERTY] for ONE YEAR and then died, וְהַבֵּן שְׁתַּיִם – AND THE SON then used it TWO years more; הָאָב שְׁתַּיִם – or, if THE FATHER used the property for TWO years and died, וְהַבֵּן שָׁנָה – AND THE SON then used it ONE YEAR more; הָאָב שָׁנָה וְהַבֵּן שָׁנָה – or, if THE FATHER used it ONE YEAR, and died, AND THE SON used it ONE YEAR and then sold it, וְהַלּוֹקֵחַ שָׁנָה – AND THE PURCHASER used it ONE YEAR more; הֲרֵי זוֹ חֲזָקָה – THIS CONSTITUTES A *CHAZAKAH*.[11] We see from this Baraisa that a purchaser can count the uncontested years of use of the previous occupants to establish a *chazakah* for himself, just as Rav ruled with regard to three successive purchasers.

NOTES

1. A sale that takes place in the presence of witnesses, without being recorded in a deed, does not generate wide publicity. Nevertheless, knowledge of it does not remain secret. A serious inquiry would certainly uncover the fact of the sale and the accompanying guarantee. A buyer is expected to investigate any possible obligations that might affect the land he is buying, and since such an investigation would have revealed the existence of the guarantee, the subsequent buyers have no one to blame but themselves if they did not know of it.

In Rav's case, however, the original owner of the land cannot be faulted for failing to discover the witnesses to the sales of the property from one holder to the next, since he had no reason to investigate the possibility of such sales. Since word does not reach him without an investigation, he has every right to assume that the three holders were unconnected. He can therefore claim that he did not bother to protest for this reason (*Rashbam*). [Had the sales been recorded, however, he would not have this claim because he would have heard of the sales even without investigating.]

2. Below, 175a.

3. I.e. real property owned by the borrower at the time of the loan and subsequently sold. This is because a loan document automatically establishes a lien upon all real estate owned by the borrower at the time of the loan. Even if no such lien is mentioned in the note, its absence is deemed an oversight by the scribe, and a lien nevertheless takes effect. However, a lender may collect from encumbered property only if the borrower has no available assets from which to collect (*Rashbam*).

4. Had the Sages considered it the buyer's responsibility to investigate the possibility of any liens on a property before buying it, there would be no difference between recorded and unrecorded loans. In either case the buyer would know of the lien. The only reason for distinguishing between them is because a buyer hears of a recorded loan even without investigation. We see from this that the Sages considered buyers responsible only for obligations which they would hear of even without inquiring.

5. While an Amora does not have the authority to dispute a Tannaic ruling, Rav, who lived during the transition from the Tannaic to the Amoraic periods, is considered to be both a Tanna and an Amora. Thus, perhaps Rav holds that purchasers *are* held responsible for failing to inquire about existing liens, and he would rule in the case of the Mishnah that a loan made before witnesses *can* be collected from buyers, even if it was not recorded.

6. The Gemara below (175b) explains that Rav and Shmuel maintain that under Biblical law, a debtor's property is not automatically mortgaged to his debt, and it requires a document to create a lien. Thus, if the debt was not recorded, any property sold by the debtor or passed on to his heirs is beyond the reach of the creditor (*Rashbam*; see below, 175b, and *Kiddushin* 13b; see also *Ritva* here).

7. Thus, not only does the Mishnah disprove Rav's contention that purchasers are expected to learn of sales made before witnesses, his own ruling regarding oral loans contradicts it as well.

8. When a person known to be in financial difficulty sells property, prospective buyers offer lower prices for it because they assume that he is desperate to sell. Therefore, when someone borrows money, he requests of the witnesses that they not publicize the loan, so that people should not realize his financial difficulties. This makes it difficult to find out about an oral loan (*Rashbam*).

9. [Once a loan is recorded in a document, however, word of it spreads despite the borrower's efforts to keep it silent.]

10. Accordingly, there are three levels of outside knowledge in regard to sales and loans. (1) A recorded *sale* or *loan* is assumed to become common knowledge by virtue of its having been recorded. [Therefore, one can collect a recorded loan or guarantee from purchasers. Similarly, the original owner of a property is assumed to have heard of its sale from one occupant to another.] (2) An unrecorded *sale* is not assumed to become common knowledge, but it is assumed to be discoverable upon investigation. [Therefore, the guarantee of an unrecorded sale may be collected from purchasers since they are expected to investigate.] (3) An unrecorded *loan*, however, is often not discoverable even upon investigation. [Therefore, it cannot be collected from purchasers.]

11. The original owner is assumed to have known that the second occupant is the son of the first; it is therefore to be expected that he should inherit from his father and occupy the property in his place. He is also assumed to have heard of the sale of the property to the purchaser, if the sale was recorded in a document. Thus, he has no excuse for his failure to protest (*Rashbam*).

אינהו אפסידו אנפשייהו ומי אמר רב הכי והתנן א) המלוה את חבירו בשטר גובה מנכסים משועבדים ע"י עדים גובה מנכסים בני חורין וכי תימא ב) רב תנא הוא ופליג והא רב ושמואל דאמרי תרוייהו ג) מלוה על פה אינו גובה לא מן היורשים ולא מן הלקוחות מלוה אזביני קא רמית מלוה כי קא יזיף בצנעא קא יזיף כי היכי דלא ליתזלו נכסיה עליה א זביני מאן דזבין ארעא בפרהסיא זבין כי היכי דליפוק לה קלא ת"ר ב אכלה האב שנה והבן שתים האב שתים והבן שנה האב שנה והבן שנה והלוקח שנה הרי זו חזקה למימרא דלוקח אית ליה קלא ורמינהי ג אכלה בפני האב שנה ובפני הבן שתים בפני האב שתים ובפני הבן שנה בפני האב שנה ובפני הבן שנה ובפני לוקח שנה הרי זו חזקה ואי סלקא דעתך לוקח אית ליה קלא אין לך מחאה גדולה מזו אמר רב פפא ד כי תניא ההיא במוכר שדותיו סתם:

מתני' ה האומנין ו והשותפין ז והאריסין ח והאפוטרופין אין להם חזקה ט לא לאיש חזקה בנכסי אשתו ולא לאשה חזקה בנכסי בעלה י ולא לאב בנכסי הבן ולא לבן בנכסי האב במה דברים אמורים במחזיק כ אבל בנותן מתנה ל והאחין שחלקו מ והמחזיק בנכסי הגר ד) נעל וגדר ופרץ כל שהוא הרי זו חזקה: גמ'

רשב"ם

אינהו אפסידו אנפשייהו. דשדו זוזייהו בכדי שהיה להם לחקור יפה אם מכר שום קרקע באחריות ולא עשו לפיכך הפסידו אבל גבי שלש לקוחות אין להפסיד המערער דכיון דליכא שטר במכירות הללו ולא יצא הקול ממילא לא היה לו לחקור דמימר אמר לפי שיראים להחזיק בקרקע שלי לא אכלוה כל אחד שלש שנים: **ומי אמר רב הכי.** דמכירת קרקע באחריות בעדים בלא שטר גובה הלוקח כשיטרפוה ממנו מנכסים משועבדים: **בשטר.** דסתם שטר לאחריות נכתב ואפילו לא נכתב קי"ל אחריות טעות סופר הוא וכמי שנכתב דמי: **מנכסים משועבדים.** מלקוחות וכגון שלא שבקו ליה ללוה בני חורין לגבות המלוה מהם: **ע"י עדים.** כלומר בלא שטר: **מנכסים בני חורין.** וכגון שמודה שלא פרעו דהא קי"ל המלוה חבירו בעדים אין צריך לפרעו בעדים אבל ממשועבדין לא יגבה דעדים בלא שטר לית להו קלא ולא אמרינן לקוחות אפסידו אנפשייהו וקשיא לרב: **מלוה על פה.** היינו מלוה את חבירו בעדים: **אינו גובה לא מן היורשין כו'.** טעמא מפרש בשלהי מכלתין שיעבודא לאו דאורייתא ומיהו לא קי"ל הכי אלא כדמפרש התם הלכתא גובה מן היורשין ולא מן הלקוחות: **יזיף איניש בצנעא.** ומבקש שלא לפרסם הדבר כדי שאם יצא למכור קרקע לא יבינו העולם שהוא דחוק לפרוע מעות ולא יקחו ממנו ביוקר הלכך מאי הוה להו ללקוחות למיעבד: **מאן דזבין בפרהסיא קזבין.** כדי שיקפצו עליה לוקחין והלכך אפסידו לקוחות אנפשייהו שאם חקרו יפה היו שומעין מפי אדם שמכר מוכר זה כבר קרקע באחריות: **אכלה האב שנה.** ומת ואכלה בנו אחריו שתים ולא מיחה המערער: **הרי זו חזקה.** שמצטרפין לשלש שנים דיורש כרעיה דאבוה הוא ולא מצי מערער למטען משום דלא אחזיק כל אחד שלש שנים לא מחיתי שהרי הכל יודעים שדרך הבן לירש את האב: **ולוקח שנה.** שמכרה לו הבן בשטר: **למימרא דלוקח.** מיורש אית ליה קלא: **ורמינהי כו'.** ולרב לא פריך לעיל דרב בלוקח מלוקח מיירי הלכך אלימא ליה טפי למיפרך ממאי דדמי ליה: **אית ליה קלא.** והיה לו למערער למחות ומשום דלא מיחה הויא חזקה: **אכלה.** המחזיק: **בפני האב.** שהיתה שלו שנה שאומר שלקחה מן האב: **ובפני הבן.** לאחר מות האב: **ובפני הלוקח.** שלקחה מן הבן ויש לו שטר: **הרי זו חזקה.** ולא מצי מפיק ליה לוקח דבן מידיה דמחזיק משום דקטעין מחזיק שטר היה לי מן האב ונזהרתי בו בשמירתו שלש שנים ועכשיו אבד הימני שלא חששתי לשמרו אחר שהחזקתי שלש שנים בלא מחאה שלא ידעתי מלקיחתך מן הבן לסוף שתי שנים דלוקח מבן לית ליה קלא ולא הויא מחאה: **אין לך מחאה גדולה מזו.** שמכרה הבן לסוף שתי שנים ללוקח זה והיה למחזיק להזהר בשטרו כל הימים עד דמרע ליה לשטרא דהאי לוקח אבל בשלש שנים אחר השטר אין די ומפקינן מידא דמחזיק אם לא נזהר בשטרו כדאמרינן בפירקין לעיל (דף לא.) אבל שית אין לך מחאה גדולה מזו: **אמר רב פפא.** לעולם אימא לך דלוקח אית ליה קלא והכא אמאי לא חשבי מחאה לקיחת הלוקח מן הבן משום דמכר לו הבן כל שדותיו סתם אותן שהיו של אביו וטוען הלוקח שגם זה השדה קניתי בכלל קרקעות כולן דאמרינן ליה כל שדותיו מכר לך חוץ מזו אבל אם מכר (א) זה השדה בפני עצמו בטלה חזקתו של מחזיק דאין לך מחאה גדולה מזו. ויש מפרשים במוכר כל שדותיו ומכר לו בפירוש גם זו עמהן ולאו מילתא היא דסתם משמע שלא פירש: **מתני' האומנין.** בעלי אומנות שמוליכין להם בביתם לתקן כלים כגון לצבוע או כובסין או חייטין או סורקי בגדים שטוענין לקוח הוא בידי: (ב) **אין להם חזקה.** ולא בחזקת שלש שנים מיירי דסתם אומן לא שייך אלא במטלטלין וחזקת שלש שנים לא נאמרה אלא במקרקעי אבל במטלטלי מי שהוא מוחזק בשל חבירו אפילו שעה אחת שאנו רואים שיוצאים מתחת ידו אע"פ שיש לחבירו עדים שהיה שלו נאמן זה המוחזק לומר לקוח הוא בידי דסתם לוקח מטלטלין מחבירו בלא עדים הוא קונה ובלא שטר חוץ מדברים העשויין להשאיל ולהשכיר ואמר לקוחין הן בידי דאינו נאמן כדקי"ל במסכת שבועות (דף מו:) וה"נ גבי אומנין אפילו דבר שאינו עשוי להשאיל ולהשכיר ועשוי לשלחו לאומן כדי לתקנו אין לו חזקה לטעון לקוח בידי מאחר שיש עדים לאידך שהיה שלו וטוען שלחתיו לך לתקנו: **שותפין.** שלקחו קרקע בשותפות והחזיק אחד בחלק חבירו ואכל כל הפירות שלש שנים אינה חזקה שכן דרך שותפין לאכול זה פירות שלש שנים או ארבע שנים ואח"כ יאכל זה כמו כן. ובסדר משנת רבינו גרשום הכי גרסי' השותפין והאפוטרופין והאריסין אבל אומנין לא קתני והכי הוה מסקנא בגמרא (ג) דכולי עלמא יש שותף שאין לו חזקה וכיון דשותף אין לו חזקה כל שכן אומן כדמפרש בגמ': **והאריסין.** שיורדין לתקן הקרקע למחצה לשליש ולרביע אם טוען שני חזקה החזקתי בקרקע ואכלתי הפירות אינה חזקה שיכול לומר המערער לאריסות הורדתיו ודמי הפירות היה משלם לי או זקפתים עליו במלוה אי נמי מנהג אריסים לעבוד קרקע עשר שנים וחמש שנים אוכלין הבעלים כל הפירות של כל השדה ואחר כך אוכלין אריסים חמש שנים כנגדן: **לא לאיש.** שאוכל פירות נכסי מלוג של אשתו חזקה בנכסי אשתו דאורחיה דבעל למיכל פירי ואם יגרשנה תטול נכסי מלוג שלה ובגמרא פריך פשיטא: **בנכסי בעלה.** אם אכלה פירות של שדה בעלה ג' שנים אינה יכולה לטעון לקוח הוא בידי דכיון דמזונות אשה על בעלה שביק לה למיכל פירי ובגמ' פריך פשיטא: **ולא לאב בנכסי הבן ולא לבן כו'.** דומיא דאפוטרופין נינהו זה בנכסיו של זה: **בד"א.** כל החזקות הללו דאינו חזקה וגם יש מהן דהויין חזקה וצריך ג' שנים: **במחזיק.** כדמפרש בגמ' בחזקה שיש עמה טענה ומחלוקת שחבירו מערער עליו: **אבל בנותן מתנה.** בפניו ומודה לו שילך ויחזיק בה וקי"ל דקרקע נקנית בכסף בשטר ובחזקה וההיא חזקה שהיא במקום קנין לקנות קרקע כיון דנעל וגדר כו' הויא חזקה לקנות: **שחלקו.** ורוצה כל אחד לזכות בשלו שלא יוכלו לחזור זה בזה: **בנכסי הגר.** שאין לו יורשין וכל הקודם להחזיק בנכסיו זכה: **נעל.** עשה דלת: **וגדר.** או גדר חומה: **ופרץ.** פירצה כדי שיכנס בה: **כל שהוא.** בגמ' מפרש: **הרי זו חזקה.** לבלתי חזור זה בזה כיון דברשות חבירו החזיק: גמ'

תוספות

מלוה על פה אינו גובה לא מן היורשין ולא מן הלקוחות. לא איצטריך אלא משום יורשין דלקוחות תנינא בהדיא וקסבר שעבודא לאו דאורייתא ומלוה בשטר שהוא גובה היינו שלא תנעול דלת בפני לוין ומכר נמי משום תקנת השוק ואע"ג דליורשין לא שייך לחלק בין מלוה על פה למלוה בשטר מ"מ כל היכא דגבי לקוחות חיישינן משום נעילת דלת כמו מלוה בשטר או מלוה הכתובה בתורה למ"ד (קדושין טו:) ככתובה בשטר דמי או כשעמד בדין או עשה עבדו אפותיקי גבי נמי מיתמי אבל מלוה על פה כיון דלא חשש לעשות שטר לגבות מלקוחות כי לא גבי נמי מיתמי ליכא נעילת דלת והא דאמרי' בפ"ק דבבא קמא (דף יא:) גבי (ד) הלכה גובין מן העבדים אמר רב נחמן לעולא אמר ר"א אפילו מיתמי לא מיניה מיניה ואפילו מגלימא דעל כתפיה שם מפורש: **בפני האב שנה כו'.** והא דאמרינן בפרק שני דכתובות (דף יח: ושם ד"ה ואמר) אמר רב הונא אין מחזיקין בנכסי קטן ואפילו הגדיל לא כמו שיש מפרש שם דיתום אפילו גדול במילי דאבוה קטן הוא ואין מועלת חזקה לגביה אפילו שהיה גדול כשמת אביו דהא הכא אמר בהדיא דהוי חזקה כשאכל בפני הבן והאב שני חזקה אלא דוקא שהיה קטן כשמת אביו אינה חזקה אע"פ שאחרי כן הגדיל. ר"י: **ואי** סלקא דעתך לוקח אית ליה קלא אין לך מחאה גדולה מזו. אור"י דהוי מצי לשנויי כאן בשטר כאן בלא שטר דאין מצטרפין אלא בשטר כדאמרינן לעיל אלא שמא דעדיפא מיניה קא משני: אבל

מסורת הש"ס

א) לקמן קמ. דף קעה. ב) [ערכין כ: כתובות מ. גיטין לח: סנהדרין פג: חולין קכב.] ג) קדושין יג: [ב"ק קד: לקמן קמ. קעה. ערכין ז:] ד) כתובות מח. בכורות מח:] ד) גיטין עז: [ועי' תוס' לקמן נג: ד"ה נעל:]

הגהות הב"ח

(א) רשב"ם ד"ה אמר רב פפא וכו' מכר זה השדה: (ב) ד"ה האומנין הד"א עם ד"ה אין להם וכו' והכא גבי אומנין וכו' כדי לתקנו נמי אין לו חזקה לטעון לקוח הוא בידי: (ג) ד"ה שותפין וכו' דלכולי עלמא: (ד) תוס' ד"ה מלוה וכו' גבי אמר רב נחמן לעולא אמר ר' אלעזר הלכה גובין מן העבדים:

ליקוטי רש"י

המלוה את חבירו בשטר. אפילו לא נכתב בו אחריות גובה מנכסים משועבדים אם אין ללוה נכסים בני חורין וגובה מלוה מן הלקוחות דאמר בשנים אוחזין (ב"מ יד.) לרבנן אחריות שלא נכתב בשטר טעות סופר הוא וכמי שנכתב בו דמי ... [רשב"ם לקמן קנז.] אין כתוב בו אחריות וגם פסקינן הלכתא בשנים אוחזין (ב"מ טו.) דאחריות טעות סופר הוא וכמי שכתוב בו דמי [שם קעה.]. **אינה גובה לא מן היורשים.** דשעבודא לאו דאורייתא ... [קידושין יג.]. **נעל.** נעל דלת ... או גדר כל שהוא. **הרי זו חזקה.** לקנות שאין המוכר יכול לחזור בו [גיטין עז.].

עין משפט נר מצוה

קטו א מיי' פי"א מהל' מלוה הל' ה סמג עשין צד טוש"ע ח"מ סי' קיא סעיף א:
קטז ב מיי' פי"ב מהל' טוען הל' ז סמג עשין צה טוש"ע ח"מ סי' קמח סעיף ג:
קיז ג ד מיי' שם הל' ח טוש"ע שם סעיף ד:
קיח ה מיי' פי"ג שם הל' א סמג שם טוש"ע ח"מ סי' קמט סעיף מ:
קיט ו מיי' שם טוש"ע שם סעיף א:
קכ ז מיי' שם טוש"ע שם וסעיף כה:
קכא ח מיי' שם טוש"ע שם סעיף א:
קכב ט מיי' שם טוש"ע שם סעיף ע:
קכג י מיי' שם טוש"ע שם סעיף ג וסעיף ו:
קכד כ מיי' פי"ג מהל' זכיה הל' ג ופ"א מהל' מכירה הל' ח סמג עשין פב טוש"ע ח"מ סי' קצב סעיף א וסי' רמא סעיף ה:
קכה ל מיי' פ"ב מהל' שכנים הל' יא ועי' בהשגות ובמ"מ ובטור ח"מ סי' קעג בשם תשובת הרא"ש ופ"א מהל' מכירה סמג שם טוש"ע ח"מ סי' קצב סעיף ה וסי' קנז סעיף ג:
קכו מ מיי' פ"א מהל' זכיה הל' א ג ופ"ב מהל' מכירה סמג שם טוש"ע ח"מ סי' קצב ... ערה סעיף יג:

רבינו גרשום

אית להו קלא שמפרסמין שקבל אחריות לזה ולא איבעיא להו לזבוני מיניה. וקשיא דרב אדרב: ומשני התם לא משום הוא טעמא גובה מנכסים דעדים אית להו קלא א) הוה להו לאסוקי אדעתייהו מקמי דליזבנו והי' להו לפשפשי ולבדוק אי משעבדי הני קרקי לאחר או לא הואיל ולא פשפשו בדבר גובה מנכסין משועבדים אבל ג' לקוחות לאחר שמכרו בעדים לא מצטרפי משום הואיל דלית להו קלא מאי הוה ליה למערער לאסוקי על דעתיה דלימחי: **ומי אמר רב הכי.** דהמוכר שדהו בעדים גובה מנכסים משועבדין כלומר דעדים אית להו קלא: **והתנן ע"י עדים גובה מנכסים בני חורין.** אלמא עדים לית להו קלא וקשיא מהני אדרב: **וכי תימא דרב תנא הוא.** דספרא רב שנאו: **ופליג.** אמתני': **מלוה על פה.** הויין בעדים ולא בשטר: **אינו גובה לא מן היורשין ולא מן הלקוחו'.** דלית להו קלא: **מלוה עביד איניש דיזיף בצנעא כי היכי דלא ליזלזלו נכסיה.** דאי הוו ידעי אינשי דהוא חייב ממון כשירצה למכור קרקע מפני חובותיו יהיו מזלזלין בנכסיו ולא יקנו ביוקר לפי שידוע שדוחקין אותו בעלי חובין ומש"ה יזיף בצנעא ומאי הוה להו ללקוחות לאסוקי אדעתייהו אם הוא חייב ממון אם לאו ולהכי אין גובה המלוה אלא מנכסין בני חורין. **אבל גבי מוכר שאני דמאן דזבין** שקונין קרקע **בפרהסיא זבין כי היכי דניפוק ליה קלא** דאינש אמיד הוא הואיל וזבין מקרקעי והואיל וכן היה לו ללוקח אחר לבדוק אם מכר לראשון באחריות שעליו לפצותו אם לא. והואיל ולא בדק ב) ולא קנה השני לפיכך גובה לוקח ראשון מנכסין משועבדין אפי' אם לקח בעדים בלא שטר: **אכלה האב.** לקרקע **שנה** ומת ואכלה **בנו** אחריו **שתים** שנה וכו' **הרי זו חזקה.** דמצטרפות לג' שנים: **והבן** אכלה **שנה.** ומכרה ללוקח ואכלה **הלוקח שנה: למימרא דלוקח אית ליה קלא.** שקונה הוא שדה פלוני והוה ליה למערער למחות בשעת לקיחה או בשעת מיתת האב והואיל ולא מיחה הויא חזקה: **ורמינהי אכלה.** המחזיק **שנה בפני האב** שהיתה הקרקע שלו **ובפני הלוקח** שלקחה מן הבן **שנה** הרי אלו מצטרפין **והוי חזקה** ואין יכול הלוקח שוב לערער ולומר לו כשם שיש לי עדים שלקחתיה מן הבן כך יש עליך להראות שטרך שקניתה מאביו מפני שיכול להשיב לו המחזיק עד ג' שנים נזהרתי בשמירת שטרי מכאן ואילך לא נזהרתי. **ואם איתא דהלוקח קלא אית ליה** יכול לומר לו הלוקח הואיל ששמעת שמכרו לי הבן **אין לך מחאה גדולה מזו** והיה לך לשמור שטרך אלא ש"מ מדקתני הרי זו חזקה מכלל דלית ליה ללוקח קלא דאם איתא דקלא אית ליה אין לך מחאה גדולה מזו ואין זו חזקה מיבעי ליה: **אמר רב פפא.** לעולם אימא לך דלוקח קלא אית ליה והכא אמאי הויא חזקה כי לית ליה שטרא משום דהבן **מכר** ללוקח **שדותיו סתם** ומכר לו זה עמהן והואיל ולא מכר לזה בפני עצמו יכול לומר המחזיק ללוקח אני הייתי סבור ששדותיו אחרות מכר לך ... **האומנין.** בעלי אומנות ... **והשותפין.** אם החזיק אחד בחלק חבירו ג' שנים **אינה חזקה** ... **והאריסין.** ... וכן **האפוטרופין** של יתומין:

חשק שלמה על רבינו גרשום א) נראה דל"ל אלא משום דהוי להו וכו'. ב) נראה דל"ל וקנה השני. ג) עי' רשב"א שכ' בשם רבינו לא גרס אומן וכ"ה במשנה שבירושלמי אבל הדבר צ"ע דהרי מוכח דרבינו היה גורס אומן במשנתינו.

The Gemara analyzes this:

לְמֵימְרָא דְלוֹקֵחַ אִית לֵיהּ קָלָא – Does this mean **to say** that the **purchase** of a property **becomes public knowledge?**[12]

The Gemara challenges this:

וּרְמִינְהִי – **A contradiction was pointed out** from the following Baraisa:[13] אֲכָלָהּ בִּפְנֵי הָאָב שָׁנָה – If ONE USED [A PROPERTY] IN THE PRESENCE OF A FATHER, who was its original owner, for A YEAR, וּבִפְנֵי הַבֵּן שְׁתַּיִם – AND following the father's death he continued using the property IN THE PRESENCE OF THE SON for TWO years more; בִּפְנֵי הָאָב שְׁתַּיִם – or, if he used the property IN THE PRESENCE OF THE FATHER for TWO years, וּבִפְנֵי הַבֵּן שָׁנָה – AND ONE YEAR more IN THE PRESENCE OF THE SON after the father's death; בִּפְנֵי הָאָב שָׁנָה וּבִפְנֵי הַבֵּן שָׁנָה – or, if he used the property ONE YEAR IN THE PRESENCE OF THE FATHER, AND then ONE YEAR IN THE PRESENCE OF THE SON, וּבִפְנֵי לוֹקֵחַ שָׁנָה – AND then ONE YEAR more IN THE PRESENCE OF A PURCHASER who bought the rights to the property from the son,[14] הֲרֵי זוֹ חֲזָקָה – THIS CONSTITUTES A *CHAZAKAH*! וְאִי סָלְקָא דַעְתָּךְ לוֹקֵחַ אִית לֵיהּ קָלָא – Now if you should think that **the purchase** of a property **becomes public knowledge,** אֵין לְךָ מְחָאָה גְדוֹלָה מִזּוֹ – **there can be no greater protest than this** act of selling the rights to the property to someone else! Thus, the son's sale should invalidate the *chazakah*! Since the Baraisa deems the *chazakah* valid, we see that the purchase of the property from the son does *not* become public knowledge.[15] – ? –

The Gemara resolves the contradiction:

אָמַר רַב פָּפָּא – **Rav Pappa said:** Indeed, a purchase does become public knowledge. כִּי תַּנְיָא הַהִיא – However, **in regard to what** case **did that** second **Baraisa state** its ruling implying that a purchase does *not* become public knowledge? בְּמוֹכֵר שְׂדוֹתָיו סְתָם – In regard to a case **in which [the son] sold all his fields without specifying** them; i.e. he sold his entire inheritance as a block, without listing the specific properties involved. Such a sale does not constitute a protest, since it does not specify which properties were sold.[16]

Mishnah

The following Mishnah lists those precluded from establishing *chazakah* by virtue of their legitimate access to other people's property:

הָאוּמָּנִין – **Craftsmen,**[17] וְהַשּׁוּתָּפִין – **partners,** וְהָאֲרִיסִין – **sharecroppers** וְהָאַפּוֹטְרוֹפִּין – **and administrators** אֵין לָהֶם חֲזָקָה – **cannot establish a *chazakah*.**[18] לֹא לְאִישׁ חֲזָקָה בְּנִכְסֵי אִשְׁתּוֹ – **A man cannot establish a *chazakah* in his wife's property,**[19] וְלֹא לְאִשָּׁה חֲזָקָה בְּנִכְסֵי בַעְלָהּ – **nor can a wife establish a *chazakah* in her husband's property;**[20] וְלֹא לְאָב בְּנִכְסֵי הַבֵּן – **nor a father in his son's property,** וְלֹא לַבֵּן בְּנִכְסֵי הָאָב – **nor a son in his father's property.**[21]

The Mishnah now delineates a basic distinction between a *chazakah* that establishes presumptive title and a *chazakah* made as an act of acquisition:[22]

NOTES

12. Literally: that a purchaser has a voice. The Gemara's question refers even to a purchase recorded in a deed.

13. In contrast to the previous Baraisa, which dealt with a succession of occupants, this Baraisa deals with a succession of people who ought to have contested the occupation of the property.

14. I.e. he purchased the land from the original owner's son (who claims that the land is his), and he has a document attesting to this purchase (*Rashbam*). The purchaser did not attempt to eject the occupant, however, but allowed him to remain upon the land without protest.

15. This contradicts not only the ruling of the previous Baraisa but also Rav's ruling regarding a *chazakah* established by a succession of purchasers. The reason the Gemara poses it specifically in regard to the Baraisa is that Rav stated his ruling with regard to one who purchased from a previous purchaser, whereas the Baraisa speaks of one who purchased from an heir. The Gemara preferred to contrast the two Baraisos, since their cases are parallel (*Rashbam*).

16. If, however, the occupied property was listed explicitly in the sale, the sale would serve as a protest, and no *chazakah* would be established (*Rashbam*).

17. Craftsmen, such as dyers, launderers, tailors, etc., who routinely accept the property of others to improve or repair, cannot demonstrate ownership of an object by their possession of it. Should a craftsman claim to have bought something, while its original owner claims to have given it to him to work on, the burden is on the craftsman to prove his claim. This stands in contrast to the general rule for movable property, in which possession of an object shifts the burden of proof to the one trying to recover it [הַמּוֹצִיא מֵחֲבֵרוֹ עָלָיו הָרְאָיָה]. This general rule does not apply in the case of craftsmen because it is normal for people to entrust their belongings to them for repair. Thus, their possession of an object is not indicative of ownership (*Rashbam*).

Accordingly, this case of the Mishnah does not deal with the three-year *chazakah* which is needed for real property, but rather with the automatic *chazakah* established by possession of movable property (*Rashbam*; cf. *Yad Ramah* and *Meiri*). The next cases of the Mishnah, however, deal with the three-year *chazakah* for real property.

18. All of these people have legitimate reasons to be present in property belonging to others. Thus, their presence does not indicate ownership, since the owner has no reason to protest their being there. For example, it is not uncommon for partners to divide the use of a jointly owned property by having one partner use the entire property for three or four years and then having the second partner do the same. For this reason, the partner who used the property for three years cannot use his occupancy as a *chazakah* to support a claim that he bought the share of the other partner (*Rashbam*). [The Gemara (42b) will define the parameters of this ruling.]

Similarly, since sharecroppers work an entire field for a landowner in return for a percentage of the crop, a sharecropper who worked a field for three years and took its produce cannot use this as a *chazakah* to claim that he bought the field from the landowner. [The Gemara below (46b) will discuss why a sharecropper cannot establish a *chazakah* if he kept all the produce of the field.]

By the same token, someone who was appointed to administer another person's estate cannot establish a *chazakah* upon that estate, since his right to enter the property in an administrative capacity, and to dispose of its produce on behalf of his wards, makes it impossible for him to prove that he purchased the estate (*Nimukei Yosef*; see *Meiri*).

19. It is customary for a wife to allow her husband to use her property and enjoy its produce. Thus, his use cannot establish a *chazakah* to prove that he bought the property from her. Should the marriage dissolve, he must return the property (*Rashbam*). [The Gemara below will ask that it is obvious on other grounds that a husband cannot establish a *chazakah* by taking the produce of his wife's property, since it is his right to do so by Rabbinic decree!]

20. A husband is required to support his wife; thus, if she is seen using the produce of his land for three years, she cannot claim a *chazakah* to prove that she bought the land from him. Rather, she is assumed to have used it with her husband's permission (*Rashbam*).

21. They are like administrators in regard to each other's property (*Rashbam*), and neither would protest the other's use (cf. *Nimukei Yosef*). Thus, no *chazakah* can be established. The Gemara (52a) will discuss whether this ruling applies even when the son is no longer being supported by his father.

22. [In addition to the *chazakah* discussed throughout this chapter, *chazakah* is also the name given to a type of *kinyan* (act of acquisition) used for acquiring real estate.] The two types of *chazakah* are completely unrelated. The Mishnah wishes to clarify that the requirements and limitations of *chazakah* mentioned earlier do not apply to the *chazakah* that is an act of acquisition (*Rashbam*).

אינהו אפסידו אנפשייהו ומי אמר רב הכי והתנן המלוה את חבירו בשטר גובה מנכסים משועבדים ע"י עדים גובה מנכסים בני חורין וכי תימא רב תנא הוא ופליג והא רב ושמואל דאמרי תרוייהו מלוה על פה אינו גובה לא מן היורשים ולא מן הלקוחות מלוה אזביני קא רמית מלוה כי קא יזיף בצנעא קא יזיף כי היכי דלא ליתזלו נכסיה עליה זביני מאן דזבין ארעא בפרהסיא זבין כי היכי דליפוק לה קלא ת"ר אכלה האב שנה והבן שתים האב שתים והבן שנה האב שנה והבן שנה והלוקח שנה הרי זו חזקה למימרא דלוקח אית ליה קלא ורמינהי אכלה בפני האב שנה ובפני הבן שתים בפני האב שתים ובפני הבן שנה בפני האב שנה ובפני הבן שנה ובפני לוקח שנה הרי זו חזקה ואי סלקא דעתך לוקח אית ליה קלא אין לך מחאה גדולה מזו אמר רב פפא כי תניא ההיא במוכר שדותיו סתם:

מתני׳ האומנין והשותפין והאריסין והאפוטרופין אין להם חזקה לא לאיש חזקה בנכסי אשתו ולא לאשה חזקה בנכסי בעלה ולא לאב בנכסי הבן ולא לבן בנכסי האב במה דברים אמורים במחזיק אבל בנותן מתנה והאחין שחלקו והמחזיק בנכסי הגר נעל וגדר ופרץ כל שהוא הרי זו חזקה:

גמ׳

אינהו אפסידו אנפשייהו. דשלו זוזייהו בכדי שהיה להם לחקור יפה אם מכר שום קרקע באחריות ולא עשו לפיכך הפסידו אבל גבי שלש לקוחות אין להפסיד המערער דכיון דליכא שטר במכירות הללו ולא יצא הקול ממילא לא היה לו לחקור דמימר אמר לפי שיראים להחזיק בקרקע שלי לא אכלוה כל אחד שלש שנים: ומי אמר רב הכי. דמכירת קרקע באחריות בעדים בלא שטר גובה הלוקח כשיטרפוה ממנו מנכסים משועבדים: בשטר. דקתני שטר לאחריות נכתב ואפילו לא נכתב קי"ל אחריות טעות סופר הוא וכמי שנכתב דמי: מנכסים משועבדים. מלקוחות וכגון שלא שבקו ליה ללוה בני חורין לגבות המלוה מהם: ע"י עדים. כלומר בלא שטר: מנכסים בני חורין. וכגון שמודה שלא פרעו דהא קי"ל המלוה חבירו בעדים אין צריך לפרעו בעדים אבל ממשועבדין לא יגבה דעדים בלא שטר לית להו קלא ולא אמרינן לקוחות אפסידו אנפשייהו וקשיא לרב: מלוה על פה. היינו מלוה את חבירו בעדים: אינו גובה לא מן היורשין כו׳. טעמא מפרש בשילהי מכילתין שיעבודא לאו דאורייתא ומיהו לא קי"ל הכי אלא כדמפרש התם הלכתא גובה מן היורשין ולא מן הלקוחות: יזיף איניש בצנעא. ומבקש שלא לפרסם הדבר כדי שאם יבא למכור קרקע לא יבינו העולם שהוא דחוק לפרוע מעות ולא יקחו ממנו ביוקר הלכך מאי הוה להו ללקוחות למיעבד: מאן דזבין בפרהסיא קזבין. כדי שיקפצו עליה לוקחין והלכך אפסידו לקוחות אנפשייהו שאם חקרו יפה היו שומעין מבני אדם שמכר מוכר זה ככר קרקע באחריות: אכלה האב שנה. ומת ואכלה בנו אחריו שתים ולא מיחה המערער: הרי זו חזקה. שמצטרפין לשלש שנים דיורש כרעיה דאבוה הוא ולא מצי מערער למטען משום דלא אחזיק כל אחד שלש שנים לא מחיתי שהרי הכל יודעים שדרך הבן לירש את האב: ולוקח שנה. שמכרה לו הבן בשטר: למימרא דלוקח. מיורש אית ליה קלא: ורמינהי כו׳. ולרב לא פריך לעיל דרב בלוקח מלוקח מיירי הלכך אלימא ליה טפי למיפרך ממאי דדמי ליה: אית ליה קלא. והיה לו למערער למחות ומשום דלא מיחה הויא חזקה: אכלה. המחזיק: בפני האב. שהיתה שלו שנה שאומר שלקחה מן האב: ובפני הבן. לאחר מות האב: ובפני הלוקח. שלקחה מן הבן ויש לו שטר: הרי זו חזקה. ולא מצי מפיק ליה לוקח דבן מידיה דמחזיק משום דקטעין מחזיק שטר היה לי מן האב ומזהרתי בו בשמירתו שלש שנים ועכשיו אבד הימני שלא חששתי לשמרו אחר שהחזקתי שלש שנים בלא מחאה שלא ידעתי מלקיחתך מן הבן לסוף שתי שנים דלוקח מבן לית ליה קלא ולא הויא מחאה: אין לך מחאה גדולה מזו. שמכרה הבן לסוף שתי שנים ללוקח זה והיה למחזיק להזהר בשטרו כל הימים עד דמרע ליה לשטרא דהאי לוקח אבל בשלש שנים אחר השטר אין די ומפקינן מידא דמחזיק אם לא נזהר בשטרו כדאמרינן בפירקין לעיל (דף לג.) אבל שית אין לך מחאה גדולה מזו: אמר רב פפא. לעולם אימא לך דלוקח אית ליה קלא והכא אמאי לא חשבי מחאה לקיחת הלוקח מן הבן משום דמכר לו הבן כל שדותיו סתם אותן שהיו של אביו וטוען הלוקח שגם זה השדה קניתי בכלל קרקעות כולן דאמרינן ליה כל שדותיו מכר לך חוץ מזו אבל אם מכר (א) זה השדה בפני עצמו בטלה חזקתו של מחזיק דאין לך מחאה גדולה מזו. ויש מפרשים במוכר כל שדותיו ומכר לו בפירוש גם זו עמהן ולאו מילתא היא דסתם משמע שלא פירש: **מתני׳** האומנין. בעלי אומנות שמוליכין להם בביתם לתקן כלים כגון צבעין או כובסין או חייטין או סורקי בגדים שטוענין לקוח הוא בידי: (ב) אין להם חזקה. ולא בחזקת שלש שנים מיירי דסתם אומן לא שייך אלא במטלטלין וחזקת שלש שנים לא נאמרה אלא במקרקעי אבל במטלטלי מי שהוא מוחזק בשל חבירו אפילו שעה אחת שאנו רואים שיוצאים מתחת ידו אע"פ שיש לחבירו עדים שהיה שלו נאמן זה המוחזק לומר לקוח הוא בידי דסתם לוקח מטלטלין מחבירו בלא עדים הוא קונה ובלא שטר חוץ מדברים העשויין להשאיל ולהשכיר ואמר לקוחין הן בידי דאינו נאמן כדקי"ל במסכת שבועות (דף מו:) וה"נ גבי אומנין אפילו דבר שאינו עשוי להשאיל ולהשכיר ועשוי לשלחו לאומן כדי לתקנו אין לו חזקה לטעון לקוח בידי מאחר שיש עדים לאידך שהיה שלו וטוען שלחתיו לך לתקנו: שותפין. שלקחו קרקע בשותפות והחזיק אחד בחלק חבירו ואכל כל הפירות שלש שנים אינה חזקה שכן דרך שותפין לאכול זה פירות שלש שנים או ארבע שנים ואח"כ יאכל זה כמו כן. ובסדר משנת רבינו גרשום הכי גרסי׳ השותפין והאפוטרופין והאריסין אבל אומנין לא קתני והכי הוה מסקנא בגמרא (ג) דכולי עלמא יש שותף שאין לו חזקה וכיון דשותף אין לו חזקה כל שכן אומן כדמפרש בגמ׳: והאריסין. שיורדין לתקן הקרקע למחצה לשליש ולרביע אם טוען שני חזקה החזקתי בקרקע ואכלתי הפירות אינה חזקה שיכול לומר המערער לאריסות הורדתיו ודמי הפירות היה משלם לי או זקפתים עליו במלוה אי נמי מנהג אריסים לעבוד קרקע עשר שנים וחמש שנים אוכלין הבעלים כל הפירות של כל השדה ואחר כך אוכלין אריסים חמש שנים כנגדן: לא לאיש. שאוכל פירות נכסי מלוג של אשתו חזקה בנכסי אשתו דאורחיה דבעל למיכל פירי ואם יגרשנה תטול נכסי מלוג שלה ובגמרא פריך פשיטא: בנכסי בעלה. אם אכלה פירות של שדה בעלה ג׳ שנים אינה יכולה לטעון לקוח הוא בידי דכיון דמזונות אשה על בעלה שביק לה למיכל פירי ובגמ׳ פריך פשיטא: ולא לאב בנכסי הבן ולא לבן כו׳. דומיא דאפוטרופין נינהו זה בנכסיו של זה: בד"א. כל החזקות הללו דאינו חזקה וגם יש מהן דהויין חזקה וצריך ג׳ שנים: במחזיק. כדמפרש בגמ׳ בחזקה שיש עמה טענה ומחלוקת שחבירו מערער עליו: אבל בנותן מתנה. בפנינו ומודה לו שילך ויחזיק בה וקי"ל דקרקע נקנית בכסף בשטר ובחזקה וההיא חזקה שהיא במקום קנין לקנות קרקע כיון דנעל וגדר כו׳ הויא חזקה לקנות: שחלקו. ורוצה כל אחד לזכות בשלו שלא יוכלו לחזור זה בזה: בנכסי הגר. שאין לו יורשין וכל הקודם להחזיק בנכסיו זכה: נעל. עשה דלת: וגדר. או גדר חומה: ופרץ. פירצה כדי שיכנס בה: כל שהוא. בגמ׳ מפרש: הרי זו חזקה. לבלתי חזור זה בזה כיון דברשות חבירו החזיק:

גמ׳

מלוה על פה אינו גובה לא מן היורשין ולא מן הלקוחות. לא איצטריך אלא משום יורשין דלקוחות תנינא בהדיא וקסבר שעבודא לאו דאורייתא ומלוה בשטר שהוא גובה היינו שלא תנעול דלת בפני לוין ומכר נמי משום תקנת השוק ואע"ג דביורשין לא שייך לחלק בין מלוה על פה למלוה בשטר מ"מ כל היכא דגבי לקוחות חיישינן משום נעילת דלת כמו מלוה בשטר או מלוה הכתובה בתורה למ"ד (קדושין כט:) ככתובה בשטר דמי או כשעמד בדין או עשה עדבו אפותיקי גבי נמי מיתמי אבל מלוה על פה כיון דלא חשש לעשות שטר לגבות מלקוחות כי לא גבי נמי מיתמי ליכא נעילת דלת והא דאמרי׳ בפ"ק דבבא קמא (דף יא:) גבי הלכה גובין מן העבדים אמר רב נחמן לעולא אמר ר"א אפילו מיתמי לא מיניה מיניה ואפילו מגלימא דעל כתפיה שם מפורש: **בפני** האב שנה כו׳. והא דאמרינן בפרק שני דכתובות (דף יח: ושם ד"ה ואמת) אמר רב הונא אין מחזיקין בנכסי קטן ואפילו הגדיל לא כמו שיש אותו מפרש שם דיתום אפילו גדול במילי דאבוה קטן הוא ואין מועלת חזקה לגביה אפילו שהיה גדול בשמת אביו דהא הכא אמר בהדיא דהוי חזקה כשאכל בפני הבן והאב שני חזקה אלא דוקא שהיה קטן כשמת אביו אינה חזקה אע"פ שאכלו כן הגדיל. ר"י: **ואי** סלקא דעתך לוקח אית ליה קלא אין לך מחאה גדולה מזו. ור"י דהוי מצי לשנויי כאן בשטר כאן בלא שטר דלאו מנטרפין אלא בשטר כדאמרינן לעיל אלא שמא דעדיפא מיניה קא משני:

אבל

בַּמֶּה דְּבָרִים אֲמוּרִים – **In regard to what** type of *chazakah* **are these** rules **stated?** בְּמַחֲזִיק – In regard **to one who establishes a *chazakah*** to prove his title to a property.[23] אֲבָל בְּנוֹתֵן מַתָּנָה – **But in the case of one who gives a gift** וְהָאַחִין שֶׁחָלְקוּ – **or brothers who divide** an estate, וְהַמַּחֲזִיק בְּנִכְסֵי הַגֵּר – **or one who takes possession of the** ownerless **property of a** deceased **convert,**[24] נָעַל וְגָדַר וּפָרַץ כָּל שֶׁהוּא – once **he locked, fenced, or breached** the property being acquired, even **to a minor extent,**[25] הֲרֵי זוֹ חֲזָקָה – **this is** considered a ***chazakah.***[26]

NOTES

23. I.e. one who holds land and wishes to establish a *chazakah* to fend off challenges to his title (Gemara 52b; see there for elaboration).

24. The property of a deceased convert who has no [Jewish] heirs is considered ownerless, and the first person to perform an act of acquisition upon it becomes its owner (*Rashbam*). [A born Jew *always* has heirs, since all Jews are related, at least distantly. A convert, however, is not considered to be related to his non-Jewish family with respect to Torah laws. Thus, if he dies without having fathered children after his conversion, he is considered to be without heirs and his property is ownerless.]

25. The Gemara (53a) will explain what this means.

26. These acts constitute the method of acquisition known as *chazakah*. Once one of these acts of *chazakah* is performed with the consent of the owner, the sale or gift is complete and neither side can retract (*Rashbam*).

אינהו אפסידו אנפשייהו ומי אמר רב הכי והתנן [ו]המלוה את חבירו בשטר גובה מנכסים משועבדים ע"י עדים גובה מנכסים בני חורין וכי תימא [ז]רב תנא הוא ופליג והא רב ושמואל דאמרי תרוייהו [ח]מלוה על פה אינו גובה לא מן היורשים ולא מן הלקוחות מלוה אזביני קא רמית מלוה כי קא יזיף בצנעא קא יזיף כי היכי דלא ליתזלו נכסיה עליה [א]זביני מאן דזבין ארעא בפרהסיא זבין כי היכי דליפוק לה קלא ת"ר [ב]אכלה האב שנה והבן שתים האב שתים והבן שנה האב שנה והבן שנה והלוקח שנה הרי זו חזקה למימרא דלוקח אית ליה קלא ורמינהי [ג]אכלה בפני האב שנה ובפני הבן שתים בפני האב שתים ובפני הבן שנה בפני האב שנה ובפני הבן שנה ובפני לוקח שנה הרי זו חזקה ואי סלקא דעתך לוקח אית ליה קלא אין לך מחאה גדולה מזו אמר רב פפא [ד]כי תניא ההיא במוכר שדותיו סתם:

מתני' [ה]האומנין [ו]והשותפין [ז]והאריסין [ח]והאפוטרופין אין להם חזקה [ט]לא לאיש חזקה בנכסי אשתו ולא לאשה חזקה בנכסי בעלה [י]ולא לאב בנכסי הבן ולא לבן בנכסי האב במה דברים אמורים במחזיק [כ]אבל בנותן מתנה [ל]והאחין שחלקו [מ]והמחזיק בנכסי הגר [נ]נעל וגדר ופרץ כל שהוא הרי זו חזקה:
גמ'

רש"י

אינהו אפסידו אנפשייהו. דשלו זוזייהו בכדי שהיה להם לחקור יפה אם מכר שום קרקע באחריות ולא עשו לפיכך הפסידו אבל גבי שלש שנים לקוחות אין להפסיד המערער דכיון דליכא שטר במכירות הללו ולא יצא הקול ממילא לא היה לו לחקור דמימר אמר לפי שירדאים להחזיק בקרקע שלי לא אכלוה כל אחד שלש שנים: ומי אמר רב הכי. דמכירת קרקע באחריות בעדים בלא שטר גובה הלוקח כשיטרפוה ממנו מנכסים משועבדים: בשטר. דסתם שטר לאחריות נכתב ואפילו לא נכתב קי"ל אחריות טעות סופר הוא וכמי שנכתב דמי: מנכסים משועבדים. מלקוחות וכגון שלא שבקו ליה ללוה בני חורין לגבות המלוה מהם: ע"י עדים. כלומר בלא שטר: מנכסים בני חורין. וכגון שמודה שלא פרעו דהא קי"ל המלוה חבירו בעדים אין צריך לפרעו בעדים אבל ממשועבדין לא יגבה דעדים בלא שטר לית להו קלא ולא אמרינן לקוחות אפסידו אנפשייהו וקשיא לרב: מלוה על פה. היינו מלוה את חבירו בעדים: אינו גובה לא מן היורשין כו'. טעמא מפרש בשילהי מכילתין שיעבודא לאו דאורייתא ומיהו לא קי"ל הכי אלא כדמפרש התם הלכתא גובה מן היורשין ולא מן הלקוחות: יזיף איניש בצנעא. ומבקש שלא לפרסם הדבר כדי שאם יצא למכור קרקע לא יזינו העולם שהוא דחוק לפרוע מעות ולא יקחו ממנו ביוקר הלכך מאי הוה להו ללקוחות למיעבד: מאן דזבין בפרהסיא קזבין. כדי שיקפצו עליה לוקחין והלכך אפסידו לקוחות אנפשייהו שאם חקרו יפה היו שומעין מבני אדם שמכר מוכר זה כבר קרקע באחריות: אכלה האב שנה. ומת ואכלה בנו אחריו שתים ולא מיחה המערער: הרי זו חזקה. שמצטרפין לשלש שנים דיורש כרעיה דאבוה הוא ולא מצי מערער למטען משום דלא אחזיק כל אחד שלש שנים לא מחיתי שהרי הכל יודעים שדרך הבן לירש את האב: ולוקח שנה. שמכרה לו הבן בשטר: למימרא דלוקח. מיורש אית ליה קלא: ורמינהי כו'. ולרב לא פריך לעיל דרב בלוקח מלוקח מיירי הלכך אלימא ליה טפי למיפרך ממאי דדמי ליה: אית ליה קלא. והיה לו למערער למחות ומשום דלא מיחה הויא חזקה: אכלה. המחזיק: בפני האב. שהיתה שלו שנה שאומר שלקחה מן האב: ובפני הבן. לאחר מות האב: ובפני הלוקח. שלקחה מן הבן ויש לו שטר: הרי זו חזקה. ולא מצי מפיק ליה לוקח דבן מידיה דמחזיק משום דקטעין מחזיק שטר היה לי מן האב ונזהרתי בו בשמירתו שלש שנים ועכשיו אבד הימני שלא חששתי לשמרו אחר שהחזקתי שלש שנים בלא מחאה שלא ידעתי מלקיחתך מן הבן לסוף שתי שנים דלוקח מבן לית ליה קלא ולא הויא מחאה: אין לך מחאה גדולה מזו. שמכרה הבן לסוף שתי שנים ללוקח זה והיה למחזיק להזהר בשטרו כל הימים עד דמרע ליה לשטרא דהאי לוקח אבל בשלש שנים אחר הסטר אין די ומפקינן מידא דמחזיק אם לא נזהר בשטרו כדאמרינן בפירקין לעיל (דף לא.) אבל שית אין לך מחאה גדולה מזו: אמר רב פפא. לעולם אימא לך דלוקח אית ליה קלא והכא אמאי לא חשבי מחאה לקיחת הלוקח מן הבן משום דמכר לו הבן כל שדותיו סתם אותן שהיו של אביו וטוען הלוקח שגם זה השדה קניתי בכלל קרקעות כולן דאמרינן ליה כל שדותיו מכר לך חוץ מזו אבל אם מכר (א) זה השדה בפני עצמו בטלה חזקתו של מחזיק דאין לך מחאה גדולה מזו. ויש מפרשים במוכר כל שדותיו ומכר לו בפירוש גם זו עמהן ולאו מילתא היא דסתם משמע שלא פירש: מתני' האומנין. בעלי אומנות שמוליכין להם בביתם לתקן כלים כגון לצבוע או כובסין או חייטין או סורקי בגדים שטוענין לקוח הוא בידי: (ב) אין להם חזקה. ולא בחזקת שלש שנים מיירי דסתם אומן לא שייך אלא במטלטלין וחזקת שלש שנים לא נאמרה אלא במקרקעי אבל במטלטלי מי שהוא מוחזק בשל חבירו אפילו שעה אחת שאנו רואים שיוצאים מתחת ידו אע"פ שיש לחבירו עדים שהיה שלו נאמן זה המוחזק לומר לקוח הוא בידי דסתם לוקח מטלטלין מחבירו בלא עדים הוא קונה ובלא שטר חוץ מדברים העשויין להשאיל ולהשכיר ואמר לקוחין הן בידי דאינו נאמן כדקי"ל במסכת שבועות (דף מו:) וה"נ גבי אומנין אפילו דבר שאינו עשוי להשאיל ולהשכיר ועשוי לשלחו לאומן כדי לתקנו אין לו חזקה לטעון לקוח בידי מאחר שיש עדים לאידך שהיה שלו וטוען שלחתיו לך לתקנו: שותפין. שלקחו קרקע בשותפות והחזיק אחד בחלק חבירו ואכל כל הפירות שלש שנים אינה חזקה שכן דרך שותפין לאכול זה פירות שלש שנים או ארבע שנים ואח"כ יאכל זה כמו כן. ובסדר משנת רבינו גרשום הכי גרסי' השותפין והאפוטרופין והאריסין אבל אומנין לא קתני והכי הוה מסקנא בגמרא (ג) דכולי עלמא יש שותף שאין לו חזקה וכיון דשותף אין לו חזקה כל שכן אומן כדמפרש בגמ': והאריסין. שיורדין לתקן הקרקע למחצה לשליש ולרביע אם טוען שני חזקה החזקתי בקרקע ואכלתי הפירות אינה חזקה שיכול לומר המערער לאריסות הורדתיו ודמי הפירות היה משלם לי או זקפתים עליו במלוה אי נמי מנהג אריסים לעבוד קרקע עשר שנים וחמש שנים אוכלין הבעלים כל הפירות של כל השדה ואחר כך אוכלין אריסים חמש שנים כנגדן: לא לאיש. שאוכל פירות נכסי מלוג של אשתו חזקה בנכסי אשתו דאורחיה דבעל למיכל פירי ואם יגרשנה תטול נכסי מלוג שלה ובגמרא פריך פשיטא: בנכסי בעלה. אם אכלה פירות של שדה בעלה ג' שנים אינה יכולה לטעון לקוח הוא בידי דכיון דמזונות אשה על בעלה שביק לה למיכל פירי ובגמ' פריך פשיטא: ולא לאב בנכסי הבן ולא לבן כו'. דומיא דאפוטרופין נינהו זה בנכסיו של זה: בד"א. כל החזקות הללו דאינו חזקה וגם יש מהן דהוויין חזקה וצריך ג' שנים: במחזיק. כדמפרש בגמ' בחזקה שיש עמה טענה ומחלוקת שחבירו מערער עליו: אבל בנותן מתנה. בפניו ומודה לו שילך ויחזיק בה וקי"ל דקרקע נקנית בכסף בשטר ובחזקה ובההיא חזקה שהיא במקום קנין לקנות קרקע כיון דנעל וגדר כו' הויא חזקה לקנות: שחלקו. ורוצה כל אחד לזכות בשלו שלא יוכלו לחזור זה בזה: בנכסי הגר. שאין לו יורשין וכל הקודם להחזיק בנכסיו זכה: נעל. עשה דלת: וגדר. או גדר חומה: ופרץ. פירצה כדי שיכנס בה: כל שהוא. בגמ' מפרש: הרי זו חזקה. לבלתי חזור זה בזה כיון דברשות חבירו החזיק:
גמ'

תוספות

מלוה על פה אינו גובה לא מן היורשין ולא מן הלקוחות. לא איצטריך אלא משום יורשין דלקוחות תניא בהדיא וקסבר שעבודא לאו דאורייתא ומלוה בשטר שהוא גובה היינו שלא תנעול דלת בפני לוין ומכר נמי משום תקנת השוק ואע"ג דיורשין לא שייך לחלק בין מלוה על פה למלוה בשטר מ"מ כל היכא דגבי לקוחות חיישינן משום נעילת דלת כמו מלוה בשטר או מלוה הכתובה בתורה למ"ד (קדושין כט.) ככתובה בשטר דמי או כשעמד בדין או עשה עבדו אפותיקי גבי נמי מיתמי אבל מלוה על פה כיון דלא חשש לעשות שטר לגבות מלקוחות כי לא גבי נמי מיתמי ליכא נעילת דלת והא דאמרי' בפ"ק דבבא קמא (דף יא:) גבי (ד) הלכה גובין מן העבדים אמר רב נחמן לעולא אמר ר"א אפילו מיתמי לא מיניה ומיניה ואפילו מגלימא דעל כתפיה שם מפורש: בפני האב שנה כו'. והא דאמרינן בפרק שני דכתובות (דף יז: ושם ד"ה ואחת) אמר רב הונא אין מחזיקין בנכסי קטן ואפילו הגדיל לא כמו שיש מפרש שם דיתום אפילו גדול במילי דאבוה קטן הוא ואין מועלת חזקה לגביה אפילו שהיה גדול כשמת אביו דהא הכא אמר בהדיא דהוי חזקה כשאכל בפני הבן והאב שני חזקה אלא דוקא שהיה קטן כשמת אביו אינה חזקה אע"פ שאחרי כן הגדיל. ר"י: ואי סלקא דעתך לוקח אית ליה קלא אין לך מחאה גדולה מזו. אור"י דהוי מצי לשנויי כאן בשטר כאן בלא שטר דאין מצטרפין אלא בשטר כדאמרינן לעיל אלא שמא דעדיפא מיניה קא משני:
אבל

מסורת הש"ס

א) לקמן קמ. ודף קעה., ב) [ערכין כ: כתובות ח. גיטין לח. סנהדרין פב: חולין קכב.], ג) קדושין יג. [ב"ק קד: לקמן קמ. קעה. ערכין ו: ז. בכורות מח.], ד) גיטין עז: [ועי' תוס' לקמן נג: ד"ה נעל].

הגהות הב"ח

(א) רשב"ם ד"ה אמר רב פפא וכו' מכר זו השדה: (ב) ד"ה האומנין הד"א עם ד"ה אין להם וכו' והכא גבי אומנין וכו' כדי לתקנו נמי אין לו חזקה לטעון לקוח הוא בידי: (ג) ד"ה שותפין וכו' דכולי עלמא: (ד) תוס' ד"ה מלוה וכו' גבי אמר עולא אמר ר' אלעזר הלכה גובין מן העבדים:

ליקוטי רש"י

המלוה את חבירו בשטר. אפילו לא נכתב בו אחריות גובה מנכסים משועבדים אם אין ללוה נכסים בני חורין וגובה מלוה מן הלקוחות דאמר בשנים אוחזין (ב"מ יד.) לרבנן אחריות שלא נכתב בשטר טעות סופר הוא וכמי שנכתב בו אחריות דמי [שם קעה.]. אינו גובה לא מן היורשים. דשיעבודא לאו דאורייתא וכ"ש מן הלקוחות אבל מלוה בשטר שיעבדו לכתב ליה בשטרו הילכך דייקי [קידושין יג.]. נעל. דלת. או גדר גדר כל שהוא. הרי זו חזקה. לקנות שאין המוכר יכול לחזור בו [גיטין עז.].

עין משפט נר מצוה

קטו א מיי' פי"א מהל' מלוה הל' ה סמג עשין צד טוש"ע ח"מ סי' קנט סעיף א:
קטז ב מיי' פי"ב מהל' טוען הל' ז סמג עשין צה טוש"ע ח"מ סי' קמד סעיף ג:
קיז ג ד מיי' שם הל' ח טוש"ע שם סעיף ד:
קיח ה מיי' פי"ג שם הל' א סמג שם טוש"ע ח"מ סי' קמט סעיף כח:
קיט ו מיי' שם טוש"ע שם סעיף ו:
קכ ז מיי' שם טוש"ע שם ובסעיף כה:
קכא ח מיי' שם טוש"ע שם סעיף טו:
קכב ט מיי' שם טוש"ע שם סעיף ע:
קכג י מיי' שם טוש"ע שם סעיף ג וסעיף ו:
קכד כ מיי' פ"ג מהל' זכיה הל' א ופ"א מהל' מכירה הל' ח סמג עשין פב טוש"ע ח"מ סי' קצב סעיף א וסי' רעה סעיף א:
קכה ל מיי' פ"ב מהל' שכנים הל' יא ועי' בהשגות ובמ"מ ובטור ח"מ סי' קעג בשם תשובת הרא"ש ופ"א מהל' מכירה סמג עשין פב טוש"ע ח"מ סי' קנז סעיף ה ובסי' קצב סעיף ג:
קכו מ מיי' פ"ב מהל' זכיה הל' א ג ה ופ"א מהל' מכירה סמג עשין פב טוש"ע ח"מ סי' קצב סעיף ו וסי' רעה סעיף יב:

רבינו גרשום

אית להו קלא שמפרסמין שקבל אחריות לזה ולא איבעיא להו לזבוני מיניה. וקשיא דרב אדרב: ומשני התם לא משום ההוא טעמא גובה מנכסים דעדים אית להו קלא (א) הוה להו לאסוקי אדעתייהו מקמי דליזבון והוי להו לפשפשי ולבדוק אי משעבדי הני קרקעי לאחר או לא הואיל ולא פשפשו בדבר גובה מנכסין משועבדים אבל ג' לקוחות לאחר שמכרו בעדים לא מצטרפי משום הואיל דלית להו קלא מאי הוה ליה למערער לאסוקי על דעתיה דלימחי: ומי אמר רב הכי. דהמוכר שדהו בעדים גובה מנכסים משועבדים דעדים אית להו קלא: והתנן ע"י עדים גובה מנכסים בני חורין. אלמא עדים לית להו קלא וקשיא מהני אדרב: וכי תימא רב תנא הוא. דספרא רב שנאו: ופליג. אמתני': מלוה על פה. הוין בעדים ולא בשטר: אינו גובה לא מן היורשין ולא מן הלקוחות. דלית להו קלא: מלוה עביד איניש דיזיף בצנעא כי היכי דלא ליזלזלו נכסיה. דאי הוו ידעי אינשי דהוא חייב ממון כשירצה למכור קרקע מפני חובותיו יהיו מזלזלין בנכסיו ולא יקנו ביוקר לפי שידעו שדוחקין אותו בעלי חובין ומש"ה יזיף בצנעא ומאי הוה להו ללקוחות לאסוקי אדעתייהו אם הוא חייב ממון אם לאו ולהכי אין גובה המלוה אלא מנכסים בני חורין. אבל גבי מוכר שאני דמאן דזבין שקונין קרקע בפרהסיא זבין כי היכי דניפוק ליה קלא דאיניש אמיד הוא הואיל

חובין מקרקעי והואיל וכן היה לו ללוקח אחר לבדוק אם מכר לראשון באחריות שעליו לפצותו אם לא. והואיל ולא בדק (ג) ולא קנה השני לפיכך גובה לוקח ראשון מנכסין משועבדין אפי' אם לקח בעדים בלא שטר: אכלה האב. [illegible]

חשק שלמה על רבינו גרשום [illegible]

גמ' אבוה דשמואל ולוי תנו שותף אין לו חזקה וכל שכן אומן שמואל תני אומן אין לו חזקה אבל שותף יש לו חזקה ואזדא שמואל לטעמיה דאמר שמואל השותפין מחזיקין זה על זה ומעידין זה על זה ונעשים שומרי שכר זה לזה רמי ליה רבי אבא לרב יהודה (א) במערתא דבי רב זכאי מי אמר שמואל שותף יש לו חזקה והאמר שמואל שותף כיורד ברשות דמי לאו למימרא דשותף אין לו חזקה לא קשיא °הא דנחית לכולה הא דנחית לפלגא °אמרי לה להאי גיסא ואמרי לה להאי גיסא רבינא אמר [א]הא והא דנחית לכולה ולא קשיא הא דאית בה דין חלוקה הא דלית בה דין חלוקה גופא אמר שמואל [ב]שותף כיורד ברשות דמי מאי קמ"ל (ב) שותפות אין לו חזקה לימא שותף אין לו חזקה אמר רב נחמן אמר רבה בר אבוה [ג]לומר שנוטל בשבח המגיע לכתפים בשדה שאינה עשויה ליטע כשדה העשויה ליטע: [ד]ומעידין זה לזה אמאי

גמ' אבוה דשמואל. וגם לוי חבירו: תנו. במתני': שותף. השותפין והאפוטרופין כו' אבל אומן לא תנו דכ"ש דאין לו חזקה דהא אין לו חלק כלל דנימא מיגו דהיה לו חלק בו קנה מחבירו את חלקו אלא ודאי לתקן ניתן לו: אבל שותף יש לו חזקה. דאם איתא דלא מכר לו חלקו היה לו לעכב את האדמה ולאכול הפירות בשותפות: מחזיקין זה (ג) לזה. אם האחד מחזיק בחלקו ובחלק חבירו ג' שנים הויא חזקה: ומעידין. זה על חלקו של זה להעמידה בידו אם בא אחד מן השוק לערער עליו ולא הוי נוגע בעדות כדמפרש לקמן: ונעשין כשומרי שכר זה לזה. שאם מבית אחד מהן נגנב דבר של שותפות חייב לשלם כשומר שכר וזהו שכרו שגם חבירו ישמור הכל כשיעור זמן שמשמר זה עכשיו: והא אמר שמואל שותף. שמחזיק בכל השדה גם בחלקו של חבירו: כיורד ברשות דמי. כלומר כאילו נתן לו חבירו רשות ולוהו להיות במקומו כדין אריס דמי: לאו למימרא דשותף אין לו חזקה. דהוי כאריס שיורד ברשות ולכך לא הויא חזקתו חזקה ולקמן מפרש דאכתי לשאר דברים קאמר שמואל כיורד ברשות דמי מדלא קאמר בהדיא שותף אין לו חזקה: דנחית לכולה. שדה שקנו שניהם: דנחית לפלגא. בחלק המובחר החזיק ואמר חלקנו והגיע זה לחלקי והחזקתי בו שלש שנים ואידך טוען עדיין לא חלקנו אלא כך התנינו בינינו שתאכל אותו חלק ג' שנים ואני אחריך כמו כן ג' שנים: אמרי לה להאי גיסא. יש מתרצים בענין זה הא דאמר שמואל שותף יש לו חזקה דנחית לכולה דמנהג שותפים ליטול בשותפות פירות כל שנה ושנה או זה יטול חצי הקרקע וזה החצי ולשנה הבאה למפרע מה שלקח זה אשתקד יקח זה עכשיו שכל אחד רוצה ליהנות בכל שנה מחלקו וזה שהניח להחזיק לחבירו ג' שנים בכל השדה ודאי מכר לו את חלקו והלכך הויא חזקה: והא דאמר שמואל אין לו חזקה דנחית לפלגא. שכן דרך שותפין לאכול זה פלגא ואידך חבריה פלגא שלש שנים או ארבע ואחר כך אוכלין למפרע בענין זה ארבע שנים אחרות: ואמרי לה להאי גיסא. היכא דנחית לכולה לא הויא חזקה שכן הוא מנהג השותפין לאכול שדה שלש שנים והלכך לא מצי טעין לקוח חלקך בידי והיכא דנחית לפלגא הויא חזקה דסברא הוא דחלקו דאם איתא דניחא ליה ליהנות מחלקו בכל שנה ולא להמתין שלש שנים או ארבע שנים אחר חבירו כמנהג שותפין לא היה לו לברר חלק אחד לבדו אלא יעשו בשותפות ויחלקו הפירות: הכי גרסי' רבינא אמר הא והא דנחית לכולה הא דאית בה דין חלוקה. ארבע אמות לזה וארבע אמות לזה הויא חזקה דכיון דיש כדי לזה וכדי לזה אינו מנהג להניח האחד להקדים לו חבירו ג' שנים אלא אם כן מכר לו חלקו: דלית בה דין חלוקה. אינה חזקה דהתם מנהג הוא לאכול זה שלש או ארבע שנים שלימות כל השדה ואחר כך זה משום דבשניהם ביחד אינו כדאי והכי קיימא לן והך עובדא דרמי בר חמא ורב עוקבא בר חמא דזבון אמהתא בשותפות מר משתמש ראשונה שלישית כו' בריש פרקין (ד) (דף כט:) ופרשינן טעמא כי היכי דלא ליחזקו אהדדי ה"ה דאי הוה כל אחד משתמש שלש שנים רצופין לא תהוי חזקה דהא לית בחדא אמתא דין חלוקה והלכך לא תהוי חזקה ואינהו דאחזוק בסירוגין משום דלמא לא ידעי העדים לסוף ג' שנים שלקחוה בשותפות ויטעון המחזיק בה שאינו שותף ותהוי חזקתו חזקה: לומר שנוטל. כדין אריס שיורד ברשות אפי' בשבח המגיע לכתפים גמר פירי כגון קמה לקצור וענבים לבצור נוטל כל החצי כדין אריסי העיר ואפילו הוא שדה שאינו עשוי ליטע אלא לזריעה ונטעה הוא נוטל כל דינו כאילו עשוי ליטע כדין היורד ברשות דאילו יורד שלא ברשות שמין לו וידו על התחתונה דאם השבח יתר על היציאה נוטל את היציאה ואם היציאה יתר על השבח נוטל יציאה שיעור שבח כדאמר בב"מ בהשואל (דף קא.) היורד לתוך שדה חבירו ונטעה שלא ברשות אמר רב שמין לו וידו על התחתונה ושמואל אומר אומדין כמה אדם רוצה ליתן על שדה זו ליטע וא"ר פפא לא פליגי כאן בשדה העשויה ליטע כאן בשדה שאינה עשויה ליטע והכא חשיב להאי שותף כיורד ברשות והלכך שקיל בשדה שאינה עשויה ליטע כבשדה העשויה ליטע ואי הוה אמר שמואל שותף אין לו חזקה הוה אמינא דידו על התחתונה הואיל ובלא רשות חבירו ירד: אמאי

אבל שותף יש לו חזקה. יש ענין לשותף דאין לו חזקה כדמפרש לקמן וא"ת א"כ ליתני במתני' שותף אין לו חזקה אע"פ שיש שותף שיש לו חזקה כי היכי דתני אריס אע"פ שאר אריס שאינו אריסי בתי אבות יש להן חזקה ויש לחלק:

שותף כיורד ברשות דמי לאו למימרא דאין לו חזקה. (ה) וא"ת מנא ליה דילמא לענין שנוטל בשבח המגיע לכתפים כדאמר בסמוך וכ"ת דמשמע ליה דכל ענין מדמי ליה לאריס דלמא כשאר אריסים קאמר שיש להן חזקה ולא כאריסי בתי אבות: שבח המגיע לכתפים. מפרש רש"י בכמה מקומות וכן רבינו שמואל דמגיע לכתפים כגון ענבים הראויין ליבצר וקשה דאמרי' בפ"ק דב"מ (דף טו:) והא מעשים בכל יום וקא מגבי שמואל לבעל חוב בשבח המגיע לכתפים ואי ס"ד היינו ענבים (ו) הראוים ליבצר א"כ בעל חוב לא גבי מינייהו כדאמר בכתובות פ' נערה (דף נ:) אמר ליה זיל הב ליה מתמרי דעל בודיא אמר ליה (ז) לא יהא אלא בעל חוב דחזו לבודיא קאמינא סוף סוף כל העומד ליגדר כגדור דמי דצריכי לדקלא קאמינא אלמא לא גבי מאותם העומדים ליגדר ולאו פירכא היא דהא רש"י נמי לא בעי למימר מאותן העומדים ליבצר מיד אלא כלומר כל דבר שסופו ליתלש כגון פגין או בוסר ור"ת מפרש מגיע לכתפים היינו דבר שבא ע"י טורח ומייתי ראיה מהא דתנן בסוף יש נוחלין (לקמן דף קלד.) האומר זה אחי אינו נאמן ויטול עמו בחלקו מת יחזירו נכסים למקומם נפלו לו נכסים ממקום אחר יירשו אחיו עמו ובעי רבא (שם קלה:) שבח ששבחו נכסים מאליהם מהו בשבח המגיע לכתפים לא תבעי לך דכי נפלו ממקום אחר דמי כי תיבעי לך בשבח שאינו מגיע לכתפים כגון דקלא ואלים ארעא ומסקא שרטון משמע שבח שאינו מגיע לכתפים היינו בא מאליו ולר' אלחנן נראה דאדרבה משם קשה לר"ת דלמה שינה בלשון דמעיקרא קאמר נכסים ששבחו מאליהם מהו ובתר הכי קאמר כי תיבעי לך בשבח שאין מגיע לכתפים דמעיקרא נמי הוה ליה למימר שבח שאין מגיע לכתפים אלא משמע דשבח המגיע לכתפים נמי הוי נכסים ששבחו מאליהם וע"ק לר"ת מאי קאמר כגון דקלא ואלים ה"ל למימר כגון פירות הבאות מאליהם ואומר רשב"א דאין תימה לפי' רש"י דשבח המגיע לכתפים היינו פירות אמאי חשיב להו כנכסים שנפלו לו ממקום אחר ויטלו אחיו עמו הלא גם להם יש פירות בארעא שהיתה כנגד זו דהא מבעי ליה בדקלא ואלים ארעא ומסקא שרטון אי חשיב כנפלו לו נכסים ממקום אחר כ"ש פירות דאית לן לאחשובינהו טפי כנפלו לו ממקום אחר כדמוכח גבי בכור (לקמן דף קכד.) דפליגי רבי ורבנן בחפירה והוו שיבלי [א](שלחופי) והוו תמרי אי בכור נוטל פי שנים אי לא ואפ"ה מודו בדקלא ואלים וארעא ומסקא שרטון דשקיל אלמא חשבינן פירות טפי בנפלו לאחר מכן מדקלא ואלים ומצינן למימר שפיר שיטלו אחיו בפירות ואע"פ שגם לקחו נגדם בחלקם דהם טרחו והם אכלו אבל מה שהמת טרח למה לא יקחו בטורח המת כמותו וכתלושים חשיבי ואי תלשם ואח"כ מת זה דבר פשוט שיטלו עמו ומיהו קשה לפי' הקונט' למה הוצרך כאן להאריך ולומר (ח) בשבח המגיע לכתפים דהיינו פירות שבכל שנה ושנה כדין אריס לא היה לו לומר אלא שנוטל בשדה שאינה עשויה ליטע כשדה העשויה ליטע דהיינו כדין אריס דיורד שלא ברשות שקיל בשדה העשויה ליטע כדין אריס כדאמר בהשואל (ב"מ דף קא.) היורד לתוך שדה חבירו שלא ברשות כו' ומסיק דבשדה העשויה ליטע אומדים כמה אדם רוצה ליתן בשדה זו ולנוטעה ופרש"י דהיינו כדין אריסי העיר אבל לפר"ת אתי שפיר דה"פ שנוטל דוקא בשבח המגיע לכתפים דהיינו בא ע"י טורח בשדה שאין עשויה ליטע כשדה העשויה ליטע כדין אריס אבל באין מגיע לכתפים לא יטול כדין אריס ואף על גב ([ג] דאדם) נוטל בשבח דאתי מעלמא ממילא כדמשמע בפ' מי שאחזו (גיטין דף עד:) הכא שיורד שלא ברשות סבר גמרא דאין לו ליטול בשבח הבא מאליו כדין אריס ומ"מ קשה דבכל מקום גרס ובשדה ([ג] שאינו שלו) בו"ו ולפירוש זה הוה ליה למימר בשדה בלא וי"ו כיון דחדא מילתא היא ויש ליישב פ"ה ונפרש ההיא דהשואל כמה אדם רוצה ליתן בשדה זו ולנוטעה דלאו היינו כדין אריס דלאריס נותנין יותר למחצה ולשליש כי עוסק בה לתקנה כמה צרכים אלא ה"פ כמה אדם רוצה ליתן לקבלן ליטע שדה זו ולא ירד בה לאריסות אלא מיד נוטל שכרו ונוטל יותר משכיר יום כי שכיר יום אין עליו לתקן אם יתקלקל והכי

עין משפט נר מצוה

קכז א מיי' פי"ג מהל' טוען ונטען הל' ח סמג עשין צה טוש"ע ח"מ סי' קמט סעיף ג ומיי' פ"ה מהל' שותפין הל' ח ובטוש"ע ח"מ סי' קעו:

קכח ב ג מיי' פ"י מהל' גזלה הל' ז סמג עשין עג טוש"ע ח"מ סי' שעה סעיף ג:

קכט ד מיי' פט"ו מהל' עדות הל' ד סמג לאוין קט טוש"ע ח"מ סי' לז סעיף ה:

רבינו גרשום

שותף אין לו חזקה. אע"ג דיכול למימר מן חבירי קניתי חלקי: וכ"ש אומן. דאיכא למימר כדי לתקן נתנו לו: מחזיקין זה על זה. שאם האחד תופש חלקו וחלק חבירו בו ג' שנים החזיק בו: ומעידין זה על זה. שאם בא אחד וערער על חלק חבירו יכול שותפו להצטרף עם עד אחר ולהעיד עליו דשל אביו היה זה או אם ערער עליו אדם יכול שותפו להצטרף עם עד אחד ולהעיד עליו שקנאו: ונעשין שומרי שכר זה לזה. שאם שומר זה מקצת הממון שבשותפות וזה מקצת ונגנב מבית אחד או אבד אינו כש"ח אלא חייב לשלם משום דש"ש הוא שבשכר ששומר לו חבירו מקצת הממון שומר לו אידך מקצתו: כיורד ברשות. חבירו לשדהו דמי דהוי כאריס שיורד לרשות לדעתו וכיון דחשיב הוא כיורד ברשות חבירו לדעתו (וכו') מכלל דאין לו חזקה: אמרי לה להאי גיסא הכי שאם ירד לפלגי לאותו חצי שלא הגיע לחלקו יש לו חזקה משום דמצי למימר המחזיק חלקך קניתי ממך וכבר החזקתי בו ואין לך בו כלום ודאי הויא חזקה אבל אי נחת לכולה ואמר כולה מוחזקת בידי אינה חזקה דאמר דמש"ה הניחה זה ברשותו ג' שנים כדי שישתמש בה נמי הוא כנגדו ג' שנים אחרות ומש"ה אינה חזקה דכיורד ברשות הוה: ואמרי לה להאי גיסא הכי האי דנחית לכולה הויא חזקה משום דמצי למימר למערער האיל שהחזקתי בכולה שני חזקה שלי היא שקניתי חלקך ממך אבל אי נחית לפלגא לא הויא חזקה משום דמצי למימר המערער חלקנו בשוה ובחלקך המגיע החזקת ובתוך שלי לא תחזיק כלל דמה שירדתי בחלקי ברשותי ירדתי: הא דאית בה דין חלוקה. ד' אמות לזה וד' אמות לזה ונחית לכולה והחזיק בה ג' שנים חזקתו חזקה משום דמצי למימר ליה חלקך קניתי ממך. אבל אי לית [בה] דין חלוקה והחזיק בה אינה חזקה משום דמצי למימר המערער הואיל דלא הוה דין חלוקה הייתי מתרצה שיהא בידך ג' שנים: לומר שנוטל בשבח המגיע לכתפים. שאם השביח עד גמר פירי שנוטלו חצי דאי הוה אמר בפירוש אין לו חזקה והיה השותף זורעה היה ידו על התחתונה ולא היה נוטל בחלקו של חבירו כלום אבל השתא דאמר שותף כיורד ברשות דמי הא אתא לאשמעי' דנוטל כאריס דמה אריס נוטל מחצה אפי' בשבח המגיע לכתפים האי נמי נוטל מחצה של חבירו וחלקו משום דהיינו ג' חלקים. איבעית אימא מש"ה תני שותף כיורד ברשות דמי ונוטל **בשדה שאינה עשויה ליטע כשדה העשויה ליטע** לומר מה שדה העשויה ליטע אם יורד בה אדם שלא ברשות חורעה ותיקנה דנוטל כפי חלקו המגיעו על מחצית השבח האי שותף נמי אם יורד בשדה שאינה עשויה ליטע חורעה והשביחה נוטל בכל מה שהשביח חלקו וחצי חלק חבירו משא"כ אדם אחר דעלמא שאם יורד שלא ברשות בשדה שאינה עשויה ליטע אם השבח יתר על ההוצאה נוטל את ההוצאה ואם היציאה יתירה על השבח נוטל את השבח דלא כהואיל שידו על התחתונה הואיל שירד שלא ברשות אבל האי שותף כיורד ברשות דמי וידו על העליונה.

מסורת הש"ס

א) [נ"ל שלחופי], ב) [נ"ל דלארים], ג) [נ"ל שאינה עשויה ליטע].

הגהות הב"ח

(א) גמ' במערתא דבי ר' זכאי: (ב) שם מאי קמ"ל שותף כל"ל ותיבות ו' מ' נמחק: (ג) רשב"ם ד"ה מחזיקין זה על זה: (ד) ד"ה דלית בה וכו' בריש פירקין. נ"ב דף כ"ט ע"ב וע"ש בתוס': (ה) תוס' ד"ה שותף וכו' וא"ת. נ"ב דף ט"ז ותימה: (ו) ד"ה שבח וכו' היינו ענבים העומדים ליבצר: (ז) בא"ד אמר ליה אביי לא יהא: (ח) בא"ד להאריך ולומר שנוטל בשבח:

גליון הש"ס

גמרא הא דנחית לכולא. עיין לקמן דף נז ע"ב תד"ה בשותפין: שם אמרי לה להאי גיסא. שבת דף קמ ע"א פסחים דף קמ ע"א גיטין דף מז ע"ב:

ליקוטי רש"י

שבח המגיע לכתפים. קרוב ליקצר אלא שעדיין צריכין לקרקע הוי להו כפירות גמורין [ב"מ טו:]. כגון תבואה שגדלה כל צרכה [ב"ק צה:]. שדה העשויה ליטע. אילנות שיפה לאין יותר מזרעים [ב"מ קא.].

Gemara The Mishnah taught that neither craftsmen nor partners can establish a *chazakah.* The Gemara now cites two variant versions of the Mishnah, each of which omits mention of one of these rulings:

אֲבוּהָ דִּשְׁמוּאֵל וְלֵוִי תָּנוּ – **The father of Shmuel, as did Levi, taught in** their versions of **the Mishnah:** שׁוּתָּף אֵין לוֹ חֲזָקָה – A PARTNER CANNOT ESTABLISH A *CHAZAKAH.* Their version considered it unnecessary to mention the case of a craftsman, וְכָל שֶׁכֵּן אוּמָּן – **for** if a partner cannot establish a *chazakah,* then **certainly a craftsman** cannot establish one.[1]

The Gemara cites the second variant version:

שְׁמוּאֵל תָּנֵי – **Shmuel taught in** his version of **the Mishnah:** אוּמָּן אֵין לוֹ חֲזָקָה – A CRAFTSMAN CANNOT ESTABLISH A *CHAZAKAH.* His version, which does not mention partners at all, implies that אֲבָל שׁוּתָּף יֵשׁ לוֹ חֲזָקָה – **a partner, however, can establish a *chazakah.***[2]

The Gemara observes:

וְאָזְדָא שְׁמוּאֵל לְטַעֲמֵיהּ – **And** in advocating his reading of the Mishnah, which implies that partners can establish a *chazakah,* **Shmuel is consistent with his opinion** stated elsewhere. דְּאָמַר שְׁמוּאֵל – **For Shmuel stated** elsewhere: הַשּׁוּתָּפִין מַחֲזִיקִין זֶה עַל זֶה – **Partners** in a property **can establish a *chazakah* one against the other,** i.e. in each other's portion of property; וּמְעִידִין זֶה עַל זֶה – **and they may testify one on behalf of the other;**[3] וְנַעֲשִׂים שׁוֹמְרֵי שָׂכָר זֶה לָזֶה – **and they become paid custodians one for the other.**[4] Thus, the first part of Shmuel's three-part ruling is consistent with Shmuel's reading of our Mishnah.

The Gemara notes a contradiction between this ruling of Shmuel and another of his rulings:

רָמֵי לֵיהּ רַבִּי אַבָּא לְרַב יְהוּדָה – **R' Abba noted the** following **contradiction to Rav Yehudah** בִּמְעַרְתָּא דְּבֵי רַב זַכַּאי – **in the burial crypt**[5] **of Rav Zakkai's estate.** מִי אָמַר שְׁמוּאֵל שׁוּתָּף יֵשׁ לוֹ חֲזָקָה – **Did Shmuel** indeed **say that a partner can establish a *chazakah,*** as cited in the Gemara above? וְהָאָמַר שְׁמוּאֵל שׁוּתָּף כְּיוֹרֵד בִּרְשׁוּת דָּמֵי – **But Shmuel said** elsewhere that **a partner** who occupies his partner's portion of the field **is considered** in regard to that portion **as one who has worked** it **with permission,** i.e. like a sharecropper.[6] לָאו לְמֵימְרָא דְּשׁוּתָּף אֵין לוֹ חֲזָקָה – Was it **not** Shmuel's intent **to say that a partner cannot establish a *chazakah*?**[7]

The Gemara resolves the contradiction:

לֹא קַשְׁיָא – There is **no difficulty.** הָא דְּנָחִית לְכוּלָּהּ הָא דְּנָחִית לְפַלְגָא – **One** statement of Shmuel refers to **where [the partner] occupied the entire** field,[8] whereas **the other** statement of Shmuel refers to **where [the partner] occupied half** the field.[9] אָמְרֵי לָהּ לְהַאי גִּיסָא – **Some explain [the resolution] one way** וְאָמְרֵי לָהּ לְהַאי גִּיסָא – **while some explain it the other way.**[10]

NOTES

1. Our version of the Mishnah (above, 42a) lists both partners and craftsmen among those who cannot establish a *chazakah.* Now, of the two rulings, the one regarding partners is the more novel, for there is reason to believe that a partner, who already owns a portion of the property, would seek to purchase his partner's share as well. [Thus, his exclusive occupancy of the property might signify complete ownership.] A craftsman, however, is not known to have owned any part of the property. Thus, his possession of the property signifies no more than that the property was entrusted to him for repair (*Rashbam*).

The version of the Mishnah taught by Shmuel's father and Levi contains only the more novel ruling that a partner cannot establish a *chazakah.* The omitted ruling, however, is taught by implication: If a partner, who is known to own part of the property, cannot establish a *chazakah,* then a craftsman surely cannot. As regards the law, then, their version of the Mishnah accords with our own.

2. Shmuel's version of the Mishnah teaches only the *less* novel law, viz. that a craftsman cannot establish a *chazakah* (see previous note). We can infer that the Tanna of the Mishnah (in Shmuel's version) did not include the more novel ruling regarding partners, because he holds, in fact, that a partner *can* establish a *chazakah.* Since [the first partner's exclusive occupancy of the property could be construed as exclusive ownership] the second partner should have made sure to utilize his portion of the property as well (*Rashbam*). Thus, Shmuel's version of the Mishnah differs with our own (and with that of his father and of Levi) with regard to whether a partner can establish a *chazakah.*

3. E.g. if one partner's title to the property was challenged, the second partner is not disqualified from testifying on his behalf that the title is genuine. The Gemara below (43a) will explain why the partner is considered an impartial witness (*Rashbam*).

4. E.g. if a commonly owned article is stolen from the house of one partner, he is liable to compensate the other, even though he has received no payment for watching the object. Although an unpaid custodian is normally exempt from paying for objects stolen from him when no negligence is involved (see *Bava Metzia* 93a, 94b), each partner is treated as a paid custodian (who is responsible for theft), for the arrangement between partners is that each takes a turn guarding the joint property. The fact that the other partner reciprocates by guarding the property for an equal amount of time is considered payment for each partner's term of custodianship; thus, both are deemed paid custodians (*Rashbam* here and to 43b).

5. *Bach* emends the text to read בְּמַעַצְרְתָּא, *in the olive press,* of R' Zakkai's estate. *Hagahos Yaavetz,* in explanation of our version, writes that the vault was used as a hiding place when persecution made it impossible to study Torah publicly.

6. [Literally: who has descended with permission.] I.e. when one partner works the entire field, we view it as if the other partner gave him permission to do so as he would a sharecropper (*Rashbam*).

7. I.e. didn't Shmuel liken a partner to a sharecropper in order to indicate that a partner cannot establish a *chazakah,* just as a sharecropper cannot [as stated explicitly in the Mishnah: Sharecroppers . . . cannot establish a *chazakah*] (*Rashbam*)? [The Gemara below will explain why Shmuel chose this way of indicating that a partner cannot establish a *chazakah,* instead of directly stating: A partner cannot establish a *chazakah* (ibid.).]

8. For three years, and seeks to use his occupancy as proof that he bought out his partner.

9. I.e. he occupied the better half of the field for three years and claims that it was this half that he received when the partnership was dissolved and the assets divided. The other partner, however, denies that the partnership was ever dissolved. He explains his partner's occupancy of the better half these three years as part of an arrangement they had, by which each partner would work one half for several years [to minimize constant moving expenses] and then exchange halves with the other partner (*Rashbam*).

10. [Literally: some say it to this side and some say it to that side.] There is a difference of opinion as to how this difference in cases accounts for the two rulings of Shmuel. Some explain that Shmuel's first ruling (a partner can establish a *chazakah*) refers to a partner who occupies the whole of a jointly owned property for three years, whereas his second ruling (a partner is like a sharecropper, who cannot establish a *chazakah*) refers to a partner who occupied the more desirable half of the property for three years. Others explain just the opposite.

According to the first approach, the reasoning runs as follows: Most partners desire an annual return on their investment. Thus, it is unlikely that one partner would allow the other exclusive use of the field for three years and delay his own benefit from the field until it is his turn to have exclusive use. Consequently, one partner's exclusive and unchallenged use of the field for three years indicates that he bought out his partner and it was regarding this case that Shmuel ruled that a partner can establish a *chazakah.* On the other hand, one partner's use of a particular half of the field for three years — even if it is a better half — is a common practice among partners, since each receives an annual return. The difference in yield obtained by the two partners will balance out when the partners switch halves during the next three years. Consequently, one partner's unchallenged use of the better half for three years does *not* indicate that he is the owner and it was regarding this case that Shmuel ruled that a partner does not establish a *chazakah.*

The second approach employs a different line of reasoning: A partner

קכז א מיי' פי"ג מהל' טוען הל' ט סמג עשין לה טוש"ע ח"מ סי' קמט סעיף ג ועי' פ"ה מהל' שותפין הל' ח וטוש"ע ח"מ סי' קעט:
קכח ב ג מיי' פ"י מהל' גזילה הל' ז סמג עשין עג טוש"ע ח"מ סי' שעה סעיף ה:
קכט ד מיי' פט"ו מהל' עדות הל' ד סמג לאוין קט טוש"ע ח"מ סי' לז סעיף א:

גמ' אבוה דשמואל ולוי תנו שותף אין לו חזקה וכל שכן אומן שמואל תני אומן אין לו חזקה אבל שותף יש לו חזקה ואזדא שמואל לטעמיה דאמר שמואל השותפין מחזיקין זה על זה ומעידין זה על זה ונעשים שומרי שכר זה לזה רמי ליה רבי אבא לרב יהודה (א) במערתא דבי רב זכאי מי אמר שמואל שותף יש לו חזקה והאמר שמואל שותף כיורד ברשות דמי לאו למימרא דשותף אין לו חזקה לא קשיא הא דנחית לכולה הא דנחית לפלגא אמרי לה להאי גיסא ואמרי לה להאי גיסא רבינא אמר הא והא דנחית לכולה ולא קשיא הא דאית בה דין חלוקה הא דלית בה דין חלוקה גופא אמר שמואל שותף כיורד ברשות דמי מאי קמ"ל (ג) שותפות אין לו חזקה לימא שותף אין לו חזקה אמר רב נחמן אמר רבה בר אבוה לומר שנוטל בשבח המגיע לכתפים בשדה שאינה עשויה ליטע כשדה העשויה ליטע: ומעידין זה לזה אמאי

רשב"ם

גמ' אבוה דשמואל. וגם לוי חבירו: תנו. במתני': שותף. השותפין והאפוטרופין כו' אבל אומן לא תנו דכ"ש דאין לו חזקה דהא אין לו חלק כלל דנימא מיגו דהיה לו חלק בו קנה מחבירו את חלקו אלא ודאי לתקן ניתן לו: אבל שותף יש לו חזקה. דאם איתא דלא מכר לו חלקו היה לו לעבוד את האדמה ולאכול הפירות בשותפות: מחזיקין זה (ג) לזה. אם האחד מחזיק בחלקו ובחלק חבירו ג' שנים הויא חזקה: ומעידין. זה על חלקו של זה להעמידה בידו אם בא אחד מן השוק לערער עליו ולא הוי נוגע בעדות כדמפרש לקמן: ונעשין כשומרי שכר זה לזה. שאם מביא אחד מהן נגנב דבר של שותפות חייב לשלם כשומר שכר והוו שכרו שגם חבירו ישמור הכל כשיעור זמן שמשמר זה עכשיו: והא אמר שמואל שותף. שמחזיק בכל השדה גם בחלקו של חבירו: כיורד ברשות דמי. כלומר כאילו נתן לו חבירו רשות ולזהו להיות במקומו כדין אריס דמי: לאו למימרא דשותף אין לו חזקה. דהוי כאריס שיורד ברשות ולכך לא הויא חזקתו חזקה ולקמן מפרש דלהכי נקט לשאר דברים קאמר שמואל כיורד ברשות דמי מלתא קאמר בהדיא שותף אין לו חזקה: דנחית לכולה. שדה שקנו שניהם: דנחית לפלגא. בחלק המובחר החזיק ואמר חלקנו והגיע לו לחלקי והחזקתי בו שלש שנים ואידך טוען עדיין לא חלקנו אלא כך התנינו ביניהו שתאכל אותו חלק ג' שנים ואני אחריך כמו כן ג' שנים: אמרי לה להאי גיסא. יש מתרצים בענין זה הא דאמר שמואל שותף יש לו חזקה דנחית לכולה דמנהג שותפים ליטול בשותפות פירות כל שנה ושנה או זה יטול חצי הקרקע וזה החצי ולשנה הבאה למפרע מה שלקח זה אשתקד יקח זה עכשיו שכל אחד רוצה ליהנות בכל שנה מחלקו וזה שהניח להחזיק לחבירו ג' שנים בכל השדה ודאי מכר לו את חלקו והלכך הויא חזקה: והא דאמר שמואל אין לו חזקה דנחית לפלגא. שכן דרך שותפין לאכול זה פלגא ואידך חבריה פלגא שלש שנים או ארבע ואחר כך אוכלין למפרע בענין זה ארבע שנים אחרות: ואמרי לה להאי גיסא. היכא דנחית לכולה לא הויא חזקה שכן הוא מנהג השותפין לאכול שדה שלש שנים והלכך לא מצי טוען לקוח חלקך בידי והיכא דנחית לפלגא הויא חזקה דסברא הוא דחלקו דאם איתא דניחא ליה ליהנות מחלקו בכל שנה ולא להמתין שלש שנים או ארבע שנים אחר חבירו כמנהג שותפין לא היה לו לברר חלק אחד לבדו אלא יעשו בשותפות ויחלקו הפירות: הכי גרסי' רבינא אמר הא והא דנחית לכולה הא דאית בה דין חלוקה. ארבע אמות לזה וארבע אמות לזה הויא חזקה דכיון דיש כדי לזה וכדי לזה אינו מנהג להניח האחד להקדים לו חבירו ג' שנים אלא אם כן מכר לו חלקו: דלית בה דין חלוקה. אינה חזקה דהתם מנהג הוא לאכול זה שלש או ארבע שנים שלימות כל השדה ואחר כך זה משום דבשניהם ביחד אינו כדאי והכי קיימא לן והך עובדא דרמי בר חמא ורב עוקבא בר חמא דזבון אמהתא בשותפות מר משתמש ראשונה שלישית כו' בריש פרקין (ד) (דף כט:) ופרשינן טעמא כי היכי דלא ליחזקו אהדדי ה"ה דאי הוה כל אחד משתמש שלש שנים רצופין לא תהוי חזקה דהא לית בחדא אמתא דין חלוקה והלכך לא תהוי חזקה ואינהו דאחזוק בסירוגין משום דלמא לא ידעי העדים לסוף ג' שנים שלקחוה בשותפות ויטעון המחזיק בה שאינו שותף ותהוי חזקתו חזקה: לומר שנוטל. כדין אריס שיורד ברשות אפי' בשבח המגיע לכתפים גמר פירי כגון קמה לקצור וענבים לבצור נוטל כל החצי כדין אריסי העיר ואפילו הוא שדה שאינו עשוי ליטע אלא לזריעה ונטעה הוא נוטל כל דינו כאילו עשוי ליטע כדין היורד ברשות דאילו יורד שלא ברשות שמין לו וידו על התחתונה דאם השבח יתר על היציאה נוטל את היציאה ואם היציאה יתר על השבח נוטל יציאה שיעור שבח כדאמר בב"מ בהשואל (דף קא.) היורד לתוך שדה חבירו ונטעה שלא ברשות אמר רב שמין לו וידו על התחתונה ושמואל אומר אומדין כמה אדם רוצה ליתן על שדה זו ליטע וא"ר פפא לא פליגי כאן בשדה העשויה ליטע כאן בשדה שאינה עשויה ליטע והכא חשיב להאי שותף כיורד ברשות והלכך שקיל בשדה שאינה עשויה ליטע כשדה העשויה ליטע ואי הוה אמר שמואל שותף אין לו חזקה הוה אמינא דידו על התחתונה הואיל ובלא רשות חבירו ירד: אמאי

תוספות

אבל שותף יש לו חזקה. יש ענין לשותף דאין לו חזקה כדמפרש לקמן וא"ת א"כ ליתני במתני' שותף אין לו חזקה אע"פ שיש שותף שיש לו חזקה כי היכי דתני אריס אע"פ שאר אריס שאינו אריסי בתי אבות יש להן חזקה ויש לחלק:

שותף כיורד ברשות דמי לאו למימרא דאין לו חזקה. (ה) וא"ת מנא ליה דילמא לענין שנוטל בשבח המגיע לכתפים כדאמר בסמוך וכ"ת דמשמע ליה דכל ענין מדמי ליה לאריס דלמא כשאר אריסים קאמר שיש להן חזקה ולא כאריסי בתי אבות: שבח המגיע לכתפים. מפרש רש"י בכמה מקומות וכן רבינו שמואל דמגיע לכתפים כגון ענבים הראוין ליבצר וקשה דאמרי' בפ"ק דב"מ (דף טו:) והא מעשים בכל יום וקא מגבי שמואל לבעל חוב בשבח המגיע לכתפים ואי ס"ד היינו ענבים (ו) הראוים ליבצר א"כ בעל חוב לא גבי מינייהו כדאמר בכתובות פ' נערה (דף נ:) אמר ליה זיל הב ליה מתמרי דעל בודיא אמר ליה (ז) לא יהא אלא בעל חוב דמזו לבודיא קאמינא סוף סוף כל העומד ליגדר כגדור דמי דלריכי לדקלא קאמינא אלמא לא גבי מאותם העומדים ליגדר ואלו פירכא היא דהא רש"י נמי לא בעי למימר מאותן העומדים ליבצר מיד אלא כלומר כל דבר שסופו ליתלש כגון פגין או בוסר ור"ת מפרש מגיע לכתפים היינו דבר שבא ע"י טורח ומייתי ראיה מהא דתנן בסוף יש נוחלין (לקמן דף קמג.) האומר זה אחי אינו נאמן ויטול עמו בחלקו מת יחזרו נכסים למקומם נפלו לו נכסים ממקום אחר יירשו אחיו עמו ובעי רבא (שם קמב:) שבח שבחו נכסים מאליהם מהו בשבח המגיע לכתפים לא תבעי לך דכי נפלו ממקום אחר דמי כי תיבעי לך בשבח שאינו מגיע לכתפים כגון דקלא ואלים ארעא ומסקא שרטון משמע שבח שאינו מגיע לכתפים היינו בא מאליו ולר' אלחנן נראה דאדרבה משם קשה לר"ת דלמה שינה בלשון דמעיקרא קאמר נכסים ששבחו מאליהם מהו ובתר הכי קאמר כי תיבעי לך בשבח שאין מגיע לכתפים מעיקרא נמי הוה ליה למימר שבח שאין מגיע לכתפים אלא משמע דשבח המגיע לכתפים נמי הוי נכסים ששבחו מאליהם וע"ק לר"ת אמאי קאמר כגון דקלא ואלים ה"ל למימר כגון פירות הבאות מאליהם ואומר רשב"א דאין תימה לפי' רש"י דשבח המגיע לכתפים היינו פירות אמאי חשיב להו כנכסים שנפלו לו ממקום אחר ויטלו אחיו עמו הלא גם להם יש פירות בארלס שהיתה כנגד זו דהא מבעי ליה בדקלא ואלים ארעא ומסקא שרטון אי חשיב כנפלו לו נכסים ממקום אחר כ"ש פירות דאית לן לאחשובינהו טפי כנפלו לו ממקום אחר כדמוכח גבי בכור (לקמן דף קכד.) דפליגי רבי ורבנן בחפירה והוו שיבלי [א] (שלחופי) והוו תמרי אי בכור נוטל פי שנים אי לא ואפ"ה מודו בדקלא ואלים וארעא ומסקא שרטון דשקיל אלמא חשבינן פירות טפי בנפלו לאחר מכן מדקלא ואלים ומצינן למימר שפיר שיטלו אחיו בפירות ואע"פ שגם לקחו נגדם בחלקם דהם טרחו והם אכלו אבל מה שהמת טרח למה לא יקחו בטורח המת כמותו וכתלושים חשיבי ואי תלשם ואח"כ מת זה דבר פשוט שיטלו עמו ומיהו קשה לפי' הקונט' למה הוצרך כאן להאריך ולומר (ח) בשבח המגיע לכתפים דהיינו פירות שבכל שנה ושנה כדין אריס לא היה לו לומר אלא שנוטל בשדה שאינה עשויה ליטע כשדה העשויה ליטע דהיינו כדין אריס דיורד שלא ברשות שקיל בשדה העשויה ליטע כדין אריס כדאמר בהשואל (ב"מ דף קא.) היורד לתוך שדה חבירו שלא ברשות כו' ומסיק דבשדה העשויה ליטע אומדים כמה אדם רוצה ליתן בשדה זו ולנוטעה ופרש"י דהיינו כדין אריסי העיר אבל לפר"ת אתי שפיר דה"פ שנוטל דוקא בשבח המגיע לכתפים דהיינו בא ע"י טורח בשדה שאין עשויה ליטע כשדה העשויה ליטע כדין אריס אבל באין מגיע לכתפים לא יטול כדין אריס ואף על גב [ג] (דאדם) נוטל בשבח דאתי מעלמא ממילא כדמשמע בפ' מי שאחזו (גיטין דף עד:) הכא שיורד שלא ברשות סבר גמרא דאין לו ליטול בשבח הבא מאליו כדין אריס ומ"מ קשה דבכל מקום גרס ובשדה ([ג] שאינו שלו) בוי"ו ולפירוש זה הוה ליה למימר בשדה בלא וי"ו כיון דחדא מילתא היא ויש ליישב פ"ה ונפרש ההיא דהשואל כמה אדם רוצה ליתן בשדה זו ולנוטעה דלאו היינו כדין אריס דלאריס נותנין יותר למחצה ולשליש כי עוסק בה לתקנה כמה נרכיס אלא ה"פ כמה אדם רוצה ליתן לקבלן ליטע שדה זו ולא ירד בה לאריסות אלא מיד נוטל שכרו ונוטל יותר משכיר יום כי שכיר יום אין עליו לתקן אם יתקלקל והכי

רבינו גרשום

שותף אין לו חזקה. אע"ג דיכול למימר מן חבירי קניתי חלקי: וכ"ש אומן. דאיכא למימר כדי לתקן נתנו לו: מחזיקין זה על זה. שאם האחד תופש חלקו וחלק חבירו ג' שנים החזיק בו: ומעידין זה על זה. שאם בא אחד וערער על חלק חבירו יכול שותפו להצטרף עם עד אחר ולהעיד עליו דשל אביו היה או אם ערער עליו אדם יכול שותפו להצטרף עם עד אחד ולהעיד עליו שקנאו: ונעשין שומרי שכר זה לזה. שאם שומר זה מקצת הממון ונגנב מבית אחד או אבד אינו כש"ח אלא חייב לשלם משום דש"ש הוא שבשכר ששומר לו חבירו מקצת הממון שומר לו איהו מקצתו: כיורד ברשות. חבירו לשדהו דמי דהוי כאריס שיורד לרשות חבירו וכיון דחשיב הוא כיורד ברשות חבירו לדעתו (וכו' לדעתו) מכלל דאין לו חזקה: אמרי לה להאי גיסא הכי שאם ירד לפלגי לאותו חצי שלא הגיע לחלקו יש לו חזקה משום דמצי למימר המחזיק חלקך קניתי ממך וכבר החזקתי בו ואין לך בו כלום ודאי הויא חזקה אבל אי נחת לכולה ואמר כולה מוחזקת בידי אינה חזקה דאמר משה"ה הניחה לו ברשותו ג' שנים כדי שישתמש בה נמי הוא כנגדו ג' שנים אחרות ומש"ה אינה חזקה דכיורד ברשות הוה: ואמרי לה להאי גיסא הכי דאי נחית לכולה הויא חזקה משום דמצי למימר למערער הואיל שהחזקתי בכולה שני חזקה שלי היא שקניתי חלקך ממך אבל אי נחית לפלגא לא הויא חזקה משום דמצי למימר המערער הואיל ובחלקך לא נחית ובחלקך המגיע לך החזקת ובתוך שלך לא תחזיק בכלל דמה שירדתי בחלקי ברשותי ירדתי: הא דאית בה דין חלוקה. ד' אמות לזה וד' אמות לזה ונחית לכולה והחזיק בה ג' שנים חזקתו חזקה משום דמצי למימר ליה חלקך קניתי ממך. אבל אי לית [בה] דין חלוקה והחזיק בה אינה חזקה משום דמצי למימר המערער הואיל דלא הוה דין חלוקה הייתי מתרצה שיהא בידך ג' שנים: לומר שנוטל בשבח המגיע לכתפים. שאם השביח עד גמר פירי שנוטל חצי דאי הוה אמר בפירותיו אין לו חזקה היה השותף זורעה היה ידו על התחתונה ולא היה נוטל בחלקו של חבירו כלום אבל השתא דאמר שותף כיורד ברשות דמי הא אתא לאשמעי' דנוטל כאריס דמה אריס נוטל מחצה אפי' בשבח המגיע לכתפים האי נמי נוטל מחצה של חבירו וחלקו משום דהיינו ג' חלקים. איבעית אימא משה"ה תני שותף כיורד ברשות דמי ונוטל **בשדה שאינה עשויה ליטע כשדה העשויה ליטע** מה שדה העשויה ליטע אם יורד בה אדם שלא ברשות וזרעה ותיקנה דנוטל כפי מחצית השבח האי שותף נמי אם יורד בשדה שאינה עשויה ליטע וזרעה והשביחה נוטל בכל מה שהשביח חלקו וחצי חלק חבירו משא"כ אדם אחר דעלמא שאם יורד שלא ברשות בשדה שאינה עשויה ליטע אם השבח יתר על ההוצאה נוטל את ההוצאה ואם היציאה יתירה על השבח נוטל את השבח דכל שעה ידו על התחתונה הואיל שירד שלא ברשות אבל האי שותף כיורד ברשות דמי וידו על העליונה.

מסורת הש"ס

א) [נ"ל שלחופי], ב) [נ"ל דלארים], ג) [נ"ל שאינה עשויה ליטע]

הגהות הב"ח

(א) גמ' במערתא דבי ר' זכאי: (ב) שם מאי קמ"ל שותף כל"ל ואות ו' נמחק: (ג) רשב"ם ד"ה מחזיקין זה על זה: (ד) ד"ה דלית בה וכו' בריש פירקין. נ"ב דף כ"ט ע"ב וע"ש בתוס': (ה) תוס' ד"ה שותף וכו' וא"ת. נ"ב ס"ל ומיהו: (ו) ד"ה שבח וכו' היינו ענבים העומדים ליבצר: (ז) בא"ד אמר ליה אבי לא יהא: (ח) בא"ד להאריך ולומר שנוטל בשבח:

גליון הש"ס

גמרא הא דנחית לכולא. עיין לקמן דף מז ע"ב תד"ה בשותפין: שם אמרי לה להאי גיסא. שבת דף קס ע"א פסחים דף קח ע"א גיטין דף מז ע"ב:

ליקוטי רש"י

שבח המגיע לכתפים. קרוב ליקצר אלא שעדיין צריכין לקרקע הוי להו כפירות גמורין [ב"מ טו:]. כגון תבואה שגדלה כל צרכה [ב"ק צה:]. שדה העשויה ליטע. אילנות שיפה לאילן יותר מזרעים [ב"מ קא.].

An alternative resolution of the contradiction in Shmuel's rulings:

רְבִינָא אָמַר – **Ravina says:** הָא וְהָא דְּנָחִית לְכוּלָּהּ – **Both** rulings of Shmuel refer to **where he** [the partner who seeks to establish a *chazakah*] **occupied the entire** field for three years וְלָא קַשְׁיָא – **and** still there is **no difficulty.** הָא דְּאִית בָּהּ דִּין חֲלוּקָה – **This** ruling, which states that partners can establish a *chazakah,* speaks of **[a field] that is** large enough to be **subject to legal division.**[11] הָא דְּלֵית בָּהּ דִּין חֲלוּקָה – **This** ruling, which states that partners cannot establish a *chazakah,* speaks of **[a field] that is not** large enough to be **subject to legal division.**[12]

The Gemara cites Shmuel's second ruling again in order to elaborate upon it:

גּוּפָא – **The matter itself** cited above: אָמַר שְׁמוּאֵל שׁוּתָּף כְּיוֹרֵד בִּרְשׁוּת דָּמֵי – **Shmuel said: A partner** who occupies his partner's portion of the field **is considered** in regard to that portion **as one who has worked** it **with permission,** i.e. like a sharecropper. מַאי קָא מַשְׁמַע לָן – **What** law **does [Shmuel]** wish to **teach us** with this statement? שׁוּתָּפוּת אֵין לוֹ חֲזָקָה – That in **a** case of **partnership,** one partner **cannot establish a *chazakah*** against the other.[13] לֵימָא שׁוּתָּף אֵין לוֹ חֲזָקָה – Then **let [Shmuel] state** directly that **a partner cannot establish a *chazakah*!** Why does he use such a roundabout means of saying it?

The Gemara answers:

אָמַר רַב נַחְמָן אָמַר רַבָּה בַּר אֲבוּהָ – **Rav Nachman said in the name of Rabbah bar Avuha:** לוֹמַר שֶׁנּוֹטֵל בְּשֶׁבַח הַמַּגִּיעַ לִכְתֵפַיִם – Shmuel worded his statement in this way **to teach that [the partner]** is entitled **to take** his share **from "yield that reaches the shoulders,"** i.e. mature produce, בְּשָׂדֶה שֶׁאֵינָהּ עֲשׂוּיָה לִיטַּע – even **in a field which is not normally used for planting,** כְּשָׂדֶה הָעֲשׂוּיָה לִיטַּע – **just as** he may take such produce from **a field that is normally used for planting.**[14] [15]

The Gemara quotes and elaborates upon a section of Shmuel's ruling (cited above) regarding partners:

וּמְעִידִין זֶה לָזֶה – Shmuel ruled that **[partners] may testify one on behalf of the other.**

NOTES

does not necessarily seek an annual return on his investment. For this reason, it *is* a common practice for a person to allow his partner exclusive use of the property for several years in return for his own exclusive use during an equivalent number of years. Consequently, one partner's exclusive and unchallenged use of the field for three years does *not* indicate that he bought out his partner and it was regarding this case that Shmuel ruled that a partner *cannot* establish a *chazakah.* However, once a partner decides that he desires an annual return, it is not likely that he would accept the inferior half for several years running; rather, he would insist on an equal sharing of the entire field every year. Consequently, one partner's unchallenged use of the better half for three years indicates that he is the owner and it was regarding this case that Shmuel ruled that a partner can establish a *chazakah* (*Rashbam*).

11. I.e. a property large enough so that, if divided, the halves would be usable in their own rights. In that case, either partner can demand dissolution of the partnership and division of the property (see Mishnah 11a). With regard to a jointly owned courtyard, the minimum size after division must be four *amos* square of open space for each partner (ibid.). With regard to jointly owned fields, the minimum size varies with the fertility of the land (Gemara 12a).

Ravina holds (as do the proponents of the first approach mentioned in the previous note) that under normal circumstances one partner would not allow the other exclusive use of their joint property for three years. This applies, however, only to a property that is large enough to be used simultaneously by both. Thus, in a property that large, one partner's exclusive and unchallenged use serves to establish a *chazakah* (*Rashbam*).

12. A field that small is not large enough to be worked simultaneously by both partners. In the case of such a field, it is common for partners to take turns working the plot and taking its yield for several years in a row. Accordingly, neither partner can establish a *chazakah* in the plot and it was to such a field that Shmuel referred when he ruled that partners cannot establish a *chazakah* (*Rashbam*).

13. The Gemara assumes at this point that the only law which Shmuel meant to teach with this statement was that partners cannot establish a *chazakah* (see note 7).

14. The Gemara in *Bava Metzia* (101a) speaks of a case in which a person planted trees in someone else's field without permission. Since the intruder has, in fact, generated profit for the owner, he receives compensation for his efforts. The amount of compensation, however, depends upon what type of field it was. If it was a field that was better suited for trees than for grains or vegetables [שָׂדֶה הָעֲשׂוּיָה לִיטַּע], then he receives whatever percentage of the profits is usually paid to sharecroppers. [Though he cultivated the field without permission, he provided a valuable service that the owner would have contracted and paid for anyway.] If, however, the field is better suited for grains or vegetables than for trees [שָׂדֶה שֶׁאֵינָהּ עֲשׂוּיָה לִיטַּע], then the intruder is simply reimbursed for his expenses (provided that they do not exceed the profit generated) and does not receive a sharecropper's portion of the profit. [Though he has provided some service for the owner, it is not a service that the owner would be expected to have had performed anyway.]

The foregoing applies when the one who worked the field did not receive permission to do so. If, however, the owner granted the person permission to work the field without specifying what should be planted, the planter receives a sharecropper's portion regardless of whether the field is usually used for trees or for other crops.

There is also a difference between an intruder and a person who works the field with permission in regard to the mature produce that was growing on the field when the person took over the field. An intruder receives no share of this produce, as the owner can claim it had already matured and required no care. A planter who entered with permission, however, receives a share even of this produce, as it is assumed that the owner wished him to tend to the produce when he granted him permission to take over the field.

Now, when a person fails in his attempt to establish a *chazakah* in a field and is ousted by the original owner, his occupancy of the field is viewed as that of an intruder; he must return the produce to the owner and is reimbursed only for his expenses. [Cf. *Rabbeinu Gershom* here and *Tosafos* to *Bava Kamma* 95a ד״ה דאתא, who discuss the possibility that he is penalized for his attempt at theft and is *not* reimbursed for expenses.] Thus, had Shmuel merely stated that "a partner cannot establish a *chazakah,*" the partner who failed in his attempt to claim the land as his own would have been assumed to be in the category of an intruder and would have been entitled only to reimbursement of his expenses. Therefore, Shmuel said that "a partner is considered as one who works a field with permission," thereby equating him not with an intruder but with one who has worked the field with the owner's permission. This gives the partner two advantages over an intruder. He takes a share in the mature produce that was on the field when he first took over the field and he receives a sharecropper's portion of the yield whether or not he planted the field's usual crop (*Rashbam* as understood by *Ramban, Nimukei Yosef*; cf. *Tosafos, Rashba* and *Meiri*).

15. An apparent difficulty still remains. Until this point, the Gemara (as explained by *Rashbam*) has assumed that the reason one partner cannot establish a *chazakah* against the other is that the challenger can claim that his colleague's occupancy of the land was based on a prearranged schedule of sharing, and he, in turn, was to use the land for the *next* three years (see note 10 above and 42a note 18). Accordingly, when the court rejects the partner's claim of *chazakah,* the assumption should be that the challenger will take his turn occupying the property during the next three years. Why, then, does the partner who has failed to establish a *chazakah* receive only a sharecropper's percentage of the profits? He should rather keep the entire yield of the preceding three years, in place of the next three years' yield, which his partner is slated to keep!

Possibly, Shmuel indeed means to introduce an additional rationale for a partner's inability to establish a *chazakah*; namely, that the challenger can claim that the occupying partner was working on behalf of *both* of them in return for an extra share of the profits. Accordingly, the intent of Shmuel's ruling is that the occupying partner, though he has failed to establish a *chazakah,* receives half the yield (his own share of the joint property) plus a sharecropper's percentage of the other partner's portion (see *Dibros Moshe* §37 for a lengthy discussion of this issue).

The Gemara questions Shmuel's ruling:

אַמַּאי – **Why** does Shmuel permit partners to testify in each other's behalf? נוֹגְעִין בְּעֵדוּתָן הֵן – **They have an interest in their testimony,** since any loss suffered by one partner will ultimately result in a loss for the second partner. Thus, they are disqualified from testifying.[1] – ? –

The Gemara answers that Shmuel's ruling applies to a specific case, one in which no benefit accrues to the testifying partner: הָכָא בְּמַאי עַסְקִינָן – **With what case is [Shmuel] dealing here?** דִּכְתַב לֵיהּ – In a case **in which [the testifying partner] wrote** a document **to [the challenged partner]** stating: דִּין וּדְבָרִים אֵין לִי עַל שָׂדֶה זוֹ – **"I** wish to **have neither claim nor argument** with respect **to this field."**[2] By handing over such a document, the testifying partner divests himself of any interest in the field. He may therefore testify about it.[3]

The Gemara questions the effectiveness of such a document:

וְכִי כָּתַב לוֹ – **But even if [the testifying partner] wrote** such a note **to [the challenged partner],** מַאי הָוֵי – of **what** consequence **is it?** וְהָתַנְיָא – **Has a Baraisa** not **taught:** הָאוֹמֵר לַחֲבֵירוֹ – IF ONE SAYS TO HIS FELLOW (i.e. partner), דִּין וּדְבָרִים אֵין לִי עַל שָׂדֶה זוֹ – "I wish to HAVE NEITHER CLAIM NOR ARGUMENT with respect TO THIS FIELD," וְאֵין לִי עֵסֶק בָּהּ – OR, "I wish to HAVE NO CONCERN WITH IT,"[4] וְיָדַי מְסוּלָּקוֹת הֵימֶנָּה – OR, "MY HANDS ARE hereby WITHDRAWN FROM IT," לֹא אָמַר כְּלוּם – HE HAS NOT SAID ANYTHING of legal consequence, and the field remains his?[5] We see from this Baraisa that such a declaration is *not* sufficient to divest a person of his holding in a jointly owned property.[6] – ? –

The Gemara responds:

הָכָא בְּמַאי עַסְקִינָן – **With what case is [Shmuel] dealing here?** כְּשֶׁקָּנוּ מִיָּדוֹ – **Where [the challenged partner] acquired** the divested share **from [the testifying partner]** with a *kinyan chalifin.*[7] Although the declaration itself is insufficient to effect transfer of the partner's holding, it can do so when coupled with a *kinyan chalifin.*[8]

The Gemara accepts this explanation, and grants that such a divestiture is effective. However, the Gemara persists in questioning Shmuel's ruling, pointing out that even after the testifying partner gives away his share, he still has a vested interest in bolstering his former partner's case:

וְכִי קָנוּ מִיָּדוֹ – **But even if [the challenged partner] acquired** the divested share **from [the testifying partner],** מַאי הָוֵי – of **what** consequence **is it?** הֲרֵי מַעֲמִידָהּ בִּפְנֵי בַּעַל חוֹבוֹ – The testifying partner still has an interest in maintaining his former partner's title to the land, for **then he makes it available to his creditor,** who may take it to satisfy an obligation.[9] Thus, he would still be an interested party, and his testimony should be disqualified. – ? –

The Gemara quotes a ruling of Shmuel to demonstrate that a witness is indeed disqualified for this reason:

דְּאָמַר רָבִין בַּר שְׁמוּאֵל מִשְּׁמֵיהּ דִּשְׁמוּאֵל – **For Ravin bar Shmuel said in the name of Shmuel:** הַמּוֹכֵר שָׂדֶה לַחֲבֵירוֹ שֶׁלֹּא בְּאַחֲרָיוּת – **If one sells a field to his fellow without a guarantee,**[10] אֵין מֵעִיד לוֹ עָלֶיהָ – **he cannot testify in [the buyer's] behalf regarding it,**[11] מִפְּנֵי שֶׁמַּעֲמִידָהּ בִּפְנֵי בַּעַל חוֹבוֹ – **because he makes it available to his creditor** by preserving it in the buyer's possession.[12] The seller is therefore considered an interested party and unfit to testify. By the same token, even if one partner divests himself of his share of a jointly owned field, he should still be barred from testifying in his partner's behalf. – ? –

The Gemara responds:

הָכָא בְּמַאי עַסְקִינָן – **With what case is [Shmuel] dealing here?** דְּקַבֵּיל עָלֵיהּ אַחֲרָיוּת – With a case **in which [the testifying partner] guaranteed** the share he signed away.[13] Thus, the testifying partner derives no benefit from keeping the land

NOTES

1. Although one partner was using the disputed land at the time of the challenge, it actually belongs to *both* partners. Thus, if a challenger is awarded half the land, for example, part of that loss will come out of the share of the partner who wishes to testify. In essence, then, the one testifying is testifying *in his own* behalf (*Rashba*).

Rashba points out that the testifying partner is not only an interested party, he is actually a co-defendant, since he owns part of the disputed land. However, the Gemara applies the broader disqualification of an "interested party" to include even cases in which the testifying partner renounces his share, as the Gemara will discuss below.

2. Although the declaration is made as a statement of fact ("I *have* no claim etc."), it is used in legal terminology to refer to the future ("I will not have any claim etc."), and therefore it can serve as a divestiture.

3. The Gemara could have answered simply that the testifying partner had given his share of the property to his co-owner with a valid *kinyan* (or had sold it to him – *Meiri*). The Gemara chooses to discuss this manner of transfer to teach us that even such a declaration is effective (*Rashbam*).

4. As if to say, "I will have no further dealings with it," implying that the entire property now belongs to the other partner (*Rashbam*).

5. This is true whether the declaration was made orally or in a document (*Kesubos* 83a, *Rashi* ד״ה תני ר׳ חייא). The reason for this is that in order to transfer property to another, one must tell him to acquire it. A declaration renouncing one's interest in a property does not do this; it merely expresses the fact that the owner wishes to be rid of his property. This is regarded as no more than a prayerful expression: "I wish this property were no longer mine!" Such a declaration is ineffective, for whether the owner wants it or not, the property is his until he gives it away formally (*Rashbam's* preferred explanation). See further, Gemara 49a.

6. Consequently, Shmuel's ruling is still problematic, since even if the partner renounced his share, his renunciation would not be effective. Thus, his testimony should be dismissed as biased.

7. Literally: an exchange. A buyer hands a seller an object of insignificant value (generally a kerchief); the seller's acceptance of it effects a legal transfer of the item or right being sold.

8. Although the declaration, "I have no claim etc.," can be interpreted merely as a wishful statement without any intent to transfer the property (see note 5), a *kinyan chalifin* is not made unless there is intent to transfer. Thus, the *kinyan chalifin* proves that the partner actually intended to give away the land (*Rashi* to *Kesubos* 83a ד״ה מהו; see *Rashbam* here).

9. If the testifying partner incurred a debt before renouncing his portion of the property, his portion is mortgaged to the debt. Thus, his creditor is entitled to take it if the debtor himself has no other assets from which to collect (see 41b note 24). This is true, however, only if the field originally belonged to the debtor. If it is established that the field *never* belonged to him, the creditor would have no right to it. This would leave the debtor in the uncomfortable position of *an evil borrower who does not pay* (*Psalms* 37:21; see Gemara below, 45a). The desire to avoid such a position, the Gemara argues, gives a person an interest in the outcome of the challenge even after divesting himself of the property (*Rashbam*).

10. I.e. with a clause added to the contract *explicitly* excluding any obligation on the part of the seller to reimburse the buyer if the field is taken from him. [In the absence of such a clause, a guarantee would be presumed to exist.]

11. He cannot testify against someone claiming that the field never belonged to the seller.

12. Should the challenger succeed in proving that the field never belonged to the seller, the seller's creditor would have no claim on it. Thus, it is in the seller's interest to preserve the property in the hands of the buyer.

Shmuel states this ruling for a seller who did not guarantee the sale. Had he guaranteed the sale, he would *certainly* be disqualified from testifying (*Rashbam*), because the loss of the property would render the seller liable to reimburse the buyer. Shmuel means to teach that bias exists *even* if no guarantee was issued.

13. He not only signed away his share of the property to his partner, but he also guaranteed to reimburse him if this share should ever be taken from him.

אמאי נוגעין בעדותן הן הכא במאי עסקינן דכתב ליה דין ודברים אין לי על שדה זו וכי כתב לו מאי הוי והתניא [א] האומר לחבירו דין ודברים אין לי על שדה זו ואין לי עסק בה וידי מסולקות הימנה לא אמר כלום [א] הכא במאי עסקינן כשקנו מידו וכי קנו מידו מאי הוי הרי מעמידה בפני בעל חובו [ג] דאמר רבין בר שמואל משמיה דשמואל [ב] המוכר שדה לחבירו שלא באחריות אין מעיד לו עליה מפני שמעמידה בפני בעל חובו הכא במאי עסקינן דקביל עליה אחריות אחריות דמאן אי נימא אחריות דעלמא כל שכן דניחא ליה [ג] אלא אחריות דאתיא ליה מחמתיה וכי מסלק נפשיה מיניה מי מסתלק והתניא [ד] בני עיר שנגנב ספר תורה שלהן אין דנין בדייני אותה העיר ואין מביאין ראיה מאנשי אותה העיר ואם איתא ליסלקו בי תרי מינייהו ולידיינו שאני ס"ת דלשמיעה קאי תא שמע האומר תנו מנה לבני עירי אין דנין בדייני אותה העיר ואין מביאין ראיה מאנשי אותה העיר אמאי ליסלקו בי תרי נפשייהו ולידיינו הכא נמי בס"ת ש [ה] האומר תנו מנה לענייי עירי אין דנין בדייני אותה העיר ואין מביאין ראיה מאנשי אותה העיר ותסברא עניים שקלי דייני מיפסלי אלא אימא אין דנין בדייני עניי אותה העיר ואין מביאין ראיה מעניי אותה העיר ואמאי לסתלקו בי תרי נפשייהו ולידיינו הכא נמי בספר תורה ואמאי קרי להו עניים דהכל אצל ספר תורה עניים הן ואיבעית אימא לעולם כדקתני עניים ממש [ו] ובענייי דראמו עלייהו והיכי דמי אי דקיץ להו ליתבו בי תרי מינייהו מאי דקיץ להו ולידיינו הכא במאי עסקינן דלא קיץ להו ואב"א [ז] לעולם דקיץ להו וניחא להו דכיון דרווח רווח: [ח] ונעשין שומרי שכר זה לזה

אמאי

אמאי. מעידין זה על זה: נוגעין בעדותן הן. דכל זמן שלא חלקו לגמרי אם יטול שום מערער כלום מן השדה יפסידו שניהם ונמלא דלעצמו מעיד: **דכתב ליה.** האי מעיד להאי מחזיק דין ודברים אין לי עמך בכל השדה ואפילו על חלקי שהלך שלך והכי משמע דין ודברים לא יהא לי על שדה זו ולשון חכמים הוא לומר אין לי במקום לא יהא לי והלכך כיון דנתן לו חלקו מעיד עליה דלא נוגע בעדות הוא והכי נמי הוה מלי למתני כשהקנה לו חלקו אלא רבותא נקט לאשמועינן דבכי האי גוונא הוי לשון מתנה: **מאי הוי.** הרי אינו לשון מתנה ואהכי נוגע בעדות הוא: **האומר לחבירו.** שותף: **ואין לי עסק בה.** כלומר לא יהא לי עסק בה ומכלל אתה שומע אלא הכל יהא שלך אלא שלא הוציא הדבר בפירוש מפיו: **וידי יהו מסולקות לא אמר כלום.** דכיון דכבר יש לו חלק בשדה והוא אומר לא יהא לי חלק בו אין זה לשון מתנה לחבירו אלא לשון תפלה הוא הלואי שלא יהא לי חלק בשדה זו וכל זמן שלא אמר יהי נתון לך שדה זו לא ילא עדיין מרשותו ואין תופס לשון זה אלא בדבר שעדיין לא זכה בו והוא מתנה עליו שלא יהא שלו כשיבוא הזמן שעתיד לזכות באותו דבר דלאין אדם זוכה בדבר בעל כרחו כדלקמן בפירקין (דף מט.) וכתובות (דף פג.) דנחלה הבאה לו לאדם לאחר מכן מתנה עליה שלא יירשנה אבל מכיון שכבר הדבר שלו הוא והוא אומר לא יהא שלי לא אמר כלום דבעל כרחו יהיה שלו כל זמן שלא יתננה לאחרים כן נראה בעיני ועיקר והכי מוכח לקמן בפירקין. וי"מ דמשום הכי לא אמר כלום דקאמר אין לי דין ודברים ולא קאמר לא יהא ונמלא שהוא מכזב שהרי יש לו חלק בו והוא אומר אין לי ושבוש הוא דאין זה לשון הגמ' לומר בשום מקום לא יהא והכי מוכח לקמן דקמשני הכא במאי עסקינן בשקנו מידו ולא קא מתרך באומר לא יהא: **כשקנו מידו.** שותף חבירו קנה מידו בקנין סודר והשתא דאיכא קנין מועיל התנאי: **וכי קנו מידו מאי הוי.**

אכתי אמאי מעיד להעמיד השדה בידו הרי נוגע הוא בעדות זו דניחא ליה שיהיה השדה ביד השותף מפני שמעמידו האי נותן לפני בעל חובו שאם יש לו שום בע"ח שהלוהו מעות קודם שהקנה לחבירו חלקו שהיה לו בשדה זו ויבא בע"ח של זה ויטרוף אותה שהרי הלוה משועבדת לו ויפטר זה הנותן מבעל חובו ולא יהיה לוה רשע ולא ישלם כדלקמן בשמעתין שאילו יטרפוה מזה עדים שיאמרו שלא היה לאלו שותפין חלק בה לא יוכל בעל חוב שלו לגבות הימנה והו"ל לוה רשע ולא ישלם: **שלא באחריות.** וכל שכן באחריות: **אין מעיד לו עליה.** אין מצטרף עם עד אחר להעמידה בידו ואע"ג דלאו הוא מפסיד לוקח לא הדר עליה למוכר: **מפני שמעמידה כו'.** ובדלית ליה ארעא אחריתי מוקמינן לה לקמן בשמעתין דלא ניחא למיהוי לוה רשע ולא ישלם: **דקביל עליה אחריות.** האי שותף לחבירו ממה שהקנה לו ולכשיטרפו ממנו יחזור עליו ולא בעי לשקורי ולהכי ניחא ליה להעמיד ביד חבירו והלכך אינו מעיד: **אחריות דעלמא.** שלא בשביל חוב חבירו אלא מערער לומר שדה זו של אבותי או שלי היא: **כל שכן דאינו מעיד.** דנוגע בעדות הוא כשמעיד להעמידו ביד זה דניחא ליה למיהוי בידו משום דלא מפיק מיניה עליה הדר: **אלא אחריות דאתא ליה מחמתיה.** אם יטרפוהו בשביל חובו שהיא חייב לאחרים יחזיר לו הדמים הלכך מעיד עליה גבי ערער דעלמא להעמידה בידו שאינו מעמידו בפני בעל חובו דמה הנאה יש לו אם יטרפנה בעל חוב מיד זה ולא יהא לוה רשע סוף סוף לוה רשע הוא שקיבל עליו אחריות ומחייב לשלם ואין לו נכסים בע"ח זה במקום בעל חוב ראשון וגם אם לא יעיד לו מה מפסיד הרי אחריות דעלמא לא קיבל וממ"נ בין יעיד בין לא יעיד לא הוא דיש לו להוי כנגדו לוה רשע ולא ישלם ולקמן בשמעתין מוכח דמיקרי לוה רשע מוכר באחריות וטרפוה מן הלוקח ואינו משלם לו: **וכי מסלק.** שום שותף נפשיה מחלקו: **מי מסתלק.** בתמיה מי הוי סילוק גמור אפילו לגבי עדות דלא הוי נוגע בעדות כלל ויכול להעיד דאוקמת ליה בשקנו מידו: **והתניא כו'.** וטעמא משום דאיכא למימר קנויא הוא לעבוד כדי שיעיד לו עליה ויעמידנה בידו ואחר כך יחזור לשותפותו: **אין דנין.** הגנב והוא טוען לקחתיו בדמים או שום טענה: **ראיה.** עדים שראוהו שגנבו או שמעידין שזהו ס"ת של אותה העיר דכולן שותפין ונוגעין בעדותן: **ליסתלקו.** יכתבו דין ודברים אין לי על ספר תורה זה ° ויקנו מידם: **דלשמיעה קאי.** ואין יכול לסלק עצמו שלא יהא נוגע בעדות שהרי נהנה בו ויוצא בשמיעתו אלא אם כן ילך לו לדור בעיר אחרת שלא יהנה בקריאתו: **לבני עירי.** לצרכי בני העיר לחומות העיר ולכל צרכי רבים: **וליסלקו בי תרי מינייהו.** שלא יהנו בו כלל ויתנו מכיסם כנגד המנה של צבור: **הכא נמי בס"ת.** שפירש תנו מנה לבני עירי לקנות בו ס"ת: **ותסברא עניים שקלי כו'.** גמרא קא פריך עלה ומתרך לה והדר מקשי מינה ושיטת הגמרא היא זו ועדיין לא סיים קושיא שלו למיפרך מינה עד לבסוף כלומר ותסברא דהכי קאמר דוקא שהדיינין יפסלו בשביל העניים והלא אין נוגעין בעדותן כלל: **דהכל אצל ספר תורה עניים הם.** שכולן צריכים לו ודרך בני אדם לקרוא בני עירו עניים כשאין להם ס"ת דעניות גדול הוא זה: **ואי בעית אימא לעולם.** כל הברייתא כדקתני דבעניים ממש מיירי ודייני העיר שאינן עניים קאמר דמפסלי ודקא קשיא לך דיינין אמאי מפסלי הרי אין נוגעין בעדות: **בעניי דרמו עלייהו.** על דייני העיר פירוש עשירי העיר וכדמפרש ואזיל דהשתא נוגעין בעדות הן: **אי דקיץ להו.** דבר קלוב לבני העיר לכל אחד כמה יתן לעניי העיר משלו בכל שנה ושנה: **ומשני דלא קיץ להו.** אלא הכל לפי הצורך ולפי מחסורן של עניים נותנין דכל זמן שיש מן המנה בעין לא יתנו הדיינין כלום: **לעולם דקיץ להו.** ואפ"ה ניחא להו לדיינין שיתן המנה לעניים: **דכיון דרווח.** שיש להם מעות רווח כלומר הרי יש להם מעות ולמה יתנו כלום כל זמן שאין צריכין:

שמירה

והכי קאמר שנוטל בשבח המגיע לכתפים כאריס שלא [א] יסלקנו אותו כמו קבלן כמו שעושין לנוטע שלא ברשות שמסלקין אותו בכך אפי' משדה העשויה ליטע ובשדה שאין עשויה ליטע כו' פי' ועוד שגם בשדה שאין עשויה ליטע נוטל כמו בעשויה ליטע מה שאין כן בנוטע שלא ברשות: **אין** לי עסק בה לא אמר כלום. וא"ת דבפרק השולח (גיטין דף מ: ושם) גבי מוכר עבדו לנכרי כו' אמר היכי דמי אונו דכתב ליה לכשתברח ממנו אין לי עסק בך אלמא אין לי עסק בך הוי לשון טוב ואור"י דלאין לי עסק בך משמע אלא תהא לעצמך וגבי עבד דמהני הרי את לעצמך מהני נמי אין לי עסק בך אבל בשדה דלא שייך למימר הרי את לעצמך כי אמר נמי אין לי עסק בך לא אמר כלום דכיון דליכא לפרושי אין לי עסק בך אלא תהא לעצמך גבי שדה כמו גבי עבד לא משמע גבי שדה אין לי עסק בה אלא סילוק דין ודברים כדמוכח בכריתות (דף כד:): **מפני** שמעמידה בפני בעל חובו. וא"ת מאי איריא מפני שמעמידה (ג) תיפוק ליה משום דלא ניחא ליה דליהוי תרעומת עליו כדאמרי' בפ"ק דב"ק (דף ח:) דאמר בעל חובו והכא ליכא לאמעון לתת באחריות שלא באחריות ואתא בעל חובו וקטריף לה מיניה דינא הוא דלאתי דאמר דינא נהדיה ולא מלי לאמעון ומשתעי דינא נהדיה ולא מלי א"נ לאו בעל דברים דידי את דהא לא ניחא לו דליהוי לאמעון תרעומת עילוי' וי"ל דאין נפסל בשביל כך לעדות א"נ הכא מיירי אפילו במוכר בה שהיא שלו דליכא תרעומת: **וליסלקו** בי תרי מינייהו ולידיינו. וא"ת והא בעינן [ג] תחילתו וסופו בכשרות והכא הוי תחילה בפסול והוי כמו קרוב ונתרחק ° ואור"י דלא שייך תחילתו בפסלות הכא כיון שאין פסלות תלוי בגוף ° אלא בממון [ז]: ה"ג **ותסברא** עניים שקלי ודיינין מיפסלי [אלא] ה"ג בספר תורה ואמאי קרי להו עניים כו':

אמאי

עין משפט נר מצוה

קל א מיי' פט"ו מהל' עדות הל' ד סמג לאוין קט טוש"ע ח"מ סי' לז סעיף ל:
קלא ב מיי' פט"ו שם הל' ג סמג שם טוש"ע שם סעיף טו:
קלב ג טוש"ע שם סעיף ל:
קלג ד מיי' שם פט"ו הל' ב סמג שם טוש"ע שם סעיף יט וסי' ז סעיף יב:
קלד ה ו ז מיי' שם הל' ג וסמג שם טוש"ע ח"מ סי' ז וסי' לז סעיף כ:
קלה ח טוש"ע ח"מ סי' קנו סעיף ח ועיין בש"ך:

רבינו גרשום

ומעידין זה על זה כדאמר לעיל: **ואמאי** מעידין הא **נוגעין בעדותן הן.** משום דאם האחד היה מאבד חלקו היה חוזר זה שאבד והיה נוטל חצי מחלקו של חבירו ולפיכך מסייע לשותפו כדי שלא יפסיד הוא עצמו: **הכא במאי עסקינן.** דמצי מעיד לו: **דכתב ליה.** כל חד לחבריה: **דין ודברים אין לי על שדה זו.** של חבירי ואפי' מאבד אחד חלקו [א]: **והא לא אמר** ולא כלום **מי שאמר** לחבירו דין ודברים אין לי בשדה זו דמש"ה לא מסתלק דהא קא חזינן דאית ליה. וכן הכי נמי להיכא דאמר ליה **אין לי עסק בה וידי מסולקות** ממנה הא קא חזינן דאית ליה חלק בה ומש"ה **לא אמר כלום** דנוגע בעדות הוא: **בשקנו מידו.** דלית ליה לחד על חבירו כלום מש"ה מעיד דלא נוגע בעדות: **וכי קנו מידו.** מעיד לו והלא נוגע בעדותו הוא מפני שמעמידה זה המעיד בפני בעל חוב שלו. דהואיל דקנו זה מזה דומה כמכרו זה לזה וכמכר לשותפו לאחר שנתחייב ממון למלוה דמשועבד לו מה שמכר ומש"ה מסייע לשותפו כדי שיבא בעל חוב שלו ויטרפנה ממנו בשביל חובו כי היכי דלא מקרי להו רשע ולא ישלם. **דאמר רבין כו'.** והני שותפין נמי כמוכרין זה לזה שאם יאבד אחד מהם חלקו שיחזור על האחר: **הכא במאי עסקינן.** דמצי מעיד **דקביל עליה אחריות: אחריות דמאן** קבלו עליהן: **אי דעלמא** אחריות של כל אדם בעולם שאם יבא שום אדם ויערער עליו ויוציאה מידו שיחזור ויטול חצי מחלקו של חבירו: **כל שכן** וכל שכן דנוגע בעדות הוא דקסבר אם מאבד חבירו חלקו יחזור עלי: **אלא שקבל עליו** בלבד **אחריות דאתיא מחמתיה.** דאי טרף לה בעל חוב דאיהו מפצי ליה וכיון דקבל לו אחריות בשביל עצמו וכל הבא מכחו לאו נוגע בעדות הוא למערער דעלמא שאין בא בשבילו ונאמן: **וכי מסלק נפשיה.** וכל מדבר של שותפו מי מסתלק ומצי מעיד: **אין דנין.** הגנב: **בדייני** העיר משום דנוגעין בדבר הן: **ואין מביאין ראיה.** עדות: **ואם איתא.** דשותף מצי מסלק: **לסתלקו תרי** מאותה העיר מחלק של ספר תורה **ולידייני.** אלא ש"מ דלא מצו לסלוקי נפשייהו מספר תורה הואיל דשותפין אינון מש"ה אין דנין הכי נמי

הגהות הב"ח

(א) תוס' ד"ה (כדף הקודם) שגם וכו' כאריס שלא יסלקו אותו כמו: (ג) ד"ה מפני וכו' מאי איריא מפני שמעמידה בפני ב"ח תיפוק:

גליון הש"ס

רשב"ם ד"ה ליסתלקו כו' ויקנו מידם. קשה לי הא קי"ל דגול ולא נתייאשו הבעלים שניהם אינם יכולים להקדישו ואם כן ל"י הקנות ובתשובה הארכתי בעזה"י. תוס' ד"ה וליסלקו כו' ואור"י. עי' בריטב"א קדושין דף מג ע"ב ד"ה והשתא ועי' נדה דף כ ע"א תוס' ד"ה וא"ת: **באד בכופו. אלא בממון.** עי' תוס' שבועות דף לג ע"א ד"ה קרובים:

ליקוטי רש"י

האומר לחבירו דין ודברים אין לי על שדה זו וכו'. כלומר לא יהא לי [רשב"ם לקמן מט.]. כגון שדה של שותפין ואמר האחד לחבירו אחד מן הלשונות הללו [בין בכתובה בין באמירה] [כתובות פג.]. שהיתה לו עמו שותפות בה. **ואין לי עסק בה.** אתה מכל לשונות הללו [גיטין עז.]. **לא אמר כלום.** דלאין כאן לשון מתנה [כתובות שם]. דמאחר שהיא שלו צריך לכתוב לשון מתנה [גיטין שם]. לשון מתנה כשמאמר לא יהא לי חלק בשלי בעל כרחו הרי הוא שלו עד שיאמר לחבירו שדי נתונה לך שדי מכורה לך שדי מופקרת לכל מי שירלה [רשב"ם שם]. ולא אבד זכותו [כריתות כד:]. **המוכר שדה שלא באחריות.** במוכר קרקע שלו שהיתה משועבדת לבעל חוב ומכרה ללוקח זה ואותו אינים מעלמא וקמערער דלא יעיד לו המוכר ללוקח מפני שבאחריותו של בעל חוב עליו למוכר לגבות מקרקע זו ולהכי ניחא ליה דמיקו ביד הלוקח דסדר לא יוכל בעל חוב שלו ליהוי מוכר לוה רשע ולא ישלם וכגנד לוקח לא ליהוי לוה רשע שהרי לא באחריות מכר לו והלכך אין מעיד דנוגע בעדות הוא [רשב"ם לקמן מד.].

חשק שלמה על רבינו גרשום

[א] נראה דל"ל ואפי' מאבד אחד חלקו לא יפסיד חבירו.

מסורת הש"ס

[א] כתובות פג. לה. גיטין עז. [לקמן מט. כריתות כד:], [ב] [לקמן מד.], [ג] [לקמן קכח.], [ד] [וע"ע תוס' נדה כ. ד"ה וכ"ת היאך]

available for his creditor, since if the creditor seizes the land, he will have to reimburse his partner for the loss. Either way, he will be in default.[14]

The Gemara, seeking to clarify this reply, asks:

אִי נֵימָא אַחֲרָיוּת – **What did he guarantee?**[15] אַחֲרָיוּת דְּמַאן דְּעָלְמָא – **If we say** he gave **a guarantee against general [claims],** i.e. against claims that the land was never his, כָּל שֶׁכֵּן דְּנִיחָא לֵיהּ – then **he would certainly prefer** that his partner retain the land, since the loss of the property would require him to make good his guarantee. Thus, his testimony would certainly be disqualified! אֶלָּא אַחֲרָיוּת דְּאַתְיָא לֵיהּ מֵחֲמָתֵיהּ – **Rather,** we must say he gave **a guarantee against [claims] resulting from his** personal debts.[16] Such a guarantee negates any benefit which would accrue to him from making his holding available to his creditor, and renders him an impartial witness.[17]

The Gemara has now concluded that if a partner divests himself of his share and issues a guarantee to his partner, he has no interest in seeing that the partner retains the land. His testimony should therefore be admissible. However, the Gemara now discusses another reason to disqualify the partner's testimony:

וְכִי מְסַלֵּק נַפְשֵׁיהּ מִינֵּיהּ – **But** even **if [the partner] formally removes himself from [the field],** מִי מִסְתַּלֵּק – **is he** truly **removed?** Perhaps he has released his share only to enable himself to testify, and his partner will return it after the lawsuit is settled.[18] – ? –

The Gemara cites a Baraisa which seemingly disallows such testimony for this very reason:

וְהָתַנְיָא – **Has a Baraisa** not **taught:** בְּנֵי עִיר שֶׁנִּגְנַב סֵפֶר תּוֹרָה שֶׁלָּהֶן – IF INHABITANTS OF A TOWN HAD THEIR TORAH SCROLL STOLEN,[19] and the thief is apprehended, אֵין דָּנִין בְּדַיָּינֵי אוֹתָהּ הָעִיר – the case MAY NOT BE TRIED BY THE JUDGES OF THAT TOWN, וְאֵין מְבִיאִין רְאָיָה מֵאַנְשֵׁי אוֹתָהּ הָעִיר – NOR MAY EVIDENCE (i.e. testimony) BE ACCEPTED FROM THE PEOPLE OF THAT TOWN.[20] וְאִם אִיתָא – **Now if it is true** that by releasing his share in a property, a partner is rendered an impartial witness, לִיסַלְּקוּ בֵּי תְּרֵי מִינַּיְיהוּ – **let two of [the town's inhabitants] withdraw from** their partnership in **[the Torah scroll],**[21] וְלִידַיְינוּ – **and try** the case![22] Since the Baraisa does not permit this, it indicates that the possibility of collusion disqualifies even judges (or witnesses) who divest themselves of their share of the disputed property. Why, then, does Shmuel allow a partner to testify once he has divested himself of his share of the challenged property?

The Gemara rejects the proof:

שָׁאנֵי סֵפֶר תּוֹרָה – The case of a stolen **Torah scroll is different,** דִּלְשְׁמִיעָה קָאֵי – **for its function is to be heard.** Each member of the town is equally obligated to hear the Torah read. Thus, in order to be considered a disinterested party, a potential judge would have to move away and hear the Torah readings elsewhere! Since this is unlikely, the Baraisa disqualifies all the inhabitants.[23]

The Gemara attempts another proof:

תָּא שְׁמַע – **Come, learn** a proof from the following Baraisa: הָאוֹמֵר תְּנוּ מָנֶה לִבְנֵי עִירִי – If [A DYING MAN] SAYS, "GIVE A *MANEH* TO THE INHABITANTS OF MY TOWN,"[24] אֵין דָּנִין בְּדַיָּינֵי אוֹתָהּ הָעִיר – the case MAY NOT BE TRIED[25] BY THE JUDGES OF THAT TOWN, וְאֵין מְבִיאִין רְאָיָה מֵאַנְשֵׁי אוֹתָהּ הָעִיר – NOR MAY EVIDENCE BE ACCEPTED FROM THE PEOPLE OF THAT TOWN. אַמַּאי – Now, **why** is this so? לִיסַלְּקוּ בֵּי תְּרֵי נַפְשַׁיְיהוּ – **Let two** of the inhabitants **remove themselves** from any share of the bequest,[26] וְלִידַיְינוּ – **and try** the case! It would seem that the Baraisa disqualifies the townspeople as judges or witnesses even after they divest themselves of their shares, due to the possibility of collusion. – ? –

The Gemara rejects this proof as well:

הָכָא נַמִּי בְּסֵפֶר תּוֹרָה – **Here, too,** the Baraisa deals **with a Torah scroll.** The bequeather specifically stated that the funds be used

NOTES

14. Making a property available to one's creditor is not a monetary benefit to a debtor, since land can be seized from the buyer only if the debtor himself has nothing left with which to repay the loan. Rather, the benefit is derived from the fact that the debtor will not be branded *an evil borrower who does not pay* (see note 9). In our case, this benefit exists for the testifying partner only when he cedes his share of the field without a guarantee, in which case he is not required to reimburse his partner if the share is seized. However, if there is a guarantee, the confiscation of the land triggers a *new* obligation – since the testifying partner must then reimburse his partner as per the guarantee. Obviously, he will not be able to fulfill this obligation (since he has no remaining assets), and he will in any case be branded a person who does not pay his obligations! This being the case, he derives no benefit from making the land available to his creditor (since he must default on *one* obligation or the other). He may thus be considered an impartial witness (*Rashbam*).

15. Literally: a guarantee against whom.

16. He guaranteed to reimburse his partner only if the property is seized as a result of an obligation incurred by the giver – but not if his title to it is proven false. Thus, the testifying partner loses nothing if the lawsuit nullifies his title to the ceded land, since he need not compensate his partner in any case. At the same time, he gains nothing by preserving it for his creditor, since if a creditor of the testifying partner seizes the land, he will have to compensate the partner. Thus, he does not stand to benefit in any way from his testimony.

17. **In summary:** Shmuel allows one partner to testify in defense of another if the following three conditions are met: 1) The testifying partner must cede his share of the property to his co-owner. 2) The divestiture of his share must be made either by a valid act of transfer, or a declaration ("I have no right to this field") accompanied by a *kinyan chalifin.* 3) The testifying partner must also guarantee reimbursement to his partner if the ceded portion of the field is seized by one of his creditors but not if his original title is proven false.

18. I.e. the testifying partner agreed to present a "gift" to the challenged partner to render his testimony acceptable, with the understanding that once the lawsuit is settled, the "gift" will be returned and the partnership continued as before (*Rashbam*).

19. It was customary for an entire town to pool their resources and purchase a communal Torah scroll, which was owned by the citizenry as a whole.

20. I.e. they may not identify the Torah scroll as the one stolen from their town, or testify about the theft itself (*Rashbam*). [The Gemara assumes that the reason for the disqualification is due to the bias of the inhabitants.]

21. By a combination of a declaration ("we have no right to this Torah scroll") and a *kinyan chalifin* (*Rashbam;* see notes 3 and 8).

22. This translation follows *Yad Ramah,* who points out that while the law is that *three* judges are required to adjudicate monetary cases, the Gemara here discusses the opinion of Shmuel who rules (*Sanhedrin* 3a) that in cases of necessity even two judges can try a case. Other Rishonim, however, (*Rashba, Ran, Meiri*) understand the Gemara to refer to *witnesses,* and render the Gemara thusly: "Let two *witnesses* withdraw, and let the case be tried *based on their testimony.*"

23. However, a partner in a field *can* relinquish his share without creating a problem for himself; therefore, once this is done, his testimony is admissible, for we do not suspect collusion.

24. The Rabbis accorded a dying man's oral bequest the force of a written document (below, 151a; see *Yad Ramah*).

The Gemara assumes that the money (a *maneh* = 100 *zuz*) was to be used for such communal needs as building the town's walls (*Rashbam*).

25. I.e. if the man's heirs contest the bequest (*Rabbeinu Gershom*).

26. By forswearing benefit from the particular project for which the money will be used, and by contributing to the town's coffers the amount they would have been required to give toward that particular project (*Rashbam* as explained by *Nachalas Moshe;* cf. *Maharam*).

אמאי נוגעין בעדותן הן הכא במאי עסקינן דכתב ליה דין ודברים אין לי על שדה זו וכי כתב לו מאי הוי והתניא [א] האומר לחבירו דין ודברים אין לי על שדה זו ואין לי עסק בה וידי מסולקות הימנה לא אמר כלום [א] הכא במאי עסקינן כשקנו מידו וכי קנו מידו מאי הוי הרי מעמידה בפני בעל חובו [ג] דאמר רבין בר שמואל משמיה דשמואל [ב] המוכר שדה לחבירו שלא באחריות אין מעיד לו עליה מפני שמעמידה בפני בעל חובו הכא במאי עסקינן דקביל עליה אחריות אחריות דמאן אי נימא אחריות דעלמא כל שכן דניחא ליה [ג] אלא אחריות דאתיא ליה מחמתיה וכי מסלק נפשיה מיניה מי מסתלק והתניא [ד] בני עיר שנגנב ספר תורה שלהן אין דנין בדייני אותה העיר ואין מביאין ראיה מאנשי אותה העיר ואם איתא ליסלקו בי תרי מינייהו ולידיינו שאני ס"ת דלשמיעה קאי תא שמע האומר תנו מנה לבני עירי אין דנין בדייני אותה העיר ואין מביאין ראיה מאנשי אותה העיר אמאי ליסלקו בי תרי נפשייהו ולידיינו הכא נמי בס"ת [ה] האומר תנו מנה לעניי עירי אין דנין בדייני אותה העיר ואין מביאין ראיה מאנשי אותה העיר ותסברא עניים שקלי דייני מיפסלי אלא אימא אין דנין בדייני עניי אותה העיר ואין מביאין ראיה מעניי אותה העיר ואמאי לסתלקו בי תרי נפשייהו ולידיינו הכא נמי בספר תורה ואמאי קרי להו עניים דהכל אצל ספר תורה עניים הן ואיבעית אימא לעולם כדקתני עניים ממש [ו] ובעניי דרמאו עלייהו והיכי דמי אי דקיץ להו ליתבו בי תרי מינייהו מאי דקיץ להו ולידיינו הכא במאי עסקינן דלא קיץ להו ואב"א [ז] לעולם דקיץ להו וניחא להו דכיון דרווח רווח: [ח] ונעשין שומרי שכר זה לזה

אמאי

רש"י

אמאי. מעידין זה על זה: נוגעין בעדותן הן. דכל זמן שלא חלקו לגמרי אם יטול שום מערער כלום מן השדה יפסידו שניהן ונמצא לעצמו מעיד: דכתב ליה. האי מעיד להאי מחזיק דין ודברים אין לי עמך בכל השדה ואפילו על חלקי שהכל שלך והכי משמע דין ודברים לא יהא לי על שדה זו ולשון חכמים הוא לומר אין לי במקום לא יהא לי והלכך כיון דנתן לו חלקו מעיד עליה דלא נוגע בעדות הוא והכי נמי הוה מצי למתני כשהקנה לו חלקו אלא רבותא נקט לאשמועינן דבכי האי גוונא הוי לשון מתנה: מאי הוי. הרי אינו לשון מתנה ולהכי נוגע בעדות הוא: האומר לחבירו. שותף: ואין לי עסק בה. כלומר לא יהא לי עסק בה ומכלל אתה שומע אלא הכל יהא שלך אלא שלא הוציא הדבר בפירוש מפיו: וידי יהו מסולקות לא אמר כלום. דכיון דכבר יש לו חלק בשדה והוא אומר לא יהא לי חלק בו אין זה לשון מתנה לחבירו אלא לשון תפלה הוא הלואי שלא יהא לי חלק בשדה זו וכל זמן שלא אמר יהי נתון לך שדה זו לא יצא מרשותו ואין תופס לשון זה אלא בדבר שעדיין לא זכה בו והוא מתנה עליו שלא יהא שלו כשיבוא הזמן שעתיד לזכות באותו דבר דאין אדם זוכה בדבר בעל כרחו כדלקמן בפירקין (דף מט.) וכתובו' (דף פג.) דנחלה הבאה לו לאדם לאחר מכן מתנה עליה שלא יירשנה אבל מכיון שכבר הדבר שלו הוא והוא אומר לא יהא שלי לא אמר כלום דבעל כרחו יהיה שלו כל זמן שלא יתננה לאחרים כן נראה בעיני ועיקר והכי מוכח לקמן בפירקין. וי"מ דמשום הכי לא אמר כלום דקאמר אין לי דין ודברים ולא קאמר לא יהא ונמצא שהוא מכזב שהרי יש לו חלק בו והוא אומר אין לי ושבוש הוא דאין זה לשון הגמ' לומר בשום מקום לא יהא והכי מוכח לקמן דקמשני הכא במאי עסקינן בשקנו מידו ולא קא מתרץ באומר לא יהא: כשקנו מידו. שותף חבירו קנה מידו בקנין סודר והשתא דאיכא קנין מועיל התנאי: וכי קנו מידו מאי הוי. הכתי אמאי מעיד להעמיד השדה בידו הרי נוגע הוא בעדות זו דניחא ליה שיהיה השדה ביד השותף מפני שמעמידו האי נותן לפני בעל חובו שאם יש לו שום בע"ח שהלוהו מעות קודם שהקנה לחבירו חלקו שהיה לו בשדה יבא בעל חוב ויטרוף אותה שהרי אליה משועבדת לו ויפטר זה הנותן מבעל חובו ולא יהיה לוה רשע ולא ישלם כדלקמן במתניתין שאילו יטרפוה מזה בעדים שיאמרו שלא היה לאלו שותפין חלק בה לא יוכל בעל חוב שלו לגבות הימנה והו"ל לוה רשע ולא ישלם: שלא באחריות. וכל שכן באחריות: אין מעיד לו עליה. אין מצטרף עם עד אחר להעמידה בידו ואע"ג דאי הוה מפסיד לוקח לא הדר עליה דמוכר: מפני שמעמידה כו'. ובדלית ליה ארעא אחריתי מוקמינן לה לקמן במתניתין דלא ניחא למיהוי לוה רשע ולא ישלם: דקביל עליה אחריות. האי שותף לחבירו ממה שהקנה לו וכדמפרש ואזיל דהשתא אינו מעמידה לפני בעל חובו והלכך מעיד: אחריות דעלמא. שלא בשביל חוב חבירו אלא מערער לומר שדה זו של אבותי או שלי היא: כל שכן דאינו מעיד. דנוגע בעדות הוא כשמעיד להעמידו ביד זה דניחא ליה דתיהוי בידו משום דלא מפיק מיניה עליה הדר: אלא אחריות דאתא ליה מחמתיה. אם יטרפוהו בשביל חובו שחייב לאחרים יחזיר לו הדמים הלכך מעיד עליה גבי ערער דעלמא להעמידה בידו שאינו מעמידו בפני בעל חובו דמה הנאה יש לו אם יטרפנה בעל חוב מיד זה ולא יהא כנגדו לוה רשע סוף סוף לוה רשע ולא ישלם הוא גבי חבירו שקיבל עליו אחריות וחייב לשלם ואין לו ונכנס בע"ח זה במקום בעל חוב ראשון וגם אם לא יעיד לו מה מפסיד הרי אחריות דעלמא לא קיבל וממ"נ בין יעיד בין לא יעיד בע"ח אחד הוא דיש לו דהוי כנגדו לוה רשע ולא ישלם ולקמן במתניתין מוכח דמיקרי לוה רשע מוכר באחריות וטרפוה מן הלוקח ואינו משלם לו: וכי מסלק. שום שותף נפשיה מחלקו: מי מסתלק. בתמיה מי הוי סילוק גמור אפילו לגבי עדות דלא הוי נוגע בעדות כלל ויכול להעיד דאוקמת ליה בשקנו מידו: והתניא כו'. וטעמא משום דאיכא למימר קנוניא הוא דעבוד כדי שיעיד לו עליה ויעמידנה בידו ואחר כך יחזור לשותפותו: אין דנין. הגנב והוא טוען לקחתיו בדמים או שום טענה: ראיה. עדים שראוהו שגנבו או שמעידין שזהו ס"ת של אותה העיר דכולן שותפין ונוגעין בעדותן: ליסתלקו. יכתבו דין ודברים אין לי על ספר תורה זה [ט] ויקנו מידם: דלשמיעה קאי. ואין יכול לסלק עצמו שלא יהא נוגע בעדות שהרי נהנה בו ויוצא בשמיעתו אלא אם כן ילך לו לדור בעיר אחרת שלא יהנה בקריאתו: לבני עירי. לצרכי בני העיר לחומות העיר ולכל צרכי רבים: וליסלקו בי תרי מינייהו. שלא יהנו בו כלל ויתנו מכיסם כנגד המנה של צבור: הכא נמי בס"ת. שפירש תנו מנה לבני עירי לקנות בו ס"ת: ותסברא עניים שקלי כו'. גמרא קא פריך עלה ומתרץ לה והדר מקשי מינה ושיטת הגמרא היא זו ועדיין לא סיים קושיא שלו למיפרך מינה עד לבסוף כלומר ותסברא דהכי קאמר דוקא שהדיינין יפסלו בשביל העניים והלא אין נוגעין בעדותן כלל: דהכל אצל ספר תורה עניים הם. שכולן צריכים לו ודרך בני אדם לקרוא בני עירו עניים כשאין להם ס"ת דעניות גדול הוא זה: ואי בעית אימא לעולם. כל הברייתא כדקתני דבעניים ממש איירי ודייני העיר שאין עניים קאמר דמפסלי ודקא קשיא לך דיינין אמאי מפסלי הרי אין נוגעין בעדות: בעניי דרמו עלייהו. על דייני העיר פירוש עשירי העיר וכדמפרש ואזיל דהשתא נוגעין בעדות הן: אי דקיץ להו. דבר קצוב לבני העיר לכל אחד כמה יתן לעניי העיר משלו בכל שנה ושנה: ומשני דלא קיץ להו. אלא הכל לפי הצורך ולפי מחסורן של עניים נותנין דכל זמן שיש מן המנה בעין לא יתנו הדיינין כלום: לעולם דקיץ להו. ואפ"ה ניחא להו לדיינין שינתן המנה לעניים: דכיון דרווח. שיש להם מעות כלומר הרי יש להם מעות ולמה יתנו כלום כל זמן שאין צריכין:

שמירה

תוספות

והכי קאמר שנוטל בשבח המגיע לכתפים לאריס שלא [א] יסלקנו אותו כמו קבלן כמו שעושין לנוטע שלא ברשות שמסלקין אותו בכך אפי' משדה העשויה ליטע ובשדה שאין עשויה ליטע כו' פי' ועוד שגם בשדה שאין עשויה ליטע נוטל כמו בעשויה ליטע מה שאין כן בנוטע שלא ברשות:

אין לי עסק בה לא אמר כלום. וא"ת דבפרק השולח (גיטין דף מג: ושם) גבי מוכר עבדו לנכרי כו' אמר היכי דמי אונו דכתב ליה לכשתברח ממנו אין לי עסק בך אלמא אין לי עסק בך הוי לשון טוב ואור"י דאין לי עסק בך משמע אלא תהא לעצמך וגבי עבד דמהכי הרי את לעצמך מהני נמי אין לי עסק בך אבל בשדה דלא שייך למימר הרי את לעצמך כי אמר נמי אין לי עסק בך לא אמר כלום דכיון דליכא לפרושי אין לי עסק בך אלא תהא לעצמך גבי שדה כמו גבי עבד לא משמע גבי שדה אין לי עסק בה אלא סילוק דין ודברים כדמוכח בכריתות (דף כד:):

מפני שמעמידה בפני בעל חובו. וא"ת מאי איריא מפני שמעמידה (ג) תיפוק ליה משום דלא ניחא ליה דליהוי תרעומת עליו כדאמרי' בפ"ק דב"ק (דף ח:) דלוקח שמכר שדה לשמעון שלא באחריות ואתא בעל חובו וקטריף לה מיניה דינא הוא דלחי רלובן ומשתעי דינא בהדיה ולא מצי א"ל לאו בעל דברים דידי את דא"ל לא ניחא לי דליהוי לשמעון תרעומת עילואי וי"ל דאין נפסל בשביל כך לעדות א"נ הכא מיירי אפילו במכר בה שהיה לא שייך תרעומת:

וליסלקו בי תרי מינייהו ולידיינו. וא"ת והא בעינן [ז] תחילתו וסופו בכשרות והכא הוי תחילה בפסול והוי כמו קרוב ונתרחק [ה] ואור"י דלא שייך תחילתו בפסלות הכא כיון שאין פסלות תלוי בגוף [ט] אלא בממון [ז]:

ה"ג **ותסברא** עניים שקלי ודיינין מיפסלי. [אלא] ה"ג בספר תורה ואמאי קרי להו עניים כו':

אמאי

עין משפט נר מצוה

קל א מיי' פט"ו מהל' עדות הל' ד סמג לאוין קט טוש"ע ח"מ סי' לז סעיף א:

קלא ב מיי' פט"ו שם הל' ג סמג שם טוש"ע שם סעיף טו:

קלב ג טוש"ע שם סעיף א:

קלג ד מיי' פט"ו שם הל' ג סמג שם טוש"ע שם סעיף יט וסי' ז סעיף יג:

קלד ה ו ז מיי' שם הל' ג וסמג שם טוש"ע ח"מ סי' ז שם וסי' לז סעיף כ:

קלה ח טוש"ע ח"מ סי' קעו סעיף ח ועיין בש"ך:

רבינו גרשום

ומעידין זה על זה כדאמר לעיל: **ואמאי** מעידין הא **נוגעין בעדותן הן.** משום דאם האחד היה מאבד חלקו היה חוזר זה שאבד והיה נוטל חצי מחלקו של חבירו ולפיכך מסייע לשותפו כדי שלא יפסיד הוא עצמו: **הכא במאי עסקינן.** דמצי מעיד לו: **דכתב ליה.** כל חד לחבריה: **דין ודברים אין לי על שדה זו.** של חבירי ואפי' מאבד אחד חלקו [א]: **והא לא אמר** ולא כלום **מי שאמר לחבירו דין ודברים אין לי בשדה זו** דמש"ה לא מסתלק דהא קא חזינן דאית ליה. וכן הכי נמי להיכא דאמר ליה **אין לי עסק בה וידי מסולקות** ממנה הא קא חזינן דאית ליה חלק בה ומש"ה **לא אמר כלום** דנוגע בעדות הוא: **בשקנו מידו.** דלית ליה לחד על חבירו כלום מש"ה מעיד דלא נוגע בעדות: **וכי קנו מידו.** מעיד לו והלא נוגע בעדותו הוא מפני **שמעמידה** זה המעיד **בפני בעל חוב שלו.** דהואיל דקנו זה מזה דומה כמכרו זה לזה וכמכר לשותפו לאחר שנתחייב ממון למלוה דמשועבד לו מה שמכר ומש"ה מסייע לשותפו כדי שיבא בעל חוב שלו ויטרפנה ממנו בשביל חובו כי היכי דלא מקרי לוה רשע ולא ישלם: **דאמר רבין כו'.** והני שותפין נמי כמוכרין זה לזה שאם יאבד אחד מהם חלקו שיחזור על האחר: **הכא במאי עסקינן.** דמצי מעיד **דקביל עליה אחריות: אחריות דמאן** קבלו עליהן. **אי דעלמא** אחריות של כל אדם בעולם שאם יבא שום אדם ויערער עליו ויוציאה מידו שיחזור ויטול חצי מחלקו של חבירו: **כל שכן** וכל שכן דנוגע בעדות הוא דקסבר אם מאבד חבירו חלקו יחזור עלי: **אלא** שקבל עליו בלבד **אחריות דאתיא מחמתיה.** דאי טרף לה בעל חוב דאיהו מפצי ליה וכיון דקבל לו אחריות בשביל עצמו וכל הבא מכחו לאו נוגע בעדות הוא למערער דעלמא שאין בא בשבילו ונאמן: **וכי מסלק נפשיה.** מכל וכל מדבר של שותפו **מי מסתלק** ומצי מעיד: **אין דנין.** הגנב: **בדייני אותה העיר** משום דנוגעין בדבר הן: **ואין מביאין ראיה.** עדות: **ואם איתא.** דשותף מצי מסלק: **לסתלקו תרי** מאותה העיר מחלק של ספר תורה **ולידייני.** אלא ש"מ דלא מצו לסלוקי נפשייהו מספר תורה הואיל דשותפין אינון מש"ה אין דנין הכי נמי להיכא דאמר השותף אין לי עסק בה היכי מסתלק: **דלשמיעה קאי.** ולא מצו לסלוקי נפשייהו דלא מצי לסתומי אודניהו שלא לשמוע מספר תורה אבל הכא גבי שדה מצו לסלוקי נפשייהו כדאמרן: **אין דנין.** ליורשין: **הכא נמי בס"ת** קאמר. **תנו מנה לבני עירי** לקנות ס"ת דלשמיעה קאי: **ותסברא.** דמתרצתא היא דמצית לאקשויי ניהליה וכי **עניים שקלי** המנה **ודייני** העיר **מיפסלי: דהכל עניים אצל ס"ת.** דכל אדם צריך לה: **ובעניים דרמו עלייהו.** על אנשי העיר לפרנסן ומש"ה אין דנין בדייני העיר משום דכל זמן שמעות מנה הזה מתקיימין אין צריכין ליתן אחרים לעניים ונוגעין בדבר הן: **אי דקיץ להו.** כמה נותן כל בעה"ב בחודש לעניים. **ניתבו בי תרי מינייהו** מאי **דקיץ להו** ובתר הכי **נידיינו** דהשתא לא נגעי: אפ"ה **ניחא להנהו דייני. דנרווחו** עניי העיר ולא יצטרכו ליתן להם כל כך ומש"ה אין דנין:

אמאי

מסורת הש"ס

א) כתובות פג. לה. גיטין עז. [לקמן מט. כריתות כד:], ב) [לקמן מד.], ג) [לקמן קכח.], ד) [עי' תוס' נדה כ. ד"ה ור"מ היא]:

הגהות הב"ח

(א) תוס' ד"ה (בדף הקודם) שבח וכו' לאריס שלא יסלקנו אותו כמו: (ג) ד"ה מפני וכו' מאי איריא מפני שמעמידה בפני ב"ח תיפוק:

גליון הש"ס

רשב"ם ד"ה ליסתלקו כו' ויקנו מידם. קשה לי הא קי"ל דגזל ונתייאשו הבעלים שניהם אינם יכולים להקדישו ואם כן א"א להקנות ותמשכנה הארכתי בגוה"ש: תוס' ד"ה וליסלקו כו' ואור"י. עי' קדושין דף מג ע"ב ד"ה השתא ועי' נדה דף ב ע"א תוס' ד"ה ור"מ: באו"ד בגופו. אלא בממון. עי' תוס' שבועות דף לג ע"א ד"ה קרובים:

ליקוטי רש"י

האומר לחבירו דין ודברים אין לי על שדה זו וכו'. כלומר לא יהא לי [רשב"ם לקמן מט.]. כגון שנים שלקחו שותפין ואמר האחד לשני שותפין מן השדות הללו [בין בכתובה בין במכירה] [כתובות פג.]. שטיפח לו עמו שותפים בה. ואין לי עסק בה. אתה מכל לשונות הללו [גיטין עז.]. לא אמר כלום. דאין כאן לשון מתנה [כתובות שם]. דמאמר שהיא שלו צריך לכתוב לך שדה מתנה [גיטין שם]. דאין זה לשון מתנה כשאמר לא יהא לי חלק בשדה בעל כרחו הוי שלו עד שיאמר לחבירו שדי נתונה לך שדי מכורה לך או כל מי שירצה [רשב"ם שם]. ולא אבד זכותו [כריתות כד:]. המוכר שדה שלא באחריות. במוכר קרקע שלו שהיתה משועבדת לבעל חוב ומכרה לאחר שלא באחריות שאם יטלוה ממנו מעלמא וקמערער דלא יעיד לו המוכר ללוקח מפני שאחריותו של בעל חוב עליו למוכר לגבות מקרקע המכורה ולא יהא לו מה שיגבה מלוקח אם ידוחק ביד הלוקח להדר עלה כגון אם לא יהיה מוכר לוה רשע ולא ישלם ולוקח ישאר כנגדו שהרי יש לו באחריות מכר ולהכי אין מעיד דנוגע בעדות הוא [רשב"ם לקמן מד.].

חשק שלמה על רבינו גרשום

א) נראה דצ"ל ואפי' מאבד אחד חלקו לא יפסיד חבירו.

to purchase a Torah scroll. Thus, none of the inhabitants can avoid the benefit which will accrue to them from the bequest, and they are therefore disqualified. Shmuel, however, speaks of partners who *can* divest themselves of their interests.

The Gemara attempts once again to prove that relinquishing one's benefits is insufficient to render his testimony impartial:

תָּא שְׁמַע – **Come, learn** a proof from the following Baraisa: הָאוֹמֵר תְּנוּ מָנֶה לַעֲנִיֵּי עִירִי – IF [A DYING MAN] SAYS, "GIVE A *MANEH* TO THE POOR OF MY TOWN," אֵין דָּנִין בְּדַיָּינֵי אוֹתָהּ הָעִיר – the case MAY NOT BE TRIED BY THE JUDGES OF THAT TOWN, וְאֵין מְבִיאִין רְאָיָה מֵאַנְשֵׁי אוֹתָהּ הָעִיר – NOR MAY EVIDENCE BE ACCEPTED FROM THE PEOPLE OF THAT TOWN.

But before the proof is developed, the Gemara interjects:

וְתִסְבְּרָא – **Now is this logical?** עֲנִיִּים שָׁקְלֵי דַּיָּינֵי מִיפְּסְלֵי – The **poor receive** the bequest, **and the judges,** who receive nothing, **are disqualified!?** This cannot be, for the judges have no reason to be biased!

The Gemara therefore emends the Baraisa:

אֶלָּא אֵימָא – **Rather, state** the Baraisa's ruling thusly: אֵין דָּנִין בְּדַיָּינֵי עֲנִיֵּי אוֹתָהּ הָעִיר – The case MAY NOT BE TRIED BY *POOR* JUDGES OF THAT TOWN, וְאֵין מְבִיאִין רְאָיָה מֵעֲנִיֵּי אוֹתָהּ הָעִיר – NOR MAY EVIDENCE BE ACCEPTED FROM THE *POOR* OF THAT TOWN, for they stand to benefit from the bequest.

The Gemara now returns to explain the proof:

וְאַמַּאי – **Now why** is this so? לִסְתַּלְּקוּ בֵּי תְּרֵי נַפְשַׁיְיהוּ – **Let two** of the town's poor **remove themselves** from their share in the bequest, וְלִידַיְינוּ – **and try** the case! It would seem that the Baraisa deems such judges biased even after they renounce their share in the benefits, presumably because of the possibility of collusion. — ? —

The Gemara rejects this proof as well:

הָכָא נַמִּי בְּסֵפֶר תּוֹרָה – **Here, too,** the Baraisa speaks of a bequest made **for** purchase of **a Torah scroll.**[27] Thus, all the citizens are perforce interested parties as explained previously.

The Gemara asks:

וְאַמַּאי קָרֵי לְהוּ עֲנִיִּים – **But** then **why did [the bequeather] call [his beneficiaries] "poor"** if his intent was to provide a Torah scroll for the entire populace?[28]

The Gemara answers:

דְּהַכֹּל אֵצֶל סֵפֶר תּוֹרָה עֲנִיִּים הֵן – **For in regard to a Torah scroll, anyone** who does not possess a share in one **is considered poor.**[29]

וְאִיבָּעִית אֵימָא – **Or, if you prefer, say:** לְעוֹלָם כִּדְקָתָנֵי – **Actually** the Baraisa can be understood exactly **as it states,** עֲנִיִּים מַמָּשׁ – as a bequest of funds to **the poor, literally.** Yet, the entire populace is disqualified from trying the case, וּבַעֲנִיֵּי דְּרָמוּ עֲלַיְיהוּ – for the Baraisa speaks of a case **in which** the responsibility for supporting **the** town's **poor rests upon [the citizens of the town]** and they therefore all stand to benefit from the bequest.[30]

The Gemara seeks to clarify this interpretation:

וְהֵיכִי דָּמֵי – **But what are the circumstances** of the Baraisa's case? אִי דְּקִיץ לְהוּ – **If [the townspeople]** were each assessed **a specific amount,** לֵיתְבוּ בֵּי תְּרֵי מִינַּיְיהוּ מַאי דְּקִיץ לְהוּ – **let two [of the townspeople] donate the amount** they were assessed, so that they derive no benefit from the bequest, וְלִידַיְינוּ – **and** then **try** the case!

The Gemara answers:

הָכָא בְּמַאי עַסְקִינַן – **With what case is [the Baraisa] dealing here?** דְּלָא קִיץ לְהוּ – **Where they were not** assessed **a specific amount.**[31]

An alternative answer:

וְאִי בָּעֵית אֵימָא – **Or, if you prefer, say:** לְעוֹלָם דְּקִיץ לְהוּ – **Actually,** the Baraisa speaks of a case **in which they were** assessed **a specific amount.** וְנִיחָא לְהוּ – **Still, [the judges] are interested** that the bequest be upheld, דְּכֵיוָן דְּרָוַוח רָוַוח – **for once there is a surplus** for the poor **there is a surplus,** and they will not be called upon to donate the fixed sum that they were previously assessed.[32] In the final analysis, the Gemara fails to prove that one's renunciation of his share in common property is insufficient to render him impartial. Thus, Shmuel's ruling that partners can testify for each other can be explained as referring to where the testifying partner ceded his share in the disputed property to his co-owner, as explained above.

The Gemara cites the next in Shmuel's previously quoted series of rulings regarding partners:

וְנַעֲשִׂין שׁוֹמְרֵי שָׂכָר זֶה לָזֶה – **And [partners] are considered paid custodians for each other.**

NOTES

27. I.e. the benefactor did not intend a bequest to the poor, but rather to the entire town. (The fact that he mentioned the poor in his bequest is discussed in the Gemara below.) Thus, the Baraisa's text no longer needs the aforementioned emendation, for the *entire* town is disqualified from trying the case, as the bequest of funds for a Torah scroll benefits *all* of the town's inhabitants.

28. The bequest was worded: "Give a *maneh* to the *poor* of my town." How can this be translated to mean a bequest of funds to purchase a Torah scroll, which obviously benefits both rich and poor alike?

29. A Torah scroll is a necessity for all, and it is a great deficiency if a town does not possess one. Thus, the bequeather aptly applies the term "poor" to his fellow citizens who lack a Torah scroll (*Rashbam*).

30. The judges (and indeed, any citizen of means) bear the responsibility of supporting the poor of the town. Thus, the income from the bequest would lessen their obligation, and result in a monetary savings for them. This is sufficient reason to regard the town's populace as interested parties (*Rashbam*).

31. Rather, contributions are solicited only when the need arises. Thus, if the bequest is secured, no collections will be made, and the judges will benefit (*Rashbam*).

32. Furthermore, even if the judges donate the sum *before* trying the case, they are disqualified, for we fear that if the bequest is secured, their money will not be needed and it will be refunded to them (*Bach, Tur Choshen Mishpat* 7:17; cf. *Lechem Mishneh* to *Rambam Hil. Eidus* 15:3).

אמאי נוגעין בעדותן הן הכא במאי עסקינן דכתב ליה דין ודברים אין לי על שדה זו וכי כתב לו מאי הוי והתניא [א] האומר לחבירו דין ודברים אין לי על שדה זו ואין לי עסק בה וידי מסולקות הימנה לא אמר כלום [א] הכא במאי עסקינן כשקנו מידו וכי קנו מידו מאי הוי הרי מעמידה בפני בעל חובו [ג] דאמר רבין בר שמואל משמיה דשמואל [ב] המוכר שדה לחבירו שלא באחריות אין מעיד לו עליה מפני שמעמידה בפני בעל חובו הכא במאי עסקינן דקביל עליה אחריות אחריות דמאן אי נימא אחריות דעלמא כל שכן דניחא ליה [ג] אלא אחריות דאתיא ליה מחמתיה וכי מסלק נפשיה מיניה מי מסתלק והתניא [ד] בני עיר שנגנב ספר תורה שלהן אין דנין בדייני אותה העיר ואין מביאין ראיה מאנשי אותה העיר ואם איתא ליסלקו בי תרי מינייהו ולידיינו שאני ס"ת דלשמיעה קאי תא שמע האומר תנו מנה לבני עירי אין דנין בדייני אותה העיר ואין מביאין ראיה מאנשי אותה העיר אמאי ליסלקו בי תרי נפשייהו ולידיינו הכא נמי בס"ת ת"ש [ה] האומר תנו מנה לענויי עירי אין דנין בדייני אותה העיר ואין מביאין ראיה מאנשי אותה העיר ותסברא עניים שקלי דייני מיפסלי אלא אימא אין דנין בדייני ענויי אותה העיר ואין מביאין ראיה מענויי אותה העיר ואמאי לסתלקו בי תרי נפשייהו ולידיינו הכא נמי בספר תורה ואמאי קרי להו עניים דהכל אצל ספר תורה עניים הן ואיבעית אימא לעולם כדקתני עניים ממש [ו] ובעניי דראמו עלייהו והיכי דמי אי דקיץ להו ליתבו בי תרי מינייהו מאי דקיץ להו ולידיינו הכא במאי עסקינן דלא קיץ להו ואב"א [ז] לעולם דקיץ להו וניחא להו דכיון דרווח רווח: [ח] ונעשין שומרי שכר זה לזה

אמאי

אמאי. מעידין זה על זה: נוגעין בעדותן הן. דכל זמן שלא חלקו לגמרי אם יטול שום מערער כלום מן השדה יפסידו שניהן ונמלא לעצמו מעיד: דכתב ליה. האי מעיד להאי מחזיק דין ודברים אין לי עמך בכל השדה ואפילו על חלקי שהכל שלך והכי משמע דין ודברים לא יהא לי על שדה זו ולשון חכמים הוא לומר אין לי במקום לא יהא לי והלכך כיון דנתן לו חלקו מעיד עליה דלא נוגע בעדות הוא והכי נמי הוה מלי לתרולי כשהקנה לו חלקו אלא רבותא נקט לאשמועינן דבכי האי גוונא הוי לשון מתנה: מאי הוי. הרי אינו לשון מתנה ולהכי נוגע בעדות הוא: האומר לחבירו. שותף: ואין לי עסק בה. כלומר לא יהא לי עסק בה ומכלל אתה שומע אלא הכל יהא שלך אלא שלא הוציא הדבר בפירוש מפיו: וידי יהו מסולקות לא אמר כלום. דכיון דכבר יש לו חלק בשדה והוא אומר לא יהא לי חלק בה אין זה לשון מתנה אלא לשון תפלה הוא הלואי שלא יהא לי חלק בשדה זו וכל זמן שלא אמר יהי נתון לך שדה זו לא יצא עדיין מרשותו ואין תופס לשון זה אלא כדבר שעדיין לא זכה בו והוא מתנה עליו שלא יהא שלו כשיבוא הזמן שעתיד לזכות באותו דבר דאין אדם זוכה בדבר בעל כרחו כדלקמן בפירקין (דף מט.) ובכתובו' (דף פג.) דנהלה הבאה לו לאדם לאחר מכן מתנה עליה שלא ירשנה אבל מכיון שכבר הדבר שלו הוא והוא אומר לא יהא שלי לא אמר כלום דבעל כרחו יהיה שלו כל זמן שלא יתננה לאחרים כן נראה בעיני ועיקר והכי מוכח לקמן בפירקין. וי"מ דמשום הכי לא אמר כלום דקאמר אין לי דין ודברים ולא קאמר לא יהא ונמלא שהוא מכזב שהרי יש לו חלק בו והוא אומר אין לי ושבוש הוא דאין זה לשון הגמ' לומר בשום מקום לא יהא והכי מוכח לקמן דקמשני הכא במאי עסקינן בשקנו מידו ולא קא מתרץ באומר לא יהא: כשקנו מידו. שותף חבירו קנה מידו בקנין סודר והשתא דאיכא קנין מועיל התנאי: וכי קנו מידו מאי הוי. אכתי אמאי מעיד להעמיד השדה בידו הרי נוגע הוא בעדות זו דניחא ליה שיהיה השדה ביד השותף מפני שמעמידו האי נותן לפני בעל חובו שאם יש לו שום בע"ח שהלוהו מעות קודם שהקנה לחבירו חלקו שהיה לו בשדה יבא בעל חוב ויטרוף אותה שהרי אליה משועבדת לו ויפטר זה הנותן מבעל חובו ולא יהיה לוה רשע ולא ישלם כדלקמן בשמעתין שאילו יטרפוה מזה בעדים שיאמרו שלא היה לאלו שותפין חלק בה לא יוכל בעל חוב שלו לגבות הימנה והו"ל לוה רשע ולא ישלם: שלא באחריות. וכל שכן באחריות: אין מעיד לו עליה. אין מצטרף עם עד אחר להעמידה בידו ואע"ג דאי הוה מפסיד לוקח לא הדר עליה דמוכר: מפני שמעמידה כו'. ובדלית ליה ארעא אחריתי מוקמינן לה לקמן בשמעתין דלא ניחא למיהוי לוה רשע ולא ישלם: דקביל עליה אחריות. האי שותף לחבירו ממה שהקנה לו וכדמפרש ואזיל דהשתא אינו מעמידה לפני בעל חובו והלכך מעיד: אחריות דעלמא. שלא בשביל חוב חבירו אלא מערער לומר שדה זו של אבותי או שלי היא: כל שכן דאינו מעיד. דנוגע בעדות הוא כשמעיד להעמידו ביד זה דניחא ליה דתיהוי בידו משום דלא מפיק מיניה עליה הדר: אלא אחריות דאתא ליה מחמתיה. אם יטרפוהו בשביל חובו שחייב לאחרים יחזיר לו הדמים הלכך מעיד עליה גבי ערער דעלמא להעמידה בידו שאינו מעמידו בפני בעל חובו דמה הנאה יש לו אם יטרפנה בעל חוב מיד זה ולא יהא כנגדו לוה רשע סוף סוף לוה רשע ולא ישלם הוא גבי חבירו שקיבל עליו אחריות וחייב לשלם ואין לו ונכנס בע"ח זה במקום בעל חוב ראשון וגם אם לא יעיד לו מה מפסיד הרי אחריות דעלמא לא קיבל וממ"נ בין יעיד בין לא יעיד בע"ח אחד הוא דיש לו להוי כנגדו לוה רשע ולא ישלם ולקמן בשמעתין מוכח דמיקרי לוה רשע מוכר באחריות וטרפוה מן הלוקח ואינו משלם לו: וכי מסלק. שום שותף נפשיה מחלקו: מי מסתלק. בתמיה מי הוי סילוק גמור אפילו לגבי עדות דלא הוי נוגע בעדות כלל ויכול להעיד דאוקמת ליה בשקנו מידו: והתניא כו'. וטעמא משום דאיכא למימר קנוניא הוא דעבוד כדי שיעיד לו עליה ויעמידנה בידו ואחר כך יחזור לשותפותו: אין דנין. הגנב והוא טוען לקחתיו בדמים או שום טענה: ראיה. עדים שראוהו שגנבו או שמעידין שזהו ס"ת של אותה העיר דכולן שותפין ונוגעין בעדותן: ליסתלקו. יכתבו דין ודברים אין לי על ספר תורה זה [ט] ויקנו מידם: דלשמיעה קאי. ואין יכול לסלק עצמו שלא יהא נוגע בעדות שהרי נהנה בו ויוצא בשמיעתו אלא אם כן ילך לו לדור בעיר אחרת שלא יהנה בקריאתו: לבני עירי. לצרכי בני העיר לחומות העיר ולכל צרכי רבים: וליסלקו בי תרי מינייהו. שלא יהנו בו כלל ויתנו מכיסם כנגד המנה של צבור: הכא נמי בס"ת. שפירש תנו מנה לבני עירי לקנות בו ס"ת: ותסברא עניים שקלי כו'. גמרא קא פריך עלה והדר מקשי מינה ושיטת הגמרא היא זו ועדיין לא סיים קושיא שלו למיפרך מינה עד לבסוף כלומר ותסברא דהכי קאמר דוקא שהדיינין יפסלו בשביל העניים והלא אין נוגעין בעדותן כלל: דהכל אצל ספר תורה עניים הם. שכולן צריכים לו ודרך בני אדם לקרוא בני עירו עניים כשאין להם ס"ת דעניות גדול הוא זה: ואי בעית אימא לעולם. כל הברייתא כדקתני דבעניים ממש מיירי ודייני העיר שאינן עניים קאמר דמפסלי ודקא קשיא לך דיינין אמאי מפסלי הרי אין נוגעין בעדות: בעניי דרמו עלייהו. על דייני העיר פירוש עשירי העיר וכדמפרש ואזיל דהשתא נוגעין בעדות הן: אי דקיץ להו. דבר קצוב לבני העיר לכל אחד כמה יתן לעניי העיר משלו בכל שנה ושנה: ומשני דלא קיץ להו. אלא הכל לפי הצורך ולפי מחסורן של עניים נותנין דכל זמן שיש מן המנה בעין לא יתנו הדיינין כלום: לעולם דקיץ להו. ואפ"ה ניחא להו לדיינין שינתן המנה לעניים: דכיון דרווח. שיש להם מעות רווח כלומר הרי יש להם מעות ולמה יתנו כלום כל זמן שאין צריכין:

שמירה

והכי קאמר שנוטל בשבח המגיע לכתפים כארים שלא (א) יסתלקו אותו כמו קבלן כמו שעושין לנוטע שלא ברשות שמסלקין אותו בכך אפי' משדה העשויה ליטע ובשדה שאין עשויה ליטע כו' פי' ועוד שגם בשדה שאין עשויה ליטע נוטל כמו בעשויה ליטע מה שאין כן בנוטע שלא ברשות:

אין לי עסק בה לא אמר כלום. וא"ת דבפרק השולח (גיטין דף מג: ושם) גבי מוכר עבדו לנכרי כו' אמר היכי דמי אונו דכתב ליה לכשתברח ממנו אין לי עסק בך הוי לשון טוב אלמא אין לי עסק בך משמע אלא תהא לעצמך וגבי עבד דמהני הרי את לעצמך מהני נמי אין לי עסק בך אבל בשדה דלא שייך למימר הרי את לעצמך כי אמר נמי אין לי עסק בך לא אמר כלום דכיון דליכא לפרושי אין לי עסק בך אלא תהא לעצמך גבי שדה כמו גבי עבד לא משמע גבי שדה אין לי עסק בה אלא סילוק דין ודברים כדמוכח בכריתות (דף ה:):

מפני שמעמידה בפני בעל חובו. וא"ת מאי אירא מפני שמעמידה (ג) תיפוק ליה משום דלא ניחא ליה דתיהוי תרעומת עליו כדאמרי' בפ"ק דב"ק (דף ח:) דאוכן שמכר שדה לשמעון שלא באחריות ואתא בעל חובו וקטריף לה מיניה דינא הוא דאתי ראובן ומשתעי דינא בהדיה ולא מצי א"ל לאו בעל דברים דידי את דא"ל לא ניחא לי דליהוי לשמעון תרעומת עילואי וי"ל דאין נפסל בשביל כך לעדות ולהכי הכא מיירי אפילו במכר בה שהיה לליכא תרעומת:

וליסלקו בי תרי מינייהו ולידיינו. וא"ת והא בעינן [ג] תחילתו וסופו בכשרות והכא הוי תחילה בפסול והוי כמו קרוב ונתרחק [ה] ואור"י דלא שייך תחילתו בפסלות הכא כיון שאין פסלות תלוי בגוף [ו] אלא בממון [ז]:

ותסברא עניים שקלי ודיינין מיפסלי ה"ג

[אלא] ה"ג בספר תורה ואמאי קרי להו עניים כו':

אמאי

להיכא דאמר השותף אין לי עסק בה היכי מסתלק: **דלשמיעה קאי.** ולא מצו לסלוקי נפשייהו דלא מצי לסתומי אודניהו שלא לשמוע מספר תורה אבל הכא גבי שדה מצו לסלוקי נפשייהו כדאמרן: **אין דנין.** ליורשין: **הכא נמי** בס"ת קאמר. **תנו מנה לבני עירי** לקנות ס"ת דלשמיעה קאי: **ותסברא.** דמתרצתא היא דמצית לאקשויי ניהליה וכי **עניים שקלי** המנה **ודייני** העיר **מיפסלי: דהכל עניים אצל ס"ת.** דכל אדם צריך לה: **ובעניים דרמו** עלייהו. על אנשי העיר לפרנסן ומש"ה אין דנין בדייני העיר משום דכל זמן שמעות מנה הזה מתקיימין אין צריכין ליתן אחרים לעניים ונוגעין בדבר הן: **אי דקיץ להו.** כמה נותן כל בעה"ב בחודש לעניים. **ניתבו בי תרי מינייהו** מאי דקיץ להו ובתר הכי נידיינו דהשתא לא נגעי: אפ"ה **ניחא להנהו דייני. דנרווחו** עניי העיר ולא יצטרכו ליתן להם כל כך ומש"ה אין דנין:

אמאי

א) כתובות פג. לה. גיטין עז. [לקמן מט. כריתות כד:], ב) [לקמן מד.], ג) [לקמן קכח.], ד) [וע"ע תוס' נדה ב. ד"ה וכ"ת היאך],

הגהות הב"ח

(א) תוס' ד"ה (בדף הקודם) שבח וכו' כארים שלא יסלקו אותו כמו: (ב) ד"ה מפני וכו' מאי אירא מפני שמעמידה בפני בע"ח תיפוק:

גליון הש"ס

רשב"ם ד"ה ליסתלקו כו' ויקנו מידם. קשה לי הא קי"ל דגזל ולא נתייאשו הבעלים שניהם אינם יכולים להקדישו ואם כן אי"ל להקנות ובתבונה הארכתי בעו"ה: תוס' ד"ה וליסלקו כו' ואור"י. עי' ברטנ"ע קדושין דף מג ע"ב ד"ה השתא ועי' נדה דף כב ע"א תוס' ד"ה ור"מ: **באיד בגופו. אלא בממון.** ע"י תוס' שבועות דף לג ע"א ד"ה קרובים:

ליקוטי רש"י

האומר לחבירו דין ודברים אין לי על שדה זו וכו'. כלומר לא יהא לי [רשב"ם לקמן מט.]. כגון שדה של שותפין ואמר האחד לחבירו אחד מן הלשונות הללו [בין כמתנה בין במכירה] [כתובות פג.]. שהיתה עמו שותפים בה. **ואין לי עסק בה.** אחת מן הלשונות הללו [גיטין עז.]. **לא אמר כלום.** דאין כאן לשון מתנה [כתובות שם]. דמאחר שהיא שלו צריך לכתוב לשון מתנה [גיטין שם]. דאין זה לשון מתנה כשאמר לא יהא לי חלק בשדה זו שהרי כבר היא שלו עד שיאמר לחבירו שדי נתונה לך שדי מכורה לך שדי מופקרת לכל מי שירצה [רשב"ם שם]. ולא אבד זכותו [כריתות כד:]. **המוכר שדה שלא באחריות.** במוכר קרקע שלו שהיתה משועבדת לבעל חוב ומכרה ללוקח זה ואתא איניש מעלמא וקמערער דלא יעיד לו המוכר ללוקח מפני שמעמידה לפני בעל חוב שלו עליו דמוכר לגבות מקרקע זו והלכך ניחא ליה דתיקום ביד הלוקח דהדר עלה בעל חוב ולא ליהוי לוה רשע ולא ישלם וכנגד לוקח לא ליהוי לוה רשע שהרי לא באחריות מכר לו והלכך אין מעיד דנוגע בעדות הוא [רשב"ם לקמן מד.].

רבינו גרשום

ומעידין זה על זה כדאמר לעיל: **ואמאי** מעידין הא **נוגעין בעדותן הן.** משום דאם האחד היה מאבד חלקו היה חוזר זה שאבד והיה נוטל חצי מחלקו של חבירו ולפיכך מסייע לשותפו כדי שלא יפסיד הוא עצמו: **הכא במאי עסקינן.** דמצי מעיד לו: **דכתב ליה.** כל חד לחבריה: **דין ודברים אין לי על שדה זו.** של חבירי ואפי' מאבד אחד חלקו א): **והא לא אמר** ולא כלום מי שאמר לחבירו דין ודברים אין לי בשדה זו דמש"ה לא מסתלק דהא קא חזינן דאית ליה. וכן הכי נמי להיכא דאמר ליה אין לי עסק בה **וידי מסולקות** ממנה הא קא חזינן דאית ליה חלק בה ומש"ה **לא אמר כלום** דנוגע בעדות הוא: **בשקנו מידו.** דלית ליה לחד על חבירו כלום מש"ה מעיד דלא נוגע בעדות: **וכי קנו מידו.** מעיד לו והלא נוגע בעדותו הוא מפני שמעמידה זה המעיד **בפני בעל חוב שלו.** דהואיל דקנו מזה דומה כמכרו זה לזה וכמכר לשותפו לאחר שנתחייב ממון למלוה דמשועבד לו מה שמכר ומש"ה מסייע לשותפו כדי שיבא בעל חוב שלו ויטרפנה ממנו בשביל חובו כך היכי דלא מקרי לוה רשע ולא ישלם. **דאמר רבין כו'.** והני שותפין נמי כמוכרין זה לזה שאם יאבד אחד מהם חלקו שיחזור על האחר: **הכא במאי עסקינן. דמצי מעיד דקביל** עליהו אחריות: **אחריות דמאן** קבלו עליהן: **אי דעלמא** אחריות של כל אדם בעולם שאם יבא שום אדם ויערער עליו ויוציאה מידו שיחזור ויטול חצי מחלקו של חבירו: **כל שכן** וכל שכן דנוגע בעדות הוא דקסבר אם מאבד חבירו חלקו יחזור עלי: **אלא** שקבל עליו בלבד **אחריות דאתיא** מחמתה. דאי טרף לה בעל חוב דאיהו מצפי ליה וכיון דקבל לו אחריות בשביל עצמו וכל הבא מכחו לאו נוגע בעדות הוא למערער דעלמא שאין בא בשבילו ונאמן: **וכי מסלק נפשיה.** מכל וכל מדבר של שותפו מי מסתלק ומצי מעיד: **אין דנין.** הגנב: **בדייני אותה העיר** משום דנוגעין בדבר הן: **ואין מביאין ראיה.** עדות: **ואם איתא.** דשותף מצי מסלק: **לסתלקו תרי** מאותה העיר מחלק של ספר תורה **ולידייני.** אלא ש"מ דלא מצו לסלוקי נפשייהו מספר תורה הואיל דשותפין אינון מש"ה אין דנין הכי נמי

חשק שלמה על רבינו גרשום

א) נראה דצ"ל ואפי' מאבד אחד חלקו לא יפסיד חבירו.

עין משפט נר מצוה

קל א מיי' פט"ו מהל' עדות הל' ד סמג לאוין קט טוש"ע ח"מ סי' לז סעיף א:
קלא ב מיי' פט"ו שם הל' ג סמג שם טוש"ע שם סעיף טו:
קלב ג טוש"ע שם סעיף א:
קלג ד מיי' פט"ו שם הל' ג סמג שם טוש"ע שם סעיף יט וסי' ז סעיף יב:
קלד ה ו ז מיי' שם הל' ג וסמג שם טוש"ע ח"מ סי' ז סעיף יב וסי' לז סעיף כ:
קלה ח טוש"ע ח"מ סי' קעו סעיף ח ועיין בש"ך:

א) [^א] אמאי שמירה בבעלים היא אמר רב פפא ב דאמר ליה שמור לי היום ואני אשמור לך למחר: תנו רבנן מכר לו בית מכר לו שדה אין מעיד לו עליה מפני שאחריותו עליו מכר לו פרה מכר לו טלית מעיד לו עליה מפני שאין אחריותו עליו מאי שנא רישא ומאי שנא סיפא אמר רב ששת רישא ג בראובן שגזל שדה משמעון ומכרה ללוי ואתא יהודה וקא מערער דלא ליזיל שמעון לאסהיד ליה ללוי דניחא ליה (א) דהדרא וכיון דאסהיד ליה דלוי הוא היכי מצי מפיק לה מיניה ד דאמר ידענא דהאי ארעא דלאו דיהודה היא ובההוא זכותא דקא מפיק לה מלוי ליפקה מיהודה דאמר ג) ה השני נוח לי הראשון קשה הימנו ואי בעית אימא כגון דאית ליה סהדי למר ואית ליה סהדי למר ואמור רבנן ארעא היכא דקיימא תיקום

תוספות

אמאי שמירה בבעלים היא. פי' אם התחילו שניהם לשמור יחד כל אחד בשעה שהוא משמר חלק חבירו חבירו נמי משמר לו חלקו ואע"פ שאין עמו במלאכה בשעת אונס כיון שהיה עמו בתחילת שמירה בעליו עמו קרינן ביה כדתניא (ב"מ דף לו.) היה עושה עמו בשעת שאלה אין צריך להיות עמו בשעת שבורה ומתה היה עמו בשעת שבורה ומתה צריך להיות עמו בשעת שאלה ואפילו לא התחילו שניהם לשמור יחד מכל מקום האחרון פטור שהראשון היה עמו במלאכה בשעה שהתחיל השני לשמור:

דאמר שמור לי היום כו'. וא"ת אכתי שמירה בבעלים היא דאמרינן בריש השואל דבעלים בשמירה גבי שואל את הפרה ובעלה עמה וי"ל שאני התם דבשמירה משעבדי עצמן ליכנס במלאכתם מיד אבל הכא לא משתעבד עד למחר וא"ת ומאי קמ"ל שמואל דנעשין שומרי שכר זה לזה מתניתין היא בהשוכר את האומנים (ב"מ דף פ:) שמור לי ואשמור לך שומר שכר וי"ל דאי מהתם הוה אמינא לפי שהם אינן שותפין אבל הכא שהם שותפין כל אחד ואחד כששומר חלק חבירו שומר גם בשביל עצמו:

וכיון דאסהיד דלוי הוא כו'. הוה מצי לשנויי כגון דאסהיד שמעון דשל אבותיו ללוי הוה ובתר הכי אתי שמעון וטוען דמלוי זבנה ואית ליה סהדי דראובן גזלה ממנו ומכרה ללוי:

כגון דאית ליה סהדי למר כו'. תימה דלא הוה ליה למימר כגון דהא מעיקרא נמי ידעינן דאית ליה לשמעון סהדי דלדידיה היא כדקתני ראובן שגזל שדה משמעון ואי לית ליה לשמעון סהדי שגזלה ראובן ממנו אם היכי ידעינן שגזלה ומכח מה הוא מערער ויהודה נמי ע"כ אית ליה סהדי דאי לאו הכי מאיזה כח מערער והכי הל"ל כיון דאית ליה סהדי למר כו' ומאי ס"ד דמקשה ואין לומר דמעיקרא ס"ד דאיירי כגון דאית ליה ליהודה עדים דשל אבותיו היא ולשמעון הנגזל אית ליה סהדי דאכלה שני חזקה וטוען מיהודה זבנה דא"כ מאי קאמר בהאי זכותא דמפיק לה מלוי ליפקה מיהודה הא בהאי זכותא דמצי לאפוקי מלוי לא מצי לאפוקי מיהודה דבעדי המעידין שגזל ראובן ממנו מצי מפיק לה מלוי שבא מכח ראובן ומיהודה לא מצי מפיק לה אלא בעדי חזקה ונראה לרשב"א דס"ד דמעיקרא דיהודה בעי לאפוקי מלוי משום דאית ליה סהדי דראובן מכר לו וללוי אין עדים וקא שמעון להעיד ללוי דשל לוי היא ומשום הכי פריך כיון דמסהיד דהאי ארעא דלוי היא היכי מפיק לה מיניה והוה מצי לשנויי דלא מסהדי בהאי לישנא דלוי היא אלא דאמר דראובן מכרה ללוי אלא דעדיפא מינה משני והשתא פריך שפיר דבההיא זכותא דמפיק לה מלוי ליפקה מיהודה דשניהם באין מכח ראובן ואם יביא שמעון עדים דראובן גזלה ממנו מצי לאפוקי מתרוייהו:

דוקא

רש"י

שמירה בבעלים היא. שכל אחד משמר קלת מן השותפות בביתו וקי"ל בב"מ בהשואל (דף לה.) שמירה בבעלים פטור ואע"ג דבשואל כתיב פטור דבעלים הא ילפינן שומר שכר התם מיניה מדכתיב וכי ישאל וי"ו מוסיף על ענין ראשון וילמד עליון מתחתון וכיון שהיה ראובן משמר מחלק שמעון בשעה שנגנבה או אבד מחלקו בבית שמעון הרי שמעון פטור מחלק ראובן שהרי ראובן עמו במלאכתו: אמר רב פפא. כגון שהתנו ביניהן כך שמור לי היום כל השדה חלקי וחלקך ואשמור לך למחר דכיון דלא שמרו שניהם יחד כלל אלא זה אחר זה ליכא שמירה בבעלים הלכך נעשו שומרי שכר זה לזה להתחייב באונסין ולאשמועינן אתא דהיינו שמירה בשכר כשמשמר כל השדה וחלק חבירו בכלל כדי שישמור לו חבירו למחר כמו כן דס"ד אמינא דשומר חנם הוא דבלאו חלק חבירו היה צריך לשמור את שלו ושמירה אחת היא בין הכל ולא ליהוי שומר שכר קמ"ל: (זה שייך לעיל. בתוספתא בהגוזל האומר תנו מאה דינר לכנסת תנו ספר תורה לכנסת יתנן לכנסת הרגיל בה ואם היה רגיל בשנים יתנו לשניהם האומר תנו לעניים יתנו לעניי אותה העיר ר' אחא אומר לעניי כל ישראל בן האוכל משל אביו ועבד האוכל משל רבו קולה ונותן פרוסה לעניים או לבנו של אוהבו ואינו חושש משום גזל שכך נהגו בעלי בתים. ע"כ): מכר לו בית. אדם לחבירו: אין מעיד לו. מוכר ללוקח להעמידה בידו שאם יבא להצטרף עם אחר ולהעיד שהוא שלו נוגע בעדות הוא: מפני שאחריותו. של בית עליו דמוכר שאם יטרפוה מן הלוקח יחזור על המוכר והלכך ניחא ליה למוכר שתעמוד ביד הלוקח ולא יצטרך לפרעו כלום הכי שמעינן ליה השתא: מכר לו פרה. לקמיה מפרש ליה ואזיל: שאין אחריותו. דלוקח עליה דמוכר אם יטלוהו הימנו מחמת המוכר שגזלה והיינו דקפריך מ"ש רישא ומ"ש סיפא מ"ש מטלטלי דלא הוי אחריות עליו ממקרקעי אם שתי מכירות הללו באחריות הוי תרוייהו אחריותו עליו ואי שלא באחריות הא תרוייהו אין אחריותו עליו: רישא בראובן שגזל שדה משמעון ומכרה ללוי ואתא יהודה. כלומר אינש מעלמא ומערער על שדה זו שביד לוי ואומר שלי היא ומביא עדים או שטר שלא יבא שמעון הנגזל ויצטרף עם אחר ויעיד שזה השדה אינו ליהודה כגון שיודע שום עדות לפסול עדות של יהודה בגזלנות וכן שטרו מפני שרוצה שמעון שיהיה השדה ביד לוי הקונה ואחרי כן היום ולמחר יביא שמעון ראיה שזו השדה שלו היה וראובן גזלו ממנו ויוציאו מיד לוי ויטלנו לעצמו דקרקע אינה נגזלת ולא מהני בה יאוש ושינוי רשות והלכך נוגע בעדות הוא דלא ניחא ליה שיטלנו יהודה דתו לא מצי שמעון לאפוקי מיניה כדמפרש לקמן דנוח לו לוי ויהודה קשה לו והלכך אין מעיד לו שמעון הנגזל ללוי עליה והכי קאמר ברייתא מכר לו בית מכר לו שדה ראובן הגזלן ללוי אין מעיד לו שמעון הנגזל ללוי לוקח עליה כנגד יהודה המערער מפני שאחריותו וסופו של נגזל עליו דלוקח להוציא הקרקע מידו והלכך נוגע הוא בעדות זו ולקמן מפרש אמאי מוקי לה בנגזל ומכר הוה שפיר מצי לאוקומה בגזלן גופיה ואתא יהודה וקמערער דלא יבא שמעון הנגזל להעיד לראובן הגזלן להעמידה בידו משום האי טעמא גופיה דניחא ליה דהדרא ליה וסיפא מפרש לקמן: ומקשינן ואכתי אמאי אינו מעיד לו עליה הא כיון דאסהיד דלוי היא. דקס"ד השתא הכי דמפקינן לה מיהודה ומוקים לה ביד לוי דקמסהיד הוא בשדה דלוי הוא ולאו דיהודה וכיון דהודה בפני בית דין דשל לוי הוא היכי מצי מפיק לה מלוי אחרי כן והלא הודאת בעל דין כמאה עדים דמי ונמצא שאינו מרויח כלום בעדות זו ואינו נוגע בעדות זו כלל ואמאי קתני דאין מעיד: ומשני דאמר ידענא דההוא ארעא לאו דיהודה היא. דפסיל לעדי יהודה בגזלנותא או דמכחיש לטענותיו בשום ענין בעולם כגון שמעיד בפני הודה לו וממילא מתוקמא השדה ביד לוי ואע"ג דלא קאמר דלוי הוא: ומקשינן אכתי אמאי אינו מעיד לו עליה. מה מפסיד שמעון אם תהיה בחזקת יהודה והא בההוא זכותא דקמפיק לה מלוי היום ולמחר דקמייתי עדים שדה שלו היא וגזלה ראובן ממנו ה"נ ליפקה מיהודה בהנהו עדים עצמן ונמצא שאין מרויח במה שמעיד ללוי כלל: ומשני משום הכי אינו מעיד דקסבר שמעון לוי נוח לי ויהודה גברא אלמא הוא וקשה ממנו ולא אוכל לדון עמו אם יבא בידו ומש"ה פסלינן ליה להאי עדות דאיכא למימר שזהו מחשבתו של שמעון ואין לנו להכשיר אלא עד דפשיטא לן דאינו נוגע בעדות כלל. הכא הוה לן למימר איפכא לוי הראשון נוח לי ויהודה השני קשה הימנו אבל לשון המשנה כך היא בכתובות (דף קט.): ואי בעית אימא. להכי לא מצי שמעון לאפוקה מיהודה כגון דאית ליה סהדי לשמעון שהשדה שלו ואית ליה סהדי ליהודה שמכחישין לאלו ואומרים שהשדה של יהודה ואמור רבנן בכל ספק דין קרקע היכא דקיימא ארעא תיקום שלא יוציאוה ב"ד מיד המחזיק בה כדאמר גבי פלוגתא דרבה ורב יוסף (לעיל לג:) היכא דקיימא ארעא תיקום לפי שנסתפק לנו הדין וכן (לעיל לד:) גבי זה אומר של אבותי אר"נ כל דאלים גבר (ס"א וכגון שאין לו עדות (ב) וחלוקה לזה יותר מזה ע"כ) ומשום דמספקא לן מי שרוצה להחזיק יחזיק ולא נוציא מידו וגבי נכסי דבר שטיא (כתובות דף כ.) אמר נמי אוקי תרי בהדי תרי ואוקי ארעא בחזקת בר שטיא והכא נמי אי מטיא לידיה דיהודה לא מצי שמעון לאפוקי מיניה בהני סהדי דמפיק לה מלוי דכיון דמן הדין אוקימנה ביד יהודה שהרי ממ"נ אין ללוי חלק בה הרי יהודה מוחזק ולא תצא עוד מידו ולא דמי להאי דאמרן לעיל בפרקין (דף לג:) הדר אייתי סהדי דאבהתיה היא א"ר נחמן אנן אחתינן ליה ואנן אסקי' ליה (ג) דאע"ג דהתם נמי איכא סהדי למר ואיכא סהדי למר ואפ"ה (ד) אחזיקניה לאחד ע"פ עדיו והדר מסלקינן ליה כשמביא חבירו עדים שלו היינו טעמא משום דכיון דשניהם באין יחד לדין ושני בעלי דינין יש להן עדים לא היה לב"ד להחזיק לאחד יותר מחבירו אלא כל דאלים גבר הלכך הדר מסלקינן ליה ויהו כבתחילה וכל דאלים גבר דשלא כדין הורידוהו לאחד מהן בקרקע

אבל

עין משפט נר מצוה

קלו א טוש"ע ח"מ סי' קעו סעיף ח:

קלז ב מיי' פ"י מהל' שכירות הל' ג סמג עשין פט טוש"ע ח"מ סם וסי' שה סעיף ו וסי' שמו סעיף ה וסעיף ח:

קלח ג ד ה מיי' פט"ז מהל' עדות הל' א ב סמג לאוין קט טוש"ע ח"מ סי' לז סעיף יז:

רבינו גרשום

אמאי שמירה בבעלים היא. דכל זמן שבעליו עמו לא ישלם ודרשי' ליה עמו בעבודתו עמו בשמירתו דכל זמן ששומר זה מקצת השותפות שומר אידך נמי שאר השותפות ואמאי נעשין כשומרי שכר זה לזה דמשלמין: ואני אשמור לך למחר. דלאו עמו בשמירתו הוא: אין מעיד לו עליה. שאם יבא אחר ויערער עליה. מוכר אינו רשאי להצטרף עם עד אחד להעיד שאינה של מערער אלא של לוקח. ולפיכך אותו מוכר נוגע בעדות הוא: מפני שאחריותו עליו. דאי טריף לה מיניה המערער חוזר הלוקח על המוכר ולהכי [אינו] מעיד לו. אבל מכר לו פרה וטלית וא' מערער עליה מעיד לו מוכר ללוקח להעמידה בידו: רישא בראובן שגזל שדה משמעון ומכרה ללוי. מפרש לקמן אמאי מוקי לה בגזל ומכר. ואתא יהודה וקא מערער על אותה קרקע מש"ה לא ליזל שמעון דנגזל הוא לאסהודי ללוי דקנאה משום דנוגע בדבר הוא משום דניחא ליה לשמעון דתיקום ארעא בידא דלוי דקסבר היום ומחר משכחנא סהדי דגזלה מינאי והדרא ליה מידא דלוי לשמעון והיינו שאחריותו עליו דיש לו תקוה ואחרית לשמעון שלאחר זמן יוציאה מיד לוי ולהכי מסייע ליה להעמידה בידו: ומקשי' אמאי הוי נוגע בעדות ואין מעיד לו. והא כיון דאסהיד שמעון דההיא ארעא דלוי היא הואיל והוא מודי דשל לוי היא במאי טענה מצי תו למיהדר ולאפוקי שמעון מידא דלוי: ומתרץ דלא אסהיד בפירוש דשלו היא אלא הכי מסהיד ואמר ידענא דהאי ארעא לא דיהודה היא דמערער עלה ולא קאמר דלוי היא והשתא נוגע בדבר הוא ולהכי אין מעיד: ומקשי' אכתי אמאי אין מעיד לו. והא בההוא זכותא באותה טענה עצמה דמפיק לה מלוי מצי לאפוקה מיהודה כלומר דמאי איכפת ליה אם תבוא בחזקת יהודה והא מצי למיטען ליהודה שדה זו שאתה מחזיק בה שלי היא שגזלה ראובן ממני והואיל וכן הוא אמאי אין מעיד ללוי מה הנאה יש לו יותר שתהא ברשות דלוי ולא ברשות יהודה. ומשני מש"ה אין מעיד דדלמא קסבר שמן השני לוי נוח לו להוציאה מידו והראשון קשה הימנו יהודה. ואע"ג דמשמע איפכא דיהודה הוי שני ולוי ראשון הכא לא דייק בהכי: ואיבעית אימא. מש"ה אינו מעיד דנוגע בדבר הוא כגון דאית ליה סהדי למר. ליהודה דשל אבותיו הוות: ואית ליה סהדי למר. לשמעון שנגזלה ממנו דאי לא הוי מסהיד שמעון וקא מפקה יהודה מלוי לא מצי תו שמעון לאפוקה מיהודה הואיל דאית ליה ליהודה סהדי ואית ליה לשמעון סהדי אמור רבנן אוקי תרי לבהדי תרי וארעא היכא דקיימא בחזקת יהודה תיקום ומש"ה אתי האי שמעון לאסהודי ללוי כי היכי דתיקום ארעא בידיה דלוי. דאוקמינן תרי סהדי דלוי דמסהדי דלאו דיהודה היא לבהדי תרי סהדי דיהודה ואוקי ארעא בחזקת מריה דהיינו לוי. ובתר הכי מייתי שמעון סהדי דנגזלה מיניה ומפיק לה מלוי. והכא לא מצי למימר אוקי תרי דלוי לבהדי תרי דשמעון דהא שמעון לא אסהיד דשדה של לוי היא אלא אסהיד דלאו דיהודה היא ומש"ה אין מעיד שמעון דנוגע בדבר הוא דמינה דלוי מצי לאפוקה כדאמרן להכי מעמידה בידו:

מסורת הש"ס

א) ב"מ פא., ב) [לעיל ל: כתובות קט.]

הגהות הב"ח

(א) גמ' דניחא ליה דתהדר ליה וכיון דאסהיד: (ב) רשב"ם ד"ה ואיבעית אימא וכו' שאין לו עדות וחזקה לזה יותר מזה: (ג) בא"ד אסקינן ליה אע"ג כצ"ל ואות ד' נמחק: (ד) בא"ד ואפ"ה כי אחזיקני' וכו':

ליקוטי רש"י

אמאי שמירה בבעלים היא. בעליו של חפץ זה שנגנב במלאכתו של שומר היה שאף הוא משמר היה לו וכתיב אם בעליו עמו לא ישלם ודרשינן לקמן עמו במלאכתו ואע"ג דבשואל כתיב לקמן דרשינן ליה נמי אכולהו שומרין בפרק השואל (ב"מ לה.). ואני אשמור לך למחר. דלאו במלאכתו הוא השתא [ב"מ פא.]. קשה הימנו. אדם חזק וקשה להוציאה מידו ונוח לי שתהא בידך שאוציאנה ממך בדין [כתובות קט.].

The Gemara assumes that the partnership arrangement calls for each partner to guard half the property in his home. Accordingly, each is a paid custodian, since each watches the common property in payment for the other's watching it for him. Based on this understanding, the Gemara raises an objection:

אַמַּאי – But **why** does Shmuel rule that partners are considered paid custodians? **שְׁמִירָה בִּבְעָלִים הִיא** – **This is** an example of **custodianship** undertaken **while the owner** of the deposit **is in the custodian's employ,** and such a custodian is exempt from liability![1] – ? –

The Gemara responds:

אָמַר רַב פָּפָּא – **Rav Pappa said:** **דְּאָמַר לֵיהּ** – Shmuel refers to an instance **where [one partner] said to [the other],** **שְׁמוֹר לִי הַיּוֹם** – **"Watch [our common property] for me today,** **וַאֲנִי אֶשְׁמוֹר לְךָ לְמָחָר** – **and I will watch it for you tomorrow."** Thus, although each partner works for the other, they do not do so *simultaneously.*[2] Thus, the aforementioned exemption does not apply.

The Gemara previously discussed disqualifying a witness from testifying regarding another's title to a property if the retention of the property is of benefit to the prospective witness. The Gemara now quotes a Baraisa which deals with this topic:

תָּנוּ רַבָּנָן – **The Rabbis taught in a Baraisa:** **מָכַר לוֹ בַּיִת** – If [ONE] SOLD [HIS FELLOW] A HOUSE, **מָכַר לוֹ שָׂדֶה** – or if HE SOLD HIM A FIELD, and the title is subsequently challenged in court,[3] **אֵין מֵעִיד לוֹ עָלֶיהָ** – [THE SELLER] MAY NOT TESTIFY ON [THE BUYER'S] BEHALF REGARDING IT,[4] **מִפְּנֵי שֶׁאַחֲרָיוּתוֹ עָלָיו** – BECAUSE ITS GUARANTEE RESTS ON HIM, and he is thus an interested party.[5] **מָכַר לוֹ פָּרָה** – If, however, HE SOLD HIM A COW, **מָכַר לוֹ טַלִּית** – or HE SOLD HIM A CLOAK, and the title was subsequently challenged, **מֵעִיד לוֹ עָלֶיהָ** – [THE SELLER] MAY TESTIFY ON [THE BUYER'S] BEHALF REGARDING IT, **מִפְּנֵי שֶׁאֵין אַחֲרָיוּתוֹ עָלָיו** – BECAUSE ITS GUARANTEE DOES NOT REST ON HIM, and he is therefore a disinterested party.

The Gemara initially assumes that the sole criterion for determining whether the seller's testimony is accepted in these instances is whether or not the seller guaranteed the disputed property. Consequently, the Gemara asks:

מַאי שְׁנָא רֵישָׁא וּמַאי שְׁנָא סֵיפָא – **What is the difference between the first case and the last case** of the Baraisa? Why does the Baraisa assume in the case of real property that the seller guaranteed the purchase and in the case of movable property that he did not guarantee it?[6]

Rav Sheishess therefore presents an entirely different interpretation of the Baraisa:

אָמַר רַב שֵׁשֶׁת – **Rav Sheishess said:** **רֵישָׁא** – **The first case** of the Baraisa speaks of a situation **בִּרְאוּבֵן שֶׁגָּזַל שָׂדֶה מִשִּׁמְעוֹן** – **in which Reuven stole a field from Shimon**[7] **וּמְכָרָהּ לְלֵוִי** – **and sold it to Levi.** **וְאָתָא יְהוּדָה וְקָא מְעַרְעֵר** – **Yehudah then came** forward **and challenged** Levi's title, maintaining that the field was never Reuven's but *his.*[8] In this case, the Baraisa rules **דְּלָא לֵיזִיל שִׁמְעוֹן לְאַסְהֵיד לֵיהּ לְלֵוִי** – **that Shimon may not go and testify on Levi's behalf,**[9] **דְּנִיחָא לֵיהּ דְּהַדְרָא** – **for [Shimon] prefers** to see the land remain in Levi's hands, **so it can** eventually **return** to him; i.e. Shimon hopes to prove someday that the man who sold Levi the field had actually stolen it from him. Thus, Shimon's testimony is prejudiced and cannot be accepted.[10]

The Gemara takes issue with this interpretation:[11]

וְכֵיוָן דְּאַסְהֵיד לֵיהּ דְּלֵוִי הוּא – **But once [Shimon] has testified that**

NOTES

1. The law is that a borrower is liable even for unavoidable accidents. The Torah, however, states (*Exodus* 22:14): אִם־בְּעָלָיו עִמּוֹ לֹא יְשַׁלֵּם, *If its* (the borrowed object's) *owner is with him* (the borrower), *he shall not pay.* Oral tradition teaches us that the definition of this law is that if the owner was working for the borrower at the time of the loan, he is exempt from payment for such accidents. Additionally, the Sages derive that this applies also to a paid custodian and exempts him from liability if the deposit is lost or stolen. In our case, then, since each partner simultaneously began "working" for the other (by guarding half of the common property), they should both be exempt from liability. How, then, can Shmuel rule that they are considered paid custodians?

2. That is, instead of each watching half the property all of the time, each watches all of the property half of the time. Thus, neither partner is working for the other upon commencing his turn as custodian.

[*Tosafos* raise the following question: The Gemara in *Bava Metzia,* 94a, rules that for this exemption to apply, the owner need not actually work for the custodian. Rather, even a verbal agreement on the part of the owner to work for the custodian is sufficient to exempt the custodian from liability. If so, Shmuel's ruling is still difficult, because each partner has verbally agreed to watch the common property for the other. *Tosafos* answer that this refers to an agreement to begin work immediately. In the case of the partners, however, the second partner agrees to guard the property only after the first partner is no longer doing so. Thus, he cannot be considered in the first partner's employ at the time of the first partner's custodianship.]

3. The challenger claims that the land was his and never belonged to the seller.

4. The seller wishes to join together with another witness (*Rashbam*) to testify that the property had, in fact, belonged to him and not to the challenger.

5. The seller has a vested interest in seeing that the buyer retains the field, since if the challenge is successful the seller will have to reimburse the buyer for the loss.

The Gemara below will explain this phrase (מִפְּנֵי שֶׁאַחֲרָיוּתוֹ עָלָיו) differently. However, at this point the Gemara understands it to refer to a guarantee (*Rashbam*).

6. The division of the Baraisa into two cases seems to imply an inherent distinction between real and movable property. Yet the *reason* given for each ruling indicates that the seller's admissibility as a witness depends on whether he guaranteed his sale, a provision which could apply to both movable and real property.

7. I.e. Shimon was overheard in court claiming that Reuven stole the field from him. Although his claim was not supported by witnesses, it is nevertheless sufficient to disqualify him from testifying in regard to this property, as the Gemara will explain (*Rashba, Chidushei HaRan*).

8. Yehudah produced documents or witnesses to support his claim (*Rashbam*).

9. Shimon claims that he can discredit Yehudah's evidence. [The Gemara below will explain the exact nature of the testimony which Shimon wishes to advance in Levi's behalf.] Accordingly, the Baraisa should be understood as follows: If [Reuven] sold a house to his fellow [Levi], a person [Shimon] who claims that the seller was a thief may not testify in behalf of the buyer [Levi] (whose title is now being challenged by Yehudah). The disqualification applies not to the seller, as the Gemara previously explained, but to the [alleged] original owner of the field, i.e. Shimon.

10. Shimon does not wish Yehudah to be awarded the land because this would make it more difficult for him to regain it, as the Gemara will explain below. Thus, his testimony in Levi's behalf is prejudiced and cannot be accepted.

In Rav Sheishess' interpretation of the Baraisa, Shimon's testimony is disqualified because of his possible designs on the field. Thus, the phrase מִפְּנֵי שֶׁאַחֲרָיוּתוֹ עָלָיו is rendered not as "because its guarantee rests on him," but rather as "because his ultimate design [אַחֲרִית] is on [the buyer]"; i.e. he ultimately plans to reclaim the land from him [Levi] (*Rashbam;* see also *Rabbeinu Gershom*).

11. The Gemara has not yet explained how Rav Sheishess's explanation answers the question raised previously; viz. the distinction between real and movable property. This will be explained below (44a). The Gemara pauses, however, to challenge Rav Sheishess's explanation of the first part of the Baraisa.

(א) א אמאי שמירה בבעלים היא אמר רב פפא ב דאמר ליה שמור לי היום ואני אשמור לך למחר: תנו רבנן מכר לו בית מכר לו שדה אין מעיד לו עליה מפני שאחריותו עליו מכר לו פרה מכר לו טלית מעיד לו עליה מפני שאין אחריותו עליו מאי שנא רישא ומאי שנא סיפא אמר רב ששת רישא ג בראובן שגזל שדה משמעון ומכרה ללוי ואתא יהודה וקא מערער דלא ליזיל שמעון לאסהיד ליה ללוי דניחא ליה (א) דהדרא וכיון דאסהיד ליה דלוי הוא היכי מצי מפיק לה מיניה ד דאמר ידענא דהאי ארעא דלאו דיהודה היא ובההוא זכותא דקא מפיק לה מלוי ליפקה מיהודה דאמר (ג) ה השני נוח לי הראשון קשה הימנו ואי בעית אימא כגון דאית ליה סהדי למר ואית ליה סהדי למר ואמור רבנן ארעא היכא דקיימא תיקום

שמירה בבעלים היא. שכל אחד משמר קצת מן השותפות בביתו וקי"ל בב"מ בהשואל (דף צה.) שמירה בבעלים פטור ואע"ג דבשואל כתיב פטור דבעלים הא יליף שומר שכר התם מיניה מדכתיב וכי ישאל וי"ו מוסיף על ענין ראשון וילמד עליון מתחתון וכיון שהיה ראובן משמר מחלק שמעון בשעה שנגנבה או אבד מחלקו בבית שמעון הרי שמעון פטור מחלק ראובן שהרי ראובן עמו במלאכתו: **אמר רב פפא.** כגון שהתנו ביניהן כך שמור לי היום כל השדה חלקי וחלקך ואשמור לך למחר דכיון דלא שמרו ביחד כלל אלא בזה אחר זה ליכא שמירה בבעלים הלכך נעשו שומרי שכר זה לזה להתחייב באונסין ולאשמועינן אתא דהיינו שמירה בשכר כשמשמר כל השדה וחלק חבירו בכלל כדי שישמור לו חבירו למחר כמו כן דס"ד אמינא דשומר חנם הוא דבלאו חלק חבירו היה צריך לשמור את שלו ושמירה אחת היא בין הכל ולא ליהוי שומר שכר קמ"ל: (זה שייך לעיל. בתוספתא דהגוזל האומר תנו מאה דינר לכנסת תנו ספר תורה לכנסת ינתן לכנסת הרגיל בה ואם היה רגיל בשנים יתנו לשניהם האומר תנו לעניים יתנו לעניי אותה העיר ר' אחא אומר לעניי כל ישראל בן האוכל משל אביו ועבד האוכל משל רבו קולה ונותן פרוסה לעניים או לבנו של אוהבו ואינו חושש משום גזל שכך נהגו בעלי בתים. ע"כ): **מכר לו בית.** אדם לחבירו: **אין מעיד לו.** מוכר ללוקח להעמידה בידו שאם יבא להצטרף עם אחר ולהעיד שהוא שלו נוגע בעדות הוא: **מפני שאחריותו.** של בית עליו דמוכר שאם יטרפוה מן הלוקח יחזור על המוכר והלכך ניחא ליה למוכר שתעמוד ביד הלוקח ולא יצטרך לפרעו כלום הכי שמעינן ליה השתא: **מכר לו פרה.** לקמיה מפרש ליה ואזיל: **שאין אחריותו.** דלוקח עליה דמוכר אם יטלוהו הימנו מחמת המוכר שגזלה והיינו דקפריך מ"ש רישא ומ"ש סיפא מ"ש מטלטלי דלא הוי אחריות עליו ממקרקעי אם שתי מכירות הללו באחריות הוי תרוייהו אחריותו עליו ואי שלא באחריות הא תרוייהו אין אחריותו עליו: **רישא בראובן** שגזל שדה משמעון ומכרה ללוי **ואתא יהודה.** כלומר איניש מעלמא ומערער על שדה זו שביד לוי ואומר שלי היא ומביא עדים או שטר שלא יבא שמעון הנגזל ויצטרף עם אחר ויעיד שזה השדה אינו ליהודה כגון שיודע שום עדות לפסול עדות של יהודה בגזלנות וכן שטרו מפני שרוצה שמעון שיהיה השדה ביד לוי הקונה ואחרי כן היום ולמחר יביא שמעון ראיה שזו השדה שלו היה וראובן גזלו ממנו ויוציאו מיד לוי ויטלנו לעצמו דקרקע אינה נגזלת ולא מהני בה יאוש ושינוי רשות והלכך נוגע בעדות הוא דלא ניחא ליה שיטלנו יהודה דתו לא מצי שמעון לאפוקי מיניה כדמפרש לקמן דנוח לו לוי ויהודה קשה לו והלכך אין מעיד לו שמעון הנגזל ללוי עליה והכי קאמר בברייתא מכר לו בית מכר לו שדה ראובן הגזלן ללוי אין מעיד לו שמעון הנגזל ללוי לוקח עליה כנגד יהודה המערער מפני שאחריותו וסופו של נגזל עליו דלוקח להוציא הקרקע מידו והלכך נוגע הוא בעדות זו ולקמן מפרש אמאי מוקי לה בנגזל ומכר הוה שפיר מצי לאוקומה בגזלן גופיה ואתא יהודה וקמערער דלא יבא שמעון הנגזל להעיד לראובן הגזלן להעמידה בידו משום האי טעמא גופיה דניחא ליה דהדרא ליה וסיפא מפרש לקמן: ומקשינן **ואכתי אמאי אינו מעיד** לו עליה **הא כיון דאסהיד דלוי היא.** דקס"ד השתא הכי דמפקינן לה מיהודה ומוקים לה ביד לוי דקמסהיד הוא בשדה דלוי הוא ולאו דיהודה וכיון דהודה בפני בית דין דשל לוי הוא היכי מצי מפיק לה מלוי אחרי כן והלא הודאת בעל דין כמאה עדים דמי ונמצא שאינו מרויח כלום בעדות זו ואינו נוגע בעדות זו כלל ואמאי קתני דאין מעיד: ומשני **דאמר ידענא דההוא ארעא לאו דיהודה היא.** דפסיל לעדי יהודה בגזלנותא או דמכחיש לטענותיו בשום ענין בעולם כגון שמעיד בפני הודה לו וממילא מתוקמא השדה ביד לוי ואע"ג דלא קאמר דלוי הוא: ומקשינן **אכתי אמאי אינו מעיד לו עליה.** מה מפסיד שמעון אם תהיה בחזקת יהודה והא בההוא זכותא דקמפיק לה מלוי היום ולמחר דקמייתי עדים שהשדה שלו היא וגזלה ראובן ממנו ה"נ ליפקה מיהודה בהנהו עדים עצמן ונמצא שאין מרויח במה שמעיד ללוי כלל: ומשני משום הכי אינו מעיד דקסבר שמעון לוי נוח לי ויהודה גברא אלמא הוא וקשה ממנו ולא אוכל לדון עמו אם יבא בידו ומש"ה פסלינן ליה להאי עדות דאיכא למימר שזהו מחשבתו של שמעון ואין לנו להכשיר אלא עד דפשיטא לן דאינו נוגע בעדות כלל. הכא הוה לן למימר איפכא לוי הראשון נוח לי ויהודה השני קשה הימנו אבל לשון המשנה כך היא בכתובות (דף קט.): **ואי בעית אימא.** להכי לא מצי שמעון לאפוקה מיהודה כגון דאית ליה סהדי לשמעון שהשדה שלו ואית ליה סהדי ליהודה שמכחישין לאלו ואומרים שהשדה של יהודה ואמור רבנן בכל ספק דין קרקע היכא דקיימא ארעא תיקום שלא יוציאוה ב"ד מיד המחזיק בה כדאמר גבי פלוגתא דרבה ורב יוסף (לעיל לג:) היכא דקיימא ארעא תיקום לפי שנסתפק לנו הדין וכן (לעיל לד:) גבי זה אומר של אבותי אר"נ כל דאלים גבר (ס"א וכגון שאין לו עדות (ג) ואלוקה לזה יותר מזה ע"כ) ומשום דמספקא לן מי שרוצה להחזיק יחזיק ולא נוציא מידו וגבי נכסי דבר שטיא (כתובות דף כ.) אמר נמי אוקי תרי בהדי תרי ואוקי ארעא בחזקת בר שטיא והכא נמי אי מטיא לידיה דיהודה לא מצי שמעון לאפוקי מיניה בהני סהדי דמפיק לה מלוי דכיון דמן הדין אוקימנה ביד יהודה שהרי ממ"נ אין ללוי חלק בה הרי יהודה מוחזק ולא תלא עוד מידו ולא דמי להאי דאמרינן לעיל בפרקין (דף לג:) הדר אייתי סהדי דאכלתה היא א"ר נחמן אנן אחתינן ליה ואנן אסקינן ליה (ג) דלאע"ג דהתם נמי איכא סהדי למר ואיכא סהדי למר ואפ"ה (ד) אחזקיה לאחד ע"פ עדיו והדר מסלקינן ליה כשמביא חבירו עדים שלו היינו טעמא משום דכיון דשניהם באין יחד לדין ושני בעלי דינין יש להן עדים לא היה לנו לב"ד להחזיק לאחד יותר מחבירו אלא כל דאלים גבר הלכך הדר מסלקינן ליה ויהו כבתחילה וכל דאלים גבר דשלא הורידוהו לאחד מהן בקרקע אבל

אמאי שמירה בבעלים היא. פי' אם התחילו שניהם לשמור יחד כל אחד בשעה שהוא משמר חלק חבירו חבירו נמי משמר לו חלקו ואע"פ שאין עמו במלאכה בשעת אונס כיון שהיה עמו בתחילת שמירה בעליו עמו קרינן ביה כדתניא (ב"מ דף צו.) היה עושה עמו בשעת שאלה אין צריך להיות עמו בשעת שבורה ומתה היה עמו בשעת שבורה ומתה צריך להיות עמו בשעת שאלה ואפילו לא התחילו שניהם לשמור יחד מכל מקום האחרון פטור שהראשון שהיה עמו במלאכה בשעה שהתחיל השני לשמור:

דאמר שמור לי היום כו'. וא"ת אכתי שמירה בבעלים היא דאמרינן בריש השואל דבעלים בשמירה גבי שואל את הפרה ובעלה עמה וי"ל שאני התם דבשמירה משעבדי עצמן ליכנס במלאכתם מיד אבל הכא לא משתעבד עד למחר וא"ת ומאי קמ"ל פשיטא דנעשין שומרי שכר זה לזה מתניתין היא בהשוכר את הפועלים (ב"מ דף פ:) שמור לי ואשמור לך שומר שכר וי"ל דאי מהתם הוה אמינא לפי שהם אינן שותפין אבל הכא שהם שותפין כל אחד ואחד כששומר חלק חבירו שומר גם בשביל עצמו:

וכיון דאסהיד דלוי הוא כו'. הוה מצי לשנויי כגון דאסהיד שמעון דשל אבותיו דלוי הוה ובתר הכי אתי שמעון וטעין דמלוי זבנה ואית ליה סהדי דראובן גזלה ממנו ומכרה ללוי: **כגון** דאית ליה סהדי למר כו'. תימה דלא הוה ליה למימר כגון דהא מעיקרא נמי ידעינן דאית ליה לשמעון סהדי דדידיה היא כדקתני ראובן שגזל שדה משמעון ואי לית ליה לשמעון סהדי שגזלה ראובן ממנו אן היכי ידעינן שגזלה ומכח מה הוא מערער ויהודה נמי ע"כ אית ליה סהדי דאי לאו הכי מאיזה כח מערער והכי הל"ל כיון דאית ליה סהדי למר כו' ומאי ס"ד דמקשה ואין לומר דמעיקרא ס"ד דאיירי כגון דאית ליה ליהודה עדים דשל אבותיו היא ולשמעון הנגזל אית ליה סהדי דאכלה שני חזקה וטעין מיהודה זבנה דא"כ מאי קאמר בהאי זכותא דמפיק לה מלוי ליפקה מיהודה הא בהאי זכותא דמצי לאפוקי מלוי לא מצי לאפוקי מיהודה דבעדי גזילה המעידין שגזל ראובן ממנו מצי מפיק לה מלוי שבא מכח ראובן ומיהודה לא מצי מפיק לה אלא בעדי חזקה ונראה לרשב"א דס"ד דמעיקרא דיהודה בעי לאפוקי מלוי משום דאית ליה סהדי דראובן מכר לו וללוי אין עדים ובא שמעון להעיד ללוי דשל לוי היא ומשום הכי פריך כיון דמסהיד דהאי ארעא דלוי היא היכי מפיק לה מיניה והוה מצי לשנויי דלא מסהדי בהאי לישנא דלוי היא אלא דאמר דראובן מכרה ללוי אלא דעדיפא מינה משני והשתא פריך שפיר דבהאי זכותא דמפיק לה מלוי ליפקה מיהודה דשניהם באין מכח ראובן ואם יביא שמעון עדים דראובן גזלה ממנו מצי לאפוקי מתרוייהו:

דוקא

עין משפט נר מצוה

קלו א טוש"ע ח"מ סי' קעו סעיף ח:
קלז ב מיי' פ"י מהל' שכירות הל' ג סמג עשין פט טוש"ע ח"מ סם וסי' שה סעיף ו וסי' שמו סעיף ה וסעיף ח:
קלח ג ד ה מיי' פט"ז מהל' עדות הל' א ג סמג לאוין קט טוש"ע ח"מ סי' לז סעיף יז:

רבינו גרשום

אמאי שמירה בבעלים היא. דכל זמן שבעליו עמו לא ישלם ודרשי' ליה עמו בעבודתו עמו בשמירתו דכל זמן ששומר זה מקצת השותפות שומר אידך נמי שאר השותפות ואמאי נעשין כשומרי שכר זה לזה דמשלמין: **ואני אשמור לך למחר.** דלאו עמו בשמירתו הוא: **אין מעיד לו עליה.** שאם יבא אחר ויערער עליה. מוכר אינו רשאי להצטרף עם עד אחד להעיד שאינה של מערער אלא של לוקח. ולפיכך אותו מוכר נוגע בעדות הוא: **מפני שאחריותו עליו.** דאי טריף לה מיניה המערער חוזר הלוקח על המוכר ולהכי [אינו] מעיד לו. אבל **מכר לו פרה וטלית** וא' מערער עליה **מעיד לו** מוכר ללוקח להעמידה בידו: **רישא בראובן שגזל שדה משמעון ומכרה ללוי.** מפרש לקמן אמאי מוקי לה בגזל ומכר. **ואתא יהודה וקא מערער** על אותה קרקע מש"ה **לא ליזיל שמעון** דנגזל הוא **לאסהודי ללוי** דקנאה משום דנוגע בדבר הוא משום **דניחא ליה** לשמעון דתיקום ארעא בידא דלוי דקסבר היום ומחר משכחנא סהדי דגזלה מינאי **והדרא ליה** מידא דלוי לשמעון והיינו שאחריותו עליו דיש לו תקוה ואחרית לשמעון שלאחר זמן יוציאה מיד לוי ולהכי מסייע ליה להעמידה בידו: ומקשי' אמאי הוי נוגע בעדות ואין מעיד לו. והא **כיון דאסהיד** שמעון דההיא ארעא **דלוי היא** הואיל והוא מודי דשל לוי היא במאי טענה מצי תו למיהדר ולאפוקי שמעון מידא דלוי: ומתרץ דלא אסהיד בפירוש דשלו היא אלא הכי מסהיד **ואמר ידענא דהאי ארעא לא דיהודה היא** דמערער עלה ולא קאמר דלוי היא והשתא נוגע בדבר הוא ולהכי אין מעיד: ומקשי' אכתי אמאי אין מעיד לו. והא **בההוא זכותא** באותה טענה עצמה **דמפיק לה מלוי** מצי **לאפוקה מיהודה** כלומר דמאי איכפת ליה אם תבוא בחזקת יהודה והא מצי למיטען ליהודה שדה זו שאתה מחזיק בה שלי היא שגזלה ראובן ממני והואיל וכן הוא אמאי אין מעיד ללוי מה הנאה יש לו יותר שתהא ברשות דלוי ולא ברשות יהודה. ומשני מש"ה אין מעיד דדלמא קסבר שמן **השני** לוי **נוח לו** להוציאה מידו **והראשון קשה הימנו** יהודה. ואע"ג דמשמע איפכא דיהודה הוי שני ולוי ראשון הכא לא דייק בהכי: **ואיבעית אימא.** מש"ה אינו מעיד בדבר הוא **כגון דאית ליה סהדי למר.** ליהודה דשל אבותיו

הוות: **ואית ליה סהדי למר.** לשמעון שנגזלה ממנו דאי לא הוי מסהיד שמעון וקא מפקא יהודה מלוי לא מצי תו שמעון לאפוקה מיהודה הואיל דאית ליה ליהודה סהדי ואית ליה לשמעון סהדי **אמור רבנן** אוקי תרי בהדי תרי **וארעא היכא דקיימא תיקום** בחזקת יהודה ומש"ה אתי האי שמעון לאסהודי ללוי כי היכי דתיקום ארעא בידיה דלוי. דאוקמינן תרי סהדי דלוי דמסהדי דלאו דיהודה היא לבהדי תרי סהדי דיהודה ואוקי ארעא בחזקת לוי היינו לוי. ולבתר הכי מייתי שמעון סהדי דנגזלה מיניה ומפיק לה מלוי. והכא לא מצי למימר אוקי תרי דלוי בהדי תרי דשמעון דהא שמעון לא אסהיד אלא דלאו דיהודה היא ומש"ה אין מעיד שמעון דנוגע בדבר הוא דמינה דלוי מצי לאפוקה כדאמרן להכי מעמידה בידו:

מסורת הש"ס

א) ב"מ צה., ב) [לעיל ג: כתובות קט.]

הגהות הב"ח

(א) גמ' דניחא ליה דהדרא ליה וכיון דאסהיד: (ב) רשב"ם ד"ה ואיבעית אימא וכו' שאין לו עדות וחזקה לזה יותר מזה: (ג) בא"ד אסקינן ליה אע"ג כצ"ל ואות ד' נמחק: (ד) בא"ד ואפ"ה כי אחזיקו' וכו':

ליקוטי רש"י

אמאי שמירה בבעלים היא. בעליו של חפץ זה שנגנב במלאכתו של שומר היה שאף הוא משמר היה לו וכתיב אם בעליו עמו לא ישלם ודרשינן לקמן עמו במלאכתו ואע"ג דבשואל כתיב לקמן אכולהו שומרין בפרק השואל [ב"מ צה.]. **ואני אשמור לך למחר.** דלאו במלאכתו הוה השתא [ב"מ פא.]. **קשה הימנו.** אדם חזק וקשה להוציא מידו ונוח לי שאהא חבירו שלוציאנו ממך בדין [כתובות קט.].

[the disputed property] belongs to Levi, הֵיכִי מָצֵי מַפֵּיק לָהּ מִינֵּיהּ – **how can he** hope to **reclaim it from [Levi]?** By his testimony, he has admitted that it belongs to Levi![12] – ? –

The Gemara replies:

דְּאָמַר יָדַעְנָא דְּהַאי אַרְעָא דְּלָאו דִּיהוּדָה הִיא – The Baraisa speaks of a case **in which [Shimon]** wishes to **testify that this land is not Yehudah's,** without identifying its actual owner; i.e. his testimony discredits Yehudah's proofs without admitting that the land belongs to Levi.[13]

The Gemara persists:

וּבְהַהוּא זְכוּתָא דְּקָא מַפֵּיק לָהּ מִלֵּוִי – **But whatever proof [Shimon]** plans eventually to **use to reclaim [the property] from Levi,** לִיפְקָהּ מִיהוּדָה – **let him** use it to **reclaim [the property] from Yehudah!** What difference does it make to him who holds the property in the interim?[14]

The Gemara replies:

דְּאָמַר – Shimon's testimony is still suspect, **for he may say** to himself: הַשֵּׁנִי נוֹחַ לִי – **The second** one (Levi) **is easier for me** to contend with, הָרִאשׁוֹן קָשֶׁה הֵימֶנּוּ – whereas **the first** one (Yehudah) **is more difficult than him.**[15] Thus, he has an interest in the outcome of his testimony and he is therefore disqualified.

The Gemara provides an alternative answer to the last question:

וְאִי בָּעִית אֵימָא – **Or, if your prefer, say** כְּגוֹן דְּאִית לֵיהּ סַהֲדֵי לְמַר וְאִית לֵיהּ סַהֲדֵי לְמַר – that the Baraisa speaks of **a case in which this one** (Shimon) **has** supporting **witnesses, and this one** (Yehudah) also **has** supporting **witnesses.** וְאָמוּר רַבָּנָן – **Now the Rabbis ruled** that when conflicting testimony from two sets of witnesses is introduced with respect to the ownership of a disputed property, אַרְעָא הֵיכָא דְּקַיְימָא תֵּיקוּם – **the land remains wherever it is,** i.e. in the possession of the current holder.[16] Thus, it is in Shimon's interest to prevent the land from ever reaching Yehudah's possession, and his testimony is therefore suspect.

NOTES

12. A person's admission is deemed legal proof and cannot be negated even by witnesses. Consequently, even if Shimon were to produce witnesses to testify to his ownership, his admission in court that the property is Levi's would carry more weight, and he would lose the property. Thus, he should be allowed to testify in Levi's behalf, for once he has done so, he cannot reclaim the land (*Rashbam*).

13. Shimon wishes to testify that Yehudah's witnesses are disqualified on personal grounds; for example, they are known thieves. Alternatively, he wishes to testify that Yehudah admitted to him that the land was not his (*Rashbam*). In this manner, Shimon can discredit Yehudah's claim without admitting that the land is Levi's. Since this leaves him free to pursue his own claim later, he is considered an interested party and is ineligible to testify.

14. Obviously, Shimon can hope to recover the property only if he can prove it is his. But if he possesses such proof, what difference does it make to him whether he sues to reclaim it from Levi or from Yehudah? His testimony on behalf of Levi against Yehudah should therefore be seen as unbiased and acceptable.

15. The statement should really have been the other way around: "The first is easier for me, whereas the second is more difficult than him," since it makes more sense to refer to Levi as the first and Yehudah as the second. This statement, however, is an expression borrowed from a Mishnah in *Kesubos* (109a), and the Gemara therefore preserves it intact (*Rashbam*).

16. When ownership of real property is in doubt, the property is left in the hands of whoever is currently holding it. If Shimon were to allow Yehudah to produce his witnesses and take the property from Levi, Yehudah would then be legally established as the holder. Shimon's subsequent introduction of testimony that the land is really his would not avail him at all, for Yehudah's witnesses would contradict this testimony and the land would remain in the hands of the current holder – Yehudah! Shimon thus wishes to disqualify Yehudah's witnesses before the land reaches his hands, with the intention of later using his own witnesses to seize the land from Levi. Once Shimon seizes the land from Levi, the situation would be reversed. Yehudah would be powerless to get it back from Shimon, since even if Yehudah were to produce witnesses that the land was his, their testimony would be contradicted by Shimon's witnesses, and the land would remain in the hands of the current holder – Shimon (*Rashbam*).

The Gemara accepts Rav Sheishess's explanation of Shimon's ulterior motive for testifying that the field belongs to Levi. However, the Gemara questions the Baraisa's case selection according to this explanation:

וְלוֹקְמָה בְּגַזְלָן – **But let [the Baraisa] teach** this law **in reference to the thief** himself? Why speak of a case in which the thief (Reuven) sold the field, and Yehudah challenged the purchaser (Levi)? It would have been simpler to give a case in which Yehudah challenged Reuven while the field was in his possession, and teach that Shimon is disqualified from testifying in Reuven's defense![1] – ? –

The Gemara responds, and in doing so, explains the distinction made by the Baraisa between real and movable property:

מִשּׁוּם דְּקָא בָּעֵי לְמִיתְנָא סֵיפָא – The Tanna of the Baraisa incorporated a sale into the case **because he wished to teach** the law of **the latter case** of the Baraisa: מָכַר לוֹ פָּרָה – If HE (Reuven) SOLD HIM (Levi) A COW, מָכַר לוֹ טַלִּית – or if HE SOLD HIM A CLOAK which Shimon claims he stole from him, Shimon *can* testify on Levi's behalf against Yehudah.[2]

The Gemara now explains why this ruling requires the property to have been *sold*:

דְּדוּקָא מָכַר – **For** this latter ruling is true **only if [Reuven] sold** the object to Levi, and Yehudah challenged him, דַּהֲוָה לֵיהּ יֵאוּשׁ וְשִׁינּוּי רְשׁוּת – **for this is** then a situation of **abandonment** followed by **a change of possession.**[3] In such a case, Shimon can no longer reclaim his property,[4] and he is therefore no longer an interested party and may testify. אֲבָל לֹא מָכַר – **But** in a case in which **[Reuven] did not sell** the object, and Yehudah challenged him, דְּהָדְרָא לֵיהּ – **in which case [the object] can** ultimately **return to [Shimon],** לֹא – he (Shimon) may **not** testify in Reuven's behalf, because he is an interested party.[5] Since the latter ruling of the Baraisa is true only if Yehudah challenged the one who bought it from the alleged thief, תָּנָא רֵישָׁא נַמִּי מָכַר – **[the Baraisa] also taught the first ruling,** regarding a field, in a case in which **[the thief] sold** the land.[6]

According to this interpretation of the Baraisa's latter ruling, the original owner of a cow or cloak (Shimon) can testify in the purchaser's (Levi) behalf because he can no longer reclaim his stolen object in any case. The Gemara questions this:

וְסֵיפָא נַמִּי – **But** in **the latter ruling, too,** נְהִי דְּמִיָּיאֵשׁ מִגּוּפֵיהּ – **although [Shimon] has abandoned** hope of recovering **the object** itself and cannot reclaim it once the thief sells it, מִדְּמֵיהּ מִי מְיָיאֵשׁ – **has he abandoned** hope of recovering **its value,** i.e. of receiving restitution from the thief?[7] Obviously not! Thus, Shimon's testimony should still be disallowed, for he may wish to prove that the object had been his, so that he can force the thief to pay him for it![8] – ? –

The Gemara answers:

לֹא צְרִיכָא דְּמִית גַּזְלָן – **[The Baraisa's ruling] applies only where the thief** (Reuven) **died** subsequent to the sale. In this case, Shimon cannot recover even the value of the stolen object.

דִּתְנַן – **For we have learned in a Mishnah:** הַגּוֹזֵל וּמַאֲכִיל אֶת בָּנָיו – If ONE STOLE something AND FED it to HIS CHILDREN, וְהִנִּיחַ לִפְנֵיהֶם – OR LEFT IT TO THEM as an inheritance, פְּטוּרִים מִלְּשַׁלֵּם – [THE CHILDREN] ARE EXEMPT FROM PAYING the owner of the object.[9] Thus, Shimon has no recourse to recover either the

NOTES

1. The Baraisa's basic point is that a person cannot testify in regard to a property which he hopes someday to recover. This point could have been taught more simply in a case in which Reuven had not sold the field, and Yehudah challenged his occupancy of it. In this case as well, Shimon would be disqualified from testifying in the thief's behalf, on the grounds that his ultimate intention is to retake the land himself. Thus, the Baraisa should have stated: "If a field or a house was stolen from a person, he may not testify on behalf of the thief [if the thief's title is challenged by a third party], because his ultimate design is [to reclaim the land] from the thief for himself" (*Rashbam;* see 43b note 11).

2. According to Rav Sheishess, the Baraisa's second ruling refers to a case in which Reuven stole a cow or cloak from Shimon and sold it to Levi. Yehudah now claims that it was his all along and Levi has no right to it. This parallels exactly the case given by Rav Sheishess for the Baraisa's first ruling regarding real property.

3. A stolen object must be returned to its owner if it is found intact. However, if the owner despaired of ever recovering it and the thief subsequently transferred the object to another, the latter acquires the stolen object by means of "abandonment and a change of possession" (from the thief to the buyer). The owner can no longer recover the object itself from the buyer; he can only recover the value of the object from the thief.

4. The Gemara now explains the Baraisa to be speaking of a case in which Shimon had already despaired of recovering the object before Reuven sold it to Levi. Therefore, although Levi bought the object from a thief, he is entitled to keep it by virtue of Shimon's abandonment and the change of possession from Reuven to Levi (*Rashbam*).

5. As long as a stolen object is still in the hands of the thief, its owner may reclaim it even if he has despaired of recovering it. Mere abandonment does not allow a thief (who came by the object illegally) to acquire the stolen object (see *Bava Kamma* 66a-67b). Therefore, if Reuven retains the stolen object, Shimon will be able to reclaim it from him at a later date. Thus, it is to Shimon's benefit that Reuven retain the object [as we have learned above], and so he cannot testify on the thief's behalf (*Rashbam*).

6. This entire line of reasoning is valid only with regard to movable objects, since it is only with regard to movables that abandonment combined with a change of possession bars the original owner from reclaiming them. Real property, however, can always be reclaimed, since the law is that land cannot be stolen (קַרְקַע אֵינָהּ נִגְזֶלֶת) [i.e. the Torah's laws of theft do not take effect in regard to land (see *Bava Kamma* 117b)]. Since Shimon can always hope to reclaim his land, he can never testify in the holder's behalf, whether that holder is the thief himself or a subsequent purchaser (*Rashbam*).

In summary: The Baraisa speaks of a case in which Reuven stole property from Shimon and sold it to Levi. Shimon had in the meantime abandoned hope of recovering his property. Yehudah now challenges Levi's right to the property. The Baraisa teaches that if the property in question is real estate, Shimon may *not* testify against Yehudah because Shimon can someday reclaim this property from Levi and he therefore stands to benefit from his testimony. However, if the property in question is movable (e.g. a cow or cloak), Shimon *may* testify against Yehudah because he can in any case never recover the stolen object. The difference between the two cases is that stolen movable property is acquired by a buyer through abandonment and change of possession, whereas stolen real property is not acquired by this means.

In a case in which Reuven stole property from Shimon and did *not* sell it, and Reuven's possession is challenged by Yehudah, Shimon *cannot* testify against Yehudah even in the case of movable property. Since the property is still in the hands of the thief, Shimon can reclaim it even after having abandoned it. Thus, it is no different than real property; in either case Shimon stands to benefit from his testimony and he is therefore ineligible to testify against Yehudah. It is for this reason that the Baraisa speaks of a case in which the property was *sold* before its possession was challenged, since it is only in this case that a distinction can be made between real and movable property (*Rashbam*).

7. The law of "abandonment and change of possession" affects only the owner's ability to recover the stolen *object* from the buyer. The thief, however, must certainly pay for what he stole.

8. If Shimon does not testify and Yehudah is awarded the object, Shimon will not be able to recoup even its value from the thief; for, if Yehudah wins the case, it will have been proven that Shimon never owned the object (*Rashbam*). Thus, the Gemara argues, Shimon's testimony against Yehudah is self-serving and should be disqualified.

9. *Bava Kamma* 111b. The Gemara there explains that the Mishnah refers to a case in which the victim of the theft abandoned hope of retrieving the object. The thief's children have no obligation to return the stolen object, either because they have acquired it by means of "abandonment and a change of possession" or because the Mishnah

ולוקמה בגזלן משום דקא בעי למיתנא סיפא מכר לו פרה מכר לו טלית [א] דדוקא מכר דהוה ליה יאוש ושינוי רשות אבל לא מכר דהדרא ליה לא תנא רישא נמי מכר וסיפא נמי נהי דמייאש מגופיה מדמיה מי מייאש לא צריכא [ב] דמית גזלן דתנן (א) [ג] הגוזל ומאכיל את בניו והניח לפניהם פטורים מלשלם ולוקמה ביורש הניחא למאן דאמר (ב) [ד] רשות יורש לאו כרשות לוקח דמי שפיר אלא למאן דאמר רשות יורש כרשות לוקח דמי מאי איכא למימר ועוד קשיא ליה לאביי מפני שאחריותו עליו ואין אחריותו עליו מפני שהיא חוזרת לו ואינה חוזרת לו מיבעי ליה אלא כדרבין בר שמואל (ג) דאמר רבין בר שמואל משמיה דשמואל המוכר שדה לחבירו שלא באחריות אין מעיד לו עליה מפני שמעמידה בפני בעל חובו ודוקא בית או שדה אבל פרה וטלית לא מיבעיא

בסתמא

אבל הכא שמעון ויהודה אינן באין לדון זה עם זה אלא לוי ויהודה ומלוי הוא דמפיק לה יהודה מן הדין דהא ודאי לוי מגזלן קנאה וכיון דמן הדין אנו מחזיקין ליהודה בהאי שדה כשיבא שמעון (א) לריב עמו דיינינן אוקי תרי לבהדי תרי ואוקי ארעא בחזקת יהודה והלכך אין מעיד לו שמעון ללוי אם יודע שום עדות שפוסל עדיו של יהודה או שמעיד הוא ואחד בפניו הודה לו דניחא ליה דתיהוי ביד לוי דהדר ומפיק לה מלוי ע"י עדיו שראו שגזלה ראובן ממנו ובתר הכי אפילו מייתי יהודה סהדי דהא ארעא דידיה היא לא מצי מפיק לה משמעון שכבר פסל שמעון עצמו ועד אחר עמו עדיו של יהודה ועוד כיון דאית ליה נמי לשמעון סהדי דהא ארעא דידיה היא אמור רבנן היכא דקיימא ארעא תיקום: ומקשינן לרב ששת דאוקמה בלוקח מן הגזלן שלא יעיד הנגזל ללוקח וליתני גזלן אם איתא להך ברייתא כדמפרש לה רב ששת למה ליה לתנא לדחוק עצמו למיתני מכר לו בית גזלן ללוקח והלא היה יכול למנות דין זה בגזלן עצמו בלא מכירה דאי אתא יהודה וקמערער עליה דגזלן ראובן אין מעיד לו שמעון הנגזל עליה משום דהוי נוגע בעדות כדפירש והכי הוה ליה למיתני בברייתא ת"ר גזל לו בית גזל לו שדה אין מעיד לו עליה מפני שאחריותו של נגזל עליה דגזלן: ופרקינן משום דבעי למיתני סיפא מכר לו פרה מכר לו טלית. מעיד לו עליה דלא משכחת לה דמעיד לו עליה אלא בגזל ומכר כגון שמכר לו ראובן הגזלן ללוי הלוקח שלא באחריות ואתא יהודה וקאמר שלי היא מעיד לו שמעון הנגזל ללוי הלוקח דלאו דיהודה היא דהא לא הדר לה שמעון ומפיק לה מיניה דלוי ואינו נוגע בעדות וכגון דשמעיניה לשמעון דאייאש בעודה בבית ראובן קודם שמכרה ללוי דהוי יאוש ביד גזלן ושינוי רשות ביד לוקח ואפילו למאן דאמר בפרק הגוזל בתרא יאוש כדי לא קני יאוש ושינוי רשות קונה וקנה הלוקח שאין בו זכות כלל לבעלים הראשונים ולפיכך מעיד לו עליה דאפילו אי מייתי נגזל עדים שגזלה ראובן ממנו לא מפיק מלוי דקנה ביאוש ושינוי רשות ואילו היה נוטלה יהודה מלוי לא מפסיד נגזל בהכי מידי דבלאו הכי לא מצי מפיק לה מלוי וכה"ג לא משכחת לה אלא בגזל ראובן ומכרה ללוי אבל אם לא מכרה ללוי אין מעיד לו לראובן שכל זמן שהן ביד ראובן הגזלן מצי מפיק להו מיניה ואע"ג דאייאש והלכך אין מעיד שמעון לראובן שאינו של יהודה כי נוגע בעדות הוא דאי לא מפיק להו יהודה מיד ראובן הוה מפיק להו מאחר שהכירו בית דין ע"פ עדיו ומשום דלא משכחת לה לסיפא אלא בגזל ומכר תנא נמי רישא בגזל ומכר ולאשמועינן אתא דבגזל ומכר יש חילוק בין מקרקעי למטלטלי דבמקרקעי אינו מעיד דהוי נוגע בעדות דהדרא ליה דאין יאוש ושינוי רשות מועיל בקרקע דקרקע אינה נגזלת ובמטלטלין מעיד דקנה להו לוקח ביאוש ושינוי רשות ולא תהדר ליה להאי מעיד דלאיכא למ"ד בהגוזל דשינוי רשות ואח"כ יאוש לא קניא אבל ביאוש ושינוי רשות הכל מודים דקנה הלוקח ולא הדרא גזילה למרה אלא מן הגזלן יטול הנגזל דמיה: ופרכינן וסיפא נמי. אמאי מעיד לו נגזל ללוקח ומפיק לה מיהודה ומוקי לה ביד לוי נהי דמייאש מגופיה דפרה וטלית ולא יוציאנה מיד לוי דהא קנייה בשינוי רשות שאחר יאוש: מדמי מי מייאש. בתמיה וכי מוחל הוא לגזלן דמי גזילתו הלא נתחייב לו הגזלן דמיה והלכך ניחא ליה שיהיו ביד לוי שיחזור ויטול הדמים מראובן שאילו היה נוטלה יהודה בעדים נמצא שלא היה לו לשמעון חלק בהך פרה וטלית ולא היה גובה מראובן כלום והלכך נוגע בעדותו הוא ולמאי מעיד: לא צריכא דמית גזלן. דהשתא אפילו מדמיה מייאש דיורשין פטורין מלשלם וכ"ש הלוקח דקנייה ביאוש ושינוי רשות דבהיתרא אתו לידיה: דתנן הגוזל כו'. והלכך מעיד דלא נוגע בעדותו הוא: ומאכיל את בניו. אע"פ שנהנו בניו עצמן מן הגזילה פטורין דלאיהו לא גזול מידי: והניח לפניהם. כלומר או שהניח לפניהם גזלה קיימת לאחר מותו פטורין דקנייה ביאוש ושינוי רשות או נמי כשאכלום כדמוקי לה התם: ומקשינן לרב ששת דלוקמה לרישא בגזל ומכר משום סיפא ולוקמה ביורש אם איתא דבגזל ומכר מיירי ובדמית גזלן א"כ מה ראה התנא לדחוק עצמו ולאוקמה בגזלן שמכר אפילו לא מכר הגזלן נמי שלא גזל ומת וכיון דמת הורים לבניו הוה יכול למתני חילוק בין רישא לסיפא כגון ראובן גזל שדה משמעון ומית גזלן וירשו לוי בנו ואתא יהודה וקמערער לא ליזל שמעון ומסהיד ללוי בן ראובן דלאו דיהודה היא דלגבי קרקע אינה נגזלת והדרא ליה מן היורש משום הכי נוגע בעדותו הוא דאי מפיק לה יהודה מיניה דיורש לא הדרא לשמעון דהיכא דקיימא ארעא תיקום אבל בסיפא שגזל ראובן טלית או פרה משמעון ומת וירשו לוי בנו ואתא יהודה וקמערער מעיד לו שמעון עליה דלאיכא יאוש ביד ראובן ושינוי רשות ביד לוי יורש דרשות יורש כרשות לוקח דמי ולא תיהדר ליה לנגזל לא פרה ולא דמיה ולא הוי נוגע בעדות והכי הו"ל למתני גזל לו בית והורים לבנו אין מעיד לו כו' גזל לו פרה והורים כו' והאי דקאמר ולוקמה ביורש לאו דוקא אלא ליתני יורש ולאג סיפא דמקשי ליה לרב ששת דמפרש ומוקי לה בגזלן קאמר ולוקמה ביורש ומיהו ביורש לא מצי לאוקומה דהא קתני מכר אלא א"כ מתרץ לה למתני הורים: הניחא למ"ד. בהגוזל בתרא עלה דהך משנה רשות יורש דגזלן לאו כרשות לוקח מגזלן דמי דלאו גבי לוקח איכא יאוש ושינוי רשות וקני לגוזל רשותא אחריתי היא ואילו יורש כרעיה דאבוה וכרשות גזלן מורישו דמי ולא קניה ביאוש גרידא דהא שינוי רשות ליכא גבי יורש וכל היכא דאיתא הדרא בעין לנגזל והך משנה דקתני והניח לפניהם פטורין מוקי לה התם כשאכלום דלא הוי גזילה קיימת והלכך לא מיתוקמא הך סיפא ביורש דלא מצי מעיד לו דגזל ליורש עליה משום דהדרא ליה פרה וטלית לנגזל אם תעמוד ביד יורש ונוגע בעדות הוא: כרשות לוקח. דקנייה ואע"פ שגזלה קיימת דקתני והניח לפניהם פטורין דמשמע אפילו גזילה קיימת: מאי איכא למימר. ליתני גזל והורים אמאי תני גזל ומכר אלא לאו ש"מ דמוקמתא נמי בתר גזלן מוקי לה רב ששת: ועוד קשיא ליה לאביי. במאי דמוקי לה רב ששת בגזל ומכר והולכך לפרש מפני שאחריותו עליו מפני אחריות חכם יש מעיד עליו לדלאיך שהוא מעיד עליו דהיינו לוקח ולא מלינו בגמרא שום אחריותו עליו מפורש כן עליו לוקח אלא עליו דמוכר מפני שאחריותו של אילך דמוכר עליו והכי הוה ליה למיתני מכר לו בית מכר לו שדה אין מעיד לו עליה מפני שאחריותו מכר לו פרה מכר לו טלית מעיד לו עליה מפני שאינה חוזרת לו: אלא כדרבין בר שמואל. אתא לאשמועינן רישא דהך ברייתא ולא בגזל ומכר מיירי ואע"ג דליכא הכי כדלעיל מיהו ברייתא לאו בהכי איירי אלא במוכר קרקע שלו שהיתה משועבדת לבעל חוב ומכרה ללוקח זה ואתא איניש עלמא וקמערער דלא יעיד לו המוכר ללוקח מפני שאחריותו של בעל חוב עליו דמוכר לגבות מקרקע זה והלכך ניחא ליה דתיקון ביד הלוקח דהדר עלה בעל חוב ולא ליהוי מוכר לוה רשע ולא ישלם וכנגד לוקח לא ליהוי לוה רשע שהרי לא באחריות מכר לו והלכך אין מעיד דנוגע בעדות הוא אבל בסיפא מכר לו פרה וטלית ללוקח ואתא איניש עלמא וקמערער מעיד לו מוכר ללוקח עליה וכגון שמכרה לו שלא באחריות מפני שאין אחריותו דבעל חוב עליו דלוה המוכר לגבות מטלטלין שמשעבד ומכר לאחרים אפילו עשאן אפותיקי לבעל חוב ואח"כ מכרן לאחרים כדרבא ואישתכח דלא נוגע בעדות הוא:

בסתמא

דוקא מכר דהוה ליה יאוש ושינוי רשות. פ"ה וכגון שמכר ראובן ללוי שלא באחריות ונראה דפירש כן משום דאי באחריות הוי שמעון נוגע בעדות דאע"ג דהוי יאוש ושינוי רשות מפיק לה שמעון מלוי כיון דאין שום הפסד ללוי שיחזור על ראובן אבל בקרקע (ב) דאינה יאוש ושינוי רשות הדרא ליה כדפ"ה דאין מועיל יאוש (ג) בקרקע וקשה לר"י דבירושל' (דכלאים פ"ז) אמר דיאוש מועיל בקרקע דאע"פ שאינה נגזלת מ"מ מהני בה יאוש וגבי עבד משמע בהשולח (גיטין דף לט:) דמהני ביה יאוש אע"ג דאיתקש לקרקע ובשמעתין דסיקריקון (שם דף נח:) אור"י דמוכח נמי כן ונראה דמיירי שלא נתייאש והוה מצי לפלוגי נמי בפרה וטלית בין לפני יאוש בין לאחר יאוש אלא מילתא דשכיחא נקט דבקרקע אין רגילין להתייאש כשישראל גזלה שאם לא יוכל להוציאה מידו משום דלא ליית דינא יוציאנה מיד בנו: **ונוקמה** ביורש. וא"ת והא יורש אין מעיד לו עליה דהדרא ליה כדאמר בהגוזל בתרא (ב"ק דף קיא:) דכל דבר המסויים כגון פרה וטלית חייבין להחזיר מפני כבוד אביהם וי"ל דהא אוקימנא בריש הגוזל קמא (שם דף צד:) כשעשה תשובה ולא הספיק להחזיר עד שמת והכא איירי בלא עשה תשובה: **אלא** כדרבין בר שמואל. ואיירי ברייתא דוקא שלא באחריות דאז יכול להעיד על פרה וטלית ומילתא דשמואל איירי בכל ענין ורבותא נקט אפי' שלא באחריות:

עשה

עין משפט נר מצוה

קלב א ב מיי' פט"ו מהל' עדות הל' ג סמג לאוין קט טוש"ע ח"מ סי' לז סעיף יז:

קמ ג מיי' פ"ה מהל' גזילה הל' ה סמג עשין עג טוש"ע ח"מ סי' שסא סעיף ז:

קמא ד מיי' שם פ"ב הל' א סמג שם טוש"ע ח"מ סי' שנג סעיף ד וסי' שסא סעיף ז וסי' שסב סעיף א:

רבינו גרשום

ומקשי' מאי דוחקיה לאוקמיה להא ברייתא בגזל ומכר **לוקמה בגזלן** לחוד. כגון ראובן שגזל שדה משמעון ואתי לוי ומערער עלה דאמר שלי היא לא ליזל שמעון ולצטרף עם עד אחד לאסהודי לראובן דאינה של לוי משום דניחא ליה לשמעון דתיקום ברשות דראובן דהדרא ליה דהיינו מפני שאחריותו עליו על ראובן שגזלה ממנו שיחזירה לו דאי לא קא מסהיד ליה שמעון ומפיק ליה לוי לראובן בכח עדים שיש לו שהשדה שלו היא אע"ג דמייתי שמעון שוב סהדי דנגזלה מיניה לא מצי מפיק לה מיניה כדאמר לעיל דאמרי' ארעא היכא דקיימא תיקום ביד לוי ולהכי נוגע בעדות הוא: ומשני מש"ה לא מצי לאוקמא בגזלן בלא מכר **משום דקא בעי למיתנא סיפא וכו'.** דבסיפא לא סגי דלא מוקמה אלא בגזל ומכר **דדוקא מכר** דמש"ה מעיד לו **דהוה ליה יאוש** בעלים ביד גזלן דשמעיניה לבעל אבידה דמייאש **ושינוי רשות** ביד לוקח. דאפי' למאן דאמר אע"ג דמייאש לא נפקא מרשותיה דנגזל היכא דאיכא יאוש ושינוי רשות מודי דנפקא לה מרשותיה דבעלים משום הכי מעיד לו עליה: **אבל אי לא מכר.** דודאי **הדרא ליה** דליכא שינוי רשות **לא** מצי לאסהודי משום דנוגע בעדות הוא מש"ה איצטריך מכר דאיכא יאוש ושינוי רשות דלא הדרא לה ולהכי מעיד עליה דאין נוגע בעדות. וכיון דאיצטריך למיתני בסיפא גזל ומכר דאיכא שינוי רשות א) אפ"ה לא מייאש שמעון דקסבר קרקע אינה נגזלת ולהכי נוגע בדבר דניחא ליה דתיקום בידא דלוי דהדרא ליה. ומקשי' **וסיפא** בפרה וטלית אמאי מעיד עליה **נהי דמגופה** של טלית **מייאש** הואיל דאיכא יאוש ושינוי רשות מן **דמיו** של טלית **מי מייאש** והא אכתי תבע ליה דמיו ונוגע בעדותו הוי דניחא ליה דתיקום ברשותא דלוי כי היכי דליפרע ליה ראובן דמי גזילתו דאי הוה מפיק לה יהודה מן לוי בראיית עדים הוה אמר ליה ראובן לשמעון מה אתה מבקש ממני והלא לא היתה שלך אלא של יהודה היא שהוציאה מן לוי בכח עדים שהיא שלו ומש"ה נוגע בעדותו הוא: **לא צריכא דמית גזלן.** דגזלה מש"ה מיאש נמי מדמים דיורשין פטורין מלשלם וה"ה ללוקח ומש"ה מצי מעיד דלא נגע בעדותו. ומקשי' ואכתי אמאי מוקים לברייתא בגזל ומכר **ונוקמיה ביורש** כגון ראובן גזל שדה משמעון והניחה ליורשו. ואתי לוי וקא מערער עלה דלא ליזל שמעון ומסהיד לבן ראובן דלאו דלוי היא דקסבר קרקע אינה נגזלת ואין יכול להניחה ליורשיו והדרא לי וכן נמי נוקמא לסיפא ביורש כגון ראובן שגזל פרה וטלית משמעון והורישה לבנו לסהיד ליה שמעון: **הא ניחא למאן דאמר רשות יורש לאו כרשות לוקח** מגזלן **דמי.** דלגבי לוקח מגזלן איכא יאוש ושנוי רשות אחריתי משא"כ גבי יורש דליכא שינוי רשות דרשות יורש כרשות גזלן דמי לא קנאה דאין כאן שינוי רשות מש"ה לא מתוקמא ביורש דאפי' לגבי פרה וטלית לא מצי מסהיד ליה דהוי ליה נוגע בעדות דעדיין לא נפקא מרשותיה דנגזל: **אלא למאן דאמר רשות יורש כרשות לוקח דמי.** דחשיב שינוי רשות **מאי איכא למימר** אכתי נוקמה ביורש וגבי רישא להכי אין מעיד אע"ג דקרקע ברשות יורש היא לא הויא שינוי רשו' דקרקע לא ניידא ואינה נגזלת ובסיפא גבי מטלטלי הוי רשות יורש שינוי רשות ולהכי מצי מעיד. **ועוד אביי מקשה קושיא** אחריתי בהאי שמעתא אי ס"ד כדקאמרת דבגזל ומכר מיירי הברייתא מאי היא דקתני רישא **מפני שאחריותו עליו** ומאי **מפני שאין אחריותו עליו** דקתני סיפא הכי **איבעי ליה** למיתני אין מעיד **מפני שחוזרת לו** לנגזל ומעיד **מפני שאינה חוזרת לו** כדקאמרת דניחא ליה דהדרא לו אלא מדלא קתני הכי ש"מ דלאו בגזלן ולא ביורש מיירי **אלא בדרבין** דאמר **רבין בר שמואל כו' מפני שמעמידה בפני בעל חוב שלו** שקרקע זו שמכר שלא באחריות היתה משועבדת לבעל חובו ועכשיו כשמכרה שלא באחריות אי אתי מערער וקא מערער לא מצי המוכר לאסהודי ליה משום דניחא לי' דקיימא ברשותיה דלוקח כדי שימצא אותה בעל חוב בידו של לוקח ויגבה אותה ממנו והיינו מפני שאחריותו עליו שאם לא היה מוצא בעל חוב לטרוף קרקע מן הלוקח היה חוזר עליו.

מסורת הש"ס

א) ב"ק קיא:, ב) [שם], ג) [לעיל מג.]

הגהות הב"ח

(א) רשב"ם ד"ה (בדף הקודם) ואב"א וכו' כשיבא שמעון לדון עמו כצ"ל והד"א: (ב) תוס' ד"ה דוקא וכו' אבל בקרקע אע"ג דליכא יאוש ושינוי רשות וכו': (ג) בא"ד דאין מועיל יאוש ושינוי רשות בקרקע:

ליקוטי רש"י

הגוזל ומאכיל וכו' והניח לפניהם. או שהניח לפניהם (הגזלה) [בגזלה] [ב"ח] קיימת. רשות יורש כרשות לוקח דמי. והוה לה כרשות אחרת וכיון דאוקימנא למתניתין לאחר יאוש קני להו יתמי ביאוש ושינוי רשות דהא יורש כדי לא קני מדלא קתני פטורה לאבוהון [ב"ק קיא.]. המוכר שדה לחבירו שלא באחריות. וכל שכן באחריות. אין מעיד לו עליה. אם מערער עם על העמידה לו ואע"ג דלא הוה מפסיד לוקח לא הדר עליה מפני שמעמידה כו'. ובדליכא ליה ארעא אחריתי מוקים לה לקמן בשמעתין דלא ניחא ליה דניהוי לוה רשע ולא ישלם [רשב"ם לעיל מג.].

חשק שלמה על רבינו גרשום

א) נראה דל"ל תני רישא נמי בגזל ומכר וס"ה לא מייאש וכו'.

stolen object or its value, and he may therefore testify about it.

The Gemara objects:

וְלוּקְמָהּ בְּיוֹרֵשׁ – But if the Baraisa's latter ruling applies only in a case in which the thief died, **let [the Baraisa] teach** this law **in reference to the** thief's **heir,** rather than a buyer. That is, if Reuven stole from Shimon and died, and Yehudah now challenges Reuven's *heir,* Shimon can testify in his behalf, since he cannot recover the object or its value in any case! Why speak of a case in which the thief *sold* the object before he died?[10]

The Gemara qualifies its question:

הָנִיחָא לְמַאן דְּאָמַר – **This is understandable according to the one who says** **רְשׁוּת יוֹרֵשׁ לָאו כִּרְשׁוּת לוֹקֵחַ דָּמֵי** – that **the possession of an heir is** ***not*** **comparable to the possession of a buyer,**[11] **שַׁפִּיר** – for then **it is clear** that the Baraisa *had* to speak of a sale, since the transfer of the stolen object to the heirs alone would not prevent Shimon from recovering the object.[12] **אֶלָּא לְמַאן דְּאָמַר** – **But according to the one who says** **רְשׁוּת יוֹרֵשׁ כִּרְשׁוּת לוֹקֵחַ דָּמֵי** – that **the possession of an heir** ***is*** **comparable to the possession of a buyer,** and the transfer to the heirs *is* sufficient to preclude Shimon's recovery of the stolen object,[13] **מַאי אִיכָּא לְמֵימַר** – **what is there to say?** Since the Baraisa's ruling must in any case speak of a case in which the thief has died,[14] why does it not state its ruling in respect to the thief's heirs, rather than a buyer?

The Gemara notes another difficulty with Rav Sheishess's interpretation of the Baraisa:

וְעוֹד קַשְׁיָא לֵיהּ לְאַבָּיֵי – **And Abaye was bothered by another difficulty** with this interpretation. **מִפְּנֵי שֶׁאַחֲרָיוּתוֹ עָלָיו וְאֵין אַחֲרָיוּתוֹ עָלָיו** – Should the Baraisa have given as its reason for allowing or disallowing the testimony: **"because his ultimate design is on him" or "his ultimate design is not on him"?**[15] **מִפְּנֵי שֶׁהִיא חוֹזֶרֶת לוֹ וְאֵינָהּ חוֹזֶרֶת לוֹ מִיבָּעֵי לֵיהּ** – **It should have** stated: **"because it** [the stolen property] **can return to him" or "because it cannot return to him"!**[16]

Because of these two difficulties, the Gemara rejects Rav Sheishess's interpretation of the Baraisa, and offers an entirely different interpretation:[17]

אֶלָּא כִּדְרַבִין בַּר שְׁמוּאֵל – **Rather,** the first ruling of the Baraisa means to teach **as Ravin bar Shmuel** taught. **דְּאָמַר רָבִין בַּר שְׁמוּאֵל מִשְּׁמֵיהּ דִּשְׁמוּאֵל** – **For Ravin bar Shmuel said in the name of Shmuel:** **הַמּוֹכֵר שָׂדֶה לַחֲבֵירוֹ שֶׁלֹּא בְּאַחֲרָיוּת** – **If one sells a field to his fellow without a guarantee,**[18] **אֵין מֵעִיד לוֹ עָלֶיהָ** – **[the seller] may not testify in [the buyer's] behalf regarding [the field],** **מִפְּנֵי שֶׁמַּעֲמִידָהּ בִּפְנֵי בַּעַל חוֹבוֹ** – **for [the seller] makes [the field] available to his creditor** by maintaining it in the buyer's possession,[19] and his testimony is therefore suspect. This is the Baraisa's teaching as well.[20]

The Gemara now explains the Baraisa's ruling regarding movable property:

וְדַוְקָא בַּיִת אוֹ שָׂדֶה – **Now** this is true **only with regard to a house or a field,** **אֲבָל פָּרָה וְטַלִּית** – **but** with regard to **a cow or a cloak,** **לֹא מִיבָּעְיָא** – it goes without saying

NOTES

speaks of a case in which the object no longer exists. They have no obligation to repay the value of the object because they did not steal it. Since only the father has an obligation to repay, the debt can be collected only from real property. Only the real property left by a person is subject to collection for the obligations he leaves behind, not his movable property. The Mishnah speaks of a case in which the father left no real estate (see Gemara there).

10. Once Rav Sheishess is forced to explain that the Baraisa is speaking of an instance in which the thief died (so that Shimon cannot recover even his money), why is it necessary for the Baraisa to speak also of a case in which the thief *sold* it? The Baraisa should have simply spoken of an instance in which the thief died and left the object to his heirs. The passage of the object to their possession should also count as a "change of possession," and this in itself should prevent Shimon from ever reclaiming it. Thus, even without a sale, the object is forever lost to Shimon, and he should be permitted to testify about it! (*Rashbam*).

11. Although a change of possession that comes about through a purchase (or gift) is sufficient to combine with the original owner's abandonment and cause the stolen object to be "acquired" by the purchaser and lost to the original owner forever, there is a dispute whether this applies to a change of possession effected by inheritance (*Bava Kamma* 111b). One opinion is that when a son takes over his father's property by inheritance, his possession is considered merely an extension of his father's possession and not a *change* of possession. The Gemara explains that according to this opinion, the preceding question does not apply (*Rashbam*).

12. Since the heir's possession is not considered a change of possession, and mere abandonment is not sufficient to prevent Shimon from reclaiming the object, Shimon would be disqualified from testifying about it. Thus, even though the Baraisa must be speaking of a case in which the thief died (to explain why Shimon cannot recover the value of the object), it also needs to speak of a case in which he sold the stolen object before he died (to explain why Shimon cannot reclaim the object itself).

[The Gemara in *Bava Kamma* (111b) explains that according to this view, the reason the Mishnah there exempts the thief's heirs from having to return anything to the victim is because it speaks of a case in which the stolen object no longer exists, having been consumed or otherwise destroyed. Thus, the only issue is one of payment, and from this they are exempt, as explained in note 9 (*Rashbam*).]

13. According to this opinion, inheritance is considered a change of possession. Thus, the inheritance, together with Shimon's abandonment, prevents him from being able to reclaim the object.

14. Since only then is Shimon unable to recoup even the value of his object (see note 9).

15. See 43b note 10.

16. According to Rav Sheishess the word עָלָיו (literally: on him) refers to the buyer; i.e. Shimon may not testify because his ultimate design is to retake the property from the buyer. This is not the standard translation of אַחֲרָיוּתוֹ עָלָיו, which usually means the responsibility is upon the seller (to make good his guarantee). The more correct way for the Baraisa to have expressed the reason for Shimon's disqualification would have been to state: "because the field can return to him," instead of referring to his ultimate designs on the buyer (*Rashbam*; see *Ritva*).

17. This is not to say that the Gemara concludes that the law stated by Rav Sheishess is incorrect. The Gemara merely concludes that the Baraisa is not dealing with this case (*Rashbam*).

Rather, the Baraisa is dealing with a simple case of one person selling something to another. The Baraisa teaches that in the case of movable property he can testify in his behalf (regarding the ownership of the object), but not in the case of real property.

18. I.e. the deed specifically stated that the sale was not guaranteed (see 43a note 10).

19. Ravin bar Shmuel's statement was explained on 43a; see notes 9, 11, 12.

20. According to this interpretation, the Baraisa speaks of a case in which the buyer's right to the field was then challenged by someone who claims that the property never belonged to the seller. The Baraisa teaches that if the seller exempted himself from future liability of *any* kind, he cannot testify on behalf of the buyer, because it is still in the seller's interest to maintain the field in the buyer's possession and thereby keep it available to his [the seller's] creditors [see 43a note 9] (*Rashbam*).

ולוקמה בגזלן משום דקא בעי למיתנא סיפא מכר לו פרה מכר לו טלית א דדוקא מכר דהוה ליה יאוש ושינוי רשות אבל לא מכר דהדרא ליה לא תנא רישא נמי מכר וסיפא נמי נהי דמייאש מגופיה מדמיה מי מייאש לא צריכא ב דמית גזלן דתנן (א) ג הגוזל ומאכיל את בניו והניח לפניהם פטורים מלשלם ולוקמה ביורש הניחא למאן דאמר (ב) ד רשות יורש לאו כרשות לוקח דמי שפיר אלא למאן דאמר רשות יורש כרשות לוקח דמי מאי איכא למימר ועוד קשיא ליה לאביי מפני שאחריותו עליו ואין אחריותו עליו מפני שהיא חוזרת לו ואינה חוזרת לו מיבעי ליה אלא כדרבין בר שמואל (ג) דאמר רבין בר שמואל משמיה דשמואל המוכר שדה לחבירו שלא באחריות אין מעיד לו עליה מפני שמעמידה בפני בעל חובו ודוקא בית או שדה אבל פרה וטלית לא מיבעיא בסתמא

אבל הכא שמעון ויהודה אינן באין לדון זה עם זה אלא לוי ויהודה ומלוי הוא דמפיק לה יהודה מן הדין דהא ודאי לוי מגזלן קנאה וכיון דמן הדין אנו מחזיקין ליהודה בהאי שדה כשיפה שמעון (א) לריב עמו דיינינן אוקי תרי לבהדי תרי ואוקי ארעא בחזקת יהודה והלכך אין מעיד לו שמעון ללוי אם לוי יודע שום עדות שפוסל עדיו של יהודה או שמעיד הוא ואחד בפניו הודה לו דניחא ליה דמיהוי ביד לוי דיהדר ומפיק לה מלוי ע"י עדיו שראו שגזלה ראובן ממנו ובתר הכי אפילו מייתי יהודה סהדי דהא ארעא דידיה היא לא מצי מפיק לה משמעון שכבר פסל שמעון עצמו ועד אחר עמו עדיו של יהודה ועוד כיון דאית ליה נמי לשמעון סהדי דהא ארעא דידיה היא אמור רבנן היכא דקיימא ארעא תיקום: ומקשינן לרב ששת דלוקמה בלוקח מן הגזלן שלא יעיד הנגזל ללוקח וליתני גזלן אם איתא להך ברייתא כדמפרש לה רב ששת למה ליה לתנא לדחוק עצמו ולמיתני מכר לו בית גזלן ללוקח והלא היה יכול למתני דין זה בגזלן עצמו בלא מכירה דאי אתא יהודה וקמערער עליה דגזלן ראובן אין מעיד לו שמעון הנגזל עליה משום דהוי נוגע בעדות כדפירש והכי הוה ליה למיתני בברייתא ת"ר גזל לו בית גזל לו שדה אין מעיד לו עליה מפני שאחריותו של נגזל עליה דגזלן: ופרקינן משום דבעי למיתני סיפא מכר לו פרה מכר לו טלית. מעיד לו עליה דלא משכחת לה דמעיד לו עליה אלא בגזל ומכר כגון שמכר לו ראובן הגזלן ללוי הלוקח שלא באחריות ואתא יהודה וקאמר שלי היא מעיד לו שמעון הנגזל ללוי הלוקח דלאו דיהודה היא דהא לא הדר שמעון ומפיק לה מיניה דלוי ואינו נוגע בעדות וכגון דשמעיניה לשמעון דאייאש בעודה בבית ראובן קודם שמכרה ללוי דהוי יאוש ביד גזלן ושינוי רשות ביד לוקח דאפילו למאן דאמר בפרק הגוזל בתרא יאוש כדי לא קני יאוש ושינוי רשות קונה וקנה הלוקח שאין בו זכות כלל לבעלים הראשונים ולפיכך מעיד לו עליה דאפילו אי מייתי נגזל סהדי שגזלה ראובן ממנו לא מפיק מלוי דקנה ביאוש ושינוי רשות ואילו היה נוטלה יהודה מלוי לא מפסיד נגזל בהכי מידי דבלאו הכי לא מצי מפיק לה מלוי וכה"ג לא משכחת לה אלא בגזל ראובן ומכרה ללוי אבל אם לא מכרה ללוי אין מעיד לו לראובן שכל זמן שהן ביד ראובן הגזלן מצי מפיק להו נגזל מיניה ואע"ג דאייאש והלכך אין מעיד שמעון לראובן שאינו של יהודה כי נוגע בעדות הוא דמיד ראובן מצי מפיק להו אבל מיד יהודה לא מצי מפיק להו מאחר שיזכוהו בית דין ע"פ עדיו ומשום דלא משכחת לה לסיפא אלא בגזל ומכר תנא נמי רישא בגזל ומכר ולאשמועינן אתא דבגזל ומכר יש חילוק בין מקרקעי למטלטלי דבמקרקעי אינו מעיד דהוי נוגע בעדות דהדרא ליה דאין יאוש ושינוי רשות מועיל בקרקע דקרקע אינה נגזלת ובמטלטלין מעיד דקנה לה לוקח ביאוש ושינוי רשות ולא תהדר ליה להאי מעיד דאיכא למ"ד בהגוזל דשינוי רשות ואפ"ה יאוש לא קניא אבל ביאוש ושינוי רשות הכל מודים דקנה הלוקח ולא הדרא גזילה למרה אלא מן הגזלן יטול הנגזל דמיה: ופרכינן **וסיפא נמי**. אמאי מעיד לו נגזל ללוקח ומפיק לה מיהודה ומוקי לה ביד לוי נהי דמייאש מגופה דפרה וטלית ולא יוציאנה מיד לוי דהא קנייה בשינוי רשות שאחר יאוש: **מדמי מי מייאש**. בתמיה וכי מוחל הוא לגזלן דמי גזילתו והלא נתחייב לו הגזלן דמיה והלכך ניחא ליה דתיקו ביד לוי שיחזור ויטול הדמים מראובן שאילו היה נוטלה יהודה בעדים נמצא שלא היה לו לשמעון חלק בהך פרה וטלית ולא היה גובה מראובן כלום והלכך נוגע בעדותו הוא ואמאי מעיד: **לא צריכא דמית גזלן**. דהשתא אפילו מדמיה מייאש דיורשין פטורין מלשלם וכ"ש הלוקח דקנייה ביאוש ושינוי רשות דבהיתרא אתו לידיה: **דתנן הגוזל כו'**. והלכך מעיד דלא נוגע בעדותו הוא: **ומאכיל את בניו**. אע"פ שנהנו בניו עצמן מן הגזילה פטורין דלאיהו לא גזול מידי: **והניח לפניהם**. כלומר או שהניח לפניהם גזילה קיימת לאחר מותו פטורין דקנייה ביאוש ושינוי רשות אי נמי כשאכלום כדמוקי לה התם: ומקשינן לרב ששת דלוקמה לרישא בגזל ומכר משום סיפא ולוקמה ביורש אם איתא דבגזל ומכר מיירי ובדמית גזלן א"כ מה ראה התנא לדחוק עצמו ולשנות שיטתו בגזלן שמכר אפילו לא מכר הגזלן נמי אלא גזל ומת וכיון דמת הוריש לבניו היה יכול למצוא חילוק בין רישא לסיפא כגון ראובן שגזל שדה משמעון ומית גזלן וירשו לוי בנו ואתא יהודה וקמערער לא ליזיל שמעון ומסהיד ללוי בן ראובן דלאו דיהודה היא דקרקע אינה נגזלת והדרא ליה מן היורש משום הכי נוגע בעדותו הוא דאי מפיק לה יהודה מיניה דיורש לא הדרא לשמעון דהיכא דקיימא ארעא תיקום אבל בסיפא שגזל ראובן טלית או פרה משמעון ומת וירשו לוי בנו ואתא יהודה וקמערער מעיד לו שמעון עליה דאיכא יאוש ביד ראובן ושינוי רשות ביד לוי יורש דרשות יורש כרשות לוקח דמי ולא תיהדר ליה לנגזל לא פרה ולא דמיה ולא הוי נוגע בעדות והכי הו"ל לתנא למיתני גזל לו בית והוריש לבנו אין מעיד כו' גזל לו פרה והוריש כו' והאי דקאמר ולוקמה ביורש לאו דוקא אלא ליתני יורש ואגב שיטפא דמקשי ליה לרב ששת דמפרש ומוקי לה בגזלן קאמר ולוקמה ביורש ומיהו ביורש לא מצי לאוקומה דהא קתני מכר אא"כ מתרץ לה למיתני הוריש: **הניחא למ"ד**. בהגוזל בתרא עלה דהך משנה רשות יורש דגזלן לאו כרשות לוקח מגזלן דמי דאילו גבי לוקח איכא יאוש ושינוי רשות וקני דלוקח רשותא אחריתי היא ואילו יורש כרעיה דאבוה וכברשות גזלן מורישו דמי ולא קניה ביאוש גרידא דהא שינוי רשות ליכא גבי יורש וכל היכא דאיתא הדרא בעין לנגזל והך משנה דקתני והניח לפניהן פטורין מוקי לה התם כשאכלום דלא הויא גזילה קיימת והלכך פטורין והלכך לא מיתוקמא הך סיפא ביורש דלא מצי למיתני ומעיד לו נגזל ליורש עליה משום דהדרא ליה פרה וטלית לנגזל אם תעמוד ביד יורש ונוגע בעדות הוא: **כרשות לוקח**. דקנייה יורש ואע"פ שגזילה קיימת והניח לפניהם פטורין כדקתני דמשמע אפילו גזילה קיימת: **מאי איכא למימר**. ליתני גזל והוריש אמאי תני גזל ומכר בלא מכר נמי מתוקמא שפיר כיון דבמית גזלן מוקי לה רב ששת: **ועוד קשיא ליה לאביי**. במאי דמוקי לה רב ששת בגזל ומכר והולך לפרש מפני שאחריותו עליו מפני שאחריות וזכות יש למעיד עליו לאידך שהוא מעיד לו דהיינו לוקח ולא מצינו בגמרא שום אחריותו עליו מפורש כן עליו דלוקח אלא עליו דמוכר מפני שאחריותו של אידך עליו דמוכר והכי הוה ליה למיתני מכר לו בית מכר לו שדה אין מעיד לו עליה מפני שחוזרת לו מכר לו פרה מכר לו טלית מעיד עליה מפני שאינה חוזרת לו: **אלא כדרבין בר שמואל**. אתא לאשמועינן רישא דהך ברייתא ולא בגזל ומכר מיירי ואע"ג דדינא הכי כדלעיל מיהו ברייתא לאו בהכי איירי אלא במוכר קרקע שלו שהיתה משועבדת לבעל חוב ומכרה ללוקח זה ואתא איניש מעלמא וקמערער דלא יעיד לו המוכר ללוקח מפני שאחריותו של בעל חוב עליו דמוכר לגבות מקרקע זה והלכך ניחא ליה דתיקו ביד הלוקח דהדר עלה בעל חוב ולא ליהוי מוכר לוה רשע ולא ישלם וכנגד לוקח לא ליהוי לוה רשע שהרי לא באחריות מכר לו והלכך אין מעיד דנוגע בעדות הוא אבל בסיפא מכר לו פרה וטלית ללוקח ואתא איניש מעלמא וקמערער מעיד לו מוכר ללוקח עליה וכגון שמכרה לו שלא באחריות מפני שאין אחריותו דבעל חוב עליו דלוה המוכר לגבות מטלטלין שמשעבד ומכר לאחרים אפילו עשאן אפותיקי לבעל חוב ואפ"ה מכרן לאחרים כדרבא ואשתכח דלא נוגע בעדות הוא:

בסתמא

דוקא מכר דהוה ליה יאוש ושינוי רשות. פ"ה וכגון שמכר ראובן ללוי שלא באחריות ונראה דפירש כן משום דאי באחריות הוי שמעון נוגע בעדות דאע"ג דהוי יאוש ושינוי רשות מפיק לה שמעון מלוי כיון דאין שום הפסד ללוי שיחזור על ראובן אבל בקרקע (ב) דליכא יאוש ושינוי רשות הדרא ליה כדפ"ה דאין מועיל יאוש (ג) בקרקע וקשה לר"י דבירושל' (דכלאים פ"ז) אמר דיאוש מועיל בקרקע דאע"פ שאינה נגזלת מ"מ מהני בה יאוש וגבי עבד משמע בהשולח (גיטין דף לט:) דמהני ביה יאוש אע"ג דאיתקש לקרקע ובשמעתין דסיקריקון (שם דף נח:) אור"י דמוכח נמי כן ונראה דמיירי שלא נתייאש והוה מצי לפלוגי נמי בפרה וטלית בין לפני יאוש בין לאחר יאוש אלא מילתא דשכיחא נקט דבקרקע אין רגילין להתייאש כשישראל גזלה שאם לא יוכל להוציאה מידו משום דלא ליית דינא יוציאנה מיד בנו: **ונוקמה** ביורש. וא"ת והא יורש אין מעיד לו עליה דהדרא ליה כדאמר בהגוזל בתרא (ב"ק דף קיא:) דכל דבר המסוים כגון פרה וטלית חייבין להחזיר מפני כבוד אביהם וי"ל דהא אוקימנא בריש הגוזל קמא (שם דף לד:) כשעשה תשובה ולא הספיק להחזיר עד שמת והכא איירי בלא עשה תשובה: **אלא** כדרבין בר שמואל. ואיירי ברייתא דוקא שלא באחריות דאז יכול להעיד על פרה וטלית ומילתא דשמואל איירי בכל ענין ורבותא נקט אפי' שלא באחריות:

עשה

מסורת הש"ס

א) ב"ק קיא:, ב) [שם], ג) [לעיל מג.]

הגהות הב"ח

(א) רשב"ם ד"ה (בדף הקודם) ואכ"א וכו' כשיפה שמעון לדין עמו כצ"ל והד"א: (ב) תוס' ד"ה דוקא וכו' אבל בקרקע אע"ג דליכא יאוש ושינוי רשות וכו': (ג) בא"ד דאין מועיל יאוש ושינוי רשות בקרקע:

ליקוטי רש"י

הגוזל ומאכיל וכו' והניח לפניהם. או שהניח לפניהם (הגזילה) [שהגזילה] [ב"ח] קיימת. רשות יורש כרשות לוקח דמי. והוא לא כרשות אחרת וכיון דאוקימנא למתניתין לאחר יאוש קני להו יתמי ביאוש ושינוי רשות [ב"ק קיא.]. המוכר שדה לחבירו שלא באחריות. וכל שכן באחריות. אין מעיד לו עליה. מפני שמעמידה כו'. ובדליכא ליה ארעא אחריתי מוקמינן לה לקמן כשמעתין דלא ניחא ליה למיהוי לוה רשע ולא ישלם [רשב"ם לעיל מג.].

חשק שלמה על רבינו גרשום

א) נראה דצ"ל תני רישא נמי בגזל ומכר ואפ"ה לא מייאש וכו'.

עין משפט נר מצוה

קלט א ב מיי' פט"ו מהל' עדות הל' ג סמג לאוין קט טוש"ע ח"מ סי' לז סעיף יז:

קמ ג מיי' פ"ה מהל' גזילה הל' ה סמג עשין עג טוש"ע ח"מ סי' שסא סעיף ז:

קמא ד מיי' שם פ"ב הל' א סמג שם טוש"ע ח"מ סי' שנג סעיף ד וסי' שסא סעיף ז וסי' שסב סעיף א:

רבינו גרשום

ומקשי' מאי דוחקיה לאוקמיה להא ברייתא בגזל ומכר לוקמה בגזלן לחוד. כגון ראובן שגזל שדה משמעון ואתי לוי ומערער עלה דאמר שלי היא לא ליזיל שמעון ולצטרף עם עד אחד לאסהודי לראובן דאינה של לוי משום דניחא ליה לשמעון דתיקום ברשות דראובן דהדרא ליה דהיינו מפני שאחריותו עליו על ראובן שגזלה ממנו שיחזירה לו דאי לא קא מסהיד ליה שמעון ומפיק לה לוי לראובן בכח עדים שיש לו שהשדה שלו היא אע"ג דמייתי שמעון שוב סהדי דנגזלה מיניה לא מצי מפיק לה מיניה כדאמר לעיל דאמרי' ארעא היכא דקיימא תיקום ביד לוי ולהכי נוגע בעדות הוא. ומשני מש"ה לא מצי לאוקמא בגזלן בלא מכר משום דקא בעי למיתנא סיפא וכו'. דבסיפא לא סגי דלא מוקמה אלא בגזל ומכר דדוקא מכר דמש"ה מעיד לו דהוה ליה יאוש בעלים ביד גזלן דשמעיניה לבעל אבידה דמייאש ושינוי רשות ביד לוקח. דאפי' למאן דאמר אע"ג דמייאש לא נפקא מרשותיה דנגזל היכא דאיכא יאוש ושינוי רשות מודי דנפקא מרשותיה דבעלים משום הכי מעיד לו עליה: אבל אי לא מכר. דהדאי הדרא ליה דליכא שינוי רשות לא מצי לאסהודי משום דנוגע בעדות הוא משה"ה איצטריך מכר דאיכא יאוש ושינוי רשות דלא הדרא לה ולהכי מעיד עליה דאין נוגע בעדות. וכיון דאיצטריך למיתני בסיפא גזל ומכר דאיכא שינוי רשות תני נמי ברישא גזל ומכר: (א) אפ"ה לא מייאש שמעון דקסבר קרקע אינה נגזלת ולהכי נוגע בדבר דניחא ליה דתיקום בידא דלוי דהדרא ליה. ומקשי' וסיפא בפרה וטלית אמאי מעיד נהי דמגופה של טלית מייאש הואיל דאיכא יאוש ושינוי רשות מן דמיו של טלית מי מייאש והא אכתי תבע ליה דמיו ונוגע בעדותו הוי דניחא ליה דתיקום ברשותא דלוי כי היכי דליפרע ליה ראובן דמי גזילתו דאי הוה מפיק לה יהודה מן לוי בראיית עדים הוה אמר ליה ראובן לשמעון מה אתה מבקש ממני והלא לא היתה שלך אלא של יהודה היא שהוציאה מן לוי בכח עדים שהיא שלו ומש"ה נוגע בעדותו הוא: לא צריכא דמית גזלן. דגזלה מש"ה מייאש נמי מדמים דיורשין פטורין מלשלם וה"ה ללוקח ומש"ה מצי מעיד דלא נגע בעדותו. ומקשי' ואכתי אמאי מוקים לברייתא בגזל ומכר ונוקמיה ביורש כגון ראובן שגזל שדה משמעון והניחו לוי לורשו. ואתי לוי

וקא מערער עלה דלא ליזיל שמעון ומסהיד לבן ראובן דלאו דלוי היא דקסבר קרקע אינה נגזלת ואין יכול להניחה ליורשיו והדרא לי וכן נמי נוקמא לסיפא ביורש כגון ראובן שגזל פרה וטלית לבנו לסהיד ליה שמעון: הא ניחא למאן דאמר רשות יורש לאו כרשות לוקח מגזלן דמי. [illegible]

בסתמא דלא משתעבדא ליה מאי טעמא מטלטלי נינהו א ומטלטלי לבע"ח לא משתעבדי ואע"ג דכתב ליה מגלימא דעל כתפיה הני מילי דאיתנהו בעינייהו אבל ליתנהו בעינייהו לא אלא ב אפילו עשאו אפותיקי נמי לא מאי טעמא כדרבא א) דאמר רבא ג עשה עבדו אפותיקי ומכרו בעל חוב גובה ממנו ד שורו וחמורו אפותיקי ב) ומכרו אין בעל חוב גובה הימנו מאי טעמא האי אית ליה קלא והא לית ליה קלא וליחוש דלמא אקני ליה מטלטלי אגב מקרקעי דאמר רבה ה אי אקני ליה מטלטלי אגב מקרקעי ג) קני מקרקעי ג) קני מטלטלי ואמר רב חסדא ו והוא דכתב ליה דלא כאסמכתא ודלא כטופסא דשטרי הכא במאי עסקינן כגון שלקח ומכר לאלתר וליחוש דילמא ז דאיקני ד) הוא שמעת מינה ה) דאיקני קנה ומכר קנה והוריש לא משתעבד לא צריכא דקאמרי עדים ידעינן ביה בהאי דלא הוה ליה ארעא מעולם והאמר רב פפא אע"ג דאמור רבנן המוכר שדה לחבירו שלא באחריות ובא בע"ח וטרפה אינו חוזר עליו נמצאת שאינה שלו חוזר עליו הכא במאי עסקינן במכיר בה שהיא בת חמורו ורב זביד אמר ח אפילו נמצאת שאינה שלו אינו חוזר עליו דא"ל להכי זבינו לך שלא באחריות גופא אמר רבין בר בר שמואל משמיה דשמואל ט המוכר שדה לחבירו שלא באחריות אין מעיד לו עליה מפני שמעמידה בפני בעל חובו היכי דמי אי

בסתמא. שלא ייחד לו פרה וטלית בפירוש דלא משתעבדא ליה לבע"ח הך פרה וטלית: **לא משתעבדי.** דלית להו קלא ולא יזהרו לקוחות דלא משתעבדי אין לך אדם שלוקח עוד מטלטלין מחבירו דלמא טרפי להו מיניה: **אלא אפילו עשאן אפותיקי.** להך פרה וטלית שיחדן לו לגבות חובו מהם אם לא יפרענו עד זמן פלוני: **אפותיקי.** פה תהא קאי: **עשה.** לוה עבדו אפותיקי לבעל חובו ומכרו אחרי כן הלוה לאיש אחר: **אית ליה קלא.** אפשר ללקוחות לאנפשייהו: **והא לית ליה קלא.** פרה וטלית ולא ידעו הלקוחות להזהר והלכך מעיד לו עליה דאין מעמידה בפני בעל חובו: ומקשינן ולכתי בפרה וטלית אמאי מעיד וניחוש דלמא אקני ליה האי מוכר מטלטלי אגב מקרקעי לבעל חובו להשתעבד לו לגבות חובו מהן אם לא יפרענו בזמנו וחזר ומכרם וכי מעיד ללוקח שהן שלו נוגע בעדות הוא מפני שמעמידן בפני בעל חובו והיכי אשכחנא דכה"ג משתעבדי מטלטלי לבעל חוב דאמר רבה כו' וגבי מטלטלי מן הלקוחות דנכסים שאין להם אחריות כגון מטלטלין נקנין עם נכסים שיש להן אחריות לענין מתנה בכסף בשטר ובחזקה והוא הדין לענין שעבוד דמיגו דחייל שעבוד אמקרקעי חייל נמי אמטלטלי אבל אקני ליה מטלטלי גרידי בסודר להשתעבד לו לכשיגיע זמנו אם לא יפרענו יגבה מהם לא קני ואפילו בלשון מתנה דכל דאי לא קני דאסמכתא היא ואסמכתא לא קניא בפרק איזהו נשך (ב"מ דף סו:): **ואמר רב חסדא והוא דכתב ליה.** בשטר השעבוד לגמרי משעבד להו למטלטלי בהדי מקרקעי: **דלא כאסמכתא כו'.** דכיון דאין זו מכירה גמורה ולא מתנה ולא משכון אלא שעבוד בעלמא ודמי לאסמכתא דקאמר ליה אם לא אפרע לך לזמן פלוני תגבה מכאן הלכך צריך לכתוב בו לאלומי שטריה דלא כאסמכתא דאסמכתא לא קניא: **טופסי דשטרי.** הוא שטר העשוי להעתיק ממנו שטרות ולא נכתב לגבות בו ואין בו ממש: **הכא במאי עסקינן.** אי

דמלי מעיד כגון שקנה הך פרה וטלית ומיד מכרה בפניו דודאי לא לוה בינתים ולא שעבדם למלוה: **וניחוש דלמא דאיקני אמר ליה.** כלומר אכתי איכא למיחש דאקני ליה להך פרה וטלית למלוה אגב מקרקעי והיכי דמי כגון דמקמי הכי כשלוה כתב למלוה בשטר משעבדנא לך אגב מקרקעי כל נכסי דקנאי ודעתיד אנא למיקני וכשלקח הפרה והטלית אחרי כן נשתעבדו לו מיד ואכתי אמאי מעיד אלא מדלא חיישת להכי איכא למשמע דמי שכותב כן דאקני האומר לחבירו נכסים שאני עתיד לקנות אני מוכר לך או משעבד לך ואחר כן קנה ומכר לאחרים או כתב לו דאיקני והוא קנה אחרי כן ומת והוריש לבניו לא משתעבד להאי שכתב לו דאין אדם מקנה לחבירו דבר שלא בא לידו אע"פ שעתיד לבא ובעיא היא לקמן בפרק מי שמת ולא איפשיטא ומשמע מהכא דלא משתעבד: **לא צריכא.** הא דקאמרי מעיד ולא חיישינן לדלמא אקני ליה מטלטלי אגב מקרקעי כגון דקאמרי עדים ידענא ביה כו' והלכך לא אקני ליה מטלטלי אגב מקרקעי שהרי לא היו לו מקרקעי והלכך מעיד דכיון שמכר לו הך פרה וטלית בלא אחריות וגם אין מעמידה בפני בעל חובו לאו נוגע בעדותו הוא כלל והשתא מתוקמא אפילו בלא לקח ומכר לאלתר והא דלא קאמר אלא לא צריכא משום דאמורא לא תירך הכי לעיל אלא סתם הגמרא תירך כן י) [ושיטה זו נוהגת ברוב המקומות]. ופירש ר"ח ידעינן ביה בהאי דלא הוה ליה ארעא מעולם צריכי לאסהודי הכי זה האיש לא נתפרש ממנו מעודו ועד היום וברי לנו במה שקנה וכי לא קנה קרקע מעולם לא במתנה ולא בקניה כגון הא דגרסינן בהאשה רבה ביבמות (דף פח.) נשאת ואחר כך בא בעלה תצא מזה ומזה אמר רב לא שנו אלא שנשאת כו' ומסקינן בה לא צריכא דאתו תרי ואמרי אנן הוינן בהדיה מכי נפק ועד השתא ואתון לא ידעיתון ליה כו': **נמצאת שאינה שלו.** שהעידו עדים שגזלה המוכר ומכרה לו ובא בעל השדה ונטלה ממנו חוזר לוקח על המוכר ולא הויא מכירה כלל דבשלמא היכא דטרפה בעל חוב הויא מכירה דעביד איניש דזבין ארעא ליומיה בשביל פירות יום אחד כדאמרינן בבבא מציעא (דף יד.) ופירות שאכל שלו הן כדאמר שמואל בפרק שנים אוחזין בטלית (שם דף טו.) בעל חוב גובה את השבח שבח אין פירי לא אבל לוקח מגזלן אמר התם (דף יד:) המוכר שדה לחבירו ונמצאת שאינה שלו אמר שמואל מעות יש לו שבח אין לו ללוקח אלא הדרא ארעא והדרי פירי וכל השבח והלכך כיון דלא מרויח מידי לאו מכר הוא כלל והכא נמי גבי פרה וטלית אמאי מעיד הא איכא למימר דנוגע בעדותו הוא דניחא ליה למוכר דתיקו ביד לוקח דאי מפיק ליה מיניה מערער בעדים שמעידין שהיא של מערער הרי נמצא שאינה שלו של מוכר אלא גזלה מהאי מערער ומכרה לזה ויחזור לוקח עליו דמוכר ואף על גב דשלא באחריות מכר: **ומשני במכיר בה.** הלוקח ומודה בפני עדים שהפרה זו בת פרתו של מוכר היא ולא גזלה מעולם וכן הטלית נארג בביתו והודאת בעל דין כמאה עדים דמי ואילך מערער בעי לאפוקה מיניה בעדי שקרים או טועים בין בהמת המערער לבהמת המוכר דהשתא לא הדר לוקח עליה דמוכר כיון דמודה דשלו היתה והלכך מעיד לו מוכר לפסול עדיו של מערער דלאו נוגע בעדותו הוא והא דנקט חמורו ולא בת פרתו משום דלקמן אמרינן הכי: **ורב זביד אמר.** אף על גב דאינו מכיר בה שהיא בת חמורו מעיד לו עליה דאפילו ודאי גזלה אינו חוזר עליו דאמר ליה להכי זביני לך כו': אי

עשה עבדו אפותיקי ומכרו כו'. אפילו אי סבר רבא דעבדי כמקרקעי דמי נקט אפותיקי לאשמועינן בין בשטר בין בעל פה: **שורו** אפותיקי ומכרו כו'. הא דלא חשיב מכר בהדי הקדש דמפקיע מידי שעבוד משום דהקדש מפקיע אפי' אקני ליה מטלטלין אגב מקרקעי מה שאין כן במכר י): **והוא** דכתב דלא כאסמכתא. מספקא לן אי במטלטלי אגב מקרקעי דוקא או אפילו במקרקעי לחודיה: **כגון** שלקח ומכר לאלתר. הוה מצי למיפרך א"ה אפי' בית ושדה נמי אלא מגופה פריך: **דלא** הוה ליה ארעא מעולם. מכאן תשובה לאומרים דמה שנהגו לכתוב בהרשאות ונתתי לו ארבע אמות בחצרי אע"ג דלית ליה קרקע משום דאין לך אדם שאין לו ארבע אמות בארץ ישראל דקרקע אינה נגזלת אי נמי דאין לך אדם שאין לו ד' אמות לקברו (א) דהכא משמע דאפשר שאין לו קרקע וכן משמע בפ' שלישי דקדושין (דף ס: ע"ש) הרי את מקודשת לי ב) על מנת שיש לי קרקע משמע דאפשר שאין לו ודוקא להעמיד בגר שאין לו חלק בארץ ועוד דא"כ לא יעשה אדם שני שטרי הקנאה שהראשון קנה ארבע אמותיו ונראה לר"ת דהיינו טעמא כיון שמודה שיש לו קרקע וחוב הוא לו שהרי על ידי קרקע מקנה לחבירו אפילו יש כמה עדים שמכחישים אותו הרי הודאת בעל דין כמאה עדים ולא חיישינן למיחזי כשיקרא כדאשכחנא (לקמן דף קמט.) גבי איסור גיורא דנפק אודיתא מבי איסור ואף על גב שהיה איסור משקר ג) הקשה מהר"ר יחזקיהו דמכל מקום ניחוש הכא דלמא אקני ליה מטלטלין אגב קרקע והודה שיש לו מקרקע אע"פ שלא היה לו מעולם ונראה דכולי האי לא חיישינן שמא שיקרו להודות ונראה לו דבזמן הזה שרגילים לכתוב והקניתי לו ארבע אמות בחצירי א"כ מילתא דשכיחא היא וא"כ מכר לו פרה וטלית אין מעיד לו עליה אע"ג דאיכא עדים דלא היה ליה ארעא מעולם: אי

עין משפט נר מצוה

קמב א מיי' פי"ח מהל' מלוה הל' ג סמג עשין לד טוש"ע ח"מ סי' קיג סעיף א:

קמג ב מיי' שם הל' ב סמג שם טוש"ע ח"מ סי' קיז סעיף ג:

קמד ג מיי' שם טוש"ע שם סעיף ה [וברב אלפס עוד בכתובות פ"י דף קיח.]:

קמה ד מיי' שם הל' ה טוש"ע שם סעיף ג:

קמו ה ו מיי' שם הל' ב סמג שם טוש"ע ח"מ סי' קיג סעיף א:

קמז ז מיי' שם וסמג שם טוש"ע ח"מ סי' קיב סעיף א:

קמח ח מיי' פי"ט מהל' מכירה הל' ח סמג לאוין קע טוש"ע ח"מ סי' רכה סעיף ב:

קמט ט מיי' פט"ו מהל' עדות הל' ב סמג לאוין קטז טוש"ע ח"מ סי' לז סעיף טו:

רבינו גרשום

אבל פרה וטלית דודאי אם מכר לו א) מצי להעיד לו דלא מיבעיא בסתמא היכא דיש לו מטלטלין סתם דלא שיעבדן לבעל חובו אבל פרה וטלית דודאי אם מכרו לאחר לא משעבדין ליה דמטלטלי לבעל חוב לא משתעבדי. אלא אפי' היכא דעשאו אפותיקי לפרה וטלית לבעל חובו לא משתעבד ליה כדרבא וכו'. האי עבד או נעשה אפותיקי לבעל חובו ולא מכרו אית ליה קלא ולא איבעי ליה לזבוניה משום דהוה ליה לאסוקי אדעתיה דהוא אפותיקי ולא מידי ומש"ה אין גובה מהן ולהכי מצי מעיד דאין מעמיד בפני בעל חובו ולאו נוגע בעדות הוא: ומקשי' וניחוש דלמא אקנה לו לבעל חובו מטלטלי אגב מקרקעי שיהיו משועבדים לו וכי האי גוונא משתעבדי ללוקח וחוזר ומכרן וכי מעיד ללוקח שהן שלו נוגע בעדות הוא מפני שמעמי' בפני בעל חובו. ומנא לן דמשתעבדי לבעל חוב דאמר רבא אקני ליה כו' ואמר רב חסדא והוא דכתב ליה כשהקנה לו אגב קרקע דלא כאסמכתא כלומר שלא בתנאי כותבן לו ולא כטופסי דשטרא כלומר לא כמו שמוצא שטר ומעתיקו דאין אדם יכול לגבות באותו טופס אלא כחומר כל השטרות שהן עיקר וכיון דכתב ליה הכי משתעבדי ליה ובדין הוא דלא מצי מעיד דנוגע הוא מפני שמעמידן בפני בעל חוב. הכא במאי עסקינן דמצי מעיד לו כגון שלקחן בפנינו ומכר לאלתר דלא משעבדין לבעל חובו ולהכי מצי מעיד: ומקשי' וניחוש דלמא הכי כתב ליה בשטר לבעל חובו דקנאי ודאיקני דמשמע כל מה שאני עתיד לקנות יהא משועבד לך ואכתי אמאי מצי מעיד אפי' כשלקח בפנינו מדלא חיישי' להכי מצי מעיד **שמעת מינה** להיכא דכתב לבעל חובו **דאיקני** יהא משועבד לך **וקנה ומכר או הוריש לא משתעבד** לבעל חוב. מהכא ליכא למישמע דאיקני אי משתעבד או לא והכא א"כ אמאי מצי מעיד **לא צריכא** משום **דקאמרי עדים ידענא ביה** בפלוני **בהאי דלא הויא ליה קרקע מעולם** וליכא למיחש דמטלטלי אגב מקרקעי הקנה לו מש"ה מעיד דאין מעמיד בפניו: **ומקשי** והיכי מצי למימר רבין בר שמואל לעיל דמש"ה מצי מעיד גבי פרה וטלית דכיון שלא באחריות מכר לו לאו לאוקמי קמיה בעל חובו קא בעי וכדמתרצינן **והאמר רב פפא אע"ג דאמור רבנן וכו' נמצאת שאינה שלו.** דאסהידי עדים שגזלה ומכרה לו ובא בעל השדה ונטלה ממנו **חוזר** הלוקח **עליו** על המוכר והכא נמי אמאי מצי מעיד הא איכא למיחש דלמא גזלה ולהכי מעיד לו דלמא כי היכי דלא מפיק לה המערער מידו דאי מפיק לה הואיל ונמצאת שאינה שלו דגזלה חוזר עליו הלוקח ואיכא למיחש שמא נוגע בעדות הוא דגזלה ואמאי מעיד: **הכא במאי עסקינן.** דמצי להעיד **במכיר בה** הלוקח **שאותה פרה בת חמורו** כלומר שבת פרתו היא ולא גזלה והכא נמי גבי טלית דמכיר זה דשלו היא ומשום הכי מצי מעיד דלאו נוגע בעדותו משום הכי נקט הכא בת חמורו ולא בת פרתו אגב דאיצטריך לן לקמן למימר בת חמורו קאמר נמי הכא ולא משום דוקא: **דאמר ליה להכי זביני לך שלא באחריות.** דלא תהדר עלי ולא נוגע בעדות הוא: **היכי דמי.** האי מוכר:

חשק שלמה על רבינו גרשום א) נראה דצ"ל אם מכר לו שלא באחריות מצי להעיד וכו'.

מסורת הש"ס

א) ב"ק יא. ודף נג: [גיטין מא.], ב) [עי' תוס' כתובות מט: ד"ה הוא ולשמון], ג) גי' רש"ל גובה [וכ"ה הגי' בב"מ בפי"ח מהל' מלוה הל' ב'], ד) ג"א א', ה) לקמן קנז., ו) גי' רש"ל, ז) [ועי' תוס' גיטין מ: ד"ה הקדש ותוס' ערכין כג: ד"ה משום], ח) [ועי' תוס' ב"ק קד: ד"ה אגב ותוס' כתובות נד: ד"ה אע"פ אם לאה].

הגהות הב"ח

(א) תוס' ד"ה דלא הוה וכו' דהכא משמע. נ"ב עיין פרק מי שמת דף קנז ע"ב:

גליון הש"ס

תוס' ד"ה דלא כו' ע"מ שיש לי קרקע. שם איתא ע"מ שיש לי בית כור עפר ואם כן צ"ל לראיה זו:

ליקוטי רש"י

אפותיקי. אם לא אפרע לך תגבה ממקום אחר הרי זה לפניך לגבות [גיטין מ:]. פה תהא קאי כלומר מזה יהא לך פרעון [ב"ק יא:]. **דאיקני קנה ומכר קנה והוריש.** היכא דכתב דאיקני וקנה ואחרי כן שעבדו למכר או במכירה או שהורישו לאחר [רשב"ם לקמן קנז.]. **נמצאת שאינה שלו.** שלא היתה של מוכר שהיתה גזולה בידו והגזול בא ומוציא מיד הלוקח [ב"מ יד:]. **המוכר שדה לחבירו שלא באחריות אין מעיד לו עליה.** במוכר קרקע שלו שהיתה משועבדת לבעל חוב ומכרה ללוקח והוא ואתא איניש מעלמא וקמערער דלא יעיד המוכר ללוקח מפני שמעמידה לבעל חוב עליו למוכר לגבות מקרקע זה והלכך ניחא ליה לתיקו ביד לוקח דהדר עלה בעל חוב ולא ליהוי מוכר לוה רשע ולא ישלם וכנגד לוקח לא ליהוי לוה רשע שהרי באחריות מכר לו והלכך אין מעיד דנוגע בעדות הוא [רשב"ם לעיל ע"א ועי"ש בליקוטי רש"י].

בִּסְתָמָא – that **where no specific mention** of a lien on the cow or cloak was made in the loan taken by the seller, דְּלָא מִשְׁתַּעְבְּדָא לֵיהּ – **that they are not mortgaged** to the debt.[1] מַאי טַעְמָא – **What is the reason?** מִטַּלְטְלֵי נִינְהוּ – Because **they are movable property,** וּמִטַּלְטְלֵי לְבַעַל חוֹב לֹא מִשְׁתַּעְבְּדֵי – **and movable property does not become mortgaged to a creditor.**[2] וְאַף עַל גַּב דִּכְתַב לֵיהּ – This is true **even though [the seller] wrote** in the loan document **to [the creditor]** מִגְּלִימָא דְּעַל כַּתְפֵּיהּ – that he is empowered to collect even **from the garment on his shoulders,** הָנֵי מִילֵּי דְּאִיתְנְהוּ בְּעֵינַיְיהוּ – because **these words** apply only **when [the movable items] are present** in the debtor's possession; אֲבָל לֵיתְנְהוּ בְּעֵינַיְיהוּ לֹא – **but when they are not present,** having been sold by the debtor, he is **not** empowered to collect them from the buyer. Thus, if no lien was specified, the seller can certainly testify about the movables he sold since his creditor cannot collect from them in any case.

אֶלָּא אֲפִילוּ עֲשָׂאוֹ אַפּוֹתִיקִי – **However, even if [the debtor] designated his [movable property] an** ***apotiki,***[3] in which case it would be expected that the creditor should be able to collect them from the buyer, נַמִּי לֹא – it is **also not** mortgaged to the debt. מַאי טַעְמָא – **What is the reason** for this? כִּדְרָבָא – The reason is **as** stated **by Rava.** דְּאָמַר רָבָא – **For Rava said:** עָשָׂה עַבְדּוֹ אַפּוֹתִיקִי – If **[a debtor] designated his slave an** ***apotiki*** וּמְכָרוֹ – **and he** then **sold him,** בַּעַל חוֹב גּוֹבֶה מִמֶּנּוּ – his **creditor can collect** the debt **from [this slave];**[4] שׁוֹרוֹ וַחֲמוֹרוֹ אַפּוֹתִיקִי – however, if he designated **his ox or donkey an** ***apotiki*** וּמְכָרוֹ – **and he** then **sold it,** אֵין בַּעַל חוֹב גּוֹבֶה הֵימֶנּוּ – his **creditor cannot collect** the debt **from [the animal].** מַאי טַעְמָא – **What is the reason** for this distinction? הַאי אִית לֵיהּ קָלָא – **This** (the designation of the slave as an *apotiki*) **becomes public knowledge,** וְהָא לֵית לֵיהּ קָלָא – **while this** (the designation of an animal) **does not become public knowledge.**[5] Since a creditor cannot collect from an animal that was sold even if it was designated an *apotiki,* the seller can testify about it because he does not stand to benefit from the buyer's retention of it.[6]

The Gemara has now explained that not even an *apotiki* lien can empower a creditor to seize a cow or cloak from a buyer,[7] and the seller therefore does not benefit from his testimony about them. The Gemara asks, however, that there is one type of lien which *could* empower the creditor to seize movable property:

וְלֵיחוּשׁ – **But let us be concerned** דִּלְמָא אַקְנֵי לֵיהּ מִטַּלְטְלֵי אַגַּב מְקַרְקְעֵי – that **perhaps [the seller] conveyed to [a creditor]** a lien on **movables along with** a lien on **real property.** Although a lien does not take effect on movable property by itself, it *does* take effect when it is executed in conjunction with a lien on real property. דְּאָמַר רַבָּה – **For Rabbah has stated:** אִי אַקְנֵי לֵיהּ מִטַּלְטְלֵי אַגַּב מְקַרְקְעֵי – **If [a debtor] conveys to [a creditor]** a lien on **movables along with** a lien on **real property,** קָנֵי מְקַרְקְעֵי – when **[the creditor] acquires** the lien on **the real property,** קָנֵי מִטַּלְטְלֵי – **he** also **acquires** the lien on **the movables!**

The Gemara interjects with a qualification of Rabbah's ruling: וְאָמַר רַב חִסְדָּא – **And Rav Chisda said:** וְהוּא דִּכְתַב לֵיהּ – **Provided [the debtor] wrote to [the creditor]** in the document establishing the lien, דְּלָא כְּאַסְמַכְתָּא – "This lien is **not a conditional commitment,**[8] וּדְלָא כְּטוֹפְסָא דִשְׁטָרֵי – **nor** is this document **a draft form,"** i.e. a document meant to serve as a form from which other documents are copied.[9]

NOTES

1. I.e. they are not subject to collection by the creditor once they have been sold.

2. The existence of a lien on movable items is difficult for a potential buyer to determine. Thus, if movable property could be collected from a purchaser to satisfy a debt, people would be reluctant to buy movables, for fear they would be seized (*Rashbam*). [The existence of a lien on real property, however, is more readily determined (since the history of a field or house is traceable, unlike that of movable property). Since a prospective buyer can avoid such property if he is unwilling to assume the risk, the existence of liens on real estate is not a barrier to commerce.] In addition, lenders themselves do not expect to be able to collect their debts from movables, because they realize that they may not be found when the loan is due. Thus, when they lend money, they rely only on real estate to insure repayment, not movables (see *Rashi* to *Bava Metzia* 67b ד״ה אין בע״ח). [For this reason, the absence of liens on movable property is not a barrier to lending.] The law therefore does not provide for a lien on movable property (see *Derishah, Choshen Mishpat* 113:1).

3. This is an acronym for אַפֹּה תְהֵא קָאֵי, *you* [the creditor] *will stand here* (*Rashbam*). It refers to property specifically designated by a debtor for collection in case the debtor is unable to pay his obligation. [It should be noted that the Greek word *hypotheke* means a "pledge" or a "property placed under obligation." The word hypothec is used even today in that legal sense. *Tosefos Anshei Shem* (*Sheviis* 10:3) writes that the Talmudic sages often provided Hebrew or Aramaic interpretations for words they knew to be of foreign origin. They did not mean these interpretations to be etymological, but explanatory.]

4. I.e. he can seize the slave from the buyer.

5. Literally: does not have a voice. Since one slave is distinguishable from another, a prospective buyer can discover the existence of an *apotiki* lien on a slave. Therefore, if he bought the slave without investigation, he has only himself to blame for his loss (*Rashbam, Chidushei HaRan*). In the case of an animal, however, one animal is often indistinguishable from another. Thus, it is difficult if not impossible for a prospective buyer to discover the existence of an *apotiki* on any given animal. We therefore do not allow the creditor to seize an animal even on the strength of an *apotiki* (*Rashbam;* see *Rashba* and *Chidushei HaRan*).

6. Thus, the difference between real and movable property is that real property in the hands of a buyer is subject to collection by a creditor; hence, the seller benefits from preserving it in the buyer's hands. Movable property in the hands of a buyer cannot be collected by a creditor; hence, the seller does not benefit from maintaining it in his hands.

7. Seemingly, there is still one more way to establish a lien for movables – by transacting for it separately with a *kinyan chalifin*. [The Gemara's earlier rejection of even an *apotiki* lien because of the lack of public knowledge applies only to a lien that takes effect as a direct consequence of the loan. This should not preclude the conveyance of a lien separately by means of a *kinyan chalifin,* which can be used to convey any type of property.] Nevertheless, a lien transacted for movables is not legally valid for the following reason. Since the lender expects to collect from real property if he is not paid and not from movables (see note 2), the lien on the movables is in effect a conditional one: If payment is not forthcoming, and real property is not available, the lender would then attempt to collect from the movables that have been sold. A conditional commitment, known as *asmachta,* is not legally binding because the person committing himself does not really expect to have to honor the commitment [see *Bava Metzia* 66b] (*Rashbam*).

This reason does not apply, however, to an ordinary lien on real property. Since the lender fully expects to be able to collect his debt from real property, and indeed his primary surety for the loan is the borrower's real property, the lien is not considered conditional. Nevertheless, if the lien on the movables was issued in conjunction with a lien on real property, it is valid because it is considered an extension of the lien on the real property, which is not conditional (*Ramban, Nimukei Yosef* et al.).

8. As explained in the previous note, a lien on movables alone is invalid because it is considered a conditional commitment. When it is issued in conjunction with a lien on real property, however, it is valid, because it is considered an *extension* of the lien on the real property, which is not conditional. To emphasize its unconditional aspect, Rav Chisda requires that the note specifically state that the lien on movables contained in this document is *not* a conditional commitment (*Rashbam*).

9. The Rishonim differ as to whether this phrase is required specifically for a lien on movables issued in conjunction with a lien on real property (see *Rashba* for more elaboration), or whether it is a standard insertion into all notes; it is mentioned here only because it was usually inserted in the note next to the words, "not a conditional commitment" (see *R' Saadiah Gaon,* quoted by *Ramban*).

בסתמא דלא משתעבדא ליה מאי טעמא מטלטלי נינהו א ומטלטלי לבע"ח לא משתעבדי ואע"ג דכתב ליה מגלימא דעל כתפיה הני מילי דאיתנהו בעינייהו אבל ליתנהו בעינייהו לא אלא ב אפילו עשאו אפותיקי נמי לא מאי טעמא כדרבא א) דאמר רבא ג עשה עבדו אפותיקי ומכרו בעל חוב גובה ממנו ד שורו וחמורו אפותיקי ג) ומכרו אין בעל חוב גובה הימנו מאי טעמא האי אית ליה קלא והא לית ליה קלא וליחוש דלמא אקני ליה מטלטלי אגב מקרקעי דאמר רבה ה אי אקני ליה מטלטלי אגב מקרקעי ג) קני מקרקעי ג) קני מטלטלי ואמר רב חסדא ו והוא דכתב ליה דלא כאסמכתא ודלא כטופסא דשטרי הכא במאי עסקינן כגון שלקח ומכר לאלתר וליחוש דילמא ז דאיקני ד) הוא שמעת מינה ה) דאיקני קנה ומכר קנה והוריש לא משתעבד לא צריכא דקאמרי עדים ידעינן ביה בהאי דלא הוה ליה ארעא מעולם והאמר רב פפא אע"ג דאמור רבנן המוכר שדה לחבירו שלא באחריות ובא בע"ח וטרפה אינו חוזר עליו נמצאת שאינה שלו חוזר עליו הכא במאי עסקינן במכיר בה שהיא בת חמורו ורב זביד אמר ח אפילו נמצאת שאינה שלו אינו חוזר עליו דא"ל להכי זבינו לך שלא באחריות גופא אמר רבין בר שמואל משמיה דשמואל ט המוכר שדה לחבירו שלא באחריות אין מעיד לו עליה מפני שמעמידה בפני בעל חובו היכי דמי אי

עשה עבדו אפותיקי ומכרו כו'. אפילו אי סבר רבא דעבדי כמקרקעי דמי נקט אפותיקי לאשמועינן בין בשטר בין בעל פה: **שורו** אפותיקי ומכרו כו'. הא דלא חשיב מכר בהדי הקדש דמפקיע מידי שעבוד משום דהקדש מפקיע אפי' אקני ליה מטלטלין אגב מקרקעי מה שאין כן במכר ו): **והוא** דכתב דלא כאסמכתא. מספקא לן אי במטלטלי אגב מקרקעי דוקא או אפילו במקרקעי לחודיה: **כגון** שלקח ומכר לאלתר. הוה מצי למיפרך א"ה אפי' בית ושדה נמי אלא מגופה פריך: **דלא** הוה ליה ארעא מעולם. מכאן תשובה לאומרים דמה שנהגו לכתוב בהרשאות ונתתי לו ארבע אמות בחצרי אע"ג דלית ליה קרקע משום דאין לך אדם שאין לו ארבע אמות בארץ ישראל דקרקע אינה נגזלת אי נמי דאין לך אדם שאין לו ד' אמות לקברו (א) דהכא משמע דאפשר שאין לו קרקע וכן משמע בפ' שלישי דקדושין (דף ס: ע"ש) הרי את מקודשת לי ה על מנת שיש לי קרקע משמע דאפשר שאין לו ודוחק להעמיד בגר שאין לו חלק בארץ ועוד דא"כ לא יעשה אדם שני שטרי הקנאה שהראשון קנה ארבע אמותיו ונראה לר"ת דהיינו טעמא כיון שמודה שיש לו קרקע וחוב הוא לו שהרי על ידי קרקע מקנה לחבירו אפילו יש כמה עדים שמכחישים אותו הרי הודאת בעל דין כמאה עדים ולא חיישינן למיחזי כשיקרא כדאשכחנא (לקמן דף קמט.) גבי איסור גיורא דנפק אודיתא מבי איסור ואף על גב שהיה איסור משקר ח) הקשה מהר"ר חזקיהו דמכל מקום ניחוש הכא דלמא אקני ליה מטלטלין אגב קרקע והודה שיש לו מקרקע אע"פ שלא היה לו מעולם ונראה דכולי האי לא חיישינן שמא שיקרו להודות ונראה לו דבזמן הזה שרגילים לכתוב והקניתי לו ארבע אמות בחצירי א"כ מילתא דשכיחא היא וא"כ מכר לו פרה וטלית אין מעיד לו עליה אע"ג דאיכא עדים דלא היה ליה ארעא מעולם: אי

בסתמא. שלא ייחד לו פרה וטלית בפירוש דלא משתעבדא ליה לבע"ח הך פרה וטלית: **לא משתעבדי.** דלית להו קלא ולא יזהרו לקוחות דלאו משתעבדי אין לך אדם שלוקח עוד מטלטלין מחבירו דלמא טרפי להו מיניה: **אלא אפילו עשאן אפותיקי.** להך פרה וטלית שיחדן לו לגבות חובו מהם אם לא יפרענו עד זמן פלוני: **אפותיקי.** פה תהא קאי: **עשה.** לוה עבדו אפותיקי לבעל חובו ומכרו אחרי כן הלוה לאיש אחר: **אית ליה קלא.** אפסידו לקוחות אנפשייהו: **והא לית ליה קלא.** פרה וטלית ולא ידעו הלקוחות להזהר והלכך מעיד לו עליה דאין מעמידה בפני בעל חובו: ומקשינן ולאכתי בפרה וטלית אמאי מעיד וניחוש דלמא אקני ליה האי מוכר מטלטלי אגב מקרקעי לבעל חובו להשתעבד לו לגבות חובו מהן אם לא יפרענו בזמנו וחזר ומכרם וכי מעיד ללוקח שהן שלו נוגע בעדות הוא מפני שמעמידן בפני בעל חובו והכי אשכחנא דכה"ג משתעבדי מטלטלי לבעל חוב דאמר רבה כו': וגבי מטלטלי מן הלקוחות דנכסים שאין להם אחריות כגון מטלטלין נקנין עם נכסים שיש להן אחריות לענין מתנה בכסף בשטר ובחזקה והוא הדין לענין שעבוד דמיגו דחייל שעבוד אמקרקעי חייל נמי אמטלטלי אבל אקני ליה מטלטלי גרידי בסודר להשתעבד לו לכשיגיע זמנו אם לא יפרענו יגבה מהם לא קני ואפילו בלשון מתנה דכל דאי לא קני לאסמכתא היא ואסמכתא לא קניא בפרק איזהו נשך (ב"מ דף סו.): **ואמר רב חסדא והוא דכתב ליה.** בשטר השעבוד דלגמרי משעבד להו למטלטלי בהדי מקרקעי: **דלא כאסמכתא** כו'. דכיון דאין זו מכירה גמורה ולא מתנה ולא משכון אלא שעבוד בעלמא ודמי לאסמכתא דקאמר ליה אם לא אפרע לך לזמן פלוני תגבה מכאן הלכך צריך לכתוב בו לאלומי שטריה דלא כאסמכתא דאסמכתא לא קניא: **טופסי דשטרי.** הוא שטר העשוי להעתיק ממנו שטרות ולא נכתב לגבות בו ואין בו ממש: **הכא במאי עסקינן.** דמאי מעיד כגון שקנה הך פרה וטלית ומיד מכרה בפניו דודאי לא לוה בינתים ולא שעבדם למלוה: **וניחוש דלמא דאיקני אמר ליה.** כלומר אכתי איכא למיחש דאקני ליה להך פרה וטלית למלוה אגב מקרקעי והיכי דמי כגון דמקמי הכי כשלוה כתב למלוה בשטר משעבדנא לך אגב מקרקעי כל נכסי דקנאי ודעתיד אנא למיקני וכשלקח הפרה והטלית אחרי כן נשתעבדו לו מיד ואכתי אמאי מעיד אלא מדלא חיישת להכי איכא למשמע דמי שכותב כן דאקני האומר לחבירו נכסים שאני עתיד לקנות אני מוכר לך או משעבד לך ואחר כן קנה ומכר לאחרים או כתב לו דאיקני והוא קנה אחרי כן ומת והוריש לבניו לא משתעבד דהאי שכתב לו דאין אדם מקנה לחבירו דבר שלא בא לידו אע"פ שעתיד לבא ובעיא היא לקמן בפרק מי שמת ולא איפשיטא ומשמע מהכא דלא משתעבד: **לא צריכא.** הא דקאמרי מעיד ולא חיישינן לדלמא אקני ליה מטלטלי אגב מקרקעי כגון דקאמרי עדים ידענא ביה כו' והלכך לא אקני ליה מטלטלי אגב מקרקעי שהרי לא היו לו מקרקעי והלכך מעיד דכיון שמכר לו הך פרה וטלית בלא אחריות וגם אין מעמידה בפני בעל חובו לאו נוגע בעדותו הוא כלל והשתא מתוקמא אפילו בלא לקח ומכר לאלתר והא דלא קאמר אלא לא צריכא משום דלאמורא לא תירץ הכי לעיל אלא סתם הגמרא תירץ כן י) [ושיטה זו נוהגת ברוב המקומות]. ופירש ר"ח ידעינן ביה בהאי דלא הוה ליה ארעא מעולם צריכי לאסהודי הכי זה האיש לא נתפרש ממנו מעודו ועד היום וברי לנו במה שקנה וכי לא קנה קרקע מעולם לא במתנה ולא בקניה כגון הא דגרסינן בהאשה רבה ביבמות (דף פח.) נשאת ואחר כך בא בעלה תצא מזה ומזה אמר רב לא שנו אלא שנשאת כו' ומסקינן בה לא צריכא דאתו תרי ואמרי אנן הוינן בהדיה מכי נפק ועד השתא ואתון לא ידעיתון ליה כו': **נמצאת שאינה שלו.** שהעידו עדים שגזלה המוכר ומכרה לו ובא בעל השדה ונטלה ממנו חוזר לוקח על המוכר ולא הויא מכירה כלל דבשלמא היכא דטרפה בעל חוב הויא מכירה דעביד איניש דזבין ארעא ליומיה בשביל פירות יום אחד כדאמרינן בבבא מציעא (דף יד.) ופירות שאכל שלו הן כדאמר שמואל בפרק שנים אוחזין בטלית (שם דף טו.) בעל חוב גובה את השבח שבח אין פירי לא אבל לוקח מגזלן אמר התם (דף יד:) המוכר שדה לחבירו ונמצאת שאינה שלו אמר שמואל מעות יש לו שבח אין לו ללוקח אלא הדרא ארעא והדרי פירי וכל השבח והלכך כיון דלא מרויח מידי לאו מכר הוא כלל והכא נמי גבי פרה וטלית אמאי מעיד הא איכא למימר דנוגע בעדותו הוא דניחא ליה למוכר דתיקו ביד לוקח דאי מפיק ליה מיניה מערער בעדים שמעידין שהיא של מערער הרי נמצא שאינה שלו של מוכר אלא גזלה מהאי מערער ומכרה לזה ויחזור לוקח עליו דמוכר ואף על גב דשלא באחריות מכר: **ומשני במכיר בה.** הלוקח ומודה בפני עדים שהפרה זו בת פרתו של מוכר היא ולא גזלה מעולם וכן הטלית נארג בביתו והודאת בעל דין כמאה עדים דמי ואידך מערער בעי לאפוקה מיניה בעדי שקרים או טועים בין בהמת המערער לבהמת המוכר דהשתא לא הדר לוקח עליה דמוכר כיון דמודה דשלו היתה והלכך מעיד לו מוכר לפסול עדיו של מערער דלאו נוגע בעדותו הוא והא דנקט חמורו ולא בת פרתו משום דלקמן אמרינן הכי: **ורב זביד אמר.** אף על גב דלאינו מכיר בה שהיא בת חמורו מעיד לו עליה דאפילו ודאי גזלה אינו חוזר עליו דאמר ליה להכי זביני לך כו': אי

מסורת הש"ס

א) ב"ק יא: ודף לג: (גיטין מא.), ב) [ער' תוס' כתובות מט: ד"ה הוא ולשמו], ג) גי' רש"ל גובה [וכ"ה הגי' במ"מ בפי"ח מהל' מלוה הל' ב'], ד) ג"א לא, ה) לקמן קמו. ו) ג' רש"ל, ז) [ועי' תוס' גיטין מ: ד"ה הקדש ותוס' ערכין כג: ד"ה משום], ח) [וע"ע תוס' ב"ק קד: ד"ה אגב ותוס' כתובות נד: ד"ה אף ע"פ אם לאו].

הגהות הב"ח

(א) תוס' ד"ה דלא הוה וכו' דהכא משמע. נ"ב עיין פרק מי שמת דף קנו ע"ב:

גליון הש"ס

תוס' ד"ה דלא כו' ע"מ שיש לי קרקע. שם איתא ע"מ שיש לי בית כור עפר ואם כן אולי לראיה זו:

ליקוטי רש"י

אפותיקי. אם לא אפרע לך תגבה חובך ממקום אחר הרי זה לפניך לגבות [גיטין מ:]. **אפס תהא קאי.** כלומר מזה יהא לך פרעון [ב"ק יא.]. **דאיקני קנה ומכר קנה והוריש.** היכא דכתב דאיקני וקנה ואחרי כן שעבדו לאחר או במכירה או שהוריש [רשב"ם לקמן קנז.]. **נמצאת שאינה שלו.** שלא היתה של מוכר שהיתה גזולה בידו והגזלן בא ומוציא מיד הלוקח [ב"מ יד.]. **המוכר שדה לחבירו שלא באחריות אין מעיד לו עליה.** במוכר קרקע שלו שהיתה משועבדת לבעל חוב ומכרה ללוקח זה ואתא איניש ומערער וקמערער ליה המוכר ללוקח מפני שמעמידו בפני בעל חובו של מוכר שאם לא יהיה שם ללוקח ניחא ליה דמיקו ביד הלוקח דהדר עלה בעל חובו ואם לא יהיה מוכר לוה רשע ולא ישלם וכנגד לוקח לא ליהוי לוה רשע שהרי לא במתנה מכר והלכך אין מעיד דנוגע בעדות הוא [רשב"ם לעיל ע"א וע"ש בליקוטי רש"י].

עין משפט נר מצוה

קמב א מיי' פי"ח מהל' מלוה הל' ב סמג עשין צד טוש"ע ח"מ סי' קיז סעיף א:

קמג ב מיי' שם הל' ה סמג שם טוש"ע ח"מ סי' קיז סעיף ג:

קמד ג מיי' שם טוש"ע שם סעיף ה [וכרב אלפס עוד בכתובות פ"י דף קיח.]:

קמה ד מיי' שם הל' ה טוש"ע שם סעיף ג:

קמו ה ו מיי' שם הל' ג סמג שם טוש"ע ח"מ סי' קיז סעיף ג:

קמז ז מיי' שם וסמג שם טוש"ע ח"מ סי' קיב סעיף א:

קמח ח מיי' פי"ט מהל' מכירה הל' ה סמג לאוין קע טוש"ע ח"מ סי' רכה סעיף ה:

קמט ט מיי' פט"ז מהל' עדות הל' ג סמג לאוין קע טוש"ע ח"מ סי' לז סעיף טו:

רבינו גרשום

אבל פרה וטלית דודאי אם מכר לו א) מצי להעיד לו **דלא מיבעיא בסתמא** היכא דיש לו מטלטלין סתם **דלא שיעבדן** לבעל חובו אותה פרה וטלית דודאי אם מכרו לאחר לא משעבדינן ליה **דמטלטלי לבעל חוב לא משתעבדי. אלא אפי' היכא דעשאו אפותיקי** לפרה וטלית לבעל חובו **לא** משתעבד ליה **כדרבא וכו'. האי עבד** אם נעשה אפותיקי לבעל חובו **אית ליה קלא** ולא איבעי ליה לזבוניה מש"ה **בעל חוב גובה הימנו** ואינו מעיד לו מפני שמעמידו בפני בעל חובו אבל **פרה** וטלית **לית ליה קלא** ולא הוה ליה לאסוקי אדעתיה ולא מידי ומש"ה **אין גובה מהן** ולהכי מצי מעיד דאין מעמיד בפני בעל חובו ולאו נוגע בעדות הוא: **ומקשי'** בפרה וטלית אמאי מעיד **וניחוש דלמא אקנה לו** לבעל חובו **מטלטלי אגב מקרקעי** שיהיו משועבדים לו וכי האי גוונא משתעבדי ללוקח וחזר ומכרן וכי מעיד ללוקח שהן שלו נוגע בעדות הוא מפני שמעמי' בפני בעל חובו. ומנא לן דמשתעבדי לבעל חוב **דאמר רבא אקני ליה וכו' ואמר רב חסדא והוא דכתב ליה** כשהקנה לו אגב קרקע **דלא כאסמכתא** כלומר שלא בתנאי כותבן לו **ולא כטופסי דשטרא** כלומר לא כמו שמוצא שטר ומעתיקו דאין אדם יכול לגבות באותו טופס אלא כחומר כל השטרות שהן עיקר וכיון דכתב ליה הכי משתעבדי ליה ובדין הוא דלא מצי מעיד דנוגע הוא דמעמידן בפני בעל חוב. **הכא במאי עסקינן** דמצי מעיד לו **כגון שלקחן** בפנינו **ומכר לאלתר** דלא משעבדין לבעל חובו ולהכי מעיד: ומקשי' **וניחוש דלמא** הכי כתב ליה בשטר לבעל חובו **דקנאי ודאיקני** דמשמע כל מה שאני עתיד לקנות יהא משועבד לך ואכתי אמאי מצי מעיד אפי' כשלקח בפנינו מדלא חיישי' להכי מצי מעיד **שמעת מינה** להיכא דכתב לבעל חובו **דאיקני** יהא משועבד לך **וקנה ומכר או הוריש לא משתעבד** לבעל חוב. מהכא ליכא למישמע דאיקני אי משתעבד או לא והכא א"כ אמאי מצי מעיד **לא צריכא** משום **דקאמרי עדים ידענא ביה** בפלוני **בהאי** לוה **דלא הויא ליה קרקע מעולם** וליכא למיחש דמטלטלי אגב מקרקעי הקנה לו מש"ה מעיד דאין מעמיד בפניו: **ומקשי** והיכי מצי למימר רבין בר שמואל לעיל דמש"ה מצי מעיד גבי פרה וטלית דכיון שלא באחריות מכר לו לאו לאוקמי קמיה בעל חובו קא בעי וכדמתרצינן **והאמר רב פפא אע"ג דאמור רבנן וכו' נמצאת שאינה שלו.** דאסהידי עדים שגזלה ומכרה לו ובא בעל השדה ונטלה ממנו **חוזר** הלוקח **עליו** על המוכר והכא נמי אמאי מצי מעיד הא איכא למיחש דלמא גזלה ולהכי מעיד לו דלמא כי היכי דלא מפיק לה המערער מידו דאי מפיק לה הואיל ונמצאת שאינה שלו דגזלה חוזר עליו הלוקח ואיכא למיחש שמא נוגע בעדות הוא דגזלה ואמאי מעיד: **הכא במאי עסקינן.** דמצי להעיד **במכיר בה** הלוקח **שאותה פרה בת חמורו** כלומר שבת פרתו היא ולא גזלה והכא נמי גבי טלית דמכיר זה דשלו היא ומשום הכי מצי מעיד דלאו נוגע בעדותו משום הכי נקט הכא בת חמורו ולא בת פרתו אגב דאיצטריך לן לקמן למימר בת חמורו קאמר נמי הכא ולא משום דוקא: **דאמר ליה להכי זביני לך שלא באחריות.** דלא תהדר עלי ולא נוגע בעדות הוא: **היכי דמי.** האי מוכר:

חשק שלמה על רבינו גרשום א) נראה דל"ל אם מכר לו שלא באחריות מצי להעיד וכו'.

Thus, the Gemara's question stands. Why does the Baraisa permit the seller to testify regarding a cow or cloak, if it is possible that his creditor can indeed collect it from the buyer in the circumstance just described?

The Gemara responds:

הָכָא בְּמַאי עַסְקִינַן – With what case **is [the Baraisa] dealing here? כְּגוֹן שֶׁלָּקַח וּמָכַר לְאַלְתַּר – In a case in which [the seller] bought** the cow or cloak in question **and sold** it **immediately.** Thus, we need not concern ourselves that he perhaps mortgaged it to a creditor, for we are certain that the seller did not take any loans during the brief time the cow or cloak was in his possession.[10]

The Gemara asks that this may still not preclude the possibility of a lien:

וְלֵחוּשׁ – But let us be concerned דִּלְמָא דְּאִיקְנֵי הוּא – that **perhaps** the seller took out a loan *before* he bought the object, and he accepted that lien **even for that which he would** subsequently **buy!**[11] This would render the seller's testimony inadmissible.

The Gemara explains the difficulty with this:

שְׁמְעַתְּ מִינָּהּ – Learn from this (the fact that the Baraisa does not concern itself with this possibility) **דְּאִיקְנֵי קָנָה וּמָכַר** – that if a debtor attaches a lien on movables **that he will purchase** subseqently, **and he** then **purchased and sold them, קָנָה וְהוֹרִישׁ** – or **he** then **purchased them and bequeathed** them to his heirs, **לֹא מִשְׁתַּעְבֵּד – they are not mortgaged** to the debt and cannot be seized by the creditor.[12] **– ? –**

The Gemara answers that this cannot be proven:

לֹא צְרִיכָא – We can say that **[the Baraisa's ruling] applies only דְּקָאָמְרֵי עֵדִים** – in a case **in which witnesses testify, יָדְעִינַן בֵּיהּ דְּלֹא הֲוָה לֵיהּ אַרְעָא בְּהַאי מֵעוֹלָם – "We know that this** man (the seller) **never possessed any land** at all."[13]

The Gemara now turns to the other premise on which the Baraisa's second ruling is based; viz. that when a movable object is sold without a guarantee, the buyer cannot recover his money from the seller.[14] The Gemara questions this:

וְהָאָמַר רַב פַּפָּא – But has Rav Pappa not **said: אַף עַל גַּב דְּאָמוּר רַבָּנַן – Even though the Rabbis have stated** that **הַמּוֹכֵר שָׂדֶה לַחֲבֵירוֹ שֶׁלֹּא בְּאַחֲרָיוּת** – if **one sells a field to his fellow without a guarantee, וּבָא בַּעַל חוֹב וְטְרָפָהּ – and a creditor comes and seizes it, אֵינוֹ חוֹזֵר עָלָיו – [the buyer] cannot return to [the seller]** to recover his money;[15] **נִמְצֵאת שֶׁאֵינָהּ שֶׁלּוֹ** – nevertheless if **[the land] is found never to have been [the seller's], חוֹזֵר עָלָיו – [the buyer] can return to him** to recover his money.[16] Since the Baraisa refers to this latter type of challenge, even one who sells a cow or cloak should not be able to testify in the buyer's behalf, according to Rav Pappa, because he would have to refund the buyer what he paid! **– ? –**

The Gemara answers:

הָכָא בְּמַאי עַסְקִינַן – According to Rav Pappa, **with what** case **is [the Baraisa] dealing here? בְּמַכִּיר בָּהּ שֶׁהִיא בַּת חֲמוֹרוֹ – Where the buyer recognizes [the animal]** and acknowledges **that it is the offspring of [the seller's] donkey.**[17] Thus, he cannot challenge the seller regardless of the outcome of the challenge. The seller may therefore testify.

The Gemara cites a dissenting opinion:

NOTES

10. The possibility that the seller borrowed money subsequent to his sale of the cow or cloak does not concern us, since the cow or cloak would not be subject to a lien established after the sale.

Tosafos point out that if the Baraisa refers to objects bought and sold immediately, testimony should be permitted even in the case of a field or house, since no lien could have been established on them either. *Tosafos* explain that the Gemara abstained from asking this question to address a more basic problem.

11. [The lien included movables in conjunction with real property, in the manner discussed above.] Whether or not a lien can be established to include property purchased after the loan is the subject of a discussion in the Gemara below, 157a-b (*Rashbam*).

12. This is a question left unresolved by the Gemara below (157a-b). However, if the interpretation given here is correct, this Baraisa would seem to prove that such a lien does not cause future purchases to be mortgaged to the debt (*Rashbam*).

13. The witnesses testify that they were constant companions of the seller and that he never bought or received any real property (*Rabbeinu Chananel*, quoted by *Rashbam*). [*Chidushei HaRan,* however, notes that such testimony is a practical impossibility. He explains the Gemara to mean that they need only testify that they knew the seller and never saw him own, buy, or receive any land. Constant surveillance, however, is not necessary for their testimony to be effective.]

Since he never owned land, the creditor could never have subjected the cow or cloak to a lien, inasmuch as a lien can only take effect for movables in conjunction with a lien on real estate. Thus, even if a lien on future purchases is effective, the Baraisa deals with a case in which we know that no such lien could have been established (*Rashbam*).

It is now no longer necessary to say that the Baraisa deals with a case in which the cow or cloak was bought and sold immediately. Even if a loan was made while the cow or cloak was in the seller's possession, they could not be subject to a lien (*Rashbam*).

In summary: The Baraisa on 43b states that if one sold a house or field to someone he cannot testify about it in his behalf, but if he sold him a cow or cloak he can testify about it. The Baraisa refers to a case in which the seller explicitly excluded any guarantee from the transaction. [Thus, he does not have to reimburse the buyer even if the property proves never to have been his (see 43a notes 10, 12).] Nevertheless, he is *ineligible* to testify regarding the house or field because he benefits from the buyer's retention of the property, which remains available to his creditor. He *is* eligible to testify regarding the cow or cloak since these can never be subject to collection by the creditor once they are sold. However, before he may testify, it is necessary to establish that he never owned any real property [to preclude the possibility that he mortgaged the movable property along with real property].

14. If the buyer could recover his money from the seller, the latter would clearly have a strong interest in defeating the challenge, and he would therefore be ineligible to testify even in the case of a cow or cloak. Thus, the Baraisa must be speaking of a case in which the seller does not have to reimburse the buyer. This was explained above (43a) to refer to a case in which the seller explicitly declined to guarantee the purchase. The Gemara will now discuss whether such a clause suffices to exempt the seller in a case in which the property is taken because it was proven never to have belonged to the seller.

15. Since he consented to purchase the field without a guarantee.

16. Since the field never belonged to the seller, the sale was never valid. He cannot exempt himself on the grounds that the sale was not guaranteed since there never really was any sale! In contrast, when a creditor seizes land, this does not negate the sale retroactively. Indeed, whatever produce or profit the buyer realized before the seizure remains his (see *Bava Metzia* 15a). Therefore, the seller has no obligation to refund the buyer's money, since he sold the property without a guarantee (*Rashbam*).

17. I.e. the buyer acknowledges that he knows the cow or cloak is the seller's property and that the challenger's claim is untrue. [The example of a donkey is relevant to the case in the Gemara below (45a) where this phrase is used in reference to a donkey. The phrase here is borrowed from there.] The buyer's admission before witnesses that the challenger's claim is spurious renders it impossible for him to seek a refund from the seller regardless of the outcome of the challenge. Thus, the seller has no personal interest and can testify (*Rashbam*).

The buyer's acknowledgment must have been known before the challenger pressed his claim; otherwise, we suspect the buyer of acknowledging it only to enable the seller to testify in his behalf (*Chidushei HaRan*).

בסתמא דלא משתעבדא ליה מאי טעמא מטלטלי נינהו ומטלטלי לבע"ח לא משתעבדי ואע"ג דכתב ליה מגלימא דעל כתפיה הני מילי דאיתנהו בעינייהו אבל ליתנהו בעינייהו לא אלא אפילו עשאו אפותיקי נמי לא מאי טעמא כדרבא דאמר רבא עשה עבדו אפותיקי ומכרו בעל חוב גובה ממנו שורו וחמורו אפותיקי ומכרו אין בעל חוב גובה הימנו מאי טעמא האי אית ליה קלא והא לית ליה קלא וליחוש דלמא אקני ליה מטלטלי אגב מקרקעי דאמר רבה אי אקני ליה מטלטלי אגב מקרקעי קני מקרקעי קני מטלטלי ואמר רב חסדא והוא דכתב ליה דלא כאסמכתא ודלא כטופסא דשטרי הכא במאי עסקינן כגון שלקח ומכר לאלתר וליחוש דילמא דאיקני הוא שמעת מינה דאיקני קנה ומכר קנה והוריש לא משתעבד לא צריכא דקאמרי עדים ידעינן ביה בהאי דלא הוה ליה ארעא מעולם והאמר רב פפא אע"ג דאמור רבנן המוכר שדה לחבירו שלא באחריות ובא בע"ח וטרפה אינו חוזר עליו נמצאת שאינה שלו חוזר עליו הכא במאי עסקינן במכיר בה שהיא בת חמורו ורב זביד אמר אפילו נמצאת שאינה שלו אינו חוזר עליו דא"ל להכי זביני לך שלא באחריות גופא אמר רבין בר שמואל משמיה דשמואל המוכר שדה לחבירו שלא באחריות אין מעיד לו עליה מפני שמעמידה בפני בעל חובו היכי דמי

אי

תוספות

עשה עבדו אפותיקי ומכרו כו'. אפילו אי סבר רבא דעבדי כמקרקעי דמי נקט אפותיקי לאשמועינן בין בשטר בין בעל פה: שורו אפותיקי ומכרו כו'. הא דלא חשיב מכר בהדי הקדש דמפקיע מידי שעבוד משום דהקדש מפקיע אפי' אקני ליה מטלטלין אגב מקרקעי מה שאין כן במכר ז): והוא דכתב דלא כאסמכתא. מספקא לן אי במטלטלי אגב מקרקעי דוקא או אפילו במקרקעי לחודיה: כגון שלקח ומכר לאלתר. הוה מצי למיפרך א"ה אפי' בית ושדה נמי אלא מגופה פריך: דלא הוה ליה ארעא מעולם. מכאן תשובה לאומרים דמה שנהגו לכתוב בהרשאות ונתתי לו ארבע אמות בחצרי אע"ג דלית ליה קרקע משום דאין לך אדם שאין לו ארבע אמות בארץ ישראל דקרקע אינה נגזלת אי נמי דאין לך אדם שאין לו ד' אמות לקברו (א) דהכא משמע דאפשר שאין לו קרקע וכן משמע בפ' שלישי דקדושין (דף ס: ע"ש) הרי את מקודשת לי ט) על מנת שיש לי קרקע משמע דאפשר שאין לו ודוחק להעמיד בגר שאין לו חלק בארץ ועוד דא"כ לא יעשה אדם שני שטרי הקנאה שהראשון קנה ארבע אמותיו ונראה לר"ת דהיינו טעמא כיון שמודה שיש לו קרקע וחוב הוא לו שהרי על ידי קרקע מקנה לחבירו אפילו יש כמה עדים שמכחישים אותו הרי הודאת בעל דין כמאה עדים ולא חיישינן למיחזי כשיקרא דלאסמכתא (לקמן דף קמט.) גבי איסור גיורא דנפק אודיתא מבי איסור ואף על גב שהיה איסור משקר ט) הקשה מהר"ר חזקיהו דמכל מקום ניחוש הכא דלמא אקני ליה מטלטלין אגב קרקע והודה שיש לו מקרקע אע"פ שלא היה לו מעולם ונראה דכולי האי לא חיישינן שמא שיקרו להודות ונראה לו דבזמן הזה שרגילים לכתוב והקניתי לו ארבע אמות בחצירי א"כ מילתא דשכיחא היא וא"כ מכר לו פרה וטלית אין מעיד לו עליה אע"ג דאיכא עדים דלא היה ליה ארעא מעולם:

אי

רש"י

בסתמא. שלא ייחד לו פרה וטלית בפירוש דלא משתעבדא ליה לבע"ח הך פרה וטלית: לא משתעבדי. דלית להו קלא ולא יזהרו לקוחות דאי משתעבדי אין לך אדם שלוקח עוד מטלטלין מחבירו דלמא טרפי להו מיניה: אלא אפילו עשאן אפותיקי. להך פרה וטלית שיחדן לו לגבות מהן חובו אם לא יפרענו עד זמן פלוני: אפותיקי. פה תהא קאי: עשה. לוה עבדו אפותיקי לבעל חובו ומכרו לאחר כו' הלוה לאיש אחר: אית ליה קלא. אפסידו לקוחות אנפשייהו: והא לית ליה קלא. פרה וטלית ולא ידעו הלקוחות להזהר והלכך מעיד לו עליה דאין מעמידה בפני בעל חובו: ומקשינן ואכתי בפרה וטלית אמאי מעיד וניחוש דלמא אקני ליה האי מוכר מטלטלי אגב מקרקעי לבעל חובו להשתעבד לו לגבות חובו מהן אם לא יפרענו בזמנו וחזר ומכרם וכי מעיד ללוקח שהן שלו נוגע בעדות הוא מפני שמעמידן בפני בעל חובו והכי אשכחנא דכה"ג משתעבדי מטלטלי לבעל חוב דאמר רבה כו' וגבי מטלטלי מן הלקוחות דנכסים שאין להם אחריות כגון מטלטלין נקנין עם נכסים שיש להן אחריות לענין מתנה בכסף בשטר ובחזקה והוא הדין לענין שעבוד דמיגו דחייל שעבוד אמקרקעי חייל נמי אמטלטלי אבל אקני ליה מטלטלי גרידי בסודר להשתעבד לו לכשיגיע זמנו אם לא יפרענו יגבה מהם לא קני ואפילו בלשון מתנה דכל דאי לא קני דלאסמכתא היא ואסמכתא לא קניא בפרק איזהו נשך (ב"מ דף סו:): ואמר רב חסדא והוא דכתב ליה. בשטר השעבוד לגמרי משעבד להו למטלטלי בהדי מקרקעי: דלא כאסמכתא כו'. דכיון דאין זו מכירה גמורה ולא מתנה ולא משכון אלא שעבוד בעלמא ודמי לאסמכתא דקאמר ליה אם לא אפרע לך לזמן פלוני תגבה מכאן הלכך צריך לכתוב בו לאלומי שטריה דלא כאסמכתא דאסמכתא לא קניא: טופסי דשטרי. הוא שטר העשוי להעתיק ממנו שטרות ולא נכתב לגבות בו ואין בו ממש: הכא במאי עסקינן. דמצי מעיד כגון שקנה הך פרה וטלית ומיד מכרה בפנינו דודאי לא לוה בינתיים ולא שעבדם למלוה: וניחוש דלמא דאיקני אמר ליה. כלומר אכתי איכא למיחש דאקני ליה להך פרה וטלית למלוה אגב מקרקעי והיכי דמי כגון דמקמי הכי כשלוה כתב למלוה בשטר משעבדנא לך אגב מקרקעי כל נכסי דקנאי ודעתיד אנא למיקני וכשלקח הפרה והטלית אחרי כן נשתעבדו לו מיד ואכתי אמאי מעיד אלא מדלא חיישת להכי איכא למשמע דמי שכותב כן דאקני האומר לחבירו נכסים שאני עתיד לקנות אני מוכר לך או משעבד לך ואחר כן קנה או שמכר לאחרים או כתב לו דאיקני והוא קנה אחרי כן ומת והוריש לבניו לא משתעבד דהאי שכתב לו דאין אדם מקנה לחבירו דבר שלא בא לידו אע"פ שעתיד לבא ובעיא היא לקמן בפרק מי שמת ולא איפשיטא ומשמע מהכא דלא משתעבד: לא צריכא. הא דקאמרי מעיד ולא חיישינן דלמא אקני ליה מטלטלי אגב מקרקעי כגון דקאמרי עדים ידעינן ביה כו' והלכך לא אקני ליה אגב מקרקעי שהרי לא היו לו מקרקעי והלכך מעיד דכיון שמכר לו הך פרה וטלית בלא אחריות וגם אין מעמידה בפני בעל חובו לאו נוגע בעדותו הוא כלל והשתא מתוקמא אפילו בלא לקח ומכר לאלתר והא דלא קאמר אלא דלא צריכא משום דלאמורא לא תירץ הכי לעיל אלא סתם הגמרא תירץ כן י) [ושיטה זו נוהגת ברוב המקומות]. ופירש ר"ח ידעינן ביה בהאי דלא הוה ליה ארעא מעולם צריכי לאסהודי הכי זה האיש לא נתפרש ממנו מעודו ועד היום וברי לנו במה שקנה וכי לא קנה קרקע מעולם ולא בקנייה כגון הא דגרסינן בהאשה רבה ביבמות (דף פח.) נשאת ואחר כך בא בעלה תצא מזה ומזה אמר רב לא שנו אלא שנשאת כו' ומסקינן בה לא צריכא דאתו תרי ואמרי אנן הוינן בהדיה מכי נפק ועד השתא ואתון לא ידעיתון ליה כו': נמצאת שאינה שלו. שהעידו עדים שגזלה המוכר ומכרה לו ובא בעל השדה ונטלה ממנו חוזר לוקח על המוכר ולא הויא מכירה כלל דבשלמא היכא דטרפה בעל חוב הויא מכירה דעביד איניש דזבין ארעא ליומיה בשביל פירות יום אחד כדאמרינן בבבא מציעא (דף יד.) ופירות שאכל שלו הן כדאמר שמואל בפרק שנים אוחזין בטלית (שם דף טו.) בעל חוב גובה את השבח שבח אין פירי לא אבל לוקח מגזלן אמר התם (דף יד:) המוכר שדה לחבירו ונמצאת שאינה שלו אמר שמואל מעות יש לו שבח אין לו ללוקח אלא הדרא ארעא והדרי פירי וכל השבח והלכך כיון דלא מרויח מידי דלאו מכר הוא כלל והכא נמי גבי פרה וטלית אמאי מעיד הא איכא למימר דנוגע בעדותו הוא דניחא ליה למוכר דתיקום ביד לוקח דאי מפיק ליה מיניה הא נמצא שאינה שלו של מוכר אלא גזלה מהאי מערער ומכרה לזה ויחזור לוקח עליו דמוכר ואף על גב דשלא באחריות מכר: ומשני במכיר בה. הלוקח ומודה בפני עדים שהפרה זו בת פרתו של מוכר היא ולא גזלה מעולם וכן הטלית נארג בביתו והודאת בעל דין כמאה עדים דמי ואידך מערער בעי לאפוקה מיניה בעדי שקרים או טועים בין בהמת המערער לבהמת המוכר דהשתא לא הדר לוקח עליה דמוכר כיון דמודה דשלו היתה והלכך מעיד לו מוכר לפסול עדיו של מערער דלאו נוגע בעדותו הוא והא דנקט חמורו ולא בת פרתו משום דלקמן אמרינן הכי: ורב זביד אמר. אף על גב דאינו מכיר בה שהיא בת חמורו מעיד לו עליה דאפילו ודאי גזלה אינו חוזר עליו דאמר ליה להכי זביני לך כו':

אי

עין משפט נר מצוה

קמב א מיי' פי"ח מהל' מלוה הל' ג סמג עשין לד טוש"ע ח"מ סי' קיג סעיף א:
קמג ב מיי' שם הל' ה סמג שם טוש"ע ח"מ סי' קיז סעיף ג:
קמד ג מיי' שם טוש"ע שם סעיף ה [וברב אלפס עוד בכתובות פ"י דף קיח.]:
קמה ד מיי' שם הל' ה טוש"ע שם סעיף ג:
קמו ה ו מיי' שם הל' ג סמג שם טוש"ע ח"מ סי' קיג סעיף א:
קמז ז מיי' שם וסמג שם טוש"ע ח"מ סי' קיב סעיף א:
קמח ח מיי' פי"ט מהל' מכירה הל' ח סמג לאוין קע טוש"ע ח"מ סי' רכה סעיף ה:
קמט ט מיי' פט"ו מהל' עדות הל' ג סמג לאוין קט טוש"ע ח"מ סי' לז סעיף טו:

רבינו גרשום

אבל פרה וטלית דודאי אם מכר לו א) מצי להעיד לו דלא מיבעיא בסתמא היכא דיש לו מטלטלין סתם דלא שיעבדן לבעל חובו אותה פרה וטלית דודאי אם מכרו לאחר לא משעבדינן ליה דמטלטלי לבעל חוב לא משתעבדי. אלא אפי' היכא דעשאו אפותיקי לפרה וטלית לבעל חובו לא משתעבד ליה כדרבא וכו'. האי עבד אם נעשה אפותיקי לבעל חובו אית ליה קלא ולא איבעי ליה לזבוניה משו"ה בעל חוב גובה הימנו ואינו מעיד לו מפני שמעמידו בפני בעל חובו אבל פרה וטלית לית ליה קלא ולא הוה ליה לאסוקי אדעתיה ולא מידי ומש"ה אין גובה מהן ולהכי מצי מעיד דאין מעמיד בפני בעל חובו ולאו נוגע בעדות הוא: ומקשי' בפרה וטלית אמאי מעיד וניחוש דלמא אקנה לו לבעל חובו מטלטלי אגב מקרקעי שיהיו משועבדים לו וכי האי גוונא משתעבדי ללוקח וחזר ומכרן וכי מעיד ללוקח שהן שלו נוגע בעדות הוא מפני שמעמי' בפני בעל חובו. ומנא לן דמשתעבדי לבעל חוב דאמר רבא אקני ליה וכו' ואמר רב חסדא והוא דכתב ליה כשהקנה לו אגב קרקע דלא כאסמכתא כלומר שלא בתנאי כותבן לו ולא כטופסי דשטרא כלומר לא כמו שמוצא שטר ומעתיקו דאין אדם יכול לגבות באותו טופס אלא כחומר כל השטרות שהן עיקר וכיון דכתב ליה הכי משתעבדי ליה ובדין הוא דלא מצי מעיד דנוגע הוא דמעמידן בפני בעל חוב. הכא במאי עסקינן דמצי מעיד לו כגון שלקחן בפנינו ומכר לאלתר דלא משעבדין לבעל חובו ולהכי מעיד: ומקשי' וניחוש דלמא הכי כתב ליה בשטר לבעל חובו דקנאי ודאיקני דמשמע כל מה שאני עתיד לקנות יהא משועבד לך ואכתי אמאי מצי מעיד אפי' כשלקח בפנינו מדלא חיישי' להכי מצי מעיד שמעת מינה להיכא דכתב לבעל חובו דאיקני יהא משועבד לך וקנה ומכר או הוריש לא משתעבד לבעל חוב. מהכא ליכא למישמע דאיקני אי משתעבד או לא והכא א"כ אמאי מצי מעיד לא צריכא משום דקאמרי עדים ידענא ביה בפלוני בהאי לוה דלא הויא ליה קרקע מעולם וליכא למיחש דמטלטלי אגב מקרקעי הקנה לו מש"ה מעיד דאין מעמיד בפניו: ומקשי והיכי מצי למימר רבין בר שמואל לעיל דמש"ה מצי מעיד גבי פרה וטלית דכיון שלא באחריות מכר לו לאו לאוקמי קמיה בעל חובו קא בעי וכדמתרצינן והאמר רב פפא אע"ג דאמור רבנן וכו' נמצאת שאינה שלו. דאסהידי עדים שגזלה ומכרה לו ובא בעל השדה ונטלה ממנו חוזר הלוקח עליו על המוכר והכא נמי אמאי מצי מעיד הא איכא למיחש דלמא גזלה ולהכי מעיד לו דלמא כי היכי דלא מפיק לה המערער מידו דאי מפיק לה הואיל ונמצאת שאינה שלו דגזלה חוזר עליו הלוקח ואיכא למיחש שמא נוגע בעדות הוא דגזלה ואמאי מעיד: הכא במאי עסקינן. דמצי להעיד במכיר בה הלוקח שאותה פרה בת חמורו כלומר שבת פרתו היא ולא גזלה והכא נמי גבי טלית דמכיר זה דשלו היא ומשום הכי מצי מעיד דלאו נוגע בעדותו משום הכי נקט הכא בת חמורו ולא בת פרתו אגב דאיצטריך לן לקמן למימר בת חמורו קאמר נמי הכא ולא משום דוקא: דאמר ליה להכי זביני לך שלא באחריות. דלא תהדר עלי ולא נוגע בעדות הוא: היכי דמי. האי מוכר:

חשק שלמה על רבינו גרשום א) נראה דצ"ל אם מכר לו שלא באחריות מצי להעיד וכו'.

מסורת הש"ס

א) ב"ק יא: ודף לג: (גיטין מא.), ב) [עי' תוס' כתובות מט: בד"ה הוא ואשתו], ג) גי' רש"ל גובה [וכ"א הגי' במ"מ בפי"ח מהל' מלוה הל' ב'], ד) נ"א א"ל, ה) לקמן קנז., ו) גי' רש"ל, ז) [ועי' תוס' גיטין מ: ד"ה הקדש ותוס' ערכין כג: ד"ה משום], ח) [וע"ע תוס' ב"ק קד: ד"ה אגב ותוס' כתובות נד: ד"ה אע"פ אם לא]:

הגהות הב"ח

(א) תוס' ד"ה דלא הוה וכו' דהכא משמע. נ"ב עיין פרק מי שמת דף קנו ע"ב:

גליון הש"ס

תוס' ד"ה דלא כו' ע"מ שיש לי קרקע. שם איתא ע"מ שיש לי בית כור עפר ואם כן אודה לראיה זו:

ליקוטי רש"י

אפותיקי. אם לא אפרע לך תגבה ממקום אחר הרי זה לפניך לגבותה [גיטין מ:]. אפה תהא קאי. כלומר מזה יהא לך פרעון [ב"ק יג:]. דאיקני קנה ומכר קנה והוריש. היכא דכתב דאיקני וקנה ואחרי כן שעבדו לאחר או במכירה או שהורישו לאחר [רשב"ם לקמן קנז.]. נמצאת שאינה שלו. שלא היתה של מוכר שהיתה גזולה בידו והנגזל בא ומוציא מיד הלוקח [ב"מ יד:]. המוכר שדה לחבירו שלא באחריות אין מעיד לו עליה. במוכר קרקע שלו שהיתה משועבדת לבעל חוב ומכרה ללוקח זה ואתא איניש מעלמא וקמערער דלא יעיד לו המוכר ללוקח מפני שאחריותו של בעל חוב עליו דמוכר לגבות מקרקע זה והלכך ניחא ליה דתיקו ביד הלוקח דהדר עלה בעל חוב ולא ליהוי מוכר לוה רשע ולא ישלם וכנגד לוקח לא ליהוי לוה רשע שהרי לא באחריות מכר לו והלכך אין מעיד דנוגע בעדות הוא [רשב"ם לעיל ע"א ועי"ש בליקוטי רש"י].

וְרַב זְבִיד אָמַר – **But Rav Zevid said:** אֲפִילוּ נִמְצֵאת שֶׁאֵינָהּ שֶׁלּוֹ – When one sells a field without a guarantee, **even if [the land] is found never to have been [the seller's],** אֵינוֹ חוֹזֵר עָלָיו – **[the buyer] can** still **not return to [the seller]** to recover his money, דְּאָמַר לֵיהּ – for **[the seller] can say to him,** לְהָכִי זַבִּינִי לָךְ שֶׁלֹּא בְּאַחֲרָיוּת – **"It was for this** very **reason that I sold you** the field **without a guarantee."**[18]

The Gemara cites and analyzes the previously quoted ruling of Ravin bar Shmuel:

גּוּפָא – **[The text] itself** stated: אָמַר רָבִין בַּר שְׁמוּאֵל מִשְּׁמֵיהּ דִּשְׁמוּאֵל – **Ravin bar Shmuel said in the name of Shmuel:** הַמּוֹכֵר שָׂדֶה לַחֲבֵירוֹ שֶׁלֹּא בְּאַחֲרָיוּת – If **one sells a field to his fellow without a guarantee,** אֵין מֵעִיד לוֹ עָלֶיהָ – **[the seller] may not testify on [the buyer's] behalf regarding [the field],** מִפְּנֵי שֶׁמַּעֲמִידָהּ בִּפְנֵי בַּעַל חוֹבוֹ – **for [the seller] makes [the field] available to his creditor** by maintaining it in the buyer's possession.[19]

The Gemara analyzes this ruling:

הֵיכִי דָּמֵי – **What are the circumstances** of the case?

NOTES

18. By specifying that the sale was not guaranteed, the seller absolved himself from responsibility to repay even if it should be proven beyond a doubt that the land was not his (*Rashbam*).

Thus, according to Rav Zevid, the Baraisa deals even with a case in which the buyer does not concede that the animal was the seller's. The seller can nonetheless testify in his behalf, since his explicit refusal to subject himself to any responsibility for the property precludes the possibility of the buyer collecting from him.

19. See above, 43a notes 9-12.

אִי דְּאִית לֵיהּ אַרְעָא אַחֲרִיתִי – **If [the seller] possesses other land** at the time he wishes to testify, עֲלֵיהּ דִּידֵיהּ הָדַר – **[his creditor] must return to him** for satisfaction of the debt.[1] Thus, the seller is not concerned whether the buyer retains the land, and his testimony should be admissible. אִי דְּלֵית לֵיהּ אַרְעָא אַחֲרִיתִי – **If [the seller] does not possess** any **other land** at the time of the testimony, מַאי נַפְקָא לֵיהּ מִינָּהּ – **what difference is there to him** if the creditor collects the field or not? He has nothing for the creditor to take from him in any case![2]

The Gemara explains:

לְעוֹלָם דְּלֵית לֵיהּ אַרְעָא אַחֲרִיתִי – **In truth,** Ravin Bar Shmuel speaks of an instance **in which [the seller] does not possess** any **other land.** Nevertheless, the seller still wishes the creditor to have property from which to collect, דְּאָמַר – **for [the seller] says** to himself: לָא נִיחָא דְּלִיהֱוֵי – "I am **not willing to be branded** "לֹוֶה רָשָׁע וְלֹא יְשַׁלֵּם" – ***a wicked borrower who does not pay.***"[3] Thus, he has a vested interest in ensuring that his creditor should be able to collect.

The Gemara questions this:

סוֹף סוֹף – But **in the final analysis,** לְגַבֵּי אִידָךְ נַמִּי: "לֹוֶה רָשָׁע וְלֹא יְשַׁלֵּם" הוּא – **with regard to the other** (the buyer) **he is also *a wicked borrower who does not pay.***[4] Thus, whether the challenge is successful or not, he will have caused financial loss to one person. Why, then, should his testimony be considered biased?

The Gemara answers that the seller is not concerned with the loss he may cause the buyer:

דְּאָמַר – **For he says** to him, לְהָכִי זַבִּינִי לָךְ שֶׁלֹּא בְּאַחֲרָיוּת – **"It is for this reason that I sold you** the land **without a guarantee,"** so that you should not have any claim against me whatsoever if the field is seized. However, with regard to his creditor, the seller *is* concerned, for if the creditor cannot collect, the seller will be considered wicked.[5]

The preceding Gemara discussed instances in which we do not allow a seller to intercede in a buyer's behalf by testifying for him. The Gemara now discusses an instance in which the seller is *required* to assist the buyer:

מַכְרִיז רָבָא וְאִיתֵּימָא רַב פָּפָּא – **Rava, and some say Rav Pappa, proclaimed:**[6] דְּסָלְקִין לְעֵילָּא – **Those going up** from Babylonia to Eretz Yisrael, וּדְנָחְתִין לְתַתָּא – **and those going down** from Eretz Yisrael to Babylonia,[7] should all be aware of the following law: הַאי בַּר יִשְׂרָאֵל – **Any Jew** דְּזַבִּין לֵיהּ חַמְרָא לְיִשְׂרָאֵל חַבְרֵיהּ – **who sells a donkey to his fellow Jew,** וְקָא אָתֵי עוֹבֵד כּוֹכָבִים וְאָנֵיס לֵיהּ מִינֵּיהּ – **and an idolater comes and takes it from [the purchaser] forcibly,** claiming it belongs to him,[8] דִּינָא הוּא דְּמִפְצֵי לֵיהּ מִינֵּיהּ – **the law is that [the seller] must attempt to retrieve**[9] **[the donkey] from [the idolater].**[10]

Rava qualifies his ruling:

וְלֹא אֲמָרָן אֶלָּא שֶׁאֵינוֹ מַכִּיר בָּהּ שֶׁהִיא בַּת חֲמוֹרוֹ – **Now we say** this **only where [the buyer] does not recognize [the seized donkey] to be the offspring of [the seller's] donkey.** In such a case, the buyer can maintain that the idolater's claim is possibly true and the seller defrauded him. אֲבָל מַכִּיר בָּהּ שֶׁהִיא בַּת חֲמוֹרוֹ – **But if [the buyer] recognizes it to be the offspring of [the seller's] donkey,** לֹא – the seller is **not** required to help to retrieve it.[11]

A second qualification:

וְלֹא אֲמָרָן אֶלָּא דְּלֹא אָנֵיס לֵיהּ לְדִידֵיהּ וּלְאוּכְפָּא – **Now** even where the buyer does *not* recognize the animal, **we say** that the seller must help retrieve it **only where [the idolater] did not forcibly take [the donkey] and** its **saddle;** rather, he took the donkey and left the saddle.[12] אֲבָל אָנֵיס לֵיהּ לְדִידֵיהּ וּלְאוּכְפָּא – **But if [the idolater] forcibly took** both **[the donkey] and** its **saddle,** לֹא – the seller is **not** required to attempt to retrieve the donkey.[13]

The Gemara cites a dissenting opinion:

אֲמֵימָר אָמַר – **Ameimar said:** אֲפִילּוּ לֵיכָּא כָּל הָנֵי – **Even where**

NOTES

1. A creditor may not collect a debt from properties that were sold as long as the debtor himself possesses other property, even if it is of inferior quality (*Rashbam*).

2. Even if the challenge is successful and the creditor cannot collect his debt from this property, the seller loses nothing since he has nothing in any case. Thus, he has no vested interest in making the disputed land available to his creditor.

Tosafos and other Rishonim point out that it is still to the seller's benefit if his obligation to the creditor is satisfied since this frees him of the debt permanently, and removes any claim against any new assets he may obtain! They explain, however, that the *possibility* of benefit in the future is insufficient grounds to disallow the testimony of one who is not benefiting at the present time.

3. *Psalms* 37:21. See 43a note 9.

4. If the seller testifies and fends off the challenge, the buyer will retain the field only to have it seized by the seller's creditor. In that case, the buyer will have lost his money and the seller will be the wicked one in regard to him!

The Gemara assumes that any financial loss caused by a person which is not reimbursed is sufficient reason for one to acquire the label of "wicked". Thus, since the seller is the cause of the buyer's loss, and he does not repay him, he will be considered wicked.

5. The Gemara concludes that the appellation, "wicked" applies only to one who defaults on an obligation. Thus, if the creditor cannot collect his debt, it would apply; the fact that the buyer cannot recover his money, however, does not merit this condemnation, since the seller never accepted the responsibility to recompense the buyer in such a situation. [Moreover, a property sold without a guarantee is sold more cheaply. One who buys such a property knows that he is taking a risk, but he accepts the risk for the benefit of the lower price. Thus, if he loses his gamble, the seller does not feel that the buyer can have any complaint against him.]

6. I.e. he taught it in a public discourse (*Rashbam*).

7. Travel from anywhere to Eretz Yisrael is referred to as "ascent," for Eretz Yisrael is higher than the surrounding lands (see *Kiddushin* 69a-b).

8. The idolater claims the donkey was stolen from him by the seller, or by someone else who subsequently sold it to the seller (*Rashbam*).

9. The root פצה means "to retrieve," as in the verse (*Psalms* 144:10): הַפּוֹצֶה אֶת־דָּוִד עַבְדּוֹ מֵחֶרֶב רָעָה, *Who retrieved David, His servant, from the evil sword* (*Rashbam*).

10. The Gemara below explains that the circumstances surrounding the seizure lend credence to the idolater's claim that the donkey is his. This obligates the seller to assist the buyer to prove otherwise. However, since the idolater collected the donkey forcibly rather than by due process, the seller is *not* required to reimburse the buyer, even if he guaranteed the sale. A guarantee assures reimbursement only in the case of a *legal* seizure (*Ritva*). The seller's obligation extends only to attempting to bring witnesses that he owned the donkey, in the hope that the idolater will obey a court order to return it (*Rashbam*).

Rava's proclamation applies only to a case in which an idolater seizes the donkey. If a Jew does so, the seller is not required to assist, since the buyer has the option of suing the robber in court. A Jew cannot seize another Jew's property without witnesses or proof that it his [and if it can be proven that he did so, the court will force him to return it despite his claim] (*Rashbam*).

11. Since the animal is clearly recognizable as being from the seller's livestock, it is almost certain that the idolater seized it illegally. It is therefore not the seller's responsibility to recover it (*Rashbam*).

12. The fact that the idolater left the saddle demonstrates that his intention was to take only what was rightfully his. This lends credence to his claim, for if he were nothing but a common thief, he would have taken the saddle as well (*Rashbam*).

13. See notes 10 and 11.

אי דאית ליה ארעא אחריתי עליה דידיה הדר אי דלית ליה ארעא אחריתי מאי נפקא ליה מינה לעולם דלית ליה ארעא אחריתי דאמר לא ניחא דליהוי א) לוה רשע ולא ישלם סוף סוף לגבי איכך נמי לוה רשע ולא ישלם הוא דאמר להכי זבינו לך שלא באחריות מכריז רבא ואיתימא רב פפא דסלקין לעילא ודנחתין לתתא האי בר ישראל דזבין ליה חמרא לישראל חבריה וקא אתי עכו"ם ואניס ליה מיניה דינא הוא דמפצי ליה מיניה ולא אמרן אלא שאינו מכיר בה שהיא בת חמורו אבל מכיר בה שהיא בת חמורו לא ולא אמרן אלא דלא אניס ליה לדידיה ולאוכפא אבל אניס ליה לדידיה ולאוכפא לא אמימר אמר א אפי' ליכא כל הני לא מאי טעמא מידע ידע דסתם עובד כוכבים אנס הוא שנא' ב) אשר פיהם דבר שוא וימינם ימין שקר: ב אומן אין לו חזקה וכו': אמר רבה ל"ש אלא שמסר לו בעדים אבל מסר לו שלא בעדים מתוך שיכול לומר לו לא היו דברים מעולם כי אמר ליה נמי לקוחה היא בידי מהימן אמר ליה אביי אי הכי ג אפילו בעדים נמי מתוך שיכול לומר לו החזרתיו לך כי אמר ליה לקוחה היא בידי מהימן אמר ליה רבה מי סברת

רש"י

אי דאית ליה. למוכר ארעא אחריתי בת חורין שיכול בע"ח לגבות הימנה עליה הדר בעל חוב דאין נפרעים מנכסים משועבדים במקום שיש נכסים בני חורין ואפי' הן זבורית ולמאי אינו מעיד הרי אין מעמידה בפני בעל חובו ואין לו למוכר לא ריוח ולא הפסד אם תעמוד ביד הלוקח ואינו נוגע בעדות זו: **מאי נפקא ליה מינה.** אם תשאר ביד הלוקח הא אפילו אי מפיק לה מערער לא מצי גבי בעל חובו מיניה דמוכר מידי דהא לית ליה: **לא ניחא ליה.** ללוה דתיפוק ארעא מיד לוקח ולא ימצא בעל חוב ממה לגבות וקרי ליה לוה בלוה רשע ולא ישלם והלכך נוגע בעדותו הוא: **סוף סוף.** מה הנאה יש לו בעדות זו דמוקי לה ביד לוקח והדר בעל חוב וגבי לה מיניה לגבי לוקח נמי הוה ליה לוה רשע שהרי הפסידו ולא הוי נוגע בעדות זו: **ומשני.** דאמר ליה להכי זבני לך שלא באחריות להפטר מכל אחריות שבעולם והלכך אינו מעיד שרוצה להעמידה בפני בעל חובו לגביה הוא דהוה ליה לוה רשע אי לא פרע ליה: **מכריז רבא.** דריש לרבים: **דסלקין לעילא.** העולין מבבל לארץ ישראל: **ודנחתי לתתא.** מא"י לבבל כולכם תדעו דין זה האי בר ישראל כו': **חמרא.** חמור: **ואנים ליה.** מיניה דלוקח דקטעין עכו"ם חמור זה נגנב ממני או מי שמכרו לך גזלו ממני ובלא עדים מאמינם הימנו וכדמפרש לקמן דלא אנים ליה לאוכפא אלא לחמור לבדו דמוכח מילתא דלדידיה הוא דקא שקיל דלאו דידיה לא בעי (א) ליה למישקל והלכך דינא הוא דמפצי ליה כמו הפוצה את דוד מחרב רעה (תהלים קמד) ויביא עדים וידון עם העכו"ם אולי יוציאו מידו (ב) דעכו"ם לייתי דינא הם ודוקא עכו"ם אבל קאנים ליה ישראל לא מפצי ליה אלא יתבעהו בדין דאין לישראל לגזול חמור מחבירו בלא עדים ובלא ראיה: **ולא אמרן.** דלריך מוכר לפצות לוקח אלא שאין מכיר בה לוקח שהיא בת חמורו של מוכר דאיכא למימר הדין עם העכו"ם: **אבל הכיר בה כו'.** לא מבעי ליה לפצותו כיון דדבר ידוע הוא שגדלה בביתו של מוכר וסתם עובד כוכבים אנס הוא מסתברא דשלא כדין אנסו העכו"ם: **ולא אמרן.** דמפצי ליה היכא דלא אנים אלא את החמור אבל אנים את החמור ואת האוכף דכיון דהניח את האוכף מסתברא דשלו הוא נוטל והלכך נקט חמור אבל פרה וטלית ליכא למימר האי חילוק דאוכף: **לא.** מפצי ליה דסתם עובד כוכבים אנס הוא: **אפילו ליכא כל הני.** אינו מכיר בה שהיא בת חמורו ולא אנים לאוכפא אפילו הכי לא מפצי ליה דסתם עובד כוכבים אנס הוא (א) [והכי קי"ל משום דאמימר בתראה הוא]: **אומן אין לו חזקה.** מתני' היא דקתני האומנין והאריסין כל הלה בבא מפרש להו והולך: **אמר רבה לא שנו.** דאין לו חזקה לטעון לקוח הוא בידי וצריך לשלם האומן לבעל הבית את בגדיו או את כליו: **אלא שמסר לו.** בעל הבית לאומן טליתו בפני עדים לתקנו והלכך אפילו אין אנו רואים עכשיו הטלית ביד האומן ובעל הבית תובעו טליתו אין האומן יכול לטעון החזרתיו לך דסבירא ליה לרבה המפקיד אצל חבירו בעדים צריך להחזיר לו בעדים כדמפרש לקמיה והיה לו להחזירו בעדים וכל שכן שאנו רואין אותו בבית האומן שאין יכול לטעון לקוח הוא בידי שהרי מעידין עדים שבתורת פקדון בא לידו שהרי בפניהם מסר לו ומיהו אי טעין החזרתיו לך בפני פלוני ופלוני והלכו למדינת הים נאמן דהכי אמרינן בשבועות (דף מא.) דאפי' למ"ד המלוה את חבירו בעדים צריך לפורעו בעדים אי טעין ואמר פרעתיך בפני פלוני ופלוני והלכו להם למדינת הים נאמן ומיהו כל זמן דלא טעין אלא החזרתיו לך שלא בעדים אינו נאמן והא דלא אמרינן מתוך שיכול לומר פרעתיך בפני פלוני ופלוני והלכו להם למדינת הים כי אמר נמי החזרתי בינו ובינך נאמן כי האי גוונא לא אמרינן מיגו דכיון דלא פרעו בפני עדים לא היה יכול לומר פרעתי בפני פלוני ופלוני והלכו להם למדינת הים דמילתא דעבידא לאיגלויי לא משקר איניש פן יעשה בדאי היום ולמחר כי הדרי עדים ממדינת הים ויאמרו לא היו דברים מעולם: **אבל מסר לו שלא בעדים.** לא מיבעיא היכא דאין אנו רואין הטלית בידו דמתוך שיכול לומר אמת אתה מסרת לי אבל החזרתי לך ונאמן דהא אין לריך עכשיו להחזיר לו בעדים אי נמי יכול לומר לא היו דברים מעולם שלא מסרת לי ויהיה נאמן בשבועת היסת כי אמר לו נמי ישנו בידי ולקוח הוא שמכרתו לי דיש לו חזקה ונאמן ע"י האי מגו אלא אפילו אם ראו עכשיו עדים הטלית ביד האומן או שתפוס בו בפנינו מתוך שיכול לומר לא היו דברים מעולם שלא מסרתו לי אבל אחר מסרו לי שמכרתו לו והוא מכרה לי כי אמר ליה נמי אתה מסרתו לי ומכרתו לי נאמן בהאי מיגו דסבירא ליה לרבה השתא דהיכא דלא מסר לו בעדים לא"ש ראה הטלית בידו עכשיו לא"ש לא ראה יש חזקה דלא מדמי ליה לדין של דברים העשויין להשאיל ולהשכיר ואמר אידך לקוחין הן בידי דאינו נאמן הואיל ויש למערער עדים שהיה שלו ואע"ג דליכא עדי מסירת שאלה או שכירות משום דשאלה ושכירות לכל שכניו אדם משאיל ומשכיר אבל הכא מאי אמר אומן אינך רגיל לתקן בגדיך אצלי והכי מוכח לקמיה דלרבה לא"ש לא ראה לא"ש ראה יש לו לאומן חזקה היכא דליכא מסירה בעדים: **אמר ליה אביי.** לרבה אמאי לא משוית שום חילוק היכא דמסר לו בעדים בין ראה עכשיו הטלית בידו בעדים ללא ראה אפילו מסר בעדים נמי היכא דלא ראה יש לו חזקה מתוך שיכול לומר לו החזרתיו לך דסבירא ליה לאביי

המפקיד

תוספות

אי דאית ליה ארעא אחריתי עליה הדר. הוה מצי לשנויי כגון שעשאה אפותיקי דלא הדר אלא אהך ארעא ואחריתי דאית ליה ואם תפול ביד המערער יפרע לו אחרת ומ"מ אינו מעיד עליה דנוגע בעדות הוא: **מאי** נפקא ליה מינה. תימה דנ"מ שיפטרו אם יתעשר ושמא בשביל כן אין לפוסלו לעדות כיון דהשתא לא מרויח מידי: **דינא** הוא דמפצי ליה. תימה לרשב"א דלימא ליה אייתי ראיה דלדין טרפה ואשלם לך דאפילו לגבי ישראל מצי למימר הכי כל שכן לגבי עכו"ם ויש לומר דמיירי כגון שבדיני עכו"ם דן עמו ובדיניהם הוא דעכו"ם הלכך חייב לפצותו: **אבל** מסר לו שלא בעדים מתוך שיכול לומר כו'. אין לפרש מתוך שהיה יכול לומר אין בידי כלל דהא ברואה מיירי כדמוכח מתקפתא דאביי דרואה עדיו אלא ה"פ מתוך שיכול לומר לא היו דברים מעולם שבא לידו בתורת אומנות אלא בתורת מכר אי נמי אתה מכרתו לאחר ואחר מכרו לי כדפי' הקונטרס ואם תאמר מאי איריא אומן דאין לו חזקה היכא דמסר לו בעדים אפי' אחר נמי כיון שיש עדים שבא לידו בתורת פקדון ואפילו לא ראה למאי דמסיק שצריך להחזיר לו בעדים ולקמן פריך לה אבל מכל מקום קשה למאי ס"ד דרבה ור"י כגון שמסר לו בעדים סתם ולא פירש בפניהם אם בתורת מכר אם בתורת פקדון ולהכי דוקא אומן אין לו חזקה דמסתמא לתקנו מסר לו כיון דלא פירש אבל אחר מדלא פירש שהוא פקדון מסתמא מכר או מתנה הוא ורב נחמן בר יצחק דפריך בסוף הסוגיא אומן הוא דאין לו חזקה הא אחר יש לו חזקה לא מסתבר ליה לרב נחמן לאוקומה ברואיה בלא ידיעה דלא שכיח כדפריך [ג) לעיל מיניה] אי דאיכא עדים ליחזו עדים מאי קאמרי דלא שכיח שימסור בפניהם ולא ידעי הקבלה והכא נמי רב נחמן בר יצחק לא פריך אלא מכח סברא זו והכי פריך אי דאיכא עדים אחר אמאי יש לו חזקה הא ע"כ ידעי עדים דבתורת פקדון אתא לידיה דלא מסתבר לאוקומה (ג) בדבר דלא ידעי דלא שכיח כלל הקשה בקונט' אמאי יש חזקה לאומן מ"מ מדברים העשויין להשאיל ולהשכיר ותירץ דדברים העשויין להשאיל ולהשכיר שייך גבי כל אדם אבל הכא מצי למימר אומן אינך רגיל אצלי לתקן ור"י אומר דאפי' רגיל לתקן אצלו יש לחלק דדברים העשויין להשאיל ולהשכיר שייך בין לגבי אדם שמכיר שהוא נאמן בין מכיר שאינו נאמן ואין יכול כל שעה להעמיד עדים כשרוצה להשאיל ולהשכיר שלא להשיא עצמו שם רע בשכיניו אבל לאומן אם צריך הוא לתקן יכול ליתן לאומן המכיר שהוא נאמן או להביא עדים לכך יש לו חזקה שלא בעדים: **אי** הכי אפי' בעדים נמי מתוך שיכול לומר החזרתיו לך כו'. פירוש בשלמא לדידי דלא מפליגנא בין יש עדים לאין עדים אלא בראה הוא דמפליגנא היכא דראה אפילו היכא דליכא עדים לא מהימן כדאמר אביי בסמוך והיכא דלא ראה אף על גב דאיכא עדים מהימן במיגו דמצי אמר החזרתיו לך אלא לדידך היכא דאיכא

עדים

מסורת הש"ס

א) רש"ל, ב) גי' רש"ל לקמן:

הגהות הב"ח

(א) רשב"ם ד"ה ואנים וכו' לא בעי למישקל כצ"ל ותיבת ליה נמחק: (ב) בא"ד יוציאו מידו בדין דעכו"ם: (ג) תוס' ד"ה אבל וכו' דלא מסתבר לאוקומה כגון דלא ידעי:

תורה אור השלם

א) לֹוֶה רָשָׁע וְלֹא יְשַׁלֵּם וְצַדִּיק חוֹנֵן וְנוֹתֵן: [תהלים לז, כא]

ב) פְּצֵנִי וְהַצִּילֵנִי מִיַּד בְּנֵי נֵכָר אֲשֶׁר פִּיהֶם דִּבֶּר שָׁוְא וִימִינָם יְמִין שָׁקֶר: [תהלים קמד, יא]

ליקוטי רש"י

אומן. בעלי אומנות שמוליכין להם בביתם לתקן כלים כגון לבעין או כובסין או חייטין או סורקי בגדים שטוענין לקוח הוא בידי. **אין לו חזקה.** ולא בחזקת שלש שנים מיירי דסתם אומן לא שייך אלא במטלטלין וחזקת שלש שנים לא נאמרה אלא במקרקעי אבל במטלטלי מי שהוא מוחזק בשל חבירו אפילו שעה אחת שאנו רואים שיוצאים מתחת ידו אע"פ שיש לחבירו עדים שהיה שלו נאמן זה המוחזק לומר לקוח הוא בידי דסתם לוקח מטלטלין מחבירו בלא עדים הוא קונה ובלא שטר חוץ מדברים העשויין להשאיל ולהשכיר ואמר לקוחין הן בידי דאינו נאמן כדקיי"ל במסכת שבועות (מו:) (וה"נ) [והכא] גבי אומנין אפילו דבר שאינו עשוי להשאיל ולהשכיר ועשוי לשלחו לאומן כדי לתקנו [נמי] אין לו חזקה לטעון לקוח [הוא] בידי מאחר שיש עדים לאידך שהיה שלו וטוען שלמחתי לך לתקנו [רשב"ם לעיל מב. ע"פ ב"ח].

עין משפט נר מצוה

קנ א מיי' פי"ט מהל' מכירה הל' ד סמג לאוין קע טוש"ע ח"מ סי' רכה סעיף ב:

קנא ב מיי' פ"ט מהל' טוען הל' א סמג עשין לה טוש"ע ח"מ סי' קלד סעיף א:

קנב ג מיי' שם הל' ב טוש"ע שם סעיף ב:

רבינו גרשום

אי דאית ליה ארעא אחריתי. חוץ מזו שמכר אמאי לא מצי מסהיד ליה והא **עליה דידיה** קא **הדר** בעל חובו וגבי מההוא קרקע דשייר לו ולא על הלוקח. **ואי דלית ליה ארעא אחריתי** אמאי לא מצי מסהיד הא לא נוגע בעדות דכיון דלית ליה קרקע **מאי נפקא ליה מיניה.** כלומר אמאי איכפת לו אם לא היה מוצא בעל חובו לגבות כלום מן הלוקח סוף סוף אין יכול בעל חובו לחזור לגבות ממנו שהרי אין לו כלום הלכך מה לו למוכר לשקר ואמאי נוגע בעדות הוא: **לעולם דלית ליה ארעא אחריתי** למוכר. ודקאמרת אי הכי מה לו לשקר אפ"ה חיישינן משום **דלא ניחא** ליה **דליקרייה לוה רשע ולא ישלם** וניחא ליה דלישכח בעל חובו למטרף מידי מן הלוקח: **סוף סוף.** כי טרף ליה בעל חובו **לגבי דלוקח** הרי לוקח קורא לו **לוה רשע ולא ישלם.** לא **דמצי אמר ליה** מוכר **להכי זבינו לך שלא באחריות** דלא ליהוי ליה עוד שום תרעומות: **דסלקין לעילא.** מבבל לא"י: **ודנחתין לתתא.** מא"י לבבל כלומר הוו ידעין הכל האי דינא. **ולא אמרן** דמפצי ליה **אלא כשאין מכיר בה** הלוקח **שהיא בת חמורו** דמוכר: **לא** מפצי ליה. דהשתא ידע דעובד כוכבים באנסות לקחה ממנו ולא בדין: **ולא אמרן.** אפי' להיכא שאין מכיר בה שהיא בת חמורו דמפצי ליה **אלא דקא אניס ליה** עובד כוכבי' **בלא אוכפא** דאיכא למימר מה שהכיר אניס ומה שלא הכיר לא אנס ומש"ה דינא הוא דמפצי ליה **אבל אניס לתרוייהו לא** מפצי ליה: **אמימר כו': פיסקא אומן** שמתקן כלים אם מבקש ממנו בעל הבית שיחזור לו את כליו אע"ג דאין רואהו בידו **אין לו חזקה** לאומן לומר לקוח הוא בידי: **אמר רבה ל"ש.** דאין לו חזקה **אלא שמסר לו** בעל הבית **בעדים** דאע"ג דלא ראהו בידו אין לו חזקה לאומן לומר לקוח הוא בידי משום דסביר ליה המפקיד אצל חבירו בעדים צריך להחזיר לו בעדים **אבל מסר לו שלא בעדים** אע"ג דראוהו בידו יש לו חזקה **דמתוך שיכול לומר לא היו דברים מעולם.** לא נתת לי שום כלי לתקן: **אמר ליה אביי אי הכי אפי' בעדים.** מסר לו כיון דלא ראוהו הרי חזקה **מתוך שיכול לומר לו כו'.** משום דמשמע לו המפקיד אצל חבירו בעדים אין צריך להחזיר לו בעדים: **אמר ליה מי סברת כו'.**

none of these disqualifying conditions **are present,**[14] לֹא – the seller is **not** required to help retrieve the donkey. מַאי טַעְמָא – **What is the reason?** מֵידַע יָדַע דִּסְתָם עוֹבֵד כּוֹכָבִים אַנָּס הוּא – **[The buyer] certainly knows that the average idolater** is a robber, שֶׁנֶּאֱמַר – **as [the verse] states** regarding them:[15] "אֲשֶׁר פִּיהֶם דִּבֶּר־שָׁוְא – ***Whose mouths speak vanity,*** וִימִינָם יְמִין שָׁקֶר" – ***and whose right hand is the right hand of falsehood.*** Thus, it can be assumed that the idolater acted illegally, and the seller has no responsibility to intercede.

The Mishnah ruled:

אוּמָּן אֵין לוֹ חֲזָקָה וכו' – A CRAFTSMAN ... DOES NOT ESTABLISH A *CHAZAKAH* in an article (known to have belonged to someone else) simply by having it in his physical possession.[16]

Rabbah qualifies the ruling of the Mishnah:

אָמַר רַבָּה – **Rabbah said:** לֹא שָׁנוּ אֶלָּא שֶׁמָּסַר לוֹ בְּעֵדִים – **The Mishnah stated** its ruling regarding a craftsman **only** in a case **where [the original owner] gave** the craftsman the article **in the presence of witnesses.**[17] In this case, since the witnesses establish that the article came into his possession in his capacity as a craftsman, he cannot use his current possession of the article to buttress his claim that the article is now his.[18] אֲבָל מָסַר לוֹ שֶׁלֹּא בְּעֵדִים – **But if [the original owner] gave the article** to the craftsman **without witnesses** being present, and the craftsman claims that he subsequently purchased the item from the original owner, then the craftsman is believed. The reason: מִתּוֹךְ שֶׁיָּכוֹל לוֹמַר לוֹ לֹא הָיוּ דְּבָרִים מֵעוֹלָם – **Since he could** as easily **have said to [the original owner], "It never happened** the way you say it did," and the craftsman would certainly have been believed,[19] כִּי אָמַר לֵיהּ נַמִּי לְקוּחָה הִיא בְּיָדִי מְהֵימָן – **even when [the craftsman] says to him** instead, **"It is a purchased** article that I now hold **in my possession," he is** also **believed.**[20]

Abaye takes issue with Rabbah:

אָמַר לֵיהּ אַבַּיֵי – **Abaye said [to Rabbah]:** אִי הָכִי – **If so,**[21] that when there are no witnesses to the initial transfer, the craftsman is believed because of the principle of *migo,* אֲפִילּוּ בְּעֵדִים נַמִּי – then **even** if the initial transfer *was* made **in the presence of witnesses,** the craftsman should also be believed. The reason: מִתּוֹךְ שֶׁיָּכוֹל לוֹמַר לוֹ הֶחֱזַרְתִּיו לָךְ – **Since he can say to [the original owner], "I returned [the article] to you,"** and deny that it is still in his possession, כִּי אָמַר לֵיהּ לְקוּחָה הִיא בְּיָדִי מְהֵימָן – even **when [the craftsman] says to him** instead, **"It is**

NOTES

14. I.e. even where the animal is not clearly recognizable as having come from the seller's stable, and the idolater took only the animal and left the saddle (*Rashbam*).

15. *Psalms* 144:8.

16. As explained in the notes to the Mishnah (42a note 17), possession of a movable article is generally proof of ownership. For example, an article that is known to have once belonged to Reuven is now found in Shimon's possession. If Shimon claims that he bought the article from Reuven, he is believed on the basis of the article's current presence in his possession. An exception to this rule is the class of articles that are habitually lent or rented by their owners. Such articles might easily have come into Shimon's possession without his having purchased them. In such a case, Shimon's possession does not furnish proof of ownership, and the article is awarded to Reuven, the last-known owner, if he contends that it is still his. Apparently, another exception to this rule is the case of a craftsman. Since a craftsman is often given articles to repair, his possession of them cannot serve as proof of ownership. [Obviously, the Mishnah refers to such articles as this craftsman would normally repair, e.g. shoes in the case of a shoemaker, clothing in the case of a tailor, etc. (*Rabbeinu Yonah* to 46a; *Choshen Mishpat* 134:1; see *Beur HaGra* ad loc.).] However, whether the case of a craftsman is indeed a true exception to the rule will now be discussed by the Gemara.

17. I.e. the witnesses hear the original owner instruct the craftsman to repair the article (*Ritva*). Alternatively, even if the witnesses do not hear the owner give the craftsman any instructions, the fact that the transfer takes place in silence indicates to us that the article was indeed given to him in his professional capacity as a craftsman (see *Tosafos*). [Had it been given to him as a gift, the owner would certainly have said so explicitly.] Now, however, the craftsman claims that he subsequently purchased the article from the original owner.

18. [The following observation will facilitate understanding the Gemara's ensuing discussion and the comments of *Rashbam*: When the Mishnah speaks of a craftsman not having a *chazakah* in an article, it obviously refers to a case in which the disputed article is currently known to be in the craftsman's possession. However, this knowledge of the article's whereabouts can come about in one of two ways. It can be that the craftsman is *forced* to concede that he still has the article (e.g. witnesses testify that he still has it). Alternatively, it is possible that we would not know that the article is still in his possession were it not that he *volunteered* that information in court.]

19. That is, the craftsman could claim that he never received the article for repair from the original owner. Rather, he initially *bought* it from the original owner (*Tosafos* ד"ה אבל). Alternatively, the craftsman could claim that he did not receive it from the original owner at all. Rather, he bought it from a third party to whom the original owner had sold it (*Rashbam*; see also *Rashba*). [It is not entirely clear, however, why *Rashbam* finds it necessary to introduce a third party instead of using *Tosafos'* simpler explanation; see *Dibros Moshe* on this point; see also *Chossen Yeshuos*.]

At any rate, if the craftsman would have made one of the above claims, he would have been believed (after taking a Rabbinic oath). [This is the law in any case where a defendant denies owing any of the money claimed by the plaintiff (כּוֹפֵר הַכֹּל). Unless the plaintiff can in some way substantiate his claim, the defendant's denial of it must be accepted.] Although the article in question is known to have belonged formerly to the original owner, the craftsman's present possession of it makes him the presumed owner. For, according to Rabbah [and this is the fundamental premise of Rabbah's position in this discussion], a craftsman can assert that it was the owner's practice to patronize other craftsmen when his articles needed repair. Since he had no professional relationship with the original owner, his occupation as a craftsman has no bearing on the case at hand. Rather, he is like any other person, whose current possession of an article supports a claim of legitimate ownership (see *Rashbam;* see also *Ritva*).

20. The craftsman in fact admits that the article came into his possession as an item given to him by the owner to repair. Consequently, his current possession of the article is insufficient to support his claim to being the legitimate owner, and by rights the original owner should be considered the presumed owner. Nevertheless, since the craftsman *could* have made the claim that he did not enter into possession of the article in a professional capacity [in which case his possession *would* have supported his claim of ownership – see note 19], his present claim is believed as well. [The foregoing is an application of the principle of *migo* (מִגּוֹ, *since*); a claim that would not have won on its own merits does win if the claimant could have advanced a different, winning claim. The claimant's actual claim is believed "since" he could have advanced a winning claim, had he wished to lie. (See above, 31a note 3.)]

Thus, Rabbah asserts that the Mishnah's ruling that a craftsman's possession of the disputed article does not grant him presumed ownership applies only when the article was initially conveyed to him in the presence of witnesses; for in that case, he cannot deny having received it in a professional capacity [see above, note 17]. But if the article was not initially conveyed in the presence of witnesses, then the Mishnah's ruling does not apply; for in that case, the craftsman could have denied receiving the article in a professional capacity. Though in fact he admits receiving it in a professional capacity, his claim of ownership gains credibility from his having voluntarily compromised his case with his admission.

21. See *Tosafos, Ramban* et al.

אי דאית ליה ארעא אחריתי עליה דידיה הדר אי דלית ליה ארעא אחריתי מאי נפקא ליה מינה לעולם דלית ליה ארעא אחריתי דאמר לא ניחא דליהוי א) לוה רשע ולא ישלם הוא סוף סוף לגבי אידך נמי לוה רשע ולא ישלם הוא דאמר להכי זביני לך שלא באחריות מכריז רבא ואיתימא רב פפא דסלקין לעילא ודנחתין לתתא האי בר ישראל דזבין ליה חמרא לישראל חבריה וקא אתי עכו"ם ואניס ליה מיניה דינא הוא דמפצי ליה מיניה ולא אמרן אלא שאינו מכיר בה שהיא בת חמורו אבל מכיר בה שהיא בת חמורו לא ולא אמרן אלא דלא אניס ליה לדידיה ולאוכפא אבל אניס ליה לדידיה ולאוכפא לא אמימר אמר א אפי' ליכא כל הני לא מאי טעמא מידע ידע דסתם עובד כוכבים אנס הוא שנא' ב) אשר פיהם דבר שוא וימינם ימין שקר: ב אומן אין לו חזקה וכו': אמר רבה ל"ש אלא שמסר לו בעדים אבל מסר לו שלא בעדים מתוך שיכול לומר לו לא היו דברים מעולם כי אמר ליה נמי לקוחה היא בידי מהימן אמר ליה אביי אי הכי ג אפילו בעדים נמי מתוך שיכול לומר לו החזרתיו לך כי אמר ליה לקוחה היא בידי מהימן אמר ליה רבה מי סברת

אי דאית ליה. למוכר ארעא אחריתי בת חורין שיכול בע"ח לגבות הימנה עליה הדר בעל חוב דאין נפרעים מנכסים משועבדים במקום שיש נכסים בני חורין ואפי' הן זבורית ולמאי אינו מעיד הרי אין מעמידה בפני בעל חובו ואין לו למוכר לא ריוח ולא הפסד אם תעמוד ביד הלוקח ואינו נוגע בעדות זו: **מאי נפקא ליה מינה.** אם תשאר ביד הלוקח או אפילו אי מפיק לה מערער לא מלי גבי בעל חובו מיניה דמוכר מידי דהא לית ליה: **לא ניחא ליה.** ללוה דמיפוק ארעא מיד לוקח ולא ימצא בעל חוב ממה לגבות וקרי ליה לוה בלוה רשע ולא ישלם והלכך נוגע בעדותו הוא: **סוף סוף.** מה הנאה יש לו בעדות זו דמוקי לה ביד לוקח והדר בעל חוב וגבי לה מיניה לגבי לוקח נמי הוי ליה לוה רשע שהרי הפסידו ולא הוי נוגע בעדות זו: **ומשני.** דאמר ליה להכי זבני לך שלא באחריות להפטר מכל אחריות שבעולם והלכך אינו מעיד שרוצה להעמידה בפני בעל חובו דלגביה הוא דהוי ליה לוה רשע אי לא פרע ליה: **מכריז רבא.** דריש לרבים: **דסלקין לעילא.** העולין מבבל לארץ ישראל: **ודנחתי לתתא.** מא"י לבבל כולכם תדעו דין זה האי בר ישראל כו': **חמרא.** חמור: **ואניס ליה.** מיניה ללוקח דקטעין עכו"ם חמור זה נגנב ממני או מי שמכרו לך גזלו ממני ובלא עדים מאנסו הימנו וכדמפרש לקמן דלא אניס ליה לאוכפא אלא החמור לבדו דמוכח מילתא דדידיה הוא דקא שקיל דלאו דידיה לא בעי (א) ליה למישקל והלכך דינא הוא דמפצי ליה כמו הפוצה את דוד עבדו מחרב רעה (תהלים קמד) ויביא עדים וידון עם העכו"ם אולי יוליאנו מידו (ב) דעכו"ם לימי דינא הם ודוקא עכו"ם אבל קאניס ליה ישראל לא מפצי ליה אלא יתבענו בדין דאין כח לישראל לגזול חמור מחבירו בלא עדים ובלא ראיה: **ולא אמרן.** דצריך מוכר לפצות לוקח אלא שאין מכיר בה לוקח שהיא בת חמורו של מוכר דליכא למימר הדין עם העכו"ם: **אבל הכיר בה כו'.** לא מבעי ליה לפצותו כיון דדבר ידוע הוא שגדלה בביתו של מוכר וסתם עובד כוכבים אנס הוא מסתברא דשלא כדין אנסו העכו"ם: **ולא אמרן.** דמפצי ליה היכא דאין מכיר בה אלא דלא אניס את החמור ואת האוכף דכיון דהניח את האוכף מסתברא דשלו הוא נוטל והלכך נקט חמור אבל פרה וטלית ליכא למימר האי חילוק דאוכף: **לא.** מפצי ליה דסתם עובד כוכבים אנס הוא: **אפילו ליכא כל הני.** אינו מכיר בה שהיא בת חמורו ולא אניס לאוכפא אפילו הכי לא מפצי ליה דסתם עובד כוכבים אנס הוא א) [והכי קי"ל משום דאמימר בתראה הוא]: **אומן אין לו חזקה.** מתני' היא דקתני האומנין והאריסין כל חדא חדא בבא מפרש להו ואזיל: **אמר רבה לא שנו.** דאין לו חזקה לטעון לקוח הוא בידי וצריך לשלם האומן לבעל הבית את בגדיו או את כליו: **אלא שמסר לו.** בעל הבית לאומן טליתו בפני עדים לתקנו והלכך אפילו אין אנו רואים עכשיו הטלית ביד האומן ובעל הבית תובעו טליתו אין האומן יכול לטעון החזרתיו לך דסבירא ליה לרבה המפקיד אצל חבירו בעדים צריך להחזיר לו בעדים כדמפרש לקמיה והיה לו להחזירו בעדים וכל שכן שאנו רואין אותו בבית האומן שאין יכול לטעון לקוח הוא בידי שהרי מעידין עדים שבתורת פקדון בא לידו שהרי בפניהם מסר לו ומיהו אי טעין החזרתיו לך בפני פלוני ופלוני והלכו למדינת הים נאמן דהכי אמרינן בשבועות (דף מא.) דאפי' למ"ד המלוה את חבירו בעדים צריך לפורעו בעדים אי טעין ואמר פרעתיך בפני פלוני ופלוני והלכו להם למדינת הים נאמן ומיהו כל זמן דלא טעין אלא החזרתיו לך שלא בעדים אינו נאמן והא דלא אמרינן מתוך שיכול לומר פרעתיך בפני פלוני ופלוני והלכו להם למדינת הים כי אמר נמי החזרתי ביני וביניך נאמן כי האי גוונא לא אמרינן מיגו דכיון דלא פרעו בפני עדים לא היה יכול לומר פרעתי בפני פלוני ופלוני והלכו להם למדינת הים דמילתא דעבידא לאיגלויי לא משקר איניש פן יעשה בדאי היום ולמחר כי הדרי עדים ממדינת הים ויאמרו לא היו דברים מעולם: **אבל מסר לו שלא בעדים.** לא מיבעיא היכא דאין אנו רואין הטלית בידו דמתוך שיכול לומר אמת אתה מסרת לי אבל החזרתי לך ונאמן דהא אין צריך עכשיו להחזיר לו בעדים אי נמי יכול לומר לא היו דברים מעולם שלא מסרת לי ויהיה נאמן בשבועת היסת כי אמר לו נמי ישנו בידי ולקוח הוא שמכרתו לי דיש לו חזקה ונאמן ע"י האי מגו אלא אפילו אם ראו עכשיו עדים הטלית ביד האומן או שתפוס בו בפנינו מתוך שיכול לומר לא היו דברים מעולם שלא מסרתו לי אבל אחר מסרו לי שמכרתו לו והוא מכרה לי כי אמר ליה נמי אתה מסרתו לי ומכרתו לי נאמן בהאי מיגו דסבירא ליה לרבה השתא דהיכא דלא מסר לו בעדים ל"ש ראה הטלית בידו עכשיו ל"ש לא ראה יש חזקה דלא מדמי ליה לדין של דברים העשוין להשאיל ולהשכיר ואמר אידך לקוחין הן בידי דאינו נאמן הואיל ויש למערער עדים שהיה שלו ואע"ג דליכא עדי מסירת שאלה או שכירות משום דשאלה ושכירות לכל שכניו אדם משאיל ומשכיר אבל הכא מאי אמר אומן איך רגיל לתקן בגדיך אצלי והכי מוכח לקמיה דלרבה ל"ש ראה ל"ש לא ראה יש לו לאומן חזקה היכא דליכא מסירה בעדים: **אמר ליה אביי.** לרבה אמאי לא משוית שום חילוק היכא דמסר לו בעדים בין ראה עכשיו הטלית בידו בעדים ללא ראה אפילו מסר בעדים נמי היכא דלא ראה יש לו חזקה מתוך שיכול לומר לו החזרתיו לך דסבירא ליה לאביי המפקיד

אי דאית ליה ארעא אחריתי עליה הדר. הוה מצי לשנויי כגון שעשאה אפותיקי דלא הדר אלא אארעא אחריתי דלית ליה ואם תפול ביד המערער יפרע לו מאחרת ומש"ה אינו מעיד עליה כנוגע בעדות הוא: **מאי נפקא מינה.** תימה דנ"מ שיפטרו אם יתעשר ושמא בשביל כן אין לפוסלו לעדות כיון דהשתא לא מרויח מידי: **דינא הוא דמפצי ליה.** תימה לרשב"א דלימא ליה איתי ראיה דדנין טרפה ואשלם לך דאפילו לגבי ישראל מצי למימר הכי כל שכן לגבי עכו"ם ויש לומר דמיירי כגון שדייני עכו"ם דנו עמו ודנייהם הוא דעכו"ם הלכך חייב לפצותו: **אבל מסר לו שלא בעדים מתוך שיכול לומר כו'.** אין לפרש מתוך שהיה יכול לומר אין בידי כלל דהא ברואה מיירי כדמוכח אתקפתא דאביי דראה עדו אלא ה"פ מתוך שיכול לומר לא היו דברים מעולם שבא לידו בתורת אומנות אלא בתורת מכר אי נמי אתה מכרתו לאחר ואחר מכרו לי כדפי' הקונטרס ואם תאמר מאי איריא אומן דאין לו חזקה היכא דמסר לו בעדים אפי' אחר נמי כיון שיש עדים שבא לידו בתורת פקדון ואפילו לא ראה למאי דמסיק שצריך להחזיר לו בעדים ולקמן פריך לה אבל מכל מקום קשה דמאי ס"ד דרבה וי"ל כגון שמסר לו בעדים סתם ולא פירש בפניהם אם בתורת מכר אם בתורת פקדון ולהכי דוקא אומן אין לו חזקה דמסתמא לתקנו מסר לו כיון דלא פירש אבל אחר מדלא פירש שהוא פקדון מסתמא מכר או מתנה הוא ורב נחמן בר יצחק דפריך בסוף הסוגיא אומן הוא דאין לו חזקה הא אחר יש לו חזקה לא מסתבר ליה לרב נחמן לאוקומה בראיה בלא ידיעה דלא שכיח כדפריך [ג) לעיל מיניה] אי דאיכא עדים ליחזו עדים מאי קאמרי דלא שכיח שימסור בפניהם ולא ידעי הקבלה והכא נמי רב נחמן בר יצחק לא פריך אלא מכח סברא זו והכי פריך אי דאיכא עדים אחר אמאי יש לו חזקה הא ע"כ ידעי עדים דבתורת פקדון אתא לידיה דלא מסתבר לאוקומה (ג) בדבר דלא ידעי דלא שכיח כלל הקשה בקונט' אמאי יש חזקה לאומן מ"ש מדברים העשויין להשאיל ולהשכיר ותירץ דדברים העשויין להשאיל ולהשכיר שייך גבי כל אדם אבל הכא מאי למימר אומן איך רגיל אצלי לתקן ור"י אומר דאפי' רגיל לתקן אצלו יש לחלק דדברים העשויין להשאיל ולהשכיר שייך בין לגבי אדם שמכיר שהוא נאמן בין מכיר שאינו נאמן ואין יכול כל שעה להעמיד עדים כשרוצה להשאיל ולהשכיר שלא להשיא עצמו שם רע בשכיניו אבל לאומן אם צריך הוא לתקן יכול ליתן לאומן המכיר שהוא נאמן או להביא עדים לכך יש לו חזקה שלא בעדים: **אי הכי אפי' בעדים נמי מתוך שיכול לומר החזרתיו לך כו'.** פירוש בשלמא לדידי דלא מפליגנא בין יש עדים לאין עדים אלא בראה הוא דמפליגנא היכא דראה אפילו היכא דליכא עדים לא מהימן כדאמר אביי בסמוך והיכא דלא ראה אף על גב דאיכא עדים מהימן במיגו דמצי אמר החזרתיו לך אלא לדידך היכא דאיכא עדים

עין משפט נר מצוה

קנ א מיי' פי"ט מהל' מכירה הל' ד סמג לאוין קע טוש"ע ח"מ סי' רכה סעיף ב:

קנא ב מיי' פ"ט מהל' טוען הל' א סמג עשין צה טוש"ע ח"מ סי' קלד סעיף א:

קנב ג מיי' שם הל' ג טוש"ע שם סעיף ג:

רבינו גרשום

אי דאית ליה ארעא אחריתי. חוץ מזו שמכר אמאי לא מצי מסהיד ליה והא **עליה דידיה** קא **הדר** בעל חובו וגבי מההוא קרקע דשייר לו ולא על הלוקח. **ואי דלית ליה ארעא אחריתי** אמאי לא מצי מסהיד הא לא נוגע בעדות דכיון דלית ליה קרקע **מאי נפקא ליה מיניה.** כלומר אמאי איכפת לו אם לא היה מוצא בעל חובו לגבות כלום מן הלוקח סוף סוף אין יכול בעל חובו לחזור לגבות ממנו שהרי אין לו כלום הלכך מה לו למוכר לשקר ואמאי נוגע בעדות הוא: **לעולם דלית ליה ארעא אחריתי** למוכר. ודקאמרת אי הכי מה לו לשקר אפ"ה חיישינן משום **דלא ניחא ליה** דליקרייה **לוה רשע ולא ישלם** וניחא ליה דלישכח בעל חובו למטרף מידי מן הלוקח: **סוף סוף.** כי טרף ליה בעל חובו **לגבי דלוקח** הרי לוקח קורא לו **לוה רשע ולא ישלם.** לא **דמצי אמר ליה** מוכר **להכי זביני לך שלא באחריות** דלא ליהוי ליה עוד שום תרעומות: **דסלקין לעילא.** מבבל לא"י: **ודנחתין לתתא.** מא"י לבבל כלומר הוו ידעין הכל האי דינא. **ולא אמרן** דמפצי ליה **אלא כשאין מכיר בה** הלוקח **שהיא בת חמורו** דמוכר: **לא** מפצי ליה. דהשתא ידע דעובד כוכבים באנסות לקחה ממנו ולא בדין: **ולא אמרן.** אפי' להיכא שאין מכיר בה שהיא בת חמורו דמפצי ליה **אלא דקא אניס ליה** עובד כוכבי' **בלא אוכפא** דאיכא למימר מה שהכיר לא אנס ומה שלא הכיר לא אנס ומש"ה דינא הוא דמפצי ליה **אבל אניס לתרווייהו לא** מפצי ליה: **אמימר** כו': **פיסקא אומן** שמתקן כלים אם מבקש ממנו בעל הבית שיחזור לו את כליו אע"ג דאין רואהו בידו **אין לו חזקה** לאומן לומר לקוח הוא בידי: **אמר רבה ל"ש.** דאין לו חזקה **אלא שמסר לו** בעל הבית **בעדים** דאע"ג דלא ראהו בידו אין לו חזקה לאומן לומר לקוח הוא בידי משום דסבירא ליה המפקיד אצל חבירו בעדים צריך להחזיר לו בעדים **אבל מסר לו שלא בעדים** אע"ג דראהו בידו יש לו חזקה **דמתוך שיכול לומר לא היו דברים מעולם.** לא נתן לי שום כלי לתקן: **אמר ליה אביי אי הכי אפי' בעדים.** מסר לו כיון דלא ראהו הוי חזקה **דמתוך שיכול לומר לו כו':** משום דמשמע לו המפקיד אצל חבירו בעדים אין צריך להחזיר לו בעדים: **אמר ליה מי סברת כו'.**

מסורת הש"ס

א) רש"ל, ב) גי' רש"ל לקמן:

הגהות הב"ח

(א) רשב"ם ד"ה ואניס וכו' לא בעי למישקל כצ"ל ותיבת ליה נמחק: (ב) בא"ד יוליאנו מידו בדין דעכו"ם: (ג) תוס' ד"ה אבל וכו' דלא מסתבר לאוקומה כגון דלא ידעי:

תורה אור השלם

א) לֹוֶה רָשָׁע וְלֹא יְשַׁלֵּם וְצַדִּיק חוֹנֵן וְנוֹתֵן: [תהלים לז, כא]

ב) פְּצֵנִי וְהַצִּילֵנִי מִיַּד בְּנֵי נֵכָר אֲשֶׁר פִּיהֶם דִּבֶּר שָׁוְא וִימִינָם יְמִין שָׁקֶר: [תהלים קמד, יא]

ליקוטי רש"י

אומן. בעלי אומנות שמוליכין להם בביתם לתקן כלים כגון לצבוע או כובסין או חייטין או סורקי בגדים שטוענין לקוח הוא בידי. **אין לו חזקה.** ולא בחזקת שלש שנים מיירי דסתם אומן לא שייך אלא במטלטלין וחזקת שלש שנים לא נאמרה אלא במקרקעי אבל במטלטלי מי שהוא מוחזק בשל חבירו אפילו שעה אחת שאנו רואים שיוצאים מתחת ידו אע"פ שיש לחבירו עדים שהיה שלו נאמן זה המוחזק לומר לקוח הוא בידי דסתם לוקח מטלטלין מחבירו בלא עדים הוא קונה ובלא שטר חוץ מדברים העשויין להשאיל ולהשכיר ואמר לקוחין הן בידי דאינו נאמן כדקי"ל במסכת שבועות (מו:) (וה"נ) [והכא] גבי אומנין אפילו דבר שאינו עשוי להשאיל ולהשכיר ועשוי לשלחו לאומן כדי לתקנו [נמי] אין לו חזקה לטעון לקוח [הוא] בידי מאחר שיש עדים לאידך שהיה שלו וטוען שלחתיו לך לתקנו [רשב"ם לעיל מב. ע"פ ב"ח].

a **purchased** article that I now hold **in my possession** [i.e. I subsequently bought the article from you]," he should also be believed.[22]

Rabbah responds to Abaye's objection:
אָמַר לֵיהּ רַבָּה – Rabbah said to [Abaye]: מִי סָבְרַת – Do you think

NOTES

22. Here, too, the principle of *migo* should apply: Since the craftsman could have retained the article entrusted to him by claiming that he had already returned it to the original owner, he should be believed even when he admits that he still has the article but claims that he subsequently purchased it.

Thus, Abaye objects as follows: Rabbah qualified the Mishnah's ruling, limiting it to cases in which the article's initial transfer to the craftsman took place in the presence of witnesses. The implication is that in *all* cases in which witnesses observed the initial transfer, the Mishnah's ruling applies. Abaye therefore asks that according to Rabbah's line of reasoning, he should have further limited the Mishnah's ruling to cases in which we see independently of the craftsman's admission that he still has the article in his possession (e.g. witnesses testify that he still has it). However, if it is only by the craftsman's admission that the article is known to still be in his possession (i.e he admits having it or he actually produces it in court), then the craftsman's claim should prevail even if witnesses observed the initial transfer, "since" he could have denied having it in his possession altogether [i.e. he could have claimed, "I already returned it to you"] (see *Rashbam*).

[Abaye's own position, however, is that a craftsman in relation to types of articles that he generally repairs is no different from ordinary people in relation to articles commonly lent or rented (see above, note 16). Despite the craftsman's claim that the original owner does not ordinarily patronize him, the current presence of the article in the craftsman's possession requires us to make the logical connection: There is a strong possibility that he received the article for repair; thus, his current possession of the article cannot confer any presumption of ownership (cf. Rabbah's opposing position, explained in note 19). In Abaye's view, the sole criterion for whether or not the craftsman is believed is whether or not the article is currently "seen" in his possession — i.e. is he *forced* to concede that he still has it or not? If he is forced to concede that he still has it (i.e. witnesses can testify that he still has it), his claim of ownership is rejected. If he voluntarily produces the article, then his claim is accepted, "since" he could have said that he already returned it to the original owner. According to Abaye, then, the Mishnah's ruling that "a craftsman cannot establish a *chazakah* [in an article that might have been entrusted to him for repair]" applies only when it is known independently of the craftsman's own admission that the article is still in his possession (*Rashbam*).]

אי דאית ליה ארעא אחריתי עליה דידיה הדר אי דלית ליה ארעא אחריתי מאי נפקא ליה מינה לעולם דלית ליה ארעא אחריתי דאמר לא ניחא דליהוי א) לוה רשע ולא ישלם סוף סוף לגבי אידך נמי לוה רשע ולא ישלם הוא דאמר להכי זבינו לך שלא באחריות מכריז רבא ואיתימא רב פפא דסלקין לעילא ודנחתין לתתא האי בר ישראל דזבין ליה חמרא לישראל חבריה וקא אתי עכו"ם ואנים ליה מיניה דינא הוא דמפצי ליה מיניה ולא אמרן אלא שאינו מכיר בה שהיא בת חמורו אבל מכיר בה שהיא בת חמורו לא ולא אמרן אלא דלא אנים ליה לדידיה ולאוכפא אבל אנים ליה לדידיה ולאוכפא לא אמימר א אפי' ליכא כל הני לא מאי טעמא מידע ידע דסתם עובד כוכבים אנס הוא שנא' ב) אשר פיהם דבר שוא וימינם ימין שקר: ב אומן אין לו חזקה וכו': אמר רבה ל"ש אלא שמסר לו בעדים אבל מסר לו שלא בעדים מתוך שיכול לומר לו לא היו דברים מעולם כי אמר ליה נמי לקוחה היא בידי מהימן אמר ליה אביי אי הכי ג אפילו בעדים נמי מתוך שיכול לומר לו החזרתיו לך כי אמר ליה לקוחה היא בידי מהימן אמר ליה רבה מי סברת

רשב"ם

אי דאית ליה. למוכר ארעא אחריתי בת חורין שיכול בע"ח לגבות הימנה עליה הדר בעל חוב דאין נפרעים מנכסים משועבדים במקום שיש נכסים בני חורין ואפי' הן זבורית ואמאי אינו מעיד הרי אין מעמידה בפני בעל חובו ואין לו למוכר לא ריוח ולא הפסד אם תעמוד ביד הלוקח ואינו נוגע בעדות זו: **מאי נפקא ליה מינה.** אם תשאר ביד הלוקח הא אפילו אי מפיק לה מערער לא מצי גבי בעל חובו מיניה דמוכר מידי דהא לית ליה: **לא ניחא ליה.** ללוה לתפיסה ארעא מיד לוקח ולא ימצא בעל חוב ממה לגבות וקס ליה לוה רשע ולא ישלם והלכך נוגע בעדותו הוא: **סוף סוף.** מה הנאה יש לו בעדות זו דמוקי לה ביד לוקח והדר בעל חוב וגבי לה מיניה לגבי לוקח נמי הוה ליה לוה רשע שהרי הפסידו ולא הוי נוגע בעדות זו: **ומשני.** דאמר ליה להכי זבני לך שלא באחריות להפטר מכל אחריות שבעולם והלכך אינו מעיד כשרוצה להעמידה בפני בעל חובו לגבגיה הוא דהוה ליה לוה רשע אי לא פרע ליה: **מכריז רבא.** דריש לרבים: **דסלקין לעילא.** העולין מבבל לארץ ישראל: **ודנחתי לתתא.** מא"י לבבל כולכם תדעו דין זה האי בר ישראל כו': **חמרא.** חמור: **ואנים ליה.** מיניה לוקח דקטעין עכו"ם חמור זה נגנב ממני או מי מכרו לך גזלו ממני ובלא עדים מאנסו הימנו וכדמפרש לקמן דלא אנים ליה לאוכפא אלא החמור לבדו דמוכח מילתא דדידיה הוא דקא שקיל דלאו דידיה לא בעי (א) ליה למישקל והלכך דינא הוא דמפצי ליה כמו הפוצה את דוד עבדו מחרב רעה (תהלים קמד) ויביא עדים וידון עם העכו"ם אולי יוציאנו מידו (ב) דעכו"ם לייתי דינא הם ודוקא עכו"ם אבל קאנים ליה ישראל לא מפצי ליה אלא יתבענו בדין דאין כח לישראל לגזול חמור מחבירו בלא עדים ובלא ראיה: **ולא אמרן.** דצריך מוכר לפצות לוקח אלא שאין מכיר בה לוקח שהיא בת חמורו של מוכר דאיכא למימר הדין עם העכו"ם: **אבל הכיר בה כו'.** לא מבעי ליה לפצותו כיון דדבר ידוע הוא שגדלה בביתו של מוכר וסתם עובד כוכבים אנס הוא מסתברא דשלא כדין אנסו העכו"ם: **ולא אמרן.** דמפצי ליה היכא דאין מכיר בה אלא דלא אנים את החמור ואת האוכף דכיון דהניח את האוכף מסתברא דשלו הוא נוטל והלכך נקט חמור אבל פרה וטלית ליכא למימר האי חילוק דאוכף: **לא.** מפצי ליה דסתם עובד כוכבים אנס הוא: **אפילו ליכא כל הני.** אינו מכיר בה שהיא בת חמורו ולא אנים לאוכפא אפילו הכי לא מפצי ליה דסתם עובד כוכבים אנס הוא [א) והכי קי"ל משום דאמימר בתראה הוא]: **אומן אין לו חזקה.** מתני' היא דקתני האומנין והאריסין כל חדא חדא בבא מפרש להו ואזיל: **אמר רבה לא שנו.** דאין לו חזקה לטעון לקוח הוא בידי וצריך לשלם האומן לבעל הבית את בגדיו או את כליו: **אלא שמסר לו.** בעל הבית לאומן טליתו בפני עדים לתקנו והלכך אפילו אין אנו רואים עכשיו הטלית ביד האומן ובעל הבית תובעו טליתו אין האומן יכול לטעון החזרתיו לך דסבירא ליה לרבה המפקיד אצל חבירו בעדים צריך להחזיר לו בעדים כדמפרש לקמיה והיה לו להחזירו בעדים וכל שכן שאנו רואין אותו בבית האומן שאין יכול לטעון לקוח הוא בידי שהרי מעידין עדים שבתורת פקדון בא לידו שהרי בפניהם מסר לו ומיהו אי טעין החזרתיו לך בפני פלוני ופלוני והלכו למדינת הים נאמן דהכי אמרינן בשבועות (דף מא.) דאפי' למ"ד המלוה את חבירו בעדים צריך לפורעו בעדים אי טעין ואמר פרעתיך בפני פלוני ופלוני והלכו להם למדינת הים נאמן ומיהו כל זמן דלא טעין אלא החזרתיו לך שלא בעדים אינו נאמן והא דלא אמרינן מתוך שיכול לומר פרעתיך בפני פלוני ופלוני והלכו להם למדינת הים כי אמר נמי החזרתי ביני ובינך נאמן כי האי גוונא לא אמרינן מיגו דכיון דלא פרעו בפני עדים לא היה יכול לומר פרעתי בפני פלוני ופלוני והלכו להם למדינת הים דמילתא דעבידא לאיגלויי לא משקר אינש פן יעשה בדאי היום ולמחר כי הדרי עדים ממדינת הים ויאמרו לא היו דברים מעולם: **אבל מסר לו שלא בעדים.** לא מיבעיא היכא דאין אנו רואין הטלית בידו דמתוך שיכול לומר אמת אתה מסרת לי אבל החזרתי לך ונאמן דהא אין צריך עכשיו להחזיר לו בעדים אי נמי יכול לומר לא היו דברים מעולם שלא מסרת לי ויהיה נאמן בשבועת היסת כי אמר לו נמי ישנו בידי ולקוח הוא שמכרתו לי דיש לו חזקה ונאמן ע"י האי מגו אלא אפילו אם ראו עכשיו עדים הטלית ביד האומן או שתפוס בו בפנינו מתוך שיכול לומר לא היו דברים מעולם שלא מסרתו לי אבל אחר מסרו לי שמכרתו לו והוא מכרה לי כי אמר ליה נמי אתה מסרתו לי ומכרתו לי נאמן בהאי מיגו דסבירא ליה לרבה השתא דהיכא דלא מסר לו בעדים ל"ש ראה הטלית בידו עכשיו ל"ש לא ראה יש חזקה דלא מדמי ליה לדין של דברים העשויין להשאיל ולהשכיר ואמר אידך לקוחין הן בידי דאינו נאמן הואיל ויש למערער עדים שהיה שלו ואע"ג דליכא עדי מסירת שאלה או שכירות משום דשאלה ושכירות לכל שכניו אדם משאיל ומשכיר אבל הכא מאי אמר אומן אינך רגיל לתקן בגדיך אצלי והכי מוכח לקמיה דלרבה ל"ש ראה ל"ש לא ראה יש לו לאומן חזקה היכא דליכא מסירה בעדים: **אמר ליה אביי.** לרבה אמאי לא משוית שום חילוק היכא דמסר לו בעדים בין ראה עכשיו הטלית בידו בעדים לא ראה אפילו מסר בעדים נמי היכא דלא ראה יש לו חזקה מתוך שיכול לומר לו החזרתיו לך דסבירא ליה לאביי

המפקיד

תוספות

אי דאית ליה ארעא אחריתי עליה הדר. הוה מצי לשנויי כגון שעשאה אפותיקי דאז לא הדר אארעא אחריתי דאית ליה ואם תפול ביד המערער יפרע לו אחרת ומש"ה אינו מעיד עליה דנוגע בעדות הוא: **מאי** נפקא מינה. תימה דנ"מ שיפטרו אם יתעשר ושמא בשביל כן אין לפוסלו לעדות כיון דהשתא לא מרויח מידי: **דינא** הוא דמפצי ליה. תימה לרשב"א דלימא ליה אייתי ראיה דבדין טרפה ואשלם לך דאפילו לגבי ישראל מצי למימר הכי כל שכן לגבי עכו"ם ויש לומר דמיירי כגון שבדיני עכו"ם דן עמו ובדייניהם הויא דעכו"ם הלכך חייב לפצותו: **אבל** מסר לו שלא בעדים מתוך שיכול לומר כו'. אין לפרש מתוך שהיה יכול לומר אין בידי כלל דהא בראה מיירי כדמוכח אתקפתא דאביי דראה עבדו אלא ה"פ מתוך שיכול לומר לא היו דברים מעולם שבא לידו בתורת אומנות אלא בתורת מכר אי נמי אתה מכרתו לאחר ואחר מכרו לי כדפי' הקונטרס ואם תאמר מאי איריא אומן דאין לו חזקה היכא דמסר לו בעדים אפי' אחר נמי כיון שיש עדים שבא לידו בתורת פקדון ואפילו לא ראה למאי דמסיק שצריך להחזיר לו בעדים ולקמן פריך לה אבל מכל מקום קשה דמאי ס"ד דרבה וי"ל כגון שמסר לו בעדים סתם ולא פירש בפניהם אם בתורת מכר אם בתורת פקדון ולהכי דוקא אומן אין לו חזקה דמסתמא לתקנו מסר לו כיון דלא פירש אבל אחר מדלא פירש שהוא פקדון מסתמא מכר או מתנה הוא ורב נחמן בר יצחק דפריך בסוף הסוגיא אומן הוא דאין לו חזקה הא אחר יש לו חזקה לא מסתבר ליה לרב נחמן לאוקומה בראיה בלא ידיעה דלא שכיח כדפריך [ג) לעיל מיניה] אי דאיכא עדים ליחזו עדים מאי קאמרי דלא שכיח שימסור בפניהם ולא ידעי הקבלה והכא נמי רב נחמן בר יצחק לא פריך אלא מכח סברא זו והכי פריך אי דאיכא עדים אחר אמאי יש לו חזקה הא ע"כ ידעי עדים דבתורת פקדון אתא לידיה דלא מסתבר לאוקומה (ג) בדבר דלא ידעי דלא שכיח כלל הקשה בקונט' אמאי יש חזקה לאומן מ"ש מדברים העשויין להשאיל ולהשכיר ותירץ דדברים העשויין להשאיל ולהשכיר שייך גבי כל אדם אבל הכא מאי למימר אומן אינך רגיל אצלי לתקן ור"י אומר דאפי' רגיל לתקן אצלו יש לחלק דדברים העשויין להשאיל ולהשכיר שייך בין לגבי אדם שמכיר שהוא נאמן בין מכיר שאינו נאמן ואין יכול כל שעה להעמיד עדים כשרוצה להשאיל ולהשכיר שלא להשיא עצמו שם רע בשכיניו אבל לאומן אם צריך הוא לתקן יכול ליתן לאומן המכיר שהוא נאמן או להביא עדים לכך יש לו חזקה שלא בעדים: **אי** הכי אפי' בעדים נמי מתוך שיכול לומר החזרתיו לך כו'. פירוש בשלמא לדידי דלא מפליגנא בין יש עדים לאין עדים אלא בראה הוא דמפליגנא היכא דראה אפילו היכא דליכא עדים לא מהימן כדאמר אביי בסמוך והיכא דלא ראה אף על גב דאיכא עדים מהימן במיגו דמצי אמר החזרתיו לך אלא לדידך היכא דאיכא

עדים

מסורת הש"ס

א) רש"ל, ב) גי' רש"ל לקמן.

הגהות הב"ח

(א) רשב"ם ד"ה ואנים וכו' לא בעי למישקל כצ"ל ותיבת ליה נמחק: (ב) בא"ד יוליאנו מידו בדין דעכו"ם: (ג) תוס' ד"ה אבל וכו' דלא מסתבר לאוקומה כגון דלא ידעי:

תורה אור השלם

א) לֹוֶה רָשָׁע וְלֹא יְשַׁלֵּם וְצַדִּיק חוֹנֵן וְנוֹתֵן: [תהלים לז, כא]

ב) פְּצֵנִי וְהַצִּילֵנִי מִיַּד בְּנֵי נֵכָר אֲשֶׁר פִּיהֶם דִּבֶּר שָׁוְא וִימִינָם יְמִין שָׁקֶר: [תהלים קמד, יא]

ליקוטי רש"י

אומן. בעלי אומנות שמוליכין להם כביסה לתקן כלים כגון לבעין או כובסין או חייטין או טורקי בגדים. **אין לו חזקה.** ולא בחזקת שלש שנים מיירי דבמטלטלין לא צריך שלש שנים אלא סתם אומן לא בעי שלא במטלטלין וחזקת שלש שנים לא נאמרה אלא בקרקעות אבל במטלטלי מי שהוא מוחזק בשל חבירו אפילו שעה אחת שאנו רואים אותן תחת ידו אע"פ שיש לחבירו עדים שהיה שלו נאמן זה המוחזק לומר לקוח הוא בידי דסתם לוקח מטלטלין מחבירו בלא עדים הוא קונה ובלא שטר חוץ מדברים העשויין להשאיל ולהשכיר ואמר לקוחין הן בידי דאינו נאמן כדקי"ל במסכת שבועות (מו:) (וה"נ) [והכא] גבי אומנין אפילו דבר שאינו עשוי להשאיל ולהשכיר ועשוי לשלחו לאומן כדי לתקנו [נמי] אין לו חזקה לטעון לקוח [הוא] בידי שיש עדים לאידך שהיה שלו וטוען שנתתיו לך לתקנו [רשב"ם לעיל מב. ע"פ ב"ח].

עין משפט נר מצוה

קנ א מיי' פי"ט מהל' מכירה הל' ד סמג לאוין קע טוש"ע ח"מ סי' רכה סעיף ג:

קנא ב מיי' פ"ט מהל' טוען הל' א סמג עשין צה טוש"ע ח"מ סי' קלד סעיף א:

קנב ג מיי' שם הל' ג טוש"ע שם סעיף ג:

רבינו גרשום

אי דאית ליה ארעא אחריתי. חוץ מזו שמכר אמאי לא מצי מסהיד ליה והא עליה דידיה קא הדר בעל חובו וגבי מההוא קרקע דשייר לו ולא על הלוקח. **ואי דלית ליה ארעא אחריתי** אמאי לא מצי מסהיד הא לא נוגע בעדות דכיון דלית ליה קרקע **מאי נפקא ליה מינה.** כלומר אמאי איכפת ליה אם לא היה מוצא בעל חובו לגבות כלום מן הלוקח סוף סוף אין יכול בעל חוב לחזור לגבות ממנו שהרי אין לו כלום הלכך מה לו למוכר לשקר ואמאי נוגע בעדות הוא: **לעולם דלית ליה ארעא אחריתי** למוכר. ודקאמרת אי הכי מה לו לשקר אפ"ה חיישינן משום **דלא ניחא ליה דליקרייה לוה רשע ולא ישלם.** וניחא ליה דלישכח בעל חובו למטרף מידי מן הלוקח: **סוף סוף.** כי טרף ליה בעל חובו **לגבי דלוקח** הרי לוקח קורא לו **לוה רשע ולא ישלם.** לא דמצי אמר ליה מוכר **להכי זבינך לך שלא באחריות** דלא ליהוי לוה רשע. עוד שום תרועות: **דסלקין לעילא.** מבבל לא"י: **ודנחתין לתתא.** מא"י לבבל כלומר הוו ידעין הכל האי דינא. **ולא אמרן** דמפצי ליה אלא כשאין מכיר בה הלוקח שהיא בת חמורו דמוכר: **לא מפצי ליה.** דהשתא ידע דעובד כוכבים באנסות לקחה ממנו ולא בדין: **ולא אמרן.** אפי' להיכא שאין מכיר בה שהיא בת חמורו דמפצי ליה **אלא דקא אנים ליה** עובד כוכ' **בלא אוכפא** דאיכא למימר מה שהכיר אניס ומה שלא הכיר לא אנס ומש"ה דינא הוא דמפצי ליה **אבל אנים לתרוייהו** לא מפצי ליה: **אמימר** כו': **פיסקא אומן** שמתקן כלים אם מבקש ממנו בעל הבית שיחזור לו את כליו אע"ג דאין רואהו בידו אין לו חזקה לאומן לומר לקוח הוא בידי: **אמר רבה ל"ש.** דאין לו חזקה **אלא שמסר לו** בעל הבית **בעדים** דאע"ג דלא ראהו בידו אין לו חזקה לאומן לומר לקוח הוא בידי משום דסביר ליה המפקיד אצל חבירו בעדים צריך להחזיר לו בעדים **אבל מסר לו שלא בעדים** אע"ג דראהו בידו יש לו חזקה **דמתוך שיכול לומר לא היו דברים מעולם.** לא נתן לי שום כלי לתקן: **אמר ליה אביי אי הכי אפי' בעדים.** מסר לו כיון דלא ראהו הוי חזקה **מתוך שיכול לומר לו** כו'. משום דמשמע לו המפקיד אצל חבירו בעדים אין צריך להחזיר לו בעדים: **אמר ליה מי סברת** כו'.

המפקיד אצל חבירו בעדים אינו צריך להחזיר לו בעדים לא ס"ד אלא המפקיד אצל חבירו בעדים צריך להחזיר לו בעדים (א) מיתיבי אביי ראה עבדו ביד אומן וטליתו ביד כובס אומר לו מה טיבו אצלך (ב) אתה מכרתו לי אתה נתתו לי במתנה לא אמר כלום בפני אמרת לו למוכרו וליתנו לו במתנה דבריו קיימין מאי שנא רישא ומאי שנא סיפא אמר רבה סיפא ביוצא מתחת ידי אחר וקאמר ליה אחר בפני אמרת לו למוכרו וליתנו במתנה מיגו דאי בעי א"ל מינך זבנתיה כי א"ל נמי בפני אמרת לו למוכרו דבריו קיימין ומהימן קתני מיהת רישא ראה היכי דמי אי דאיכא עדים למה לי ראה ניתי עדים ונשקול אלא לאו דליכא עדים וכי ראה מיהא תפיס ליה לא לעולם דאיכא עדים והוא ראה והא את הוא דאמרת המפקיד אצל חבירו בעדים צריך לפורעו בעדים אמר ליה הדרי בי מתיב רבא לסיועי לרבה (א) הנותן טליתו לאומן אומן אומר שתים קצצת לי והלה אומר לא קצצתי לך אלא אחת כל זמן שהטלית ביד אומן על בעה"ב להביא ראיה נתנה לו בזמנו נשבע ונוטל עבר זמנו המוציא מחבירו עליו הראיה ה"ד אי דאיכא עדים ליחזי עדים מאי קאמרי אלא

רש"י

המפקיד אצל חבירו בעדים אין צריך להחזיר לו בעדים כי א"ל נמי לקוח הוא בידי מהימן ולא משכחת מתני' דקתני אומן אין לו חזקה אלא היכא דראה לא שנא מסר בעדים לא שנא לא מסר למסירה לא חיים אביי דעכשיו אינו יכול לטעון החזרתיו לך דהא קא חזינן ליה בידו וגם אינו יכול לטעון לא מסרתו לי דלמי לדברים העשויין להשאיל ולהשכיר ואמר לקוחה היא בידי דלאו נאמן אע"ג דליכא עדי מסירה וכה"ג לחוד הוא דס"ל לאביי דאומן אין לו חזקה והכי הוא מסקנא דשמעתין כאביי: ראה עבדו ביד אומן. שמלמדו אומנות והך ראה בעדים היא שאינו יכול לטעון לא ראית וכגון שהחזיק בו שלש שנים דאי בפחות מג' שנים למה לי דנקט אומן דמשמע אבל בא"ח אחר הוי חזקתו חזקה והאמר ר"ל (לעיל דף לו.) הגודרות אין להן חזקה ואוקימנן אין להן חזקה לאלתר אבל יש להן חזקה לאחר ג' שנים: וטליתו ביד כובס. ואפילו שעה אחת: לא אמר כלום. דאומן אין לו חזקה: בפני אמרת. לפלוני למוכרו וליתנו לו במתנה: דבריו. של (ג) גלון קיימין הכי קס"ד השתא והיינו דקפריך מאי שנא רישא כו': אמר רבא כו'. ברישא מפרש לה והדר מפרש תיובתא: ביוצא. הטלית מתחת ידי אחר שטוען שלקחו מן האומן וקאמר ליה אחר לבעל הבית התובעו ואמר לו מה טיבו אצלך והלא מסרתיו לאומן לתקנו והוא משיב מן האומן קניתיו ובמלותך מכרו לי שבפני אמרת לו למוכרו הרי הוא כמי שטוען ממך לקחתי דמיגו דאי א"ל האי מחזיק לבעה"ב מינך זבנתי ומהימן הוא דהא לאו אומן הוא כי א"ל נמי יודע אני דזבינתה ניהליה לאומן וזבנה אומן ניהלי מהימן דהיינו כדאמרן לעיל דאי א"ל דזבנה מינך קמאי דידי מהימן: אי דאיכא עדים. שמסר לו למה לי ראה הא את הוא דאמרת ל"ש אלא שמסר לו בעדים ל"ש ראה ל"ש לא ראה אמרת דאין אומן מהימן משום דכיון דהפקידוהו בעדים צריך להחזירו בעדים ואמאי קתני דכי ראה אינו נאמן אבל אם לא ראה מהימן דמשמע דאין צריך להחזיר לו בעדים: וכי ראה אותו ביד האומן מיהא תפיס ליה. בעה"ב ומוליאו מידו אלמא היכא דראה אפילו לא מסר בעדים לא מהימן אומן וקשיא לרבה דאמר דהיכא דמסר שלא בעדים ל"ש ראה ל"ש לא ראה מהימן אומן: ומשני רבה לא לעולם היכא דלא מסר בעדים אומן מהימן ואפילו ראה כדאמרינן והכא מיירי כגון דאיכא עדים שמסר לו וגם ראה הטלית בידו דכיון דאיכא תרתי עדים וראה לא מצי לאחזוקי ביה ולמימר לקוח הוא בידי שהרי בתורת פקדון בא לידו ומיגו ליכא למימר דהא לא מצי למימר החזרתיו לך שהרי רואין אותו עכשיו בידו ועכשיו חזר בו רבה בעל כרחו ממאי דאוקי למתני' במסירת עדים אע"ג דלא ראה אין לו חזקה לאומן והשתא ס"ל דהיכא דאיכא תרתי עדים וראה אין לו חזקה אבל עדים ולא ראה או ראה ולא עדים יש לו חזקה שיכול לטעון החזרתיו לך היכא דלא ראה ואע"ג דמסר בעדים דהדר ביה ממאי דאמר לעיל צריך להחזיר לו בעדים וכ"ש היכא דליכא לא עדים ולא ראה דיש לו חזקה ולאביי בראה לחוד תליא מילתא אם ראה ביד אומן אין לו חזקה ואם לא ראה יש חזקה ולמסירה לא חיישינן בין בעדים בין בלא עדים: והאמרת כו'. וכיון דאיכא עדים למה לי ראה: מתיב רבא. לאביי: לסיועי לרבה. נראה בעיני דבלשון הזה אמר רבא בבית המדרש תניא כוותיה דרבה ותיובתא דאביי: על בעה"ב להביא ראיה. עדים משום דאומן מהימן מיגו דמצי למימר לקוח הוא בידי יכול לטעון עד כדי דמיו כדאמרי' גבי הנהו עיזי דאכלי חושלי בנהרדעא (לעיל דף לו.): בזמנו נשבע ונוטל. כלומר אם בזמנו תובעו בדין נשבע ונוטל דהיינו מן הנשבעין ונוטלין שכיר בזמנו נשבע ונוטל וטעמא בשבועות משום דבעל הבית טרוד בפועליו הימנוהו לשכיר: עבר זמנו. אחר ששקעה החמה: המוציא מחבירו. שכיר: אי דאיכא עדים. שמסר לאומן בפניהם ומסתמא גם בפניהם קצץ השכירות: ליחזי. דיינין עדים מאי קאמרי: אלא

תוספות

עדים אפי' לא ראה דלא מהימנא אמאי אינו נאמן במיגו דאי בעי אמר החזרתיו לך ומיהו קשה ללשון אי הכי אפילו בעדים נמי לא משמע הכי אלא משמע אי הכי דשלא בעדים נאמן במיגו בעדים נמי הוה לך למימר מיגו בשלמא לדידי דלית לי מיגו אלא שלא בעדים בעדים נמי לית לי מיגו אלא לדידך קשה ור"ת דחק לפרש ואין נראה כלל לר"י:

המפקיד אצל חבירו בעדים צריך להחזיר לו בעדים. וא"ת אמאי לא הימניה במיגו דלאי בעי אמר נאנסו כדאמרינן בסוף המוכר את הבית (לקמן דף ע. ושם) גבי מפקיד אצל חבירו בשטר ואפי' מאן דפליג התם היינו משום דשטרך בידי מאי בעי ותירץ ר"ת דודאי הוה מצי אביי למיפרך ליה אי הכי בעדים נמי להימניה במיגו דלאי בעי אמר נאנסו אלא דלא אסיק אדעתיה ואותביה מברייתא ואודי ליה דברייתא איירי מתני' ומו ליכא למפרך מידי אנאנסו וי"מ דהא דקאמר הכא דצריך להחזיר לו בעדים היינו אם רוצה להיות פטור משבועה אבל בשבועה נאמן במיגו דנאנסו (ג) ואין מחזיר לו בעדים והכי פי' לעיל לא שנו דאומן אין לו חזקה בלא שבועה אלא שמסר לו בעדים אבל מסר לו שלא בעדים נאמן בלא שבועה במיגו דאי בעי אמר לא היו דברים מעולם ומיירי קודם שנתקנה שבועת היסת ולכך כי אמר לא היו דברים מעולם אין צריך שבועה אי נמי לאחר שנתקנה ולישנא דבעי בשבועה דרכא דממונא ולא חשיב הכא דרכא דממונא דאמר לא בא לידי בתורת אומנות ואין מודה שנתחייב בו מעולם ולא חשיב דרכא דממונא אלא מנה לי בידך וא"ל הן למחר א"ל תנהו לי וא"ל נתתיו לך שמודה שנתחייב ועל פירוש זה קשה לר"ת דמאי פריך לקמן מראה עבדו ביד אומן אי דאיכא עדים למה לי ראה לייתי עדים ולישקול הא מהני ראה דאפילו בשבועה לא יהא נאמן דאין לו מיגו דבלא ראה נאמן הוא בשבועה במיגו דנאנסו וברייתא משמע דלא אמר כלום דאפילו בשבועה אינו נאמן ונראה לו לתרץ דהכא לא חשיב מיגו דטעמא דמ"ד דצריך להחזיר בעדים משום דכיון דלא הימניה בשבועה כדאמר בשבועות (דף מא: ושם) דהויא כאילו א"ל בהדיא אל תחזיר לי אלא בעדים הלכך לא מהימן במיגו דהוי דלהפקיד אנפשיה אבל התם בהמוכר סבר דאין צריך להחזיר לו בעדים ולא חשיב כאילו אמר אל תחזירני אלא בעדים ולכך נאמן במיגו אבל אין נראה דאפילו מאן דלית ליה צריך להחזיר לו בעדים כי איכא מיגו מהימן דאי לאו הכי תקשי מאי פריך ליה אביי מההיא דראה עבדו ביד אומן דסברא דאין צריך להחזיר לו בעדים הא איכא תנא בשבועות דלית ליה המלוה את חבירו בעדים צריך להחזיר לו בעדים ויסבור רבה כוותיה אלא משום דאפילו ההוא תנא דשבועות מודה בפקדון דאיכא מיגו דנאנסו דאין צריך להחזיר לו בעדים לכך נראה כפי' ר"ת:

נתנה לו בזמנו נשבע ונוטל. וא"ת והא אמר בפ' המקבל (ב"מ דף קיב: ושם) אומן אומר שתים קצצת לי והלה אומר לא קצצתי לך אלא אחת המוציא מחבירו עליו הראיה דקיילא מידע ידיע ובפ' כל הנשבעין (שבועות דף מו. ושם) פריך ליה ומשני דהך דהכא כרבי יהודה דקיילא נמי לא דכיר דטרוד הוא בפועליו וא"ת א"כ לאחר זמנו נמי אמאי אמר המע"ה הוה לן למימר נשבע ונוטל דמאי טעמא אמרינן בעלמא לאחר זמנו דאין נשבע ונוטל כדמפרש בריש כל הנשבעין דחזקה דאין שכיר משהה שכרו ואין בעה"ב עובר בבל תלין והכא הרי שהה שכיר ובעה"ב עבר דמודה שקצץ לו אחת ועדיין חייב לו וליכא למימר דמיירי כגון דאמר לא קצצתי לך אלא אחת ופרעתי לך דא"כ בזמנו אמאי נשבע ונוטל הא כרבי יהודה מוקמי לה ואיהו בעי הודאה במקצת ואין לתרץ נמי כגון שאומר אותה אחת שקצצתי לך ברשותך השהיתי דלא עבר בבל תלין דמ"מ חזקה דאין שכיר משהה שכרו ליכא דהרי שיהה אחת ודוחק לומר דמאי דחזינן דשיהה שיהה ומאי דלא חזינן (ג) דלא שיהה לא שיהה: **אי** דאיכא עדים ליחזי עדים מאי קאמרי. דודאי ידעי הקיילא דרגילות הוא תימה לר"י דעדיפא מינה הוה ליה למיפרך דאי איכא עדים וראה דהכתי לא מסיק אדעתיה לאוקמה בלא ראה אם כן אמאי מהימן אומן שהטלית בידו והכי הוה ליה למימר בשלמא לרבה במיגו אלא לאביי במאי מוקי לה בין דאיכא עדים בין דליכא עדים לא מהימן במיגו ויש לומר דהכי קאמר אי דאיכא עדים ואתא לאשמועינן דאע"ג דאיכא עדים אומן מהימן וכגון דלא ראה ליחזי עדים מאי קאמרי אלא לאו דליכא עדים דתו לא מצית לאוקומי בדלא ראה דאם כן מאי קא משמע לן פשיטא דכי ליכא עדים ולא ראה דמהימן

עין משפט נר מצוה

קנג א מיי' פ"ט מהל' טוען הל' ב סמג עשין לה טוש"ע ח"מ סי' לב סעיף א: ב ג וסי' לב סעיף ה:
קנד ב טוש"ע ח"מ סי' קלד סעיף ד:
קנה ג מיי' פ"ו מהל' פקדון הלכה ד ופ"ט מהל' טוען הל' ב סמג שם טוש"ע ח"מ סי' קלד סעיף א וסי' רלו [רלה] סעיף א:
קנו ד מיי' פ"ט מהל' טוען הל' ב ופי"א מהלכות שכירות הל' ח סמג עשין פח טוש"ע ח"מ סי' פט סעיף ד [ה]:

הגהות הב"ח

(א) גמ' מיתיביה אביי לרבה ראה עבדו וכו': (ב) שם מה טיבו אצלך א"ל אתה: (ג) תוס' ד"ה נתנה וכו' דלא חזינן דשיהה וכו' כצ"ל ותיבת דלא נמחק:

ליקוטי רש"י

כל זמן שהטלית ביד אומן. דבעל הבית הוי המוציא מחבירו עליו הראיה להביא עדים שלא קצץ אלא אחת [שבועות מו.]. בזמנו. אם תבעו בתוך זמן גבייתו. עבר זמנו המוציא מחבירו. היינו אומן. עליו הראיה. צריך להביא עדים ולא יהא נאמן בשבועה [שם מה:].

מסורת הש"ס

א) ב"מ קיב: שבועות מו., ב) נ"א אומן, ג) נ"א ולפי' אין:

רבינו גרשום

אמר רב' מפרש לה לסיפא א) **ביוצאת** העדות **מתחת ידי אחר** ולא מתחת ידי אומן וכי אמר ליה המערער להאי אחר מה טיבו אצלך **אמר לו בפני אמרת לו** לאומן **למוכרו** למי שירצה ואני קניתיו ממנו דבריו קיימין מיגו כו' כי אמר ליה נמי זבינתה ניהליה **ובפני אמרת לו שימכרהו** או יתנהו למי שירצה מהימן: **אי דאיכא עדים.** שראוהו שמסר לו **למה ליה ראה** בידו אע"ג דלא ראה בידו לא אמר כלום האומן **דנייתי עדים** שהפקידו אצלו **ונפיק** לדבריך דאמרת המפקיד אצל חבירו בעדים צריך להחזיר לו בעדים. **אלא לאו** הכא במאי עסקינן **דליכא עדים** ומש"ה דוקא ראה **וכי ראה** המפקיד ביד האומן **מיהא תפיס** מן האומן דלא מהימן הוא דלית ליה חזקה וקשיא לרבה דאמר היכא דמסר לו שלא בעדים אע"ג דראהו מהימן האומן והא הכא קתני דאינו נאמן אע"ג דליכא עדים הואיל דראהו. ומשני **לא לעולם** מש"ה אינו נאמן האומן **דאיכא עדים** שמסרו לו **והוא דראה** המפקיד דוקא. מש"ה הואיל דאיכא תרתי עדים וראה אינו נאמן. אבל לעולם אי ליכא עדים אע"ג דראה בידו מהימן האומן וכן הכי נמי אי איכא עדים הואיל דלא ראהו המפקיד מהימן האומן ויש לו חזקה. ומקשה ליה אביי והיכי מצית למימר משום דאיתנייהו תרוייהו אינו נאמן הא ליתנייהו תרוייהו נאמן **והא את הוא דאמרת המפקיד אצל חבירו בעדים** אע"ג דלא ראהו **צריך להחזיר לו בעדים** ולא מהימן האומן אע"ג דליתנייהו תרוייהו: **א"ל הדרי בי.** דסבירא ליה המפקיד אצל חבירו בעדים א"צ להחזיר לו בעדים והואיל שלא ראהו מהימן האומן והכי קתני לה אמר רבה ל"ש דאין לו חזקה אלא שמסר לו בעדים וראהו בידו אבל אם לא ראהו מהימן האומן משום דסבירא ליה המפקיד אצל חבירו בעדים א"צ להחזיר לו בעדים ואם מסר לו שלא בעדים נמי אע"ג דראהו מהימן האומן מתוך שיכול כו' ואביי ס"ל אע"ג דליכא עדים הואיל שראהו מיהא תפיס דלאו אומן מהימן. ואי איכא נמי עדים הואיל שלא ראהו בידו נאמן האומן משום דס"ל המפקיד אצל חבירו בעדים א"צ להחזיר לו בעדים ואביי עביד ראיה עיקר בלא עדים ורבה ס"ל דאינו נאמן עד דאיכא תרתי: **הנותן טליתו לאומן.** לתקנה וראה אותה בידו: **אומן אומר.** ב' מעות **קצצת לי** בשכירותי: **להביא ראיה.** בעדים: **נתנה לו.** האומן לבעה"ב: **בזמנו.** היינו כל היום שהחזירה לו: **נשבע.** האומן **ונוטל** מבעה"ב דשכיר בזמנו נשבע ונוטל: **עבר זמנו המוציא מחבירו עליו הראיה.** בעדים: **אי דאיכא עדים.** שקצץ לו בפניהן: אלא

חשק שלמה על רבינו גרשום

א) נראה דל"ל ביוצא הטלית.

הַמַּפְקִיד אֵצֶל חֲבֵירוֹ בְּעֵדִים – that if **someone deposits** an article **with his fellow in the presence of witnesses,** אֵינוֹ צָרִיךְ לְהַחֲזִיר לוֹ בְּעֵדִים – **[the custodian] does not have to return it in front of witnesses?**[1] לֹא סָלְקָא דַּעְתָּךְ – **Do not think so!** אֶלָּא הַמַּפְקִיד אֵצֶל חֲבֵירוֹ בְּעֵדִים – **Rather,** if **someone deposits** an article **with his fellow in the presence of witnesses,** צָרִיךְ לְהַחֲזִיר לוֹ בְּעֵדִים – **[the custodian] must,** likewise, **return it in the presence of witnesses.**[2] Thus, the basis for Abaye's objection is removed. For if the article was deposited with the craftsman in the presence of witnesses, he has no *migo* to support his actual claim ["I still have the article, but I subsequently purchased it"], since he could not have claimed that he already returned it.

Abaye raises another objection:

מֵיתִיבֵי אַבַּיֵי – **Abaye challenged** Rabbah **from the** following **Baraisa:**[3] רָאָה עַבְדּוֹ בְּיַד אוּמָּן – A PERSON SAW HIS SLAVE IN THE POSSESSION OF A CRAFTSMAN וְטַלִּיתוֹ בְּיַד כּוֹבֵס – OR HIS CLOAK IN THE POSSESSION OF A LAUNDERER,[4] אוֹמֵר לוֹ מַה טִּיבוֹ אֶצְלְךָ – and [THE OWNER] SAYS TO HIM [the craftsman]: "WHAT IS THE NATURE OF ITS PRESENCE IN YOUR POSSESSION?" I.e. in what capacity do you claim to hold the slave or cloak? As my custodian or as its owner? אָמַר לוֹ אַתָּה מְכַרְתּוֹ לִי אַתָּה נְתַתּוֹ לִי בְּמַתָּנָה – If HE ANSWERS, "YOU SOLD IT TO ME," or "YOU GAVE IT TO ME AS A GIFT," לֹא אָמַר כְּלוּם – HE HAS SAID NOTHING. I.e. the craftsman cannot use his current possession of the slave or cloak to prove that it is his.[5] בִּפְנַי אָמַרְתָּ לוֹ לְמוֹכְרוֹ וְלִיתְּנוֹ לוֹ בְּמַתָּנָה – But if he says, "YOU TOLD HIM [i.e. a third person] IN MY PRESENCE TO SELL IT OR TO GIFT IT TO HIM (i.e. me)." דְּבָרָיו קַיָּימִין – HIS WORDS STAND, i.e. his claim is accepted.[6]

Before explaining how this Baraisa presents a challenge to Rabbah, the Gemara pauses to ascertain the exact meaning of the Baraisa. Towards this end the Gemara asks:

מַאי שְׁנָא רֵישָׁא וּמַאי שְׁנָא סֵיפָא – **What is the difference between the** craftsman's claim described in the **first case** of the Baraisa **and** that described in **the latter case?** There seems to be no substantive difference. In both cases, the craftsman claims that he bought the article from the original owner — whether directly or through the owner's agent. Why, then, is the craftsman believed in the second case and not in the first?

The Gemara therefore reinterprets the second case of the Baraisa:

אָמַר רַבָּה – **Rabbah said:** סֵיפָא בְּיוֹצֵא מִתַּחַת יְדֵי אַחֵר – **The second case refers to where [the article]** presently **emerges from someone else's possession.** I.e. neither the original owner nor the craftsman currently has the article. Rather, a third party has it and claims it as his own.[7] וְקָאָמַר לֵיהּ אַחֵר – **And** this **someone else says to [the original owner]:** בְּפָנַי אָמַרְתָּ לוֹ לְמוֹכְרוֹ וְלִיתְּנוֹ בְּמַתָּנָה – **"In my presence did you instruct [the craftsman] to sell it or to gift it** to me."[8] This third party is believed for the following reason: מִיגּוֹ דְּאִי בָּעֵי אָמַר לֵיהּ מִינָּךְ זְבַנְתֵּיהּ – **Since he could have said** instead **to [the original owner]: "I bought it** directly **from you,"** and he would have been believed, since he is not a craftsman, and we would not have attributed his possession of the article to having received it in a professional capacity,[9] כִּי אָמַר לֵיהּ נַמִּי בְּפָנַי אָמַרְתָּ לוֹ לְמוֹכְרוֹ דְּבָרָיו קַיָּימִין וּמְהֵימַן – **even when he says, "In my presence did you tell [the craftsman] to sell [the article]** to me," **his words stand and he is believed.**[10]

Having clarified the meaning of the Baraisa, the Gemara now returns to elaborate Abaye's objection:

קָתָנֵי מִיהַת רֵישָׁא רָאָה – **At any rate, the first part** of the Baraisa **states** a case in which **"[the original owner] saw"** his article in the craftsman's possession [i.e. there are witnesses that the craftsman still has it]. Apparently, then, incontrovertible evidence

NOTES

1. [Abaye's objection is based on this premise. For if an article entrusted in the presence of witnesses would likewise have to be returned in the presence of witnesses (see next note), then the craftsman would *not* have had the option of claiming that he had already returned it to the original owner. Since the article is still, in fact, in the craftsman's possession, there are certainly no witnesses to substantiate the claimed return.]

2. Since the depositor took the precaution of securing witnesses that he gave a deposit to the custodian, it is implicit in the terms of the custodianship that the custodian cannot terminate his obligations by claiming that he returned the deposit unless he can produce witnesses to that effect (*Tosafos* ד"ה המפקיד, from *Shevuos* 41b).

3. [*Bach* emends the text to read: אֵיתִיבֵיהּ אַבַּיֵי, which is the grammatically correct form.]

4. [In the course of this discussion, when it is said that the person "saw" his article in the craftsman's possession,] the meaning is that witnesses were with him when he saw his article there, so that the craftsman cannot deny that the person has indeed seen it there (*Rashbam*). [The person claims that] he had apprenticed his slave to the craftsman to be taught his craft (*Rashbam*) or that he had deposited his cloak with the cleaner for cleaning.

[The Baraisa thus lists two cases of an article (slave or cloak) claimed to have been delivered to a craftsman (teacher or launderer) in his professional capacity (to teach the slave or clean the cloak). For the sake of simplicity, we will in the ensuing discussion generally refer simply to the "craftsman" and the "article," rather than to the specific nature of the craft or article.]

5. When the Baraisa discusses here whether or not the craftsman has a *chazakah* based on his possession of the slave or cloak, the reference is to a *chazakah* that is appropriate for the particular object. In the case of the cloak, the *chazakah* (when effective) would be immediate, as is the law in regard to all inanimate movables, current possession of the article is generally construed as current ownership. In the case of the slave, however, who can wander of his own accord, the *chazakah* (when effective) would require possession of the slave for three years, as is the law in regard to mobile creatures [see above, 36a] (*Rashbam*).

6. The Gemara initially understands this latter case of the Baraisa as follows: The craftsman does not assert that he bought the article (or received it as a gift) directly from the owner. Rather, the craftsman asserts that he bought it (or received it as a gift) from the owner's agent and that he has personal knowledge that the owner authorized the agent to do so. In this case, the craftsman is believed. Based on this understanding of the case, the Gemara asks its next question (*Rashbam*; *Ritva*).

7. According to the Gemara's new explanation, the latter case of the Baraisa discusses the owner's dispute with a third party rather than with the craftsman. The original owner sees a third party with an article that he had initially entrusted to a craftsman's care and now confronts that third party.

8. Thus, all agree that the original owner indeed entrusted the article to the craftsman's care. However, this third party asserts that in his very presence the original owner subsequently instructed the craftsman to sell or gift the article to him (see *Rashbam* and *Rashash*).

9. Rather, as with any other ordinary person, his very possession of an article would support his claim to legitimate ownership, even though the article is known to have belonged to someone else.

10. The principle of *migo* causes us to accept his actual claim, because he could have offered instead a different, winning claim.

[Were it not for the principle of *migo,* however, this third party would not have won with his present claim (that the original owner instructed the craftsman to sell or gift the article to him). Although this third party is not a craftsman himself, he admits that he received the article from a craftsman. Since the craftsman's possession of the article does not constitute proof of ownership, neither does the possession of one who received the article from the craftsman. The third party wins his case only because he has a *migo* — he could have claimed that he received the article directly from the original owner, a claim that would be supported by his current possession of the article.]

קנג א מיי' פ"ט מהל' טוען הל' ב סמג עשין צה טוש"ע ח"מ סי' רלו סעיף א ב וסי' רלז סעיף ה:

קנד ב טוש"ע ח"מ סי' קלג סעיף ד:

קנה ג מיי' פ"ו מהל' פקדון הלכה ד ופ"ט מהל' טוען הל' ג סמג שם טוש"ע ח"מ סי' קלג סעיף א וסי' רלו [רלז] סעיף א:

קנו ד מיי' פ"ט מהל' טוען הל' ג ופי"א מהלכות שכירות הל' ו סמג עשין צה טוש"ע ח"מ סי' פט סעיף ד [ה]:

א) ב"מ קיב: שבועות מה., ב) ג"א אומן, ג) ג"א ולפי' אין:

אהמפקיד אצל חבירו בעדים אינו צריך להחזיר לו בעדים לס"ד אלא המפקיד אצל חבירו בעדים צריך להחזיר לו בעדים (א) מיתיבי אביי ראה עבדו ביד אומן וטליתו ביד כובס אומר לו מה טיבו אצלך (ב) אתה מכרתו לי אתה נתתו לי במתנה לא אמר כלום בפני אמרת לו למוכרו וליתנו לו במתנה דבריו קיימין מאי שנא רישא ומאי שנא סיפא אמר רבה סיפא בביוצא מתחת ידי אחר וקאמר ליה אחר בפני אמרת לו למוכרו וליתנו במתנה מיגו דאי בעי א"ל מינך זבנתיה כי א"ל נמי בפני אמרת לו למוכרו דבריו קיימין ומהימן קתני מיהת רישא ראה היכי דמי אי דאיכא עדים למה לי ראה ניתי עדים ונשקול אלא לאו דליכא עדים וכי ראה מיהא תפים ליה לא גלעולם דאיכא עדים והוא דראה והא את הוא דאמרת המפקיד אצל חבירו בעדים צריך לפורעו בעדים אמר ליה הדרי בי מתיב רבא לסיועי לרבה דהנותן טליתו לאומן אומן אומר שתים קצצת לי והלה אומר לא קצצתי לך אלא אחת כל זמן שהטלית ביד אומן על בעה"ב להביא ראיה נתנה לו בזמנו נשבע ונוטל עבר זמנו המוציא מחבירו עליו הראיה ה"ד אי דאיכא עדים ליחזי עדים מאי קאמרי אלא

עדים אפי' לא ראה דלא מהימנא אמאי אינו נאמן במיגו דאי בעי אמר החזרתיו לך ותימה קשה דלשון אי הכי אפילו בעדים נמי לא משמע הכי אלא משמע אי הכי דשלא בעדים נאמן במיגו בעדים נמי הוה לך למימר מיגו בשלמא לדידי דלית לי מיגו שלא בעדים בעדים נמי לית לי מיגו אלא לדידך קשה ור"ת דחק לפרש ואין נראה כלל לר"י:

המפקיד אצל חבירו בעדים צריך להחזיר לו בעדים. וא"ת אמאי להימניה במיגו דאי בעי אמר נאנסו כדאמרינן בסוף המוכר את הבית (לקמן דף ע. ושם) גבי מפקיד אצל חבירו בשטר ואפי' מאן דפליג התם היינו משום דשטרך בידי מאי בעי ותירץ ר"ת דודאי הוה מצי אביי למיפרך ליה אי הכי בעדים נמי להימניה במיגו דאי בעי אמר נאנסו אלא דלא אסיק אדעתיה ואותביה מברייתא ואודי ליה דברייתא איירי מתני' ותו ליכא למיפרך מידי אנאנסו וי"מ דהא דקאמר הכא דצריך להחזיר לו בעדים היינו אם רוצה להיות פטור משבועה אבל בשבועה נאמן במיגו דנאנסו (ג) ואין מחזיר לו בעדים והכי פי' לעיל לא שנו דאומן אין לו חזקה בלא שבועה אלא שמסר לו בעדים אבל מסר לו שלא בעדים נאמן בלא שבועה במיגו דאי בעי אמר לא היו דברים מעולם ומיירי קודם שנתקנה שבועת היסת ולכך כי אמר לא היו דברים מעולם אין צריך שבועה אי נמי לאחר שנתקנה ולישנא דבעי בשבועה דרך דממונא ולא חשיב הכא דרך דממונא דאמר לא בא לידי בתורת אומנות ואין מודה שנתחייב בו מעולם ולא חשיב דרך דממונא אלא מנה לי בידך וא"ל הן למחר א"ל תנהו לי וא"ל נתתיו לך שמודה שנתחייב ועל פירוש זה קשה לר"ת דמאי פריך לקמן מראה עבדו ביד אומן אי דאיכא עדים למה לי ראה לייתי עדים ולישקול הא מהני ראה דאפילו בשבועה לא יהא נאמן דאין לו מיגו דבלא ראה מהימן הוא בשבועה במיגו דנאנסו ובריית' משמע דלא אמר כלום דאפילו בשבועה אינו נאמן ונראה לו לתרץ דהכא לא חשיב מיגו דטעמא דמ"ד דצריך להחזיר בעדים משום דכיון דלא הימניה בשבועה כדאמר בשבועות (דף מא: ושם) דהויא כאילו א"ל בהדיא אל תחזיר לי אלא בעדים הלכך לא מהימן במיגו דאיהו דאפסיד אנפשיה אבל התם בהמוכר סבר דאין צריך להחזיר לו בעדים ולא חשיב כאילו אמר אל תחזירני אלא בעדים ולכך נאמן במיגו אבל אין נראה דאפילו מאן דאית ליה צריך להחזיר לו בעדים כי איכא מיגו מהימן דאי לאו הכי תקשי מאי פריך ליה אביי מההיא דראה עבדו ביד אומן דסברא דאין צריך להחזיר לו בעדים הא איכא תנא בשבועות דאית ליה המלוה את חבירו בעדים צריך להחזיר לו בעדים ויסבור רבה כוותיה אלא משום דאפילו ההוא תנא דשבועות מודה בפקדון דאיכא מיגו דנאנסו דאין צריך להחזיר לו בעדים לכך נראה כפי' ר"ת:

נתנה לו בזמנו נשבע ונוטל. וא"ת והא אמר בפ' המקבל (ב"מ דף קיב: ושם) אומן אומר שתים קצצת לי והלה אומר לא קצצתי לך אלא אחת המוציא מחבירו עליו הראיה דקיילא מידע ידיע ובפ' כל הנשבעין (שבועות דף מו. ושם) פריך ליה ומשני דהך דהכא כרבי יהודה דקיילא נמי לא דכיר דטרוד הוא בפועליו וא"ת א"כ לאחר זמנו נמי אמאי אמר המע"ה הוה לן למימר נשבע ונוטל דמאי טעמא אמרינן בעלמא לאחר זמנו דאין נשבע ונוטל כדמפרש בריש כל הנשבעין דחזקה דאין שכיר משהה שכרו ואין בעה"ב עובר בבל תלין והכא הרי שהה שכיר ובעה"ב עבר דמודה שקצץ לו אחת ועדיין חייב לו וליכא למימר דמיירי כגון דאמר לא קצצתי לך אלא אחת ופרעתי לך דא"כ בזמנו אמאי נשבע ונוטל הא כרבי יהודה מוקמי לה ואיהו בעי הודאה במקצת ואין לתרץ נמי כגון שאומר אותה אחת שקצצתי לך ברשותך השהיתי דלא עבר בבל תלין דמ"מ חזקה דאין שכיר משהה שכרו ליכא דהרי שיהה אחת ודוחק לומר דמאי דחזינן דשיהה שיהה ומאי דלא חזינן (ג) דלא שיהה לא שיהה:

אי דאיכא עדים ליחזי עדים מאי קאמרי. דודאי ידעי הקציצה דרגילות הוא תימה לר"י דעדיפא מינה הוה ליה למיפרך דאי איכא עדים וראה דהכתי לא מסיק אדעתיה לאוקמה בלא ראה אם כן אמאי מהימן אומן שהטלית בידו והכי הוה ליה למימר בשלמא לרב' מוקי לה בדליכא עדים דמהימן לרבא במיגו אלא לאביי במאי מוקי לה בין דאיכא עדים בין דליכא עדים לא מהימן במיגו ויש לומר דהכי קאמר אי דאיכא עדים ואתא לאשמועינן דאע"ג דאיכא עדים אומן מהימן וכגון דלא ראה ליחזי עדים מאי קאמרי אלא לאו דליכא עדים דתו לא מצית לאוקומי בדלא ראה דאם כן מאי קא משמע לן פשיטא דכי ליכא עדים ולא ראה דמהימן

המפקיד אצל חבירו בעדים אין צריך להחזיר לו בעדים כי א"ל נמי לקוח הוא בידי מהימן ולא משכחת מתני' דקתני אומן אין לו חזקה אלא היכא דראה לא שנא מסר בעדים לא שנא מסר שלא בעדים דלמסירה לא חיישי אביי דעכשיו אינו יכול לטעון החזרתיו לך דהא קא חזינן ליה בידו וגם אינו יכול לטעון לא מסרתו לי דדמי לדברים העשויין להשאיל ולהשכיר ואמר לקוחה היא בידי דאינו נאמן אע"ג דליכא עדי מסירה ובכה"ג לחוד הוא דס"ל לאביי דאומן אין לו חזקה והכי הויא מסקנא דשמעתין כאביי: **ראה עבדו ביד אומן.** שמלמדו אומנות והכן ראוהו בעדים היא שאינו יכול לטעון לא ראית וכגון שהחזיק בו שלש שנים דלאו בפחות מג' שנים למה לי דנקט אומן דמשמע אבל באדם אחר הויא חזקתו חזקה והאמר ר"ל (לעיל דף לו.) הגודרות אין להן חזקה ואוקימנן אין להן חזקה לאלתר אבל יש להן חזקה לאחר ג' שנים: **וטליתו ביד כובס.** ואפילו שעה אחת: **לא אמר כלום.** דאומן אין לו חזקה: **בפני אמרת.** לפלוני למוכרו וליתנו לו במתנה: **דבריו.** של (ג) גזלן קיימין הכי קס"ד השתא והיינו דקפריך מאי שנא רישא כו': **אמר רבא כו'.** ברישא מפרש לה והדר מפרש תיובתא: **ביוצא.** הטלית מתחת ידי אחר שטוען שלקחו מן האומן וקאמר ליה אחר לבעל הבית התובעו ואמר לו מה טיבו אצלך והלא מסרתיו לאומן לתקנו והוא משיב מן האומן קניתיו ובמלותך מכרו לי שבפני אמרת לו למוכרו הרי הוא כמי שטוען ממך לקחתי דמיגו דאי א"ל האי מחזיק לבעה"ב מנך זבנתי ומהימן הוא דהא לאו אומן הוא כי א"ל נמי יודע אני דזבינתה ניהליה לאומן וזבנה אומן ניהלי מהימן דהיינו כדאמרן לעיל דאי א"ל דזבנה מינך קמאי דידי מהימן: **אי דאיכא עדים.** שמסר לו למה לי ראה הא את הוא דאמרת ל"ש אלא שמסר לו בעדים ל"ש ראה ל"ש לא ראה אמרת דאין אומן מהימן משום דכיון דהפקידוהו בעדים צריך להחזירו בעדים ואמאי קתני דכי ראה אינו נאמן אבל אם לא ראה מהימן דמשמע דאין צריך להחזיר לו בעדים: **וכי ראה אותו ביד האומן מיהא תפים ליה.** בעה"ב ומוציאו מידו אלמא היכא דראה אפילו לא מסר בעדים לא מהימן אומן וקשיא לרבה דאמר דהיכא דמסר שלא בעדים ל"ש ראה לא שנא לא ראה מהימן אומן: ומשני רבה לא לעולם היכא דלא מסר בעדים אומן מהימן ואפילו ראה כדאמרינן והכא מיירי כגון דאיכא עדים שמסר לו וגם ראה הטלית בידו דכיון דאיכא תרתי עדים וראה לא מצי לאחזוקי ביה ולמימר לקוח הוא בידי שהרי בתורת פקדון בא לידו ומיגו ליכא למימר דהא לא מצי למימר החזרתיו לך שהרי רואין אותו עכשיו בידו ועכשיו חזר בו רבה בעל כרחו ממאי דאוקי למתני' במסירת עדים אע"ג דלא ראה אין לו חזקה לאומן והשתא ס"ל דהיכא דאיכא תרתי עדים וראה אין לו חזקה אבל עדים ולא ראה או ראה ולא עדים יש לו חזקה שיכול לטעון החזרתיו לך היכא דלא ראה ואע"ג דמסר בעדים דהדר ביה ממאי דאמר לעיל צריך להחזיר לו בעדים וכ"ש היכא דליכא לא עדים ולא ראה דיש לו חזקה ולאביי בראה לחוד תליא מילתא אם ראה ביד אומן אין לו חזקה ואם לא ראה יש חזקה ולמסירה לא חיישינן בין בעדים בין בלא עדים: **והאמרת כו'.** וכיון דאיכא עדים למה לי ראה: **מתיב רבא.** לאביי: **לסיועי לרבה.** נראה בעיני דבלשון הזה אמר רבא בבית המדרש תניא כוותיה דרבה ותיובתא דאביי: **על בעה"ב להביא ראיה.** עדים משום דאומן מהימן מיגו דמצי למימר לקוח הוא בידי יכול לטעון עד כדי דמיו כדאמרי' גבי הנהו עיזי דאכלי חושלי בנהרדעא (לעיל דף לו.): **בזמנו נשבע ונוטל.** כלומר אם בזמנו תובעו בדין נשבע ונוטל דהיינו מן הנשבעין ונוטלין שכיר בזמנו נשבע ונוטל וטעמא בשבועות משום דבעל הבית טרוד בפועליו הימנוהו לשכיר: **עבר זמנו.** אחר ששקעה החמה: **המוציא** מחבירו. שכיר: **אי דאיכא עדים.** שמסר לאומן בפניהם ומסתמא גם בפניהם קצץ השכירות: **ליחזי.** דיינין עדים מאי קאמרי: אלא

מינה הוה ליה למיפרך דאי איכא עדים וראה דהכתי לא מסיק אדעתיה לאוקמה בלא ראה אם כן אמאי מהימן אומן שהטלית בידו והכי הוה ליה למימר בשלמא לרב' מוקי לה בדליכא עדים דמהימן לרבא במיגו אלא לאביי במאי מוקי לה בין דאיכא עדים בין דליכא עדים לא מהימן במיגו ויש לומר דהכי קאמר אי דאיכא עדים ואתא לאשמועינן דאע"ג דאיכא עדים אומן מהימן וכגון דלא ראה ליחזי עדים מאי קאמרי אלא לאו דליכא עדים דתו לא מצית לאוקומי בדלא ראה דאם כן מאי קא משמע לן פשיטא דכי ליכא עדים ולא ראה דמהימן

הגהות הב"ח

(א) גמ' מיתיביה אביי לרבה ראה עבדו וכו': (ב) שם מה טיבו אצלך א"ל אתה: (ג) תוס' ד"ה נתנה וכו' דלא חזינן דשיהה לא חזינן כצ"ל ותיבת דלא נמחק:

ליקוטי רש"י

כל זמן שהטלית ביד אומן. דבעל הבית הוי המוציא מחבירו עליו הראיה להביא עדים שלא קצץ אלא אחת [שבועות מו.]. בזמנו. אם תבעו בתוך זמן גבייתו. עבר זמנו המוציא מחבירו. היינו אומן. עליו הראיה. צריך להביא עדים ולא יהא נאמן בשבועה [שם מה:].

רבינו גרשום

אמר רב' מפרש לה לסיפא (א) ביוצאת העדות מחמת ידי אחר ולא מחמת ידי אומן וכי אמר ליה המערער להאי אחר מה טיבו אצלך אמר לו בפני אמרת לו לאומן למוכרו למי שירצה ואני קניתיו ממנו דבריו קיימין מיגו כו' כי אמר ליה נמי זבינתה ניהליה ובפני אמרת לו שימכרהו או יתנהו למי שירצה מהימן: אי דאיכא עדים. שראוהו שמסר לו למה ליה ראה בידו אע"ג דלא ראה בידו לא אמר כלום האומן דנייתי עדים שהפקידו אצלו ונפיק לדבריך דאמרת המפקיד אצל חבירו בעדים צריך להחזיר לו בעדים. אלא לאו הכא במאי עסקינן דליכא עדים ומש"ה דוקא ראה וכי ראה המפקיד ביד האומן מיהא תפים מן האומן דלא מהימן הוא דלית ליה חזקה וקשיא לרבה דאמר היכא דמסר לו שלא בעדים אע"ג דראהו מהימן האומן והא הכא קתני דאינו נאמן אע"ג דליכא עדים הואיל דראהו. ומשני לא לעולם משה"ה אינו נאמן האומן דאיכא עדים שמסרו לו והוא דראה המפקיד דוקא. מש"ה הואיל דאיכא תרתי עדים וראה אינו נאמן. אבל לעולם אי ליכא עדים אע"ג דראה בידו מהימן האומן וכן הכי נמי אי איכא עדים הואיל דלא ראהו המפקיד מהימן האומן ויש לו חזקה. ומקשה ליה אביי והיכי מצית למימר משום דאיתנהו תרוייהו אינו נאמן הא ליתנהו תרוייהו נאמן והא את הוא דאמרת המפקיד אצל חבירו בעדים אע"ג דלא ראהו צריך להחזיר לו בעדים ולא מהימן האומן אע"ג דליתנהו תרווייהו. א"ל הדרי בי. דסבירא ליה המפקיד אצל חבירו בעדים א"צ להחזיר לו בעדים והואיל שלא ראהו מהימן האומן והכי קתני לה אמר רבה ל"ש דאין לו חזקה אלא שמסר לו בעדים וראהו בידו אבל אם לא ראהו מהימן האומן משום דסבירא ליה המפקיד אצל חבירו בעדים א"צ להחזיר לו בעדים ואם מסר לו שלא בעדים נמי אע"ג דראהו מהימן מתוך שיכול כו' ואביי ס"ל אע"ג דליכא עדים הואיל שראהו מיהא תפיס דלאו אומן מהימן. ואי איכא נמי עדים הואיל שלא ראהו בידו נאמן האומן משום דס"ל המפקיד אצל חבירו בעדים א"צ להחזיר לו בעדים ואביי עביד ראיה עיקר בלא עדים ורבה ס"ל דאינו נאמן עד דאיכא תרתי: הנותן טליתו לאומן. לתקנה וראה אותה בידו: אומן אומר. ב' מעות קצצת לי בשכירותי: להביא ראיה. בעדים: נתנה לו. האומן לבעה"ב: בזמנו. היינו כל היום שהחזירה לו: נשבע. האומן ונוטל מבעה"ב דשכיר בזמנו נשבע ונוטל: עבר זמנו המוציא מחבירו עליו הראיה. בעדים: אי דאיכא עדים. שקצץ לו בפניהן: אלא

חשק שלמה על רבינו גרשום

א) נראה דצ"ל ביוצא הטלית.

דמהימן

that the article is still in the craftsman's possession is an essential component of the case. הֵיכִי דָּמֵי – Now, **how is it?** What is the exact case? אִי דְּאִיכָּא עֵדִים – **If** the case is one in which **there are witnesses** who saw the original owner deposit the article with the craftsman in his professional capacity, לָמָּה לִי רָאָה – then **what need is there for [the original owner] to have seen** the article in the craftsman's possession? Even if it is not known whether the article is still in the craftsman's possession, נֵיתֵי עֵדִים וְנִשְׁקוֹל – **let [the owner]** simply **produce** the **witnesses** to the original deposit, **and take** back his article.[11] אֶלָּא לָאו דְּלֵיכָּא עֵדִים – **Rather, is it not that** the Baraisa speaks of a case in which **there are no witnesses** to the original deposit? וְכִי רָאָה מִיהָא תָּפִיס לֵיהּ – **Nonetheless, when [the original owner] has seen** the article still in the craftsman's possession, **[the original owner] may seize it** from the craftsman, as the Baraisa rules in this case that the craftsman's claim amounts to nothing. This contradicts Rabbah's opinion that in the absence of witnesses to the original deposit, the craftsman can *always* lay claim to the article.[12] – ? –

Rabbah responds to Abaye's objection:

לֹא לְעוֹלָם דְּאִיכָּא עֵדִים – **No, in fact** the Baraisa refers to a case in which **there *are* witnesses** to the original deposit. וְהוּא דְּרָאָה – **Nevertheless,** the craftsman loses the case **only if [the original owner] has seen** that the article is still in the craftsman's possession. But if the article has *not* been seen there, the craftsman is believed by force of a *migo,* since he could have claimed that he already returned the article.

Abaye asks the obvious question:

וְהָא אַתְּ הוּא דְּאָמְרַתְּ – **But you,** Rabbah, **are the one who said** previously that הַמַּפְקִיד אֵצֶל חֲבֵירוֹ בְּעֵדִים צָרִיךְ לְפוֹרְעוֹ בְּעֵדִים – if **someone deposits** an article **with his fellow in the presence of witnesses, [the custodian] must,** likewise, **return it in the presence of witnesses!** How, then, would the custodian have been believed to say that he already returned the article?

Rabbah responds:

אֲמַר לֵיהּ הֲדַרִי בִּי – **[Rabbah] said to [Abaye], I retract** my earlier ruling on that point. Rather, I agree that a custodian need not return the deposit in the presence of witnesses, even though it was initially entrusted to him in that manner.[13]

מְתִיב רָבָא לְסִיּוּעֵי לְרַבָּה – **Rava challenged [Abaye] from a Baraisa,** which seems **to support Rabbah.** The Baraisa discusses the law in the following case: הַנּוֹתֵן טַלִּיתוֹ לְאוּמָן – ONE WHO GIVES HIS CLOAK TO A CRAFTSMAN to repair, and after the repair was completed the owner and the craftsman disagree over what wages were originally set; אוּמָן אוֹמֵר שְׁתַּיִם קָצַצְתָּ לִי – THE CRAFTSMAN SAYS, "YOU AGREED TO PAY ME TWO dinars," וְהַלָּה אוֹמֵר לֹא קָצַצְתִּי לְךָ אֶלָּא אַחַת – BUT [THE OWNER] SAYS, "I AGREED TO PAY YOU ONLY ONE." The law is as follows: כָּל זְמַן שֶׁהַטַּלִּית בְּיַד אוּמָן עַל בַּעַל הַבַּיִת לְהָבִיא רְאָיָה – AS LONG AS THE CRAFTSMAN STILL HOLDS THE CLOAK, THE BURDEN OF PROOF RESTS UPON THE OWNER, because the craftsman has a *migo.*[14] נְתָנָהּ לוֹ – BUT IF [THE CRAFTSMAN] HAS ALREADY GIVEN [THE CLOAK] BACK to the owner, and thus no longer has a *migo,* then the law depends on when the craftsman claims his wages: בִּזְמַנּוֹ נִשְׁבַּע וְנוֹטֵל – If he claims his wages ON TIME, i.e. on the day that he returns the cloak,[15] then HE SWEARS AND COLLECTS.[16] עָבַר זְמַנּוֹ הַמּוֹצִיא מֵחֲבֵירוֹ עָלָיו הָרְאָיָה – But if he claims his wages AFTER THE TIME

NOTES

11. As Rabbah himself stated above, if someone deposits an article with a custodian in the presence of witnesses, the custodian is obligated to return the object in the presence of witnesses. Now, the custodian in our case obviously has no witnesses that he returned the article (since in point of fact he still has it). Therefore, he would be forced to surrender the article (or its monetary equivalent) even if the article was *not* seen in his possession. Why, then, does the Baraisa stipulate that the article *was* seen in his possession?

12. As Rabbah stated on 45a.

13. To summarize the Gemara up to this point: Two rulings emerge from Rabbah's original qualification of our Mishnah. 1) If there are witnesses that the craftsman initially took possession of the article as a deposit, then the craftsman must surrender the article (or its value) whether or not the article is still seen in his possession. [He does not have a *migo* that he could have claimed that he already returned the article, because he is obligated to return it in the presence of witnesses.] 2) If there are no witnesses that the craftsman initially took possession of the article as a deposit, then the craftsman is believed even if the article is currently seen in his possession. [Since there are no witnesses that the original transfer was a deposit, the craftsman has a *migo* that he could have claimed to have initially bought the article from the original owner or from a third party – see 45a note 20.]

Abaye, however, produced a Baraisa which in effect states that the craftsman's claim is rejected *only* if the article is currently seen in his possession. This perforce contradicts one of Rabbah's two rulings: If the Baraisa refers to a case in which there are witnesses that the craftsman initially took possession of the article as a deposit, then Rabbah's first ruling is contradicted. [According to that ruling, once there are witnesses that the original transfer was a deposit, the craftsman is not believed even if the article is not currently seen in his possession.] And if the Baraisa refers to a case in which there are no witnesses that the craftsman initially took possession of the article as a deposit, then Rabbah's second ruling is contradicted. [According to that ruling, when there are no witnesses that the original transfer was a deposit, the craftsman is believed even if the article is currently seen in his possession.] Faced with this dilemma, Rabbah retracts and asserts that the Baraisa refers to a case in which there were witnesses that the craftsman initially took possession of the article as a deposit. [Had there not been witnesses, even though the article is currently seen in the craftsman's possession, he could effectively claim to have initially *bought* the article from the owner.] Though there are witnesses that the original transfer was a deposit, the craftsman loses his case only if the article is currently seen in his possession. But if he volunteers that he still has it, then his claim to legitimate ownership is accepted, since he could have said that he already returned it.

Thus, Rabbah and Abaye are now divided on only one issue: Is the craftsman believed when there are no witnesses that he initially took possession of the article as a deposit but the article is currently seen in his possession? According to Rabbah, he is believed [since he can say that he initially bought it from the owner; the article found in his possession is not automatically assumed to have come there in his professional capacity as a craftsman – see 45a note 19]. Abaye, on the other hand, holds that the craftsman is not believed. [The article found in his possession *is* automatically assumed to have come there in his professional capacity as a craftsman – see 45a note 22] (see *Rashbam*).

14. The craftsman could have won with the claim that he *bought* the cloak from the owner, which would have been supported by his current possession of it. Therefore, through the principle of *migo,* he is believed regarding any claim he makes about the stipulated price of repair, up to the value of the cloak (*Rashbam*; see Gemara 46a; cf. *Rashi* to *Shevuos* 46a ד״ה כל זמן שהטלית).

15. The Torah commands that an employer pay wages on time (*Deuteronomy* 24:15 et al.). A worker hired for the day must be paid sometime that night; one hired for the night must be paid sometime the following day. A craftsman who returns the completed article to the owner during the day must be paid sometime before sunset (see *Rambam, Hil. Sechirus* 11:1-3).

16. In this case, the Rabbis legislated that the employee be believed under oath. The Rabbis reasoned that on the day that the wages are due, the employer's recollection of the agreed wages is not to be relied upon, since he is burdened with his many obligations to various different workers; thus, he may genuinely think that he agreed to pay the craftsman only one *dinar* when in fact he agreed to pay two (see *Rashbam*). [The craftsman, on the other hand, generally has a clearer

א המפקיד אצל חבירו בעדים אינו צריך להחזיר לו בעדים לא ס"ד אלא המפקיד אצל חבירו בעדים צריך להחזיר לו בעדים (א) מיתיבי אביי ראה עבדו ביד אומן וטליתו ביד כובס אומר לו מה טיבו אצלך (ג) אתה מכרתו לי אתה נתתו לי במתנה לא אמר כלום בפני אמרת לו למוכרו וליתנו לו במתנה דבריו קיימין מאי שנא רישא ומאי שנא סיפא אמר רבה סיפא ב ביוצא מתחת ידי אחר וקאמר ליה אחר בפני אמרת לו למוכרו וליתנו במתנה מיגו דאי בעי א"ל מינך זבנתיה כי א"ל נמי בפני אמרת לו למוכרו דבריו קיימין ומהימן קתני מיהת רישא ראה היכי דמי אי דאיכא עדים למה לי ראה ניתי עדים ונשקול אלא לאו דליכא עדים וכי ראה מיהא תפים ליה לא ג לעולם דאיכא עדים והוא דראה והא את הוא דאמרת המפקיד אצל חבירו בעדים צריך לפורעו בעדים אמר ליה הדרי בי מתיב רבא לסיועי לרבה (א) ד הנותן טליתו לאומן אומן אומר שתים קצצת לי והלה אומר לא קצצתי לך אלא אחת כל זמן שהטלית ביד אומן על בעה"ב להביא ראיה נתנה לו בזמנו נשבע ונוטל עבר זמנו המוציא מחבירו עליו הראיה ה"ד אי דאיכא עדים ליחזי עדים מאי קאמרי אלא

רש"י

המפקיד אצל חבירו בעדים אין צריך להחזיר לו בעדים כי א"ל נמי לקוח הוא בידי מהימן ולא משכחת מתני' דקתני אומן אין לו חזקה אלא היכא דראה לא שנא מסר בעדים לא שנא לא מסר דלמסירה לא חייש אביי דעכשיו אינו יכול לטעון החזרתיו לך דהא קא חזינן ליה בידו וגם אינו יכול לטעון לא מסרתו לי דדמי לדברים העשויין להשאיל ולהשכיר ואמר לקוחה היא בידי דאינו נאמן אע"ג דליכא עדי מסירה ובכה"ג לחוד הוא דס"ל לאביי דאומן אין לו חזקה והכי הויא מסקנא דשמעתין כאביי: ראה עבדו ביד אומן. שמלמדו אומנות והך ראיה בעדים היא שאינו יכול לטעון לא ראית וכגון שהחזיק בו שלש שנים דאי בפחות מג' שנים למה לי דנקט אומן דמשמע אבל באדם אחר הויא חזקתו חזקה והאמר ר"ל (לעיל דף לו.) הגודרות אין להן חזקה ואוקימנן אין להן חזקה לאלתר אבל יש להן חזקה לאחר ג' שנים: וטליתו ביד כובס. ואפילו שעה אחת: לא אמר כלום. דאומן אין לו חזקה: בפני אמרת. לפלוני למוכרו וליתנו לו במתנה: דבריו. של [ג] גזלן קיימין הכי קס"ד השתא והיינו דקפריך מאי שנא רישא כו': אמר רבא כו'. ברישא מפרש לה והדר מפרש תיובתא: ביוצא. הטלית מתחת ידי אחר שטוען שלקחו מן האומן וקאמר ליה אחר לבעל הבית המוכרו ואמר לו מה טיבו אצלך והלא מסרתיו לאומן לתקנו והוא משיב מן האומן קניתיו ובמלותך מכרו לי שבפני אמרת לו למוכרו הרי הוא כמי שטוען ממך לקחתי דמיגו דאי א"ל האי מחזיק לבעה"ב מנך זבנתי ומהימן הוא דהא לאו אומן הוא כי א"ל נמי יודע אני דזבינתה ניהליה לאומן וזבנה אומן ניהלי מהימן דהיינו כדאמרן לעיל דאי א"ל דזבנה מינך קמאי לידי מהימן: אי דאיכא עדים. שמסר לו למה לי ראה הא את הוא דאמרת ל"ש אלא שמסר לו בעדים ל"ש ראה ל"ש לא ראה אמרת דאין אומן מהימן משום דכיון דהפקידוהו בעדים צריך להחזירו בעדים ואמאי קתני דכי ראה אינו נאמן אבל אם לא ראה הוא מהימן דמשמע דאין צריך להחזיר לו בעדים: וכי ראה אותו ביד האומן מיהא תפים ליה. בעה"ב ומוציאו מידו דלמא היכא דלא ראה אפילו לא מסר בעדים לא מהימן אומן וקשיא לרבה דאמר דהיכא דמסר שלא בעדים ל"ש ראה ל"ש לא ראה מהימן אומן: ומשני רבה לא לעולם היכא דלא מסר בעדים אומן מהימן ואפילו ראה כדאמרינן והכא מיירי כגון דאיכא עדים שמסר לו וגם ראה הטלית בידו דכיון דאיכא תרתי עדים וראה לא מצי לאחזוקי ביה ולמימר לקוח הוא בידי שהרי בתורת פקדון בא לידו ומיגו ליכא למימר דהא לא מצי למימר החזרתיו לך שהרי רואין אותו עכשיו בידו ועכשיו חזר בו רבה בעל כרחו ממאי דאוקי למתני' במסירת עדים אע"ג דלא ראה אין לו חזקה לאומן והשתא ס"ל דהיכא דאיכא תרתי עדים וראה אין לו חזקה אבל עדים ולא ראה או ראה ולא עדים יש לו חזקה שיכול לטעון החזרתיו לך היכא דלא ראה ואע"ג דמסר בעדים דהדר ביה ממאי דאמר לעיל צריך להחזיר לו בעדים וכ"ש היכא דליכא לא עדים ולא ראה דיש לו חזקה ולאביי בראה לחוד תליא מילתא אם ראה ביד אומן אין לו חזקה ואם לא ראה יש לו חזקה ולמסירה לא חיישינן בין בעדים בין בלא עדים: והאמרת כו'. וכיון דאיכא עדים למה לי ראה: מתיב רבא. לאביי: לסיועי לרבה. נראה בעיני דבלשון הזה אמר רבא בבית המדרש תניא כוותיה דרבה ותיובתא לאביי: על בעה"ב להביא ראיה. עדים משום דאומן מהימן מיגו דמצי למימר לקוח הוא בידי יכול לטעון עד כדי דמיו כדאמרי' גבי הנהו עיזי דאכלי חושלי בנהרדעא (לעיל דף לו.): בזמנו נשבע ונוטל. כלומר אם בזמנו תובעו בדין נשבע ונוטל דהיינו מן הנשבעין ונוטלין שכיר בזמנו נשבע ונוטל וטעמא בשבועות משום דבעל הבית טרוד בפועליו הימנוהו לשכיר: עבר זמנו. אחר ששקעה החמה: המוציא מחבירו. שכיר: אי דאיכא עדים. שמסר לאומן בפניהם ומסתמא גם בפניהם קצץ השכירות: ליחזי. דיינן עדים מאי קאמרי: אלא

תוספות

עדים אפי' לא ראה דלא מהימנא אמאי אינו נאמן במיגו דאי בעי אמר החזרתיו לך ומיהו קשה דלשון אי הכי אפילו בעדים נמי לא משמע הכי אלא משמע אי הכי דשלא בעדים נאמן במיגו בעדים נמי הוה לך למימר מיגו בשלמא לדידי דלית לי מיגו שלא בעדים בעדים נמי לית לי מיגו אלא לדידך קשה ור"ת דחק לפרש ואין נראה כלל לר"י: **המפקיד** אצל חבירו בעדים צריך להחזיר לו בעדים. וא"ת אכתי להימניה במיגו דאי בעי אמר נאנסו כדאמרינן בסוף המוכר את הבית (לקמן דף ע. ושם) גבי מפקיד אצל חבירו בשטר ואפי' מאן דפליג התם היינו משום דשטרך בידי מאי בעי ותירץ ר"ת דודאי הוה מצי אביי למיפרך ליה אי הכי בעדים נמי להימניה במיגו דאי בעי אמר נאנסו אלא דלא אסיק אדעתיה ואותביה מברייתא ואודי ליה דבראה איירי מתני' ותו ליכא למפרך מידי אנאנסו וי"מ דהא דקאמר הכא דצריך להחזיר לו בעדים היינו אם רוצה להיות פטור משבועה אבל בשבועה נאמן במיגו דנאנסו [ג] ואין מחזיר לו בעדים והכי פי' לעיל לא שנו דאומן אין לו חזקה בלא שבועה אלא שמסר לו בעדים אבל מסר לו שלא בעדים נאמן בלא שבועה במיגו דאי בעי אמר לא היו דברים מעולם ומיירי קודם שנתקנה שבועת היסת ולכך כי אמר לא היו דברים מעולם אין צריך שבועה אי נמי לאחר שנתקנה ולישנא דבעי בשבועה דרך דממונא ולא חשיב הכא דרך דממונא דאמר לא בא לידי בתורת אומנות ואין מודה שנתחייב בו מעולם ולא חשיב דרך דממונא אלא מנה לי בידך וא"ל הן למחר א"ל תנהו לי וא"ל נתתיו לך שמודה שנתחייב ועל פירוש זה קשה לר"ת דמאי פריך לקמן מראה עבדו ביד אומן למה לי ראה לייתי עדים וליסקול הא מהני ראה דאפילו בשבועה לא יהא נאמן דאין לו מיגו דבלא ראה מהימן הוא בשבועה במיגו דנאנסו וברייתא משמע דלא אמר כלום דאפילו בשבועה אינו נאמן ונראה לתרץ דהכא לא חשיב מיגו דטעמא דמ"ד דצריך להחזיר בעדים משום דכיון דלא הימניה בשבועה כדאמר בשבועות (דף מה: ושם) דהוי כאילו א"ל בהדיא אל תחזיר לי אלא בעדים ולהכי לא מהימן במיגו דאיהו דאפסיד אנפשיה אבל התם בהמוכר סבר דאין צריך להחזיר לו בעדים ולא חשיב כאילו אמר אל תחזירני אלא בעדים ולכך נאמן במיגו אבל אין נראה דאפילו מאן דלית ליה צריך להחזיר לו בעדים כי איכא מיגו מהימן דלאו הכי מקשי מאי פריך ליה אביי מהבריא דראה עבדו ביד אומן דקסבר דאין צריך להחזיר לו בעדים הא איכא תנא דשבועות דלית ליה המלוה את חבירו בעדים צריך להחזיר לו בעדים ויסבור רבה כוותיה אלא משום דאפילו ההוא תנא דשבועות מודה בפקדון דאיכא מיגו דנאנסו דאין צריך להחזיר לו בעדים לכך נראה כפי' ר"ת:

נתנה לו בזמנו נשבע ונוטל. וא"ת והא אמר בפ' המקבל (ב"מ דף קיב: ושם) אומן אומר שתים קצצת לי והלה אומר לא קצצתי לך אלא אחת המוציא מחבירו עליו הראיה דקאלה מידע ידיע ובפ' כל הנשבעין (שבועות דף מו. ושם) פריך ליה ומשני דהך דהכא כרבי יהודה דקאלה נמי לא דכיר דטרוד הוא בפועליו וא"ת א"כ לאחר זמנו נמי אמאי אמר המע"ה הוה לן למימר נשבע ונוטל דמאי טעמא אמרינן בעלמא לאחר זמנו דאין נשבע ונוטל כדמפרש בריש כל הנשבעין דחזקה דאין שכיר משהה שכרו ואין בעה"ב עובר בבל תלין והכא הרי שהה שכיר ובעה"ב עבר דמודה שקצץ לו אחת ועדיין חייב לו וליכא למימר דמיירי כגון דאמר לא קצצתי לך אלא אחת ופרעתי לך דא"כ בזמנו אמאי נשבע ונוטל הא כרבי יהודה מוקמי לה ואיהו בעי הודאה במקצת ואין לתרץ נמי כגון שאומר אותה אחת שקצצתי לך ברשותך השהיתי דלא עבר בבל תלין דמ"מ חזקה דאין שכיר משהה שכרו ליכא דהרי שיהה אחת ודוחק לומר דמאי דחזינן דשיהה שיהה ומאי דלא חזינן (ג) דלא שיהה לא שיהה: **אי** דאיכא עדים ליחזי עדים מאי קאמרי. דודאי ידעי הקצילה דרגילות הוא תימה לר"י דעדיפא מינה הוה ליה למיפרך דאי איכא עדים וראה דאכתי לא מסיק אדעתיה לאוקמה בלא ראה אם כן אמאי מהימן אומן שהטלית בידו והכי הוה ליה למימר בשלמא לרב' מוקי לה בדליכא עדים דמהימן לרבא במיגו אלא לאביי במאי מוקי לה בין דאיכא עדים בין דליכא עדים לא מהימן במיגו ויש לומר דהכי קאמר אי דאיכא עדים ואתא לאשמועינן דאע"ג דאיכא עדים אומן מהימן וכגון דלא ראה ליחזי עדים מאי קאמרי אלא לאו דליכא עדים דתו לא מצית לאוקומי בדלא ראה דאם כן מאי קא משמע לן פשיטא דכי ליכא עדים ולא ראה דמהימן

עין משפט נר מצוה

קנג א מיי' פ"ט מהל' טוען הל' ב סמג עשין צה טוש"ע ח"מ סי' רצו סעיף א ב וסי' רלו [רלז] סעיף א:
קנד ב טוש"ע ח"מ סי' קלד סעיף ז:
קנה ג מיי' פ"ו מהל' פקדון הלכה ד ופ"ט מהל' טוען הל' ב סמג שם טוש"ע ח"מ סי' קלד סעיף א וסי' רלו [רלז] סעיף א:
קנו ד מיי' פ"ט מהל' טוען הל' ב ופי"א מהלכות שכירות הל' ח סמג עשין צה טוש"ע ח"מ סי' פט סעיף ד [ה]:

הגהות הב"ח

(א) גמ' מיתיביה אביי לרבה ראה עבדו וכו': (ב) שם מה טיבו אצלך א"ל אתה: (ג) תוס' ד"ה נתנה וכו' דלא חזינן דשיהה לא שיהה כצ"ל ותיבת דלא נמחק:

ליקוטי רש"י

כל זמן שהטלית ביד אומן. דבעל הבית הוי המוציא מחבירו עליו הראיה להביא עדים שלא קצץ אלא אחת [שבועות מו.]. בזמנו. אם תבעו בתוך זמן גבייתו. עבר זמנו המוציא מחבירו. היינו אומן. עליו הראיה. צריך להביא עדים ולא נאמן בשבועה [שם מה:].

מסורת הש"ס

א) ב"מ קיב: שבועות מו., ב) נ"א אומן, ג) נ"א ואפי' אין:

רבינו גרשום

אמר רב' מפרש לה לסיפא א) ביוצאת העדות מחמת ידי אחר ולא מחמת ידי אומן וכי אמר ליה המערער להאי אחר מה טיבו אצלך אמר לו בפני אמרת לו לאומן למוכרו למי שירצה ואני קניתיו ממנו דבריו קיימין מיגו כו' כי אמר ליה נמי זבינתה ניהליה ובפני אמרת לו שימכרהו או יתנהו למי שירצה מהימן: אי דאיכא עדים. שראוהו שמסר לו למה ליה ראה בידו אע"ג דלא ראה בידו לא אמר כלום האומן דנייתי עדים שהפקידו אצלו ונפיק לדבריך דאמרת המפקיד אצל חבירו בעדים צריך להחזיר לו בעדים. אלא לאו הכא במאי עסקינן דליכא עדים ומש"ה דוקא ראה וכי ראה המפקיד ביד האומן מיהא תפיס מן האומן דלא מהימן הוא דלית ליה חזקה וקשיא לרבה דאמר היכא דמסר לו שלא בעדים אע"ג דראהו מהימן האומן והא הכא קתני דאינו נאמן אע"ג דליכא עדים הואיל דראהו. ומשני לא לעולם מש"ה אינו נאמן האומן דאיכא עדים שמסרו לו והוא דראה המפקיד דוקא. מש"ה הואיל דאיכא תרתי עדים וראה אינו נאמן. אבל לעולם אי ליכא עדים אע"ג דראה בידו מהימן האומן וכן הכי נמי אי איכא עדים הואיל דלא ראהו המפקיד מהימן האומן ויש לו חזקה. ומקשה ליה אביי והיכי מצית למימר משום דאיתנייהו תרוייהו אינו נאמן הא ליתנייהו תרוייהו נאמן והא את הוא דאמרת המפקיד אצל חבירו בעדים אע"ג דלא ראהו צריך להחזיר לו בעדים ולא מהימן האומן אע"ג דליתנייהו תרוייהו: א"ל הדרי בי. דסבירא ליה המפקיד אצל חבירו בעדים א"צ להחזיר לו בעדים והואיל שלא ראהו מהימן האומן והכי קתני לה אמר רבה דל"ש דאין לו חזקה אלא שמסר לו בעדים וראהו בידו אבל אם לא ראהו מהימן האומן משום דסבירא ליה המפקיד אצל חבירו בעדים א"צ להחזיר לו בעדים ואם מסר לו שלא בעדים נמי אע"ג דראהו מהימן האומן מתוך שיכול כו' ואביי ס"ל אע"ג דליכא עדים הואיל שראהו מיהא תפיס דלאו אומן מהימן: ואי איכא נמי עדים הואיל שלא ראהו בידו נאמן האומן משום דס"ל המפקיד אצל חבירו בעדים א"צ להחזיר לו בעדים ואביי עביד ראיה עיקר בלא עדים ורבה ס"ל דאינו נאמן עד דאיכא תרתי: הנותן טליתו לאומן. לתקנה וראה אותה בידו: אומן אומר. ב' מעות קצצת לי בשכירותי: להביא ראיה. בעדים: נתנה לו. האומן לבעה"ב: בזמנו. היינו כל היום שהחזירה לו: נשבע. האומן ונוטל מבעה"ב דשכיר בזמנו נשבע ונוטל: עבר זמנו המוציא מחבירו עליו הראיה. בעדים: אי דאיכא עדים. שקצץ לו בפניהן: אלא

חשק שלמה על רבינו גרשום

א) נראה דל"ל ביוצא הטלית.

of payment **HAS PASSED**, i.e. after sunset, then **THE BURDEN OF PROOF RESTS UPON** the craftsman, since he is **THE ONE WHO SEEKS TO EXACT** payment **FROM HIS FELLOW.**[17] הֵיכִי דָּמֵי – Now, **how is it?** What is the Baraisa's exact case? אִי דְּאִיכָּא עֵדִים – **If** it deals with a case in which **there are witnesses** who saw the owner deposit the cloak with the craftsman, לֵיחֲזֵי עֵדִים מַאי קָאָמְרֵי – then **let [the court]** simply **see what the witnesses say** about the amount of wages stipulated.[18]

NOTES

recollection, since he relies on his wage for his very sustenance (*Rambam, Hil. Sechirus* 11:6).]

[Were it not for this special Rabbinic enactment, however, the craftsman, who is the one seeking to exact payment from his litigant, would not be able to collect without producing witnesses that can substantiate his claim of two *dinars.* In the absence of such witnesses, the employer would be believed (albeit only after taking the oath of *modeh bemiktzas,* which the Torah imposes upon a defendant who admits partial liability [see Mishnah *Shevuos* 38b]; in this case, the employer admits to owing half of what is claimed by the employee).]

17. [Since the day has passed, the employer is no longer burdened with his many obligations, and there is no longer any reason to mistrust his recollection. Therefore, the basis for the special Rabbinic enactment is removed, and the law reverts to the basic statute that the burden of proof rests upon the one who seeks to exact payment — in this case, the employee. As explained at the end of the previous note, this means that unless the employee can produce witnesses who substantiate his claim, the employer is believed after taking the oath of *modeh bemiktzas.*]

[Though not necessary for understanding the Gemara's present discussion, it is worthwhile noting that this Baraisa represents the minority view of R' Yehudah, who questions the employer's recollection even in regard to the amount of wages fixed. According to other Tannaic views, however, the employer's recollection is mistrusted only in regard to whether or not he already paid the employee; but it is not assumed that the employer is ever confused about the amount he agreed to pay. See Mishnah *Shevuos* 44b and Gemara there 45a-46a. See also *Tosafos* here.]

18. If witnesses were present at the original deposit, they should be able to tell us what wages were stipulated at the time.

אֶלָּא לָאו דְּלֵיכָּא עֵדִים – **Rather, is it not that** the Baraisa discusses a case in which **there are no witnesses** to the original deposit? וְקָתָנֵי אוּמָּן מְהֵימָן – **Yet, the Baraisa rules that the craftsman is believed** as long as he still holds the cloak – apparently, for the following reason: מִיגּוֹ דְּאִי בָּעֵי אָמַר לֵיהּ לְקוּחָה הִיא בְּיָדִי – **Since he could have said, "It is** a **purchased** cloak that I hold **in my possession,"** מְהֵימָן נַמִּי אַאַגְרֵיהּ – **he is also believed regarding his wages.**[1] This supports Rabbah's position[2] and poses a challenge to the dissenting opinion of Abaye. – ? –

The Gemara rebuts Rava's objection:

לֹא לְעוֹלָם דְּלֵיכָּא עֵדִים – **No;** it is not a proof. **Indeed** the Baraisa speaks of a case in which **there are no witnesses** to the original deposit, as Rava has proved. However, וְהוּא דְּלֹא רָאָה – the Baraisa might speak **only** of a case **where [the original owner] did not see** the cloak in the craftsman's possession;[3] rather, the craftsman volunteered the information that he has the cloak. In such a case, everyone agrees that he has a *migo,* for he could have altogether denied ever receiving the cloak. Therefore, his claim regarding his wages is believed.

The Gemara raises a final objection against Rabbah:

מְתִיב רַב נַחְמָן בַּר יִצְחָק – **Rav Nachman bar Yitzchak challenged** Rabbah's view. אוּמָּן אֵין לוֹ חֲזָקָה – Our Mishnah states that A CRAFTSMAN ... DOES NOT ESTABLISH A *CHAZAKAH* in an article (known to have belonged to someone else) simply because it is now in his physical possession. The implication is that אוּמָּן הוּא דְּאֵין לוֹ חֲזָקָה – **it is only a craftsman who does not establish a** ***chazakah*** in an article based on his possession of it, הָא אַחֵר יֵשׁ לוֹ חֲזָקָה – **but another person** who is not a craftsman **does establish a** ***chazakah*** in the article in an analogous situation. הֵיכִי דָּמֵי – Now, **what is the case** of the Mishnah? אִי דְּאִיכָּא עֵדִים – **If** it is a case in which **there are witnesses** that the original owner deposited the article with the craftsman in order to repair it,[4] אַחֵר אַמַּאי יֵשׁ לוֹ חֲזָקָה – then **why would another person** who is not a craftsman **establish a** ***chazakah*** in the article in an analogous situation? If there are witnesses that the article came into his possession as a deposit, of what value is his current possession of the article in establishing ownership? אֶלָּא לָאו דְּלֵיכָּא עֵדִים – **Rather, is it not that** the Mishnah speaks of a case in which **there are no witnesses** to the original deposit?[5] וְקָתָנֵי אוּמָּן אֵין לוֹ חֲזָקָה – **Accordingly, the Mishnah states that** even in the absence of witnesses to the original deposit, A CRAFTSMAN ... DOES NOT ESTABLISH A *CHAZAKAH* in an article (known to have belonged to someone else) simply because it is now in his possession; for we must naturally assume that it came into his possession in his professional capacity of a craftsman, not as a sale or a gift.[6] תְּיוּבְתָּא דְּרַבָּה תְּיוּבְתָּא – **This is a refutation of Rabbah;**[7] indeed, **it is a refutation.**

The Gemara begins discussion of a new topic concerning articles deposited with a craftsman:

תָּנוּ רַבָּנָן – **The Rabbis taught in a Baraisa:** נִתְחַלְּפוּ לוֹ כֵּלִים בְּכֵלִים בְּבֵית הָאוּמָּן – If SOMEONE'S GARMENTS WERE EXCHANGED FOR DIFFERENT GARMENTS IN A CRAFTSMAN'S SHOP,[8] הֲרֵי זֶה יִשְׁתַּמֵּשׁ בָּהֶן – HE IS PERMITTED TO USE [THE GARMENTS] that he was given, even though they do not belong to him, עַד שֶׁיָּבֹא הַלָּה וְיִטּוֹל אֶת שֶׁלּוֹ – UNTIL THE OTHER fellow COMES AND TAKES WHAT IS HIS.[9] בְּבֵית הָאֵבֶל אוֹ בְּבֵית הַמִּשְׁתֶּה – But if the exchange was made IN A MOURNER'S HOUSE OR AT A FEAST,[10] הֲרֵי זֶה לֹא יִשְׁתַּמֵּשׁ בָּהֶן – HE MAY NOT USE THEM; עַד שֶׁיָּבֹא הַלָּה וְיִטּוֹל אֶת שֶׁלּוֹ – rather, he must wait UNTIL THE OTHER fellow COMES AND TAKES WHAT IS HIS.

The Gemara analyzes this Baraisa:

מַאי שְׁנָא רֵישָׁא וּמַאי שְׁנָא סֵיפָא – **What** substantive **difference is there between** the cases in **the former and latter clauses** of the Baraisa that the law should be different in each? Why may the person use what was exchanged in the craftsman's shop but not what was exchanged elsewhere? אָמַר רַב – **Rav said:** הֲוָה יָתֵיבְנָא קַמֵּיהּ דַּחֲבִיבִי – **I was sitting in front of my uncle** [R' Chiya] וְאָמַר לִי וְכִי אֵין אָדָם עָשׂוּי לוֹמַר לְאוּמָּן מְכוֹר לִי טַלִּיתִי – **and he explained to me: Is a person not apt to say to a craftsman, "Sell my cloak for me"?** Since people often do so, we can assume that the craftsman intentionally gave him a cloak that he had been commissioned to sell; therefore, he may use it.[11]

The Gemara qualifies the ruling of the Baraisa:

אָמַר רַב חִיָּיא בְּרֵיהּ דְּרַב נַחְמָן – **Rav Chiya the son of Rav**

NOTES

1. The Gemara assumes that the Baraisa speaks of a case in which the craftsman cannot deny that the cloak is in his possession [it is currently "seen" there] (see *Tosafos* to 45b ד״ה אי for why the Gemara assumes this). Hence, his only *migo* is that he could have claimed to have initially bought the cloak.

2. That in the absence of evidence that the cloak came into the craftsman's possession as a deposit, he is believed to say that he bought the cloak, since his current possession of it substantiates that claim.

3. Unlike the assumption made above – see note 1. [See 45b, beginning of note 4.]

4. And the article is known to still be in the craftsman's possession.

But if it is the craftsman who volunteers that he still has it, then he would be awarded the object, since he could have claimed that he already returned it. [For the Gemara above has already concluded that both Rabbah and Abaye agree that a deposit given in the presence of witnesses need not be returned in the presence of witnesses] (*Rashbam*).

5. Only in that case is a craftsman not the presumed owner of the article, whereas a non-craftsman is.

6. [Unless, of course, it is he who volunteers that he has the article in his possession, in which case he is believed by virtue of the *migo* that he could have denied current possession of the article altogether. Obviously, then, the Mishnah could not be discussing a case in which the craftsman volunteers that he has the article.]

7. For Rabbah said that it is only when there are witnesses to the original deposit that a craftsman is not the presumed owner of the article in his possession.

8. When the person [whom we will call "Reuven"] came to pick up his repaired garments from the shop, the craftsman gave him someone else's garments instead [which Reuven realized only later] (*Rashbam*).

9. I.e. until the other fellow, who was given Reuven's garments by mistake, returns it and takes his own back (*Rashbam*). [It is assumed that the craftsman mistakenly gave Reuven's garments to someone else. Subsequently, when Reuven came to retrieve his garments, the craftsman said nothing of the matter, but simply gave him the other person's garments instead (see *Rashbam* below, and note 11 and 12).]

10. [I.e. when leaving the gathering, the person was accidentally given someone else's cloak instead of his own.]

11. That is, we can assume that the exchange came about when the craftsman was commissioned by a different customer to sell his cloak, but he sold Reuven's cloak by mistake. When Reuven came to pick up his cloak, the craftsman (who realized his mistake) simply gave Reuven the cloak that was supposed to have been sold, figuring that Reuven would use the substitute until the mistake could be corrected. [See note 12, where it is explained why we assume that this is what transpired.] Since the craftsman intentionally gave Reuven a cloak that was earmarked for sale, there is no reason that Reuven should not be able to use it (*Rashbam*).

In the Baraisa's latter case, however, the cloak that Reuven has mistakenly taken from the gathering clearly belongs to someone else. Therefore, he may not use it without the owner's permission [even though it is likely that the owner has – and may even be using – Reuven's cloak].

אלא לאו דליכא עדים וקתני אומן מהימן מיגו דאי בעי א"ל לקוחה היא בידי מהימן נמי אאגריה לא [א]לעולם דליכא עדים והוא דלא ראה מתיב ר"נ בר יצחק אומן אין לו חזקה אומן הוא דאין לו חזקה הא אחר יש לו חזקה ה"ד אי דאיכא עדים אחר אמאי יש לו חזקה אלא לאו דליכא עדים וקתני אומן אין לו חזקה תיובתא דרבה תיובתא: ת"ר [א] [ב] נתחלפו לו כלים בכלים בבית האומן הרי זה ישתמש בהן עד שיבא הלה ויטול את שלו [ג] בבית האבל או בבית המשתה הרי זה לא ישתמש בהן עד שיבא הלה ויטול את שלו מאי שנא רישא ומאי שנא סיפא (א) אמר רב הוה יתיבנא קמיה דחביבי ואמר לי וכי אין אדם עשוי לומר לאומן מכור לי טליתי אמר רב חייא בריה דר"נ [ד] לא שנו אלא הוא אבל אשתו ובניו לא והוא נמי לא אמרן [ה] אלא דא"ל טלית סתם אבל טליתך לא האי לאו טלית דידיה הוא א"ל אביי לרבא תא אחוי לך רמאי דפומבדיתא מאי עבדי א"ל הב לי סרבלאי (ב) לא היו דברים מעולם הא אית לי סהדי דחזיוה גבך אמר ליה ההוא אחרינא הוה אפקיניה ונחזינהו אמר ליה איברא לא מפיקנא ליה אמר רבא [ו] שפיר קאמר ליה (ג)

אלא לאו דליכא עדים. עדי מסירה ואע"ג דראה: **וקתני אומן מהימן.** דקתני על בעה"ב להביא ראיה כרבה ותיובתא דאביי דאמר לא מהימן היכא דראה: **דליכא עדים ולא ראה.** ודברי הכל מהימן דמצי אמר לא היו דברים מעולם: **הא אחר.** איירי בעלמא דלאו אומן: **היכי דמי.** דבאומן אין לו חזקה ואחר יש לו חזקה: **אי דאיכא עדים.** שמסר בעה"ב לאומן בפניהם והוא דראה הטלית עכשיו בידו א"כ היאך דייקינן אחר יש לו חזקה הא כיון דאיכא עדים דבתורת פקדון בא לידו וגם רואין אותו עכשיו בידו דלא מצי למימר החזרתיו לך הא ודאי לא מהימן לומר לקוח הוא בידי דמאי שנא מארים ואפוטרופוס שאין יכולין לומר לקוח הוא בידי והא ליכא למימר דבדאיכא עדים ולא ראה מיירי והלכך אחר מהימן דהא אפילו אומן נמי מהימן לדברי הכל דהא אוקמינן לעיל המפקיד אצל חבירו בעדים אין צריך להחזיר לו בעדים ומיגו דמצי אמר החזרתיו לך כי אמר נמי לקוח הוא בידי מהימן: **אלא לאו דליכא עדים.** בשעת מסירה והלכך אע"ג דרואין אנו בידו דאחר יש לו חזקה דכיון דלאו אומן יכול לומר לקוח הוא בידי כדין כל הקונין מטלטלין מחבריהן שאין צריכין עדים אלא מכיון שהוא מוחזק בו יכול לומר שלי הוא שלקחתיו ממך: **וקתני אומן אין לו חזקה.** היכא דליכא עדים ואיכא ראה כאביי: **תיובתא דרבה.** דאמר לעולם מהימן אומן עד דאיכא תרתי. והשתא שמעינן מהכא דהמפקיד אצל חבירו בעדים אין צריך להחזיר לו בעדים דהא הדר ביה רבה לגבי דאביי ובהמוכר את הבית לקמן (דף ע.) פסקינן שאפילו המפקיד אצל חבירו בשטר אין צריך להחזיר לו בעדים ומדקאמר גמרא אי דאיכא עדים אחר אמאי מהימן מיניה שמעינן שהמפקיד אצל חבירו בעדים ועדיין ישנו לפקדון בידו לפנינו שאינו יכול לטעון החזרתיו לך (ד) ולטעון שמכרו לי אח"כ [ג] אינו נאמן וה"מ בשראה ותפס אבל אם לא ראה (ותפס) מהימן מיגו דאי בעי אמר החזרתיו לך כי אמר מכרת אותם לי נאמן ובשבועה וה"מ שהפקיד אצלו בעדים אבל אם ראה טליתו ביד חבירו ומכירין בו עדים שהיה של זה הטוען לזה מה טיבו אצלך ואמר לו לקוח הוא בידי הוא נאמן דאין זה נאמן לומר הפקדתיו אצלך מאחר שאין לו עדים וה"מ שמצא טליתו ביד חבירו שאינו אומן אבל ראה טליתו ביד אומן ואמר אומן לקוח הוא בידי אינו נאמן אא"כ יש לו עדים שלקחו מזה בפניהם (ובא הלה ונטל את שלו) ואע"פ שלא מסר לו בעדים אבל אם לא ראהו בידו נאמן האומן לומר לקוח הוא בידי ואע"פ שמסר לו בעדים דמיגו דמצי טעין החזרתיו לך כי אמר נמי לקוח הוא בידי נאמן וה"מ דאומן אין לו חזקה בכלים שאותו אומן ראוי לתקן כגון לצבע בגד לצבוע וטלית לכובס וכן חלוק וכל בגדים בני כיבוס ולעבדן עורות וה"מ שיש חילוק בין אומן לבעל הבית בדברים שאין עשויין להשאיל ולהשכיר אבל דברים העשויין להשאיל ולהשכיר ל"ש אומן ול"ש כל אדם אם אמר לקוחין הן בידי אינו נאמן במס' שבועות (דף מו:): **בבית האומן.** שנתן לו האומן טלית של אדם אחר: **ה"ז ישתמש בהן.** עד שיבא הלה אותו שנטל טליתו של זה [ג] האומן ולא הוי שואל שלא מדעת כדמפרש לקמיה דאיכא למימר האומן נתן לו זה מדעת: **אמר רב חייא.** טעם דרישא בא לפרש מאי שנא מסיפא וכי אין אדם עשוי כו' והלכך איכא למימר שהאומן מכר טלית (ה) אחת שהוא מתקן במלות בעל הבית שלוה לו למוכרו וטעה האומן ומכר טליתו של זה ונתן לו טלית זו מדעת עד שיחזיר לו את שלו וכיון דמדעתו נתן לו מותר להשתמש בה מה שאין כן בבית האבל ובבית המשתה: **ל"ש.** דמותר להשתמש אלא שנתן לו האומן עצמו דאיכא למימר מדעת עשה: **אבל.** אם נתנו לו לזה אשתו ובניו של אומן לא ישתמש דאיכא למימר מיטעא טעו: **והוא נמי.** אומן: **לא אמרן.** דאם נתן הוא מותר להשתמש בו אלא דאמר ליה הילך טלית זו דאיכא למימר דלהכי לא אמר ליה טליתך שאין זו שלו ומדעת נתן לו חליפי טליתו שלו: **אבל אם אמר לו הילך טליתך.** כסבור הוא שזו היא שלו וטעות הוא ואסור להשתמש שלא מדעת וכן הלכה: **רמאי דפומבדיתא.** האומנין שמביאין להן בגדים לתקן כדאמרינן התם (חולין דף קכז.) פומבדיתא לויך אשני אושפיזך: **אמר ליה.** בעל הבית (ו): **הב לי סרבלאי.** טליתי שמסרתי לך לתקן: **דחזיוה גבך.** בגד אחד ראו והוא שלי ומיהו העדים אין מכירין בו יפה אם זה הוא: **אפקיניה ונחזינהו.** הוצא אותו שיראו עדים שאתה אומר אחרינא הוא ואמת דבריך והוציא עצמך מן החשד: **איברא לא מפיקנא ליה.** באמת לא אוציאנו בשביל טענותיך של הבל אראה לך ממון אחרים וזהו הרמאות דלא לשם שמים מתכוין אלא לגנוב את טלית חבירו מתכוין: **שפיר קאמר ליה.** האומן כך השיב רבא לאביי שאע"פ שרמאים הן הדין עמם דאפי' כשרים שבישראל יכולין לטעון כן:

רמה

דמהימן ואין כאן שום חידוש אלא ודאי איירי בראה ואפ"ה אומן מהימן ומשני לעולם בדליכא עדים ולא ראה ולא תני לרישא לשום חידוש אלא משום סיפא דבעי לאשמועינן דינא בנתנה לו תנא נמי רישא כל זמן שהטלית ביד אומן אע"ג דפשיטא היא ואין להקשות במאי דמשני אביי אמאי נקט בסיפא נתנה לו הוה ליה למיתני ראהו בידו אע"פ שהטלית ביד אומן דהא לא נחת תנא לאשמועינן מידי בדינא דראה ולהכי קתני נתנה לו והוא הדין דראה נמי כנתנה דמי שהיה צריך ליתנה לו על כרחו:

אלא לאו דליכא עדים. הקשה ריב"ם דהיכי מצי [ד] לאוריי בדליכא עדים אם כן אמאי בזמנו נשבע ונוטל הא אמרינן בריש כל הנשבעין (שבועות דף מה: ושם) דאם שכרו שלא בעדים מתוך שיכול לומר לא שכרתיך מעולם יכול לומר לו שכרתיך ונתתי לך שכרך [ה] ואור"י דלא קשה מידי דהדא דפלוגתא היא התם ועוד דהכא ליכא האי מיגו כיון שמודה במקצת ואי אמר לא שכרתיך מעולם הוי כופר בכל וחזקה דאין אדם מעיז פניו בפני בעל חובו:

אי דאיכא עדים אחר אמאי יש לו חזקה. ונראה דבראה מיירי דאי בלא ראה אומן נמי יש לו חזקה מיגו דאי בעי אמר החזרתיו לך דאין צריך להחזיר לו בעדים אלא ודאי בראה מיירי א"כ אחר אמאי יש לו חזקה כיון דאיכא עדים דבתורת פקדון בא לידו ולא מצי למיטען נמי החזרתי לך שהרי ראה ופר"ת נראה לר"י מאד רחוק על כן לא כתבתיו:

וכי אין אדם עשוי לומר לאומן מכור לי טליתי. וטעה אומן ומכר את של זה שהיה סבור למכור את של חבירו ונתן לו את של חבירו תחתיו אבל אם לא היה עשוי לומר לאומן למכור לא היה מותר מחמת שטעה אומן ונתן את שלו לחבירו דהוי כנתחלפו לו בבית האבל או בבית המשתה וסופו שיחזיר חבירו את שלו לאומן ויחזור ויתבע ממנו טליתו:

הא אית לי סהדי דחזיוה גבך. פי' טלית שהיו בו סימנים כעין שלי ולא שהיה להם טביעות עין שהיו מכירים שהיא שלו:

שפיר קאמר ליה דלא משוי ראה מ"ט דראה תניא. תימה לרשב"א דמאי בעי למימר אי בעי למימר שפיר קאמר דלא משוי ליה ראה דלא בעי לאפוקי דנחזייה דמה צריך למימר עלה ראה תניא פשיטא דאי מפיק ליה ויכירוה שהיא שלו דחייב להחזיר שהרי כפר ואמר לא היו דברים מעולם ונראה לו לפרש הכי שפיר קאמר כלומר שטוען טענה זו לא היו דברים מעולם דעל ידי כך לא משוי ליה ראה הואיל ולעדים לא היה בה טביעות עין ויכול לומר אחר היה אבל אי הוה טעין לקוח הוא בידי לא היה נאמן דאין לו עוד מיגו דאי בעי אמר החזרתיו לך או לא היו דברים מעולם דירא לומר כן הואיל ויש עדים שראו טלית כאותו שהוא שלו בידו והשתא אתי שפיר דקאמר מ"ט ראה תניא כלומר אע"פ שאינה ראיה גמורה של טביעות עין אלא שהיו בה סימנין כמו שלו דראה דקתני בברייתא משמע ליה בכל ענין ראיה [ו] (גמורה) אינו נאמן לומר לקוח הוא בידי:

שלא

רבינו גרשום

אלא לאו דליכא עדים וקתני דאומן מהימן באגריה. היכא דלית ליה עדים וראיה לבעל הבית ברישא. ותיובתא דאביי דאמר דהיכא דליכא עדים כי ראה מהימן בעל הבית ותפיס ליה והא הכא אע"ג דראה בעל הבית ביד האומן לא תפיס דהאומן מהימן. וסייעתא לרבה דאמר הואיל דאיכא תרתי אבל ראה לחוד מהימן האומן דהכא נמי ליכא אלא ראה לחוד: **לא לעולם דליכא עדים** ולא ראה. משה"ה האומן מהימן אבל אי ראה אע"ג דליכא עדים מצי תפיס דלא מהימן האומן וכדאביי: **הא אחר.** כגון סותר יש לו חזקה: **היכי דמי אי דאיכא עדים.** בידי אחר **אמאי יש לו חזקה. אלא לאו דליכא** עדים אע"ג דליכא עדים וראה אחר יש לו חזקה אבל אומן אין לו חזקה ואע"ג דראה אע"ג דליכא עדים. דבאיכא עדים לא מצית לה לאוקמי דמשום דאיכא למיפרך אחר אמאי יש לו חזקה הואיל דאיכא עדים בשלמא לאביי ניחא מיהא תפיס דאין לו חזקה לאומן אלא לרבה דאמר משה"ה אין לו חזקה אבל אי ליכא עדים אע"ג דראה יש לו חזקה והא קתני דאין לו חזקה קשיא: **נתחלפו כלים בכלים בבית האומן.** שהחזיר לו האומן כליו של אחר: **הרי זה ישתמש בה.** זה באותו כלי עד שיבא הלה ויטול את שלו ויחזיר לו את שלו אבל אם נתחלפו לו בבית האבל כו': **אמר רב חייא.** מפרש מאי איכא בין רישא לסיפא: **וכי אין אדם עשוי לומר לאומן מכור לי טליתי.** למי שמבקשו ממך ודאי עשוי לומר לו וכסבור היה האומן למכור אותו טלית של אחר ומכר טליתו של זה בשגגה ומדעתו נתן לו לזה טלית שאינה שלו עד שיפשפש ויראה אחר שלו שמכר. ומשה"ה מותר להשתמש בה דמדעתו נתן לו משא"כ בבית האבל ובבית המשתה: **ל"ש.** דמותר להשתמש **אלא** שנתן לו האומן הוא בעצמו. **אבל** נתנו לו אשתו ובניו אין משתמש בהן דשלא מדעת יהבי ניהלה: **והוא נמי.** האומן אי יהיב ליה: **לא אמרן.** דמשתמש בה: **אלא דאמר ליה** הא לך טלית זו סתם. משמע דמדעת יהביה ניהליה דקא ידע דלא דידיה היא נתנה לו לישתמש בה: **סרבלי.** טלית: **לא היו דברים מעולם.** שאין בידי טליתך: **אפקיניה.** טלית אחרינא דאמרת דלא דידי הוא ונחזיה: **אמר איברא.** כלומר בודאי שלא אוציא לך טליתך:

שפיר

מסורת הש"ס

א) [תוספתא ב"ק פ"י ע"ש], ב) לו מסכנו. רש"ג, ג) נ"ל מהאומן, ד) נ"א לאוקמי. ר"מ, ה) ר"מ מ"ז:

עין משפט נר מצוה

קנז א מיי' פ"ט מהל' טוען הל' ב סמג עשין צה טוש"ע ח"מ סי' פט סעיף ד [ה]:

קנח ב מיי' פ"ו מהל' גזילה הל' ו סמג עשין עג טוש"ע ח"מ סי' קלו סעיף א:

קנט ג מיי' שם טוש"ע שם סעיף ב:

קס ד ה מיי' שם טוש"ע שם סעיף א:

קסא ו מיי' פ"ט מהל' טוען הל' א [ב] סמג עשין צה טוש"ע ח"מ סי' קלד סעיף ב [א]:

הגהות הב"ח

(א) גמ' [אמר רב הוה יתיבנא קמיה דחביבי ואמר לי וכו'] תא"מ ונ"ב ס"א והיא גי' רשב"ס אמר רבי חייא וכו' וכו': (ב) שם הב לי סרבלאי א"ל לא היו: (ג) שם שפיר קאמר ליה מ"ט ראה. נ"ב גי' תוס' דלא משוי ליה ראה: (ד) רשב"ם ד"ה תיובתא וכו' החזרתיו לך וטוען שמכרו לי אח"כ אי מכשנו בידי אינו נאמן: (ה) ד"ה אמר (רב) [רבי] חייא וכו' טלית אחד שהוא: (ו) ד"ה בעל הבית לאומן הס"ד:

גליון הש"ס

תוס' ד"ה אלא כו' ואור"י דלק"מ. קשה לי הא מה קשה במתניתין דקתני ר"י"א עד שיהא שם מקצת הודאה וקשה הא יש לו מגו דכפר הכל וא"ל מוכח מירושלמי השני וצ"ע:

ליקוטי רש"י

קמיה דחביבי. ר' חייא דודו של רב כדאמרינן בסנהדרין [ה.] דרב בר אחוה דר"ח ובר אחתיה דר"ח [רשב"ם לעיל מא.]. ר' חייא שהוא אחי אביו ואמו של רב [עירובין יב:]. רבי חייא שהוא דודו אחי אביו [כתובות נב.]. רמאי דפומבדיתא. שגנבים מומחין הם [חולין קכז.].

Nachman said: לֹא שָׁנוּ אֶלָּא הוּא – **[The Baraisa] taught** that the person can use the exchanged cloak **only** in a case where the craftsman **himself** gave it to him; only then do we assume that the wrong cloak was given to him deliberately. אֲבָל אִשְׁתּוֹ וּבָנָיו לֹא – **But** if **[the craftsman's] wife or children** gave him the wrong cloak, then he may **not** use it, since it is quite possible that they made a mistake. וְהוּא נַמִּי – **Furthermore, even** in a case where the craftsman **himself** gave him the wrong cloak, לֹא אֲמָרַן אֶלָּא דְּאָמַר לֵיהּ טַלִּית סְתָם – **we say** that the person may use the exchanged cloak **only where [the craftsman] said to him** upon handing it to him, "Here is **'a' cloak."** אֲבָל טַלִּיתְךָ לֹא – **But** if the craftsman said, "Here is **'your' cloak,"** then he may **not** use the cloak, since הַאי לָאו טַלִּית דִּידֵיהּ הוּא – **this is not,** in fact, **his cloak.** We must therefore consider the possibility that the craftsman inadvertently gave him the wrong cloak.[12]

The Gemara recounts an exchange between Abaye and Rava that has bearing on our Mishnah:

אָמַר לֵיהּ אַבַּיֵּי לְרָבָא – **Abaye said to Rava:** תָּא אַחְוִי לָךְ רַמָּאֵי דְּפוּמְבְּדִיתָא – **Come, I will show you** the practice of **the cheats of Pumpedisa.** [These cheats are craftsmen.] מַאי עָבְדֵי – **What do they do?** אָמַר לֵיהּ הַב לִי סַרְבְּלָאִי – **If someone says to one of them, "Give me** back **my cloak,** which I gave you to repair," he answers, לֹא הָיוּ דְבָרִים מֵעוֹלָם – **"It never happened,"** i.e. you never gave me a cloak. הָא אִית לִי סָהֲדֵי דְּחַזְיוּהָ גַּבָּךְ – And if the claimant persists, **"But I have witnesses who saw it in your possession!"**[13] אָמַר לֵיהּ הַהוּא אַחֲרִינָא הֲוָה – he retorts, **"That** cloak which they saw **was a different one."** אַפְּקִינֵיהּ וְנֶחֱזִינְהוּ – And if the claimant says, **"Produce [the cloak]** that the witnesses saw, **in order that we can see it** and ascertain whether it is, in fact, mine," אָמַר לֵיהּ אִיבְרָא לֹא מַפִּיקְנָא לֵיהּ – **[the craftsman] says to him, "Indeed, I will not produce [the cloak]!** Why should I allow you to inspect someone else's property because of your unfounded claims? That would be unfair to its owner!"[14]

אָמַר רָבָא – **Rava said [to Abaye]:** שַׁפִּיר קָאָמַר לֵיהּ – Technically, what **[the craftsman] says to him** is **right.**[15] Legally, we cannot force the craftsman to produce the cloak for inspection;

NOTES

12. It is the craftsman's curious use of the vague expression "a cloak" instead of the expected "your cloak" that leads us to assume that he deliberately gave the wrong cloak to Reuven (*Rashbam*). Once we assume that it was deliberate, the logical explanation is that Reuven's own cloak was mistakenly sold in place of one that had been given to the craftsman for sale. [There is no reason to impute any base motives to the craftsman.]

Alternatively, we assume this scenario for the following reason: The craftsman has certainly mistaken one garment for another. On balance, it is far more likely that he has made the mistake of selling a wrong cloak rather than the mistake of returning the wrong one, since craftsmen are generally more careful to ascertain the identity of an article when returning it to its owner than when selling it (see *Ritva*).

13. I.e. the witnesses cannot say with certainty that it was the claimant's cloak which they saw, but they testify that the craftsman holds a cloak that resembles the claimant's (see *Rashbam* and *Tosafos*).

14. Thus, he is a cheat and a dissembler; for he pretends to be protecting the privacy of the fictitious "real" owner of the cloak, while he is, in fact, using his pious argument as a front to cover his theft (*Rashbam*).

15. It is a claim that even an honest craftsman could make [though we are fairly convinced that this particular craftsman is a thief] (*Rashbam*).

אלא לאו דליכא עדים וקתני אומן מהימן מיגו דאי בעי א"ל לקוחה היא בידי מהימן נמי אאגריה לא אלעולם דליכא עדים והוא דלא ראה מתיב ר"נ בר יצחק אומן אין לו חזקה אומן הוא דאין לו חזקה הא אחר יש לו חזקה ה"ד אי דאיכא עדים אחר אמאי יש לו חזקה אלא לאו דליכא עדים וקתני אומן אין לו חזקה תיובתא דרבה תיובתא: ת"ר (א) בנתחלפו לו כלים בכלים בבית האומן הרי זה ישתמש בהן עד שיבא הלה ויטול את שלו גבבית האבל או בבית המשתה הרי זה לא ישתמש בהן עד שיבא הלה ויטול את שלו מאי שנא רישא ומאי שנא סיפא (א) אמר רב הוה יתיבנא קמיה דחביבי ואמר לי וכי אין אדם עשוי לומר לאומן מכור לי טליתי אמר רב חייא בריה דר"נ דלא שנו אלא הוא אבל אשתו ובניו לא והוא נמי לא אמרן האלא דא"ל טלית סתם אבל טליתך לא האי לאו טלית דידיה הוא א"ל אביי לרבא תא אחוי לך רמאי דפומבדיתא מאי עבדי א"ל הב לי סרבלאי (ב) לא היו דברים מעולם הא אית לי סהדי דחזיוה גבך אמר ליה ההוא אחרינא הוה אפקיניה ונחזינהו אמר ליה איברא לא מפיקנא ליה אמר רבא ושפיר קאמר ליה (ג)

רש"י

אלא לאו דליכא עדים. עדי מסירה ואע"ג דראה: **וקתני אומן מהימן.** דקתני על בעה"ב להביא ראיה כרבה ותיובתא דאביי דאמר לא מהימן היכא דראה: **דליכא עדים ולא ראה.** ודברי הכל מהימן דמלי אמר לא היו דברים מעולם: **הא אחר.** איניש בעלמא דלאו אומן: **היכי דמי.** דבאומן אין לו חזקה ואחר יש לו חזקה: **אי דאיכא עדים.** שמסר בעה"ב לאומן בפניהם והוא דראה הטלית עכשיו בידו א"כ היאך דייקינן אחר יש לו חזקה הא כיון דאיכא עדים דבתורת פקדון בא לידו וגם רואין אותו עכשיו בידו דלא מלי למימר החזרתיו לך הא ודאי לא מהימן לומר לקוח הוא בידי דמאי שנא מאריס ואפוטרופוס שאין יכולין לומר לקוח הוא בידי והא ליכא למימר דבדליכא עדים ולא ראה מיירי והלכך אחר מהימן דהא אפילו אומן נמי מהימן לדברי הכל דהא אוקמינן לעיל המפקיד אצל חבירו בעדים אין צריך להחזיר לו בעדים ומיגו דמלי אמר החזרתיו לך כי אמר נמי לקוח הוא בידי מהימן: **אלא לאו דליכא עדים.** בשעת מסירה והלכך אע"ג דרואין אותו בידו לאחר יש לו חזקה דכיון דלאו אומן יכול לומר לקוח הוא בידי כדין כל הקונין מטלטלין מחבריהן שאין צריכין עדים אלא מכיון שהוא מוחזק בו יכול לומר שלי הוא שלקחתיו ממך: **וקתני אומן אין לו חזקה.** היכא דליכא עדים ואיכא ראה כאביי: **תיובתא דרבה.** דאמר לעולם מהימן האומן עד דאיכא תרתי. והשתא שמעינן מהכא דהמפקיד אצל חבירו בעדים אין צריך להחזיר לו בעדים דהא הדר ביה רבה לגבי דאביי ובהמוכר את הבית לקמן (דף ע.) פסקינן שאפילו המפקיד אצל חבירו בשטר אין צריך להחזיר לו בעדים ומדקאמר גמרא אי דאיכא עדים אחר אמאי מהימן מיניה שמעינן שהמפקיד אצל חבירו בעדים ועדיין ישנו לפקדון בידו לפנינו שאינו יכול לטעון החזרתיו לך (ד) ולטעון שמכרו לי אח"כ (ה) אינו נאמן וה"מ בשראה ותפס אבל אם לא ראה (ותפס) מהימן מיגו דאי בעי אמר החזרתיו לך כי אמר מכרת אותם לי נאמן ובשבועה וה"מ שהפקיד אצלו בעדים אבל אם ראה טליתו ביד חבירו ומכירין בו עדים שהיה של זה הטוען לזה מה טיבו אצלך ואמר לו לקוח הוא בידי הוא נאמן דאין זה נאמן לומר הפקדתיו אצלך מאחר שאין לו עדים וה"מ שמצא טליתו ביד חבירו שאינו אומן אבל ראה טליתו ביד אומן ואמר אומן לקוח הוא בידי אינו נאמן אא"כ יש לו עדים שלקחו מזה בפניהם (ובא הלה ונטל את שלו) ואע"פ שלא מסר לו בעדים אבל אם לא ראהו בידו נאמן האומן לומר לקוח הוא בידי ואע"פ שמסר לו בעדים דמיגו דמלי טעין החזרתיו לך כי אמר נמי לקוח הוא בידי נאמן וה"מ דהאומן אין לו חזקה בכלים שאותו אומן ראוי לתקן כגון לצבע בגד לצבוע וטלית לכובס וכן חלוק וכל בגדים בני כיבוס ולעבדן עורות וה"מ שיש חילוק בין אומן לבעל הבית בדברים שאין עשויין להשאיל ולהשכיר אבל דברים העשויין להשאיל ולהשכיר לא שנא אומן ולא שנא כל אדם אם אמר לקוחין הן בידי אינו נאמן כמס' שבועות (דף מו:): **בבית האומן.** שנתן לו האומן טלית של אדם אחר: **ה"ז ישתמש בהן.** עד שיבא הלה אותו שנטל טליתו של זה (ג) האומן ולא הוי שואל שלא מדעת כדמפרש לקמיה דאיכא למימר האומן נתן לו זה מדעת: **אמר רב חייא.** טעם דרישא בא לפרש מאי שנא מסיפא וכי אין אדם עשוי כו' והלכך איכא למימר שהאומן מכר טלית (ה) אחת שהוא מתקן במלאכה שבעל הבית שלוה לו למוכרו וטעה האומן ומכר טליתו של זה ונתן לו טלית זו מדעת עד שיחזיר לו את שלו וכיון דמדעתו נתן לו מותר להשתמש בה מה שאין כן בבית האבל ובבית המשתה: **ל"ש.** דמותר להשתמש אלא שנתן לו האומן עצמו דליכא למימר מדעת עשה: **אבל.** אם נתנו לו לזה אשתו ובניו של אומן לא ישתמש דאיכא למימר מיטעא טעו: **והוא נמי.** אומן: **לא אמרן.** דאם נתן הוא מותר להשתמש בו אלא דאמר ליה הילך טלית זו דאיכא למימר דלהכי לא אמר ליה טליתך שאין זו שלו ומדעת נתן לו חליפי טליתו שלו: **אבל אם אמר לו הילך טליתך.** כסבור הוא שזו היא שלו וטעות הוא ואסור להשתמש שלא מדעת וכן הלכה: **רמאי דפומבדיתא.** האומנין שמביאין להן בגדים לתקן כדאמרינן התם (חולין דף קכז.) פומבדיתא לויך אשני אושפיזך: **אמר ליה.** בעל הבית (ו): **הב לי סרבלאי.** טליתי שמסרתי לך לתקן: **דחזיוה גבך.** בגד אחד ראו והוא שלי ומיהו העדים אין מכירין בו יפה אם זה הוא: **אפקיניה ונחזינהו.** הוצא אותו שיראו עדים שאתה אומר אחרינא הוא ואמת דבריך והוציא עצמך מן החשד: **איברא לא מפיקנא ליה.** באמת לא אוציאנו בשביל טענותיך של הבל אראה לך ממון אחרים וזהו הרמאות דלא לשם שמים מתכוין אלא לגנוב את טלית חבירו מתכוין: **שפיר קאמר ליה.** האומן כך השיב רבא לאביי שאע"פ שרמאים הן הדין עמם דאפי' כשרים שבישראל יכולין לטעון כן:

ראה

תוספות

דמהימן ואין כאן שום חידוש אלא ודאי איירי בראה ואפ"ה אומן מהימן ומשני לעולם בדליכא עדים ולא ראה ולא תני ברישא לשום חידוש אלא משום סיפא דבעי לאשמועינן דינא בנתנה לו תנא נמי רישא כל זמן שהטלית ביד אומן אע"ג דפשיטא היא ואין להקשות במאי דמשני אביי אמאי נקט בסיפא נתנה לו הוה ליה למיתני ראהו בידו אע"פ שהטלית ביד אומן דהא לא נתן תנא לאשמועינן מידי בדליכא דראה ולהכי קתני נתנה לו והוא הדין נמי כנתנה לו דמי שהיה צריך ליתנה לו על כרחו:

אלא לאו דליכא עדים. הקשה ריב"ם דהיכי מצי ד) לאוקמי בדליכא עדים אם כן אמאי בזמנו נשבע ונוטל הא אמרינן בריש כל הנשבעין (שבועות דף מה: ושם) דאם שכרו שלא בעדים מתוך שיכול לומר לא שכרתיך מעולם יכול לומר לו שכרתיך ונתתי לך שכרך ה ואור"י דלא קשה מידי דהא דפלוגתא היא התם ועוד דהכא ליכא האי מיגו כיון שמודה במקצת ואי אמר לא שכרתיך מעולם הוי כופר בכל וחזקה דאין אדם מעיז פניו בפני בעל חובו:

אי דאיכא עדים אחר אמאי יש לו חזקה. ונראה דבראה מיירי דאי בלא ראה אומן נמי יש לו חזקה מיגו דאי בעי אמר החזרתיו לך דאין צריך להחזיר לו בעדים אלא ודאי בראה מיירי א"כ אחר אמאי יש לו חזקה כיון דאיכא עדים דבתורת פקדון בא לידו ולא מצי למיטען נמי החזרתי לך שהרי ראה ופר"ת נראה לר"י מאד רחוק על כן לא כתבתיו:

וכי אין אדם עשוי לומר לאומן מכור לי טליתי. וטעה אומן ומכר את של זה שהיה סבור למכור את של חבירו ונתן לו את של חבירו תחתיו אבל אם לא היה עשוי לומר לאומן למכור לא היה מותר מחמת שטעה אומן ונתן את שלו לחבירו דהוי כנתחלפו לו בבית האבל או בבית המשתה וסופו שיחזיר חבירו את שלו לאומן ויחזור ויתבע ממנו טליתו:

הא אית לי סהדי דחזיוה גבך. פי' טלית שהיו בו סימנים כעין שלי ולא שהיה להם טביעות עין שהיו מכירים שהיא שלו:

שפיר קאמר ליה דלא משוי ראה מ"ט דראה תניא. תימה לרשב"א דמאי בעי למימר אי בעי למימר שפיר קאמר דלא משוי ליה ראה דלא בעי לאפוקי דנחזייה דמה צריך למימר עלה ראה תניא פשיטא דאי מפיק ליה ויכירוה שהיא שלו דחייב להחזיר שהרי כפר ואמר לא היו דברים מעולם ונראה לו לפרש הכי שפיר קאמר כלומר שטוען טענה זו לא היו דברים מעולם דעל ידי כך לא משוי ליה ראה הואיל ולעדים לא היה בה טביעות עין ויכול לומר אחר היה אבל אי הוה טעין לקוח הוא בידי לא היה נאמן דאין לו עוד מיגו דאי בעי אמר החזרתיו לך או לא היו דברים מעולם דירא לומר כן הואיל ויש עדים שראו טלית כאותו שהוא שלו בידו והשתא אתי שפיר דקאמר מ"ט ראה תניא כלומר אע"פ שאינה ראיה גמורה של טביעות עין אלא שהיו בה סימנין כמו שלו דראה דקתני בברייתא משמע ליה בכל ענין ראיה ה) (גמורה) אינו נאמן לומר לקוח הוא בידי:

שלא

מסורת הש"ס

א) [תוספתא ב"ק פ"י ע"ש], ב) או משכנו. רש"ל, ג) ל"ל מהאומן, ד) נ"א לאוקמי. ר"מ, ה) ר"מ מ"ז:

רבינו גרשום

אלא לאו דליכא עדים וקתני דאומן מהימן באגריה. היכא דלית ליה עדים וראיה לבעל הבית ברישא. ותיובתא דאביי דאמר דהיכא דליכא עדים כי ראה מהימן בעל הבית ותפיס ליה והא הכא אע"ג דראה בעל הבית ביד האומן לא תפיס דהאומן מהימן. וסייעתא לרבה דאמר הואיל דאיכא תרתי אבל ראה לחוד מהימן האומן דהכא נמי ליכא אלא ראה לחוד: **לא לעולם דליכא עדים ולא ראה.** מש"ה האומן מהימן אבל אי ראה אע"ג דליכא עדים מצי תפיס דלא מהימן האומן וכדאביי: **הא אחר.** כגון סוחר **יש לו חזקה: היכי דמי אי דאיכא עדים.** שהפקידה אצלו וראה בידי אחר אמאי **יש לו חזקה. אלא לאו דליכא עדים** אע"ג דליכא עדים וראה אחר יש לו חזקה אבל **אומן אין לו חזקה** הואיל דראה אע"ג דליכא עדים. דבאיכא עדים לא מצית לה לאוקמי דמשום דאיכא למיפרך אחר אמאי יש לו חזקה הואיל דאיכא עדים בשלמא לאביי ניחא משום דליכא עדים וראה מיהא תפיס דאין לו חזקה לאומן **אלא לרבה** דאמר דבעינן תרתי עדים וראה מש"ה אין לו חזקה אבל אי ליכא עדים אע"ג דראה יש לו חזקה והא קתני דאין לו חזקה קשיא: **נתחלפו כלים בכלים בבית האומן.** שהחזיר לו האומן כליו של אחר: **הרי זה ישתמש בה.** זה באותו כלי **עד שיבא הלה ויטול את שלו** ויחזיר לו את שלו אבל אם נתחלפו לו **בבית האבל כו': אמר רב חייא.** מפרש מאי איכא בין רישא לסיפא: **וכי אין אדם עשוי לומר לאומן מכור לי טליתי.** למי שמבקשו ממך ודאי עשוי לומר לו וכסבור היה האומן למכור אותו טלית של אחר ומכר טליתו של זה בשגגה ומדעתו נתן לו לזה טלית שאינה שלו עד שיפשפש ויראה אחר שלו שמכר. ומש"ה מותר להשתמש בה מדעתו נתן לו משא"כ בבית האבל ובבית המשתה: **ל"ש.** דמותר להשתמש **אלא** שנתן לו האומן **הוא** בעצמו. **אבל** נתנו לו **אשתו ובניו** אין משתמש בהן דשלא מדעת יהבי ניהלה: **והוא נמי.** האומן אי יהיב לו: **לא אמרן.** דמשתמש בה: **אלא דאמר ליה** הא לך **טלית** זו **סתם.** משמע דמדעת יהביה ניהליה דקא ידע דלא דידיה היא ונתנה לו לישתמש בה: **סרבלי.** טלית: **לא היו דברים מעולם.** שאין בידי טליתך: **אפקיניה.** טלית אחרינא דאמרת דלא דידי הוא **ונחזינה: אמר איברא.** כלומר בוודאי שלא אוציא לך טליתך:

שפיר

עין משפט נר מצוה

קנז א מיי' פ"ט מהל' טוען הל' ב סמג עשין צה טוש"ע ח"מ סי' פט סעיף ד [ה]:

קנח ב מיי' פ"ט מהל' גזילה הל' ו סמג עשין עג טוש"ע ח"מ סי' קלו סעיף א:

קנט ג מיי' שם טוש"ע שם סעיף ב:

קס ד ה מיי' שם טוש"ע שם סעיף א:

קסא ו מיי' פ"ט מהל' טוען הל' א [ג] סמג עשין צה טוש"ע ח"מ סי' קלג סעיף ג [א]:

הגהות הב"ח

(א) גמ' (אמר רב הוה יתיבנא קמיה דחביבי ואמר לי וכו') תא"מ ונ"ב ס"א והיא גי' רשב"ם אמר רבי חייא וכו' וכו': (ב) שם הב לי סרבלאי א"ל לא היו: (ג) שם שפיר קאמר ליה מ"ט ראה. נ"ב גי' תוס' דלא משוי ליה ראה: (ד) רשב"ם ד"ה תיובתא וכו' החזרתיו לך וטוען שמכרו לי א"נ לא משכנו בידי אינו נאמן: (ה) ד"ה אמר (רב) [רבי] חייא וכו' טלית אחד שהוא: (ו) ד"ה אמר ליה בעל הבית לאומן הס"ד:

גליון הש"ס

תוס' ד"ה אלא כו' ואור"י דלק"מ. קשה לי הא מה קשה כמתניתין דקתני רי"ב עד שיטה שם מקלת הודאה וקשה הא יש לו מגו דכפר הכל ול"ל מוכח מירוש השני ול"ע:

ליקוטי רש"י

קמיה דחביבי. ר' חייא דודו של רב כדאמרינן בסנהדרין (ה.) דרב בר אחוה דר"ח ובר אחתיה דר"ח [רשב"ם לעיל מא.]. ר' חייא שהוא אחי אביו ואמו של רב [עירובין יב:]. רבי חייא שהוא דודו אחי אביו [כתובות נב.]. רמאי דפומבדיתא. שגנבים מומחין הם [חולין קכז.].

ראה תניא אמר רב אשי ואי חכים משוי ליה ראה דאמר ליה אמאי תפיסת ליה לאו משום דאית לך גבאי השתא (א) אפקינהו ושימינהו שקול את דידך ואשקול אנא דידי א"ל רב אחא בריה דרב אויא לרב אשי מצי א"ל לא צריכנא לשומא דידך כבר שמוה קמאי דקמך: אריס אין לו חזקה: א אמאי עד האידנא פלגא והשתא כולה א"ר יוחנן ב באריסי בתי אבות אמר רב נחמן ג אריס שהוריד אריסין תחתיו יש לו חזקה מאי טעמא דלא עביד איניש דנחתי אריסי לארעיה ושתיק א"ר יוחנן ד אריס שחלק לאריסין אין לו חזקה מאי טעמא אימור א) הרמניא בעלמא שויוה שלח ליה ר"נ בר רב חסדא לר"נ בר יעקב ילמדנו רבינו אריס מעיד או אינו מעיד הוה יתיב רב יוסף קמיה אמר ליה הכי אמר שמואל ה אריס מעיד והתניא אינו מעיד לא קשיא ו הא דאיכא פירא בארעא והא דליכא פירא בארעא (עמלק סימן) תנו רבנן ז ערב מעיד ללוה והוא דאית ליה ארעא אחריתי ח מלוה מעיד ללוה והוא דאית ליה ארעא אחריתי ט לוקח ראשון מעיד ללוקח שני והוא דאית ליה ארעא אחריתי

קבלן

רשב"ם

ראה תניא. ראה טליתו ביד האומן שרואה עכשיו ובעדים אבל זה אינו רואה טליתו ביד זה האומן וגם העדים שבראוהו לא הכירוהו אם זה הוא: ואי חכים. התובע מאי משוי ליה ראה שיאמר לו להאומן בדברים עד שיראהו לו בפני עדים וכיון שיראהו יוכל להוציאו ממנו דלאומן אין לו חזקה היכא דראה: דא"ל. דרך ערמה במשאל: אמאי תפסת. טלית דידי: לאו משום דאית לך. זוזי גבאי ואתה ירא שלא אכפור בך איני כופר בך ואף אתה אל תכפור לי ולעכבה בהיתר כנגד מה שאני חייב לך אפקה בפני בני אדם שבקיאין בשומא ונשיימיה ושקול דידך והחזר לי המותר אם יש יותר: מצי א"ל כו'. כלומר גם האומן כ"ש שיהא ערום ומכיר בערמתו ויאמר לא צריכנא לשומא דידך כבר שיימוה ראשונים לפני בואך ואין שוה כלום יותר מן החוב שאתה חייב לי: אריס. שיודעין בו שבאריסות ירד לשדה זו אין לו חזקה: אמאי. אין לו חזקה והלא עד האידנא שהיה באריסות פלגא היה נוטל כדין אריס והשתא אכלה כולה שלש שנים ואין זה דרך אריסים והיה לו לבעל השדה למחות: א"ר יוחנן. מתני' באריסי בתי אבות מיירי שרגילין לשמור שדות של משפחה זו מעולם הן ואבותיהן באריסות ולא היו יכולים להחליפו באריסים אחרים ואותן אריסים נוהגים לאכול כל הפירות ב' וג' שנים ואחרי כן יאכלו הבעלים כמו כן הלכך אין להם חזקה אבל שאר אריסין יש להן חזקה: אריס. של בתי אבות שהוריד אריסין תחתיו אותן ג' שנים שהיה לו לאכול והוא לא עשה עמהן כלום: יש לו חזקה. דלא עביד בעה"ב דנחתי אריסין נכרים בארעיה בלא רשותו ושתיק שמא יקלקלו שדותיו אא"כ עושה האריס עצמו עמהן ורואה מה הם עושים כדלקמיה: אריס. של בתי אבות: שחלק לאריסין. לכל אחד מסר לעשות חלקו בשדה וגם הוא עושה עמהן: אין לו חזקה. דאע"ג דהיכא דהוריד תחתיו יש לו חזקה הכא אין לו חזקה דהכ"ג לא קפיד בעל השדה מאחר שגם הוא עושה עמהן: ואיכא למימר הרמניא שויוה. רשות נתנו לו להוריד אריסין עמו אם טורח הוא לו לעשות לבדו: אריס. שהורידהו ראובן ובא שמעון לערער עליו מי מצי אריס להעיד לו לראובן להעמיד בידו מי הוי נוגע בעדות משום דנהנה מן פירות השדה או לא: א"ל. רב יוסף דיתיב קמיה הכי אמר שמואל כו': הא דאיכא פירא בארעא. שעדיין לא נטל האריס חלקו אינו מעיד דניחא ליה דתיקו ביד ראובן דאי שקיל ליה שמעון יטול גם הפירות כדין נגזל: דליכא פירא בארעא. וגם לא טרח בה האריס כלום בשנה זו מצי להעיד דלא מרויח מידי בהאי עדות ואם משום שאם נשאר הקרקע ביד ראובן היה מורידו באריסות הרבה (ב) ימצא שדה באריסות וגם מי יודע אם יעשנו אריס שלו אם ירצה יעשה ואם ירצה יחדל: ערב. של לוה כנגד המלוה מעיד ללוה על קרקע שלו להוציאה מן המערער ואימת מעיד: והוא דאית ליה. ללוה: ארעא אחריתי. שיוכל המלוה לגבות הימנה את חובו ויפטר הערב ונמצא שאין הערב מרויח כלום במה שמעמיד שדה זו ביד לוה והא ליכא למימר דלכך מתכוין הערב דניחא ליה שיהו שדות הרבה ביד הלוה שאם חייב הלוה עדיין לבעל חוב אחר שיגבה תחלה קרקע האחת ויגבה הערב קרקע השנית ונוגע בעדותו הוא ליכא למימר הכי דכולי האי לא חייש שמא לא יפרע הלוה בזמנו ואת"ל לא יפרע שמא יבא מלוה אחר ויגבה ואח"כ יבא מלוה זה ויפרע ממנו שני חששות לא חייש והלכך לאו נוגע בעדות הוא וכי האי גוונא איכא לתרולי גבי מלוה מעיד ללוה: לוקח ראשון מעיד ללוקח שני. כגון ראובן שמכר שדה אחת ללוי ואחר כך שדה אחרת ליהודה ואתא איניש מעלמא ומערער על של יהודה לומר גזלה ראובן ממני מעיד לו לוי ליהודה דהיינו לוקח ראשון ללוקח שני ומעיד לו שהיא שלו ולא של מערער והוא דאית ליה ליהודה עוד קרקע אחרת שלקח מראובן שיוכל בעל חוב דראובן לגבות חובו הימנה כדין בעל חוב שגובה מלוקח אחרון ואם אין לו גובה משלפניו והלכך כיון דאית ליה ליהודה עוד קרקע אחרת המשועבדת לבעל חוב דראובן אי נמי יש לו לראובן קרקע אחרת בת חורין דליהדר עלה בעל חוב דידיה מאי לוי לאסהודי ליהודה אהך קרקע דלאו נוגע בעדותו הוא דהא אפי' מפיק ליה מערער מיהודה לא אתי בעל חוב דראובן וטריף מלוי אלא מקרקע אחרת שיש לו ליהודה מראובן או לקרקע אחרת שיש לו לראובן עוד אבל אי ליכא קרקע אחרת לא מסהיד לוי ליהודה מפני שמעמידה לוי בפני בעל חוב דראובן פן יבא ויטרוף הימנו. ודוקא לוקח ראשון אין מעיד ללוקח שני [ג) היכא דלית ליה ארעא אחריתי] אבל לוקח שני מעיד ללוקח ראשון אפילו היכא דלית ליה למוכר קרקע אחרת דהא בעל חוב דמוכר לעולם אלוקח שני הדר בין שיש קרקע ללוקח ראשון ובין אין לו והלכך לא מרויח מידי בעדותו וכגון שמכר מוכר ללוקח ראשון שלא באחריות אבל אם מכר לו באחריות לא מסהיד ליה שני לראשון אלא אם כן יש לו קרקע למוכר דליהדר לוקח ראשון עלויה דנוגע בעדותו הוא דחייש דאי מפקי ליה מלוקח ראשון הדר לוקח ראשון עילוואי שקניתי אחריו קרקע המשועבדת לו כן נראה בעיני:

קבלן

תוספות

שלח ליה ר"נ בר רב חסדא לרב נחמן בר יעקב. ר"נ סתם שבכל גמרא הוא ר"נ בר יעקב ג) תדע דבכל הגמ' לא תמצא ר"נ בר יעקב נזכר שמו ושם אביו אא"כ יש ר"נ אחר אצלו כי הכא ובירושל' פליגי בכל מקום רב נחמן בר יעקב ורב ששת משמע דהוא ר"נ סתם דהוא בר פלוגתיה דרב ששת בגמ' שלנו ולא כמו שמשמע מתוך פירוש הקונטרס בסוף פרק כל הגט (גיטין דף לא: ושם ד"ה אנא) דרב נחמן בר יצחק הוה חתניה דבי נשיאה דהיינו רב נחמן סתם כדמוכח בהעור והרוטב (חולין דף קכד.) ועוד דאמרינן בהשולח (גיטין דף לט:) אמר ר"נ בר יצחק אנא אמינא [אין] הלכה ורבנן דאתו ממחוזא אמרי משמיה דר"נ הלכה אלמא ר"נ סתם לאו היינו ר"נ בר יצחק ובפרק מי שהוציאוהו (עירובין דף מג: ושם ד"ה יתיב) אמר יתיב ר"נ בר יצחק אחורי דרבא ויתיב רבא קמיה דר"נ וכן בכמה מקומות אמר רבא אמר רב נחמן ורב נחמן בר יצחק הוה תלמידיה דרבא כדמשמע בלא יחפור (לעיל דף כב.) ואין להאריך ד):

הא דאית ליה פירא בארעא. לא יעיד דנוגע בעדות הוא לפי שהיה נותן לו למחצה לשליש ולרביע ואם יזכה המערער הרי שלא ברשותו ירד וידו על התחתונה אבל לית ליה פירא בארעא לא חייש אם יסלקוהו דכמה שדות ימצא באריסות:

לוקח ראשון מעיד ללוקח שני והוא דאית ליה ארעא אחריתי אבל לית ליה ארעא אחריתי לא יעיד. פ"ה משום דחייש שמא יבא בע"ח ויטרוף ממנו ולא יהא לו ממה לגבות מן המוכר וקשה לר"י דא"כ אפילו אית ליה ארעא אחריתי נמי דכי היכי דחייש לבע"ח קטן ה"נ ניחוש לבעל חוב גדול שיהא חובו כנגד שני קרקעות אלא נראה לר"י דאע"ג דלעיל (דף מד.) גבי מוכר שדה שלא באחריות אמרינן שאין מעיד לו עליה מפני שמעמידה בפני בעל חובו התם ודאי חיישינן לבעל חוב לפי שאדם יודע אם יש לו בעלי חובים אם לאו וכשאנו רואים שבא להעיד אנו חוששים שלכך מעיד לפי שרוצה להעמידה בפני בע"ח והתם אפילו אית ליה ארעא אחריתי לא יעיד דחיישינן שמא יש לו בעל חוב גדול וכן אומר רשב"ם דמשמע לעיל כי פריך וכי קנו מידו מאי הוי הרי מעמידה בפני בע"ח ולא משני כגון דאית ליה ארעא אחריתי והא דקאמר לעיל אי דאית ליה ארעא אחריתי עליה הדר לא תקשי היאך הדר עליה שמא יש לו בעל חוב גדול דה"פ אי אית ליה ארעא אחריתי כדי כל החוב עליה הדר ואי לית ליה ארעא אחריתי כדי כל החוב מאי נפקא מינה אבל אין לחוש שהלוקח מעיד לפי שיהיה לבע"ח של מוכר ממה לגבות דאין הלוקח יודע אם יש למוכר שום בע"ח אלא היינו טעמא דאין הלוקח ראשון מעיד ללוקח שני אע"ג דלא חייש לבע"ח מיהו חייש שמא קרקע גזולה היא והיום או למחר יבא הנגזל ויקחנה ולא יהיה לו ממה לחזור על המוכר היכא דלית ליה ארעא אחריתי למוכר וא"ת ומלוה וערב (והלוקח) אמאי מעידים ללוה אע"ג דאית ליה ארעא אחריתי ניחוש שמא היא גזולה וכשיבא נגזל ויקחנה לא יהיה לו ממה לגבות כדחיישינן לחד נגזל גבי לוקח ה"נ ניחוש גבי ערב ומלוה וי"ל דבשום מקום אין המלוה וערב והלוקח חוששין כל זמן שאחריות שלהן קיים:

לוקח ראשון מעיד ללוקח שני. קשה לרשב"א אמאי לא קאמר לוקח מעיד למוכר והוא דאית ליה ארעא אחריתי בין ה) (לפרש"י) בין לפר"י:

קבלן

עין משפט נר מצוה

קסב א ב מיי' פי"ג מהל' טוען הל' ה סמג עשין לה טוש"ע ח"מ סי' קמט סעיף כה:
קסג ג ד מיי' שם הל' ו טוש"ע שם סעיף כו:
קסד ה ו מיי' פט"ו מהל' עדות הל' ה סמג לאוין קט טוש"ע ח"מ סי' לז סעיף ג:
קסה ז ח מיי' שם הל' ו טוש"ע שם סעיף יג:
קסו ט מיי' שם ועי' בהשגות טוש"ע שם סעיף יד:

רבינו גרשום

שפיר קאמר דראה תניא. דכל זמן שלא ראה נאמן המחזיק: אי חכים התובע מצי משוי ליה ראה. כלומר כי היכי דכי ראהו בידו אין האומן נאמן הכי נמי יכול לשדלו בדברים עד דמשוי ליה ראה ויכול להוציאה דאמר ליה דרך הערמה אמאי תפשית האי טלית דידי לאו משום דאית לך גבאי כך וכך זוזי איני כופר לך ואף אתה אל תכפור לי שאני יודע שזה שאתה אומר לא היו דברים מעולם בעבור שאתה (חושבה) [תופסה] כנגד מה שאני חייב לך: אפקיה. דנישום ושקול דידך והב דידי וכן יכול לטוענו שיוציאה: א"ל רב אחא. אי משום הא לא דמצי טעין האי לא צריך לשומא דידך שאני יודע שומתה: פיסקא אריס. (שידוע) אין לו חזקה לומר שלי היא כבר אכלתיה ג' שנים: אמאי. אין לו חזקה ולימא ליה האריס עד האידנא אכלתיה פלגא כדין אריס והשתא אכלתיה כולה ג' שני חזקה ודילי הוא שקניתיה: הכא באריסי בתי אבות עסקינן. כגון משפחה אחת שמתחברין וכל אחד נותן לאריס שדה אחת כולה ג' שנים או ה' כדי שיזרענה ויאכל פירותיה ובאותו שכר ישמור כל השדות של משפחה ולאחר ג' שנים או ה' מחזירה לבעליה וחוזר שני של אותה משפחה ונותן לו שדה אחת לג' שנים שיהיו כל הפירות שלו כדי שישמור כל שאר שדותיו ושדות כל המשפחה וכן עושין כולם. היה לו שדה אחת כולה כל ימי אריסותיו אין לו חזקה בה דהשתא לא מצי למיטען עד האידנא פלגא והשתא כולה דמעיקרא נמי לאוכלה כולה הקצוה לו: אריס שהוריד אריסין תחתיו על אותה שדה שקבל מן בתי אבות והוריד אריסין לחצי השדה למחצה מפירות וחצי השדה החזיק בידו בשביל שכר השדה והוריד בחציה אריסין ג' שנים יש לו חזקה באותו חצי שהוריד בה האריסין לומר שלי היא ואין יכולין לומר לו בתי אבות כולה הלוינוך בשכירות משום דלא עביד אינש דמחתי כלל: אריס שהיו לו שדות הרבה לעבוד ולא היה מספיק לבדו והקים עליהן אריסין לסייעו והיה מחלק להם משכר אריסותו בין מאותן שדות שקבל ובין מאותן שדות שייחדו לו לשכירותו אם טוען ואמר החזקתי באותו חלק שהורדתי האריסין לא הויא חזקה. דאימור בהרמנא בעלמא שוי' נתנו לו רשות בעלי השדות להורידן. דהואיל דנפישי אריסין מתעסקי טפי בשדות ומינטרן טפי וניחא להו: אריס וכו'. להעיד לבעל השדה שקנאה לדחות מעליו המערער או לא. מי אמרי' דנוגע בעדות הוא הואיל דמתהני מפירותיה או לא: הכי אמר שמואל מעיד. הואיל דאין לו בגוף קרקע: הא דאיכא פירי בארעא. שעדיין לא נטל האריס חלקו נוגע בעדות הוא: הא דליכא פירי בארעא. דכבר לקט חלקו מעיד: ערב מעיד ללוה. אע"ג דמשעבדי לערב שדותיו של לוה. ואימת מעיד והוא דאית ליה ארעא אחריתי ללוה חוץ מזו שמעיד עליה שוה שיעור החוב שנתערב בשבילו: מלוה נמי מעיד ללוה. דהבין ההוא קרקע דלא אמרי' דהאי קרקע משועבד למלוה נוגע בעדות הוא. דכיון דאית ליה ארעא אחריתי [illegible]: לוקח ראשון מעיד ללוקח שני. [illegible] ממנו:

מסורת הש"ס

א) [גירסת הערוך קהרמנא פי' אפוטרופוס], ב) מהרש"א, ג) וכמס' קדושין דף לג. משמע דסתם ר"נ הוא ר"נ בר אבא [ועי' בתשובת סוט השני סי' כ' שרוצה לומר דתרי רב נחמן הוו וחד מיניהו ר"נ בר אבא], ד) [ועי' תוס' עירובין יח: ד"ה מתקיף ועוד שם מג: ד"ה יתיב ותוס' גיטין לא: ד"ה אנא], ה) [צ"ל לפי' רשב"ם].

הגהות הב"ח

(א) גמ' השתא אפקיה ולשיימיה שקול את דידך: (ב) רשב"ם ד"ה דליכא פירא וכו' הרבה שדות ימצא באריסות וגם:

ליקוטי רש"י

אריס אין לו חזקה. שיורדין לתקן קרקע למחצה לשליש ולרביע אם טוען שני חזקה החזקתי בקרקע ואכלתי פירותיה אינה חזקה שיכול לומר המערער הורדתיו ולמי הפירות היה משלם לי או וקפתים עליו באלוה אי נמי מנהג אריסים לעבוד קרקע עשר שנים וחמש שנים אוכלין הבעלים כל הפירות של כל השדה ואחר כך אוכלין אריסים חמש שנים כנגדן [רשב"ם לעיל מב.].

רָאָה תַּנְיָא – for the Baraisa[1] states specifically that [a person] *saw* his article in the craftsman's possession. Only then can the owner demand it from the craftsman, but not if he lacks definite proof that the craftsman has it.[2]

Rav Ashi suggests a strategy to deal with such cheats:

אָמַר רַב אַשִׁי – **Rav Ashi said:** וְאִי חֲכִים מַשְׁוֵי לֵיהּ רָאָה – **If [the claimant] is shrewd, he can** trick the cheat into **making [the cloak] "seen"** in his possession. דְּאָמַר לֵיהּ אַמַּאי תְּפִיסַת לֵיהּ – **For he can say** deceitfully **to [the cheat], "Why are you holding on to [my cloak]?** לָאו מִשּׁוּם דְּאִית לָךְ גַּבַּאי – **Is it not because you have** an outstanding claim **against me** for money that I owe you?[3] הַשְׁתָּא אַפְּקִינְהוּ וְשַׁיְּמִינְהוּ – **Now, bring out [the cloak] and let us assess its value;**[4] שְׁקוֹל אַתְּ דִּידָךְ וְאֶשְׁקוֹל אֲנָא דִּידִי – **take** whatever portion of the cloak is rightfully **yours and I will take** the rest, which is **mine."**[5]

Rav Acha rejects this suggestion:

אָמַר לֵיהּ רַב אַחָא בְּרֵיהּ דְּרַב אַוְיָא לְרַב אַשִׁי – **Rav Acha the son of Rav Avya said to Rav Ashi:** מָצֵי אָמַר לֵיהּ – **[The craftsman]** will certainly see through the ruse and **can say [to the claimant],** לָא צְרִיכְנָא לְשׁוּמָא דִּידָךְ – **"I do not need your assessment** of the cloak. כְּבָר שָׁמוּהָ קַמָּאֵי דְּקַמָּךְ – **The predecessors of your predecessor have already assessed it."** I.e. the cloak (that I have in my possession – though I insist that it only looks like yours but is not[6]) was already assessed as having no greater value than the amount of the debt and there is therefore no need for me to produce it.

The Gemara now discusses the Mishnah's statement:

אָרִיס אֵין לוֹ חֲזָקָה – A SHARECROPPER ... DOES NOT ESTABLISH A *CHAZAKAH* by virtue of three years' unchallenged use of a field that is known to have been given to him to work as a sharecropper.[7]

The Gemara questions this ruling:

אַמַּאי – **Why** should the sharecropper not establish a ***chazakah?*** עַד הָאִידָּנָא פַּלְגָא וְהַשְׁתָּא כּוּלֵּהּ – After all, **until now** (i.e. until three years ago) he took only **half** the yield of the field for himself,[8] **whereas now** (i.e. for the past three years) he has been taking **its entire** yield for himself![9] Since for the past three years he has been consuming more than a sharecropper would and there has been no protest from the original owner, why does the Mishnah not allow the sharecropper to use these three years as proof that he, in fact, purchased the field?

The Gemara answers:

אָמַר רַבִּי יוֹחָנָן – **R' Yochanan said:** בַּאֲרִיסֵי בָּתֵּי אָבוֹת – The Mishnah refers to **ancestral sharecroppers,** i.e. sharecroppers whose families have been with the owner's family for generations. Such established sharecroppers often have an arrangement whereby rather than split the harvest with the owner every year, they keep the entire harvest for several years running, and then give the entire harvest to the owner for several years running.[10] It is in regard to sharecroppers such as these that the Mishnah rules that their consumption of the harvest for three consecutive years cannot furnish proof of ownership.

The Gemara cites a new teaching.

אָמַר רַב נַחְמָן – **Rav Nachman said:** אָרִיס שֶׁהוֹרִיד אֲרִיסִין תַּחְתָּיו – **An** ancestral **sharecropper who** in turn **installed** other **sharecroppers in his stead** יֵשׁ לוֹ חֲזָקָה – **does establish a *chazakah*** in that field by virtue of his subcontractors working the field for three years without protest from the original owner.[11] מַאי טַעְמָא – **What is the reason?** Why does the subcontractors' occupancy establish a *chazakah* where the sharecropper's own occupancy would not? דְּלָא עָבִיד אִינִישׁ דְּנָחְתֵי אֲרִיסֵי לְאַרְעֵיהּ וְשָׁתִיק – **Because a person is not apt to remain silent while** other **sharecroppers are installed in his land** without his permission.[12]

NOTES

1. Rava refers to the Baraisa cited above (45b), which reads: *A person saw his slave in the possession of a craftsman or his cloak in the possession of a cleaner etc.*

2. The Baraisa there, which specifically describes a case in which the original owner has *seen* his article in the craftsman's possession [i.e. he has witnesses who can attest that the craftsman still has it – see note 4 there], clearly implies that in no other circumstance will the craftsman be required to surrender the article. Thus, if the article is not actually *seen* there – even if there is some evidence to suggest that he might have it – his claim of not having it must be accepted and we cannot force him to produce his articles for inspection (see *Rashbam;* see also *Tosafos* 46a ד״ה שפיר).

3. He is careful to say this to the craftsman quietly, so as not to be overheard [and thus avoid having to explain away his false admission in court] (*Rashbam*).

4. [Literally: bring them out and assess them. Our translation, however, follows *Bach's* emendation: אַפְּקֵיהּ וְלִישַׁיְּמֵיהּ.]

5. I.e. return to me the amount that the cloak is worth in excess of the debt that I owe you (*Rashbam*). [By this subterfuge, the claimant seeks to tempt the craftsman into producing the cloak in front of witnesses. Once the craftsman does so, and the cloak is indeed identified as having belonged to the claimant, he can recover his cloak on the principle (established by the Gemara above) that a craftsman cannot establish a *chazakah* in an article seen in his possession. Moreover, the claimant's position will prevail simply because the craftsman will have been proven to be a liar, since he denied having the cloak altogether (see *Tosafos* to 46a ד״ה שפיר). The claimant's admission of debt will have no legal standing, since it was not heard by witnesses.]

6. See *Ritva.*

7. The Mishnah refers to a case in which it is known that the sharecropper initially occupied the field under a sharecropping arrangement, whereby the sharecropper works the field in return for a percentage of its yield, the rest of the yield being delivered to the owner. However, the sharecropper has worked the field and kept its entire yield for himself for three years without any protest from the original owner. The Mishnah rules that the sharecropper cannot use his total occupancy of the field as proof that he terminated the sharecropping arrangement and bought the field from the original owner, since it is possible that this total occupancy was merely an extension of the initial sharecropping arrangement.

8. [The Gemara uses the example of a sharecropper who is given half the yield in return for his work.]

9. [He could hardly lay claim to the field on the basis of three years' occupancy if during those three years he had been relinquishing half the yield to the original owner.]

10. Such old established sharecroppers cannot be fired and will thus continue to be with the employer for the long term. Therefore, it is common for the employer to enter into long-term arrangements regarding allocation of the yield with the sharecropper, instead of sharing the yield with them on a year by year basis (see *Rashbam* and *Nimukei Yosef*).

11. In this case, the ancestral sharecropper subcontracted the work to other sharecroppers, who take a percentage of the yield for themselves and give the rest to the ancestral sharecropper, not to the original owner. Although the ancestral sharecropper could not have established a *chazakah* in the field by virtue of his own absolute three-year occupancy (as the Mishnah ruled), Rav Nachman teaches that he can establish a *chazakah* by virtue of his subcontractors' occupancy. [Although the subcontractor is the one actually working the field, the occupancy is credited to his employer – the ancestral sharecropper – for an owner's utilization of his property can take either the form of personal use or of leasing the property to tenants; see Gemara 29a.]

12. Since he does not trust them to work the field independently without damaging it. Thus, the field's owner would be expected to

קסב א ב מיי' פי"ג מהל' טוען הל' ה סמג עשין לה טוש"ע ח"מ סי' קמט סעיף כה:

קסג ג ד מיי' שם הל' ו טוש"ע שם סעיף כו:

קסד ה ו מיי' פט"ו מהל' עדות הל' ה סמג לאוין קט טוש"ע ח"מ סי' לז סעיף ב:

קסה ז ח מיי' שם הל' ו טוש"ע שם סעיף יג:

קסו ט מיי' שם ועי' בהגהות טוש"ע שם סעיף יד:

ראה תניא אמר רב אשי ואי חכם משוי ליה ראה דאמר ליה אמאי תפיסת ליה לאו משום דאית לך גבאי השתא (א) אפקינהו ושימנהו שקול את דידך ואשקול אנא דידי א"ל רב אחא בריה דרב אויא לרב אשי מצי א"ל לא צריכנא לשומא דידך כבר שמוה קמאי דקמך: אריס אין לו חזקה: א אמאי עד האידנא פלגא והשתא כולה א"ר יוחנן ב באריסי בתי אבות אמר רב נחמן ג אריס שהוריד אריסין תחתיו יש לו חזקה מאי טעמא דלא עביד איניש דנחתי אריסי לארעיה ושתיק א"ר יוחנן ד אריס שחלק לאריסין אין לו חזקה מאי טעמא אימור ו הרמנא בעלמא שויה שלח ליה ר"נ בר רב חסדא לר"נ בר יעקב ילמדנו רבינו אריס מעיד או אינו מעיד הוה יתיב רב יוסף קמיה אמר ליה הכי אמר שמואל ה אריס מעיד והתניא אינו מעיד לא קשיא ו הא דאיכא פירא בארעא והא דליכא פירא בארעא (עמלק סימן) תנו רבנן ז ערב מעיד ללוה והוא דאית ליה ארעא אחריתי ח מלוה מעיד ללוה והוא דאית ליה ארעא אחריתי ט לוקח ראשון מעיד ללוקח שני והוא דאית ליה ארעא אחריתי קבלן

ראה תניא. ראה טליתו ביד האומן שרואה עכשיו ובעדים אבל זה אינו רואה טליתו ביד זה האומן וגם העדים כשראוהו לא הכירוהו אם זה הוא: **ואי חכם.** המוכר מצי משוי ליה ראה לשתול לאומן בדברים עד שיראהו לו בפני עדים וכיון שיראהו יוכל להוציאו ממנו דלאומן אין לו חזקה היכא דראה: **דא"ל.** דרך ערמה בחשאי: **אמאי תפסת.** טלית דידי: **לאו משום דאית לך.** זוזי גבאי ואתה ירא שלא תפסיד בך אני כופר בך ואף אתה אל תכפור לי ולעכבה בהיתר כנגד מה שאני חייב לך אפקה בפני בני אדם שבקיאין בשומא ושיימיה ושקול דידך והחזר לי המותר אם יש יותר: **מצי א"ל כו'.** כלומר גם האומן ר"ל שיהא ערום ומכיר בערמומו ויאמר לא צריכנא לשומא דידך כבר שימוה ראשונים לפני בואך ואין שוה כלום יותר מן החוב שאתה חייב לי: **אריס.** שיודעין בו שבאריסות ירד לשדה זו אין לו חזקה: **אמאי.** אין לו חזקה והלא עד האידנא שהיה באריסות פלגא היה נוטל כדין אריס והשתא אכלה כולה שלש שנים ואין זה דרך אריסים והיה לו לבעל השדה למחות: **א"ר יוחנן.** מתני' באריסי בתי אבות מיירי שרגילין לשמור שדות של משפחה זו מעולם הן ואבותיהן באריסות ולא היו יכולים להחליפו באריסים אחרים ואותן אריסים נוהגים לאכול כל הפירות ב' וג' שנים ואחרי כן יאכלו הבעלים כמו כן הלכך אין להם חזקה אבל שאר אריסין יש להן חזקה: **אריס.** של בתי אבות שהוריד אריסין תחתיו אותן ג' שנים שהיה לו לאכול והוא לא עשה עמהן כלום: **יש לו חזקה.** דלא עביד בעה"ב דנחתי אריסין נכרים בארעיה בלא רשותו ושתיק שמא יקלקלו שדותיו אא"כ עושה האריס עצמו עמהן ורואה מה הם עושים כדלקמיה: **אריס.** של בתי אבות: **שחלק לאריסין.** לכל אחד מסר חלקו בשדה וגם הוא עושה עמהן: **אין לו חזקה.** דאע"ג דהיכא דהוריד תחתיו יש לו חזקה הכא אין לו חזקה דהכא לא קפיד בעל השדה מאחר שגם הוא עושה עמהן: **ואיכא למימר הרמנא שויה.** רשות נתנו לו להוריד אריסין עמו אם טורח הוא לו לעשות לבדו: **אריס.** שהורידהו ראובן ובא שמעון לערער עליו מי מצי אריס להעיד לו לראובן להעמיד בידו מי הוי נוגע בעדות משום דנהנה מן פירות השדה או לא: **א"ל.** רב יוסף דיתיב קמיה הכי אמר שמואל כו': **הא דאיכא פירא בארעא.** שעדיין לא נטל האריס חלקו אינו מעיד דניחא ליה דתיקו ביד ראובן דאי שקיל ליה שמעון יטול גם הפירות כדין נגזל: **דליכא פירא בארעא.** וגם לא טרח בה האריס כלום בשנה זו מצי להעיד דלא מרויח מידי בהאי עדות ואם משום שאם נשאר הקרקע ביד ראובן היה מורידו באריסות הרבה (ג) ימצא שדה באריסות וגם מי יודע אם יעשנו אריס שלו אם ירצה יעשה ואם ירצה יחדל: **ערב.** של לוה כנגד המלוה מעיד ללוה על קרקע שלו להוציאה מן המערער ואימת מעיד: **והוא דאית ליה.** ללוה: **ארעא אחריתי.** שיוכל המלוה לגבות הימנה את חובו ויפטר הערב ונמצא שאין הערב מרויח כלום במה שמעמיד שדה זו ביד לוה והא ליכא למימר דלכך מתכוין הערב דניחא ליה שיהו שדות הרבה ביד הלוה שאם חייב הלוה עדיין לבעל חוב אחר שיגבה תחלה קרקע האחת ויגבה הערב קרקע השנית ונוגע בעדותו הוא ליכא למימר הכי דכולי האי לא חייש שמא לא יפרע הלוה בזמנו ואת"ל לא יפרע שמא יבא מלוה אחר ויגבה ואח"כ יבא מלוה זה ויפרע ממנו שני חששות לא חייש והלכך לאו נוגע בעדות הוא וכי האי גוונא איכא לתרוצי גבי מלוה מעיד ללוה: **לוקח ראשון מעיד ללוקח שני.** כגון ראובן שמכר שדה אחת ללוי ואחר כך שדה אחרת ליהודה ואתא איניש מעלמא ומערער על של יהודה לומר גזלה ראובן ממני מעיד לו לוי ליהודה דהיינו לוקח ראשון ללוקח שני ומעיד לו שהיא שלו ולא של מערער והוא דאית ליה ליהודה עוד קרקע אחרת שלקח מראובן שיוכל בעל חוב דראובן לגבות חובו הימנה כדין בעל חוב שגובה מלוקח אחרון ואם אין לו גובה משלפניו והלכך כיון דאית ליה ליהודה עוד קרקע אחרת המשועבדת לבעל חוב דראובן אי נמי יש לו לראובן קרקע אחרת בת חורין דליהדר עלה בעל חוב דידיה מצי לוי לאסהודי ליהודה אהך קרקע דלאו נוגע בעדותו הוא דהא אפי' מפיק ליה מערער מיהודה לא אתי בעל חוב דראובן וטריף מלוי אלא מקרקע אחרת שיש לו ליהודה מראובן או לקרקע אחרת שיש לו לראובן עוד אבל אי ליכא קרקע אחרת לא מסהיד לוי ליהודה מפני שמעמידה לוי בפני בעל חוב דראובן פן יבא ויטרוף הימנו. ודוקא לוקח ראשון אין מעיד ללוקח שני [ו) היכא דלית ליה ארעא אחריתי] אבל לוקח שני מעיד ללוקח ראשון אפילו היכא דלית ליה למוכר קרקע אחרת דהא בעל חוב דמוכר לעולם אלוקח שני הדר בין שיש קרקע ללוקח ראשון ובין אין לו והלכך לא מרויח מידי בעדותו וכגון שמכר מוכר ללוקח ראשון שלא באחריות אבל אם מכר לו באחריות לא מסהיד ליה שני לראשון אלא אם כן יש לו קרקע למוכר דליהדר לוקח ראשון עלויה דנוגע בעדותו הוא דחייש דאי מפקי ליה מלוקח ראשון הדר לוקח ראשון עילוואי שקניתי אחריו קרקע המשועבדת לו כן נראה בעיני: קבלן

שלח ליה ר"נ בר רב חסדא לרב נחמן בר יעקב. ר"ת פסק שבכל גמרא הוא ר"נ בר יעקב ג) תדע דבכל הגמ' לא תמצא ר"נ בר יעקב נזכר שמו ושם אביו אלא א"כ יש ר"נ אחר אצלו כי הכא ובירושלמי פליגי בכל מקום רב נחמן בר יעקב ורב ששת משמע דהוא ר"נ סתם דהוא בר פלוגתיה דרב ששת בגמ' שלנו ולא כמו שמשמע מתוך פירוש הקונטרס בסוף פרק כל הגט (גיטין דף לג: ושם ד"ה אמר) דרב נחמן בר יצחק הוה מתניה דבי נשיאה דהיינו רב נחמן סתם כדמוכח בהעור והרוטב (חולין דף קכד.) ועוד דאמרינן בהשולח (גיטין דף לג:) אמר ר"נ בר יצחק אנא אמינא [אין] הלכה ורבנן דאתו ממחוזא אמרי משמיה דר"נ הלכה אלמא ר"נ סתם לאו היינו ר"נ בר יצחק ובפרק מי שהוציאוהו (עירובין דף מג: ושם ד"ה יתיב) אמר יתיב ר"נ בר יצחק אחורי דרבא ויתיב רבא קמיה דר"נ וכן בכמה מקומות אמר רבא אמר רב נחמן ורב נחמן בר יצחק הוה תלמידיה דרבא כדמשמע בלא יחפור (לעיל דף כב.) ואין להאריך ד):

הא דאית ליה פירא בארעא. לא יעיד דנוגע בעדות הוא לפי שהיה נותן לו למחצה לשליש ולרביע ואם יזכה המערער הרי שלא ברשותו ירד ודינו על התבואה הלא לית ליה פירא בארעא לא חיים אם יסלקוהו דכמה שדות ימצא באריסות:

לוקח ראשון מעיד ללוקח שני והוא דאית ליה ארעא אחריתי אבל לית ליה לא יעיד. פ"ה משום דחיים שמא יבא בע"ח ויטרוף ממנו ולא יהא לו ממה לגבות מן המוכר וקשה לר"י דא"כ אפילו אית ליה ארעא אחריתי נמי דכי היכי דחיים לבע"ח קטן ה"נ ניחוש לבעל חוב גדול שיהא חובו כנגד שני קרקעות אלא נראה לר"י דאע"ג דלעיל (דף מד.) גבי מוכר שדה שלא באחריות אמרינן שאין מעיד לו עליה מפני שמעמידה בפני בעל חובו הכא ודאי חיישינן לבעל חוב לפי שאדם יודע אם יש לו בעלי חובים אם לאו וכשאנו רואים שבא להעיד אנו חוששים שלכך מעיד לפי שרוצה להעמידה בפני בע"ח והתם אפילו אית ליה ארעא אחריתי לא יעיד דחיישינן שמא יש לו בעל חוב גדול וכן אומר רשב"א דמשמע לעיל כי פריך וכי קנו מידו מאי הוי הרי מעמידה בפני בע"ח ולא משני כגון דאית ליה ארעא אחריתי והא דקאמר לעיל אי דאית ליה ארעא אחריתי עליה הדר לא תקשי היאך הדר עליה שמא יש לו בעל חוב גדול דה"פ אי אית ליה ארעא אחריתי כדי כל החוב עליה הדר ואי לית ליה ארעא אחריתי כדי כל החוב מאי נפקא מינה אבל אין לחוש שהלוקח מעיד לפי שיהיה לבע"ח של מוכר ממה לגבות דאין הלוקח יודע אם יש למוכר שום בע"ח אלא היינו טעמא דאין הלוקח ראשון מעיד ללוקח שני אע"ג דלא חייש לבע"ח מיהו חייש שמא קרקע גזולה היא והיום או למחר יבא הנגזל ויקחנה ולא יהיה לו ממה לחזור על המוכר היכא דלית ליה ארעא אחריתי למוכר וא"ת ומלוה וערב (והלוקח) אמאי מעידים ללוה אע"ג דאית ליה ארעא אחריתי ניחוש שמא היא גזולה וכשיבא נגזל ויקחנה לא יהיה לו ממה לגבות כדחיישינן לחד נגזל גבי לוקח ה"נ ניחוש גבי ערב ומלוה וי"ל דבשום מקום אין המלוה וערב והלוקח חוששין כל זמן שאחריות שלהן קיים:

לוקח ראשון מעיד ללוקח שני. קשה לרשב"א אמאי לא קאמר לוקח מעיד למוכר והוא דאית ליה ארעא אחריתי בין ה) (לפרש"י) בין לפר"י: קבלן

א) [גירסת הערוך קהרמנא פי' אפוטרופוס, ב) מהרש"א], ג) ובמס' קדושין דף לג. משמע דסתם ר"נ הוא ר"נ בר אבא [ועי' בתשובות השני סי' שרוצה לומר דבר רב נחמן הוא ונזכר מיניה ר"נ בר אבא], ד) [ועי' תוס' ערכין יח: ד"ה מתקיף ועוד שם מג: ד"ה יתיב ותוס' גיטין לג: ד"ה אמר], ה) [צ"ל לפר"י רשב"ם]:

הגהות הב"ח

(א) גמ' השתא אפקיה ולשיימיה שקול את דידך: (ב) רשב"ם ד"ה שלכא וכו': (ג) רשב"ם ד"ה ליכא פירא וכו' הרבה שדות ימצא לאריסים וגם:

ליקוטי רש"י

אריס אין לו חזקה. שיורדין לתוך הקרקע למחצה לשליש ולרביע אם טוען שני חזקה החזקתי בקרקע ואכלתי הפירות אינה חזקה שיכול לומר המערער לאריסות הורדתיו ולמי הפירות היה משלם לי או זקפתיו עליו במלוה או נמי מנהג אריסים לעבוד קרקע עשר שנים ותחת שנים אוכלין הבעלים כל הפירות של כל השדה ואחר כך אוכלין אריסים ממש שנים כנגדן [רשב"ם לעיל מב.].

רבינו גרשום

שפיר קאמר דראה תניא. דכל זמן שלא ראה נאמן המחזיק: **אי חכם התובע מצי משוי ליה ראה.** כלומר כי היכי דראהו בידו אין האומן נאמן הכי נמי אינו יכול לשדלו בדברים עד דמשוי ליה ראה ויכול להוציאה **דאמר ליה** דרך הערמה **אמאי תפשת** האי טלית דידי **לאו משום דאית לך גבאי** כך וכך זוזי אינך כופר לך ואף אתה אל תכפור לך שאני חייב לך שאתה אומר לא היו דברים מעולם בעבור שאתה [חושבה] [תופסה] כנגד מה שאני חייב לך: **אפקיה.** דנישום ונשקול דידך והב דידי וכן יכול לטעון שיוציאה: **א"ל רב אחא.** אי משום הא לא דמצי טעין האי לא צריך לשומא דידך שאני יודע שומתה: **פיסקא אריס.** (שידוע) אין לו חזקה לומר שלי היא כבר אכלתיה ג' שנים: **אמאי.** אין לו חזקה וליהוי ליה האריס **עד האידנא** אכלתיה **פלגא** כדין אריס **והשתא כולה** אכלתיה ג' שני וזהו חזקה ודילי הוא שקניתיה: **הכא באריסי בתי אבות עסקינן.** כגון משפחה אחת שמתחברין וכל אחד נותן לאריס שדה אחת כולה ג' שנים או ה' כדי שיורענה ויאכל פירותיה ובאותו שכר ישמור כל השדות של משפחה ולאחר ג' שנים מחזירה לבעליה וחוזר שני של אותה משפחה ונותן לו שדה אחת לג' שנים שיהיו כל הפירות שלו כדי שישמור כל שאר שדותיו ושדות כל המשפחה וכן עושין כולם. היה לו שדה אחת כולה כל ימי אריסותיו אין לו חזקה בה דהשתא לא מצי למיטען עד האידנא פלגא והשתא כולה דמעיקרא נמי לאוכלה כולה הקצוה לו: **אריס שהוריד אריסין תחתיו** על אותה שדה שקבל מן בתי אבות והוריד אריסין לחצי השדה למחצה פירות וחצי השדה החזיק בידו בשביל שכר השדה והוריד בחציה אריסין ג' שנים **יש לו חזקה** באותו חצי שהוריד בה האריסין לומר שלי היא ואין יכולין לומר לו בתי אבות כולה הלוינך בשכירות משום **דלא עביד איניש דמחתי** כלל: **אריס** שהיו לו שדות הרבה לעבוד ולא היה מספיק לבדו והקים עליהן **אריסין** לסייעו והיה **מחלק** להם משכר אריסותו בין מאותן שדות שקבל ובין מאותן שדות שכירותו אם טוען ואמר החזקתי באותו חלק שהורדתי האריסין **לא הויא חזקה. דאימור בהרמנא בעלמא שוי'** נתנו לו רשות בעלי השדות להוריד. דהואיל דנפישי אריסין מתעסקי טפי בשדות ומינטרן טפי וניחא להו: **אריס וכו'.** **להעיד** לבעל השדה שקנאה לדחות מעליו המערער **או לא**. מי אמרי' דנוגע בעדות הוא הואיל דמתהני מפירותיה או לא: **הכי אמר שמואל מעיד.** הואיל דאין לו בגוף קרקע: **הא דאיכא פירי בארעא.** שעדיין לא נטל האריס חלקו אינו מעיד דנוגע הוא. ואי **ליכא פירי בארעא** דכבר לקט חלקו המגיע מעיד: **ערב מעיד ללוה.** דשלו היא הקרקע שקנאה אע"ג דמשעבדי לערב שדותיו של לוה. ואימת מעיד **והוא דאית ליה ארעא אחריתי** ללוה חוץ מזו שמעיד עליה שוה שיעור החוב שנתערב בשבילו: **מלוה** נמי **מעיד ללוה.** דזבין ההוא קרקע דלא אמרי' הואיל דהאי קרקע משועבד למלוה נוגע בעדות הוא. דכיון **דאית ליה** ללוה **ארעא אחריתי** דמצי למיגבי מינה מלוה שיעור הלואתו לאו נוגע בעדות הוא: **לוקח ראשון מעיד ללוקח שני.** כגון ראובן לוה משמעון מנה ושוב מכר ב' שדותיו אחת ללוי באחריות ואחת ליהודה השתא שדה זו שמכר ליהוד' משועבדת ללוי מפני שקיבל ללוי אחריות שאם יבא שמעון ויטרוף את לוי שיחזור לוי ויגבה ממה ששייר ראובן שלא מכר ללוי עכשיו אם רוצה לערער על שדה שקנה יהודה שמשועבדת ללוי יכול לוי שהוא לוקח ראשון להעיד על יהודה שקנאה ולא אמרי' נוגע בעדותו הוא משום דמשועבדת לו אינו רוצה שתצא מידו. ואימתי מעיד לו **והוא דאית לו** לראובן או ליהודה **קרקע אחריתי** שאם היה שמעון טורף את לוי שיכול לוי לחזור או על ראובן שמכר לו או על יהודה שקנה מה שמשועבד לו דהשת' לא נוגע בעדות הוא דעדיין יש לו מקום לגבות ממנו:

Another ruling of Rav Yochanan:

אָמַר רַבִּי יוֹחָנָן – **R' Yochanan said:** אָרִיס שֶׁחָלַק לַאֲרִיסִין – **An** ancestral **sharecropper who apportioned** some of his work **to** other **sharecroppers** אֵין לוֹ חֲזָקָה – **does not establish a *chazakah*** in that field.[13] מַאי טַעְמָא – **What is the reason?** Why is this different from the previous case? אֵימוּר הַרְמַנְיָא בְּעָלְמָא שַׁוְיֵהּ – Because where the sharecropper assists his subcontractors, **I can say that [the field's owners] gave [the sharecropper] permission to** act as **a supervisor.**[14]

The Gemara now addresses another issue concerning sharecroppers:

שְׁלַח לֵיהּ רַב נַחְמָן בַּר רַב חִסְדָּא לְרַב נַחְמָן בַּר יַעֲקֹב – **Rav Nachman bar Rav Chisda sent** the following query **to Rav Nachman bar Yaakov:** יְלַמְּדֵנוּ רַבֵּינוּ – **Will our master please teach us** whether אָרִיס מֵעִיד אוֹ אֵינוֹ מֵעִיד – **a sharecropper can or cannot testify** on behalf of his employer? Should someone contest the employer's title to the field, is the sharecropper legally qualified to support his employer's claim?[15] הֲוָה יָתִיב רַב יוֹסֵף קַמֵּיהּ – **Rav Yosef was sitting in front of [Rav Nachman bar Yaakov]** when the query arrived אָמַר לֵיהּ – **and said to him:** הָכִי אָמַר שְׁמוּאֵל – **Thus did Shmuel say:** אָרִיס מֵעִיד – **A sharecropper can testify** on his employer's behalf. וְהָתַנְיָא אֵינוֹ מֵעִיד – **But it has been taught in a Baraisa that** HE CANNOT TESTIFY for his employer! לָא קַשְׁיָא – There is **no conflict.** הָא דְּאִיכָּא פֵּירָא בְּאַרְעָא – **This** case of the Baraisa refers to **where there is** unharvested **fruit in the field.** In such a case, the sharecropper has a material interest in testifying on behalf of his employer, because if someone else should prove to be the real owner of the field the sharecropper will not collect his full share of the unharvested fruit.[16] וְהָא דְּלֵיכָּא פֵּירָא בְּאַרְעָא – **But this** case of Shmuel refers to **where there is no fruit in the field.**[17] In that case, the sharecropper can testify on his employer's behalf.

The Gemara discusses four other cases of people who may or may not testify in cases of disputed land ownership:

(עמלק סִימָן – עמלק **is the mnemonic** for these four cases.)

תָּנוּ רַבָּנָן – **The Rabbis taught in a Baraisa:** עָרֵב מֵעִיד לַלֹּוֶה – THE GUARANTOR MAY TESTIFY ON BEHALF OF THE BORROWER that a contested piece of land indeed belongs to him,[18] וְהוּא דְּאִית לֵיהּ אַרְעָא אַחֲרִיתִי – PROVIDED THAT [THE BORROWER] OWNS SOME OTHER LAND as well.[19] מַלְוֶה מֵעִיד לַלֹּוֶה – Similarly, THE LENDER MAY TESTIFY ON BEHALF OF THE BORROWER that a contested piece of land indeed belongs to him, וְהוּא דְּאִית לֵיהּ אַרְעָא אַחֲרִיתִי – PROVIDED THAT [THE BORROWER] OWNS SOME OTHER LAND as well.[20] לוֹקֵחַ רִאשׁוֹן מֵעִיד לְלוֹקֵחַ שֵׁנִי – Similarly,

NOTES

protest subcontractors working his field; and since he has not protested for three years, it can be assumed that he sold the field to the sharecropper, as the sharecropper indeed claims (*Rashbam*).

13. Unlike Rav Nachman's case, in which the sharecropper completely subcontracted the work to other sharecroppers, this case deals with a sharecropper who delegates some of the work to other workers, but also participates with them in working the field (*Rashbam;* cf. *Shitah Mekubetzes* for other explanations).

14. I.e. it is assumed that a field owner, though he does not want subcontractors to work the field on their own, does not mind if his hand-picked sharecropper delegates some of his work to others. Since the sharecropper of his choice participates in working the field, the owner is confident that the sharecropper will supervise the subcontractors' work and prevent them from damaging the field. Therefore, no inference can be drawn from the original owner's silence these past three years (*Rashbam*).

15. A person is disqualified from testifying in a matter in which he has a material interest. Now, the sharecropper stands to benefit from his employer's continued control of a contested field, since, for example, the sharecropper thereby has a source of income (see *Rashbam* below, ד״ה דליכא פירא). The question here is: Do the benefits that the sharecropper has constitute sufficient material interest to disqualify him from testifying in support of his employer's claim to the field? (*Rashbam*).

16. If it turns out that his employer was a squatter, the true owner will retrieve his field and its yield, in accordance with the rule that a stolen field is returned to its owner together with the fruit it has produced. Thus, the sharecropper will lose the percentage of the fruit that would have otherwise been his fee (*Rashbam*). Although the restored owner will have to reimburse the sharecropper for his expenses in cultivating the field (even though he had never commissioned the sharecropper to do so), this amount is usually less than what a commissioned sharecropper takes (see *Tosafos;* cf. *Ritva*).

17. [I.e. the sharecropper has already harvested the fruit and taken his share, but] he has not [yet] invested any effort in cultivating this [coming] year's crop. In such a case, the sharecropper has no material interest in the outcome of the case. Though advancing his employer's cause might protect his own job as a sharecropper in this field, he knows that there are many other sharecropping jobs available to him; moreover, he knows that his employer is under no obligation to continue to employ him. Therefore, the sharecropper's interest in the outcome of the case is negligible and does not disqualify him from testifying (see *Rashbam*).

One might still object that should the sharecropper's employer lose his case, the restored owner of the field will then extract from the sharecropper reimbursement for all the produce that he took from the field in years past, and that this should give the sharecropper a material interest in the case. See *Rabbeinu Yonah,* who discusses this issue.

18. The guarantor has guaranteed repayment of the borrower's loan. Thus, if the borrower defaults on the loan and has no assets for the lender to collect, the guarantor must repay the lender. In the Baraisa's case, the borrower's ownership of a piece of land is contested. Now, it is in the guarantor's best interests that the borrower should retain title to the contested piece of land, since the guarantor does not have to repay the loan if the borrower has sufficient collectible assets. Nevertheless, the Baraisa rules that the guarantor is not disqualified from testifying that the land belongs to the borrower.

19. Since the borrower owns other land, which can be collected by the lender in case of default, the guarantor's interests are protected in any event. Thus, he remains qualified to testify on behalf of the borrower (*Rashbam*).

Now, it is true that it is in the guarantor's best interests that the borrower should own additional property. For it is possible that there is some other creditor who will collect the uncontested field owned by the borrower, leaving him with no assets other than this contested field, thereby exposing the guarantor to liability should the contested field indeed be awarded to the contester. However, that eventuality is too remote to figure in the guarantor's calculations — the borrower would first have to default on his loan and his other property would then have to be collected by some other creditor whose claim precedes that of the lender. Since the guarantor is not assumed to be concerned about such remote possibilities, he remains qualified to testify on the borrower's behalf (*Rashbam*).

20. Although it is advantageous to the lender that the borrower should retain title to the contested property as well, (for if some other creditor collects the borrower's remaining assets, the lender will be able to collect the contested field), nevertheless, the lender remains qualified to testify on the borrower's behalf, since the eventuality of the lender having to resort to the contested land for collection of his debt is too remote to figure in his calculations, as explained previously in regard to the guarantor (*Rashbam*).

ראה תניא אמר רב אשי ואי חכים משוי ליה ראה דאמר ליה אמאי תפיסת ליה לאו משום דאית לך גבאי השתא (א) אפקינהו ושימינהו שקול את דידך ואשקול אנא דידי א"ל רב אחא בריה דרב אויא לרב אשי מצי א"ל לא צריכנא לשומא דידך כבר שמוה קמאי דקמך: אריס אין לו חזקה: אאמאי עד האידנא פלגא והשתא כולה א"ר יוחנן בבאריסי בתי אבות אמר רב נחמן גאריס שהוריד אריסין תחתיו יש לו חזקה מאי טעמא דלא עביד איניש דנחתי אריסי לארעיה ושתיק א"ר יוחנן דאריס שחלק לאריסין אין לו חזקה מאי טעמא אימור (א) הרמניא בעלמא שוויה שלח ליה ר"נ בר רב חסדא לר"נ בר יעקב ילמדנו רבינו אריס מעיד או אינו מעיד הוה יתיב רב יוסף קמיה אמר ליה הכי אמר שמואל האריס מעיד והתניא אינו מעיד לא קשיא והא דאיכא פירא בארעא והא דליכא פירא בארעא (עמלק סימן) תנו רבנן זערב מעיד ללוה והוא דאית ליה ארעא אחריתי חמלוה מעיד ללוה והוא דאית ליה ארעא אחריתי טלוקח ראשון מעיד ללוקח שני והוא דאית ליה ארעא אחריתי

רש"י

ראה תניא. ראה טליתו ביד האומן שרואה עכשיו ובעדים אבל זה אינו רואה טליתו ביד זה האומן וגם העדים כשראוהו לא הכירוהו אם זה הוא: ואי חכים. התובע מצי משוי ליה ראה יכול לישתדל לאומן בדברים עד שירוהו לו בפני עדים וכיון שירוהו יוכל להוציאו ממנו דהאומן אין לו חזקה היכא דראה: דא"ל. דרך ערמה כשאלו אמאי תפסת. טלית דידי: לאו משום דאית לך. זוזי גבאי ואתה ירא שלא תכפור בך אני כופר בך ואף אתה אל תכפור לי ולעכבה בהיתר כנגד מה שאני חייב לך אפקה בפני בני אדם שבקיאין בשומא ונשיימיה ושקול דידך והחזר לי המותר אם יש יותר: מצי א"ל כו'. כלומר גם האומן כ"ש שיהא ערום ומכיר בערמתו ויאמר לא צריכנא לשומא דידך כבר שיימוה ראשונים לפני בואך ואין שוה כלום יותר מן החוב שאתה חייב לי: אריס. שיודעין בו שבאריסות ירד לשדה זו אין לו חזקה: אמאי. אין לו חזקה והלא עד האידנא שהיה באריסות פלגא היה נוטל לדין אריס והשתא אכלה כולה שלש שנים ואין זה דרך אריסים והיה לו לבעל השדה למחות: א"ר יוחנן. מתני' באריסי בתי אבות מיירי שרגילין לשמור שדות של משפחה זו מעולם הן ואבותיהן באריסות ולא היו יכולים להחליפו באריסים אחרים ואותן אריסים נוהגים לאכול כל הפירות ג' וד' שנים ואחרי כן יאכלו הבעלים כמו כן הלכך אין להם חזקה אבל שאר אריסין יש להן חזקה: אריס. של בתי אבות שהוריד אריסין תחתיו אותן ג' שנים שהיה לו לאכול והוא לא עשה עמהן כלום: יש לו חזקה. דלא עביד בעה"ב דנחתי אריסין נכרים בארעיה בלא רשותו ושתיק שמא יקלקלו שדותיו אא"כ עושה האריס עצמו עמהן ורואה מה הם עושים כדלקמיה: אריס. של בתי אבות: שחלק לאריסין. לכל אחד מסר לעשות חלקו בשדה וגם הוא עושה עמהן: אין לו חזקה. דאע"ג דהיכא דהוריד תחתיו יש לו חזקה הכא אין לו חזקה דהכ"ג לא קפיד בעל השדה מאחר שגם הוא עושה עמהן: ואיכא למימר הרמניא שוויה. רשות נתנו לו להוריד אריסין עמו אם טורח הוא לו לעשות לבדו: אריס. שהורידהו ראובן ובא שמעון לערער עליו מי מצי אריס להעיד לו לראובן להעמיד בידו או הוי נוגע בעדות משום דנהנה מן פירות השדה או לא: א"ל. רב יוסף דיתיב קמיה הכי אמר שמואל כו': הא דאיכא פירא בארעא. שעדיין לא נטל האריס חלקו אינו מעיד דניחא ליה דתיקו ביד ראובן דלא שקיל ליה שמעון יטול גם הפירות מדין נגזל: דליכא פירא בארעא. וגם לא טרח בה האריס כלום בשנה זו מצי להעיד דלא מרויח מידי בהאי עדות ואם משום שאם נשאר הקרקע ביד ראובן היה מורידו באריסות הרבה (ב) ימצא שדה באריסות וגם מי יודע אם יעשנו אריס שלו אם ירצה יעשה ואם ירצה יחדל: ערב. של לוה כנגד המלוה מעיד ללוה על קרקע שלו להוציאה מן המערער ואימת מעיד: והוא דאית ליה. ללוה: ארעא אחריתי. שיוכל המלוה לגבות הימנה את חובו ויפטר הערב ונמצא שאין הערב מרויח כלום במה שמעמיד שדה זו ביד לוה והא ליכא למימר דלכך מתכוין הערב דניחא ליה שיהו שדות הרבה ביד הלוה שאם חייב הלוה עדיין לבעל חוב אחר שיגבה תחלה קרקע האחת ויגבה הערב קרקע השנית ונוגע בעדותו הוא ליכא למימר הכי דכולי האי לא חייש שמא לא יפרע הלוה בזמנו ואת"ל לא יפרע שמא יבא מלוה אחר ויגבה ואח"כ יבא מלוה זה ויפרע ממנו שני חששות לא חייש והלכך לאו נוגע בעדות הוא וכי האי גוונא איכא לתרוצי גבי מלוה מעיד ללוה: לוקח ראשון מעיד ללוקח שני. כגון ראובן שמכר שדה אחת ללוי ואחר כך שדה אחרת ליהודה ואתא איניש מעלמא ומערער על של יהודה לומר גזלה ראובן ממני מעיד לו לוי ליהודה דהיינו לוקח ראשון ללוקח שני ומעיד לו שהיא שלו ולא של מערער והוא דאית ליה ליהודה עוד קרקע אחרת שלקח מראובן שיוכל בעל חוב דראובן לגבות חובו הימנה כדין בעל חוב שגובה מלוקח אחרון ואם אין לו גובה משלפניו והלכך כיון דאית ליה ליהודה עוד קרקע אחרת המשועבדת לבעל חוב דראובן אי נמי יש לו לראובן קרקע אחרת בת חורין דליהדר עלה בעל חוב דידיה מאי לוי לאסהודי ליהודה אהך קרקע דלאו נוגע בעדותו הוא דהא אפי' מפיק ליה מערער מיהודה לא אתי בעל חוב דראובן וטריף מלוי אלא מקרקע אחרת שיש לו ליהודה מראובן או לקרקע אחרת שיש לו לראובן עוד אבל אי ליכא קרקע אחרת לא מסהיד לוי ליהודה מפני שמעמידה לוי בפני בעל חוב דראובן פן יבא ויטרוף הימנו. ודוקא לוקח ראשון אין מעיד ללוקח שני [(ג) היכא דלית ליה ארעא אחריתי] אבל לוקח שני מעיד ללוקח ראשון אפילו היכא דלית ליה למוכר קרקע אחרת דהא בעל חוב דמוכר לעולם אלוקח שני הדר בין שיש קרקע ללוקח ראשון ובין אין לו והלכך לא מרויח מידי בעדותו וכגון שמכר מוכר ללוקח ראשון שלא באחריות אבל אם מכר לו באחריות לא מסהיד ליה שני לראשון אלא אם כן יש לו קרקע למוכר דליהדר לוקח ראשון עליה דנוגע בעדותו הוא דחייש דאי מפקי ליה מלוקח ראשון הדר לוקח ראשון עילוואי שקניתי אחריו קרקע המשועבדת לו כן נראה בעיני:

תוספות

שלח ליה ר"נ בר רב חסדא לרב נחמן בר יעקב. ר"ת פסק שבכל גמרא הוא ר"נ בר יעקב (ג) מדע דבכל הגמ' לא תמצא ר"נ בר יעקב מזכר שמו ושם אביו אא"כ יש ר"נ אחר אצלו כי הכא ובירושל' פליגי בכל מקום רב נחמן בר יעקב ורב ששת משמע דהוא ר"נ סתם דהוא בר פלוגתיה דרב ששת בגמ' שלנו ולא כמו שמשמע מתוך פירוש הקונטרס בסוף פרק כל הגט (גיטין דף לג. ושם ד"ה אמר) דרב נחמן בר יצחק הוה מתניה דבי נשיאה דהיינו רב נחמן סתם כדמוכח בהעור והרוטב (חולין דף קכב.) ועוד דאמרינן בהשולח (גיטין דף לג:) אמר ר"נ בר יצחק אנא אמינא [אין] הלכה ורבנן דאתו ממחוזא אמרי משמיה דר"נ הלכה אלמא ר"נ סתם לאו היינו ר"נ בר יצחק ובפרק מי שהוציאוהו (עירובין דף מג: ושם ד"ה יתיב) אמר יתיב ר"נ בר יצחק אחורי דרבא ויתיב רבא קמיה דר"נ וכן בכמה מקומות אמר רבא אמר רב נחמן ורב נחמן בר יצחק הוה תלמידיה דרבא כדמשמע בלא יתפור (לעיל דף כב.) ואין להאריך (ד):

הא דאית ליה פירא בארעא. לא יעיד דנוגע בעדות הוא לפי שהיה נותן לו למחצה לשליש ולרביע ואם יזכה המערער הרי שלא ברשותו ירד וידו על התחתונה אבל לית ליה פירא בארעא לא חייש אם יסלקוהו דכמה שדות ימצא באריסות:

לוקח ראשון מעיד ללוקח שני והוא דאית ליה ארעא אחריתי אבל לית ליה ארעא אחריתי לא יעיד. פ"ה משום דחייש שמא יבא בע"ח ויטרוף ממנו ולא יהא לו ממה לגבות מן המוכר וקשה לר"י דא"כ אפילו אית ליה ארעא אחריתי נמי דכי היכי דחייש לבע"ח קטן ה"נ ניחוש לבעל חוב גדול שיהא חובו כנגד שני קרקעות אלא נראה לר"י דאע"ג דלעיל (דף מד.) גבי מוכר שדה שלא באחריות אמרינן שאין מעיד לו עליה מפני שמעמידה בפני בעל חובו התם ודאי חיישינן לבעל חוב לפי שאדם יודע אם יש לו בעלי חובים אם לאו וכשאנו רואים שבא להעיד אנו חוששים שלכך מעיד לפי שרוצה להעמידה בפני בע"ח והתם אפילו אית ליה ארעא אחריתי לא יעיד דחיישינן שמא יש לו בעל חוב גדול וכן אומר רשב"א דמשמע לעיל כי פריך וכי קנו מידו מאי הוי הרי מעמידה בפני בע"ח ולא משני כגון דאית ליה ארעא אחריתי והא דקאמר לעיל אי דאית ליה ארעא אחריתי עליה הדר לא תקשי היאך הדר עליה שמא יש לו בעל חוב גדול דה"פ אי אית ליה ארעא אחריתי כדי כל החוב עליה הדר ואי לית ליה ארעא אחריתי כדי כל החוב מאי נפקא מינה אבל אין לחוש שהלוקח מעיד לפי שיהיה לבע"ח של מוכר ממה לגבות דאין הלוקח יודע אם יש למוכר שום בע"ח אלא היינו טעמא דאין הלוקח ראשון מעיד ללוקח שני אע"ג דלא חייש לבע"ח מיהו חייש שמא קרקע גזולה היא והיום או למחר יבא הנגזל ויקחנה ולא יהיה לו ממה לחזור על המוכר היכא דלית ליה ארעא אחריתי למוכר וא"ת ומלוה וערב (והלוקח) אמאי מעידים ללוה אע"ג דאית ליה ארעא אחריתי ניחוש שמא היא גזולה וכשיבא נגזל ויקחנה לא יהיה לו ממה לגבות כדחיישינן לחד נגזל גבי לוקח ה"נ ניחוש גבי ערב ומלוה וי"ל דבשום מקום אין המלוה וערב והלוקח חוששין כל זמן שאחריות שלהן קיים:

לוקח ראשון מעיד ללוקח שני. קשה לרשב"א אמאי לא קאמר לוקח מעיד למוכר והוא דאית ליה ארעא אחריתי בין (ה) (לפרש"י) בין לפר"י:

עין משפט נר מצוה

קפב א ב מיי' פי"ג מהל' טוען הל' ה סמג עשין לה טוש"ע ח"מ סי' קמט סעיף כה:
קפג ג ד מיי' שם הל' ו טוש"ע שם סעיף כו:
קפד ה ו מיי' פט"ו מהל' עדות הל' ה סמג לאוין קטן טוש"ע ח"מ סי' לז סעיף ג:
קפה ז ח מיי' שם הל' ו טוש"ע שם סעיף יג:
קפו ט מיי' שם ועי' בהשגות טוש"ע שם סעיף יד:

רבינו גרשום

שפיר קאמר דראה תניא. דכל זמן שלא ראה נאמן המחזיק: אי חכים התובע מצי משוי ליה ראה. כלומר כי היכי דכי ראהו בידו אין האומן נאמן הכי נמי יכול לשדלו בדברים עד דמשוי ליה ראה ויכול להוציאה דאמר ליה דרך הערמה אמאי תפשית האי טלית דידי לאו משום דאית לך גבאי כך וכך זוזי איני כופר לך ואף אתה אל תכפור לי שאני יודע שזה שאתה אומר לא היו דברים מעולם בעבור שאתה (חושבה) [תופסה] כנגד מה שאני חייב לך: אפקיה. דנישום ושקול דידך והב דידי וכן יכול לטוענו שיוציאה: א"ל רב אחא. אי משום הא לא דמצי טעין האי לא צריך לשומא דידך שאני יודע שומתה: פיסקא אריס. (שידוע) אין לו חזקה לומר שלי היא כבר אכלתיה ג' שנים: אמאי. אין לו חזקה ולימא ליה האריס עד האידנא אכלתיה פלגא כדין אריס והשתא אכלתיה כולה ג' שני חזקה ודילי הוא שקניתיה: הכא באריסי בתי אבות עסקינן. כגון משפחה אחת שמתחברין וכל אחד נותן לאריס שדה אחת כולה ג' שנים או ה' כדי שיזרענה ויאכל פירותיה ובאותו שכר ישמור כל השדות של משפחה ולאחר ג' שנים או ה' מחזירה לבעליה וחוזר שני של אותה משפחה ונותן לו שדה אחת לג' שנים שיהיו כל הפירות שלו כדי שישמור כל שאר שדותיו ושדות כל המשפחה וכן עושין כולם. היה לו שדה אחת כולה כל ימי אריסותיו אין לו חזקה בה דהשתא לא מצי למיטען עד האידנא פלגא והשתא כולה דמעיקרא נמי לאוכלה כולה הקצוה לו: אריס שהוריד אריסין תחתיו על אותה שדה שקבל מן בתי אבות והוריד אריסין לחצי השדה למחצה מפירות וחצי השדה החזיק בידו בשביל שכר השדה והוריד בחציה אריסין ג' שנים יש לו חזקה באותו חצי שהוריד בה האריסין לומר שלי היא ואין יכולין לומר לו בתי אבות כולה הלוינוך בשכירות משום דלא עביד אינש דמחתי כלל: אריס שהיו לו שדות הרבה לעבוד ולא היה מספיק לבדו והקים עליהן אריסין לסייעו והיה מחלק להם משכר אריסותו בין מאותן שדות שקבל ובין מאותן שדות שייחדו לו לשכירותו אם טוען ואמר החזקתי באותו חלק שהורדתי האריסין לא הויא חזקה. דאימור הרמנא בעלמא שוי' נתנו לו רשות בעלי השדות להורידן. דהואיל דנפישי אריסין מתעסקי טפי בשדות ומינטרן טפי וניחא להו: אריס וכו'. להעיד לבעל השדה שקנאה לדחות מעליו המערער או לא. מי אמרי' דנוגע בעדות הוא הואיל דמתהני מפירותיה או לא: הכי אמר שמואל מעיד. הואיל דאין לו בגוף קרקע: הא דאיכא פירי בארעא. שעדיין לא נטל האריס חלקו אינו מעיד דנוגע הוא. ואי ליכא פירי בארעא דכבר לקט חלקו המגיע מעיד: ערב מעיד ללוה. דשלו היא הקרקע שקנאה אע"פ דמשעבדי לערב שדותיו של לוה. ואימת מעיד והוא דאית ליה ארעא אחריתי ללוה חוץ מזו שמעיד עליה שוה שיעור החוב שנתערב בשבילו: מלוה נמי מעיד ללוה. דזבין ההוא קרקע דלא אמרי' הואיל דהאי קרקע משועבד למלוה נוגע בעדות הוא. דכיון דאית ליה ללוה ארעא אחריתי דמצי למיגבי מינה מלוה שיעור הלואתו לאו נוגע בעדות הוא: לוקח ראשון מעיד ללוקח שני. כגון ראובן לוה משמעון מנה ושוב מכר ב' שדותיו אחת ללוי באחריות ואחת ליהודה השתא שדה זו שמכר ליהוד' משועבדת ללוי מפני שקיבל ללוי אחריות שאם יבא שמעון ויטרוף את לוי שיחזור לוי ויגבה ממה ששייר ראובן שלא מכר ללוי עכשיו אם רוצה לערער על שדה שקנה יהודה שמשועבדת ללוי ורוצה לוי להעיד על יהודה שקנאה ולא אמרי' נוגע בעדותו הוא משום דמשועבדת לו אינו רוצה שתצא מידו. ואימתי מעיד לו והוא דאית לו לראובן או ליהודה קרקע אחריתי שאם היה שמעון טורף את לוי שיכול לוי לחזור על ראובן שמכר לו או על יהודה שקנה מה שמשועבד לו דהשתא לא נוגע בעדות הוא דעדיין יש לו מקום לגבות ממנו:

מסורת הש"ס

א) [גירסת הערוך קהרמנא פי' אפטורופוס], ב) מהרש"א, ג) ובמס' קדושין דף לג. משמע דפסק ר"נ הוא ר"נ בר אבא [ועי' בתשובת מוהר"ם השני סי' ב' שרוצה לומר דתרי רב נחמן הוו וחד מינייהו ר"נ בר אבא], ד) [ועי' תוס' עירובין יח: ד"ה מתקיף ועוד שם מג: ד"ה יתיב ותוס' גיטין לג. ד"ה אמר], ה) [נ"ל לפר' רשב"ם]:

הגהות הב"ח

(א) גמ' השתא אפקיה ולשיימיה שקול את דידך: (ב) רשב"ם ד"ה דליכא פירא וכו' הרבה שדות ימצא באריסות וגם:

ליקוטי רש"י

אריס אין לו חזקה. שיורדין לתוך הקרקע למחצה לשליש ולרביע אם טוען שני חזקה החזקתי בקרקע ואכלתי הפירות אינה חזקה שיכול לומר המערער לאריסות הורדתיו ודמי הפירות היה משלם לי או זקפתים עליו במלוה אי נמי מנהג אריסים לעבוד קרקע עשר שנים וחמש שנים אוכלין הבעלים כל הפירות של כל השדה ואחר כך אוכלין אריסים חמש שנים כנגדן [רשב"ם לעיל מב:].

AN EARLIER PURCHASER MAY TESTIFY ON BEHALF OF A LATER PURCHASER,[21] וְהוּא דְאִית לֵיהּ אַרְעָא אַחֲרִיתִי – **PROVIDED THAT [THE LATER PURCHASER] HAS OTHER LAND** that he purchased from the seller as well.[22]

NOTES

21. In this case, a seller sold one property to one buyer and then a second property to a second buyer. Later, a contester lays claim to the second property, claiming that the seller had stolen it from him and thus had no legal right to sell it. The Baraisa rules that the first buyer is qualified to testify on the second buyer's behalf that the second property indeed belonged to the seller. Now, the first buyer actually has a vested interest in advancing the second buyer's cause. For the seller's land is mortgaged to any recorded loans that he might have incurred prior to the sale of the land. If the seller defaults on those loans, the creditors can collect the mortgaged lands even if they have since been sold. The law is that when the debtor has no assets from which to collect, the last piece of mortgaged land sold is the first to be collected. Thus, if the seller's original title to the second property is upheld (thereby validating its sale to the second buyer), there will be one additional property standing in the way of the first buyer losing his purchase to the seller's creditors. Nevertheless, the Baraisa rules that this interest does not disqualify the first buyer from testifying on the second buyer's behalf.

22. If the second buyer has other land that he bought from the seller subsequent to the first buyer's purchase, the loss of the contested property does not affect the first buyer so directly, for (similar to the situations described in the Baraisa's earlier cases) the risk to the security of the first buyer's property is remote. First, the seller will have to default on a loan and have no assets to be collected. Then, other creditors will have to appear on the scene, rendering the second buyer's uncontested purchase from the seller insufficient to satisfy the claims of all the seller's creditors; only then will creditors have recourse to the first buyer's purchase. This eventuality is too remote to figure in the first buyer's calculations; hence, he remains qualified to testify on the second buyer's behalf (see *Rashbam;* cf. *Tosafos*). [Even if the second buyer does not have other land that he purchased from the seller, the first buyer remains qualified to testify if the seller himself has other land. For the seller's other land also precedes the first buyer's purchase in the succession of lands that can be collected by the seller's creditors (*Rashbam*).]

קַבְּלָן – Regarding a ***kablan*** **guarantor,**[1] אָמְרֵי לֵהּ מֵעִיד – **some maintain that he may testify** on the borrower's behalf, וְאָמְרֵי לֵהּ אֵינוֹ מֵעִיד – **whereas others maintain that he may not testify.** אָמְרֵי לֵהּ מֵעִיד כְּעָרֵב דָּמֵי – **Some say that he may testify** on the borrower's behalf – provided that the borrower has additional property – **for he is like** any other **guarantor.**[2] וְאָמְרֵי לֵהּ אֵינוֹ מֵעִיד – **But others say that he may not testify** on the borrower's behalf, even though the borrower has other properties, דְּנִיחָא לֵיהּ דְּלֶהֱווּ בִּידֵיהּ תַּרְוַויְיהוּ – **since he prefers that [the borrower] should** continue to **own both** properties – the disputed property as well as the undisputed property – דְּכִי אָתֵי בַּעַל חוֹב מַאי דְּבָעֵי שָׁקִיל – **so that when the lender comes** to collect his debt, **he should** have the option to **seize whichever** of the borrower's properties **he desires.** The more properties the borrower has, the more likely it is that the lender will be satisfied to collect from those properties and not resort to the *kablan* guarantor for payment.[3]

The Gemara now returns to the Mishnah's topic of which people do not establish a *chazakah* by virtue of their possession of property:[4]

אָמַר רַבִּי יוֹחָנָן – **R' Yochanan said:** אוּמָּן אֵין לוֹ חֲזָקָה – **A craftsman cannot establish a *chazakah*** by virtue of his possession,[5] בֶּן אוּמָּן יֵשׁ לוֹ חֲזָקָה – **but a craftsman's son** who is not a craftsman himself **can establish a *chazakah.***[6] אָרִיס אֵין לוֹ חֲזָקָה – **A sharecropper cannot establish a *chazakah*** by virtue of his possession,[7] בֶּן אָרִיס יֵשׁ לוֹ חֲזָקָה – **but the son of a sharecropper** who is not a sharecropper himself **can establish a *chazakah.***[6] גַּזְלָן וּבֶן גַּזְלָן אֵין לָהֶן חֲזָקָה – **Neither a robber nor the son of a robber** (though he is not a robber himself) **can establish a *chazakah*** by virtue of his possession, בֶּן בְּנוֹ שֶׁל גַּזְלָן יֵשׁ לוֹ חֲזָקָה – **but the grandson of a robber can establish a *chazakah.***[6]

The Gemara analyzes R' Yochanan's rulings:

הֵיכִי דָּמֵי – **How is it?** What claim do the sons enumerated above lay to the object in question? אִי אָתוּ בְּטַעֲנְתָא דַּאֲבוּהוֹן – **If they come with their fathers' claim** to the object, i.e. they claim simply that the object was among the father's property when they inherited his estate, אֲפִילוּ הָנָךְ נַמֵּי לֹא – then **even those** first two sons – the son of the craftsman or sharecropper – **should not** have a *chazakah* in those objects.[8] אִי דְּלֹא אָתוּ בְּטַעֲנְתָא דַּאֲבוּהוֹן – And **if they do not come with their fathers' claim,** rather they claim to have personally purchased the objects in question, אֲפִילוּ בֶּן גַּזְלָן נַמֵּי – then **even the son of a robber** should have a *chazakah* by virtue of such possession.[9] – ? –

The Gemara explains:

לֹא צְרִיכָא דְּקָא אָמְרֵי עֵדִים בְּפָנֵינוּ הוֹדָה לוֹ – **No, [the distinction] applies where witnesses testify, "In our presence did [the challenger] admit to [the father]** that he sold him the object in question."[10] הָנָךְ אִיכָּא לְמֵימַר קוּשְׁטָא קָא אָמְרֵי – In the case of **those** first two sons – the son of a craftsman or sharecropper – **it can be said that they** [the sons] **tell the truth** when they assert that their father bought the object, since that claim is supported by the witnesses. הַאי אַף עַל גַּב דְּאוֹדֵי נַמֵּי לֹא מְהֵימַן – But in the case of **this** son of a robber, **even though [the challenger] has admitted** in the presence of witnesses that he sold the object to the robber, **[the son] is not believed** when he claims that the object is his, כִּדְרַב כַּהֲנָא – **as Rav Kahana** taught; דְּאָמַר רַב כַּהֲנָא – **for Rav Kahana said:** אִי לָאו דְּאוֹדֵי לֵיהּ – **Had [the original owner] not admitted [to the robber]** that he sold him the item, הֲוָה מַמְטֵי לֵיהּ וּלְחַמְרֵיהּ לַשְׁחְוָור – **[the robber] would have handed him and his donkey over to the requisitioner.**[11]

NOTES

1. A *kablan* guarantor is a guarantor who personally receives [קבל] the loan from the lender and conveys it to the borrower (*Rashbam*; cf. *Rabbeinu Gershom*). Unlike an ordinary guarantor, the *kablan* guarantor is as responsible as the borrower is to the lender. Whereas a lender has recourse to the ordinary guarantor only if unable to collect the loan from the borrower, the lender can resort to the *kablan* guarantor for payment even *initially,* and does not have to first try and collect his loan from the borrower (*Rashbam;* see *Rashash* and *Shach* to *Choshen Mishpat* 37:17).

2. Like any other guarantor, the *kablan* guarantor is qualified to testify on behalf of the borrower, as long as the borrower has – in addition to the land in dispute – some other land sufficient to cover the amount of the loan. Since, regardless of the outcome of the case, the borrower will still be left with enough land to cover the loan, the *kablan* guarantor has no material interest in the outcome and is qualified to testify that the contested land belongs to the borrower (*Rabbeinu Gershom*).

3. The following example illustrates a situation in which the *kablan* guarantor benefits from having the borrower possess additional properties: The borrower has two fields, both sufficient in value to cover the loan. However, one of the fields is of average quality; the other is of inferior quality. The borrower's title to the average field is contested. Now, if the borrower retains title to the average field, the *kablan* guarantor might be able to persuade the lender to collect that field in payment of his debt, rather than take an average field of the *kablan.* [Where a debtor owns a variety of properties, the lender has the right to demand land of average quality for payment of his debt.] However, if the borrower loses title to the average field and is left only with the inferior one, the lender will resort to the *kablan's* average field, since he prefers land of average quality to that of inferior grade. Accordingly, the *kablan* guarantor has a material interest in having the borrower retain title to his second field (*Rashbam*; see *Rabbeinu Yonah*).

On the other hand, an ordinary guarantor would remain qualified to testify on the borrower's behalf in an analogous situation. For a lender has recourse to an ordinary guarantor *only* if he cannot collect his debt from the borrower. But if the borrower has collectible property – albeit of inferior quality – the lender must be satisfied with that property and cannot resort to the guarantor simply to obtain choicer property. Accordingly, an ordinary guarantor has no material interest in having the borrower retain title to the better field (*Rashbam*).

4. [In the case of chattels, by virtue of present possession; in the case of land, by virtue of continuous and unchallenged possession over three years' time.]

5. As explained in the Mishnah (42a) and the Gemara (45a-46a).

6. As will be explained below.

7. As explained in the Mishnah (42a) and the Gemara (46b).

8. Their claim, which derives from their father's possession of the object, is certainly no better than the claim of the father himself. If he does not have a *chazakah* in the object, neither do they.

For example: A launderer's son holds a suit claimed by the original owner, who maintains that he gave it to the father to clean. The launderer himself, being a craftsman, would not have been believed had he claimed to have purchased the suit. If the son's sole justification is that his father told him that the suit was purchased, then his claim has no greater weight than his father's.

9. Since he lays claim to the object in his own right and he is not a robber, there should be no impediment to his using his possession as proof of ownership.

10. R' Yochanan indeed refers to a case in which the sons come with their fathers' claims and as such the claims should be rejected (see note 8). However, the sons also produce witnesses who testify that the original owners admitted to the fathers that they had sold the fathers the object in question.

11. The understanding is that an admission made to a robber is not to be relied upon. The original owner might have felt coerced into making a false admission for fear that the robber (who is usually a powerful and ruthless person) might otherwise [falsely accuse him of some misdeed and] hand him and his possessions over to the government requisitioner for impressment into government service (*Rashbam*).

Thus, R' Yochanan rules that the son of a craftsman or sharecropper retains ownership of a disputed item in his possession if witnesses testify that the challenger admitted selling it to the father. A robber's son does not retain ownership under these circumstances. However, the robber's grandson does; that is, if a robber's grandson claims that he inherited the

קבלן אמרי לה מעיד ואמרי לה [א]אינו מעיד
אמרי לה מעיד כערב דמי ואמרי לה אינו
מעיד דניחא ליה דלהוו בידיה תרוייהו דכי
אתי בע"ח מאי דבעי שקיל אמר רבי יוחנן
אומן אין לו חזקה [ב]בן אומן יש לו חזקה
ארים אין לו חזקה [ג]בן ארים יש לו חזקה
גזלן [ד]ובן גזלן אין להן חזקה [ה]בן בנו של
גזלן יש לו חזקה היכי דמי אי (א) אתו בטענתא
דאבוהון [ו]אפילו הנך נמי לא אי דלא אתו
בטענתא דאבוהון אפילו בן גזלן נמי לא
צריכא [ז]דקא אמרי עדים בפנינו הודה לו
הנך איכא למימר קושטא קא אמרי האי
אע"ג דאודי נמי לא מהימן כדרב כהנא
דאמר רב כהנא אי לאו דאודי ליה הוה ממטי
ליה (ב) ולחמריה לשחוור אמר רבא [ח]פעמים
שאפילו בן בנו של גזלן נמי אין לו חזקה
היכי דמי כגון דקא אתי בטענתא דאבא
דאבוה היכי דמי גזלן אמר רבי יוחנן [ט]כגון
שהוחזק על שדה זו בגזלנותא ורב חסדא
אמר [י]כגון דבית פלוני שהורגין נפשות על
עסקי ממון: תנו רבנן [כ]אומן אין לו חזקה ירד
מאומנותו יש לו חזקה ארים אין לו חזקה
[ל]ירד מאריסותו יש לו חזקה (א) [מ]בן שחלק
ואשה שנתגרשה הרי הן כשאר כל אדם
בשלמא בן שחלק איצטריך סלקא דעתך
אמינא (ג) אחולי אחיל גביה קמ"ל דלא אלא
אשה שנתגרשה פשיטא [נ]לא צריכא
במגורשת

רש"י

קבלן. ערב קבלן שקבל המעות מידו של מלוה ונתן לידו של לוה וזהו דינו דממי שירצה המלוה יפרע תחלה אבל ערב סתמא אין תובעין לערב תחלה עד שיעמיד מלוה ללוה בדין ויחייבוהו לשלם ואין לו מה לפרוע ואז יגבה מן הערב: אמרי לה מעיד. כמו ערב: ואמרי לה אינו מעיד. דלאכי נוגע בעדות הוא דניחא ליה דנוקמא תרוייהו ארעתא בידיה דלוה כי היכי דליהוו ליה ארעי טובא זיבורית ובינונית דכי אתא מלוה למגבי בינונית דקבלן כדין בע"ח שדינו בבינונית לימא ליה אמתן לך בינונית דלוה והלכך הוה נוגע בעדות דאי לא הוה ללוה בינונית לא ליגבי מלוה אלא מבינונית דקבלן דהכי הוי דינא דלכל מאן דבעי תבע ברישא אבל בערב סתם ליכא למימר הכי דלכל כמה דאית ליה ללוה למיפרע מידי ואפי' זיבורית לאו כל כמיניה דמלוה למיהדר גבי ערב כדקי"ל במכילתין (לקמן דף קעג.) לא יתבע לערב תחלה: אומן אין לו חזקה. כדקתני מתני': אבל בן. של אומן וכגון שאין הבן אומן יש לו חזקה וכדמפרש לקמן: גזלן. לקמן מפרש היכי דמי יש שמפרש שהוחזק בגזלנות על שדה זו ובהאי שדה הוא דאין לו חזקה ויש שמפרש לקמן כגון רוצח נפשות על עסקי ממון והלכך אין לו חזקה על שום קרקע של אחרים בעולם: אי דאתו. הנך בנים בטענתא דאבוהון דאמרי אבינו הורישה לנו ומש"ה בן גזלן אין לו חזקה דכי האי גוונא אין טוענין ליורש דכיון דמכח גזלן קאתי ואיהו לא טעין מאבי אני יורש דזבנה מינך קמאי דידי דליהמניה ע"י מיגו דמצי אמר (ד) זבנית מינך הלכך חזקה שאין עמה טענה היא שהרי אין לאבא חזקה וגם הבן הבא מכחו אין חזקתו חזקה וכיון דמכח אבוהון קאתו אפילו הנך בן אומן ובן אריס נמי לא ליהוי להו חזקה: אלא בטענה דנפשייהו. אנא זבנתה מינך: לא צריכא. דקאתו בטענתא דאבוהון וכגון דאמרו עדים בפנינו הודה לו המערער לאביהן של אלו שמכרו להם הלכך הנך בן אריס ובן אומן איכא למימר קושטא קאמרי כשטוענין אבינו לקחו ממך שהרי הודה והודאת בעל דין כמאה עדים אבל בן גזלן אע"ג דאודי האי מערער לאביו לא מהימן לומר לקוח הוא ביד אבי ואפי' בחיי אביו אם נתנו לבן שהרי הוא מתוך פחד הודה לו לגזלן כדרב כהנא כו' אבל בן בנו של גזלן יש לו חזקה אי אתי בטענה דאבוה דטעין מאבי ירשתי ואבי לא היה גזלן וכי האי גוונא טוענין ליורש דאילו היה אביו קיים הוה טעין מינך זבנתה ולא הוה אתי בטענתא דאבוה אף אנו נטעון בשביל היורש וריש' דקתני אומן אין לו חזקה בדליכא עדי הודאה דלאלדין קתני: אי לאו דאודי ליה. נגזל לגזלן: הוה ממטי ליה לדידיה ולחמריה לשחוור. היה מוסר אותו ואת חמורו לפקיד כדמתרגמינן (במדבר טז) [לא חמור אחד מהם נשאתי] לא חמרא דחד מנהון שחרית דסתם גזלן גברא אלמא הוא: פעמים שאפילו בן גזלן יש לו חזקה. ואע"ג דלא אתי בטענה דנפשיה היכי דמי כגון דקא אתי בטענתא דאבא דאבוה שטוען מאבי אבי אני יורש ואיהו לא היה גזלן ומיגו דמצי אמר זבנתה מינך כי אמר נמי זקני הורישה לאבי ואבי הורישני נאמן דחזקה שיש עמה טענה מעלייתא היא: ל"א כתוב בספרים פעמים שבן בנו של גזלן נמי אין לו חזקה וכגון דאתי בטענתא דאבא דאבוה. שאבי אביו גזלן היה ושניהם מתו אבל הראשון נראה שאמר רבא ולא האחרון: היכי דמי גזלן. אותו שאין לו חזקה: על שדה זו. ובההוא שדה הוא דאין לו חזקה אבל בשאר שדות יש לו חזקה: כגון של בית פלוני שהורגין כו'. אנשי רשעים היו שהיה מכיר בהן רב חסדא שהורגין נפשות על עסקי ממון אין להן חזקה בשום קרקע בעולם שכל אדם ירא למחות בהן וקי"ל כתרוייהו: ירד מאומנותו. ושוב מחזיק בה יש לו חזקה: בן שחלק. הפליג מאביו ואין סמוך עוד על שולחנו כגון שנשא אשה ואין משתדל עוד בנכסי אביו הרי הן ככל אדם אע"ג דתנן (לעיל דף מב.) לא לאיש חזקה בנכסי אשתו ולא לאשה בנכסי בעלה ולא האב בנכסי הבן ולא הבן כו' הנך כיון שהופלגו זה מזה יש להן חזקה זה על זה: סלקא דעתך אמינא אחולי אחיל. האב גבי דבן פירות שאכל בשלש שנים ולפיכך לא ערער ולא תיהוי חזקה קמ"ל דלא מחיל: אלא אשה שנתגרשה פשיטא. דמחזקת בנכסי בעלה וכן בעלה מחזיק בנכסיה שהרי שונאין זה את זה והיה להן למחות:
מגורשת

תוספות

קבלן אמרי לה אינו מעיד. אע"ג דאית ליה ארעא אחריתי תימה דמאי נפקא מינה דלאי אתי מלוה וטריף את של קבלן אתי קבלן וקטריף את של לוה כיון דאית ליה ארעא אחריתי ואין נראה לומר כגון שיש לקבלן בינונית והיא ארעא שרוצה להעיד עליה נמי בינונית אבל ארעא אחריתי דאית ליה ללוה היא זיבורית דמפסיד כשיבא מלוה וטריף את שלו דלא יהיה לו לגבות אלא מזיבורית דא"כ מלוה נמי לא יעיד ללוה אפילו אית ליה ארעא אחריתי כענין זה ועוד דבכל ענין משמע דאינו מעיד דלא מפליג בין היא בינונית בין היא זיבורית ועוד דל"ע בהניזקין (גיטין דף מט:) דנראה דמוכח התם דאם אין ללוה אלא זיבורית גם קבלן לא יתן לו אלא זיבורית ונראה דהיינו טעמא דקבלן אינו מעיד ללוה אע"ג דאית ליה ארעא אחריתי משום דטריחא ליה מילתא למיקם עליה בדינא ודיינא וכשיהיו ללוה קרקעות הרבה לא יגבה המלוה מן הקבלן הואיל ויכול לגבות מן הלוה בהרווחה אבל מלוה מעיד ללוה בכל ענין אפילו אותה שמעיד עליה היא בינונית ואחריתי זיבורית דמשום איחלופי בינונית לזיבורית לא יעיד שקר דמכל מקום יש לו שוה בשוה אי נמי ארעא אחריתי דכולה שמעתין כיוצא בו קאמר:

ה"ג כגון דקאמר בפנינו הודה. פי' בן אריס בן אומן בן גזלן ומש"ה אומן אין לו חזקה אבל בן יש לו חזקה כשטוען קמי דידי הודית לאבי שמכרת לו נאמן במיגו דאי בעי אמר מינך זבנתה אבל בן גזלן אין לו חזקה דהודאה שהודה לגזלן לאו הודאה היא דאי לאו דאודי ליה שמכרה לו הוה ממטי ליה ולחמריה לשחוור אבל לא גרסינן כגון דקאמרי עדים דהא אי איכא עדים דאודי ליה דמיניה זבנה א"כ אומן ואריס גופייהו יהו נאמנים ועוד כיון דאיכא עדים בן אריס בן אומן למה צריכים להחזיק בלא חזקה נמי מוקמינן לה בידייהו כיון דאיכא סהדי. ר"ת:

פעמים שבן בן גזלן אין לו חזקה כגון דקאתי בטענתא דאבא דאבוה. תימה לר"י דלמאי אין לו חזקה הא טוענין ליורש והוה ליה למימר דלמא אי הוה אביו קיים דהיינו בן גזלן הוה טעין אנא הדר זבינתה מינך ונראה לר"י דגרס פעמים שבן גזלן יש לו חזקה כגון דקאתי בטענתא דאבא דאבוה דהוא אבי הגזלן וקמ"ל דאע"ג שהיתה ביד מי שאין לו חזקה דהיינו אביו הגזלן מ"מ יש לו חזקה כיון שאמר שהיתה של אבי אביו ויש לייש' גירסא ראשונה פעמי' דבן בן גזלן אין לו חזקה והכי פירושה כגון דאתא בטענתא דאבא דאבוה ואומר שאמר לו אביו דהיינו בן הגזלן שהניחה לו הגזלן אביו דאם איתא דהדר (ה) זבנתה מינך הוה א"ל אנא זבינא אי נמי נראה לר"י דלא טענינן ליורש כי האי גוונא דמילתא דלא שכיחא היא כי היכי דאמר בסוף המוכר את הבית (לקמן דף ע: ושם ד"ה מאן) דלא טענינן ליתמי נאנסו משום דמילתא דלא שכיחא היא והא דקאמר לעיל [בן] בן גזלן בן אומן יש לו חזקה היינו דוקא משום דאמר בפנינו הודה ואדרבה משם יש להוכיח דמשמע הא לאו הכי אין לו חזקה כיון דמעיקרא בתורת אומנות ואריסות וגזלנות אתא לידיה:

ירד מאומנותו יש לו חזקה. מלינו לפרש מאותן כלים שנתן לו לאחר שירד מאומנותו דומיא דאריס שירד מאריסותו אי נמי אפילו אותן כלים שנתנו לו בשעה שהיה עדיין אומן והוא ששהו אחר אומנותו כ"כ שהוא רגילות שמחזירם לבעלים ונראה דבן אומן נמי דאמר לעיל דיש לו חזקה כי אמר (ו) בפנינו הודה היינו אחר ששהה אחר מות אביו דאי לאו הכי אין נראה שיהא נאמן במיגו דאי בעי אמר לקוח הוא בידי דאי טעין נמי לקחתיה ממך לא היה נאמן:
מגורשת

מסורת הש"ס

א) [לקמן נב.]

הגהות הב"ח

(א) גמ' אי דאתו בטענתא וכו' אי דלא אתו בטענתא דאבוהון אלא בטענתא דנפשייהו אפי' בן גזלן נמי. נ"ב ע"ל דף נב בתוס' ד"ה ומודה לי: (ב) שם ממטי ליה לדידיה ולחמריה: (ג) שם סלקא דעתך אמינא אב לבן אחולי: (ד) רשב"ם ד"ה אי דאתו וכו' דמצי אמר אנא זבנית: (ה) תוס' ד"ה פעמים וכו' דאם איתא דהדר זבנה מיניה הוה אמר: (ו) ד"ה ירד וכו' כי אמר בפנינו הודה:

עין משפט נר מצוה

קנז א מיי' פט"ו מהל' עדות הל' ו ועי' כ"מ סמג לאוין קט טוש"ע ח"מ סי' לז סעיף יג בהגה"ה:
קנח ב ג ד ה ו ז ח מיי' פי"ד מהל' טוען הל' ג ד סמג עשין צה טוש"ע ח"מ סי' קמט סעיף יד:
קנט ט י מיי' פ"ג שם הל' יא סמג שם טוש"ע ח"מ סי' קמט סעיף יג:
קס כ מיי' שם הל' ד טוש"ע שם סעיף כה:
קסא ל מיי' שם הל' ו טוש"ע שם סעיף טז:
קסב מ מיי' שם הל' ט טוש"ע שם סעיף ז:
קסג נ מיי' שם טוש"ע שם סעיף י ועיין בטוש"ע אה"ע סי' פז:

רבינו גרשום

קבלן מאי. דדיניה דקבלן שאמר למלוה הלוהו ואני קבלן יכול המלוה לפרוע מן הקבלן ועכשיו כל שדותיו של לוה משועבדים לקבלן עד שיפרע חובו: אמרי לה מעיד. ללוה והוא שיש ללוה שדה אחרת כשיעור החוב חוץ מה שעוררין עליה דהשתא לאו נוגע הוא: ואמרי לה דאפ"ה אין מעיד. דניחא ליה לקבלן דלוקמי מן הני קרקע תרווייהו בידא דלוה שיהא לו יותר ממה לפרוע: בן אומן. ובן אריס הרי הן כאחר ויש להן חזקה: אי דקאתי הני בנים בטענה דאבוהון. דאמרי אבינו הורישה לנו. מאי איריא בן גזלן דאין לו חזקה אפי' הנך בן אומן ובן אריס נמי לא ליהוי חזקה. ואי דאתי בטענה דנפשייהו דאמרי זבנינה אפי' בן מגזלן נמי ליהוי ליה חזקה: בפנינו הודה לו. המוכר לבן אומן ולבן אריס ולבן גזלן דזבינה ניהליה לאבוהון מש"ה איכא למימר בבן אומן ובן אריס כי אתו בטענה דאבוהון דקושטא קאמרי דהמוכר (בכ"י הנעתק הוא בכאן מקום פנוי כמו חצי שורה ואולי חסר כאן איזה תיבות) [זבן] ניהליה. והאי בן גזלן אע"ג דאיכא עדים שהודה המוכר לגזלן שמכרה לו לא הויא חזקה דמחמת ביעתותא הוא דאודי ליה דהוי מסתפי דאי לא מודי ליה הוי מלשין עליה: וממטי ליה ולחמריה לשחור. שילך עם חמור באנגרא לשליחו' עבודת השלטון כדמתרגמינן לא חמור א' [מהם] נשאתי לא חמרא דחד מנהון שחרית. וכמו נוח לתשחורת. ולא גמר והקנה לו. אבל בן בנו של גזלן אי אתי בטענה דאבוה יש לו חזקה דאביו לאו גזלן הוה: ירד מאומנותו. ושוב מחזיק בה יש לו חזקה: בן שחלק. שנתן לו אביו חלקו בחייו והוא מחזיק בשדה אחת יותר על חלקו שנתן לו אביו ג' שנים וכן אשה שנתגרשה והחזיקה שוב בשדה בעלה ג' שנים: הרי הן ככל אדם. ויש להן חזקה: סד"א אחולי אחיל ליה. א) היה הפירות דלא מערער ולא תהוי חזקה:

חשק שלמה על רבינו גרשום

א) אולי צ"ל הפירות שאכל הבן ולא מערער וכו'.

Rava qualifies R' Yochanan's ruling:

אָמַר רָבָא – **Rava said:** פְּעָמִים שֶׁאֲפִילוּ בֶּן בְּנוֹ שֶׁל גַּזְלָן נַמִּי אֵין לוֹ חֲזָקָה – **There are times when even the grandson of a robber cannot establish a** ***chazakah*** by virtue of his possession. הֵיכִי דָּמֵי – **How so?** כְּגוֹן דְּקָא אָתֵי בְּטַעְנְתָא דְּאַבָּא דַּאֲבוּהַ – **In a case where he comes with his grandfather's claim.** I.e. he bases his claim to the object on his grandfather's possession of it; that is, the grandson says that his father (the robber's son) told him that he had inherited the object from the grandfather.[12]

The Gemara explains the case of "a robber" mentioned above:

הֵיכִי דָּמֵי גַּזְלָן – **What is the case of "a robber"?** Under what circumstances does he not have a *chazakah*?[13] אָמַר רַבִּי יוֹחָנָן – **R' Yochanan said:** כְּגוֹן שֶׁהוּחְזַק עַל שָׂדֶה זוּ בְּגַזְלָנוּתָא – **In a case where it has been established that he stole this** particular **field.**[14] וְרַב חִסְדָּא אָמַר – **And Rav Chisda says:** כְּגוֹן דְּבֵית פְּלוֹנִי שֶׁהוֹרְגִין נְפָשׁוֹת עַל עִסְקֵי מָמוֹן – No *chazakah* is established by a robber **like those of a certain family, who murder for financial considerations.**[15]

The Gemara cites a Baraisa that discusses when certain people who cannot establish a *chazakah* resume the capacity to do so:

תָּנוּ רַבָּנָן – **The Rabbis taught in a Baraisa:** אוּמָּן אֵין לוֹ חֲזָקָה – A CRAFTSMAN CANNOT ESTABLISH A *CHAZAKAH*;[16] יָרַד מֵאוּמְנוּתוֹ יֵשׁ לוֹ חֲזָקָה – however, if HE QUIT HIS PROFESSION, HE CAN ESTABLISH A *CHAZAKAH*.[17] אָרִיס אֵין לוֹ חֲזָקָה – A SHARECROPPER CANNOT ESTABLISH A *CHAZAKAH*;[16] יָרַד מֵאֲרִיסוּתוֹ יֵשׁ לוֹ חֲזָקָה – however, if HE QUIT SHARECROPPING, HE CAN ESTABLISH A *CHAZAKAH*.[18] בֵּן שֶׁחָלַק – In the cases of A SON WHO HAS SEPARATED from his father and set up house for himself וְאִשָּׁה שֶׁנִּתְגָּרְשָׁה – AND A WOMAN WHO HAS BEEN DIVORCED from her husband, הֲרֵי הֵן כִּשְׁאָר כָּל אָדָם – THEY [the separated parties] ARE now LIKE ANY OTHER PERSON with regard to *chazakah*.[19]

The Gemara questions the necessity of the Baraisa's final ruling:

בִּשְׁלָמָא בֵּן שֶׁחָלַק אִיצְטְרִיךְ – Now, **it is understandable** that the ruling concerning **a son who separated is needed;** for without it, סָלְקָא דַּעְתָּךְ אָמִינָא אַחוּלֵי אַחִיל גַּבֵּיהּ – **you might have thought to say that [a father] forgoes his rights in favor of [his son]** and

NOTES

disputed object in his possession from his father, he has a *chazakah* and retains the object. In this latter case, the rationale is that we advance claims on behalf of orphans (טַעֲנִינָן לְיַתְמֵי). [An orphan is usually insufficiently aware of his deceased father's affairs to be able to offer any definite defense against claims brought against the estate. Therefore, the court assumes the role of defender and advances any defense that the father, had he still been alive, might conceivably have advanced. Though the defense offered by the court is merely speculative (שֶׁמָּא) — they have no way of knowing whether the father would have asserted such a claim — it is accorded the status of a definite defense (בָּרִי).] The robber's son, had he been alive, might have asserted that he *personally* bought the object from the challenger, in which case his personal claim to the object, supported by his *chazakah,* would have been believed. Since the son is not here to assert such a claim, the court advances the claim on behalf of the grandson, whose *chazakah* therefore prevails (*Rashbam*).

The foregoing explanation of the Gemara (offered by *Rashbam*) entails several difficulties (as pointed out by *Tosafos*). If the sons' *chazakah* prevails because there are witnesses that the challenger admitted selling the object to the fathers, then why should the fathers' *chazakah* not prevail as well? Why, then, does R' Yochanan state that the sons have a *chazakah,* but the fathers do not? Moreover, what need is there for a *chazakah* altogether? If there are witnesses that the challenger admitted selling the object, no further evidence is needed to refute his challenge. Why, then, does R' Yochanan say that the sons "have a *chazakah*"? It is not their *chazakah* that prevails, but the testimony of the witnesses! Furthermore (as pointed out by *Rabbeinu Yonah* and *Ritva*), the Gemara's expression: "It can be said that they [the sons] tell the truth," which implies that there remains an element of uncertainty, would seem to be out of place if there are witnesses who corroborate the sons' claims. *Rashbam* addresses the first difficulty by explaining that the respective cases of R' Yochanan's ruling (fathers versus sons) do not refer to the same circumstances. Rather, the fathers have no *chazakah* when there are no witnesses to refute the challenger; the sons have a *chazakah* when there are witnesses. [The difficulty remains, however, that R' Yochanan did not have to introduce the case of sons to illustrate this distinction. He could have said simply that a craftsman or sharecropper has no *chazakah* when not supported by witnesses, but does have when supported by witnesses; a robber has no *chazakah* in either case (cf. *Ran*).]

Because of these difficulties, *Tosafos* adopt a variant reading of the Gemara text. See, however, *Rabbeinu Yonah,* who asserts that *Rashbam's* reading is indeed the authentic reading as found in the Gaonic texts, and who resolves the major difficulties by explaining the Gemara somewhat differently than *Rashbam.*

12. Since the possession of the grandfather, who was a robber, proves nothing, neither does the continued possession of his heirs (see *Tosafos*).

Had the grandson's father not told him anything about how the disputed object came into the family's possession, the grandson would have a *chazakah* in it, since we would advance on his behalf the claim that his father (who was not a robber) bought the object from the original owner (as explained above in note 11). In this case, however, since the father has told him that he inherited the object from *his* father, he has in effect admitted that he did not personally buy the object. Consequently, we certainly cannot advance such a claim on his son's behalf (ibid.; see there for an alternative explanation; see also *Rabbeinu Yonah*).

[We have followed the Gemara text as it appears in our editions. *Rashbam,* though he concedes that the law taught by this version is true, considers it likely that an alternative version is the authentic one — see *Rashbam* and *Tosafos*.]

13. [Certainly, the intent is not that a person who was once convicted of robbery can never establish a *chazakah* in objects that are in his possession.]

14. [Literally: where he has been established on this field in robbery.] According to R' Yochanan, a robber cannot establish a *chazakah* only in the very object he is known to have stolen. But in that object, he can *never* establish a *chazakah.* Thus, even if the stolen property has since been restored to the owner, the robber has no *chazakah* in the object if it again appears in his possession. We are concerned that just as he stole it once, he has stolen it again (*Rashba, Ritva, Ran*). A robber can, however, establish a *chazakah* in an identical item that he has not previously stolen (*Rashbam*), even if that identical item belonged to the very person from whom he had stolen the other one (*Rabbeinu Yonah; Ritva*).

[Though this robber is not suspect in regard to other properties, in regard to the property that he has once stolen he is suspect to go so far as to deliver the owner to the requisitioner if he does not concede ownership to him (*Rabbeinu Yonah*).]

15. Rav Chisda had in mind a particular family whose members were known to him to be guilty of murder for financial gain. Such people are precluded from establishing ownership by virtue of possession even in regard to properties that they are not known to have stolen, since victims are afraid to protest the lawless actions of such people (*Rashbam*). [Thus, their unchallenged possession of an object proves nothing.]

R' Yochanan and Rav Chisda are not in disagreement. They merely state different situtations in which a robber has no *chazakah* (*Rashbam; Ritva*).

16. As explained in the Mishnah and Gemara above.

17. In items that he took possession of subsequent to his retirement (*Tosafos*; see there for an alternative approach).

18. That is, in a property that he begins to occupy after retiring from sharecropping (*Tosafos*; cf. *Rambam, Hil. To'ein VeNitan* 13:6).

19. The Mishnah (42a) taught that a dependent son cannot establish a *chazakah* in his father's property by occupying it and taking its yield nor a wife in her husband's property, and vice versa (since it is usual for such related people to occupy each other's properties). The Baraisa

קבלן אמרי לה מעיד ואמרי לה [א]אינו מעיד אמרי לה מעיד כערב דמי ואמרי לה אינו מעיד דניחא ליה דלהוו בידיה תרוייהו דכי אתי בע"ח מאי דבעי שקיל אמר רבי יוחנן אומן אין לו חזקה [ב]בן אומן יש לו חזקה ארים אין לו חזקה [ג]בן ארים יש לו חזקה גזלן [ד]ובן גזלן אין להן חזקה [ה]בן בנו של גזלן יש לו חזקה היכי דמי אי (א) אתו בטענתא דאבוהון [ו]אפילו הנך נמי לא אי דלא אתו בטענתא דאבוהון אפילו בן גזלן נמי לא צריכא [ז]דקא אמרי עדים בפנינו הודה לו הנך איכא למימר קושטא קא אמרי האי אע"ג דאודי נמי לא מהימן כדרב כהנא דאמר רב כהנא אי לאו דאודי ליה הוה ממטי ליה (ב) ולחמריה לשחוור אמר רבא [ח]פעמים שאפילו בן בנו של גזלן נמי אין לו חזקה היכי דמי כגון דקא אתי בטענתא דאבא דאבוה היכי דמי גזלן אמר רבי יוחנן [ט]כגון שהוחזק על שדה זו בגזלנותא ורב חסדא אמר [י]כגון דבית פלוני שהורגין נפשות על עסקי ממון: תנו רבנן [כ]אומן אין לו חזקה ירד מאומנותו יש לו חזקה ארים אין לו חזקה [ל]ירד מאריסותו יש לו חזקה (א) [מ]בן שחלק ואשה שנתגרשה הרי הן כשאר כל אדם בשלמא בן שחלק איצטריך סלקא דעתך אמינא (ג) אחולי אחיל גביה קמ"ל דלא אלא אשה שנתגרשה פשיטא [נ]לא צריכא במגורשת

רש"י

קבלן. ערב קבלן שקבל המעות מידו של מלוה ונתן לידו של לוה וזהו דינו דממי שירצה המלוה יפרע תחלה אבל ערב סתמא אין תובעין לערב תחלה עד שיעמיד מלוה ללוה בדין ויחייבוהו לשלם ואין לו מה לפרוע ואז יגבה מן הערב: **אמרי לה מעיד.** כמו ערב: **ואמרי לה אינו מעיד.** דאכתי נוגע בעדות הוא דניחא ליה דלוקמא תרווייהו ארעתא בידיה דלוה כי היכי דליהוו ליה ארעי טובא זיבורית ובינונית דכי אתא מלוה למגבי בינונית דקבלן כדין בע"ח שדינו בבינונית לימא ליה אתן לך בינונית דלוה והלכך הוה נוגע בעדות דאי לא הוה ללוה בינונית לא ליגבי מלוה אלא מבינונית דקבלן דהכי הוי דינא דלכל מאן דבעי תבע ברישא אבל בערב סתם ליכא למימר הכי דלכל כמה דאית ליה ללוה למיפרע מידי ואפי' זיבורית לאו כל כמיניה דמלוה למיהדר גבי ערב כדקי"ל במכילתין (לקמן דף קעג.) לא יתבע לערב תחלה: **אומן אין לו חזקה.** כדקתני מתני': **אבל בן.** של אומן וכגון שאין הבן אומן יש לו חזקה וכדמפרש לקמן: **גזלן.** לקמן מפרש היכי דמי יש שמפרש שהוחזק בגזלנות על שדה זו ובהאי שדה הוא דאין לו חזקה ויש שמפרש לקמן כגון רוצח נפשות על עסקי ממון והלכך אין לו חזקה על שום קרקע של אחרים בעולם: **אי דאתו.** הנך בנים בטענתא דאבוהון דאמרי אבינו הורישה לנו ומש"ה בן גזלן אין לו חזקה דכי האי גוונא אין טוענין ליורש דכיון דמכח גזלן קאתי ואיהו לא טעין מאבי אני יורש דזבנה מינך קמאי דידי דליהמניה ע"י מיגו דמצי אמר (ד) זבנית מינך הלכך חזקה שאין עמה טענה היא שהרי אין לאבא חזקה וגם הבן הבא מכחו אין חזקתו חזקה וכיון דמכח אבוהון קאתו אפילו הנך בן אומן ובן ארים נמי לא ליהוי להו חזקה: **אלא בטענה דנפשייהו.** אנא זבנתה מינך: **לא צריכא.** דקאתו בטענתא דאבוהון וכגון דאמרו עדים בפנינו הודה לו המערער לאביהן של אלו שמכרו להם הלכך הנך בן ארים ובן אומן איכא למימר קושטא קאמרי כשטוענין אבינו לקחו ממך שהרי הודה והודאת בעל דין כמאה עדים אבל בן גזלן אע"ג דאודי האי מערער לאביו לא מהימן לומר לקוח הוא ביד אבי ואפי' בחיי אביו אם נתנו לבן שהרי הוא מתוך פחד הודה לו לגזלן כדרב כהנא כו' אבל בן בנו של גזלן יש לו חזקה אי אתי בטענה דאבוה דטעין מאבי ירשתי ואבי לא היה גזלן וכי האי גוונא טוענין ליורש דאילו היה אביו קיים הוה טעין מינך זבנתה ולא הוה אתי בטענתא דאבוה אף אנו נטעון בשביל היורש ורישא דקתני אומן אין לו חזקה בדליכא עדי הודאה דלאדדין קתני: **אי לאו דאודי ליה.** נגזל לגזלן: **הוה ממטי ליה לדידיה ולחמריה לשחוור.** היה מוסר אותו ואת חמורו לפקיד כדמתרגמינן (במדבר טז) [לא חמור אחד מהם נשאתי] לא חמרא דחד מנהון שחרית דסתם גזלן גברא אלמא הוא: **פעמים שאפילו בן גזלן יש לו חזקה.** ואע"ג דלא אתי בטענה דנפשיה היכי דמי כגון דקא אתי בטענתא דאבא דאבוה שטוען מאבי אבי אני יורש ואיהו לא היה גזלן ומיגו דמצי אמר זבנתה מינך כי אמר נמי זקני הורישה לאבי ואבי הורישני נאמן דחזקה שיש עמה טענה מעלייתא היא: ל"א כתוב בספרים פעמים **שבן בנו של גזלן נמי אין לו חזקה וכגון דאתי בטענתא דאבא דאבוה.** שאבי אביו גזלן היה ושניהם אמת אבל הראשון נראה שאמר רבא ולא האחרון: **היכי דמי גזלן.** אותו שאין לו חזקה: **על שדה זו.** ובהאי שדה הוא דאין לו חזקה אבל בשאר שדות יש לו חזקה: **כגון של בית פלוני שהורגין כו'.** אנשי רשעים היו שהיה מכיר בהן רב חסדא שהורגין נפשות על עסקי ממון אין להן חזקה בשום קרקע בעולם שכל אדם ירא למחות בהן וקי"ל כתרוייהו: **ירד מאומנותו.** ושוב מחזיק בה יש לו חזקה: **בן שחלק.** הפליג מאביו ואין סמוך עוד על שולחנו כגון שנשא אשה ואין משתדל עוד בנכסי אביו הרי הן ככל אדם אע"ג דתנן (לעיל דף מב.) לא לאיש חזקה בנכסי אשתו ולא לאשה בנכסי בעלה ולא האב בנכסי הבן ולא הבן כו' הנך כיון שהופלגו זה מזה יש להן חזקה זה על זה: **סלקא דעתך אמינא אחולי אחיל.** האב גבי דבן פירות שאכל בשלש שנים ולפיכך לא ערער ולא תיהוי חזקה קמ"ל דלא מחיל: **אלא אשה שנתגרשה פשיטא.** דמחזקת בנכסי בעלה וכן בעלה מחזיק בנכסיה שהרי שונאין זה את זה והיה להן למחות:

מגורשת

תוספות

קבלן אמרי לה אינו מעיד. אע"ג דאית ליה ארעא אחריתי תימה דמאי נפקא מינה דאי אתי מלוה וטריף את של קבלן אתי קבלן וקטריף את של לוה כיון דאית ליה ארעא אחריתי ואין נראה לומר כגון שיש לקבלן בינונית והיא ארעא שרוצה להעיד עליה נמי בינונית אבל ארעא אחריתי דאית ליה ללוה היא זיבורית דמפסיד כשיבא מלוה וטריף את שלו דלא יהיה לו לגבות אלא מזיבורית דא"כ מלוה נמי לא יעיד ללוה אפילו אית ליה ארעא אחריתי כענין זה ועוד בכל ענין משמע דאינו מעיד דלא מפליג בין היא בינונית בין היא זיבורית ועוד דל"ע בהניזקין (גיטין דף מט:) דנראה דמוכח התם דאם אין ללוה אלא זיבורית גם קבלן לא יתן לו אלא זיבורית ונראה דהיינו טעמא דקבלן אינו מעיד ללוה אע"ג דאית ליה ארעא אחריתי משום דטריחא ליה מילתא למיקם עליה בדינא ודיינא וכשיהיו ללוה קרקעות הרבה לא יגבה המלוה מן הקבלן הואיל ויכול לגבות מן הלוה בהרווחה אבל מלוה מעיד ללוה בכל ענין אפילו אותה שמעיד עליה היא בינונית ואחריתי זיבורית דמשום איחלופי בינונית לזיבורית לא יעיד שקר דמכל מקום יש לו שום בשוה אי נמי ארעא אחריתי דלוה שמעתין כיוצא בו קאמר:

ה"ג **כגון** דקאמר בפנינו הודה. פי' בן ארים בן אומן בן גזלן ומש"ה אומן אין לו חזקה אבל בן יש לו חזקה כשטוען קמי דידי הודית לאבי שמכרת לו ונאמן במיגו דאי בעי אמר מינך זבנתה אבל בן גזלן אין לו חזקה דהודאה שהודה לגזלן לאו הודאה היא דאי לאו דאודי ליה שמכרה לו הוה ממטי ליה ולחמריה לשחוור אבל לא גרסינן כגון דקאמרי עדים דהא אי איכא עדים דאודי ליה דמיניה זבנה א"כ אומן וארים גופייהו יהו נאמנים ועוד כיון דאיכא עדים בן ארים בן אומן למה צריכים להחזיק בלא חזקה נמי מוקמינן לה בידייהו כיון דאיכא סהדי. ר"ת:

פעמים שבן בן גזלן אין לו חזקה כגון דקאתי בטענתא דאבא דאבוה. תימה לר"י דאמאי אין לו חזקה הא טוענין ליורש והוה ליה למימר דלמא אי הוה אביו קיים דהיינו בן גזלן הוה טעין אנא הדר זבינתה מינך ונראה לר"י דגרס פעמים שבן גזלן יש לו חזקה כגון דקאתי בטענתא דאבא דאבוה דהוא אבי הגזלן וקמ"ל דאע"ג שהיתה ביד מי שאין לו חזקה דהיינו אביו הגזלן מ"מ יש לו חזקה כיון שאמר שהיתה של אבי אביו ויש ליישב גירסא ראשונה פעמי' דבן בן גזלן אין לו חזקה והכי פירושה כגון דאתא בטענתא דאבא דאבוה ואומר שאמר לו אביו דהיינו בן הגזלן שהניחה לו הגזלן אביו דאם איתא דהדר (ה) זבנתה מינך הוה א"ל אנא זבינא אי נמי נראה לר"י דלא טענינן ליורש כי האי גוונא דמילתא דלא שכיחא היא כי היכי דאמר בסוף המוכר את הבית (לקמן דף ע: ושם ד"ה מאן) דלא טענינן ליתמי נאנסו משום דמילתא דלא שכיחא היא והא דקאמר לעיל [בן] בן גזלן בן אומן יש לו חזקה היינו דוקא משום דאמר בפנינו הודה ואדרבה משם יש להוכיח דמשמע הא לאו הכי אין לו חזקה כיון דמעיקרא בתורת אומנות ואריסות וגזלנות אתא לידיה:

ירד מאומנותו יש לו חזקה. מצינו לפרש מאותן כלים שנתן לו לאחר שירד מאומנותו דומיא דארים שירד מאריסותו אי נמי אפילו אותן כלים שנתנו לו בשעה שהיה עדיין אומן והוא שהוא אחר אומנותו כ"כ שהוא רגילות שמחזירם לבעלים ונראה דבן אומן נמי דאמר לעיל דיש לו חזקה כי אמר (ו) בפנינו הודה היינו אחר שהאב אחר מות אביו דאי לאו הכי אין נראה שיהא נאמן במיגו דאי בעי אמר לקוח הוא בידי דאי טעין נמי לקחתיה ממך לא היה נאמן:

מגורשת

עין משפט נר מצוה

קמז א מיי' פט"ו מהל' עדות הל' ו ועי' כ"מ סמג לאוין קט טוש"ע ח"מ סי' לז סעיף יג בהג"ה:

קמח ב ג ד ה ו ז ח מיי' פי"ד מהל' טוען הל' ג ד סמג עשין צה טוש"ע ח"מ סי' קנב:

קמט ט י מיי' פי"ג שם הל' יא סמג שם טוש"ע ח"מ סי' קמט סעיף יג:

קנ כ מיי' שם הל' ד טוש"ע שם סעיף כח:

קנא ל מיי' שם הל' ו טוש"ע שם סעיף מ:

קנב מ מיי' שם הל' ט טוש"ע שם סעיף ז:

קנג נ מיי' שם טוש"ע שם סעיף י ועיין בטוש"ע אה"ע סי' פז:

רבינו גרשום

קבלן מאי. דדיניה דקבלן שאמר למלוה הלוהו ואני קבלן יכול המלוה לפרוע מן הקבלן ועכשיו כל שדותיו של לוה משועבדים לקבלן עד שיפרע חובו: **אמרי לה מעיד.** ללוה והוא שיש ללוה שדה אחרת כשיעור החוב חוץ מה שעוררין עליה דהשתא לאו נוגע הוא: **ואמרי לה** דאפ"ה **אין מעיד. דניחא ליה** לקבלן **דלוקמי** מן הני קרקע **תרוייהו בידא** דלוה שיהא לו יותר ממה לפרוע: **בן אומן. ובן אריס** הרי הן כאחר **ויש להן חזקה: אי דקאתי** הני בנים **בטענה דאבוהון.** דאמרי אבינו הורישה לנו. מאי איריא בן גזלן דאין לו חזקה **אפי' הנך** בן אומן ובן אריס **נמי לא** ליהוי חזקה. **ואי דאתי בטענה דנפשייהו** דאמרי זבנינה **אפי' בן מגזלן נמי** ליהוי ליה חזקה: **בפנינו הודה לו.** המוכר לבן אומן ולבן אריס ולבן גזלן דזבניה ניהלייהו לאבוהון מש"ה **איכא למימר** בבן אומן ובן אריס כי אתו בטענה דאבוהון **דקושטא קאמרי** דהמוכר (בכ"י הנעתק הוא בכאן מקום פנוי כמו חצי שורה ואולי חסר כאן איזה תיבות) [זבן] ניהלייהו. **והאי בן גזלן אע"ג** דאיכא עדים **שהודה** המוכר לגזלן שמכרה לו לא הויא חזקה דמחמת ביעתותא הוא דאודי ליה דהוי מסתפי דאי לא מודי ליה הוי מלשין עליה: **וממטי ליה ולחמריה לשחוור.** שילך עם חמורו באנגרא לשליחו' עבודות השלטון כדמתרגמינן לא חמור א' [מהם] נשאתי לא חמרא דחד מנהון שחרית. וכמו נוח לתשחורות. ולא גמר והקנה לו. **אבל בן בנו של גזלן אי אתי בטענה דאבוה יש לו חזקה** דאביו לאו גזלן הוה: **ירד מאומנותו.** ושוב מחזיק בה **יש לו חזקה: בן שחלק.** שנתן לו אביו חלקו בחייו והוא מחזיק בשדה אחת יותר על חלקו שנתן לו אביו ג' שנים וכן **אשה שנתגרשה** והחזיקה שוב בשדה בעלה ג' שנים: **הרי הן ככל אדם.** ויש להן חזקה: **סד"א אחולי אחיל ליה.** א) היה הפירות דלא מערער ולא תהוי חזקה:

חשק שלמה על רבינו גרשום

א) אולי צ"ל הפירות שאכל הבן ולא מערער וכו'.

מסורת הש"ס

א) [לקמן נב.]

הגהות הב"ח

(א) גמ' אי דאתו בטענתא וכו' אי דלא אתו בטענתא דאבוהון אלא בטענתא דנפשייהו אפי' בן גזלן נמי. נ"ב ע"ל דף נב ע"ב ד"ה ומודה לי: (ב) שם ממטי ליה לדידיה ולחמריה: (ג) שם סלקא דעתך אמינא אב לבן אחולי: (ד) רשב"ם ד"ה אי דאתו וכו' דמצי אמר אנא זבנית: (ה) תוס' ד"ה פעמים וכו' דאם איתא דהדר זבנה מיניה הוה אמר: (ו) ד"ה ירד וכו' כי אמר בפני הודה:

allows his son to occupy and appropriate the yield of his property even after the son has become independent.[20] קָא מַשְׁמַע לָן דְּלֹא – The Baraisa therefore **informs us that** this is **not** so.[21] אֶלָּא אִשָּׁה שֶׁנִּתְגָּרְשָׁה פְּשִׁיטָא – **But** the Baraisa's ruling concerning **a woman who was divorced is obvious!** Certainly, there is now animosity between the two and it is obvious that neither would brook the other's unwarranted use of his or her property and appropriation of its yield. Why, then, did the Baraisa find it necessary to teach that the divorced spouses can establish a *chazakah* in each other's property?

The Gemara answers:

לֹא צְרִיכָא – **No,** the ruling is not always obvious, for **it is necessary**

NOTES

teaches that if the son becomes independent (e.g. he marries and conducts his own affairs) or the wife is divorced, the now separated parties are like unrelated people with no inherent connection to each other's property. Thus, they can establish a *chazakah* in each other's property (*Rashbam*).

20. *Rashbam*; see also *Hagahos HaBach*.

21. As explained on 29a, the establishment of a *chazakah* in real property is based on the assumption that a property owner would not fail to protest a squatter's unwarranted use of his property and appropriation of its yield. One could think that this rationale does not apply when the squatter is the owner's son. Therefore, the Baraisa must teach that it indeed applies in that case as well [for a father is not assumed to be quite so generous with his financially independent son].

קבלן אמרי לה מעיד ואמרי לה [א]אינו מעיד אמרי לה מעיד כערב דמי ואמרי לה אינו מעיד דניחא ליה דלהוו בידיה תרווייהו דכי אתי בע"ח מאי דבעי שקיל אמר רבי יוחנן אומן אין לו חזקה [ב]בן אומן יש לו חזקה ארים אין לו חזקה [ג]בן ארים יש לו חזקה גזלן [ד]ובן גזלן אין להן חזקה [ה]בן בנו של גזלן יש לו חזקה היכי דמי אי (א) אתו בטענתא דאבוהון [ו]אפילו הנך נמי לא אי דלא אתו בטענתא דאבוהון אפילו בן גזלן נמי לא צריכא [ז]דקא אמרי עדים בפנינו הודה לו הנך איכא למימר קושטא קא אמרי האי אע"ג דאודי נמי לא מהימן כדרב כהנא דאמר רב כהנא אי לאו דאודי ליה הוה ממטי ליה (ב) ולחמריה לשחוור אמר רבא [ח]פעמים שאפילו בן בנו של גזלן נמי אין לו חזקה היכי דמי כגון דקא אתי בטענתא דאבא דאבוה היכי דמי גזלן אמר רבי יוחנן [ט]כגון שהוחזק על שדה זו בגזלנותא ורב חסדא אמר [י]כגון דבית פלוני שהורגין נפשות על עסקי ממון: תנו רבנן [כ]אומן אין לו חזקה ירד מאומנותו יש לו חזקה ארים אין לו חזקה [ל]ירד מאריסותו יש לו חזקה (א) [מ]בן שחלק ואשה שנתגרשה הרי הן כשאר כל אדם בשלמא בן שחלק איצטריך סלקא דעתך אמינא (ג) אחולי אחיל גביה קמ"ל דלא אלא אשה שנתגרשה פשיטא [נ]לא צריכא במגורשת

רשב"ם

קבלן. ערב קבלן שקבל המעות מידו של מלוה ונתן לידו של לוה וזהו דינו דממי שירצה המלוה יפרע תחלה אבל ערב סתמא אין תובעין לערב תחלה עד שיעמיד מלוה ללוה בדין ויחייבוהו לשלם ואין לו מה לפרוע ואז יגבה מן הערב: **אמרי לה מעיד.** כמו ערב: **ואמרי לה אינו מעיד.** דלהכי נוגע בעדות הוא דניחא ליה דנוקמא תרוייהו ארעתא בידיה דלוה כי היכי דליהוו ליה ארעי טובא זיבורית ובינונית דכי אתא מלוה למגבי בינונית דקבלן כדין בע"ח שדינו בבינונית לימא ליה אתה לך בינונית דלוה והלכך הוה נוגע בעדות דאי לא הוה ללוה בינונית לא ליגבי מלוה אלא מבינונית דקבלן דהכי הוי דינא דלכל מאן דבעי תבע ברישא אבל בערב סתם ליכא למימר הכי דלכל כמה דאית ליה ללוה למיפרע מידי ואפי' זיבורית לאו כל כמיניה דמלוה למיהדר גבי ערב כדקי"ל במכילתין (לקמן דף קעד.) לא יתבע לערב תחלה: **אומן אין לו חזקה.** כדקתני מתני': **אבל בן.** של אומן וכגון שאין הבן אומן יש לו חזקה וכדמפרש לקמן: **גזלן.** לקמן מפרש היכי דמי יש שמפרש שהוחזק בגזלנות על שדה זו ובהאי שדה הוא דאין לו חזקה ויש שמפרש לקמן כגון רוצח נפשות על עסקי ממון והלכך אין לו חזקה על שום קרקע של אחרים בעולם: **אי דאתו.** הנך בנים בטענתא דאבוהון דאמרי אבינו הורישה לנו ומש"ה בן גזלן אין לו חזקה דכי האי גוונא אין טוענין ליורש דכיון דמכח גזלן קאתי ואיהו לא טעין מאבי אני יורש דזבנה מינך קמאי דידי דליהמניה ע"י מיגו דמצי אמר (ד) זבנית מינך הלכך חזקה שאין עמה טענה היא שהרי אין לאבא חזקה וגם הבן הבא מכחו אין חזקתו חזקה וכיון דמכח אבוהון קאתו אפילו הנך בן אומן ובן ארים נמי לא ליהוי להו חזקה: **אלא בטענה דנפשייהו.** אנא זבנתה מינך: **לא צריכא.** דקאתו בטענתא דאבוהון וכגון דאמרו עדים בפנינו הודה לו המערער לאביהן של אלו שמכרו להם הלכך הנך בן אריס ובן אומן איכא למימר קושטא קאמרי כשטוענין אבינו לקחו ממך שהרי הודה והודאת בעל דין כמאה עדים אבל בן גזלן אע"ג דאודי האי מערער לאביו לא מהימן לומר לקוח הוא ביד אבי ואפי' בחיי אביו אם נתנו לבן שהרי הוא מתוך פחד הודה לו לגזלן כדרב כהנא כו' אבל בן בנו של גזלן יש לו חזקה אי אתי בטענה דאבוה דטעין מאבי ירשתי ואבי לא היה גזלן וכי האי גוונא טוענין ליורש דאילו היה אביו קיים הוה טעין מינך זבנתה ולא הוה אתי בטענתא דאבוה אף אנו נטעון בשביל היורש ורישא דקתני אומן אין לו חזקה בדליכא עדי הודאה דלגלדין קתני: **אי לאו דאודי ליה.** נגזל לגזלן: **הוה ממטי ליה לדידיה ולחמריה לשחוור.** היה מוסר אותו ואת חמורו לפקיד כדמתרגמינן (במדבר טז) [לא חמור אחד מהם נשאתי] לא חמרא דחד מנהון שחרית דסתם גזלן גברא אלמא הוא: **פעמים שאפילו בן גזלן יש לו חזקה.** ואע"ג דלא אתי בטענה דנפשיה היכי דמי כגון דקא אתי בטענתא דאבא דאבוה שטוען מאבי אבי אני יורש ואיהו לא היה גזלן ומיגו דמצי אמר זבנתה מינך כי אמר נמי זקני הורישה לאבי ואבי הורישני נאמן דחזקה שיש עמה טענה מעלייתא היא: ל"א כתוב בספרים **פעמים שבן בנו של גזלן נמי אין לו חזקה וכגון דאתי בטענתא דאבא דאבוה.** שאבי אביו גזלן היה ושניהם אמת אבל הראשון נראה שאמר רבא ולא האחרון: **היכי דמי גזלן.** אותו שאין לו חזקה: **על שדה זו.** ובההוא שדה הוא דאין לו חזקה אבל בשאר שדות יש לו חזקה: **כגון של בית פלוני שהורגין כו'.** אנשי רשעים היו שהיה מכיר בהן רב חסדא שהורגין נפשות על עסקי ממון אין להן חזקה בשום קרקע בעולם שכל אדם ירא למחות בהן וקי"ל כתרוייהו: **ירד מאומנותו.** ושוב מחזיק בה יש לו חזקה: **בן שחלק.** הפליג מאביו ואין סמוך עוד על שולחנו כגון שנשא אשה ואין משתדל עוד בנכסי אביו הרי הן ככל אדם אע"ג דתנן (לעיל דף מב.) לא לאיש חזקה בנכסי אשתו ולא לאשה בנכסי בעלה ולא האב בנכסי הבן ולא הבן כו' הנך כיון שהופלגו זה מזה יש להן חזקה זה על זה: **סלקא דעתך אמינא אחולי אחיל.** האב גבי דבן פירות שאכל בשלש שנים ולפיכך לא ערער ולא תיהוי חזקה קמ"ל דלא מחיל: **אלא אשה שנתגרשה פשיטא.** דמחזקת בנכסי בעלה וכן בעלה מחזיק בנכסיה שהרי שונאין זה את זה והיה להן למחות:

תוספות

קבלן אמרי לה אינו מעיד. אע"ג דאית ליה ארעא אחריתי תימה דמאי נפקא מינה דאי אתי מלוה וטריף את של קבלן אתי קבלן וקטריף את של לוה כיון דאית ליה ארעא אחריתי ואין נראה לומר כגון שיש לקבלן בינונית והיא ארעא שרוצה להעיד עליה נמי בינונית אבל ארעא אחריתי דאית ליה ללוה היא זיבורית דמפסיד כשיבא מלוה וטריף את שלו דלא יהיה לו לגבות אלא מזיבורית דא"כ מלוה נמי לא יעיד ללוה אפילו אית ליה ארעא אחריתי כענין זה ועוד דבכל ענין משמע דאינו מעיד דלא מפליג בין היא בינונית בין היא זיבורית ועוד דל"ע בהניזקין (גיטין דף מט:) דנראה דמוכח התם דאם אין ללוה אלא זיבורית גם קבלן לא יתן לו אלא זיבורית ונראה דהיינו טעמא דקבלן אינו מעיד ללוה אע"ג דאית ליה ארעא אחריתי משום דטריחא ליה מילתא למיקם עליה בדינא ודינא וכשיש ללוה קרקעות הרבה לא יגבה המלוה מן הקבלן הואיל ויכול לגבות מן הלוה בהרווחה אבל מלוה מעיד ללוה בכל ענין אפילו אותה שמעיד עליה היא בינונית ואחריתי זיבורית דמשום איחלופי בינונית לזיבורית לא יעיד שקר דמכל מקום יש לו שום בשום אי נמי ארעא אחריתי דכולה שמעתין ביוצא בו קאמר:

כגון דקאמר בפנינו הודה. ה"ג פי' בן ארים בן אומן בן גזלן ומש"ה אומן אין לו חזקה אבל בן יש לו חזקה כשטוען קמי דידי הודית לאבי שמכרת לו נאמן במיגו דאי בעי אמר מינך זבנתה אבל בן גזלן אין לו חזקה דהודאה שהודה לגזלן לאו הודאה היא דאי לאו דאודי ליה שמכרה לו הוה ממטי ליה ולחמריה לשחוור אבל לא גרסינן כגון דקאמרי עדים דהא אי איכא עדים דאודי ליה דמיניה זבנה א"כ אומן ואריס גופייהו יהו נאמנים ועוד כיון דאיכא עדים בן ארים בן אומן למה צריכים להחזיק בלא חזקה נמי מוקמינן לה בידייהו כיון דאיכא סהדי. ר"ת:

פעמים שבן בן גזלן אין לו חזקה כגון דקאתי בטענתא דאבא דאבוה. תימה לר"י דלמאי אין לו חזקה הא טוענין ליורש והוה ליה למימר דלמא אי הוה אביו קיים דהיינו בן גזלן הוה טעין אנא הדר זבינתה מינך ונראה לר"י דגרס פעמים שבן גזלן יש לו חזקה כגון דקאתי בטענתא דאבא דאבוה דהוא אבי הגזלן וקמ"ל דאע"ג שהיתה ביד מי שאין לו חזקה דהיינו אביו הגזלן מ"מ יש לו חזקה כיון שאמר שהיתה של אבי אביו ויש ליישב גירסא ראשונה פעמי' דבן בן גזלן אין לו חזקה והכי פירושה כגון דאתא בטענתא דאבא דאבוה ואומר שאמר לו אביו דהיינו בן הגזלן שהניחה לו הגזלן אביו דאם איתא דהדר (ה) זבנתה מינך הוה א"ל אנא זבינא אי נמי נראה לר"י דלא טענינן ליורש כי האי גוונא דמילתא דלא שכיחא היא כי היכי דאמר בסוף המוכר את הבית (לקמן דף ע: ושם ד"ה מאן) דלא טענינן ליתמי נאנסו משום דמילתא דלא שכיחא היא והא דקאמר לעיל [בן] בן גזלן בן אומן יש לו חזקה היינו דוקא משום דאמר בפנינו הודה ואדרבה מהם יש להוכיח דמשמע הא לאו הכי אין לו חזקה כיון דמעיקרא בתורת אומנות ואריסות וגזלנות אתא לידיה:

ירד מאומנותו יש לו חזקה. מצינו לפרש מאותן כלים שנתן לו לאחר שירד מאומנותו דומיא דארים שירד מאריסותו אי נמי אפילו אותן כלים שנתנו לו בשעה שהיה עדיין אומן והוא ששהו אחר אומנותו כ"כ שהוא רגילות שמחזירם לבעלים ונראה דבן אומן נמי דאמר לעיל דיש לו חזקה כי אמר (ו) בפנינו הודה היינו אחר ששהה אחר מות אביו דאי לאו הכי אין נראה שיהא נאמן במיגו דאי בעי אמר לקוח הוא בידי דאי טעין נמי לקחתיה ממך לא היה נאמן:

מסורת הש"ס

א) [לקמן נג.]:

הגהות הב"ח

(א) גמ' אי דאתו בטענתא וכו' אי דלא אתו בטענתא דאבוהון אלא בטענתא דנפשייהו אפי' בן גזלן נמי. נ"ב ע"ל דף נג בתוס' ד"ה ומודה לי: (ב) שם ממטי ליה לדידיה ולחמריה: (ג) שם סלקא דעתך אמינא אב לבן אחולי: (ד) רשב"ם ד"ה אי דאתו וכו' דמצי אמר אנא זבנית: (ה) תוס' ד"ה פעמים וכו' דאם איתא דהדר זבנה מיניה הוה אמר: (ו) ד"ה ירד וכו' כי אמר בפני הודה:

עין משפט נר מצוה

קסז א מיי' פט"ו מהל' עדות הל' ו ועי' כ"מ סמג לאוין קט טוש"ע ח"מ סי' לז סעיף יג בהג"ה:
קסח ב ג ד ה ו ז ח מיי' פי"ד מהל' טוען הל' ג ד סמג עשין לה טוש"ע ח"מ סי' קנג:
קסט ט י מיי' פי"ג שם הל' יא סמג שם טוש"ע ח"מ סי' קמט סעיף יג:
קע כ מיי' שם הל' ד טוש"ע שם סעיף כח:
קעא ל מיי' שם הל' ו טוש"ע שם סעיף כז:
קעב מ מיי' שם הל' ט טוש"ע שם סעיף ד:
קעג נ מיי' שם טוש"ע שם סעיף י ועיין בטוש"ע אה"ע סי' פז:

רבינו גרשום

קבלן מאי. דדיניה דקבלן שאמר למלוה הלוהו ואני קבלן יכול המלוה לפרוע מן הקבלן ועכשיו כל שדותיו של לוה משועבדים לקבלן עד שיפרע חובו: **אמרי לה מעיד.** ללוה והוא שיש ללוה שדה אחרת כשיעור החוב חוץ מה שעוררין עליה דהשתא לאו נוגע הוא: **ואמרי לה** דאפ"ה **אין מעיד. דניחא ליה** לקבלן **דלוקמי** מן הני קרקע **תרוייהו בידא** דלוה שיהא לו יותר ממה לפרוע: **בן אומן. ובן אריס** הרי הן כאחר **ויש להן חזקה: אי דקאתי** הני בנים **בטענה דאבוהון.** דאמרי אבינו הורישה לנו. מאי איריא בן גזלן דאין לו חזקה **אפי' הנך** בן אומן ובן אריס **נמי לא** ליהוי חזקה. **ואי דאתי בטענה דנפשייהו** דאמרי זבנינה **אפי' בן מגזלן נמי** ליהוי ליה חזקה: **בפנינו הודה לו.** המוכר לבן אומן ולבן אריס ולבן גזלן דזבניה ניהלייהו לאבוהון מש"ה **איכא למימר** בבן אומן ובן אריס כי אתו בטענה דאבוהון **דקושטא קאמרי** דהמוכר (בכ"י הנעתק הוא בכאן מקום פנוי כמו חצי שורה ואולי חסר כאן איזה תיבות) [זבן] ניהלייהו. **והאי בן גזלן אע"ג** דאיכא עדים **שהודה** המוכר לגזלן שמכרה לו לא הויא חזקה דמחמת ביעתותא הוא דאודי ליה דהוי מסתפי דאי לא מודי ליה הוי מלשין עליה: **וממטי ליה ולחמריה לשחוור.** שילך עם חמורו באנגרא לשליחו' עבודות השלטון כדמתרגמינן לא חמור א' [מהם] נשאתי לא חמרא דחד מנהון שחרית. וכמו נוח לתשחורת. ולא גמר והקנה לו. **אבל בן בנו של גזלן אי אתי בטענה דאבוה יש לו חזקה** דאביו לאו גזלן הוה: **ירד מאומנותו.** ושוב מחזיק בה **יש לו חזקה: בן שחלק.** שנתן לו אביו חלקו בחייו והוא מחזיק בשדה אחת יותר על חלקו שנתן לו אביו ג' שנים וכן **אשה שנתגרשה** והחזיקה שוב בשדה בעלה ג' שנים: **הרי הן ככל אדם.** ויש להן חזקה: **סד"א אחולי אחיל ליה.** א) היה הפירות דלא מערער ולא תהוי חזקה:

חשק שלמה על רבינו גרשום

א) אולי צ"ל הפירות שאכל הבן ולא מערער וכו'.

במגורשת ואינה מגורשת וכדרבי זירא [א]דאמר ר' זירא אמר ר' ירמיה בר אבא אמר שמואל [א]כל מקום שאמרו חכמים מגורשת ואינה מגורשת בעלה חייב במזונותיה אמר רב נחמן אמר לי הונא [ב]כולן שהביאו ראיה ראייתן ראיה ומעמידין שדה בידן גזלן שהביא ראיה אין ראייתו ראיה ואין מעמידין שדה בידו מאי קמ"ל תנינא [ג]לקח מסיקריקון וחזר ולקח מבעל הבית מקחו בטל לאפוקי מדרב דאמר [ד]רב לא שנו אלא דאמר ליה לך חזק וקני אבל בשטר קנה קמ"ל כדשמואל דאמר [ה]אף בשטר נמי לא קנה ורב ביבי מסיים בה משמיה דרב נחמן [ו]קרקע אין לו אבל מעות יש לו בד"א [ז]שאמרו עדים בפנינו מנה לו אבל אמרו עדים בפנינו הודה לו לא כדרב כהנא דאמר (א) אי לאו דאודי ליה הוה ממטי ליה לדידיה ולחמריה לשחוור אמר רב הונא [ח]תליוהו וזבין זביניה זביני מ"ט כל דמזבין איניש אי לאו דאנים לא הוה מזבין ואפילו הכי זביניה זביני ודילמא שאני אונסא דנפשיה מאונסא דאחריני אלא (ב) [ט]כדתניא

יקריב

רש"י

מגורשת ואינה מגורשת. כגון זרק לה גט ספק קרוב לה ספק קרוב לו דבעלה חייב במזונותיה עד דיהיב לה גט ודאי כדר' זירא ואיכא למימר כיון דמגורשת ואינה מגורשת אשתו היא וחייב במזונותיה והניח לה בעל קרקע זו בידה כדי שתזון מפירותיה ולא הויא חזקה קמ"ל דהויא חזקה דכיון דהתחיל בגירושין והוא שונא לה לא יחד לה קרקע למזונותיה כי בטורח יתן לה מזונות בצמצום כשיתחייבוהו ב"ד: חייב במזונותיה. דאכתי אגידא ביה: וכולן. אומן ואריס וכל הנך דלעיל דאמרן אין להן חזקה: ראיה. שטר מכירה או עדי מכירה: ראייתן ראיה. מילתא דפשיטא היא ומשום סיפא נקט לה: גזלן שהביא ראיה. עדי מכירה או עדי הודאה אבל מתן מעות לא ראו: אין ראייתו ראיה. כדרב כהנא דאי לאו דאודי ליה או שכתב לו שטר מכירה הוה ממטי ליה ולחמריה לשחוור אבל אם נתן לו הגזלן מעות בפני עדים ראייתו ראיה כדרב הונא לקמיה דאמר תליוהו וזבין זביניה זביני ואע"ג דרב ביבי מוקי לה לקמן להא אפילו בשנתן מעות הגזלן לנגזל ואפ"ה לא קנה גזלן הא אמרינן לקמן בשמעתין דרב ביבי מימרא היא ומימרא לרב הונא לא סבירא ליה וכדרב הונא קיימא לן בשמעתין: ואין מעמידין שדה בידו. ולא לכל הבא מכחו כגון בן גזלן או לוקח מגזלן: מאי קמ"ל. רב הונא דגזלן וכל הבא מכחו אין ראייתו ראיה ולא קנה: תנינא. במסכת גיטין בהניזקין: לקח מסיקריקון. מגזלן נכרי הורג נפשות על עסקי ממון שאומר לו שא קרקע זו והניחני ומתנה זו לא הויא מתנה דאפילו למ"ד תליוהו וזבין זביניה זביני תליוהו ויהב לא הויא מתנה וטעמא מפרש בגיטין ג' גזירות גזרו [קמייתא כל דלא קטיל ליקטיל מציעתא כל דקטיל לייתי ארבע זוזי] בתרייתא כל דקטיל ליקטלינהו קמייתא ומציעתא כיון דקטלי נכרים לישראל אגב אונסיה גמר ומקני בתרייתא אמרי האידנא ליסקול ולמחר תבענא ליה בדינא והלכך לא קנה הסיקריקון דהא לא נתן מעות אלא גזלה בחנם והלוקח (ג) נמי ממנו לא קנה דקרקע אינה נגזלת ואכתי ברשותא דמריה קמא איתא ואפילו חזר ולקח מבעל הבית שכתב לו שטר כדמפרש לקמן או במתנה או בשטר מכירה בלא מעות דאילו נתן מעות לבעל הבית קנה כרב הונא דהא אפילו סיקריקון עצמו היה קונה אם נתן לו מעות לנגזל והכי מוכח לקמן בשמעתין גבי מילתיה דרב הונא דאית ליה תליוהו וזבין כו' אפילו הכי לא קנה לוקח דמחמת פחד דסיקריקון הקנה לו ללוקח וכיון דאין ראיית הלוקח מגזלן ראיה אפילו כי הדר וזבין מבעל הבית כל שכן וכל שכן דאין ראיית הגזלן עצמו ראיה דמחמת פחד כתב לו השטר ומעולם לא קיבל דמים מן הגזלן דנימא זביניה זביני: ומשני לאפוקי מדרב. אתא רב הונא: דאמר רב. עלה דההיא משנה: לא שנו. דחזר ולקח מבעה"ב מקחו בטל אלא דאמר לו בפני עדים (ד) חזק וקני ומעות לא קיבל בפני עדים דנימא זביניה זביני כדלקמן וגם שטר לא כתב לו בעל הבית ללוקח אבל אם כתב לו שטר ודאי אקני ליה ואתא רב הונא למימר דגזלן שהביא ראיה אפילו בשטר אין ראייתו ראיה כדשמואל: אף בשטר לא קנה. דמאימת סיקריקון כתב לו: ורב ביבי מסיים. בהא מלתא דאמר רב נחמן א"ל הונא: משמיה דרב נחמן. שהיה מוסיף בה רב נחמן דבר זה מדעתו ומיהו רב הונא לא סבירא ליה האי תוספתא כדלקמן בשמעתין דכל היכא דאיכא מתן מעות סבר ליה לרב הונא דהוו זביני ולאו אדרב ושמואל קאי דבמסכת גיטין בהניזקין דאיתא לפלוגתייהו לא איירי רב ביבי כלל התם: קרקע אין לו. לגזלן כמו שאמרנו אין מעמידין שדה בידו: אבל מעות. שנתן לו הגזלן לנגזל בדמי קרקע זו יש לו שיחזירם לו הנגזל ולא קנסינן ליה לגזלן לאבד מעותיו ושמעינן מהכא דסבירא ליה לרב ביבי תליוהו וזבין לאו זביניה זביני והיינו דאמרינן לקמן דרב הונא לית ליה דרב ביבי: בד"א. דמעות יש לו כגון שאמרו עדים בפנינו מנה לו הגזלן לנגזל ונתן לו המעות או שכתבו בשטר אנו ראינו שנתן לו המעות דמשום פחד דסיקריקון דגזלן לא מסהדי וכתבו עדים שיקרא: אבל אמרו עדים בפנינו הודה לו. נגזל לגזלן שקיבל ממנו הדמים או שכתבו בשטר המכירה וכך אמר לנו הוו עלי עדים שקיבלתי ממנו הדמים ומכרתי לו לא יחזיר לו מעות לגזלן: כדרב כהנא כו'. ומסקנא דמילתא דרב ביבי היא: תליוהו וזבין. מי שתלו אותו או עשו לו יסורין עד שמכר וקיבל הדמים ואומר רוצה אני: זביניה זביני. ולא יוכל לחזור בו וטעמא מפרש ואזיל: ואית דגרס תלוה. ורבינו חננאל כתב תליוהו. ודוקא מכר אבל מתנה לא הויא מתנה דכיון דלא מקבל מידי לא גמר ומקני כדמוכח לקמן דאמרינן מודה שמואל היכא דיהב זוזי: דכל דמזבין איניש. רוב חפצים וכלי ביתו וטליתו שאדם מוכר אי לאו דאנים ודחיק במעות לא הוה מזבין ואפ"ה הוה זביניה זביני בעל כרחו אפילו לא גמר ומקני שלא נתנה תורה חילוק במקח וממכר בין דברים הצריכין לו ומכרן לדברים שאין צריכין לו אלא כולהו קונה לוקח וה"נ אע"ג דאנים מוכר קונה לוקח הואיל וקיבל דמים אע"ג דלא גמר ומקני: שאני אונס דנפשיה. שצריך למעות ומתוך כך מוכר חפציו מדעתו דהתם איכא למימר גמר ומקני: מאונסא דאחריני. שמכריחין אותו למכור דהתם לא גמר ומקני:

יקריב

תוספות

מגורשת ואינה מגורשת בעלה חייב במזונותיה. וכגון שייחד לה ארעא אחריתי דאי לאו הכי אין (ז) לו חזקה דכיון דלית לה מזוני מזוני הוא דקא אכלה כדאמרי' לקמן:

ראייתן ראיה ומעמידין שדה בידן. נראה לרשב"א דנקט תרוייהו איידי דבעי למיתני גבי גזלן אין ראייתו ראיה ואין מעמידין שדה בידו דהשתא איצטריך תרוייהו דאי לא תנא אלא אין ראייתו ראיה הוה אמינא דאין ראייתו ראיה לגבי הא שאין מעמידין שדה בידו אבל מעות יש לו דלא ה"א טעמא אי לאו דאודי ליה הוה ממטי ליה ולחמריה לשחוור אלא הוה מפרשינן טעמא משום דתליוהו וזבין לא הוו זביניה זביני אפי' מנה לו מעות הלכך קאמרי תרוייהו דאין ראייתו ראיה כלל דאפי' מעות אין לו דטעמא הוא משום דאי לאו דאודי ליה כו' והאי כולן נראה לרשב"א דקאי נמי אבן שלא חלק ואשה שלא נתגרשה ואע"ג דאמר לקמן [גבי אשה בנכסי בעלה] דלגלויי זוזי הוא דבעי כיון דאוקימנא בהודאה לא שייך בה גלויי זוזי ועוד דמשמע לקמן דסבירא להו לרב הונא ולרב נחמן דלא אמר לגלויי זוזי הוא דבעי: **ומעמידין** שדה בידן. גבי אומן נמי שייך שדה כגון אם הוא בנאי: **אבל** בשטר קנה. אלקח מן האיש וחזר ולקח מן האשה נמי קאי כדמוכח במתני' בהניזקין (גיטין דף נה: ושם) וקשה דתניא בסוף מי שהיה נשוי (כתובות דף נה. ושם ד"ה וכתבה) כתב לראשון ולא חתמה לו לשני וחתמה לו איבדה כתובתה דוקא משום דלא חתמה לראשון אבל אי חתמה לראשון לא איבדה כתובתה כדמוכח התם אע"פ שכתבה שטר ונראה לר"י דהא דקאמר רב בשטר קנה יש להעמיד בשטר הראיה שאחר הקנין דכיון שאחר הקנין עשתה שטר שייפתה כחו כל כך קנה והתם דכתובות מיירי בשטר מתנה בלא קנין אחר אלא שטר א"נ חתמה דהתם לשון גמר כמו חתמו גבי תורף דגיטין וכמו תורה חתומה ניתנה בהניזקין (גיטין דף ס.) כלומר שגמרה מקח ונתרצתה בעל פה אי נמי חתמה ממש ובשטר של בעל והא דאמר רב בשטר קנה שעשתה שטר מכירה בשמה ומסתבר דטעמא דרב כטעמא דשמואל דאמר בהניזקין (שם דף נח. ושם ד"ה אבל) אף בשטר לא קנה עד שתכתוב לו אחריות ושמואל לטעמיה דאמר בפ"ק דב"מ (דף יד. ושם) אחריות לאו טעות סופר בשטרי מקח וממכר ורב סבר אחריות טעות סופר הוא אבל קצת קשה דלקמן פריך לרב הונא דאמר תליוהו וזבין זביניה זביני מהא דאמר שמואל אף בשטר לא קנה ואי תלוי הדבר באחריות מאי קשה ליה משמואל טפי מרב: **ורב** ביבי מסיים בה כו'. ק"ק הלשון דהא רב ביבי פליג כדאמרי' לקמן ורב הונא לא מיירי בהכי אלא בהודה ולא במנה:

אלימא

עין משפט נר מצוה

קעד א מיי' פי"מ מהל' אישות הלכה כה סמג עשין מח טוש"ע אה"ע סי' לג סעיף ב:

קעה ב מיי' פי"ד מהל' טוען הל' א סמג עשין צה טוש"ע ח"מ סי' קנא סעיף א:

קעו ג טוש"ע ח"מ סי' רלו סעיף ד:

קעז ד מיי' פי"ד מהל' טוען הל' ג ועיין כמ"מ סמג שם טוש"ע שם וסי' קנא סעיף ג:

קעח ה ו מיי' פי"ד מהל' טוען הל' ג סמג שם טוש"ע ח"מ סי' קנא סעיף ג:

קעט ז מיי' פ"י מהל' מכירה הל' א ועי' בהשגות ובמ"מ סמג עשין פב טוש"ע ח"מ סי' קנה סעיף ג בהג"ה וסי' רה סעיף א [וכרב אלפס עוד בגיטין פ"ה דף קנ.]:

רבינו גרשום

מגורשת ואינ' מגורשת. כגון זרק לה גט ספק קרוב לו דבעלה חייב במזונותיה עד דיהיב לה גט ודאי ואיכא למימר (א) דיל ספק מגורשת דאם איתא דגרשה אית ליה בהדה איבה ולא היה מייחד לה קרקע למזונות כי אם מקום אחר יהיב לה מזונות בצמצום והויא חזקה: וכולן. בין אומן ובין אריס וכל הני דלעיל שהביאו ראיה. עדות שקנו אותה קרקע ראייתן ראיה והוי חזקה: לקח מן סיקריקון. זהו גזלן שאמרו לו בני אדם מחמת שהוא אנס שא קרקע זו והניחנו ואח"כ לקח מבעה"ב (ב) שתפיס לו קנין הנגזל ללוקח שוב שסיקריקון מקחו בטל דבעל כרחיה אודי ליה ולא גמר ומקני ליה אלמא דראיה של גזלן אינה ראיה. ומשני הך ברייתא איצטריך למתני לאפוקי מדרב דאמר לא שנו דמקחו בטל אלא דאמר לו בעה"ב לך חזק בקרקע וקני משה"ה לא קני דלא מצי לאחזוקי בה משום דבעל כרחיה קאמר אבל אי כתב ליה בעל הבית שטר מכירה קנה: קמ"ל. רב נחמן דאפ"ה לא קנה כדשמואל וכו': אחריות. דלא מפיק ליה מידיה: ורב ביבי מסיים בה משמיה דרב נחמן. להיכא דחזר ולקח מבעל הבית מקחו בטל דקרקע אין לו ללוקח אבל מעות שנתן יש לו בד"א. דמעות יש לו כגון שאמרו עדים בפנינו מנה לו המעות לבעה"ב אבל אמרו העדים בפנינו הודה לו המוכר להסיקריקון ולא ראו נתינת המעות אפי' מעות אין לו דהאי דאודי ליה כדרב כהנא וכו': אמר רב הונא. אי אמרו ואיימו לאיש תלוהו בעץ אי לא מזבין לו שדהו וזבין מחמת יראה זביניה זביני אע"ג דאנסוהו: אי לאו דאניס. שאין לו מעות להוציא לצרכיו:

מסורת הש"ס

א) ב"מ יב: ע"ש גיטין עד. ע"ש כתובות מז: ע"ש, ב) גיטין נה: ג) [שם נח.], ד) [שם], ה) [לקמן מח.], ו) ב"ק סב. [לקמן מח:], ז) ערכין כא. קדושין ג. יבמות קו. ר"ה ו, ח) בפ"ק לה:

הגהות הב"ח

(א) גמ' דאמר רב כהנא אי לאו דאודי: (ב) שם אלא מדתניא יקריב: (ג) רשב"ם ד"ה לקח וכו' והלוקח ממנו נמי לא קנה: (ד) ד"ה דאמר רב וכו' בפני עדים לך חזק:

ליקוטי רש"י

כל מקום שאמרו חכמים מגורשת ואינה מגורשת. כגון זרק לה גיטו ספק קרוב לה ספק קרוב לו ברשות הרבים [ב"מ יב:]. בעלה חייב במזונותיה. בחיים [ואשמעינן מתני' דדוקא בחיים מזונותיה מעוכבת בשבילו להנשא אבל לאחר מיתה לא דדלמא גרושין הוו ואין לה מזונות דמספיקא לא מפקי' ממונא [כתובות צז:]. לקח מסיקריקון. בשעה שישראל מופקרין להריגה ואמר לעובד כוכבים שלא קרקע זו או עבד זה והניחני [גיטין מד:]. סיקריקון עובד כוכבים רוצח שנותן לו ישראל קרקע בפדיון נפשו ואומר לו שא קרקע זו או תמיתני. מקחו בטל. דאמרי' מירמא עבד לי נמי השני נוח לי והראשון קשה [שם נה:]. לא שנו. דמקחו בטל. אלא דאמר ליה. בעלים שלקח מסיקריקון. לך חזק וקני. בחזקה קנה לדיבורא בעלמא הוא איכא למימר השני נוח לי. אבל. אם כתב ליה שטר בשטר. קני. דטלי הא לא הוה ליה למיעבד אי לאו דגמר ומקני. אחריות. לשטר לו מיניה לגביה דמי ארעא [שם נח.].

חשק שלמה על רבינו גרשום

(א) אולי צ"ל ואיכא למימר דאין לה חזקה קמ"ל כיון דהתחיל בגירושין אית ליה וכו'. ב) אולי צ"ל שאמר לו הגזלן ללוקח לך חזק וקני והודה לו שוב שסיקריקון קרקע וכו'.

בִּמְגוֹרֶשֶׁת וְאֵינָהּ מְגוֹרֶשֶׁת – where she is divorced and yet not divorced, i.e. in a case of questionable divorce,[1] **וְכִדְרַבִּי זֵירָא – and in accordance with** what **R' Zeira** taught; **דְּאָמַר ר׳ זֵירָא אָמַר ר׳ יִרְמְיָה בַּר אַבָּא אָמַר שְׁמוּאֵל – for R' Zeira said in the name of R' Yirmiyah bar Abba, who said in the name of Shmuel: כָּל מָקוֹם שֶׁאָמְרוּ חֲכָמִים מְגוֹרֶשֶׁת וְאֵינָהּ מְגוֹרֶשֶׁת – Wherever the Sages said** that a woman is **"divorced and yet not divorced,"** i.e. in cases of questionable divorce, **בַּעְלָהּ חַיָּיב בִּמְזוֹנוֹתֶיהָ – her husband remains obligated in her support,** i.e. to provide her with food.[2] In that case, one might think that the wife's subsequent occupancy of her husband's property proves nothing, since the husband might have let her use the property and take its yield in lieu of the support that he is obligated to give her. Therefore, the Baraisa must teach us otherwise.[3]

The Gemara quotes a ruling concerning the abovementioned cases of craftsmen, sharecroppers and all others who do not establish a *chazakah*:

אָמַר רַב נַחְמָן – Rav Nachman said: אָמַר לִי הוּנָא – Huna[4] **said to me** that **כּוּלָּן שֶׁהֵבִיאוּ רְאָיָה – all of them** [the craftsman, sharecropper, etc.] **– if they bring** proper **proof** (other than *chazakah*) that they are the disputed property's legitimate owners **– רְאָיָיתָן רְאָיָה – their proof is** an acceptable **proof וּמַעֲמִידִין שָׂדֶה בְּיָדָן – and we place the** disputed **field in their hands.**[5] There is, however, one exception: **גַּזְלָן שֶׁהֵבִיא רְאָיָה – If a robber brings proof,**[6] **אֵין רְאָיָיתוֹ רְאָיָה – his proof is not** an acceptable **proof וְאֵין מַעֲמִידִין שָׂדֶה בְּיָדוֹ – and we do not place the field in his hands.**[7]

The Gemara questions the need for Rav Huna to teach even this ruling concerning a robber who brings proof:

מַאי קָא מַשְׁמַע לָן – What new ruling **is he teaching us? תְּנֵינָא – We have** already **learned** this **in a Mishnah:**[8] **לָקַח מִסִּיקְרִיקוֹן – If ONE ACQUIRED** stolen property **FROM AN EXTORTIONIST,**[9] **וְחָזַר וְלָקַח מִבַּעַל הַבַּיִת – EVEN IF HE IN TURN ACQUIRED** it **FROM THE OWNER** as well, **מִקָּחוֹ בָּטֵל – HIS ACQUISITION IS VOID.**[10] Thus, we see from this Mishnah that where there is reason to believe that the owner ceded his property out of fear of reprisals, his transfer of the property is void. Why, then, does Rav Huna have to reiterate this rule in his teaching that a robber's proof of acquisition is meaningless?[11]

The Gemara answers:

לְאַפּוּקֵי מִדְּרַב – Rav Huna stated his ruling **in order to take exception to** the ruling **of Rav. דְּאָמַר רַב – For Rav said: לֹא שָׁנוּ אֶלָּא דְּאָמַר לֵיהּ לֵךְ חֲזֵק וּקְנֵי – The Mishnah** cited above **taught** its rule that the acquisition is void **only where the owner** merely **said to [the extortionist's buyer], "Go, perform a proprietary act and acquire** the land," but the owner did not draw up a document certifying the transfer. **אֲבָל בִּשְׁטָר קָנָה – But** if the owner conveyed the property to the buyer **with a document** certifying the transaction, **[the buyer] does acquire** the property.[12] **קָא מַשְׁמַע לָן כִּדְשְׁמוּאֵל – [Rav Huna]** therefore **informs us** that his own view is **in accordance with that of Shmuel, דְּאָמַר אַף בִּשְׁטָר נַמִּי לֹא קָנָה – who says that even** when the owner conveys the property **with a document, [the buyer] does not acquire** the property,[13] **עַד שֶׁיִּכְתּוֹב אַחֲרָיוּת נְכָסִים – unless [the owner] writes** in the document a clause that issues **a property-backed guarantee,** which secures the owner's properties as surety for the present transfer.[14] Rav Huna, who states that a

NOTES

1. For instance, her husband threw her bill of divorce near her in a public domain and it is uncertain if the bill fell closer to her or to him. The law states that the divorce is valid only if the bill fell closer to her [see *Gittin* 78a-b]. Since we are not certain if that was the case, her status as a divorcee is in doubt (see *Rashbam*).

2. A husband is obligated to support his wife. If he divorces her in a way that is questionable, he remains obligated to support her until he divorces her in an unquestionably valid manner (*Rashbam*).

3. For a husband who has attempted to divorce his wife obviously hates her and is assumed to fulfill his support obligations only grudgingly and sparingly, and even then only after receiving a court order to do so. He would not, however, allow her to have complete possession and utilization of his property (*Rashbam*; cf. *Tosafos*).

4. [Rav Nachman was a colleague of Rav Huna and would call him by his name without the honorific "Rav" (see *Bava Kamma* 96b).]

5. That is, if any of the people who cannot establish a *chazakah* brings proof of ownership, such as witnesses, the court accepts that proof and awards the disputed property to them. This portion of the ruling is, of course, obvious; it is stated only because of the concluding portion, cited next, which is not obvious (*Rashbam*).

6. I.e. witnesses who testify that they saw the original owner convey ownership of the field to the robber or that they heard the owner admit that the field now belongs to the robber (*Rashbam*).

7. As the Gemara explains on 47a and below, citing Rav Kahana, it is not that the witnesses' integrity is in question; rather, we are concerned that the owner's conveyance or admission might have been made under duress, for fear that the robber would otherwise hand him and his possessions over to the requisitioner for impressment into government service (*Rashbam*). [As the Gemara will state below, Rav Huna invalidates conveyance under duress only if the owner does *not* receive payment (ibid.).]

8. *Gittin* 55b.

9. I.e. a gentile thug who threatens to kill the owner if he does not cede him his property (see *Rashbam*).

10. Even if the person who buys the property from the extortionist then approaches the victim and acquires the property from him through a valid *kinyan,* his acquisition is null and void. For there is reason to believe that the owner conveyed ownership to the buyer only because he was afraid that the extortionist would harm him if he did not confirm the transfer to the buyer (see *Rabbeinu Yonah*). Thus, the conveyance has been made under duress and is null and void.

[Actually, the Mishnah there also discusses a case in which conveyance under duress to an extortionist is legally valid — namely, when the government sanctions such extortion from Jews and the owner will therefore have no legal recourse. In that case, the owner — albeit under duress — knowingly cedes his property to the extortionist, fully aware that he will never retrieve it. The conscious and *permanent* nature of that conveyance invests it with legal validity; the owner might not *want* to convey his property, but he willingly does so in order to avoid bodily harm. In the case cited here, however, the government does not sanction extortion. Thus, the owner feels that he will eventually be able to appeal to the authorities and retrieve his property from the extortionist. Therefore, though he goes through the motions of conveying the property to the extortionist, he does not mean to cede it to him permanently. Accordingly, the conveyance is void (see *Rashbam*).]

11. If the Mishnah there voids even the conveyance made by the owner to the extortionist's *buyer* [since even that is attributed to the owner's fear of the extortionist], then certainly a conveyance or admission to the robber himself, which is what Rav Huna discusses, has no legal standing (*Rashbam*).

12. Rav holds that the owner's fear of reprisal will explain only his verbal acquiescence to a transfer of his property. But the owner's issuing a document of transfer [which has not been demanded by the extortionist] indicates that he really does consent to the transfer (see *Rashbam*; cf. *Tosafos* to 48a ד״ה הא איתמר עלה).

13. Even the unsolicited recording and transfer of a document can be attributed to the owner's fear of reprisal, in Shmuel's view.

14. According to the terms of this guarantee, if the property now being conveyed is subsequently taken away from the buyer by the owner's previous creditors and the owner cannot pay him back, the buyer's lien on the owner's other properties allows him to collect them as his refund, even though they have subsequently been sold to others. Shmuel agrees that the unsolicited inclusion of the guarantee clause in the document indicates that the owner really does consent to the transfer (see *Ritva* and *Nimukei Yosef*).

במגורשת ואינה מגורשת וכדרבי זירא (א) דאמר ר' זירא אמר ר' ירמיה בר אבא אמר שמואל (א) כל מקום שאמרו חכמים מגורשת ואינה מגורשת בעלה חייב במזונותיה אמר רב נחמן אמר לי הונא (ב) כולן שהביאו ראיה ראייתן ראיה ומעמידין שדה בידן גזלן שהביא ראיה אין ראייתו ראיה ואין מעמידין שדה בידו מאי קמ"ל תנינא (ג) (ג) לקח מסיקריקון וחזר ולקח מבעל הבית מקחו בטל לאפוקי מדרב דאמר (ג) רב לא שנו אלא דאמר ליה לך חזק וקני אבל בשטר קנה קמ"ל כדשמואל דאמר (ד) אף בשטר נמי לא קנה עד שיכתוב אחריות נכסים (ה) ורב ביבי מסיים בה משמיה דרב נחמן (ו) קרקע אין לו אבל מעות יש לו בד"א (ו) שאמרו עדים בפנינו מנה לו אבל אמרו עדים בפנינו הודה לו לא כדרב כהנא דאמר (א) אי לאו דאודי ליה הוה ממטי ליה לדידיה ולחמריה לשחוור אמר רב הונא (ז) תליוהו וזבין זביניה זביני מ"ט כל דמזבין איניש אי לאו דאניס לא הוה מזבין ואפילו הכי זביניה זביני ודילמא שאני אונסא דנפשיה מאונסא דאחריני אלא (ג) כדתניא

יקריב

רשב"ם

מגורשת ואינה מגורשת. כגון זרק לה גט ספק קרוב לה ספק קרוב לו דבעלה חייב במזונותיה עד דיהיב לה גט ודאי ואיכא למימר כיון דמגורשת ואינה מגורשת אשתו היא וחייב במזונותיה והניח לה בעל קרקע זו בידה כדי שתיזון מפירותיה ולא הויא חזקה קמ"ל דהויא חזקה דכיון דהתחיל בגירושין והוא שונא לה לא יחד לה קרקע למזונותיה כי בטורח יתן לה מזונות בגלמוס כשיתחייבוהו ב"ד: **חייב במזונותיה.** דלאכי לגדלה ביה: **וכולן.** אומן ואריס וכל הנך דלעיל דאמרן אין להן חזקה: **ראיה.** שטר מכירה או עדי מכירה: **ראייתן ראיה.** מילתא דפשיטא היא ומשום סיפא נקט לה: **גזלן שהביא ראיה.** עדי מכירה או עדי הודאה אבל מתן מעות לא ראו: **אין ראייתו ראיה.** כדרב כהנא דאי לאו דאודי ליה או שכתב לו שטר מכירה הוה ממטי ליה ולחמריה לשחוור אבל אם נתן לו הגזלן מעות בפני עדים ראייתו ראיה כדרב הונא לקמיה דאמר תליוהו וזבין זביניה זביני ואע"ג דרב ביבי מוקי לה לקמן להא אפילו בשנתן מעות הגזלן לנגזל ואפ"ה לא קנה גזלן הא אמרינן לקמן בשמעתין דרב ביבי מימרא היא ומימרא לרב הונא לא סבירא ליה וכדרב הונא קיימא לן בשמעתין: **ואין מעמידין שדה בידו.** ולא לכל הבא מכחו כגון בן גזלן או לוקח מגזלן: **מאי קמ"ל.** רב הונא דגזלן דלייתו ראיה ולא קנה: **תנינא.** במסכת גיטין בהניזקין: **לקח מסיקריקון.** מגזלן נכרי הורג נפשות על עסקי ממון שאומר לו שא קרקע זו והניחני ומתנה זו לא הויא מתנה דאפילו למ"ד תליוהו וזבין זביניה זביני תליוהו ויהב לא הויא מתנה וטעמא מפרש בגיטין ג' גזירות גזרו [קמייתא כל דלא קטיל ליקטיל מליעתא כל דקטיל לייתי ארבע זוזי] בתרייתא כל דקטיל ליקטלינהו קמייתא ומליעתא כיון דקטלי נכרים לישראל אגב אונסיה גמר ומקני בתרייתא אמרי האידנא לישקול ולמחר תבענא ליה בדינא והלכך לא קנה הסיקריקון דהא לא נתן מעות אלא גזלה בחנם והלוקח (ג) נמי ממנו לא קנה דקרקע אינה נגזלת ואכתי ברשותא דמריה קמא איתא ואפילו חזר ולקח מבעל הבית שכתב לו שטר כדמפרש לקמן או במתנה או בשטר מכירה בלא מעות דאילו נתן מעות לבעל הבית קנה כרב הונא דהא אפילו סיקריקון עצמו היה קונה אם נתן לו מעות לנגזל והכי מוכח לקמן בשמעתין גבי מילתיה דרב הונא דאית ליה תליוהו וזבין כו' אפילו הכי לא קנה לוקח דמחמת פחד דסיקריקון הקנה לו ללוקח וכיון דאין ראיית הלוקח מגזלן ראיה אפילו כי הדר וזבין מבעל הבית כל שכן וכל שכן דאין ראיית הגזלן עצמו ראיה דמחמת פחד כתב לו השטר ומעולם לא קיבל דמים מן הגזלן דנימא זביניה זביני: ומשני **לאפוקי מדרב.** אתא רב הונא: **דאמר רב.** עלה דההיא משנה: **לא שנו.** דחזר ולקח מבעה"ב מקחו בטל אלא דאמר לו בפני עדים (ד) חזק וקני ומעות לא קיבל בפני עדים דנימא זביניה זביני כדלקמן וגם שטר לא כתב לו בעל הבית ללוקח אבל אם כתב לו שטר ודאי אקני ליה ואתא רב הונא למימר דגזלן שהביא ראיה אפילו בשטר אין ראייתו ראיה כדשמואל: **אף בשטר לא קנה.** דמאימת סיקריקון כתב לו: **ורב ביבי מסיים.** בהא מלתא דאמר רב נחמן א"ל הונא: **משמיה דרב נחמן.** שהיה מוסיף בה רב נחמן דבר זה מדעתו ומיהו רב הונא לא סבירא ליה האי תוספתא כדלקמן בשמעתין דכל היכא דאיכא מתן מעות סבר ליה לרב הונא דהוו זביני ולאו אדרב ושמואל קאי דבמסכת גיטין בהניזקין דאיתא לפלוגתייהו לא איירי רב ביבי כלל התם: **קרקע אין לו.** לגזלן כמו שאמרנו אין מעמידין שדה בידו: **אבל מעות.** שנתן לו הגזלן לנגזל בדמי קרקע זו יש לו שיחזירם לו הנגזל ולא קנסינן ליה לגזלן לאבד מעותיו ושמעינן מהכא דסבירא ליה לרב ביבי תליוהו וזבין לאו זביניה זביני והיינו דאמרינן לקמן דרב הונא לית ליה דרב ביבי: **בד"א.** דמעות יש לו כגון שאמרו עדים בפנינו מנה לו הגזלן לנגזל ונתן לו המעות או שכתבו בשטר אנו ראינו שנתן לו המעות דמשום פחד דסיקריקון דגזלן לא מסהדי וכתבו עדים שיקרא: **אבל אמרו עדים בפנינו הודה לו.** נגזל לגזלן שקיבל ממנו הדמים או שכתבו בשטר המכירה וכך אמר לנו הוו עלי עדים שקיבלתי ממנו הדמים ומכרתי לו לא יחזיר לו מעות לגזלן: **כדרב כהנא כו'.** ומסקנא דמילתא דרב ביבי היא: **תליוהו וזבין.** מי שתלו אותו או עשו לו יסורין עד שמכר וקיבל הדמים ואומר רוצה אני: **זביניה זביני.** ולא יוכל לחזור בו וטעמא מפרש ואזיל: **ואית דגרס תלוה.** ורבינו חננאל כתב תליוהו. ודוקא מכר אבל מתנה לא הויא מתנה דכיון דלא מקבל מידי לא גמר ומקני כדמוכח לקמן דאמרינן מודה שמואל היכא דיהב זוזי: **דכל דמזבין איניש.** רוב חפצים וכלי ביתו וטליתו שאדם מוכר אי לאו דאניס ודחיק במעות לא הוה מזבין ואפ"ה הוה זביניה זביני בעל כרחו אפילו לא גמר ומקני שלא נתנה תורה חילוק במקח וממכר בין דברים הצריכין לו ומכרן לדברים שאין צריכין לו אלא כולהו קונה לוקח וה"נ אע"ג דאניס מוכר קונה לוקח הואיל וקיבל דמים אע"ג דלא גמר ומקני: **שאני אונס דנפשיה.** שצריך למעות ומתוך כך מוכר חפציו מדעתו דהתם איכא למימר גמר ומקני: **מאונסא דאחריני.** שמכריחין אותו למכור דהתם לא גמר ומקני:

יקריב

תוספות

מגורשת ואינה מגורשת בעלה חייב במזונותיה. וכגון שייחד לה ארעא אחריתי דאי לאו הכי אין (ח) לו חזקה דכיון דאית לה מזוני מזוני הוא דקא אכלה כדאמרי' לקמן:

ראייתן ראיה ומעמידין שדה בידן. נראה לרשב"א דנקט תרוייהו אידי דבעי למיתני גבי גזלן אין ראייתו ראיה ואין מעמידין שדה בידו דהשתא איצטריך תרוייהו דאי לא תנא אלא אין ראייתו ראיה הוה אמינא דאין ראייתו ראיה לגבי הא שאין מעמידין שדה בידו אבל מעות יש לו דלא ה"א טעמא אי לאו דאודי ליה הוה ממטי ליה ולחמריה לשחוור אלא הוה מפרשינן טעמא משום דתליוהו וזבין לא הוו זביניה זביני אפי' מנה לו מעות הלכך קאמרי תרוייהו דאין ראייתו ראיה כלל דאפי' מעות אין לו דטעמא הוא משום דאי לאו דאודי ליה כו' והאי כולן נראה לרשב"א דקאי נמי אבן שחלק ואשה שחלקה ושנתגרשה ואע"ג דאמר לקמן [גבי אשה בנכסי בעלה] דלגלויי זוזי הוא דבעי כיון דאוקימנא בהודאה לא שייך בה גלויי זוזי ועוד דמשמע לקמן דסבירא להו לרב הונא ולרב נחמן דלא אמר לגלויי זוזי הוא דבעי: **ומעמידין** שדה בידן. גבי אומן נמי שייך שדה כגון אם הוא בנאי: **אבל** בשטר קנה. אלקח מן האיש וחזר ולקח מן האשה נמי קאי כדמוכח במתני' בהניזקין (גיטין דף נח: ושם) וקשה דתניא בסוף מי שהיה נשוי (כתובות דף צה. ושם ד"ה וכתבה) כתב לראשון ולא חתמה לו לשני וחתמה לו איבדה כתובתה דוקא משום דלא חתמה לראשון אבל אי חתמה לראשון לא איבדה כתובתה כדמוכח התם אע"פ שכתבה שטר ונראה לר"י דהא דקאמר רב בשטר קנה יש להעמיד בשטר הראיה שאחר הקנין דכיון שאחר הקנין עשתה שטר שייפתה כחו כל כך קנה וההיא דכתובות מיירי בשטר מתנה בלא קנין אחר אלא שטר א"נ חתמה דהתם לשון גמר כמו חתמו גבי תורף דגיטין וכמו תורה חתומה ניתנה בהניזקין (גיטין דף ס.) כלומר שגמרה מקח ונתרצתה בעל פה אי נמי חתמה ממש ובשטר של בעל והא דאמר רב בשטר קנה שעשתה שטר מכירה בשמה ומסתבר דטעמא דרב כטעמא דשמואל דאמר בהניזקין (שם דף נח. ושם ד"ה אבל) אף בשטר לא קנה עד שתכתוב לו אחריות ושמואל לטעמיה דאמר בפ"ק דב"מ (דף יד. ושם) אחריות לאו טעות סופר בשטרי מקח וממכר ורב סבר אחריות טעות סופר הוא אבל קצת קשה דלקמן פריך לרב הונא דאמר תליוהו וזבין זביניה זביני מהא דאמר שמואל אף בשטר לא קנה ואי תלוי הדבר באחריות מאי קשה ליה משמואל טפי מרב: **ורב** ביבי מסיים בה כו'. ק"ק הלשון דהא רב ביבי פליג כדאמרי' לקמן ורב הונא לא איירי בהכי אלא בהודה ולא במנה:

אלימא

עין משפט נר מצוה

קעד א מיי' פי"ח מהל' אישות הלכה כה סמג עשין מח טוש"ע אה"ע סי' לג סעיף ג:

קעה ב מיי' פי"ד מהל' טוען הל' א סמג עשין נה טוש"ע ח"מ סי' קנא סעיף א:

קעו ג טוש"ע ח"מ סי' רלו סעיף ד:

קעז ד מיי' פי"ד מהל' טוען הל' ג ועיין במ"מ סמג שם טוש"ע שם וסי' קנא סעיף ג:

קעח ה ו מיי' שם וסמג שם טוש"ע ח"מ סי' קנא סעיף ג:

קעט ז מיי' פ"י מהל' מכירה הל' א ועי' בהשגות ובמ"מ סמג עשין פב טוש"ע ח"מ סי' קנג סעיף א בהג"ה וסי' רה סעיף א [ונכרא אלפס עוד בגיטין פ"ה דף קט.]:

רבינו גרשום

מגורשת ואינ' מגורשת. כגון זרק לה גט ספק קרוב לו דבעלה חייב במזונותיה עד דיהיב לה גט ודאי ואיכא למימר (א) דכ"ל ספק מגורשת דאם איתא דגרשה אית ליה בהדה איבה ולא היה מייחד לה קרקע למזונות כי אם ממקום אחר יהיב לה מזונות בצמצום והויא חזקה: וכולן. בין אומן ובין אריס וכל הני דלעיל שהביאו ראיה. עדות שקנו אותה קרקע ראייתן ראיה והוי חזקה: לקח מן סיקריקון. והוא גזלן שאמרו לו בני אדם מחמת שהוא אנס שא קרקע זו והניחני: וחזר ולקח מבעה"ב (ב) שתפיש לו קנין הנגזל ללוקח שוב שהקרקע של סיקריקון מקחו בטל דבעל כרחיה אודי ליה ולא גמר ומקני ליה אלמא דראיה של גזלן אינה ראיה. ומשני הך ברייתא איצטריך למתני לאפוקי מדרב דאמר לא שנו דמקחו בטל אלא דאמר לו בעה"ב לך חזק בקרקע וקני משו"ה מצי לאחזוקי בה משום דבעל כרחיה קאמר אבל אי כתב ליה בעל הבית שטר מכירה קנה: קמ"ל. רב נחמן דאפ"ה לא קנה כדשמואל וכו' אחריות. דלא מפיק ליה מידיה: ורב ביבי מסיים בה משמיה דרב נחמן. להיכא דחזר ולקח מבעל הבית מקחו בטל דקרקע אין לו ללוקח אבל מעות יש לו: בד"א. דמעות יש לו ללוקח כגון שאמרו עדים בפנינו מנה לו המעות לבעה"ב אבל אמרו העדים בפנינו הודה לו המוכר להסיקריקון ולא ראו נתינת המעות אפי' מעות אין לו דהאי דאודי ליה כדרב כהנא וכו'. אמר רב הונא. אי אמרו ואיימו לאיש תלוהו בעץ אי לא מזבין לו שדהו חזבין מחמת יראה זביניה זביני אע"ג דאנסוהו: אי לאו דאניס. שאין לו מעות להוציא לצרכיו:

מסורת הש"ס

א) ב"מ יב: ע"ש גיטין עד. ע"ש כתובות לז: ע"ש, ב) גיטין נה:, ג) [שם נח.], ד) [שם], ה) [לקמן מח.], ו) ב"ק סב. [לקמן מח:], ז) ערכין כא. קדושין נ. יבמות קו. כ"ה ו, ח) בס"י לה:

הגהות הב"ח

(א) גמ' דאמר רב כהנא אי לאו דאודי: (ב) שם אלא מדמנינא יקריב: (ג) רשב"ם ד"ה לקח וכו' והלוקח ממנו נמי לא קנה: (ד) ד"ה דאמר רב וכו' בפני עדים לך חזק:

ליקוטי רש"י

כל מקום שאמרו חכמים מגורשת ואינה מגורשת. כגון זרק לה גיטה ספק קרוב לה ספק קרוב לו ברשות הרבים [ב"מ יב:]. בעלה חייב במזונותיה. בחיין [ולשמעינן מתני' דוקא בחיין] משום דמעוכבת בשבילו להנשא אבל לאחר מיתה לא דדלמא גרושה הוו ואין לה מזונות דמספיקא לא מפקי' ממונא [כתובות צז:]. לקח מסיקריקון. בשעה שישראל מופקרין להריגה ואמר לעובד כוכבים שא קרקע זו או עבד זה והניחני [גיטין מד.]. סיקריקון. עובד כוכבים רוצח שנותן לו ישראל קרקע בפדיון נפשו ואומר לו שא קרקע זו ואל תמיתני. מקחו בטל. דאמרי' מירמא הוא דאי נמי השני טוח לי והראשון קשה [שם נח:]. לא שנו. דמקחו בטל. אלא דאמר ליה. בעלים לזה שלקח מסיקריקון. לך חזק וקני. בקנין דיבורא בעלמא הוא איכא למימר השני טוח לי. אבל. אי כתב ליה בשטר בשמיה. קני. דכולי האי לא הוה ליה למיעבד אי לאו דזבנה ליה מכר גמור ומדעת. דאי טרפה לה מיניה לגביה דמי ארעא [שם נח.].

חשק שלמה על רבינו גרשום

א) אולי צ"ל ואיכא למימר דאין לה חזקה קמ"ל כיון דהתחיל בגירושין וכו'. ב) אולי צ"ל שאמר לו הנגזל ללוקח לך חזק וקני והודה לו שוב שהקרקע שלו וכו'.

robber's proof of ownership is not acceptable, means to teach that even if he produces a document attesting to his ownership of the property, his claim is rejected. For the owner might have felt compelled to issue the document, as Shmuel taught.

Concerning this statement of Rav Huna that a robber's proof of acquisition is disregarded and the field is not placed in his hands, the Gemara observes:

וְרַב בִּיבִי מְסַיֵּים בָּהּ מִשְּׁמֵיהּ דְּרַב נַחְמָן – And Rav Bivi concludes it in the name of Rav Nachman himself:[15] **קַרְקַע אֵין לוֹ – [The robber] does not get** the **land,** **אֲבָל מָעוֹת יֵשׁ לוֹ – but** his **money is** refunded **to him.** I.e. if the robber paid the owner for the land that he extorted from him, the owner, upon retrieving his land through the courts, must return the robber's money. We do not penalize the robber by depriving him of that money.[16]

Rav Bivi continues:

בַּמֶּה דְּבָרִים אֲמוּרִים – When does this ruling (that the owner must refund the robber's money) **apply?**[17] **שֶׁאָמְרוּ עֵדִים בְּפָנֵינוּ מָנָה לוֹ – Where witnesses say,** either in oral deposition or in the signed document itself, **"[The robber] counted** out **the money to him in our presence."**[18] **אֲבָל אָמְרוּ עֵדִים בְּפָנֵינוּ הוֹדָה לוֹ – However, if the witnesses say,** either in oral deposition or in the signed document itself, **"[The owner] admitted to [the robber] in our presence** that he received payment,**"** **לֹא** – then the robber does **not** receive that money upon restoring the property to its owner. We do not rely on the owner's admission in this matter, **כִּדְרַב כַּהֲנָא דְּאָמַר – in accordance with Rav Kahana, who says:** **אִי לָאו דְּאוֹדֵי לֵיהּ – Had [the original owner] not admitted [to the robber]** what he demanded of him, **הֲוָה מַמְטֵי לֵיהּ לְדִידֵיהּ וּלְחַמְרֵיהּ לְשַׁחְווּר – [the robber] would have handed him and his donkey over to the requisitioner.**[19] Thus, we cannot rely on the owner's admission, since it might have been motivated by fear of reprisals.

The Gemara cites another ruling of Rav Huna:

אָמַר רַב הוּנָא – Rav Huna said: **תַּלְיוּהוּ וְזַבִּין – If they hung him up** or otherwise subjected him to distress **until he** finally relented and **sold** to them what they demanded, **זְבִינֵיהּ זְבִינֵי – his sale is a** valid **sale.** Though he sold it under duress, he cannot retract. **מַאי טַעְמָא – What is the rationale** for this rule? **כָּל דְּמִזַּבֵּין אִינִישׁ – Whatever** personal effects **a person sells,** **אִי לָאו דְּאָנִיס לֹא הֲוָה מְזַבֵּין – were it not that he was pressed** for money, **he would not sell;** **וַאֲפִילּוּ הָכִי זְבִינֵיהּ זְבִינֵי – nevertheless, his sale is a** valid **sale.**[20] Just as a sale compelled by financial distress is valid, so too is a sale compelled by physical distress a valid sale.

The Gemara challenges this comparison:

וְדִילְמָא שָׁאנֵי אוּנְסָא דְּנַפְשֵׁיהּ מֵאוּנְסָא דְּאַחֲרִינֵי – But perhaps self-coercion is different from external coercion.[21] **– ? –**

The Gemara concedes this objection and seeks another source for Rav Huna's validation of a forced sale:

אֶלָּא כִּדְתַנְיָא – Rather, the source that a forced sale is valid is **as was taught in a Baraisa:**

NOTES

15. Rav Bivi reports that after Rav Nachman cited the above ruling in the name of Rav Huna, Rav Nachman concluded with the following remarks of his own (*Rashbam*).

16. This addendum is strictly the view of Rav Nachman, not of Rav Huna. For, as the Gemara will cite shortly, Rav Huna is of the opinion that a *sale* under duress is valid. Accordingly, Rav Huna's ruling above that the robber's proof of acquisition is meaningless referred solely to where the robber did *not* pay the owner for his property. Rav Nachman, who concludes that the robber gets his money back, argues with Rav Huna on this point and extends Rav Huna's ruling invalidating the acquisition of a robber even to cases in which the robber does pay the owner for his property. Rav Nachman adds, however, that the robber does get his money back upon the property's return to its owner (*Rashbam*).

17. That is, how are we to know whether or not the robber actually paid the owner?

18. We accept at face value their testimony that the robber paid and do not suspect that they are so intimidated by the robber that they would testify falsely (*Rashbam*).

19. See above, 47a and beginning of note 11 there.

20. The Torah makes no distinction between a person's sale of items that he would really prefer to retain and items that he does not need. Either sale is equally valid. Thus, we see that a sale is valid even if the seller acquiesced only under some form of pressure (see *Rashbam*).

[According to Rav Huna, the Mishnah cited above, which invalidates an extortionist's acquisition, refers only to a case in which he did not pay the owner for the field. Similarly, when the Mishnah there speaks of someone buying the field from the extortionist and then acquiring it from the original owner, the intent is that the extortionist's buyer did not pay anything to the original owner, but merely sought to have him cede the property to him through some act of *kinyan*. Had either the extortionist or his buyer paid the original owner for the land, the situation would be one of sale under duress, which is valid in Rav Huna's view (*Rashbam* above ד״ה לקח מסקריקון).]

[Rav Huna rules only that a *sale* under duress is valid, since in the final analysis the seller agrees to the transaction and receives payment. But Rav Huna agrees that a *gift* under duress is not a valid gift, since the donor has received nothing in return (*Rashbam*; cf. note 10 above). See 48a for further elaboration.]

21. Possibly, it is only when no one else's will is being imposed upon the person that, in the final analysis, he sells a treasured item with genuine consent, although circumstances have compelled him to sell. But when others coerce him to sell, perhaps there is no genuine consent on his part (*Rashbam*).

The Torah states concerning sacrificial offerings that a person has become obligated to bring through a vow: "יַקְרִיב אֹתוֹ" – *HE SHALL BRING IT;*[1] מְלַמֵּד שֶׁכּוֹפִין אוֹתוֹ – THIS TEACHES THAT WE COMPEL HIM to fulfill his obligation to bring the offering.[2] יָכוֹל בְּעַל כָּרְחוֹ – Were that all the Torah stated, IT WOULD BE POSSIBLE to infer that he must bring it even AGAINST HIS WILL. תַּלְמוּד לוֹמַר לִרְצוֹנוֹ – Therefore, THE TORAH STATES: *WILLINGLY,* to teach that he must bring the sacrifice willingly. הָא כֵּיצַד – HOW IS THIS? What is the situation in which he is compelled to bring it, yet he brings it willingly? כּוֹפִין אוֹתוֹ עַד שֶׁיֹּאמַר רוֹצֶה אֲנִי – WE COMPEL HIM UNTIL HE SAYS, "I AM WILLING to bring it." Thus, we see that consent obtained by the use of force is deemed consent with regard to sacrificial law. Rav Huna applies this principle to the laws of acquisition and rules that a sale is valid even if the seller was forced to consent to it.[3]

The Gemara rejects this as a source for Rav Huna's ruling: וְדִלְמָא שָׁאנֵי הָתָם – **But perhaps it is different there** in the case of a sacrifice, דְּנִיחָא לֵיהּ דְּתֶיהֱוֵי לֵיהּ כַּפָּרָה – **for he is content that [the offering] should be an atonement for him.**[4] Only in such a case is his forced consent deemed genuine, since there is an objective reason for him to want what he is being forced to do.[5] We cannot prove from here, however, that forced consent is deemed genuine in a case of forced sale, where the person, though he loses nothing by the transaction, does not profit either. – ? –

The Gemara proposes a new source for Rav Huna's validation of a forced sale:

וְאֶלָּא מִסֵּיפָא – **Rather,** this can be derived **from the latter portion** of the Baraisa just cited, which states: וְכֵן אַתָּה אוֹמֵר בְּגִיטֵּי נָשִׁים – AND SIMILARLY DO YOU SAY this rule IN REGARD TO BILLS OF DIVORCE, where a recalcitrant husband refuses to grant a divorce:[6] כּוֹפִין אוֹתוֹ עַד שֶׁיֹּאמַר רוֹצֶה אֲנִי – WE COMPEL HIM UNTIL HE SAYS, "I AM WILLING to grant the divorce." Although a bill of divorce is not valid without the husband's consent,[7] nevertheless a forced consent is sufficient. Thus, we see that a forced consent is deemed genuine and the same should apply in regard to a forced sale.[8]

The Gemara rejects this source as well:

וְדִלְמָא שָׁאנֵי הָתָם – **But perhaps it is different there** in the case of divorce, דְּמִצְוָה לִשְׁמוֹעַ דִּבְרֵי חֲכָמִים – **for it is a religious obligation to heed the directives of the Sages,** who ordained in this particular situation that the husband should divorce his wife. Thus, there is an objective reason for him to consent to the forced divorce,[9] which is not the case in regard to a forced sale. – ? –

The Gemara provides another source for Rav Huna's ruling:

אֶלָּא סְבָרָא הוּא – **Rather, it is** derived by **logic:** אַגַּב אוּנְסֵיהּ גָּמַר וּמַקְנֶה – **Because of his duress, he decides to convey ownership** willingly.[10]

Rav Yehudah challenges this reasoning:

מוֹתִיב רַב יְהוּדָה – **Rav Yehudah challenged** this reasoning from a Mishnah, which states: גֵּט הַמְעוּשֶּׂה – A COERCED DIVORCE – בְּיִשְׂרָאֵל כָּשֵׁר – if it was obtained BY JEWISH [AUTHORITIES], acting in accordance with Jewish law – IS VALID, if the husband finally relents and says, "I am willing." וּבְעוֹבְדֵי כּוֹכָבִים פָּסוּל – BUT if it was obtained BY IDOLATERS, the divorce IS NOT VALID.[11] וּבְעוֹבְדֵי כּוֹכָבִים – AND IF the Jewish court wishes to employ IDOLATERS as agents to force compliance with the directives of the Jewish court, חוֹבְטִין אוֹתוֹ וְאוֹמְרִין לוֹ – then the idolatrous enforcers are instructed to STRIKE [THE RECALCITRANT HUSBAND] WHILE SAYING TO HIM, עֲשֵׂה מַה שֶּׁיִּשְׂרָאֵל אוֹמֵר לְךָ – "DO AS THE JEWISH [AUTHORITIES] DIRECT YOU to do," and the divorce is then valid.[12] Having cited this Mishnah, Rav Yehudah concludes his challenge: וְאַמַּאי – **Now, why** is the divorce not valid if coerced by idolaters on their own? הָתָם נַמִּי נֵימָא אַגַּב אוּנְסֵיהּ גָּמַר וּמְגָרֵשׁ – **There, too, let us say that because of his duress, he decides to divorce** willingly.[13] – ? –

NOTES

1. *Leviticus* 1:3. The complete verse reads: אִם־עֹלָה קָרְבָּנוֹ מִן־הַבָּקָר זָכָר תָּמִים יַקְרִיבֶנּוּ אֶל־פֶּתַח אֹהֶל מוֹעֵד יַקְרִיב אֹתוֹ לִרְצֹנוֹ לִפְנֵי ה׳, *If his sacrifice is an olah of cattle, an unblemished male shall he bring it; to the entrance of the Tabernacle he shall bring it, willingly, to Hashem.*

2. The Torah could have left out the words יַקְרִיב אֹתוֹ altogether (*Rashbam*). Their appearance, therefore, is intended to teach us some new law; namely, *he shall bring it* – whether he wants to or not. [*Malbim* (ad loc.) explains that the Baraisa expounds the extraneous expression "he shall bring it" as an exhortation to the court.]

3. [As explained above, Rav Huna validates only a forced sale, but not a forced gift. The rationale for that distinction is that the coerced person does not really lose anything in the case of a sale, since he receives monetary compensation; therefore, his consent, though obtained under duress, is deemed genuine. In the case of a forced gift, however, the coerced person is losing by the transaction; hence, we cannot assert that his forced consent is genuine, and the transaction is void. The case of a forced offering, though it is one in which the vower loses an animal, is nevertheless comparable to a case of forced sale. For although the vower does not receive any *monetary* compensation, he receives in return the fulfilment of his religious obligation (see *Tosafos* ד״ה אילימא and *Rashbam* below ד״ה התם נמי נימא).]

4. Although the verse cited by the Baraisa deals with a voluntarily offered *olah* sacrifice, rather than with the expiatory *chatas* offering, the concept of "atonement" is still applicable, since by bringing the offering he avoids violating the vow he made to offer it (*Tosafos* ד״ה יקריב).

5. See below, note 9.

6. The Mishnah in *Kesubos* 77a lists the cases in which the court compels a husband to grant his wife a divorce.

7. For the Torah (*Deuteronomy* 24:1) prescribes that וְנָתַן בְּיָדָהּ, *[the husband] places [the bill of divorce] in her hand,* which implies that he must do so willingly (*Rashbam*).

8. [The case of a forced divorce is comparable to that of a forced sale, not to that of a forced gift (which Rav Huna agrees is not valid). See below, note 13.]

9. As *Rambam* explains in *Hil. Gerushin* 2:20, we assume that every Jew who wishes to remain with that designation actually desires to heed the words of the Rabbis, and it is only the influence of his evil inclination that incites him to do otherwise. Thus, when this external desire is overcome by force, the person's declaration that he wants to comply with the law is an expression of his true will.

10. Rav Huna considers it logical to assume that the combination of distress [which the person seeks to alleviate] and the receipt of money causes the person to relent and genuinely consent to the sale that is being forced upon him, since in the final analysis he does not lose anything by it (*Rashbam*).

11. Even if the husband finally relented and said, "I am willing." Apparently, the divorce is not valid in this case because the factor of heeding the words of the Rabbis is lacking (*Rashbam*). [It is from this ruling of the Mishnah that Rav Yehudah challenges Rav Huna – see *Tosafos.*]

12. In this latter case, the coercion is being done under the auspices of the Jewish court, with the idolaters simply being used as the agents of that coercion. The husband is indeed duty bound to fulfill the directives of the Sages by divorcing his wife and the factor of his fulfillment of his religious obligation is present.

13. Even when there is no religious obligation for the husband to divorce his wife, he loses nothing by divorcing her, for the wife who sues for divorce obviously hates her husband and will not remain with him even if the divorce is not granted. The bill of divorce simply gives legal force to a separation that is already a practical reality and allows her to remarry. Consequently, the situation is comparable to one of forced sale [see above, note 3] and the divorce should be valid, according to Rav Huna's logic, if the husband finally relents and says, "I am willing" (*Rashbam*).

(ד) **אילימא** מהא דתניא יקריב אותו מלמד שכופין אותו יכול בעל כרחו תלמוד לומר לרצונו הא כיצד [א] כופין אותו עד שיאמר רוצה אני ודלמא שאני התם דניחא ליה דתיהוי ליה כפרה ואלא מסיפא [א] וכן אתה אומר בגיטי נשים [ב] כופין אותו עד שיאמר רוצה אני ודלמא שאני התם [ג] דמצוה לשמוע דברי חכמים אלא סברא הוא אגב אונסיה גמר ומקנה מותיב רב יהודה [ג] גט המעושה בישראל כשר (א) ובעכו"ם פסול [ד] ובעכו"ם חובטין אותו ואומרין לו עשה מה שישראל אומר לך ואמאי התם נמי נימא אגב אונסיה גמר ומגרש הא איתמר עלה [ז] אמר רב משרשיא דבר תורה אפילו בעכו"ם (ב) כשר ומה טעם אמרו בעכו"ם פסול כדי שלא תהא כל אחת ואחת הולכת ותולה עצמה ביד עכו"ם ומפקעת עצמה מיד בעלה מותיב רב המנונא [ה] לקח מסיקריקון וחזר ולקח מבעל הבית מקחו בטל ואמאי התם נמי נימא אגב אונסיה גמר ומקני הא אתמר עלה [ו] אמר רב לא שנו אלא דאמר ליה לך חזק וקני אבל בשטר קנה ולשמואל דאמר אף בשטר נמי לא קנה מאי איכא למימר מודה שמואל היכא דיהיב זוזי [ח] ולרב ביבי דמסיים בה משמיה דרב נחמן קרקע אין לו מעות יש לו מאי איכא למימר רב ביבי [ט] מימרא הוא ומימרא לרב הונא לא סבירא ליה אמר רבא הלכתא תליוהו וזבין זביניה זביני ולא אמרן אלא בשדה

רש"י

יקריב אותו. קרא יתירא דהא כתיב לעיל זכר תמים יקריבנו ומלי למיכתב יקריבנו אל פתח אהל מועד לרצונו לפני ה': **מלמד שכופין אותו.** להקריב מה שנדר: **עד שיאמר רוצה אני.** אלמא היכא דכופין אותו עד דאמר מתוך יסורין רוצה אני קרינא ביה לרצונו דגמר בלבו להקריב והוא הדין לזביני אם אמר רוצה אני הוי זביני דגמר בלבו להקנות: **דתיהוי ליה כפרה.** וכי אמר רוצה אני ודאי בלב שלם קאמר: **וכן אתה אומר בגיטי נשים.** בהכך דתנן (כתובות עז.) ואלו שכופין אותו להוציא מוכה שחין ובעל פוליפוס דכופין ומכין אותו עד שיאמר רוצה אני דנותן מדעתו משמע: **דלמא.** התם נמי כי אמר רוצה אני גמר בלבו לגרשה דמצוה קעביד מאחר שחייבוהו חכמים להוציא: **אלא.** רב הונא מסברא דידיה קאמר דמתוך יסורים גמר בלבו ומקני הואיל ואיכא תרתי יסורים ומתן מעות דלא מפסיד מידי: **גט המעושה.** שכופין אותו לבעל להוציא אם בישראל הוא כשר שכפוהו ישראל וכגון דאמר רוצה אני: **בעכו"ם פסול.** ואע"ג דאמר רוצה אני וקא ס"ד דמקשה דבישראל כשר משום דמצוה לשמוע דברי חכמים ובעכו"ם פסול כיון דליכא מצוה אגב אונסי' לא גמר (ג) ומקנה ומגרש וקשיא לרב הונא דכיון דליכא מצוה לא מקני אגב אונסיה: **ובעכו"ם.** אם אנו רוצים לכופו על ידי עכו"ם ויהיה הגט כשר מלמדים אנו לעכו"ם שיאמרו לו עשה מה שישראל אומר לך דהשתא נמי מצוה לשמוע דברי חכמים: **התם נמי נימא אגב אונסי' גמר ומגרש.** דהא לא מפסיד מידי דומיא דזביני שמקבל דמי שדהו דכיון דאשתו שונאתו ובלא גט נמי לא תעמוד אצלו וגט זה אינו אלא להתירה לאחרי' לא מפסיד כלום: **אפילו בעכו"ם כשר.** דאגב אונסיה גמר וגרש דלא מפסיד מידי כדפרישית: **פסול.** מדרבנן וצריכה גט אחר ומיהו אם פשטה ידה וקבלה קדושין מאחר צריכה גט מזה ומזה: **ותולה עצמה ביד עכו"ם.** להחניף לו ולזנות עמו עד שיכריח את בעלה לגרשה: **נימא אגב אונסיה.** דסיקריקון גמר ומקני בעל הבית כיון דיהיב ליה זוזי ולא מפסיד מידי דהיינו תליוהו וזבין: **מודה שמואל דהיכא דיהיב ליה זוזי.** זה הלוקח מן הסיקריקון כשחזר ולקח מבעל הבית יהב ליה זוזי לבעל הבית דאגב דמקבל זוזי גמר ומקני דהיינו תליוהו וזבין אבל בלא מעות לא גמר ומקני דהא רב הונא נמי תליוהו וזבין קאמר אבל תליוהו ויהיב לא הוי מתנה: **ולרב ביבי דמסיים בה לעיל.** במילתיה דרב נחמן דאמר גזלן שהביא ראיה אין לאיתויי ראיה ואין מעמידין שדה בידו ואוסיף רב ביבי אבל מעות יש לו לגזלן שנתן לנגזל אלמא ס"ל לרב ביבי דאפי' נתן הגזלן לנגזל מעות לא קנה דתליוהו וזבין לא הוי זביני והוא הדין להך משנה דסיקריקון דאי נתן הסיקריקון או הלוקח ממנו לבעל הבית מעות דמי השדה לא קנה וקשיא לרב הונא: **מימרא הוא.** שהיה אומר משום אחרים ואינה לא משנה ולא ברייתא ואי הוה אמר לה רב ביבי משמיה דנפשיה הוה מהדר גמרא גברא אגברא קרמית בתמיה:

תוספות

(ד) **אילימא מהא דתניא יקריב אותו.** וא"ת אי מהכא גמר אפילו תליוהו ויהיב נמי מתנה הוי והא"ל דסיקריקון מוכח דלאינה מתנה ויש לומר רוצה לתרץ דהכא הוי כמו מכר דהא יש לו כפרה תחת הקרבן וקונה הכפרה ומגיטי נשים דבעי למיגמר מינייהו הוי נמי כמו מכר שנפטר על ידי כך משאר כסות ועונה אבל אי אפשר לומר כן דא"כ גט מעושה שלא כדין נמי יהא כשר ובהמגרש (גיטין דף פח:) (שם) אמר שמואל דפסול ותירץ ר"י דכל דבר שהוא מחוייב לעשות הוי כמו מכר והכא הרי הוא מחויב להביא קרבן ולקמן נמי מחויב הוא לגרש את אשתו דמיירי דהנהו שכופין אותן להוציא אבל שלא כדין הוה כמו תליוהו ויהיב דלא הויא מתנה:

יקריב אותו מלמד שכופין אותו. לא דמי להא דאמר בפ' שור שנגח ארבעה וחמשה (ב"ק דף מ.) חייבי חטאות ואשמות אין ממשכנין אותן משום דכיון דלכפרה קאתו לא בעי משכוני דדוקא חטאות ואשמות שבאות על חטא לא בעי משכוני שרוצה שמאותו חטא יהיה לו כפרה אבל הכא נדר או נדבה אין מכפרים והא דקאמר ניחא ליה דתיהוי ליה כפרה היינו ממה שנדר שאם לא ישלם נדרו עונו ישא והא דאמר בתורת כהנים ובזבחים (דף ו.) וביומא (דף לו.) דעולה מכפרת על חייבי עשה הא אמר בפ"ק דזבחים (דף ז:) דעולה דורון היא ולא מכפרת מקופיא (ה) מכפרת מקיבעא לא מכפרת [ט]:

אלא סברא הוא דאגב אונסיה גמר ומקני. וא"ת כיון דמסברא ידעינן דאגב אונסיה גמר ומקני אמאי איצטריך קרא גבי קרבן למיכתב דכופין אותו וי"ל דאי לאו קרא הוה אמינא אע"ג דגמר ומקני כיון דאינו מתרצה אלא על ידי כפייה פסול הוא לגבי מזבח דזבח רשעים הוא קמ"ל שהקרבן נרצה: **גט מעושה בישראל כשר** (א) **בעכו"ם פסול.** בסיפא מסיים ובעכו"ם חובטין אותו ואומרים לו עשה מה שישראל אומר לך ויש מפרשים דהוי פירושא דרישא כילד בעכו"ם פסול (ו) חובטין אותו ואומרים לו כו' ואין נראה דא"כ אדפריך ליה הכא מסיפא ליסייעיה מרישא דקתני ובישראל כשר דאגב אונסי' גמר ומקני וכי תימא (ז) דבישראל כשר משום דמצוה לשמוע דברי חכמים דא"כ בעכו"ם נמי אמאי פסול והא חובטין אותו לעשות דברי חכמים ונראה לר"י דהכי קאמר דבעכו"ם נמי כשר וכגון שאומר לו עשה מה שישראל (ח) אומר לך וכן מפרש בהלכות גדולות והכי מוכח בתוספתא דקתני ובעכו"ם חובטין אותו ואומר לו עשה מה שפלוני אומר לך משמע דעל פי ר' פלוני שהוא חכם חובטין אותו וכשר הוא שהוא אומר להם לחובטו וכן משמע [י] בירושלמי דגיטין דקאמר התם רב אמר ישראל שעשה כמעשה עכו"ם כשר באומר איני זן ואיני מפרנס תנא ר' חייא עכו"ם שעשו כמעשה ישראל פסול ואפי' אמר איני זן ואיני מפרנס הדא מתני' אמרה כן ובעכו"ם חובטין אותו ואומר לו עשה מה שישראל אומר לך ולא מה שאני אומר לך והא דאמר בגיטין (דף פח:) לפניהם ולא לפני עכו"ם כיון שהעישוי על פי דייני ישראל לאו היינו לפני עכו"ם דלפני עכו"ם היינו כשהעישוי נעשה על פי דייני עכו"ם [כ]:

דבר תורה אפילו בעכו"ם כשר. דכיון דבדין מעשים כאותן שכופין אותו להוציא דבישראל נמי אי שלא כדין מעשה פסול כדאמר שמואל בהמגרש (גיטין דף פח: ושם) וא"ת ומאי נפקא מינה אם תולה בעכו"ם ומפקעת עצמה מיד בעלה דכיון דבדין עבדה וגם חכמים היו כופין אותו להוציא וי"ל דגזרו כדין אטו שלא כדין וא"ת להוה טעמא דמפרש בהמגרש דבעכו"ם פסול דבר תורה משום לפניהם ולא לפני עכו"ם ועכו"ם לאו בני עישוי נינהו תקשה ליה לרב הונא אמאי פסול נימא דאגב אונסיה גמר ומגרש וי"ל כיון שעל ידי כפיית עכו"ם נותנו הוי שלא כדין ושלא כדין הוי כמו מתנה כדפרישית לעיל וא"ת ואמאי מייתי הכא דרב משרשיא ההוא דהתם הוה ליה לאיתויי (ט) דהא אמר התם דהא דרב משרשיא בדותא היא וי"ל דלפי סברת המקשה דחשיב עכו"ם בני עישוי מתרץ לו דפריך ליה בעכו"ם אמאי פסול ואי לאו דבני עישוי נינהו לא הוה פריך ולא מידי דהוי כמו מתנה ולסברתו משני ליה כדרב משרשיא: **הא איתמר עלה אמר רב לא שנו.** תימה לרשב"א דמשמע דלא אמר רב הונא תליוהו וזבין זביניה זביני אלא בשטר אבל בלך חזק וקני לא וכיון דאגב אונסיה גמר ומקני מה לי האי ומה לי האי ועוד הקשה דקאמר ומודה שמואל היכא דיהיב זוזי משמע דלרב קני אפי' לא יהיב זוזי ואמאי והא תליוהו ויהיב לא הוי מתנה ותירץ דהכי פליגי רב ושמואל דקסבר רב דאי לאו דיהיב זוזי לא הוה עביד שטר ושמואל סבר דמחמת אונס עביד שטר אבל אחריות לא היה מקבל כדאמר בהנזקין (שם דף נח.) עד שיכתוב לו אחריות נכסים: **אמר רבא הלכתא תליוהו וזבין זביניה זביני.** לאו דוקא נקט תליוהו דאפילו בלא יסורין אלא מחמת אונס ממון כי ההוא מעשה דפרדיסא (לעיל דף מ:) הוו זביני ואם מסר מודעא לא הוו זביני דקיימא לן כרב הונא [דכתבינן] מודעא אזביני כדפירש הקונטרס ודוקא מכר אבל מתנה תליוהו ויהיב לא הויא מתנה אפילו לא מסר מודעא אי דידעי עדים אונסיה והיכא דמסר מודעא אפי' לא ידעי אונסיה כתבינן וכן בגיטין והיכא

מסורת הש"ס

א) [יבמות קו.] קדושין נ. ע"ש ערכין כא., ב) [יבמות כ. וש"נ], ג) גיטין פח., ד) [שם], ה) [שם נה:], ו) [שם מז.], ז) [לעיל מז:], ח) [גיטין מב:], ט) [וע' תוס' ר"ה ו. ד"ה יקריב], י) [בתוס' גיטין פח: ד"ה ובעכו"ם מייתו הירושלמי בהיפך ועי' מהרש"ם], כ) [ועי' תוס' גיטין פח: ד"ה ובעכו"ם מוכחין].

הגהות הב"ח

(א) גמ' בישראל כשר ובעכו"ם כצ"ל ואות ו' נמחק: (ב) שם דבר תורה אפילו בעכו"ם נמי כשר: (ג) רשב"ם ד"ה בעכו"ם פסול וכו' לא גמר ומגרש וכו' ותיבת ומקנה נמחק: (ד) תוס' ד"ה אלא דלמא דתניא יקריב: (ה) ד"ה יקריב וכו' מקופיא. נ"ב פי' כפרה מכפרת אבל עדיין קפויה ונפה עי' פ"ק דזבחים: (ו) ד"ה גט וכו' כילד בעכו"ם פסול כגון שם חובטין אותו: (ז) בא"ד וכי תימא דבעמעת דבישראל כשר: (ח) בא"ד עשה מה שישראל פלוני אומר לך וכו' דעל פי רב פלוני: (ט) ד"ה דבר וכו' הוה ליה לאיתויי הכא דהא אמר:

תורה אור השלם

א) אִם עֹלָה קָרְבָּנוֹ מִן הַבָּקָר זָכָר תָּמִים יַקְרִיבֶנּוּ אֶל פֶּתַח אֹהֶל מוֹעֵד יַקְרִיב אֹתוֹ לִרְצֹנוֹ לִפְנֵי יְיָ: [ויקרא א, ג]

ליקוטי רש"י

יקריב אותו וכו'. קרא יתירא הוא דהא כתיב ברישא דקרא זכר תמים יקריבנו. שכופין אותו. לקיים דברי נדרו. דמצוה לשמוע דברי חכמים. ואית לן לאחזוקיה בחזקת מקיים מלוה וגמר בלבו לקיים דברי בית דין [קידושין נ.]. גט המעושה. בחזקה. ותולה עצמה ביד עכו"ם. שכולת עובד כוכבים אנס לכוף בעלה לגרשה ובאה עליו בעקיפין [גיטין פח:]. לקח מסיקריקון. עיין ליקוטי רש"י לעיל מז:. ולרב ביבי דמסיים בה. בהא מלתא דאמר רב נחמן. משמיה דרב נחמן. שהיה מוסיף בה רב נחמן דבר זה מדעתו ומיהו רב הונא לא סבירא ליה הא תוספתא כלל דלקמן בשמעתין דכל היכא דליכא מתן מעות סבר ליה לרב הונא דהוו זביני ולאו אדרב הונא קאי דבמסכת גיטין בהניזקין דאיתא לפלוגתייהו לא איירי רב ביבי כלל [רשב"ם לעיל מז:]. מימרא הוא. בעלמא היא ואינה לא משנה ולא ברייתא [גיטין מב:]. תליוהו וזבין. מי שתלו אותו עד שנתרצה לו למכור ומכר ואפילו הכי קיבל הדמים אלמא גמר ומקני [רשב"ם שם].

עין משפט נר מצוה

קפא א מיי' פי"ד מהל' מעשה קרבנות הל' טז סמג לאוין קנא:
קפב ב ג מיי' פ"ב מהל' גירושין הל' כ סמג עשין נ טוש"ע אה"ע סי' קלד סעיף ה וסי' קנד סעיף כא:
קפג ד מיי' שם וסמג שם טוש"ע שם סי' קלד סעיף ח:
קפד ה מיי' שם טוש"ע שם סעיף ט:

רבינו גרשום

יקריב אותו. דלגבי עולה אותו יתירא הוא וקאמר מלמד דכופין אותו להקריב כשנדר. דניחא ליה דתיהוי ליה כפרה בקרבנו וגמר ומתרצה: כופין אותו. ליתן גט לאותן שכופין אותן להוציא כגון מוכה שחין ובעל [פוליפוס] כו': התם נמי סבר. האי מוכה שחין מצוה לשמוע דברי חכמים שגזרו כן ומתרצה. אלא סברא דכי אמר תליוהו וזבין דזביניה זביני דאגב אונסי' גמר ומקני: גט המעושה. ע"י ב"ד ישראל כשר: תולה עצמה בעכו"ם א) שאנס עצמה לגרשה. התם נמי נימא אגב אונסיה גמר בעל הבית ומקני ליה: מודה שמואל היכא דיהיב זוזי. דגמר ומקני ליה: מאי איכא למימר. אמאי אפי' קרקע בדין הוא דיש לו דאגב אונסיה גמר ומקני. אין ודאי יש לו קרקע. והא דרב ביבי מימרא היא ואינה עיקר דאינה לא משנה ולא ברייתא כי אם מימרא בעלמא.

חשק שלמה על רבינו גרשום

א) נראה דל"ל שאנס את בעלה לגרשה.

The Gemara answers:

הָא אִיתְּמַר עֲלָהּ – **It was indeed said** in elaboration **upon [that Mishnah]:** אָמַר רַב מְשַׁרְשִׁיָּא דְּבַר תּוֹרָה אֲפִילוּ בְּעוֹבְדֵי כּוֹכָבִים כָּשֵׁר – **Rav Mesharshiya said: Under** the strict dictates of **Biblical law, even** a divorce extracted from the husband **by idolaters is valid,** as indeed follows from Rav Huna's logic.[14] וּמַה טַּעַם אָמְרוּ בְּעוֹבְדֵי כּוֹכָבִים פָּסוּל – **And for what reason did [the Rabbis]** say that a divorce extracted **by idolaters is invalid?** כְּדֵי שֶׁלֹּא תְּהֵא כָּל אַחַת וְאַחַת הוֹלֶכֶת וְתוֹלָה עַצְמָהּ בְּיַד עוֹבְדֵי כּוֹכָבִים – **So that every [disaffected wife] not attach herself to idolaters**[15] וּמַפְקַעַת עַצְמָהּ מִיַּד בַּעְלָהּ – **and thereby wrest herself away from her husband.** To prevent this immoral and anarchic situation from arising, the Rabbis invalidated a divorce obtained by coercion except where it is done under the auspices of the Jewish court.

Another challenge to Rav Huna:

מוֹתִיב רַב הַמְנוּנָא – **Rav Hamnuna challenged** Rav Huna's contention from the following Mishnah:[16] לָקַח מִסִּיקְרִיקוֹן – IF ONE ACQUIRED stolen property FROM AN EXTORTIONIST, וְחָזַר וְלָקַח מִבַּעַל הַבַּיִת – EVEN IF HE IN TURN ACQUIRED it FROM THE OWNER as well, מִקָּחוֹ בָּטֵל – HIS ACQUISITION IS VOID.[17] Rav Hamnuna explains his challenge: וְאַמַּאי – **But why** is the purchase not valid, according to Rav Huna? הָתָם נַמִּי נֵימָא אַגַּב אוּנְסֵיהּ גָּמַר וּמַקְנֵי – **There, too, let us say that because of his duress, he decides to convey ownership** willingly. Apparently, the Mishnah there discusses a case of sale (i.e. one in which either the extortionist or his buyer pays the owner for the land). Why, then, does the Mishnah rule the transaction null and void?

The Gemara answers:

הָא אִיתְּמַר עֲלָהּ – **It was indeed said** in elaboration **upon [that Mishnah]:** אָמַר רַב לֹא שָׁנוּ אֶלָּא דְּאָמַר לֵיהּ לֵךְ חֲזֵק וּקְנֵי – **Rav said that the Mishnah taught** its rule that the acquisition is void **only where [the owner]** merely **said to [the extortionist's buyer], "Go, perform a proprietary act and acquire** the land," but the owner did not draw up a document certifying the transfer. אֲבָל בִּשְׁטָר קָנָה – **But** if the owner conveyed the land to the buyer **with a document** certifying the transaction, **[the buyer] does acquire** the property.[18]

The Gemara asks:

וְלִשְׁמוּאֵל דְּאָמַר אַף בִּשְׁטָר נַמִּי לֹא קָנָה – **But according to Shmuel who says** that **even** if the owner conveyed the land to the buyer **with a document, [the buyer] does not acquire** the land, מַאי אִיכָּא לְמֵימַר – **what is there to say?**[19]

The Gemara answers:

מוֹדֶה שְׁמוּאֵל הֵיכָא דְּיָהַב זוּזֵי – **Shmuel agrees** in a case **where [the buyer] gave money** to the owner that the sale is valid.[20] Thus, his view is compatible with that of Rav Huna.

The Gemara asks:

וּלְרַב בִּיבִי דִּמְסַיֵּים בָּהּ מִשְּׁמֵיהּ דְּרַב נַחְמָן – **But according to Rav Bivi, who concludes [the teaching] in the name of Rav Nachman** himself[21] with the qualification: קַרְקַע אֵין לוֹ מָעוֹת יֵשׁ לוֹ – **[The robber] does not get** the **land** that he extorted, **but** his **money is** refunded **to him,** מַאי אִיכָּא לְמֵימַר – **what is there to say?** Obviously, Rav Bivi attributes to Rav Nachman the view that the forced transfer to the robber is void even if he has paid money, which contradicts the view of Rav Huna. – **?** –

The Gemara answers:

רַב בִּיבִי מֵימְרָא הוּא – That which **Rav Bivi** said **is** not a Mishnah or Baraisa, but only **an Amoraic ruling** of Rav Nachman, וּמֵימְרָא לְרַב הוּנָא לָא סְבִירָא לֵיהּ – **and Rav Huna does not hold of that Amoraic ruling.**[22]

The Gemara continues its discussion regarding the rules of a forced sale:

אָמַר רָבָא – **Rava said:** הִלְכְתָא – **The halachah is** that תַּלְיוּהוּ וְזַבִּין זְבִינֵיהּ זְבִינֵי – if **they hung him** up or otherwise subjected him to distress **until he** finally relented and **sold** to them what they demanded, **his sale is a** valid **sale,** as Rav Huna ruled.

Rava, however, qualifies this ruling:

וְלָא אֲמָרַן אֶלָּא – But we say this only

NOTES

14. For the husband loses nothing by doing so [as explained in the previous note] (*Rashbam*). [*Tosafos* prove that a divorce coerced by idolaters is valid under Biblical law only if the situation is one in which Jewish law would require the husband to issue a divorce.]

15. To induce them by means of cajolery and the conferment of personal favors to strong-arm her husband into granting her a divorce (*Rashbam*).

16. *Gittin* 55b. [This Mishnah was already cited and explained on 47b.]

17. Even if the person who buys the property from the extortionist then approaches the victim and acquires the property from him through a valid *kinyan,* his acquisition is null and void. For there is reason to believe that the owner conveyed ownership to the buyer only because he was afraid that the extortionist would harm him if he did not confirm the transfer to the extortionist's buyer (see *Rabbeinu Yonah* to 47b). Thus, the conveyance has been made under duress and is null and void.

18. The Gemara now assumes that Rav's main distinction is whether the owner received payment for his land or not. If witnesses see the owner say nothing more than, "Go, perform a proprietary act and acquire," and do not see any payment of funds, the assumption is that the owner was not compensated; rather, he consented under duress to convey the land as a gift. Hence, the transfer is not valid. [As explained above (see note 3), even Rav Huna concedes that a forced *gift* is void.] However, it is assumed that the owner would not go so far as to convey the land with a document unless he received payment for the land. Consequently, when the owner conveys the land with a document, the transfer is valid since a forced *sale* is valid, as Rav Huna asserts (*Tosafos*; see *Nachalas Moshe*).

19. [As explained in the previous note, the Gemara now reasons that the significance of a document is that it indicates that the owner received compensation; otherwise, he would not have issued a document.] Apparently, then, Shmuel voids the forced transaction even if the owner receives compensation, which contradicts Rav Huna's view.

Although Rav Huna is authorized to disagree with Shmuel [see *Tosafos* to *Chullin* 13a ד״ה בעא מיניה], it would be preferable to reconcile his view with that of Shmuel since the halachah generally follows Shmuel in financial law. Moreover, the Gemara above (47b) explained that Rav Huna follows Shmuel's view in this matter (*Ritva*).

20. [The Gemara now backs away from its earlier assumption that the issue between Rav and Shmuel in interpreting the Mishnah has anything to do with whether or not the owner was compensated. Both might agree that the Mishnah refers exclusively to a case in which the owner never received compensation — neither from the extortionist nor from his buyer. Rather, their point of disagreement is whether despite the lack of compensation, the owner's voluntary conveyance of a document indicates genuine consent on his part (as explained above, 47a notes 11 and 12). See *Nachalas Moshe.*]

21. This was cited and explained above, 47b — see note 15 there.

22. Rather, Rav Huna would rule in a situation where the robber paid the owner that the robber would indeed be awarded the land (see above, 47b note 16).

א) יקריב אותו מלמד שכופין אותו יכול בעל כרחו תלמוד לומר לרצונו הא כיצד א) כופין אותו עד שיאמר רוצה אני ודלמא שאני התם דניחא ליה דתיהוי ליה כפרה ואלא מסיפא ב) וכן אתה אומר בגיטי נשים ב) כופין אותו עד שיאמר רוצה אני ודלמא שאני התם ג) דמצוה לשמוע דברי חכמים אלא סברא הוא אגב אונסיה גמר ומקנה מותיב רב יהודה ג) גט המעושה בישראל כשר (א) ד) ובעכו"ם פסול ה) ובעכו"ם חובטין אותו ואומרין לו עשה מה שישראל אומר לך ואמאי התם נמי נימא אגב אונסיה גמר ומגרש הא איתמר עלה ו) אמר רב משרשיא דבר תורה אפילו בעכו"ם (ב) כשר ומה טעם אמרו בעכו"ם פסול כדי שלא תהא כל אחת ואחת הולכת ותולה עצמה ביד עכו"ם ומפקעת עצמה מיד בעלה מותיב רב המנונא ח) לקח מסיקריקון וחזר ולקח מבעל הבית מקחו בטל ואמאי התם נמי נימא אגב אונסיה גמר ומקני הא אתמר עלה י) אמר רב לא שנו אלא דאמר ליה לך חזק וקני אבל בשטר קנה ולשמואל דאמר אף בשטר נמי לא קנה מאי איכא למימר מודה שמואל היכא דיהיב זוזי ז) ולרב ביבי דמסיים בה משמיה דרב נחמן קרקע אין לו מעות יש לו מאי איכא למימר רב ביבי ט) מימרא הוא ומימרא לרב הונא לא סבירא ליה אמר רבא הלכתא תליוהו וזבין זביניה זביני ולא אמרן אלא בשדה

רש"י

יקריב אותו. קרא יתירא דהא כתיב לעיל זכר תמים יקריבנו ומלי למיכתב יקריבנו אל פתח אהל מועד לרלונו לפני ה': **מלמד שכופין אותו.** להקריב מה שנדר: **עד שיאמר רוצה אני.** אלמא היכא דכופין אותו עד דאמר מתוך יסורין רולה אני קרינא ביה לרלונו דגמר בלבו להקריב והוא הדין לזביני אם אמר רולה אני הוי זביני דגמר בלבו להקנות: דתיהוי ליה כפרה. וכי אמר רולה אני ודאי בלב שלם קאמר: **וכן אתה אומר בגיטי נשים.** בהנך דתנן (כתובות עז.) ואלו שכופין אותו להוליא מוכה שחין ובעל פוליפוס דכופין ומכין אותו עד שיאמר רולה אני דונתן מדעתו משמע: **דלמא.** התם נמי כי אמר רולה אני גמר בלבו לגרשה דמלוה קעביד מאחר שחייבוהו חכמים להוליא: **אלא.** רב הונא מסברא דידיה קאמר דמתוך יסורים גמר בלבו ומקני הואיל ואיכא תרתי יסורים ומתן מעות דלא מפסיד מידי: **גט המעושה.** שכופין אותו לבעל להוליא אם בישראל הוא כשר שכפוהו ישראל וכגון דאמר רולה אני: **בעכו"ם פסול.** ואע"ג דאמר רולה אני וקא ס"ד דמקשה דבישראל כשר משום דמלוה לשמוע דברי חכמים ובעכו"ס פסול כיון דליכא מלוה אגב אונסי' לא גמר (ג) ומקנה ומגרש וקשיא לרב הונא דכיון דליכא מלוה לא מקני אגב אונסיה: **ובעכו"ם.** אם אנו רולים לכופו על ידי עכו"ס ויהיה הגט כשר מלמדים אנו לעכו"ס שיאמרו לו עשה מה שישראל אומר לך דהשתא נמי מלוה לשמוע דברי חכמים: **התם נמי נימא אגב אונסי' גמר ומגרש.** דהא לא מפסיד מידי דומיא דזביני שמקבל דמי שדהו דכיון שאשתו שונאתו ובלא גט נמי לא תעמוד אללו וגט זה אינו אלא להתירה לאחרי' לא מפסיד כלום: **אפילו בעכו"ם כשר.** דאגב אונסיה גמר וגרש דלא מפסיד מידי כדפרישית: **פסול.** מדרבנן ולריכה גט אחר ומיהו אם פשטה ידה וקבלה קדושין מאחר לריכה גט מזה ומזה: **ותולה עצמה ביד עכו"ם.** להחניף לו ולזנות עמו עד שיכריח את בעלה לגרשה: **נימא אגב אונסיה.** דסיקריקון גמר ומקני בעל הבית כיון דיהיב ליה זוזי ולא מפסיד מידי דהיינו תליוהו וזבין: **מודה שמואל דהיכא דיהיב ליה זוזי.** זה הלוקח מן הסיקריקון כשחזר ולקח מבעל הבית יהב ליה זוזי לבעל הבית דאגב דמקבל זוזי גמר ומקני דהיינו תליוהו וזבין אבל בלא מעות לא גמר ומקני דהא רב הונא נמי תליוהו וזבין קאמר אבל תליוהו ויהיב לא הוי מתנה: **ולרב ביבי דמסיים לעיל.** במילתיה דרב נחמן דאמר גזלן שהביא ראיה אין ראייתו ראיה ואין מעמידין שדה בידו ואוסיף רב ביבי אבל מעות יש לו לגזלן שנתן לנגזל אלמא ס"ל לרב ביבי דאפי' נתן הגזלן לנגזל מעות לא קנה דתליוהו וזבין לא הוי זביני והוא הדין לסיקריקון דאי נתן הסיקריקון או הלוקח ממנו לבעל הבית מעות דמי השדה לא קנה וקשיא לרב הונא: **מימרא הוא.** שהיה אומר משום אחרים ואינה לא משנה ולא ברייתא ואי הוה אמר לה רב ביבי משמיה דנפשיה הוה מהדר גמרא גמרא אגמרא קרמית בתמיה:

תוספות

(ד) **אילימא** מהא דתניא יקריב אותו. וא"ת אי מהכא גמר אפילו תליוהו ויהיב נמי מתנה הוי והשיא דסיקריקון מוכח דאינה מתנה והיה ר"י רולה לתרץ דהכא הוי כמו מכר דהא יש לו כפרה תחת הקרבן וקונה הכפרה ומגיטי נשים דבעי למיגמר מינייהו הוי נמי כמו מכר שנפטר על ידי כך משאר כסות ועונה אבל אי אפשר לומר כן דא"כ גט מעושה שלא כדין נמי יהא כשר ובהמגרש (גיטין דף פח: ושם) אמר שמואל דפסול ותירץ ר"י דכל דבר שהוא מחוייב לעשות הוי כמו מכר והכא הרי הוא מחויב להביא קרבן ולקמן נמי מחויב הוא לגרש את אשתו דמיירי בהנהו שכופין אותן להוליא אבל שלא כדין הוה כמו תליוהו ויהיב דלא הויא מתנה:

יקריב אותו מלמד שכופין אותו. לא דמי להא דאמר בפ' שור שנגח ארבעה וחמשה (ב"ק דף מ.) חייבי חטאות ואשמות אין ממשכנין אותן משום דכיון דלכפרה קאתו לא בעי משכוני דדוקא חטאות ואשמות שבאות על חטא לא בעי משכוני שרולה שמאותו חטא יהיה לו כפרה אבל הכא נדר או נדבה אין מכפרים והא דקאמר ניחא ליה דתיהוי ליה כפרה היינו ממה שנדר שאם לא ישלם נדרו עונו ישא והא דאמר בתורת כהנים ובזבחים (דף ו.) ובזימא (דף לו.) דעולה מכפרת על חייבי עשה הא אמר בפ"ק דזבחים (דף ז:) דעולה דורון היא ולא מכפרת מקופיא (ה) מכפרת מקיבלת לא מכפרת ט):

אלא סברא הוא דאגב אונסיה גמר ומקני. וא"ת כיון דמסברא ידעינן דאגב אונסיה גמר ומקני אמאי אילטריך קרא גבי קרבן למיכתב דכופין אותו וי"ל דאי לאו קרא הוה אמינא אע"ג דגמר ומקני כיון דלאו מתרצה אלא על ידי כפייה פסול לגבי מזבח דזבח רשעים הוא קמ"ל שהקרבן כשר נרצה:

גט מעושה בישראל כשר ובעכו"ם פסול. בסיפא מסיים ובעכו"ם חובטין אותו ואומרים לו עשה מה שישראל אומר לך ויש מפרשים דהוי פירושא דרישא כילד בעכו"ם פסול (ו) חובטין אותו ואומרים לו כו' ואין נראה דא"כ אדפריך ליה הכא מסיפא ליסייעיה מרישא דקתני ובישראל כשר דאגב אונסי' גמר ומקני ועוד קשה (ז) דבישראל כשר משום דמצוה לשמוע דברי חכמים דא"כ בעכו"ם נמי כשר אמאי פסול והא חובטין אותו לעשות דברי חכמים ונראה לר"י דהכי קאמר דבעכו"ם נמי כשר וכגון שאומר לו עשה מה שישראל (ח) אומר לך וכן מפרש בהלכות גדולות והכי מוכח בתוספתא דקתני ובעכו"ם חובטין אותו ואומר לו עשה מה שפלוני אומר לך משמע דעל פי ר' פלוני שהוא חכם חובטין אותו וכשר הוא שהוא אומר להם לחובטו וכן משמע י) בירושלמי דגיטין דקאמר התם רב אמר ישראל שעשה כמעשה עכו"ם כשר בשאומר איני זן ואיני מפרנס תנא ר' חייא עכו"ם שעשו כמעשה ישראל פסול ואפי' אמר איני זן ואיני מפרנס הדא מתני' אמרה כן ובעכו"ם חובטין אותו ואומר לו עשה מה שישראל אומר לך ולא מה שאני אומר לך והא דאמר בגיטין (דף פח:) לפניהם ולא לפני עכו"ם היינו לפני דייני ישראל לאו היינו לפני עכו"ם דלפני עכו"ם היינו כשהעישוי נעשה על פי דייני עכו"ם כ):

דבר תורה אפילו בעכו"ם כשר. דכיון דבדין שכופין אותו להוליא דבישראל נמי אי שלא כדין מעשה פסול כדאמר שמואל בהמגרש (גיטין דף פח: ושם) וא"ת ומאי נפקא מינה אם תולה בעכו"ם ומפקעת עצמה מיד בעלה דכיון דבדין עבדה וגם חכמים היו כופין אותו להוליא וי"ל דגזרו כדין אטו שלא כדין וא"ת ולהוהוא טעמא דמפרש בהמגרש דבעכו"ם פסול דבר תורה משום לפניהם ולא לפני עכו"ם ועכו"ם לאו בני עישוי ניהו תקשה ליה לרב הונא אמאי פסול נימא דאגב אונסיה גמר ומגרש וי"ל כיון שעל ידי כפיית עכו"ם נותנו הוי שלא כדין ושלא כדין הוי כמו מתנה כדפרישית לעיל וא"ת ואמאי מייתי הכא לדרב משרשיא ההוא דהתם הוה ליה לאיתויי (ט) דהא אמר התם דהא דרב משרשיא בדותא היא וי"ל דלפי סברת המקשה דחשיב עכו"ם בני עישוי מתוך ליה שפיר לפרוך ליה ולא הוה פריך ולא מידי דהוי כמו מתנה ולסברתו משני ליה כדרב משרשיא:

הא איתמר עלה אמר רב לא שנו. תימה לרשב"א דמשמע דלא אמר רב הונא תליוהו וזבין זביניה זביני אלא בשטר אבל בלא שטר חזק וקני לא וכיון דאגב אונסיה גמר ומקני מה לי הכי ומה לי הכי ועוד הקשה דקאמר ומודה שמואל היכא דיהיב זוזי אלמא דתליוהו ויהיב לאו מתנה ותירץ דבהכי פליגי רב ושמואל דקסבר רב דלאו דליהיב זוזי לא הוה עביד שטר ושמואל סבר דמחמת אונס עביד שטר אבל אחריות לא היה מקבל כדאמר בהנזקין (שם דף מח.) עד שיכתוב לו אחריות נכסים:

אמר רבא הלכתא תליוהו וזבין זביניה זביני. לאו דוקא נקט תליוהו דאפילו בלא יסורין אלא מחמת אונס ממון כי ההוא עובדא דפרדיסא (לעיל דף מ:) הוו זביני ואם מסר מודעא לא הוו זביני דקיימא לן כרב הונא [דלכתבינן] מודעא אזביני כדפירש הקונטרס ודוקא מכר אבל מתנה תליוהו ויהיב לא הויא מתנה אפילו לא מסר מודעא אי ידעי עדים אונסיה והיכא דמסר מודעא אפי' לא ידעי אונסיה כדתנן ובגיטין והיכא

מסורת הש"ס

א) [יבמות קו.] קדושין נ. ע"ש ערכין כא., ב) [יבמות כ. וש"נ], ג) גיטין פח:, ד) [שם], ה) [שם נה:], ו) [שם נח.], ז) [לעיל מז:], ח) [גיטין מב:], ט) [וע' תוס' ר"ה ו. ד"ה יקריב], י) [בתוס' דגיטין פח: ד"ה ובעכו"ם מייתו הירושלמי בהיפך ועי' מהר"ם], כ) [ועי' תוס' גיטין פח: בד"ה ובעכו"ם חובטין]:

הגהות הב"ח

(א) גמ' בישראל כשר בעכו"ם כצ"ל ואות ו' נמחק: (ב) **שם** דבר תורה אפילו בעכו"ם נמי כשר: (ג) **רשב"ם** ד"ה בעכו"ם פסול וכו' לא גמר ומגרש כצ"ל ותיבת ומקנה נמחק: (ד) **תוס'** ד"ה אלא מהא דתניא יקריב: (ה) **ד"ה** יקריב וכו' מקופיא. נ"ב פי' כפרה מכפרת אבל עדיין קפויה ולפה עי' פ"ק דזבחים: (ו) **ד"ה** גט וכו' כילד בעכו"ם פסול כגון אם חובטין אותו: (ז) **בא"ד** וכי תימא דטעמא דבישראל כשר: (ח) **בא"ד** עשה מה שישראל פלוני אומר לך וכו' דעל פי רב פלוני: (ט) **ד"ה** דבר וכו' הוה ליה לאיתויי הכא דהא אמר:

תורה אור השלם

א) אִם עֹלָה קָרְבָּנוֹ מִן הַבָּקָר זָכָר תָּמִים יַקְרִיבֶנּוּ אֶל פֶּתַח אֹהֶל מוֹעֵד יַקְרִיב אֹתוֹ לִרְצֹנוֹ לִפְנֵי יְיָ: [ויקרא א, ג]

ליקוטי רש"י

יקריב אותו וכו'. קרא יתירא הוא דהא כתיב ברישא דקרא זכר תמים יקריבנו. **שכופין אותו.** לקיים דברי נדרו. **דמצוה לשמוע דברי חכמים.** ואית לן לאחזוקיה בחזקת מקיים מלוה וגמר בלבו לקיים דברי בית דין [קידושין נ.]. **גט המעושה.** בחזקה. **ותולה עצמה ביד עכו"ם.** שוכרת עובד כוכבים אנס לכוף בעלה לגרשה ובאה עליו בעקיפין [גיטין פח:]. **לקח מסיקריקון.** עיין ליקוטי רש"י לעיל מז:. **ולרב ביבי דמסיים בה.** בהא מלתא דאמר רב נחמן א"ל הונא. **משמיה דרב נחמן.** שהיה מוסיף בה רב נחמן דבר זה מדעתו ומיהו רב הונא לא סבירא ליה האי תוספתא כדלקמן בשמעתין דכל היכא דאיכא מתן מעות סבר ליה לרב הונא דהוו זביני ולאו אדרב ושמואל קאי דבמסכת גיטין בהניזקין דאיתא לפלוגתייהו לא איירי רב ביבי כלל התם [רשב"ם לעיל מז:]. **מימרא הוא.** בעלמא היא ואינה לא משנה ולא ברייתא [גיטין מב:]. **תליוהו וזבין.** מי שתלו אותו או עשו לו יסורין עד שמכר וקיבל הדמים ואומר רולה אני [רשב"ם שם].

עין משפט נר מצוה

קפ א מיי' פי"ד מהל' מעשה קרבנות הל' טז סמג לאוין קלא:

קפא ב ג מיי' פ"ב מהל' גירושין הל' כ סמג עשין נ טוש"ע אה"ע סי' קלד סעיף ה וסי' קנד סעיף כא:

קפב ד מיי' שם וסמג שם טוש"ע שם סי' קלד סעיף ח:

קפג ה מיי' שם טוש"ע שם סעיף ט:

רבינו גרשום

יקריב אותו. דלגבי עולה אותו יתירא הוא וקאמר **מלמד דכופין אותו** להקריב כשנדר. **דניחא ליה דתיהוי ליה כפרה** בקרבנו וגמר ומתרצה: **כופין אותו.** ליתן גט לאותן שכופין אותן להוציא כגון מוכה שחין ובעל [פוליפוס] כו': **התם** נמי סבר. האי מוכה שחין **מצוה לשמוע דברי חכמים** שגזרו כן ומתרצה. **אלא סברא** דכי אמר תליוהו וזבין דזביניה זביני **דאגב אונסי' גמר ומקני: גט המעושה.** ע"י ב"ד **ישראל כש': תולה עצמה בעכו"ם** א) שאנס עצמה לגרשה. **התם נמי נימא אגב אונסיה גמר** בעל הבית **ומקני** ליה: **מודה שמואל היכא דיהיב זוזי.** דגמר ומקני ליה: **מאי איכא למימר.** אמאי אפי' קרקע בדין הוא דיש לו דאגב אונסיה גמר ומקני. אין ודאי יש לו קרקע. והא **דרב ביבי מימרא היא** ואינה עיקר דאינה לא משנה ולא ברייתא כי אם מימרא בעלמא.

חשק שלמה על רבינו גרשום

א) נראה דצ"ל שיאנס את בעלה לגרשה.

עין משפט
נר מצוה

קפד א מיי' פ"י מהל' מכירה הל' א ועיין בהשגות ובמגיד משנה סמג עשין פב טוש"ע ח"מ סי' רה סעיף א [וברב אלפס עוד בגיטין ד' קע.]:
קפה ב ג מיי' פ"ד מהל' אישות הלכה א ועיין בהשגות ובמגיד משנה סמג עשין מח טוש"ע אה"ע סי' מב סעיף א:
קפו ד מיי' פ"י מהל' מכירה הלכה ו סמג עשין פב טוש"ע ח"מ סי' רה סעיף ט:

רבינו גרשום

והני מילי בשדה סתם. כלומר שאם כופהו בפירוש שימכור לו שדה שלו משום הכי גמר ומקני ליה שדה שיתן לו שדה פחותה שלו. **אבל** אי אמר **שדה זו** מכור לי בפירוש אגב אונסיה אודי **ולא** גמר ומקני ליה: **דלא ארצי זוזי.** שלא רצה לבדוק המעות אם טובות הן אם לאו משמע דמחמת כעס לא מעיין ולא גמר ומקני **אבל ארצי זוזי** זביניה זביני: **אבל הוה לי' לאישתמוטי.** מיניה בשום ענין ומכר זביניה זביני: **תליוה.** שאנסו האשה **שתתקדש** לו: **התינח דקדיש בכספא.** דהיינו קדושין דרבנן משום הכי מצי לאפקועי רבנן מדרבנן. **אבל קדיש בביאה** בעל כרחה. א) דביאה היינו קדושי דאורייתא והיא בעולת בעל **מאי איכא למימר: אמר ליה.** אפי' הכי לא הוויין קדושיה קדושין משום **דשויוה רבנן** למאן דקדיש בביאה **לבעילתו בעילת זנות** דחוצפא קא עביד הואיל דתקינו קדושי כספא מצי לאפקועי קדושי ביאה: **אכינרא.** על אותו עץ שכך נקרא שמו עד דזבין ליה קרקע שלו: **אמודעא** דבעל כרחו זבין: **ואאשקלתא.** זהו שטר מכירה שחתם עליו שמכרו: **הכי קאמר אי לאו דחתם אמודעא מאי דחתם אאשקלתא שפיר חתם** דזביניה באונס הוי זביני: והיכי מצי רבה בר בר חנה למיחתם אמודעא מאחר דחתם אאשקלתא **והאמר רב נחמן עדים שאמרו אמנה היה דברינו** כגון שטר שכתוב כי פלוני לוה מפלו' מנה וחתומין עליו העדים אם אמרו העדים בפנינו לא הלוהו אלא נדר לו להלוותו והאמין לו הלוה למלוה שיקיים דיבורו ואמר לנו כתבו לו שטר שלוויתי ממנו מנה אבל אנו לא ראינו ההלוואה והלוה טוען לא הלוני שוב. **אינן נאמנים** דודאי לא הוו משווי נפשיהו רשיעי דחתמי שטרא אי לא חזו ההלוואה.

חשק שלמה
על רבינו גרשום

א) עי' בפירשב"ם כאן בד"ה תינח.

והיכא דבטל מודעא בשעת זביני מהני ביטול דאגב אונסיה גמר ומבטל כדאמרינן בפ' האומר משקלי (ערכין דף כא:) ובקונט' הביאה לעיל ואפילו אמר בשעת מודעא כל מה שאבטל לא יהא ביטול אינו כלום דמ"מ לבסוף כשמבטל כל מה שאמר קודם לכן יהא מבוטל דאגב אונסי' גמר ומבטל אבל במתנה אי ידעינן באונסיה לא מהני ביטול ולא גמר ומבטל ומיהו אי לא ידעינן באונסיה ומבטל מודעא מדעתו נראה שבטולו ביטול ולכך כתבינן בשטרי מתנה ביטול מודעי:

אבל שדה זו לא. והא דאמרי' נהרדעי לעיל (דף מ:) כל מודעא דלא כתב בה (ח) אנא ידענא ביה באונסין דפלוני לאו מודעא היא לא משכחת אליבא דרבה לעיל אלא כי הוה מעשה דפרדיסא דבשדה סתם לא מהניא מודעה ובשדה זו לא צריך מודעה אלא לידעו אונסיה:

ואפי' בשדה זו לא אמרינן אלא דלא ארצי זוזי. לפי הספרים דגרסי לא ארצי ליה משמע דבעי למימר דכי אמרי עדים בפנינו מנה לו הוי זביני אפי' בשדה זו וכי קאמר רבה דלא הוי זביני היינו כי אמרו בפנינו הודה לו שלא רצו נתינת המעות וא"כ משמע דבשדה סתם אפילו כי אמרו בפנינו הודה שלא רצו נתינת המעות הוי זביני ואין נראה דבהודאה לא שייך לחלק בין שדה סתם לשדה זו דבתרוייהו שייך למימר אי לאו דאודי ליה הוה ממטי ליה ולחמרי' לשחור ע"כ נראה דגרסינן ולא ארצי זוזי ולא גרסינן ליה וכן פירש בקונטרס:

תינח דקדיש בכספא. הכא לא קאמר כל דמקדש אדעתא דרבנן מקדש וכן בפרק בית שמאי (יבמות דף קי. ושם ד"ה לפיקן) גבי עובדא דנרש דקדשה כשהיא קטנה וגדלה ואתא איניש אחרינא וחטפה מיניה כדאמר בריש כתובות (דף ג. ושם ד"ה תינח) ובהשולח (גיטין דף לג. ושם) משום דהכא ובפ' בית שמאי לא קדש אדעתא דרבנן כדקאמר הוא עשה שלא כהוגן וצריך לומר דסבר הכא דיש כח ביד חכמים לעקור דבר מן התורה כיון דאפקעינהו רבנן לקדושין מיניה ואע"ג דלא קדש אדעתם והכי פירושא בשלמא דקדיש בכספא מצו רבנן להפקיר הכסף ולאת במתנה לאשה אלא דקדיש בביאה אע"ג דיש כח ביד חכמים לעקור דבר מן התורה היינו היכא דליכא עבירה כגון (יבמות פט.) ההוא גריוא דהדר לטיבלא אבל ביאה וכי יעשו חכמים ביאתו ביאת עבירה ומשני אין ודאי דשויוה ביאתו ביאת זנות ובהאיבה דכתובות (שם) ובהשולח (שם) לכאורה פליגי אהך דשמעתין דאיצטריך למימר טעמא דאדעתא דרבנן מקדש משמע דאי לאו דאדעתא דרבנן מקדש לא היה כח בידם להפקיע הקדושין ומיהו נראה דלא פליגי ואיצטריך טעמא דאדעתא דרבנן מקדש משום דהתם כיון דקדושין נעשו כהוגן לא היה כח לחכמים להפקיעם אי לאו משום דאדעתא דרבנן מקדש:

קדיש בביאה מאי איכא למימר. תימה לרשב"א דקדיש בביאה בלא הפקעה לא להוו קדושין דהוי תליוהו ויהיב דכנגד גופה שקנוי לו אינו נותן לה כלום ודוחק לומר לפי שיש לה הנאת ביאה ועוד דאם כן הא דאמר אמימר תליוה וקדיש קדושיו קדושין לא הוי אלא דקדיש בכסף או בביאה אבל בשטר לא דהוי כמו תליוהו ויהיב וי"ל דכנגד גופה שקנוי לו מתחייב לה שאר כסות ועונה ואע"ג דפרי' לעיל גבי גט דלא חשיב זביני מה שהבעל נפטר משאר כסות ועונה ה"מ גבי בעל שהיה נותנם ברצון ולא היה מגרשה:

אמר רב הונא מאן דחתים אמודעא שפיר חתים. הא דרב הונא פליגא אדרבא דאמר (לעיל מ:) דלא כתבינן מודעא אזביני:

אמר רב נחמן עדים שאמרו אמנה היו דברינו אין נאמנין. על כרחך באין כתב ידם יוצא ממקום אחר איירי דאי יוצא ממקום אחר פשיטא דהכי פריך בפ' שני דכתובות (דף יט. ושם: ד"ה אמר) גבי האומר שטר אמנה הוא זה אינו נאמן דקאמר מאן אי דקאמרי עדים אי כתב ידן יוצא ממקום אחר פשיטא ועוד דמר בר רב אשי דקאמר אמנה היו דברינו אינו נאמן משום דלא ניתן ליכתב ואי כתב ידן יוצא ממקום אחר אפי' ניתן ליכתב אינו נאמן וקשה דאמאי לא מהימני במיגו דאי בעו אמרי אין זה כתב ידינו דהא רב נחמן גופיה אית ליה מיגו לפסול השטר בפ' שני דכתובות (שם) דקאמר כי אתו לקמן לדינא אמינא להו זילו קיימו שטרייכו וחותו לדינא דמהימן לומר פרוע הוא מיגו דאי בעי אמר מזויף הוא וכ"ש עדים דאלימי לאורועי שטרא דהכי אמר בהדיא בפרק מי שמת (לקמן דף קנד. ושם) ותי' ר"י דהיינו טעמא דמודעא ואמנה לר"נ הואיל ואמר שהשטר נכתב ונמסר כהלכתו שוב לא אתי על פה ומרע לשטרא אפילו במיגו ודמי נמי למחזרין ומגידין הואיל שחתמו על השטר כדין ומדאורייתא עדים החתומין על השטר נעשה כנחקרה עדותן בבית דין ומדרבנן הוא דאצרכוהו קיום דוקא כי טוען מזויף אבל

בשדה סתם אבל בשדה זו לא ובשדה זו נמי לא אמרן אלא דלא ארצי זוזי אבל ארצי זוזי לא ולא אמרן אלא דלא הוה (א) לאישתמוטי אבל הוה ליה לאישתמוטי לא [א] והלכתא בכולהו דהוו זביניה זביני ואפי' בשדה זו דהא אשה כשדה זו דמיא (ג) ואמר אמימר [ב] תליוה וקדיש קדושיו קדושין מר בר רב אשי אמר [ג] באשה ודאי קדושין לא הוו הוא עשה שלא כהוגן לפיכך עשו עמו שלא כהוגן ואפקעינהו רבנן לקידושיה מיניה אמר ליה רבינא לרב אשי [א] תינח דקדיש בכספא קדיש בביאה מאי איכא למימר אמר ליה שויוה רבנן לבעילתו בעילת זנות טאבי תלא לפאפי אכינרא וזבין חתם רבה בר בר חנה אמודעא ואאשקלתא אמר רב הונא [ד] מאן דחתים אמודעא שפיר חתים ומאן דחתים אאשקלתא שפיר חתים מה נפשך אי מודעא לא אשקלתא ואי אשקלתא לא מודעא ה"ק אי לאו מודעא מאן דחתים אאשקלתא שפיר חתים רב הונא לטעמיה [ה] דאמר רב הונא תליוהו וזבין זביניה זביני [ו] והא"ר נחמן העדים שאמרו אמנה היו דברינו אין

בשדה סתם. שהכריחוהו למכור אחת משדותיו והוא בירר מעצמו ומכר את זאת דכיון דמדעתו בירר רעה שבהן בירר (ג) שאינו חושש בה כל כך וגמר ומקני: בשדה זו. הכריחוהו למכור שדה זו ואותה מכר: **דלא ארצי זוזי.** לא מנה המעות גילה דעתו דבעל כרחו מקבל: ואפי' בשדה זו ולא ארצי זוזי לא אמרן דלא הוי זביני אלא דלא הוה ליה להאי לאישתמוטי מן התולה (ד) בשום דיחוי שבעולם כגון המתמן לי עד למחר או עד שתבוא אשתי או שום דיחוי שיכול לטעות בו האנס: **והלכתא בכולהו הוו זביניה זביני ואפי' בשדה זו.** ולא ארצי זוזי ולא הוה ליה לאישתמוטי דהוי אונס גמור וכגון דאמר רוצה אני: **דהא אשה.** כשמכריחה אדם לקבל קדושיו והתקדשה לו: **כשדה זו דמיא.** שאינו חפץ כי אם בזה: **ואמר** (ה) **אמימר.** כלומר קיימא לן הכי: **תליוה וקדיש.** קבלה קדושין קדושיה קדושין דלדמי לזביני שמוכרת עצמה לזה: **מר בר רב אשי אמר.** במכר מודינא דהוו זביני אבל גבי אשה תקון רבנן דלא ליהוו קדושין דהוא עשה שלא כהוגן שהכריחה לפיכך נעשה עמו שלא כהוגן שלא כדין דאע"ג דמן התורה ליהוו קידושין רבנן עקרינהו והפקירו אותן ועשו מעות מתנה ובמקום אחר מפרש דכל דמקדש אדעתא דרבנן מקדש כדת משה וישראל ורבנן אמור לא ליהוו קדושין נמצא שלא קדשה זה שהרי בדעת חכמים תלה והם אינם חפצים בקדושין הללו: **תינח דקדיש בכספא.** יכולין חכמים להפקיע הקידושין דהפקר ב"ד הפקר גבי ממון ואילו קדשה בגזל ובחמס דמיא דלא הוו קדושין אבל קדיש בביאה שעשה מעשה בגופה היאך יאמרו חכמים שלא תהא ביאה הרי בעל כרחנו ביאה היא: **ואית דמפרש** תינח דקדיש בכספא דקידושי כסף דרבנן הם שאמרו והם אמרו וקידושין דדרבנן יכולין לעקור אבל קדיש בביאה דהוו קידושי דאורייתא מאי איכא למימר וטעות הוא בידם דמגזירה שוה ילפינן לקידושי כסף במסכת קדושין (דף ב.) וגם לכל דבר אתקוש הוויות להדדי ואמרינן בכריתות (דף ה.) אל תהי גזירה שוה קלה בעיניך שהרי נותר אחד מגופי תורה ולא למדה הכתוב אלא בגזירה שוה ועוד מאי האי דקמהדר ליה שויוה רבנן לבעילתו בעילת זנות הא כיון דמדאורייתא היא היאך יכולין לעשות ביאתו זנות אלא כיון דאדעתא דרבנן מקדש לא הוי קידושין דאמרי רבנן לא ליהוו קידושין ומתוך כך (ו) נמצאת מעלמה בעילת זנות: **טבי.** גברא אלמא הוי: **תלי' לפפי.** באילן שהוא מירג למכור לו שדהו: לא תלה אותו בשביל הכירגלא שימכרנו לו: **וזבין.** כלומר וכן עשה שמכרה לו: **חתם רבה בר בר חנה.** על מודעא שמסר לעדים מקודם ואח"כ מסר מקדם לשם המכירה: **ואאשקלתא.** זהו על שטר המכירה חתם: **מאן דחתם אמודעא שפיר חתם.** דלאע"ג דתליוהו חזין זביניה זביני הני מילי היכא דלא מסר מודעא אבל המודעא שכתב בה מבטל את המכירה: **ומאן דחתם אאשקלת' שפיר חתם.** דתליוהו חזין זביניה זביני ודמסתיק לקמיה: **רב הונא לטעמיה כו'.** מהכא שמעינן דכתבינן מודעא אזביני אפילו בתליוהו וזבין ודלא כרבא דאמר לעיל (דף מ:) לא כתבינן מודעא אזביני כדפרישית בפירקין לעיל אלא היכא דאניס כמעשה דפרדיסא והכא אפי' בתליוהו וזבין כתבי מודעא ונ"כ נראין הדברים שהרי פסקינהו של רבה לא עמדו מאי דפסיק לעיל בתליוהו וזבין [ז] [לא אמרן אלא בשדה סתם] שאחר פסק שלו אמר (ז) לא כתבינן מודעא אזביני כדפרישי' לעיל: **איני.** כלומר היאך בטלה מודעה שחתם בה רבה בר בר חנה את האשקלתא שחתם הוא עצמו בה: **והא אמר רב נחמן כו'.** והכא נמי רבה בר בר חנה קמסהיד עכשיו על האשקלתא מודעא היו דברינו ואמאי נאמן: **עדים.** החתומין בשטר: **ואמרו אמנה היו דברינו.** לא הלוהו כלום אלא כתבנו לו ולכשיצטרך ילוה בו והאמינו לוה למלוה שלא יוציא עליו שטר מלוה זו לגבות הימנו עד שעבד לו כספו מעכשיו אם ילוה אפי' לאחר זמן דלאו מוקדם הוא לטרוף שלא כדין:

אין

מסורת הש"ס

א) כתובות ג. יבמות ל: קי. גיטין לג. עג., ב) [לעיל מז: וש"נ], ג) כתובות דף יט:, ד) מהרש"ל:

הגהות הב"ח

(א) גמ' דלא הוה ליה לאישתמוטי: (ב) שם כשדה זו דמיא (ואמר אמימר) תא"מ ונ"ב ג"י רשב"ם והרא"ש ואמר מר: (ג) רשב"ם ד"ה בשדה וכו' רעה שבהן בירר גלי דעתיה שאינו חושש: (ד) ד"ה ואפי' בשדה וכו' מן התולה אותו בשום דיחוי בעולם וכו' שיכול להטעות בו: (ה) ד"ה ואמר מר כלומר קיימא לן: (ו) ד"ה ואית דמפרש וכו' ומתוך כך נעשית מעלמה בעילת זנות: (ז) ד"ה רב הונא וכו' בתליוהו חזין שאחר פסק שלו אמר כתבינן כצ"ל ותיבת לא נמחק: (ח) תוס' ד"ה אבל וכו' דלא כתב בה אנן ידעינן ביה באונסיה דפלוני:

ליקוטי רש"י

ואפקעינהו רבנן לקידושיה מיניה. כל המקדש אשה על דעת שהנהיגו חכמי ישראל בישראל הוא מקדשה שיהיו קיימין קידושין לפי דברי חכמים ויהיו בטילים לפי דברי חכמים [כתובות ג.]. ושויוהו למעות קידושין מתנה למפרע דהפקר ב"ד היה הפקר [יבמות צ:]. דכל דמקדש תולה בדעת חכמים הוא דהא כדת משה וישראל קאמרינן ניהוי קידושין [יבמות קי.]. כל דמקדש אדעתא דרבנן מקדש ליהוי קידושין אלין כדת משה וישראל שהנהיגו חכמי ישראל והרי הם אמרו שיפקיעו וכו' היילך פקעי שעל מנת כן קידשה [גיטין לג.]. **תינח דקדיש בכספא.** מיגח למימר אפקעתא דכדקדיש בכספא דנימא וכו' זה עוקר הקידושין ועושה מעות מתנה מעיקרן [כתובות שם]. איכא למימר אפקעינהו לקידושין וכו' ואמרו ליהוי מעות למפרע מתנה וממילא פקעו שהרי כשקידש ע"מ כן קידש [גיטין שם]. איכא למימר אפקעתא דשויוהו למעות מתנה [יבמות צ:]. **קדיש בביאה.** דקיימא לן בקידושין (ד:) מכי יקח איש אשה ובעלה דאשה מתקדשת נמי בביאה [גיטין שם]. **מאי איכא למימר.** מאי אפקעתא מעיקרא איכא בשלמא על ידי גט כשר אע"פ שהקידושין קיימים עד עכשיו גוזרים הכתוב היא שהגט כורתו ומתיר איסורו מכאן ולהבא וכו' ואי קדיש בביאה ואתא עוקר קידושין למפרע מה תהא על ביאתו [כתובות שם]. מאי אפקעתא איכא למימר בהא ביאה [גיטין שם]. מאי הפקר ב"ד איכא למימר [יבמות קי.]. מאי אפקעתא איכא למימר האי ביאה מאי שויה [שם צ:]. **א"ל שויוה רבנן לבעילתו בעילת זנות.** כיון דבדעתא דרבנן תלה ורבנן אמור וכו' תבטל ביאה דתיהוי בעילת זנות ואית דאמרי תינח קדיש בכספא דקידושי כסף דרבנן קדיש בביאה דקידושין דמדאורייתא נינהו מאי

איכא למימר וטעות גדול הוא בידם דקידושי כסף דאורייתא נינהו ומג"ש דקיחה קיחה משדה עפרון גמר להו במסכת קידושין (ג.) וג"ש בסיני נאמרה וכל י"ג מדות ואי קידושי כסף מדרבנן מי קטלינן נפשא עלייהו דבעל ארוסה בסקילה ועוד מאי שינויא דשני שויוה רבנן כו' הא קשיא ליה היכי מצו רבנן לאפקועי מידי דאורייתא ומשני שויוה רבנן להא דאפקעת היא [יבמות צ:]. שויוה רבנן להביה ביאה למפרע וכו' בעילת זנות דאפקעו שם קידושין מינה ויש בהן כח לכך שהרי כשקידש על מנהג חוק דתם קידש כך אני מפרש בכל מקום מלבי ומרבותי קבלתי כל דמקדש אדעתא דרבנן מקדש [illegible] עפרון והיינו דקפריך תינח דקדיש בכספא קדיש בביאה דכתיב בהדיא (דברים כד) כי יקח איש אשה ובעלה [illegible] כדאמר התם (קידושין יב:) רב מנגיד אמאן דמקדש בביאה משום פריצותא ותשובות קשות יש בדבר חדא [illegible] המאורסה נהרגת בקדושי כסף ואי דרבנן מי מיקטלא ועוד דקמשני שויוה רבנן לבעילתו בעילת זנות היכי [illegible]

בְּשָׂדֶה סְתָם – where they demand some **unspecified field** and it is the owner who chooses which field to cede to them.[1] אֲבָל בְּשָׂדֶה זוּ לֹא – **However, where a specified field** is demanded by the extortionists, then the sale is **not** valid. וּבְשָׂדֶה זוּ נַמִּי לֹא אָמְרָן אֶלָּא דְּלָא אַרְצֵי זוּזֵי – **And even where a specified field** is demanded by the extortionists, **we say** that the sale is void **only where [the owner] did not count** the **money** that they paid him for his field, thereby indicating that he remains steadfastly opposed to the sale. אֲבָל אַרְצֵי זוּזֵי לֹא – **But if he counted** the **money,** the sale is **not** void.[2] וְלָא אָמְרָן אֶלָּא דְּלָא הֲוָה לְאִישְׁתַּמּוּטֵי – **And we say** that failure to count the money is an indication of the owner's continued dissent (in the case of a specified field) **only where [the owner] had no way to evade** the extortionists. אֲבָל הֲוָה לֵיהּ לְאִישְׁתַּמּוּטֵי לֹא – **But if he had a way to evade** the extortionists,[3] the sale is **not** void, because we regard his failure to evade them as evidence of his genuine consent, even though he has not counted the money that was given to him.

The Gemara's conclusion, however, is unlike Rava's:

וְהִלְכְתָא בְּכוּלְּהוּ דַּהֲווּ זְבִינֵיהּ זְבִינֵי – **But the** final **halachah in all** the cases mentioned above **is that his** forced **sale is a** valid **sale,** וַאֲפִילּוּ בְּשָׂדֶה זוּ – **even where a specified field** is demanded by the extortionists;[4] דְּהָא אִשָּׁה כְּשָׂדֶה זוּ דָּמְיָא – **for** the case of **a woman** who is forced into marriage **is analogous to** the case of **a specified field,**[5] וְאָמַר אֲמֵימַר תַּלְיוּהָ וְקַדֵּישׁ קִדּוּשָׁיו קִדּוּשִׁין – **and Ameimar said: If they hung [a woman] up** or otherwise subjected her to distress **until** she consented that **he betroth**[6] her, **his betrothal** of her **is a** valid **betrothal.**[7] Thus, we see that even the coerced sale of a specified article is deemed a valid sale.[8]

The Gemara records a dissenting opinion in regard to forced betrothal:

מָר בַּר רַב אַשִׁי אָמַר – **Mar bar Rav Ashi says:** בְּאִשָּׁה וַדַּאי קִדּוּשִׁין לֹא הָווּ – **In** the case of **a woman** forced to accept betrothal money, **it is definitely not a** valid **betrothal,** by special Rabbinic enactment.[9] הוּא עָשָׂה שֶׁלֹּא כְּהוֹגֶן – Since **he acted improperly** by forcing the woman to accept betrothal, לְפִיכָךְ עָשׂוּ עִמּוֹ שֶׁלֹּא כְּהוֹגֶן – **therefore they** [the Rabbis] **acted with him improperly** (i.e. they exceeded the bounds of normative law) וְאַפְקְעִינְהוּ רַבָּנָן לְקִידוּשֵׁיהּ מִינֵּיהּ – **and the Rabbis abrogated his** technically valid **betrothal.**[10]

The Gemara asks:

אָמַר לֵיהּ רָבִינָא לְרַב אַשִׁי – **Ravina said to Rav Ashi:** תֵּינַח דְּקַדֵּישׁ בְּכַסְפָּא – **That would rest well where he betrothed** her **with money.** We could then understand the mechanism by which the Rabbis abrogated his betrothal.[11] קַדֵּישׁ בְּבִיאָה מַאי אִיכָּא לְמֵימַר – **But what can be said of where he betrothed** her **through cohabitation?**[12]

The Gemara answers:

אָמַר לֵיהּ – **[Rav Ashi] said to [Ravina]:** שַׁוְיוּהָ רַבָּנָן לִבְעִילָתוֹ בְּעִילַת זְנוּת – **The Rabbis rendered his cohabitation** an act of **non-marital cohabitation,** thereby nullifying it as a valid act of betrothal.[13]

The Gemara records an incident concerning a forced sale:

טָאבִי תָּלָא לְפָאפֵּי אַכִּינְרָא וְזַבִּין – **Tabbi hung Pappi up on a** ***kinera*** tree **until he** relented and **sold** him what he demanded.[14] חָתֵם רַבָּה בַּר בַּר חָנָה אַמּוֹדָעָא – **Rabbah bar bar Chanah signed the notification** (that Pappi had drawn up surreptitiously) declaring the sale to be one executed under duress[15] וְאַאַשְׁקַלְתָּא – **as well as the document of sale.** Rabbah bar bar Chanah affixed his signature to the two contradictory notes. אָמַר רַב הוּנָא – **Rav Huna said:** מַאן דְּחָתֵים אַמּוֹדָעָא שַׁפִּיר חָתֵים – **The one who signed the notification signed properly,** i.e. his signature gives the document legal force, as the notification indeed nullifies the forced sale, וּמַאן דְּחָתֵים אַאַשְׁקַלְתָּא שַׁפִּיר חָתֵים – **and the one**

NOTES

1. When the extortionists do not demand a specific field, since it is the owner himself who has chosen the field, he probably chose his most inferior one and decided, in the final analysis, to consent to the sale (*Rashbam; cf. Hagahos HaBach*).

2. [Rava, who voids the forced sale of a *specified* field, does so only when there is some indication of the owner's continued dissent; otherwise, the forced sale is valid.]

3. E.g. he could have stalled for time by asking the extortionists to wait until the morrow or until his wife returns or by using some other pretext (*Rashbam*).

4. And he did not count the money nor were any evasive maneuvers possible. Though the sale is completely forced, it is valid, as long as the owner finally relents and says, "I am willing" (*Rashbam*).

5. The coercer demands the specific woman he is coercing into marriage (*Rashbam*).

6. [For lack of a better English term, we use "betrothal" (which usually denotes mere engagement) to correspond to the Hebrew term *kiddushin,* which refers to the first stage of actual marriage. After a woman accepts *kiddushin* money from a man, she is legally bound to him in regard to most laws. The marriage is ultimately consummated by the process of *nisuin,* whereupon the couple is fully married.]

7. Betrothal is analogous to sale, since in return for the betrothal the woman receives not only the minimal *kiddushin* money but the benefits of being a married woman (see *Rashba; cf. Tosafos* ד״ה קדיש בביאה).

8. The Gemara's analogy to the case of forced betrothal proves only that a forced sale can be valid even in the case of a specified field. But that the forced sale of a specified field is valid even when the owner did not count the money and no evasive maneuvers were possible is not indicated by the case of betrothal; rather, the Gemara reached that conclusion on the basis of its own reasoning (*Ritva*).

9. Mar bar Rav Ashi agrees that a forced sale is valid and that technically the same should be true of a forced betrothal. However, he maintains that there is a special Rabbinic enactment that invalidates a forced betrothal (*Rashbam*).

10. [The Gemara will discuss the legal mechanism of this abrogation.]

11. There is the principle of הֶפְקֵר בֵּית דִּין הֶפְקֵר, *whatever is [declared] ownerless by the court is ownerless,* whereby the Torah authorizes the Rabbis to declare property ownerless (see *Gittin* 36b). Thus, as a penalty for the improper conduct of the coercer in forcing the woman to marry him, the Rabbis could declare that the money he gives her for the betrothal is ownerless; thus, he has given her nothing of his own and the betrothal is consequently void.

12. In addition to the standard means of betrothal through the giving of money, betrothal can also be effected through the act of cohabitation. When the coercer has used cohabitation as his means of betrothal, with what legal mechanism can the Rabbis abrogate his betrothal?

13. When a man betroths a woman, he ties the betrothal's validity to the approval of the Torah authorities. (This is reflected in the betrothal declaration, wherein the man declares: "You are hereby betrothed to me . . . in accordance with the law of Moses and Israel.") The Rabbis thus have the authority to declare invalid any act of betrothal that does not meet their approval. As a result of the Rabbis' abrogation of the coerced betrothal, the act of cohabitation (through which the man sought to effect betrothal) is in effect rendered a non-marital act of cohabitation, having no power to effect acquisition (*Rashbam,* interpreting the Gemara's statement to mean that his cohabitation is rendered a non-marital act as the *result* of the Rabbis' abrogation rather than as a description of legal mechanism by which they did so).

14. Alternatively, Tabbi hung Pappi up with regard to a *kinera* tree; that is, he subjected him to duress until he sold him the *kinera* tree that he demanded (*Rashbam*).

15. Prior to writing a document of sale, Pappi composed a formal notification declaring his unwillingness to sell. According to our Gemara, this advance notification invalidates the subsequent sale even if the sale otherwise conforms to the conditions necessary for a forced sale to be valid (see *Rashbam* ד״ה רב הונא and Gemara above, 40b).

עין משפט
נר מצוה

קפד א מיי' פ"י מהל' מכירה הל' א ועיין בהשגות ובמגיד משנה סמג עשין פב טוש"ע ח"מ סי' רה סעיף א [וברב אלפס עוד בגיטין ד' קע.]:
קפה ב ג מיי' פ"ד מהל' אישות הלכה א ועיין בהשגות ובמגיד משנה סמג עשין מח טוש"ע אה"ע סי' מב סעיף א:
קפו ד מיי' פ"י מהל' מכירה הלכה ו סמג עשין פב טוש"ע ח"מ סי' רה סעיף ט:

רבינו גרשום

והני מילי בשדה סתם. כלומר שאם כופהו בפירוש שימכור לו שדה שלו משום הכי גמר ומקני ליה שדה שיתן לו שדה פחותה שלו. **אבל** אי אמר **שדה זו** מכור לי בפירוש אגב אונסיה אודי **ולא** גמר ומקני ליה: **דלא ארצי זוזי.** שלא רצה לבדוק המעות אם טובות הן אם לאו משמע דמחמת כעס לא מעיין ולא גמר ומקני **אבל ארצי זוזי** זביניה זביני: **אבל הוה לי' לאישתמוטי.** מיניה בשום ענין ומכר זביניה זביני: **תליוה.** שאנסו האשה **שתתקדש** לו: **התינח דקדיש בכספא.** דהיינו קדושין דרבנן משום הכי מצי לאפקועי רבנן מדרבנן. אבל **קדיש בביאה** בעל כרחה. א) דביאה היינו קדושי דאורייתא והיא בעולת בעל **מאי איכא למימר:** **אמר ליה.** אפי' הכי לא הוויין קדושיה קדושין משום **דשויוה רבנן** למאן דקדיש בביאה **לבעילתו בעילת זנות** דחוצפא קא עביד הואיל דתקינו קדושי כספא מצי לאפקועי קדושי ביאה: **אכינרא.** על אותו עץ שכך נקרא שמו עד דזבין ליה קרקע שלו: **אמודעא** דבעל כרחו זבין: **ואאשקלתא.** זהו שטר מכירה שחתם עליו שמכרו: **הכי קאמר אי לאו דחתם אמודעא מאי דחתם אאשקלתא שפיר חתם** דזביניה באונס הוי זביני: והיכי מצי רבה בר בר חנה למיחתם אמודעא מאחר דחתם אאשקלתא **והאמר** רב נחמן עדים שאמרו אמנה היה דברינו כגון שטר שכתבו כי פלוני לוה מפלוני מנה והעדים אם אמרו העדים בפנינו לא הלוהו אלא נדר לו להלוותו והאמין לו הלוה למלוה שיקיים דיבורו ואמר לנו כתבו לו שטר שלוויתי ממנו מנה אבל אנו לא ראינו ההלוואה והלוה טוען לא **אינן נאמנים** דודאי לא הוו משווי נפשיה רשיעי דחתמי שטרא אי לא חזו ההלואה.

חשק שלמה על רבינו גרשום
א) עי' בשיטמ"ק כאן כד"ה תינח.

בשדה סתם אבל בשדה זו לא ובשדה זו נמי לא אמרן אלא דלא ארצי זוזי אבל ארצי זוזי לא ולא אמרן אלא דלא הוה (א) לאישתמוטי אבל הוה ליה לאישתמוטי לא [א] והלכתא בכולהו דהוו זביניה זביני ואפי' בשדה זו דהא אשה כשדה זו דמיא (ב) ואמר אמימר [ב] תליוה וקדיש קדושיו קדושין מר בר רב אשי אמר [ג] באשה ודאי קדושין לא הוו הוא עשה שלא כהוגן לפיכך עשו עמו שלא כהוגן ואפקעינהו רבנן לקידושיה מיניה אמר ליה רבינא לרב אשי [א] תינח דקדיש בכספא קדיש בביאה מאי איכא למימר אמר ליה שויוה רבנן לבעילתו בעילת זנות טאבי תלא לפאפי אכינרא וזבין חתם רבה בר בר חנה אמודעא ואאשקלתא אמר רב הונא [ד] מאן דחתים אמודעא שפיר חתים ומאן דחתים אאשקלתא שפיר חתים מה נפשך אי מודעא לא אשקלתא ואי אשקלתא לא מודעא ה"ק אי לאו מודעא מאן דחתים אאשקלתא שפיר חתים רב הונא לטעמיה [ה] דאמר רב הונא תליוהו וזבין זביניה זביני [ו] והא"ר נחמן העדים שאמרו אמנה היו דברינו אין

והיכא דבטל מודעא בשעת זביני מהני ביטול דאגב אונסיה גמר ומבטל כדאמרינן בפ' האומר משקלי (ערכין דף כא:) ובקונט' הביאה לעיל ואפילו אמר בשעת מודעא כל מה שאבטל לא יהא ביטול אינו כלום דמ"מ לבסוף כשמבטל כל מה שאמר קודם לכן יהא מבוטל דאגב אונסי' גמר ומבטל אבל במתנה אי ידעינן באונסיה לא מהני ביטול ולא גמר ומבטל ומיהו אי לא ידעינן באונסיה ומבטל מודעא מדעתו נראה שבטולו ביטול ולכן כתבינן בשטרי מתנה ביטול מודעי:

אבל שדה זו לא. והא דאמרי נהרדעי לעיל (דף מ.) כל מודעא דלא כתב בה (ח) אנא ידענא ביה באונסין דפלוני לאו מודעא היא לא משכחת אליבא דרבא לעיל אלא כי ההוא מעשה דפרדיסא דבסתם שדה לא מהניא מודעא ובשדה זו לא צריך מודעא אלא לידעו אונסיה:

ואפי' בשדה זו לא אמרינן אלא דלא ארצי זוזי. לפי הספרים דגרסי לא ארצי ליה משמע דבעי למימר דכי אמרי עדים בפנינו מנה לו הוי זביני אפי' בשדה זו וכי קאמר רבא דלא הוי זביני היינו כי אמרו בפנינו הודה לו שלא ראו נתינת המעות וא"כ משמע דבשדה סתם אפילו כי אמרו בפנינו הודה שלא ראו נתינת המעות הוי זביני ואין נראה דבהודאה לא שייך לחלק בין שדה סתם לשדה זו דבתרוייהו שייך למימר אי לאו דאודי ליה הוה ממטי ליה ולאחרי' לשחור ע"כ נראה דגרסינן ולא ארצי זוזי ולא גרסינן ליה וכן פירש בקונטרס:

תינח דקדיש בכספא. הכא לא קאמר כל דמקדש אדעתא דרבנן מקדש וכן בפרק בית שמאי (יבמות דף קי. ושם ד"ה לפיכך) גבי עובדא דנרש דקדשה כשהיא קטנה וגדלה ואתא אינש אחרינא וחטפה מיניה כדאמר בריש כתובות (דף ג. ושם ד"ה תינח) ובהשולח (גיטין דף לג. ושם) משום דהכא ובפ' בית שמאי לא קדש אדעתא דרבנן כדקאמר הוא עשה שלא כהוגן וצריך לומר דסבר הכא דיש כח ביד חכמים לעקור דבר מן התורה כיון דאפקעינהו רבנן לקדושין מיניה ואע"ג דלא קדש אדעתא והכי פירושא בשלמא דקדיש בכספא מצו רבנן להפקיר הכסף ולתת במתנה לאשה אלא דקדיש בביאה אע"ג דיש כח ביד חכמים לעקור דבר מן התורה היינו היכא דליכא עבירה כגון (יבמות פט.) ההוא גריוא דהדר לטיבלא אבל ביאה וכי יעשו חכמים ביאתו ביאת עבירה ומשני אין ודאי דשוויה ביאתו ביאת זנות ובההיא דכתובות (שם) ובהשולח (שם) לכאורה פליגי אהך דשמעתין דאיצטריך למימר טעמא דאדעתא דרבנן מקדש משמע דאי לאו דאדעתא דרבנן מקדש לא היה כח בידם להפקיע הקדושין ומיהו נראה דלא פליגי ואיצטריך טעמא דאדעתא דרבנן מקדש משום דהתם כיון דקדושין נעשו כהוגן לא היה כח לחכמים להפקיעם אי לאו משום דאדעתא דרבנן מקדש:

קדיש בביאה מאי איכא למימר. תימה לרשב"א דקדיש בביאה בלא הפקעה לא להוו קדושין דהוי תליוהו ויהיב דכנגד גופה שקנוי לו אינו נותן לה כלום ודוחק לומר לפי שיש לה הנאת ביאה ועוד דאם כן הא דאמר אמימר תליוה וקדיש קדושיו קדושין לא הוי אלא דקדיש בכסף או בביאה אבל בשטר לא דהוי כמו תליוהו ויהיב וי"ל דכנגד גופה שקנוי לו מתחייב לה שאר כסות ועונה ואע"ג דפרי' לעיל גבי גט דלא חשיב זביני מה שהבעל נפטר משאר כסות ועונה ה"מ גבי בעל שהיה נותנם ברצון ולא היה מגרשה:

אמר רב הונא מאן דחתים אמודעא שפיר חתים. הא דרב הונא פליגא אדרבה דאמר (לעיל מ:) דלא כתבינן מודעא אזביני:

אמר רב נחמן עדים שאמרו אמנה היו דברינו אין נאמנין. על כרחך באין כתב ידם יוצא ממקום אחר איירי דאי יוצא ממקום אחר פשיטא דהכי פריך בפ' שני דכתובות (דף יט. ושם ד"ה אמר) גבי האומר שטר אמנה הוא וכו' זה אינו נאמן דקאמר מאן אי דקאמרי עדים אי כתב ידן יוצא ממקום אחר פשיטא ועוד דמר בר רב אשי דקאמר אמנה היו דברינו אינו נאמן משום דלא ניתן ליכתב ואי כתב ידן יוצא ממקום אחר אפי' ניתן ליכתב אינו נאמן וקשה דלמאי לא מהימני במיגו דאי בעו אמרי אין זה כתב ידינו דהא רב נחמן גופיה אית ליה מיגו לפסול השטר בפ' שני דכתובות (שם) דקאמר כי אתו לקמן לדינא אמינא להו זילו קיימו שטרייכו ותו דלדינא דמהימן לומר פרוע הוא מיגו הוא וכ"ש עדים דלאלימי לאורועי שטרא דהכי אמר בהדיא בפרק מי שמת (לקמן דף קנד.) ותי' ר"י דהיינו טעמא דמודעא ואמנה לר"ל דהשטר נכתב ונמסר כהלכתו שוב לא אתי על פה ומרע לשטרא אפילו במיגו ודמי נמי לחוזרין ומגידין הואיל ואמרו שחתמו על השטר כדין ומדאורייתא עדים החתומין על השטר נעשה כנחקרה עדותן בב"ד ודין הוא דלהכרחו קיום דוקא כי עיין מוזיף אבל

בשדה סתם. שהכריחוהו למכור אחת משדותיו והוא בירר מעצמו ומכר את זאת דכיון דמדעתו בירר רעה שבהן בירר (ג) שאינו חושש בה כל כך וגמר ומקני: **בשדה זו.** הכריחוהו למכור שדה זו ואותה מכר: **דלא ארצי זוזי.** לא מנה המעות גילה דעתו דבעל כרחו מקבל: **ואפי' בשדה זו** ולא ארצי זוזי לא אמרן דלא הוי זביני אלא דלא הוה ליה להאי לאישתמוטי מן התולה (ד) בשום דיחוי שבעולם כגון המתן לי עד למחר או עד שתבוא אשתי או שום דיחוי שיכול לטעות בו האנס: **והלכתא בכולהו הוו זביניה זביני ואפי' בשדה זו.** ולא ארצי זוזי ולא הוה ליה לאישתמוטי דהוי אונס גמור וכגון דאמר רוצה אני: **דהא אשה.** כשמכריחה אדם לקבל קדושיו ולהתקדש לו: **כשדה זו דמיא.** שאינו חפץ כי אם בה: **ואמר** (ה) **אמימר.** כלומר קיימא לן הכי: **תליוה וקדיש.** קבלה קדושין קדושיה קדושין דדמי לזביני שמוכרת עצמה לזה: **מר בר רב אשי אמר.** במכר מודינא דהוו זביני אבל גבי אשה תקון רבנן דלא ליהוו קדושין דהוא עשה שלא כהוגן שהכריחה לפיכך נעשה עמו שלא כהוגן שלא כדין דאע"ג דמן התורה ליהוו קידושין רבנן עקרינהו והפקירו אותן ועשו מעות מתנה ובמקום אחר מפרש דכל דמקדש אדעתא דרבנן מקדש כדת משה וישראל ורבנן אמור לא ליהוו קדושין נמצא שלא קדשה זה שהרי בדעת חכמים תלה והם אינם חפצים בקידושין הללו: **תינח דקדיש בכספא.** יכולין חכמים להפקיע הקדושין דהפקר ב"ד הפקר גבי ממון וכאילו קדשה בגזל ובאתם דמיא דלא הוו קדושין אבל קדיש בביאה שעשה מעשה בגופה היאך יאמרו חכמים שלא תהא ביאה הרי בעל כרחנו ביאה היא: **ואית דמפרש** תינח דקדיש בכספא דקידושי כסף דרבנן הם אמרו והם אמרו וקידושין דדרבנן יכולין לעקור אבל קדיש בביאה דהוו קידושי דאורייתא מאי איכא למימר וטעות הוא בידם דמגזירה שוה ילפינן לקידושי כסף במסכת קדושין (דף ב.) וגם לכל דבר אתקוש הוויות להדדי ואמרינן בכריתות (דף ה.) אל תהי גזירה שוה קלה בעיניך שהרי נותר אחד מגופי תורה ולא למדה הכתוב אלא בגזירה שוה ועוד מאי האי דקמהדר ליה שויוה רבנן לבעילתו בעילת זנות הא כיון דמדאורייתא היא היאך יכולין לעשות ביאתו זנות אלא כיון דאדעתא דרבנן מקדש לא הוי קידושין דאמרי רבנן לא ליהוו קידושין ומתוך כך (ו) נמצאת מעלמה בעילת זנות: **טבי.** גברא אלמא הוי: **תלי' לפפי.** באילן ששמו כינרא למכור לו שדהו. ל"א תלה אותו בשביל הכינרא שימכרנו לו: **וזבין.** כלומר וכן עשה שמכרה לו: **חתם רבה בר בר חנה.** ועד אחר עמו אמודעא שמסר פפי קודם שנכתב שטר המכירה: **ואאשקלתא.** וגם על שטר המכירה חתם: **מאן דחתם אמודעא שפיר חתם.** דאע"ג דתליוהו וזבין זביניה זביני הני מילי היכא דלא מסר מודעא אבל המודעא שכתב בה תבטל המכירה: **ומאן דחתם אאשקלת' שפיר חתם.** דתליוהו וזבין זביניה זביני ודמסיק לקמיה: **רב הונא לטעמיה כו'.** מהכא שמעינן דכתבינן מודעא אזביני אפילו בתליוהו וזבין ודלא כרבא דאמר לעיל (דף מ:) לא כתבינן מודעא אזביני כדפרישית בפירקין לעיל אלא היכא דאנים כמעשה דפרדיסא והכא חזינן עובדא אפי' בתליוהו וזבין דכתבי מודעא וג"כ נראין הדברים שהרי פסקותיו של רבא לא עמדו מאי דפסיק לעיל בתליוהו וזבין [ז] [לא אמרן אלא בשדה סתם] שאחר פסק שלו אמר (ז) לא כתבינן מודעא אזביני כדפרישי' לעיל: **איני.** כלומר היאך בטלה מודעא שחתם בה רבה בר בר חנה את האשקלתא שחתם הוא עצמו בה: **והא אמר רב נחמן כו'.** והכא נמי רבה בר בר חנה קמסהיד עכשיו על האשקלתא מודעא היו דברינו ואמאי נאמן: **עדים.** החתומין בשטר: **ואמרו אמנה היו דברינו.** לא הלוהו כלום אלא כתבנו לו ולכשיצטרך ילוה בו והאמינו לוה למלוה שלא יוציא עליו שטר מלוה זו לגבות הימנו אא"כ ילוה לו וזה שעבד לו נכסיו מעכשיו אם ילוה אפי' לאחר זמן דלאו מוקדם הוא לטרוף שלא כדין:

אין

מסורת הש"ס

א) כתובות ג. יבמות ל: קי. גיטין לג. עג., ב) [לעיל מז: וש"נ], ג) כתובות דף יט., ד) מהרש"ל:

הגהות הב"ח

(א) גמ' דלא הוה ליה לאישתמוטי: (ב) שם כשדה זו דמיא (ואמר אמימר) תא"מ ונ"ב ג"י רשב"ם והרא"ש ואמר מר: (ג) רשב"ם ד"ה בשדה וכו' רעה שבהן בירר גלי דעתיה שאינו חושש: (ד) ד"ה ואפי' בשדה וכו' מן התולה אותו בשום דיחוי בעולם וכו' שיכול לטעות בו: (ה) ד"ה ואמר מר כלומר קיימא לן: (ו) ד"ה ולא למפרע וכו' ומתוך כך נעשית מעלמה בעילת זנות: (ז) ד"ה רב הונא וכו' לתליוהו וזבין שאחר פסק שלו אמר כצ"ל ותיבת לא נמחק: (ח) תוס' ד"ה אבל וכו' דלא כתב בה אנא ידענא ביה באונסיה דפלוני:

ליקוטי רש"י

ואפקעינהו רבנן לקידושיה מיניה. כל המקדש אשה על דעת שהנהיגו חכמי ישראל הוא מקדשה שיהיו קיימין קידושין לפי דברי חכמים ויהיו בטילים לפי דברי חכמים [כתובות ג.]. ושויוה למעות קידושין מתנה למפרע הפקר ב"ד היה הפקר [יבמות צ:]. דכל המקדש אדעתא דרבנן מקדש להיות קידושין תלוין בדת משה וישראל שהנהיגו חכמי ישראל והרי הם אמרו שיפקיעו וכו' והולך פקעי שעל מנת כן קידשה [גיטין לג.]. **תינח דקדיש בכספא.** מינח למימר אפקעתא דקדושין בכספא דמעות וכו' זה עוקר הקידושין ועושה מעות מתנה מעיקרן [כתובות שם]. איכא למימר אפקעינהו לקידושין וכו' ואמרו ליהוי מעות למפרע מתנה ומעלמה פקעו שהרי כשקידש ע"מ כן קידש [גיטין לג.]. איכא למימר דהא אפקעתא דשויוה למעות מתנה [יבמות צ:]. **קדיש בביאה.** דקיימא לן בקידושין (ד:) מכי יקח איש אשה ובעלה דאשה מתקדשת בביאה [גיטין שם]. **מאי איכא למימר.** מאי אפקעתא איכא בשלמא על ידי כסף עשאום מתנה וכו' שהרי גוזרים הכתוב היא שהגט כורתו ומתיר איסורו מכאן והוא הפקר וכו' ואי קדיש בביאה ואתא עוקר קידושין למפרע מה תהא על ביאתו [כתובות שם]. מאי אפקעתא איכא למימר בהא ביאה [גיטין שם]. מאי אפקעתא איכא למימר בהא [יבמות קי.]. מאי אפקעתא איכא למימר האי ביאה מאי שויוה [שם צ:]. **א"ל שויוה רבנן לבעילתו בעילת זנות.** כיון דבדעתא דרבנן תלה ורבנן אמור ליהוי קידושין בכספא וכו' בעילת זנות ואית דאמרי תינח קידושי כסף דמדאורייתא נינהו קדושין בביאה דמדאורייתא נינהו ומאי

א) למימר ועכשיו גדול הוא בידם דקידושי כסף דאורייתא נינהו ומג"ש בקיחה קיחה משדה עפרון גמר לה במסכת קידושין (ב.) וג"ש בשני אמהמה וכל י"ג מדות ואי קידושי כסף מדרבנן מאי קטלינן עלייהו ובדבל ארוסה בסקילה ועוד מאי שינויא דשני שויוה רבנן כו' הא קשיא ליה היכי מצו רבנן לאפקועי מידי דאורייתא ומשני דכל דמקדש אדעתא דרבנן מקדש הא נמי אפקעתא היא [יבמות צ:]. שויוה רבנן להאיך ביאה לבעילת זנות דהא קא בעיל לה למפרע וכו' בעילת זנות לא הפקעתא מיהו שם קדושין מינה ויש כח בהן כל דבר שיהא אמרו ואמר לא להוי כסף קדושין אשר מקדש על דעתם ואם לא הפקירו לא ידעינן אמרה דנקיט דאי מקדש על מנהג מקום כל מאן דמקדש אדעתא דרבנן מקדש אמר דקדושי כסף דרבנן דלא כתיב בהדיא אלא אמרינן קיחה קיחה משדה עפרון והיינו דאקשינן אי מקדש תינח דקדיש בכספא אלא דקדיש בביאה דהיינו קדושי דאורייתא שבביאה משום פירושא ותוספות קשות וכו' בעילת זנות אי הוי קדושין דהוו דבר הלמד מג"ש כגוף תורה הוא דגרסינן להו שאר בעל אלא מגזירה שוה ומעשר אמר ולא הוא דאמר בגמרא כדאמרינן ביבמות וכו' בעילתו בעילת זנות והוא היכי אמרו רבנן שויוה לבעילתו בעילת זנות היא דאורייתא היא וכו' גבי הפקירו ביאה בעל אם קדושי כסף המגרשת נהרגת בקדושין ובו' אם דלא גרסינן אלא דהכא דמשמע דבלא הפקירו וכו' על כרחיה והא ודאי לא מהני בלא דעתו וכו' אם מקדש בכסף וכו' דקדושי ביאה דאורייתא בביאה היא אם לאו ודאי בעי שום הפקעה וכו' הלכך על כרחך אנן מפקעינן ביאה דעתא דידהו [גיטין שם]. שמעתי של רבותי מפרשי לה בגמ' כיון דקידושי כסף נמי דאורייתא נינהו ואי אפשר להם בדבריהם ליהוי הפקר והא לא דלא למיעבד וכו'

who signed the sale document signed properly, i.e. his signature gives the document legal force, as a forced sale is indeed valid.

Rav Huna's statement seems self-contradictory. Thus, the Gemara asks:

מַה נַּפְשָׁךְ – **What is your opinion?** אִי מוֹדָעָא לֹא אַשְׁקַלְתָּא – **If the notification is** legitimate, **then the sale document is not** legitimate. וְאִי אַשְׁקַלְתָּא לֹא מוֹדָעָא – **And if the sale document is** legitimate, **then the notification is not** legitimate. Certainly they cannot *both* have legal force. – ? –

The Gemara answers:

הָכִי קָאָמַר – **This is what [Rav Huna] was saying:** אִי לָאו מוֹדָעָא – **If not** for **the notification,** מַאן דְּחָתִים אַאַשְׁקַלְתָּא שַׁפִּיר חָתִים – then **the one who signs the sale document would be signing properly,** since a forced sale – in the absence of a notification of coercion – is valid.[16]

The Gemara observes:

רַב הוּנָא לְטַעֲמֵיהּ – **Rav Huna,** who says that in the absence of a disclaimer a forced sale is valid, **is consistent with his own view** stated elsewhere, דְּאָמַר רַב הוּנָא – **for Rav Huna said** elsewhere:[17] תַּלְיוּהוּ וְזַבֵּין זְבִינֵיהּ זְבִינֵי – **If they hung him up until he** finally relented and **sold** to them what they demanded, **his sale is a** valid **sale.**

At any rate, Rav Huna agreed that Rabbah bar bar Chanah's signing of the notification succeeded in nullifying the forced sale. Accordingly, the Gemara asks: אִינִי – **Is that so?** וְהָא אָמַר רַב נַחְמָן – **But Rav Nachman said:** הָעֵדִים שֶׁאָמְרוּ אֲמָנָה הָיוּ דְּבָרֵינוּ – Witnesses signed on a document, **who** later **said, "Our** written **words** of testimony in the loan document **were** actually referring to **a** document written on **trust,"**[18]

NOTES

16. The Gemara explains that Rav Huna certainly did not mean that both documents are valid *simultaneously.* Rather, he meant that the sale document would be valid were it not for the notification that nullifies it.

17. Above, 47b.

18. A loan document states that the witnesses (signed below) observed the lender lend money to the borrower. Thus, when the lender produces the loan document, it stands in the place of actual testimony that he indeed lent money to the borrower. Rav Nachman considers a case where the witnesses who signed the document later claim that they did not witness any loan. Rather, they prepared the document in anticipation of a loan (with the "borrower's" approval) so that the document would be ready in the lender's possession when he actually lends the money to the borrower. This is called a "document written on trust," since the "borrower" trusts the lender not to seek to collect on the basis of the document unless a loan is actually made (*Rashbam*).

אֵין נֶאֱמָנִים – **are not believed,** and the document remains effective.[1] מוֹדָעָא הָיוּ דְּבָרֵינוּ אֵין נֶאֱמָנִין – Similarly, witnesses signed on a sale document who say, **"Our words** of testimony in the document **were** preceded by **a notification** made to us by the owner,"[2] **are not believed** and the sale remains valid.[3] How, then, could Rav Huna rule that the notification signed by Rabbah bar bar Chanah nullifies the sale document that he signed?

The Gemara answers:

הָנֵי מִילֵּי עַל פֶּה – **This** ruling of Rav Nachman rejecting the notification **applies** only when the witnesses testify about the notification **orally,** דְּלֹא אָתֵי עַל פֶּה וּמַרְעָא לִשְׁטָרָא – **for** then we say that **the** subsequent **oral [testimony] cannot come and undermine** their testimony given in **the document.** אֲבָל בִּשְׁטָרָא – **But** when their testimony about the notification is recorded **in a document** that precedes the document of sale, אָתֵי שְׁטָרָא וּמַרְעָא לִשְׁטָרָא – then **the** earlier testimony of the notification **document comes and undermines** the later testimony of **the** sale **document.**[4]

The Gemara now cites Rav Nachman's ruling again, in order to record a dissenting view:

גּוּפָא – **The matter itself** cited above: אָמַר רַב נַחְמָן אֲמָנָה הָיוּ דְּבָרֵינוּ אֵין נֶאֱמָנִין – **Rav Nachman said:** Witnesses signed on a document, who later said, **"Our** written **words** of testimony in the loan document **were** actually referring to **a** document written on **trust," are not believed.** מוֹדָעָא הָיוּ דְּבָרֵינוּ אֵין נֶאֱמָנִין – Similarly, if witnesses signed on a sale document say, **"Our words** of testimony in the document **were** preceded by **a notification** made to us by the owner," **they are not believed.** וּמַר בַּר רַב אַשִׁי אָמַר – **But Mar bar Rav Ashi says:** אֲמָנָה הָיוּ דְּבָרֵינוּ אֵין נֶאֱמָנִין – True, witnesses signed on a loan document who say, **"Our words** of testimony in the document **were** referring to **a** document written on **trust," are not believed,** as Rav Nachman asserts. מוֹדָעָא הָיוּ דְּבָרֵינוּ נֶאֱמָנִין – But witnesses signed on a sale document who say, **"Our words** of testimony in the document **were** preceded by **a notification** made to us by the owner," **are believed** and the sale is nullified. מַאי טַעֲמָא – **What is the reason** to distinguish between the two cases? שֶׁזֶּה נִיתָּן לִיכָּתֵב – **For this** sale document that was preceded by the owner's notification **is allowed to be written,** i.e. the witnesses who heard the notification acted properly in proceeding to compose the bogus document of sale, since they thereby relieved the owner of the distress to which he was being subjected. Hence, the testimony of the witnesses is not self-incriminating and is accepted. וְזֶה לֹא נִיתָּן לִיכָּתֵב – **But this** loan document written on trust **is not allowed to be written.**[5] Hence, the testimony of the witnesses is self-incriminating and is rejected.[6]

The Gemara considers the Mishnah's next ruling, which states: וְלֹא לְאִישׁ חֲזָקָה בְּנִכְסֵי אִשְׁתּוֹ וכו׳ – A MAN CANNOT ESTABLISH A *CHAZAKAH* IN THE PROPERTY OF HIS WIFE **etc.**[7]

The Gemara questions the need for this ruling:

פְּשִׁיטָא – **This is obvious!** כֵּיוָן דְּאִית לֵיהּ לְפֵירָא – **Since [the**

NOTES

1. *Rashbam* gives two reasons for this ruling. First, a fundamental principle in the laws of testimony is כֵּיוָן שֶׁהִגִּיד שׁוּב אֵינוֹ חוֹזֵר וּמַגִּיד, *once [a witness] has submitted testimony, he cannot recant and submit [conflicting] testimony.* This applies whether the testimony is submitted personally in court or in a document (when witnesses affix their signatures to a document, it is as if they have testified in court as to what is stated in the document) [see *Shevuos* 31b and *Kesubos* 18b with *Rashi*]. Thus, when the witnesses who signed on a document later declare that the document was written on trust, we cannot accept their new testimony, since that would in effect constitute allowing them to retract what they testified in the document — namely, that a loan did actually occur on the said date. Second, it is prohibited for a lender to hold a loan document written on trust [so that he not be tempted to break his trust and use the document to collect even in the absence of an actual loan]. Thus, the drawing up and signing of such a document is itself an improper act and the witnesses who declare that they did just that are not believed, in keeping with the principle that self-incriminating testimony is not accepted [אֵין אָדָם מֵשִׂים עַצְמוֹ רָשָׁע].

2. I.e. the witnesses signed on the document now testify that before they signed the document the owner showed them how he was being forced to sell and made the disclaimer that he did not want the sale to be effective (*Rashbam*).

3. In this case, too, their new testimony concerning a notification that preceded the sale document conflicts with their earlier testimony in the document, which attests to a bona fide sale. Thus, we cannot accept their retraction of their earlier testimony (*Rashbam*).

4. The principle that testimony cannot be recanted invalidates the witnesses' *later* testimony regarding the case. Now, in Rav Nachman's case, the oral testimony concerning the notification is given *after* that of the sale document (which testifies as of the date of the document). Therefore, the notification testimony, since it is the later testimony, is rejected. In Rav Huna's case, however, the notification testimony recorded in the earlier document precedes the sale testimony recorded in the later one. Therefore, it is the sale testimony that is rejected.

5. As explained in note 1.

6. Unlike Rav Nachman (see above, note 1), Mar bar Rav Ashi holds that the later statements of a document's witnesses clarifying the circumstances under which the document was written as either a situation of trust or of notification do *not* constitute a retraction of their original testimony in the document. It is true that their subsequent testimony serves to nullify the *effects* of that earlier testimony; but since this is done by adding additional information rather than by denying any part of the earlier testimony, it does not fall within the category of recanted testimony. (Mar bar Rav Ashi would agree, however, that if a document's witnesses later claim that the very composition of the document was flawed — e.g. they were minors when they signed it or they signed falsely under duress — they are not believed, since such later statements constitute a retraction of their testimony in the document.) Thus, the sole consideration when the witnesses claim that the document was written on trust or preceded by a notification is whether the witnesses acted properly in composing the impotent document. In the case of a document now claimed to have been written on trust, the witnesses will have acted improperly in being party to such a document (as explained in note 1). Hence, the principle that self-incriminating testimony is not accepted requires us to reject their testimony that the document was written on trust. In the case of a document now claimed to have been preceded by a notification, however, the witnesses were right in signing the impotent document, since that was the only way the owner would be released by his coercers. Hence, their present claim is not at all incriminating and is accepted as a new testimony clarifying the circumstances surrounding their earlier one (*Rashbam*; cf *Tosafos*).

7. A woman can bring her property into a marriage in one of two ways. One way is to have its value appraised and fixed for her at the time of the marriage, and the sum recorded and added to her *kesubah*. In the event of her divorce or widowhood she receives that amount of money, regardless of the actual value of the property at that time. Property brought into the marriage in such a fashion is known as נִכְסֵי צֹאן בַּרְזֶל, *tzon barzel* (literally: iron sheep) *property*. This, in effect, becomes the husband's property, since any increase or decrease in its value accrues to him and he is responsible to pay her (in case of divorce or death) only the value fixed at the time of the marriage. A woman may also decide to bring her property into the marriage and have it remain hers, to be returned to her intact in case of divorce or widowhood. In this case, any increase or decrease in the value of the property during the years of the marriage accrues to her. Nevertheless, the husband has the right to use this property and keep whatever crops or income it produces for as long as the marriage lasts. Such property is known as נִכְסֵי מְלוֹג, *melog* (literally: plucking) *property*.

The Mishnah's ruling refers to this latter type of property (*Rashbam*). The reason for this is that there is no practical difference to a *chazakah* in regard to *tzon barzel* property, inasmuch as the property is his in any case, and he must certainly repay her the value recorded in her *kesubah* if the marriage should dissolve.

אין נאמנים מודעא היו דברינו אין נאמנין ה"מ על פה דלא אתי על פה ומרע לשטרא אבל בשטרא אתי שטרא ומרע לשטרא גופא אמר רב נחמן אמנה היו דברינו אין נאמנין מודעא היו דברינו אין נאמנין (א) ומר בר רב אשי אמר א אמנה היו דברינו אין נאמנין מודעא היו דברינו נאמנין מאי טעמא שזה ניתן ליכתב וזה לא ניתן ליכתב: ב ולא לאיש חזקה בנכסי אשתו וכו': פשיטא כיון דאית ליה לפירא פירא הוא דקאכיל לא צריכא ג דכתב לה דין ודברים אין לי בנכסייך וכי כתב לה מאי הוי והתניא ג) האומר לחבירו דין ודברים אין לי על שדה זו ואין לי עסק בה וידי מסולקות ממנה לא אמר כלום אמרי לה דבי רבי ינאי ד מתניתין בכותב לה ועודה ארוסה וכדרב כהנא דאמר רב כהנא

נחלה

אין נאמנים. לא מבעיא אם כתב ידן יוצא ממקום אחר דלא מהימני לעקרו דלאו הפה שאסר הוא הפה שהתיר איכא אלא אפילו (א) הן עצמם מקיימים אותו ואומרים חתמנו אבל אמנה היו דברינו אין נאמנים דמאחר שהודו שבכשרות נכתב הרי חתימת השטר כאילו העידו בב"ד כל מה שכתוב בשטר שהלוהו מלוה ללוה וכיון שהגיד שוב אינו חוזר ומגיד כדאמרינן בכתובות בפרק האשה שנתארמלה (דף יח:) א"ל רבא כיון שהגיד שוב אינו חוזר ומגיד וכי תימא ה"מ על פה אבל בשטר לא הא אמר ר"ל עדים החתומים על השטר נעשו כמי שנחקרה עדותן בב"ד וה"נ מפרש התם דטעמא דר"נ משום דעקר ליה לשטרא דבעא מיניה רבא מר"נ תנאי היו דברינו מהו מודעא ואמנה טעמא מאי אין נאמנים דקמעקר ליה לשטרא וכו' ועוד יש טעם אחר גבי אמנה היו דברינו אמאי אין נאמנים כדאמר נמי התם אמר רב האומר שטר אמנה הוא זה אינו נאמן ואמרי' דקאמר מאן אילימא דקאמר לוה כו' עד אלא דקאמרי עדים אי דכתב ידם יוצא ממקום אחר פשיטא דלא מהימני ואי דאין כתב ידן יוצא ממקום אחר אמאי לא מהימני והא איכא למימר הפה שאסר הוא הפה שהתיר דאי בעו אמרו לא חתמנו ומסקינן אמר רב אשי לעולם דאמרי עדים ודאין כתב ידן יוצא ממקום אחר ודקאמרת אמאי לא מהימני כדרב כהנא דאמר רב כהנא אסור לאדם שישהה שטר אמנה בתוך ביתו משום שנאמר אל תשכן באהלך עולה וכיון דעולה היא עדים אעולה לא חתמי וכי אמר חתמתי אינו נאמן דאין אדם נאמן בעדות כשמשים עצמו רשע בעדות זו כדאמר התם: **מודעא היו דברינו.** אם שטר מכר הוא ואמרו עדים החתומים בו המוכר מסר מודעא בפנינו והראינו אנסו והכרנו בו אין נאמנין דתרוייהו מודו דשטרא מעליא הוא ועכשיו באין לבטלו ע"י עדות מודעא וקרוי זה חוזר ומגיד וכיון שהגיד עדות שבשטר אינו חוזר ומגיד לבטלו. וה"נ אמאי ביטל רב הונא האשקלתא בשביל המודעא שהרי רבה בר בר חנה הוא העד שאומר מודעא היו דברינו ואינו נאמן: **ומשני ה"מ.** דאין נאמנין על פה שמעידין עכשיו מודעא היו דברינו ובאים לבטל עדות שבשטר שנעשה כמי שנחקרה עדותן בבית דין משעה שנכתב ונחתם ואין עדות אחרון מבטל את הראשון דכיון שהגיד שוב אינו חוזר ומגיד לא אתי על פה דהשתא ומרע לשטרא דקדים אבל בשטרא שנכתב המודעא בשטר וחתמו עליה העדים כי הך דרבה בר בר חנה שקדמה לאשקלתא אתי שטרא דמודעא דקדים ומרע לשטרא דאשקלתא דבתריה: **ומר בר רב אשי אמר אמנה היו דברינו אין נאמנים.** כדמפרש לקמיה שלא ניתן ליכתב כדפרישית לעיל משום דכתיב אל תשכן באהלך עולה ועדים אעולה לא חתמי וכשמעיד חתמתי אינו נאמן דאין אדם משים עצמו רשע והלכך אפי' אין כתב ידן יוצא ממקום אחר אין נאמנין דאין נאמן לעשות עצמו רשע אבל לעקירת שטר לא חייש מר בר רב אשי דא"כ גבי מודעא אמאי נאמנים: **מודעא היו דברינו נאמנים.** שהרי ניתן ליכתב דמלוה קעבדי כדי להציל האנוס מאנסו ואפי' כתב ידן יוצא ממקום אחר נאמנים דאין זה חוזר ומגיד אלא מילתא אחריתי קמסהדי כדאמרינן נמי התם חתמנו אבל תנאי היו דברינו ולא נתקיים התנאי דמילתא אחריתי היא ונאמנים שעל השטר מעידין שכשר וגם מעידים שאין חייב לו כלום והיכי דמי חוזר ומגיד כדתנן התם פסולים היינו אנוסין היינו קטנים היינו אם כתב ידן יוצא ממקום אחר אין נאמנים שהרי פוסלין את השטר לגמרי דקאמרי בפסלות נחתם הוא דפסלין לעדותם משום חוזר ומגיד: **אין לאיש חזקה בנכסי אשתו.** שאם החזיק בנכסי מלוג של אשתו שנפלו לה מבית אביה בירושה ג' שנים אינה חזקה לומר מאשתי לקחתיה ואבדתי שטרי דאין דרך אשה למחות על בעלה כשמחזיק בנכסיה ואוכל את הפירות מאחר שזן אותה: **פשיטא.** דאין יכול לטעון לקוח הוא בידי: **דכיון דאית ליה פירא.** בתקנת חכמים שתקנו פירות של נכסי אשה לבעל תחת פרקונה אותן פירי הוא דקאכיל ואין לו בגוף הקרקע כלום ואין צריכה למחות שהכל יודעין שבתורת פירות ירד לקרקע זו ולא דמי למשכנתא דסורא דאמרן דצריך למחות בסוף כל ג' דהתם היינו טעמא שמא לסוף זמן מרובה לא יהו עדים זכורים שבתורת משכון באה לידו ויכול לטעון לקוח הוא בידי אבל נכסי אשה לבעלה כל העולם יודעין שפירות יש לו בקרקע אשתו ולא תהיה לו חזקה בחייה: **דין ודברים אין לי.** כלומר לא יהא לי ואפילו הכי אין לאיש חזקה דאין אשתו מקפדת אם יאכל הפירות שלא כדין: **לא אמר כלום.** דאין זה לשון מתנה כשאמר לא יהא לי חלק בשלי דעל כרחו הרי הוא שלו עד שיאמר לחבירו שדי נתונה לך שדי מכורה לך שדי מופקרת לכל מי שירצה: **מתני' בכותב לה.** דין ודברים אין לי בנכסייך: **בעודה ארוסה.** דהיינו קודם שיזכה בנכסי אשתו דאינו זוכה בפירות עד שעת נשואין וכדמסיק ואזיל דירושות הבאות לאדם בתקנת חכמים יכול לעקרן אם מתנה עליה קודם הזמן בעוד שלא באו לידו ואומר לא יהא לי חלק באותו ממון העתיד לבא לי בתקנת חכמים דאין מזכין לו לאדם בעל כרחו: **וכדרב כהנא.** הוא דמועיל תנאי זה:

נחלה

אבל כשאומר שהשטר נכתב ונמסר כהלכתו אין נאמן לומר מודעא ואמנה היו דברינו במיגו דמזוייף ולא דמי לקטנים ואנוסים היינו דמתני' בפ"ב דכתובות (דף יח: ושם ד"ה הרי) דאין מודין כלל שהשטר נכתב כדין שאומרים שאנוסים וקטנים ופסולים היו ולא נכתב מעולם כדין הלכך מיגו מהני דלא שייך כאן לומר לא אתי על פה ומרע לשטרא שהרי אין מודים שהיה שטר כדין והא דאית ליה בפ' שני דכתובות (דף יט.) דנאמן לומר פרוע הוא במיגו דמזוייף התם נמי לא מרע לשטרא כלל ורב הונא דקאמר התם מודה בשטר שכתבו א"צ לקיימו סבר דאפילו פרוע הוא אינו נאמן לומר במיגו אע"ג דלא מרע לשטרא אלא א"כ טוען מזוייף וא"ת כיון דר"נ מודה דאין נאמן לומר שהוא שטר אמנה ומודעא מאי קא"ל לרב הונא דאמר א"צ לקיימו גנובה גנבי למה לך אי סבירא לך כר"מ אימא הלכה כר"מ דלמא רב הונא נמי אאמנה ומודעא קאמר דא"צ לקיימו דמודה ביה ר"נ וי"ל דרב הונא אפי' אטענת פרוע קאמר דא"צ לקיימו מדלא מפליג מידי והשתא לר"נ אפילו לרבנן דפליגי אר"מ התם באמנה ומודעא מודו והכיא ברייתא דתניא פ' מי שמת (לקמן דף קנד: ושם) האומר דשטר אמנה הוא זה אינו נאמן ובעי לאוקומה בפלוגתא דר"מ ורבנן ורב נחמן הוי מוקי לה כדברי הכל: **מר** בר רב אשי אמר מודעא היו דברינו נאמנין. דלא דמי לחוזרין ומגידין שאינם אלא מוסיפין על עדותם אע"ג דכשכתב ידן יוצא ממקום אחר אין נאמנין ולא אמרינן דמוסיפין על עדותן הן מ"מ כשאין כתב ידן יוצא ממקום אחר נאמנין במיגו הואיל ואין חוזרין לגמרי מעדותם: **דכתב** לה דין ודברים אין לי בנכסייך. וצריך לומר דכתב לה נמי ובפירותיהן כדתנן בהכותב (כתובות דף פג.) דאי לא כתב לה אלא בנכסייך אכתי אוכל פירות ולא מהני בנכסייך אלא שאם מכרה ונתנה קיים: **בכתב** לה בעודה ארוסה. והוי מצי למימר שכתב לה בלשון טוב על מנת שאין לבעלה רשות בה או שנתן לה בעלה לקמן קנתה ואין הבעל אוכל פירות: **וכדרב** כהנא. תימה דמאי מייתי ראיה מדרב כהנא אי דמייתי דמהני לשון דין ודברים אע"פ שהוא לשון גרוע דלמא כל הנהו דמייתי מיירי (ב) בלשון טוב ועוד דאי אפשי דמייתי הוא לשון טוב כדמוכח בפ' בתרא דכריתות (דף כד.) ויש מפרשים (ג) מדקאמרינן נחלה הבאה לו לאדם דוקא ולא הבאה לו כבר מכלל דבלשון גרוע מיירי דאי בלשון טוב אפי' באה לו כבר נמי למה לא יוכל להתנות עליה ולר"י נראה דמייתי ראיה דלאע"ג דקיי"ל דאין אדם מקנה דבר שלא בא לעולם מ"מ יכול להסתלק מדבר שלא בא לעולם ואם תאמר לרב כהנא מאי מייתי דמדבר שלא בא לעולם יכול להסתלק מידי דהוה אשאר כסות ועונה (לקמן קכו:) דאר"י בדבר שבממון תנאו קיים ואפי' ר"מ לא פליג אלא משום דקסבר מתנה על מה שכתוב בתורה תנאו בטל וי"ל דשאני התם שעושה תנאי גמור אבל הכא מיירי שאינו אומר דרך תנאי אלא שאומר דין ודברים אין לי בנכסייך ועוד דהכא שאומר מעצמו ואין האשה מבקשת ממנו ס"ד דהוי פטומי מילי בעלמא כדאמרינן גבי נשך (ב"מ דף סו. ושם) דלאשה איבעי לה לאתנויי ועוד קא מתני ומייתי נמי מדרב כהנא דהסילוק מועיל נמי כדרבא דאמר כלומר באותו נחלה מועיל התנאי באותה שבאה לו על ידי תקנת חכמים כדרבא נחלה דאורייתא כגון דין ודברים אין לי בירושתך לא יועיל כלום ודרב הונא מייתי דטעמא דיכול להסתלק משום דכיון דלטובתו תקנו יכול לומר אי אפשי בטובה (ג) בלשון דין ודברים לא צריך לאיתויי ראיה דסברא הוא דכיון דלא בא לידו (ד) דשייך לשון דין ודברים כמו בעלמא לישנא מעליא והא דאיצטריך לכדרב כהנא לאו משום דרבי ינאי איצטריך דאיהו סבירא ליה בהאשה רבה (יבמות דף לג. ושם)

דלאדם

עין משפט נר מצוה

קפז א מיי' פ"ג מהל' עדות הלכה ז סמג לאוין קט טוש"ע ח"מ סי' מו סעיף לז:

קפח ב ג ד מיי' פי"ג מהל' טוען הל' א ופי"ד הלכה א ופכ"ג מהלכות אישות הלכה טו סמג עשין לה ועשין מח טוש"ע ח"מ סי' קמט סעי' ט וטוש"ע אה"ע סי' צב סעי' א:

רבינו גרשום

מודעא היו דברינו. כלומר אע"פ שחתמנו על שטר המכירה שמעיד שברצונו מכר אעפ"כ יודעים אנו שאנוס היה ואין נאמנין והיכי מצי חתים רבה אמודעא. והכי משמע השתא דמאי דאמרין מודעא היו דברינו דחתמי נמי אמודעא: ומשני הני מילי דאין נאמנין להיכא דאמרי עדים על פה יודעין אנו שבאונס מכר דודאי לא אתא על פה ומרע לשטר דכתוב ביה דברצון מכר אבל היכא דכתבו המודעא בשטר וחתומה הויא מודעא דאתי שטר מודעא ומרע ליה לשטר מכירה ומשום הכי שפיר חתם רבה בר בר הונא אמודעא שבשטר ואי לאו דחתים אמודעא מאי חתים אאשקלתא שפיר חתם: מאי טעמא מודעא היו דברינו נאמנין. דזה מודעא ניתן ליכתב שטר מסירת מודעא וניתנה נמי ליחתם ואפי' הכי יכולין לחתום עדי מודעא גופייהו על שטר מכירה ונאמנין. והאי שטר אמנה לא ניתן ליכתב כלומר מאחר שחתמו על השטר שכתב בו פלוני לוה מפלוני מנה ודאי משמע דאי לאו דחזו דהלוהו לא הוו חתמי והשתא אי הוו כתבו בשטר אחר אמנה היו דברינו הוו מיחזו עדים שקרים. הלכך אין נאמנין דלא ניתן ליכתב דאין אדם משים עצמו רשע לחתום שקר: פיס'. אין לאיש חזקה בנכסי אשתו של מלוג דאם החזיק לבדו בנכסים ג' שנים אין לו חזקה. פשיטא דלא הוי חזקה דכיון דנכסי מלוג משתעבדי ליה לפירי פירי הוא דקאכיל ואין הגוף שלו ואין לו חזקה: אין לי בנכסייך. דמשמע לגמרי דהשתא לא אכיל לפירי וסד"א הואיל דכתב לה הכי והחזיק בנכסיה תיהוי חזקה קמ"ל דלא דמצא למימר נחת רוח עשיתי לבעלי שלא מחיתי בנכסיו: לא אמר כלום. דהא חזינן דמתנקש ברשותו הוי: ועודה ארוסה. דעדיין לא היו נכסיה ברשותו:

מסורת הש"ס

א) [כתובות דף יט:], ב) [לעיל מג.], כתובות פג. פה. גיטין עז. כריתות כד:, ג) צ"ל אלשון, ד) ר"מ:

הגהות הב"ח

(א) רשב"ם ד"ה אין נאמנים וכו' אפי' אם הן עצמם: (ב) תוס' ד"ה וכדרב כהנא וכו' מיירי דלאמר בלשון טוב: (ג) בא"ד ויש מפרשים דמדקאמר נחלה הבאה: (ד) בא"ד הסיכה דלא בא לידו מהני לשון דין ודברים:

ליקוטי רש"י

[illegible]

[ע"כ שייך לדף מח:] מודעא היו דברינו. אם שטר מכר הוא ואמרו עדים החתומים בו המוכר מסר מודעא בפנינו והראינו אונסו והכרנו בו. מודעא. [illegible] [כתובות יט.]. האומר לחבירו. שותף [רשב"ם לעיל מג.]. [illegible] [כתובות פג.]. על שדה זו. [illegible] [גיטין עז.]. לא אמר כלום. דאין כאן לשון מתנה [כתובות שם]. [illegible] [כריתות כד.]. [illegible]

[illegible] לאדם לאחר מכן יכול להתנות עליה שלא יירשנה אבל מכיון שכבר הדבר שלו הוא והוא אומר לא יהא שלי לא אמר כלום דבעל כרחו יהיה שלו כל זמן שלא יתננה לאחרים כן נראה בעיני ועיקר והכי מוכח לקמן בפירקין וי"מ דמשום הכי לא [illegible] אמר כלום כדקאמר אין לי דין ודברים ולא קאמר לא יהא ונמצא שהוא מכזב שהרי יש לו חלק בו והוא אומר אין לי ושבוש הוא דאין זה לשון הגמ' לומר בשום מקום לא יהא והכי מוכח לקמן דקמשני הכא במאי עסקינן בשקנו מידו [illegible] לא יהא [רשב"ם שם]. מתניתין בכותב לה ועודה ארוסה. ודאי מי שהקרקע שלו ובא ליתנו לחבירו צריך לשון מתנה ומתניתין בכותב לה עד שלא זכה בנכסים ומתנה עמה שלא יזכה בהן לכשישאנה ולא [illegible] לשון מתנה שהרי אין לו עכשיו רשות בהן [כתובות פג.]. בכותב לה דין ודברים כו' בעודה ארוסה קודם שזוכה בנכסים וא"צ לכתוב לשון מתנה דיכול להתנות כדרב כהנא [גיטין עז.].

husband] has a right to **the produce** of his wife's property, פֵּירָא הוּא דְּקָאָכִיל – it is merely **the produce** to which he is entitled **that he has consumed!** Quite obviously, his consumption of it cannot prove that he acquired the field from his wife. Why should the Mishnah state such a self-evident ruling?[8]

The Gemara answers:

לֹא צְרִיכָא – **[The Mishnah's ruling] is needed only** דְּכָתַב לָהּ דִּין וּדְבָרִים אֵין לִי בִּנְכָסַיִךְ – **where [the husband] wrote** a document **to [his wife]** stating: **I** wish to **have neither claim nor argument** with respect **to your property.**[9] The Mishnah teaches that even after a husband waives his right to the produce of his wife's property, his use of the property can still not establish a *chazakah* for him to support his claim of having bought it from her.[10]

The Gemara asks:

וְכִי כָתַב לָהּ מַאי הָוֵי – **But even if he wrote** this declaration **to her, what does it** accomplish? וְהָתַנְיָא – **Have we** not **learned in a Baraisa:** הָאוֹמֵר לַחֲבֵירוֹ דִּין וּדְבָרִים אֵין לִי עַל שָׂדֶה זוֹ – IF ONE SAYS TO HIS FELLOW: I wish to HAVE NEITHER CLAIM NOR ARGUMENT with respect TO THIS FIELD of mine, וְאֵין לִי עֵסֶק בָּהּ – OR, I wish to HAVE NO CONCERN WITH IT, וְיָדַי מְסוּלָּקוֹת מִמֶּנָּה – OR, MY HANDS ARE hereby WITHDRAWN FROM IT, לֹא אָמַר כְּלוּם – HE HAS NOT SAID ANYTHING, i.e. his statement is of no legal consequence?[11] Thus, the right to take the produce remains his despite the declaration! – ? –

The Gemara answers:

אָמְרֵי לָהּ דְּבֵי רַבִּי יַנַּאי – **The academy of R' Yannai answered:** מַתְנִיתִין בְּכוֹתֵב לָהּ וְעוֹדָהּ אֲרוּסָה – **Our Mishnah** refers to a case in **which he writes** this document **to her while she is still betrothed** to him, when he has not yet acquired the right to use her property.[12] וְכִדְרַב כַּהֲנָא – **And** this explanation of the Mishnah **follows** the ruling of **Rav Kahana.** דְּאָמַר רַב כַּהֲנָא – **For Rav Kahana said:**

NOTES

8. It is perfectly obvious that if a husband has the right to take the produce of his wife's property, his wife has no reason to protest his taking it. She has a right to expect that everyone understands he is taking the produce of the field only by the right granted to all husbands to use their wives' property (*Rashbam*). [This right is by Rabbinic enactment, in exchange for an obligation on the husband to ransom his wife should she be taken captive (*Rashbam* from *Kesubos* 47b).]

9. The Gemara here gives an abbreviated form of this declaration. In practice, he must say that he waives his right to her property *and its produce* (*Tosafos*, based on *Kesubos* 83a).

10. Once a man relinquishes his right to the produce of his wife's field, he has no more right to it than a stranger. It should follow, therefore, that if after waiving his right, the husband used the field for three years without eliciting any protest from his wife, this should establish that she sold it to him. The Mishnah teaches that even so, his use of her field does not constitute a *chazakah*. Since her husband supports her, a wife is likely to allow him to take produce that belongs to her even when he is not legally entitled to it (*Rashbam*).

11. In order for a person to relinquish ownership of his property, he must formally transfer it, either by selling it, giving it away to someone, or declaring it ownerless (הֶפְקֵר, *hefker*). Merely stating that he wishes to have nothing further to do with his property is not effective because it is neither the wording of a gift (since he does not tell his friend to acquire it) nor of *hefker* (since he does not state that it is available for anyone to acquire); it is merely a wishful prayer. Thus, the property remains his despite his declaration (*Rashbam* 43a).

Accordingly, even if the husband gives his wife a document stating that he wishes to have no right or claim to her property, the right is still his (*Rashbam*). Therefore, even if he did make this declaration, it is still obvious that he can have no *chazakah* in the property of his wife!

12. Marriage takes place in two stages. The first is known as *erusin* (betrothal). During this stage, the couple is legally 'married' and the prohibition of adultery is in effect. A regular divorce is required to dissolve the marriage. Nevertheless, the couple does not live together as husband and wife until the completion of the marriage, which is known as *nisuin*. The Rabbinic enactment that a husband may take the produce of his wife's property does not take effect until the *nisuin* stage of the marriage. Thus, if the husband renounces his right to the produce before *nisuin*, during the *erusin* (betrothal) period, his renunciation precedes his acquisition of the right, and is effective even without a formal transaction, as the Gemara will now explain (*Rashbam*).

[The contemporary custom is for the *erusin* (commonly effected by giving the wedding ring) and *nisuin* (effected by means of the *chupah*) to take place one immediately after the other. In earlier times, however, these were performed separately, with as much as a year intervening.]

Although the Gemara speaks of a case in which he recorded the waiver in a legal document, it is effective even if it is only declared orally (Gemara, *Kesubos* 83a; *Even HaEzer* 92:1).

[The Gemara speaks of his renouncing his future right during their betrothal (*erusin*). Before they are betrothed, however, his renunciation of the produce is of no consequence (*Rama, Even HaEzer* 92:1; see *Chelkas Mechokek* ad loc. for an explanation).]

אין נאמנים מודעא היו דברינו אין נאמנין ה״מ על פה דלא אתי על פה ומרע לשטרא אבל בשטרא אתי שטרא ומרע לשטרא גופא אמר רב נחמן אמנה היו דברינו אין נאמנין מודעא היו דברינו אין נאמנין (א) ומר בר רב אשי אמר א אמנה היו דברינו אין נאמנין מודעא היו דברינו נאמנין מאי טעמא שזה ניתן ליכתב וזה לא ניתן ליכתב: ב ולא לאיש חזקה בנכסי אשתו וכו׳: פשיטא כיון דאית ליה לפירא פירא הוא דקאכיל לא צריכא ג דכתב לה דין ודברים אין לי בנכסייך וכי כתב לה מאי הוי והתניא ג) האומר לחבירו דין ודברים אין לי על שדה זו ואין לי עסק בה וידי מסולקות ממנה לא אמר כלום אמרי דבי רבי ינאי ד מתניתין בכותב לה ועודה ארוסה וכדרב כהנא דאמר רב כהנא נחלה

אין נאמנים. לא מבעיא אם כתב ידן יוצא ממקום אחר דלא מהימני לעקרו דלאו הפה שאסר הוא הפה שהתיר איכא אלא אפילו (א) הן עצמם מקיימים אותו ואומרים חתמנו אבל אמנה היו דברינו אין נאמנים למאמר שהודו שבכשרות נכתב הרי חתימת השטר כאילו העידו בב״ד כל מה שכתוב בשטר שהלוהו מלוה לזה וכיון שהגיד שוב אינו חוזר ומגיד כדאמרינן בכתובות בפרק האשה שנתארמלה (דף יח:) א״ל רבא כיון שהגיד שוב אינו חוזר ומגיד וכי תימא ה״מ על פה אבל בשטר לא והא אמר ר״ל עדים החתומים על השטר נעשו כמי שנחקרה עדותן בב״ד וה״נ מפרש התם דטעמא דר״ל משום דעקר ליה לשטרא דבעלמא מייתי רבה מר״ל תנאי היו דברינו מהו מודעא ואמנה טעמא מאי אין נאמנים דקמעקר ליה לשטרא וכו׳ ועוד יש טעם אחר גבי אמנה היו דברינו אמאי אין נאמנים כדאמר נמי התם אמר רב הא דאמר שטר אמנה הוא זה אינו נאמן ואמרי׳ דקאמר מאן אילימא דקאמר לוה כו׳ עד אלא דקאמרי עדים אי דכתב ידם יוצא ממקום אחר פשיטא דלא מהימני ואי דאין כתב ידן יוצא ממקום אחר אמאי לא מהימני והא איכא למימר הפה שאסר הוא הפה שהתיר דאי בעו אמרו לא חתמנו ומסקינן אמר רב אשי לעולם דאמרי עדים ודאין כתב ידן יוצא ממקום אחר ודקאמרת אמאי לא מהימני מדרב כהנא דאמר רב כהנא אסור לאדם שיהא שטר אמנה בתוך ביתו משום שנאמר אל תשכן באהלך עולה וכיון דעולה היא ועדים אעולה לא חתמי וכי אמר חתמתי אינו נאמן דאין אדם נאמן לשים עצמו רשע בעדות זו כדאמר התם: **מודעא היו דברינו.** אם שטר מכר הוא ואמרו עדים החתומים בו המוכר מסר מודעא בפנינו והכרחו אנסו והכריחו בו אין נאמנין דהדריהו מודו דשטרא מעליא הוא ועכשיו באין לבטלו ע״י עדות מודעא וקרוי זה חוזר ומגיד וכיון שהגיד עדות שבשטר אינו חוזר ומגיד לבטלו. וה״נ אמאי ביטל רב הונא האשקלתא בשביל המודעא שהרי רבה בר בר חנה הוא העד שאומר מודעא היו דברינו ואינו נאמן: **ומשני ה״מ.** דאין נאמנין על פה שמעידין עכשיו מודעא היו דברינו ובאים לבטל עדות שבשטר שנעשה כמי שנחקרה עדותן בבית דין משעה שנכתב ונחתם ואין עדות אחרון מבטל את הראשון דכיון שהגיד שוב אינו חוזר ומגיד לא אתא על פה להשתא ומרע לשטרא קדים אבל בשטרא שנכתב המודעא בשטר וחתמו עליה העדים כי הך דרבה בר בר חנה שקדמה לאשקלתא אתי שטרא דמודעא דקדים ומרע לשטרא דאשקלתא דבתריה: **ומר בר רב אשי אמר אמנה היו דברינו אין נאמנים.** כדמפרש לקמיה שלא ניתן ליכתב כדפרישית לעיל משום דכתיב אל תשכן באהלך עולה ועדים אעולה לא חתמי וכשמעיד חתמתי אינו נאמן דאין אדם משים עצמו רשע והלכך אפי׳ אין כתב ידן יוצא ממקום אחר אין נאמנין דאין נאמן לעשות עצמו רשע אבל לעקירת שטר לא חיים מר בר רב אשי דא״כ גבי מודעא אמאי נאמנים: **מודעא היו דברינו נאמנים.** שהרי ניתן ליכתב דמצוה קעבדי כדי להציל האנוס מאונסו ואפי׳ כתב ידן יוצא ממקום אחר נאמנים דאין זה חוזר ומגיד אלא מילתא אחריתי קמסהדי כדאמרינן נמי התם חתמנו אבל תנאי היו דברינו ולא נתקיים התנאי דמילתא אחריתי היא ונאמנים שעל השטר מעידין שכשר וגם מעידים שאין חייב לו כלום והיכי דמי חוזר ומגיד כדתנן התם פסולים היינו אנוסין היינו קטנים היינו אם כתב ידן יוצא ממקום אחר אין נאמנים שהרי פוסלין את השטר לגמרי דקאמרי בפסלות נחתם הוא דפסלינן לעדותם משום חוזר ומגיד: **אין לאיש חזקה בנכסי אשתו.** שאם החזיק בנכסי מלוג של אשתו שנפלו לה מבית אביה בירושה ג׳ שנים אינה חזקה לומר מאשתי לקחתיה ואבדתי שטרי דאין דרך אשה למחות על בעלה כשמחזיק בנכסיה ואוכל את הפירות מאחר שזן אותה: **פשיטא.** דאין יכול לטעון לקוח הוא בידי: **דכיון דאית ליה פירא.** בתקנת חכמים שתקנו פירות של נכסי אשה לבעל תחת פרקונה אותן פירי הוא דקאכיל ואין לו בגוף הקרקע כלום ואין צריכה למחות שהכל יודעין שבתורת פירות ירד לקרקע זו ולא דמי למשכנתא דסורא דאמרן דצריך למחות בסוף כל ג׳ דהתם היינו טעמא שמא לסוף זמן מרובה לא יהו עדים זכורים שבתורת משכון באה לידו ויכול לטעון לקוח הוא בידי אבל נכסי אשה לבעלה כל העולם יודעין שפירות יש לו בקרקע אשתו ולא תהיה לו חזקה בחייה: **דין ודברים אין לי.** כלומר לא יהא לי ואפילו הכי אין לאיש חזקה דאין אשתו מקפדת אם יאכל הפירות שלא כדין: **לא אמר כלום.** דאין זה לשון מתנה כשאמר לא יהא לי חלק בשלי דעל כרחו הרי הוא שלו עד שיאמר לחבירו שדי נתונה לך שדי מכורה לך שדי מופקרת לכל מי שירצה: **מתני׳ בכותב לה.** דין ודברים אין לי בנכסייך: **בעודה ארוסה.** דהיינו קודם שזכה בנכסי אשתו דאינו זוכה בפירות עד שעת נשואין וכדמסיק ואזיל דירושות הבאות לאדם בתקנת חכמים יכול לעקרן אם מתנה עליה קודם הזמן בעוד שלא באו לידו ואומר לא יהא לי חלק באותו ממון העתיד לבא לי בתקנת חכמים דאין מזכין לו לאדם בעל כרחו: **וכדרב כהנא.** הוא דמועיל תנאי זה:

אבל כשאומר שהשטר נכתב ונמסר כהלכתו אין נאמן לומר מודעא ואמנה היו דבריהם מיגו דמזויף ולא דמי לקטנים ואנוסים היינו דמתני׳ בפ״ב דכתובות (דף יח: ושם ד״ה הרי) דאין מודין כלל שהשטר נכתב כדין שאומרים שאנוסים וקטנים ופסולים היו ולא נכתב מעולם כדין הלכך מיגו מהני דלא שייך כאן לומר לא אתי על פה ומרע לשטרא שהרי אין מודים שהיה שטר כדין והא דאית ליה בפ׳ שני דכתובות (דף יט.) דנאמן לומר פרוע הוא במיגו דמזויף התם נמי לא מרע לשטרא כלל ורב הונא דקאמר התם מודה בשטר שכתבו א״צ לקיימו סבר דאפילו פרוע הוא אינו נאמן לומר במיגו אע״ג דלא מרע לשטרא אלא א״כ טוען מזויף וא״ת כיון דר״נ מודה דאין נאמן לומר שהוא שטר אמנה ומודעא מאי קא״ל לרב הונא דאמר א״צ לקיימו גנובה למה לך אי סבירא לך כר״מ אימא הלכה כר״מ דלמא רב הונא נמי לאמנה ומודעא קאמר דא״צ לקיימו דמודה ביה ר״נ וי״ל דרב הונא אפי׳ לטענת פרוע קאמר דא״צ לקיימו מלהא מפליג מידי והשתא לר״נ אפילו לרבנן דפליגי אר״מ התם באמנה ומודעא מודו והשתא ברייתא דתניא פ׳ מי שמת (לקמן דף קנד: ושם) זה האומר דשטר אמנה הוא זה אינו נאמן ובעי לאוקומה כפלוגתא דר״מ ורבנן רב נחמן הוי מוקי לה כדברי הכל: **מר בר רב אשי אמר מודעא היו דברינו נאמנין.** דלא דמי לחוזרין ומגידין שאינם אלא מוסיפין על עדותם אע״ג דכשכתב ידן יוצא ממקום אחר אין נאמנין ולא אמרינן דמוסיפין על עדותן הן מ״מ כשאין כתב ידן יוצא ממקום אחר נאמנין במיגו הואיל ואין חוזרין לגמרי מעדותם: **דכתב** לה דין ודברים אין לי בנכסייך. וצריך לומר דלדכתב לה ופירותיהן כדתנן בהכותב (כתובות דף פג. ושם) דלאו כי כתב לה אלא בנכסייך הכי אכיל פירות ולא מהני בנכסייך אלא אם מכרה ונתנה קיים: **בכתב** לה בעודה ארוסה. והוה מצי למימר שכתב לה בלשון טוב אי נמי שנתנו לה על מנת שאין לבעלה רשות בה או שנתן לה בעלה דאמר לקמן קנתה ואין הבעל אוכל פירות: **וכדרב** כהנא. תימה דמאי מייתי ראיה מדרב כהנא לא מייתי מדמהני לשון דין ודברים אע״פ שהוא לשון גרוע דלמא כל הנהו דמייתי מיירי (ג) בלשון טוב ועוד דלאו אפשי דמייתי הוא לשון טוב כדמוכח בפ׳ בתרא דכריתות (דף כד.) ויש מפרשים (ג) מדקאמרינן נחלה הבאה לו לאדם לו דוקא ולא הבאה לו כבר מכלל דבלשון גרוע מיירי דאי בלשון טוב אפי׳ באה לו כבר נמי למה לא יוכל להתנות עליה ולר״י נראה דמייתי ראיה דאע״ג דקיי״ל דאין אדם מקנה דבר שלא בא לעולם מ״מ יכול להסתלק מדבר שלא בא לעולם ואם תאמר בלא רב כהנא מאי מייתי מדבר שלא בא לעולם יכול להסתלק מידי דהוה אשאר כסות ועונה (לקמן קכו:) דאר״י בדבר שבממון תנאו קיים ואפי׳ ר״מ לא פליג אלא משום דקסבר מתנה על מה שכתוב בתורה תנאו בטל וי״ל שאני התם שעושה תנאי גמור אבל הכא מיירי שאינו אומר דרך תנאי אלא שאומר דין ודברים אין לי בנכסייך ועוד דהכא שאומר מעצמו ואין האשה מבקשת ממנו ס״ד דהוי פטומי דמילי בעלמא כדאמרינן באיזהו נשך (ב״מ דף סו. ושם) דלאשה איבעי לה לאתנויי ובעל קא מתני ומייתי מדרב כהנא דבסילוק מועיל ומייתי נמי כדרבא כלומר באיזו נחלה מועיל התנאי באותה שבאה לו על ידי תקנת חכמים כדרבא אבל בנחלה דאורייתא כגון דין ודברים אין לי בירושת אבי לא יועיל כלום ודרב הונא מייתי דטעמא דיכול להסתלק משום דכיון דלטובתו תקנו יכול לומר איני חפץ באותה טובה אבל (ג) בלשון דין ודברים לא צריך לאיתויי ראיה דסברא הוא דהיכא דלא בא לידו (ד) דשייך לשון דין ודברים כמו בעלמא לישנא מעליא והא דאיצטריך לכדרב כהנא לאו משום דרבי ינאי איצטריך דאיהו סבירא ליה בהאשה רבה (יבמות דף לג. ושם) דאדם

מסורת הש״ס

א) [כתובות דף יט:], ב) [לעיל מב.] כתובות פג. לה. גיטין עז. [כריתות כד:], ג) נ״ל אלעזר, ר״מ:

הגהות הב״ח

(א) רשב״ם ד״ה אין נאמנים וכו׳ אפי׳ אם הן עצמם: (ב) תוס׳ ד״ה וכדרב כהנא וכו׳ מיירי דאמר בלשון טוב: (ג) בא״ד ויש מפרשים מדקאמר נחלה הבאה: (ד) בא״ד דהיכא דלא בא לידו מהני לשון דין ודברים:

ליקוטי רש״י

היה קונה קונה משדה עפרון (קידושין ג.). וכל הלמד מגזירה שוה כמו שכתוב מפורש הוא לכל דבר ועוד אי דרבנן ניכנסו היאך מוקלין על ידי ומבטלין עולין לעזרה על שגגתן ואין סוף כי קא משמע שויה רבנן לבעילתו בעילת זנות על כרחך צריך לאו לפרש כמו שפירשתי שמקדושין נעקרין מעיקרן ולא מכאן והבא והמפרש לומר שויה רבנן לכל מקדשי בביאה בעילתו זנות טעות גמור הוא ולא לאסור אשת איש המתקדשת בביאה בלא גט מן הטעם הזה ולא מצינו זאת בתלמוד [כתובות שם]. **העדים.** החתומים בשטר ואמרו העדים היו בשטר לא הלויה כלום אלא שאמרו לו לכשיצטרך ילוה לו הוא שיעבד לך נכסיו עכשיו אם יבא ליפרע לאחר זמן דלאו מוקדם ליהוי ולטרוף שלא כדין [כתובות יט:]. [ע״כ שייך לדף מח:] **מודעא היו דברינו.** אם שטר מכר הוא ואמרו עדים החתומים בו המוכר מסר מודעא בפנינו והכרחו אנסו והכריחו בו. **מודעא.** ניתן לכתוב את השטר כדי להציל האנוס מאונסו אמנה לא ניתן להכתב דעולה הוא וכי אמרו חתמנו אבל אמנה היו דברינו רשעים ואין אדם נאמן לשום עצמו רשע [כתובות יט.]. **האומר לחבירו.** שותף [רשב״ם לעיל מג.] כגון שדה של שותפין ואמר האחד לחבירו דין ודברים אין לי עליה כגון מן הלשונות הללו [בין בכתיבה בין באמירה] [כתובות פג.]. **על שדה זו.** שהיא לו עמו שותפות בה. **ואין לי עסק בה.** ואין אחת מכל לשונות הללו [גיטין עז.] כלומר לא יהא לי עסק בה ומכלל זה שמע שלא יהא לי חלק בה [ו]מהכל שלא הוציא הדבר בפירות מפיו [רשב״ם שם]. **לא אמר כלום.** דאין כאן מתנה [כתובות שם]. דמאמר שהיא שלו צריך לכתוב לו לשון מתנה [גיטין שם]. ולא אבד זכותו [כריתות כד.]. דכיון דכבר יש לו חלק בשדה והוא אומר לא יהא לי חלק בו אין זה לשון מתנה לחבירו אלא לשון תפלה הוא הגולה לא יהא לי חלק בשדה זו ולא יהי נתון לך שדה זו ולא עדיין מרשותו ואין מופס לשון מתנה כלל לא זכה לא בדבר שעליו שלא יהא שלו כשיבוא הזמן שעתיד לבוא באותו דבר דאין אדם זוכה בדבר בעל כרחו כדלקמן בפירקין (ומסתבר) (פג.) דנחלה הבאה לו לאדם לאמר מכן מתנה

עליה שלא יירשנה אבל מכיון שכבר הדבר שלו הוא והוא אומר לא יהא שלי לא אמר כלום דבעל כרחו יהיה שלו כל זמן שלא יתננה לאחרים כן נראה בעיני ועיקר והכי מוכח לקמן בפירקין וי״מ דמשום הכי לא קאמר לי דין ודברים ולא קאמר לא יהא ונמלא שהוא מכזב שהרי יש לו חלק בו והוא אומר אין לי ושבוש הוא דאין זה לשון הגמ׳ לומר בשום מקום לא יהא והכי מוכח לקמן דקמשני הכא במאי עסקינן בשקנו מידו ולא קא [רשב״ם שם]. **מתניתין בכותב לה ועודה ארוסה.** ודאי מי שהקרקע שלו ובא ליתנו לחבירו צריך לשון מתנה ומתניתין בכותב לה עד שלא זכה בנכסים ומתנה עמה שלא יזכה בהן לכשישאנה ואין צריך לשון מתנה שהרי אין לו עכשיו רשות בהן [כתובות פג.]. **בכותב לה דין ודברים** כו׳ בעודה ארוסה קודם שזכה בנכסים וא״צ לכתוב לשון מתנה דיכול להתנות כדרב כהנא [גיטין עז.].

עין משפט נר מצוה

קפז א מיי׳ פ״ג מהל׳ עדות הלכה ז סמג לאוין קט טוש״ע ח״מ סי׳ מו סעיף לז:

קפח ב ג ד מיי׳ פי״ג מהל׳ טוען הל׳ א ופי״ד הלכה א ופכ״ב מהלכות אישות הלכה טו סמג עשין לה ועשין מח טוש״ע ח״מ סי׳ קמט סעי׳ ט וטוש״ע אה״ע סי׳ פז סעי׳ א:

רבינו גרשום

מודעא היו דברינו. כלומר אע״פ שחתמנו על שטר המכירה שמעיד שברצונו מכר אעפ״כ יודעים אנו שאנוס היה **ואין נאמנין** והיכי מצי חתים רבה אמודעא. והכי משמע השתא דמאי דאמרין מודעא היו דברינו דחתמי נמי אמודעא: ומשני **הני מילי** דאין נאמנין להיכא דאמרי עדים **על פה** יודעין אנו שבאונס מכר דודאי **לא אתא על פה ומרע לשטר** דכתוב ביה דברצון מכר **אבל** אי כתבו המודעא **בשטר** וחתומה הויא מודעא **דאתי שטר** מודעא **ומרע ליה לשטר** מכירה ומשום הכי שפיר חתם רבה בר רב הונא אמודעא שבשטר ואי לאו דחתים אמודעא מאי דחתים אאשקלתא שפיר חתם: **מאי טעמא מודעא היו דברינו נאמנין. דזה** מודעא **ניתן ליכתב** שטר מסירת מודעא וניתנה נמי ליחתם ואפי׳ הכי יכולין לחתום עדי מודעא גופייהו על שטר מכירה ונאמנין. **והאי שטר אמנה לא ניתן ליכתב** כלומר מאחר שחתמו על השטר שכתב בו פלוני לוה מפלוני מנה ודאי משמע דאי לאו דחזו דהלוהו לא הוו חתמי והשתא אי הוו כתבו בשטר אחר אמנה היו דברינו הוו מיחזו עדים שקרים. הלכך אין נאמנין דלא ניתן ליכתב דאין אדם משים עצמו רשע לחתום שקר: **פים׳. אין לאיש חזקה בנכסי אשתו** של מלוג דאם החזיק לבדו בנכסים ג׳ שנים אין לו חזקה. **פשיטא** דלא הוי חזקה דכיון דנכסי מלוג משתעבדי ליה לפירי **פירי הוא דקאכיל** ואין הגוף שלו ואין לו חזקה: **אין לי בנכסיך.** דמשמע לגמרי דהשתא לא אכיל לפירי וסד״א הואיל דכתב לה הכי והחזיק בנכסיה תיהוי חזקה קמ״ל דלא דמציא לימר נחת רוח עשיתי לבעלי שלא מחיתי בנכסיו: **לא אמר כלום.** דהא חזינן דמתעסק בה וברשותו הוי: **ועודה ארוסה.** דעדיין לא היו נכסיה ברשותו:

עין משפט
נר מצוה

קפט **א** מיי' פכ"ג מהל' אישות הלכה א ועיין במ"מ סמג עשין מח טוש"ע אה"ע סי' לב סעי' א וסעי' ג וסעי' ז וסי' סט סעי' ז:

קצ **ב** מיי' פי"ט מהל' מלוה הלכה ו:

קצא **ג** מיי' פי"ב מהל' אישות הלכה ד סמג עשין מח טוש"ע אה"ע סי' סט סעי' ד וסי' פ סעי' טו בהג"ה וסי' פא סעי' א בהג"ה:

קצב **ד** מיי' פכ"ב מהל' אישות הל' טו ועיין בהשגות ובמגיד משנה ופי"ז שם הל' יא ופ"ל מהל' מכירה הלכה ג ועיין במ"מ סמג שם טוש"ע אה"ע סי' צ סעי' יז:

קצג **ה ו ז** מיי' פכ"ב מהל' אישות הל' יח ופ"ל מהל' מכירה הלכה ג ופי"ד מהל' טוען הלכה א סמג שם וסי' צה טוש"ע שם וטוש"ע ח"מ סי' קנא סעי' א:

ליקוטי רש"י

נחלה הבאה לו לאדם ממקום אחר. שאינה ירושת אבותיו מן התורה מתנה עליה קודם שזכה [גיטין עז.]. שאינה ירושת אבותיו אלא ע"י מעשיו תבא לו כגון נחלת אשתו הבאה לו ע"י נשואין שלו דהואיל ומשום תקנתא דידיה תקון רבנן והוא בא למחול עליה מוחל וכדרב הונא [כתובות פג.]. **דאמר רבא וכו'.** אמילתא אחריתי אמרה רבא [גיטין שם:]. **אי אפשי בתקנת חכמים.** שתיקנו לטובתי ואינה טובה לי. **כגון זו.** לקמן מפרש אהייא אתמר [כתובות שם]. **שומעין לו.** הואיל והתקנה לצורכו נעשית יכול לומר כלום עשו אלא להנאתי אני אי אפשי בהנאה זו. **מאי כגון זו.** אהייא אמרה רבא [גיטין שם]. **כדרב הונא.** אמזונות שתיקנו לאשה תחת מעשה ידיה ואי אמרה אי אפשי בתקנה זו שתיקנו חכמים לטובתי שחשו לכל הנשים דמנין דלא ספקי להו מזונות במעשה ידיהן ותקנו להן מזונות ומעשה ידיהן לבעל אני איני צריכה לכך מעונגת אני ואי אפשי לעשות מלאכה אמלא לי מזונות או יש לי אומנות יקרה יתר על כדי מזונותי [כתובות שם]. **איני ניזונת.** משל בעלי [גיטין שם]. משלך [ב"ק ח:]. **ואיני עושה.** לו מלאכה דכי תקון רבנן מזוני להנאתה תקון זמנין דלא ספקה במעשה ידיה ואחר כך תקנו מעשה ידיה לבעלה משום איבה הלכך יכולה לומר אי אפשי [גיטין שם]. מלאכה דמשום תקנתא דידי דדלמא לא ספקי לי מזונות במעשה ידי תקינו לי רבנן מזונות משלך תחת מעשה ידי בהיא תקנתא לא ניחא לי [ב"ק שם]. **מקחו בטל.** דאמרה נחת רוח עשיתי לבעלי [גיטין נה:]. משמע לגמרי ואפי' בחיי הבעל [כתובות צה.].

דאדם מקנה דבר שלא בא לעולם אלא משום דלדידן קי"ל דאין אדם מקנה ובמילתיה דרבא לחודיה לא סגי שלא בא לעולם. ר' יוסף בהכא דאמר מלהכא אל תהא שמעינן שיכול להתנות בדבר שלא בא לעולם דאע"ג דרבא קאי אמזונות שלא באו לעולם התם אינו חידוש מאי שאין לה מזונות דאטו יש לה ליטול מזונות בעל כרחה דכשרוצה חוזרת [א] בה ולא קמ"ל רב הונא אלא שיכולה להפקיע מעשה ידיה מבעלה ולא"ת רב דפסיק בפ' הכותב (כתובות דף פד: ושם) כרשב"ג דאמר אם מתה יירשנה אפי' כתב לה דין ודברים אין לי בנכסיך בחייך ובמותך ולאו מטעמיה דאיהו סבר ירושת הבעל דאורייתא ורב סבר ירושת הבעל דרבנן וחכמים עשו חיזוק לדבריהם כשל תורה מאי שנא דמפירות יכול להסתלק משום דהוו דרבנן ויש לומר דשאני ירושה דנפלה קמיה דבעל דיורשי האשה כנכרים הם באותה ירושה לגבי בעל ולכך אין יכול להסתלק אבל הכא מנכסי מלוג יכול להסתלק שישארו ביד מי שהן עכשיו דהיינו ביד האשה ועוד מצינן למימר דלא עשו חיזוק אלא בדבר שיש לו שורש מן התורה כגון ירושה דאיכא ירושה דאורייתא אבל בדבר דליכא כוותיה בדאורייתא לא עבוד רבנן חיזוק אי נמי פירות דלא שכיחי לא עבוד חיזוק כדאמרינן בריש אע"פ (שם דף נו.) לכל יש כתובה ולא לכל יש פירות דלא שכיחי כמו ירושה דאין לך אשה שאין לה נכסי צאן ברזל שיירש הבעל דאפי' במשיאים יתומה תנן (כתובות דף סז.) לא יפחתו לה מנ' זוז הלכך ירושת צאן ברזל שכיח ולא פלוג רבנן בירושת הבעל לכל ירושות אין יכול להתנות אבל פירות דלא שכיחי דליכא טובא שאין להם נכסי מלוג לא עשו חיזוק:

נחלה הבאה [א] נחלה הבאה לו לאדם ממקום אחר אדם מתנה עליה שלא יירשנה וכדרבא [א] דאמר רבא [ב] כל האומר אי אפשי בתקנת חכמים כגון זאת שומעין לו מאי כגון זאת כדרב הונא אמר רב [ג] דאמר רב הונא אמר רב [ג] יכולה אשה שתאמר לבעלה איני ניזונת ואיני עושה הא ראיה יש תימא נחת רוח עשיתי לבעלי מי לא תנן [ג] [ד] לקח מן האשה מקחו בטל אלמא אמרה נחת רוח עשיתי לבעלי [ה] הכא נמי תימא נחת רוח עשיתי לבעלי [ו] הא איתמר עלה אמר רבה בר רב הונא לא נצרכה אלא [ז] באותן ג' שדות אחת שכתב לה בכתובתה ואחת

נחלה הבאה לו. העתידה לבא לו כגון נחלה דרבנן כדמפרש לקמן אדם יכול להתנות עליה קודם שתבא שלא יירשנה כגון דקאמר דין ודברים אין לי על אותה נחלה העתידה לבא לי כלומר לא יהא לי דין ודברים: **וכדרבא.** כלומר ובאיזו נחלה מועיל התנאי בנחלה הבאה לו בתקנת חכמים כדרבא אבל בנחלה דאורייתא כגון דין ודברים אין לי בירושת אבי כשימות לא יועיל התנאי דבעל כרחו שלו יהא אא"כ יתננה לאחרים בלשון מתנה: **אי אפשי בתקנת חכמים.** שעשו להנאתי: **כגון זאת.** לקמן מפרש: **שומעין לו.** דבעל כרחו דאיניש לא יזכוהו חכמים שאם אינו חושש בטובה שעשו לו חכמים לא ניתן לו בעל כרחו שלדעתו תקנו חכמים: **מאי כגון זאת.** באיזו תקנת חכמים היו מדברים בבהמ"ד שעליה אמר רבא כל האומר אי אפשי בתקנת חכמים כגון זאת התקנה שאנו מדברים בה שומעין לו: **כדרב הונא אמר רב.** כלומר מתקנת מזונות שהבעל נותן לאשה היו עסוקים בבית המדרש והוא נוטל מלאכת ידיה תחתיהן וע"ז אמר רבא כגון זאת התקנה שתקנו חכמים מזונות האשה לטובתה אם אומרת אי אפשי בתקנת חכמים בזו התקנה שתקנו לטובתי דהא לדידי אינה טובה דמלאכת ידי עדיף על מזונותי אזון משלי ואעשה מלאכה לעצמי שומעין לה ואתא לאשמועינן כרב הונא אמר רב שיכולה אשה לומר לבעלה איני ניזונת משלך ואיני עושה מלאכה לך כי אם לעצמי כדמפרש טעמא בכתובות (דף נח:) קסבר מזוני עיקר כלומר תחלה תקנו עיקר מזונות לאשה מן הבעל בע"כ בין לא תעשה בין תעשה ואח"כ תקנו מלאכה תחת מזונות שלא תהיה לה איבה וכיון דלטובתה נתכוונו לתקן לה מזונות תחלה והיא עוקרת לומר איני חפילה בתקנה זו איני חוששת למזונותיו הרשות בידה וכיון דעקרה תקנת המזונות גם תקנת מלאכת ידיה לבעלה בטלה ממילא דכיון דמזונות אין לה גם הבעל לא יטול מלאכת ידיה והיינו נחלה הבאה לו לאדם לאחר מכאן שהמזונות עתידים לבא בכל יום וה"ה לפירות של נכסי מלוג שתקנו חכמים לבעל פירותיה תחת פרקונה כ"ש וכ"ש שאם אמר איני מקבל עלי תקנת פרקונה ואיני חושש בפירות נכסי מלוג שתקנו לי דמועיל התנאי בעודה ארוסה שעדיין לא זכה בקרקעותיה לפירות והיינו דאצטריך במתני' למיתני דאין לאיש חזקה בנכסי אשתו לומר לקוח הוא בידי דאע"ג דכתב לה בעודה ארוסה שלא יטול כלום בפירותיה אפי' הכי שתקה ולא מיחתה לבעלה דמצי אמרה נחת רוח עשיתי לבעלי ששתקתי אבל מעולם לא מכרתי לו: ומקשי גמרא **הא ראיה יש.** דקתני מתני' אין לאיש חזקה שאין חזקה מועלת לו לקיים מקחו אבל ראיית עדים או שטר תועיל לו לקיים מכירתה דאם מכרה לו אשתו נכסי מלוג שלה קנה: **תימא נחת רוח עשיתי לבעלי.** שמכרתי לו שלא יכעוס עלי אבל לא היה בדעתי להקנותו דלא דמי לתליוהו וזבין דזביניה זביני דאגב אונסי' גמר ומקני אבל הכא דליכא אונס כ"כ לא גמרה ואקנייה: **מי לא תנן.** דכי הך טענה יכולה אשה לטעון לאחרים שקנו מבעלה וכ"ש (א) שמכרה לבעלה עצמו: **לקח מן האיש.** מן הבעל כל קרקעותיו משועבדים לכתובת אשתו והיום ולמחר אם ימות או יגרשנה תטרוף מלקוחות אם לא תמצא בני חורין שכן כתב לה כל נכסי אחראין וערבאין לכתובתיך במס' כתובות (דף נא.): **וחזר.** זה הלוקח ולקח מן האשה נתן לה דבר מועט והקנתו לו כדי שלא תטרוף ממנו חוב כתובתה: **מקחו בטל.** לא בטל בטל ממש שכל זמן שיחיה הבעל יאכל זה הלוקח את הפירות שהרי המוכר מכר לו כ"ז שלא תתגרש האשה ולא יבא זמן גיבוי כתובתה שהרי משנה זו בכל נכסים וקרקעות שיש לו לבעל מיירי כדמוכח לקמן בסמוך דאמרי' למעוטי מאי אילימא למעוטי שאר נכסים כו' ובכולן אי אתה יכול לומר מקחו בטל לגמרי דאמר בפ' האשה שנפלו לה נכסים בסופה דאי לא תימא הכי סיפא דקתני לא יאמר אדם לאשתו הרי כתובתיך מונחת על השולחן אלא כל נכסי אחראין לכתובתיך ואי בעי לזבוני ה"נ לא מצי מזבין בתמיה מכאן אנו למדין שהמכר קיים ואע"פ שמשועבדין לאשה אלא דלהכי אהני שעבוד שתוכל לטרוף מהן כשיגיע זמנה לגבות כתובתה הלכך האי מקחו בטל אחזר ולקח מן האשה קאי דהוי בטל לגמרי ההוא מקח וכשתבא לגבות כתובתה תטרוף ממנו דמצי אמרה נחת רוח עשיתי לבעלי למכור לך קרקע המשועבד לי ולא גמרתי בלבי להקנות לך: ומשני **הא איתמר עלה.** דההיא דחזר ולקח מן האשה אמר רבה בר רב הונא לא נצרכה למיתני מקחו בטל היכא דחזר ולקח מן האשה אלא באותן ג' שדות המשועבדות לה יותר משאר נכסים ודעתה סמכא עילוייהו טפי דהוי מקחן בטל דודאי לא גמרה ואקניי' אלא נחת רוח עשתה לבעלה ולקמיה מפרש למעוטי מאי דלא ליהוי מקח בטל: **אחת שכתב לה בכתובתה.** כלומר אחת מן הג' שדות הוא שדה בשטר הכתובה ששיעבד לה בפי' והזכיר ההוא שדה שמעבד לה וסמכא דעתה עליה טפי משאר נכסים מיהו כל נכסיו נמי שעבד לה שכך כתב לה כל נכסי אחראין לכתובתיך ומיהו לא הזכיר ולא סיים מכולם בפי' בתוך שטר הכתובה כי אם זה לבדו:

ואחת

יכולה אשה שתאמר לבעלה כו'. פי' בקונטרס וכי קאמר נמי איני מקבל (ג) פרקונה ואיני חושש בפירות נכסי מלוג שלה שתקנו לי דמועיל התנאי בעודה ארוסה שעדיין לא זכה בקרקעותיה לפירות וקשה היא נראה לרשב"א דהכא ראיה לדבריו מדתניא פ' נערה שנתפתתה (שם דף מז: ושם ד"ה זימנין) תקנו פרקונה תחת פירות ש"מ דפירי עיקר ויכול לומר כן דהא בפ' אע"פ (שם דף נח: ושם) פריך אמילתא דרב הונא דהכא מהא דקתני תקנו מזונות תחת מעשה ידיה ומשני אימא תקנו מעשה ידיה תחת מזונות ומ"מ (ג) אומר רשב"א דאי אפשר לומר כן דלדרבא פרקונה עיקר כמו שמדקדק ר"י בכתובות פ' נערה (דף מז:) דאמר מאי לפיכך בעל אוכל פירות מהו דתימא מיכל לא ניכלינהו אנותי ניכנינהו כו' קמ"ל דהא עדיפא דזימנין דלא מלו ופריך לה מדידיה וקאמר נמי התם לעיל בשלמא בעל תקינו ליה רבנן פירות דאי לישתבקי הויא ליה איבה ומימנע ולא פריק משמע דלטובת האשה נתקן ובירושל' פ' נערה קאמר בהדיא אהא דתנן נשאת יתר עליו הבעל שאוכל פירות בחייה בעל שאמר אי אפשי לאכול ולא לפרוק אין שומעין לו והא דתנן פרקונה תחת פירות אע"ג דפרקונה עיקר תני הכי לאשמועינן שלא תוכל האשה לומר איני נפדית ואיני נותנת פירות ואע"ג דלטובתה נתקן שלא תשתקע בין העובדי כוכבים ועוד דלא דמי למזונות שיכולה לומר איני ניזונת ואיני עושה דהתם לא מפקעת תקנת מעשה ידיה שאם אינה עושה ואינה ניזונת היום למחר תעשה ותהא ניזונת אבל אם אמרה איני נפדית ואיני נותנת פירות הרי מפקעת לגמרי תקנת פירות דפירות של כל ימיה הם תחת פרקונה א"נ שאני פירות משום דידו כידה שהוא זוכה בגוף הקרקע אבל מעשה ידיה היאך יזכה בהן שאינן בעין דלא שייך למימר שיזכה בגוף הידים וכענין זה מצינו דר"ל דפליג ארב הונא בפ' אע"פ וסבר דמעשה ידיה עיקר ואינו מגיה הברייתא אלא תני תקנו מזונות תחת מעשה ידיה כדקתני אפ"ה אומר ר"ת דאין הבעל יכול לומר לה היכא דלא ספקה לאי מעשה ידיך למזונותיך כדמוכח בהדיא בפ"ק דגיטין (דף יב.) וברים המדיר (כתובות דף ע.) דפריך אי דלא ספקה הדרא קושיא לדוכתה כיון דמשעבד לה היכי מצי מדיר לה: **ה"ג** בפי' ר"ח **ואחת שהכניס לה שום משלו.** וה"פ אחת שכתב לה בכתובה במנה ומאתים וכמה שאדם נותן משלו שייך לשון כתיבה ולא לשון יחוד כגון הכותב כל נכסיו לבניו ואחת שיחד לה בכתובתה תחת הנדוניא שהביאה מבית אביה כי נדוניא נמי נקראת כתובה דבפ' נערה שנתפתתה (שם דף מז: ושם) קתני קבורתה תחת כתובתה דהיינו תחת נדונייתה דתחת מנה מאתים לא קאמרי' דבסוף ההוא פירקא (דף נג.) קאמרי' דארוס' (ד) אית לה קבורה ואחת שהכניס לה שום משלו שאם לה שדה כנגד תוספת שהוסיף לה משלו על מנה ומאתים וג' עניני ממון אלו כותבין בכתובה בסדר זה תחלה מנה ומאתים ואח"כ נדוניא שמביאה עמה דהנעלת ליה ואחר כך ולבי חתן והוסיף לה מדיליה כו' ובקונט' לא פירש כן:

אילימא

מסורת הש"ס

א) ב"ק ח: גיטין עז. כתובות פג., ב) כתובות נח: ע. פג. קז: ע"ש [ב"ק ח:], ג) כתובות נא. גיטין נה:, ד) [צ"ל לית]:

הגהות הב"ח

(א) **רשב"ם** ד"ה מי לא וכו' וכ"ש כשמכרה: (ב) **תוס'** ד"ה יכולה וכו' איני מקבל עלי תקנת פרקונה: (ג) **בא"ד** אומר רשב"א דאי אפשר לומר כן. נ"ב עיין בש"ח ב"ח סי' רל"ב דכתב דגם כן דעת רשב"ם כך והוא ט"ס וצ"ל [והשאר חסר]:

הגהות הגר"א

[א] בתוס' (ד"ה בע"א) **דכשרוצה חוזרת.** ויש חולקין (הר"ן פ"ה דכתובות בשם הרא"ה והובא בהא"ע סי' ס"ט ס"ד בהגה"ה):

רבינו גרשום

ממקום אחר. כגון נכסי מלוג דאשתו: **איני ניזונית.** איני מבקשת ממך מזונות **ואיני עושה** לך מלאכה. שתיקנו חכמים מזונותיה תחת מעשה ידיה ופירות נכסי מלוג שלה תחת קבורתה. ואם מתנה איני מבקש מפירותיה ואיני קוברה **שומעין לו.** וכיון דכתב לה הכי ואפי' הכי מחזיק בעל בנכסיה ס"ד תיהוי חזקה קמ"ל דלא דיכולה היא שתאמר נחת רוח עשיתי לבעלי ששתקתי, ומקשי' **הא ראיה יש.** כלומר חזקה אין לאיש בנכסי אשתו הא ראיה יש לו דאי מייתי בעל ראיה שטר דזבנה ניהלי': **[תימא] דנחת רוח עשיתי לו.** שפיים ממני למוכרה לו ולא גמרתי בלבי להקנותה לו: **לא נצרכה.** דמצי למימר נחת רוח עשיתי לבעלי ומקחו בטל: **באותן ג' שדות אחת שכתב לה בכתובתה.** שהיתה לו שדה גדולה ששוה יותר משיעור כתובה וכתב לה שתגבה שיעור כתובתה מאותה שדה **ואחת שיחד לה בכתובתה** ששוה כנגד כתובתה שתגבה ממנו כתובתה. **ואחת שהכניס לה שום משלו** לתוספת כנגד נדונייתה. דהיך ג' שדות שייחד לה בעלה אם מביא הבעל ראיה שמכרה לו אינו כלום דיכולה למחות ולומר נחת רוח עשיתי לבעלי. ומקשי' **למעוטי מאי** שאם א) מירי ומכרה היא דמקחו קיים.

חשק שלמה
על רבינו גרשום

א) אולי צ"ל שאם מודה האשה שמכרה לו דמקחו קיים.

נַחֲלָה הַבָּאָה לוֹ לְאָדָם מִמָּקוֹם אַחֵר – With respect to **an inheritance coming to a person from another source,**[1] **אָדָם מַתְנֶה עָלֶיהָ שֶׁלֹּא יִירָשֶׁנָּה** – **a person may stipulate about it** in advance **that he should not inherit it.**[2]

The Gemara explains the basis of Rav Kahana's ruling:

וּכְדְרָבָא – **And** this ruling of Rav Kahana is **in accord with** a ruling of **Rava. דְּאָמַר רָבָא** – **For Rava said: כָּל הָאוֹמֵר אִי אֶפְשִׁי בְּתַקָּנַת חֲכָמִים** – **"Whoever declares, 'I do not wish** to make use of a **Rabbinic enactment** instituted for my benefit,' **כְּגוֹן זֹאת** – **in a case such as this,**[3] **שׁוֹמְעִין לוֹ** – **we comply with his** wishes."[4]

The Gemara elaborates on Rava's original statement: **מַאי כְּגוֹן זֹאת** – To **what** did Rava refer when he said "in a case **such as this**"?[5] **כִּדְרַב הוּנָא אָמַר רַב** – He referred to a case such **as the one** discussed **by Rav Huna in the name of Rav. דְּאָמַר רַב הוּנָא אָמַר רַב** – **For Rav Huna said in the name of Rav: יְכוֹלָה אִשָּׁה שֶׁתֹּאמַר לְבַעְלָהּ** – **A woman may say to her husband, אֵינִי נִיזּוֹנֶת וְאֵינִי עוֹשָׂה** – "I will not receive food** from you, **and I will not work** and give you my income."[6]

The Gemara now returns to the Mishnah's ruling that a husband cannot establish a *chazakah* over property that belonged to his wife:

הָא רְאָיָה יֵשׁ – **This implies that** if he has **proof** that he acquired the field, it **is effective,** and the sale is considered binding.[7]

The Gemara questions why this should be so:

תֵּימָא נַחַת רוּחַ עָשִׂיתִי לְבַעְלִי – **She should be able to argue:**[8] **"I did** this (i.e. consented to the sale) only **to please my husband**, but I did not really want to sell it."[9]

The Gemara demonstrates that such an argument can nullify a sale:

מִי לֹא תְנַן – **Have we not learned in a Mishnah: לָקַח מִן הָאִישׁ וְחָזַר וְלָקַח מִן הָאִשָּׁה** – If ONE BOUGHT a property FROM THE

NOTES

1. I.e. a property [or right] that a person is destined to receive, but which does not come to him automatically by virtue of the Torah's laws of inheritance. Rather, it comes to him by virtue of a Rabbinic enactment (*Rashi* to *Gittin* 77a ד״ה ממקום אחר; *Rashbam;* see also *Rashi* to *Kesubos* 83a). This will be explained further in note 4.

2. Once a person is in possession of something [even by Rabbinic law], he cannot withdraw his ownership of it merely by declaring that he no longer desires it; he must either give it away or formally declare it ownerless (*hefker*). However, if one is not yet the legal owner of a property, but it is destined to become his by Rabbinic law, he can prevent it from becoming his merely by stating that he does not wish to acquire it.

Accordingly, since a husband is not entitled to the produce of his wife's property until they are fully married (i.e. until after *nisuin*), he may effectively renounce his right to the produce during the *erusin* period by declaring to his betrothed, "I wish to have neither claim nor argument with respect to the produce of your fields." It is to such a case that our Mishnah refers when it teaches that despite the waiver, the husband cannot establish a *chazakah* in his wife's property [see 49a note 9] (*Rashbam*).

3. I.e. in cases similar to the Rabbinic enactment that was under discussion in the academy when Rava made his statement. The Gemara will explain which enactment this was (*Rashbam*).

4. Since this enactment was made for his benefit, the Rabbis did not intend that he should be forced to accept it. Accordingly, if he declares that he wishes to waive this benefit, the enactment does not take effect for him (*Rashbam*). [Needless to say, a person does not have the power to free himself of general Rabbinic enactments; the Gemara speaks here only of enactments intended for someone's personal benefit, as in the case the Gemara cites below.]

Since a husband's right to the produce of his wife's property is a Rabbinic enactment, as explained above (49a note 8), he may waive it if he so desires. However, a person cannot waive – even in advance – a property or right which he is to receive under Biblical law, such as an inheritance from his father. Since these are Biblically decreed, [they take effect even against a person's will, and] one can only rid himself of them by making a formal gift of them (*Rashbam;* see *Tos. Rid*).

5. Which Rabbinic enactment was being discussed in the academy when Rava ruled that one may waive a Rabbinic enactment instituted for his benefit?

6. The academy was discussing the Rabbinical enactment that a husband must feed his wife, for which he receives in return any income generated by her handiwork. The primary intention of the Rabbis was that the wife should be supported. Therefore, says Rava, in a case such as this, the woman has the option of declining the benefit instituted on her behalf and keeping her own income. A woman may prefer such an arrangement when her earnings far surpass what she receives in food support. She therefore wishes to pay for her own support and keep the residue of her income.

This is an example of an "inheritance" that comes to a person from another source. [The term "inheritance" is used here as a metaphor for any property or benefit that is destined to come to a particular person.] A woman may make this declaration even during her marriage, because her food support is due her each day anew and she is thus always renouncing only what she has not yet received (*Rashbam*; cf. *Tosafos*). [This is quite different from a husband's renunciation of the benefit of his wife's property. In that instance the right to the produce takes the form of a partial ownership of the land (קַרְקַע לְפֵירוֹת), i.e. he holds an interest in the land that entitles him to its produce for the duration of the marriage. Thus, once the marriage has been finalized, the husband has acquired this interest and he can no longer simply waive it. This interest is what entitles him to the produce on an ongoing basis. The obligation to feed one's wife, however, does not give her any interest in her husband's property; it is merely an obligation that is constantly renewed. Thus, she may simply waive that obligation at any time, since she has not yet acquired the assets to cover her future support (see *Rashbam*).]

[*Rashbam* states that the renunciation of the right to the produce takes the form of renouncing his responsibility to ransom his wife and thereby withdrawing from the associated right to the produce of his wife's property. This implies that the enactment was primarily designed to give the husband the produce, in return for which he must ransom her should that become necessary. *Tosafos* dispute this and maintain that the primary intention of the Rabbis was to ensure the wife's ransom should she be taken captive. The husband, if he wishes, may nonetheless renounce his right to the produce, but this does not diminish his obligation to ransom his wife (see *Kos HaYeshuos*).]

7. I.e. if the husband can produce a bill of sale or witnesses to testify to his purchase of his wife's *melog* property, the sale would stand. By stating that a three-year possession of the land does not suffice to prove that his wife sold it to him, the Mishnah implies that conclusive evidence, such as witnesses or a bill of sale, would suffice to establish his ownership (*Rashbam*).

8. Literally: let her say.

9. I.e. she agreed to the sale only so that her husband should not become angry with her, but her agreement was not wholehearted. Since the purchase lacked the full agreement of the seller, it should be declared void.

This is different from the case of a person who was subjected to physical punishment until he agreed to sell, in which case we learned that the sale stands (see 47b, 48a). In that case, because the pressure on him is very great, we may presume that he in the end agrees wholeheartedly to the sale in order to gain his release. [I.e. he is happy in the end to be able to rid himself of his tormentor by selling him the property.] But in the case of a wife agreeing to sell her *melog* property to her husband, the pressure on her is not so great that we should presume that she transferred ownership to her property to him wholeheartedly. [I.e. even at the moment of the sale she was not happy with it.] (*Rashbam*).

Other commentators maintain that the difference between the two cases is not, as *Rashbam* suggests, whether the compelling force is great or not, but rather whether the woman received payment or not. In the case on 47b, the person received payment and we therefore assume that he wholeheartedly agreed to the sale even though it was under duress. However, in this case, there is no evidence that the wife received payment for her *melog* property. Therefore, we say that even under pressure she did not wholeheartedly agree to the sale (*Rashba; Ritva*).

עין משפט
נר מצוה

קפט א מיי' פכ"ג מהל' אישות הלכה ה ועיין במ"מ סמג עשין מח טוש"ע אה"ע סי' סט סעי' ג וסעי' ה וסי' סט סעי' ז:

קצ ב מיי' פי"ט מהל' מלוה הלכה ו:

קצא ג מיי' פי"ב מהל' אישות הלכה ד סמג עשין מח טוש"ע אה"ע סי' סט סעי' ד וסי' פא סעי' ב בהג"ה:

קצב ד מיי' פי"ב מהל' אישות הל' טו ועיין בהשגות ובמגיד משנה ופי"ט מהל' מכירה הלכה ו ועיין במ"מ סמג שם טוש"ע אה"ע סי' צ סעי' יח:

קצג ה ו ז מיי' פכ"ב מהל' אישות הל' יח ופ"ל מהל' מכירה הלכה ג ופי"ד מהל' טוען הלכה ג סמג שם וסי' טוש"ע שם וטוש"ע ח"מ סי' קנח סעי' ה:

מסורת הש"ס

א) ב"ק ח: גיטין עז. כתובות פג., ב) כתובות נח: ע. פג. קז: ע"ש [ב"ק ח:], ג) כתובות נה. גיטין נה: ד) [צ"ל לין].

אנחלה הבאה לו לאדם ממקום אחר אדם מתנה עליה שלא יירשנה וכדרבא (א) דאמר רבא בכל האומר אי אפשי בתקנת חכמים כגון זאת שומעין לו מאי כגון זאת כדרב הונא אמר רב (ג) דאמר רב הונא אמר רב גיכולה אשה שתאמר לבעלה איני ניזונת ואיני עושה הא ראיה יש תימא נחת רוח עשיתי לבעלי מי לא תנן (ג) דלקח מן האיש וחזר ולקח מן האשה מקחו בטל אלמא אמרה נחת רוח עשיתי לבעלי ההכא נמי תימא נחת רוח עשיתי לבעלי והא איתמר עלה אמר רבה בר רב הונא לא נצרכה אלא זבאותן ג' שדות אחת שכתב לה בכתובתה ואחת

תוספות

דאדם מקנה דבר שלא בא לעולם אלא משום דלדידן קיי"ל דאין אדם מקנה ובמילתיה דרבא לחודיה לא סגי בלא רב כהנא דמדרבא לא הוה שמעינן שיוכל להתנות בדבר שלא בא לעולם דאע"ג דרבא קאי אמזונות שלא באו לעולם התם אינו חידוש מאי שאין לה מזונות דאטו יש לה ליטול מזונות בעל כרחה דכשרוצה חוזרת [א] בה ולא קמ"ל רב הונא אלא שיכולה להפקיע מעשה ידיה מבעלה וא"ת רב דפסיק בפ' הכותב (כתובות דף פד: ושם) כרשב"ג דאמר אם מתה יירשנה אפי' כתב לה דין ודברים אין לי בנכסייך בחייך ובמותך ולאו מטעמיה דאיהו סבר ירושת הבעל דאורייתא ורב סבר ירושת הבעל דרבנן וחכמים עשו חיזוק לדבריהם כשל תורה מאי שנא דמפירות יכול להסתלק משום דהוו דרבנן ויש לומר דשאני ירושה דנפלה קמיה דבעל דיורשי האשה כנכרים הם באותה ירושה לגבי בעל ולכך אין יכול להסתלק אבל הכא מנכסי מלוג יכול להסתלק שישארו ביד מי שהן עכשיו דהיינו ביד האשה ועוד מצינן למימר דלא עשו חיזוק אלא בדבר שיש לו שורש מן התורה כגון ירושה דאיכא ירושה דאורייתא אבל בדבר דליכא כוותיה בדאורייתא לא עבוד רבנן חיזוק אי נמי פירות דלא שכיחי לא עבוד חיזוק כדאמרינן בריש אע"פ (שם דף נו:) לכל יש כתובה ולא לכל יש פירות דלא שכיחי כמו ירושה דאין לך אשה שאין לה נכסי צאן ברזל שיירש הבעל דאפי' במשיאים יתומה תנן (כתובות דף סז.) לא יפחתו לה מנ' זוז הלכך ירושת צאן ברזל שכיח ולא פלוג רבנן בירושת הבעל דכל ירושות אין יכול להתנות אבל פירות דלא שכיחי דאיכא טובא שאין להם נכסי מלוג לא עשו חיזוק:

יכולה אשה שתאמר לבעלה כו'. פי' בקונטרס וכי קאמר נמי איני מקבל (ג) פרקונה ואיני חושש בפירות נכסי מלוג שלה שתקנו לי דמועיל התנאי בעודה ארוסה שעדיין לא זכה בקרקעותיה לפירות וקצת היה נראה לרשב"א להביא ראיה לדבריו מדתניא פ' נערה שנתפתתה (שם דף מז: ושם ד"ה זימנין) תקנו פרקונה תחת פירות ש"מ דפירי עיקר ויכול לומר כן דהא בפ' אע"פ (שם דף נח: ושם) פריך אמילתא דרב הונא דהכא מהא דקתני תקנו מזונות תחת מעשה ידיה ומשני אימא תקנו מעשה ידיה תחת מזונות ומ"מ (ג) אומר רשב"א דאי אפשר לומר כן דאדרבה פרקונה עיקר כמו שמדקדק ר"י בכתובות פ' נערה (דף מז:) דאמר מאי לפיכך בעל אוכל פירות מהו דתימא מיכל לא ניכלינהו אנוחי ניינחינהו כו' קמ"ל דהא עדיפא דזימנין דלא מלו ופריק לה מדידיה וקאמר נמי התם לעיל בשלמא בעל תקינו ליה רבנן פירות דאי אישתבאי הויא ליה איבה ומימנע ולא פריק משמע דלטובת האשה נתקן ובירושל' פ' נערה קאמר בהדיא אהא דתנן נשאת יתר עליו הבעל שאוכל פירות בחייה בעל שאמר אי אפשי לאכול ולא לפרוק אין שומעין לו והא דתנן פרקונה תחת פירות אע"ג דפרקונה עיקר לא תני הכא אלא לאשמועי' שלא תוכל האשה לומר איני נפדית ואיני נותנת פירות ואע"ג דלטובתה נתקן שלא תטמע בין העובדי כוכבים ועוד דלא דמי למזונות שיכולה לומר איני ניזונת ואיני עושה דהכא לא מפקעת תקנת מעשה ידיה שאם אינה עושה ואינה ניזונת היום למחר תעשה ותהא ניזונת אבל אם אמרה איני נפדית ואיני נותנת פירות הרי מפקעת לגמרי תקנת פירות דפירות של כל ימיה הם תחת פרקונה א"נ שאני פירות משום דידו כידה שהוא זוכה בגוף הקרקע אבל מעשה ידיה היאך יזכה בהן שאינן בעין דלא שייך למימר שיזכה בגוף הידים וכענין זה מצינו דר"ל דפליג ארב הונא בפ' אע"פ (שם) וסבר דמעשה ידיה עיקר ואינו מגיה הברייתא אלא תני תקנו מזונות תחת מעשה ידיה כדקתני אפ"ה אומר ר"ת דאין הבעל יכול לומר לה היכא דלא ספקה צאי מעשה ידיך למזונותיך כדמוכח בהדיא בפ"ק דגיטין (דף יב.) ובריש המדיר (כתובות דף ע:) דפריך אי דלא ספקה הדרא קושיא לדוכתה כיון דמשעבד לה היכי מצי מדיר לה:

ה"ג בפי' ר"ח ואחת שהכניס לה שום משלו. וה"פ אחת שכתב לה בכתובה במנה ומאתים ובמה שאדם נותן משלו שייך לשון כתיבה ולא לשון יחוד כגון הכותב כל נכסיו לבניו [illegible] שייחד לה בכתובתה תחת הנדוניא שהביאה מבית אביה כי נדוניא נמי נקראת כתובה דבפ' נערה שנתפתתה (שם דף מז: ושם) קתני קבורתה תחת כתובתה דהיינו תחת נדונייתה דתחת מנה מאתים לא קאמרי' דבסוף הסוגיא פירקה (דף נג.) קאמרי' דארוס (ד) אית לה קבורה ואחת שהכניס לה שום משלו שם לה שדה כנגד תוספת שהוסיף לה משלו על מנה ומאתים וג' עניני ממון אלו כותבין בכתובה כסדר זה תחלה מנה ומאתים ואח"כ נדוניא שמביאה עמה הנעשית ליה ואחר כך ובכי תתן והוסיף לה מדיליה כו' ובקונט' לא פירש כן:

אלימא

רשב"ם

נחלה הבאה לו. העתידה לבא לו כגון נחלה דרבנן כדמפרש לקמן אדם יכול להתנות עליה קודם שתבא שלא יירשנה כגון דקאמר דין ודברים אין לי על אותה נחלה העתידה לבא לי כלומר לא יהא לי דין ודברים: וכדרבא. כלומר ובאיזו נחלה מועיל התנאי בנחלה הבאה לו בתקנת חכמים כדרבא אבל בנחלה דאורייתא כגון דין ודברים אין לי בירושת אבי כשימות לא יועיל התנאי דבעל כרחו שלו יהא אא"כ יתננה לאחרים בלשון מתנה: אי אפשי בתקנת חכמים. שעשו להנאתי: כגון זאת. דלקמן דמדרבנן היא: שומעין לו. דבעל כרחו דאינשי לא יזכוהו חכמים שאם אינו חושש בטובה שעשו לו חכמים לא ניתן לו בעל כרחו שלדעתו תקנוה חכמים: מאי כגון זאת. באיזו תקנת חכמים היו מדברים בבהמ"ד שעליה אמר רבא כל האומר אי אפשי בתקנת חכמים כגון זאת התקנה שאנו מדברים בה שומעין לו: כדרב הונא אמר רב. כלומר מתקנת מזונות שהבעל נותן לאשה היו עסוקים בבית המדרש והוא נוטל מלאכת ידיה תחתיהן וע"ז אמר רבא כגון זאת התקנה שתקנו חכמים מזונות האשה לטובתה אם אומרת אי אפשי בתקנת חכמים בזו התקנה שתקנו לטובתי דהא לדידי אינה טובה דמלאכת ידי עדיף על מזונותי אזון משלי ואעשה מלאכה לעצמי שומעין לה ואתא לאשמועינן כרב הונא אמר רב שיכולה אשה לומר לבעלה איני ניזונת משלך ואיני עושה מלאכה לך כי אם לעצמי כדמפרש טעמא בכתובות (דף נח:) קסבר מזוני עיקר כלומר תחלה תקנו עיקר מזונות לאשה מן הבעל בע"כ בין לא תעשה ואח"כ תקנו מלאכה תחת מזונות שלא תהיה לה איבה וכיון דלטובתה נתכוונו לתקן לה מזונות תחלה והיא עוקרת לומר איני חפילה בתקנה זו איני חוששת למזונותיו הרשות בידה וכיון דעקרה תקנת המזונות גם תקנת מלאכת ידיה לבעלה בטלה ממילא דכיון דמזונות אין לה גם הבעל לא יטול מלאכת ידיה והיינו נחלה הבאה לו לאדם לאחר מכאן שהמזונות עתידים לבא בכל יום וה"ה לפירות של נכסי מלוג שתקנו חכמים לבעל פירותיה תחת פרקונה כ"ש וכ"ש שאם אמר איני מקבל עלי תקנת פרקונה ואיני חושש בפירות נכסי מלוג שתקנו לי דמועיל התנאי בעודה ארוסה שעדיין לא זכה בקרקעותיה לפירות והיינו דאצטריך במתני' למיתני דאין לאיש חזקה בנכסי אשתו לומר לקוח הוא בידי דאע"ג דכתב לה בעודה ארוסה שלא יטול כלום בפירותיה אפי' הכי שתקה ולא מיחתה לבעלה דמלי אמרה נחת רוח עשיתי לבעלי ששתקתי אבל מעולם לא מכרתי לו: ומקשי גמרא הא ראיה יש. דקתני מתני' אין לאיש חזקה שאין חזקה מועלת לו לקיים מקחו אבל ראיית עדים או שטר תועיל לו לקיים מכירתה דאם מכרה לו אשתו נכסי מלוג שלה קנה: תימא נחת רוח עשיתי לבעלי. שמכרתי לו שלא יכעוס עלי אבל לא היה בדעתי להקנותו דלא דמי לתליוהו וזבין דזביניה זביני דאגב אונסי' גמר ומקני אבל הכא ליכא אונס כ"כ לא גמרה ואקניה: מי לא תנן. דכי הך טענה יכולה אשה לטעון לאחרים שקנו מבעלה וכ"ש (א) שמכרה לבעלה עצמו: לקח מן האיש. מן הבעל כל קרקעותיו משועבדים לכתובת אשתו והיום ולמחר אם ימות או יגרשנה תטרוף מלקוחות דאנן סהדי דעל מנת כן בני חורין שכן כתב לה כל נכסי אחראין וערבאין לכתובתיך במס' כתובות (דף נא.): וחזר. זה הלוקח ולקח מן האשה נתן לה דבר מועט והקנתה לו כדי שלא תטרוף ממנו חוב כתובתה: מקחו בטל. לא בטל ממש שכל זמן שיחיה הבעל יאכל זה הלוקח את הפירות שהרי המוכר מכר לו כ"ז שלא תתגרש האשה ולא יבא זמן גוביינא כתובתה שהרי משנה זו בכל נכסים וקרקעות שיש לו לבעל מיירי כדמוכח לקמן בסמוך דאמרי' למעוטי מאי אילימא למעוטי שאר נכסים כו' ובכולן אי אתה יכול לומר מקחו בטל לגמרי דאמר בפ' האשה שנפלו לה נכסים בסופה דאי לא תימא הכי סיפא דקתני לא יאמר אדם לאשתו הרי כתובתיך מונחת על השולחן אלא כל נכסי אחראין לכתובתיך ואי בעי לזבוני ה"נ לא מצי מזבין בתמיה אלא משם אנו למדין שהמכר קיים ואע"פ שמשועבדין לאשה אלא שלהכי אהני שעבוד שתוכל לטרוף מהן כשיגיע זמנה לגבות כתובתה הלכך האי מקחו בטל בטל לגמרי הוא ולקח מן האשה קאי דהוי בטל לגמרי הוא מקח וכשתבא לגבות כתובתה תטרוף ממנו דמצי אמרה נחת רוח עשיתי לבעלי למכור לך קרקע המשועבד לי ולא גמרתי בלבי להקנות לך: ומשני הא איתמר עלה. דהאי לחזור ולקח מן האשה אמר רבה בר רב הונא לא נצרכה למיתני מקחו בטל היכא דחזר ולקח מן האשה אלא באותן ג' שדות המשועבדות לה יותר משאר נכסים ודעתה סמכה עלייהו טפי דהוי מקחו בטל דודאי לא גמרה ואקני' אלא נחת רוח עשתה לבעלה ולקמיה מפרש למעוטי מאי דלא ליהוי מקח בטל: אחת שכתב לה בכתובתה. כלומר אחת מן הג' שדות הוא שדה שעשאה לה בפי' והזכיר הבעל בשטר הכתובה שדה שיעבד לה וסמכה דעתה עליה טפי משאר נכסים מיהו כל נכסיו נמי שעבד לה שכן כתב לה כל נכסי אחראין לכתובתיך ומיהו לא הזכיר ולא סיים מכלום בפי' בתוך שטר הכתובה כי אם זה לבדו: ואחת

ליקוטי רש"י

נחלה הבאה לו לאדם ממקום אחר. שאינה ירושת אבותיו מן התורה מתנה עליה קודם שזכה [גיטין עז.]. שאינה ירושת אבותיו אלא ע"י מעשיו הבאה לו כגון נכסי אשתו הבאה לו ע"י נשואין שלו דהואיל ומשום תקנתא דידיה תקון רבנן יכול למחול עליה מוחל וכדרב הונא [כתובות פג.]. דאמר רבא וכו'. ממילתא אחריתי אמרה רבא [גיטין שם]. אי אפשי בתקנת חכמים. שתיקנו לטובתי ואינה טובה לי. כגון זו. לקמן מפרש היא מאי [כתובות שם]. שומעין לו. הואיל והתקנה לצורכו נעשית יכול לומר כלום [illegible] אלא להנאתי אני אי אפשי בהנאה זו. מאי כגון זו. אהייא אמרה רבא [גיטין שם]. כדרב הונא. למזונות שתיקנו לאשה תחת מעשה ידיה ואי אמרה אי אפשי בתקנה זו שתיקנו חכמים לטובתי שמשו [illegible] זמנין דלא ספיק להו מזונות במעשה ידיהן ותיקנו להן מזונות ומעשה ידיהן [illegible] לבעל [illegible] מעוגנת [illegible] לעשות מלאכה [illegible] [כתובות שם]. איני ניזונת. משל בעלי [גיטין שם]. משלך [ב"ק ח:]. ואיני עושה. לו מלאכה [illegible] מעשה ידיה [illegible] יכולה לומר לא אפשי [גיטין שם]. [illegible] מקחו בטל. דאמרה נחת רוח עשיתי לבעלי [גיטין נה:]. [illegible] [כתובות צה.].

הגהות הב"ח

(א) רשב"ם ד"ה מי לא וכו' וכ"ש כשמכרה: (ב) תוס' ד"ה יכולה וכו' איני מקבל עלי תקנת פרקונה: (ג) בא"ד אומר רשב"א דאי אפשר לומר כן. נ"ב עיין בש"ך ח"מ סי' [illegible] דכתב דגם כן דעת רשב"ם והוא ט"ס וצ"ל [illegible] (והשאר חסר):

הגהות הגר"א

[א] בתוס' (ד"ה בעא) דכשרוצה חוזרת. ויש חולקין (הר"ן פ"ה כתובות בשם הרא"ה והובא בש"ע סי' ס"ט בהגה"ה):

רבינו גרשום

ממקום אחר. כגון נכסי מלוג דאשתו: איני ניזונת. איני מבקשת ממך מזונות ואיני עושה לך מלאכה. שתיקנו חכמים מזונותיה תחת מעשה ידיה ופירות נכסי מלוג שלה תחת קבורתה. ואם מתה איני מבקש מפירותיה ואיני קוברה שומעין לו. וכיון דכתב לה הכי ואפ"ה הכי מחזיק בעל בנכסיה ס"ד תיהוי חזקה קמ"ל דלא דיכולה לומר נחת רוח עשיתי לבעלי ששתקתי, ומקשי' הא ראיה יש. כלומר חזקה אין לאיש בנכסי אשתו הא ראיה יש לו דאי מייתי בעל ראיה שטר דזבינה ניהלי: [תימא] דנחת רוח עשיתי לו. שפיס ממני למוכרה לו ולא גמרתי בלבי להקנותו לו: לא נצרכה. דמצי למימר נחת רוח עשיתי לבעלי ומקחו בטל: באותן ג' שדות שכתב לה בכתובתה. שהיתה לו שדה גדולה שוה יותר משיעור כתובה וכתב לה שתגבה שיעור כתובתה מאותה שדה. ואחת שיחד לה בכתובתה ששוה כנגד כתובתה שתגבה ממנו כתובתה. ואחת שהכניס לה שום משלו לתוספת כנגד נדונייתה. דהיך ג' שדות שייחד לה בעלה אם מביא הבעל ראיה שמכרה לו אינו כלום דיכולה למחות ולומר נחת רוח עשיתי לבעלי. ומקשי' למעוטי מאי שאם מכרה לו מירי ומכרה היא דמקחו קיים.

חשק שלמה על רבינו גרשום

א) אולי צ"ל שאם מודה האשה שמכרה לו מקחו קיים.

HUSBAND AND THEN BOUGHT it **FROM HIS WIFE,** to acquire her lien on it,[10] מִקְחוֹ בָּטֵל – **HIS PURCHASE IS VOID.**[11] אַלְמָא אָמְרָה נַחַת רוּחַ עָשִׂיתִי לְבַעְלִי – **We see** from this that **[a wife] can argue** that **"I did** this (consented to the transaction) only **to please my husband,"** and thereby nullify the sale to the outsider. הָכָא נַמִּי תֵּימָא נַחַת רוּחַ עָשִׂיתִי לְבַעְלִי – By the same logic we should say that **here, too, she should be able to argue: "I did** this (consented to sell my property to my husband) only **to please my husband,"** and thereby nullify the sale to her husband![12] – **?** –

The Gemara answers that the Mishnah's ruling does not apply in all cases:[13]

הָא אִיתְּמַר עֲלָהּ – **But** the following qualification **has been stated in regard to that** Mishnah: אָמַר רַבָּה בַּר רַב הוּנָא – **Rabbah bar Rav Huna said:** לֹא נִצְרְכָה אֶלָּא בְּאוֹתָן ג׳ שָׂדוֹת – **That** Mishnah's ruling voiding the wife's sale of the lien **is necessary only for those three** instances of **fields** which are *specifically* assigned to the payment of the *kesubah.*[14] These are: אַחַת שֶׁכָּתַב לָהּ בִּכְתוּבָּתָהּ – **One is** land **which [the husband] specified for her *kesubah* and recorded** in its text;[15]

NOTES

10. When a man marries, all his property becomes mortgaged to his wife's *kesubah* (*Kesubos* 51a). Should the husband die or divorce his wife and leave no property from which to collect the *kesubah,* she is authorized to seize in payment for her *kesubah* any properties that he sold or gave away since their marriage. This is pledged by the husband in the text of the *kesubah*, which reads: "All properties I own are surety for your *kesubah"* (see *Kesubos* 51a).

The Mishnah here speaks of a property mortgaged for a woman's *kesubah*. After buying the land from the husband, the buyer made a payment to the wife so that she should relinquish her right to collect her *kesubah* from this property (*Rashbam*).

11. *Gittin* 55b. I.e. the purchase of the lien from the wife is void, because she can claim that she consented to it unwillingly, only in order to please her husband. However, the purchase of the field from the husband is valid. Thus, the purchaser may use the field for as long as the marriage lasts, but if the woman's husband dies or divorces her, she can collect her *kesubah* from this field (if the husband left no other property).

12. Yet our Mishnah implies that she cannot void the sale to her husband, and it is only necessary for him to prove conclusively that she sold it to him, as explained above.

13. I.e. we do not always disallow a transaction because of the assumption that the woman consented to it only to please her husband. This assumption applies only in the cases which the Gemara will now elaborate.

14. When a husband designates specific properties for the *kesubah's* payment, the wife relies primarily on those properties to guarantee her *kesubah*. Therefore, even if she consents to their sale, we assume that she did not consent wholeheartedly, but only to please her husband. The Gemara will soon analyze what types of property are excluded by Rabbah bar Rav Huna's qualification of the Mishnah (*Rashbam*).

15. Although the *kesubah* states that all a husband's property is surety for the *kesubah,* the woman relies more on this field because it was designated for collection in her *kesubah*. Therefore, it is safe to say that she would never willingly agree to sell her lien on this field. We may then assume that if she did agree, it was not done wholeheartedly, but only to please her husband (*Rashbam*).

וְאַחַת שֶׁיִּחֵד לָהּ בִּכְתוּבָּתָהּ – **one is** land **which he designated for her *kesubah*** orally, in the presence of witnesses, without recording it in the *kesubah;*[1] וְאַחַת שֶׁהִכְנִיסָה לוֹ שׁוּם מִשֶּׁלָּהּ – **and one is** land of **her own which she brought** into the marriage **for him** as **assessed [property].**[2]

Rabbah bar Rav Huna's statement would seem to indicate that the Mishnah's ruling voiding the wife's sale of her rights holds true only for the three cases just listed. In all other cases, a wife's agreement to sell her rights would be considered binding. The Gemara now analyzes this:

לְמַעוּטֵי מַאי – **What** properties does Rabbah bar Rav Huna mean **to exclude** when he states that the Mishnah's ruling applies to these fields? אִילֵימָא לְמַעוּטֵי שְׁאָר נְכָסִים – **If you say** he means to exclude all **other properties** owned by the husband, which, though they are also surety for the payment of the *kesubah,* were not specifically designated for that purpose,[3] this cannot be, כָּל שֶׁכֵּן דְּהָוְיָא לֵיהּ אֵיבָה – because her refusal to forgo the lien on them **would certainly arouse** her husband's **antagonism towards her;**[4] דְּאָמַר לָהּ – **for he would say to her:** עֵינַיךְ נָתַתְּ בְּגֵירוּשִׁין וּבְמִיתָה – **You are anticipating** our **divorce or** my **demise!**[5] Since it would have been very difficult for her to refuse to sell her lien, the sale should not be binding.

The Gemara therefore suggests a different exclusion:

אֶלָּא לְמַעוּטֵי נִכְסֵי מְלוֹג – **Rather,** Rabbah bar Rav Huna means **to exclude** the sale of ***melog* property** and to teach that a wife's sale of her rights to these is considered binding. Similarly, our Mishnah also refers to *melog* property when it implies that a wife's sale to her husband is binding.[6]

The Gemara challenges this explanation as well:

הָאָמַר אֲמֵימַר – **But Ameimar has said:** אִישׁ וְאִשָּׁה שֶׁמָּכְרוּ בְּנִכְסֵי מְלוֹג – **A husband and wife who sold *melog* property** לֹא עָשׂוּ וְלֹא כְלוּם – **have not done anything** of legal consequence, i.e. the sale is void.[7] – ? –

The Gemara answers that our Mishnah indeed considers a wife's sale of her *melog* property to her husband binding, and Ameimar's statement must be understood to mean something else:

כִּי אִיתְמַר דַּאֲמֵימַר – In regard to **what was [the ruling] of Ameimar said?** Not in regard to a case where the husband and wife *both* sold their rights to the *melog* property, as we originally thought, but rather in regard to cases where one or the other of them sold;[8] הֵיכָא דְּזַבִּין אִיהוּ וּמִית – for example, **where [the husband] sold** his rights to the *melog* property **and** then **died,** אַתְיָא אִיהִי וּמַפְּקָא – Ameimar teaches that **[the wife] can come and take** the property **away** from the purchaser.[9] אִי נַמִי –

NOTES

1. After they were married, the husband designated one of his fields as a source of payment for her *kesubah.* As we explained above (49b notes 10 and 15), all of a husband's property is surety for payment of the *kesubah.* Nevertheless, a woman feels more assured by this field because it was specifically designated for this purpose. Consequently, she would never wholeheartedly agree to sell her lien on it (*Rashbam*).

2. Such property is known as נִכְסֵי צֹאן בַּרְזֶל, *tzon barzel property* (see 49a note 7). It is assessed at the time of the marriage and its value is recorded in the *kesubah.* The husband assumes the responsibility to repay the assessed value of these properties in the event of his death or their divorce. In effect, this property now belongs to the husband [since his only responsibility is to repay its value, not to return the property itself], and it is mortgaged to the *kesubah* the same as all his other properties. Nevertheless, a woman relies on such a property more for her *kesubah* because she brought it into the marriage from her father's estate. Thus, she would not willingly sell her right to collect from it (*Rashbam*).

3. I.e. perhaps Rabbah bar Rav Huna means to say that if a buyer purchased from the husband any property other than the three listed above, and then purchased from the wife her lien on the property, the sale is valid. The assumption that a woman would not willingly sell the lien guaranteeing her *kesubah* holds true, according to this suggested interpretation, only for those properties specifically assigned for the collection of the *kesubah* (*Rashbam*).

4. See emendation of *Bach.*

5. I.e. he might interpret her refusal to relinquish the lien as a sign that she hoped to collect her *kesubah* in the near future. [Her refusal is critical to him because a buyer is understandably reluctant to buy a property with a lien on it. Thus, unless she waives her lien, it would be difficult for him to sell the property, and certainly to obtain full value for it. Her refusal might therefore arouse his anger and suspicion.] To avoid such an accusation, a woman might well feel pressured into giving up her lien on the non-designated property of her husband, and the sale should therefore be void.

Accordingly, we must say that when Rabbah bar Rav Huna explains that the Mishnah's rule voiding her sale refers to the three designated fields, he does not mean to say that it applies only to these three. On the contrary, he means to teach that it applies *even* to these three fields. It could be argued that since the husband himself designated them for her *kesubah* he would understand her refusal to part with them; thus, if she agreed to sell her rights to these three properties, the sale should be binding and she should not be able to argue that she sold them unwillingly. Rabbah bar Rav Huna therefore teaches that even the sale of these properties is void, because although a wife has the understandable right to reject such a sale, she is nevertheless embarrassed to do so (*Rashbam*).

6. As we learned above (49a note 7), *melog* property remains the property of the wife, with the husband receiving its produce for the duration of the marriage. A husband may sell this right; the property then remains in the hands of the buyer for the duration of the marriage. Should the husband die before his wife or divorce her, the property reverts to the wife.

Because of this, a buyer who wishes to be assured of keeping the property must purchase the permanent rights to it from the wife. Rabbah bar Rav Huna teaches that if a buyer first bought *melog* property from the husband (i.e. the right to its produce) and then bought from the wife her title to the property, the purchase stands. In such a case the wife would not have to fear offending her husband by refusing to sell her permanent right to the property because the husband recognizes that the property belongs to the wife.

We may then say that when our Mishnah implies that a husband's purchase of property from his wife is binding (if he can produce a bill of sale or witnesses that he bought it), he refers to *melog* property. Since the title to this property is hers, she is not afraid to refuse to sell it to him; and if she does sell it to him, we must assume that she did so wholeheartedly (*Rashbam*).

7. The Gemara now assumes that Ameimar means that if the husband sells someone his rights to a *melog* property (the produce), and his wife subsequently sells that same person her rights in that *melog* property (the title), the sale is void, because the wife can claim that she consented only to please her husband. It follows that if she sold these rights to her husband, she should certainly be able to void the sale with this argument. How then can you explain our Mishnah to mean that such a sale would be valid? (*Rashbam*).

8. I.e. when Ameimar speaks of a husband and wife selling *melog* property, he is not teaching the law for a single case in which both sold the same property; rather, he is teaching the law for two distinct cases, one in which the husband alone sold his rights to the *melog* property, and another in which the wife alone sold her rights. In both these cases, Ameimar teaches, the sale by one in no way diminishes the rights of the other, as the Gemara will now elaborate.

9. A purchaser can buy from the husband only those rights which the husband himself possesses. The rights of a husband to *melog* property are limited to its produce and the right to inherit the property should his wife die first. Should he die first, however, the property and its produce automatically revert to the wife. Therefore, the purchaser, too, loses his rights to the property if the husband dies before the wife.

Accordingly, when Ameimar said that a husband who sells *melog* property has not done anything of legal consequence, he meant that he has done nothing to change the ultimate disposition of the property. Should the husband die before the wife, the property and its produce revert back to the wife (*Rashbam*; cf. *Rosh, Ritva, Chidushei HaRan*).

ואחת שיחד לה בכתובתה ואחת שהכניסה לו שום משלה למעוטי מאי אילימא למעוטי שאר נכסים כל שכן דהויא (א) ליה איבה דאמר לה עיניך נתת בגירושין ובמיתה אלא למעוטי נכסי מלוג האמר (ה) אמימר א איש ואשה שמכרו בנכסי מלוג לא עשו ולא כלום כי איתמר דאמימר ב היכא דזבין איהו ומית אתיא איהי ומפקא א"נ זבנה איהי ומתה אתא איהו ומפיק בתקנתא דרבנן וכדר' יוסי בר חנינא ג) דאמר רבי יוסי בר חנינא באושא התקינו ג האשה שמכרה בנכסי מלוג ומתה הבעל מוציא מיד הלקוחות אבל ד היכא דזבינו תרוייהו לעלמא ה א"נ זבנה איהי לדידיה זבינה זביני ואיבעית אימא אמימר דאמר כר' אלעזר דתניא ג) המוכר את עבדו ופסק עמו שישמשנו שלשים יום ר' מאיר אומר הראשון ישנו בדין א) יום או יומים מפני שהוא תחתיו והשני אינו בדין יום או יומים מפני שאינו תחתיו קסבר ז) קנין פירות כקנין הגוף דמי ר' יהודה אומר השני ישנו בדין יום או יומים מפני שהוא כספו הראשון אינו בדין יום או יומים מפני שאינו כספו קסבר קנין פירות לאו כקנין הגוף דמי ר' יוסי אומר שניהם

ואחת שיחד לה בכתובתה. לא נכתב בתוך השטר אלא לאחר נישואין ייחד לה אחת משדותיו ועשאה אפותיקי לגבות ממנה כתובתה ומיהו כל שדותיו משועבדים לה בתוך שטר הכתובה אלא על זה בוטחת יותר הואיל וייחדו לה בפני עדים: ה"ג **ואחת שהכניסה לו שום משלה.** שדה שהכניסה לו מבית אביה ושמו אותו וכתבו שווי בשטר הכתובה שקבלו עליו הבעל בדמים והן נכסי צאן ברזל שאם פחתו פחתו לו ואם הותירו הותירו לו והוו שכותבים ודא נדוניא דהנעלת ליה מבית אבוה כך וכך ממון סך הכל קיבל עליו החתן בכך וכך דינרין וגם זה השדה משעבד לה עם שאר נכסיו של בעל אלא שעל זה בוטחת יותר משעבודו הואיל ומבית אביה הכניסתו ומג' שדות הללו אם חזר ולקח מן האשה מקחו בטל דאמרה נחת רוח עשיתי לבעלי. והמתרץ עצמו מפרש והולך לקיים פירוש שלו למעוטי מאי כלומר ולמעוטי מאי נקט ג' שדות הללו דהוי מקחו בטל ולא שדה אחרת אילימא למעוטי שאר נכסים וקרקעות של בעל המשועבדין לה דאם חזר ולקח מן האשה יהא מקחו קיים ולא תאמר נחת רוח עשיתי לבעלי והכי קאמר רבה בר רב הונא לא נצרכה כו' כלומר אין משנה זו מדברת בשאר נכסים אלא בהנך ג' שדות דכיון דמשועבדין לה כל כך שהן מיוחדין לה ודאי לא גמרה ואקנייה אלא נחת רוח עשתה לבעלה אבל בשאר שדות שאין משועבדין לה כל כך שאין מיוחדים לה ודאי גמרה ואקנייה ולא מצית אמרה נחת רוח עשיתי לבעלי והוו מקחו קיים: **כל שכן.** דמצית אמרה נחת רוח עשיתי לבעלי: **דהויא לה איבה.** אם לא תמכור לו ללוקח מבעלה וכל שכן דהוי מקחו בטל ותטרוף האשה ממנו כתובתה כשתתגרש או ימות בעלה דאי לא כתבה ליה ללוקח אמר לה בעלה עיניך נתת בגירושין או במיתה וסבורה את לגבות כתובתך כשאמות או אגרשך ולכך אין את מנחת למכור מנכסי כלום אבל בהנך ג' שדות לא אמר לה בעל הכי דמאחר שייחדם לה דין הוא שתערער במכירתן והלכך רבותא הוא דקאמר לא נצרכה האי דתני מקחו בטל לא מבעיא בשאר נכסים דמילתא דפשיטא היא דמצית אמרה נחת רוח עשיתי לבעלי כדי שלא יאמר עיניך נתת בגירושין ובמיתה אלא אפי' בהנך ג' שדות דליכא למימר הכי אפ"ה מקחו בטל דכיון דמ"מ אינן שלה לגמרי כי אם של בעל מצית אמרה נחת רוח עשיתי לבעלי: **אלא ודאי למעוטי נכסי מלוג.** אתא רבה בר רב הונא דבהנהו אמר אם לקח מן האיש וחזר ולקח מן האשה מקחו קיים דכיון דשלה הן אינה יגורה מבעלה ויכולה למחות לבעלה שלא ימכור ולא מצית אמרה נחת רוח עשיתי לבעלי ומתני' נמי דקתני אין לאיש חזקה בנכסי אשתו הא ראיה יש בנכסי מלוג מיירי דכיון דהנכסים שלה לא מצית אמרה נחת רוח עשיתי לבעלי: ה"ג **והא** (ג) **אמימר כו'.** וקס"ד השתא דהכי קאמר איש שמכר ואחריו האשה לא עשו כלום דמצית אמרה נחת רוח כו' וכל שכן אי זבנה לבעלה דנחת רוח עבדה ולמאי קדייקא מתניתין הא ראיה יש: **ומשני כי איתמר דאמימר.** לא שמכרו שניהם ביחד אלא איש או אשה קאמר כגון היכא דזבין איהו לאחר ומית דאתיא איהי האשה ומפקא מן הלקוחות גוף הקרקע והפירות מכאן ואילך שבעל אין יכול למכור אלא הפירות שהן שלו בחייו וגם הגוף אם תמות אשתו ויירשנה הוא אבל אם ימות הוא היא תיטול נכסי מלוג שלה הלכך האיש שמכר לא עשה ולא כלום לגבי הכי שאם ימות בחיי אשתו היא תקח נכסי מלוג שלה א"נ אם מכרה היא גוף הקרקע בלא פירות שהרי הפירות של בעל הן תחת פרקונה ואח"כ מתה לא עשתה ולא כלום ולא נאמר מאחר שמתה אין לבעל עוד פירות שהרי לא יפדנה עוד וגם גוף הקרקע לא ירש מאשתו אע"פ שהבעל יורש את אשתו שהרי מכרה גוף הקרקע בחייה אי אפשר לומר כן אלא אתי בעל ומפיק כמו שהתקינו באושא כשהיתה סנהדרין לשם באחת מי' גליות שגלתה סנהדרין כדאיתא בראש השנה (דף לא.) וכדר' יוסי בר' חנינא כו': **הבעל מוציא מיד הלקוחות.** כדמפרש טעמא בב"ק (דף פ.) דאלמוהו רבנן לשעבודא דבעל משום איבה ועשאוהו לוקח ראשון ומיהו להכי אהני מכירת האשה שאם ימות בעלה בחייה יטלם הלוקח: **אבל היכא דזבינו תרוייהו לעלמא.** הוא מכר את הפירות והיא מכרה את הגוף: **א"נ זבנה איהי לדידיה.** לבעלה: **זבינייהו זביני.** ולא מצית אמרה נחת רוח עשיתי לבעלי דשלה לא עבדה נחת רוח דלא קפיד עליה בעל והלכך שפיר קדייקא מתני' הא ראיה יש שאם יש לו שטר או עדים שמכרה לו אשתו נכסי מלוג שלה הוי המקח קיים: **ואי בעית אימא אמימר.** (ג) כשמכרו שניהם ביחד לאדם אחד קאמר דלא עשו ולא כלום ואפילו לקח תחלה מן האיש וחזר ולקח מן האשה וכ"ש היכא דמכרה היא לבעלה דלא הויא מכר ומיהו לא תקשי ממתניתין דדייקא דהוי מכר דאמימר דאמר כר' אלעזר ויליף טעמא מקראי דדבר של שני שותפין שהגוף לזה והפירות לזה אין כח לשניהם למכור דלא זה קרוי בעליו ולא זה קרוי בעליו ומתני' רבנן דפליגי עליה דר' אלעזר: **שישמשנו.** למוכר: **הראשון.** אם הכהו ומת לסוף שני ימים מחמת הכאה זו: **ישנו בדין יום או יומים.** יעמד לא יוקם (שמות כא) ופטור דאילו מכה לישראל חבירו אם מחמת מכה זו מת אפילו לסוף שנה נהרג כדנפקא לן מונקה המכה מלמד שחובשים אותו כו' (סנהדרין דף עח:): **מפני שהוא תחתיו.** עדיין כל ל' יום וכתיב ומת תחת ידו (שם) ותחת קרינא ביה אבל השני הלוקח אינו בדין יום או יומים אם הכהו ומת אלא הורגין אותו דעבד כנעני כבר ישראל הוא לכל דבריו דגמר לה לה מאשה: **קסבר.** רבי מאיר קנין פירות דהיינו תשמיש דעבד כל שלשים יום: **בקנין הגוף דמי.** כלומר כאילו קנה גופו ואותו שאין לו פירות אין קנין הגוף שיש לו בעבד כלום דאין גופו עומד אלא לפירותיו והלכך ראשון קרוי אדון: **רבי יהודה.** דייק סיפיה דקרא לא יוקם כי כספו הוא למי שהוא קנוי לגופו הוי עבד:

שניהם

אילימא למעוטי שאר נכסים. בפ' האשה שנפלו (כתובות דף פא.) גבי הרוצה למכור בנכסי אחיו פ"ה דהא דתנן בהניזקין (גיטין דף נה:) לקח מן האיש וחזר ולקח מן האשה מקחו בטל הא אוקימנא בג' שדות והקשה ה"ר שמואל דכ"ש בשאר נכסים איירי כדמשמע הכא לכך נראה לר"י לפרש מקחו בטל משעת טריפה וג' שדות לאו למעוטי שאר נכסים ואפילו בג' שדות מקחו קיים עד שעת טריפה ויש ליישב פ"ה דמקחו בטל משמע בטל לגמרי וה"ק למעוטי מאי דלא מצית אמרה נחת רוח עשיתי לבעלי אילימא למעוטי שאר נכסים דלא תטרוף לגמרי כ"ש דהויא לה איבה והא דלא קאמר למעוטי שאר נכסים דאין מקחו בטל לגמרי דמשום הא לא הוה צריך למימר לא נצרכה אלא לאותן ג' שדות דפשיטא הוא דאין מקח בטל אלא באותן ג' שדות דהא כל אדם מוכר קרקע המשועבדת אלא ודאי לא איצטריך לאוקומי באותן שלש שדות אלא למעוטי שאר נכסים דלא טרפה כלל ° אבל קשיא לרשב"א דהיכי מצית למימר דפשיטא ליה דבשאר נכסים אין מקחו בטל לגמרי הא מקמי דמוקי לה הכא באותן ג' שדות הוה ס"ד דמיירי בשאר נכסים ואע"ג דקתני מקחו בטל: **המוכר** עבדו ע"מ שישמשנו ל' יום. הא דלא נקט המוכר עבדו לפירות כדנקט בהשולח (גיטין דף מז:) המוכר שדהו לפירות משום דאין דרך למכור עבד כענין זה אלא משכיר אותו לעשות מלאכה:

ישנו בדין יום או יומים. אין להקשות השתא בעמידת יום לא יוקם כ"ש ביומים דרש"י פי' בפרשת ואלה המשפטים איזהו יום שהוא כיומים הוי אומר מעת לעת: **קסבר** קנין פירות כקנין הגוף דמי. דאי משום דדריש תחתיו ה"נ כתיב כספו ומנא ליה דתחתיו דוקא טפי מכספו אלא משום דסבירא ליה קנין פירות כקנין הגוף דמי וא"ת א"כ הוה ליה למימר שניהם אינן בדין יום או יומים כדאשכחן בהחובל (ב"ק דף פט: ושם) דתני חדא עבדי מלוג יוצאין בשן ועין לאשה אבל לא לאיש ותניא אידך לא לאיש ולא לאשה ומסיק דכ"ע לית להו תקנת אושא ובקנין פירות כקנין הגוף דמי קמיפלגי מר סבר כקנין הגוף דמי ומר סבר לאו כקנין הגוף דמי אלמא הא דחשיב קנין פירות כקנין הגוף דמי לא מהני שיצא לאיש אלא לענין שלא יצא לאשה ור"י בר ברוך ל"ג ובקנין פירות כקנין הגוף דמי קמיפלגי אלא ה"ג דכ"ע לית להו תקנה ובפלוגתא דהני תנאי כו' והא דקתני לאשה אבל לא לאיש כר' יהודה והיא דקתני לא לאיש ולא לאשה כר' אלעזר דאמר שניהם אינן בדין יום או יומים ואפילו שניהם יחד אין יכולין לשחרר ומשום הכי לית להו תקנת אושא דלר' אלעזר אין מכירתו כלום הלכך לא שייך לר' אלעזר תקנת אושא דתקנו שהבעל מוציא מיד הלקוחות ולדידיה אין כאן מכירה כלל ויש לתרץ בדוחק גירסת הספרים דהתם סברא הוא שלא יועיל קנין פירות להיות כקנין הגוף אלא לענין שלא יצא בשן ועין לאשה אבל לענין שיצא לאיש לא דלא אלים להפקיע קנין פירותיו את קנין גוף דאשה שיצאו לו לחרות אי נמי דלא דמי קנין פירות דבעל שלא היה

קצד א ב מיי' פכ"ב מהל' אישות הל' טו [טוו] ופוסק מכרן קיום סמג עשין מח טוש"ע אה"ע סי' צ סעי' יג וסעי' טו:

קצה ג מיי' שם הל' יז טוש"ע שם ס"ע:

קצו ד שם סעי' יח:

קצז ה מיי' שם הל' ח ופי"ד מהל' טוען הלכה א סמג שם ועי' לח טוש"ע שם וטוש"ע ח"מ סי' קנא סעיף א:

ליקוטי רש"י

באושא התקינו. כמה שנים אחר חורבן כדאמרינן בראש השנה (לא.) גבי עשרה מסעות נסעה שכינה [שבת טו.]. כשיצאו סנהדרין גזית באושא היא אחת מעשר גליות שגלתה סנהדרין כדאמר בר"ה (לא.) [כתובות מט: וכעי"ז ב"מ לה.]. **האשה שמכרה בנכסי מלוג.** להיות הבעל אוכל פירות בחייה וגוף הקרקע יהיה ללוקח לכשתמות ומתה [ב"ק שם]. הקרן [כתובות נ.]. האשה שמכרה נכסי מלוג בחיי בעלה שאם ימות בעלה יזכה בהן ואם תמות היא ויירשנה בעל יעכב ונכסי מלוג הן נכסים שנפלו לה מבית אביה שהכניסה קרקעות שלא שומה בכתובתה ולא קיבל בעל עליו אחריות ואוכל פירותיהן בחייה כתקנת חכמים תחת מזונות ולהכי מיקרי מלוג שמולגן ומחסרן בעל שאוכל הפירות כמליגת הראש [רשב"ם לקמן קלט:]. **ומתה.** ובעל יורש אשתו דבר תורה [ב"ם צו:]. **הבעל מוציא.** גוף הקרקע מיד הלקוחות והכי מוקי לה בפרק קמא דכתובות (עח.) תקנת אושא בגופה של קרקע לאחר מיתה דאלמא ללוקח שויוה רבנן כיורש ואומר לא לקחתי דאי לאו דשויוה רבנן יורש [illegible] [שם לה.]. דשויוה רבנן ללוקח והוה לוקח ראשון [כתובות שם]. דלאו"ג בדעלמא [קנין פירות] לאו כקנין הגוף דמי בעל בנכסי אשתו אלמוה רבנן לשעבודיה משום איבה והוי לוקח ראשון [ב"ק פח:]. **ואיבעית אימא.** אפי' מכרו שניהם כאחד [illegible] **המוכר את עבדו.** עבד כנעני לאחר. **ופסק.** המוכר עם הלוקח ע"מ שישמשנו עוד שלשים יום. **הראשון ישנו בדין יום או יומים.** אם הכהו בתוך שלשים יום הללו ולא מת תחת ידו אלא עמד יום או יומים [illegible] [ב"ק צ.].

א) [ב"ק נ.], ב) ב"ק פט: ב"מ לה. נו: לקמן קלט: כתובות נ. עח: ג) ב"ק נ. ד) [שבת קלה. וש"נ].

הגהות הב"ח

(א) גמ' דהויא לה איבה: (ב) רשב"ם ד"ה ה"ג והא אמר אמימר וכו' עבדה ליה ולמאי: (ג) ד"ה ולימעיות אימא אמימר אפילו כשמכרו:

גליון הש"ס

תוס' ד"ה אילימא כו' אבל קשה להרשב"א. קשה לי דהיכן פסיקא להו דהמקשן הוי מוקי לה בשאר נכסים. דלמא הוי דמלישנא בעל מוכח דלא מיירי בשאר נכסים אלא דהוי מוקי לה בג' שדות ובנכסי מלוג חו רק בג' שדות ומדמי מקבלת כ"מ בג' שדות לענין נ"ר והתרלן חידש לו למדברי רבה בר ר"ה דע"כ לא למעט דנכי ר"מ לא אמרי נ"ר וכ"ע:

רבינו גרשום

אילימא למעוטי שאר נכסים דידיה כל שכן. הוא דמקחו בטל דמצית למימר נחת רוח עשיתי לבעלי דאי לא שבקתיה למזבן ליה מכנסיה מידי הוא איבה ליה לבעלי איבה בהכי. דאמר לי הכי את מקנטת אותי שאין את מנחת לי למכור כלום כדי שאגרשך ותטול כתובתך מהן ואי רצונך שאמות בחייך כדי שתטול כתובה מהן ולהכי לא מחית ומכרה בטל: אלא למעוטי נכסי מלוג. שאם מכרן הבעל בפניה ושתקה מקחו קיים דאין יכולה לומר נחת רוח עשיתי לבעלי משום הואיל דהגוף שלה ולא של בעל אינה לה למחוי: והאמר אמימר איש או אשה שמכרו נכסי מלוג לא עשו ולא כלום: דאמר כר' אלעזר: ופסק עמו. המוכר ללוקח: ראשון ישנו בדין יום או יומים. שאם הכהו ומת לאחר יום או יומים לא יוקם: שני. אם הכהו בתוך אותן ל' יום אע"פ שמת לאחר יום או יומים יהרג המכה והבעבד כנעני (גר) קמיירי: קסבר. ר' מאיר להכי ראשון ישנו בדין יום או יומים משום דסבירא ליה קנין פירות שיש לו לעבודת ל' יום (דהיינו) כקנין הגוף דמי מה קנין הגוף כשהוא עבדו לגמרי וחבל בו דישנו בו ביום או יומים כן הכי נמי קנין פירות: ר' יהודה אומר. אם חבל בו שני באותן ל' יום ישנו ביום או יומים מפני שהוא כספו שקנאו:

תורה אור השלם

א) אַךְ אִם יוֹם אוֹ יוֹמַיִם יַעֲמֹד לֹא יֻקָּם כִּי כַסְפּוֹ הוּא: [שמות כא, כא]

Additionally, Ameimar teaches that זַבְנָה אִיהִי וּמֵתָה – where **[the wife] sold** the title to the land **and then died,** אָתָא אִיהוּ וּמַפִּיק – **[the husband] may come and take** the land **away** from the purchaser בְּתַקַּנְתָּא דְּרַבָּנָן – **by** the power granted to him in **a Rabbinical enactment,**[10] וְכִדְר׳ יוֹסֵי בַּר חֲנִינָא – **as** stated by **R' Yose bar Chanina.** דְּאָמַר רַבִּי יוֹסֵי בַּר חֲנִינָא – **For R' Yose bar Chanina said:** בְּאוּשָׁא הִתְקִינוּ – **[The Sages] enacted in Usha**[11] הָאִשָּׁה שֶׁמָּכְרָה בְּנִכְסֵי מְלוֹג – that **if a woman sells** ***melog*** **property** during her husband's lifetime וּמֵתָה – **and she** then **died,** הַבַּעַל מוֹצִיא מִיַּד הַלָּקוֹחוֹת – **the husband may take** the property **out of the hands of the purchasers.**[12] אֲבָל הֵיכָא דְּזַבִּינוּ תַּרְוַיְיהוּ לְעָלְמָא – **But where they both sold** the *melog* property **to someone else,**[13] אִי נַמִּי זַבְנָה אִיהִי לְדִידֵיהּ – **or if [the wife] sold it to [the husband],** זְבִינָהּ זְבִינֵי – **the sale stands.**[14]

The Gemara offers another interpretation of Ameimar's ruling:[15]

וְאִיבָּעִית אֵימָא – **If you prefer, say** that Ameimar's ruling is indeed not in agreement with our Mishnah; אֲמֵימַר דְּאָמַר כְּר׳ אֶלְעָזָר – however, **Ameimar stated** his ruling **following** the opinion of **R' Elazar.** דְּתַנְיָא – **For a Bariasa has taught:** הַמּוֹכֵר אֶת עַבְדּוֹ – If ONE SELLS HIS SLAVE וּפָסַק עִמּוֹ – AND STIPULATES WITH [THE BUYER] שֶׁיְּשַׁמְּשֶׁנּוּ שְׁלֹשִׁים יוֹם – THAT [THE SLAVE] SHOULD continue to SERVE HIM FOR THIRTY DAYS, ר׳ מֵאִיר אוֹמֵר – R' MEIR SAYS: הָרִאשׁוֹן – THE FIRST, i.e. original owner, יֶשְׁנוֹ בְּדִין יוֹם אוֹ יוֹמַיִם – IS SUBJECT TO THE RULE OF *A DAY OR TWO* if he should strike the slave and cause his death,[16] מִפְּנֵי שֶׁהוּא תַּחְתָּיו – BECAUSE [THE SLAVE] IS still UNDER [HIS AUTHORITY]; וְהַשֵּׁנִי – WHEREAS THE SECOND owner, the one who bought the slave, אֵינוֹ בְּדִין יוֹם אוֹ יוֹמַיִם – IS NOT SUBJECT TO THE RULE OF *A DAY OR TWO,* מִפְּנֵי שֶׁאֵינוֹ תַּחְתָּיו – BECAUSE [THE SLAVE] IS NOT UNDER [HIS AUTHORITY].[17] The Gemara interrupts the Baraisa to explain R' Meir's view. קָסָבַר – **[R' Meir] maintains** קִנְיַן פֵּירוֹת כְּקִנְיַן הַגּוּף דָּמֵי – that **ownership** of the **produce** of a thing **is tantamount to ownership of the** thing's **essence.**[18]

The Baraisa resumes:

ר׳ יְהוּדָה אוֹמֵר – R' YEHUDAH SAYS: הַשֵּׁנִי – THE SECOND owner יֶשְׁנוֹ בְּדִין יוֹם אוֹ יוֹמַיִם – IS SUBJECT TO THE RULE OF *A DAY OR TWO,* מִפְּנֵי שֶׁהוּא כַּסְפּוֹ – BECAUSE [THE SLAVE] IS HIS PROPERTY,[19] הָרִאשׁוֹן – whereas THE FIRST owner אֵינוֹ בְּדִין יוֹם אוֹ יוֹמַיִם – IS

NOTES

10. Accordingly, when Ameimar said that the wife's sale of her *melog* property accomplishes nothing, he meant that it does not alter her husband's prospects, because if she dies before her husband, he still inherits the property she sold (*Rashbam*).

11. Usha was one of a series of ten sites to which the Great Sanhedrin relocated after it left the Temple (*Rashbam,* from *Rosh Hashanah* 31a-b).

12. Strictly speaking, if a wife sold the title to her *melog* property before she died, the husband has no claim to inherit it since it is no longer part of her estate. Moreover, he loses the rights even to the produce, because there is no longer any need to insure that the husband will ransom his wife. Nevertheless, there is a Rabbinical enactment that a husband whose wife has died receives title to his wife's *melog* property even if she sold it before her death. This enactment treated the husband as the first buyer of the property. It is viewed as if husband and wife had agreed at the time of their marriage that the husband would receive the profits of the property during her lifetime and, if she should die first, he would receive the title itself retroactively. Thus, his right to the *melog* property predates that of any other purchaser, and he therefore takes title away from the buyer upon his wife's death. The Sages strengthened the position of the husband in this way to prevent antagonism between husband and wife. Thus, the only practical effect of a wife's sale of her *melog* property is that if the husband dies first, the property goes to the buyer rather than to the wife (*Rashbam*).

13. I.e. the wife sold the title to the land itself and the husband sold the right to the produce (*Rashbam*).

14. Because a woman cannot claim that she agreed to sell her *melog* property only to please her husband, as explained above (note 6).

15. According to the previous interpretation, we were compelled to say that Ameimar referred to cases in which either the husband alone sold the *melog* property or the wife did. But if the wife and husband both sold their rights to the same person, the sale would stand.

The Gemara now offers a second explanation, according to which Ameimar indeed invalidates the sale of *melog* property even if both husband and wife sell it together, and indeed even if the wife sells it to her husband. Although this contradicts the implied ruling of our Mishnah, Ameimar follows the view of another Tanna, who in fact disputes our Mishnah's ruling (*Rashbam*).

16. The Torah states (*Exodus* 21:20-21): וְכִי־יַכֶּה אִישׁ אֶת־עַבְדּוֹ אוֹ אֶת־אֲמָתוֹ בַּשֵּׁבֶט וּמֵת תַּחַת יָדוֹ נָקֹם יִנָּקֵם. אַךְ אִם־יוֹם אוֹ יוֹמַיִם יַעֲמֹד לֹא יֻקַּם כִּי כַסְפּוֹ הוּא, *If a man strikes his male or female slave with a rod and he dies under his hand, [the death] shall surely be avenged. However, if [the slave] survives for a day or two, [the death] shall not be avenged, for he is his property.*

These verses deal with a Canaanite slave. Should his Jewish master strike him and kill him, he is liable to the death penalty. In general, one is liable for murder even if the victim does not die until sometime later, as long as death results from the aggressor's blow. In the case of a master, however, the Torah decrees that he is liable for murder only if the slave dies within twenty-four hours of being struck. If the slave survives more than twenty-four hours, the master is exempt from punishment. [The words "for a day *or two*" are meant to teach that the day spoken of is a full twenty-four-hour period, even if it overlaps two days of the week (*Rashi* to the verse, citing *Mechilta; Rambam Hil. Rotzei'ach* 2:12).] This exception applies only to the master. Should anyone else strike the slave, he would be subject to the death penalty even if the slave died more than twenty-four hours after the blow.

17. R' Meir rules that although the first owner sold the slave, his right to his services for thirty days qualifies him as the owner in regard to the law of a death occurring more than twenty-four hours after a blow. This may be seen from the verse which states: *If a man strikes his. . .slave with a rod and he dies under his hand.* The phrase *under his hand* indicates that the verse is giving the rule for a slave who is *under* (i.e. subject to) *his authority* – even if he does not hold title to the slave. Since the slave in question is still bound to work for the original owner for thirty days, he is under his authority rather than under the authority of his new owner. Therefore, if the new master strikes the slave during the thirty-day period and the slave dies more than twenty-four hours afterwards, the new master is liable to the death penalty (*Rashbam*).

18. I.e. the one who owns the produce of a property is the one to whom we apply any special laws that pertain to the owner of a property.

In this case, the ownership of the slave is divided between the buyer, who holds title to him, and the original owner, who holds the right to his labor for thirty days. Thus, the buyer owns the essence of the slave, whereas the original owner continues (for thirty days) to own his produce. R' Meir maintains that the one who receives the fruits of the slave's labor is the one who is subject to all the laws that pertain specifically to the master. Accordingly, only the original owner is subject to the leniency of *a day or two* and not the buyer (*Rashbam*).

This is the primary reason for R' Meir's ruling. His allusion to the verse of *under his hand* is only to neutralize a counter-indication from the verse cited below by R' Yehudah; see note 21 (*Tosafos; Toras Chaim*).

19. R' Yehudah alludes to the verse's explanation of the exemption: *for he* [the slave] *is his property.* This indicates to R' Yehudah that these verses refer to the master who has monetary possession of the slave, not just a right to his labor (*Rashbam*). Thus, R' Yehudah rules that the buyer is not subject to the death penalty if he strikes the slave and he dies more than twenty-four hours later, even though the slave is still bound to work for his original owner. However, if the original owner strikes the slave, he is liable to the death penalty even if the slave survives for more than twenty-four hours.

ואחת שיחד לה בכתובתה ואחת שהכניסה לו שום משלה להו למעוטי מאי אילימא למעוטי שאר נכסים כל שכן דהויא (א) ליה איבה דאמר לה עיניך נתת בגירושין ובמיתה אלא למעוטי נכסי מלוג האמר אמימר איש ואשה שמכרו בנכסי מלוג לא עשו ולא כלום כי איתמר דאמימר היכא דזבין איהו ומית אתיא איהי ומפקא א"נ זבנה איהי ומתה אתא איהו ומפיק בתקנתא דרבנן וכדר' יוסי בר חנינא דאמר רבי יוסי בר חנינא באושא התקינו האשה שמכרה בנכסי מלוג ומתה הבעל מוציא מיד הלקוחות אבל היכא דזבינו תרוייהו לעלמא א"נ זבנה איהי לדידיה זבינה זביני ואיבעית אימא אמימר דאמר כר' אלעזר דתניא המוכר את עבדו ופסק עמו שישמשנו שלשים יום ר' מאיר אומר הראשון ישנו בדין א) יום או יומים מפני שהוא תחתיו והשני אינו בדין יום או יומים מפני שאינו תחתיו קסבר קנין פירות כקנין הגוף דמי ר' יהודה אומר השני ישנו בדין יום או יומים מפני שהוא כספו הראשון אינו בדין יום או יומים מפני שאינו כספו קסבר קנין פירות לאו כקנין הגוף דמי ר' יוסי אומר שניהם

רשב"ם

ואחת שיחד לה בכתובתה. לא נכתב בתוך השטר אלא לאחר נישואין ייחד לה אחת משדותיו ועשאה אפותיקי לגבות ממנה כתובתה ומיהו כל שדותיו משועבדים לה בתוך שטר הכתובה אלא על זה בוטחת יותר הואיל ויחדו לה בפני עדים: ה"ג ואחת שהכניסה לו שום משלה. שדה שהכניסה לו מבית אביה ושמו אותו וכתבו שוויו בשטר הכתובה שקבלו עליו הבעל בדמים והן נכסי צאן ברזל שאם פחתו פחתו לו ואם הותירו הותירו לו והוו שכותבים ולא נדוניא דהנעלת ליה מבית אבוה כך וכך ממון סך הכל קיבל עליו החתן בכך וכך דינרין וגם זה השדה משעבד לה עם שאר נכסיו של בעל אלא שעל זה בוטחת יותר בשעבודו הואיל ומבית אביה הכניסתו ומג' שדות הללו אם חזר ולקח מן האשה מקחו בטל דאמרה נחת רוח עשיתי לבעלי. והתלמוד עצמו מפרש והולך לקיים פירוש שלו למעוטי מאי כלומר ולמעוטי מאי נקטו ג' שדות הללו דהוי מקחו בטל ולא שדה אחרת אילימא למעוטי שאר נכסים וקרקעות של בעל שאין משועבדין לה דאם חזר ולקח מן האשה יהא מקחו קיים ולא תאמר נחת רוח עשיתי לבעלי והכי קאמר רבה בר רב הונא לא נכרכה כו' כלומר אין משנה זו מדברת בשאר נכסים אלא בהנך ג' שדות דכיון דמשועבדין לה כל כך שהן מיוחדין לה ודאי לא גמרה ואקנייה אלא נחת רוח עשתה לבעלה אבל בשאר שדות שאין משועבדין לה כל כך שאין מיוחדים לה ודאי גמרה ואקנייה ולא מצית אמרה נחת רוח עשיתי לבעלי והוו מקחו קיים: כל שכן. דמצית אמרה נחת רוח עשיתי לבעלי: דהויא לה איבה. אם לא תמכור לו ללוקח מבעלה וכל שכן דהוי מקחו בטל ותטרוף האשה ממנו כתובתה כשתתגרש או ימות בעלה דאי לא כתבה ליה ללוקח אמר לה בעלה עיניך נתת בגירושין או במיתה וסבורה את לגבות כתובתך כשאמות או אגרשך ולכך אין את מנחת למכור מנכסי כלום אבל בהנך ג' שדות לא אמר לה בעל הכי דמאחר שייחדם לה דין הוא שתערער במכירתן והלכך רבותא הוא דקאמר לא נכרכה האי דתני מקחו בטל לא מבעיא בשאר נכסים דמילתא דפשיטא היא דמצית אמרה נחת רוח עשיתי לבעלי כדי שלא יאמר עיניך נתת בגירושין ובמיתה אלא אפי' בהנך ג' שדות דליכא למימר הכי אפ"ה מקחו בטל דכיון דמ"מ אינן שלה לגמרי כי אם של בעל מצית אמרה נחת רוח עשיתי לבעלי: אלא ודאי למעוטי נכסי מלוג. אתא רבה בר רב הונא דבהנהו אמר אם לקח מן האיש וחזר ולקח מן האשה מקחו קיים דכיון דשלה הן אינה יגורה מבעלה ויכולה למחות לבעלה שלא ימכור ולא מצית אמרה נחת רוח עשיתי לבעלי ומתני' נמי דקתני אין לאיש חזקה בנכסי אשתו הא ראיה יש בנכסי מלוג מיירי דכיון דהנכסים שלה לא מצית אמרה נחת רוח עשיתי לבעלי: ה"ג והא (ב) אמימר כו'. וקס"ד השתא דהכי קאמר איש שמכר ואחריו האשה לא עשו כלום דמצית אמרה נחת רוח כו' וכל שכן אי זבנה לבעלה דנחת רוח עבדה ואמאי קדייקא מתניתין הא ראיה יש: ומשני כי איתמר דאמימר. לא שמכרו שניהם ביחד אלא איש או אשה קאמר כגון היכא דזבין איהו לאחר ומית דאתיא איהי האשה ומפקא מן הלקוחות גוף הקרקע והפירות מכאן ואילך שבעל אין יכול למכור אלא הפירות שהן שלו בחייו וגם הגוף אם תמות אשתו ויירשנה הוא אבל אם ימות הוא היא תיטול נכסי מלוג שלה הלכך האיש שמכר לא עשה ולא כלום לגבי הכי שאם ימות בחיי אשתו היא תקח נכסי מלוג שלה א"נ אם מכרה היא גוף הקרקע בלא פירות שהרי הפירות של בעל הן תחת פרקונה ואח"כ מתה לא עשתה ולא כלום ולא נאמר מאחר שמתה אין לבעל עוד פירות שהרי לא יפדנה עוד וגם גוף הקרקע לא ירש מאשתו אע"פ שהבעל יורש את אשתו שהרי מכרה גוף הקרקע בחייה אי אפשר לומר כן אלא אתי בעל ומפיק כמו שהתקינו באושא כשהיתה סנהדרין לשם באחת מי' גליות שגלתה סנהדרין כדאיתא בראש השנה (דף לא.) וכדר' יוסי בר' חנינא כו': הבעל מוציא מיד הלקוחות. כדמפרש טעמא בב"ק (דף פ.) דאלמוהו רבנן לשעבודא דבעל משום איבה ועשאוהו לוקח ראשון ומיהו להכי אהני מכירת האשה שאם ימות בעלה בחייה יטלם הלוקח: אבל היכא דזבינו תרווייהו לעלמא. הוא מכר את הפירות והיא מכרה את הגוף: א"נ זבנה איהי לדידיה. לבעלה: זביניהו זביני. ולא מצית אמרה נחת רוח עשיתי לבעלי דבשלה לא עבדה נחת רוח דלא קפיד עליה בעל והלכך שפיר קדייקא מתני' הא ראיה יש שאם יש לו שטר או עדים שמכרה לו אשתו נכסי מלוג שלה הוי המקח קיים: ואי בעית אימא אמימר. (ג) כשמכרו שניהם ביחד לאדם אחד קאמר דלא עשו ולא כלום ואפילו לקח תחלה מן האיש וחזר ולקח מן האשה וכ"ש היכא דמכרה היא לבעלה דלא הויא מכר ומיהו לא תקשי ממתניתין דדייקא דהוי מכר דאמימר דאמר כר' אלעזר ויליף טעמא מקראי דדבר של שני שותפין שהגוף לזה והפירות לזה אין כח לשניהם למכור דלא זה קרוי בעליו ולא זה קרוי בעליו ומתני' רבנן דפליגי עליה דר' אלעזר: שישמשנו. למוכר: הראשון. אם הכהו ומת לסוף שני ימים מחמת הכאה זו: ישנו בדין יום או יומים. יעמד לא יוקם (שמות כא) ופטור דאילו מכה לישראל חבירו אם מחמת מכה זו מת אפילו לסוף שנה נהרג כדנפקא לן מונקה המכה מלמד שחובשים אותו כו' (סנהדרין דף עח:): מפני שהוא תחתיו. עדיין כל ל' יום וכתיב ומת תחת ידו (שם) ותחת קרינא ביה אבל השני הלוקח אינו בדין יום או יומים אם הכהו ומת אלא הורגין אותו דעבד כנעני כבר ישראל הוא לכל דבריו דגמר לה לה מאשה: קסבר. רבי מאיר קנין פירות דהיינו תשמיש דעבד כל שלשים יום: כקנין הגוף דמי. כלומר כאילו קנה גופו ואותו שאין לו פירות אין קנין הגוף שיש לו בעבד כלום דאין גופו עומד אלא לפירותיו והלכך ראשון קרוי אדון: רבי יהודה. דייק סיפיה דקרא לא יוקם כי כספו הוא למי שהוא קנוי לגופו הוי עבד:

שניהם

תוספות

אילימא למעוטי שאר נכסים. בפ' האשה שנפלו (כתובות דף פא.) גבי הרוצה למכור בנכסי אחיו פ"ה דהא דתנן בהניזקין (גיטין דף נה:) לקח מן האיש וחזר ולקח מן האשה מקחו בטל הא אוקמינן בג' שדות והקשה ה"ר שמואל דכ"ש בשאר נכסים איירי כדמשמע הכא לכך נראה לר"י לפרש מקחו בטל משעת טריפה וג' שדות לאו למעוטי שאר נכסים ואפילו בג' שדות מקחו קיים עד שעת טריפה ויש ליישב פ"ה דמקחו בטל משמע בטל לגמרי והכא והכי למעוטי מאי דלא מצית אמרה נחת רוח עשיתי לבעלי אילימא למעוטי שאר נכסים דלא מטרוף לגמרי כ"ש דהויא לה איבה והא דלא קאמר למעוטי שאר נכסים דאין מקחו בטל לגמרי דמשום הא לא הוה צריך למימר לא נכרכה אלא באותן ג' שדות דפשיטא הוא דאין מקח בטל אלא באותן ג' שדות דהא כל אדם מוכר קרקע המשועבדת אלא ודאי לא איצטריך לאוקומי באותן שלש שדות אלא למעוטי שאר נכסים דלא טרפה כלל ° אבל קשיא לרשב"א דהיכי מצית למימר דפשיטא ליה דבשאר נכסים אין מקחו בטל לגמרי דהא מקמי דמוקי לה הכא באותן ג' שדות הוה ס"ד דמיירי בשאר נכסים ואע"ג דקתני מקחו בטל: המוכר עבדו ע"מ שישמשנו ל' יום. הא דלא נקט המוכר עבדו לפירות כדנקט בהשולח (גיטין דף מז:) המוכר שדהו לפירות משום דאין דרך למכור עבד כענין זה אלא משכיר אותו לעשות מלאכה:

ישנו בדין יום או יומים. אין להקשות השתא בעמידת יום לא יוקם כ"ש ביומים דרש"י פי' בפרשת ואלה המשפטים איזהו יום שהוא כיומים הוי אומר מעת לעת: קסבר קנין פירות כקנין הגוף דמי. דאי משום דדריש תחתיו ה"נ כתיב כספו ומנא ליה דתחתיו דוקא טפי מכספו אלא משום דסבירא ליה קנין פירות כקנין הגוף דמי וא"ת א"כ הוה ליה למימר שניהם אינן בדין יום או יומים כדאשכחן בהחובל (ב"ק דף פט: ושם) דתני חדא עבדי מלוג יוצאין בשן ועין לאשה אבל לא לאיש ותניא אידך לא לאיש ולא לאשה ומסיק דכ"ע לית להו תקנת אושא ובקנין פירות כקנין הגוף דמי קמיפלגי מר סבר כקנין הגוף דמי ומר סבר לאו כקנין הגוף דמי אלמא הא דחשיב קנין פירות כקנין הגוף דמי לא מהני שיצא לאיש אלא לענין שלא יצא לאשה ור"י בר ברוך ל"ג ובקנין פירות כקנין הגוף דמי קמיפלגי אלא ה"ג דכ"ע לית להו תקנה ובפלוגתא דהני תנאי כו' והא דקתני לאשה אבל לא לאיש כר' יהודה וההיא דקתני לא לאיש ולא לאשה כר' אלעזר דאמר שניהם אינן בדין יום או יומים ואפילו שניהם יחד אין יכולין לשחרר ומשום הכי לית להו תקנת אושא דלר' אלעזר אין מכירתו כלום הלכך לא שייך לר' אלעזר תקנת אושא דתקנו שהבעל מוציא מיד הלקוחות ולדידיה אין כאן מכירה כלל ויש לתרץ בדוחק גירסת הספרים דהתם סברא הוא שלא יועיל קנין פירות להיות כקנין הגוף אלא לענין שלא יצא בשן ועין לאשה אבל לענין שיצא לאיש לא דלא אלים להפקיע קנין פירותיו את קנין גוף דאשה שיצאו לו לחרות אי נמי דלא דמי קנין פירות דבעל שלא

היה

מסורת הש"ס

א) [ב"ק ל.], ב) ב"ק פח: ב"מ לה. לו: לקמן קלט: כתובות נ. עח:, ג) ב"ק ל., ד) [שבת קלה. וש"נ]:

הגהות הב"ח

(א) גמ' דהויא לה איבה: (ב) רשב"ם ד"ה ה"ג והא אמר אמימר וכו' עבדה ליה ואמאי: (ג) ד"ה ואיבעית אימא אמימר אפילו כשמכרו:

גליון הש"ס

תוס' ד"ה אילימא כו' אבל קשה להרשב"א. קשה לי דהיכן פסיקא להו דהמקשן היה מוקי לה בשאר נכסים. דלמא ידע דמליצתא בטל מוכח דלא מיירי בשאר נכסים אלא דהיה מוקי (בג' שדות ובנכסי מלוג וזו) רק בג' שדות ומדמי מסברא נ"מ לג' שדות לענין נ"ר והתרצן חידש לו דמדברי רבה בר ר"ה דע"כ בא למעט דבנ"מ לא אמרי' נ"ר ול"ע:

רבינו גרשום

אילימא למעוטי שאר נכסים דידיה כל שכן. הוא דמקחו בטל דמצית למימר נחת רוח עשיתי לבעלי דאי לא שבקתיה למזבן ליה מנכסיה מידי הויא ליה לבעלי איבה בהכי. דאמר לי להכי את מקנטת אותי שאין את מנחת לי למכור כלום כדי שאגרשך ותטול כתובתך מהן או רצונך שאמות בחייך כדי שתטול כתובה מהן ולהכי לא מחיתי ומכרו בטל: אלא למעוטי נכסי מלוג. שאם מכרן הבעל בפניה ושתקה מקחו קיים דאין יכולה לומר נחת רוח עשיתי לבעלי משום הואיל דהגוף שלה ולא של בעל איבעי לה למחויי: והאמר אמימר איש או אשה שמכרו נכסי מלוג לא עשו ולא כלום: דאמר כר' אלעזר: ופסק עמו. המוכר ללוקח: ראשון ישנו בדין יום או יומים. שאם הכהו ומת לאחר יום או יומים לא יוקם: שני. אם הכהו בתוך אותן ל' יום אע"פ שמת לאחר יום או יומים יהרג המכה ובעבד כנעני (גר) קמיירי: קסבר. ר' מאיר להכי ראשון ישנו בדין יום או יומים משום דסבירא ליה קנין פירות שיש לו בעבודות ל' יום (דהיינו) כקנין הגוף דמי מה קנין הגוף כשהוא עבדו לגמרי וחבל בו דישנו ביום או יומים כן הכי נמי קנין פירות: ר' יהודה אומר. אם חבל בו שני באותן ל' יום ישנו ביום או יומים מפני שהוא כספו שקנאו:

תורה אור השלם

א) אַךְ אִם יוֹם אוֹ יוֹמַיִם יַעֲמֹד לֹא יֻקַּם כִּי כַסְפּוֹ הוּא: [שמות כא, כא]

עין משפט נר מצוה

קצד א ב מיי' פכ"ב מהל' אישות הל' טו [טו] ופוסק מכרן קיים סמג עשין מח טוש"ע אה"ע סי' צ סעי' יג וסעי' טז:
קצה ג מיי' שם הל' ז טוש"ע שם ס"ט:
קצו ד שם סעי' יז:
קצז ה מיי' שם הל' יח ופי"ד מהל' טוען ונטען הלכה א סמג שם וסי' לה טוש"ע שם וטוש"ע ח"מ סי' קנא סעיף א:

ליקוטי רש"י

באושא התקינו. כמה שנים אחר חורבן כדאמרינן בראש השנה (לא.) גבי עשרה מסעות נסעה שכינה [שבת טו:]. כשישבו סנהדרי גזית באושא שהיא אחת מעשר גליות שגלתה סנהדרין כדאמר בר"ה (לא.) [כתובות מט: וכעי"ז ב"מ לה.]. האשה שמכרה בנכסי מלוג. להיות הבעל אוכל פירות בחייה וגוף הקרקע יהיה ללוקח לכשתמות ומתה [ב"מ שם]. הקרן [כתובות נ.]. האשה שמכרה נכסי מלוג בחיי בעלה שאם ימות בעלה יזכה בהן ואם תמות היא ויירשנה בעל יפסידו ונכסי מלוג הן נכסים שנפלו לה מבית אביה או שהכניסה קרקעות שלא נשומו בכתובתה ולא קיבל בעל עליו אחריות ואוכל פירותיהן בחייה כתקנת חכמים תחת פרקונה ולהכי מיקרי מלוג שמולגן ומחסרן בעל שאוכל הפירות כמליגת הראש [רשב"ם לקמן קלט:]. ומתה. ובעל יורש אשתו דבר תורה [ב"מ צו:]. הבעל מוציא. גוף הקרקע מיד הלקוחות והכי מוקי לה בפרק האשה בכתובות (עח:) תקנת אושא בגופה של קרקע לאחר מיתה אלמא כלוקח שויוהו רבנן ואומר לו אני לקחתי ראשון דאי כשאר יורש שויוהו רבנן יורש שמכר אביו נכסיו בחייו אין לו ירושה בהן [שם לה.]. דשויוהו רבנן כלוקח והוא לוקח ראשון [כתובות שם]. דאע"ג דבעלמא [קנין פירות] לאו כקנין הגוף דמי בעל בנכסי אשתו אלמוה רבנן לשעבודיה משום איבה והוי כלוקח ראשון [ב"ק פח:]. ואיבעית אימא. אפי' מכרו שניהם כאחד לא עשו ולא כלום שאינו לא לזה ולא לזה ואם מת אחד מהם זה הנשאר מוציא מידי הלקוחות ולא דמו לשותפין דעלמא דהתם יש לזה חלק בכולו ליטול חצי וכן לזה אבל הכא כולן קנויין לה לגוף וכולן קנויין לו לפירות וליכא מיוחד לא לזה ולא לזה. המוכר את עבדו. עבד כנעני לאחר. ופסק. המוכר עם הלוקח ע"מ שישמשנו עוד שלשים יום. הראשון ישנו בדין יום או יומים. אם הכהו בתוך שלשים יום הללו ולא מת תחת ידו אלא עמד יום או יומים חי אינו נהרג דכתיב (שמות כא) אך אם יום או יומים וגו' אבל שני אם הכהו בתוך שלשים יום הללו שהיה בבית ראשון אינו בדין יום או יומים ונהרג עליו אפי' מת מחולי זה לסוף שלש שנים דקנין פירות שהוא קנין לראשון כקנין הגוף דמי ולאו דשני הוא [ב"ק צ.].

שֶׁאֵינוֹ כַּסְפּוֹ – NOT SUBJECT TO THE RULE OF *A DAY OR TWO,* BECAUSE [THE SLAVE] IS NOT HIS PROPERTY.[20]

The Gemara explains R' Yehudah's view:

קָסָבַר – **[R' Yehudah] maintains** קִנְיַן פֵּירוֹת לָאו כְּקִנְיַן הַגּוּף דָּמֵי – that **ownership of** the **produce** of a thing **is not tantamount to ownership of the** thing's **essence.**[21]

The Baraisa resumes:

ר׳ יוֹסֵי אוֹמֵר – R' YOSE SAYS:

NOTES

20. I.e. the "owner" is defined as the one who holds the title to the essence of the thing rather than the right to its produce. Thus, whenever ownership of a thing is divided between one person who holds title to the thing and another who has the right to its produce, R' Yehudah rules that the special laws associated with the "owner" apply to the holder of the title, not the holder of the right to the produce.

21. This is R' Yehudah's primary reason for ruling that the original owner can no longer be deemed the slave's master even though the slave is still working for him. R' Yehudah cites the verse's statement: *for he is his property,* because it could otherwise be argued that the phrase cited earlier by R' Meir – *under his hand* – demonstrates that the Torah grants the exemption from the death penalty to the one for whom he must labor. To negate this, R' Yehudah points out the verse also states *for he is his property,* which implies that the criterion that determines who is considered the master is based on who has the legal title to the slave. Similarly, R' Meir makes reference to the phrase *under his hand* to neutralize the argument that the phrase *for he is his property* proves R' Yehudah's view. In essence, however, the dispute between R' Meir and R' Yehudah does not center on Scriptural interpretations but on the conceptual question of whether "ownership of the produce of a thing is tantamount to the ownership of the thing's essence" (*Toras Chaim*).

ואחת שיחד לה בכתובתה ואחת שהכניסה לו שום משלה למעוטי מאי אילימא למעוטי שאר נכסים כל שכן דהויא (א) ליה איבה דאמר לה עיניך נתת בגירושין ובמיתה אלא למעוטי נכסי מלוג האמר [ו] אמימר [א] איש ואשה שמכרו בנכסי מלוג לא עשו ולא כלום כי איתמר דאמימר [ב] היכא דזבין איהו ומית אתיא איהי ומפקא א"נ זבנה איהי ומתה אתא איהו ומפיק בתקנתא דרבנן וכדר' יוסי בר חנינא [ג] דאמר רבי יוסי בר חנינא באושא התקינו [ג] האשה שמכרה בנכסי מלוג ומתה הבעל מוציא מיד הלקוחות אבל [ד] היכא דזבינו תרוייהו לעלמא [ה] א"נ זבנה איהי לדידיה זבינה זביני ואיבעית אימא אמימר דאמר כר' אלעזר דתניא [ו] המוכר את עבדו ופסק עמו שישמשנו שלשים יום ר' מאיר אומר הראשון ישנו בדין [א] יום או יומים מפני שהוא תחתיו והשני אינו בדין יום או יומים מפני שאינו תחתיו קסבר [ז] קנין פירות כקנין הגוף דמי ר' יהודה אומר השני ישנו בדין יום או יומים מפני שהוא כספו הראשון אינו בדין יום או יומים שאינו כספו קסבר קנין פירות לאו כקנין הגוף דמי ר' יוסי אומר שניהם

ואחת שיחד לה בכתובתה. לא נכתב בתוך השטר אלא לאחר נישואין ייחד לה אחת משדותיו ועשאה אפותיקי לגבות ממנה כתובתה ומיהו כל שדותיו משועבדים לה בתוך שטר הכתובה אלא על זה בוטחת יותר הואיל ויחדו לה בפני עדים: ה"ג **ואחת שהכניסה לו שום משלה.** שדה שהכניסה לו מבית אביה ושמו אותו וכתבו שווין בשטר הכתובה שקבלן עליו הבעל בדמים והן נכסי צאן ברזל שאם פחתו פחתו לו ואם הותירו הותירו לו וזהו שכותבים ודא נדוניא דהנעלת ליה מבית אבוה כך וכך ממון סך הכל קיבל עליו החתן בכך וכך דינרין וגם זה השדה משעבד לה עם שאר נכסיו של בעל אלא שעל זה בוטחת יותר משעבודו הואיל ומבית אביה הכניסתו ומג' שדות הללו אם חזר ולקח מן האשה מקחו בטל דאמרה נחת רוח עשיתי לבעלי. והמתרך עצמו מפרש והולך לקיים פירוש שלו למעוטי מאי כלומר ולמעוטי מאי נקט ג' שדות הללו דהוי מקחו בטל ולא שדה אחרת אילימא למעוטי שאר נכסים וקרקעות של בעל המשועבדין לה דאם חזר ולקח מן האשה יהא מקחו קיים ולא תאמר נחת רוח עשיתי לבעלי והכי קאמר רבה בר רב הונא לא נצרכה כו' כלומר אין משנה זו מדברת בשאר נכסים אלא בהנך ג' שדות דכיון דמשועבדין לה כל כך שהן מיוחדין לה ודאי לא גמרה ואקנייה אלא נחת רוח עשתה לבעלה אבל בשאר שדות שאין משועבדין לה כל כך שאין מיוחדים לה ודאי גמרה ואקנייה ולא מצית אמרה נחת רוח עשיתי לבעלי והוו מקחו קיים. **כל שכן.** דמצית אמרה נחת רוח עשיתי לבעלי: **דהויא לה איבה.** אם לא תמכור לו ללוקח מבעלה וכל שכן דהוי מקחו בטל ותטרוף האשה ממנו כתובתה כשתתגרש או ימות בעלה דאי לא כתבה ליה ללוקח אמר לה בעלה עיניך נתת בגירושין או במיתה וסבורה את לגבות כתובתך כשתמות או אגרשך ולכך אין את מנחת למכור מנכסי כלום אבל בהנך ג' שדות לא אמר לה בעל הכי דמאחר שייחדם לה דין הוא שתעער במכירתן והלכך רבותא הוא דקאמר לא נצרכה האי דתני מקחו בטל לא מבעיא בשאר נכסים דמילתא דפשיטא היא דמצית אמרה נחת רוח עשיתי לבעלי כדי שלא יאמר עיניך נתת בגירושין ובמיתה אלא אפי' בהנך ג' שדות דליכא למימר הכי אפ"ה מקחו בטל דכיון דמ"מ אינן שלה לגמרי כי אם של בעל מצית אמרה נחת רוח עשיתי לבעלי: **אלא ודאי למעוטי נכסי מלוג.** אתא רבה בר רב הונא דבהנהו אמר אם לקח מן האיש וחזר ולקח מן האשה מקחו קיים דכיון דשלה הן אינה יגורה מבעלה ויכולה למחות לבעלה שלא ימכור ולא מצית אמרה נחת רוח עשיתי לבעלי ומתני' נמי דקתני אין לאיש חזקה בנכסי אשתו הא ראיה יש בנכסי מלוג מיירי דכיון דהכניסם שלה לא מצית אמרה נחת רוח עשיתי לבעלי: ה"ג **והא** (ב) **אמימר כו'.** וקס"ד השתא דהכי קאמר איש שמכר ואחריו האשה לא עשו כלום דמצית אמרה נחת רוח כו' וכל שכן אי זבנה לבעלה דנחת רוח עבדה ואמאי קדייקא מתניתין הא ראיה יש: **ומשני כי איתמר דאמימר.** לא שמכרו שניהם ביחד אלא איש או אשה קאמר כגון היכא דזבין איהו לאחר ומית דאתיא איהי האשה ומפקא מן הלקוחות גוף הקרקע והפירות מכאן ואילך שבעל אין יכול למכור אלא הפירות שהן שלו בחייו וגם הגוף אם תמות אשתו ויירשנה הוא אבל אם ימות הוא היא תיטול נכסי מלוג שלה הלכך האיש שמכר לא עשה ולא כלום לגבי הכי שאם ימות בחיי אשתו היא תקח נכסי מלוג שלה א"נ אם מכרה היא גוף הקרקע בלא פירות שהרי הפירות של בעל הן תחת פרקונה ואח"כ מתה לא עשתה ולא כלום ולא נאמר מאחר שמתה אין לבעל עוד פירות שהרי לא יפדנה עוד וגם גוף הקרקע לא ירש מאשתו אע"פ שהבעל יורש את אשתו שהרי מכרה גוף הקרקע בחייה אי אפשר לומר כן אלא אתי בעל ומפיק כמו שהתקינו באושא כשהיתה סנהדרין לשם באחת מי' גליות שגלתה סנהדרין כדאיתא בראש השנה (דף לא.) וכדר' יוסי בר' חנינא כו': **הבעל מוציא מיד הלקוחות.** כדמפרש טעמא בב"ק (דף פ.) דאלמוהו רבנן לשעבודא דבעל משום איבה ועשאוהו לוקח ראשון ומיהו להכי אהני מכירת האשה שאם ימות בעלה בחייה יטלם הלוקח: **אבל היכא דזבינו תרוייהו לעלמא.** הוא מכר את הפירות והיא מכרה את הגוף: **א"נ זבנה איהי לדידיה.** לבעלה: **זביניהו זביני.** ולא מצית אמרה נחת רוח עשיתי לבעלי דבשלה לא עבדה נחת רוח דלא קפיד עליה בעל והלכך שפיר קדייקא מתני' הא ראיה יש שאם יש לו שטר או עדים שמכרה לו אשתו נכסי מלוג שלה הוי המקח קיים: **ואי בעית אימא אמימר.** (ג) כשמכרו שניהם ביחד לאדם אחד קאמר דלא עשו ולא כלום ואפילו לקח תחלה מן האיש וחזר ולקח מן האשה וכ"ש היכא דמכרה היא לבעלה דלא הוי מכר ומיהו לא תקשי ממתניתין דדייקא דהוי מכר דאמימר דאמר כר' אלעזר ויליף טעמא מקראי דדבר של שני שותפין שהגוף לזה והפירות לזה אין כח לשניהם למכור דלא זה קרוי בעליו ולא זה קרוי בעליו ומתני' רבנן דפליגי עליה דר' אלעזר: **שישמשנו.** למוכר: **הראשון.** אם הכהו ומת לסוף שני ימים מחמת הכאה זו: **ישנו בדין יום או יומים.** יעמד לא יוקם (שמות כא) ופטור דאילו מכה לישראל חבירו אם מחמת מכה זו מת אפילו לסוף שנה נהרג כדנפקא לן מונקה המכה מלמד שחובשים אותו כו' (סנהדרין דף עח:): **מפני שהוא תחתיו.** עדיין כל ל' יום וכתיב ומת תחת ידו (שם) ותחת קרינא ביה אבל השני הלוקח אינו בדין יום או יומים אם הכהו ומת אלא הורגין אותו דעבד כנעני כבר ישראל הוא לכל דבריו דגמר לה לה מאשה: **קסבר.** רבי מאיר קנין פירות דהיינו תשמיש דעבד כל שלשים יום: **כקנין הגוף דמי.** כלומר כאילו קנה גופו ואותו שאין לו פירות אין קנין הגוף שיש לו בעבד כלום דאין גופו עומד אלא לפירותיו והלכך ראשון קרוי אדון: **רבי יהודה.** דייק סיפיה דקרא לא יוקם כי כספו הוא למי שהוא קנוי לגופו הוי עבד: שניהם

אילימא למעוטי שאר נכסים. בפ' האשה שנפלו (כתובות דף פא.) גבי הרוצה למכור בנכסי אחיו פ"ה דהא דתנן בהניזקין (גיטין דף נה:) לקח מן האיש וחזר ולקח מן האשה מקחו בטל הא אוקמינן בג' שדות והקשה ה"ר שמואל דכ"ש בשאר נכסים איירי כדמשמע הכא לכך נראה לר"י לפרש מקחו בטל משעת טריפה וג' שדות לאו למעוטי שאר נכסים ואפילו בג' שדות מקחו קיים עד שעת טריפה ויש ליישב פ"ה דמקחו בטל משמע בטל לגמרי וה"פ למעוטי מאי דלא מצית אמרה נחת רוח עשיתי לבעלי אילימא למעוטי שאר נכסים דלא תטרוף לגמרי כ"ש דהויא לה איבה והא דלא קאמר למעוטי שאר נכסים דאין מקחו בטל לגמרי משום הא לא הוה צריך למימר לא נצרכה אלא לאותן ג' שדות דפשיטא הוא דאין מקח בטל אלא באותן ג' שדות דהא כל אדם מוכר קרקע המשועבדת אלא ודאי לא איצטריך לאוקומי באותן שלש שדות אלא למעוטי שאר נכסים דלא טרפה כלל [ז] אבל קשיא לרשב"א דהיכי מצית למימר דפשיטא ליה דבשאר נכסים אין מקחו בטל לגמרי הא מקמי דמוקי לה הכא באותן ג' שדות הוה ס"ד דמיירי בשאר נכסים ואפ"ה קתני מקחו בטל: **המוכר** עבדו ע"מ שישמשנו ל' יום. הא דלא נקט המוכר עבדו לפירות כדנקט בהשולח (גיטין דף מז:) המוכר שדהו לפירות משום דאין דרך למכור עבד כענין זה אלא משכיר אותו לעשות מלאכה:

ישנו בדין יום או יומים. אין להקשות השתא בעמידת יום לא יוקם כ"ש ביומים דרש"י פי' בפרשת ואלה המשפטים איזהו יום שהוא כיומים הוי אומר מעת לעת: **קסבר** קנין פירות כקנין הגוף דמי. דאי משום דדריש תחתיו ה"נ כתיב כספו ומנא ליה דתחתיו דוקא טפי מכספו אלא משום דסבירא ליה קנין פירות כקנין הגוף דמי וא"ת א"כ הוה ליה למימר שניהם אין בדין יום או יומים כדאשכחן בהחובל (ב"ק דף פט: ושם) דתני חדא עבדי מלוג יוצאין בשן ועין לאשה אבל לא לאיש ותניא אידך לא לאיש ולא לאשה ומסיק דכ"ע לית להו תקנת אושא ובקנין פירות כקנין הגוף דמי קמיפלגי מר סבר כקנין הגוף דמי ומר סבר לאו כקנין הגוף דמי אלמא הא דחשיב קנין פירות כקנין הגוף דמי לא מהני שיהא לאיש אלא לענין שלא יצא לאשה ור"י בר ברוך ל"ג ובקנין פירות כקנין הגוף דמי קמיפלגי אלא ה"ג דכ"ע לית להו תקנה ובפלוגתא דהני תנאי כו' והא דקתני לאשה אבל לא לאיש כר' יהודה והא דקתני לא לאיש ולא לאשה כר' אלעזר דאמר שניהם אינן בדין יום או יומים ואפילו שניהם יחד אין יכולין לשחרר ומשום הכי לית להו תקנת אושא דלר' אלעזר אין מכירתו כלום הלכך לא שייך לר' אלעזר תקנת אושא דתקנו שהבעל מוציא מיד הלקוחות ולדידיה אין כאן מכירה כלל ויש לתרץ בדוחק גירסת הספרים דהתם סברא הוא שלא יועיל קנין פירות להיות כקנין הגוף אלא לענין שלא יצא בשן ועין לאשה אבל לענין שיצא לאיש לא דלא אליס להפקיע קנין פירותיו את קנין גוף דאשה שיצאו לו לחרות אי נמי דלא דמי קנין פירות דבעל שלא היה

מסורת הש"ס

א) [ב"ק נ.], ב) ב"ק פח. ב"מ לה. נו: לקמן קלט: כתובות נ. עח. ג) ב"ק נ. ד) [שבת קלה. וש"נ].

הגהות הב"ח

(א) גמ' דהויא לה איבה: (ב) רשב"ם ד"ה ה"ג והא אמר אמימר וכו' עבדה ליה ולמאי: (ג) ד"ה ואיבעית אימא אמימר אפילו כשמכרו:

גליון הש"ס

תוס' ד"ה אילימא כו' אבל קשה להרשב"א. קשה לי דהיכן פסיקא להו דהמקשן היה מוקי לה בשאר נכסים. דלמא ידע דמליגאה בטל מוכח דלא מיירי בשאר נכסים אלא דהיה מוקי (בג' שדות ובנכסי מלוג וחן) רק בג' שדות ותמדמי מסברא כ"מ בג' שדות לענין נ"ר והתלן חידש דבכ"ה לתלביי רבה בר ר"ה דע"כ בא למעט דבנ"מ לא אמרי' נ"ר ול"ע:

רבינו גרשום

אילימא למעוטי שאר נכסים דידיה כל שכן. הוא דמקחו בטל דמצית למימר נחת רוח עשיתי לבעלי דאי לא שבקתיה למזבן ליה מנכסיה מידי הויא ליה לבעלי איבה בהכי. דאמר לי להכי את מקנטת אותי שאין את מנחת לי למכור כלום כדי שאגרשך ותטול כתובתך מהן או רצונך שאמות בחייך כדי שתטול כתובה מהן ולהכי לא מחיתי ומכרו בטל: אלא למעוטי נכסי מלוג. שאם מכרן הבעל בפניה ושתקה מקחו קיים דאין יכולה לומר נחת רוח עשיתי לבעלי משום הואיל דהגוף שלה ולא של בעל איבעי לה למחויי: והאמר אמימר איש או אשה שמכרו נכסי מלוג לא עשו ולא כלום: דאמר כר' אלעזר: ופסק עמו. המוכר ללוקח: ראשון ישנו בדין יום או יומים. שאם הכהו ומת לאחר יום או יומים לא יוקם: שני. אם הכהו בתוך אותן ל' יום אע"פ שמת לאחר יום או יומים יהרג המכה ובעבד כנעני (גר) קמיירי: קסבר. ר' מאיר להכי ראשון ישנו בדין יום או יומים משום דסבירא ליה קנין פירות שיש לו בעבודות ל' יום (דהיינו) כקנין הגוף דמי מה קנין הגוף כשהוא עבדו לגמרי וחבל בו דישנו ביום או יומים כן הכי נמי קנין פירות: ר' יהודה אומר. אם חבל בו שני באותן ל' יום ישנו ביום או יומים משום שהוא כספו שקנאו:

תורה אור השלם

א) אַךְ אִם יוֹם אוֹ יוֹמַיִם יַעֲמֹד לֹא יֻקַּם כִּי כַסְפּוֹ הוּא: [שמות כא, כא]

עין משפט נר מצוה

קצד א ב מיי' פכ"ג מהל' אישות הל' טז [טו] ופוסק מכרן קיים סמג עשין מח טוש"ע אה"ע סי' צ סעי' יג וסעי' טז:
קצה ג מיי' שם הל' ז טוש"ע שם ס"ט:
קצו ד שם סעי' ח:
קצז ה מיי' שם הל' יח ופי"ד מהל' טוען הלכה א סמג שם וסי' לה טוש"ע שם וטוש"ע ח"מ סי' קנא סעיף א:

ליקוטי רש"י

באושא התקינו. כמה שנים אחר חורבן כדאמרינן בראש השנה (לא.) גבי עשרה מסעות נסעה שכינה [שבת טו:]. כשישבו סנהדרי גזית באושא שהיא אחת מעשר גליות שגלתה סנהדרין כדאמר בר"ה (לא.) [כתובות מט: ובעי"ז ב"מ לה.]. האשה שמכרה בנכסי מלוג. להיות הבעל אוכל פירות בחייה וגוף הקרקע יהיה ללוקח לכשתמות ומתה [ב"מ שם]. הקרן [כתובות נ.]. האשה שמכרה נכסי מלוג בחיי בעלה שאם ימות בעלה יזכה בהן ואם תמות היא ויירשה בעל יפסידו ונכסי מלוג הן נכסים שנפלו לה מבית אביה או שהכניסה קרקעות שלא נשומו בכתובתה ולא קיבל בעל עליו אחריות ואוכל פירותיהן בחייה כתקנת חכמים תחת פרקונה ולהכי מיקרי מלוג שמולגן ומחסרן בעל שאוכל הפירות כמליגת הראש [רשב"ם לקמן קלט.]. ומתה. ובעל יורש אשתו דבר תורה [ב"מ צו:]. הבעל מוציא. גוף הקרקע מיד הלקוחות והכי מוקי לה בפרק המפקיד בכתובות (עח:) תקנת אושא בגופה של קרקע לאחר מיתה אלמה כשהיו שוויה רבנן כלוקח ראשון ואומר לו לפי לקוחתי ראשון דאי בשאר יורש שוויה רבנן כיורש שמכר אביו נכסי כבחיין הם לו ירושה בהן [שם לה.]. דשוויה רבנן כלוקח והוא לוקח ראשון [כתובות שם]. דלאו"ג דבעלמא [קנין פירות] לאו כקנין הגוף דמי בעל בנכסי אשתו אלמוה רבנן לשעבודיה משום איבה והוי כלוקח ראשון [ב"ק פח:]. ואיבעית אימא. אפי' מכרו שניהם כאחד לא עשו ולא כלום שאינו לא לזה ולא לזה ואם מת אחד מהם זה הנשאר מוציא מידי הלקוחות ולא דמו לשותפין דבעלמא דהתם יש לזה חלק בכולו ויכול למכור בו וזה כחו בגוף וזה כחו בפירות ואינו מיוחד כל זמן שהוא מיוחד לו לפירות וליכא. המוכר את עבדו. עבד כנעני לאחר. ופסק. המוכר עם הלוקח ע"מ שישמשנו עוד שלשים יום. הראשון ישנו בדין יום או יומים. אם הכהו בתוך שלשים יום הללו ולא מת תחת ידו אלא עמד יום או יומים ומת אינו נהרג דכתיב (שמות כא) אך אם יום או יומים יעמד לא יקם ואם הכהו בתוך שלשים יום הללו שהיה בבית ראשון אינו בדין יום או יומים ונהרג עליו אף שאין כאן מתחת ידו זה לסוף שלא עד שנים קנין פירות ולא קנין גוף הראשון כקנין הגוף דמי ולא דמי הוא [ב"ק צ.].

עין משפט
נר מצוה

קצח א מיי' פ"ב מהל' רוצח ושמירת נפש הלכה טו:
קצט ב מיי' פי"ד מהל' טוען הל' יא סמג עשין לה טוש"ע ח"מ סי' קמט סעיף יא וטוש"ע אה"ע סי' פז סעיף ג:
ר ג טוש"ע ח"מ סי' קמט סעי' ע בהגה"ה:
רא ד מיי' שם הל' יא וסמג שם טוש"ע אה"ע סימן פז סעי' ג:

שניהם ישנן בדין יום או יומים זה מפני שהוא תחתיו וזה מפני שהוא כספו ומספקא ליה אי קנין פירות כקנין הגוף דמי אי לאו כקנין הגוף דמי [א] וספק נפשות להקל רבי אלעזר אומר [א] שניהם אינן בדין יום או יומים זה לפי שאינו תחתיו וזה לפי שאינו כספו ואמר רבא מאי טעמא דרבי אלעזר אמר קרא [א] לא יוקם כי כספו הוא כספו המיוחד לו: ולא לאיש חזקה בנכסי אשתו: והאמר רב אשת איש צריכה למחות במאן אילימא באחר והאמר רב [ב] אין מחזיקין בנכסי אשת איש אלא לאו בבעל אמר רבא לעולם בבעל [ג] וכגון שחפר בה בורות שיחין ומערות [ג] והאמר רב נחמן אמר רבה בר אבוה אין חזקה לנזקין אימא אין דין חזקה לנזקין אי בעית אימא (א) לאו איתמר עלה [ג] רב מרי אמר בקוטרא רב זביד אמר בבית הכסא רב יוסף אמר לעולם באחר [ד] וכגון שאכלה מקצת חזקה בחיי הבעל ושלש לאחר מיתת הבעל מיגו דאי בעי אמר (ב) ליה אנא זבינתה מינך כי א"ל נמי את זבינתה ליה וזבנה ניהלי מהימן גופא אמר רב אין מחזיקין בנכסי אשת איש

ודייני

שניהם ישנן כו'. ופטורין דספק נפשות דבעלים שהכוהו ומי נהרג מהם להקל דנפקא לן מושפטו העדה והצילו העדה (במדבר לה): **שניהם.** כלומר שניהם שהכוהו נהרגין: **זה.** אחרון לפי שאינו תחתיו: **וזה.** הראשון לפי שאינו עכשיו כספו שהרי מכרו: **כי כספו הוא.** מיותר הוא דמה נתינת טעם היה צריך ליתן בדבר ולומר לא יוקם לפי שכספו הוא אי נמי מדמצי למיכתב כי כסף הוא ומש"ה נמי יליף אמימר לגבי נכסי מלוג דכיון דאינו מיוחד לא לאיש ולא לאשה אינו קרוי שדה האיש ולא שדה האשה והלכך אם מכרו שניהן מכרן בטל ויכולין לחזור בה כאדם המוכר דבר שאינו שלו דלא (ג) ליהוי מכר: **וקמתמה גמרא ולא לאיש חזקה בנכסי אשתו.** בתמיה אלמא אינה צריכה למחות בבעלה הואיל ולית ליה חזקה: **אשת איש.** שהחזיק אחר בנכסי מלוג שלה צריכה למחות משום דההוא אחר יש לו חזקה ואם לא מיחתה הפסידה: **במאן.** צריכה למחות מי הוא המחזיק: **אילימא באחר.** שאינו בעלה וכל זה סיום הקושיא הוא: **אין מחזיקין בנכסי אשת איש.** דמצית אמרה על בעלי סמכתי שהוא ימחה ויערער ולכך שתקתי ובאחר בני אדם דלא בבעל קאמר רב דאין מחזיקין שכן משמע אין מחזיקין לשון רבים ועוד דאי בבעל קאמר דאין מחזיקין היינו מתניתין לא לאיש חזקה בנכסי אשתו ומאי אתא לאשמועינן: **אלא לאו בבעל.** אלמא יש חזקה וקשיא מתני' לרב: **לעולם בבעל.** שהחזיק בנכסי אשתו קאמר רב דצריכה למחות שיש חזקה לבעל ואפי' הכי לא תקשי ליה מתניתין דהך חזקה דקאמר רב כגון שחפר בה הבעל בורות שיחין ומערות דלפירות הוא דאשתעבד ליה נכסי מלוג דאשתו ולא לקלקל הקרקע לחפירת בורות וכגון שדה שאינה עשויה לבורות והלכך יש לו חזקה דודאי קנאה מאשתו והלכך מקלקל לה לצרכו וכי האי גוונא הוא דקאמר רב צריכה למחות: **אין חזקה לנזקין.** כלומר היכא דמזיק לחבירו אין יכול לטעון לקוחה היא בידי שהרי החזקתי בה ג' שנים בחפירת בורות שיחין ומערות דכי האי גוונא לא הויא חזקה דמאי טעין אידך משום דלא אחזקת כדמחזקי אינשי לא חששתי למחות: **אימא אין דין חזקה.** להצטרך ג' שנים לנזקין היכא דחזקתו ע"י נזקין אלא לאלתר הויא חזקה דאין אדם רואה ד) (שמחזיקין) קרקע שלו ושותק אלא מוחה מיד והיכא דלא מחה הפסיד והלכך אשת איש דקאמר רב צריכה למחות מיד הוא דצריכה למחות מאחר שחופר בה בעל בורות שאין אדם רואה היזקו ושותק והלכך כי האי גוונא יש לו חזקה: ה"ג **ואי בעית אימא הא איתמר עלה רב מרי אמר כו'.** כלומר ואיבעית אימא לעולם חזקת ג' שנים בעינן אפי' היכא דחפר בו בורות כדאוקימנן למילתיה דרב והא דקאמר רב נחמן אין חזקה לנזקין לא בחזקת ג' שנים בקרקע חבירו איירי אלא בעושה היזק לחבירו אפי' בבית של עצמו כגון עשן וריח רע ואתא לאורויי שלא יזיק לחבירו ואפי' החזיק ימים רבים אין חזקה מועלת לו להזיק חבירו: **רב מרי אמר כו'.** כבר פירשנו בלא יחפור: **רב יוסף אמר.** מתני' לא תקשי לרב דמאי דקאמר רב אשת איש צריכה למחות לאו בבעל קאמר דהא אין לאיש חזקה בנכסי אשתו כדקתני מתני' אלא לעולם באחר שהחזיק בנכסיה קאמר רב דצריכה למחות ודקשיא לך האמר רב אין מחזיקין בנכסי אשת איש לא תקשי דה"מ דאין מחזיקין בחיי הבעל שאם החזיק בנכסי' בחיי הבעל ג' שנים אינה חזקה ואינה צריכה למחות דמצית אמרה על בעלי סמכתי א"נ דוקא פירות שהיו לבעלי בנכסים שלי אותן מכר לך אבל הגוף שהוא שלי לא היית יכול לקנות שגם הוא אין לו חזקה בנכסיי באכילת פרי דכיון דאית ליה פרי הכל יודעין דפרי הוא דקאכיל ולכך לא חששתי למחות אבל הכא במאי עסקינן כגון שאכל הלוקח מקצת חזקה בחיי הבעל שמכר לו וג' שנים שלימות לאחר מיתת הבעל כי האי גוונא קאמר רב דצריכה למחות כדמפרש טעמא לקמיה והכי קאמר רב אשת איש שמכר בעלה לאחר נכסי מלוג שלה צריכה למחות לאחר מיתתו דסד"א כיון דהכל יודעין שהבעל מכרם לו ולא היא וגם הוא מודה כמו כן שהבעל מכרם לו לא תועיל חזקתו אף לאחר מיתת הבעל כלום שהרי לא יכול לטעון לאשה מינך זבנתה אחרי כן ואכלתיה שני חזקה דכיון דמתחלה הבעל מכרה לו ופירות הוא דהוי ליה לבעל באותה שדה ואותן מכר לזה הרי זה כאריס שיורד לקרקע באריסות לפירות שאינו יכול לטעון אחרי כן לקחתיה הימנך והלכך לא איצטרך למחות קמ"ל רב דצריכה למחות לאחר מות בעלה קודם שיחזיק בה ההוא אחר ג' שנים דודאי אע"פ שמתחלה היתה קנויה לו מן הבעל יכול לטעון הבעל מכר לי הגוף אם יירשך ואם ימות קודם לך פירות מיהא קניתי ומיד כשמת הרי נסתלקתי ממקחי ולכך קניתי ממך שהרי עתה נעשה השדה שלך והלכך מיגו דאי בעי אמר אנא זבנתה מינך אחר מות בעליך ואכלתיה שני חזקה כי קאמר יודע אני דזבינתיה לבעליך ואחרי כן זבין ניהלי מהימן ולא דמי לאריס שאין יכול לטעון לקחתיו אחרי כן משום דסתם אריס אין זמן לאריסותו אלא כל הימים בתורת אריסותו עומד אבל זה שלוקחה מן האיש על מנת שאם ימות יפסיד מקחו שתטול האשה נכסי מלוג שלה התם ודאי כשמת הבעל הרי זה כאילו יורד עכשיו מחדש לשדה אשה זו והיא שותקת שלש שנים איכא למימר דזבוני זבינה ליה:

ודייני

היה לו בגוף כלום מעולם לקנין פירות דמוכר עבדו ע"מ שישמשנו שלשים יום שתחלה היה הכל שלו ועדיין לא יצא מתחת ידו שהפירות שלו וכעין זה מחלקין גבי בהמת ארנונא בפ"ק דפסחים (דף ו.) ומה שהיה קשה עליה מבכורות שם מפורש וכן נ"ל דאין לומר כלל דלר"מ דסבר הכא קנין פירות כקנין הגוף דמי וסבר שם לאיש אבל לא לאשה דהא דיבמות בפרק אלמנה (דף סו. ושם) פליגי במכנסת שום לבעלה היא אומרת כלי אני נוטל בכתובתי והוא המגרש אומר דמים אני נותן לך ר' אמי אמר הדין עמו רב יהודה אמר הדין עמה ואמרינן תניא כותיה דר' אמי עבדי לאן ברזל יוצאין בשן ועין לאיש אבל לא לאשה ומאי קושיא לרב יהודה דלמא אע"ג דהדין עמה יוצאין לאיש ולא לאשה דקסבר קנין פירות כקנין הגוף דמי ואפילו בנכסי מלוג נמי הוי דינא הכי לרבי מאיר אלא ודאי לא מהני כלל קנין פירות להיות כקנין הגוף לאחד לאיש כדפרישית: **קנין פירות לאו כקנין הגוף דמי כו'.** קשה דבסוף השולח (גיטין דף מח. ושם) מסיק אפלוגתא דרבי יהודה ור"ש דכ"ע קנין פירות כקנין הגוף דמי וי"ל דהתם לא קאמר אלא דמהכא ליכא למילף מינה ובערכין (דף כו:) גרס לעולם אימא לך לרבי שמעון כקנין הגוף ול"ג דכ"ע והא דלא מייתי בהשולח הך דהכא משום דניחא ליה לאיתויי תנאי היא דפליגי בשדה דומיא דפלוגתא דרבי יוחנן ור"ל דהתם:

וספק נפשות להקל. פי' בקונטרס משום דכתיב ושפטו העדה והצילו העדה ואין נראה דבלאו הכי נמי לא קטלי מספיקא דאפילו ממונא לא מפקינן מספיקא: **רבי אלעזר אומר שניהם אינן בדין יום או יומים.** הקשה ריב"א דהיכי מדמי אמימר מכירה לדין יום או יומים דא"כ שותפים לא יוכלו למכור לעולם דהא אמר בהחובל (ב"ק דף צ. ושם) מאן תנא להא דתנו רבנן מי שחציו עבד וחציו בן חורין וכן עבד של שני שותפין אין יוצאין בראשי אברים כמאן כר' אלעזר וא"כ הכא נמי דעבד של שני שותפין אין יכולים למכרו וי"ל דהתם מיירי בשני שותפין שלהם גוף ולהם פירות דומיא דמוכר עבדו ע"מ שישמשנו שלשים יום וחציו עבד וחציו בן חורין כגון שנתן כל דמיו ואינו מעוכב אלא גט שחרור להיות מותר בבת חורין דאין לו בגופו כלום אבל אם מקצת גוף של זה ומקצת של זה אז היה יוצא בראשי אברים והיה מפסיד חלקו אם הפיל את שינו או סימא את עינו כמו שיכול למכרו והא דקאמר התם לאו א"ר אלעזר כספו המיוחד לו ה"נ עבדו המיוחד לו ולאו מקרא יליף דבלאו קרא יליף לראשי אברים מדין יום או יומים כי היכי דילפינן לענין מכירה אלא גמרא דתלמודא קאמר כלומר בעינן שיהא עבדו המיוחד לו: **במאן אילימא באחר והאמר רב אין מחזיקין כו'.** תימה לרשב"א דמאי קשיא דילמא לעולם באחר והא דקאמר ה) (צריך) למחות כשכתב לה דין ודברים אין לי בנכסיך ובפירותיהם שאין לבעל פירות ולכך צריכה למחות שאינה סומכת עליו ונראה לו דמ"מ סומכת עליו כיון שאם מתה יורשה דאפילו כתב לה בחייך ובמותך קיימא לן כרשב"ג דאם מתה יורשה בפרק הכותב (כתובות דף פג.): **כגון שאכלה מקצת חזקה בחיי הבעל ושלש שנים לאחר מיתת הבעל.** אבל מקצת בחיי הבעל ומקצת לאחר מיתת הבעל לא ולא דמי לאכלה בפני האב שנה ובפני הבן שתים (לעיל דף מב.) דהתם אם היה אוכל שלש שנים בחיי האב היתה חזקה: **מיגו דאי בעי אמר מינך זבינתה כו'.** תימה ומאי נקט כי האי גוונא דזבינתיה ניהליה וחבנה ניהלי הוה"ל דנאמן לומר דמינך זבינתיה דאי מילתא דפשיטא היא דמהימן א"כ השתא נמי מילתא דפשיטא היא דמהימן במיגו:

הא

רבינו גרשום

וספק נפשות. להקל דמספקא ליה אי כקנין הגוף דמי אי כקנין פירות: **להקל.** דלא יוקם (העבד) דהיינו קילותא דתרווייהו ישנן בדין יום או יומים ולא יוקם. **ר' אלעזר אומר** וכו'. דאינו לא של זה לגמרי ולא של זה לגמרי והכי נמי סבירא ליה לאמימר דשניהן אם מכרו בנכסי מלוג לא עשו ולא כלום משום דאין לאשה בפירות כלום ולאיש אין בגוף הקרקע כלום אבל אי זביני תרוייהו לעלמא אי נמי היכא דזבנה איהי לדידיה הוו זביניה זביני ולעולם ראיה בעי: **כי כספו הוא כספו המיוחד לו.** וזה עבד אינו מיוחד באותן ל' יום לא לזה ולא לזה: **פיס' האמר רב אשת איש צריכה למחות.** במי שמחזיק בקרקע שלה אלמא דיש לו חזקה בנכסיה אם לא מיחתה: **במאן.** צריכה למחות: **אילימא באחר.** שמחזיק בנכסיה: **והאמר רב אין מחזיקין בנכסי אשת איש.** אע"ג דאכלה שני חזקה לא הויא חזקה דמגו דיש לה בעל סמכה עליה ולא מיחתה: **וכגון שחפר בה בורות שיחין ומערות.** דמזיק לה לארעא דבעל אין לו בנכסי אשתו אלא פירות בלבד ולא לחפור בה כלום הלכך אם חפר בה צריכה למחות ואם לא מיחתה החזיק בהן: **והאמר רב נחמן אין חזקה לנזקין.** לומר הרי שימשתי בזה נזק כמה שנים ושלי היא הקרקע ואמאי צריכה למחות: **אימא.** הא דאמר רב נחמן הכי **אין דין חזקה לניזקין** דלאלתר הויא חזקה אם ראה ולא מיחה ולא צריך ג' שנים ומשום הכי צריכה למחות לאלתר בחפר בה: **איבעית אימא** הא דאמר רב נחמן אין חזקה לניזקין **בקוטרא ובית הכסא.** דאפי' שתיק אינש לא מחיל אבל בורות שיחין ומערות אם לא מיחתה והחזיק הבעל הוי חזקה: **ורב יוסף אמר לעולם באחר.** ודקשיא לך אין מחזיקין **כגון שאכלה מקצת שני חזקה בחיי בעלה** כשהיא אשת איש **וג' שנים לאחר מיתת הבעל** דבתר דמית ליה לא סמכא דעתה על בעלה והיה לה למחות **ומיגו דאי בעי אמר לה מינך זבינתה** ואכלתיה שני חזקה **כי אמר לה נמי זבינתה לבעלך וזבנה ניהלי מהימן** דהיינו דקאמר רב אשת איש צריכה למחות כלומר אשת איש שהתחיל אחד להחזיק בנכסיה בחיי בעלה ומת בעלה צריכה למחות שוב שלא

מסורת הש"ס

א) [שבת קכט. וש"נ], ב) לעיל כג., ג) [שם], ד) [צ"ל שמזיקין], ה) [צ"ל צריכה]:

הגהות הב"ח

(א) גמ' איבעית אימא הא איתמר עלה: (ב) שם מיגו דאי בעי אמר אנא כצ"ל ותיבת ליה נמחק: (ג) רשב"ם ד"ה כי כספו וכו' דלא הוי מכר:

תורה אור השלם

א) אַךְ אִם יוֹם אוֹ יוֹמַיִם יַעֲמֹד לֹא יֻקַּם כִּי כַסְפּוֹ הוּא: [שמות כא, כא]

ליקוטי רש"י

ספק נפשות להקל. דיני נפשות להקל דהא והצילו העדה כתיב (במדבר לה) [כתובות טו. וכעי"ז ב"ק מד:]. **בקוטרא.** עשן. **בבית הכסא.** שעל גבי קרקע ונראה לעינים שכך היו בתי כסאות שלהן [לעיל כג.].

שְׁנֵיהֶם יֶשְׁנָן בְּדִין יוֹם אוֹ יוֹמַיִם – BOTH ARE SUBJECT TO THE RULE OF *A DAY OR TWO,*[1] זֶה מִפְּנֵי שֶׁהוּא תַּחְתָּיו – THIS ONE [the original owner] BECAUSE [THE SLAVE] IS UNDER [HIS AUTHORITY], וְזֶה מִפְּנֵי שֶׁהוּא כַּסְפּוֹ – AND THIS ONE [the buyer] BECAUSE [THE SLAVE] IS HIS PROPERTY. The Gemara explains R' Yose's view. וּמִסְפְּקָא לֵיהּ – **[R' Yose] is uncertain** אִי קִנְיַן פֵּירוֹת כְּקִנְיַן הַגּוּף דָּמֵי – **whether ownership of** the **produce** of a thing **is tantamount to ownership of the** thing's **essence,** אִי לָאו כְּקִנְיַן הַגּוּף דָּמֵי – **or whether it is not tantamount to ownership of the** thing's **essence.** וְסָפֵק נְפָשׁוֹת לְהָקֵל – **Therefore,** he applies the rule that where there is **a doubt regarding capital punishment,** we **rule leniently,**[2] and exempt both the original owner and the buyer.

The Baraisa resumes:

רַבִּי אֶלְעָזָר אוֹמֵר – R' ELAZAR SAYS: שְׁנֵיהֶם אֵינָן בְּדִין יוֹם אוֹ יוֹמַיִם – NEITHER IS SUBJECT TO THE RULE OF *A DAY OR TWO,*[3] זֶה לְפִי שֶׁאֵינוֹ תַּחְתָּיו – THIS ONE [the buyer] BECAUSE [THE SLAVE] IS NOT UNDER [HIS AUTHORITY], וְזֶה לְפִי שֶׁאֵינוֹ כַּסְפּוֹ – AND THIS ONE [the original owner] BECAUSE [THE SLAVE] IS NOT HIS PROPERTY.

The Gemara explains R' Elazar's ruling. This explanation furnishes the basis for the Gemara's statement above (50a) that R' Elazar disagrees with the Tanna of our Mishnah:

וְאָמַר רָבָא – **Now Rava said:** מַאי טַעְמָא דְּרַבִּי אֶלְעָזָר – **What is R' Elazar's reason** for ruling that neither one is exempt from the death penalty? אָמַר קְרָא – Because **the verse states:**[4] "לֹא יֻקַּם כִּי כַסְפּוֹ הוּא" – *[The death] shall not be avenged for he is his property.* כַּסְפּוֹ הַמְיוּחָד לוֹ – The words "*his* property" imply that he must be **his sole property** before the twenty-four-hour leniency applies.[5] Since in this case the slave does not belong entirely to either the old master or the new, neither master can claim the twenty-four-hour leniency. By the same token, R' Elazar would invalidate the sale of *melog* property, because neither the husband nor the wife holds full ownership of it, as Ameimar ruled.[6]

The Gemara continues to examine the Mishnah's ruling:

וְלֹא לְאִישׁ חֲזָקָה בְּנִכְסֵי אִשְׁתּוֹ – A MAN HAS NO *CHAZAKAH* IN THE PROPERTY OF HIS WIFE:

The Gemara questions how it is possible to say this:

וְהָאָמַר רַב – **But Rav has said:** אֵשֶׁת אִישׁ צְרִיכָה לִמְחוֹת – **A married woman must protest** before witnesses any attempt to establish a *chazakah* on her *melog* property.[7] בְּמַאן – Now **against whom** did Rav require a married woman to protest? אִילֵימָא בְּאַחֵר – **If you say against a stranger** (i.e. anyone other than her husband), וְהָאָמַר רַב אֵין מַחֲזִיקִין בְּנִכְסֵי אֵשֶׁת אִישׁ – this cannot be, **for Rav has said that one cannot establish a *chazakah* in the property of a married woman.**[8] Thus, there is no need for her to protest. אֶלָּא לָאו בְּבַעַל – **Rather,** are we **not** compelled to say that when Rav said that a married woman must protest, he meant that she must protest **against her husband,** to prevent him from establishing a *chazakah?*[9] This conflicts with the Mishnah's ruling that a husband cannot establish a *chazakah* in his wife's property.[10] – ? –

The Gemara reconciles the view of Rav with the Mishnah:

אָמַר רָבָא – **Rava said:** לְעוֹלָם בְּבַעַל – **In fact,** it is as you said, that Rav requires a married woman to protest **against** her **husband's** attempt to establish a *chazakah* in her *melog* property. Yet this does not conflict with the Mishnah וּכְגוֹן שֶׁחָפַר בָּהּ בּוֹרוֹת שִׁיחִין וּמְעָרוֹת – because Rav refers **to a case in which [the husband] dug pits, ditches or vaults** in her field. Since a husband has no right to alter the physical structure of his wife's property, if he does so it demonstrates that the property is now his. Thus, the wife must protest if she wishes to prevent him from

NOTES

1. I.e. neither the original owner nor the buyer is liable to the death penalty if the slave lives twenty-four hours after being struck.

2. This is derived from the verses וְשָׁפְטוּ הָעֵדָה, *the congregation shall judge,* and וְהִצִּילוּ הָעֵדָה, *the congregation shall rescue* (*Numbers* 35:24,25). [I.e. even when judging, they must rescue the defendant if it is not clear that he deserves the death penalty.] Since R' Yose is in doubt as to whether the original owner is deemed the master or the buyer is deemed the master, he rules that we cannot impose the death penalty on either (*Rashbam*; see *Pesachim* 12a).

Tosafos question the need to cite any verse for withholding capital punishment in cases of doubt. It would seem obvious that since we do not even deprive a person of money when we are in doubt as to how to rule, we certainly do not deprive him of his life (*Tosafos*).

3. I.e. if either one of them strikes the slave, he is liable to the death penalty even if the slave dies more than twenty-four hours after the blow (*Rashbam*).

4. *Exodus* 21:21.

5. The Torah could have explained the leniency by stating כִּי כֶסֶף הוּא, *because he is property*. By adding the pronoun *his,* the Torah emphasizes that this leniency applies only to a master who has total ownership over his slave. Alternatively, there was no need for the verse to offer any reason. Its inclusion is therefore understood by R' Elazar to emphasize the requirement of total ownership (*Rashbam*).

6. Ameimar ruled that if a husband and his wife sell *melog* property, they have done nothing. Although the Gemara earlier offered another explanation of his statement, its simple meaning is that even if they *both* sell their rights to the property, the sale is void. This does not agree with the view of the Tanna of our Mishnah, who rules (by implication) that a wife *can* sell her ownership of *melog* property to her husband, as explained on 50a. Nevertheless, the Gemara explains now, Ameimar's statement is consistent with the view of R' Elazar who states here that if one person owns the right to the produce of a property and another owns the title to it, neither one has sufficient ownership to rank as its absolute owner. Ameimar applies this rationale to the case of *melog* property to rule that since the husband owns the produce and the wife owns title to the land, neither has sufficient ownership to contract a sale (*Rashbam*).

This is quite different from a standard partnership, in which even R' Elazar and Ameimar would agree that each partner can sell his share. This is so because each partner has a claim to fifty percent of everything [title and produce]. Since each one's ownership relates to the whole item, R' Elazar would concur that each has a sufficient degree of ownership to contract a sale of his share of the item. In the case of *melog* property, however, the husband's ownership is limited solely to the produce with no share in the land itself, and the wife's ownership is limited to the land with no rights to the produce. No one has a proprietorship that relates to the property as a whole; therefore (according to Ameimar and R' Elazar) no one has the power to sell it (*Rashi* to *Bava Kamma* 90a).

7. This implies that if she does not protest the use of her *melog* property, the occupant will establish a *chazakah* and be able to prove his acquisition of it (*Rashbam*).

8. A married woman can always argue that she did not protest because she thought her husband would protest for her (*Rashbam*). [Since his rights to the produce of her property are being violated, and his chance of inheriting it is being threatened by the unlawful occupation and resulting *chazakah,* it would be natural for him to protest (see *Tosafos* ד״ה במאן).]

9. Since Rav requires a woman to protest her husband's attempt to establish a *chazakah* on her *melog* property, it is clear that if she fails to protest, he does establish a *chazakah* (*Rashbam*). [Rav's ruling would apply in a case in which the husband renounced all claim to the produce of her field; should he subsequently attempt to use it, Rav requires the wife to protest to prevent him from establishing a *chazakah.* (If the husband did not renounce his rights, however, there is no question that she need not protest, since he is merely taking the produce that is his by right, as the Gemara explained on 49a.)]

10. [Even in a case in which he renounced his rights to the produce, as the Gemara explained on 49a.]

שניהם ישנן בדין יום או יומים זה מפני שהוא תחתיו וזה מפני שהוא כספו ומספקא ליה אי קנין פירות כקנין הגוף דמי אי לאו כקנין הגוף דמי א) וספק נפשות להקל רבי אלעזר אומר א שניהם אינן בדין יום או יומים זה לפי שאינו תחתיו וזה לפי שאינו כספו ואמר רבא מאי טעמא דרבי אלעזר אמר קרא א) לא יוקם כי כספו הוא כספו המיוחד לו: ולא לאיש חזקה בנכסי אשתו: והאמר רב אשת איש צריכה למחות במאן אילימא באחר והאמר רב ב אין מחזיקין בנכסי אשת איש אלא לאו בבעל אמר רבא לעולם בבעל ג וכגון שחפר בה בורות שיחין ומערות ב) והאמר רב נחמן אמר רבה בר אבוה אין חזקה לנזקין אימא אין דין חזקה לנזקין אי בעית אימא (א) לאו איתמר עלה ג) רב מרי אמר בקוטרא רב זביד אמר בבית הכסא רב יוסף אמר לעולם באחר ד וכגון שאכלה מקצת חזקה בחיי הבעל ושלש לאחר מיתת הבעל מיגו דאי בעי אמר (ב) ליה אנא זבינתה מינך כי א"ל נמי את זבינתה ליה וזבנה ניהלי מהימן גופא אמר רב אין מחזיקין בנכסי אשת איש ודייני

רשב"ם

שניהם ישנן כו'. ופטורין דספק נפשות דבעלים שהכוהו ומי נהרג מהם להקל דנפקא לן מושפטו העדה והצילו העדה (במדבר לה): שניהם. כלומר שניהם שהכוהו נהרגין: זה. אחרון לפי שאינו תחתיו: וזה. הראשון לפי שאינו עכשיו כספו שהרי מכרו: כי כספו הוא. מיותר הוא דמה נתינת טעם היה צריך ליתן בדבר ולומר לא יוקם לפי שכספו הוא אי נמי מדמלי למיכתב כי כסף הוא ומש"ה נמי יליף אמימר לגבי נכסי מלוג דכיון דאינו מיוחד לא לאיש ולא לאשה אינו קרוי שדה האיש ולא שדה האשה והלכך אם מכרו שניהן מכרן בטל ויכולין לחזור בם כאדם המוכר דבר שאינו שלו דלא (ג) ליהוי מכר: וקמתמה גמרא ולא לאיש חזקה בנכסי אשתו. בתמיה אלמא אינה צריכה למחות בבעלה הואיל ולית ליה חזקה: אשת איש. שהחזיק אחר בנכסי מלוג שלה צריכה למחות משום דההוא אחר יש לו חזקה ואם לא מיחתה הפסידה: במאן. צריכה למחות מי הוא המחזיק: אילימא באחר. שאינו בעלה וכל זה סיום הקושיא הוא: אין מחזיקין בנכסי אשת איש. דמצית אמרה על בעלי סמכתי שהוא ימחה ויערער ולכך שתקתי ובשאר בני אדם דלא בעל קאמר רב דאין מחזיקין שכן משמע אין מחזיקין לשון רבים ועוד דאי בבעל קאמר דאין מחזיקין היינו מתניתין לא לאיש חזקה בנכסי אשתו ומאי אתא לאשמועינן: אלא לאו בבעל. אלמא יש חזקה וקשיא מתני' לרב: לעולם בבעל. שהחזיק בנכסי אשתו קאמר רב דצריכה למחות שיש חזקה לבעל ואפי' הכי לא תקשי ליה מתניתין דהך חזקה דקאמר רב כגון שחפר בה הבעל בורות שיחין ומערות דלפירות הוא דאשתעבד ליה נכסי מלוג דאשתו ולא לקלקל הקרקע לחפירת בורות וכגון שדה שאינה עשויה לבורות והלכך יש לו חזקה דודאי קנאה מאשתו והלכך מקלקל לה לצרכו וכי האי גוונא הוא דקאמר רב צריכה למחות: אין חזקה לנזקין. כלומר היכא דמזיק לחבירו אין יכול לטעון לקוחה היא בידי שהרי החזקתי בה ג' שנים בחפירת בורות שיחין ומערות דכי האי גוונא לא הויא חזקה דמצי טוען אידך משום דלא אחזקת דמחזקי אינשי לא חששתי למחות: אימא אין דין חזקה. להצטרך ג' שנים לנזקין היכא דחזקתו ע"י נזקין אלא לאלתר הויא חזקה דאין אדם רואה ד) (שמחזיקין) קרקע שלו ושותק אלא מוחה מיד והיכא דלא מחה הפסיד והלכך אשת איש דקאמר רב צריכה למחות מיד הוא דצריכה למחות מאחר שחופר בה בעל בורות שאין אדם רואה היזקו ושותק והלכך כי האי גוונא יש לו חזקה: ה"ג ואי בעית אימא הא איתמר עלה רב מרי אמר כו'. כלומר ואיבעית אימא לעולם חזקת ג' שנים בעינן ואפי' היכא דחפר בו בורות דלאוקימנן למילתיה דרב והא דקאמר רב נחמן אין חזקה לנזקין לא בחזקת ג' שנים בקרקע חבירו איירי אלא בעושה היזק לחבירו אפי' בבית של עצמו כגון עשן וריח רע ואתא לאורויי שלא יזיק לחבירו ואפי' החזיק ימים רבים אין חזקה מועלת לו להזיק חבירו: רב מרי אמר כו'. כבר פירשנו בלא יחפור: רב יוסף אמר. מתני' לא תקשי לרב דמאי דקאמר רב אשת איש צריכה למחות לאו בבעל קאמר דהא אין לאיש חזקה בנכסי אשתו כדקתני מתני' אלא לעולם באחר שהחזיק בנכסיה קאמר רב דצריכה למחות ודקשיא לך האמר רב אין מחזיקין בנכסי אשת איש לא תקשי דה"מ דאין מחזיקין בחיי הבעל שאם החזיק בנכסי' בחיי הבעל ג' שנים אינה חזקה ואינה צריכה למחות דמצית אמרה על בעלי סמכתי א"נ דוקא פירות שהיו לבעלי בנכסים שלי אותן מכר לך אבל הגוף שהוא שלי לא היית יכול לקנות שגם הוא אין לו חזקה בנכסיי באכילת פרי דכיון דאית ליה פרי הכל יודעין דפרי הוא דקאכיל ולכך לא חששתי למחות אבל הכא במאי עסקינן כגון שאכל הלוקח מקצת חזקה בחיי הבעל שמכר לו וג' שנים שלימות לאחר מיתת הבעל כי האי גוונא קאמר רב דצריכה למחות כדמפרש טעמא לקמיה והכי קאמר רב אשת איש שמכר בעלה לאחר נכסי מלוג שלה צריכה למחות לאחר מיתתו דסד"א כיון דהכל יודעין שהבעל מכרם לו ולא היא וגם הוא מודה כמו כן שהבעל מכרם לו לא תועיל חזקתו אף לאחר מיתת הבעל כלום שהרי לא יכול לטעון לאשה מינך זבנתה אחרי כן ואכלתיה שני חזקה דכיון דמתחלה הבעל מכרה לו ופירות הוא דהוי ליה לבעל באותה שדה ואותן מכר לזה הרי זה כאריס שיורד לקרקע באריסות לפירות שאינו יכול לטעון אחרי כן לקחתיה הימנך והלכך לא איצטרך למחות קמ"ל רב דצריכה למחות לאחר מות בעלה קודם שיחזיק בה ההוא אחר ג' שנים דודאי אע"פ שמתחלה היתה קניה לו מן הבעל יכול לטעון הבעל מכר לי הגוף אם יירשך ואם ימות קודם לך פירות מיהא קניתי ומיד כשמת הרי נסתלקתי ממקחי ולכך קניתי ממך שהרי עתה נעשה השדה שלך והלכך מיגו דאי בעי אמר אנא זבנתה מינך אחר מות בעליך ואכלתיה שני חזקה כי קאמר יודע אני דזבינתיה לבעליך ואחרי כן זבין ניהלי מהימן ולא דמי לאריס שאין יכול לטעון לקחתיו אחרי כן משום דסתם אריס אין זמן לאריסותו אלא כל הימים בתורת אריסותו עומד אבל זה שלוקחה מן האיש על מנת שאם ימות יפסיד מקחו שתטול האשה נכסי מלוג שלה התם ודאי כשמת הבעל הרי זה כאילו יורד עכשיו מחדש לשדה אשה זו והיא שותקת שלש שנים איכא למימר דזבוני זבינה ליה:

ודייני

תוספות

היה לו בגוף כלום מעולם לקנין פירות דמוכר עבדו ע"מ שישמשנו שלשים יום שתחלה היה הכל שלו ועדיין לא יצא מתחת ידו שהפירות שלו וכעין זה מחלקין גבי בהמת ארנונא בפ"ק דפסחים (דף ו.) ומה שהיה קשה עליה מבכורות שם מפורש וכן נ"ל דאין לומר כלל דלר"מ דסבר הכא קנין פירות כקנין הגוף דמי וסבר שם לאיש אבל לא לאשה דהא ביבמות בפרק אלמנה (דף סו. ושם) פליגי במכנסת שום לבעלה היא אומרת כלי אני נוטל בכתובתי והוא המגרש אומר דמים אני נותן לך ר' אמי אמר הדין עמו רב יהודה אמר הדין עמה ומתריץ תניא כותיה דר' אמי עבדי צאן ברזל יוצאין בשן ועין לאיש אבל לא לאשה ומאי קושיא לרב יהודה דלמא אע"ג דהדין עמה יוצאין לאיש ולא לאשה דקסבר קנין פירות כקנין הגוף דמי ואפילו בנכסי מלוג נמי הוי דינא הכי לרבי מאיר אלא ודאי לא מהני כלל קנין פירות להיות כקנין הגוף לצאת לאיש כדפרישית: **קנין** פירות לאו כקנין הגוף דמי כו'. קשה דבסוף השולח (גיטין דף מח. ושם) מסיק אפלוגתא דרבי יהודה ור"ש דכ"ע קנין פירות כקנין הגוף דמי וי"ל דהתם לא קאמר אלא דמהכא ליכא למילף מינה ובערכין (דף טו:) גרס לעולם אימא לך לרבי שמעון כקנין הגוף ול"ג דכ"ע והא דלא מייתי בהשולח הך דהכא משום דניחא ליה לאיתויי תנאי היא דפליגי בשדה דומיא דפלוגתא דרבי יוחנן ור"ל דהתם:

וספק נפשות להקל. פי' בקונטרס משום דכתיב ושפטו העדה והצילו העדה ואין נראה דבלאו הכי נמי לא קטלי מספיקא דאפילו ממונא לא מפקינן מספיקא: **רבי** אלעזר אומר שניהם אינן בדין יום או יומים. הקשה ריב"א דהיכי מדמי אמימר מכירה לדין יום או יומים דא"כ שותפים לא יוכלו למכור לעולם דהא אמר בהחובל (ב"ק דף צ. ושם) מאן תנא להא דתנו רבנן מי שחציו עבד וחציו בן חורין וכן עבד של שני שותפין אין יוצאין בראשי אברים כמאן כר' אלעזר וא"כ הכא נמי לעבד של שני שותפין אין יכולים למכרו וי"ל דהתם מיירי בשני שותפין שלזה גוף ולזה פירות דומיא דמוכר עבדו ע"מ שישמשנו שלשים יום וחציו עבד וחציו בן חורין כגון שנתן כל דמיו ואינו מעוכב אלא גט שחרור להיות מותר בבת חורין דאין לו בגופו כלום אבל אם מקצת גוף של זה ומקצת של זה אז היה יוצא בראשי אברים והיה מפסיד חלקו אם הפיל את שינו או סימא את עינו כמו שיכול למכרו והא דקאמר התם לאו א"ר אלעזר כספו המיוחד לו ה"נ עבדו המיוחד לו לאו מקרא יליף דבלאו קרא יליף לראשי אברים מדין יום או יומים כי היכי דילפינן לענין מכירה אלא גמרא דתלמודא קאמר כלומר בעינן שיהא עבדו המיוחד לו: **במאן** אילימא באחר והאמר רב אין מחזיקין כו'. תימה לרשב"א דמאי קשיא נימא לעולם באחר והא דקאמר ה) (לריך) למחות כשכתב לה דין ודברים אין לי בנכסיך ובפירותיהם שאין לבעל פירות ולכך צריכה למחות שאינה סומכת עליו ונראה לו דמ"מ סומכת עליו כיון שאם מתה יורשה דאפילו כתב לה בחייך ובמותך קיימא לן כרשב"ג דאם מתה יורשה בפרק הכותב (כתובות דף פג:): **כגון** שאכלה מקצת חזקה בחיי הבעל ושלש שנים לאחר מיתת הבעל. אבל מקצת בחיי הבעל ומקצת לאחר מיתת הבעל לא ולא דמי לאכלה בפני האב שנה ובפני הבן שתים (לעיל דף מב.) דהתם אם היה אוכל שלש שנים בחיי האב היתה חזקה: **מיגו** דאי בעי אמר מינך זבינתה כו'. תימה ומאי נקט כי האי גוונא דזבינתיה ניהליה וזבנה ניהלי הו"ל דנאמן לומר דמינך זבינתיה דאי מילתא דפשיטא היא דמהימן א"כ השתא נמי מילתא דפשיטא היא דמהימן במיגו:

הא

עין משפט נר מצוה

קצח א מיי' פ"ג מהל' רוצח ושמירת נפש הלכה טו:

קצט ב מיי' פי"ד מהל' טוען הל' יא סמג עשין לה טוש"ע ח"מ סי' קמט סעיף יא וטוש"ע אה"ע סי' פז סעיף ג:

ר ג טוש"ע ח"מ סי' קמט סעי' ט בהגה"ה:

רא ד מיי' שם הל' יא וסמג שם טוש"ע אה"ע סימן פז סעי' ג:

רבינו גרשום

וספק נפשות. להקל דמספקא ליה אי כקנין הגוף דמי אי כקנין פירות: להקל. דלא יוקם (העבד) דהיינו קילותא דתרווייהו ישנן בדין יום או יומים ולא יוקם. ר' אלעזר אומר וכו'. דאינו לא של זה לגמרי ולא של זה לגמרי והכי נמי סבירא ליה לאמימר דשניהן אם מכרו בנכסי מלוג לא עשו ולא כלום משום דאין לאשה בפירות כלום ולאיש אין בגוף הקרקע כלום אבל אי זביני תרווייהו לעלמא אי נמי היכא דזבנה איהי לדידיה הוו זביניה זביני ולעולם ראיה בעי: כי כספו הוא כספו המיוחד לו. וזה עבד אינו מיוחד באותן ל' יום לא לזה ולא לזה: פיס' האמר רב אשת איש צריכה למחות. במי שמחזיק בקרקע שלה אלמא דיש לו חזקה בנכסיה אם לא מיחתה: במאן. צריכה למחות: אילימא באחר. שמחזיק בנכסיה: והאמר רב אין מחזיקין בנכסי אשת איש. אע"ג דאכלה שני חזקה לא הויא חזקה דמגו דיש לה בעל סמכה עליה ולא מיחתה: וכגון שחפר בה בורות שיחין ומערות. דמזיק לה לארעא דבעל אין לו בנכסי אשתו אלא פירות בלבד ולא לחפור בה כלום הלכך אם חפר בה צריכה למחות ואם לא מיחתה החזיק בהן: והאמר רב נחמן אין חזקה לנזקין. לומר הרי שימשתי בזה נזק כמה שנים ושלי היא הקרקע ואמאי צריכה למחות: אימא. הא דאמר רב נחמן הכי אין דין חזקה לניזקין דלאלתר הויא חזקה אם ראה ולא מיחה ולא צריך ג' שנים ומשום הכי צריכה למחות לאלתר בחפר בה: איבעית אימא הא דאמר רב נחמן אין חזקה לניזקין בקוטרא ובית הכסא. דאפי' שתיק אינש לא מחיל אבל בורות שיחין ומערות אם לא מיחתה והחזיק הבעל הוי חזקה: ורב יוסף אמר לעולם באחר. ודקשיא לך אין מחזיקין כגון שאכלה מקצת שני חזקה בחיי בעלה כשהיא אשת איש וג' שנים לאחר מיתת הבעל דבתר דמית ליה לא סמכא דעתה על בעלה והיה לה למחות ומיגו דאי בעי אמר לה מינך זבינתה ואכלתיה שני חזקה כי אמר לה נמי זבינתה לבעלך וזבנה ניהלי מהימן דהיינו דקאמר רב אשת איש צריכה למחות כלומר אשת איש שהתחיל אחד להחזיק בנכסיה בחיי בעלה ומת בעלה צריכה למחות שוב שלא

מסורת הש"ס

א) [שבת קכט. וש"נ], ב) לעיל כג., ג) [שם], ד) [צ"ל שמזיקין], ה) [צ"ל צריכה]:

הגהות הב"ח

(א) גמ' איבעית אימא הא איתמר עלה: (ב) שם מיגו דאי בעי אמר אנא כצ"ל ותיבת ליה נמחק: (ג) רשב"ם ד"ה כי כספו וכו' דלא הוי מכר:

תורה אור השלם

א) אַךְ אִם יוֹם אוֹ יוֹמַיִם יַעֲמֹד לֹא יֻקַּם כִּי כַסְפּוֹ הוּא: [שמות כא, כא]

ליקוטי רש"י

ספק נפשות להקל. דיני נפשות להקל דהא והצילו העדה כתיב (במדבר לה) [כתובות טו. וכעי"ז ב"ק מד:]. בקוטרא. עשן. בבית הכסא. שעל גבי קרקע ונראה לעינים שכן היו בתי כסאות שלהן [לעיל כג.].

establishing a *chazakah* by means of these excavations.[11]

The Gemara question this:

וְהָאָמַר רַב נַחְמָן אָמַר רַבָּה בַּר אֲבוּהָ – But did Rav Nachman not **say in the name of Rabbah bar Avuha: אֵין חֲזָקָה לִנְזָקִין – There is no *chazakah* for damage?**[12]

The Gemara answers:

אֵימָא אֵין דִּין חֲזָקָה לִנְזָקִין – Say that what Rav Nachman means is that **there is no** three-year **rule of *chazakah* in the case of damage,** but there is certainly a *chazakah.*[13] Thus, a wife must protest her husband's digging to prevent him from establishing a *chazakah.*

The Gemara offers another explanation of Rav Nachman's statement that "there is no *chazakah* for damage":

אִי בָּעֵית אֵימָא – If you prefer, say that Rav Nachman's ruling does not refer to establishing a *chazakah* through damage, but to establishing a right to do things that are detrimental to others,[14] as the Gemara now illustrates. **לָאו אִיתְּמַר עֲלָהּ – Was it not said about this** ruling of Rav Nachman: **רַב מָרִי אָמַר בְּקוּטְרָא – Rav Mari said** it applies **to smoke.**[15] **רַב זְבִיד אָמַר בְּבֵית הַכִּסֵּא – Rav Zevid said** it applies **to an outhouse.**[16]

The Gemara now returns to its earlier problem — the contradiction between Rav's ruling that a married woman must protest to prevent a *chazakah* from being established in her property, and the Mishnah's ruling that a husband cannot establish a *chazakah* in his wife's property. The Gemara suggests another way of reconciling the two rulings:[17]

רַב יוֹסֵף אָמַר – Rav Yosef said: לְעוֹלָם בְּאַחֵר – In fact, Rav means that a married woman must protest **against a stranger's** attempt to establish a *chazakah* on her *melog* property but not against her husband. Thus, he does not contradict the Mishnah's ruling.[18] **וּכְגוֹן שֶׁאֲכָלָהּ מִקְצָת חֲזָקָה בְּחַיֵּי הַבַּעַל** – Nor does he contradict his other ruling, because Rav speaks here of **a case in which [the occupant] used [the land]** for **part of a *chazakah*** period **while the husband was still alive, וְשָׁלֹשׁ לְאַחַר מִיתַת הַבַּעַל – and** then for another **three** years **after the husband's death.**[19] The occupant says he bought the land from the husband, who bought it from the wife. Rav rules that if the wife did not protest the occupant's use of her land for three years following her husband's death, the occupant's claim is believed for the following reason: **מִיגּוֹ דְּאִי בָּעֵי אָמַר לֵיהּ – Since [the occupant] could** now **say** to the wife,[20] if he wished to lie, **אֲנָא זְבִינְתָּהּ מִינָּךְ**

NOTES

11. Rav agrees with the Mishnah that a husband cannot establish a *chazakah* on his wife's property by taking its produce for three years, since it is his by right and because even where it is not, a wife generally allows her husband to take it in any case (as the Gemara explained above). However, if he dug ditches in the land or otherwise damaged it, she is likely to protest. If she does not, Rav rules that his *chazakah* is valid, and the husband can claim that he acquired the field from her (*Rashbam*).

This establishes a *chazakah,* however, only in fields in which pits etc. are not normally dug. In fields where they are dug, however, digging them does not establish a *chazakah* [since it is part of the normal use of the field, and it would not arouse her protest] (see *Rashbam*).

12. The Gemara now understands this to mean that a person cannot establish a *chazakah* by damaging a field over a period of three years, for example, by digging ditches in the land. The lack of a protest, the Gemara now assumes, is not evidence of a sale, since the original owner may claim that he kept silent only because he did not view this abnormal usage as a legal challenge to his ownership of the property (*Rashbam*).

13. Although it generally takes three years to establish a *chazakah,* Rav Nachman teaches (according to this explanation) that when someone damages another person's property and that person does not protest at once, a *chazakah* is established *immediately.* The assumption is that no owner would stand by for even a moment and watch his property being destroyed without raising a protest. [Accordingly, when Rav stated that a woman must protest her husband's use of her property to prevent him from establishing a *chazakah,* he meant that she must protest immediately.]

Where a *chazakah* is established through damage, the occupant of the property is believed that he lost the bill of sale even though less than three years have elapsed. He can argue that since it was incumbent upon the owner to protest immediately and he did not, he assumed that he would never protest, and he was therefore not careful with the bill of sale (*Rashbah;* cf. *Ramban*).

14. I.e. doing things in one's own property that are damaging to a neighbor.

15. For example, installing a kiln that emits heavy smoke. Rav Nachman rules that even if one has been doing so for many days without any protest by the neighbor, he cannot claim that he has established a *chazakah* for the right to continue. Rather, his neighbor can protest at any time and block the further use of the furnace (*Rashbam*).

16. It applies to an outhouse in which the waste remains above ground (*Tosafos* above 23a ד״ה בקוטרא). If the odor from it disturbs a neighbor, he can block the further use of the outhouse. Rav Nachman rules that the owner of the outhouse *cannot* successfully claim that since the neighbor did not previously protest its placement, he has established a *chazakah* to permit him to continue using it (*Rashbam*).

Thus, Rav Nachman's ruling that there is no *chazakah* for damage means that one cannot establish a permanent right to engage in activities damaging to a neighbor. Rav Nachman, however, agrees that a person can establish a *chazakah* to prove his ownership of a property by using it in a way that damages it, for example, by digging ditches in it. But to do so, he must use the property for three years (*Rashbam*). [This is a point of difference between the two explanations of Rav Nachman's statement. According to the previous explanation, a *chazakah* established by damaging a property is established immediately if the previous owner does not protest.]

17. Previously the Gemara interpreted Rav's ruling to refer to a husband's attempt to establish a *chazakah.* To reconcile this with the Mishnah, the Gemara was forced to explain that Rav speaks of a damaging use. The explanation the Gemara will now offer returns to the assumption that Rav speaks of an ordinary type of use.

The Mishnah and Rav's Two Statements

Mishnah: A husband cannot establish a *chazakah* in his wife's property.

Rav 1: A married woman must protest the unauthorized use of her property.

Rav 2: One cannot establish a *chazakah* in the property of a married woman.

18. Since Rav agrees with the Mishnah that a man cannot establish a *chazakah* in his wife's property.

19. Thus, Rav does not contradict his other ruling (2) that one cannot establish a *chazakah* in the property of a married woman. In that ruling he referred to establishing a *chazakah* during the husband's lifetime. In such a case the woman can properly claim that she did not protest because she expected her husband to protest for her. Moreover, even if it is known that her husband sold the land to the occupant, she can argue that it was still not necessary for her to protest. Since it was clear that her husband had the right only to the produce, it was equally clear (to her) that he had sold nothing more than the right to the produce.

The case in which Rav rules that a married woman must protest is where the husband sold her *melog* property and died, and the buyer continued to occupy it. If the woman does not protest for three years after her husband's death, the occupant can win the land by claiming that he knows that the wife sold her title to the land to her husband, and that the husband sold it in turn to him, when he bought the right to the produce. The Gemara will now explain why this claim would be accepted (*Rashbam*).

20. *Bach* deletes the word לֵיהּ, *to him* [since we are dealing with what the occupant could have said to the wife].

שניהם ישנן בדין יום או יומים זה מפני שהוא תחתיו וזה מפני שהוא כספו ומספקא ליה אי קנין פירות כקנין הגוף דמי אי לאו כקנין הגוף דמי [ה] וספק נפשות להקל רבי אלעזר אומר [א] שניהם אינן בדין יום או יומים זה לפי שאינו תחתיו וזה לפי שאינו כספו ואמר רבא מאי טעמא דרבי אלעזר אמר קרא [א] לא יוקם כי כספו הוא כספו המיוחד לו: ולא לאיש חזקה בנכסי אשתו: והאמר רב אשת איש צריכה למחות במאן אילימא באחר והאמר רב [ב] אין מחזיקין בנכסי אשת איש אלא לאו בבעל אמר רבא לעולם בבעל [ג] וכגון שחפר בה בורות שיחין ומערות [ג] והאמר רב נחמן אמר רבה בר אבוה אין חזקה לנזקין אימא אין דין חזקה לנזקין אי בעית אימא (א) לאו איתמר עלה [ג] רב מרי אמר בקוטרא רב זביד אמר בבית הכסא רב יוסף אמר לעולם באחר [ד] וכגון שאכלה מקצת חזקה בחיי הבעל ושלש לאחר מיתת הבעל מיגו דאי בעי אמר (ב) ליה אנא זבינתה מינך כי א"ל נמי את זבינתה ליה וזבנה ניהלי מהימן גופא אמר רב אין מחזיקין בנכסי אשת איש ודייני

רשב"ם

שניהם ישנן כו'. ופטורין דספק נפשות דבעל"ס שהכוהו ומי נהרג מהם להקל דנפקא לן מושפטו העדה והצילו העדה (במדבר לה): שניהם. כלומר שניהם שהכוהו נהרגין: זה. אחרון לפי שהוא תחתיו: וזה. הראשון לפי שהוא עכשיו כספו שהרי מכרו: כי כספו הוא. מיותר הוא דמה נתינת טעם היה צריך ליתן בדבר ולומר לא יוקם לפי שכספו הוא אי נמי מדמצי למיכתב כי כסף הוא ומש"ה נמי יליף אמימר לגבי נכסי מלוג דכיון דאינו מיוחד לא לאיש ולא לאשה אינו קרוי שדה האיש ולא שדה האשה והלכך אם מכרו שניהן מכרן בטל ויכולין לחזור בם כאדם המוכר דבר שאינו שלו דלא (ג) ליהוי מכר: וקמתמה גמרא ולא לאיש חזקה בנכסי אשתו. בתמיה אלמא אינה צריכה למחות בבעלה הואיל ולית ליה חזקה: אשת איש. שהחזיק אחר בנכסי מלוג שלה צריכה למחות משום דההוא אחר יש לו חזקה ואם לא מיחתה הפסידה: במאן. צריכה למחות מי הוא המחזיק: אילימא באחר. שאינו בעלה וכל זה סיום הקושיא הוא: אין מחזיקין בנכסי אשת איש. דמצית אמרה על בעלי סמכתי שהוא ימחה ויערער ולכך שתקתי והשאר בני אדם דלא בעל קאמר רב דאין מחזיקין שכן משמע אין מחזיקין לשון רבים ועוד דאי בבעל קאמר דאין מחזיקין היינו מתניתין לא לאיש חזקה בנכסי אשתו ומאי אתא לאשמועינן: אלא לאו בבעל. אלמא יש חזקה וקשיא מתני' לרב: לעולם בבעל. שהחזיק בנכסי אשתו קאמר רב דצריכה למחות שיש חזקה לבעל ואפי' הכי לא תקשי ליה מתניתין דהך חזקה דקאמר רב כגון שחפר בה הבעל בורות שיחין ומערות דלפירות הוא דאשתעבד ליה נכסי מלוג ולא לקלקל הקרקע לחפירת בורות וכגון שדה שאינה עשויה לבורות והלכך יש לו חזקה דודאי קנאה מאשתו והלכך מקלקל לה לצרכו וכי האי גוונא הוא דקאמר רב צריכה למחות: אין חזקה לנזקין. כלומר היכא דמזיק לחבירו אין יכול לטעון לקוחה היא בידי שהרי החזקתי בה ג' שנים בחפירת בורות שיחין ומערות דכי האי גוונא לא הויא חזקה דמצי טעין איך משום דלא אחזקת לממחזקי איניש לא חששתי למחות: אימא אין דין חזקה. להצטרך ג' שנים לנזקין היכא דחזקתו ע"י נזקין אלא לאלתר הויא חזקה דאין אדם רואה [ד] (שמחזיקין) קרקע שלו ושותק אלא מוחה מיד והיכא דלא מחה הפסיד והלכך אשת איש דקאמר רב צריכה למחות מיד הוא דצריכה למחות מאחר שחופר בה בעל בורות שאין אדם רואה היזקו ושותק והלכך כי האי גוונא יש לו חזקה: ה"ג ואי בעית אימא הא איתמר עלה רב מרי אמר כו'. כלומר ולאיבעית אימא לעולם חזקת ג' שנים ואפי' היכא דחפר בו בורות דלאוקימנן למילתיה דרב והא דקאמר רב נחמן אין חזקה לנזקין לא בחזקת ג' שנים בקרקע מיירי אלא בעושה היזק לחבירו אפי' בבית של עצמו כגון עשן וריח רע ואתא לאורויי שלא יזיק לחבירו ואפי' החזיק ימים רבים אין חזקה מועלת לו להזיק חבירו: רב מרי אמר כו'. כבר פירשנו בלא יחפור: רב יוסף אמר. מתני' לא תקשי לרב דמאי דקאמר רב אשת איש צריכה למחות לאו בבעל קאמר דהא אין לאיש חזקה בנכסי אשתו כדקתני מתני' אלא לעולם באחר שהחזיק בנכסיה קאמר רב דצריכה למחות ודקשיא לך האמר רב אין מחזיקין בנכסי אשת איש לא תקשי דה"מ דאין מחזיקין בחיי הבעל שאם החזיק בנכסי' בחיי הבעל ג' שנים אינה חזקה ואינה צריכה למחות דמצית אמרה על בעלי סמכתי א"נ דוקא פירות שהיו לבעלי בנכסים שלי אותן מכר לך אבל הגוף שהוא שלי לא היית יכול לקנות שגם הוא אין לו חזקה בנכסיי באכילת פרי דכיון דאית ליה פרי הכל יודעין דפרי הוא דקאכיל ולכך לא חששי למחות אבל הכא במאי עסקינן כגון שאכל הלוקח מקצת חזקה בחיי הבעל שמכר לו וג' שנים שלימות לאחר מיתת הבעל כי האי גוונא קאמר רב דצריכה למחות כדמפרש טעמא לקמיה והכי קאמר רב אשת איש שמכר בעלה לאחר נכסי מלוג שלה צריכה למחות לאחר מיתתו דסד"א כיון דהכל יודעין שהבעל מכרם לו ולא היא וגם הוא מודה כמו כן שהבעל מכרם לו לא תועיל חזקתו אף לאחר מיתת הבעל כלום שהרי לא יכול לטעון לאשה מינך זבנתה אחרי כן ואכלתיה שני חזקה דכיון דמתחלה הבעל מכרה לו ופירות הוא דהוי ליה לבעל באותה שדה ואותן מכר לזה הרי זה כאריס שיורד לקרקע באריסות לפירות שאינו יכול לטעון אחרי כן לקחתיה הימנך והלכך לא איצטרך למחות קמ"ל רב דצריכה למחות לאחר מות בעלה קודם שיחזיק בה ההוא אחר ג' שנים דודאי אע"פ שמתחלה היתה קנויה לו מן הבעל יכול לטעון הבעל מכר לי הגוף אם יירשך ואם ימות קודם לך פירות מיהא קניתי ומיד כשמת הרי נסתלקתי ממקחי ולכך קניתי ממך שהרי עתה נעשה השדה שלך והלכך מיגו דאי בעי אמר אנא זבנתה מינך אחר מות בעליך ואכלתיה שני חזקה כי קאמר יודע אני דזבינתיה לבעליך ואחרי כן זבין ניהלי מהימן ולא דמי לאריס שאין יכול לטעון לקחתיו אחרי כן משום דסתם אריס אין זמן לאריסותו אלא כל הימים בתורת אריסותו עומד אבל זה שלוקחה מן האיש על מנת שאם ימות יפסיד מקחו שתטול האשה נכסי מלוג שלה התם ודאי כשמת הבעל הרי זה כאילו יורד עכשיו מחדש לשדה אשה זו והיא שותקת שלש שנים איכא למימר דזבוני זבינה ליה:

ודייני

תוספות

היה לו בגוף כלום מעולם לקנין פירות דמוכר עבדו ע"מ שישמשנו שלשים יום שמתחלה היה הכל שלו ועדיין לא יצא מתחת ידו שהפירות שלו וכעין זה מחלקין גבי בהמת ארנונה בפ"ק דפסחים (דף ו.) ומה שהיה קשה עליה מבכורות שם מפורש וכן צ"ל דאין לומר כלל דלר"מ דסבר הכא קנין פירות כקנין הגוף דמי וסבר שם לאיש אבל לא לאשה דהא ביבמות בפרק אלמנה (דף סו. ושם) פליגי במכנסת שום לבעלה היא אומרת כלי אני נוטל בכתובתי והוא המגרש אומר דמים אני נותן לך ר' אמי אמר הדין עמו רב יהודה אמר הדין עמה ומקשינן תניא כוותיה דר' אמי עבדי מלוג יוצאין בשן ועין לאיש אבל לא לאשה ומאי קושיא לרב יהודה דלמא אע"ג דהדין עמה יוצאין לאיש ולא לאשה דקסבר קנין פירות כקנין הגוף דמי ואפילו בנכסי מלוג נמי הוי דינא הכי לרבי מאיר אלא ודאי לא מהני כלל קנין פירות להיות כקנין הגוף לענין לאיש כדפרישית: **קנין** פירות לאו כקנין הגוף דמי כו'. קשה דבסוף השולח (גיטין דף מח. ושם) מסיק אפלוגתא דרבי יהודה ור"ש דכ"ע קנין פירות כקנין הגוף דמי וי"ל דהתם לא קאמר אלא דמהכא ליכא למילף מינה ובערכין (דף טו:) גרס לעולם אימא לך לרבי שמעון כקנין הגוף ול"ג דכ"ע והא דלא מייתי בהשולח הך דהכא משום דניחא ליה לאיתויי תנאי היא דפליגי בשדה דומיא דפלוגתא דרבי יוחנן ור"ל דהתם:

וספק נפשות להקל. פי' בקונטרס משום דכתיב ושפטו העדה והצילו העדה ואין נראה דבלאו הכי נמי לא קטלי מספיקא דאפילו ממונא לא מפקינן מספיקא: **רבי** אלעזר אומר שניהם אינן בדין יום או יומים. הקשה ריב"א דהיכי מדמי אמימר מכירה לדין יום או יומים דא"כ שותפים לא יוכלו למכור לעולם דהא אמר בהחובל (ב"ק דף צ. ושם) מאן תנא להא דתנו רבנן מי שחציו עבד וחציו בן חורין וכן עבד של שני שותפין אין יוצאין בראשי אברים כמאן כר' אלעזר וא"כ הכא נמי לעבד של שני שותפין אין יכולים למכרו וי"ל דהתם מיירי בשני שותפין שלזה גוף ולזה פירות דומיא דמוכר עבדו ע"מ שישמשנו שלשים יום וחציו עבד וחציו בן חורין כגון שנתן כל דמיו ואינו מעוכב אלא גט שחרור להיות מותר בבת חורין דאין לו בגופו כלום אבל אם מקצת גוף של זה ומקצת של זה אז היה יוצא בראשי אברים והיה מפסיד חלקו אם הפיל את שינו או סימא את עינו כמו שיכול למכרו והא דקאמר התם לאו א"ר אלעזר כספו המיוחד לו ה"נ עבדו המיוחד לו לאו מקרא יליף דבלאו קרא יליף לראשי אברים מדין יום או יומים כי היכי דילפינן לענין מכירה אלא גמרא דתלמודא קאמר כלומר בעינן שיהא עבדו המיוחד לו: **במאן** אילימא באחר והאמר רב אין מחזיקין כו'. תימה לרשב"א דמאי קשיא נימא לעולם באחר והא דקאמר [ה] (צריך) למחות כשכתבה לו דין ודברים אין לי בנכסייך ובפירותיהם שאין לבעל בה פירות ולכך צריכה למחות שאינה סומכת עליו ונראה לו דמ"מ סומכת עליו כיון שאם מתה יורשה דאפילו כתב לה בחייך ובמותך קיימא לן כרשב"ג דאם מתה יורשה בפרק הכותב (כתובות דף פג.): **כגון** שאכלה מקצת חזקה בחיי הבעל ושלש שנים לאחר מיתת הבעל. אבל מקצת בחיי הבעל ומקצת לאחר מיתת הבעל לא ולא דמי לאכלה בפני האב שנה ובפני הבן שתים (לעיל דף מג.) דהתם אם היה אוכל שלש שנים בחיי האב היתה חזקה: **מיגו** דאי בעי אמר מינך זבינתה כו'. תימה ומאי נקט כי האי גוונא דזבינתיה ניהליה וזבנה ניהלי הו"ל דנאמן לומר דמינך זבינתיה דאי מילתא דפשיטא היא דמהימן א"כ השתא נמי מילתא דפשיטא היא דמהימן במיגו:

הא

עין משפט נר מצוה

קצח א מיי' פ"ב מהל' רוצח ושמירת נפש הלכה טו:

קצט ב מיי' פ"ד מהל' טוען ונטען הל' יא סמג עשין צה טוש"ע ח"מ סי' קמט סעיף יא וטוש"ע אה"ע סי' פה סעיף ג:

ר ג טוש"ע ח"מ סי' קמט סעי' ט בהגה"ה:

רא ד מיי' שם הל' יא וסמג שם טוש"ע אה"ע סימן פז סעי' ג:

רבינו גרשום

וספק נפשות. להקל דמספקא ליה אי כקנין הגוף דמי אי כקנין פירות: **להקל.** דלא יוקם (העבד) דהיינו קילותא דתרוייהו ישנן בדין יום או יומים ולא יוקם. **ר' אלעזר אומר** וכו'. דאינו לא של זה לגמרי ולא של זה לגמרי והכי נמי סבירא ליה לאמימר דשניהן אם מכרו בנכסי מלוג לא עשו ולא כלום משום דאין לאשה בפירות כלום ולאיש אין בגוף הקרקע כלום אבל אי זביני תרוייהו לעלמא אי נמי היכא דזבנה איהי לדידיה הוו זביניה זביני ולעולם ראיה בעי: **כי כספו הוא כספו המיוחד לו.** וזה עבד אינו מיוחד באותן ל' יום לא לזה ולא לזה: **פיס' האמר רב אשת איש צריכה למחות.** במי שמחזיק בקרקע שלה אלמא דיש לו חזקה בנכסיה אם לא מיחתה: **במאן.** צריכה למחות: **אילימא באחר.** שמחזיק בנכסיה: **והאמר רב אין מחזיקין בנכסי אשת איש.** אע"ג דאכלה שני חזקה לא הויא חזקה דמגו דיש לה בעל סמכה עליה ולא מיחתה: **וכגון שחפר בה בורות שיחין ומערות.** דמזיק לה לארעא דבעל אין לו בנכסי אשתו אלא פירות בלבד ולא לחפור בה כלום הלכך אם חפר בה צריכה למחות ואם לא מיחתה החזיק בהן: **והאמר רב נחמן אין חזקה לנזקין.** לומר הרי שימשתי בזה נזק כמה שנים ושלי היא הקרקע ואמאי צריכה למחות: **אימא.** האי דאמר רב נחמן הכי אין דין חזקה לנזיקין דלאלתר הויא חזקה דאם ראה ולא מיחה ולא צריך ג' שנים הלכך הכי נמי צריכה למחות לאלתר בחפר בה: **איבעית אימא** הא דאמר רב נחמן אין חזקה לנזיקין **בקוטרא ובית הכסא.** דאפי' שתיק איניש לא מחיל אבל בורות שיחין ומערות אם לא מיחתה והחזיק הבעל הוי חזקה: **ורב יוסף אמר לעולם באחר.** ודקשיא לך אין מחזיקין **כגון שאכלה מקצת שני חזקה בחיי בעלה** כשהיא אשת איש **וג' שנים לאחר מיתת הבעל** דבתר דמית ליה לא סמכא דעתה על בעלה והיה לה למחות **ומיגו דאי בעי אמר לה מינך זבינתה** ואכלתיה שני חזקה **כי אמר לה נמי זבינתה לבעלך וזבנה ניהלי מהימן** דהיינו דקאמר רב אשת איש צריכה למחות כלומר אשת איש שהתחיל אחד להחזיק בנכסיה בחיי בעלה ומת בעלה צריכה למחות שוב שלא

מסורת הש"ס

א) [שבת קטו. וש"נ], ב) לעיל כג., ג) [שם], ד) [צ"ל שמחזיקין], ה) [צ"ל צריכה]

הגהות הב"ח

(א) גמ' איבעית אימא הא איתמר עלה: (ב) שם מיגו דאי בעי אמר אנא כצ"ל ותיבת ליה נמחק: (ג) רשב"ם ד"ה כי כספו וכו' דלא הוי מכר:

תורה אור השלם

א) אַךְ אִם יוֹם אוֹ יוֹמַיִם יַעֲמֹד לֹא יֻקַּם כִּי כַסְפּוֹ הוּא: [שמות כא, כא]

ליקוטי רש"י

ספק נפשות להקל. דיני נפשות להקל דהא והצילו העדה כתיב (במדבר לה) [כתובות טו.]. **בקוטרא.** עשן. **בבית הכסא.** שעל גבי קרקע ונראה לעינים שכן היו בתי כסאות שלהן [לעיל כג.].

– **"I bought [the title]** directly **from you,"**[21] כִּי אָמַר לָהּ נַמִּי – therefore, **even when he says to her,** אַתְּ זַבִּינְתָּה לֵיהּ וְזַבְנָה נִיהֲלִי – **"You sold [the land] to [your husband] and he sold it to me,"** מְהֵימָן – **he is believed.**[22]

The Gemara records a dispute in regard to Rav's ruling:

גּוּפָא – **The text** cited above stated: אָמַר רַב – **Rav said:** אֵין מַחֲזִיקִין בְּנִכְסֵי אֵשֶׁת אִישׁ – **One cannot establish a *chazakah* in the property of a married woman.**

NOTES

21. I.e. when your husband died and the property reverted to you, I went and bought it back from you [and I now own both the title and the produce] (*Rashbam*).

22. The force of this *migo* argument is that had the occupant wished to lie, he could have opted for the less complicated lie of saying that he bought the land directly from the woman after the death of her husband. His uncontested use of the land for three years after the husband's death would have enabled him to win with this claim. Thus, there was no reason for him to concoct the more elaborate claim that he bought the title from the husband who had previously bought it from the wife. Since he nonetheless makes this more elaborate claim, we must assume that he is telling the truth.

In conclusion: According to Rav Yosef, Rav teaches that "*a married woman* whose husband died *must protest* the continued use of her *melog* property" in order to prevent the occupant from establishing a *chazakah.* If she fails to do so, and the buyer continues to use it for three years after the husband's death, he is believed if he claims that he bought the title to the land from the wife, or if he claims that the husband bought the title from the wife and then sold it to him.

The novelty of this ruling is as follows: Ordinarily, when a person takes control of a property by obtaining the right to its produce, he can never use his occupancy to establish a *chazakah* to prove that he owns the land. This is because the original owner can always claim that he did not protest the use of the property because he had sold the occupant the right to its produce. For this reason a sharecropper can never claim a *chazakah* on the land he contracted to farm, as we learned in the Mishnah (42a). By the same token, it would seem logical to assume that someone who bought the rights to the produce of a *melog* field from a husband can never establish a *chazakah* on that field to prove his title to it!

Indeed, this is so for as long as the husband is alive. Rav teaches that once the husband dies this is no longer true. There is a basic difference between sharecropping and the use of *melog* property. A sharecropping arrangement may last many years, even a lifetime. Therefore, at any given time the fact that the sharecropper is taking the produce for himself is not evidence that he owns the field. However, a husband's rights to his wife's *melog* property cease when he dies, and so do any rights sold by him. Hence, once the husband dies, if the occupant remains in the land, we view it as if he had entered the property anew, and if the woman does not protest for three years, we accept his claim that she sold the field to him [or sold it to her husband who then sold it to him] (*Rashbam*).

וְדַיָּינֵי גוֹלָה אָמְרוּ – **However, the judges of the Diaspora**[1] **said:** מַחֲזִיקִין – **One can establish a *chazakah*** in the property of a married woman.[2] אָמַר רַב – **Rav said:** הֲלָכָה כְּדַיָּינֵי גוֹלָה – **The halachah is according to the judges of the Diaspora.** אָמְרוּ לֵיהּ רַב כָּהֲנָא וְרַב אַסִּי לְרַב – **Rav Kahana and Rav Assi said to Rav:** הָדַר בֵּיהּ מָר מִשְּׁמַעְתֵּיהּ – **Did the master retract his** earlier **teaching?** אָמַר לְהוּ – **He replied to them:** מִסְתַּבְּרָא אָמְרִי כִּדְרַב יוֹסֵף – **I meant** that their view **seems probable in the case of Rav Yosef.**[3]

Our Mishnah states:
וְלֹא לְאִשָּׁה בְּנִכְסֵי בַּעְלָהּ וכו׳ – NOR CAN A WIFE establish a *chazakah* IN THE PROPERTY OF HER HUSBAND **etc.**[4]

The Gemara asks:
פְּשִׁיטָא – **This** ruling of the Mishnah **is obvious!** כֵּיוָן דְּאִית לָהּ מְזוֹנֵי – **Since she has** the right to receive **food** from her husband, מְזוֹנֵי הוּא דְּקָא אָכְלָה – **it is merely** her **food** allowance that she is taking from her husband's property! Thus, this action cannot establish a *chazakah*.[5] – ? –

The Gemara answers:
לֹא צְרִיכָא – **[The Mishnah's ruling] is necessary only** in a case דְּיִחֵד לָהּ אַרְעָא אַחֲרִיתִי לִמְזוֹנָהּ – **in which [the husband] designated for her a different** section of **land for her food.** Thus, her taking produce from this field cannot be attributed to her right to receive food. The Mishnah teaches that, nevertheless, her use of the produce of the undesignated field does not establish a *chazakah*.[6]

The Mishnah ruled that a wife cannot establish a *chazakah* in her husband's property to prove that he sold her the field. The Gemara analyzes the implication of this ruling:
הָא רְאָיָה יֵשׁ – **This implies** that if she has **proof** that she purchased the property from her husband, it **is effective,** and the sale stands.[7] Why is this so? לֵימָא – **[The husband] should be able to say** that when he accepted money from her it was not his intention to transact a sale, לְגַלּוּיֵי זוּזֵי הוּא דְּבָעֵי – rather **his intention was** only **to uncover** and recover **money** she had taken from him and hidden.[8] Since the Mishnah implies that a sale is binding, שְׁמַעְתְּ מִינָּהּ – one should **learn from this** Mishnah that הַמּוֹכֵר שָׂדֶה לְאִשְׁתּוֹ – if **one sells a field to his wife,** קָנְתָה – **she** indeed **acquires** the field, וְלֹא אָמְרִינַן – **and we do *not* say** that when he accepted the money לְגַלּוּיֵי זוּזֵי הוּא דְּבָעֵי – **his intention was** only **to uncover** and recover **money** that had been hidden from him.[9]

The Gemara rejects this inference by suggesting a different implication:
לֹא – **No,** do not infer from the Mishnah that a proof of sale would entitle her to keep the field. אֵימָא – Rather, **say** that הָא רְאָיָה יֵשׁ – **this** [the Mishnah] **implies that** if she has **proof** of a transfer of ownership it **is effective** בִּשְׁטַר מַתָּנָה – in a case **in which** she produces **a document of gift,** i.e. a document that the husband gave her the property as a gift.[10]

The Gemara continues its discussion of whether a husband can claim that he pretended to sell property to his wife only to uncover money hidden from him:
אָמַר לֵיהּ רַב נַחְמָן לְרַב הוּנָא – **Rav Nachman told Rav Huna:** לֹא הֲוָה מָר גַּבָּן בְּאוּרְתָּא בִּתְחוּמָא – You, **master, were not with us last evening** in the study hall **at the** town's ***techum*** **boundary**[11]

NOTES

1. This is a reference to Shmuel and Karna (*Rashbam* from *Sanhedrin* 17b). [The Gemara there applies this appellation to Karna, but does not mention Shmuel. It seems that *Rashbam* had the reading there "Shmuel and Karna" (see *Mesoras HaShas* there).]

2. Since she should have protested the illegal occupation of her property (*Rashbam*).

3. I.e. when Rav inclined towards the view of Shmuel and Karna and ruled that one can establish a *chazakah* in the *melog* property of a married woman, he did so only for the case in which the occupant took control of the property while the husband was still alive and continued using it for three years after his death. Rav, however, continues to maintain that one cannot establish a *chazakah* in the property of a married woman while the husband is still alive. This is only Rav's view, however. The judges of the Diaspora in fact dispute Rav's ruling in all cases, and allow a *chazakah* to be established even during the husband's lifetime (*Rashbam*).

Rav could not actually have used the words: "in the case of Rav Yosef," inasmuch as Rav Yosef lived many years after Rav. Rav described the case in full; the Gemara merely paraphrased Rav's reply in that way for the sake of brevity (*Rashbam*).

4. That is, even if a woman takes all the produce of her husband's property for three years, this does not constitute *chazakah,* and she cannot claim that she purchased the property from him.

5. Since her use of the produce is not evidence of anything more than a husband's obligation to feed his wife, there was no reason for her husband to protest it. Thus, the use cannot establish a *chazakah* (*Rashbam*).

6. It is assumed that although the husband designated a specific section of land for her food, he is not particular about this, and he allows her to take additional food from other sections of land. Accordingly, there was no reason to expect him to protest, and her taking produce from this undesignated field does not constitute a *chazakah* (*Rashbam*).

7. The Mishnah rules only that her use cannot establish a *chazakah* to prove her claim. This implies that if she could produce acceptable proof of the purchase, such as a bill of sale, she would be granted the property (*Rashbam*).

8. *Rashbam*. Others explain that the husband intended to uncover monies that she had found or earned from her handiwork, which are legally his [see Mishnah *Kesubos* 46b] (*Ramban*). In any case, since the husband accepted the money without any intention of giving away the property, the sale is invalid (*Rashbam*).

[Ordinarily, a seller would not be believed if he claimed that he had accepted money without any intention of giving away the object of the sale, since if this were the case, he would have to return the money.] In the case of a husband, however, he would not need to return the money to her, since there is an assumption that whatever money a woman has belongs to her husband unless proven otherwise (see *Bach* to *Even HaEzer* 85 ד״ה מכר לה). This is because a husband has at least the right to take and invest any money brought into the marriage and keep the profits, as well as a right to keep any money earned or found by his wife. There are only rare instances in which a woman can have money to which her husband is not in some way entitled (see 51b note 16), and these would likely be provable. Thus, in the absence of evidence to the contrary, it is probable that whatever funds she has belong to her husband (*Chazon Ish, Choshen Mishpat, Likutim* 5:1).

9. There is an Amoraic dispute regarding this point (on 51b). Our Mishnah would seem to prove that such an argument is *not* accepted (*Rashbam;* see *Maharsha*). See note 12.

10. Since the husband received no money, the transaction could only have been for the purpose of giving her the property. Thus, if she can prove that he gave it to her as a gift, e.g. by producing the gift document, she may keep the property. When the Mishnah implies that a woman can enforce a transfer of property from her husband to herself with documentary proof of the transaction, it refers to a *gift*. However, if she has proof that he *sold* her a property, she cannot enforce the transaction (according to this view) because the husband can argue that he did not mean to sell it but only to recover money she had taken and hidden from him.

11. *Techum* is a legal boundary that extends two-thousand *amos* beyond the edge of a town or encampment. Its relevance is primarily to the laws of the Sabbath, which prohibit a person from passing beyond the *techum* of his place of residence on the Sabbath. For this reason, it was common in Talmudic times to locate the *beis hamedrash* (study hall) not in town, but outside town, at a point where the *techum* boundaries of several towns overlap. This enabled people from all the surrounding towns to walk to the *beis hamidrash* on the Sabbath. Rav Nachman therefore referred to the study hall as the *techum* (*Rashbam;* cf. *Rashi* to *Bava Kamma* 20a; see also *Aruch,* cited in *Mesoras HaShas* ad loc.).

ודייני גולה אמרו מחזיקין אמר רב הלכה כדייני גולה אמרו ליה רב כהנא ורב אסי לרב הדר ביה מר משמעתיה אמר להו מסתברא אמרי כדרב יוסף: ולא לאשה בנכסי בעלה וכו': פשיטא כיון דאית לה מזוני מזוני הוא דקא אכלה לא צריכא [א]דיחד לה ארעא אחריתי למזונה הא ראיה יש לימא לגלויי זוזי הוא דבעי שמעת מינה המוכר שדה לאשתו קנתה ולא אמרינן לגלויי זוזי הוא דבעי לא אימא הא ראיה יש בשטר מתנה אמר ליה רב נחמן לרב הונא [א]) לא הוה מר גבן באורתא בתחומא דאמרינן מילי מעלייתא אמר ליה מאי מילי מעלייתא אמריתו המוכר שדה לאשתו קנתה ולא אמרינן לגלויי זוזי הוא דבעי אמר ליה פשיטא דל זוזי מהכא ותיקני בשטרא מי לא תנן [ב]) נכסים שיש להן אחריות נקנין בכסף ובשטר ובחזקה אמר ליה ולאו איתמר עלה אמר שמואל לא שנו אלא בשטר מתנה [ג]אבל בשטר מכר לא קנה עד שיתן לו דמיה ולאו מותיב רב המנונא [ד]בשטר כיצד כתב לו על הנייר או על החרס אע"פ שאין בו שוה פרוטה שדי מכורה לך שדי [א]) קנויה לך הרי זו מכורה ונתונה ולאו הוא מותיב לה והוא מפרק לה [ה]במוכר שדהו מפני רעתה [ו]) (רב ביבי מסיים בה משמיה דרב נחמן) ורב אשי אמר במתנה בקש ליתנה לו ולמה כתב לו בלשון מכר כדי ליפות כחו מיתיבי [ז]לוה מן העבד ושחררו מן האשה וגרשה אין להן עליו כלום מאי טעמא לאו משום דאמרינן לגלויי זוזי הוא דבעי שאני התם דלא ניחא ליה לשווייה נפשיה [א]) עבד לוה לאיש מלוה שלח רב הונא בר אבין המוכר שדה לאשתו קנתה ובעל

רש"י

ודייני גולה. שמואל וקרנא בפרק ראשון דסנהדרין (דף יז: ע"ש): מחזיקין. (ג) והיה לה למחות: מסתברא אמרי. היכא דהויא מקצת חזקה בחיי בעלה ושלש לאחר מיתת הבעל כמו שפירש רב יוסף לעיל התם הוא דמסתברא דמחזיקין דהא רב גופיה ה"ק לעיל אשת איש צריכה למחות דמשמע דמחזיקין ומיהו דייני גולה (ג) בכל ענין פליגי אדרב כדרב יוסף. גמרא הוא שקילר דברי רב אבל רב לא הזכיר רב יוסף שהרי קדם לו רב הרבה דורות: כיון דאית לה מזוני. מהבעל: מזוני הוא דקאכלה. הכל יודעין לפירות יורדת והלכך לא מיחה בעל: דיחד לה. בעל קרקע אחריתי למזונות ואפי' הכי לא קפיד בעל אי אכלה טפי והלכך לית לה חזקה: ודייק חזקה הוא דלית לה. בלא שטר: הא ראיה יש. אם יש לה שטר מכירה מבעל הוי מקחה קיים: לימא. הבעל אע"פ שהקרקע נקנה בכסף מעות הללו שקבלתי ממנה לא קני לה הקרקע: לגלויי זוזי בעינא. מעות הטמינה ממני ונתכוונתי לגלות לי מעותיה ובחזקת מעות שלי לקחתים מידה ולא לשם מכר ולא לדעת קנין מכירה קבלתי' ולא גמרתי והקניתי: שמעת מינה המוכר כו'. ופלוגתא היא לקמן: אימא. דוק הכי: הא ראיה יש. אם יש לה שטר מתנה דהתם גמר ונתן לה דליכא גלויי זוזי: בתחומא. בתי מדרשות שלהן בסוף התחום היו כדי שיוכלו לבא שם בשבת מן העיירות שמסביב: א"ל. היכא דליכא שטר מכירה אפילו לגלויי זוזי מיכוין בקבלת המעות הוי קנין גמור דדל זוזי מהכא ותיקני בשטר מכירה דגבי מעות הוא דאיכא למימר קבלת מעות הללו לא ליקני דלגלויי זוזי נתכוין ולעצמו קבלם אבל גבי שטר המכירה לא שייך למימר הכי אלא הרי הוא כשטר מתנה דהכל מודין בו לקמן דקנתה דמה ריוח יש לו בכתיבת שטר המכירה אלא ודאי גמר ואקני לה והא ליכא למימר דאי לא כתב לה שטר לא הוה יהבה זוזי ולגלויי זוזי נתכוין גם בכתיבת השטר דכל כך לא מסיק איניש אדעתיה: מי לא תנן כו'. וקס"ד דאפי' בשטר מכירה קאמר דקני בלא נתינת מעות דכיון דכתב לו שטר מכירה אין יכולין עוד לחזור זה בזה ומעות חייב לו הלוקח למוכר: ולאו איתמר עלה. דבשטר מתנה מיירי אבל שטר מכר לא קנה. וא"ל רב הונא לרב נחמן ולאו מותיב רב המנונא לשמואל כו' אלמא שטר מכר נמי קנה והכתי מאי מילי מעלייתא: הרי זו מכורה או נתונה. ואמר ליה רב נחמן לאו אמרינן התם בפרק ראשון דקדושין דרב המנונא מותיב לה וגם מפרק לה דהך ברייתא דקתני שטר מכר קונה במוכר שדהו מפני רעתה קרקע רעה דבההיא ודאי גמר ומקנה מיד בשטר ומעות ליהוו מלוה גבי דלוקח עד דתבע ליה אבל בשאר קרקעות לא קנו בשטר עד דיהיב זוזי כשמואל והכתי איכא מילי מעלייתא: ה"ג במסכת קדושין רב אשי אמר במתנה ביקש ליתן לו כו'. ואאתקפתא דהך ברייתא דהוה קשיא לשמואל קאי ובא רב אשי לומר דהך ברייתא לא בשטר מכר איירי כלל אלא בשטר מתנה ודבר הרגיל הוא שכותבין בשטר מתנה לשון מכר ליפות כחו דמקבל מתנה שאם יערערו עליו יבא הנותן לפצותו כדין מוכר דלא ליהוי תרעומת עילויה וה"ק שדי מכורה לך וגם נתונה תהיה לך הרי זו מכורה להיות אחריותה על הנותן כדין מוכר וגם נתונה היא ולית בה משום דינא דבר מצרא דאמרינן בבבא מציעא (דף קח:) מתנה לית בה משום דינא דבר מצרא והיינו דאיכא ייפוי כח דמכר ודמתנה: ה"ג ורב אשי אמר במתנה כו': לוה מן העבד. וכתב שטר מלוה ושיעבד לו נכסיו: לגלויי זוזי הוא. דשיעבד לו נכסיו: דלא משוי נפשיה כו'. אין סהדי דשום אדם לא יהיה ברצונו עבד לוה אם יכול להפטר בשום ענין והלכך איכא למימר לגלויי זוזי הוא דבעי אבל גבי מכר גמר ומקנה שהרי אינו נעשה עבד לוה בהך שטר מכירה כלל ואפילו קבל עליו אחריות עדיין לא נטרפה מן הלוקח דליהוי עבד לוה לגבי לוקח: שלח רב הונא בר אבא. לתלמידי בית המדרש: והבעל

תוספות

הא ראיה יש בשטר מתנה. ה"ה דה"מ למימר בשטר הודאה דלא שייך ביה גלויי זוזי: דל זוזי מהכא ותיקני ליה בשטר. במקום שכותבין שטר היו וקאמר דבמקום הזה לא מהניא מעותיה מידי אע"ג דמהניא במקום שאין כותבין ומיהו אף במקום שכותבין שייך למימר דנפקא מינה להיכא דאמר אי (ד) בעינן בשטרא איקני ואי בעינן בכספא איקני דקני בכספא אע"פ שלא כתב לו השטר אי נמי כגון שכתב השטר תחלה ואח"כ נתנה דמים דאי אמר לגלויי זוזי הוא דבעי לא קנתה:

כתב לו על הנייר או על החרס. וכן תניא לענין קידושין כתב לה על הנייר או על החרס אע"פ שאין בו שוה פרוטה בתך מקודשת לי כו'. אומר ר"ת דלאו דוקא כר"א דאמר עדי מסירה כרתי דלר' מאיר כיון שצריך שיחתמו עדים בשטר קידושין כדאמר בפ"ב דקידושין (דף מח. ושם) אמר ר"ג כגון דקדשה בשטר שאין עליו עדים ור"מ לטעמיה דאמר עדי חתימה כרתי א"כ לא מהניא חתימה על דבר שיכול להזדייף כדתנן בפ"ב דגיטין (דף כב:) אין כותבין לא על הנייר כו' ואפי' איכא עדי מסירה לא מהני לר"מ דצריך שיהא מוכיח מתוכו כדאמר בריש כל הגט (שם דף כו:) גבי כתב לגרש את הגדולה דלר"מ אפילו גדולה לא מני מגרש משום דאין מוכח מתוכו הי מינייהו מגרש וא"ת והא אמר בפ"ב דגיטין (דף כב:) דלא הכשיר ר' אלעזר אלא בגיטין ולא הכשיר אלא לאלתר אבל בשאר שטרות (ה) משמע דלא הכשיר אפילו לאלתר וי"ל דהכי בעי למימר דלא הכשיר רבי אלעזר אלא בגיטין ודכותייהו כמו שדה מכורה לך דהכא וכן ההיא דקידושין דלא נכתבו אלא לקנות שדה והאשה דומיא דגיטי שאין עשויין עיקרן לראיה אלא להתגרש אבל שטרות העומדים לראיה לא ועי"ל דהכא ובקידושין לא איירי אלא בכתב ידו כדאמר הוליא עליו כתב ידו כו' וזה אינו יכול להזדייף שהיה ניכר שאין זה כתב ידו:

אע"פ שאין בו שוה פרוטה. תימה דמאי רבותא הוא שוה פרוטה בשלמא גבי קדושין נקט כתב לה על הנייר או על החרס אע"פ שאין בו שוה פרוטה דרבותא היא דאע"פ שאינה מקודשת מתורת כסף כיון שאין בו שוה פרוטה מקודשת מתורת שטר אבל הכא גבי מוכר אפי' יש בו שוה פרוטה אינו קונה מתורת כסף שהרי מוכר נותן שטר ולא לוקח ואין קרקע נקנה אגב כסף:

ולמה כתב בלשון מכר כדי ליפות את כחו. להיות אחריות על הנותן כדין מוכר ופ"ה שכתב לו בשטר כל זה שדי מכורה לך וגם שדי נתונה וכתב לשון מתנה משום דינא דבר מצרא וקשה דאמר בהמקבל (ב"מ דף קח:) מתנה דאית בה אחריות יש בה משום דינא דבר מצרא ועוד קשה לר"ת שדי שדי תרי זימני למה לי ואור"ת וכן ר"י דלא איירי בשכותב שניהן אלא בשכותב מכורה או נתונה וקאמר אפי' בשכתב מכורה במתנה בקש ליתנה לו והא דכתב בלשון מכר כדי לייפות את כחו שמקבל עליו אחריות ועי"ל דשני שטרות כותב לו באחד לשון מכירה ובאחד לשון נתינה ואם יצטרך לדינא דבר מצרא יראה של נתינה ולא של מכירה ואם צריך לאחריות יראה של מכירה ועי"ל דאפי' כתיבי תרוייהו בשטר אחד יפה כחו מה שכתב בלשון מתנה לענין הא דתנן לקמן בהמוכר את הבית (דף עא.) בד"א במוכר אבל בנותן נותן את כולן והכי איתא בירושלמי פ"ק דקידושין ועי"ל דנפקא מינה מה שכתב בלשון מתנה שאין צריך ליתן דמים ומיהו קשה לטעם זה דאמאי בעי בשטר באיקני סגי:

לוה מן העבד ושחררו כו'. תימה דמאי רבותא נקט ושחררו וגרשה פשיטא דאי אין להם עליו כלום בעודו תחתיו גם כשיולאין אין להם עליו כלום ויש לומר דסלקא דעתיה דגמר ומקני להו שיקנו לאחר שיתשחרר ותתגרש:

לא

מסורת הש"ס

א) [ב"ק כ. עמ"ש על הגליון בשם הערוך], ב) קדושין כו. [לקמן פו.], ג) קדושין כו., ד) רש"ל מ"ז.

הגהות הב"ח

(א) גמ' שדי מכורה לך שדי נתונה לך: (ב) רשב"ם ד"ה מחזיקין היהי: (ג) ד"ה מסתברא וכו' בכל ענין פליגי: (ד) תוס' ד"ה דל וכו' אי בעינא בשטרא איקני ואי בעינא: (ה) ד"ה כתב וכו' בשאר שטרות לא משמע:

תורה אור השלם

א) עָשִׁיר בְּרָשִׁים יִמְשׁוֹל וְעֶבֶד לֹוֶה לְאִישׁ מַלְוֶה: [משלי כב, ז]

ליקוטי רש"י

לא הוה מר גבן באורתא בתחומא. לא היית קרוב אללנו שמואל לבא לבית המדרש רלשון שמעתי ב"ק כ.. כלומר אבל על הוא היית אתה עמנו בשבת אללנו בתוך התחום שמואל לבא לבית המדרש ולשמוע [זבחים ב:]. נכסים שיש להן אחריות וכו'. קרקעות [כתובות לד:] היינו קרקעות שאחריות כל אדם הלוה והנושא נתמכרו עליהן לפי שקיימין ועומדין ושוקין נסמכין עליהן [קידושין כו.] והקרקעות אחריות כל מלוה והנושא והוא סומכין עליהן לפי שאין לוקיה שולטת בהן ואינן אובדין [רשב"ם לקמן קנ.] שקיימין לעולם. בכסף. במתן מעות. בשטר. אם כתב לו שדי מכורה לך או נתונה לך ומסר לו את השטר. ובחזקה. נעל וגדר ופרץ כל שהוא [קידושין דף כו.]. יליף טעמא מקראי [רשב"ם שם פו.]. רפק כיס אמלרי לו דיש אמלרי או נעל או פרץ כל שהוא. עד שיתן לו דמיה. דלא גמר מוכר ומקנה עד דקביל דמים ואע"ג דקביל דמים בעי שטרא אלא היכא דפרש ודאמרינן לעיל. הרי זו מכורה ונתונה. קא סלקא דעתך או או קאני. מפני רעתה. דמשום הכי לא איכפת ליה שטרא ללוקח כי היכי דלא מצי למיהדר ביה. רב אשי אמר. הך מתני' בנותן מתנה מיירי וכולה חדא היא ולאו או או קתני אלא כך וכך כתב לו שדי מכורה ונתונה לך לייפות את כחו שאם יגזלנה בעל חוב של נותן ממנה ישוב עליו לתבוע ממנו דמים המפורשים [קידושין שם].

עין משפט נר מצוה

רב א מיי' פי"ג מהל' טוען ונטען הלכה ח סמג עשין לה טוש"ע ח"מ סי' קמט סעיף ט:
רג ב מיי' פ"א מהל' מכירה הל' ג וב"ש מהל' זכייה הל' ג סמג עשין פב טוש"ע ח"מ סי' קצ סעי' א וסי' רמא סעיף ב:
רד ג מיי' פ"א מהל' מכירה הלכה ז סמג שם טוש"ע ח"מ סי' קצא סעיף ב:
רה ד מיי' שם טוש"ע שם ס"א:
רו ה מיי' שם טוש"ע שם ס"ב:
רז ו מיי' פ"ד מהל' מלוה הלכה ח טוש"ע אה"ע סי' פו סעי' ג:

רבינו גרשום

יחזיק לאחר מיתת בעלה ג' שנים: דייני גולה. שמואל וקרנא: הדר ביה מר משמעתא. דאמר לעיל האמר רב אין מחזיקין: מסתבר טעמייהו אמרי. משום דס"ל כתירוץ דרב יוסף דאמר לעולם באחר וכו' פיס': מזוני הוא דקא אכלה. ולא משום דמוחזקת היא בה: לא צריכא כגון דיחד לה ארע' אחריתי למזונותי'. והחזיקה באחרת אפילו הכי לא הויא חזקה דבעל גבי אשתו שתיק: הא מייתי ראיה. דזבנה ניהלה יש לה חזקה אמאי נימא הבעל משום הכי זבינתה ניהלה כדי לגלויי לי זוזי דחזו לה דהות מטמרא מינאי ולהכי זבינתה ניהלה ולא משום מכירה גמורה דהא מה שקנתה אשה קנה בעלה. ש"מ מדלא מצי למימר הכי איכא למשמע מינה דהמוכר שדהו לאשתו קנתה ולא אמרי' לגלויי זוזי הוא דבעי. ואי מייתא ראיה לא הויא חזקה. לעולם המוכר לאשתו א) קנתה ולא אמרי' לגלויי זוזי הוא דבעי. והאי דדייקת הא ראיה יש לה היינו בשטר מתנה דאי מייתא ראיה דיהבה לה במתנה ראייתה ראייה: בתחומא. בבית המדרש: אמר ליה. המוכר שדהו לאשתו וכו' ולא אמרי' לגלויי זוזי בעי: אמר ליה מאי מעלייתא. פשיטא דקנתה: דל זוזי מהכא. דאפי' לא יהבה ניהליה זוזי אפי' הכי קנתה בשטר דקא גמר ומקנה לה בשטר. דתנן כו' בכסף בלא שטר ובשטר בלא כסף ולא מצי למיהדר בהן: עד שיתן דמים. ג) ואי אמרי' הכא לא קנתה היינו טעמא משום דלגלויי זוזי בעי. ומקשי' ולא. דלא קנה עד דיהיב זוזי. ומתיב וכו' הרי זה מכורה ונתונה. ואע"ג דלא נתן דמים אלמא משום דנתינת השטר קנה. הכא נמי דל זוזי מהכא ותקני בשטרא: במוכר שדהו מפני רעתה. שאין בה תועלת ומחמת שהיא רעה קא גמר ויהבה ניהליה אע"ג דלא קיבל דמים. אבל בעלמא לא קנה עד שיתן דמים. והכי נמי אמר שדהו לאשתו לא קנתה דמצי אמר לגלויי זוזי הוא דעבדי משום הכי איצטריך להו למימר בתחומא דקנתה ולא מצי אמר לגלויי זוזי

חשק שלמה על רבינו גרשום

א) נראה דל"ל לא קנתה דאמרינן דלגלויי זוזי וכו'. ב) נראה דל"ל ומשו"ה אי אמרינן דקנתה היינו טעמא משום דלא אמרינן לגלויי זוזי בעי.

עבדא. ורב ביבי מסיים בה משמיה דרב נחמן המוכר שדהו לאשתו קנתה משום האי טעמא משום דבמתנה בקש ליתן לה ולמה כתב לה בלשון מכירה כדי ליפות כחה דעתו קרובה אצלה. דבשטר מכירה כותבין בו אחריות. ובמסכת קדושין כתב רב אשי אמר במתנה בקש ליתן לו וקאי אמוכר שדהו מפני רעתה: אין להן עליו כלום. דפטור מלשלם: מאי טעמא לאו משום דאמרינן לגלויי זוזי הוא דעביד דלוה מהן ולא גמר לפרוע להן. ומקשי' לרב נחמן דאמר לא אמרינן לגלויי זוזי עבד. לגבי הלואה שאני דלא גמר לשעבודי נפשיה למיהוי עבד לאשתו או לעבדו. דמידע ידע דעבד לוה לאיש מלוה ולא עבד

דְּאָמְרִינַן מִילֵּי מַעַלְיָיתָא – **when we said** some **outstanding things.** אָמַר לֵיהּ – **[Rav Huna] asked him:** מַאי מִילֵּי מַעַלְיָיתָא אֲמַרִיתוּ – **What outstanding things did you say?** הַמּוֹכֵר שָׂדֶה לְאִשְׁתּוֹ – Rav Nachman repeated what had been said: If **one sells a field to his wife,** קָנְתָה – **she acquires** the field, וְלֹא אָמְרִינַן – **for we do *not* say** that when he accepted money from her לְגַלּוּיֵי זוּזֵי הוּא דְּבָעֵי – **his intention was** only **to uncover money** she had hidden from him.[12]

Rav Huna questions the novelty of this "outstanding" statement:

אָמַר לֵיהּ – **[Rav Huna] said to him:** פְּשִׁיטָא – **This ruling is obvious!** דַּל זוּזֵי מֵהָכָא – **Eliminate the money from this** consideration, וְתִיקְנֵי בִּשְׁטָרָא – **and let her** still **acquire** the field **with the deed.** I.e. even if his acceptance of the money cannot serve as the basis of the transaction, his giving her a deed suffices by itself to effect the transaction, as the Gemara will now demonstrate.[13] מִי לֹא תְּנַן – **Have we not learned in a Mishnah:**[14] נְכָסִים שֶׁיֵּשׁ לָהֶן אַחֲרָיוּת – REAL PROPERTY,[15] i.e. land or houses, נִקְנִין בְּכֶסֶף וּבִשְׁטָר וּבַחֲזָקָה – MAY BE ACQUIRED BY means of MONEY, A DOCUMENT, OR A PROPRIETARY ACT.[16] Thus, in our case, even if she cannot acquire the field with the money she gives her husband, she should be able to acquire it with the document itself.[17]

Rav Nachman responds:

אָמַר לֵיהּ – **[Rav Nachman] said to him:** וְלָאו אִיתְּמַר עֲלָהּ – **Was it not stated in reference to that** Mishnah that אָמַר שְׁמוּאֵל – **Shmuel said:** לֹא שָׁנוּ אֶלָּא בִּשְׁטַר מַתָּנָה – **They taught** in the Mishnah that real property is acquired solely by means of a document **only in regard to a document of gift,** אֲבָל בִּשְׁטַר מֶכֶר – **but in regard to a document of sale** (i.e. a deed), לֹא קָנָה עַד שֶׁיִּתֵּן לוֹ דָּמֶיהָ – **one does not acquire** the property **until he gives [the seller] the money.**[18] Hence, in our case, if we discount the money, she could not acquire the field solely with the document. Thus, the ruling that a sale by a husband to his wife is binding is indeed novel and outstanding – even where the transaction was concluded with a deed.

Rav Huna challenges Rav Nachman's response:

וְלָאו מוֹתִיב רַב הַמְנוּנָא – **But did not Rav Hamnuna challenge** this ruling of Shmuel from a Baraisa that states the following:[19] בִּשְׁטָר כֵּיצַד – HOW is acquisition accomplished WITH A DOCUMENT? כָּתַב לוֹ עַל הַנְּיָיר אוֹ עַל הַחֶרֶס – If HE WROTE FOR [THE PERSON ACQUIRING HIS FIELD] UPON A PAPYRUS OR UPON A SHARD, אַף עַל פִּי שֶׁאֵין בּוֹ שָׁוֶה פְּרוּטָה – EVEN IF [THE PAPYRUS OR SHARD] DOES NOT HAVE THE VALUE OF A *PERUTAH*,[20] שָׂדִי מְכוּרָה לָךְ – "MY FIELD IS SOLD TO YOU," שָׂדִי קְנוּיָה לָךְ – or "MY FIELD IS GIVEN TO YOU as a gift,"[21] הֲרֵי זוֹ מְכוּרָה וּנְתוּנָה – THEN [THE FIELD] IS SOLD OR GIVEN.[22] Clearly, the Baraisa considers a document effective even for the sale of real property, contrary to Shmuel's ruling!

Rav Nachman retorted:

וְלָאו הוּא מוֹתִיב לָהּ וְהוּא מְפָרֵק לָהּ – **But did not [Rav Hamnuna] present the challenge** from the Baraisa **and** also **resolve it** himself as follows: בְּמוֹכֵר שָׂדֵהוּ מִפְּנֵי רָעָתָהּ – The Baraisa refers to a case **in which one sells the field because of its poor quality.** Shmuel would agree in that case that the sale would be transacted with the document alone.[23] Generally, however, a document is insufficient to finalize a sale, as Shmuel maintained.[24]

NOTES

12. Although the money is likely his, a husband prefers not to create an atmosphere of mistrust in his marriage by taking money from his wife by deception. Since he nonetheless sold her the property, we assume that he decided not to contest her right to the money but intended to sell her the land (*Chazon Ish, Choshen Mishpat, Likutim* 5:1).

13. Since fields are often sold with a deed, it is reasonable to assume that Rav Nachman refers even to such a case (see *Tosafos* ד״ה דל). Rav Huna points out that in such a case, there is nothing "outstanding" or novel about Rav Nachman's statement. Even if we accept the husband's argument that the money he took from his wife was actually his to begin with, it is also true he gave her a bill of sale. Accordingly, she should acquire the property with her reception of the bill of sale (*Rashbam;* cf. *Ramban*).

Theoretically, one could argue that the husband believed that if he had not given a bill of sale, she would not have agreed to buy the property from him. Thus, even his giving her the bill of sale could be attributed to his plan to recover his money and it should not be effective. However, the assumption is that a husband does not think he has to resort to such extremes. Thus, we must assume he gave her the document to enable her to acquire the field (*Rashbam*).

14. *Kiddushin* 26a.

15. Literally: properties that have responsibility. When one incurs a debt and that debt is recorded in a legal document [מִלְוָה בִּשְׁטָר], a lien automatically takes effect on any real property owned by the debtor at that time. This lien remains in effect even if the debtor subsequently sells the property; should the debtor default on his obligation, the creditor can seize the property from the buyer to satisfy the debt. For this reason, real property (land and houses) is said to have "responsibility," since it will always be there for the lender to collect from it [unlike movable property] (*Rashi* ad loc.; see also *Rashbam* below, 86a). The fact that real property has "responsibility" is not pertinent to the point discussed here. The term *properties that have responsibility* is merely the Mishnah's idiom for "real property," a way of characterizing the legal difference between real and movable property.

16. Any of these three methods of acquisition (*kinyan*) serves to formalize the transfer of ownership for real property:

Money – the buyer gives the seller money to acquire the property.

Document – the owner draws up a bill of sale (or gift) stating that he is selling (or giving) the property defined therein to the buyer (or recipient). By handing the document over to the buyer (or recipient), the sale (or gift) is effected without any payment.

Proprietary act [chazakah] – the buyer performs an act in the property that demonstrates his assumption of ownership. This act is generally one that improves the land; for example, plowing a small part of the field, locking the gate, or breaking open an entrance in its fence (*Rashi* ad loc.; see below, 52b).

17. The Gemara at this point assumes that the Mishnah's ruling applies not only to a gift of real property, but even to a sale. Giving a document of sale to the buyer without accepting money from him finalizes the transfer of ownership [in which case the buyer owes the seller the money for the field, and neither party can renege] (*Rashbam* ד״ה מי לא תנן).

18. The reason for this is that the seller does not fully resolve to give the buyer title to the land until he receives payment (*Rashi* to *Kiddushin* 26a; see Gemara there).

19. Rav Hamnuna's challenge, as well as his and Rav Ashi's resolutions (see below), are quoted from *Kiddushin* 26a.

20. *Perutah* – the smallest coin of Talmudic currency; the minimum value considered "money" (see *Kiddushin* 2a, 12a). [For an explanation of why the Baraisa feels compelled to state that the document need not be worth a *perutah,* see our edition of *Kiddushin,* 26a note 18.]

21. Our translation follows *Bach's* emendation – שָׂדִי נְתוּנָה לָךְ in place of שָׂדִי קְנוּיָה לָךְ. This is the version found in *Kiddushin* 26a as well.

22. The Gemara now understands the conjunctive *"vav"* (ו) in the words מְכוּרָה וּנְתוּנָה to mean "or" (not "and"). Thus, the Baraisa is clearly referring to two separate transactions, one a sale and the other a gift (*Rashi* to *Kiddushin*).

23. Generally, a seller does not fully resolve to give the buyer title to land until he receives payment, as was explained above. However, when someone sells a field because of its poor quality, he resolves to give the buyer title even before receiving payment for it, since he wishes the sale to become binding as soon as possible (*Rashi* to *Kiddushin*). Thus, he is content to finalize the sale immediately and allow the buyer to owe the money temporarily (*Rashbam*).

24. Thus, in the case of a husband who sold property to his wife, if we were to eliminate the money from our consideration and consider only

א) [ב"ק כ. עמ"ש על הגליון בשם הערוך], ב) קדושין ט. [לקמן פו.], ג) קדושין כו., ד) רש"ל מ"ז.

הגהות הב"ח

(א) גמ' שדי מכורה לך שדי נתונה לך: (ב) רשב"ם ד"ה מחזיקין דהיה: (ג) ד"ה מסתברא וכו' בכל ענין פליגי: (ד) תוס' ד"ה דל וכו' אי בעינא בשטרא איקני ואי בעינא: (ה) ד"ה כתב וכו' בשאר שטרות לא משמע:

תורה אור השלם

א) עָשִׁיר בְּרָשִׁים יִמְשׁוֹל וְעֶבֶד לֹוֶה לְאִישׁ מַלְוֶה: [משלי כב, ז]

ליקוטי רש"י

לא הוה מר גבן באורתא בתחומא. שהולך לבית קרוב אלינו שהולך בא בתחומא לבית המדרש ראשון שמעתי [ב"ק כ.]. כלומר הכל על שלא היה אמש בשבת אלנו בתוך התחום שהולך לבא לבית המדרש ולשמוע [זבחים ב:]. נכסים שיש להן אחריות וכו'. קרקעות [כתובות לד:]. היינו קרקעות שאחריות כל אדם הלוה והנושא בחבירו עליהן לפי שקיימין ועומדין לפיכך נסמכין עליהן [קידושין כו.]. והקרקעות אחריות כל מלוה ושוב וכתובה נסמכין עליהן שאין קרקע לוקה שולטת בהן ואין אובדין [רשב"ם לקמן קנ:]. קיימין לעולם. בכסף. במתן מעות. בשטר. אם כתב לו שדי מכורה לך או נתונה לך ומסר לו את השטר. ובחזקה. נעל וגדר ופרץ כל שהוא והתם (קידושין כו.) יליף טעמא מקראי [רשב"ם שם סו.]. רפק ביה פורתא או דיש בה פורתא או פרץ כל שהוא. עד שיתן לו דמיה. לא גמר מוכר ומקנה עד דקביל דמים ואע"ג דקביל דמים בעי שטרא אלא איכא דפריש ובדאמרינן לעיל. הרי זו מכורה ונתונה. לא קא סלקא דעתך או לא קמני. מפני רעתה. דימלא ליה לדקנייה ליה שטרא ללוקח כי היכי דלא מצי למיהדר ביה. רב אשי אמר. הך מתני' בנותן מתנה מיירי וכולה מדה היא ולאו או או קתני אלא הכי קאמר שדי מכורה ונתונה לך לייפות את כחו שאם יגבנה בעל חוב שלו עליו מתנה ישוב עליו לתבוע ממנו דמים המפורשים [קידושין שם].

חשק שלמה על רבינו גרשום

א) נראה דצ"ל לא קנתה דאמרינן לגלויי זוזי וכו'. ב) נראה דצ"ל ומשו"ה אי קנתה היינו טעמא משום דלא אמרינן לגלויי זוזי בעי.

ודייני גולה אמרו מחזיקין אמר רב הלכה כדייני גולה אמרו ליה רב כהנא ורב אסי לרב הדר ביה מר משמעתיה אמר להו מסתברא אמרי כדרב יוסף: ולא לאשה בנכסי בעלה וכו': פשיטא כיון דאית לה מזוני מזוני הוא דקא אכלה לא צריכא דיחד לה ארעא אחריתי למזונה הא ראיה יש לימא לגלויי זוזי הוא דבעי שמעת מינה המוכר שדה לאשתו קנתה ולא אמרינן לגלויי זוזי הוא דבעי לא אימא הא ראיה יש בשטר מתנה אמר ליה רב נחמן לרב הונא לא הוה מר גבן באורתא בתחומא דאמרינן מילי מעלייתא אמר ליה מאי מילי מעלייתא אמריתו המוכר שדה לאשתו קנתה ולא אמרינן לגלויי זוזי הוא דבעי אמר ליה פשיטא דל זוזי מהכא ותיקני בשטרא מי לא תנן נכסים שיש להן אחריות נקנין בכסף ובשטר ובחזקה אמר ליה ולאו איתמר עלה אמר שמואל לא שנו אלא בשטר מתנה אבל בשטר מכר לא קנה עד שיתן לו דמיה ולאו מותיב רב המנונא בשטר כיצד כתב לו על הנייר או על החרס אע"פ שאין בו שוה פרוטה קנויה (א) לך שדי מכורה לך שדי נתונה לך הרי זו מכורה ונתונה ולאו הוא מותיב לה והוא מפרק לה במוכר שדהו מפני רעתה (רב ביבי מסיים בה משמיה דרב נחמן) ורב אשי אמר במתנה בקש ליתנה לו ולמה כתב לו בלשון מכר כדי ליפות כחו מיתיבי לוה מן העבד ושחררו מן האשה וגרשה אין להן עליו כלום מאי טעמא לאו משום דאמרינן לגלויי זוזי הוא דבעי שאני התם דלא ניחא ליה לשווייה נפשיה עבד לוה לאיש מלוה שלח רב הונא בר אבין המוכר שדה לאשתו קנתה ובעל

רשב"ם

ודייני גולה. שמואל וקרנא בפרק ראשון דסנהדרין (דף יז: ע"ש): מחזיקין. (ב) והיה לה למחות: מסתברא אמרי. היכא דהויא מקלת חזקה בחיי בעלה ושלש לאחר מיתת הבעל כמו שפירש רב יוסף לעיל התם הוא דמסתברא דמחזיקין דהא רב גופיה ה"ק לעיל אשת איש צריכה למחות דמשמע דמחזיקין ומיהו דייני גולה (ג) בכל ענינן פליגי אדרב: כדרב יוסף. גמרא הוא שקיבל דברי רב אבל רב לא הזכיר רב יוסף שהרי קדם לו רב הרבה דורות: כיון דאית לה מזוני. מהבעל: מזוני הוא דקאכלה. הכל יודעין לפירות יורדת והלכך לא מיחה בעל: דיחד לה. בעל קרקע אחריתי למזונות ואפ"ה הכי לא קפיד בעל אי אכלה טפי והלכך לית לה חזקה: ודייק חזקה הוא דלית לה. בלא שטר: הא ראיה יש. אם יש לה שטר מכירה מבעל הוי מקחה קיים: לימא. הבעל אע"פ שהקרקע נקנה בכסף מעות הללו שקבלתי ממנה לא קני לה הקרקע: לגלויי זוזי בעינא. מעות הטמינה ממני ונתכוונתי לגלות לי מעותיה ובחזקת מעות שלי לקחתים מידה ולא לשם מכר ולא לדעת קנין מכירה קבלתי' ולא גמרתי והקניתי: שמעת מינה המוכר כו'. ופלוגתא היא לקמן: אימא. דוק הכי: הא ראיה יש. אם יש לה שטר מתנה דהתם גמר ונתן לה דליכא גלויי זוזי: בתחומא. בתי מדרשות שלהן בסוף התחום היו כדי שיוכלו לבא שם בשבת מן העיירות שסביביו: א"ל. היכא דאיכא שטר מכירה אפילו לגלויי זוזי מיכוין בקבלת המעות הוי קנין גמור דדל זוזי מהכא ותיקני בשטר מכירה דגבי מעות הוא דאיכא למימר קבלת מעות הללו לא ליקני דלגלויי זוזי נתכוין ולעצמו קבלם אבל גבי שטר המכירה לא שייך למימר הכי אלא הרי הוא כשטר מתנה דהכל מודין בו לקמן דקנתה דמה ריוח יש לו בכתיבת שטר המכירה אלא ודאי גמר ואקני לה והא ליכא למימר דאי לא כתב לה שטר לא הוה יהבה זוזי ולגלויי זוזי נתכוין גם בכתיבת השטר דכל כך לא מסיק איניש אדעתיה: מי לא תנן כו'. וקס"ד דאפי' בשטר מכירה קאמר דקני בלא נתינת מעות דכיון דכתב לו שטר מכירה אין יכולין עוד לחזור זה בזה ומעות חייב לו הלוקח למוכר: ולאו איתמר עלה. דבשטר מתנה מיירי אבל שטר מכר לא קנה. וא"ל רב הונא לרב נחמן ולאו מותיב רב המנונא לשמואל כו' אלמא שטר מכר נמי קנה ואכתי מאי מילי מעלייתא: הרי זו מכורה או נתונה. ואמר ליה רב נחמן לאו אמרינן התם בפרק ראשון דקדושין דרב המנונא מותיב לה וגם מפרק לה דהך ברייתא דקתני שטר מכר קונה במוכר שדהו מפני רעתה קרקע רעה דבההיא ודאי גמר ומקנה מיד בשטר ומעות ליהוו מלוה גבי לוקח עד דתבע ליה אבל בשאר קרקעות לא קנו בשטר עד דיהיב זוזי כשמואל ואכתי איכא מילי מעלייתא: ה"ג במסכת קדושין רב אשי אמר במתנה ביקש ליתן לו כו'. ואאתקפתא דהך ברייתא דהוה קשיא לשמואל קאי ובא רב אשי לומר דהך ברייתא לא בשטר מכר איירי כלל אלא בשטר מתנה ודבר הרגיל הוא שכותבין בשטר מתנה לשון מכר ליפות כחו דמקבל מתנה שאם יערערו עליו יבא הנותן לפצותו כדין מוכר דלא ליהוי תרעומת עילויה וה"ק שדי מכורה לך וגם נתונה תהיה לך הרי זו מכורה להיות אחריותה על הנותן כדין מוכר וגם נתונה היא ולית בה משום דינא דבר מצרא דאמרינן בבבא מציעא (דף קח:) מתנה לית בה משום דינא דבר מצרא והיינו דאיכא ייפוי כח דמכר ודמתנה: ה"ג ורב אשי אמר במתנה כו': לוה מן העבד. וכתב שטר מלוה ושיעבד לו נכסיו: לגלויי זוזי הוא. דשיעבד לו נכסיו: דלא משוי נפשיה כו'. אין סהדי דשום אדם לא יהיה ברצונו עבד לוה אם יכול להפטר בשום ענין והלכך איכא למימר לגלויי זוזי הוא דבעי אבל גבי מכר גמר ומקנה שהרי אינו נעשה עבד לוה בהך שטר מכירה כלל ואפילו קבל עליו אחריות עדיין לא נטרפה מן הלוקח דליהוי עבד לוה לגבי לוקח: שלח רב הונא בר אבא. לתלמידי בית המדרש:

והבעל

תוספות

הא ראיה יש בשטר מתנה. ה"ה דה"מ למימר בשטר הודאה דלא שייך ביה גלויי זוזי: דל זוזי מהכא ותיקני ליה בשטר. במקום שכותבין שטר היו וקאמר דבמקום הזה לא מהניא שמעתיה מידי אע"ג דמהניא במקום שאין כותבין ומיהו אף במקום שכותבין שייך למימר דנפקא מינה להיכא דאמר אי (ד) בעינן בשטרא איקני ואי בעינן בכספא איקני דקני בכספא אע"פ שלא כתב לו השטר אי נמי כגון שכתב השטר תחלה ואח"כ נתנה דמים דאי אמר לגלויי זוזי הוא דבעי לא קנתה: כתב לו על הנייר או על החרס. וכן תניא לענין קידושין כתב לה על הנייר או על החרס אע"פ שאין בו שוה פרוטה בתך מקודשת לי כו'. אומר ר"ת דאתי כר"א דאמר עדי מסירה כרתי דלר' מאיר כיון שצריך שיחתמו עדים בשטר קידושין כדאמר בפ"ב דקידושין (דף מח. ושם) אמר ר"נ כגון דקדשה בשטר שאין עליו עדים ור"מ לטעמיה דאמר עדי חתימה כרתי א"כ לא מהניא חתימה על דבר שיכול להזדייף כדתנן בפ"ב דגיטין (דף כא:) אין כותבין לא על הנייר כו' ואפי' איכא עדי מסירה לא מהני לר"מ דצריך שיהא מוכיח מתוכו כדאמר בריש כל הגט (שם דף כד:) גבי כתב לגרש את הגדולה דלר"מ אפילו גדולה לא מצי מגרש משום דאין מוכח מתוכו הי מינייהו מגרש וא"ת והא אמר בפ"ב דגיטין (דף כב:) דלא הכשיר ר' אלעזר אלא בגיטין ולא הכשיר אלא לאלתר אבל בשאר שטרות (ה) משמע דלא הכשיר אפילו לאלתר וי"ל דהכי בעי למימר דלא הכשיר רבי אלעזר אלא בגיטין ודכוותייהו כמו שדה מכורה לך דהכא וכן ההיא דקידושין דלא נכתבו אלא לקנות שדה והאשה דומיא דגיטי שאינן עשויין עיקרן לראיה אלא להתגרש אבל שטרות העומדים לראיה לא ועי"ל דהכא ובקידושין לא איירי אלא בכתב ידו כדאמר הוציא עליו כתב ידו כו' וזה אינו יכול להזדייף שהיה ניכר שאין זה כתב ידו: אע"פ שאין בו שוה פרוטה. תימה דמאי רבותא הוא שוה פרוטה בשלמא גבי קדושין נקט כתב לה על הנייר או על החרס אע"פ שאין בו שוה פרוטה דרבותא היא דאע"פ שאינה מקודשת מתורת כסף כיון שאין בו שוה פרוטה מקודשת מתורת שטר אבל הכא גבי מוכר אפי' יש בו שוה פרוטה אינו קונה מתורת כסף שהרי מוכר נותן שטר ולא לוקח ואין קרקע נקנה אגב כסף: ולמה כתב בלשון מכר כדי ליפות את כחו. להיות אחריות על הנותן כדין מוכר ופ"ה שכתב לו בשטר כל זה שדי מכורה לך וגם שדי נתונה וכתב לשון מתנה משום דינא דבר מצרא וקשה דאמר בהמקבל (ב"מ דף קח:) מתנה דאית בה אחריות יש בה משום דינא דבר מצרא ועוד קשה לר"ת שדי שדי תרי זימני למה לי ואור"ת וכן ר"י דלא מיירי בשכותב שניהן אלא בשכותב מכורה או נתונה וקאמר אפי' בשכתב מכורה במתנה בקש ליתנה לו והא דכתב בלשון מכר כדי לייפות את כחו שמקבל עליו אחריות ועי"ל דשני שטרות כותב לו באחד לשון מכירה ובאחד לשון נתינה ואם יצטרך לדינא דבר מצרא יראה של נתינה ולא של מכירה ואם צריך לאחריות יראה של מכירה ועי"ל דאפי' כתיבי תרוייהו בשטר אחד יפה כחו מה שכתב בלשון מתנה לענין הא דתנן לקמן בהמוכר את הבית (דף עא.) בד"א במוכר אבל בנותן נותן את כולן והכי איתא בירושלמי פ"ק דקידושין ועי"ל דנפקא מינה מה שכתב בלשון מתנה שאין צריך ליתן דמים ומיהו קשה לטעם זה דלמאי בעי בשטר באיקני סגי: לוה מן העבד ושחררו כו'. תימה דמאי רבותא נקט ושחררו וגרשה פשיטא דאי אין להם עליו כלום בעודו תחתיו גם לכשיוצאין אין להם עליו כלום ויש לומר דסלקא דעתיה דגמר ומקני להו שיקנו לאחר שישתחרר ותתגרש:

לא

עין משפט נר מצוה

רב א מיי' פי"ג מהל' טוען ונטען הלכה ח סמג עשין צה טוש"ע ח"מ סי' קמט סעיף ט:

רג ב מיי' פ"א מהל' מכירה הל' ג ופ"ב מהל' זכיה הל' א סמג עשין פב טוש"ע ח"מ סי' קצ סעי' א וסי' רמא סעיף א:

רד ג מיי' פ"א מהל' מכירה הלכה ז סמג שם טוש"ע ח"מ סי' קצא סעיף ג:

רה ד מיי' שם טוש"ע שם ס"א:

רו ה מיי' שם טוש"ע שם ס"ב:

רז ו מיי' פ"ב מהל' מלוה הלכה ח טוש"ע אה"ע סי' פו סעי' ג:

רבינו גרשום

יחזיק לאחר מיתת בעלה ג' שנים: **דייני גולה.** שמואל וקרנא: **הדר ביה מר משמעתא.** דאמר לעיל האמר רב אין מחזיקין: **מסתבר טעמייהו אמרי.** משום דס"ל כתירוץ **דרב יוסף** דאמר לעולם באחר וכו': פיס' **מזוני הוא דקא אכלה.** ולא משום דמוחזקת היא בה: **לא צריכא** כגון **דיחד לה ארע' אחריתי למזונותי'.** והחזיקה באחרת אפילו הכי לא הויא חזקה דבעל גבי אשתו שתיק: **הא מייתי ראיה.** דזבונה ניהלה **יש** לה חזקה אמאי **נימא** הבעל משום הכי זבינתה ניהלה כדי **לגלויי לי זוזי** דחזו לה דהות מטמרא מינאי ולהכי זבינתה ניהלה ולא משום מכירה גמורה דהא מה שקנתה אשה קנה בעלה. ש"מ מדלא מצי למימר הכי איכא למישמע מינה **דהמוכר שדהו לאשתו** קנתה **ולא אמרי' לגלויי זוזי הוא דבעי** ואי מייתא ראיה הויא חזקה. לעולם המוכר לאשתו א) קנתה ולא אמרי' לגלויי זוזי הוא דבעי. והאי דדייקת **הא ראיה יש לה** היינו **בשטר מתנה** דאי מייתא ראיה דיהבה לה במתנה ראייתה ראייה: **בתחומא.** בבית המדרש: **אמר ליה.** **המוכר שדהו לאשתו וכו' ולא אמרי' לגלויי זוזי בעי: אמר ליה** מאי מעלייתא. **פשיטא** דקנתה: **דל זוזי מהכא.** דאפי' לא יהבה ניהליה זוזי אפי' הכי **קנתה בשטר** דקא גמר ומקנה לה בשטר. **דתנן כו'** בכסף בלא שטר **ובשטר** בלא כסף ולא מצי למיהדר בהן: **עד שיתן דמים.** ג) ואי אמרי' הכא לא קנתה היינו טעמא משום דלגלויי זוזי בעי. ומקשי' **ולא.** דלא קנה עד דיהיב זוזי. ומתיב וכו' **הרי זה מכורה ונתונה.** ואע"ג דלא נתן דמים אלמא משום דנתינות השטר קנה. הכא נמי דל זוזי מהכא ותקני בשטרא: **במוכר שדהו מפני רעתה.** שאין בה תועלת ומחמת שהיא רעה קא גמר ויהבה ניהליה אע"ג דלא קיבל דמים. אבל בעלמא לא קנה עד שיתן דמים. והכי נמי במוכר שדהו לאשתו לא קנתה דמצי אמר לגלויי זוזי הוא דעבדי משום הכי איצטריך להו למימר בתחומא דקנתה ולא מצי אמר לגלויי זוזי

The Gemara presents another solution to Rav Hamnuna's challenge to Shmuel from the Baraisa:

(רב ביבי מסיים בה משמה דרב נחמן) וְרַב אָשֵׁי אָמַר – **And Rav Ashi said** that the Baraisa is referring to a case in which בְּמַתָּנָה בִּקֵּשׁ לִיתְּנָהּ לוֹ – **he wished to give him [the field] as a gift,** and in the document making over the gift to the recipient he wrote, "My field is sold to you *and* my field is given to you."[25] וְלָמָּה כָּתַב לוֹ בִּלְשׁוֹן מֶכֶר – **Then why did he record** this gift **for him in the language of a sale?** כְּדֵי לְיַפּוֹת כֹּחוֹ – **In order to enhance [the recipient's] rights** by giving him the prerogatives of a buyer.[26] The ruling of the Baraisa, then, is not contrary to Shmuel's ruling, for the Baraisa speaks not of a sale, but rather of a gift. A document of gift may indeed effect a gift without anything else. Shmuel, however, teaches that a sale cannot be effected by a document alone without payment.[27]

Rav Nachman stated above that if a man sold a field to his wife, he cannot claim that he accepted the money only to recover what she had hidden from him. The Gemara now questions this:

מֵיתִיבֵי – **They challenged** Rav Nachman's ruling **from the** following **Baraisa:** לָוָה מִן הָעֶבֶד – If ONE BORROWED money FROM [HIS] Canaanite SLAVE, and recorded the loan in a document,[28] וְשִׁחְרְרוֹ – AND HE subsequently EMANCIPATED HIM, מִן הָאִשָּׁה – or if he borrowed money FROM [HIS WIFE] and recorded the loan, וְגֵרְשָׁהּ – AND HE subsequently DIVORCED HER, אֵין לָהֶן עָלָיו כְּלוּם – THEY HAVE NO monetary claim AGAINST HIM; i.e. they cannot collect the money from him. מַאי טַעְמָא – **What is the reason** for this? לָאו מִשּׁוּם דְּאָמְרִינַן – **Is it not because we say** that לְגַלּוּיֵי זוּזֵי הוּא דְּבָעֵי – **he intended** only **to uncover money** they had hidden from him and never assumed a commitment to repay them? This contradicts Rav Nachman's ruling, which rejects the attempt to void a transaction with such a claim.[29] – ? –

The Gemara answers:

שָׁאנֵי הָתָם – **There,** in the case of the Baraisa, which deals with borrowing, **it is different,** דְּלָא נִיחָא לֵיהּ לְשַׁוּוּיֵיהּ נַפְשֵׁיהּ – **because it is disagreeable to him to place himself** in the position of being "עֶבֶד לֹוֶה לְאִישׁ מַלְוֶה" – ***a borrower*** who ***is a servant to the lender.***[30] Thus, it is unlikely that he would agree to subject himself to a debt after uncovering money he could claim as his own. Rav Nachman, however, deals with a sale, which does not place the seller in this uncomfortable position. Therefore, it is possible he intended to let his wife keep the property.[31]

Rav Nachman ruled that if a man sells a field to his wife, the sale stands. The Gemara now examines the status of such a field:

שְׁלַח רַב הוּנָא בַּר אָבִין – **Rav Huna bar Avin sent** the following message to the students of the academy: הַמּוֹכֵר שָׂדֶה לְאִשְׁתּוֹ – If **one sells a field to his wife,** קָנְתָה – **she acquires** the field,

NOTES

the document, as Rav Huna suggested, the sale could not be considered valid. Therefore, when they stated in the *beis hamedrash* that the husband's sale is binding it was indeed a novel ruling.

25. According to Rav Ashi, when the Baraisa says: שָׂדִי מְכוּרָה לָךְ שָׂדִי נְתוּנָה לָךְ, *My field is sold to you, my field is given to you*, the Baraisa is not giving the text for two different transactions, as previously thought (see note 22). Rather, it means that both these statements appeared in one document in reference to a single transaction. Thus, it is not to be rendered as, "My field is sold to you," *or* "My field is given to you," but rather as, "My field is sold to you *and* my field is given to you," as the Gemara will now explain (*Rashbam; Rashi* ibid.).

26. When someone sells a field, and the field is later seized by the seller's creditors, the buyer has recourse; he may sue the seller to pay him for the lost land. However, the recipient of a gift has no recourse, since he paid nothing for the property and thus lost nothing. It is for this reason that a person giving a gift would add the words, "My field is sold to you." By doing so, he obligates himself to compensate the recipient [as if he were a buyer] should he lose the field to a creditor.

Were this the sole consideration, the seller would simply write in the document, "My field is sold to you"; there would be no need for him to add anything about its being a gift. The reason he does so is to protect the recipient in regard to דִּינָא דְּבַר מִצְרָא, *the law pertaining to the owner of the adjacent property.* This rule states that when a person sells his property and the owner of an adjacent property wishes to buy it, the neighbor has first claim. Even if the land is sold to someone else, the neighbor may simply reimburse the buyer and take over the property (above 5a, *Bava Metzia* 108a; *Choshen Mishpat* 175:6). This rule applies only with respect to a sale, not a gift. If one gives property as a gift, the neighbor cannot force the recipient to sell it to him. In our case, had the benefactor recorded the gift strictly as a sale, the property would have been subject to this rule. He thus records it as a gift as well (*Rashbam;* cf. *Tosafos*).

27. The entire discussion here of Shmuel's ruling is an almost verbatim quote from the Gemara in Kiddushin (26a). Rav Huna and Rav Nachman quoted that discussion in connection with their own discussion. Rav Nachman, of course, did not quote Rav Ashi's answer, since Rav Ashi had not yet been born when the discussion with Rav Huna took place. The Gemara nevertheless quotes Rav Ashi's interpretation as an answer to the challenge posed to Shmuel from the Baraisa (see *Rashbam*). [Though Rav Nachman did not quote Rav Ashi's answer, that answer nonetheless allays the challenge from the Baraisa and preserves Shmuel's ruling. Thus, even according to Rav Ashi's answer, Rav Nachman was correct in stating that the ruling stated in the *beis hamedrash* was novel and "outstanding."]

28. He thereby mortgaged his property to this loan (*Rashbam*). See next note.

29. [The Baraisa speaks even in a case in which the husband or master mortgaged his property to this loan (by recording it in a document). Had he not mortgaged his property, there would be no question that he need not repay the loan. Since the husband or master now holds the money, and he claims that the money which was "lent" him was actually his to begin with, it would be up to the wife or slave to prove otherwise. (As noted above, the husband's claim is quite plausible, because it is rare for a woman to have money which is not (at least) under her husband's control; see note 8. This is all the more true in the case of a slave.) However, the Baraisa refers even to a case in which he did mortgage his property to the loan by recording it in a document. To exempt himself now, he must void the lien on his property. Since the Baraisa states that he is exempt, we see that the argument that he entered the transaction in order to recover money that was really his is sufficiently strong even to undo a transaction freely undertaken. This contradicts Rav Nachman's assertion that a husband cannot void the sale of property to his wife with such a claim.]

30. *Proverbs* 22:7.

31. Since the burden of a debt weighs heavily on a borrower, a person would never subject himself to this burden if he could avoid it (*Rashbam*). [Thus, since he can simply take the money from his wife or slave on the grounds that it was probably his to begin with (see note 8), he would not subject himself to being in their debt simply to avoid contention. In the case of a sale, however, it is possible that he prefers not to make an issue over the money and allow her to buy the field from him, as explained in note 12. Thus, the evidence for voiding the sale is not definitive. See *Chazon Ish, Choshen Mishpat, Likutim* 5:1.] See *Rabbeinu Gershom* for another explanation.

ודייני גולה אמרו מחזיקין אמר רב הלכה כדייני גולה אמרו ליה רב כהנא ורב אסי לרב הדר ביה מר משמעתיה אמר להו מסתברא אמרי כדרב יוסף: ולא לאשה בנכסי בעלה וכו': פשיטא כיון דאית לה מזוני מזוני הוא דקא אכלה לא צריכא א דיחד לה ארעא אחריתי למזונה הא ראיה יש לימא לגלויי זוזי הוא דבעי שמעת מינה המוכר שדה לאשתו קנתה ולא אמרינן לגלויי זוזי הוא דבעי לא אימא הא ראיה יש בשטר מתנה אמר ליה רב נחמן לרב הונא א) לא הוה מר גבן באורתא בתחומא דאמרינן מילי מעלייתא אמר ליה מאי מילי מעלייתא אמריתו המוכר שדה לאשתו קנתה ולא אמרינן לגלויי זוזי הוא דבעי אמר ליה פשיטא דל זוזי מהכא ותיקני בשטרא מי לא תנן ג) ב נכסים שיש להן אחריות נקנין בכסף ובשטר ובחזקה אמר ליה ולאו איתמר עלה אמר שמואל לא שנו אלא בשטר מתנה ג אבל בשטר מכר לא קנה עד שיתן לו דמיה ולאו מותיב רב המנונא ג) ד בשטר כיצד כתב לו על הנייר או על החרס אע"פ שאין בו שוה פרוטה שדי מכורה לך שדי (א) קנויה לך הרי זו מכורה ונתונה ולאו הוא מותיב לה והוא מפרק לה ה במוכר שדהו מפני רעתה ד) (רב ביבי מסיים בה משמיה דרב נחמן) ורב אשי אמר במתנה בקש ליתנה לו ולמה כתב לו בלשון מכר כדי ליפות כחו מיתיבי ו לוה מן העבד ושחררו מן האשה וגרשה אין להן עליו כלום מאי טעמא לאו משום דאמרינן לגלויי זוזי הוא דבעי שאני התם דלא ניחא ליה לשווייה נפשיה א) עבד לוה לאיש מלוה שלח רב הונא בר אבין המוכר שדה לאשתו קנתה ובעל

רשב"ם

ודייני גולה. שמואל וקרנא בפרק ראשון דסנהדרין (דף יז: ע"ש): מחזיקין. (ג) והיא לה למחות: מסתברא אמרי. היכא דהויא מקלת חזקה בחיי בעלה ושלש לאחר מיתת הבעל כמו שפירש רב יוסף לעיל התם הוא דמסתברא דמחזיקין דהא רב גופיה ה"ק לעיל אשת איש צריכה למחות דמשמע דמחזיקין ומיהו דייני גולה (ג) בכל ענין פליגי אדרב: כדרב יוסף. גמרא הוא שקילר דברי רב אבל רב לא הזכיר רב יוסף שהרי קדם לו רב הרבה דורות: כיון דאית לה מזוני. מהבעל: מזוני הוא דקאכלה. הכל יודעין לפירות יורדת והלכך לא מיחה בעל: דיחד לה. בעל קרקע אחריתי למזונות ואפי' הכי לא קפיד בעל אי אכלה טפי והלכך לית לה חזקה: ודייק חזקה הוא דלית לה. בלא שטר: הא ראיה יש. אם יש לה שטר מכירה מבעל הוי מקחה קיים: לימא. הבעל אע"פ שהקרקע נקנה בכסף מעות הללו שקבלתי ממנה לא קני לה הקרקע: לגלויי זוזי בעינא. מעות הטמינה ממני ונתכוונתי לגלות לי מעותיה ובחזקת מעות שלי לקחתים מידה ולא לשם מכר ולא לדעת קנין מכירה קבלתי' ולא גמרתי והקניתי: שמעת מינה המוכר כו'. ופלוגתא היא לקמן: אימא. דוק הכי: הא ראיה יש. אם יש לה שטר מתנה דהתם גמר ונתן לה דליכא גלויי זוזי: בתחומא. בתי מדרשות שלהן בסוף התחום היו כדי שיוכלו לבא שם בשבת מן העיירות שמסביב: א"ל. היכא דליכא שטר מכירה אפילו לגלויי זוזי מיכוין בקבלת המעות הוי קנין גמור דל זוזי מהכא ותיקני בשטר מכירה דגבי מעות הוא דאיכא למימר קבלת מעות הללו לא ליקני לגלויי זוזי נתכוין ולעצמו קבלם אבל גבי שטר המכירה לא שייך למימר הכי אלא הרי הוא כשטר מתנה דהכל מודין בו לקמן דקנתה דמה ריוח יש לו בכתיבת שטר המכירה אלא ודאי גמר והקנה לה והא ליכא למימר דאי לא כתב לך לא הוה יהבה זוזי ולגלויי זוזי נתכוין גם בכתיבת השטר דכל כך לא מסיק אינש אדעתיה: מי לא תנן כו'. וקס"ד דאפי' בשטר מכירה קאמר דקני בלא נתינת מעות דכיון דכתב לו שטר מכירה אין יכולין עוד לחזור זה בזה ומעות חייב לו הלוקח למוכר: ולאו איתמר עלה. דבשטר מתנה מיירי אבל שטר מכר לא קנה. וא"ל רב הונא לרב נחמן ולאו מותיב רב המנונא לשמואל כו' אלמא שטר מכר נמי קנה והכתי מאי מילי מעלייתא: הרי זו מכורה או נתונה. ואמר ליה רב נחמן לאו אמרינן התם בפרק ראשון דקידושין דרב המנונא מותיב לה וגם מפרק לה דהך ברייתא דקתני שטר מכר קונה במוכר שדהו מפני רעתה דבההיא ודאי גמר ומקנה מיד בשטר ומעות ליהוו מלוה גבי דלוקח עד דמטבע ליה אבל בשאר קרקעות לא קנו בשטר עד דיהיב זוזי כשמואל והכתי היכא מילי מעלייתא: ה"ג במסכת קידושין רב אשי אמר במתנה ביקש ליתן לו כו'. ואתקפתא דהך ברייתא דהויה קשיא לשמואל קאי ובא רב אשי לומר דהך ברייתא לא בשטר מכר איירי כלל אלא בשטר מתנה ודבר הרגיל הוא שכותבין בשטר מתנה לשון מכר ליפות כחו של מקבל מתנה שאם יערערו עליו יבא הנותן לפצותו כדין מוכר דלא ליהוי תרעומת עילויה וה"ק שדי מכורה לך וגם נתונה תהיה לך הרי זו מכורה להיות אחריותה על הנותן כדין מוכר וגם נתונה היא וליח בה משום דינא דבר מצרא דאמרינן בבבא מציעא (דף קח:) מתנה לית בה משום דינא דבר מצרא והיינו דליכא יפוי כח למכר ומתנה: ה"ג ורב אשי אמר במתנה כו': לוה מן העבד. וכתב שטר מלוה ושיעבד לו נכסיו: לגלויי זוזי הוא. לשיעבד לו נכסיו: דלא משוי נפשיה כו'. אין סהדי דשום אדם לא יהיה ברצונו עבד לוה אם יכול להפטר בשום ענין והלכך ליכא למימר לגלויי זוזי הוא דבעי אבל גבי מכר גמר ומקנה שהרי אינו נעשה עבד לוה בהך שטר מכירה כלל ואפילו קבל עליו אחריות עדיין לא נטרפה מן הלוקח דליהוי עבד לוה לגבי לוקח: שלח רב הונא בר אבא. לתלמידי בית המדרש:

והבעל

תוספות

הא ראיה יש בשטר מתנה. ה"ה דה"מ למימר בשטר הודאה דלא שייך ביה גלויי זוזי: דל זוזי מהכא ותיקני ליה בשטר. במקום שכותבין שטר היו וקאמר דבמקום הזה לא מהניא שמעתיה מידי אע"ג דמהניא במקום שאין כותבין ומיהו אף במקום שכותבין שייך למימר דנפקא מינה היכא דאמר אי בעינן בשטרא איקני ואי בעינן (ד) בכספא איקני דקני בכספא אע"פ שלא כתב לו השטר אי נמי כגון שכתב השטר תחלה ואח"כ נתנה דמים דלא אמר לגלויי זוזי הוא דבעי לא קנתה: כתב לו על הנייר או על החרס. וכן תניא לענין קידושין כתב לה על הנייר או על החרס אע"פ שאין בו שוה פרוטה בתך מקודשת לי כו'. אומר ר"ת דלאו דוקא דאמר עדי מסירה כרתי דלר' מאיר כיון שצריך שיחתמו עדים בשטר קידושין כדאמר בפ"ב דקידושין (דף מח. ושם) אמר ר"ל כגון שקדשה בשטר שאין עליו עדים ור"מ לטעמיה דאמר עדי חתימה כרתי א"כ לא מהניא חתימה על דבר שיכול להזדייף כדתנן בפ"ב דגיטין (דף כב:) אין כותבין לא על הנייר כו' ואפי' איכא עדי מסירה לא מהני לר"מ דלריך שיהא מוכיח מתוכו כדאמר בריש כל הגט (שם דף כד:) גבי כתב לגרש את הגדולה דלר"מ אפילו גדולה לא מצי מגרש משום דאין מוכח מתוכו הי מינייהו מגרש ואי"מ והא אמר בפ"ב דגיטין (דף כב:) דלא הכשיר ר' אלעזר אלא בגיטין ולא הכשיר אלא לאלתר אבל בשאר שטרות (ה) משמע דלא הכשיר אפילו לאלתר וי"ל דהכי בעי למימר דלא הכשיר רבי אלעזר אלא בגיטין ודכותייהו כמו שדה מכורה לך דהכא וכן ההיא דקידושין דלא נכתבו אלא לקנות שדה והאשה דומיא דגיטי שאין עשויין עיקרן לראיה אלא להתגרש אבל שטרות העומדים לראיה לא ועי"ל דהכא ובקידושין לא איירי אלא בכתב ידו כדאמר הוליא עליו כתב ידו כו' וזה אינו יכול להזדייף שהיה ניכר שאין זה כתב ידו: אע"פ שאין בו שוה פרוטה. תימה דמאי רבותא הוא שוה פרוטה בשלמא גבי קידושין נקט כתב לה על הנייר או על החרס אע"פ שאין בו שוה פרוטה דרבותא היא דאע"פ שאינה מקודשת מתורת כסף כיון שאין בו שוה פרוטה מקודשת מתורת שטר אבל הכא גבי מוכר אפי' יש בו שוה פרוטה אינו קונה מתורת כסף שהרי מוכר נותן שטר ולא לוקח ואין קרקע נקנה אגב כסף: ולמה כתב בלשון מכר כדי ליפות את כחו. להיות אחריות על הנותן כדין מוכר ופ"ה שכתב לו בשטר כל זה שדי מכורה לך וגם שדי נתונה וכתב לשון מתנה משום דינא דבר מצרא וקשה דאמר בהמקבל (ב"מ דף קח:) מתנה דאית בה אחריות יש בה משום דינא דבר מצרא ועוד קשה לר"ת שדי שדי תרי זימני למה לי ואור"ת וכן ר"י דלא מיירי בשכותב שניהן אלא בשכותב מכורה או נתונה וקאמר אפי' בשכתב מכורה במתנה בקש ליתנה לו והא דכתב בלשון מכר כדי לייפות את כחו שמקבל עליו אחריות ועי"ל דשני שטרות כותב לו בחד לשון מכירה ובחד לשון נתינה ואם יצטרך לדינא דבר מצרא יראה של נתינה ולא של מכירה ואם צריך לאחריות יראה של מכירה ועי"ל דאפי' כתיבי תרוייהו בשטר אחד יפה כחו מה שכתב בלשון מתנה לענין הא דתנן לקמן בהמוכר את הבית (דף עא.) בד"א במוכר אבל בנותן נותן את כולן והכי איתא בירושלמי פ"ק דקידושין ועי"ל דנפקא מינה מה שכתב בלשון מתנה שאין צריך ליתן דמים ומיהו קשה לטעם זה דלמאי בעי בשטר באיקני סגי: לוה מן העבד ושחררו כו'. תימה דמאי רבותא נקט ושחררו וגרשה פשיטא דאי אין להם עליו כלום בעודו תחתיו גם לכשיולאין אין להם עליו כלום ויש לומר דסלקא דעתיה דגמר ומקני להו שיקנו לאחר שישתחרר ותתגרש:

לא

עין משפט נר מצוה

רב א מיי' פי"ג מהל' טוען הלכה ח סמג עשין לה טוש"ע ח"מ סי' קמט סעיף ט:

רג ב מיי' פ"א מהל' מכירה הל' ג ופ"ג מהל' זכייה הל' א סמג עשין פב טוש"ע ח"מ סי' קל סעי' א וסי' רמא סעיף א:

רד ג מיי' פ"א מהל' מכירה הלכה ז סמג שם טוש"ע ח"מ סי' קלא סעיף ב:

רה ד מיי' שם טוש"ע שם ס"א:

רו ה מיי' שם טוש"ע שם ס"ב:

רז ו מיי' פ"ב מהל' מלוה הלכה ח טוש"ע אה"ע סי' פו סעי' ב:

רבינו גרשום

יחזיק לאחר מיתת בעלה ג' שנים: דייני גולה. שמואל וקרנא: הדר ביה מר משמעתא. דאמר לעיל האמר רב אין מחזיקין: מסתבר טעמייהו אמרי. משום דס"ל כתירוץ דרב יוסף דאמר לעולם באחר וכו': פיס' מזוני הוא דקא אכלה. ולא משום דמוחזקת היא בה: לא צריכא כגון דיחד לה ארע' אחריתי למזונותי'. והחזיקה באחרת אפילו הכי לא הויא חזקה דבעל גבי אשתו שתיק: הא מייתי ראיה. דזבנה ניהלה יש לה חזקה אמאי נימא הבעל משום הכי זבינתה ניהלה כדי לגלויי לי זוזי דחזו לה דהות מטמרא מינאי ולהכי זבינתה ניהלה ולא משום מכירה גמורה דהא מה שקנתה אשה קנה בעלה. ש"מ מדלא מצי למימר הכי איכא למישמע מינה דהמוכר שדהו לאשתו קנתה ולא אמרי' לגלויי זוזי הוא דבעי ואי מייתא ראיה הויא חזקה. לעולם המוכר לאשתו א) קנתה ולא אמרי' לגלויי זוזי הוא דבעי. והאי דדייקת הא ראיה יש לה היינו בשטר מתנה דאי מייתא ראיה דיהבה לה במתנה ראייתה ראייה: בתחומא. בבית המדרש: אמר ליה. המוכר שדהו לאשתו וכו' ולא אמרי' לגלויי זוזי בעי: אמר ליה מאי מעלייתא. פשיטא דקנתה: דל זוזי מהכא. דאפי' לא יהבה ניהליה זוזי אפי' הכי קנתה בשטר דקא גמר ומקנה לה בשטר. דתנן כו' בכסף בלא שטר ובשטר בלא כסף ולא מצי למיהדר בהן: עד שיתן דמים. ב) ואי אמרי' הכא לא קנתה היינו טעמא משום דלגלויי זוזי בעי. ומקשי' ולא. דלא קנה עד דיהיב זוזי. ומתיב וכו' הרי זה מכורה ונתונה. ואע"ג דלא נתן דמים אלמא משום דנתינת השטר קנה. הכא נמי דל זוזי מהכא ותקני בשטרא: במוכר שדהו מפני רעתה. שאין בה תועלת ומחמת שהיא רעה קא גמר ויהבה ניהליה אע"ג דלא קיבל דמים. אבל בעלמא לא קנה עד שיתן דמים. והכי נמי במוכר שדהו לאשתו לא קנתה דמצי אמר לגלויי זוזי הוא דעבדי משום הכי איצטריך להו למימר בתחומא דקנתה ולא מצי אמר לגלויי זוזי

עבדא. ורב ביבי מסיים בה משמיה דרב נחמן דהמוכר שדהו לאשתו קנתה משום האי טעמא משום דבמתנה ביקש ליתן לה ולמה כתב לה בלשון מכירה כדי ליפות כחה דדעתו קרובה אצלה. דבשטר מכירה כותבין בו אחריות. ובמסכת קידושין כתב ורב אשי אמר במתנה בקש ליתן לו וכו' וקאי אמוכר שדהו מפני רעתה: אין להן עליו כלום. דפטור מלשלם: מאי טעמא לאו משום דאמרינן לגלויי זוזי הוא דבעיד דלוה מהן ולא גמר לפרוע להן. ומקשי' לרב נחמן דאמר לא אמרינן לגלויי זוזי עבד. לגבי הלוואה שאני דלא גמר לשעביד נפשיה למיהוי עבד לאשתו או לעבדו. דמידע ידע דעבד לוה לאיש מלוה ולא עבד

מסורת הש"ס

א) [ב"ק כ. עמ"ש על הגליון בשם הערוך], ב) קדושין כו. [לקמן פו.], ג) קדושין כו., ד) רש"ל מ"ז:

הגהות הב"ח

(א) גמ' שדי מכורה לך שדי נתונה לך: (ב) רשב"ם ד"ה מחזיקין דהיא: (ג) ד"ה מסתברא וכו' בכל ענין פליגי: (ד) תוס' ד"ה דל וכו' אי בעינא בשטרא איקני ואי בעינא: (ה) ד"ה כתב וכו' בשאר שטרות לא משמע:

תורה אור השלם

א) עָשִׁיר בְּרָשִׁים יִמְשׁוֹל וְעֶבֶד לֹוֶה לְאִישׁ מַלְוֶה: [משלי כב, ז]

ליקוטי רש"י

לא הוה מר גבן באורתא בתחומא. לא היית קרוב אללנו שתוכל לבא לי"א בתחומא בבית המדרש ראשון שמעתי [ב"ק כ.]. כלומר אבל על שלא היית אמש בשבת אללנו בתוך התחום שתוכל לבא לבית המדרש ולשמוע [זבחים ב:]. נכסים שיש להן אחריות וכו'. קרקעות [כתובות לד:]. היינו קרקעות שאחריות כל אדם הלוה והנושא בחבירו עליהן לפי שקיימין ועומדין לפיכך נסמכין עליהן [קידושין כו.]. והקרקעות אחריות כל מלוה וחוב וכתובה נסמכין עליהן לפי שאין לקיה שולטת בהן ואין אובדין [רשב"ם לקמן קנ:]. שקיימין לעולם. בכסף. בממון מעות. בשטר. אם כתב לו שדי מכורה לך או נתונה לך ומסר לו את השטר. ובחזקה. נעל וגדר ופרץ כל שהוא והתם (קידושין דף כו.) יליף טעמא מקראי [רשב"ם שם פו.]. רפק ביה פורתא או דיש אמלרי או נעל או פרץ כל שהוא. עד שיתן לו דמיה. דלא גמר מוכר ומקנה עד דקביל דמים ואע"ג דקביל דמים בעי שטרא אלא היכא דפריש ודאמרינן לעיל. הרי זו מכורה ונתונה. קא סלקא דעתך או או קתני. מפני רעתה. דניחא ליה דלקנייה ליה שטרא ללוקח כי היכי דלא מצי למיהדר ביה. רב אשי אמר. הך מתני' בנותן מתנה מיירי וכולה חדא היא ולאו או או קתני אלא כך וכך כתב לו שדי מכורה ונתונה לך לייפות את כחו שאם יגבנה בעל חוב של נותן מתנה ישוב עליו לתבוע ממנו דמים המפורשים [קידושין שם].

חשק שלמה על רבינו גרשום

א) נראה דל"ל לא קנתה דאמרינן לגלויי זוזי וכו'. ב) נראה דל"ל ומשו"ה אי אמרינן דקנתה היינו טעמא משום דלא אמרינן לגלויי זוזי בעי.

ובעל אוכל פירות ברם רבי אבא ורבי אבהו וכל גדולי הדור אמרו במתנה בקש ליתנו לה ולמה כתב לה [א] לשום מכר כדי ליפות את כחה מיתיבי לוה מן העבד ושחררו מן האשה וגרשה אין להן עליו כלום מ"ט לאו משום דאמרי לגלויי זוזי הוא דבעא שאני התם דלא (א) לישוי איניש עבד לוה לאיש מלוה אמר רב המוכר שדה לאשתו קנתה והבעל אוכל פירות במתנה קנתה ואין הבעל אוכל פירות ורבי אלעזר אמר אחד זה ואחד זה קנתה ואין הבעל אוכל פירות עבד רב חסדא עובדא כרבי אלעזר אמרו ליה [ב] רבן עוקבא [ג] ורבן נחמיה בני בנתיה דרב (ב) לרב חסדא שביק מר רברבי ועביד כזוטרי א"ל (ג) ואנא נמי כרברבי עבדי דכי אתא רבין אמר ר' יוחנן אחד זה ואחד זה קנתה ואין הבעל אוכל פירות אמר רבא הלכתא [א] המוכר שדה לאשתו לא קנתה והבעל אוכל פירות [ב] במתנה קנתה ואין הבעל אוכל פירות תרתי לא קשיא [ג] כאן במעות טמונין כאן במעות שאין טמונין דאמר רב יהודה מעות טמונין לא קנתה מעות שאינן טמונין קנתה: ת"ר [ד] אין מקבלין פקדונות לא מן הנשים ולא מן העבדים ולא מן התינוקות קבל מן האשה יחזיר לאשה ואם מתה יחזיר לבעלה קבל מן העבד יחזיר לעבד ואם מת יחזיר לרבו

קבל

רשב"ם

והבעל אוכל פירות. דלא גרע מנכסים שנפלו לה בירושה: במתנה בקש ליתן לה. ולא יאכל פירות כדאמרי' לקמן במתנה קנתה ואין הבעל אוכל פירות ומיהו במוכר לחבירו אין לומר כן שאינו אוהבו כל כך: מיתיבי כו'. הכיא קשיא לדעיל ולשני המימרות נקשית בבית המדרש: במתנה קנתה ואין הבעל אוכל פירות. דעתו בעין יפה נותן: רברבי. רב שקדם לרבי יוחנן רבו של רבי אלעזר כדאיתא בשמעתא בחולין (דף נד.) דלכל זמן שהיה רב קיים הוה שלח ליה רבי יוחנן לקדם רבינו שבבבל ועוד דאמר ליה לריש לקיש [ז] שכל אותן הימים היה הוא בישיבה ואני בעמידה ועוד דאמרי' בעירובין (דף יג: ע"ש) אמר [ע"ש] רב הלל (ד) דממדדן מתגרביה טפי משום דחזיתיה לרבי מאיר מאחוריה: כזוטרי. ר' אלעזר שהיה תלמידו של רבי יוחנן ואע"ג דרבי אבא ורבי אבהו וכל גדולי הדור חבריהם דאמרי' לעיל במתנה בקש ליתן לה כו' סבירא להו כר' אלעזר דאין הבעל אוכל פירות אינהו נמי זוטרי נינהו לגבי רב שתלמידי רבי יוחנן היו: כרברבי עבדי. ר' יוחנן שהיה חבירו של רב: תרתי. בתמיה שני דבריו של רבא סותרין זה את זה לא קנתה משמע לא גוף ולא פירות דלגלויי זוזי הוא דבעי והבעל אוכל פירות משמע שקנתה גוף הקרקע דלאו לגלויי זוזי הוא דבעי: במעות טמונין. שלא היו ידועין ומפורסמים לבעל לא קנתה דלגלויי זוזי הוא דבעי: מעות שאין טמונין. קנתה והבעל אוכל פירות דליכא גלויי זוזי שהרי גלויין ועומדין הן: לא מן הנשים כו'. דאיכא למימר גנבום לבעליהן ולאדוניהם ותינוקות נמי שמא גנבו מבית בעל הבית שהם דרים שם ואסור לסייע ידי עוברי עבירה וכשלא יקבלו מהם יחזירו למקום שגנבו (ה) שם: יחזיר לאשה. ולא לבעל דאין לנו להחזיקה בגנבתה: יחזיר לבעלה. שאפי' אם ניתן לה ממון זה על מנת שאין לבעלה רשות בה מכיון שמתה יורשה בעלה שהבעל יורש את אשתו והלכך יחזיר לבעל דממה נפשך עכשיו הרי הוא של בעלה: יחזיר לרבו. דמסתמא כל מה שקנה עבד קנה רבו ונראה בעיני דהוא הדין אם נשתחרר העבד ואח"כ מת יחזיר לרבו שהרי עבד היה כשהפקיד לזה וסתם עבדים גזלנין הן אבל אם נתגרשה האשה ואחר כך מתה יחזיר ליורשיה ולא לבעלה דמשנתגרשה אין הבעל יורשה:

קבל

תוספות

[י] **לא** ניחא ליה דליהוי עבד לוה כו'. ודוקא נקט לוה אבל מכר לא ומשום אשה הוא דנקט לוה אבל גבי עבד אין חילוק בין לוה למכר דמה שקנה עבד קנה רבו: **[ברם]** רבינו תם לא גריס ברם ר' אבא אלא גריס ר' אבא ורבי אבהו וכל גדולי הדור כו' כדי ליפות את כחו. ולא גרים את כחה אלא ליפות את כחו ופירש שיאכל הוא את הפירות והשתא מייתי רב הונא בר אבין סייעתא לדבריו דתימה הוא לומר שהיה שולא שכל גדולי הדור חולקין עליו שאם כן אין ממש בדבריו ואין מתיישב לר"י גירסתו דא"כ מה צריך לומר במתנה בקש ליתן לה ונראה לר"י גירסת הספרים (ו) ברם ר' אבא וליפות כחה ופליגי עליה וסברי דמוכר לאשתו לא קנתה דלגלויי זוזי הוא דבעי וסברי כרב הונא דאמר דל זוזי מהכא ותיקני בשטר ומה שקונה בשטר אינו אלא מתנה כיון דלגלויי זוזי הוא דבעי ולא קנתה בזוזי ומה שכתב בלשון מכר לא כתב אלא ליפות את כחה ופירוש רבינו תם יש ליישב ולפרש בקש ליתן לה לענין זה שבמתנה (ז) נתן את כולן ועוד יש ליישב פירוש ר"ת במתנה בקש כו' דאפילו למאן דאמר קנתה במוכר לאשתו ולא אמר לגלויי זוזי הוא דבעי לא קנתה אלא משום דבמתנה נתן לה דהא אין כאן מכר שלא נתנה לו כלום שהדמים הן שלו בלאו הכי ואע"פ שאין יכול להוציא ממנה בדין מ"מ אם תקף ממנה או הוציא מידה דרך ערמה הם שלו כדאמרינן בסמוך וא"כ השתא שהוציאן דרך מכר הם שלו ואין כאן מכר והלכך למ"ד קנתה לא קנתה אלא משום דבמתנה בקש לתת לה והא דכתב לה בלשון מכר כדי ליפות את כחו לענין שיאכל הפירות כי המכר מבטל הקנין דהא אין כאן מכר כדפי' ולענין שדה הויא מתנה וקנתה ולענין פירות הוי מכר ולא קנתה: **במתנה** קנתה ואין הבעל אוכל פירות. תימה דאמר בגיטין בפ' הזורק (דף עז: ושם ד"ה מה) גבי ההוא שכיב מרע דכתיב גט לדביתהו בהדי פניא דמעלי שבתא כו' אתא לקמיה דרבא אמר ליקני לה ההוא אתרא דאית בה גיטא כו' אמר רב עילש מה שקנתה אשה קנה בעלה איכסיף ומאי קושיא והא במתנה אין הבעל אוכל פירות א"כ לא קנה בעלה ואומר רבינו תם דאין תלוי באכילת פירות למיקרי חצרה דהא רבא סבר כריש לקיש (לקמן דף קלו:) דקנין פירות לאו כקנין הגוף דמי ואפילו יש לבעל פירות אינו מפקיע כח האשה שהגוף שלה ומתגרשת שפיר אלא בהא תליא מילתא דלא מיקרי חצרה לענין זכיה אלא כשמוכרת ונותנת קיים הלכך כשנתן לה הבעל אע"ג דאין אוכל פירות כיון שאם מכרה ונתנה אינו קיים לא מיקרי חצרה דאדעתא דהכי שתמכור ותתן לא יהיב לה ומייתי ראיה דהתם בריש הזורק גבי זרק לה בחצרה פריך חצרה מה שקנתה אשה קנה בעלה ומשני כגון שכתב לה דין ודברים אין לי בנכסיך אע"ג דכשכתב לה נמי הכי יש לבעל פירי עד שיכתוב לה ובפירותיהן כדתנן בכתובות (כתובות דף פג.) אפילו הכי חשיב חצרה כיון שאם מכרה ונתנה קיים כדתנן בהכותב ומיהו אינה ראיה דאע"ג דאינו מזכיר ובפירותיהן הכי בעי למימר כדאשכחן לעיל [ז] גבי אין לאיש חזקה בנכסי אשתו וא"ת אע"ג דאינה יכולה למכור (ח) תקני לה לגט מידי דהוה אשכירות דאמר (במסכת מע"ש פ"ה מ"ט) גבי ר"ג מעשר (שני) נתון ליהושע ומקומו מושכר לו ובהמוכר את הספינה (לקמן דף פד:) מדד ולא משך לא קנה ואם היה פיקח שוכר את מקומו ואומר רבינו תם דגדול קנינו של שוכר מזה שאפי' מת בתוך הזמן המקום מושכר ליורשיו עד הזמן משא"כ באשה שאם מכרה ונתנה הבעל מוציא מיד הלקוחות ובירושלמי לא משמע כפר"ת דפריך בריש הזורק (גיטין דף עז.) וגנתה וחצרה אינן משתעבדות לאיש לאכילת פירות ומשני ר' יוחנן בשם ר' ינאי עד שיכתוב לה דין ודברים אין לי בנכסיך ובפירותיהן ומשמע מדפריך מפירות דבפירות הדבר תלוי ולא במה שאינה יכולה למכור ור"י אמר דאפי' תלויה הזכייה בפירות מ"מ פריך שפיר התם מה שקנתה אשה קנה בעלה שלא היה נותן לה הבעל מקום הגט אלא משאיל ודוקא במתנה הוא דקאמר דקנתה ואין הבעל אוכל פירות ועוד אומר ר"י דהא דאמר הכא במתנה קנתה ואין הבעל אוכל פירות היינו דוקא שאינו אוכלם אבל כנכסי מלוג הם אותם פירות וילקח בהם קרקע ויאכל הפירות ומשום הכי פריך התם שפיר מה שקנתה אשה קנה בעלה:

קבל מן האשה יחזיר לאשה. נראה דאם אמרה האשה תן לפלוני שהם שלו דנותן לו דנאמנת היא במיגו דאי בעיא שקלה איהי מיניה ויהבה ליה ואפי' אומר הבעל שהממון שלו אין לו כח להוציא מידה מדקאמר יחזיר לאשה דהוה ליה למימר יודיע לבעל (ט) דאם היה כח ביד הבעל להוציא מידה כשאומר שהוא שלו והא דמפליג בסמוך בדביתהו דרבה בר בר חנה בין מהימנא בין לא מהימנא הנ"מ בשעת מיתתה דלית לה מיגו דאי בעי שקלה מיניה ויהבה למי שרוצה ואם תקף הבעל מידה שוב אינה יכולה להוציא מידו ולומר של פלוני הם כדאמר לעיל לוה מן האשה וגרשה אין לה עליו כלום ואם היתה נאמנת לומר של פלוני הם תהא (י) נאמנת לומר שלי הם במיגו דאי בעי אמרה אחרים הפקידו בידי דאינה צריכה לומר מי הם האחרים וישאר הממון לעולם בידה ודוקא במעות טמונות דלוה מן האשה דלעיל במעות טמונות איירי מדקאמר לגלויי זוזי הוא דבעי אבל מעות שאינן טמונות יש לה עליו וכן אם תקף מוציאין מידו ועוד מדקאמר רבא דבמעות שאינן טמונות קנתה משמע דאם תקף מוציאין אותן מידו דאם אין מוציאין אמאי קנתה הא יכול לומר להוציא מידה נתכוונתי כי לא יכולתי להוציא מידה בענין אחר ואפי' בב"ד ואם היא נושאת ונותנת בתוך הבית אינה נאמנת לומר לא שלי ולא של פלוני הם כדאמר לקמן (דף נב:) וכן האשה שהיא נושאת ונותנת כו' ואמרה שלי הם עליה להביא ראיה ולא מהימנינן לה במיגו דאי בעיא אמרה שהיא נפקדת משל אחרים ומיהו היכא שאינה נושאת ונותנת בחיי בעלה וממון בעלה מצוי בידה יש להסתפק אם חשבינן לה כאילו נושאת ונותנת אם לאו:

קבל

עין משפט נר מצוה

רח א מיי' פכ"ב מהל' אישות הל' כט סמג עשין מח טוש"ע אה"ע סי' פה סעי' ט:

רט ב מיי' שם הל' כ טוש"ע שם סעי' ז:

רי ג מיי' שם הלכה כט טוש"ע שם ס"ט:

ריא ד מיי' פ"ו מהל' פקדון הלכה י ופכ"ב מהלכות אישות הל' לב סמג עשין פה טוש"ע חו"מ סי' פו סעי' א ועיין בטור [וברב אלפס עוד בב"ק דף פז.]:

רבינו גרשום

עבד אלא דבעי לגלויי ליה זוזיהו: וכל גדולי הדור אמרו. ודאי קנתה דלא אמרינן לגלויי זוזי עבד משום דבמתנה בקש ליתן לה: ובעל אוכל פירות. כנכסי מלוג: קנתה ואין הבעל אוכל פירות. משום דכולה שדה בין גוף ובין פירות יהיב לה: שבק מר רברבי. דהיינו רב ורב הונא דאמרי לעיל דקנתה ובעל אוכל פירות: ועבדת כזוטרי. כר' אלעזר דהוה תלמידיה דרב: כרברבי. כר' יוחנן: תרתי. קאמר והלא חדא סתרא לאידך דאי לא קנתה אמאי איצטריך למימר הבעל אוכל פירות אפי' גוף הקרקע נמי שלו הוה: במעות טמונים. שטמנתם ממנו לא קנתה והכל שלו משום דלגלויי זוזי הוא דעבד. אבל במעות שאינם טמונים קנתה והבעל אוכל פירות: לא מן הנשים וכו'. דאיכא למימר גנבין לבעליהן ולאדוניהם:

מסורת הש"ס

א) [ס"א לשון], ב) [נ"ל רבנא וכ"א לקמן בתוס' קמט. ד"ה רב ובחולין נג.], ג) [נ"ל ורבנא], ד) [חולין נד.], ה) הוא רבי ולא רב ועיין רש"ג, ו) שייך לעמוד הקודם, ז) [דף מט. ושם ד"ה דכתבן]:

הגהות הב"ח

(א) גמ' שאני התם דלא משוי איניש נפשיה עבד: (ב) שם בני בנתיה דרב חסדא לרב חסדא: (ג) שם א"ל אנא נמי כנ"ל ואות ו' נמחק: (ד) רשב"ם ד"ה רברבי וכו' אמר רב הא דממדדנא. נ"ב כך הוא בפ"ק דעירובין דף י"ג אבל הסמ"ג בסוף הלכות י"ט מביא מן הירושלמי דרבי הוא שאמר כן ע"ש: (ה) ד"ה לא מן וכו' שגנבו משם הס"ד: (ו) תוס' ד"ה ברם וכו' ונראה לר"י גי' הספרים דגרסי רבי אבא אמר וליפות כחה: (ז) בא"ד לענין זה שבמתנה נתן. נ"ב כדתנן לקמן המוכר את הבית והתוס' הביאו בדף זה סוף ע"א: (ח) ד"ה במתנה וכו' וא"ת אע"ג דאינה יכולה למכור מכל מקום תקני לה: (ט) ד"ה קבל וכו' ולא ידיע לבעל בה כל"ל ואות ד' נמחק: (י) בא"ד דהא נמי נאמנת לומר שלי:

ליקוטי רש"י

ובעל אוכל פירות. מה שקנתה אשה קנה בעלה. לפירות להשתמש בה [גיטין עז.].

וּבַעַל אוֹכֵל פֵּירוֹת – **and the husband receives produce.**[1] בְּרַם רַבִּי אַבָּא וְרַבִּי אַבָּהוּ וְכָל גְּדוֹלֵי הַדּוֹר אָמְרוּ – **However, R' Abba, R' Abahu and all the great** Torah scholars **of the generation said** that the husband is not entitled to eat the produce, בְּמַתָּנָה בִּקֵּשׁ לִיתְּנוֹ לָהּ – for we assume that **he** actually **wished to give her [the field] as a gift,** and a husband does not receive produce from the gifts he bestows on his wife. וְלָמָּה כָּתַב לָהּ לְשׁוּם מֶכֶר – If so, **why did he record** it **for her as a sale?** כְּדֵי לְיַפּוֹת אֶת כֹּחָהּ – **In order to enhance her rights** and give her the prerogatives of a buyer.[2]

Rav Huna bar Avin and the other scholars differ whether the transaction is to be construed as a sale or as a gift. All agree, however, that it is binding. Clearly, they hold that we do not accept the argument that the husband intended only to recover money that had been hidden from him.[3] The Gemara questions this:

מֵיתִיבֵי – **They challenged this from the** following **Baraisa:** לָוָה מִן הָעֶבֶד – If ONE BORROWED money FROM [HIS] Canaanite SLAVE and recorded the loan in a document, וְשִׁחְרְרוֹ – AND HE subsequently EMANCIPATED HIM, מִן הָאִשָּׁה – or if he borrowed money FROM [HIS WIFE] and recorded the loan, וְגֵרְשָׁהּ – AND HE subsequently DIVORCED HER: אֵין לָהֶן עָלָיו כְּלוּם – THEY HAVE NO monetary claim AGAINST HIM, i.e. they cannot collect from him. מַאי טַעְמָא – **What is the reason** for this? לָאו מִשּׁוּם דְּאָמְרִי – **Is it not because we say** that לְגַלּוּיֵי זוּזֵי הוּא דִּבְעָא – **he intended** only **to uncover money** they had hidden from him, but he never meant to commit himself to repay? This Baraisa appears to contradict the underlying assumption of all these Amoraim. – ? –

The Gemara answers:

שָׁאנֵי הָתָם – **There,** in the case of the Baraisa, which deals with borrowing, **it is different,** i.e. the assumption that he never meant to commit himself is more plausible, דְּלָא לִישַׁוֵּי אִינִישׁ – **so that we should not** have to **characterize the person as** someone who would make himself, "עֶבֶד לֹוֶה לְאִישׁ מַלְוֶה" – ***a borrower*** who ***is a servant to the lender.***[4]

The Gemara records other statements regarding this issue:

אָמַר רַב – **Rav said:** הַמּוֹכֵר שָׂדֶה לְאִשְׁתּוֹ – **If one sells a field to his wife,** קָנְתָה – **she acquires** the field, וְהַבַּעַל אוֹכֵל פֵּירוֹת – **and the husband receives produce,** as Rav Huna bar Avin said.[5] בְּמַתָּנָה – If, however, he gave her the field **as a gift,** קָנְתָה – **she acquires** the field, וְאֵין הַבַּעַל אוֹכֵל פֵּירוֹת – **and the husband does not receive produce.**[6] וְרַבִּי אֶלְעָזָר אָמַר – **But R' Elazar says:** אֶחָד זֶה וְאֶחָד זֶה – **In either case,** קָנְתָה – **she acquires** the field, וְאֵין הַבַּעַל אוֹכֵל פֵּירוֹת – **and the husband does not receive produce.**[7]

The Gemara relates:

עָבַד רַב חִסְדָּא עוּבְדָא כְּרַבִּי אֶלְעָזָר – **Rav Chisda decided a case** that came before him **in accordance with R' Elazar's** ruling.[8] אָמְרוּ לֵיהּ רַבָּן עוּקְבָא וְרַבָּן נְחֶמְיָה בְּנֵי בְּנָתֵיהּ דְּרַב לְרַב חִסְדָּא – **Rabban Ukva and Rabban Nechemiah, the sons of Rav's daughter, said to Rav Chisda:** שָׁבִיק מַר רַבְרְבֵי – **The master has abandoned the greater** scholars (Rav) וְעָבֵיד כְּזוּטְרֵי – **and decided in favor of the lesser** scholars (R' Elazar)![9] You should have ruled in accordance with Rav that the husband does receive produce, because the transaction is presumed to have been a sale. אָמַר לְהוּ – **[Rav Chisda] answered them:** וַאֲנָא נַמִּי כְּרַבְרְבֵי עֲבַדִּי – **I too decided** the case in accordance **with great** scholars. דְּכִי אֲתָא רָבִין אָמַר רַבִּי יוֹחָנָן – **For when Ravin came** to Babylonia from Eretz Yisrael, **he said in the name of R' Yochanan:** אֶחָד זֶה וְאֶחָד זֶה – **In either case,** i.e. whether the transaction was a sale or a gift, קָנְתָה – **she acquires** the field, וְאֵין הַבַּעַל אוֹכֵל פֵּירוֹת – **and the husband does not receive produce.**[10]

The Gemara records the halachah:

אָמַר רָבָא – **Rava said:** הִלְכְתָא – **The halachah is** that הַמּוֹכֵר שָׂדֶה לְאִשְׁתּוֹ – if **one sells a field to his wife,** לֹא קָנְתָה – **she does not acquire** the field, וְהַבַּעַל אוֹכֵל פֵּירוֹת – **and the husband receives produce.** בְּמַתָּנָה – If, however, he gives her the field **as a gift,** קָנְתָה – **she acquires** the field, וְאֵין הַבַּעַל אוֹכֵל פֵּירוֹת – **and the husband does not receive produce.**

Rava made two statements with regard to a sale: (1) The woman does not acquire the field, and (2) the husband receives its produce. The Gemara points out that these statements are contradictory:

תַּרְתֵּי – Is it possible for **both** of these to be true? The statement that she does not acquire the field makes it clear that she acquires nothing, whereas the statement that the husband receives produce implies that she acquires the field.[11] – ? –

The Gemara answers:

לֹא קַשְׁיָא – This is **not a difficulty,** for the two statements were actually referring to two different cases. כָּאן – **Here,** where Rava stated that she does not acquire the field whatsoever, it is referring

NOTES

1. The Rabbinic decree granting a husband the right to the produce of his wife's property applies both to property she owned at the time of her marriage as well as to property she acquires during the marriage (e.g. through purchase or inheritance). Thus, if she purchases a property from her husband, he has the right to its produce (*Rashbam*).

2. Should the field ever be seized to satisfy a debt of his, the characterization of the gift as a sale would entitle her to recover her loss from him. See 51a note 25.

3. *Rabbeinu Gershom;* cf. *Ri* cited by *Tosafos.*

4. *Proverbs* 22:7. See 51a note 31 for the explanation.

The Gemara above (51a) asked the same question and gave the same answer. The question and answer are repeated here because Rav Nachman's statement (51a) and those of Rav Huna bar Avin and R' Abba etc. were discussed in the academy at different times, and the Baraisa was cited as a challenge each time (*Rashbam*).

5. Rav does not accept the argument that he engaged in the transaction only to recover hidden money. Thus, he considers a sale binding. The husband receives the produce as he would from any other land she bought during the marriage.

6. It is assumed that one who gives a gift, gives it generously, with the rights to the produce as well (*Rashbam*).

7. R' Elazar agrees with R' Abba, R' Abahu and the other scholars that the transaction is presumed to have been a gift with the enhancements of a sale. Thus, regardless of what the document says, the transaction is a gift and the husband is not entitled to produce.

8. A woman produced a bill of sale for a field she bought from her husband, and Rav Chisda ruled that the husband was not entitled to produce because the field had been a gift.

9. R' Yochanan was R' Elazar's teacher, and Rav was older than R' Yochanan. Indeed, R' Yochanan would address his letters to Rav with the title, "our teacher" (see *Chullin* 95b). Thus [based on the tenet that the earlier generations were generally greater, especially in the case of teachers and their disciples], Rav was clearly more distinguished than R' Elazar.

Similarly, although R' Abba, R' Abahu and all the great scholars of their generation concurred with R' Elazar's ruling, Rav was more distinguished than all of them, since they were all students of R' Yochanan. Thus, all of them were considered scholars of lesser stature relative to Rav (*Rashbam*).

10. [Although he afforded Rav the title of "our teacher,"] R' Yochanan was in fact Rav's colleague and was considered a scholar of equal caliber as him (*Rashbam*). [Indeed, the rule is that whenever there is a dispute between Rav and R' Yochanan, the halachah follows R' Yochanan.] Since R' Yochanan concurred with R' Elazar's position, Rav Chisda followed their ruling.

11. Or, to look at it another way, the statement that she does not acquire the field implies that we accept the argument that he never intended to sell, but only to uncover hidden money. The statement that the husband receives produce indicates that we reject this argument and consider the sale binding (*Rashbam*).

עין משפט נר מצוה

רח א מיי' פכ"ב מהל' אישות הל' כט סמג עשין מח טוש"ע אה"ע סי' פה סעי' ט:

רט ב מיי' שם הל' ס טוש"ע שם סעי' ז:

רי ג מיי' שם הלכה כט טוש"ע שם ס"ט:

ריא ד מיי' פ"ז מהל' פקדון הלכה י ופכ"ב מהלכות אישות הל' לב סמג עשין פה טוש"ע אה"ע סי' פו סעי' א ועיין בטור [וברב אלפס עוד בב"מ פ"ג דף פז.]:

רבינו גרשום

עבד אלא דבעי לגלויי ליה זוזיהו: **וכל גדולי הדור אמרו.** ודאי קנתה דלא אמרינן לגלויי זוזי עבד משום **דבמתנה בקש ליתן לה**: **ובעל אוכל פירות.** בנכסי מלוג: **קנתה ואין הבעל אוכל פירות.** משום דכולה שדה בין גוף ובין פירות יהיב לה: **שבק מר רברבי.** דהיינו רב ורב הונא דאמרי לעיל דקנתה ובעל אוכל פירות: **ועבדת כזוטרי.** כר' אלעזר דהוה תלמידיה דרב: **כרברבי.** ר' יוחנן: **תרתי.** קאמר והלא חדא סתרא לאידך דאי לא קנתה אמאי איצטריך למימר הבעל אוכל פירות אפי' גוף הקרקע נמי שלו הוה: **במעות טמונים.** שמטמנת ממנו **לא קנתה** והכל שלו משום דלגלויי זוזי הוא דעבד. אבל **במעות שאינם טמונים קנתה** והבעל אוכל פירות: **לא מן הנשים וכו'.** דאיכא למימר גונבין לבעליהן ולאדוניהם:

גמרא

ובעל אוכל פירות ברם רבי אבא ורבי אבהו וכל גדולי הדור אמרו במתנה בקש ליתנו לה ולמה כתב לה [א] לשום מכר כדי ליפות את כחה מיתיבי לוה מן העבד ושחררו מן האשה וגרשה אין להן עליו כלום מ"ט לאו משום דאמרי לגלויי זוזי הוא דבעא שאני התם דלא (א) לישוי איניש עבד לוה לאיש מלוה אמר רב המוכר שדה לאשתו קנתה והבעל אוכל פירות במתנה קנתה ואין הבעל אוכל פירות ורבי אלעזר אמר אחד זה ואחד זה קנתה ואין הבעל אוכל פירות עבד רב חסדא עובדא כרבי אלעזר אמרו ליה [ב] רבן עוקבא [ג] ורבן נחמיה בני בנתיה דרב (ב) לרב חסדא שביק מר רברבי ועביד כזוטרי א"ל (ג) ואנא נמי כרברבי עבדי דכי אתא רבין אמר ר' יוחנן אחד זה ואחד זה קנתה ואין הבעל אוכל פירות אמר רבא הלכתא א המוכר שדה לאשתו לא קנתה והבעל אוכל פירות ב במתנה קנתה ואין הבעל אוכל פירות תרתי לא קשיא ג כאן במעות טמונין כאן במעות שאין טמונין דאמר רב יהודה מעות טמונין לא קנתה מעות שאינן טמונין קנתה: ת"ר ד אין מקבלין פקדונות לא מן הנשים ולא מן העבדים ולא מן התינוקות קבל מן האשה יחזיר לאשה ואם מתה יחזיר לבעלה קבל מן העבד יחזיר לעבד ואם מת יחזיר לרבו

קבל

רשב"ם

והבעל אוכל פירות. דלא גרע מנכסים שנפלו לה בירושה: במתנה בקש ליתן לה. ולא יאכל פירות כדאמרי' לקמן במתנה קנתה ואין הבעל אוכל פירות ומיהו במוכר לחבירו אין לומר כן שאינו אוהבו כל כך: מיתיבי כו'. ההיא קשיא דלעיל ולשני המימרות נקשית בבית המדרש: במתנה קנתה ואין הבעל אוכל פירות. דעתן בעין יפה נותן: רברבי. רב שקדם לרבי יוחנן רבו של רבי אלעזר כדאיתא בשחיטת חולין (דף לה:) דכל זמן שהיה רב קיים היה שולח ליה רבי יוחנן לקדם רבינו שבבבל ועוד דאמר ליה לריש לקיש [ד] שכל אותן הימים היה הוא בישיבה ואני בעמידה ועוד דאמרי' בעירובין (דף יג: ע"ש) אמר [ה] רב האי (ד) דמחדדן מחבריא טפי משום דחזיתיה לרבי מאיר מאחוריה: כזוטרי. ר' אלעזר שהיה תלמידו של רבי יוחנן ואע"ג דרבי אבא ורבי אבהו וכל גדולי הדור חבריהם דאמרי לעיל במתנה בקש ליתן לה כו' סבירא להו כר' אלעזר דאין הבעל אוכל פירות אינהו נמי זוטרי נינהו לגבי רב שתלמידי רבי יוחנן היו: כרברבי עבדי. ר' יוחנן שהיה חבירו של רב: תרתי. בתמיה שני דברים של רבא סותרין זה את זה לא קנתה משמע לא גוף ולא פירות דלגלויי זוזי הוא דבעי והבעל אוכל פירות משמע שקנתה גוף הקרקע דלאו לגלויי זוזי הוא דבעי: במעות טמונין. שלא היו ידועין ומפורסמים לבעל לא קנתה דלגלויי זוזי הוא דבעי: מעות שאין טמונין. קנתה והבעל אוכל פירות דליכא גלויי זוזי שהרי גלויין ועומדין הן: לא מן הנשים כו'. דאיכא למימר גנבום לבעליהן ולאדוניהם ותינוקות נמי שמא גנבו מבית בעל הבית שהם דרים שם ואסור לסייע ידי עוברי עבירה וכשלא יקבלו מהם יחזירו למקום שגנבו (ה) שם: יחזיר לאשה. ולא לבעל דאין לנו להחזיקה בגנבתה: יחזיר לבעלה. שאפי' אם ניתן לה ממון זה על מנת שאין לבעלה רשות בה מכיון שמתה יורשה בעלה שהבעל יורש את אשתו והלכך יחזיר לבעל דממה נפשך עכשיו הרי הוא של בעלה: יחזיר לרבו. דמסתמא כל מה שקנה עבד קנה רבו ונראה בעיני דהוא הדין אם נשתחרר העבד ואח"כ מת יחזיר לרבו שהרי עבד היה כשהפקיד לזה וסתם עבדים גזלנין הן אבל אם נתגרשה האשה ואחר כך מתה יחזיר ליורשיה ולא לבעלה דמשנתגרשה אין הבעל יורשה:

קבל

תוספות

[י] לא ניחא ליה דליהוי עבד לוה כו'. ודוקא נקט לוה אבל מכר לא ומשום אשה הוא דנקט לוה אבל גבי עבד אין חילוק בין לוה למכר דמה שקנה עבד קנה רבו: [ברם] רבינו תם לא גריס ברם ר' אבא אלא גריס ר' אבא ורבי אבהו וכל גדולי הדור כו' כדי ליפות את כחו. ולא גריס את כחה אלא ליפות את כחו ופירש שיאכל הוא את הפירות והשתא מייתי רב הונא בר אבין סייעתא לדבריו דתימה הוא לומר שהיה שולח שכל גדולי הדור חולקין עליו שאם כן אין ממש בדבריו ואין מתיישב לר"י גירסתו דא"כ מה צריך לומר במתנה בקש ליתן לה ונראה לר"י גירסת הספרים (ו) ברם ר' אבא וליפות כחה ופליגי עליה וסברי דמוכר לאשתו לא קנתה דלגלויי זוזי הוא דבעי וסברי כרב הונא דאמר דל זוזי מהכא ותיקני בשטר ומה שקונה בשטר אינו אלא מתנה כיון דלגלויי זוזי הוא דבעי ולא קנתה בזוזי ומה שכתב בלשון מכר לא כתב אלא ליפות את כחה ופירוש רבינו תם יש ליישב ולפרש בקש ליתן לה לענין זה שבמתנה (ז) נתן את כולן ועוד יש ליישב פירוש ר"ת במתנה בקש כו' דאפילו למאן דאמר קנתה במוכר לאשתו ולא אמר לגלויי זוזי הוא דבעי לא קנתה אלא משום דבמתנה נתן לה דהא אין כאן מכר שלא נתנה לו כלום שהדמים הן שלו בלאו הכי ואע"פ שאין יכול להוציא ממנה דבין מ"מ אם תקף ממנה או הוציא מידה לכך ערמה הם שלו כדאמרינן בסמוך וא"כ השתא שהוציאן דרך מכר הם שלו ואין כאן מכר והלכך למ"ד קנתה לא קנתה אלא משום דבמתנה בקש לתת לה והא דכתב לה בלשון מכר כדי ליפות את כחו לענין שיאכל הפירות כי המכר מבטל הקנין דהא אין כאן מכר כדפי' ולענין שדה הויא מתנה וקנתה ולענין פירות הוי מכר ולא קנתה: **במתנה** קנתה ואין הבעל אוכל פירות. תימה דאמר בגיטין בפ' הזורק (דף עז: ושם ד"ה מה) גבי ההוא שכיב מרע דכתיב גט לדביתהו בהדי פניא דמעלי שבתא כו' אתא לקמיה דרבא אמר ליקני לה ההוא אתרא דאית בה גיטא כו' אמר רב עילים מה שקנתה אשה קנה בעלה איכסיף ומאי קושיא והא במתנה אין הבעל אוכל פירות א"כ לא קנה בעלה ואומר רבינו תם דאין תלוי באכילת פירות למיקרי חצרה דהא רבא סבר כריש לקיש (לקמן דף קלו:) דקנין פירות לאו כקנין הגוף דמי ואפילו יש לבעל פירות אינו מפקיע כח האשה שהגוף שלה ומתגרשת שפיר אלא בהא תליא מילתא דלא מיקרי חצרה לענין זכיה אלא כשמוכרת ונותנת קיים הלכך כשנתן לה הבעל אע"ג דאין אוכל פירות כיון שאם מכרה ונתנה אינו קיים לא מיקרי חצרה דאדעתא דהכי שתמכור ותתן לא יהיב לה ומייתי ראיה דהתם בריש הזורק גבי זרק לה בחצרה פריך חצרה מה שקנתה אשה קנה בעלה ומשני כגון שכתב לה דין ודברים אין לי בנכסיך אע"ג דכשכתב לה נמי הכי יש לבעל פירי עד שיכתוב לה ובפירותיהן כדתנן בהכותב (כתובות דף פג.) אפילו הכי חשיב חצרה כיון שאם מכרה ונתנה קיים כדתנן בהכותב ומיהו אינה ראיה דאע"ג דאינו מזכיר ובפירותיהן הכי בעי למימר כדאשכחן לעיל [י] גבי אין לאיש חזקה בנכסי אשתו וא"ת אע"ג דאינה יכולה למכור (ח) תקני לה לגט מידי דהוה אשכירות דאמר (במסכת מע"ש פ"ה מ"ט) גבי ר"ג מעשר (שני) נתון ליהושע ומקומו מושכר לו ובהמוכר את הספינה (לקמן דף פד:) מדד ולא משך לא קנה ואם היה פיקח שוכר את מקומו ואומר רבינו תם דגדול קנינו של שוכר מזה שאפי' מת בתוך הזמן המקום מושכר ליורשיו עד הזמן משא"כ באשה שאם מכרה ונתנה הבעל מוציא מיד הלקוחות ובירושלמי לא משמע כפר"ת דפריך בריש הזורק (גיטין דף עז.) וגנתה וחצרה אינן משתעבדות לאיש לאכילת פירות ומשני ר' יוחנן בשם ר' ינאי עד שיכתוב לה דין ודברים אין לי בנכסיך ובפירותיהן ומשמע מדפריך מפירות דבפירות הדבר תלוי ולא במה שאינה יכולה למכור ור"י אמר דאפי' תלויה הזכייה בפירות מ"מ פריך שפיר התם מה שקנתה אשה קנה בעלה שלא היה נותן לה הבעל מקום הגט אלא משאיל ודוקא במתנה הוא דקאמר דקנתה ואין הבעל אוכל פירות ועוד אומר ר"י דהא דאמר הכא במתנה קנתה ואין הבעל אוכל פירות היינו דוקא שאינו אוכלם אבל כנכסי מלוג הם אותם פירות וילקח בהם קרקע ויאכל הפירות ומשום הכי פריך התם שפיר מה שקנתה אשה קנה בעלה:

קבל מן האשה יחזיר לאשה. נראה דאם אמרה האשה תן לפלוני שהם שלו דנותן לו דנאמנת היא במיגו דאי בעיא שקלה איהי מיניה ויהבה ליה ואפי' אומר הבעל שהממון שלו אין לו כח להוציא מידה מדקאמר יחזיר לאשה דהוה ליה למימר יודיע לבעל (ט) דאם היה כח ביד הבעל להוציא מידה כשאומר שהוא שלו והא דמפליג בסמוך בדביתהו דרבה בר בר חנה בין מהימנא בין לא מהימנא הנ"מ בשעת מיתתה דלית לה מיגו דאי בעי שקלה מיניה ויהבה למי שרוצה ואם תקף הבעל מידה שוב אינה יכולה להוציא מידו ולומר של פלוני הם כדאמר לעיל לוה מן האשה וגרשה אין לה עליו כלום ואם היתה נאמנת לומר של פלוני הם תהא (י) נאמנת לומר שלי הם במיגו דאי בעי אמרה אחרים הפקידו בידי דאינה צריכה לומר מי הם האחרים וישאר הממון לעולם בידה ודוקא במעות טמונות דלוה מן האשה דלעיל במעות טמונות איירי מדקאמר לגלויי זוזי הוא דבעי אבל מעות שאינן טמונות יש לה עליו וכן אם תקף מוציאין מידו ועוד מדקאמר רבא דבמעות שאינן טמונות קנתה משמע דאם תקף מוציאין אותן מידו דאם אין מוציאין אמאי קנתה הא יכול לומר להוציא מידה נתכוונתי כי לא יכולתי להוציא מידה בענין אחר ואפי' בב"ד ואם היא נושאת ונותנת בתוך הבית אינה נאמנת לומר לא שלי ולא של פלוני הם כדאמר לקמן (דף נב:) וכן האשה שהיא נושאת ונותנת כו' ואמרה שלי הם עליה להביא ראיה ולא מהימנינן לה במיגו דאי בעיא אמרה שהיא נפקדת משל אחרים ומיהו היכא שאינה נושאת ונותנת בחיי בעלה וממון בעלה מצוי בידה יש להסתפק אם חשבינן לה כאילו נושאת ונותנת אם לאו:

קבל

מסורת הש"ס

א) [ס"א לשון], ב) [נ"ל רבנא וכ"א לקמן בתוס' קמט. ד"ה רב ובחולין נב.], ג) [נ"ל ורבנא], ד) [חולין נד.], ה) הוא רבי ולא רב ועיין רש"ל, ו) שייך לעמוד הקודם, ז) [דף מט. ושם ד"ה דכתב]:

הגהות הב"ח

(א) גמ' שאני התם דלא משוי איניש נפשיה עבד: (ב) שם בני בנתיה דרב חסדא לרב חסדא: (ג) שם א"ל אנא נמי כצ"ל ואות ו' נמחק: (ד) רשב"ם ד"ה רברבי וכו' אמר רב הא דמחדדנא. נ"ב כך הוא בפ"ק דעירובין בדף י"ג אבל הסמ"ג בסוף הלכות י"ט מביא מן הירושלמי דרבי הוא שאמר כך ע"ש: (ה) ד"ה לא מן וכו' שגנבו משם הס"ד: (ו) תוס' ד"ה ברם וכו' ונראה לר"י גי' הספרים דגרסי רבי אבא אמר וליפות כחה: (ז) בא"ד לענין זה שבמתנה נתן. נ"ב כדתנן לקמן בהמוכר את הבית והתוס' הביאו בדף זה סוף ע"א: (ח) ד"ה במתנה וכו' וא"ת אע"ג דאינה יכולה למכור מכל מקום תקני לה: (ט) ד"ה קבל וכו' יודיע לבעל אם כצ"ל ואות ד' נמחק: (י) בא"ד תהא נמי נאמנת לומר שלי:

ליקוטי רש"י

ובעל אוכל פירות. מה שקנתה אשה קנה בעלה. לפירות להשתמש בה [גיטין עז.].

to a case in which she purchased the field בְּמָעוֹת טְמוּנִין – **with money that was hidden,** i.e. money she was not known to possess.[12] In such a case Rava assumes that the husband never intended to sell her the field but merely to uncover his money. כַּאן – **Here,** where Rava stated that the husband receives produce, implying that the wife acquires the field itself, it is referring to a case in which she purchased the field בְּמָעוֹת שֶׁאֵין טְמוּנִין – **with money that was not hidden,** i.e. money her husband knew she possessed.[13] In such a case, we do not assume that he entered into the transaction only to recover money from her. Rather, we assume he intended to sell to her.

דְּאָמַר רַב יְהוּדָה – This distinction is indeed valid, **for Rav Yehudah said:** מָעוֹת טְמוּנִין לֹא קָנְתָה – If she purchased the field with **money that was hidden, she does not acquire** it; מָעוֹת שֶׁאֵינָן טְמוּנִין קָנְתָה – but if she purchased it **with money that was not hidden, she acquires** it.

The Gemara quotes a Baraisa:[14]

תָּנוּ רַבָּנָן – **The Rabbis taught in a Baraisa:** אֵין מְקַבְּלִין פִּקְדוֹנוֹת – WE DO NOT ACCEPT DEPOSITS לֹא מִן הַנָּשִׁים – FROM married WOMEN, וְלֹא מִן הָעֲבָדִים – OR FROM Canaanite SLAVES, וְלֹא מִן הַתִּינוֹקוֹת – OR FROM SMALL CHILDREN, for we suspect that they may have stolen the money.[15] קִבֵּל מִן הָאִשָּׁה – If ONE did, in fact, ACCEPT a deposit FROM a married WOMAN, יַחֲזִיר לָאִשָּׁה – HE SHOULD RETURN it TO THE WOMAN, for we cannot assume she is a thief.[16] וְאִם מֵתָה – IF SHE DIED while the money was in the custodian's possession, יַחֲזִיר לְבַעְלָהּ – HE SHOULD RETURN the money TO HER HUSBAND.[17] קִבֵּל מִן הָעֶבֶד – If ONE did, in fact, ACCEPT a deposit FROM A Canaanite SLAVE, יַחֲזִיר לָעֶבֶד – HE SHOULD RETURN it TO THE SLAVE, for we cannot assume he is a thief.[18] וְאִם מֵת – IF [THE SLAVE] DIED while the money was in the custodian's possession, יַחֲזִיר לְרַבּוֹ – HE SHOULD RETURN it TO [THE SLAVE'S] MASTER.[19]

NOTES

12. If there is any question, the husband is believed that he did not know of this money, unless the wife can prove otherwise (*Ramah* cited by *Tur, Choshen Mishpat* 85).

13. This refers to any money held exclusively and openly by her in her husband's house (*Chazon Ish, Choshen Mishpat, Likutim* 5:2).

According to some, such money is assumed to belong to her, even if the husband claims to know definitely that it is his (*Rosh,* cited by *Tur, Even Haezer* 86). Others maintain that we would accept his claim even without proof. Rava means only that we do not accept his claim that he sold a field to his wife only in order to recover such money. Since this money was both known and accessible to him, and he could have recovered it without going through a sale, we do not believe that he transacted the sale merely to recover the money (*Ri,* cited by *Tur* ibid.).

14. This Baraisa is quoted here because it too deals with the issue of whether money held by a woman is assumed to belong to her husband.

15. That is, the woman may have unlawfully taken the object from her husband, and the slave from his master. Similarly, these children may have stolen the objects from the people with whom they reside. One may not accept a stolen object as a deposit because caring for it is considered מְסַיֵּיעַ לִידֵי עוֹבְרֵי עֲבֵירָה, *being an accomplice to sinners,* which is forbidden. On the contrary, by not accepting the deposit, we encourage them to return it to the rightful owner (*Rashbam*).

Rashbam's explanation of the Baraisa [which speaks of money the children may have taken from their hosts] indicates that he understands the Baraisa to be referring to orphans rather than ordinary children. Seemingly, the case could just as well refer to ordinary children who may have stolen from their fathers. Indeed, *Yad Ramah* and *Tur* explain the case this way. *Chasdei David* (to *Yerushalmi, Bava Kamma* 9:7) explains that the wording of the end of the Baraisa leads *Rashbam* to believe that the case was dealing with orphans. The Baraisa later states that if one did, in fact, accept a deposit from a child and the child died, he must return it to the child's heirs. Since the Baraisa does not say that he should return it to the child's father, *Rashbam* concluded that the Baraisa was referring to orphans. [It is interesting that our Baraisa appears in *Tosefta* (*Bava Kamma* 11:1), with some variations, one of which is that *Tosefta* states that he should return it to the child's father.]

16. Although we do not accept a deposit from a married woman because of the *possibility* that she stole it, we can also not assume with *certainty* that she did in fact steal it. Therefore, once one accepted a deposit from a married woman, one cannot return it to her husband but must return it to her (*Rashbam*). Since the money is in her possession [with the custodian holding it on her behalf], we must accept her claim and maintain it in her possession until it is proven not to belong to her (*Rabbeinu Yonah*). [This is based on the principle of *muchzak;* see General Introduction.]

[It is possible for a woman to own money to which her husband has no rights in a case in which a third party gave it to her on the condition that her husband not have any right to it (*Rashbam* ד״ה יחזיר לבעלה, from *Kiddushin* 23b; see *Rambam Hil. Zechiyah U'Matanah* 3:13,14).]

17. Once the woman dies, we may certainly return it to her husband, since if she stole it, it was his all along, and if it was actually hers, he now inherits it from her [see below, 108a] (*Rashbam*).

Such would not be the case if the woman had been divorced before she died, since he would then not be in line to inherit her estate. Rather, in such a case, the object would be returned to her sons or other heirs (*Rashbam* ד״ה יחזיר לרבו).

18. Here too, it is possible that the object belonged to the slave because a third party gave it to him on the condition that his master have no rights to it (see note 16). Accordingly, we cannot assume that he is a thief.

19. In general, whatever a slave acquires, his master acquires automatically. [The only exception to this would be in the case set forth in the previous note. Such a case is most unlikely.] Thus, any money the slave has in his possession should be assumed to belong to his master and to have been stolen from him. Moreover, slaves are commonly thieves. We therefore return the deposit to the master.

It follows, then, that even if the slave was emancipated before he died, his former master is nonetheless entitled to the money upon the slave's death. For at the time that the object came into the custodian's possession, the object is assumed to have been stolen from the master (*Rashbam*).

Rashbam's explanation is difficult to understand. If there is an assumption that the slave is a thief, the money should be returned to the master even during the slave's lifetime. The only reason it is not, is because the slave's possession of it requires us to leave it with him unless it can be proven that he is a thief. If so, the slave is no different than a wife except in one respect: A slave does not have legal heirs while a woman does.

It should follow from this that if the slave fathers children *after* his emancipation, the deposit should be returned to them since they are his legal heirs. Yet *Rashbam's* distinction between a woman who was divorced (note 17) and a slave who was emancipated implies that in the case of a slave, the deposit is returned to the owner even if he left free children! Indeed, *Tosefos Rid* disagrees with *Rashbam* for this very reason and rules that if the slave fathered children after his emancipation, the deposit is returned to them just as with a woman who was divorced (see also *Hagahos Maimonios Hil. She'alah U'Pikadon* 7:10). See *Chazon Ish* (*Even HaEzer* 72:20) who grapples with this problem.

קִבֵּל מִן הַקָּטָן – If ONE did, in fact, ACCEPT a deposit FROM A CHILD, יַעֲשֶׂה לוֹ סְגוּלָּה – HE SHOULD SET UP A TRUST FOR HIM.[1] וְאִם מֵת – IF [THE CHILD] DIED while the object was still in the custodian's possession, יַחֲזִיר לְיוֹרְשָׁיו – [THE CUSTODIAN] should RETURN the object TO [THE CHILD'S] HEIRS.

וְכוּלָּן – AND ANY OF THEM שֶׁאָמְרוּ בִּשְׁעַת מִיתָתָן – WHO SAID AT THE TIME OF THEIR DEATHS שֶׁל פְּלוֹנִי הֵן – that [THE OBJECTS] BELONG TO SO-AND-SO,[2] יַעֲשֶׂה כְּפֵירוּשָׁן – [THE CUSTODIAN] SHOULD ACT ACCORDING TO THEIR SPECIFICATION; i.e. he should return it to the person specified.[3] וְאִם לָאו – BUT IF the custodian does NOT believe them, but believes that it actually belongs to the husband or master, יַעֲשֶׂה פֵּירוּשׁ לְפֵירוּשָׁן – HE SHOULD MAKE his own SPECIFICATION TO supersede THEIR SPECIFICATION, and return it to the husband or master.[4]

The Gemara relates an incident in conjunction with this last ruling of the Baraisa:

דְּבֵיתְהוּ דְּרַבָּה בַּר בַּר חָנָה כִּי קָא שָׁכְבָה – When Rabbah bar bar Chanah's wife was dying, אָמְרָה – she said: הָנֵי כִּיפֵי – "These earrings דְּמַרְתָּא וּבְנֵי בְּרַתָּא – belong to Marta and his daughter's children, who gave them to me to hold."[5] **אֲתָא לְקַמֵּיהּ דְּרַב – He came before Rav** to decide whether to give the earrings to Marta. **אָמַר לֵיהּ – [Rav] said to [Rabbah bar bar Chanah]: אִי מְהֵימְנָא לָךְ – If she is trustworthy to you,** and you feel that she would not have stolen from you, **עֲשֵׂה כְּפֵירוּשָׁהּ – act according to her specification** and give the earrings to Marta; **וְאִי לֹא – but if** you are **not** convinced of her trustworthiness, **עֲשֵׂה פֵּירוּשׁ לְפֵירוּשָׁהּ – make your own specification to** supersede **her specification;** i.e. keep them for yourself.[6] **וְאִיכָּא דְּאָמְרֵי – Others say** that **הָכִי אָמַר לֵיהּ – this is what [Rav] said to [Rabbah bar bar Chanah]: אִי אֲמִידָא לָךְ – If** Marta and his family appear **wealthy** enough **to you** to have owned such expensive earrings, **עֲשֵׂה כְּפֵירוּשָׁהּ – act according to her specification** and give them to Marta. **וְאִי לֹא – But if** they do **not** appear wealthy enough to have owned such earrings, **עֲשֵׂה פֵּירוּשׁ לְפֵירוּשָׁהּ – make** your own **specification to** supersede **her specification;** i.e. keep them for yourself.[7]

The Baraisa stated:

מִן הַקָּטָן יַעֲשֶׂה לוֹ סְגוּלָּה – If one did, in fact, accept a deposit FROM A CHILD, HE SHOULD SET UP A TRUST FOR HIM.

The Gemara clarifies the Baraisa:

מַאי סְגוּלָּה – What is meant by **a trust? רַב חִסְדָּא אָמַר – Rav Chisda says: סֵפֶר תּוֹרָה – A Torah scroll;** the custodian should purchase a Torah scroll from which the child can study. **רַבָּה בַּר רַב הוּנָא אָמַר – Rabbah bar Rav Huna said: דִּיקְלָא – A palm tree, דְּאָכַל מִינֵּיהּ תַּמְרֵי – from which the child can eat the dates.**[8]

The Gemara cites the next section of the Mishnah and analyzes it:

וְלֹא לָאָב בְּנִכְסֵי הַבֵּן – NOR can A FATHER establish a *chazakah* IN HIS SON'S PROPERTY, וְלֹא לַבֵּן בְּנִכְסֵי הָאָב – NOR can A SON establish a *chazakah* IN HIS FATHER'S PROPERTY.

The Gemara discusses when the Mishnah's ruling applies:[9]

אָמַר רַב יוֹסֵף – Rav Yosef said: אֲפִילּוּ חָלְקוּ – The ruling applies **even if [a father and son] separated,** i.e. the son is no longer being supported by the father.[10] **רָבָא אָמַר – Rava,** however, **said: חָלְקוּ לֹא – If they separated,** the Mishnah's ruling does

NOTES

1. Although we suspect the child may have taken the money from his host, we have no right to conclude that he is a thief. Thus, once we are holding it for him we must assume that it is perhaps something that he found (*Tosafos*). [See 51b note 16.]

Accordingly, the custodian should, in theory, return the money to him. However, since children are irresponsible, the custodian cannot discharge his obligation by returning it to him. Thus, he must set up a trust for the child until he grows up (*Rashbam;* cf. *Rashba* who explains that the custodian may, according to the strict letter of the law, return the money to the child; he must set up a trust only to fulfill a heavenly obligation).

The Gemara (below) will explain what type of trust the custodian sets up for the child.

2. I.e. they admitted on their deathbeds that the object was not theirs, but belonged to a certain person who had given it to them to hold.

3. The Baraisa's ruling applies equally to a case in which they were healthy and instructed the custodian to return the object to the third party. However, it would be unusual for them to do so in this case because they could simply reclaim the object and return it themselves without having to admit that it was never theirs. The Baraisa therefore speaks of the more likely case (*Rashbam*). *Ramban,* however, explains the reason we follow their instruction is because a person generally does not lie on his deathbed. Thus, the Baraisa's ruling refers only to dying people (quoted by *Rashba*).

[*Rashbam* (ד״ה וכולן) notes that the Baraisa's ruling that the custodian must follow their instructions applies even to the case of the child. *Kovetz Shiurim* (*Bava Basra* §235) deduces from this that *Rashbam* interprets the Baraisa to refer to a child who reached the age of פְּעוּטוֹת (literally: *talkers*), at which time certain of his transactions are [Rabbinically] effective. (This stage begins between the ages of six and ten, depending on the child's mental maturity – see *Gittin* 59a.) The instructions of a child who had not reached this stage would be considered meaningless. *Rashba* and *Yad Ramah*, however, explain the Baraisa to be dealing only with children who have not yet reached the stage of פְּעוּטוֹת. Had they reached this stage, the Baraisa would not have ruled that the custodian should not return it to the children, since they are considered responsible. According to this view, when the Baraisa rules that the custodian must follow 'their' instructions, it must refer only to a woman and a slave, not a child.]

4. I.e. the custodian does not believe the deathbed identification but suspects that they stole it and identified this other person as the owner to avoid the embarrassment of being discovered (*Rashbam*). [A person does not want to be known as a thief even after he is dead – see *Bava Metzia* 16a, and *Rashi* there ד״ה סוף סוף. Were they to die without disposing of the property, it would be returned to the proper owner, who would then realize the theft.]

5. Marta was the name of a scholar. He was the brother of R' Chiya (*Rashbam*, from *Sanhedrin* 5a).

6. Since Rabbah bar bar Chanah held the earrings in his possession, he was the *muchzak*. Therefore, as long as there was any doubt as to the true owner, he did not have to return them (*Chazon Ish, Choshen Mishpat, Likutim* 5:17, end).

7. According to this version, Rav disagrees with the Baraisa's ruling (*Hagahos HaGra, Even HaEzer* 86:3) [inasmuch as the Baraisa bases the decision entirely on her credibility, whereas according to this version of Rav's ruling, it depends on an assessment of the third party's wealth].

8. In this manner, the principal of the deposit is protected and the child has the benefit of the fruit as well. A palm tree is chosen as an example of a safe investment which produces profit (*Ritva*). [It served as a common source of food in Babylonia (see *Taanis* 9b).] Rav Chisda also agrees with this perspective, but considers the educational benefit provided to be of equal advantage (*Rambam, Hil. She'eilah U'Pikadon* 7:10; see *Taz Choshen Mishpat* 424:7). One should not, however, invest the money in a business, since the principal might then be lost (*Rashbam*).

9. The Mishnah taught that a son cannot establish a *chazakah* in his father's property and vice versa, since it is usual for a father and son to occupy each other's properties and take its yield. The Gemara now discusses whether this still applies after the son has become financially independent.

10. Rav Yosef maintains that even after a son becomes financially independent, a father or son would not object to the other's using his property (*Rashbam*). Thus, fathers and sons can never establish a *chazakah* in each other's property.

קבל מן הקטן יעשה לו סגולה ואם מת יחזיר ליורשיו וכולן שאמרו בשעת מיתתן של פלוני הן יעשה כפירושן ואם לאו יעשה פירוש לפירושן דביתהו דרבה בר בר חנה כי קא שכבה אמרה הני כיפי דמרתא ובני ברתא אתא לקמיה דרב א"ל [א] אי מהימנא לך עשה כפירושה ואי לא עשה פירוש לפירושה ואיכא דאמרי הכי א"ל אי אמידא לך עשה כפירושה ואי לא עשה פירוש לפירושה: מן הקטן יעשה לו סגולה: מאי סגולה רב חסדא אמר ספר תורה [ב] רבה בר רב הונא אמר [ג] דיקלא דאכל מיניה תמרי: ולא לאב בנכסי הבן ולא לבן בנכסי האב: אמר רב יוסף אפילו חלקו (א) רבא אמר חלקו לא אמר רב ירמיה מדפתי עבד רב פפי עובדא חלקו לא כרבא אמר רב נחמן בר יצחק אישתעי לי רב חייא מהורמיז ארדשיר דאישתעי ליה רב אחא בר יעקב משמיה דרב נחמן בר יעקב חלקו לא והלכתא חלקו לא תניא נמי הכי [ג] בן שחלק ואשתו שנתגרשה הרי הן כשאר כל אדם: איתמר אחד מן האחין שהיה נושא ונותן בתוך הבית והיו אונות ושטרות יוצאין על שמו ואמר שלי הם שנפלו לי מבית אבי אמא אמר רב [ד] עליו להביא ראיה ושמואל אמר על האחין להביא ראיה אמר שמואל [ה] מודה לי אבא שאם מת על האחין להביא ראיה מתקיף לה רב פפא כלום טענינן להו ליתמי מידי דלא טען להו אבוהון והא [ו] רבא אפיק [ז] זוגא דסרבלא וספרא דאגדתא מיתמי בלא ראיה בדברים העשוים להשאיל ולהשכיר

כדשלח

רש"י

קבל מן הקטן. לא יחזיר לו שהרי אין יודע לשמור וכמשליך לאיבוד דמי מי שהחזיר לו אלא יעשה לו סגולה אוצר עד שיגדל ויחזיר לו ולקמן מפרש מאי סגולה: ואם מת. קטן יחזיר ליורשיו: וכולן שאמרו. אפי' קטן: בשעת מיתתן. אורחא למילתא נקט דכשהן בריאין אם רוצים להחזיר לבעלים יטלו שלהן מיד הנפקד ויחזירו לבעליהן דמה להן לגלות הדבר: יעשה כפירושן. יחזיר הנפקד לאותו פלוני שפירשו אלו: ה"ג ואם לאו יעשה פירוש לפירושן. כלומר ואם לא מהימן להאי להאומר שהפקדון של אותו פלוני הוא אלא של בעלים שלהם הוא ומתוך בושה אינם רוצים לומר שהוא של בעלים דלא ליתחזקו כגזלנים וגנבים יעשה הנפקד פירוש אחר לפירושו שיחזור לבעליהן של אלו ולא לאותו פלוני וכי האי גוונא אמרינן בסמוך בההיא עובדא דדביתהו דרבה בר בר חנה. ויש מפרשים ואם לאו יעשה פירוש לפירושן כלומר אם לא פירשו בשעת מיתה יעשה (ב) פירוש למה שהם היו צריכין לפרש שיחזיר לבעליהן ולא נהירא דא"כ היינו רישא ואם מתו יחזיר לבעליהן ואם מת יחזיר לירתו דמיירי בשמת ולא פירש למי יחזיר וקאמר דיחזיר לבעלים ותרי זימני למה לי. ואית ספרים דכתב בהו ואיכא דאמרי יעשה פירוש לפירושו כלומר לא יעשה כמה שפירשו הן אלא יחזיר לבעלים ולא נהירא דא"כ רב דאמר אי מהימן לך כו' דאמר כמאן לא כרישא ולא כסיפא: כיפי. עגילים אנו"ש כדאמרינן בעלמא (עירובין דף נו:) כיפי תלא ליה עגילים תלה באזניהם: דמרתא. שם חכם אחיו של ר' חייא כדאמרינן (סנהדרין דף ה.) מרתא ואייבו וחנה ור' חייא כו': ובני ברתא. של מרתא ושל בני בתו: אי מהימנא לך. שלא גנבה ממך כלום: עשה פירוש לפירושה. עכב לעצמך: אי אמידא לך. אותם שהיא אומרת שהם שלהם אם עשירים הם וראוין להפקיד כיפי ושאר חפצים עשה כפירושה והחזירם להם. אי נמי אי אמידא לך אשתך שיש לה אוהבים שנתנו לה ממון ע"מ שלא יהא לך חלק בו ומתנה (ג) זו שנותנת לקרוביה משלה עשה כפירושה: ס"ת. ללמוד בו הרי פירות והקרן קיים: דאכיל מיניה. הקטן תמרי והקרן קיים אבל בעיסקא לא שמא יארע בה דבר תקלה ותאבד: אפי' חלקו. נתפרדו האב והבן שאין הבן סמוך על שולחן אביו ואין הבן (ד) בנכסי אביו כלום אפ"ה אין מחזיקין זה על זה דלא קפדי אהדדי: חלקו לא. כלומר בחלקו לא מיירי מתני' אלא כיון דחלקו יש להן חזקה זה על זה: הכי גרסינן עבד רב פפי עובדא חלקו לא. כלומר כרבא עשה דהיכא דחלקו לא דברה משנתנו אלא ודאי יש להן חזקה: הכי גרסינן בפירוש רבינו חננאל איתמר אחד מן האחין שהיה נושא ונותן כו'. אחד מן האחין כגון גדול אחין לאחר מות האב: אונות. שטרי מכירות לשון כחי וראשית אוני (בראשית מט): ושטרות. של הלואה: יוצאין על שמו. שבשמו נכתבו שהוא לקח (ה) והלוה: שלי הן. ואין לאחי חלק בהן שנפלו לי הממונות שהלויתי וקניתי בהן קרקעות הללו מבית אבי אמא ואין אתם יורשים עמי והלכך נקט אבי אמא דאילו מבית אבא כולן יורשין בשוה דבאחין מן האב עסקינן שכולן יורשין ממון של אביהן ביחד ולא יטול זה יותר מזה והלכך מאין לו ממון זה לבדו אם לא ירשו מאמו וכגון שאינם בני אם אחת: עליו להביא ראיה. שהממון שלו אע"פ שכתובין השטרות בשמו דכיון שהיה הוא לבדו נושא ונותן בנכסים שנכתבו על שמו וכדמפרש לקמיה שאין חלוקין אפי' בעיסקתן דכיון דלא נודע מעולם מאיזה צד יצא לו ממון בלא אחיו אין לתלות השטרות אלא בממון האב ואינו יכול להוציא הממון מחזקת האב ולקמן מפרש ראיה במאי: על האחין להביא ראיה. שהשטרות הללו מממון אביהן דמאי דכתב בשטר סמכינן והרי על שמו נכתב ואע"ג דהלכתא כשמואל בדיני בהא הלכתא כרב דתניא לקמן כוותיה ורב חסדא ורבה ורב ששת נמי כרב סבירא להו דמפרשי מילתיה לקמן: אבא. רב כך היה שמו (ז) כדקרי ליה בשחיטת חולין (דף קלז:) אבא אריכא דאמרינן מאן ריש סדרא בבבל אבא אריכא ואמרינן במסכת נדה (דף כד:) רב ארוך בדורו היה והאי דקרי ליה רב כמו שקורין לר' יהודה הנשיא רבי בארץ ישראל קרו ליה נמי בבבל רב וכן מצאתי בספר ערוך [ח] המוגה מרומה: שאם מת. ויש לו בנים ליורשו על האחין להביא ראיה דכיון דיתמי לאו בני איתויי ראיה נינהו ואין יודעין לחפש זכותן וגם השטר מוכיח (ו) שהיה ממון של אביהן על שכנגדו להביא ראיה אבל כשהאח עצמו קיים היה מטיל רב עליו להביא ראיה דאם איתא דשלו הוא ממון זה יכול לחפש ולמצוא ראיה ואם לא ימצא ראיה הפסיד: מתקיף לה רב פפא. למאי דאמר שמואל מודי לי אבא: כלום טענינן להו ליתמי כו'. בתמיה אילו היה אביהן קיים היינו מחזיקין הממון ביד אחין עד שיביא ראיה שאינו שלהן ולפי שמת יפה כחן של יתומין ממנו ויפסידו אחין בתמיה ואע"ג דאמרינן (לעיל דף מא:) טוענין ליורש גבי חזקת ג' שנים שאע"פ שלא דר בו אביו אלא יום אחד וזה החזיק ג' שנים אחרי כן הויא חזקה ואע"ג דאבוהון לא מהניא ליה חזקת שלש שנים לומר לקוח הוא בידי אלא א"כ יש עמה טענה אתה מכרתו לי אתה נתתו לי במתנה וגבי בנו לא בעינן טענה זו אלא מאבי ירשתי אלמא טענינן ליתמי מאי דלא מצי אבוהון למטען לא דמי דהתם נמי אין טוענין בשביל היתומים אלא שאביהן קנאה מן המערער כמו שהיה הוא האב יכול לטעון ולפיכך הויא חזקה אע"ג דלא טענו מידי אבל הכא האב לא מצי טעין לאחין שיביאו ראיה ואנן היכי נטעון במקום היתומים כן: והא רבא אפיק כו'. סיומא דאתקפתא דרב פפא היא: זוגא דסרבלא. זוג מספריים של סורקי בגדים שגוזזין בהם הסרבלים: בלא ראיה. הבעלים שהיו להם עדים שהן שלהן הוציאום מן היתומים בלא ראיה ועדים שיעידו שהשאילו לאביהן של יתומים לפי שהן עשוין להשאיל ולהשכיר שאם אמר אביהן לקוחין הם בידי עליו להביא ראיה אף היתומין עליהן להביא ראיה שלקחן אביהן מן הבעלים וכיון דלית להו ראיה החזירם רבא לבעלים ולא נאמר כיון שמת האב על הבעלים להביא ראיה:

כדשלח

תוספות

קבל מן הקטן יעשה לו סגולה. דמשבא לידו איסור מציאה אשכח ולכך הוי דקטן ויעשה לו סגולה אבל מכל מקום לכתחלה אין מקבלין: ומודה לי אבא שאם מת על האחין להביא ראיה. אומר רשב"א אין לומר משום דטענינן ליתמי דאי הוה אבוהון קיים הוה מייתי ראיה דלעיל (דף מז.) פריך (ז) דאי הוה אתי בטענתא דאבוהון אפי' הנך נמי משמע דפשיטא ליה דבן אומן ובן אריס דאתו בטענתא דאבוהון דאין להן חזקה ומאין פשיט לו כל כך הא לרב יש חזקה לבן אריס אע"פ שאריס עצמו אין לו חזקה ומיהו י"ל דהתם (ח) מבן גזלן פריך כלומר אפי' הנך נמי הוו כבן גזלן אבל מ"מ אין לפרש כן דהא תנן (לעיל דף מא.) הבא מחמת ירושה אין צריך טענה הא חזקה בעי ואמאי דלמא אם היה אביו קיים היה מביא עדים שלקחה אלא נראה דהכא דוקא הוא דקאמר רב על האחין להביא ראיה אם מת משום דאונות ושטרות יוצאים על שמו דמוכחא מילתא דשלו הן אלא בחייו הוא דקאמר רב עליו להביא ראיה דלא סמכינן אמאי דיוצאין על שמו דאם איתא דנפלו לו מבית אבי אמו היו לו עדים בדבר אבל בבנו דליכא למימר הכי סמכינן אמאי דיוצאין על שמו ונראה דרב מודה במאי דאפיק רבא זוגא דסרבלא מיתמי ולרב פפא דפריך מינה נראה לו לדמותה לאונות ושטרות יוצאין על שמו:

דברים

עין משפט נר מצוה

ריב א מיי' פ"ז מהל' פקדון הל' י ופכ"ב מהלכות אישות הל' לב סמג עשין פה טוש"ע אה"ע סי' פו סעי' א [וברב אלפס עוד בב"מ פ"ג דף פז.]:

ריג ב ג מיי' שם וסמג שם טור אה"ע שם:

ריד ד ה מיי' פ"ט מהלכות נחלות הל' ז ח סמג עשין לז וסי' פח טוש"ע ח"מ סי' סב:

רבינו גרשום

קבל פקדון מן הקטן. אין יכול להחזיר לו לפי שאין יד לקטן אלא יעשה לו ממנו סגולה ויחזיר לו כשיגדל: וכולן. בין נשים ועבדים ותינוקות: שאמרו בשעת מיתתן של פלוני הן הפקדון יעשה כפירושן. ויחזיר לאותו פלוני: ואם לא פירשו יעשה. א) מי שהפקדון בידו פירוש לפירושן שהן היו צריכין לפרוש. ושל אשה יחזיר לבעל ושל עבד יחזיר לאדונו: הני כיפי. עגילים: דמרתא. של אשת פלוני: ובני ברתא. של שתיהן הוה: אי מהימנא לך. שלא גנבה מינך כלום: עשה כפירושה. ותן להם: אי אמידא לך. שאותה שהיא אומרת עשירה ומפקדת פקדוני' עשה כפירושה: ואי לא עשה פירוש לפירושה. ויהיה שלך: ספר תורה. כי היכי דלא מיכליא קרנא: פיסקא ולא לאב בנכסי הבן. בנכסים שקנה הבן: ואפילו חלקו. שהאב תופס לעצמו מה שקנה והבן תופס מה שקנה ושב והחזיק זה בשל זה לא הויא חזקה משום דאבא לגבי ברא וברא לגבי אבא אחולי אחלי הפירות זה לזה: רבא אמר חלקו לא אמרינן דלא הויא חזקה דודאי הויא חזקה משום דהבן שחלק הרי הוא כשאר כל אדם: מהורמיז ארדשיר. שהוא מן כרך שולטנות דארדשיר: אונות. כותות כגון הרשאות: ושטרות. דהלואות ומכירות: מבית אבי אמא. שאינן בני אם אחת: ואמר שלי הוא. רב אמר עליו להביא ראיה שאף ע"פ שנכתבין על שמו כיון שלא חלק והוא נושא ונותן בממון כולו הרי הן בחזקת האחין ועליו להביא ראיה שהוא רוצה להוציא ממון מחזקתו: ושמואל אמר. כיון דנכתבין על שמו והוא תופס על האחין להביא ראיה שלא יהא כדבריו: אבא. קרי לרב: על האחין להביא ראיה. שאין מוציאין מיתומים אלא בראיה: מתקיף לה רב פפא. וכי היכי טענינן בשביל יתומי מאי דלא מצי אבוהון למטען: דאילו הוה אבוהון קיים עליו היה להביא ראיה ולא על האחין ואנן היכי מטענינן ליתמי דלימרו דעל האחין להביא ראיה בשביל דאינון יתמי: והא רבא אפיק זוגי דסרבלא. מקטורן כפול וכו' מיתמי. דהיינו דברים העשוים להשאיל ולהשכיר דאע"ג דאמרי לקוחות הן בידי משום דאילו הוה אבוהון קיים לא

מסורת הש"ס

א) ב"ק פז., ב) [נ"א רבא בר הונא], ג) לעיל מז., ד) שבועות מו: ב"מ קיז., ה) [בערוך ערך זוז איתא זווא פי' שני סרבלים], ו) ושם פי' זמים וכן עיקר, ז) [עי' תוס' חולין לח. ד"ה אצטריך ליה לאבא], ח) [בערך אבא ובערך אביי]:

הגהות הב"ח

(א) גמ' רבה אמר חלקו לא וכו' לא כרבה: (ב) רשב"ם ד"ה ה"ג וכו' יעשה הוא פירוש למה: (ג) ד"ה אי אמידא וכו' ומתנה היא זו: (ד) ד"ה אפילו חלקו וכו' ואין הבן מתעסק בנכסי אביו: (ה) ד"ה יוצאין וכו' שהוא לקח או הלוה: (ו) ד"ה שאם מת וכו' השטר מוכיח שהממון היה של אביהן: (ז) תוס' ד"ה מודה וכו' פריך אי דאתו: (ח) באו"ד י"ל דהתם מכח בן גזלן:

ליקוטי רש"י

כיפי. מרגליות לישנא אחרינא נזמים וכן עיקר [עירובין צו:]. נזמים [כתובות פא:]. בן שחלק ואשה שנתגרשה הרי הן ככל אדם. הפליג מאביו ואין סמוך עוד על שולחנו כגון שנשא אשה ואין משתדל עוד בנכסי אביו הרי הן ככל אדם אע"ג דתנן (לעיל מב.) לא לאיש חזקה בנכסי אשתו ולא לאשה בנכסי בעלה ולא האב בנכסי הבן ולא הבן כו' הנך כיון שהופלגו זה מזה יש להן חזקה זה על זה [רשב"ם לעיל מז.]. מודה לי אבא. לרב הוה קרי ליה שמואל הכי משום כבוד [חולין לח. ועי"ש בתוס' ד"ה איצטריך]. משום דקשיש מיניה קרי ליה אבא כמו לשון נשיאי ורבי [יבמות נז:]. ושמואל היה קורא לרב אב לכבודו [ברכות מז.]. זוגא דסרבלא. מספריים של סורקי בגדים [שבועות מו:]. מספרים שגוזזין בהן למר [ב"מ קטז.]. מיתמי. שהביא המופקד עדים שהן שלו ואמר שהשאילם לאבי היתומים ומדאפקינהו רבא מיתמי ש"מ דסבירא ליה אי הוה אבוהון קמן ואמר לקוחין הן בידי אינו נאמן בשבועה דאי מהימן אנן הוינן טוענין בשביל יתמי אביהם לקחם ממך ודוקא ספרי דאגדתא שאין אדם עשוי ללמוד אלא בשל אחר שכל ספרים אינן עשוין להשאיל ולהשכיר לפי שמתקלקלין כמו ששנינו במוצא ספרים לא יקרא בהן לכתחלה ולא ילמוד אחר עמו ויכול לומר לקוחין הן בידי ואין צריך לכתוב עליהן שטר מכירה אלא לרווחא דמילתא שלא יצטרך לשבע ואין קבלני מכר כיון דאיכא ליה זוגא דסרבלי [שבועות מו:]. שהביאו הבעלים עדים שהיו שלהן ולאביהם של אלו ואפקינהו רבא מינייהו משום דברים העשוין להשאיל ולהשכיר [ב"מ שם].

חשק שלמה על רבינו גרשום א) עי' ברשב"ם ויש מפרשים וכו' כלומר אם לא פירשו בשעת מיתה וכו' ונראה דכוון לפי' רבינו ז"ל.

not apply. Once the son is financially independent, either he or his father can establish a *chazakah* upon the other's property.[11]

The Gemara cites a decision that supports Rava's view:

אָמַר רַב יִרְמְיָה מִדִּפְתִּי – **Rav Yirmiyah of Difti said:** עֲבַד רַב פַּפִּי עוּבְדָא – **Rav Pappi ruled concerning an** actual **case** חָלְקוּ לֹא – that if a father and son **separated,** the Mishnah's ruling does **not** apply, i.e. a *chazakah* can be established, כְּרָבָא – **in accordance with Rava's** opinion.

Another support for Rava's view:

אָמַר רַב נַחְמָן בַּר יִצְחָק – **Rav Nachman bar Yitzchak said:** אִישְׁתָּעֵי לִי רַב חִיָּיא מֵהוּרְמִיז אַרְדְּשִׁיר – **Rav Chiya from** the town of **Hurmiz Ardeshid told me** דְּאִישְׁתָּעֵי לֵיהּ רַב אַחָא בַּר יַעֲקֹב – **that Rav Acha bar Yaakov told him** מִשְּׁמֵיהּ דְּרַב נַחְמָן בַּר יַעֲקֹב – **in the name of Rav Nachman bar Yaakov:** חָלְקוּ לֹא – If a father and son **separated,** the Mishnah's ruling does **not** apply.

The Gemara decides the issue:

וְהִלְכְתָא חָלְקוּ לֹא – **And the halachah is** that if a father and son **separated,** the Mishnah's ruling does **not** apply.

The Gemara cites a Baraisa that supports its decision:

תַּנְיָא נַמִּי הָכִי – **This has also been taught in a Baraisa:** בֵּן שֶׁחָלַק – In the case of A SON WHO SEPARATED from his father and set up house for himself, וְאִשְׁתּוֹ שֶׁנִּתְגָּרְשָׁה – OR A WIFE WHO WAS DIVORCED from her husband, הֲרֵי הֵן כִּשְׁאָר כָּל אָדָם – THEY [the separated parties] ARE LIKE ANY OTHER PERSON with regard to *chazakah.*[12] The Baraisa thus supports Rava's interpretation of the Mishnah.[13]

The Gemara previously precluded certain people from establishing a *chazakah* in property because their position of trust allows them constant access to it. The Gemara now discusses a similar issue – the criteria for establishing title to property in which a person has legal authority to act on behalf of another:

אִיתְּמַר – **It was stated:** אֶחָד מִן הָאַחִין – **One of** a group of **brothers** שֶׁהָיָה נוֹשֵׂא וְנוֹתֵן בְּתוֹךְ הַבַּיִת – **who had been managing** the affairs of **[his late father's] estate**[14] on behalf of all the brothers, וְהָיוּ אוֹנוֹת וּשְׁטָרוֹת יוֹצְאִין עַל שְׁמוֹ – **and bills of sale and** loan **documents**[15] **appear in [the brother's] name;**[16] וְאָמַר שֶׁלִּי הֵם – **he claims, "These** assets **represent my own** holdings, שֶׁנָּפְלוּ לִי מִבֵּית אֲבִי אִמָּא – **which I inherited from my maternal grandfather."**[17] It is unclear, however, whether this is true. אָמַר רַב – **Rav said:** עָלָיו לְהָבִיא רְאָיָה – **The burden is on [the managing brother] to prove** that he used his own money to acquire the assets.[18] וּשְׁמוּאֵל אָמַר – **But Shmuel said:** עַל הָאַחִין לְהָבִיא רְאָיָה – **The burden is upon the brothers to prove** that the managing brother purchased the asset with money from their estate.[19] אָמַר שְׁמוּאֵל – **Shmuel** further **stated:** מוֹדֶה לִי אַבָּא – Even **Abba,**[20] i.e. Rav, **agrees with me** שֶׁאִם מֵת – **that if [the managing brother] died** and the other brothers claim that he used the estate's money, עַל הָאַחִין לְהָבִיא רְאָיָה – **the burden is upon the brothers to prove** their claim. Unless they can prove that the dead brother used their money, they are not awarded a portion of the purchased property or money owned on the loans.[21]

The Gemara objects:

מַתְקִיף לָהּ רַב פָּפָּא – **Rav Pappa challenged [Shmuel's statement]:** כְּלוּם טָעֲנִינַן לְהוּ לְיַתְמֵי – **Do we then advance any plea for orphans** מִידֵי דְּלֹא טָעַן לְהוּ אֲבוּהוֹן – **that their father would be unable to plead?** Certainly not! Why, then, would Rav require the other brothers to prove their claim if the managing brother died? He would not have required them to do so during the managing brother's lifetime.[22] – ? –

NOTES

11. According to Rava, it is common for a father and son to use each other's property only so long as the son is still being supported. Once he becomes financially independent, however, this no longer holds true and a *chazakah* can be established.

12. That is, once the son becomes independent or the wife is divorced, the now separated parties are like unrelated people, with no inherent connection to each other's property. Thus, they can establish a *chazakah* in each other's property.

13. That if the father and son separated (i.e. the son became financially independent), each can establish a *chazakah* on the other's property.

The *Yerushalmi* (cited in *Rashbam* to 52b) states that if either the son or the father died, the survivor can then establish a *chazakah* in the estate of the deceased party as well [for death is the ultimate separation]. Similarly, a wife can establish a *chazakah* on her late husband's property (or vice versa).

14. When a group of brothers inherit their father's estate, it is common for one of them (usually the oldest – see 139a) to manage the estate until it is actually divided (*Rashbam*).

15. [When a person holds a bill of sale naming him as purchaser, this generally proves that he has bought the property mentioned in the document.] Bills of sale are therefore called אוֹנוֹת (the plural of אוֹן, which means strength – see *Genesis* 49:3), because they strengthen the holder's legal position (*Rashbam*).

16. That is, the documents state that he purchased property or lent money (*Rashbam*).

17. Our Gemara discusses a case in which the managing brother was born of a different mother than the other brothers. In addition to inheriting his father's estate along with the other brothers, he claims to have inherited property from his maternal grandfather. A dispute then arose between him and the other brothers concerning the property or loans mentioned in the documents. He claimed that he purchased the property or advanced the loans with money he inherited from his maternal grandfather. According to him, the purchased property or money due on the loans is all his (*Rashbam*). The other brothers, however, challenged his claim, maintaining that he purchased the property or advanced the loan with money from the estate. They therefore demand a share in the property or the money due on the loans.

18. Otherwise, we assume that it belonged to the estate. The Gemara below (52b) elucidates the case concerning which Rav and Shmuel ruled. According to the Gemara, their rulings concern a brother who managed the estate alone and had no apparent source of income. Thus, even though the documents name him as the purchaser or creditor, still Rav maintains that he presumably used money from his father's estate to make the purchase or advance the loan. He must therefore divide it with the other brothers unless he proves that it is all his.

The Gemara below (ibid.) will discuss the nature of the required proof (*Rashbam*).

19. According to Shmuel, we are bound to follow the wording of the documents in question. Since the documents name the managing brother as the purchaser or creditor, we assume that he purchased the property or advanced the loan with his own money, unless his brother can prove otherwise (*Rashbam*).

20. Rav's name was actually Abba (*Chullin* 137b); "Rav" was merely an honorific accorded him in Babylonia, just as R' Yehudah HaNasi was accorded the title "Rebbe" in Eretz Yisrael (*Rashbam*, citing *Aruch*).

21. Shmuel argues that even according to Rav, who maintains that the burden of proof is on the managing brother, still, once he dies, the burden of proof shifts to the other brothers, for the following reason. If the managing brother is telling the truth (that he used his own money to acquire the assets), he should be able to prove this, since he acquired them himself. His failure to do so would thus suggest that he might be lying. His orphans, on the other hand, are not expected to have familiarized themselves with their father's transactions. Moreover, the wording of the document does indicate that their father used his own money (since it names him as purchaser or creditor). Therefore, once the managing brother dies, his orphans are not expected to prove that he was telling the truth, and the burden of proof shifts to the other brothers (*Rashbam*).

22. Rav maintains that as long as the managing brother is living, he is presumed to have purchased the property or advanced the loans with money from his father's estate, unless he can prove otherwise. He cannot

קבל מן הקטן יעשה לו סגולה ואם מת יחזיר ליורשיו וכולן שאמרו בשעת מיתתן של פלוני הן יעשה כפירושן ואם לאו יעשה פירוש לפירושן דביתהו דרבה בר בר חנה כי קא שכבה אמרה הני כיפי דמרתא ובני ברתא אתא לקמיה דרב א"ל א אי מהימנא לך עשה כפירושה ואי לא עשה פירוש לפירושה ואיכא דאמרי הכי א"ל אי אמידא לך עשה כפירושה ואי לא עשה פירוש לפירושה: מן הקטן יעשה לו סגולה: א) מאי סגולה רב חסדא אמר ב ספר תורה ב) רבה בר רב הונא אמר ג דיקלא דאכל מיניה תמרי: ולא לאב בנכסי הבן ולא לבן בנכסי האב: אמר רב יוסף אפילו חלקו (א) רבא אמר חלקו לא אמר רב ירמיה מדפתי עבד רב פפי עובדא חלקו לא כרבא אמר רב נחמן בר יצחק אישתעי לי רב חייא מהורמיז ארדשיר דאישתעי ליה רב אחא בר יעקב משמיה דרב נחמן בר יעקב חלקו לא והלכתא חלקו לא תניא נמי הכי ג) בן שחלק ואשתו שנתגרשה הרי הן כשאר כל אדם: איתמר אחד מן האחין שהיה נושא ונותן בתוך הבית והיו אונות ושטרות יוצאין על שמו ואמר שלי הם שנפלו לי מבית אבי אמא אמר רב ד עליו להביא ראיה ושמואל אמר על האחין להביא ראיה אמר שמואל ה מודה לי אבא שאם מת על האחין להביא ראיה מתקיף לה רב פפא כלום טענינן להו ליתמי מידי דלא טען להו אבוהון והא ד) רבא אפיק ה) זוגא דסרבלא וספרא דאגדתא מיתמי בלא ראיה בדברים העשוים להשאיל ולהשכיר
כדשלח

קבל מן הקטן יעשה לו סגולה. דמשבא לידו איסור מיאה אשכח ולכך הוו דקטן ויעשה לו סגולה אבל מכל מקום לכתחלה אין מקבלין: **ומודה** לי אבא שאם מת על האחין להביא ראיה. אומר רשב"א אין לומר משום דטענינן ליתמי דאי הוה אבוהון קיים הוה מייתי ראיה דלעיל (דף מז.) פריך (ז) דאי הוה אתי בטענתא דאבוהון אפי' הנך נמי משמע דפשיטא ליה דבן אומן ובן אריס דאתו בטענתא דאבוהון דאין להן חזקה ומאין פשיט לו כל כך הא לרב יש חזקה לבן אריס אע"פ שלאריס עצמו אין לו חזקה ומיהו י"ל דהתם (ח) מבן גזלן פריך כלומר אפי' הנך נמי הוו כבן גזלן אבל מ"מ אין לפרש כן דהא תנן (לעיל דף מא.) הבא מחמת ירושה אין צריך טענה הא חזקה בעי ואמאי דלמא אם היה אביו קיים היה מביא עדים שלקחה אלא נראה דהכא דוקא הוא דקאמר רב על האחין להביא ראיה אם מת משום דאונות ושטרות יוצאים על שמו דמוכחא מילתא דשלו הן אלא בחייו הוא דקאמר רב עליו להביא ראיה דלא סמכינן אמאי דיוצאין על שמו דאם איתא דנפלו לו מבית אבי אמו היו לו עדים בדבר אבל בבנו דליכא למימר הכי סמכינן אמאי דיוצאין על שמו ונראה דרב מודה במאי דאפיק רבא זוגא דסרבלא מיתמי ולרב פפא דפריך מינה נראה לו לדמותה לאונות ושטרות יוצאין על שמו:
דברים

קבל מן הקטן. לא יחזיר לו שהרי אין יודע לשמור וכמשליך לאיבוד דמי מי שהחזיר לו אלא יעשה לו סגולה אוצר עד שיגדל ויחזיר לו ולקמן מפרש מאי סגולה: **ואם מת.** קטן יחזיר ליורשיו: **וכולן שאמרו.** אפי' קטן: **בשעת מיתתן.** אורחא דמילתא נקט דכשהן בריאין אם רוצים להחזיר לבעלים יטלו שלהן מיד הנפקד ויחזירו לבעליהן דמה להן לגלות הדבר: **יעשה כפירושן.** יחזיר הנפקד לאותו פלוני שפירשו אלו: ה"ג **ואם לאו יעשה פירוש לפירושן.** כלומר ואם לא מהימן להו נפקד שהפקדון של אותו פלוני הוא אלא של בעלים שלהם הוא ומתוך בושה אינם רוצים לומר שהוא של בעלים דלא ליתחזקו כגזלנים וגנבים יעשה הנפקד פירוש אחר לפירושו שיחזור לבעליהן של אלו ולא לאותו פלוני וכי האי גוונא אמרינן בסמוך בההיא עובדא דביתהו דרבה בר בר חנה. ויש מפרשים ואם לאו יעשה פירוש לפירושן כלומר אם לא פירשו בשעת מיתה יעשה (ב) פירוש למה שהם היו צריכין לפרש שיחזיר לבעליהן ולא נהירא דא"כ היינו רישא ואם מתו יחזיר לבעליהן ואם מת יחזיר לרבו דמיירי בשמת ולא פירש למי יחזיר וקאמר דיחזיר לבעלים ותרי זימני למה לי. ואית ספרים דכתב בהו ואיכא דאמרי יעשה פירוש לפירושו כלומר לא יעשה כמה שפירשו הן אלא יחזיר לבעלים ולא נהירא דא"כ רב דאמר אי מהימן לך כו' דאמר כמאן לא כרישא ולא כסיפא: **כיפי.** עגילים אנור"ש כדאמרינן בעלמא (עירובין דף נו:) ו) כיפי תלא ליה עגילים תלה באזניהם: **דמרתא.** שם חכם אחיו של ר' חייא כדאמרינן (סנהדרין דף ה.) מרתא ואייבו ותנא ור' חייא כו': **ובני ברתא.** של מרתא ושל בני בתו: **אי מהימנא לך.** שלא גנבה ממך כלום: **עשה פירוש לפירושה.** כיפי ושאר חפצים עשה כפירושה והחזירם להם. אי נמי אי אמידה לך אשתך שיש לה אוהבים שנתנו לה ממון ע"מ שלא יהא לך חלק בו ומתנה (ג) זו שנותנת לקרוביה משלה עשה כפירושה: **ס"ת.** ללמוד בו הרי פירות והקרן קיים: **דאכיל מיניה.** הקטן תמרי והקרן קיים אבל בעיסקא לא שמא יארע בה דבר תקלה ותאבד: **אפי' חלקו.** נתפרדו האב והבן שאין הבן סמוך על שולחן אביו ואין הבן (ד) בנכסי אביו כלום אפ"ה אין מחזיקין זה על זה דלא קפדי אהדדי: **חלקו לא.** כלומר בחלקו לא מיירי מתני' אלא כיון דחלקו יש להן חזקה זה על זה: הכי גרסינן **עבד רב פפי עובדא חלקו לא.** כלומר כרבא עשה דהיכא דחלקו לא דברה משנתנו אלא ודאי יש להן חזקה: הכי גרסינן בפירוש רבינו חננאל **איתמר אחד מן האחין שהיה נושא ונותן כו'.** אחד מן האחין כגון גדול אחין לאחר מות האב: **אונות.** שטרי מכירות לשון כחי וראשית אוני (בראשית מט): **ושטרות.** של הלואה: **יוצאין על שמו.** שבשמו נכתבו שהוא לקח (ה) והלוה: **שלי הן.** ואין לאחי חלק בהן שנפלו לי הממונות שלוויתי וקניתי בהן קרקעות הללו מבית אבי אמא דאילו מבית אבא כולן יורשין בשוה דבאחין מן האב עסקינן שכולן יורשין ממון של אביהן ביחד ולא יטול זה יותר מזה ולהכי נקט אבי אמא דאילו מבית אבא לא היה לו לבדו ממון זה מאחין לו ממון זה לבדו אם לא ירשו מאמו וכגון שאינם בני אם אחת: **עליו להביא ראיה.** שהממון שלו אע"פ שכתובין השטרות בשמו דכיון שהיה הוא לבדו נושא ונותן בנכסים שנכתבו על שמו וכדמפרש לקמיה שאין חלוקין אפי' בעיסקתן דכיון דלא נודע מעולם מאיזה צד יבא לו ממון בלא אחיו אין לתלות השטרות אלא בממון האב ואינו יכול להוציא הממון מחזקת האב ולקמן מפרש ראיה במאי: **על האחין להביא ראיה.** שהשטרות הללו מממון אביהן דאמאי דכתב בשטר סמכינן והרי על שמו נכתב ואע"ג דהלכתא כשמואל בדיני בהא הלכתא כרב דתניא לקמן כוותיה ורב חסדא ורבה ורב ששת נמי כרב סבירא להו דמפרשי מילתיה לקמן: **אבא.** רב כך היה שמו ז) כדקרי ליה בשחיטת חולין (דף קלז:) אבא אריכא דאמרינן מאן ריש סדרא בבבל אבא אריכא ואמרינן במסכת נדה (דף כד:) רב ארוך בדורו היה והאי דקרי ליה רב כמו שקורין לר' יהודה הנשיא רבי בארץ ישראל קרו ליה נמי בבבל רב וכן מצאתי בספר ערוך ח) המוגה מרומא: **שאם מת.** ויש לו בנים ליורשו על האחין להביא ראיה דכיון דיתמי לאו בני איתויי ראיה נינהו ואין יודעין לחפש זכותן וגם השטר מוכיח (ו) שהיה ממון של אביהן על שכנגדו להביא ראיה אבל כשהאח עצמו קיים היה מטיל רב עליו להביא ראיה דאם איתא דשלו הוא ממון זה יכול לחפש ולמצוא ראיה ואם לא ימצא ראיה הפסיד: **מתקיף לה רב פפא.** למאי דאמר שמואל מודי לי אבא: **כלום טענינן להו ליתמי כו'.** בתמיה אילו היה אביהן קיים היינו מחזיקין הממון ביד אחין עד שיביא ראיה שאינו שלהן ולפי שמת יפה כחן של יתומין ממנו ויפסידו אחין בתמיה ואע"ג דאמרינן (לעיל דף מא:) טוענין ליורש גבי חזקת ג' שנים שאע"פ שלא דר בו אביו אלא יום אחד וזה החזיק ג' שנים אחרי כן הויא חזקה ואע"ג דאבוהון לא מהניא ליה חזקת שלש שנים לומר לקוח הוא בידי אלא א"כ יש עמה טענה אתה מכרתו לי אתה נתתו לי במתנה וגבי בנו לא בעינן טענה זו אלא מאבי ירשתי אלמא טענינן ליתמי מאי דלא מצי אבוהון למטען לא דמי דהתם נמי אין טוענין בשביל היתומים אלא שאביהן קנאה מן המערער כמו שהיה הוא האב יכול לטעון ולפיכך הויא חזקה אע"ג דלא טענו מידי אבל הכא האב לא מצי טעין לאחין שיביאו ראיה ואנן היכי נטעון במקום היתומים כן: **והא רבא אפיק כו'.** סיומא דאתקפתא דרב פפא היא: **זוגא דסרבלא.** זוג מספריים של סורקי בגדים שגוזזין בהם הסרבלים: **בלא ראיה.** הבעלים שהיו להם עדים שהן שלהן הוציאום מן היתומים בלא ראיה ועדים שיעידו שהשאילו לאביהן של יתומים לפי שהן עשוין להשאיל ולהשכיר שאם אמר אביהן לקוחין הם בידי עליו להביא ראיה אף היתומין עליהן להביא ראיה שלקחום אביהן מן הבעלים וכיון דלית להו ראיה החזירום לבעלים ולא נאמר כיון שמת האב על האחין להביא ראיה:
כדשלח

א) ב"ק פז:, ב) [ג"א רבא בר הונא], ג) לעיל מז., ד) שבועות מו:, ה) ב"מ קיז., ו) [בערוך ערך זו איתא זווא פי' שני סרבלים], ז) וכן פי' ממים וכן עיקר, ח) [עי' תוס' חולין לח: ד"ה אצטריך ליה לאבא], ט) [בערוך אבא ובערך אבין]:

הגהות הב"ח

(א) גמ' רבא אמר חלקו לא כרבה: (ב) רשב"ם ד"ה ה"ג וכו' יעשה הוא פירוש למה: (ג) ד"ה אי אמידא וכו' ומתנה היא זו: (ד) ד"ה אפילו חלקו וכו' ואין הבן מתעסק בנכסי אביו: (ה) ד"ה יוצאין וכו' שהוא לקח או הלוה: (ו) ד"ה שאם מת וכו' השטר מוכיח שהממון היה של אביהן: (ז) תוס' ד"ה מודה וכו' פריך לה דאי הוה: (ח) בא"ד י"ל דהתם מכח בן גזלן:

ליקוטי רש"י

כיפי. מרגליות לישנא אחרינא נזמים וכן עיקר [עירובין צו.]. נזמים [כתובות סא:]. **בן שחלק ואשה שנתגרשה הרי הן ככל אדם.** הפליג מאביו ואין סמוך עוד על שולחנו כגון שנשא אשה ואין מתעסק עוד בנכסי אביו הרי הן ככל אדם אע"ג דתנן (לעיל מב.) לא לאשה בנכסי בעלה ולא לאב בנכסי הבן ולא לבן בנכסי האב ולאיש חזקה בנכסי אשתו זה אם זה יש להן חזקה זה על זה [רשב"ם לעיל מז.]. **לרב קרי ליה אבא.** לרב הוה קרי ליה שמואל הכי משום כבוד [חולין לח.]. ועי' רש"י חולין לח. ד"ה איצטריך]. משום דקשיש מיניה קרי ליה אבא כמו לשון נשיאי ורבי [יבמות נו:]. ושמואל היה קורא לרב אב לכבודו [ברכות מז.]. **זוגא דסרבלא.** מספריים של סורקי בגדים [שבועות מו:]. מספריים שגוזזין בהן למר [ב"מ קטז.]. **מיתמי.** שהיה מופיע עדים שהן שלו ואמר שהשאילם לאבי היתומים ואפקינהו רבא מיתמי מ"ט דקיימא ליה דאי הוה אבוהון קמן לא נאמן לקוחין הן בידי דאינו נאמן בכשעונה דלאי מהימן אלא לא הוינן טוענין בשביל יתמי אביהם לקחם ממך ודוקא ספרי דאגדתא שאין אדם עשוי ללמוד בהן תדיר אבל שאר ספרים אין עשוין להשאיל ולהשכיר לפי שמתקלקלין ...

ריב א מיי' פ"ז מהל' פקדון הל' י ופכ"ב מהלכות אישות הל' לב סמג עשין פה טוש"ע אה"ע סי' פו סעי' א [וברב אלפס עוד בב"מ פ"ג דף פז.]:
ריג ב ג מיי' שם וסמג שם טור אה"ע שם:
ריד ד ה מיי' פ"ט מהלכות נחלות הל' ה סמג עשין לג וסי' פח טוש"ע ח"מ סי' קנ:

רבינו גרשום

קבל פקדון מן הקטן. אין יכול להחזיר לו לפי שאין יד לקטן אלא יעשה לו ממנו סגולה ויחזיר לו כשיגדל: וכולן. בין נשים ועבדים ותינוקות: שאמרו בשעת מיתתן של פלוני הן הפקדון יעשה כפירושן. יחזיר לאותו פלוני: ואם לא פירש יעשה. א) מי שהפקדון בידו פירוש לפירושן שהן היו צריכין לפרש. ושל אשה יחזיר לבעל ושל עבד יחזיר לאדונו: הני כיפי. עגילים: דמרתא. של אשת פלוני: ובני ברתא. של שתיהן הוה: אי מהימנא לך. שלא גנבה מינך כלום: עשה כפירושה. ותן להם: אי אמידא לך. שאותה שהיא אומרת עשירה ומפקדת פקדונ' עשה כפירושה. ואי לא עשה פירוש לפירושה. ויהיה שלך: ספר תורה. כי היכי דלא מיכליא קרנא: פיסקא ולא לאב בנכסי הבן. בנכסים שקנה הבן: ואפילו חלקו. שהאב תופס לעצמו מה שקנה והבן תופס מה שקנה ושב והחזיק זה בשל זה לא הויא חזקה משום דאבא לגבי ברא וברא לגבי אבא אחולי אחלי הפירות זה לזה: רבא אמר חלקו לא אמרינן דלא הויא חזקה דודאי הויא חזקה משום דהבן שחלק הרי הוא כשאר כל אדם: מהורמיז ארדשיר. שהוא מן כרך שולטניות דארדשיר: אונות. כותות כגון הרשאות: ושטרות. דהלואות ומכירות: מבית אבי אמא. שאינן בני אם אחת: ואמר שלי הם. רב אמר עליו להביא ראיה שאף ע"פ שנכתבין על שמו כיון שלא חלק והוא נושא ונותן בממון כולו הרי הן בכח האחין ועליו להביא ראיה שהוא רוצה להוציא ממון מחזקתו: ושמואל אמר. כיון דנכתבין על שמו והוא תפוס על האחין להביא ראיה שלא יהא כדבריו: אבא. קרי לרב: על האחין להביא ראיה. שאין מוציאין מיתומים אלא בראיה: מתקיף לה רב פפא. וכי היכי טענינן בשביל יתמי מאי דלא מצי אבוהון למטען. דאילו הוה אבוהון קיים עליו היה להביא ראיה על האחין ואנן היכי מטענינן ליתמי דלימור דעל האחין להביא ראיה בשביל דאינון יתמי: והא רבא אפיק זוגי דסרבלא. מקטרן כפול וכו' מיתמי. דהיינו דברים העשוים להשאיל ולהשכיר דאע"ג דאמרי לקוחות הן בידינו משום דאילו הוה אבוהון קיים לא

חשק שלמה על רבינו גרשום א) עי' ברשב"ם ד"ה ויש מפרשים וכו' כלומר אם לא פירשו בשעת מיתה וכו' ונראה דכוון לפי' רבינו ז"ל.

Rav Pappa cites a decision that supports his argument: וְהָא רָבָא אַפִּיק זוּגָא דְסַרְבְּלָא – **But did Rava** not **seize a pair of cloakmaker's scissors**[23] וְסִפְרָא דְאַגַּדְתָּא – **and a book of** ***agaddah***[24] מִיַּתְמֵי – **from orphans** and award them to their previous owner[25] בְּלֹא רְאָיָה – **without proof** that he still owned them? בִּדְבָרִים הָעֲשׂוּיִם לְהַשְׁאִיל וּלְהַשְׂכִּיר – He did so **since** these **things are apt to be lent or rented** to others[26]

NOTES

force the other brothers to prove that he used the estate's money before they take a share of these assets. Hence, if we in fact do not advance a claim for orphans that was unavailable to the father, as our Gemara maintains, the brothers should not be required to produce such proof after the managing brother died either (*Rashbam*).

Rashbam questions the Gemara's contention (that we do not advance a claim for orphans that was unavailable to their father) from an earlier Gemara. According to the Gemara on 41b, if we know that someone inherited a field from his father and used it for three continuous years, he need only prove that the father occupied the field for one day. If he can do this, the court then enters a plea on the claimant's behalf that he inherited the field from his father and awards him the field. If his father had occupied the field for three years, however, the court would not have awarded it to him unless he also claimed to have bought it or to have received it as a gift from the previous owner. This apparently contradicts Rav Pappa's rule that we do not enter a plea for orphans if the plea was unavailable to their father.

Rashbam answers that the above case differs from ours. In that case, we merely enter a plea that the father himself could have entered if he were alive, i.e. that the father purchased the field. In our case, on the other hand, the father could not have demanded that the brothers prove their claim. Rav Pappa therefore argues that the orphans should not be able to make such a demand either.

23. Cloak makers used these scissors to cut loose strands off the cloak (*Rashbam; cf. Rabbeinu Gershom*).

24. A book of the Sages' homiletic discourses – see glossary.

25. In Rava's case, the last known owner of the objects in question claimed to have lent them to the orphans' father but produced no evidence to support the claim (*Rashbam*).

26. Normally, if someone claims to own movable articles that are in someone else's possession, the burden of proof falls upon the one wishing to take the property away from the person in possession of it. However, if someone holds in his possession articles that are apt to be lent or rented, the burden of proof falls upon the holder to prove that they are not merely rented or borrowed from the true owner.

In our case, after someone possessing such articles died, Rava seized them from the orphans' possession and awarded them to the previous owner. He did not enter a plea that the orphans' father had purchased these items, just as he would not have accepted such an unsubstantiated claim from their father. This supports Rav Pappa's argument (*Rashbam*).

קבל מן הקטן יעשה לו סגולה ואם מת יחזיר ליורשיו וכולן שאמרו בשעת מיתתן של פלוני הן יעשה כפירושן ואם לאו יעשה פירוש לפירושן דביתהו דרבה בר בר חנה כי קא שכבה אמרה הני כיפי דמרתא ובני ברתא אתא לקמיה דרב א"ל אי מהימנא לך עשה כפירושה ואי לא עשה פירוש לפירושה ואיכא דאמרי הכי א"ל אי אמידא לך עשה כפירושה ואי לא עשה פירוש לפירושה: מן הקטן יעשה לו סגולה: מאי סגולה רב חסדא אמר ספר תורה רבה בר רב הונא אמר דיקלא דאכל מיניה תמרי: ולא לאב בנכסי הבן ולא לבן בנכסי האב: אמר רב יוסף אפילו חלקו רבא אמר חלקו לא אמר רב ירמיה מדפתי עבד רב פפי עובדא חלקו לא כרבא אמר רב נחמן בר יצחק אישתעי לי רב חייא מהורמיז ארדשיר דאישתעי ליה רב אחא בר יעקב משמיה דרב נחמן בר יעקב חלקו לא והלכתא חלקו לא תניא נמי הכי בן שחלק ואשתו שנתגרשה הרי הן כשאר כל אדם: איתמר אחד מן האחין שהיה נושא ונותן בתוך הבית והיו אונות ושטרות יוצאין על שמו ואמר שלי הם שנפלו לי מבית אבי אמא אמר רב עליו להביא ראיה ושמואל אמר על האחין להביא ראיה אמר שמואל מודה לי אבא שאם מת על האחין להביא ראיה מתקיף לה רב פפא כלום טענינן להו ליתמי מידי דלא טען להו אבוהון והא רבא אפיק זוגא דסרבלא וספרא דאגדתא מיתמי בלא ראיה בדברים העשוים להשאיל ולהשכיר

כדשלח

רש"י

קבל מן הקטן. לא יחזיר לו שהרי אין יודע לשמור וכמשליך לאיבוד דמי מי שהחזיר לו אלא יעשה לו סגולה אוצר עד שיגדל ויחזיר לו ולקמן מפרש מאי סגולה: ואם מת. קטן יחזיר ליורשיו: וכולן שאמרו. אפי' קטן: בשעת מיתתן. אורחא דמילתא נקט דכשהן בריאין אם רוצים להחזיר לבעלים יטלו שלהן מיד הנפקד ויחזירו לבעליהן דמה להן לגלות הדבר: יעשה כפירושן. יחזיר הנפקד לאותו פלוני שפירשו אלו: ה"ג ואם לאו יעשה פירוש לפירושן. כלומר ואם לא מהימן להאי נפקד שהפקדון של אותו פלוני הוא אלא של בעלים שלהם הוא ומתוך בושה אינם רוצים לומר שהוא של בעלים דלא ליתחזקו כגזלנים וגנבים יעשה הנפקד פירוש אחר לפירושו שיחזור לבעליהן של אלו ולא לאותו פלוני וכי האי גוונא אמרינן בסמוך בהכיא עובדא דביתהו דרבה בר בר חנה. ויש מפרשים ואם לאו יעשה פירוש לפירושן כלומר אם לא פירשו בשעת מיתה יעשה (ב) פירוש למה שהם היו צריכין לפרש שיחזיר לבעליהן ולא נהירא דא"כ היינו רישא ואם מתו יחזיר לבעליהן ואם מת יחזיר לרבו דמיירי בשמת ולא פירש למי יחזיר וקאמר דיחזיר לבעלים ותרי זימני למה לי. ואית ספרים דכתב בהו ואיכא דאמרי יעשה פירוש לפירושו כלומר לא יעשה כמה שפירשו הן אלא יחזיר לבעלים ולא נהירא דא"כ רב דאמר אי מהימן לך כו' דאמר כמאן לא כרישא ולא כסיפא: כיפי. עגילים אנור"ש כדאמרינן בעלמא (עירובין דף נו:) כיפי תלא ליה עגילים תלה באזניהם: דמרתא. שם חכם אחיו של ר' חייא כדאמרינן (סנהדרין דף ה.) מרתא ואייבו ותנא ור' חייא כו': ובני ברתא. של מרתא ושל בני בתו: אי מהימנא לך. שלא גנבה ממך כלום: עשה פירוש לפירושה. עכב לעצמך: אי אמידא לך. אותה שהיא אומרת שהם שלהם אם עשירים הם וראוין להפקיד כיפי ושאר חפצים עשה כפירושה והחזירם להם. אי נמי אי אמידא לך אשתך שיש לה אוהבים שנתנו לה ממון ע"מ שלא יהא לך חלק בו ומתנה (ג) זו שנותנת לקרוביה משלה עשה כפירושה: ס"ת. ללמוד בו הרי פירות והקרן קיים: דאכיל מיניה. הקטן תמרי והקרן קיים אבל בעיסקא לא שמא יארע בה דבר תקלה ותאבד: אפי' חלקו. נתפרדו האב והבן שאין הבן סמוך על שולחן אביו ואין הבן (ד) בנכסי אביו כלום אפ"ה אין מחזיקין זה על זה דלא קפדי אהדדי: חלקו לא. כלומר בחלקו לא מיירי מתני' אלא כיון דחלקו יש להן חזקה זה על זה: הכי גרסינן עבד רב פפי עובדא חלקו לא. כלומר כרבא עשה דהיכא דחלקו לא דברה משנתנו אלא ודאי יש להן חזקה: הכי גרסינן בפירוש רבינו חננאל איתמר אחד מן האחין שהיה נושא ונותן כו'. אחד מן האחין כגון גדול אחין לאחר מות האב: אונות. שטרי מכירות לשון כחי וראשית אוני (בראשית מט): ושטרות. של הלואה: יוצאין על שמו. שבשמו נכתבו שהוא לקח (ה) והלוה: שלי הן. ואין לאחי חלק בהן שנפלו לי הממונות שהלויתי וקניתי בהן קרקעות הללו מבית אבי אמא ואין אתם יורשים עמי והלכך נקט אבי אמא דאילו מבית אבא כולן יורשין בשוה דבאחין מן האב עסקינן שכולן יורשין ממון של אביהן ביחד ולא יטול זה יותר מזה והלכך מאין לו ממון זה לבדו אם לא ירשו מאמו וכגון שאינם בני אם אחת: עליו להביא ראיה. שהממון שלו אע"פ שכתובין השטרות בשמו דכיון שהיה הוא לבדו נושא ונותן בנכסים שנכתבו על שמו וכדמפרש לקמיה שאין חלוקין אפי' בעיסקתן דכיון דלא נודע מעולם מאיזה צד יבא לו ממון בלא אחיו אין לתלות השטרות אלא בממון האב ואינו יכול להוציא הממון מחזקת האב ולקמן מפרש ראיה במאי: על האחין להביא ראיה. שהשטרות הללו מממון אביהן דאמאי דכתב בשטר סמכינן והרי על שמו נכתב ואע"ג דהלכתא כשמואל בדיני בהא הלכתא כרב דתניא לקמן כוותיה ורב חסדא ורבה ורב ששת נמי כרב סבירא להו דמפרשי מילתיה לקמן: אבא. רב כך היה שמו כדקרי ליה בשחיטת חולין (דף קלז:) אבא אריכא דאמרינן מאן ריש סדרא בבבל אבא אריכא ואמרינן במסכת נדה (דף כד:) רב ארוך בדורו היה והאי דקרי ליה רב כמו שקורין לר' יהודה הנשיא רבי בארץ ישראל קרו ליה נמי בבבל רב וכן מצאתי בספר ערוך המוגה מרומא: שאם מת. ויש לו בנים ליורשו על האחין להביא ראיה דכיון דיתמי לאו בני איתויי ראיה נינהו ואין יודעין לחפש זכותן וגם השטר מוכיח (ו) שהיה ממון של אביהן על שכנגדו להביא ראיה אבל כשהאח עצמו קיים היה מטיל רב עליו להביא ראיה דאם איתא דשלו הוא ממון זה יכול לחפש ולמצוא ראיה ואם לא ימצא ראיה הפסיד: מתקיף לה רב פפא. למאי דאמר שמואל מודי לי אבא: כלום טענינן להו ליתמי כו'. בתמיה אילו היה אביהן קיים היינו מחזיקין הממון ביד אחין עד שיביא ראיה שאינו שלהן ולפי שמת יפה כחן של יתומין ממנו ויפסידו אחין בתמיה ואע"ג דאמרינן (לעיל דף מא:) טוענין ליורש גבי חזקת ג' שנים שאע"פ שלא דר בו אביו אלא יום אחד וזה החזיק ג' שנים אחרי כן הויא חזקה ואע"ג דאבוהון לא מהניא ליה חזקת שלש שנים לומר לקוח הוא בידי אלא א"כ יש עמה טענה אתה מכרתו לי אתה נתתו לי במתנה וגבי בנו לא בעינן טענה זו אלא מאבי ירשתי אלמא טענינן ליתמי מאי דלא מצי אבוהון למטען לא דמי דהתם נמי אין טוענין בשביל היתומים אלא שאביהן קנאה מן המערער כמו שהיה הוא האב יכול לטעון ולפיכך הויא חזקה אע"ג דלא טענו מידי אבל הכא האב לא מצי טעין לאחין שיביאו ראיה ואנן היכי נטעון במקום היתומים כן: והא רבא אפיק כו'. סיומא לאתקפתא דרב פפא היא: זוגא דסרבלא. זוג מספריים של סורקי בגדים שגוזזין בהם הסרבלים: בלא ראיה. הבעלים שהיו להם עדים שהן שלהן הוציאום מן היתומים בלא ראיה ועדים שיעידו שהשאילו לאביהן של יתומים לפי שהן עשוין להשאיל ולהשכיר שאם אמר אביהן לקוחין הם בידי עליו להביא ראיה אף היתומין עליהן להביא ראיה שאביהן קנאן מן הבעלים וכיון דלית להו ראיה החזירם לבעלים ולא נאמר כיון שמת האב על האחין להביא ראיה:

כדשלח

תוספות

קבל מן הקטן יעשה לו סגולה. דמשמע לידו אימור מציאה אשכח ולכך הוו דקטן ויעשה לו סגולה אבל מכל מקום לכתחלה אין מקבלין: ומודה לי אבא שאם מת על האחין להביא ראיה. אומר רשב"א אין לומר משום דטענינן ליתמי דלא הוה אבוהון קיים הוה מייתי ראיה לעיל (דף מו.) פריך (ז) דלא הוה אתי בטענתא דאבוהון אפי' הכך נמי משמע דפשיטא ליה דבן אומן ובן אריס דאתו בטענתא דאבוהון דאין להן חזקה ומאין פשיט לו כל כך הא לרב יש חזקה לבן אריס אע"פ שלאריס עצמו אין לו חזקה ומיהו י"ל דהתם (ח) מבן גזלן פריך כלומר אפי' הכך נמי הוו כבן גזלן אבל מ"מ אין לפרש כן דהא תנן (לעיל דף מא.) הבא מחמת ירושה אין צריך טענה הא חזקה בעי ואמאי דלמא אם היה אביו קיים היה מביא עדים שלקחה אלא נראה דהכא דוקא הוא דקאמר רב על האחין להביא ראיה אם מת משום דאונות ושטרות יוצאים על שמו דמוכחא מילתא דשלו הן אלא בחייו הוא דקאמר רב עליו להביא ראיה דלא סמכינן אמאי דיוצאין על שמו דאם איתא דנפלו לו מבית אבי אמו היו לו עדים בדבר שבנו לא ליכא למימר הכי סמכינן אמאי דיוצאין על שמו ונראה דרב מודה במאי דאפיק רבא זוגא דסרבלא מיתמי ולרב פפא דפריך מינה נראה לו לדמותה לאונות ושטרות יוצאין על שמו:

רבינו גרשום

קבל פקדון מן הקטן. אין יכול להחזיר לו לפי שאין יד לקטן אלא יעשה לו ממנו סגולה ויחזיר לו כשיגדל: וכולן. בין נשים ועבדים ותינוקות: שאמרו בשעת מיתתן של פלוני הן הפקדון יעשה כפירושן. ויחזיר לאותו פלוני: ואם לא פירשו יעשה. א) מי שהפקדון בידו פירוש לפירושן שהן היו צריכין לפרוש. ושל אשה יחזיר לבעל ושל עבד יחזיר לאדונו: הני כיפי. עגילים: דמרתא. של אשת פלוני: ובני ברתא. של שתיהן הוה: אי מהימנא לך. שלא גנבה מינך כלום: עשה כפירושה. ותן להם: אי אמידא לך. שאותה שהיא אומרת עשירה ומפקדת פקדוני' עשה כפירושה: ואי לא עשה פירוש לפירושה. ויהיה שלך: ספר תורה. כי היכי דלא מיכליא קרנא: פיסקא ולא לאב בנכסי הבן. בנכסים שקנה הבן: ואפילו חלקו. שהאב תופס לעצמו מה שקנה והבן תופס מה שקנה ושב והחזיק זה בשל זה לא הויא חזקה משום דאבא לגבי ברא וברא לגבי אבא אחולי אחלי הפירות זה לזה: רבא אמר חלקו לא אמרינן דלא הויא חזקה דודאי הויא חזקה משום דהבן שחלק הרי הוא כשאר כל אדם: מהורמיז ארדשיר. שהוא מן כרך שולטניות דארדשיר: אונות. כוחות כגון הרשאות: ושטרות. דהלואות ומכירות: מבית אבי אמא. שאינן בני אם אחת: ואמר שלי הוא. רב אמר עליו להביא ראיה שאף ע"פ שנכתבין על שמו כיון שלא חלק והוא נושא ונותן בממון כולו הרי הן בכח האחין ועליו להביא ראיה שהוא רוצה להוציא ממון מחזקתו: ושמואל אמר. כיון דנכתבין על שמו והוא תפוס על האחין להביא ראיה שלא יהא כדבריו: אבא. קרי לרב: על האחין להביא ראיה. שאין מוציאין מיתומים אלא בראיה: מתקיף לה רב פפא. וכי היכי טענינן בשביל יתמי מאי דלא מצי אבוהון למטען. דאילו הוה אבוהון קיים עליו היה להביא ראיה ולא על האחין ואנן היכי מטענינן ליתמי דלימרו דעל האחין להביא ראיה בשביל דאינן יתמי: והא רבא אפיק זוגי דסרבלא. מקטורן כפול וכו' מיתמי. דהיינו דברים העשוים להשאיל ולהשכיר דאע"ג דאמרי לקוחות הן בידי משום דאילו הוה אבוהון קיים לא

עין משפט נר מצוה

ריב א מיי' פ"ז מהל' פקדון הל' י ופכ"ב מהלכות אישות הל' לב סמג עשין פח טוש"ע אה"ע סי' פו סעי' א [וברב אלפס עוד בב"מ פ"ג דף פו.]:
ריג ב ג מיי' שם וסמג שם טור אה"ע שם:
ריד ד ה מיי' פ"ט מהלכות נחלות הל' ז ח סמג עשין צו ופי' פח טוש"ע ח"מ סי' סב:

מסורת הש"ס

א) ב"ק פז:, ב) [ג"א רבא בר הונא], ג) לעיל מז., ד) שבועות מו: ב"מ קח., ה) [בערוך ערך זה איתא זווא פי' שני סרבלים], ו) וכן פי' ממים וכן עיקר, ז) [עי' תוס' חולין לז. ד"ה אצטריך ליה לאבא], ח) [בערך אבא ובערך אבין]:

הגהות הב"ח

(א) גמ' רבא אמר חלקו לא וכו' לא כרבא: (ב) רשב"ם ד"ה ה"ג וכו' יעשה הוא פירוש למה: (ג) ד"ה אי אמידא וכו' ומתנה היא זו: (ד) ד"ה אפילו חלקו וכו' ואין הבן מתעסק בנכסי אביו: (ה) ד"ה יוצאין וכו' שהוא לקח או הלוה: (ו) ד"ה שאם מת וכו' השטר מוכיח שהממון היה של אביהן: (ז) תוס' ד"ה מודה וכו' פריך אי דלאו: (ח) בא"ד י"ל דהתם מבן גזלן:

ליקוטי רש"י

כיפי. מרגליות לשונה אחרונה אנוש"ט וכן עיקר [עירובין נו:]. ממים [כתובות פא:]. בן שחלק ואשה שנתגרשה הרי הן ככל אדם. הפליג מאביו ואין סמוך עוד על שולחנו כגון שנשא אשה ואין מתפרנס עוד מנכסי אביו הרי הן ככל אדם.

כדשלח רב הונא בר אבין [א]דברים העשוין להשאיל ולהשכיר ואמר לקוחין הן בידי אינו נאמן קשיא: אמר רב חסדא [ב]לא שנו אלא דאין חלוקין בעיסתן אבל חלוקים בעיסתן אימור מעיסתו קימץ ראיה במאי רבה אמר [ג]ראיה בעדים רב ששת אמר ראיה בקיום השטר אמר ליה רבא לרב נחמן הא רב והא שמואל הא רבה והא רב ששת מר כמאן סבירא ליה א"ל אנא מתניתא ידענא דתניא אחד מן האחין שהיה נותן ונושא בתוך הבית והיו אונות ושטרות יוצאין על שמו ואמר שלי הן שנפלו לי מבית אבי אמא עליו להביא ראיה וכן [ד]האשה שהיא נושאת ונותנת בתוך הבית והיו אונות ושטרות יוצאין על שמה ואמרה שלי הן שנפלו לי מבית אבי אבא או מבית אבי אמא עליה להביא ראיה מאי וכן מהו דתימא אשה כיון דשביחא לה מילתא דאמרי קא טרחא קמי יתמי לא גזלה מיתמי קא משמע לן: במה דברים אמורים במחזיק אבל בנותן מתנה והאחין שחלקו וכו': אטו כל הני דאמרינן לאו בני חזקה נינהו חסורי מחסרא והכי קתני במה דברים אמורים בחזקה שיש עמה טענה כגון מוכר אומר לא מכרתי ולוקח אומר לקחתי אבל חזקה שאין עמה טענה כגון נותן מתנה והאחין שחלקו והמחזיק בנכסי הגר דלמקני בעלמא הוא (א) נעל גדר פרץ כל שהוא הרי זו חזקה תני רב [א]הושעיא בקדושין דבי לוי [ב]נעל גדר פרץ כל שהוא בפניו הרי זו חזקה בפניו אין שלא בפניו לא אמר רבא [ה]הכי קאמר בפניו לא צריך למימר ליה לך חזק וקני שלא

רשב"ם

כדשלח רב הונא כו'. כלומר להכי אפקינהו רבא משום דדברים העשוין להשאיל ולהשכיר אין אדם נאמן לומר לקוח הוא בידי כדשלח רב הונא: קשיא. לדידן קשיא אמאי אמר שמואל מודי לי אבא כו': ופסק ר' חננאל דהלכתא כשמואל דהיכא דמית על האחין להביא ראיה וכן פירש נקטינן מרבותי ז"ל כל היכא דאמר בגמ' תיובתא דפלוני תיובתא בטלו דברי מי שהתיובתא עליו לגמרי אבל היכא דעלתה בקשיא כי הך דשמואל לא בטלו דבריו דאמרינן לא הוה ברירא להן דבטלה שמועה זו לגמרי אלא לא אשתכח פירוקא בההוא שעתא דתליא וקיימא ואעפ"כ אין נראה בעיני דלא שנא תיובתא ולא שנא קשיא דקאי אמילתא דאמוראי חדא היא ולא הויא עיקר אלא לגבי תיובת' ממשנה או מברייתא שייך לומר תיובתא [ס]ומפירכא דאמוראי שייך למימר קשיא והא דשמואל נראה בעיני דלא סמכינן עליה כל עיקר וכן בפי' ר"ח כתב מרי"ש גאון כי זה שאמר שמואל ומודי לי אבא שאם מת על האחין להביא ראיה אין הלכה כמותו: **לא שנו.** הא דקאמר רב עליו להביא ראיה: **אלא שאין חלוקין.** בשום דבר בעולם אפי' בעיסתן הלכך מאין לו לזה כלום בלא אחיו: **קימץ.** עצרן ביותר ולכך נתעשר והיה לו ממון לבדו שאין לאחיו חלק בו ומהממון ההוא לקח קרקעות והלוה לאחרים: **ראיה במאי.** אדרב קאי שהלכה כמותו דאי אדשמואל היכי אמר רב ששת ראיה בקיום השטר והרי לשמואל דאית ליה על האחין להביא ראיה צריך להן לפסול שטרו של זה ולא לקיימו: **ראיה בעדים.** על בעל השטר להביא ראיה דמעיסתו קימץ או מאבי אמו ירש והיה ממון של שטרות הללו שלו: **בקיום השטר.** שכתבו לו בית דין הנפק על שטר זה (ב) וכיון דקיימוהו ב"ד בדקו השטר וחקרו ועמדו על אמיתת הדבר שכל הכתוב בשטר אמת הוא והשטר הרי כתוב בשמו של זה: **הא רבה והא רב ששת.** דפליגי אליבא דרב ואי כרב סבירא לך ראיה במאי אי כרבה אי כרב ששת: **מתניתא ידענא.** כרב ומיהו לא פירש לי אי כרבה אי כרב ששת: ורבינו חננאל פסק בעדים צריך להביא ראיה ולא בקיום השטר דהא אפי' רב ששת מודי דראיה בעדים שוה יותר מקיום השטר: **וכן האשה.** אלמנה: **מבית אבי אבא.** ה"נ מצי למימר מבית אבא ומשום רישא דקתני מבית אבי אמא קתני נמי סיפא מבית אבי אבא: **מאי וכן.** דמשמע ואפי' האשה דינה כן (ג) ומאי רבותא איכא טפי דקתני וכן הכי הוה ליה למיתני אשה שהיתה נושאת ונותנת כו' ודרך תנא לומר שני דברים שוין וזימנין דאמרינן דצריכי תרוייהו אבל הכא דקתני וכן משמע דבלא זו אף זו קתני: **דשביחא לה מילתא.** חשיבות היא לה שמאמינין אותה בית דין לעשותה אפוטרופוס בשל יתומין וגם משבחין אותה בני אדם על כך ומקושי גדול תאמר על שלהן שהוא שלה וסד"א דליהמנה קא משמע לן: בבבא בתרא ירושלמי' אין לאיש חזקה בנכסי אשתו בחיי אשתו אבל לאחר מיתת אשתו יש לו חזקה ולא לאשה בחיי בעלה בנכסי בעל אבל לאחר מיתת בעלה יש לה חזקה ולא לאב בנכסי הבן בחיי הבן אבל לאחר מיתת הבן יש לו חזקה ולא לבן בנכסי האב בחיי האב אבל לאחר מיתת האב יש לו חזקה ואיכא לדמויי להך דתניא לעיל בן שחלק ואשה שנתגרשה כו': במתני' לא גרסינן ופרץ בפניו דהא נכסי הגר לא שייך ביה בפניו דהא מית ליה הגר: **אטו כל הני.** דאמרינן לקמן במתני' נותן מתנה ואחין שחלקו לאו על ידי חזקה דנעל גדר הן קונין כדקתני מתני' בתמיה: **במה דברים אמורים.** דבעינן ג' שנים: **בחזקה שיש עמה טענה.** כלומר ערעור: **אבל בחזקה שאין עמה טענה.** שבעל הקרקע מודה לו ליטלה כגון נותן מתנה כו' כיון דנעל גדר ופרץ כל שהוא בפני עדים הויא חזקה לקנות שלא יוכל לחזור עוד זה בזה: **בקדושין דבי לוי.** בתוספתא (ד) בברייתא דמס' קדושין שסידר לוי כמו שסידרו ר' חייא ור' אושעיא: **נעל וגדר ופרץ בפניו.** במקח וממכר מיירי דתנן בקידושין (דף כו.) דקרקע נקנית בחזקה: ומתמה גמ' **בפניו הוא** דהוי חזקה **אבל שלא בפניו.** דמוכר אם נעל וגדר שלא בפניו לא תיהוי חזקה בתמיה: **ה"ק.** אם גדר ופרץ לוקח בפניו דמוכר לא צריך למימר ליה מוכר ללוקח לך חזק וקני אלא מכיון שנתרצה לו למכרה בכך וכך מעות והחזיק זה בפניו הויא חזקה דניחא ליה בהך חזקה והלכך שתיק ולא יוכל מוכר לחזור בו עוד והלוקח נתחייב לו דמי מקחו: שלא

תוספות

דברים העשוין להשאיל ולהשכיר ואמר לקוחים הן בידי אינו נאמן. וקשה דאמר בפ' כל הנשבעין (שבועות דף מו. ושם) א"ר יהודה ראוהו שהטמין כלים תחת כנפיו ויצא ואמר לקוחין הן בידי אין נאמן ולא אמרן אלא בבעל הבית שאינו עשוי למכור כליו ולא אמרן אלא בדברים שאין עשוין להטמין ולא אמרן אלא בדברי' העשוין להשאיל ולהשכיר אלמא דאפילו בדברים העשוין להשאיל ולהשכיר נאמן אי ליכא כל הני מילי דקאמר שאין עשוי למכור כליו וכלים שאין דרכן להטמין ונראה לר"ת דגרס התם ובכולהו נמי כי ליתנהו לא אמרן אלא בדברים שאין עשוין להשאיל ולהשכיר אבל דברים העשוין להשאיל ולהשכיר אפי' ליתנהו לחד מהני אין נאמן וכן גורס רב האי בשערים (שער מ) וכן ר"ח וכן מוכח בשילהי המקבל (ב"מ דף קטז.) וא"ת (ה) דתנא בהגוזל בתרא (ב"ק דף קיד:) המכיר כליו וספריו ביד אחר ויצא שם גנבה בעיר ישבע כמה הוציא ויטול והשתא אפי' לא יצא שם גנבה יהא נאמן לומר שגנבוה מיגו דאי בעי אמר השאלתי לך דספרים הן עשוין להשאיל דאפי' ספרא דאגדתא אמר הכא דעשוין להשאיל כ"ש שאר ספרים כדאמר בנערה שנתפתתה (כתובות דף נ.) ולדקתו עומדת לעד זה הכותב ספרים ומשאילן לאחרים ואין לומר דלא מהימן במיגו לומר דגנובים (ו) משום דלאחזוקי אינשי בגנבי לא מחזקינן כדאמר בכל הנשבעין (שבועות דף מו:) דלא דמי דהתם ודאי אינו נאמן לאחזוקי ההוא גברא בגנבי אפי' במיגו אבל הכא שאינו אומר פלוני גנבם אלא שהם גנובים מהימן שפיר דכמה גנבים יש בעולם ואין לומר נמי דלאו מיגו הוא שאינו טוען ברצון השאלתי לך לפי שאותו יודע בו שהוא משקר דהא לעיל (דף לא.) אמר דנאמן לומר של אבותי הוא שלקחוה מאבותיך במיגו דאי בעי אמר מינך זבינתיה אע"פ שהוא יודע דלאו מיניה זבנה וכן בפרק שני דכתובות (דף טו: וע"ש בתוס' ד"ה ומודה) תנן דנאמן לומר שדה זו של אביך היתה ולקחתיה הימנו במיגו דאי בעי אמר לא היתה של אביך מעולם אע"פ שהבן יודע שהיתה של אביו ומהנהו עזי דאכלי חושלי בנהרדעא לעיל (דף לו.) אין ראיה דאיכא למימר כגון שמכחישו ואומר שלא אכלו כל כך דהשתא הוי מיגו טוב ותירץ ר"ת דהתם מיירי באדם שאין (ז) עשוין להשאיל ולהשכיר לזה שקנאם כגון דלא גיים ביה ולפי זה אם עשוי להשאיל לו אפי' לא יצא לו שם גנבה נאמן לומר שהם גנובים במיגו ולמה"ר (ח) דודי נראה דלא מהימן במיגו דהוי מיגו להוציא אע"פ שנוטל דמים שהוציא:

אימא מעיסתו קימץ. אע"ג דלא טעין הכי אלא אומר מבית אבי אמא מ"מ נאמן במיגו דאי בעי אמר מעיסתי קמצתי:

דטרחא קמי יתמי אימא לא גזלה מיתמי. קשה לרשב"א דאדרבה מהאי טעמא דטרחא קמי יתמי גזלה מיתמי כדאמר בהשולח (גיטין דף לה.) בההוא הנאה דטרחא קמי יתמי אתיא לאורויי ותירץ דה"נ קאמר הכא קמ"ל דלא אמרינן דלא גזלה אלא אדרבה אתיא לאורויי כדאמר בגיטין:

נעל וגדר כל שהוא כו'. בגמרא פר"ש דהאי נעל היינו שקבע מנעול בדלת דהוי בנין אבל סגר הדלת ונעל במפתח בנכסי הגר דליכא דמסר ליה לא הוי חזקה דאין זה אלא כמבריח ארי מנכסי חבירו אע"ג דבריש פסחים (דף ד. ושם ד"ה אם) אמר דמשמסר לו מפתח הוי הבית בחזקת שוכר לבדקו וה"ה לקנותו ה"מ

עין משפט נר מצוה

רטו א מיי' פ"ח מהל' טוען הלכה ג סמג עשין פט טוש"ע ח"מ סי' עב סעיף יח וסי' קלג ס"ה:

רטז ב ג מיי' פ"ט מהל' נחלות הלכה ח סמג לאוין פא טוש"ע ח"מ סי' סב:

ריז ד מיי' שם ופכ"ב מהל' אישות הל' ל סמג שם טוש"ע שם וטוש"ע אה"ע סי' פו סעי' ג וע"ש בהג"ה:

ריח ה מיי' פ"א מהל' מכירה הלכה ח סמג עשין פב טוש"ע ח"מ סי' קלב סעיף ב:

ליקוטי רש"י

דברים העשוין להשאיל ולהשכיר וכו'. אבל דברים שאין עשוין להשאיל שהבעלים חסים עליהם לפי שמתקלקלין נאמן לשבע שלקחם ואין נראין דברי האומר השאלתים לו [שבועות מו:]. **אונות.** שטרי מכירות לשון כחי וראשית אוני (בראשית מט). **ושטרות.** של הלואה [רשב"ם לעיל ע"א]. **נעל.** דלת או גדר פרלה או פרץ גדר כל שהוא [גיטין עז:]. עשה דלת. **וגדר.** או גדר חומה. **פרץ.** פירלה כדי שיכנס בה [רשב"ם לעיל מב.]. **הרי זו חזקה.** לקנות שאין המוכר יכול לחזור בו [גיטין שם]. לבלתי חזור זה בזה כיון דברשות חבירו החזיק [רשב"ם שם].

רבינו גרשום

מצי טעין **לקוחות הן בידי** אינהו נמי לא מצי טעני **וקשיא: אמר רב חסדא לא שנו.** הא דאמרן דאינו נאמן דעליו להביא ראיה שהן שלו **אלא שאין חלוקין בעיסתן.** כלומר שעדיין לא חלקו ירושתן ואוכלין יחד מעיסה אחת: **אבל חלוקין בעיסתן.** שכבר חלקו ואעפ"כ נושא ונותן בחלקם ודאי על האחין להביא ראיה דאינו שלו דאי לא מייתו ראיה א) מוחזק זה בזה **דאימור מעיסתו קיבץ.** כלומר ממזונותיו צמצם וקיבץ ממון ועשה אלו אונות ושטרות ולהכי כתובין על שמו: **בעדים.** שיודעין שהם שלו: **בקיום דשטר.** שאם קיימו בית דין אלו שטרות על שמו דכתבי הכי שטרא של פלוני נפק לקדמנא ודאי שלו הן דבית דין לא הוי מקיימי על שמו אי לא דבקיאי דהן שלו: **הא רב ושמואל הא רבה ורב ששת.** כולהו גילו טעמיהו בדבר זה: **מר כמאן סבירא ליה.** כלומר מה דעתך בזה: **וכן אשה** אלמנה **שנושאת ונותנת בתוך הבית.** של יתומין דעדיין לא נסתלקה מהם: **שנפלו לי מבית אבי אמא.** והוא הדין שנפלו לה מאביה עצמה לאחר מיתת בעלה דהכי יכולה למימר: **אימא לא גזלה מיתמי.** ותהא מהימנא ועל היתומים לאיתויי ראיה. **קמ"ל** דאפי' הכי לא מהימנא אי לא מייתא ראיה: **פיסקא במה דברים אמורים.** דצריך חזקה ג' שנים: **במחזיק.** כלומר כגון כל הני דאמרן לעיל **דזה המחזיק טוען לקחתי והמערער אומר לא מכרתי** דאינו מודה לו **אבל** היכא דמכר או **נותן מתנה** צריך כל אחד להחזיק בחלקו כדי שלא יהיו יכולין לחזור בהן. וכן **המחזיק בנכסי הגר** שמת אינן צריכין ג' שנים לחזקה. אלא **נעל** שסתם פתח כל שהוא או **פרץ** בו מעט או **גדר כל שהוא** לאלתר **הוי חזקה: בקדושין דבי לוי.** במסכת קדושין בבית המדרש של לוי: **בפניו לא צריך למימר ליה לך חזק וקני.** כלומר אם המקבל הוא שם בפני הנותן לא צריך למימר ליה הנותן לך חזק וקני אע"ג דלא קאמר ליה אי מחזיק מקבל בנעל וגדר כל שהוא קני. אבל **שלא בפניו** כגון שהקרקע בעיר אחרת

מסורת הש"ס

א) [גי' הרא"ש שרביא ועי' תוס' לקמן נג. ד"ה נעל וכ"א בשאלתות פ' מסעי סימן קלט], ב) [תוספתא דקידושין פ"א]:

הגהות הב"ח

(א) גמ' דלמקני בעלמא הוא דבעי נעל וגדר ופרץ וכו' תני רב שרביא בקידושין דבי לוי נעל וגדר ופרץ: (ב) רשב"ם ד"ה בקיום וכו' שטר זה דכיון: (ג) ד"ה מאי וכן וכו' ומאי רבותא. נ"ב וכה"ג פרש"י בב"ק דף קיד ע"ב: (ד) ד"ה בקידושין דבי לוי בתוספתא (בברייתא) תז"מ ונ"ב הגהה היא: (ה) תוס' ד"ה דברים וכו' וא"ת הא דתנא וכו' ויצא לו שם גניבה: (ו) בא"ד דגנובים הם משום: (ז) בא"ד באדם שאין עשוי להשאיל: (ח) בא"ד ולמה"ר דוד נראה:

גליון הש"ס

רשב"ם ד"ה ופסק כו' ומפירכא דאמוראי שייך לומר קשיא. עי' סנהדרין דף עב ע"א ברש"י ד"ה קשיא ושם דף קיב ע"א ברש"י ד"ה קשיא ובבאר שבע שם ועי' לקמן דף קמו ע"א ברשב"ם ד"ה קשיא ובפלפולא חריפתא שם על הרא"ש ובמו"ק דף ג' ע"ב בתוספות ד"ה חייב שתים:

לעזי רש"י

אנור"ש. פירוש עגילים, נזמים (רש"י עירובין דף נו סוע"ב וכתובות דף פא ע"ב וב"מ דף לה ע"א ודף נא ע"א ועיין רש"י במדבר לא, נ ויחזקאל טז, יב), טבעות. רומ"א. פירוש העיר רומא (הבירה של מדינת איטליה):

חשק שלמה על רבינו גרשום

א) נ"ל אין מוליאין ממוחזקו דמוחזק זה בזה.

כִּדְשָׁלַח רַב הוּנָא בַּר אָבִין – **in accordance with** the following law **reported by Rav Huna bar Avin:** דְּבָרִים הָעֲשׂוּיִן לְהַשְׁאִיל וּלְהַשְׂכִּיר – If a person has **things that are apt to be lent or rented** in his possession, וְאָמַר לְקוּחִין הֵן בְּיָדִי – **and he says,** "They are mine, for **I purchased them,"** אֵינוֹ נֶאֱמָן – **he is not believed.** Thus, Rava's ruling supports Rav Pappa's contention that we do not enter a plea on behalf of orphans if it was unavailable to their father.[1]

The Gemara concludes:

קַשְׁיָא – This is indeed **a difficulty.**[2]

The Gemara qualifies the ruling of Rav which was cited above:

אָמַר רַב חִסְדָּא – **Rav Chisda said:** לֹא שָׁנוּ אֶלָּא דְּאֵין חֲלוּקִין בְּעִיסְקָן – **[Rav's ruling] was taught only in a case in which they were not divided** even **in their food expenditures,** i.e. their food (and all other expenses) are paid for communally,[3] אֲבָל חֲלוּקִים בְּעִיסְקָן – **but if** they were divided in **their food expenditures,**[4] אֵימוּר מֵעִיסְקָתוֹ קִימֵּץ – **say** that **perhaps he skimped on his food allotment** and used the money saved for independent investments.[5]

The Gemara discusses how the managing brother proves that he invested his own money:[6]

רְאָיָה בְּמַאי – **What** type of **proof** must he produce? רַבָּה אָמַר – **Rabbah said:** רְאָיָה בְּעֵדִים – **A proof** consisting **of witnesses** who corroborate his claim.[7] רַב שֵׁשֶׁת אָמַר – **Rav Sheishess,** however, **said:** רְאָיָה בְּקִיּוּם הַשְּׁטָר – **A proof** consisting **of** a court's **certification of the** disputed **document,** i.e. the disputed bill of sale or loan document, suffices;[8] he need not produce witnesses.

The Gemara elicits Rav Nachman's opinion concerning the two aforementioned disputes:

אָמַר לֵיהּ רָבָא לְרַב נַחְמָן – Rava said to Rav Nachman: הָא רַב וְהָא שְׁמוּאֵל – **Here** we have **Rav and here** we have **Shmuel** disagreeing over who has the burden of proof. הָא רַבָּה וְהָא רַב שֵׁשֶׁת – **Here** we have **Rabbah and here** we have **Rav Sheishess** disagreeing over what type of proof must be brought. מַר כְּמַאן סְבִירָא לֵיהּ – **With whom does master agree?**[9]

Rav Nachman gives his opinion on the first question:

אָמַר לֵיהּ – **[Rav Nachman] said to [Rava]:** אֲנָא מַתְנִיתָא יָדַעְנָא – **I know a Baraisa** that supports Rav's position, דְּתַנְיָא – **for it was taught in a Baraisa:** אֶחָד מִן הָאַחִין – ONE OF a group of BROTHERS שֶׁהָיָה נוֹתֵן וְנוֹשֵׂא בְּתוֹךְ הַבַּיִת – WHO HAD BEEN MANAGING the affairs of [HIS LATE FATHER'S] ESTATE on behalf of all the brothers וְהָיוּ אוֹנוֹת וּשְׁטָרוֹת יוֹצְאִין עַל שְׁמוֹ – AND BILLS OF SALE AND loan DOCUMENTS APPEAR IN HIS NAME; וְאָמַר שֶׁלִּי הֵן – HE CLAIMS, "THESE assets represent MY OWN holdings, שֶׁנָּפְלוּ לִי מִבֵּית אֲבִי אִמָּא – WHICH I INHERITED FROM MY MATERNAL GRANDFATHER." It is unclear, however, whether this is true. עָלָיו לְהָבִיא רְאָיָה – THE BURDEN OF PROOF IS UPON HIM to prove that he acquired the assets with his own money.[10]

The Gemara continues to quote the remainder of the Baraisa:

וְכֵן הָאִשָּׁה – AND SIMILARLY, A widowed WOMAN שֶׁהִיא נוֹשֵׂאת וְנוֹתֶנֶת בְּתוֹךְ הַבַּיִת – WHO HAD BEEN MANAGING THE AFFAIRS OF [HER LATE HUSBAND'S] ESTATE וְהָיוּ אוֹנוֹת וּשְׁטָרוֹת יוֹצְאִין עַל שְׁמָהּ – AND BILLS OF SALE AND loan DOCUMENTS APPEARED IN HER NAME; וְאָמְרָה שֶׁלִּי הֵן – SHE CLAIMS, "THESE assets represent MY OWN holdings, שֶׁנָּפְלוּ לִי מִבֵּית אֲבִי אַבָּא – WHICH I INHERITED FROM MY PATERNAL GRANDFATHER אוֹ מִבֵּית אֲבִי אִמָּא – OR FROM MY MATERNAL GRANDFATHER."[11] It is unclear, however, whether this is true. עָלֶיהָ לְהָבִיא רְאָיָה – In such a case, THE BURDEN OF PROOF IS UPON HER to prove that she purchased the assets with her own money.

The Gemara objects to the wording of this last clause:

מַאי וְכֵן – **What** is the reason that the clause begins with the phrase **"and similarly"?** Why is the ruling of this clause more novel than that of the first clause?[12]

NOTES

1. Rav Pappa therefore disputed Shmuel's qualification of Rav's ruling, maintaining instead that even if the managing brother died, his orphans must prove that their father made the purchases or advanced the money with his own money.

2. I.e., we do not know how to to defend Shmuel's statement (*Rashbam*).

3. That is, whenever a brother incurred an expense, it was paid directly from the estate. They were not granted allowances from which to pay their expenses. Thus, no brother has money which belongs exclusively to him and is not part of the estate (*Rashbam*).

4. That is, the expenses were not paid directly from the estate. Rather, each brother was allotted a given allowance for his expenses (e.g. a food allowance). Thus, if one brother spent less on food than the others, he could save money and later invest it.

5. Even according to Rav, then, he need not prove that he purchased the property or advanced the loans with his own money, because there is a plausible explanation for how he had money to invest.

Tosafos note that the managing brother never claimed to have invested money from his share of the estate; rather, he claimed to have inherited money from his maternal grandfather. Nevertheless, *Tosafos* explains, we accept his claim because of the *migo* principle: If he had wanted to lie he could have claimed that he saved money from his food allowance and his claim would have been accepted as true. Hence, we believe him even when he claims to have inherited money from his grandfather.

6. The following discussion refers to Rav's ruling that the burden of proof is upon the managing brother. The Gemara now defines what the proof must consist of. It does not define what the proof must consist of according to Shmuel's ruling, since the halachah is not in accordance with his view (see *Rashbam*).

7. That is, they testify either that he saved money from his food allowance or that he inherited money from his maternal grandfather (*Rashbam*).

8. That is, he need only take the document to court and have them append a *henpeik* (certification) to it. Before doing so, the court will investigate the document's authenticity and ascertain the veracity of everything written in it. Now, the document names only the managing brother as the purchaser or creditor. Hence, if the court certifies the document, we are assured that he indeed used his own money to make the purchase or advance the loan (*Rashbam*).

Rashbam notes that Rav Sheishess's opinion reflects Rav's view that the managing brother must prove that he spent his own money to acquire the assets mentioned in the documents. When the brother certifies the document, he indeed proves this, as explained above. According to Shmuel, on the other hand, it is the other brothers who must prove that the managing brother spent the estate's money. It would thus be counterproductive for them to certify the document (cf. *Rashba* and *Ramban*).

9. Does master side with Rav or Shmuel? If master sides with Rav (that the burden of proof is upon the managing brother), what type of proof must he produce? Must he produce witnesses (as Rabbah requires) or only a certified document (as Rav Sheishess maintains)? (*Rashbam;* cf. *Ramban* and *Rashba*).

10. Since the Baraisa clearly supports Rav's view, Rav Nachman accepted it. He did not offer an opinion, however, about the issue over which Rabbah and Rav Sheishess disagreed.

11. When a woman inherits money from any of her ancestors, her children have no claim to it. In our case, then, the Baraisa could have stated simply that the widow inherited money from her father. Nonetheless, it presents a claim stated to parallel the former case (*Rashbam*).

12. The Mishnah usually uses the connective phrase וְכֵן, *and similarly*, to introduce a ruling that is more novel than the previous one. Hence, our Baraisa's second clause, which begins with וְכֵן, implies that its second ruling (concerning a woman who manages her late husband's estate) is more novel than its first ruling (concerning one brother managing his father's estate). Why, asks the Gemara, should this be so? (*Rashbam*).

כדשלח רב הונא בר אבין [א] דברים העשוין להשאיל ולהשכיר ואמר לקוחין הן בידי אינו נאמן קשיא: אמר רב חסדא [ב] לא שנו אלא דאין חלוקין בעיסתן אבל חלוקים בעיסתן אימור מעיסתו קימץ ראיה במאי אמר רבה אמר [ג] ראיה בעדים רב ששת אמר ראיה בקיום השטר אמר ליה רבא לרב נחמן הא רב והא שמואל הא רבה והא רב ששת מר כמאן סבירא ליה א"ל אנא מתניתא ידענא דתניא אחד מן האחין שהיה נותן ונושא בתוך הבית והיו אונות ושטרות יוצאין על שמו ואמר שלי הן שנפלו לי מבית אבי אמא עליו להביא ראיה וכן [ד] האשה שהיא נושאת ונותנת בתוך הבית והיו אונות ושטרות יוצאין על שמה ואמרה שלי הן שנפלו לי מבית אבי אבא או מבית אבי אמא עליה להביא ראיה מאי וכן מהו דתימא אשה כיון דשביחא לה מילתא דאמרי קא טרחא קמי יתמי לא גזלה מיתמי קא משמע לן: במה דברים אמורים במחזיק אבל בנותן מתנה והאחין שחלקו וכו': אטו כל הני דאמרינן לאו בני חזקה נינהו חסורי מחסרא והכי קתני במה דברים אמורים בחזקה שיש עמה טענה כגון מוכר אומר לא מכרתי ולוקח אומר לקחתי אבל חזקה שאין עמה טענה כגון נותן מתנה והאחין שחלקו והמחזיק בנכסי הגר דלמקני בעלמא הוא (א) נעל גדר פרץ כל שהוא הרי זו חזקה תני רב [ו] הושעיא בקדושין דבי לוי [ג] נעל גדר פרץ כל שהוא בפניו הרי זו חזקה בפניו אין שלא בפניו לא אמר רבא [ה] הכי קאמר בפניו לא צריך למימר ליה לך חזק וקני שלא

רשב"ם

כדשלח רב הונא כו'. כלומר להכי אפקינהו רבא משום דדברים העשוין להשאיל ולהשכיר אין אדם נאמן לומר לקוח הוא בידי כדשלח רב הונא: קשיא. לדידן קשיא אמאי אמר שמואל מודי לי אבא כו': ופסק ר' חננאל דהלכתא כשמואל דהיכא דמית על האחין להביא ראיה וכן פירש נקטינן מרבותי ז"ל כל היכא דאמר בגמ' תיובתא דפלוני תיובתא בטלו דברי מי שהתיובתא עליו לגמרי אבל היכא דעלתה בקשיא כי הך דשמואל לא בטלו דבריו דאמרינן לא הוה ברירא להו דבטלה שמועה זו לגמרי אלא לא אשתכח פירוקא בההיא שעתא דתליא וקיימא ואעפ"כ אין נראה בעיני דלא שנא תיובתא ולא שנא קשיא דקאי אמילתא דאמוראי חדא היא ולא הויא עיקר אלא לגבי תיובתא ממשנה או מברייתא שייך לומר תיובתא [ג] ומפירכא דאמוראי שייך למימר קשיא והא דשמואל נראה בעיני דלא סמכינן עליה כל עיקר וכן פי' ר"ח כתב מרי"ש גאון כי זה שאמר שמואל ומודי לי אבא שאם מת על האחין להביא ראיה אין הלכה כמותו: לא שנו. הא דקאמר רב עליו להביא ראיה: אלא שאין חלוקין. בשום דבר בעולם אפי' בעיסתן הלכך מאין לו לזה כלום בלא אחיו: קימץ. עלכן ביותר ולכך נתעשר והיה לו ממון לבדו שאין לאחיו חלק בו והממון הוא לקח קרקעות והלוה לאחרים: ראיה במאי. לדרב קאי שהלכה כמותו דאי לדשמואל היכי אמר רב ששת בקיום השטר והרי לשמואל דאית ליה על האחין להביא ראיה צריך להן לפסול שטרו של זה ולא לקיימו: ראיה בעדים. על בעל השטר להביא ראיה למעיסתו קימץ או מאבי אמו ירש והיה ממון של שטרות הללו שלו: בקיום השטר. שכתבו לו בית דין הנפק על שטר זה (ב) וכיון דקיימוהו ב"ד בדקו השטר וחקרו ועמדו על אמיתת הדבר שכל הכתוב בשטר אמת הוא והשטר הרי כתוב בשמו של זה: הא רבה והא רב ששת. דפליגי אליבא דרב ואי כרב סבירא לך ראיה במאי אי כרבה אי כרב ששת: מתניתא ידענא. כרב ומיהו לא פירש לי אי כרבה אי כרב ששת: ורבינו חננאל פסק בעדים צריך להביא ראיה ולא בקיום השטר דהא אפי' רב ששת מודי דראיה בעדים שוה יותר מקיום השטר: וכן האשה. אלמנה: מבית אבי אבא. ה"נ מצי למימר מבית אבא ומשום רישא דקתני מבית אבי אמא קתני נמי סיפא מבית אבי אבא: מאי וכן. דמשמע ואפי' האשה דינה כן (ג) ומאי רבותא איכא טפי דקתני וכן הכי הוה ליה למיתני אשה שהיתה נושאת ונותנת כו' ודרך תנא לומר שני דברים שוין וזימנין דאמרינן דצריכי תרוייהו אבל הכא דקתני וכן משמע דבלא זו אף זו קתני: דשביחא לה מילתא. חשיבות היא לה שמאמינין אותה בית דין לעשותה אפוטרופוס בשל יתומין וגם משבחין אותה בני אדם על כך ומקושי גדול תאמר על שלהן שהוא שלה וסד"א דליהמנה קא משמע לן: בבבא בתרא ירושלמי' אין לאיש חזקה בנכסי אשתו בחיי אשתו אבל לאחר מיתת אשתו יש לו חזקה ולא לאשה בחיי בעלה בנכסי בעל אבל לאחר מיתת בעלה יש לה חזקה ולא לאב בנכסי הבן בחיי הבן אבל לאחר מיתת הבן יש לו חזקה ולא לבן בנכסי האב בחיי האב אבל לאחר מיתת האב יש לו חזקה ואיכא לדמויי להך דתניא לעיל בן שחלק ואשה שנתגרשה כו': במתני' לא גרסינן ופרץ בפניו דהא נכסי הגר לא שייך ביה בפניו דהא מית ליה הגר: אטו כל הני. דאמרינן לקמן במתני' נותן מתנה ואחין שחלקו לאו על ידי חזקה דנעל גדר הן קונין כדקתני מתני' בתמיה: במה דברים אמורים. דבעינן ג' שנים: בחזקה שיש עמה טענה. כלומר ערעור: אבל בחזקה שאין עמה טענה. שבעל הקרקע מודה לו ליטלה כגון נותן מתנה כו' כיון דנעל גדר ופרץ כל שהוא בפני עדים הויא חזקה לקנות שלא יוכל לחזור עוד זה בזה: בקדושין דבי לוי. בתוספתא (ד) בברייתא דמס' קדושין שסידר לוי כמו שסידרו ר' חייא ור' אושעיא: נעל וגדר ופרץ בפניו. במקח וממכר מיירי דתנן בקידושין (דף כו.) דקרקע נקנית בחזקה: ומתמה גמ' בפניו הוא דהוי חזקה אבל שלא בפניו. דמוכר אם נעל וגדר שלא בפניו לא תיהוי חזקה בתמיה: ה"ק. אם גדר ופרץ לוקח בפניו דמוכר לא צריך למימר ליה מוכר ללוקח לך חזק וקני אלא מכיון שנתרצה לו למכרה בכך וכך מעות והחזיק זה בפניו הויא חזקה דניחא ליה בהך חזקה והלכך שתיק ולא יוכל מוכר לחזור בו עוד והלוקח נתחייב לו דמי מקחו: שלא

תוספות

דברים העשוין להשאיל ולהשכיר ואמר לקוחים הן בידי אינו נאמן. וקשה דאמר בפ' כל הנשבעין (שבועות דף מו. ושם) א"ר יהודה ראוהו שהטמין כלים תחת כנפיו ויצא ואמר לקוחין הן בידי אין נאמן ולא אמרן אלא בבעל הבית שאינו עשוי למכור כליו ולא אמרן אלא בדברים שאין עשוין להטמין ולא אמרן אלא בדברי' העשוין להשאיל ולהשכיר אלמא דאפילו בדברים העשוין להשאיל ולהשכיר נאמן אי ליכא כל הני מילי דקאמר שאין עשוי למכור כליו וכלים שאין דרכן להטמין ונראה לר"ת דגרס התם ובכולהו נמי כי ליתנהו לא אמרן אלא בדברים שאין עשוין להשאיל ולהשכיר אבל דברים העשוין להשאיל ולהשכיר אפי' ליתנהו לחד מהני אין נאמן וכן גורס רב האי בשערים (שער מ) וכן ר"ח וכן מוכח בשילהי המקבל (ב"מ דף קטז.) וא"ת (ה) דתנא בהגוזל בתרא (ב"ק דף קיד:) המכיר כליו וספריו ביד אחר ויצא שם גנבה בעיר ישבע כמה הוציא ויטול והשתא אפי' לא יצא שם גנבה יהא נאמן לומר שגנבוה מיגו דאי בעי אמר השאלתי לך דספרים הן עשוין להשאיל דאפי' ספרא דאגדתא אמר הכא דעשוין להשאיל כ"ש שאר ספרים כדאמר בנערה שנתפתתה (כתובות דף נ.) ולדקתו עומדת לעד זה הכותב ספרים ומשאילן לאחרים ואין לומר דלא מהימן במיגו לומר דגנובים (ו) משום דלאחזוקי אינשי בגנבי לא מחזקינן כדאמר בכל הנשבעין (שבועות דף מו:) דלא דמי דהתם ודאי אינו נאמן לאחזוקי ההוא גברא בגנבי אפי' במיגו אבל הכא שאינו אומר פלוני גנבם אלא שהם גנובים מהימן שפיר דכמה גנבים יש בעולם ואין לומר נמי דלאו מיגו הוא שאינו טוען ברצון השאלתי לך לפי שאותו יודע בו שהוא משקר דהא לעיל (דף לג.) אמר דנאמן לומר של אבותי הוא שלקחוה מאבותיך במיגו דאי בעי אמר מינך זבינתיה אע"פ שהוא יודע דלאו מיניה זבנה וכן בפרק שני דכתובות (דף טו: וע"ש בתוס' ד"ה ומודה) תנן דנאמן לומר שדה זו של אביך היתה ולקחתיה הימנו במיגו דאי בעי אמר לא היתה של אביך מעולם אע"פ שהבן יודע שהיתה של אביו ומהנהו עזי דאכלי חושלי בנהרדעא לעיל (דף לו.) אין ראיה דאיכא למימר כגון שמכחישו ואומר שלא אכלו כל כך דהשתא הוי מיגו טוב ותירץ ר"ת דהתם מיירי באדם שאין (ז) עשוין להשאיל ולהשכיר לזה שקנאם כגון דלא גיים ביה ולפי זה אם עשוי להשאיל לו אפי' לא יצא לו שם גנבה נאמן לומר שהם גנובים במיגו ולמה"ר (ח) דודי נראה דלא מהימן במיגו דהוי מיגו להוציא אע"פ שנוטל דמים שהוציא:

אימא מעיסתו קימץ. אע"ג דלא טעין הכי אלא אומר מבית אבי אמא מ"מ נאמן במיגו דאי בעי אמר מעיסתי קמצתי:

דטרחא קמי יתמי אימא לא גזלה מיתמי. קשה לרשב"א דאדרבה מהאי טעמא דטרחא קמי יתמי גזלה מיתמי כדאמר בשילהי (גיטין דף לה.) בההוא הנאה דטרחא קמי יתמי אתיא לאורויי ותירץ דה"נ קאמר הכא קמ"ל דלא אמרינן דלא גזלה אלא אדרבה אתיא לאורויי כדאמר בגיטין:

נעל וגדר כל שהוא כו'. בגמרא פרש"ם דהאי נעל היינו שקבע מנעול בדלת דהוי בנין אבל סגר הדלת ונעל במפתח בנכסי הגר דליכא דמסר ליה לא הוי חזקה דאין זה אלא כמבריח ארי מנכסי חבירו אע"ג דברים פסחים (דף ד. ושם ד"ה אם) אמר דמשמסר לו מפתח הוי הבית בחזקת שוכר לבדקו וה"ה לקנותו ה"מ

רטו א מיי' פ"ח מהל' טוען הלכה ב סמג עשין פט טוש"ע ח"מ סי' עב סעיף יח וסי' קלג ס"ה:
רטז ב ג מיי' פ"ט מהל' נחלות הלכה ח סמג לאוין פא טוש"ע ח"מ סי' סב:
ריז ד מיי' שם ופכ"ב מהל' אישות הל' ל סמג שם טוש"ע שם וטוש"ע אה"ע סי' פו סעי' ג וע"ש בהג"ה:
ריח ה מיי' פ"א מהל' מכירה הלכה ח סמג עשין פב טוש"ע ח"מ סי' קלב סעיף ג:

ליקוטי רש"י

דברים העשוין להשאיל ולהשכיר וכו'. אבל דברים שאין עשוין להשאיל שהבעלים חסים עליהם לפי שמתקלקלין נאמן לשבע שלקחם ואין נראין דברי האומר השאלתים לו [שבועות מו:]. אונות. שטרי מכירות לשון כתי ולאשית אוני (בראשית מט). ושטרות. של הלואה [רשב"ם לעיל ע"א]. נעל. דלת או גדר פרצה או פרץ גדר כל שהוא [גיטין עז.]. עשה דלת. וגדר. או גדר חומה. פרץ. פירצה כדי שיכנס בה [רשב"ם לעיל מב.]. הרי זו חזקה. לקנות שאין המוכר יכול לחזור בו [גיטין שם]. לגלגלי חזור זה בזה כיון דברשות חבירו המחזיק [רשב"ם שם].

רבינו גרשום

מצי טעין לקוחות הן בידי אינהו נמי לא מצי טעני וקשיא: אמר רב חסדא לא שנו. הא דאמרן דאינו נאמן דעליו להביא ראיה שהן שלו אלא שאין חלוקין בעיסתן. כלומר שעדיין לא חלקו ירושתן ואוכלין יחד מעיסה אחת: אבל חלוקין בעיסתן. שכבר חלקו ואעפ"כ נושא ונותן בחלקם ודאי על האחין להביא ראיה דאינו שלו דאי לא מייתו ראיה (א) מוחזק זה בזה דאימור מעיסתו קיבץ. כלומר ממזונותיו צמצם וקיבץ ממון ועשה אלו אונות ושטרות ולהכי כתובין על שמו: בעדים. שיודעין שהם שלו: בקיום דשטר. שאם קיימו בית דין אלו שטרות על שמו דכתבי הכי שטרא של פלוני נפק לקדמנא ודאי שלו הן דבית דין לא הוי מקיימי על שמו אי לא דבקיאי דהן שלו: הא רב ושמואל הא רבה ורב ששת. כולהו גילו טעמיהו בדבר זה: מר כמאן סבירא ליה. כלומר מה דעתך בזה: וכן אשה אלמנה שנושאת ונותנת בתוך הבית. של יתומין דעדיין לא נסתלקה מהם: שנפלו לי מבית אבי אמא. והוא הדין שנפלו לה מאביה עצמה לאחר מיתת בעלה דהכי יכולה למימר: אימא לא גזלה מיתמי. ותהא מהימנא ועל היתומים לאיתויי ראיה. קמ"ל דאפי' הכי לא מהימנא אי לא מייתא ראיה: פיסקא במה דברים אמורים. דצריך חזקה ג' שנים: במחזיק. כלומר כגון כל הני דאמרן לעיל דזה המחזיק טוען לקחתי והמערער אומר לא מכרתי דאינו מודה לו אבל היכא דמכר או נותן מתנה צריך כל אחד להחזיק בחלקו כדי שלא יהיו יכולין לחזור בהן. וכן המחזיק בנכסי הגר שמת אינן צריכין ג' שנים לחזקה. אלא נעל שסתם פתח כל שהוא או פרץ בו מעט או גדר כל שהוא לאלתר הוי חזקה: בקדושין דבי לוי. במסכת קדושין בבית המדרש של לוי: בפניו לא צריך למימר ליה לך חזק וקני. כלומר אם המקבל הוא שם בפני הנותן לא צריך למימר ליה הנותן לך חזק וקני אע"ג דלא קאמר ליה אי מחזיק מקבל בנעל וגדר כל שהוא קני. אבל שלא בפניו כגון שהקרקע בעיר אחרת

א) [גי' הרא"ש שרביא ועי' תוס' לקמן נג. ד"ה נעל וכו"א בשאלתות פ' מסעי סימן קלט], ב) [תוספתא דקידושין פ"א]:

הגהות הב"ח

(א) גמ' דלמקני בעלמא הוא דבעי נעל וגדר ופרץ וכו' תני רב שרביא בקידושין דבי לוי נעל וגדר ופרץ: (ב) רשב"ם ד"ה בקיום וכו' שטר זה דכיון: (ג) ד"ה מאי וכן וכו' ומאי רבותא. נ"ב וכה"ג פרש"י בב"ק דף קיד ע"ב: (ד) ד"ה בקידושין דבי לוי בתוספתא (בברייתא) תז"מ ונ"ב הגהה היא: (ה) תוס' ד"ה דברים וכו' וא"ת הא דתנא וכו' ויצא לו שם גניבה: (ו) בא"ד דגנובים הם משום: (ז) בא"ד באדם שאין עשוי להשאיל: (ח) בא"ד ולמה"ר דוד נראה:

גליון הש"ס

רשב"ם ד"ה ופסק כו' ומפירכא דאמוראי שייך לומר קשיא. עי' סנהדרין דף עב ע"א ברש"י ד"ה קשיא ושם דף קיב ע"א ברש"י ד"ה קשיא ובבאר שבע שם ועי' לקמן דף קמ ע"א ברשב"ם ד"ה קשיא ובפלפולא חריפתא שם על הרא"ש ובמו"ק דף ג' ע"ב בתוספות ד"ה חייב שתים:

לעזי רש"י

אנור"ש. פירוש עגילים, נזמים (רש"י עירובין דף נו סוע"ב וכתובות דף סח ע"ב וב"מ דף לה ע"א ודף נא ע"א ועיין רש"י במדבר לא, נ ויחזקאל טז, יב), טבעות. רומ"א. פירוש העיר רומא (הבירה של מדינת איטליה):

חשק שלמה על רבינו גרשום

א) נ"ל אין מוציאין מחזקתו דמוחזק זה בזה.

The Gemara explains the novelty of the second clause's ruling: מַהוּ דְתֵימָא – If the Baraisa had taught only the first ruling (concerning a brother) but not the second (concerning a widow), **I might have said** that the ruling does not apply to a widow for the following reason. אִשָּׁה – In the case of a widowed **woman,** כֵּיוָן דִּשְׁבִיחָא לָהּ מִילְּתָא – **since she is honored to manage the orphans' affairs** דְּאָמְרֵי קָא טָרְחָא קַמֵּי יַתְמֵי – **because [people] say** that **she is toiling for the orphans,** לֹא גָזְלָה מִיַּתְמֵי – **she would** certainly **not steal from the orphans.**[13] I would therefore have said that she need not prove that she acquired assets with her own money. קָא מַשְׁמַע לָן – **[The Baraisa] therefore informs us** that in spite of her dedication, still she must prove her claim.[14]

The Gemara quotes the final section of the Mishnah:

בַּמֶּה דְּבָרִים אֲמוּרִים – IN REGARD TO WHAT type of *chazakah* ARE THESE RULES STATED? בְּמַחֲזִיק – IN REGARD TO ONE WHO ESTABLISHES A *CHAZAKAH.* אֲבָל בְּנוֹתֵן מַתָּנָה – BUT IN THE CASE OF ONE WHO GIVES A GIFT, וְהָאַחִין שֶׁחָלְקוּ וכו׳ – OR BROTHERS WHO DIVIDE an estate, etc.

The Mishnah implies that people such as "one who gives a gift, or brothers who divide, etc.," do not establish or execute a *chazakah.* The Gemara questions this:

אָטוּ כָּל הָנֵי דְּאָמְרִינַן – **But all these** people **that are mentioned** in the Mishnah (one who gives a gift, brothers, etc.), לָאו בְּנֵי חֲזָקָה נִינְהוּ – **do they not acquire** property **through** an act of ***chazakah,*** e.g. locking, fencing, etc.?[15]

The Gemara answers:

חַסּוֹרֵי מִחַסְּרָא – It is as if **[the Mishnah] is missing words,** וְהָכִי קָתָנֵי – **and this is what [the Mishnah] is saying:** בַּמֶּה דְּבָרִים אֲמוּרִים – IN REGARD TO WHAT ARE THESE RULES STATED? בַּחֲזָקָה שֶׁיֵּשׁ עִמָּהּ טַעֲנָה – IN REGARD TO A *CHAZAKAH* AGAINST WHICH THERE IS A CHALLENGE: כְּגוֹן מוֹכֵר אוֹמֵר לֹא מָכַרְתִּי – **For instance,** a case where **the seller,** i.e. the previous owner **claims, "I did not sell** the land," וְלוֹקֵחַ אוֹמֵר לָקַחְתִּי – **and the purchaser,** i.e. the occupant, **claims, "I purchased** it." This is the *chazakah* of proving title, which requires three years to take effect.[16] אֲבָל חֲזָקָה שֶׁאֵין עִמָּהּ טַעֲנָה – BUT REGARDING A *CHAZAKAH* AGAINST WHICH THERE IS NO CHALLENGE: כְּגוֹן נוֹתֵן מַתָּנָה – FOR EXAMPLE, ONE WHO GIVES A GIFT, וְהָאַחִין שֶׁחָלְקוּ – OR BROTHERS WHO DIVIDE an estate, וְהַמַּחֲזִיק בְּנִכְסֵי הַגֵּר – OR ONE WHO TAKES POSSESSION OF THE ownerless PROPERTY OF A deceased CONVERT, דִּלְמִקְנֵי בְּעָלְמָא הוּא – **where it** [the purpose of the *chazakah*] **is merely to *acquire*** the property in question, and no challenge is raised against it, נָעַל גָּדַר פָּרַץ כָּל שֶׁהוּא – IF HE LOCKED, FENCED, OR BREACHED EVEN TO A MINOR EXTENT, הֲרֵי זוֹ חֲזָקָה – THIS IS CONSIDERED A *CHAZAKAH.*

The Gemara discusses the *second* type of *chazakah* mentioned in the Mishnah — a proprietary act by means of which property is acquired:

תָּנֵי רַב הוֹשַׁעְיָא – **Rav Hoshaiah taught the** following **Baraisa,** בְּקִדּוּשִׁין דְּבֵי לֵוִי – which is included **in** the corpus of Baraisos to tractate ***Kiddushin*** compiled **by the academy of Levi:** נָעַל גָּדַר פָּרַץ כָּל שֶׁהוּא בְּפָנָיו – IF [THE PURCHASER] FENCED, LOCKED, OR BREACHED some property, EVEN TO A MINOR EXTENT, IN [THE SELLER'S] PRESENCE, הֲרֵי זוֹ חֲזָקָה – THIS IS CONSIDERED A *CHAZAKAH.*

The Gemara questions the Baraisa's mention of the seller's presence:

בְּפָנָיו אִין – Can it be that if the *chazakah* is performed **in [the seller's] presence,** it is **indeed** valid, שֶׁלֹּא בְּפָנָיו לֹא – but if it is performed **in his absence,** it is **not** valid?! Why should the seller's presence be required?

The Gemara explains the Baraisa's ruling:

אָמַר רָבָא – **Rava said,** הָכִי קָאָמַר – **This is what [the Baraisa] is saying:** בְּפָנָיו – If the *chazakah* is performed **in [the seller's] presence,** לֹא צָרִיךְ לְמֵימַר לֵיהּ – **it is not necessary for [the seller] to say to [the buyer],** לֵךְ חֲזֵק וּקְנֵי – **"Go, perform an act of *chazakah* and** thereby **acquire** the property." His presence alone indicates his acquiescence to the buyer's actions.[17]

NOTES

13. It is an honor for a woman to manage her late husband's estate because this shows that the courts trust her. Moreover, people praise her for this work. She would therefore be very reluctant to embezzle money from the estate [and ruin her good name] (*Rashbam*).

14. Since she indeed works diligently managing the estate, she might well embezzle money from it, rationalizing that her hard work entitles her to the money (*Tosafos*).

15. Literally: are they not persons [who perform] *chazakah* (cf. *Ritva*).

16. In contrast to its initial assumption that the term מַחֲזִיק in our Mishnah includes the act of acquisition as well, and that the Mishnah excludes the people mentioned in the concluding clause, it is now understood that even these people are termed *ones who execute a chazakah.* The Gemara now defines מַחֲזִיק as exclusively meaning *one who is proving title,* and calls it a "*chazakah* against which there is a challenge," because the purpose of such a *chazakah* is to support the current occupier's claim to some land against the challenge of another (see *Rashbam*).

This definition of חֲזָקָה שֶׁיֵּשׁ עִמָּהּ טַעֲנָה is not the usual meaning of the phrase. Normally it is understood to mean a *chazakah* with a supporting claim. *Meiri* explains the Gemara in such a way that the meaning of this term conforms to its meaning elsewhere, as follows: The term מַחֲזִיק (one who establishes a *chazakah*) refers to one who makes חֲזָקָה שֶׁיֵּשׁ עִמָּהּ טַעֲנָה, *a chazakah with a supporting claim* (i.e. the *purchaser* who claims, "I bought the land"). This is in contrast to the *chazakah* of acquisition, which does not require a supporting claim.

17. Normally, even after a price has been agreed upon, some indication of a seller's readiness to transfer a property is necessary. This can be accomplished by the seller instructing the buyer to go and perform an act of *chazakah* upon the land. But where the seller is present, this is not necessary, for his silence alone indicates his acquiescence to the transfer (*Rashbam*).

שֶׁלֹּא בְּפָנָיו – If, however, the *chazakah* was performed **in the absence of [the seller],** צָרִיךְ לְמֵימַר לֵיהּ – **it is necessary** for the seller **to say to [the buyer],** לֵךְ חֲזֵק וּקְנֵי – **"Go, perform an act of *chazakah* and** thereby **acquire** the property."[1]

The Gemara discusses whether this limitation (viz. an act of *chazakah* is not effective in the seller's absence unless the seller had explicitly told the buyer to perform an act of *chazakah*) applies only to purchases or to gifts as well:

בָּעֵי רַב – **Rav asked:** מַתָּנָה הֵיאַךְ – **How** would the Baraisa rule regarding **a gift?** Does a *chazakah* performed by a recipient of a gift in the absence of the giver require the giver's instruction?[2]

Shmuel rejects Rav's question:

אָמַר שְׁמוּאֵל – **Shmuel replied:** מַאי תִּבָּעֵי לֵיהּ לְאַבָּא – **What is Abba's**[3] **question?!** הַשְׁתָּא וּמַה מֶּכֶר – **Now, if** regarding **a sale,** דְּקָא יָהִיב לֵיהּ זוּזֵי – **where [the buyer] is giving [the seller] money**[4] for the property, אִי אָמַר לֵיהּ לֵךְ חֲזֵק וּקְנֵי – the Baraisa nevertheless rules that **if [the seller] says to [the buyer], "Go, perform an act of *chazakah*, and** thereby **acquire** the land," אִין – it is **indeed** a valid *chazakah*, אִי לֹא לֹא – **but if** the seller does **not** give this instruction, it is **not** a valid *chazakah*; מַתָּנָה לֹא כָּל שֶׁכֵּן – **is it not certain** that **regarding a gift,** where the giver receives nothing in return,[5] the giver's instruction is required where the *chazakah* is performed in his absence?!

The Gemara now gives the basis for Rav's inquiry:

וְרַב סָבַר – **But Rav holds** that מַאן דְּיָהִיב מַתָּנָה בְּעַיִן יָפָה יָהִיב – **one who gives a gift does so generously,** out of his fondness for the recipient. Hence, it is possible that, although he receives no money for the property, his instruction is not required even where the *chazakah* is performed in his absence.[6]

It was stated above[7] that if the buyer locked, fenced, or breached even to "a minor extent," the entire property is acquired thereby. The Gemara defines what is meant by fencing and breaching to "a minor extent":

וְכַמָּה כָּל שֶׁהוּא – **And how much** fencing or breaching **is** considered **"a minor extent"?** כִּדְשְׁמוּאֵל – **It is as Shmuel** said. דְּאָמַר שְׁמוּאֵל – **For Shmuel said:** גָּדַר גָּדֵר – If one **added to** an existing **fence**[8] וְהִשְׁלִימוֹ לַעֲשָׂרָה – **and completed it to** a height of **ten** *tefachim*,[9] וּפָרַץ פִּרְצָה – **or if** he **widened** an existing **breach**[10] כְּדֵי שֶׁיִּכָּנֵס וְיֵצֵא בָהּ – **so that one can enter and exit through [the breach],** הֲרֵי זוּ חֲזָקָה – **this is a** valid ***chazakah.***

The Gemara seeks to define Shmuel's ruling concerning a fence:

הַאי גָּדֵר הֵיכִי דָּמֵי – **What are the circumstances of this fence?** אִילֵימָא – **If you will say** דְּמֵעִיקָּרָא לֹא הֲוו סָלְקֵי לָהּ – that Shmuel refers to a case **where** even **before** the addition to the fence **one could not scale it,**[11] וְהַשְׁתָּא נַמִּי לֹא סָלְקֵי לָהּ – **and now too,** after the addition, **one cannot scale it,** מַאי עָבַד – **what has he** [the person who added to the fence] **accomplished?**[12] וְאֶלָּא – **And** if you will say **instead** that Shmuel refers to a case דְּמֵעִיקָּרָא הֲוו סָלְקֵי לָהּ – **where before** the addition to the fence **one could scale [the fence],** וְהַשְׁתָּא לֹא סָלְקֵי לָהּ – **and now,** after the addition, **one cannot scale it,** why is this called fencing to "a minor extent"? טוּבָא עָבַד – **He has accomplished a great deal!**[13] – ? –

The Gemara responds:

לֹא – This **not** a difficulty. צְרִיכָא – The description of "fencing to a minor extent" is **relevant** in a case דְּמֵעִיקָּרָא הֲוו סָלְקֵי לָהּ בִּרְוָוחָא – **where before** the addition to the fence **one could scale it with ease,** וְהַשְׁתָּא קָא סָלְקֵי לָהּ בִּדְוחְקָא – **and now,** after the addition, **one** can **scale it** only **with difficulty.** Shmuel teaches that even such a minimally effective fencing is considered a proprietary act.[14]

The Gemara now seeks to define Shmuel's ruling concerning a breach:

הַאי פִּרְצָה הֵיכִי דָּמֵי – **What are the circumstances of this breach?** אִילֵימָא – **If you will say** that Shmuel refers to a case דְּמֵעִיקָּרָא הֲוו עָיְילֵי בָּהּ – **where** even **before** the widening of the breach **one could enter through it,** וְהַשְׁתָּא נַמִּי עָיְילֵי בָּהּ – **and now too,** after the widening, **one can enter through it,** מַאי עָבַד – **what has he accomplished?**[15] וְאֶלָּא – **And** if you will say **instead** that Shmuel refers to a case דְּמֵעִיקָּרָא לֹא הֲוו עָיְילֵי בָּהּ – **where before** the widening of the breach **one could not**

NOTES

1. [If the seller had not given this instruction, the *chazakah* is ineffective.] In certain circumstances, this instruction is necessary even if the buyer has already paid for the land. For although land can be acquired through payment of money (*Kiddushin* 26a), this applies only in those localities where it is not the custom to write deeds of sale. Where the custom is to write deeds of sale, payment alone does *not* acquire the land, unless the buyer and seller made a stipulation that money alone will effect the transfer (ibid.). However, *chazakah* is effected even without a deed, regardless of the custom (*Rashbam*).

2. I.e. perhaps the Baraisa's ruling applies only to sales, but with regard to gifts, once the giver says to the recipient, "I am giving you this land," no further instruction is necessary and *chazakah* can be performed even in the giver's absence. The Gemara below explains why a gift might be different from a sale.

3. See 52a note 20.

4. Either he has already paid the seller (and nevertheless, a *chazakah* is necessary to finalize the sale – see note 1), or, he has not yet paid, and the act of *chazakah* will render him liable to pay. In either case, through the *chazakah*, the seller receives full payment for the field (*Rashbam*).

5. He may therefore wish to renege upon the gift before it is finalized (*Rashbam*).

6. Actually, Shmuel also agrees that one who gives a gift does so generously. But in his view, this concept serves only to define the *extent* of a gift which has already been given. In the present case, however, the question is not the *extent* of the gift, but whether it is a gift in the first place. Since, in this case, it is possible that no gift is being given (if the giver wishes to renege), Shmuel holds that the generous nature of gift givers is not a determining factor, and thus he requires the giver's specific instruction (*Rashbam*).

7. Mishnah 42a; Baraisa 52b.

8. Literally: he fenced a fence.

9. Generally, a fence of this height is sufficient to prevent people from entering the land (*Rashbam*; see above, 6b).

10. Literally: or he breached a breach.

11. For example, the fence was slanted, or it was built on sloping ground (*Rashbam*).

12. [He has not added to the security of the field at all!] An act of construction that does not accomplish a definable purpose is not considered a *chazakah* (*Rashbam*).

13. For although the amount of construction was minor, the improvement caused thereby is major. The minute addition rendered the heretofore ineffective fence an effective barrier (*Rashbam*).

14. Although access is rendered difficult, it is still possible for someone to climb over the fence and enter the field. This is considered "fencing to a minor extent," for the resulting improvement is only minor (*Rashbam*).

According to this interpretation, Shmuel's ruling would apply even in a case where the fence was completed to a height of *less* than ten *tefachim*, as long as the addition restricted access somewhat. Shmuel specifies ten *tefachim* only because, generally speaking, a fence that is less than ten *tefachim* high can be negotiated with ease and one that is ten *tefachim* high can be scaled only with difficulty (*Rashbam*).

15. See note 12.

שלא בפניו צריך למימר ליה לך חזק וקני בעי רב מתנה היאך אמר שמואל מאי תבעי ליה לאבא א השתא ומה מכר דקא יהיב ליה זוזי אי א"ל לך חזק וקני אין אי לא לא מתנה לא כל שכן ורב סבר ב) מאן דיהיב מתנה בעין יפה יהיב וכמה כל שהוא כדשמואל דאמר שמואל ב גדר גדר והשלימו לעשרה ג ופרץ פרצה כדי שיכנס ויצא בה הרי זו חזקה האי גדר היכי דמי אילימא דמעיקרא לא הוו סלקי לה והשתא נמי לא סלקי לה מאי עבד ואלא דמעיקרא הוו סלקי לה והשתא לא סלקי לה טובא עבד לא צריכא ד דמעיקרא הוו סלקי לה ברווחא והשתא קא סלקי לה בדוחקא האי פרצה ה"ד אילימא דמעיקרא הוו עיילי בה והשתא נמי עיילי בה מאי עבד ואלא דמעיקרא לא הוו עיילי בה והשתא קא עיילי בה טובא עבד לא צריכא ה דמעיקרא הוו עיילי בה בדוחקא והשתא עיילי בה ברווחא א"ר אסי א"ר יוחנן נתן צרור והועיל נטל צרור והועיל ה"ז חזקה מאי נתן ומאי נטל אילימא נתן צרור וסכר מיא מינה נטל צרור ואפיק מיא מינה האי ג) מבריח ארי מנכסי חברו הוא אלא ו נתן צרור דצמד (א) לה מיא נטל צרור וארוה לה מיא ואמר רב אסי א"ר יוחנן ז שתי שדות ומצר אחד ביניהן החזיק באחת מהן לקנותה קנאה לקנות

שלא בפניו צ"ל כו'. אם בא להחזיק שלא בפניו דמוכר כגון בעיר אחרת או אפי' באותה העיר שלא מדעתו של מוכר לא הויא חזקה אלא א"כ א"ל מוכר ללוקח לך חזק וקני ואפי' אם נתן לו מעות כגון בעיר שכותבין שטר דאין הכסף מועיל עד שיחזיק או עד שיכתוב השטר כדאמרי' בפ"ק דקדושין (דף כו.) עלה דהך משנה נכסים שיש להם אחריות נקנין בכסף כו' אמר רב ל"ש אלא במקום שאין כותבין את השטר אבל במקום שכותבין את השטר לא קנה עד שיכתוב לו את השטר ואי פריש פירש בכסף אקנה קנין גמור בלא חזקה ושטר אבל מסתמא לא קני במעות עד דמחזיק: **בעי רב.** הך ברייתא הוה שמיעא ליה דקתני בפניו אבל שלא בפניו לא הויא חזקה עד דא"ל בהדיא לך חזק וקני וקמבעיא ליה מי לימא דבמכירה איירי אבל במתנה מכיון שאמר לו (ב) נותנני לו קרקע זו והלך והחזיק שלא בפניו הויא חזקה ואע"ג דלא א"ל לך חזק וקני ולמפרש טעמא לקמיה דנותן בעין יפה נותן או דלמא לא שנא: **מאי תיבעי ליה לאבא.** במתנה טפי ממכר ק"ו הוא דלא קני עד דא"ל לך חזק וקני: **ומה מכר דקיהיב ליה זוזי.** לוקח למוכר היום ולמחר לאחר שיחזיק שהרי ע"מ כן הוא מחזיק כדי לפרוע דמים למוכר דמוכר לא מפסיד כיון ג) דקבל כל הדמים א"נ יהיב ליה (ג) מקמי דמחזיק זוזי לא קנה כדפרישית לעיל וכגון במקום שכותבין את השטר כדתניא בקדושין (דף כו.) מכר לו י' שדות בי' מדינות כיון שהחזיק בשדה אחת קנה כולן מה שאין בשניהן בד"א שנתן לו דמי כולן כו' אלמא אחר נתינת דמים בעינן חזקה ואפ"ה אי א"ל מוכר ללוקח לך חזק וקני הוי חזקה ואי לא לא: **מתנה.** דאין לו כי אם חסרון ממונו לא כל שכן דצריך למימר ליה לך חזק וקני ולא ליהוי חזקה עד דא"ל דדלמא לכשירצה להחזיק כבר חזר בו ממתנתו: **ורב.** דקבעי לה סבר איכא למימר מאן דיהיב מתנה בעין יפה יהיב שמחמת חיבה נתן לו והלכך ניחא ליה שילך ויחזיק ואיכא למימר דכמאן דא"ל דמי והלכך מספקא ליה. ושמואל נמי דפשיטא ליה ס"ל היכא אמרינן בעין יפה נותן ה"מ כגון לאחר שהחזיק ונתקיימה המתנה הוא דאמרינן בעין יפה נותן לו מכל וכל שלא שייר לעצמו במתנה זו (ד) דאמרן לעיל [מט:] המוכר שדהו לאשתו קנתה והבעל אוכל פירות במתנה קנתה ואין הבעל אוכל פירות אבל כל זמן דמספקא לן אי גמר להקנות המתנה או לא מספק אין לנו לומר שנתן את שלו במתנה עד דמפרש ואומר לך חזק וקני: **דאמר שמואל (ה) גדר גדר.** שהיה גבוה פחות מי' והשלימו לעשרה לפי שלא יוכלו לעלות עליו וליכנס בשדה: **פרץ פרצה.** הרחיב הפרצה: **דמעיקרא.** כשהיה פחות מי' לא הוו סלקי לה אין יכולין לעלות דרך עליו ליכנס בשדה כגון שהיה עשוי בשיפוע או היה בנוי על מקום מדרון: **והשתא נמי לא סלקי לה מאי קעביד.** ואמאי הוי חזקה דכל בנין בלא צורך לא הויא חזקה: **ואלא דמעיקרא הוו סלקי לה.** מיהא בדוחק והשתא שהשלימו לעשרה לא סלקי לה לכלל טובה עביד ואין זה ראוי לקרות כל שהוא ואע"פ שבנין כל שהוא גדר: **והשתא סלקי לה בדוחקא.** והיינו כל שהוא דכל שהוא אהני דהא אכתי סלקי לה קצת והאי דנקט שמואל והשלימו לעשרה לאו דוקא דה"ה לפחות מי' (והוא) דהשתא אהני להכי דסלקי בדוחקא ומעיקרא הוו סלקי לה ברווחא ואורחא דמילתא נקט דסתם השלימו לעשרה מעיקרא סלקי לה ברווחא והשתא סלקי לה בדוחקא: **והשתא קעיילי לה ברווחא.** דפורתא אהני ולא בעי לתרוצי דמעיקרא לא עיילי לה כלל והשתא עיילי לה בדוחק דטובא עבד דשוייה פתח. וגבי נעל כל שהוא נמי איכא לפרושי כה"ג שסתם פתח סתימה כל שהוא דמעיקרא עיילי לה ברווחא והשתא עיילי לה בדוחקא א"נ קבע מנעול בדלת לנעול בו דהיינו בנין. אבל סגר את הדלת ונעל במפתח בנכסי הגר אינה חזקה דאין זה אלא עושה מלוה לשמור בית חבירו ומבריח ארי מנכסי חבירו הוא כדלקמן בשמעתין ואע"ג דגבי שכירות בתים אמרי' בפסחים (דף ד.) משמסר לו מפתחות הוי בחזקת שוכר וה"ה לגבי לקנותו ה"מ במוכר ומשכיר לחבירו אבל בנכסי הגר מי מסר לו מפתחות שיקנה הלכך צריך בנין כל שהוא: **נתן צרור.** בחור שבגדר השדה וכולה שמעתי' אנכסי הגר קאי וה"ה לקונה דבר מחבירו: **נטל צרור.** מן הגדר ועשה בו נקב: **ה"ז חזקה.** וכגון דמהני לשדה כדמפרש ואזיל: **מאי נתן כו'.** למאי אהני האי נתינה ונטילה ליהוי חזקה: **אילימא נתן צרור וסכר מיא.** דאיכא נהר סמוך ורוצה ליכנס דרך נקב זה וסתם את הנקב בצרור וסכר את המים מן השדה שלא יכנסו בו (ו) שלא ישטפו את השדה: **ואפיק מינה מיא.** שנאספו בה בצד האחד ועשה נקב בצד השני כדי שילכו לחוץ: **האי מבריח ארי וכו'.** הא למה זה דומה למשיב אבידה דכל ישראל מצווין להציל ממון חביריהם מן הזיק ואין קרוי חזקה אלא דומיא דגודר ופורץ שעושה בו בנין או כל תיקון הצריך לו לשדה כגון משקה מים או זומר או זורע או חורש: **דצמד לה מיא.** כמו צמיד פתיל (במדבר יט) ויצמדו לבעל פעור (תהלים קו) חיבר (ז) המים שבתוכו שלא ילכו לחוץ וזהו כמו משקה את השדה דומיא דחורש שמתקן את השדה ומייפו בהשקאה זו: **דפתח ליה מיא.** ע"י נטילת צרור נכנסו המים מן הנהר דרך חור שבכותל: **וא"ר אסי אר"י ב' שדות.** של גר הסמוכין זה לזה אלא שיש מצר אחד ביניהן: **החזיק באחת מהן.** כגון דרפק בה (ח) כדלקמן ונתכוין לקנותה לבדה ולחברתה לא נתן לב לקנות קנאה לאותה שדה לבדה ואי לא הוה מצר בינתיים הוה קנה את כולם מסתמא במחזיק כל שהוא: לקנות

ה"מ במוכר ומשכיר לחבירו דאיכא דמסר ליה לליקני אבל בנכסי הגר מאן מסר ליה לליקני ואין נראה לר"י דבהדיא אמר בפרק הפרה (ב"ק דף נב. ושם ד"ה כיון) דלא קנה במסירת מפתח ולא מהני מסירת מפתח אלא שלא יצטרך לומר לו לך חזק וקני ודוקא גבי בדיקת חמץ הוא דמהני במסירת מפתח דמי שמפתח בידו עליו לבדוק לפי שבידו ליכנס ולבדוק ומה שפי' נמי דלא קני בנעילת דלת לא משמע כן בגיטין בהזורק (דף עז: ושם) דקאמר תיזיל איהי ותיחוד ותפתח אלמא בנעילה לחודה קניא שלא היתה יכולה לעשות מנעול דבשבת היה ואפי' לאסור לקנות בשבת בשכ"מ שרי שלא תטרף דעתו עליו כדאמר לקמן ולא דמי נעילת דלת למבריח ארי דלודקא נתן צרור דסכר מינה מיא הוא דאמר בסמוך דהוי מבריח ארי אבל הכא שנועל בפני כל אדם ואין מניח אדם ליכנס מוכח מילתא שהבית הוא שלו וקני בנעילה לחוד וכן מוכח לקמן (דף נז.) גבי הא דתנן אלו דברים שיש להן חזקה ואלו דברים שאין להם חזקה ופריך בגמ' מ"ש רישא ומ"ש סיפא ואמר עולא כל שאלו בנכסי הגר לא קנה כו' וקתני סיפא הכנים תרנגולין בתוך הבית ה"ז חזקה וקנה נמי בנכסי הגר וה"ט דהכא דקנה משום דמסתמא כשמכנס שם תרנגולין נעל דלת לשמרן אלמא דקנה בנעילה אבל קשה לרשב"א דאמר לקמן הבונה פלטרין בנכסי הגר ובא אחר והעמיד להן דלתות קנה והתם מיירי בנעל דאי לא נעל אמאי קנה הא לבני בעלמא הוא דאפיך כמו קמא שכל אדם יכול ליכנס כשלא נעל אלא ודאי בנעל איירי ומשמע דוקא שהעמיד דלתות אבל לא העמיד דלתות לא קנה בנעילה: **(לעיל) נעל כל שהוא.** פ"ה דל"ג בפניו משום דבנכסי הגר לא שייך לפניו והיא קשיא דאיכא למימר משום דנותן מתנה ואחין שחלקו נקט בפניו ומיהו ל"ג ליה דדייק בגמ' אברייתא דרב שרביא בפניו אין שלא בפניו לא ואמתני' ה"ל למידק ועוד דבעי רב במתנה היאך תפשוט ממתני' דלנותן מתנה קתני בפניו אי גרס לה: **(לעיל) אמר כל הני לאו בני חזקה נינהו.** פירוש דמשמע ליה בד"א במחזיק הוא דבעי ג"ש חזקה כלומר במידי דשייך חזקה אבל בנותן כו' מש"ה פריך אטו הני כגון נותן מתנה והאחין שחלקו לאו בני חזקת ג"ש נינהו: **אמר שמואל ומאי תבעי ליה לאבא ומה מכר כו'.** אע"ג דשמואל אית ליה בפ"ק דב"מ (דף טו.) דיפה כח מתנה מכח מכר לענין דלא טריף מיניה את השבח היינו אחר שכבר נתקיימה המתנה כדפ"ה: **האי פרצה היכי דמי אילימא דמעיקרא לא עיילי בה והשתא נמי לא עיילי בה מאי עבד.** נראה דל"ג (ט) דהיכי מצינן למימר השתא נמי לא עיילי הא כדי שיכנס ויצא בה קאמר לכך נראה כספרים דגרסינן דמעיקרא לא עיילי בה והשתא עיילי בה טובא עבד: **טובא עבד.** ואין זה כל שהוא אלא כו' ונעל נמי כל שהוא צריך ליישב כענין הני: אותה

מסורת הש"ס

א) [לקמן סה. ע"א], ב) [נדרים נג. ב"ק נח.], ג) [צ"ל דמקבל].

הגהות הב"ח

(א) גמ' דצמד ליה מיא נטל צרור דפתח ליה מיא: (ב) רשב"ם ד"ה בעי רב וכו' מכיון שאמר לו נותני לו: (ג) ד"ה ומה מכר וכו' א"נ יהיב ליה זוזי מקמי דמחזיק לא קנה: ושם בא"ד מה שאין בשניהן. נ"ב פי' בכסף ובשטר אין מועיל קנין שדה אחת לשאר שדות: (ד) ד"ה ורב דקבעי וכו' במתנה זו כלום כדאמרינן: (ה) ד"ה דאמר שמואל גבי גדר שהיה: (ו) ד"ה אילימא וכו' שלא יכנסו בו כדי שלא: (ז) ד"ה דצמד וכו' חיבר את המים: (ח) ד"ה החזיק וכו' דרפק בה פורתא כדלקמן: (ט) תוס' ד"ה האי וכו' דל"ג ליה דהיכי מצי למימר וכו' לא עיילו בה הא וכו' כספרים דגרסי דמעיקרא:

ליקוטי רש"י

מאן דיהיב מתנה בעין יפה יהיב. נותן מתנה כיון דרגיל ליתן בעין יפה וכו' אבל מוכר זוזי אנסוהו [רשב"ם לקמן עא.]. **מבריח ארי.** [ב"ק נח.]. **שתי שדות ומצר אחד ביניהן וכו'.** בנכסי הגר קאי דלא מקבל ליה מעות הלכך לא קנה אלא אותו שהחזיק [הואיל ואין מי שמוכר לו ואומר לו לך חזק וקני] [רשב"ם לקמן סז.].

עין משפט נר מצוה

ריט א מיי' פ"א מהל' מכירה הל' ח סמג עשין פב טוש"ע ח"מ סי' קלב סעיף ג:
רכ ב מיי' שם הל' יא טוש"ע שם ס"ד ועיין בטור ובב"י:
רכא ג מיי' שם טוש"ע שם סעיף ה:
רכב ד מיי' שם טוש"ע שם סעיף ה:
רכג ה מיי' שם טוש"ע שם סעיף ה:
רכד ו מיי' שם הל' יב טוש"ע שם סעיף ד:
רכה ז מיי' פ"א מהל' זכייה הלכה ז סמג שם טוש"ע ח"מ סי' ערה סעיף ח:

רבינו גרשום

אע"ג דמחזיק המקבל לא קני עד דאמר ליה המוכר לך חזק וקנה: **במתנה היאך.** צריך למימר ליה לך חזק וקנה או לא. מי אמרינן בעין יפה נותן וקנה המקבל אע"ג דלא אמר ליה לך חזק וקנה: **גדר גדר.** שהיה קרוב לעשרה **והשלימו** המקבל **לעשרה: שיכנס ויצא בה.** דרך אותה פירצה **הויא חזקה: דמעיקרא** כשגדרה הנותן **הוו סלקי ליה** אינשי על אותו גדר ועכשיו הגביהו זה מקבל **דלא יכלי אינשי למיסלק לה: טובא עבד.** ואמאי קרי ליה כל שהוא: אי נימא **נתן דסכר מיניה מיא.** כלומר שראה מים שהיו באין דרך חור אחד לשטוף את השדה ונתן צרור באותו חור כדי שיעכב המים שלא ישטפו את השדה: **נטל דאפיק מיא מיניה.** שהיה כל השדה מלאה ולא היו יכולין לצאת ממנה ונטל זה צרור אחד מפצת השדה ויצאו המים דרך נטילת הצרור: **האי מבריח ארי.** כלומר מה חזקה הויא זו הא מצי למימר ליה הנותן או אחד מן האחין מצוה עבדת שהצלת נכסי כי כן חובה לכל ישראל להציל ממון חבירו ולא הויא חזקה: **אלא נתן צרור דצמד לה מיא.** שהיתה שדה בית השלחין דצריך לה מים הרבה וצמד לה. שסכך בצרור דרך צאת המים שלא יצאו מן השדה ולא סגי לה בלי מים: **נטל דפתח לה מיא.** שנטל צרור א' ועשה דרך למים ליכנס דרך נטילת אותו צרור דבענין זה ודאי [הוי] חזקה: **ב' שדות.** של נכסי הגר:

enter through it, וְהַשְׁתָּא קָא עָיְילֵי בָּהּ – and **now,** after the widening, **one can enter through it,** why is this called breaching to "a minor extent"? טוּבָא עָבַד – **He has accomplished a great deal!**[16] – ? –

The Gemara responds:

לֹא – This is **not** a difficulty. צְרִיכָא – The description of "breaching to a minor extent" is **relevant** in a case דְּמֵעִיקָּרָא הֲוו עָיְילֵי בָּהּ בְּדוֹחְקָא – **where before** the widening of the breach, **one could enter through it** only **with difficulty,** וְהַשְׁתָּא עָיְילֵי בָּהּ בְּרַוְוחָא – **and now,** after the widening, **one can enter through it with ease.** Shmuel teaches that even such a minimally effective breaching is considered a proprietary act.[17]

The Gemara discusses other acts besides those mentioned in the Mishnah that can serve as proprietary acts by means of which property is acquired:

אָמַר רַבִּי אַסִּי אָמַר רַבִּי יוֹחָנָן – **R' Assi said in the name of R' Yochanan:** נָתַן צְרוֹר – If **one places a stone,** וְהוֹעִיל – **and benefits** the land thereby, נָטַל צְרוֹר – or **if he removes a stone,** וְהוֹעִיל – **and benefits** the land thereby, הֲרֵי זוֹ חֲזָקָה – **this is** considered **a proprietary act.**

The Gemara seeks to clarify R' Assi's teaching:

מַאי נָתַן – **What** benefit **is** caused by **placing** a stone, וּמַאי נָטַל – **and what** benefit **is** caused by **removing** a stone? אִילֵימָא – **If you will say** נָתַן צְרוֹר – that **he placed a stone** in a dike וְסָכַר מַיָּא מִינָּהּ – **and** thereby **prevented water from** entering **[the field],**[18] נָטַל צְרוֹר – **or he removed a stone** from a dike וְאַפֵּיק מַיָּא מִינָּהּ – **and** thereby **let water out of [a field],**[19] הַאי מַבְרִיחַ אֲרִי מִנִּכְסֵי חֲבֵרוֹ הוּא – **that is** tantamount **to chasing away a lion from another's property!** Such acts are not considered proprietary in nature, for it is one's duty to prevent damage to the property of another.[20] Thus R' Assi could not have been referring to such instances. – ? –

The Gemara answers:

אֶלָּא – **Rather,** R' Assi refers to the following cases: נָתַן צְרוֹר – **He placed a stone** in a dike דְּקָמַד לַהּ מַיָּא – and **thereby sealed water in [the field],** to keep it irrigated, נָטַל צְרוֹר – or **he removed a stone** from a dike וְאַרְוַח לַהּ מַיָּא – **and** thereby **increased the** amount of **the water in [the field]** by allowing water from a river to enter. Since these acts improve the field, they are considered proprietary acts.

Another teaching by R' Assi in the name of R' Yochanan:

וְאָמַר רַבִּי אַסִּי אָמַר רַבִּי יוֹחָנָן – **And R' Assi said in the name of R' Yochanan:** שְׁתֵּי שָׂדוֹת וּמֵצַר אֶחָד בֵּינֵיהֶן – Concerning **two** ownerless **fields**[21] **with a single boundary**[22] **between them:** הֶחֱזִיק בְּאַחַת מֵהֶן לִקְנוֹתָהּ – If **one performed a proprietary act**[23] on **one of them in order to acquire it,** but had no intention to acquire the other field, קְנָאָהּ – **he acquires [that field]** but not the other one.[24]

NOTES

16. See note 13.

17. Widening a breach to allow easier access is considered "breaching to a minor extent."

The Gemara could not have answered that Shmuel speaks of a case where prior to the widening of the breach the property was completely inaccessible, and afterwards it can be entered with difficulty. This is because such an improvement would be considered major, for it is tantamount to creating a door to the field, which would definitely acquire the property (*Rashbam*).

The third type of *chazakah* mentioned in the Mishnah – "locking" – can also be explained in a similar fashion: If one filled in an existing breach in a manner that restricts access only partially, he has established *chazakah.* Alternatively, the Mishnah speaks of one who affixed a lock to an existing door (*Rashbam*).

However, closing an existing door and locking it does not establish *chazakah,* for this is a protective rather than a proprietary act, and protective acts do not establish *chazakah*, as the Gemara explains below (*Rashbam*).

18. He saw water from an overflowing river heading towards the field and he prevented it from entering the field and swamping it by sealing a crack that was in a dike adjacent to the field (*Rashbam*).

19. Water had collected in the field, and, by removing a stone from a dike, he created an opening through which the water can drain out (see *Rashbam*).

20. Rather, they are analogous to the return of lost property. A proprietary act is one which improves the property in some way (*Rashbam*).

21. The property of a deceased convert who has no [Jewish] heirs is considered ownerless, and the first person to perform an act of acquisition upon it becomes its owner (*Rashbam*). [A born Jew *always* has heirs, since all Jews are related, at least distantly. A convert, however, is not considered to be related to his non-Jewish family with respect to Torah laws. Thus, if he dies without having fathered children after his conversion, he is considered to be without heirs and his property is ownerless.]

22. In Talmudic times, fields were generally separated by narrow strips of land that were higher or lower than the fields themselves (*Rashbam* to 53b ד״ה או).

23. E.g. digging (*Rashbam*). [Digging improves the field by preparing it for planting and is therefore considered a proprietary act.]

24. If there was no boundary (see note 22) between the two fields, digging in just one of the fields would effect the acquisition of both fields (as long as there was no specific intention not to acquire the second field) (*Rashbam*).

שלא בפניו צריך למימר ליה לך חזק וקני
בעי רב מתנה היאך אמר שמואל מאי תבעי
ליה לאבא [א]השתא ומה מכר דקא יהיב ליה
זוזי אי א"ל לך חזק וקני אין אי לא לא מתנה
לא כל שכן ורב סבר (א) מאן דיהיב מתנה בעין
יפה יהיב וכמה כל שהוא כדשמואל דאמר
שמואל [ב]גדר גדר והשלימו לעשרה [ג]ופרץ
פרצה כדי שיכנס ויצא בה הרי זו חזקה האי
גדר היכי דמי אילימא דמעיקרא לא הוו
סלקי לה והשתא נמי לא סלקי לה מאי עבד
ואלא דמעיקרא הוו סלקי לה והשתא לא
סלקי לה טובא עבד לא צריכא [ד]דמעיקרא
הוו סלקי לה ברווחא והשתא קא סלקי לה
בדוחקא האי פרצה ה"ד אילימא דמעיקרא
הוו עיילי בה והשתא נמי עיילי בה מאי
עבד ואלא דמעיקרא לא הוו עיילי בה
והשתא קא עיילי בה טובא עבד לא צריכא
[ה]דמעיקרא הוו עיילי בה בדוחקא והשתא
עיילי בה ברווחא א"ר אסי א"ר יוחנן נתן
צרור והועיל נטל צרור והועיל ה"ז חזקה
מאי נתן ומאי נטל אילימא נתן צרור וסכר
מיא מינה נטל צרור ואפיק מיא מינה האי
(ב) מבריח ארי מנכסי חברו הוא אלא [ו]נתן צרור
דצמד (א) לה מיא נטל צרור וארוח לה מיא
ואמר רב אסי א"ר יוחנן [ז]שתי שדות ומצר
אחד ביניהן החזיק באחת מהן לקנותה קנאה
לקנות

רש"י

שלא בפניו צ"ל כו'. אם בא להחזיק שלא בפניו דמוכר כגון בעיר אחרת או אפי' באותה העיר שלא מדעתו של מוכר לא הויא חזקה אלא א"כ א"ל מוכר ללוקח לך חזק וקני ואפי' אם נתן לו מעות לא קני במעות כגון בעיר שכותבין שטר דאין הכסף מועיל עד שיחזיק או עד שיכתוב השטר כדאמרי' בפ"ק דקדושין (דף כו.) עלה דהך משנה נכסים שיש להם אחריות נקנין בכסף כו' אמר רב ל"ש אלא במקום שאין כותבין את השטר אבל במקום שכותבין את השטר לא קנה עד שיכתוב לו את השטר ואי פריש פריש שפירש בכסף אקנה קנין גמור בלא חזקה ושטר אבל מסתמא לא קני במעות עד דמחזיק: בעי רב. הך ברייתא הוה שמיעא ליה דקתני בפניו אבל שלא בפניו לא הויא חזקה עד דא"ל בהדיא לך חזק וקני וקמבעיא ליה מי לימא דבמכירה איירי אבל במתנה מכיון שאמר לו (ב) נותנני לו קרקע זו והלך והחזיק שלא בפניו הויא חזקה ואע"ג דלא א"ל לך חזק וקני וכדמפרש טעמא לקמיה דנותן בעין יפה נותן או דלמא לא שנא: מאי תיבעי ליה לאבא. במתנה טפי ממכר ק"ו הוא דלא קני עד דא"ל לך חזק וקני: ומה מכר דקיהיב ליה זוזי. לוקח למוכר היום ולמחר לאחר שיחזיק שהרי ע"מ כן הוא מחזיק כדי לפרוע דמים למוכר דמוכר לא מפסיד כיון [ג]דקבל כל הדמים א"כ יהיב ליה (ג) מקמי דמחזיק זוזי לא קנה כדפרישית לעיל וכגון במקום שכותבין את השטר כדתניא בקדושין (דף מ.) מכר לו י' שדות בי' מדינות כיון שהחזיק בשדה אחת קנה כולן מה שאין בשניהן בד"א שנתן לו דמי כולן כו' אלמא אחר נתינת דמים בעינן חזקה ואפ"ה אי א"ל מוכר ללוקח לך חזק וקני הוי חזקה ואי לא לא: מתנה. דאין לו כי אם חסרון ממונו לא כל שכן דצריך למימר ליה לך חזק וקני ולא ליהוי חזקה עד דא"ל דדלמא לכשירצה להחזיק כבר חזר בו ממתנתו: ורב. דקבעי לה סבר איכא למימר מאן דיהב מתנה בעין יפה יהיב שמחמת חיבה נתן לו והלכך ניחא ליה שילך ויחזיק ואיכא למימר דכמאן דא"ל דמי והלכך מספקא ליה. ושמואל נמי דפשיטא ליה ס"ל היכא אמרינן בעין יפה נותן ה"מ כגון לאחר שהחזיק ונתקיימה המתנה הוא דאמרינן בעין יפה נותן לו מכל וכל שלא שייר לעצמו במתנה זו (ד) דאמרן לעיל [נא:] המוכר שדהו לאשתו קנתה והבעל אוכל פירות במתנה קנתה ואין הבעל אוכל פירות אבל כל זמן דמספקא לן אי גמר להקנות המתנה או לא מספק אין לנו לומר שנתן את שלו במתנה עד דמפרש ואומר לך חזק וקני: דאמר שמואל (ה) גדר גדר. שהיה בנוי פחות מי' והשלימו לעשרה לפי שלא יוכלו לעלות עליו וליכנס בשדה: פרץ פרצה. הרחיב הפרצה: דמעיקרא. כשהיה פחות מי' לא הוו סלקי לה אין יכולין לעלות דרך עליו ליכנס בשדה כגון שהיה עשוי בשיפוע או היה בנוי על מקום מדרון: והשתא נמי לא סלקי לה מאי קעביד. ואמאי הוי חזקה דכל בנין בלא צורך לא הויא חזקה: ואלא דמעיקרא הוו סלקי לה. מיהא בדוחק והשתא שהשלימו לעשרה לא סלקי לה כלל טובא עביד ואין זה ראוי לקרות כל שהוא ואע"פ שבנין כל שהוא גדר: והשתא סלקי לה בדוחקא. והיינו כל שהוא דכל שהוא אהני דהא אכתי סלקי לה קצת והאי דנקט שמואל והשלימו לעשרה לאו דוקא דה"ה לפחות מי' (והוא) דהשתא אהני להכי דסלקי בדוחקא ומעיקרא הוו סלקי לה ברווחא ואורחא דמילתא נקט דסתם השלימו לעשרה מעיקרא סלקי לה ברווחא והשתא סלקי לה בדוחקא: והשתא קעיילי לה ברווחא. דפורתא אהני ולא בעי לתרוצי דמעיקרא לא עיילי לה כלל והשתא עיילי לה בדוחק דטובא עבד דשוייה פתח. וגבי נעל כל שהוא נמי איכא לפרושי כה"ג שסתם פתח סתימה כל שהוא דמעיקרא עיילי לה ברווחא והשתא עיילי לה בדוחקא א"נ שקבע מנעול בדלת לנעול בו דהיינו בנין. אבל סגר את הדלת ונעל במפתח בנכסי הגר אינה חזקה דאין זה אלא עושה מצוה לשמור בית חבירו ומבריח ארי מנכסי חבירו הוא כדלקמן בשמעתין ואע"ג דגבי שכירות בתים אמרי' בפסחים (דף ד.) משמסר לו מפתחות הוי בחזקת שוכר וה"ה לגבי לקנותו ה"מ במוכר ומשכיר לחבירו אבל בנכסי הגר מי מסר לו מפתחות שיקנה הלכך צריך בנין כל שהוא: נתן צרור. בחור שבגדר השדה וכולה שמעתי' אנכסי הגר קאי וה"ה לקונה דבר מחבירו: נטל צרור. מן הגדר ועשה בו נקב: ה"ז חזקה. וכגון דמהני לשדה כדמפרש ואזיל: מאי נתן כו'. למאי אהני האי נתינה ונטילה דליהוי חזקה: אילימא נתן צרור וסכר מיא. ראה נהר שוטף ורוצה ליכנס דרך נקב ובא זה וסתם את הנקב בצרור וסכר את המים מן השדה שלא יכנסו בו (ו) שלא ישטפו את השדה: ואפיק מינה מיא. שנאספו לה מים בצד האחד ועשה נקב בצד השני כדי שיצאו לחוץ: האי מבריח ארי וכו'. הא למה זה דומה למשיב אבידה דכל ישראל מצווין להציל ממון חביריהם מן ההיזק ואין קרוי חזקה אלא דומיא דגדר ופרץ שעושה בו בנין או כל תיקון הצריך לו לשדה כגון משקה מים או זומר או זורע או חורש: דצמד לה מיא. כמו צמיד פתיל (במדבר יט) ויצמדו לבעל פעור (תהלים קו) חיבר (ז) המים שבתוכו שלא יצאו לחוץ וזהו כמו משקה את השדה דומיא לחורש שמתקן את השדה ומייפו בהשקאה זו: דפתח ליה מיא. ע"י נטילת צרור נכנסו המים מן הנהר דרך חור שבכותל: וא"ר אסי אר"י ב' שדות. של גר הסמוכין זה לזה אלא שיש מצר אחד ביניהן: החזיק באחת מהן. כגון דרפק בה (ח) כדלקמן ונתכוין לקנותה לבדה ולחברתה לא נתן לב לקנות קנאה לאותה שדה לבדה ואי לא הוה מצר בינתיים הוה קנה את כולם מסתמא בחפירה כל שהוא:
לקנות

תוספות

ה"מ במוכר ומשכיר לחבירו דאיכא דמסר ליה דליקני אבל בנכסי הגר מאן מסר ליה דליקני ואין נראה לר"י דבהדיא אמר בפרק הספינה (ב"ק דף נג. ושם ד"ה מיון) דלא קנה במסירת מפתח ולא מהני מסירת מפתח אלא שלא יצטרך לומר לו לך חזק וקני ודוקא גבי בדיקת חמץ הוא דתלי במסירת מפתח דמי שמפתח בידו עליו לבדוק לפי שבידו ליכנס ולבדוק ומה שפי' נמי דלא קני בנעילת דלת לא משמע כן בגיטין בהזורק (דף עז: ושם) דקאמר תזיל איהי ותיחוד ותפתח אלמא בנעילה לחודה קניא שלא היתה יכולה לעשות מנעול דבשבת היה ואפי' דאסור לקנות בשבת בשכ"מ שרי שלא תטרף דעתו עליו כדאמר לקמן ולא דמי נעילת דלת למבריח ארי דדוקא נתן צרור דסכר מינה מיא הוא דאמר בסמוך דהוי מבריח ארי אבל הכא שנועל בפני כל אדם ואין מניח אדם ליכנס מוכח מילתא שהבית הוא שלו וקני בנעילה לחוד וכן מוכח לקמן (דף נז.) גבי הא דתנן אלו דברים שיש להן חזקה ואלו דברים שאין להם חזקה ופריך בגמ' מ"ש רישא ומ"ש סיפא אמר עולא כל שאילו בנכסי הגר לא קנה כו' וקתני סיפא הכניס תרנגולין בתוך הבית ה"ז חזקה וקנה נמי בנכסי הגר וה"ט דהתם דקנה משום דמסתמא כשנתן שם תרנגולין נעל דלת לשמרן אלמא דקנה בנעילה אבל קשה לרשב"א דאמר לקמן הבונה פלטרין בנכסי הגר ובא אחר והעמיד להן דלתות קנה והתם מיירי בנעל דאי לא נעל אמאי קנה הא לבני בעלמא הוא דאפיך כמו קמא שכל אדם יכול ליכנס כשלא נעל אלא ודאי בנעל איירי ומשמע דוקא שהעמיד דלתות אבל לא העמיד דלתות לא קנה בנעילה: **נעל** (לעיל) וגדר ופרץ כל שהוא. פ"ה דל"ג בפניו משום דבנכסי הגר לא שייך לפניו ואינה קשיא דאיכא למימר משום דנותן מתנה ואחין שחלקו נקט בפניו ומיהו ל"ג ליה דדייק בגמ' אברייתא דרב שרביא בפניו אין שלא בפניו לא ואמתני' ה"ל למידק ועוד דבעי רב במתנה היאך תפשוט ממתני' דאנותן מתנה קתני בפניו אי גרס לה: **אטו** (לעיל) כל הני לאו בני חזקה נינהו. פירוש דמשמע ליה בד"א במחזיק הוא דבעי ג"ש חזקה כלומר במידי דשייך חזקה אבל בנותן כו' מש"ה פריך אטו הני כגון נותן מתנה והאחין שחלקו לאו בני חזקת ג"ש נינהו: **אמר** שמואל ומאי תבעי ליה לאבא ומה מכר כו'. אע"ג דשמואל אית ליה ספ"ק דב"מ (דף טו.) דיפה כח מתנה מכח מכר לענין דלא טריף מיניה את השבח היינו אחר שכבר נתקיימה המתנה כדפ"ה: **האי** פרצה היכי דמי אילימא דמעיקרא לא עיילי בה והשתא נמי לא עיילי בה מאי עבד. נראה דל"ג (ט) דהיכי מצינן למימר השתא נמי לא עיילי הא כדי שיכנס ויצא בה קאמר לכך נראה כספרים דגרסינן דמעיקרא לא עיילי בה והשתא עיילי בה טובא עבד: **טובא** עבד. ואין זה כל שהוא אלא כו' ונעל נמי כל שהוא צריך לפרש כעין הני:
אותה

עין משפט נר מצוה

ריט א מיי' פ"א מהל' מכירה הל' ח סמג עשין פב טוש"ע ח"מ סי' קצב סעיף ג:
רכ ב מיי' שם פ"ב הל' יא טוש"ע שם ס"ד ועיין בטור ובב"י:
רכא ג מיי' שם טוש"ע שם סעיף ה:
רכב ד מיי' שם טוש"ע שם סעיף ד:
רכג ה מיי' שם טוש"ע שם סעיף ה:
רכד ו מיי' שם פ"ב הל' יג טוש"ע שם סעיף ו:
רכה ז מיי' פ"א מהל' זכייה הלכה ז סמג שם טוש"ע ח"מ סי' ערה סעיף ח:

רבינו גרשום

אע"ג דמחזיק המקבל לא קני עד דאמר ליה המוכר לך חזק וקנה: במתנה היאך. צריך למימר ליה לך חזק וקנה או לא. מי אמרינן בעין יפה נותן וקנה המקבל אע"ג דלא אמר ליה לך חזק וקנה: גדר גדר. שהיה קרוב לעשרה והשלימו המקבל לעשרה: שיכנס ויצא בה. דרך אותה פירצה הויא חזקה: דמעיקרא כשגדרה הגוזלן הוו סלקי ליה אינשי על אותו גדר ועכשיו הגביהו זה מקבל דלא יכלי אינשי למיסלק לה: טובא עבד. ואמאי קרי ליה כל שהוא: אי נימא נתן דסכר מיניה מיא. כלומר שראה מים שהיו באין דרך חור אחד לשטוף את השדה ונתן צרור באותו חור כדי שיעכב המים שלא ישטפו את השדה: נטל דאפיק מיא מיניה. שהיה כל השדה מלאה ולא היו יכולין לצאת ממנה ונטל זה צרור אחד מפתח השדה ויצאו המים דרך נטילת הצרור: האי מבריח ארי. כלומר מה חזקה הויא זו הא מצי למימר ליה הנותן או אחד מן האחין מצוה עבדת שהצלת נכסי כי כן חובה לכל ישראל להציל ממון חבירו ולא הויא חזקה: אלא נתן צרור דצמד לה מיא. שהיתה שדה בית השלחין דצריך לה מים הרבה וצמד לה. שסכר בצרור דרך צאת המים שלא יצאו מן השדה ולא סגי לה בלי מים: נטל דפתח לה מיא. שנטל צרור א' ועשה דרך ליכנס דרך נטילת אותו צרור דבעינן זה ודאי [הוין] חזקה: ב' שדות. של נכסי הגר:

מסורת הש"ס

א) [לקמן סה. ע"ש], ב) [נדרים לג. ב"ק נח.], ג) [נ"ל דמקבל].

הגהות הב"ח

(א) גמ' דצמד ליה מיא נטל צרור דפתח ליה מיא: (ב) רשב"ם ד"ה בעי רב וכו' מכיון שאמר לו נותני לו: (ג) ד"ה ומה מכר וכו' א"כ יהיב ליה זוזי מקמי דמחזיק לא קנה: ושם בא"ד מה שאין בשניהן. נ"ב פי' בכסף ובשטר אין מועיל קנין שדה אחת ולא לשאר שדות: (ד) ד"ה ורב דקבעי וכו' במתנה זו כלום כדאמרינן: (ה) ד"ה דאמר שמואל גבי גדר שהיה: (ו) ד"ה אילימא וכו' שלא יכנסו בו כדי שלא: (ז) ד"ה דצמד וכו' חיבר את המים: (ח) ד"ה החזיק וכו' דרפק בה פורתא כדלקמן: (ט) תוס' ד"ה האי וכו' דל"ג ליה דהיכי מצי למימר וכו' לא עיילי בה הא וכו' כספרים דגרסי דמעיקרא:

ליקוטי רש"י

מאן דיהיב מתנה בעין יפה יהיב. נותן מתנה כיון דרגיל ליתן זוזי אנפשיה [רשב"ם לקמן עא.]. מבריח ארי. [ב"ק נח.]. שתי שדות ומצר אחד ביניהן וכו'. בנכסי הגר קאי דממילא קא קני בלא מתן מעות הלכך לא קנה אלא אותו שהחזיק [הואיל ואין מי שמוסר לו ואומר לו לך חזק וקני] [רשב"ם לקמן סו.].

[א] לקנות אותה ואת חברתה אותה קנה חברתה לא קנה לקנות את חברתה אף אותה לא קנה בעי רבי זירא החזיק באחת מהן לקנות אותה ואת המצר ואת חברתה מהו מי אמרינן (א) מצר דארעא חד הוא וקני או דלמא האי לחודיה קאי והאי לחודיה קאי [ב] תיקו בעי רבי אלעזר החזיק במצר לקנות שתיהן מהו מי אמרינן האי מצר אפסרא דארעא הוא וקני או דלמא האי לחודיה קאי והאי לחודיה קאי [ג] תיקו א"ר נחמן אמר רבה בר אבוה [ד] שני בתים זה לפנים מזה החזיק בחיצון לקנותו קנאו לקנות אותו ואת הפנימי חיצון קנה פנימי לא קנה לקנות את הפנימי אף חיצון נמי לא קנה החזיק בפנימי לקנותו קנאו לקנות אותו ואת החיצון קנה שניהן לקנות את החיצון אף פנימי לא קנה (ב) א"ר נחמן אמר רבה בר אבוה [ה] הבונה פלטרין גדולים בנכסי הגר ובא אחר והעמיד להן דלתות קנה מאי טעמא קמא לבני בעלמא הוא דאפיך אמר רב דימי בר יוסף א"ר אלעזר [ו] המוצא פלטרין בנכסי הגר וסד בהן סיוד אחד או כיור אחד קנאן וכמה אמר רב יוסף [ז] אמה אמר רב חסדא [ח] וכנגד הפתח אמר רב עמרם האי מילתא אמר לן רב ששת ואנהרינהו (ג) עיינין ממתניתא [ט] המציע מצעות בנכסי הגר קנה ואנהרינהו עיינין ממתניתא מאי היא דתניא (א) [י] כיצד בחזקה נעל לו מנעלו או התיר לו מנעלו או שהוליך כליו אחריו לבית המרחץ והפשיטו והרחיצו [כ] סכו גרדו והלבישו והנעילו והגביהו קנאו אמר ר"ש לא תהא חזקה גדולה מהגבהה שהגבהה קונה בכל מקום מאי קאמר הכי קאמר הגביהו לרבו קנאו הגביה רבו לו לא קנאו אמר ר"ש [ל] לא תהא חזקה גדולה מהגבהה שהגבהה קונה בכל מקום [מ] א"ר ירמיה ביראה אמר רב יהודה האי מאן

דשדא

לקנות אותה ואת חברתה. כשמחזיק באחת נתכוין לקנות בחזקה זו את שתיהן: **אותה קנה.** לבדה אבל חברתה לא קנה דמצר מפסיק כדאמר ר' יוסי בר חנינא לקמן בשמעתי' [נה. ע"ש] המצר והחלב מפסיקין בנכסי הגר ודוקא נכסי הגר דממילא קני הלכך אין בו כח לקנות אלא אותה שדה שהחזיק בה אבל במכר מודי ר' יוחנן שאם החזיק באח' מהן קנה כולן כדאמרינן בפ' ראשון דב"ק (דף יב.) ולקמן בהמוכר את הבית (דף סז.) אמר שמואל מכר לו י' שדות בעשר מדינות החזיק באחת מהן קנה כולן ותניא בהדיא כוותיה דשמואל בפ"ק דקדושין (דף כז:) ומפרש טעמא דסלקא דארעא חד הוא וכדמפרש התם בברייתא בד"א שקנה כולן שנתן לו לוקח למוכר דמי כולן דכולהו אשתעבוד ליה ללוקח בשביל מעותיו אהני חזקת אחת מהן לקנות כולן אבל לא נתן לו דמי כולן לא קנה אלא כנגד מעותיו והלכך גבי נכסי הגר נמי דליכא מתן מעות לא קני אלא ההיא שדה דאחזיק בה: **אף אותה לא קנה.** דלא נתכוין להחזיק בה ואין חזקה אלא מדעתו דאין אדם קונה שלא מדעתו: **בעי ר' זירא החזיק באחת מהן לקנות אותה והמצר כו'.** מי לימא האי דלר' יוחנן לא קנה חברתה בחזקתה דאידך היינו משום שלא נתכוין להחזיק במצר וכיון שהוא מפסיק לא תועיל חזקה לשדה אחר שאינו מחובר לה אבל הכא דמתכוין לקנות גם את המצר עם חברתה מאי מי אמרי' האי מצר דהאי ארעא שהחזיק בה הוא וקנה גם המצר והאי ארעא [ד] של מצר שני גם הוא ויקנה גם אותה: **או דלמא האי לחודיה קאי והאי לחודיה קאי.** המצר מופלג מן השדה גבוה או נמוך וכל אחד (ד) מקום חשוב בפני עצמו הוא מצר לבד ושדה לבד ולא מבעיא דחברתה לא קנה אלא אפילו המצר לא קנה והאי דא"ר יוחנן חברתה לא קנה הוא הדין דאפילו מצר לא יכול לקנות בחזקת השדה אלא אורחא דמילתא נקט שאין חוששין בני אדם בקניית המצר כי אם בקנין השדה: **והחזיק במצר.** דרפק ביה פורתא: **לקנות שתיהן.** השדות דמכאן ומכאן: **מהו.** דאם תמצי לומר החזיק בשדה לא קנה המצר התם היינו טעמא שאין המצר צריך מן השדה ואין זקוק לו כלל אבל המצר משועבד הוא לשדה לשמרו כמו שהאפסר משמר את הבהמה ואמרינן בקדושין (שם) תדע אילו מכר לו עשר בהמות באפסר אחד מי לא קנה הבהמות בשביל שמחזיק באפסר והאי מצר נמי אפסרא דארעא הוא וכמי שמחזיק בשדות דמי: **או דלמא האי לחודיה קאי.** המצר לגמרי ולא דמי לאפסר של בהמות כדאמרי' נמי בקדושין מי דמי התם אגודו בידו הכא לא אגודו בידו: **זה לפנים מזה.** והפנימי יש לו דריסת הרגל על החיצון לצאת לרה"ר דרך עליו: **פנימי לא קנה.** דאין פנימי משועבד לחיצון כלל דליהוי חזקה שלו: ה"ג לקנות אותו ואת החיצון קנה שתיהן: **לקנות את החיצון.** לבדו לכך החזיק בפנימי אף פנימי לא קנה: **קמא לבני בעלמא הוא דאפיך.** הפך לבנים בעלמא וסדרן זה על זה לכל זמן שלא העמיד דלתות מאי קעביד מעיקרא עיילי ברווחא והשתא נמי עיילי לה ברווחא דתחלת בנין אינו עיקר אלא גמרו ודתנן (לעיל דף מב.) נעל וגדר דהיינו העמדת דלתות אבל בנה כל שהוא לא קתני: **המוצא פלטרין.** בנויין ואין חסר כלום ואין לו מה לחדש בבית שתהיה חזקה: גדולים לא גרסינן: **סיוד.** טיח בסיד: **כיור.** ציורין מתוקין על הקיר: **וכמה.** הוי ייפוי להחזיק: **וכנגד הפתח.** דרך כניסת פתח הבית בכותל שכנגדו דשם נראה יותר לנוי אבל במקום אחר טפי מאמה בעי: **הא מילתא.** דלקמן אמר לן רב ששת מדעתו: **ואנהרינהו לעיינין ממתניתא.** והאיר עינינו להביא לנו ראיה לדבריו ממתניתא דלקמן: **הציע מצעות.** ושכב שם על הקרקע בנכסי הגר קנה ואף על גב דלא היינו נעל וגדר ופרץ שלא תיקן שום תיקון בקרקע אלא שנהנה גופו מן הקרקע שמשתמש בקרקע הוי חזקה. ונראה בעיני דמהכא ילפינן דנפקא לן קרקע נקנה בחזקה בקדושין מהאי קרא ושבו בעריכם אשר תפשתם במה תפשתם בישיבה ועוד מדכתיב וירשתם אותה וישבתם בה במה ירשתם בישיבה והיינו בכלל ישיבה כששוכב על הקרקע: **כיצד בחזקה.** אעבד כנעני קאי דתנן בקדושין שנקנה בחזקה קאי: **נעל לו.** עבד לרבו שימש העבד לרבו הויא חזקה וכן כולן אף הציע מצעות שמשתמש הקרקע קנה: **והנעילו.** היינו נעל לו מנעלו דרישא ולאגב שיטפא דהלבישו אמר נמי הנעילו: **גרדו.** כמו ויקח לו חרש להתגרד בו (איוב ב) **והגביהו קנאו.** לקמיה מפרש מי הגביה למי: **אמר ר"ש כו'.** לקמיה מפרש: **מאי קאמר.** הגביהו דקאמר ת"ק מי הגביה למי ומאי קמהדר ליה ר"ש לפום ריהטא משמע דהיינו ת"ק: **הגביה העבד לרבו.** כגון שהיה צריך להגבהה זו כגון להעלותו למטתו קנאו לעבד בהגבהה זו שהרי שימש לרבו שנסמך עליו והיינו דומיא דהציע בנכסי הגר דכיון שנסמך ונשען בשכיבתו על הקרקע קנאה: **הגביה רבו לו לא קנאו.** דלא שייכא הגבהה כי אם במטלטלי שאין דרך להגביה בני אדם: **לא תהא חזקה.** דהנעיל והלביש והרחיץ והפשיט גדולה מהגבהת רב לעבד וקנה רב לעבד שהרי הגבהה חמורה היא דקונה אפילו ברשות מוכר מה שאין כן במשיכה ומסירה וגם קונה ברשות הרבים ובסימטא:

דעלא

אותה קנה וחברתה לא קנה. והא דאמרי' בפ"ק דקדושין (דף כו.) גבי עשר שדות בעשר מדינות החזיק באחת מהן קנה כולן התם בנותן לו דמי כולן והכא בנכסי הגר או במתנה ואע"ג דאין מחוסרין דמים מכל מקום לא הוי כמכר שנתן לו דמי כולן:

ליבני בעלמא הוא דאפיך. ואע"ג דרפק בה פורתא כשבנה יסוד לא מהני מידי אלא בקרקע העומד לחרישה ולא דמי למוצא פלטרין בנויין וסד בהן סיוד אחד דקני דהתם משביח הוא בנכסי הגר דהיינו פלטרין אבל הכא מה הן נכסי הגר הוא קרקע והיא לא נשתבחה שאין ראוי לדור שם כל זמן שאין דלתות וא"ת והא יש בה גג וראוי ליכנס בה בחמה מפני החמה ובגשמים מפני הגשמים וי"ל דמ"מ לא חזיא לדירת קבע כל זמן שאין בה דלתות דאדרבה קילקלה דמעיקרא חזיא לזריעה והשתא לא חזיא לזריעה:

המציע מצעות בנכסי הגר קנה. ודוקא הציע אבל הלך בבית או שכב לא קנה ואפי' מלא מטות מוצעות ושכב עליהם משמע דלא קנה [ה] דהגבהה חשובה בעינן: **הרחיצו** וסכו. בפרק כירה (שבת דף מא.) דאמר רחץ ולא סך מעיקרא ולא גרסינן מעיקרא דהכא משמע דסיכה היא בתר רחיצה דליכא למימר שתי סיכות היו עושין דא"כ אמאי לא חשיב ליה הכא ההיא דקודם רחיצה ומקרא דורחצת וסכת אין ראיה דההיא סיכה איכא למימר במיני בשמים דההיא סיכה ודאי שהיא להתבסם ולריח טוב היא אחר רחיצה שלא יעבירו המים את הבשמים:

אדעתא

עין משפט נר מצוה

רכו א מיי' פ"א מהל' זכייה הלכה ז סמג עשין פב טוש"ע ח"מ סי' ערה סעיף ח:

רכז ב ג מיי' שם טוש"ע שם ס"ט:

רכח ד מיי' שם הל' ח טוש"ע שם סעי' י:

רכט ה מיי' שם פ"ב הלכה ט סמג עשין פב טוש"ע ח"מ שם סעי' כא:

רל ו ז ח מיי' שם הל"ג טוש"ע שם סעי' יג:

רלא ט מיי' שם הל' ד טוש"ע שם סעיף טו:

רלב י כ מיי' פ"ב מהל' מכירה הל' ב ועיין בהשגות ובכסף משנה סמג עשין עג טוש"ע ח"מ סי' קצו סעיף ג:

מסורת הש"ס

א) קדושין כב:, ב) [נ"ל וסכו], ג) ערובין כה., ד) [נ"ל מלר של שני], ה) נ"א דחזקה:

הגהות הב"ח

(א) גמ' מי אמרינן מצר דארעא חד. נ"ב ס"א האי מצר דהאי ארעא ודהאי ארעא הוא וקני וכו': (ב) שם פנימי לא קנה וא"ר נחמן: (ג) שם ואנהרינהו לעיינין וכו' והרחיצו וסכו וגרדו וכו': (ד) רשב"ם ד"ה או דילמא וכו' וכל אחד חשוב מקום בפני עצמו:

ליקוטי רש"י

התיר לו מנעלו. העבד ללוקח. **גרדו.** גראט"ר בלע"ז. **והגביהו.** העבד את הלוקח. **מאי קאמר.** מה ענין הגבהה דעלמא להגבהה דהכא הגבהה דעלמא לוקח מגביה החפץ והכא אמרינן שהעבד מגביהו משום עבודה שהלוקח משעבד בו לקנותו בחזקה [קידושין כב:]. **א"ר ירמיה ביראה.** כך שמו [גיטין לד.]. דמן בירי [מגילה ד.].

רבינו גרשום

לקנות אותה ואת חברתה. דלא החזיק אלא באחת ובעי למיקני מהחזקת האחת שתי השדות דסבר הואיל והמצר עולה לשתיהן כשדה אחת דמי. אעפ"כ לא קני אלא **אותה** שהחזיק בה: **לקנות את חברתה.** כלומר דלא נתכוין לקנות אותה שהחזיק אלא חברתה: **אף אותה.** שהחזיק בה: **לא קנה.** משום דלא נתכוין לה כל שכן חברתה דלא קנה: **לקנות אותו ואת הפנימי.** בחזקת החיצון דסבר הואיל ואית ליה דרך החיצון לא צריך להחזיק אלא בחיצון ובההוא חזקה אקנה שתיהן. אפילו הכי לא **קני** אלא **חיצון**: החזיק בו **לקנות את הפנימי** דהחזיק בחיצון ולא נתכוין לקנות החיצון אלא בחזקת חיצון סבר לקנות פנימי. לא תימא דפנימי לא קנה הואיל דלא החזיק בו. אלא **אף חיצון** דאחזיק **לא קנהו** הואיל דלא נתכוין לקנותו אלא לפנימי. **החזיק בפנימי** והי' קמכוין ומבין **לקנות אותו ואת החיצון קנה** שתיהן הואיל ויש דרך לפנימי על החיצון. **החזיק בפנימי** ולא לדעת לקנות את הפנימי אלא **לקנות** באותה חזקה **את החיצון. אף פנימי לא קנה** וכל שכן חיצון דמאחר דלא קנה פנימי לא קנה חיצון: **לבני בעלמא הוא דאפיך.** כאדם שמהפך לבנים ממקום למקום דלא חשוב עיקר בנין כ"ז שלא העמיד הדלתות כדאמר נעל דהיינו עיקר: **סיוד.** בסיד: **וכיור.** צייר בו ציור **אחד** בכותל מן הסיד על שמי קורה כמו שעושין בפלטין **וכנגד הפתח** הוי חשוב דניכר: **המציע מצעותיו** של נכרי בנכסי הגר אע"ג דלא הוי לא נעל ולא גדר הוי חזקה: **ואנהר לעיינין.** שהראה לנו ראיה לדבריו מן המשנה דחזקה כל שהוא היא חזקה: **הגביהו העבד לרבו קנאו.** דהיינו קצת שימוש: ה"ק **אגביהה** איהו **לרביה קנייה** דהיינו חזקה דקצת שימוש: **הגביהו רבו לעבדו.** היינו טפי עיקר מחזקה **דהגבהה קונה** בכ"מ אפי' ברשות של חבירו ואפי' לא שכר המקום: (נוסחא א') ואם שכר מקומו והגביהו והניחו שם קנה.

לִקְנוֹת אוֹתָהּ וְאֶת חֲבֶרְתָּהּ – If he performs a proprietary act in one of the fields with intent **to acquire** both **it and the adjacent [field],**[1] אוֹתָהּ קָנָה – **he acquires it** (the field in which he performs the proprietary act), חֲבֶרְתָּהּ לֹא קָנָה – but **he does not acquire the adjacent [field].**[2] לִקְנוֹת אֶת חֲבֶרְתָּהּ – If he performs a proprietary act in one field with intent **to acquire** *only* **the adjacent [field],** אַף אוֹתָהּ לֹא קָנָה – **he does not even acquire that [field]** in which he performed the proprietary act.[3]

A related query:
בָּעֵי רַבִּי זֵירָא – **R' Zeira inquired:** הֶחֱזִיק בְּאַחַת מֵהֶן – **If he performed a proprietary act in one of [the two fields],** לִקְנוֹת אוֹתָהּ – with intent **to acquire it** וְאֶת הַמֵּצַר – *and* **the boundary divider** וְאֶת חֲבֶרְתָּהּ – *and* **the adjacent field,** מַהוּ – **what is [the law]?** מִי אַמְרִינַן – **Do we say,** מֵצַר דְּאַרְעָא חַד הוּא – **the boundary divider of** each **land is one** and the same, וְקָנֵי – **and** therefore, by performing a proprietary act with intent to acquire both fields and the divider, **he acquires** them all?[4] אוֹ דִלְמָא – **Or perhaps** we say, הַאי לְחוּדֵיהּ קָאֵי – **[the field] stands alone** וְהַאי לְחוּדֵיהּ קָאֵי – **and [the boundary divider] stands alone,** and it is thus impossible to acquire the divider *or* the adjacent field with a proprietary act in the one field.[5]

The Gemara has no satisfactory resolution to the question and concludes:
תֵּיקוּ – **[The question] stands.**[6]

A second, related question:
בָּעֵי רַבִּי אֶלְעָזָר – **R' Elazar inquired:** הֶחֱזִיק בְּמֵצַר – **If he performed a proprietary act in the boundary divider** between the two ownerless fields,[7] לִקְנוֹת שְׁתֵּיהֶן – with intent **to acquire both** fields,[8] מַהוּ – **what is [the law]?** מִי אַמְרִינַן – **Do we say** הַאי מֵצַר אַפְסָרָא דְּאַרְעָא הוּא – that **this boundary divider is** considered like **the "reins" of the land,**[9] וְקָנֵי – **and he** therefore **acquires** the fields by performing a proprietary act in the divider?[10] אוֹ דִלְמָא – **Or perhaps** we say, הַאי לְחוּדֵיהּ קָאֵי – **[the boundary divider] stands alone,** וְהַאי לְחוּדֵיהּ קָאֵי – **and [each of the two fields] stands alone.**[11]

The Gemara cannot resolve this inquiry either, and concludes:
תֵּיקוּ – **[The question] stands.**[12]

The Gemara quotes another ruling concerning the performance of proprietary acts with intent to acquire adjacent properties:
אָמַר רַב נַחְמָן אָמַר רַבָּה בַּר אֲבוּהָ – **Rav Nachman said in the name of Rabbah bar Avuha:** שְׁנֵי בָתִּים זֶה לִפְנִים מִזֶּה – If there are **two** ownerless **apartments,** arranged **one behind the other,**[13] הֶחֱזִיק בַּחִיצוֹן לִקְנוֹתוֹ – and [one] **performs a proprietary act in the outer** apartment with intent **to acquire it** alone, קְנָאוֹ – **he has acquired it.** לִקְנוֹת אוֹתוֹ וְאֶת הַפְּנִימִי – If he performs the proprietary act with intent **to acquire it** *and* **the inner** apartment as well, חִיצוֹן קָנָה – **he has acquired the outer** apartment, פְּנִימִי לֹא קָנָה – but **has not acquired the inner** one.[14] לִקְנוֹת אֶת הַפְּנִימִי – If his intent was **to acquire** *only* **the inner** apartment, אַף חִיצוֹן נַמִּי לֹא קָנָה – **he does not acquire even the outer** one.[15]

Rav Nachman continues, considering the reverse case:
הֶחֱזִיק בִּפְנִימִי לִקְנוֹתוֹ – If **he performs a proprietary act in the inner** apartment with intent **to acquire it** alone, קְנָאוֹ – **he has acquired it.** לִקְנוֹת אוֹתוֹ וְאֶת הַחִיצוֹן – If he performs the act with intent **to acquire it** *and* **the outer** apartment, קָנָה שְׁנֵיהֶן – **he has acquired both.**[16] לִקְנוֹת אֶת הַחִיצוֹן – If his intent was **to**

NOTES

1. Literally: and its fellow.

2. For the intervening boundary divider renders each field a separate parcel.

This limitation applies only to acquisition of fields that are ownerless (such as the property of a deceased convert). Regarding a *sale* of fields, however, performing a proprietary act in one field suffices to acquire *all* the fields. The reason for this distinction is as follows: The Gemara below (67a) explains that since *all* fields are, in a sense, connected — for all land on the earth is part of one mass — a proprietary act performed in one field is effective for the others. However, the Gemara (*Kiddushin* 27b) rules that this law is true only if the buyer already paid for all the fields, so that the money tendered obligates the seller to transfer title of all of them to the buyer. It follows, then, that the acquisition of ownerless property, for which money has obviously not been tendered, is similar to a case of a sale in which full payment was not yet made. Thus, a proprietary act in one field is ineffective for the other (*Rashbam*).

3. He does not acquire the adjacent field, for he has not performed a proprietary act in it; nor does he acquire the field in which he performed the proprietary act, for he had no intent to acquire it (*Rashbam*).

4. I.e. do we say that a boundary divider prevents acquisition of an adjacent field only where one did not intend to acquire the boundary divider, but if one had intention to do so, he would also acquire the boundary divider and the adjacent field, for they are contiguous with the field in which he performs the proprietary act? (*Rashbam*).

5. That is, perhaps a boundary divider is per se considered a separate parcel, since it is not level with the surface of the field. (Boundary dividers were usually slightly higher or lower than the fields they bound.) Thus, if one performs a proprietary act in one of the fields with the specific intention to acquire the divider, he does not acquire it, nor, consequently, the adjacent field.

If this view is correct, R' Yochanan's ruling above — that one cannot acquire a field by performing a proprietary act in an adjacent field — refers not only to the adjacent field but also to the boundary divider between the fields. R' Yochanan, though, formulated his ruling only for an adjacent field, because people are generally unconcerned with whether or not they acquire the boundary divider (*Rashbam*).

6. Thus, it is uncertain whether the second field has been acquired, and if another man were to subsequently come and occupy that field, it would be allowed to remain in his hands (*Rambam, Hil. Zechiyah U'Matanah* 1:7).

7. I.e. by digging in it a bit (*Rashbam*).

8. And the boundary divider itself (See *Ramban, Chidushei HaRan*).

9. Just as the reins of an animal serve to control the animal and prevent it from running away, so does a boundary divider protect the field it surrounds (*Rashbam*).

10. The law is that a group of animals joined to each other by reins can be acquired by having the seller hand over the reins to the buyer (*Kiddushin* 27b). Similarly, if we regard the boundary divider as the "reins" of the fields it surrounds, then performing a proprietary act in the divider should serve as a *kinyan* for the fields (*Rashbam*).

Rashbam explains that R' Elazar's query is a follow-up to that posed by R' Zeira. That is, even if we assume that performing a proprietary act in a field is ineffective for acquiring the divider, perhaps performing a proprietary act upon the *divider* is effective for the field, since the divider is considered the "reins" of the land.

11. Aside from serving to guard the animals, the reins are physically attached to them. Thus, one who takes up the reins holds, to a large degree, the attached animals. A proprietary act upon the boundary divider, on the other hand, although it is a valid *kinyan,* cannot cause us to view the person performing it as "holding" the pieces of land adjacent to the boundary (*Rashbam* from *Kiddushin* 27b).

12. See above, note 6.

13. In order for the residents of the inner apartment to enter and exit, they must pass through the outer apartment (*Rashbam*).

14. Since the owner of an outer apartment has no rights in the inner apartment at all, there is no reason why a proprietary act in the outer one should serve to acquire the inner one (*Rashbam*).

15. See note 3.

16. The outer apartment is in a sense subordinate to the inner one, as the only access to the inner apartment is through the outer one. Thus, when one performs a *kinyan* in the "main," inner apartment, he simultaneously performs a *kinyan* on the outside, "secondary" one (see *Rashbam*).

It should be noted that most Rishonim (*Rif, Nimukei Yosef, Rambam,*

רכו א מיי' פ"א מהל' זכיה הלכה ז סמג עשין פב טוש"ע ח"מ סי' ערה סעיף ט:
רכז ב ג מיי' שם טוש"ע שם ס"ט:
רכח ד מיי' שם הל' ח טוש"ע שם סעי' י:
רכט ה מיי' שם פ"ב הלכה ב סמג עשין פב טוש"ע ח"מ סעי' כא:
רל ו ז ח מיי' שם הל"ג טוש"ע שם סעי' יג:
רלא ט מיי' שם הל' ד טוש"ע שם סעיף טו:
רלב י כ מיי' פ"ב מהל' מכירה הל' ב ועיין בהשגות ובכסף משנה סמג עשין עב טוש"ע ח"מ סי' קצו סעיף ג:

[א] לקנות אותה ואת חברתה אותה קנה חברתה לא קנה לקנות את חברתה אף אותה לא קנה בעי רבי זירא החזיק באחת מהן לקנות אותה ואת המצר ואת חברתה מהו מי אמרינן (א) מצר דארעא חד הוא וקני או דלמא האי לחודיה קאי והאי לחודיה קאי [ב] תיקו בעי רבי אלעזר החזיק במצר לקנות שתיהן מהו מי אמרינן האי מצר אפסרא דארעא הוא וקני או דלמא האי לחודיה קאי והאי לחודיה קאי [ג] תיקו א"ר נחמן אמר רבה בר אבוה [ד] שני בתים זה לפנים מזה החזיק בחיצון לקנותו קנאו לקנות אותו ואת הפנימי חיצון קנה פנימי לא קנה לקנות את הפנימי אף חיצון נמי לא קנה החזיק בפנימי לקנותו קנאו לקנות אותו ואת החיצון קנה שניהן לקנות את החיצון אף פנימי לא קנה (ב) א"ר נחמן אמר רבה בר אבוה [ה] הבונה פלטרין גדולים בנכסי הגר ובא אחר והעמיד להן דלתות קנה מאי טעמא קמא לבני בעלמא הוא דאפיך אמר רב דימי בר יוסף א"ר אלעזר [ו] המוצא פלטרין בנכסי הגר וסד בהן סיוד אחד או כיור אחד קנאן וכמה אמר רב יוסף [ז] אמה אמר רב חסדא [ח] וכנגד הפתח אמר רב עמרם האי מילתא אמר לן רב ששת ואנהרינהו (ג) עיינין ממתניתא [ט] המציע מצעות בנכסי הגר קנה ואנהרינהו עיינין ממתניתא מאי היא דתניא [י] כיצד בחזקה נעל לו מנעלו או התיר לו מנעלו או שהוליך כליו אחריו לבית המרחץ והפשיטו והרחיצו [כ] סכו גרדו והלבישו והנעילו והגביהו קנאו אמר ר"ש לא תהא חזקה גדולה מהגבהה שהגבהה קונה בכל מקום מאי קאמר הכי קאמר הגביהו לרבו קנאו הגביה רבו לו לא קנאו אמר ר"ש [ל] לא תהא חזקה גדולה מהגבהה שהגבהה קונה בכל מקום [מ] א"ר ירמיה ביראה אמר רב יהודה האי מאן דשדא

אותה קנה וחברתה לא קנה. והא דאמרי' בפ"ק דקדושין (דף כו.) גבי עשר שדות בעשר מדינות החזיק באחת מהן קנה כולן התם בנותן לו דמי כולן והכא בנכסי הגר או במתנה ואע"ג דאין מחוסרין דמים מכל מקום לא הוי כמכר שנתן לו דמי כולן:

ליבני בעלמא הוא דאפיך. ואע"ג דרפק בה פורתא כשבנה יסוד לא מהני מידי אלא בקרקע העומד לחרישה ולא דמי למוצא פלטרין בנויין וסד בהן סיוד אחד דקני דהתם משביח הוא בנכסי הגר דהיינו פלטרין אבל הכא מה הן נכסי הגר הוא קרקע והיא לא נשתבחה שאין ראוי לדור שם כל זמן שאין דלתות וא"ת והא יש בה גג וראוי ליכנס בה בהמה מפני החמה ובגשמים מפני הגשמים וי"ל דמ"מ לא חזיא לדירת קבע כל זמן שאין בה דלתות דלדרכה קילקלה דמעיקרא חזיא לזריעה והשתא לא חזיא לזריעה:

המציע מצעות בנכסי הגר קנה. ודוקא הציע אבל הלך בבית או שכב לא קנה ואפי' אלא מטות מוצעות ושכב עליהם משמע דלא קנה (ז) דהגבהה חשובה בעינן:

הרחיצו וסכו. בפרק כירה (שבת דף מא.) דאמר רחץ ולא סך מעיקרא ולא גרסינן מעיקרא דהכא משמע דסיכה היא בתר רחיצה דליכא למימר דהא חזינן שהיו עושין דא"כ אמאי לא חשיב ליה הכא ההיא קודם רחיצה ומקרא דורחצת וסכת אין ראיה דהיא סיכה איכא למימר במיני בשמים דהיא סיכה ודאי שהיא להתכנס ולריח טוב היא אחר רחיצה שלא יעבירו המים את הבשמים: לדעתא

לקנות אותה ואת חברתה. כשמחזיק באחת נתכוין לקנות בחזקה זו את שתיהן: **אותה קנה.** לבדה אבל חברתה לא קנה דמצר מפסיק כדאמר ר' יוסי בר חנינא לקמן בשמעתי' [נה. ע"ש] המצר והחצב מפסיקין בנכסי הגר ודוקא נכסי הגר דממילא קני הלכך אין בו כח לקנות אלא אותה שדה שהחזיק בה אבל במכר מודי ר' יוחנן שאם החזיק באח' מהן קנה כולן כדאמרינן בפ' ראשון דב"ק (דף יב.) ולקמן בהמוכר את הבית (דף סו.) אמר שמואל מכר לו י' שדות בעשר מדינות החזיק באחת מהן קנה כולן ותניא בהדיא כוותיה דשמואל בפ"ק דקדושין (דף כו:) ומפרש טעמא דסדנא דארעא חד הוא וכדמפרש התם בברייתא בד"א שקנה כולן שנתן לו לוקח למוכר דמי כולן דכולהו אשתעבוד ליה ללוקח בשביל מעותיו אהני חזקת אחת מהן לקנות כולן אבל לא נתן לו דמי כולן לא קנה אלא כנגד מעותיו והלכך גבי נכסי הגר נמי דליכא מתן מעות לא קני אלא ההיא שדה דאחזיק בה: **אף אותה לא קנה.** דלא נתכוין להחזיק בה ואין חזקה אלא מדעתו דאין אדם קונה שלא מדעתו: **בעי ר' זירא החזיק באחת מהן לקנות אותה והמצר כו'.** מי לימא האי דלר' יוחנן לא קנה חברתה בחזקתה דאידך היינו משום שלא נתכוין להחזיק במצר וכיון שהוא מפסיק לא תועיל חזקה לשדה אחר שאינו מחובר לה אבל הכא דמתכוין לקנות גם את המצר עם חברתה מאי מי אמרי' האי מצר דהאי ארעא שהחזיק בה הוא וקנה גם המצר ודהאי ארעא (ד) של מצר שני גם הוא ויקנה גם אותה: **או דלמא האי לחודיה קאי והאי לחודיה קאי.** המצר מופלג מן השדה גבוה או נמוך וכל אחד (ד) מקום חשוב בפני עצמו הוא מצר לבד ושדה לבד ולא מבעיא דחברתה לא קנה אלא אפילו המצר לא קנה והאי דא"ר יוחנן חברתה לא קנה הוא הדין דאפילו מצר לא יכול לקנות בחזקת השדה אלא אורחא דמילתא נקט שאין חוששין בני אדם בקניית המצר כי אם בקנין השדה: **והחזיק במצר.** דרפק ביה פורתא: **לקנות שתיהן.** השדות דמכאן ומכאן: **מהו.** דאם תמצי לומר החזיק בשדה לא קנה המצר התם היינו טעמא שאין המצר צריך מן השדה ואין זקוק לו כלל אבל המצר משועבד הוא לשדה לשמרו כמו שהאפסר משמר את הבהמה ואמרינן בקדושין (שם) תדע אילו מכר לו עשר בהמות באפסר אחד מי לא קנה הבהמות בשביל שמחזיק באפסר והאי מצר נמי אפסרא דארעא הוא וכמי שמחזיק בשדות דמי: **או דלמא האי לחודיה קאי.** המצר לגמרי ולא דמי לאפסר של בהמות כדאמרי' נמי בקדושין מי דמי התם אגודו בידו הכא לא אגודו בידו: **זה לפנים מזה.** והפנימי יש לו דריסת הרגל על החיצון לצאת לרה"ר דרך עליו: **פנימי לא קנה.** דאין פנימי משועבד לחיצון כלל דליהני חזקה שלו: **ה"ג לקנות אותו ואת החיצון קנה שתיהן:** **לקנות את החיצון.** לבדו לכך החזיק בפנימי אף פנימי לא קנה: **קמא לבני בעלמא הוא דאפיך.** הפך לבנים בעלמא וסדרן זה על זה דכל זמן שלא העמיד דלתות מאי קעביד מעיקרא עיילי ברוותא והשתא נמי עיילי לה ברוותא דתחלת בנין אינו עיקר אלא גמרו וכדתנן (לעיל דף מב.) נעל וגדר דהיינו העמדת דלתות אבל בנה כל שהוא לא קתני: **המוצא פלטרין.** בנויין ואין חסר כלום ואין לו מה לחדש בבית שתהיה חזקה: **גדולים לא גרסינן:** **סיוד.** טיח בסיד: **כיור.** ציורין מחוקקין על הקיר: **וכמה.** הוי ייפוי להחזיק: **וכנגד הפתח.** דרך כניסת פתח הבית בכותל שכנגדו דשם נראה יותר נוי אבל במקום אחר טפי מאמה בעי: **הא מילתא.** דלקמן אמר לן רב ששת מדעתו: **ואנהרינהו לעיינין ממתניתא.** והאיר עינינו להביא לנו ראיה לדבריו ממתניתא דלקמן: **הציע מצעות.** ושכב שם על הקרקע בנכסי הגר קנה ואף על גב דלא היינו נעל וגדר ופרץ שלא תיקן שום תיקון בקרקע אלא שנהנה גופו מן הקרקע שמשתו הקרקע הוי חזקה. ונראה בעיני דמהכא ילפינן דנפקא לן קרקע נקנה בחזקה בקדושין מהאי קרא ושבו בעריכם אשר תפשתם במה תפשתם בישיבה ועוד מדכתיב וירשתם אותה וישבתם בה במה ירשתם בישיבה והיינו בכלל ישיבה כששוכב על הקרקע: **כיצד בחזקה.** אעבד כנעני דתנן בקדושין שנקנה בחזקה קאי: **נעל לו.** עבד לרבו שימש העבד לרבו הויא חזקה וכן כולן אף הציע מלעות שמשתו הקרקע קנה: **והנעילו.** היינו נעל לו מנעלו דרישא ואגב שיטפא דהלבישו אמר נמי הנעילו: **גרדו.** כמו ויקח לו חרש להתגרד בו (איוב ב): **והגביהו קנאו.** לקמיה מפרש מי הגביה למי: **אמר ר"ש כו'.** לקמיה מפרש: **מאי קאמר.** הגביהו דקאמר ת"ק מי הגביה למי ומאי קמהדר ליה ר"ש דלפום ריהטא משמע דהיינו ת"ק: **הגביה העבד לרבו.** כגון שהיה צריך להגבהה זו כגון להעלותו למטתו קנאו לעבד בהגבהה זו שהרי שימש לרבו שנסמך עליו והיינו דומיא דהציע בנכסי הגר דכיון שנסמך ונשען בשכיבתו על הקרקע קנאה: **הגביה רבו לו לא קנאו.** דלא שייכא הגבהה כי אם במטלטלי שאין דרך להגביה בני אדם: **לא תהא חזקה.** דהנעיל והלביש והרחיץ והפשיט גדולה מהגבהת רב לעבד וקנה רב לעבד שהרי הגבהה חמורה היא דקונה אפילו ברשות מוכר מה שאין כן במשיכה ומסירה וגם קונה ברשות הרבים ובסימטא: דשדא

רבינו גרשום

לקנות אותה ואת חברתה. דלא החזיק אלא באחת ובעי למיקני מהחזקת האחת שתי השדות דסבר הואיל והמצר עולה לשתיהן כשדה אחת דמי. אעפ"כ לא קני אלא **אותה** שהחזיק בה: **לקנות את חברתה.** כלומר דלא נתכוין לקנות אותה שהחזיק אלא חברתה: **אף אותה.** שהחזיק בה: **לא קנה.** משום דלא נתכוין לה כל שכן חברתה דלא קנה: **לקנות אותו ואת הפנימי.** בחזקת החיצון דסבר הואיל ואית ליה דרך החיצון לא צריך להחזיק אלא בחיצון ובההוא חזקה אקנה שתיהן. אפילו הכי לא קני אלא **חיצון:** **החזיק בו לקנות את הפנימי** דהחזיק בחיצון ולא נתכוין לקנות החיצון אלא בחזקת חיצון סבר לקנות פנימי. לא תימא הפנימי לא קנה הואיל ולא החזיק בו. אלא **אף חיצון** דאחזיק **לא קנהו** הואיל ולא נתכוין לקנותו אלא לפנימי. **החזיק בפנימי** והוי קמכוין ומבין **לקנות אותו ואת החיצון** קנה שתיהן הואיל ויש דרך לפנימי על החיצון. **החזיק בפנימי** ולא לדעת **לקנות** את הפנימי אלא לקנות באותה חזקה את החיצון: **אף פנימי לא קנה** וכל שכן חיצון דמאחר דלא קנה פנימי לא קנה חיצון: **לבני בעלמא הוא דאפיך.** כאדם שהמפך לבנים ממקום למקום דלא חשוב עיקר בנין כ"ז שלא העמיד הדלתות כדאמר נעל דהיינו עיקר: **סיוד.** בסיד: **וכיור.** צייר בו ציור **אחד** בכותל מן הסיד על שמי קורה כמו שעושין בפלטין: **וכנגד הפתח** הוי חשוב דניכר: **המציע מצעותיו** של נכרי **בנכסי הגר** אע"ג דלא הוי לא נעל ולא גדר הוי **חזקה:** **ואנהר לעיינין.** שהראה לנו ראיה לדבריו מן המשנה דחזקה כל שהוא הויא חזקה: **הגביהו** העבד **לרב קנאו.** דהיינו קצת שימוש: הי"ק אגבהיה איהו לרביה קנייה. דהיינו חזקה דקצת שימוש: **הגביהו רבו לעבדו.** היינו טפי עיקר מחזקה דהגבהה קונה בכ"מ אפי' ברשות חבירו ואפי' לא שכר המקום: (נוסחא א') ואם שכר מקומו והגביהו והניחו שם קונה.

א) קדושין כו:, ב) [נ"ל וסכו], ג) עירובין כה., ד) [נ"ל מלר של שני], ה) נ"ל למזוקה.

הגהות הב"ח

(א) גמ' מי אמרינן מצר דארעא חד. נ"ב ס"א האי מצר דהאי ארעא ודהאי ארעא הוא וקני וכו': (ב) שם פנימי לא קנה וא"ר נחמן: (ג) שם ואנהרינהו לעיינין וכו' והרחיצו וסכו וגרדו וכו': (ד) רשב"ם ד"ה או דלמא וכו' וכל אחד חשוב מקום בפני עצמו:

ליקוטי רש"י

התיר לו מנעלו. העבד ללוקח. **גרדו.** גרלט"ר בלע"ז. **והגביהו.** העבד את הלוקח. **מאי קאמר.** מה ענין הגבהה דעלמא להגבהה דהכא הגבהה דעלמא לוקח מגביה החפץ והכא אמרינן שהעבד מגביהו משום עבודה שהלוקח משעבד בו לקנותו בחזקה [קידושין כב:]. **א"ר ירמיה ביראה.** כך שמו [גיטין לד.]. ומן בירי [מגילה ד.].

acquire *only* **the outer** apartment, **אַף פְּנִימִי לֹא קָנָה – he does not acquire even the inner** apartment.[17]

The Gemara proceeds to rule on the effectiveness of various acts as far as acquiring ownerless property of a deceased convert: **אָמַר רַב נַחְמָן אָמַר רַבָּה בַּר אֲבוּהּ – Rav Nachman** further **said in the name of Rabbah bar Avuha: הַבּוֹנֶה פַּלְטְרִין גְּדוֹלִים בְּנִכְסֵי הַגֵּר – If one erects a large mansion upon the** ownerless **property of a** deceased **convert, וּבָא אַחֵר – and another comes וְהֶעֱמִיד לָהֶן דְּלָתוֹת – and installs the doors on it,**[18] **קָנָה – [the second person] has acquired** the property.

The Gemara asks:

מַאי טַעְמָא – What is the reason for this? Why does the construction of the mansion itself not constitute a proprietary act?

The Gemara answers:

קַמָּא לִבְנֵי בְּעָלְמָא הוּא דְּאַפִּיךְ – The first person **merely rearranged** some **bricks** but did not do anything meaningful enough to constitute a proprietary act.[19]

Another such ruling:

אָמַר רַב דִּימִי בַּר יוֹסֵף אָמַר רַבִּי אֶלְעָזָר – Rav Dimi bar Yosef said in R' Elazar's name: הַמּוֹצֵא פַּלְטְרִין בְּנִכְסֵי הַגֵּר – If one comes across a fully constructed **mansion in the** ownerless **property of a** deceased **convert, וְסָד בָּהֶן סִיּוּד אֶחָד – and he plasters one of** its walls **with a single swath of lime, אוֹ כִּיּוּר אֶחָד – or** he engraves **a single design** upon the wall,[20] **קְנָאָן – he has acquired [the mansion].**[21]

The Gemara clarifies Rav Dimi's ruling:

וְכַמָּה – And how much area must be covered by the lime or the design? **אָמַר רַב יוֹסֵף – Rav Yosef said: אַמָּה – A** square ***amah.***[22] **אָמַר רַב חִסְדָּא – Rav Chisda added: וּכְנֶגֶד הַפֶּתַח – And** the square *amah* must be **opposite the doorway.**[23]

A third ruling:

הַאי מִילְּתָא אֲמַר לָן רַב שֵׁשֶׁת – אָמַר רַב עַמְרָם – Rav Amram said: – [The following] ruling[24] **was told to us by Rav Sheishess, וְאַנְהֲרִינְהוּ עֵינִין מִמַּתְנִיתָא – and he enlightened our eyes** by adducing proof to it **from a Baraisa.**

The ruling:

הַמַּצִּיעַ מַצָּעוֹת בְּנִכְסֵי הַגֵּר – One who spreads out mats on the ownerless **land of a** deceased **convert** and lies down upon them **קָנָה – has acquired** the land.[25]

The corroborative Baraisa:

וְאַנְהֲרִינְהוּ עֵינִין מִמַּתְנִיתָא – And [Rav Sheishess] enlightened our eyes by adducing a proof to his law **from a Baraisa. מַאי הִיא – What** Baraisa **is this? דְּתַנְיָא – As it was taught in a Baraisa: כֵּיצַד בַּחֲזָקָה – HOW** does one acquire a Canaanite slave **BY** means of **A PROPRIETARY ACT?**[26] **נָעַל לוֹ מִנְעָלוֹ – IF [THE SLAVE] PUT [A MAN'S] SHOE ON FOR HIM, אוֹ הִתִּיר לוֹ מִנְעָלוֹ – OR REMOVED HIS SHOE FOR HIM, אוֹ שֶׁהוֹלִיךְ כֵּלָיו אַחֲרָיו לְבֵית הַמֶּרְחָץ – OR CARRIED HIS CLOTHING AFTER HIM TO THE BATHHOUSE, וְהִפְשִׁיטוֹ – OR REMOVED HIS CLOTHING FOR HIM, וְהִרְחִיצוֹ – OR WASHED HIM, סָכוֹ – OR RUBBED HIM** with oil,[27] **גְּרָדוֹ – OR SCRAPED** his skin,[28] **וְהִלְבִּישׁוֹ – OR DRESSED HIM, וְהִנְעִילוֹ – OR PUT ON HIS SHOE FOR HIM,**[29] **וְהִגְבִּיהוֹ – OR LIFTED HIM**[30] **– קְנָאוֹ –** if the slave performed any of these servile acts, **[THE PERSON]** seeking to acquire the slave **HAS ACQUIRED HIM.**[31] **אָמַר רַבִּי שִׁמְעוֹן – R' SHIMON SAID: לֹא תְּהֵא חֲזָקָה גְּדוֹלָה מֵהַגְבָּהָה – A PROPRIETARY ACT SHOULD NOT BE SUPERIOR TO "LIFTING"** the object, **שֶׁהַגְבָּהָה קוֹנָה בְּכָל מָקוֹם – FOR "LIFTING" EFFECTS ACQUISITION IN EVERY PLACE.**[32]

The Gemara seeks to clarify the last segment of the Baraisa and asks:

מַאי קָאָמַר – What does [the Baraisa] mean to **say** when it discusses lifting?[33]

NOTES

Hil. Zechiyah U'Matanah 1:8) dispute this ruling and maintain that the outer apartment is *not* acquired in the case discussed here. This ruling is based upon an alternate text of the Gemara, which states that if the one performing the proprietary act meant to acquire both apartments, he nevertheless does not receive the outer one.

17. See note 3.

18. The first man did all the construction except for installing doors and the second man installed the doors.

19. Until the doors are installed, no new use has been added to the land. Thus, although the first man did most of the construction, he has not performed a valid *kinyan.* Installing the doors, however, completes the edifice and renders it useful. Thus, although it is a relatively small act, it effects a *kinyan,* similar to locking and fencing (*Rashbam*).

Even if a foundation was excavated for the mansion, the digging involved does not serve to acquire the land, for digging is only considered a proprietary act if it prepares the land for seeding (*Tosafos; Ramban*). Other Rishonim, however, disagree, and explain that our Gemara refers to a mansion that was built without an excavated foundation (*Ri Migash* cited by *Rashba;* see *Rambam, Hil. Zechiyah* 2:9).

20. E.g. he engraved a design or a flower (*Rashbam* 54a ד״ה בנכסי).

21. Since the design and the lime beautify the building, they constitute a proprietary act (*Rashbam*).

22. *Meiri, Rashash.*

23. As it is most noticeable there. If, however, the plastering or designing is done elsewhere in the house, the area required to effect acquisition is greater than an *amah* (*Rashbam*).

24. Literally: this matter.

25. Although by lying on the ground he has not improved it, physically benefiting from the land can also effect the *kinyan,* for having the land "serve" him, as it were, indicates his ownership. This differs from using a field's produce, which is not a valid proprietary act, for in using the produce one does not use the land directly. [Actually, one benefits from the land by lying even on the ground *itself* (without a mat). However, since it is not considered a usual method of benefit such an act is perhaps not considered proprietary (*Ran Nimukei Yosef*).] *Rashbam* postulates that the source for this seemingly novel law is the pair of verses cited by the Gemara in *Kiddushin* (26a) to derive that a proprietary act effects a *kinyan.* Both verses adduced there describe the proprietary act as יְשִׁיבָה, *dwelling.* We see, therefore, that even mere dwelling constitutes a proprietary act.

Other Rishonim reject this approach and explain that the mats beautify the land, and the proprietary act involved is thus similar to that discussed by Rav Dimi bar Yosef above. According to this interpretation, it is not necessary to *lie* upon the mats to acquire the land (see *Rashba, Meiri, Ri Migash*).

26. One who wishes to acquire a Canaanite slave can do so by means of any of the three methods of acquisition which can be used to acquire real estate; i.e. tendering money, delivering a document, or performing a proprietary act (*Kiddushin* 22b). The Baraisa cited explains what is considered a proprietary act that can acquire such a slave.

27. It was customary to apply oil to the skin after bathing (see *Tosafos*).

28. In Mishnaic times, it was customary to scrape the skin at the bath with a curved implement made for this purpose (see Mishnah, *Shabbos* 147a and *Rashi* there ד״ה ולא מתגררין).

29. This is identical to the first case mentioned in the Baraisa. It is mentioned again here because after dressing his master, the slave would normally put on the master's shoes for him as well (*Rashbam*). [The text of the Baraisa quoted in *Kiddushin* 22b does not contain the first case.]

30. The Gemara below will explain who lifted whom.

31. All the services listed in this Baraisa are acts of servitude and thus qualify as a proprietary act in the slave (see *Rambam, Hil. Mechirah* 2:2 and *Kesef Mishnah* there).

32. The Gemara below will explain R' Shimon's statement.

33. What does the Tanna Kamma mean by lifting — who lifted whom? Additionally, what does R' Shimon mean to add, for at first glance, he appears to concur with the Tanna Kamma's ruling? (*Rashbam*).

^אלקנות אותה ואת חברתה ואת חברתה אותה קנה חברתה
לא קנה לקנות את חברתה אף אותה לא קנה
בעי רבי זירא החזיק באחת מהן לקנות אותה
ואת המצר ואת חברתה מהו מי אמרינן
(א) מצר דארעא חד הוא וקני או דלמא האי
לחודיה קאי והאי לחודיה קאי ^בתיקו בעי רבי
אלעזר החזיק במצר לקנות שתיהן מהו מי
אמרינן האי מצר אפסרא דארעא הוא וקני או
דלמא האי לחודיה קאי והאי לחודיה קאי
^גתיקו א"ר נחמן אמר רבה בר אבוה ^דשני בתים
זה לפנים מזה החזיק בחיצון לקנותו קנאו
לקנות אותו ואת הפנימי חיצון קנה פנימי לא
קנה לקנות את הפנימי אף חיצון נמי לא קנה
החזיק בפנימי לקנותו קנאו לקנות אותו ואת
החיצון קנה שניהן לקנות את החיצון אף
פנימי לא קנה (ב) א"ר נחמן אמר רבה בר אבוה
^ההבונה פלטרין גדולים בנכסי הגר ובא אחר
והעמיד להן דלתות קנה מאי טעמא קמא
לבני בעלמא הוא דאפיך אמר רב דימי בר
יוסף א"ר אלעזר ^והמוצא פלטרין בנכסי הגר
וסד בהן סיוד אחד או כיור אחד קנאן וכמה
אמר רב יוסף ^זאמה אמר רב חסדא ^חוכנגד
הפתח אמר רב עמרם האי מילתא אמר לן רב
ששת ואנהרינהו (ג) עינין ממתניתא ^טהמציע
מצעות בנכסי הגר קנה ואנהרינהו עינין
ממתניתא מאי היא דתניא ^א) ^יכיצד בחזקה
נעל לו מנעלו או התיר לו מנעלו או שהוליך
כליו אחריו לבית המרחץ והפשיטו והרחיצו
^ב) סכו גרדו והלבישו והנעילו והגביהו קנאו אמר ר"ש לא תהא חזקה גדולה
מהגבהה שהגבהה קונה בכל מקום מאי קאמר הכי קאמר הגביהו לרבו
קנאו הגביה רבו לו לא קנאו אמר ר"ש ^כלא תהא חזקה גדולה מהגבהה
שהגבהה קונה בכל מקום ^ג) א"ר ירמיה ביראה אמר רב יהודה האי מאן
דשדא

לקנות אותה ואת חברתה. כשמחזיק באחת נתכוון לקנות בחזקה זו את שתיהן: אותה קנה. לבדה אבל חברתה לא קנה שהרי המצר מפסיק כדאמר ר' יוסי בר חנינא לקמן בשמעתין [נד. ע"ש] המצר והשלב מפסיקין בנכסי הגר ודוקא נכסי הגר דממילא קני הלכך אין בו כח לקנות אלא אותה שדה שהחזיק בה אבל במכר מודי ר' יוחנן שאם החזיק באחת מהן קנה כולן כדאמרינן בפ' ראשון דק"ק (דף כו.) ולקמן בהמוכר את הבית (דף סג.) אמר שמואל מכר לו י' שדות בעשר מדינות החזיק באחת מהן קנה כולן ותניא נמי בהדיא כוותיה דשמואל בפ"ק דקדושין (דף כז:) ומפרש טעמא דסלקא לארעא חד הוא וכדמפרש התם בברייתא בד"א שקנה כולן שנתן לו לוקח למוכר דמי כולן דכולהו אשתעבוד ליה ללוקח בשביל מעותיו אהני חזקת אחת מהן לקנות כולן אבל לא נתן לו דמי כולן לא קנה אלא כנגד מעותיו והלכך גבי נכסי הגר נמי דליכא מתן מעות לא קני אלא ההיא שדה דהמחזיק בה: אף אותה לא קנה. דלא נתכוין להחזיק בה ואין חזקה אלא מדעתו דאין אדם קונה שלא מדעתו: בעי ר' זירא החזיק באחת מהן לקנות אותה והמצר כו'. מי לימא האי דלר' יוחנן לא קנה חברתה בחזקתה דלידך היינו משום שלא נתכוין להחזיק במצר וכיון שהוא מפסיק לא מועיל חזקה לשדה אחר שאינו מחובר לה אבל הכא דמתכוין לקנות גם את המצר עם חברתה מאי מי אמרי' האי מצר דהאי ארעא שהחזיק בה הוא וקונה גם המצר ודהאי ארעא (ד) של מצר שני גם הוא ויקנה גם אותה: או דלמא האי לחודיה קאי והאי לחודיה קאי. המצר מופלג מן השדה גבוה או נמוך וכל אחד (ד) מקום חשוב בפני עצמו הוא מצר לבד ושדה לבד ולא מבעיא דחברתה לא קנה אלא אפילו המצר לא קנה והאי דלר' יוחנן חברתה לא קנה הוא הדין דאפילו מצר לא יכול לקנות בחזקת השדה אלא אורחא דמילתא נקט שאין חופשין בני אדם בקנין השדה: והחזיק במצר. דרפק ביה פורתא: לקנות שתיהן. השדות דמכאן ומכאן: מהו. דאם תמצי לומר החזיק בשדה לא קנה המצר התם היינו טעמא שאין המצר צריך מן השדה ואין זקוק לו כלל אבל המצר משועבד הוא לשדה לשמרו כמו שהאפסר משמר את הבהמה ואמרינן בקדושין (שם) תדע אילו מכר לו עשר בהמות באפסר אחד מי לא קנה הבהמות בשביל שמחזיק באפסר והאי מצר נמי אפסרא דארעא הוא וכמי שמחזיק בשדות דמי: או דלמא האי לחודיה קאי. המצר לגמרי ולא דמי לאפסר של בהמות כדאמרי' נמי בקדושין מי דמי התם אגודו בידו הכא לא אגודו בידו: זה לפנים מזה. והפנימי יש לו דריסת הרגל על החיצון לצאת לרה"ר דרך עליו: פנימי לא קנה. דאין פנימי משועבד לחיצון כלל דליהני חזקה שלו: ה"ג לקנות אותו ואת החיצון קנה שתיהן: לקנות את החיצון. לבדו לכך החזיק בפנימי אף פנימי לא קנה: קמא לבני בעלמא הוא דאפיך. הפך לבנים בעלמא וסדרן זה על זה דכל זמן שלא העמיד דלתות מאי קעביד מעיקרא עיילי ברווחא והשתא נמי עיילי לה ברווחא דתחלת בנין אינו עיקר אלא גמרו וכדתנן (לעיל דף מב.) נעל וגדר דהיינו העמדת דלתות אבל בנה כל שהוא לא קתני: המוצא פלטרין. בנויין ואין חסר כלום ואין לו מה לחדש בבית שתהיה חזקה: גדולים לא גרסינן: סיוד. טיח בסיד: כיור. ציורין מחוקין על הקיר: וכמה. הוי ייפוי להחזיק: וכנגד הפתח. דרך כניסת פתח הבית בכותל שכנגדו דשם נראה יותר לנוי אבל במקום אחר טפי מאמה בעי: הא מילתא. דלקמן אמר לן רב ששת מדעתו: ואנהרינהו לעיינין ממתניתא. והאיר עינינו להביא לנו ראיה לדבריו ממתניתא דלקמן: הציע מצעות. ושכב שם על הקרקע בנכסי הגר קנה ואף על גב דלא היינו נעל וגדר ופרץ שלא תיקן שום תיקון בקרקע אלא שנהנה גופו מן הקרקע שמשמשו הקרקע הוי חזקה. ונראה בעיני דמהכא ילפינן דנפקא לן קרקע נקנה בחזקה בקדושין מהאי קרא ושבו בעריכם אשר תפשתם במה תפשתם בישיבה ועוד מדכתיב וירשתם אותה וישבתם בה במה ירשתם בישיבה והיינו בכלל ישיבה כששוכב על הקרקע: כיצד בחזקה. אעבד כנעני דתנן בקדושין שנקנה בחזקה קאי: נעל לו. עבד לרבו שימש העבד לרבו הויא חזקה וכן כולן אף הציע מצעות שמשמשו הקרקע קנה: והנעילו. היינו נעל לו מנעלו דרישא ואגב שיטפא דהלבישו אמר נמי הנעילו: גרדו. כמו ויקח לו חרש להתגרד בו (איוב ב): והגביהו קנאו. לקמיה מפרש מי הגביה למי: אמר ר"ש כו'. לקמיה מפרש: מאי קאמר. הגביהו דקאמר ת"ק מי הגביה למי ומאי קמהדר ליה ר"ש דלפום ריהטא משמע דהיינו ת"ק: הגביה העבד לרבו. כגון שהיה צריך להגבהה זו כגון להעלותו למטתו קנאו לעבד בהגבהה זו שהרי שימש לרבו שנסמך עליו והיינו דומיא דהציע בנכסי הגר דכיון שנסמך ונשען בשכיבתו על הקרקע קנאה: הגביה רבו לו לא קנאו. דלא שייכא הגבהה כי אם במטלטלי שאין דרך להגביה בני אדם: לא תהא חזקה. דהנעיל והלביש והרחיץ והפשיט גדולה מהגבהת רב לעבד וקונה רב לעבד שהרי הגבהה חמורה היא דקונה אפילו ברשות מוכר מה שאין כן במשיכה ומסירה וגם קונה ברשות הרבים ובסימטא:

דשדא

אותה קנה וחברתה לא קנה. והא דאמרי' בפ"ק דקדושין (דף כו.) גבי עשר שדות בעשר מדינות החזיק באחת מהן קנה כולן התם בנותן לו דמי כולן והכא בנכסי הגר או במתנה ואע"ג דאין מחוסרין דמים מכל מקום לא הוי כמכר שנתן לו דמי כולן: ליבני בעלמא הוא דאפיך. ואע"ג דרפק בה פורתא כשבנה יסוד לא מהני מידי אלא בקרקע העומד לחרישה ולא דמי למולא פלטורין בנויין וסד בהן סיוד אחד דקני דהתם משבח הוא בנכסי הגר דהיינו פלטורין אבל הכא מה הן נכסי הגר הוא קרקע והיא לא נשתבחה שאין ראוי לדור שם כל זמן שאין דלתות וא"ת והא יש בה גג וראוי ליכנס בה בחמה מפני החמה ובגשמים מפני הגשמים וי"ל דמ"מ לא חזיא לדירת קבע כל זמן שאין בה דלתות דאדרבה קילקלה דמעיקרא חזיא לזריעה והשתא לא חזיא לזריעה: המציע מצעות בנכסי הגר קנה. ודוקא הציע אבל הלך בבית או שכב לא קנה ואפי' מלא מטות מוצעות ושכב עליהם משמע דלא קנה ^ה) דהגבהה חשובה בעינן: והרחיצו וסכו. בפרק כירה (שבת דף מא.) דאמר רחץ ולא סך מעיקרא ולא גרסינן מעיקרא דהכא משמע דסיכה היא בתר רחיצה דליכא למימר שתי סיכות היו עושין דא"כ אמאי לא חשיב ליה הכא הסיכה דקודם רחיצה ומקרא דורשת וסכת אין ראיה דההיא סיכה איכא למימר במיני בשמים דהסיכה סיכה ודאי שהיא להתבשם ולריח טוב היא אחר רחיצה שלא יעבירו המים את הבשמים:

אלעתא

עין משפט נר מצוה

רכו א מיי' פ"א מהל' זכייה הלכה ז סמג עשין פב טוש"ע ח"מ סי' ערה סעיף ח:

רכז ב ג מיי' שם טוש"ע שם ס"ט:

רכח ד מיי' שם הל' ח טוש"ע שם סעי' י:

רכט ה מיי' שם פ"ב הלכה ט סמג עשין פב טוש"ע ח"מ שם סעי' כא:

רל ו ז ח מיי' שם הל"ג טוש"ע שם סעי' יג:

רלא ט מיי' שם הל' ד טוש"ע שם סעיף טו:

רלב י כ מיי' פ"ב מהל' מכירה הל' ג ועיין בהשגות ובכסף משנה סמג עשין עג טוש"ע ח"מ סי' קצו סעיף ג:

הגהות הב"ח

(א) גמ' מי אמרינן מצר דארעא חד. נ"ב ס"א האי מצר דהאי ארעא ודהאי ארעא הוא וקני וכו': (ב) שם פנימי לא קנה וא"ר נחמן: (ג) שם ואנהרינהו לעיינין וכו' והרחיצו וסכו וגרדו וכו': (ד) רשב"ם ד"ה או דילמא וכו' וכל אחד חשוב מקום בפני עצמו:

ליקוטי רש"י

התיר לו מנעלו. העבד ללוקח. גרדו. גרא"ט"ר בלע"ז. והגביהו. העבד את הלוקח. מאי קאמר. מה ענין הגבהה דעלמא להגבהה דהכא הגבהה דעלמא לוקח מגביה החפץ והכא אמרינן שהעבד מגביהו משום עבודה שהלוקח משעבד בו לקנותו בחזקה [קידושין כב:]. א"ר ירמיה ביראה. כך שמו [גיטין לד.]. דמן בירי [מגילה ד.].

מסורת הש"ס

א) קדושין כב:, ב) [נ"א וסכו], ג) עירובין כה., ד) [נ"א מצר של שני], ה) נ"א דמזקה:

רבינו גרשום

לקנות אותה ואת חברתה. דלא החזיק אלא באחת ובעי למיקני מהחזקת האחת שתי השדות דסבר הואיל והמצר עולה לשתיהן כשדה אחת דמי. אעפ"כ לא קני אלא אותה שהחזיק בה: לקנות את חברתה. כלומר דלא נתכוין לקנות אותה שהחזיק אלא חברתה: אף אותה. שהחזיק בה: לא קנה. משום דלא נתכוין לה כל שכן חברתה דלא קנה: לקנות אותו ואת הפנימי. בחזקת החיצון דסבר הואיל ואית ליה דרך החיצון לא צריך להחזיק אלא בחיצון ובההוא חזקה אקנה שתיהן. אפילו הכי לא קני אלא חיצון: החזיק בו לקנות את הפנימי דהחזיק בחיצון ולא נתכוין לקנות החיצון אלא בחזקת חיצון סבר לקנות פנימי. לא תימא דפנימי לא קנה הואיל דלא החזיק בו. אלא אף חיצון דאחזיק לא קנהו הואיל דלא נתכוין לקנותו אלא לפנימי. החזיק בפנימי והי' קמכוין ומבין לקנות אותו ואת החיצון קנה שתיהן הואיל ויש דרך לפנימי על החיצון. החזיק בפנימי ולא לדעת לקנות את הפנימי אלא לקנות באותה חזקה את החיצון. אף פנימי לא קנה וכל שכן חיצון דמאחר דלא קנה פנימי לא קנה חיצון: לבני בעלמא הוא דאפיך. כאדם שמהפך לבנים ממקום למקום דלא חשוב עיקר בנין כ"ז שלא העמיד הדלתות כדאמר נעל דהיינו עיקר: סיוד. בסיד: וכיור. צייר בו ציור אחד בכותל מן הסיד על שמי קורה כמו שעושין בפלטין וכנגד הפתח הוי חשוב דניכר: המציע מצעותיו של נכרי בנכסי הגר אע"ג דלא הוי לא נעל ולא גדר הוי חזקה: ואנהר לעיינין. שהראה לנו ראיה לדבריו מן המשנה דחזקה כל שהוא הויא חזקה: הגביהו העבד לרב קנאו. דהיינו קצת שימוש: ה"ק אגבהיה איהו לרביה קנייה. דהיינו חזקה דקצת שימוש: הגביהו רבו לעבדו. היינו טפי עיקר מחזקה דהגבהה קונה בכ"מ אפי' ברשות של חבירו ואפי' לא שכר המקום: (נוסחא א') ואם שכר מקומו והגביהו והניחו שם קונה.

The Gemara answers:

הָכִי קָאָמַר – This is what [the Baraisa] means to **say: הִגְבִּיהוֹ לְרַבּוֹ קְנָאוֹ – If [the slave] lifted** the one seeking to become **his master, [that person] has acquired [the slave];**[34] **הִגְבִּיהַּ רַבּוֹ לֹא קְנָאוֹ –** but if the one seeking to become **his master lifted him, [that person] has not acquired [the slave].**[35] Accordingly, **אָמַר רַבִּי שִׁמְעוֹן – R' Shimon** disagreed with the Tanna Kamma and **said: לֹא תְהֵא חֲזָקָה גְּדוֹלָה מֵהַגְבָּהָה – A proprietary act should not be superior to "lifting," שֶׁהַגְבָּהָה קוֹנָה בְּכָל מָקוֹם – for "lifting" effects acquisition in every place.**[36] Thus, the slave would be acquired even if the master lifts the slave.

Rav Sheishess adduces the following proof: The Baraisa indicates that having the slave support the weight of the man seeking to acquire him constitutes a proprietary act on the slave. Similarly, then, using land to support one's weight by spreading mats on it and lying on them constitutes a proprietary act on the land.[37]

Another such ruling:

אָמַר רַבִּי יִרְמְיָה בִּירָאָה אָמַר רַב יְהוּדָה – R' Yirmiyah Bira'ah said in Rav Yehudah's name, הַאי מַאן – One

NOTES

34. For the slave has served him by lifting him. This ruling refers to where the lifting demonstrates servility to the man seeking to acquire him, e.g. he lifted the man into bed (*Rashbam*).

35. As the *kinyan* of "lifting" is only appropriate to movable objects, which are usually lifted. It is not common practice, however, to lift people (*Rashbam*).

36. Unlike other *kinyanim*, such as *meshichah* and *mesirah, hagbahah* effects acquisition even when performed in the domain of the seller. (*Meshichah* and *mesirah* require at least a neutral domain.) Thus, R' Shimon argues that the powerful *kinyan* of *hagbahah*, which effects acquisition in any place, should certainly be the equal of a proprietary act and effect acquisition of a Canaanite slave (*Rashbam*).

37. *Rashbam.* Other Rishonim understand this proof differently (see note 25).

דְשָׁדָא לִיפְתָּא בֵּי פִּילֵי – **who threw a turnip into a crack**[1] דְּאַרְעָא דְּגֵר – **in the field of a convert** who died without heirs.[2] לֹא הָוֵי חֲזָקָה – The law is that **[his action] is not a** valid **proprietary act** and he has not acquired the ownerless field. מַאי טַעְמָא – **What is the reason** that he does not acquire the field with this act? בְּעִידְנָא דְשָׁדָא – **At the time that he threw** the turnip into the ground, לֹא הָוֵי שְׁבָחָא – **there was no improvement** in the property, since nothing grew immediately.[3] הַשְׁתָּא דְּקָא שָׁבַח – **Now that [the property] has improved,** as the turnip takes root and grows, מִמֵּילָא קָא שָׁבַח – **it has improved on its own** without any action on the part of the person who threw the turnip there. Since the improvement occurred on its own, it does not effect acquisition on behalf of the one who caused it.[4]

The Gemara cites a series of related rulings authored by Shmuel:[5]

אָמַר שְׁמוּאֵל – **Shmuel said:** הַאי מַאן דְּפָשַׁח דִּיקְלָא – Concerning **a person who removed branches from a palm tree,** and later claimed that his intent was to acquire the tree thereby, the law is as follows: אַדַּעְתָּא דְּדִיקְלָא – If he removed the branches **for the sake of** improving **the tree,**[6] קָנֵי – **he has acquired** the tree. אַדַּעְתָּא דְּחֵיוָתָא – But if he removed them **for the sake of** procuring food for his **animals,** לֹא קָנֵי – **he has not acquired** the tree.[7] הֵיכִי דָּמֵי – **What are the circumstances?** How can we tell whether he removed the branches for the sake of the tree or for the sake of procuring fodder?[8] שָׁקַל מֵהַאי גִּיסָא וּמֵהַאי גִּיסָא – If **he took** branches **from all sides**[9] of the tree, אַדַּעְתָּא דְּדִיקְלָא – we assume that he removed them **for the sake of** improving **the tree.**[10] כּוּלָּא מֵחַד גִּיסָא – But if **all** the branches he took were **from one side** of the tree, אַדַּעְתָּא דְּחֵיוָתָא – it is evident that he removed them **for the sake of** procuring fodder for **animals.**[11]

Shmuel's second ruling:

וְאָמַר שְׁמוּאֵל – **And Shmuel** also **said:** הַאי מַאן דְּזָבֵי זִיבְּיָא – Concerning **a person who swept debris** (e.g. weeds and twigs) from a parcel of land, and later claimed that it was his intent to acquire the land thereby, the law is as follows: אַדַּעְתָּא דְּאַרְעָא – If he swept **for the sake of** improving **the land,**[12] קָנֵי – **he has acquired** the land. אַדַּעְתָּא דְּצִיבֵי – But if he swept **for the sake of** gathering **wood** for fuel, לֹא קָנֵי – **he has not acquired** the land.[13] הֵיכִי דָּמֵי – **What are the circumstances** that reveal his intention? שָׁקַל רַבְרְבֵי וְזוּטְרֵי – If **he took** both **large and small [twigs],** אַדַּעְתָּא דְּאַרְעָא – we assume that he removed them **for the sake of** improving **the land.** שָׁקַל רַבְרְבֵי – But if **he took** only the **large ones** וְשָׁבַק זוּטְרֵי – **and left** the **small ones,** אַדַּעְתָּא דְּצִיבֵי – it is evident that he removed them **for the sake of** gathering **wood.**

Shmuel's third ruling:

וְאָמַר שְׁמוּאֵל – **And Shmuel** also **said:** הַאי מַאן דְּאַתְקִיל תִּיקְלָא – Concerning **a person who removed obstacles** (piles of dirt, holes) from a parcel of land to level its surface, and later claimed that his intent was to acquire the land thereby, the law is as follows: אַדַּעְתָּא דְּאַרְעָא – If he leveled the ground **for the sake of** improving **the land,**[14] קָנֵי – **he has acquired** the land.[15] אַדַּעְתָּא דְּבֵי דָּרֵי – But if he leveled the ground **for the sake of** creating **a** temporary **threshing floor,** לֹא קָנֵי – **he has not acquired** the land.[16] הֵיכִי דָּמֵי – **What are the circumstances that** reveal his intention? שָׁקַל מוּלְיָא וְשָׁדָא בְּנַצָּא – If he **took the heaps** of dirt **and threw** them **into the holes,** אַדַּעְתָּא דְּאַרְעָא – we assume that he leveled the ground **for the sake of** improving **the land.** מוּלְיָא בְּמוּלְיָא – But if he leveled the ground by flattening **the heaps** to some extent וְנַצָּא בְּנַצָּא – **and filling in the holes** to some extent,[17] אַדַּעְתָּא דְּבֵי דָּרֵי – it is evident that he

NOTES

1. I.e. he planted a turnip by throwing it into a fissure in the ground, without plowing the land beforehand or covering the turnip with earth afterwards. Thus, he did not improve the land with his actions (*Rashbam*; see note 4).

2. As explained on 42a (see note 24 there), a convert has no legal heirs unless he fathers children from a Jewish wife subsequent to his conversion. If he dies without Jewish issue, his property becomes ownerless and can be acquired by anyone who performs an act of acquisition in it.

3. A proprietary act, such as plowing, is one that *improves* the land. In the case of plowing, the land is improved in that it is now ready to be planted. The planting of a turnip, however does not ready the land for anything, and is thus not considered an act of improvement (*Rashbam*).

4. Even the subsequent harvest and consumption of the turnip crop does not constitute a proprietary act that effects acquisition of the field, though it is an act that establishes a *chazakah* (i.e. presumption of ownership). For there is a basic distinction between the criteria of a proprietary act needed to effect the acquisition of a field and the act of *chazakah* needed to create the presumption of existing title to the field. An act of acquisition must effect some improvement to the land itself. Harvesting and consuming the crop does not meet that criterion. Presumptive ownership, however, is established by simply using the field as an owner would. This is indeed accomplished by harvesting and consuming the field's crop (*Rashbam;* see Gemara below, 57a).

5. These rulings apply equally to a buyer, a recipient of a gift and one who wishes to acquire the ownerless property of a deceased convert (*Rashbam* ד"ה אדעתא דבי דרי).

6. I.e. to prune it. [Since pruning enhances the tree's growth, it is considered an act of *chazakah*.]

7. Although by removing branches he improves the tree, this act does not effect acquisition. Since he did not have intent to improve the tree, he has not performed a proprietary act. He is no better than one who proclaims, "I wish to acquire this land" without performing any proprietary act (*Rashbam*).

8. If there is no way of determining what his intention was, he could claim later that his intent was to improve the tree (see *Rashbam*).

9. Literally: from this side and from that side. He trimmed the tree all around, in the manner of pruners (*Rashbam*).

10. [And he thereby acquires the tree.] It is *possible* that even in such a case his intent was to procure fodder. However, as a rule, when a person performs an ambiguous act, we assume that his intent was to perform the act that is valid to effect acquisition. Therefore, in the present case, we assume that he [also] intended to improve the tree and thereby acquire it (*Rashbam*).

11. Removing branches from only one side of a tree is detrimental to the tree. Therefore, it is clear that in such a case his intent was to procure fodder. If he should claim later that his intent was to improve the tree, he is not believed, for his actions belie his claim (*Rashbam*).

12. So that it will be easier to plow (*Rashbam*).

13. This is no different than harvesting crops, which is not a proprietary act (*Rashbam; see note 4*).

14. So that the plow will not be obstructed and damaged (*Rashbam*).

15. This is similar to plowing [which is an act of *chazakah* inasmuch as it improves the land] (*Rashbam*).

16. The field in question stands to be used for planting rather than threshing. Therefore, after the threshing floor has been used, it will be plowed over to prepare the field for planting. Since this threshing floor will eventually be removed, its creation is classified as a destructive act, by means of which one cannot acquire a field. (However, the establishment of a *permanent* threshing floor is considered a constructive act, through which one can acquire a field) (*Rashbam*).

17. Literally: a heap in a heap, and a hole in a hole. He flattened the heaps by taking the dirt off the top of each heap and spreading it around the heap. Similarly, he filled in the holes by pushing the dirt at the pit's lip into the pit. This does not make the entire field level. The heaps and holes themselves are leveled somewhat, but the heaps are still higher and the holes lower than the general surface. For a temporary threshing floor, such a surface suffices. But to prepare the ground for plowing, the entire field must be level (*Rashbam*).

דשדא ליפתא בי פילי דארעא דגר לא הוי חזקה מאי טעמא בעידנא דשדא לא הוי שבחא השתא דקא שבח ממילא קא שבח אמר שמואל (א) ב האי מאן דפשח דיקלא אדעתא דדיקלא קני אדעתא דחיותא לא קני (ה"ד) שקל מהאי גיסא ומהאי גיסא אדעתא דדיקלא כולא מחד גיסא אדעתא דחיותא ואמר שמואל ד האי מאן דזכי זיכיא אדעתא דארעא קני אדעתא דציבי לא קני (ג) היכי דמי ה שקל רברבי וזוטרי אדעתא דארעא שקל רברבי ושבק זוטרי אדעתא דציבי ואמר שמואל ו האי מאן דאתקיל תיקלא אדעתא דארעא קני אדעתא דבי דרי לא קני היכי דמי ז שקל מוליא (א) ושדא בנצא אדעתא דארעא מוליא במוליא ונצא בנצא אדעתא דבי דרי ואמר שמואל ח האי מאן דפתח מיא בארעא אדעתא דארעא קני אדעתא דכוורי לא קני היכי דמי ט פתח תרי בבי חד מעייל וחד מפיק אדעתא דכוורי חד בבא אדעתא דארעא י ההיא איתתא דאכלה דיקלא בתפשיחא תליסר שנין אתא ההוא (ג) רפיק תותיה פורתא אתא לקמיה דלוי ואמרי לה קמיה דמר עוקבא כ אוקמיה בידיה אתאי קא צווחא קמיה אמר לה מאי אעביד לך דלא אחזיקת כדמחזקי אינשי אמר רב ל הצר צורה בנכסי הגר קנה דרב לא קני לגנתא דבי רב אלא י בצורתא: איתמר שדה המסויימת במצריה אמר רב הונא אמר רב מ כיון שהכיש בה מכוש אחד קנה כולה ושמואל אמר לא קנה אלא מקום מכושו בלבד

ושאינה

דשדא ליפתא בי פילי. זורע לפת בתוך נקעים של קרקע הגר ולא כיסה עפר ולא עשה כלום כי אם זריקת הלפת בתוך החריץ לא הויא חזקה שהרי לא עשה שום תיקון בקרקע והשלכת זרע בקרקע אינו מעשה אלא אם כן זורע ואח"כ מכסהו (ג) ואע"פ שגדל הלפת ונשרש בקרקע היום ולמחר ממילא הוא דקשבא ולא דמי לרפק בה פורתא דמעשה קעביד בגוף הקרקע ומשביח הקרקע מיד בחרישה זו וכן למד לה מילא דלמכן לעיל הרי משקה את השדה ומנגב את הקרקע אבל האי מאי קעביד ואכילת הלפת נמי אינה חזקה דאכילת פירות אינו קונה ולא הויא חזקה לקנות שהרי אינו עושה בלקיטת הפירות ולא באכילתם שום תיקון בקרקע שיהא דומה לנעל גדר ופרץ וגם לא להציע מלעות בנכסי הגר דהתם קמיתהני גופו מן הקרקע וקמשתמשא ליה קרקע כעבד לרב והכי נמי אמרינן לקמן בשמעתין והרי אכילת פירות דבנכסי חבירו קנה לענין חזקת שלש שנים להיות אכילת הפירות של שלש שנים עומדים במקום שטר ובנכסי הגר לא קנה כלומר לגבי לקנות קרקע מיד כדין קרקע שנקנית בכסף בשטר ובחזקה דנעל וגדר לא הויא חזקה: **פילי.** כמו פילא: **דפשח דיקלא.** כמו ויפשחני (איכה ג) נוטל מן הענפים ויש שמפשחין אותו לצורך הדקל לפי שענפיו מרובים ואין מניחין אותו ליגדל ומהניא ליה הפשיחה כזימור בכרם: **אדעתא דדיקלא.** כדי שיגדל (ד): **קני.** הדקל: **אדעתא דחיותא.** אם מפשיחו לצורך בהמותיו להאכילן ואינו מתכוין להנאת הדקל ומיהו בלקיטת הענפים מתכוין הוא להחזיק בדקל ולקנותו בחזקה זו לא קני ואע"ג דממילא מהני לדקל כיון דאינו מתכוין לתקן הקרקע דומיא דנעל וגדר אלא ללקיטת פירות מתכוין לא הויא חזקה וכמחזיק שלא מדעת דמי וכי קאמר מתכוין אני לקנות בלקיטה זו הרי הוא כמי שהולך בשוק ואומר רוצה אני להחזיק בשדה פלוני דבדיבור בלא מעשה לא הויא חזקה דתרתי בעינן שיעשה תיקון בקרקע בידים ובאותו תיקון יהא מתכוין לשם תיקון כדי להחזיק: **היכי דמי.** מנא ידעינן אי אדעתא דדיקלא או אדעתא דחיותא עבד שלא יוכל לכפור ולטעון אדעתא דדיקלא עבדי: **מהאי גיסא ומהאי גיסא.** אם מכל צדדין ליקט כאן מעט וכאן מעט אדעתא דדיקלא שכן מנהג לעשות דכי האי גוונא הוא דאיכא למימר אדעתא דדיקלא ואע"ג דאיכא למימר נמי אדעתא דחיותא מסתמא כל אדם אדעתא להחזיק מתכוין וכל היכא דאיכא למימר הכי והכי אמרינן אדעתא למיקני מכוין: **כולה מחד גיסא.** מקלקל הוא את האילן שמגלהו כולו מצד אחד והוא ודאי אדעתא דחיותא לחוד מכוין דלאילן לא חייש: **האי מאן דזכי זיכיא.** מכבד ומטהר את השדה מקיסמים ועשבים רעים: **אדעתא דארעא.** שתהא נוחה לחרוש: **אדעתא דציבי.** ללקט עצים לשרוף לא קני דכל לקיטת פירות לא קני: **שקל רברבי וזוטרי.** איכא למיתלי אדעתא דארעא אבל שבק זוטרי ליכא למיתלי אלא אדעתא דציבי לחוד דגדולים הראוין לשריפה מלקט: **דאתקיל תיקלא.** מסיר המכשולות ומשוה פני הקרקע שתהא חלקה ולא תכשל המחרישה ותשבר: **קני.** דדמי למורש: **דבי דרי.** גורן לדוש שם תבואה דכיון דקרקע זה לחרישה עומד ולא לגורן ואף לאחר שיסליקנו לגורן ויחבוט שם חטין יהא צריך (ה) שם לחרוש ולזרוע נמצא שאין גורן זה כאן כי אם קלקול ואין זה מתקן השדה כי אם מקלקל וכל תיקון שסופו לסתור אינו אלא קלקול ומעיקרא לא מתקן הוא ולא דמי לנעל וגדר ורפק ביה פורתא והשקאת מים שכל דברים הללו אין סופן לסתרן אבל גורן זה סופו לקלקלו ולסתרו דעיקר דארעא לחרישה קיימא אבל אם רצה לעשות שם גורן קבוע לעולם נראה בעיני דקני דלאין לך חזקה גדולה מזו: **מוליא.** תל: **נצא.** גומא: **שקל מוליא ושדא בנצא אדעתא דארעא.** לקח התל והשליך בגומא נמצא שהשוה כל הקרקע איכא למימר דלחרוש עשה שלא תתעכב המחרישה: **מוליא במוליא ונצא בנצא.** התל הרחיב במקומו והשפילו ונותן מגבהו סביבתו לצדדין שלא יהא זקוף כל כך וכן נמי בגמא שפתי הגומות השפיל (ו) וגדר לאמצעיתה ונעשית הגומא חלקה הרי הגומות לבד והתלים לבד והרי יש כאן מקומות מקומות חלקים כל אחד לבדו: **אדעתא דבי דרי.** ראוי הוא לחבוט חטים ולא לחרישה וכל החזקות הללו בין בנכסי הגר בין במתנה בין במכר והאחין שחלקו: **דפתח מיא.** שיכנסו בשדה: **פתח תרי בבי.** אחד לצד הנהר ליכנס המים ואחד לצד שני לצאת: **אדעתא דכוורי.** לצוד דגים נתכוין ולא להשקות השדה דאי להשקות השדה מתכוין היה לו לעשות פתח אחד ויתעכבו שם המים וגם הדגים יהו נצודין שם מאיליהן: **בתפשיחא.** כדאמרן לעיל דפשח דיקלא אדעתא דחיותא כולה מחד גיסא: **רפק תותיה פורתא.** דהיינו עודר תחת האילן דמהני ליה כחורש לזריעה: **כדמחזקי אינשי.** אדעתא דדיקלא דהיינו מהאי גיסא ומהאי גיסא: **הצר צורה.** צורת חיה או עוף: **בנכסי הגר.** בכתלי הבית אבל סיוד וכיור דאמר לעיל (דף נג:) אמה כנגד הפתח לאו היינו צורת בריה אלא ציורים בעלמא מעשה צלועים ופרחים אבל צורת חיה או עוף חשובה ודי באחד ולא בעינן אמה ולא כנגד הפתח: **דרב לא קנה לגינתא דבי רב.** גינה הסמוכה לבית מדרשו והיתה של גר ומת וקנאה רב בכך שעשה בה צורה להחזיק בה ומכללא דהך מעשה איתמר הך דרב: **המסויימת במצריה.** שיש לה מצר בארבע רוחותיה: **כיון שהכיש בה.** וחפר במרא מכוש אחד הכאה אחת בקרקע קנה כולה דהיינו רפק בה פורתא וכגון קרקע שעומד לחרישה. אבל בבית לא הוי חזקה ול"ש מכר ול"ש נכסי הגר קנה כולה: **לא קנה אלא מקום מכושו בלבד.** ודוקא נכסי הגר אבל מכר וקבל זוזי אפילו עשר שדות בעשר מדינות והחזיק באחת מהן קנה כולן כדאמר שמואל בפרקי קמאי בב"ק וקדושין וכדפרישית לעיל (דף נג.) ובהך פלוגתא הלכתא כרב דהא ר"נ עבד עובדא כוותיה דרב לקמן בשמעתין:

ושאינה

אדעתא דציבי לא קני. ואע"פ שמתקן הקרקע וכן פשח דיקלא אדעתא דחיותא אע"פ שהדקל מיתקן בכך לעולם לא קני אלא אם כן מתכוין לקנות כדאמרינן לעיל לקנות את חבירתה אף אותה לא קנה כיון שלא נתכוין לקנותה וביבמות פרק ר"ג (דף נג:) אמר הא למה זה דומה לעודר בנכסי הגר וכסבור שלו הן דלא קנה ובהפרה (ב"ק דף מט: ושם) אמר דהמחזיק בשטרותיו של גר מהו מאן דמחזיק בשטרא אדעתא דארעא הוא מחזיק ובארעא הא לא אחזיק ושטרא נמי לא קנה דלאו דעתיה אשטרא או דלמא דעתיה נמי אשטרא ואין להקשות דלע"ג דאין דעתיה אשטרא אמאי אין ידו קונה לו שלא מדעתו כמו חצרו דחצר מתורת יד איתרבאי דהא חצר קונה לו שלא מדעתו היינו שאינו יודע אם הוא בחצרו ואם היה יודע היה רוצה לקנות ° אבל אם יודע ואין מתכוין לקנות לא קני ול"ת מלא בגד או כותל ישן דתנן באלו מליאות (ב"מ דף כה:) הרי אלו שלו מפני שיכול לומר של אמוריים הוא אמאי לא קניא ליה חצרו וי"ל דבדבר שאין הווה שימצא לא קנה חצרו שלא מדעת:

מוליא במוליא כו'. הקשה ה"ר יוסף דאורלינ"ש (ו) משמע שצריך קרקע שוה יותר מלדישה ואמן שהדי לדישה צריך הרבה יותר שוה וחלק ומה שפירש נמי בקונט' דאם עושה אדעתא דגורן קבוע קני היכי ידעינן אי עבד אדעתא דגורן קבוע או אינו קבוע והיה מפרש דבי דרי דהכא היינו להעמיד שם בהמות כמו אבי דרי חושבנא (שבת דף לב.) דלקמן (דף מ.) תנן דבהעמדת בהמה לא קני ור"ת השיב לו שהם היו דשים במוריגים ולא היו צריכין להשוות קרקע כל כך:

ושאינה

עין משפט נר מצוה

רלג א מיי' פ"ב מהל' זכיה ומתנה הל' י סמג עשין עב טוש"ע ח"מ סי' ערה סעיף כב:
רלד ב ג מיי' שם הל' ד ה טוש"ע שם סעיף יז:
רלה ד ה מיי' שם הל' ה ו טוש"ע שם סעיף יח:
רלו ו ז מיי' שם הל' ו ז טוש"ע שם סעיף יט:
רלז ח ט מיי' שם הל' ז ח טוש"ע שם סעיף כ:
רלח י כ מיי' שם הל' ג סמג שם טוש"ע שם סעיף יב:
רלט ל מיי' שם הל' ד טוש"ע שם סעיף יד:
רמ מ מיי' שם פ"א הלכה י סמג שם טוש"ע שם סעיף ג:

רבינו גרשום

לפת בפילי ארעא דגר. ששתל לפת בארעיה דגר בנקעיה דבאותה שעה **לא** שבח **דליהוי חזקה: דפשח דיקלא.** שעוקר קצת הענפים של דקל של גר: **אדעתא דדיקלא.** אם לצורך הדקל מתכוין שיגדיל יותר וישביח הוי חזקה **וקני:** אם לצורך **חיותא.** להאכיל הענפין והלולבין לבהמתו **לא** קני הדקל: **דזכי זכיא.** שמכבד ומזכי את השדה **אדעתא דארעא** כדי שתהא נוחה לחרוש ולזרוע **קני:** אבל אם **אדעתא דציבי.** ללקט העצים להסקה **לא קני: דתקיל תיקלא.** למשוי קרקע השדה: **אדעתא דארעא.** שתהא נוחה לחרוש ולזרוע **קני: אדעתא דבי דרי.** לחבוט שם חטים: **מוליא.** תל: **נצא.** חריץ: **שקל מוליא במוליא.** שנוטל ראש המוליא ונותן סביב התל כדי להרחיבו. **נצא בנצא** שנוטל מצידי הגומא ומשליך למטה בקרקעית' כדי להשוותה ולהרחיבה א) היינו **אדעתא דארעא.** ב) כמו אמת המים שמשקה בכל השדה: **פתח תרי בבי.** שפעמים סוכר האחד ומוציא המים באחר היינו **אדעתא דכוורי: בתפשיחא.** בנכסי הגר ולא היתה לנקות כל האילן ביחד אלא כדאמר לעיל: **אתא חד גברא רפק ביה.** חפר תחתיו שעידרו כמו שחופרין תחת האילנות: **אלא בצורתא.** בציור שצייר בכותליה: **המסוימת.** המסומנת שניכרת בין השדות שהמצרים גבוהין סביבה והיא של גר: **ניכוש.** חפירת יד:

חשק שלמה על רבינו גרשום

א) עי' בתוס' מו"ק דף י' ע"ב ד"ה מוליא במוליא כו' דג"ר לא אלפס דמוליא במוליא לאדעתא דארעא ואינו כן בזה רבינו כתבו להיפך ול"ע. ב) נראה דחסר כאן ול"ל האי מאן דפתח מיא. כמו אמת המים וכו'.

מסורת הש"ס

א) מו"ק י., ב) [שם], ג) שם, ד) [שם ע"ש], ה) עירובין כה., ו) [ע' תוס' יומא נד: בד"ה כרובים], ז) [וע' תוס' מו"ק י: ד"ה מוליא].

הגהות הב"ח

(א) גמ' ושדא בנלא אדעתא דארעא. נ"ב ובמס' מו"ק דף י' ע"ב איתא להדיא איפכא: (ב) שם אתא ההוא גברא רפיק: (ג) רשב"ם ד"ה דשדא וכו' מכסהו עפר ואע"פ וכו' משקה את השדה ומטיב ומנגב: (ד) ד"ה אדעתא דדיקלא כדי שיגדל הדקל כצ"ל ותיבת קני נמחק: (ה) ד"ה דבי דרי וכו' יהא צריך לחרוש שם ולזרוע: (ו) ד"ה מוליא במוליא וכו' השפיל וגירר לאמצעיתה: (ז) תוס' ד"ה מוליא וכו' הר"י דאורלינ"ש הכא משמע וכו' מלדישה צריך הרבה. נ"ב תימה על התוס' שלא הרגישו דבמו"ק דף י' ע"ב איתא להדיא איפכא ונראה שכאן הוא ט"ס וצ"ל איפכא:

גליון הש"ס

תוס' ד"ה אדעתא כו' אבל אם יודע ואינו מכוין לקנות. עיין גיטין דף עז ע"ח תוס' ד"ה ליקני:

ליקוטי רש"י

דשדא ליפתא בי פילי. נטע לפת בגומא שמלא בקרקע הגר ולא חפרה הוא דאי חפרה במכוש ראשון קנה. **לא הוי שבחא.** ואלו חזקה היא ואכן נעל גדר ופרץ כל שהוא תנן [ב"ב מב.] מידי דמהני הוי חזקה. **ממילא קא שבח.** והויא שעתא לאו איהו מחזיק בה אלא לפת הוא דשבח וגדל [עירובין כה.]. **האי מאן דפשח דיקלא.** שוזמר הדקל מן הענפים שבו. **אדעתא דחיותא.** דלאוין למאכל בהמה דנקט מן הענפים דמחד גיסא בין לאין בין יבשין לצורך מאכל בהמה היינו דחיותא. **שקל מהאי גיסא.** דיקלא ומהאי גיסא ענפים יבשין שבו היינו אדעתא דדיקלא. **האי מאן דזכי זיכיא.** שמכבד את הקרקע מעלים קטנים שעליה שנוטלם. **אדעתא דארעא.** דלהכי ליקטן שרולה לזרוע הקרקע שלוקט גדולים וקטנים. **אדעתא דציבי.** אם ליקטן אדעתא דעלים להסיקן דנקט רברבי ושבק זוטרי. **אדעתא דארעא.** שמוסר שדהו לצורך זריעה. **שקל מוליא.** שנוטל הקרקע ממקום גבוה דבי דרי. שמוסר מסם האדמה לצורך הגורן לחבוט שם חטין. [מו"ק י:]. גבשושית [ב"מ קט. וכעי"ז רשב"ם לקמן קלז.]. **ושדא בנצא.** במקום נמוך. **מוליא במוליא.** שנוטל הקרקע ממקום גבוה ומניחו שם על גבי מקום גבוה היינו מוליא במוליא. **או נצא בנצא.** שחופר במקום נמוך ומניחו במקום נמוך. **האי מאן דפתח בארעא וכו' אדעתא דכוורי.** שעושין המים שיולאין מן הגומא של ניבר לחוץ אם לצורך שילאו המים ושתיירו הדגים. **פתח תרי בבי.** חד שבו נכנסין המים לגומא ובכנסין אף הדגים לגומא וחד שהמים יולאין חוץ לגומא והדגים משתיירים בתוכה ולוקחים אותם כו' דהיינו אדעתא דכוורי. **חד בבא.** דפתח חד בבא שבו נכנסים המים לגומא ולידך פתח שבו יולאין המים לחוץ לא פתח. **אדעתא דארעא.** שכשהגומא מליאה מים יולאין המים למעלה ומשקין כל השדה. [מו"ק שם].

leveled the ground **for the sake of** creating **a** temporary **threshing floor.**

Shmuel's fourth ruling:

וְאָמַר שְׁמוּאֵל – **And Shmuel** also **said:** הַאי מַאן דְּפָתַח מַיָּא בְּאַרְעָא – Concerning **a person who made an opening for water to** enter a parcel of **land,** and later claimed that it was his intent to acquire the land thereby, the law is as follows: אַדַּעְתָּא דְּאַרְעָא – If he made the opening **for the sake of** irrigating **the land,** קָנֵי – **he has acquired** the land. אַדַּעְתָּא דְּכַוּורֵי – But if he made the opening **for the sake of** catching **fish,**[18] לֹא קָנֵי – **he has not acquired** the land.[19] הֵיכִי דָּמֵי – **What are the circumstances** that reveal his intention? פָּתַח תְּרֵי בָּבֵי – If **he opened two holes** for the water, חַד מְעַיֵּיל וְחַד מַפִּיק – **one that allows** the **entry** of water into the field **and one that allows** the **exit** of water from the field אַדַּעְתָּא דְּכַוּורֵי – it is evident that he made the openings **for the sake of** catching **fish.** חַד בָּבָא – But if he made only **one opening,** אַדַּעְתָּא דְּאַרְעָא – we assume that he let the water in **for the sake of** irrigating **the land.**

The Gemara cites an incident that illustrates Shmuel's first ruling:

הַהִיא אִיתְּתָא דְּאָכְלָה דִּיקְלָא בְּתַפְשִׁיחָא – **There was a certain woman who consumed** the fruit of **a palm by removing branches** from one side of the tree[20] תְּלֵיסַר שְׁנִין – for **thirteen years.** אֲתָא הַהוּא רְפִיק תּוּתֵיהּ פּוּרְתָּא – **Then a certain [man] came and dug a little under [the tree].**[21] אֲתָא לְקַמֵּיהּ דְּלֵוִי – **He came before Levi,** וְאָמְרֵי לַהּ קַמֵּיהּ דְּמַר עוּקְבָא – **and some say before Mar Ukva,** to inquire whether he had acquired the palm. אוֹקְמֵיהּ בְּיָדֵיהּ – **[Levi] ruled that [the tree] is his.**[22] The man had made a valid act of acquisition whereas the woman had not. אֲתַאי קָא צָוְוחָא קַמֵּיהּ – **[The woman] then came and shouted before [Levi]** in protest. אָמַר לַהּ – **[Levi] said to her:** מַאי אֶעֱבִיד לָךְ – **What can I do for you** דְּלֹא אַחְזִיקַת כִּדְמַחְזְקֵי אִינָשֵׁי – seeing **that you did not take possession** of the property **in the manner that people** usually **take possession?** Removing branches from only one side of a tree is not an acceptable method of acquisition, as Shmuel ruled above.

The Gemara concludes this series of rulings with a similar law: אָמַר רַב – **Rav said** הַצָּר צוּרָה בְּנִכְסֵי הַגֵּר – that **one who draws a picture**[23] **upon the** ownerless **property of a** deceased **convert** קָנָה – **acquires** the property.

The Gemara explains that Rav's opinion was not stated explicitly, rather it was inferred from the following incident: דְּרַב לֹא קָנֵי לְגִנְתָא דְּבֵי רַב – **For Rav did not acquire the garden adjoining his academy,** which had belonged to a convert who died without leaving heirs, אֶלָּא בְּצוּרְתָא – **except by** drawing **a picture** on it.

The Gemara continues its discussion concerning the acquisition of a deceased convert's ownerless land:

אִיתְּמַר – **It was stated:** שָׂדֶה הַמְסוּיֶּימֶת בְּמִצְרֶיהָ – Regarding **a field that is demarcated by its boundary dividers,**[24] אָמַר רַב הוּנָא אָמַר רַב – **Rav Huna said in the name of Rav** כֵּיוָן שֶׁהִכִּישׁ בָּהּ מַכּוֹשׁ אֶחָד – that **as soon as one makes a single insertion** of the spade **in [the field],** קָנָה כּוּלָּהּ – **he has acquired the entire** field. וּשְׁמוּאֵל אָמַר לֹא קָנָה אֶלָּא מְקוֹם מַכּוֹשׁוֹ בִּלְבָד – **But Shmuel says** that **he has acquired only the place of his insertion.**[25]

NOTES

18. I.e. his intention was to bring water containing fish into the confines of the field, and then allow the water to drain out of the field, leaving the fish behind.

19. See note 13.

20. [The tree was ownerless, and the woman assumed that she had acquired it through this act.]

21. Digging under a tree aerates its roots and thereby enhances its growth. This is, therefore, a valid act of acquisition.

22. Literally: he placed it in his possession.

23. For example, he draws a picture of an animal or bird upon the wall of a building.

Although the Gemara said above (53b) that an act of plastering or painting acquires the property of a deceased convert only if the decorated portion measures one *amah* square and is situated opposite the door of the building, that applies only to patterns or solid colors. A picture of an animal or bird, however, is considered a significant decoration, and its creation serves to acquire the building regardless of the picture's size or location (*Rashbam*).

24. I.e. boundary dividers mark off the borders of field on all four sides (*Rashbam*).

25. Shmuel's ruling here applies only to ownerless property, such as that of a convert who has died without heirs. However, if one purchases land and tenders payment to the seller, Shmuel explicitly ruled elsewhere that even a single proprietary act performed in just one of several purchased fields serves to acquire for the buyer all of the fields, even if some are in a different country (*Rashbam*; see above, 53b note 2).

א) מו"ק י, ב) [שם], ג) שם, ד) [שם ע"ש], ה) עירובין כה, ו) [עי' תוס' יומא נד: ד"ה כרובים], ז) [עי' תוס' מו"ק י: ד"ה מולין].

רלג א מיי' פ"ב מהל' זכיה ומתנה הל' י סמג עשין עג טוש"ע ח"מ סי' ערה סעיף כב:
רלד ב ג מיי' שם הל' ה טוש"ע שם סעיף יז:
רלה ד ה מיי' שם הל' ו טוש"ע שם סעיף יח:
רלו ו ז מיי' שם הל' ז טוש"ע שם סעיף יט:
רלז ח ט מיי' שם הל' ח טוש"ע שם סעיף כ:
רלח י כ מיי' שם הל' ג סמג שם טוש"ע שם סעיף יב:
רלט ל מיי' שם הל' ד טוש"ע שם סעיף יד:
רמ מ מיי' שם פ"א הלכה י סמג שם טוש"ע שם סעיף ג:

[א]דשדא ליפתא בי פילי דארעא דגר לא הוי חזקה מאי טעמא בעידנא דשדא לא הוי שבחא השתא דקא שבח ממילא קא שבח אמר שמואל (א) [ב]האי מאן דפשח דיקלא אדעתא דדיקלא קני אדעתא דחיותא לא קני [ג] ה"ד [ג]שקל מהאי גיסא ומהאי גיסא אדעתא דדיקלא כולא מחד גיסא אדעתא דחיותא ואמר שמואל [ד]האי מאן דזכי זיכיא אדעתא דארעא קני אדעתא דציבי לא קני [ג]היכי דמי [ה]שקל רברבי וזוטרי אדעתא דארעא שקל רברבי ושבק זוטרי אדעתא דציבי ואמר שמואל [ו]האי מאן דאתקיל תיקלא אדעתא דארעא קני אדעתא דבי דרי לא קני היכי דמי [ז]שקל מוליא (א) ושדא בנצא אדעתא דארעא מוליא במוליא ונצא בנצא אדעתא דבי דרי ואמר שמואל [ח]האי מאן דפתח מיא בארעא אדעתא דארעא קני אדעתא דכוורי לא קני היכי דמי (ז) [ט]פתח תרי בבי חד מעייל וחד מפיק אדעתא דכוורי חד בבא אדעתא דארעא [י]ההיא איתתא דאכלה דיקלא בתפשיחא תליסר שנין אתא ההוא (ב) [ס]רפיק תותיה פורתא אתא לקמיה דלוי ואמרי לה קמיה דמר עוקבא [כ]אוקמיה בידיה אתאי קא צווחא קמיה אמר לה מאי אעביד לך דלא אחזיקת כדמחזקי אינשי אמר רב [ל]הצר צורה בנכסי הגר קנה דרב לא קני לגנתא דבי רב אלא [י]בצורתא: איתמר שדה המסויימת במצריה אמר רב הונא אמר רב [מ]כיון שהכיש בה מכוש אחד קנה כולה ושמואל אמר לא קנה אלא מקום מכושו בלבד ושאינה

דשדא ליפתא בי פילי. שזרע לפת בתוך נקעים של קרקע הגר ולא כיסה עפר ולא עשה כלום כי אם זריקת הלפת בתוך החריץ לא הויא חזקה שהרי לא עשה שום תיקון בקרקע והשלכת זרע בקרקע אינו מעשה אלא אם כן זורע ואח"כ מכסהו (ג) ואע"פ שגדל הלפת ונשרש בקרקע היום ולמחר ממילא הוא דקשבח ולא דמי לרפק בה פורתא למעשה קעביד בגוף הקרקע ומשביח הקרקע מיד בחרישה זו וכן נמד לה מיא דאמרן לעיל הרי משקה את השדה ומנגב את הקרקע אבל האי מאי קעביד ואכילת הלפת נמי אינה חזקה דאכילת פירות אינו קונה ולא הויא חזקה לקנות שהרי אינו עושה בלקיטת הפירות ולא באכילתם שום תיקון בקרקע שיהא דומה לנעל גדר ופרץ וגם לא להציע מצעות בנכסי הגר דהתם קמיתהני גופו מן הקרקע וקמשמשא ליה קרקע כעבד לרב והכי נמי אמרינן לקמן בשמעתין והרי אכילת פירות דבנכסי חבירו קנה לענין חזקת שלש שנים להיות אכילת הפירות של שלש שנים עומדים במקום שטר ובנכסי הגר לא קנה כלומר לגבי לקנות קרקע מיד כדין קרקע שנקנית בכסף בשטר ובחזקה דנעל וגדר לא הויא חזקה: **פילי.** כמו פילאי: **דפשח דיקלא.** כמו ויפשחני (איכה ג) נוטל מן הענפים ויש שמפשחין אותו לצורך הדקל לפי שענפיו מרובים ואין מניחין אותו ליגדל ומהניא ליה הפשיחא כזימור בכרם: **אדעתא דדיקלא.** כדי שיגדל (ד) הדקל: **קני.** **אדעתא דחיותא.** אם מפשיחו לצורך בהמותיו להאכילן ואינו מתכוין להנאת הדקל ומיהו בלקיטת הענפים מתכוין הוא להחזיק בדקל ולקנותו בחזקה זו לא קני ואע"ג דממילא מהני לדקל כיון דאינו מתכוין לתקן הקרקע דומיא דנעל וגדר אלא ללקיטת פירות מתכוין לא הויא חזקה וכמחזיק שלא מדעת דמי וכי קאמר מתכוין אני לקנות בלקיטה זו הרי הוא כמי שהולך בשוק ואומר רוצה אני להחזיק בשדה פלוני דבדיבור בלא מעשה לא הויא חזקה דתרתי בעינן שיעשה תיקון בקרקע בידים ובאותו תיקון יהא מתכוין לשם תיקון כדי להחזיק: **היכי דמי.** מנא ידעינן אי אדעתא דדיקלא או אדעתא דחיותא עבד שלא יוכל לכפור ולטעון אדעתא דדיקלא עבדי: **מהאי גיסא ומהאי גיסא.** אם מכל צדדין ליקט כאן מעט וכאן מעט אדעתא דדיקלא שכן מנהג לעשות דכי האי גוונא הוא דאיכא למימר אדעתא דדיקלא ואע"ג דאיכא למימר נמי אדעתא דחיותא מסתמא כל אדם אדעתא להחזיק מתכוין וכל היכא דאיכא למימר הכי והכי אמרינן אדעתא למיקני מכוין: **כולא מחד גיסא.** מקלקל הוא את האילן שמגלהו כולו מצד אחד והשני ודאי אדעתא דחיותא לחוד מכוין דלאילן לא חייס: **האי מאן דזכי זיכיא.** מכבד ומטהר את השדה מקיסמים ועשבים רעים: **אדעתא דארעא.** שתהא נוחה לחרוש: **אדעתא דציבי.** ללקט עצים לשרוף לא קני דלא לקיטת פירות לא קני: **שקל רברבי וזוטרי.** איכא למיתלי אדעתא דארעא אבל שבק זוטרי ליכא למיתלי אלא אדעתא דציבי לחוד דגדולים הראוין לשריפה מלקט: **דאתקיל תיקלא.** מסיר המכשולות ומשוה פני הקרקע שתהא חלקה ולא תכשל המחרישה ותשבר: **קני.** דלמי לחורש: **דבי דרי.** גורן לדוש שם תבואה דכיון דקרקע זה לחרישה עומד ולא לגורן ואף לאחר שיליקטנו לגורן ויחבוט שם חטין יהא צריך (ה) שם לחרוש ולזרוע נמצא שאין גורן זה כאן כי אם קלקול ואין זה מתקן השדה כי אם מקלקל וכל תיקון שסופו לסתור אינו אלא קלקול ועיקרא לא מתקן הוא ולא דמי לנעל וגדר ופרץ ורפק ביה פורתא והשקאת מים שכל דברים הללו אין סופן לסתרן אבל גורן זה סופו לקלקלו ולסתרו דעיקר לארעא לחרישה קיימא אבל אם רצה לעשות שם גורן קבוע לעולם בעיני דקני דלאין לך חזקה גדולה מזו: **מוליא.** תל: **נצא.** גומא: **שקל מוליא ושדא בנצא אדעתא דארעא.** לקח התל והשליך בגומא נמצא שהשוה כל הקרקע איכא למימר לחרוש עשה שלא תתעכב המחרישה: **מוליא במוליא ונצא בנצא.** התל הרחיב במקומו והשפילו ונותן מגבהו סביבותיו לצדדין שלא יהא זקוף כל כך וכן נמי הגומא השפיל (ו) וגדר למלאותיה ועשית הגומא חלקה הרי הגומות לבד והתלים לבד והרי יש כאן מקומות מקומות חלקים כל אחד לבדו: **אדעתא דבי דרי.** ראוי הוא לחבוט חטים ולא לחרישה וכל החזקות הללו בין בנכסי הגר בין במכר ובמתנה בין בסקל והאמן שמלקטן: **דפתח מיא.** שיכנסו בשדה: **פתח תרי בבי.** אחד לצד הנהר ליכנס המים ואחד לצד שני לצאת: **אדעתא דכוורי.** לצוד דגים נתכוין ולא להשקות השדה דאי להשקות השדה מתכוין היה לו לעשות פתח אחד ויתעכבו שם המים וגם הדגים יהו נעודין שם מאליהן: **בתפשיחא.** כדאמרן לעיל דפשח דיקלא אדעתא דחיותא כולה מחד גיסא: **רפק תותיה פורתא.** דהיינו עודר תחת האילן דמהני ליה כחורש לזריעה: **כדמחזקי אינשי.** אדעתא דדיקלא דהיינו מהאי גיסא ומהאי גיסא: **הצר צורה.** צורת חיה או עוף: **בנכסי הגר.** בכותלי הבית אבל סיוד וכיור דאמר לעיל (דף נג.) אמה כנגד הפתח לאו היינו צורת בריה אלא ציורים בעלמא מעשה צבעונים ופרחים אבל צורת חיה או עוף חשובה ודי באחד ולא בעינן אמה ולא כנגד הפתח: **דרב לא קנה לגינתא דבי רב.** גינה הסמוכה לבית מדרשו והיתה של גר ומת וקנאה רב בכך שעשה בה צורה להחזיק בה ומכללא דהך מעשה איתמר הך דרב: **המסויימת במצריה.** שיש לה מצר מארבע רוחותיה: **כיון שהכיש בה.** וחפר במרא מכוש אחד הכאה אחת בקרקע קנה כולה דהיינו רפק בה פורתא וכגון קרקע שעומד לחרישה. אבל בבית לא הוי חזקה ול"ש מכר ול"ש נכסי הגר קנה כולה: **לא קנה אלא מקום מכושו בלבד.** ודוקא נכסי הגר אבל מכר וקבל זוזי אפילו עשר שדות בעשר מדינות ואחזיק באחת מהן קנה כולן כדאמר שמואל בפרקי קמאי בב"ק וקדושין ודפרישית לעיל (דף נג.) והך פלוגתא הלכתא כרב דהא ר"נ עבד עובדא כוותיה לקמן בשמעתין: ושאינה

אדעתא דציבי לא קני. ואע"פ שמתקן הקרקע וכן פשח דיקלא אדעתא דחיותא אע"פ שהדקל מיתקן בכך דלעולם לא קני אלא אם כן מתכוין לקנות כדאמרינן לעיל לקנות את חבירתה אף אותה לא קנה כיון שלא נתכוין לקנותה וביבמות פרק ר"ג (דף נג:) אמר הא למה זה דומה לעודר בנכסי הגר וכסבור שלו הן דלא קנה ובהפרה (ב"ק דף מט: ושם) אמר דהמחזיק בשטרותיו של גר מהו מאן דמחזיק בשטרא אדעתא דארעא הוא מחזיק ובארעא הא לא אחזיק ושטרא נמי לא קנה דלאו דעתיה אשטרא או דלאו דעתיה נמי אשטרא ואין להקשות דאע"ג דאין דעתיה אשטרא אמאי אין ידו קונה לו שלא מדעתו כמו חצרו דחצר מתורת יד איתרבאי דהא דחצר קונה לו שלא מדעתו היינו שאינו יודע אם הוא בחצרו ואם היה יודע היה רוצה לקנות [ס]אבל אם יודע ואין מתכוין לקנות לא קני וא"ת מצא בגל או בכותל ישן דתנן באלו מציאות (ב"מ דף כה:) הרי אלו שלו מפני שיכול לומר של אמוריים הוא אמאי לא קניא ליה חצרו וי"ל דבדבר שאין הווה שימצא לא קנה חצרו שלא מדעת:

מוליא במוליא כו'. הקשה ה"ר יוסף דאורליינ"ש (ז) משמע שצריך קרקע שוה לחרישה יותר מלדישה ואנן סהדי דלדישה צריך הרבה יותר שוה וחלק ומה שפירש נמי בקונט' דאם עושה אדעתא דגורן קבוע קני היכי ידעינן אי עבד אדעתא דגורן קבוע או אינו קבוע והיה מפרש דבי דרי דהכא היינו להעמיד שם בהמות כמו אבי דרי חושבנא (שבת דף לב.) דלקמן (דף נז.) תנן דבהעמדת בהמה לא קני ור"ת השיב לו שהם היו דשים במוריגים ולא היו צריכין להשוות קרקע כל כך": ושאינה

עין משפט נר מצוה

רבינו גרשום

לפת בפילי ארעא דגר. ששתל לפת בארעיה דגר בנקעיה דבואתה שעה לא שבח דליהוי חזקה: **דפשח דיקלא.** שעוקר קצת הענפים של דקל של גר: **אדעתא דדיקלא.** אם לצורך הדקל מתכוין שיגדיל יותר ושביחה הוי חזקה וקני: אם לצורך **חיותא.** להאכיל הענפין והלולבין לבהמתו לא קני הדקל: **דזכי זכיא.** שמכבד ומזכי את השדה יותר **אדעתא דארעא** כדי שתהא נוחה לחרוש ולזרוע קני: אבל אם **אדעתא דציבי.** ללקט העצים להסקה **לא קני: דתקיל תיקלא.** אם משוי קרקע השדה: **אדעתא דארעא.** שתהא נוחה לחרוש ולזרוע קני: **אדעתא דבי דרי.** לחבוט שם חטים: **מוליא.** תל: **נצא.** חריץ: **שקל מוליא במוליא.** שנוטל ראש המוליא ונותן סביב התל כדי להרחיבו: **נצא בנצא.** שנוטל מצידי הגומא ומשליך למטה בקרקעית כדי להשוותה ולהרחיבה א) היינו **אדעתא דארעא.** ב) כמו אמת המים שמשקה בכל השדה: **פתח תרי בבי.** שפעמים סוכר האחד ומוציא המים באחר היינו **אדעתא דכוורי: בתפשיחא.** בנכסי הגר ולא היתה לנקות כל האילן ביחד אלא כדאמר לעיל: **אתא חד גברא רפק ביה.** חפר תחתיו שיעדרו כמו שחופרין תחת האילנות: **אלא בצורתא.** בציור שצייר בכותליה: **המסוימת.** המסומנת שניכרת בין השדות שהמצרים גבוהין סביבה והיא של גר: **מכוש.** חפירת יד:

חשק שלמה על רבינו גרשום

א) עי' בתוס' מו"ק דף י ע"ב ד"ה מולא במולא ונלא כו' גי' רב אלפס דמוליא במוליא אדעתא דארעא ולכן בזה רבינו כתב להיפך וצ"ע. ב) נראה דחסר כאן וצ"ל האי מאן דפתח מיא. כמו אמת המים וכו'.

הגהות הב"ח

(א) גמ' ושדא בנצא אדעתא דארעא. נ"ב ובתמ' מו"ק דף י' ע"ב איתא להדיא איפכא: (ב) שם אתא הוא גברא רפיק: (ג) רשב"ם ד"ה דשדא וכו' מכסהו עפר ואע"פ וכו' משקה את השדה ומנגב: (ד) ד"ה אדעתא דדיקלא כדי שיגדל הדקל כל"ל ותיבת קני נמחק: (ה) ד"ה דבי דרי וכו' יהא צריך לחרוש שם ולזרוע: (ו) ד"ה מולא וכו' השפיל וגדר למלאותיה: (ז) תוס' ד"ה מולא וכו' הר"י דאורלינ"ש הכא משמע וכו' לדישה צריך הרבה. נ"ב תימה על התוס' שלא הרגישו דבמו"ק דף י' ע"ב איתא להדיא איפכא ונראה שכן היה ע"ס וצ"ל איפכא.

גליון הש"ס

תוס' ד"ה אדעתא כו' אבל אם יודע ואינו מכוין לקנות. עיין גיטין דף מ ע"א תוס' ד"ה ליקני:

ליקוטי רש"י

דשדא ליפתא בי פילי. נטע לפת בתוך גומא שמצא בקרקע הגר ולא חפרה הוא דלאו מעשה הוא. **לא הוי שבחא.** ולאו חזקה היא ואין נעל גדר ופרץ כל שהו קנה [ב"מ קג.]. מידי דמהני הוי חזקה. **ממילא קא שבח.** שהוא לא עשה כלום כי אם מחזיק בה אלא לפת שבא דקבלת ואכיל [עירובין כה.]. **האי מאן דפשח דיקלא.** שומר הדקל מן הענפים שבו. **אדעתא דחיותא.** דלאוין למאכל בהמה לקטן מן הענפים ממעד גיסא בין לחין בין יבשין לצורך מאכל בהמה היינו אדעתא דחיותא. **שקל מהאי גיסא.** דיקלא ומהאי גיסא ענפים יבשין שבו היינו אדעתא דדיקלא. **האי מאן דזכי זיכיא.** שמכבד את הקרקע מעצים קטנים שעליה שנוטלם. **אדעתא דארעא.** דלהכי ליקטן הקרקע שלוקט לזרוע בה עצים גדולים וקטנים. **אדעתא דציבי.** אם ליקטן אדעתא דעצים להסקן דנקט רברבי ושבק זוטרי. **אדעתא דארעא.** שמוסר שדהו לצורך זריעה. **שקל מוליא.** שנוטל הקרקע ממקום גבוה. **דבי דרי.** שמוסר מסם המהמה לצורך הגורן שבו חטין [מו"ק י.]. גבשושית [ב"מ קז.]. **ושדא בנצא.** במקום נמוך. **מוליא במוליא.** נוטל הקרקע ממקום גבוה ומניחו על גבי מקום גבוה היינו מוליא במוליא. **או נצא בנצא.** שחופר במקום נמוך ומניחו במקום נמוך. **האי מאן דפתח בארעא וכו' אדעתא דכוורי.** שעושין המים שיוצאין מן הגומא של נהר לתוך אם לצורך שיצאו המים ויעמידו הדגים. **פתח תרי בבי.** חד שבו נכנסין המים לגומא ונכנסין אף הדגים בגומא וחד שהמים יוצאין מן הגומא והדגים מעכבים ונשארים בתוך. **חד בבא.** דפתח חד בבא שבו נכנסים המים לגומא ואין שם פתח אחר לצאת. **אדעתא דארעא.** שכשהגומא מליאה מים יוצאין המים למעלה ומשקין כל השדה. [מו"ק שם].

עין משפט נר מצוה | מסורת הש"ס

ושאינה מסויימת במצריה עד כמה אמר רב פפא א כדאזיל תיירא (א) דשורי והדר אמר רב יהודה אמר שמואל ב נכסי עובד כוכבים הרי הן כמדבר כל המחזיק בהן זכה בהן מ"ט עובד כוכבים מכי מטו זוזי לידיה אסתלק ליה ישראל לא קני ג עד דמטי שטרא לידיה הלכך הרי הן כמדבר וכל המחזיק בהן זכה בהן א"ל אביי לרב יוסף מי אמר שמואל הכי (ב) והאמר שמואל ד דינא דמלכותא דינא ומלכא אמר לא ליקני ארעא אלא באיגרתא אמר ליה ה אנא לא ידענא (ג) עובדא הוה בדורא דרעותא בישראל דזבן ארעא מעובד כוכבי' ואתא ישראל אחרינא רפיק בה פורתא אתא לקמיה דרב יהודה אוקמה בידא דשני א"ל דורא דרעותא קאמרת התם באגי מטמרי הוו דאינהו גופייהו לא הוו יהבי טסקא למלכא ומלכא אמר מאן דיהיב טסקא ליכול ארעא רב הונא זבן ארעא מעובד כוכבים אתא ישראל אחר רפיק בה פורתא אתא לקמיה דרב נחמן אוקמה בידיה א"ל מאי דעתיך דאמר שמואל נכסי עובד כוכבים הרי הן כמדבר וכל המחזיק בהם זכה ליעבד

ושאינה מסויימת במצריה. אלא בקעה גדולה ופתוחה לשדות אחרים או לרשות הרבים עד כמה צריך לחפור ויקנה כולה אליבא דרב דהא ודאי לשמואל לא חשיבה מסוימת טפי משאינה מסוימת דאפילו במסוימת קאמר לא קנה אלא (ג) מכושו וכ"ש בשאינה מסוימת. יש מפרשים בעניין אחרים ולא נהירא לי כלל: **כדאזיל תיירא דתורי והדר.** כשיחרוש צמד בקר שורה אחת מקצה גבול השדה ועד קצהו והדר ובחזרתו יעשה עוד שורה אחרת דהיינו שתי שורות על פני כל השדה משפתו אל שפתו ממזרח למערב מתוך כך קנה כל השדה גם מן הצפון לדרום דכיון דחרש שתי שורות על פני כל אורך השדה או על כל רחבו כאילו חרש כולו שהרי החזיק בו מראשו ועד סופו כן נראה בעיני: **אמר רב יהודה אמר שמואל נכסי העובד כוכבים.** שמכרם עובד כוכבים לישראל שקבל העובד כוכבים הדמים ממנו ועדיין לא החזיק בה ישראל זה הקונה אותם: **הרי הן כמדבר.** הפקר כדמפרש לקמן שאם קדם ישראל אחר והחזיק בם קנה כאילו הן נכסי הגר שמת ויש מפרשין דמעות מיהא יחזיר ללוקח ראשון ולי אין נראה כלל דא"כ מאי הרי הן כמדבר אלא זכה בהן לגמרי ואם יכול לוקח ראשון לדון עם העובד כוכבי' ולהוציא ממנו מעותיו יעשה ואם לאו יפסיד ומיהו נראה בעיני ° דהאי שני רשע מיקרי דכיון דיהב לוקח ראשון זוזי לא גרע מעני המהפך בחררה ובא אחר ונטלה דמיקרי רשע ההוא אחר ופירש רבינו חננאל דלית הלכתא כשמואל ומשום דמקשי עלה אביי אידך דשמואל דאמר דינא דמלכותא דינא ובא רב יוסף לתרץ והקשהו אביי ואמר דמעולם לא אמרה שמואל דא"כ קשיא דשמואל אדשמואל דאמר דינא דמלכותא דינא ולי נראה דהלכתא כשמואל דהא רב נחמן דדיינא הוי והלכתא כוותיה בדיני דן כוותיה לקמיה וגם הרבה אמוראים כשמואל ס"ל לקמן וסליק שמעתין בהכי והא דאמר שמואל דינא דמלכותא דינא רב יוסף עצמו היה יודע תירוץ לדבר (ד) דא"ל לאביי אנא לא ידענא עובדא היכי הוה כו' לא חשש לתרץ מאחר דהוה מייתי ראיה מעובדא: **כי מטו זוזי לידיה.** מן הלוקח: **אסתלק ליה.** העובד כוכבים שהרי כל קנינו של עובד כוכבים בכסף כדאמרי' בפ"ק דקדושין (דף יד:) ומשקבל המעות לגבי דידיה הויא מכירה גמורה שאין יכולין עוד לחזור זה בזה וישראל לא קני במתן מעות עד דאתא שטרא לידיה כדאמרינן בקדושין וכדפרישית לעיל דאפילו מישראל חבריה לא קני בזוזי עד שיכתוב לו את השטר וכ"ש מעובד כוכבים דסתם עובדי כוכבים אנסים הם ואין בדעתו לקנות בלא שטר והלכך אי אתא ישראל אחרינא רפק ביה פורתא מקמי האי קנה ודוקא בלוקח מעובד כוכבים אבל לוקח מישראל חבירו נהי דלא קני לוקח עד דאתי שטרא לידיה אחר מיהא אין יכול לקדם ולהחזיק שהרי עדיין ברשות מוכר קיימא שכל זמן שלא החזיק הלוקח או לא בא השטר לידו יכולין שניהם לחזור זה בזה: **מי אמר שמואל הכי.** דקני ליה (ה) שני לארעא דעובד כוכבים בחזקה בלא שטר מן העובד כוכבים: **והאמר שמואל דינא דמלכותא דינא.** כל מסים וארנוניות ומנהגות של משפטי מלכים שרגילים להנהיג במלכותם דינא הוא שכל בני המלכות מקבלים עליהם מרצונם חוקי המלך ומשפטיו והלכך דין גמור הוא ואין למחזיק בממון חבירו ע"פ חוק המלך הנהוג בעיר משום גזל: **ומלכא אמר.** לא ליכול ארעא שום מחזיק בארעא אלא א"כ יש בידו שטר מכירה מן המוכר והיאך יקנה זה המחזיק הואיל ואין לו שטר מן העובד כוכבים אלא לוקח ראשון יקנה בדינא דמלכותא לכי אתי שטריה דעובד כוכבים לידיה: **אמר ליה אנא לא ידענא.** רב יוסף נמי כי נ"כ הוה ידע להא דאמר שמואל דינא דמלכותא דינא והא דקמהדר ליה לאביי אנא לא ידענא כו' ודאי היה יודע תירוץ לדבר אלא דעדיף ליה למימר עובדא ולכך לא חשש לתרץ ולאביי מהדר ליה דמההוא עובדא ליכא לאיתויי ראיה ומיהו רב יוסף לא חזר בו אם דמכל מקום שמואל אמרה כדאמר בסמוך והאי דקשיא ליה דינא דמלכותא דינא רב יוסף לא ס"ל האי דאמר אביי ומלכא אמר לא ליכול ארעא אלא בשטרא דלאו דינא דמלכותא הוא אלא בחזקה נמי ליכול: **בדורא דרעותא.** שם מקום אלא כפר של רועים: **אתא לקמיה דרב יהודה.** ורוב מעשיו שמע משמואל רבו: **דורא דרעותא קאמרת.** בתמיה וכי משם אתה מביא ראיה דנכסי העובד כוכבים הרי הן כמדבר: **באגי מיטמרי.** שדות טמונות שלא היו הבעלים נותנין את המס למלך אלא מבריחין עצמן: **דאינהו גופייהו.** בעלים ראשונים לא הוו יהבי טסקא ומדינא דמלכותא לא היו בידם של הבעלים כח למכור ומכרן בטל והם השני שמחזיק קנה בדינא דמלכותא שהמלך לא נתן אותה אלא לנותן את הטסקא למלך ומלכא אמר מאן דיהיב טסקא ליכול ארעא מחזקה בלא שטרא דלא ליכול ארעא אבל בקרקע שהיא ירושה לעובד כוכבים מאבותיו ומכרה לעולם אימא לך אם בא אחר והחזיק בה מוציאין אותה מידו ומחזירין לראשון כשיהיה לו השטר מן המוכר:

ליעבד

ושאינה מסוימת במצריה עד כמה. פי' כמה יקנה במקום אחד כדאזיל תיירא דתורי והדר פירוש כשיעור מדת תלם (ו) והן היו יודעים מדת התלם כמה היא אורך שלו דבשדה גדולה לא היו חורשים במענה אחד כל אורך השדה ולא כפ"ה כשיחרוש צמד בקר שורה אחת מקצה גבול שדהו עד קצהו ומתוך כך קונה כל השדה חדא דלישנא לא משמע הכי ועוד דלאמאי בעי והדר רק כשיחרוש פעם אחת אע"ג דלא הדר: **עובד כוכבים** מכי מטי זוזי לידיה אסתלק ליה. פ"ה משום דכל קנינו של עובד כוכבים בכסף כדאמרינן בפ"ק דקדושין (ד' יד: ושם) דאשכחן עובד כוכבים דכל קנינו בכסף ולאו ראיה היא דלפי' ר"ת דמפרש התם דוקא בעבד עברי קאמר שאין בו קנין אחר דשטר לא ידעינן ביה אפי' בישראל אלא מדהוקש לאמה העבריה ואמה העבריה לאחרת אבל בעובד כוכבים דלא שייך ביה קדושין ליכא למילף מאחרת ועוד תניא התם מכסף מקנתו בכסף מקנתו הוא נקנה ואינו נקנה בתבואה וכלים דהיינו חליפין משמע דה"ה בשטר אינו נקנה דאפילו כל שוה כסף הוה ממעט התם מכסף אי לאו דכתיב ישיב לרבות שוה כסף ככסף אבל בעלמא אור"ת דאדרבה אין קנינו של עובד כוכבים בכסף אלא במשיכה וכדר' יוחנן ק"ל דדריש (בכורות דף יג:) מיד עמיתך בכסף הא מיד עובד כוכבים במשיכה וכן בפ' בתרא דע"ז (דף עא. ושם ד"ה רב) מסיק דמשיכה לעובד כוכבים קונה והא דקאמר הכא ועובד כוכבים מכי מטו זוזי לידיה אסתלק ליה היינו משום דמלינו בעובד כוכבים קנין כסף בעפרון ושטר ודאי לא קנה בעובד כוכבים משום דישראל גופיה לא קנה בשטרא אלא מספר המקנה דירמיה והתם ישראל הוה: **וישראל** לא קנה עד דמטי שטרא לידיה. שהיו עומדים במקום שכותבין את השטר וקשיא לרבינו שמשון בן אברהם דאמאי לא קנה בכסף גרידא מעפרון בק"ו מגופו באחת ממונו בשתים כדאמרינן בבכורות בפ"ב (דף יג. ושם) דליכא למימר שאינו גומר בדעתו לקנות עד שיהיה בשטר דמאחר שהעובד כוכבים מסתלק למה לא יגמור בדעתו לקנות ויניחנו להיות הפקר והוה לן למימר דהוי כאילו פירש אי בעינא בכספא איקני מה"ט דפרישית וי"ל דאנן סהדי שלא היה בדעתו אלא כמות שהוא רגיל לקנות עם ישראל דהיינו בשטר מדלא פירש אי בעינא בכספא איקני אבל קשיא לרבינו שמשון בן אברהם דבפרק ב' דבכורות (שם) א"ר יצחק ישראל שנתן מעות לעובד כוכבים בבהמה בדיניהן אע"פ שלא משך קנה וחייבת בבכורה ואמאי לא אמרינן אע"ג דקנה מן התורה כדאמר אביי התם בדיניהם שפסקה להן תורה מיד עמיתך במשיכה הא מיד עובד כוכבים בכסף מ"מ אין בדעתו לקנות אלא עד שימשוך כמו שהוא רגיל לקנות עם ישראל כדאמרינן הכא וי"ל דהתם בדיניהם קאמר ונראה דשרי לישראל לתבוע (ז) מינייהו מעותיו אע"פ שמתוך כך יחזיר העובד כוכבים ויגזול את המחזיק דבדין קא תבע ליה דלא נתן לו מעות אלא ע"מ שתבא הקרקע לידו ואם המחזיק יכול לישמט מן העובד כוכבים ישמט אע"פ שהלוקח מפסיד אך אם המחזיק בעי לפרוע לו מעותיו אם (ח) יפקיענו הראשון הקרקע מידו ע"י עובד כוכבים נראה דה"ל מסור ממש: **באגי** דמטמרי הוו כו'. והא דאמר בהניזקין (גיטין דף נח: ושם ד"ה אגן) לאזול מרוותייהו דבאגי ואזיל גידול בר רעילאי ויהיב טסקא לתלת שנין ולבתר אתו מרוותייהו הדרא להו ולא אמרי' כיון דלא יהבי טסקא הופקעה מידם וזכה בה גידול בר רעילאי דהתם מיירי כגון שאמרו מרוותייהו לבני באגי שיחרשו הקרקע ויזרעו ויאכלו פירות ויפרעו טסקא עד שיחזרו ונתרצו להם בני באגי ונתנוה לגידול הלכך לא הופקעה מידם וכשיחזרו חזרו להן אבל הכא הוו מטמרי בשביל המס שלא רצו לפרוע:

רמא א מיי' פ"א מהל' זכיה ומתנה הל' י סמג עשין עב טוש"ע ח"מ סי' ערה סעיף ג:

רמב ב מיי' שם הל' יד סמג עשין פב טוש"ע ח"מ סי' קצד סעיף ג וסי' רעד:

רמג ג מיי' שם ופ"ה מהל' מכירה הלכה ו [ח] סמג שם טוש"ע ח"מ סי' קצד סעיף ג [א]:

רמד ד מיי' פ"ה מהל' זכיה הל' טו ופ"ה מהל' גזילה הל' יא סמג שם וסי' עג טוש"ע שם וסי' שסט סעיף ב ז ח ט:

רבינו גרשום

ושאינה מסוימת. אלא בקעה גדולה היא: עד כמה. קנה בה: תיירא דתורי והדר. כלומר כמו שהולך צמד בקר של מחרישה בתלם וחוזר ועושה תלם אחר כשיעור אותן שני תלמים קני ולא יותר: כל המחזיק בהן זכה בהן. כגון שאם מכר עובד כוכבים שדהו לישראל אחד ונתן לו מעות ובא ישראל אחר והחזיק בה קודם שיכתוב לו שטר זכה בהן זה שני בלבד שיחזיר מעותיו לראשון: מי אמר שמואל הכי. דהאי שני זכה בלא שטר. והאמר שמואל דינא דמלכותא דינא. דכל מי שבא מחמת עובד כוכבים יש לידון בדין מלכות: אלא באיגרתא. בשטר: בדורא דרעותא. בכפר של רועים: התם באגי מטמרי. שדות טמונות היו בידי עובדי כוכבים שהיו מבריחין מן המס ואמטול להכי לא הוי צריך למיקני מינייהו בשטרא דלא הוו דידהו לגמרי אלא משועבדים הן למס המלך. והואיל ורצו להבריח המס יכול להחזיק בהן מי שירצה בדינא דמלכותא ובלבד שיתן המס של שדה דהיינו טסקא. אבל בעלמא דלאו באגי מטמרי אימא דלא קני המחזיק בהן אלא בשטר:

א) [לקמן נה.] ב"ק קיג. גיטין י: נדרים כח.

הגהות הב"ח

(א) גמ' תיירא דתורי והדר: (ב) שם לא ידענא אלא עובדא הוה: (ג) רשב"ם ד"ה ושאינה וכו' אלא מקום מכושו: (ד) ד"ה הרי וכו' תירוץ לדבר והא דא"ל לאביי אנא לא ידענא אלא עובדא הכי הוה: (ה) ד"ה מי אמר וכו' דקני ליה האי שני: (ו) תוס' ד"ה ושאינה וכו' מדת תלם והם היו כו' ולא כפ"ה שפי' כשיחרוש וכו' מקצה גבול השדה ועד קצהו: (ז) ד"ה וישראל וכו' לתבוע מיניה מעותיו: (ח) בא"ד אם יפקיע הראשון:

גליון הש"ס

גמרא אנא לא ידענא. עירובין דף ז ע"ב וש"נ: רשב"ם ד"ה הרי הן כמדבר כו' דהאי שני רשע מקרי. עי' לעיל דף כא ע"ב תוס' ד"ה מרחיקין:

ליקוטי רש"י

דינא דמלכותא דינא. בהגוזל (קמא) [בתרא] (ב"ק קיג:) אמר תדע דקטלי דיקלי וגשרי גשרי ועברינן עלייהו [רשב"ם לקמן נה.]. של עובדי כוכבים [גיטין י:]. באגי. בקעה בקעה [ב"ק קיג:]. טסקא. מס קרקע [גיטין נח: ובכו"ז ב"מ עג: וקדו.]. לא הוו יהבי טסקא למלכא. לפרוע מס הקרקע למלך [כתובות מד.].

The Gemara inquires:

וְשֶׁאֵינָהּ מְסוּיֶּימֶת בִּמְצָרֶיהָ עַד כַּמָּה – **And a field that is not demarcated by its boundary dividers, how much?** I.e. how extensive must the act of acquisition be in order to acquire the entire field?[1] אָמַר רַב פָּפָּא כִּדְאָזִיל תְּיָירָא דְּתוֹרֵי וְהָדַר – **Rav Pappa said:** The person must plow the field as much **as a yoke of oxen goes and returns.**[2]

A situation similar to that of one who performs an act of acquisition in the ownerless property of a deceased convert:

אָמַר רַב יְהוּדָה אָמַר שְׁמוּאֵל – **Rav Yehudah said in the name of Shmuel:** נִכְסֵי עוֹבֵד כּוֹכָבִים הֲרֵי הֵן כְּמִדְבָּר – **An idolater's** real **properties** that he sells to a Jew **are** ownerless **like a desert;** כָּל הַמַּחֲזִיק בָּהֶן זָכָה בָּהֶן – **whoever performs a proprietary act in them has acquired them.**[3] מַאי טַעְמָא – **What is the reason?** עוֹבֵד כּוֹכָבִים מִכִּי מָטוּ זוּזֵי לִידֵיהּ אִסְתַּלֵּק לֵיהּ – As regards **the idolater, as soon as the** purchase **money reaches his hand, he is removed** from the property.[4] יִשְׂרָאֵל לָא קָנֵי עַד דְּמָטֵי שְׁטָרָא לִידֵיהּ – **The Jew** purchasing the land, however, **does not acquire** it **until the deed reaches his hand.**[5] הִלְכָּךְ הֲרֵי הֵן כְּמִדְבָּר – **Therefore,** in the interim, **[the properties] are** ownerless **like a desert,** וְכָל הַמַּחֲזִיק בָּהֶן זָכָה בָּהֶן – **and whoever performs a proprietary act in them has acquired them.**[6]

Abaye questions this ruling:

מִי אָמַר – אָמַר לֵיהּ אַבָּיֵי לְרַב יוֹסֵף – **Abaye said to Rav Yosef:** שְׁמוּאֵל הָכִי – **Did Shmuel** really **say so?**[7] וְהָאָמַר שְׁמוּאֵל – **But Shmuel said:** דִּינָא דְּמַלְכוּתָא דִּינָא – **The law of the kingdom is the law!**[8] וּמַלְכָּא אָמַר – **And the king has decreed:** לָא לִיקְנֵי אַרְעָא אֶלָּא בְּאִיגַּרְתָּא – **One cannot acquire land except with a document.**[9] – ? –

Rav Yosef replies:

אָמַר לֵיהּ – **He said to [Abaye]:** אֲנָא לָא יָדַעְנָא – **I do not know** about that statement regarding the legal force of secular law, but I do know that עוּבְדָּא הֲוָה בְּדוּרָא דְּרַעֲוָתָא – **there was an incident in a shepherds' village**[10] בְּיִשְׂרָאֵל דִּזְבַן אַרְעָא מֵעוֹבֵד כּוֹכָבִים – **concerning a Jew who bought land from an idolater** וְאָתָא יִשְׂרָאֵל אַחֲרִינָא רָפִיק בָּהּ פּוּרְתָּא – **and another Jew came along and dug a little in it,** thereby performing a proprietary act.[11] אֲתָא לְקַמֵּיהּ דְּרַב יְהוּדָה – **[The case] came before Rav Yehudah,** אוֹקְמָהּ בִּידָא דְּשֵׁנִי – **who placed [the land] in the possession of the second one.** Thus, Rav Yehudah indeed ruled that the second Jew could take advantage of the proprietary vacuum that existed between the idolater's receipt of the money and the Jewish buyer's receipt of the deed. And since Rav Yehudah was a prime disciple of Shmuel, we can certainly infer that his ruling in the matter was one that he heard from his master, Shmuel.[12]

NOTES

1. *Rashbam*; cf. *Tosafos*.

This inquiry assumes the view of Rav, who rules that a single dig serves to acquire an entire ownerless field whose borders are demarcated by boundary dividers. The Gemara therefore inquires as to what is necessary, in Rav's view, to acquire an entire ownerless field whose borders are *not* demarcated (see *Rashbam*).

2. I.e. if the person plows two furrows in this field from end to end (either north to south or east to west), he acquires the entire field (*Rashbam*).

3. Normally, when a person buys a piece of land, he pays the money to the seller and then performs a proprietary act in the land or receives a deed from the seller. It is not the seller's receipt of the money that legally effects the acquisition of the land, but rather the buyer's proprietary act or receipt of the deed (see note 5). Shmuel teaches us here that when one buys a piece of land from an idolater, that land is legally in an ownerless state (like a desert) for the time that elapses between the seller's receipt of the money and the buyer's act of acquisition. Consequently, anyone who performs a proprietary act to the land during that time period acquires it (see *Rashbam*).

4. In Torah law, the only act of acquisition that effects transfer for a non-Jew in commercial transactions is the payment or receipt of money. Thus, as soon as the idolater receives the purchase money for his land, the sale is final from his end and the land is no longer his (*Rashbam*). Now, were the buyer also an idolater, the sale would be complete from his end as well (since payment of money is his sole instrument of transfer) and the buyer would assume ownership of the land at the very moment the seller's ownership is concluded. In Shmuel's case, however, where the buyer is a Jew, the law is different, as the Gemara proceeds to explain.

5. In Torah law, a Jew does not acquire land that he buys simply by giving the money to the seller. Even after the money has been paid, the transfer of ownership has not yet occurred and the sale is not final (see *Kiddushin* 26a and *Tosafos* here). (At this point, either the buyer or [Jewish] seller can technically still back out of the transaction.) The transfer of ownership occurs only when the buyer receives the deed from the seller or performs a proprietary act. Now, this is true even in the case of a Jew who buys land from another Jew. Certainly, then, it is true where the Jew buys land from an idolater, since idolaters are often lawless and the Jew therefore does not rely on the finality of the sale until he receives the deed proving his purchase of the land. [The reliance of the buyer on the finality of the sale is essential for the *kinyan* (act of acquisition) to formalize the transfer] (*Rashbam*).

6. Shmuel is teaching only the strict dictates of the law, not sanctioning the actions of an interloper. For though one who intrudes and takes possession of this ownerless land has acted within his legal rights, his actions are morally reprehensible, since he has snatched away from the buyer a property that he was in the process of obtaining. His actions are similar to those described in the classic example of עָנִי הַמְהַפֵּךְ בַּחֲרָרָה, *a poor man who is striving for a griddle cake,* and another poor man intrudes and pre-empts it. The Gemara in *Kiddushin* (59a) characterizes the intruder as a רָשָׁע, *wicked person* (*Rashbam*; cf. *Tosafos* above, 21b ד״ה מרחיקין).

[Thus, the proprietary vacuum generated by the idolater's receipt of money is analogous to that created by a convert who dies without heirs, which was discussed in the Gemara above.]

[*Rashbam* adds that the Jewish buyer (who was preempted by the intruder) should seek to obtain a refund from the seller. *Rosh* dissents, however, arguing that the seller has legally acquired the purchase money and there is no reason for him to refund it.]

7. I.e. did Shmuel really say that the second Jew can acquire land by performing a proprietary act without receiving a document from the idolater? (*Rashbam*).

8. I.e. all tax and civil laws that prevail in a country have legal force, since the country's citizenry voluntarily accepts upon itself to abide by the government's laws. Thus, a Jew who takes possession of property according to the provisions of local law is not guilty of theft even if Torah law would consider the property as belonging to another Jew (*Rashbam*).

9. [*Rashbam's* reading here is apparently: לָא לִיכוּל אַרְעָא, as in the Gemara below; there is no substantive difference in meaning.]

The legal rationale for allowing an intruder to take possession of the land in between the idolater's receipt of the money and the Jewish buyer's receipt of the deed holds true only under Torah law. But according to the secular law that prevailed in Babylonia at the time, which did not recognize real estate transactions without deeds, the intruder could not take possession of the property without receiving a deed from the seller. Therefore, the buyer could take possession of the land upon receiving the deed from the seller [even though Jewish law would consider the intruder to be the owner, as a result of his proprietary act]. How, then, can you say that Shmuel ruled that the intruder acquires the land? (*Rashbam*).

10. [Alternatively, דוּרָא דְּרַעֲוָתָא is the proper name of a place (*Rashbam*).]

11. [See above, 54a.]

12. Since most of his rulings were based on what he had learned from Shmuel (*Rashbam*). Thus, you cannot dispute the authenticity of the ruling cited above in the name of Shmuel because of its apparent

ושאינה מסויימת במצריה עד כמה אמר רב פפא [א] כדאזיל תיירא (א) דשורי והדר אמר רב יהודה אמר שמואל [ב] נכסי עובד כוכבים הרי הן כמדבר כל המחזיק בהן זכה בהן מ"ט עובד כוכבים מכי מטו זוזי לידיה אסתלק ליה ישראל לא קני [ג] עד דמטי שטרא לידיה הלכך הרי הן כמדבר וכל המחזיק בהן זכה בהן א"ל אביי לרב יוסף מי אמר שמואל הכי (א) והאמר שמואל [ד] דינא דמלכותא דינא ומלכא אמר לא ליקני ארעא אלא באיגרתא אמר ליה ° אנא לא ידענא (ב) עובדא הוה בדורא דרעותא בישראל דזבן ארעא מעובד כוכבי' ואתא ישראל אחרינא רפיק בה פורתא אתא לקמיה דרב יהודה אוקמה בידא דשני א"ל דורא דרעותא קאמרת התם באגי מטמרי הוו דאינהו גופייהו לא הוו יהבי טסקא למלכא ומלכא אמר מאן דיהיב טסקא ליכול ארעא רב הונא זבן ארעא מעובד כוכבים אתא ישראל אחר רפיק בה פורתא אתא לקמיה דרב נחמן אוקמה בידיה א"ל מאי דעתיך דאמר שמואל נכסי עובד כוכבים הרי הן כמדבר וכל המחזיק בהם זכה

ליעבד

רשב"ם

ושאינה מסויימת במצריה. אלא בקעה גדולה ופתוחה לשדות אחרים או לרשות הרבים עד כמה צריך לחפור ויקנה כולה אליבא דרב דהא ודאי לשמואל לא חשיבא מסוימת טפי משאינה מסוימת דאפילו במסוימת קאמר לא קנה אלא (ג) מכושו וכ"ש בשאינה מסוימת. יש מפרשים בעניין אחרים ולא נהירא לי כלל: **כדאזיל תיירא דתורי והדר.** כשיחרוש צמד בקר שורה אחת מקצה גבול השדה ועד קצהו והדר ובחזרתו יעשה עוד שורה אחרת דהיינו שתי שורות על פני כל השדה משפתו אל שפתו ממזרח למערב מתוך כך קנה כל השדה גם מן הצפון לדרום דכיון דחרש שתי שורות על פני כל אורך השדה או על כל רחבו כאילו חרש כולו שהרי החזיק בו מראשו ועד סופו כן נראה בעיני: **אמר רב יהודה אמר שמואל נכסי העובד כוכבים.** שמכרם עובד כוכבים לישראל שקבל העובד כוכבים הדמים ממנו ועדיין לא החזיק בה ישראל זה הקונה אותם: **הרי הן כמדבר.** הפקר כדמפרש לקמן שאם קדם ישראל אחר והחזיק בם קנה כאילו הן נכסי הגר שמת ויש מפרשין דמעות מיהא יחזיר ללוקח ראשון ולי אין נראה כלל דא"כ מאי הרי הן כמדבר אלא זכה בהן לגמרי ואם יכול לוקח ראשון לדון עם העובד כוכבי' ולהוציא ממנו מעותיו יעשה ואם לאו יפסיד ומיהו נראה בעיני ° דהאי שני רשע מיקרי דכיון דיהב לוקח ראשון זוזי לא גרע מעני המהפך בחררה ובא אחר ונטלה דמיקרי רשע ההוא אחר ופירש רבינו חננאל דלית הלכתא כשמואל ומשום דמקשי עלה אביי אידך דשמואל דאמר דינא דמלכותא דינא ובא רב יוסף לתרץ והקשהו אביי ואמר דמעולם לא אמרה שמואל דא"כ קשיא דשמואל אדשמואל דאמר דינא דמלכותא דינא ולי נראה הלכתא כשמואל דהא רב נחמן דדינא הוי והלכתא כוותיה בדיני דן כוותיה לקמיה וגם הרבה אמוראים כשמואל ס"ל לקמן ופליק שמעתין בהכי והא דאמר שמואל דינא דמלכותא דינא רב יוסף עצמו היה יודע תירוץ לדבר (ד) דא"ל לאביי אנא לא ידענא עובדא היכי הוה כו' לא חשש לתרץ מאחר דהוה מייתי ראיה מעובדא: **כי מטו זוזי לידיה.** מן הלוקח: **אסתלק ליה.** העובד כוכבים שהרי כל קניינו של עובד כוכבים בכסף כדאמרי' בפ"ק דקדושין (דף יד:) ומשקבל המעות לגבי דידיה הויא מכירה גמורה שאין יכולין עוד לחזור זה בזה וישראל לא קני בממון מעות עד דאתא שטרא לידיה כדאמרינן בקדושין וכדפרישית לעיל דאפילו מישראל חבריה לא קני בזוזי עד שיכתוב לו את השטר וכ"ש מעובד כוכבים דסתם עובדי כוכבים אנסים הם ואין בדעתו לקנות בלא שטר והלכך אי אתא ישראל אחרינא רפק ביה פורתא מקמי האי קנה ודוקא בלוקח מעובד כוכבים אבל לוקח מישראל חבירו נהי דלא קני לוקח עד דאתי שטרא לידיה אחר מיהא אין יכול לקדם ולהחזיק שהרי עדיין ברשות מוכר קיימא שכל זמן שלא החזיק הלוקח או לא בא השטר לידו יכולין שניהם לחזור זה בזה: **מי אמר שמואל הכי.** דקני ליה (ה) שני לארעא דעובד כוכבים בחזקה בלא שטר מן העובד כוכבים: **והאמר שמואל דינא דמלכותא דינא.** כל מסים וארנוניות ומנהגות של משפטי מלכים שרגילים להנהיג במלכותם דינא הוא שכל בני המלכות מקבלים עליהם מרצונם חוקי המלך ומשפטיו והלכך דין גמור הוא ואין למחזיק בממון חבירו ע"פ חוק המלך הנהוג בעיר משום גזל: **ומלכא אמר.** לא ליכול שום מחזיק בארעא אלא א"כ יש בידו שטר מכירה מן המוכר והילך יקנה זה המחזיק הואיל ואין לו שטר מן העובד כוכבים אלא לוקח ראשון יקנה בדינא דמלכותא לכי אתי שטריה דעובד כוכבים לידיה: **אמר ליה אנא לא ידענא.** רב יוסף נמי בע"כ הוה ידע להא דאמר שמואל דינא דמלכותא דינא והא דקמהדר ליה לאביי אנא לא ידענא כו' ודאי היה יודע תירוץ לדבר אלא דעדיף ליה למימר עובדא ולכך לא חשש לתרץ ואביי מהדר ליה דמההוא עובדא ליכא לאיתויי ראיה ומיהו רב יוסף לא חזר בו דמכל מקום שמואל אמרה כדאמר בסמוך והאי דקשיא ליה דינא דמלכותא דינא רב יוסף לא ס"ל האי דאמר אביי ומלכא אמר לא ליכול ארעא אלא בשטרא דלאו דינא דמלכותא הוא אלא בחזקה נמי ליכול: **בדורא דרעותא.** שם מקום אי נמי כפר של רועים: **אתא לקמיה דרב יהודה.** ורוב מעשיו שמע משמואל רבו: **דורא דרעותא קאמרת.** בתמיה וכי משם אתה מביא ראיה דנכסי העובד כוכבים הרי הן כמדבר: **באגי מיטמרי.** שדות טמונות שלא היו הבעלים נותנין את המס למלך אלא מבריחין עצמן: **דאינהו גופייהו.** בעלים ראשונים לא הוו יהבי טסקא ומדינא דמלכותא לא היה בידם דבעלים כח למכור ומכרן בטל וזה השני שהחזיק קנה בדינא דמלכותא שהתנה בחזקתו על מנת ליתן את הטסקא למלך ומלכא אמר מאן דיהיב טסקא ליכול ארעא בחזקה בלא שטרא אבל בקרקע שהיא ירושה לעובד כוכבים מאבותיו ומכרה לעולם אימא לך אם בא אחר והחזיק בה מוציאין אותה מידו ומחזירין לראשון כשיהיה לו השטר מן המוכר:

תוספות

ושאינה מסוימת במצריה עד כמה. פי' כמה יקנה במכוש אחד כדאזיל תיירא דתורי והדר פירוש כשיעור מדת תלם (ו) וכן היו יודעים מדת התלם כמה היה אורך שלו דבשדה גדולה לא היו חורשים במענה אחד כל אורך השדה ולא כפ"ה כשיחרוש צמד בקר שורה אחת מקצה גבול שדהו עד קצהו ומתוך כך קונה כל השדה חדא דלישנא לא משמע הכי ועוד דאמאי בעי והדר רק כשיחרוש פעם אחת אע"ג דלא הדר: **עובד** כוכבים מכי מטי זוזי לידיה אסתלק ליה. פ"ה משום דכל קניינו של עובד כוכבים בכסף כדאמרינן בפ"ק דקדושין (ד' יד: ושם) אשכחן עובד כוכבים דכל קניינו בכסף ולאו ראיה היא לפי' ר"ת דמפרש התם דוקא בעבד עברי קאמר שאין בו קנין אחר דשטר לא ידעינן ביה אפי' בישראל אלא מדהוקש לאמה העבריה ואמה העבריה לאחרת אבל בעובד כוכבים דלא שייך ביה קדושין ליכא למילף מאחרת ועוד תניא התם מכסף מקנתו בכסף הוא נקנה ואינו נקנה בתבואה וכלים דהיינו חליפין משמע דה"ה בשטר אינו נקנה דאפילו כל שוה כסף הוה ממעט התם מכסף אי לאו דכתיב ישיב לרבות שוה כסף ככסף אבל בעלמא אור"ת דאדרבה אין קנינו של עובד כוכבים בכסף אלא במשיכה וכדר' יוחנן קי"ל דדריש (בכורות דף יג:) מיד עמיתך בכסף הא מיד עובד כוכבים במשיכה וכן בפ' בתרא דע"ז (דף עא. ושם ד"ה רב) מסיק דמשיכה לעובד כוכבים קונה והא דקאמר הכא ועובד כוכבים מכי מטו זוזי לידיה אסתלק ליה היינו משום דמלינו בעובד כוכבים קנין כסף בעפרון ושטר ודאי לא קנה בעובד כוכבים משום דישראל גופיה לא קנה בשטרא אלא מספר המקנה דירמיה והתם ישראל הוה: **וישראל** לא קנה עד דמטי שטרא לידיה. שהיו עומדים במקום שכותבין את השטר וקשיא לרבינו שמשון בן אברהם דאמאי לא קנה בכסף גרידא מעפרון בק"ו מגופו ממנו באחת ממנו בשתים כדאמרינן בבכורות בפ"ב (דף יג. ושם) דליכא למימר שאינו גומר בדעתו לקנות עד שיהיה בשטר דמאחר שהעובד כוכבים מסתלק למה לא יגמור בדעתו לקנות ויניחנו להיות הפקר והוה לן למימר דהוי כאילו פירש אי בעינא בכספא איקני מה"ט דפרישית וי"ל דאין סהדי שלא היה בדעתו אלא כמות שהוא רגיל לקנות עם ישראל דהיינו בשטר מדלא פירש אי בעינא בכספא איקני אבל קשיא לרבינו שמשון בן אברהם דבפרק ב' דבכורות (שם) א"ר יצחק ישראל שנתן מעות לעובד כוכבים בבהמה בדייהן אע"פ שלא משך קנה וחייבת בבכורה ואמאי לא אמרינן אע"ג דקנה מן התורה כדאמר אביי התם בדייהם שפסקה להן תורה מיד עמיתך במשיכה הא מיד עובד כוכבים בכסף מ"מ אין בדעתו לקנות אלא עד שימשוך כמו שהוא רגיל לקנות עם ישראל כדאמרינן הכא וי"ל דהתם בדייהם קאמר ונראה דשרי לישראל לתבוע (ז) מינייהו מעותיו אע"פ שמתוך כך יחזיר העובד כוכבים ויגזול את המחזיק דבדין קא תבע ליה דלא נתן לו מעות אלא ע"מ שתבא הקרקע לידו ואם המחזיק יכול לישמט מן העובד כוכבים ישמט אע"פ שהלוקח מפסיד אך אם המחזיק בעי לפרוע לו מעותיו אם (ח) יפקיעו הראשון הקרקע מידו ע"י עובד כוכבים נראה דה"ל מסור ממש: **באגי** דמטמרי הוו כו'. והא דאמר בהניזקין (גיטין דף נח: ושם ד"ה מגן) דאזול מרוותייהו דבאגי ואזיל גידול בר רעילאי ויהיב טסקא דתלת שנין ולכי אתו מרוותייהו הדרא להו ולא אמרי' כיון דלא יהבי טסקא הופקעה מידם וזכה בה גידול בר רעילאי דהתם מיירי כגון שאמרו מרוותייהו לבני באגי שיחרשו הקרקע ויזרעו ויאכלו פירות ויפרעו טסקא עד שיחזרו ונתרצו להם בני באגי ונתנוה לגידול הלכך לא הופקעה מידם וכשיחזרו חזרו להן אבל הכא הוו מטמרי בשביל המס שלא רצו לפרוע:

אם

עין משפט נר מצוה

רמא א מיי' פ"א מהל' זכיה ומתנה הל' י סמג עשין עג טוש"ע ח"מ סי' ערה סעיף ג:

רמב ב מיי' שם הל' יד סמג עשין פה טוש"ע ח"מ סי' קלד סעיף ג וסי' רעד:

רמג ג מיי' שם ופ"א מהל' מכירה הלכה ז [ח] סמג שם טוש"ע ח"מ סי' קלד סעיף ג [א]:

רמד ד מיי' פ"א מהל' זכיה הל' טו ופ"ה מהל' גזילה הל' יא סמג שם וסי' עג טוש"ע שם וסי' שסט סעיף ב ז ח ט:

רבינו גרשום

ושאינה מסוימת. אלא בקעה גדולה היא: **עד כמה.** קנה בה: **תיירא דתורי והדר.** כלומר כמו שהולך צמד בקר של מחרישה בתלם וחוזר ועושה תלם אחר כשיעור אותן שני תלמים קני ולא יותר: **כל המחזיק בהן זכה בהן.** כגון שאם מכר עובד כוכבים שדהו לישראל אחד ונתן לו מעות ובא ישראל אחר והחזיק בה קודם שיכתוב לו שטר זכה בהן זה שני ובלבד שיחזיר מעותיו לראשון: **מי אמר שמואל הכי.** דהאי שני זכה בלא שטר: **והאמר שמואל דינא דמלכותא דינא.** דכל מי שבא מחמת עובד כוכבים יש לידון בדין מלכות: **אלא באיגרתא.** בשטר: **בדורא דרעותא.** בכפר של רועים: **התם באגי מטמרי.** שדות טמונות היו בידי עובדי כוכבים שהיו מבריחין מן המס ואמטיל להכי לא הוי צריך למיקני מינייהו בשטרא דלא הוו דידהו לגמרי אלא משועבדים הן למס המלך. והואיל ורצו להבריח המס יכול להחזיק בהן מי שירצה בדינא דמלכותא ובלבד שיתן המס של שדה דהיינו טסקא. אבל בעלמא דלאו באגי מטמרי אימא דלא קני המחזיק בהן אלא בשטר:

מסורת הש"ס

א) [לקמן נה.] ב"ק קיג. גיטין י: נדרים כח.:

הגהות הב"ח

(א) גמ' תיירא דתורי והדר: (ב) שם לא ידענא אלא עובדא הוה: (ג) רשב"ם ד"ה ושאינה וכו' אלא מקום מכושו: (ד) ד"ה הרי הן וכו' תירוץ לדבר והא דא"ל לאביי אנא לא ידענא אלא עובדא הכי הוה: (ה) ד"ה מי אמר וכו' דקני ליה האי שני: (ו) תוס' ד"ה ושאינה וכו' מדת תלם והם היו כו' ולא כפ"ה שפי' כשיחרוש וכו' מקצה גבול השדה ועד קצהו: (ז) ד"ה וישראל וכו' לתבוע מיניה מעותיו: (ח) בא"ד אם יפקיע הראשון:

גליון הש"ס

גמרא אנא לא ידענא. עירובין דף ז ע"ב וש"נ: רשב"ם ד"ה הרי הן כמדבר כו' דהאי שני רשע מקרי. עי' לעיל דף כא ע"ב תוס' ד"ה מרחיקין:

ליקוטי רש"י

דינא דמלכותא דינא. בהגוזל (קמא) [בתרא] (ב"ק קיג:) אמר מדע דקטילו דיקלי וגשרי גשרי ועברינן עלייהו [רשב"ם לקמן נה.]. של עובדי כוכבים [גיטין י:]. **באגי.** באגא בקעה [ב"ק קיג:] **טסקא.** מס קרקע [גיטין נח: וכעי"ז ב"מ עג: וקח.]. **לא הוו יהבי טסקא למלכא.** לפרוע מס הקרקע למלך [כתובות מד.].

Abaye rebuts Rav Yosef's proof:

אָמַר לֵיהּ – **He said to [Rav Yosef]:** דוּרָא דְרַעֲוָתָא קָאָמְרַתְּ – **Do you** mean to **say** that any proof can be brought from the incident in **a shepherds' village?** הָתָם בַּאגֵי מִטַּמְרֵי הֲווּ – **There** the lands involved **were fields undisclosed** to the authorities, דְּאִינְהוּ גּוּפַיְיהוּ לֹא הֲווּ יָהֲבֵי טַסְקָא לְמַלְכָּא – **for** which **they [the original owners] themselves did not pay property taxes to the king,** וּמַלְכָּא אָמַר מַאן דְּיָהֵיב טַסְקָא לֵיכוּל אַרְעָא – **and the king has decreed: The one who pays the** delinquent **property taxes** due on a piece of land **shall possess that land.**[13] Consequently, the original owner, who had evaded the taxes, was not legally empowered to sell it and its sale to the Jewish buyer was void. Rather, the second Jew, who performed the proprietary act of digging in the land, acquired it.[14]

A similar incident:

רַב הוּנָא זְבַן אַרְעָא מֵעוֹבֵד כּוֹכָבִים – **Rav Huna bought land from an idolater.** אֲתָא יִשְׂרָאֵל אַחֵר רָפִיק בָּהּ פּוּרְתָּא – **Another Jew came along and dug a little in it.** אֲתָא לְקַמֵּיהּ דְּרַב נַחְמָן – **[The case] came before Rav Nachman,** אוֹקְמַהּ בִּידֵיהּ – **who placed [the land] in his possession,** i.e. in the possession of the one who had dug in the land, thereby pre-empting Rav Huna. אָמַר לֵיהּ מַאי דַּעְתֵּיךְ – **[Rav Huna] said to [Rav Nachman]: What is your rationale** for ruling so? דְּאָמַר שְׁמוּאֵל נִכְסֵי עוֹבֵד כּוֹכָבִים הֲרֵי הֵן כְּמִדְבָּר וְכָל הַמַּחֲזִיק בָּהֶם זָכָה – Is it not **that Shmuel said: An idolater's** real **properties** that he sells to a Jew **are** ownerless **like a desert; whoever performs a proprietary act in them has acquired them?**

NOTES

incompatibility with Shmuel's other dictum regarding the binding nature of secular law. Shmuel certainly handed down that first ruling.

Rav Yosef's rejoinder, "I do not know [about that statement regarding the legal force of secular law, but I do know that] there was an incident . . ." should not be misconstrued as indicating that Rav Yosef questioned whether Shmuel really said that "the law of the kingdom is the law." Certainly, Rav Yosef knew that Shmuel said that as well. However, Rav Yosef's aim was not to reconcile the two statements of Shmuel for Abaye, but rather to emphasize the unquestionable authenticity of Shmuel's first ruling. Thus, Rav Yosef in effect told Abaye that regardless of any other pronouncements that Shmuel might have made, it cannot be doubted that Shmuel did indeed hand down the first ruling attributed to him above by Rav Yehudah (*Rashbam*). [As to how Rav Yosef in fact reconciled the two rulings of Shmuel, *Rashbam* explains that Rav Yosef maintained that secular law did *not* require a deed for the acquisition of land.]

13. [Literally: shall eat the land.] Those who pay the taxes acquire the property simply by taking possession of it and they do not require the usual receipt of a deed that the royal decree ordinarily demands (*Rashbam*).

14. For he stipulated upon performing the proprietary act that he would pay the taxes due on the property (*Rashbam*).

Accordingly, Rav Yehudah's ruling regarding the case in the shepherds' village in no way reflects the first ruling attributed to Shmuel above, since the seller in the shepherds' village had lost the title to his land by royal edict. Abaye, therefore, remains opposed to the first ruling attributed to Shmuel above, since it runs counter to Shmuel's other dictum: The law of the kingdom is the law. [Rav Yosef, however, sees no contradiction between the two rulings, as explained above in note 12.]

לִיעֲבַד לִי מָר כְּאִידַךְ דִּשְׁמוּאֵל – By the same token, **let the master rule for me in accordance with Shmuel's other ruling;** דְּאָמַר שְׁמוּאֵל לֹא קָנָה אֶלָּא מְקוֹם מַכּוֹשׁוֹ בִּלְבַד – **for Shmuel said:** When one digs in an ownerless field, **he has acquired solely the place of his dig.**[1] Consequently, the intruder should be awarded only the actual place of his digging and the rest of the field should belong to me.

Rav Nachman explains his verdict:

אָמַר לֵיהּ – **[Rav Nachman] said to [Rav Huna]:** בְּהַאי אֲנָא כִּשְׁמַעְתִּין סְבִירָא לִי – **In this** matter of digging in an ownerless field, **I hold in accordance with our tradition;**[2] דְּאָמַר רַב הוּנָא אָמַר רַב – **for Rav Huna said in the name of Rav:** כֵּיוָן שֶׁנִּיכֵּשׁ בָּהּ מַכּוֹשׁ אֶחָד – When one digs in an ownerless field, **as soon as he makes a single dig,** קָנָה כּוּלָּהּ – **he has acquired the entire [field].**[3] Therefore, the intruder has acquired the entire field.

שְׁלַח רַב הוּנָא בַּר אָבִין – **Rav Huna bar Avin sent** the following report: יִשְׂרָאֵל שֶׁלָּקַח שָׂדֶה מֵעוֹבֵד כּוֹכָבִים – **"If a Jew bought a field from an idolater,** וּבָא יִשְׂרָאֵל אַחֵר וְהֶחֱזִיק בָּהּ – **and another Jew came along and performed a proprietary act in it** in the interim between the idolater's receipt of the money and the buyer's receipt of the deed, אֵין מוֹצִיאִים אוֹתָהּ מִיָּדוֹ – **we do not remove [the field] from [the intruder's] possession** (precisely as Shmuel ruled). וְכֵן הָיָה ר׳ אָבִין וְר׳ אִילְעָא וְכָל רַבּוֹתֵינוּ שָׁוִין בַּדָּבָר – **And so were R' Avin and R' Ila'a and all our teachers** in Eretz Yisrael **agreed in this matter."**

The Gemara now cites a report concerning the legal force of secular law:

אָמַר רַבָּה הָנֵי תְּלָת מִילֵּי אִישְׁתָּעֵי לִי עוּקְבָן בַּר נְחֶמְיָה רֵישׁ גָּלוּתָא מִשְּׁמֵיהּ דִּשְׁמוּאֵל – **Rabbah said: Ukvan bar Nechemiah, the** ***Reish Galusa,***[4] **told me the following three things in the name of Shmuel:** דִּינָא דְּמַלְכוּתָא דִּינָא – 1) **The law of the kingdom is the law;**[5] וַאֲרִיסוּתָא דְּפַרְסָאֵי עַד מ׳ שְׁנִין – 2) **the** ***chazakah*** **of the Persians is** not effective **until forty years** have elapsed;[6] וְהָנֵי זַהֲרוּרֵי דְּזָבִין אַרְעָא לְטַסְקָא – **and** 3) regarding **the wealthy heirs who acquire land by** paying its **property taxes,** זְבִינְהוּ זְבִינֵי – **their acquisition** of the land **is a** valid **acquisition.**[7]

The Gemara qualifies this last ruling:[8]

וְהָנֵי מִילֵּי לְטַסְקָא – **However, this** latter **ruling applies only to** one who acquires the land by paying **the** delinquent **property tax,** אֲבָל לְכַרְגָּא לֹא – **but not to** one who acquires it by paying **the** delinquent **head tax.** מַאי טַעְמָא – **What is the reason** for this distinction? כַּרְגָּא אַקַּרְקַף דְּגַבְרֵי מְנַח – **The head tax is placed upon the heads of the** obligated **persons,** and the law does not subject the delinquents' lands to confiscation.[9]

A dissenting opinion:

רַב הוּנָא בְּרֵיהּ דְּרַב יְהוֹשֻׁעַ אָמַר – **Rav Huna the son of Rav Yehoshua says:** אֲפִילוּ שַׂעֲרֵי דְּכַדָּא מִשְׁתַּעְבְּדֵי לְכַרְגָּא – **Even** chattel such as **barley in a jug is subject to** collection for **the head tax.** Certainly, then, land is also subject to confiscation.[10]

Rav Huna the son of Rav Yehoshua's view is questioned:

אָמַר רַב אַשִׁי – **Rav Ashi said:** אָמַר לִי הוּנָא בַּר נָתָן – **Huna bar Nassan said to me** that קַשְׁיָא בָּהּ אַמֵּימָר – **Ameimar had** the following **difficulty with [the view of Rav Huna the son of Rav Yehoshua]:** אִם כֵּן בִּטַּלְתָּ יְרוּשַּׁת בְּנוֹ הַבְּכוֹר – **If so, you have nullified** the law relating to **the inheritance of one's firstborn son!**[11] דַּהֲוָה לֵיהּ רָאוּי – **For** according to the view of Rav Huna

NOTES

1. [Shmuel's ruling in this matter is cited above on 54a.]

2. [*Hagahos Yavetz* emends the text to read: כִּשְׁמַעְתִּיךְ, *in accordance with your tradition.*]

3. [This, too, has been cited above on 54a.] Thus, Rav Nachman explained that although he rules in accordance with Shmuel's verdict that an intruder can take advantage of the lapse of ownership that occurs when a Jew buys a field from an idolater, he follows Rav's view in the matter of acquiring an entire ownerless field by virtue of a single act of digging.

4. The *Reish Galusa* ("Exilarch" or "Head of the Exile") was a descendant of the Davidic dynasty who ruled over the Jews in Babylonia.

5. [As explained above, 54b.] *Rashbam* adds that the Gemara (*Bava Kamma* 113b) proves that this rule is universally accepted from the fact that we use public works built by the government with requisitioned materials (e.g. bridges constructed with appropriated lumber). If Torah law did not recognize the government's law as binding on its citizens, then use of these public works would constitute use of stolen property and would be forbidden. Since it is the universally accepted practice to use such public works, it is evidently accepted that Torah law does recognize the government's right of eminent domain (*Rashbam*).

6. Although according to normative Torah law a *chazakah* on a field is established with an occupancy of only three years, in Persia an occupancy of forty years is required, since that is the law of the land there (*Rashbam,* second explanation).

Alternatively, Persian law, though it ordinarily recognizes only recorded real estate transactions as valid (see Gemara above), considers anyone who has occupied a property for forty years to be its legitimate owner. Accordingly, a Jew in Persia may buy real estate from an idolater who has occupied it for forty years, even if another Jew claims that the idolater stole it from him. Even if the other Jew's claim is true, the idolater has acquired the land under Persian law by occupying it for forty years (*Rashbam,* first explanation). [According to this explanation, the word עַד, *until,* must apparently be deleted from the Gemara text.]

7. I.e. if the poor people are delinquent in paying their real estate taxes, the government confiscates their land and offers it to anyone willing to pay the taxes. Thus, the wealthy heirs who pay the delinquent taxes assume legal title to the land. Even if the original owners subsequently obtain sufficient funds and are willing to reimburse the new owners for the amount of taxes paid, the new owners have no obligation to relinquish the land, which has become rightfully theirs under secular law (*Rashbam*). These, then, are the three laws that Shmuel told Ukvan bar Nechemiah, the *Reish Galusa* — the general principle that the law of the land is the law and two manifestations of that principle (ibid.; cf. *Ritva* cited in next note).

8. *Rashbam.* [See, however, *Ritva,* who explains that this qualification is the *third* ruling cited by Ukvan bar Nechemiah; the first ruling "the law of the kingdom is the law" is not counted among the three, as it is the general principle from which the three rulings are derived.]

9. Under secular law, the individual head tax is but a personal obligation; the tax collector is empowered to imprison the delinquent until the tax is paid, but he is not empowered to confiscate his property. Therefore, if the tax collector [exceeded his authority and] confiscated a person's land in lieu of the delinquent head tax, one may not acquire the illegally confiscated property from him (*Rashbam*). This is unlike the situation in the case of delinquent property taxes, where the secular law does allow confiscation of the delinquent's property.

10. Rav Huna the son of Rav Yehoshua maintains that secular law *does* authorize confiscation of property for a delinquency in paying the head tax. Therefore, the tax collector's actions have legal force in regard to both taxes (*Rashbam*).

[The Rishonim question why the Amoraim debate the particulars of secular law. Why not simply ask the secular authorities what the law is? The Rishonim answer that the dictum "the law of the kingdom is the law" applies only to those laws that are sanctioned by the constitution of the country. Oftentimes, however, the monarchy exceeds its constitutional authority and appropriates property by force. The legality of such appropriations are *not* recognized by Torah law. (For this reason, the Talmud states that "the law of the *kingdom* is the law," rather than "the law of the *king* is the law.") In cases such as those discussed by our Gemara, the constitutionality of certain government practices is unclear even to the secular jurists and indeed falls within the province of Amoraic consideration (see *Ramban* et al.).]

11. The Torah rules that a firstborn son takes a double portion of his father's inheritance, as the verse states (*Deuteronomy* 21:17): כִּי אֶת־הַבְּכֹר . . . יַכִּיר לָתֶת לוֹ פִּי שְׁנַיִם בְּכֹל אֲשֶׁר־יִמָּצֵא לוֹ, *For the firstborn . . . he shall*

ליעבד לי מר כאידך דשמואל דאמר שמואל לא קנה אלא מקום מכושו בלבד א"ל בהאי אנא א) כשמעתין סבירא לי דאמר רב הונא אמר רב כיון שניכש בה מכוש אחד קנה כולה שלח רב הונא בר אבין ישראל שלקח שדה מעובד כוכבים ובא ישראל אחר והחזיק בה אין מוציאים אותה מידו וכן היה ר' אבין ור' אילעא וכל רבותינו שוין בדבר אמר ב) רבה הני תלת מילי אישתעי לי עוקבן בר נחמיה ריש גלותא משמיה דשמואל ג) דינא דמלכותא דינא ד) ואריסותא דפרסאי עד מ' שנין א והני זהרורי דזבין ארעא לטסקא זבינהו זביני וה"מ לטסקא ב אבל לכרגא לא מ"ט כרגא אקרקף דגברי מנח רב הונא בריה דרב יהושע אמר אפילו שערי דכדא משתעבדי לכרגא אמר רב אשי אמר לי הונא בר נתן קשי בה אמימר ג א"כ בטלת ירושת בנו הבכור דהוה ליה ראוי ו) ואין הבכור נוטל בראוי כבמוחזק א"ל אי הכי אפילו טסקא נמי אלא מה אית לך למימר דיהיב טסקא ומית הכא נמי דיהיב כרגא ומית אמר רב אשי אמר לי הונא בר נתן שאילתינהו לספרי דרבא ואמרו לי הלכתא כרב הונא בריה דרב יהושע ולא היא התם לאוקומי מילתיה הוא דאמר ואמר רב אשי ד פרדכת מסייע מתא וה"מ דאצילתיה מתא ה אבל אנדיסקי סיעתא דשמיא היא אמר רב אסי א"ר יוחנן ו) המצר והחצב מפסיקין בנכסי הגר ז אבל לענין פאה וטומאה לא כי אתא רבין אמר רבי יוחנן אפילו לפאה וטומאה פאה מאי היא דתנן ז) ח ואלו מפסיקין לפאה הנחל והשלולית ודרך

רש"י

ליעבד לי מר כאידך דשמואל. כיון דכשמואל סבירא לך ולא ליקני אלא ההוא פורתא דרפק והא לא מצי למימר ליעבד לי מר כאידך דשמואל דאמר דינא דמלכותא דינא ולא ליקני אלא בשטר דכיון דמודי רב הונא דשמואל אמרה להא דנכסי הגר הרי הן כמדבר על כרחך זקוק אתה לתרץ דלא תקשי שמואל אדשמואל וכדפרישית לעיל: אין מוציאין כו'. כשמואל: וכן היו רבותינו כו'. כל זה שלח רב הונא בר אבין: דינא דמלכותא דינא. בהגוזל (א) קמא (ב"ק דף קיג:) אמר תדע דקטלי דיקלי וגשרי גשרי ועברינן עלייהו: דאריסא דפרסאי ארבעין שנין. חזקת פרסיים מ' שנים היא ע"י דינא דמלכותא דלאע"ג דלא קני איניש אלא בשטר מיהו אם החזיק בה עכו"ם מ' שנים ובא ישראל וקנה ממנו הוי קנין גמור ולא יוכל ישראל אחר לומר שלי היא שגזולה עכו"ם ממני ואע"ג דאמרינן (לעיל דף לה:) ישראל הבא מחמת העכו"ם הרי הוא כעכו"ם ואין לו חזקה אלא בההוא שטרא שמכרה ישראל לעכו"ם הכא יש לו חזקה. אי נמי אתא לאשמועינן דאע"ג דבשאר מקומות הויא חזקה לישראל בג' שנים בארץ פרס אינה חזקה בפחות ממ' שנים דדינא דמלכותא הוא שם כן: הני זהרורי. בעלי נחלות העשירים קונים מעבדי המלך שדות עניי העיר שאין יכולין ליתן הטסקא למלך והן פורעין את המס ומחזיקין בקרקעות בשביל המס שכן דינא דמלכותא דמאן דיהיב טסקא ליכול ארעא כדאמר לעיל: זבינייהו זביני. מה שקונין הקרקע מעבדי המלך בשביל המס שנותנים מכרן קיים דדינא דמלכותא דינא ואם יחזרו בעלים ראשונים או יתעשרו ויאמרו להחזיר המס להני זהרורי לא יוכלו לערער על הני זהרורי כלל לזבינייהו זביני: זהרורי. על שם נחלה שקרוי זיהרא לקמן בפרק המוכר את הבית (דף סח:) ואי א"נ זיהרא אפילו בוסתני ופרדסי והילך תלת מילי קמייתא דינא דמלכותא דינא ובאריסא דפרסאי והני זהרורי שתלויין בדינא דמלכותא דינא הרי תלת: והני מילי. דזבינייהו זביני אי זבין לטסקא בשביל מס הקרקע שלא נתנו הבעלים: אבל לכרגא. בשביל כסף גולגלתא שלא פרעו מכרו להם עבדי המלך קרקעותיו של זה לא הוו זביני דלאין זה דינא דמלכותא לגבות הקרקע בשביל מס הראש כי אם בשביל מס הקרקע: אקרקפתא דגברא מנח. או יתפשוהו עד שיתן מאליו או יברח מן העיר והך מלתא גמרא קאמר ליה: אפי' שערי דכדא. שכבר נתלשו מן הקרקע ומונחין בכדו וכל שכן קרקע עצמה ולא שנא זבין ארעא לטסקא או לכרגא זבינייהו זביני דהכי הוי דינא דמלכותא: שערי דכדא. כלומר כל מטלטלין שיש לו בעולם משועבדין למלך בשביל מס ראשו והיכא דלא פרע נתחייב כל אשר לו ומי שיקנה מעבדי המלך בין קרקעות בין מטלטלין זבינייהו זביני: אם כן. דאפילו שערי דכדא משתעבדי לכרגא היכי יתקיים הכתוב דכתיב (דברים כא) בכל אשר ימצא לו הרי באותה המלכות בטלת ירושת בנו הבכור דכל ממון האב אם מת ולא פרע עדיין כרגא דשנה זו הוה ליה ממונו ראוי דאינו מוחזק בו כלל כי אם המלך דשעבוד המלך עדיף משאר שעבודין וכגבוי דמי ומיהו לאו אתקפתא מעלייתא היא דאיכא למימר אין הכי נמי תבטל ותבטל לשם ובשאר מקומות יתקיים דשבקיה לקרא דאיהו דחיק ומוקי אנפשיה: אי הכי אפי' טסקא נמי. רב אשי הוא דקפריך עליה דאמימר הכי דכיון דקשיא ליה לאמימר הכי אפילו כי אמרינן ארעא לטסקא אשתעבדא לדברי הכל א"כ בטלת בקרקעות ירושת בנו הבכור: אלא מאי אית לך למימר. היכי דמי דלא תבטל כגון דיהיב טסקא של אותה שנה בתחלת השנה ומית דעד סוף השנה אינה משועבדת למלך עוד והוה ליה מוחזק ויטול בה בכור פי שנים ה"נ וכו': ולא היא (ב) התם. לית הלכתא כרב הונא בריה דרב יהושע דלא משתעבדי לא קרקעות ולא מטלטלין לכרגא ואי זבון לכרגא לא הוו זבינייהו זביני דכרגא אקרקפתא דגברא מנח ואינהו ספרי דרבא דאמרי הלכתא כרב הונא לאוקומי מלתייהו בעו לקיים מעשיהם ושטרות שכתבו על מכירת קרקעות שנמכרו לכרגא ובאו לומר דמשתעבדי לכרגא כדי שיהו המכירות והשטרות קיימין ומיהו שלא כדין נכתבו השטרות ונמכרו הקרקעות והדרי זביני: פרדכת. אדם בטל ממלאכה ומלמוד ומדלך ארך ואין עוסק בישובו של עולם כלל: מסייע מתא. הוא חייב בעול הקהל ואף על פי שהוא אינו עושה ריוח בעיר: והני מילי. דמסייע ליתן במס הקהל: כגון דאצילתיה מתא. עבדי המלך היו תובעים לו לבדו והם הצילוהו והקלו במשאו בטענותם שאמרו עליו שאין לו ממון ומתוך כך נתרצה מס שלהן והכביד עולן יותר כגון שהמלך רגיל ליקח מכולן מס קצוב לשנה ובאו לתבוע לכל אחד כפי אומד דעתם עד שיעלה גיבוייס לחשבון מס הקצוב והיו שואלין לזה יותר מדאי והם הפלוהו ופטרוהו ומה שפחתו מזה יגבו מן השאר: אבל אנדיסקי. ממונין של מלך הרגילין לגבות מכל בית ובית מכל איש ואיש עד שיעלה החשבון למס הקצוב ושכחוהו לזה או לא רצו לשאול לו כלום בשביל שהוא אדם בטל וסבורין היו שאין לו ממון וגבו כל המס מכל השאר אף על פי שהכביד עליהם המס כדי שהיה לו לזה ליתן פטור דסייעתא דשמיא הוא שמחלו לו: המצר והחצב כו'. ב' שדות של גר ומלר אחד ביניהן החזיק באחת מהן לא קנה את חבירתה אלא האי דאחזיק ביה לבדו קנה כדאמר רבי יוסי בר חנינא לעיל בשמעתא י) והוא הדין אם אין שם מלר אבל יש חלב נטוע בינתים מפסיק: חצב. הוא אילן או עשב שבו תיחס יהושע את ארץ ישראל לפי שיורד ויונק לא מכאן ולא מכאן כדאמר (ביצה דף כה:) חלוקא מקטע רגליהון דרשעים שמשיגין גבול רעיהן וזה אינו משיג גבול אחר: אבל לענין פאה או טומאה לא. הוי הפסק לחשבן ב' שדות אלא יניח פאה אחת על שניהם הואיל וסמוכין זה לזה דמן התורה אין מלר מפליג קרקע המחוברת לחייבה שתי פאות ומיהו לגבי חזקה די לנו אם יקנה במכוש אחד שדה אחת דהא אפילו בשדה אחת איכא למ"ד לא קנה אלא מקום מכושו וכל שכן בשתי שדות לדברי הכל דלא קנה אלא מה שהחזיק וסברא בעלמא הוא לחזקה מעלייתא בעינן שיחזיק בכל השדות: פאה וטומאה. לקמיה מפרש מאי נפקא מינה בין שדה אחת לשתים: אפי' לפאה ולטומאה. דמאי שנא מחזקה: פאה מאי היא. לגבי מאי מהני הפסק: דתנן. דהפסק מחייב להניח פאה בכל אחת: הנחל. (ג) כנחל איתן אשר לא יעבד בו ולא יזרע קרקע קשה מלא צרורות ואבנים שאין ראוי לזריעה: והשלולית. קבולת מי גשמים בהכונס לגן לדיר (ב"ק דף סא.) מאי שלולית אמר רב יהודה אמר שמואל מקום (ד) ששוללין מי גשמים שם רב ביבי א"ר יוחנן אמת המים המחלקת שלל לאגפיה:

דרך

תוספות

אם כן בטלת ירושת בנו. דבשלמא מכל אדם שיש עליו כתובת אשה ובעל חוב אף על פי שנכסים משועבדין להן מ"מ אין ירושת בני הבכור בטילה משום דמלוה ואשה מחסרי גוביינא וצריכי אדרכתא ואכרזתא ושומא אבל למס המלך אפילו קרקע שוה אלף זוז משועבדת לדבר מועט והקרקעות עיקר הן של המלך וכבר הוא מוחזק ולא מחסרי גוביינא. ר"י ור"ת:

אנדיסקי. פי' כותבי שטרות המלך לדיסקא הוא שטר כדאמר בהגוזל בתרא (ב"ק דף קיג:) האי מאן דנקיט דיסקא מב"ד הגדול ובפרק השולח (גיטין דף לו.) מעיקרא במאי אפקינהו בדיסקי:

רבינו גרשום

באריסותא דפרסאי. דחזקה של פרסיים לא הויא חזקה אא"כ החזיק ארבעין שנין: הני זיהרורי. בעלי נחלות: דזבין ארעא לטסקא. שקנו שדה של אדם שנטלוה ממנו מחמת שהבריח מס שלה: זביניה זביני. משום דדינא דמלכותא דינא דאמר דמאן דיהיב טסקא ליכול ארעא. אבל שדהו של אדם שנטלוה ממנו בשביל שלא נתן כרגא. מס גולגלתו אינן רשאין לקנות משום דכרגא אקרקף גברי מנח. כלומר ראש האיש עצמו משתעבד לכרגא ולא שדהו דלא היה להם ליטול שדהו בשביל מס הכרגא: אפי' שערי דכדא משעבד לכרגא. וכ"ש שדהו. ואפי' מכרו שדהו מפני הברחת כרגא הויא מכורה: א"כ בטלת ירושת בנו הבכור. וא"כ הוא דכל נכסין משעבדי לכרגא אפי' שערי דכדא א"כ כל זמן דלא יהב כרגא אינן מוחזקין נכסיו בידו וא"כ לא יירש מהן הבכור פי שנים משום דאין הבכור נוטל בראוי כבמוחזק: אי הכי אפי' טסקא נמי. אם מת ולא יהב טסקא אינה מוחזקת הקרקע בידו א"כ אין הבכור נוטל פי שנים בה: אלא דיהיב טסקא ומית בו ביום. בההוא יומא מצי שקיל פי שנים דמההוא שעתא דיהיב טסקא וכרגא הוחזקו בידו: ואמרו לי הלכתא כרב הונא בריה דרב יהושע. דאמר אפי' שערי דכדא משעבד לכרגא: ולא היא. אין הלכה כרב הונא בריה דרב יהושע. והאי דקאמרי ספרי דהלכ' כוותיה לאוקמי מלתא הוא דבעי. כלומר להחזיק דבריהן לפי שהן רגילין לכתוב שטרי מכירה לאותן הלוקחין מן המוכסין דגבו ארעא לכרגא ומש"ה אמרו הלכה כוותיה כדי לקיים שטרי כתיבתן להרבות שכרן ולעולם אמרי' אין הלכה כרב הונא: פרדכת מסייעא מתא. אדם בטל דלית ליה שדות לעסוק בהן ואין מתעסק בשום דבר אלא בבטלנות היינו פרדכת. מסייעא מתא. שצריך לו לאותו פרדכת ליתן חלקו בעול בני העיר לשעבוד שר העיר: וה"מ. דצריך ליתן חלק: דאצילתיה מתא. שהצילוהו בני העיר בדבריהם מיד השר שאמרו לשר אין לזה כלום ליתן לך ושמע להן והניחו על פיהן וניצל על פיהן. חייב לסייעם: אבל אנדיסקי. היינו שר העיר מעצמו נותן לו לאותו פרדכת שאמר איני חושש ליקח מזה כלום סייעתא דשמיא הוא דרחמי עליה ואינו צריך ליתן עמהם לסייעם: המצר. זהו חריץ או גדר העשוי סביב השדה להיכרא בין שדות אחרות: והחצב. שם אילן ואין נוטין שרשיו לכאן ולכאן אלא במקום שנוטעין אותו יורדין עד התהום ומש"ה נוטעין אותן על הגבולין בין שדה לחבירתה לפסוק. ומש"ה אמר מפסיקין בנכסי הגר [שאם הי'] באחת משדות הגר מופסקת בין כל אחת במצר או בחצב לא קנה אלא עד מקום המצר או עד מקום החצב: אבל לפאה ולטומאה לא. אין מפסיקין. כיצד לפאה שאם היה מצר או חצב בשדה אינו מפסיק שיהא צריך להניח שתי פאות משום אותו הפסק אלא יקצור כל השדה ויניח פאה אחת על כולו ולטומאה נמי אינו הפסק. כיצד כדמפרש לקמן הלכתי למקום הלז בשדה זו והטומאה היתה ממצר להלן או מחצב להלן ואמר איני יודע אם נכנסתי למקום הטומאה מעבר למצר או לחצב אמרי' דספיקו טמא דלא הוי הפסק לטומאה האי מצר וחצב: אפי' לפאה ולטומאה. הוי הפסק האי מצר וחצב כדתנן אלו מפסיקין לפאה א) ולשדי' דצריך להניח שתי פאות דכשתי שדות דמי: שלולית. כעין אמת המים ומקום שמי גשמים שוללין שם:

חשק שלמה על רבינו גרשום א) נראה דל"ל לשתי שדות.

עין משפט נר מצוה

רמה א ב מיי' פ"ה מהל' גזלה הל' יח סמג עשין עג טוש"ע ח"מ סי' שסט סעיף ט:
רמו ג טוש"ע ח"מ סי' רעה סעיף ה בהגה:
רמז ד ה טוש"ע ח"מ סי' קסג סעיף ו וע"ש כל דיני המסים:
רמח ו מיי' פ"א מהל' זכיה ומתנה הל' י סמג עשין פב טוש"ע ח"מ סי' ערה סעיף ז:
רמט ז ח מיי' פ"ג מהל' מתנות עניים הלכה ב ג:

מסורת הש"ס

א) [נ"ל כשמעתיך יעב"ן], ב) [גי' רי"ף ורא"ש רבא], ג) [לעיל נד: וש"נ], ד) [נ"ל ארישן פי' חזקה דפרסאי בלא שטר מ' שנין. ערוך ערך אריס א'], ה) [לקמן קיט. קכג: קכה: בכורות נא:], ו) ב"ק סא. [פאה פ"ב מ"א] מנחות עא:, ז) [לעיל נג: ע"ש הגי' רב אסי א"ר יוחנן]:

הגהות הב"ח

(א) רשב"ם ד"ה דינא וכו' בהגוזל בתרא אמר רבא תדע: (ב) ד"ה ולא היא לית כצ"ל ותיבת התם נמחק: (ג) ד"ה הנחל כגון נחל איתן: (ד) ד"ה והשלולית וכו' מקום שמי גשמים שוללין שם וכו' שמחלקת שלל לאגפיה:

ליקוטי רש"י

לא קנה אלא מקום מכושו בלבד. ודוקא נכסי הגר אבל מכר וקבל זוזי אפילו עשר שדות בעשר מדינות והחזיק באחת מהן קנה כולן כדאמר שמואל בפרקי קמאי בב"ק (יב.) וקדושין (כז.) וכדפרישית לעיל (נג:). מכוש אחד. הכאה אחת בקרקע קנה כולה דהיינו רפק בה פורתא וכגון קרקע שעומד לחרישה אבל בבית לא הוי חזקה ול"ש מכר ול"ש נכסי הגר קנה כולה. ובהך פלוגתא הלכתא כרב הואיל ורב הונא עבד עובדא כותיה דרב [רשב"ם לעיל נד.]. דינא דמלכותא. של עובדי כוכבים [גיטין י:]. כרגא. כסף גולגלתא שהיה על היהודים כל אחד נותן כסף גולגלתו למלך [ב"מ עג:]. ואין הבכור נוטל בראוי כבמוחזק. חלק בכורה בממון הראוי לבא לאחר מיתת אביו אלא במה שמוחזק ביד אביו ביום מותו כדכתיב בכל אשר ימצא לו (דברים כא) [יבמות כד.]. בנכסים שלא היו אביהן מוחזק בשעת מיתתו אבל לאויין היו להן לאחר זמן אין הבכור נוטל פי שנים [בכורות נא:]. והחצב. עשב שעושים גבולין בין שדה לשדה לפי ששרשיו נוקבין ויורדין בעומק ואין מתפשטין לצדדין כלל ונוטעין אותו בין גבולי שדות ובו תיחס יהושע לישראל את הארץ [ביצה כה:]. עשב שמשרש בעומק כנגדו ואין שרשיו מתפשטין ובו תיחס יהושע את הארץ לישראל [שבת קכח.]. ואלו מפסיקין לפאה. להניח פאה מכל אחד ואחד [ב"ק סא.]. לתת שתי פאות [מנחות עא:]. הנחל. שדה מכאן ושדה מכאן ונחל עמוק באמצע חייב להניח פאה מכל אחד ואחד [ב"ק שם]. והשלולית. מקום שמי גשמים שוללים שם ואם יש שם זריעה מכאן ומכאן נותן פאה לכל אחד ואחד דהאיך שלולית מפסקא להו [מנחות שם]. שוללין. מתקבצין כמו מן השלל של ביצים (ביצה ז.) דבר אחר לשון שלל ומלקוט (במדבר לא) דבר המקובץ [ב"ק שם].

the son of Rav Yehoshua, **[the father's estate] is** regarded as **prospective** assets,[12] וְאֵין הַבְּכוֹר נוֹטֵל בְּרָאוּי כִּבְמוּחְזָק – **and a firstborn son does not take** a double portion **in prospective** assets **as** he does **in** assets already **possessed.**[13] – ? –

Rav Ashi answers:

אָמַר לֵיהּ – **[Rav Ashi] said to [Huna bar Nassan]:** אִי הָכִי – **If** it is **so,** as Ameimar asserts, that the royal lien on property causes the property to be classified as prospective assets, אֲפִילוּ טַסְקָא נַמִּי – then **even the property tax** should present this difficulty.[14] אֶלָּא מָה אִית לָךְ לְמֵימַר – **Rather, what can you say** to resolve this difficulty according to Ameimar's own view? דְּיָהֵיב טַסְקָא וּמִית – **That** the law of the firstborn's inheritance is relevant where **[the father] paid the property tax** for that year **and** then **he died,** hence releasing the royal lien from his property. הָכָא נַמִּי – **Here too,** in regard to the head tax, Rav Huna the son of Rav Yehoshua will explain that the law of the firstborn's inheritance is relevant דְּיָהֵיב כְּרָגָא וּמִית – **where [the father] paid the head tax** for that year **and** then **he died,** hence removing the royal lien from his property.

The Gemara presents the final halachah in this matter:

אָמַר רַב אַשִׁי – **Rav Ashi said:** אָמַר לִי הוּנָא בַּר נָתָן – **Huna bar Nassan said to me:** שְׁאֵילְתִּינְהוּ לְסַפְרֵי דְּרָבָא – **I asked Rava's scribes,** who draw up legal documents for his court, וְאָמְרוּ לִי הִלְכְתָא כְּרַב הוּנָא בְּרֵיהּ דְּרַב יְהוֹשֻׁעַ – **and they said to me that the halachah** in this matter **follows Rav Huna the son of Rav Yehoshua,** who maintains that all a person's property is subject to the royal lien for payment of the head tax.

The Gemara concludes, however:

וְלֹא הִיא – **But it is not so** as Rava's scribes assert. הָתָם לְאוֹקוּמֵי מִילְּתֵיהּ הוּא דְּאָמַר – **There, they said this** ruling in order **to uphold** the validity of **their actions.**[15]

Another ruling stated by Rav Ashi:

וְאָמַר רַב אַשִׁי – **And Rav Ashi said:** פַּרְדַּכְתְּ מְסַיֵּיעַ מָתָא – **A loafer must assist the city** of his residence with its tax burden.[16] וְהָנֵי מִילֵּי דְּאַצִּילְתֵּיהּ מָתָא – **However, this applies only where the city saved him** from his share of the tax.[17] אֲבָל אַנְדִּיסְקֵי סַיַּעְתָּא דִּשְׁמַיָּא הִיא – **But** if **the state officials** exempted him, **it is Divine** rather than human **assistance** that he has received and he does not have to reimburse the city's taxpayers.[18]

The Gemara returns to its discussion concerning the acquisition of ownerless properties of a deceased convert:[19]

אָמַר רַב אַסִּי אָמַר רַבִּי יוֹחָנָן – **Rav Assi said in the name of R' Yochanan:** הַמֵּצַר וְהֶחָצָב מַפְסִיקִין בְּנִכְסֵי הַגֵּר – **The boundary and the *chatzav* plant divide** a field **in regard to the estate of a convert** who died without heirs,[20] אֲבָל לְעִנְיַן פֵּאָה וְטוּמְאָה לֹא – **but not in regard to *pe'ah***[21] **and *tumah*.**[22]

NOTES

acknowledge to give him a double portion in all that is found of his. As indicated by the words "in all that *is found* of his," the law applies only to assets that are possessed by the father at the time of his death, not to assets that are realized only later (e.g. a loan repaid to the father posthumously). Thus, if the father's debtor repays the loan only after the father dies, the firstborn son does not receive a double portion of that repayment, but it is divided equally among the brothers.

12. According to Rav Huna the son of Rav Yehoshua, who maintains that all a person's property is subject to the royal lien for the collection of the head tax, if the father dies without having paid his head tax for the year, none of the property he leaves over is actually his, but only potentially so. For (unlike ordinary liens) the royal lien encumbering the entire estate is so strong as to render the estate the property of the king. Only potentially does the estate belong to the father — a potential realized when the head tax is paid and the royal lien is released (*Rashbam*; cf. *Ritva*).

13. Thus, taken to its logical conclusion, Rav Huna the son of Rav Yehoshua's view would yield the untenable result that the law of the firstborn's inheritance is no longer applicable, as it is superseded by the law of the land, which provides for a royal lien on all property for payment of the head tax.

Rashbam observes, however, that the issue raised by Ameimar is not really a difficulty, since the law of the firstborn's inheritance will apply in other countries, where the law does not provide for a royal lien on all properties for payment of the head tax. [The Gemara nevertheless succeeds in resolving the difficulty in a different way.] Cf. *Ritva*.

14. Ameimar certainly agrees that the law of the land provides for a royal lien on all land for the payment of the property tax. Accordingly, the law of the firstborn's inheritance does not apply to land, since the royal lien on the land for unpaid property taxes renders the land prospective rather than actual assets (*Rashbam*). [It is nearly as untenable to say that the law of the firstborn's inheritance does not apply to land as it is to say that it does not apply to any assets.] Thus, quite apart from Rav Huna the son of Rav Yehoshua's view, there must be some way to resolve Ameimar's difficulty, and that resolution will in all likelihood serve to defend Rav Huna the son of Rav Yehoshua's position as well.

15. [Literally: he said this to uphold his action. It appears, however, that many Rishonim had a plural reading.]

In fact, the law does not follow Rav Huna the son of Rav Yehoshua. Rather, a person's property — real or movable — is *not* subject to the royal lien for payment of the head tax; thus, a person may not acquire from the tax collector property confiscated for collection of the head tax. Rava's scribes, however, had been in the habit of drawing up documents to record the acquisition of such properties from the tax collectors. In an effort to uphold the validity of their documents, they asserted that the halachah follows Rav Huna the son of Rav Yehoshua, according to whom such acquisitions from the tax collector are legally recognized. But in point of fact, such acquisitions are not legal; the documents attesting to them are null and void and the land reverts to its original owner (*Rashbam*).

16. Even a person who is idle from work, study or any productive activity must bear his share of the communal tax burden, though he does not earn any money in that city (*Rashbam*; see *Aruch HaShulchan, Choshen Mishpat* 163:16). The case involves a tax levied upon an entire city, with the burden spread among its various residents. This loafer did not pay his share of tax, thereby slightly increasing the burden of each of the taxpayers. Rav Ashi rules that the loafer is obligated to reimburse the taxpayers for the increased tax that they in effect paid for him.

17. I.e. the ruling applies in a case where the tax collector assesses what share of the total tax each particular resident should contribute. The collector assessed the loafer for a certain amount, but the gainfully employed residents of the city succeeded in convincing the collector that the loafer had no money and that he should not, therefore, be required to pay any tax. Since their defense of the loafer has added to the amount of tax that they must pay, he is obligated to reimburse them for it (*Rashbam*).

18. I.e. if the tax officials skipped the loafer of their own accord — either inadvertently or because they thought he had no money — he does not have to reimburse the taxpayers for their increased burden. For the loafer's exemption has been a direct gift from Heaven rather than the result of his fellow residents' intervention on his behalf (see *Rashbam*; *Rabbeinu Gershom*).

19. [This discussion had been interrupted on 54b.]

20. As stated on 53a-b, Rav Assi taught in the name of R' Yochanan that a boundary divider partitions a deceased convert's ownerless property, so that an act of acquisition performed on one side of the boundary does not effect acquisition of the property that is on the other side of the boundary. Here, Rav Assi adds that in regard to this law, even the *chatzav* plant serves to partition the property. The *chatzav* plant is either a shrub or an herb whose roots extend directly downward without veering to the side, and which was used by Joshua to demarcate property boundaries when the Jews took possession of Eretz Yisrael (*Rashbam*; see below, 56a).

21. *Pe'ah,* literally: *corner,* is the portion of the crop that the Torah requires be left for the poor. It is left standing in the field for the poor to harvest themselves (see *Leviticus* 19:9-10; 23:22).

22. The Gemara will explain these cases shortly.

ליעבד לי מר כאידך דשמואל דאמר שמואל לא קנה אלא מקום מכושו בלבד א"ל בהאי אנא א) כשמעתין סבירא לי דאמר רב הונא אמר רב כיון שניכש בה מכוש אחד קנה כולה שלח רב הונא בר אבין ישראל שלקח שדה מעובד כוכבים ובא ישראל אחר והחזיק בה אין מוציאים אותה מידו וכן היה ר' אבין ור' אילעא וכל רבותינו שוין בדבר אמר ב) רבה הני תלת מילי אישתעי לי עוקבן בר נחמיה ריש גלותא משמיה דשמואל ג) דינא דמלכותא דינא ד) ואריסותא דפרסאי עד מ' שנין א והני זהרורי דזבין ארעא לטסקא זבינהו זביני וה"מ לטסקא ב אבל לכרגא לא מ"ט כרגא אקרקף דגברי מנח רב הונא בריה דרב יהושע אמר אפילו שערי דכדא משתעבדי לכרגא אמר רב אשי אמר לי הונא בר נתן קשי בה אמימר ג א"כ בטלת ירושת בנו הבכור דהוה ליה ראוי ה) ואין הבכור נוטל בראוי כבמוחזק א"ל אי הכי אפילו טסקא נמי אלא מה אית לך למימר דיהיב טסקא ומית הכא נמי דיהיב כרגא ומית אמר רב אשי אמר לי הונא בר נתן שאילתינהו לספרי דרבא ואמרו לי הלכתא כרב הונא בריה דרב יהושע ולא היא התם לאוקומי מילתיה הוא דאמר ואמר רב אשי ד פרדכת מסייע מתא וה"מ דאצילתיה מתא ה אבל אנדיסקי סיעתא דשמיא היא אמר רב אסי א"ר יוחנן ו) המצר והחצב מפסיקין בנכסי הגר ז אבל לענין פאה וטומאה לא כי אתא רבין אמר רבי יוחנן אפילו לפאה וטומאה פאה מאי היא דתנן ח ז) ואלו מפסיקין לפאה הנחל והשלולית ודרך

ליעבד לי מר כאידך דשמואל. כיון דכשמואל סבירא לך ולא ליקני אלא הסוה פורתא דרפק והא לא מצי למימר ליעבד לי מר כאידך דשמואל דאמר דינא דמלכותא דינא ולא ליקני אלא בשטר דכיון דמודי רב הונא דשמואל אמרה להיות לנכסי הגר הרי הן כמדבר על כרחך זקוק אתה לתרך דלא תקשי שמואל אדשמואל ולכדפרישית לעיל: **אין מוציאין כו'.** כשמואל: וכן היו רבותינו כו'. כל זה שלח רב הונא בר אבין: **דינא דמלכותא דינא.** בהגוזל (א) קמא (ב"ק דף קיג:) אמר תדע דקטלי דיקלי וגשרי גשרי ועברינן עלייהו: **דאריסא דפרסאי ארבעין שנין.** חזקת פרסיים מ' שנים היא ע"י דינא דמלכותא דלאע"ג דלא קני אינים אלא בשטר מיהו אם החזיק בה עכו"ם מ' שנים ובא ישראל וקנה ממנו הוי קנין גמור ולא יוכל ישראל אחר לומר שלי היא שגזלה עכו"ם ממני ואע"ג דאמרינן (לעיל דף לה:) ישראל הבא מחמת העכו"ם הרי הוא כעכו"ם ואין לו חזקה אלא בההוא שטרא שמכרה ישראל לעכו"ם הכא יש לו חזקה. אי נמי אתא לאשמועינן דאע"ג דבשאר מקומות הויא חזקה לישראל בג' שנים האכא פרס אינה חזקה בפחות ממ' שנים לדינא דמלכותא הוא שם כן: **הני זהרורי.** בעלי נחלות העשירים קונים מעבדי המלך שדות עני העיר שאין יכולין ליתן הטסקא למלך והן פורעין את המס ומחזיקין בקרקעות בשביל המס שכן דינא למלכותא דמאן דיהיב טסקא ליכול ארעא כדאמר לעיל: **זבינייהו זביני.** מה שקונין הקרקע מעבדי המלך בשביל המס שנותנים מכרן קיים דדינא למלכותא דינא ואם לא יחזרו בעלים ראשונים או יתעשרו ויאמרו להחזיר המס להני זהרורי לא יוכלו לערער על הני זהרורי כלל דזבינייהו זביני: **זהרורי.** על שם נחלה שקרוי זיהרא לקמן בפרק המוכר את הבית (דף סא:) ולי א"ל זיהרא אפילו בוסתני ופרדסי והילך תלת מילי קמייתא דינא דמלכותא דינא ודאריסא דפרסאי והני זהרורי שתלויין בדינא דמלכותא דינא הרי תלת: **והני מילי.** דזבינייהו זביני אי זבין לטסקא בשביל מס הקרקע שלא נתנו הבעלים: **אבל לכרגא.** בשביל כסף גולגלתא שלא פרעו מכרו להם עבדי המלך קרקעותיו של זה לא הוו זביני דאין זה דינא דמלכותא לגבות הקרקע בשביל מס הראש כי אם בשביל מס הקרקע: **אקרקפתא דגברא מנח.** או יתפסוהו עד שיתן מאליו או יברח מן העיר והך מלתא גמרא קאמר ליה: **אפי' שערי דכדא.** שכבר נתלשו מן הקרקע ומונחין בכדו וכל שכן קרקע עצמה ולא שנא זבין ארעא לטסקא או לכרגא זבינייהו זביני דהכי הוי דינא למלכותא: **שערי דכדא.** כלומר כל מטלטלין שיש לו בעולם משועבדין למלך בשביל מס ראשו והיכא דלא פרע נתחייב כל אשר לו ומי שיקנה מעבדי המלך בין קרקעות בין מטלטלין זבינייהו זביני: **אם כן.** דאפילו שערי דכדא משתעבדי לכרגא היכי יתקיים הכתוב דכתיב (דברים כא) בכל אשר ימצא לו הרי באותה המלכות בטלת ירושת בנו הבכור דכל ממון האב אם מת ולא פרע עדיין כרגא דשנה זו הוה ליה ממונו ראוי דאינו מוחזק בו כלל כי אם המלך דשעבוד המלך עדיף משאר שעבודין וגבוי דמי ומיהו לאו אתקפתא מעלייתא היא דאיכא למימר אין הכי נמי תבטל ותבטל לשם ובשאר מקומות יתקיים דשבקיה לקרא דאיהו דחיק ומוקי אנפשיה: **אי הכי אפי' טסקא נמי.** רב אשי הוא דקפריך עליה דאמימר הכי דכיון דקשיא ליה לאמימר הכי אפילו כי אמרינן דארעא לטסקא משתעבדא לדברי הכל א"כ בטלת ירושת בנו הבכור: **אלא מאי אית לך למימר.** היכי דמי דלא תבטל כגון דיהיב טסקא של אותה שנה בתחלת השנה ומית קודם סוף השנה דאין משועבדת למלך עוד והוה ליה מוחזק ויטול בה בכור פי שנים ה"נ וכו': **ולא היא** (ב) **התם.** לית הלכתא כרב הונא בריה דרב יהושע דלא הוו מטלטלין לכרגא ולא זבין לא הוו זבינייהו זביני דכרגא אקרקפתא דגברא מנח ואינהו ספרי דרבא דאמרי הלכתא כרב הונא לאוקומי מלתיהו בעו לקיים מעשיהם ושטרות שכתבו על מכירת קרקעות שנמכרו לכרגא ובאו לומר דמשתעבדי לכרגא כדי שיהו המכירות והשטרות קיימין ותיהוי שלא כדין נכתבו השטרות ונמכרו הקרקעות והדרי זביני: **פרדכת.** אדם בטל ממלאכה ומלמוד ומדרך ארץ ואין עוסק בישובו של עולם כלל: **מסייע מתא.** הוא חייב בעול הקהל ואף על פי שהוא אינו עושה ריוח בעיר: **והני מילי.** דמסייע ליתן במס הקהל: **כגון דאצילתיה מתא.** עבדי המלך היו תובעים לו לבדו והם הצילוהו והקלו במשאו בטענותם שאמרו עליו שאין לו ממון ומתוך כך נתרבה מס שלהן והכביד עולן יותר כגון שהמלך רגיל ליקח מכולן מס קצוב לשנה ובאו לתבוע לכל אחד כפי אומד דעתם עד שיעלה גיבויים לחשבון מס הקצוב והיו שואלין לזה יותר מדאי והם הפלוהו ופטרוהו ומה שפחתו מזה יגבו מן השאר: **אבל אנדיסקי.** ממונין של מלך הרגילין לגבות מכל בית ובית מכל איש ואיש עד שיעלה החשבון למס הקצוב ושכחוהו לזה או לא רצו לשאול לו כלום בשביל שהוא אדם בטל וסבורין היו שאין לו ממון וגבו כל המס מכל השאר אף על פי שהכביד עליהם המס כדי שהיה לו לזה ליתן פטור דסייעתא דשמיא הוא שמחלו לו: **המצר והחצב כו'.** ב' שדות של גר ומצר אחד ביניהן החזיק באחת מהן לא קנה את חבירתה אלא ההיא דאחזיק ביה לבדו קנה כדאמר רבי יוסי בר חנינא לעיל בשמעתא ז) והוא הדין אם אין שם מצר אבל יש חצב נטוע ביניהם מפסיק: **חצב.** הוא אילן או עשב שבו תיחם יהושע את ארץ ישראל לפי שיורד ויונק לא מכאן ולא מכאן כדאמר (ביצה דף כה:) חצובא מקטע רגליהון דרשעים שמשיגין גבול רעיהן וזה אינו משיג גבול אחר: **אבל לענין פאה או טומאה לא.** הוי הפסק לחשבן ב' שדות אלא יניח פאה אחת על שניהם הואיל וסמוכין זה לזה דמן התורה אין מצר מפליג קרקע המחוברת לחייבה שתי פאות ומיהו לגבי חזקה די לנו אם יקנה במכוש אחד שדה אחת דהא אפילו בשדה אחת איכא למ"ד לא קנה אלא מקום מכושו וכל שכן בשתי שדות לדברי הכל דלא קנה אלא מה שהחזיק וסברא בעלמא הוא דחזקה מעלייתא בעינן שיחזיק בכל השדות: **פאה וטומאה.** לקמיה מפרש מאי נפקא מינה בין שדה אחת לשתים: **אפי' לפאה ולטומאה.** דמאי שנא מחזקה: **פאה מאי היא.** לגבי מאי מהני הפסק: **דתנן.** דהפסק מחייב להניח פאה בכל אחת: **הנחל.** (ג) כנחל איתן אשר לא יעבד בו ולא יזרע קרקע קשה מלא צרורות ואבנים שאין ראוי לזריעה: **והשלולית.** קבוצת מי גשמים בהכונס לאן לדיר (ב"ק דף סא.) מאי שלולית אמר רב יהודה אמר שמואל מקום (ד) ששוללין מי גשמים שם רב ביבי א"ר יוחנן אמת המים המחלקת שלל לאגפיה:
דרך

אם כן בטלת ירושת בנו. דבשלמא מכל אדם שיש עליו כתובת אשה ובעל חוב אף על פי שנכסים משועבדין להן מ"מ אין ירושת בני הבכור בטילה משום דמלוה ואשה מחסרי גוביינא וצריכי אדרכתא ואכרזתא ושומא אבל למס המלך אפילו קרקע שוה אלף זוז משועבדת לדבר מועט והקרקעות עיקר הן של המלך וכבר הוא מוחזק ולא מחסרי גוביינא. ר"י ור"ת: **אנדיסקי.** פי' כותבי שטרות המלך דדיסקא הוא שטר כדאמר בהגוזל בתרא (ב"ק דף קיז:) האי מאן דנקיט דיסקא מב"ד הגדול ובפרק השולח (גיטין דף לו.) מעיקרא במאי אפקינהו בדיסקי:
דרך

עין משפט נר מצוה

רמה א ב מיי' פ"ה מהל' גזלה הל' יד סמג עשין עג טוש"ע ח"מ סי' שסט סעיף ט:
רמו ג טוש"ע ח"מ סי' רעה סעיף כג:
רמז ד ה טוש"ע ח"מ סי' קסג סעיף ג ועי"ש כל דיני המסים:
רמח ו מיי' פ"א מהל' זכיה ומתנה הל' י סמג עשין פב טוש"ע ח"מ סי' ערה סעיף ד:
רמט ז ח מיי' פ"ג מהל' מתנות עניים הלכה ג:

רבינו גרשום

באריסותא דפרסאי. דחזקה של פרסיים לא הויא חזקה אא"כ החזיק ארבעין שנין: **הני זיהרורי.** בעלי נחלות: **דזבין ארעא לטסקא.** שקנו שדה של אדם שנטלוה ממנו מחמת שהבריח מס שלה: **זביניה זביני.** משום דדינא דמלכותא דינא דאמר דמאן דיהיב טסקא ליכול ארעא. **אבל** שדהו של אדם שנטלוה ממנו בשביל שלא נתן **כרגא.** מס גולגלתו אינן רשאין לקנות משום **דכרגא אקרקף גברי מנח.** כלומר ראש האיש עצמו משתעבד לכרגא ולא שדהו דלא היה להם ליטול שדהו בשביל מס הכרגא: **אפי' שערי דכדא משעבד לכרגא.** וכ"ש שדהו. ואפי' מכרו שדהו מפני הברחת כרגא הויא מכורה: **א"כ בטלת ירושת בנו הבכור.** וא"כ הוא דכל נכסין משעבדי לכרגא אפי' שערי דכדא א"כ כל זמן דלא יהב כרגא אינן מוחזקין נכסיו בידו וא"כ לא יירש מהן הבכור פי שנים משום **דאין הבכור נוטל בראוי כבמוחזק: אי הכי אפי' טסקא נמי.** אם מת ולא יהב טסקא אינה מוחזקת הקרקע בידו א"כ אין הבכור נוטל פי שנים בה: **אלא דיהב טסקא ומית בו ביום.** בההוא יומא מצי שקיל פי שנים דמההוא שעתא דיהב טסקא וכרגא הוחזקו בידו: **ואמרו לי הלכתא כרב הונא בריה דרב יהושע.** דאמר אפי' שערי דכדא משעבד לכרגא: **ולא היא.** אין הלכה כרב הונא בריה דרב יהושע. והאי דקאמרי ספרי דהלכה כוותיה לאוקמי מלתא הוא דבעי. כלומר להחזיק דבריהן לפי שהן רגילין לכתוב שטרי מכירה לאותן הלוקחין מן המוכסין דגבו ארעא לכרגא ומש"ה אמרו הלכה כוותיה כדי לקיים שטרי כתיבתן להרבות שכרן ולעולם אמרי' אין הלכה כרב הונא: **פרדכת מסייעא מתא.** אדם בטל דלית ליה שדות ולא עסק בהן ואין מתעסק בשום דבר אלא בבטלנות היינו פרדכת. **מסייעא מתא.** שצריך לו לאותו פרדכת ליתן חלקו בעול העיר לשעבוד שר העיר: **וה"מ.** דצריך ליתן חלק: **דאצילתיה מתא.** שהצילוהו בני העיר בדבריהם מיד השר שאמרו לשר אין לזה כלום ליתן לך ושמע להן והניחו על פיהן וניצל על פיהן. חייב לסייעם: **אבל אנדיסקי.** היינו שר העיר שאמר מעצמו נותן לו לאותו פרדכת שאמר איני חושש ליקח מזה כלום **סייעתא דשמיא הוא** דרחמי עליה ואינו צריך ליתן עמהם לסייעם: **המצר.** זהו חריץ או גדר העשוי סביב השדה להיכרא בין שדות אחרות: **והחצב.** שם אילן שאין שרשיו הולכין לכאן ולכאן אלא במקום שנוטעין אותו יורדין עד התהום ומש"ה נוטעין אותן על הגבולין בין שדה לחבירתה לפסוק. ומש"ה אמר **מפסיקין בנכסי הגר** [שאם הי'] באחת משדות הגר מופסקת בין כל אחת במצר או בחצב לא קנה אלא אחת או עד מקום המצר או עד מקום החצב: **אבל לפאה ולטומאה לא.** אין מפסיקין. כיצד לפאה שאם היה מצר או חצב בשדה אינו מפסיק שיהא צריך להניח שתי פאות משום אותו הפסק אלא יקצור כל השדה ויניח פאה אחת על כולו ולטומאה נמי אינו הפסק. כיצד כדמפרש לקמן הלכתי למקום הלז בשדה זו והטומאה היתה ממצר להלן או מחצב להלן ואמר איני יודע אם נכנסתי למקום הטומאה מעבר למצר או לחצב אמרי' דספיקו טמא דלא הוי הפסק האי מצר וחצב: **אפי' לפאה ולטומאה.** הוי הפסק האי מצר וחצב כדתנן אלו מפסיקין לפאה א) ולשדי' דצריך להניח שתי פאות דכשתי שדות דמי: **שלולית.** כעין אמת המים ומקום שמי גשמים שוללין שם:

חשק שלמה על רבינו גרשום א) נראה דצ"ל לשני שדות.

מסורת הש"ס

א) [ע"ל כשמעתיך יעב"ן], ב) [גי' רי"ף ורא"ש רבא], ג) [לעיל נד: וש"נ], ד) [ע"ל ארישן], ה) [עי' תוס' חזקה דפרסאי בלא שטר מ' שנין. ערוך ערך ארס א'], ו) [לקמן קיט. קכב. בכורות נא:], ו) ב"ק קיג. [מגלה פ"ב מ"א] מנחות עא., ז) [לעיל נג: ע"ש הגי' רב אסי א"ר יוחנן]

הגהות הב"ח

(א) רשב"ם ד"ה דינא וכו' בהגוזל בתרא אמר רבא תדע: (ב) ד"ה ולא היא ליה כצ"ל ותיבת התם נמחק: (ג) ד"ה הנחל כגון נחל איתן: (ד) ד"ה והשלולית וכו' מקום שמי גשמים שוללין שם וכו' המחלקת שלל לאגפיה:

ליקוטי רש"י

לא קנה אלא מקום מכושו בלבד. דוקא קנה הגר אבל מכר וקבל וזכי אפילו עשר שדות בעשר מדינות והחזיק באחת מהן קנה כולן כדאמר בפרק קמא דקידושין (כו.) וכדפרישית לעיל (נג.). **מכוש אחד.** הכא אתא בקרקע קנה כולה דסיימו רפק בה מכוש וכגון קרקע שעומד לחרישה אבל בנין לא הוי חזקה וכו' ע"ש נכסי הגר קנה כולה. וכהן פלוגתא הלכתא כרב דהא ר"ג עבד עובדא כוותיה דרב. [רשב"ם לעיל נד.]. **דינא דמלכותא.** של עובדי כוכבים [גיטין י:]. **כרגא.** כסף גולגלתא שהיו היהודים כל אחד נותן כסף גולגלתו למלך. **ואין הבכור נוטל בראוי כבמוחזק.** חלק בכורה בנחלה הבאה ליורשים לאחר מיתת אביהן אלא במה שמוחזק ביד אביהן ביום מותו דכתיב בכל אשר ימצא לו (דברים כא) [יבמות כה:]. בנכסים שלא היה אביהן מוחזק בשעת מיתתו אבל כלווין היו לו ביד אחרים ונפלו להן לאחר זמן אין הבכור נוטל פי שנים [בכורות נא:]. **והחצב.** עשב ששרשיו נוקבין ויורדין בעומק ואין מתפשטין לצדדין כלל ונוטעין אותו בין גבולי שדות ובו תיחם יהושע לישראל את הארץ [ביצה כה:]. עשב שמשרש בעומק כנגדו ואין שרשיו מתפשטין ובו תיחם יהושע את הארץ לישראל [שבת קכח.]. **ואלו מפסיקין לפאה.** לתת שתי פאות [ב"ק סא.]. שדה מכאן ושדה מכאן ונחל עמוק באמצע חייב להניח פאה מכל אחד ואחד [ב"ק שם]. **והשלולית.** מקום שמי גשמים שוללין שם ואם יש שם זריעה מכאן ומכאן נותן פאה לכל אחד ואחד דהויא שלולית מפסקא להו [מנחות שם]. **שוללין.** מתקבצין כמו מן השלל של ביליס (ביצה ז.) דבר אחר לשון שלל ומלקוט (במדבר לא) דבר המקובץ [ב"ק שם].

A conflicting report of R' Yochanan's view:
כִּי אֲתָא רָבִין אָמַר רַבִּי יוֹחָנָן – **When Ravin came** to Babylonia from Eretz Yisrael, where he had studied under R' Yochanan, **he said in the name of R' Yochanan:** אֲפִילוּ לְפֵאָה וְטוּמְאָה – They divide a field **even in regard to *pe'ah* and *tumah*.**

The Gemara explains:
פֵּאָה מַאי הִיא – **What is** the case of ***pe'ah*** to which a boundary divider in the field has relevance? דִּתְנַן וְאֵלוּ מַפְסִיקִין לְפֵאָה – It is **that** which **we learned in a Mishnah:**[23] THE FOLLOWING DIVIDE a field FOR *PE'AH*:[24] הַנַּחַל – A RAVINE,[25] וְהַשְּׁלוּלִית – A WATER-FILLED DITCH,[26]

NOTES

23. *Pe'ah* 2:1.

24. The law is that a separate *pe'ah* must be left for each field. This Mishnah enumerates the separations that serve to partition an otherwise continuous expanse of land into distinct fields, each requiring its own area of *pe'ah*.

25. I.e. a rocky, untillable strip of land (*Rashbam*). [Alternatively, נַחַל means *a river* (see *Rav* to *Pe'ah* ad loc.; see also *Tos. R' Akiva* there.]

26. There is a dispute in *Bava Kamma* (61a) whether this refers to a pond of rainwater or to a main irrigation canal that distributes water to the laterals that branch off into the fields (*Rashbam*).

ליעבד לי מר כאידך דשמואל דאמר שמואל לא קנה אלא מקום מכושו בלבד א"ל בהאי אנא כשמעתין סבירא לי דאמר רב הונא אמר רב כיון שניכש בה מכוש אחד קנה כולה שלח רב הונא בר אבין ישראל שלקח שדה מעובד כוכבים ובא ישראל אחר והחזיק בה אין מוציאים אותה מידו וכן היה ר' אבין ור' אילעא וכל רבותינו שוין בדבר אמר רבה הני תלת מילי אישתעי לי עוקבן בר נחמיה ריש גלותא משמיה דשמואל דינא דמלכותא דינא ואריסותא דפרסאי עד מ' שנין והני זהרורי דזבין ארעא לטסקא זבינהו זביני וה"מ לטסקא אבל לכרגא לא מ"ט כרגא אקרקף דגברי מנח רב הונא בריה דרב יהושע אמר אפילו שערי דכדא משתעבדי לכרגא אמר רב אשי אמר לי הונא בר נתן קשי בה אמימר א"כ בטלת ירושת בנו הבכור דהוה ליה ראוי ואין הבכור נוטל בראוי כבמוחזק א"ל אי הכי אפילו טסקא נמי אלא מה אית לך למימר דיהיב טסקא ומית הכא נמי דיהיב כרגא ומית אמר רב אשי אמר לי הונא בר נתן שאילתינהו לספרי דרבא ואמרו לי הלכתא כרב הונא בריה דרב יהושע ולא היא התם לאוקומי מילתיה הוא דאמר ואמר רב אשי פרדכת מסייע מתא וה"מ דאצילתיה מתא אבל אנדיסקי סיעתא דשמיא היא אמר רב אסי א"ר יוחנן המצר והחצב מפסיקין בנכסי הגר אבל לענין פאה וטומאה לא כי אתא רבין אמר רבי יוחנן אפילו לפאה וטומאה פאה מאי היא דתנן ואלו מפסיקין לפאה הנחל והשלולית ודרך

ליעבד לי מר כאידך דשמואל. כיון דכשמואל סבירא לך ולא ליקני אלא ההוא פורתא דרפק והא לא מצי למימר ליעבד לי מר כאידך דשמואל דאמר דינא דמלכותא דינא ולא ליקני אלא בשטר דכיון דמודי רב הונא דשמואל אמרה להאי דנכסי הגר הרי הן כמדבר על כרחך זקוק אתה לתרץ דלא תקשי שמואל אדשמואל וכדפרישית לעיל: אין מוציאין כו'. כשמואל: וכן היו רבותינו כו'. כל זה שלח רב הונא בר אבין: דינא דמלכותא דינא. בהגוזל (א) קמא (ב"ק דף קיג:) אמר תדע דקטלו דיקלי וגשרי גשרי ועברינן עלייהו: דאריסא דפרסאי ארבעין שנין. חזקת פרסיים מ' שנים היא ע"י דינא דמלכותא דאע"ג דלא קני אינים אלא בשטר מיהו אם החזיק בה עכו"ם מ' שנים ובא ישראל וקנה ממנו הוי קנין גמור ולא יוכל ישראל אחר לומר שלי היא שגזלה עכו"ם ממני ואע"ג דאמרינן (לעיל דף לה:) ישראל הבא מחמת העכו"ם הרי הוא כעכו"ם ואין לו חזקה אלא בההוא שטרא שמכרה ישראל לעכו"ם הכא יש לו חזקה. אי נמי אתא לאשמועינן דאע"ג דבשאר מקומות הויא חזקה לישראל בג' שנים בארץ פרס אינה חזקה בפחות ממ' שנים דדינא דמלכותא הוא שם כן: הני זהרורי. בעלי נחלות העשירים קונים מעבדי המלך שדות עניי העיר שאין יכולין ליתן הטסקא למלך והן פורעין את המס ומחזיקין בקרקעות בשביל המס שכן דינא דמלכותא דמאן דיהיב טסקא ליכול ארעא כדאמר לעיל: זביניהו זביני. מה שקונין הקרקע מעבדי המלך בשביל המס שנותנים מכרן קיים דדינא דמלכותא דינא ואם יחזרו בעלים ראשונים או יתעשרו ויאמרו להחזיר המס להני זהרורי לא יוכלו לערער על הני זהרורי כלל דזביניהו זביני: זהרורי. על שם נחלה שקרוי זיהרא לקמן בפרק המוכר את הבית (דף סח:) ואי א"ל זיהרא אפילו בוסתני ופרדסי והילך תלת מילי קמייתא דינא דמלכותא דינא ודאריסא דפרסאי והני זהרורי שתלויין בדינא דמלכותא דינא הרי תלת: והני מילי. דזביניהו זביני אי זבין לטסקא בשביל מס הקרקע שלא נתנו הבעלים: אבל לכרגא. בשביל כסף גולגלתא שלא פרעו מכרו להם עבדי המלך קרקעותיו של זה לא הוו זביני דאין זה דינא דמלכותא לגבות הקרקע בשביל מס הראש כי אם בשביל מס הקרקע: אקרקפתא דגברא מנח. או יתפשוהו עד שיתן מאליו או יברח מן העיר והך מלתא גמרא קאמר ליה: אפי' שערי דכדא. שכבר נתלשו מן הקרקע ומונחין בכדו וכל שכן קרקע עצמה ולא שנא זבין ארעא לטסקא או לכרגא זביניהו זביני דהכי הוי דינא דמלכותא: שערי דכדא. כלומר כל מטלטלין שיש לו בעולם משועבדין למלך בשביל מס ראשו והיכא דלא פרע נתחייב כל אשר לו ומי שיקנה מעבדי המלך בין קרקעות בין מטלטלין זביניהו זביני: אם כן. דאפילו שערי דכדא משתעבדי לכרגא היכי מתקיים הכתוב דכתיב (דברים כא) בכל אשר ימצא לו הרי באותה המלכות בטלת ירושת בנו הבכור דכל ממון האב אם מת ולא פרע עדיין כרגא דשנה זו הוה ליה ממונו ראוי דאינו מוחזק בו כלל כי אם המלך דשעבוד המלך עדיף משאר שעבודין וכגבוי דמי ומיהו לאו אתקפתא מעלייתא היא דאיכא למימר אין הכי נמי תבטל ותבטל לשם ובשאר מקומות יתקיים דשבקיה לקרא דאיהו דחיק ומוקי אנפשיה: אי הכי אפי' טסקא נמי. רב אשי הוא דקפריך עליה דאמימר הכי דכיון דקשיא ליה לאמימר הכי אפילו כי אמרינן ארעא לטסקא אשתעבדא לדברי הכל א"כ בטלת בקרקעות ירושת בנו הבכור: אלא מאי אית לך למימר. היכי דמי דלא תבטל כגון דיהיב טסקא של אותה שנה בתחלת השנה ומית דעד סוף השנה אינה משועבדת למלך עוד והוה ליה מוחזק ויטול בה בכור פי שנים ה"נ וכו': ולא היא (ב) התם. לית הלכתא כרב הונא בריה דרב יהושע דלא משתעבדי לא קרקעות ולא מטלטלין לכרגא ואי זבון לכרגא לא הוו זביניהו זביני דכרגא אקרקפתא דגברא מנח ואינהו ספרי דרבא דאמרי הלכתא כרב הונא לאוקומי מלתייהו בעו לקיים מעשיהם ושטרות שכתבו על מכירת קרקעות שנמכרו לכרגא ובאו לומר דמשתעבדי לכרגא כדי שיהו המכירות והשטרות קיימין ומיהו שלא כדין נכתבו השטרות ונמכרו הקרקעות והדרי זביני: פרדכת. אדם בטל ממלאכה ומלמוד ומדלך ארץ ואין עוסק בישובו של עולם כלל: מסייע מתא. הוא חייב בעול הקהל ואף על פי שהוא אינו עושה ריוח בעיר: והני מילי. דמסייע ליתן במס הקהל: כגון דאצילתיה מתא. עבדי המלך היו תובעים לו לבדו והם הצילוהו והקלו במשאו בטענותם שאמרו עליו שאין לו ממון ומתוך כך נתרצה מס שלהן והכביד עולן יותר כגון שהמלך רגיל ליקח מכולן מס קצוב לשנה ובאו לתבוע לכל אחד כפי אומד דעתם עד שיעלה גיבויים לחשבון מס הקצוב והיו שואלין לזה יותר מדאי והם הפלוהו ופטרוהו ומה שפחתו מזה יגבו מן השאר: אבל אנדיסקי. ממונין של מלך הרגילין לגבות מכל בית ובית מכל איש ואיש עד שיעלה החשבון למס הקצוב ושכחוהו לזה או לא רצו לשאול לו כלום בשביל שהוא אדם בטל וסבורין היו שאין לו ממון וגבו כל המס מכל השאר אף על פי שהכביד עליהם המס כדי שיהיה לו לזה ליתן פטור דסייעתא דשמיא הוא שמחלו לו: המצר והחצב כו'. ב' שדות של גר ומצר אחד ביניהן החזיק באחת מהן לא קנה את חבירתה אלא האי דאחזיק ביה לבדו קנה כדאמר רבי יוסי בר חנינא לעיל בשמעתא והוא הדין אם אין שם מצר אבל יש חצב נטוע ביניהם מפסיק: חצב. הוא אילן או עשב שבו תיחם יהושע את ארץ ישראל לפי שיורד ויונק כנגדו ואינו יונק לא מכאן ולא מכאן כדאמר (ביצה דף כה:) חצובא מקטע רגליהון דרשעים שמשיגין גבול רעיהן וזה אינו משיג גבול אחר: אבל לענין פאה או טומאה לא. הוי הפסק לחשבן ב' שדות אלא יניח פאה אחת על שניהם הואיל וסמוכין זה לזה דמן התורה אין מצר מפליג קרקע המחוברת לחייבה שתי פאות ומיהו לגבי חזקה די לנו אם יקנה במכוש אחד שדה אחת דהא אפילו בשדה אחת איכא למ"ד לא קנה אלא מקום מכושו וכל שכן בשתי שדות לדברי הכל דלא קנה אלא מה שהחזיק וסברא בעלמא הוא דחזקה מעלייתא בעינן שיחזיק בכל השדות: פאה וטומאה. לקמיה מפרש מאי נפקא מינה בין שדה אחת לשתים: אפי' לפאה ולטומאה. דמאי שנא מחזקה: פאה מאי היא. לגבי מאי מהני הפסק: דתנן. להפסק מחייב להניח פאה בכל אחת: הנחל. (ג) כנחל איתן אשר לא יעבד בו ולא יזרע קרקע קשה מלא צרורות ואבנים שאין ראוי לזריעה: והשלולית. קבוצת מי גשמים בהכוש שאין לדיר (ב"ק דף סא.) מאי שלולית אמר רב יהודה אמר שמואל מקום (ד) ששוללין מי גשמים שם רב ביבי א"ר יוחנן אמת המים המחלקת שלא לאנפיה:

דרך

אם כן בטלת ירושת בנו. דבשלמא מכל אדם שיש עליו כתובת אשה ובעל חוב אף על פי שנכסים משועבדין להן מ"מ אין ירושת בני הבכור בטילה משום דמלוה ואשה מחסרי גוביינא וצריכי אדרכתא ואכרזתא ושומא אבל למס המלך אפילו קרקע שוה אלף זוז משועבדת לדבר מועט והקרקעות עיקר הן של המלך וכבר הוא מוחזק ולא מחסרי גוביינא. ר"י ור"ת: אנדיסקי. פי' כותבי שטרות המלך דדיסקא הוא שטר כדאמר בהגוזל בתרא (ב"ק דף קיז:) האי מאן דנקיט דיסקא מב"ד הגדול ובפרק השולח (גיטין דף לו.) מעיקרא במאי אפקינהו בדיסקי:

דרך

עין משפט נר מצוה

רמה א ב מיי' פ"ח מהל' גזילה הל' יח סמג עשין עג טוש"ע ח"מ סי' שסט סעיף ט:

רמו ג טוש"ע ח"מ סי' רעה סעיף י בהגה"ה:

רמז ד ה טוש"ע ח"מ סי' קסג סעיף ג וע"ש כל דיני המסים:

רמח ו מיי' פ"א מהל' זכיה ומתנה הל' י סמג עשין פב טוש"ע ח"מ סי' רעה סעיף ד:

רמט ז ח מיי' פ"ג מהל' מתנות עניים הלכה ג:

רבינו גרשום

בארישתא דפרסאי. דחזקה של פרסיים לא הויא חזקה אא"כ החזיק ארבעין שנין: הני זיהרורי. בעלי נחלות: דזבין ארעא לטסקא. שקנו שדה של אדם שנטלוה ממנו מחמת שהבריחה מס שלה: זביניה זביני. משום דדינא דמלכותא דינא דאמר דמאן דיהיב טסקא ליכול ארעא. אבל שדהו של אדם שנטלוה ממנו בשביל שלא נתן כרגא. מס גולגלתו אינן רשאין לקנות משום דכרגא אקרקף גברי מנח. כלומר ראש האיש עצמו משתעבד לכרגא ולא שדהו דלא היה להם ליטול שדהו בשביל מס הכרגא: אפי' שערי דכדא משעבד לכרגא. וכ"ש שדהו. ואפי' מכרו שדהו מפני הברחת כרגא הויא מכורה: א"כ בטלת ירושת בנו הבכור. וא"כ הוא דהכל נכסין משעבדי לכרגא אפי' שערי דכדא א"כ כל זמן דלא יהב כרגא אינן מוחזקין בנכסיו בידו וא"כ לא יירש מהן הבכור פי שנים משום דאין הבכור נוטל בראוי כבמוחזק: אי הכי אפי' טסקא נמי. אם מת ולא יהב טסקא אינה מוחזקת הקרקע בידו וא"כ אין הבכור נוטל פי שנים בה: אלא דיהיב טסקא ומית ביו ביום. בההוא יומא מצי שקיל פי שנים דמההוא שעתא דיהיב טסקא וכרגא הוחזק בידו: ואמרו לי הלכתא כרב הונא בריה דרב יהושע. דאמר אפי' שערי דכדא משעבד לכרגא: ולא היא. אין הלכה כרב הונא בריה דרב יהושע. והאי דקאמרי ספרי דהלכ' כוותיה לאוקומי מלתא הוא דבעי. כלומר להחזיק דבריהן לפי שהן רגילין לכתוב שטרי מכירה לאותן הלוקחין מן המוכסין דבגו ארעא לכרגא ומשו"ה אמרו הלכה כוותיה כדי לקיים שטרי כתיבתן להרבות שכרן ולעולם אמרי' אין הלכה כרב הונא: פרדכת מסייעא מתא. אדם בטל דלית ליה שדות לעסוק בהן ואין מתעסק בשום דבר אלא בבטלנות היינו פרדכת. מסייעא מתא. שצריך לו לאותו פרדכת ליתן חלקו בעול בני העיר לשעבוד שר העיר: וה"מ. דצריך ליתן חלק: דאצילתיה מתא. שהצילוהו בני העיר בדבריהם מיד השר שאמרו לשר שאין לזה כלום ליתן לך ושמע להן והניחו על פיהן וניצל על פיהן: חייב לסייעם: אבל אנדיסקי. היינו שר העיר מעצמו נותן לו לאותו פרדכת שאמר איני חושש ליקח מזה כלום סייעתא דשמיא הוא דרחמי עליה ואינו צריך ליתן עמהם לסייעם: המצר. זהו חריץ או גדר העשוי סביב השדה להיכרא בין שדה לשדה אחרות: והחצב. שם אילן ואין נוטע שרשיו לכאן ולכאן אלא במקום שנוטעין אותו יורדין עד התהום ומש"ה נוטעין אותן על הגבולין בין שדה לחבירתה להפסק. ומש"ה אמר מפסיקין בנכסי הגר [שאם הי'] באחת משדות הגר מופסקת בין כל אחת מצר או חצב לא קנה אלא עד מקום המצר או עד מקום החצב: אבל לפאה ולטומאה לא. אין מפסיקין. כיצד לפאה שאם היה מצר או חצב בשדה אינו מפסיק שיהא צריך להניח שתי פאות משום אותו הפסק אלא יקצור כל השדה ויניח פאה אחת על כולו וטומאה נמי אינו הפסק. כיצד כדמפרש לקמן הלכתי למקום הלז בשדה זו והטומאה היתה מקום להלן או מכאן ואמר איני יודע אם נכנסתי למקום הטומאה מעבר המצר או לא דספיקו טמא דלא הוי הפסק לטומאה האי מצר וחצב: אפי' לפאה ולטומאה. הוי הפסק האי מצר וחצב דלשדה דצריך להניח שתי פאות (א) דכשתי שדות דמי ובספק טומאה אמרינן דלא נכנס: שלולית. כעין אמת המים ומקום שמי גשמים שוללין שם:

חשק שלמה על רבינו גרשום (א) נראה דצ"ל לשתי שדות.

מסורת הש"ס

א) [צ"ל כשמעתיך יעב"ץ], ב) [גי' ר"ח ורא"ש רבא], ג) [לעיל נד: וש"נ], ד) [צ"ל ארישן פי' חזקה דפרסאי בלא שטר מ' שנין. ערוך ערך אריש א'], ה) [לקמן קיט. קכג: בכורות נא:], ו) ב"ק פא. [פאה פ"ב מ"א] מנחות עא:, ז) [לעיל נג: ע"ש גי' רב אסי א"ר יוחנן].

הגהות הב"ח

(א) רשב"ם ד"ה דינא וכו' בהגוזל בתרא אמר רבא תדע: (ב) ד"ה ולא היא ליה כל"ל ותיבת התם נמחק: (ג) ד"ה הנחל כגון נחל איתן: (ד) ד"ה והשלולית וכו' מקום שמי גשמים שוללין שם וכו' אמת המים המחלקת שלא לאנפיה:

ליקוטי רש"י

לא קנה אלא מקום מכושו בלבד. ודוקא נכסי הגר אבל מכר וקבל זוזי אפילו עשר שדות בעשר מדינות והחזיק באחת מהן קנה כולן כדאמר שמואל בפרקין קמא [ב"ק יב.] וקידושין (כז:) וכדפרישית לעיל [נג:]. מכוש אחד. הכאה אחת בקרקע קנה כולה דסייעיה רפק בה פורתא וכגון קרקע שעומד לחרישה אבל בנין לא הוי חזקה [לעיל נד.]. ול"ש נכסי הגר ול"ש מכר קנה כולה. ובהא פלוגתא הלכתא כרב דהא ר"י עבד עובדא כוותיה דרב [רשב"ם לעיל נד.]. דינא דמלכותא. של עובדי כוכבים [גיטין י:]. כרגא. כסף גולגלתא שהיו כל היהודים כל אחד נותן למלך כסף גולגלתו [ב"מ עג:]. ואין הבכור נוטל בראוי כבמוחזק. חלק בכורה בנכסים הראויים לבא לאב אחר מיתת אביהן אלא במה שמוחזק ביד אביהן ביום מותו דכתיב בכל אשר ימצא לו [דברים כא] [יבמות כו:]. נכסים שלא היה אביהן מוחזק בשעת מיתתו אלא שראוים היו ליפול לו בירושה ונפלו להן לאחר זמן אין הבכור נוטל פי שנים [בכורות נא:]. והחצב. עשב שרשיו נוקבין ויורדין בעומק ואין מתפשט לצדדין כלל ונוטעין אותו בין גבולי שדות ובו תיחם יהושע לישראל את הארץ [ביצה כה:]. עשב שמשריש בעומק כנגדו ואין שרשיו מתפשטין ובו תיחם יהושע הארץ לישראל [שבת קכח.]. ואלו מפסיקין לפאה. להניח פאה מכל אחד ואחד [ב"ק סא.]. להניח שתי פאות [מנחות עא:]. הנחל. שדה מכאן ושדה מכאן ונחל עמוק באמצע חייב להניח פאה מכל אחד ואחד [ב"ק שם]. והשלולית. מקום שמי גשמים שוללים שם ואם יש שם זריעה מכאן ומכאן נותן פאה לכל אחד ואחד דהכא שלולית מפסקא להו [מנחות שם]. שוללין. מתקבצין כמו מן השלל כי ביזים (ביצה ז.) דבר אחר לשון שלל ומלקוח (במדבר לא) דבר המקובץ [ב"ק שם].

עין משפט נר מצוה

רנ א מיי' פ"ב מהל' שאר אבות הטומאה הלכה ט:

רנא ב מיי' פי"ח מהל' שבת הלכה כד:

ודרך הרבים ודרך היחיד ושביל הרבים ושביל היחיד הקבוע בין בימות החמה ובין בימות הגשמים טומאה מאי היא דתנן [א]הנכנס לבקעה בימות הגשמים וטומאה בשדה פלונית ואמר הלכתי למקום הלז ואיני יודע אם נכנסתי לאותו מקום ואם לאו ר"א מטהר וחכמים מטמאין [ב]שהיה ר"א אומר ספק ביאה טהור ספק מגע טומאה טמא אבל לשבת לא רבא אמר אפילו לענין שבת דתניא [ג]הוציא חצי גרוגרת לרשות הרבים והניחה וחזר והוציא חצי גרוגרת אחרת בהעלם אחד חייב בשני העלמות פטור רבי יוסי אומר [ב]בהעלם אחד ברשות

דרך הרבים. ט"ז אמה רוחב דרך היחיד (א) ד' אמות ולא זו אף זו קתני: שביל הרבים. שהולכין שם רבים ברגליהן אבל דרך הרבים מקום הילוך העגלות והסוסים וכולה לא זו אף זו קתני: הקבוע בין בימות החמה. ואפילו בימות הגשמים שאין רגילים להלך בבקעה מהלכין שם שאין חרישה וזריעה לשם: טומאה מאי היא. מאי הפסק שייך בשדה לענין טומאה: דתנן כו'. ואליבא דר"א הוא דשייך הפסק כדמפרש ואזיל: בימות הגשמים. הויא רה"י לטומאה וספיקה טמא שהרי אין מהלכין בה בני אדם שלא לקלקל הזריעה: הלכתי למקום הלז. נכנסתי בבקעה זו: וחכמים מטמאים. דסוף סוף מה לי שדה אחת מה לי ב' שדות חדא ספיקא היא שמא הלך עד הקבר והאהיל שמא לא הלך וספיקו טמא: ספק ביאה טהור. היכא דמספקא ליה אם נכנס באותה שדה ואם תמצא לומר נכנס ספק אם בא עד מקום (ב) טומאה אם לאו וספק ספיקא הוא וטהור אבל היכא דליכא אלא ספק מגע דפשיטא ליה דנכנס באותה שדה אלא שספק לו אם נגע בקבר אם לאו חדא ספיקא הוא וטמא והלכך לרבי אליעזר אי מפסיק מצר וחלק בינתים וטומאה באחת מהן ואין יודע באיזה מהן נכנס ספק ביאה הוא וטהור ואי ליכא מצר בינתים ספק מגע איכא ולא ספק ביאה דכולהו שדה אחת הן וטמא: וקדייק גמרא דלרבנן אמר רבי יוחנן דוקא פאה וטומאה אבל לשבת לא הוי הפסק אי מפסיק מצר וחלק בין שני רה"ר והוציא חצי גרוגרת בזה ואחר כך הוציא חצי גרוגרת בשני חייב דאפילו לרבי יוסי דפטר בשני רשויות (ג) דאין המצר מפסיקן לשני רשויות: במסכת שבת תנן המוציא אוכלין חייב בגרוגרת דשבת מלאכת מחשבת אסרה תורה ולא חשיבא הוצאת דבר (ד) חשוב בפחות מכגרוגרת: בהעלם אחד חייב. שלא נודע לו בינתים שהוא שבת דידיעה מחלקת: ברשות

דרך היחיד ודרך הרבים. (ה) בירושלמי פריך אמאי איצטריך למיתני דרך הרבים דכיון דתנא דדרך היחיד מפסיק כ"ש דרך הרבים ומשני משום סיפא נקטינן דקתני הכל מפסיק לזרעים ואין מפסיק לאילנות אלא גדר כו' וקמ"ל דאפילו דרך הרבים לא מפסיק לאילן ומפרש נמי אמאי תנא שביל הרבים כיון דתנא שביל היחיד מפסיק דמשום אילן לא צריך למיתנייה כיון דאשמועינן דאפי' דרך הרבים לא מפסיק לאילן כל שכן שביל הרבים אלא אתא לאשמועינן דשביל הרבים נמי בעינן שיהא קבוע בימות החמה ובימות הגשמים והשתא איצטריך למיתני כולהו שביל היחיד לאשמועינן דמפסיק לזרעים אע"ג דגריע מכולהו ודרך הרבים אשמועינן דלא מפסיק לאילן ודרך היחיד אשמועינן דלא בעינן קבוע ושביל הרבים אשמועינן דבעינן קבוע ואין להקשות דלא ליתני שביל הרבים ואנא ידענא דבעינן קבוע מדתנן דרך היחיד דאי לא בעי לא ליתני דרך היחיד אלא ליתני שביל הרבים דהוי רבותא טפי או איפכא דלא ליתני דרך היחיד ואנא ידענא דלא בעינן קבוע מדתנן שביל הרבים ולא תנא דרך היחיד דהוי רבותא טפי דהא אי לאו דתנא תרוייהו לא הוה ידענא הי מינייהו (ו) מפסיק טפי דרך היחיד רחב טפי ושביל הרבים בקעי ביה רבים: רבי אליעזר מטהר. רשב"ם פירש דפליגי דרבי אליעזר חשיב ליה ספק ספיקא ורבנן לא חשיבי ליה אלא ספיקא אחת ורש"י פירש בפרק בתרא דע"ז (דף ע. ושם) דאיירי בשדה מלאה טומאה ופליגי דר"א סבר אע"ג דליכא אלא חדא ספיקא כיון דליכא ספק מגע אלא ספק ביאה טהור והיינו טעמא דטומאה מסוטה גמרינן וגבי סוטה הוי ספק מגע ולא ספק ביאה דודאי [ד](נטהרה) וחכמים מטמאין כיון דאין כאן אלא ספיקא אחת וסוגיא דע"ז מוכחת כפרש"י דר"א מטהר אפילו בספיקא אחת דקאמר עובדא הוה בנהרדעא ואמר שמואל חמרא שרי כמאן כרבי אליעזר דאמר ספק ביאה טהור פי' דמטעם רוב גנבי ישראל נינהו לא מצינן למימר דשרא שמואל כדשרא רבא לעיל בעובדא דפומבדיתא דדוקא בפומבדיתא הוו רוב גנבי ישראל דרעים היו כדאמרינן לעיל (דף מו.) תא אחוי לך רמאי דפומבדיתא ואמרינן (חולין דף קכז.) פומבדיתאי לוויך אשני אושפיזך ומשני (ז) לא שאני התם כיון דאיכא דפתחי לשם ממונא הוה ליה ספק ספיקא פי' ספק גנבי עכו"ם ספק גנבי ישראל ואם תמצי לומר עכו"ם אימור לא נגעי כיון דידעי ע"י ריח שהיה יין לא היו חוששין כו' משמע דלמאי דהוה בעי לאוקומי כרבי אליעזר דסלקא דעתך דלא פתחי לשם ממונא ובודאי נגע הוי שרי אף על גב דליכא אלא חדא ספיקא אם עכו"ם אם ישראלים משום דהוי ספק ביאה אם באו עכו"ם לשם או לאו ומיהו קשה מההוא פולמוס (ע"ז דף ע:) דסליק לנהרדעא ושרייה ר"א וקאמר רב דימי לא ידענא אי משום דסבר כר"א דסבר ספק ביאה טהור אי משום רוב דאתו בהדי דפולמוס ישראל נינהו ופריך ספק ביאה ספק מגע הוא ומשני כיון (ח) דפתוח חביות טובא אימור אדעתא דממונא פתח וכספק ביאה דמי ואע"ג דתלינן אדעתא דממונא והוי ס"ס אפ"ה לא שרי אלא לר"א (ט) ולעיל שרי שמואל בהאי טעמא אפילו לרבנן ופרש"י התם גנבי נהרדעא לא הוו ידעי אם רוב עכו"ם או רוב ישראלים ושרי אפילו לרבנן דספק ספיקא היא אבל הנהו דאזלי בתר פולמוס הוה ידע רבי אליעזר (י) דשרא אם רוב ישראל הם אם רוב עכו"ם הלכך אף על גב דאיכא למימר דאתו אדעתא דממונא ליכא אלא חדא ספיקא אם היו רוב עכו"ם ושרי לרבי אליעזר כיון דפתוח חביות טובא דמוכחא מילתא דלשם ממון באו ולא מנסכי דהוי כבולשת שנכנסה לעיר בשעת מלחמה דקתני אלו ואלו מותרות הלכך אף על גב דספק מגע הוא כיון דמוכחא מילתא לקולא כספק ביאה דמי ומיהו קשה לר"ת לשני הפירושים דבמסכת טהרות (פ"ו מ"ד) מוכח דרבנן מטמאין אפי' בספק ספיקא דתנן כל שאתה יכול לרבות ספיקות וספיקי ספיקות ברה"י טמא ברה"ר טהור כיצד כו' ואח"כ קתני הנכנס לבקעה בימות הגשמים דמייתי הכא ומיהו ההוא דע"ז נוכל לפרש כשיטת רש"י דר"א שרי אפי' בספיקא אחת כדמוכח (כ) הסוגיא ורבנן נהי דבטומאה מחמירי לטמאות אפי' בספק ספיקא ביין נסך שריא ספק ספיקא ור"ת מפרש דפליגי דרבנן מטמאו אפילו בכמה ספיקות משום דמן הדין אפילו בחדא ספיקא טהור דלוקמה אחזקיה וילפינן מסוטה דטמא וא"כ מה לי חדא ספיקא מה לי תרי ספיקי דהא אפי' בחדא ספיקא הוה לן למימר דטהור ור"א סבר אין לך בו אלא חידושו ודוקא חדא ספיקא טמא ואתי שפיר ההוא דפולמוס דמשמע דמודו רבנן אפילו בספק ספיקא לא שרי אלא לר"א ובההיא עובדא דנהרדעא לא גרים ר"א דוקא לר"א לא שאני התם כו' דלהאי גירסא משמע דמודו רבנן דבספק ספיקא שרי ור"א שרי אפילו בספיקא אחת ובההיא דפולמוס מפרש ר"ת כמאן כר"א במיעוטא גרים והדר גרים האי ספק ביאה ספק מגע הוא ולאו דוקא ספק מגע קאמר דלדרבה ספק ביאה הוא דספק אם באו עכו"ם שם אם לאו דאימור ישראל נינהו אלא לספיקא אחת קרי ספק מגע דספק ביאה דר"א היינו ספק ספיקא והכי פריך והא ספיקא אחת היא ואפי' לר"א לא שרי בספיקא אחת וא"ת ומנ"ל דלרבנן אפילו ביין נסך אסרי בספק ספיקא ויש לומר דבכמה דוכתי מדמה במס' ע"ז טומאה דטהרות: רבי אליעזר מטהר. נראה דגרסינן רבי אלעזר דאי ר' אליעזר היכי בעי למימר בפ' בתרא דע"ז (דף ע. ושם) דשמואל ורבי אלעזר כר' אליעזר והא שמואל ור' אלעזר אית להו סוף פ"ק דנדה (דף ח.) דאין הלכה כר' אליעזר בסדר טהרות אלא בד' והך בסדר טהרות היא: בהעלם אחד חייב. אפילו בשתי רשויות ותימה דאמר רבא בפ' המוציא יין (שבת דף פ. ושם) הוציא חצי גרוגרת והניחה וחזר והוציא חצי גרוגרת והעבירה דרך עליה חייב מה צריך דרך עליה הא לא בעי הכא (ל) אלא לרשות אחת אפילו רחוקות זו מזו ויש לומר דודאי בלא דרך עליה חייב והא דנקט דרך עליה לאשמועינן דאם העביר תוך ג' לאותו חצי גרוגרת המונחת דחייב אע"ג דלא הוי תוך ג' לקרקע והקשה ר"ת לרבי יוסי דב' רשויות אמאי פטור והאמר בפ' הבונה (שם דף קד:) כתב אות אחת בטבריא ואות אחת בצפורי חייב מחוסר קריבה לאו כמחוסר מעשה דמי וגרס ר"ת מרשות אחת חייב משתי רשויות פטור אם הוציא חצי גרוגרת לרשות הרבים אחת אבל ברשות אחת אם הוציא לקחה אפילו חלקה והוציאה לשתי רשויות חייב דמחוסר קריבה לאו כמחוסר מעשה דמי ולר"י נראה דלאו פירכא היא דלא דמי דהתם שם המלאכה (מ) כתיבה וכתיבה נגמרה כשיכתוב שתי אותיות ואפי' רחוקות זו מזו אבל הכא שם המלאכה היא הוצאה וכשהוציא לשתי רשויות אכתי לא נגמרה הוצאה עד שיקרבם: אבל

רבינו גרשום

דרך היחיד. היינו מצר שבין שדותיו כשהולך בו משדה לשדה: דרך הרבים. היינו מצר שבין שדהו לשדות של רבים: שביל. שביל ממש אלא של יחיד קצר ושל רבים רחב: הקבוע בימות החמה ובימות הגשמים. דבימות הגשמים מונעים דריסת הרגל מן השדות משום דזורעין (א) ואותו שביל דמפסיק אע"כ הוי קבוע חשיב בימות החמה ובימות הגשמים. קאמר מיהת דרך היחיד היינו מצר דמפסיק לפאה וה"ה לחצב: טומאה. נמי מפסיק מצר וחצב דתנן הנכנס לבקעה בימות הגשמים משה"כ נסיב ימות הגשמים כדאמרן דבימות הגשמים מונעין דריסת הרגל והוי כרה"י וקי"ל ספק טומאה ברה"י ספיקו טמא דגמרינן מסוטה ואפ"ה אם אמר הלכתי למקום פלוני בבקעה זו והטומאה היתה מעבר למצר או לחצב ואמר איני יודע אם נכנסתי למקום הטומאה שמעבר לחצב או לא ר"א מטהר דהוי הפסק: אבל לשבת לא. דלאו הפסק לשבת דלא הוי כשתי רשויות: רבא אמר. אפי' לשבת הוי הפסק כדאמר לקמן אפי' פיסלא: לרשות אחת שתיהן. כגון מרה"י לרה"ר: חייב דמצטרפי: לשתי רשויות פטור. היינו שתי רשויות כגון אם היה עומד בבית דיש לו שני פתחים לשני רשויות אחד פתוח לרשות הרבים ואחד פתוח לרשות אחר והוציא חצי גרוגרת בפתח זה וחצי גרוגרת בפתח זה:

חשק שלמה על רבינו גרשום

(א) לכאורה צ"ל ואותו שביל דמונעין ממנו בימות הגשמים לא חשיב להפסיק אא"כ הוי קבוע וכו'.

מסורת הש"ס

א) טהרות פ"ו [מ"ה] פסחים י. ע"ז ע., ב) [עי' טהרות שם מ"ד], ג) שבת פ. כריתות יז, ד) [צ"ל נטהרה].

הגהות הב"ח

(א) רשב"ם ד"ה דרך וכו' ד' אמות. נ"ב בפ' המוכר פירות דף ק' איתא דדרך היחיד הוא שני גמדין ומחצה פי' שתי אמות קטנות ומחצה וע"ש: (ב) ד"ה ספק וכו' אם בא עד מקום הקבר אם לאו: (ג) ד"ה וקדייק וכו' דפטר בשני רשויות הכא חייב דאין המצר: (ד) ד"ה במס' שבת וכו' ולא חשיבא הוצאת דבר מאכל חשוב: (ה) תוס' ד"ה דרך היחיד ודרך הרבים שביל היחיד ושביל הרבים הקבוע וכו' בירושלמי פריך וכו' משום סיפא נקטיה קתני: (ו) בא"ד או מיניהו עדיף דדרך היחיד רחב: (ז) ד"ה ר' אליעזר וכו' ומשני לא שאני: (ח) בא"ד ומשני כיון דפתחו חביות וכו' וכספק ביאה דמי אלמא אע"ג: (ט) בא"ד אלא לר"א דוקא ולעיל שרי שמואל בהאי לישנא אפי' לרבנן: (י) בא"ד הוה ידע ר"א דשרייה אם רוב עובדי ישראלים או רוב עובדי כוכבים: (כ) בא"ד כדמוכח התם הסוגיא: (ל) ד"ה בהעלם וכו' לא בעי הכא רבי יוסי אלא לרשות אחת: (מ) בא"ד שם המלאכה היינו כתיבה וכתיבה נגמרה:

ליקוטי רש"י

ודרך הרבים. ט"ז אמה. ודרך היחיד. ארבע אמות [מנחות צא. וב"ב ק.]. ושביל היחיד הקבוע. אי לא קביע לא מפסיק דמקום זר הוא ולא חשוב [מנחות שם]. הנכנס לבקעה. שדות הרבה קנפורי"א בלע"ז [שבת ו.]. הרבה שדות הסמוכים יחד קרי בקעה [פסחים י.]. בימות הגשמים. שזרועה היא ואין רבים דורסין אותה והוי רשות היחיד לטומאה וספיקה שאירעה בה הוי ספיקו טמא [ע"ז ע.]. הוא לבקעה רשות היחיד לטומאה מפני שכבר צמח הזרע ואין רשות לכל אדם ליכנס לה וקיימא לן ספק טומאה ברשות היחיד ספיקו טמא. בשדה פלונית. כלומר באחת השדות ויודעין אנו באיזו היא. שדה מקויימת בגלויה [פסחים שם]. באחת מן השדות ואין אנו יודעין באיזו היא [ע"ז שם]. הלכתי במקום הלז. בבקעה זו [פסחים וע"ז שם]. וחכמים מטמאין. דהוה ליה ספק טומאה ברשות היחיד ור' אליעזר לא אסר כן נכנס לשדה אבל אינו יודע אם האהיל אם לא אבל הטמאה הוה ליה ספק ספיקא [פסחים שם]. וכי פליגי רבנן עליה דר"א היכי דמליאה שדה טומאה דאי על לה לא אפשר דלא האהיל דליכא אלא כל ספק [ע"ז שם]. ספק מגע טומאה טמא. דלאמר נכנסתי לשדה שהטומאה בה ואיני יודע אם נגעתי בטומאה אם לאו [ע"ז שם]. בשני העלמות פטור. (ויש) [דיש] ידיעה לחצי שיעור [כריתות יז. ע"פ שטמ"ק].

וְדֶרֶךְ הָרַבִּים וְדֶרֶךְ הַיָּחִיד – A PUBLIC ROAD AND A PRIVATE ROAD,[1] וּשְׁבִיל הָרַבִּים וּשְׁבִיל הַיָּחִיד הַקָּבוּעַ בֵּין בִּימוֹת הַחַמָּה וּבֵין בִּימוֹת הַגְּשָׁמִים – AND A PUBLIC PATH OR PRIVATE PATH THAT IS IN CONSTANT USE, BOTH DURING THE HOT SEASON AND THE RAINY SEASON.[2]

טוּמְאָה מַאי הִיא – What is the case of ***tumah*** to which a divider in the field has relevance? דִּתְנַן הַנִּכְנָס לְבִקְעָה בִּימוֹת הַגְּשָׁמִים – It is **that** which **we learned in a Mishnah:**[3] If ONE ENTERS AN EXPANSE OF FIELDS DURING THE RAINY SEASON, when few people walk in the fields, so as not to trample the growing crops, וְטוּמְאָה בְּשָׂדֶה פְּלוֹנִית – AND THERE IS *TUMAH* IN A CERTAIN FIELD within this expanse of fields,[4] וְאָמַר הָלַכְתִּי לְמָקוֹם הַלָּז – AND HE SAID: "I WENT TO THAT PLACE, i.e. to the expanse that includes the field containing the grave, וְאֵינִי יוֹדֵעַ אִם נִכְנַסְתִּי לְאוֹתוֹ מָקוֹם וְאִם לָאו – BUT I DO NOT KNOW WHETHER I ENTERED THAT particular PLACE, i.e. the field containing the grave, OR NOT."[5] What is the law? רַבִּי אֱלִיעֶזֶר מְטַהֵר וַחֲכָמִים מְטַמְּאִין – R' ELIEZER[6] DECLARES HIM *TAHOR,* WHEREAS THE SAGES DECLARE HIM *TAMEI;* שֶׁהָיָה רַבִּי אֱלִיעֶזֶר אוֹמֵר – FOR R' ELIEZER WAS WONT TO SAY: סָפֵק בִּיאָה טָהוֹר – In a case where the doubt is A DOUBT OF ENTRY, the person IS *TAHOR.*[7] סָפֵק מַגָּע טוּמְאָה טָמֵא – In a case where the doubt is A DOUBT OF CONTACT WITH THE *TUMAH*, the person IS *TAMEI.*[8] Thus, according to R' Eliezer, field division is significant in regard to the laws of *tumah,* and what constitutes a divider in a field is indeed relevant.[9]

According to Rav Assi, neither a boundary divider nor the *chatzav* plant serves to divide a field in regard to *pe'ah* or *tumah,*[10] whereas according to Ravin they do divide.

The Gemara now infers that even Ravin considers a boundary divider and the *chatzav* plant as separators *only* in regard to the property of a deceased convert, *pe'ah* and *tumah*:

אֲבָל לְשַׁבָּת לֹא – **But not in regard to the Sabbath.**[11] רָבָא אָמַר – **Rava says:** אֲפִילוּ לְעִנְיַן שַׁבָּת – They are considered separators **even in regard to the Sabbath.** What is the relevance of separators in a field to the laws of the Sabbath? דְּתַנְיָא – **For it was taught in a Baraisa:** הוֹצִיא חֲצִי גְרוֹגֶרֶת לִרְשׁוּת הָרַבִּים וְהִנִּיחָהּ – If ONE CARRIED OUT the equivalent of HALF A DRIED FIG INTO A PUBLIC DOMAIN AND DEPOSITED IT there, וְחָזַר וְהוֹצִיא חֲצִי גְרוֹגֶרֶת אַחֶרֶת – AND THEN CARRIED OUT ANOTHER equivalent of HALF A DRIED FIG[12] – בְּהֶעְלֵם

NOTES

1. A "private road" is a route between fields that [is used for pedestrian, animal and vehicular traffic and] is at least four *amos* wide. If the road is sixteen *amos* or wider, it is a "public road" (see *Rashbam* from Mishnah below, 99b; *Rosh* to *Pe'ah* ad loc.; cf. *Rabbeinu Gershom*). If either kind of road bisects a field, it divides the field into two distinct areas for purposes of *pe'ah*.

The Mishnah could have simply stated that the narrower private road divides a field and we would have known that the wider public road certainly does. Nevertheless, the Mishnah states both and places the more obvious law first, in keeping with the style known as לֹא זוּ אַף זוּ, *not only this but also this* (*Rashbam*; cf. *Tosafos*).

2. In contrast to a public road, which is used for travel by wagons or animals, a public *path* is a route used solely for pedestrian traffic. The Mishnah teaches that these paths do not divide a field unless they are used as paths year round – even during the rainy season. That is, even when the crops are planted in the fields during the rainy season, these paths are left uncultivated to serve as paths across the fields (see *Rashbam* and *Tosafos*).

3. *Tohoros* 6:5.

4. I.e. one of the fields in this expanse contains a grave. If a person touches [מַגָּע] or even extends part of his body over the grave [אֹהֶל], he becomes *tamei.*

5. Thus, the person is in doubt whether or not he walked over the grave, thereby contracting *tumah* from it. Ordinarily, the law regarding a doubtful case of *tumah* is that when the doubtful situation arises in a private domain, the person is *tamei*; when the doubtful situation arises in a public domain, the person remains *tahor.* In regard to this law, an open expanse of fields is regarded as a private domain during the rainy season, since people seldom enter at that time.

6. [According to *Tosafos,* this should read: ר' אֶלְעָזָר, *R' Elazar.*]

7. I.e. when the doubt is whether the person even entered the field that contains the grave, he is *tahor,* even though the doubt has arisen in a private domain. For in this case, there is a double doubt [סְפֵק סְפֵיקָא]. First, there is a doubt whether the person even entered the field in question. And second, even if he did enter the field, there is a doubt whether he came into contact with the grave that is in it. Therefore, R' Eliezer declares the person *tahor*; for in a case of double doubt, the person is *tahor* even if the doubt arises in a private domain (*Rashbam*; cf. *Tosafos*).

The Sages, however, argue that the division of the expanse into distinct fields is of no significance. In the final analysis, only a single doubt exists: The person has definitely entered an expanse of fields containing a grave and the sole question is whether or not he came into contact with that grave (ibid.).

8. I.e. when the person definitely entered the field in question and the only doubt is whether or not he came into contact with the grave, even R' Eliezer concedes that the person is *tamei.* For in that case, there is only a single doubt; and the law is that doubtful *tumah* in a private domain is adjudged to be a situation of definite *tumah.*

9. Thus, according to R' Eliezer, if a field bisected by a legal divider contains a grave and a person entered the field but does not know which half, he is *tahor* even during the rainy season (at which time the field is a private domain). For there exists a double doubt: he may not have entered that half of the field which contains the grave; and even if he did, he may not have come into contact with the grave (*Rashbam*).

10. In Rav Assi's view, since the fields are in fact contiguous, relatively insignificant separators (such as boundary dividers and the *chatzav* plant) are not sufficient to render the fields separate in regard to the laws of *pe'ah* and *tumah.* As regards acquisition of an ownerless field, however, it is already somewhat of a novelty that the act of digging in one place acquires the entire field for the person, as evidenced by the fact that Shmuel indeed rules that it acquires no more than the place of the actual digging (54a). Although Rav disagrees and rules that the act of digging does acquire the entire field, he concedes that there is some degree of legal merit to Shmuel's position. Rav would therefore agree that where even an insignificant separator, such as a boundary divider or *chatzav* plant, divides the field, the act of digging cannot affect what is beyond the divider. Rather, a proper act of acquisition is required for each part of the divided field (*Rashbam* to 55a ד״ה אבל לענין פאה).

11. To what this refers will be explained by the Gemara shortly.

12. One of the thirty-nine categories of activity forbidden on the Sabbath is carrying an object from one domain to another. Thus, a person who takes an object from a private domain and sets it down in a public domain has desecrated the Sabbath. If his sin was premeditated, he incurs the death penalty; if inadvertent [he forgot that it was the Sabbath or that such acts are forbidden on the Sabbath], then he must atone for his deed by offering a *chatas.* In order for liability to be incurred, the transported object must be at least marginally significant. In regard to most foodstuffs, this means that the object must be at least the size of a dried fig (see *Shabbos* 76a).

This Baraisa discusses the case of a person who inadvertently carried out the equivalent of half a dried fig from a private to a public domain and then carried out another half. If the two acts of carrying are viewed as distinct, he is exempt from bringing a *chatas,* since on neither occasion has he carried out the equivalent of a dried fig. If, however, the second act of carrying is viewed as a continuation of the first, then he is liable to bring a *chatas,* since in the course of this combined act of carrying he has carried out the equivalent of a dried fig. The Baraisa considers various factors that determine whether the two acts of carrying are viewed as distinct or as combined (see *Rashbam*).

עין משפט
נר מצוה

רנ א מיי' פ"כ מהל' שאר אבות הטומאה הלכה ט:

רנא ב מיי' פי"ח מהל' שבת הלכה כד:

רבינו גרשום

דרך היחיד. היינו מצר שבין שדותיו כשהולך בו משדה לשדה: **דרך הרבים.** היינו מצר שבין שדהו לשדות של רבים: **שביל.** שביל ממש אלא של **יחיד** קצר ושל **רבים** רחב: **הקבוע בימות החמה ובימות הגשמים.** דבימות הגשמים מונעים דריסת הרגל מן השדות משום דזורעין (א) ואותו שביל דמפסיק דמונעין לא חשיב אא"כ הוי קבוע בימות החמה ובימות הגשמים. קאמר מיהת דרך היחיד דהיינו מצר דמפסיק לפאה וה"ה לחצב: **טומאה.** נמי מפסיק מצר וחצב **דתנן הנכנס לבקעה בימות הגשמים** מש"ה נסיב ימות הגשמים כדאמרן דבימות הגשמים מונעין דריסת הרגל והוי כרה"י וקי"ל ספק טומאה ברה"י ספיקו טמא דגמרינן מסוטה ואפ"ה אם **אמר הלכתי למקום הלז** בבקעה זו והטומאה היתה מעבר למצר או לחצב ואמר **איני יודע אם נכנסתי למקום הטומאה** שמעבר לחצב **ר"א מטהר** דהוי הפסק: **אבל לשבת לא.** דלאו הפסק לשבת דלא הוי כשתי רשויות: **רבא אמר. אפי' לשבת** הוי הפסק כדאמר לקמן אפי' פיסלא: **לרשות אחת** שתיהן. כגון מרה"י לרה"ר **חייב** דמצטרפי: **לשתי רשויות פטור.** היינו לשתי רשויות כגון אם היה עומד בבית דיש לו שני פתחים אחד פתוח לרשות הרבים ואחד פתוח לרשות אחר והוציא חצי גרוגרת בפתח זה וחצי גרוגרת בפתח זה:

חשק שלמה על רבינו גרשום
(א) לכאורה צ"ל ואותו שביל דמונעין מתוך בימות הגשמים לא חשיב להפסיק אא"כ הוי קבוע וכו'.

ודרך הרבים ודרך היחיד ושביל הרבים ושביל היחיד הקבוע בין בימות החמה ובין בימות הגשמים טומאה מאי היא דתנן (א) הנכנס לבקעה בימות הגשמים וטומאה בשדה פלונית ואמר הלכתי למקום הלז ואיני יודע אם נכנסתי לאותו מקום ואם לאו ר"א מטהר וחכמים (א) מטמאין (ג) שהיה ר"א אומר ספק ביאה טהור ספק מגע טומאה טמא אבל לשבת לא רבא אמר אפילו לענין שבת דתניא (ג) הוציא חצי גרוגרת לרשות הרבים והניחה וחזר והוציא חצי גרוגרת אחרת בהעלם אחד חייב בשני העלמות פטור רבי יוסי אומר (ב) בהעלם אחד ברשות

דרך הרבים. ט"ז אמה רוחב דרך היחיד (א) ד' אמות ולא זו אף זו קתני: **שביל הרבים.** שהולכין שם רבים ברגליהן אבל דרך הרבים מקום הילוך העגלות והסוסים וכולה לא זו אף זו קתני: **הקבוע בין בימות החמה.** ואפילו בימות הגשמים שאין רגילים להלך בבקעה מהלכין שם שאין חרישה וזריעה לשם: **טומאה מאי היא.** מאי הפסק שייך בשדה לענין טומאה: **דתנן כו'.** ואליבא דר"א הוא דשייך הפסק כדמפרש ואזיל: **בימות הגשמים.** הויא רה"י לטומאה וספיקה טמא שהרי אין מהלכין בה בני אדם אלא לקלקל הזריעה: **הלכתי למקום הלז.** נכנסתי בבקעה זו: **וחכמים מטמאים.** דסוף סוף מה לי שדה אחת מה לי ב' שדות חדא ספיקא היא שמא הלך עד הקבר והאהיל שמא לא הלך וספיקו טמא: **ספק ביאה טהור.** היכא דמספקא ליה אם נכנס באותה שדה ואם תמצא לומר נכנס ספק אם בא עד מקום (ג) טומאה אם לאו וספק ספיקא הוא וטהור אבל היכא דליכא אלא ספק מגע דפשיטא ליה דנכנס באותה שדה אלא שספק לו אם נגע בקבר אם לאו חדא ספיקא הוא וטמא והלכך לרבי אליעזר אי מפסיק מצר וחצב בינתיים וטומאה באחת מהן ואין יודע באיזה מהן נכנס ספק ביאה הוא וטהור ואי ליכא מצר בינתים ספק מגע איכא ולא ספק ביאה דכולהו שדה אחת הן וטמא: וקדייק גמרא דלרבנן אמר רבי יוחנן דוקא פאה וטומאה אבל לשבת לא הוי הפסק אי מפסיק מצר וחצב בין שני רה"ר והוציא חצי גרוגרת בזה ואחר כך הוציא חצי גרוגרת בשני חייב דאפילו לרבי יוסי דפטר בשני רשויות (ג) דאין המצר מפסיקן לשני רשויות: במסכת שבת תנן המוציא אוכלין חייב בגרוגרת דבשבת מלאכת מחשבת אסרה תורה ולא חשיבא הוצאת דבר (ד) חשוב בפחות מכגרוגרת: **בהעלם אחד חייב.** שלא נודע לו בינתיים שהוא שבת דידיעה מחלקת:

דרך היחיד ודרך הרבים. (ה) בירושלמי פריך אמאי איצטריך למיתני דרך הרבים דכיון דתנא דדרך היחיד מפסיק כ"ש דרך הרבים ומשני משום סיפא נקטינן דקתני הכל מפסיק לזרעים ואין מפסיק לאילנות אלא גדר כו' וקמ"ל דאפילו דרך הרבים לא מפסיק לאילן ומפרש נמי אמאי תנא שביל הרבים כיון דתנא שביל היחיד מפסיק דמשום אילן לא צריך למיתנייה כיון דאשמועינן דאפי' דרך הרבים לא מפסיק לאילן כל שכן שביל הרבים אלא אתא לאשמועינן דשביל הרבים נמי בעינן שיהא קבוע בימות החמה ובימות הגשמים והשתא איצטריך למיתני כולהו שביל היחיד לאשמועינן דמפסיק לזרעים אע"ג דגריע מכולהו ודרך הרבים אשמועינן דלא מפסיק לאילן ודרך היחיד אשמועינן דלא בעינן קבוע ושביל הרבים אשמועינן דבעינן קבוע ואין להקשות דלא ליתני שביל הרבים ואנא ידענא דבעינן קבוע מדתנן דרך היחיד דאי לא בעי לא ליתני דרך היחיד אלא ליתני שביל הרבים דהוי רבותא טפי או איפכא דלא ליתני דרך היחיד ואנא ידענא דלא בעינן קבוע מדתנן שביל הרבים ולא תנא דרך היחיד דהוי רבותא טפי דהא אי לאו דתנא תרוייהו לא הוה ידענא (ו) מפסיק טפי דהא אי מינייהו דרך היחיד רחב טפי ושביל הרבים בקעי ביה רבים: **רבי** אליעזר מטהר. רשב"ם פירש דפליגי דרבי אליעזר חשיב ליה ספק ספיקא ורבנן לא חשיבי ליה אלא ספיקא אחת והר"ם פירש בפרק בתרא דע"ז (דף ע. ושם) דאיירי בשדה מלאה טומאה ופליגי דר"א סבר אע"ג דליכא אלא ספיקא כיון דליכא ספק מגע אלא ספק ביאה טהור והיינו טעמא דטומאה מסוטה גמרינן וגבי סוטה הוי ספק מגע ולא ספק ביאה דודאי (ז) (נטהרה) וחכמים מטמאין כיון דאין כאן אלא ספיקא אחת וסוגיא דע"ז מוכחת כפרש"י דר"א מטהר אפילו בספיקא אחת דקאמר עובדא הוה בנהרדעא ואמר שמואל חמרא שרי מאן כרבי אליעזר דאמר ספק ביאה טהור פי' דמטעם רוב גנבי ישראל ניהו לא מצינן למימר דשרא שמואל כדשרא רבה לעיל בעובדא דפומבדיתא דדוקא בפומבדיתא הוו רוב גנבי ישראל דרעים היו כדאמרינן לעיל (דף מו.) תא אחוי לך דמאי דפומבדיתא ואמרינן (חולין דף קכז.) פומבדיתאי לוויך אשני אושפיזך ומשני (ז) לה שאני התם כיון דליכא דפתחי לשם ספק ספיקא פי' ספק גנבי עכו"ם ספק גנבי ישראל ואם תמצי לומר עכו"ם איסור לא נגעי כיון דידעי ע"י ריח שהיה יין לא היו חוששין כו' משמע דלמאי דהוה בעי לאוקומי כרבי אליעזר דסלקא דעתך דלא פתחי לשם ממונא ובודאי נגע הוי שרי אף על גב דליכא אלא חדא ספיקא אם עכו"ם אם ישראלים משום דהוי ספק ביאה אם באו עכו"ם לשם או לאו ומיהו קשה מההוא פולמוס (ע"ז דף ע:) דסליק לנהרדעא ושרייה ר"א וקאמר רב דימי לא ידענא אי משום דסבר כר"א דספק ביאה טהור או משום רוב דלאו בהדי דפולמוס ישראל ניהו ופריך ספק ביאה ספק מגע הוא ומשני כיון (ח) דפתוח חביות טובא איסור לדעתא דממונא פתח וכספק ביאה דמי ואע"ג דתלינן לדעתא דממונא והוי ס"ס אפ"ה לא שרי אלא לר"א (ט) ולעיל שרי שמואל בהאי טעמא אפילו לרבנן ופרש"י התם גנבי נהרדעא לא הוו ידעי אם רוב עכו"ם או רוב ישראלים ושרי אפילו לרבנן דספק ספיקא היא אבל הכא בתר פולמוס הוה דודאי ידע רבי אליעזר (י) דשרא אם רוב ישראל הם אם רוב עכו"ם הלכך אף על גב דליכא למימר דלאו לדעתא דממונא ליכא אלא חדא ספיקא אם היו רוב עכו"ם ושרי לרבי אליעזר כיון דפתוח חביות טובא דמוכחא מילתא דלשם ממון באו ולא מנכסי דהוי כבולשת שנכנסה לעיר בשעת מלחמה דקתני אלו ואלו מותרות הלכך אף על גב דספק מגע הוא כיון דמוכחא מילתא לקולא כספק ביאה דמי ומיהו קשה לר"ת לשני הפירושים דבמסכת טהרות (פ"ו מ"ד) מוכח דרבנן מטמאין אפי' בספק ספיקא דתנן כל שאתה יכול לרבות ספיקות וספיקי ספיקות ברה"י טמא ברה"ר טהור כיצד כו' ואח"כ קתני הנכנס לבקעה בימות הגשמים דמייתי הכא ומיהו ההוא לא תוכל לפרש כשיטת רש"י דר"א שרי אפי' בספיקא אחת דמוכח (כ) הסוגיא ורבנן נהי דבטומאה מחמירי לטמאות אפי' בספק ספיקא ר"ת מפרש דפליגי דרבנן מטמאו אפילו בכמה ספיקות משום דמן הדין אפילו בחדא ספיקא טהור דלוקמה אחזקיה ויליפינן מסוטה דטמא ואמ"כ מה לי חדא ספיקא מה לי תרי ספיקי דהא אפי' בחדא ספיקא הוה לן למימר דטהור ור"א סבר אין לך בו אלא חידושו ודוקא חדא ספיקא טמא ואתי שפיר ההוא דפולמוס דמשמע אפילו בספק ספיקא לא שרי אלא לר"א דוקא לר"א לא גרים ר"ת לא שאני התם כו' דלהאי גירסא משמע דמודו רבנן דבספק ספיקא שרי ור"א שרי אפילו בספיקא אחת אלא מפרש ר"ת כמאן כר"א בניחותא גרים והדר גרים האי ספק ביאה ספק מגע הוא ולאו דוקא ספק מגע קאמר דלדרבה ספק ביאה הוא דספק אם באו עכו"ם שם אם לאו לספיקא אחת קרי ספק מגע דספק ביאה דר"א היינו ספק ספיקא והא ספיקא אחת היא ואפי' לר"א לא שרי בספיקא אחת וא"ת ומנ"ל לרבנן אפילו ביין נסך אסרי בספק ספיקא ויש לומר דבכמה דוכתי מדמה במס' ע"ז חומרא דיין נסך לחומרא דטהרות: **רבי אליעזר מטהר.** נראה דגרסינן רבי אליעזר דלא ר' אלעזר דהיכי בעי למימר בפ' בתרא דע"ז (דף ע. ושם) דשמואל ורבי אלעזר כר' אליעזר והא שמואל ור' אלעזר אית להו סוף פ"ק דנדה (דף ח.) דאין הלכה כר' אליעזר בסדר טהרות אלא בד' והך בסדר טהרות היא: **בהעלם אחד חייב.** אפילו בשתי רשויות ותימה דאמר רבא בפ' המוציא יין (שבת דף פ. ושם) הוציא חצי גרוגרת והניחה וחזר והוציא חצי גרוגרת והעבירה דרך עליה חייב מה צריך דרך עליה הא לא בעי הכא (ל) אלא לרשות אחת אפילו רחוקות זו מזו ויש לומר דודאי בלא דרך עליה חייב והא דנקט דרך עליה לאשמועינן דאם העביר תוך ג' לחצי גרוגרת המונחת דחייב אע"ג דלא הוי תוך ג' לקרקע והקשה ר"ת לרבי יוסי דד' רשויות אמאי פטור והאמר בפ' הבונה (שם דף קד:) כתב אות אחת בטבריא ואות אחת בצפורי חייב מחוסר קריבה לאו כמחוסר מעשה דמי וגרס ר"ת מרשות אחת חייב משתי רשויות פטור אם הוציא חצי גרוגרת משתי רשויות לרשות הרבים פטור אבל אם ברשות אחת לקחה אפילו חלקה והוציאה לשתי רשויות חייב דמחוסר קריבה לאו כמחוסר מעשה דמי ולר"י נראה דלאו פירכא היא דלא דמי דהתם שם המלאכה (מ) כתיבה וכתיבה נגמרה כשיכתוב שתי אותיות ואפי' רחוקות זו מזו אבל הכא שם המלאכה היא הוצאה וכשהוציא לשתי רשויות אכתי לא נגמרה הוצאה עד שיקרבם:

אבל

מסורת הש"ס

א) טהרות פ"ו [מ"ה] פסחים י. ע"ז ע., ב) [עי' טהרות שם מ"ד], ג) שבת פ. כריתות יז., ד) [נ"ל נסתרה]:

הגהות הב"ח

(א) רשב"ם ד"ה דרך וכו' ד' אמות. נ"ב בפ' המוכר פירות דף ק' איתא דרך היחיד הוא שני גמדין ומחצה פי' שתי אמות קטנות ומחצה וע"ש: (ב) ד"ה ספק וכו' אם בא עד מקום הקבר אם לאו: (ג) ד"ה וקדייק וכו' דפטר בשתי רשויות הכא חייב דאין המצר: (ד) ד"ה במס' שבת וכו' ולא חשיבא הוצאת דבר מאכל חשוב: (ה) תוס' ד"ה דרך היחיד ודרך הרבים שביל היחיד ושביל הרבים הקבוע וכו' בירושלמי פריך וכו' משום סיפא נקטיה דקתני: (ו) בא"ד הי מינייהו עדיף דדרך היחיד רחב: (ז) ד"ה ר' אליעזר וכו' ומשני לה שאני: (ח) בא"ד ומשני כיון דפתחו חביות וכו' וכספק ביאה דמי אלמא אע"ג: (ט) בא"ד אלא לר"א דוקא ולעיל שרי שמואל בהאי לישנא אפי' לרבנן: (י) בא"ד הוה ידע ר"א דשרייה אם הם רוב ישראלים או רוב עודדי כוכבים: (כ) בא"ד כדמוכח התם הסוגיא: (ל) ד"ה בהעלם וכו' לא בעי הכא רבי יוסי אלא לרשות אחת: (מ) בא"ד שם המלאכה היינו כתיבה והכתיבה נגמרה:

ליקוטי רש"י

ודרך הרבים. ט"ז אמה. **ודרך היחיד.** ארבע אמות [מנחות עא: וב"ק סא.]. **ושביל היחיד הקבוע.** אי לא קביע לא מפסיק דמקום צר הוא ולא חשוב [מנחות שם]. **הנכנס לבקעה.** שדות הרבה קנפני"א בלע"ז [שבת ו.]. הרבה שדות הסמוכים יחד קרי בקעה [פסחים י.]. **בימות הגשמים.** שזרועה היא ואין רבים דורסין אותה והוי רשות היחיד לטומאה וספיקא שאירעה בה הוי ספיקא טמא [ע"ז ע.]. הויא בקעה רשות היחיד לטומאה מפני שכבר צמח הזרע ואין רשות לכל אדם ליכנס לה וקיימא לן ספק טומאה ברשות היחיד ספקו טמא. **בשדה פלונית.** כלומר באחת השדות ויודעין אנו באיזו היא וכל שדה ושדה מסויימת במצריה [פסחים שם]. באחת מן השדות ואין אנו יודעין איזו היא [ע"ז שם]. **הלכתי במקום הלז.** בבקעה זו [פסחים וע"ז שם]. **וחכמים מטמאין.** דהויא ליה ספק טומאה ברשות היחיד ור' אליעזר לא חשיב לה ספק טומאה אלא אם כן נכנס לשדה אבל אינו יודע אם האהיל אם לא אבל השתא הוה ליה ספק ספיקא [פסחים שם]. וכי פליגי רבנן עליה דר"א היכי דמליא שדה טומאה דאי על לה לא אפשר דלא האהיל דליכא אלא כד ספק [ע"ז שם]. **ספק מגע טומאה טמא.** דאמר נכנסתי לשדה שהטומאה בה ואיני יודע אם נגעתי בטומאה אם לאו [ע"ז שם]. **בשני העלמות פטור.** (ויש) [דיש] ידיעה לחצי שיעור [כריתות יז. ע"פ שטמ"ק].

אֶחָד חַיָּיב – if he did this **IN ONE PERIOD OF FORGETFULNESS, HE IS LIABLE** for a *chatas* offering;[13] בִּשְׁנֵי הָעֲלָמוֹת פָּטוּר – if he did so **IN TWO PERIODS OF FORGETFULNESS, HE IS EXEMPT** from the offering.[14] רַבִּי יוֹסֵי אוֹמֵר – **R' YOSE SAYS:** בְּהֶעְלֵם אֶחָד – Even **IN ONE PERIOD OF FORGETFULNESS,**

NOTES

13. I.e. the two acts of carrying were committed under the mistaken impression that the day was a weekday and the person did not become aware in between that the day was in fact the Sabbath (*Rashbam*). Therefore, the two acts of carrying combine and the person is liable for a *chatas*.

14. I.e. in between the two acts of carrying, the person became aware that the day was indeed the Sabbath, but forgot again and committed the second act of carrying in a second episode of forgetfulness. Awareness is deemed a "separator" between the two acts of carrying; thus, they do not combine to form a single act and no *chatas* obligation is incurred (*Rashbam*).

בִּרְשׁוּת אַחַת חַיָּיב – it is only if he placed both halves IN ONE DOMAIN that HE IS LIABLE for a *chatas*; בִּשְׁתֵּי רְשׁוּיוֹת פָּטוּר – but if he placed them IN TWO DOMAINS, HE IS EXEMPT.[1] וְאָמַר רַבָּה – **And** regarding what constitutes two separate public domains in R' Yose's view, **Rabbah said:** וְהוּא שֶׁיֵּשׁ חִיּוּב חַטָּאת בֵּינֵיהֶם – **Provided that there is between [the two public domains]** an area that can create **a *chatas* liability;**[2] אֲבָל כַּרְמְלִית לֹא – **but** if the two domains are separated only by **a *karmelis,*** they are **not** considered separate.[3] אַבָּיֵי אָמַר אֲפִילּוּ כַּרְמְלִית – **Abaye** disagrees and **says: Even** when separated by **a *karmelis,*** the two domains are considered separate, אֲבָל פִּיסְלָא לֹא – **but not** when they are separated merely by **a block of wood.**[4] רָבָא אָמַר אֲפִילּוּ פִּיסְלָא – **Rava** disagrees and **says: Even** when they are separated merely by **a block of wood,** they are considered separate domains in R' Yose's view.[5]

The Gemara observes:

וְאַזְדָא רָבָא לְטַעְמֵיהּ – **And Rava** (who considers a boundary divider, a *chatzav* plant or a block of wood a separator in regard to Sabbath law[6]) **is consistent with his opinion** stated elsewhere; דְּאָמַר רָבָא רְשׁוּת שַׁבָּת כִּרְשׁוּת גִּיטִּין דָּמֵי – **for Rava said** elsewhere: **The domain in regard to the Sabbath is like the domain in regard to divorce** law.[7]

The Gemara resumes its original discussion about acquiring the ownerless property of a deceased convert. R' Yochanan had ruled that a proprietary act performed in one part of the ownerless field acquires the field for the person up until the boundary divider or *chatzav* plant. The Gemara now inquires: אֵין שָׁם לֹא מֵצַר וְלֹא חָצָב מַאי – **If there is neither a boundary divider nor a *chatzav*** breaking up the convert's field into smaller parcels, **what** is the law? How extensive must the act of acquisition be in order to acquire the entire field?[8] פֵּירֵשׁ רַבִּי מְרִינוּס מִשְּׁמוֹ – **R' Merinos explained in his** [R' Yochanan's] **name:**[9] כָּל שֶׁנִּקְרֵאת עַל שְׁמוֹ – **As much** of a field **as is called by his name.**[10]

The Gemara illustrates this condition:

הֵיכִי דָּמֵי – **How so?** אָמַר רַב פָּפָּא דְּקָרוּ לֵיהּ בֵּי גַּרְגּוּתָא דִּפְלָנְיָא – **Rav Pappa said: "That they call it the field of So-and-so's waterhole."**[11]

A ruling similar to that of R' Yochanan:

יָתִיב רַב אַחָא בַּר עַוְיָא קַמֵּיהּ דְּרַב אַסִּי – **Rav Acha bar Avya was sitting before Rav Assi** וְיָתִיב וְקָאָמַר מִשְּׁמֵיהּ דְּרַב אַסִּי בַּר חֲנִינָא – **and he sat and said in the name of Rav Assi bar Chanina:** חֲצוּבָא מַפְסִיק בְּנִכְסֵי הַגֵּר – ***Chatzuva*** [i.e. *chatzav*] divides a field **in regard to the estate of a convert** who died without heirs.

The Gemara inquires:

מַאי חֲצוּבָא – **What is *chatzuva*?**[12] אָמַר רַב יְהוּדָה אָמַר רַב שֶׁבוֹ

NOTES

1. According to R' Yose, the two acts of carrying combine only if the person placed both halves in the same public domain. But if he placed them in two separate public domains, then they do not combine. For in R' Yose's opinion, domains "separate" for purposes of *chatas* liability (*Rashbam*).

2. I.e. a private domain. [For purposes of the Sabbath laws, a private domain is an area at least four *tefachim* square enclosed by partitions that are at least ten *tefachim* high.] A private domain situated between two public ones is said to be "[an area that can create] a *chatas* liability," since one who inadvertently carries between one of the public domains and the private one is liable for a *chatas* (*Rashbam*). Therefore [since the intervening private domain is so different from the public domains on either side of it that a person carrying from one to the other incurs *chatas* liability], the intervening private domain is considered a significant separator, which serves to divide the public domains into two distinct areas (ibid.).

3. [A *karmelis* is an area of at least four *tefachim* by four *tefachim* that is neither a public domain nor a private one (e.g. an open field). Though Rabbinic law treats a *karmelis* like a domain that is at the same time both public and private, Biblical law considers it a non-domain; thus, if one carries between the *karmelis* and a public or private domain, he does not incur any *chatas* liability.] Under Biblical law [which views a *karmelis* as a non-domain], the intervening *karmelis* is considered auxiliary to the public domain on either side of it (*Rashbam*). [Therefore, the *karmelis* does not interrupt the two public domains and they are deemed as one in regard to *chatas* liability.]

4. I.e. a block that is not four *tefachim* wide. Since it lacks even the minimally significant width of four *tefachim*, the block of wood is deemed a *mekom petur* [an exempt area], which is absolutely auxiliary to the public domains on either side of it. (Even under Rabbinic law, it is permitted to carry between a public [or private] domain and the *mekom petur* that borders upon it, since it is considered absolutely auxiliary to the adjoining domain.) Therefore, the block of wood does not legally divide the public domain into two distinct areas (*Rashbam*; cf. *Tosafos*).

5. Rava's view here is identical to that which he stated above (55b) that even a boundary divider or *chatzav* plant are separators in regard to the laws of the Sabbath; that is, if one of them bisects a public domain, it effectively creates two distinct areas in regard to *chatas* liability (see *Rashbam*). Thus, according to R' Yose, if a person inadvertently placed half a dried fig on one side of the separator and another half on the other side of the separator, there is no *chatas* liability incurred.

As the Gemara above (55b) infers, however, Ravin disagrees and does not consider a boundary divider or *chatzav* plant a separator in regard to the laws of Sabbath (i.e. *chatas* liability, according to R' Yose's view).

6. See *Rashbam*; cf. *Maharshal* and *Maharsha*.

7. The reference is to a law taught in *Gittin* 77b, regarding a husband who lends a yard to his wife so that she should have a domain into which her bill of divorce can be deposited. [A divorce is effected by the husband placing the bill of divorce in his wife's hand or domain (ibid. 77a).] The husband tossed the bill into the loaned yard, but it landed on a block of wood narrower than four *tefachim* rather than on the ground. The Gemara there rules that the surface of the block is considered a domain distinct from that of the yard. And since the husband lent his wife the yard, not the block of wood, the bill has not been deposited in her domain and the divorce has not been effected. Referring to this law, Rava stated that the domain in regard to the Sabbath is like the domain in regard to divorce: Just as the block of wood is viewed as a domain distinct from the yard in the case of divorce, so too is a block of wood considered distinct from the public domain in R' Yose's case of two public domains. Hence, as a distinct domain, the block of wood serves to separate an otherwise contiguous public domain into two distinct areas; if half a dried fig is deposited in the public domain on one side of the block and half on the other, the acts do not combine in regard to *chatas* liability (*Rashbam*; *Rabbeinu Gershom*).

8. [The Gemara above (54b) has already given an answer to such a query according to Rav's view. Here, the Gemara seeks an answer according to the view of R' Yochanan, who disputes Rav (*Rashbam*; cf. *Ritva*).]

9. [This follows *Rashbam,* who understands that R' Merinos cited here is an Amora, a contemporary of R' Yochanan. See, however, *Tosafos,* who adduce strong evidence to support their contention that the Gemara means to cite an explanation that the Tanna R' Merinos said in the name of R' Eliezer in regard to the laws of *tumah.*]

10. I.e. whatever land is called by the same field name as the place of the proprietary act – "So-and-so's *field*" (singular). But the further reaches of the convert's estate that are known by a different field name are not acquired by virtue of this proprietary act. Thus, if an unbroken expanse of the convert's estate is referred to as "So-and-so's *fields*" (plural), the entire expanse cannot be acquired simply by performing a proprietary act in one place. The proprietary act extends to whatever is part of that field as defined by its name, but does not extend to the next field, even though there is no physical demarcation between the two (*Rashbam*).

11. The convert owned an expanse of land that he irrigated from a single reservoir within it. The entire expanse is considered a single field, since it is called "the expanse irrigated by So-and-so from his waterhole" (see *Rashbam*).

12. I.e. what is it and what is its significance that it should serve to demarcate boundaries? (*Rashbam*).

ברשות אחת חייב בשתי רשויות פטור (א) ואמר רבה (א) והוא שיש חיוב חטאת ביניהם אבל כרמלית לא אביי אמר אפילו כרמלית אבל פיסלא לא רבא אמר אפי' פיסלא ואזדא רבא לטעמיה דאמר רבא רשות שבת כרשות גיטין דמי אין שם לא מצר ולא חצב מאי פירש רבי מרינוס משמו (ב) כל שנקראת על שמו היכי דמי אמר רב פפא דקרו ליה בי גרגותא דפלניא יתיב רב אחא בר עויא קמיה דר' אסי ויתיב וקאמר משמיה דר' אסי בר חנינא חצובא מפסיק בנכסי הגר מאי חצובא אמר רב יהודה אמר רב שבו תיחם יהושע לישראל את הארץ ואמר רב יהודה אמר רב לא מנה יהושע אלא עיירות העומדות על הגבולין אמר רב יהודה אמר שמואל (ג) כל שהראהו הקב"ה למשה חייב במעשר לאפוקי מאי לאפוקי קיני קניזי וקדמוני תניא רבי מאיר אומר נפתוחא ערבאה ושלמאה רבי יהודה אומר הר שעיר עמון ומואב רבי שמעון אומר ערדיסקים אסיא ואספמיא: **מתני'** (ד) היו שנים מעידין אותו שאכלה שלש שנים ונמצאו זוממים משלמין לו את הכל שנים בראשונה שנים בשניה ושנים בשלישית משלשין

ברשות אחת. ברה"ר עלמה שהוליא בה חלי גרוגרת לאותה עלמו הוליא האחרון: **בשתי רשויות.** הרבים המופלגים זה מזה פטור דרשויות מחלקות ס"ל: **ואמר רבה.** אימתי חשיבי שתי רשויות: **והוא שיש חיוב חטאת ביניהן.** שיש רה"י בין שתי רה"ר שאם הוליא ממנו לכאן או מהן הכניס לו חייב חטאת הלכך חשיב הפסק לעשותן שתים: **אבל כרמלית.** כגון בקעה שבינתים לא מחלקא להו דבטל מן התורה להכא ולהכא: **אבל פיסלא לא.** כגון חתיכת עץ או עמוד שאין גבוה י' (א) אמות ואין רוחב ד' א"נ גבוה י' אלא שאין רוחב ד' דהוי מקום פטור דאפילו מדרבנן מותר לטלטל מתוכו לרה"ר ומרה"ר לתוכו וכן מתוכו לרה"י ומרה"י לתוכו וכיון דבטל לגמרי להכא ולהכא אפילו מדרבנן דליכא מקום חשוב של ד' טפחים הלכך לא הוי הפסק: **רבא אמר אפילו פיסלא.** מחלקת הרשויות לפטרו מחיוב שבת דלא גרע ממצר וחצב: **ואזדא רבא לטעמיה.** דאמר לעיל אפי' לענין שבת: **כרשות גיטין דמי.** דאמרי' במס' גיטין בהזורק (דף עז.) דאם הקנה לה חצרו להתגרש וזרק לה גט ונפל על הפיסלא שבחצר אינה מגורשת דהא פיסלא מקום אחר הוא בפני עצמו ואינו בכלל חצר וחצר הקנה לה ולא פיסלא דחד מקום מושלי אינש תרי מקומות לא מושלי אינש הכי מפרשינן לה התם וקאמר רבה רשות שבת דומה לרשות גיטין דה"נ לענין שבת הויא הך פיסלא מקום חשוב בפני עצמו ומחלק רשויות אם הוא ממוצע בינתים דכי היכי דלא בטיל פיסלא לגבי חצר ה"נ לא בטיל הכא לענין שבת לגבי רה"ר: וקבעי גמרא לר' יוחנן דאמר המצר והחצב מפסיקין בנכסי הגר שלא יקנה בחזקת חבירו עד שיחזיק בשתיהן ואם אין שם לא מצר ולא חצב דאינה מסויימת במצרים מה לי אמר רבי יוחנן כמה צריך להחזיק שיקנה הכל דאילו רב ושמואל אמרו לעיל (ג) כדאזיל תיירא דתורי והדר אלא משום דשמעינן ליה לרבי יוחנן שיעור אחר קבעי ליה: **פירש רבי מרינוס משמו.** של רבי יוחנן: **כל שנקראת על שמו.** כל שנקראת (ב) על שדה אחד בלשון יחיד על שמו שקורין לה שדה פלוני שאין אומר שדות פלוני קנה הכל במכוש אחד: **בי גרגותא דפלניא.** כל השדה שהיה הגר משקה מבורו קנה הכל במכוש אחד: **מאי חצובא.** איזה דבר הוא ומאי חשיבותו להחשב כמצר: **שבו תיחם.** בין שבט לשבט בין איש לאיש לפי שאינו יונק לא מכאן ולא מכאן: **לא מנה יהושע כו'.** כדאמר בפ"ק (לעיל דף יד:) יהושע כתב ספרו: **על הגבולין.** כדי להראות התחומין ופשטיה דקרא אתא לאשמועינן מה טעם חשב אותן עיירות: **כל שהראהו הקדוש ברוך הוא למשה.** בשעת מיתתו כדכתיב ויראהו ה' את כל הארץ את הגלעד עד דן (דברים לד): **חייב במעשר.** דהא הם ז' עממים הכתובים בכל מקום אבל קיני קניזי וקדמוני שנתנו לאברהם אבינו (ג) בין הבתרים לא יתחייבו במעשר לעתיד לבא כשיחזירם לנו לעתיד כדאמר בב"ר אי נמי אם כבשו ישראל מהם אחרי מות יהושע כולן פטורין מן המעשר דכתיב התם זאת הארץ אשר נשבעתי וגו' (שם) זאת למעוטי הני שנתוספו לאברהם על השבועה כן נראה בעיני ואף על גב דרפאים נמי כתיב באברהם לא ממעטינן ליה דהיינו חוי דלא כתיב התם ומלינו שכבשם משה דכתיב (דברים ג) ההוא יקרא ארץ רפאים כלומר היינו רפאים שניתן לאברהם (ג) בין הבתרים: **תניא ר"מ אומר כו'.** כולהו הני תנאי בפירוש דקיני קניזי וקדמוני פליגי: **מתני'** **נמצאו זוממין.** שבאו ב' ואמרו להם היאך ראיתם חזקה זו והלא באותו הזמן עמנו הייתם במקום פלוני: **משלמין לו את הכל.** כפי דמי קרקע שהיו רוצים להפסידו יגבה מהן כדכתיב (דברים יט) כאשר זמם ולא כאשר עשה לבד קרקע שלו שיטול מן המחזיק: **שנים בראשונה כו'.** דהיינו ג' כתות לג' השנים כת לשנה כת אם נמצאו זוממים כולם: (ג) **משלשין ביניהן.** כל כת תתן השליש דג' כתות הם וקי"ל (ד) מכות ה:) אין עדים נעשים זוממין עד שיזומו כולם:

שלש

אבל פיסלא לא. הקשה ריב"א והלא פיסלא היא כרמלית דבהזורק (גיטין דף עז: ושם ד"ה פליג) מפרש דפיסלא דהוי גבי גט רשות לעצמה כגון דלא גבוה י' א"כ משמע דגבוהה ג' ומסתמא איירי ברחבה ארבעה דלא אשכחן רשות בפני עצמו שהוא חשיב בפחות מארבעה ועמוד גבוה ג' ורחב ד' ברה"ר הוי כרמלית וא"כ אמאי קאמר אבל פיסלא לא וי"ל דמ"מ הואיל וקטן הוא כל כך ומטלטל לא חשיבא לאביי להפסיק בין ב' רשויות בכרמלית: **אין** שם לא מצר כו'. אטומאה קאי כדמוכח בהדיא בתוספתא דטהרות (פ"ז) דקתני הנכנס לבקעה בימות הגשמים וטומאה בשדה פלוני אמרו לפני רבי אליעזר הרי היא של רה"י פירש ר' מרינוס משמו כל שיש לה שם בפני עצמה כו' ולא כפ"ה דפירש משמו דקאמר רבי מרינוס היינו משמו של רבי יוחנן:

העומדות על הגבולים. אין לפרש על הגבולים של א"י דכמה עיירות חשיב שהם באמצע א"י אלא בגבולים דכל שבט ושבט וכו': **כל** שהראהו כו'. טפי הוה ליה למינקט מה שתיאם באלה מסעי שמונה עיירות של המצר ושם מפורש היטב תחום של ארץ ישראל: **חייב** במעשר. וא"ת וכללא הוא והלא הרבה כרכים כבשום עולי מצרים ולא כבשום עולי בבל ולא נתחייבו במעשר אע"פ שהראם למשה וי"ל דקסבר קדושה ראשונה קידשה לשעתה וקידשה לעתיד לבא והשתא ניחא שלא תקשי כל לאתויי מאי דאתא לאתויי כרכים שכבשו עולי מצרים ולא כבשו עולי בבל: **לאפוקי** מאי. תימה מאי קאמר לאפוקי מאי והא כל קאמר דמשמע לאתויי וי"ל (ד) דמשהראהו דייק דמשמע לאפוקי וא"ת ולימא לאפוקי חו"ל וי"ל דאין זה חידוש ולכך אמר לאפוקי קיני וקניזי וקדמוני אף על גב דמא"י הם: **הר** שעיר עמון ומואב. תימה דמשמע דעמון ומואב לא כבשום עולי מצרים ובספ"ק דיבמות (דף טז. ושם) אמרינן עמון ומואב מעשרין מעשר עני בשביעית דאמר מר הרבה כרכים כבשו כו' וקסבר קדושה ראשונה לא קידשה לעתיד והניחום שיסמכו עליהם עניים בשביעית ואין לומר דהתם בעמון ומואב שטהרו בסיחון דהתם נהג שביעית דהיינו עבר הירדן דאמרינן בפסחים (דף נב.) ג' ארצות לביעור יהודה ועבר הירדן והגליל ואומר ר"ת דעבר הירדן היינו ארץ סיחון ועוג שלא היתה מעמון ומואב ועוד מתרץ ר"ת דיבמות נמי איירי בעמון ומואב שלא טהרו בסיחון כדהכא ולא בא לפרש התם אמאי אין שביעית נוהגת שם דהא חוצה לארץ היא אלא לפרש למה מעשרין מעשר עני ולא מעשרין מעשר שני שלא לשנות סדר השנים דבמס' ידים (פ"ד משנה ג) איכא פלוגתא דר' אלעזר בן עזריה גזר שיעשרו מעשר שני כמו בבבל שלא לשנות מסדר השנים ור"ט גזר שיעשרו מעשר עני כמו במצרים שהיא קרובה מעשרין מעשר עני כדי שיהו עניי ישראל נסמכים עליהם אף עמון ומואב שהם קרובים כו' וא"ת ואמאי לא מייתי ביבמות ההוא טעמא דמצרים דתנן במסכת ידים (שם) וי"ל דניחא ליה למימר טפי הרבה כרכים כו' דלמ"ד לא קידשה הניחו אפי' מא"י עצמה ליכבש מפני סמך עניים וזה התירוץ עיקר דבהכי מיתרצא דלא קשיא דר"א אדר"א ורבי יהושע אדרבי יהושע ואין להאריך: **ערדיסקים** אסיא כו'. תימה דמשמע אסיא בחו"ל היא וא"כ היכי קאמר בפ' זה בורר (סנהדרין דף כו. ושם) רבי חייא בר זרונקי ור"ש בן יהוצדק הוו קאזלי לעבר השנה בעסיא והתניא בפ"ק דסנהדרין (דף יא: ושם ד"ה אין) דאין מעברין אלא ביהודה ובשלמא ר"מ דעיבר שנה בעסיא (מגילה יח:) איכא למימר דלא הניח כמותו בא"י כדאמרינן בברכות (דף סג.) אר"ע אלא ר' חייא ור"ש ליכא למימר דלא הניחו כמותן דהא ר"ל הוי קרי להו רועי בקר וחשודים על השביעית וי"ל דההוא לעבר היינו חישוב כמו ועיבר שלש שנים זו אחר זו דפרק קמא דהתם (דף יב.) תדע דהא שנה שביעית היתה ותני התם (סוף פ"ק) (דף יב.) דאין מעברין שנים בשביעית:

משלשין

מסורת הש"ס

א) [שבת פ.], ב) [דף נד:], ג) שייך לע"ב, ד) [חגיגה טז:]:

הגהות הב"ח

(א) רשב"ם ד"ה אבל פיסלא וכו' שאין גבוה עשרה ואין רוחב כצ"ל ותיבת אמות נמחק: (ב) ד"ה כל וכו' שנקראת שדה א' כצ"ל ותיבת על נמחק: (ג) ד"ה חייב וכו' לאברהם אבינו בברית בין הבתרים: (ד) תוס' ד"ה לאפוקי וכו' וי"ל דמה שהראהו:

ליקוטי רש"י

בשתי רשויות. ושתיהן רשות הרבים אלא שיש הפסק ביניהם. [שבת פ.]. **פטור.** דרשויות מחלקות [כריתות יז.]. **והוא שיש חיוב חטאת ביניהם.** שמופסקות ברשות היחיד אבל אם היה כרמלית מפסיקן כגון קרפף יותר מבית סאתים או בקעה ושני בתים פתוחים אחד לרשות הרבים זה ואחד לזה והוליא חלי גרוגרת מבית זה לרשות זה וחלי גרוגרת מבית זה לרשות זה שהיא פתוחה לה חייב דכיון דלא מפסיק לה רשות היחיד חדא רשותא הוא [שבת שם]. **אבל כרמלית לא.** כרמלית לשון יערו וכרמלו (ישעיה י) שאינו לא הילוך תמיד לרבים ולא תשמיש רשות היחיד [שם ג:]. כרמל. יער גבוה [ישעיה י, יח]. **פיסלא.** עץ שוכב לרחבו של רשות הרבים וממלא כל רחבו והוליא חלי גרוגרת מביתו מכאן וחלי גרוגרת מכאן [שבת פ.]. פיסלא. חתיכת עץ [גיטין עז:]. **כרשות גיטין דמי.** ולענין גיטין פיסלא רשות לנפשיה הוא כדאמרן בהזורק (גטין עז:) ההוא גברא דזרק גיטא לדביתהו בחצירו איגנדר גיטא ונפל בפיסלא ואוקי התם שהשאיל לה מקום בחצירו חד מקום מושלי אינשי תרי מקומות לא מושלי אינשי [שבת שם]. **חצובא.** עשב ששרשיו נוקבין ויורדין בעומק ואין מתפשטין לצדדין כלל ונוטעין אותו בין גבולי שדות ובו תיחם יהושע לישראל את הארץ [ביצה כה: וכעי"ז פסחים קיא:]. עשב שמשתרש בעומק כנגדו ואין שרשיו מתפשטין ובו תיחם יהושע את הארץ לישראל [שבת קכח.]. הוא אילן או עשב שבו תיחם יהושע את ארץ ישראל לפי שיורד ויונק כנגדו ואינו יונק לא מכאן ולא מכאן כדאמר (ביצה כה:) תגובה מקצע רגליהון דרשעים שמשיגין גבול לחבריהן וזה אינו משיג גבול אחר [רשב"ם לעיל נה.]. **נמצאו זוממין.** כילד דין זוממין דקתני במתני' אבל אמרו להם המזימים היאך אתם מעידים עדות זה והלא באותו היום עמנו הייתם במקום פלוני כו' [מכות ב.].

עין משפט נר מצוה

רנב א מיי' פי"ח מהל' שבת הלכה כד:
רנג ב מיי' פ"א מהל' זכיה הל' יג ועי' בהשגות ובמ"מ ובל"מ טוש"ע ח"מ סי' ערה סעיף ז:
רנד ג מיי' פ"א מהל' תרומות וע"ש כל הפרק:
רנה ד מיי' פכ"א מהל' עדות הלכה ז טור ח"מ סי' לח:

רבינו גרשום

אמר רבה. היכא אמרי' לשתי רשויות פטור **הוא שיש חיוב חטאת ביניהן** כגון מקום שהוא רה"י בין אלו ב' רשויות הרבים כגון עמוד גבוה י' ורחב ד' מפסיק בין אלו ב' רשויות הואיל דהוא מקום חשוב שאם היה מוציא גרוגרת שלם ביחד מתוכו לרה"ר חייב חטאת להכי יש לו כח להפסיקו כשהוציאן לחצאין דפטור: **אבל כרמלית לא.** הוי הפסק ומצטרפין וחייב: **אפי' פיסלא.** הוי הפסק לשבת ולא מצטרפי: **פיסלא.** היינו חתיכה של עץ שנמוכה מי' ואינה רחבה ד' דהיינו כל שהוא כעין מצר וחצב: **רשות שבת כרשות גיטין דמי.** מה לענין גט מפסיק שאם זרק לה גט על הפיסלא והיא עומדת על הקרקע או עומדת על הפיסלא וזרק הגט על הקרקע אינו גט עד שיהיו היא וגיטה במקום אחד כך מפסיק נמי לענין שבת בין שני חצאי גרוגרת לפוטרו: **אין שם לא מצר ולא חצב.** בנכסי הגר והחזיק בה אחד במכושו: **מאי.** עד היכן קנה: **כל שנקראת על שמו** של גר זכה: **היכי דמי** נקראת על שמו: כל היכא **דקרו ליה בי גרגותא דפלניא** גר. כל השדה שהיה משקה הגר מבורו זכה זה בה: **שבו תיחם.** בין איש לחבירו: **לא מנה יהושע** בספרו. **אלא עיירות העומדות על הגבולים** של א"י מכלל דאחריני הוי טובא שלא היה יכול להזכירן: **קיני וקניזי וקדמוני.** דכרת הקב"ה לאברהם אבינו. פטור ממעשר דלא ראם משה דאינן מז' עממין והיינו נמי דרבי מאיר ור"י ור' שמעון: **פיסקא שנים. מעידים אותו בראשונה. שאכלה** שנה ראשונה: **ושנים בשנה** שניה **ושנים בשלישי'** ונמצאו זוממין.

תִּיהֵם יְהוֹשֻׁעַ לְיִשְׂרָאֵל אֶת הָאָרֶץ – **Rav Yehudah said in the name of Rav:** It is the plant **with which Joshua demarcated** the various portions of **the Land for** the people of **Israel.**[13]

The Gemara now quotes other statements by Rav Yehudah concerning the boundaries of Eretz Yisrael:

וְאָמַר רַב יְהוּדָה אָמַר רַב – **And Rav Yehudah said in the name of Rav:** לֹא מָנָה יְהוֹשֻׁעַ אֶלָּא עֲיָירוֹת הָעוֹמְדוֹת עַל הַגְּבוּלִין – **Joshua enumerated** in the Book of *Joshua* **only those cities situated on the boundaries.**[14]

Another statement:

אָמַר רַב יְהוּדָה אָמַר שְׁמוּאֵל – **Rav Yehudah said in the name of Shmuel:** כָּל שֶׁהֶרְאָהוּ הַקָּדוֹשׁ בָּרוּךְ הוּא לְמֹשֶׁה חַיָּיב בְּמַעֲשֵׂר – **Whatever** land **the Holy One, Blessed is He, showed Moses** before his death **is obligated in tithes.**[15] לְאַפּוּקֵי מַאי – **What** land does Rav Yehudah mean **to exclude?** לְאַפּוּקֵי קֵינִי קְנִיזִי וְקַדְמוֹנִי – He means **to exclude** the lands of **the Kenites, Kenizzites and Kadmonites.**[16]

The Gemara presents various Tannaic views regarding the precise identity of the lands of the Kenites, Kenizzites and Kadmonites:

תַּנְיָא רַבִּי מֵאִיר אוֹמֵר נַפְּתוּחָא עַרְבָאָה וְשַׁלְמָאָה – **It was taught in a Baraisa: R' MEIR SAYS:** They are, respectively: **THE NAPHTUCHIM, ARABIANS AND SHALMAITES.** רַבִּי יְהוּדָה אוֹמֵר הַר שֵׂעִיר עַמּוֹן וּמוֹאָב – **R' YEHUDAH SAYS:** They are the regions of **MOUNT SEIR, AMMON AND MOAB.**[17] רַבִּי שִׁמְעוֹן אוֹמֵר עַרְדִּיסְקִיס אַסְיָא וְאַסְפַּמְיָא – **R' SHIMON SAYS:** They are the regions of **DAMASCUS, ASIA MINOR AND ASPAMIA.**

Mishnah

הָיוּ שְׁנַיִם מְעִידִין אוֹתוֹ שֶׁאֲכָלָהּ שָׁלֹשׁ שָׁנִים – If **two** witnesses **testified on behalf [of a person] that he used [a property] for three years**[18] וְנִמְצְאוּ זוֹמְמִים – **and they are found to be** ***zomemim,*** מְשַׁלְּמִין לוֹ אֶת הַכֹּל – **they pay [the original owner] everything.**[19] שְׁנַיִם בָּרִאשׁוֹנָה שְׁנַיִם בַּשְּׁנִיָּה וּשְׁנַיִם בַּשְּׁלִישִׁית – If **two** witnesses testified **concerning the first** year's use, **two** others testified **concerning the second** year's use **and two** others testified **concerning the third** year's use, and they were found to be *zomemim,*[20]

NOTES

13. When Joshua apportioned the conquered land of Canaan to the Israelites, he had the *chatzav* planted along the borders between tribe and tribe, as well as between individual estates within a given tribe. He used this plant because its roots grow straight down and do not spread out, and siphon off nutrients from the adjoining land, as other plants do (*Rashbam*). Joshua thereby indicated to the landowners that they should emulate the ways of the *chatzav* and not encroach on their neighbor's property (*Rashbam* and *Ritva* to 55a ד״ה המצר והחצב, citing a related statement in *Beitzah* 25b).

14. Rav Yehudah is explaining why only certain cities appear in the lists recorded in the Book of *Joshua* (a book that was written by Joshua himself – see above, 14b). He explains that Scripture enumerated only those cities that demarcated the boundaries (*Rashbam*). [Though some of the cities listed are unquestionably interior cities, these, too, demarcated the boundaries between one tribe and the next (*Tosafos*; cf. *Rabbeinu Gershom*).]

15. Moses was denied the privilege of entering Eretz Yisrael. However, as stated in *Deuteronomy* (34:1-3), God took him up to Mount Nevo and showed him all of Eretz Yisrael. Moses was shown the land of the seven Canaanite nations mentioned often in the Torah [i.e. the Canaanites, Perizzites, Hittites, Hivvites, Girgashites, Emorites and Jebusites] (*Rashbam*). These lands compose Eretz Yisrael proper, and *terumos* and *maasros* must be separated from produce that is grown there.

16. These are the lands of three additional nations that God promised to Abraham at the Covenant between the Parts (*Genesis* 15:19). [The other seven nations mentioned in that context (vs. 20-21) are the standard Seven Canaanite Nations, the Rephaim being identical with the Hivvites.] These three additional lands were not shown to Moses. Rav Yehudah teaches us that although these three additional lands will eventually become the property of the Jewish nation, as promised to Abraham, their produce will not be obligated in tithes. Similarly, he teaches us that even if some parts of these lands were conquered by the Jews subsequent to Joshua's death, they are exempt from tithes (see *Rashbam;* see also *Kovetz Shiurim*).

17. Elsewhere in the Talmud, we find that parts of Ammon and Moab were conquered by Sichon, king of the Emorites, whose lands were in turn conquered by the Israelites, and that tithes were required from the produce of those lands. This does not represent a contradiction of R' Yehudah's view in this Baraisa, since he refers to the majority of Ammon and Moab, which was *not* conquered by Sichon or the Israelites (see *Ritva* and *Tosafos*).

18. A person has held a field for three years without protest from the original owner. Now, the original owner claims that the occupant in fact stole the field from him. The occupant is unable to produce the deed, but he does produce witnesses who substantiate his three-year occupancy of the premises. If the witnesses are believed, then the occupant has established his *chazakah* and is awarded title to the field.

19. I.e. other witnesses come and testify that the first pair could not possibly know whether or not the occupant lived in the field for those three years, since the first pair was in their company during that time in a distant place.

Ordinarily, when two pairs of witnesses offer conflicting testimony, the result is a stalemate; the court does not know which pair to believe (see above, 31b). However, the Torah decrees that when the second pair does not directly contradict facts asserted by the first pair, but rather impugns the first pair's ability to have witnessed the event altogether – i.e. the second pair testifies that at the time of the alleged event, the first pair was in their company in a distant place, where it was impossible for them to witness what they claim transpired – then the testimony of the second pair is accepted. The first witnesses are designated as *zomemim* [plotters], who have sought to impose a liability on their victim through false testimony. The Torah decrees that whatever penalty the *zomemim* sought to impose upon their victim be assessed against them, be it financial liability or physical punishment (see *Deuteronomy* 19:16-21 and *Makkos,* chapter 1).

In the case of our Mishnah, then, the *zomemim* sought to deprive the original owner of his field by falsely testifying that the occupant had established a *chazakah.* Accordingly, they must pay the value of that field to the owner, who receives these punitive damages in addition to the field itself, which he retrieves from the occupant (*Rashbam*).

20. I.e. there were three pairs of witnesses, each testifying concerning a different one of the occupant's three years of occupancy. Thus, the occupant's *chazakah* is established through the combined testimony of three pairs of witnesses. After testifying, all three pairs were found to be *zomemim* (*Rashbam*).

ברשות אחת חייב בשתי רשויות פטור (א) ואמר רבה (א) והוא שיש חיוב חטאת ביניהם אבל כרמלית לא אביי אמר אפילו כרמלית אבל פיסלא לא רבא אמר אפי' פיסלא ואזדא רבא לטעמיה דאמר רבא רשות שבת כרשות גיטין דמי אין שם לא מצר ולא חצב מאי פירש רבי מריניס משמו (ב) כל שנקראת על שמו היכי דמי אמר רב פפא דקרו ליה בי גרגותא דפלניא יתיב רב אחא בר עויא קמיה דר' אסי ויתיב וקאמר משמיה דר' אסי בר חנינא חצובא מפסיק בנכסי הגר מאי חצובא אמר רב יהודה אמר רב שבו תיחם יהושע לישראל את הארץ ואמר רב יהודה אמר רב לא מנה יהושע אלא עיירות העומדות על הגבולין אמר רב יהודה אמר שמואל (ג) כל שהראהו הקב"ה למשה חייב במעשר לאפוקי מאי לאפוקי קיני קניזי וקדמוני תניא רבי מאיר אומר נפתוחא ערבאה ושלמאה רבי יהודה אומר הר שעיר עמון ומואב רבי שמעון אומר ערדיסקים אסיא ואספמיא: **מתני'** (ד) היו שנים מעידין אותו שאכלה שלש שנים ונמצאו זוממים משלמין לו את הכל שנים בראשונה שנים בשניה ושנים בשלישית משלשין

ברשות אחת. ברה"ר עלמה שהוליא בה חלי גרוגרת ולאשון באותה עלמו הוליא האחרון: **בשתי רשויות.** הרבים המופלגים זה מזה פטור דרשויות מחלקות ס"ל: **ואמר רבה.** אימתי חשיבי שתי רשויות: **והוא שיש חיוב חטאת ביניהן.** שיש רה"י בין שתי רה"ר שאם הוליא ממנו להן או מהן הכניס לו חייב חטאת הלכך חשיב הפסק לעשותן שתים: **אבל כרמלית.** כגון בקעה שביניהם לא מחלקא להו דבטל מן התורה להכא ולהכא: **אבל פיסלא לא.** כגון חתיכת עץ או עמוד שאין גבוה י' (א) אמות ואין רוחב ד' א"נ גבוה י' אלא שאין רוחב ד' דהוי מקום פטור דאפילו מדרבנן מותר לטלטל מתוכו לרה"ר ומרה"ר לתוכו וכן מתוכו לרה"י ומרה"י לתוכו וכיון דבטל לגמרי להכא ולהכא אפילו מדרבנן ליכא מקום חשוב של ד' טפחים הלכך לא הוי הפסק: **רבא אמר אפילו פיסלא.** מחלקת הרשויות לפטרו מחיוב שבת דלא גרע ממלר וחלב: **ואזדא רבא לטעמיה.** דאמר לעיל אפי' לענין שבת: **כרשות גיטין דמי.** דאמרי' במס' גיטין בזורק (דף עז.) דאם הקנה לה חלרו להתגרש וזרק לה גט ונפל על הפיסלא שבחלר אינה מגורשת דהא פיסלא מקום אחר הוא בפני עלמו ואינו בכלל חלר וחלר הקנה לה ולא פיסלא דחד מקום מושיל איניש תרי מקומות לא מושיל איניש הכי מפרשינן לה התם וקאמר רבא רשות שבת דומה לרשות גיטין דס"ל לענין שבת הויא הך פיסלא מקום חשוב בפני עלמו ומחלק רשויות אם הוא ממולע ביניהם דכי היכי דלא בטיל פיסלא לגבי חלר ה"נ לא בטיל הכא לענין שבת לגבי רה"ר: וקבעי גמרא לר' יוחנן דאמר המילר והחלב מפסיקין בנכסי הגר שלא יקנה בחזקת חבירו עד שיחזיק בשתיהן ואם אין שם לא מלר ולא חלב דאינה מסויימת במלריה מה לי אמר רבי יוחנן כמה לריך להחזיק שיקנה הכל דאילו רב ושמואל אמרו לעיל (ב) כדאזיל תירלא דתורי והדר אלא משום דשמעינן ליה לרבי יוחנן שיעור אחר קבעי ליה: **פירש רבי מריניס משמו.** של רבי יוחנן: **כל שנקראת על שמו.** כל שנקראת (ג) על שדה אחד בלשון יחיד על שמו שקורין לה שדה פלוני שאין אומר שדות פלוני קנה הכל במכוש אחד: **בי גרגותא דפלניא.** כל השדה שהיה הגר משקה מבורו קנה הכל במכוש אחד: **מאי חצובא.** איזה דבר הוא ומאי חשיבותו להחשב כמלר: **שבו תיחם.** בין שבט לשבט בין איש לאיש לפי שאינו יונק לא מכאן ולא מכאן: **לא מנה יהושע כו'.** כדאמר בפ"ק (לעיל דף יד:) יהושע כתב ספרו: **על הגבולין.** כדי להראות התחומין ושביטה דקרא אתא לאשמועינן מה טעם חשב אותן עיירות: **כל שהראהו הקדוש ברוך הוא למשה.** בשעת מיתתו כדכתיב ויראהו ה' את כל הארץ את הגלעד עד דן (דברים לד): **חייב במעשר.** דהא הם ז' עממים הכתובים בכל מקום אבל קיני קניזי וקדמוני שנתנו לאברהם אבינו (ג) בין הבתרים לא יתחייבו במעשר לעתיד לבא כשיחזירום לנו לעתיד כדאמר בב"ר לי נמי אם כבשו ישראל מהם אחרי מות יהושע כולן פטורין מן המעשר דכתיב התם זאת הארץ אשר נשבעתי וגו' (שם) זאת למעוטי הני שנתוספו לאברהם על השבעה כן נראה בעיני ואף על גב דרפאים נמי כתיב באברהם לא ממעטינן ליה דהיינו חוי דלא כתיב התם ומלינו שכבשם משה דכתיב (דברים ג) ההוא יקרא ארץ רפאים כלומר היינו רפאים שניתן לאברהם (ג) בין הבתרים: **תניא ר"מ אומר כו'.** כולהו הני תנאי בפירוש דקיני קניזי וקדמוני פליגי: **מתני' נמצאו זוממין.** שבאו ב' ואמרו להם היאך לאיתם חזקה זו והלא באותו הזמן עמנו הייתם במקום פלוני: **משלמין לו את הכל.** כפי דמי קרקע שהיו רולים להפסידו יגבה מהן דכתיב (דברים יט) כאשר זמם ולא כאשר עשה לבד קרקע שלו שיטול מן המחזיק: **שנים בראשונה כו'.** דהיינו ג' כתות לג' השנים כת לשנה כת לשנה אם נמלאו זוממים כולם: (ג) **משלשין ביניהן.** כל כת תתן השליש דג' כתות הם וקי"ל (מכות ה:) אין עדים נעשים זוממין עד שיזומו כולם:

שלם

אבל פיסלא לא. הקשה ריב"א והלא פיסלא היא כרמלית דבזורק (גיטין דף עז: ושם ד"ה פליג) מפרש דפיסלא דהוי גבי גט רשות לעצמה כגון דלא גבוה י' א"כ משמע דגבוהה ג' ומסתמא איירי ברחבה ארבעה דלא אשכחן רשות בפני עצמו שהוא חשיב בפחות מארבעה ועמוד גבוה ג' ורחב ד' ברה"ר הוי כרמלית וא"כ מאי קאמר אבל פיסלא לא וי"ל דמ"מ הואיל וקטן הוא כל כך ומטלטל לא חשיבא לאביי להפסיק בין ב' רשויות ככרמלית: **אין שם לא מצר כו'.** לטומאה קאי כדמוכח בהדיא בתוספתא דטהרות (פ"ו) דקתני הנכנס לבקעה בימות הגשמים וטומאה בשדה פלוני אמרו לפני רבי אליעזר הרי היא של רה"י פירש ר' מריניס משמו כל שיש לה שם בפני עצמה כו' ולא כפ"ה דפירש משמו דקאמר רבי מריניס היינו משמו של רבי יוחנן: **העומדות על הגבולים.** אין לפרש על הגבולים של א"י דכמה עיירות חשיב שהם באמצע א"י אלא גבולים לכל שבט ושבט: **כל שהראהו כו'.** אפי' הוה ליה למינקט מה שתיחם באלה מסעי שמונה עיירות של המצר ושם מפורש היטב תחום של ארץ ישראל: **חייב במעשר.** וא"ת וכללא הוא והלא הרבה כרכים כבשום עולי מצרים ולא כבשום עולי בבל ולא נתחייבו במעשר אע"פ שהראם למשה וי"ל דקסבר קדושה ראשונה קידשה לשעתה וקידשה לעתיד לבא והשתא ניחא שלא תקשי כל לאתויי מאי דאתא לאתויי כרכים שכבשו עולי מצרים ולא כבשו עולי בבל: **לאפוקי** מאי. תימה מאי קאמר לאפוקי מאי והא כל קאמר דמשמע לאתויי וי"ל (ד) דמשהראהו דייק דמשמע לאפוקי וא"ת ולימא לאפוקי חו"ל וי"ל דאין זה חידוש ולכך אמר לאפוקי קיני וקניזי וקדמוני אף על גב דמא"י הם: **הר** שעיר עמון ומואב. תימה דמשמע דעמון ומואב לא כבשום עולי מצרים ובספ"ק דיבמות (דף טז. ושם) אמרינן עמון ומואב מעשרין מעשר עני בשביעית דאמר מר הרבה כרכים כבשו כו' וקסבר קדושה ראשונה לא קידשה לעתיד והניחום שיסמכו עליהם עניים בשביעית ואין לומר דהתם בעמון ומואב שטהרו בסיחון דהתם נהג שביעית דהיינו עבר הירדן דאמרינן בפסחים (דף נב.) ג' ארצות לביעור יהודה ועבר הירדן והגליל ואומר ר"ת דעבר הירדן היינו ארץ סיחון ועוג שלא היתה מעמון ומואב ועוד מתרץ ר"ת דיבמות נמי איירי בעמון ומואב שלא טהרו בסיחון כדהכא ולא בא לפרש התם אמאי אין שביעית נוהגת שם דהא חוצה לארץ היא אלא לפרש למה מעשרין מעשר עני ולא מעשרין מעשר שני שלא לשנות סדר השנים דבמס' ידים (פ"ד משנה ג) איכא פלוגתא דר' אלעזר בן עזריה גזר שיעשרו מעשר שני כמו בבבל שלא לשנות מסדר השנים ור"ט גזר שיעשרו מעשר עני כמו במצרים שהיא קרובה מעשרין מעשר עני כדי שיהו עניי ישראל נסמכים עליהם אף עמון ומואב שהם קרובים כו' וא"ת ואמאי לא מייתי ביבמות ההוא טעמא דמצרים דתנן במסכת ידים (שם) וי"ל דניחא ליה למימר טפי הרבה כרכים כו' דלמ"ד לא קידשה הניחו אפי' מא"י עצמה ליכבש מפני סמך עניים וזה התירוץ עיקר דבהכי מיתרצא דלא קשיא דר"א אדר"א ורבי יהושע אדרבי יהושע ואין להאריך: **ערדיסקים** אסיא כו'. תימה דמשמע אסיא בחו"ל היא וא"כ היכי קאמר בפ' זה בורר (סנהדרין דף כו. ושם) רבי חייא בר זרנוקי ור"ש בן יהוצדק הוו קאזלי לעבר השנה בעסיא והתניא בפ"ק דסנהדרין (דף יא: ושם ד"ה אין) דאין מעברין אלא ביהודה ובשלמא ר"מ דעיבר שנה בעסיא (מגילה יח:) איכא למימר דלא הניח כמותו בא"י כדאמרינן בברכות (דף סג.) אר"ע אלא ר' חייא ור"ש ליכא למימר דלא הניחו כמותן דהא ר"ל הוי קרי להו רועי בקר וחשודים על השביעית וי"ל דההוא לעבר היינו חישוב כמו ועיבר שלש שנים זו אחר זו דפרק קמא דהתם (דף יב.) תדע דהא שנה שביעית היתה ותני התם (סוף פ"ק) (דף יב.) דאין מעברין שנים בשביעית:

משלשין

מסורת הש"ס

א) [שבת פ.], ב) [דף נד:], ג) שייך לע"ב, ד) [חגיגה טז:]:

הגהות הב"ח

(א) רשב"ם ד"ה אבל פיסלא וכו' שאין גבוה עשרה ואין רוחב כצ"ל ותיבת אמות נמחק: (ב) ד"ה כל וכו' שנקראת שדה א' כצ"ל ותיבת על נמחק: (ג) ד"ה חייב וכו' לאברהם אבינו בברית בין הבתרים: (ד) תוס' ד"ה לאפוקי וכו' וי"ל דמה שהראהו:

ליקוטי רש"י

בשתי רשויות. ושתיהן רשות הרבים אלא שיש הפסק ביניהם [שבת פ.]. **פטור.** דרשויות מחלקות [כריתות יז.]. **והוא שיש חיוב חטאת ביניהם.** שמופסקות ברשות היחיד אבל אם היה כרמלית מפסיקן כגון קרפף יותר מבית סאתים או בקעה ושני בתים פתוחים אחד לרשות הרבים זה ואחד לזה והוציא חצי גרוגרת מבית זה לרשות זה וחצי גרוגרת מבית זה לרשות זה שהיא פתוחה לה חייב דכיון דלא מפסיק לה רשות היחיד חדא רשותא הוא [שבת שם]. **אבל כרמלית לא.** כרמלית לשון יערו וכרמלו (ישעיה י) שאינו לא הילוך תמיד לרבים ולא תשמיש רשות היחיד [שם ג:]. כרמל. יער גבוה [ישעיה י, יח]. **פיסלא.** עץ שוכב לרחבו של רשות הרבים וממלא כל רחבו והוציא חצי גרוגרת מביתו מכאן וחצי גרוגרת מכאן [שבת פ.]. פיסלא. חתיכת עץ [גיטין עז:]. **כרשות גיטין דמי.** ולענין גיטין פיסלא רשות לנפשיה הוא כדאמרן בהזורק (גיטין עז:) ההוא גברא דזרק גיטא לדביתהו בחצירו איגנדר גיטא ונפל בפיסלא ואוקי התם שהשאיל לה מקום בחצירו חד מקום מושלי איניש תרי מקומות לא מושלי איניש [שבת שם]. **חצובא.** עשב ששרשיו נוקבין ויורדין בעומק ואין מתפשטין לצדדין כלל ונוטעין אותו בין גבולי שדות וכן תיחם יהושע ליה לישראל את הארץ [ביצה כה: וכעי"ז פסחים קיא:]. עשב שמשרש בעומק כנגדו ואין שרשיו מתפשטין וכו תיחם יהושע את הארץ לישראל [שבת קכח.]. הוא אילן או עשב שבו תיחם יהושע את ארץ ישראל לפי שיורד ויונק כנגדו ואינו יונק לא מכאן ולא מכאן כדאמר (ביצה כה:) חצובא מקטע רגליהון דרשעים שמשיגין גבול רעיהן וזה אינו משיג גבול אחר [רשב"ם לעיל נה.]. **נמצאו זוממין.** כיצד דין זוממין דקתני במתני' אבל אמרו להם המזומים היאך אתם מעידים עדות זה והלא הייתם עמנו אותו היום במקום פלוני כו' [מכות ב.].

עין משפט נר מצוה

רנב א מיי' פי"ח מהל' שבת הלכה כד:
רנג ב מיי' פ"א מהל' זכיה הל' יג ועי' בהשגות ובמ"מ ובל"מ טוש"ע ח"מ סי' ערה סעיף ז:
רנד ג מיי' פ"א מהל' תרומות וע"ש כל הפרק:
רנה ד מיי' פכ"א מהל' עדות הלכה ז טור ח"מ סי' לח:

רבינו גרשום

אמר רבה. היכא אמרי' לשתי רשויות פטור **הוא שיש חיוב חטאת ביניהן** כגון מקום שהוא רה"י בין אלו ב' רשויות הרבים כגון עמוד גבוה י' ורחב ד' מפסיק בין אלו ב' רשויות הואיל דהוא מקום חשוב שאם היה מוציא גרוגרת שלם ביחד מתוכו לרה"ר חייב חטאת להכי יש לו כח להפסיק כשהוציאן לחצאין דפטור: **אבל כרמלית לא.** הוי הפסק ומצטרפין וחייב: **אפי' פיסלא.** הוי הפסק לשבת ולא מצטרפי: **פיסלא.** היינו חתיכה של עץ שנמוכה מי' ואינה רחבה ד' דהיינו כל שהוא כעין מצר וחצב: **רשות שבת כרשות גיטין דמי.** מה לענין גט מפסיק שאם זרק לה גט על הפיסלא והיא עומדת על הקרקע או עומדת על הפיסלא וזרק הגט על הקרקע אינו גט עד שיהיו היא וגיטה במקום אחד כך מפסיק נמי לענין שבת בין שני חצאי גרוגרת לפוטרו: **אין שם לא מצר ולא חצב.** בנכסי הגר והחזיק בה אחד במכושו: **מאי.** עד היכן קנה: **כל שנקראת על שמו** של גר זכה: **היכי דמי** נקראת על שמו: כל היכא **דקרו ליה בי גרגותא דפלניא** גר. כל השדה שהיה משקה הגר מבורו זכה זה בה: **שבו תיחם.** בין איש לחבירו: **לא מנה יהושע** בספרו. **אלא עיירות העומדות על הגבולים** של א"י מכלל דאחריני הוי טובא שלא היה יכול להזכירן: **קיני וקניזי וקדמוני.** דכרת הקב"ה לאברהם אבינו. פטור ממעשר דלא ראם משה דאינן מז' עממין והיינו נמי דרבי מאיר ור"י ור' שמעון: **פיסקא שנים. מעידים אותו בראשונה. שאכלה** שנה ראשונה: **ושנים** בשנה שניה **ושנים בשלישי'** ונמצאו זוממין.

משלשין ביניהם (א) א שלשה אחים ואחד מצטרף עמהם הרי אלו שלש עדיות והן עדות אחת להזמה: **גמ'** מתני' דלא כרבי עקיבא דתניא ב א"ר יוסי כשהלך אבא חלפתא אצל רבי יוחנן בן נורי ללמוד תורה ואמרי לה ר' יוחנן בן נורי אצל אבא חלפתא ללמוד תורה אמר לו הרי שאכלה שנה ראשונה בפני שנים שניה בפני שנים שלישית בפני שנים מהו אמר לו ב הרי זו חזקה אמר לו אף אני אומר כן אלא שר"ע חולק בדבר זה שהיה ר"ע אומר (א) דבר ג ולא חצי דבר ורבנן האי דבר ולא חצי דבר מאי עבדי ליה אילימא ג למעוטי אחד אומר אחת בגבה ואחד אומר אחת בכריסה האי חצי דבר (א) וחצי עדות היא ד אלא למעוטי שנים אומרים אחת בגבה ושנים אומרים אחת בכריסה אמר רב יהודה ה אחד אומר אכלה חטים ואחד אומר אכלה שעורים הרי זו חזקה מתקיף לה ר"נ אלא מעתה אחד אומר אכלה ראשונה שלישית וחמישית ואחד אומר אכלה שניה רביעית וששית הכי נמי דהויא חזקה א"ל רב יהודה הכי השתא ו התם בשתא דקא מסהיד מר לא קא מסהיד מר הכא תרוייהו בחדא שתא קא מסהדי מאי איכא למימר בין חיטי לשערי לאו אדעתייהו דאינשי: שלשה אחין ואחד מצטרף עמהן הרי אלו שלש עדיות והן עדות אחת להזמה: ההוא

שלשה אחים ואחד מצטרף עמהם. דהיינו אח לשנה אח לשנה ואחד עם האח שאותו אחד מעיד עם כולן: **הרי אלו ג' עדיות.** ולהכי כשר עדותן לאשתא דקא מסהיד האי לא קמסהיד האי ואין כאן שני עדים קרובים בעדות אחת: **והן עדות אחת להזמה.** שאם הוזמו משלשין ביניהן וגם אין ניזומין עד שיזומו כולן: **גמ' מתני'.** דקתני ג' כתות של עדים עדות אחת לשלש שני חזקה: **דלא כר"ע.** דלר"ע לא מהני עדותן כלל הואיל וכל אחד אין מעיד על חזקה שלימה דשלש שנים אלא על שליש חזקה והיינו חצי דבר: **אבא חלפתא.** אבי חלפתא דר' יוסי שמו: **דבר.** היינו רבי יוסי בן חלפתא: **שהיה ר"ע אומר דבר.** על פי שנים עדים יקום דבר שלם שישתלם כל הממון ע"פ עדים השנים: **ולא חצי דבר.** כל כת וכת אינה מעידה אלא על שליש החזקה והיינו שליש דבר ולא דבר שלם הואיל ואין שני עדים מעידים על כל הג' שנים: **ה"ג אילימא למעוטי אחד כו'.** במס' נדה (דף נב:) אמר ב' שערות שאמרו אפי' אחת בגבה ואחת בכריסה: **בכריסה.** באותו מקום: **חצי עדות הוא.** דאין כאן אלא עד אחד לכל שיער ועד אחד אינו נאמן לעשותה בת עונשין לחייבה וקרא חצי דבר אתא למעוטי שהרי דבר כתיב וחצי עדות למעוטי לא איצטריך קרא דבהדיא כתיב לא יקום עד אחד וגו': **אלא.** האי דבר למעוטי חצי דבר (ב) דכי האי גוונא כגון שנים אומרים אחת בגבה ראינו ולא בדקנו יותר ושנים אומרים אנו בדקנו מלפניה וראינו אחת בכריסה ואי לאו מיעוטא דקרא דבר ולא חצי דבר לא היה לנו לפסול עדות זה דעדות זה כשר הוא מאחר שיש ב' עדים על כל שיער שהרי אין מכחישין כלל זה את זה אלא כת זו בדקו מגבה וכת שניה בדקו מלפניה ובשעה אחת ראו ב' (ג) שערות אלו מכאן ואלו מכאן דליכא למימר שומא נינהו השתא דכתיב דבר עדותן בטלה דב' שערות דבר אחד הוא ואין מועילין אלא כשהן ביחד בבת אחת שאם נראה אחד היום מכאן ולמחר גדל שני במקום אחר וכבר נשר הראשון אמרינן שומא נינהו (ד) ואין כלום אלא אם כן ישנן ביחד וכל כת וכת יכול לראות ב' השערות דהא ביחד היו נמצא שכל כת עדות של חצי דבר מעידין וכל אחד אינו מעיד שהיא גדולה אלא חצי סימני גדלות ראינו אבל ג' שני חזקה דמתני' שאין יכולין להיות כי אם בזה אחר זה ומי שרואה אכילת שנה זו אינו יכול לראות של שנה שניה אלא אם כן שוהה שנה שניה בזה המלכות הלכך כל שנה ושנה וכל יום ויום חשיב דבר שלם בפני עצמו דעל כרחך כיון דקרא למעוטי אתא ומיעוט אחד הוא דליכא (ד) למימר) אין לך למעט כי אם (ה) חצי דבר דמסתבר טפי למעוטי דהיינו עדות דב' שערות בשתי כתות: **ואחד אומר.** אותן ג' שנים שאתה אומר אכלה חטין אני מעיד כמותך שאכלה אבל אכילת שעורים היתה הרי זו חזקה וטעמא מפרש לקמיה: **מתקיף לה ר"נ אלא מעתה כו'.** ר"נ לא היה יודע טעמו של רב יהודה המפורש לפנינו דבין חטין ושעורין טעו אינשי אלא ס"ל דהא דקאמר רב יהודה אחד אומר אכלה חטין ואחד אומר אכלה שעורין כו' לאו באותן ג' שנים דקמסהיד האי מסהיד האי דא"כ עדות מוכחשת היא ותיבטל אלא ס"ל לר"נ דה"ק רב יהודה אחד אומר אכלה חטין ג' שנים כפי מנהג עובדי אדמה ואחד אומר אכלה שעורים שלש שנים כפי מנהג עובדי אדמה והיינו שש שנים בדילוג ושאלתי לעובדי האדמה ואמרו לי שלעולם כך הוא המנהג שנה אחת חטין ושנה אחת שעורין כן כל הימים ואינה צריכה שביתה כלום ה"ז חזקה שהרי אין מכחישים זה את זה כלל וממ"נ כל אחד מעיד שאכלה שני חזקה והלכך הויא חזקה דדמיא להא דר' יהושע בן קרחה דאמרי' בפירקין לעיל (דף לג.) אין עדותם מצטרפת עד שיראו שניהם כאחד ר' יהושע בן קרחה אומר אפי' בזה אחר זה וטעמא דר' יהושע מפורש בסנהדרין בפ' זה בורר דאע"ג דאמנה דקמסהיד האי לא מסהיד האי מיהו תרוייהו אמנה קמסהדי והכא נמי תרוייהו אחזקה קמסהדי: **אלא מעתה אחד אומר אכלה ראשונה שלישית כו'.** דהיינו כרב יהודה הכי נמי דתיהוי חזקה הא ודאי לא תיהוי חזקה דלא דמיא כלל לר' יהושע בן קרחה אלא היכא דאחד אומר אכלה ראשונה ושניה ושלישית ואחד אומר אכלה ד' ה' ו' דתרוייהו אחזקה מעלייתא (ו) קמסהדי אבל הכא לא זה ולא זה מעידים על חזקה רצופה דחזקה בדילוג אינה כלום וכן עיקרה של שיטה זו כמו שפירשתיה: **א"ל רב יהודה הכי השתא התם כו'.** וכיון דליכא אלא עד אחד לשנה חצי עדות הוא הכא תרוייהו בחדא שתא מסהדי כשזה אומר אכלה חטין וזה אומר אכלה שעורים אין לנו לחוש ולומר דלמא בדילוג קא מסהדי אלא מסתמא על אותם שלש שזה מעיד השני נמי מעיד וכיון דעדות שלימה יש על השלש שנים מה יש פסול (ז) עוד אי משום דזה אומר אכלה שעורים: **בין חיטי ושערי לאו אדעתייהו דאינשי.** אין מבינין יפה בין קמת חטים לקמת שעורים: ההוא

משלשין ביניהם. הכא לא שייך למיפרך ולימרו הנך קמאי אנן מנא ידעינן דכל דקאי בדי דינא לאסהודי אהאי ארעא אנן לחיובי מחזיק פירות קאתינן כדפריך בפרק כיצד הרגל (ב"ק דף כד: ושם) גבי שור ולימרו הנך (ה) קמאי כו' אנן לחיובי פלגא ניזקא קאתינן דכיון דמחזיק מביאן לב"ד ודאי לטובתו באו כדי להחזיקו בקרקע ולא כדי לחייבו פירות: **הרי** אלו ג' עדיות. שהרי העד שהעיד בראשונה הוא עצמו יכול להעיד בשניה ולא אמרינן אדם קרוב אצל עצמו כמו כן אחיו יכול להעיד בשניה: **והן** עדות אחת. דאין משלמין עד שיזומו כולן: **ורבנן** האי דבר ולא חצי דבר מאי עבדי ליה. וא"ת דהכא כ"ע דרשי דבר ולא חצי דבר ובפ' מרובה (שם דף עא:) אמרינן חמשה בקר אמר רחמנא ואפי' ה' חצאי בקר וי"ל דהכא משום דדבר מיותר הוא וא"ת והא איצטריך לדבר דבר ממון לאשמועינן דאין דבר שבערוה פחות משנים (גיטין דף ב.) וי"ל דדבר דגבי ערוה מופנה הוא ואפילו למ"ד דלמידין ומשיבין שמא ליכא למיפרך מידי ואי איכא למיפרך י"ל דלאו מדבר דריש אלא מעל פי שנים יקום (ח) דמשמע יקום כל העדות ולא חצי אבל גבי ממון מה לי ממון גדול ומה לי ממון קטן לפי מה שגנב ישלם להכי אין סברא למעט חצאי בקר והא דדרשינן בפרק ד' וה' (ב"ק דף מ. ושם) גבי שור של שני שותפין כופר (ט) ולא חצי כופר שאני התם דלכפרה אתי דאין אדם מביא חצי כפרה חצי חטאת וחצי אשם והא דאמרינן התם (גיטין מג:) גבי חציו עבד וחציו בן חורין דמשלם חצי כופר התם כל וחשיב כופר שלם דלא הרג אלא חצי בן חורין ובפרק יש בכור (בכורות דף מח: ושם ד"ה דרשי) דרשי' חמש ולא חצי חמש התם נמי מצות פדיונו ה' סלעים ולא מקיימא מצוה בפחות: **אלא** למעוטי שנים אומרים אחת בגבה. אומר רשב"א דאין צריך לחלק כפירוש הקונט' דאפילו [היתה] תשובה גדולה כשבדקו שני עדים היום בכל מקום ולא ראו כי אם אחת בגבה ובדקו למחר אותם עדים עצמן ולא ראו כי אם אחת בכריסה בשתי כתי עדים חשיב חצי דבר אע"פ שראו כל מה שיכולין (י) ולא דמי לעדות חזקה דהכא אין עדותן עדות בלא עדות ב' אחרונים (כ) ואין מועיל לשום דבר בעולם לכך הוי חצי דבר אבל שנים בראשונה אע"פ שאין עדות מועיל לענין חזקה מכל מקום נפקא מינה בעדותן לשלומי פירי ודבר שלם הוא: **אלא** מעתה אחד אומר אכלה ראשונה שלישית כו'. פי' הקונט' דר"נ היה סבור דרב יהודה איירי באחד אומר אכלה חטים היינו ראשונה שלישית וחמישית ואין נראה דא"כ מאי פריך אלא מעתה אכלה ראשונה כו' אין ה"נ דלסברתו אמר רב יהודה דהוי חזקה והכי הוה ליה למיפרך אמאי הוי חזקה והא אין שום אדם אומר שאכלה רצופין ולא דמי לר' יהושע בן קרחה ונראה לפרש דר"נ ידע דתרוייהו אחדא שתא קמסהדי וה"פ כיון דאמר דהויא חזקה אע"ג דמכחשי אהדדי משום דתרוייהו אחזקה קמסהדי אלא מעתה אחד אומר אכלה ראשונה שלישית וחמישית ושנית ורביעית וששית הניחה בורה כדרך מוברי באגי ואחד אומר לא כי אלא אכלה (ל) שנית רביעית וששית וראשונה שלישית וחמישית הניחה בורה ה"נ דהוה חזקה אע"ג דמכחשי אהדדי כיון דתרוייהו מיהא אחזקה קא מסהדי ומשני

עין משפט נר מצוה

רנו א ב מיי' פכ"א מהל' עדות הל' ז טור ח"מ סי' לח:

רנז ג ד מיי' פ"ד מהל' עדות הל' ז סמג לאוין קט טוש"ע ח"מ סי' ל סעיף יג:

רנח ה ו מיי' פט"ו מהל' טוען ונטען הל' ג סמג עשין לה טוש"ע ח"מ סי' קמה סעיף א:

רבינו גרשום

משלשין ביניהן. כל כת משלמת לו שליש דמי הקרקע: **שלשה אחין.** מעידין כל אחד שאכלה שנה: **ואחד.** עד נכרי: **מצטרף.** להעיד עמהן עם כל א' וא': **הרי אלו ג' עדיות.** שכל מה שמעיד אח זה אין מעיד אח זה וכשר הוא העדות: **והן עדות אחת.** הואיל וכל אחת מצטרף עם זה נכרי אם הוזם זה נכרי או אחד מן האחין שמצטרף עמו בטל כל העדות של חזקה זו הואיל וזה נכרי מעיד עם כולן ומשלמין בין ארבעתם: על פי שנים עדים יקום **דבר.** שלם **ולא חצי דבר** וזה השנים אין מעידין אלא שליש דבר: **ורבנן** דמתני' דקא סברי ה"ז חזקה **[דבר] ולא חצי דבר מאי עבדי ליה** למעוטי מאי: **האי חצי עדות.** דאחד בלבד אמר בגבה: **אלא שנים אמרו אחת בגבה.** היינו שנים מעידין חצי דבר וכן נמי **שנים אומרין אחת בכריסה** דלא מצרפינן לסהדותייהו דהאי כת דמעיד על נימא אחת בלבד אכתי משוו לה קטנה. וכן נמי כת אחרת משוו לה קטנה ולא ידעת איזו חזיא ברישא: **אחד אומר.** שזרעה **לאכלה** ג' שנים **חטים** וא' אומר שעורין אכלה ג' שנים הרי זה חזקה: **בין חטי לשערי** לא דייקי. אינשי ועדותן עדות והויא חזקה:

מסורת הש"ס

א) [סנהדרין דף כח.], ב) ב"ק ע. [תוספתא ב"ב פ"ב], ג) ב"ק ע: סנהדרין ל: ודף פו., ד) רש"ל מ"ז, ה) [צ"ל בתרא], ו) [וע"ע תוס' סנהדרין פו. ד"ה דבר ותוס' ב"ק מ. ד"ה כופר]:

הגהות הב"ח

(א) גמ' האי חצי דבר חצי עדות כצ"ל ואות ו' נמחק: (ב) רשב"ם ד"ה אלא האי וכו' בכי האי גוונא וכו': (ג) בא"ד ראו ב' השערות אלו אחת מכאן ואלו אחת מכאן וכו': (ד) בא"ד ואין כלום וכו' וכל כת וכת היה יכול וכו': (ה) בא"ד למעט כי אם אותו חצי דבר: (ו) ד"ה אלא מעתה וכו' מעלייתא רצופה קמסהדי: (ז) ד"ה א"ל רב יהודה וכו' מה יש פסול עדות עוד אי משום דזה אומר אכלה חטים וזה אומר אכלה שעורים: (ח) תוס' ד"ה ורבנן וכו' יקום דבר דמשמע: (ט) בא"ד כופר שלם ולא חצי כופר: (י) ד"ה אלא למעוטי וכו' כל מה שיכולין לראות ולא דמי: (כ) בא"ד ואין מועיל. נ"ב עי' ברי"ף: (ל) ד"ה אלא מעתה וכו' אלא אכלה שניה רביעית:

תורה אור השלם

א) לֹא יָקוּם עֵד אֶחָד בְּאִישׁ לְכָל עָוֹן וּלְכָל חַטָּאת בְּכָל חֵטְא אֲשֶׁר יֶחֱטָא עַל פִּי שְׁנֵי עֵדִים אוֹ עַל פִּי שְׁלֹשָׁה עֵדִים יָקוּם דָּבָר: [דברים יט, טו]

ליקוטי רש"י

שלשה אחים ואחד מצטרף עמהם. מן השוק עם כל אחד ואחד מעידים על אכילת שני חזקה של קרקע של אדם מן השוק ומעיד אחד מן האחין והבא מן השוק על שנה ראשונה ואחד מן האחין והבא מן השוק על שנה שניה והשלישי על השלישית והרי אלו שלש עדיות והחזקה קיימת ולא אמרינן עדות אחת היא והרי העדים קרובים אלא שלש עדיות נינהו לאשתא דקא מסהיד האי לא מסהיד האי. **והן עדות אחת להזמה.** דעד דמתזמי כולהו לא משלמי ממונא דהא לא הוה מתוקמא בידא לגוקא אלא בסהדותא דכולהו [סנהדרין כח.]. **אבא חלפתא.** אבא של ר' יוסי חלפתא שמו [שבת קטו. ב"ק ע: מעילה יז:]. שהכל יודעין שהוא חסיד [סנהדרין פ.]. **למעוטי אחד אומר אחת בגבה.** וקאמר לשויה גדולה לענין עונשין או לענין שיהו קידושיה קידושין. **בגבה.** שיער ראיתי בקשרי אצבעותיה [ב"ק שם]. בין קשרי אצבעותיה [סנהדרין ל:]. אחת אותו מקום [נדה נב: ע"ש]. **חצי דבר.** שיער אחד. **וחצי עדות.** עד אחד יש לשער ופשיטא דלאו עדות היא [ב"ק שם]. עד אחד חצי עדות הוא שיער אחת הוא חצי דבר. [סנהדרין שם].

מְשַׁלְּשִׁין בֵּינֵיהֶם – THEY DIVIDE the penalty IN THREE AMONG THEM.[1] שְׁלֹשָׁה אַחִים – If THREE BROTHERS testified, each to one year's use וְאֶחָד מִצְטָרֵף עִמָּהֶם – AND ONE unrelated witness, who observed the entire three years' use, JOINED WITH each of THEM,[2] הֲרֵי אֵלּוּ שָׁלֹשׁ עֵדִיּוֹת – THESE ARE considered THREE separate TESTIMONIES and they can establish a *chazakah*.[3] וְהֵן עֵדוּת אַחַת לַהֲזָמָה – NEVERTHELESS, THEY ARE considered ONE TESTIMONY WITH REGARD TO the laws of *HAZAMAH*.[4]

Gemara מַתְנִיתִין דְּלָא כְּרַבִּי עֲקִיבָא – **The Mishnah does not follow** the view of **R' Akiva,**[5] דְּתַנְיָא – **for it was taught in a Baraisa:** אָמַר רַבִּי יוֹסֵי – R' YOSE SAID: כְּשֶׁהָלַךְ אַבָּא חֲלַפְתָּא אֵצֶל רַבִּי יוֹחָנָן בֶּן נוּרִי לִלְמוֹד תּוֹרָה – WHEN my FATHER CHALAFTA[6] WENT TO R' YOCHANAN BEN NURI TO STUDY TORAH וְאָמְרֵי לָהּ – (AND OTHERS HAVE IT: ר' יוֹחָנָן בֶּן נוּרִי אֵצֶל אַבָּא חֲלַפְתָּא לִלְמוֹד תּוֹרָה – R' YOCHANAN BEN NURI WENT TO my FATHER CHALAFTA TO STUDY TORAH); אָמַר לוֹ – [R' YOCHANAN BEN NURI] SAID TO [MY FATHER], הֲרֵי שֶׁאֲכָלָהּ שָׁנָה רִאשׁוֹנָה בִּפְנֵי שְׁנַיִם – "SUPPOSE AN OCCUPANT USED [A PROPERTY] for three years, THE FIRST YEAR BEFORE TWO witnesses, שְׁנִיָּה בִּפְנֵי שְׁנַיִם – THE SECOND YEAR BEFORE another TWO witnesses שְׁלִישִׁית בִּפְנֵי שְׁנַיִם – AND THE THIRD BEFORE still another TWO witnesses, מַהוּ – WHAT IS [THE LAW]? Can the three testimonies be combined to establish a *chazakah* or not?" אָמַר לוֹ – [MY FATHER] SAID TO [R' YOCHANAN BEN NURI], הֲרֵי זוֹ חֲזָקָה – "THIS IS A *CHAZAKAH*, as the testimonies can be combined."[7] אָמַר לוֹ – [R' YOCHANAN BEN NURI] SAID TO [MY FATHER], אַף אֲנִי אוֹמֵר כֵּן – "I, TOO, SAY THAT THIS IS SO. אֶלָּא שֶׁרַבִּי עֲקִיבָא חוֹלֵק בְּדָבָר זֶה – HOWEVER, R' AKIVA DIFFERS IN THIS MATTER, שֶׁהָיָה רַבִּי עֲקִיבָא אוֹמֵר – FOR R' AKIVA WAS WONT TO SAY, ,,דָּבָר" – 'Scripture states:[8] *By the testimony of two witnesses . . . shall a matter be established*, and the Rabbis expound: A full *MATTER* וְלֹא חֲצִי דָבָר – BUT NOT HALF A MATTER; i.e. to be admissible, witnesses' testimony must *by itself* directly affect some legal matter.' "[9] Thus, the Mishnah, which allows for establishment of *chazakah* based on the combination of three sets of witnesses who each observed only part of the occupancy, does not accord with R' Akiva's view.[10]

The Gemara asks:

וְרַבָּנָן – **And the Rabbis,**[11] הַאי ,,דָּבָר" וְלֹא חֲצִי דָבָר מַאי עָבְדֵי לֵיהּ – **how do they apply** this rule of **"*a matter* but not half a matter"?** What manner of incomplete testimony would *they* disqualify?[12]

The Gemara suggests an answer but immediately rejects it:

אִילֵימָא לְמַעוּטֵי – **If** we are **to say** that the Rabbis apply this rule **to exclude** the following testimony: אֶחָד אוֹמֵר אַחַת בְּגַבָּהּ – If **one** witness, testifying to the adult status of a girl,[13] **says, "One** hair was present **on her back,"**[14] וְאֶחָד אוֹמֵר אַחַת בִּכְרֵיסָהּ – **and one** witness **says, "One** hair was present **on her abdomen,"**[15] and the Rabbis say that their testimony would be disallowed, as each witness testifies to only half of the matter being proved. הַאי חֲצִי דָבָר וַחֲצִי עֵדוּת הִיא – This exclusion would be unnecessary, as

NOTES

1. The *hazamah* penalty is not assessed unless all three sets of witnesses are declared *zomemim (Rashbam* from *Makkos* 5b). All three sets are therefore guilty of a combined conspiracy attempt to defraud the original owner of his land, and all must share equally in the reciprocal penalty which is imposed upon *zomemim* witnesses.

Each pair cannot claim that their sole intent in testifying was not to harm the owner but to enable him to collect for the produce the occupant consumed, for since it was the occupant who brought them to court, they clearly intended to support his claim (*Tosafos;* cf. *Yad Ramah; Ran*).

2. This fourth witness combines in turn with each of the three brothers to form a separate pair testifying in regard to each of the three years of *chazakah* (*Rashbam*).

3. Although brothers normally are disqualified from testifying together, in this instance their testimony is accepted, because each testifies in regard to a different year of use and their testimonies do not overlap. Thus, although they all testify in behalf of the occupant, their testimonies are valid (*Rashbam*).

4. [One of the rules of *zomemim* witnesses is that all who testify together must be shown to be *zomemim* before the penalty for *hazamah* can be applied to any of them (Mishnah *Makkos* 5b). In our case, therefore, since none of their testimonies could have established a *chazakah* except in conjunction with the other,] they are considered as one testimony in regard to the laws of *hazamah,* and unless all three brothers as well as the fourth, unrelated witness have been declared *zomemim*, none of them is subject to punishment. If this occurs, the assessed penalty is divided among the three pairs (*Rashbam*). Accordingly, each brother would be liable for one-sixth of the value of the property, while the unrelated witness would be liable for a full half of the value (*Meiri; Rambam, Hilchos Eidus* 21:7).

5. As the Gemara explains below, R' Akiva requires that one pair of witnesses testify to all three years of *chazakah.* He is thus in disagreement with our Mishnah that allows three pairs to testify, each to one year of *chazakah* (*Rashbam*).

6. [R' Akiva Eiger puzzles over how R' Yose can refer to his father by name, in seeming violation of the law that forbids this (*Chidushei R' Akiva Eiger* to *Yoreh De'ah* 240:2). *Aruch HaShulchan* (ibid. 15) suggests that perhaps this restriction does not apply where the son adds the title "father," as in this case "my father Chalafta."]

7. R' Chalafta thus echoed the ruling of the Mishnah, which allows *chazakah* to be established in such an instance.

8. *Deuteronomy* 19:15.

9. But any testimony which by itself has no legal consequences and is relevant only in conjunction with that of other witnesses regarding the same aspect of the case is not valid at all.

10. For "a full matter" in this case is a full three-year *chazakah.* Thus, testifying to only one year's use is testifying to only a third of a matter and is not a valid testimony.

11. I.e. those Sages who disagree with R' Akiva's view, namely R' Yochanan ben Nuri, R' Chalafta and the Tanna of our Mishnah.

12. The Gemara assumes that there is no argument whether such a principle exists, for all agree that the word "matter" is superfluous in the aforementioned verse and is therefore expounded in this manner (see *Tosafos*). The dispute centers only on when to apply the principle.

13. An underage girl is considered to have entered *naarus,* the intermediate state of adulthood, once two conditions are fulfilled: 1) She must have reached twelve year of age, and 2) she must have grown at least two body hairs. Generally, it is sufficient for one woman to attest to the physical conditions that establish a girl's adulthood. However, there are instances where this does not suffice and the testimony of two witnesses is necessary. Our Gemara discusses such instances (*Kovetz Shiurim* §253). [The back and abdomen are actually oblique references to different parts of the pubic area (*Rashbam*, *Rashi* to *Niddah* 52b ד"ה אחת בגבה.]

The Gemara in *Niddah* (52b) states that according to some Tannaim, the two hairs need not be close together or even visible together. These Tannaim also do not require them to be pubic hairs. Accordingly, even if one hair was on the back of her person and the second in front, they nevertheless fulfill the requirement of two hairs. Our Gemara follows their view. [*Rambam* (*Ishus* 2:17), however, rules that pubic hairs are required to establish adulthood, in contradiction of these Tannaim. See *Ramban* and *Rashba* to *Niddah* 52b, *Rambam's* commentators and especially *Shulchan Aruch Even HaEzer* 155:17 with *Beur HaGra.*]

14. The first witness did not inspect the front of the girl's person; [he did not, therefore, offer any testimony as to the presence (or absence) of a hair in that location] (*Rashbam*).

15. Both witnesses saw the hairs they attested to at one time; thus, a combination of the two testimonies would indicate that the girl had grown two hairs at that point in time. [Testimonies to two single hairs during consecutive time periods, however, would be insufficient evidence of *naarus*, for if the first hair had fallen out before the second

נו: חזקת הבתים פרק שלישי בבא בתרא

משלשין ביניהם: (א) שלשה אחים ואחד מצטרף עמהם הרי אלו שלש עדיות והן עדות אחת להזמה: **גמ'** מתני' דלא כרבי עקיבא דתניא (ב) א"ר יוסי כשהלך אבא חלפתא אצל רבי יוחנן בן נורי ללמוד תורה ואמרי לה ר' יוחנן בן נורי אצל אבא חלפתא ללמוד תורה אמר לו הרי שאכלה שנה ראשונה בפני שנים שניה בפני שנים שלישית בפני שנים מהו אמר לו (ג) הרי זו חזקה אמר לו אף אני אומר כן אלא שר"ע חולק בדבר זה שהיה ר"ע אומר (א) דבר (ד) ולא חצי דבר ורבנן האי דבר ולא חצי דבר מאי עבדי ליה אילימא למעוטי אחד אומר אחת בגבה ואחד אומר אחת בכריסה האי חצי דבר (ב) וחצי עדות היא אלא למעוטי שנים אומרים אחת בגבה ושנים אומרים אחת בכריסה אמר רב יהודה (ה) אחד אומר אכלה חטים ואחד אומר אכלה שעורים הרי זו חזקה מתקיף לה ר"נ אלא מעתה אחד אומר אכלה ראשונה שלישית וחמישית ואחד אומר אכלה שניה רביעית וששית הכי נמי דהויא חזקה א"ל רב יהודה הכי השתא (ו) התם בשתא דקא מסהיד מר לא קא מסהיד מר הכא תרוייהו בחדא שתא קא מסהדי מאי איכא למימר בין חיטי לשערי לאו אדעתייהו דאינשי: שלשה אחין ואחד מצטרף עמהן הרי אלו שלש עדיות והן עדות אחת להזמה: ההוא

שלשה אחים ואחד מצטרף עמהם. דהיינו את לשנה את לשנה ואחד עם האב שאותו אחד מעיד עם כולן: **הרי אלו ג' עדיות.** ולהכי כשר עדותן דלשתא דקא מסהיד האי לא קמסהיד האי ואין כאן שני עדים קרובים בעדות אחת: **והן עדות אחת להזמה.** שאם הוזמו משלשין ביניהן וגם אין נוזמין עד שיוזמו כולן: **גמ' מתני'.** דקתני ג' כתות של ג' שנים עדות אחת לשלש שני חזקה: **דלא כר"ע.** דלר"ע לא מהני עדותן כלל הואיל וכל אחד אין מעיד על חזקה שלימה דשלש שנים אלא על שליש חזקה והיינו חצי דבר: **אבא חלפתא.** אבי חלפתא דר' יוסי שאם היינו רבי יוסי בן חלפתא: **שהיה ר"ע אומר דבר.** על פי שנים עדים יקום דבר שלם שישתלם כל הממון ע"פ עדים השנים: **ולא חצי דבר.** כל כת וכת אינה מעידה אלא על שליש החזקה והיינו שליש דבר ולא דבר שלם הואיל ואין שני עדים מעידים על כל הג' שנים: **ה"ג אילימא למעוטי אחד כו'.** במס' נדה (דף נב:) אמר ב' שערות שאמרו אפי' אחת בגבה ואחת בכריסה: **בכריסה.** באותו מקום: **חצי עדות הוא.** דאין כאן אלא עד אחד לכל שיער ועד אחד אינו נאמן לעשותה בת עונשין לחייבה וקרא חצי דבר אתא למעוטי שהרי דבר כתיב וחצי עדות למעוטי לא איצטריך קרא דבהדיא כתיב לא יקום עד אחד וגו': **אלא.** האי דבר למעוטי חצי דבר (ג) דכי האי גוונא כגון שנים אומרים אחת בגבה ראינו ולא בדקנו יותר ושנים אומרים אנו בדקנו מלפניה וראינו אחת בכריסה ואי לאו מיעוטא דקרא דבר ולא חצי דבר לא היה לנו לפסול עדות זה דעדות זה כשר הוא מאחר שיש ב' עדים על כל שיער שהרי אין מכחישין כלל זה את זה אלא את זו בדקו מגבה וכת שניה בדקו מלפניה ובשעה אחת ראו ב' (ג) שערות אלו מכאן ואלו מכאן דליכא למימר שומא ניהו השתא דכתיב דבר עדותן בטלה דב' שערות דבר אחד הוא ואין מועילין אלא כשהן ביחד בבת אחת שאם נראה אחד היום מכאן ולמחר גדל שני במקום אחר וכבר נשר הראשון אמרינן שומא ניהו (ד) ואין כלום אלא אם כן ישנן ביחד וכל כת וכת יכול לראות ב' השערות דהא ביחד היו נמצא שכל כת עדות של חצי דבר מעידין וכל אחד אינו מעיד שהיא גדולה אלא חצי סימני גדלות ראינו אבל ג' שני חזקה דמתני' שאין יכולין להיות כי אם בזה אחר זה ומי שרואה אכילת שנה זו אינו יכול לראות של שנה שניה אלא אם כן שוהה שנה שניה בזה המלכות הלכך כל שנה ושנה וכל יום ויום חשיב דבר שלם בפני עצמו דעל כרחך כיון דקרא למעוטי אתא ומיעוט אחד הוא דאיכא (למימר) אין לך למעט כי אם (ה) חצי דבר דמסתבר טפי למעוטי דהיינו עדות דב' שערות בשתי כתות: **ואחד אומר.** אותן ג' שנים שאתה אומר אכלה חטין אני מעיד כמותך שאכלה אבל אכילת שעורים היתה הרי זו חזקה וטעמא מפרש לקמיה: **מתקיף לה ר"נ אלא מעתה כו'.** ר"נ לא היה יודע טעמו של רב יהודה המפורש לפנינו דבין חטין ושעורין טעו אינשי אלא ס"ל דהא דקאמר רב יהודה אחד אומר אכלה חטין ואחד אומר אכלה שעורין כו' לאו באותן ג' שנים דקמסהיד האי מסהיד האי דא"כ עדות מוכחשת היא ותיבטל אלא ס"ל לר"נ דה"ק רב יהודה אחד אומר אכלה חטין ג' שנים כפי מנהג עובדי אדמה ואחד אומר אכלה שעורים שלש שנים כפי מנהג עובדי אדמה והיינו שש שנים בדילוג ושאלתי לעובדי האדמה ואמרו לי שלעולם כך הוא המנהג שנה אחת חטין ושנה אחת שעורין כן כל הימים ואינה צריכה שביתה כלום ה"ז חזקה שהרי אין מכחישים זה את זה כלל ומ"מ כל אחד מעיד שאכלה שני חזקה והלכך הויא חזקה דדמיא להא דר' יהושע בן קרחה דאמרי' בפירקין לעיל (דף לג.) אין עדותם מצטרפת עד שיראו שניהם כאחד ר' יהושע בן קרחה אומר אפי' בזה אחר זה וטעמא דר' יהושע מפורש בסנהדרין בפ' זה בורר דאע"ג דאמנה דקמסהיד האי לא מסהיד האי מיהו אמנה קמסהדי והכא נמי תרוייהו אחזקה קמסהדי: **אלא מעתה אחד אומר אכלה ראשונה שלישית כו'.** הכי נמי דתיהוי חזקה הא ודאי לא תיהוי חזקה דלא דמיא כלל לר' יהושע בן קרחה אלא היכא דאחד אומר אכלה ראשונה ושניה ושלישית ואחד אומר אכלה ד' ה' ו' דתרוייהו אחזקה מעלייתא (ו) קמסהדי אבל הכא לא זה ולא זה מעידים על חזקה רצופה דחזקה בדילוג אינה כלום וכן עיקרה של שיטה זו כמו שפירשתיה: **א"ל רב יהודה הכי השתא התם כו'.** וכיון דליכא אלא עד אחד לשנה הכא תרוייהו בחדא שתא מסהדי כשזה אומר אכלה חטין וזה אומר אכלה שעורים אין לנו לחוש ולומר דלמא בדילוג קא מסהדי אלא מסתמא על אותם שלש שזה מעיד השני נמי מעיד וכיון דעדות שלימה יש על השלש שנים מה יש פסול (ז) עוד אי משום דזה אומר אכלה שעורים: **בין חיטי ושערי לאו אדעתייהו דאינשי.** אין מבינין יפה בין קמת חטים לקמת שעורים: ההוא

משלשין ביניהם. הכא לא שייך למיפרך ולימרו הנך קמאי אנן מנא ידעינן דכל דקאי בדי דינא לאסהודי אתי אהאי ארעא אנן לחיובי מחזיק פירות קאתינן כדפריך בפרק כיצד הרגל (ב"ק דף כד: ושם) גבי שור ולימרו הנך (ט) קמאי כו' אנן לחיובי פלגא נזקא קאתינן דכיון דמחזיק מגילו לב"ד ודאי לטובתו באו כדי להחזיקו בקרקע ולא כדי לחייבו פירות: **הרי** אלו ג' עדיות. שהרי העד שהעיד בראשונה הוא עצמו יכול להעיד בשניה ולא אמרינן אדם קרוב אצל עצמו כמו כן אחיו יכול להעיד בשניה: **והן** עדות אחת. דאין משלמין עד שיוזמו כולן: **ורבנן** האי דבר ולא חצי דבר מאי עבדי ליה. וא"ת דהכא כ"ע דרשי דבר ולא חצי דבר ובפ' מרובה (שם דף עא.) אמרינן חמשה בקר אמר רחמנא ולא ארבעה בקר והשתא ה' חצאי בקר וי"ל דהכא משום דדבר מיותר הוא וא"ת והא איצטריך לדבר ממון לאשמועינן דאין דבר שבערוה פחות משנים (גיטין דף ב:) וי"ל דדבר דגבי ערוה מופנה הוא ואפילו למ"ד דלמידין ומשיבין שמא ליכא למיפרך מידי ואי איכא למיפרך י"ל דלאו מדבר דריש אלא מעל פי שנים יקום (ח) דמשמע יקום כל העדות ולא חצי אבל גבי ממון מה לי ממון גדול ומה לי ממון קטן ולפי מה שגנב ישלם להכי אין סברא למעט חצאי בקר והא דדרשינן בפרק ד' וה' (ב"ק דף מ. ושם) גבי שור של שני שותפין כופר (ט) ולא חצי כופר שאני התם לכפרה אתי דאין אדם מביא חצי כפרה חצי חטאת וחצי אשם והא דאמרינן התם (גיטין מב:) גבי חציו עבד וחציו בן חורין דמשלם חצי כופר התם כל הכופר דשייך בו משלם וחשיב כופר שלם דלא הרג אלא חצי בן חורין ובפרק יש בכור (בכורות דף מח: ושם ד"ה דרשי) דרשי' חמש ולא חצי חמש התם נמי מלות פדיונו ה' סלעים ולא מקיימא מלוה בפחות (י): **אלא** למעוטי שנים אומרים אחת בגבה. אומר רשב"א דאין צריך לחלק כפירוש הקונט' דאפילו [היתה] חשובה גדולה כשבדקו שני עדים היום בכל מקום ולא ראו כי אם אחת בגבה ובדקו למחר אותם עדים עצמן ולא ראו כי אם אחת בכריסה בשתי כתי עדים חשיב חצי דבר אע"פ שראו כל מה שיכולין (י) ולא דמי לעדות חזקה דהכא אין עדותן עדות בלא עדות ב' אחרונים (כ) ואין מועיל לשום דבר בעולם לכך הוי חצי דבר אבל שנים בראשונה אע"פ שאין עדות מועיל לענין חזקה מכל מקום נפקא מינה בעדותן לשלומי פירי ודבר שלם הוא: **אלא** מעתה אחד אומר אכלה ראשונה שלישית כו'. פי' הקונט' דר"נ היה סבור דרב יהודה איירי באחד אומר אכלה חטים היינו ראשונה שלישית וחמישית ואין נראה דא"כ מאי פריך אלא מעתה אכלה ראשונה כו' אין ה"נ דלסברתו אמר רב יהודה דהוי חזקה והכי הוה ליה למיפרך אמאי הוי חזקה והא אין שום אדם אומר שאכלה רצופין ולא דמי לר' יהושע בן קרחה ונראה לפרש דר"נ ידע דתרוייהו בחדא שתא קמסהדי וה"פ כיון דאמר דהויא חזקה אע"ג דמכחשי אהדדי משום דתרוייהו אחזקה קמסהדי אלא מעתה אחד אומר אכלה ראשונה שלישית וחמישית ושנית ורביעית וששית הניחה בורה ואחד אומר לא כי אלא אכלה (ג) שנית רביעית וששית וראשונה שלישית וחמישית הניחה בורה ה"נ דהוה חזקה אע"ג דמכחשי אהדדי כיון דתרוייהו מיהא אחזקה קא מסהדי ומשני

עין משפט נר מצוה

רנו א ב מיי' פט"ו מהל' עדות הל' ז טור ח"מ סי' לה:

רנז ג ד מיי' פ"ד מהל' עדות הל' ז סמג לאוין קט טוש"ע ח"מ סי' ל סעיף יג:

רנח ה ו מיי' פט"ו מהל' טוען ונטען הל' ג סמג עשין לה טוש"ע ח"מ סי' קמה סעיף ח:

רבינו גרשום

משלשין ביניהן. כל כת משלמת לו שליש דמי הקרקע: שלשה אחין. מעידין כל אחד שאכלה שנה: ואחד. עד נכרי: מצטרף. להעיד עמהן עם כל א' וא': הרי אלו ג' עדיות. שכל מה שמעיד את זה אין מעיד את זה וכשר הוא העדות: והן עדות אחת. הואיל וכל אחת מצטרף עם הזה נכרי אם הוזם זה נכרי או אחד מן האחין שמצטרף עמו בטל כל העדות של חזקה זו הואיל וזה נכרי מעיד עם כולם ומשלמין בין ארבעתם: על פי שנים עדים יקום דבר. שלם ולא חצי דבר וזה הוי חצי דבר שהרי אין מעידין אלא שליש דבר: ורבנן דמתני' דקא סברי ה"ז חזקה [דבר] ולא חצי דבר מאי עבדי ליה למעוטי מאי: האי חצי עדות. אחד אומר אחת בגבה. אלא שנים אומרים אחת בגבה. היינו שנים מעידין חצי דבר וכן נמי שנים אומרים אחת בכריסה דלא מצרפינן לסהדותייהו דהאי כת דמעיד על נימא אחת בלבד אכתי משום לה קטנה. וכן נמי כת אחרת משום לה קטנה ולא ידעת איזו חזיא ברישא: אחד אומר. שזרעה לאכלה ג' שנים חטים וא' אומר שעורין אכלה ג' שנים הרי זה חזקה: בין חטי לשעורי לא דייקי אינשי ועדותן עדות והויא חזקה:

מסורת הש"ס

א) [סנהדרין דף כח.], ב) ב"ק ע. [תוספתא ב"ב פ"ב], ג) ב"ק ע: סנהדרין ל: ודף פו., ד) רש"ל מ"ז, ה) [ע"ל בתרא], ו) [וע"ע תוס' סנהדרין ל. ד"ה דבר ותוס' ב"ק מ. ד"ה כופר].

הגהות הב"ח

(א) גמ' האי חצי דבר חצי עדות כצ"ל ואות ו' נמחק: (ב) רשב"ם ד"ה אלא האי וכו' בכי האי גוונא וכו': (ג) בא"ד ראו ב' השערות אלו אחת מכאן ואלו אחת מכאן וכו': (ד) בא"ד ואין כלום וכו' ולכל כת וכת היה יכול וכו': (ה) בא"ד למעט כי אם אותו חצי דבר: (ו) ד"ה אלא מעתה וכו' מצטרפות לרופה קמסהדי: (ז) ד"ה א"ל רב יהודה וכו' מה יש פסול עדות עוד אי משום דזה אומר אכלה חטים וזה אומר אכלה שעורים: (ח) תוס' ד"ה ורבנן וכו' יקום דבר דמשמע: (ט) בא"ד כופר שלם ולא חצי כופר: (י) ד"ה אלא למעוטי וכו' כל מה שיכולין לראות ולא דמי: (כ) בא"ד ואין מועיל. נ"ב עי' בכר"ן: (ג) ד"ה אלא מעתה וכו' אלא אכלה שניה רביעית:

תורה אור השלם

א) לֹא יָקוּם עֵד אֶחָד בְּאִישׁ לְכָל עָוֹן וּלְכָל חַטָּאת בְּכָל חֵטְא אֲשֶׁר יֶחֱטָא עַל פִּי שְׁנֵי עֵדִים אוֹ עַל פִּי שְׁלשָׁה עֵדִים יָקוּם דָּבָר: [דברים יט, טו]

ליקוטי רש"י

שלשה אחים ואחד מצטרף עמהם. מן השוק עם כל אחד ואחד מעידים על אכילת שני חזקה של קרקע של אדם מן השוק ומעיד אחד מן האחין והכא עם השוק על שנה ראשונה ואחד מן האחין והכא מן השוק על שנה שניה והשלישי על השלישית והרי אלו שלש עדיות והחזקה קיימת ולא אמרינן עדות אחת היא והרי העדים קרובים אלא שלש עדיות ניהו דשתא דקא מסהיד האי לא מסהיד האי. והן עדות אחת להזמה. דעד דמזמזי כולהו לא משלמי ממונא דהא לא הוה מתוקמא בידא לפוקא בסהדותא דלכולהו [סנהדרין כח.]. אבא חלפתא. אבא של ר' יוסי חלפתא שמו [שבת קטו. ב"ק ע: מעילה יז:]. שהכל יודעין שהוא חסיד [סנהדרין פ.]. למעוטי אחד אומר אחת בגבה. וקתני לשויה גדולה לענין עונשין או לענין חליצה או לענין שיהו קידושיה קדושין. בגבה. שיער ראיתי בקשרי אצבעותיה [ב"ק שם]. או בין קשרי אצבעותיה [סנהדרין ל:]. מתם מקום [נדה נב:]. חצי דבר. שיער אחד. וחצי עדות. עד אחד יש לשער ופשיטא דלאו עדות היא [ב"ק שם]. עד אחד הוא חצי עדות שיער אחת הוא חצי דבר. [סנהדרין שם].

[such testimony] is not only **half a matter,** it is **also half the** necessary **testimony,** for *two* witnesses must attest to the presence of *each* hair! Thus, the word "matter" is not needed to exclude this testimony.

The Gemara answers:

אֶלָּא לְמְעוּטֵי – Rather, in the view of the Rabbis, the rule of "a matter but not half a matter" comes **to exclude** שְׁנַיִם אוֹמְרִים אַחַת בְּגַבָּהּ – an instance in which **two** witnesses **say,** "We observed **one** hair **on her back,"**[16] וּשְׁנַיִם אוֹמְרִים אַחַת בִּכְרֵיסָהּ – **and two** other witnesses **say,** "We observed **one** hair **on her abdomen."**[17] In this instance, all the necessary testimony is present, for two witnesses attest to the presence of each hair. Nevertheless, since neither set of witnesses viewed both hairs, their testimony is disqualified, as it addresses only "half a matter."[18]

The Gemara discusses another instance where testimonies are combined to establish a *chazakah:*

אָמַר רַב יְהוּדָה – **Rav Yehudah stated:** אֶחָד אוֹמֵר אֲכָלָהּ חִטִּים – If **one witness says** that **[the occupant] used [the land]** to cultivate **wheat** for three years, וְאֶחָד אוֹמֵר אֲכָלָהּ שְׂעוֹרִים – **and one witness says** that **he used it** to cultivate **barley** for three years, הֲרֵי זוּ חֲזָקָה – **this is a** valid ***chazakah,*** as the two testimonies can be combined.[19]

Rav Nachman assumed that the two witnesses do not testify about the same years.[20] Rather, they testify to alternate years of occupation; i.e. the first witness testifies that the occupant cultivated wheat in the first, third and fifth years, and the second witness testifies that he cultivated barley in the second, fourth and sixth years.[21] Based on this assumption, Rav Nachman posed the following question:

מַתְקִיף לָהּ רַב נַחְמָן – **Rav Nachman challenged [Rav Yehudah's ruling]:** אֶלָּא מֵעַתָּה – **But now,** אֶחָד אוֹמֵר אֲכָלָהּ רִאשׁוֹנָה שְׁלִישִׁית וַחֲמִישִׁית – if **one** witness **testifies** that **[an occupant] used [a property]** for the **first, third and fifth** years, וְאֶחָד אוֹמֵר אֲכָלָהּ שְׁנִיָּה רְבִיעִית וְשִׁשִּׁית – **and one** witness **testifies** that **he used it** for the **second, fourth and sixth** years, הָכִי נַמִּי דְּהָוְיָא חֲזָקָה – **would a *chazakah* also be established** in such a case? Obviously not![22] How, then, can you rule that a *chazakah* is established in what is essentially this very case![23]

Rav Yehudah, realizing that Rav Nachman had misunderstood his ruling, clarified his position:

אָמַר לֵיהּ רַב יְהוּדָה – **Rav Yehudah replied to [Rav Nachman]:** הָכִי הַשְׁתָּא – **How can these** two instances **be compared!?** הָתָם – **There,** in the instance you mentioned (where one witness testifies to occupancy in years one, three and five, while the other testifies to occupancy in years two, four and six) בְּשַׁתָּא דְּקָא מַסְהִיד מַר – **regarding the year** about **which one witness testifies,**[24] לָא קָא מַסְהִיד מַר – **the other witness does not testify** at all. Thus, obviously no *chazakah* can be established, for two witnesses have not testified to any one period of occupancy![25] הָכָא – **Here,** (in the case of my ruling, where one witness testifies to cultivation of wheat and the other testifies to cultivation of barley) תַּרְוַייהוּ בַּחֲדָא שַׁתָּא קָא מַסְהֲדֵה – **both** witnesses **testify about the same time** and a *chazakah* can therefore be established based upon their testimony.[26] מַאי אִיכָּא לְמֵימַר – **What is there to say;** i.e. what problem can be raised with my ruling —

NOTES

sprouted, both would be regarded as aberrations resulting from moles, and not indicative of *naarus*] (*Rashbam*).

16. See note 13.

17. See note 15.

18. Thus, although these Sages maintain that testimony to a portion of a three-year period of *chazakah* is not considered attesting to half a matter, testifying to one of two existing hairs on the girl's person is so considered. *Rashbam* explains the distinction as follows: The witnesses to a portion of a *chazakah* have attested to all that transpired within the year about which they testify; nothing was omitted or left incomplete. Thus, their testimony is considered an entire unit and is acceptable. It can then be combined with two other similar testimonies to establish a *chazakah*. In the case of the testimony regarding the *naarah*, however, each pair of witnesses does not attest to the entire situation which presented itself at the time of their testimony, for they could have inspected the girl's entire person, and did not do so. Their testimony is therefore deemed incomplete, and is invalidated by virtue of its being considered testimony to only half a matter. (However, see *Rashba* who questions this explanation; see also *Rif* and Rishonim who offer various other explanations of the distinction.)

19. The rationale for this ruling is explained in the Gemara below.

20. For in that case their testimonies would conflict and offset each other (*Rashbam*).

21. It was the common practice of grain farmers to alternate crops in this manner, for such crop rotation prevents the earth from becoming nutrient-deficient and eliminates the need to allow the land to lie fallow between plantings (*Rashbam*; see however, *Rashi* to *Bava Metzia* 107a ד״ה ליזרעה).

22. Since a *chazakah* can only be established by three *consecutive* years of occupancy, as the Gemara stated previously, 29a (*Rashbam*).

23. [*Tosafos* reject this explanation of Rav Nachman's challenge, for if Rav Yehudah had truly stated that testimony to alternate consumption of wheat and barley constitutes a *chazakah*, he perforce contends that *chazakah* can be established in Rav Nachman's hypothetical case as well! *Tosafos* therefore explain the entire discussion differently (see also *Nimukei Yosef* and *Chidushei HaRan*).]

An apparent difficulty: Why did Rav Nachman not challenge Rav Yehudah's ruling by asking the obvious question: If only one witness testifies to each period of the *chazakah*, how can a *chazakah* be established? Without two witnesses testifying to the same period of occupancy, it is impossible to establish a *chazakah*!

Rashbam explains that Rav Nachman understood Rav Yehudah's logic to be as follows: The Gemara above (32a) cited the view of R' Yehoshua ben Korchah that if one witness testifies that Shimon borrowed a sum of money from Reuven on Sunday, and another testifies that he borrowed a like sum on Monday, their testimonies may be combined to render Shimon liable to pay that amount. The reason for R' Yehoshua's ruling is that although the witnesses do not testify to the same loan, both agree that Shimon owes a like sum of money. Rav Nachman assumed that Rav Yehudah subscribes to similar logic here; i.e. although each witness attests to a different three-year period, both agree that the occupant has established a *chazakah*. Rav Nachman's challenge is then understood as follows: Even if we grant that testimonies to two different occupancies can result in a *chazakah*, this is true only if either *chazakah* would be valid if attested to by two witnesses (Thus, if, for example, one witness testified to occupancy during years 1,2 and 3, and the second testified to occupancy during years 4,5 and 6, a *chazakah* would be established, for both agree that the occupant used the land in a manner able to effect a *chazakah*). However, when each witness attests to alternate years, neither occupancy would establish *chazakah* even if proven, since *chazakah* years must be consecutive. How, then, can the two testimonies be combined to form a *chazakah?*

24. Literally: the master testifies.

25. Rav Yehudah means: As you, Rav Nachman, argued, neither witness testifies to having seen a *chazakah,* for each claims to have seen the occupant use the land in alternate years, which does not establish a *chazakah.* However, if we could believe both witnesses, we would know that the occupant used the land consecutively for six years, which is more than enough to establish a *chazakah*. But since each witness does not corroborate the testimony of the other, we have only one witness to each year's use! Hence, their testimony is useless.

26. Rav Yehudah states that Rav Nachman misunderstood his ruling; i.e. the witnesses do not testify about alternate years — they testify about the *same* three years (see *"Rashi"* to *Rif* here. *Rashbam*,

משלשין ביניהם א שלשה אחים ואחד מצטרף עמהם הרי אלו שלש עדיות והן עדות אחת להזמה: גמ' מתני' דלא כרבי עקיבא דתניא ב א"ר יוסי כשהלך אבא חלפתא אצל רבי יוחנן בן נורי ללמוד תורה ואמרי לה ר' יוחנן בן נורי אצל אבא חלפתא ללמוד תורה אמר לו הרי שאכלה שנה ראשונה בפני שנים שנייה בפני שנים שלישית בפני שנים מהו אמר לו ג הרי זו חזקה אמר לו אף אני אומר כן אלא שר"ע חולק בדבר זה שהיה ר"ע אומר א דבר ולא חצי דבר ורבנן האי דבר ולא חצי דבר מאי עבדי ליה אילימא ד למעוטי אחד אומר אחת בגבה ואחד אומר אחת בכריסה האי חצי דבר (א) וחצי עדות היא ה אלא למעוטי שנים אומרים אחת בגבה ושנים אומרים אחת בכריסה אמר רב יהודה ו אחד אומר אכלה חטים ואחד אומר אכלה שעורים הרי זו חזקה מתקיף לה ר"נ אלא מעתה אחד אומר אכלה ראשונה שלישית וחמישית ואחד אומר אכלה שנה רביעית וששית הכי נמי דהויא חזקה א"ל רב יהודה הכי השתא ז התם בשתא דקא מסהיד מר לא קא מסהיד מר הכא תרוייהו בחדא שתא קא מסהדי מאי איכא למימר בין חיטי לשערי לאו אדעתייהו דאינשי: שלשה אחין ואחד מצטרף עמהן הרי אלו שלש עדיות והן עדות אחת להזמה: ההוא

רשב"ם

שלשה אחים ואחד מצטרף עמהם. דהיינו אח לשנה אח לשנה ואחד עם האח שאותו אחד מעיד עם כולן: הרי אלו ג' עדיות. ולהכי כשר עדותן דלשתא דקא מסהיד האי לא קמסהיד האי ואין כאן שני עדים קרובים בעדות אחת: והן עדות אחת להזמה. שאם הוזמו משלשין ביניהן וגם אין ניזומין עד שיוזמו כולן: גמ' מתני'. דכתיב לג' כתות של עדים עדות אחת לשלש שני חזקה: דלא כר"ע. דלר"ע לא מהני עדותן כלל הואיל וכל אחד אין מעיד על חזקה שלימה דשלש שנים אלא על שליש חזקה והיינו חצי דבר: אבא חלפתא. אבי חלפתא דר' יוסי סתם היינו רבי יוסי בן חלפתא: שהיה ר"ע אומר דבר. על פי שנים עדים יקום דבר שלם ישתלם כל הממון ע"פ עדים השנים: ולא חצי דבר. כל כת וכת אינה מעידה אלא על שליש החזקה והיינו שליש דבר ולא דבר שלם הואיל ואין שני עדים מעידים על כל הג' שנים: ה"ג אילימא למעוטי אחד כו'. במס' נדה (דף נב:) אמר ב' שערות שאמרו אפי' אחת בגבה ואחת בכריסה: בכריסה. באותו מקום: חצי עדות הוא. דאין כאן אלא עד אחד לכל שיער ועד אחד אינו נאמן לעשותה בת עונשין לחייבה וקרא חצי דבר אתא למעוטי שהרי דבר כתיב וחצי עדות למעוטי לא איצטריך קרא דבהדיא כתיב לא יקום עד אחד וגו': אלא. האי דבר למעוטי חצי דבר (ב) דכי האי גוונא כגון שנים אומרים אחת בגבה ראינו ולא בדקנו יותר ושנים אומרים אנו בדקנו מלפניה וראינו אחת בכריסה ואי לאו מיעוטא דקרא דבר ולא חצי דבר לא היה לנו לפסול עדות זה דעדות זה כשר הוא מאחר שיש ב' עדים על כל שיער שהרי אין מכחישין כלל זה את זה אלא כת זו בדקו מגבה וכת שניה בדקו מלפניה ובשעה אחת ראו ב' (ג) שערות אלו מכאן ואלו מכאן דליכא למימר שומא ניהו השתא דכתיב דבר עדותן בטלה דב' שערות דבר אחד הוא ואין מועילין אלא כשהן ביחד בבת אחת שאם נראה אחד היום מכאן ולמחר גדל אחר במקום אחר וכבר נשר הראשון אמרינן שומא ניהו (ד) ואין כלום אלא אם כן ישנן ביחד וכל כת וכת יכול לראות ב' השערות דהא ביחד היו נמצא שכל כת עדות של חצי דבר מעידין וכל אחד אינו מעיד שהיא גדולה אלא חצי סימני גדלות ראינו אבל ג' שני חזקה דמתני' שאין יכולין להיות כי אם בזה אחר זה ומי שרואה אכילת שנה זו אינו יכול לראות של שנה שניה אלא אם כן שוהה שנה שניה בזה המלכות הלכך כל שנה ושנה וכל יום ויום חשיב דבר שלם בפני עצמו דעל כרחך כיון דקרא למעוטי אתא ומיעוט אחד הוא דאיכא (ד) למימר) אין לך למעט כי אם (ה) חצי דבר דמסתבר טפי למעוטי דהיינו עדות דב' שערות בשתי כתות: ואחד אומר. אותן ג' שנים שאתה אומר אכלה חטין אני מעיד כמותך שאכלה אבל אכילת שעורים היתה הרי זו חזקה וטעמא מפרש לקמיה: מתקיף לה ר"נ אלא מעתה כו'. ר"נ לא היה יודע טעמו של רב יהודה המפורש לפנינו דבין חטין ושעורין טעו אינשי אלא ס"ל דהא דקאמר רב יהודה אחד אומר אכלה חטין ואחד אומר אכלה שעורין כו' לאו באותן ג' שנים דקמסהיד האי מסהיד האי דא"כ עדות מוכחשת היא ותיבטל אלא ס"ל לר"נ דה"ק רב יהודה אחד אומר אכלה חטין ג' שנים כפי מנהג עובדי אדמה ואחד אומר אכלה שעורים שלש שנים כפי מנהג עובדי אדמה והיינו שש שנים בדילוג ושאלתי לעובדי האדמה ואמרו לי שלעולם כך הוא המנהג שנה אחת חטין ושנה אחת שעורין כן כל הימים ואינה צריכה שביתה כלום ה"ז חזקה שהרי אין מכחישים זה את זה כלל וממ"נ כל אחד מעיד שאכלה שני חזקה והלכך הויא חזקה דדמיא להא דר' יהושע בן קרחה דאמרי' בפירקין לעיל (דף לג.) אין עדותם מצטרפת עד שיראו שניהם כאחד ר' יהושע בן קרחה אומר אפי' בזה אחר זה וטעמא דר' יהושע מפורש בסנהדרין בפ' זה בורר דאע"ג דאמנה דקמסהיד האי לא מסהיד האי מיהו תרוייהו אמנה קמסהדי והכא נמי תרוייהו אחזקה קמסהדי: אלא מעתה אחד אומר אכלה ראשונה שלישית כו'. דהיינו כרב יהודה הכי נמי דתיהוי חזקה הא ודאי לא תיהוי חזקה דלא דמיא כלל לר' יהושע בן קרחה דליכא היכא דאחד אומר אכלה ראשונה ושניה ושלישית ואחד אומר אכלה ד' ה' ו' דתרוייהו אחזקה מעלייתא (ו) קמסהדי אבל הכא לא זה ולא זה מעידים על חזקה רצופה דחזקה בדילוג אינה כלום וכן עיקרה של שיטה זו כמו שפירשתיה: א"ל רב יהודה הכי השתא התם כו'. וכיון דליכא אלא עד אחד לשנה חצי עדות הוא הכא תרוייהו בחדא שתא מסהדי כשזה אומר אכלה חטין וזה אומר אכלה שעורים אין לנו לחוש ולומר דלמא בדילוג קא מסהדי אלא מסתמא על אותם שלש שזה מעיד השני נמי מעיד וכיון דלעדות שלימה יש על השלש שנים מה יש פסול (ז) עוד אי משום דזה אומר אכלה שעורים: בין חיטי ושערי לאו אדעתייהו דאינשי. אין מבינין יפה בין קמת חטים לקמת שעורים:
ההוא

תוספות

משלשין בינידם. הכא לא שייך למיפרך ולימרו הנך קמאי אנן מנא ידעינן דכל דקמי דינא לאסהודי אתי אהאי ארעא אנן לחיובי מחזיק פירות קאתינן כדפריך בפרק כיצד הרגל (ב"ק דף כד: ושם) גבי שור ולימרו הנך (א) קמאי כו' אנן לחיובי פלגא ניזקא קאתינן דכיון דמחזיק מביאן לב"ד ודאי לטובתו באו כדי להחזיקו בקרקע ולא כדי לחייבו פירות: הרי אלו ג' עדיות. שהרי העד שהעיד בראשונה הוא עצמו יכול להעיד בשניה ולא אמרינן אדם קרוב אצל עצמו כמו כן אחיו יכול להעיד בשניה: והן עדות אחת. דאין משלמין עד שיוזמו כולן: ורבנן האי דבר ולא חצי דבר מאי עבדי ליה. וא"ת דהכא כ"ע דרשי דבר ולא חצי דבר ובפ' מרובה (שם דף עא:) אמרינן חמשה בקר אמר רחמנא ואפי' ה' חצאי בקר וי"ל דהכא משום דדבר מיותר הוא וא"ת והא איצטריך לדבר דבר ממון לאשמועינן דאין דבר שבערוה פחות משנים (גיטין דף ב.) וי"ל דדבר דגבי ערוה מופנה הוא ואפילו למ"ד דלמידין ומשיבין שמא ליכא למיפרך מידי ואי איכא למיפרך י"ל דלאו מדבר דריש אלא מעל פי שנים יקום (ח) דמשמע יקום כל העדות ולא חצי אבל גבי ממון מה לי ממון גדול ומה לי ממון קטן לפי מה שגנב ישלם להכי אין סברא למעט חצאי בקר והא דדרשינן בפרק ד' וה' (ב"ק דף מ. ושם) גבי שור של שני שותפין כופר (ט) ולא חצי כופר שאני התם דלכפרה אתי דאין אדם מביא חצי כפרה חצי חטאת וחצי אשם והא דאמרינן התם (גיטין מב:) גבי חציו עבד וחציו בן חורין משלם חצי כופר התם וחשיב כופר שלם דלא הרג אלא חצי בן חורין ובפרק יש בכור (בכורות דף מח: ושם ד"ה דרבי) דרשי' חמש ולא חצי חמש התם נמי מצות פדיונו ה' סלעים ולא מקיימא מצוה בפחות (י) מכן: אלא למעוטי שנים אומרים אחת בגבה. אומר רשב"א דאין צריך לחלק כפירוש הקונט' דאפילו [היתה] תשובה גדולה כשבדקו שני עדים היום בכל מקום ולא ראו כי אם אחת בגבה ובדקו למחר אותם עדים עצמן ולא ראו כי אם אחת בכריסה בשתי כתי עדים חשיב חצי דבר אע"פ שראו כל מה שיכולין (י) ולא דמי לעדות חזקה דהכא אין עדותן עדות בלא עדות ב' אחרונים (כ) ואין מועיל לשום דבר בעולם לכך הוי חצי דבר אבל שנים בראשונה אע"פ שאין עדות מועיל לענין חזקה מכל מקום נפקא מינה בעדותן לשלומי פירי ודבר שלם הוא: אלא מעתה אחד אומר אכלה ראשונה שלישית כו'. פי' הקונט' דר"נ היה סבור דרב יהודה איירי באחד אומר אכלה חטים היינו ראשונה שלישית וחמישית ואין נראה דא"כ מאי פריך אלא מעתה אכלה ראשונה כו' אין ה"נ לסברתו אמר רב יהודה דהוי חזקה והכי הוה ליה למיפרך מאי הוי חזקה והא אין שום אדם אומר שאכלה רצופין ולא דמי לר' יהושע בן קרחה ונראה לפרש דר"נ ידע דתרוייהו אחדא שתא קמסהדי וה"פ כיון דאמר דהויא חזקה אע"ג דמכחשי אהדדי משום דתרוייהו אחזקה קמסהדי אלא מעתה אחד אומר אכלה ראשונה שלישית וחמישית ושנית ורביעית וששית הניחה בורה כדרך מוברי באגי ואחד אומר לא כי אלא אכלה (ל) שנית רביעית וששית וראשונה שלישית וחמישית הניחה בורה ה"נ דהוה חזקה אע"ג דמכחשי אהדדי כיון דתרוייהו מיהא אחזקה קא מסהדי
ומשני

עין משפט נר מצוה

רנו א ב מיי' פכ"א מהל' עדות הל' ז טור ח"מ סי' לח:

רנז ג ד מיי' פ"ד מהל' עדות הל' ז סמג לאוין קט טוש"ע ח"מ סי' ל סעיף יג:

רנח ה ו מיי' פט"ו מהל' טוען ונטען הל' ב סמג עשין לה טוש"ע ח"מ סי' קמה סעיף א:

רבינו גרשום

משלשין ביניהן. כל כת משלמת לו שליש דמי הקרקע: שלשה אחין. מעידין כל אחד שאכלה שנה: ואחד. עד נכרי: מצטרף. להעיד עמהן עם כל א' וא': הרי אלו ג' עדיות. שכל מה שמעיד אח זה אין מעיד אח זה וכשר הוא העדות: והן עדות אחת. הואיל וכל אחת מצטרף עם זה נכרי אם הוזם זה נכרי או אחד מן האחין שמצטרף עמו בטל כל העדות של חזקה זו הואיל וזה נכרי מעיד עם כולן ומשלמין בין ארבעתם: על פי שנים עדים יקום דבר. שלם ולא חצי דבר וזה השנים אין מעידין אלא שליש דבר: ורבנן דמתני' דקא סברי ה"ז חזקה [דבר] ולא חצי דבר מאי עבדי ליה למעוטי מאי: האי חצי עדות. דאחד בלבד אמר בגבה: אלא שנים אמרו אחת בגבה. היינו שנים מעידין חצי דבר וכן נמי שנים אומרין אחת בכריסה דלא מצרפינן לסהדותייהו דהאי כת דמעיד על נימא אחת בלבד אכתי משוו לה קטנה. וכן נמי כת אחרת משוו לה קטנה ולא ידעת איזו חזיא ברישא: אחד אומר. שזרעה לאכלה ג' שנים חטים וא' אומר שעורין אכלה ג' שנים הרי זה חזקה: בין חטי לשערי לא דייקי אינשי. ועדותן עדות והויא חזקה:

מסורת הש"ס

א) [סנהדרין דף כח.], ב) ב"ק ע. [תוספתא ב"ב פ"ב], ג) ב"ק ע: סנהדרין ל: ודף פו., ד) רש"א מ"ז, ה) [נ"ל בתרא], ו) [וע"ע תוס' סנהדרין פו. ד"ה דבר ותוס' ב"ק מ. ד"ה כופר]:

הגהות הב"ח

(א) גמ' האי חצי דבר חצי עדות כצ"ל ואות ו' נמחק: (ב) רשב"ם ד"ה אלא האי וכו' בכי האי גוונא וכו': (ג) בא"ד ראו ב' השערות אלו אחת מכאן ואלו אחת מכאן וכו': (ד) בא"ד ואין כלום וכו' וכל כת וכת היה יכול וכו': (ה) בא"ד למעט כי אם אותו חצי דבר: (ו) ד"ה אלא מעתה וכו' מעלייתא רצופה קמסהדי: (ז) ד"ה א"ל רב יהודה וכו' מה יש פסול עדות עוד אי משום דזה אומר אכלה חטים וזה אומר אכלה שעורים: (ח) תוס' ד"ה ורבנן וכו' יקום דבר דמשמע: (ט) בא"ד כופר שלם ולא חצי כופר: (י) ד"ה אלא למעוטי וכו' כל מה שיכולין לראות ולא דמי: (כ) בא"ד ואין מועיל. נ"ב ע' ברי"ף: (ל) ד"ה אלא מעתה וכו' אלא אכלה שניה רביעית:

תורה אור השלם

א) לֹא יָקוּם עֵד אֶחָד בְּאִישׁ לְכָל עָוֹן וּלְכָל חַטָּאת בְּכָל חֵטְא אֲשֶׁר יֶחֱטָא עַל פִּי שְׁנֵי עֵדִים אוֹ עַל פִּי שְׁלֹשָׁה עֵדִים יָקוּם דָּבָר: [דברים יט, טו]

ליקוטי רש"י

שלשה אחים ואחד מצטרף עמהם. מן השוק עם כל אחד ואחד מעידים על אכילת שני חזקה של קרקע של אדם מן השוק ומעיד אחד מן האחין והבא מן השוק על שנה ראשונה ואחד מן האחין והבא מן השוק על שנה שניה והשלישי על השלישית והרי אלו שלש עדיות והחזקה קיימת ולא אמרינן עדות אחת היא והרי העדים קרובים אלא שלש עדיות ניהו דלשתא דקא מסהיד האי לא מסהיד האי. והן עדות אחת להזמה. דעד דמזמזי כולהו לא משלמי ממונא דהא לא הוה מתוקמא בידא דלוקח אלא בסהדותא דכולהו [סנהדרין כח.]. אבא חלפתא. אבא של ר' יוסי חלפתא שמו [שבת קטו. ב"ק ע: מעילה יז:]. שהכל יודעין שהוא חסיד [סנהדרין פ.]. למעוטי אחד אומר אחת בגבה. וקאתו לשויה גדולה לענין עונשין או לענין שיהו קידושיה קדושין. בגבה. שיער ראיתי בקשרי אצבעותיה [ב"ק שם]. בין קשרי אצבעותיה [סנהדרין ל:]. אותו מקום [נדה נב: ע"ש]. חצי דבר. שיער אחד. וחצי עדות. עד אחד יש לשער ופשיטא דלאו עדות היא [ב"ק שם]. עד אחד הוא חצי עדות שיער אחת הוא חצי דבר.

the fact that the two witnesses' testimonies conflict as to what type of grain the occupant cultivated? That is of no consequence, for בֵּין חִיטֵּי לְשַׂעְרֵי לָאו אַדַּעְתַּיְיהוּ דְּאִינְשֵׁי – **people do not** easily **discern between wheat and barley.**[27]

The Gemara cites the final section of the Mishnah:

שְׁלֹשָׁה אַחִין וְאֶחָד מִצְטָרֵף עִמָּהֶן – If **THREE BROTHERS** testified each to one year's use, **AND ONE** unrelated witness **JOINED WITH** each of **THEM,** הֲרֵי אֵלּוּ שָׁלֹשׁ עֵדֻיּוֹת – **THESE ARE** considered **THREE** separate **TESTIMONIES.** וְהֵן עֵדוּת אַחַת לְהֲזָמָה – **NEVERTHELESS, THEY ARE** considered **ONE TESTIMONY WITH REGARD TO** the laws of ***HAZAMAH.***

NOTES

however, explains that each witness was vague as to exactly which three years' consumption he witnessed. Rav Yehudah argues that there is no reason not to assume that they refer to the same three years – see *Chossen Yeshuos.*)

27. Thus, the conflicting testimony on this detail is ignored, and a *chazakah* is established.

The Gemara discusses another instance in which brothers testify regarding different facets of the same case:

דַּהֲוָה חַתִימֵי ‏ הַהוּא שְׁטָרָא – There was **a certain** loan **document** עֲלֵיהּ בֵּי תְרֵי – **on which two witnesses were signed.** The lender wished to certify the document by having the witnesses who signed it verify their signatures.[1] שְׁכִיב חַד מִינַּיְיהוּ – However, **one of [the witnesses] died,** and therefore could not verify his signature. Consequently, two new witnesses were required to verify the second signature.[2] אֲתָא אֲחוּהָ דְּהַאי דְּקָאֵי – **A brother of the surviving [witness] came** forward, וְחַד אַחֲרִינָא – **along with another** witness, לְאַסְהוּדֵי אַחֲתִימַת יְדֵיהּ דְּאִידָךְ – **to testify to** the authenticity of **[the deceased witness'] signature.** Thus, the surviving witness verified his own signature, while his brother along with another witness verified the deceased witness' signature.

The question presented itself whether both brothers can participate in certifying the document:

סָבַר רָבִינָא לְמֵימַר – **Ravina thought to say:** הַיְינוּ מַתְנִיתִין – **This is** analogous to the ruling in **our Mishnah,** which states: ג׳ אַחִין וְאֶחָד מִצְטָרֵף עִמָּהֶן – If **THREE BROTHERS** testified, each to one year's use, **AND ONE** unrelated witness who observed the entire three years' use **JOINED WITH** each of **THEM,** their testimony establishes a *chazakah.* It seems from the Mishnah that two brothers may testify in the same case, as long as their testimonies relate to different facets of the case.

The Gemara rejects the comparison:

אָמַר לֵיהּ רַב אַשִׁי – **Rav Ashi said to [Ravina]:** מִי דָּמֵי – **Are these** two cases truly **analogous?** הָתָם – **There,** in the Mishnah's case, לֹא נָפִיק נְבֵי רִיבְעָא דְּמָמוֹנָא אַפּוּמָא דְּאַחֵי – **three quarters of the money is not exacted through the testimony of brothers,** as the combined testimony of the brothers supplies only half of the evidence necessary to establish a *chazakah.*[3] הָכָא – **Here,** in the instance of the loan document, however, נָפִיק נְבֵי רִיבְעָא דְּמָמוֹנָא אַפּוּמָא דְּאַחֵי – **three quarters of the money is exacted through the testimony of brothers.**[4] Thus, although testimony of brothers is accepted in the Mishnah's case, it is inadmissible with regard to the document.[5]

Mishnah The law has already been established that unchallenged use of a property for three years by consuming its produce establishes the occupant's *chazakah* on the premises. As long as he asserts a legitimate claim of ownership, he prevails against an unsubstantiated challenge to his title brought by the original owner. The Mishnah now considers which usages of a property — though they do not indicate that the user is the owner of the property itself — indicate that he has acquired the rights to those usages from the property's owner. If the activities that indicate acquisition of the rights are performed by the user in the property for three years without challenge from the property's owner, he will have established a *chazakah* with respect to those specific activities and his claim that he acquired those rights legitimately will be accepted by the court.[6]

אֵלּוּ דְבָרִים שֶׁיֵּשׁ לָהֶן חֲזָקָה – **These are the activities regarding which a *chazakah* can be established**[7] וְאֵלּוּ דְבָרִים שֶׁאֵין לָהֶן חֲזָקָה – **and these are the activities regarding which a *chazakah* cannot be established.** First, the Mishnah lists those activities for which no *chazakah* is established: הָיָה מַעֲמִיד בְּהֵמָה בֶּחָצֵר – If **[a person] would place an animal in a courtyard** belonging to someone else, תַּנּוּר רֵיחַיִם וְכִירַיִים – or if he would place **an oven, millstones or a stove** in the courtyard,[8] וּמְגַדֵּל תַּרְנְגוֹלִים – or if **he would raise chickens** וְנוֹתֵן זִבְלוֹ – **or deposit**

NOTES

1. When a note is presented by a creditor for payment, the debtor may deny having borrowed, arguing that the witnesses' signatures are forged. The creditor then cannot collect unless he can prove to the court that the signatures are genuine. If he succeeds, the court appends to the document a paragraph attesting to the authenticity of the signatures, and the judges sign their names below. This certification is called a הֶנְפֵּק.

One of the ways in which a creditor can prove the note's authenticity is to bring to the court the witnesses who signed on the document, who then verify their signatures. Although the rule for monetary law is that a minimum of two witnesses is required, in this case it is not necessary for each witness to testify to *both* signatures on the note. Rather, each one's testimony to his *own* signature is sufficient. This is because we regard the witnesses as testifying to the actual loan rather than merely to the authenticity of the signatures. By certifying the note, then, the witnesses testify that they saw the loan and signed on the document. Hence, in essence, rather than having one witness on each signature, we have two witnesses to the loan (*Rashbam,* following the opinion of the Rabbis as explained in *Kesubos* 21a).

2. The Torah declares, *"By the testimony of two witnesses . . . shall a matter be established"* (*Deuteronomy* 19:15). The Sages understand this not only to require a minimum of two witnesses to obligate a man monetarily (the simple meaning of the verse), but also to require that no one witness play more than half the role in the total testimony.

In the case here, then, it goes without saying that we may not certify the document by accepting verification of both signatures from the surviving witness, for we would then be exacting all the money upon the testimony of one witness. Additionally, however, we may not allow him to verify his own signature and join with a second witness to verify the second signature, because we would then be exacting three-quarters of the money upon the testimony of one witness; i.e. by single-handedly verifying his own signature he exacts half the money, and by joining another witness to verify the second signature he exacts another quarter. Rather, he may verify only his own signature, and the creditor must seek two witnesses to verify the second signature (*Rashbam* from *Kesubos* 21a).

3. In disqualifying the testimony of relatives who testify together, the Torah is, in essence, regarding them both as if they were only one witness. In our Mishnah, then, where each witness testifies to only one year's occupancy, a total of six witnesses is needed to establish the full three-year *chazakah* — two witnesses for each year. Since the three brothers each testify to only one year, half of the claim is established by "one" witness, and the other half is established by the single unrelated witness who testifies to all three years of occupancy. This complies with the law mentioned in the previous note that no one witness may effect more than half the outcome of the litigation (*Rashbam*).

4. The witness who verifies his own signature requires no supporting testimony, and thus is considered to have imposed upon the borrower half of the liability for the loan. Additionally, since he is the brother of one of the witnesses who verify the second signature, it is as if he imposed yet another quarter of the liability, for both brothers are viewed by the Torah as one. This violates the rule that no one witness may impose more than half the liability (*Rashbam*).

5. [The Gemara means only that *this* method of certifying the document is ineffective. However, there is a simple, alternate method of certification: The surviving witness can sign his name before the court and the judges can then compare it to the signature in the document. In this way, it will be the court and not the surviving witness who verifies his signature, and he (or his brother) is free to join the other, unrelated witness to verify the second signature. In this way, no single witness imposes more than half the obligation on the borrower (*Tosafos* from *Kesubos* 21a).]

6. [The above follows *Rashbam,* who understands the Mishnah to refer to *chazakah* based on three years of use and a claim of acquisition. Cf. *Rambam* and *Meiri,* citing Geonim, who explain the Mishnah differently; see also *Rambam, Hil. Shecheinim* 5:5 *Tur, Choshen Mishpat* 140:19..]

7. Literally: these things have a *chazakah.*

8. These items are not affixed to the ground and can be removed. (The millstones referred to are those of a hand mill.) Thus, their presence

א) [נ"ל דאחין]

הגהות הב"ח

(א) תוס' ד"ה (בדף הקודם) אלא מעתה כו' לשלם כאותו מנה: (ב) ד"ה הכא נפיק כולה ממונא נכי ריבעא:

ההוא שטרא דהוה חתימי עליה בי תרי שכיב חד מינייהו אתא אחוה דהאי דקאי וחד אחרינא לאסהודי אחתימת ידיה דאידך סבר רבינא למימר היינו מתני' ג' אחין ואחד מצטרף עמהן אמר ליה רב אשי א) מי דמי התם לא נפיק נכי ריבעא דממונא אפומא דאחי הכא נפיק נכי ריבעא דממונא אפומא דאחי: **מתני'** אלו דברים שיש להן חזקה ואלו דברים שאין להן חזקה ב) היה מעמיד בהמה בחצר תנור וכירים וריחים ומגדל תרנגולים ונותן זבלו בחצר אינה חזקה אבל עשה מחיצה לבהמתו גבוה עשרה טפחים וכן לתנור וכן לכיריים וכן לריחים הכנים תרנגולין לתוך הבית ועשה מקום לזבלו עמוק שלשה או גבוה שלשה הרי זו חזקה: **גמ'** מאי שנא רישא ומאי שנא סיפא אמר עולא כל שאילו בנכסי הגר קנה בנכסי חבירו קנה כל שאילו בנכסי הגר לא קנה בנכסי חבירו לא קנה מתקיף לה רב ששת וכללא הוא והרי ניר דבנכסי הגר קנה בנכסי חבירו לא קנה והרי אכילת פירות דבנכסי חבירו קנה בנכסי הגר לא קנה אלא אמר רב נחמן אמר רבה בר אבוה הכא

ההוא שטרא. והולך המלוה לקיימו: **שכיב חד מינייהו.** מת אחד מהן קודם שנתקיים השטר ואילו לא מת היה כל אחד בא ומעיד לבדו על חתימת ידו ואין צריך לצרף עמו אחר אלא נאמן לומר זה כתב ידי כדתנן בפ"ב דכתובות (דף כ:) זה אומר זה כתב ידי וזה אומר זה כתב ידי כו' וחכמים אומרים אין צריכין לצרף עמהן אחר אלא נאמן לומר זה כתב ידי ואמרינן בגמ' לדברי חכמים על מנה שבשטר הן מעידין אנחנו ראינו המלוה ותחתנו הלכך בתרי סגי ולא צריך חד מינייהו לאסהודי אדחבריה והיכא דמת אחד מהן אמרינן התם אליבא דרבנן דצריך שנים מן השוק להעיד על חתימת יד המת והחי יעיד הוא לבדו על חתימת ידו אבל להעיד החי לא יצטרף עם אחר מן השוק להעיד על חתימת המת דכיון דעל מנה שבשטר הן מעידין וכי אמר זה כתב ידי נפק פלגא דממונא אפומיה שהרי הוא לבדו מעיד על חתימתו ואין צריך אחר להעיד עמו וכי הדר מצטרף עם ההוא מן השוק להעיד על חתימת המת הדר נפיק ריבעא דממונא על פומיה אשתכח דכוליה ממונא נכי ריבעא נפק אפומיה ואנן על פי שנים עדים בעינן חצי דבר על פיו של זה וחצי דבר על פיו של זה והלכך הכא דשכיב חד מינייהו אין עד החי יכול להצטרף עם אחר מן השוק להעיד על חתימת יד המת אלא צריך שנים מן השוק להעיד עליו: **אתא אחוה דהאי דקאי.** אחיו של עד החי בא להצטרף עם אחד מן השוק להעיד על חתימתו כדפרישית דצריך שנים מן השוק להעיד על חתימת דאידך המת: **היינו מתניתין.** דתנן גבי דשני אחין פסולין לעדות אחת דלא חשיבי אלא כחד אפילו הכי מכשרא להו מתניתין לשלשה אחין בעדות קרקע אחד מאחר מאחר שאין זה מעיד על אותה שנה שזה מעיד אף כאן העד החי מעיד על החתימה שלו ואחיו על חתימת יד המת: **התם.** במתניתין לא קנפיק כל הממון: **נכי ריבעא.** חסר רביע דהיינו שלשה חלקים ממון אפומא דאחי אלא פלגא הוא דנפיק אפומא דעד נכרי ופלגא נפיק אפומא דאחי והלכך כשירין לעדות זו דטעמא דפסיל רחמנא קרובים בעדות אחת לפי שאינן חשובין אלא כאיש אחד ולגבי חזקת שלש שנים כאיש אחד דמו שהרי איש אחר שמצטרף עמהן מועיל בשלשתן אם ראה החזקה שלש שנים: **אבל הכא.** גבי שטרא נפיק נכי רבעא דממונא דהיינו שלש חלקי הממון אפומא דאחי וכי חשבת לאחי כעד אחד נמצא עד אחד מגבה שלשה חלקים והאחד רביע ולא קרינא על פי שנים עדים וגו': **מתני' אלו דברים שיש להם חזקה.** כלומר אלו מיני תשמישין דאמרינן לקמן שאדם משתמש בשל חבירו שאם משתמש שלש שנים ולא מיחה בו חבירו יש לו חזקה לזה המחזיק ויכול לטעון אתה נתתו לי לתשמיש זה במתנה או מכרתו לי כגון תשמישין קבועין כדמפרש לקמן שאדם מקפיד עליהן אם נעשין שלא ברשותו והלכך בשלש שנים הויא חזקה דומיא דבורות שיחין ומערות ובית השלחין וכל הנך דלעיל דכיון דקביעות תשמיש הוא כדמחזיק בגופה של קרקע חבירו דמי והויא חזקה בשלש שנים. ורבינו חננאל פירש אלו דברים שיש להם חזקה כאשר כבר פירשנו ולא נהירא אלא לקמיה קאי כדפרישית דאי לעיל קאי ומסקנא דמתני' דלעיל היא אריכות לשון של הבל הוא בלא צורך ועוד דהכי תנינן לקמן יש להם חזקה טובא כללא דמילתא כל הני יש להן חזקה דתנן במתניתין עד סוף הפרק בחזקת שלש שנים מיירי כדמוכח בברייתא (לקמן נט:) בא לפני רבי חייא אמר לו יגעת בני יגעת: **היה מעמיד בהמה כו'.** כל הנך דברים המיטלטלין הן ואינן תשמיש של קביעות ואין בעל חצר מקפיד עד ארבע וחמש שנים ולכך אין לו חזקה למחזיק לומר מדוע לא מחית בידי דאמר ליה בעל חצר לא חששתי למחות דלא מחזקת בגוף הקרקע כדמחזקי אינשי ולא הייתי נפסד כלום ומעתה אני מקפיד: **תנור וכירים.** מטלטלין הן וכן ריחים בריחיא דידא: **אבל עשה מחיצה בחצר כו'.** הרי זה גדר והרי זו חזקה כל מקום תוך המחילות שעשה יכול לטעון לקוח הוא בידי: **הכנים תרנגולין לתוך הבית.** של חבירו שלש שנים גם על זאת ודאי מקפיד אינש ואם לא מיחה הפסיד דודאי על פיו עשה וברשותו: **ועשה מקום.** עמוק שלשה: **או עשה מקום כו'.** כדי שלא יתפזר: **או גבוה שלשה.** מחילה גבוהה שלשה: **גמ' מאי שנא רישא.** דבהעמדת בהמה כדי בלא מחילה אין זו חזקה: **ומ"ש סיפא.** דבעשיית מחילה קנה וקא ס"ד השתא דבאינש בעלמא שאינו בר חצר זו קאמר דאין זו חזקה והלכך קשיא ליה מ"ש רישא מסיפא הא ודאי מקפידין בני חצר על איש נכרי שיבא כאן בהמותיו ומדלא מיחו ודאי הקנו לו מקום בחצר זה להעמיד בהמותיו ואמאי אין לו חזקה ולקמן מתרך לה בשותפין: **אמר עולא.** כל חזקה רעועה דלא קנה אם בא לעשותה בנכסי הגר לקנותה מיד והוא הדין לענין קונה קרקע מחבירו וא"ל לך חזק וקני והלך והחזיק חזקה רעועה דלא קנה כגון העמדת שם בהמתו או תנור וכירים דאין זה נעל וגדר דלא עשה שום תיקון בגוף הקרקע: **בנכסי חבירו נמי לא קנה.** כלומר לענין חזקת שלש שנים שלוקח אומר לקחתי ומוכר אומר לא מכרתי אינה קרויה חזקה להיות במקום עדי מכירה דהא לא עבד ולא מידי: **כל שאילו בנכסי הגר קנה.** כגון עשיית מחילה ורפק בה פורתא: **בנכסי חבירו נמי קנה.** כלומר הויא חזקה ומיהו הקנין ע"י מעות או מתנה היא ומיהו הכנים תרנגולין לתוך הבית דקתני סיפא דהוי חזקה בנכסי הגר לא הויא חזקה והאי דלא פריך לה משום דעדיפא מינה קפריך רב ששת. ואית דמפרש דהכנים תרנגולין נמי הוי חזקה בנכסי הגר דהיינו נעל שנעל את הדלת בפניהם ולאו מילתא היא דנעילת דלת לאו חזקה היא דאינו דומה אלא למבריח ארי כדאמרן לעיל (נג.) ונעל דלת בבנין מיירי שעשה דלת או סתימה: **וכללא הוא.** בתמיה דקא מדמית חזקת שלש שנים שתלוי בקפידא לחזקת קנין נכסי הגר שתלוי בתקון הקרקע: **ניר.** אמרינן בפירקין דלעיל (דף נג:) דלכולי עלמא ניר לא הוי חזקה דבנכסי הגר קנה אפי' רפק בה פורתא ובנכסי חבירו לענין שלש שנים לא קנה בחזקה זו לפי שהכל תלוי באכילת הפירות שאם יחרוש ולא יאכל אין בעל הקרקע מפסיד שהרי יזרע ואחר יאכל: **והרי אכילת פירות.** לקיטת הפירות דבנכסי חבירו קנה אם אכל הפירות שלש שנים דהויא אכילת שלש שנים במקום עדות שקנה הקרקע זו מן הבעלים כדאמרן בכוליה פירקין: **ובנכסי הגר לא קנה.** דאין זה נעל וגדר כדאמרן לעיל (דף נג.) האי מאן דפסח דיקלא אדעתא דחיותא לא קני: **אלא אמר רב נחמן אמר רבה בר אבוה.** לעולם גבי איש נכרי שבא להעמיד בהמה בחצר אחרים שאין לו בה שותפות לא שנא רישא ולא שנא סיפא דהויא חזקה שאין בני חצר מניחין לנכרי להשתמש תשמישין הללו בחצר שלהן אלא אם כן נטלו רשות מהן ואם לא מיחו בתוך שלש שנים הויא חזקה:

והכא

תוספות

ומשני דהכא לא מכחשי אהדדי דבין חיטי ושערי לא דייקי אינשי אע"ג דדייקי בין מנה שחור למנה לבן בזה בורר (סנהדרין דף ל:) התם צריכי למידק שחייב לשלם (א) אותו מנה שלוה אבל הכא לא דייקי דבכל ענין שיאכלנה חטין או שעורים הוא חזקה ומיהו זה אומר אכלה חטין וזה קטנית עדותן בטלה דאפי' בלא דקדוק אין אדם טועה בין חטין לקטנית: **הכא נפיק** (ב) **נכי רבעא [דממונא] אפומא** א) **דחד.** ואע"ג דיש תקנה כדאמרינן בפרק ב' דכתובות (דף כא. ושם) דאם מת אחד מן החתומין ואין שנים מן השוק להעיד עליו לכתוב חתימת ידיה אחספא ושדי לבי דינא ומחזקי ליה כו' הכי נמי הכא אלא דרבינא בעי למימר דבלאו הכי יכול אחיו להעיד והוה מדמה למתני':

בשותפין

עין משפט נר מצוה

רנט **א** מיי' פ"ז מהל' עדות הל' ד סמג עשין קיז טוש"ע ח"מ סי' מו סעיף יג:

רס **ב** מיי' פי"ב מהל' טוען ונטען הל' יד ופ"ה מהל' שכנים הל' ה סמג עשין לה וסי' פב טוש"ע ח"מ סי' קמ סעיף טו וסי' קסא סעיף ה ועי' בב"י:

רבינו גרשום

אחתימת ידא דאידך. דמית: **היינו מתני'.** דא' יכול ליצטרף עם אחין להעיד: **התם.** במתני' **לא נפיק.** אלא פלגא ממונא **אפומי דאחי** ופלגא אפומא [דאחר]: **הכא נפיק נכי ריבעא אפומא דאחי.** שאותו אח הנחתם מעיד על חצי הממון ואח השני ואחד מעידין על חתימת המת נמצא אח שני מעיד על רביע הממון והאחד שעמו מעיד על הרביע: **פיסקא היה מעמיד בהמה. בחצר** חבירו: או מעמיד **תנור וכירים וכו'.** אלו דבר המטלטל הן **אינה חזקה** דהואיל דלא קביע לא קפיד בעל חצר: **אבל עשה מחיצות.** דהיינו בנין קבוע או **הכניס תרנגולין לתוך הבית** של בעל חצר שמשתמש בביתו או **עשה מקום לזבלו** בחצר ושתיק בעל חצר **הרי זו חזקה: כל שאילו בנכסי הגר קנה.** כגון נעל גדר ופרץ היינו דומיא דסיפא דגדר ועשה מחיצה: **כל שבנכסי הגר לא קנה.** כגון הני דרישא דלא עבד ולא מידי בגוף הקרקע: **והרי נירא דבנכסי הגר קנה.** כדאמר לעיל אתא ההוא גברא רפיק ביה פורתא ואוקמיה בידיה: **ובנכסי חבירו לא קנה.** כדאמר בפירקין דלעיל אלא דכולי עלמא ניר לא הוי חזקה: **והרי אכילת פירות.** אילן חבירו ג' שנים הויא חזקה: **ובנכסי הגר לא קנה.** כדאמר לעיל בההיא איתתא דאכלה תליסר שנין ולא קנתה בהכי: **אלא אמר רב נחמן אמר רבה בר אבוה.** לאו היינו טעמא דמתני' כדקאמרת אלא מתני'

his manure בֶּחָצֵר – **in the courtyard,** אֵינָהּ חֲזָקָה – **it is not a *chazakah*,** even though the courtyard's owner has not protested this person's use of his property for three years.[9] The Mishnah now lists the activities for which a *chazakah* can be established: אֲבָל עָשָׂה מְחִיצָה לִבְהֶמְתּוֹ – **But if [the user] made a partition for his animal** גָּבוֹהַּ עֲשָׂרָה טְפָחִים – **ten *tefachim* high,** וְכֵן לְתַנּוּר וְכֵן לְכִירַיִים וְכֵן לְרֵיחַיִם – **and similarly,** if he erected such a partition **for an oven, stove or millstones;**[10] הִכְנִיס תַּרְנְגוֹלִין לְתוֹךְ הַבַּיִת – or **if he brought chickens into the** owner's **house,**[11] וְעָשָׂה מָקוֹם לְזִבְלוֹ עָמוֹק שְׁלֹשָׁה אוֹ גָּבוֹהַּ שְׁלֹשָׁה – or **if he made for his manure** in the courtyard **a place** either **three *tefachim* deep or three *tefachim* high,**[12] הֲרֵי זוֹ חֲזָקָה – **this is a *chazakah*.**[13]

Gemara

The Gemara asks:

מַאי שְׁנָא רֵישָׁא וּמַאי שְׁנָא סֵיפָא – **Why is the former clause** of the Mishnah **different from the latter clause?** Surely a person would object to an intruder performing any of the activities listed in the Mishnah, even if the intruder does not partition the area that he uses. Why, then, does the user not establish a *chazakah* in the cases of the Mishnah's former clause?

The Gemara answers:

אָמַר עוּלָּא – **Ulla said:** כָּל שֶׁאִילּוּ בְּנִכְסֵי הַגֵּר קָנָה – **Any** proprietary act **which,** if performed **in the** ownerless **property of a** deceased **convert, would acquire** it[14] בְּנִכְסֵי חֲבֵירוֹ קָנָה – **acquires,** i.e. establishes a *chazakah,* when performed **in the property of one's fellow.**[15] כָּל שֶׁאִילּוּ בְּנִכְסֵי הַגֵּר לֹא קָנָה – **Any** proprietary act **which,** if performed **in the** ownerless **property of a** deceased **convert, would not acquire** it[16] בְּנִכְסֵי חֲבֵירוֹ לֹא קָנָה – **does not acquire,** i.e. establish a *chazakah,* when performed **in the property of one's fellow.** Thus the first list of activities in the Mishnah cannot effect *chazakah* while those in the latter clause can.[17]

The Gemara asks:

מַתְקִיף לָהּ רַב שֵׁשֶׁת – **Rav Sheishess challenged [Ulla's rule]:** וּכְלָלָא הוּא – **But is this a** hard and fast **rule** that you present? וַהֲרֵי נִיר – **But there is** the act of **plowing** of a field, דִּבְנִכְסֵי הַגֵּר קָנָה – **which,** if performed **in the** ownerless **property of a** deceased **convert, would acquire** it,[18] בְּנִכְסֵי חֲבֵירוֹ לֹא קָנָה – **yet,** if performed **in the property of one's fellow, does not acquire** (i.e. establish a *chazakah* in) it.[19] וַהֲרֵי אֲכִילַת פֵּירוֹת – **And there is** also the **consumption of** a field's **produce,** דִּבְנִכְסֵי חֲבֵירוֹ קָנָה – **which, in** regard to **the property of one's fellow, does acquire,** i.e. serve to establish a *chazakah* in that property,[20] בְּנִכְסֵי הַגֵּר לֹא קָנָה – **yet, in** regard to **the** ownerless **property of a** deceased **convert, does not** serve to **acquire it.**[21] Obviously, the criteria for acquiring a proselyte's property and establishing *chazakah* are not identical.[22] – ? –

The Gemara concedes this objection and offers another explanation for the rulings of our Mishnah:

אֶלָּא אָמַר רַב נַחְמָן אָמַר רַבָּה בַּר אֲבוּהַּ – **Rather, Rav Nachman said in the name of Rabbah bar Avuha:**

NOTES

does not constitute an activity that an owner would definitely be expected to protest (*Rashbam*).

9. The property owner can claim that he saw no harm in allowing these items to remain, as long as they did not inconvenience him. Thus, unless the user can prove that he acquired from the owner the right to use the courtyard for these purposes, the owner can oust him.

10. This constitutes a *chazakah* in the area within the partitions, since the user has performed the proprietary act of partitioning the property (*Rashbam*). [*Rashbam* is apparently explaining the Mishnah according to the view of Ulla (below in the Gemara), who states that performing a proprietary act in a property serves to establish a *chazakah* in it. However, the Gemara eventually rejects this view. According to the accepted explanation of Rabbah bar Avuha (see Gemara below), we must apparently explain that although use of someone's property for the items listed here might be tolerated, enclosing the area for these purposes is quite another matter. If an intruder were to set off part of a property for his personal use, one would surely expect the owner to protest. His failure to protest indicates that he has granted the user that right and enables the user to establish a *chazakah* (see *Meiri*).]

11. The owner would certainly protest such unauthorized use of his property.

12. I.e. he dug a three-*tefach* pit for the manure (so that it would not scatter) or he erected a three-*tefach* partition around it (*Rashbam*).

13. If the owner did not protest these uses of his property for three years, the user has established a *chazakah,* which supports his claim that he acquired the right to use the property for these purposes from the owner.

14. As explained in the Mishnah 42a (see note 24 there), if a convert dies without Jewish heirs, his property becomes ownerless and the first person to perform an act of acquisition in them acquires them. Among the acts of acquisition by which a person can acquire the ownerless property are digging in the land or partitioning it (*Rashbam*).

15. I.e. if these activities are performed in a person's property and he does not protest, the one performing the activity can establish a *chazakah* on that basis. Thus, if he has performed that activity for three years without protest, he can use the lack of protest as proof of his claim that the owner had conveyed rights of use in the property to him (see *Rashbam*).

16. Only acts that in some way improve the property itself effect acquisition of a convert's ownerless property. However, uses of the property that do not improve it, such as placing an oven or stove in the property, do not serve to acquire the property [as discussed in the Gemara above — 53b-54a] (*Rashbam*).

17. [Apparently, Ulla means to say that an owner will protest only those unauthorized uses of his property that in some way alter the property itself, but not those uses which do not.]

Actually, the Gemara could have disproven Ulla's explanation of the Mishnah by pointing to the fact that the Mishnah considers the bringing of chickens into the house an act that establishes a *chazakah,* even though it is not an act that would serve to acquire the ownerless house of a convert. Nevertheless, the Gemara opts for an even better way of disproving Ulla's explanation (*Rashbam*).

18. Since plowing improves the land [by preparing it for planting]. Indeed, even a small amount of digging can acquire a deceased convert's ownerless property (*Rashbam*; see above, 54a).

19. As established in the Gemara above (36b), simply plowing a field for three years does not establish a *chazakah*; rather, the occupant must also plant the field and take its crop (see *Rashbam*).

20. As has been established throughout the entire chapter, consumption of a property's yield for three years without challenge is in place of testimony that the property was acquired legally (*Rashbam*).

21. As the Gemara states on 54a, if a person removed branches from an ownerless palm tree in order to feed them to his animals (an act of "consumption of produce"), he does not thereby acquire the palm tree (*Rashbam*).

22. Rav Sheishess cited these two examples to show that the criterion for establishing a *chazakah* is completely different from the criterion for acquiring the ownerless property of a deceased convert. The criterion for establishing a *chazakah* is whether an owner would be expected to protest such unauthorized activity in his property. The criterion for acquiring ownerless property is whether the act is one that improves the property itself. Thus, Ulla's rule, which equates the two laws, is unacceptable (*Rashbam*).

מסורת הש"ס

א) [נ"ל דאחי]:

הגהות הב"ח

(א) תוס' ד"ה (בדף הקודם) אלא מעתה כו' לשלם כאותו מנה: (ג) ד"ה הכא נפיק כולה ממונא נכי ריבעא:

ההוא שטרא דהוה חתימי עליה בי תרי שכיב חד מינייהו אתא אחוה דהאי דקאי וחד אחרינא לאסהודי אחתימת ידיה דאידך סבר רבינא למימר היינו מתני' ג' אחין ואחד מצטרף עמהן אמר ליה רב אשי א מי דמי התם לא נפיק נכי ריבעא דממונא אפומא דאחי הכא נפיק נכי ריבעא דממונא אפומא דאחי: **מתני'** אלו דברים שיש להן חזקה ואלו דברים שאין להן חזקה ב היה מעמיד בהמה בחצר תנור ריחים וכיריים ומגדל תרנגולים ונותן זבלו בחצר אינה חזקה אבל עשה מחיצה לבהמתו גבוה עשרה טפחים וכן לתנור וכן לכיריים וכן לריחים הכנים תרנגולין לתוך הבית ועשה מקום לזבלו עמוק שלשה או גבוה שלשה הרי זו חזקה: **גמ'** מאי שנא רישא ומאי שנא סיפא אמר עולא כל שאילו בנכסי הגר קנה בנכסי חבירו קנה כל שאילו בנכסי הגר לא קנה בנכסי חבירו לא קנה מתקיף לה רב ששת וכללא הוא והרי ניר דבנכסי הגר קנה בנכסי חבירו לא קנה והרי אכילת פירות דבנכסי חבירו קנה בנכסי הגר לא קנה אלא אמר רב נחמן אמר רבה בר אבוה הכא

ההוא שטרא. והולך המלוה לקיימו: **שכיב חד מינייהו.** מת אחד מהן קודם שנתקיים השטר ואילו לא מת היה כל אחד בא ומעיד לבדו על חתימת ידו ואין צריך לצרף עמו אחר אלא נאמן לומר זה כתב ידי כדתנן בפ"ב דכתובות (דף כ:) זה אומר זה כתב ידי וזה אומר זה כתב ידי כו' וחכמים אומרים אין צריכין לצרף עמהן אחר אלא נאמן לומר זה כתב ידי ואמרינן בגמ' לדברי חכמים על מנה שבשטר הן מעידין אנחנו ראינו המלוה וחתמנו הלכך בתרי סגי ולא צריך חד מינייהו לאסהודי אדחבריה והיכא דמת אחד מהן אמרינן התם אליבא דרבנן דצריך שנים מן השוק להעיד על חתימת יד המת והחי יעיד הוא לבדו על חתימת ידו אבל העד החי לא יצטרף עם אחר מן השוק להעיד על חתימת המת דכיון דעל מנה שבשטר הן מעידין וכי אמר זה כתב ידי נפק פלגא דממונא אפומיה שהרי הוא לבדו מעיד על חתימתו ואין צריך אחר להעיד עמו וכי הדר מצטרף עם ההוא מן השוק להעיד על חתימת המת הדר נפיק ריבעא דממונא על פומיה אשתכח דכוליה ממונא נכי ריבעא נפק אפומיה ואין על פי שנים עדים בעינן חצי דבר על פיו של זה וחצי דבר על פיו של זה והלכך הכא דשכיב חד מינייה אין עד החי יכול להצטרף עם אחר מן השוק להעיד על חתימת יד המת אלא צריך שנים מן השוק להעיד עליו: **אתא אחוה דהאי דקאי.** אחיו של עד החי בא להצטרף עם אחד מן השוק להעיד על חתימתו כדפרישית דצריך שנים מן השוק להעיד על חתימת דאידך המת: **היינו מתניתין.** דאף על גב דשני אחין פסולין לעדות אחת דלא חשיבי אלא כחד אפילו הכי מכשרא להו מתניתין לשלשה אחין בעדות קרקע אחד מאחר שאין זה מעיד על אותה שנה שזה מעיד אף כאן העד החי מעיד על החתימה שלו ואחיו על חתימת יד המת: **התם.** במתניתין לא קנפיק כל הממון: **נכי ריבעא.** חסר רביע דהיינו שלשת חלקים ממון אפומא דאחי אלא פלגא הוא דנפיק אפומא דעד נכרי ופלגא נפיק אפומא דאחי והלכך כשירין לעדות זו דטעמא דפסיל רחמנא קרובים בעדות אחת לפי שאינן חשובין אלא כאיש אחד ולגבי חזקת שלש שנים כאיש אחד דמו שהרי איש אחר שמצטרף עמהן מועיל בשלשתן אם ראה החזקה שלש שנים: **אבל הכא.** גבי שטרא נפיק נכי רבעא דממונא דהיינו שלש חלקי הממון אפומא דאחי וכי חשבת לאחי כעד אחד נמצא עד אחד מגבה שלשה חלקים והאחד רביע ולא קרינא על פי שנים עדים וגו': **מתני' אלו דברים שיש להם חזקה.** כלומר אלו מיני תשמישין דאמרינן לקמן שאדם משתמש בשל חבירו שאם משתמש שלש שנים ולא מיחה בו חבירו יש לו חזקה לזה המחזיק ויכול לטעון אתה נתתו לי לתשמיש זה במתנה או מכרתו לי כגון תשמישין קבועין כדמפרש לקמן שאדם מקפיד עליהן אם נעשין שלא ברשותו והלכך בשלש שנים הויא חזקה דומיא דבורות שיחין ומערות ובית השלחין וכל הנך דלעיל דכיון דקביעות תשמיש הוא כמחזיק בגופה של קרקע חבירו דמי והויא חזקה בשלש שנים. ורבינו חננאל פירש אלו דברים שיש להם חזקה כאשר כבר פירשנו ולא נהירא אלא לקמיה קאי כדפרישית דאי לעיל קאי ומסקנא דמתני' דלעיל היא אריכות לשון של הבל הוא בלא צורך ועוד דהכי תנינן לקמן יש להן חזקה דתנן במתניתין עד סוף הפרק בחזקת שלש שנים מיירי כדמוכח בברייתא (לקמן נט:) בא לפני רבי חייא אמר לו יגעת בני יגעת: **היה מעמיד בהמה כו'.** כל הנך דברים המיטלטלין הן ואין תשמיש של קביעות ואין בעל חצר מקפיד עד ארבע וחמש שנים ולכך אין לו חזקה למחזיק לומר מדוע לא מחית בידי דאמר ליה בעל חצר לא חששתי למחות דלא מחזקת בגוף הקרקע כדמחזקי אינשי ולא הייתי נפסד כלום ומעתה אני מקפיד: **תנור וכירים.** מטלטלין הן וכן ריחים בריחיא דידא: **אבל עשה מחיצה בחצר כו'.** הרי זה גדר והרי זו חזקה כל מקום תוך המחילות שעשה יכול לטעון לקוח הוא בידי: **הכנים תרנגולין לתוך הבית.** של חבירו שלש שנים גם על זאת ודאי מקפיד איניש ואם לא מיחה הפסיד דודאי על פיו עשה וברשותו: **ועשה מקום כו'.** או עשה מקום: **עמוק שלשה.** כדי שלא יתפזר: **או גבוה שלשה.** מחילה גבוהה שלשה: **גמ' מאי שנא רישא.** דבהעמדת בהמה כדי בלא מחילה אין זו חזקה: **ומ"ש סיפא.** דבעשיית מחילה קנה וקא ס"ד השתא דבאינים בעלמא שאינו בר חצר זו קאמר דאין זו חזקה והלכך קשיא ליה מ"ש רישא מסיפא הא ודאי מקפידין בני חצר על איש נכרי שיביא כאן בהמותיו ומדלא מיחו ודאי הקנו לו מקום בחצר זה להעמיד בהמותיו ואמאי אין לו חזקה ולקמן מתרץ לה בשותפין: **אמר עולא.** כל חזקה רעועה דלא קנה אם בא לעשותה בנכסי הגר לקנותה מיד והוא הדין לענין קונה קרקע מחבירו וא"ל לך חזק וקני והלך והחזיק חזקה רעועה דלא קנה כגון העמדת שם בהמתו או תנור וכירים דאין זה נעל וגדר דלא עשה שום תיקון בגוף הקרקע: **בנכסי חבירו נמי לא קנה.** כלומר לענין חזקת שלש שנים שלוקח אומר לקחתי ומוכר אומר לא מכרתי אינה קרויה חזקה להיות במקום עדי מכירה דהא לא עבד ולא מידי: **כל שאילו בנכסי הגר קנה.** כגון עשיית מחילה ורפק בה פורתא: **בנכסי חבירו נמי קנה.** כלומר הויא חזקה ומיהו הקנין ע"י מעות או מתנה היא ומיהו הכנים תרנגולין לתוך הבית דקתני סיפא דהוי חזקה בנכסי הגר לא הויא חזקה והאי דלא פריך לה משום דעדיפא מינה קפריך רב ששת. ואית דמפרש דהכנים תרנגולין נמי הוי חזקה בנכסי הגר דהיינו נעל שנעל את הדלת בפניהם ולאו מילתא היא דנעילת דלת לאו חזקה היא דאינו דומה אלא למבריח ארי כדאמרן לעיל (נג.) ונעל דלת דבנין מיירי שעשה דלת או סתימה: **וכללא הוא.** בתמיה דקא מדמית חזקת שלש שנים שתלוי בקפידא לחזקת קנין נכסי הגר שתלוי בתקון הקרקע: **ניר.** אמרינן בפירקין לעיל (דף נג:) דלכולי עלמא ניר לא הוי חזקה דבנכסי הגר קנה אפי' רפק בה פורתא ובנכסי חבירו לענין שלש שנים לא קנה בחזקה זו לפי שהכל תלוי באכילת הפירות שאם יחרוש ולא יאכל אין בעל הקרקע מפסיד שהרי יזרע ואחר יאכל: **והרי אכילת פירות.** לקיטת הפירות דבנכסי חבירו קנה אם אכל הפירות שלש שנים דהויא אכילת שלש שנים במקום עדות שקנה הקרקע זו מן הבעלים כדאמרן בכוליה פירקין: **ובנכסי הגר לא קנה.** דאין זה נעל וגדר כדאמרן לעיל (דף נג.) האי מאן דפשט דיקלא לדעתא דחיותא לא קני: **אלא אמר רב נחמן אמר רבה בר אבוה.** לעולם גבי איש נכרי שבא להעמיד בהמה בחצר אחרים שאין לו בה שותפות ולא שנא רישא ולא שנא סיפא דהויא חזקה שאין בני חצר מניחין לנכרי להשתמש תשמישין הללו בחצר שלהן אלא אם כן נטלו רשות מהן ואם לא מיחו בתוך שלש שנים הויא חזקה:

והכא

ומשני דהכא לא מכחשי אהדדי דבין חיטי ושערי לא דייקי אינשי וא"ג דדייקי בין מנה שחור למנה לבן בזה בורר (סנהדרין דף ל:) התם צריך למידק שחייב לשלם (א) אותו מנה שלוה אבל הכא לא דייקי דבכל ענין שיאכלנה חטין או שעורים הויא חזקה ומיהו זה אומר אכלה חטין וזה קטנית עדותן בטלה דלפי' בלא לדקדק אין אדם טועה בין חטין לקטנית: **הכא נפיק** (ג) **נכי רבעא [דממונא] אפומא** (א) **דאחי.** וא"ג דיש תקנה כדאמרינן בפרק ב' דכתובות (דף כא. ושם) דאם מת אחד מן החתומין ואין שנים מן השוק להעיד עליו לכתוב חתימת ידיה אחספא ושדי לבי דינא ומחזקי ליה כו' הכי נמי הכא אלא דלרבינא בעי למימר דבלאו הכי יכול אחיו להעיד והוה מדמה למתני':

בשותפין

עין משפט
נר מצוה

רנט א מיי' פ"ז מהל' עדות הל' ד סמג עשין קיז טוש"ע ח"מ סי' מו סעיף יג:
רס ב מיי' פי"ג מהל' טוען ונטען הל' יד ופ"ה מהל' שכנים הל' ה סמג עשין לה וסי' פב טוש"ע ח"מ סי' קמ סעיף טו וסי' קסא סעיף ה ועי' בב"י:

רבינו גרשום

אחתימת ידא דאידך. דמית: **היינו מתני'.** דא' יכול ליצטרף עם אחין להעיד: **התם.** במתני' **לא נפיק.** אלא פלגא ממונא **אפומי דאחי** ופלגא אפומא [דאחר]: **הכא נפיק נכי ריבעא אפומא דאחי.** שאותו אח הנחתם מעיד על חצי הממון ואח השני ואחד מעידין על חתימת המת נמצא אח שני מעיד על רביע הממון והאחד שעמו מעיד על הרביע: **פיסקא היה מעמיד בהמה. בחצר** חבירו: או מעמיד **תנור וכירים וכו'.** אלו דבר המטלטל הן **אינה חזקה** דהואיל דלא קביע לא קפיד בעל חצר: **אבל עשה מחיצות.** דהיינו בנין קבוע או **הכניס תרנגולין לתוך הבית** של בעל חצר שמשתמש בביתו או **עשה מקום לזבלו** בחצר ושתיק בעל חצר **הרי זו חזקה: כל שאילו בנכסי הגר קנה.** כגון נעל גדר ופרץ היינו דומיא דסיפא דגדר ועשה מחיצה: **כל שבנכסי הגר לא קנה.** כגון הני דרישא דלא עבד ולא מידי בגוף הקרקע: **והרי נירא דבנכסי הגר קנה.** כדאמר לעיל אתא ההוא גברא רפיק ביה פורתא ואוקמיה בידיה: **ובנכסי חבירו לא קנה.** כדאמר בפירקין דלעיל אלא דכולי עלמא ניר לא הוי חזקה: **והרי אכילת פירות.** אילן חבירו ג' שנים הויא חזקה: **ובנכסי הגר לא קנה.** כדאמר לעיל בההיא איתתא דאכלה תליסר שנין ולא קנתה בהכי: **אלא אמר רב נחמן אמר רבה בר אבוה.** לאו היינו טעמא דמתני' כדקאמרת אלא מתני'

עין משפט
נר מצוה

רסא א מיי' פ"ה מהל' שכנים הל' ה סמג עשין פב טוש"ע ח"מ סי' קסא סעיף ה ועי' בטור ובב"י ובמ"מ:
רסב ב ג מיי' פ"ז מהל' נדרים הל' ד סמג לאוין רמב טוש"ע י"ד סי' רכו סעיף א ואין הלכה כן וטוש"ע ח"מ סי' קפ:
רסג ד מיי' פכ"א מהל' איסורי ביאה הל' כא סמג לאוין קכ טוש"ע אה"ע סי' כא סעיף א:
רסד ה מיי' פ"ה מהל' דעות הלכה ט:
רסה ו (מיי' שם הל' ג):

א הכא בחצר השותפין עסקינן דבהעמדה כדי לא קפדי אמחיצה קפדי ובהעמדה כדי לא קפדי והא א) תנן ב השותפין שנדרו הנאה זה מזה אסורין ליכנס לחצר אלא אמר רב נחמן אמר רבה בר אבוה הכא ברחבה של אחורי בתים עסקינן דבהעמדה כדי ג לא קפדי ואמחיצה קפדי רב פפא אמר אידי ואידי בחצר השותפין ואיכא דקפדי ואיכא דלא קפדי גבי ג ממונא לקולא גבי איסורא לחומרא רבינא אמר לעולם לא קפדי ג והא מני ר' אליעזר היא דתניא ד ר' אליעזר אומר אפילו ויתור אסור במודר הנאה א"ר יוחנן משום ר' בנאה בכל שותפין מעכבין זה את זה חוץ מן הכביסה שאין דרכן של בנות ישראל להתבזות על הכביסה א ועוצם עיניו מראות ברע ה א"ר חייא בר אבא ד זה שאין מסתכל בנשים בשעה שעומדות על הכביסה היכי דמי אי דאיכא דרכא אחריתא רשע הוא אי דליכא דרכא אחריתא אנוס הוא לעולם דליכא דרכא אחריתא ואפ"ה מיבעי ליה למינס נפשיה בעא מיניה ר' יוחנן מרבי בנאה ה חלוק של ת"ח כיצד ה כל שאין בשרו נראה מתחתיו טלית של ת"ח כיצד כל שאין חלוקו נראה מתחתיו טפח ו שלחן של ת"ח כיצד שני שלישי גדיל ושליש גלאי ועליו קערות וירק וטבעתו מבחוץ והא תניא טבעתו מבפנים לא קשיא הא דאיכא ינוקא הא דליכא ינוקא ואי בעית אימא הא והא דליכא ינוקא ולא קשיא הא דאיכא שמעא הא דליכא שמעא ואי בעית אימא הא והא דאיכא שמעא ולא קשיא הא ביממא הא בליליא ושל עם הארץ דומה למדורה

תוספות

בשותפין עסקינן דבהעמדה כדי לא קפדי. תימה דאמר הכא דהיכא דקפדי קני והאמר לעיל (דף מג:) דשותפין אין מחזיקין זה על זה דפעמים מניח האחד להשתמש לחברו ג' שנים ואח"כ ישתמש הוא וי"ל הא דנחית לפלגא והא דנחית לכולא להאי גיסא או להאי גיסא כדאמר לעיל ועוד נראה דיש לחלק בין שדה לחצר דהכא מיירי שבתים אלו פתוחין לחצר זה דכיון שהוא יולא ונכנס דרך חצר זה היכא דקפדי אין מניח לו לעשות אי לאו דזבנה מיניה: **אסור** ליכנס בחצר. בגמ' מוקי לה בין בחצר שיש בה דין חלוקה בין אין בה ואע"ג דבאין בה דין חלוקה אין יכול למחות בו מליכנס בחצר מ"מ יכול לאסור עליו מידי דהוה אמשכיר בית לחברו שיכול המשכיר להקדישו כדאמר בפ' האומר משקלי עלי (ערכין דף כא. ושם) אע"פ שאין יכול למחות בידו של שוכר מליכנס בו ומיהו היא גופה תימה דמ"מ מבעל חוב דאם הקדיש שדהו דאתי בעל חוב וטריף (שם כג:) (ב) אלא משום דרבי אבהו שלא יאמרו הקדש יוצא בלא פדיון הלכך מוסיף דינר וי"ל דאתי בע"ח שגוף הקרקע יוצא מתחת יד מקדיש אבל התם אין גוף הקרקע יוצא מתחת יד משכיר לעולם: **רבינא** אמר לעולם לא קפדי. משמע הכא (ג) דכולי עלמא קפדי אינשי אדריסת הרגל דלפי רבינא לא קאמר אלא בשותפין ותימה דתנן בפ"ק דמגילה (דף ח. ושם ד"ה דריסה) אין בין המודר הנאה מחבירו למודר הימנו מאכל אלא דריסת הרגל וכלים שאין עושין בהן אוכל נפש ופריך בגמ' דריסת הרגל הא לא קפדי ומפרש ר"ת דהתם משמע ליה לגמרא דמתני' איירי בבקעה דלא קפדי לאי בחצר דקפדי אפילו מודר הימנו מאכל אסור דכיון דקפדי א"כ כיולא בו משכירים ותנן בפרק אין בין המודר (נדרים דף לג.) דכיולא בו משכירים אסור אפילו כלים שאין עושין בהן אוכל נפש והכי פריך כיון דעל כרחך איירי בדריסת הרגל בבקעה דלא קפדי אם כן אפילו מודר הימנו הנאה אמאי אסור והוא הדין דהוי מצי למיפרך כלים הא לא קפדי ו):

רשב"ם

והכא בחצר השותפין עסקינן. שאחד מן השותפין עלמו העמיד בהמותיו ותנור ואשפה שלו בחצר ג' שנים ולא מיחו בו ואחס חצר לכניסה ויליאה הוא ולא להעמיד שם בהמותיו ואפילו זמן מרובה והלכך בהעמדת בהמותיו גרידא בלא בנין לא הויא חזקה דבהעמדה כדי לא קפדי שותפין זה על זה עד שעה שילטרכו לאותו מקום (א) וכשילטרכו יקפידו ויסלק זה חפליו דאין לו חזקה בשתיקתן: **אמחיצה קפדי.** ומדשתקינו ולא מיחו ודאי ברשותו עשה והויא חזקה: **אסורין ליכנס לחצר.** שכל זמן שלא חלקו את החצר נכנס כל אחד בחלק חבירו וקא ליה בלא יחל דברו שהרי נהנה מחבירו שעומד בחצרו דבהעמדה קפדי דאם איתא דלא קפדי מותר לעמוד בחצר חבירו אע"פ שמודר ממנו הנאה דכיון דלא קפיד בעמידה הרי הפקיר את החצר לכל בני החצר לעמוד בו ולגבי עמידה אין לו חלק בו: **הכא ברחבה כו'.** מתני' ברחבה שאחורי הבתים דאינו מקפיד כל כך אבל בחצר שלפני הבתים צריך שיהא מקום פנוי לביאה ויליאה והלכך קפדי בהעמדה כדי: **אידי ואידי.** מתני' דהכא ודנדרים: **איכא דקפיד.** בהעמדה כדי: **גבי ממונא.** לענין חזקה: **לקולא.** יש לנו לילך להקל ולומר שאין השותפין מקפידין זה על זה ומותר להעמיד זה בהמותיו בחצר כל זמן שאין חבירו מעכב עליו והיינו קולא שאנו מתירין לזה מסתמא להעמיד שם בהמותיו אף על פי שלא נטל רשות מחבירו ובדוכתא אחרינא (ב"מ דף מא.) אמרינן דשואל שלא מדעת גזלן הוי והכא בלא דעת יכול להכניס בהמותיו והלכך לא הוי חזקה דהא לא קפדי ומאיזה טעם נאמר כך משום דא"ל שותף לחבריה המחזיק אנא מהנך דלא קפדי אנא והלכך שתקתי ואין חזקתך חזקה ואם רצונך להחזיק אייתי ראיה דמהנך דקפדי אנא ותיהוי חזקתך חזקה והלכך לא הויא חזקה שכל מקום שיש טענה למערער למה לא מיחה לא הויא חזקתו של מחזיק חזקה: **גבי איסורא.** השותפין שנדרו: **לחומרא.** ואסורין ליכנס לחצר דדלמא מהנך דקפדי נינהו וכל ספק איסורא דאורייתא לחומרא: **לעולם לא קפדי.** בהעמדה כדי כדתנן דלא הויא חזקה וגבי נדרים נמי מותרין ליכנס לחצר: **והא דקתני אסורין רבי אליעזר היא.** דמחמיר בנדרים טפי דאפילו דבר שאינו הנאה כל כך אסר: **אפילו ויתור אסור.** כגון בעה"ב שמודר הנאה מחנוני ושלח לו בעל הבית פרוטה לחנוני לקנות ממנו מאה אגוזים בפרוטה והוסיף לו חנוני אחת יתירה או שתים אסור בעל הבית באותו ויתור שהותיר לו חנוני דמתנה הוא ואף על פי שלשאר לוקחים נמי הוסיף כמו כן ומיהו רבנן שרו דמ"מ בשביל המקח הוא מוסיף לזה על החשבון הקצוב לפרוטה שאילו לא היה לוקח ממנו בדמים לא היה נותן לו חנוני לבעל הבית כלום: **בכל שותפין מעכבין כו'.** בכל תשמישין הקבועין בחצר דומיא להעמדת בהמות תנור וכיריים שממעטין אויר החצר יכולין לעכב אם האחד רוצה לעשות לבדו וחביריו אין רוצים לעשות כן: **חוץ מן הכביסה.** שתקנו לו חכמים שיעשה בחצר בעל כרחן של שותפין חביריו: **לפי שאין דרכן כו' להתבזות.** שלריכות לעמוד שם יחיפות לגלות שוק לעמוד בנהר: **שאין מסתכל.** כשהוא הולך על שפת הנהר: **היכי דמי.** דמשתבח ביה קרא אם עולם עיניו דמשמע שאם לא יעלים עיניו אינו לא לדיק ולא רשע: **אי דאיכא דרכא אחרינא.** ואזיל בהך: **רשע הוא.** ואף על פי שעולם עיניו שלא היה לו לקרב אלא להרחיק מן העבירה דקיימא לן (דף מד:) הרחק מן הכיעור: **אנוס הוא.** אם מסתכל דרך הליכתו ואונס רחמנא פטריה ולמה מזקיקו הכתוב להעלים עיניו דמדמשתבח ביה קרא שמעינן דלריך לעלום עיניו: **למינס נפשיה.** להטות עיניו ללד אחר והיינו דמשתבח ביה קרא דלאי אניס נפשיה חסיד הוא: **בעא מיניה ר' יוחנן מרבי בנאה.** שמעתין דרבי בנאה קחשיב ואזיל אגב גררא דהך דלעיל: **כל שאין בשרו נראה מתחתיו.** שיהא ארוך עד פיסת רגלו שלא יראה כשילך יחף: **טלית.** מקטורן שמתכסה בו על כל בגדים שהוא לובש: **שאין נראה כו'.** וכל שכן דלאי קאי עד להדי חלוק דאיכא לניעות טפי: **שני שלישי גדיל ושליש גלאי.** שני שלישי רוחב השלחן מכוסה במפה מצד האוכלין לקנח את פיהן ולתת עליה את הפת ושליש החיצון מגולה להניח עליו קערות וכוסות שלא ילכלכו המפה ויתבזו האוכלין. ואית דמפרשי שליש גלאי באמצע שני שלישי גדיל דהיינו מפה מבחוץ ומבפנים כל סביב השלחן ואמצעיתו מגולה. גדיל קרי המפה על שם שארוגה ולשון נח הוא: **וטבעתו.** של שלחן שהיו רגילין לעשות בשפתו לתלותו בו יהיה מבחוץ ולא מבפנים מצד האוכלין וכדמפרש ואזיל: **מבפנים.** בצד הסמוך לו: **היכא דאיכא ינוקא.** שיושב אצל אביו לאכול צריך להושיב השלחן שיהא צד שבו קבוע הטבעת מבחוץ פן ילחוק התינוק בטבעת וינענע השלחן: **ואי ליכא ינוקא.** יעשה מבפנים ולא יהפכנה מבחוץ פן יכשל בה השמש שהולך ובא סביב השלחן: **הא דאיכא שמעא.** שמש יעשה מבפנים פן יכשל בה השמש: **והא דליכא שמעא.** יעשה מבחוץ ולא מבפנים פן יוזקו בה האוכלין ומיהו היכא דאיכא שמעא יעשה מבפנים מצד היושבין ולא מבחוץ שיכולין להזהר מן הטבעת יותר מן השמש שהוא הולך והן יושבין: **הא ביממא.** יהיה מבחוץ שיוכל השמש להזהר ולא מבפנים דמזיק לאוכלין שאר להם המקום:

רבינו גרשום

בחצר השותפין עסקינן. שמעמיד בה אחד מן השותפין בהמה או תנור וכירים ואמאי לא הויא חזקה משום דשותפין אהעמדה כדי גרידא **לא קפדי** כו': **אסורין ליכנס לחצר.** דהיינו הנאה משום דקפדי אהדדי אלמא דאהעמדה כדי קפדי ואמאי לא קנה בשלא מיחה: **אלא הכא.** מתני' דקתני היה מעמיד בהמתו בחצר **ברחבה שאחורי הבתים** מיירי **דאהעמדה כדי לא קפדי: גבי ממונא.** לענין חזקה: **לקולא.** דאזלינן בתר דלא קפיד ולא הוי חזקה: **גבי איסורא.** דנדר: **לחומרא.** דאסורין ליכנס: **רבינא אמר לעולם** בחצר [השותפין] אהעמדה **לא קפדי.** ואמאי שותפין שנדרו אסורין בהנאה: **ר"א היא דאמר אפי' ויתור אסור.** מה שמוסיף חנוני לקונה אגוז אחד או תפוח א' אם הקונה **מודר הנאה** מחנוני אסור לאותו תוספת אע"פ שאינו נותנו לו אלא מחמת מכירה. ולר' אליעזר דמחמיר א) הכא הוא מחמיר דאסור ליכנס ולא דברי הכל היא: **בכל שותפין מעכבין זה לזה.** שלא יעשה מלאכה בחצר שאין חבירו עושה: **חוץ מן הכביסה.** שאם האחד מכבס בגדיו בחצר וא' אינו רוצה לכבס בה אינו יכול לכופו לזה שלא יכבס בחצר: **לפי שאין דרכן של בנות ישראל להתבזות.** על גבי הנהר לכבס שם: **שעומדות על הכביסה.** בנהר אפי' נכריות משום שעומדות יחיפות ומגלות זרועותיהן שלא יגרה בעצמו יצה"ר: **אנוס הוא.** אי מסתכל דרך הליכה: **אפ"ה איבעי ליה למינס נפשי'.** לכוף עצמו שלא יסתכל: **כל שאין בשרו נראה מתחתיו.** שיהא ארוך עד פיסת רגלו שלא יראה רגלו כשהוא הולך יחף: **וטלית של תלמידי חכמים.** מקטורן שלו שיהא רחב כל כך שלא יהא חלוקו נראה מתחתיו אלא טפח: **שני שלישי גדיל.** מכוסה במפה מדבר שהוא עשוי בגדיל ארוג מקום שמשים הלחם עליו: **שליש גלוי.** בלא מפה שעליו מניחין קערות וכוסות שלא ילכלכו המפה ויקלקל הסעודה: **וטבעתו.** של שלחן שתולין אותו בה תהא קבועה **מבחוץ** שלא באותו צד שהוא יושב אלא מבחוץ מצד האחר: **והתניא מבפנים.** באותו צד שהוא סמוך לו: **לא קשיא הא דאיכא ינוקא.** שיושב אצלו יחזיר השלחן שיהא הטבעת מבחוץ שאם היה הטבעת מבפנים בסמוך שהוא יושב הוה איכא למיחש שמא יחזיק התינוק בטבעת וינענע השלחן ויהפוך אותו ואי **ליכא ינוקא** יהא מבפנים: **אי איכא שמעא.** שעומד לפני השלחן ומשמשו יחזיר הטבעת מבפנים סמוך לו שלא יזיק לשמש לשעומד לצד האחר: **הא ביממא.** יכול להחזירו שיהא הטבעת מבחוץ לפי שרואהו ויכול לשמור שלא יגע בו:

חשק שלמה על רבינו גרשום א) נראה דל"ל ולר"א דמחמיר התם הוא מחמיר הכא דאסור ליכנס וכו'.

מסורת הש"ס

א) ב"ק נא: ביצה לט: נדרים מה:, ב) מגילה ח., ג) [כתובות עג: וש"נ], ד) [מגילה ח. נדרים לב: לג. מח:], ה) סוטה כד., ו) [וע"ע תוס' ב"ק נא: ד"ה זה].

הגהות הב"ח

(א) רשב"ם ד"ה והכא וכו' עד שעה שילטרכו לאותו מקום וכשילטרכו יקפידו: (ב) תוס' ד"ה אסור וכו' הקדיש שדהו דאתי בע"ח וטריף אי לאו משום דר' אבהו: (ג) ד"ה רבינא וכו' משמע הכא דלכולי עלמא:

גליון הש"ס

גמרא חלוק של ת"ח. ע' תענית דף י ע"ב:

תורה אור השלם

א) הֹלֵךְ צְדָקוֹת וְדֹבֵר מֵישָׁרִים מֹאֵס בְּבֶצַע מַעֲשַׁקּוֹת נֹעֵר כַּפָּיו מִתְּמֹךְ בַּשֹּׁחַד אֹטֵם אָזְנוֹ מִשְּׁמֹעַ דָּמִים וְעֹצֵם עֵינָיו מֵרְאוֹת בְּרָע: [ישעיה לג, טו]

ליקוטי רש"י

השותפין שנדרו הנאה זה מזה אסורין ליכנס לחצר. בחצר של שניהן לכל חד אסור בדריסת הרגל של חבירו וקא סבר אין ברירה דאימור האי לחלק חבירו עייל והאי לחלק חבירו עייל [נדרים מה:]. אפילו ויתור. ויתור דבר שהיה מוותר לכל אדם ולאינו מקפיד עליו [מגילה ח.]. ויתור זהו כגון שלוקח מדה של תפוחים ולאחר שמדד לו המדה מוסיף לו שתים או שלשה והוא דרך של חנונין להוסיף על המדות משלהן הואיל ובלא תנאי נותן לו מיחזי כמתנה בעלמא ולאיכא דרבי אליעזר אסור המודר באותו הויתור של מדידת פירות הכא נמי אף על גב דדריסת הרגל לא הויא הנאה גמורה הוא [נדרים לב:]. ויתור מה שדרכן של מוכרים לוותר ללוקחין שמוסיפין לו פירות אחד או שנים לאותו ויתור אסור במודר הנאה ואע"ג דהוי כמו דבר המחול דרמי על אפיה הלכך דריסת הרגל אסור אע"ג דלא קפדי בה אינשי אסור במודר הנאה [ר"ן שם]. ועוצם. סוגר וכן (ישעיהו כט) ויעצם את עיניכם [ישעיה לג, טו]. חלוק של תלמיד חכם וכו' טלית של תלמיד חכם וכו'. ולמעוטה יתירתא הוא [רשב"ם לקמן צח.].

הָכָא בְּחָצֵר הַשּׁוּתָּפִין עָסְקִינַן – **Here** in the Mishnah, **we are dealing with** activities performed by one of the residents in **a jointly owned courtyard.**[1] דִּבְהַעֲמָדָה כְּדִי לָא קָפְדִי – The first part of the Mishnah rules that no *chazakah* is established **because [the other residents] do not object** when a fellow resident **merely places** an item (such as an animal or stove) in the courtyard.[2] אַמְּחִיצָה קָפְדִי – **But they do object to** the construction of **a partition.**[3] Therefore, the second part of the Mishnah rules that if one of the residents walls off part of the courtyard and there is no protest from the other residents for three years, he has established a *chazakah* in that part of the courtyard.[4]

The Gemara asks:

וּבְהַעֲמָדָה כְּדִי לָא קָפְדִי – **Is it** true **that [the other residents] do not object** when a fellow resident **merely places** an item in the courtyard? וְהָא תְּנַן – **But we have learned in a Mishnah:**[5] הַשּׁוּתָּפִין שֶׁנָּדְרוּ הֲנָאָה זֶה מִזֶּה – PARTNERS WHO HAVE VOWED not to derive BENEFIT ONE FROM THE OTHER אֲסוּרִין לִיכָּנֵס לֶחָצֵר – ARE FORBIDDEN TO ENTER THE COURTYARD that they own jointly.[6] This would not be forbidden if people would generally not object to a co-owner standing in the property without permission.[7] We see, therefore, from the Mishnah that people *do* object; certainly, then, they object to a co-owner's unauthorized placement of his items in the common courtyard. – ? –

The Gemara modifies its answer:

אֶלָּא אָמַר רַב נַחְמָן אָמַר רַבָּה בַּר אֲבוּהָ – **Rather, Rav Nachman said in the name of Rabbah Bar Avuha:** הָכָא בְּרַחֲבָה שֶׁל אֲחוֹרֵי בָתִּים עָסְקִינַן – **Here** in the Mishnah, **we are dealing with** activities performed by one of the residents in **a** jointly owned **expanse** that is **behind the houses.**[8] דִּבְהַעֲמָדָה כְּדִי לָא קָפְדִי – **For** in that expanse, **[the other residents] do not object** when a fellow resident **merely places** an item there, וְאַמְּחִיצָה קָפְדִי – **but they do object to** the construction of **a partition.**[9]

An alternative reconciliation of the two Mishnahs:

רַב פַּפָּא אָמַר – **Rav Pappa says:** אִידִי וְאִידִי בְּחָצֵר הַשּׁוּתָּפִין – **Both** Mishnahs **refer to a jointly owned courtyard.** וְאִיכָּא דְּקָפְדֵי וְאִיכָּא דְּלָא קָפְדֵי – **And** the fact is that **there are some** people **who object** to co-residents placing items or even walking there, **while some** people **do not object** to such activities. This range of attitude gives rise to the apparently conflicting laws stated in the two Mishnahs: גַּבֵּי מָמוֹנָא – **With regard to monetary** matters (i.e. in the Mishnah here, where it is simply a question of property rights), לְקוּלָּא – we must assume **the lenient** possibility that the owners are not the type to object to their fellow resident's placement of his items in the courtyard. Therefore, a *chazakah* cannot be established with regard to those activities.[10] גַּבֵּי אִיסּוּרָא – **However, with regard to prohibitory** matters (i.e. in the Mishnah concerning vows), לְחוּמְרָא – we must assume **the stringent** possibility that the owners are the type to object to their fellow resident's standing in the courtyard; we cannot allow either vowing partner to enter the courtyard, for he might thereby be in violation of his vow.[11]

Ravina offers a third possible resolution to the contradiction between the two Mishnahs:

רָבִינָא אָמַר – **Ravina says:** לְעוֹלָם לָא קָפְדֵי – **Actually, [people] do not object** to a fellow resident's placement of objects in the common courtyard, as long as no partitions are erected. This explains the distinction made in the Mishnah here. וְהָא מַנִּי – **And whose opinion is** reflected in **this** Mishnah concerning vows, which forbids the vowing partners from entering the joint courtyard? ר׳ אֱלִיעֶזֶר הִיא – **It** reflects the opinion of **R' Eliezer,** דְּתַנְיָא – **for it was taught in a Baraisa:** ר׳ אֱלִיעֶזֶר אוֹמֵר – R' ELIEZER SAYS, אֲפִילּוּ וִיתּוּר אָסוּר בְּמוּדָּר הֲנָאָה – EVEN GRATUITIES ARE FORBIDDEN TO ONE PROHIBITED by vow FROM BENEFIT.[12] Since R' Eliezer forbids to a vower even gratuities that are

NOTES

1. [Certainly, an owner would not tolerate a stranger using his courtyard for *any* of the activities listed in the Mishnah.] Our Mishnah, however, refers to activities done in the courtyard by one of the joint owners. The Mishnah distinguishes between those activities that might be tolerated by fellow residents in the courtyard and those that would not (*Rashbam*).

2. The common courtyard is supposed to serve as an open passageway to and from the individual houses [and as a place to load and unload animals (see above 11a)]. Thus, it was not customary to cook or perform similar activities there, as the courtyard had to be kept uncluttered to allow for unrestricted movement. Nevertheless, if one of the residents does place some of his items in the courtyard, he cannot establish a *chazakah* in regard to that use, for the other residents do not object to such use by a fellow resident. Since the item is not fixed in place, the other residents know that it can always be removed if the space is needed (*Rashbam*). Thus, if the other residents in the courtyard later insist that the items be removed, it is upon the user to prove that he acquired the right to use the courtyard for this purpose from his fellow residents.

3. See 57a note 10.

4. This *chazakah* supports his claim that he acquired the right to use that portion of the courtyard from his fellow residents (*Rashbam*).

5. *Nedarim* 45b.

6. [Every section of a jointly owned courtyard is owned by both of the partners (see *Nedarim* 45b with *Ran*). Thus,] neither partner can set foot in the courtyard, for he is treading on his partner's land, thereby deriving benefit from his partner's property (*Rashbam*).

7. If a person would ordinarily not object to his partner's unauthorized walking through a jointly owned property, it would be considered as if each owner relinquished his rights to the property in regard to his co-owner's unrestricted access to the property. Accordingly, a partner entering the property would not be considered as benefiting from the other owners, since their rights to the property in regard to that entry have already been relinquished. The fact that the Mishnah forbids the vowing partners from entering the joint courtyard proves that people do ordinarily object to co-owners entering the joint property without authorization (*Rashbam*; cf. *Rashash* and *Kovetz Shiurim*).

8. I.e. a backyard — in contrast to the courtyard, which was generally in front of the houses (see *Rashi* to 6b ד״ה אבל רחבא).

[Though the Mishnah here speaks explicitly of placing the animal etc. in "a courtyard," it uses the word "courtyard" in a loose sense; the actual reference is to a backyard.]

9. Unlike a front courtyard, which must be kept open as a passageway, a backyard does not have to be kept as free of clutter. Therefore, owners of a backyard do not object to a fellow resident placing his items in there, unless he partitions the area of his use (*Rashbam*).

[The Mishnah in *Nedarim,* however, refers specifically to a jointly owned *courtyard.* In the case of a jointly owned backyard, however, the vower would indeed be permitted to walk there, since one co-owner generally does not mind the other one being there.]

10. Even if one partner places items in the courtyard for three years without protest, his co-owner can claim that he was not the type to protest such activities. This claim effectively negates the *chazakah,* for that co-owner's silence does not prove the user's claim to having acquired the rights of usage [unless it can be *proven* that the other owner does normally object to such usage] (*Rashbam*). [This possibility is termed the "lenient" possibility, since it posits that the resident was permitted to make unauthorized use of the joint property — something that would be tantamount to theft were it assumed that the other owner does object (see *Rashbam* and *Pnei Shlomo*).]

11. This is in keeping with the principle that when an action might possibly violate a Biblical prohibition, we must be stringent and avoid that action (*Rashbam*).

12. "Gratuities" here refers to the premium that a vendor commonly adds gratis to the amount specified by the customer. If a person has vowed not to receive any benefit from a particular vendor, he may not use the premium that the vendor has added on to his purchase. Though the vendor automatically adds this amount gratis to every customer's purchase, it is still considered a benefit, from which this customer has

עין משפט נר מצוה

רסא א מיי' פ"ה מהל' שכנים הל' ה סמג עשין פב טוש"ע ח"מ סי' קסא סעיף ה ועי' בטור ובב"י ובמ"מ:

רסב ב ג מיי' פ"ז מהל' נדרים הל' ד סמג לאוין רמב טוש"ע י"ד סי' רכו סעיף א ואין הלכה כן וטוש"ע ח"מ סי' קפ:

רסג ד מיי' פכ"א מהל' איסורי ביאה הל' כא סמג לאוין קכ טוש"ע אה"ע סי' כא סעיף א:

רסד ה מיי' פ"ה מהל' דעות הלכה ט:

רסה ו (מיי' שם הל' ג):

מסורת הש"ס

א) ב"ק נא: ביצה לט: נדרים מה:, ב) מגילה ח., ג) [כתובות עג: וש"נ], ד) [מגילה ח. נדרים לב: לג. מח:], ה) מכות כד., ו) [וע"ע תוס' ב"ק נא: ד"ה זה]:

א הכא בחצר השותפין עסקינן דבהעמדה כדי לא קפדי אמחיצה קפדי ובהעמדה כדי לא קפדי והא א) תנן ב השותפין שנדרו הנאה זה מזה אסורין ליכנס לחצר אלא אמר רב נחמן אמר רבה בר אבוה הכא ברחבה של אחורי בתים עסקינן דבהעמדה כדי ג לא קפדי ואמחיצה קפדי רב פפא אמר אידי ואידי בחצר השותפין ואיכא דקפדי ואיכא דלא קפדי גבי ב) ממונא לקולא גבי איסורא לחומרא רבינא אמר לעולם לא קפדי ג והא מני ר' אליעזר היא דתניא ד) ר' אליעזר אומר אפילו ויתור אסור במודר הנאה א"ר יוחנן משום ר' בנאה בכל שותפין מעכבין זה את זה חוץ מן הכביסה שאין דרכן של בנות ישראל להתבזות על הכביסה א) ועוצם עיניו מראות ברע ה) א"ר חייא בר אבא ד זה שאין מסתכל בנשים בשעה שעומדות על הכביסה היכי דמי אי דאיכא דרכא אחריתא רשע הוא אי דליכא דרכא אחריתא אנוס הוא לעולם דליכא דרכא אחריתא ואפ"ה מיבעי ליה למינס נפשיה בעא מיניה ר' יוחנן מרבי בנאה ° חלוק של ת"ח כיצד ה כל שאין בשרו נראה מתחתיו טלית של ת"ח כיצד כל שאין חלוקו נראה מתחתיו טפח ו שלחן של ת"ח כיצד שני שלישי גדיל ושליש גלאי ועליו קערות וירק וטבעתו מבחוץ והא תניא טבעתו מבפנים לא קשיא הא דאיכא ינוקא הא דליכא ינוקא ואי בעית אימא הא והא דליכא ינוקא ולא קשיא הא דאיכא שמעא הא דליכא שמעא ואי בעית אימא הא והא דאיכא שמעא ולא קשיא הא ביממא הא בליליא ושל עם הארץ דומה למדורה

רשב"ם

והכא בחצר השותפין עסקינן. שאחד מן השותפין עצמו העמיד בהמותיו ותנור ואשפה שלו בחצר ג' שנים ולא מיחו בו ולא סתם חצר לכניסה ויציאה הוא ולא להעמיד שם בהמותיו וחפציו זמן מרובה והלכך בהעמדת בהמותיו גרידא בלא בנין לא הויא חזקה דבהעמדה כדי לא קפדי שותפין זה על זה עד שעה שיצטרכו לאותו מקום (א) וכשיצטרכו יקפידו ויסלק זה חפציו דאין לו חזקה בשתיקתן: אמחיצה קפדי. ומדשתקו ולא מיחו ודאי ברצונם עשה והויא חזקה: אסורין ליכנס לחצר. שכל זמן שלא חלקו את החצר נכנס כל אחד בחלק חבירו וקם ליה בלא יחל דברו שהרי נהנה מחבירו שעומד בחלקו דבהעמדה קפדי דאם איתא דלא קפדי מותר לעמוד בחצר חבירו אע"פ שמודר ממנו הנאה דכיון דלא קפיד בעמידה הרי הפקיר את החצר לכל בני החצר לעמוד בו ולגבי עמידה אין לו חלק בו: הכא ברחבה כו'. מתני' ברחבה שאחורי הבתים דאינו מקפיד כל כך אבל בחצר שלפני הבתים צריך שיהא מקום פנוי לביאה ויציאה והלכך קפדי בהעמדה כדי: אידי ואידי. מתני' דהכא ודנדרים: איכא דקפיד. בהעמדה כדי: גבי ממונא. לענין חזקה: לקולא. יש לנו לילך להקל ולומר שאין השותפין מקפידין זה על זה ומותר להעמיד זה בהמותיו בחצר כל זמן שאין חבירו מעכב עליו והיינו קולא שאנו מתירין לזה מסתמא להעמיד שם בהמותיו אף על פי שלא נטל רשות מחבירו ובדוכתא אחרינא (ב"מ דף מא.) אמרינן דשואל שלא מדעת גזלן הוי והכא בלא דעת יכול להכניס בהמותיו והלכך לא הוי חזקה דהא לא קפדי ומאחר דעל כן נאמר כך משום דס"ל שותף לחבריה ממחיק אנא מהנך דלא קפדי אנא והלכך שתקתי ואין חזקתך חזקה ואם רצונך להחזיק אייתי ראיה דמהנך דקפדי אנא ותיהוי חזקתך חזקה והלכך לא הויא חזקה שכל מקום שיש טענה למערער למה לא מיחה לא הויא חזקתו של מחזיק חזקה: גבי איסורא. השותפין שנדרו: לחומרא. ואסורין ליכנס לחצר דדלמא מהנך דקפדי נינהו וכל ספק איסורא דאורייתא לחומרא: לעולם לא קפדי. בהעמדה כדי כדתנן דלא הויא חזקה וגבי נדרים נמי מותרין ליכנס לחצר:

והא דקתני אסורין רבי אליעזר היא. דמחמיר בנדרים טפי דאפילו דבר שאינו הנאה כל כך אסר: אפילו ויתור אסור. כגון בעה"ב שמודר הנאה מחנוני ושלח לו בעל הבית פרוטה לחנוני לקנות ממנו מאה אגוזים בפרוטה והוסיף לו חנוני אחת יתירה או שתים אסור בעל הבית באותו ויתור שהותיר לו חנוני דמתנה הוא ואף על פי שלשאר לוקחים נמי הוסיף כמו כן ומיהו רבנן שרו דמ"מ בשביל המקח הוא מוסיף לזה על החשבון הקצוב לפרוטה שאילו לא היה לוקח ממנו בדמים לא היה נותן לו חנוני לבעל הבית כלום: בכל שותפין מעכבין כו'. בכל תשמישין הקבועין בחצר דומיא להעמדת בהמות תנור וכיריים שממעטין אויר החצר יכולין לעכב אם האחד רוצה לעשות לבדו וחביריו אין רוצים לעשות כן: חוץ מן הכביסה. שתקנו לו חכמים שיעשה בחצר בעל כרחן של שותפין חביריו: לפי שאין דרכן כו' להתבזות. שצריכות לעמוד שם יחיפות לגלות שוק לעמוד בנהר: שאין מסתכל. כשהוא הולך על שפת הנהר: היכי דמי. דמשתבח ביה קרא אם עוצם עיניו אינו לא צדיק ולא רשע: אי דאיכא דרכא אחרינא. ואזיל בהך: רשע הוא. ואף על פי שעוצם עיניו שלא היה לו לקרב אלא להרחיק מן העבירה דקיימא לן (חולין דף מד:) הרחק מן הכיעור: אנוס הוא. אם מסתכל דרך הליכתו ואונס רחמנא פטריה ולמה מזקיקו הכתוב להעלים עיניו דמדמשתבח ביה קרא שמעינן דצריך לעצום עיניו: למינס נפשיה. להטות עיניו לצד אחר והיינו דמשתבח ביה קרא דאי אניס נפשיה חסיד הוא: בעא מיניה ר' יוחנן מרבי בנאה. שמעתין דרבי בנאה קחשיב ואזיל אגב גררא דהך דלעיל: כל שאין בשרו נראה מתחתיו. שיהא ארוך עד פיסת רגלו שלא יראה כשילך יחף: טלית. מקטורן שמתכסה בו על כל בגדים שהוא לובש: שאין נראה כו'. וכל שכן דלאו קאי עד להדי חלוק דאיכא צניעות טפי: שני שלישי גדיל ושליש גלאי. שני שלישי רוחב השלחן מכוסה במפה מצד האוכלין לקנח את פיהן ולתת עליה את הפת ושליש החיצון מגולה להניח עליו קערות וכוסות שלא ילכלכו המפה ויתבזו האוכלין. ואית דמפרשי שליש גלאי באמצע שני שלישי גדיל דהיינו מפה מבחוץ ומבפנים כל סביב השלחן ואמצעיתו מגולה. גדיל קרי המפה על שם שארוגה ולשון לה הוא: וטבעתו. של שלחן שהיו רגילין לעשות בשפתו לתלותו בו יהיה מבחוץ ולא מבפנים מצד האוכלין וכדמפרש ואזיל: מבפנים. בצד הסמוך לו: היכא דאיכא ינוקא. שיושב אצל אביו לאכול צריך להושיב השלחן שיהא צד שבו קבוע הטבעת מבחוץ פן ילחוק התינוק בטבעת ויגנע השלחן: ואי ליכא ינוקא. יעשה מבפנים ולא יהפכנה מבחוץ פן יכשל בה השמש שהולך ובא סביב השלחן: הא דאיכא שמעא. שמש יעשה מבפנים פן יכשל בה השמש: והא דליכא שמעא. יעשה מבחוץ ולא מבפנים פן יוזקו בה האוכלין ומיהו היכא דאיכא שמעא יעשה מבפנים מצד היושבין ולא מבחוץ שיכולין להזהר מן הטבעת יותר מן השמש שהוא הולך והן יושבין: הא ביממא. יהיה מבחוץ שיכול השמש להזהר ולא מבפנים דמזיק לאוכלין שצר להם המקום: למדורה

תוספות

בשותפין עסקינן דבהעמדה כדי לא קפדי. תימה דלמאי דמסיק הכא דהיכא דקפדי קני והאמר לעיל (דף מב:) דשותפין אין מחזיקין זה על זה דפעמים מניח האחד להשתמש לחבירו ג' שנים ואח"כ ישתמש הוא י"ל הא דנקיט לפלגא והא דנקיט לכולא להאי גיסא או להאי גיסא כדאמר לעיל ועוד נראה דיש לחלק בין שדה לחצר דהכא מיירי שבתים אלו פתוחין לחצר זה דכיון שהוא יוצא ונכנס דרך חצר זה היכא דקפדי אין מניח לו לעשות אי לאו דזבנה מיניה: אסור ליכנס בחצר. בגמ' מוקי לה בין בחצר שיש בה דין חלוקה בין אין בה ואע"ג דבאין בה דין חלוקה אין יכול למחות בו מליכנס בחצר מ"מ אין יכול לאסור עליו מידי דהוה אמשכיר בית לחבירו שיכול המשכיר להקדישו כדאמר בפ' האומר משקלי עלי (ערכין דף כא. ושם) ואע"פ שאין יכול למחות בידו של שוכר מליכנס בו ומיהו היא גופא תימה דמ"ש מבעל חוב דאם הקדיש שדהו דאתי בעל חוב וטריף (שם כג:) (ב) אלא משום דרבי אבהו שלא יאמרו הקדש יוצא לחולין בלא פדיון מוסיף דינר וי"ל דשאני בע"ח שגוף הקרקע יוצא מתחת יד מקדיש אבל התם אין גוף הקרקע יוצא מתחת יד משכיר לעולם: רבינא אמר לעולם לא קפדי. משמע הכא (ג) דכולי עלמא קפדי אינשי אדריסת הרגל דאפי' רבינא לא קאמר אלא בשותפין ותימה דתנן בפ"ק דמגילה (דף ח. ושם ד"ה דריסת) אין בין המודר הנאה מחבירו למודר הימנו מאכל אלא דריסת הרגל וכלים שאין עושין בהן אוכל נפש ופריך בגמ' דריסת הרגל הא לא קפדי ומפרש ר"ת דהתם משמע ליה לגמרא דמתני' איירי בבקעה דלא קפדי דאי בחצר דקפדי אפילו מודר הימנו מאכל אסור דכיון דקפדי א"כ כיוצא בו משכירים ותנן בפרק אין בין המודר (נדרים דף לג.) דכיוצא בו משכירים אסור אפילו כלים שאין עושין בהן אוכל נפש ולהכי פריך כיון דעל כרחך איירי בדריסת הרגל בבקעה דלא קפדי אם כן אפילו מודר הימנו הנאה אמאי אסור והוא הדין דהוי מצי למיפרך כלים הא לא קפדי ו): מליין

רבינו גרשום

בחצר השותפין עסקינן. שמעמיד בה אחד מן השותפין בהמה או תנור וכירים ואמאי לא הויא חזקה משום דשותפין אהעמדה כדי גרידא לא קפדי כו': אסורין ליכנס לחצר. דהיינו הנאה משום דקפדי אהדדי אלמא דאהעמדה כדי קפדי ואמאי לא קנה בשלא מיחה: אלא הכא. מתני' דקתני היה מעמיד בהמתו בחצר ברחבה שאחורי הבתים מיירי דאהעמדה כדי לא קפדי: גבי ממונא. לענין חזקה: לקולא. דאזלינן בתר דלא קפיד ולא הוי חזקה: גבי איסורא. דנדר: לחומרא. דאסורין ליכנס: רבינא אמר לעולם בחצר [השותפין] אהעמדה לא קפדי. ואמאי שותפין שנדרו אסורין בהנאה: ר"א היא דאמר אפי' ויתור אסור. מה שמוסיף חנוני לקונה אגוז אחד או תפוח א' אם הקונה מודר הנאה מחנוני אסור לאותו תוספת אע"פ שאינו נותנו לו אלא מחמת מכירה. ולר' אליעזר דמחמיר א) הכא הוא מחמיר דאסור ליכנס ולא דברי הכל היא: בכל שותפין מעכבין זה לזה. שלא יעשה מלאכה בחצר שאין חבירו עושה: חוץ מן הכביסה. שאם האחד מכבס בגדיו בחצר וא' אינו רוצה לכבס בה אינו יכול לכופו זה שלא יכבסו לו בחצר: לפי שאין דרכן של בנות ישראל להתבזות. על גבי הנהר לכבס שם: שעומדות על הכביסה. בנהר אפי' נכריות משום שעומדות יחיפות ומגלות זרועותיהן שאין יצר הרע מצוי בעצמו יצה"ר: אנוס הוא. אי מסתכל דרך הליכה: אפ"ה איבעי ליה למינס נפשיה. לכוף עצמו שלא יסתכל: כל שאין בשרו נראה מתחתיו. שיהא ארוך עד פיסת רגלו שלא יראה רגלו כשהוא הולך יחף: וטלית של חלוק של חכמים. מקטורן שלו שיהא רחב כל כך שלא יהא חלוקו נראה מתחתיו אלא טפח: שני שלישי גדיל. מכוסה במפה מדבר שהוא עשוי בגדיל ארוג מקום שמשים הלחם עליו: שליש גלוי. בלא מפה שעליו מניחין קערות וכוסות שלא ילכלכו המפה ויקלקל הסעודה: וטבעתו. של שלחן שתולין אותו בו תהא קבועה מבחוץ שלא באותו צד שהוא יושב אלא מבחוץ מצד האחר: והתניא מבפנים. באותו צד שהוא סמוך לו: לא קשיא הא דאיכא ינוקא. שיושב אצלו יחזיר השלחן שיהא הטבעת מבחוץ שאם היה הטבעת מבפנים בסמוך שהוא יושב הוה איכא למיחש שמא יחזיק התינוק בטבעת וינענע השלחן ויהפוך אותו ואי ליכא ינוקא יהא מבפנים: אי איכא שמעא. שעומד לפני השלחן ומשמשו יחזיר הטבעת מבפנים סמוך לו שלא יזיק לשמש לשעומד לצד האחר: הא ביממא. יכול להחזירו שיהא הטבעת מבחוץ לפי שרואהו ויכול לשמור שלא יגע בו:

חשק שלמה על רבינו גרשום א) נראה דל"ל ולר"א דמחמיר התם הוא מחמיר הכא דאסור ליכנס וכו'.

הגהות הב"ח

(א) רשב"ם ד"ה והכא וכו' עד שעה שיצטרכו לאותו מקום וכשיצטרכו יקפידו: (ב) תוס' ד"ה אסור וכו' הקדיש שדהו דאתי בע"ח וטריף אי לאו משום דר' אבהו: (ג) ד"ה רבינא וכו' משמע הכא דלכולי עלמא:

גליון הש"ס

גמרא חלוק של ת"ח. עי' תענית דף י ע"ב:

תורה אור השלם

א) הֹלֵךְ צְדָקוֹת וְדֹבֵר מֵישָׁרִים מֹאֵס בְּבֶצַע מַעֲשַׁקּוֹת נֹעֵר כַּפָּיו מִתְּמֹךְ בַּשֹּׁחַד אֹטֵם אָזְנוֹ מִשְּׁמֹעַ דָּמִים וְעֹצֵם עֵינָיו מֵרְאוֹת בְּרָע: [ישעיה לג, טו]

ליקוטי רש"י

השותפין שנדרו הנאה זה מזה אסורין ליכנס לחצר. בחצר של שניהן דכל חד אסור בדריסת הרגל של חבירו. וקא סבר אין ברירה דלימור האי לחלק חבירו עייל והאי לחלק חבירו עייל [נדרים מה:]. אפילו ויתור. ויתור דבר שהיה מותר לכל אדם ואינו מקפיד עליו [מגילה ח.]. ויתור זהו כגון שלקח מדה של תפוחים בפרוטה ולאחר שמדד לו המדה מוסיף לו שתים או שלשה וזהו דרך של חנונין להוסיף על המדות משלהן הואיל ובלא תנאי נותן לו לא מיחזי כמתנה אלא כמקח ולהכי אסר רבי אליעזר אסור המודר באותו הויתור של מדת פירות הכא אף על גב דדריסת הרגל לא הויא הנאה גמורה [נדרים לב:]. ויתור מה שדרכן של מוכרים לוותר ללוקחין שמוסיפין להם בלוקחין פירות אחד או שנים אותו ויתור אסור במודר הנאה ואע"ג דדמי לאפיה הלכך דריסת הרגל אסור אע"ג דלא קפדי בה לחלק מיהו אסור במודר הנאה [ר"ן שם]. ועוצם. סוגר וכן (ישעיה כט) ויעצם את עיניכם [ישעיה לג, טו]. חלוק של תלמיד חכם וכו' טלית של תלמיד חכם וכו'. ולניעותא יתירתא הוא [רשב"ם לקמן צח.].

conferred as a matter of course, he surely forbids either vowing partner to traverse their jointly owned courtyard, though it is a benefit that one resident confers on the other as a matter of course.[13]

The Gemara now states an activity that the other residents *must* allow their fellow resident to perform in the jointly owned courtyard.

אָמַר רַבִּי יוֹחָנָן מִשּׁוּם ר׳ בָּנָאָה – **R' Yochanan said in the name of R' Bana'ah:** בַּכֹּל שׁוּתָּפִין מְעַכְּבִין זֶה אֶת זֶה – **In** regard to **all** disruptive activities, **[residents] can prevent each other** from performing them in the jointly owned courtyard,[14] חוּץ מִן הַכְּבִיסָה – **except for** the **washing** of clothes, which can be performed regularly by any partner in the courtyard, even if his partner objects. שֶׁאֵין דַּרְכָּן שֶׁל בְּנוֹת יִשְׂרָאֵל לְהִתְבַּזּוֹת עַל הַכְּבִיסָה – **For it is not the practice of the daughters of Israel to debase themselves by washing** clothes in public.[15]

The Gemara cites a related exposition:

וְעֹצֵם עֵינָיו מֵרְאוֹת בְּרָע – The verse states:[16] ***and he who averts his eyes from seeing evil.*** אָמַר רַבִּי חִיָּיא בַּר אַבָּא – **R' Chiya bar Abba expounded:** זֶה שֶׁאֵין מִסְתַּכֵּל בְּנָשִׁים בְּשָׁעָה שֶׁעוֹמְדוֹת עַל הַכְּבִיסָה – **This is** a reference to **one who does not gaze at women at the time that they are engaged in** the **washing** of clothing.[17]

The Gemara asks:

הֵיכִי דָּמֵי – **What are the circumstances?**[18] אִי דְּאִיכָּא דַּרְכָּא אַחֲרִיתָא – **If there is an alternate route** for the traveler to take, which does not entail his passing by the women, and he takes the river route instead, רָשָׁע הוּא – then **he is a sinful person** even if he averts his gaze, for he deliberately exposes himself to a situation in which he might be tempted to sin. אִי דְּלֵיכָּא דַּרְכָּא אַחֲרִיתָא – And **if there is no alternate route** for him to take, אָנוּס הוּא – then **he is forced** by circumstances to see the women as he passes by the river. How can the verse urge him not to look?[19]

The Gemara answers:

לְעוֹלָם דְּלֵיכָּא דַּרְכָּא אַחֲרִיתָא – **Actually,** the case is one in which **there is no alternate route.** וַאֲפִילוּ הָכִי מִיבָּעֵי לֵיהּ לְמֵינַס נַפְשֵׁיהּ – **Nevertheless, [a person] should force himself** to avert his gaze.[20]

The Gemara quotes other teachings of R' Bana'ah:

בְּעָא מִינֵּיהּ ר׳ יוֹחָנָן מֵרַבִּי בָּנָאָה – **R' Yochanan inquired of R' Bana'ah:** חָלוּק שֶׁל תַּלְמִיד חָכָם כֵּיצַד – **How long should the tunic of a Torah scholar be?**[21] R' Bana'ah replied: כָּל שֶׁאֵין בְּשָׂרוֹ נִרְאֶה מִתַּחְתָּיו – Long enough **so that his flesh should not be visible below** the hem of **[the tunic].**[22]

R' Yochanan inquired further:

טַלִּית שֶׁל תַּלְמִיד חָכָם כֵּיצַד – And **how** long **should the outer cloak of a Torah scholar be?** R' Bana'ah replied: כָּל שֶׁאֵין חֲלוּקוֹ נִרְאֶה מִתַּחְתָּיו טֶפַח – Long enough **so that a *tefach* of his tunic does not show below** the hem of **[the outer cloak].**[23]

R' Yochanan inquired regarding other utensils of a Torah scholar:

שֻׁלְחָן שֶׁל תַּלְמִיד חָכָם כֵּיצַד – **How should the table of a Torah scholar be** set? R' Bana'ah replied: שְׁנֵי שְׁלִישֵׁי גְּדִיל – **Two-thirds** of the table's width should be **covered with a cloth,**[24] וּשְׁלִישׁ גְּלַאי – **and** the remaining **third** left **uncovered;** וְעָלָיו קְעָרוֹת וְיָרָק – **and** the **dishes and vegetables** should be placed **upon [the uncovered section].**[25]

NOTES

vowed to abstain. Thus, R' Eliezer forbids the vower to derive even an insignificant benefit from the person whose benefit is forbidden to him. Similarly, R' Eliezer would hold that even the insignificant benefit enjoyed by a partner passing through a jointly owned courtyard is considered a benefit from which a vower is enjoined (*Rashbam*).

[The Sages, however, disagree with R' Eliezer, and hold that the gratuity is permitted to the vower, since the vendor would have given that gratuity to *any* customer. In their view, a benefit freely bestowed upon all is not a benefit forbidden to a vower (see *Rashbam*).]

13. [According to *Rashbam,* who explained above (see note 7) that co-residents who do not object to each other's unauthorized use of the common courtyard are deemed to have relinquished their rights in the courtyard in regard to that use, it is difficult to understand why entry into the courtyard should be forbidden according to R' Eliezer. Though R' Eliezer forbids even gratuities, benefiting from a relinquished right is not considered benefiting in any way from the former holder of that right. *Turei Even* (to *Megillah* 8a) and *Chossen Yeshuos* explain instead that co-residents who do not object to each other's use are not assumed to have actually *relinquished* their rights in that regard; rather, such use is in the category of a gratuity — one that they confer freely upon all fellow residents. Thus, such use would be forbidden to vowing partners, according to R' Eliezer (who forbids gratuities to a vower), but permitted to the vowing partners according to the Sages (who permit gratuities to a vower).]

14. If one partner wishes to perform in the courtyard any activity that will take up space (such as the placement of an oven or a stove), the other partners may prevent him from doing so (*Rashbam*).

15. The washing of clothes in a river was a practice avoided by Jewish women whenever possible, as it entailed exposing their legs as they stood in the river. The Rabbis thus decreed that women who wished to wash their clothing in their courtyards could not be stopped from doing so [even if the other owners of the courtyard did not wish to avail themselves of the same right] (*Rashbam*).

16. *Isaiah* 33:15. The verse extols the virtues of a righteous man.

17. I.e. while he is traveling alongside the river, he averts his eyes so as not to gaze at the women who are doing their laundry there (*Rashbam*). [Since their legs are partially exposed, he averts his gaze so as to avoid sinful thoughts.]

18. The fact that the verse especially praises the man who averts his eyes indicates that one who does *not* do so is considered neither especially virtuous nor sinful (*Rashbam*). The Gemara seeks to identify the situation in which this would hold true.

19. Though (according to R' Chiya bar Abba's exposition) the verse does not *require* the passerby to avert his gaze, it praises one who does so, which implies that doing so is the proper course to follow. How can we say that the verse makes a near-impossible demand on a person? (*Rashbam*).

20. Although it is difficult to travel in this manner, one should make every effort to do so. If he succeeds, he is a truly pious and praiseworthy man (*Rashbam*).

21. Torah scholars, who represent God's Torah, must dress in a dignified manner (see *Shabbos* 114a and *Berachos* 43b for further discussion). R' Yochanan asked R' Bana'ah to describe the tunic that would be fitting for Torah scholars to wear.

22. I.e. the hem of the tunic should extend to the scholar's feet, so that they are not visible when he walks barefoot (*Rashbam*). [Cf. *Rambam, Hil. De'os* 5:9 with *Kesef Mishneh,* who understands the Gemara as referring to the *thickness* of the garment; i.e. the tunic should be sufficiently thick so that the tunic is opaque. See also *Yad Ramah* and *Meiri.*]

23. An outer cloak that long is considered modest attire. An even more modest attire would be an outer cloak that extends to the very bottom of the tunic (*Rashbam*).

24. The word גְּדִיל literally means *braided*; here it refers to the [woven] tablecovering (*Rashbam*).

25. The diners sat on one side of the table along its length. The two-thirds of the table's width closest to the diners were covered with a cloth, upon which the bread was placed. The diners were also able to use the edge of the cloth as a napkin (*Rashbam*). Platters of food and goblets were placed upon the uncovered third of the table's width, so that the drippings from the food would not soil the tablecloth and cause the diners to be demeaned [since they would not be able to use the soiled cloth as a napkin] (*Rashbam's* first explanation).

א הכא בחצר השותפין עסקינן דבהעמדה כדי לא קפדי אמחיצה קפדי ובהעמדה כדי לא קפדי והא א) תנן ב השותפין שנדרו הנאה זה מזה אסורין ליכנס לחצר אלא אמר רב נחמן אמר רבה בר אבוה הכא ברחבה של אחורי בתים עסקינן דבהעמדה כדי ג) לא קפדי ואמחיצה קפדי רב פפא אמר אידי ואידי בחצר השותפין ואיכא דקפדי ואיכא דלא קפדי גבי ג ממונא לקולא גבי איסורא לחומרא רבינא אמר לעולם לא קפדי ד והא מני ר' אליעזר היא דתניא ד) ר' אליעזר אומר אפילו ויתור אסור במודר הנאה א"ר יוחנן משום ר' בנאה בכל שותפין מעכבין זה את זה חוץ מן הכביסה שאין דרכן של בנות ישראל להתבזות על הכביסה א) ועוצם עיניו מראות ברע ה) א"ר חייא בר אבא ה זה שאין מסתכל בנשים בשעה שעומדות על הכביסה היכי דמי אי דאיכא דרכא אחריתא רשע הוא אי דליכא דרכא אחריתא אנוס הוא לעולם דליכא דרכא אחריתא ואפ"ה מיבעי ליה למינס נפשיה בעא מיניה ר' יוחנן מרבי בנאה ° חלוק של ת"ח כיצד ה כל שאין בשרו נראה מתחתיו טלית של ת"ח כיצד כל שאין חלוקו נראה מתחתיו טפח ו שלחן של ת"ח כיצד שני שלישי גדיל ושליש גלאי ועליו קערות וירק וטבעתו מבחוץ והא תניא טבעתו מבפנים לא קשיא הא דאיכא ינוקא הא דליכא ינוקא ואי בעית אימא הא והא דליכא ינוקא ולא קשיא הא דאיכא שמעא הא דליכא שמעא ואי בעית אימא הא והא דאיכא שמעא ולא קשיא הא ביממא הא בליליא ושל עם הארץ דומה למדורה

והכא בחצר השותפין עסקינן. שאחד מן השותפין עצמו העמיד בהמותיו ותנור ואשפה שלו בחצר ג' שנים ולא מיחו בו וקתני חצר לכניסה ויציאה הוא ולא להעמיד שם בהמותיו וחפציו זמן מרובה והלכך בהעמדת בהמותיו גרידא בלא בנין לא הויא חזקה דבהעמדה כדי לא קפדי שותפין זה על זה עד שעה שיצטרכו לאותו מקום (א) וכשיצטרכו יקפידו ויסלק זה חפציו דאין לו חזקה בשתיקתן: **אמחיצה קפדי.** ומדשתקו ולא מיחו ודאי ברשותו עשה והויא חזקה: **אסורין ליכנס לחצר.** שכל זמן שלא חלקו את החצר נכנס כל אחד בחלק חבירו וקם ליה בלא יחל דברו שהרי נהנה מחבירו שעומד בחלקו דבהעמדה קפדי דאם איתא דלא קפדי מותר לעמוד בחצר חבירו אע"פ שמודר ממנו הנאה דכיון דלא קפיד בעמידה הרי הפקיר את החצר לכל בני החצר לעמוד בו ולגבי עמידה אין לו חלק בו: **הכא ברחבה כו'.** מתני' ברחבה שאחורי הבתים דאינו מקפיד כל כך אבל בחצר שלפני הבתים צריך שיהא מקום פנוי לביאה ויציאה והלכך קפדי בהעמדה כדי: **אידי ואידי.** מתני' דהכא ודנדרים: **איכא דקפיד.** בהעמדה כדי: **גבי ממונא.** לענין חזקה: **לקולא.** יש לנו לילך להקל ולומר שאין השותפין מקפידין זה על זה ומותר להעמיד זה בהמותיו בחצר כל זמן שאין חבירו מעכב עליו והיינו קולא שאנו מתירין לזה מתחלה להעמיד שם בהמותיו אף על פי שלא נטל רשות מחבירו ובדוכתא אחרינא (ב"מ דף מא.) אמרינן דשואל שלא מדעת גזלן הוי והכא בלא דעת יכול להכניס בהמותיו והלכך לא הוי חזקה דהא לא קפדי ומאיזה טעם נאמר כך משום דלא"ל שותף לחבריה המחזיק אנא מהנך דלא קפדי אנא והלכך שתקתי ואין חזקתך חזקה ואם רצונך להחזיק אייתי ראיה דמהנך דקפדי אנא ותיהוי חזקתך חזקה והלכך לא הויא חזקה שכל מקום שיש טענה למערער למה לא מיחה לא הויא חזקתו של מחזיק חזקה: **גבי איסורא.** השותפין שנדרו: **לחומרא.** ואסורין ליכנס לחצר דדלמא מהנך דקפדי נינהו וכל ספק איסורא דאורייתא לחומרא: **לעולם לא קפדי.** בהעמדה כדי כדתנן דלא הויא חזקה וגבי נדרים נמי מותרין ליכנס לחצר: **והא דקתני אסורין רבי אליעזר היא.** דמחמיר בנדרים טפי דאפילו דבר שאינו הנאה כל כך אסר: **אפילו ויתור אסור.** כגון בעה"ב שמודר הנאה מחנוני ושלח לו בעל הבית פרוטה לחנוני לקנות ממנו מאה אגוזים בפרוטה והוסיף לו חנוני אחת יתירה או שתים אסור בעל הבית באותו ויתור שהותיר לו חנוני דמתנה הוא ואף על פי שלשאר לוקחים נמי הוסיף כמו כן ומיהו רבנן שרו דמ"מ בשביל המקח הוא מוסיף לזה על החשבון הקצוב לפרוטה שאילו לא היה לוקח ממנו בדמים לא היה נותן לו חנוני לבעל הבית כלום: **בכל שותפין מעכבין כו'.** בכל תשמישין הקבועין בחצר דומיא דהעמדת בהמות תנור וכירים שממעטין אויר החצר יכולין לעכב אם האחד רוצה לעשות לבדו וחביריו אין רוצים לעשות כן: **חוץ מן הכביסה.** שתקנו לו חכמים שיעשה בחצר בעל כרחן של שותפין חביריו: **לפי שאין דרכן כו' להתבזות.** שצריכות לעמוד שם יחיפות לגלות שוק לעמוד בנהר: **שאין מסתכל.** כשהוא הולך על שפת הנהר: **היכי דמי.** דמשתבח ביה קרא אם עוצם עיניו דמשמע שאם לא יעצים עיניו אינו לא צדיק ולא רשע: **אי דאיכא דרכא אחרינא.** ואזיל בהך: **רשע הוא.** ואף על פי שעוצם עיניו שלא היה לו לקרב אלא להרחיק מן העבירה דקיימא לן חולין (דף מד:) הרחק מן הכיעור: **אנוס הוא.** אם מסתכל דרך הליכתו ואונס רחמנא פטריה ולמה מזקיקו הכתוב להעצים עיניו דמלדמשתבח ביה קרא שמעינן דצריך לעצום עיניו: **למינס נפשיה.** להטות עיניו לצד אחר והיינו דמשתבח ביה קרא דאי אניס נפשיה חסיד הוא: **בעא מיניה ר' יוחנן מרבי בנאה.** שמעתין דרבי בנאה קחשיב ואזיל אגב גררא דהך דלעיל: **כל שאין בשרו נראה מתחתיו.** שיהא ארוך עד פיסת רגלו שלא יראה כשילך יחף: **טלית.** מקטורן שמתכסה בו על כל בגדים שהוא לובש: **שאין נראה כו'.** וכל שכן דאי קאי עד להדי חלוק דאיכא לניעות טפי: **שני שלישי גדיל ושליש גלאי.** שני שלישי רוחב השלחן מכוסה במפה מצד האוכלין לקנח את פיהן ולתת עליה את הפת ושליש החיצון מגולה להניח עליו קערות וכוסות שלא ילכלכו המפה ויתבזו האוכלין. ואית דמפרשי שליש גלאי באמצע שני שלישי גדיל דהיינו מפה מבחוץ ומבפנים כל סביב השלחן ואמצעיתו מגולה. גדיל קרי המפה על שם שארוגה ולשון לא הוא: **וטבעתו.** של שלחן שהיו רגילין לעשות בשפתו לתלותו בו יהיה מבחוץ ולא מבפנים מצד האוכלין וכדמפרש ואזיל: **מבפנים.** בצד הסמוך לו: **היכא דאיכא ינוקא.** שיושב אצל אביו לאכול צריך להושיב השלחן שיהא צד שבו קבוע הטבעת מבחוץ פן יאחוז התינוק בטבעת וינענע השלחן: **ואי ליכא ינוקא.** יעשה מבפנים ולא יהפכנה מבחוץ פן יכשל בה השמש שהולך ובא סביב השלחן: **הא דאיכא שמעא.** שמש יעשה מבפנים פן יכשל בה השמש: **והא דליכא שמעא.** יעשה מבחוץ ולא מבפנים פן יוזקו בה האוכלין ומיהו היכא דאיכא שמעא יעשה מבפנים מצד היושבין ולא מבחוץ שיכולין להזהר מן הטבעת יותר מן השמש שהוא הולך והן יושבין: **הא ביממא.** יהיה מבחוץ שיוכל השמש להזהר ולא מבפנים דמזיק לאוכלין שאר להם המקום:

בשותפין עסקינן דבהעמדה כדי לא קפדי. תימה דלמר הכא דהיכא דקפדי קני והאמר לעיל (דף מב:) דשותפין אין מחזיקין זה על זה דפעמים מניח האחד להשתמש לחברו ג' שנים ואח"כ ישתמש הוא וי"ל הא דנחית לפלגא והא דנחית לכולא להאי גיסא או להאי גיסא כדאמר לעיל ועוד נראה דיש לחלק בין שדה לחצר דהכא מיירי שבתים אלו פתוחין לחצר זה דכיון שהוא יוצא ונכנס דרך חצר זה היכא דקפדי אין מניח לו לעשות אי לאו דזכנה מיניה: **אסור ליכנס בחצר.** בגמ' מוקי לה בין בחצר שיש בה דין חלוקה בין אין בה ואע"ג דבאין בה דין חלוקה אין יכול למחות בו מליכנס בחצר מ"מ יכול לאסור עליו מידי דהוה אמשכיר בית לחברו שיכול המשכיר להקדישו כדאמר בפ' האומר משקלי עלי (ערכין דף כא. ושם) אע"פ שאין יכול למחות בידו של שוכר מליכנס בו ומיהו היא גופא תימה דמ"ש מבעל חוב דאם הקדיש שדהו דלאתי בעל חוב ושקיל (שם כג:) (ג) אלא משום דרבי אבהו שלא יאמרו הקדש יוצא לחולין בלא פדיון מוסיף דינר וי"ל דלאתי בע"ח שגוף הקרקע יוצא מתחת יד מקדיש אבל התם אין גוף הקרקע יוצא מתחת יד משכיר לעולם: **רבינא אמר לעולם לא קפדי.** משמע הכא (ג) דכולי עלמא קפדי אינשי אדריסת הרגל דאפי' רבינא לא קאמר אלא בשותפין ותימה דתנן בפ"ק דמגילה (דף ח. ושם ד"ה דריסת) אין בין המודר הנאה מחבירו למודר הימנו מאכל אלא דריסת הרגל וכלים שאין עושין בהן אוכל נפש ופריך בגמ' דריסת הרגל הא לא קפדי ומפרש ר"ת דהתם משמע ליה לגמרא דמתני' איירי בבקעה דלא קפדי דאי בחצר דקפדי אפילו מודר הימנו מאכל אסור דכיון דקפדי א"כ כיוצא בו משכירים ותנן בפרק אין בין המודר (נדרים דף לג.) דכיוצא בו משכירים אסור אפילו כלים שאין עושין בהן אוכל נפש והכי פריך כיון דעל כרחך איירי בדריסת הרגל בבקעה דלא קפדי אם כן אפילו מודר הימנו הנאה אמאי אסור והוא הדין דהוי מצי למיפרך כלים הא לא קפדי ז):

מליין

עין משפט נר מצוה

רסא א מיי' פ"ה מהל' שכנים הל' ה סמג עשין פב טוש"ע ח"מ סי' קסא סעיף ה ועי' בטור ובב"י ובמ"מ:
רסב ב ג מיי' פ"ז מהל' נדרים הל' ד סמג לאוין רמב טוש"ע י"ד סי' רכו סעיף א ואין הלכה כן וטוש"ע ח"מ סי' קפ:
רסג ד מיי' פכ"א מהל' איסורי ביאה הל' כא סמג לאוין קכ טוש"ע אה"ע סי' כא סעיף א:
רסד ה מיי' פ"ה מהל' דעות הלכה ט:
רסה ו (מיי' שם הל' ג):

רבינו גרשום

בחצר השותפין עסקינן. שמעמיד בה אחד מן השותפין בהמה או תנור וכירים ואמאי לא הויא חזקה משום דשותפין **אהעמדה כדי** גרידא **לא קפדי** כו': **אסורין ליכנס לחצר.** דהיינו הנאה משום דקפדי אהדדי אלמא דאהעמדה כדי קפדי ואמאי לא קנה בשלא מיחה: **אלא הכא.** מתני' דקתני היה מעמיד בהמתו בחצר **ברחבה שאחורי הבתים** מיירי **דאהעמדה כדי לא קפדי: גבי ממונא.** לענין חזקה: **לקולא.** דאזלינן בתר דלא קפיד ולא הוי חזקה: **גבי איסורא.** דנדר: **לחומרא.** דאסורין ליכנס: **רבינא אמר לעולם** בחצר [השותפין] אהעמדה **לא קפדי.** ואמאי שותפין שנדרו אסורין בהנאה: **ר"א היא דאמר אפי' ויתור אסור.** מה שמוסיף חנוני לקונה אגוז אחד או תפוח א' אם הקונה **מודר הנאה** מחנוני אסור לאותו תוספת אע"פ שאינו נותנו לו אלא מחמת מכירה. ולר' אליעזר דמחמיר א) הכא הוא מחמיר דאסור ליכנס ולא דברי הכל היא: **בכל שותפין מעכבין זה לזה.** שלא יעשה מלאכה בחצר שאין חבירו עושה: **חוץ מן הכביסה.** שאם האחד מכבס בגדיו בחצר וא' אינו רוצה לכבס בה אינו יכול לכופו זה שלא יכבסו לו בחצר: **לפי שאין דרכן של בנות ישראל להתבזות.** על גבי הנהר לכבס שם: **שעומדות על הכביסה.** בנהר אפי' נכריות משום שעומדות יחיפות ומגלות זרועותיהן שלא יגרה בעצמו יצה"ר: **אנוס הוא.** אי מסתכל דרך הליכה: **אפ"ה איבעי ליה למינס נפשי'.** לכוף עצמו שלא יסתכל: **כל שאין בשרו נראה מתחתיו.** שיהא ארוך עד פיסת רגלו שלא יראה רגלו כשהוא הולך יחף: **וטלית של תלמידי חכמים.** מקטורן שלו שיהא רחב כל כך **שלא יהא חלוקו נראה מתחתיו** אלא **טפח: שני שלישי גדיל.** מכוסה במפה מדבר שהוא עשוי בגדיל ארוג מקום שמשים הלחם עליו: **שליש גלוי.** בלא מפה **שעליו** מניחין **קערות** וכוסות שלא ילכלכו המפה ויקלקל הסעודה: **וטבעת.** של שלחן שתולין אותו בו תהא קבועה **מבחוץ** שלא באותו צד שהוא יושב אלא מבחוץ מצד האחר: **והתניא מבפנים.** באותו צד שהוא סמוך לו: **לא קשיא הא דאיכא ינוקא.** שיושב אצלו יחזיר השלחן שיהא הטבעת מבחוץ שאם היה הטבעת מבפנים בסמוך שהוא יושב הוה איכא למיחש שמא יחזיק התינוק בטבעת וינענע השלחן ויהפוך אותו ואי **ליכא ינוקא** יהא מבפנים: **אי איכא שמעא.** שעומד לפני השלחן ומשמשו יחזיר הטבעת מבפנים סמוך לו שלא יזיק לשמש לשעומד לצד האחר: **הא ביממא.** יכול להחזירו שיהא הטבעת מבחוץ לפי שרואהו ויכול לשמור שלא יגע בו:

חשק שלמה על רבינו גרשום א) נראה דל"ל ולר"א דמחמיר התם הוא מחמיר הכא דאסור ליכנס וכו'.

מסורת הש"ס

א) ב"ק נא: ביצה לט: נדרים מה:, ב) מגילה ח., ג) [כתובות עג: וש"נ], ד) [מגילה ח. נדרים לב: לג. מח:], ה) מכות כד., ו) [וע"ע תוס' ב"ק נא: ד"ה זה]:

הגהות הב"ח

(א) רשב"ם ד"ה והכא וכו' עד שעה שיצטרכו לאותו מקום וכשיצטרכו יקפידו: (ב) תוס' ד"ה אסור וכו' הקדיש שדהו דלאתי בע"ח ושקיל אי לאו משום דר' אבהו: (ג) ד"ה רבינא וכו' משמע הכא דלכולי עלמא:

גליון הש"ס

גמרא חלוק של ת"ח. עי' תענית דף י ע"ב:

תורה אור השלם

א) הֹלֵךְ צְדָקוֹת וְדֹבֵר מֵישָׁרִים מֹאֵס בְּבֶצַע מַעֲשַׁקּוֹת נֹעֵר כַּפָּיו מִתְּמֹךְ בַּשֹּׁחַד אֹטֵם אָזְנוֹ מִשְּׁמֹעַ דָּמִים וְעֹצֵם עֵינָיו מֵרְאוֹת בְּרָע: [ישעיה לג, טו]

ליקוטי רש"י

השותפין שנדרו הנאה זה מזה אסורין ליכנס לחצר. בחצר של שניהן דכל חד אסור בדריסת הרגל של חבירו. וקא סבר אין ברירה דלימור האי לחלק חבירו עייל והאי לחלק חבירו עייל [נדרים מה:]. **אפילו ויתור.** ויתור דבר שהיה מוותר לכל אדם ואינו מקפיד עליו [מגילה ח.]. ויתור זהו כגון שלקח מדה של תפוחים בפרוטה ולאחר שמדד לו המדה מוסיף לו שתים או שלשה וזהו דרך של חנונין להוסיף על המדות משלהן הואיל ובלא תנאי נותן לו לא מיחזי כמקח אלא כמתנה ואליבא דרבי אליעזר אסור המודר באותו הויתור של מדידת פירות הכא נמי אף על גב דדריסת הרגל לא הויא הנאה גמורה אסור [נדרים לב:]. ויתור מה שדרכן של מוכרים לוותר ללוקחין שמוסיפין להם כשלוקחין פירות אחד או שנים אפילו אותו ויתור אסור במודר הנאה ואע"ג דהוי זבינא דרמי על אפיה הלכך דריסת הרגל אסור אע"ג דלא קפדי בה אינשי אסור במודר הנאה [ר"ן שם]. **ועוצם.** סוגר וכן (ישעיהו כט) ויעצם את עיניכם [ישעיה לג, טו]. **חלוק של תלמיד חכם וכו' טלית של תלמיד חכם וכו'.** ולניעותא יתירתא הוא [רשב"ם לקמן צח.].

R' Bana'ah discussed the proper positioning of the table itself: וְטַבַּעְתּוֹ מִבַּחוּץ – **And [the table's] ring**[26] **should be** positioned **on the outside** of the table, opposite the side at which the diners are seated.[27]

R' Bana'ah's statement regarding the table's ring is challenged: וְהָא תַּנְיָא – **But a Baraisa has stated:** טַבַּעְתּוֹ מִבִּפְנִים – [A TABLE'S] RING SHOULD BE attached ON THE INSIDE of the tabletop, on the diners' side. – ? –

The Gemara offers three resolutions to this contradiction. The first resolution:

לָא קַשְׁיָא – **This is not a difficulty.** הָא דְּאִיכָּא יְנוּקָא – **This** statement of R' Bana'ah refers to **where there is a child** present; the ring is then placed on the outside, so that the child will not play with it and shake the table. הָא דְּלֵיכָּא יְנוּקָא – **This** statement of the Baraisa refers to **where there is no child** present; the ring is then placed on the inside of the tabletop, so that the waiter will not accidentally injure himself while serving.[28]

The second resolution:

וְאִי בָּעֵית אֵימָא – **Or, if you prefer, say** הָא וְהָא דְּלֵיכָּא יְנוּקָא – **both** statements refer to **where there is no child** present; וְלָא קַשְׁיָא – **and** still **there is no difficulty.** הָא דְּאִיכָּא שַׁמְּעָא – **This** statement of the Baraisa refers to **where there is a waiter** serving; the ring is then placed on the inside, so that the waiter will not injure himself. הָא דְּלֵיכָּא שַׁמְּעָא – **This** statement of R' Bana'ah refers to **where there is no waiter** serving.

The third resolution:

וְאִי בָּעֵית אֵימָא – **Or, if you prefer, say** הָא וְהָא דְּאִיכָּא שַׁמְּעָא – **both** statements refer to **where there is a waiter** serving; וְלָא קַשְׁיָא – **and** still **there is no difficulty.** הָא בִּימָמָא – **This** statement of R' Bana'ah refers to a table used **by day,** הָא בְּלֵילְיָא – while **this** statement of the Baraisa refers to a table used **at night.**[29]

R' Bana'ah contrasts the unlearned person's table with that of the scholar described above:

וְשֶׁל עַם הָאָרֶץ דּוֹמָה – **But [the table] of an unlearned person is like**

NOTES

26. A ring was usually attached to the side of the tabletop. The tabletop was hung by this ring [when not in use] (*Rashbam*). [The tables in Talmudic times were small and tray-like. They would, as a rule, be removed after the meal (see *Tosafos* to *Pesachim* 100b ד״ה שאין).]

27. So that the diners should not accidentally injure themselves by bumping into it (see *Rashbam* ד״ה והא).

28. It is easier for the seated diners to avoid injuring themselves on the ring than the waiter, who moves to and fro (*Rashbam* ד״ה והא דליכא שמעא).

29. When the table is used during the day, the waiter can see the ring and avoid it. The ring is then placed on the outside of the table, so as not to inconvenience the diners, whose seating space will be limited by the protruding ring. If, however, the meal is being served at night, the concern for possible injury to the waiter outweighs the comfort of the diners, and the ring is placed on the inside of the table (*Rashbam*).

לִמְדוּרָה וּקְדֵרוֹת מַקִּיפוֹת אוֹתָהּ – **a cooking fire with pots all around it.**[1]

R' Bana'ah continued his description of the accoutrements of a Torah scholar:

מִטָּה שֶׁל תַּלְמִידֵי חֲכָמִים כֵּיצַד – **How does the bed of Torah scholars** look? כָּל שֶׁאֵין תַּחְתֶּיהָ – **Any [bed] that has nothing** stored **beneath it** אֶלָּא סַנְדָּלִין בִּימוֹת הַחַמָּה – **except hard-leather shoes during the summer season** וּמִנְעָלִין בִּימוֹת הַגְּשָׁמִים – **and soft-leather shoes during the rainy season**[2] can be recognized as the bed of a Torah scholar.[3] וְשֶׁל עַם הָאָרֶץ – **But** the area underneath the bed **of an unlearned person** דּוֹמָה לְאוֹצָר בָּלוּס – **is like a jumbled storeroom.**[4]

The Gemara relates a series of incidents involving R' Bana'ah:

רַבִּי בְּנָאָה הֲוָה קָא מְצַיֵּין מְעָרָתָא – **R' Bana'ah would mark** the boundaries of burial **crypts,** so that people would not inadvertently walk over them and contract *tumah.*[5] כִּי מְטָא לִמְעַרְתָּא דְּאַבְרָהָם – **When he reached the crypt of Abraham** and sought to enter in order to measure its dimensions,[6] אַשְׁכְּחֵיהּ לֶאֱלִיעֶזֶר עֶבֶד אַבְרָהָם – **he found Eliezer,** the **servant of Abraham,** דְּקָאֵי קַמֵּי בָּבָא – **standing in front of the entrance** to the crypt.[7] אֲמַר לֵיהּ – **[R' Bana'ah] said to [Eliezer],** מַאי קָא עָבֵיד אַבְרָהָם – **"What is Abraham doing?"**[8] אֲמַר לֵיהּ – **[Eliezer] replied to [R' Bana'ah],** גָּאנֵי בְּכַנְפָהּ דְּשָׂרָה וְקָא מְעַיְּינָא לֵיהּ בְּרֵישֵׁיהּ – **"He is lying in the arms of Sarah, and she is peering at his head."**[9] אֲמַר לֵיהּ – **[R' Bana'ah] said to [Eliezer],** זִיל אֵימָא לֵיהּ בְּנָאָה קָאֵי אַבָּבָא – **"Go and tell [Abraham] that Bana'ah is standing at the entrance."** אֲמַר לֵיהּ לֵיעוּל – Eliezer announced R' Bana'ah and **[Abraham] said to him, "Let him enter.** מִידַע יְדִיעַ דְּיֵצֶר בְּהַאי עָלְמָא לֵיכָּא – **It is well known that there is no physical desire in this world."**[10] עַיֵּיל עַיֵּין וְנָפַק – **[R' Bana'ah] entered** the crypt, **surveyed** its dimensions **and departed.**[11] כִּי מְטָא לִמְעַרְתָּא דְּאָדָם הָרִאשׁוֹן – **When he reached** the nearby **crypt of Adam,** and attempted to enter to measure its dimensions, יָצְתָה בַּת קוֹל וְאָמְרָה – **a Heavenly voice came forth and proclaimed,** נִסְתַּכַּלְתָּ בִּדְמוּת דְּיוּקְנִי – **"You have gazed at the likeness of My image** [i.e. at the form of Jacob].[12] בִּדְיוּקְנִי עַצְמָהּ אַל תִּסְתַּכֵּל – **Do not gaze at My image itself** [i.e. at Adam]!"[13]

R' Bana'ah replied:

הָא בְּעִינָא לְצִיּוּנֵי מְעַרְתָּא – **But I want to mark** the extent of **the crypt** above the ground and I must enter the crypt in order to ascertain the precise dimensions.

The Heavenly voice responded:

כְּמִדַּת הַחִיצוֹנָה כָּךְ מִדַּת הַפְּנִימִית – **As the dimensions of the outer** crypt (where the Patriarchs and three of the Matriarchs are buried), whose size you have already determined, **so are the dimensions of the inner** crypt, in which Adam is buried. There is thus no need for you to enter and measure.[14] וּלְמַאן דְּאָמַר שְׁנֵי בָתִּים זוֹ לְמַעְלָה מִזּוֹ – **And according to the one who says** that the "double" cave of Machpelah was configured as **two rooms, one atop the other,**[15] the Heavenly voice responded: כְּמִדַּת עֶלְיוֹנָה כָּךְ מִדַּת הַתַּחְתּוֹנָה – **As the dimensions of the upper** room, in which the Patriarchs are buried, **so are the dimensions of the lower** room, in which Adam is buried. Thus, no additional

NOTES

1. Just as a cooking fire has pots arranged around its periphery, the table of an ignorant person is set with the bread laid upon the covered center of the table, and platters of food arranged around its uncovered perimeter (*Rashbam*; see *Maharsha*).

2. [Definitions of סַנְדָּל and מִנְעָל follow *Rashi* to *Yevamos* 101a.] In Talmudic times, hard-leather shoes were worn during the rainy season, when the roads were muddy, and soft-leather shoes were worn only during the drier summer months. A Torah scholar would keep only his out-of-season footwear under his bed (see *Rashbam*).

3. It was considered a breach of modesty for a Torah scholar to keep household implements and other utensils beneath his bed, as conceivably this could result in a member of the household entering the bedchamber at an inopportune time (*Meiri*). Additionally, food placed under a bed — even if enclosed within a container — becomes contaminated by a רוּחַ רָעָה, *evil spirit* (*Rashbam* from *Pesachim* 112a).

4. A jumble of various objects, utensils and even food are to be found under the bed of an unlearned person (*Rashbam*).

The word בָּלוּס connotes a mixture of varied objects, as in the term עִיסָּה בְּלוּסָה, a "jumbled" dough composed of many types of grain [*Shabbos* 76b] (*Rashbam*).

5. A human corpse renders *tamei* a person who walks over it (since the person thereby forms a "tent" over the corpse). To prevent people from accidentally contracting corpse *tumah,* R' Bana'ah would enter burial crypts to determine their dimensions and then outline with lime the corresponding surfaces of the ground above. People would see the markings and detour around the crypts, thereby avoiding *tumah.*

6. Abraham is buried in the מְעָרַת הַמַּכְפֵּלָה, *Cave of Machpelah,* which (as explained in the Gemara, *Eruvin* 53a) was a double crypt containing the graves of Adam and Eve, Abraham and Sarah, Isaac and Rebeccah, Jacob and Leah (ibid.).

The crypts of the righteous are hallowed places and people are generally barred from entering them. R' Bana'ah, however, was permitted to do so, due to his extreme piety (*Rashbam*).

For a variety of considerations, *Ben Yehoyada* insists that the following account involving R' Bana'ah in the crypts of the Cave of Machpelah is actually the Gemara's record of a vision that was shown to R' Bana'ah in a dream. For the symbolism of this dream and the teaching it was meant to convey, see there and in *Maharal* at length. See also *Chidushei HaGeonim* in *Ein Yaakov.*

7. Eliezer, the servant of Abraham, is one of the seven righteous people who never died (*Rashbam,* citing tractate *Derech Eretz*; see *Derech Eretz Zuta,* end of Ch. 1, where the reading is "*nine* righteous people." See tractate *Kallah Rabbasi,* end of Ch. 3, where the reading is "seven ...").

8. R' Bana'ah assumed that Eliezer was guarding the entrance to the crypt to prevent Abraham from being disturbed. He therefore asked Eliezer if Abraham was engaged in an activity (such as prayer) that could not be disturbed (*Maharsha*).

9. This symbolizes the true union of Abraham and Sarah, which transcended the physical limitations of their earthly marriage (see *Maharal* at length).

10. There is thus no concern that what he will see inside will be misconstrued as something immodest and there is no need for me to conceal myself from him (*Rashbam*).

[It is evident from this Aggadic narrative that it is improper for a husband and wife to embrace or otherwise make physical displays of their affection in the view of others (*Nimukei Yosef*).]

11. He then marked the outline of the crypt on the ground above (*Rashbam*).

12. As the *Gemara* states below, Jacob was possessed of a beauty second only to that of Adam himself (*Rashbam*). [Jacob was buried in the same crypt as Abraham and Isaac and the three Matriarchs; thus, R' Bana'ah had seen him when he saw Abraham (see *Rashbam* ד"ה כמדת החיצונה).]

13. The Torah (*Genesis* 1:27) relates that Adam was created in the image of God; that is, in the special image that God had prepared for man [similar to the Divine representation that God shows to the prophets; God Himself, however, has no form or image] (see *Rashi* ad loc. and commentaries). Since Adam was the only human personally formed by God, he was the only one to possess the very image that God had prepared for man. All subsequent people, however, possessed only a likeness of that original image (see *Mizrachi* ad loc.).

14. Since you have already measured and marked off the dimensions of the outer crypt, you need only mark off an identical portion of the ground behind it.

15. The Gemara in *Eruvin* (53a) records a dispute between Rav and Shmuel whether the two chambers of the Cave of Machpelah were one behind the other or one on top of the other. According to the latter opinion, Adam and Eve were buried in a crypt situated *beneath* the crypt in which the Patriarchs were buried, and the Heavenly voice could not have spoken of "inner" and "outer" crypts.

למדורה וקדרות מקיפות אותה מטה של תלמידי חכמים כיצד כל שאין תחתיה אלא סנדלין בימות החמה ומנעלין בימות הגשמים ושל עם הארץ דומה לאוצר בלום: ר' בנאה הוה קא מציין מערתא כי מטא למערתא דאברהם אשכחיה לאליעזר עבד אברהם דקאי קמי בבא א"ל מאי קא עביד אברהם א"ל גאני בכנפה דשרה וקא מעיינא ליה ברישיה א"ל זיל אימא ליה בנאה קאי אבבא א"ל ליעול מידע ידיע דיצר בהאי עלמא ליכא עייל עיין ונפק כי מטא למערתא דאדם הראשון יצתה בת קול ואמרה נסתכלת בדמות דיוקני בדיוקני עצמה אל תסתכל הא בעינא לציוני מערתא כמדת החיצונה כך מדת הפנימית ולמ"ד [א] שני בתים זו למעלה מזו כמדת עליונה כך מדת התחתונה א"ר בנאה נסתכלתי בשני עקיביו ודומים לשני גלגלי חמה הכל בפני שרה כקוף בפני אדם שרה בפני חוה כקוף בפני אדם חוה בפני אדם כקוף בפני אדם אדם בפני שכינה כקוף בפני אדם [ג] שופריה דרב כהנא [ג] (מעין שופריה דרב) שופריה דרב מעין שופריה דרבי אבהו שופריה דר' אבהו מעין שופריה דיעקב אבינו שופריה דיעקב אבינו מעין שופריה דאדם הראשון ההוא אמגושא דהוה חטיט שכבי כי מטא אמערתא דרב טובי בר מתנה תפשיה (א) בדיקניה אתא אביי א"ל במטותא מינך שבקיה לשנה אחריתי הדר אתא תפשיה בדיקניה אתא אביי לא שבקיה עד דאייתי מספרא וגזיא לדיקניה ההוא דאמר להו חביתא דעפרא לחד בראי חביתא דגרמי לחד בראי חביתא [ד] דאודרא לחד בראי לא הוו ידעי מאי קאמר להו אתו לקמיה דרבי בנאה אמר להו אית לכו ארעא אמרו ליה אין אית לכו חיותא (ב) אין אית לכו בסתרקי אין אי הכי קאמר לכו ההוא גברא דשמעה לדביתהו דקא אמרה לברתה אמאי לא צניעת באיסורא הך איתתא עשרה בני אית לה ולית לי מאבוך אלא חד כי שכיב אמר להו כל נכסי לחד ברא לא ידעי להי מינייהו אתו לקמיה דרבי בנאה אמר להו זילו [ה] חבוטו קברא דאבוכון עד דקאי ומגלי לכו להי מינייכו שבקא אזלו כולהו ההוא דבריה הוה לא אזל אמר להו כולהו נכסי דהאי אזלו אכלו קורצא בי מלכא אמרי איכא גברא חד ביהודאי דקא מפיק ממונא מאנשי בלא סהדי ובלא (ג) מידי אתיוהו חבשוהו אזלא דביתהו אמרה להו עבדא חד הוה לי פסקו לרישיה ופשטו למשכיה ואכלו בישריה וקא מלו ביה מיא ומשקו ביה לחברייא ולא קא יהבי לי דמי ולא אגריה לא ידעי מאי קא אמרה להו אמרי ניתו לחכימא דיהודאי ולימא קריוהו לר' בנאה אמר להו זרנוקא אמרה לכו אמרי הואיל וחכים כולי האי ליתיב אבבא ונידון דינא חזא דהוה כתיב באבולא כל דיין דמתקרי לדין לא שמיה דיין אמר להו אלא מעתה אתא איניש מעלמא ומזמין

רש"י: למדורה. שמוקפת קדירות והאש באמלע אף כאן המטה והאדם באמלע והקערות סביב: כל שאין תחתיה כו'. דאמרינן בפסחים (דף קיב.) אוכלין תחת המטה אפי' מחופין בכלי ברזל רוח רעה שורה עליהן: לרך לנעול מנעלין בימות החמה וסנדלים בימות הגשמים בשביל הטיט: אלא סנדלים בימות החמה. שמניחים שם עד ימות הגשמים שילטרך להם: לאולר בלום. בסמ"ך כמו עיסה בלוסה במסכת שבת בפרק כלל גדול (דף עו:) עיסה מעורבת ממינין הרבה וכן אולר בלום (גיטין דף סז.) מינין הרבה מעורבין בתוכה ביחד וכן מיטת עם הארץ כל דבר מניחין תחת מטתן אוכלין וכלים: רבי בנאה. אדם גדול וחשוב היה לפיכך ניתן לו רשות ליכנס בקברי לדיקים אבל אחר לא כדאמרי' (חולין דף ז:) גדולים לדיקים במיתתן יותר מבחייהן והיה נכנס במערות ומודד מדת ארכן מבפנים ואח"כ מודד מבחוץ כנגדן ועשה שם ליון סיד כדי להכיר מקום הטומאה ולא יאכלו טהרות לרך כאן שלא יאהיל על הקבר: אשכחיה לאליעזר. דתניא במסכת דרך ארץ לשבעה לדיקים קיימין שלא מתו וקא חשיב בהדייהו אליעזר עבד אברהם: בכנפה. בין זרועותיו: א"ל. רבי בנאה לאליעזר: זיל אימא ליה. לאברהם: בנאה קאי אבבא. ותן לו רשות ליכנס: אמר ליה ליעול. דאין כאן תופסת לאיגירא באגפיה בכנפה דשרה: דמידע ידיע דיצר הרע בהאי עלמא ליכא. ולא לריכנא לאיטנועי מיניה: ה"ג על עיין ונפק. נכנס ר' בנאה ונסתכל מדת אורך המערה ויצא ואח"כ ליין מבחוץ: למערתא דאדם הראשון. כדדרשינן בעירובין (דף נג.) ממרא קרית ארבע א"ר ילחק קרית ארבע זוגות אדם וחוה אברהם ושרה ילחק ורבקה יעקב ולאה: בדמות דיוקני. יעקב דאמרינן בסמוך שופריה דיעקב מעין שופריה דאדם הראשון: בדיוקני עצמה. דהיינו אדם הראשון דכתיב ביה (בראשית א) בללם אלהים ברא אותו: הא בעינא לציוני. מבחוץ ולפיכך לריך אני למדוד תחלה מבפנים: כמדת החיצונה. שבה ג' אבות ואמהות כך מדת הפנימית וכמאן דדריש מכפלה שני בתים זה לפנים מזה ופלוגתא דרב ושמואל היא בכילד מעברין (עירובין דף נג.): כך מדת התחתונה. ודי לך בליון עליונה: בשני עקיביו של אדם הראשון כו'. והאי דכתיב כי עפר אתה ואל עפר תשוב הא פרכינן ליה במסכת שבת בפרק שואל (דף קנב:) ומוקמינן לה בההוא שעה אחת קודם תחיית המתים: שופריה דר' אבהו מעין שופריה דיעקב. ובהשוכר את הפועלים פריך וליחשוב נמי ר' יוחנן ומשני הדרת פנים לא הואי ליה: אמגושא. מכשף: חטיט שכבי. חופר המתים להפשיטם בגדיהם: אתא אביי כו'. בשביל שהיה העובד כוכבים אוהבו: ההוא דאמר להו. מלוה מחמת מיתה היה ומחלק נכסיו לבניו על פיו: חביתא דעפרא. אני מניח לאחד מבני ודרך חכמה אמר שלא ידעו הכל שהוא עשיר ובעל נכסים: חביתא דגרמי. חבית מלא עלמות: אודרא. מוכין: אית לכו ארעא. נשתייר לכם קרקע מאביכם דאם כן היינו חביתא דעפרא והבהמות שיש בהן עלמות זהו חביתא דגרמי: בוסתרקי. כל מיני בגדים עשויין ממוכין: לחד ברא. לאחד מבני אותו שיבררו בית דין: חבוטו. הכו הכאות על קברו ולנסותן נתכוין שאותן שהן ממזרים הן עזי פנים וילכו לחבוט: אמר להו כולהו נכסי דהאי. שלא רלה לחבוט על קברו של אביו שזה הוא הלנוע שבכלם א] ומסתברא דלזה אהב יותר ויפה דן רבי בנאה דלא שייך הכא אלא שודא דדייני והיינו שודא שלא רלה לחבוט והכי נמי אמרינן גבי ההוא דאמר נכסי לטוביה כו' (כתובות דף פה:): אזלו. תשעה האחין: אכלו ביה קורצא. הלשינו עליו: אזלא דביתהו. דרבי בנאה ללעוק אל בית המלך בלשון חכמה כדי שלא יבינו הם אלא על ידי בעלה: ואכלו בישריה. של עבד: וקמלו ביה מיא. שואבים בו מים בעורו ומשקו ביה בעורו לחברייא לבני הישיבה: לחכימא דיהודאי. לרבי בנאה: זרנוקא. נוד של עור וכך אמרה תיש הוה לי וגזלוהו ממני ושחטוהו ואכלו את הבשר ומן העור עשו חמת ושואבין בו מים ושותין בו: באבולא. על דלתות השער היה כתוב כדי שילמדו מסס בני אדם: כל דיין. המיוחד לדון דיני העיר וזימנין דמיתקרי לדינא שתובעין אותו לדין על ממון שתובעין ממנו: לא שמיה דיין. ופסול לדון דכיון דאוהב בלע הוא יקבל שוחד:

ומזמין

תוספות: מציין מערתא. משום (ד) דקבר סתום טומאה בוקעת ועולה כדאמר בכמה דוכתי וא"ת והא אין קברי עובדי כוכבים מטמאים באהל משום דאין קרויין אדם ואפילו רבנן דפליגי אר' שמעון (יבמות סא.) ואמרי דמטמאים באהל מ"מ בקבר שלפני הדיבור לא מרבה לה בנזיר (דף נד.) אלא לענין נגיעה או בקבר לרבות קבר שלפני הדיבור ומקרא דכתב גבי נגיעה מרבי לה התם ויש לומר דאברהם נקרא אדם דכתיב האדם הגדול וכן אדם הראשון והכי אין למעטם מקרא דאדם [וע"ע תוס' יבמות סא. ד"ה קברי]:

רבינו גרשום: למדורה. שיושבין סביבה קדרות כך מניח גלוי מכאן ומכאן ומקיף קערות סביב המפה: כל שאין תחתיה אלא סנדלין בימות החמה. לפי שבימות החמה שאין טיט נועלין מנעלין ומשמרין הסנדלין עד לימות הגשמים ואותן סנדלין יהיו מונחין תחתיהן בימות החמה ולא יותר. וכן בימות הגשמים [משמרין] המנעלים לפי שאסור להניח אוכלין ומשקין וכלים אחרים תחת המטה מפני שרוח רעה שורה עליהן: ושל ע"ה. שאינו מקפיד מניח הכל תחת מטתו ודומה לאוצר בלום כאוצר המאכל שמניחין בו רוב מינין: הוה מציין מערתא (אתא) היה נכנס במערה ומדד ארכה ורחבה וכמה מקום תפיסת הכוכין שבתוכה והיה יוצא חוץ על גבה מן הפתח ומכוין באיזה מקום מונחין הקברים בתוכה ומציין אותו מקום שלא יכנסו שם כהנים ויאכלו טהרות מפני שטומאה בוקעת ועולה ושאר מקום המערה שלא היו הקברים כנגדה מותר לעבור על גבה: דיצר בהאי עלמא ליכא. דאינו צריך להניח מפני שרה שלא יכנס: בדמות דיוקני. שדמותו של אברהם כדמות אדם הראשון: בדיוקני עצמה. של אדם הראשון. אל תסתכל שנברא בצלם של מעלה: א"ר בנאה והא בעינא ליכנס למערה שלו בשביל לציין: אמרה לו בת קול אין את צריך כמדת החיצונה שאברהם מונח בה כך מדת הפנימית של אדם לפי שאברהם האדם הגדול כאדם הראשון. ולמ"ד דמערת המכפלה שהיתה כפולה בית ועליה היו הכי קאמרי לר' בנאה כמדת העליונה ששם אברהם כך מדת התחתונה ששם אדם הראשון: דאודרי. דבר העשוי ממוכין צמר שגוררין מן הבגדים: בסתרקי. כרים וכסתות ומצעות עשוין מאודרין: באיסורא. דזנות: אזלא דביתהו לבי מלכא אמרה להו עבדא הוי לי וכו': אמר להו זרנוקא. עבדא היינו בהמה ששחטו אותה ופסקו ראשה והפשיטו העור שלה ועשו ממנו נוד לשאוב בו מים מן הבור: הואיל וחכים כולי האי ליתיב אבבא. דחצר המלך: באבולא. על גב השער.

מסורת הש"ס: א) [עירובין נג.], ב) ב"מ פד., ג) ס"א ל"ג, ד) [גי' הערוך דאודרא פי' עלמן]:

הגהות הב"ח
(א) גמ' דרב טובי בר מתנה תפשיה אתא אביי כל"ל ותיבת בדיקניה נמחק: (ב) שם אית לכו חיותא א"ל אין אית לכו בסתרקי א"ל אין: (ג) שם בלא סהדי ובלא ראיה אתיוהו: (ד) תוס' ד"ה מציין מערתא משום דקא סבר טומאה רצוצה בוקעת ועולה:

גליון הש"ס
גמרא חבוטו קיברא. עיין אליה רבה או"ח סימן תקפט ס"ק ט"ו:

הגהות מהר"ב רנשבורג
א] רשב"ם ד"ה אמר להו כלהו נכסי דהאי כו' ומסתברא דלזה אהב יותר. נ"ב ע' בינה לעתים דפוס ברלין חלק ב' דרוש כ"ב דף לג ע"א ד"ה ההוא גברא כו'. יעוי"ש ודו"ק:

ליקוטי רש"ש
כל שאין תחתיה אלא סנדלין בימות החמה וכו'. אלהו מטה של תלמידי חכמים שאין תחתיה אלא מנעלים של בעל הבית בימות החמה וסנדלים בימות הגשמים שם כשהוא בא לשכב וליכן הולך בין מנעלין ונותנן תחת המטה דרכים אחרים גנאי הוא לו שמרגיל בני הבית לשם כשהוא בא לשכב ולשון אוצר בלום. בלוס. סתום כמו אולר בלום (ב"ב נח.) [ר"ן נדרים סו.] ונראה בעיני אולר בלוס סגור מקבוצות לבדן מחילות מחילות כמו שעושין בתיבות גדולות ליתן מינין מכאן ושורין מכאן עדשים מכאן כמו פיר בלוס וכו' בבכורות (מ:) קלוסי"א בלע"ז [גיטין סז. וער"ש תוס' וער' רש"י חולין קז:] שופריה. וזכרוני תולדו וקירון [עור] פניו [ב"מ פד.]. אמגושא. מכשף [יומא לה. וסנהדרין לט.].

marking is necessary.[16]

אָמַר רַבִּי בְּנָאָה – **R' Bana'ah said:** נִסְתַּכַּלְתִּי בִּשְׁנֵי עֲקֵיבָיו – **"I glimpsed [Adam's] two heels** from outside the crypt, וְדוֹמִים לִשְׁנֵי גַלְגַּלֵּי חַמָּה – **and they were like two orbs of the sun,** so radiant was the skin."[17]

The Gemara cites a related teaching:

הַכֹּל בִּפְנֵי שָׂרָה – **The radiance of any** other person's countenance **in comparison to** that of **Sarah** כְּקוֹף בִּפְנֵי אָדָם – **is like** that of **a monkey in comparison to** that of **a human being.** שָׂרָה בִּפְנֵי חַוָּה – The radiance of the countenance of **Sarah in comparison to** that of **Eve** כְּקוֹף בִּפְנֵי אָדָם – **is like** that of **a monkey in comparison to** that of **a human being.** חַוָּה בִּפְנֵי אָדָם – The radiance of the countenance of **Eve in comparison to** that of **Adam** כְּקוֹף בִּפְנֵי אָדָם – **is like** that of **a monkey in comparison to** that of **a human being.** אָדָם בִּפְנֵי שְׁכִינָה – The radiance of the countenance of **Adam in comparison to** that of **the** ***Shechinah***[18] כְּקוֹף בִּפְנֵי אָדָם – **is like** that of **a monkey in comparison to** that of **a human being.**

The Gemara describes Adam's great beauty of form:[19]

שׁוּפְרֵיהּ דְּרַב כַּהֲנָא (מֵעֵין שׁוּפְרֵיהּ) – **The beauty of Rav Kahana** דְּרַב שׁוּפְרֵיהּ דְּרַב – **was a semblance of the beauty of Rav. The beauty of Rav)** מֵעֵין שׁוּפְרֵיהּ דְּרַבִּי אַבָּהוּ – **was a semblance of the beauty of R' Abahu.** שׁוּפְרֵיהּ דְּר׳ אַבָּהוּ – **The beauty of R' Abahu** מֵעֵין שׁוּפְרֵיהּ דְּיַעֲקֹב אָבִינוּ – **was a semblance of the beauty of our forefather Jacob.** שׁוּפְרֵיהּ דְּיַעֲקֹב אָבִינוּ – **The beauty of our forefather Jacob** מֵעֵין שׁוּפְרֵיהּ דְּאָדָם הָרִאשׁוֹן – **was a semblance of the beauty of Adam.**

The Gemara recounts another incident involving burial crypts:[20]

הַהוּא אַמְגּוּשָׁא – There was a **certain magician**[21] דַּהֲוָה חָטִיט שְׁכָבֵי – **who would dig up corpses** and strip them of their clothes. כִּי מָטָא אַמְעַרְתָּא דְּרַב טוֹבִי בַּר מַתְנָה – **When he reached the crypt of Rav Tuvi bar Masnah** and attempted to strip the corpse, תַּפְשֵׂיהּ בִּדִיקְנֵיהּ – **[the corpse] seized him by his beard,** and would not release him. אֲתָא אַבַּיֵי – **Abaye,** who was the magician's friend, **came to the crypt** אָמַר לֵיהּ – and **said to [Rav Tuvi's corpse],** בְּמָטוּתָא מִינָּךְ שַׁבְקֵיהּ – **"I beg of you – release him."** The magician was released. לְשָׁנָה אַחֲרִיתִי – **The following year,** הֲדַר אָתָא – **[the magician] came** once **again,** attempting to strip Rav Tuvi's corpse. תַּפְשֵׂיהּ בִּדִיקְנֵיהּ – **[The corpse] seized him by his beard** once more. אָתָא אַבַּיֵי – **Abaye came** again to plead for his release, but to no avail; לֹא שַׁבְקֵיהּ – **[the corpse] would not release him,** עַד דְּאַיְיתִי מַסְפְּרָא וְגַזְיָא לְדִיקְנֵיהּ – **until [Abaye] brought a pair of scissors and cut [the magician's] beard.**

The Gemara returns to incidents involving R' Bana'ah:

הַהוּא דְּאָמַר לְהוּ – There was **a certain man who said** on his deathbed **to [his sons]:** חֲבִיתָא דְעַפְרָא לְחַד בְּרַאי – **"I bequeath a keg of earth to one** of my **sons,** חֲבִיתָא דְגַרְמֵי לְחַד בְּרַאי – **a keg of bones to one** of my **sons** חֲבִיתָא דְאוּדְרָא לְחַד בְּרַאי – and **a keg of cotton**[22] to **one** of my **sons."** לֹא הֲווּ יָדְעֵי מַאי קָאָמַר לְהוּ – **[The sons] did not understand what [their father] had said** to them, and were uncertain how to divide their father's estate.[23] אָתוּ לְקַמֵּיהּ דְּרַבִּי בְּנָאָה – **They came before R' Bana'ah** for counsel. אָמַר לְהוּ – **[R' Bana'ah] said to them:** אִית לְכוּ אַרְעָא – **"Do you have land** left to you by your father?" אָמְרוּ לֵיהּ אִין – **They told him, "Yes."** אִית לְכוּ חֵיוָתָא – **"Do you have livestock** left to you by your father?" אִין – Again they replied, **"Yes."** אִית לְכוּ בִּסְתַּרְקֵי – **"Do you have quilts** left to you by your father?" אִין – Again they answered, **"Yes."** R' Bana'ah thereupon told them: אִי הָכִי – **"If so,** that all of these items were part of your father's estate, הָכִי קָאָמַר לְכוּ – then **these are** the items about which **he was telling you."** The "keg of earth" referred to the land, the "keg of bones" referred to the livestock and the "keg of cotton" referred to the quilts.

Another incident involving R' Bana'ah:

הַהוּא גַּבְרָא – There was a **certain man** דִּשְׁמַעָהּ לְדְבֵיתְהוּ דְּקָא אָמְרָה לִבְרַתָּהּ – **who overheard his wife saying to her daughter,** אַמַּאי לֹא צְנִיעַת בְּאִיסּוּרָא – **"Why are you not discreet when you do forbidden** things?[24] הָךְ אִיתְּתָא עֲשָׂרָה בְּנֵי אִית לָהּ – **This woman** (she said, referring to herself) **has ten sons,** וְלֵית לִי מֵאֲבוּךְ אֶלָּא חַד – **and only one of them is by your father!"**[25] כִּי שָׁכִיב – **When [the father] was dying,** אָמַר לְהוּ – **he said to [his family],** כָּל נְכָסַי לְחַד בְּרָא – **"I bequeath all** my **possessions to my one son."**[26] לֹא יָדְעֵי לְהֵי מִינַּיְיהוּ – **[The sons] did not know to which of them** the father had referred. אָתוּ לְקַמֵּיהּ דְּרַבִּי בְּנָאָה – **They came before R' Bana'ah** for counsel. אָמַר לְהוּ – **[R' Bana'ah] said to them:** זִילוּ חַבּוּטוּ קִבְרָא דַּאֲבוּכוֹן – **"Go and bang upon the grave of your father,** עַד דְּקָאֵי וּמְגַלֵּי לְכוּ לְהֵי מִינַּיְיכוּ שָׁבְקָא – **until he rises and reveals to you to which of you he left** his estate."[27] אָזְלוּ כּוּלְּהוּ – **They all went** to do as R' Bana'ah suggested, הַהוּא דִּבְרֵיהּ הֲוָה לֹא אָזַל – except for **the one who was** actually **his son,** who **did not go**

NOTES

16. R' Bana'ah had been concerned that the lower crypt might extend beyond the upper. The heavenly voice responded that they were equal in size; thus, the marking of the upper crypt effectively marked the lower one as well.

17. Although God told Adam that he would return to dust (*Genesis* 3:19), that refers to a moment before the resurrection of the dead (*Rashbam* from *Shabbos* 152b).

18. I.e. the radiant light created by God to signify His presence.

19. The previous Gemara listed people of exceptional radiance. The present Gemara lists people of exceptional beauty of form (*Maharsha*).

20. [The following incident is mentioned here tangentially, since it, too, deals with a crypt whose occupant exhibited attributes of the living.]

21. [The word אַמְגּוּשִׁי or אַמְגּוּשָׁא often refers to a magician, as it is indeed rendered here by *Rashbam*. Sometimes, the term can refer to a Magus, one of the Persian priestly caste of the Magi. See also *Shabbos* 75a with *Rashi* and *Tosafos*.]

22. [*Rashbam* renders: מוֹכִין, which refers to cotton-like tufts of soft fibers, whether of cotton, unprocessed wool or old garments (see *Rashi* to *Shabbos* 47b ד״ה מוכין).]

23. He wanted to make his wishes known as to how his estate should be allocated among his children, but he spoke cryptically so that people would not realize that he was actually a wealthy man (*Rashbam*; cf. *Maharsha*).

24. I.e. when you have illicit affairs.

25. [She thereby proved that she had been very discreet during her sinful life, since her husband had never discovered anything.]

26. The father was unaware which son was truly his son. Therefore, by declaring that his estate should be awarded to "his one son," he effectively appointed the court as arbiter to decide which of his sons was most deserving of the bequest (*Rashbam* ד״ה אמר; see *Kesubos* 85b; see also following note).

27. R' Bana'ah meant to isolate the true son by seeing which one was the least brazen. His test was based on the Gemara's observation that *mamzerim* [children of an adulterous or incestuous union] are generally brazen (see *Kiddushin* 71b). Now, nine of the ten sons were in fact *mamzerim,* as they were born of their married mother's adulterous unions. It was R' Bana'ah's hope that the one legitimate son would refrain from the disrespectful act of banging on his father's grave. Additionally, the father probably favored the son most solicitous of his honor and that would be sufficient reason for the court to exercise its mandate to arbitrate and award the estate to that son (*Rashbam*; see *Rashbam* to 35a ד״ה שורא).

למדורה וקדרות מקיפות אותה מטה של תלמידי חכמים כיצד כל שאין תחתיה אלא סנדלין בימות החמה ומנעלין בימות הגשמים ושל עם הארץ דומה לאוצר בלום: ר' בנאה הוה קא מציין מערתא כי מטא למערתא דאברהם אשכחיה לאליעזר עבד אברהם דקאי קמי בבא א"ל מאי קא עביד אברהם א"ל גאני בכנפה דשרה וקא מעיינא ליה ברישיה א"ל זיל אימא ליה בנאה קאי אבבא א"ל ליעול מידע ידיע דיצר בהאי עלמא ליכא עייל עיין ונפק כי מטא למערתא דאדם הראשון יצתה בת קול ואמרה נסתכלת בדמות דיוקני בדיוקני עצמה אל תסתכל הא בעינא לציוני מערתא כמדת החיצונה כך מדת הפנימית ולמ"ד [א] שני בתים זו למעלה מזו כמדת עליונה כך מדת התחתונה א"ר בנאה נסתכלתי בשני עקיביו ודומים לשני גלגלי חמה הכל בפני שרה כקוף בפני אדם שרה בפני חוה כקוף בפני אדם חוה בפני אדם כקוף בפני אדם אדם בפני שכינה כקוף בפני אדם [ג] שופריה דרב כהנא [ג] (מעין שופריה דרב שופריה דרב) מעין שופריה דרבי אבהו שופריה דר' אבהו מעין שופריה דיעקב אבינו שופריה דיעקב אבינו מעין שופריה דאדם הראשון ההוא אמגושא דהוה חטיט שכבי כי מטא אמערתא דרב טובי בר מתנה תפשיה (א) בדיקניה אתא אביי א"ל במטותא מינך שבקיה לשנה אחריתי הדר אתא תפשיה בדיקניה אתא אביי לא שבקיה עד דאייתי מספרא וגזיא לדיקניה ההוא דאמר להו חביתא דעפרא לחד בראי חביתא דגרמי לחד בראי חביתא [ד] דאודרא לחד בראי לא הוו ידעי מאי קאמר להו אתו לקמיה דרבי בנאה אמר להו אית לכו ארעא אמרו ליה אין אית לכו חיותא (ב) אין אית לכו בסתרקי אין אי הכי קאמר לכו ההוא גברא דשמעה לדביתהו דקא אמרה לברתה אמאי לא צניעת באיסורא הך איתתא עשרה בני אית לה ולית לי מאבוך אלא חד כי שכיב אמר להו כל נכסי לחד ברא לא ידעי להי מינייהו אתו לקמיה דרבי בנאה אמר להו זילו [ה] חבוטו קברא דאבוכון עד דקאי ומגלי לכו להי מינייכו שבקא אזלו כולהו ההוא דבריה הוה לא אזל אמר להו כולהו נכסי דהאי אזלו אכלו קורצא בי מלכא אמרי איכא גברא חד ביהודאי דקא מפיק ממונא מאנשי בלא סהדי ובלא (ג) מידי אתיוהו חבשוהו אזלא דביתהו אמרה להו עבדא חד הוה לי פסקו לרישיה ופשטו למשכיה ואכלו בישריה וקא מלו ביה מיא ומשקו ביה לחברייא ולא קא יהבי לי דמי ולא אגריה לא ידעי מאי קא אמרה להו אמרי ניתו לחכימא דיהודאי ולימא קריוהו לר' בנאה אמר להו זרנוקא אמרה לכו אמרי הואיל וחכים כולי האי ליתיב אבבא ונידון דינא חזא דהוה כתיב באבולא כל דיין דמתקרי לדין לא שמיה דיין אמר להו אלא מעתה אתא איניש מעלמא ומזמין

רשב"ם

למדורה. שמוקפת קדירות והאש באמצע אף כאן המטה והאלפס באמצע והקערות סביב: כל שאין תחתיה כו'. דאמרינן בפסחים (דף קיא:) אוכלין תחת המטה אפי' מחופין בכלי ברזל רוח רעה שורה עליהן: דרך לנעול מנעלין בימות החמה וסנדלים בימות הגשמים בשביל הטיט: אלא סנדלים בימות החמה. שמניחים שם עד ימות הגשמים שיצטרך להם: לאוצר בלום. בסמ"ך כמו עיסה בלוסה במסכת שבת בפרק כלל גדול (דף עו:) עיסה מעורבת ממינין הרבה וכן אוצר בלום (גיטין דף סז.) מינין הרבה מעורבין בתוכה ביחד וכן מיטות עם הארץ כל דבר מניחין תחת מטתן אוכלין וכלים: רבי בנאה. אדם גדול וחשוב היה לפיכך ניתן לו רשות ליכנס בקברי צדיקים אבל אחר לא כדאמרי' (חולין דף ז:) גדולים צדיקים במיתתן יותר מבחייהן והיה נכנס במערות ומודד מדת ארכן מבפנים ואח"כ מודד מבחוץ כנגדן ועשה שם ציון סיד כדי להכיר מקום הטומאה ולא יביאו טהרות דרך כאן שלא יאהיל על הקבר: אשכחיה לאליעזר. דתניא במסכת דרך ארץ דשבעה צדיקים קיימין שלא מתו וקא חשיב בהדייהו אליעזר עבד אברהם: בכנפה. בין זרועותיה: א"ל. רבי בנאה לאליעזר: זיל אימא ליה. לאברהם: בנאה קאי אבבא. ותן לו רשות ליכנס: אמר ליה ליעול. דאין כאן חולפא לאיצנינא באנפיה בכנפה דשרה: דמידע ידיע דיצר הרע בהאי עלמא ליכא. ולא צריכנא לאיצטנועי מיניה: ה"ג על עיין ונפיק. נכנס ר' בנאה ונסתכל מדת אורך המערה ויצא ואח"כ ציין מבחוץ: למערתא דאדם הראשון. כדדרשינן בעירובין (דף נג.) ממרא קרית ארבע א"ר יצחק קרית ארבע זוגות אדם וחוה אברהם ושרה יצחק ורבקה יעקב ולאה: בדמות דיוקני. יעקב דאמרינן בסמוך שופריה דיעקב מעין שופריה דאדם הראשון: בדיוקני עצמה. דהיינו אדם הראשון דכתיב ביה (בראשית א) בצלם אלהים ברא אותו: הא בעינא לציוני. מבחוץ ולפיכך צריך אני למדוד תחלה מבפנים: כמדת החיצונה. שבה ג' אבות ואמהות כך מדת הפנימית וכמאן דדריש מכפלה שני בתים זה לפנים מזה ופלוגתא דרב ושמואל היא בפרק מעברין (עירובין דף נג.): כך מדת התחתונה. ודי לך בציון עליונה: בשני עקיביו של אדם הראשון כו'. והאי דכתיב כי עפר אתה ואל עפר תשוב הא פרכינן ליה במסכת שבת בפרק שואל (דף קנב:) ומוקמינן לה ההוא שעה אחת קודם תחיית המתים: שופריה דר' אבהו מעין שופריה דיעקב. ובהשוכר את הפועלים פריך וליחשוב נמי ר' יוחנן ומשני הדרת פנים לא הויא ליה: אמגושא. מכשף: חטיט שכבי. חופר המתים להפשיטם בגדיהם: אתא אביי כו'. בשביל שהיה העובד כוכבים אוהבו: ההוא דאמר להו. מלוה מחמת מיתה היה ומחלק נכסיו לבניו על פיו: חביתא דעפרא. אני מניח לאחד מבני ודרך חכמה אמר שלא ידעו הכל שהוא עשיר ובעל נכסים: חביתא דגרמי. חבית מלא עצמות: אודרא. מוכין: אית לכו ארעא. נשתייר לכם קרקע מאביכם דאם כן היינו חביתא דעפרא והבהמות שיש בהן עצמות זהו חביתא דגרמי: בוסתרקי. כל מיני בגדים עשויין ממוכין: לחד ברא. לאחד מבני אותו שיבררו בית דין: חבוטו. הכו הכאות על קברו ולנסותן נתכוין שאותן שהן ממזרים הן עזי פנים וילכו לחבוט: אמר להו כולהו נכסי דהאי. שלא רצה לחבוט על קברו של אביו שזה הוא הצנוע שבכם א] ומסתברא דלזה אהב יותר ויפה דן רבי בנאה דלא שייך הכא אלא שודא דדייני והיינו שודא שלא רצה לחבוט והכי נמי אמרינן גבי ההוא דאמר נכסי לטוביה כו' (כתובות דף פה:): אזלו. תשעה האחין: אכלו ביה קורצא. הלשינו עליו: אזלא דביתהו. דרבי בנאה לצעוק אל בית המלך בלשון חכמה כדי שלא יבינו הם אלא על ידי בעלה: ואכלו בישריה. של עבד: וקמלו ביה מיא. שואבים בו מים בעורו ומשקו ביה בעורו לחברייא לבני הישיבה: לחכימא דיהודאי. לרבי בנאה: זרנוקא. נוד של עור וכך אמרה תיש הוה לי וגזלוהו ממני ושחטוהו ואכלו את הבשר ומן העור עשו חמת ושואבין בו מים ושותין בו: באבולא. על דלתות השער היה כתוב כדי שילמדו משם בני אדם: כל דיין. המיוחד לדון דיני העיר וזימנין דמיתקרי לדינא שתובעין אותו לדין על ממון שתובעין ממנו: לא שמיה דיין. ופסול לדון דכיון דאוהב בצע הוא יקבל שוחד:

ומזמין

תוספות

מציין מערתא. משום (ד) דקבר סתום טומאה בוקעת ועולה כדאמר בכמה דוכתי וא"ת והא אין קברי עובדי כוכבים מטמאים באהל משום דאין קרויין אדם ואפילו רבנן דפליגי אר' שמעון (יבמות סא.) ואמרי דמטמאים באהל מ"מ בקבר שלפני הדיבור לא מרבה לה בנזיר (דף נד.) אלא לענין נגיעה או בקבר לרבות קבר שלפני הדיבור ומקרא דכתב גבי נגיעה מרבי לה התם ויש לומר דאברהם נקרא אדם דכתיב האדם הגדול וכן אדם הראשון והכי אין למעטם מקרא דאדם (וע"ע תוס' יבמות סא. ד"ה קברי):

רבינו גרשום

למדורה. שיושבין סביבה קדרות כך מניח גלוי מכאן ומכאן ומקיף קערות סביב המפה: כל שאין תחתיה אלא סנדלין בימות החמה. לפי שבימות החמה שאין טיט נועלין מנעלין ומשמרין הסנדלין עד לימות הגשמים ואותן סנדלין יהיו מונחין תחתיהן בימות החמה ולא יותר. וכן בימות הגשמים [משמרין] המנעלים לפי שאסור להניח אוכלין ומשקין וכלים אחרים תחת המטה מפני שרוח רעה שורה עליהן: ושל ע"ה. שאינו מקפיד מניח הכל תחת מטתו ודומה לאוצר בלום כאוצר המאכל שמניחין בו רוב מינין: הוה מציין מערתא (אתא) היה נכנס במערה ומודד ארכה ורחבה וכמה מקום תפיסת הכוכין שבתוכה והיה יוצא חרץ על גבה מן הפתח ומכוין באיזה מקום מונחין הקברים בתוכה ומציין אותו מקום שלא יכנסו שם כהנים ויאכלו טהרות מפני שטומאה בוקעת ועולה ושאר מקום המערה שלא היו הקברים כנגדה מותר לעבור על גבה: דיצר בהאי עלמא ליכא. דאינו צריך להניח מפני שרה שלא יכנס: בדמות דיוקני. שדמותו של אברהם כדמות אדם הראשון: בדיוקני עצמה. של אדם הראשון. אל תסתכל שנברא בצלם של מעלה: א"ר בנאה והא בעינא ליכנס למערה שלו בשביל לציין. אמרה לו בת קול אין את צריך כמדת החיצונה שאברהם מונח בה כך מדת הפנימית של אדם לפי שאברהם האדם הגדול כאדם הראשון. ולמ"ד דמערת המכפלה שהיתה כפולה בית ועליה היו הכי קאמרי לר' בנאה כמדת העליונה ששם אברהם כך מדת התחתונה ששם אדם הראשון: אודרי. דבר העשוי ממוכין צמר שגוררין מן הבגדים: בסתרקי. כרים וכסתות ומצעות עשויין מאודרין: באיסורא. דונות: אזלא דביתהו לבי מלכא אמרה להו עבדא הוי לי וכו': אמר להו זרנוקא. עבדא היינו בהמה ששחטו אותה ופסקו ראשה והפשיטו העור שלה ועשו ממנו נוד לשאוב בו מים מן הבור: הואיל וחכים כולי האי ליתיב אבבא. דחצר המלך: באבולא. על גב השער.

מסורת הש"ס

א) [עירובין נג.], ב) ב"מ פד., ג) ס"א ל"ג, ד) [גי' הערוך דאודרא פי' מוכין]:

הגהות הב"ח

(א) גמ' דרב טובי בר מתנה תפשיה אתא אביי כצ"ל ותיבת בדיקניה נמחק: (ב) שם אית לכו חיותא א"ל אין אית לכו בסתרקי א"ל אין: (ג) שם בלא סהדי ובלא ראיה אתיוהו: (ד) תוס' ד"ה מציין מערתא משום דקא סבר טומאה רצוצה בוקעת ועולה:

גליון הש"ס

גמרא חבוטו קיברא. עיין אליה רבה א"ח סימן תקפח ס"ק ט"ו:

הגהות מהר"ב רנשבורג

א] רשב"ם ד"ה אמר להו כולהו נכסי דהאי כו' ומסתברא דלזה אהב יותר. ע"ע בינה לעתים דפוס ברלין חלק ב' דרוש כ"ב דף לג ע"א ד"ה חבוטו קברא כו'. יעוש"ה ודו"ק:

ליקוטי רש"י

כל שאין תחתיה אלא סנדלין בימות החמה וכו'. אותו מטה של תלמידי חכמים כל שאין תחתיה אלא מנעלים של נעל הבית בימות החמה וסנדלים בימות הגשמים שנותנים שם כשהוא בא לשכב ולישן הוא חולץ מנעליו ונותנן תחת מטתו ואין לתת תחתיה דברים אחרים כגון גגלי הוא לו שמרגיל בני הבית לשם [סוכה כא.]. לאוצר בלום. בלום. סתום כמו אוצר בלום (ב"ב נח.) [ר"ן נדרים סו.]. ונראה בעיני אוצר בלום סגור מסגירות לבדק מחיצות מחיצות כמו שעושין בתיבות גדולות ליתן חטין מכאן שעורין מכאן עדשים מכאן כמו פיו בלום וגלוי מבלומות בבכורות (מ:) קלוטי"ש בלע"ז [גיטין סז. וע"יש תוס' ועי' רש"י חולין קז:]. שופריה. זיהרורי תואריו וקירון [עור] פניו [ב"מ פד.]. אמגושא. מכשף [יומא לה. וסנהדרין לט.].

bang on the grave, out of concern for his father's honor.[28] אָמַר לְהוּ – **R' Bana'ah said to them:** כּוּלְהוּ נִכְסֵי דְּהַאי – **"All the possessions belong to this** brother, who did not go and bang on the grave; he is the true heir." אָזְלוּ אָכְלוּ קוּרְצָא בֵּי מַלְכָּא – **[The remaining nine]** thereupon **went and informed on**[29] **[R' Bana'ah] in the royal palace.** אָמְרֵי – **They said** to the king's agents, אִיכָּא גַּבְרָא חַד בִּיהוּדָאֵי – **"There is one man among the Jews** דְּקָא מַפִּיק מָמוֹנָא מֵאִינָשֵׁי – **who exacts money from people** בְּלָא סָהֲדֵי וּבְלָא מִידֵי – **without** supporting **testimony and without any** other **proof."** אַתְיוּהוּ חַבְשׁוּהוּ – **[The king's agents] brought [R' Bana'ah]** to them **and imprisoned him.**

R' Bana'ah's wife devised a stratagem to effect her husband's release:[30]

אָזְלָא דְּבֵיתְהוּ – **[R' Bana'ah's] wife came before the king's court** אָמְרָה לְהוּ – and **said to them:** עַבְדָּא חַד הֲוָה לִי – **"I had a slave** פְּסַקוּ לְרֵישֵׁיהּ – and **[robbers] cut off his head,** וּפָשְׁטוּ לְמַשְׁכֵּיהּ – **stripped his hide** וְאָכְלוּ בִּישְׂרֵיהּ – **and ate his flesh.** וְקָא מָלוּ בֵּיהּ מַיָּא – **And they would draw water with [the hide]** וּמַשְׁקוּ בֵּיהּ לְחַבְרַיָּיא – **and give students to drink from it,** וְלֹא קָא יָהֲבֵי לִי דְּמֵי – **and they have not paid me its worth** וְלֹא אַגְרֵיהּ – **or its rental!"**

As R' Bana'ah's wife had intended, the king's judges were mystified:

לֹא יָדְעֵי מַאי קָא אָמְרָה לְהוּ – **They did not know what she was saying to them.** אָמְרֵי – So, **they said:** נֵיתוּ לְחַכִּימָא דִּיהוּדָאֵי – **"Let us summon the wise man of the Jews,** i.e. R' Bana'ah, וְלֵימָא – **and let him tell** us the meaning of this woman's complaint." קָרְיוּהוּ לְר׳ בְּנָאָה – **They summoned R' Bana'ah** to the court, and repeated to him the narrative. אָמַר לְהוּ – **[R' Bana'ah] said to them,** זַרְנוּקָא אָמְרָה לְכוּ – **"She spoke to you** about **a skin bottle."**[31]

The king's judges were impressed with R' Bana'ah's wisdom: אָמְרֵי – **They said:** הוֹאִיל וְחַכִּים כּוּלֵּי הַאי – **"Since he is so wise,** לֵיתֵיב אַבָּבָא וְנִידוּן דִּינָא – **let him sit** as a judge **at the entrance** to the king's courtyard **and render judgments."**[32]

R' Bana'ah took notice of his new surroundings:

חָזָא דַּהֲוָה כְּתִיב בְּאֵבוּלָא – **He saw** that the following aphorism was **inscribed on** the doors of **the entrance:**[33] כָּל דַּיָּין דְּמִתְקְרֵי לְדִין – **"Any judge who is summoned to court** to answer monetary claims brought against him לֹא שְׁמֵיהּ דַּיָּין – **cannot** in truth **be called a judge** and is unfit for that role, for his integrity is suspect."[34]

R' Bana'ah objected to this teaching:

אָמַר לְהוּ – **He said to [the king's judges],** אֶלָּא מֵעַתָּה – **"But now,** if a mere complaint is sufficient to impugn a judge's standing, אָתָא אִינִישׁ מֵעָלְמָא – then **if a man comes** in **off the street**

NOTES

28. Although this child did not know that he was the true son, he did not have the brazenness of his *mamzer* half-brothers that would have allowed him to commit this disrespectful act.

29. אָכְלוּ קוּרְצָא is an idiomatic expression for informing on someone (see *Daniel* 3:8; see *Rashi* to *Leviticus* 19:16 and *Ramban* there).

30. Her plan, which the Gemara proceeds to relate, was to appear before the judges with a complaint that she knew they would not comprehend, in the hope that they would summon the wise R' Bana'ah from prison to interpret her statement (*Rashbam*).

31. I.e. she meant that her goat had been stolen, slaughtered, skinned and eaten, and its hide fashioned into a water bottle. [The robbers neither paid her for the goat nor paid her rental for the use of the skin bottle] (*Rashbam*). [Cf. *Maharsha,* who questions her description of the goat as a "slave" and who interprets this as a veiled reference to R' Bana'ah himself.]

32. [Thus, his release from prison was obtained.]

33. The inscription had been placed there for the edification of visitors to the courtyard (*Rashbam*).

34. Since [the charges brought against him indicate that] he seeks illicit wealth, he is suspect to accept bribes and pervert justice (*Rashbam*).

למדורה וקדרות מקיפות אותה מטה של תלמידי חכמים כיצד כל שאין תחתיה אלא סנדלין בימות החמה ומנעלין בימות הגשמים ושל עם הארץ דומה לאוצר בלום: ר' בנאה הוה קא מציין מערתא כי מטא למערתא דאברהם אשכחיה לאליעזר עבד אברהם דקאי קמי בבא א"ל מאי קא עביד אברהם א"ל גאני בכנפה דשרה וקא מעיינא ליה ברישיה א"ל זיל אימא ליה בנאה קאי אבבא א"ל ליעול מידע ידיע דיצר בהאי עלמא ליכא עייל עיין ונפק כי מטא למערתא דאדם הראשון יצתה בת קול ואמרה נסתכלת בדמות דיוקני בדיוקני עצמה אל תסתכל הא בעינא לציוני מערתא כמדת החיצונה כך מדת הפנימית ולמ"ד [א] שני בתים זו למעלה מזו כמדת עליונה כך מדת התחתונה א"ר בנאה נסתכלתי בשני עקיביו ודומים לשני גלגלי חמה הכל בפני שרה כקוף בפני אדם שרה בפני חוה כקוף בפני אדם חוה בפני אדם כקוף בפני אדם אדם בפני שכינה כקוף בפני אדם [ג] שופריה דרב כהנא [ג] (מעין שופריה דרב שופריה דרב) מעין שופריה דרבי אבהו שופריה דר' אבהו מעין שופריה דיעקב אבינו שופריה דיעקב אבינו מעין שופריה דאדם הראשון ההוא אמגושא דהוה חטיט שכבי כי מטא אמערתא דרב טובי בר מתנה תפשיה (א) בדיקניה אתא אביי א"ל במטותא מינך שבקיה לשנה אחריתי הדר אתא תפשיה בדיקניה אתא אביי לא שבקיה עד דאייתי מספרא וגזיא לדיקניה ההוא דאמר להו חביתא דעפרא לחד בראי חביתא דגרמי לחד בראי חביתא [ז] דאודרא לחד בראי לא הוו ידעי מאי קאמר להו אתו לקמיה דרבי בנאה אמר להו אית לכו ארעא אמרו ליה אין אית לכו חיותא (ב) אין אית לכו בסתרקי אין אי הכי הכי קאמר לכו ההוא גברא דשמעה לדביתהו דקא אמרה לברתה אמאי לא צניעת באיסורא הך איתתא עשרה בני אית לה ולית לי מאבוך אלא חד כי שכיב אמר להו כל נכסי לחד ברא לא ידעי להי מינייהו אתו לקמיה דרבי בנאה אמר להו זילו [*] חבוטו קברא דאבוכון עד דקאי ומגלי לכו להי מינייכו שבקא אזלו כולהו ההוא דבריה הוה לא אזל אמר להו כולהו נכסי דהאי אזלו אכלו קורצא בי מלכא אמרי איכא גברא חד ביהודאי דקא מפיק ממונא מאנשי בלא סהדי ובלא (ג) מידי אתיוהו חבשוהו אזלא דביתהו אמרה להו עבדא חד הוה לי פסקו לרישיה ופשטו למשכיה ואכלו בישריה וקא מלו ביה מיא ומשקו ביה לחברייא ולא קא יהבי לי דמי ולא אגריה לא ידעי מאי קא אמרה להו אמרי ניתו לחכימא דיהודאי ולימא קריוהו לר' בנאה אמר להו זרנוקא אמרה לכו אמרי הואיל וחכים כולי האי ליתיב אבבא ונידון דינא חזא דהוה כתיב באבולא כל דיין דמתקרי לדין לא שמיה דיין אמר להו אלא מעתה אתא איניש מעלמא ומזמין

מציין מערתא. משום (ד) דקבר סתום טומאה בוקעת ועולה כדאמר בכמה דוכתי וא"ת והא אין קברי עובדי כוכבים מטמאים באהל משום דאין קרויין אדם ואפילו רבנן דפליגי אר' שמעון (יבמות סא.) ואמרי דמטמאים באהל מ"מ בקבר שלפני הדיבור לא מרבה לה בנזיר (דף נד.) אלא לענין נגיעה או בקבר לרבות קבר שלפני הדיבור ומקרא דכתב גבי נגיעה מרבי לה התם ויש לומר דאברהם נקרא אדם דכתיב האדם הגדול וכן אדם הראשון ולהכי אין למעטם מקרא דאדם [וע"ע תוס' יבמות סא. ד"ה קברי]:

למדורה. שמוקפת קדירות והאש באמצע אף כאן המטה והכלים באמצע והקערות סביב: **כל שאין תחתיה כו'.** דאמרינן בפסחים (דף קיב.) אוכלין תחת המטה אפי' מחופין בכלי ברזל רוח רעה שורה עליהן: דרך לנעול מנעלין בימות החמה וסנדלים בימות הגשמים בשביל הטיט: **אלא סנדלים בימות החמה.** שמניחים שם עד ימות הגשמים שילבשו להם: **לאוצר בלום.** בסמ"ך כמו עיסה בלוסה במסכת שבת בפרק כלל גדול (דף עו:) עיסה מעורבת ממינין הרבה וכן אוצר בלוס (גיטין דף סז.) מינין הרבה מעורבין בתוכה ביחד וכן מיטת עם הארץ כל דבר מניחין תחת מטתן אוכלין וכלים: **רבי בנאה.** אדם גדול וחשוב היה לפיכך ניתן לו רשות ליכנס בקברי צדיקים אבל אחר לא כדאמרי' (חולין דף ז:) גדולים צדיקים במיתתן יותר מבחייהן והיה נכנס במערות ומודד מדת ארכן מבפנים ואח"כ מודד מבחוץ כנגדן ועשה שם ציון סיד כדי להכיר מקום הטומאה ולא יביאו טהרות דרך כאן שלא יאהיל על הקבר: **אשכחיה לאליעזר.** דתניא במסכת דרך ארץ דשבעה צדיקים קיימין שלא מתו וקא חשיב בהדייהו אליעזר עבד אברהם: **בכנפה.** בין זרועותיה: **א"ל.** רבי בנאה לאליעזר: **זיל אימא ליה.** לאברהם: **בנאה קאי אבבא.** ותן לו רשות ליכנס: **אמר ליה ליעול.** דאין כאן חולפא דאיגנינא באנפיה בכנפה דשרה: **דמידע ידיע דיצר הרע בהאי עלמא ליכא.** ולא צריכנא לאיטנועי מיניה: ה"ג **על עיין ונפיק.** נכנס ר' בנאה ונסתכל מדת אורך המערה ויצא ואח"כ ציין מבחוץ: **למערתא דאדם הראשון.** כדדרשינן בעירובין (דף נג.) ממרא קרית ארבע א"ר יצחק קרית ארבע זוגות אדם וחוה אברהם ושרה יצחק ורבקה יעקב ולאה: **בדמות דיוקני.** יעקב דאמרינן בסמוך שופריה דיעקב מעין שופריה דאדם הראשון: **בדיוקני עצמה.** דהיינו אדם הראשון דכתיב ביה (בראשית א) בצלם אלהים ברא אותו: **הא בעינא לציוני.** מבחוץ ולפיכך צריך אני למדוד תחלה מבפנים: **כמדת החיצונה.** שבה ג' אבות ואמהות כך מדת הפנימית וכמאן דדריש מכפלה שני בתים זה לפנים מזה ופלוגתא היא בכילד מעברין (עירובין דף נג.): **כך מדת התחתונה.** ודי לך בציון עליונה: **בשני עקיביו של אדם הראשון כו'.** והאי דכתיב כי עפר אתה ואל עפר תשוב הא פרכינן ליה במסכת שבת בפרק שואל (דף קנב:) ומוקמינן לה ההוא שעה אחת קודם תחיית המתים: **שופריה דר' אבהו מעין שופריה דיעקב.** ובהשוכר את הפועלים פריך וליחשוב נמי ר' יוחנן ומשני הדרת פנים לא הויא ליה: **אמגושא.** מכשף: **חטיט שכבי.** חופר המתים להפשיטם בגדיהם: **אתא אביי כו'.** בשביל שהיה העובד כוכבים אוהבו: **ההוא דאמר להו.** מלוה מחמת מיתה היה ומחלק נכסיו לבניו על פיו: **חביתא דעפרא.** אני מניח לאחד מבני ודרך חכמה אמר שלא ידעו הכל שהוא עשיר ובעל נכסים: **חביתא דגרמי.** חבית מלא עצמות: **אודרא.** מוכין: **אית לכו ארעא.** נשתייר לכם קרקע מאביכם דאם כן היינו חביתא דעפרא והבהמות שיש בהן עצמות זהו חביתא דגרמי: **בוסתרקי.** כל מיני בגדים עשויין ממוכין: **לחד ברא.** לאחד מבני אותו שיבררו בית דין: **חבוטו.** הכו הכאות על קברו ולנסותן נתכוין שאותן שהן ממזרים הן עזי פנים וילכו לחבוט: **אמר להו כולהו נכסי דהאי.** שלא רצה לחבוט על קברו של אביו שזה הוא הצנוע שבכם א] ומסתברא דלזה אהב יותר ויפה דן רבי בנאה דלא שייך הכא אלא שודא דדייני והיינו שודא שלא רצה לחבוט והכי נמי אמרינן גבי ההוא דאמר נכסי לטוביה כו' (כתובות דף פה:): **אזלו.** תשעה האחין: **אכלו ביה קורצא.** הלשינו עליו: **אזלא דביתהו.** דרבי בנאה לצעוק אל בית המלך בלשון חכמה כדי שלא יבינו הם אלא על ידי בעלה: של עבד: **וקמלו ביה מיא.** שואבים בו מים בעורו ומשקו ביה בעורו לחברייא לבני הישיבה: **לחכימא דיהודאי.** לרבי בנאה: **זרנוקא.** נוד של עור וכך אמרה תייש הוה לי וגזלוהו ממני ושחטוהו ואכלו את הבשר ומן העור עשו חמת ושואבין בו מים ושותין בו: **באבולא.** על דלתות השער היה כתוב כדי שילמדו מהם בני אדם: **כל דיין.** המיוחד לדון דיני העיר וזימנין דמיתקרי לדינא שתובעין אותו לדין על ממון שתובעין ממנו: **לא שמיה דיין.** ופסול לדון דכיון דאוהב בצע הוא יקבל שוחד:

ומזמין

רבינו גרשום

למדורה. שיושבין סביבה **קדרות** כך מניח גלוי מכאן ומכאן **ומקיף** קערות סביב המפה: **כל שאין תחתיה אלא סנדלין בימות החמה.** לפי שבימות החמה שאין טיט נועלין מנעלין ומשמרין הסנדלין עד לימות הגשמים ואותן סנדלין יהיו מונחין תחתיהן בימות החמה ולא יותר. וכן **בימות הגשמים** [משמרין] **המנעלים** לפי שאסור להניח אוכלין ומשקין וכלים אחרים תחת המטה מפני שרוח רעה שורה עליהן: **ושל ע"ה.** שאינו מקפיד מניח הכל תחת מטתו **ודומה לאוצר בלום** כאוצר המאכל שמניחין בו רוב מינין: **הוה מציין מערתא** (אתא) היה נכנס במערה ומדד ארכה ורחבה וכמה מקום תפיסת הכוכין שבתוכה והיה יוצא חוץ על גבה מן הפתח ומכוין באיזה מקום מונחין הקברים בתוכה ומציין אותו מקום שלא יכנסו שם כהנים ויאכלו טהרות מפני שטומאה בוקעת ועולה ושאר מקום המערה שלא היו הקברים כנגדה מותר לעבור על גבה: **דיצר בהאי עלמא ליכא.** דאינו צריך להניח מפני שרה שלא יכנס: **בדמות דיוקני.** שדמותו של אברהם כדמות אדם הראשון: **בדיוקני עצמה.** של אדם הראשון. **אל תסתכל** שנברא בצלם של מעלה: א"ר בנאה **והא בעינא** ליכנס למערה שלו בשביל **לציין:** אמרה לו בת קול אין את צריך **כמדת החיצונה** שאברהם מונח בה **כך מדת הפנימית** של אדם לפי שאברהם האדם הגדול כאדם הראשון. **ולמ"ד** דמערת המכפלה שהיתה כפולה **בית ועליה** היו הכי קאמרי לר' בנאה **כמדת העליונה** ששם אברהם **כך מדת התחתונה** ששם אדם הראשון: **דאודרי.** דבר העשוי ממוכין צמר שגוררין מן הבגדים: **בסתרקי.** כרים וכסתות ומצעות עשוין מאודרין: **באיסורא.** דזנות: **אזלא דביתהו** לבי מלכא **אמרה להו עבדא הוי לי וכו'.** **אמר להו זרנוקא.** עבדא היינו בהמה ששחטו אותה ופסקו ראשה והפשיטו העור שלה ועשו ממנו נוד לשאוב בו מים מן הבור: **הואיל וחכים כולי האי ליתיב אבבא.** דחצר המלך: **באבולא.** על גב השער.

מסורת הש"ס

א) [עירובין נג.], ב) ב"מ פד., ג) ב"מ ל"ג, ד) [גי' הערוך דאודרא פי' עלה]:

הגהות הב"ח

(א) גמ' דרב טובי בר מתנה תפשיה אתא אביי כצ"ל ותיבת בדיקניה נמחק: (ב) שם אית לכו חיותא א"ל אין אית לכו בסתרקי א"ל אין: (ג) שם בלא סהדי ובלא ראיה אתיוהו: (ד) תוס' ד"ה מציין מערתא משום דקא סבר טומאה רצוצה בוקעת ועולה:

גליון הש"ס

גמרא חבוטו קיברא. עיין אליה רבה א"ח סימן תקפט ס"ק ט"ו:

הגהות מהר"ב רנשבורג

א] רשב"ם ד"ה אמר להו כלהו נכסי דהאי כו' ומסתברא דלזה אהב יותר. נ"ב עי' בינה לעתים דרוש ברלין חלק ב' דרוש כ"ב דף לג ע"א ד"ה ההוא גברא כו'. יעוש"ה ודו"ק:

ליקוטי רש"י

כל שאין תחתיה אלא סנדלין בימות החמה וכו'. איזהו מטה של תלמידי חכמים כל שאין תחתיה אלא מנעלים של בעל הבית בימות החמה וסנדלים בימות הגשמים שמניחים שם כשהולך בא לשכב וליכין הולך במנעליו ונותנן תחת מטתו אבל לא תחת מטתה דברים אחרים דגנאי הוא לו שמרגיל בני הבית לשם [סוכה כא.]. **לאוצר בלום.** בלוס. סתום כמו אוצר בלוס [ב"ב נח.] [ר"ן נדרים כה:]. ונראה בעיני אוצר בלוס סגור מקבירות לבלבן מחילות מחילות כמו שעושין בתיבות גדולות ליתן חטין מכאן שעורין מכאן עדשים מכאן כמו פיו בלום ובגלוי מבלומות בבכורות (מ:) [קלוטי"ש בלע"ז] [גיטין סז. ועי' רש"י תוס' ועי' רש"י חולין קו:]. **שופריה.** זיהורי תוארו וקירון [עור] פניו [ב"מ פד.]. **אמגושא.** מכשף [יומא לה. וסנהדרין לט.].

ומזמין (א) להו לדינא פסליה אלא כל דיין דמתקרי לדין ומפקין מיניה ממונא בדין לאו שמיה דיין כתבו הכי ברם סאבי דיהודאי אמרי כל דיין דמתקרי לדין ומפקין מיניה ממונא בדין לאו שמיה דיין חזא (ב) דכתיב בראש כל מותא אנא דם בראש כל חיין אנא חמר אלא מעתה דנפיל מאיגרא ומית ודנפיל מדיקלא ומית דמא קטליה ותו מן דדרכיה למימת משקו ליה חמרא וחיי אלא הכי בעי למכתב בראש כל מרעין אנא דם בראש כל אסוון אנא חמר כתבו הכי ברם סאבי דיהודאי אמרי בראש כל מרעין אנא דם בראש כל אסוון אנא חמר באתר דלית חמר תמן מתבעו סמנין כתיב אפיתחא דקפוטקיא אנפק אנבג אנטל ואיזהו אנטל זהו רביעית של תורה:

מתני' א המרזב אין לו חזקה ויש למקומו חזקה המזחילה יש לה חזקה ב סולם המצרי אין לו חזקה ולצורי יש לו חזקה ג חלון המצרית אין לה חזקה ולצורית יש לה חזקה איזו היא חלון המצרית ד כל שאין ראשו של אדם יכול ליכנס לתוכה רבי יהודה אומר אם יש לה מלבן אף על פי שאין ראשו של אדם יכול ליכנס לתוכה הרי זו חזקה:

גמ' מאי המרזב אין לו חזקה ויש למקומו חזקה אמר רב יהודה אמר שמואל ה הכי קאמר המרזב אין לו חזקה מרוח אחת ויש למקומו חזקה משתי רוחות רבי חנינא אמר המרזב אין לו חזקה ו שאם היה ארוך מקצרו ויש למקומו חזקה שאם בא לעוקרו אינו עוקרו רב ירמיה בר אבא אמר ז המרזב אין לו חזקה שאם רוצה לבנות תחתיו בונה ויש למקומו חזקה שאם בא לעוקרו אינו עוקרו

תנן

ומזמין ליה לדינא. שלא כדין ושלא מן הדין זכאי: **ומפקין מיניה ממונא בדינא לא שמיה דיין.** דגזלן פסול לדין שיעות הדין בשביל שוחד: **בריש כל מותא אנא דם.** ראש לכל המיתות הוא דם שאין אדם מת אלא ע"י רוב דם שלא הקיז דם בזמן הראוי לו: **בריש כל חיין אנא חמר.** שהיין מחיה כל שותיו: **דדרכיה למימת.** כגון גוסס: **בריש כל מרעין אנא דם.** כל תחלואי האדם על הדם הם שמתרבה עליו: **בריש כל אסוון אנא חמר.** שאם ישתה יין כהלכה וכראוי לא יבא לידי חולי: **תמן מתבען סממנין.** שם מבקשין סממנים לרפואה שבמקום שאין יין מצויין תחלואין: **כתיב אפיתחא דקפוטקיא.** מילתא באנפי נפשה היא ואגב גררא נקטה וללמוד בני העיר מהם כתבו שלשה שמות הללו מדה אחת הן ונפקא מינה למקח וממכר שאם התנה למכור לחבירו מלא מדה זו באיזה לשון שיאמר יתן שיעור אחד ומקומות מקומות יש שקורין אנפק או אנטל או אנבג וכדאמר בקדושין (דף ע.) לישתי מר אנבגא א"ל מי סני מר אספרגוס כדאמרי אינשי או אנטל כדקריוהו רבנן: **ואיזהו אנטל** [ג]. גמרא קאמר ליה כלומר ואיזהו שיעורו של אנטל: **רביעית של תורה.** רביעית הלוג דהיינו ביצה ומחצה ומשום דארבעה כוסות של פסח שיעורן ברביעית ומלאו להן חכמים סמך מן התורה מד' כוסות האמורים במצרים מד' לשוני גאולה האמורים בפ' והוצאתי (ג והצלתי ולקחתי והבאתי) לפיכך קרי ליה רביעית של תורה וכן רביעית של יין לנזיר הלכה למשה מסיני ובמסכת נזיר (דף לח.) חשיב עשר רביעית הן שמן התורה שיעורן בכך רביעית והכי נמי אמרינן (חולין דף קז.) דשיעור אנטל היינו רביעית דאתקין ר' יעקב מנהר פקוד נטלא בת רביעתא: **מתני' המרזב.** צינור קטן ורגילין לתלותו לסוף צינור גדול ההולך על פני כל הגג ורגילין להפכו לכל ראש שירצו ומרחיק קילוח מים מן הכותל ולשון מרזב טפה של מים זו דרך שם כדכתיב (ישעיה מ) כמר מדלי לשון טפה והלכך אין לו חזקה דאינו דבר קבוע ואם החזיק בו בעל הגג ג' שנים ותלה אותו באויר חצר חבירו אינו יכול לטעון החזקתי דכיון דלאו מילתא דקביעותא הוא לא קפיד בעל חצר ושתיק שנתים ושלש: **אבל יש למקומו חזקה.** בגמ' מפרש לה: **המזחילה.** הוא צינור הגדול מחזיק כל אורך הגג ומילתא דקביעות הוא הלכך יש לו חזקה דלא עביד איניש דשתיק אלא קפיד ומדשתיק איכא למימר הדין עם המחזיק דודאי נתרצה [ד] עלמו בדמים: **סולם המצרי.** קטן הוא הלכך אין לו חזקה דכיון דלאו מילתא דקביעותא הוא לא קפיד ולא חש למחות והלכך אם נתן סולמו בחצר חבירו לעלות לגגו ולשובכו אינה חזקה: **ולצורי.** סולם גדול: **חלון המצרית.** קטנה היא אין לה חזקה אם עשה חלון בכותל ביתו להביט דרך שם ולשמור פרדסו וגינתו והחלון פתוח לחצר חבירו והחזיק בה שלש שנים אינה חזקה דכיון דלאו מילתא דקביעותא הוא לא חש למחות אבל אם עשאו להאיר שלא היה לו אורה מצד אחר כי אם מכאן יש לו חזקה דלשם קביעות עשאו דאינו יכול להשתמש בביתו בלא אורה וכל מידי דקביעות הוי חזקה והכי אמר שמואל בגמ' ולאורה אפילו כל שהוא הוי חזקה: **מלבן.** הוא משקוף החלון מלמעלה ולמטה מימין ומשמאל כעין פתח: **גמ' אין לו חזקה מרוח אחת.** אם המרזב מונח בראש דרומי של מזחילה ושופך שם מים והחזיק בו ג' שנים אינה חזקה ואם צריך בעל חצר להשתמש שם צריך זה לעקור מרזבו מכאן ולהניח בראש השני של מזחילה דאין בעל הגג מפסיד בכך כלום והלכך אין כאן קביעות להיות מונח לעולמים לרוח זה והלכך לא חש בעל חצר למחות: **אבל יש למקומו חזקה.** באחת משתי רוחות או לפוני או דרומי שאם יעקרנו מצד זה יניחו בצד אחר ואין בעל חצר יכול לעקרו לגמרי מן החצר שהרי החזיק מיהא בתוך החצר דלגבי אחת משתי רוחות הוי מרזב מילתא דקביעותא דסתם בית אי אפשר בלא מרזב וכשעשה זה מרזב בתחלה בחצר לשם קביעות עשאו והיה לו לבעל החצר למחות בתוך שלש ומדלא מיחה הפסיד: **שאם היה ארוך.** יותר מכדי צרכו ותופס באויר חצר הרבה מקצרו והיינו אין לו חזקה לארכו אבל יש למקומו שהוא מונח שם חזקה דלא יעקרנו ממקומו כלל אפילו מצד זה לצד אחר אלא באותו רוח שהחזיק ובאותו מקום הויא חזקה: **שאם רוצה.** בעל החצר לבנות תחתיו בונה בנינו עד שמגיע למרזב ולא מצי טעין בעל הגג כי היכי דאחזיקי במקום המרזב אחזיקי נמי במה שתחתיו שאם נותן רשות לתלות מרזבו באויר לא נתן לו קרקע שלו שתחת המרזב ולא שעבדו לו לבלתי עשות בו צרכיו בין בנין בין כל דבר הצריך לו אבל אם בא לעקרו ולהגביה בנינו במקום שהיה המרזב אינו יכול לעקרו דלמקומו מיהא יש לו חזקה:

תנן

כל דיין דמתקרי לדינא ומפקי מיניה כו'. כגון אם כפר והוציאו ממנו בעדים אבל אם חייבוהו שבועה ולא רצה לישבע ושילם משום הכי לא מיפסל לדינא: **אנבג אנפק אנטל.** אומר הר"ר חיים דאנבג ואנפק הם משקים דרפואה והיינו אספרגוס דאמר (ה) בפ' כל הבשר (חולין דף קי וסם) אנפקא אספרגוס שיפה ללב כדמשמע בפרק עשרה יוחסין (קדושין דף ע.) וה"ק הכא מה שקורין אנבג ואנפק צריך לשתותו כשיעור אנטל שהוא רביעית והיינו דאמר בפרק גיד הנשה (חולין דף לד. וסם) אנפקא חייא משמע שהוא אספרגוס כדאמר בברכות דאספרגוס אין שותין אלא מי והא דלא חשיב בברכות (דף נא. ע"ש) גבי ה' דברים שנאמרו באספרגוס שצריך לשתותו כשיעור רביעית משום שאינו חושש לחשוב מה שתלוי בשיעור והא דאמר בפרק שמונה שרצים (שבת דף קט:) (ו) וליסקליה עד דקאי אאנפקא משמע דהוא מדה י"ל עד דקאי אשיעור (ז) שתיה אנפקא קאמר אי נמי כלי נמי קרי אנפקא על שם ששותים אותו באותו שיעור: **המרזב אין לו חזקה מרוח אחת.** פי' שאם הוא במזרח יכול לומר לו תנהו במערב אבל לסלקו לגמרי מב' רוחות לא ותימה דמזחילה היאך יש לה חזקה והלא כשמניח המרזב בראש אחד של המזחילה גם המזחילה צריך לזוזה ולהגביה ראש אחד ולהנמיך ראש האחר שנותן שם המרזב והיכי קאמר דמרזב אין לו חזקה והמזחילה יש לה חזקה והלא לעולם לא יזיז המרזב אם לא יזיז גם המזחילה וי"ל דמ"מ יש לה חזקה לענין שאין צריך לעוקרה לגמרי ממקומה כמו שצריך לעקור המרזב אי נמי כגון שהמזחילה שוה ואין גבוה צד זה יותר מצד זה דהשתא לעולם אין צריך לזוזה ממקומה אלא לסתום לצד שמסיר ממנו המרזב וה"ר יוסף פירש דמרזב שאין לו חזקה מרוח אחת שיוכל להטות ראש המרזב לצד צפון או לצד דרום כשהוא מונח במזרח יש לו חזקה משתי רוחות שאין יכול לדוחקו להסיר לראש לצד אחד של מזחילה וכענין זה פירש רבינו חננאל שאם המרזב קבוע באמצע רוח מזרחי יכול בעל החצר לעקרו מן האמצע ולקבעו בשליש הגג או ברביע ובכל אותה רוח בכל מקום שירצה אבל לרוח אחרת אין יכול לסלקו לפי שיש לו חזקה:

במזחילה

עין משפט נר מצוה

רסו א מיי' פ"ח מהל' שכנים הל' ה סמג עשין פב טוש"ע ח"מ סי' קנג סעיף ו:
רסז ב מיי' שם הל' ד טוש"ע שם סעיף יג:
רסח ג ד מיי' שם פ"ז הל' ז סמג שם טוש"ע ח"מ סי' קנד סעיף י:
רסט ה ו מיי' שם פ"ח הל' ה ועי' בהשגות ובמ"מ סמג שם טוש"ע ח"מ סי' קנג סעיף ז:
ער ז מיי' שם טוש"ע שם סעיף ח:

רבינו גרשום

בראש כל מותא אנא דם. מי שאחזו הדם שאינו מקיז מסתכן ומת. כלומר דכל מיתות מחמת דם הן: **אלא בריש כל מרעין.** עיקר חולי מחמת רוב דמין באין. ועיקר רפואה היא חמרא: **אנבג אנפק אנטל.** כלומר אותו כלי אספרגוס ששותין בשחרית משום רפואה היו קורין אותו בלשונם אנפק והיינו אנבג והיינו אנטל כלומר שיעורו באותו כלי שנוטלין ממנו לידים. ושיעורו **כרביעית של תורה** ביצה ומחצה: **פיסקא המרזב אין לו חזקה.** היינו צינור קטן כמו שתים או שלש אמות שתולין אותו בסוף צינור גדול כדי שיקלחו מימיו ברחוק מן הכותל. וכשתולי' בסוף הצינור גדול (רגליו) יכולין להחזירו לאותו מרזב לקלח מימיו או לימין או לשמאל: **ויש למקומו חזקה.** מפרש בגמ' מאי קאמר הכי קאמר **אין לו חזקה** בחצר אם שופכין מימיו לחצר חבירו אם הוא נטוי תדיר **לצד אחד** דאיכא למימר הואיל ואין לו רשות להטותו לאיזה צד שירצה ברשות בעל חצר בעה"ב תלוהו שם ואימתי שירצה יכול לעכב עליו: **ויש לו למקומו חזקה מב' רוחות.** כלומר ואם בעל המרזב מחזירו פעמים לצד זה ופעמים לצד זה ברור שיש לו למקומו לשפיכת מימיו חזקה בחצר. איכא דאמר **אין לו חזקה** בחצר **מרוח אחת.** כשלא תלה אלא מרזב אחד בראש אחד של צינור אבל תלה שני מרזבין משני ראשין והחזירן לחצר היינו משתי רוחותיו **ויש למקומו חזקה.** ור' חנינא מתרץ למתני' אין לו חזקה שיכול בעל חצר לקצר למרזב: **שאם בא לבנות.** בנין תחת המרזב בונה ומקבל מימיו כמה שרוצה: **ויש למקומו חזקה.** שאם בא לעקור ולהגביה בנינו ולעקרו למרזב אינו רשאי: המזחילה

מסורת הש"ס

א) [צ"ל ליה], ב) עי' בר"מ מכשירין פ"ו מ"ב וכר"ן סוף עירובין ד"ה בור הגולה, ג) [צ"ל והצלתי וגאלתי ולקחתי וכ"ה במדרש רבה פרשה פ"ח ועי' רש"י פסחים קט:], ד) [צ"ל עמון], ה) [צ"ל בברכות נא.], ו) [צ"ל ונישלוקינהו], ז) [צ"ל שתיית].

הגהות הב"ח

(א) גמ' חזא דהוה כתיב בראש:

ליקוטי רש"י

אנפק. והוא רביעית הלוג [שבת קט:]. כוס של רביעית ולשון אנפק היה שגור בפיהם. **אנבג.** כוס שהוא רביעית [קידושין ע.]. **המזחילה.** מזחילה הוא צינור גדול כעין קנקל"א שלנו ומונחת לאורך הכותל על הכותל ומי הגג זבין לתוכה והיא מקלחתם לחצר [לעיל כב:]. גגין שלהן חלקים היו וטחים בטיט ומרזבין קטנים הרבה היו בגג להוליך המים ומוקמין למטה מהם דף כנגד אורך הכותל בשיפוע וכל המרזבין שופכין עליו והוא מוליך כל המים ויוקו למקום אחד שלא יזיקו את הכותל [עירובין צה:].

וּמַזְמִין (להו) [לֵיהּ] לְדִינָא – and summons [a judge] to court with some spurious claim, **פַּסְלֵיהּ – will he have disqualifed [the judge]** even though the judge is found not liable for the claims brought against him?"[1] **אֶלָּא – Rather,** R' Bana'ah recommended, the aphorism should read as follows: **כָּל דַּיָּין דְּמִתְקְרֵי לְדִין – "Any judge who is summoned to court** to answer charges **וּמַפְּקִין מִינֵּיהּ מָמוֹנָא בְּדִין – and money is exacted from him in judgment לָאו שְׁמֵיהּ דַּיָּין – cannot be called a judge"** and he is unfit to continue in that role.[2]

The judges accepted R' Bana'ah's recommendation: **כָּתְבוּ הָכִי – [They] wrote the following** addendum to the inscription on the doors: **בְּרַם סָאבֵי דִיהוּדָאֵי אָמְרֵי – "However, the** wise **elders of the Jews say: כָּל דַּיָּין דְּמִתְקְרֵי לְדִין – Any judge who is summoned to court וּמַפְּקִין מִינֵּיהּ מָמוֹנָא בְּדִין – and money is exacted from him in judgment לָאו שְׁמֵיהּ דַּיָּין – cannot be called a judge."**

R' Bana'ah noticed another inscription:

חֲזָא דִּכְתִיב – He further **saw that it was inscribed** on the doors to the court: **בְּרֹאשׁ כָּל מוֹתָא אֲנָא דָם – "At the head of all death am I, blood;**[3] **בְּרֹאשׁ כָּל חַיִּין אֲנָא חֲמַר – at the head of all life am I, wine."**[4]

R' Bana'ah objected to this aphorism as well:

אֶלָּא מֵעַתָּה דְּנָפִיל מֵאִיגְרָא וּמִית – But now, one who falls from a roof and dies, וּדְנָפִיל מִדִּיקְלָא וּמִית – or one who falls from a palm tree and dies, דָּמָא קַטְלֵיהּ – has a surplus of **blood killed him? וְתוּ – And furthermore, מַן דְּדַרְבֵּיהּ לְמֵימַת – one who is about to die, מַשְׁקוּ לֵיהּ חַמְרָא וְחַיֵּי – do they give him wine to drink and vivify him?** Obviously, then, blood and wine do not control life and death!

R' Bana'ah again suggested a revised version of the aphorism: **אֶלָּא הָכִי בָּעֵי לְמִכְתַּב – Rather, this is what should be inscribed** upon the doors: **בְּרֹאשׁ כָּל מַרְעִין אֲנָא דָם – "At the head of all illness am I, blood;**[5] **בְּרֹאשׁ כָּל אַסְוָון אֲנָא חֲמַר – at the head of all cures**[6] **am I, wine."**

The judges concurred:

כָּתְבוּ הָכִי – They wrote the following addendum to the inscription upon the doors: **בְּרַם סָאבֵי דִיהוּדָאֵי אָמְרֵי – "However,** the wise **elders of the Jews say: בְּרֹאשׁ כָּל מַרְעִין אֲנָא דָם – At the head of all illnesses am I, blood; בְּרֹאשׁ כָּל אַסְוָון אֲנָא חֲמַר – at the head of all cures am I, wine. בַּאֲתַר דְּלֵית חֲמַר – In a place where there is no wine, תַּמָּן מִתְבָּעוּ סַמָּנִין – there** medicinal **herbs will be required** to cure diseases."[7]

The Gemara mentions another aphorism that was inscribed on an entranceway:

כְּתִיב אַפִּיתְחָא דְקַפּוּטְקַיָא – [The following] was inscribed on **the entrance of Kaputkaya:**[8] **אַנְפַּק אַנְבַּג אַנְטַל – *"Anpak anbag antal."*** The purpose of this inscription was to teach that the three units of measure known by these names were in fact identical in size.[9]

The Gemara provides the known equivalent of these measures:

וְאֵיזֶהוּ אַנְטַל – And what is the volume of **an *antal*? זֶהוּ רְבִיעִית שֶׁל תּוֹרָה – It is the *reviis* required by the Torah.**[10]

Mishnah

The Mishnah continues the delineation, begun in the previous Mishnah, of which usages establish *chazakah:*[11]

הַמַּרְזֵב – A drainspout[12] **אֵין לוֹ חֲזָקָה – has no *chazakah*,**[13] **וְיֵשׁ לִמְקוֹמוֹ חֲזָקָה – but its place has a *chazakah*.**[14] **הַמַּזְחִילָה יֵשׁ לָהּ חֲזָקָה – A gutter,**[15] however, **does have a *chazakah*.**[16] **סוּלָּם הַמִּצְרִי אֵין לוֹ חֲזָקָה – An Egyptian ladder has no *chazakah*.**[17] **וְלַצּוֹרִי יֵשׁ לוֹ חֲזָקָה – But a Tyrean** ladder **does**

NOTES

1. This would not be logical, for accordingly, any person wishing to destroy a judge's career could simply bring some spurious claim against him and thereby disqualify him! Obviously, merely being sued in court should not undermine a judge's reputation.

2. The judge has been convicted of financial improprieties. He is thus unfit to judge, as he may accept a bribe to pervert justice (*Rashbam*).

3. I.e. the chief cause of death is a surplus of blood in the body, caused by a failure to have blood let in a timely fashion (see *Rashbam*).

4. I.e. the chief life-giving substance is wine, which vitalizes all who drink it (*Rashbam*).

5. I.e. most diseases can be traced to a surplus of blood in the body. [Physical injury, however, obviously cannot be attributed to a surplus of blood] (*Rashbam*; cf. *Maharsha*, who explains the Gemara as referring to psychological disorders).

6. I.e. wine is the ultimate preventive medicine, as proper consumption of wine ensures good health (*Rashbam*).

7. This was added to the inscription, to clarify that wine is a preventive medicine.

8. Cappadocia, an ancient country in the eastern end of the peninsula of Asia Minor, included in modern-day Turkey (*Mosaf HaAruch* ד״ה קפודקיא).

9. *Rashbam*; cf. *Tosafos*.

10. I.e. the "quarter" of a *log* which is the minimum volume of liquid for certain Biblical laws, such as the amount of wine for whose consumption a *nazir* incurs lashes and the amount of wine needed for each of the four cups of wine that are drunk on the night of Passover. (Although the requirement of the four cups is actually a Rabbinic enactment, it is called "required by the Torah" since the Rabbis tied their requirement to drink the four cups to the four expressions of redemption found in the verses describing the exodus from Egypt.) A *reviis* is equal to the volume of one-and-a-half average chicken eggs (*Rashbam*; see also *Nazir* 38a).

11. The previous Mishnah was explained by the Gemara (57b) as referring to a jointly owned courtyard, with the activities described in the Mishnah being performed by one of the owners. This Mishnah, however, refers to two neighbors, with one neighbor creating a situation that affects the other neighbor. The Mishnah discusses whether the continual existence of these situations for three years without protest establishes a *chazakah*, which would allow their further continuation.

12. I.e. a leader; the pipe at the end of a gutter through which the water flows to the ground.

13. The Mishnah speaks of a case where the homeowner placed the drainspout on his roof in such a way that it projected over his neighbor's courtyard [and water ran through it into his neighbor's courtyard] (*Rashbam*).

Generally speaking, in Talmudic times, a drainspout was not permanently fixed in place; rather, it was constructed so that it could easily be moved. Therefore, the neighbor might tolerate its presence even for several years (*Rashbam*). Thus, the neighbor's silence for three years does not create a *chazakah*.

14. The Gemara explains the meaning of this.

15. I.e. the pipe which runs along the entire length of the roof and collects rainwater that drips from the roof.

16. A gutter is generally a permanent fixture; thus, if one is put in place and remains there for three years without any protest from the neighbor, it can be assumed that the gutter's owner had paid for the right to project his gutter over his neighbor's courtyard. [Otherwise, the neighbor would surely have protested] (*Rashbam*).

17. An Egyptian ladder is defined in the Gemara below (59a) as a small ladder which was three rungs or less. Such a ladder is portable; therefore, if one placed it in his neighbor's courtyard in order to climb up to a low roof or dovecote, that does not establish a *chazakah* which allows him to continue to keep it there. The reason is that since the ladder can be removed easily, the neighbor might tolerate its presence

כל דיין דמתקרי לדינא ומפקי מיניה כו׳. כגון אם כפר והוליאו ממנו בעדים אבל אם חייבוהו שבועה ולא רלה לישבע ושילם משום הכי לא מיפסל לדינא: **אנבג אנפק אנטל.** אומר הר״ר חיים דאנבג ואנפק הם משקים דרפואה והיינו אספרגוס דאמר (ט) בפ׳ כל הבשר (חולין דף קי ושם) אנפק אספרגוס שיפה ללב כדמשמע בפרק עשרה יוחסין (קדושין דף ע.) וה״ק הכא מה שקורין אנבג ואנפק צריך לשתותו כשיעור רביעית אנטל שהוא רביעית והיינו דאמר בפרק גיד הנשה (חולין דף לב. ושם) אנפקא חייא משמע שהוא אספרגוס כדאמר בברכות דאספרגוס אין שותין אלא מי והא דלא חשיב בברכות (דף נא. ע״ש) גבי י׳ דברים שנאמרו באספרגוס שצריך לשתותו כשיעור רביעית משום שאינו חושש לחשוב מה שתלוי בשיעור והא דאמר בפרק שמנה שרצים (שבת דף קט:) (ו) ולישקליה עד דקאי אאנפקא משמע דהוא מדה י״ל עד דקאי אשיעור (ז) שתיה אנפקא קאמר אי נמי כלי נמי קרי אנפקא על שם ששומים אותו באותו שיעור: **המרזב** אין לו חזקה מרוח אחת. פי׳ שאם הוא במזרח יכול לומר לו תנהו במערב אבל לסלקו לגמרי מב׳ רוחות לא ותימה דמזחילה היאך יש לה חזקה והלא כשמניח המרזב בראש אחר של המזחילה גם המזחילה צריך לזוח ולהגביה ראש אחד ולהנמיך ראש האחר שנותן שם המרזב והיכי קאמר דמרזב אין לו חזקה והמזחילה יש לה חזקה והלא לעולם לא יזיז המרזב אם לא יזיז גם המזחילה וי״ל דמ״מ יש לה חזקה לענין שאין צריך לעוקרה לגמרי ממקומה כמו שצריך לעקור המרזב אי נמי כגון שהמזחילה שוה ואין גבוה לד זה יותר מלד זה דהשתא לעולם אין צריך לזוחה ממקומה אלא לסתום לצד שמסיר ממנו המרזב וה״ר יוסף פירש דמרזב שאין לו חזקה מרוח אחת שיוכל להטות ראש המרזב לצד צפון או לצד דרום כשהוא מונח במזרח יש לו חזקה משתי רוחות שאין יכול לדוחקו להסיר לראש לצד אחד של מזחילה וכענין זה פירש רבינו חננאל שאם המרזב קבוע באמצע רוח מזרחי יכול בעל החצר לעקרו מן האמצע ולקבעו בשליש הגג או ברביע ובכל אותה רוח בכל מקום שירצה אבל לרוח אחרת אין יכול לסלקו לפי שיש לו חזקה:

ומזמין (א) להו לדינא פסליה אלא כל דיין דמתקרי לדין ומפקין מיניה ממונא בדין לאו שמיה דיין כתבו הכי ברם סאבי דיהודאי אמרי כל דיין דמתקרי לדין ומפקין מיניה ממונא בדין לאו שמיה דיין חזא (א) דכתיב בראש כל מותא אנא דם בראש כל חיין אנא חמר אלא מעתה דנפיל מאיגרא ומית ודנפיל מדיקלא ומית דמא קטליה ותו מן דדרכיה למימת משקו ליה חמרא וחיי אלא הכי בעי למכתב בראש כל מרעין אנא דם בראש כל אסוון אנא חמר כתבו הכי ברם סאבי דיהודאי אמרי בראש כל מרעין אנא דם בראש כל אסוון אנא חמר באתר דלית חמר תמן מתבעו סמנין כתיב אפיתחא דקפוטקיא אנפק אנבג אנטל ואיזהו אנטל זהו רביעית של תורה: **מתני׳** [א] המרזב אין לו חזקה ויש למקומו חזקה המזחילה יש לה חזקה [ב] סולם המצרי אין לו חזקה ולצורי יש לו חזקה [ג] חלון המצרית אין לה חזקה ולצורית יש לה חזקה איזו היא חלון המצרית [ד] כל שאין ראשו של אדם יכול ליכנס לתוכה רבי יהודה אומר אם יש לה מלבן אף על פי שאין ראשו של אדם יכול ליכנס לתוכה הרי זו חזקה: **גמ׳** מאי המרזב אין לו חזקה ויש למקומו חזקה אמר רב יהודה אמר שמואל [ה] הכי קאמר המרזב אין לו חזקה מרוח אחת ויש למקומו חזקה משתי רוחות רבי חנינא אמר המרזב אין לו חזקה [ו] שאם היה ארוך מקצרו ויש למקומו חזקה שאם בא לעוקרו אינו עוקרו רב ירמיה בר אבא אמר [ז] המרזב אין לו חזקה שאם רוצה לבנות תחתיו בונה ויש למקומו חזקה שאם בא לעוקרו אינו עוקרו תנן

ומזמין ליה לדינא. שלא כדין ושלא מן הדין זכאי: ומפקין מיניה ממונא בדינא לא שמיה דיין. דגזלן פסול לדין שיעוות הדין בשביל שוחד: בריש כל מותא אנא דם. ראש לכל המיתות הוא דם שאין אדם מת אלא ע״י רוב דם שלא הקיז בזמן הראוי לו: בריש כל חיין אנא חמר. שהיין מחיה כל שותיו: דדרכיה למימת. כגון גוסס: בריש כל מרעין אנא דם. כל תחלואי האדם על הדם הם שמתרבה עליו: בריש כל אסוון אנא חמר. שאם ישתה יין כהלכה וכראוי לא יבא לידי חולי: תמן מתבעו סמנין. שם מבקשין סממנים לרפואה שבמקום שאין יין מצויין מתחלואין: **כתיב אפיתחא דקפוטקיא.** מילתא באנפי נפשה היא ואגב גררא נסבה וללמוד בני העיר מהם שכתבו שלשה שמות הללו מדה אחת הן ונפקא מינה למקח וממכר שאם התנה למכור לחבירו מלא מדה זו באיזה לשון שיאמר יתן שיעור אחד ומקומות מקומות יש שקורין אנפק או אנטל או אנבג וכדאמר בקדושין (דף ע.) לישתי מר אנבגא א״ל מי סני מר אספרגוס כדאמרי אינשי או אנטל כדקריוהו רבנן: ואיזהו אנטל [ג]. גמרא קאמר ליה כלומר ואיזהו שיעורו של אנטל: **רביעית של תורה.** רביעית הלוג דהיינו ביצה ומחצה ומשום דארבעה כוסות של פסח שיעורן ברביעית ומלאו להן חכמים סמך מן התורה מד׳ כוסות האמורים במצרים מד׳ לשוני גאולה האמורים בפ׳ והוצאתי (ג) וגאלתי ולקחתי והצלתי) לפיכך קרי ליה רביעית של תורה וכן רביעית של יין לנזיר הלכה למשה מסיני ובמסכת נזיר (דף לח.) חשיב עשר רביעית הן שמן התורה שיעורן בכך רביעית והכי נמי אמרינן (חולין דף קז.) דשיעור אנטל היינו רביעית דאתקין ר׳ יעקב מנהר פקוד נטלא בת רביעתא: **מתני׳** המרזב. צינור קטן ורגילין לתלותו לסוף צינור גדול ההולך על פני כל הגג ורגילין להפכו לכל ראש שירצו ומרחיק קילוח מים מן הכותל ולשון מרזב טפה של מים זב דרך שם כדכתיב (ישעיה מ) כמר מדלי לשון טפה והלכך אין לו חזקה דאינו דבר קבוע ואם החזיק בו בעל הגג ג׳ שנים ותלה אותו באויר חצר חבירו אינו יכול לטעון החזקתי דכיון דלאו מילתא דקביעותא הוא לא קפיד בעל חצר ושתיק שנתים ושלש: **אבל יש למקומו חזקה.** במזחילה בגמ׳ מפרש לה: **המזחילה.** הוא צינור הגדול מחזיק כל אורך הגג ומילתא דקביעות הוא הלכך יש לו חזקה דלא עביד איניש דשתיק אלא קפיד ומדשתיק איכא למימר הדין עם המחזיק דודאי נתרצה [ז] עלמו בדמים: **סולם המצרי.** קטן הוא הלכך אין לו חזקה דכיון דלאו מילתא דקביעותא הוא לא קפיד ולא חש למחות והלכך אם נתן סולמו בחצר חבירו לעלות לגגו ולשובכו אינה חזקה: **ולצורי.** סולם גדול: **חלון המצרית.** קטנה היא אין לה חזקה אם עשה חלון בכותל ביתו להביט דרך שם ולשמור פרדסו וגינתו והחלון פתוח לחצר חבירו והחזיק בה שלש שנים אינה חזקה דכיון דלאו מילתא דקביעותא הוא לא חש למחות אבל אם עשאו להאיר שלא היה לו אורה מצד אחר כי אם מכאן יש לו חזקה דלשם קביעות עשאו דאינו יכול להשתמש בביתו בלא אורה וכל מידי דקביעות הוי חזקה והכי אמר שמואל בגמ׳ ולאורה אפילו כל שהוא הוי חזקה: **מלבן.** הוא משקוף החלון מלמעלה ולמטה מימין ומשמאל כעין פתח: **גמ׳ אין לו חזקה מרוח אחת.** אם המרזב מונח בראש דרומי של מזחילה ושופך שם מים והחזיק בו ג׳ שנים אינה חזקה ואם צריך בעל חצר להשתמש שם צריך זה לעקור מרזבו מכאן ולהניח בראש השני של מזחילה דאין בעל הגג מפסיד בכך כלום והלכך אין כאן קביעות להיות מונח לעולמים לרוח זה והלכך לא חש בעל חצר למחות: **אבל יש למקומו חזקה.** באחת משתי רוחות או לפוני או דרומי שאם יעקרנו מצד זה יניחו בצד אחר ואין בעל חצר יכול לעקרו לגמרי מן החצר שהרי החזיק מיהא בתוך החצר דלגבי אחת משתי רוחות הוי מרזב מילתא דקביעותא דסתם בית אי אפשר בלא מרזב וכשעשה זה מרזב בתחלה בחצר לשם קביעות עשאו והיה לו לבעל החצר למחות בתוך שלש ומדלא מיחה הפסיד: **שאם היה ארוך.** יותר מכדי צרכו ותופס באויר חצר הרבה מקצרו והיינו אין לו חזקה לארכו אבל יש למקומו שהוא מונח שם חזקה דלא יעקרנו ממקומו כלל אפילו מצד זה לצד אחר אלא באותו רוח שהחזיק ובאותו מקום הויא חזקה: **שאם רוצה.** בעל החצר לבנות תחתיו בונה בנינו עד שמגיע למרזב ולא מצי טוען בעל הגג כי היכי דאחזיקי במקום המרזב אחזיקי נמי במה שתחתיו שאם נותן רשות לתלות מרזבו באויר לא נתן לו קרקע שלו שתחת המרזב ולא שעבדו לו לבלתי עשות בו צרכיו בין בנין בין כל דבר הצריך לו אבל אם בא לעקרו ולהגביה בנינו במקום שהיה המרזב אינו יכול לעקרו דלמקומו מיהא יש לו חזקה:

תנן

עין משפט נר מצוה

רסו א מיי׳ פ״ח מהל׳ שכנים הל׳ ה סמג עשין פב טוש״ע ח״מ סי׳ קנג סעיף ו:
רסז ב מיי׳ שם הל׳ ד טוש״ע שם סעיף יג:
רסח ג ד מיי׳ שם פ״ז הל׳ ז סמג שם טוש״ע ח״מ סי׳ קנד סעיף י:
רסט ה ו מיי׳ שם פ״ח הל׳ ה ועי׳ בהשגות ובמ״מ סמג שם טוש״ע ח״מ סי׳ קנג סעיף ז:
ער ז מיי׳ שם טוש״ע שם סעיף ח:

רבינו גרשום

בראש כל מותא אנא דם. מי שאחזו הדם שאינו מקיז מסתכן ומת. כלומר דכל מיתות מחמת דם הן: **אלא בריש כל מרעין.** עיקר חולי מחמת רוב דמין באין. ועיקר רפואה היא חמרא: **אנבג אנפק אנטל.** כלומר אותו כלי אספרגוס ששותין בשחרית משום רפואה היו קורין אותו בלשונם אנפק והיינו אנבג והיינו אנטל כלומר שיעורו באותו כלי שנוטלין ממנו לידים. ושיעורו **כרביעית של תורה** ביצה ומחצה: **פיסקא המרזב אין לו חזקה.** היינו צינור קטן כמו שתים או שלש אמות שתולין אותו בסוף צינור גדול כדי שיקלחו מימיו ברחוק מן הכותל. וכשתלוי בסוף הצינור גדול (רגליו) יכולין להחזירו לאותו מרזב לקלח מימיו או לימין או לשמאל: **ויש למקומו חזקה.** מפרש בגמ׳ מאי קאמר הכי קאמר **אין לו חזקה** בחצר אם שופכין מימיו לחצר חבירו אם הוא נטוי תדיר **לצד אחד** דאיכא למימר הואיל ואין לו רשות להטותו לאיזה צד שירצה ברשות בעל חצר בעה״ב תלוהו שם ואימתי שירצה יכול לעכב עליו: **ויש לו למקומו חזקה מב׳ רוחות.** כלומר ואם בעל המרזב מחזירו פעמים לצד זה ופעמים לצד זה ברור שיש לו למקומו לשפיכת מימיו חזקה בחצר. איכא דאמר **אין לו חזקה** בחצר **מרוח אחת.** כשלא תלה אלא מרזב אחד בראש אחד של צינור אבל תלה שני מרזבין משני ראשין והחזירן לחצר היינו **משתי רוחותיו ויש למקומו חזקה. ור׳ חנינא** מתרץ למתני׳ **אין לו חזקה** שיכול בעל חצר **לקצר** למרזב: **שאם בא לבנות.** בנין תחת המרזב בונה ומקבל מימיו כמה שרוצה: **ויש למקומו חזקה. שאם בא לעקור** שאם רוצה להגביה בנינו ולעקרו למרזב אינו רשאי: המזחילה

מסורת הש״ס

א) [צ״ל ליה], ב) עי׳ בר״ש מכשירין פ״ו מ״ב ובר״ן סוף עירובין ד״ה בור הגולה, ג) [צ״ל והצלתי וגאלתי ולקחתי וכ״ה במדרש רבה פרשה פ״ח ועי׳ רש״י פסחים לט:], ד) [צ״ל עמו], ה) [צ״ל בברכות נא.], ו) [צ״ל ונישלוקינהו], ז) [צ״ל שתיית]:

הגהות הב״ח

(א) גמ׳ חזא דהוה כתיב בראש:

ליקוטי רש״י

אנפק. והיא רביעית הלוג [שבת קט:]. כוס של רביעית ולשון אנפק היה שגור בפיהם. **אנבג.** כוס שהוא רביעית [קידושין ע.]. **המזחילה.** מזחילה הוא צינור גדול כעין קנעל״א שלנו ומונחת לאורך הכותל על הכותל ומי הגג זבין לתוכה והיא מקלחתם לארץ [לעיל כב:]. גגין שלהן חלקים היו וטחים בטיט ומרזבין קטנים הרבה היו לגג להוציא המים ונותנין למטה מהם דף כנגד אורך הכותל בשיפוע וכל המרזבין שופכין עליו והוא מביא כל המים למקום אחד שלא יזיקו את הכותל [עירובין צט:].

have a *chazakah*.[18]

חַלּוֹן הַמִּצְרִית אֵין לָהּ חֲזָקָה – An Egyptian window has no *chazakah*.[19] **וְלַצּוֹרִית יֵשׁ לָהּ חֲזָקָה – But a Tyrean** window **does have a *chazakah*.**[20]

The Mishnah defines an Egyptian window:[21]

אֵיזוֹ הִיא חַלּוֹן הַמִּצְרִית – What is an Egyptian window? כָּל שֶׁאֵין רֹאשׁוֹ שֶׁל אָדָם יָכוֹל לִיכָּנֵס לְתוֹכָהּ – Any window **which** is so small that **a man's head cannot enter through it.**

R' Yehudah qualifies the ruling that an Egyptian window has no *chazakah*:

רַבִּי יְהוּדָה אוֹמֵר – R' Yehudah says: אִם יֵשׁ לָהּ מַלְבֵּן – If [the window] has a frame, אַף עַל פִּי שֶׁאֵין רֹאשׁוֹ שֶׁל אָדָם יָכוֹל לִיכָּנֵס לְתוֹכָהּ – even though the window is so small that **a person's head cannot enter through it, הֲרֵי זוֹ חֲזָקָה – it has a *chazakah*.**[22]

Gemara The Gemara analyzes the first rulings of the Mishnah:

מַאי הַמַּרְזֵב אֵין לוֹ חֲזָקָה וְיֵשׁ לִמְקוֹמוֹ חֲזָקָה – What is meant by the Mishnah's statement: A DRAINSPOUT HAS NO *CHAZAKAH* BUT ITS PLACE HAS A *CHAZAKAH*? If the drainspout itself must be removed, what is the practical consequence of a *chazakah* for "its place"?

The Gemara offers three interpretations:

אָמַר רַב יְהוּדָה אָמַר שְׁמוּאֵל – Rav Yehudah said in the name of Shmuel: הָכִי קָאָמַר – This is what [the Mishnah] is saying: הַמַּרְזֵב אֵין לוֹ חֲזָקָה – A DRAINSPOUT HAS NO *CHAZAKAH*. **מֵרוּחַ אַחַת** – This means that no *chazakah* is established that entitles the owner to keep his drainspout **on one** particular **side** of the gutter.[23] וְיֵשׁ לִמְקוֹמוֹ חֲזָקָה – BUT ITS PLACE HAS A *CHAZAKAH*. **מִשְּׁתֵּי רוּחוֹת** – This means that a *chazakah* is established that entitles the owner to place his drainspout **on** either one of the **two sides** of the gutter, whichever side is preferred by the neighbor.[24]

The second interpretation:

רַבִּי חֲנִינָא אָמַר – R' Chanina says: הַמַּרְזֵב אֵין לוֹ חֲזָקָה – A DRAINSPOUT HAS NO *CHAZAKAH*. **שֶׁאִם הָיָה אָרוֹךְ מְקַצְּרוֹ** – This means **that if [the drainspout] was long, [the neighbor] may shorten it.**[25] וְיֵשׁ לִמְקוֹמוֹ חֲזָקָה – BUT ITS PLACE HAS A *CHAZAKAH*. **שֶׁאִם בָּא לְעוֹקְרוֹ** – This means **that if [the neighbor] wishes to remove [the drainspout] entirely, אֵינוֹ עוֹקְרוֹ – he may not remove it.**[26]

The third interpretation:

רַב יִרְמְיָה בַּר אַבָּא אָמַר – Rav Yirmiyah bar Abba says: הַמַּרְזֵב אֵין לוֹ חֲזָקָה – A DRAINSPOUT HAS NO *CHAZAKAH*. **שֶׁאִם רוֹצֶה לִבְנוֹת תַּחְתָּיו** – This means **that if [the neighbor] wishes to build beneath [the drainspout], בּוֹנֶה – he may build** there.[27] וְיֵשׁ לִמְקוֹמוֹ חֲזָקָה – BUT ITS PLACE HAS A *CHAZAKAH*. **שֶׁאִם בָּא לְעוֹקְרוֹ** – This means **that if [the neighbor] wishes to remove [the drainspout] entirely, אֵינוֹ עוֹקְרוֹ – he may not remove it.**[28]

NOTES

and not make a protest (*Rashbam*; cf. *Yad Ramah* and *Tur, Choshen Mishpat* 153:20).

18. A Tyrean ladder is larger and more difficult to move than an Egyptian ladder. Its placement is therefore considered more permanent, and if a neighbor allows it to remain in place for three years without protest, a *chazakah* is established which allows the owner of the ladder to keep it there.

19. An Egyptian window is very small (its size is defined in the Mishnah below). Such a window, if opened for the purpose of viewing one's properties, is not considered a permanent fixture. Thus, it might be accepted by the neighbor without protest even though it infringes upon his privacy; therefore, its unprotested presence for even a three-year period does not establish a *chazakah*.

Rashbam (59a ד"ה למעלה) asserts that one does not have the right to force his neighbor to close up an Egyptian window, even if the window is at ground level. If so, the ruling that one does not establish a *chazakah* for such a window does not mean (as it does in other cases) that the use under discussion must be discontinued if the neighbor protests; it must mean, rather, that the neighbor may build a wall in his property that blocks the window. The owner of the window cannot contend that he has a *chazakah,* which – if granted validity – would force the neighbor to draw his wall back (see *Rashbam* there). *Ramban,* however, writes that *Rashbam's* position is not correct and that one must block up even an Egyptian window upon his neighbor's protest. If so, the ruling that "it does not have a *chazakah*" means that the owner of the window has no right to retain it and must close it up.

This law applies only if the window was opened for viewing purposes. If it was opened by a homeowner to allow light into a dark section of his home, it is considered a permanent fixture, for it is essential to him inasmuch as it enables him to use his house. Accordingly, such a window can establish *chazakah,* regardless of its size (*Rashbam*, from Gemara 59a; see also *Ritva* here).

20. The (larger) Tyrean windows are considered a permanent fixture and their opening (even if merely for viewing purposes) would normally be protested. If such protest is not forthcoming within three years, a *chazakah* is established and the neighbor is no longer entitled to ask that the window be closed up or to block the window (see previous note).

21. The Gemara below (59a) explains why the Mishnah does not define Egyptian ladders.

22. Framing a window indicates that it is intended as a permanent fixture. Therefore, whatever the window's size, the neighbor whose courtyard it overlooks would be expected to issue a protest, and his failure to do so creates a *chazakah (Meiri)*.

23. If the drainspout had been located, even for three years, on one particular side of the gutter, its owner is not entitled to keep it there. The neighbor can insist that it be moved to the other end of the gutter. Since the choice of side on which the drainspout is placed is not a significant matter to the owner, the neighbor reasoned that its presence on one particular side is not permanent and therefore did not feel that it was necessary to lodge a protest (*Rashbam*).

24. Although the *location* of a drainspout is not considered permanent, its *existence* is permanent, for houses generally require drainspouts. Therefore, if the neighbor does not want a drainspout to project over his property, he should protest. If he does not protest, a *chazakah* is established which allows the owner of the drainspout to place it at one of the ends of his gutter. Its exact position, however, can be determined by the neighbor (*Rashbam*).

25. Although his lack of protest allows the drainspout's owner to leave it in place, the neighbor can nevertheless prevent the drainspout from projecting further into his property than necessary (*Rashbam*).

26. According to R' Chanina, the location of the drainspout cannot be shifted at all, even from one end of the gutter to the other (*Rashbam*).

27. The *chazakah* established by the drainspout only affords its owner the right to project it over the neighbor's property, and the right to channel water into his neighbor's courtyard. It does not give him any rights in the land beneath the drainspout, and the neighbor may do what he wishes with the land (*Rashbam*).

28. If the neighbor wishes to erect a structure which would necessitate removal of the drainspout, the *chazakah* prevents him from doing so (*Rashbam*).

The Gemara challenges the third interpretation:

תְּנַן – **We learned in the Mishnah:** הַמַּזְחִילָה יֵשׁ לָהּ חֲזָקָה – **A GUTTER HAS A** ***CHAZAKAH.*** בִּשְׁלָמָא לְמַאן דְּאָמַר הָנָךְ תַּרְתֵּי שַׁפִּיר – Now, **this is perfectly in order according to** either **one** of the Amoraim [Shmuel and R' Chanina] **who advanced those** first **two** interpretations.[1] אֶלָּא לְמַאן דְּאָמַר – **But according to the one** [Rav Yirmiyah bar Abba] **who said** that the meaning of the Mishnah's ruling was שֶׁאִם רָצָה לִבְנוֹת תַּחְתָּיו בּוֹנֶה – **that if [the neighbor] wishes to build beneath [the drainspout], he may build** there, then when the Mishnah states that a gutter does have a *chazakah,* it means that the owner of the courtyard may *not* build underneath it. מַאי נַפְקָא לֵיהּ מִינָּהּ – But **what difference does it make to [the owner of the gutter]** whether the owner of the courtyard builds underneath the gutter? He is not harmed in any way by this![2] – ? –

The Gemara answers:

הָכָא בְּמַזְחִילָה שֶׁל בִּנְיָן עֲסָקִינַן – The Mishnah deals **here with a gutter of** stone **construction.** In such a case, once a *chazakah* has been established, the neighbor can be barred from building below the gutter, דְּאָמַר לֵיהּ – **for [the gutter's owner] can say to him:** לָא נִיחָא לִי – **"It** [your building] **is not acceptable to me,** דְּתִיתְרַע אֲשִׁיתַאי – **for it** will **damage my** gutter's **walls."**[3]

The Mishnah teaches that a *chazakah* can be established allowing a person to channel water into a neighbor's property. The Gemara now addresses the question of whether the neighbor can in turn establish a *chazakah* giving him the right to prevent the flow of water into his land from being interrupted:

אָמַר רַב יְהוּדָה אָמַר שְׁמוּאֵל – **Rav Yehudah said in the name of Shmuel:** צִינּוֹר הַמְקַלֵּחַ מַיִם לַחֲצַר חֲבֵרוֹ – If **a pipe** belonging to one person **pours water** from his roof **into the courtyard of his neighbor,**[4] וּבָא בַּעַל הַגָּג לְסוֹתְמוֹ – **and the roof's owner came to seal [the pipe],** בַּעַל הֶחָצֵר מְעַכֵּב עָלָיו – **the owner of the courtyard can prevent him** from doing so, דְּאָמַר לֵיהּ – **for he can say to [the pipe's owner]:** כִּי הֵיכִי דְּאַתְּ קָנִית לָךְ חָצֵר דִּידִי – **"Just as you have acquired** a right in **my courtyard,** לְמִשְׁדָּא בֵּיהּ מַיָּא – **to discharge water into it,** לְדִידִי נַמִּי קְנֵי לִי מַיָּא דְּאִיגְּרָךְ – **I have also acquired** the rights to **the water** that runs **from your roof.**[5] Therefore, you have no right to interrupt the water's flow."

The Gemara cites a dispute regarding this very point:

אִיתְּמַר – **It was stated:** רַבִּי אוֹשַׁעְיָא אָמַר – **R' Oshaya said:** מְעַכֵּב – **[The courtyard owner] can prevent** the owner of the pipe from sealing the pipe. רַבִּי חָמָא אָמַר – **R' Chama,** the father of R' Oshaya, **said:** אֵינוֹ מְעַכֵּב – **[The courtyard owner] cannot prevent** the owner of the pipe from sealing it.[6]

The opinion of R' Bissa, the father of R' Chama, was solicited:

אָזַל שַׁיְילֵיהּ לְרַבִּי בִּיסָא – **They went and asked R' Bissa** for his opinion. אָמַר לְהוּ – **He said to them:** מְעַכֵּב – **[The courtyard owner] can prevent** the owner of the pipe from sealing it.

The Gemara comments on R' Oshaya:

קְרֵי עֲלֵיהּ רָמִי בַּר חָמָא – **Rami bar Chama applied the** following **verse to him:** "וְהַחוּט הַמְשֻׁלָּשׁ לֹא בִמְהֵרָה יִנָּתֵק" – ***And the three-ply cord is not easily severed.***[7] זֶה רַבִּי אוֹשַׁעְיָא – **This refers to R' Oshaya,** בְּנוֹ שֶׁל רַבִּי חָמָא – **the son of R' Chama,** בְּנוֹ שֶׁל רַבִּי בִּיסָא – **the son of R' Bissa.**[8]

The Gemara cites the next section of the Mishnah:

סוּלָּם הַמִּצְרִי אֵין לוֹ חֲזָקָה – **AN EGYPTIAN LADDER HAS NO** ***CHAZAKAH.***

The Gemara defines an "Egyptian ladder":

הֵיכִי דָּמֵי סוּלָּם הַמִּצְרִי – **What is an "Egyptian ladder"?** אָמְרֵי דְּבֵי רַבִּי יַנַּאי – **It was taught in the academy of R' Yannai:** כָּל שֶׁאֵין לוֹ אַרְבָּעָה חֲווּקִין – **Any** ladder **that does not have four rungs.**[9]

The next section of the Mishnah stated:

חַלּוֹן הַמִּצְרִית אֵין לָהּ חֲזָקָה כו' – **AN EGYPTIAN WINDOW HAS NO** ***CHAZAKAH*** **etc.** But a Tyrean window does have a *chazakah.*

The Gemara asks:

מַאי שְׁנָא גַּבֵּי סוּלָּם – **What is the difference** between **ladders,** דְּלָא מְפָרֵשׁ – which **[the Tanna] does not define,** וּמַאי שְׁנָא גַּבֵּי חַלּוֹן – **and windows,**[10] דִּמְפָרֵשׁ – **which [the Tanna] does define?** Why is it that the Mishnah explains the difference between Egyptian and Tyrean *windows* but not between Egyptian and Tyrean *ladders?*

The Gemara answers:

מִשּׁוּם דְּקָא בָּעֵי אִיפְּלוּגֵי רַבִּי יְהוּדָה בְּסֵיפָא – The Tanna defined

NOTES

1. According to the first interpretation, the presence of a drainspout does not establish a *chazakah* with regard to its exact location. According to the second interpretation, it does not establish a *chazakah* with regard to size. If one follows either of these views, the Mishnah's distinction between a drainspout and a gutter is easily understood: A gutter, unlike a drainspout, is not moved from one place to another [nor is its size diminished], and therefore its presence can establish a *chazakah* which allows it to remain in place, undisturbed and undiminished (*Rashbam*).

2. Consequently, the silence of the yard owner regarding the gutter shows only that he gave his neighbor the right to hang his gutter over the yard. It shows nothing about the use of the land beneath it. Therefore, he has no *chazakah* regarding the use of that land (*Rashbam).*

3. The vibrations caused by your construction could make my gutter collapse (*Rashbam*; cf. *Rabbeinu Gershom).*

Thus, the gutter's owner can claim that when he erected the gutter, the neighbor should have realized that his acquiescence to the gutter's presence would constitute not only acceptance of the gutter itself, but also agreement not to build underneath it. Hence, if the neighbor is silent for three years, he forfeits even his right to build below the gutter.

This law applies only to a gutter. A drainspout is usually constructed of wood, which is unaffected by the vibrations of construction. Thus, even after a *chazakah* has been established, it is permitted to build beneath a drainspout (*Rashbam, Tosafos).*

4. The pipe had been in place for more than three years: Thus, a *chazakah* had already been established with regard to its continued use.

5. The neighbor may want to give the water to his animals.

The rationale for Shmuel's ruling is as follows: The owner of the courtyard can claim that his acquiesence to the gutter's presence was based on the expectation that the water flowing from the gutter would be his. Thus, while the gutter's owner established a *chazakah* to channel water into his neighbor's property, his neighbor simultaneously acquired a *chazakah* to use the water from the gutter. Accordingly, the neighbor can claim that although the gutter's owner may no longer wish to continue using the gutter, he is still entitled to receive the water (*Rashbam*).

6. R' Chama agrees that the owner of the courtyard is entitled to use the water that flows from the gutter. However, in his view, this right exists only as long as the gutter expresses water (*Rashbam*).

It is unusual for the opinion of a son [R' Oshaya] to be recorded before that of his father [R' Chama]. However, an exception was made in this case, since R' Oshaya was such an outstanding scholar (*Tosafos*; cf. *Tosafos* to *Bava Metzia* 4b ד"ה אין).

7. *Ecclesiastes* 4:12.

8. For R' Oshaya had advanced an opinion that was corroborated by his grandfather (*Rashbam*).

Alternatively: Although many families boast several generations of Torah scholars, it was unusual for three generations of Torah scholars to attain stature contemporaneously (*Tosafos*).

9. Since it is so small, the placement of such a ladder does not establish a *chazakah* (see 58b note 17).

10. Literally: and what is different regarding a window.

תנן המזחילה יש לה חזקה בשלמא למאן דאמר הנך תרתי שפיר אלא למאן דאמר שאם רצה לבנות תחתיו בונה מאי נפקא ליה מינה הכא במזחילה של בנין עסקינן דאמר ליה לא ניחא לי דתיתרע אשיתאי אמר רב יהודה אמר שמואל א צינור המקלח מים לחצר חברו ובא בעל הגג לסותמו בעל החצר מעכב עליו דאמר ליה כי היכי דאת קנית לך חצר דידי למשדא ביה מיא לדידי נמי קני לי מיא דאיגרך איתמר רבי אושעיא אמר מעכב ר' חמא אמר אינו מעכב א) אזל שייליה לרבי ביסא אמר להו מעכב ב) קרי עליה רמי בר חמא א) והחוט המשולש לא במהרה ינתק זה רבי אושעיא בנו של רבי חמא בנו של רבי ביסא: סולם המצרי אין לו חזקה: ב היכי דמי סולם המצרי אמרי דבי ר' ינאי כל שאין לו ארבעה חווקין: חלון המצרית אין לה חזקה כו': מאי שנא גבי סולם דלא מפרש ומאי שנא גבי חלון דמפרש משום דקא בעי איפלוגי רבי יהודה בסיפא אמר רבי זירא למטה מד' אמות יש לו חזקה ויכול למחות למעלה מארבע אמות אין לו חזקה ואינו יכול למחות ורבי אילעא אמר ג אפילו למעלה מארבע אמות אין לו חזקה ויכול למחות ג) לימא בכופין על מדת סדום קא מיפלגי דמר סבר כופין ומר סבר אין כופין לא דכולי עלמא כופין ושאני הכא ד דאמר ליה זימנין דמותבת שרשיפא תותך וקיימת וקא חזית ההוא דאתא לקמיה דר' אמי שדריה לקמיה דרבי אבא בר ממל אמר ליה עביד ליה כרבי אילעא אמר שמואל ה ולאורה אפי' כל שהוא יש לו חזקה:

מתני' ו הזיז עד טפח יש לו חזקה ויכול

תנן המזחילה יש לה חזקה. ובמאי דקתני המרזב אין לו חזקה קאמר אבל המזחילה יש לה חזקה: **בשלמא למאן דאמר הנך תרתי שפיר.** דלשמואל דאמר אין לו חזקה מרזב אחת שפיר איצטריך למימר אבל המזחילה יש לה חזקה לדבר קביעות הוא ואין רגילין לעקרה ממקום למקום וכן דר' חנינא שאם היה ארוך מקצרו אבל המזחילה יש לה חזקה ואין מקצרין אותה: **אלא למאן דאמר.** גבי מרזב דלהכי אין לו חזקה שאם רצה לבנות תחתיו בונה מאי שנא מזחילה דקאמר יש לו חזקה שאין בונין תחתיה מאי נפקא ליה מינה לבעל מזחילה אי בני בעל חצר תותה הא לא מפסיד מידי ובעל חצר לא שעבד לו תחתיו למזחילתו לדבר שאינו מזיק לו: **של בנין.** אבנים: **דאמר לא ניחא לי.** שתבנה תחתיה: **דתיתרע אשיתאי.** כלומר מזחילה שלי תפול לקול מקבות והגרזן וכל כלי ברזל בהבנות בניינך אבל גבי מרזב (א) לא חשיב כל כך אפילו הוי של בנין בונה תחתיו אי נמי האי דקא מפליג בין מרזב למזחילה היינו משום דסתם מרזב של עץ וסתם מזחילה של אבנים: **צינור.** של שופכין: **לדידי נמי קני לי מיא דאיגרך.** להשקות בהמותי שעל מנת כן נתרצתי לך ודמי למקח וממכר שאני שעבדתי לך חצירי בשביל מימך ואם אתה חוזר בך אני לא אחזור בי: **מעכב.** על בעל הגג: **אינו מעכב.** דלא שעבד לו מימיו אלא כל ימי שיהיו יורדין לחצירו: **אזול שיילוה לרבי ביסא.** אביו של ר' חמא וזקנו של רבי אושעיא: **לא במהרה ינתק.** כדדרשינן נמי (ב"מ דף פה.) מפי זרעך ומפי זרע זרעך וגו' מדור שלישי ואילך תורה מחזרת על אכסניא שלה: **זה ר' אושעיא.** שאמר כזקנו: **חווקין.** שליבות אשקלוני"ש: וקבעי גמרא מ"ש גבי **סולם דלא קמפרש.** מתני' שיעורא כי היכי דקמפרש גבי חלון: **משום דקבעי לאיפלוגי רבי יהודה** . גבי חלון הוצרך ת"ק לפרש שיעורו: **א"ר זירא למטה מד' אמות.** מקרקע הבית קתני מתני' דחלון צורי יש לו חזקה דכיון דאיכא תרתי שהוא גדול ונמוך ויכולין להסתכל ממנו בחצר יש לו חזקה שלא היה זה מניחו לעשות אלא ודאי ברשותו עשה ואם בא שכנו לבנות הדין להתרחק כדתנן (לעיל דף כב.) החלונות מלמעלן ומלמטן ומכנגדן ד' אמות ואם בא עכשיו אחד מהן לפתוח חלון צורי למטה מד' אמות מקרקע הבית שכנו יכול למחות בידו ומעכבו שלא יפתח: **למעלה מד' אמות.** מקרקע הבית אין לו חזקה דאין חבירו מקפיד וכשבונה שכנו אינו יכול לעכב עליו ולומר לו הרחק בניינך מן החלון שלי שלא תאפיל עלי שיכול לומר לו סתום אותו שאין לך חזקה ואם אין לו חלון שם וביקש עכשיו לפתוח חלון למעלה מד' אמות אין יכול שכנו למחות בידו ולמנעו ודוקא חלון צורי אבל חלון המצרי בין מלמעלה מד"א בין מלמטה אין לו חזקה וגם אין יכול השכן למחות: **ור' אילעא אמר אפילו למעלה מד' אמות.** אע"ג דלית ליה חזקה יכול למחות לבלתי עשות שכנו שם חלון כדמפרש טעמא לקמיה זימנין דמותבת שרשיפא וקא חזית בביתי ור' זירא לא חייש להכי דלא חליפי אינשי כולי האי למיעבד הכי: **מדת סדום.** אין מהנה לחבירו אע"פ שאין חסר בכך כלום. לר"ז כופין דלמעלה מד' אין מניחין אותו למחות שהרי אינו חסר כלום ולרבי אילעא אין כופין ויכול למחות: **ושאני הכא.** דאיכא חסרון: **שרשיפא.** ספסל: **ההוא דאתא וכו'.** רוצה היה לעשות חלון צורי למעלה מד' אמות וחבירו היה מוחה בידו: **עביד ליה כר' אילעא.** אלמא הכי הלכתא: **אמר שמואל ולאורה אפילו כל שהוא יש לו חזקה.** חלון העשוי ליכנס ממנו אור במקום אפל לא בעינן חלון צורי אלא אפילו כל שהוא יש לו חזקה דחלון העשוי לאורה מילתא דקביעותא דכל הימים אדם צריך לאורה וכיון שעשה חלון זה לכל הימים עשאו והיה לו לבעל חצר למחות בתוך ג' ומדלא מיחה איכא למימר דברשותו עשה ומתני' לאו בחלון העשוי לאורה איירי אלא בחלון העשוי לשמור גנות ופרדסים דרך החלון: **מתני' הזיז עד טפח יש לו חזקה.** מי שיש לו כותל סמוך לחצר חבירו והוציא זיז טפח בולט מכותלו לחצר חבירו הויא חזקה ואין בעל החצר יכול לבנות שם בנין לסתור את הזיז דכולי האי לא הוה שביק ליה בעל החצר להוציא זיז טפח בחצרו בלא רשותו שהרי יכול למחות כדקתני ואזיל ומדלא מיחה בתוך ג' איכא למימר דברשותו הוציא:

במזחילה של בנין עסקינן. אבל מרזב סתמו של עץ ואין עושין אותו של בנין וא"ת וליפלוג במזחילה עצמה בין של בנין לשל עץ וי"ל דניחא ליה במתניתין לאשמועינן במרזב דיש לו חזקה: **והחוט** המשולש לא במהרה ינתק. כמה היו שהן תלמידי חכמים ולאבות אבותיהם היו ואבותיהם ולא קאמר עליהם החוט המשולש אלא הכא היינו טעמא לפי שלשתן ראו זה את זה והא דמזכיר ר' אושעיא קודם רבי חמא אביו במחלוקת לפי שהיה גדול יותר מאביו כדאמר (עירובין דף נג.) לבן של ד) (ראשונים) כפתח [היכל] זה ר' אושעיא ואמר נמי ר' אושעיא בדורו כר"מ בדורו שלא יכלו חביריו לעמוד על סוף דעתו:

למטה מד' יש לו חזקה. ר"ת מפרש דאיירי בחלון מצרית אבל בחלון צורי או שעשוי לאורה שהוא דבר קביעות אפילו למעלה מארבע אמות יש לו חזקה והביא ראיה מדתניא לעיל (דף כב:) החלונות בין מלמעלה בין מלמטה ד"א ותני עלה מלמטה שלא יעמוד ויראה אלמא אפי' למעלה מד' אמות יש לו חזקה כיון דהוי דבר קביעות ואומר רשב"א דאין נראה משם ראיה דאף על פי שהוא יותר מד' אמות לעומד בחוץ לעומד בפנים לא הוי למעלה מארבע אמות כגון שאותן חלונות בעלייה אי נמי מיירי כגון שיש לו עדים או שטר:

עד טפח יש לו חזקה ויכול למחות. אפילו בעל הגג בבעל החצר דאין לומר דוקא בעל החצר בבעל הגג אבל בעל הגג בבעל החצר לא יוכל למחות דהא קתני בסיפא פחות מטפח אין יכול למחות ומפרש רב הונא היינו בעל הגג בבעל החצר אבל בעל החצר בבעל הגג יכול למחות אלא על כרחך בטפח אפילו בעל הגג יכול למחות בבעל החצר וטעמא דבטפח יכול לתלות דברים גדולים המכבידים על הכותל או אם יניח עליו כלי מלא מים וישפך ויתקלקל הכותל ובעל החצר יכול למחות משום היזק ראיה ולמאי דס"ד בגמרא למימר דרב יהודה לית ליה היזק ראיה מכל מקום כשיש כלי מלא מים פעמים שיפול ויטשטש כל החצר ופעמים שיפול על ראש בעל החצר ומיירי תוך ג' אבל אחר שהחזיק אין יכול למחות בעל החצר בבעל הגג ועוד יש לפרש דדוקא אחר ג' איירי ויכול למחות בעל הגג בבעל החצר ולא מטעם דפריסית אלא משום דיש לו תשמיש לבעל הגג על הזיז רוצה להשתמש בו כל שעה ולא יניח את בעל החצר להשתמש בו אבל בתוך ג' שלא החזיק אין יכול למחות בבעל החצר אבל בעל החצר בבעל הגג יכול למחות והוי כמו לרב הונא בפחות מטפח והא דמפליג בין טפח לפחות הא בהא תליא דבטפח דמהני ביה חזקה יכול למחות בבעל החצר אבל בפחות מטפח דלא הויא חזקה אין יכול למחות: ואפילו

מסורת הש"ס

א) [אזלו שיילוהו. יעב"ץ], ב) כתובות סב:, ג) [לעיל יב: וש"נ] לקמן קסח., ד) [נ"ל אחרונים]:

הגהות הב"ח

(א) רשב"ם ד"ה דתיתרע כו' דלא חשיב כל כך אפי' אי הוי:

תורה אור השלם

א) וְאִם יִתְקְפוֹ הָאֶחָד הַשְּׁנַיִם יַעַמְדוּ נֶגְדּוֹ וְהַחוּט הַמְשֻׁלָּשׁ לֹא בִמְהֵרָה יִנָּתֵק: [קהלת ד, יב]

ליקוטי רש"י

והחוט המשולש לא במהרה ינתק. מי שהוא ת"ח ובנו ובן בנו שוב אין תורה פוסקת מזרעו וכן הוא אומר (ישעיה נט) לא ימושו מפיך ומפי זרעך ומפי זרע זרעך [קהלת ד, יב]. **כופין על מדת סדום.** זה נהנה וזה לא חסר [לעיל יב:]. דאפילו מידי דלא חסר ביה לא מהני לחבריה. מדת סדום. שלי שלי [עירובין מט.]. זה נהנה וזה לא חסר לא היו עושין טובה [כתובות קג.]. כדתנן (אבות פ"ה מ"י) האומר שלי שלי שלך שלך זו מדה בינונית ויש אומרים זו מדת סדום [רשב"ם לקמן קסח.]. **הזיז.** כל עץ היוצא מן הכותל קרוי זיז [שבת ד:].

עין משפט נר מצוה

רעא א מיי' פ"ח מהל' שכנים הל' ה סמג עשין פב טוש"ע ח"מ סי' קנג סעיף ז:

רעב ב מיי' שם הל' ד טוש"ע שם סעיף יג:

רעג ג מיי' פ"ז הל' ה סמג עשין לה טוש"ע ח"מ סי' קנד סעיף י:

רעד ד מיי' שם טוש"ע שם סעיף ו:

רעה ה מיי' שם הל' ז וע"ש טוש"ע שם סעיף י:

רעו ו מיי' שם פ"ח הל' ג סמג עשין פב טוש"ע ח"מ סי' קנג סעיף ג:

רבינו גרשום

המזחילה. היינו צנור גדול שמונח כנגד כל הבית אם מקלחת מים לחצר חבירו **יש לו חזקה** לפי שהיא גדולה: **בשלמא להני תרי** לישני קמאי **שפיר.** דלמרזב אין לו חזקה מרוח אחת ושאם היה ארוך מקצרו משא"כ במזחילה שיש לה חזקה: **אלא למ"ד שאם בא לבנות תחתיו.** של מרזב: **מאי נפקא ליה מינה.** לבעל המזחילה והלא מקבל הוא מימיו שלו בתוך של בנינו: **הכא במזחילה של בנין.** שעשויה מן אבנים ומן סיד **עסקינן דאמר ליה** בעל המזחילה **לא ניחא לי דתיתרע אשיתאי.** שאם יגע בנינך למזחילה יקלקל אותה. ואם לא יהיה ריוח למים לקלח ולצאת ישתהו שם במזחילה ויקלקלו הכותל: **לדידי קני לי ממיא דאיגרך.** לקבלן ולעשות מהן צרכי: **רבי אושעיא אומר מעכב.** לו שלא לסותמו זה: ר' אושעיא שאמר דמעכב כמו שאמר **ר' ביסא זקינו** שהוא שלישי לו: **שאין לו ד' חווקין.** מעלות: **אין לו חזקה:** אם יש לו מלבן בחצר חבירו כמו שפה מתחתיה שמשפע בחצר: **מ"ש גבי סולם דלא קמפרש.** במתני' איזהו סולם: **ר' זירא אמר** אדר' יהודה דמתני' קאי ואמר **למטה מד' אמות** אי איכא חלון בחצר חבירו **יש לו חזקה ויכול למחות** משום היזק ראיה ואי לא מיחה יש לו חזקה: ואי **למעלה מד' אמות** קאי. דליכא היזק ראיה **אין לו חזקה** מפני **שאין יכול למחות** האי הואיל דלא מזיק ליה הלכך אין לו חזקה מפני שאין יכול למחות לכך שתק אבל לא מחיל: **ור' אילעא אמר אפי' למעלה מד' אמות אין לו חזקה.** דלכך שתיק דלא מזיק ליה. **ויכול למחות** ולעכב לו מתי שירצה: **בכופין על מדת סדום.** דבר שאין מזיק לו ומועיל לחבירו כגון חלון למעלה מד' אמות **דר' זירא סבר כופין** שלא יעכב ולהכי קאמר שאין יכול למחות **ור' אילעא סבר** יכול למחות קסבר **דאין כופין: דכולי עלמא.** ואפי' ר' אילעא אמר דכופין: אי הכי אמאי אמר דיכול למחות. **דאמר ליה זימנין דמותבת** מידי תותך עד **דקיימת** להדי חלון

וחזית מינאי ומסתכל כלום מה שבחצירי: **ההוא דאתא לקמיה דר' אמי.** שהיה לו חלון בחצר חבירו למעלה מד' אמות: **כר' אילעא.** דאין לו חזקה ויכול למחות: **אמר שמואל ולאורה אפי' כל שהוא הרי זו חזקה.** כלומר אם פתח חלון בחצר חבירו למעלה מד' אמות לצורך אורה בפני חבירו ולא מיחה אפי' כל שהוא שאין ראש אדם נכנס בו ואע"פ שאין לו מלבן הריא חזקה ואין יכול בעל חצר לסותמה ולא להאפיל עליו: **פיסקא הזיז עד טפח.** שאם יש לו לאדם זיז יוצא מכותלו לחצר חבירו עד טפח יש לו חזקה בחצר חבירו כשיעור טפח. שאלמלא שיש לו חזקה בחצר לא היה מניחו להוציא בה זיז כשיעור טפח: **מפני שיכול** למחות

an Egyptian window only **because he wished to include the dissenting opinion of Rabbi Yehudah in the final clause of the Mishnah.** In order to demonstrate that R' Yehudah refers to an Egyptian window, it was necessary to define an Egyptian window.[11]

The Gemara presents a dispute that concerns the ruling in our Mishnah that a Tyrean window has a *chazakah*:[12]

אָמַר רַבִּי זֵירָא – R' Zeira said: לְמַטָּה מֵאַרְבַּע אַמּוֹת – If the window was opened at a height of **less than four *amos*** from the ground, יֵשׁ לוֹ חֲזָקָה – **it has a *chazakah*.**[13] וְיָכוֹל לִמְחוֹת – Therefore, at any time during the first three years, **[the neighbor] can protest** the presence of such a window.[14] לְמַעְלָה מֵאַרְבַּע אַמּוֹת – If, however, the window was opened at a height of **more than four *amos*** from the ground, אֵין לוֹ חֲזָקָה – **it has no *chazakah*.**[15] וְאֵינוֹ יָכוֹל לִמְחוֹת – Therefore, **[the neighbor] cannot protest** the presence of such a window.[16]

The dissenting opinion:

וְרַבִּי אִילְעָא אָמַר – **R' Ila'a said:** אֲפִילּוּ לְמַעְלָה מֵאַרְבַּע אַמּוֹת – **Even** if the window was opened at a height of **more than four *amos*** from the ground, אֵין לוֹ חֲזָקָה – granted that **it has no *chazakah*,** וְיָכוֹל לִמְחוֹת – nevertheless **[the neighbor] can protest** such a window.[17]

The Gemara attempts to define the point of contention between the disputants:

לֵימָא בְּכוֹפִין עַל מִדַּת סְדוֹם קָא מִיפַּלְגֵי – **Shall we say that [R' Zeira and R' Ila'a] argue about whether we coerce** people **not to emulate the behavior of Sodom,** i.e. whether we compel people to benefit others when no loss is involved to themselves?[18] דְּמַר סָבַר כּוֹפִין – **One master** [R' Zeira] **holds** that **we do coerce** people not to emulate the behavior of Sodom. Since the neighbor loses nothing by the presence of the window, he cannot have it closed.[19] וּמַר סָבַר אֵין כּוֹפִין – **And** the other **master** [R' Ila'a] **holds** that **we do not coerce** people not to emulate the behavior of Sodom. Although the presence of the window causes the neighbor no loss, he is empowered to have it closed.

The Gemara rejects this interpretation of this dispute:

לֹא – This is **not** necessarily correct. דְּכוּלֵּי עָלְמָא כּוֹפִין – It is possible that, in the opinion of **all, we do coerce** people not to emulate the behavior of Sodom. וְשָׁאנֵי הָכָא – **This case,** however, **is different,** דְּאָמַר לֵיהּ – **for [the neighbor] can say to him** [the one who wants to open the window]: זִימְנִין דְּמוֹתְבַתְּ שַׁרְשִׁיפָא תּוּתָךְ – **"At times you might put a bench to support yourself**[20] beneath the window, וְקַיְימַתְּ וְקָא חָזֵית – **stand on it and look** into my courtyard!" Neither R' Zeira nor R' Ila'a dispute that we do coerce people not to emulate the behavior of Sodom. Rather, they argue whether this principle is relevant in this case. R' Ila'a contends that the opening of even a high window can be detrimental to the neighbor and therefore the neighbor is within his rights to have it sealed.[21]

The Gemara cites a related incident:

הַהוּא דְּאָתָא לְקַמֵּיהּ דְּרַבִּי אַמִּי – **There was a** certain **man** (whose neighbor sought to prevent him from opening a window higher than four *amos* from the ground) **who came before R' Ami.** שַׁדְרֵיהּ לְקַמֵּיהּ דְּרַבִּי אַבָּא בַּר מַמָּל – **[R' Ami] sent [the man] to R' Abba bar Mamal,** אֲמַר לֵיהּ – and **instructed [R' Abba]:** עֲבֵיד לֵיהּ כְּרַבִּי אִילְעָא – **"Decide** the law[22] **in accordance with** the view **of R' Ila'a** [i.e. do not allow him to open the window]!"

The Gemara states an exception to the Mishnah's ruling that a small window has no *chazakah:*

NOTES

11. R' Yehudah said that if a window has a frame, even though "it is so small that a man's head cannot enter through it," it has a *chazakah.* He did not refer to such a window as an "Egyptian window." Therefore, it was necessary for the Mishnah to define an Egyptian window in order to clarify the connection between R' Yehudah's statement and the first part of the Mishnah.

12. Our elucidation follows *Rashbam,* who interprets the Gemara's following discussion as referring to Tyrean windows. *Tosafos* and *Rambam* (*Hil. Shecheinim* 7:6), however, interpret the Gemara as referring to Egyptian windows. In their view, the opening of Tyrean windows always establishes *chazakah,* even if they are at a height of four *amos* above the ground.

A second point of contention among the Rishonim concerns the nature of the damage which the windows mentioned in the Mishnah are liable to cause. According to *Rashbam,* the Mishnah refers to a window overlooking a courtyard and it deals with the issue of privacy (see also *Ramban*). Other Rishonim, however, maintain that the right to privacy cannot be compromised even by a failure to protest. In their opinion, even one who remained silent for three years may claim that he originally thought he could bear the loss of privacy but now realizes that he was mistaken. According to the latter view, the Mishnah is discussing only windows which pose no threat to privacy — such as those which do not overlook a courtyard — and which threaten only the property owner's right to build in front of the windows (*Rif, Ritva;* see *Choshen Mishpat* 155:36; see 59b note 26).

13. Since it is a large (Tyrean) window, *and* it is placed within four *amos* of the floor, the owner of the courtyard would definitely have protested had he been opposed to it. His lack of protest for three years is taken as evidence that the window was opened with his permission. If he then wishes to build a wall opposite the window, he must distance the wall from the window in accordance with the laws set in forth in the Mishnah on 22a (*Rashbam*).

14. I.e. since silence on the part of the courtyard's owner will result in the establishment of a *chazakah,* he is within his rights to protest the opening of the window.

15. Since the owner of a courtyard does not usually object to the opening of such a high window [as it poses no threat to his privacy], his silence does not create a *chazakah.* Therefore, even after three years, he may build a wall that blocks the window (*Rashbam*).

16. The Gemara below discusses the reason for this view.

17. The Gemara below explains the reason for this view.

The dispute between R' Zeira and R' Ila'a applies only to Tyrean windows. Egyptian windows do not establish *chazakah* regardless of the height at which they are opened, and the owner of the courtyard cannot protest them (*Rashbam;* see 58b note 19).

18. Sodomites would not allow a person to benefit from their property even when this entailed no cost whatsoever to them (see *Avos* 5:10).

19. The window does not create any inconvenience for the neighbor. Therefore, it would be behavior befitting a resident of Sodom to have the window sealed in the meantime. (*Rashbam*). [Nor can the neighbor claim that he wishes to prevent the establishment of a *chazakah* for the window, since this window will not have a *chazakah* and the neighbor will be free to build opposite it (see *Chidushei HaRashba*).]

20. Literally: beneath you.

21. However, even R' Ila'a agrees that the lack of such a protest does not create a *chazakah*, for the neighbor could claim that he did not suspect his neighbor of violating his privacy (see *Yad Ramah*).

R' Zeira, however, does not allow the courtyard owner to protest the opening of the window, as he contends that no one would have the impudence to bring a bench and stand upon it to gaze into his neighbor's courtyard (*Rashbam*).

The Mishnah in the first chapter (5a) rules that a four-*amah* wall is sufficient to prevent a person from gazing into his neighbor's courtyard, and does not entertain the possibility of a person standing upon a stool to do so. The Rishonim explain that this does not constitute a contradiction to R' Ila'a, as that Mishnah refers to an open courtyard, where benches are not at hand (*Rashba*). Furthermore, it is unlikely that a person would perform such an act in a courtyard, where he is liable to be observed (*Chidushei HaRan*).

22. Literally: do for him.

גמרא

תנן המזחילה יש לה חזקה בשלמא למאן דאמר הנך תרתי שפיר אלא למאן דאמר שאם רצה לבנות תחתיו בונה מאי נפקא ליה מינה הכא במזחילה של בנין עסקינן דאמר ליה לא ניחא לי דתיתרע אשיתאי אמר רב יהודה אמר שמואל א צינור המקלח מים לחצר חברו ובא בעל הגג לסותמו בעל החצר מעכב עליו דאמר ליה כי היכי דאת קנית לך חצר דידי למשדא ביה מיא לדידי נמי קני לי מיא דאיגרך איתמר רבי אושעיא אמר מעכב ר' חמא אמר אינו מעכב א) אזל שייליה לרבי ביסא אמר להו מעכב ב קרי עליה רמי בר חמא א) והחוט המשולש לא במהרה ינתק זה רבי אושעיא בנו של רבי חמא בנו של רבי ביסא: סולם המצרי אין לו חזקה: ב היכי דמי סולם המצרי אמרי דבי ר' ינאי כל שאין לו ארבעה חווקין: חלון המצרית אין לה חזקה כו': מאי שנא גבי סולם דלא מפרש ומאי שנא גבי חלון דמפרש משום דקא בעי איפלוגי רבי יהודה בסיפא אמר רבי זירא למטה מד' אמות יש לו חזקה ויכול למחות למעלה מארבע אמות אין לו חזקה ואינו יכול למחות ורבי אילעא אמר ג אפילו למעלה מארבע אמות אין לו חזקה ויכול למחות ג) לימא בכופין על מדת סדום קא מיפלגי דמר סבר כופין ומר סבר אין כופין לא דכולי עלמא כופין ושאני הכא ד דאמר ליה זימנין דמותבת שרשיפא תותך וקיימת וקא חזית ההוא דאתא לקמיה דר' אמי שדריה לקמיה דרבי אבא בר ממל אמר ליה עביד ליה כרבי אילעא אמר שמואל ה ולאורה אפי' כל שהוא יש לו חזקה:

מתני' ו הזיז עד טפח יש לו חזקה ויכול

רש"י

במזחילה של בנין עסקינן. שהיא ארוך מקלח מים ואינו שוב את המים כמי שמבור מזיק תן דר' חנינא שאם היה ארוך מקרו אבל המזחילה יש לה חזקה ואין מקלקלין אותה: אלא למאן דאמר. גבי מרזב דלהכי אין לו חזקה שאם רצה לבנות תחתיו בונה מאי שנא מזחילה דקאמר יש לו חזקה שאין בונין תחתיה מאי נפקא ליה מינה לבעל מזחילה אי בני בעל חצר תותה הא לא מפסיד מידי ובעל חצר לא שעבד לו חבירו למזחילתו לדבר שאינו מזיק לו: של בנין. אבנים: דאמר לא ניחא לי. שתבנה תחתיה: דתיתרע אשיתאי. כלומר מזחילה שלי תפול לקול מקבות והגרזן וכל כלי ברזל בהבנות בנינך אבל גבי מרזב (א) לא חשיב כל כך אפילו הוי של בנין בונה תחתיו אי נמי האי דקא מפליג בין מרזב למזחילה היינו משום דסתם מרזב של עץ וסתם מזחילה של אבנים: צינור. של שופכין: לדידי נמי קני לי מיא דאיגרך. להשקות בהמותיי שעל מנת כן נתרציתי לך ודמי למקח וממכר שאני שעבדתי לך חצירי בשביל מימיך ואם אתה חוזר בך אני לא אחזור בי: מעכב. על בעל הגג: אינו מעכב. דלא שעבד לו מימיו אלא כל ימי שיהיו יורדין לחצירו: אזול שייליה לרבי ביסא. אביו של ר' חמא וזקנו של רבי אושעיא: לא במהרה ינתק. כדדרשינן נמי (ב"מ דף פה.) מפי זרעך ומפי זרע זרעך וגו' מדור שלישי ואילך תורה מחזרת על אכסניא שלה: זה ר' אושעיא. שאמר כזקנו: חווקין. שליבות אשקלוויי"ש: וקבעי גמרא מ"ש גבי סולם דלא קמפרש. מתני' שיעורא כי היכי דקמפרש גבי חלון: משום דקבעי לאיפלוגי רבי יהודה. גבי חלון הוצרך ת"ק לפרש שיעורו: א"ר זירא למטה מד' אמות. מקרקע הבית קתני מתני' דחלון צורי יש לו חזקה דכיון דאיכא תרתי שהוא גדול ונמוך ויכולין להסתכל ממנו בחצר יש לו חזקה שלא היה זה מניחו לעשות אלא ודאי ברשותו עשה ואם בא שכנו לבנות הדין להתרחק כדתנן (לעיל דף כב.) החלונות מלמעלן ומלמטן ומכנגדן ד' אמות ואם בא עכשיו אחד מהן לפתוח חלון צורי למטה מד' אמות מקרקע הבית שכנו יכול למחות בידו ומעכבו שלא יפתח: למעלה מד' אמות. מקרקע הבית אין לו חזקה דאין חבירו מקפיד וכשבונה שכנו אינו יכול לעכב עליו ולומר לו הרחק בנינך מן החלון שלי שלא תאפיל עלי שיכול לומר לו סתום אותו שאין לך חזקה ואם אין לו חלון שם וביקש עכשיו לפתוח חלון למעלה מד' אמות אין יכול שכנו למחות בידו ולמנעו ודוקא חלון צורי אבל חלון המצרי בין מלמעלה מד"א בין מלמטה אין לו חזקה וגם אין יכול השכן למחות: ור' אילעא אמר אפילו למעלה מד' אמות. אע"ג דלית ליה חזקה יכול למחות לבלתי עשות שכנו שם חלון כדמפרש טעמא לקמיה זימנין דמותבת שרשיפא וקא חזית בביתי ור' זירא לא חייש להכי דלא חציפי אינשי כולי האי למיעבד הכי: מדת סדום. אין מהנה לחבירו אע"פ שאין חסר בכך כלום. לר"ז כופין דלמעלה מד' אין מניחין אותו למחות שהרי אינו חסר כלום ולרבי אילעא אין כופין ויכול למחות: ושאני הכא. דאיכא חסרון: שרשיפא. ספסל: ההוא דאתא וכו'. רוצה היה לעשות חלון צורי למעלה מד' אמות וחבירו היה מוחה בידו: עביד ליה כר' אילעא. אלמא הכי הלכתא: אמר שמואל ולאורה אפילו כל שהוא יש לו חזקה. חלון העשוי ליכנס ממנו אור במקום אפל לא בעינן חלון צורי אלא אפילו כל שהוא יש לו חזקה דחלון העשוי לאורה מילתא דקביעותא דכל הימים אדם צריך לאורה וכיון שעשה חלון זה לכל הימים עשאו והיה לו לבעל חצר למחות בתוך ג' ומדלא מיחה איכא למימר דברשותו עשה ומתני' לאו בחלון העשוי לאורה מיירי אלא בחלון העשוי לשמור גנות ופרדסים דרך החלון: מתני' הזיז עד טפח יש לו חזקה. מי שיש לו כותל סמוך לחצר חבירו והוציא זיז טפח בולט מכתלו לחצר חבירו הויא חזקה ואין בעל החצר יכול לבנות שם בנין לסתור את הזיז דכולי האי לא הוה שביק ליה בעל החצר להוציא זיז טפח בחצרו בלא רשותו שהרי יכול למחות כדקתני ואזיל ומדלא מיחה בתוך ג' איכא למימר דברשותו הוציא:

תוספות

במזחילה של בנין עסקינן. אבל מרזב סתמו של עץ ואין עושין אותו של בנין וא"ת וליפלוג במזחילה עצמה בין של בנין לשל עץ וי"ל דניחא ליה במתמיתין לאשמועינן במרזב דיש לו מקומו חזקה: **והחוט** המשולש לא במהרה ינתק. כמה היו שכן ולאבותיהם ולאבות אבותיהם היו תלמידי חכמים ולא קאמר עליהם החוט המשולש אלא הכא היינו טעמא לפי שנשלשתן ראו זה את זה והא דמזכיר ר' אושעיא קודם רבי חמא אביו במחלוקת לפי שהיה גדול יותר מאביו כדאמר (עירובין דף נג.) לבן של ד) (ראשונים) כפתח [היכל] זה ר' אושעיא ואמר נמי ר' אושעיא בדורו כר"מ בדורו שלא יכלו חביריו לעמוד על סוף דעתו:

למטה מד' יש לו חזקה. ר"ת מפרש דאיירי בחלון צורי או שעשוי לאורה שהוא דבר קביעות אפילו למעלה מארבע אמות יש לו חזקה והביא ראיה מדתניא לעיל (דף כב:) החלונות בין מלמטה בין מלמעלה ד"א ותני עלה מלמטה שלא יעמוד ויראה אלמא אפי' למעלה מד' אמות יש לו חזקה כיון דהוי דבר קביעות ואומר רשב"א דאין נראה משם ראיה דאף על פי שהוא יותר מד' אמות לעומד בחוץ לעומד בפנים לא הוי למעלה מארבע אמות כגון שאותן חלונות בעלייה אי נמי מיירי כגון שיש לו עדים או שטר:

עד טפח יש לו חזקה ויכול למחות. אפילו בעל הגג בבעל החצר דאין לומר דוקא בעל החצר בבעל הגג אבל בעל הגג בבעל החצר לא יכול למחות דהא קתני בסיפא פחות מטפח אין יכול למחות ומפרש רב הונא היינו בעל הגג בבעל החצר אבל בעל החצר בבעל הגג יכול למחות אלא על כרחך בטפח אפילו בעל הגג יכול למחות בבעל החצר וטעמא דבטפח יכול לתלות דברים גדולים המכבידים על הכותל או אם יניח עליו כלי מלא מים וישפך ויתקלקל הכותל ובעל החצר יכול למחות משום היזק ראיה ולמאי דס"ד בגמרא למימר דרב יהודה לית ליה היזק ראיה מכל מקום כשיש כלי מלא מים פעמים שיפול ויטשטש כל החצר ופעמים שיפול על ראש בעל החצר ומיירי תוך ג' אבל אחר שהחזיק אין יכול למחות בעל הגג בבעל החצר ועוד יש לפרש דדוקא אחר ג' איירי ויכול למחות בעל הגג בבעל החצר ולא מטעם דפרישית אלא משום דיש לו תשמיש לבעל הגג על הזיז רוצה להשתמש בו כל שעה ולא יניח את בעל החצר להשתמש בו אבל בתוך ג' שלא החזיק אין יכול למחות בבעל החצר אבל בעל החצר בבעל הגג יכול למחות והוי כמו לרב הונא בפחות מטפח והא דמפליג בין טפח לפחות הא בהא תליא דבטפח דמהני ביה חזקה יכול למחות בבעל החצר אבל בפחות מטפח דלא הויא חזקה אין יכול למחות:

ואפילו

מסורת הש"ס

א) [אולי שיילוהו. יעב"ץ], ב) כתובות סב:, ג) [לעיל יב: וש"נ] לקמן קסח., ד) [צ"ל אחרונים].

הגהות הב"ח

(א) רשב"ם ד"ה דמיתרע כו' דלא חשיב כל כך אפי' אי הוי:

תורה אור השלם

א) וְאִם יִתְקְפוֹ הָאֶחָד הַשְּׁנַיִם יַעַמְדוּ נֶגְדּוֹ וְהַחוּט הַמְשֻׁלָּשׁ לֹא בִמְהֵרָה יִנָּתֵק: [קהלת ד, יב]

ליקוטי רש"י

והחוט המשולש לא במהרה ינתק. מי שהוא ת"ח ובנו ובן בנו שוב אין תורה פוסקת מזרעו וכן הוא אומר (ישעיה נט) לא ימושו מפיך ומפי זרעך ומפי זרע זרעך [קהלת ד, יב]. כופין על מדת סדום. זה נהנה וזה לא חסר [לעיל יב:]. דאפילו מידי דלא חסר ביה לא מהני לחבריה. מדת סדום. שלי שלי [עירובין מט.]. זה נהנה וזה לא חסר דלא הוי עושין טובה [כתובות קג.]. האומר שלי שלי ושלך שלך זו מדה בינונית ויש אומרים כלתה מדת סדום [רשב"ם לקמן קסח.]. הזיז. כל עץ היוצא מן הכותל קרוי זיז [שבת ד:].

עין משפט נר מצוה

רעא א מיי' פ"ח מהל' שכנים הל' ה סמג עשין פב טוש"ע ח"מ סי' קנג סעיף ז:

רעב ב מיי' שם הל' ד טוש"ע שם סעיף יג:

רעג ג מיי' שם פ"ז הל' ה סמג עשין לה טוש"ע ח"מ סי' קנד סעיף י:

רעד ד מיי' שם טוש"ע שם סעיף ט:

רעה ה מיי' שם הל' ז וטוש"ע שם סעיף י:

רעו ו מיי' שם פ"ח הל' ב סמג עשין פב טוש"ע ח"מ סי' קנג סעיף ג:

רבינו גרשום

המזחילה. היינו צנור גדול שמונח כנגד כל הבית אם מקלחת מים לחצר חבירו יש לו חזקה לפי שהיא גדולה: בשלמא להני תרי לישני קמאי שפיר. דלמרזב אין לו חזקה מרוח אחת ושאם היה ארוך מקצרו משא"כ במזחילה שיש לה חזקה: אלא למ"ד שאם בא לבנות תחתיו. של מרזב: מאי נפקא ליה מינה. לבעל המזחילה והלא מקבל הוא מימיו שלו בחצר של בנינו: הכא במזחילה של בנין. שעשויה מן אבנים ומן סיד עסקינן דאמר ליה בעל המזחילה לא ניחא לי דתיתרע אשיתאי. שאם יגע בבנינך למזחילה יקלקל אותה. ואם לא יהיה ריוח למים לקלוח ולצאת ישהיו שם במזחילה ויקלקלו הכותל: לדידי קני לי ממיא דאיגרך. לקבלן ולעשות מהן צרכי: רבי אושעיא אומר מעכב. לו שלא לסותמו זה: ר' אושעיא שאמר דמעכב כמו שאמר ר' ביסא זקינו שהוא שלישי לו: שאין לו ד' חווקין. מעלות: אין לו חזקה: אם יש לו מלבן בחצר חבירו כמו שפה מתחתיה שמשפע בחצר: מ"ש גבי סולם דלא קמפרש. במתני' איזהו סולם: ר' זירא אמר אדר' יהודה דמתני' קאי ואמר למטה מד' אמות אי איכא חלון בחצר חבירו יש לו חזקה ויכול למחות משום היזק ראיה ואי לא מיחה יש לו חזקה: ואי למעלה מד' אמות קאי. דליכא היזק ראיה אין לו חזקה מפני שאין יכול למחות האי הואיל דלא מזיק ליה הלכך אין לו חזקה מפני שאין יכול למחות לכך שתק אבל לא מחיל: ור' אילעא אמר אפי' למעלה מד' אמות אין לו חזקה. דלכך שתיק דלא מזיק ליה. ויכול למחות ולעכב לו מתי שירצה: בכופין על מדת סדום. דבר שאין מזיק לו ומועיל לחבירו כגון חלון למעלה מד' אמות דר' זירא סבר כופין שלא יעכב ולהכי קאמר שאין יכול למחות ור' אילעא סבר יכול למחות וקסבר דאין כופין: דכולי עלמא. ואפי' ר' אילעא אמר דכופין: אי הכי אמאי אמר דיכול למחות. דאמר ליה זימנין דמותבת מידי תותך עד דקיימת להדי חלון

וחזית מינאי ואסתכל כלום מה שבחצירי: ההוא דאתא לקמיה דר' אמי. שהיה לו חלון בחצר חבירו למעלה מד' אמות: כר' אילעא. דאין לו חזקה ויכול למחות: אמר שמואל ולאורה אפי' כל שהוא הרי זו חזקה. כלומר אם פתח חלון בחצר חבירו למעלה מד' אמות לצורך אורה בפני חבירו ולא מיחה אפי' כל שהוא שאין אדם ראש אדם נכנס בו ואע"פ שאין לו מלבן הויא חזקה ואין יכול בעל חצר לסותמה ולא להאפיל עליו: פיסקא הזיז עד טפח. שאם יש לו לאדם זיז יוצא מכותלו לחצר חבירו עד טפח יש לו חזקה בחצר חבירו כשיעור טפח. שאלמלא שיש לו חזקה בחצר לא היה מניחו להוציא בה זיז כשיעור טפח: מפני שיכול למחות

אָמַר שְׁמוּאֵל – Shmuel said: וּלְאוֹרָה – But if the window was opened **to provide light** for a dark room, **אֲפִילוּ כָּל שֶׁהוּא – even** if the window is **minuscule, יֵשׁ לוֹ חֲזָקָה – it has a *chazakah.***[23]

Mishnah The next Mishnah speaks of establishing a *chazakah* in the airspace of a neighbor's courtyard: **הַזִּיז – A beam**[24] that protrudes into a neighbor's courtyard **עַד טֶפַח – at least a *tefach***[25] **יֵשׁ לוֹ חֲזָקָה – has a *chazakah.***[26]

NOTES

23. A window opened to let light into a dark room is definitely intended to be permanent. Thus, the owner of the neighboring courtyard should have protested, and his silence indicates that the window was opened with his permission (*Rashbam*). [Our Mishnah does not speak of a window opened for light; rather, it deals with a window that a person opened for the purposes of viewing his distant properties (see 58b note 19).]

Rashbam understands Shmuel's ruling as referring only to a window opened to let light into a dark room, which has no light from another source (cf. *Ritva*).

24. I.e. a board or the end of a beam that projects from a roof or wall and extends into the airspace of a neighbor's courtyard. Objects are hung on the beam (*Rashbam* 59b ד״ה זיז; cf. *Yad Ramah*).

25. Literally: to a *tefach.* I.e. even a board as small as a *tefach,* and certainly a larger one.

26. A courtyard owner can be expected to object to a beam protruding into his courtyard. His lack of protest for three years is taken as evidence that the beam was placed with his permission. The resultant *chazakah* allows the owner of the beam to continue using it, and prevents the courtyard's owner from undertaking any construction that would require removal of the beam (*Rashbam*).

תנן המזחילה יש לה חזקה בשלמא למאן דאמר הנך תרתי שפיר אלא למאן דאמר שאם רצה לבנות תחתיו בונה מאי נפקא ליה מינה הכא במזחילה של בנין עסקינן דאמר ליה לא ניחא לי דתיתרע אשיתאי אמר רב יהודה אמר שמואל [א]צינור המקלח מים לחצר חברו ובא בעל הגג לסותמו בעל החצר מעכב עליו דאמר ליה כי היכי דאת קנית לך חצר דידי למשדא ביה מיא לדידי נמי קני לי מיא דאיגרך איתמר רבי אושעיא אמר מעכב ר' חמא אמר אינו מעכב [א]אזל שייליה לרבי ביסא אמר להו מעכב [ג]קרי עליה רמי בר חמא [א]והחוט המשולש לא במהרה ינתק זה רבי אושעיא בנו של רבי חמא בנו של רבי ביסא: סולם המצרי אין לו חזקה: [ב]היכי דמי סולם המצרי אמרי דבי ר' ינאי כל שאין לו ארבעה חווקין: חלון המצרית אין לה חזקה כו': מאי שנא גבי סולם דלא מפרש ומאי שנא גבי חלון דמפרש משום דקא בעי איפלוגי רבי יהודה בסיפא אמר רבי זירא למטה מד' אמות יש לו חזקה ויכול למחות למעלה מארבע אמות אין לו חזקה ואינו יכול למחות ורבי אילעא אמר [ג]אפילו למעלה מארבע אמות אין לו חזקה ויכול למחות [ג]לימא בכופין על מדת סדום קא מיפלגי דמר סבר כופין ומר סבר אין כופין לא דכולי עלמא כופין ושאני הכא [ד]דאמר ליה זימנין דמותבת שרשיפא תותך וקיימת וקא חזית ההוא דאתא לקמיה דר' אמי שדריה לקמיה דרבי אבא בר ממל אמר ליה עביד ליה כרבי אילעא אמר שמואל [ה]ולאורה אפי' כל שהוא יש לו חזקה: מתני' [ו]הזיז עד טפח יש לו חזקה ויכול

תנן המזחילה יש לה חזקה. ובמאי דקתני המרזב אין לו חזקה קאמר אבל המזחילה יש לה חזקה: בשלמא למאן דאמר הנך תרתי שפיר. דלשמואל דאמר אין לו חזקה מרזב אחת שפיר איצטריך למימר אבל המזחילה יש לה חזקה דדבר קביעות הוא ואין רגילין לעקרה ממקום למקום וכן לדר' חנינא שאם היה ארוך מקצרו אבל המזחילה יש לה חזקה ואין מקצרין אותה: אלא למאן דאמר. גבי מרזב דלהכי אין לו חזקה שאם רצה לבנות תחתיו בונה מאי שנא מזחילה דקאמר יש לו חזקה שאין בונין תחתיה מאי נפקא ליה מינה לבעל מזחילה אי בני בעל חצר תותה הא לא מפסיד מידי ובעל חצר לא שעבד לו חצירו למזחילתו לדבר שאינו מזיק לו: של בנין. אבנים: דאמר לא ניחא לי. שתבנה תחתיה: דתיתרע אשיתאי. כלומר מזחילה שלי תפול לקול מקבות והגרזן וכל כלי ברזל בהבנות בנינך אבל גבי מרזב (א) לא חשיב כל כך אפילו הוי של בנין בונה תחתיו אי נמי האי דקא מפליג בין מרזב למזחילה היינו משום דסתם מרזב של עץ וסתם מזחילה של אבנים: צינור. של שופכין: לדידי נמי קני לי מיא דאיגרך. להשקות בהמותי שעל מנת כן נתרציתי לך ודמי למקח וממכר שאני שעבדתי לך חצירי בשביל מימך ואם אתה חוזר בך אני לא אחזור בי: מעכב. על בעל הגג: אינו מעכב. דלא שעבד לו מימיו אלא כל ימי שיהיו יורדין לחצירו: אזול שייליה לרבי ביסא. אביו של ר' חמא וזקנו של רבי אושעיא: לא במהרה ינתק. כדדרשינן נמי (ב"מ דף פה.) מפי זרעך ומפי זרע זרעך וגו' מדור שלישי ואילך תורה מחזרת על אכסניא שלה: זה ר' אושעיא. שאמר מעכב: זקנו: חווקין. שליבות אשקלוני"ש: וקבעי גמרא מ"ש גבי סולם דלא קמפרש. מתני' שיעורא כי היכי דקמפרש גבי חלון: משום דקבעי לאיפלוגי רבי יהודה. גבי חלון הוצרך ת"ק לפרש שיעורו: א"ר זירא למטה מד' אמות. מקרקע הבית קתני מתני' דחלון צורי יש לו חזקה דכיון דאיכא תרתי שהוא גדול ונמוך ויכולין להסתכל ממנו בחצר יש לו חזקה שלא היה זה מניחו לעשות אלא ודאי ברשותו ואם בא שכנו לבנות הדין להתרחק כדתנן (לעיל דף כב:) החלונות מלמעלן ומלמטן ומכנגדן ד' אמות ואם בא עכשיו אחד מהן לפתוח חלון צורי למטה מד' אמות מקרקע הבית שכנו יכול למחות בידו ומעכבו שלא יפתח: למעלה מד' אמות. מקרקע הבית אין לו חזקה דאין חבירו מקפיד וכשבונה שכנו אינו יכול לעכב עליו ולומר לו הרחק בנינך מן החלון שלי שלא תאפיל עלי שיכול לומר לו סתום אותו שאין לך חזקה ואם אין לו חלון שם ובקש עכשיו לפתוח חלון למעלה מד' אמות אין יכול שכנו למחות בידו ולמנעו ודוקא חלון צורי אבל חלון המצרי בין מלמעלה מד"א בין מלמטה אין לו חזקה וגם אין יכול השכן למחות: ור' אילעא אמר אפילו למעלה מד' אמות. אע"ג דלית ליה חזקה יכול למחות לבלתי עשות שכנו שם חלון כדמפרש טעמא לקמיה זימנין דמותבת שרשיפא וקא חזית בביתי ור' זירא לא חייש להכי דלא חציפי אינשי כולי האי למיעבד הכי: מדת סדום. אין מהנה לחבירו אע"פ שאין חסר בכך כלום. לר"ז כופין דלמעלה מד' אין מניחין אותו למחות שהרי אינו חסר כלום ולרבי אילעא אין כופין ויכול למחות: ושאני הכא. דאיכא חסרון: שרשיפא. ספסל: ההוא דאתא וכו'. רוצה היה לעשות חלון צורי למעלה מד' אמות וחבירו היה מוחה בידו: עביד ליה כר' אילעא. אלמא הכי הלכתא: אמר שמואל ולאורה אפילו כל שהוא יש לו חזקה. חלון העשוי ליכנס ממנו אור במקום אפל לא בעינן חלון צורי אלא אפילו כל שהוא יש לו חזקה דחלון העשוי לאורה מילתא דקביעותא דכל הימים אדם צריך לאורה וכיון שעשה חלון זה לכל הימים עשאו והיה לו לבעל חצר למחות בתוך ג' ומדלא מיחה איכא למימר דברשותו עשה ומתני' לאו בחלון העשוי לאורה מיירי אלא בחלון העשוי לשמור גנות ופרדסים דרך החלון: מתני' הזיז עד טפח יש לו חזקה. מי שיש לו כותל סמוך לחצר חבירו והוציא זיז טפח בולט מכותלו לחצר חבירו הויא חזקה ואין בעל החצר יכול לבנות שם בנין לסתור את הזיז דכולי האי לא הוה שביק ליה בעל החצר להוציא זיז טפח בחצרו בלא רשותו שהרי יכול למחות כדקתני ואזיל ומדלא מיחה בתוך ג' איכא למימר דברשותו הוציא: ויכול

במזחילה של בנין עסקינן. אבל מרזב סתמו של עץ ואין עושין אותו של בנין וא"ת וליפלוג במזחילה עצמה בין של בנין לשל עץ וי"ל דניחא ליה במתניתין לאשמועינן במרזב דיש למקומו חזקה: והחוט המשולש לא במהרה ינתק. כמה היו שהן תלמידי חכמים ואבותיהם ואבות אבותיהם היו תלמידי חכמים ולא קאמר עליהם החוט המשולש אלא הכא היינו טעמא לפי שנשתכן ראו זה את זה והא דמזכיר ר' אושעיא קודם רבי חמא אביו במחלוקת לפי שהיה גדול יותר מאביו כדאמר (עירובין דף נג.) לבן של [ד](ראשונים) כפתח [היכל] זה ר' אושעיא ואמר נמי ר' אושעיא בדורו כר"מ בדורו שלא יכלו חביריו לעמוד על סוף דעתו: למטה מד' יש לו חזקה. ר"ת מפרש דאיירי בחלון מצרית אבל בחלון צורי או שעשוי לאורה שהוא דבר קביעות אפילו למעלה מארבע אמות יש לו חזקה והביא ראיה מדתניא לעיל (דף כב:) החלונות בין מלמעלה בין מלמטה ד"א ותני עלה מלמטה שלא יעמוד ויראה אלמא אפי' למעלה מד' אמות יש לו חזקה כיון דהוי דבר קביעות ואומר רשב"א דאין נראה משם ראיה דאף על פי שהוא יותר מד' אמות לעומד בחוץ לעומד בפנים לא הוי למעלה מארבע אמות כגון שאותן חלונות בעלייה אי נמי מיירי כגון שיש לו עדים או שטר: עד טפח יש לו חזקה ויכול למחות. אפילו בעל הגג בבעל החצר דאין לומר דוקא בעל החצר בבעל הגג אבל בעל הגג בבעל החצר לא יוכל למחות דהא קתני בסיפא פחות מטפח אין יכול למחות ומפרש רב הונא היינו בעל הגג בבעל החצר אבל בעל החצר בבעל הגג יכול למחות אלא על כרחך בטפח אפילו בעל הגג יכול למחות בבעל החצר וטעמא דבטפח יכול לתלות דברים גדולים המכבידים על הכותל או אם יניח עליו כלי מלא מים וישפך ויתקלקל הכותל ובעל החצר יכול למחות משום היזק ראיה ולמאי דס"ד בגמרא למימר דרב יהודה לית ליה היזק ראיה מכל מקום כשיש כלי מלא מים פעמים שיפול ויטשטש כל החצר ופעמים שיפול על ראש בעל החצר ומיירי תוך ג' אבל אחר שהחזיק אין יכול למחות בעל החצר בבעל הגג ועוד יש לפרש דדוקא אחר ג' איירי ויכול למחות בעל הגג בבעל החצר ולא מטעם דפרישית אלא משום דיש לו תשמיש לבעל הגג על הזיז רוצה להשתמש בו כל שעה ולא יניח את בעל החצר להשתמש בו אבל בתוך ג' שלא החזיק אין יכול למחות בבעל החצר אבל בעל החצר בבעל הגג יכול למחות והוי כמו לרב הונא בפחות מטפח והא דמפליג בין טפח לפחות הא בהא תליא דבטפח דמהני ביה חזקה יכול למחות בבעל החצר אבל בפחות מטפח דלא הויא חזקה אין יכול למחות: ואפילו

מסורת הש"ס

א) [אולי שיילוהו. יעב"ץ], ב) כתובות סב., ג) [לעיל יב: וש"נ] לקמן קסח., ד) [צ"ל אחרונים].

הגהות הב"ח

(א) רשב"ם ד"ה דמיתרע כו' דלא חשיב כל כך אפי' אי הוי:

תורה אור השלם

א) וְאִם יִתְקְפוֹ הָאֶחָד הַשְּׁנַיִם יַעַמְדוּ נֶגְדּוֹ וְהַחוּט הַמְשֻׁלָּשׁ לֹא בִמְהֵרָה יִנָּתֵק: [קהלת ד, יב]

ליקוטי רש"י

והחוט המשולש לא במהרה ינתק. מי שהוא ת"ח ובנו ובן בנו שוב אין תורה פוסקת מזרעו וכן הוא אומר (ישעיה נט) לא ימושו מפיך ומפי זרעך ומפי זרע זרעך [קהלת ד, יב]. כופין על מדת סדום. זה נהנה וזה לא חסר [לעיל יב:]. דאפילו מידי דלא חסר ביה לא מהני לחבריה. מדת סדום. [ערכין ל:]. דלפילו מידי דלא חסר ביה לא מהני לחבריה. זה נהנה וזה לא חסר לא היו עושין טובה [כתובות קג.]. (אבות פ"ה מ"י) האומר שלי שלי ושלך שלך זו מדה בינונית ויש אומרים זו מדת סדום [רשב"ם לקמן קסח.]. הזיז. כל עץ היוצא מן הכותל קרי זיז [שבת ד:].

עין משפט נר מצוה

רעא א מיי' פ"ה מהל' שכנים הל' ה סמג עשין פב טוש"ע ח"מ סי' קנג סעיף ז:
רעב ב מיי' שם הל' ד טוש"ע שם סעיף יג:
רעג ג מיי' שם פ"ז הל' ה סמג עשין לה טוש"ע ח"מ סי' קנד סעיף ז:
רעד ד מיי' שם טוש"ע שם סעיף ו:
רעה ה מיי' שם פ"ה הל' ז וע"ש טוש"ע שם סעיף י:
רעו ו מיי' שם פ"ה הל' ג סמג עשין פב טוש"ע ח"מ סי' קנג סעיף ג:

רבינו גרשום

המזחילה. היינו צנור גדול שמונח כנגד כל הבית אם מקלחת מים לחצר חבירו יש לו חזקה לפי שהיא גדולה: בשלמא להני תרי לישני קמאי שפיר. דלמרזב אין לו חזקה מרוח אחת ושאם היה ארוך מקצרו משא"כ במזחילה שיש לה חזקה: אלא למ"ד שאם בא לבנות תחתיו. של מרזב: מאי נפקא ליה מינה. לבעל המזחילה והלא מקבל הוא מימיו שלו בתוך של בנינו: הכא במזחילה של בנין. שעשויה מן אבנים ומן סיד עסקינן דאמר ליה בעל המזחילה לא ניחא לי דתיתרע אשיתאי. שאם יגע בנינך למזחילה יקלקל אותה. ואם לא יהיה ריוח למים לקלח ולצאת ישתהו שם במזחילה ויקלקלו הכותל: לדידי קני לי ממיא דאיגרך. לקבלן ולעשות מהן צרכי: רבי אושעיא אומר מעכב. לו שלא לסותמו זה: ר' אושעיא שאמר דמעכב כמו שאמר ר' ביסא זקינו שהוא שלישי לו: שאין לו ד' חווקין. מעלות: אין לו חזקה: אם יש לו מלבן בחצר חבירו כמו שפה מתחתיה שמשפע בחצר: מ"ש גבי סולם דלא קמפרש. במתני' איזהו סולם: ר' זירא אמר אדר' יהודה דמתני' קאי ואמר למטה מד' אמות אי איכא חלון בחצר חבירו יש לו חזקה ויכול למחות משום היזק ראיה ואי לא מיחה יש לו חזקה: ואי למעלה מד' אמות קאי. דליכא היזק ראיה אין לו חזקה מפני שאין יכול למחות האי הואיל דלא מזיק ליה הלכך אין לו חזקה מפני שאין יכול למחות לכך שתק אבל לא מחיל: ור' אילעא אמר אפי' למעלה מד' אמות אין לו חזקה. דלכך שתיק דלא מזיק ליה. ויכול למחות ולעכב לו מתי שירצה: בכופין על מדת סדום. דבר שאין מזיק לו ומועיל לחבירו כגון חלון למעלה מד' אמות דר' זירא סבר כופין שלא יעכב ולהכי קאמר שאין יכול למחות ור' אילעא סבר יכול למחות קסבר דאין כופין: דכולי עלמא. ואפי' ר' אילעא אמר דכופין: אי הכי אמאי אמר דיכול למחות. דאמר ליה זימנין דמותבת מידי תותך עד דקיימת להדי חלון וחזית מינאי ותסתכל כלום מה שבחצירי: ההוא דאתא לקמיה דר' אמי. שהיה לו חלון בחצר חבירו למעלה מד' אמות: כר' אילעא. דאין לו חזקה ויכול למחות: אמר שמואל ולאורה אפי' כל שהוא הרי זו חזקה. כלומר אם פתח חלון בחצר חבירו למעלה מד' אמות לצורך אורה בפני חבירו ולא מיחה אפי' כל שהוא שאין ראש אדם נכנס בו ואע"פ שאין לו מלבן הויא חזקה ואין יכול בעל חצר לסותמה ולא להאפיל עליו: פיסקא הזיז עד טפח. שאם יש לו לאדם זיז יוצא מכותלו לחצר חבירו עד טפח יש לו חזקה. שאלמלא שיש לו חזקה בחצר לא היה מניחו להוציא בה זיז כשיעור טפח: מפני שיכול למחות

עין משפט נר מצוה

רעז א מיי' פ"ח מהל' שכנים הל' ג ועי' בהשגות ובמ"מ סמג עשין פב טוש"ע ח"מ סי' קנג סעיף ד:
רעח ב מיי' שם הל' א טוש"ע שם סעיף ה:
רעט ג מיי' פ"ה הל' ו סמג שם טוש"ע ח"מ סי' קנד סעיף ה:
רפ ד ה מיי' שם הל' ח טור ש"ע שם סעיף ו:
רפא ו מיי' שם פ"ה הל' ו סמג שם טוש"ע שם סעיף ג:
רפב ז מיי' שם פ"ה הל' ו סמג שם טוש"ע שם:

ויכול למחות פחות מטפח אין לו חזקה ואין יכול למחות: **גמ'** אמר רבי אסי אמר רבי מני ואמרי לה אמר רבי יעקב אמר רבי מני החזיק בטפח החזיק בד' מאי קאמר אמר אביי ה"ק א החזיק רוחב טפח במשך ארבע החזיק ברוחב ארבע: פחות מטפח אין לו חזקה ואינו יכול למחות: אמר רב הונא לא שנו אלא בעל הגג בבעל החצר ב אבל בעל החצר בבעל הגג יכול למחות ורב יהודה אמר אפילו בעל חצר בבעל הגג אינו יכול למחות לימא (א) בהיזק ראיה קמיפלגי דמר סבר שמיה היזק ומר סבר לאו שמיה היזק לא דכולי עלמא שמיה היזק ושאני הכא דאמר ליה לתשמישתא לא חזי למאי חזי למתלא ביה מידי מהדרנא אפאי ותלינא ביה ואידך א"ל זימנין דבעיתת: **מתני'** ג לא יפתח אדם חלונותיו לחצר השותפין ד לקח בית בחצר אחרת לא יפתחנה בחצר השותפין ה בנה עלייה על גבי ביתו לא יפתחנה לחצר השותפין אלא אם רצה בונה את החדר לפנים מביתו ובונה עלייה על גבי ביתו ופותחה לתוך ביתו: **גמ'** מאי איריא לחצר השותפין אפילו לחצר חבירו נמי לא לא מיבעיא קאמר ו לא מיבעיא לחצר חברו דלא אבל לחצר השותפין דא"ל סוף סוף הא קא בעית אצטנועי מינאי בחצר קא משמע לן דאמר ליה עד האידנא בחצר הוה בעינא אצטנועי מינך השתא אפי' בבית נמי בעינא אצטנועי מינך ת"ר מעשה באדם אחד שפתח חלוניו לחצר השותפין ובא לפני ר' ישמעאל בר רבי יוסי אמר לו החזקת בני החזקת ובא לפני רבי חייא אמר יגעת ופתחת (א) ז יגע וסתום אמר רב נחמן

ויכול למחות. כלומר הבא להוציא זיז טפח בתחלה לחצר חבירו יכול למחות בו בעל חצר שלא למלאות אויר חבירו ולא אמרינן זה נהנה וזה אינו חסר דודאי איכא חסרון כדאמרינן בגמרא גבי זיז פחות מטפח דמגו דמשתמש בעל הגג בזיז רואה בחצר ואיכא היזק ראיה: פחות מטפח אין לו חזקה. שאם ירצה בעל החצר לבנות שם בונה משום דלא קפיד דבציר מטפח לא חשיב: ואינו יכול למחות. בגמרא מפרש מי אינו יכול למחות במי: זיז. הוא כעין נסר או ראש קורה הבולט מן העלייה לחוץ וראוי לתלות בו חפציו: גמ' מאי קאמר. דמשמע דהכי קאמר שאם החזיק בהוצאת זיז ארוך טפח יכול להוציא כמו כן זיז ארבעה דכיון דהחזיק בזיז טפח החזיק נמי בארבעה ומילתא בלא טעמא הוא שאם נתרצה לו בעל החצר בטפח לא נתרצה לו בארבעה: הכי קאמר החזיק. בזיז שהוא רוחב טפח באורך ד' טפחים בולט מן הכותל לחוץ החזיק נמי בזיז שהוא רחב בד' על ד' אורך דכיון דהניח לו אורך של מקום חשוב נתרצה לו נמי ברחבו דאין מקום חשוב בפחות מד' על ד' והוא הדין שאם החזיק ברחב טפח במשך עשרה לא החזיק כי אם ברחב ד' אבל אם החזיק ברחב טפח במשך ג' לא החזיק ברחב ג' אלא מה שהחזיק החזיק ולא יותר: אמר רב הונא לא שנו. דאין יכול למחות: אלא בעל הגג. שהוא בעל הזיז: בבעל החצר. דאינו יכול למחות בו ולומר אל תשתמש בזיז שלי דמה הפסיד בעל הגג הלא כשישתמש בעל החצר ויתלה בזיז חפציו לא יראהו לבעל הגג שהרי הוא תחתון לו וליכא היזק ראיה ואי משום דממלא מקום הזיז שעכשיו אין יכול בעל הגג לתלות בו חפציו להא לא חיישינן דכיון דאין לו חזקה ויכול זה בעל חצר לחתכו לזיז אם יצטרך כל שכן שישתמש בו בעודנו תלוי באויר שלו אי נמי הכי קאמרה מתני' אין לו חזקה לבעל הגג וגם אינו יכול למחות בבעל החצר אם בא לקבוע זיזין סמוך לכתלו דהא ליכא היזק ראיה: אבל בעל החצר. יכול למחות בבעל הגג שלא יוציא זיז פחות מטפח בתחלה אי נמי שלא ישתמש בזיז שהוציא כבר מפני שהוא עליון וכשיבא להשתמש יראה בעלילה זו בחצר ואיכא היזק ראיה: ורב יהודה אומר כו'. טעמא מפרש לקמיה: ומר סבר לא שמיה היזק. רב יהודה והלכך אינו יכול למחות בעל החצר בבעל הגג: ושאני הכא דא"ל. בעל הגג לבעל החצר לשום תשמיש לא חזי לי האי זיז כל שהוא שאלך ואעמוד עליו ואראה בחצירך בעלילה זו ולא חזי אלא למתלי בי חפצי וכשארצה לתלות מהדרנא אפאי ואושיט זרועי ואתלה דכיון דיכולני לתלות בחזרת פנים אם אסתכל בחצירך אהא נתפס כגנב והלכך ליכא היזק ראיה ורב הונא [א"ל] זימנין דבעיתת ליפול מן הגג כשתעמוד בשפת הגג ותשוח לתלות דבר על הזיז ולא תהדר אפך ולא תבוש מלהסתכל בחצירי ולא תהא נתפס כגנב דאפילו כי לא בעיתת תטעון כך ותאמר מחמת ביעתותא לא אהדרנא אפאי והלכך איכא היזק ראיה: מתני' לא יפתח אדם חלונותיו לחצר. שיש לו בשותפות משום היזק ראיה וכל שכן לחצר חבירו כדמפרש בגמרא: לקח בית בחצר אחרת. הסמוך לזה החצר: לא יפתחנו לחצר השותפין. דאע"ג דיש לו חלק בחצר אינו יכול לרבות עליהם אכסנאין: לא יפתחנה. שהרי הוסיף דיורין בחצר ומטריח על בני החצר שמרבה עליהן דריסת הרגל: ופותחה לתוך ביתו. דכיון דדרך פתח שלו יוצאין לחצר אין טורח לבני החצר שאינו מרבה עליהן דיורין וכדמפרש בגמרא שלא הוסיף על ביתו כלום אלא חולקה לשנים שהרי כל ביתו יכול למלאות אכסנאין אם ירצה: גמ' מאי איריא לחצר השותפין. הרבים דלא יפתח דמשמע מפני שהן רבים חיישינן שלא יעשה להן היזק ראיה אפילו יחיד (ב) ראיה נמי אסור להזיקו והלכך אפילו לחצר חבירו נמי לא: אבל לחצר השותפין. איכא למימר דשרי לפתוח דבלאו הכי בעי אילטנועי מחבירו בחצר שזה יכול לראותו דרך פתח ביתו הפתוח לחצר ולא מזקי ליה חלונות מידי קמ"ל מתניתין דקתני לא יפתח דא"ל האי לבעל החלונות עד האידנא כי הוה משתמשנא בחצר הוה בעינא לאילטנועי מינך שלא תראני דרך פתח ביתך (ג) ואי הוינא בבית לא הוה בעינא לאילטנועי מינך שהרי לא היו עושין פתח כנגד פתח לכדקתני מתניתין אבל השתא אפי' בבית בעינא לאילטנועי מינך כדי שלא תראני דרך חלונותיך שהן גבוהות א"נ עד האידנא כי הוית בחצר בעינא לאילטנועי מינך כי הוית בבית לא בעינא לאילטנועי מינך השתא אפילו כשאתה בבית (ד) בעינא לאילטנועי מינך: שפתח חלונותיו. והיה טוען שעשה ברשות בני חצר: החזקת. סבר לה דאמר הוי חזקה דכיון דבפניו החזיק ושתק אם איתא דשלא ברשות עשה היה לו למחות והיינו דאמרן בפירקין לעיל (דף מא.) כמאן כרבי יהודה וכר' ישמעאל (ז) וכרבי יוסי דאמרי כל בפניו לאלתר הוי חזקה ואין הלכה כן: יגע וסתום. דלא הוי חזקה עד שלש שנים: ולסתום

ואפילו בעל החצר בבעל הגג אין יכול למחות. אע"ג דגבי זיז [שלפני] החלון דיוצא לרשות הרבים לא שרינן במסכת עירובין (דף לח:) להניח עליו אלא כלים הנשברים משום דחיישינן דלמא נפיל ואתי לאתויי והכא לא חיישינן שמא יפול על ראשו של בעל החצר שאינו עומד כל שעה תחת הזיז א"נ התם לא אסר אלא להניח עליו אבל הכא איירי למיתלא ביה דבדבר התלוי לא חיישינן לנפילה וא"ת והיאך יכול בעל הגג להשתמש בזיז והא איכא מעקה דאמר בפ"ק (לעיל ו:) גג הסמוך לחצר חברו עושה לו מעקה גבוה ארבע אמות וי"ל כגון דהזיז בקרן זוית בסוף המעקה: **מאי** איריא לחצר השותפין. פ"ה מאי איריא לחצר השותפין שמזיק לשנים משמע מתוך פירושו שהוא אינו שותף באותה חצר וקשה לר"י לפירושו מדמסיק בתר הכי אלא אפילו לחצר השותפין דאמר ליה סוף סוף בעית לאילטנועי מינאי משמע שהוא שותף ונראה לר"י לפרש מאי איריא לחצר השותפין שהוא מזיק לו משני מקומות אפילו לחצר חבירו שאינו מזיק לו אלא מכאן נמי ולפי' קשה לרשב"א דא"כ אמאי קאמר עד האידנא הוה בעית כו' הוה ליה למימר קא משמע לן דבשני מקומות לא מצינא לאילטנועי מינך ונראה לי דמעיקרא דפריך מאי איריא לא סלקא דעתיה שיש לו שותפות בחצר: **בבית** לא בעינא לאיצטנועי מינך. פירוש כשאתה בבית אבל פירוש אחר שפ"ה כשאני בבית אין נראה לרשב"א דהשתא נמי לא בעי לאילטנועי בתשמיש הבית דהא האי חלון דפתח אינו לא כנגד הפתח ולא כנגד החלון דהא תנן (לקמן דף ס.) אין פותחין חלון כנגד החלון כו': לקח

מסורת הש"ס

א) [לעיל ג:], ב) [ל"ל בר רבין]:

הגהות הב"ח

(א) גמ' ופתחת לך יגע: (ב) רשב"ם ד"ה מאי איריא וכו' אפי' יחיד נמי כצ"ל ותיבת ראיה נמחק: (ג) ד"ה אבל וכו' ביתך וכי הוינא וכו' לא הוה בעינא וכו': (ד) בא"ד כשאתה בבית נמי בעינא:

לעזי רש"י

אשקלויינ"ש. פירוש חווקין, שליבות, מעלות (רש"י ב"מ דף כה ע"ב ד"ה כסולם; רש"י שמות כ, כג, מדרגות (רש"י יחזקאל מ, כו; שה"ש ב, יד):

רבינו גרשום

למחות. ולעכב אדם בחבירו שלא יוציא בחצירו זיז טפח ואם פחות מטפח הוא אין לו חזקה בחצר שאינו חשוב. ואין יכול למחות בידו בעל החצר שלא יוציא בחצירו פחות מטפח שכיון שאין לו חזקה בכך מאי איכפת ליה: הכי קאמר. החזיק בטפח שיש לו בחצר חבירו זיז רחב טפח ובמשך ארכו ד' יש לו חזקה בחצר ברוחב ד' כנגד אורך כל הכותל שכיון שלא מיחה בו בעל חצר בזיז חשוב כזה בידוע שיש לו חזקה בחצר כנגד כל הכותל ברוחב אותו זיז: לא שנו. שאין יכול למחות אלא בעל הגג בבעל חצר שאין יכול בעל הגג לעכב לבעל החצר שלא ישים בחור שבכותלו זיז פחות מטפח אם הוא צריך לו שכבר אין לו חזקה: אבל בעל חצר בבעל הגג יכול למחות. שלא יוציא זיז פחות מטפח בחצירו בכותלו: מר סבר. רב הונא: שמיה היזק. להכי מעכב בעל חצר לבעל הגג שאבב שישחה אם ראש גגו וישתמש באותו זיז פחות מטפח שיקשור בו חבל או יתלה עליו [יסתכל] כלום ממנו בחצר ור"י סבר לאו שמיה היזק: ושאני הכא דאמר ליה בעל הגג לבעל חצר לתשמיש לא חזי ההוא זיז פחות מטפח שאין ראוי לעמוד עליו ולא חזי אלא למתלי ביה שום חפץ: כי תלינא ביה מידי מהדרנא אפאי ותלינא. ולא אסתכל בחצירך: ואידך. בעל חצר אמר זימנין דבעיתת שלא יהא תלוי או קשור בזיז יפה ומעיינת ואגב הכי תסתכל בחצירי: פיסקא לא יפתח אדם חלונותיו לחצר השותפין. חצר שיש לו שותפות בה אם אין לשאר שותפין שם חלונות. אפי' לחצר חבירו. של יחיד אין רשאי לפתוח משום היזק ראיה: לא מבעיא לחצר חבירו דלא. משום דאין לו חלק בה: אבל לחצר שותפין. שיש לו חלק בה:

הא מצי אמר ליה סוף סוף הא בעית איצטנועי מינאי כשאני נכנס ויוצא בחצר כך הצנע עצמך כשלחלונותי פתוחין: קמ"ל. דמצי א"ל השותף עד האידנא קודם פתיחת החלונות כשאתה בחצר הייתי צריך להצנע ממך וכשהייתה בבית לא הייתי צריך להצנע. עכשיו אפי' כשאתה בבית צריך אני להצנע ממך בחצר מפני חלונותיך: שפתח. לחצר השותפין ולא מיחו ושב מיחו: לך יגע וסתום. שאין חזקה עד ג' שנים: אמר רב נחמן ולסתום

וְיָכוֹל לִמְחוֹת — and [the courtyard owner] can protest the initial placement of the beam.[1] **פָּחוֹת מִטֶּפַח** — If the beam projects **less than a *tefach*, אֵין לוֹ חֲזָקָה — it has no *chazakah*,**[2] **וְאֵין יָכוֹל לִמְחוֹת — and he cannot protest.**[3]

Gemara The Gemara cites a ruling that expands the scope of a *chazakah* created by a projecting beam:

אָמַר רַבִּי אַסִּי אָמַר רַבִּי מָנִי — R' Assi said in the name of R' Mani, וְאָמְרֵי לָהּ — and some say אָמַר רַבִּי יַעֲקֹב אָמַר רַבִּי מָנִי — R' Yaakov said in the name of R' Mani: הֶחֱזִיק בְּטֶפַח — If one established a *chazakah* for a beam of **[one] *tefach*, הֶחֱזִיק בְּאַרְבָּעָה — he has established a *chazakah* for four *tefachim*.**

The Gemara is puzzled by this cryptic statement:

מַאי קָאָמַר — What did [R' Mani] say? Why should the beam's owner have a *chazakah* greater than that actually established?[4]

The Gemara explains the ruling:

אָמַר אַבָּיֵי — Abaye said: הָכִי קָאָמַר — [R' Mani] said thus: הֶחֱזִיק רוֹחַב טֶפַח — If [the beam's owner] established a ***chazakah*** for **a width of [one] *tefach* בְּמֶשֶׁךְ אַרְבָּעָה — at a length of four** *tefachim*,[5] **הֶחֱזִיק בְּרוֹחַב אַרְבָּעָה — he has** automatically **established** a ***chazakah* for a width of four** *tefachim*.[6]

The Gemara cites the latter ruling of the Mishnah:

פָּחוֹת מִטֶּפַח — If the beam projects LESS THAN A *TEFACH*, **אֵין לוֹ חֲזָקָה — IT HAS NO *CHAZAKAH*, וְאֵינוֹ יָכוֹל לִמְחוֹת — AND HE CANNOT PROTEST** the initial placement of the beam.

Amoraim argue over the identity of the subject of this last ruling:

אָמַר רַב הוּנָא — Rav Huna said: לֹא שָׁנוּ אֶלָּא בַּעַל הַגַּג בְּבַעַל הֶחָצֵר — They taught only that **the owner of the roof** from which the beam protruded may not protest **against the owner of the courtyard.**[7] **אֲבָל בַּעַל הֶחָצֵר בְּבַעַל הַגַּג יָכוֹל לִמְחוֹת — But the owner of the courtyard may protest against the owner of the roof** if the latter attempts to project a beam even less than a *tefach* over his courtyard.[8]

The dissenting opinion:

וְרַב יְהוּדָה אָמַר — But Rav Yehudah said: אֲפִילוּ בַּעַל חָצֵר בְּבַעַל הַגַּג אֵינוֹ יָכוֹל לִמְחוֹת — Nor can the owner of the courtyard protest against the owner of the roof.[9]

The Gemara attempts to define the point of contention between the disputants:

לֵימָא בְּהֶיזֵּק רְאִיָּה קָמִיפַּלְגֵי — Shall we say that [Rav Huna and Rav Yehudah] argue on the issue of **visual trespass,**[10] **דְּמָר סָבַר שְׁמֵיהּ הֶיזֵּק — as one master** (Rav Huna, who permits the courtyard owner to protest) **is of the opinion that visual trespass is considered damage, וּמָר סָבַר לָאו שְׁמֵיהּ הֶיזֵּק — and** the other **master** (Rav Yehudah, who enjoins the courtyard owner from protesting) **is of the opinion that visual trespass is not considered damage?**

The Gemara rejects this interpretation:

לֹא — This is **not** necessarily true. **דְּכוּלֵּי עָלְמָא שְׁמֵיהּ הֶיזֵּק** — For perhaps **everyone** agrees that visual trespass is **considered damage, וְשָׁאנֵי הָכָא — and** yet the situation **here is different, דְּאָמַר לֵיהּ — for [the roof owner] can say to [the courtyard owner]: לְתַשְׁמִישְׁתָּא לֹא חֲזֵי — "[This tiny beam] is unsuitable for** any normal **use;** hence, I cannot go out and stand upon it as a pretext for gazing into your courtyard. **לְמַאי חֲזֵי — For what** use **is it suitable? לְמִתְלָא בֵּיהּ מִידֵי** — Only **to hang objects upon it. מְהַדַּרְנָא אַפַּאי — I shall turn my face away** from your courtyard, stretch out my arm **וְתָלֵינָא בֵּיהּ — and hang** my objects **upon it!"**[11] Thus, Rav Yehudah does not empower the courtyard owner to protest the projection of a small beam, since no visual trespass will result from its use.

The Gemara inquires why Rav Huna rejects this reasoning:

וְאִידָךְ — And the other disputant? Why does Rav Huna authorize the courtyard owner to lodge a protest?

The Gemara answers:

אָמַר לֵיהּ — [The courtyard owner] can retort to [the roof owner]: זִימְנִין דְּבָעִיתַתְּ — "At times, as you stand at the edge of your roof and bend over to hang things on the beam, **you will be afraid** of losing your balance, and you will not turn your face away from my courtyard."[12] The courtyard owner is therefore empowered to protest the projection of the beam, since it is possible that he will suffer a loss of privacy on its account.

NOTES

1. The Gemara explains below that while using the beam its owner can gaze into the courtyard, thereby depriving the courtyard's owner of his privacy. Hence, the latter is entitled to protest the placement of the beam (*Rashbam*).

2. A beam so small is insignificant, and the owner of the courtyard will not object to its presence. Thus, his silence does not create a *chazakah;* and if he later wishes to build a wall upon his property and the beam impedes the construction, he may remove it (*Rashbam*).

3. The Gemara will discuss who is the subject of this ruling and what he wishes to protest.

4. The Gemara initially understands R' Mani to mean that one who has established a *chazakah* to project a beam one *tefach* long has the right to project a longer beam, even one of four *tefachim.* But this interpretation is illogical! The Gemara is therefore puzzled by R' Mani's statement (*Rashbam*).

5. I.e. the beam was one *tefach* wide and extended four *tefachim* over the courtyard (*Rashbam*).

6. I.e. he is entitled to extend a beam four *tefachim* wide and four *tefachim* long over the courtyard. For R' Mani maintains that once the courtyard's owner has allowed the beam to occupy a length of four *tefachim,* which is the minimum length of מָקוֹם חָשׁוּב, *a significant space,* he has thereby given his consent for a projecting beam to occupy the entire area of a "significant space." Hence, once one establishes a *chazakah* to project a beam four *tefachim* or more in length, he is automatically entitled to project a beam of up to four *tefachim* in width (*Rashbam;* cf. *Rabbeinu Gershom*).

7. I.e. the owner of the roof may not prevent the courtyard's owner from using the former's projecting beam for hanging objects therefrom. Since the courtyard owner is located below, he cannot see onto his neighbor's roof when using the beam, and therefore does not commit visual trespass. Further, the beam's owner cannot complain that the courtyard owner preempts his use of the beam, for the former has established no *chazakah* to extend the beam into the latter's airspace, and the latter may even cut down the beam if he needs the space. Certainly, then, he may make use of the beam whenever he wishes (*Rashbam,* first explanation).

8. Or if he attempts to use an existing beam. For since the beam's owner occupies the higher ground, the courtyard owner is justified in fearing that his neighbor will take advantage of the time spent using the beam to gaze into the courtyard, thus committing visual trespass (*Rashbam*).

Although we learned above (2b) that the owner of a roof that overlooks a courtyard must build a fence four *amos* high along his roof to protect against visual trespass, this fence does not prevent the roof's owner from using the projecting beam, for in our case the beam projects from the corner of the roof. The roof's owner can therefore reach around the edge of his fence and hang objects on the beam (*Tosafos*).

9. The Gemara below explains Rav Yehudah's reasoning.

10. The question of whether visual trespass is considered damaging is the subject of a major discussion at the beginning of this tractate (2a-3a).

11. Thus, since the beam can be used in this innocuous manner, the roof owner would not risk looking into the courtyard, for if caught doing so it would be obvious that he was intentionally committing visual trespass (*Rashbam*).

12. Thus, it is possible that the roof owner will intentionally gaze into the courtyard when he uses the beam, for since he can falsely claim that

ויכול למחות פחות מטפח אין לו חזקה ואין יכול למחות: **גמ'** אמר רבי אסי אמר רבי מני ואמרי לה אמר רבי יעקב אמר רבי מני החזיק בטפח החזיק בד' מאי קאמר אמר אביי ה"ק [א] החזיק רוחב טפח במשך ארבע החזיק ברוחב ארבע: פחות מטפח אין לו חזקה ואינו יכול למחות: אמר רב הונא לא שנו אלא בעל הגג בבעל החצר [ב] אבל בעל החצר בבעל הגג יכול למחות ורב יהודה אמר אפילו בעל חצר בבעל הגג אינו יכול למחות לימא (א) בהיזק ראיה קמיפלגי דמר סבר שמיה היזק ומר סבר לאו שמיה היזק לא דכולי עלמא שמיה היזק ושאני הכא דאמר ליה לתשמישתא לא חזי למאי חזי למתלא ביה מידי מהדרנא אפאי ותלינא ביה ואידך א"ל זימנין דבעיתת: **מתני'** [ג] לא יפתח אדם חלונותיו לחצר השותפין [ד] לקח בית בחצר אחרת לא יפתחנה בחצר השותפין [ה] בנה עלייה על גבי ביתו לא יפתחנה לחצר השותפין אלא אם רצה בונה את החדר לפנים מביתו ובונה עלייה על גבי ביתו ופותחה לתוך ביתו: **גמ'** מאי איריא לחצר השותפין אפילו לחצר חבירו נמי לא לא מיבעיא קאמר [ו] לא מיבעיא לחצר חברו דלא אבל לחצר השותפין דא"ל סוף סוף הא קא בעית אצטנועי מינאי בחצר קא משמע לן דאמר ליה עד האידנא בחצר הוה בעינא אצטנועי מינך השתא אפי' בבית נמי בעינא אצטנועי מינך ת"ר מעשה באדם אחד שפתח חלוניו לחצר השותפין ובא לפני ר' ישמעאל בר רבי יוסי אמר לו החזקת בני החזקת ובא לפני רבי חייא אמר יגעת ופתחת (א) [ז] יגע וסתום אמר רב נחמן

רשב"ם

ויכול למחות. כלומר הבא להוציא זיז טפח בתחלה לחצר חבירו יכול למחות בו בעל חצר שלא למלאות אויר חצירו ולא אמרינן זה נהנה וזה אינו חסר דודאי איכא חסרון כדאמרינן בגמרא גבי זיז פחות מטפח דמגו דמשתמש בעל הגג בזיז רואה בחצר ואיכא היזק ראיה: **פחות מטפח אין לו חזקה.** שאם ירצה בעל החצר לבנות שם בונה משום דלא קפיד דבציר מטפח לא חשיב: **ואינו יכול למחות.** בגמרא מפרש מי אינו יכול למחות במי: **זיז.** הוא כעין נסר או ראש קורה הבולט מן העלייה לחוץ וראוי לתלות בו חפציו: **גמ' מאי קאמר.** דמשמע דהכי קאמר שאם החזיק בהוצאת זיז ארוך טפח יכול להוציא כמו כן זיז ארבעה דכיון דהחזיק בזיז טפח החזיק נמי בארבעה ומילתא בלא טעמא הוא שאם נתרצה לו בעל החצר בטפח לא נתרצה לו בארבעה: **הכי קאמר החזיק.** בזיז שהוא רוחב טפח באורך ד' טפחים בולט מן הכותל לחוץ החזיק נמי בזיז שהוא רחב בד' על ד' אורך דכיון דהניח לו אורך של מקום חשוב נתרצה לו נמי ברחבו דאין מקום חשוב בפחות מד' על ד' והוא הדין שאם החזיק ברחב טפח במשך עשרה לא החזיק כי אם ברחב ד' אבל אם החזיק ברחב טפח במשך ג' לא החזיק ברחב ג' אלא מה שהחזיק החזיק ולא יותר: **אמר רב הונא לא שנו.** דאין יכול למחות: **אלא בעל הגג.** שהוא בעל הזיז: **בבעל החצר.** דאינו יכול למחות בו ולומר אל תשתמש בזיז שלי דמה הפסיד בעל הגג הלא כשישתמש בעל החצר ויתלה בזיז חפציו לא יראהו לבעל הגג שהרי הוא תחתון לו וליכא היזק ראיה ואי משום דממלא מקום הזיז שעכשיו אין יכול בעל הגג לתלות בו חפציו להא לא חיישינן דכיון דאין לו חזקה ויכול זה בעל חצר לחתכו לזיז אם יצטרך כל שכן שישתמש בו בעודנו תלוי באויר שלו אי נמי הכי קאמרה מתני' אין לו חזקה לבעל הגג וגם אינו יכול למחות בבעל החצר אם בא לקבוע זיזין סמוך לכתלו דהא ליכא היזק ראיה: **אבל בעל החצר.** יכול למחות בבעל הגג שלא יוציא זיז פחות מטפח בתחלה אי נמי שלא ישתמש בזיז שהוציא כבר מפני שהוא עליון וכשיבא להשתמש יראה בעלילה זו בחצר ואיכא היזק ראיה: **ורב יהודה אומר כו'.** טעמא מפרש לקמיה: **ומר סבר לא שמיה היזק.** רב יהודה והלכך אינו יכול למחות בעל החצר בבעל הגג: **ושאני הכא דא"ל.** בעל הגג לבעל החצר לשום תשמיש לא חזי לי האי זיז כל שהוא שאלך ואעמוד עליו ואראה בחצירך ולא חזי אלא למתלי בי חפצי וכשארצה לתלות מהדרנא אפאי ואושיט זרועי ואתלה דכיון דיכולני לתלות בחזרת פנים אם אסתכל בחצירך אהא נתפס כגנב והלכך ליכא היזק ראיה ורב הונא [א"ל] זימנין דבעיתת ליפול מן הגג כשתעמוד בשפת הגג לתלות דבר על הזיז ולא תהדר אפך ולא תבוש מלהסתכל בחצירי ולא תהא נתפס כגנב דאפילו כי לא בעיתת תטעון כך ותאמר מחמת ביעותא לא אהדרנא אפאי והלכך איכא היזק ראיה: **מתני' לא יפתח אדם חלונותיו לחצר.** שיש בו שותפות משום היזק ראיה וכל שכן לחצר חבירו כדמפרש בגמרא: **לקח בית בחצר אחרת.** הסמוך לזה החצר: **לא יפתחנו לחצר השותפין.** דאע"ג דיש לו חלק בחצר אינו יכול לרבות עליהם אכסנאין: **לא יפתחנה.** שהרי הוסיף דיורין בחצר ומטריח על בני החצר שמרבה עליהן דריסת הרגל: **ופותחה לתוך ביתו.** דכיון דדרך פתח שלו יוצאין לחצר אין טורח לבני החצר שאינו מרבה עליהן דיורין וכדמפרש בגמרא שלא הוסיף על ביתו כלום אלא חולקה לשנים שהרי כל ביתו יכול למלאות אכסנאין אם ירצה: **גמ' מאי איריא לחצר השותפין.** הרבים דלא יפתח דמשמע מפני שהן רבים חיישינן שלא יעשה להן היזק ראיה אפילו יחיד (ב) נמי אסור להזיקו והלכך אפילו לחצר חבירו נמי לא: **אבל לחצר השותפין.** איכא למימר דשרי לפתוח דבלאו הכי בעי איצטנועי מחבירו בחצר שזה יכול לראותו דרך פתח ביתו הפתוח לחצר ולא מזקי ליה חלונות מידי קמ"ל מתניתין דקתני לא יפתח דא"ל האי לבעל החלונות עד האידנא כי הוה משתמשנא בחצר הוה בעינא לאיצטנועי מינך שלא תראני דרך פתח ביתך (ג) ואי הוינא בבית לא הוה בעינא לאיצטנועי מינך שהרי לא היו עושין פתח כנגד פתח כדקתני מתניתין אבל השתא אפי' בבית בעינא לאיצטנועי מינך כדי שלא תראני מחלונותיך שהן גבוהות א"נ עד האידנא כי הוית בחצר בעינא לאיצטנועי מינך כי הוית בבית לא בעינא לאיצטנועי מינך השתא אפילו כשאתה בבית (ד) בעינא לאיצטנועי מינך: **שפתח חלונותיו.** והיה טוען שעשה ברשות בני חצר: **החזקת.** סבר לה לאלתר הויא חזקה דכיון דבפניו החזיק ושתק אם איתא דשלא ברשות עשה היה לו למחות והיינו דאמרן בפירקין לעיל (דף מא.) כמאן כרבי יהודה וכר' ישמעאל (ג) וכרבי יוסי דאמרי כל בפניו לאלתר הויא חזקה ואין הלכה כן: **לך יגע וסתום.** דלא הויא חזקה עד שלש שנים:

ולסתום

תוספות

ואפילו בעל החצר בבעל הגג אין יכול למחות. אע"ג דגבי זיז [שלפני] החלון דיוצא לרשות הרבים לא שרינן במסכת עירובין (דף נח:) להניח עליו אלא כלים הנשברים משום דחיישינן דלמא נפיל ואתי לאתויי והכא לא חיישינן שמא יפול על ראשו של בעל החצר שאינו עומד כל שעה תחת הזיז א"נ התם לא אסר אלא להניח עליו אבל הכא איירי למיתלא ביה דבדבר התלוי לא חיישינן לנפילה וא"ת והיאך יכול בעל הגג להשתמש בזיז והא איכא מעקה דאמר בפ"ק (לעיל ו:) גג הסמוך לחצר חברו עושה לו מעקה גבוה ארבע אמות וי"ל כגון דהזיז בקרן זוית בסוף המעקה: **מאי** איריא לחצר השותפין. פ"ה מאי איריא לחצר השותפין שמזיק לשנים משמע מתוך פירושו שהוא אינו שותף באותה חצר וקשה לר"י לפירושו מדמסיק בתר הכי אלא אפילו לחצר השותפין דאמר ליה סוף סוף בעית לאיצטנועי מינאי משמע שהוא שותף ונראה לר"י לפרש מאי איריא לחצר השותפין שהוא מזיק לו משני מקומות אפילו לחצר חבירו שאינו מזיק לו אלא מכאן נמי ולפי' קשה לרשב"א דא"כ אמאי קאמר עד האידנא הוה בעית כו' הוה ליה למימר קא משמע לן דבשני מקומות לא מצינא לאיצטנועי מינך ונראה לי דמעיקרא דפריך מאי איריא לא סלקא דעתיה שיש לו שותפות בחצר: **בבית** לא בעינא לאיצטנועי מינך. פירוש כשאתה בבית אבל פירוש אחר שפ"ה כשאני בבית אין נראה לרשב"א דהשתא נמי לא בעי לאיצטנועי בתשמיש הבית דהא האי חלון דפתח אינו לא כנגד הפתח ולא כנגד החלון דהא תנן (לקמן דף ס.) אין פותחין חלון כנגד החלון כו':

לקח

עין משפט נר מצוה

רעז א מיי' פ"ח מהל' שכנים הל' ג ועי' בהשגות ובמ"מ סמג עשין פב טוש"ע ח"מ סי' קנג סעיף ד:

רעח ב מיי' שם הל' ה טוש"ע שם סעיף ה:

רעט ג מיי' שם פ"ה הל' ו סמג שם טוש"ע ח"מ סי' קנד סעיף ג:

רפ ד ה מיי' שם הל' ה טור ש"ע שם סעיף ג:

רפא ו מיי' שם פ"ו הל' ג סמג שם טוש"ע שם סעיף ד:

רפב ז מיי' שם פ"ה הל' ו סמג שם טוש"ע שם:

רבינו גרשום

למחות. ולעכב אדם בחבירו שלא יוציא בחצירו זיז טפח ואם פחות מטפח הוא אין לו חזקה בחצר שאינו חשוב. ואין יכול למחות בידו בעל החצר שלא יוציא בחצירו פחות מטפח שכיון שאין לו חזקה בכך מאי איכפת ליה: הכי קאמר. החזיק בטפח שיש לו בחצר חבירו זיז רחב טפח ובמשך ארכו ד' יש לו חזקה בחצר ברוחב ד' כנגד אורך כל הכותל שכיון שלא מיחה בו בעל חצר בזיז חשוב כזה בידוע שיש לו חזקה בחצר כנגד כל הכותל ברוחב אותו זיז: לא שנו. שאין יכול למחות אלא בעל הגג בבעל חצר שאין יכול בעל הגג לעכב לבעל החצר שלא ישים בחור שבכותלו זיז פחות מטפח אם הוא צריך לו שכבר אין לו חזקה: אבל בעל חצר בבעל הגג יכול למחות. שלא יוציא זיז פחות מטפח בחצירו בכותלו: מר סבר. רב הונא: שמיה היזק. להכי מעכב בעל חצר לבעל הגג שאגב שישהה מראש גגו וישתמש באותו זיז פחות מטפח שיקשור בו חבל או יתלה עליו [יסתכל] כלום ממנו בחצר ור"י סבר לאו שמיה היזק: ושאני הכא דאמר ליה בעל הגג לבעל חצר לתשמיש לא חזי ההוא זיז פחות מטפח שאין ראוי לעמוד עליו ולא חזי אלא למיתלי ביה שום חפץ: כי תלינא ביה מידי מהדרנא אפאי ותלינא. ולא אסתכל בחצירך: ואידך. בעל חצר אמר זימנין דבעיתת שלא יהא תלוי אקשר בזיז יפה ומעיינת ואגב הכי תסתכל בחצירי: פיסקא לא יפתח אדם חלונותיו לחצר השותפין. בחצר שיש לו שותפות בה אם אין לאשר שותפין בה חלונות: אפי' לחצר חבירו. של יחיד אין ראשי לפתוח משום היזק ראיה: לא מבעיא לחצר חבירו דלא. משום דאין לו חלק בה: אבל לחצר שותפין. שיש לו חלק בה: הא מצי אמר ליה סוף סוף הא בעית איצטנועי מינאי כשאני נכנס ויוצא בחצר כך הצנע עצמך כשחלונותי פתוחין: קמ"ל. דמצי א"ל השותף עד האידנא קודם פתיחת החלונות כשאתה בחצר הייתי צריך להצנע ממך וכשהייתה בבית לא הייתי צריך להצנע. עכשיו אפי' כשאתה בבית צריך אני להצנע ממך בחצר מפני חלונותיך: שפתח. לחצר השותפין ולא מיחו ושוב מיחו: לך יגע וסתום. שאין חזקה עד ג' שנים: אמר רב נחמן

ולסתום

מסורת הש"ס

א) [לעיל ב:], ב) [נ"ל בר רבין]:

הגהות הב"ח

(א) גמ' ופתחת לך יגע: (ב) רשב"ם ד"ה מאי איריא וכו' אפי' יחיד נמי כצ"ל ותיבת ראיה נמחק: (ג) ד"ה אבל וכו' ביתך ואי הוינא וכו' לא הוה בעינא וכו': (ד) בא"ד כשאתה בבית נמי בעינא:

לעזי רש"י

אשקליינ"ש. פירוש חווקין, שליבות, מעלות (רש"י ב"מ דף כה ע"א ד"ה כסולם; רש"י שמות כ, כג), מדרגות (רש"י יחזקאל מג, כ; שה"ש ב, יד):

Mishnah The Mishnah restricts renovations to property that adversely affect one's neighbors: לֹא יִפְתַּח אָדָם חַלּוֹנוֹתָיו – **A person may not open his windows** לַחֲצַר הַשּׁוּתָּפִין – **onto a jointly owned courtyard.**[13]

לָקַח בַּיִת בְּחָצֵר אַחֶרֶת – **If one purchased a house in another** adjoining **courtyard,**[14] לֹא יִפְתְּחֶנָּה בַּחֲצַר הַשּׁוּתָּפִין – **he may not open it into a jointly owned courtyard.**[15] בָּנָה עֲלִיָּיה עַל גַּבֵּי בֵיתוֹ – **If he built an attic atop his house,** לֹא יִפְתְּחֶנָּה לַחֲצַר הַשּׁוּתָּפִין – **he may not open [the attic] onto a jointly owned courtyard.**[16] אֶלָּא אִם רָצָה – **But if he wishes,** בּוֹנֶה אֶת הַחֶדֶר לִפְנִים מִבֵּיתוֹ – **he may build a room within his house,** וּבוֹנֶה עֲלִיָּיה עַל גַּבֵּי בֵיתוֹ – **or build an attic atop his house,** וּפוֹתְחָהּ לְתוֹךְ בֵּיתוֹ – **and open it into his house.**[17]

Gemara The Gemara questions the first ruling of the Mishnah:

מַאי אִירְיָא לַחֲצַר הַשּׁוּתָּפִין – **Why does [the Mishnah] single out** the case of opening windows **onto a jointly owned courtyard?** אֲפִילוּ לַחֲצַר חֲבֵירוֹ נַמִּי לֹא – **Even onto a neighbor's courtyard one may not** open a window![18]

The Gemara answers:

לֹא מִיבַּעְיָא קָאָמַר – **[The Tanna] formulates** the Mishnah according to the principle that **there is no need** to state the more obvious case. לֹא מִיבַּעְיָא לַחֲצַר חֲבֵרוֹ דְּלֹא – **There is no need** to rule that one may **not** open windows **onto a neighbor's courtyard,** for a damaging visual trespass will surely result. אֲבָל לַחֲצַר הַשּׁוּתָּפִין – **But** as for opening windows **onto a jointly owned courtyard,** דְּאָמַר לֵיהּ – **where [the person opening the window] can say to [his partner],** סוֹף סוֹף – **"In any event,** הָא קָא בָּעֵית אִצְטְנוּעֵי מִינָּאִי בֶּחָצֵר – **you need to conceal your actions from me in the courtyard,"**[19] one might conclude that opening windows would be permitted, since no additional visual trespass will result therefrom. קָא מַשְׁמַע לָן – **[The Mishnah]** therefore **informs us** that opening windows is nonetheless forbidden, דְּאָמַר לֵיהּ – **for [the partner] can say to him,** עַד הָאִידָּנָא – **"Until now** when no windows existed בֶּחָצֵר הֲוָה בְּעֵינָא אִצְטְנוּעֵי מִינָּךְ – **I needed to conceal myself from you** only while you were **in the courtyard;**[20] הַשְׁתָּא – but **now,** if you open a window to the courtyard, אֲפִילוּ בְּבַיִת נַמִּי – **even** when you are **in your house** בְּעֵינָא אִצְטְנוּעֵי מִינָּךְ – **I need to conceal myself from you."**[21] Since a window increases the opportunities for visual trespass, the affected partner may protest the opening of a new one.

The Gemara continues to discuss the subject of opening windows onto a jointly owned courtyard:

תָּנוּ רַבָּנָן – **The Rabbis taught in a Baraisa:** מַעֲשֶׂה בְּאָדָם אֶחָד – There was once AN INCIDENT INVOLVING AN INDIVIDUAL שֶׁפָּתַח חַלּוֹנָיו לַחֲצַר הַשּׁוּתָּפִין – WHO OPENED HIS WINDOWS ONTO A JOINTLY OWNED COURTYARD, claiming that he acted with the permission of the residents of the courtyard. וּבָא לִפְנֵי ר׳ יִשְׁמָעֵאל בַּר רַבִּי יוֹסֵי – HE CAME BEFORE R' YISHMAEL BAR R' YOSE to defend his right to retain the windows.[22] אָמַר לוֹ – [R' YISHMAEL] SAID TO HIM: הֶחֱזַקְתָּ בְּנִי הֶחֱזַקְתָּ – "YOU HAVE INDEED ESTABLISHED A *CHAZAKAH,* MY SON."[23]

A dissenting opinion is issued:

וּבָא לִפְנֵי רַבִּי חִיָּיא – [THE MAN] then CAME BEFORE R' CHIYA.[24] אָמַר – [R' CHIYA] SAID to him: יָגַעְתָּ וּפָתַחְתָּ – "YOU TOILED AND OPENED the windows; יְגַע וּסְתוֹם – Go[25] TOIL AND CLOSE them, for you have not established a *chazakah."*[26]

The Gemara issues a related ruling:

אָמַר רַב נַחְמָן – **Rav Nachman said:**

NOTES

he feared he would fall from the roof and for that reason failed to turn away, he does not risk exposure as an intentional visual trespasser (*Rashbam*).

13. Since he will be able to observe the activities of his partners in the courtyard below without their knowledge, thereby committing visual trespass. The prohibition certainly applies when he opens his windows onto the courtyard of a stranger (*Rashbam*).

14. And the house was located on the side common to both courtyards.

15. I.e. the buyer may not open a back door in that house, for it will allow the residents access to the first courtyard. For even though the buyer is a partner in the first courtyard, he is not allowed to increase the flow of traffic there from another residence (*Rashbam;* see Gemara below, 60a, and *Nimukei Yosef*).

16. If a person adds an upper story to his house, he may not build a separate entrance from it to the courtyard below. For if he rents the addition to another family, he will be inconveniencing his neighbors by increasing traffic in the courtyard (*Rashbam*).

17. The Gemara below (60a) will explain how these cases differ and why such construction is permitted.

18. The Gemara assumes that, since the Mishnah speaks of a courtyard owned by *many* people, it prohibits visual trespass only when *several* neighbors are affected. The Gemara therefore asserts that violating the privacy of even one person is also forbidden (*Rashbam*).

19. Since I can observe your activities whenever I am in the courtyard (*Rashbam*, second explanation).

20. But if you were in your house and your door was closed, I was able to use the courtyard for private activities (*Rashbam*).

The translation follows *Rashbam's* second explanation; see *Tosafos,* who challenge *Rashbam's* first explanation.

21. For even while you are inside your house you can observe me from the window (*Rashbam*). [Thus, I will never be assured of privacy, for I cannot know when you are watching me.]

22. Initially, the residents of the courtyard did not protest his opening the windows; later [before three years had elapsed], they did voice their opposition (*Rabbeinu Gershom;* see *Rashbam*).

23. Literally: you have established a *chazakah,* my son, you have established a *chazakah*. R' Yishmael was of the opinion that a *chazakah* is established *immediately* if it is clear that the residents of the courtyard were aware of the individual's actions and did not protest. The individual need not maintain the windows for three years. Thus, R' Yishmael ruled that the failure of the courtyard residents to protest immediately is proof that the individual acted with their consent.

R' Yishmael's position extends even to establishing a *chazakah* on real property. Thus, if one occupied a field in its owner's presence for even a single day and the owner remained silent, R' Yishmael would award the occupant control of the field. [R' Yishmael's ruling here is the primary statement of his position on *chazakah;* see also above, 41a, and *Rashbam* to 39a ד״ה אלא.] The halachah does not follow R' Yishmael's view (*Rashbam*).

24. The residents of the courtyard apparently did not accept R' Yishmael's ruling (see previous note), and the matter came before R' Chiya. Perhaps they did not appear together with the owner of the window before R' Yishmael in a legal proceeding, and were therefore not constrained to accept his ruling on the matter.

25. *Bach* and *Rashbam* add the word לֵךְ, *go,* to the text.

26. For the halachah is that a *chazakah* cannot be established in less than three years (*Rashbam*).

Other Rishonim (*Rif, Rashba* and *Ramban*), however, deduce from the fact that R' Chiya did not ascertain how long the windows had been in place that a *chazakah* can never be established for a window that infringes on a neighbor's privacy. They maintain that visual trespass damages a neighbor's *person,* and not his *property,* and thus is analogous to damage caused by smoke or an outhouse, for which no *chazakah* can be established (above, 23a).

וְלִסְתּוֹם – But if a person acts **to seal** his neighbor's window by building a wall within it,[1] לְאַלְתַּר הָוֵי חֲזָקָה – **an immediate *chazakah* is established** for the builder of the wall[2] if the owner of the window does not protest at once. שֶׁאֵין אָדָם עָשׂוּי שֶׁסּוֹתְמִים אוֹרוֹ בְּפָנָיו וְשׁוֹתֵק – **For a person is not inclined** to witness **[others] obstructing his light and remain silent.**[3]

The Gemara cites the next ruling of the Mishnah:

לָקַח בַּיִת בְּחָצֵר אַחֶרֶת – IF ONE PURCHASED A HOUSE IN ANOTHER, adjoining COURTYARD, לֹא יִפְתָּחֶנּוּ לַחֲצַר הַשּׁוּתָּפִין – **he may not open it into a jointly owned courtyard.**

The Gemara asks:

מַאי טַעְמָא – **What is the reason** for this ruling?[4]

The Gemara replies:

מִפְּנֵי שֶׁמַּרְבֶּה עֲלֵיהֶם אֶת הַדֶּרֶךְ – **Because** by opening a new door **he increases traffic for [his neighbors]** in the courtyard.[5]

The Gemara challenges this explanation:

אֵימָא סֵיפָא – But **cite the latter section** of the Mishnah, which states: אֶלָּא אִם רָצָה – BUT IF HE WISHES, בּוֹנֶה אֶת הַחֶדֶר לִפְנִים מִבֵּיתוֹ – HE MAY BUILD A ROOM WITHIN HIS HOUSE, וּבוֹנֶה עֲלִיָּיה עַל גַּבֵּי בֵיתוֹ – OR BUILD AN ATTIC ATOP HIS HOUSE. These rulings imply that he may enlarge his own house and let others live in the addition, so long as he does not create a new entrance to the courtyard. וְהָלֹא מַרְבֶּה עָלָיו אֶת הַדֶּרֶךְ – **But will he not increase the traffic for [the residents]** in the courtyard? These latter rulings would seem to indicate that increased traffic in the courtyard is not a just cause for complaint – ? –

The Gemara replies:

אָמַר רַב הוּנָא – **Rav Huna said:** מַאי חֶדֶר – **What** does the Mishnah mean when it permits the construction of **"a room"?** שֶׁחֲלָקוֹ בִּשְׁנַיִם – **That [the house's owner] divided [the interior]** of his dwelling **in two.**[6] וּמַאי עֲלִיָּיה – **And what** does the Mishnah mean when it permits the construction of **"an attic"?** אַפְּתָאִי – It means splitting a room into two **low compartments.**[7] Thus, in each of these cases the overall size of the house was not increased, and so the other courtyard residents have no grounds to block construction.[8]

Mishnah

The Mishnah continues to expound the laws of opening windows and doors into a jointly owned courtyard:

לֹא יִפְתַּח אָדָם לַחֲצַר הַשּׁוּתָּפִין – **A person may not open into a jointly owned courtyard** פֶּתַח כְּנֶגֶד פֶּתַח – **a doorway opposite a doorway**[9] וְחַלּוֹן כְּנֶגֶד חַלּוֹן – or **a window opposite**[10] **a window.**[11] הָיָה קָטָן – Also, **if it** [the doorway or window] **was small,** לֹא יַעֲשֶׂנּוּ גָּדוֹל – **one may not enlarge it;** אֶחָד לֹא יַעֲשֶׂנּוּ שְׁנַיִם – or if there was **one** doorway or window, **one may not convert it into two.**[12] אֲבָל פּוֹתֵחַ הוּא לִרְשׁוּת הָרַבִּים – **But one may open into the public domain** (i.e the street) פֶּתַח כְּנֶגֶד פֶּתַח – **a doorway opposite a doorway,** וְחַלּוֹן כְּנֶגֶד חַלּוֹן – **or a window opposite a window.** הָיָה קָטָן – Also, **if it** [the doorway or window facing the street] **was small,** עוֹשֶׂה אוֹתוֹ גָּדוֹל – one **may enlarge it;** וְאֶחָד עוֹשֶׂה אוֹתוֹ שְׁנַיִם – **or** if there was **one** doorway or window, **one may convert it into two.**

NOTES

1. *Rashbam;* cf. *Nimukei Yosef.* This "person" is the resident of a courtyard onto which the window opens.

2. In the sense that the window may not be reopened unless the builder of the wall, whose privacy is compromised by the window, expressly allows it (*Rashbam*).

3. This ruling applies when the window had been open for three years and its owner had therefore established a *chazakah* for it. Thus, if the owner is silent when the wall is constructed, his *chazakah* is nullified, for his silence is construed as an admission that he originally opened the window without obtaining permission from the residents of the courtyard (*Rashbam*).

4. Since he owns a share in the courtyard, why is he not entitled to open a door into it?

5. Since more people will pass through the courtyard than before, the residents of the courtyard will suffer a loss of privacy. [Hence, they are entitled to prevent the creation of a new door] (*Rashbam*).

6. Thus, he did not enlarge his house; he merely constructed interior partitions and allowed others to dwell in one of the newly created rooms. Although he thereby increases traffic in the courtyard, the homeowner is permitted to take this action, for there is no limit to the number of people one may shelter in his home (*Rashbam;* see note 8 below).

7. The Gemara below (61a) describes an אַפְּתָאִי as a low structure attached to the side or rear of a house. In the case of the Mishnah the owner divided a room horizontally to create two low compartments. The upper compartment was accessed through an aperture in the ceiling of the lower compartment (*Rashbam;* see *Maharsha* and *Rashash*).

8. This explanation follows the view of *Rashbam* and *Rabbeinu Gershom*. According to them, building an *addition* to a house is forbidden regardless of whether it opens into the courtyard or only into the house. However, many Rishonim (*Ramban, Rashba* and others) explain the Gemara differently. They maintain that the chief criterion for determining the permissibility of an addition is if it will become rental property. Accordingly, they understand the Gemara's answer as follows: Dividing a house is permissible, for access to the subdivided rooms is from within the house; hence, these rooms will be used for storage rather than rental, since the owner will be loath to allow strangers to walk through his house. Thus, there will be no increased traffic (and resultant loss of privacy) in the courtyard. According to this explanation, it is permissible even to enlarge a house (e.g. with the addition of a full attic), so long as no door is created from the addition to the courtyard. The halachah follows this view (see *Choshen Mishpat* 154:1-3, and *Rambam Hil. Shecheinim* 5:8).

9. The reason for this law is to preserve the privacy of the dwellings (*Rashbam*). This law is derived from Scripture, as the Gemara will demonstrate.

10. But if the proposed window is removed even a minute distance from opposite the other window, one may open it (*Rashbam*; cf. *Nimukei Yosef, Tur Choshen Mishpat* 154). Similarly, one may open a doorway to a courtyard if it is not directly opposite another's doorway or window (*Ritva*). The Mishnah is concerned only about the loss of privacy that results if a neighbor is able to look inadvertently into one's doorway or window while going about his daily household activities, and this is possible only when the facing windows or doorways are directly aligned. The halachah does not seek to protect against a neighbor's deliberate gazing into one's doorway or window at an angle, since if he wishes he can spy on anyone from the courtyard itself. Consequently, it is not necessary to remove a doorway or window four *amos* from a direct alignment with a facing doorway or window (*Rashba, Ritva*).

11. The Mishnah (above, 59b) has already categorically prohibited the opening of a window onto a courtyard; why, then, is it necessary to prohibit opening a window opposite a window that is across the courtyard? *Rashbam* explains that our Mishnah teaches that even if one has a presumptive right (*chazakah*) to have a window directly opposite his neighbor's (i.e. such a situation has already existed for three years; see *Choshen Mishpat* 153:2), he must nonetheless seal his window (*Rashbam*). Even those who maintain that a *chazakah* allows one to continue a practice that may cause visual trespass [הֶיזֵּק רְאִיָּה] (see *Choshen Mishpat* 154:7) concede that the circumstance of directly facing windows invites too serious a breach of privacy for *chazakah* to be effective (*Hagahos Derishah U'Perishah* to *Tur Choshen Mishpat* 154 §10; cf. *Chidushei Hagahos* there). Thus, when the Mishnah prohibits *opening* a window, it actually means not to *leave one open* (*Hagahos Derishah U'Perishah* ibid.). Some explain that the Mishnah speaks of where one was granted permission by his neighbors to open a doorway or window onto the courtyard. Nevertheless, the Mishnah teaches, this permission does not extend to opening the window or doorway *directly opposite* a neighbor's window or doorway (*Nimukei Yosef*).

12. The Gemara will explain the reason for this.

ולסתום. אם החזיק בחלון ג' שנים בחצר השותפין ובא חבירו וסתמו שבנה כותל כנגדו והוא שתק לאלתר הוי חזקה לזה הסותם שלא יפתח עוד חבירו אלא ברשותו וחזקת ג' שנים שהיה חלונו פתוח אינה כלום מאחר ששתק כשסתמו זה: **שאין אדם עשוי שסותמין אורו בפניו ושותק.** ומדשתק אודויי אודי ליה דשלא כדין החזיק מעיקרא: **שמרבה עליהן את הדרך.** שרוב בני אדם יוצאין ונכנסין עכשיו בחצר יותר מבתחלה וליכא לניעות כדמעיקרא: **והלא מרבה עליהן את הדרך.** דבנין עלייה זו שלא היתה שם קודם לכן והוא מכניס לתוכה דיורין לבד דיורין שבביתו

לקח בית בחצר אחרת **לא יפתחנה** לחצר השותפין. פירוש אפילו לביתו כדי (ו) שלא יכנס ממנו לחצר השותפין: **ראוין** הללו שתשרה שכינה עליהם. מסיפיה דקרא דריש דכתיב ותהי עליו רוח אלהים:
נפלה

א ולסתום לאלתר הוי חזקה שאין אדם עשוי שסותמים אורו בפניו ושותק: לקח בית בחצר אחרת לא יפתחנו לחצר השותפין: מאי טעמא ב מפני שמרבה עליהם את הדרך אימא סיפא אלא אם רצה בונה את החדר לפנים מביתו ובונה עלייה על גבי ביתו והלא מרבה עליו את הדרך אמר רב הונא ג מאי חדר שחלקו (א) בשנים ומאי עלייה אפתאי: **מתני'** ד לא יפתח אדם לחצר השותפין פתח כנגד פתח וחלון כנגד חלון ה היה קטן לא יעשנו גדול אחד לא יעשנו שנים ו אבל פותח הוא לרה"ר פתח כנגד פתח וחלון כנגד חלון ז היה קטן עושה אותו גדול ואחד עושה אותו שנים: **גמ'** מנהני מילי א"ר יוחנן דאמר קרא א) וישא בלעם את עיניו וירא את ישראל שוכן לשבטיו מה ראה ראה שאין פתחי אהליהם מכוונין זה לזה אמר ראוין הללו שתשרה עליהם שכינה: היה קטן לא יעשנו גדול: סבר רמי בר חמא למימר בר ד' לא לישוייה בר תמניא דקא שקיל תמניא בחצר אבל בר תרתי לישוייה בר ארבעה שפיר דמי א"ל רבא ח מצי א"ל בפיתחא זוטרא מצינא לאצטנועי מינך בפיתחא רבה לא מצינא אצטנועי מינך: אחד לא יעשנו שנים: סבר רמי בר חמא למימר בר ארבעי לא לישוייה תרי בני תרתי תרתי דקא שקיל תמני בחצר אבל בר תמני לישוייה בני ארבעי ארבעי שפיר דמי א"ל רבא ט מצי אמר ליה בחד פיתחא מצינא אצטנועי מינך בתרי לא מצינא אצטנועי מינך: אבל פותח הוא לרה"ר פתח כנגד פתח: דא"ל סוף סוף הא בעית אצטנועי מבני רה"ר: **מתני'** א) י אין עושין חלל תחת רה"ר בורות שיחין ומערות ◦ ר"א מתיר כדי שתהא עגלה מהלכת וטעונה אבנים כ אין מוציאין זיזין וגזוזטראות לרה"ר אלא אם רצה כונס לתוך שלו ומוציא ג) ל לקח חצר ובה זיזין וגזוזטראות הרי זו בחזקתה: **גמ'** ורבנן ג) מ זימנין דמפחית ולאו אדעתיה: אין מוציאין זיזין וגזוזטראות וכו': ר' אמי הוה ליה זיזא דהוה נפיק למבואה והוא גברא נמי הוה ליה זיזא דהוה מפיק לרה"ר ד) (הוו קא מעכבי עליה בני רה"ר) אתא לקמיה דר' אמי א"ל זיל קוץ אמר ליה והא מר נמי אית ליה (ג) דידי למבואה מפיק בני מבואה מחלין גבאי דידך לרשות הרבים מפיק מאן מחיל גבך: ר' ינאי הוה ליה אילן הנוטה לרשות הרבים הוה ההוא גברא דהוה ליה נמי אילן הנוטה לרשות הרבים אתו בני רשות הרבים הוו קא מעכבי עילויה אתא לקמיה דר' ינאי א"ל זיל

דיורין לבד דיורין שבביתו אע"פ שכולן נכנסין ויוצאין דרך פתח ביתו הרי נתרבו נכנסין ויוצאין בחצר: **מאי.** בונה החדר דקתני מתני' לא בונה ממש כדקאמרת אלא שחלקו לחדר שלו לשנים שעשה מחיצה באמצעיתו להושיב שם דיורין מרובין דבדבר זה יש לו רשות שיכול למלאות כל ביתו דיורין: **ומאי עלייה אפתא.** יליע מפרשי לקמן (פרק המוכר את הבית) אפתא ואמרינן ג' שמות יש לה יליע צלע ותא ומוכח התם מקראי דהיינו בנין נמוך בצדי הבית או מאחוריו ואינו שוה לגג הבית ומתני' הכי קתני ובונה עלייה על גביו דהיינו חדר שלפנים מביתו דהיינו נמי שחלקו בגובהו ועולה דרך ארובה מן החדר להאי עלייה דהיינו יליע שהרי אחורי הבית הוא והלכך קרוי יליע וגם גבי יליע אשכחן כי האי גוונא תחתיים שניים ושלישים כדכתיב הצלע התיכונה וכתיב ובלולים יעלו על התיכונה ומן התיכונה וגו' (מלכים א ו) והלכך אין כאן תוספת בנין כלל לא בחדר ולא בעלייה דחדר היינו שחלק רחבו של חדר ועשאו שני חדרים קצרים וכן עלייה שבנה באמצעית גובהו של חדר ונמלאת עלייה בנויה מאליה: **מתני' לא יפתח אדם לחצר השותפין.** אפילו היכא דיש לו חזקה: חלון **כנגד חלון.** אלא משהו ירחיקנו זה שלא כנגד זה וטעם משום צניעות כולה מתני' מפרש בגמ': **גמ' וירא את ישראל** שוכן. ראה היאך שוכנים ולפיכך אמר מה טובו אהליך וגו' שאין פתחי אהליהם מכוונים ומתנה ישראל בחצר השותפין דמי דלא היה

רה"ר אלא במחנה לויה כדאמרינן במס' שבת (דף צו:): **אמר ראוין הללו כו'.** מדכתיב התם מה טובו אהליך קדייק: **סבר רמי בר חמא למימר.** דמאי דקתני היה קטן לא יעשנו גדול היינו דאי הוה פתח בר ד' אמות רחב לא ירחיבנו לח' אמות דקמפסיד לבעלי החצר דקשקיל השתא תמני אמות בחצר כנגד כל הפתח באורך ארבע אמות רחוק מן הפתח כדאמרינן בפרק ראשון (לעיל יא.) היה רחב שמנה אמות נוטל שמנה אמות באורך החצר כנגד רוחב כל הפתח ואילו מעיקרא לא הוה שקיל אלא ארבע אמות אבל לצניעותא לא הוה חייש רמי בר חמא דכי היכי דמצטנעי מפתח קטן מצטנעי (ג) מפתח גדול: **בר תרתי.** דשקיל נמי ד' אמות בחצר כבר ארבעי כדאמרי' נוטן לכל פתח ארבע אמות: **לישוייה בר ארבעי.** דלא מפסיד לחבריה מידי דמעיקרא נמי הוה שקיל ד' אמות בחצר: **לישוייה תרין בני ארבעי.** השתא נמי לא שקיל אלא תמני בחצר כמעיקרא ולאיצטנועי נמי לא חיישינן דמה לי ח' אמות בפתח אחד מה לי ח' אמות חלוקות לב' פתחים בשני מקומות מ"מ ח' אמות יש לו פתוחות לחצר: **בחד פיתחא מצינא איצטנועי.** כשהוא נעול יכולני להשתמש בחצר אע"ג להשתמש שלא כנגדו אבל בשני פתחים לא מצינא לאיצטנועי כל כך דלפני אם האחד נעול השני יהיה פתוח: **סוף סוף הא בעית איצטנועי מבני רה"ר.** שרואין בביתך דרך פתח הבית ורוכבי סוסים וגמלים רואין בתוך (ד) חלונותיו: **מתני' אין עושין חלל תחת רה"ר.** ואע"ג דמקבל עליה כל היזקא דלאתי מחמתיה שאין רצונם של בני אדם ליזוק ולילך לדין על עסקי ממונו ומפרש ואזיל מה הוא אותו חלל בורות שיחין ומערות: **ר"א מתיר.** אלא שיכסהו כיסוי חזק כדי שתהא עגלה מהלכת דר"א אזיל בתר השתא ולא חייש לשמא היום ולמחר יכלה הכיסוי ויפול והכי אמרינן בבבא קמא (דף נ:): **זיזין.** קורות קטנות: **גזוזטראות.** קורות גדולות הבולטות מן הבית לחוץ וליכא למיחש פן יכשלו בהם בני רה"ר והלכך אין מוציאין דהא כל בני רה"ר ליתנהו גביה דלימחלו: **כונס לתוך** קרקע שלו. את כותלו ומניח מקרקעו לחוץ כשיעור הוצאת זיזין ומוציא: **ובה זיזין וגזוזטראות.** הבולטות לרשות הרבים: **הרי זו בחזקתה.** דטענינן ללוקח ואומרים אימר כונס לתוך שלו היה אבל המוכרה לו שהוציא הזיזין הוא היה צריך להביא עדים שכנס לתוך שלו או שיטעון שני חזקה החזקתי וכנסתי לתוך שלי דהויא לה חזקה שיש עמה טענה אבל לוקח לא צריך למיטען מידי אלא כך לקחתיה וא"נ לטעון היאך הוציא המוכר את הזיזין לחוץ לרה"ר דטוענין ליורש וטוענין ללוקח: **גמ' ורבנן.** דאסרי סברי לא אזלינן בתר השתא וחיישינן משום דזימנין דמתליע מתוכו ויפחות ולאו אדעתיה דעובר ברה"ר ויעבור ויפול: **מפיק למבואה.** מוציא (ה) למבואה והמבוי מקום הלוך כל בני החצירות הוא: **הוו מעכבי עילויה בני רה"ר.** שנופיו מזיקין לגמל ורוכבו:

א) לעיל מ:, ב) [לעיל כג.], ג) [לעיל מ:], ד) מ"מ מ"ו וכן ברי"ף ורא"ש ליתא:

הגהות הב"ח

(א) גמ' שחלקו לשנים: (ב) שם אמר נמי אית ליה א"ל דידי: (ג) רשב"ם ד"ה סבר וכו' מלטנעי נמי מפתח גדול: (ד) ד"ה סוף וכו' חלונותיו הס"ד: (ה) ד"ה מפיק וכו' מוליא למבוי והמבוי מקום: (ו) תוס' ד"ה לקח בית וכו' כדי שיכנס כל"ל ותיבת שלא נמחק:

גליון הש"ס

מתני' ר"א מתיר. עיין בר"ש ריש בכורים:

תורה אור השלם

א) וַיִּשָּׂא בִלְעָם אֶת עֵינָיו וַיַּרְא אֶת יִשְׂרָאֵל שֹׁכֵן לִשְׁבָטָיו וַתְּהִי עָלָיו רוּחַ אֱלֹהִים: [במדבר כד, ב]

ליקוטי רש"י

אפתאי. אפנטמ"ר בנין נמוך אצל הבית מצדו או מאחוריו [רשב"ם לקמן סא.]. **שוכן לשבטיו.** ראה כל שבט ושבט שוכן לעצמו ואינן מעורבין ראה שאין פתחיהם מכוונין זה כנגד זה שלא יציץ לתוך אהל חבירו [במדבר כד, ב]. **כדי שתהא עגלה מהלכת.** אם הקרקה חזקה כל כך מותר ואע"ג שסופה שתתליע ותפחת [לעיל כ:]. **לקח חצר ובה זיזין וגזוזטראות וכו'.** אדם הבונה בית לא יוציא ראשי קורותיו מקרתו לרה"ר אבל אם רוצה כונס בניינו לתוך שלו ובונה ויוציא ראשי קורותיו לחוץ ואם לקח חצר ובה זיזין וגזוזטראות יוצאים לרה"ר הרי הוא בחזקתו שבית דין טוענין לו שהראשון כנס לתוך שלו או נתפייסו עם הרבים [שם כג.].

רפג א מיי' פ"ז מהל' שכנים הל' ז סמג עשין פב טוש"ע ח"מ סי' קנד סעיף יג:
רפד ב ג מיי' פ"ה שם הל' ח סמג שם טוש"ע שם סעיף א:
רפה ד מיי' שם הל' ו טוש"ע שם סעיף ג:
רפו ה מיי' שם הל' ו טוש"ע שם סעיף א:
רפז ו מיי' שם הל' ו טוש"ע שם סעיף ג:
רפח ז ח מיי' שם הל' י יא טוש"ע שם סעיף ד:
רפט י מיי' פי"ג מהל' נזקי ממון הל' כג סמג עשין סח טוש"ע ח"מ סי' תט סעיף א:
רצ כ מיי' שם הל' כד טוש"ע שם סעיף ג:
רצא ל מיי' שם הל' כה טוש"ע שם סעיף א:
רצב מ מיי' שם הל' כג טוש"ע שם סעיף א:

רבינו גרשום

ולסתום. שאם יש לאדם חלון בחצר חבירו ובונה בעל חצר כנגדו וסותמו בפנים. אם לא מיחה לאלתר בעל חלון (שעה) **לאלתר הוי חזקה** לבעל חצר לסותמו: **לקח.** אחד מן השותפין: **בית בחצר אחרת לא יפתח לחצר השותפין. מפני שמרבה** על השותפין דריסת רגל של אותן שיהיו דרין באותו בית מה שלא היה שם קודם לכן: בנה עלייה על גבי ביתו ורוצה לשוכרה לבית דירה לא יפתח לה פתח בחצר השותפין **מפני שמרבה עליהם הדרך: אלא אם רוצה** כו'. מפרש בגמ'. **והלא מרבה על הדרך.** דהשתא בונה עלייה מה שלא היתה שם קודם לכן ומשים בה דיורין אע"פ שפותחה בתוך ביתו מרבה עליהם הדרכים. אלא **מאי** בונה את החדר ואת העלייה דקאמר לא עלייה ממש אלא **שחלק** חדרו **לשנים** וחלק החיצון קרוי חדר **ומאי עלייה** דקאמר **אפתא** שקורין אפלדי"ץ והיינו חלק הפנימי ושוכר האחר לדירה. ואי אמרת והלא מרבה עליהם הדרכים לא מצי אמרת דכשם שאם היו לו בני בית לזה יותר מן השותפין אחרים לא היו יכולין לעכבן שלא יכנסו ושלא יצאו בחצר כך עכשיו כיון שלא בנה בנין יותר אלא שהיה כמו שהיה וחלקו לשנים והכניס דיורין בחלק האחד אין יכולין לעכבו: **פיסקא. שלא היו מכוונין זה כנגד זה.** מפני היזק ראיה: **אם היה קטן.** הפתח: א) דקא שקיל ח' אמות בחצר דאיכא ביה שיעור ב' פתחים: **אבל בר תרי** (טפח בכ"י) אמות. **לישויה בר ארבע** אמות (טפח בכ"י) רוחב **שפיר דמי** דסוף סוף לא שקיל אלא ד' אמות ככל פתח שהוא פחות מח' אמות (טפח בכ"י). ואם הפתח פחות מח' וחלקן לשני פתחים לכל פתח יש לו ד' אמות ושהוא בו ח' אע"פ שלא נחלק לשנים יש ח' אמות: **אבל בר תמני.** שיש לו ח' אמות **לישויה תרי פתחים** שפיר דמי דסוף סוף לא שקלי אלא ח' אמות בחצר כדמעיקרא: **מצי אמר ליה. בחד פיתחא מצינא דאיצטנועי מינך** שאני משתמש כשהוא נעול: **בתרי** פתחי **לא מצינא איצטנועי.** שכשהאחד נעול השני פתוח: **אבל פותח הוא לרה"ר פתח כנגד פתח דא"ל סוף סוף כו': פיסקא ור"א מתיר.** ובלבד שיכסנו כסוי חזק **כדי שתהא עגלה כו': ורבנן.** דאסרי מאי טעמא והלא הכסוי חזק סברי **דזימנין דמיפחת.** שיתליע מתוכו **ולאו אדעתיה** דהאי שיהא רעוע: **זיזין.** יברונ"ש: **גזוזטראות.** קורות: **לרה"ר.** דליתנייהו כל בני רה"ר גבי הדדי דלימחלי ליה: **לקח חצר ובה זיזין וגזוזטראות** שיוצאין לרה"ר **הרי זו בחזקתה** ואין צריך לקוץ: **מחלין לי בני מבואה.** דיחידים נינהו ומצי מחלי: **הוו מעכבי עילויה.** בני רה"ר שנופיו מזיקין לגמל ורוכבו:

חשק שלמה על רבינו גרשום א) נראה דהוא ליון על הגמ' דסבר רמי בר חמא למימר דבר ד' לא לישוייה בר תמניא דקא שקיל וכו'.

Gemara The Mishnah rules that one may not open a doorway opposite a doorway or a window opposite a window. The Gemara now inquires what the source for this ruling is:

מְנָהָנֵי מִילֵי – **From where** in Scripture **is [this ruling] derived?** אָמַר רַבִּי יוֹחָנָן – **R' Yochanan said:** דְּאָמַר קְרָא – **For Scripture says:**[13] "וַיִּשָּׂא בִלְעָם אֶת־עֵינָיו וַיַּרְא אֶת־יִשְׂרָאֵל שֹׁכֵן לִשְׁבָטָיו" – ***And Bilam raised his eyes and saw Israel dwelling tribe by tribe*** and proceeded to bless them. מָה רָאָה – **What did [Bilam] see?**[14] רָאָה שֶׁאֵין פִּתְחֵי אָהֳלֵיהֶם מְכוּוָּנִין זֶה לָזֶה – **He saw that the openings of their tents were not aligned one opposite the other,** אָמַר רְאוּיִן הַלָּלוּ שֶׁתִּשְׁרֶה עֲלֵיהֶם שְׁכִינָה – and so **he said: These** people **are worthy that the Divine Presence rest upon them.**[15]

The Gemara cites a segment of our Mishnah and expounds upon it:

הָיָה קָטָן לֹא יַעֲשֶׂנּוּ גָּדוֹל – IF IT WAS SMALL, ONE MAY NOT ENLARGE IT. סָבַר רָמִי בַּר חָמָא לְמֵימַר – **Rami bar Chama thought it plausible to interpret** this prohibition as it applies to a doorway as meaning only that בַּר ד׳ לֹא לִישַׁוְיֵיהּ בַּר תְּמַנְיָא – **one may not convert a four-*amah*-wide [doorway] into an eight-*amah*-wide [doorway],** דְּקָא שָׁקִיל תְּמַנְיָא בְּחָצֵר – **for he would** then be entitled to **take** an **eight-*amah*-**wide swath of land **in the courtyard** opposite his doorway if the joint ownership of the courtyard were to be dissolved.[16] אֲבָל בַּר תַּרְתֵּי לִישַׁוְיֵיהּ בַּר אַרְבְּעָה שַׁפִּיר דָּמֵי – **But,** according to this line of reasoning, **to convert a two-*amah*--wide [doorway] into a four-*amah*-wide [doorway] is permissible,**[17] since he gains nothing should the courtyard later be divided among its owners.[18]

Rava disagrees with Rami:

אָמַר לֵיהּ רָבָא – **Rava responded to [Rami bar Chama]:** מָצֵי אָמַר לֵיהּ – Your reasoning is flawed, for **[a neighbor] may say to [the partner]** who seeks to widen his doorway: בְּפִיתְחָא זוּטְרָא מָצֵינָא לְאִצְטְנוּעֵי מִינָּךְ – If you have **a small doorway I am able to conceal my** actions **from you;**[19] בְּפִיתְחָא רַבָּה לֹא מָצֵינָא אִצְטְנוּעֵי מִינָּךְ – but if you have **a large doorway, I am unable to conceal my** actions **from you.**[20]

The Gemara cites another segment of our Mishnah and expounds upon it:

אֶחָד לֹא יַעֲשֶׂנּוּ שְׁנַיִם – If there was ONE doorway, ONE MAY NOT CONVERT IT INTO TWO.

סָבַר רָמִי בַּר חָמָא לְמֵימַר – **Rami bar Chama thought it plausible to interpret** this prohibition of the Mishnah as meaning only that בַּר אַרְבְּעֵי לֹא לִישַׁוְיֵיהּ תְּרֵי בְּנֵי תַּרְתֵּי תַּרְתֵּי – if it was **a four-*amah*-wide [doorway] one may not convert it into two two-*amah*-wide [doorways],** דְּקָא שָׁקִיל תַּמְנֵי בְּחָצֵר – **for he will** now be entitled to **take eight *amos*** of land **in the courtyard** for his two doorways if the joint ownership of the courtyard were to be dissolved.[21] אֲבָל בַּר תַּמְנֵי לִישַׁוְיֵיהּ בְּנֵי אַרְבְּעֵי אַרְבְּעֵי שַׁפִּיר דָּמֵי – **But to convert an eight-*amah*-wide [doorway] into** two **four--*amah*-wide [doorways] is permissible,** since he gains nothing should the courtyard later be divided among its owners.[22]

Rava disagrees with Rami:

אָמַר לֵיהּ רָבָא – **Rava responded to [Rami bar Chama]:** מָצֵי אָמַר לֵיהּ – Your reasoning is flawed, for **[a neighbor] may say to [the partner]** who seeks to split his doorway: בְּחַד פִּיתְחָא מָצֵינָא אִצְטְנוּעֵי מִינָּךְ – If you have only **one doorway, I am able to conceal my** actions **from you;** בִּתְרֵי לֹא מָצֵינָא אִצְטְנוּעֵי מִינָּךְ – but if you have **two [doorways], I am unable to conceal my** actions **from you.**[23]

The Gemara cites and explains another segment of the Mishnah:

אֲבָל פּוֹתֵחַ הוּא לִרְשׁוּת הָרַבִּים פֶּתַח כְּנֶגֶד פֶּתַח – BUT ONE MAY OPEN

NOTES

13. *Numbers* 24:2.

14. I.e. what sight caused him to bless Israel.

15. It was this arrangement of the tents that prompted Bilam to exclaim, appropriately (*Numbers* 24:5): *How goodly are your tents* [and to bless Israel. The fact that the prophet Bilam extolled the virtue of respecting another's privacy and that his words are inscribed in the Torah demonstrate how highly the Torah values privacy]. The "goodness" of which Bilam spoke was the *Shechinah,* which he saw in "the tents of Jacob" (*Rashbam*; cf. *Rif, Tosafos, Rosh* and *Maharsha*).

The entire Israelite camp fell into the category of a jointly owned courtyard; hence, it was imperative for the Jews to respect the privacy of their neighbors. The only area of the camp that qualified as a public domain was the Levite camp, as explained in *Shabbos* 96b (*Rashbam*; cf. *Ritva*).

16. The Gemara (above, 11a) states that when a jointly owned courtyard is divided, each partner is entitled to retain an area in front of his doorway along the entire width of the doorway and measuring four *amos* into the courtyard. Furthermore, one is entitled to such an area in front of each doorway he owns. It is this law that serves as the background for the Mishnah's ruling, according to Rami. One may not widen an existing doorway that opens into a courtyard, because he will then be entitled to a wider area, corresponding to the new width of the doorway, should the courtyard be divided (*Rashbam*). [According to this view, the Mishnah's ruling applies to doorways, but not to windows.]

Rosh (above, 1:38) explains that, of course, one may not profit from widening a doorway. Any division of the courtyard must accurately reflect each partner's share of the whole. Although the needs of an owner having a wider doorway must be taken into consideration, this owner must nonetheless compensate his partners either monetarily [or by ceding to them a commensurate amount of land elsewhere in the courtyard].

17. Even a doorway two *amos* wide entitles one to an area four *amos* squared before it, and for a doorway four *amos* wide he receives the same amount of land. Hence, widening a doorway from two to four *amos* does not entitle the owner to a greater share in the courtyard (*Rashbam*).

18. Rami maintains that widening a doorway does not adversely affect the neighbors' privacy, for they realize that their actions can be observed even through a narrow doorway (*Rashbam*).

19. Literally: I am able to hide myself.

20. Although a great amount of privacy is lost by the mere existence of a doorway (regardless of its size), widening the doorway nonetheless causes a further loss of privacy, inasmuch as new areas of the courtyard come into view. It is to prevent this additional loss of privacy — however slight — that the Mishnah prohibited the widening of existing doorways.

Since, according to Rava, the prohibition against widening doorways is based on considerations of privacy, the prohibition also applies to the widening of windows; see *Choshen Mishpat* 154:4 with *Shach*.

21. Since for every doorway (even if it is only two *amos* wide) one is entitled to four *amos* squared in the courtyard (see above, note 17), splitting a doorway into two would entitle the owner to an area of eight *amos* by four *amos*. The other partners of the courtyard can therefore prevent him from gaining this advantage (*Rashbam*).

22. In this case no advantage accrues to the owner of the doorway, since he is entitled to an area eight *amos* by four *amos* regardless of whether he splits his doorway [for one is entitled to an area as wide as the width of his doorway (see above, note 16)]. Rami also maintains that the users of the courtyard incur no loss of privacy (as is the case when a doorway is widened; see Gemara above), because there is no difference, as far as privacy is concerned, whether an eight-*amah* opening is split into two doorways or remains one unbroken doorway (*Rashbam*). [Rami believes that even Rava, who objects to the widening of a doorway on the grounds that it would cause a diminution of the neighbors' privacy, might here concede that loss of privacy is not an issue; cf. *Ritva*.]

23. The partners are justified in claiming that their privacy is compromised by the splitting of the doorway. For if there is only one door, they are able to enjoy private use of the courtyard when that door is closed. When there are two doors, however, one may remain open even when the other is closed (*Rashbam*).

ולסתום. אם החזיק בחלון ג' שנים בחצר השותפין ובא חבירו וסתמו שבנה כותל כנגדו והוא שתק לאלתר הויא חזקה לזה הסותם שלא יפתח עוד חבירו אלא ברשותו וחזקת ג' שנים שהיה חלונו פתוח אינה כלום מאחר ששתק כשסתמו זה: **שאין אדם עשוי שסותמין אורו בפניו ושותק.** ומדשתק אודויי אודי ליה דשלא כדין החזיק מעיקרא: **שמרבה עליהן את הדרך.** שרוב בני אדם יוצאין ונכנסין עכשיו בחצר יותר מבתחלה וליכא לניעות כדמעיקרא: **והלא מרבה עליהן את הדרך.** דבנין עלייה זו שלא היתה שם קודם לכן והוא מכניס לתוכה דיורין לבד דיורין שבביתו אע"פ שכולן נכנסין ויוצאין דרך פתח ביתו הרי נתרבו נכנסין ויוצאין בחצר: **מאי.** בונה החדר דקתני מתני' לא בונה ממש כדקאמרת אלא שחלקו לחדר שלו לשנים שעשה מחיצה באמצעיתו להושיב שם דיורין מרווחין דבדבר זה יש לו רשות שיכול למלאות כל ביתו דיורין: **ומאי עלייה אפתא.** יציע מפרשי לקמן (פרק המוכר את הבית) אפתא ואמרינן ג' שמות יש לה יציע צלע ותא ומוכח התם מקראי דהיינו בנין נמוך בצדי הבית או מאחוריו ואינו שוה לגג הבית ומתני' הכי קתני ובונה עלייה על גביו דההוא חדר שלפנים מביתו דהיינו נמי שחלקו בגגהו ועולה דרך ארובה מן החדר להיא עלייה דהיינו יציע שהרי אחורי הבית הוא והלכך קרוי יציע וגם גבי יציע אשכחן כי האי גוונא תחתיים שניים ושלישים דכתיב הצלע התיכונה וכתיב ובלולים יעלו על התיכונה ומן התיכונה וגו' (מלכים א ו) והלכך אין כאן תוספת בנין כלל לא בחדר ולא בעלייה דחדר היינו שחלק רחבו של חדר ועשאו שני חדרים קצרים וכן עלייה שבנה מעזיבה באמצעית גבהו של חדר ונמצאת עלייה בנויה מאיליה: **מתני' לא יפתח אדם לחצר השותפין.** אפילו היכא דיש לו חזקה: **חלון כנגד חלון.** אלא משהו ירחיק זה שלא כנגד זה וטעם משום לניעות כולה מתני' מפרש בגמ': **גמ' וירא את ישראל שוכן.** ראה היאך שוכנים ולפיכך אמר מה טובו אהליך וגו' שאין פתחי אהליהם מכוונים ומחנה ישראל כחצר השותפין דמי דלא היה רה"ר אלא במחנה לויה כדאמרינן במס' שבת (דף צו:): **אמר ראוין הללו כו'.** מדכתיב התם מה טובו אהליך קדייק: **סבר רמי בר חמא למימר.** דמאי דקתני היה קטן לא יעשנו גדול היינו דאי הוה פתח בר ד' אמות רחב לא ירחיבנו לח' אמות דקמפסיד לבעלי החצר דקשקיל השתא תמני אמות בחצר כנגד כל הפתח באורך ארבע אמות רחוק מן הפתח כדאמרינן בפרק ראשון (לעיל יא.) היה רחב שמנה נוטל שמנה אמות באורך החצר כנגד רוחב כל הפתח ואילו מעיקרא לא הוה שקיל אלא ארבע אמות אבל לצניעותא לא הוה חייש רמי בר חמא דכי היכי דמצטנעי מפתח קטן מצטנעי (ג) מפתח גדול: **בר תרתי.** דשקיל נמי ד' אמות בחצר כבר ארבעי כדאמרי' נותן לכל פתח ארבע אמות: **לישוייה בר ארבעי.** דלא מפסיד לחבריה מידי דמעיקרא נמי הוה שקיל ד' אמות בחצר: **לישוייה תרין בני ארבעי.** דהשתא נמי לא שקיל אלא תמני בחצר כמעיקרא ולאיצטנועי נמי לא חיישינן דמה לי ח' אמות בפתח אחד מה לי ח' אמות חלוקות לב' פתחים בשני מקומות מ"מ ח' אמות יש לו פתוחות לחצר: **בחד פיתחא מצינא איצטנועי.** כשהוא נעול יכולני להשתמש בחצר א"נ להשתמש שלא כנגדו אבל בשני פתחים לא מצינא לאיצטנועי כל כך דאפי' אם האחד נעול השני יהיה פתוח: **סוף סוף הא בעית איצטנועי מבני רה"ר.** שרואין בביתך דרך פתח הבית ורוכבי סוסים וגמלים רואין בתוך (ד) חלונותיו: **מתני' אין עושין חלל תחת רה"ר.** ואע"ג דמקבל עליה כל היזקא דאתי מחמתיה שאין רצונם של בני אדם ליזוק ולירד לדין על עסקי ממונו ומפרש ואזיל מה הוא אותו חלל בורות שיחין ומערות: **ר"א מתיר.** אלא שיכסהו כיסוי חזק כדי שתהא עגלה מהלכת דר"א אזל בתר השתא ולא חייש לשמא היום ולמחר יכלה הכיסוי ויפול והכי אמרינן בבבא קמא (דף נ:): **זיזין.** קורות קטנות: **גזוזטראות.** קורות גדולות הבולטות מן הבית לחוץ ואיכא למיחש פן יכשלו בהם בני רה"ר והלכך אין מוציאין דהא כל בני רה"ר ליתנהו גביה דלימחלו: **כונס לתוך קרקע שלו.** את כותלו ומניח מקרקעו לחוץ כשיעור הוצאת זיזין ומוציא: **ובה זיזין וגזוזטראות.** הבולטות לרשות הרבים: **הרי זו בחזקתה.** דטענינן ללוקח ואומרים אימר כונס לתוך שלו היה אבל המוכרה לו שהוציא הזיזין הוא היה צריך להביא עדים שכנס לתוך שלו או שיטעון שני חזקה החזקתי וכנסתי לתוך שלי דהויא לה חזקה שיש עמה טענה אבל לוקח לא צריך למיטען מידי אלא כך לקחתיה וא"צ לטעון היאך הוציא המוכר את הזיזין לחוץ לרה"ר דטוענין ליורש וטוענין ללוקח: **גמ' ורבנן.** דאסרי סברי לא אזלינן בתר השתא וחיישינן משום דזימנין דמתליע מתוכו ויפחות ולאו אדעתיה דעובר ברה"ר ויעבור ויפול: **מפיק למבואה.** מוציא (ה) למבואה והמבוי מקום הלוך כל בני החצירות הוא: **הוו מעכבי עילויה בני רה"ר.** שנופיו מזיקין לגמל ורוכבו: זיל

א ולסתום לאלתר הוי חזקה שאין אדם עשוי שסותמים אורו בפניו ושותק: **לקח** בית בחצר אחרת לא יפתחנו לחצר השותפין: מאי טעמא ב מפני שמרבה עליהם את הדרך אימא סיפא אלא אם רצה בונה את החדר לפנים מביתו ובונה עלייה על גבי ביתו והלא מרבה עליו את הדרך אמר רב הונא ג מאי חדר שחלקו (א) בשנים ומאי עלייה אפתאי: **מתני'** ד לא יפתח אדם לחצר השותפין פתח כנגד פתח וחלון כנגד חלון ה היה קטן לא יעשנו גדול אחד לא יעשנו שנים ו אבל פותח הוא לרה"ר פתח כנגד פתח וחלון כנגד חלון ז היה קטן עושה אותו גדול ואחד עושה אותו שנים: **גמ'** מנהני מילי א"ר יוחנן דאמר קרא א) וישא בלעם את עיניו וירא את ישראל שוכן לשבטיו מה ראה ראה שאין פתחי אהליהם מכוונין זה לזה אמר ראוין הללו שתשרה עליהם שכינה: היה קטן לא יעשנו גדול: סבר רמי בר חמא למימר בר ד' לא לישוייה בר תמניא דקא שקיל תמניא בחצר אבל בר תרתי לישוייה בר ארבעה שפיר דמי א"ל רבא ח מצי א"ל בפיתחא זוטרא מצינא לאצטנועי מינך בפיתחא רבה לא מצינא אצטנועי מינך: אחד לא יעשנו שנים: סבר רמי בר חמא למימר בר ארבעי לא לישוייה תרי בני תרתי תרתי דקא שקיל תמני בחצר אבל בר תמני לישוייה בני ארבעי ארבעי שפיר דמי א"ל רבא ט מצי אמר ליה בחד פיתחא מצינא אצטנועי מינך בתרי לא מצינא אצטנועי מינך: אבל פותח הוא לרה"ר פתח כנגד פתח: דא"ל סוף סוף הא בעית אצטנועי מבני רה"ר: **מתני'** (א) י אין עושין חלל תחת רה"ר בורות שיחין ומערות ר"א מתיר כדי שתהא עגלה מהלכת וטעונה אבנים כ אין מוציאין זיזין וגזוזטראות לרה"ר אלא אם רצה כונס לתוך שלו ומוציא ל לקח חצר ובה זיזין וגזוזטראות הרי זו בחזקתה: **גמ'** ורבנן מ זימנין דמפחית ולאו אדעתיה: אין מוציאין זיזין וגזוזטראות וכו': ר' אמי הוה ליה זיזא דהוה נפיק למבואה וההוא גברא נמי הוה ליה זיזא דהוה מפיק לרה"ר (הוו קא מעכבי עליה בני רה"ר) אתא לקמיה דר' אמי א"ל זיל קוץ אמר ליה והא מר נמי אית ליה (ב) דידי למבואה מפיק בני מבואה מחלין גבאי דידך לרשות הרבים מפיק מאן מחיל גבך: ר' ינאי הוה ליה אילן הנוטה לרשות הרבים הוה ההוא גברא דהוה ליה נמי אילן הנוטה לרשות הרבים אתו בני רשות הרבים הוו קא מעכבי עילויה אתא לקמיה דר' ינאי א"ל זיל

לקח בית בחצר אחרת לא יפתחנה לחצר השותפין. פירוש אפילו לביתו כדי (ו) שלא יכנס ממנו לחצר השותפין: **ראוין הללו שתשרה שכינה עליהם.** מקפיד דקרא דריש דכתיב ותהי עליו רוח אלהים: נפלה

עין משפט נר מצוה

רפג **א** מיי' פ"ז מהל' שכנים הל' ז סמג עשין פב טוש"ע ח"מ סי' קנד סעיף יג:

רפד **ב ג** מיי' פ"ה שם הל' ח סמג שם טוש"ע שם סעיף א:

רפה **ד** מיי' שם הל' ו טוש"ע שם סעיף ג:

רפו **ה** מיי' שם הל' י טוש"ע שם סעיף ד:

רפז **ו** מיי' שם הל' ו טוש"ע שם סעיף ג:

רפח **ז ח ט** מיי' שם הל' יא טוש"ע שם סעיף ד:

רפט **י** מיי' פי"ג מהל' נזקי ממון הל' כג סמג עשין שם טוש"ע ח"מ סי' תח סעיף א:

רצ **כ** מיי' שם הל' כד טוש"ע שם סעיף ב:

רצא **ל** מיי' שם הל' כה טוש"ע שם סעיף ג:

רצב **מ** מיי' שם הל' כג טוש"ע שם סעיף א:

רבינו גרשום

ולסתום. שאם יש לאדם חלון בחצר חבירו ובונה בעל חצר כנגדו וסותמו בפנים. אם לא מיחה לאלתר בעל חלון (שעה) לאלתר הוי חזקה לבעל חצר לסותמו: **לקח.** אחד מן השותפין: **בית בחצר אחרת לא יפתח לחצר השותפין. מפני שמרבה** על השותפין דריסת רגל של אותן שיהיו דרין באותו בית מה שלא היה שם קודם לכן: בנה עלייה על גבי ביתו ורוצה לשוכרה לבית דירה לא יפתח לה פתח בחצר השותפין **מפני שמרבה עליהם הדרך: אלא אם רוצה כו'.** מפרש בגמ'. **והלא מרבה על הדרך.** דהשתא בונה עלייה מה שלא היתה שם קודם לכן ומשים בה דיורין אע"פ שפותחה בתוך ביתו מרבה עליהם הדרכים. אלא **מאי** בונה את החדר ואת העלייה דקאמר לא עלייה ממש אלא **שחלק** חדרו **לשנים** וחלק החיצון קרוי חדר **ומאי עלייה** דקאמר **אפתא** שקורין אפלדי"ץ והיינו חלק הפנימי ושוכר האחר לדירה. ואי אמרת והלא מרבה עליהם הדרכים לא מצי אמרת דכשם שאם היו לו בני בית לזה יותר מן השותפין אחרים לא היו יכולין לעכבן שלא יכנסו ושלא יצאו בחצר כך עכשיו כיון שלא בנה בנין יותר אלא שהיה כמו שהיה וחלקו לשנים והכניס דיורין בחלק האחד אין יכולין לעכבו: **פיסקא. שלא היו מכוונין זה כנגד זה.** מפני היזק ראיה: **אם היה קטן.** הפתח: א) דקא שקיל ח' אמות בחצר דאיכא ביה שיעור ב' פתחים: **אבל בר תרי** (טפח בכ"י) אמות. **לישויה בר ארבע** אמות (טפח בכ"י) רוחב **שפיר דמי** דסוף סוף לא שקיל אלא ד' אמות ככל פתח שהוא פחות מח' אמות (טפח בכ"י). ואם הפתח פחות מח' וחלקן לשני פתחים לכל פתח יש לו ד' אמות ושהוא בו ח' אמות: **אבל בר תמני.** שיש לו ח' אמות **לישויה תרי פתחים** שפיר דמי דסוף סוף לא שקיל אלא ח' אמות בחצר כדמעיקרא: מצי אמר ליה. **בחד פיתחא מצינא דאיצטנועי מינך** שאני משתמש כשהוא נעול: **בתרי** פתחי **לא מצינא איצטנועי.** שכשהאחד נעול השני פתוח: **אבל פותח הוא לרה"ר פתח כנגד פתח דא"ל סוף סוף כו': פיסקא** ור"א מתיר. ובלבד שיכסנו כסוי חזק **כדי שתהא עגלה כו': ורבנן.** דאסרי מאי טעמא והלא הכסוי חזק סברי **דזימנין דמיפחת.** שיתליע מתוכו **ולאו אדעתיה** דהאי שיהא רעוע: **זיזין.** יברונ"ש: **גזוזטראות.** קורות: **לרה"ר.** דליתנייהו כל בני רה"ר גבי הדדי דלימחלי ליה: **לקח חצר ובה זיזין וגזוזטראות** שיוצאין לרה"ר **הרי זו בחזקתה** ואין צריך לקוץ: **מחלין לי בני מבואה.** דיחידים נינהו ומצי מחלי: **הוו מעכבי עילויה.** בני רה"ר שנופיו מזיקין לגמל ורוכבו:

מסורת הש"ס

א) לעיל מ:, ב) [לעיל כג.], ג) [לעיל מ:], ד) ת"מ מ"ז וכן ברי"ף ורא"ש ליתא:

הגהות הב"ח

(א) גמ' שחלקו לשנים: (ב) שם מר נמי אית ליה א"ל דידי: (ג) רשב"ם ד"ה סבר וכו' מלטנעי נמי מפתח גדול: (ד) ד"ה סוף וכו' חלונותיך הס"ד: (ה) ד"ה מפיק וכו' מוליא למבוי והמבוי מקום: (ו) תוס' ד"ה לקח בית וכו' כדי שיכנס כצ"ל ותיבת שלא נמחק:

גליון הש"ס

מתני' ר"א מתיר. עיין בר"ש ריש בכורים:

תורה אור השלם

א) וַיִּשָּׂא בִלְעָם אֶת עֵינָיו וַיַּרְא אֶת יִשְׂרָאֵל שֹׁכֵן לִשְׁבָטָיו וַתְּהִי עָלָיו רוּחַ אֱלֹהִים: [במדבר כד, ב]

ליקוטי רש"י

אפתאי. אפנטמ"ן בנין נמוך אצל הבית מצדו או מאחוריו [רשב"ם לקמן סא.]. **שוכן לשבטיו.** ראה כל שבט ושבט שוכן לעצמו ואינן מעורבין ראה שאין פתחיהם מכוונין זה כנגד זה שלא יציץ לתוך אהל חבירו [במדבר כד, ב]. **כדי שתהא עגלה מהלכת.** אם תקרתה חזקה כל כך מותר ואע"ג שסופה שתתליע ותפחת [לעיל כז:]. **לקח חצר ובה זיזין וגזוזטראות וכו'.** אדם הבונה בית לא יוציא לפני קורותיו לחוץ לרה"ר אבל אם רצה כונס בנינו לתוך שלו ובונה ולקח חצר ובה זיזין וגזוזטראות יוצאים לפני קורותיו לחוץ הרי הוא בחזקתה שבית דין טוענין לו שהכונס כנס לתוך שלו ונתפייס עם הרבים [שם כג.].

חשק שלמה על רבינו גרשום א) נראה דהוא ליון על הגמ' דסבר רמי בר חמא למימר דבר ד' לא לישוייה בר תמניא דקא שקיל וכו'.

INTO THE PUBLIC DOMAIN A DOORWAY OPPOSITE A DOORWAY. דְּאָמַר לֵיהּ – In this case there is no concern for privacy, **for [the person opening the doorway] may say to [his neighbor]:** סוֹף הָא בָּעֵית אִצְטְנוּעֵי מִבְּנֵי רְשׁוּת הָרַבִּים – **Ultimately, you will have to conceal your** actions **from the people in the public domain.**[24]

Mishnah אֵין עוֹשִׂין חָלָל תַּחַת רְשׁוּת הָרַבִּים – **One may not make a cavity beneath the public domain,** בּוֹרוֹת שִׁיחִין וּמְעָרוֹת – e.g. **pits, ditches or vaults.**[25] רַבִּי אֱלִיעֶזֶר מַתִּיר – **R' Eliezer permits** this כְּדֵי שֶׁתְּהֵא עֲגָלָה מְהַלֶּכֶת וּטְעוּנָה אֲבָנִים – as long as **[the cavity's cover]** is strong **enough for a wagon laden with stones to pass** over it.[26]

אֵין מוֹצִיאִין זִיזִין וּגְזוּזְטְרָאוֹת לִרְשׁוּת הָרַבִּים – **One may not extend ledges or balconies into the public domain.**[27] אֶלָּא אִם רָצָה – **However, if he wishes,** כּוֹנֵס לְתוֹךְ שֶׁלּוֹ וּמוֹצִיא – **he may draw** the wall of his house **back into his own** property **and extend** the ledges or balconies.[28] לָקַח חָצֵר וּבָהּ זִיזִין וּגְזוּזְטְרָאוֹת – **If one purchased a courtyard in which there are** houses that have **ledges and balconies** protruding into the public domain, הֲרֵי זוֹ בְחֶזְקָתָהּ – **[the courtyard] retains its status** and he may keep the ledges or balconies.[29]

Gemara The Gemara examines the position of the Rabbis, i.e. the Tanna Kamma, who prohibit excavating a cavity beneath the public domain even if its covering is strong enough to bear the traffic of the street:

וְרַבָּנָן – **And the Rabbis?** What is their reasoning?[30]

The Gemara explains:

זִימְנִין דִּמְפַחִית וְלָאו אַדַּעְתֵּיהּ – The Rabbis are concerned that **sometimes [the covering] will rot and [a passerby] may not be aware of it.**[31]

The Gemara cites a passage of our Mishnah:

אֵין מוֹצִיאִין זִיזִין וּגְזוּזְטְרָאוֹת וכו׳ – ONE MAY NOT EXTEND LEDGES OR BALCONIES ETC. into the public domain.

The Gemara relates an episode that clarifies the ruling of the Mishnah:

ר׳ אַמֵּי הֲוָה לֵיהּ זִיזָא דַּהֲוָה נָפִיק לִמְבוֹאָה – **R' Ami had a ledge that protruded** from his house **into an alleyway.**[32] וְהַהוּא גַּבְרָא נַמִּי הֲוָה לֵיהּ זִיזָא דַּהֲוָה מַפִּיק לִרְשׁוּת הָרַבִּים – **And a certain person also had a ledge that protruded** from his house, but his protruded **into the public domain.** (הֲווּ קָא מְעַכְּבֵי עֲלֵיהּ בְּנֵי רְשׁוּת הָרַבִּים – **The public objected to his** use of the public space.) אֲתָא לְקַמֵּיהּ דְּר׳ אַמֵּי – **He appeared before R' Ami** to seek a ruling from him on this matter. אָמַר לֵיהּ זִיל קוֹץ – **[R' Ami] said to [the person]: Go and cut** your ledge down! אָמַר לֵיהּ וְהָא מַר נַמִּי אִית לֵיהּ – **[The person] protested to [R' Ami]: But master also has** a ledge protruding from his house. Why must mine be destroyed and not yours? דִּידִי לִמְבוֹאָה מַפִּיק – R' Ami explained: **Mine protrudes into an alleyway,** בְּנֵי מְבוֹאָה מַחֲלִין גַּבַּאי – and **the people of the alleyway allow me** to extend my ledge. דִּידָךְ לִרְשׁוּת הָרַבִּים מַפִּיק – However, **yours protrudes into the public domain.** מַאן מָחִיל גַּבָּךְ – **Who allows you** to extend your ledge?[33]

The Gemara relates a similar episode:

ר׳ יַנַּאי הֲוָה לֵיהּ אִילָן הַנּוֹטֶה לִרְשׁוּת הָרַבִּים – **R' Yannai had a tree that extended into the public domain,** הֲוָה הַהוּא גַּבְרָא דַּהֲוָה לֵיהּ נַמִּי אִילָן הַנּוֹטֶה לִרְשׁוּת הָרַבִּים – and **there was a certain person who also had a tree that extended into the public domain.** אָתוּ בְּנֵי רְשׁוּת הָרַבִּים הֲווּ קָא מְעַכְּבֵי עִילָוֵיהּ – **The public came** and **objected to his** violation of the public space.[34] אֲתָא לְקַמֵּיהּ דְּר׳ יַנַּאי – **He appeared before R' Yannai** to seek a ruling from him on this matter. אָמַר לֵיהּ – **[R' Yannai] said to [the person]:**

NOTES

24. In any event the people in the street can gaze into your doorway, and riders on camels and horses can look into your windows (*Rashbam*). Thus, the widening of a doorway or window does not result in a further loss of privacy in this particular case.

25. Even if one formally assumes the obligation to pay for any damage that may be occasioned by a subsequent collapse of the cavity's cover, he can be prevented from digging the cavity, for — justifiably — people do not want to sustain damages and then have to litigate in order to recover their losses (*Rashbam*). [Without a formal declaration that one assumes responsibility for any future damage, one is not even liable to pay for such damage. For the Mishnah (*Bava Kamma* 52a) rules that if one dug a pit in the public domain and covered it adequately, he is not liable if the cover later deteriorates and collapses.]

26. R' Eliezer holds that we need not be concerned about future deterioration of the cavity's cover so long as it is now solid [and will presumably endure] (*Rashbam*, from Gemara above, 27b).

27. So that people will not stumble over them (*Rashbam*), or hurt themselves on their account (*Nimukei Yosef*). However, if they are situated so high above the street that a camel with its rider can pass underneath them, one may extend them (*Rif, Rosh*; see Mishnah above, 27b).

28. He need not be concerned that traffic from the street will overflow into the recessed space and passersby will suffer injury (*Tosefos Yom Tov*).

29. I.e. he may retain the ledges or balconies even if he does not know if the seller drew back from the street line; it is sufficient for him to claim that he purchased the house with the ledges or balconies already in place. Although the seller would either have to produce witnesses that he drew back from the street line or claim that he did so and establish a *chazakah* of having the ledge or balcony in place for [three] years, the buyer retains his property's status without definite evidence and without a definite claim. Since he cannot be expected to know the particulars of the extension of the ledge or balcony, the court enters a plea for him to the effect that the extension was legal. The court's action involves the well-known legal principle (see above, 23a et al.) that a court pleads on behalf of buyers or heirs regarding matters of which they are necessarily ignorant (*Rashbam*).

30. Why are the Rabbis not satisfied if a sturdy covering is placed over the cavity?

31. The covering may rot from the inside, and a passerby, unaware of its present condition, may fall into the cavity and injure himself. Therefore, [in this case] the Rabbis are not satisfied with a covering that is adequate *now* (*Rashbam*). Although the Rabbis are not ordinarily concerned with the possibility of future damage if there is no danger of damage *now*, relying instead that future dangers will be eliminated when they become evident, they are nonetheless concerned in this case because the future deterioration will not necessarily be evident; see above, 27b.

32. An alleyway, or *mavoi*, is designated primarily for the use of the courtyards that open into it (see *Rashbam*).

33. Surely the entire public was not there when you extended your ledge (see *Rashbam* to Mishnah ד״ה גזוזטראות).

34. The tree's branches posed a danger to camels and their riders (*Rashbam*). The Mishnah (above, 27b) rules that tree branches overhanging the public domain must be cut unless their height exceeds the height of a camel and its rider.

ולסתום. אם החזיק בחלון ג' שנים בחצר השותפין ובא חבירו וסתמו שבנה כותל כנגדו והוא שתק לאלתר הויא חזקה לזה הסותם שלא יפתח עוד חבירו אלא ברשותו וחזקת ג' שנים שהיה חלונו פתוח אינה כלום מאחר ששתק כשסתמו זה: שאין אדם עשוי שסותמין אורו בפניו ושותק. ומדשתק אודויי אודי ליה דשלא כדין החזיק מעיקרא: שמרבה עליהן את הדרך. שרוב בני אדם יוצאין ונכנסין עכשיו בחצר יותר מבתחלה וליכא לניעות כדמעיקרא: והלא מרבה עליהן את הדרך. דבנין עלייה זו שלא היתה שם קודם לכן והוא מכניס לתוכה דיורין לבד דיורין שבביתו

א ולסתום לאלתר הוי חזקה שאין אדם עשוי שסותמים אורו בפניו ושותק: לקח בית בחצר אחרת לא יפתחנו לחצר השותפין: מאי טעמא ב מפני שמרבה עליהם את הדרך אימא סיפא אלא אם רצה בונה את החדר לפנים מביתו ובונה עלייה על גבי ביתו והלא מרבה עליו את הדרך אמר רב הונא ג מאי חדר שחלקו (א) בשנים ומאי עלייה אפתאי: מתני' ד לא יפתח אדם לחצר השותפין פתח כנגד פתח וחלון כנגד חלון ה היה קטן לא יעשנו גדול אחד לא יעשנו שנים ו אבל פותח הוא לרה"ר פתח כנגד פתח וחלון כנגד חלון ז היה קטן עושה אותו גדול ואחד עושה אותו שנים: גמ' מנהני מילי א"ר יוחנן דאמר קרא א) וישא בלעם את עיניו וירא את ישראל שוכן לשבטיו מה ראה ראה שאין פתחי אהליהם מכוונין זה לזה אמר ראוין הללו שתשרה עליהם שכינה: היה קטן לא יעשנו גדול: סבר רמי בר חמא למימר בר ד' לא לישוייה בר תמניא דקא שקיל תמניא בחצר אבל בר תרתי לישוייה בר ארבעה שפיר דמי א"ל רבא ח מצי א"ל בפיתחא זוטרא מצינא לאצטנועי מינך בפיתחא רבה לא מצינא אצטנועי מינך: אחד לא יעשנו שנים: סבר רמי בר חמא למימר בר ארבעי לא לישוייה תרי בני תרתי תרתי דקא שקיל תמני בחצר אבל בר תמני לישוייה בני ארבעי ארבעי שפיר דמי א"ל רבא ט מצי אמר ליה בחד פיתחא מצינא אצטנועי מינך בתרי לא מצינא אצטנועי מינך: אבל פותח הוא לרה"ר פתח כנגד פתח: דא"ל סוף סוף הא בעית אצטנועי מבני רה"ר: מתני' א) י אין עושין חלל תחת רה"ר בורות שיחין ומערות ר"א מתיר כדי שתהא עגלה מהלכת וטעונה אבנים כ אין מוציאין זיזין וגזוזטראות לרה"ר אלא אם רצה כונס לתוך שלו ומוציא ב) ל לקח חצר ובה זיזין וגזוזטראות הרי זו בחזקתה: גמ' ורבנן ג) מ זימנין דמפחית ולאו אדעתיה: אין מוציאין זיזין וגזוזטראות וכו': ר' אמי הוה ליה זיזא דהוה נפיק למבואה וההוא גברא נמי הוה ליה זיזא דהוה מפיק לרה"ר ד) (הוו קא מעכבי עליה בני רה"ר) אתא לקמיה דר' אמי א"ל זיל קוץ אמר ליה והא מר נמי אית ליה (ב) דידי למבואה מפיק בני מבואה מחלין גבאי דידך לרשות הרבים מפיק מאן מחיל גבך: ר' ינאי הוה ליה אילן הנוטה לרשות הרבים הוה ההוא גברא דהוה ליה נמי אילן הנוטה לרשות הרבים אתו בני רשות הרבים הוו קא מעכבי עילויה אתא לקמיה דר' ינאי א"ל זיל

רש"י

לתוכה דיורין לבד דיורין שבביתו אע"פ שכולן נכנסין ויוצאין דרך פתח ביתו הרי נתרבו נכנסין ויוצאין בחצר: מאי. בונה החדר דקתני מתני' לא בונה ממש כדקאמרת אלא שחלקו לחדר שלו לשנים שעשה מחיצה באמצעיתו להושיב שם דיורין מרווחין דבדבר זה יש לו רשות שיכול למלאות כל ביתו דיורין: ומאי עלייה אפתא. יליע מפרשי לקמן (פרק המוכר את הבית) אפתא ואמרינן ג' שמות יש לה יליע ותא ומוכח התם מקראי דהיינו בנין נמוך בלדי הבית או מאחוריו ואינו שוה לגג הבית ומתני' הכי קתני ובונה עלייה על גביו דההוא חדר שלפנים מביתו דהיינו נמי שחלקו בגבהו ועולה דרך ארובה מן החדר להיא עלייה דהיינו יליע שהרי אחורי הבית הוא והלכך קרי יליע וגם גבי יליע אשכחן כי האי גוונא תחתיים שניים ושלישים כדכתיב הצלע התיכונה וכתיב ובלולים יעלו על התיכונה ומן התיכונה וגו' (מלכים א ו) והלכך אין כאן תוספת בנין כלל לא בחדר ולא בעלייה דחדר היינו שחלק רחבו של חדר ועשאו שני חדרים קצרים וכן עלייה שבנה מעזיבה באמצעית גבהו של חדר ונמצאת עלייה בנויה מאליה: מתני' לא יפתח אדם לחצר השותפין. אפילו היכא דיש לו חזקה: חלון כנגד חלון. אלא משהו ירחיק זה שלא כנגד זה וטעם משום צניעות כולה מתני' מפרש בגמ': גמ' וירא את ישראל שוכן. ראה היאך שוכנים ולפיכך אמר מה טובו אהליך וגו' שאין פתחי אהליהם מכוונים ומחנה ישראל כחצר השותפין דמי דלא היה רה"ר אלא במחנה לויה כדאמרינן במס' שבת (דף צו:): אמר ראוין הללו כו'. מדכתיב התם מה טובו אהליך קדייק: סבר רמי בר חמא למימר. דמאי דקתני היה קטן לא יעשנו גדול היינו דאי הוה פתח בר ד' אמות רחב לא ירחיבנו לח' אמות דקמפסיד לבעלי החצר דקשקיל השתא תמני אמות בחצר כנגד כל הפתח באורך ארבע אמות רחוק מן הפתח כדאמרינן בפרק ראשון (לעיל יא.) היה רחב שמנה נוטל שמנה אמות באורך החצר כנגד רוחב כל הפתח ואילו מעיקרא לא הוה שקיל אלא ארבע אמות אבל לצניעותא לא הוה חייש רמי בר חמא דכי היכי דמצטנעי מפתח קטן מצטנעי (ג) מפתח גדול: בר תרתי. דשקיל נמי ד' אמות בחצר כבר ארבעי כדאמרי' נותן לכל פתח ארבע אמות: לישוייה בר ארבעי. דלא מפסיד לחבריה מידי דמעיקרא נמי הוה שקיל ד' אמות בחצר: לישוייה תרין בני ארבעי. דהשתא נמי לא שקיל אלא תמני בחצר כמעיקרא ולאיצטנועי נמי לא חיישינן דמה לי ח' אמות בפתח אחד מה לי ח' אמות חלוקות לב' פתחים בשני מקומות מ"מ ח' אמות יש לו פתוחות לחצר: בחד פיתחא מצינא איצטנועי. כשהוא נעול יכולני להשתמש בחצר אע"ג להשתמש שלא כנגדו אבל בשני פתחים לא מצינא לאיצטנועי כל כך דלפי' אם האחד נעול השני יהיה פתוח: סוף סוף הא בעית איצטנועי מבני רה"ר. שרואין בביתך דרך פתח הבית ורוכבי סוסים וגמלים רואין בתוך (ד) חלונותיו: מתני' אין עושין חלל תחת רה"ר. ואע"ג דמקבל עליה כל היזקא דאתי מחמתיה שאין רצונם של בני אדם ליזוק ולירד לדין על עסקי ממונו ומפרש ואזיל מה הוא אותו חלל בורות שיחין ומערות: ר"א מתיר. אלא שיכסהו כיסוי חזק כדי שתהא עגלה מהלכת דר"א אזל בתר השתא ולא חייש לשמא היום ולמחר יכלה הכיסוי ויפול והכי אמרינן בבבא קמא (דף נ:): זיזין. קורות קטנות: גזוזטראות. קורות גדולות הבולטות מן הבית לחוץ ואיכא למיחש פן יכשלו בהם בני רה"ר והלכך אין מוציאין דהא כל בני רה"ר ליתנהו גביה דלימחלו: כונס לתוך קרקע שלו. את כותלו ומניח מקרקעו לחוץ כשיעור הוצאת זיזין ומוציא: ובה זיזין וגזוזטראות. הבולטות לרשות הרבים: הרי זו בחזקתה. דטענינן ללוקח ואומרים אימר כונס לתוך שלו היה אבל המוכרה לו שהוציא הזיזין הוא היה צריך להביא עדים שכנס לתוך שלו או שיטעון שני חזקה החזקתי וכנסתי לתוך שלי דהויא לה חזקה שיש עמה טענה אבל לוקח לא צריך למיטען מידי אלא כך לקחתיה וא"נ לטעון היאך הוציא המוכר את הזיזין לחוץ לרה"ר דטוענין ליורש וטוענין ללוקח: גמ' ורבנן. דאסרי סברי לא אזלינן בתר השתא וחיישינן משום דזימנין דמתליע מתוכו ויפחות ולאו אדעתיה דעובר ברה"ר ויעבור ויפול: מפיק למבואה. מוציא (ה) למבואה והמבוי מקום הלוך כל בני החצירות הוא: הוו מעכבי עילויה בני רה"ר. שנופיו מזיקין לגמל ורוכבו: זיל

תוספות

לקח בית בחצר אחרת לא יפתחנה לחצר השותפין. פירוש אפילו לביתו כדי (ו) שלא יכנס ממנו לחצר השותפין: ראוין הללו שתשרה שכינה עליהם. מסיפיה דקרא דריש דכתיב ותהי עליו רוח אלהים: נפלה

מסורת הש"ס

א) לעיל ס:, ב) [לעיל כג.], ג) [לעיל מ:], ד) ח"מ מ"ו וכן ברי"ף ורא"ש ליתא:

הגהות הב"ח

(א) גמ' שחלקו לשנים: (ב) שם מר נמי אית ליה א"ל דידי: (ג) רשב"ם ד"ה סבר וכו' מצטנעי נמי מפתח גדול: (ד) ד"ה סוף וכו' חלונותיך הס"ד: (ה) ד"ה מפיק וכו' מוציא למבוי והמבוי מקום: (ו) תום' ד"ה לקח בית וכו' כדי שיכנס כצ"ל ותיבת שלא נמחק:

גליון הש"ס

מתני' ר"א מתיר. עיין בר"ש ריש בכורים:

תורה אור השלם

א) וַיִּשָּׂא בִלְעָם אֶת עֵינָיו וַיַּרְא אֶת יִשְׂרָאֵל שֹׁכֵן לִשְׁבָטָיו וַתְּהִי עָלָיו רוּחַ אֱלֹהִים: [במדבר כד, ב]

ליקוטי רש"י

אפתאי. אפטמנט בנין נמוך מצדו או מאחוריו [רשב"ם לקמן סא.]. שוכן לשבטיו. ראה כל שבט ושבט שוכן לעצמו ואינן מעורבין ראה שאין פתחיהם מכוונין זה כנגד זה שלא יציץ לתוך אהל חבירו [במדבר כד, ב]. כדי שתהא עגלה מהלכת. אם מקרקעה חזקה כל כך מותר ואע"ג שסופה שתתליע ותפחות [לעיל כ:]. לקח חצר ובה זיזין וגזוזטראות וכו'. אדם הבונה בית לא יוציא ראשי קורות מקרקעו לרה"ר אבל אם רוצה כונס בניינו לתוך שלו ובונה ומוציא הזיזין לחוץ ואם לקח חצר ובה זיזין וגזוזטראות יוצאים לרה"ר הרי הוא בחזקתה שבית דין טוענין לו שמא לתוך שלו או נתפייסו עם הרבים [שם כג.].

עין משפט נר מצוה

רפג א מיי' פי"ג מהל' שכנים הל' ז סמג עשין פב טוש"ע ח"מ סי' קנד סעיף יג:
רפד ב ג מיי' פ"ה מהל' שם הל' ח סמג שם טוש"ע שם סעיף א:
רפה ד מיי' שם הל' ו טוש"ע שם סעיף ג:
רפו ה מיי' שם הל' ו טוש"ע שם סעיף ד:
רפז ו מיי' שם הל' ו טוש"ע שם סעיף ג:
רפח ז ח ט מיי' שם הל' יא טוש"ע שם סעיף ד:
רפט י מיי' פי"ג מהל' נזקי ממון הל' כג סמג עשין עה טוש"ע ח"מ סי' תיז סעיף א:
רצ כ מיי' שם הל' כד טוש"ע שם סעיף ג:
רצא ל מיי' שם הל' כה טוש"ע שם סעיף ג:
רצב מ מיי' שם הל' כג טוש"ע שם סעיף א:

רבינו גרשום

ולסתום. שאם יש לאדם חלון בחצר חבירו ובונה בעל חצר כנגדו וסותמו בפניו. אם לא מיחה לאלתר בעל חלון (שעה) לאלתר הוי חזקה לבעל חצר לסותמו: לקח. אחד מן השותפין: בית בחצר אחרת לא יפתח לחצר השותפין. מפני שמרבה על השותפין דריסת רגל של אותן שיהיו דרין באותו בית מה שלא היה שם קודם לכן: בנה עלייה על גבי ביתו ורוצה לשוכרה לבית דירה לא יפתח לה פתח בחצר השותפין מפני שמרבה עליהם הדרך: אלא אם רוצה כו'. מפרש בגמ': והלא מרבה על הדרך. דהשתא בונה עלייה מה שלא היתה שם קודם לכן ומשים בה דיורין אע"פ שפותחה בתוך ביתו מרבה עליהם הדרכים: אלא מאי בונה את החדר ואת העלייה דקאמר לא עלייה ממש אלא שחלק חדרו לשנים וחלק החיצון קורי חדר ומאי עלייה דקאמר אפתא שקורין אפלדרין והיינו חלק הפנימי ושוכר האחר לדירה. ואי אמרת והלא מרבה עליהם הדרכים לא מצי אמרת דכשם שאם היו לו בני בית לזה יותר מן השותפין אחרים לא היו יכולין לעכבן שלא יכנסו ושלא יצאו בחצר כך עכשיו כיון שלא בנה בנין יותר אלא שהיה כמו שהיה וחלקו לשנים והכניס דיורין בחלק האחד אין יכולין לעכבו: פיסקא. שלא יהו מכוונין זה כנגד זה. מפני היזק ראיה: אם היה קטן. הפתח: א) דקא שקיל ח' אמות בחצר דאיכא ביה שיעור ב' פתחים: אבל בר תרי (טפח בכ"י) אמות. לישוייה בר ארבע אמות (טפח בכ"י) רוחב שפיר דמי דסוף סוף לא שקיל אלא ד' אמות ככל פתח שהוא פחות מח' אמות (טפח בכ"י). ואם הפתח פחות מח' וחלקן לשני פתחים לכל פתח יש לו ד' אמות ושהוא בו ח' אע"פ שלא נחלק לשנים יש לו ח' אמות: אבל בר תמני. שיש לו ח' אמות לישויה תרי פתחים שפיר דמי דסוף סוף לא שקלי אלא ח' אמות בחצר כדמעיקרא: מצי אמר ליה. בחד פיתחא מצינא דאיצטנועי מינך שאני משתמש כשהוא נעול: בתרי פתחי לא מצינא איצטנועי. שכשהאחד נעול השני פתוח: אבל פותח הוא לרה"ר פתח כנגד פתח דא"ל סוף סוף כו': פיסקא ור"א מתיר. ובלבד שיכסנו כסוי חזק כדי שתהא עגלה כו': ורבנן. דאסרי מאי טעמא והלא הכסוי חזק סברי דזימנין דמפחת. שיתליע מתוכו ולאו אדעתיה דהאי שהוא רעוע: זיזין. יבר"ש: גזוזטראות. קורות: לרה"ר. דליתנייהו כל בני רה"ר גבי דלימחלו ליה: לקח חצר ובה זיזין וגזוזטראות שיוצאין לרה"ר הרי זו בחזקתה ואין צריך לקרקן: מחלין לי בני מבואה. דיחידים נינהו ומצו מחלי: הוו מעכבי עילויה. בני רה"ר שנופיו מזיקין לגמל ורוכבו:

חשק שלמה על רבינו גרשום א) נראה דהוא ציון על הגמ' דסבר רמי בר חמא למימר דבר ד' לא לישוייה בר תמניא דקא שקיל וכו'.

עין משפט
נר מצוה

רצג א ב ג מיי' פ"ג מהל' נזקי ממון הל' כד סמג שם טוש"ע ח"מ סי' קנח סעיף ג:
רצד ד מיי' שם הל' כה טוש"ע שם סעיף ג:
רצה ה ו ז ח מיי' פ"ה מהל' תעניות הל' יג סמג עשין מד"ס ג טוש"ע או"ח סי' תקס סעיף א:
רצו י כ ל מיי' שם טוש"ע שם סעיף ב [וברב אלפס תענית דף קעט:]:
רצז נ טוש"ע או"ח סי' תקנד סעיף כה:
רצח ם מיי' פ"ב מהל' ממרים הלכה ה סמג עשין קיא:

לעזי רש"י

טנפ"ל. פירוש לדע, רקה (רש"י שופטים ד, כב), לד המלא שליד האוזן:

זיל האידנא ותא למחר בליליא שדר קצייה להההוא דידיה למחר אתא לקמיה א"ל זיל קוץ א"ל הא מר נמי אית ליה א"ל זיל חזי אי קוץ דידי קוץ דידך אי לא קוץ דידי לא תקוץ את מעיקרא מאי סבר ולבסוף מאי סבר מעיקרא סבר ניחא להו לבני רה"ר דיתבי בטוליה כיון דחזא דקא מעכבי שדר קצייה ולימא ליה זיל קוץ דידך והדר אקוץ דידי משום דריש לקיש דאמר א) התקוששו וקושו קשוט עצמך ואח"כ קשוט אחרים: אבל אם רצה כונס לתוך שלו ומוציא: איבעיא להו כנס ולא הוציא מהו שיחזור ויוציא ר' יוחנן אמר כנס מוציא וריש לקיש אמר כנס אינו מוציא א"ל רבי יעקב לר' ירמיה בר תחליפא אסברה לך להוציא כ"ע לא פליגי דמוציא כי פליגי להחזיר כתלים למקומן ואיפכא איתמר ר' יוחנן אמר אינו מחזיר וריש לקיש אמר מחזיר ר' יוחנן אמר אינו מחזיר משום דרב יהודה דאמר רב יהודה מצר שהחזיקו בו רבים אסור לקלקלו וריש לקיש אמר מחזיר הני מילי היכא דליכא רווחא הכא הא איכא רווחא: לקח חצר ובה זיזין וגזוזטראות הרי היא בחזקתה: אמר רב הונא נפלה חוזר ובונה אותה מיתיבי אין מסיידין ואין מכיירין ואין מפייחין בזמן הזה לקח חצר מסוידת מכוירת מפויחת הרי זו בחזקתה נפלה אינו חוזר ובונה אותה איסורא שאני ת"ר לא יסוד אדם את ביתו בסיד ואם עירב בו חול או תבן מותר ר"י אומר עירב בו חול הרי זה טרכסיד ואסור תבן מותר ת"ר כשחרב הבית בשניה רבו פרושין בישראל שלא לאכול בשר ושלא לשתות יין נטפל להן ר' יהושע אמר להן בני מפני מה אי אתם אוכלין בשר ואין אתם שותין יין אמרו לו נאכל בשר שממנו מקריבין על גבי מזבח ועכשיו בטל נשתה יין שמנסכין על גבי המזבח ועכשיו בטל אמר להם א"כ לחם לא נאכל שכבר בטלו מנחות אפשר בפירות פירות לא נאכל שכבר בטלו בכורים אפשר בפירות אחרים מים לא נשתה שכבר בטל ניסוך המים שתקו אמר להן בני בואו ואומר לכם שלא להתאבל כל עיקר אי אפשר שכבר נגזרה גזרה ולהתאבל יותר מדאי אי אפשר שאין גוזרין גזירה על הצבור אא"כ רוב צבור יכולין לעמוד בה דכתיב ב) במארה אתם נארים ואותי אתם קובעים הגוי כולו אלא כך אמרו חכמים סד אדם את ביתו בסיד ומשייר בו דבר מועט וכמה אמר רב יוסף אמה על אמה אמר רב חסדא כנגד הפתח עושה אדם כל צרכי סעודה ומשייר דבר מועט מאי היא אמר רב פפא כסא דהרסנא עושה אשה כל תכשיטיה ומשיירת דבר מועט מאי היא אמר רב בת צדעא שנאמר ג) אם אשכחך ירושלים תשכח ימיני תדבק לשוני לחכי וגו' מאי על ראש שמחתי אמר רב יצחק זה אפר מקלה שבראש חתנים א"ל רב פפא לאביי היכא מנח לה במקום תפילין שנאמר ד) לשום לאבלי ציון לתת להם פאר תחת אפר וכל המתאבל על ירושלים זוכה ורואה בשמחתה שנאמר ה) שמחו את ירושלים וגו' תניא אמר ר' ישמעאל בן אלישע מיום שחרב בית המקדש דין הוא שנגזור על עצמנו שלא לאכול בשר ולא לשתות יין אלא אין גוזרין גזרה על הצבור אא"כ רוב צבור יכולין לעמוד בה ומיום שפשטה מלכות הרשעה שגוזרת עלינו גזירות רעות וקשות ומבטלת ממנו תורה ומצות ואין מנחת אותנו ליכנס לשבוע הבן ואמרי לה לישוע הבן דין הוא שנגזור על עצמנו שלא לישא אשה ולהוליד בנים ונמצא זרעו של אברהם אבינו כלה מאליו אלא הנח להם לישראל מוטב שיהיו שוגגין ואל יהיו מזידין:

הדרן עלך חזקת הבתים

נפלה אינו חוזר ובונה אותה. השתא ס"ד דבית שבנה בזמן שבהמ"ק קיים ונפלה חוזר ובונה וכשלקח חצר המסוידת הרי זו בחזקתה לכל זמן שהיא קיימת יש לנו לתלות שבהיתר עשה בזמן שבהמ"ק קיים אבל כשנפלה תלינן שבאיסור נעשית לאחר חורבן ומ"ה פריך ארב הונא אמאי חוזר ובונה אותה כיון דנפלה אית לן למימר שבאיסור הוציא ומשני איסורא שאני דאפי' ודאי נבנה בהיתר כי נפלה אסור לבנותו ולסייד: **מים לא** נשתה [וכו'] שתקו. וא"ת אמאי לא אהדרו דאפשר במי בורות דפסולין לניסוך כדמשמע בסוכה (דף מח.) ואומר ר"י דדבר דהוי ממין שעושין בו ניסוך חשיב כמו דבר עצמו דאי לאו הכי תקשה דישתו יין מבושל דפסול לנסכים ואין להקשות דאפשר במי תותים ויין תפוחים שלא היו יכולין לסבול (ג) שלא לשתות בלא מים: **דין** הוא שנגזור על עצמנו שלא לישא נשים. תימה הכתיב פרו ורבו ושמא על אותן שכבר קיימו פריה ורביה קאמר והיינו זרעו של אברהם כלה שלא יוליד אלא בן ובת: **מוטב** שיהיו שוגגין ואל יהיו מזידין. בדבר שאין ידוע אם יקבלו כשנמחה בהן אם לאו צריך למחות כדמוכח בפ' במה [בהמה] (שבת דף נה. ושם ד"ה ואע"ג) דלאמרה מדת הדין (ג) אם לפניך גלוי לפניהם מי גלוי ונענשו אבל בדבר שאנו יודעים בבירור שלא יקבלו אמרינן מוטב שיהיו שוגגין וכו'(ס):

הדרן עלך חזקת הבתים

זיל האידנא. שהיה רוצה לקצוץ עצמו תחלה כדלקמן: **אי קוץ דידי.** אם שלי קצוץ כבר: **כיון דחזא דמעכבי.** הבין שבשביל כבודו שותקין על שלו: **ולימא ליה זיל קוץ כו'.** ולמאי א"ל זיל האידנא כו': **התקוששו.** הסר קש מבין עיניך תחלה כמו לקושש קש (שמות ה) כלומר קשוט עצמך: **איבעיא להו כנס.** לתוך שלו ולא הוציא עכשיו זיזין מהו שיחזור ויוציא לאחר זמן מי אמרינן דויתרה לבני רה"ר ולאבד כחו או לא: (א) **וריש לקיש אמר כנס אינו מוציא.** קס"ד לא יוציא עוד זיזין לאבד כחו: **ואיפכא איתמר.** דמוקמינן לרבי יוחנן כר' יהודה דהלכתא כוותיה וקי"ל כרב יהודה בהך: **מצר.** שבין שתי שדות שהחזיקו בו והכא נמי הרי החזיקו בהך כניסה: **איכא רווחא.** כשיחזיר כתלים למקומן אכתי איכא כל רוחב רה"ר וסתם רה"ר מרווח הוא: **ה"ג אמר רב הונא נפלה כו'.** אי נמי ואם נפלה ולא גרס שאם נפלה: **חוזר ובונה אותה.** להוציא זיזין כבתחלה: **אין מסיידין.** בית משום אבל בית המקדש: **ואין מכיירין.** צורות שלר בסיד. וי"מ דהיינו נמי סיוד אלא שהכיור לבן יותר: **מפייחין.** צורות של מיני צבעונים: **נפלה אינו חוזר כו'.** אלמא כל בנין שאינו רשאי לעשות בתחלה אם היה לו ונפל אינו חוזר ובונה וגבי הוצאת זיזין לרה"ר נמי כיון דלאו אפשר להוציא בתחלה אם נפל אינו חוזר ומוציא: **איסורא שאני.** מהזיקא: **חול או תבן.** מכהה לבנונו: **טרכסיד.** בנין חזק וטוב ואף על פי שמשחיר קצת אסור: **אפשר בפירות.** ויפה אמרת ונפרוש גם מן הלחם: **בפירות אחרים.** שאין מביאים ביכורים אלא מז' המינין: **שכבר נגזרה גזירה.** חורבן ונתחייבנו להתאבל דכתיב שישו אתה משוש כל המתאבלים עליה (ישעיה סו): **במארה אתם נארים.** קבלתם עליכם בגזירת ארור להביא המעשר אל בית האוצר דכתיב במלאכי (ג) הביאו את כל המעשר וגו' ואעפ"כ ואותי אתם קובעים אתם גוזלים את המעשר ואת התרומה כדכתיב התם ולמעלה במה קבענוך המעשר והתרומה: **הגוי כולו.** כלומר וכל הקהל כולו קיבלו את הגזירה ומתמהא כלומר אם לא היו כולן יכולין לעמוד בה לא היו מסכימין ורובן כולן אלמא לא חשיבא גזירה אא"כ רובן יכולין לעמוד בה: **אלא כך אמרו חכמים כו'.** מסקנא למילתיה דרבי יהושע היא: **כסא דהרסנא.** קערה של מאכל דגים מטוגנין בשמנן בסולת: **בת צידעא.** טנפ"ל שרגילות לסוד שם ולהסיר שערן: **שנאמר אם אשכחך וגו'.** אכולהו קאי: **אפר מקלה.** אפר הסירה השרופה באש קרוי כן ומשום דליכא אפר פרה נמי הולך לפרש כן: **פאר תחת אפר.** מכלל שהיו רגילין ליתן אפר במקום פאר דהיינו תפילין דכתיב פארך חבוש עליך (יחזקאל כד): **לשבוע הבן.** מילה שהיא לסוף ז': **ונמצא זרעו של אברהם אבינו כלה מאליו.** בענין טוב ולא ע"י עובדי כוכבים ומלות לא יבטלו עוד: **אלא הנח להם לישראל מוטב שיהיו שוגגין.** במה שלוקחין נשים שאינם סבורים שיש איסור בדבר: **ואל יהיו מזידין.** דמשום דלא יוכלו לעמוד בה יבטלוה ונמצאו מזידין הלכך לא גזרין: הדרן עלך חזקת הבתים

מסורת הש"ס

א) סנהדרין יח. יט. ב"מ קז:, ב) ב"ק כח. לעיל יב. כו: לקמן ק., ג) שבת פ: [תוספתא סוטה פט"ו], ד) [תוספתא שם], ה) ע"ז לו. הוריות ג: [ב"ק עט:], ו) [תוספתא פ"ב], ז) [תענית טז.], ח) [מיבת שנאמר ליתא ברב אלפס], ט) [שם בתוספתא תענית ל:], י) [שבת קמח. ביצה ל.], כ) [וע"ע תוס' ע"ז ד. ד"ה שהיה בידם]:

הגהות הב"ח

(א) רשב"ם ד"ה וריש לקיש אמר כנס אינו מוציא. נ"ב [חסר ההתחלה ונשאר זה הלשון] ומאן דקא מיבעי ליה נמי לא קא מיבעי ליה אלא בלהחזיר כו' והכי קא מיבעי ליה הא דתנן אלא אם רצה כונס לתוך שלו ומוציא ומשכנס מחל לבני רה"ר ושוב אינו יכול להחזיר כתלים למקומן אלא מוציא זיזים בלחוד או דלמא ה"ק כונס לתוך שלו ומוציא והתם הוא כיון דכבר הוציא זיזין אינו מחזיר כתלים למקומן דכבר מחל לבני רה"ר אבל אם לא הוציא הזיזין עדיין אלא כנס בלבד מחזיר כתלים למקומן ומאי דקאמר מהו שיחזור ויוציא ה"פ מי נימא דמוציא זיזין וא"כ שוב לא יחזיר הכתלים למקומן או דלמא אינו מוציא לפי שמחזיר הכתלים למקומן וממילא אם הוציא שוב אין יכול להחזיר וזה לא נצטרך לפרש דמאי דקאמר ואיפכא איתמר משום דר' יוחנן מוקמינן כרב יהודה כמו שפירש רשב"ם: (ב) תוס' ד"ה מים וכו' שלא היו יכולין לסבול בלא שתיית מים הס"ד: (ג) ד"ה מוטב וכו' דלאמרה מדת הדין רבש"ע אם לפניך:

תורה אור השלם

א) הִתְקוֹשְׁשׁוּ וָקוֹשּׁוּ הַגּוֹי לֹא נִכְסָף: [צפניה ב, א]

ב) בַּמְּאֵרָה אַתֶּם נֵאָרִים וְאֹתִי אַתֶּם קֹבְעִים הַגּוֹי כֻּלּוֹ: [מלאכי ג, ט]

ג) אִם אֶשְׁכָּחֵךְ יְרוּשָׁלָםִ תִּשְׁכַּח יְמִינִי: תִּדְבַּק לְשׁוֹנִי לְחִכִּי אִם לֹא אֶזְכְּרֵכִי אִם לֹא אַעֲלֶה אֶת יְרוּשָׁלַםִ עַל רֹאשׁ שִׂמְחָתִי: [תהלים קלז, ה-ו]

ד) לָשׂוּם לַאֲבֵלֵי צִיּוֹן לָתֵת לָהֶם פְּאֵר תַּחַת אֵפֶר שֶׁמֶן שָׂשׂוֹן תַּחַת אֵבֶל מַעֲטֵה תְהִלָּה תַּחַת רוּחַ כֵּהָה וְקֹרָא לָהֶם אֵילֵי הַצֶּדֶק מַטַּע יְיָ לְהִתְפָּאֵר: [ישעיה סא, ג]

ה) שִׂמְחוּ אֶת יְרוּשָׁלַםִ וְגִילוּ בָהּ כָּל אֹהֲבֶיהָ שִׂישׂוּ אִתָּהּ מָשׂוֹשׂ כָּל הַמִּתְאַבְּלִים עָלֶיהָ: [ישעיה סו, י]

ליקוטי רש"י

התקוששו. התלקטו ואספו יחד כמו לקושש קש (שמות ה). וקושו. מעשיכם השוו מעשיכם לדעת קונכם ורז"ל דרשו קשוט עצמך ואח"כ קשוט אחרים עשו שיהם לשון היקש אדם המשוה עצמו ומישר דרכו [צפניה ב, א]. **מצר שהחזיקו בו רבים אסור לקלקלו.** לעשותו להן דרך אסור לקלקלו אע"פ שהוא של יחיד [לעיל כו:]. שהשווהו ותקנוהו להילוך והבעלים ידעו ושתקו אסור לקלקלו דודאי לרבים מחל [רשב"ם לקמן ק.]. **לא יסוד אדם את ביתו בסיד.** לאחר שחרב הבית שלא יהא לבן כל צרכו. **טרכסיד.** סיד חזק ומתקשה יותר משאם לא עירב בו [שבת פ:]. **על ראש שמחתי.** את זכרון אבל מורנה אעלה להזכירו בראש כל שמחתי [תהלים קלז ו]. **פאר תחת אפר.** שמע מינה במקום תפילין דכתיב בהו (יחזקאל כד) פארך חבוש עליך ואמרינן (ברכות יא.) אלו תפילין ומתרגמינן נמי טוטפתך הוין עלך והיכא מניחין תפילין במקום שמוחו של תינוק רופף [תענית טז.]. **הנח להם לישראל.** בדבר שהרגילו בו ולא יחזרו בהם. **מוטב שיהיו שוגגין ואל יהיו מזידין.** לעבור כשידעו ולא יניחו בכך [ביצה ל.].

רבינו גרשום

כיון דחזי דמעכבי. להאי אמר ש"מ דלא ניחא להו ומשום יקרא דידי שתקו: **איבעיא להו כנס** לתוך שלו **ולא הוציא.** זיזין באותה פעם באותה כניסה **מהו שיחזור ויוציא** לאחר זמן. מי אמרי' כיון דלא הוציא בתחלה בההיא כניסה ויתרה לבני רה"ר אי לא: **ר' יוחנן אמר.** לרשותו **מוציא** בה זיזין כל זמן שירצה. **וריש לקיש אמר כנס** ולא הוציא לאלתר **אינו מוציא** שוב: **להחזיר כתלים למקומן.** כמו שהיה: אבל רה"ר **מצר שהחזיקו בו [רבים].** שכבר דשין באותה כניסה: **ה"מ.** דאסור לקלקלו **היכא דליכא רווחא** טפי ברה"ר: **אין מכיירין.** שאין עושין ציור מן הסיד עצמו כמו שעושין בנאין: **אין מפייחין.** שאין מלבין הבית לאחר שמצויר בזמן הזה מפני איבול בהמ"ק: **אין חוזר ובונה אותה.** באותו סיד וכיור: **איסורא שאני.** שאסרו חכמים מפני איבול: אבל אם (כן) **עירב בו חול.** שלא יהא לבן כל כך: **הרי זה טרכסיד.** השביחו מפני שאע"פ ששחור כמעט נעשה חזק ונדבק ביותר: **אפשר בפירות אחרים.** שלא היו מביאין בכורים אלא משבעת המינין: **שתקו.** שא"א לחיות בלא מים: **במארה אתם נארים.** כשאתם גוזרים מארה גזרה **ואותי אתם** קובעין בהם בהסכמתכם. אי איכא **הגוי כולו** שיכולין לעמוד בה אין. מקוימת הגזירה ואי לא לא: **בת צדעא.** א) שלא תזבין צדעא בשרק שלא תיתפור ממנה שיער: **כנגד הפתח.** כדי שתהא נראה: **לשבוע הבן.** שעושין לסוף שבעה: **שיהיו שוגגין.** שיבטלו אותו דין בשוגג **ואל יהיו מזידין** שאם נגזור גזירה יהיו מבטלין אותה במזיד שלא יהיו יכולין לעמוד בה שלא לישא אשה:

הדרן עלך חזקת הבתים

חשק שלמה
על רבינו גרשום

א) אולי צ"ל שלא תעביר לדעא בשרק כדי שתיפול ממנה שער.

זיל הָאִידְנָא וְתָא לְמָחָר – Go for now and come back **tomorrow.**[1] **בְּלֵילְיָא שָׁדַר קַצְיֵיה לְהַהוּא דִּידֵיהּ – At night [R' Yannai] sent** someone, who **cut down his own [tree].** **לְמָחָר אֲתָא לְקַמֵּיהּ – On the morrow [the person]** again **came before [R' Yannai].** **אָמַר לֵיהּ זיל קוֹץ – [R' Yannai] said to him: Go and cut down** the tree. **אָמַר לֵיהּ הָא מַר נַמֵּי אִית לֵיהּ – [The person] protested to [R' Yannai]: But master also has** a tree extending into the public domain. Why must mine be cut down while yours is left standing? **אָמַר לֵיהּ זיל חֲזִי אִי קוֹץ דִּידִי קוֹץ דִּידָךְ – [R' Yannai] said to him: Go see; if my [tree] is cut down,** then **cut down yours** as well, **אִי לֹא קוֹץ דִּידִי לֹא תָּקוֹץ אַתְּ – but if my [tree] is not cut down, you should not cut down** yours.

The Gemara points out the inconsistency of R' Yannai's conduct:

מֵעִיקָּרָא מַאי סָבַר – What did [R' Yannai] hold initially when he allowed his tree's branches to extend over the public domain, **וּלְבַסּוֹף מַאי סָבַר – and what did he hold in the end** when he cut the branches?[2]

R' Yannai's conduct is justified:

מֵעִיקָּרָא סָבַר – Initially he held that **נִיחָא לְהוּ לִבְנֵי רְשׁוּת הָרַבִּים דְּיָתְבֵי בְּטוּלֵיהּ – the public was pleased** that his tree's branches extended over the street, **for** they were then able to **sit in its shade.** **כֵּיוָן דַּחֲזָא דְּקָא מְעַכְּבֵי – However, once he saw that [the public] objected** to the other person's overhanging branches, **שָׁדַר קַצְיֵיהּ – he sent** someone **[who] cut down** his own branches.[3]

The Gemara finds yet another difficulty with R' Yannai's conduct:

וְלֵימָא לֵיהּ – But let [R' Yannai] say to [the person]: **זיל קוֹץ דִּידָךְ וְהָדַר אָקוּץ דִּידִי – Go, cut off your [branches] and then I shall cut mine** as well. Why did R' Yannai postpone his directive to the other person until *after* he had cut off his own branches?

The Gemara explains R' Yannai's conduct:

מִשּׁוּם דְּרֵישׁ לָקִישׁ – R' Yannai acted as he did **because of Reish Lakish's** exposition of a verse. **דְּאָמַר: "הִתְקוֹשְׁשׁוּ וָקוֹשׁוּ" – For [Reish Lakish] said:** The Scriptures say, ***Clean yourselves of straw and clean others of straw,***[4] which we interpret to mean: **קְשׁוֹט עַצְמְךָ וְאַחַר כָּךְ קְשׁוֹט אֲחֵרִים –** First **adorn yourself** (i.e. cleanse yourself of sin), **and** only **then adorn others.**[5]

A segment of the Mishnah is cited and commented upon:

אֲבָל אִם רָצָה כּוֹנֵס לְתוֹךְ שֶׁלּוֹ וּמוֹצִיא – One may not extend ledges or balconies into the public domain. **HOWEVER, IF HE WISHES, HE MAY DRAW BACK INTO HIS OWN AND EXTEND** the ledges or balconies. **אִיבַּעְיָא לְהוּ – [The scholars]** of the academy **inquired:** **כָּנַס וְלֹא הוֹצִיא – If one drew** the wall of his house **back** into his own property **but did not extend** his ledges at that time, **מַהוּ שֶׁיַּחֲזוֹר וְיוֹצִיא – may he subsequently extend** them?[6] **ר׳ יוֹחָנָן אָמַר כָּנַס מוֹצִיא – R' Yochanan said: If one drew back** and did not immediately extend his ledges, **he may extend** them at a later date. **וְרֵישׁ לָקִישׁ אָמַר כָּנַס אֵינוֹ מוֹצִיא – But Reish Lakish said: If one drew back** and did not immediately extend his ledges, **he may not extend** them at a later date.

The Gemara records an Amora's explanation of this dispute, together with his own version of it:

אָמַר לֵיהּ רַבִּי יַעֲקֹב לְר׳ יִרְמְיָה בַּר תַּחְלִיפָא – R' Yaakov said to R' Yirmiyah bar Tachalifa: **אַסְבְּרָה לָךְ – I shall explain [this dispute] to you.** **לְהוֹצִיא –** Regarding whether or not it is permitted **to extend** the beams, **כּוּלֵּי עָלְמָא לֹא פְּלִיגֵי דְּמוֹצִיא – all agree that one may extend** them.[7] **כִּי פְּלִיגֵי –** Regarding **what,** then, **do [R' Yochanan and Reish Lakish] disagree?** **לְהַחֲזִיר כְּתָלִים לִמְקוֹמָן –** Regarding whether it is permissible **to return the walls to their** original **place.**[8]

R' Yaakov presents his version of the dispute:

וְאִיפְּכָא אִיתְּמַר – And the positions of R' Yochanan and Reish Lakish **were stated in the reverse,** as follows:[9] **ר׳ יוֹחָנָן אָמַר אֵינוֹ מַחֲזִיר – R' Yochanan said: He may not return** the walls to their original place, **וְרֵישׁ לָקִישׁ אָמַר מַחֲזִיר – but Reish Lakish said: He may return** the walls to their original place.

R' Yaakov now explains the two positions:

ר׳ יוֹחָנָן אָמַר אֵינוֹ מַחֲזִיר מִשּׁוּם דְּרַב יְהוּדָה – R' Yochanan said that he may not return the walls because of [the principle] of Rav Yehudah. **דְּאָמַר רַב יְהוּדָה – For Rav Yehudah said:** **מֵצַר שֶׁהֶחֱזִיקוּ בּוֹ רַבִּים אָסוּר לְקַלְקְלוֹ – A** private **boundary** strip on **which the public established** a right-of-way **may not be ruined** by the owner.[10] Here, too, the space left vacant by the withdrawal of the wall has now become part of the public thoroughfare, and the owner may not now deprive the public of the use of this space by returning the wall to its original place. **וְרֵישׁ לָקִישׁ אָמַר מַחֲזִיר – But Reish Lakish said that he may return** the wall to its original place, for **הָנֵי מִילֵּי הֵיכָא דְּלֵיכָּא רַוְוחָא –** regarding the prohibition against ruining a public right-of-way, **that ruling** is applicable **only where there is no place** for the public to pass if the right-of-way is revoked; **הָכָא הָא אִיכָּא רַוְוחָא –** but **here, however, there is space** for the public even if the walls are returned to their original place.[11]

Another segment of the Mishnah is cited:

לָקַח חָצֵר וּבָהּ זִיזִין וּגְזוּזְטְרָאוֹת הֲרֵי הִיא בְּחֶזְקָתָהּ – IF ONE PURCHASED A COURTYARD IN WHICH THERE ARE LEDGES AND BALCONIES, [THE COURTYARD] RETAINS ITS STATUS and he may keep the ledges or balconies.

NOTES

1. R' Yannai wanted to cut off the branches of his own tree before ordering the person to cut off his branches (*Rashbam*).

2. Surely R' Yannai knew the ruling of the Mishnah (above, 27b), that tree branches overhanging the public domain may be cut off to allow for the passage of a camel and its rider. If he had reason to assume that this law did not apply to him, why did he later change his mind and cut them off?

3. R' Yannai realized that the public's silence did not derive from their being pleased with the shade from his overhanging branches. Rather, it was due to their respect for R' Yannai (*Rashbam*). Had they been pleased with the shade, they would not have objected to the other person's branches either. Once he realized this he hurried to have them removed (*Meiri*).

4. *Zephaniah* 2:1. We have followed *Rashbam's* interpretation of the phrase; the root of the verbs הִתְקוֹשְׁשׁוּ וָקוֹשׁוּ derives from קַשׁ, *straw* or *stubble.* The commentators to the verse give various interpretations to these words. See *Ibn Ezra,* whose interpretation comes close to the sense the Gemara imparts to the phrase.

5. Alternatively: The root קשט can also be rendered *truth.* I.e. rectify yourselves and then rectify others.

6. Do we assume that by drawing his walls back and not extending his beams he has relinquished the resulting space in favor of the public, so that he may not subsequently retract his offering and extend the ledges? Or do we not interpret his inaction as a relinquishment, so that his right to extend remains intact? (*Rashbam*).

7. Everyone — R' Yochanan and Reish Lakish — agree that we do not interpret a person's inaction as indicating relinquishment, and thus rule that his right to extend remains intact.

8. Thus, R' Yaakov disagrees with the version of the dispute quoted above.

9. We have followed the apparent meaning of the Gemara, that R' Yaakov presents a version of the dispute that differs from that recorded initially. But see *Maharshal, Maharsha* and *Hagahos HaBach,* who offer various interpretations that avoid emending the first version of the dispute.

10. Rather, it is assumed that the owner ceded to the public the right to use the strip of land as a path.

11. Usually the street is wide enough to accommodate all the traffic, and by reclaiming his space the owner is not impeding the public (*Rashbam*).

עין משפט נר מצוה

רצג א ב ג מיי' פי"ג מהל' נזקי ממון הל' כד סמג שם טוש"ע ח"מ סי' קנג סעיף ג:
רצד ד מיי' שם הל' כה טוש"ע שם סעיף ג:
רצה ה ו ז ח מיי' פ"ה מהל' תענית הל' יב סמג עשין מד"ס ג טוש"ע או"ח סי' תקס סעיף א:
רצו י כ ל מ מיי' שם הל' יג טוש"ע שם סעיף ב [וברב אלפס תענית דף קעט:]:
רצז נ טוש"ע או"ח סי' תקנד סעיף כה:
רצח ס מיי' פ"ב מהל' ממרים הלכה ה סמג עשין קיא:

לעזי רש"י

טנפ"ל. פירוש לעז, רקה (רש"י שופטים ד, כב, לד המלת שליד האוזן).

רבינו גרשום

כיון דחזי דמעכבי. להאי אמר ש"מ דלא ניחא להו משום הקוץ דידי שתקו: איבעיא להו כנס לתוך שלו ולא הוציא. זיזין באותה פעם באותה כניסה מהו שיחזור ויוציא לאחר זמן. מי אמרי כיון דלא הוציא בתחלה בההיא כניסה ויתרה לבני רה"ר או לא: ר' יוחנן אמר. לרשותו מוציא בה זיזין כל זמן שירצה. וריש לקיש אמר כנס ולא הוציא לאחר אינו מוציא שוב: להחזיר כתלים למקומן. כמו שהיה: אבל רה"ר מצר שהחזיקו בו [רבים]. שכבר דשין באותה כניסה: ה"מ. דאסור לקלקלו היכא דליכא רווחא טפי בהה"ר: אין מכיירין. שאין עושין ציור מן הסיד עצמו כמו שעושין בבנאין: אין מפייחין. שאין מלבנין הבית לאחר שמצויר בזמן הזה מפני אבילו בהמ"ק: אין חוזר ובונה אותה. באותו סיד וכיור: איסורא שאני. שאסרו חכמים מפני איבול: אבל אם (כן) עירב בו חול. שלא יהא לבן כל כך: הרי זה טרכסיד. השבחו מפני שאע"פ שחור כמעט נעשה חזק ונדבק ביותר: אפשר בפירות אחרים. שלא היו מביאין בכורים אלא משבעת המינין: שתקו. שא"א לחיות בלא מים: במארה אתם נארים. כשאתם גוזרים מארה גזרה ואותי אתם קובעין בהם בהסכמתכם. אי איכא הגוי כולו שיכולין לעמוד בה אין. קיימת הגזירה ואי לא לא: בת צדעא. א) שלא תובין צדעא בשרק שלא תיתפור ממנה שיער: כנגד הפתח. כדי שתהא נראה: לשבוע הבן. שעושין לסוף שבעה: שיהיו שוגגין. שיבטלו אותו דין בשוגג ואל יהיו מזידין שאם נגזור גזירה יהיו מבטלין אותה במזיד כדי שלא יהיו יכולין לעמוד בה שלא לישא אשה:

הדרן עלך חזקת הבתים

חשק שלמה על רבינו גרשום

א) אולי צ"ל שלא תעביר לדעת בשרק כדי שתיפול ממנה שער.

נפלה אינו חוזר ובונה אותה. השתא ס"ד דבית שבנה בזמן שבהמ"ק קיים ונפלה חוזר ובונה וכשלקח חצר המסוידת הרי זו בחזקתה דכל זמן שהיא קיימת יש לנו לתלות שבהיתר עשה בזמן שבהמ"ק קיים אבל כשנפלה תלינן שבאיסור נעשית לאחר חורבן ומש"ה פריך ארב הונא אמאי חוזר ובונה אותה כיון דנפלה אית לן למיתלי שבאיסור הוצא ומשני איסורא שאני דאפי' ודאי נבנה בהיתר כי נפלה אסור לבנותה ולסייד: **מים** לא נשתה [וכו'] שתקו. וא"ת אמאי לא אהדרו דאפשר במי בורות דפסולין לניסוך כדמשמע בסוכה (דף מח.) ואומר ר"י דדבר דהוי ממין שעושין בו ניסוך חשיב כמו דבר עצמו דאי לאו הכי תקשה דישתו יין מבושל דפסול לנסכים ואין להקשות דאפשר במי תותים ויין תפוחים שלא היו יכולין לסבול (ב) שלא לשתות בלא מים: **דין** הוא שנגזור על עצמנו שלא לישא נשים. תימה הכתיב פרו ורבו ושמא על אותן שכבר קיימו פריה ורביה קאמר והיינו זרעו של אברהם כלה שלא יוליד אלא בן ובת: **מוטב** שיהיו שוגגין ואל יהיו מזידין. בדבר שאין ידוע אם יקבלו כשנמחה בהן אם לאו צריך למחות כדמוכח בפ' במה [בהמה] (שבת דף נה. ושם ד"ה ואע"ג) דאמרה מדת הדין (ג) אם לפניך גלוי לפניהם מי גלוי ונענשו אבל בדבר שאנו יודעים בבירור שלא יקבלו אמרינן מוטב שיהיו שוגגין וכו' (ד):

הדרן עלך חזקת הבתים

זיל האידנא ותא למחר בליליא שדר קצייה להההוא דידיה למחר אתא לקמיה א"ל זיל קוץ א"ל הא מר נמי אית ליה א"ל זיל חזי אי קוץ דידי קוץ דידך אי לא קוץ דידי לא תקוץ את מעיקרא מאי סבר ולבסוף מאי סבר מעיקרא סבר ניחא להו לבני רה"ר דיתבי בטוליה כיון דחזא דקא מעכבי שדר קצייה ולימא ליה זיל קוץ דידך והדר אקוץ דידי משום דריש לקיש דאמר א) התקוששו וקושו קשוט עצמך ואח"כ קשוט אחרים: אבל אם רצה כונס לתוך שלו ומוציא: איבעיא להו כנס ולא הוציא מהו שיחזור ויוציא ר' יוחנן אמר א כנס מוציא וריש לקיש אמר כנס אינו מוציא א"ל רבי יעקב לר' ירמיה בר תחליפא אסברה לך להוציא כ"ע לא פליגי דמוציא כי פליגי להחזיר כתלים למקומן ואיפכא איתמר ר' יוחנן אמר אינו מחזיר וריש לקיש אמר מחזיר ר' יוחנן אמר ב אינו מחזיר משום דרב יהודה דאמר רב יהודה ג מצר שהחזיקו בו רבים אסור לקלקלו וריש לקיש אמר מחזיר הני מילי היכא דליכא רווחא הכא הא איכא רווחא: לקח חצר ובה זיזין וגזוזטראות הרי היא בחזקתה: אמר רב הונא ד נפלה חוזר ובונה אותה מיתיבי ה אין מסיידין ואין מכיירין ואין מפייחין בזמן הזה ו לקח חצר מסוידת מכוירת מפויחת הרי זו בחזקתה נפלה אינו חוזר ובונה אותה איסורא שאני ת"ר לא יסוד אדם את ביתו בסיד ואם עירב בו חול או תבן מותר ר"י אומר עירב בו חול הרי זה טרכסיד ואסור תבן מותר ת"ר ז כשחרב הבית בשניה רבו פרושין בישראל שלא לאכול בשר ושלא לשתות יין נטפל להן ר' יהושע אמר להן בני מפני מה אי אתם אוכלין בשר ואין אתם שותין יין אמרו לו נאכל בשר שממנו מקריבין על גבי מזבח ועכשיו בטל נשתה יין שמנסכין על גבי המזבח ועכשיו בטל אמר להם א"כ לחם לא נאכל שכבר בטלו מנחות אפשר בפירות פירות לא נאכל שכבר בטלו בכורים אפשר בפירות אחרים מים לא נשתה שכבר בטל ניסוך המים שתקו אמר להן בני בואו ואומר לכם שלא להתאבל כל עיקר אי אפשר שכבר נגזרה גזרה ולהתאבל יותר מדאי אי אפשר ח שאין גוזרין גזירה על הצבור אא"כ רוב צבור יכולין לעמוד בה דכתיב ב) במארה אתם נארים ואותי אתם קובעים הגוי כולו אלא כך אמרו חכמים ט סד אדם את ביתו בסיד ומשייר בו דבר מועט וכמה אמר רב יוסף י אמה על אמה אמר רב חסדא כ כנגד הפתח ל עושה אדם כל צרכי סעודה ומשייר דבר מועט מאי היא אמר רב פפא כסא דהרסנא מ עושה אשה כל תכשיטיה ומשיירת דבר מועט מאי היא אמר רב בת צדעא שנאמר ג) אם אשכחך ירושלים תשכח ימיני תדבק לשוני לחכי וגו' מאי על ראש שמחתי אמר רב יצחק נ זה אפר מקלה שבראש חתנים א"ל רב פפא לאביי היכא מנח לה ס במקום תפילין שנאמר ד) לשום לאבלי ציון לתת להם פאר תחת אפר ע וכל המתאבל על ירושלים זוכה ורואה בשמחתה שנאמר ה) שמחו את ירושלים וגו' תניא אמר ר' ישמעאל בן אלישע מיום שחרב בית המקדש דין הוא שנגזור על עצמנו שלא לאכול בשר ולא לשתות יין אלא פ אין גוזרין גזרה על הצבור אא"כ רוב צבור יכולין לעמוד בה ומיום שפשטה מלכות הרשעה שגוזרת עלינו גזירות רעות וקשות ומבטלת ממנו תורה ומצות ואין מנחת אותנו ליכנס לשבוע הבן ואמרי לה לישוע הבן דין הוא שנגזור על עצמנו שלא לישא אשה ולהוליד בנים ונמצא זרעו של אברהם אבינו כלה מאליו אלא צ הנח להם לישראל מוטב שיהיו שוגגין ואל יהיו מזידין:

הדרן עלך חזקת הבתים

זיל האידנא. שהיה רוצה לקשט עצמו תחלה כדלקמן: אי קוץ דידי. אם שלי קצוץ כבר: כיון דחזא דמעכבי. הבין שבשביל כבודו שותקין על שלו: ולימא ליה זיל קוץ כו'. ואמאי א"ל זיל האידנא כו': התקוששו. הסר קש מבין עיניך תחלה כמו לקושש קש (שמות ה) כלומר קשוט עצמך: איבעיא להו כנס. לתוך שלו ולא הוציא עכשיו זיזין מהו שיחזור ויוציא לאחר זמן מי אמרינן דויתרה לבני רה"ר ואבד כחו או לא: (א) וריש לקיש אמר כנס אינו מוציא. קס"ד לא יוציא עוד זיזין דאבד כחו: ואיפכא איתמר. דמוקמינן לרבי יוחנן כר"י דהלכתא כוותיה וקי"ל כרב יהודה בהך: מצר. שבין שתי שדות שהחזיקו בו והלכו נמי הרי החזיקו בהך כניסה: איכא רווחא. כשיחזיר כתלים למקומן אכתי איכא כל רוחב רה"ר וכשם רה"ר מרווח הוא: ה"ג אמר רב הונא נפלה כו'. אי נמי ואם נפלה ולא גרס שאם נפלה: חוזר ובונה אותה. להוציא זיזין כבתחלה: אין מסיידין. בית משום אבל בית המקדש: ואין מכיירין. צורות שלר בסיד. וי"מ דהיינו נמי סיד אלא שמכיור לבן יותר: מפייחין. צורות של מיני צבעונים: נפלה אינו חוזר כו'. אלמא כל בנין שאינו ראשי לעשות בתחלה אם היה לו ונפל אינו חוזר ובונה וגבי הוצאת זיזין לרה"ר נמי כיון דלאי אפשר להוציא בתחלה אם נפל אינו חוזר ומוציא: איסורא שאני. מהזיקה: חול או תבן. מכהה לבנונו: טרכסיד. בנין חזק וטוב ואף על פי שמשחיר קצת אסור: אפשר בפירות. ויפה אמרת ונפרוש גם מן הלחם: בפירות אחרים. שאין מביאים ביכורים אלא מז' המינין: שכבר נגזרה גזירה. חורבן ונתחייבנו להתאבל דכתיב שישו אתה משוש כל המתאבלים עליה (ישעיה סו): במארה אתם נארים. קבלתם עליכם בגזירת ארור להביא המעשר אל בית האוצר דכתיב במלאכי (ג) הביאו את כל המעשר וגו' ואעפ"כ ואותי אתם קובעים אתם גוזלים את המעשר ואת התרומה דכתיב התם ואמרתם במה קבענוך המעשר והתרומה: הגוי כולו. כלומר וכל הקהל כולו קיבלו את הגזירה ומסתמא אם לא היו כולן יכולין לעמוד בה לא היו מסכימין ורובן ככולן אלמא לא חשיבא גזירה אלא"כ רובן יכולין לעמוד בה: אלא כך אמרו חכמים כו'. מסקנא למילתיה דרבי יהושע היא: כסא דהרסנא. קערה של מאכל דגים מטוגנין בשמנן בסולת: בת צידעא. טנפ"ל שרגילות לסוד שם ולהסיר שערן: שנאמר אם אשכחך וגו'. אכולהו קאי: אפר מקלה. אפר הכירה השרופה באש קרוי כן ומשום דאיכא אפר פרה נמי הוצרך לפרש כן: פאר תחת אפר. מכלל שהיו רגילין ליתן אפר במקום פאר דהיינו תפילין דכתיב פארך חבוש עליך (יחזקאל כד): לשבוע הבן. מילה שהיא לסוף ז': ונמצא זרעו של אברהם אבינו כלה מאליו. בענין טוב ולא ע"י עובדי כוכבים ומלות לא יבטלו עוד: אלא הנח להם לישראל מוטב שיהיו שוגגין. כמה שלוקחין נשים שאינם סבורים שיש איסור בדבר: ואל יהיו מזידין. דמשום דלא יוכלו לעמוד בה יבטלוה ונמצאו מזידין הלכך לא גזרינן: הדרן עלך חזקת הבתים

מסורת הש"ס

א) סנהדרין יח. יט. ב"מ קז:, ב) ב"ק כח. לעיל יב. כו:, ג) לקמן ק., ד) שבת פ: [תוספתא סוטה פט"ו], ה) [תוספתא שם], ו) ע"ז לו. הוריות ג: [ע"ש], ז) [תוספתא פ"ב], ח) [מגילה עט.] [תענית טו.], ט) [תוספתא שנאמר ליתא ברב אלפס], י) [שם בתוספתא תענית ל:], כ) [שבת קמח. ביצה ל.], ל) [וע"ע תוס' ע"ז ד. ד"ה שהיה בידם].

הגהות הב"ח

(א) רשב"ם ד"ה וריש לקיש אמר כנס אינו מוציא. נ"ב [חסר הסתלה ונשאר זה הלשון] ומאן דקא מיבעי ליה נמי לא קא מיבעי ליה אלא בלהחזיר אבל כי הכי קא מיבעי ליה הא דתנן אלא אם רצה כונס לתוך שלו ומוציא ומשכחת מחל לבני רה"ר ושוב אינו יכול להחזיר כתלים למקומן אלא מוציא זיזים בלחוד הוא דלמא ה"ק כונס לתוך שלו ומוציא והסם הוא כיון דכבר הוציא זיזין אינו מחזיר כתלים למקומן דכבר מחל לבני רה"ר אם לא הוציא הזיזין עדיין אלא כנס בלבד שוב מחזיר כתלים למקומן ומאי דקאמר מהו שיחזור ויוציא ה"פ מי נימא דמוציא זיזין וא"כ שוב לא יחזיר הכתלים למקומן או דלמא אינו מוציא לפי שמחזיר הכתלים למקומן וממילא אם הוציא שוב אין יכול להחזיר וכזה לא נצטרך לפרש דמאי דקאמר ואיפכא איתמר משום דר' יוחנן מוקמינן כרב יהודה כמו שפירש רשב"ם: (ב) תוס' ד"ה מים וכו' שלא היו יכולין לסבול בלא שתיית מים הס"ד: (ג) ד"ה מוטב וכו' דאמרה מדת הדין רבש"ע אם לפניך:

תורה אור השלם

א) הִתְקוֹשְׁשׁוּ וָקוֹשּׁוּ הַגּוֹי לֹא נִכְסָף: [צפניה ב, א]
ב) בַּמְּאֵרָה אַתֶּם נֵאָרִים וְאֹתִי אַתֶּם קֹבְעִים הַגּוֹי כֻּלּוֹ: [מלאכי ג, ט]
ג) אִם אֶשְׁכָּחֵךְ יְרוּשָׁלָ͏ִם תִּשְׁכַּח יְמִינִי: תִּדְבַּק לְשׁוֹנִי לְחִכִּי אִם לֹא אֶזְכְּרֵכִי אִם לֹא אַעֲלֶה אֶת יְרוּשָׁלַ͏ִם עַל רֹאשׁ שִׂמְחָתִי: [תהלים קלז, ה-ו]
ד) לָשׂוּם לַאֲבֵלֵי צִיּוֹן לָתֵת לָהֶם פְּאֵר תַּחַת אֵפֶר שֶׁמֶן שָׂשׂוֹן תַּחַת אֵבֶל מַעֲטֵה תְהִלָּה תַּחַת רוּחַ כֵּהָה וְקֹרָא לָהֶם אֵילֵי הַצֶּדֶק מַטַּע יְיָ לְהִתְפָּאֵר: [ישעיה סא, ג]
ה) שִׂמְחוּ אֶת יְרוּשָׁלַ͏ִם וְגִילוּ בָהּ כָּל אֹהֲבֶיהָ שִׂישׂוּ אִתָּהּ מָשׂוֹשׂ כָּל הַמִּתְאַבְּלִים עָלֶיהָ: [ישעיה סו, י]

ליקוטי רש"י

התקוששו. התלקטו ואספו יחד כמו לקושש קש (שמות ה). וקושו. מעשיכם השוו מעשיכם לדעת קונכם ורז"ל דרשו קשוט עצמך ואח"כ קשוט אחרים עשו שניהם לשון היקש אדם המשוה עצמו ומישר דרכו [צפניה ב, א]. מצר שהחזיקו בו רבים אסור לקלקלו. לעשותו להן דרך אסור לקלקלו אע"פ שהוא של יחיד [לעיל כו:]. שהשווהו ותקנוהו להילוך והבעלים ידעו ושתקו אסור לקלקלו דודאי לרבים מחל [רשב"ם לקמן ק.]. לא יסוד אדם את ביתו בסיד. לאחר חורבן משום אבילות של ירושלים. חול או תבן. שלא יהא לבן כל צרכו. טרכסיד. סיד חזק ומתקשה יותר משאם לא עירב בו [שבת פ:]. על ראש שמחתי. אם זכרון אבל חורבנה אעלה להזכירו בראש כל שמחתי [תהלים קלז ו]. פאר תחת אפר. שמע מינה במקום תפילין דכתיב בהו (יחזקאל כד) פארך חבוש עליך ואמרינן (ברכות יא.) אלו תפילין ומתרגמינן נמי טוטפתך הוין עלך והיכא מניחין תפילין במקום שמוחו של תינוק רופף [תענית טז.]. הנח להם לישראל. בדבר שהרגילו בו ולא יחזרו בהם. מוטב שיהיו שוגגין ואל יהיו מזידין. לעבור כשידעו ולא ימחו בכך [ביצה ל.].

אָמַר רַב הוּנָא – **Rav Huna said:** נָפְלָה חוֹזֵר וּבוֹנֶה אוֹתָהּ – **If** [a **house**] in the courtyard **collapsed, one may rebuild it** as it was before, with ledges and balconies extending from it.[12]

Rav Huna's ruling is challenged:

מֵיתִיבֵי – **[The scholars of the academy] pointed out a contradiction:** אֵין מְסַיְּידִין וְאֵין מְכַיְּירִין וְאֵין מְפַיְּיחִין בַּזְּמַן הַזֶּה – WE MAY NOT PLASTER a wall WITH LIME,[13] NOR ORNAMENT[14] OR PAINT[15] it IN OUR TIMES (i.e. in the post-Temple era). לָקַח חָצֵר מְסוּיֶּדֶת מְכוּיֶּרֶת מְפוּיַּחַת – However, IF ONE PURCHASED A COURTYARD whose houses are already PLASTERED WITH LIME, ORNAMENTED or PAINTED, הֲרֵי זוֹ בְּחֶזְקָתָהּ – [THE COURTYARD] RETAINS ITS STATUS.[16] נָפְלָה אֵינוֹ חוֹזֵר וּבוֹנֶה אוֹתָהּ – But if [A WALL OR HOUSE] in the courtyard COLLAPSED, ONE MAY NOT REBUILD IT as it was before. Rather, one must leave its walls unornamented and unpainted; nor may he plaster them with lime. Thus, we see that a wall does not retain its prior status if it collapses and is rebuilt, contrary to Rav Huna's ruling.[17] – ? –

The Gemara answers:

אִיסוּרָא שַׁאנֵי – **Prohibitory law differs** from monetary law. While prior status is of no avail in cases of prohibitory law [so ruled the Baraisa, which spoke of *prohibitions* for the post-Temple era], it is controlling in cases of monetary law [as indicated by Rav Huna's ruling].[18]

The Gemara clarifies the current prohibition against plastering the walls of a house with lime:

תָּנוּ רַבָּנָן – **The Rabbis taught in a Baraisa:** לֹא יָסוּד אָדָם אֶת בֵּיתוֹ בְּסִיד – ONE MAY NOT PLASTER the walls of HIS HOUSE WITH LIME in the post-Temple era, וְאִם עֵירַב בּוֹ חוֹל אוֹ תֶּבֶן מוּתָּר – BUT IF HE MIXED SAND OR STRAW WITH [THE LIME], [PLASTERING] IS PERMITTED.[19] ר׳ יְהוּדָה אוֹמֵר – R' YEHUDAH SAYS: עֵירַב בּוֹ חוֹל – IF HE MIXED SAND WITH IT, הֲרֵי זֶה טַרְכְּסִיד וְאָסוּר – [THE MIXTURE] IS VERY STRONG PLASTER AND IT IS PROHIBITED for use as a building material.[20] תֶּבֶן מוּתָּר – But if he mixed STRAW with the lime, [PLASTERING] IS PERMITTED.[21]

תָּנוּ רַבָּנָן – **The Rabbis taught in a Baraisa:** כְּשֶׁחָרַב הַבַּיִת בַּשְּׁנִיָּה – WHEN THE TEMPLE WAS DESTROYED THE SECOND TIME,[22] רַבּוּ פְּרוּשִׁין בְּיִשְׂרָאֵל – MANY JEWS BECAME ASCETICS שֶׁלֹּא לֶאֱכוֹל בָּשָׂר וְשֶׁלֹּא לִשְׁתּוֹת יַיִן – and resolved NOT TO EAT MEAT AND NOT TO DRINK WINE, as an expression of mourning for the destruction of the Temple. נִטְפַּל לָהֶן ר׳ יְהוֹשֻׁעַ – Seeking to dissuade them, R' YEHOSHUA ENGAGED THEM in conversation. אָמַר לָהֶן – HE SAID TO THEM: בָּנַי – MY SONS! מִפְּנֵי מָה אִי אַתֶּם אוֹכְלִין בָּשָׂר וְאֵין אַתֶּם שׁוֹתִין יַיִן – FOR WHAT [REASON] DO YOU NOT EAT MEAT OR DRINK WINE?

The ascetics replied:

אָמְרוּ לוֹ – THEY SAID TO HIM: נֹאכַל בָּשָׂר – How can you ask such a question?! SHALL WE, then, EAT MEAT? שֶׁמִּמֶּנּוּ מַקְרִיבִין עַל גַּבֵּי מִזְבֵּחַ – Why, THEY USED TO OFFER UP [MEAT] ON THE ALTAR in the Temple as part of the sacred sacrifices, וְעַכְשָׁיו בָּטֵל – AND NOW IT IS NO MORE, for the Temple has been destroyed. Is it proper that we should enjoy meat while the sacred Altar is deprived of it? Certainly not! נִשְׁתֶּה יַיִן – Similarly, SHALL WE DRINK WINE? שֶׁמְּנַסְּכִין עַל גַּבֵּי הַמִּזְבֵּחַ – THEY USED TO POUR WINE ON THE ALTAR as part of the Temple service, וְעַכְשָׁיו בָּטֵל – AND NOW IT IS NO MORE. Is it proper that we enjoy wine while the sacred Altar cannot? Certainly not!

R' Yehoshua countered:

אָמַר לָהֶם – [R' YEHOSHUA] SAID TO THEM: אִם כֵּן לֶחֶם לֹא נֹאכַל – IF SO, WE SHOULD NOT EAT BREAD, שֶׁכְּבָר בָּטְלוּ מְנָחוֹת – FOR THE MEAL OFFERINGS that were offered on the Altar ARE likewise NO MORE![23] אֶפְשָׁר בְּפֵירוֹת – The ascetics agreed that, indeed, it was proper to abstain from bread. Reasoning that bread is not a necessity of life, they proposed: IT IS POSSIBLE to subsist ON FRUIT.[24]

NOTES

12. It is assumed that initially the ledges and balconies were extended legally, i.e. that the wall was drawn back from the street. Hence, the buyer has a legal right to extend again the ledges and balconies (see *Tosafos*).

13. All of the practices listed here were proscribed as an expression of mourning for the Temple (*Rashbam*). Any embellishment not necessary for structural purposes, but which is done only for aesthetic reasons, is proscribed (*Meiri*). However, a Baraisa cited below narrows the first prohibition to instances where the whole house is plastered with lime. If an area of one *amah* square is left unplastered, it is permissible to plaster the rest of the house (*Tur Orach Chaim* 560). *Rambam's* view on this differs; see *Beis Yosef, Bach* and *Mishnah Berurah* there.

14. With figures and patterns that are impressed in the plaster (*Rashbam*).

15. With pictures or forms that are painted on the walls (*Rashbam*).

16. The lime, ornaments or paint need not be removed.

17. The Gemara initially assumes that the prohibition covers only houses built after the destruction of the Temple. Hence, if one *purchased* a house he need not remove the lime or decorations, since it is assumed that the house was built prior to the Temple's destruction and the lime and decorations were applied legally. However, this assumption only prevents the removal of already existing lime. If a house *collapsed* and the question is now whether to *apply* lime *anew,* the assumption is not valid, and one must consider that perhaps the house was built after the Temple's destruction and that the lime was applied illegally. Thus, its reapplication is forbidden.

The Gemara now draws an analogy to the issue discussed by Rav Huna – whether we allow one to re-extend ledges when one rebuilds a collapsed wall. That is, just as we do not assume that lime was applied legally to a collapsed house, so we should not assume that ledges were extended legally in the case of a collapsed wall. The implication of the Baraisa thus contradicts Rav Huna, who ruled that it is permitted to rebuild a collapsed wall as before (*Tosafos;* cf. *Ritva*).

18. The Gemara now retreats from its initial position and asserts that in the case of prohibitory law prior status is not valid; a house built in the pre-Destruction era, too, may not be plastered anew in the post-Temple era. The prohibition against plastering a house rebuilt in post-Temple days is not, as previously thought, due to a consideration that perhaps the house was initially built and plastered in the post-Temple era. Thus, this law does not contradict the ruling made by Rav Huna regarding monetary law, i.e. that one may re-extend ledges when rebuilding a wall that had collapsed. In that case Rav Huna ruled that we should assume that the extension was initially made legally, and allowed the re-extension (*Tosafos;* cf. *Ritva*).

[The difference between prohibitory law and monetary law in this instance is not intrinsic to these two genres of law; rather, it is due to the individual natures of the specific laws under discussion.]

19. The sand or straw diminishes the whiteness of the lime, and renders plastering permissible (*Rashbam*).

20. Since the loss of whiteness is offset by an enhancement of the lime's strength, plastering is prohibited (*Rashbam*).

21. Since the loss of whiteness is not offset by an enhancement, plastering is permitted even according to R' Yehudah.

22. *Ben Yehoyada* explains that prophets had forewarned the people about the destruction of the first Temple, but explicitly promised that it would be rebuilt within a century, as indeed it was. Since the people knew that the period of desolation would be relatively short lived, they did not enact measures of self-denial in mourning for the Temple. However, no prophet stepped forward after the second destruction to promise a speedy redemption. Thus, many feared – correctly, as it turned out – that the Temple site might remain desolate for centuries. As a result, many people felt it proper to enact measures of self-denial to express their mourning. 23. The various meal offerings consisted of flour mixed with oil or water, and thus were akin to bread; see *Leviticus* 2, 5, 6, 23 and 24, and *Numbers* 5 and 15.

24. This follows *Rashbam,* but see *Maharsha.*

זיל האידנא ותא למחר בליליא שדר קצייה להההוא דידיה למחר אתא לקמיה א"ל זיל קוץ א"ל הא מר נמי אית ליה א"ל זיל חזי אי קוץ דידי קוץ דידך אי לא קוץ דידי לא תקוץ את מעיקרא מאי סבר ולבסוף מאי סבר מעיקרא סבר ניחא להו לבני רה"ר דיתבי בטוליה כיון דחזא דקא מעכבי שדר קצייה ולימא ליה זיל קוץ דידך והדר אקוץ דידי משום דריש לקיש [ו] דאמר [א] התקוששו וקושו קשוט עצמך ואח"כ קשוט אחרים: אבל אם רצה כונס לתוך שלו ומוציא: איבעיא להו כנס ולא הוציא מהו שיחזור ויוציא ר' יוחנן אמר [א] כנס מוציא וריש לקיש אמר כנס אינו מוציא א"ל רבי יעקב לר' ירמיה בר תחליפא אסברה לך להוציא כ"ע לא פליגי דמוציא כי פליגי להחזיר כתלים למקומן ואיפכא איתמר ר' יוחנן אמר אינו מחזיר וריש לקיש אמר מחזיר ר' יוחנן אמר [ב] אינו מחזיר משום דרב יהודה [ג] דאמר רב יהודה [ג] מצר שהחזיקו בו רבים אסור לקלקלו וריש לקיש אמר מחזיר הני מילי היכא דליכא רווחא הכא הא איכא רווחא: לקח חצר ובה זיזין וגזוזטראות הרי היא בחזקתה: אמר רב הונא [ד] נפלה חוזר ובונה אותה מיתיבי [ה] אין מסיידין ואין מכיירין ואין מפייחין בזמן הזה [ו] לקח חצר מסוידת מכוירת מפויחת הרי זו בחזקתה נפלה אינו חוזר ובונה אותה איסורא שאני ת"ר [ג] לא יסוד אדם את ביתו בסיד ואם עירב בו חול או תבן מותר ר"י אומר עירב בו חול הרי זה טרכסיד ואסור תבן מותר ת"ר [ד] כשחרב הבית בשניה רבו פרושין בישראל שלא לאכול בשר ושלא לשתות יין נטפל להן ר' יהושע אמר להן בני מפני מה אי אתם אוכלין בשר ואין אתם שותין יין אמרו לו נאכל בשר שממנו מקריבין על גבי מזבח ועכשיו בטל נשתה יין שמנסכין על גבי המזבח ועכשיו בטל אמר להם א"כ לחם לא נאכל שכבר בטלו מנחות אפשר בפירות פירות לא נאכל שכבר בטלו בכורים אפשר בפירות אחרים מים לא נשתה שכבר בטל ניסוך המים שתקו אמר להן בני בואו ואומר לכם שלא להתאבל כל עיקר אי אפשר שכבר נגזרה גזרה ולהתאבל יותר מדאי אי אפשר [ה] שאין גוזרין גזירה על הצבור אא"כ רוב צבור יכולין לעמוד בה דכתיב [ב] במארה אתם נארים ואותי אתם קובעים הגוי כולו אלא כך אמרו חכמים [ו] סד אדם את ביתו בסיד ומשייר בו דבר מועט וכמה אמר רב יוסף [ח] אמה על אמה אמר רב חסדא [ט] כנגד הפתח [י] עושה אדם כל צרכי סעודה ומשייר דבר מועט מאי היא אמר רב פפא כסא דהרסנא [כ] עושה אשה כל תכשיטיה ומשיירת דבר מועט מאי היא אמר רב בת צדעא שנאמר [ג] אם אשכחך ירושלים תשכח ימיני תדבק לשוני לחכי וגו' מאי על ראש שמחתי אמר רב יצחק [ל] זה אפר מקלה שבראש חתנים א"ל רב פפא לאביי [ו] היכא מנח לה [מ] במקום תפילין [ז] שנאמר [ד] לשום לאבלי ציון לתת להם פאר תחת אפר [ט] וכל המתאבל על ירושלים זוכה ורואה בשמחתה שנאמר [ה] שמחו את ירושלים וגו' תניא אמר ר' ישמעאל בן אלישע מיום שחרב בית המקדש דין הוא שנגזור על עצמנו שלא לאכול בשר ולא לשתות יין אלא [ס] אין גוזרין גזרה על הצבור אא"כ רוב צבור יכולין לעמוד בה ומיום שפשטה מלכות הרשעה שגוזרת עלינו גזירות רעות וקשות ומבטלת ממנו תורה ומצות ואין מנחת אותנו ליכנס לשבוע הבן ואמרי לה לישוע הבן דין הוא שנגזור על עצמנו שלא לישא אשה ולהוליד בנים ונמצא זרעו של אברהם אבינו כלה מאליו אלא [י] הנח להם לישראל מוטב שיהיו שוגגין ואל יהיו מזידין:

הדרן עלך חזקת הבתים

נפלה אינו חוזר ובונה אותה. השתא ס"ד דבית שבנה בזמן שבהמ"ק קיים ונפלה חוזר ובונה וכשלקח חצר המסוידת הרי זו בחזקתה לכל זמן שהיא קיימת יש לנו לתלות שבהיתר עשה בזמן שבהמ"ק קיים אבל כשנפלה תלינן שבאיסור נעשית לאחר חורבן ומש"ה פריך אהא דרב הונא דאמר חוזר ובונה אותה כיון דנפלה אית לן למימרי שבאיסור הוציא ומשני איסורא שאני דאפי' ודאי נבנה בהיתר כי נפלה אסור לבנותה ולסייד: **מים** לא נשתה [וכו'] שתקו. וא"ת אמאי לא אהדרו לאשתר במי בורות דפסולין לניסוך כדמשמע בסוכה (דף מח.) ואומר ר"י דדבר דהוי ממין שעושין בו ניסוך חשיב כמו דבר עצמו דאי לאו הכי תקשה דישתו יין מבושל דפסול לנסכים ואין הקשות לאפשר במי תותים ויין תפוחים שלא היו יכולין לסבול (ב) שלא לשתות בלא מים: **דין** הוא שנגזור על עצמנו שלא לישא נשים. תימה דהכתיב פרו ורבו ושמא על אותן שכבר קיימו פריה ורביה קאמר והיינו זרעו של אברהם כלה שלא יוליד אלא בן ובת: **מוטב** שיהיו שוגגין ואל יהיו מזידין. בדבר שאין ידוע אם יקבלו כשנמחה בהן אם לאו צריך למחות כדמוכח בפ' במה [בהמה] (שבת דף נה. ושם ד"ה ואע"ג) דאמרה מדת הדין (ג) אם לפניך גלוי לפניהם מי גלוי וענשו אבל בדבר שאנו יודעים בבירור שלא יקבלו אמרינן מוטב שיהיו שוגגין וכו':

הדרן עלך חזקת הבתים

זיל האידנא. שהיה רוצה לקשט עצמו תחלה כדלקמן: **אי קוץ דידי.** אם שלי קוצץ כבר: **כיון דחזא דמעכבי.** הבין שבשביל כבודו שותקין על שלו: **ולימא ליה זיל קוץ כו'.** ולמאי א"ל זיל האידנא כו': **התקוששו.** הסר קש מבין עיניך תחלה כמו לקושש קש (שמות ה) כלומר קשוט עצמך: **איבעיא להו כנס.** לתוך שלו ולא הוציא עכשיו זיזין מהו שיחזור ויוציא לאחר זמן מי אמרינן דויתרה לבני רה"ר ולאבד כמו לא לו: (א) **וריש לקיש אמר כנס אינו מוציא.** קס"ד לא יוציא עוד זיזין לאבד כמו: **ואיפכא איתמר.** דמוקמינן לרבי יוחנן כר' יהודה דהלכתא כוותיה וקי"ל כרב יהודה בהך: **מצר.** שבין שתי שדות שהחזיקו בו והכא נמי הרי החזיקו בהך כניסה: **איכא רווחא.** כשיחזיר כתלים למקומן אכתי איכא כל רוחב רה"ר וכסס רה"ר מרווח הוא: ה"ג **אמר רב הונא נפלה כו'.** אי נמי ואם נפלה ולא גרם שאם נפלה: **חוזר ובונה אותה.** להוציא זיזין כבתחלה: **אין מסיידין.** בית משום אבל בית המקדש: **ואין מכיירין.** צורות שאר בסיד. וי"מ דהיינו נמי סיוד אלא שהכיור לבן יותר: **מפייחין.** צורות של מיני צבעונים: **נפלה אינו חוזר כו'.** אלמא כל בנין שאינו רשאי לעשות בתחלה אם היה לו ונפל אינו חוזר ובונה וגבי הוצאת זיזין לרה"ר נמי כיון דאי אפשר להוציא בתחלה אם נפל אינו חוזר ומוציא: **איסורא שאני.** מהיזיקא: **חול או תבן.** מכהה לבנונו: **טרכסיד.** בנין חזק וטוב ואף על פי שמשחיר קצת אסור: **אפשר בפירות.** ויפה אמרת ונפרוש גם מן הלחם: **בפירות אחרים.** שאין מביאים ביכורים אלא מז' המינין: **שכבר נגזרה גזירה.** חורבן ונתחייבנו להתאבל דכתיב שישו אתה משוש כל המתאבלים עליה (ישעיה סו): **במארה אתם נארים.** קבלתם עליכם בגזירת ארור להביא המעשר אל בית האוצר כדכתיב במלאכי (ג) הביאו את כל המעשר וגו' ואעפ"כ ואותי אתם קובעים אתם גוזלים את המעשר ואת התרומה כדכתיב התם ואמרתם במה קבענוך המעשר והתרומה: **הגוי כולו.** כלומר וכל הקהל כולו קיבלו את הגזירה ומסתמא אם לא היו כולן יכולין לעמוד בה לא היו מסכימין ורובן ככולן אלמא לא חשיבא גזירה אא"כ רובן יכולין לעמוד בה: **אלא כך אמרו חכמים כו'.** מסקנא דמילתיה דרבי יהושע היא: **כסא דהרסנא.** קערה של מאכל דגים מטוגנין בשמנן בסולת: **בת צידעא.** טופ"ל שרגילות לסוד שם ולהסיר שערן: **שנאמר אם אשכחך וגו'.** אכולהו קאי: **אפר מקלה.** אפר הכירה השרופה באש קרוי כן ומשום דאיכא אפר פרה נמי הוצרך לפרש כן: **פאר תחת אפר.** מכלל שהיו רגילין ליתן אפר במקום פאר דהיינו תפילין כדכתיב פארך חבוש עליך (יחזקאל כד): **לשבוע הבן.** מילה שהיא לסוף ז': **ונמצא זרעו של אברהם אבינו כלה מאליו.** בענין טוב ולא ע"י עובדי כוכבים ומלות לא יבטלו עוד: **אלא הנח להם לישראל מוטב שיהיו שוגגין.** במה שלוקחין נשים שאינם סבורים שיש איסור בדבר: **ואל יהיו מזידין.** דמשום דלא יוכלו לעמוד בה יבטלוה ונמצאו מזידין הלכך לא גזרינן: **הדרן עלך חזקת הבתים**

מעשיכם השוו מעשיכם לדעת קונכם ורז"ל דרשו קשוט עצמך ואח"כ קשוט אחרים עשו שניהם לשון היקש אדם המשוה עצמו ומישר דרכו [צפניה ב, א]. **מצר שהחזיקו בו רבים אסור לקלקלו.** לעשותו להן דרך אסור לקלקלו אע"פ שהוא של יחיד [לעיל כו:]. שהשווהו ותקנוהו להילוך והבעלים ידעו ושתקו אסור לקלקלו דודאי לרבים מחל [רשב"ם לקמן ק.]. **לא יסוד אדם את ביתו בסיד.** לאחר חורבן משום אבילות של ירושלים. שלא יהא לבן כל צרכו. **טרכסיד.** סיד חזק ומתקשה יותר משאם לא עירב בו [שבת פ:]. **על ראש שמחתי.** את זכרון אבל חורבנה אעלה להזכירו בראש כל שמחתי [תהלים קלז ו]. **פאר תחת אפר.** שמע מינה במקום תפילין דכתיב בהו (יחזקאל כד) פארך חבוש עליך ואמרינן (ברכות יא.) אלו תפילין ומתרגמינן נמי טוטפתך הוין עלך והיכא מניחין תפילין במקום שמוחו של תינוק רופף [תענית טז.]. **הנח להם לישראל.** בדבר שהרגילו בו ולא יחזרו בהם. מוטב שיהיו שוגגין ואל יהיו מזידין. לעבור כשידעו ולא יניחו בכך [ביצה ל.].

עין משפט נר מצוה

רצג א ב ג מיי' פי"ג מהל' נזקי ממון הל' כד סמג שם טוש"ע ח"מ סי' תיז סעיף ג:
רצד ד מיי' שם הל' כה טוש"ע שם סעיף ג:
רצה ה ו ז ח ט מיי' פ"ה מהל' תענית הל' יב סמג עשין מד"ס ג טוש"ע או"ח סי' תקס סעיף א:
רצו י כ ל מ מיי' שם הל' יג טוש"ע שם סעיף ב [וברב אלפס תענית דף קטע:]:
רצז נ טוש"ע או"ח סי' תקנד סעיף כה:
רחצ ס מיי' פ"ב מהל' ממרים הלכה ה סמג עשין קיא:

לעזי רש"י

טנפ"ל. פירוש לדע, רקה (רש"י שופטים ד, כב), לד המלח שליד האוזן:

רבינו גרשום

כיון דחזי דמעכבי. להאי אמר ש"מ דלא ניחא להו ומשום יקרא דידי שתקו: **איבעיא להו כנס** לתוך שלו **ולא הוציא.** זיזין באותה פעם באותה כניסה **מהו שיחזור ויוציא** לאחר זמן. מי אמרי' כיון דלא הוציא בתחלה בההיא כניסה ויתרה לבני רה"ר אי לא: **ר' יוחנן אמר.** לרשותו **מוציא** בה זיזין כל זמן שירצה. **וריש לקיש אמר כנס** ולא הוציא לאלתר **אינו מוציא** שוב: **להחזיר כתלים למקומן.** כמו שהיה: אבל רה"ר **מצר שהחזיקו בו [רבים].** שכבר דשין באותה כניסה: **ה"מ.** דאסור לקלקלו **היכא דליכא רווחא** טפי ברה"ר: **אין מכיירין.** שאין עושין ציור מן הסיד עצמו כמו שעושין בנאין: **אין מפייחין.** שאין מלבין הבית לאחר שמצויר בזמן הזה מפני איבול בהמ"ק: **אין חוזר ובונה אותה.** באותו סיד וכיור: **איסורא שאני.** שאסרו חכמים מפני איבול: **אבל אם (כן) עירב בו חול.** שלא יהא לבן כל כך: **הרי זה טרכסיד.** השביחו מפני שאע"פ ששחור כמעט נעשה חזק ונדבק ביותר: **אפשר בפירות אחרים.** שלא היו מביאין בכורים אלא משבעת המינין: **שתקו.** שא"א לחיות בלא מים: **במארה אתם נארים.** מארה גזרה ואותי אתם קובעין בהם בהסכמתכם. אי איכא **הגוי כולו** שיכולין לעמוד בה אין. מקיימת הגזירה ואי לא לא: **בת צדעא.** (א) שלא תזבין צדעא בשרק שלא תיתפור ממנה שיער: **כנגד הפתח.** כדי שתהא נראה: **לשבוע הבן.** שעושין לסוף שבעה: **שיהיו שוגגין.** שיבטלו אותו דין בשוגג ואל יהיו מזידין שאם נגזור גזירה יהיו מבטלין אותה במזיד שלא יהו יכולין לעמוד בה שלא לישא אשה:

הדרן עלך חזקת הבתים

חשק שלמה על רבינו גרשום

א) אולי צ"ל שלא תעביר לדעת בסרק כדי שתיפול ממנה שער.

מסורת הש"ס

א) סנהדרין יח. יט. ב"מ קז:, ב) ב"ק כח. לעיל יב. כו:, ג) לקמן ק., ד) שבת פ: [תוספתא סוטה פט"ו], ה) [תוספתא שם], ו) ע"ז לו. הוריות ג: [ב"ק עט:], ז) [תוספתא פ"ב], ח) [תענית טז.], ט) [תענית ... שנאמר ליתא ברב אלפס], ו) [שם בתוספתא תענית ל:], י) [שבת קמח: ביצה ל.], כ) [וע"ע תוס' ע"ז ד. ד"ה שהיה בידם].

הגהות הב"ח

(א) רשב"ם ד"ה וריש לקיש אמר כנס אינו מוציא. נ"ב [חסר] ההתחלה ונשאר זה הלשון ומאן דקא מיבעי ליה נמי לא קא מיבעיא ליה אלא בלהחזיר כו' והכי קא מיבעי ליה הא דתנן אלא אם רצה כונס לתוך שלו ומוציא ומכניס מהו לבני רה"ר ושוב אינו יכול להחזיר כתלים למקומן אלא מוציא זיזים בלבד או דלמא ה"ק כונס לתוך שלו ומוציא והשתא הוא לבני דבכה הוציא זיזין עדיין מחזיר כתלים למקומן דכבר מחל לבני רה"ר אבל אם לא הוציא הזיזין עדיין אלא כנס בלבד כבר מחזיר כתלים למקומן ומאי דקאמר מהו שיחזיר ויוציא ה"ק מי נימא דלא נמחל מדשיחזור ויוציא ואח"כ שוב לא יחזיר הכתלים למקומן או דלמא אינו מוציא לפי שמחזיר הכתלים למקומן וממילא אם הוציא שוב אין יכול להחזיר וזהו לא נלפרך לפרש דקאמר ואיפכא איתמר משום דר' יוחנן מוקמינן כרב יהודה כמו שפירש רשב"ם: (ב) תוס' ד"ה מים וכו' שלא היו יכולין לסבול בלא שתיית מים הס"ד: (ג) ד"ה מוטב וכו' דאמרה מדת הדין רבש"ע אם לפניך:

תורה אור השלם

א) הִתְקוֹשְׁשׁוּ וָקוֹשּׁוּ הַגּוֹי לֹא נִכְסָף: [צפניה ב, א]
ב) בַּמְּאֵרָה אַתֶּם נֵאָרִים וְאֹתִי אַתֶּם קֹבְעִים הַגּוֹי כֻּלּוֹ: [מלאכי ג, ט]
ג) אִם אֶשְׁכָּחֵךְ יְרוּשָׁלָ‍ִם תִּשְׁכַּח יְמִינִי: תִּדְבַּק לְשׁוֹנִי לְחִכִּי אִם לֹא אֶזְכְּרֵכִי אִם לֹא אַעֲלֶה אֶת יְרוּשָׁלַ‍ִם עַל רֹאשׁ שִׂמְחָתִי: [תהלים קלז, ה-ו]
ד) לָשׂוּם לַאֲבֵלֵי צִיּוֹן לָתֵת לָהֶם פְּאֵר תַּחַת אֵפֶר שֶׁמֶן שָׂשׂוֹן תַּחַת אֵבֶל מַעֲטֵה תְהִלָּה תַּחַת רוּחַ כֵּהָה וְקֹרָא לָהֶם אֵילֵי הַצֶּדֶק מַטַּע יְיָ לְהִתְפָּאֵר: [ישעיה סא, ג]
ה) שִׂמְחוּ אֶת יְרוּשָׁלַ‍ִם וְגִילוּ בָהּ כָּל אֹהֲבֶיהָ שִׂישׂוּ אִתָּהּ מָשׂוֹשׂ כָּל הַמִּתְאַבְּלִים עָלֶיהָ: [ישעיה סו, י]

ליקוטי רש"י

התקוששו. התלקטו ואספו יחד כמו לקושש קש (שמות ה). וקושו.

R' Yehoshua again countered:

פֵּירוֹת לֹא נֹאכַל – But WE SHOULD NOT EAT FRUIT either, שֶׁכְּבָר בָּטְלוּ בִכּוּרִים – FOR now that the Temple has been destroyed, THE "FIRST FRUITS" ARE NO MORE,[25] and it is not proper that we enjoy fruit while the Temple cannot. אֶפְשָׁר בְּפֵירוֹת אֲחֵרִים – The ascetics agreed that, indeed, it was proper to abstain from eating those species that had been offered as "first fruits." Nevertheless, they proposed: IT IS still POSSIBLE to subsist ON OTHER types of FRUIT, i.e. those species that were not brought as "first fruits."[26]

R' Yehoshua delivered the coup de grace:

מַיִם לֹא נִשְׁתֶּה – He said to them: But according to your reasoning, WE SHOULD NOT DRINK WATER either, שֶׁכְּבָר בָּטֵל נִיסּוּךְ הַמַּיִם – FOR THE WATER LIBATION IS NO MORE,[27] and it is not proper that we enjoy water while the Temple cannot. שָׁתְקוּ – [THE ASCETICS] WERE SILENT, for they realized that it is impossible to live without water,[28] and that R' Yehoshua had demonstrated the impossibility of abstaining from every type of food or drink that had been used in the Temple.

R' Yehoshua then instructed the ascetics how to mourn for the Temple:

אָמַר לָהֶן – [R' YEHOSHUA] SAID TO THEM: בָּנַי – MY CHILDREN! בּוֹאוּ וְאוֹמַר לָכֶם – COME here AND I WILL EXPLAIN TO YOU the proper way to mourn for the Temple. שֶׁלֹּא לְהִתְאַבֵּל כָּל עִיקָּר אִי אֶפְשָׁר – NOT TO MOURN AT ALL IS IMPOSSIBLE, שֶׁכְּבָר נִגְזְרָה גְּזֵרָה – FOR THE DECREE of destruction HAS BEEN PROMULGATED,[29] and we must mourn for the catastrophe in some manner. וּלְהִתְאַבֵּל יוֹתֵר מִדַּאי אִי אֶפְשָׁר – AND TO MOURN EXCESSIVELY IS also IMPOSSIBLE, שֶׁאֵין גּוֹזְרִין גְּזֵירָה עַל הַצִּבּוּר – FOR WE MAY NOT IMPOSE A DECREE UPON THE PUBLIC אֶלָּא אִם כֵּן רוֹב צִבּוּר יְכוֹלִין לַעֲמוֹד בָּהּ – UNLESS THE MAJORITY OF THE PUBLIC IS ABLE TO COMPLY WITH [THAT DECREE],[30] דִּכְתִיב: ,,בַּמְּאֵרָה אַתֶּם נֵאָרִים וְאֹתִי אַתֶּם קֹבְעִים הַגּוֹי כֻּלּוֹ" – AS IT IS WRITTEN: *YOU ARE CURSED WITH A CURSE, YET YOU ROB ME, THE ENTIRE NATION.*[31] אֶלָּא כָּךְ אָמְרוּ חֲכָמִים – RATHER, THUS SAID THE SAGES: The proper way to mourn for the Temple is that when סָד אָדָם אֶת בֵּיתוֹ בְּסִיד – A MAN APPLIES PLASTER TO HIS HOUSE, וּמְשַׁיֵּיר בּוֹ דָּבָר מוּעָט – HE SHOULD LEAVE A SMALL [AREA] OF IT unplastered.

The Gemara momentarily digresses to provide a clarification of this instruction:

וְכַמָּה – And how much should be left unplastered? אָמַר רַב יוֹסֵף אַמָּה עַל אַמָּה – Rav Yosef said: An area of [one] *amah* by [one] *amah*.[32] אָמַר רַב חִסְדָּא – Rav Chisda said: כְּנֶגֶד הַפֶּתַח – The proper location of the unplastered area is opposite the door.[33]

The Gemara resumes its account of R' Yehoshua's instructions:

עוֹשֶׂה אָדָם כָּל צָרְכֵי סְעוּדָה – A MAN MAY PREPARE A MEAL, וּמְשַׁיֵּיר דָּבָר מוּעָט – BUT HE SHOULD LEAVE OUT SOME SMALL PART, i.e. one item on the menu.

The Gemara seeks a clarification:

מַאי הִיא – What is [an example] of such an item?

The Gemara answers:

אָמַר רַב פָּפָּא כַּסָּא דְּהַרְסְנָא – Rav Pappa said: A pie of fish hash.[34]

R' Yehoshua teaches a third way to mourn for the Temple:

עוֹשָׂה אִשָּׁה כָּל תַּכְשִׁיטֶיהָ – A WOMAN MAY APPLY ALL OF HER usual ADORNMENTS, וּמְשַׁיֶּירֶת דָּבָר מוּעָט – BUT SHE SHOULD OMIT SOME SMALL [ADORNMENT].[35]

The Gemara seeks a clarification:

מַאי הִיא – What is [an example] of such an adornment?

The Gemara answers:

אָמַר רַב בַּת צְדָעָא – Rav said: The hair on her temple.[36]

R' Yehoshua provides a Scriptural basis for instituting these practices as expressions of mourning for the destruction of the Holy Temple:

שֶׁנֶּאֱמַר: ,,אִם־אֶשְׁכָּחֵךְ יְרוּשָׁלָםִ תִּשְׁכַּח יְמִינִי תִּדְבַּק לְשׁוֹנִי לְחִכִּי וגו׳" –

NOTES

25. *Exodus* 23:19 and *Deuteronomy* 26:1-11 mandate that each year, between the festivals of Shavuos and Succos, every Jewish farmer in Eretz Yisrael bring a gift of "first fruits" to the Temple. These were the first ripenings of his wheat, barley, grape, fig, pomegranate, olive and date harvests. After placing them before the Altar and reciting the Biblical passage of the "first fruits" (*Deuteronomy* 26:5-10), he presented them to the Kohanim. When the Temple was destroyed, the offering of "first fruits" was discontinued.

26. I.e. any fruits other than the seven species listed in the preceding note. Since these other fruits are never offered in the Temple, there was no reason to abstain from eating them after the Temple was destroyed.

27. The Mishnah (*Succah* 42b) teaches that on each of the seven days of Succos, water was ceremoniously poured on the Altar in the Temple (see Gemara there 48a-b for a description of the service). In *Rosh Hashanah* (16a) the Sages teach that the purpose of this ceremony was to entreat God for a favorable judgment concerning rainfall for the coming year.

28. Although, strictly speaking, it is possible to abstain from water and instead drink the juice of permitted fruits, such a severe abstinence was considered too difficult even for the ascetics (*Tosafos*).

29. I.e. the destruction of the Temple and of Jerusalem, decreed by Heaven, has occurred (*Rashbam*).

Alternatively, the decree to mourn for the Temple has already been issued by the Sages (*Rashash;* see *Maharsha*).

30. And to require the entire Jewish people to abstain from such basic foods as bread, meat and wine would be to impose an intolerable burden on the majority of Jews.

31. *Malachi* 3:9. God, through the prophet Malachi, censures the Jewish people for their faithlessness. The passage in its entirety (verses 8-10) reads as follows: *Will a man rob God? Yet you rob Me! But you say, "How have we robbed You?" In tithes and terumah offerings! You are cursed with a curse, yet you rob Me, the entire nation. Bring the whole tithe into the storehouse, that there may be food in My house...* The prophet records that the Jews accepted with a curse their obligation to bring all the prescribed agricultural offerings to the proper *storehouse* in the Temple from where it would be distributed to the recipients – i.e. to the Kohen or the Levi (see *Nechemiah* 10:38-40). That is, the entire Jewish people pronounced a curse upon anyone who did not fulfill these obligations. Nevertheless, the people did not act properly, but kept the food for themselves, thereby "robbing" God. They were therefore subject to the curse that they had pronounced upon themselves.

The point here is that "the entire nation" pronounced the curse, and most probably they would not have agreed to do so if they felt they could not meet their responsibilities. Thus, from here we learn that a decree is not binding unless a majority of the nation can tolerate it [for in halachah a majority has the force of the entirety, רובו ככולו] (*Rashbam*).

32. An *amah* is 22.8 inches/58 cm. (*Chazon Ish*), or 18.9 inches/48 cm. (*R' A.C. Naeh*).

33. I.e. on the wall a person faces when he enters the house (*Mishnah Berurah* 560:3; see *Shaarei Teshuvah* there).

34. A dish consisting of fish fried in its own oil and flour (*Rashbam*), or cooked in flour and vinegar (*Aruch* ד״ה הרסנא).

35. *Ben Yehoyada* explains that R' Yehoshua's three examples are symbolic of three features lost with the destruction of the Temple: Leaving part of the house unplastered recalls the destroyed House, the Temple building itself; withholding a dish from the dinner table recalls the destroyed Altar, where foodstuffs were offered as sacrifices; and omitting an adornment recalls the priestly vestments, which are considered the Kohen's adornments.

36. It is a sign of mourning for a woman to let the hair on her temples grow. Ordinarily, it was fashionable to remove such hair with a depilatory (*Rashbam*).

See, however, *Aruch* (ד״ה בת צידעא), who explains that it was the fashion for wealthier women to apply a scented gel to the hair on the

עין משפט נר מצוה

רצג א ב ג מיי' פי"ג מהל' נזקי ממון הל' כד סמג שם טוש"ע ח"מ סי' קיז סעיף ב:
רצד ד מיי' שם הל' כה טוש"ע שם סעיף ג:
רצה ה ו ז ח ט מיי' פ"ה מהל' תענית הל' יב סמג עשין מד"ם ג טוש"ע או"ח סי' תקס סעיף א:
רצו י כ ל מ מיי' שם הל' יג טוש"ע שם סעיף ב [וברב אלפס תענית דף קעט:]:
רצז נ טוש"ע או"ח סי' תקנד סעיף כה:
רחצ ס מיי' פ"ב מהל' ממרים הלכה ה סמג עשין קיא:

נפלה אינו חוזר ובונה אותה. השתא ס"ד דבית שבנה בזמן שבהמ"ק קיים ונפלה חוזר ובונה ולכשלקח חצר המסוידת הרי זו בחזקתה דכל זמן שהיא קיימת יש לנו לתלות שנסיד עסה בזמן שבהמ"ק קיים אבל כשנפלה תלינן שבאיסור נעשית לאחר חורבן ומש"ה פריך ארבא הונא ואמאי חוזר ובונה אותה כיון דנפלה אית לן למיתלי שבאיסור הוציא ומשני איסורא שאני דאפי' ודאי נבנה בהיתר כי נפלה אסור לבנותה ולסייד: מים לא נשתה [וכו'] שתקו. וא"ת אמאי לא אהדרו לאפשר במי בורות דפסולין לניסוך כדמשמע בסוכה (דף מח.) ואומר ר"י דדבר דהוי ממון שעושין בו ניסוך חשיב כמו דבר עצמו דאי לאו הכי תקשה להו יין מבושל דפסול לנסכים ואין להקשות דאפשר במי מותים ויין פסולים שלא היו יכולין לסבול (ב) שלא לשתות בלא מים: דין הוא שנגזור על עצמנו שלא לישא נשים. תימה הכתיב פרו ורבו ושמא על אותן שכבר קיימו פריה ורביה קאמר והיינו זרעו של אברהם כלה שלא יוליד אלא בן ובת: מוטב שיהיו שוגגין ואל יהיו מזידין. בדבר שאין ידוע אם יקבלו כשנמחה בהן אם לאו צריך למחות כדמוכח בפ' במה [בהמה] (שבת דף נה. ושם ד"ה ואע"ג) דאמרה מדת הדין (ג) אם לפניך גלוי לפניהם מי גלוי ונענשו אבל בדבר שאנו יודעים בבירור שלא יקבלו אמרינן מוטב שיהיו שוגגין וכו'(ך):

הדרן עלך חזקת הבתים

זיל האידנא ותא למחר בליליא שדר קצייה להההוא דידיה למחר אתא לקמיה א"ל זיל קוץ א"ל הא מר נמי אית ליה א"ל זיל חזי אי קוץ דידי קוץ דידך אי לא קוץ דידי לא תקוץ את מעיקרא מאי סבר ולבסוף מאי סבר מעיקרא סבר ניחא להו לבני רה"ר דיתבי בטוליה כיון דחזא דקא מעכבי שדר קצייה ולימא ליה זיל קוץ דידך והדר אקוץ דידי משום דריש לקיש דאמר התקוששו וקושו קשוט עצמך ואח"כ קשוט אחרים: אבל אם רצה כונס לתוך שלו ומוציא: איבעיא להו כנס ולא הוציא מהו שיחזור ויוציא ר' יוחנן אמר כנס מוציא וריש לקיש אמר כנס אינו מוציא א"ל רבי יעקב לר' ירמיה בר תחליפא אסברה לך להוציא כ"ע לא פליגי דמוציא כי פליגי להחזיר כתלים למקומן ואיפכא איתמר ר' יוחנן אמר אינו מחזיר וריש לקיש אמר מחזיר ר' יוחנן אמר אינו מחזיר משום דרב יהודה דאמר רב יהודה מצר שהחזיקו בו רבים אסור לקלקלו וריש לקיש אמר מחזיר הני מילי היכא דליכא רווחא הכא הא איכא רווחא: לקח חצר ובה זיזין וגזוזטראות הרי היא בחזקתה: אמר רב הונא נפלה חוזר ובונה אותה מיתיבי אין מסיידין ואין מכיירין ואין מפייחין בזמן הזה לקח חצר מסוידת מכוירת מפויחת הרי זו בחזקתה נפלה אינו חוזר ובונה אותה איסורא שאני ת"ר לא יסוד אדם את ביתו בסיד ואם עירב בו חול או תבן מותר ר"י אומר עירב בו חול הרי זה טרכסיד ואסור תבן מותר ת"ר כשחרב הבית בשניה רבו פרושין בישראל שלא לאכול בשר ושלא לשתות יין נטפל להן ר' יהושע אמר להן בני מפני מה אי אתם אוכלין בשר ואין אתם שותין יין אמרו לו נאכל בשר שממנו מקריבין על גבי מזבח ועכשיו בטל נשתה יין שמנסכין על גבי המזבח ועכשיו בטל אמר להם א"כ לחם לא נאכל שכבר בטלו מנחות אפשר בפירות פירות לא נאכל שכבר בטלו בכורים אפשר בפירות אחרים מים לא נשתה שכבר בטל ניסוך המים שתקו אמר להן בני בואו ואומר לכם שלא להתאבל כל עיקר אי אפשר שכבר נגזרה גזרה ולהתאבל יותר מדאי אי אפשר שאין גוזרין גזירה על הצבור אא"כ רוב צבור יכולין לעמוד בה דכתיב במארה אתם נארים ואותי אתם קובעים הגוי כולו אלא כך אמרו חכמים סד אדם את ביתו בסיד ומשייר בו דבר מועט וכמה אמר רב יוסף אמה על אמה אמר רב חסדא כנגד הפתח עושה אדם כל צרכי סעודה ומשייר דבר מועט מאי היא אמר רב פפא כסא דהרסנא עושה אשה כל תכשיטיה ומשיירת דבר מועט מאי היא אמר רב בת צדעא שנאמר אם אשכחך ירושלים תשכח ימיני תדבק לשוני לחכי וגו' מאי על ראש שמחתי אמר רב יצחק זה אפר מקלה שבראש חתנים א"ל רב פפא לאביי היכא מנח לה במקום תפילין שנאמר לשום לאבלי ציון לתת להם פאר תחת אפר וכל המתאבל על ירושלים זוכה ורואה בשמחתה שנאמר שמחו את ירושלים וגו' תניא אמר ר' ישמעאל בן אלישע מיום שחרב בית המקדש דין הוא שנגזור על עצמנו שלא לאכול בשר ולא לשתות יין אלא אין גוזרין גזרה על הצבור אא"כ רוב צבור יכולין לעמוד בה ומיום שפשטה מלכות הרשעה שגוזרת עלינו גזירות רעות וקשות ומבטלת ממנו תורה ומצות ואין מניחות אותנו ליכנס לשבוע הבן ואמרי לה לישוע הבן דין הוא שנגזור על עצמנו שלא לישא אשה ולהוליד בנים ונמצא זרעו של אברהם אבינו כלה מאליו אלא הנח להם לישראל מוטב שיהיו שוגגין ואל יהיו מזידין:

הדרן עלך חזקת הבתים

זיל האידנא. שהיה רוצה לקשט עצמו תחלה כדלקמן: אי קוץ דידי. אם שלי קצוץ כבר: כיון דחזא דמעכבי. הבין שבשביל כבודו שותקין על שלו: ולימא ליה זיל קוץ כו'. ולמאי א"ל זיל האידנא כו': התקוששו. הסר קש מבין עיניך תחלה כמו לקושש קש (שמות ה) כלומר קשוט עצמך: איבעיא להו כנס. לתוך שלו ולא הוציא עכשיו זיזין מהו שיחזור ויוציא לאחר זמן מי אמרינן דויתרה לבני רה"ר ולאבד כחו או לא: (א) וריש לקיש אמר כנס אינו מוציא. קס"ד לא יוציא עוד זיזין לאבד כחו: ואיפכא איתמר. דמוקמינן לרבי יוחנן כר' יהודה דהלכתא כוותיה וקי"ל כרב יהודה בהכן: מצר. שבין שתי שדות שהחזיקו בו רבים והכא נמי הרי החזיקו בהך כניסה: איכא רווחא. כשיחזיר כתלים למקומן אכתי איכא כל רוחב רה"ר וסתם רה"ר מרווח הוא: ה"ג אמר רב הונא נפלה כו'. אי נמי ואם נפלה ולא גרס שאם נפלה: חוזר ובונה אותה. להוציא זיזין כבתחלה: אין מסיידין. בית משום אבל בית המקדש: ואין מכיירין. צורות שלר בסיד. וי"מ דהיינו נמי סיד אלא שהסיור לבן יותר: מפייחין. צורות של מיני צבעונים: נפלה אינו חוזר כו'. אלמא כל בנין שאינו רשאי לעשות בתחלה אם היה לו ונפל אינו חוזר ובונה וגבי הוצאת זיזין לרה"ר נמי כיון דאי אפשר להוציא בתחלה אם נפל אינו חוזר ומוציא: איסורא שאני. מהיזיקא: חול או תבן. מכהה לבנונו: טרכסיד. בנין חזק וטוב ואף על פי שמשחיר קלת אסור: אפשר בפירות. ויפה אמרת ונפרוש גם מן הלחם: בפירות אחרים. שאין מביאים ביכורים אלא מז' המינין: שכבר נגזרה גזירה. חורבן ונתחייבנו להתאבל דכתיב שישו אתה משוש כל המתאבלים עליה (ישעיה סו): במארה אתם נארים. קבלתם עליכם בגזירת ארור להביא המעשר אל בית האוצר כדכתיב במלאכי (ג) הביאו את כל המעשר וגו' ואעפ"כ ואותי אתם קובעים אתם גוזלים את המעשר ואת התרומה כדכתיב התם ואמרתם במה קבענוך המעשר והתרומה: הגוי כולו. כלומר וכל הקהל כולו קיבלו את הגזירה ומסתמא אם לא היו כולן יכולין לעמוד בה לא היו מסכימין ורובן ככולן אלמא לא חשיבא גזירה אא"כ רובן יכולין לעמוד בה: אלא כך אמרו חכמים כו'. מסקנא דמילתיה דרבי יהושע היא: כסא דהרסנא. קערה של מאכל דגים מטוגנין בשמן בסולת: בת צידעא. טנפ"ל שרגילות לסוד שם ולהשיר שערן: שנאמר אם אשכחך וגו'. אכולהו קאי: אפר מקלה. אפר הכירה השרופה באש קרוי כן ומשום דאיכא אפר פרה נמי הוצרך לפרש כן: פאר תחת אפר. מכלל שהיו רגילין ליתן אפר במקום פאר דהיינו תפילין כדכתיב פארך חבוש עליך (יחזקאל כד): לשבוע הבן. מילה שהיא לסוף ז': ונמצא זרעו של אברהם אבינו כלה מאליו. בענין טוב ולא ע"י עובדי כוכבים ומלות לא יבטלו עוד: אלא הנח להם לישראל מוטב שיהיו שוגגין. במה שלוקחין נשים שאינם סבורים שיש איסור בדבר: ואל יהיו מזידין. דמשום דלא יוכלו לעמוד בה יבטלוה ונמצאו מזידין הלכך לא גזרינן: הדרן עלך חזקת הבתים

מסורת הש"ס

א) סנהדרין יח. יט. ב"מ קז:, ב) ב"ק כח. לעיל יב. כו: לקמן ק., ג) שבת פ: [תוספתא סוטה פט"ו], ד) [תוספתא שם], ה) ע"ז לו. הוריות ג: [ב"ק עט:], ו) [תוספתא פ"ב], ז) [תענית טז.], ח) [תיבת שנאמר ליתא ברב אלפס], ט) [שם בתוספתא תענית ל:], י) [שבת קמח. ביצה ל.], כ) [וע"ע תוס' ע"ז ד. ד"ה שהיה בידם]:

הגהות הב"ח

(א) רשב"ם ד"ה וריש לקיש אמר כנס אינו מוציא. נ"ב [חסר ההתחלה ונשאר זה הלשון] ומאן דקא מיבעי ליה נמי לא קא מיבעי ליה אלא בלהחזיר כו' והכי קא מיבעי ליה הא דתנן אלא אם רצה כונס לתוך שלו ומוציא ומשכנס מחל לבני רה"ר ושוב אינו יכול להחזיר כתלים למקומן אלא מוציא זיזים בלחוד או דלמא ה"ק כונס לתוך שלו ומוציא והתם הוא כיון דכבר הוציא זיזין אינו מחזיר כתלים למקומן דכבר מחל לבני רה"ר אבל אם לא הוציא הזיזין עדיין אלא כנס בלבד מחזיר כתלים למקומן ומאי דקאמר מהו שיחזור ויוציא ה"פ מי נימא דמוציא זיזין וא"כ שוב לא יחזיר הכתלים למקומן או דלמא אינו מוציא לפי שמחזיר הכתלים למקומן וממילא אם הוציא שוב אין יכול להחזיר וזה לא נצטרך לפרש דמאי דקאמר ואיפכא איתמר משום דר' יוחנן מוקמינן כרב יהודה כמו שפירש רשב"ם: (ב) תוס' ד"ה מים וכו' שלא היו יכולין לסבול בלא שתיית מים הס"ד: (ג) ד"ה מוטב וכו' דאמרה מדת הדין רבש"ע אם לפניך:

תורה אור השלם

א) הִתְקוֹשְׁשׁוּ וָקוֹשּׁוּ הַגּוֹי לֹא נִכְסָף: [צפניה ב, א]
ב) בַּמְּאֵרָה אַתֶּם נֵאָרִים וְאֹתִי אַתֶּם קֹבְעִים הַגּוֹי כֻּלּוֹ: [מלאכי ג, ט]
ג) אִם אֶשְׁכָּחֵךְ יְרוּשָׁלָ‍ִם תִּשְׁכַּח יְמִינִי: תִּדְבַּק לְשׁוֹנִי לְחִכִּי אִם לֹא אֶזְכְּרֵכִי אִם לֹא אַעֲלֶה אֶת יְרוּשָׁלַ‍ִם עַל רֹאשׁ שִׂמְחָתִי: [תהלים קלז, ה-ו]
ד) לָשׂוּם לַאֲבֵלֵי צִיּוֹן לָתֵת לָהֶם פְּאֵר תַּחַת אֵפֶר שֶׁמֶן שָׂשׂוֹן תַּחַת אֵבֶל מַעֲטֵה תְהִלָּה תַּחַת רוּחַ כֵּהָה וְקֹרָא לָהֶם אֵילֵי הַצֶּדֶק מַטַּע יְיָ לְהִתְפָּאֵר: [ישעיה סא, ג]
ה) שִׂמְחוּ אֶת יְרוּשָׁלַ‍ִם וְגִילוּ בָהּ כָּל אֹהֲבֶיהָ שִׂישׂוּ אִתָּהּ מָשׂוֹשׂ כָּל הַמִּתְאַבְּלִים עָלֶיהָ: [ישעיה סו, י]

לעזי רש"י

טנפ"ל. פירוש לדע, רקה (רש"י שופטים ד, כב), לד המלח שליד האוזן:

רבינו גרשום

כיון דחזי דמעכבי. להאי אמר ש"מ דלא ניחא להו ומשום יקרא דידי שתקו: איבעיא להו כנס לתוך שלו ולא הוציא. זיזין באותה פעם באותה כניסה מהו שיחזור ויוציא לאחר זמן. מי אמרי' כיון דלא הוציא בתחלה בההיא כניסה ויתרה לבני רה"ר אי לא: ר' יוחנן אמר. לרשותו מוציא בה זיזין כל זמן שירצה. וריש לקיש אמר כנס ולא הוציא לאלתר אינו מוציא שוב: להחזיר כתלים למקומן. כמו שהיה: אבל רה"ר מצר שהחזיקו בו [רבים]. שכבר דשין באותה כניסה: ה"מ. דאסור לקלקלו היכא דליכא רווחא טפי ברה"ר: אין מכיירין. שאין עושין ציור מן הסיד עצמו כמו שעושין בנאין: אין מפייחין. שאין מלבין הבית לאחר שמצויר בזמן הזה מפני איבול בהמ"ק: אין חוזר ובונה אותה. באותו סיד וכיור: איסורא שאני. שאסרו חכמים מפני איבול: אבל אם (כן) עירב בו חול. שלא יהא לבן כל כך: הרי זה טרכסיד. השביחו מפני שאע"פ ששחור במעט נעשה חזק ודבק ביותר: אפשר בפירות אחרים. שלא היו מביאין בכורים אלא משבעת המינין: שתקו. שא"א לחיות בלא מים: במארה אתם נארים. כשאתם גוזרים מארה גזרה ואותי אתם קובעין בהם בהסכמתכם. אי איכא הגוי כולו שיכולין לעמוד בה אין. מקיימת הגזירה ואי לא לא: בת צדעא. א) שלא תזבין צדעא בשוק כדי שלא תיפתור ממנה שיער: כנגד הפתח. כדי שתהא נראה: לשבוע הבן. שעושין לסוף שבעה: שיהיו שוגגין. שיבטלו אותו דין בשוגג ואל יהיו מזידין שאם נגזור גזירה יהיו מבטלין אותה במזיד שלא יהיו יכולין לעמוד בה שלא לישא אשה:

הדרן עלך חזקת הבתים

חשק שלמה על רבינו גרשום

א) אולי צ"ל שלא תעביר לדעת בשוק כדי שתיפול ממנה שער.

ליקוטי רש"י

התקוששו. התלקטו ואספו ועשו קשוט כמו וקושו קש (שמות ה). וקושו. מעשיכם השוו מעשיכם לדעת קונכם ורז"ל דרשו קשוט עצמך ואח"כ קשוט אחרים עשו שניהם לשון היקש אדם המשוה עצמו ומישר דרכו [צפניה ב, א]. מצר שהחזיקו בו רבים אסור לקלקלו. לעשותו להן דרך אסור לקלקלו אע"פ שהוא של יחיד [לעיל כו:]. שהשווהו ותקנוהו להילוך והבעלים ידעו ושתקו אסור לקלקלו דודאי לרבים מחל [רשב"ם לקמן ק.]. לא יסוד אדם את ביתו בסיד. לאחר חורבן משום אבילות של ירושלים. חול או תבן. שלא יהא לבן כל צרכו. טרכסיד. סיד חזק ומתקשה יותר משאם לא עירב בו [שבת פ:]. על ראש שמחתי. את זכרון אבל חורבנה אעלה להזכירו בראש כל שמחתי [תהלים קלז ו]. פאר תחת אפר. שמע מינה במקום תפילין דכתיב בהו (יחזקאל כד) פארך חבוש עליך ואמרינן (ברכות יא.) אלו תפילין ומתרגמינן נמי טוטפתך הוין עלך והיכא מניחין תפילין במקום שמוחו של תינוק רופס [תענית טז.]. הנח להם לישראל. בדבר שהרגילו בו ולא יחזרו בהם. מוטב שיהיו שוגגין ואל יהיו מזידין. לעבור כשידעו ולא יניחו בכך [ביצה ל.].

FOR IT IS STATED:[37] *IF I FORGET YOU, O JERUSALEM, MAY MY RIGHT HAND WITHER! MAY MY TONGUE CLEAVE TO THE ROOF OF MY MOUTH if I do not remember you, if I do not set Jerusalem above my highest joy!*

The Gemara asks:

מַאי: ,,עַל רֹאשׁ שִׂמְחָתִי" – **What is** the meaning of *if I do not set Jerusalem* ***above my highest joy?***

The Gemara asnwers:

אָמַר רַב יִצְחָק – **Rav Yitzchak said:** זֶה אֵפֶר מִקְלֶה שֶׁבְּרֹאשׁ חֲתָנִים – **This** refers to **ashes**[38] **that** are placed **on the heads of bridegrooms** at their weddings as a sign of mourning for the destruction of Jerusalem and the Temple.[39]

A clarification is sought:

אָמַר לֵיהּ רַב פָּפָּא לְאַבַּיֵי – **Rav Pappa said to Abaye:** הֵיכָא מַנַּח לֵהּ – **Where** exactly on the head **does [the bridegroom] place [the ashes]?**

The Gemara answers:

בִּמְקוֹם תְּפִילִּין – Abaye answered: **In the place where the** head **tefillin** are worn, שֶׁנֶּאֱמַר: ,,לָשׂוּם לַאֲבֵלֵי צִיּוֹן לָתֵת לָהֶם פְּאֵר תַּחַת אֵפֶר" – **as it is stated:** ***To appoint for the mourners of Zion, to give them adornment in place of ashes.***[40]

R' Yehoshua's final words:

וְכָל הַמִּתְאַבֵּל עַל יְרוּשָׁלַיִם – AND WHOEVER MOURNS FOR JERUSALEM זוֹכֶה וְרוֹאֶה בְּשִׂמְחָתָהּ – WILL MERIT TO WITNESS ITS reconstruction and the attendant REJOICING, שֶׁנֶּאֱמַר: ,,שִׂמְחוּ אֶת־יְרוּשָׁלַםִ וגו׳" – AS IS STATED: *REJOICE WITH JERUSALEM* ETC.[41]

Another Tanna echoes the sentiments of R' Yehoshua:

תַּנְיָא – **It was taught in a Baraisa:** אָמַר ר׳ יִשְׁמָעֵאל בֶּן אֱלִישָׁע – R' YISHMAEL BEN ELISHA SAID: מִיּוֹם שֶׁחָרַב בֵּית הַמִּקְדָּשׁ – EVER SINCE THE DAY THE HOLY TEMPLE WAS DESTROYED, דִּין הוּא שֶׁנִּגְזוֹר עַל עַצְמֵנוּ – IT WOULD BE PROPER THAT WE DECREE UPON OURSELVES שֶׁלֹּא לֶאֱכוֹל בָּשָׂר וְלֹא לִשְׁתּוֹת יַיִן – NOT TO EAT MEAT AND NOT TO DRINK WINE, as a sign of mourning for the Temple and Jerusalem. אֶלָּא אֵין גּוֹזְרִין גְּזֵרָה עַל הַצִּבּוּר – HOWEVER, WE NEVER IMPOSE A DECREE UPON THE PUBLIC אֶלָּא אִם כֵּן רוֹב צִבּוּר יְכוֹלִין לַעֲמוֹד בָּהּ – UNLESS THE MAJORITY OF THE PUBLIC IS ABLE TO COMPLY WITH [THAT DECREE], and most Jews are not able to abstain from meat and wine. וּמִיּוֹם שֶׁפָּשְׁטָה מַלְכוּת הָרְשָׁעָה שֶׁגּוֹזֶרֶת עָלֵינוּ גְּזֵירוֹת רָעוֹת וְקָשׁוֹת – AND, similarly, EVER SINCE THE DAY THE WICKED KINGDOM (i.e. the Roman Empire) THAT DECREES UPON US EVIL AND HARSH DECREES EXTENDED its dominion over the Jewish people, וּמְבַטֶּלֶת מִמֶּנּוּ תּוֹרָה וּמִצְוֹת – AND DEPRIVES US OF the opportunity to study TORAH AND observe the COMMANDMENTS, וְאֵין מַנַּחַת אוֹתָנוּ לִיכָּנֵס לִשְׁבוּעַ הַבֵּן – AND, furthermore, DO NOT ALLOW US TO ATTEND CIRCUMCISIONS,[42] וְאָמְרֵי לָהּ לִישׁוּעַ הַבֵּן – AND SOME SAY REDEMPTIONS OF THE FIRSTBORN,[43] דִּין הוּא שֶׁנִּגְזוֹר עַל עַצְמֵנוּ – IT WOULD BE PROPER THAT WE DECREE UPON OURSELVES שֶׁלֹּא לִישָּׂא אִשָּׁה וּלְהוֹלִיד בָּנִים – NOT TO TAKE A WIFE AND FATHER CHILDREN, וְנִמְצָא זַרְעוֹ שֶׁל אַבְרָהָם אָבִינוּ כָּלֶה מֵאֵלָיו – AND IT WOULD TRANSPIRE that OUR FOREFATHER ABRAHAM'S SEED, the Jewish people, WOULD EXPIRE ON ITS OWN, instead of being annihilated by the Romans.[44] אֶלָּא הַנַּח לָהֶם לְיִשְׂרָאֵל – HOWEVER, LET THE JEWS continue to marry and father children, since in any event they will not cease to do so, even if we were to prohibit it. מוּטָב שֶׁיִּהְיוּ שׁוֹגְגִין – For IT IS PREFERABLE THAT THEY BE UNINTENTIONAL [VIOLATORS], וְאַל יִהְיוּ מְזִידִין – AND NOT BE DELIBERATE [VIOLATORS].[45]

הדרן עלך חזקת הבתים

WE SHALL RETURN TO YOU, CHEZKAS HABATIM

NOTES

sides of their heads, and to comb their hair in a certain manner. It was this hairstyle that was discontinued as an expression of mourning for the Temple.

37. *Psalms* 137:5-6.

38. Literally: burnt ashes. The adjective, מִקְלֶה, *burnt*, is added to indicate ashes from a fire in a stove, as opposed to the ashes of a burnt red cow (*Rashbam*).

39. Ashes placed on the head, at the highest point of the rejoicing bridegroom's body, is a symbolic fulfillment of [*setting*] *Jerusalem above my highest joy.*

40. *Isaiah* 61:3. The word פְּאֵר, *adornment,* can refer to tefillin (see *Targum* to *Ezekiel* 24:17, where the verse, פְּאֵרְךָ חֲבוֹשׁ עָלֶיךָ, *bind your adornment upon you,* is translated: טוֹטְפָתָךְ יְהֶוְיָן עֲלָךְ, *your tefillin shall be upon you;* see also *Berachos* 11a).

Isaiah prophesied that in the Messianic era tefillin will be worn on the head, where ashes were once placed as a sign of mourning for Zion. It is thus evident that placing ashes where the head tefillin are usually worn constitutes a sign of mourning.

Head tefillin are positioned at the point where the top of an infant's head is soft — i.e. at the fontanel [the membrane-covered gap in an infant's skull] (*Eruvin* 95b; see *Rashi* there).

41. *Isaiah* 66:10, which states in its entirety: *Rejoice with Jerusalem and be glad with her, all who love her; rejoice for joy with her, all who mourn for her.*

42. I.e. the Romans executed not only one who circumcised his child, but also anyone who attended the circumcision ceremony (see *Ben Yehoyada*). [During the reign of the emperor Hadrian, the Romans prohibited circumcision on pain of death; see *Doros HaRishonim* IV, 27.]

The literal translation of לִיכָּנֵס לִשְׁבוּעַ הַבֵּן is: to enter [a house or synagogue where] a circumcision [is being celebrated]. שְׁבוּעַ הַבֵּן literally means "the week of the son," i.e. the circumcision that is performed at the end of seven full days following the birth of the son (*Rashbam*).

Some commentators explain that it was customary to celebrate the entire week following the birth of a child. These celebrations took place at the home of the parents. Hence, according to this understanding, the Gemara means that the Romans did not permit any Jew to enter such a house (see *Margolios HaYam* to *Sanhedrin* 32b).

43. The word יֵשׁוּעַ is rendered by *Targum Onkelos* as פרק, *saving* or *redemption;* see, for example, *Exodus* 14:30. Accordingly, *Rashi* (*Bava Kamma* 80a) and *Aruch* translate יֵשׁוּעַ הַבֵּן as *the redemption of the son* — that is, the ceremony during which the father redeems his firstborn son by giving redemption money to a Kohen, as prescribed in *Exodus* 13:13. The Romans would not permit any Jew to attend this ceremony and its accompanying feast (cf. *Rabbeinu Tam* ibid.).

44. I.e. it would be preferable not to father a son than to have a son and not circumcise him (*Rashbam*).

According to *Tosafos,* R' Yishmael was referring only to persons who already had children and had thereby fulfilled the Biblical obligation to procreate (*Genesis* 1:28). However, see *Iyun Yaakov*.

Ben Yehoyada explains that R' Yishmael did not actually intend for the Jewish people to disappear. Rather, he expected the Roman religious persecution to end one day (as, indeed, it did; see *Doros HaRishonim* IV, 706-12), and then the people could resume their normal lives.

45. The Sages adopted this policy only when they were absolutely certain that the people would not desist from the activity the Sages wished to proscribe (*Tosafos*).

Glossary

Scriptural Index

Glossary

Adar — twelfth month of the Hebrew calendar.

Adar Sheni — lit. the second **Adar.** When it is deemed necessary for a leap year to be designated, an extra month is added. This thirteenth month is placed between **Adar** and **Nissan** and is called *Adar Sheni.*

agav — see **kinyan agav.**

agency — the principle that an agent may act as a proxy of a principal and have his actions legally accepted on behalf of the principal.

Aggadah, aggadata — the homiletical teachings of the Sages and all non-halachic Rabbinic literature found in the Talmud.

ailonis — an adult woman who never developed the physical signs of female maturity; she is therefore assumed to be incapable of bearing children.

akum — idolater.

Altar — the great *Altar,* which stands in the Courtyard of the **Beis HaMikdash.** Certain portions of every offering are burnt on the **Altar.** The blood of most offerings is applied to the walls of the **Altar.**

amah [pl. **amos**] — cubit; a linear measure equaling six **tefachim.** Opinions regarding its modern equivalent range between 18 and 22.9 inches.

am haaretz [pl. **amei haaretz**] — common, ignorant person.

Amora [pl. **Amoraim**] — sage of the **Gemara;** cf. **Tanna.**

amud — one side of the **daf** in the **Gemara.**

Anshei Knesses HaGedolah — see **Men of the Great Assembly.**

aravos — see **four species**.

arusah — a woman who is only betrothed and not yet fully married. See **erusin.**

asham [pl. **ashamos**] — guilt offering, an offering brought to atone for one of several specific sins, as well as a part of certain purification offerings. It is one of the **kodshei kodashim.**

asham gezeilos — **asham** of theft. If a defendant denies, under oath, a monetary claim against him and then admits that he perjured himself, he must pay the debt plus a fifth to the plaintiff and offer an **asham** sacrifice. This **asham** is known as *asham gezeilos.*

asmachta — (a) a conditional commitment made by a party who does not really expect to have to honor it; (b) a verse cited by the **Gemara** not as a Scriptural basis for the law but as an allusion to a Rabbinic law.

Av — fifth month of the Hebrew calendar.

av beis din — chief of the court. This position was second in importance to the **nasi** who served as head of the **Sanhedrin.**

av [pl. **avos**] — see **melachah.**

av [pl. **avos**] **hatumah** — primary source of **tumah,** such as an object or person possessing a degree of **tumah** sufficient to contaminate a person or utensil. Examples include **metzora, neveilah,** et al.

avi avos hatumah — a human corpse, which is the most severe source of **tumah.**

avodah [pl. **avodos**] — the sacrificial service, or any facet of it. There are four critical *avodos* to the sacrificial service. They are **shechitah, kabbalah, holachah** and **zerikah.**

avodah zarah — idol worship, idolatry.

ayin hara — evil eye (jealousy).

Baraisa [pl. **Baraisos**] — the statements of **Tannaim** not included by **Rebbi** in the **Mishnah.** R' Chiya and R' Oshaya, the students of **Rebbi,** researched and reviewed the *Baraisos* and compiled an authoritative collection of them, based on the teachings of **Rebbi.**

bechor — (a) firstborn male child; (b) a firstborn male kosher animal. Such an animal is born with sacrificial sanctity, and must be offered as a *bechor* sacrifice in the **Temple.** Unlike other sacrifices, the *bechor* is automatically sacred from birth even without designation.

bedek habayis — **Temple** treasury.

bedi'avad — after the fact. See **lechatchilah.**

beheimah — domestic species, livestock. In regard to various laws, the Torah distinguishes between two categories of animals: (a) *beheimah:* domestic species; e.g. cattle, sheep, goats; (b) **chayah:** wild species; e.g. deer, antelope.

bein hashemashos — the twilight period preceding night. The legal status of *bein hashemashos* as day or night is uncertain.

beis din — court, Rabbinical court. See also **Sanhedrin.**

beis hamidrash — a **Torah** study hall.

Beis HaMikdash — Holy **Temple** in Jerusalem. The Temple edifice comprised (a) the Antechamber; (b) the **Holy** or **Heichal;** and (c) the **Holy of Holies.**

beis kor — lit. house of a *kor.* Parcel size needed to plant a **kor** of barley seeds. It measures 75,000 square **amos.**

bikkurim — The first-ripening fruits of any of the seven species (wheat, barley, grapes, figs, pomegranates, olives, dates), with which the **Torah** praises **Eretz Yisrael.** They are brought to the **Temple** and given to the **Kohanim.**

binyan av — one of the thirteen principles of Biblical hermeneutics. This principle dictates that whenever a commonality of law or essence is found in two separate areas of **Torah** law, analogies may be drawn from one area to the other, and the laws that apply to one can be applied to the other as well.

Bircas Kohanim — see **Priestly Blessing.**

bris milah — ritual circumcision.

chadash — new crop of any of the **five grains;** *chadash* may not be eaten until the **omer** offering is brought on the second day of **Pesach,** the sixteenth of **Nissan.**

chagigah offering — festival offering. Every adult Jewish male is required to bring a *chagigah* offering on the first day of the festivals of **Pesach, Shavuos** and **Succos.** It is one of the **kodashim kalim,** specifically a type of **shelamim** offering.

chalifin — see **kinyan chalifin.**

chalitzah — procedure [taking off the shoe] by which a **yevamah** can be released from her attachment to her brothers-in-law. See **yibum.**

challah — portion removed from a dough of the **five grains,** given to a **Kohen;** if *challah* is not taken, the dough is **tevel** and may not be eaten. The minimum amount of dough from which *challah* must be separated is the volume-equivalent of 43.2 eggs which is one **issaron.** Nowadays the *challah* is removed and burned. This is one of the three special mitzvos for women.

chametz — leaven. *Chametz* is forbidden on **Pesach.**

Chanukah — Festival of Lights. The holiday that commemorates the Maccabean victory over the Greeks. It begins on the 25th of **Kislev** and lasts for eight days.

chatas [pl. **chataos**] — sin offering; an offering generally brought in atonement for the inadvertent transgression of a **kares**-bearing sin. A **chatas** is also brought as one of various purification offerings. It is one of the **kodshei kodashim.**

chatzitzah — lit. an interposition. Foreign matter attached or adhering to the person or object to be immersed in the **mikveh.** The foreign matter does not allow the water to come into contact with the whole of their surface; this invalidates the **tevilah.**

chaver [pl. **chaverim**] — a) one who observes the laws of ritual purity even regarding non-consecrated foodstuffs; b) Torah scholar, scrupulous in his observance of mitzvos. Regarding tithes and other matters, he is accorded a special degree of trustworthiness.

chayah — see **beheimah.**

chazakah — (a) legal presumption that conditions remain unchanged unless proven otherwise; (b) one of the methods of acquiring real estate by performing an act of improving the property, such as enclosing it with a fence or plowing it in preparation for planting; c) "established rights;" uncontested usage of another's property establishes the right to such usage; since the owner registered no protest, acquiescence is assumed; d) uncontested holding of real property for three years as a basis for claiming acquisition of title from the prior owner.

cheilev — animal fats forbidden for human consumption. See **shuman.**

Cheshvan — eighth month of the Hebrew calendar.

Chol HaMoed — the Intermediate Days of the Festivals of **Pesach** and **Succos,** which enjoy a quasi-**Yom Tov** status.

chullin — any substance that is not sanctified. See **kodesh.**

chuppah — (a) the bridal canopy; (b) a procedure for effecting **nisuin,** the final stage of marriage.

Cuthites — a non-Jewish tribe brought by the Assyrians to settle the part of **Eretz Yisrael** left vacant by the exile of the Ten Tribes; their subsequent conversion to Judaism was considered questionable and their observance of many laws was lax.

daf — folio (two sides) in the Gemara.

days of counting — see **metzora.**

decapitated cow — If a person is found murdered between two cities and his murderer is not known, the elders of the **Sanhedrin** must measure the distance to the surrounding cities to determine the city closest to the corpse. The elders of that city must then bring a female calf and decapitate it in an untilled valley, in accordance with the procedure outlined in *Deuteronomy* 21:1-9.

demai — lit. what is this; produce of **Eretz Yisrael** that is obtained from an unlearned person. By Rabbinic enactment it must be tithed since it is uncertain whether it was tithed.

dinar — a coin. The silver content of the coin was equivalent to ninety-six grains of barley. It was worth 1/25 the value of a *gold dinar.*

double payment — a punative fine. A thief must both return the stolen property and pay the owner a fine equal to the value of the stolen object.

eglah arufah — see **decapitated cow.**

Elul — sixth month of the Hebrew calendar.

emurin — the portions of an animal offering burnt on the **Altar.**

encumbered property — land owned by a debtor at the time he incurred a debt, but which he later sold or gave to a third party. Such land is encumbered by the debt; the creditor can collect it from the current owner to satisfy the debt, if the debtor defaults.

ephah [pl. **ephos**] — a measure of volume equal to three **se'ah.**

Eretz Yisrael — Land of Israel.

erev Pesach — the day before the Passover holiday. It is the day on which the **pesach offering** is sacrificed to be eaten that night.

erusin — betrothal, the first stage of marriage. This is effected by the man giving the woman an object of value, in the presence of witnesses, to betroth her. At this point the couple is not yet permitted to have conjugal relations, but is nonetheless considered legally married in most respects.

eruv — popular contraction of **eruvei tavshilin, eruvei techumin** or **eruvei chatzeiros.**

eruvei chatzeiros — a legal device which merges several separate ownerships **(reshus hayachid)** into a single joint ownership. This procedure allows us to view all the houses opening into the courtyard as the property of a single consortium (composed of all the residents of the courtyard). This permits all the contributing residents of the *chatzeir* to carry items during the Sabbath from the houses into the *chatzeir* and from one house to another.

eruvei tavshilin — the prepared food set aside prior to a **Yom Tov** that falls on Friday to serve as token food for the Sabbath that follows. Once this token food has been set aside, the person is allowed to complete his preparations for Sabbath on **Yom Tov.** Such preparation is generally forbidden.

eruvei techumin — a legal device that allows a person to shift his Sabbath residence from which the 2,000-**amah techum** is measured. This is accomplished by placing a specific amount of food at the desired location before the start of the Sabbath. The place where the food has been placed is then viewed as his Sabbath residence, and his **techum**-limit is measured from there.

ervah [pl. **arayos**] — sexual relationships forbidden under penalty of **kares** or death, as enumerated in *Leviticus* ch. 18.

esrog — see **four species**.

fingerbreadth — There are three definitions of fingerbreadth: (a) thumb (1/4 **tefach**); (b) index finger (1/5 **tefach**); (c) little finger (1/6 **tefach**).

five grains — wheat, barley, oats, spelt and rye.

forbidden labors of the Sabbath — see **avos melachah.**

four species — (a) **aravos** — willow branches; (b) **esrog** — citron; (c) **hadasim** — myrtle branches; (d) **lulav** — palm branch; we are commanded to hold these *four species* in hand on the Festival of **Succos.**

Gan Eden — Garden of Eden, place where souls receive reward after death.

Gaon [pl. **Geonim**] — (a) title accorded the heads of the academies in Sura and Pumbedisa, the two Babylonian seats of Jewish learning, from the late 6th to mid-11th centuries C.E; they served as the link in the chain of Torah tradition that joined the **Rishonim** to the **Amoraim;** (b) later used to describe any brilliant Torah scholar.

Gehinnom — a metaphysical realm where souls are punished.

Gemara — portion of the Talmud which discusses the **Mishnah;** also, loosely, a synonym for the Talmud as a whole.

gematria — the numeric valuation of the Hebrew alphabet.

get [pl. **gittin**] — (a) bill of divorce; the document that effects the dissolution of a marriage when it is placed in the wife's possession; (b) any document.

gezeirah shavah — one of the thirteen principles of Biblical hermeneuticals. If a similar word or phrase occurs in two otherwise unrelated passages in the Torah, the principle of *gezeirah shavah* teaches that these passages are linked to one another, and the laws of one passage are applied to the other. Only those words which are designated by the **Oral Sinaitic Law** for this purpose may serve as a basis for a *gezeirah shavah.*

gid hanasheh — sciatic nerve. This portion of an animal is prohibited even if the animal has undergone valid ritual slaughter.

gifts to the poor — these include **leket, shich'chah, pe'ah, peret; Maaser ani** is also a *gift to the poor.*

Golden Altar — see **Inner Altar**.

Great Court — see **Sanhedrin**.

gud or agud — lit. you set or I will set; a formula for the disssolution of a partnership. A partner proposes *"gud or agud,"* meaning "either you set a price for my share and buy it or I will set a price for your share and buy it."

g'vil — (a) rough unplaned stones — rough edged stones (*g'vil*).

(b) parchment prepared using the entire thickness of the hide with just the hair removed.

hadas – see **four species.**

hagbahah – lifting. One of the methods of acquisition, used for movable property.

halachah [pl. **halachos**] – (a) a Torah law; (b) [cap.] the body of Torah law; (c) in cases of dispute, the position accepted as definitive by the later authorities and followed in practice; (d) a **Halachah LeMoshe MiSinai.**

Halachah LeMoshe MiSinai – laws taught orally to Moses at Sinai, which cannot be derived from the Written Torah.

Hashem – lit. the Name; an expression used to refer to God without pronouncing His Ineffable Name.

Havdalah – lit. distinction. The blessing recited at the conclusion of the Sabbath.

hazamah – the process by which witnesses are proven false by testimony that places them elsewhere at the time of the alleged incident. Such witnesses are punished with the consequences their testimony would have inflicted upon their intended victim.

Hebrew maidservant – Jewish girl between the age of six and twelve sold by her father into servitude. See **yiud.**

Hebrew servant – a Jewish man sold as an indentured servant, generally for a period of six years, for reasons of poverty or because he was convicted of stealing and lacks the funds to repay his theft.

hechsher l'tumah – rendering a food susceptible to **tumah** contamination by contact with one of seven liquids – water, dew, milk, bee honey, oil, wine or blood.

hefker – ownerless

Heichal – See **Beis HaMikdash.**

hekdesh – (a) items consecrated to the **Temple** treasury or as offerings; (b) the state of consecration; (c) the **Temple** treasury.

hekeish – Scriptural analogy. Two subjects that are juxtaposed are compared to each other in the manner of a **gezeirah shavah.** This rule of exegesis is termed *hekeish.*

henpeik – statement of certification, written onto a document by **beis din,** validating the authenticity of the signatures appearing in the document.

hesess – a special oath imposed by the post-Mishnaic Rabbis on one who totally denies a monetary claim. It is imposed on the assumption that a plaintiff would not make a totally frivolous claim.

holachah – one of the four essential blood **avodos.** It involves carrying the blood of the offering to the **Altar.**

Holy – anterior chamber of the Temple edifice containing the **Shulchan, Inner Altar** and **Menorah.**

Holy Ark – the Ark containing the Tablets of the Ten Commandments and the Torah Scroll written by Moses; it stood in the **Holy of Holies.**

Holy of Holies – interior chamber of the Temple edifice. During most of the First Temple era, it contained the **Holy Ark;** later it was empty of any utensil. Even the **Kohen Gadol** is prohibited from entering there except on **Yom Kippur.**

Hoshana Rabbah – the seventh day of **Succos.** It is the custom to take a willow branch in hand and beat it against the ground on this day.

Inner Altar – the gold-plated Altar which stood in the **Sanctuary.** It was used for the daily incense service and for the blood applications of inner **chataos.**

ir ha'nidachas – the city led astray (to idol worship). If at least a majority of the inhabitants of a city is seduced by proselytizers into committing idolatry, the entire population is executed by **beis din** through the method of sword, and the city and property within it are burned.

Israelites' Courtyard – an area in the Temple Courtyard, extending eleven **amah** from the eastern Courtyard wall inward into the Courtyard, and abutted on its west side by the **Kohanim's Courtyard.** It reached across the entire width of the Courtyard from north to south.

issaron – a dry measure equal to one-tenth of an **ephah** or approximately (depending on the conversion factor) eleven or twenty-one cups.

Iyar – second month of the Hebrew calendar.

Jubilee – see **Yovel.**

kabbalah – (a) term used throughout the Talmud to refer to the Books of the Prophets; (b) receiving the blood of a sacrificial animal that is slaughtered; one of the four blood **avodos.**

kablan guarantor – a guarantor who personally receives the loan from the lender and conveys it to the borrower. He is as responsible to the lender as is the borrower.

kallah – a public lecture given on the Sabbath preceding each of the **pilgrimage** festivals.

kal vachomer – lit. light and heavy, or lenient and stringent; an *a fortiori* argument. One of the thirteen principles of Biblical hermeneutics. It involves the following reasoning: If a particular stringency applies in a usually lenient case, it must certainly apply in a more serious case; the converse of this argument is also a *kal vachomer.*

kares – excision. Divinely imposed premature death decreed by the Torah for certain classes of transgression.

karpaf – large enclosure designated for non-residential use.

kav [pl. **kabim]** – a (Talmudic) measure equal to four **luggin.**

Kehunah – priesthood; the state of being a **Kohen.**

keifel – see **double payment.**

kemitzah – the first of the four essential services of a **minchah** offering, in which the **Kohen,** using the three middle fingers of his right hand, scoops out flour from the **minchah** to burn on the Altar.

kesubah – (a) marriage contract; the legal commitments of a husband to his wife upon their marriage, the foremost feature of which is the payment awarded her in the event of their divorce or his death; (b) document in which this agreement is recorded.

Kesuvim – Holy Writings – 11 books – *Psalms, Proverbs, Job, Song of Songs, Ruth, Lamentations, Ecclesiastes, Esther, Daniel, Ezra-Nehemiah, Chronicles.*

kezayis – an olive's volume [lit. as an olive]. Minimum amount of food whose consumption is legally considered "eating."

kiddush – the benediction recited over wine before the evening and morning meals on the **Sabbath** and **Yom Tov.**

kiddushin [betrothal] – Jewish marriage consists of two stages – **erusin** and **nisuin.** *Kiddushin* is the procedure which establishes the first stage of marriage **[erusin].**

kilayim – various forbidden mixtures, including: **shaatnez** (cloth made from a blend of wool and linen); cross-breeding of animals; cross-breeding (or side-by-side planting) of certain food crops; working with different species of animals yoked together; and mixtures of the vineyard.

kilei hakerem – forbidden mixtures of the vineyard; see **kilayim.**

kinyan [pl. **kinyanim]** – formal act of acquisition. An action that causes an agreement or exchange to be legally binding.

kinyan agav – lit. acquisition by dint of; the term for the acquisition of movable property by means of the acquisition of land. The **kinyan** used for the land serves for the movable property.

kinyan chalifin – lit. acquisition by exchange. (a) Even exchange: an exchange of two items of comparable value, in which each item serves as payment for the other. The acquisition of any of the items automatically effects the acquisition of the other. (b) Uneven exchange: An item of relatively negligible value is given in order to effect the acquisition of the item for sale. A handkerchief or the like is traditionally used.

kinyan chatzeir — the acquisition of movable property by virtue of it being in the premises of the person acquiring it.

kinyan chazakah — see **chazakah** (b).

Kislev — ninth month of the Hebrew calendar.

kodashim kalim — offerings of lesser holiness (one of the two classifications of sacrifical offerings). They include the **todah, shelamim, bechor, maaser** and **pesach offerings.** This category of offerings are not subject to the stringencies applied to **kodshei kodashim.**

kodesh — (a) any consecrated object; (b) the anterior chamber of the **Temple** — the **Holy;** (c) portions of sacrificial offerings.

kodshei kodashim — most-holy offerings — one of the two classifications of sacrificial offerings. They include the **chatas, olah, asham** and communal **shelamim.** These are subject to greater stringencies than **kodashim kalim** and may be eaten in the **Temple Courtyard** only by the **Kohanim** on the day they are offered and the following night.

Kohanim's Courtyard — eleven-**amah**-wide area in the Courtyard of the **Beis HaMikdash** abutting the **Israelites' Courtyard** on its east side, and the **Altar** on its west side. It reached across the entire width of the Courtyard from north to south.

Kohen [pl. **Kohanim**] — member of the priestly family descended in the male line from Aaron. The *Kohen* is accorded the special priestly duties and privileges associated with the **Temple** service and is bound by special laws of sanctity.

Kohen Gadol — High Priest.

kol d'alim g'var — lit. let he who is stronger prevail. In a case where neither litigant advances conclusive proof to support his claim and neither is in possession of the disputed property, the court (in certain cases and when certain criteria exist) withdraws and allows the stronger party to take possession.

kometz — see **kemitzah.**

korah — crossbeam.

korban — a sacrificial offering brought in the **Beis HaMikdash.**

kor — large dry measure; a measure of volume consisting of thirty **se'ah.**

kri u'ksiv — a word in Scripture written one way but read differently by special directive to Moses at Sinai.

lashes — see **malkus** and **makkas mardus.**

lavud — a **Halachah Le'Moshe MiSinai** that allows a gap of less than three **tefachim** (as between two sections of a wall) to be viewed as if it were actually closed.

leaning — see **semichah.**

lechatchilah — (a) before the fact; (b) performance of a mitzvah or procedure in the proper manner.

lechem hapanim — shewbread, see **Shulchan**.

leket — gleanings. One or two stalks of grain that fall from the sickle or the reaper's hand when he gathers the harvest. The Torah grants these to the poor. See **shichchah, pe'ah.**

lessach — one half of a **kor.** It is one-sixtieth the size of a **beis kor.**

Levi [pl. **Leviim**] — Male descendant of the tribe of *Levi* in the male line, who is sanctified for auxiliary services in the **Beis HaMikdash.** The *Leviim* were the recipients of **maaser rishon.**

log [pl. **luggin**] — a liquid measure equal to the volume of six eggs.

lulav — see **four species**.

ma'ah — the smallest silver unit in Talmudic coinage. Thirty-two copper **perutahs** equal one *ma'ahs* and six *ma'ah* equal a silver **dinar.**

Maariv — the evening prayer service.

maaser [pl. **maaseros**] — tithe; it is a Biblical obligation to give two tithes, each known as *maaser,* from the produce of the Land of Israel. The first tithe (**maaser rishon**) is given to a **Levi.** The second tithe (**maaser sheini**) is taken to Jerusalem and eaten there or else is redeemed with coins which are then taken to Jerusalem for the purchase of food to be eaten there. In the third and sixth years of the **shemittah** cycle, the *maaser sheini* obligation is replaced with **maaser ani,** the tithe for the poor.

maaser ani — see **maaser.**

maaser beheimah — the animal tithe. The newborn kosher animals (specifically sheep, goats) born to one's herds and flocks are gathered into a pen and made to pass through an opening one at a time. Every tenth animal is designated as *maaser*. It is brought as an offering in the Temple and is eaten by the owner.

maaser rishon — see **maaser.**

maaser sheini — see **maaser.**

mah matzinu — a **binyan av** from one verse. Just as one particular law possesses aspect A and aspect B, so any other law that possesses aspect A should also possess aspect B.

makkas mardus — lashes for rebelliousness. This is the term used for Rabbinically authorized lashes.

malkus — the thirty-nine lashes imposed by the court for violations of Biblical prohibitions.

mamzer [pl. **mamzerim**] [f. **mamzeress**] — (a) offspring of most illicit relationships punishable by **kares** or capital punishment; (b) offspring of a *mamzer* or *mamzeress.*

maneh — (a) equivalent to 100 **zuz** or ***dinar*;** (b) a measure of weight, equal to 17 ounces.

Marcheshvan — see **Cheshvan.**

matanos [or matnos kehunah] — lit. gifts. The Torah commands that we give the right forceps, jaws and maw of an ox, sheep or goat that are slaughtered (for non-sacrifical purposes) to the **Kohen.** These are referred to as the "gifts."

matzah — unleavened bread; any loaf made from dough that has not been allowed to ferment or rise. One is Biblically obligated to eat **matzah** on the night of the 15th of Nissan.

mavoi — alley; specifically an alley into which courtyards open. See **shitufei mevo'os.**

mazal — fortune.

mechitzah — a division or partition.

mei chatas — springwater consecrated by the addition of ashes of a **parah adumah.** This was used to purify individuals or objects of **tumas meis.**

me'ilah — unlawfully benefiting from **Temple** property or removing such property from the **Temple** ownership.

melachah [pl. **melachos**] — labor; specifically, one of the 39 labor categories whose performance is forbidden by the Torah on the Sabbath and **Yom Tov.**

melikah — the unique manner in which bird offerings were slaughtered. The **Kohen** pierces the back of a bird's neck with his right thumbnail and cuts through the neck. Only birds for sacrificial purposes may be slaughtered by **melikah**. See **shechitah.**

melog — a married woman's property in which she retains ownership of the property itself, but her husband enjoys the right of usufruct, i.e. he owns the yield of that property.

menachos — see **minchah.**

Men of the Great Assembly — a group of 120 sages active at the end of the Babylonian exile and during the early years of the Second Temple. They were responsible for the formulation of our prayers and many other enactments.

Menorah — the seven-branched gold candelabrum which stood in the **Holy.**

meshichah — pulling, or otherwise causing an object to move. One of the methods of acquisition used for movable property.

mesirah — handing over; transferring the animal to a buyer by handing him its reins or mane; a means of acquisition used for articles too heavy to be acquired via **meshichah** or **hagbahah.**

metzora — A **metzora** is a person who has contacted **tzaraas** (erroneously described as leprosy), an affliction mentioned in *Leviticus* (Ch. 13,14). **Tzaraas** manifests itself (on people) as white or light-colored spots on the body. A **Kohen** must examine any such spots to determine if they are indeed **tzaraas;** if he so determines, the **metzora** is called a **muchlat** — confirmed — and is rendered **tamei**. The purification of a **metzora** whose spots have receded (certain guidelines exist — see *Leviticus* ch. 13) consists of several steps. First, the **Kohen** performs an act of purification with two birds (*Leviticus* 14:1-8). This ritual is known as **taharas hatzipporim,** and is followed by a seven-day waiting period, during which the **metzora** is still encumbered by certain restrictions. This is the period called **"days of counting."** After these days pass, a second act of purification, involving various rituals and sacrifices (see *Leviticus* 14:10-32), is performed, following which the status of *metzora* is completely removed.

mezuzah [pl. **mezuzos**] — a small scroll, containing the passages of *Deuteronomy* 6:4-9 and 11:13-21, that is affixed to the right doorpost.

migo — literally: since; a rule of procedure. If one makes a claim that on its own merits, the court would reject, it nonetheless will be accepted "since" had he wished to tell an untruth he would have chosen a claim that certainly is acceptable to the court.

mikveh — ritualarium; a body of standing water containing at least forty **se'ah.** It is used to purify (by immersion) people and utensils of their **tumah**-contamination. A **mikveh** consists of waters naturally collected,without direct human intervention. Water drawn in a vessel is not valid for a *mikveh.*

minchah — (a) [cap.] the afternoon prayer service; (b) [pl.**menachos**] a flour offering, generally consisting of fine wheat flour, oil and frankincense, part of which is burnt on the **Altar.** See **kemitzah.**

minyan — quorum of ten adult Jewish males necessary for the communal prayer service and other matters.

mishmar [pl. **mishmaros**] — lit. watch; one of the twenty-four watches of **Kohanim** and **Leviim** who served in the Temple for a week at a time on a rotating basis.

Mishnah [pl. **Mishnahs**] — (a) the organized teachings of the **Tannaim** compiled by **R' Yehudah HaNasi;** (b) a paragraph of that work.

mi'un — By Rabbinic enactment, an underaged orphan girl may be given in marriage by her mother or brothers. She may annul the marriage anytime before reaching majority by declaring, before a **beis din** of three judges, her unwillingness to continue in the marriage. This declaration and process is called *mi'un.*

mixtures of the vineyard — see **kilayim.**

mohel — one who performs ritual circumcisions.

monetary law — law dealing with financial matters rather than matters of ritual prohibition.

movables, movable property — property that is transportable; in contrast to real estate.

muad — lit. warned one. A bull that gores three times and whose owner was duly warned after each incident to take precautions is considered a *muad* bull. The owner must pay full damages for the fourth and all subsequent incidents. See **tam**.

muchlat — see **metzora.**

muchzak — one who has the assumed legal possession of an object.

muktzeh — lit. set aside. (a) a class of objects which, in the normal course of events, do not stand to be used on the Sabbath or **Yom Tov.** The Rabbis prohibited moving such objects on the Sabbath or **Yom Tov;** (b) an animal set aside to be sacrificed for idolatry.

mussaf — (a) additional sacrifices offered on the Sabbath, Rosh Chodesh, or **Yom Tov;** (b) [cap] the prayer service which is recited in lieu of these sacrifices.

naarah — a girl at least 12 years old who has sprouted at least two pubic hairs. This marks her coming of age as an adult.

naarus — the state of being a **naarah.**

nasi — the prince. He serves as the head of the **Sanhedrin** and de facto as the spiritual leader of the people.

nazir [f. **nezirah**] — a person who takes the vow of **nezirus,** which prohibits him to drink wine, eat grapes, cut his hair or contaminate himself with the **tumah** of a corpse.

negaim — **tzaraas** spots.

nesachim — a libation, generally of wine, which is poured upon the **Altar.**

nesech wine — wine poured as a libation in idolatrous service; a Jew is prohibited to drink or derive any benefit from it. The Rabbis added to this a decree regarding wine touched or poured by a gentile, even not as a libation to an idol.

nesin [pl. **nesinim**] — descendant of the Gibeonites, who deceptively concluded a peace treaty with Joshua (*Joshua* 9:3-27) and converted to Judaism.

neveilah — the carcass of an animal that was not slaughtered according to procedure prescribed by the Torah. A *neveilah* may not be eaten. It is an **av hatumah.** The term **neveilah** is sometimes used generically for forbidden food.

Neviim — Prophets — the following books: *Joshua, Judges, Samuel, Kings, Jeremiah, Ezekiel, Isaiah, The Twelve Prophets.*

nezirus — the state of being a **nazir.**

niddah — a woman who has menstruated but has not yet completed her purification process, which concludes with immersion in a **mikveh.**

Nissan — first month of the Hebrew calander.

nisuin — second stage of marriage. It is effected by a procedure called **chuppah.** See **kiddushin.**

Noahide laws — the seven commandments given to Noah and his sons, which are binding upon all gentiles. These laws include the obligation to have a body of civil law, and the prohibitions against idolatry, immorality, bloodshed, blasphemy, stealing and robbing, and eating limbs from a live animal.

nossar — part of a **korban** left over after the time to eat it has passed.

oath of modeh b'miktzas — A Biblical oath administered to one who partially admits to a monetary claim.

olah [pl. **olos**] — burnt or elevation offering; an offering which is consumed in its entirety by the **Altar** fire. It is one of the **kodshei kodashim.**

omer — an obligatory **minchah** offering brought on the sixteenth of **Nissan.** It was forbidden to eat from the new grain crop (**chadash**) before this offering was brought.

onein [f. **onenes**] — a person on the day of the death of a close relative. Special laws of bereavement apply to an *onein.*

Oral Sinaitic Law — **Halachah LeMoshe MiSinai.**

orlah — fruit that grows on a tree during its first three years. The Torah prohibits any benefit from such fruit.

Outer Altar — the great **Altar** built of stone which stands in the Courtyard of the **Beis HaMikdash,** to which the blood of most offerings is applied, and on which the offerings are burned.

paid custodian — a **shomer** who receives remuneration for his services. He is obligated to make restitution even in the event of theft or loss.

parah adumah — lit. red cow. The ashes of the *parah adumah* are mixed with spring water. The resulting mixture is known as

mei chatas and is used in the purification process of people or objects who have contracted **tumah** from a human corpse.

paroches — curtain; specifically, the curtain which divided the **Holy** from the **Holy of Holies.**

parsah [pl. **parsaos**] — measure of length equal to eight thousand **amos.**

peace offering — see **shelamim.**

pe'ah — the portion of the crop, generally the corner of the field, that must be left unreaped as a gift to the poor. See *Leviticus* 19:9, 23:22. See **shichchah, leket, peret.**

peret — individual grapes which fell during harvesting. The Torah grants these to the poor.

perutah — smallest coin used in Talmudic times. In most cases its value is the minimum that is legally significant.

Pesach — Passover. The **Yom Tov** that celebrates the Exodus of the Jewish nation from Egypt.

pesach offering — sacrifice offered on the afternoon of the 14th day of **Nissan** to be eaten after nightfall. It is one of the **kodashim kalim.**

piggul — an offering which was made unfit by means of incorrect intent during one of the four **avodos.** The intention was present to eat of it or place it on the **Altar** after the allotted time.

pikadon — an object deposited with a custodian for safekeeping.

pilgrimage — a title designated for the holidays of **Pesach, Shavuos** and **Succos,** when all Jewish males were obligated to appear at the **Beis HaMikdash** in Jerusalem.

positive commandment — a Torah commandment expressed as a requirement *to do.*

poskim — authoritative decisors of Torah law.

Priestly Blessing — the blessing the **Kohanim** are obligated to confer upon the congregation. It contains the Scriptural verses designated for the blessing in the Torah (*Numbers* 6:24-26), and is recited aloud by the **Kohanim,** toward the conclusion of the **Shemoneh Esrei,** while they keep their hands raised.

prohibition — a negative commandment, which the Torah expresses as a command *not to do.*

prohibitory law — refers to the category of Torah law which deals with questions of permissible or forbidden status, as opposed to questions of **monetary law.**

prosbul — The Torah requires all loans to be canceled by **shemittah.** The Rabbis enacted a law allowing for loans to be collected after the Sabbatical year through a process whereby the lender authorizes the court to collect all his debts. The document which authorizes the court to assume responsibility for the collection of those debts is called a *prosbul.*

pundyon — a coin.

purification waters — See **mei chatas.**

R' — Rabbi; specifically a **Tanna,** or **Amora** of **Eretz Yisrael.**

Rebbi — R' Yehudah HaNasi; prince or president of the Supreme **Sanhedrin.** He was the redactor of the **Mishnah.**

red cow — see **parah adumah.**

reshus harabim — lit. public domain: any unroofed, commonly used street, public area or highway at least sixteen **amos** wide and open at both ends. According to some, it must be used by at least 600,000 people.

reshus hayachid — lit. private domain: any area measuring at least four **tefachim** by four **tefachim** and enclosed by partitions at least ten **tefachim** high. According to most opinions, it needs to be enclosed only on three sides to qualify as a *reshus hayachid*. Private ownership is not a prerequisite.

Rishon [pl. **Rishonim**] — a Torah authority of the period following the **Geonim** (approx. 1000-1500 C.E.).

rishon l'tumah — a **tamei** of the first degree. He can transmit **tumah** to food and drink but not to other people or utensils.

Rosh Chodesh — (a) festival celebrating the new month; (b) the first of the month.

Rosh Hashanah — the **Yom Tov** which celebrates the new year. It falls on the first and second days of **Tishrei.**

Sadducees — heretical sect active during the Second Temple era named after Tzaddok, a disciple of Antigonas of Socho. They denied the validity of the Oral Law and refused to accept the Sages' interpretation of the Torah.

Sages — (a) the collective body of Torah authorities in the Mishnaic era; (b) the anonymous majority opinion in a **Mishnah** or **Baraisa;** (c) [lower case] Torah scholar and authority.

Sanctuary — a term applied to the **Temple** edifice, consisting of the **Holy** and the **Holy of Holies.**

Sanhedrin — (a) the High Court of Israel; the Supreme Court consisting of seventy-one judges whose decisions on questions of Torah law are definitive and binding on all courts; (b) a lesser High Court of twenty-three judges authorized to inflict capital and corporal punishment.

saris — (a) a male who is incapable of maturing sexually; (b) a person who was castrated.

se'ah — a Mishnaic measure of volume; six **kav.**

Seder [pl. **Sedarim**] — lit. order. (a) The Mishnah is divided into six *sedarim*: *Zeraim* (Plants), *Moed* (Festivals), *Nashim* (Women), *Nezikim* (Damages), *Kodashim* (Sacred Things) and *Tohoros* (Ritual Purities); (b) [lower case] festive meal on **Pesach.**

sela — a silver coin having the weight of 384 barleycorns. This is the equivalent of four **dinars.**

semichah — (a) Rabbinical ordination empowering one to serve as a judge; (b) a rite performed with almost all personal sacrificial offerings. The owner of the offering places both his hands on the animal's head and presses down with all his might. In the case of a **chatas,** or an **asham,** he makes his confession during *semichah*. In the case of a **shelamim** or **todah** offering, he praises and thanks God.

Seventeenth of Tammuz — a fast day.

shaatnez — see **kilayim.**

Shabbos — (a) the Sabbath; (b) the Talmudic tractate that deals with the laws of the Sabbath.

Shacharis — the morning prayer service.

Shavuos — Pentecost; the festival that celebrates the giving of the Torah to the Jewish nation on Mount Sinai.

Shechinah — Divine Presence.

shechitah — (a) ritual slaughter; the method prescribed by the Torah for killing a kosher animal for consumption; it consists of cutting through most of the esophagus and windpipe from the front of the neck with a specially sharpened knife that is free of nicks; (b) one of the four essential blood **avodos.**

shekel — Scriptural coin equivalent to the Aramaic **sela** or four **dinars.** In Mishnaic terminology, the Scriptural half-*shekel* is called a **shekel,** and the Scriptural **shekel** is called by its Aramaic name, **sela.**

shelamim — peace offering; generally brought by an individual on a voluntary basis. Part is burnt on the **Altar,** part is eaten by a **Kohen** (and the members of his household) and part is eaten by the owner. It is one of the **kodashim kalim.**

shelichus — see **agency.**

Shemini Atzeres — the eighth and concluding day of the **Succos** celebration. In many respects, it is a **Yom Tov** in its own right.

shemittah — the Sabbatical year, occurring every seventh year, during which the land of **Eretz Yisrael** may not be cultivated. See also **prosbul.**

Shemoneh Esrei — the silent, standing prayer, which is one of the main features of the daily prayer services.

sheretz [pl. **sheratzim**] – one of eight rodents or reptiles, listed by the Torah, whose carcasses transmit **tumah.**

Shevat – eleventh month of the Hebrew calendar.

sheviis – see **shemittah.**

shichchah – forgotten sheaves. The Torah grants these to the poor. See **leket, pe'ah.**

shituf – see **shitufei mevo'os.**

shitufei mevo'os – incorporation of the alleys; a provision similar to **eruvei chatzeiros,** instituted to permit carrying from a courtyard into an alley on the Sabbath. It merges the different courtyards in a common ownership of a **mavoi.**

shliach tzibur – lit. messenger of the congregation. The individual leading the prayer service.

shofar – trumpet formed from the horn of a ram or certain other animals. It is a Biblical obligation to hear the blowing of a *shofar* on **Rosh Hashanah.**

shomer – One who has assumed custodial responsibility for another's property.

shtar [pl. **shtaros**] – legal document.

Shulchan – literally, table; the golden Table for the **lechem hapanim,** located in the **Holy.**

shuman – those animal fats that are permitted for consumption. See **cheilev.**

Sifra – lit. the book; the primary collection of Tannaic exegesis, mainly halachic in nature, on the Book of *Leviticus.* It is also known as *Toras Kohanim.*

Sifri (or **Sifrei**) – lit. the books; the counterpart of the **Sifra,** it expounds on the Books of *Numbers* and *Deuteronomy.*

Sivan – third month of the Hebrew calendar.

sotah – an adulteress or a woman whose behavior has made her suspect of adultery. The Torah prescribes, under specific circumstances, that her guilt or innocence be established by having her drink specially prepared water. (See **Numbers** ch. 5.)

sprinkling – see **haza'ah.**

succah – (a) the temporary dwelling in which one must live during the festival of **Succos;** (b) [cap.] the Talmudic tractate that deals with the laws that pertain to the festival of **Succos.**

Succos – one of the three **pilgrimage festivals,** during which one must dwell in a **succah.**

Tabernacle – a portable **Sanctuary** for the sacrificial service during the forty years of national wandering in the Wilderness and the first fourteen years after entry into Eretz Yisrael.

taharah – a halachically defined state of ritual purity; the absence of **tumah**-contamination.

taharas hatzipporim – see **metzora.**

tahor – person or object in a state of **taharah.**

tam – lit. ordinary; a bull the first three times it gores another animal. See **muad.**

tamei – person or object that has been contaminated by **tumah.**

tamid – communal **olah,** offered twice daily.

Tammuz – fourth month of the Hebrew calendar.

Tanna [pl. **Tannaim**] – Sage of the Mishnaic period whose view is recorded in a **Mishnah** or **Baraisa.**

Tanna Kamma – the anonymous first opinion of a **Mishnah** or **Baraisa.**

Targum – lit. translation; the Aramaic interpretive translation of Scripture.

techias hameisim – the future resurrection of the dead.

techum [pl. **techumim**] – Sabbath boundary; the distance of 2,000 **amos** from a person's place of residence which he is permitted to travel on the Sabbath or **Yom Tov.**

tefach [pl. **tefachim**] – handbreadth; a measure of length equal to the width of four thumbs.

tefillah – (a) prayer, specifically the daily prayer services and the additions added on the Sabbath and Festivals; (b) in Talmudic usage, **tefillah** invariably refers to **Shemoneh Esrei.**

tefillin – phylacteries. Two black leather casings, each of which contains Torah passages written on parchment. It is a mitzvah for adult males to wear one on the head and one on the arm.

Temple – See **Beis HaMikdash.**

Temple Mount – the site of the Holy **Temple.** See **Beis HaMikdash.**

terumah [pl. **terumos**] – the first portion of the crop separated and given to a **Kohen,** usually between 1/40 and 1/60 of the total crop. Terumah may not be eaten by a non-**Kohen,** or by a **Kohen** in a state of **tumah.** It is separated prior to **maaser.**

terumas maaser – the tithe portion separated by the **Levi** from **maaser rishon** and given to a **Kohen.**

tevel – produce of **Eretz Yisrael** that has become subject to the obligation of **terumah** and **tithes;** it is forbidden for consumption until *terumah* and all tithes have been designated.

Teves – tenth month of the Hebrew calendar.

tevilah – immersion in a **mikveh** for the purpose of purification from **tumah**-contamination.

tevul yom – people or utensils that had been **tamei** and underwent immersion in a **mikveh** but still retain a vestige of their **tumah** until nightfall.

Tishah B'Av – lit. the Ninth of Av; the fast day that commemorates the destruction of the First **Beis HaMikdash** and the Second one, as well as other national tragedies.

Tishrei – seventh month of the Hebrew calendar.

todah – thanksgiving offering brought when a person survives a potentially life-threatening situation.

tofes – see **toref.**

toladah [pl. **tolados**] – subcategory of an **av** (pl. **avos**).

Torah – the five books of Moses; the Chumash or Pentateuch.

toref – a document's essence, specifying its date, the names of the principals and the pertinent facts particular to the document. The document's form – the **tofes** – contains the rest of the document's text including a summary of all the significant information contained in the *toref* except for the document's date.

Tosefta – a written collection of **Baraisos**.

treifah – a person, animal, or bird possessing one of a well-defined group of life-threatening body defects.

tumah – legally defined state of ritual impurity inherent in certain people (e.g. a **niddah**) or objects (e.g. a corpse). Under specific conditions, this contamination can be transmitted to other people or objects, with the degree of *tumah* generally declining with each transmission. People or utensils in a state of **tumah** are restricted from contact and certain other forms of interaction with holy objects by a body of intricate and complex laws. People or utensils that are **tamei** can become **tahor** by being immersed in a **mikveh.**

tumas meis – the **tumah** of a human corpse.

tumas ohel – lit. roof **tumah;** the **tumah** conveyed to objects or persons when they are under the same roof as certain **tumah** conveyors, generally a human corpse.

Twelve Prophets – the final book of the Prophets consists of twelve short prophetic works: *Hosea, Joel, Amos, Obadiah, Jonah, Micah, Nahum, Habakkuk, Zephaniah, Haggai, Zechariah, Malachi.*

tzaraas – see **metzora.**

tzitzis – the fringes that by Torah law must be placed on a four--cornered garment.

tzon-barzel – lit. iron-sheep; the portion of a woman's dowry assessed prior to the marriage; its value is recorded in the **kesubah.** Should the marriage end, reimbursement is made to the woman at the property's assessed value, even if in the interim it was lost or damaged. Thus, the property's value remains preserved for the wife like *iron*.

unpaid custodian – a **shomer** who receives no remuneration for his services.

yavam – see **yibum.**

yetzer hara – Evil Inclination.

yevamah – see **yibum.**

yibum – levirate marriage. When a man dies childless, the Torah provides for one of his brothers to marry the widow. This marriage is called *yibum*. The surviving brother, upon whom the obligation to perform the mitzvah of **yibum** falls, is called the **yavam.** The widow is called the **yevamah. Yibum** is effected only through cohabitation. See **chalitzah.**

Yisrael [pl. **Yisraelim**] – (a) Jew; (b) Israelite (in contradistinction to **Kohen** or **Levi**).

Yom Kippur – Day of Atonement; a day of prayer, penitence, fasting and abstention from **melachah.**

Yom Tov [pl. **Yamim Tovim**] – holiday; the festival days on which the Torah prohibits **melachah.** Specifically, it refers to the first and last days of **Pesach,** the first day of **Succos, Shemini Atzeres, Shavuos, Yom Kippur** and two days of **Rosh Hashanah.** Outside of **Eretz Yisrael,** an additional day of **Yom Tov** is added to each of these festivals, except **Yom Kippur** and **Rosh Hashanah.**

Yovel – fiftieth year [Jubilee]; the year following the conclusion of a set of seven **shemittah** cycles. On **Yom Kippur** of that year, the **shofar** is sounded to proclaim freedom for the Jewish servants, and to signal the return of fields sold in Eretz Yisrael during the previous forty-nine years to their original owner. **Yovel** is observed only at times when most of the Jewish nation resides in **Eretz Yisrael.**

zav [pl. **zavim**] – a man who has become **tamei** because of a specific type of seminal emission. If three emissions were experienced during a three-day period, the man must bring offerings upon his purification.

zavah – After a woman concludes her seven days of **niddah,** there is an eleven-day period during which any evidence of vaginal bleeding renders her a *minor zavah.* If the menstruation lasts for three consecutive days, she is a *major* **zavah** and must bring offerings upon her purification.

zechiyah – rule which states that one can act as a person's agent without his prior knowledge or consent if the act is clearly advantageous to the beneficiary.

zechus – unqualified benefit.

zerikah – throwing; applying the blood of an offering to the **Altar.** It is one of the four essential blood **avodos.**

zivah – the type of discharge which causes one to be a **zavah** or **zav.**

zomeim [pl. **zomemim**] – witnesses proven false through **hazamah.**

zuz – (a) monetary unit equal to a **dinar;** (b) a coin of that value; (c) the weight of a **zuz** coin.

Scriptural Index